# WORLD
# CHRISTIAN
# ENCYCLOPEDIA

# WORLD
# CHRISTIAN
# ENCYCLOPEDIA

A comparative study of churches and
religions in the modern world
AD 1900–2000

EDITED BY

## DAVID B. BARRETT

NAIROBI
**OXFORD UNIVERSITY PRESS 1982**
OXFORD   NEW YORK

*Oxford University Press*

OXFORD LONDON GLASGOW
NEW YORK TORONTO MELBOURNE AUCKLAND
NAIROBI DAR ES SALAAM CAPE TOWN
KUALA LUMPUR SINGAPORE HONG KONG TOKYO
DELHI BOMBAY CALCUTTA MADRAS KARACHI

ISBN 0 19 572435 6
© Oxford University Press 1982

*Published by Oxford University Press, East and Central Africa,
Science House, Monrovia Street, P.O. Box 72532, Nairobi;
typeset and filmed by Quality Typesetters Limited,
Lusaka Road, P.O. Box 42913, Nairobi*

*Printed in the United States of America*

# PREFACE

In 1968, a group of church demographers met and decided that the time was ripe to undertake, for possibly the first time in Christian history, a comprehensive survey of all branches of global Christianity. It was expected that the task of compiling this resulting encyclopedia would take about three years; in the event, it has taken twelve years. The reason for this lengthy period was that all those originally involved, including the editor, seriously underestimated the immense size and complexity of the Christian world. The number of denominations was found to be four times as numerous as the estimates made in 1968. Vast areas of Christian activity proved to be undocumented in the literature and had to be surveyed by means of visits to every country in the world. The survey proceeded through such visits, through an extensive correspondence, and through the part-time investigations of a modest network of specialists in every country.

Perhaps the first impression to strike the reader will be of the enormous diversity and fragmentation of Christianity. The proliferation of 20,800 denominations is sure to cause unfavourable comment. Some will see it as sectarianism run riot. But here several points to the contrary can be noted. Diversity—divergences in faith and practice from one denomination to another—is not divisiveness; it is what we would expect when Christianity is being spread among some 8,990 peoples speaking 7,010 languages in the modern world. Amongst other things, this diversity has made it far more difficult for hostile regimes to comprehend the phenomenon of Christianity in order to control it, suppress it, or eradicate it.

Fragmentation—multiplicity of denominations—seems to be more obviously wrong, even disastrous. But our response as Christians cannot be censorious. The United Nations' *Universal Declaration of Human Rights* (1948) states that every human being has the right to embrace the religion or belief of his choice, including no religion. In consequence, Christians should respect this human right by granting and showing genuine religious toleration to, at the least, all other expressions of faith in Christ, including those expressed in deviations. Such toleration does not, of course, imply that Christians should deny their convictions about Christ and his church, or abandon proclamation, evangelism or conversion; it means only that we recognize the right of others to adhere to whatever religion they choose, although we may believe those religions false or inadequate and may attempt to win them to faith in Jesus Christ as we understand it.

Again, the problem of fragmentation recedes when members of this great variety of denominations find themselves working together on a common task. In our case, Christians of every persuasion willingly co-operated in collecting accurate data about their own co-religionists. Fragmented they may be still, but these widely scattered individual believers, several thousand in number, have helped to produce a survey in which global Christianity emerges as a single whole, even as the Body of Christ.

The reader's second impression may well be of vast numbers confronting him at every turn. There are two pitfalls that we should avoid in interpreting large demographic tables and totals involving Christians. The first is triumphalism. We are well aware that a survey which describes church statistics as being startlingly larger than most currently-held stereotypes can easily be labelled by the superficial reader (whether he be Christian, secularist or atheist) as mere triumphalism. Massive church growth is often misinterpreted in this way. Spectacular growth or numerical success do not in themselves spell spiritual depth or significant progress. We need therefore continually to disavow any vestige of triumphalism, and to replace it by service in the name of Christ. As Hans Küng has put it, 'The Church must not conquer but serve the world religions'. Neither should we fall into the trap of equating the fortunes of organized Christianity and institutionalized religion with the fortunes of the Kingdom of God.

The other pitfall when examining these tables is to regard them as depersonalizing, and to allege that they treat human beings as mere cyphers of little individual worth. One must admit that statistics of enormous numbers of people, well into the billions, have a numbing effect on many of us. We need to remember Jesus' teaching that God's love for every individual is proved by his counting every last detail about us: 'Even the hairs of your head have all been counted' (Matthew 10.30). It is salutary therefore to view the statistical tables given here as vignettes or portraits of a scene in which every one of us features personally. If you belong to a church whose members are here given as 72,836, you are included in that total; without you the total would be 72,835. If you are a pastor in a country with 75 ordained ministers, you are one of the 75; without you it would have been 74. In fact, if you are a Christian of any sort, you personally appear (as a single digit, to be sure) in some 760 distinct absolute numbers (excluding percentages) in this encyclopedia's statistics. Every Christian also appears, though not as obviously as one digit, in some 570 percentages, and also in around 450 further derived figures (averages, etc). In several tables, you as a Christian of a particular type are included in over 100 numbers and percentages in each table. If you and your family are charismatic Christians (or Evangelicals, or a similar tradition), you all feature in a total of 780 absolute numbers here. If in addition you are a Christian worker, you feature as an individual in an additional 35 sets of absolute numbers. If you are a worker in a foreign land, you feature in a further 20. And so on. Since you and I permeate these statistical tables to that extent, they cannot be so impersonal after all.

*Nairobi, 1981*

David B. Barrett

# TABLE OF CONTENTS

PART 1    STATUS

An illustrated and numerical survey summarizing 20th-century global religious trends
documented in this Encyclopedia, including tables showing the spread of Christianity across the
world; non-Christian religions; the rise and spread of secularization, Communism, secularism
and atheism; missions, evangelization and conversion; the effect of population explosion, and
the shift in the Christian numerical centre of gravity towards the Third World; and present
trends extrapolated to the year AD 2000.

PART 2    CHRONOLOGY

The historical background to world Christianity.

PART 3    METHODOLOGY

A comprehensive description and analysis of the varieties and problems of comparative
Christian enumeration, embodying a detailed explanation, illustrated by photographs, of the
new methodology employed in the construction of the Encyclopedia's statistical tables, the
sources used, the assumptions made, classifications and codes, and how data have been selected
where a choice was available.

PART 4    CULTURE

Evolving a detailed listing of mankind's 5 races, 7 stylized racial colours, 13 geographical races,
71 ethnolinguistic families, and 432 major peoples, with classification of 8,990 major
constituent peoples, sub-peoples and cultures, 7,010 languages, 17,000 dialects, and 80,000
alternative names in use.

PART 5    EVANGELIZATION

The concepts of evangelization and world evangelization, and their definition, description,
quantification, and enumeration.

PART 6    CODEBOOK

A quick-reference alphabetic codebook covering all religious and religious activities, for the
various series of national and international statistical tables in this Encyclopedia, especially in
the Survey immediately following.

PART 7    SURVEY

This survey gives, for every country in the world (in a single alphabetical listing, A-Z), (a) brief
secular data, (b) a standardized statistical table 1 'Religious adherents in each country, AD
1900-2000' presenting overall religious adherents, profession (preference), affiliation and
practice in the 20th century, with annual change during the decade 1970-80; and presenting

also government statistics of religion, and polls of religion and church attendance; (c) an illustrated text describing the present religious situation, non-Christian religions (described in order of numerical size), the current status of Christianity, description of the major churches (in order of size), the churches and development, church and society, church-state relations, interdenominational organizations, and religious broadcasting; (d) a listing of any major bibliographical items describing churches and religions in the country; and (e) a standardized statistical table 2 'Organized churches and denominations in each country' presenting statistics and description of organized Christianity—every church, denomination and diocese in each nation, including indigenous churches, banned churches, suppressed churches, underground churches, radio churches, refugee churches, migrant churches, diaspora churches, uniting churches, para-churches, micro-churches, alternative churches, etc., with totals and projections covering the decade 1970-1980; together with data on organized Christian activity including evangelization, foreign missionaries, institutions, periodicals, personnel, religious libraries, scripture distribution, and service agencies.

# LIST OF GLOBAL TABLES

## *In Part 1, STATUS*



## *In Part 8, STATISTICS*



# LIST OF MAPS

The Encyclopedia contains 3 varieties of maps: (1) on the masthead title of each country's article in Part 7, a small continental map locating the country; (2) for most countries, a second map in each article's text, partly contemporary and partly historical (20th century), showing boundaries, main cities (with current or recent spellings) and surrounding countries; and (3) the following maps in Part 11.

# LIST OF NATIONS AND COUNTRIES
## Shortened, full and official names for all countries

1. Names in capitals below form this Encyclopedia's definitive alphabetized geographical listing in English of all 223 sovereign and non-sovereign nations, countries and territories in the world, as existing in 1981, with a handful of territories whose status has recently been in dispute (Palestine, Sahara, Sikkim, Timor, et alia). It is based on the official listing utilized by the United Nations, using the official terminology requested of the UN by each member country; but it modifies this terminology by changing nations alphabetized by the UN under 'Republic of...' or 'Democratic...' or 'Socialist...' to their recognized or normally-employed geographical terms. Full details of names, including names in their own languages, are given under SECULAR DATA at the start of each country's article on the page indicated below. In addition to the official UN names in English, all UN members also have official names in the other 5 of the 6 official UN languages (Arabic, Chinese, English, French, Russian, Spanish).

2. Page numbers below refer only to the main article on each country, found in the Survey, Part 7. Further extensive data on each country can be found, arranged alphabetically, in Global Table 31 and in the Directory, Part 13.

3. All member countries of the United Nations (shown below preceded by an asterisk, *) are here given their definitive shortened names (shown in capitals), which are the shortest English official forms agreed to with the UN by the countries

concerned. The only exceptions are the following countries which insist on UN use of their full English titles but which we here, in the interests of standardization and ease of reference, reduce to their normally-employed geographical terms, as follows: Cameroon, Kampuchea, Korea (North), Korea (South), Laos, Libya, Syria, Tanzania, Viet Nam, Yemen (North), Yemen (South). In all these cases, however, we follow this geographical term below after a semi-colon by the shortest official form, also in capital letters; and then by the full official name if different.

4. Words in upper/lowercase following a capitalized name, after a comma, form the rest of the full official name of the country concerned (except words in parentheses). If there are no such additional words (as e.g. for Ireland), this indicates that for UN purposes the full official name is the same as the shortest official form.

5. Words in upper/lowercase following a capitalized name, after a colon, form the full official name and indicate that it has formal priority over the shortest official form (e.g. Spain is officially called The Spanish State, France is The French Republic, Greece is The Hellenic Republic, Switzerland is The Swiss Confederation, etc).

6. Names in parentheses are not part of official titles but have widespread popular use. Details of other names in use are given under SECULAR DATA.

7. Entries below not in capitals but in upper/lower

case only do not form part of our definitive listing; they are alternative forms of title, popular names, older names still in use, or names of territories which are, or have now (1981) become part of some larger unit, to all of which the reader is referred.

8. The word 'see' refers the reader from an abbreviation or alternative or popular or widely-used or incorrect name to the fuller or correct or shortest official form of the name or its geographical equivalent as employed in our listing.

9. The word 'now' indicates that although an older name is still in use in some international or national circles, correctly or incorrectly, the newer name indicated has now officially replaced it.

10. The word 'under' indicates that a territory is or is now part of the larger nation or country indicated.

11. The 9 Homelands or Bantustans which claim political independence from the Republic of South Africa have not been recognized as independent republics by the wider world, hence are excluded from our listing of 223 countries, although listed below in upper/lowercase. They, and their statistics, are included here under South Africa. To illustrate this problem, however, we include an article on the Republic of the Transkei, although its statistics are included under South Africa in all the Global Tables.

# EDITORS AND CONSULTANTS

*Editor:*    David B. Barrett, MA, BD, STM, PhD

*Associate Editors:*

      Georges Deroy, Lic. Sci. Relig., FERES
      François Houtart, PhD, Catholic University of Louvain
      Malcolm J. McVeigh, BD, STM, PhD, United Methodist Church
      T. John Padwick, MA, Church Missionary Society

*Editor Emeritus:*

      Sir Kenneth Grubb, CMG, LLD

*Assistant Editor:*

      Mary Linda Hronek, PhD

*Consultants:*

      Rev. Michael A. Bourdeaux, Keston College
      Rev. Canon Jean Bruls, *Eglise Vivante*
      Edward R. Dayton, MARC, WVI
      Dr David A. Fraser, MTRC
      Rev. Dr Willi Henkel, OMI, Librarian, SC Propaganda
      Dr James D. Holway, Islam in Africa Project
      Patrick J. St G. Johnstone, *Operation World*, WEC
      Dr Donald A. McGavran, Fuller Theological Seminary
      Bishop Stephen C. Neill, *World Christian Books*
      Dr Donald Tinder, *Christianity Today*, New College
      Dr Bryan R. Wilson, All Souls College, Oxford

*Produced by:*

      CSWE (Centre for the Study of World Evangelization/World Christian Encyclopedia, Nairobi, Kenya).

*Co-operating research institutions:*

      FERES (International Federation of Institutes for Socio-Religious Research, Louvain-la-Neuve, Belgium).
      MARC (Missions Advanced Research & Communication Center, Monrovia, California, USA).

*Country Text Compilers:*

      Georges Deroy, Malcolm J. McVeigh

*Photographic, Cartographic & Statistical Editor:*

      David B. Barrett

# COLLABORATORS, CONTRIBUTORS AND LOCAL EDITORS

Names of collaborators, contributors and local editors listed below are followed in most cases by initials of their organization or style at the time of their contribution (see index of Christian Abbreviations, Acronyms and Initials), or their profession, and in parentheses the country or countries of their contribution, expertise or residence, or in a few cases their subject. The listing excludes a number of experts who have requested anonymity, but includes a few requested pseudonyms.

Bishop I.A. Adetosoye, NAAC Aladura (Nigeria)
Dr Tokunboh Adeyemo, AEAM (Nigeria)
Rev. Dr Jean Albertini, Aumônier Militaire (Niger)
Rev. Canon Roger G. Allison, MBE (Israel)
Bishop Oliver C. Allison, CMS (Sudan)
Rev. Dr Johannes Althausen (German DR)
Rev. S.G. Andrews (Fiji)
Rev. Charles Antoine, DIAL (Brazil)
Paul Arnold (France)
Rev. Dr A.G. Baan, OFM (Indonesia)
Rev. Brian H. Bailey, BCC (Botswana)
J.F. Bango, sociologist (Hungary, Romania)
Rev. E.E. Barde, EEM (Morocco)
Dr John Barrett (UK)
Pam Barrett (Kenya)
Rev. P. Basile, OFM Cap (Comoros)
Albert Bastenier, CRSR (Belgium)
Peter Bayes, FEBA (UK)
Bertha Beachy, EMBMC (Somalia)
Nadia Benjamin, GICC (Grenada)
Dr Walter W. Benjamin (USA)
Rev. Joseph-Roger de Benoist, WF (Benin)
Rev. Augusto Beuzeville F. (Peru)
Rev. William E. Biernatzki, SJ (N. & S. Korea)
Dr R. Biernazek (Poland)
Gordon Bishop, SIM (Niger)
Rev. Joseph L. Blackett (Belize)
Dr C. Boeke, Interreligio (Netherlands)
Dr Hugo Bogensberger, IKS (Austria)
Rev. A. Boland (Laos, Thailand)
Jean-Charles Bonenfant (Canada)
Professor David J. Bosch, UNISA (South Africa)
Rev. Wallace Boulton, CMS (UK)
Msgr J.E. Bourke, FCEO (Australia)
Rev. Malcolm R. Bradshaw, OMF (Singapore)
Rev. W.G.M. Brandful, CCG (Ghana)
Dr Rodolphe A. Bréchet, SAM (Angola)
Huguette Breil (Morocco)
Rev. H. Briand, FMI (St Lucia)
Leslie Brierley, IRRO/WEC (Guinea Bissau)
Helen Brown, TWR (UK)
Rev. Elden M. Buck, UCC (Pacific Islands)
Dr Aldo Büntig (Argentina)
Rev. Canon Samuel R. Burgoyne, UMN (Nepal)
Dr Edgar H. Burks, SBC (Nigeria)
Rev. Palle Burla (Faeroe Islands)
Rev. A.J. Butler (Botswana)
Rev. James Byrne, SMA (Liberia)
Rev. Pierre Cadier, PEMS (Dahomey/Benin)
Rev. Giuseppe Caffaratto (Italy)
Bishop Michel Callens, WF (Tunisia)
Rev. Michael Campbell-Johnston, SJ (Guyana)
Rev. Humberto Capo, CEE (Spain)
Bishop Edmund M.H. Capper, CPSA (St Helena)
Archdeacon Jack Cattell (Bermuda)
Rev. Dr Rafael Cepeda, CIEC (Cuba)
Rev. Carlos Manuel de Cespedes, CEC (Cuba)
Rev. Ricardo Cetrulo, SJ, CER (Uruguay)
Rev. Marc Chambron, LWF (France)
Dr Maxwell Charlesworth, ANU (Australia)
Rev. F.E. Charman (St Kitts-Nevis-Anguilla)
Carlos Chiesa (Argentina)
Franco Chittolina, sociologist (Italy)
Msgr Damian Ciacci (Saudi Arabia, Gulf)
Sister Peter Claver, OP, CARA (USA)
Geraldine Coldham, BFBS (Names for God)

Rev. Tom S. Colvin, CSC/CCM (Malawi)
Rev. W.H. Conrad (Costa Rica)
Dr Frank L. Cooley, DGI (Indonesia)
Rev. Jean Corbon (Lebanon)
Rev. Richard G. Cote, OMI (Lesotho)
Rev. J.B.D. Cotter (Bahrain)
Very Rev. W. Frank Curtis, C of E (UK)
Rev. Dr Marthinus L. Daneel, AICC (Zimbabwe)
Bishop Michel Darmancier, SM (Wallis & Futuna Is)
Nabih Kamel David (Egypt)
Brother Joseph M. Davis, SM, NOBC (USA)
John Dean, UBS (Scripture distribution)
Rev. M. Defresne (Japan)
Rev. Natale Del Mistro (Iran)
Rev. Dr Raymond Deniel, INADES (Upper Volta)
Dr Duncan Derrett (India)
Rev. M. Dhavamony, SJ (India)
Dr F. Dingjan (Netherlands)
Rev. Max Dominique, CSSp (Central African Rep)
Rev. T.F. Doust, MMS (Benin)
Rev. du Noyer, BLASC (Madagascar)
Rev. Willehad Paul Eckert (FR Germany)
Bishop Sigurbjörn Einarsson (Iceland)
Mercedes Massi Elizalde (Argentina)
Edward A. Elliott, Living Bibles (USA)
M.F. Elliott-Binns, General Synod C of E (UK)
Rev. Edgar J. Elliston, CMF (Ethiopia)
Rev. Eulogio V. Enrique, SJ, CBIES (Philippines)
Dr Juan Estruch (Spain)
Rev. Gareth M. Evans, *Sobornost* (UK)
Rev. John B. Finger (Bahamas)
Rev. Guillermo Flores (Guatemala)
Msgr Jean Foradaris (Cyprus)
Rev. A.D. Fowler (Brunei)
Bishop Hendrik Hubert Frehen, SMM (Iceland)
Joachim W.H. Freitag, WEC (Mauritania)
L. Andrew Friend (Mozambique)
Rev. Paul D. Fueter (Switzerland)
Lcdo. Euclides J. Fuguet, CEV (Venezuela)
Bishop Hyacinthe Gad (Greece)
George Gallup Jr, AIPO (Polls)
Rev. Anthony M. Gann, USPG (Lesotho)
Bishop Manuel J. Gaxiola, CINCOMEX (Mexico)
Helmut Geller, sociologist (FR Germany)
Pastor Dr Roswith Gerloff (UK Black churches)
Rev. Jean-Paul Gladu, CSC (Haiti)
Dr Walter Goddijn (Netherlands)
Bishop William Gomes (India)
Rev. Dr José-Maria Gonzalez-Ruiz, SJ (Spain)
Rev. P. Grégoire, OP (Denmark)
Rev. Paul Grillou, WF, ISTR (France)
Rev. Guilbert Guérin, SJ (China/Taiwan)
Bishop R.L. Guilly, SJ (Guyana)
Dr Berndt Gustafsson, RIS (Sweden)
Rev. Dr J. Harry Haines, UMC (PR China)
Rev. Joseph Hajjar, Melkite Patriarchate (Syria)
Rev. Richard Haller (Switzerland)
Rev. E.I. Hamelberg, CSSp (Sierra Leone)
Rev. Clive Handford, JEM (Syria)
Dr W.E. Ted Haney, FEBC (USA)
Rev. James T. Hardyman, LMS (Madagascar)
Rev. Patricia J. Harrison, CRC (Australia)
Robert W. Harvie, UPUSA (India)
Bishop Ralph P. Hatendi, UBS (Zambia)
Rev. Stephen Hayes, CPSA (Namibia)
Bishop Edward G. Haynsworth, PECUSA (Nicaragua)

Archdeacon Frank M.M. Haythornthwaite (Namibia)
Rev. Roger E. Hedlund, CBFMS (Italy)
Rev. André Heiderscheid (Luxembourg)
Rev. Jean Heinrichs, SJ (Sikkim)
Dr Guy Hermet (Spain)
Javier Solis Herrera (Costa Rica)
Dr Horst Herrmann (FR Germany)
John Hickey, sociologist (UK)
Rev. John A. Hinchey, SJ (Cayman Islands)
Bishop H. Hofmann, OFM Cap (Djibouti)
Dr Sibenda M. Holsteyn, CCN (Netherlands)
Rev. Dr T.E. Floyd Honey, CCC (Canada)
Rev. Dr Norman A. Horner, UPUSA (Lebanon)
Rev. John F. Hotchkin, NCCB (USA)
Rev. C. Hulsen, SMA (Ghana)
Rev. Robert A. Humphreys (Australia)
Dr R.G.W. Huysmans (Netherlands)
Rev. Dr David Hynd, CBE (Swaziland)
Rev. Xavier Jacob, AA (Turkey)
Rev. Gustavo Amigo Jansen, SJ (Dominican Rep)
S.J. Jegasothy, NCCSL (Sri Lanka)
Rev. Alfred E. Johnson, WEC (Venezuela)
R. Boyd Johnson, MARC (USA)
Rev. Bernard Joinet, WF, TPRI (Tanzania)
Rev. Enrique Jorda, SJ, ISET (Bolivia)
François Joyaux (PR China)
Rev. Jean Julien (Martinique)
Basile Jultsis (Greece)
Janet Kalven (USA)
Lusanga Kanyinda (Zaire)
Rev. John Kelly (St Helena)
Rev. Joseph Kelly, CSSp, AMECEA (Kenya)
Dr Jocelyn C. Kelsey (UK)
Oberkirchenrat Claus Kemper, EKD (FR Germany)
Sister Anne Marie Kernéis, UISG (Italy)
Rev. Pierre Kerzoncuf, OMI (Channel Islands)
Rev. John Key, MCC (Papua New Guinea)
Dr A. Khoury (FR Germany)
Pastor R. Buana Kibongi, EEC (Congo)
Rev. Karlo Kjaer, ELFD (Denmark)
Dr A.M.J. Kloosterman (Cook Islands)
Josip Kolanovic (Yugoslavia)
Dr Elfriede Kreuzeder, ECCA (Austria)
Rev. Philip F. Kurts, SJ (Papua New Guinea)
Rev. Oscar Lacroix (Guadeloupe)
Rev. Victor A. Lamont (UK; photographic)
Dr Aldo Landi (Italy)
Gordon Landreth, EAGB (UK)
Rev. Gilles Langevin, SJ (Canada)
Bishop Neville Langford-Smith, CMS (Australia)
Rev. Bill Lasley (Senegal)
Rev. Professor René Laurentin, OP (Evangelization)
Rev. Angelo S. Lazzarotto, PIME (PR China)
Roger Lee, SDA (Macau)
Rev. A. Lemaire, OP (Finland)
Raymond Lemieux, CRSR (Canada)
Rev. James Lennon, RDU (Ireland)
Rev. David Chia-En Liao (Taiwan)
Archdeacon Ralph A. Lindley, ECJME (Qatar, UAE)
Rev. Melvin T. Long (USA)
Emily Kalled Lovell (USA, Canada)
Arthur M. Lundblad, ECZ (Zaire)
Rev. P. Lunot (Mauritania)
Rev. Gilles Lussier, PME (Honduras)
Rev. Finn Lynge, OMI (Greenland)
Rev. Brian J. Macdonald-Milne (Solomon Islands)

Rev. Luiz Machado de Abreu (Mozambique)
Rev. W. Mackey, SJ (Bhutan)
Sister Janice McLaughlin, MM (Kenya)
Rev. Noel McNeill, ACOP (Canada)
Marion McVeigh, UMC (Canada)
Dr Enrique Miret Magdalena (Spain)
Msgr J.P. Mahony (Isle of Man)
Eric Maillefer, AEAM (Kenya)
Rev. Canon Dr Josef Majka (Poland)
Rev. Carl Major (Antigua)
Hilkka Malaska, CoN (Finland)
George K. Mambo, AACC (Kenya)
Rev. Edward F. Mann, SJ (Nepal)
Adele Manzi (Lebanon)
Bishop Antonious Markos, See of St Mark (Egypt)
Rev. Bill F. Marsters, CICC (Cook Islands)
Dr Marie-Louise Martin, EJCSK (Zaire)
Rev. Antonio Martins (Portugal)
Jonathan Marzeki, ICC (Iran)
Rev. Louis Mascarenhas, OFM, IRSS (Pakistan)
Rev. Dr Joseph Masson, SJ (Missiology)
Kathleen Matchett, CSRC (USSR)
Senator Gordon Matthews, WHC (Barbados)
Bishop François-Joseph Maurer, CSSp (St Pierre & M)
Rev. J.-B. Mayté (Mali)
Rev. Professor John S. Mbiti, WCC (Uganda)
Rev. Dr Otto Meinardus (Egypt, Greece)
Rev. Clifford S. Michelsen (Cameroon)
Rev. Dr David I. Mitchell (Trinidad & Tobago)
Rev. Dr Samuel H. Moffett (Korea)
Bishop Michael Moloney, CSSp (Gambia)
Lic. Vital H. Moreno G. (Panama)
Rev. Professor Charlie F.D. Moule, Cambridge U
Rev. Roger Muller (FTAI)
Rev. José Miguel Munarriz, CEP (Paraguay)
Rev. Paul Munier, MEP (Malaysia, Singapore)
Rev. Edward F. Murphy (Colombia)
Msgr Amédée Nagapen (Mauritius)
Rev. Albert Nambiaparambil, CMI (India)
Rev. Juhani Natri, FMS (Finland)
Rev. Louis de Naurois (France)
Bishop Justin Ndandali, CPR (Rwanda)
William A. Needham, MARC (USA)
Rev. Charles A. Nelson (US Virgin Islands)
Rev. Jean Nenonene, EET (Togo)
Dr Arnaldo Nesti (Italy)
Rev. Gilbert Nichols, SBC (Paraguay)
Dr Elisa Juan de Nieves (Puerto Rico)
Paul H. Nilson, ABS (Turkey)
Rev. Dr Loren E. Noren (Hong Kong)
John J. Nquku, LACS (Swaziland)
Rt Rev. Ildefonso Obama Obono (Equatorial Guinea)
Rev. Gilbert W. Olson (Sierra Leone)
Rev. Dr J.M. Ondra (Czechoslavakia)
Rev. Adolphe Ouédraogo, CEHV (Upper Volta)
Rev. Michel de Paillerets, OP (Sweden)
Rev. Peyton Palmore III, UCCJ (Japan)

Rev. Angelo Panigati (Afghanistan)
Archbishop G. Anthony Pantin, CSSp (Trinidad)
Balwant A.M. Paradkar (India)
Rev. Ramon Pardo, OMI (Sahara)
Julia Campos Parise (Uruguay)
Rev. Dr Janos Pasztor (Hungary)
Rev. Celestin Patock, OSA (USSR)
Rev. Zdzislaw Pawlik (Poland)
Rt Rev. W.L.A. Don Peter (Sri Lanka)
Cardinal Sergio Pignedoli, Roman Curia (Statistics)
Rev. Renato Poblete, SJ (Chile)
Rev. John R. Pritchard, MMS (Ivory Coast)
Professor Paul A. Puchkov, Akademii Nauk SSSR
Rev. Pedro Puentes (Chile)
Rev. Roland Quesnel, CSSp (Propaganda data)
Thomas E. Quigley, USCC (USA)
Rev. Jean Rabemanahaka (Comoro Islands)
Rev. J.-P. Ramanankilana (Madagascar)
Lic. Manuel R. Gonzalez Ramirez, SJ, IMES (Mexico)
Dr Michael Raske (FR Germany)
Bishop Derek A. Rawcliffe, CPM (New Hebrides)
Rev. Dr William R. Read, UPUSA (Brazil)
Pastor Pierre Regard (Belgium, Luxembourg)
Rev. Dr H.-Diether Reimer, EZW (FR Germany)
Reginald E. Reimer, CMA (Viet Nam)
Bishop Charles Reiterer, MHM (Brunei)
Rev. Norman G. Riddle, EBCO (Zaire)
Rev. Istvan Rigo (Hungary)
Dr C.A. Rijk, SIDIC (Italy)
Rev. Antonio Rivera Rodriguez (Puerto Rico)
Jean Robert (pseudonym) (German Democratic Rep)
Rev. M.A.Z. Rolston, NCCI (India)
Pastor Jean de Rougemont, AdD (Upper Volta)
André Rousseau, sociologist (France)
François Routhier, CRSR (Canada)
Dr Michael Rowe, U of Glasgow (USSR)
Bishop Jean Rupp (Monaco)
William Ryan, USCC (USA)
Rev. Réginald de Sa, OP, IDEO (Egypt)
Professor Todor Sabev, WCC (Bulgaria)
Luis Alberto Saenz (Costa Rica)
Sister M.-B. Salmon, SIDIC (France)
Bishop Samuel, See of St Mark (Egypt)
Rev. Kirkley Caleb Sands (Turks & Caicos Is)
Msgr Victor San Miguel, OCD (Kuwait)
Rev. Giuseppe Scapino (Italy)
Rev. Joseph B. Schuyler, SJ (Nigeria)
J. Sayer, sociologist (FR Germany)
Rev. Herbert Seignoret, CSSp, AEC (Jamaica)
Rev. E.R. Simmons (New Zealand)
Rev. Adrian B. Smith, WF (Zambia)
Rev. Erwin L. Spruth, LCMS (Papua New Guinea)
Rev. Harvey Staal, RCA (Kuwait, Oman)
Rev. Gunnar Stalsett, LWF (Norway)
Dr Roland C. Stevenson, UBS (Sudan)
Rev. Fred E. Stock (Pakistan)
Bishop Daniel Stuyvenberg, SM (Solomon Islands)

Rev. Lloyd Swantz, ELCT (Tanzania)
Pastor K. Tabuariki, SDA (Gilbert & Ellice Is)
Rev. Norman W. Taggart, ICC (Ireland)
Rabbi Marc H. Tannenbaum (USA)
Cardinal Pio Taofinu'u, SM (Western Samoa)
Michael A. Tarrant, WEC (Guinea Bissau)
Rev. David M. Taylor, NCCNZ (New Zealand)
Rev. Canon Ronald J. Taylor, CMSNZ (Tanzania)
Bishop Henri Teissier (Algeria)
Dr O. ter Reegen (Netherlands)
Pastor Randall L. Thetford (Guam)
Rev. John Thetgyi, BCC (Burma)
Harvey Thomas, NLEA (UK)
Dr Lars Thunberg (Sweden)
Rev. Canon Benjamin Tonna, SEDOS (Malta)
Rev. Dr T. Michael Traber, WACC (Zimbabwe)
Dr Garry Trompf, Univ of Sydney (Melanesia)
Rev. Dr Harold W. Turner, PRONERM (UK)
Mady Vaillant, WEC (Upper Volta)
Rev. Roger Velasquez Valle (El Salvador)
Rev. G. van den Asdonk (Malawi)
Rev. J. Van Hecken, CICM (Mongolia)
Rev. Juan Ramon Vega (El Salvador)
Rev. Rodney Venberg, CLB (Chad)
Dr Ad F. Vermeulen (Netherlands)
Rev. Canon Trevor Verryn, UNISA (South Africa)
Canon Jacques Verscheure, CISR (France)
Rev. Modeste Vesin (Seychelles)
Dr Ignacio Palacios Videla (Argentina)
Dr Ernst K. Vilaghy (Bulgaria)
Jeanne-Françoise Vincent, anthropologist (Congo)
Rev. Edvard Vogt (Norway)
Rev. Paul M. Volz, LCMS (Kenya)
Rev. Dr J.D.J. Waardenburg, WF (Netherlands)
Rev. Professor C. Peter Wagner (Bolivia)
Rev. Peter Wanko (Uganda)
Rev. Wichean Watakeecharoen, CCT (Thailand)
Rev. Stanford A. Webley (Jamaica)
Dr Erika Weinzierl, IKZ (Austria)
Benjamin M. Weir (Lebanon)
Dr Martin E. West, SACC (South Africa)
Rev. Francis J. Westhoff, MSC (Gilbert & Ellice Is)
Rev. Frank E. Wilcox, UMN (Nepal)
Dr J. Christy Wilson, Jr (Afghanistan)
Rev. W. Wipfler, NCCCUSA (Dominican Republic)
Rev. Joseph C. Wold (Liberia)
Rev. Canon James Yui Kok Wong (Singapore)
Chester Woodhall, CCGB (Zambia)
Jean Woods, CMS (bibliography)
Prälat Wilhelm Wöste (FR Germany)
Sister Gertrude Wright, MMS (Gambia)
Akiko Yamaguchi, NCCJ (Japan)
Rev. Y. Yamatoa (Niue)
Antonio Ybarra, sociologist (Nicaragua)
Msgr L. Zichem, CSSR (Surinam)
Bishop Antonio Silvio Zocchetta (Somalia)
Rev. Francisco Zuluaga, SJ, CIAS (Colombia)

# INTRODUCTION

This encyclopedia is descended from a long series of some 40 major surveys and atlases of Christianity and missions. A number have been denominational or confessional; others have been interdenominational or ecumenical. The series begins with Cosmas Indicopleustes, an intrepid Nestorian theologian and geographer who travelled the world and then, from AD 535 to 547, produced a survey, *Topographia Christiana*, in twelve Books. It contained one of the earliest and most famous of global maps. Little else systematic was published during the Middle Ages or the Reformation period until the modern Protestant missionary movement began. Then in 1792 came William Carey's survey, *An enquiry into the obligations of Christians to use means for the conversion of the heathens*. From the first, this new Protestant emphasis produced estimates of global statistics, then later ventured into ambitious statistical tables. Further factual Protestant surveys were published in 1818 (Hall & Newell), 1823, 1836, 1854, 1888, 1896, and 1900 (John R. Mott). More comprehensive global surveys followed with H.P. Beach's *A geography and atlas of Protestant missions* (1906), and further detailed missionary atlases in 1910, 1925 and 1938. On the Roman Catholic side, K. Streit's statistical surveys and atlases of 1906, 1913 and 1929 were the pioneers. From 1930 to 1960, a number of detailed country-by-country surveys appeared, including the prolific World Dominion series by Anglicans and Protestants, and later the many FERES publications by their Roman Catholic counterparts.

The genesis of this encyclopedia goes back to the *World Christian handbook*, an Anglican and Protestant publication which appeared on average every five years from 1949 to 1968, and to the similar Roman Catholic publication *Bilan du Monde: encyclopédie catholique du monde chrétien*, which had editions in 1958 and 1964. The present volume embodies the traditions of both these former publications. However, it takes an entirely new and more comprehensive form, and a quite new format. The encyclopedia covers many aspects of the Christian and religious worlds hitherto undescribed in the literature. It includes information on all the types and activities of organized Christianity, gives the data in an interdenominational or ecumenical presentation, and sets the whole in the context of all other religions including new religions and atheism. The encyclopedia surveys most of the quantifiable aspects of church life. It also attempts to interpret the data and to assess present global trends as revealed by this mass of information, most of it published here for the first time.

This study shares with its more recent predecessors a critical, scholarly, and scientific approach to data describing the Christian world. In the main, it uses existing data collected by the churches for their own purposes. The annual enquiries of several thousand denominations must be, in aggregate, the world's most mammoth statistical operation. All statistics resulting have been checked and counter-checked, sources investigated, and documents verified. A large computerized database was created to hold the information gathered. Use of a computer to compile all national and global statistical tables also enabled a large number of checks to be run for consistency, plausibility, probability and so on. Details of the methodology evolved are given in Part 3.

The scope of this book has been made as comprehensive as possible. It is clearly impossible, however, to cover every aspect of Christianity within a single volume. Thus it does not attempt to deal with subjects like the archaeology of Christianity, nor its philosophical system, evolution of dogma, ethics or liturgy.

In order not to fragment the subject unnecessarily by forcing the material into the artificial mould of a single A–Z alphabetical sequence throughout, this volume divides its treatment of the subject into the fourteen major topics shown in the Table of Contents. Each of these subjects is examined comprehensively and systematically by employing several alphabetical sequences for the world's 223 countries, for names of churches, organizations, cultures and languages, bibliographies, and various subject indexes. Statistical and other data are presented in a standard format and order for every country, religion and church. The advantage of this topical approach (as contrasted with an A–Z listing of articles) is that it enables the reader to grasp both the local detail and the global entirety of the various subjects treated, as well as allowing him to immediately compare the situation in one country with that in another, one culture with another, one religious tradition with another, one church or denomination with another. The book is, therefore, in the main a comparative and topical encyclopedia.

Organized Christianity is studied here mainly by describing the structures of the organized churches and denominations of the world. But there is also a vast complex of unorganized or unstructured Christian activity, better described perhaps as spontaneous Christianity, which is much more difficult to document or delineate. The task is attempted here by describing its more visible incipient or embryonic structures. These include reform movements, revivals, renewals, protest movements and charismatic movements. The concrete reality of these is documented in words, in photographs, and in the Topical Directory with names and addresses of all such spontaneous activities as have crystallized to the point of having an identity and a location.

It should be realized at this point that this encyclopedia is a descriptive survey first and foremost; it is not, and cannot be, a theological assessment or evaluation of the significance, relevance or authenticity of the present-day Christian enterprise across the world. This task must be left to those theologians and missiologists who may be interested. What is attempted here is description rather than evaluation.

# HOW TO USE THIS ENCYCLOPEDIA

*Fourteen major topics*
This is a topical encyclopedia, and not solely an alphabetical one. The Table of Contents sets out the 14 topics under which all material is systematically presented. Within 8 of them—Parts 4, 6, 7, 9, 10, 12, 13 and 14—material is arranged alphabetically in one, two or more sets of listings. All major categories or items of information are then indexed in Part 14.

*Alphabetization*
All lists are alphabetized to a standard pattern, counting and including spaces between words. In the alphabetizing sequence, a space always precedes all letters; thus the entries 'Church of England' and 'church statistics' always precede 'Churches of Christ' and 'churches of silence'. Three almost identical schemes of alphabetization are adopted here. In all Tables 2, churches and denominations with lengthy names have them shortened using standard abbreviations, but they remain always alphabetized on their unabbreviated versions, as described on page 77. The indexes in Part 14 use slightly different systems; inter alia, they ignore whether or not letters are uppercase or lowercase.

*A ruler is necessary*
All tables are closely printed in Times New Roman 6 point type (12 lines to the inch vertically) in order to provide the reader with as complete an overview as possible, in as compact a space as possible. To find your way around these tables quickly and accurately, use a ruler or straight edge.

## HOW TO FIND WHAT YOU WANT

1. **To locate a particular country's data.** Locate the country's main survey article from the *List of nations and countries* (page viii). This list includes official names of all countries, and also their full names, shortened names, popular names and partial names. Coded data on every country are also given in Global Table 31 (page 799).

2. **To locate known categories in a known country.** To find a particular religion, examine the country's Table 1, where religions are listed by order of number of adherents in 1970. Detailed footnotes and a plain-English narrative describing major religions usually follow. To locate a particular known denomination, examine the alphabetical listing in the country's Table 2. To locate other types of category, consult the *Standard and definitive locations index* (page 1005).

3. **To locate comparative data for known categories in known countries.** Find each category's standardized location (repeated for all countries) from the *Standard and definitive locations index* (page 1005). A quicker way, for 107 variables, is to examine Global Table 31 (page 799), where all countries are listed alphabetically on 2 facing pages.

4. **To locate unknown denominations in a known country.** Four examples can be given. (a) To find a denomination of a given ecclesiastical tradition (e.g. Lutheran), or all such denominations, place a vertical rule against Table 2's column 3, then look down the column for that tradition's 3-letter code (in this case, 'Lut'), as given in the Codebook (page 123). (b) To find all denominations begun before a given year (e.g. '1940'), examine Table 2's column 2. (c) To find all denominations which are members of a given council of churches (e.g. 'World Council of Churches'), look for the council's code (in this case, 'W') in Table 2's column 4, second sub-column. (d) To locate denominations served by a known foreign missionary society, look for the latter's initials in Table 2's column 8, or (for Roman Catholic jurisdictions) in column 4, sub-columns 2-5.

5. **To locate all countries with particular given characteristics.** To locate all countries subjected to severe religious persecution, or those closed to foreign missions, or those under 10% literate, et alia, examine Global Table 31 (page 799). From that page's list of categories, or from the Codebook (page 123), find the relevant column and code and read off names of all countries involved.

6. **To locate global totals for known categories.** Consult the *List of global tables* (page ix), or, for more exact detail, entries ending in the word 'total' in the *Standard and definitive locations index* (page 1005).

7. **To obtain visual data on known categories and subjects.** Consult the *List of maps* (page x), and the *Photographic index* (page 999).

8. **To identify an unfamiliar ethnolinguistic name.** First obtain its code from the *Index of peoples and languages* (page 988). Then use this code to locate its descriptive line in the classification Peoples of the World (pages 112-115). The size of population involved can likewise be found from Global Table 24 (page 786).

9. **To identify an unfamiliar set of initials.** Use the index *Christian abbreviations, acronyms and initials*, on page 993, which lists bodies of significance at national or wider levels. In a particular country, initials of denominations may be found in Table 2, beginning of column 8.

10. **To locate an organization whose initials only are known.** First use the index on page 993 to obtain the full name required. Then use the *Topical directory subject index* on page 900 to find the directory topic and location. Scan the organizations listed there until you locate the required organization, its country and its address.

11. **To locate major organizations related to a known topic.** Use the *Topical directory subject index* (page 900) to locate whichever of the Directory's 76 topics cover your topic. Turn to that topic or those topics in the Topical Directory (Part 13), which will then list names and addresses of relevant major organizations in the various countries.

12. **To locate further or parallel references to a given category.** Cross-references have been kept to a minimum (given as 'See page x', or 'q.v.'). To locate references, return to the *Standard and definitive locations index* (page 1005).

# PART 1

# STATUS

The expansion and status of Christianity
in the 20th century

*The Kingdom of God is like a grain of mustard seed, which is the smallest of all the seeds on earth; yet when it is sown it grows up and becomes the greatest of all shrubs.*
—Mark 4.30–32, Revised Standard Version.

## Arrangement of Part 1

The object of Part 1 is to give, in the following 17 pages, a highly condensed global over-view of the fortunes of Christianity in the 20th century. There are 4 parts to this description. (1) A narrative text is given on the next 9 right-hand pages. For an immediate overview, this can be read as a continuous whole, and can be read without the reader looking at photographs or tables. (2) Twelve global statistical tables are added, one on the opening page opposite and all the rest on left-hand pages facing any narrative interpretation of them. These are given to provide the necessary documentary support for the narrative, and to assist the reader who wants to digress at any point into more detail. (3) Illustrations are added at various points in Part 1 to support major features of the narrative. (4) After the first page, these materials—text, tables, illustrations—are divided into 8 pairs of facing pages. On each, one or more distinct topics are described using the 3 kinds of material on each pair of pages.

## Introduction to Global Tables in Parts 1 and 8

These form a series of 31 interconnected statistical tables. Twelve shorter or overall tables are given here in Part 1. The remaining 19 tables are longer or more detailed, and are given without commentary in Part 8. For the complete listing of all 31, see the list of Global Tables after the Table of Contents.

Most figures in these tables are given to the nearest 1,000 or 100 or 10. Many, however, are given to the last digit, in order that all totals and sub-totals should add up exactly, and be seen to add up exactly. Without this their comprehensibility and credibility would be less satisfactory. When using or quoting all such individual figures, therefore, especially for publication elsewhere, the reader is advised to round them off to the nearest 100, 1,000, 10,000 or 100,000 or even million, as may best serve his purpose.

These tables are built on precisely defined and exactly delimited definitions, which should be carefully examined when particular figures are wanted or are to be used or quoted elsewhere. In particular, our fundamental statistical distinction between 'global Christianity' (world total of all Christians of all categories) and 'global church membership' (world total of Christians affiliated to churches) should be borne in mind throughout.

Also to be remembered throughout is that all figures, especially those of change or changing situations, report *nett* totals of the categories concerned, i.e. births minus deaths, gains minus losses, immigrants minus emigrants, conversions minus defections, and so on.

# CHRISTIANITY IN THE TWENTIETH CENTURY

## A GLOBAL OVERVIEW

### Christianity over 20 centuries

The fortunes of Christianity as a global religion have fluctuated widely since the crucifixion and resurrection of Jesus Christ in AD 30. Over the first 19 centuries, it gradually increased its size and influence, in a series of 9 massive pulsations or epochs. Of these, 5 were times of advance for the Christian faith and 4 were times of retreat. Already by AD 500, 22% of mankind were believers in Jesus Christ, but by AD 1500 the figure had fallen to only 19%. This is illustrated here in Global Table 1 (see also Chronology in Part 2 for further details). Throughout 18 centuries, Christians were predominantly (over 90%) Caucasian by race, and from 1500-1900 were predominantly Whites (93-81%). By the year 1900, one third of humanity were Christians, and one half were aware of Christianity and had become influenced by it. Optimism for rapid completion of the task of global evangelization was high. From 1889-1914 the great Protestant and Anglican communions of Europe and North America promoted the Watchword that summarized this optimism in the objective 'The Evangelization of the World in This Generation'. In 1900, the pioneer of the modern ecumenical movement, John R. Mott, summed it all up in a masterly book of the same title.

The 20th century itself, however, has proved to be startlingly different from these expectations. Certainly the total of Christians has grown enormously, from 558 millions in 1900 to 1,433 millions by 1980. Certainly also, since 1900 Christianity has become massively accepted as the religion of developing countries in the so-called Third World, Africa in particular. But no-one in 1900 expected the massive defections from Christianity that subsequently took place in Western Europe due to secularism, in Russia and later Eastern Europe due to Communism, and in the Americas due to materialism.

### Global Christianity today

At the beginning of the 1980s, Christians of all kinds numbered 1,432,686,500, which is 32.8% of the world's population. This percentage Christian had increased rapidly during the Great Century from 1815–1914 at a rate of 1.2% per decade, then after 1914 reverted to a catastrophic decline of 0.4% per decade which by 1980 had worsened to 1.0% per decade. Despite this, the absolute number of Christians increases at 21.6 million a year. Global Table 2 gives the overall picture. It shows that Christianity has surged ahead in the world's less-developed countries from 83 millions in 1900 to 643 millions by 1980. During the 20th century, in fact, Christianity has become the most extensive and universal religion in history. There are today Christians and organized Christian churches in

every inhabited country on earth. The church is therefore now, for the first time in history, ecumenical in the literal meaning of the word: its boundaries are coextensive with the *oikumene*, the whole inhabited world.

In two-thirds of the world's 223 countries, Christians now form the majority (over 50%); in one third, the minority. This spread is very uneven, though (see Global Map 1). Christians number over 90% in 100 countries, less than 10% in 51 countries, less than 1% in 24 countries, and less than 0.1% in 6 countries: Afghanistan, Bhutan, Nepal, Somalia, North Yemen and South Yemen.

Of all Christians, 1,323,390,000 are church members affiliated to 7 ecclesiastico-cultural major blocs, also to some 156 different ecclesiastical traditions, and also to (in 1980) 20,780 distinct Christian denominations across the world. Of these Christians, 1,018,355,000 are active, practising church members.

**Worshipping Christians.** Sunday worship in Naulakha Church, Lahore (Pakistan). In 1980, the world contained 1,018 million such active, practising, worshipping church members.

## CHRISTIANITY IN THE GLOBAL SECULAR CONTEXT

### The secular background

The 1970s and 1980s have seen the emergence of a vast variety of types of modern state. Of the world's 223 countries in 1980, 69 were multi-party democratic states, 50 were one-party states, 56 were no-party dependencies or colonies, 28 were no-party countries under military rule, and 20 were autocracies or dictatorships (see Global Table 13 in Part 8). Marxist states have increased rapidly in numbers since 1960, and in 1980 numbered 38, of which 30 were fully-organized Communist states. In United Nations' terminology of development, 51 of the 223 were more developed countries, and 172 were less developed countries. In terms of political alignment, 35 countries belonged to the Western world, 30 to the Communist world, and 158 to the Third World. Fuller details of secular background data for the world are given in the totals to Global Table 31.

**Children too can be practising Christians.** Bible charade in Katanga (Zaire): Jesus (in white) calls Zaccheus down from the tree. Some 570 million Christians are children under 15 years of age.

### The demography of Christianity

As Global Table 2 (overleaf) illustrates, Christians are scattered throughout this world of variegated nations. They have followers on all 8 continents (or on all 8 of the major regional-continental areas defined by the United Nations), in all 24 UN-defined major regions, as well as being found in all 223 countries. Something like 524 million Christians are under 15 years of age. Some 196 million of them are infants and children under 5 years of age; the percentage is 9.3% of all Christians in developed countries, 15.4% in developing countries. Life expectancy (expectation of life at birth) among Christians averages 72 years in more developed regions, with a peak of 74.7 years in Sweden (and 77.3 years for women in Sweden); but in less developed regions, it averages only 55 years, falling to 38 years for 9 African nations and a world nadir of 35.8 years for Bangladesh.

### Christianity and urbanization

Some 41.1% of the world in 1980 were urban dwellers. Christians as a whole are more urbanized: by 1980, 843 million Christians (59.0% of global Christianity) were living in cities and urban areas. The evolution of this situation on 8 continents across the 20th century is shown in Global Table 21.

### Christianity and literacy

The number of literate adults in the world has multiplied sixfold during this century, climbing from 287 million (27.9% of the world) in 1900 to 1,774 million by 1980 (65.7%). Christians have always and almost everywhere been proportionately greatly more literate than average. In 1900, 60.8% of all Christian adults were literate, rising to 87.6% (927 million adults) by 1980. This latter total is increasing at 1.48% per year; every year the churches increase by a nett total of 12.5 million new Christian adult literates. This evolution is set out in Global Table 22.

Paralleling this mushrooming growth of literacy, the number of new book titles of all kinds published each year has increased twentyfold since 1900. It now stands at around 648,000 distinct new titles a year (Global Table 12). Some 22,200 of them are new religious books, and of these 17,000 are specifically Christian titles. There are also around 22,980 Christian periodicals; of these, 41% are published in the English language, 16% in German, 10% in Spanish, 9% in French, 7% in Italian, 3% in Portuguese and 14% in several hundred other languages, Dutch in particular.

Global Table 1. CHRISTIANS AMONG THE PEOPLES OF THE WORLD, AD 30-2000.

| | Year | AD 30 | 100 | 500 | 1000 | 1500 | 1800 | 1900 | 1980 | 1985 | 2000 |
|---|---|---|---|---|---|---|---|---|---|---|---|
| **1. *Christians and population*** | | | | | | | | | | | |
| Population (millions) | | 169.7 | 181.5 | 193.4 | 269.2 | 425.3 | 902.6 | 1619.9 | 4373.9 | 4781.1 | 6259.6 |
| Christians (millions) | | 0.0 | 1.0 | 43.4 | 50.4 | 81.0 | 208.2 | 558.1 | 1432.7 | 1548.6 | 2019.9 |
| % Christian | | 0.0 | 0.6 | 22.4 | 18.7 | 19.0 | 23.1 | 34.4 | 32.8 | 32.4 | 32.3 |
| **2. *Christians by race, %*** | | | | | | | | | | | |
| Australoid | | 0 | 0 | 0 | 0 | 0 | 0.0 | 0.1 | 0.5 | 0.5 | 0.6 |
| Capoid | | 0 | 0 | 0 | 0 | 0 | 0.0 | 0.0 | 0.0 | 0.0 | 0.0 |
| Caucasoid | | 99.9 | 99.9 | 97.0 | 90.0 | 98.7 | 91.0 | 88.7 | 70.0 | 68.2 | 63.0 |
| Mongoloid | | 0.0 | 0.0 | 3.0 | 10.0 | 1.0 | 6.0 | 6.6 | 11.2 | 11.8 | 13.1 |
| Negroid | | 0.0 | 0.0 | 0.0 | 0.0 | 0.3 | 3.0 | 4.6 | 18.3 | 19.5 | 23.2 |
| **3. *Christians by colour, %*** | | | | | | | | | | | |
| Black | | 0.0 | 0.0 | 0.0 | 0.0 | 0.3 | 3.0 | 4.5 | 18.0 | 19.3 | 22.9 |
| Brown | | 0.0 | 0.5 | 1.4 | 2.4 | 1.5 | 3.0 | 5.1 | 10.8 | 11.6 | 13.0 |
| Grey | | 0 | 0 | 0 | 0 | 0.0 | 0.0 | 0.1 | 0.2 | 0.2 | 0.3 |
| Red | | 0 | 0 | 0 | 0 | 0.1 | 3.0 | 1.7 | 3.1 | 3.3 | 3.8 |
| Tan | | 95.0 | 69.5 | 59.5 | 28.6 | 4.8 | 2.2 | 5.0 | 10.6 | 11.0 | 11.8 |
| White | | 5.0 | 30.0 | 38.1 | 61.0 | 92.6 | 86.5 | 81.1 | 50.5 | 47.4 | 39.8 |
| Yellow | | 0 | 0 | 1.0 | 8.0 | 0.7 | 2.3 | 2.5 | 6.8 | 7.2 | 8.4 |

Global Table 2.   GLOBAL CHRISTIANITY: CHRISTIANS ON 8 CONTINENTS, AD 1900-2000.

| Continent | 1900 Adherents | % | % | mid-1970 Adherents | % | % | Annual change 1970-1985 Natural | Conversion | Total | Rate | mid-1975 Adherents | % | % | mid-1980 Adherents | % | % | mid-1985 Adherents | % | % | 2000 Adherents | % | % | Countries (in 1980) |
|---|---|---|---|---|---|---|---|---|---|---|---|---|---|---|---|---|---|---|---|---|---|---|---|
| Africa | 9,938,448 | 1.8 | 0.6 | 142,962,732 | 11.8 | 4.0 | 4,586,648 | 1,466,149 | 6,052,797 | 3.55 | 170,702,570 | 13.0 | 4.3 | 203,490,710 | 14.2 | 4.7 | 236,278,850 | 15.3 | 4.9 | 393,326,210 | 19.5 | 6.3 | 53 |
| East Asia | 2,179,350 | 0.4 | 0.1 | 12,668,243 | 1.0 | 0.4 | 276,181 | 359,622 | 635,803 | 4.04 | 15,727,850 | 1.2 | 0.4 | 19,026,270 | 1.3 | 0.4 | 22,324,690 | 1.4 | 0.5 | 32,337,300 | 1.6 | 0.5 | 8 |
| Europe | 278,383,690 | 49.9 | 17.2 | 405,132,656 | 33.3 | 11.2 | 2,197,458 | -1,150,645 | 1,046,813 | 0.26 | 410,275,220 | 31.2 | 10.3 | 415,600,780 | 29.0 | 9.5 | 420,926,340 | 27.2 | 8.8 | 431,403,570 | 21.4 | 6.9 | 37 |
| Latin America | 62,002,115 | 11.1 | 3.8 | 267,383,563 | 22.0 | 7.4 | 8,419,292 | -291,821 | 8,127,471 | 2.66 | 305,111,930 | 23.2 | 7.7 | 348,658,275 | 24.3 | 8.0 | 392,204,600 | 25.3 | 8.2 | 571,157,820 | 28.3 | 9.1 | 27 |
| Northern America | 78,811,810 | 14.1 | 4.9 | 206,443,460 | 17.0 | 5.7 | 2,008,880 | -669,881 | 1,338,999 | 0.63 | 212,429,330 | 16.1 | 5.4 | 219,833,450 | 15.3 | 5.0 | 227,237,570 | 14.7 | 4.8 | 253,589,450 | 12.6 | 4.1 | 5 |
| Oceania | 4,827,450 | 0.9 | 0.3 | 17,851,851 | 1.5 | 0.5 | 372,894 | -128,200 | 244,694 | 1.28 | 19,060,096 | 1.4 | 0.5 | 20,298,794 | 1.4 | 0.5 | 21,537,492 | 1.4 | 0.5 | 27,741,966 | 1.4 | 0.4 | 20 |
| South Asia | 16,920,469 | 3.0 | 1.0 | 78,124,616 | 6.4 | 2.2 | 2,645,668 | 447,043 | 3,092,711 | 3.35 | 92,188,835 | 7.0 | 2.3 | 109,051,740 | 7.6 | 2.5 | 125,914,645 | 8.1 | 2.6 | 192,264,050 | 9.5 | 3.1 | 72 |
| USSR | 104,993,000 | 18.8 | 6.5 | 86,012,300 | 7.1 | 2.4 | 907,238 | 164,182 | 1,071,420 | 1.17 | 91,285,000 | 6.9 | 2.3 | 96,726,500 | 6.7 | 2.2 | 102,168,000 | 6.6 | 2.1 | 118,101,000 | 5.8 | 1.9 | 1 |
| **POLITICAL ALIGNMENT:** | | | | | | | | | | | | | | | | | | | | | | | |
| Western world | 470,991,120 | 84.4 | 29.1 | 526,141,240 | 43.2 | 14.6 | 3,761,782 | -1,706,852 | 2,054,930 | 0.38 | 535,703,030 | 40.7 | 13.5 | 546,690,540 | 38.2 | 12.5 | 557,678,050 | 36.0 | 11.7 | 592,155,430 | 29.3 | 9.5 | 35 |
| Communist world | 0 | 0.0 | 0.0 | 195,172,881 | 16.0 | 5.4 | 1,784,400 | 4,108,633 | 5,893,033 | 2.90 | 202,902,300 | 15.4 | 5.1 | 254,103,210 | 17.7 | 5.8 | 305,304,210 | 19.7 | 6.4 | 443,861,700 | 22.0 | 7.1 | 30 |
| Third World | 87,065,212 | 15.6 | 5.4 | 495,265,300 | 40.7 | 13.7 | 15,868,077 | -2,205,332 | 13,662,745 | 2.36 | 578,175,521 | 43.9 | 14.6 | 631,892,769 | 44.1 | 14.4 | 685,610,017 | 44.3 | 14.3 | 983,904,236 | 48.7 | 15.7 | 158 |
| **DEVELOPMENT:** | | | | | | | | | | | | | | | | | | | | | | | |
| More developed regions | 474,627,335 | 85.0 | 29.3 | 748,366,431 | 61.5 | 20.7 | 5,935,101 | -1,803,369 | 4,131,732 | 0.54 | 768,115,295 | 58.3 | 19.4 | 789,683,745 | 55.1 | 18.1 | 811,252,195 | 52.4 | 17.0 | 875,976,170 | 43.4 | 14.0 | 51 |
| Less developed regions | 83,428,997 | 15.0 | 5.1 | 468,212,990 | 38.5 | 13.0 | 15,479,158 | 1,999,818 | 17,478,976 | 3.19 | 548,665,556 | 41.7 | 13.8 | 643,002,774 | 44.9 | 14.7 | 737,339,992 | 47.6 | 15.4 | 1,143,945,196 | 56.6 | 18.3 | 172 |
| **GLOBAL CHRISTIANITY** | 558,056,332 | 100.0 | 34.4 | 1,216,579,421 | 100.0 | 33.7 | 21,414,259 | 196,449 | 21,610,708 | 1.64 | 1,316,780,851 | 100.0 | 33.2 | 1,432,686,519 | 100.0 | 32.8 | 1,548,592,187 | 100.0 | 32.4 | 2,019,921,366 | 100.0 | 32.3 | 223 |
| **WORLD POPULATION** | 1,619,886,760 | — | 100.0 | 3,610,034,405 | — | 100.0 | 76,388,313 | 0 | 76,388,313 | 1.93 | 3,966,711,095 | — | 100.0 | 4,373,917,535 | — | 100.0 | 4,781,123,975 | — | 100.0 | 6,259,642,000 | — | 100.0 | 223 |

1. All figures in this table refer to Christians except (for purposes of comparison) the last line which refers to total world population. Note that the Communist world did not exist in 1900, and in the 1970s and 1980s was rapidly increasing in number of countries and hence in apparent annual Christian conversions (new Christians). Likewise, the concept 'Third World' only emerged after 1945 and hence for 1900 is somewhat vague.
2. Of the 2 adjacent columns of percentages, the first gives the preceding absolute number of Christians as a percentage of all Christians (global Christianity), and the second as a percentage of that continent's total population. A third variety (Christians as a percentage of their continent's total population) is given in Global Table 23. Note that totals of percentages may not always add up exactly (e.g. to 100.0%), due to rounding.
3. The categories 'more developed' and 'less developed' refer to the United Nations-defined categories of those names.

Global Table 3.   THE UNDERGROUND CHURCH: CHRISTIANS LIVING UNDER HOSTILE REGIMES OR POLITICO-RELIGIOUS RESTRICTIONS, AD 1970-1980.

| Types of religio-political restrictions | Countries 1980 | Christians 1970 | Christians 1980 | % of all Christians 1970 | % of all Christians 1980 | Total population 1970 | Total population 1980 | Source |
|---|---|---|---|---|---|---|---|---|
| 1. Christians in countries without full political freedom or full civil rights | 149 | 682,977,700 | 866,574,400 | 56.1 | 60.6 | 2,850,577,800 | 3,521,257,700 | Global Table 14 |
| 2. Christians living under political restrictions on religious liberty | 79 | 488,285,100 | 605,098,900 | 40.1 | 42.3 | 1,832,435,000 | 2,214,408,000 | Global Table 16 |
| 3. Christians living under military rule or dictatorships | 48 | 284,878,200 | 356,430,600 | 21.8 | 24.9 | 584,759,500 | 762,642,500 | Global Table 13 |
| 4. Christians living in countries which restrict foreign missionary aid | 67 | 295,761,800 | 351,351,600 | 24.3 | 24.6 | 2,515,557,600 | 3,068,683,600 | Global Table 17 |
| 5. Christians living in countries with no political freedom or adequate civil liberties | 68 | 291,564,210 | 345,530,300 | 24.0 | 24.2 | 1,598,799,300 | 1,904,308,200 | Global Table 14 |
| 6. Christians living under anti-Christian regimes | 59 | 205,924,500 | 269,699,400 | 16.9 | 18.9 | 1,536,982,000 | 1,948,948,500 | Global Table 15 |
| 7. Christians living under atheistic regimes | 30 | 193,311,400 | 254,103,200 | 15.9 | 17.8 | 1,156,793,000 | 1,488,355,500 | Global Table 15 |
| 8. Christians experiencing severe state interference in religion, obstruction or harassment | 37 | 198,636,700 | 224,445,200 | 16.3 | 15.7 | 1,414,211,000 | 1,675,039,000 | Global Table 16 |
| 9. Christians living in closed countries which prohibit foreign missionary aid | 25 | 143,459,100 | 155,543,900 | 11.8 | 10.9 | 1,126,718,100 | 1,306,316,100 | Global Table 17 |
| 10. Crypto-Christians (secret believers unknown to or unrecognized by the state) | 65 | 55,699,700 | 70,395,000 | 4.6 | 4.9 | 775,314,000 | | Global Table 4 |
| 11. Christians in states committed to total suppression or eradication of religion | 3 | 2,316,600 | 319,300 | 0.2 | 0.02 | 22,626,000 | | Global Table 16 |
| **GLOBAL CHRISTIANITY/WORLD POPULATION** | 223 | 1,216,579,400 | 1,429,589,300 | 100.0 | 100.0 | 3,610,034,600 | 4,373,917,700 | Global Table 4 |

1. Christians living under hostile political regimes, or experiencing severely-curtailed political and religious liberties, are often said to constitute the so-called 'underground church', or 'the church of silence'. There are several different ways of enumerating this phenomenon. Eleven such ways are set out in tabular form below, in ascending order of curtailment of civil and religious freedoms and rights.
2. The column headed 'Countries' enumerates the number of states or countries involved in 1980; the next 4 columns give the total Christians involved (as absolute numbers and as percentages of global Christianity), and the next 2 the total populations involved. The last column gives the relevant Global Tables where the figures quoted may be found in the context of fuller definitions and global statistics. The last row gives global totals (not totals of the preceding 11 rows), for purposes of comparison.

**Absolute poverty.** Scene of Anglican work in Bangladesh, world's poorest country (GNP per capita, US$ 90 per year). Worldwide, some 190 million Christians live in similar absolute poverty.

### Christianity and poverty

Some 46% of the world, 2.0 billion people, eke out a living in 26 countries each with a per capita income of under UK£100 (US$235) per year. In the world's 172 less developed countries, 780 million live in absolute poverty, a clearly-defined category that represents 'a condition of life so characterized by malnutrition, illiteracy and disease as to be beneath any reasonable definition of human decency' (World Bank, 1980). This total increases annually as the gap between affluence and poverty widens rapidly almost everywhere. Among the consequences are: permanently unsettled refugees, now 16 million, increase in number each year; 20% of the Third World, and 33% in several countries, suffer from severe protein-calorie malnutrition; 40% remain without adequate shelter; 80% do not have access to adequate water supply; 850 million have little or no access to schools; and 500 million exist on the edge of starvation. Altogether, some 1.5 billion human beings on earth are malnourished. A further consequence is seething unrest, anger, hatred towards the affluent world, and revolutionary goals.

Christians suffer along with others in this predicament. Some 109 million Christians live in the 26 poorest countries. In all developing countries, Christians living in absolute poverty number 190 million (24% of the 780 million absolutely poor, or 13.3% of all Christians); half of them live in Latin America, a third in Africa, the rest in South and Southeast Asia. This is 'the church of the poor'. By the world's standards, they have nothing. They are far from being spiritual paupers, however. Some of the most dynamic forms of Christianity today, and the most rapid church growth, are found in these areas of material poverty and destitution.

It is not surprising, then, that the church, entrusted with the gospel of Christ's compassion for the poor, should have become heavily involved in correcting the injustices of poverty (see Part 13, especially Topic 17).

**Riches out of poverty.** Although 28% of sub-Saharan Africans live in absolute poverty, rich and dynamic new forms of faith in Christ emerge continually; as here, in Zimbabwe.

## CHURCH & STATE, FREEDOM & PERSECUTION

### Christians and political freedom

Using an objective and non-partisan typology, we can classify 74 countries in 1980 as politically free, 81 as partially politically free, and 68 as politically not free (see Global Table 14). The first category embraces 853 million people and 566 million Christians (39.6% of all Christians). The rest have to live under regimes practising varying degrees of political repression.

### State attitudes to religion

In the year 1900, there were 145 religious countries (countries regarding themselves as officially religious), 78 secular countries, and no officially atheistic ones (Global Table 15 and Global Map 3). With increasing secularization, religious countries fell to 114 by 1970 and to 101 by 1980. Secular countries increased somewhat to 92. Atheistic states mushroomed from nil to 17 in 1970 and to 30 by 1980 (38 if one includes states that are Marxist but not or not yet Communist).

In 1980, 1,307 million people lived in these religious countries, 1,579 millions under secular regimes, and 1,488 millions under atheistic regimes. Of all Christians, 662 millions lived in religious countries, 513 millions under secular regimes, and 254 millions under atheistic regimes.

### Religious liberty and persecution

Religious freedom in a country may be quite different, de facto, to what the state professes about it and what it purports to guarantee in its constitution. In fact, in 79 countries some 2.2 billion people (50.6% of the world in 1980) live under restrictions on their religious freedom, despite the guarantees in those countries' constitutions and in the 1948 United Nations' *Universal Declaration of Human Rights* (see Global Map 4, and Global Tables 16 and 31 for fuller details). The worst recent case of persecution has been the 1966–67 Great Proletarian Revolution in China. This was history's most systematic attempt ever, by a single nation, to eradicate and destroy Christianity and all religion. In this it failed.

### The 'underground church'

There are several different ways of enumerating the so-called 'underground' church, or the 'churches of silence', by which is meant Christians living under hostile or unfavourable regimes or circumstances. Eleven such ways may be seen set out in tabular form in Global Table 3, in ascending order of curtailment of their civil or religious freedoms. At the top of the scale, one can see that 60.4% of all Christians live in countries where civil liberties are curtailed. Lower down, we see that 16% of all Christians (224 million) live under severe state interference and harassment in religion. Towards the bottom end, some 4.9% of all Christians exist as crypto-Christians, refusing to publicize their religious beliefs or divulge them to the state, in order to protect their rights from hostile states. At the bottom of the scale live a tiny handful—319,300 in 1980—who have to endure living for Christ in states committed to the total suppression or eradication of Christianity and all religion.

As the World Council of Churches resolved at its 1975 Nairobi Assembly: 'No-one—imprisoned, tortured, harassed or persecuted—should escape the vigilance of the praying church'.

## CHRISTIANITY IN THE GLOBAL RELIGIOUS CONTEXT

### Religious pluralism today

Global Table 4 sets out the fortunes of the world's 20 distinct major religions, religious systems or quasi-religions across the 20th century. Almost all of these religions have expanded numerically during these 8 decades. Most have also expanded geographically: thus, Muslims now form significantly large communities in 162 countries, Hindus in 84 countries, Buddhists in 84 also, Jews in 112 countries, whilst Baha'is have planted their faith significantly in no less than 192 countries.

### Erosion of Christianity's numerical strength

Global Table 4 also summarizes in statistical form the fortunes of Christianity in the 20th century in its total global context. It shows the enormous numerical increases of almost all categories of Christians—those professing in censuses (sometimes called 'confessing Christians'), those who are affiliated church members

**Decline and resurgence.** *Above.* Theravada Buddhists in Burma. Buddhism worldwide is losing a nett 900,000 persons a year to agnosticism, yet has recently spread to 84 countries.

on the churches' rolls, and those who regularly practise their faith. But it also shows the gradual numerical decline of these categories when expressed as percentages of the world's total population.

### Decline within all world religions

This gradual decline of Christianity must however be seen in context. It is not Christianity alone which is in decline; it is the entire phenomenon of religion. All the other major world religions have suffered similarly, some catastrophically. At the same time, revivals of religion are taking place in widespread secularized areas. One must therefore be careful not to exaggerate the progress of secularization. The best way to portray the trends is to quote the actual figures, as obtainable from Global Table 4: whilst the proportion of religionists of all kinds has declined from 80.4% of the world in 1970 to 79.2% in 1980, their absolute numbers have increased over that period from 2,902 millions to 3,463 millions.

### The persistence of tribal religion

Startling evidence of religion's power to survive in an anti-religious world can be found in the persistence since 1900 of tribal religions. These are the faiths which are also termed primal religions, traditional religions, or local religions, and which cover animism, shamanism, and the like. The expectation in 1900 was that these religions, more than any others, were doomed and would disappear completely within a generation. Not only would Christianity provide an irresistible alternative; secular advances also—in education, science, technology, colonialism, communications—would destroy them in a decade or two. The prognosis of the World Missionary Conference (Edinburgh 1910) concerning the so-called primitive peoples was:

> Most of these peoples will have lost their ancient faiths within a generation, and will accept that culture-religion with which they first come into contact.

The ancient faiths did not disappear as expected. Despite secularization, and despite vast numbers of conversions from their ranks to Christianity, Hinduism and Islam, the absolute numbers of tribal religionists including shamanists have increased markedly and regularly in many countries from 1900-1980. In the year 2000 there will very likely be 110 million of them across the world, almost the same as their total of 117 million in 1900.

### The meteoric rise of secular quasi-religions

Equally startling has been the meteoric growth of secularism in its religious forms. Two immense quasi-religious systems have emerged at the expense of the world religions: agnosticism (also termed secularism, materialism, non-religion, etc) and atheism (also termed anti-religion or irreligion). Variations include secularism, scientific materialism, atheistic communism, nationalism, nazism, fascism, Maoism, liberal humanism and numerous constructed or fabricated pseudo-religions. From a miniscule presence in 1900, a mere 0.2% of the globe, these systems have mushroomed to 20.8% of the globe by 1980. They are today increasing at the extraordinary rate of 8.5 million new converts each year, and are likely to reach one billion adherents by the year 1984. A large percentage of their members are the children, grandchildren or great-grandchildren of persons who in their lifetimes were practising Christians. No Christian strategist in 1900 had envisaged such a massive rate of defection from Christianity within its 19th-century heartlands.

Global Table 4. GLOBAL ADHERENTS OF ALL RELIGIONS, AD 1900-2000.

| Year: | 1900 | | mid-1970 | | Annual change, 1970-1985 | | | | mid-1975 | | mid-1980 | | mid-1985 | | 2000 | | Countries |
|---|---|---|---|---|---|---|---|---|---|---|---|---|---|---|---|---|---|
| | *Adherents* | % | *Adherents* | % | *Natural* | *Conversion* | *Total* | *Rate* | *Adherents* | % | *Adherents* | % | *Adherents* | % | *Adherents* | % | |
| **Christians** | **558,056,332** | **34.4** | **1,216,579,421** | **33.7** | **21,414,259** | **196,449** | **21,610,708** | **1.64** | **1,316,780,851** | **33.2** | **1,432,686,519** | **32.8** | **1,548,592,187** | **32.4** | **2,019,921,366** | **32.3** | **223** |
| crypto-Christians | 3,572,357 | 0.2 | 55,699,695 | 1.5 | 886,385 | 583,146 | 1,469,531 | 2.35 | 62,605,240 | 1.6 | 70,395,020 | 1.6 | 78,184,800 | 1.6 | 106,208,730 | 1.7 | 65 |
| professing | 554,483,975 | 34.2 | 1,160,879,726 | 32.2 | 20,527,874 | −386,697 | 20,141,177 | 1.61 | 1,254,175,611 | 31.6 | 1,362,291,499 | 31.1 | 1,470,407,387 | 30.8 | 1,913,712,636 | 30.6 | 221 |
| Roman Catholics | 271,990,786 | 16.8 | 668,023,829 | 18.5 | 13,782,658 | 330,662 | 14,133,320 | 1.92 | 734,092,076 | 18.5 | 809,157,029 | 18.5 | 884,221,982 | 18.5 | 1,169,462,660 | 18.7 | 218 |
| Spiritist Catholics | 5,859,700 | 0.4 | 21,859,500 | 0.6 | 644,477 | 186,089 | 830,566 | 3.24 | 25,643,670 | 0.6 | 30,165,160 | 0.7 | 34,686,650 | 0.7 | 53,672,300 | 0.9 | 13 |
| Evangelical Catholics | 960,430 | 0.1 | 16,648,380 | 0.5 | 587,362 | 241,371 | 828,733 | 4.06 | 20,431,410 | 0.5 | 24,935,710 | 0.6 | 29,440,010 | 0.6 | 48,052,180 | 0.8 | 31 |
| Christo-pagans | 8,322,900 | 0.5 | 12,919,660 | 0.4 | 415,021 | −137,097 | 277,924 | 1.95 | 14,266,400 | 0.4 | 15,698,900 | 0.4 | 17,131,400 | 0.4 | 20,239,700 | 0.3 | 16 |
| Protestants | 119,662,529 | 7.4 | 259,044,841 | 7.2 | 3,312,646 | −1,182,331 | 2,130,315 | 0.80 | 267,962,303 | 6.8 | 280,348,001 | 6.4 | 292,733,699 | 6.1 | 357,489,414 | 5.7 | 209 |
| Orthodox | 121 245,310 | 7.5 | 111,898,590 | 3.1 | 1,346,056 | −93,992 | 1,252,064 | 1.06 | 118,001,080 | 3.0 | 124,419,230 | 2.8 | 130,837,380 | 2.7 | 153,051,810 | 2.4 | 96 |
| Anglicans | 33,030,340 | 2.0 | 59,914,871 | 1.7 | 742,794 | −213,445 | 529,349 | 0.85 | 62,368,507 | 1.6 | 65,208,364 | 1.5 | 68,048,221 | 1.4 | 82,801,482 | 1.3 | 144 |
| Non-White indigenous | 7,241,010 | 0.4 | 49,022,430 | 1.4 | 1,167,779 | 643,089 | 1,810,868 | 3.16 | 57,365,720 | 1.4 | 67,131,110 | 1.5 | 76,896,500 | 1.6 | 124,917,260 | 2.0 | 90 |
| Marginal Protestants | 1,040,150 | 0.1 | 10,168,545 | 0.3 | 143,880 | 142,287 | 286,167 | 2.49 | 11,494,935 | 0.3 | 13,030,205 | 0.3 | 14,565,475 | 0.3 | 22,150,680 | 0.4 | 90 |
| Catholics (non-Roman) | 273,850 | 0.0 | 2,806,620 | 0.1 | 32,061 | −12,967 | 19,094 | 0.66 | 2,890,990 | 0.1 | 2,997,560 | 0.1 | 3,104,130 | 0.1 | 3,839,330 | 0.1 | 35 |
| nominal | 36,493,151 | 2.2 | 84,769,841 | 2.3 | 1,658,769 | 793,920 | 2,452,689 | 2.56 | 95,928,718 | 2.4 | 109,296,794 | 2.5 | 122,664,870 | 2.6 | 175,307,174 | 2.8 | 157 |
| affiliated | 521,563,181 | 32.2 | 1,131,809,580 | 31.4 | 19,755,490 | −597,471 | 19,158,019 | 1.57 | 1,220,852,133 | 30.8 | 1,323,389,725 | 30.3 | 1,425,927,317 | 29.8 | 1,844,614,192 | 29.5 | 221 |
| doubly-affiliated | −3,020 510 | −0.2 | −26,711,568 | −0.7 | −737,099 | −221,973 | −959,072 | 3.08 | −31,099,120 | −0.8 | −36,302,280 | −0.8 | −41,505,440 | −0.9 | −62,275,880 | −1.0 | 34 |
| disaffiliated | −182,400 | −0.0 | −10,848,188 | −0.3 | −95,013 | −356,720 | −451,733 | 3.42 | −13,226,950 | −0.3 | −15,365,510 | −0.4 | −17,504,070 | −0.4 | −14,797,500 | −0.2 | 9 |
| total practising | 469,259,773 | *90* | 884,021,780 | *78* | 14,995,485 | −1,562,133 | 13,433,352 | 1.42 | 946,362,223 | *77* | 1,018,355,317 | *77* | 1,090,348,411 | *76* | 1,330,325,057 | *72* | 221 |
| non-practising | 52,303,418 | *10* | 247,787,776 | *22* | 4,760,005 | 964,662 | 5,724,667 | 2.09 | 274,489,905 | *23* | 305,034,408 | *23* | 335,578,911 | *24* | 514,289,155 | *28* | 221 |
| Roman Catholics | 266,419,407 | 16.4 | 672,319,062 | 18.6 | 13,605,375 | −571,280 | 13,034,095 | 1.78 | 733,215,226 | 18.5 | 802,659,956 | 18.4 | 872,104,686 | 18.2 | 1,132,541,508 | 18.1 | 219 |
| Catholic pentecostals | 0 | 0.0 | 238,500 | 0.0 | 26,134 | 427,155 | 453,289 | 22.71 | 1,995,730 | 0.0 | 4,771,390 | 0.1 | 7,547,050 | 0.2 | 23,101,300 | 0.4 | 75 |
| Protestants | 103,056,655 | 6.4 | 233,424,245 | 6.5 | 3,028,904 | −155,570 | 2,873,334 | 1.17 | 246,401,095 | 6.2 | 262,157,585 | 6.0 | 277,914,075 | 5.8 | 345,709,110 | 5.5 | 212 |
| Evangelicals | 52,135,480 | 3.2 | 124,775,274 | 3.5 | 2,087,863 | 1,124,125 | 3,211,988 | 2.30 | 139,588,110 | 3.5 | 156,895,150 | 3.6 | 174,202,190 | 3.6 | 247,664,830 | 4.0 | 192 |
| Neo-pentecostals | 0 | 0.0 | 824,100 | 0.0 | 29,182 | 317,088 | 346,270 | 16.39 | 2,112,700 | 0.1 | 4,286,800 | 0.1 | 6,460,900 | 0.1 | 10,818,000 | 0.2 | 38 |
| Orthodox | 115,897,704 | 7.2 | 143,402,488 | 4.0 | 1,712,059 | 21,487 | 1,733,546 | 1.14 | 151,827,165 | 3.8 | 160,737,930 | 3.7 | 169,648,695 | 3.5 | 199,819,040 | 3.2 | 107 |
| Orthodox pentecostals | 0 | 0.0 | 15,200 | 0.0 | 661 | 13,519 | 14,180 | 19.42 | 73,000 | 0.0 | 157,000 | 0.0 | 241,000 | 0.0 | 680,000 | 0.0 | 6 |
| Non-White indigenous | 7,743,060 | 0.5 | 58,701,960 | 1.6 | 1,530,638 | 817,269 | 2,347,907 | 3.38 | 69,564,535 | 1.8 | 82,181,070 | 1.9 | 94,797,605 | 2.0 | 154,140,440 | 2.5 | 145 |
| Evangelicals | 5,320,000 | 0.3 | 13,551,000 | 0.4 | 129,090 | 39,910 | 169,000 | 1.18 | 14,333,000 | 0.4 | 15,241,000 | 0.3 | 16,149,000 | 0.3 | 18,775,000 | 0.3 | 1 |
| Black neo-pentecostals | 0 | 0.0 | 400,000 | 0.0 | 6,500 | 23,500 | 30,000 | 5.45 | 550,000 | 0.0 | 700,000 | 0.0 | 850,000 | 0.0 | 1,600,000 | 0.0 | 1 |
| Anglicans | 30,573,665 | 1.9 | 47,556,975 | 1.3 | 518,392 | −293,687 | 224,705 | 0.46 | 48,507,937 | 1.2 | 49,804,014 | 1.1 | 51,100,091 | 1.1 | 61,037,174 | 1.0 | 165 |
| Evangelicals | 14,690,910 | 0.9 | 15,088,700 | 0.4 | 244,848 | 97,682 | 342,530 | 2.06 | 16,662,100 | 0.4 | 18,514,000 | 0.4 | 20,365,900 | 0.4 | 29,062,300 | 0.5 | 27 |
| Anglican pentecostals | 0 | 0.0 | 109,900 | 0.0 | 4,672 | 93,358 | 98,030 | 18.86 | 519,650 | 0.0 | 1,090,200 | 0.0 | 1,660,750 | 0.0 | 2,662,200 | 0.0 | 18 |
| Marginal Protestants | 927,580 | 0.1 | 10,830,221 | 0.3 | 158,251 | 166,481 | 324,732 | 2.62 | 12,384,245 | 0.3 | 14,077,520 | 0.3 | 15,770,795 | 0.3 | 24,106,170 | 0.4 | 176 |
| Catholics (non-Roman) | 276,020 | 0.0 | 3,134,385 | 0.1 | 33,983 | −3,478 | 30,505 | 0.93 | 3,278,000 | 0.1 | 3,439,440 | 0.1 | 3,600,880 | 0.1 | 4,334,130 | 0.1 | 59 |
| **Muslims** | **200,102,284** | **12.4** | **550,919,011** | **15.3** | **17,063,381** | **140,371** | **17,203,752** | **2.74** | **628,847,789** | **15.9** | **722,956,504** | **16.5** | **817,065,219** | **17.1** | **1,200,653,040** | **19.2** | **162** |
| Sunnis | 173,111,354 | 10.7 | 465,826,991 | 12.9 | 14,584,781 | −249,680 | 14,335,101 | 2.70 | 530,500,789 | 13.4 | 609,178,000 | 13.9 | 680,855,211 | 14.2 | 999,826,320 | 16.0 | 157 |
| Hanafites | 106,611,354 | 6.6 | 238,500,991 | 6.6 | 8,179,481 | −723,780 | 7,455,701 | 2.77 | 268,780,789 | 6.8 | 313,058,000 | 7.2 | 350,335,211 | 7.3 | 508,226,320 | 8.1 | 106 |
| Shafiites | 39,000,000 | 2.4 | 112,000,000 | 3.1 | 3,551,800 | 233,900 | 3,785,700 | 2.89 | 130,900,000 | 3.3 | 149,857,000 | 3.4 | 168,814,000 | 3.5 | 248,800,000 | 4.0 | 83 |
| Malikites | 27,000,000 | 1.7 | 114,186,000 | 3.2 | 2,817,700 | 240,000 | 3,057,700 | 2.36 | 129,500,000 | 3.3 | 144,763,000 | 3.3 | 160,026,000 | 3.3 | 240,300,000 | 3.8 | 51 |
| Hanbalites | 500,000 | 0.0 | 1,140,000 | 0.0 | 35,800 | 200 | 36,000 | 2.73 | 1,320,000 | 0.0 | 1,500,000 | 0.0 | 1,680,000 | 0.0 | 2,500,000 | 0.0 | 18 |
| Shias | 26,000,000 | 1.6 | 79,500,000 | 2.2 | 2,291,800 | 318,200 | 2,610,000 | 2.85 | 91,462,000 | 2.3 | 105,600,000 | 2.4 | 126,738,000 | 2.7 | 185,000,000 | 3.0 | 60 |
| Ithna-Asharis | 22,250,000 | 1.4 | 65,270,000 | 1.8 | 1,770,800 | 304,900 | 2,075,700 | 2.78 | 74,561,000 | 1.9 | 86,027,000 | 2.0 | 104,493,000 | 2.2 | 151,700,000 | 2.4 | 54 |
| Ismailis | 2,300,000 | 0.1 | 9,700,000 | 0.3 | 376,100 | 13,900 | 390,000 | 3.35 | 11,650,000 | 0.3 | 13,600,000 | 0.3 | 15,550,000 | 0.3 | 23,500,000 | 0.4 | 35 |
| Zaydis | 1,200,000 | 0.1 | 3,760,000 | 0.1 | 120,300 | −500 | 119,800 | 2.75 | 4,359,000 | 0.1 | 4,958,000 | 0.1 | 5,557,000 | 0.1 | 8,200,000 | 0.1 | 8 |
| Alawites | 250,000 | 0.0 | 770,000 | 0.0 | 24,600 | −100 | 24,500 | 2.75 | 892,000 | 0.0 | 1,015,000 | 0.0 | 1,138,000 | 0.0 | 1,600,000 | 0.0 | 11 |
| Schismatics | 990,930 | 0.1 | 5,592,020 | 0.2 | 186,800 | 71,851 | 258,651 | 3.76 | 6,885,000 | 0.2 | 8,178,504 | 0.2 | 9,472,008 | 0.2 | 15,826,720 | 0.3 | 85 |
| Ahmadis | 70,030 | 0.0 | 2,635,220 | 0.1 | 97,383 | 38,581 | 135,964 | 4.18 | 3,255,980 | 0.1 | 3,994,860 | 0.1 | 4,733,740 | 0.1 | 9,216,720 | 0.1 | 56 |
| Kharijites | 320,000 | 0.0 | 780,000 | 0.0 | 26,000 | −1,650 | 24,350 | 2.70 | 901,800 | 0.0 | 1,023,500 | 0.0 | 1,145,200 | 0.0 | 1,700,000 | 0.0 | 7 |
| Druzes | 71,000 | 0.0 | 374,800 | 0.0 | 14,000 | −970 | 13,030 | 2.96 | 440,000 | 0.0 | 505,100 | 0.0 | 570,200 | 0.0 | 810,000 | 0.0 | 8 |
| Black Muslims | 0 | 0.0 | 200,000 | 0.0 | 4,500 | 55,500 | 60,000 | 12.00 | 500,000 | 0.0 | 800,000 | 0.0 | 1,100,000 | 0.0 | 1,700,000 | 0.0 | 3 |
| Yazidis | 29,900 | 0.0 | 102,000 | 0.0 | 3,600 | −100 | 3,500 | 2.93 | 119,500 | 0.0 | 137,000 | 0.0 | 154,500 | 0.0 | 200,000 | 0.0 | 4 |
| Other sectarians | 500,000 | 0.0 | 1,500,000 | 0.0 | 41,317 | −19,510 | 21,807 | 1.31 | 1,667,720 | 0.0 | 1,718,044 | 0.0 | 1,768,368 | 0.0 | 2,200,000 | 0.0 | 20 |
| **Non-religious** | **2,923,330** | **0.2** | **543,065,287** | **15.0** | **9,314,352** | **7,969,260** | **17,283,612** | **2.76** | **626,017,979** | **15.8** | **715,901,416** | **16.4** | **805,784,853** | **16.9** | **1,071,888,370** | **17.1** | **177** |
| **Hindus** | **203,033,330** | **12.5** | **465,784,832** | **12.8** | **12,144,744** | **−248,235** | **11,896,509** | **2.30** | **517,932,375** | **13.1** | **582,749,920** | **13.3** | **647,567,465** | **13.5** | **859,252,260** | **13.7** | **84** |
| Vaishnavites | 143,183,330 | 8.8 | 324,649,000 | 9.0 | 8,452,144 | −224,544 | 8,227,600 | 2.28 | 360,452,475 | 9.1 | 406,925,000 | 9.3 | 453,397,525 | 9.5 | 595,752,260 | 9.5 | 66 |
| Shaivites | 52,800,000 | 3.3 | 115,946,000 | 3.2 | 3,067,400 | −93,300 | 2,974,100 | 2.27 | 130,816,000 | 3.3 | 145,687,000 | 3.3 | 160,558,000 | 3.4 | 214,800,000 | 3.4 | 42 |
| Saktists | 6,700,000 | 0.4 | 13,932,832 | 0.4 | 367,900 | −16,491 | 351,409 | 2.24 | 15,689,900 | 0.4 | 17,446,920 | 0.4 | 19,203,940 | 0.4 | 22,500,000 | 0.4 | 25 |
| Neo-Hindus | 100,000 | 0.0 | 6,957,000 | 0.2 | 195,800 | 82,600 | 278,400 | 3.33 | 8,349,000 | 0.2 | 9,741,000 | 0.2 | 11,133,000 | 0.2 | 21,000,000 | 0.3 | 47 |
| Reformed Hindus | 250,000 | 0.0 | 2,300,000 | 0.1 | 61,500 | 3,500 | 65,000 | 2.48 | 2,625,000 | 0.1 | 2,950,000 | 0.1 | 3,275,000 | 0.1 | 5,200,000 | 0.1 | 22 |
| **Buddhists** | **127,158,971** | **7.8** | **231,672,189** | **6.4** | **5,112,463** | **−908,123** | **4,204,340** | **1.67** | **251,860,400** | **6.3** | **273,715,590** | **6.3** | **295,570,780** | **6.2** | **359,092,100** | **5.7** | **84** |
| Mahayana | 71,558,971 | 4.4 | 130,140,189 | 3.6 | 2,865,473 | −503,733 | 2,361,740 | 1.67 | 141,160,400 | 3.6 | 153,757,590 | 3.5 | 166,354,780 | 3.5 | 201,842,100 | 3.2 | 77 |
| Theravada | 48,100,000 | 3.0 | 87,700,000 | 2.4 | 1,940,490 | −349,690 | 1,590,800 | 1.66 | 95,600,000 | 2.4 | 103,608,000 | 2.4 | 111,616,000 | 2.3 | 135,850,000 | 2.2 | 18 |
| Tantrayana | 7,500,000 | 0.5 | 13,832,000 | 0.4 | 306,500 | −54,700 | 251,800 | 1.67 | 15,100,000 | 0.4 | 16,350,000 | 0.4 | 17,600,000 | 0.4 | 21,400,000 | 0.3 | 19 |
| Chinese folk-religionists | 380,403,738 | 23.5 | 214,391,509 | 5.9 | 3,443,710 | −5,103,324 | −1,659,614 | −0.80 | 207,596,706 | 5.2 | 197,795,366 | 4.5 | 187,994,026 | 3.9 | 158,470,664 | 2.5 | 55 |
| Atheists | 225,620 | 0.0 | 165,288,500 | 4.6 | 2,446,459 | 536,627 | 2,983,086 | 1.66 | 179,595,180 | 4.5 | 195,119,360 | 4.5 | 210,643,540 | 4.4 | 262,447,550 | 4.2 | 113 |
| Tribal religionists | 106,339,595 | 6.6 | 88,077,403 | 2.4 | 2,374,577 | 2,185,971 | 188,606 | 0.21 | 88,796,520 | 2.2 | 89,963,450 | 2.1 | 91,130,380 | 1.9 | 100,535,850 | 1.6 | 93 |
| New-Religionists | 5,910,000 | 0.4 | 76,443,120 | 2.1 | 1,830,567 | 127,301 | 1,957,868 | 2.28 | 85,726,000 | 2.2 | 96,021,800 | 2.2 | 106,317,600 | 2.2 | 138,263,800 | 2.2 | 22 |
| Shamanists | 11,341,020 | 0.7 | 15,927,300 | 0.4 | 308,883 | −551,336 | −242,453 | 0.41 | 14,840,060 | 0.4 | 13,502,770 | 0.4 | 12,165,480 | 0.4 | 9,946,530 | 0.3 | 7 |
| Jews | 12,269,790 | 0.8 | 15,185,936 | 0.4 | 185,873 | −10,644 | 175,229 | 1.09 | 16,038,400 | 0.4 | 16,938,230 | 0.4 | 17,838,060 | 0.4 | 20,173,560 | 0.3 | 112 |
| Ashkenazis | 10,920,000 | 0.7 | 12,756,000 | 0.4 | 156,000 | −8,600 | 147,400 | 1.09 | 13,470,000 | 0.3 | 14,230,000 | 0.3 | 14,990,000 | 0.3 | 19,946,000 | 0.3 | 108 |
| Orientals | 700,000 | 0.0 | 1,520,000 | 0.0 | 18,600 | −1,200 | 17,400 | 1.08 | 1,604,000 | 0.0 | 1,694,000 | 0.0 | 1,784,000 | 0.0 | 2,017,000 | 0.0 | 20 |
| Sefardis | 300,000 | 0.0 | 607,000 | 0.0 | 7,500 | −450 | 7,050 | 1.10 | 641,500 | 0.0 | 677,500 | 0.0 | 713,500 | 0.0 | 807,000 | 0.0 | 65 |
| Karaites | 13,400 | 0.0 | 15,500 | 0.0 | 160 | 0 | 160 | 0.98 | 16,300 | 0.0 | 17,100 | 0.0 | 17,900 | 0.0 | 20,500 | 0.0 | 2 |
| Sikhs | 2,960,600 | 0.2 | 10,612,200 | 0.3 | 333,367 | 29,849 | 363,216 | 2.94 | 12,338,830 | 0.3 | 14,244,360 | 0.3 | 16,149,890 | 0.3 | 23,831,700 | 0.4 | 19 |
| Confucians | 640,000 | 0.0 | 4,516,000 | 0.1 | 94,125 | −47,725 | 46,400 | 0.98 | 4,753,000 | 0.1 | 4,980,000 | 0.1 | 5,207,000 | 0.1 | 5,356,000 | 0.1 | 1 |
| Shintoists | 6,720,000 | 0.4 | 4,173,000 | 0.1 | 46,252 | −110,914 | −64,662 | −1.66 | 3,889,200 | 0.1 | 3,526,380 | 0.1 | 3,163,560 | 0.1 | 2,658,000 | 0.1 | 1 |
| Baha'is | 9,025 | 0.0 | 2,659,426 | 0.1 | 78,906 | 37,413 | 116,319 | 3.63 | 3,202,675 | 0.1 | 3,822,630 | 0.1 | 4,442,585 | 0.1 | 7,649,150 | 0.1 | 194 |
| Jains | 1,323,100 | 0.1 | 2,616,300 | 0.1 | 67,123 | −4,373 | 62,750 | 2.00 | 3,138,500 | 0.1 | 3,243,800 | 0.1 | 3,349,100 | 0.1 | 4,303,800 | 0.1 | 5 |
| Afro-American spiritists | 246,940 | 0.0 | 1,777,100 | 0.0 | 65,072 | 67,257 | 132,329 | 5.54 | 2,390,460 | 0.1 | 3,100,390 | 0.1 | 3,810,320 | 0.1 | 7,132,900 | 0.1 | 21 |
| Spiritists | 58,600 | 0.0 | 1,384,900 | 0.0 | 50,597 | 48,357 | 98,954 | 5.35 | 1,850,770 | 0.0 | 2,374,440 | 0.1 | 2,898,110 | 0.1 | 5,605,700 | 0.1 | 13 |
| Parsis | 108,290 | 0.0 | 120,970 | 0.0 | 3,339 | −14 | 3,325 | 2.43 | 136,640 | 0.0 | 154,220 | 0.0 | 171,800 | 0.0 | 218,700 | 0.0 | 10 |
| Mandaeans | 8,000 | 0.0 | 23,000 | 0.0 | 908 | −88 | 820 | 3.03 | 27,100 | 0.0 | 31,200 | 0.0 | 35,300 | 0.0 | 49,000 | 0.0 | 2 |
| Other religionists | 48,195 | 0.0 | 817,001 | 0.0 | 9,356 | 17,863 | 27,219 | 2.86 | 951,660 | 0.0 | 1,089,190 | 0.0 | 1,226,720 | 0.0 | 2,191,960 | 0.0 | 98 |
| **WORLD POPULATION** | **1,619,886,760** | **100.0** | **3,610,034,405** | **100.0** | **76,388,313** | **0** | **76,388,313** | **1.93** | **3,966,711,095** | **100.0** | **4,373,917,535** | **100.0** | **4,781,123,975** | **100.0** | **6,259,642,000** | **100.0** | **223** |
| Western world | 487,886,760 | 30.1 | 575,159,150 | 15.9 | 4,361,005 | −16 | 4,360,989 | 0.73 | 596,490,095 | 15.0 | 618,769,035 | 14.1 | 641,048,000 | 13.4 | 708,510,000 | 11.3 | 35 |
| Communist world | 0 | 0.0 | 1,189,066,000 | 32.9 | 18,272,200 | 11,656,750 | 29,928,950 | 2.32 | 1,289,256,000 | 32.5 | 1,488,355,500 | 34.0 | 1,596,797,500 | 33.4 | 2,090,000,000 | 33.4 | 30 |
| Third World | 1,132,000,000 | 69.9 | 1,845,809,255 | 51.1 | 53,755,108 | −11,656,734 | 42,098,374 | 2.02 | 2,080,965,000 | 52.5 | 2,266,793,000 | 51.8 | 2,543,278,475 | 53.2 | 3,461,132,000 | 55.3 | 158 |

## DYNAMICS OF RELIGIOUS CHANGE TODAY

### Great complexity, with dynamic change

These tables depict a situation of enormous religious complexity in today's world. Moreover, the situation is anything but static. Every year millions of people are changing their religious profession or their Christian affiliation. Mass defections are occurring from stagnant majority religions to newer religions. Mass conversions under way in many countries are accruing primarily to missionary religions aggressively engaged in proselytism. Our tables document these phenomena by analysing in detail the decade 1970-1980, and by giving, for all religions and for the different categories of Christians, the annual numerical change divided into natural increase and conversion change.

### Natural increase among Christians

A large part of this change is demographic increase due to the so-called population explosion. Over the decade 1970-1980, this accounted for an average of 21,414,000 new Christians each year (58,700 a day). By 1981 this rate had increased to 23,353,000 a year (64,000 a day). These are nett totals; in fact, births among Christians are markedly higher at 39,113,000 a year (107,200 a day), offset by 15,760,000 deaths a year (43,200 Christians die every day).

### Massive gains offset by massive losses

From the Christian standpoint, the overall situation presents a mixed picture. On the one hand, Christianity has experienced massive gains across the Third World throughout the 20th century. In Africa, Christians have mushroomed from 9.9 million in 1900 (0.6% of the world's population then) to 203 million in 1980 (4.7%). The present nett increase on that continent is 6 million new Christians a year (16,400 a day), of which 1.5 million are nett new converts (converts minus defections or apostasies). Sizeable nett conversions are also taking place in East Asia (360,000 a year), and in South Asia (447,000). A major reason for this expansion across the continents of the Third World is the attracting power of the Christian gospel of justice and the love of God for the poor and oppressed.

But on the other hand, Christianity has experienced massive losses in the Western and Communist worlds over the last 60 years. In the Soviet Union, Christians have fallen from 83.6% in 1900 to 36.1% today. In Europe and North America, nett defections from Christianity—converts to other religions or to irreligion—are now running at 1,820,500 former Christians a year. This loss is much higher if we consider only church members: 2,224,800 a year (6,000 a day). It is even higher if we are speaking of only church attenders: every year, some 2,765,100 church attenders in Europe and North America cease to be practising Christians within the 12-month period, an average loss of 7,600 every day (Global Table 23).

At the global level, these losses from Christianity in the Western and Communist worlds slightly outweigh the gains in the Third World. This can be observed by examining the trends in percentages over the period 1900-1980. In 1900, Christians numbered 34.4% of the world (37.8%, if adults only are counted; see Global Table 22). This percentage has fallen gradually over the decades until Christians in 1980 numbered 32.8% of the world (34.4% of the world's adults). Likewise, practising Christians have fallen from 29.0% of the world's population in 1900 to 23.3% today.

**Natural increase.** *Above.* Baptism of new infants in Hussite Church, Czechoslovakia. Every day, 107,200 new Christians are born worldwide, whilst 43,200 other Christians die.

**Massive conversion increase.** A 7-year comparison from Korea. (1) *Below.* 1973: crowd of 1,150,000 people on Yoido Plaza, Seoul, hear evangelist Billy Graham (5-day attendance was 3 million). (2) *Above right.* 1980: crowd of 2,700,000 persons on same site at Here's Life Korea (4-day attendance was 16.5 million); largest preaching service in history.

Global Table 5.    CHRISTIAN CULTURES AND ETHNOLINGUISTIC PEOPLES, AD 1900-2000.

1. The table divides world population, and global church membership, into the 5 races, 17 geographical races, and 7 stylized colours of mankind. Note that 'global church membership' is not identical to 'global Christianity' as enumerated in Global Table 2 et alia.
2. Totals for the 5 races, or 17 geographical races, add up to only 99.7% of the actual totals, the remainder being due to small populations too minute to classify under the countries' coded data.
3. For detailed meanings of codes, see Part 4. Culture, which also gives the 71 families and 432 peoples shown below, in its classification PEOPLES OF THE WORLD.
4. For meanings of columns for 1900-2000, see Codebook (Part 6) concerning Tables 1. Note that 'Rate' = % per year.

## 1. WORLD POPULATION

*Cultures = Families / Peoples / Groups. Annual change, 1970-1980 = Natural / Conversion / Total / Rate.*

| Race / Geographical race | Code | Families | Peoples | Groups | 1900 Adherents | % | Natural | Conversion | Total | Rate | mid-1970 Adherents | % | mid-1975 Adherents | % | mid-1980 Adherents | % | mid-1985 Adherents | % | 2000 Adherents | % |
|---|---|---|---|---|---|---|---|---|---|---|---|---|---|---|---|---|---|---|---|---|
| AUSTRALOID | A | 10 | 35 | 1,953 | 12,120,074 | 0.7 | 906,126 | 0 | 906,126 | 2.57 | 31,143,281 | 0.9 | 35,299,814 | 0.9 | 40,204,554 | 0.9 | 45,109,294 | 0.9 | 63,347,855 | 1.0 |
| Austro-Asiatic | AUG | 7 | 21 | 515 | 10,151,351 | 0.6 | 768,998 | 0 | 768,998 | 2.58 | 26,296,533 | 0.7 | 29,820,904 | 0.8 | 33,986,518 | 0.8 | 38,152,132 | 0.8 | 53,517,123 | 0.9 |
| Oceanic | AON | 3 | 14 | 1,438 | 1,968,723 | 0.1 | 137,128 | 0 | 137,128 | 2.50 | 4,846,748 | 0.1 | 5,478,910 | 0.1 | 6,218,036 | 0.1 | 6,957,162 | 0.1 | 9,830,732 | 0.2 |
| CAPOID | B | 2 | 6 | 64 | 133,390 | 0.0 | 12,420 | 0 | 12,420 | 2.60 | 422,815 | 0.0 | 478,554 | 0.0 | 547,014 | 0.0 | 615,474 | 0.0 | 960,973 | 0.0 |
| Early African | BYG | 2 | 6 | 64 | 133,390 | 0.0 | 12,420 | 0 | 12,420 | 2.60 | 422,815 | 0.0 | 478,554 | 0.0 | 547,014 | 0.0 | 615,474 | 0.0 | 960,973 | 0.0 |
| CAUCASIAN | C | 24 | 135 | 1,047 | 839,778,705 | 51.8 | 38,420,756 | 0 | 38,420,756 | 1.84 | 1,910,873,319 | 52.9 | 2,088,144,990 | 52.6 | 2,295,080,557 | 52.5 | 2,502,016,132 | 52.3 | 3,273,710,981 | 52.3 |
| European | CEW | 10 | 69 | 253 | 439,218,888 | 27.1 | 6,989,704 | 0 | 6,989,704 | 0.81 | 824,646,164 | 22.8 | 858,749,573 | 21.6 | 894,542,934 | 20.5 | 930,336,301 | 19.5 | 1,034,662,165 | 16.5 |
| Indo-Iranian—1 | CNN | 26 | 26 | 317 | 284,225,889 | 17.5 | 18,980,735 | 0 | 18,980,735 | 2.49 | 676,284,231 | 18.7 | 762,213,602 | 19.2 | 866,091,524 | 19.8 | 969,969,448 | 20.3 | 1,351,293,421 | 21.6 |
| Indo-Iranian—2 | CNT | 2 | 9 | 131 | 17,793,682 | 1.1 | 1,659,550 | 0 | 1,659,550 | 2.84 | 51,000,332 | 1.4 | 58,512,596 | 1.5 | 67,595,802 | 1.5 | 76,679,008 | 1.6 | 114,153,330 | 1.8 |
| Latin American—1 | CLT | 2 | 2 | 18 | 21,653,838 | 1.3 | 2,873,053 | 0 | 2,873,053 | 2.46 | 103,241,638 | 2.9 | 116,668,258 | 2.9 | 131,972,184 | 3.0 | 147,276,110 | 3.1 | 208,526,084 | 3.3 |
| Latin American—2 | CLN | 2 | 2 | 26 | 25,934,511 | 1.6 | 3,066,259 | 0 | 3,066,259 | 2.74 | 97,900,150 | 2.7 | 112,030,094 | 2.8 | 128,562,743 | 2.9 | 145,095,392 | 3.0 | 216,516,215 | 3.5 |
| Middle Eastern | CMT | 7 | 27 | 302 | 50,951,897 | 3.1 | 4,851,455 | 0 | 4,851,455 | 2.70 | 157,800,804 | 4.4 | 179,970,867 | 4.5 | 206,315,370 | 4.7 | 232,659,873 | 4.9 | 348,559,766 | 5.6 |
| MONGOLIAN | M | 19 | 137 | 3,653 | 671,131,638 | 41.4 | 27,675,821 | 0 | 27,675,821 | 1.87 | 1,344,159,968 | 37.2 | 1,476,707,833 | 37.2 | 1,620,918,083 | 37.1 | 1,765,128,337 | 36.9 | 2,206,707,932 | 35.3 |
| American Indian | MIR | 1 | 20 | 2,136 | 9,940,928 | 0.6 | 1,171,629 | 0 | 1,171,629 | 2.90 | 35,073,985 | 1.0 | 40,444,191 | 1.0 | 46,790,283 | 1.1 | 53,136,375 | 1.1 | 81,790,337 | 1.3 |
| Arctic-Mongoloid | MRY | 1 | 3 | 12 | 14,847 | 0.0 | 1,266 | 0 | 1,266 | 1.86 | 60,956 | 0.0 | 67,888 | 0.0 | 73,618 | 0.0 | 80,384 | 0.0 | 93,311 | 0.0 |
| Asian—1 | MSY | 11 | 80 | 1,360 | 647,268,903 | 40.0 | 26,304,845 | 0 | 26,304,845 | 1.86 | 1,284,399,320 | 35.6 | 1,410,605,997 | 35.6 | 1,547,447,659 | 35.4 | 1,684,289,320 | 35.2 | 2,094,391,547 | 33.5 |
| Asian—2 | MSW | 1 | 13 | 53 | 13,337,900 | 0.8 | 125,922 | 0 | 125,922 | 0.55 | 2,388,508 | 0.1 | 23,017,293 | 0.6 | 23,647,761 | 0.5 | 24,278,230 | 0.5 | 25,618,431 | 0.4 |
| Pacific | MPY | 3 | 21 | 92 | 569,060 | 0.0 | 72,159 | 0 | 72,159 | 2.81 | 2,237,199 | 0.1 | 2,572,464 | 0.1 | 2,958,762 | 0.1 | 3,345,064 | 0.1 | 4,814,306 | 0.1 |
| NEGRO | N | 16 | 119 | 2,276 | 90,692,308 | 5.6 | 9,134,772 | 0 | 9,134,772 | 2.59 | 311,719,305 | 8.6 | 353,228,716 | 8.9 | 403,066,942 | 9.2 | 452,905,165 | 9.5 | 695,425,668 | 11.1 |
| African—1 | NAB | 10 | 103 | 2,167 | 67,582,935 | 4.2 | 7,068,308 | 0 | 7,068,308 | 2.74 | 226,352,973 | 6.3 | 258,244,806 | 6.5 | 297,036,020 | 6.8 | 335,827,232 | 7.0 | 533,984,556 | 8.5 |
| African—2 | NAN | 1 | 1 | 20 | 868,574 | 0.1 | 91,270 | 0 | 91,270 | 2.56 | 3,135,998 | 0.1 | 3,558,671 | 0.1 | 4,048,691 | 0.1 | 4,538,710 | 0.1 | 6,653,951 | 0.1 |
| Afro-American | NFB | 5 | 15 | 89 | 22,240,799 | 1.4 | 1,975,194 | 0 | 1,975,194 | 2.16 | 82,230,334 | 2.3 | 91,425,239 | 2.3 | 101,982,231 | 2.3 | 112,539,223 | 2.4 | 154,787,161 | 2.5 |
| WORLD POPULATION | | 71 | 432 | 8,993 | 1,619,886,760 | 100.0 | 76,388,313 | 0 | 76,388,313 | 1.93 | 3,610,034,405 | 100.0 | 3,966,711,095 | 100.0 | 4,373,917,535 | 100.0 | 4,781,123,975 | 100.0 | 6,259,642,000 | 100.0 |

## 2. GLOBAL CHURCH MEMBERSHIP

*Christian cultures = Families / Peoples / Groups. Annual change, 1970-1980 = Natural / Conversion / Total / Rate.*

| Race / Geographical race | Code | Families | Peoples | Groups | 1900 Adherents | % | Natural | Conversion | Total | Rate | mid-1970 Adherents | % | mid-1975 Adherents | % | mid-1980 Adherents | % | mid-1985 Adherents | % | 2000 Adherents | % |
|---|---|---|---|---|---|---|---|---|---|---|---|---|---|---|---|---|---|---|---|---|
| AUSTRALOID | A | 5 | 14 | 1,375 | 570,570 | 0.1 | 153,506 | 49,438 | 202,940 | 3.27 | 5,282,398 | 0.5 | 6,199,484 | 0.5 | 7,311,826 | 0.6 | 8,424,157 | 0.6 | 13,147,235 | 0.7 |
| Austro-Asiatic | AUG | 2 | 2 | 305 | 348,246 | 0.1 | 52,708 | 15,224 | 67,932 | 3.13 | 1,872,845 | 0.2 | 2,168,073 | 0.2 | 2,552,182 | 0.2 | 2,936,288 | 0.2 | 4,705,091 | 0.3 |
| Oceanic | AON | 3 | 12 | 1,070 | 222,324 | 0.0 | 100,798 | 34,214 | 135,008 | 3.35 | 3,409,553 | 0.3 | 4,031,411 | 0.3 | 4,759,644 | 0.4 | 5,487,869 | 0.4 | 8,442,144 | 0.5 |
| CAPOID | B | 1 | 4 | 30 | 2,117 | 0.0 | 4,525 | 1,272 | 5,796 | 3.27 | 150,552 | 0.0 | 177,348 | 0.0 | 208,507 | 0.0 | 239,668 | 0.0 | 388,562 | 0.0 |
| Early African | BYG | 1 | 4 | 30 | 2,117 | 0.0 | 4,525 | 1,272 | 5,796 | 3.27 | 150,552 | 0.0 | 177,348 | 0.0 | 208,507 | 0.0 | 239,668 | 0.0 | 388,668 | 0.0 |
| CAUCASIAN | C | 15 | 70 | 298 | 465,191,992 | 89.2 | 11,547,179 | -2,105,228 | 9,351,950 | 1.05 | 846,591,923 | 74.8 | 890,659,601 | 73.0 | 940,111,451 | 71.0 | 989,563,289 | 69.4 | 1,178,892,553 | 63.9 |
| European | CEW | 6 | 60 | 218 | 410,211,056 | 78.7 | 4,722,783 | -2,007,242 | 2,715,538 | 0.43 | 617,726,564 | 54.6 | 631,013,661 | 51.7 | 644,882,029 | 48.7 | 658,750,384 | 46.2 | 702,201,247 | 38.1 |
| Indo-Iranian—1 | CNN | 0 | 0 | 0 | 5,185,961 | 1.0 | 615,882 | 152,599 | 768,478 | 3.14 | 21,043,758 | 1.9 | 24,483,529 | 2.0 | 28,728,545 | 2.2 | 32,973,562 | 2.3 | 50,914,786 | 2.8 |
| Indo-Iranian—2 | CNT | 0 | 0 | 15 | 197,418 | 0.0 | 2,429 | 348 | 2,776 | 1.36 | 190,317 | 0.0 | 203,986 | 0.0 | 218,075 | 0.0 | 218,075 | 0.0 | 280,782 | 0.0 |
| Latin American—1 | CLT | 2 | 2 | 17 | 20,252,239 | 3.9 | 2,656,353 | -155,558 | 2,500,796 | 2.35 | 94,902,307 | 8.4 | 106,610,592 | 8.7 | 119,910,259 | 9.1 | 133,209,925 | 9.3 | 184,588,310 | 10.0 |
| Latin American—2 | CLN | 2 | 2 | 22 | 23,053,073 | 4.4 | 2,903,490 | -124,649 | 2,778,843 | 2.68 | 90,979,164 | 8.0 | 103,841,322 | 8.5 | 118,767,568 | 9.0 | 133,693,818 | 9.4 | 196,357,988 | 10.6 |
| Middle Eastern | CMT | 3 | 6 | 26 | 6,292,245 | 1.2 | 556,242 | 29,274 | 585,519 | 2.39 | 21,749,813 | 1.9 | 24,506,511 | 2.0 | 27,604,975 | 2.1 | 30,703,436 | 2.2 | 44,549,440 | 2.4 |
| MONGOLIAN | M | 9 | 60 | 1,632 | 43,942,931 | 8.4 | 3,354,640 | 511,671 | 3,866,304 | 2.87 | 116,645,810 | 10.3 | 134,488,318 | 11.0 | 155,308,837 | 11.7 | 176,129,341 | 12.4 | 253,347,751 | 13.7 |
| American Indian | MIR | 9 | 17 | 1,297 | 31,988,649 | 6.1 | 1,077,697 | -39,398 | 1,038,302 | 2.82 | 31,988,649 | 2.8 | 36,773,918 | 3.0 | 42,371,619 | 3.2 | 47,969,317 | 3.4 | 72,645,338 | 3.9 |
| Arctic-Mongoloid | MRY | 1 | 1 | 3 | 12,515 | 0.0 | 894 | -49 | 845 | 1.75 | 43,708 | 0.0 | 48,379 | 0.0 | 52,163 | 0.0 | 55,946 | 0.0 | 64,312 | 0.0 |
| Asian—1 | MSY | 1 | 11 | 11 | 11,960,673 | 2.3 | 2,122,838 | 600,148 | 2,722,979 | 3.51 | 64,954,746 | 5.7 | 77,509,198 | 6.3 | 92,184,541 | 7.0 | 106,859,878 | 7.5 | 158,019,849 | 8.6 |
| Asian—2 | MSW | 14 | 220 | 220 | 12,691,596 | 2.4 | 88,531 | -45,993 | 42,535 | 0.24 | 17,692,521 | 1.6 | 17,906,176 | 1.5 | 18,117,895 | 1.4 | 18,329,606 | 1.3 | 18,512,621 | 1.1 |
| Pacific | MPY | 3 | 20 | 17 | 461,925 | 0.1 | 64,680 | -3,037 | 61,643 | 2.74 | 1,966,186 | 0.2 | 2,250,647 | 0.2 | 2,582,619 | 0.2 | 2,914,594 | 0.2 | 4,105,631 | 0.2 |
| NEGRO | N | 7 | 47 | 712 | 20,854,198 | 4.0 | 4,724,326 | 942,362 | 5,666,698 | 3.04 | 160,397,110 | 14.2 | 186,288,541 | 15.3 | 217,064,039 | 16.4 | 247,839,543 | 17.4 | 393,620,628 | 21.3 |
| African—1 | NAB | 1 | 31 | 610 | 1,763,881 | 0.3 | 2,869,954 | 1,105,052 | 3,975,011 | 3.80 | 86,533,144 | 7.6 | 104,528,570 | 8.6 | 126,283,189 | 9.5 | 148,037,807 | 10.4 | 257,748,745 | 14.0 |
| African—2 | NAN | 1 | 1 | 17 | 365,928 | 0.1 | 70,859 | 5,777 | 76,639 | 2.67 | 2,512,976 | 0.2 | 2,867,053 | 0.2 | 3,279,350 | 0.2 | 3,691,646 | 0.3 | 5,519,093 | 0.3 |
| Afro-American | NFB | 5 | 15 | 85 | 18,724,389 | 3.6 | 1,783,513 | -168,467 | 1,615,048 | 2.05 | 71,350,990 | 6.3 | 78,892,918 | 6.5 | 87,501,500 | 6.6 | 96,110,090 | 6.7 | 130,352,790 | 7.1 |
| GLOBAL CHURCH MEMBERSHIP | | 37 | 195 | 4,047 | 521,563,181 | 100.0 | 19,755,490 | -597,471 | 19,158,019 | 1.57 | 1,131,809,580 | 100.0 | 1,220,852,133 | 100.0 | 1,323,389,725 | 100.0 | 1,425,927,317 | 100.0 | 1,844,614,192 | 100.0 |

## CHRISTIAN CULTURES AND ETHNOLINGUISTIC PEOPLES

Yet further insights into the fortunes of Christianity today can be derived by using, not political or religious criteria, but the criteria of race, ethnic group and language. This approach shows us the world of Homo Sapiens divided into the 5 races of mankind. 13 geographical races and 4 sub-races, 7 stylized skin colours, 71 ethnolinguistic families, 432 major ethnolinguistic peoples, 7,010 languages, and 8,990 distinct people groups or cultures. Of the 5 races, the Caucasian predominates with a global population in 1980 of 2,295 million (52.5% of the globe).

Christian cultures are found across the face of the earth. If we define a Christian culture as an ethnolinguistic population in which over 50% are church members, there are some 4,050 such cultures today. The largest racial groupings of these are 1,280 cultures among American Indians and 1,190 cultures among Oceanic peoples (Global Table 5).

*Ethnolinguistic changes, 1900-2000*
The composition of the Christian world has changed markedly since the year 1900. At the turn of the century, Christians were 88.7% Caucasian (Caucasoid) by race and 81.1% White by colour (Global Table 1). By 1980, massive church growth in the Third World had reduced these proportions to 70.0% Caucasian and to as low as 50.5% White. By 1981, Non-Whites formed a majority of all Christians for the first time for twelve hundred years. And by AD 2000, Non-Whites are expected to account for 60.1% of all Christians.

Again, there has been a major shift concerning the location of the largest single Christian ethnolinguistic people (using our definitions). In 1900, the Christian world's largest single ethnolinguistic group was to be found in Russia, shortly to become the heart of the Communist world; this largest group was the Russians themselves, who then had 59 million church members. By 1980, the largest group was in North America: USA Whites, with 108 million church members. But by the year 2000, the largest single ethnolinguistic group will be found in the Third World, namely the Spanish-speaking Mestizos of Latin America, with 173 million church members (see Global Table 24). Harbingers of this massive shift of centre of gravity from Europe in 1900 to North America in 1980 and then by 2000 to the Third World are large numbers of Third-World population groups. Of the 67 major ethnolinguistic peoples in the world that are most heavily christianized (each with over 90% church members by 1980), only 23 (34%) are of the predominant Caucasian stock whilst 44 (66%) are Non-White or Third-World peoples and tribes (Global Table 25). Likewise, of the 131 major ethnolinguistic peoples among whom church members number 70% or more by 1980, only 57 (44%) are Caucasian, whilst 74 (56%) are Non-White or Third-World peoples and tribes. Inexorably, the centre of gravity of committed Christianity continues its century-long shift from the Western world's capitals of London, Rome, Geneva and New York southwards to Third-World cities like Mexico City, São Paulo, Manila, Seoul, Madras, Nairobi and Kinshasa.

**A century-long shift.** (1) In 1900, the largest Christian culture was that of the Russians; by 1930 it had been smashed by militant atheism (and ridiculed, *above left*, on Orthodox monastery street walls).

(2) By 2000, the largest Christian culture will be Spanish-speaking Mestizos in Latin America, as heralded by (*above right*) vast procession of Methodist Pentecostal Church through Santiago (Chile).

**A Christian culture.** *Below.* A thousand schoolboys and (top left) schoolgirls of the Ruanda tribe at a youth service in Rwaza Mission (Rwanda). Entirely animists in 1900, the Ruanda are now 69.5% church members.

Global Table 6.    WORLD POPULATION RANKED BY 271 LANGUAGES EACH WITH OVER 1 MILLION NATIVE SPEAKERS, AD 1980.

1. The table ranks the world's largest languages, i.e. those with over a million native (mother-tongue) speakers in 1980.
2. A number of large languages have constituent dialects or sub-languages, and so their peoples can correctly be described as 'mother-tongue speakers' of both (e.g. Chinese and Wu, French and Provençal, Punjabi and Lahnda). There is therefore a certain amount of duplication in figures of this sort that are often quoted in the literature because certain languages can be subsumed under larger groupings; e.g. Wu native speakers are also Chinese native speakers; Provençal native speakers are also French native speakers; Lahnda is the Western dialect of Punjabi; etc. In this table, this is clarified below first by indentation of the sub-divisions of Chinese, each being followed by an asterisk; and thereafter by asterisk alone. The symbol * after a name thus indicates that the language's native speakers form a sub-division of a larger mother-tongue language grouping already listed above. The table's sub-total at the end, 'Languages over 1 million', is therefore the sum of the previous lines' statistics excluding those of asterisked * languages.

3. This table and the one following refer to each language by a single name only, that mainly used in English (anglicized) usage. There are also many variant or alternate names, but these are not given here. For further clarification or to locate an alternate language name not given here, see the classification PEOPLES OF THE WORLD in Part 4, and the Index of Peoples and Languages in Part 14.

| Language | Native speakers |
|---|---|
| Chinese | 886,376,100 |
|   Mandarin* | 551,716,000 |
|   Wu* | 75,638,000 |
|   Cantonese* | 59,500,000 |
|   Hsiang* | 44,493,000 |
|   Hakka* | 35,800,000 |
|   Min* | 35,600,000 |
|   Minnan* | 23,100,000 |
|   Kan* | 22,250,000 |
|   Taiwanese* | 13,416,000 |
| English | 265,095,800 |
| Spanish | 227,951,900 |
| Hindi | 168,327,500 |
| Arabic | 144,309,400 |
| Russian | 142,596,100 |
| Bengali | 138,404,400 |
| Portuguese | 135,610,900 |
| Japanese | 117,409,200 |
| German | 90,040,100 |
| Punjabi | 80,136,000 |
| French | 67,827,200 |
| Javanese | 65,628,200 |
| Italian | 63,762,200 |
| Marathi | 62,487,800 |
| Tamil | 58,471,600 |
| Korean | 58,179,400 |
| Telugu | 55,042,300 |
| Ukrainian | 44,829,700 |
| Turkish | 43,240,800 |
| Vietnamese | 42,932,300 |
| Polish | 39,294,700 |
| Urdu | 38,057,100 |
| Kosali* | 38,000,000 |
| Kannada | 37,537,700 |
| Gujarati | 34,829,600 |
| Rajasthani | 32,798,400 |
| Bihari | 28,944,900 |
| Oriya | 27,772,400 |
| Malayalam | 27,217,100 |
| Thai | 27,210,200 |
| Awadhi-Bagheli* | 26,500,000 |
| Burmese | 25,263,600 |
| Sundanese | 21,062,200 |
| Dutch | 20,866,800 |
| Pushtu | 19,469,200 |
| Lahnda* | 19,200,000 |
| Romanian | 19,076,300 |
| Dekini* | 18,530,000 |
| Bhojpuri* | 18,326,500 |
| Assamese | 18,243,200 |
| Persian | 17,763,900 |
| Serbo-Croatian | 17,172,100 |
| Hausa | 14,826,800 |
| Quechua | 14,785,300 |
| Braj Bhasa* | 14,690,000 |
| Cebuano | 14,616,800 |
| Lao | 14,157,800 |
| Uzbek | 14,037,500 |
| Malay | 14,011,500 |
| Hungarian | 13,940,400 |
| Yoruba | 13,725,100 |
| Provençal* | 13,550,000 |
| Ibo | 12,799,500 |
| Galla | 12,655,900 |
| Sindhi | 12,534,900 |
| Fulani | 11,954,000 |
| Azeri | 11,789,100 |
| Greek | 11,449,000 |
| Tagalog | 11,191,300 |
| Sinhala | 11,034,700 |
| Madurese | 10,840,800 |
| Bundeli* | 10,220,000 |
| Czech | 10,095,700 |
| Nepali | 10,092,500 |
| Byelorussian | 9,864,000 |
| Chuang | 9,788,500 |
| Kurdish | 9,368,900 |
| Malagasy | 9,195,400 |
| Tadzhik | 9,158,400 |
| Khmer | 9,115,100 |
| Kharwari* | 8,940,000 |
| Swedish | 8,857,500 |
| Chhatisgarhi* | 8,550,000 |
| Marwari* | 7,977,000 |
| Amharic | 7,944,300 |
| Bulgarian | 7,907,500 |
| Kanauji* | 7,670,000 |
| Kazakh | 7,667,500 |
| Benarsi* | 7,650,000 |
| Yiddish | 6,500,000 |
| Sotho | 6,476,200 |
| Tatar | 6,465,900 |
| Catalan | 6,445,600 |
| Varhadi* | 6,390,000 |
| Maithili* | 6,371,000 |
| Ilocano | 6,346,600 |
| Kashmiri | 5,969,200 |
| Somali | 5,924,800 |
| Shona | 5,821,000 |
| Armenian | 5,812,600 |
| Santali | 5,733,400 |
| Hebrew | 5,600,000 |
| Zulu | 5,564,000 |
| Hiligaynon | 5,429,000 |
| Ruanda | 5,400,000 |
| Uighur | 5,385,000 |
| Yi | 5,340,000 |
| Xhosa | 5,222,000 |
| Danish | 5,203,600 |
| Minangkabau | 5,184,000 |
| Romany | 5,135,600 |
| Bangaru* | 5,100,600 |
| Slovak | 5,056,400 |
| Finnish | 4,999,200 |
| Norwegian | 4,957,900 |
| Creole | 4,931,200 |
| Rundi | 4,800,000 |
| Kanuri | 4,621,300 |
| Batak | 4,491,200 |
| Mongo | 4,472,300 |
| Tibetan | 4,449,300 |
| Nahuatl | 4,422,000 |
| Buginese | 4,364,300 |
| Shangaan | 4,266,700 |
| Albanian | 4,229,900 |
| Moré | 4,200,000 |
| Gondi | 4,165,900 |
| Bicol | 4,071,800 |
| Miao | 4,019,000 |
| Nyamwezi | 4,000,000 |
| Mongolian | 3,949,900 |
| Karen | 3,893,400 |
| Georgian | 3,889,700 |
| Sotho | 3,836,200 |
| Magahi* | 3,599,000 |
| Galician | 3,589,500 |
| Manchu | 3,559,500 |
| Turkmen | 3,548,900 |
| Bhili | 3,471,500 |
| Lithuanian | 3,422,100 |
| Luba | 3,418,900 |
| Efik | 3,412,000 |
| Mandingo | 3,305,900 |
| Makua | 3,278,500 |
| Balinese | 3,252,200 |
| Kongo | 3,200,000 |
| Kikuyu | 3,153,300 |
| Baluchi | 3,101,400 |
| Achinese | 3,097,000 |
| Chewa | 3,075,000 |
| Moldavian | 2,949,300 |
| Tswana | 2,938,700 |
| Swahili | 2,900,000 |
| Sidamo | 2,837,000 |
| Afrikaans | 2,792,500 |
| Luo | 2,723,000 |
| Aymara | 2,689,500 |
| Edo | 2,613,500 |
| Tiv | 2,600,000 |
| Shan | 2,562,600 |
| Western Pahari* | 2,550,000 |
| Nagpuri* | 2,490,000 |
| Dayak | 2,477,900 |
| Mbundu | 2,450,000 |
| Kammyang* | 2,410,000 |
| Dinka | 2,356,200 |
| Kermanji* | 2,353,000 |
| Sukuma | 2,346,800 |
| Azande | 2,329,700 |
| Banjarese | 2,323,000 |
| Bambara | 2,280,000 |
| Ewe | 2,276,900 |
| Shilha | 2,262,600 |
| Gilaki | 2,233,000 |
| Senufo | 2,213,000 |
| Yuan | 2,200,000 |
| Yao | 2,159,000 |
| Ganda | 2,155,200 |
| Wolof | 2,150,000 |
| Pedi | 2,140,000 |
| Samareño | 2,100,000 |
| Tamazigt | 2,099,600 |
| Luhya | 2,086,500 |
| Otomí | 2,043,200 |
| Kabyle | 2,042,300 |
| Slovenian | 2,025,100 |
| Puyi | 1,950,000 |
| Salale* | 1,946,000 |
| Kirgiz | 1,920,900 |
| Tigrinya | 1,891,300 |
| Chuvash | 1,876,800 |
| Wallega* | 1,869,000 |
| Makassarese | 1,858,400 |
| Guarani | 1,840,000 |
| Fon | 1,772,600 |
| Mazanderani | 1,771,000 |
| Ronga | 1,750,000 |
| Kamba | 1,725,700 |
| Macedonian | 1,700,600 |
| Kru | 1,671,900 |
| Pampango | 1,670,500 |
| Dogri* | 1,659,000 |
| Kimbundu | 1,652,000 |
| Garhwali* | 1,632,000 |
| Baya | 1,625,500 |
| Chung-chia | 1,620,000 |
| Sasak | 1,611,000 |
| Zapotec | 1,609,200 |
| Kalenjin | 1,584,500 |
| Fang | 1,550,000 |
| Lamani* | 1,538,000 |
| Ashanti | 1,522,000 |
| Afar | 1,488,000 |
| Alsatian | 1,487,800 |
| Tulu | 1,480,000 |
| Manipuri | 1,473,400 |
| Pangasinan | 1,461,700 |
| Malvi* | 1,459,000 |
| Ijaw | 1,451,900 |
| Nupe | 1,451,000 |
| Latvian | 1,404,000 |
| Konkani | 1,401,800 |
| Puyi | 1,401,000 |
| Kumaoni* | 1,400,000 |
| Mixtec | 1,399,300 |
| Toraja | 1,393,800 |
| Ho | 1,388,600 |
| Mundari | 1,388,000 |
| Oraon | 1,386,000 |
| Bagri* | 1,348,000 |
| Mordvinian | 1,340,600 |
| Bashkir | 1,340,000 |
| Arusi* | 1,331,000 |
| Teso | 1,328,700 |
| Luri | 1,309,000 |
| Khandesi* | 1,300,000 |
| Fante | 1,293,000 |
| Breton | 1,269,900 |
| Sardinian | 1,239,000 |
| Sena | 1,234,600 |
| Bura | 1,234,100 |
| Rif | 1,202,700 |
| Ngala | 1,200,000 |
| Estonian | 1,184,700 |
| Songhai | 1,184,100 |
| Nuer | 1,165,600 |
| Swazi | 1,160,000 |
| Welsh | 1,136,300 |
| Temne | 1,120,000 |
| Baule | 1,115,800 |
| Lubu | 1,110,000 |
| Dong | 1,110,000 |
| Losengo | 1,100,000 |
| Beja | 1,099,000 |
| Kwottu* | 1,077,000 |
| Nkole | 1,071,000 |
| Li | 1,060,000 |
| Ryukyuan | 1,057,900 |
| Kui | 1,050,000 |
| Bai | 1,050,000 |
| Mende | 1,048,100 |
| Ndebele | 1,039,000 |
| T'ung | 1,032,000 |
| Soga | 1,031,300 |
| Basque | 1,016,900 |
| Nimadi* | 1,015,000 |
| Kharchin* | 1,010,000 |
| Minahasan | 1,007,500 |
| Ruthenian | 1,006,800 |
| Gusii | 1,004,000 |
| Quiché | 1,001,000 |

Sub-totals;
Languages over 1 million.....95.6%   4,179,992,600
Languages under 1 million.....4.4%   193,924,900

WORLD POPULATION..........100.0%   4,373,917,500

Global Table 7.    AFFILIATED CHRISTIANS (CHURCH MEMBERS) RANKED BY 96 LANGUAGES EACH WITH OVER A MILLION NATIVE SPEAKERS, AD 1980.

The introductory notes at the beginning of the previous table, Global Table 6, apply to the present table also. In this table, the third column 'Church members' refers to affiliated Christians who are native (mother-tongue) speakers of the languages shown, excluding Christians who speak them as second language, etc. The languages given here are ranked from 1–96 in order to give an idea of comparative numerical importance.

| Rank | Language | Church members |
|---|---|---|
| 1 | Spanish | 206,594,100 |
| 2 | English | 196,051,800 |
| 3 | Portuguese | 127,972,600 |
| 4 | German | 84,995,000 |
| 5 | French | 56,205,100 |
| 6 | Italian | 52,929,500 |
| 7 | Russian | 44,788,600 |
| 8 | Polish | 35,558,000 |
| 9 | Ukrainian | 30,964,100 |
| 10 | Dutch | 16,777,900 |
| 11 | Romanian | 15,999,900 |
| 12 | Quechua | 14,631,100 |
| 13 | Cebuano | 13,500,000 |
| 14 | Serbo-Croatian | 12,552,200 |
| 15 | Hungarian | 11,227,500 |
| 16 | Provençal* | 11,200,000 |
| 17 | Tagalog | 10,957,700 |
| 18 | Greek | 10,813,500 |
| 19 | Korean | 10,711,200 |
| 20 | Arabic | 10,480,000 |
| 21 | Malayalam | 8,586,900 |
| 22 | Czech | 7,984,700 |
| 23 | Amharic | 7,712,000 |
| 24 | Ibo | 7,367,000 |
| 25 | Chinese | 6,965,600 |
| 26 | Byelorussian | 6,962,500 |
| 27 | Swedish | 6,430,300 |
| 28 | Catalan | 6,213,300 |
| 29 | Ilocano | 5,666,000 |
| 30 | Bulgarian | 5,606,900 |
| 31 | Tamil | 5,589,000 |
| 32 | Danish | 4,920,000 |
| 33 | Hiligaynon | 4,880,700 |
| 34 | Creole | 4,652,400 |
| 35 | Norwegian | 4,613,800 |
| 36 | Mongo | 4,595,600 |
| 37 | Finnish | 4,357,600 |
| 38 | Malagasy | 4,331,200 |
| 39 | Batak | 4,233,700 |
| 40 | Galla | 4,231,800 |
| 41 | Yoruba | 4,097,500 |
| 42 | Nahuatl | 4,073,400 |
| 43 | Slovak | 4,038,600 |
| 44 | Ruanda | 3,780,000 |
| 45 | Bicol | 3,660,500 |
| 46 | Rundi | 3,600,000 |
| 47 | Telugu | 3,480,800 |
| 48 | Galician | 3,454,500 |
| 49 | Luba | 3,350,000 |
| 50 | Zulu | 3,304,000 |
| 51 | Sotho | 3,247,800 |
| 52 | Xhosa | 3,238,700 |
| 53 | Vietnamese | 3,180,100 |
| 54 | Armenian | 2,965,600 |
| 55 | Lithuanian | 2,854,600 |
| 56 | Japanese | 2,732,600 |
| 57 | Aymara | 2,523,700 |
| 58 | Shona | 2,510,200 |
| 59 | Chewa | 2,400,000 |
| 60 | Afrikaans | 2,210,500 |
| 61 | Kongo | 2,200,000 |
| 62 | Kikuyu | 2,169,000 |
| 63 | Luo | 2,149,000 |
| 64 | Mbundu | 2,100,000 |
| 65 | Efik | 2,061,700 |
| 66 | Tiv | 2,021,000 |
| 67 | Romany | 2,011,300 |
| 68 | Shangaan | 1,984,500 |
| 69 | Slovene | 1,927,900 |
| 70 | Otomi | 1,856,300 |
| 71 | Luhya | 1,838,300 |
| 72 | Tswana | 1,824,800 |
| 73 | Guaraní | 1,810,000 |
| 74 | Moldavian | 1,741,100 |
| 75 | Samareño | 1,700,000 |
| 76 | Tigrinya | 1,675,800 |
| 77 | Javanese | 1,571,500 |
| 78 | Punjabi | 1,560,500 |
| 79 | Macedonian | 1,542,000 |
| 80 | Pampango | 1,501,800 |
| 81 | Zapotec | 1,499,800 |
| 82 | Ganda | 1,490,200 |
| 83 | Latvian | 1,398,000 |
| 84 | Marathi | 1,353,900 |
| 85 | Pangasinan | 1,314,000 |
| 86 | Mixtec | 1,304,100 |
| 87 | Kimbundu | 1,300,000 |
| 88 | Ewe | 1,234,400 |
| 89 | Fang | 1,200,000 |
| 90 | Alsatian | 1,191,000 |
| 91 | Kannada | 1,166,100 |
| 92 | Pedi | 1,100,000 |
| 93 | Breton | 1,058,700 |
| 94 | Ashanti | 1,050,000 |
| 95 | Sardinian | 1,036,300 |
| 96 | Minahasan | 1,007,100 |

Sub-totals:
Languages over 1 million.....90.8%   1,201,244,300
Languages under 1 million.....9.2%   122,145,400

GLOBAL CHURCH MEMBERSHIP 100.0%   1,323,389,700

## MAJOR CHRISTIAN LANGUAGES

The idea of 'Christian languages' can usefully be quantified in several ways. One could approach the task linguistically (based on the importance of Christian words and ideas); or, as we do here, demographically (based on the number of speakers who are Christians). Again, rankings of languages on the latter criterion differ depending on whether we are speaking of languages which are Christians' mother tongues (first languages), or their second languages, or their state languages, and so on. Here, we describe three of these approaches.

Ninety-six languages have over a million affiliated Christians (church members) each as native (mother-tongue) speakers (see Global Table 7 and Global Map 1). The 6 largest Christian languages, defined in this way, are the 6 major European languages used throughout this survey's Tables 2 (Part 7) and in the Topical Directory (Part 13). They are, in order of magnitude: Spanish (207 million church-member native speakers in 1980), English (196 million), Portuguese (128 million), German (85 million), French (56 million), and Italian (53 million). What we may call the 20 largest Christian languages are therefore these 6 followed by (in order of size): Russian, Polish, Ukrainian, Dutch, Romanian, Quechua, Cebuano, Serbo-Croatian, Hungarian, Provençal, Tagalog, Greek, Korean and Arabic. Each had over 10 million church-member native speakers in 1980.

Alternatively, we could take the view that what matters in world Christianity (e.g. at international conferences, in international service agencies, or in secular international affairs) is what official state languages have the most Christians. We can therefore rank languages by the numbers of Christians who live under the world's 76 official state languages (Global Table 20). This time, English comes out first: 516 million Christians live in countries with English as their official language. The next few, in order, are: Spanish (255 million), French (142 million), Portuguese (138 million), then Russian, German, Italian, Filipino, Polish, Hindi, Afrikaans, Dutch, Swahili, Romanian, Amharic, Quechua and Indonesian.

Lastly, we could enumerate radio/TV usage of the various languages. English and Spanish far outrun all other languages in this respect. Of the world's regular radio/TV audience listening to or viewing Christian programmes, in 1980 412 million live in countries with English as official language, and 176 million live in countries with Spanish as official language.

**Largest Christian language.** Since 1970, the largest Christian language has been Spanish, with 207 million church-member native speakers in 1980. *Above.* Two Penzotti Institute workers in Guatemala explain Illustrated Luke's Gospel to telegraph messenger cyclist (left). *Below left.* Spanish-language Christian radio/TV programmes (as here, featuring (right) evangelist Luis Palau) are now heard by a regular audience of 176 million worldwide.

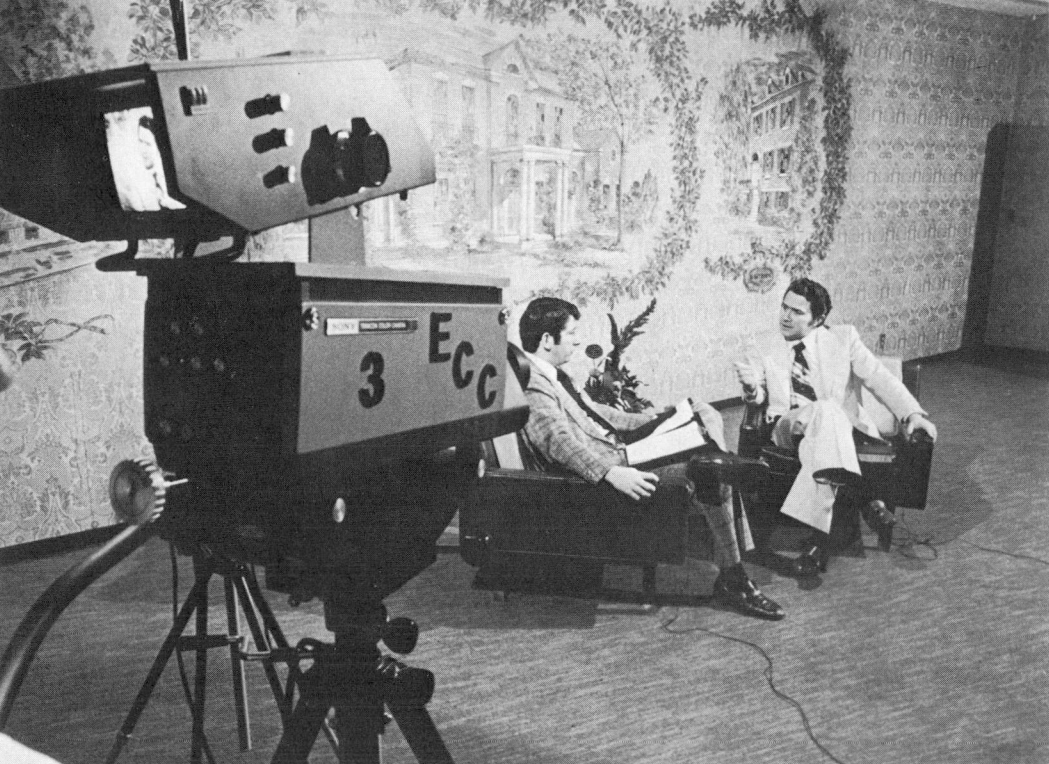

**Interpreters.** *Below.* For large Christian meetings, 2, 3, 4 or more interpreters are increasingly essential. In this East African Revival convention, 4 languages are used in rapid-fire sentence-by-sentence translation.

Global Table 8.    CULTURES, LANGUAGES AND AVAILABILITY OF THE SCRIPTURES ON 8 CONTINENTS AND FOR 17 RACES, AD 1900-1980.

A. The table is divided into 2 parts. (1) The first, upper, part takes 20 global totals of languages with or without Scripture translations and analyses them by the world's 8 continents. (2) The second, lower, part takes the same 20 columns and analyses them instead by the world's 5 races, 13 geographical races, 17 races or racial types, and 7 stylized colours. These races, colours, etc are as derived and presented here in our classification PEOPLES OF THE WORLD in Part 4.

B. The data come from the Encyclopedia's computerized database, itself based at this point on Scriptures of the World (UBS, 1978), Ethnologue (WBT, 1978), et alia. Each source contains data on several languages not reported in the other sources.

C. Columns. These have the same meanings for the 2 parts of the table. The meaning of each column, and of the abbreviations used, may be explained as follows.

1. People groups. The total number of all distinct or separate component ethnolinguistic peoples and people groups or cultures making up each race named below, or found on each continent shown.

LANGUAGES. Columns 2-3 give total of distinct mother-tongue languages and/or dialects sufficiently distinct for separate translations of the Scriptures to be considered necessary or essential, whether or not such translations have yet been attempted.

2. Unduplicated. Totals of languages where each is counted only once, even if spoken in several countries.

3. Duplicated. Totals of languages significant in any country, with any language counted as many times as it occurs significantly in any country (source: Global Table 31, column 13).

LANGUAGE TOTALS BASED ON CRITERIA OF SCRIPTURE TRANSLATION (Columns 4-20). These columns analyse the unduplicated totals in column 2.

LANGUAGES WITHOUT SCRIPTURES (i.e. with translations absent) (columns 4-10):

4. NO TRANSLATION. Languages enumerated in column 2 without Scriptures in 1900, or (column 5) in 1980.
NO WORK BEGUN YET (Columns 6-9). Languages without Scriptures and in which neither translation nor preparation for translation has yet begun.

6. Definite need. Languages which definitely need first Bible translation because speakers cannot be adequately reached through any other language (as determined by Ethnologue, 1978).

7. Possible need. Languages which possibly or probably need first Bible translation, though the extent of bilingualism, or of related dialects with Scriptures, is incompletely known (Ethnologue).

8. No need, because bilingual. Languages which, even though sufficiently different or distinct from others to warrant their own translations, can have them dispensed with because their speakers are extremely bilingual in a second language with its own Scriptures (usually the national language) (Ethnologue).

9. No need, because nearly extinct. Languages which do not need Bible translation because nearly extinct (only a few elderly speakers left) or extinct (no longer any speakers, the ethnic group using another language).

10. PROJECTS. Languages in which first translation work or analysis is actually in progress (in 1980).

LANGUAGES WITH SCRIPTURES (i.e. with translations present) (columns 11-20):

11. PROJECTS. Languages in which work is in progress (in 1980) on revising or retranslating an existing Bible or New Testament, or on first translation of some part of the Bible.
NO WORK IN PROGRESS (columns 12-14). Languages with Scriptures in which additional or further translation work is needed but not yet begun.

12. Definite need. Languages which definitely need further translation of Scriptures (Ethnologue).

13. Possible need. Languages which possibly or probably need further translation of Scriptures (Ethnologue).

14. Revision need. Languages in which an existing Bible or New Testament is recognized as requiring either revision or an entirely new translation.
EXISTING TRANSLATIONS (columns 15-20).

15. Portion. Languages into which portions of Scripture (a Gospel or other whole book) had been translated by the end of the year 1900, and (column 16) by 1980.

17. New Testament. Languages with the New Testament translated by the end of 1900, and (column 18) by 1980.

19. Bible. Languages with the whole Bible translated by the end of 1900, and (column 20) by 1980.

**Column key (SCRIPTURE TRANSLATIONS):** (1) People groups · (2) Languages Unduplicated · (3) Languages Duplicated · ABSENT — No translation: (4) 1900, (5) 1980 · No work begun yet: (6) Definite need, (7) Possible need, (8) Bilingual, (9) Extinct · (10) Projects · PRESENT — (11) Projects · No work in progress: (12) Definite need, (13) Possible need, (14) Revision need · Existing translations — Portion: (15) 1900, (16) 1980 · NT: (17) 1900, (18) 1980 · Bible: (19) 1900, (20) 1980

## 1. GEOGRAPHICAL DISTRIBUTION

| Continent | 1 | 2 | 3 | 4 | 5 | 6 | 7 | 8 | 9 | 10 | 11 | 12 | 13 | 14 | 15 | 16 | 17 | 18 | 19 | 20 |
|---|---|---|---|---|---|---|---|---|---|---|---|---|---|---|---|---|---|---|---|---|
| Africa | 2,511 | 1,883 | 3,052 | 1,770 | 1,357 | 155 | 879 | 5 | 24 | 93 | 164 | 38 | 92 | 7 | 113 | 526 | 40 | 253 | 14 | 99 |
| East Asia | 210 | 193 | 327 | 161 | 131 | 4 | 58 | 3 | 0 | 1 | 3 | 0 | 4 | 0 | 32 | 62 | 21 | 34 | 7 | 18 |
| Europe | 216 | 169 | 759 | 49 | 21 | 0 | 10 | 0 | 4 | 7 | 30 | 1 | 2 | 1 | 120 | 148 | 48 | 57 | 39 | 44 |
| Latin America | 2,011 | 1,538 | 1,626 | 1,520 | 1,248 | 77 | 123 | 58 | 64 | 93 | 155 | 4 | 6 | 3 | 18 | 290 | 4 | 106 | 2 | 3 |
| Northern America | 272 | 250 | 383 | 216 | 180 | 3 | 69 | 69 | 73 | 19 | 22 | 4 | 0 | 2 | 34 | 70 | 15 | 24 | 7 | 7 |
| Oceania | 1,277 | 1,253 | 1,702 | 1,195 | 987 | 164 | 465 | 22 | 72 | 102 | 73 | 19 | 37 | 11 | 58 | 266 | 22 | 93 | 9 | 21 |
| South Asia | 2,331 | 1,596 | 3,925 | 1,475 | 1,201 | 121 | 794 | 11 | 14 | 69 | 131 | 31 | 63 | 9 | 121 | 395 | 71 | 170 | 37 | 72 |
| USSR | 165 | 128 | 150 | 87 | 74 | 11 | 48 | 0 | 0 | 6 | 18 | 11 | 4 | 0 | 41 | 54 | 18 | 22 | 9 | 12 |
| **WORLD TOTALS** | **8,993** | **7,010** | **11,924** | **6,473** | **5,199** | **535** | **2,446** | **168** | **251** | **390** | **596** | **108** | **208** | **33** | **537** | **1,811** | **239** | **759** | **124** | **276** |

## 2. ETHNOLINGUISTIC DISTRIBUTION

*(e = Families, f = Peoples, 1 = Groups, 2 = Languages Unduplicated, 3 = Duplicated)*

| Race / Geographical race | Code | Colour | e | f | 1 | 2 | 3 | 4 | 5 | 6 | 7 | 8 | 9 | 10 | 11 | 12 | 13 | 14 | 15 | 16 | 17 | 18 | 19 | 20 |
|---|---|---|---|---|---|---|---|---|---|---|---|---|---|---|---|---|---|---|---|---|---|---|---|---|
| **AUSTRALOID** | A | | 10 | 35 | 1,953 | 1,684 | — | 1,625 | 1,369 | 235 | 721 | 24 | 74 | 130 | 84 | 26 | 47 | 9 | 59 | 315 | 15 | 100 | 4 | 18 |
| Austro-Asiatic | AUG | Grey | 7 | 21 | 515 | 500 | — | 480 | 418 | 27 | 159 | 2 | 26 | 23 | 25 | 10 | 7 | 0 | 20 | 82 | 6 | 26 | 1 | 7 |
| Oceanic | AON | Brown | 3 | 14 | 1,438 | 1,184 | — | 1,145 | 951 | 208 | 562 | 22 | 48 | 107 | 59 | 16 | 40 | 9 | 39 | 233 | 9 | 74 | 3 | 11 |
| **CAPOID** | B | | 2 | 6 | 64 | 59 | — | 58 | 55 | 1 | 43 | 0 | 3 | 0 | 1 | 0 | 1 | 0 | 1 | 4 | 1 | 1 | 0 | 1 |
| Early African | BYG | Grey | 2 | 6 | 64 | 59 | — | 58 | 55 | 1 | 43 | 0 | 3 | 0 | 1 | 0 | 1 | 0 | 1 | 4 | 1 | 1 | 0 | 1 |
| **CAUCASIAN** | C | | 24 | 135 | 1,047 | 664 | — | 452 | 359 | 32 | 230 | 2 | 10 | 27 | 71 | 5 | 19 | 7 | 212 | 305 | 109 | 141 | 69 | 84 |
| European | CEW | White | 10 | 69 | 253 | 198 | — | 73 | 44 | 4 | 27 | 1 | 5 | 9 | 33 | 5 | 3 | 7 | 125 | 154 | 53 | 66 | 43 | 51 |
| Indo-Iranian—1 | CNN | Brown | 1 | 26 | 317 | 243 | — | 191 | 163 | 9 | 123 | 1 | 2 | 5 | 23 | 0 | 11 | 0 | 52 | 80 | 37 | 41 | 14 | 17 |
| Indo-Iranian—2 | CNT | Tan | 2 | 9 | 131 | 48 | — | 42 | 38 | 9 | 30 | 0 | 0 | 3 | 5 | 0 | 0 | 0 | 6 | 10 | 3 | 2 | 2 | 2 |
| Latin American—1 | CLT | Tan | 2 | 2 | 18 | 3 | — | 3 | 0 | 0 | 0 | 0 | 0 | 0 | 0 | 0 | 0 | 0 | 1 | 1 | 1 | 3 | 1 | 1 |
| Latin American—2 | CLN | Brown | 2 | 2 | 26 | 3 | — | 0 | 0 | 0 | 0 | 0 | 0 | 0 | 0 | 0 | 0 | 0 | 1 | 4 | 1 | 3 | 1 | 1 |
| Middle Eastern | CMT | Tan | 7 | 27 | 302 | 170 | — | 143 | 114 | 10 | 50 | 0 | 3 | 10 | 10 | 0 | 5 | 0 | 27 | 56 | 14 | 26 | 8 | 12 |
| **MONGOLIAN** | M | | 19 | 137 | 3,653 | 2,868 | — | 2,702 | 2,172 | 130 | 647 | 137 | 146 | 149 | 282 | 41 | 51 | 11 | 166 | 696 | 79 | 280 | 40 | 82 |
| American Indian | MIR | Red | 3 | 20 | 2,136 | 1,706 | — | 1,667 | 1,382 | 78 | 117 | 124 | 137 | 108 | 169 | 6 | 5 | 4 | 39 | 324 | 12 | 115 | 4 | 5 |
| Arctic Mongoloid | MRY | Yellow | 1 | 3 | 12 | 11 | — | 6 | 0 | 0 | 0 | 0 | 0 | 0 | 6 | 1 | 0 | 1 | 5 | 0 | 2 | 0 | 2 | 2 |
| Asian—1 | MSY | Yellow | 11 | 80 | 1,360 | 1,043 | — | 957 | 734 | 45 | 501 | 10 | 6 | 36 | 93 | 27 | 43 | 3 | 86 | 309 | 44 | 132 | 22 | 59 |
| Asian—2 | MSW | White | 1 | 13 | 53 | 41 | — | 22 | 20 | 6 | 10 | 0 | 0 | 1 | 2 | 3 | 0 | 0 | 19 | 31 | 8 | 20 | 5 | 5 |
| Pacific | MPY | Yellow | 3 | 21 | 92 | 67 | — | 50 | 36 | 1 | 19 | 3 | 3 | 4 | 12 | 4 | 3 | 3 | 17 | 32 | 13 | 13 | 7 | 11 |
| **NEGRO** | N | | 16 | 119 | 2,276 | 1,735 | — | 1,636 | 1,244 | 137 | 805 | 5 | 18 | 84 | 158 | 36 | 90 | 6 | 99 | 491 | 35 | 237 | 11 | 91 |
| African—1 | NAB | Black | 10 | 103 | 2,167 | 1,660 | — | 1,567 | 1,187 | 135 | 786 | 4 | 18 | 83 | 153 | 36 | 85 | 6 | 93 | 473 | 33 | 233 | 11 | 91 |
| African—2 | NAN | Brown | 1 | 1 | 20 | 13 | — | 12 | 8 | 2 | 4 | 1 | 0 | 0 | 1 | 0 | 4 | 0 | 1 | 5 | 0 | 0 | 0 | 0 |
| Afro-American | NFB | Black | 5 | 15 | 89 | 62 | — | 57 | 49 | 0 | 15 | 0 | 0 | 1 | 4 | 0 | 1 | 0 | 5 | 13 | 2 | 4 | 0 | 0 |
| **WORLD TOTALS** | | | **71** | **432** | **8,993** | **7,010** | **—** | **6,473** | **5,199** | **535** | **2,446** | **168** | **251** | **390** | **596** | **108** | **208** | **33** | **537** | **1,811** | **239** | **759** | **124** | **276** |

## GLOBAL AVAILABILITY OF THE SCRIPTURES

The world of the 20th century has some 7,010 distinct and different languages in it, defining the term 'language' from the Christian viewpoint as explained here in Part 4. Of these, by the year 1900 the Christian Scriptures had become available, in whole or in part, in 537 languages. Through prodigious efforts, this total rose by 1980 to 1,811 languages with Scriptures. This leaves 5,200 languages with no translations as yet—a staggering challenge to global Christianity. Native speakers of these languages in 1980 numbered some 185 million — 4.2% of the world with no access to the Scriptures in their mother tongue. Translation projects are therefore in progress in 986 languages: first translations in 390 of them, further translation in an additional 596 (see Global Table 8). Despite this monumental translation work by the churches worldwide, it is calculated that at least 3,297 further languages have a definite need for immediate Bible translation, or at the least a probable or possible need; but up to the present no-one has begun the necessary work in them.

Annual distribution of Scriptures continues to increase each year. In the year 1900, 5.4 million whole Bibles were sold or distributed; by 1980, this had risen to 36.8 million (Global Tables 12 and 31). By 1980 also, Scripture selections distributed annually by the United Bible Societies' members had reached 432 million, or one per person for 10% of the world's population.

**World's smallest language: Hixkaryana.** *Above.* The smallest living language possessing its own New Testament (excluding virtually extinct languages) is this Cariban language which has only 150 speakers; this tribe lives in northwest Brazil. Pictured are translators at work on Mark's Gospel (1966); the New Testament followed in 1976.
**World's largest language: Chinese.** *Below.* With 886 million native (mother-tongue) speakers, Chinese consists of some 68 different languages, dialects or versions, into 29 of which Scriptures have been translated. Pictured is a Bible used in the Chinese Methodist Church, Telak Ayer, Singapore.

Global Table 9.    ORGANIZED CHRISTIANITY: GLOBAL MEMBERSHIPS RANKED BY 7 ECCLESIASTICAL BLOCS AND 92 MAJOR TRADITIONS, AD 1970-1985.

Notes describing this table are placed at the bottom of the facing page (page 15).

| Bloc Tradition Code Name | | Congs 1970 | Adults 1970 | Affiliated (total membership, total community) | | | | Sig | Denominations Total | | | | Coun- tries |
|---|---|---|---|---|---|---|---|---|---|---|---|---|---|
| | | | | 1970 | 1975 | 1980 | 1985 | | 1970 | 1975 | 1980 | 1985 | |
| 1 2 | 3 | 4 | 5 | 6 | 7 | 8 | 9 | 10 | 11 | 12 | 13 | 14 | 15 |
| ROMAN CATHOLIC | | 247,118 | 432,125,990 | 672,319,062 | 733,215,181 | 802,659,904 | 872,104,646 | 222 | 222 | 222 | 222 | 223 | 220 |
| Lat | Latin-rite local church | 116,236 | 203,922,520 | 337,889,866 | 379,208,614 | 427,199,552 | 475,190,504 | 194 | | | | | |
| | Latin-rite Catholics | 242,329 | 427,735,090 | 665,234,769 | 725,317,386 | 793,860,613 | 862,421,866 | 2,453 | | | | | |
| LEr | Latin/Eastern-rite local church | 130,882 | 228,203,470 | 334,429,196 | 354,006,567 | 375,460,352 | 396,914,142 | 28 | | | | | |
| | Eastern-rite Catholics: | 4,789 | 4,390,900 | 7,084,293 | 7,897,795 | 8,799,291 | 9,682,780 | 153 | | | | | |
| SyM | Syro-Malabarese | 1,272 | 1,190,020 | 2,017,046 | 2,405,470 | 2,811,066 | 3,216,663 | 16 | | | | | |
| Ukr | Ukrainian (3 million suppressed) | 607 | 941,300 | 1,381,513 | 1,447,631 | 1,523,311 | 1,598,991 | 18 | | | | | |
| Mar | Maronite | 889 | 653,800 | 1,130,389 | 1,258,851 | 1,417,659 | 1,576,462 | 17 | | | | | |
| Rom | Romanian (totally suppressed) | 1,794 | 600,000 | 900,000 | 910,000 | 920,000 | 930,000 | 5 | | | | | |
| Mel | Melkite | 463 | 372,350 | 650,212 | 733,642 | 830,424 | 927,202 | 20 | | | | | |
| Cha | Chaldean | 177 | 152,200 | 280,456 | 312,195 | 345,680 | 379,171 | 22 | | | | | |
| Rut | Ruthenian | 205 | 192,400 | 279,615 | 283,126 | 286,649 | 290,170 | 4 | | | | | |
| Hun | Hungarian | 149 | 202,100 | 269,100 | 272,731 | 276,136 | 279,542 | 2 | | | | | |
| Ori | plural Oriental rites | 30 | 134,800 | 209,000 | 228,237 | 249,173 | 270,110 | 3 | | | | | |
| Mal | Syro-Malankarese | 255 | 119,000 | 201,589 | 240,409 | 280,945 | 321,482 | 2 | | | | | |
| Slo | Slovak | 201 | 128,000 | 176,000 | 179,940 | 183,899 | 187,859 | 1 | | | | | |
| Cop | Coptic | 175 | 64,150 | 109,500 | 121,769 | 133,544 | 145,320 | 5 | | | | | |
| PROTESTANT | | 724,825 | 139,668,088 | 233,424,245 | 246,399,497 | 262,155,904 | 277,912,513 | 3,294 | 6,920 | 7,389 | 7,889 | 8,196 | 212 |
| uni | united (including Lutheran/Reformed) | 102,247 | 38,220,824 | 60,000,899 | 61,433,986 | 63,298,983 | 65,163,979 | 64 | | | | | |
| Lut | Lutheran (excluding united) | 59,994 | 23,347,633 | 39,650,970 | 40,865,277 | 42,202,147 | 43,539,026 | 217 | | | | | |
| Ref | Reformed (Presbyterian) | 77,479 | 18,989,088 | 32,434,522 | 34,449,841 | 36,866,788 | 39,283,735 | 286 | | | | | |
| Bap | Baptist | 102,124 | 18,982,612 | 29,418,833 | 31,177,158 | 33,306,814 | 35,436,498 | 321 | | | | | |
| Met | Methodist | 80,112 | 13,452,545 | 21,795,923 | 23,056,024 | 24,562,647 | 26,069,273 | 117 | | | | | |
| Pen | Pentecostal (6 types) | 94,201 | 8,730,868 | 16,647,128 | 19,034,889 | 21,909,778 | 24,784,725 | 652 | | | | | |
| Dis | Disciples (Restorationist) | 33,866 | 5,270,388 | 7,876,091 | 8,165,957 | 8,474,567 | 8,783,192 | 118 | | | | | |
| Hol | Holiness (Perfectionist) | 32,430 | 1,865,299 | 4,188,938 | 4,605,748 | 5,186,276 | 5,766,841 | 300 | | | | | |
| Adv | Adventist | 20,980 | 2,143,086 | 4,077,940 | 4,703,668 | 5,445,372 | 6,187,077 | 193 | | | | | |
| Sal | Salvationist | 16,678 | 1,425,965 | 2,936,406 | 3,238,471 | 3,633,818 | 4,029,163 | 78 | | | | | |
| int | interdenominational | 12,522 | 776,942 | 2,094,177 | 2,431,231 | 2,953,705 | 3,476,191 | 199 | | | | | |
| Con | Congregationalist | 11,495 | 1,042,950 | 2,004,792 | 2,103,500 | 2,230,023 | 2,356,553 | 91 | | | | | |
| rad | isolated radio-church | 40,248 | 1,110,750 | 1,611,500 | 1,785,533 | 1,941,672 | 2,097,807 | 9 | | | | | |
| sin | single-congregation | 4,500 | 750,000 | 1,500,000 | 1,493,967 | 1,486,534 | 1,479,101 | 2 | | | | | |
| ind | independent evangelical | 4,775 | 664,853 | 1,320,280 | 1,409,198 | 1,508,585 | 1,607,986 | 125 | | | | | |
| CBr | Christian Brethren (Open) | 9,720 | 534,240 | 1,255,627 | 1,357,486 | 1,484,817 | 1,612,151 | 117 | | | | | |
| Men | Mennonite (Anabaptist) | 5,499 | 522,017 | 947,484 | 1,032,777 | 1,141,439 | 1,250,111 | 91 | | | | | |
| Dun | Dunker (German Baptist) | 2,075 | 305,436 | 513,800 | 562,182 | 619,068 | 675,958 | 10 | | | | | |
| Mor | Moravian | 1,045 | 224,443 | 469,518 | 547,259 | 643,572 | 739,885 | 26 | | | | | |
| Qua | Friends (Quaker) | 3,610 | 207,710 | 377,246 | 413,268 | 457,877 | 502,486 | 50 | | | | | |
| EBr | Exclusive Brethren | 1,704 | 91,640 | 187,000 | 182,721 | 177,195 | 171,668 | 21 | | | | | |
| ORTHODOX | | 99,716 | 97,237,333 | 143,402,488 | 151,826,987 | 160,737,744 | 169,648,520 | 424 | 523 | 534 | 550 | 580 | 107 |
| Sla | Slavonic | 12,777 | 54,810,710 | 79,071,581 | 83,428,031 | 87,976,007 | 92,523,987 | 115 | | | | | |
| Rum | Romanian | 11,873 | 11,596,050 | 16,158,850 | 16,792,312 | 17,376,315 | 17,960,324 | 19 | | | | | |
| Gre | Greek (New Calendar) | 31,112 | 8,664,873 | 12,348,972 | 12,682,054 | 13,055,760 | 13,429,465 | 71 | | | | | |
| Eth | Ethiopian | 15,063 | 7,041,830 | 11,931,400 | 13,578,730 | 15,455,876 | 17,333,022 | 10 | | | | | |
| Ser | Serbian | 2,985 | 5,031,700 | 7,405,075 | 7,632,997 | 7,868,093 | 8,103,190 | 18 | | | | | |
| Cop | Coptic | 2,019 | 3,491,750 | 6,027,850 | 6,643,483 | 7,281,016 | 7,918,552 | 16 | | | | | |
| Arm | Armenian (Gregorian) | 874 | 1,795,540 | 2,826,198 | 2,993,983 | 3,172,309 | 3,350,626 | 37 | | | | | |
| OBe | Old Believer (Old Ritualist) | 616 | 1,596,900 | 2,274,000 | 2,405,785 | 2,543,809 | 2,681,833 | 11 | | | | | |
| SyM | Syro-Malabarese/Syrian | 942 | 834,680 | 1,415,932 | 1,496,433 | 1,580,969 | 1,665,504 | 5 | | | | | |
| Geo | Georgian | 80 | 500,000 | 800,000 | 846,803 | 895,926 | 945,050 | 1 | | | | | |
| Ara | Arabic | 792 | 445,000 | 772,400 | 854,119 | 945,259 | 1,036,406 | 28 | | | | | |
| Pol | Polish | 305 | 345,000 | 547,000 | 569,660 | 592,821 | 615,982 | 2 | | | | | |
| sub | sub-Orthodox (Russian) | 1,525 | 202,600 | 388,300 | 411,136 | 435,447 | 459,763 | 12 | | | | | |
| Tru | True Orthodox | 18,100 | 176,000 | 253,000 | 267,800 | 283,335 | 298,870 | 4 | | | | | |
| OCd | Old Calendarist (Authentic Orthodox) | 188 | 105,500 | 209,000 | 211,944 | 215,364 | 218,783 | 5 | | | | | |
| Syr | Syrian | 94 | 113,160 | 204,830 | 216,507 | 230,132 | 243,757 | 19 | | | | | |
| Cze | Czech | 141 | 147,000 | 200,000 | 204,000 | 208,000 | 212,000 | 1 | | | | | |
| Alb | Albanian | 535 | 110,500 | 172,150 | 170,672 | 169,314 | 169,954 | 4 | | | | | |
| Nes | Assyrian (Nestorian) | 52 | 83,240 | 144,050 | 155,322 | 167,684 | 180,049 | 16 | | | | | |
| NON-WHITE INDIGENOUS | | 209,521 | 33,174,946 | 58,701,960 | 69,563,886 | 82,180,415 | 94,796,927 | 1,365 | 8,733 | 9,365 | 10,065 | 10,956 | 145 |
| pen | pentecostal (6 types) | 66,308 | 9,963,170 | 20,146,882 | 24,278,527 | 29,257,409 | 34,215,137 | 588 | | | | | |
| Bap | Baptist | 51,045 | 10,708,922 | 12,980,718 | 13,601,469 | 14,243,449 | 14,885,425 | 48 | | | | | |
| Met | Methodist | 17,574 | 2,949,757 | 4,417,828 | 4,791,113 | 5,219,670 | 5,648,235 | 71 | | | | | |
| ReC | Reformed Catholic | 3,423 | 1,877,700 | 3,551,500 | 4,446,316 | 5,453,844 | 6,461,373 | 8 | | | | | |
| ind | independent evangelical | 10,181 | 1,218,146 | 3,414,945 | 4,282,035 | 5,292,272 | 6,302,497 | 160 | | | | | |
| CCa | Conservative Catholic | 1,853 | 1,192,741 | 2,457,626 | 3,062,487 | 3,794,103 | 4,525,723 | 29 | | | | | |
| mar | marginal | 4,688 | 948,278 | 2,427,465 | 3,276,758 | 4,182,967 | 5,089,178 | 53 | | | | | |
| Ref | Reformed (Presbyterian) | 5,817 | 820,088 | 1,760,512 | 2,523,631 | 3,342,713 | 4,161,785 | 68 | | | | | |
| rad | isolated radio-church | 34,020 | 600,670 | 1,274,730 | 1,561,357 | 1,888,552 | 2,215,746 | 58 | | | | | |
| Lut | Lutheran | 2,400 | 353,700 | 764,684 | 955,647 | 1,158,229 | 1,360,811 | 23 | | | | | |
| Ang | Anglican | 3,591 | 387,876 | 732,077 | 921,859 | 1,160,426 | 1,398,990 | 40 | | | | | |
| ReO | Reformed Orthodox | 909 | 238,640 | 401,797 | 474,583 | 569,503 | 664,424 | 16 | | | | | |
| Con | Congregationalist | 479 | 128,314 | 285,888 | 350,083 | 429,606 | 509,128 | 12 | | | | | |
| EBr | Exclusive Brethren | 1,764 | 75,600 | 152,300 | 179,373 | 207,250 | 235,128 | 8 | | | | | |
| non | no-church (anti-church) | 903 | 50,100 | 150,300 | 184,190 | 222,215 | 260,241 | 3 | | | | | |
| uni | united | 100 | 75,000 | 150,000 | 176,545 | 207,626 | 238,706 | 2 | | | | | |
| CBr | Christian Brethren (Open) | 620 | 29,730 | 144,110 | 171,617 | 206,963 | 242,307 | 15 | | | | | |
| Hol | Holiness | 944 | 53,759 | 143,386 | 200,798 | 262,810 | 324,829 | 22 | | | | | |
| Sal | Salvationist | 185 | 51,477 | 114,000 | 138,011 | 167,882 | 197,753 | 8 | | | | | |
| Spi | Spiritualist | 53,500 | | 107,000 | 134,032 | 164,456 | 194,882 | 3 | | | | | |
| ANGLICAN | | 67,698 | 16,403,751 | 47,556,975 | 48,507,912 | 49,803,974 | 51,100,061 | 182 | 194 | 210 | 225 | 240 | 165 |
| plu | plural-tradition | 39,139 | 13,544,976 | 37,316,303 | 37,012,655 | 36,751,370 | 36,490,086 | 41 | | | | | |
| Low | Low Church | 7,065 | 617,862 | 3,614,546 | 4,064,383 | 4,650,854 | 5,237,319 | 14 | | | | | |
| Hig | High Church (Prayer Book Catholic) | 8,303 | 949,386 | 2,915,362 | 3,015,089 | 3,131,604 | 3,248,124 | 31 | | | | | |
| Eva | Evangelical | 9,072 | 689,763 | 2,338,551 | 2,902,210 | 3,610,370 | 4,318,535 | 10 | | | | | |
| ACa | Anglo-Catholic | 2,658 | 368,083 | 909,553 | 1,009,237 | 1,114,591 | 1,219,948 | 37 | | | | | |
| Cen | Central (Broad Church) | 908 | 177,049 | 358,416 | 400,507 | 441,578 | 482,659 | 33 | | | | | |
| MARGINAL PROTESTANT | | 52,452 | 5,900,032 | 10,830,221 | 12,384,056 | 14,077,333 | 15,770,614 | 448 | 1,107 | 1,220 | 1,345 | 1,490 | 176 |
| Jeh | Jehovah's Witnesses (Russellite) | 26,268 | 1,662,719 | 4,012,405 | 4,706,291 | 5,487,303 | 6,268,327 | 181 | | | | | |
| LdS | Latter-day Saints (Mormon) | 7,843 | 2,367,076 | 3,097,068 | 3,527,037 | 4,001,263 | 4,475,484 | 82 | | | | | |
| Sci | Religious Science (Christian Science) | 3,819 | 623,579 | 1,340,140 | 1,496,039 | 1,654,546 | 1,813,048 | 61 | | | | | |
| Unt | Unitarian (Free Christian) | 1,908 | 274,398 | 469,256 | 517,526 | 566,792 | 616,069 | 29 | | | | | |
| Spi | Spiritualist | 1,471 | 216,887 | 356,522 | 393,613 | 430,910 | 468,208 | 21 | | | | | |
| BrI | British-Israelite | 551 | 104,500 | 228,000 | 253,692 | 279,918 | 306,142 | 4 | | | | | |
| CATHOLIC (NON-ROMAN) | | 10,610 | 2,024,208 | 3,134,385 | 3,277,933 | 3,439,375 | 3,600,810 | 176 | 463 | 474 | 485 | 504 | 59 |
| CAp | Catholic Apostolic | 7,161 | 1,005,660 | 1,610,105 | 1,743,771 | 1,887,279 | 2,030,790 | 68 | | | | | |
| ReC | Reformed Catholic | 1,530 | 478,050 | 657,700 | 665,650 | 681,527 | 697,403 | 7 | | | | | |
| OCa | Old Catholic | 723 | 307,145 | 445,900 | 444,686 | 443,578 | 442,741 | 20 | | | | | |
| CCa | Conservative Catholic | 512 | 175,381 | 273,529 | 272,831 | 272,544 | 272,249 | 29 | | | | | |
| Doubly-affiliated | | | −15,859,171 | −26,711,568 | −31,099,112 | −36,302,272 | −41,505,432 | — | | | | | 34 |
| Disaffiliated | | | −7,276,400 | −10,848,188 | −13,226,950 | −15,365,510 | −17,504,070 | — | | | | | 9 |
| GLOBAL CHURCH MEMBERSHIP | | 1,411,940 | 703,398,777 | 1,131,809,580 | 1,220,849,390 | 1,323,386,867 | 1,425,924,589 | 6,111 | 18,162 | 19,414 | 20,781 | 22,189 | 220 |
| More developed countries | | 877,490 | 434,019,987 | 698,364,049 | 714,252,735 | 730,264,530 | 747,032,825 | | | | | | 51 |
| Less developed countries | | 534,450 | 269,378,790 | 433,445,531 | 506,596,655 | 592,744,337 | 678,891,764 | | | | | | 172 |

## ORGANIZED CHRISTIANITY:
## 7 MAJOR BLOCS

So far we have outlined the fortunes of Christianity considered as a whole. We should now subdivide organized Christianity into its 7 major constituent ecclesiastical blocs and compare their differing fortunes. This is done and shown in Global Tables 4 and 9, inter alia.

One of the more startling findings documented in this survey is the existence of a whole new bloc of global Christianity unrelated to either Western or Eastern Christendom: this is termed here Non-White indigenous Christianity. Parts of it have been known about for many decades; but no-one realized its formidable collective zeal and its immense aggregate size—82 million affiliated church members in 1980.

From Global Table 4 also we can see that whilst Orthodoxy has suffered drastic numerical setbacks during the 20th century—mainly due to the 65-year assault of Communism on the Russian Orthodox —the other 6 major blocs have all increased in numbers. Three have increased spectacularly over 80 years: marginal Protestantism and Catholicism (non-Roman) originating in the Western world, and Non-White indigenous Christianity in the Third World. The remaining 3 mainline Western European/North American blocs—Roman Catholicism, Anglicanism and Protestantism—have barely held their own, as their percentages show, against the immense tide of demographic increase.

Two other features of church membership in the 20th century need comment. First, the overlap between blocs has grown markedly—persons counted as members by a majority church or an established church (usually the Roman Catholic Church) and also by another denomination (usually a Pentecostal or an Evangelical minority church). These doubly-affiliated persons have increased from 3 million in 1900 to 36 million by 1980.

A second feature is defection from the churches, yet unacknowledged by and unrecognized by the churches. We term this the phenomenon of disaffiliation; it is restricted mainly to Latin Europe and Latin America. These disaffiliated are baptized persons counted as members by the churches long after they have abandoned their church affiliation completely, and in fact any Christian profession, replacing it by agnosticism or atheism. Since 1900 such disaffiliated persons have mushroomed from 283,000 to over 15 million in 1980.

### 156 MAJOR ECCLESIASTICAL TRADITIONS

The 7 major blocs making up world Christianity can, in their turn, be divided into a large number of major ecclesiastical traditions. The 92 largest of these—all those with over 100,000 affiliated members in 1970—are shown in Global Table 9. An expanded listing of 156 significant traditions, large and small, is given in Global Table 27.

The 4 largest traditions in 1980 were as follows: 794 million Latin-rite Roman Catholics; 88 million Slavonic-rite Orthodox; 63 million Protestants in united churches formed as unions of several older Protestant traditions; and 51 million Pentecostals in Pentecostal denominations (including those in Non-White indigenous bodies).

### 1.8 MILLION WORSHIP CENTRES

Full acceptance of the gospel and claims of Christ involves Christianity manifesting itself in some sort of community. Consequently a vast network of Christian communities has arisen across the globe— sharing communities, eucharistic communities, basic communities, charismatic communities, and a host of others. Large numbers remain spontaneous and unstructured, though most are structured. Statistics of the growth of these communities are startling.

Global Table 27 enumerates 1,506,400 congregations or worship centres in 1970; by 1975, they had grown to 1,599,100; by 1980, to 1,718,400; with a projected 1,840,000 by 1985. These are nett figures, incorporating large numbers of closures each year in the Western and Communist worlds. They indicate a nett increase of 23,900 congregations each year (460 a week, or 65 nett new congregations a day).

### WORSHIPPING CHRISTIANS

Based on these centres are, as we have noted, 1,018 million active, practising church members. Of these latter, some 12% attend worship services daily, 27% only weekly (on Sundays but not on weekdays), 23% only fortnightly, 13% only monthly, 6% over radio/TV only (mostly sick or handicapped or elderly or isolated Christians), 6% at festivals only, 6% only occasionally, and 6% only annually to fulfil their church's minimum membership requirements.

Another important aspect of practising Christianity is worshippers on the move as religious tourists, travellers and pilgrims. Very large numbers of local, national and international shrines and pilgrimage centres exist. Christian pilgrims today exceed 94 million annually; in other words, 7% of all Christians are on the move as pilgrims every year. Particularly in Communist and anti-Christian lands, this represents a major form of witness and, to their regimes, a disconcertingly effective demonstration of the latent power of Christianity should they attempt to interfere with it.

**Pilgrims.** Russian Orthodox pilgrims visit Zagorsk monastery for a large open-air service. In foreground are bishops (crowned) and priests in procession. Christian pilgrims worldwide exceed 90 million every year.

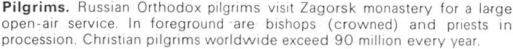

**One of 65 new churches a day.** *Below.* Joyous scene in Kenya as new AIPC church (African Independent Pentecostal Church of Africa) is opened by state President Jomo Kenyatta, who helped found this huge indigenous denomination in 1925. A nett total of 65 such new churches worldwide are being opened every day, most being in the Third World.

---

Introduction to Global Table 9 (opposite).

1. This table gives statistics of congregations and membership belonging to the world's 20,800 organized churches and denominations. The Christian world's 7 ecclesiastical blocs (shown in capitals) are listed in order of size; and the world's 92 largest ecclesiastical traditions (all those with over 100,000 affiliated members in 1970, as shown in column 6) out of the global total of 156 traditions, are also listed in order of size below their related blocs. For full details of definitions, exact meanings, explanations, codes, etc, see Parts 3, 6, and 9. A more complete table listing the 156 ecclesiastical traditions is given in Part 8 (Global Table 27).
2. Note that this table refers primarily to organized denominations

of these various types, and secondarily to dioceses or other jurisdictions. All the figures in column 10 refer to denominations, except those in italics (under ROMAN CATHOLIC) which refer to dioceses and jurisdictions. These 2 meanings produce widely differing statistics. Thus under 'ROMAN CATHOLIC' below, 'Latin-rite local church' in column 3 refers to the 194 Roman Catholic local (nationwide) Churches which are solely Latin-rite, whilst 'Latin-rite Catholics' refers to the more-numerous members of the 2,453 solely Latin-rite dioceses and jurisdictions. Similarly 'Latin/Eastern-rite local church' refers to the 28 Churches which include both Latin-rite and Eastern-rite dioceses, with 375 million Catholics in 1980;

whilst Catholics in the Eastern-rite jurisdictions alone numbered only 8,800,000 in 1980. Likewise, under 'ANGLICAN', the 6 traditions listed below it here refer only to the dominant tradition of Anglican Churches in various countries, as a whole; the totals do not here refer to dioceses of those traditions. Thus the tradition 'Evangelical' here refers to those 10 Anglican Churches which regard themselves specifically as Evangelical, whereas there were 50 Anglican Evangelical dioceses with 6,800,000 affiliated in 1970, and a world total of 15,089,000 individual affiliated Anglican Evangelicals in 1970 (Global Table 4). The reader needs therefore to specify exactly what categories he needs.

**Rapid growth in non-Christian countries.** Two countries with very rapid church growth (over 4% per year) in predominantly non-Christian populations :
(1) **South Korea** (still 69% non-Christian). *Above*. Largest Christian conference in history, EXPLO-74 (2nd Training Conference on Evangelism) attracted 323,419 residents for a week in 1974 in Seoul, Korea. In Korea, also, non-conciliarism is widespread ; conciliarism attracts little interest.
(2) **Togo** (still 63% non-Christian). *Below*. Festive procession through a Togo village for first mass celebrated by young Roman Catholic priest (centre).

## CHURCH GROWTH

In vast areas of the world, the church of Jesus Christ is growing rapidly. In many other areas, it is declining gradually, and in a few other areas it is declining catastrophically. Any realistic measure of the status of the global church today must enumerate not solely the church's successful growth in the former areas, but also its declining fortunes in the latter areas. What counts therefore are the nett figures—growth minus decline. Again, many widely-publicized instances of massive growth of particular denominations are accompanied by unpublicized massive decline in neighbouring denominations. Members are simply transferring their allegiance from one Christian body to another. To be a valid and realistic indicator of Christian progress in a particular area or people or country, nett church growth statistics are needed which indicate the overall nett growth of the church by enumerating overall nett conversions from non-Christian religions and milieux as well as nett biological and transfer growth.

Employing this criterion, Global Map 2 depicts the world situation with regard to church growth. In 1980, very rapid church growth (defined as over 4% per year) is taking place in 28 countries. Rapid church growth (from 3% to 4% per year) is found in 42 countries. Moderate church growth (defined as from 1% to 3% per year) is occurring in 77 countries. Little or no church growth (defined as under 1% per year, down to zero) is found in 48 countries. And nett decline, or less than zero growth (defined as any negative rate per year), is the unfortunate lot of the church in 26 countries.

### GROWTH OF DENOMINATIONS

Church growth in the Third World since 1950 has been to a large degree the result of 2 developments, both fully documented in this Encyclopedia. First, hundreds of Western denominations have opened work in scores of countries new to them across the world. And second, a massive proliferation of newly-formed Non-White indigenous denominations has taken place. The former unconsciously perpetuate in the Third World the milieux and controversies from which they originated in the Western world. The latter usually spring directly out of local disagreements in how to indigenize and inculturate the Christian faith. The inevitable result has been a vast increase in the number of distinct, discrete, separate and divergent Christian denominations in many countries of the world. Global Table 26 illustrates the magnitude of the problem that this has created. In 1900 there was a global total of 1,900 denominations; but this has subsequently proliferated to 18,160 in 1970, 19,410 in 1975, 20,780 in 1980, with a projected 22,190 by 1985. The present nett increase is 270 new denominations each year (5 new ones a week). In many countries this produces serious overlapping, competition, rivalries, clashes, violence, and even lawsuits and protracted litigation. The confusion and even scandal that this vast fragmentation generates in non-Christian lands, or in the minds of non-Christians anywhere, is portrayed in our cartoon below.

## COUNCILS AND CONCILIARISM

Up to AD 1900, there were no multidenominational councils of churches at the national level, nor any at regional, continental or international levels except the World Evangelical Alliance (begun 1846). There were then only 7 confessional councils: the Lambeth Conference (Anglican, begun 1867), Alliance of Reformed Churches (1875), World Methodist Conference (1876), International Old Catholic Bishops' Conference (1889), and the International Congregational Council (1891); together with ongoing Roman Catholic deliberations since the Ecumenical Council of 1869 (Vatican I), and scattered Orthodox attempts at confessional co-ordination. As the numbers of denominations then began to mushroom uncontrollably, churches felt the urgent need to take counsel together and to work with each other in permanent ongoing relationships. Thus by 1980 there had been created across the world a vast transconfessional network of some 550 national or nationwide councils of churches, 55 regional or subcontinental councils, 27 continent-wide councils of churches, and 3 international or world ecclesiastical councils of denominations. The latter were open, at least in theory, to all churches in the world. Further, there had also arisen 45 distinct world confessional councils, and 1 pan-global Conference of Secretaries of Christian World Communions representing 1,770 denominations with 1,179,200,000 church members. The detailed statistics are set out in Global Table 28.

### NON-CONCILIARISM

Despite this massive growth in organized ecclesiastical conciliarism, large numbers of denominations nevertheless opt not to participate. Thus of the world's 6,111 numerically-significant denominations in 1980, 2,033 denominations with 66 million church members were unaffiliated or unrelated to any confessional council. Similarly, 3,840 denominations with 144 million church members were unrelated to any world or international council or synod; 4,815 denominations with 315 million church members were unrelated to any continental council; 5,799 denominations with 1,273 million church members were unrelated to any regional council; and 4,161 denominations with 157 million church members were unrelated to any national council or alliance of churches. If we now include in our total the vast number of smaller denominations, we find that of the world's 20,780 organized Christian denominations in 1980, some 16,100 denominations with over 42 million members have no conciliar ties of any sort. The reason for this is partly the geographical, political, cultural or social isolation often enforced on so many denominations; and partly that the secretariats of councils have tended to adopt radical political or theological stances or programmes alien to the local interests of their constituent members.

Over the last 3 decades, the pattern of denominations joining councils, or refraining from joining, indicates 3 findings. Firstly, rapidly-expanding denominations in areas of full religious liberty only join existing councils in small numbers; they can, and do, flourish without them. It can almost be set down as a variant of the maxim: 'Those who are engaged in making Christian history rarely have time to write it'. The variant is: 'Those who are caught up in massive numerical expansion rarely have time to join councils, or to co-operate with other churches, or to enumerate their own progress, or even to collect statistics of membership'. Secondly, hard-pressed denominations—isolated, declining or persecuted churches under Marxist or other anti-Christian harassment or repression—increasingly find in conciliar membership a new avenue of identity, fellowship, security, new contacts, new service, new witness and, in short, new life. Thirdly, 2 or 3 decades after their formation most councils seem to find their final level in the total numbers of denominations who want to join. Thereafter, only a handful of new churches join by comparison with the vast numbers of new denominations coming into existence each year.

### CHRISTIANS AND THE STATUS OF FOREIGN MISSIONS

During the 20th century, it has become increasingly difficult for foreign missionary societies or personnel to enter or operate in a number of non-Christian countries. By 1980, 25 countries had become closed to foreign missions, and 24 were partially-closed, depriving their 1.3-billion-strong populations of the ministrations of cross-cultural Christianity (see Global Table 17 and Global Map 5). Some 18 other countries restricted missionary entry with varying degrees of severity. This makes a total of 67 countries with 3.1 billion inhabitants beyond the reach of unrestricted cross-cultural witness and service in the name of Christ (Global Tables 3 and 17). Despite this gradual worsening of the global mission of the churches, remaining countries of the world could in 1980 be categorized as 99 receiving, 35 receiving/sending, 10 sending, and 12 sharing; the latter being defined as countries where foreign missionaries sent out are greater than those received from other countries and where both are more numerous than 100 missionaries per million inhabitants.

Full-time Christian personnel, nationals plus aliens, numbered some 3,199,000 in 1980. They vary in density from 3,200 per million population in sending countries to under 90 per million in closed countries. At the global level, they average 676 per million, and of these, foreign missionaries account for only 9% (62 per million), as Global Table 17 shows.

Foreign missionaries and personnel in 1980 number 249,000. As with the changing fortunes of the churches themselves, their absolute number increases slightly each year. The total sent out from Europe and North America, Roman Catholics in particular, continues the gradual decline that began after 1965. This is, however, offset by growth among foreign missionaries and personnel sent out by Third-World churches. These Third-World foreign missionaries, by definition all citizens sent out by developing countries outside the Western and Communist worlds, now number over 32,500. They are rapidly increasing each year in numbers and in the geographical extent of their service.

Global Table 10.    CHRISTIAN OUTREACH AND WORLD EVANGELIZATION, AD 30-2000.

For details of methodology and documentation, see the enlarged version of this table found in Global Table 29, in Part 8.

| Year | AD 30 | 100 | 500 | 1000 | 1500 | 1800 | 1900 | 1975 | 1980 | 1985 | 2000 |
|---|---|---|---|---|---|---|---|---|---|---|---|
| Population (millions) | 169.7 | 181.5 | 193.4 | 269.2 | 425.3 | 902.6 | 1619.6 | 4373.9 | 4373.9 | 4781.1 | 6259.6 |
| Christians (millions) | 0.0 | 1.0 | 43.4 | 50.4 | 81.0 | 208.2 | 558.1 | | 1432.7 | 1548.6 | 2019.9 |
| Evangelized (millions) | 0.3 | 50.8 | 81.2 | 67.3 | 89.3 | 245.8 | 831.8 | | 2993.8 | 3451.8 | 5221.1 |
| *% Christian* | *0.0* | *0.6* | *22.4* | *18.7* | *19.0* | *23.1* | *34.4* | | *32.8* | *32.4* | *32.3* |
| *% evangelized* | *0.2* | *28.0* | *42.0* | *25.0* | *21.0* | *27.2* | *50.7* | | *64.8* | *72.2* | *80.0* |
| Ratio Evangelized/Christians | 200.0 | 50.8 | 1.9 | 1.3 | 1.1 | 1.2 | 1.5 | | 2.1 | 2.2 | 2.6 |

Global Table 11.    EVANGELIZED, UNEVANGELIZED, AND EVANGELIZING GLOBAL POPULATIONS, AD 1900-2000.

**Notes on rows and columns**

1. *Rows.* Each successive indentation below divides up the un-indented category immediately above it. Thus, world population is divided below into 2 categories, Unevangelized and Evangelized; the latter is then divided into the 2 categories, Evangelized non-Christians, and Christians; and so on.

2. *Columns.* The heading *%* in all cases throughout this table refers to the preceding absolute number as a percentage of world population at that date.

3. *Natural.* This component of annual numerical change refers, for the first 7 rows, to natural (biological plus transfer) growth.

4. *Conversion.* This component of annual numerical change

refers to change of allegiance or status to or from the category indicated.

5. *Total.* This column refers to the nett total of annual numerical change, equal to the sum of the 2 preceding columns.

6. *Rate.* The preceding column, divided by the following column, multiplied by 100, and hence expressed as a percent increase per year.

7. *Christian workers and personnel.* For these 3 rows, the column 'Natural' refers to the annual nett increase; the column 'Natural' refers to that component of annual numerical increase which is more demographic, rational, explainable, due to the expectable or anticipated effect of existing large numbers on new vocations,

such as family or church environments or pressures; the column 'Conversion' refers to that component which is less rational, i.e. new vocations which are unexpected because unrelated to family or church environments or pressures.

8. *Foreign personnel.* Foreign missionaries and personnel serving abroad. 'Natural' increase refers to new vocations from within the existing foreign missionary community (children of former missionaries, etc); 'Conversion' refers to new vocations from outside the existing foreign missionary community (new converts, persons from non-Christian backgrounds, etc).

| | 1900 Adherents | % | 1970 Adherents | % | Annual change, 1970-1985 Natural | Conversion | Total | Rate |
|---|---|---|---|---|---|---|---|---|
| World population | 1,619,866,760 | 100.0 | 3,610,034,405 | 100.0 | 76,388,313 | 0 | 76,388,313 | 1.93 |
| Unevangelized | 788,158,970 | 48.7 | 1,391,955,988 | 38.6 | 28,344,594 | -29,482,570 | -1,137,976 | -0.08 |
| Evangelized | 831,727,790 | 51.3 | 2,218,078,417 | 61.4 | 48,043,719 | 29,482,570 | 77,526,289 | 3.01 |
| Evangelized non-Christians | 273,671,458 | 16.9 | 1,001,498,996 | 27.7 | 26,629,460 | 29,286,121 | 55,915,581 | 4.45 |
| Christians | 558,056,332 | 34.4 | 1,216,557,421 | 33.7 | 21,414,259 | 2,196,449 | 1,610,708 | 1.64 |
| Non-evangelizing Christians | 88,796,559 | 5.5 | 332,557,641 | 9.2 | 6,418,774 | 1,758,582 | 8,177,356 | 2.21 |
| Evangelizing Christians | 469,259,773 | 29.0 | 884,021,780 | 24.5 | 14,995,485 | -1,562,133 | 13,433,352 | 1.42 |
| Full-time Christian workers | 1,112,000 | 0.1 | 2,575,600 | 0.1 | 56,370 | 5,970 | 62,340 | 2.13 |
| National personnel | 1,050,000 | 0.1 | 2,330,000 | 0.1 | 51,600 | 10,400 | 62,000 | 2.31 |
| Foreign personnel | 62,000 | 0.0 | 245,600 | 0.0 | 4,770 | -4,430 | 340 | 0.14 |

Global Table 12.    SELECTED GLOBAL CHRISTIAN RESOURCES, ORGANIZATIONS, INSTITUTIONS, PERSONNEL AND ACTIVITIES, AD 1900-1980.

The table presents data on a small selection from the whole range of Christian organizational and institutional activity not already tabulated in earlier Global Tables. It is condensed from Global Table 31, where much fuller data are tabulated. Under PERSONNEL, the global total of all ordained persons (bishops, priests, ministers, clergy, pastors) is about 850,000.

| | GLOBAL TOTALS | | | | CONTINENTAL TOTALS, 1975 | | | | | | | |
|---|---|---|---|---|---|---|---|---|---|---|---|---|
| | 1900 | 1975 | 1980 | Africa | East Asia | Europe | Latin America | % | Northern America | Oceania | South Asia | USSR |
| **ORGANIZATIONS** | | | | | | | | | | | | |
| Service agencies | 1,500 | 15,811 | 17,500 | 1,994 | 582 | 6,304 | 2,078 | 100.0 | 2,664 | 600 | 1,469 | 120 |
| Institutions | 9,500 | 85,953 | 91,000 | 12,335 | 1,816 | 38,525 | 11,421 | 35.1 | 7,656 | 1,908 | 12,212 | 80 |
| **PERSONNEL** | | | | | | | | | | | | |
| Christian workers resident: | | | | | | | | | | | | |
| Nationals (citizens) | 1,112,000 | 2,928,112 | 3,199,000 | 431,321 | 46,319 | 1,059,742 | 253,712 | 64.9 | 776,749 | 64,437 | 235,102 | 60,730 |
| Foreigners (aliens) | 1,050,000 | 2,680,349 | 2,950,000 | 373,469 | 35,080 | 1,013,639 | 180,967 | 64.9 | 754,892 | 53,163 | 208,439 | 60,700 |
| Christian workers (nationals) sent abroad | 62,000 | 247,763 | 249,000 | 57,852 | 11,239 | 46,103 | 72,745 | 31.7 | 21,889 | 11,274 | 26,663 | 30 |
| | 62,000 | 247,763 | 249,000 | 4,268 | 1,533 | 149,544 | 13,002 | 33.2 | 67,387 | 5,505 | 6,399 | 157 |
| **BOOKS & PERIODICALS** | | | | | | | | | | | | |
| New book titles per year: | | | | | | | | | | | | |
| Total all subjects | 28,000 | 583,565 | 648,000 | 10,918 | 54,900 | 275,241 | 28,084 | 23.9 | 87,870 | 5,308 | 41,048 | 80,196 |
| Religious subjects | 3,100 | 22,199 | 24,500 | 1,187 | 2,459 | 11,059 | 1,170 | 0.1 | 2,271 | 245 | 3,586 | 222 |
| Christian periodicals | 3,500 | 22,978 | 22,500 | 983 | 658 | 10,885 | 1,884 | 0.1 | 5,963 | 561 | 1,575 | 70 |
| Christian libraries | 4,000 | 13,002 | 13,300 | | 401 | 5,702 | 1,410 | 0.0 | 2,951 | 210 | 1,273 | 72 |
| **SCRIPTURE DISTRIBUTION** | | | | | | | | | | | | |
| Bibles per year: | | | | | | | | | | | | |
| Free | 5,000 | 1,335,899 | 2,100,000 | 30,780 | 4,600 | 105,915 | 27,260 | 100.0 | 938,434 | 14,290 | 161,620 | 53,000 |
| Subsidized | 1,747,626 | 6,258,167 | 9,100,000 | 1,666,530 | 704,037 | 1,546,815 | 993,567 | 35.1 | 759,476 | 233,624 | 344,118 | 10,000 |
| Commercial | 3,700,000 | 22,117,995 | 25,600,000 | 182,810 | 77,100 | 5,096,580 | 1,073,675 | 64.9 | 15,450,200 | 49,500 | 187,130 | 1,000 |
| Total | 5,452,626 | 30,034,491 | 36,800,000 | 1,919,120 | 785,737 | 6,749,310 | 2,388,732 | 31.7 | 17,148,110 | 297,414 | 682,068 | 64,000 |
| New Testaments per year | 7,300,000 | 51,049,054 | 57,500,000 | 2,091,916 | 4,863,381 | 7,180,647 | 5,534,573 | 32.5 | 26,556,796 | 693,937 | 3,981,804 | 146,000 |
| Portions per year | 4,500,000 | 27,377,619 | 46,814,000 | 3,511,254 | 2,503,261 | 3,211,818 | 4,837,849 | 23.9 | 5,579,697 | 761,767 | 6,969,973 | 2,000 |
| **CHRISTIAN BROADCASTING** | | | | | | | | | | | | |
| Christian radio/TV stations | 0 | 1,332 | 1,450 | 6 | 14 | 56 | 436 | 0.1 | 780 | 8 | 32 | 0 |
| Monthly listeners/viewers: | | | | | | | | | | | | |
| For Christian stations | 0 | 270,950,700 | 291,810,500 | 19,163,400 | 37,765,700 | 16,374,600 | 21,936,000 | 0.1 | 126,631,400 | 314,700 | 28,106,800 | 53,000,000 |
| For secular stations | 0 | 770,799,500 | 834,068,900 | 37,719,200 | 43,504,700 | 237,531,700 | 148,714,400 | 0.0 | 186,011,700 | 11,682,200 | 105,635,600 | 20,658,100 |
| Total audience (excluding overlap) | 0 | 913,360,400 | 990,474,400 | 55,667,300 | 80,687,700 | 250,173,400 | 165,353,700 | 0.0 | 197,620,700 | 11,912,400 | 131,287,100 | 20,658,100 |

| | 1975 Adherents | % | 1980 Adherents | % | 1985 Adherents | % | 2000 Adherents | % |
|---|---|---|---|---|---|---|---|---|
| World population | 3,966,711,095 | 100.0 | 4,373,917,535 | 100.0 | 4,781,123,975 | 100.0 | 6,259,642,000 | 100.0 |
| Unevangelized | 1,393,053,600 | 35.1 | 1,380,576,225 | 31.6 | 1,335,212,151 | 27.9 | 1,038,819,110 | 16.6 |
| Evangelized | 2,573,657,495 | 64.9 | 2,993,341,310 | 68.4 | 3,445,911,824 | 72.1 | 5,220,822,890 | 83.4 |
| Evangelized non-Christians | 1,256,876,644 | 31.7 | 1,560,654,791 | 35.7 | 1,897,319,637 | 39.7 | 3,200,901,524 | 51.1 |
| Christians | 1,316,780,851 | 33.2 | 1,432,686,519 | 32.8 | 1,548,592,187 | 32.4 | 2,019,921,366 | 32.3 |
| Non-evangelizing Christians | 370,418,628 | 9.3 | 414,331,202 | 9.5 | 458,243,776 | 9.6 | 689,596,309 | 11.0 |
| Evangelizing Christians | 946,362,223 | 23.9 | 1,018,355,317 | 23.3 | 1,090,348,411 | 22.8 | 1,330,325,057 | 21.3 |
| Full-time Christian workers | 2,928,112 | 0.1 | 3,199,000 | 0.1 | 3,470,000 | 0.1 | 4,980,000 | 0.1 |
| National personnel | 2,680,349 | 0.1 | 2,950,000 | 0.1 | 3,219,700 | 0.1 | 4,630,000 | 0.1 |
| Foreign personnel | 247,763 | 0.0 | 249,000 | 0.0 | 250,300 | 0.0 | 350,000 | 0.0 |

## CHRISTIAN OUTREACH AND WORLD EVANGELIZATION

The expansion of Christianity and world evangelization over 20 centuries is outlined in Global Tables 1 and 10, and is depicted in more detail in Global Table 29. It illustrates how Christians as a percentage of world population have gone up and down several times throughout their history. Now in the 20th century, the global percentage Christian is once again decreasing each year. But the 20th century is notable in respect of the church's outreach. In 1900, the evangelized population of the world was, at 51%, higher than at any previous period in history, and it has since increased with every subsequent year to 68% by 1980 and a projected 72% by 1985. The contrast is depicted in Global Maps 7 and 8. At the same time, the global ratio of evangelized persons to Christians has increased markedly from 1.5 in 1900 to 2.2 today. This means that, on average, each Christian today is reaching and evangelizing 2.4 times as many non-Christians as the average Christian in 1900. So we have the paradoxical situation that, although the percentage of Christians in the world has fallen regularly since 1900, the outreach, impact and influence of Christianity have risen spectacularly by something like 140%. The dimensions of the unfinished task of world evangelization are in fact very much smaller than contemporary Protestant and Catholic missionary organizations realize.

### EVANGELIZERS

Not all Christians, by any means, are involved in the evangelization of non-Christians around them. A sizeable proportion are unconcerned or uninterested. A large percentage however are involved in the many varieties of Christian outreach, and these active, practising, attending, worshipping, believing, and committed Christians are termed here evangelizers, or evangelizing Christians. In 1980 they numbered 1,018 million, or 23.3% of the world. As Global Table 11 shows, this percentage is decreasing gradually as some 1.6 million persons defect from their ranks each year.

**Evangelizers.** In Tahan (Burma), Lushai Christians form a YCA (Young Christians Association; Methodist) to spread the gospel far and wide.

### THE UNEVANGELIZED

Using the precise definitions evolved for this Encyclopedia, the global total of evangelized populations in 1980 is 2,993 million. The evangelized can be further divided into 1,433 million Christians, who by definition either profess Christ or are part of his church; and 1,561 millions whom we here term evangelized non-Christians—persons who are not Christians in any recognized sense but who have become aware of Christianity, Christ and the gospel, and yet have not, or not yet, responded positively by accepting them.

This leaves 1,381 million as unevangelized persons, unaware of Christianity, Christ and the gospel. The exact whereabouts of these millions can be determined from Global Tables 30 (by continents) and 31 (by nations). The 9 least evangelized countries in the world, each with under 20% of its population adequately evangelized, are (listed in order, the least being last); Libya, Afghanistan, Bhutan, Guinea, Oman, North Yemen, Mauritania, Maldives, and Sahara. We define them here as unreached countries. In 1980, their total population was 41,281,200. Their unreached status is not the result of neglect by the churches, for despite hostile receptions some 468 Christian foreign missionaries work in these countries (see Global Table 31, column 44).

## UNREACHED PEOPLES AND HIDDEN PEOPLES

As we noted earlier, there are in the world some 4,050 Christian cultures (with church members over 50%) and 4,940 non-Christian cultures (with church members under 50%). Of the latter, around 2,800 have been extensively exposed to the gospel and evangelized by numerous means including Scripture translation into their languages; response however has been meagre.

This leaves some 2,100 distinct ethnolinguistic people groups or cultures who are still in varying degrees unevangelized, which on our definition means with populations of whom less than 60% have been evangelized. These cultures are not however totally unreached by the gospel; many are found in largely christianized countries, one in four already have Scripture translations in their own languages, many are exposed to Christian broadcasting in their languages, and many have small but significant churches of their own people. Less than half of these are unreached peoples. On our definition, the only people groups who can correctly be called unreached are the one thousand or so whose populations are each less than 20% evangelized.

What is remarkable about the situation of these unreached peoples is how close many of them live to related unevangelized peoples who nevertheless already have the Scriptures in their own languages. This can be shown by a brief numerical overview. The least christianized of these people groups, living in the world's least-christianized countries, can be characterized as follows (see Global Table 25). Eighty-one major peoples (19% of the world's 432 major peoples) each have less than 1% of their population as church members; their total population is 1,700 million; they consist of 976 people groups, speaking 527 languages of which 169 have Scripture translations available. Fifty-eight of these same 81 major peoples each have less than 0.1% as church members; their population is 309 million; they consist of 636 people groups, speaking 336 languages of which 89 have Scripture translations available. Lastly, the least-christianized 43 of all major peoples each have less than 0.01% as church members; their population is 140 million; they consist of 394 people groups, speaking 220 languages of which 54 have Scripture translations available.

Even a church as small as 0.1% of a people can be a significantly evangelizing church; there are plenty of examples in history of a thousand Christians evangelizing their group or culture of a million people. But below this figure, the church is so small that it cannot reach very far by itself. This is the case with the 636 people groups just described. They have each no numerically significant evangelizing church, and they each live in countries with only a miniscule Christian presence. The gospel is therefore effectively hidden from them until outside influences can be brought to bear. For this reason they are sometimes referred to as 'hidden peoples'. Their locations and sizes may be approximately determined here from Global Tables 5, 8, 24 and 25.

As the figures above indicate, most of the world's cultures have already been effectively exposed to the gospel. The Scriptures in particular permeate not only the non-Christian world, but also the unevangelized world of unreached and hidden peoples.

## CHRISTIAN ORGANIZATIONS, RESOURCES AND ACTIVITIES

The last table set out here in Part 1 gives a summary and overview of global Christian resources, organizations, institutions, personnel and activities across the 20th century (see Global Table 12). A greatly expanded version, covering all 223 countries and ranging across 107 variables, is given at the end of Part 8 as Global Table 31. These tables demonstrate that almost all categories of Christian resources and activities have multiplied startlingly over the 8 decades since the year 1900. The single most massive development is probably that of Christian broadcasting. Non-existent in 1900, this phenomenon came into existence in 1921; by 1980, the total monthly audience listening regularly to Christian radio and TV programmes had climbed to a staggering 990 million, which is 22.6% of the world (see Global Map 6, and Global Table 31).

**Radio/TV broadcasting.** Christian programmes now regularly reach 23% of the world's population. *Above.* Programmer/announcer in East Africa.

### CONCLUSION

We can sum up as follows. The status of Christianity at this point in history presents a striking paradox. On the one hand, the 20th century has seen a marked decline in the number of Christianity's committed adherents in proportion to the world. But on the other hand, the impact and influence of those adherents on the world scene has expanded phenomenally. In Jesus' day, the rapid growth of a mustard seed startled his followers; in the same way today, the vast expansion of the influence of the Kingdom of God exceeds all the expectations of earlier generations of Christians.

NOTE ON SOURCES.
The sources of all data on religions in this essay are Tables 1 and 2 in Part 7 of this Encyclopedia, together with their summaries in Global Tables 1 to 31 here and in Part 8.
Sources for totals of secular data are, again, data presented in Part 7. References to their own sources are given in Methodology (Part 3). Global secular totals in the section 'Christianity and poverty' above come from *World development report, 1980* (World Bank, 1980).
The delineation here of socialism, Communism, atheism, secularism, fascism, nationalism, etc as 'secular quasi-religions' is due to Paul Tillich, as developed in his 1962 Bampton Lectures, *Christianity and the encounter of the world religions.*

**Hidden peoples.** 3 unreached Saharan peoples around Timbuktu, who are still hidden from the Christian gospel behind centuries of culture and custom. *Left.* Ahaggaren Tuareg (= 'The Forsaken Ones'), whose men are permanently veiled day and night. *Centre.* The warlike Aulliminden. *Right.* Voltaic Negro masked for pagan rites.

# PART 2
# CHRONOLOGY
A chronology of world evangelization,
AD 27-1983

*The doctrine of the Saviour has irradiated the whole Oikumene.*
    —Eusebius, *Ecclesiastical history* 2.3.1, AD 310.

This chronology provides a historical background to the study of contemporary Christianity by listing a selection of the major or most significant events in the growth and spread of Christianity across 20 centuries and across the world; in evangelism; and in the evangelization of peoples and nations across the globe, with particular emphasis on statistical enumeration. It sets forth the 9 major epochs or pulsations in Christian history (shown as sub-titles in capitals) using the terminology coined by the historian K.S. Latourette; the origin of the 7 major ecclesiastical blocs and over 150 ecclesiastical traditions detailed in this Encyclopedia; the founding of Christian work in every continent, nation, country and territory; the conversion or christianization of whole peoples; notable foreign missionary enterprises to other lands; the founding of major missionary societies and orders; statistics of Christian expansion; revival and renewal movements; major recessions or setbacks to Christianity, schisms and apostasies, church unions, mass movements into the churches; major international evangelistic campaigns, translations of the Bible into the world's languages; major technological innovations facilitating evangelization; and other significant events in the history of the spread of Christianity. Most of these events are noted in Tables 2 or in the texts on countries in Part 7. The presentation and language used are standardized to a large degree; note in particular that the spelling '1st', '2nd', '3rd', etc refers to the official titles of a series of regular conferences, whereas the spelling 'First', 'Second', 'Third', etc refers to all other types of situation.

In Global Table 29 (Part 8) is a statistical table showing the numerical expansion of both evangelization (evangelized peoples) and of Christianity (total Christians) across the continents of the world throughout these 20 centuries, at regular intervals through historical time. These statistics are repeated in the chronology at 29 historical turning-points or watersheds at which we summarize the **Global status** (printed in boldface type for quick identification) of Christianity and world evangelization.

The chronology and its format are designed to display with clarity 3 particular emphases: (1) expansion over time, i.e. over the whole period of Christian history, illustrated by the 9 major epochs or pulsations in Christian history; (2) expansion in numbers, i.e. the numerical growth of evangelization and of Christians, churches, dioceses, movements, et alia, especially for those few occasions before the year 1800 where detailed statistics were collected; and (3) geographical expansion to all nations and peoples. To give an overview of this latter emphasis (3), the chronology gives in italics, once only, the name of every country in the world (as existing in 1980, with frontiers as today) with the year when Christianity first reached it and ongoing or definitive evangelization began (i.e. arrival of the first resident Christians or missionaries, excluding any earlier temporary or short visits), giving details, in parentheses, of the agents involved.

At the end of the chronology, a diagram sets out the patterns of fission and fusion which have characterized Christianity over its 20 centuries of history.

# A CHRONOLOGY OF WORLD EVANGELIZATION, AD 27–1983

## MINISTRY OF JESUS

BC 4 Birth of Jesus of Nazareth.

AD

27 Roman empire (33 million, 50% slaves) has 2.3 million Jews (7% of population), a large proportion being proselytes; in Palestine, 580,000 Jews and 220,000 Gentiles.

Beginning of public ministry of Jesus of Nazareth.

28 Jesus proclaims nearness and imminence of the rule of God: 'The Kingdom of God is at hand' (Mark 1.15).

29 Jesus envisages lightning spread of the gospel to all nations within one single generation: 'This Good News of the Kingdom will be proclaimed to the whole oikumene as a witness to all nations. And then the end will come' (Matthew 24.14, Jerusalem Bible. Oikumene = Graeco-Roman inhabited world; 'the end' probably = Fall of Jerusalem in AD 70).

30 Crucifixion of Jesus, followed by resurrection and ascension.

Appearance of risen Jesus to over 500 disciples on one occasion in Galilee (1 Corinthians 15.6).

Jesus' Great Commission: 'Go to all peoples everywhere and make them my disciples' (Matthew 28.19, GNB).

Epoch I:
**CHRISTIANITY WINS THE ROMAN EMPIRE AD 30–500**

*AD 30-80 The Apostolic Age*

30 **Global status:** during 40 days' Appearances of the Risen Christ, total of Jesus' disciples = about 4,000, total evangelized = whole of Palestine (800,000).

Day of Pentecost in Jerusalem: 3,000 converted among Diaspora Jews and Gentiles from 'every nation under heaven', from North Africa to Persia.

*Palestine.* First Christians, in Jerusalem.

*Israel.* First Christians, from Jerusalem on Day of Pentecost, return to homes across Judaea.

*Egypt.* First Christians (returning from Jerusalem after Day of Pentecost).

*Lebanon* (then Phoenicia). First Christians (returning from Jerusalem after Day of Pentecost).

*Jordan* (Transjordan). First Christians (returning from Jerusalem after Day of Pentecost).

*Libya.* First Christians (returning from Jerusalem after Day of Pentecost).

*Syria.* First Christians (returning from Jerusalem after Day of Pentecost).

*Italy.* First Christians (returning home soon after Day of Pentecost).

Large-scale people movement of families and villages into the church: 'More than ever believers were added to the Lord, multitudes both of men and of women' (Acts 5.14).

31 Apostles begin evangelizing widely: several remain in Jerusalem for a decade or two, several travel outside, but most evangelize only Jews until AD 36 (Peter), 43 (Paul), and after AD 50 (others).

32 'The number of the disciples multiplied greatly in Jerusalem, and a great many of the priests were obedient to the faith' (Acts 6.7).

c 33 *Turkey* (then called Asia Minor). First Christians (in Antioch, returned from Jerusalem after Day of Pentecost).

34 Martydom of Stephen. Believers scattered throughout Judaea and Samaria.

*Sudan.* First Christians; gospel taken to Nubia (Meroe) by Ethiopian eunuch baptized by Philip.

Mission extended to Samaritans by Philip; fresh persecution.

Conversion of Saul of Tarsus (age 24), a Roman citizen; departs to Arabia, then to Jerusalem and Tarsus; later renamed Paul.

35 Church throughout Judaea, Galilee and Samaria multiplied (Acts 9.31).

c 35 Armenia (now *USSR*). First Christians (returned from Jerusalem after Day of Pentecost); c 80, traditionally evangelized by Thaddeus and Bartholomew.

36 Commission to evangelize pagan Gentiles as Gentiles first forced on consciousness of Jewish church, through baptism by Peter of Cornelius, a God-fearer but not a Jewish proselyte (Acts 10.1–48).

c 36 Large influx of Italians (Cohors II Italica Civium Romanorum) converted through ministry of Apostle Peter at Caesarea (Acts 10.48).

c 37 Antioch: wider mission to Gentiles inaugurated.

c 40 *Greece.* First Judeo-Christians.

*Holy See* (at that time, Rome). First Christians in capital of Roman empire.

42 Mark the Evangelist arrives in Alexandria, founds Coptic church.

Phoenicia, Cyprus, Antioch: 'A great number that believed turned to the Lord' (Acts 11.21).

43 Paul and Barnabas at Antioch, new centre for Hellenistic Christians, 500 strong; believers first called Christians, in derision (Acts 11.26).

44 Persecution in Jerusalem under king Herod Agrippa I; James brother of John executed, imprisonment and escape of Peter.

45–49 Paul's 1st missionary journey: Antioch, Cyprus, Pamphilia, Pisidia, Lycaonia.

46 *Cyprus.* First missionaries (Apostles Paul and Barnabas).

49 Apostolic Council of Jerusalem: converts from paganism exempted from Jewish Law; Paul recognized as apostle to non-Jews.

c 50 Jews and Christians banished from Rome.

*Iraq* (then termed Media, et alia). First Christians (Assyrians, with Apostle Thomas, evangelizing Jewish colonies).

*Iran* (at that time Persia). First Christians (Assyrians).

Assyrian Christians found Church of the East (later Nestorian).

50–52 Paul's 2nd missionary journey: Phrygia, Galatia, Greece, Athens.

50 Paul begins evangelization of 3 important Roman provinces: Macedonia, Achaia and Asia (Acts 16.6).

52 *India.* First missionaries (Apostle Thomas, and others, in the south).

53–58 Paul's 3rd missionary journey: Ephesus (2 years, 3 months), Corinth, Macedonia, Philippi.

54 1st imperial Roman persecution of Christians, under emperor Nero.

55 Roman province of Asia (500 cities) evangelized from capital Ephesus, seat of the proconsul. In 2 years, 'All the residents of Asia heard the word of the Lord' (Acts 19.10).

57 Paul's *Letter to the Romans* sent to about 3,000 Christians in 5 congregations in Rome (population 800,000).

Paul describes spread of the gospel: 'The sound of their voice went out to all the world; their words reached the ends of the earth (oikumene)' (Romans 10.18, GNB).

Greek (eastern) half of Roman empire already evangelized by Paul: 'From Jerusalem and as far round as Illyricum (1,800 miles) I have fully preached the gospel of Christ' (Romans 15.19).

58 Paul arrested in Jerusalem.

60 Paul sent for trial to Rome.

*Malta.* First missionary (shipwrecked Apostle Paul, and others).

c 60 *Yugoslavia* (at that time Dalmatia, Illyricum). First Christians (among Diaspora Jews).

61 Paul in Rome under military guard; gospel proclaimed in capital of empire.

Paul writes: 'The Good News which has reached you is spreading all over the world' (Colossians 1.6, Jerusalem); 'The Good News, which you have heard, has been preached to the whole human race' (Colossians 1.23; Greek 'to all creation under the sky').

*Britain* (later UK). First resident Christians (Roman soldiers, merchants); origins of Celtic church.

63 Paul freed in Rome, visits Spain, Greece, Asia Minor.

Martyrdom of Apostle Mark in Baucalis near Alexandria.

*Spain.* First Christians (Roman soldiers, merchants, evangelized by Paul).

64 Great Fire of Rome; Apostles Peter and Paul martyred, thousands of Christians burned or killed by emperor Nero.

65 Revelation of John the Divine: 'I saw another angel flying high in the air, with an eternal message of Good News to announce to the peoples of the earth, to every race, tribe, language and nation' (Rev. 14.6, GNB).

66 Evangelist Luke concludes his 2-volume narrative (Luke-Acts): The worlds of the empire and Judaism have now been evangelized, the Gospel is now known throughout them, and the Great Commission there largely completed.

Anti-Jewish riots and pogroms in Egypt: 50,000 killed in Alexandria, 60,000 elsewhere.

67 Vespasian with 60,000 troops quells Jewish insurrection, reconquers Galilee.

69 All 4 million Jews throughout diaspora now evangelized, 'having been destined to hear the good news before judgement falls'.

70 **Global status:** One generation after Christ, world is 0.1% Christians (85% of them being Non-Whites, 15% Whites), 15% evangelized; with scriptures translated into 5 languages.

Destruction of Jerusalem by Titus with 4 legions; 600,000 killed in Judaea, 10,000 Jews crucified, 90,000 Jews to Rome as slaves; Jews and Jewish Christians scattered abroad.

Destruction of Jewish Christianity and end of the Judaizers.

After fall of Jerusalem, Antioch becomes Christian centre of eastern half of Roman empire.

c 70 *Albania* (then Macedonia). First Christians (among Diaspora Jews).

71 Colosseum built in Rome; large numbers of Christians thrown to beasts or otherwise martyred.

*AD 80–130 The Sub-Apostolic Age*

c 80 *Tunisia* (then termed Roman province of Africa). First Christians.

Missionary centre of Christianity shifts to Ephesus under the Apostle John.

*France.* First Christians (from Italy).

81 2nd imperial Roman persecution, under Domitian.

c 85 Writings of the Apostolic Fathers (Apostolici), Greek Christian writers from 85–150: Barnabas, Clement, Hermas, Ignatius, Papias, Polycarp.

90 Rise of Gnosticism, a dualistic rationalistic heresy.

c 90 First of a vast number of amateur Scripture translations in Old Latin.

c 90 *West Germany.* First Christians (merchants and Roman soldiers).

94 Clement of Rome maintains that under the apostle Paul the entire Roman empire became evangelized.

98 Roman emperor Trajan extends empire to include Arabia, Iraq, Armenia, Romania, Hungary.

3rd imperial persecution, under Trajan.

100 **Global status:** 2 generations after Christ, world is 0.6% Christians (70% of them being Non-Whites, 30% Whites), 28.0% evangelized; with scriptures translated into 6 languages.

c 100 *Monaco.* First Christians (soldiers, traders).

*Algeria* (at that time Roman province of Mauretania). First Christians (Latin-speaking).

*Romania.* First Christians (in Roman province of Dacia).

Christianity predominantly urban throughout Roman cities, spreading from city to city along trade routes.

100 *Saudi Arabia.* First Christians; later eradicated in 7th century by Islam.

c 100 *Sri Lanka* (then Ceylon). First Christians (Christians of St Thomas from India; Nestorians).

115 Martyrdom of Ignatius bishop of Antioch.

117 Roman emperor Hadrian codifies laws of Rome, establishes postal system throughout empire.

*AD 130–313 Pre-Constantinian Post-Apostolic Era.*

132 Second Jewish rebellion under Bar Kokeba; second destruction of Jerusalem by Romans in 134; almost entire Jewish population of Palestine died or fled.

136 Hadrian refounds Jerusalem; temple of Jupiter built on site of Solomon's temple.

c 140 Hermas writes: 'The Son of God. . . has been preached to the ends of the earth' (*Shepherd of Hermas*).

c 150 The 4 Gospels available written in Old Syriac as harmony or continuous narrative in the *Diatessaron* of the Gnostic Tatian.

Mandaeanism, a Jewish-Christian Gnostic syncretistic religion, begun in Iran.

*Morocco* (then part of Roman province of Mauretania). First Christians (4 bishoprics in Tangier-Rabat-Fez area before 200).

150 Phrygia: rise of Montanism, a puritanical prophetic charismatic movement.

c 150 *Bulgaria* (at that time Roman provinces of Moesia and Thracia). First Christians (churches at Anchialus and Debeltum, and along Black Sea).

*Portugal* (then Roman province of Lusitania). First Christians (Romans).

Justin Martyr writes: 'The first Apostles, twelve in number, in the power of God went out and proclaimed Christ to every race of men'; and 'There is not one single race of men, whether barbarians, or Greeks, or whatever they may be called, nomads, or vagrants, or herdsmen dwelling in tents, among whom prayers and giving of thanks are not offered through the name of the Crucified Jesus'.

156 Death at the stake of Polycarp bishop of Smyrna.

161 4th imperial Roman persecution, under Marcus Aurelius.

c 170 Portions of scripture in Coptic translated.

174 *Austria.* First Christians.

180 Christians now found in all provinces of the Roman empire and in Mesopotamia.

c 180 Pantaenus founds missionary training school in Alexandria (Egypt).

189 Christian activity reported from Malabar (South India) through visit of Pantaenus of Alexandria.

c 190 Widespread turning to Christianity, with vast numbers, in North Africa.

193 5th imperial Roman persecution, under Septimius Severus.

197 Tertullian writes: 'The blood of the martyrs is seed', and 'There is no nation indeed which is not Christian'.

200 **Global status:** 6 generations after Christ, world is 3.4% Christians (68.0% of them being Non-Whites, 32.0% Whites), 32.0% evangelized; with scriptures translated into 7 languages.

c 200 Most of New Testament available in Sahidic Coptic (Upper Egypt), later in Bohairic/Memphitic Coptic (Coastal or Lower Egypt round Alexandria).

200 Vicious persecutions in Egypt with thousands martyred.

c 200 *Switzerland* (then called Roman province of Raetia). First Christians (Roman soldiers, merchants).

*Sahara* (later Spanish, Western). First Christians; eradicated during later Muslim rule.

*Belgium.* First Christians (during Roman occupation).

New Testament in Latin completed.

200 First permanent church buildings constructed (all worship previously in homes).

c 200 Edessa (now Urfa) first city-state to make Christianity its state religion.

c 205 Clement of Alexandria writes: 'The whole world, with Athens and Greece, (has) already become the domain of the Word'.

c 210 *Qatar* (then Persian province of Beit Qatraiye). First Christians (first documents AD 224).

c 220 Origen writes: 'The gospel of Jesus Christ has been preached in all creation under heaven, to Greeks and barbarians, to wise and foolish. . . It is impossible to see any race of men which has avoided accepting the teaching of Jesus'; 'The divine goodness of Our Lord and Saviour is equally diffused among the Britons, the Africans, and other nations of the world'; and 'The preaching of the gospel through the whole Oikumene shows that the church is receiving divine support'; but also 'Many people, not only barbarians, but even in the

Empire, have not yet heard the word of Christ'; and 'The gospel has not yet been preached to all nations, since it has not reached the Chinese or the Ethiopians beyond the river, and only small parts of the more remote and barbarous tribes'.

225 Over 20 Assyrian bishoprics of the Church of the East, in Tigris-Euphrates region and to Caspian Sea and Bahrain.

235 6th imperial Roman persecution, under Maximinus.

c 240 Gregory Thaumaturgos made bishop in Pontus, a majority pagan diocese; mass movement begins, 95% converted before his death in 270.

244 Christian hierarchy already established in northwest Arabia.

249 7th imperial Roman persecution, under military ruler Decius; systematic state attempt to destroy Christianity.

250 Over 100 bishoprics in southern Italy.

c 250 *Hungary* (at that time Roman provinces of Pannonia and Valeria). First Christians (Arian, Roman and Orthodox missionaries).

Church founded in Chersonesus (Sebastopol), Crimea, Ukraine.

*Bahrain.* First Christians, with a bishopric.

Peshitta (Simple), Syriac version of Bible, completed.

*Luxembourg.* First Christians (Roman soldiers).

251 City of Rome: 30,000 Christians (3% of population of 1 million), 46 presbyters, 7 deacons, 42 acolytes, 52 exorcists, 1,500 widows and persons in distress.

252 Catastrophic plague epidemic strikes Mediterranean world, kills 25% of entire population of Roman empire over 20 years; 50% die in Alexandria; in Carthage, bishop Cyprian organizes medical aid.

253 8th imperial Roman persecution, under Valerian.

260 Number of Christians in Roman empire about 40%, increasing very rapidly.

261 First basilicas (rectangular churches) built.

270 9th imperial Roman persecution, under Aurelian.

Rise of Manicheism, a dualistic hierarchical rival religion to Christianity.

c 270 Rise of monasticism in Egypt: (1) eremitical (Anthony of Egypt), (2) cenobitic (Pachomius); widespread over next 2 centuries.

285 Baptism of converts at Lake Zurich (Switzerland).

287 Mass conversion of Armenia under Gregory the Illuminator; Christianity declared its state religion.

290 Roman empire reorganized by emperor Diocletian into 4 prefectures, 15 (secular) dioceses, 120 provinces.

295 David of Basra evangelizes in India.

300 **Global status:** 9 generations after Christ, world is 10.4% Christians (66.4% of them being Non-Whites, 33.6% Whites), 35.0% evangelized; with scriptures translated into 10 languages.

300 Missionary activity under way in Georgia.

c 300 *Afghanistan* (then Khorasan). First Christians, with Nestorian bishop of Herat.

300 Roman empire: areas of strongest Christian development: Syria, Asia Minor, Egypt, North Africa, also Rome, Lyons. Chief numerical strength in east; no area in empire entirely unevangelized.

300 Over 200 dioceses already established in Italy.

303 10th and last imperial Roman persecution, under Diocletian; destruction of all church buildings and scriptures ordered. Around 500,000 Christians executed in 10 years of systematic slaughter.

c 310 Gaul still 70% pagan.

Eusebius of Caesarea's apologetic works: *Praeparatio evangelica* (refuting paganism), *Demonstratio evangelica* (fulfilment of Hebrew prophecy in Christ).

Eusebius writes: 'The doctrine of the Saviour has irradiated the whole Oikumene (whole inhabited earth)'.

Beginning of Arianism (Christ a created being, not truly divine).

311 Donatist schism in North Africa; rigorists, opposing leniency towards those who lapsed under persecution.

312 Constantine marches on Rome, sees sign 'In hoc signo vinces/By this sign conquer'.

313 Constantine at Milan issues Edict of Toleration legalizing Christianity throughout Roman empire.

314 3 British bishops attend council of Arles in France.

319 Pagan sacrifices prohibited throughout Roman empire.

325 Council of Nicea I (1st Ecumenical Council): Arianism condemned.

330 **Global status:** 10 generations after Christ, world is 12% Christians (65.7% of them being Non-Whites, 34.3% Whites), 36% evangelized; with scriptures translated into 10 languages.

Constantine moves capital of Roman empire to Byzantium, and renames it Constantinople.

332 *Ethiopia.* First Christians (shipwrecked Syrian slave Frumentius, in Axum; later bishop). Origin of Ethiopian Orthodox Church.

339 Severe persecution of Christians in Persia, until 379; intermittent vicious persecution by Sassanian rulers until 640 conquest by Islam.

c 340 Coptic Orthodox bishoprics under pope Athanasius number 100 in Egypt.

341 Ulfilas, an Arian, bishop of the Goths and later in Moesia II; creates German alphabet and translates Bible into Visigothic.

345 Persecution in East Syria and Persia drives 400 Nestorians with a bishop to settle in Malabar, India.

c 350 *South Yemen.* First Christians (church built at Aden).

Nestorians on Socotra island, with own bishop from 5th to 15th centuries.

Sudan: Coptic Orthodox traders active from Egypt. On breakup of kingdom of Meroe over next 100 years, its 3 successor states become officially Christian.

350 *Ireland* (then Hibernia). First Christians (monks from Crete).

Apogee of Arianism: whole of East now Arian.

361 Julian the Apostate emperor: last attempt to restore paganism throughout Roman empire.

367 Canon of New Testament finally agreed on, the 27 books being listed in Athanasius' Easter Letter (367) for the East, and by the Synod of Carthage (397) for the West.

374 A layman, Ambrose of Milan, acclaimed bishop by crowds.

378 Goths and northern barbarians begin conquest of Roman empire.

Jerome writes: 'From India to Britain, all nations resound with the death and resurrection of Christ' (*Isaiam cliv, Epistol. xiii ad Paulinum*); estimates 1.9 million Christians to have been martyred since AD 30.

380 City of Antioch: of 500,000 population, 50% Christians, increasing rapidly.

Theodosius emperor of the East makes Christianity the state religion and decrees that all subjects of the Roman empire must become Christians.

381 Council of Constantinople I (2nd Ecumenical Council); creed of Nicaea reaffirmed; Macedonianism and Apollinarianism condemned.

Constantinople recognized as first among the eastern patriarchates.

c 390 Collapse of Arianism throught Roman empire; continues among some German tribes until c 700.

395 Roman empire permanently divided: western empire ruled from Rome (sacked 410, 455, 476), eastern from Constantinople.

400 **Global status:** 12 generations after Christ, world is 17.1% Christians (64.0% of them being Non-Whites, 36.0% Whites), 39.0% evangelized; with scriptures translated into 11 languages.

c 400 John Chrysostom founds training school for native Gothic evangelists; writes, '"Go and make disciples of all nations" was not said for the Apostles only, but for us also'.

Persia (Tigris/Euphrates, and highlands) a strong Christian area: Persians now 25% Christians (Syriac-speaking, but no Persian liturgy or scriptures).

Several millions of Christians known to have been buried in catacombs near Rome over 3 centuries by this date.

*Spanish North Africa* (Ceuta, Melilla; then in Roman province of Mauretania). First Christians (Romans).

Scriptures being translated into Ethiopic by monks from Egypt.

404 Vulgate (Latin translation of Bible) completed by Jerome after 22 years' work from original Hebrew and Greek, living in Palestine.

409 Arian Visigoths overrun Iberian peninsula.

410 Fall of Rome to barbarian Alaric and his Visigoths.

c 410 Alphabet and Bible in Armenian completed by Mesrob, later patriarch.

410 Synod of Seleucia uniting Persian and Greek churches.

424 Assyrian bishop of Seleucia-Ctesiphon becomes independent of Antioch.

426 Augustine of Hippo (North Africa) completes treatise *The City of God.*

431 Council of Ephesus (3rd Ecumenical Council): Nestorius patriarch of Constantinople condemned as heretic, also Pelagianism.

432 Ireland evangelized by Patrick.

438 Theodosian Code, codifying Roman law.

441 *San Marino.* First Christians (hermitage built).

442 *Isle of Man.* First Christians.

c 450 Conversion to Christianity becomes mainly by communities, led by their kings or princes.

*Liechtenstein.* First Christians (merchants and Roman soldiers).

6 Nestorian bishoprics in Arabia, under metropolitan of Kashkar.

Caucasus begins to be converted to Christianity.

451 Council of Chalcedon (4th Ecumenical Council): Tome of Leo approved, definition of faith against Apollinarianism, Nestorianism and Eutychianism.

After Chalcedon, Copts of Egypt divided, most becoming Monophysites.

476 Sack of Rome: end of Roman empire in the West, largely due to demographic pressure (overpopulation).

490 Assyrian church in Persia declares itself Nestorian, opposing churches of Roman empire.

Climax of first major epoch of advance: Christianity wins at least 80% of Roman empire.

c 495 Nestorian metropolitan provinces in Persia number 7, with several bishoprics abroad (Arabia, India).

496 Clovis king of the Franks baptized with 3,000 warriors at Rheims.

498 Christianity spreading widely in Central Asia, with whole tribes converted; Nestorians active in Turkestan until eliminated c1350.

499 Task of translating Jesus' message into Greek and Latin cultures virtually completed, after 16 generations.

## Epoch II: **THE GREAT RECESSION** (The Dark Ages) **AD 500–950**

500 **Global status:** 16 generations after Christ, world is 22.4% Christians (61.9% of them being Non-Whites, 38.1% Whites), 42.0% evangelized; with scriptures translated into 13 languages.

The so-called Dark Ages begin (AD 500–1000, early medieval period in Western Europe): no emperor in West, frequent warfare, virtual disappearance of urban life.

First Bantu cultivators, expanding from Nigeria, reach Africa's east coast, and in south cross river Limpopo.

c 500 *North Yemen.* First Christians, later eradicated by Islam.

500 The Nine Saints (Syrian Orthodox) establish monastery in northern Ethiopia and secure monophysite character of Ethiopian church.

c 510 Irish Peregrini (unorganized wandering hermits and preachers) begin to migrate across Europe for next 400 years, to the Alps, Germany, Danube, Italy, also to Orkneys, Faeroes, Iceland.

512 West Syrian church becomes formally Monophysite under patriarch Severus.

520 Nestorians (Syriac evangelists) reported on island of Ceylon, with many converts, also in Malabar under a Persian bishop, and in the Ganges region.

523 Massacre of Arab Christians in Najran and Himyar (Arabia) by Jewish Arab king.

525 Christianity firmly established in Arabian peninsula until Islam conquers in 7th century.

526 King of Axum (Abyssinia) sends expeditionary force to Yemen to protect persecuted Christians.

250,000 including many Christians killed by earthquake in Antioch, Syria.

529 Justinian I closes ancient schools of philosophy at Athens.

Rule of Benedict of Nursia begun in Monte Cassino monastery, Italy; rise of Western monasticism.

535 Cosmas Indicopleustes, Nestorian merchant missionary over most of world, retires to monastery and in 547 completes his survey *Topographia Christiana* in 12 Books.

c 540 Emperor Justinian orders 70,000 persons forcibly baptized in Asia Minor.

542 Over 100,000 priests secretly ordained by Jacob Baradaeus as West Syrian bishop of Edessa till 578; rapid expansion of Syrian Orthodoxy (Jacobites).

543 Melkite missionaries sent by emperor Justinian to Nubia (Sudan), but wife sends Monophysite Julian who converted king of Nobatae (Nubia); Monophysitism holds sway till AD 1000; Christians also in Darfur and Kordofan.

549 Nestorian patriarch sends bishop to Hephthalite Huns.

c 550 *Channel Islands.* First Christians (Breton settlers).

Egypt: Coptic bishops number 168 in 4 ecclesiastical provinces.

553 Council of Constantinople II (5th Ecumenical Council): Three Chapters controversy.

563 Scotland evangelized by Columba from Ireland; Iona monastery founded, influence spreads to the English, Franks, and Swiss.

589 Arian Visigoths in Spain converted to Catholicism, declared state religion at Toledo.

596 Augustine sent by Roman pope to England; 597 baptizes king and 10,000 Saxons at Canterbury; parliament adopts the faith.

c 600 *Andorra.* First Christian settlers.

622 Rise of Islam: Hegira, flight of prophet Muhammad from Mecca to Medina.

Armenian patriarchate established in Jerusalem.

630 **Global status:** 20 generations after Christ, world is 22.5% Christians (58% of them being Non-Whites, 42% Whites), 39% evangelized; with scriptures translated into 14 languages.

632 Muslim Arabs sweep across Palestine, Syria; death of Muhammad.

635 *China* (then richest and most civilized nation on earth). First missionary (Alopen, a Nestorian from Syria) reaches capital Ch'ang-an (Hsian).

638 Jerusalem falls to Muslims.

639 Arabs (Saracens, Moors) invade Egypt, establish Islam and Arabic language.

c 640 Christians in Persia about one million before Muslim conquest of Sassanid empire.

c 640 Egypt: 3 million Coptic and 200,000 Chalcedonian Christians.

640 80% of 6.5 million Berbers across North Africa (2.6 million urbanized) now Christians; but by 950 all converted to Islam.

646 Mesopotamia (Iraq) conquered by Muslims.

c 650 *Netherlands.* First organized Christians (St Martin's Church, Utrecht).

650 Yeshuyab III Nestorian patriarch of Seleucia-Ctesiphon.

c 650 Nestorian metropolitan of Merv converts many Turks.

c 650 *Niger.* First Christians (North African Berber Christians driven south by Islam).

c 650 Psalms translated into Anglo-Saxon by bishop Aldhelm.

c 650 *Indonesia* (then East Indies). First Christians (Catholic community on Sumatra).

c 650 *Mongolia.* First missionaries (Nestorians); 300 years later, Christianity disappears finally.

c 651 Death of Aidan, missionary to York.

c 660 Mass conversions of Egyptians from Christianity to Islam.

c 670 Earliest Old English (Anglo-Saxon) scripture version: metrical Paraphrases, sung by Caedmon.

680 Council of Constantinople III (6th Ecumenical Council): Monothelitism condemned.

687 Conversion of England completed under Wilfrid; christianizes Sussex and Isle of Wight, last important centres of Anglo-Saxon paganism.

690 Frisians and Netherlands evangelized by Willibrord from Ripon, England.

692 'The light of Christ illuminates the whole world' (*Liturgy of the Presanctified*).

697 Carthage captured by Muslims; North Africa in Muslim hands.

711 Muslim Arabs defeat Arian Visigoths in Portugal and in 715 eliminate them from Spain.

716 South and central Germany evangelized by Winfrith (Boniface) from Crediton, England.

720 Bede's Anglo-Saxon translations of John's Gospel.

724 Boniface fells pagan sacred oak of Thor at Geismar in Hesse (Germany); collapse of German paganism.

730 *Church history of the English people* compiled by Bede, monk at Jarrow on Tyne, England, describing conversion of the Anglo-Saxons.

732 Muslims defeated by Charles Martel between Tours and Poitiers; they retreat from Europe.

c 740 *Iceland.* First missionaries (from Ireland).

c 750 Expansion of Christianity in India renewed.

*Faeroe Islands.* First missionaries (monks from Iceland); monasteries destroyed a century later.

Yemen: Nestorian missionaries in Sana and Socotra.

*Pakistan* (then Punjab). First Christians (Nestorian missionaries); later eradicated.

First Bible version in Arabic.

772 *East Germany.* First Christians (through Charlemagne's violent conquest of Saxons).

775 Nestorian patriarchal see moved from Seleucia-Ctesiphon to Baghdad.

c 780 Forced baptism of the Saxon race by Charlemagne: 4,500 executed in one day.

781 Hsian inscription indicates Syriac New Testament known in China.

784 Last major revolt of pagan Frisians.

787 Council of Nicaea II (7th Ecumenical Council, last recognized by Eastern Orthodox): iconoclasm condemned.

796 Pippin destroys Avar power; conversion of Avars follows.

797 Tibet: Nestorian metropolitan see, appointed from Baghdad.

800 **Global status:** 26 generations after Christ, world is 22.5% Christians (51.0% of them being Non-Whites, 49.0% Whites), 31.0% evangelized; with scriptures translated into 15 languages.

Christianity becoming dominant religion from the Caspian to Sinkiang (China).

Charlemagne crowned Roman emperor in Rome by pope.

825 Party of Persian Christians with 2 Nestorian bishops emigrate to Malabar.

826 *Denmark.* First missionary (Anskar, monk of Flanders, apostle of the north).

828 *Czechoslovakia.* First missionaries (Franks).

829 *Sweden.* First missionary (Anskar). Many Swedish noblemen converted after his visits.

837 Egypt: Christian education prohibited, also celebration of festivals; all new churches demolished by Muslims, and Christians ordered to wear 5-pound crosses around their necks.

845 Baptism of 14 Czech princes.
Severe persecution of Nestorians and Buddhists in China by Taoist emperor Wu Tsung; 44,000 temples and monasteries destroyed or closed.
c 850 Nestorian Christianity finally eradicated in Arabia.
First Scriptures translated into Norman French.
851 Ireland: pagan kingdom set up in Dublin for 3 centuries by Norwegian Olaf the White.
861 Conversions of Slavs under way through Cyril and Methodius, sent to Moravia (Bohemia) at request of Rastislav; by 900, Christianity strong in Moravia.
864 Baptism of Boris king of the Bulgars; 870, conversion of the Bulgars, with a Bulgar consecrated as archbishop. Basil I, emperor 866–886, forced baptism on Serbs of Narenta Valley.
869 Council of Constantinople IV: Photian schism condemned.
880 Slavonic Bible translated by Methodius; Psalms translated into Anglo-Saxon by king Alfred of England.
c 900 *Norway.* First mission (from Bremen-Hamburg archbishopric). Later, Norwegian kings educated in England return to evangelize their people.
900 Magyars now evangelized.
c 900 Continuous apostasies of Christians to Islam in Middle East and North Africa.
902 Sicily subjugated by Muslims after 75 years, also coastal areas of southern Italy.
c 920 *Burma.* First Christians (Nestorian bishopric at Pegu).
926 Revival of Western monasticism under Odo abbot of Cluny, France.
927 Conversion of Bulgars completed; death of Simeon.
c 949 50% of all former Christendom now captured by Islam, including nomadic Berbers of Mauretania.

Epoch III:
## RESURGENCE AND ADVANCE AD 950–1350

950 **Global status:** 31 generations after Christ, world is 19.0% Christians (58.8% of them being Whites, 41.2% Non-Whites), 26.0% evangelized; with scriptures translated into 17 languages.
c 950 *Poland.* First Christians; 966, king baptized.
950 Conversion of the Scandinavians (Northmen) under way across Denmark, Norway and Sweden.
c 950 Rise of Bogomilism in Bulgarian Orthodox Church; dualist, perfectionist.
Egypt: Coptic bishops decline in numbers to 110 (from 168 in AD 550).
954 Olga regent of Kiev baptized; conversion of Russia begun.
962 Holy Roman Empire founded by Otto I, king of Germany, crowned by pope John XII; 10 million by AD 1000, 16 million by 1200, 29 million by 1800; finally abolished in 1806.
966 Duke of Mieszka (Poland) converted to Christianity by his wife; first Polish bishopric established at Poznan (Posen) 2 years later; rapid expansion of the faith.
987 Muslim rulers in Iraq assume right to appoint the Nestorian catholicos.
987 Conversion and baptism of archduke Vladimir of Kiev (Russia) by Greeks; Orthodoxy introduced into Russia, mass conversion of Russia under way.
c 990 *Greenland.* First Christians (Norse settlement; priest brought by founder's son Lief).
991 Whole population of Novgorod (Russia) baptized by bishop from Crimea.
996 Egypt: caliph El Hakim destroys 3,000 churches and forcibly converts thousands of Copts to Islam in violent persecution.
997 Mass conversion of the Magyars (Hungarians) under Stephen.
Prussians, last remaining heathens in Europe, evangelized; Adalbert martyred.
999 Bohemia: evangelization and christianization completed.

1000 **Global status:** 32 generations after Christ, world is 18.7% Christians (61.0% of them being Whites), 25% evangelized; with scriptures translated into 17 languages.
1000 Most of North African Christianity wiped out: the Land of the Vanished Church.
c1000 Nestorian (East Syrian) Church most extensive in world, with 250 dioceses across Asia and 12 million adherents.
Nestorian metropolitan provinces within Arab caliphate (Persia) number 15, with 5 abroad including India and China.
1000 Patriarchate of Constantinople has authority over 624 dioceses around eastern Mediterranean.
Conversion of northern Europe by Latin church completed.
Nubian bishop (Sudan) reintroduces Orthodox Melkite tradition, provoking split between church in Nubia and Copts in Egypt.
c1000 Emergence of Christian kingdoms in Denmark, England, Hungary, Norway, Poland, Sweden, Scotland.
1005 Iceland: 2 dioceses, many monasteries and abbeys.
1009 Northern Mongolia: Nestorians convert prince and 200,000 Keraits (a Turkish tribe) in capital Karakorum; also Namians and Merkites.
c1010 Lief Ericson, Norse Christian leader from Greenland, makes first European and Christian contact with North America.
1015 Russia permanently christianized; all 3 bishops and most clergy Greeks; numerous monasteries.
c1016 Iceland only country to accept Christianity by genuine democratic process.
c1020 Nestorians over 50% of population in Syria, Iraq and Khorasan (south of Oxus).
c1050 King in Nubia erects many churches and monasteries.
Egypt: Coptic bishops decline in numbers to 47 (from 168 in AD 550).
1054 Great Schism between western (Rome) and eastern (Constantinople) Christianity; Roman cardinal Humbart places bull of excommunication on altar of Santa Sophia cathedral in Constantinople. Church of Byzantium declines; no further missionary outreach implemented.
1061 Norman (Christian) conquest of Sicily, completed by 1091.
1066 Evangelization and conversion of Western Europe completed with Norman conquest of Saxons and Celts.
1071 Overthrow of Byzantine army at Manzikert (Anatolia) by Turkish sultan Alp Arslan; inrush of Turkish tribes follows.
1073 Papacy of Gregory VII (Hildebrand), till 1085.
1076 Last contact between Roman pope and bishop of Carthage.

1078 Suppression of Bulgarian patriarchate by Byzantine emperor; re-established 1235.
1081 Muslim Turks dominant in most of Armenia and Asia Minor.
1095 Crusades to liberate Holy Land launched by pope Urban II.
1096 Start of First Crusade with 30,000 French and Italian crusaders invading Seljuk Turk empire: 'Deus vult' (God wills it); 1099 Jerusalem sacked.
1099 Latin patriarchate of Jerusalem established.
1100 Sweden: christianization completed.
Poland: christianization completed.
c1100 *Finland.* First Christians (seamen and merchants).
1100 Hungarians accept Christianity as national religion.
c1100 Armenian church split by Paulician separatists.
1119 Military religious order of Knights Templar founded with headquarters near temple site in Jerusalem.
1121 Abelard: *Sic et Non* (scholasticism).
1123 Council of Lateran I: subject, investiture controversy.
1139 Council of Lateran II: against pseudo-popes, and on points of discipline.
1146 Jews of Spain forcibly converted to Christianity; further force used, 1391.
c1150 Widest expansion of West Syrian (Jacobite) church: 20 metropolitan sees, 103 bishoprics in Syria, Mesopotamia, Cyprus, et alia, and 2 million adherents.
1150 College of Cardinals established in Rome by pope.
1166 Waldensian movement begins under reformer Peter Waldo at Lyons.
1168 Danes destroy paganism among Wends of Rügen.
1179 Council of Lateran III: no Christian should be subjected to slavery.
1181 Roman Catholic uniate churches begin to emerge (Syria).
1189 Third Crusade launched, capturing Acre.
c1190 Rise of demand for vernacular versions of scriptures; poetical and prose versions in French, Italian, Spanish.

1200 **Global status:** 39 generations after Christ, world is 19.4% Christians (64.3% of them being Whites), 26% evangelized; with scriptures translated into 22 languages.
Apex of medieval papacy, under Innocent III (1198–1216).
Europe entirely christianized except for Wends, Prussians, Lithuanians and other Baltic races.
1202 Fourth Crusade launched against Egypt under Innocent III, also capturing Constantinople from Greeks in 1204.
1208 20,000 Albigensians massacred as heretics at papal order.
1209 Francis of Assisi begins travelling preachers (Franciscans), largest of the mendicant orders (OFM).
1211 Genghiz Khan, Universal Emperor of the Mongols (whose mother was a Nestorian), attacks China (with army of only 129,000) and massacres 35 million in a decade.
1212 Children's Crusade, a disastrous venture by over 20,000 children, many of whom ended as slaves in Egypt.
1215 Council of Lateran IV: against Waldensians, Albigensians, et alii.
Dominic founds Order of Preachers (OP, Dominicans) in southern France.
1219 Independent Serbian Orthodox Church formed.
Francis of Assisi preaches the gospel before sultan of Egypt.
c1220 German scripture translations available.
1220 Genghiz Khan massacres 25% of population in Iran and Iraq; dies 1227.
1221 Ukraine entered by Dominicans; 1228, diocese under Rome created.
1229 Vernacular scriptures prohibited by Synod of Toulouse, also (1233) at Tarragona, Spain.
1240 Dominicans begin mission in Tiflis, Georgia.
1244 Jerusalem finally recaptured by Muslims.
1249 Conquest and conversion of Finland by Jarl Birger Magnusson; christianized through English bishop, Henry of Uppsala.
c1250 Nubia: many new mosques erected, Christianity waning.
Nestorian influence strong across Asia, still with over 250 bishoprics.
Central Asia: Uighurs, Keraits, Onguts, Mongols and all other major peoples partially christianized.
Height of the Catholic church's political power.
All Prussians forcibly baptized and pagan worship eradicated.
Portions of Bible available in Italian (Tuscan, Lombardic), Polish, Spanish or Catalan.
1254 Council of Lyons I: against Frederick II.
*Introduction* to abbot Joachim's Eternal Gospel issued by Gerard of Borgo San Domino (a 3rd age replacing OT and NT eras).
1258 Baghdad and (1260) Damascus sacked by Mongols in attempt to destroy Muslim world.
1260 Thomas Aquinas (1225–74): 'Africa is a fertile ground for schism'.
1266 Mongol ruler Kublai Khan requests Roman pope: 'Send me 100 men skilled in your religion . . . and so I shall be baptized, and then all my barons and great men, and then their subjects. And so there will be more Christians here than there are in your parts'; 2 Dominicans sent, but turned back; then 1278, pope sent 5 Franciscans; greatest missed opportunity in Christian history.
1271 Rijmbijbel (scriptures in poetical Dutch) written.
1274 Council of Lyons II (for RCs, 14th Ecumenical Council): attempt to unite Greek and Roman churches; proliferation of mendicant orders discouraged.
1275 Nestorian archbishopric established in Cambaluc (Khanbalik/Peking), and hierarchy restored throughout central Asia.
1281 Mongolian monk Marcus elected Nestorian catholicos Yabalaha III (died 1317).
1290 Expulsion of Jews from England.
1291 Fall of Acre, in Syria, last Crusader stronghold; Crusaders driven from Middle East by Muslims.
1293 Armenian catholicate of Cilicia transferred to Sis.
1294 Italian Franciscan John of Montecorvino arrives in Cambaluc (Peking); bitter opposition from Nestorians.
1295 Ghazan Khan, a Muslim, becomes ruler of Mongols in Persia.
1300 Mongol world (Russia, Persia, Turkestan) gradually being converted to Islam.
Franciscans at work in 17 stations throughout Mongol empire, with a monastery in Cambaluc.
1301 Egypt: all churches ordered closed or destroyed by Mamluk dynasty (1250–1517).
1306 Expulsion of Jews from France.
John of Montecorvino builds 2 churches in Cambaluc with 6,000 converts, translates New Testament into Ongut.

1309 Papacy moved from Rome to Avignon (France).
*Gibraltar.* First Christians (Spanish Catholic soldiers, capturing Rock from Muslims).
c1310 Persia: large proportion Christian, but Mongol rulers still undecided.
1311 Council of Vienna: abolition of Templars, condemnation of various heresies.
1315 Ramon Lull, Franciscan, stoned to death at Bugia (Algeria) by Muslims.
1321 Egypt: most of remaining Coptic churches and monasteries destroyed.
1323 Franciscan contacts in Sumatra, Java and Borneo.
1330 Jordanus (a Dominican) sent by Roman pope as a bishop to Quilon, south India, to convert Malabar Nestorians.
c1330 Scripture historical books translated into Norwegian.
1345 Serbian Orthodox patriarchate established; later suppressed in 1459 and 1765.
1347 Black Death (bubonic plague pandemic) from Crimea (origin Mongolia), sweeps across Europe killing 33% of 60 million population (including 40% of England); 99% of all victims Christians; ends 1353.
1349 Jews expelled from Hungary over 11-year period.
30,000 Christians in Mongol empire in China, mostly Mongols.
Apogee of Nestorian expansion across Asia, geographically more extensive and more prosperous than ever before or since; 25 metropolitans (each with 6–12 suffragan bishops) in 250 dioceses in China, India, Kashgar, Samarkand, Turkestan, et alia, with total of over 15 million Nestorians.

Epoch IV:
## THE SECOND RECESSION: CONFUSION AND CORRUPTION 1350–1500

1350 **Global status:** 44 generations after Christ, world is 24.1% Christians (67.6% of them being Whites), 28% evangelized; with scriptures translated into 28 languages.
Rapid shrinking of geographical frontiers of Christianity begins, especially in Asia, and continues for 150 years.
c1350 Recrudescence of anti-Christian paganism in the European Renaissance.
1350 Rupture between European church in East and West finally complete.
c1350 Strong Christian communities in South India; Nestorians scattered across subcontinent.
Komi-Perm peoples of Russia evangelized by Stephen of Perm.
First Middle Persian (Pahlavi) version of scriptures.
1355 12,000 Jews massacred by Christian mob in Toledo, Spain.
1357 Maronite Church, which had separated from Greek Orthodoxy in 7th century, unites with Rome.
1358 Mongol emperor Tamerlane begins to destroy Christian civilization from China and north India to Mediterranean.
c1365 Christian influence in Afghanistan terminated by Turkish Muslim emperor, Tamerlane.
1368 Ming dynasty ousts Mongol dynasty in China; Christianity disappears.
1370 John of Trevisa completes translation of whole Bible in Anglo-Norman (Middle English).
c1370 Conversion of Mongolia from Nestorian influence to Buddhism.
1376 Bible translated into English by John Wycliffe and followers; NT 1378; Bible completed 1382.
1377 End of Babylonian Captivity (popes living at Avignon).
1378 Beginning of Great Schism of the West: up to 3 rival popes at a time, until 1417.
1380 Mongol hordes under Tamerlane (died 1405) destroy Nestorian church and missions throughout Asia; 70,000 heads piled on ruins of Isfahan, 90,000 in Baghdad; extinction of Christianity in central Asia, reduced to remnants in Mesopotamia, Kurdistan, South India.
1384 John Wycliffe produces first complete English Bible.
1386 Baptism of Jagiello king of Lithuanians; end of European paganism as an organized religion.
1391 Start of anti-Semitic massacres in Spain and Portugal; 4,000 Jews killed in Seville.
1396 Bulgaria falls to Muslim invaders, Ottoman Turks.
c1400 Nubia: Christianity widespread, with 7 bishoprics in the north and 400 churches in the south.
1400 Continued northeastward expansion of Orthodoxy across Russia through monks.
c1400 First Russian indigenous movements: Strigolniks (Barbers) from Pskov form schismatic groups out of Russian Orthodox Church, protesting against charging of fees for sacraments.
Western Europe becomes main centre of Christianity worldwide.
Scriptures translated into Icelandic.
1402 Ottoman Empire 6.3 million, rising to 28 million by 1580; then continuous decline until 1922 dissolution.
c1410 Hungarian translation of Bible.
1414 Council of Constance: condemnation of reformers Wycliffe, Hus, et alii; 1415, Hus burned at stake as heretic.
1415 Capture of Ceuta in Morocco by Portuguese under Henry the Navigator.
1431 Council of Basle: question of papal supremacy, and the Hussite heresy.
1438 Council of Florence: union with Greeks attempted.
1441 Armenian patriarchate moved from Sis (Cilicia) to Echmiadzin.
1445 *Senegal.* First Christians (Portuguese explorers); 1486, Senegalese chief baptized.
*Guinea Bissau.* First Christians (Portuguese trading centre; Catholic missionaries 1462).
*Equatorial Guinea.* First Christians (Portuguese traders).
1448 *Mauritania.* First Christians (Portuguese, French, Dutch and English traders).
Russian Orthodox Church becomes autocephalous patriarchate.
c1449 Scriptures: languages possessing some translated portions of the Bible number 33, just prior to invention of printing.
1450 Invention of printing (typography and the printing press) by Johan Gutenberg at Mainz, Germany; more than 100 editions of the Bible produced by 1500.
c1450 Dechristianizing forces strong in Europe: Renaissance, humanism, recrudescence of paganism, obsession with wealth.
1452 St Peter's basilica in Rome planned as world's largest church, after 1453 to replace Santa Sophia (Con-

stantinople); 1506, foundation stone laid; 1626, completed.

1453 Fall of Constantinople to Muslim Ottoman Turks; end of Byzantine empire. Fleeing scholars take Greek text of Bible to the West.

1455 Thomas à Kempis: *Imitation of Christ.*

1456 Latin (Gutenberg) Bible: first printed scripture edition and first large printed book in Europe (4 years being printed in Mainz): 500 copies printed.

1457 Turkish Muslims conquer peoples of Yugoslavia.

Unitas Fratrum (Moravians) establish Christian village in Moravia.

1461 Armenian patriarchate established in Constantinople.

1462 *Cape Verde Islands.* First mission (Portuguese Catholics).

1466 High German Bible printed: first in any modern language.

1471 *Ghana* (then Gold Coast). First Christians (Portuguese soldiers).

First Italian printed Bible.

1477 First Dutch printed Old Testament.

First French printed New Testament.

1478 First Spanish printed Bible.

Spanish Inquisition established to ferret out crypto-Jews and hidden Muslims; 120,000 Spanish intellectuals executed from 1481-98.

1480 Russia expels Mongol Muslim rulers, becomes Christian state, spreads gospel across northern Asia.

1482 *Zaire* (then Congo). First Christians (Portuguese explorers); 1491, first missionaries (Franciscans, Dominicans).

1485 *São Tomé & Principe.* First Christians (Portuguese settlement).

1487 First French printed Bible.

*Nigeria.* First Christians (Portuguese Catholics); 1491, king of Benin baptized.

1491 *Angola* (then Congo kingdom). First mission (Catholics at São Salvador). First church building built by Portuguese Jesuits.

*Congo* (Brazzaville). First mission (Portuguese Catholics); collapsed and not revived until 1883.

1492 Christopher Columbus sails to the New World, discovers America.

Capture of Granada, last Muslim stronghold in Spain.

Expulsion of 180,000 Jews from Spain; 300,000 others forcibly converted to Christianity and remain in Spain as Marranos (Conversos, Crypto-Jews), though 20,000 burned as heretics by Inquisition.

Rodrigo Borgia made pope as Alexander VI; nadir in morality of Renaissance papacy.

1493 Pope issues Demarcation Bull, giving Portugal authority over Africa, much of Asia and later Brazil; Spain given authority over rest of world west of a north-south line 345 miles west of the Azores.

*Haiti* (then Santo Domingo). First mission (Spanish Catholics).

1494 *Dominican Republic* (then Santo Domingo). First missionaries (Spanish Catholics).

1497 All 200,000 Jews in Portugal (20% of population) forced to either accept Christianity as Marranos (Conversos) or be deported.

1498 *Kenya.* First Christians (Vasco da Gama and Portuguese explorers). By 1597, 600 African converts.

c1499 Gradual extinction of Christianity in Nubia.

Christianity extinguished in China, Central Asia and across the Muslim world.

Steady shrinking of Christian influence. Outlook for Christianity as a world religion decidedly unfavourable.

Up to this date, almost no contact between the 3 races of mankind (Caucasoid, Mongoloid, Negroid).

## Epoch V: **REFORM AND EXPANSION** **1500-1750**

1500 **Global status:** 49 generations after Christ, world is 19.0% Christians (92.6% of them being Whites), 21.0% evangelized; with printed scriptures available in 12 languages.

c1500 Printing presses in Europe now number 40, with 8 million volumes printed, a large proportion being Christian works (98 distinct editions of the Vulgate).

About 1,000 books a year worldwide published with newly-invented movable type.

1500 *Brazil.* First Christians (Portuguese explorers).

c1500 Moscow declared to be Third Rome, successor to heretical Rome and Muslim Constantinople.

1500 Several African chiefs on west coast and in Congo baptized by Portuguese.

Portuguese discover 100,000-strong Christians of St Thomas (Syrian Orthodox) in Kerala, south India.

Worldwide expansion of Christianity commences again, mainly through Spanish and Portuguese Catholics.

1501 *South Africa.* First Christians (Catholic church built at Mossel Bay, Natal, by Portuguese).

1502 *Tanzania* (then Tanganyika, Zanzibar). First Christians (Portuguese, at Kilwa); c1550, first Jesuit and Dominican missionaries.

All Jews of Rhodes (Greece) forcibly converted, expelled or taken into slavery.

1503 Franciscan college begun in Haiti.

1506 *Mozambique.* First mission (Portuguese Dominicans).

Massacre of Lisbon: thousands of 'New Christians' (baptized Jews and Muslims) killed.

1508 *Oman.* First Christians (Portuguese port at Muscat).

1509 *Puerto Rico.* First Christians (Spanish settlement).

*Jamaica.* First Christians (Spanish Catholic plantation owners).

1511 *Timor.* First Christians (Portuguese sailors); 1561, king baptized.

*Singapore.* First mission (Portuguese Dominicans).

*Malaysia.* First missionaries (Portuguese Catholics).

First Catholic diocese of New World established at Puerto Rico.

1512 Council of Lateran V: reform of the church.

*Cuba.* First mission (Dominicans).

*Colombia.* First Christians (Spanish explorers).

1513 *Venezuela.* First missionaries (Spanish Dominicans and Franciscans).

*Panama.* First Christians (Spanish settlement).

*Trinidad & Tobago.* First missionaries (2 Dominicans).

1514 Pope Leo X accorded kings of Portugal right of patronage (padroado) in Asia.

*Costa Rica.* First mission (Catholic).

1516 Erasmus produces first printed Greek New Testament (by which time over 100 Latin versions already printed).

1517 *Comoro Islands.* First Christians (French settlers).

*Mayotte.* First Christians (Portuguese).

*Nicaragua.* First Christians (Spanish settlement).

Martin Luther's 95 Theses nailed to church door in Wittenberg; Protestant Reformation begins.

1518 *Mexico.* First Christians (Cortés and Spanish conquistadores).

1519 Huldreich Zwingli installed as people's priest in Zurich; reformation spreads across Switzerland.

1520 Protestant inertia in missions for 275 years begins because, having dispensed with monasticism (major method of mission from 4th-16th centuries), no knowledge of how to prosecute a missionary endeavour (Harnack).

Luther's classic '*The Liberty of a Christian Man*'.

c1520 Luther writes: 'The gospel will always be preached... It has gone out throughout the length and the breadth of the world... It is made known farther and farther, to those who have not heard it before', and 'The gospel preached by the Apostles in various languages, sounds forth even now till the end of time'.

Climax of Ottoman Turk expansion into Christian Europe; mass conversions of Christians to Islam.

1521 *Philippines.* First Christians (Magellan and Spanish explorers; first mass celebrated; 1565, first missionaries).

1522 Spanish expedition under Magellan first to circumnavigate globe.

Luther's translation of New Testament into German; Bible in 1534.

1523 Spanish monarch orders Cortés to enforce mass conversion of Mexican Indians.

*Guadeloupe.* First missionaries (Catholics; massacred by Caribs).

1524 *Paraguay.* First Christians (Spanish settlement).

*Guatemala.* First Christians (Spanish soldiers).

*Honduras.* First Christians (Spanish settlement).

1525 *El Salvador.* First mission (Spanish Catholic priests).

William Tyndale produces (in Worms) first printed English New Testament; burned at stake in 1536 near Brussels.

30,000 Anabaptists in Europe executed (by Catholics and Lutherans, later by Calvinists).

1526 *USA* (then America). First missionaries (Spanish Catholic priests to Indians in California, Florida, Texas et alia).

*Ecuador.* First Christians (Spanish settlers).

1527 Sweden adopts Lutheran Confession.

*Argentina.* First Christians (Spanish fort erected); 1539 first mission (Franciscans).

First Baptist church established in Zurich.

Ethiopia: Muslim tribal leader Ahmad Gran destroys Amharic Orthodox churches and monasteries in 15 years' savage pillaging.

1530 *Viet Nam.* First missionaries (Portuguese priests on merchant ships from Goa and Macao).

Confession of Augsburg produced by Melancthon and signed by Protestant princes.

c1530 Luther and Calvin teach that the Great Commission (Mark 16.15) was the work of the 1st-century Apostles only and expired with them.

*Panama Canal Zone* (then Panama). First Christians (Spaniards).

1530 Bartholomew de Las Casas supports rights of indigenous peoples of Central America; before death in 1566, charges 15 million Indians killed by Spanish conquistadores.

1531 Death of Zwingli in battle attempting to force Zurich Protestantism on Catholic cantons.

In Mexico, Franciscans baptize one million Amerindians in 12 years since conquest, often at a rate of 7,000 a day per missionary.

1532 *Peru.* First Christians (Spanish colonists).

1533 Goa on Indian coast made a Catholic bishopric by Portuguese.

1534 *Canada.* First Christians (French soldiers).

British Supremacy Act makes British monarch (then Henry VIII) head of Church of England.

Portuguese Catholic missionaries arrive in Moluccas.

Ignatius Loyola at University of Paris founds Society of Jesus, made into an order in 1539; spearhead of Catholic Reformation.

1535 First English Bible printed, translated by Myles Coverdale.

John Calvin (age 26) publishes his *Institutes of the Christian Religion.*

1536 John Calvin as reformer in Geneva; 1538 banished, 1541 returns to make it centre of Reformed faith and life.

Nearly 5 million Amerindians baptized in Mexico since 1519.

*Bangladesh* (then East Bengal). First Christians (Portuguese traders in Chittagong).

Denmark, Norway, Sweden adopt Lutheranism as state religion by 1540.

10,000-strong Bharatha (Parava) fishing caste of Coromandel coast (Kerala) baptized en masse by Portuguese, then ignored until Xavier's arrival in 1542.

1537 *Bolivia.* First Christians (Spanish colonists).

Bolivia: Catholic diocese formed to include work among Parias and Charcas.

English king declared head of church in Ireland.

1540 *Madagascar.* First mission (Catholic).

1541 Ignatius Loyola first general of Jesuit order.

*Chile.* First mission (one Catholic priest).

1542 Francis Xavier, Jesuit, arrives in India; 1546, Malacca; then carries the faith throughout the Far East (1549, Japan) until his death in 1552.

Congregation of Universal Inquisition established by Holy See.

1544 Xavier begins mission at Travancore, baptizes 10,000 Mukuvas in one month (and 15,000 others later).

Roman Catholics in Burma: Portuguese, with Franciscan missionaries.

1545 Augsburg Confession adopted by Hungarian Lutheran church.

Council of Trent (Counter-Reformation) 19th Ecumenical Council: Protestantism condemned. 25 sessions 1545-63 during lives of 3 popes.

1546 First of several Amerindian anti-Catholic religious movements of revolt in Ecuador: Quimbaya (also 1576 Sobce, 1603).

1547 Severe persecution of Protestants in France; 72,000 executed.

1548 *Guyana* (later British Guiana). First mission (Portuguese Catholic).

1549 Brazil: beginning of Catholic missions among Amerindians by first Jesuits in South America.

*Japan.* First missionary (Francis Xavier, Spanish Jesuit). By 1580, 150,000 Christians (1% of Japan) and 200 churches; by 1600, 300,000.

1550 **Global status:** 51 generations after Christ, world is 19.5% Christians (89.5% of them being Whites), 22% evangelized; with printed scriptures available in 28 languages.

c1550 *Kuwait.* First Christians (Portuguese sailors and traders).

800,000 Peruvian Amerindians confirmed by one Catholic archbishop of Lima.

*Netherlands Antilles.* First missionaries (Catholic priests from Santo Domingo).

*Martinique.* First Christians (Dominican, Jesuit and Capuchin missionaries).

1550 Lutheranism proclaimed state religion of Iceland.

At least 30,000 witches burned by Roman Inquisition over previous 150 years.

1551 Converts from Assyrian Church of the East in Iraq and Persia submit to Rome as Chaldean Catholic Church, with patriarchate in Babylon.

1552 Council of Lima (Peru): Amerindians may receive Catholic baptism, matrimony and penance, but not communion or ordination.

1553 Roman Catholicism restored in England under queen Mary; 300 Reformed leaders including Cranmer archbishop of Canterbury burned at stake.

In 3 years, 300 Protestants burned as heretics in Europe.

1554 *Thailand* (then Siam). First Christians (Portuguese soldiers at royal court, 2 Dominican chaplains, 1,500 Thai converts).

1555 *Kampuchea* (Cambodia). First missions (Jesuits and Dominicans).

1556 Calvin sends first and only Reformed missionary party of 18 French Huguenots to Brazil, off Rio de Janeiro; work collapsed.

Jesuits arrive in Paraguay, establish about 100 Christian settlements (reductions) among Guaraní Amerindians.

World's worst earthquake disaster: 830,000 killed in Shensi province, China.

At death of Loyola, Jesuits number 1,000 and become the outstanding Catholic missionary society.

1557 *Macao.* First Christians (Portuguese settlement).

France: 33% of population reputed to be Protestants (known as Huguenots); 1559, create Reformed Church (72 congregations, 400,000 adherents).

1558 Spain: Protestants virtually wiped out by Inquisition by burning at the stake.

1560 Philippines christianized by Spaniards; by 1600, 70% Christians.

c1560 Anabaptists the only Reformation grouping to deliberately work for and obey Jesus' Great Commission, especially through Hutterian Brethren's itinerant evangelism.

1560 India: 300,000 Roman Catholic converts in Kerala.

1561 *Zimbabwe* (later Southern Rhodesia). First missionary (Portuguese Jesuit); king of Monomotapa baptized.

*St Helena.* First Christians (Dutch settlers).

*Malawi* (later Nyasaland). First missionaries (Catholics from Mozambique).

1562 3,000 French Protestants (Huguenots) massacred at Toulouse.

1564 Index Tridentinus of prohibited books.

1565 First permanent USA Catholic community begun at St Augustine, Florida.

1566 First Unitarian churches founded: in Hungary, Romania, Poland.

1567 Second Helvetic Confession adopted by Hungarian Reformed Church.

1569 80,000 Christians in East Indies under Jesuit missions.

1570 Santiago, Chiriguano prophet and reformer, appears in Bolivia.

1571 Japan: mass movement begins under Omura Sumitada; 50,000 converted.

1572 70,000 Huguenots massacred in France.

1575 First German pietist missionaries begin in Tranquebar, India.

1576 China re-entered by Catholics with Macao made a Portuguese diocese.

1578 First Anglicans in North America (California, then Virginia).

1580 *Surinam.* First Christians (Dutch settlement).

1581 Claudio Aquaviva elected 5th general of Society of Jesus; by his death in 1615 Jesuits have increased from 5,000 to 13,000.

1582 Matteo Ricci, Jesuit, begins his mission in Macao, then on to Peking and south China.

Japan: 200 churches and 150,000 Christians; 1588, Japan made a Catholic diocese.

1586 Total baptized Filipinos over 400,000 since start of Spanish conquest a decade earlier.

Jesuit priest Alonso Sánchez drafts evangelistic scheme for the invasion and military conquest of China.

1588 Anglican parish priest Hadrian Saravia (1531-1613), one of first non-Roman advocates of foreign missions.

1589 Russian Orthodox patriarchate instituted (the Third Rome); suppressed 1764.

1592 *South Korea.* First Christians (invading army from Japan, with Catholic general and Jesuit priest).

1594 Jesuits reach court of Mongol emperor Akbar; construction of first Christian church in Lahore permitted, though few conversions.

1598 *Mauritius.* First Christians (Dutch).

*French Guiana.* First Christians (French settlements).

Edict of Nantes ending French wars of religion, allowing religious liberty and civil equality to Huguenots in France.

Smallpox and measles responsible for killing millions in Latin America during preceding 100 years.

1600 **Global status:** 52 generations after Christ, world is 20.7% Christians (86.0% of them being Whites), 24.0% evangelized; with printed scriptures available in 36 languages.

c1600 Jesuit reductions (co-operative Amerindian villages) in Bolivia among Moxos and Chiquitos.

Nkimba and Kimpasi in Congo, syncretistic prophet movements based on Jesuit institutions.

*North Korea.* First Christians.

Philippines now 70% christianized.

*Svalbard & Jan Mayen Islands.* First Christians (European whaling centre.)

*Brunei.* First Christians (Spanish trading centre).

1600 Christians in Japan number 750,000 (3.4% of the population), including most of Nagasaki area, with 300,000 being baptized Roman Catholics.

Scriptures: languages possessing some printed portions of Bible now number 41.

c1600 Nubia: final extinction of Christianity.

1602 Orthodox bishopric erected at Astrakhan near mouth of Volga.
Dutch government sends missionaries to convert the Malays in its East Indies domains.
1603 Roman Catholics in England and Wales number 1.5 million, declining to 69,376 by 1780.
1604 *St Pierre & Miquelon.* First Christians (French Catholic settlers).
1605 Armenian Catholic Church (Uniate) created through Dominican activity in Iran.
Catholic missionaries expelled by Dutch from Indonesia, replaced by Dutch Reformed chaplains of Dutch East India Company.
Robert de Nobili (Jesuit) arrives in Madura, south India.
1607 USA: Anglicans begin evangelization with foundation of Virginia Colony at Jamestown.
1608 Canada: Roman Catholic work begun among Micmac Indians.
1609 *Bermuda.* First Christians (English sailors; Anglicans).
Philip II of Spain expels all Moriscos (Spanish Muslims forcibly baptized); 300,000 flee to Algeria, Morocco and Tunisia.
1610 Catholics in Peking number 2,000 at death of Jesuit superior Matteo Ricci.
1611 King James Version (KJV) or Authorized Version (AV) of English Bible published.
British East India Company begin trade in Surat, Bombay.
1612 Anglican clergy first serve as chaplains with East India Company.
322,400 Filipino Christians on Luzon alone.
1613 Major missionary work by Thomas à Jesu, *De procuranda salute omnium gentium*, urges and envisages the conversion of the entire world to Christ.
1614 Japanese edict prohibiting Christianity, then 3.5% of the population; churches destroyed, Jesuits and other missionaries deported, over 40,000 Christians massacred.
1616 *Uruguay.* First missionaries (Spanish Franciscans and Jesuits).
First Baptist congregation in England (London); known as General Baptists.
1619 Dutch colonize East Indies (Indonesia).
Over last 100 years since Conquest, Spaniards reduce Meso-Americans from 20 million to 4 million through war, disease, starvation, forced labour.
1620 Pilgrim Fathers from England cross Atlantic to America to found New England.
Bohemia forcibly made Roman Catholic by Austrian armies; 30,000 Protestants expelled, others massacred.
1621 *China* (*Taiwan*, Formosa). First mission (Dominicans from Philippines).
1622 Sacred Congregation for the Propagation of the Faith (Propaganda) founded by pope Gregory XV.
1623 *St Kitts-Nevis.* First Christians (British settlers).
German Lutherans arrive in New York, organizing a congregation by 1649.
23 Jesuit reductions (settlements), with 100,000 population, in Paraguay.
1626 *Barbados.* First Christians (English settlers with Anglican clergy).
1627 Alexander de Rhodes baptizes 6,700 in North Viet Nam.
1628 Dutch in New York organize first Christian Reformed Church on Manhattan island.
Revival in Ireland under Blair and Livingstone.
1629 Matthew's Gospel printed in Malay: first evangelistic portion in a non-European language.
1630 *Laos.* First mission (Catholics).
Catholicism in Japan totally destroyed after 16 years' persecution, with 1,900 martyrs crucified; remnants continue underground.
1632 *Montserrat.* First Christians (Irish settlers).
1634 Bavaria: Oberammergau Passion Play begun by amateurs in fulfilment of a vow.
Lord Baltimore founds Maryland for Roman Catholic settlers in North America.
*Antigua.* First Christians (English settlers, Anglicans).
1635 Public letter post introduced in England as first in world.
1637 *Ivory Coast.* First Christians (Portuguese traders).
1639 Roger Williams founds first Baptist church in USA at Providence, Rhode Island.
c1640 North America; 4,000 Indians converted and nurtured in 14 settlements under John Eliot who produced the Mohican Bible, first Indian translation.
1641 Massacre of thousands of Protestants in Ulster by Irish Catholics.
1642 *Dominica.* First mission (RC Dominican priests).
1643 Catholic missionaries in China appeal to Rome over rites controversy; 1742, final papal bull rejecting Ricci's methods.
1644 Heir to Chinese throne baptized by Jesuits with name Constantine.
1645 Capuchins in Congo and Angola baptize 600,000 Africans (mainly infants) by 1700.
1648 *US Virgin Islands.* First Christians (French settlers).
Russian expansion eastwards reaches Pacific Ocean.
*St Lucia.* First Christians (French settlers).
100,000 Jews murdered in Chmielnicki massacres by Christians in Poland.
*British Virgin Islands.* First Christians (Dutch settlers).
1649 *Reunion.* First Christians (French settlement).
Christians far more widely spread geographically than ever previously, but less numerous proportionately than in AD 500.

1650 **Global status:** 54 generations after Christ, world is 21.2% Christians (83.1% of them being Whites), 24.7% evangelized; with printed scriptures available in 45 languages.
China: Manchu conquest kills 25 million Chinese.
German pioneers of Pietistic evangelism: Voetius (1588-1676), von Lodenstein, de Labadie, Untereyck, Spener, Francke.
c1650 *St Vincent.* First Christians (French, Dutch, British settlers).
Russian Orthodoxy reaches across Siberia to Bering Strait.
*Grenada.* First Christians (French settlers).
*Belize.* First Christians (Spanish settlement).
*Anguilla.* First Christians (British Anglicans).
Egypt: Coptic bishops decline in number to only 17 (from 168 in AD 550).
Syrian Orthodox Church declines to 20 dioceses from 103 dioceses in 1150.
1651 Dutch control Cape Colony, South Africa.
*Gambia.* First Christians (British soldiers).
1652 Large numbers of White and Little Russian Orthodox submit to Rome as the Podcarpathian Ruthenians.
1653 Metropolitan Ahatalla of Syrian Church of India intercepted at sea, then allegedly burned alive by Jesuits at Goa. Malabar Church comes under Rome.
1658 Ceylon: Dutch finally drive out Portuguese, ban Catholicism with its 300,000 Catholics.
Viet Nam: 300,000 Catholics (including many death-bed baptisms).
1659 *French Polynesia.* First mission (Catholics); further attempts 1772, 1831 et alia.
1660 Founding of Society of Foreign Missions in Paris (MEP); Roman Catholic missions to east and southeast Asia.
Britain: 13,000 Quakers imprisoned under Charles II from 1660–85.
1662 Schism ex Church of England: 300,000 communicants follow ministers ejected under Act of Uniformity.
1663 *Chad.* First mission (RC, Capuchins); then abandoned until 1929.
1664 Baptized Catholics in Chinese empire grow from 150,000 in 1650 to 254,980 in 1664 (including vast numbers of children baptized in articulo mortis).
1665 Plague and fire devastate London; 75,000 die of plague.
1666 15,000 Protestants expelled by archbishop of Salzburg from his principality.
Old Ritualist schism ex Russian Orthodox Church.
1668 *Pacific Islands* (Micronesia). First mission (Spanish Catholics).
*Guam.* First mission (Spanish Jesuits).
1670 Bengal: 20,000 Namasudra (outcaste Hindus) in Dacca converted to Catholicism.
*Cayman Islands.* First Christians (British settlers).
c1670 *Bahamas.* First Christians (English settlers, Anglicans).
1670 Devotional evangelistic meetings at Frankfurt, Germany (Philip Jakob Spener).
1671 Anton Horneck, Pietistic evangelist, founds first Vestry Society in England.
1673 *Gabon.* First mission (Italian Capuchins).
1675 Germany: Lutheran Pietism and missionary outreach begun, led by Philip Spener.
1676 Compton Census in England: first census of church affiliation (Anglicans, Nonconformists, Roman Catholics).
1680 *Benin* (then Dahomey). First Christians (Portuguese settlers).
1681 Religious toleration accorded to Hungarian Protestants.
1685 Edict of Nantes revoked by Louis XIV; 400,000 Huguenots flee from France to England, South Africa and elsewhere.
1686 Russian Orthodox chaplains accompany cossacks to Peking; 1715, Orthodox mission begun.
1688 First Bible translation in South East Asia: NT translated into Malay; Bible in 1734 (Roman script) and 1759 (Arabic script).
1689 Student revival at Leipzig, Germany.
1690 West African slave trade accelerates; 5,500,000 slaves traded up to year 1800; grand total eventually 9.5 million Africans to the Americas.
1692 China decrees freedom of worship to all Christians (totalling 300,000, found in every province).
1697 Finland: crop failure and famine kill 100,000, 35% of population.
1698 First 2 non-Roman missionary societies formed, by Church of England: Society for Promoting Christian Knowledge (SPCK), and (1701) Society for the Propagation of the Gospel in Foreign Parts (SPG).

1700 **Global status:** 56 generations after Christ, world is 21.7% Christians (84.1% of them being Whites), 25.2% evangelized; with printed scriptures available in 52 languages.
1700 Christians in Portuguese possessions number 500,000.
2,000 Quakers from England settle in Pennsylvania.
Hochenau's evangelistic campaigns, Germany (1700–1721).
Wittgenstein revival movement in Germany (till 1750).
Swabian Pietistic Fathers (Germany): Bengel, Rieger, Hiller, Steinhofer, Storr, et alii.
Roman Catholic baptisms in Congo and Angola average 12,000 a year (mainly infants).
Peter the Great orders christianization of Siberia.
Dutch East Indies: 100,000 Protestants on Java, 40,000 on Ambon.
Catholics found in all provinces of China, numbering 250,000.
1701 200,000 Romanian Orthodox, with their clergy, submit to Rome as uniate church.
Russia: in Middle Volga, 3,638 pagan Cheremis (Mari) baptized by 1705.
1702 Congo: first attempt to found church independent of Rome in Black Africa: 22-year-old prophetess Donna Béatrice founded Antonian sect with as followers most of Congo kingdom; 1706 Béatrice burned alive by king Pedro VI.
Filofey bishop of Tobolsk increases churches from 160 to 448 and baptizes 40,000 Ostyaks, Voguls and Yakuts by 1721.
1703 St Petersburg (Petrograd) built as imperial capital of Russia by Peter the Great, at cost of lives of 100,000 labourers (Orthodox and others).
200,000 Indian converts to Jesuit mission around Madura, South India.
1704 China: persecution begins throughout empire.
1706 USA: Presbyterians form first organized church; origin of Presbyterian Church in the USA.
Danish Halle Foreign Mission begun.
Protestant missions begun in India with arrival of Danish Halle Lutherans, Ziegenbalg and Plütschau, on coast of Tranquebar.
1710 Canstein House printing press, Halle (Germany) with Bible society founded by Count von Canstein: 3 million Bibles and NTs printed in 80 years.
1715 *Nepal.* First mission in Kathmandu (Capuchins); 1769 all Christians finally left.
1716 William Tennent evangelizes in American colonies.
1717 August Hermann Francke's evangelistic campaign in Germany.
1721 Lutheran Church of Greenland recognized as integral part of Evangelical Lutheran Church of Denmark.
Peter the Great abolishes Russian Orthodox patriarchate, establishes synod of bishops and tsar-appointed oberprocurator, enabling tsars to rule church through synod until 1917.
Hans Egede (Norway) begins Protestant mission to Greenland Eskimos.
1722 Moravian (Herrnhut) Pietism begun, led by Zinzendorf.
In Ceylon, Protestants number 424,392 (21% of the population) through forced conversion by Dutch Reformed Church.
1724 Melkite (Greek Catholic) patriarchate of Antioch (in Beirut) established.
1727 Jews expelled from Russia; repeated in 1747.
Irkutsk in Siberia an independent Russian Orthodox diocese.
Treaty of Kiachta: China permits 4 Russian priests to begin Peking mission.
1732 Moravian Brethren send mission to Danish West Indies, and 1733 to Greenland.
1734 The Great Awakening, revival in New England (USA) spreading throughout the 13 Colonies; mass conversions of dechristianized European populations in North America; led by Jonathan Edwards.
1735 Christians in the Philippines reach 837,182; over a million by 1750.
John and Charles Wesley travel to Georgia (North America) as SPG missionaries, but meet hostility and return in 1737.
George Whitefield's conversion experience; 1736, begins evangelistic travels.
1737 300,000 killed in Calcutta by storm surge of Hooghly river.
1738 George Whitefield's evangelistic campaigns in North America (1738–1770); heard by 80% of entire population.
Conversion of Charles Wesley; commences writing Evangelical hymns, totalling 7,270 original compositions in all.
Conversion of John Wesley at Aldersgate (UK); beginning of 18th-century Evangelical Revival and rise of Methodism under the Wesleys.
1739 First evangelistic open-air sermons in England for centuries: George Whitefield (17 February), John Wesley (2 April).
John Wesley's evangelistic travels in Britain average 8,000 miles a year on horseback until his death in 1791.
1740 Armenian Catholic patriarchate of Cilicia established.
c1740 Bavarian Pietists: Rehberger (1716–1769), Urlsperger, Kieszling, Schöner.
1741 Oldest USA Indian independent church formed, Narraganset Indian Church in Charleston, Rhode Island.
Mass baptisms of pagans in Russia: 1741–62, 430,550 Chuvash, Cheremis, Ostyaks, et alii baptized; no pagans left in Middle Volga.
1742 Juan Santos Atahuallpa appears as Quechua messiah in eastern Peru.
*Seychelles.* First Christians (French Catholic settlers).
1746 Widespread and severe persecution of Christians begins in China, lasts 38 years.
1749 England: 10,000 Particular or Exclusive Baptists, 15,000 Congregationalists; 50,000 Nonconformists.

## Epoch VI: REPUDIATION AND REVIVAL 1750–1815

1750 **Global status:** 57 generations after Christ, world is 22.2% Christians (85.2% of them being Whites), 25.8% evangelized; with printed scriptures available in 60 languages.
c1750 Christianity now the prevailing religion of the West Indies.
c1750 *Turks & Caicos Islands.* First Christians (British Loyalist settlers from America).
1750 North American Whites (the 13 Colonies) about 95% professing Christians (50% Congregationalists, 30% baptized Anglicans, 10% Presbyterians), though only 5% affiliated as church members.
Moravian mission to Labrador begun.
Most peoples of Kamchatka christianized by Russians.
1759 Suppression of Jesuit order throughout Portugal and Portuguese domains; also 1764 in France and its colonies; 1767 Spain, Italy; 1773 order dissolved by pope; 1814 ban lifted throughout world.
1763 North America (USA): 24,000 Roman Catholics, growing to 35,000 by 1789, 150,000 by 1800 and 6,231,417 by 1890.
1764 *Falkland Islands.* First Christians (French settlers).
1766 First Methodist society in New World formed in North America.
Planters from Scotland begin Presbytery of British Guiana.
1767 First complete church membership returns published (by Methodists, in Britain).
1770 East African slave trade rapidly increases; 1,250,000 slaves traded at coast by Muslim Arabs up to 1897 abolition of slavery.
1772 Slavery ruled illegal in Britain (but not in colonies), but Atlantic slave trade delivers average of 75,000 a year from 1750-1800.
Polish Orthodox united with Russian Orthodox Church until 1918.
1773 First independent USA Black Baptist congregation is formed near Augusta, Georgia.
Pope Clement XIV dissolves Society of Jesus (22,589 members including 11,293 priests); 3,000 Jesuit overseas missionaries recalled.
Syrian Catholic patriarchate established.
1775 Industrialization and urbanization accelerate in Britain; working classes alienated from churches.
1778 USA Universalists organize their first church in 1778, Unitarians following with their own church in 1796.
1780 Edict of Toleration of Joseph II of Austria guaranteeing religious freedom.
Tupac Amarú II leads Quechua religious revolt against Spanish in Peru; crushed and executed.
Deutsche Christentumsgesellschaft begun.
Sunday schools popularized by Robert Raikes of Gloucester; 1786, 200,000 children enrolled in England. 1789 in Wales, then to Scotland, Ireland and America.
*Pitcairn Island.* First Christians (British mutineers).
c1780 Viet Nam: 200,000 Catholics, 28 European priests and 47 local priests.
1780 Roman Catholics in England number 70,000.
1783 Native Baptist Church, first Jamaican Afro-Christian movement, begun by ex-slave; played a significant political role 80 years later.
1783 Eclectic Society and Clapham Sect formed in England.
Charles Simeon starts Evangelical student movement in Cambridge, England.
1784 Methodists in the 13 Colonies multiply from 500 in 1771 to 15,000 in 13 years, then to 1,324,000 by 1850.
Russian Orthodox mission to Alaska begun.
1785 *Sierra Leone.* First Christians (Black settlers from Nova Scotia).

*New Zealand.* First Christians (European commercial base).
Evangelical awakenings (revivals) throughout Wales: 1785 Brynengan, 1786 Trecastle, 1791 Bala, 1805 Aberystwyth, 1810 Llangeitho, 1817 Beddgelert, 1821 Denbighshire, 1822 Anglesey, 1828 Carmarthenshire, 1832 Caernarvonshire, 1840 Merionethshire, 1849 South Wales, et alia.
c1785 Christianity reintroduced into Korea; prospers for a while, then exterminated.
1787 Revival in Virginia, North America.
First USA Black Methodist dissidents appear, with officially-organized African Methodist Episcopal Church emerging by 1816.
Moravian foreign mission formed: Society for Propagating the Gospel among the Heathen.
1788 Revival among Bavarian Catholics, led by Sailer, Feneberg, Boos, Goszner, Lindl.
*Australia.* First Christians (English convicts and Anglican chaplains).
*Norfolk Island.* First Christians (Australian convict colony).
Large colonies of German Mennonites and farmers settle in Black Earth region of Russia; origin of Stundists.
1789 Roman Catholics in USA number 35,000, half in Maryland, quarter in Philadelphia. First diocese erected in Baltimore (Maryland).
French Revolution: church/state separation and religious liberty proclaimed in France.
1790 Methodists in Great Britain number 71,668.
1792 Second Great Awakening among Congregationalist and other New England churches (USA), lasting 30 years.
8 Russian Orthodox missionary monks arrive on island of Kodiak (Alaska), baptize 2,500 shamanist Eskimos in following 2 years, and 10,000 in 1795.
1793 William Carey sails for India under Baptist Missionary Society (formed 1792); at Serampore, initiates modern era of Protestant world missions.
1794 First Catholic ordination of Amerindian priests in Latin America (3 persons).
1795 London Missionary Society (LMS) founded (interdenominational, later Congregationalist).
Methodists in Britain separate from Church of England after John Wesley's death in 1791.
Mass movement in Cape Comorin (South India): 5,000 Nadars (Shanars) baptized by SPCK missionaries in 10 years.
1796 First LMS missionaries sent to South Pacific (Tahiti).
Edinburgh Tract Society, Edinburgh Missionary Society, formed in Scotland.
Over 2 million Uniate Ruthenians in Poland return to Russian Orthodox Church.
Founding of Scottish Missionary Society and Glasgow Missionary Society.
Ceylon: British drive out Dutch forces, find 67,000 Ceylonese still Roman Catholics despite 140 years' ban.
Norwegian Revival, under Hans Nielsen Hauge.
1797 *Tonga.* First missionaries (LMS), also 1822, then 1825.
Netherlands Missionary Society (NZG) founded in Rotterdam.
1799 Elberfeld-Barmen Missionary Society begun.
New Religion of the Iroquois founded by Handsome Lake, a Seneca Indian in Great Lakes region (USA).
Religious Tract Society (RTS) founded (UK).
Church Missionary Society (CMS) founded by Anglicans in London.

1800 **Global status:** 59 generations after Christ, world is 23.1% Christians (86.5% of them being Whites), 27.2% evangelized; with printed scriptures available in 67 languages.
Widespread evangelistic camp meetings begin in USA: Kentucky Revival awakening, with crowds of up to 25,000, sweeps over Kentucky, Tennessee and the Carolinas.
Protestant foreign missionaries number 100.
c1800 *Papua New Guinea.* First Christians (European trading post).
1800 Congo and Angola: no trace of former Catholic missions remaining.
China: about 200,000 baptized Roman Catholics remaining.
c1800 Old Believers in many parts of northern Russia number half population.
1800 Beginnings of local awakenings (revivals) in Scotland: Lewis, Harris, Perthshire.
1801 Protestants in Ceylon number 342,000 (Dutch Reformed), or 14% of the population; through neglect, most lapse to Buddhism by 1830.
1802 320,000 Catholics in Viet Nam, with 3 European bishops, 15 missionary and 119 Vietnamese priests.
1804 First German Bible society.
*Fiji Islands.* First Christians (escaped convicts from Australia).
British & Foreign Bible Society (BFBS) founded (London).
1805 *Namibia* (South West Africa). First mission (LMS, among Hottentots).
1806 Napoleon abolishes Holy Roman Empire.
Britain: revivals secede from Methodism — 1806 Independent Methodists, 1810 Camp Meeting Methodists, joining in 1812 as Primitive Methodists.
1807 Slave trade prohibited by British parliament.
Robert Morrison (LMS), first Protestant missionary to China, arrives in Macao, translates Bible into Chinese by 1818, dictionary by 1821; died in 1834, seeing only 10 baptisms of Chinese.
1809 Sweden: Evangeliska Sällskapet (for Bibles and tracts) founded.
1810 Britain: 312,000 Nonconformists (including 30,000 Particular or Exclusive Baptists).
China: 215,000 native Catholics, 6 bishops, 2 coadjutors, 23 missionaries, 80 native agents.
German evangelist T. Grenz spreads gospel among Lithuanians.
c1810 Revival in Russian Orthodox Church; 1813 Russian Bible Society founded, printing in 30 languages (17 new) with 600,000 copies; 1827 disbanded.
1810 American Board of Commissioners for Foreign Missions organized (USA Congregationalists).
Evangelical awakenings (revivals) in Switzerland (Robert Haldane), France, Low Countries, Germany.
1811 Henry Martyn, Anglican chaplain (CMS), begins in Persia translating Bible.
1812 Wuppertal Tract Society formed (Germany).
1813 Burma: arrival of American Baptist missionary Adoniram Judson.
1814 Society of Jesus re-established by pope Pius VII after 40 years' ban.
American Baptist Missionary Union founded (USA); later ABFMS.
New Zealand: Protestant missions to Maoris begin.
Prussian Bible Society founded.

Epoch VII:
**THE GREAT CENTURY**
**1815–1914**

1815 **Global status:** 60 generations after Christ, world is 24.4% Christians (86.1% of them being Whites), 30.3% evangelized; with printed scriptures available in 86 languages.
Beginning of the Great Century of worldwide Christian expansion, from end of Napoleonic wars to 1914.
Printed Bible available in 44 languages, New Testament in 59, portions in 86; Bible-publishing societies now begun in a number of countries.
Over 80% of all North American Indians still non-Christians, despite extensive missions.
Basel Evangelical Missionary Society founded (Switzerland).
Vast proliferation begins in number of Roman Catholic orders and congregations.
1816 *Botswana* (then Bechuanaland). First mission (LMS).
Elberfeld revivals in western Germany: 1816 first revival, 1820 second.
American Bible Society (ABS) founded.
1817 Proposal (by Hall and Newell of ABCFM) to convert the millions of heathens in the world through sending 30,000 Protestant missionaries from the USA and Europe in 21 years, at a cost of US$4 from each Protestant and Anglican communicant in Christendom.
Robert Moffat begins 50-year ministry among Tswana of Southern Africa; 1857 completes Tswana Bible.
1818 Wesleyan Methodist Missionary Society begun (London); later MMS.
'The Conversion of the World: or the Claims of 600 Millions, and the Ability and Duty of the Churches Respecting Them': pamphlet by G. Hall & S. Newell (ABCFM, India).
Madagascar: first Protestants (LMS) begin work.
1819 Settlers' Meeting (Creoles) secedes from Wesleyan Mission in Freetown (Sierra Leone); first ecclesiastical schism south of the Sahara.
1820 Protestant mission begins in Argentina (BFBS).
Revival in Pomerania, Germany.
London Jews Society make first British missionary contact in Iraq.
c1820 Georgian Orthodox Church forcibly assimilated by Russian Orthodox Church.
1821 Chile: first Protestant missionary (BFBS) opens schools.
84-year-old ecumenical patriarch robed in vestments by Turks then hanged with other bishops in Constantinople; 23,000 Greeks and 12,000 Turks massacred.
Danish Missionary Society founded.
1822 *Liberia.* First Christians (Black settlers from USA; Baptists and Methodists).
Paris Evangelical Missionary Society founded (France).
Province Baptist Church in Monrovia (Liberia), oldest Baptist congregation in Africa, begun by first USA missionary to Africa, Lott Carey, a Black slave from Virginia.
Society for the Propagation of the Faith begun in Lyons (France).
1823 Josiah Pratt's annual Survey of the World (CMS, London) headed 'The Conversion of the World dependent on the more abundant influence of the Holy Spirit'.
*Cook Islands.* First mission (LMS).
German Lutherans emigrate from Germany to Brazil.
1824 Coptic Catholic patriarchate established (Egypt).
Berlin Missionary Society formed.
USA: beginnings of interdenominational city-wide co-operative evangelism.
First Anglican bishoprics in Caribbean established in Jamaica and Barbados.
1825 Bombay Missionary Union formed in India for prayer and discussion among Anglican, Brethren, Congregationalist and Presbyterian missionaries, eventually producing the principle of comity.
Hawaii: Hapu syncretistic cult announces imminent end of world; temple then burned to ground by Protestant missionaries.
*Swaziland.* First missionaries (Methodists from South Africa).
Colombia: BFBS agent arrives as first Protestant missionary.
American Tract Society founded.
Church of Scotland Mission (Presbyterian) begun.
British Honduras: Methodists (MMS) begin Protestant work; 1840 British colony declared.
1826 *Cocos (Keeling) Islands.* First Christians (British settlement).
Massive apostasies from Russian Orthodox missions: 299,300 in Kazan, 95% of 14,800 new Tartar converts, 233,500 Chuvash, et alii.
New Zealand: Hau Hau (Good News of Peace) syncretistic cult among the Maoris; 1865 full-scale uprising against British.
33 of the 38 RC bishoprics in Spanish America vacant or inactive due to reluctance of Rome to recognize state appointments.
1827 Siegen-Dillkreis revival, western Germany.
*Western Samoa.* First mission (Methodist).
*American Samoa.* First mission (Methodist).
John Darby, Anglican clergyman, begins Brethren movement in Dublin.
Netherlands Missionary Society begins work in Celebes.
1828 *Transkei.* First Christians (Moravians).
Rhenish Missionary Society (RMG) formed (Germany); begins work among Dayaks of Borneo.
Mamaia (Flock of God) cult founded in Society Islands by prophet Teau, a Christian from Panavia, protesting harsh mission destruction of paganism.
England: emancipation of Nonconformists, and 1829 of Roman Catholics.
1830 *New Hebrides.* First Christians (small sandalwood trading centres).
USA: widespread campaigns through evangelists Andrew, Barnes, Burchard, Baker, Caughey, Griffith, Inskip, Knapp, Maffit, Swan.
Joseph Smith at Fayette, NY (USA), has visions which lead to establishment of Church of Jesus Christ of Latter-day Saints (Mormons); 1844 murdered by mob.
Reveil (French-speaking Reformed Church awakening) sweeps Netherlands.
1831 Massacres of Nestorians by Kurds; also in 1843, 1846.
*New Caledonia.* First mission (Tongans, from Tonga).
1832 Tract Society of Lausanne and Eszlingen begun.
American Baptist Home Missionary Society formed.
Revival sweeps Hawaii until 1843.
London City Mission founded.
Iran entered by American Board (ABCFM) as first Protestant mission, under name Mission to the Nestorians.
1833 Slavery abolished in British empire; owners of 700,000 freed slaves compensated.
Church of Greece proclaims its autocephality in defiance of Ecumenical Patriarchate of Constantinople; latter eventually recognizing it in 1850.
*Lesotho* (then Basutoland). First mission (Paris Mission, PEMS).
1834 Religious orders in Portugal suppressed.
1835 Finland: the Österbottenväckelse, evangelical awakening in the west, active for 15 years; also revival under Laestadius.
Attempt to eradicate Christianity in Madagascar by queen Ranavalona; large numbers of Christians killed from 1835 to 1861.
Swedish Missionary Society founded.
1836 *Wallis & Futuna Islands.* First mission (French Marist priests).
Booklet: 'The Duty of the Present Generation to Evangelize the World: An Appeal from the Missionaries at the Sandwich Islands to their Friends in the United States'.
Leipzig Evangelical Lutheran Mission formed (Germany).
1837 *Gilbert Islands.* First Christians (European trading centre).
Great Awakening in Hawaii, until 1842: 27,000 Protestant adult converts (20% of population).
Electric telegraph invented.
1838 Turkey: small-scale revivals among Armenians in Nicomedia and (1841) Adabazar, through ABCFM (USA); and later in Aintab and Aleppo.
Tenrikyo (Religion of Divine Wisdom), a Shinto/Christian amalgam, founded in Japan as first of the Shinko Shukyo (New Religious Movements).
1839 New Hebrides: missionary pioneer John Williams (LMS) martyred on island of Eromanga; Catholic missionaries also arrive, but systematic missions not begun until 1887.
Scottish Highlands Awakening for 4 years: Oban, islands, also Lowlands.
1840 Penny post introduced in England as first in world.
Philippines: Confraternity of St Joseph founded by Tagalogs to seize autonomy; crushed by Spaniards.
1841 *Hong Kong.* First missions (Catholic, Anglican, Baptist).
Edinburgh Medical Missionary Society founded in Scotland.
Anglican bishopric in Jerusalem established.
UK: 22,000 converted over 7 years through preaching of James Caughey of New York.
1842 Treaty of Nanking, following Opium War, cedes Hong Kong to Britain and opens territory to missions.
Gossner Mission Society begun in Berlin.
Revival spreads through state church of Norway; Norwegian Mission Society (Stavanger) begun.
Dahomey: MMS (UK) missionaries arrive at Fon kingdom, Abomey.
1843 Great Peaceful Heavenly Kingdom (Tai Ping Tien Kueh: Society of Worshippers of the True God/Celestial Kingdom of Great Peace) begun in China as quasi-Christian sect with Hakka founder and leaders strongly influenced by New Testament; 1853, rebels capture Nanking, rule south China; 1862, suppressed, 35 million killed.
Hermannsburg revival, western Germany.
20,000 Nestorians massacred in Kurdistan by Muslim Kurds.
Sierra Leonian former slave Samuel Crowther sent as missionary to Nigeria; 1864, consecrated as first non-European Anglican bishop.
Goanese (Roman Catholic) schism in India; 600 untrained Indians ordained; later, Latin-rite schism, Independent Catholic Church of Ceylon, Goa and India, existing until 1950.
1844 Seventh-day Adventist movement begun in USA.
CMS missionary J.L. Krapf first to begin modern missionary work in Kenya; wife and child die of malaria in Mombasa.
Young Men's Christian Association (YMCA) founded in London.
Christadelphians founded by John Thomas in Birmingham (UK) and London.
Persia: revival among Nestorians around ABCFM station Urumiah; other revivals in 1849, 1850.
1845 *Solomon Islands.* First missionaries (Marists, with bishop killed on landing).
*Cameroon.* First mission (Baptist Missionary Society, UK).
Potato blight from America devastates Ireland, with a million killed by famine and typhus, resulting in another million Irish migrating to Britain, USA and Australia, markedly influencing development of Catholicism there.
Southern Baptist Convention, largest USA Baptist church, comes into being in reaction against ABFMS refusing to accept slave-owners as missionaries.
Oxford Movement in England: 60 prominent Anglicans and 250 clergy enter Church of Rome by 1862.
1846 World Evangelical Alliance (WEA) formed in London to further unity among Evangelicals worldwide.
Mormons under Brigham Young leave Nauvoo City for Great Salt Lake; 1847, Salt Lake City founded.
*Niue Island.* First missionaries (a returning Niuean, and a Samoan).
1847 Latin patriarchate of Jerusalem restored.
'The light of Christ illuminates the whole world' — last words of Macarius Glukharev, apostle to the Altai (1792–1847).
1848 Karl Marx and Friedrich Engels publish *Communist Manifesto* in Germany, calling for violent overthrow of the established order including religion.
1849 Charles G. Finney's evangelistic campaigns in Britain, 1849–51 and 1859–61.
Ludwigsburg evangelists' school founded in Germany; 1856, moved to Krischenhardthof.
Thailand: all foreign missionaries ordered out.
Brazil: total Black slaves from Africa 5.5 million over 1550–1850.

1850 **Global status:** 61 generations after Christ, world is 27.2% Christians (85.2% of them being Whites), 38.1% evangelized; with printed scriptures available in 205 languages.
Cult of the Holy Cross, Yucatan (Mexico).

c1850 *British Indian Ocean Territory.* First Christians (from Mauritius).

1851 Spanish concordat with Holy See.
England & Wales: first (and only) state Census of Religious Worship; 61% of entire population attend church every Sunday.
Edict of Tu Du of Viet Nam, following French intervention (1843); persecution of Christians results in death of 115 priests and 70,000 Catholics, and in 1884 French declaration of protectorate over territory.
Anglicans and Protestants in Indian subcontinent (150 million population): 91,092 adherents (51,300 in Tinnevelly (CMS) and South Travancore (LMS)), 14,661 communicants; 339 ordained missionaries in 19 societies; members expand tenfold by mass movements from 1851–1901.

1852 Canada: Anglican church separated from state.

1853 Society for Itinerant Preachers founded in Germany.
Norway: first Home Mission (Indremisjon) begun within state church.
David Livingstone (LMS) passes through Zambia on way to Luanda.
Catholic hierarchy re-established in Netherlands.
Open Air Mission founded (UK).

1854 International missionary conference in New York, USA, guided by Alexander Duff: 'To what extent are we authorized by the Word of God to expect the conversion of the world to Christ?'

1855 East Africa: 20,000 Black slaves a year exported by Arabs.

1856 Stonemason Grünewald spreads gospel using colporteurs in western Germany.
Sweden: Evangeliska Fosterlands-Stiftelsen founded within state church.

1857 Mass secession from Mexican Roman Catholic Church leads to formation of Iglesia de Jesus, ultimately becoming Episcopal Church of Mexico.
Society for Home Preachers in Schleswig-Holstein (Germany) formed.
USA: evangelist D.L. Moody (1837–99) in Chicago; other evangelists R.A. Torrey (1856–1928), Billy Sunday (1862–1925), Robert P. Wilder (1863–1938); beginnings of large-scale lay-centred evangelism.
Evangelical Awakening in USA (under Charles Grandison Finney et alii; one million converts in 2 years), spreading to Europe and the other 4 continents (1859 India, 1860 China).

c1858 *Johnston Island.* First Christians (USA guano-digging company).

1858 Apparition at Lourdes, France, with site subsequently becoming a world-famous Catholic pilgrimage and healing centre.
India: first of over 150 attempts to establish indigenous Hindu-Christian movements or churches: Hindu Church of the Lord Jesus (Tinnevelly).
David Livingstone begins exploration of Zambesi and Shire rivers, attracting others to begin missionary work in Nyasaland.
Townsend treaty between USA and Japan opening Japan to Christian missionaries.
Religious freedom and impartiality in India proclaimed by queen Victoria: 'Relying ourselves on the truth of Christianity . . . we have no desire to impose our convictions on any of our subjects'.
India: over one million Roman Catholics, 100,000 Protestants and Anglicans.

1859 Second Evangelical Awakening in Britain, reaching over 3 million with 1.1 million converts: 100,000 in Wales, 300,000 in Scotland, 100,000 in Ulster, over 500,000 in England.

1860 Korea: Chondogyo (Religion of the Heavenly Way), a blend of shamanistic, Buddhist, Confucian and Christian elements, emerges as a reaction against Western, especially Catholic, influence.
Revival in Ukraine; 1884–1904, persecution of Evangelicals.

c1860 *Togo.* First Christians (Methodist immigrants from Gold Coast).
Revival in South Africa erupts under Andrew Murray (Dutch Reformed), sweeping the Afrikaner churches.
Liverpool Conference on Missions, as aftermath of 1859 Awakening in UK; 126 attenders; first world missionary conference.

1861 Great Christian Revival (Great Awakening) in Jamaica, resulting in rapid spread of Native Baptist Church (now Revival Zion); wild dancing, trances.
Ellice Island (*Tuvalu*). First Christians (Samoan pastors of the LMS).
*Tokelau Island.* First mission (LMS).
Cornish Revivals, in Britain for 2 years.
110 North American Blacks settle in Haiti and establish Episcopal Church.
Universities Mission to Central Africa (UMCA) begun in Britain.
Madagascar: after 25 years' vicious persecution, Christians found to have multiplied twenty-fold.
Batak church in Sumatra (HKBP) grows from 52 Christians (1866) to 2,056 (1876), 7,500 (1881), 103,525 (1911), 380,000 (1941), 1,044,382 (1970), and to 1,160,000 (1976).
Russian Orthodox monk Nicolai (Ivan Kasatkin) arrives in Japan, 1868 baptizes 3 converts, 1880 made bishop and 1906 archbishop in Tokyo; dies in 1912 with 30,000 converts made.
USA: 620,000 killed, mostly by disease, in 1861–65 Civil War between North and South over slavery issue.

1862 *Djibouti.* First Christians (French colonists).
Methodist Society, a Fanti schism ex Wesleyan Methodists near Cape Coast, Gold Coast.

1863 Samoa: syncretistic cult begun by local preacher Sio-vili; vast crowds.

1864 USA: first Greek Orthodox church organized in New Orleans, Louisiana.

1865 *Bhutan.* First Christians (British troops).
From 1820–65, nearly 2 million Roman Catholics from Ireland emigrate to USA.
Salvation Army founded by William Booth in England.
Paraguay: one million killed in 5-year war with Brazil and Uruguay.
China Inland Mission (CIM) founded as faith mission by Hudson Taylor; 1950, renamed OMF.

1866 Korea: severe persecution of the 25,000 Catholics; 10,000 Koreans martyred, including 2 bishops and 7 priests.

1867 *Midway Islands.* First Christians (USA).
Anglican Church ceases to be state religion in Ireland.
Archbishop of Canterbury convenes first decennial Lambeth Conference of all bishops of Anglican Communion (London); 76 bishops present.
Invention of typewriter (Sholes, Remington).
Finland: crop failure kills 8% of population.

1868 White Fathers (Missionaries of Our Lady of Africa) begun by cardinal Lavigerie.
Catholic Action begun in Bologna (Italy).

1869 Council of Vatican I, in Rome: papal infallibility defined, widening gulf between Rome and rest of Christendom.

c1870 *Canton and Enderbury Islands.* First Christians (British guano-digging companies).

1870 Ghost Dance among American Indians begun by prophet Wodziwob; 1890 spreads to Paiute, Cheyenne, Kiowa, Sioux and other tribes.
Unification of Italy under Victor Emmanuel I; annexes Rome and papal states, makes Rome its capital.
Heyday of British evangelists: William Booth (1829–1912), C. H. Spurgeon (1834–1892), Henry Drummond (1851–1897), Wilson Carlile (1847–1942), Gipsy Smith (1860–1947).
Jehovah's Witnesses (then called Watch Tower) begun in USA through Charles T. Russell.
Punjab: mass movement of 50% of Hindu Chuhras in Sialkot to American Presbyterian mission begins; continuing revival up to 1912.
South India: mass movement brings one million Telugu outcastes into Baptist, Lutheran and Methodist churches in 30 years.
Kugu Sorta (Great Candle), anti-Russian and anti-missionary cult after Cheremis forcibly converted to Christianity.
Native American (Peyote) Church, large USA Amerindian church, takes shape.
Orthodox Missionary Society organized in Russia; branches in 55 Russian dioceses.

1871 Great Fire of Chicago: 50 churches and missions destroyed.
USA: beginnings of large-scale team evangelism; 1871–99, D.L. Moody & Ira D. Sankey.

1872 Revivals in Japan; also 1883.
Angola: Kiyoka (Burning) anti-sorcery prophetic movement sweeps across the north.
First indigenous church movement in southern Africa: secession from Herman congregation, Paris Mission, Basutoland.
8th International Statistical Congress, held at St Petersburg (Russia), urges inclusion of item on religion in every national census.

1873 Dwight L. Moody's evangelistic campaigns in England: first 1873–75, second 1882–84, third 1891–92.
India: Roman Catholic mass movement among aboriginal Kols; 79,000 baptized by 1891.

1874 Guatemala: Catholic religious orders and congregations dissolved.

1875 Japan: Doshisha University founded.
*Uganda.* First resident evangelist (Dallington Maftaa, Anglican from Nyasaland).
Alliance of Reformed Churches (Presbyterian); first confessional council to be formed (London). 1970, as WARC, merger with International Congregational Council.
Arya Samaj founded in India for purification of Hinduism; anti-Christian.
USA: Bible conference movement begun as Believers' Meeting for Bible Study, later Niagara Bible Conference, dominated by premillennialists.
Society of the Divine Word (Germany) inaugurated.
Keswick Convention for higher spiritual life begun (UK), under theme 'All One in Christ Jesus'.

1876 World Methodist Conference (WMC) founded.
Invention of electric telephone (Bell).
Sweden: evangelical awakening in state church under Skogsbergh and Waldenström.

1877 *Guinea* (French). First mission (French CSSp).
Shanghai, China: foreign missions conference, with 473 missionaries from 20 Protestant missionary societies.

1878 BMS(UK) open São Salvador station in northern Angola.
Thailand: Edict of Religious Toleration proclaimed by king Chulalongkorn.
USA: First American Bible and Prophetic Conference, New York City.
2nd Lambeth Conference; 100 bishops present.

1879 Death of J. Veniaminov (born 1797), prominent Russian Orthodox missionary.
First Church of Christ, Scientist, founded in Boston by Mary Baker Eddy as worldwide movement centering on spiritual healing.
Scripture Union (SU) founded; 300,000 members in UK alone by 1887.
*Burundi* (then Urundi). First mission (White Fathers).

1880 Thirty Years' Revival in Germany (till 1910): several hundred thousand converted in state churches.

1881 300,000 killed in Indochina by typhoon.
Shakerism and Indian Shaker Church begun by John Slocum among Puget Sound Amerindians.
*Somalia.* First mission (Catholic).
First of 40 International Eucharistic Congresses, held in Lille (France) with 800 present; growing to the 41st (1976) in Philadelphia (USA) with one million present.

1882 India: Anglicans and Protestants number 500,000.
Britain: International Bible Reading Association (IBRA) founded; 100,000 members by 1886.
Korean treaty with USA ensures religious freedom in Korea; Presbyterian and Methodist missionaries enter 3 years later.
Church Army (Anglican) founded by Wilson Carlile (UK).

1883 Fourth Evangelical Awakening (of the century) in Norway, especially in Skien.
Japan: first Japanese Catholic priests ordained: 15 by 1891, 33 by 1910.
General Conference of Protestant Missionaries of Japan; several revivals; 'Japan is now embracing Christianity with a rapidity unexampled since the days of Constantine . . . will be predominantly Christian within 20 years'.

1884 German Evangelization Society founded.
City-wide evangelists in USA: Samuel Porter Jones & E.O. Excell (1885–1906, 25 million attenders and 500,000 converts, most in South), B. Fay Mills, J. Wilbur Chapman.

1885 First African ordinations to Anglican ministry in Kenya.
*Zambia* (Northern Rhodesia). First mission (Paris Mission, PEMS).
Violent persecution in Indochina: 100,000 Catholics (16% of total) and 115 local priests killed.
Uganda martyrs: around 250 Catholic and Anglican Christians executed by king Mwanga at Namugongo.
Wesleyan Forward Movement in UK Methodism under Hugh Price Hughes of West London Mission, founding central halls and stressing social evangelism.

1886 *Sikkim.* First mission (Church of Scotland).
More indigenous movements and churches in India opposing Western missions: 1886 National Church of Madras, 1887 Calcutta Christo Samaj.
Church of God (Cleveland) begun as study and fellowship group in Cleveland, Tennessee; later became first Pentecostal church in USA, from 1906.

1887 900,000 drowned in Honan, China, by Yellow river flood.
First scripture translation in Philippines: Gospel of Luke in Pangasinan.
Canada: evangelistic campaigns in cities under evangelists Crossley and Hunter.
*Maldives.* First Christians (under British protectorate).

1888 German Association for Evangelism and Christian Fellowship (Gnadauer Band) formed at Gnadau.
Student Volunteer Movement for Foreign Missions formed in USA, with watchword 'The Evangelization of the World in this Generation'.
*Christmas Island.* First Christians (British administrators).
*Nauru.* First mission (LMS).
India: Mar Thoma Syrian Christian Evangelistic Association of Malabar formed for non-Syrian outcaste converts; large annual conventions.
Native Baptist Church secedes in Lagos (Nigeria) and Douala (Cameroon), from Southern Baptists and Basel Mission.
Invention of Edison motion-picture camera (Kinetograph).
Centenary Conference on Foreign Missions, London; 1,576 missionaries and representatives of 140 agencies; first of the great international conferences.
3rd Lambeth Conference; 145 bishops present.

1889 Gipsy Smith's evangelistic campaigns in USA.
Largest USA non-Chalcedonian church established: Armenian Church of North America, under Catholicate of Echmiadzin.
Japan: 500 Japanese students at Student Conference send telegram to SVM Conference, Northfield (USA), urging 'Make Jesus King'.
1st International Old Catholic Bishops' Conference, Utrecht (Dutch, German and Swiss churches).
North Africa Mission enters Tripoli as first Protestant mission in Libya.
*Rwanda.* First mission (White Fathers).
Brazil: republic proclaimed and Catholic church formally separated from state.

1890 China: 500,000 baptized Catholics, 639 foreign priests, 369 Chinese priests.
Shanghai: foreign missions conference, with 1,295 missionaries present.
Philippine Independent Church founded by Catholic priest Gregorio Aglipay; 1902 organized as schism taking 45% of all Roman Catholics.
Nevius method introduced in Korea (Bible-training for lay members).

1891 Japan: Roman Catholic hierarchy constituted; Catholics 44,500, rising to 63,000 by 1910.
International Congregational Council formed in London.

1892 *United Arab Emirates* (then Trucial Oman). First Christians (British officials, Indian merchants).

1893 Papua New Guinea: Cult of the Prophet Tokerau at Milne Bay, first of over 120 distinct cargo cult movements over next 80 years.
National Spiritualist Association of Churches founded, in USA.
World Parliament of Religions, in Chicago.

1894 Madagascar: first indigenous church, Malagasy Protestant Church (ex LMS).
Soatanana Revival begins among Lutheran and LMS churches in Madagascar, lasting 80 years (Fifohazana, Revivalists).
*Central African Republic* (then Ubangi-Chari). First mission (Roman Catholic).

1895 *Mali.* First mission (White Fathers from Senegal).
Massacres of Armenian Christians by Turks: 1895, 80,000 in Trebizond; Christmas 1895, 1,200 burned alive in Urfa cathedral; 1896, 6,000 in Istanbul; total killed 1895–96, 200,000; 1905, 20,000 in Cilicia; 1909, 30,000 in district of Adana; 1915, 600,000 in Anatolia; and in 1920, 30,000 at Marash and Hadjin.
Church of God in Christ formed in USA; later became Black pentecostals.
Coptic Catholic patriarchate of Alexandria erected by Roman pope (earlier attempt 1824).
Christian Endeavour movement numbers 38,000 societies across world, with 2,225,000 members.

1896 German Student Volunteer Movement begun.
'Make Jesus King': International Students Missionary Conference, Liverpool; 800 students from 24 nations.
T. Herzl publishes his *Der Judenstaat* (The Jewish State); rise of global Zionist movement (Hibbat Zion, 'Love of Zion').

1897 Ross's discovery of cause of malaria; missionary fatalities in Africa decline.
Lott Carey Baptist Foreign Mission Convention (Black American) formed.
USA: largest Catholic (non-Roman) church established: Polish National Catholic Church, formed over conflict between Polish Catholics and Irish Catholic hierarchy.
4th Lambeth Conference; 194 bishops present.

1898 50,000 Nestorians in Urmia diocese (Iran) converted to Russian Orthodoxy; 1914, annihilated by Turks.
Nyasaland: Providence Industrial Mission founded by US Blacks, later leading to 1915 Chilembwe uprising.
Church and state separated in Cuba on independence from Spain.

1899 *Wake Island.* First Christians (USA cable station).

1900 **Global status:** 62 generations after Christ, world is 34.4% Christians (81.1% of them being Whites), 51.3% evangelized; with printed scriptures available in 537 languages.
*Upper Volta.* First mission (French White Fathers).
First cinemas in fair sideshows; 1905 first cinema theatre.
Boxer revolt in China kills 47,000 Catholics (out of 1.2 million) with 5 bishops and 31 priests, and 2,000

Protestants with 186 missionaries and children.

In Hawaii, catastrophic decline of Aboriginal population through disease from 200,000 (in 1775) to 70,000 (1850) to 35,000 (1900).

Peak of massive Roman Catholic immigration from Europe to USA.

*Northern Solomons* (Bougainville). First mission (Roman Catholic).

New York Ecumenical Missionary Conference; 2,500 members, 200,000 attenders.

International Council of Unitarian and other Liberal Religious Thinkers and Workers, founded in USA; 1910, renamed International Congress of Free Christians and other Religious Liberals; 1930, renamed International Association for Liberal Christianity and Religious Freedom (IARF).

John R. Mott's classic, *The evangelization of the world in this generation*, published.

Minahasa (north of Celebes) entirely christianized.

1901 First Atlantic wireless signal sent by Marconi from Poldhu Cornwall (UK) to St Johns, Newfoundland.

Pentecostalism in USA begun at Topeka Bible College (Kansas).

UK: BFBS grand total of Scriptures issued since 1808: 46,030,124 Bibles, 71,178,373 NTs, 52,763,047 portions.

1902 Pakistan (then India): Hindu outcaste mass movement into Methodist church begins.

Adolf von Harnack publishes his *The mission and expansion of Christianity during the first 3 centuries*.

Team evangelism: 1902–08, R.A. Torrey & C.M. Alexander, with 130,000 converts.

1904 Conversion of Indian evangelist and mystic, Sadhu Sundar Singh; 1929, vanishes in Tibet.

Welsh revival through ministry of Evan Roberts, with 100,000 converts in Wales in 6 months; short-lived (1904–06), but literally swept the world; led to worldwide Pentecostal movement in 1906.

1905 Baptist World Alliance (BWA) founded.

In France, Catholic church separated from state.

Evangelical awakenings in Denmark, Finland, Sweden, Germany, Russia, Madagascar, India (Assam, Kerala, Sialkot through Praying Hyde), China.

Evangelistic Faith Missions (USA) formed.

Evangelistic Council of London sponsors Greater London crusade with Torrey & Alexander team; 202 meetings, 1.1 million attenders, 14,000 conversions.

1906 Beginnings of world Pentecostalism: Black revival in Azuza Street, Los Angeles, USA, with simultaneous spontaneous revivals elsewhere across world.

First indigenous schism in China, the China Jesus Independent Church.

1907 Massive revival in Korea: phenomenal growth of churches spreading also into Manchuria and China.

First pentecostal movement within Church of England (parish in Sunderland).

USA: peak immigration rate of 1,285,000 Europeans in one year; immigrants from 1845–1914 total 33 million.

1908 Manchurian Revival, at Changte under Jonathan Goforth.

Nyasaland: Elliott Kamwana baptizes 10,000 Lakeside Tonga, start of major separatist church in Central Africa (Church of the Watch Tower).

J. Wilbur Chapman's 6-week evangelistic campaign in Philadelphia (USA): 400 churches, 1.5 million attenders, 7,000 enquirers.

5th Lambeth Conference; 242 bishops present.

1909 Pentecostal movement begins in Chile: Iglesia Metodista Pentecostal splits ex USA Methodists.

1910 Beginnings of Faith and Order Movement, on initiative of Protestant Episcopal Church in Cincinnati, USA.

World Missionary Conference, Edinburgh, Scotland (previously called 3rd Ecumenical Missionary Conference until 1908 change); 1,355 delegates; beginning of the 20th-century ecumenical movement.

Protestant and Anglican missionaries worldwide number 45,000.

Anti-church laws of Mexico, though aimed at Catholic Church, result in decline of older Protestant churches.

Million Souls Movement, Korea (aiming at one million converts).

USA team evangelism: 1910–30, Billy Sunday & H. Rodeheaver; former preacher to 100 million, with 1 million converts.

1911 Watch Tower movement (USA) enters Northern Rhodesia from Nyasaland to meet with extraordinary success, with over 800,000 Zambians estimated to have belonged at one time or another by 1970.

1912 *International review of missions* begins publication; editor J.H. Oldham.

USA team evangelism: 1912–45, Mordecai Ham & W.J. Ramsay.

Burma: Self-Supporting Karen Baptist Missionary Society splits ex ABFMS.

1913 Liberian Grebo prophet William Wadé Harris preaches in Ivory Coast resulting in 120,000 converts by 1915.

Worldwide Evangelization Crusade (WEC) founded by C.T. Studd (England).

Fédération Protestant de France (FPF) founded.

Highwater mark of influence of Watchword 'The Evangelization of the World in this Generation' on Protestant missions; decline thereafter.

## Epoch VIII: **VIGOUR AMIDST STORM** **1914–1950**

1914 **Global status:** 63 generations after Christ, world is 34.9% Christians (76.2% of them being Whites), 52.5% evangelized; with printed scriptures available in 676 languages.

World War I begins, with 42 million men mobilized by Allies versus 23 million by Central Powers. By its end in 1918, 8.4 million killed (5 million Allied, including 1.7 million lost by Russia and 1.3 million by France; 3.4 million Central Powers, including 1.7 million by Germany and 1.25 million by 50-million Austro-Hungarian Empire); combatants wounded, 21 million.

Uganda: mass revival, Society of the One Almighty God (KOAB), or Malakite Church, secedes ex CMS with 91,740 Ganda adherents by 1921.

Nomiya Luo Mission, first of Kenya's independent indigenous churches, begun in Nyanza as schism from Anglican Church.

Protestants in Latin America total over 500,000 communicants.

Joazeiro movement begun in Brazil by Padre Cicero Romão Baptista, declaring holy war against authorities.

First motion pictures with sound showings: Photo-Drama of Creation (Watch Tower), seen by 35,000 daily.

Foreign missionaries in Africa: 4,273 Protestants, 5,977 Roman Catholics.

Protestants in Japan grow to 103,000 from only 10 in 1872.

Roman Catholic bishops worldwide still all of European origin, except for 4 Indians in Kerala elevated in 1896.

China: Protestant and Anglican missionaries number 5,462 including 1,652 wives.

45% of all North American Indians now affiliated to churches (25% Protestant).

1915 Third major massacre of Armenians by Turks; at least 600,000 perish, with a further 600,000 fleeing or deported from Turkey.

1916 Kenya: mass movement begins into all churches.

1st Evangelical Congress, Panama City.

*Bibliotheca Missionum* periodical begun by SC Propaganda (Rome), covering all mission literature in past centuries; discontinued 1974.

1917 Apparition at Fatima, Portugal, bringing about religious renewal reinforcing conservatism of Portuguese Catholicism.

Balfour Declaration (UK) recognizes Palestine as national homeland of the Jews.

20,000 Nestorians massacred by Turks and Kurds on Turko-Persian frontier after withdrawal of Russian army.

Bolshevik Revolution in Russia, followed by civil war: 1.5 million, mostly Christians, killed; 1918, decree on separation of church and state; 1.5 million flee abroad as refugees.

True Jesus Church begun in China, a charismatic schism ex Apostolic Faith Movement.

1918 Global influenza pandemic, the most deadly in history, sweeps the world in 3 waves over 2 years, killing around 40 million (20 million in India, over 500,000 in USA), via migratory birds and domestic animal reservoirs; 10 other global pandemics since 1700.

Nigeria: influenza epidemic (part of worldwide swine flu epidemic) brings about formation of prayer and healing groups which later grow into large indigenous churches: Cherubim and Seraphim, Church of the Lord (Aladura), and Christ Apostolic Church.

Hungarian Lutheran Church loses half a million members with reduction of Hungary in size and dispersal of population to non-Lutheran areas.

Movement into churches in Congo takes on massive proportions.

Fundamentalism/modernism controversy erupts within USA Protestantism, until 1931, splitting every major denomination; premillennialism now a major part of all revivalist preaching.

1919 World's Conference on Christian Fundamentals, Philadelphia, USA; over 6,000 attenders.

World's Christian Fundamentals Association (WCFA) founded in New York; premillennialist Protestants opposing modernism; active until 1950s.

Cao Daist Missionary Church founded by Le Van Trung in Viet Nam, a syncretistic mixture of popular Buddhism, Confucian ethics, the ancestral cult, and Catholic-type organization, with a membership of about 2.8 million by 1975.

1920 First World Conference of Friends (Quakers) held in London.

USSR: 28 Orthodox bishops and 1,290 priests killed in first years of Bolshevik regime.

Evangelization Society chartered in USA (Pittsburgh Bible Institute).

6th Lambeth Conference; 252 bishops present.

1921 USSR: civilian deaths in 1921–23 due to Civil War, other wars and famine, 13 million, mostly Christians.

USSR, 1921–1960: deaths in slave labour camps 19 million, mostly Christians.

First broadcast of a church worship service: Sunday evening, 2 January, from Calvary Episcopal Church, Pittsburgh (USA).

International Missionary Council (IMC) founded at Lake Mohonk, NY (USA).

First Baptist radio broadcast in USA.

Simon Kimbangu's revival in Lower Congo leads to mass conversions, persecutions, jailings, and by 1960 a massive indigenous church (EJCSK).

Oxford Group in Britain (1921–38), later renamed Moral Re-armament (MRA).

Pentecostal World Conference formed, in Amsterdam.

1922 National Christian Council of China founded.

10,000 Orthodox bishops, priests, monks and nuns in USSR executed by Bolsheviks under Stalin.

Aliança Evangélica de Angola founded.

70% of all USA Protestant foreign missionaries now premillennialists.

Britain: Bible Reading Fellowship (BRF) founded, for Anglicans.

1923 2nd Meeting of International Missionary Council, Oxford, England.

143,000 killed as earthquake destroys Yokohama, Japan, and half Tokyo.

BBC (Britain) commences broadcasting, including daily Christian programmes.

1.5 million Greek Orthodox in Turkey deported to Greece, and 400,000 Muslim Turks in Greece deported to Turkey.

1924 Near East Christian Council (NECC) founded, at Mount of Olives, Jerusalem.

First international Christian radio station, NCRV (Netherlands); Dutch Protestants.

1925 Mennonite World Conference formed in Basel.

Spirit Movement (Aladura) in Nigeria; charismatic revivals within Anglican Church lead to major indigenous churches: Cherubim & Seprahim, Christ Apostolic Church, Church of the Lord (Aladura).

Universal Christian Conference on Life and Work, Stockholm, Sweden.

United Church of Canada formed (union of Methodists, Presbyterians and Congregationalists).

1926 German Association for Mass Evangelism begun.

Unevangelized Tribes Mission of Borneo formed (USA).

Assembly Hall Churches (Little Flock; indigenous) begun by Watchman Nee in China.

Famine in northwest China: 8 million die of starvation in 3 years.

Largest schism in Mexico from Roman Catholic Church, leading to formation of Orthodox Catholic Apostolic Mexican Church, by 1970 with 10 bishops and 60,000 members.

1927 East African Revival movement (Balokole) emerges in Ruanda, moves rapidly across Uganda, East Africa, Zaire, later to Sudan and Malawi.

Stalin threatens to execute entire Orthodox clergy of Russia (146,000 including monks and nuns); acting patriarch capitulates.

USA: 50 radio stations now licensed to religious bodies.

China: 20 million killed in civil wars, 1927–49.

Anti-Christian movement in China; 5,000 of the 8,000 Protestant missionaries leave.

Church of Christ in China founded, uniting 7 Protestant denominations.

1st World Conference on Faith and Order, Lausanne.

1928 Unevangelized Africa Mission founded (1947, merged in CBFMS), also Unevangelized Tribes Mission of Africa, both in USA.

USA: National Conference of Christians and Jews formed in New York City to combat religious and social prejudice; member of International Council of Christians and Jews.

Anglican evangelist Bryan Green begins 50 years of ministry as a diocesan missioner in Britain, USA, Canada, South Africa, Australia and elsewhere.

3rd Meeting of International Missionary Council, Jerusalem; 231 members.

1929 Lateran Agreements signed by Italian government and Roman Catholic Church, creating Vatican City as an independent sovereign state known as the Holy See.

First major international Protestant radio station, Voice of the Andes (HCJB), founded at Quito, Ecuador; first broadcast on Christmas Day 1931.

First experimental television (BBC, London).

2nd Evangelical Congress, Havana, Cuba.

Armenian catholicate of Sis transferred to Antelias, Lebanon.

China: Five Year Movement begun by National Christian Council of China, supported by most churches (mass evangelism).

1930 Japan: Kingdom of God Movement begun under evangelist Toyohiko Kagawa, reaching over one million (75% non-Christian) in 2 years; concluded 1934.

Christian Businessmen's Committee International formed.

Mass movement into churches begins in Burundi.

Movement for World Evangelization (Mildmay Movement) begun in England.

Prophetic movements in French Congo: 1930 Matswa, 1953 Lassyism (Bougie), 1964 Croix-Koma.

Independent Church of India, schism ex Indo-Burma Pioneer Mission.

'Lutheran Hour' broadcasts begun by Missouri Synod (USA); 1931, heard by 5 million a week; after 1945, worldwide to 20 million a week.

Formation of World Council for Life and Work.

7th Lambeth Conference; 307 bishops present.

1931 Unevangelized Fields Mission (UFM) founded in London, UK.

Spain: church separated from state; thousands of priests and Catholics murdered and churches burned in mob riots.

Radio Vatican inaugurated in Rome by Pius XI; entrusted to Jesuits.

Catholicism spreads from Dahomey to Niger.

1932 Charismatic revival ex American Methodists in Southern Rhodesia, led by Johane Maranke, forms massive indigenous church (AACJM).

USSR: League of Militant Godless numbers 7 million, plus 1.5 million children.

China: flood kills one million.

India: All-India Forward Movement in Evangelism launched in Nagpur.

Dutch East Indies (Indonesia): 30,000 Muslims converted around Modjowarno, East Java.

1933 USSR: collectivization drive and famine kill 7 million kulaks and others, mainly Christians in the Ukraine.

Shanghai Christian Broadcasting Association organized (XMHD), covering entire Far East; also 1935 XLKA (Peking).

*Bibliografia Missionaria* periodical begun by SC Propaganda (Rome), covering contemporary mission literature.

1934 USSR: Stalin attempts liquidation of entire Christian church.

*Jesus Christ and world evangelization* published by Alexander McLeish (World Dominion Press).

Confederação Evangélica do Brasil founded.

Variant of SVMU Watchword: 'Evangelize to a finish to bring back the King'.

1936 Japan: Nation-Wide United Evangelistic Movement launched (Toyohiko Kagawa).

Civil war in Spain; one million Catholic Spaniards on both sides killed or emigrated before Franco victory in 1939.

BBC (Britain) begins first television broadcasting, including worship services and (1937) the Coronation of George VI.

USA: International General Assembly of Spiritualists formed.

1937 K.S. Latourette's 7-volume *A history of the expansion of Christianity* published 1937–45.

Ethiopia: after expulsion of missionaries by Italian invaders, widespread revival erupts among Protestant (SIM) churches in south.

Japan's largest indigenous Christian church, Spirit of Jesus Church, formed as split from Assemblies of God.

2nd World Conference on Faith and Order, Edinburgh, Scotland.

2nd World Conference on Life and Work, Oxford, England: 'Church, community and state'.

1938 Hendrik Kraemer's *The Christian message in a non-Christian world;* powerful statement of traditional views of mission.

World Council of Churches 'in process of formation', Utrecht, Netherlands.

4th World Missionary Conference/Meeting of International Missionary Council, Tambaram, Madras, India; 471 delegates from 69 countries.

Muscat and Oman: RCA mission (USA) reports winning 5 converts in 50 years.

Scotland: Iona Community founded by clergy and laymen of Church of Scotland.

1939 Protestant international radio station PRA7 begun in Brazil.

Radio Vatican begins broadcasting in 10 languages.

Portuguese Guinea: Protestantism introduced by World-

wide Evangelization Crusade (WEC).
1st World Conference of Christian Youth, Amsterdam, Netherlands.
Scriptures: languages possessing some printed portions of Bible now number 969.
World War II: by its end in 1945 around 55 million killed: Poland 5.8 million including 3.2 million Jews; USSR 11 million combatants, 7 million civilians; Germany 3.5 million combatants/780,000 civilians; China 1,310,224 combatants/around 22 million civilians; Japan 1.3 million/672,000; Yugoslavia 305,000/1,200,000; UK 264,443/92,673; and USA 292,131/6,000.
The Holocaust 1939-1945: murder of 5.7 million Ashkenazi Jews by German Nazis and their European collaborators.

1940 Extermination of 400,000 Gypsies, mostly Christians, by Nazi Germany over 4 years.
Formation of Kyodan ordered by Japanese government to include all Protestant churches in a United Church of Christ.
John Frum cargo cults begun on Tanna Island, New Hebrides, growing in strength with arrival of USA military personnel with extensive material possessions.
Algeria: Evangelical Mission Council begun.
Estonia, Latvia, Lithuania conquered by Red Army (USSR); 200,000 deported to labour camps in Siberia; most bishops, church leaders and clergy shot or deported; 1944-53, 500,000 more deported.

1941 Origin of large-scale international Bible correspondence course organizations: Emmaus Bible School founded in Toronto, Canada.
Extensive mass revival in Orthodox churches in German-occupied USSR.
Siege of Leningrad by Nazis begun, lasting 880 days; 1.4 million (50% Christians) perish.
National Council of Churches in New Zealand founded.
Gemeinde für Evangelisation und Erweckung founded in Zürich, Switzerland.

1942 William Temple at Canterbury enthronement refers to worldwide Christianity as 'the great new fact of our time'.
British Council of Churches (BCC) founded.
Sumatra: Christ's Witnesses spread Simalungun Church north of Lake Toba.

1943 China: 5 million perish in Honan province in worst famine in modern history.
Worker-priest movement begun in France; finally dissolved in 1959.
USA: National Religious Broadcasters of North America formed.
Britain: Christian Commando Campaigns 1943–47, led by Methodists, in London, Edinburgh, Glasgow et alia.

1944 Canadian Council of Churches (CCC) founded.
Protestant monastic community of Taizé founded near Cluny.
200,000 Muslim Meskhetians deported by Stalin to Central Asia; 30,000 die (November).

1945 Atomic bomb on Nagasaki kills 40,000 including 10,000 Catholics at once; end of World War II.
Germany: 12.5 million Germans resident abroad forcibly expelled to Germany as refugees.
Viet Nam: 2,791 Cao Daists massacred by communists.
Archbishops' report *Towards the conversion of England* published by Church of England.
Evangelical academies and student associations begun in Germany.
Mass international tourism begins, with package tours (Thomas Cook, Britain).
Refugees (fugitives, expellees) increase vastly in numbers across globe, totalling 45 million over next 3 decades.

1946 African Orthodox Church (independent Kenyan body) accepted into communion by Greek Orthodox patriarchate of Alexandria.
North Korea: Christian organizations suppressed.
Europe: widespread evangelistic experiments in state and majority churches (Kerk en Wereld in Holland, worker-priests in France, MRA, etc).
South West Africa: massive Nama Hottentot schism ex Rhenish Mission.
Australian Council of Churches (ACC) begun.
Revised Standard Version (RSV) of NT published in USA.
International radio station IKOR begun in Netherlands.
United Bible Societies (UBS) formed as a federation and fellowship of autonomous Bible societies.

1947 5th Meeting of International Missionary Council, Whitby, Toronto, Canada; 112 delegates from 40 countries.
Conference on Evangelism, Geneva, sponsored by WCC in formation (February).
Church of South India inaugurated by merger of Methodists and Anglicans with earlier-united Reformed and Congregationalist bodies.
2nd World Conference of Christian Youth, Oslo, Norway.
Southern Baptist evangelist Billy Graham begins global ministry, preaching face-to-face to 50,780,505 by 1976, in 229 crusades, with 1,526,729 enquirers.
Partition of India: 9 million Muslims flee to Pakistan, 9 million Hindus and Sikhs flee Pakistan for India, the greatest population transfer in history; 1.1 million massacred or starved to death en route.
Lutheran World Federation (LWF) founded; 1st Assembly, at Lund, Sweden.
1st Pentecostal World Conference, Zürich, Switzerland: 100 present, from 20 countries.
Evangelize China Fellowship founded in Shanghai by Andrew Gih.

1948 Radio Vatican now broadcasting in 19 languages.
Byzantine-rite Uniate Catholic Church of Romania declared dissolved by a few priests, rejoining Romanian Orthodox Church.
8th Lambeth Conference; 329 bishops present.
Kirchenkreis-Evangelisation begun in Germany.
World Council of Churches (WCC) inaugurated at Amsterdam by 147 churches from 44 countries; 351 delegates and 238 alternates.
International radio stations begun: FEBC (Philippines), TIFC (Costa Rica).
La Violencia, civil war in Colombia; 100,000 killed, Protestants persecuted till 1952.
Evangelistic mission in St John the Divine Episcopal Cathedral, New York; beginning of mass evangelism in USA after World War II.
Far East Broadcasting Corporation (USA) opens Radio DZAS in Philippines.

1949 *French Southern & Antarctic Territories.* First resident Christians (French scientists).
2nd Pentecostal World Conference, Paris.
WCC study 'The Evangelization of Man in Modern Mass Society'; surveys done in Ceylon, Finland, France, Germany, Holland, India, Latin America, Scotland, USA.
Burma Christian Council formed.
Joint IMC/WCC Conference, in preparation for forming of EACC, in Bangkok, Thailand.
After Communist victory, China expels 5,496 Catholic, 3,745 Protestant and 198 Anglican foreign missionaries over next 3 years.
Los Angeles, USA: first major Billy Graham crusade; 441,000 attenders, 5,700 enquirers.
Japanese Evangelical Missionary Society formed (USA, Tokyo) to send Japanese abroad.
Kirchentag begun in Germany as annual evangelistic mass event: 1949 Hanover, 1950 Essen, 1951 Berlin, 1952 Stuttgart.
Organized churches present in all countries of the world except Afghanistan, Saudi Arabia and Tibet.
1st Latin American Evangelical Conference (CELA I), Buenos Aires, Argentina.

Epoch IX:
**SURGE IN THE THIRD WORLD**
**1950–1980**

1950 **Global status:** 64 generations after Christ, world is 34.1% Christians (63.5% of them being Whites), 57.0% evangelized; with printed scriptures available in 1,052 languages.
Black Africa: Christians number about 44 million, increasing rapidly by 1.8 million a year.
China: 24,700,000 killed over next 10 years through purges, famine, deaths in slave labour camps, Tibet revolt, including large numbers of Christians; over 40 million imprisoned in labour camps.
Hungary: 53 Catholic religious orders and congregations forcibly dissolved.
International Christian radio stations now 10 in number.
British Guiana: 'Guiana for God' one-year evangelistic campaign under Christian Council, with Roman Catholic, Protestant and Anglican workers.
1st Assembly of World Council of Christian Education and Sunday School Association (WCCESSA), Toronto, Canada.
Haiti Great Commission Crusades (Haiti Inland Mission): 10 crusades over decade 1950–60.
USA: beginnings of evangelistic association evangelism (Billy Graham Evangelistic Association, et alia).

c1950 *British Antarctic Territory.* First resident Christians (British scientists).

1951 World Evangelical Fellowship (WEF) formed at Zeist, Netherlands.
Three Self Reform Movement in China, to eradicate imperialism in churches.
Alianza Evangélica Costarricense formed.
'Cuba for Christ' 2-week campaign in all Methodist churches of Cuba; 2,100 first decisions.
USSR: all 7,000 Jehovah's Witnesses arrested and forcibly scattered across Siberia and Far North labour camps.

1952 3rd World Conference of Christian Youth, at Travancore, India.
3rd World Conference on Faith and Order, at Lund, Sweden.
6th Meeting of International Missionary Council, at Willingen, Germany; 190 delegates.
3rd Pentecostal World Conference, in London.

1954 2nd Assembly of World Council of Churches, in Evanston, USA: 'Christ the Hope of the World'; 502 delegates.
5th Kirchentag held in Lepizig (East Germany), draws 650,000 for closing rally.
International radio stations begun: ELWA (Liberia), TWR (Tangier, later closed).
USA: World Conference on Missionary Radio formed.

1955 Radio IBRA (Swedish Pentecostal) begins in Tangier in 20 languages.
Jesus Family, indigenous movement in China begun 1921, virtually obliterated by communists.
4th Pentecostal World Conference, in Stockholm, Sweden.

1956 Catholicate of Cilicia (Lebanon) ceases to acknowledge primacy of catholicate of Echmiadzin (USSR) in dispute over appointment of new catholicos.

1957 National Patriotic Catholic Association formed in China; anti-Vatican.
Conference of European Churches (CEC) formed, at Liselund, Denmark.
Conference of World Confessional Families founded.
East Asia Christian Conference (EACC) founded at Prapat, Sumatra, Indonesia.

1958 5th Pentecostal World Conference, in Toronto, Canada.
International Christian radio stations now 20 in number.
Federación Argentina de Iglesias Evangélicas (FAIE) founded.
First Ethiopian national consecrated patriarch of Ethiopian Orthodox Church: Basilios.
Brazil: neo-pentecostal (charismatic) renewal begins among Baptist pastors.
9th Lambeth Conference; 310 bishops present.
Final Assembly of International Missionary Council, Accra, Ghana; 215 delegates.
Establishment of Theological Education Fund (TEF), in Ghana.
First All African Christian Conference held at Ibadan, Nigeria.
253,922 attend Jehovah's Witnesses 'Divine Will' international convention in New York City, USA, with 7,136 baptized.
Christian peace movement begun in Prague.

1959 USSR: wave of persecution of churches under Krushchev regime, continuing until 1964.
Communist revolution in Cuba; 500,000 Cubans flee to USA, Catholic priests declining from 725 to 231 in 3 years.
1st Assembly, Conference of European Churches (CEC), Nyborg, Denmark.

1960 IFMA Congress on World Missions, Chicago; resurgence among conservative Evangelicals of the Watchword 'The Evangelization of the World in this Generation'.
Secretariat for Christian Unity established by pope John XXIII in preparation for Vatican II.
USA: charismatic (neo-pentecostal) renewal begins among Episcopal and Protestant churches.
Continuation Committee of Pacific Churches' Conference launched at Malua, Samoa.
750,000 Cubans flee Cuba after Communist regime installed.

1961 3rd Assembly of WCC, in New Delhi, India; integration of WCC and IMC, latter emerging as Division of World Mission and Evangelism (DWME and CWME).
Joint Action for Mission launched by DWME of WCC; but resistance from confessional and institutional structures of churches and missionary agencies.
International Christian radio stations now number 30.
2nd Latin American Evangelical Conference (CELA II), Lima, Peru.
HCJB-TV (Quito, Ecuador) becomes pioneer missionary telecaster.
6th Pentecostal World Conference, in Jerusalem.
First religious TV station opened, in USA: Christian Broadcasting Network.

1962 850,000 French Catholics flee Algeria for France.
Charismatic renewal in Church of England recommences (after 1907 beginning had lapsed).
Vatican Council II (21st Ecumenical Council, for Roman Catholics) meets in Rome, 1962–65; 2,200 attending RC bishops.
6 churches in USSR become members of WCC (1962–65).

1963 2nd Meeting of Commission on World Mission and Evangelism (CWME), Mexico City: 'Mission to Six Continents'; 200 delegates.
RVOG (Radio Voice of the Gospel) founded in Addis Ababa, Ethiopia, by Lutheran World Federation.
4th World Conference on Faith and Order, Montreal, Canada.
Foundation of All Africa Conference of Churches (AACC), in Kampala, Uganda.
New Life for All 10-year campaign in Nigeria begun.
International Christian Broadcasters (ICB) formed (USA Evangelicals).

1964 7th Pentecostal World Conference, Helsinki, Finland (June).
Provisional Commission for Latin American Evangelical Unity (UNELAM) founded at Montevideo, Uruguay.
Papal journeys on international scale begun: Holy Land 1964, Bombay 1964, New York City and United Nations 1965, Fatima 1967, Constantinople and Ephesus 1967, Bogotá 1968, Geneva (WCC and ILO) 1969, Kampala 1969, Far East and Australia 1970.
Meeting in Jerusalem of Paul VI and Athenagoras of Constantinople, first meeting of pope and ecumenical patriarch in 900 years.
Secretariat for Non-Christians formed by Paul VI.
Egyptian bishop (later Pope Shenouda III) commences evangelistic newspaper *Al Keraza* (Spreading of the Word).
Fiji Council of Churches founded.
First superpower missionary radio station: TWR Bonaire.
International Christian radio stations now 40 in number.

1965 Oriental Orthodox Churches Conference, in Addis Ababa; first conference of heads of Armenian, Coptic, Ethiopian and Syrian churches.
Rome and Constantinople withdraw mutual excommunication of AD 1054.
DWME consultation of Yaoundé, Cameroon: 'The Evangelisation of West Africa Today', preceded by 4-month survey.
Indonesia: Communist coup thwarted, 250,000 massacred; mass revivals begin, producing 2.5 million Protestant and Catholic converts within 15 years.
Decree 'Ad Gentes' on the Missions promulgated by Vatican II on its final day (7 December).

1966 Asociación Nacional de Bolivia (ANDEB) formed.
Christian Council of Botswana begun.
Evangelical Congress on 'The Church's Worldwide Mission', Wheaton, IL, USA (April).
Burma expels 250 Protestant and Anglican foreign missionaries.
'Christ pour Tous' national campaign in Zaire begins, for 2 years.
World Congress on Evangelism, Berlin: 'One race, one gospel, one task'; 1,200 delegates from 100 countries.
Great Proletarian Cultural Revolution in China: over 11 million Red Guards suppress all churches and temples, destroy churches and scriptures.
Total elimination of religion begun in Albania as world's first atheist state.
World Conference on Church and Society, Geneva: 'Christians in the technical and social revolutions of our time'.
1st Assembly of Pacific Conference of Churches, in Lifou, Loyalty Islands.

1967 Communist purges in USSR over the 50 years 1917–67 estimated at 21.5 million executed or killed (about 16 million being Christians).
Far East Broadcasting Associates (UK) open FEBA in Seychelles.
Macedonian Orthodox Church unilaterally declares full independence from Serbian Orthodox Church.
SC Propaganda (Rome) renamed SC for the Evangelization of Peoples.
Guinea: foreign missionaries expelled except for 26 CMA missionaries.
Catholic charismatic renewal begun, first at Duquesne University, USA.
International Congress on Religion, Architecture & the Visual Arts, New York (August).
1st Synod of Bishops in Rome: Dangers to the Faith, Canon Law, Liturgy.
8th Pentecostal World Conference, in Rio de Janeiro, Brazil.
Solomon Islands Christian Association (SICA) founded.

1968 2nd General Conference of CELAM (Latin American Catholic hierarchy), at Medellín, Colombia.
10th Lambeth Conference; 459 bishops present.
Major schisms occur in Pakistan among Presbyterians, Methodists and Anglicans, influenced by ICCC.
4th Assembly of WCC, in Uppsala, Sweden: 'Behold, I make all things new'; 2,741 participants (704 delegates, 750 press).
West Africa Congress on Evangelism.
Southeast Asia/South Pacific Congress on Evangelism, Singapore; 1,100 delegates from 24 nations (November).

1969 Pope Paul VI visits Kampala, Uganda, and canonizes 22 of Namugongo Catholic martyrs.
Extraordinary Synod of Bishops in Rome: Relations between the Holy See and Episcopal Conferences.
Congo Congress on Evangelism.

Zagorsk Conference of All Religions in the USSR.

Congo-Brazzaville declares itself first Marxist-Leninist state in Africa.

Barbados: disestablishment of Anglican state church.

3rd Latin American Evangelical Conference (CELA III), Buenos Aires, Argentina.

Jehovah's Witnesses hold series of 5-day 'Peace on Earth' International Assemblies in 13 cities (Denmark, France, Germany, Italy, UK, USA) with 840,572 attenders (25% non-JWs) and 27,442 publicly baptized.

Paul VI first pope to visit World Council of Churches, Geneva.

1st Latin American Congress on Evangelism (CLADE I), Bogotá, Colombia: 'Action in Christ for a Continent in Crisis'; 920 delegates from 25 countries (November).

2nd Assembly of AACC, Abidjan, Ivory Coast.

First USA Congress on Evangelism, Minneapolis: 'Much is given — much is required'; over 5,000 delegates (September).

African indigenous churches (AICM) now number over 5,800 denominations, with 17 million adherents growing by 960,000 each year.

1970 **Global status:** 64.7 generations after Christ, world is 33.7% Christians (56.4% of them being Whites), 61.4% evangelized; with printed scriptures available in 1,490 languages.

Pontifical Commission for the Pastoral Care of Migrants and Tourists formed in Vatican.

Thailand Congress on Evangelism.

Church of North India inaugurated through merger of Anglican, Baptist, Brethren, Disciples, Methodist and United churches.

Orthodox Church in America (USA) granted autocephalous status by Moscow patriarchate.

WCC allocates first grants to 19 anti-racist organizations throughout world for humanitarian work.

Nestorian patriarch Mar Shimun Isayi, in exile in USA since 1933, permitted to visit Iraq; later assassinated by Assyrian dissident (1975).

Sodoin Dendo (total saturation evangelism) mass campaigns begun for various areas of Japan.

Fédération des Eglises et Missions Evangéliques du Cameroun formed.

International Communications Congress (ICB, USA).

India Congress on Evangelism.

Euro-70 Crusade, largest evangelistic campaign in Europe, using radio/TV; 839,000 attenders.

Philippines Congress on Evangelism.

Frankfurt Declaration on Mission, promulgated by 14 Conservative Evangelical Lutheran theologians in Germany.

Canada Congress on Evangelism.

1st World Conference on Religion and Peace, Kyoto, Japan; 1,600 delegates from 22 world religions (October).

500,000 killed by cyclone in Bangladesh (November 12–13).

9th Pentecostal World Conference, Dallas, USA (November).

World circulation of subsidized scriptures doubles from 80 million in 1966 to 173 million in 1970.

Oberammergau Passion Play (Bavaria) draws 530,000 attenders; repeated every 10 years since 1634.

From Samoa, Paul VI sends out Missionary Message to the World, urging spreading of the gospel.

Total languages with printed scriptures: Bible 249, NT 578, portions 1,431; covering 97% of world's population.

1971 Taiwan Congress on Evangelism.

2nd Synod of Bishops in Rome: Priesthood, Justice in the Modern World.

Over 500 indigenous churches in Zaire deprived of legal recognition as official recognition is given to 3 churches only: Roman Catholic Church, EJCSK, ECZ (Greek Orthodox added in 1972).

European Congress on Evangelism, Amsterdam; 1,064 participants from 36 European nations.

1st Ecumenical Pentecost Meeting in Augsburg (Germany) for Catholics and Protestants (June).

World Assembly of World Council of Christian Education, Lima, Peru; 1972, WCCE integrated in WCC.

International Catechetical Congress, Rome (September).

World Evangelization Strategy Consultation, White Sulphur Springs, Georgia, USA (December).

1972 World Conference and Assembly of CWME, Bangkok, Thailand: 'Salvation Today'.

Abolition of 'special position' of Catholic Church in Ireland.

Publication of 3-volume history of Catholic Missions 1622–1972: *Sacrae Congregationis de Propaganda Fide Memoria Rerum.*

EXPLO–72 in Dallas, Texas; 1st Training Congress on Evangelism (Campus Crusade for Christ); 80,000 for one week (June), 200,000 for final day.

Consultation on the Gospel and Frontier Peoples, Chicago (December).

Letter of Paul VI to International Missionary Congress at Lyons (France).

1973 ECCLA III: 3rd Latin American Catholic Charismatic Leaders Conference; 250 delegates from 25 countries, including 8 bishops; in Aguas Buenas, Puerto Rico.

Massive Jehovah's Witnesses assemblies across world on theme 'Divine Victory' (including Dusseldorf with 67,950 attenders, Munich with 78,792).

Caribbean Conference of Churches (CCC) founded in Kingston, Jamaica.

28 Christian denominations banned in Uganda, resulting in some coming under wing of Anglican Church, others going underground.

Key '73 evangelistic campaign in USA.

Finland Congress on Evangelism.

SPRE-E 73: youth rallies at Earl's Court, UK (August).

Largest preaching service in history: 1.1 million at one rally in Seoul, Korea, hear evangelist Billy Graham during 5-day Crusade.

All-Asia Mission Consultation, Seoul, Korea.

10th Pentecostal World Conference, Seoul, Korea: 'Anointed to preach'.

Urbana 73: 10th Inter-Varsity Missionary Convention, Chicago; 17,000 attend (December).

1974 1.5 million persons worldwide mobilized to pray for Lausanne Congress on World Evangelization later in year.

Construction of first Muslim mosque in Rome sanctioned by Holy See.

1st Plenary Assembly, Federation of Asian Bishops' Conferences (FABC), in Taipei: 'Evangelization in Modern Day Asia' (April).

3rd Assembly of AACC, Lusaka, Zambia: 'Living no longer for ourselves, but for Christ' (May).

Orthodox Consultation on 'Confessing Christ Today', Bucharest (June).

Japan Congress on Evangelism, Kyoto (June).

Iberian Congress on Evangelism, Madrid, Spain (June).

International Congress on World Evangelization (ICOWE), Lausanne, Switzerland (July), on 'Let the Earth hear His Voice'; 2,700 delegates, from 150 countries.

EXPLO-74 in Seoul, Korea: 2nd Training Congress on Evangelism (Campus Crusade for Christ); 323,419 residents for one week, evening meetings 800,000 daily, with one rally drawing a new world record of 1.5 million (90% responding to invitation to commitment to Christ); biggest Christian conference in history (August).

3rd Synod of Bishops in Rome, on 'The Evangelization of the Modern World'.

1975 **Global status:** 64.8 generations after Christ, world is 33.2% Christians (53.5% of them being Whites), 64.9% evangelized; with printed scriptures available in 1,630 languages.

Asia Missions Association formed, in Seoul, Korea; Seoul Declaration on Christian Mission promulgated.

Paul VI's Apostolic Exhortation *Evangelii Nuntiandi* published (8 December) as the major Catholic statement on evangelization.

75 million in all Latin American countries hear or see Luis Palau 3-week mission in Nicaragua over radio/TV.

Foreign missionaries expelled from Cambodia, later from Viet Nam.

Brazil Congress on Evangelism, Rio de Janeiro (January).

13th meeting of Baptist World Alliance (BWA), in Stockholm.

4th International Christian Television Festival, Brighton England (sponsored by WACC/UNDA).

International Catholic Charismatic Conference in Rome; 10,000 pilgrims addressed by pope Paul VI in St Peter's Basilica (May).

Here's Life, America (2-year media campaign in over 200 major cities): 179 million in USA exposed to gospel, 543,000 recorded decisions.

Consultation of United Churches held in Toronto, Canada (June); 24 united and uniting churches present from several countries.

Euro-fest, Brussels (July).

1st Nigeria National Congress on Evangelization, Ile-Ife; 800 participants.

World Conference on the Holy Spirit and Holy Land Pilgrimage, Jerusalem (October).

5th International Congress of Christian Physicians (ICCP), Singapore. (Also 1963 Amsterdam, 1966 Oxford, 1969 Oslo, 1972 Toronto).

2nd World Conference on the Holy Spirit, Jerusalem (November).

4th Assembly of WCC, in Nairobi, Kenya: 'Jesus Christ frees and unites'; 2,085 participants (850 delegates, 600 press).

Bible translators at work in over 300 of world's remaining 5,200 languages as yet with no portion of Bible (4% of world's population). Bible revisions and new translations under way in 500 languages (representing 80% of world's population).

1976 Guatemala: catastrophic earthquake kills 24,000, 77,000 injured, over 500 Protestant churches destroyed (February).

Since 1917 Revolution in USSR, 60 million (over half Christians) killed directly or indirectly, 40% being executed or killed by communist officials.

First Latin American Amerindian in history consecrated as bishop: Mario Marino, a Mataco in Argentina (Anglican).

China: 1.4 million victims of widespread catastrophic earthquakes; 655,237 killed in Tangshan alone.

1st Pan-orthodox Preconciliar Conference, Chambésy Switzerland.

World Congress of Fundamentalists: first 8-day USA-dominated meeting in Edinburgh; 2,000 in attendance.

41st International Eucharistic Congress, Philadelphia, USA (August); one million Catholics participate.

11th Pentecostal World Conference, Albert Hall, London: 'The Spirit of Truth'.

Pan-African Christian Leadership Assembly (PACLA), in Nairobi; 700 delegates (December).

Christmas: over 1.3 billion people hear pope Paul VI over radio/TV.

1977 ECCLA V, Fifth Latin American Catholic Charismatic Renewal Leaders Conference, in Caracas, Venezuela; leaders from almost all Latin American countries (January).

2nd National Evangelical Anglican Congress, Nottingham University (April), following first congress at Keele University, 1967.

1st Conference on the Charismatic Renewal in the Christian Churches; ecumenical, embracing all pentecostal traditions, in Kansas City, USA; 50,000 present (July).

Romania: catastrophic earthquake destroys or damages 1,200 churches.

4th Synod of Bishops in Rome, on 'Catechetics in Our Time', dealing with evangelization of children and youth (September).

World Conference on Audio-Visuals and Evangelization, Munich (November).

Here's Life, World (saturation and total mobilization evangelization campaign), organized by Campus Crusade for Christ, launched in over 100 countries, on every continent.

500 million hear or see one-hour radio/TV gospel service broadcast from Jerusalem on Christmas Eve in 7 languages simultaneously (Rex Humbard).

Burma: 6,200 converts baptized by Kachin Baptist Convention at largest single baptismal service in recent Christian history.

1978 World Mission 1978–1981 begun: World Methodist Council's 4-year plan of global evangelism.

Congress on Evangelism for Malaysia and Singapore (COEMAS); 300 leaders (April).

International Conference on the Charismatic Renewal in the Catholic Church, in Dublin: 'You shall be My Witnesses'; 15,000 participants (June).

8th International Convention on Missionary Medicine, Wheaton, USA (June).

11th Lambeth Conference, Canterbury, England: 'Today's church in today's world'; 420 Anglican bishops (July/August).

2nd Nigeria National Congress on Evangelization, Ile-Ife; 1,000 participants (August).

Rhodesia: National Christian Leadership Assembly (NACLA), in September.

Death of pope Paul VI; succeeded by an Italian, John Paul I; on his death 34 days later, cardinals elect a Pole, first non-Italian for 450 years: John Paul II (October).

Latin American Council of Churches (in formation) (CLAI) created at Oaxtepec, Mexico (September): 340 representatives.

International convention series of Jehovah's Witnesses produce 100 'Victorious Faith' assemblies in 45 countries, averaging 25,000 attenders at each.

World Congress of Mission and Migration, Rome (October).

Asian Leadership Conference on Evangelism (ALCOE), Singapore: 'Together obeying Christ for Asia's harvest'; 280 participants (November).

1979 3rd General Conference of CELAM, in Puebla, Mexico: 'Evangelization in Latin America now and in the Future' (January).

Over 10,000 pilgrims attend International Charismatic Pilgrimage to Lourdes on Shrine's 100th anniversary (July).

12th Pentecostal World Conference, in Vancouver, Canada: 'The Holy Spirit in the last days' (October).

2nd Latin American Congress on Evangelization (CLADE II), Huampani, Lima, Peru (October); 266 delegates from 21 countries.

Canadian Congress on World Evangelization.

Asiatic New Religions (New Religious Movements) continue to grow rapidly, with 94 million adherents growing by 2 million a year.

1980 **Global status:** 65 generations after Christ, world is 32.8% Christians (50.5% of them being Whites), 68.4% evangelized; with printed scriptures available in 1,811 languages.

Africa: Christians number 203,490,000 in 59 countries, increasing at 6 million a year.

Pope John Paul II undertakes global travels over last 2 years: Mexico, Poland, Ireland, USA, Africa, Brazil et alia.

International Consultation on Simple Life-Style, London (March).

7th General Assembly, World Evangelical Fellowship, High Leigh, UK; delegates from 50 countries (March).

World Missionary Conference of CWME (WCC), in Melbourne, Australia: 'Your Kingdom come'; 600 delegates from 82 countries (May).

Consultation on World Evangelization (COWE) in Bangkok: 'How shall they hear?'; 875 delegates (June).

World Evangelization Crusade, Seoul, Korea: 16,500,000 attendances, including largest single meeting in Christian history (2.7 million).

5th Synod of Bishops in Rome, on the Catholic family.

United States Festival of World Evangelization; 50,000 participants (September).

International Congress on Evangelization and Atheism, Urbanian University, Rome (October).

World Consultation on Frontier Missions, Edinburgh: 'A Church for every People by the Year 2000'; 270 delegates (October).

1981 4th Assembly of AACC, Nairobi: 'Following the Light of Jesus Christ'.

Chinese Congress on World Evangelization, Singapore.

UBS Common Language translations now available: 107 Bibles, 136 New Testaments.

1982 13th Pentecostal World Conference, Nairobi (Sept).

Old Catholic Congress, in Vienna (September).

1983 5th Assembly of WCC in Vancouver, Canada (August).

APPENDIX

# FISSION AND FUSION IN WORLD CHRISTIAN TRADITIONS, AD 30-1985

# FISSION AND FUSION IN WORLD CHRISTIAN TRADITIONS, AD 30-1985

## The rise and expansion of the major Christian traditions

The flow chart or development diagram opposite illustrates the chronology on the previous pages. It shows the expansion of Christianity over the centuries, and sketches its fragmentation or fission into 7 major blocs or streams, 156 different ecclesiastical traditions and 20,800 separate and distinct denominations or churches. It also illustrates the recent movement towards church reunion or fusion. The diagram should be studied in conjunction with the detailed statistics of the evolution of these phenomena given in Global Tables 1, 2, 9, 26, and 27. The various concepts and schemata in this diagram may be explained as follows.

THE 7 MAJOR BLOCS. As set forth in this Encyclopedia, all Christians can be divided into the following 7 major blocs or streams of Christianity: Orthodox, Roman Catholics, Protestants, Anglicans, Catholics (non-Roman), Non-White indigenous Christians, and marginal Protestants. In the diagram, the boundaries of these blocs are shown by heavy full lines.

THE 156 TRADITIONS. The 7 major blocs can be further sub-divided into around 156 ecclesiastical traditions, by which are meant the various confessions, families or types of Christianity. In the diagram, the boundaries of a selection of these traditions are shown by light full lines.

MAJOR DENOMINATIONS. Within the 156 traditions there have been formed over 20,800 separate autonomous denominations or churches. A detailed analysis of the location of these denominations by bloc and continent is given in Global Table 26; but this evolution is not shown here.

CHURCH REUNIONS. Since the year 1900, at least 180 denominations including some of the largest have merged to form over 60 united churches. The growth of this new tradition is briefly sketched.

ORIGINS. The diagram depicts the origins and development of blocs and traditions on the world scene over 20 centuries, shows where they came from and how they have fared, and indicates, schematically and relatively, the numerical strength of each over the centuries up to the year 1985.

CHRONOLOGY. The horizontal scale represents time, or chronology. The diagram covers, from left to right, the period from AD 30 to 1985.

NUMERICAL SIZE. Vertical scale represents, approximately or schematically, the numerical size of Christians affiliated to the various traditions or blocs at any particular year up to the present.

CENTRALIZATION. Across the centre of the page a horizontal axis can be envisaged, which represents the concept of centralization, including the concepts of uniformity, collaboration, mergers, church union. It represents schematically the position of churches with centralized structure, centralized hierarchy, centralized organization, centralized administration, and centralized tradition, doctrine, ritual and liturgy. As the most centralized of all churches, the Roman Catholic Church therefore straddles this axis in the diagram.

DECENTRALIZATION. The position of a tradition (or bloc, or denomination) above or below this central axis represents the concept of decentralization, which includes the concepts of departure from centralization, ruptures of relations, splits, schismatic movements. Traditions (or blocs, or denominations) which have separated from or moved away from the Church of Rome in order to decentralize some aspect of their church life are thus found above or below the central axis, and the same is true for subsequent divisions from other churches.

STRUCTURALISM. The position of a bloc or body vertically on the diagram also stands for what may be called the concept of relative ecclesiastical or structural conservatism or liberalism: from conservative at the top to liberal at the bottom. At the top are right-wing or conservative structures such as the Oriental Orthodox or monophysite churches which still largely use ancient dead languages in worship. Along the central axis is the Roman Catholic Church. Below the axis are Protestant churches and others in what may be called left-wing or liberal structures adapted to their eras. Going down the page are found increasingly left-wing or liberal or radical traditions rejecting centralization or uniformity of structure, hierarchy, tradition, doctrine, ritual or liturgy. Next below follows the range of Non-White indigenous churches across the world which have rejected Western and Eastern Christianity along with all attempts at control by these latter blocs. Finally, along the extreme lower edge of the diagram is a fringe of free-thinking or radically heterodox bodies originating in the Western Protestant world, here termed marginal Protestant bodies because of their peripheral nature in this schematic presentation of mainstream or main-line or orthodox Christianity.

EVOLUTION. Lines across the diagram from left to right indicate evolution, i.e. the way in which the 7 major blocs (separated by heavy lines) and the 156 traditions (separated by light lines) have evolved and crystallized out over the centuries. At first the lines are sometimes dotted, illustrating how new traditions begin to form with existing traditions and exist therein for a time before rupture of relations with the parent or adjacent traditions takes place. Sometimes a dotted line means the first stage in the parting of the ways when a large body begins to divide into two. If and when a rupture or schism eventually takes place, this is shown at that point by the line changing from dotted to full. If the rupture is later healed, and the schism is reabsorbed into the parent, the line stops at that point in its movement across the page. Church unions or mergers can be illustrated by such lines, with the original separate traditions shown bounded by full lines; then after union the lines are dotted until the traditions begin to lose their original identity in the new united body and eventually disappear.

SCHISMS OR FISSIONS. Full lines drawn vertically indicate the clearcut formation of a relatively small schismatic or separate body out of a large existing body, or the breaking of communion. In most cases such schisms have been a small or minority part of the existing body. When a large parent body splits into 2 or more parts of comparable size, however, the vertical line covers all of the parts.

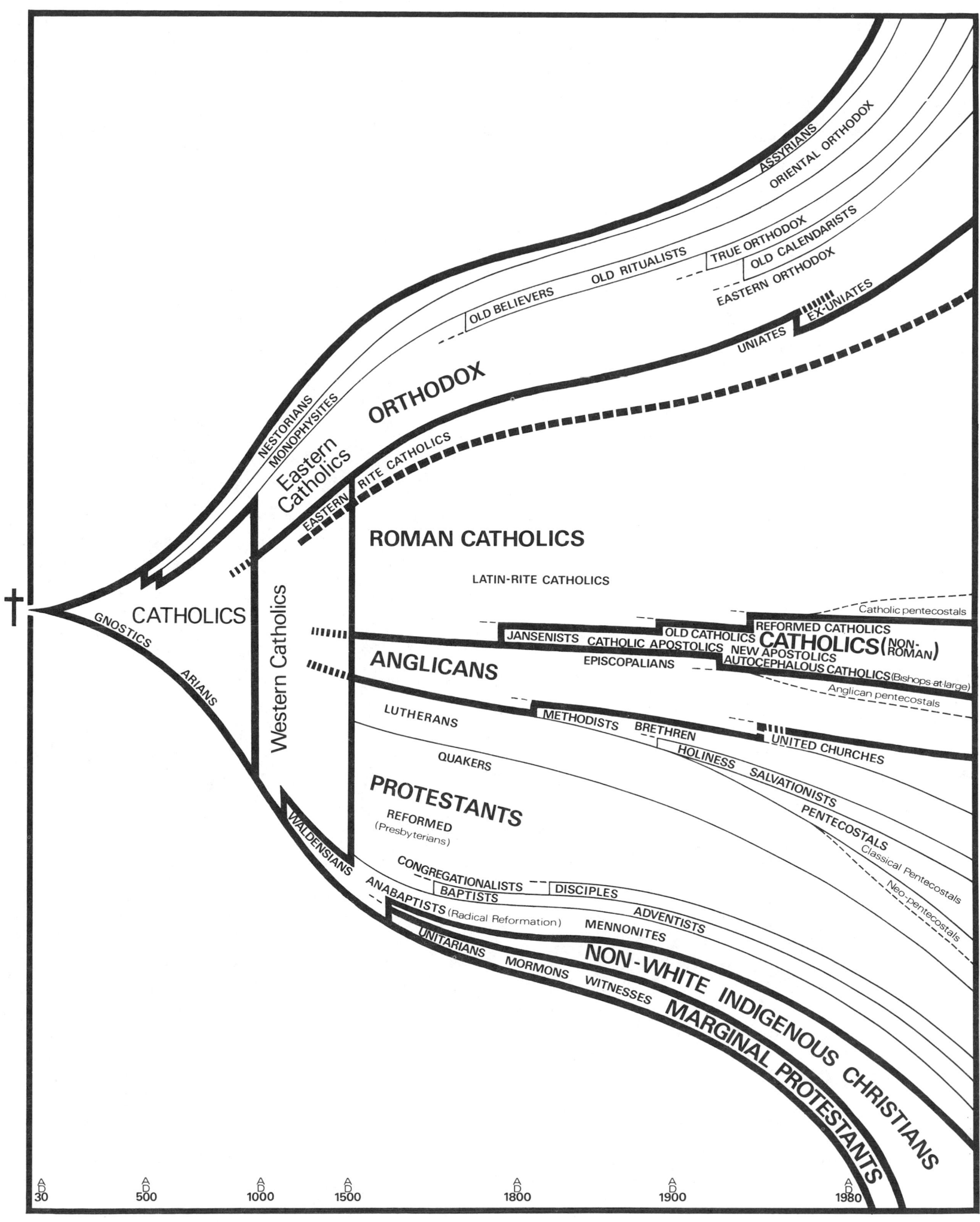

# PART 3

# METHODOLOGY

Enumerating Christianity and religions:
methodology, sources, classifications and codes

*The immemorial experience of mankind, that new knowledge can only be won through breaking a taboo, that all autonomous thinking is accompanied by a consciousness of guilt, has been a fundamental experience of my own life.*

—Paul Tillich (1886–1977).

New knowledge is built on new understanding, new insights, new information, new data and new methods. In the case of global Christianity, new methods are called for because of its vast size and hitherto unrealized complexity. These methods are described in this part.

# ENUMERATING CHRISTIANITY AND RELIGIONS

In this section of the Encyclopedia, we are concerned with explaining how this survey was conducted. In particular we explain how those various aspects of Christianity and religions which can be quantified have in fact been enumerated here. Before we begin on this explanation, though, we must first ask whether such surveys are legitimate or useful or even necessary at all from the Christian standpoint and whether in fact there is any theological justification for such endeavour. Our answer here cannot be termed an adequate theological statement, but only a pointer towards such a theology of enumeration.

## A THEOLOGY OF CHRISTIAN ENUMERATION

### The Great Commission
The background to this survey is the theology of the Christian mission as evidenced in its basic statement and starting-point, the command of the risen Jesus to his disciples recorded in the Gospels: 'Go forth therefore and make all nations my disciples; baptize men everywhere' (Matthew 28.19, NEB), or 'Go forth to every part of the world, and proclaim the Good News to the whole creation' (Mark 16.15, NEB). It is this Great Commission which has inspired Christian missionary endeavour over the centuries since the Apostolic era. It is this mandate also which demands the global perspective utilized throughout the present survey.

**The Great Commission.** Jesus Christ, Lord of the Church, commands his disciples (in Latin) 'Ite'—Go, and evangelize all peoples of the earth. (Miniature from Abdinghoven Gospel, AD 1060).

### Why do surveys?
From the spiritual and theological standpoints, queries have often been raised concerning the legitimacy of surveying Christian work. Is it right? Is it wrong? Is it compatible with faith? Is it possible? Is it of any value? Is it essential? How can one survey the work of God the Holy Spirit, who is the Evangelizer and Missionary par excellence? What priority if any does such endeavour have for the churches? and so on. A first, immediate answer derives from the Great Commission described above. The main justification for surveys of Christianity in its world mission is that they help the followers of Christ to see to what extent they have been faithful to that commission; to perceive the magnitude of their unfinished task; and to discern at what points

to commit their resources in order to implement their commission.

### Numbers
The earliest known view of number is the Pythagorean contention that number is the sole inner reality of each thing, e.g. justice is 4, perfection is 10. The article on 'Number' in the *New Catholic encyclopedia* (1967:10.565) continues:

> Number is a way of knowing the quantity, intensity, order, or structure of material reality. With the aid of statistics and probability, number affords scientists the opportunity of predicting and controlling countable or measurable things or events with varying degrees of probability and success.

### Numbers in the Bible
The decimal scale of notation and system of counting were used by the Israelites, Assyrians, Babylonians, Egyptians, Greeks and Romans. They all reckoned by units, tens, hundreds, etc. One book of the Bible is called Numbers (in the Greek Septuagint, 'Arithmoi') because of its emphasis on censuses and enumeration. Numbers occur widely, and are extensively used, elsewhere in the Bible also. There are 3 main usages, as follows.

1. *Exact numbers.* Most usage of numbers in the Bible is simple enumeration, i.e. for simple expression of numerical values. Numbers are used to depict the exact, factual situation, such as the actual number of fighting men available. Such numbers are usually given to the last digit; an example is the 153 fish caught by the Apostles in John 21.11.

2. *Round numbers.* Usage of numbers can also be for rhetorical purposes. As in most languages, biblical Hebrew used 'round numbers', i.e. exact tens, hundreds, thousands, or 20,000 (the highest single number), on the understanding that they were only approximately accurate. Hebrew usage preferred concrete rather than abstract forms of expression, using a definite number when only an approximation was intended. Thus in 1 Corinthians 14.19, Paul says: 'In church I would rather speak five words with my mind than ten thousand words in a tongue'. Numbers are therefore used in the Bible as rhetorical indications of the general order of magnitude, in which case they are given rounded (i.e. with several zeros at the end). In Revelation 9.16, the seer is told the number of mounted troops he sees: 200 million. This is the biggest number in the Bible.

3. *Symbolic numbers.* Several numbers developed special meanings of theological significance in the Bible. These included: 1 (unity), 2 (division), 3 (sacred; trinity), 4 (completion), 5 (sufficiency), 6 (man; imperfection), 7 (especially sacred; perfection), 8, 10 (a round or complete number), 12 (election), 40 (the average length in years of a generation), 70, 100; et alia. In Revelation 7.4, the total number of the saved is said to be 144,000, which is the number 12 (the number of election), squared, and multiplied by a thousand (an indefinitely large number). It therefore symbolizes the full number of God's saints, the elect. And in Revelation 13.18, the seer calls on his readers to 'work out the meaning of the number of the beast, because the number stands for a man's name. Its number is 666'. The article on 'Numbers' in the *Encyclopedia of religion and ethics* (1916:9.406–417) concludes with the warning:

> It is easy to be led into extravagance in attempting to interpret the significance of numbers; allegorical arithmetic has called forth fantastic absurdities from both Jewish and Christian writers.

### Surveys in the Bible
The Old Testament contains many references to surveys, connected either with the journeyings of the people of Israel; or with the armed forces, military service and military operations; or with religious personnel and the Tabernacle and Temple. Censuses in Egypt are known to have begun as early as BC 2500. Detailed surveys and censuses were made by

Moses, as a former Egyptian official, immediately before and after the 40 years' wandering in the wilderness. Later, censuses were taken by Joshua, Saul, David, Joab, Solomon, Ahab, Jehoram, Amaziah, Ezra, Nehemiah and other Old Testament prophets, priests and kings. The Old Testament can therefore be seen as a storehouse of census information. The Old Testament narrators are at pains to make it clear that, in so doing, these men were obeying the direct command of the LORD (Yahweh, Jehovah) as part of His evolving plan for His people and for the world: 'The LORD spoke to Moses, saying, "Take a census of all the congregation of the people of Israel, by families"'. (Numbers 1.1-2, RSV). As the New English Bible version at this point makes clear, this was to be done in great detail: 'The LORD spoke to Moses in these words: "Number the whole community of Israel by families... You and Aaron are to make a detailed list of them by their tribal hosts"'. Exact counts were to be kept not only of the Israelites but also of prisoners and booty: 'The LORD spoke to Moses and said, "Count all that has been captured, man or beast"'. (Numbers 31.26). Exact records of their journeyings were meticulously kept: 'Moses recorded their starting-points stage by stage as the LORD commanded him' (Numbers 33.2). Elsewhere we read of numerous population censuses at different stages in the Israelites journeyings; a survey of the Promised Land (Numbers 13); a census of all aliens resident in Israel (2 Chronicles 2.17); a survey of the houses of Jerusalem (Isaiah 22.10); a survey of the heavenly temple (Ezekiel 40-48); and a variety of other topics in addition to civil, military or religious censuses of the Israelite population. The Old Testament record of the results of all these surveys runs into many thousands of words.

When we come to the New Testament, we are in the era of the Roman empire, in which official state censuses were taken on average every 5 years. In the reign of Augustus, 3 empire-wide censuses were taken, in BC 28, BC 8 and AD 14.

### Numerical growth in the New Testament
The New Testament records present a healthy interest in numbers, statistics, and their relation to the growth of the church. The Acts of the Apostles records the early history of the church. It is usually recognized that the author, Luke, divided his narrative up into 7 parts, at the end of each of which he appended a summary statement of the progress of the gospel to that point. These summaries are: 'The disciples multiplied greatly' (Acts 6.7, RSV), 'The church was multiplied' (9.31), 'The word of God grew and multiplied' (12.24), 'The churches increased in numbers daily' (16.5), 'The word of the Lord grew and prevailed mightily' (19.20), 'They came in great numbers to Paul... preaching and teaching openly and unhindered' (28.23, 31).

### Why enumerate or quantify?
The human mind can only comprehend and make sense of a limited number of people, names, populations or situations at any one time. It is usually estimated that the average person can handle at once only up to 500 face-to-face relationships. A pastor can know intimately the names and situations of only 500 parishioners; a bishop can know 500 of his clergy; a headmaster 500 of his pupils; and so on. Exceptional individuals may manage to comprehend more, even up to 1,000; but beyond that number, in order to comprehend the dimensions of their situation, they must resort to enumeration. Christians wanting to understand the numerical dimensions of their task of world evangelization have therefore to come to terms with statistics. Without enumeration, they may be able to comprehend a small community, or a small parish, or a small tribe, or a single-language situation. But for anything larger, as when many

communities are involved, or scores of parishes, or numerous peoples, or hundreds of tribes and languages, or thousands of cities and towns, or tens of thousands of Christian denominations, or millions of church personnel or billions of human beings, they must quantify, and quantify with great precision, in order to have even the remotest idea as to what is going on.

Enumeration is defined as spelling-out or describing in detail, listing in order, counting, numbering, often meaning a count or census. Quantification is defined as measuring an item's quantity or number, or transforming qualitative data into quantitative. Together, these 2 procedures can assist the Christian mission by providing a simple way of describing otherwise incomprehensibly-large situations or processes. In so doing they can help us to comprehend the stark realities of a situation.

### Statistics as self-knowledge

One value of surveys to the Christian cause is that they form an application of the principle enunciated by Jesus as one that should guide his disciples' lives: 'You shall know the truth, and the truth will set you free' (John 8.32, NEB). Ignorance cripples; knowledge (especially self-knowledge) liberates. Christians have nothing to fear from the truth, whether it is palatable or unpalatable, exhilarating or alarming. Taking an objective missionary survey may be compared to a person undergoing a routine medical checkup, or receiving a bank statement of his balance of account, or having his car serviced, or having a public-opinion poll conducted into his political party's fortunes. The results are always a valuable corrective to either excessive optimism or undue pessimism, since they tell us with objective precision about a situation where our impressionistic hunches, guesswork and even wishful thinking may be seriously, even dangerously, misleading. Some such thoughts would have been in the mind of Pope John XXIII when he addressed the priests of the Diocese of Rome during the Roman Synod of 24–31 January 1960 with these words:

> Beloved parish priests, pay attention, we beg you, to accurate and well-studied statistics. They are a very important task in governing a parish.

### Wrong use of numbers

A number of Christian traditions refuse to publish their statistics, or even to count their membership. Part of the reason is that the best-known reference to a census in the Bible is a negative case, a classic instance of the wrong use of statistics: king David's numbering of the people in BC 1017 (2 Samuel 24). According to eminent demographers, David's census 'had the effect of delaying the adoption of the census in England and in Christian Europe for many years' (H. Alterman, *Counting people: the census in history*, New York, 1969:26). Against the advice of his senior officers, the king ordered a census of his army and his kingdom. His motives appear to have been, not the glory of God but personal pride, the desire for aggrandisement, the worship of national greatness, through the enforcement of new taxation and forced labour schemes. Although 'The LORD gave him orders that Israel and Judah should be counted' (NEB), the narrative explains that this was in order to teach the king a lesson in spiritual humility. The census was clearly not in the same category as those undertaken by Moses. This case therefore does not prove that, in the Bible, numbering and censuses in themselves are unspiritual activities; it merely indicates that numbering, like most other human activities, can be used for good or ill, and that we should therefore be aware of the possibility of the wrong use, or even deliberate misuse, of such activity.

### The folly of triumphalism

Our present survey, with its massive totals of Christians of many kinds, almost all increasing rapidly every year, is clearly open to the dangers of triumphalism. This is the dogma that large and numerically-expanding churches must necessarily be in themselves good, right, spiritually successful and, in short, what God and the world need most. Instead, these vast totals should have a sobering effect on all Christians: for if the churches are to be effective in serving the rapidly-overpopulating world, they must first of all come to terms with their own staggering population problems.

The observer who succumbs to triumphalistic statistical statements taken by themselves is as shortsighted as an advocate of mass megabirths who ignores the resultant problems of overcrowding,

infant mortality, undernutrition, scarcity of schools, unemployment and the like. What we are attempting to do here is less ambitious. It is to present an objective and empirical picture of numerical expansion and decline within their total context. The result is an attempt to measure the progress or decline of the churches in so far as progress or decline can be measured by comparative statistics. Subsequent theological assessment and judgement can then later be attempted by others.

### Statistics as signs from God

In order to serve the world, the church must first discover and comprehend the total environment and total situation in which the peoples of the world find themselves. This gives us as Christians a 3-fold task: (a) to understand the total human situation in which all the peoples of the world corporately live, namely the secular and religious environments surrounding them and conditioning them and often oppressing them; (b) to know who and where these peoples are individually, what their particular secular characteristics and differentia are, and what their individual problems and needs are; and (c) to then interpret

**'Statistics are signs from God'.** The existence of 273 million handicapped children in the world (like these youngsters at Port Reitz school, Kenya) is both a sign and a call from God to all who seek to serve God and man.

these peoples' religious situations (from the standpoints of evangelization, conversion, christianization, church growth or decline, and so on) in this secular and religious context. In this task, statistical data, and even a single isolated statistical fact (e.g. 'The Turkana tribe is 99% illiterate', or 'This ethnic group has the highest mortality rate in the world') can become for us direct pointers to a people's predicament and how they can best be served. In this sense, statistical and other information can alert theologians to new problems as they emerge. It is this spiritual significance of statistical data that prompts the Brothers of Taizé to echo their Prior Roger Schutz in affirming:

> Les chiffres sont les signes de Dieu — Statistics are signs from God.

If this is so, then it both explains and justifies the prodigious amount of effort put into the production of church statistics every year by millions of pastors and congregations, thousands of denominations, hundreds of international Christian organizations, and scores of major confessions and Christian councils around the world. Intuitively in the main, most of them have realized that statistics can be signs from

God, in which case enumerating and quantifying are important activities to be taken seriously by all Christians.

### The limits to quantification

Ultimately, it is impossible to quantify the totality of the Christian situation, because numbers usually describe quantity only and cannot normally delineate quality except over a series of clearly-defined gradations. One cannot quantify the faith of a Christian martyr in Albania, or the witness of an imprisoned pastor in Siberia, or the selfless service of relief workers after an earthquake. For this reason it is best to regard statistics only as signs or pointers, or at any rate as concrete starting-points from which qualitative assessments may begin.

But even enumeration pure and simple has its limits: there are some numbers too enormous to be counted at all with any meaning. The Old Testament prophets foresaw a time in the future when the People of God would be too big to be counted: 'The Israelites shall become countless as the sands of the sea which can neither be measured nor numbered' (Hosea 1.10). The same theme recurs right up to the last book of the Bible, where the seer hears the voice of countless angels: 'Myriads upon myriads there were, thousands upon thousands. . .' (Revelation 5.11); he sees 'a vast throng, which no-one could count, from every nation, of all tribes, peoples and languages, standing in front of the throne and before the Lamb' (Revelation 7.9); and the hosts of evil also are 'countless as the sands of the sea' (Revelation 20.8).

## STATISTICS IN PROFESSIONAL USAGE

### What are statistics?

Information presented in abstract numerical form is described as statistics. Originally, statistics had nothing to do with numbers. The word originated in German in the 18th century, when Achenwall first coined the term *Statistik* to refer to 'the political science of the several countries', that is, the study of practical politics. The English term first appeared in a 1770 translation from the German (R.A. Bauer, ed, *Social indicators*, 1966:75). 'Statistics' is derived etymologically from the Latin *ratio status* and could well be translated as 'state of the nation'. For several hundred years the primary concern of men who called themselves statisticians was to set up a system of social indicators by which to judge the performance of the society with respect to its norms, values, and goals (Bauer 1966:22). By information as to the 'state' of the nation they meant those statistical measurements that revealed the current situation of the nation, its population and its economy. Today the term has evolved somewhat: the subject of statistics is 'the association and bringing together of those facts which are calculated to illustrate the conditions and prospects of society' (American Statistical Association, 1962). The full definition of the term is: '1. a science dealing with the collection, analysis, interpretation, and presentation of masses of numerical data; 2. a collection of quantitative data' (*Webster's third new international dictionary*, 1971).

With the years the purpose of statistics has sharpened also. In the USA, the decennial census originated as the basis for apportioning representation in the House of Representatives. Statistics in the sense of numbers nowadays are gathered because it is presumed that they will be guides to planning and action.

### Quantification and enumeration

Quantification was not an essential element in the definition of statistics until fairly recently. The term has several meanings; the one we are chiefly interested in is: quantification is 'the transformation of qualitative into quantitative data in scientific methodology' (*Webster's* 1971). Quantification is sound policy, a necessary corrective, because we cannot really see the dimensions of a complex problem until we quantify it. This process is as helpful as the placing of milestones along a trunk road or continental highway; travellers can immediately assess the progress of their journeying. Enumeration is counting up and totalling with specific and clear treatment of each item. It is defined by Webster as: '1a. The act of listing one after the other; 1b. an itemized list; 2a. the act of counting or numbering; 2b. a count of something (as of a population), a census'.

### Methods of counting

A full description and analysis of methods of counting peoples and of censuses throughout history is given in H. Alterman, *Counting people: the census in history*, 1969. This study begins with the Babylonians, Egyptians, and censuses in the Bible. Censuses usually count heads throughout the whole population, using large numbers of enumerators. Either they count everybody, or they enumerate a small random sample, usually 5%. Where such expensive methods are impossible, estimates are made. There is an interesting parallel here with modern methods of counting large herds of wild animals, which aim to measure total numbers, size and structure of population, distribution and migratory movements. These methods have revealed that counting error increases with counting rate, always in the direction of under-counting: 'It must always be remembered that even highly experienced observers consistently undercount the numbers of animals in a group by as much as 40%' (M. Norton-Griffiths, *Counting animals*, Nairobi, 1975:46). The same error occurs in human demography too: 'All evidence points to universal underenumeration' (H. Alterman, op. cit., 1969: 326).

### Statistical indicators

For many of the important topics on which social critics blithely pass judgement, and on which policies are made, there are no yardsticks by which to know whether things are getting better or worse (Bauer 1966:20). This is just as true in the fields of religion and church life. To assist at this point, indicators must be found. Social indicators — statistics, statistical series, and all other forms of evidence — enable us to assess where we stand and are going with respect to our values and goals, and to evaluate specific programmes and determine their impact. An information system is needed consisting of 2 parts: (1) regular trend series of social indicators, whereby comparisons from time to time and across societies can be made; and (2) special mechanisms for gathering data on new developments falling outside those regular trend series (ibid. 21).

It must not be imagined that indicators must always be standard types of statistics. Expert judgements by knowledgeable persons can also be valuable indicators. The science of appraising conditions is well organized in welfare, mortgage banking, and other occupational areas.

### Multidimensional definitions and scales

Statistical indicators have often been combined to form 'dimensions' or aspects of religion in people's lives. Multidimensional definitions of religion have been widely accepted in the social scientific study of religion since the work of Allport and of Glock in 1954. Analysts have traced 4, 5 or even up to 13 such dimensions, usually revolving around people's beliefs, credos, behaviour, affiliation, and religious profession. In this Encyclopedia, we do not investigate such dimensions in detail, since we are mainly concerned with documenting the basic data upon which such scales can later be built.

### Does Christian work need statistics?

The question is often asked: why do the Churches need to bother with statistics at all? From time to time, a handful of theologians attacks any form of preoccupation with numbers in Christian work. One such attempt was H.R. Weber's 'God's arithmetic' (*Frontier*, VI (1963), 298ff). The argument usually revolves around the assertion that one cannot measure God nor his activities or work, which are concerned only with spiritual affairs. Especially in Muslim areas, as an Anglican bishop put it, 'No mission is constituted in its success and none therefore is invalidated by numerical failure. Mission is not a calculus of success but an obligation in love. Statistics do not make it nor can they unmake it' (K. Cragg, *The call of the minaret*, London, 1964:339).

We will shortly be detailing the positive side of the subject. Meanwhile, it should be said that we reject stereotyped statements of the form 'Church statistics are meaningless and notoriously unreliable'. If church statistics have been so in the past, this has been due to error and carelessness on the part of compilers, collators and editors, rather than due to defects in the basic data themselves.

The shortest answer to this question is that virtually every established Christian denomination takes enormous pains, goes to no mean expense, and makes very considerable demands on its overburdened clergy and officers, in order to produce each year such statistics. The most detailed and voluminous statistics of all come annually from the Church of Rome, and from the Evangelical Church of Germany (EKD). Exceptions to this generalization are the new and rapidly-growing pentecostal and other indigenous churches of the Third World, which are too busy expanding to stop and record the fact. In terms of efforts and time accorded to this work, though, we can fairly assert that establishing the exact numerical size of its membership is one of the major activities of the empirical Church. This fact alone justifies the present survey and analysis.

## THE VALUE OF CHURCH STATISTICS

### Statistics as objective descriptions

Statistics are valuable in describing a situation because they offer us probably the quickest, most scientific and most objective way of presenting large amounts of highly-condensed and accurate information, and

**Statistics with a human face.** Behind the dry bones of all bare statistics are human beings with needs and feelings. *Above.* Child (one of 4 million refugees in Africa) awaits milk donated by Swiss Evangelical Churches. *Below.* 45% of all Bangladeshis are under 15 years old. Their life expectancy is the world's lowest: 35.8 years.

of describing large groupings of peoples and their activities at particular points in time. This term however has 2 usages: (1) it refers to numeral, numerical or quantitative data, or numerical facts systematically collected (*Concise Oxford dictionary*), and (2) it also refers to the science of collecting and classifying numerical data, or that branch of applied mathematics that actually arranges, describes and draws inferences from sets of numerical data. In this Encyclopedia the term is used primarily in the first sense; interested analysts can then move on to the second sense.

### The quality of the data

The present volume demonstrates the reliability and value of the large volume of church statistics which it presents and analyses. To generalize, we regard these statistics on a comparative basis as surprisingly, even remarkably, reliable. For the first time it has now been possible to relate all religious statistics closely to demographic statistics of countries and ethnolinguistic groups, and in particular to government censuses of religion in over half the countries of the world. The result is that religious statistics can be seen to be often more reliable and more detailed than their secular counterparts.

### Putting flesh on the bones

Statistical facts for many people are merely lifeless dry bones. This sparseness, or this cut-and-dried and standardized nature, is indeed one of their values. We go even further in this direction here by standardizing all our statistical categories so that they have exactly the same definition in every country of the world. However, in each country we put a certain amount of flesh on these bones by supplying, under Tables 1 and 2, copious and detailed footnotes elaborating on those statistical facts in the tables where such amplification is needed.

### Statistics with a human face

The majority of the statistics reported in this Encyclopedia are statistics of people. People are human beings and not merely cyphers or figures. Statistics may assist us to comprehend certain features about a population, but it should never be forgotten that behind the bare statistics are scores, or hundreds, or thousands, or millions, or billions, of human souls with human needs and feelings. To emphasize this point, we have included a large number of demographic photographs illustrating large crowds of Christians, and of people in general, in various activities across the world. These illustrations assist the data presented here to be seen not merely as 'statistics' but as 'statistics with a human face'.

### One man one religion

There is a considerable ideological overlap, or overlap of belief and culture, between several of the 19 major world religions or philosophies into which we have divided the world in our Tables 1. In Thailand, a Christian may consider himself to be 70% Buddhist also, and vice versa. In India, a Christian may regard himself as also a Hindu. In the USA, Hebrew Christians regard themselves as both Christians and Jews. In Europe, dilettantes may regard themselves as followers of the best aspects of several religions at once. Nevertheless, the overwhelming majority of individuals in the world can be said to have and to profess one single predominant religion or philosophy. In this survey, therefore, we consider every person to be a coherent individual with one single religion or none.

### Statistical compassion

Overall statistics of churches and countries are provided here so that the totality of each situation, and of its human populations and their activities and needs, may be grasped. It is comparatively easy for a local church, or a local mission, or a local group of Christians to show Christian compassion to a few score of needy persons visible and tangible immediately around them; but this is often only a tiny fraction of the total population and of the total need, and there may be thousands of other needy persons who remain invisible and unreached beyond them. The church of Jesus Christ is concerned not just with a favoured, visible, minority but with the world's invisible populations in their totality. The statistics in this Encyclopedia have been compiled therefore to assist Christians to exercise a world ministry, and to be concerned not only for individuals but also for the world's populations as a whole. To this concern we may give the name 'statistical compassion'.

### Statistics must be read in context

One virtue of statistical facts is that they can stand alone or in isolation and still be correct. However, their value for interpreting a particular situation is considerably enhanced if they are presented and studied, not in isolation, but in a much wider context which we term here the historico-social, photographico-cartographical global context. In other words, statistical facts about people in churches and religions in a particular country need to be read both in the verbal context of a narrative describing history and society in that country, and also in the pictorial or visual context of photographs illustrating concrete statistical situations and maps showing the human environment in which those people live. Further, a country's statistics need to be seen in the light of parallel statistics from other countries and of the total global context. The bigger the numbers of people involved, and the newer or more startling the statistics presented, the more important this wider context is for correctly interpreting the totality of the situation and for convincing readers sceptical of vast numbers and staggering trends. It is for this reason that this survey places its complex statistical tables in this wider historico-socio-photographico-cartographical global context.

**Statistical compassion.** Statistics of huge numbers enable Christians to grasp, and minister to, the totality of a situation. Here, Pope Pius XII greets 300,000 pilgrims from balcony of St Peter's Basilica, where arrangements have been made to minister to them all.

### What do church statistics mean?

As already noted, vast efforts are put into the collection of statistics by the over 20,000 churches and denominations across the world and their 1.7 million constituent congregations of believers. This raises again the familiar fundamental questions: Do these statistics mean anything at all? Are they worth the churches' time and effort involved in collecting them? Do they in any sense assist the churches in realistic planning for mission in the modern world? After compiling this Encyclopedia, we would wish to answer all 3 questions clearly in the affirmative. We would however point out that, through inadequate analysis by the churches in almost all countries of the world, the true implications of church statistics have almost everywhere not yet even begun to be investigated. Further, proper analysis is only rarely being attempted. This is therefore the place to issue a call to a fresh approach to the collection, use and creative analysis of church statistics. To help churches put the right value on their statistics, and to encourage their proper evaluation, we suggest that such statistics have 3 major types of use to the churches: they assist in understanding of the past, in analysis of the present, and in planning for the future. These can be elaborated as follows.

1. *Understanding the past.* The first use of church statistics, and the most widely employed today, is towards understanding a church's development in the past. Up to the present time, the collection and presentation of church statistics seem to have been of most value to church and mission historians and others writing up the history of the church or denomination concerned; or comparing the church life of a former generation with that of the present; or discussing expansion and other trends from the past to the present. We use statistics ourselves in this way in this survey's Tables 1 by giving figures of all religions and Christian blocs in the years 1900 and 1970, thus enabling long-term trends of decline or increase to be detected.

2. *Analysing the present.* Secondly, statistics are often of considerable contemporary value to church officials and administrators. This is so in that they enable them to compare the present situation of their church with its immediate past (e.g. the previous year or two), to find out how that situation is changing. For large organizations, it is primarily an urgent or immediate question of logistics (the planning, handling and implementation of large quantities of personnel, material and facilities). The Billy Graham Evangelistic Association, for instance, requires detailed statistics of previous campaigns in order to plan how many chairs, ushers, hymnbooks, etc, are needed for a large campaign, how much literature to produce, how much car parking space needs to be procured, and so on and so forth (their largest single meeting has had 1.1 million physically in attendance). For organized churches and denominations, 3 less immediate but equally profitable areas of analysis are: (1) numerical decline of membership, where this is happening, and the problems it raises (e.g. redundant buildings), (2) numerical growth of membership, where this is happening, and the problems it raises (e.g. inadequate buildings or supplies of hymn books), and (3) adult baptisms as an indicator of the impact being made, if any, on the secular or non-Christian world around. By careful analysis of relevant statistics the effectiveness of the churches' organization can be assessed, points of weakness located, and reorganization effected.

There is, however, another and far more valuable type of contemporary analysis which is only rarely being done as yet. This involves relating a church's statistics to current secular statistics concerning the social situation, and social change, in its own country or area. In most parts of the world, a vast amount of secular statistical data is now available. This covers demography, population increase or decline, urban growth, industrialization, migration, age-groups, ethnic groups, social classes, occupational groups, employment, tourism, transportation, mobility, education, sickness and health, the handicapped, incomes, standards of living, socio-economic status, housing, land use, literacy, publishing, book sales, leisure, radio and TV sets and listening habits, and

so on. Much of this is available to the enquirer in printed form, sometimes in the form of pictorial charts, and sometimes in the form of maps. A church or denomination which relates its own statistics to this wealth of secular data can form a realistic appraisal of its own contribution and progress and can gain valuable insights into the present effectiveness of its various ministries.

Such data are widely available both at the international level (published by UN, UNESCO, FAO, WHO, ILO, et alia), and also at the national level (from government census and statistical offices, and national public-opinion and planning organizations). In this present survey in Tables 1, we relate church statistics to demographic data at these 2 levels. Moreover, in many countries, there is also a steady flow of detailed secular data available at sub-national levels, namely those of region, province, state, county, municipality, city, district, borough, local authority or ward, down to the secular equivalent of the local church parish or congregation. If a denomination collects and organizes its own data not only at the national level but also broken down by these secular regions and local areas, then immediate comparison and creative analysis at those levels also become possible.

There is a widespread problem here concerning areas of ecclesiastical jurisdiction. In many denominations and in most countries of the world, the boundaries of dioceses, synods, conferences, districts, parishes, presbyteries, circuits and so on bear little or no relation to the local secular or political administrative boundaries within which secular statistics are collected. This means that direct comparisons of church data and secular data are often difficult or impossible. There is a simple remedy, however. By a simple process of adjusting beforehand the areas within which the church collects its statistics, or by totalling or dividing them up to fit the secular boundaries after their collection, church statistical areas can be brought into line with secular areas, and direct comparison is then possible.

3. *Planning for the future.* Using church statistics for strategic forward-planning, i.e. to plan church development and activities in both the immediate future and the long-range foreseeable future, is a novel exercise for most denominations. Statistical data about both the church and the environment are indispensable for effective planning. Again, the starting-point is secular planning in the church's locality, region or nation. In many countries, ambitious 5-year or 10-year development plans are being drafted, not only at the national level but also for standard socio-economic planning regions and even for small local areas. The fundamental or base data in all such cases are demographic estimates or projections of the size of the population over the

**Analysing the present.** Evangelist Billy Graham preaches at interfaith service in 1970 at Lincoln Memorial, Washington (USA). For such mass meetings, statistics provide answers to questions of logistics, including how many chairs, ushers, hymn sheets, refreshments, etc are needed.

next 5 or 10 years, often divided up into small geographical areas and also by sex (male/female), age-groups, and ethnic or language groups. Such data often include also projections concerning employment trends, literacy, education, leisure patterns, and so on. Population projection into the future is no longer a matter of guesswork or speculation but is now a well-developed science, and in this Encyclopedia's Tables 1 we use the United Nations Population Division's population projections for all countries of the world for the years 1970–2000. Similarly, a church or group of churches could use regional projections to plan new congregations, manpower deployment, youth ministries, literature evangelism and the like. Another important by-product of such analysis is that churches known to be making use of secular planning data are often invited by secular authorities to take part themselves in the on-going secular planning process.

The indicators and indexes given here enable interested persons to assess the various purely numerical and hence relatively objective criteria involved in any decision about priorities, and hence to plan realistically for the future.

*Maps and religious geography*
Another important aspect of this analysis of the past, present and future is the relating of religious statistics to geography. A church's membership and manpower (past, present, future) can be charted on a map (in particular on government maps with secular data) to provide visual analysis of the church's situation vis-a-vis the secular world, development and social change. The best type of maps to use in this connection are human environment maps, i.e. maps which depict not only topography but also population density, urbanization, political divisions, land resources and land use, communications, transportation and traffic (on air, land and sea), and so on. In this survey we give human environment maps of this type in the World Atlas of Christianity and Religions (Part 11). On these maps will be found most of the places, areas, regions, ecclesiastical or diocesan headquarters, and so on, referred to in this survey. The geographical location of most churches can be found on them by using addresses in the Topical Directory of World Christianity (Part 13). Churches interested in similar maps in their own countries will often find that a wide range is available from their government's department of survey or planning, or from local university departments of geography; or from professional international bodies located elsewhere.

*Improving your church's statistics*
With such creative possibilities before us, small improvements in your church's statistical procedures could yield enormous benefits. Churches and denominations, with their administrative officers and planning staff, should therefore realize that their statistics, which are already of considerable value to many other churches and Christian groups of which they themselves may be unaware, could be made of immeasurably greater value, both to themselves, to their sister churches of like tradition, and to the wider Christian world (as well as to the world at large), if the following modifications were made to their procedures.

(1) Each church or denomination should examine the existing statistical categories it uses, and, for the benefit of readers from other churches, confessions or countries, should add to its published figures and reports the fullest definitions of exactly what those categories are measuring, from the standpoints of time (the date the statistics refer to) and geographical area or boundaries. They should make clear which of the following groups are included or excluded in each category: adults and children or infants (defining the ages covered by each group), de jure or de facto members, citizens or aliens, residents or non-residents, immigrants and refugees, Blacks and Whites (and all other racial, ethnic and linguistic groups), peasants, farmers, office workers, students (and other occupational groups where known); and so on. When a church official from another country or confession, or any other Christian observer, reads your church's statistical report, the answers to all such queries should be immediately clear to him.

(2) Each church should ensure that the statistics it collects include the following strategic information: (a) some measure of annual decline or growth in membership; (b) some measure of practising Christians, either weekly or monthly church attenders, or attenders at Easter or Christmas; (c) some measure of the participation or presence of children and infants,

i.e. annual baptisms or dedications of infants, and Sunday-school enrolments or weekly attendances; and (d) some measure of conversions from (or losses to) the secular or non-Christian society around, e.g. the year's adult baptisms (indicating from what age it is administered to children), stating in addition what their previous religious backgrounds were (agnostics, atheists, Buddhists, and so on). With this concrete statistical data in hand, your church can then immediately assess its strategic situation.

(3) Each church should consider collecting additional statistics about its membership and its ministries which can be compared directly, for purposes of self-analysis and forward-planning, with the secular or general social statistics regularly collected and published in its own country at national, regional, and local levels, concerning social change in the country and the present and future socio-economic situations.

(4) Each church should then adjust the boundaries of the areas for which it collects its statistics, so that they coincide with secular or political boundaries at national, regional, and local levels, to enable its statistics to be directly comparable with the secular statistics. No doubt it would cause too great a structural upheaval to alter the actual boundaries of the jurisdictions themselves, which are often hallowed by years, decades or even centuries of existence. There should however be little difficulty in ensuring that the church's statistics are gathered and collated within the boundaries of standard socio-economic planning areas used by local and national governments. Again, all such boundaries implicit in the church's statistical reports need to be clearly described for the benefit of other users.

(5) Each church, finally, might very well consider taking this process to its logical conclusion by redefining and standardizing its own ecclesiastical categories to approach, or even coincide with, some overall worldwide interdenominational or ecumenical system (such as that proposed and followed in this Encyclopedia). This means that it should consider adopting some agreed standardized criteria for enumerating membership and ministry, so that its statistics then become directly comparable both with those of its sister churches of similar denomination, and also with those of other denominations.

A series of standardized questionnaires was in fact evolved to collect data for the present survey, using the major European languages. Each questionnaire asked not only for a denomination's data but also their own exact definitions used, and the relevant date (year). The actual questions asked have resulted in the precise definitions given here in each country's Tables 1 and 2.

## A MACROECCLESIOGRAPHICAL APPROACH

*Macromissiography*
The standpoint or discipline from which the statistical presentation in this Encyclopedia has been compiled may be described as that of missiography (descriptive analysis of the Christian world mission) and ecclesiography (descriptive analysis of the churches). In particular, the discipline followed is that of macromissiography, which is defined here as descriptive and numerical analysis of the entire Christian world mission set in and related to the total global demographic, sociographic, ecological, secular and world religious, non-religious and anti-religious contexts. A parallel term for describing this survey in its totality would be macroecclesiography, the statistical aspect of which could also be termed ecclesiastical macrodemography. Missiography is a new term in English, although for many years the Pontifical Gregorian University in Rome has offered degree courses entitled Missiographia. Though related, all these disciplines are not the same as, and should therefore be distinguished from, either missiology (the science of missions, missionary history, missionary thought and missionary methods) or ecclesiology (the doctrine of the church) or micromissiography (descriptive analysis in detail of a single or a local missionary situation).

*Research in macroevangelistics*
From another point of view, our approach may be described as research in the science of evangelistics. As described by *Webster's third new international dictionary*, evangelistics is 'the science of the propagation of Christianity'. A science is defined as (a) a branch of study concerned with observation and classification of facts, and (b) accumulated and

accepted knowledge that has been systematized and formulated with reference to the discovery of general truths or the operation of general laws (*Webster's*). Research is defined as (a) careful, diligent or close searching, and (b) critical and exhaustive investigation or experimentation having for its aim the discovery of new facts and their correct interpretation or the revision of accepted conclusions (*Webster's*). Our research methodology here has been to collect a vast body of facts and then to evolve from them one particular area in evangelistics, regarded as a science, for which we may coin the term macroevangelistics, meaning the scientific study, at the global level, of the propagation of Christianity.

*Range of data available*
Surveying the world in a sentence or two, we find that at least 7 varieties of religious statistics are kept and compiled by churches in one country or another. These are: (1) demographic and sociographic statistics on Christian population in particular areas and peoples; (2) statistics of religious behaviour and Christian practice; (3) statistics of ecclesiastical jurisdiction and structures; (4) statistics of church personnel and lay workers; (5) statistics of social and cultural institutions (schools, hospitals, etc); (6) statistics of church prosperity and finance; and (7) statistics of religious psychology, beliefs, motivation and attitudes. Most but not all of these are handled in the present survey.

*Geopolitico-religious analysis*
When it comes to analysing the mass of statistical data assembled for this survey, we do so by regarding the world as an aggregate of 223 countries, each of which has certain geographical, socio-economic, political, cultural and religious characteristics, and which may be classified in various ways, one of which is into the Western (or Capitalist) world, the Communist (or Socialist) world, and the Third (or Non-aligned) World. This process is described here as geopolitico-religiocultural analysis, or, a shorter term, geopolitico-religious analysis.

## SURVEYING THE GLOBE

*A survey of 223 countries*
Part 7 contains a survey in a standardized format of the de facto situation in each of the 223 distinct and separate countries in the world in 1980, based on the list of countries published quarterly and annually by the United Nations (see *Population and vital statistics report*, UN, January 1978, and *UN demographic yearbook*, 1978). This definition of 'country' covers both all sovereign independent nations, and also all non-sovereign dependencies and territories with over 50 inhabitants which do not form a subject, organic or federal part of some larger nation (i.e. dependencies which are self-governing, or governed separately). Because the UN listing is politically conditioned, the listing used in this Encyclopedia differs slightly from it. We attempt a more exact description of the de facto situation by (1) accepting as definitive the divided state of Germany, Korea and certain other states; (2) including as distinct and separate countries China (Taiwan), Spanish North Africa, and a small number of other disputed territories with de facto or contested separate existence (Northern Solomons, Palestine, Sahara, Sikkim, Timor), unless the dispute is now over 15 years old and has been settled de facto (e.g. Goa, Kashmir); and (3) excluding certain territories (though listed separately by the UN) on the grounds that each forms part of a larger nation, namely Ascension, Asian Turkey, Byelorussian SSR, East Berlin, England, European Turkey, Northern Ireland, Scotland, Tanganyika, Tristan da Cunha, Ukrainian SSR, Wales, West Berlin, West Irian, Zanzibar. In this Encyclopedia, the adjectives 'national' and 'nation-wide' and also the noun 'national' (meaning a citizen as opposed to an alien) are used to mean pertaining to the countries in our listing.

*Future changes in nation status*
Our present format permits a number of future political changes to be quickly catered for. If 2 of our 223 countries merge, or if a large nation absorbs a smaller territory (such as India absorbing Sikkim), the reader can work out the new Tables 1 and 2 for the new entities simply by adding these together for both of the countries involved.

*Statistics are for one country only*
The statistics given in Tables 2, as with Tables 1,

always refer only and exclusively to the country indicated in the table's title. Many churches or dioceses are not found exclusively within the boundaries of a single country, but may spread over into adjacent countries. For such churches or dioceses, the statistics in Tables 2 are always divided among the various countries. This may occasion misunderstandings if the reader is familiar with a particular church's statistics but does not realize that the body in question may cover more than one country.

*Mutually exclusive listings*
The listings of religions and organized churches presented in Tables 1 and 2, respectively, are mutually exclusive and non-overlapping, in that the vast majority of persons belong each to only one religion or church, except in Table 1 where clearly indicated by indentation of categories. This means that in Tables 1 every individual in the world is enumerated only once under only one religion (though he may occur again under an indented category like 'Total practising Christians' and also in the last line's totals); and in Tables 2 every affiliated Christian in the world is enumerated only once, under only one church or denomination (though he may occur again under an indented diocese or other jurisdiction, and also in the last 3 lines' totals, and occasionally also, as explained below, if in the category of doubly-affiliated persons).

*Major areas and regions*
Traditionally the world has been divided up into 5 or 6 continents. However, this concept has lost much of its significance for modern purposes, since several countries overlap the boundaries of the traditional continents. This survey therefore uses the scheme of regionalization adopted by the United Nations (*World population prospects as assessed in 1963*, p. 16). Under this scheme, the world is divided into 8 major areas roughly equivalent to continents, and 6 of the 8 are further sub-divided into 22 regions, or 24 regions for the whole world including the 2 undivided major areas (see Part 11). All national statistics obtained in Tables 1 and 2 are then summarized by these 8 major areas and 24 regions (see Part 8).

*Large aggregates mask smaller variations*
This survey demonstrates that, at every level, large aggregate totals can mask or hide significant smaller-scale variations. Consider the question of the expansion of Christianity. At the world level, the totals here in Part 1 show that Christianity is expanding at a rate of 21,611,000 each year. Of this, however, 21,414,000 is natural increase (births minus deaths), and there is a nett gain of 196,000 by conversions from other religions. But this latter total is itself composed of (a) nett continental increases by conversion from other religions of 2,437,000 a year, particularly in Africa and Asia, and (b) nett continental decreases or losses to other religions or to irreligion of 2,241,000 a year, mainly in Europe and socialist countries. Again, the 2,437,000 includes converts to rapidly-growing traditions like classical Pentecostalism as well as to slower-growing traditions like Lutheranism. Classical Pentecostal growth in its turn consists of areas and nations with remarkable growth (Brazil, Colombia, Romania) and areas of numerical stagnation (Sweden, Britain). National totals in turn often mask great differences from one denomination to the next. And lastly, within a single denomination, there are often great differences in growth from one area to another, from one ethnic group to another, from one social class to another, from one homogeneous group to the next, and from one age group to another; and so on right down to the level of a single congregation or a sub-group within it. In general, further new insights can always be obtained by breaking down large aggregates into their component parts, especially if these latter form each sc me kind of homogeneous unit either ethnically, racially, linguistically, culturally, socially, politically or geographically.

All of this does not lessen the value of large aggregate totals; it depends on what particular level the reader is interested in. But it does mean that, whatever level is examined and analysed, that analysis by itself can only tell part of the whole story of massive flux, of ebb and flow, of conversion and apostasy, and of rapid growth here and rapid decline there.

*Countries as homogeneous units*
This survey attempts to describe the world in terms of homogeneous population units (sometimes also called sub-cultures). These may be defined as population groups, strata, societies or segments of societies within each of which a number of characteristics or interests are held in common by all members, with a common self-consciousness (referring to themselves as 'we', in contrast to others around them as 'they'). It is usual to regard as the clearest example of these groups the world's 432 ethnolinguistic peoples, or even the 8,990 or so smaller ethnolinguistic units (tribes, peoples, cultures, languages) that exist in the world today. Other types of homogeneous units are also found in traditional castes, clans or lineages, or in occupational groups such as industrial workers or truck drivers, or in political units or groups (refugees, political prisoners, etc), or in geographical units (cities, districts, regions), or in age-groups, educational groups, socio-economic groups, and so on. Whilst in this survey we accept this position, we must also point out 2 important considerations. (1) Firstly, there is nothing absolute or final about ethnolinguistic or any other types of homogeneous groups, because each of these groups is itself composed of sub-groups, sub-populations and other sub-groups that are even more homogeneous than the parent group. Every homogeneous unit is itself a mosaic of different strata, language groups divided up by dialects, tribes into clans, monolingual populations into social classes or castes, and so on. (2) Secondly, larger units or groupings made up of numbers of these homogeneous units (e.g. nations, countries, continents, the 3 Worlds, and the entire globe itself) may themselves be regarded from one perfectly-valid point of view as homogeneous units, relatively or comparatively speaking. A nation or country, composed as it usually is of a number of homogeneous ethnolinguistic units, itself has a population that is united or unified by all or many of the following 25 shared characteristics held in common: citizenship, patriotism, geographical contiguity, the national name and flag, national territory, national language, national history, a rich heritage of memories, shared historical experience, a common struggle for self-determination (political independence), national consciousness, national traditions, national culture, a joint national inheritance, a national literature, common social institutions, national values, national standards, national political aspirations, national pride, national economic life, common economic interests, national government, perhaps also a national or state religion. For this reason, throughout this survey we regard countries, treated relatively or comparatively, as homogeneous units. Even a vast country with such disparate ethnic groups as India (and among whom vastly different responses to Christianity have taken place) can still legitimately be regarded as a relatively homogeneous group (unified by the entire spectrum of specifically 'Indian' characteristics) by comparison with France, or Brazil, or Zaire, or any other country. If the reader wishes to conduct a more detailed analysis than we attempt here, the next subdivided level of homogeneous unit is not the 432 ethnolinguistic peoples as such (e.g. Bengalis, or Tamils, or Chinese) but these 432 as divided by national boundaries, i.e. ethnolinguistic-peoples-within-national-boundaries (e.g. Chinese in China, Chinese in Japan, Chinese in the USA, etc). In the same way, in the context of God's entire creation of vast numbers of living species, the human population of the globe itself is composed of one single species, Homo Sapiens, members of which by contrast with other species have a large number of unique characteristics in common (physical traits, erect stance, self-consciousness, rational thought, speech and language, ability to read and write, religious consciousness, and so on). From this point of view, therefore, the human population of the world itself composes a single homogeneous unit.

There is theological justification also for the importance we attach to these homogeneous units. In the Bible, the idea and concept of a people carries with it the thought of the solidarity of the community with its leaders and its followers, its rich and its poor, its old and its young, its learned and its ignorant. Particularly in the Old Testament, the people or community is the primary entity, and individuals have no separate importance or existence but derive their being from the larger community. God then deals with people primarily as communities, and only secondarily as isolated individuals.

*Geographical, political and ethnic sub-divisions*
The present survey of religions and churches uses as its main unit the country, and the statistical tables in Part 7 each deal only with a single entire country and so give data mainly at the national or country-wide level. However, it is possible for any reader interested in smaller sub-national groups to take this analysis further and to use the same method to derive similar tables for those smaller groups; and this paragraph will explain how. As has just been noted, countries' tables mask considerable internal variation. Few if any countries or nations are homogeneous geographically, politically, or ethnically. Most consist of several regions, or provinces, or states, or counties, or ethnic groups, or social classes or strata, or other homogeneous units, or urban and rural areas, or other politically or geographically distinct areas, in which the religious situation may differ widely from one region to the next. In many cases, though, there are sufficient data available in the literature (often that reported at the end of each country's article) to enable new tables in the formats of Tables 1 and 2 to be compiled for any sub-division the reader is interested in. Considering Egypt as an example, its census of 22-23.XI.1976 reported population and Christians both at the national level and also divided amongst the country's 25 governorates; thus one could construct a Table 1 for each governorate. Considering the United Kingdom (Britain) as a second example, it would be possible to divide Tables 1 and 2, as they appear here in Part 7, into 4 similar pairs of tables analysing separately the situation in England, Wales, Scotland and Northern Ireland. The same could be done for the city of London, or for Black immigrants in the UK, or for the working classes (70% of the UK population), or for men and women separately, or for young people aged 15–25 years, or for any other groups for which the basic demographic data (the last line in Table 1) are readily available from government population census reports or statistical abstracts. Even if exact data on a number of churches and religions were not available divided among the 4 UK regions (for example), each figure in the UK Table 1 could be divided among the 4 by making reasonable assumptions and estimates. Once the statistics for the new Tables 1 have been completed using the methodology described below, the reader can begin to analyse and interpret the figures. Clearly, much greater insight into a specific country's situation can be obtained by dividing national totals up by sex, geography, age-groups, social classes, occupations, income-groups, education, literacy, ethnolinguistic groups, and so on. To do this here for all countries is beyond the scope of this Encyclopedia; we therefore give only the country-wide totals in Tables 1 and 2.

## THE PRESENT SURVEY

*Two standardized tables*
For every country, the survey in Part 7 gives 2 statistical tables, preceded by a section SECULAR DATA which gives the background secular statistical data against which our religious data can be evaluated. Table 1, *Religious adherents*, presents an overview of the adherents of all religions in the country, both organized and unorganized, across the 20th century, in a standardized classification and layout. Table 2, *Organized churches and denominations*, presents an overview of all organized churches in the country and all Christians affiliated to them. These are the national tables from which the world and continental totals in Parts 1 and 8 are derived. These are followed by Global Table 31, *Geopolitico-religious data for all countries*. In the interests of clarity, the methodology employed in these tables, and all purely methodological considerations, have been kept out of the tables and articles as far as is possible, and are restricted to the present chapter, Part 3. In the pages that follow, we now describe the methodology behind this survey, the sources employed, the layout of the tables, and the classifications, categories and codes used in them. These are then condensed and summarized in a quick-reference alphabetical *Codebook* (Part 6).

*A ruler is necessary*
Tables 1 and 2 (also Global Tables and all other tables and charts) are closely printed in order to provide the reader with a complete overview in as compact a space as possible. To get the best use out of these tables, the reader will need to have a straight edge or ruler handy (preferably a transparent ruler) for use in the following ways.

(1) *Horizontally*. By placing the ruler horizontally under a line across the page, the reader can see at a glance (a) in Tables 1, the numerical development

or evolution of any religion or Christian bloc from AD 1900–2000; or (b) in Tables 2, the size and characteristics of any organized church or denomination in the 1970s.

(2) *Vertically*. By placing the ruler vertically up the table, to the right of a column he is interested in, the reader can see at a glance (a) in Tables 1, the comparative sizes of all religions and Christian blocs at any particular year; or (b) in Tables 2, comparative sizes or dates of origin for all organized churches and denominations. Also in Tables 2, a vertical ruler placed to the right of column 3 (Type) will show the reader at a glance the blocs and traditions of all churches. For example, if he wants to find Orthodox churches, he can place the ruler to the right of the first (single-letter) sub-column, and look down the ruler's edge until he finds where these bodies are, coded 'O'. If he wishes to find Methodist bodies, he can move the ruler to the right of the second sub-column and look down the ruler's edge until he finds the code 'Met'. In the same way in Tables 2, a vertical ruler placed to the immediate right of column 4 (Councils) will show the reader at a glance which churches belong to which Christian councils, if any, for its 5 sub-columns which represent (in order) confessional, international, continental, regional, and national conciliarism. For example, to find which denominations are full members of the World Council of Churches, place the ruler to the immediate right of the 2nd sub-column and find which denominations have the code W there.

A ruler should also be used for the reader to find his way rapidly around all other large tables in this Encyclopedia.

*Statistics for 1981–85*
The tables enable the reader to obtain figures at certain precise points in time during the 20th century, namely the years 1900, mid-1970, mid-1975, mid-1980 and the year 2000. Figures for intermediate years can easily be obtained by extrapolation.

The reader who wants a figure, or figures, for Christians or other religionists in the year 1981, or 1982, etcetera, can obtain them from the appropriate Tables 1 as follows. To get a figure for mid-1981, take the mid-1980 figure shown and simply add the figure under 'Annual change' in the column 'Total'. For mid-1982, add the figure 'Total' twice; for mid-1983, three times; and so on. For mid-1979, subtract 'Total' once. And so on.

From Tables 2, the reader can get approximate projections for 1980–85 by multiplying a denomination's total Christian community by various combinations of the last 3 lines of totals (those for 1970, 1975 and 1980).

*Statistics for 1985–2000*
For projections after 1985, one may assume even or linear change from 1980 to 2000 in Tables 1. Thus if the reader wants a quick estimate for a figure for 1990, he should add the figures for 1980 and 2000 and then divide by 2.

*Quantifying 80 categories*
In this survey we quantify a total of at least 80 different categories for a number of denominations and countries, i.e. for those traditions which produce statistics of them. On the world scale, we quantify some 40 different categories for every nation and denominational tradition. Of our scale of stages in Christian commitment (see Part 9), we give quantified statistics of at least 22. What this all means is that a very substantial part of the entire range of Christian activity in the modern world has been quantified by one tradition or another, and hence can be reproduced here.

*We either list or quantify*
The principle used throughout this survey is that we attempt to describe the whole spectrum — all religions, all churches and denominations, all parachurch agencies, and all varieties of Christian work and activities. This we do either by listing by name all significant items present in a particular country, or, where they are too numerous to list, by quantifying and counting them. If any category proves too lengthy, we quantify it and give a statistical total. Thus Tables 1 and 2 list most religions and churches in each country, the significant ones at least, but often end their listings with 'Other religionists' (in Tables 1) or 'Other Protestant denominations', 'Other Orthodox churches', etc (in Tables 2). Similarly with other bodies and activities in the footnotes: if these are few, we describe them all by name. But if these are too numerous we always total them, as with seminaries, periodicals, libraries, institutions and agencies.

## SOURCES

The sources used in this survey were so numerous and diverse (often a different one for each number in a table) that it has proved impossible to insert them or document them in either the text or the tables. In most cases, the most authoritative local sources, published or unpublished, were available and so were used. The published documentation used is presented in this volume in the form of 3 separate bibliographies. (a) A 500-title *Bibliography of World Christianity* (or, *of the Christian world*) is presented here as a series of short bibliographies appended to the descriptive texts in Part 7 for most countries, giving descriptive works significant on the national level, i.e. listing for each country the major titles describing Christianity and religions in that country (and usually restricted to only that country). (b) A 346-title *World Bibliography of Christian Directories* (see end of Part 13) lists national, international, confessional, denominational, topical and other types of reference directory significant within their own contexts but not necessarily so at the global level. Lastly, (c) the *Selective World Bibliography of Christianity* (Part 10) lists the major reference works on Christianity (not only world Christianity or Christianity as a world phenomenon) which are significant at the international or world or global level.

Most of the materials collected for this survey, however, relate to original and previously unpublished enquiries. A large majority of the data came from field work, unpublished reports, and private communications from the collaborators listed after our title page. The major physical collections of data built up may be summarized here under 12 heads: (1) around 5,000 statistical questionnaires returned by churches and national collaborators over the period 1968–76; (2) field surveys and interviews on the spot in over 200 countries conducted by the editors, who over the years 1965–75 visited (especially the statistical editor) virtually every country in the world; (3) extensive correspondence over the last 16 years; (4) a mass of unpublished documentation for all countries, collected on the field, including reports, memoranda, fascimiles, photocopies, photographs, maps, statistical summaries and historical documents; (5) a large collection of primary published documents of limited circulation; (6) the collection just described of 300 directories of denominations, Christian councils, confessions and topics; (7) a collection of 400 printed contemporary descriptions of the churches, describing denominations, movements, countries and confessions; (8) officially-published reports of 500 government-organized national censuses of population each including the question on religion, in over 120 countries, covering most decades over the period 1900–1976; (9) unpublished reports and data concerning 50 government censuses of population by religion which were unprocessed or had remained incomplete, and which the editors then completed; (10) unpublished computer searches and computerized surveys of 8,000 dissertations on Christianity and religion, using 40 keywords ('Christian', 'Catholic', 'Protestant', etc); (11) systematic bibliographical listings from searches (including computerized enquiries on keywords) in a number of major libraries including those of the British Library (London), Library of Congress (Washington), Propaganda (Rome), Missionary Research Library (New York), and a score of universities; and (12) a series of in-depth focused interviews with bishops, church leaders, theologians and others (of Catholic, Protestant, Orthodox, Anglican and all other traditions), focusing specifically on the meaning, understanding, quantification and interpretation of (a) keywords in use in the propagation of Christianity (evangelization, mission, development, conversion, etc) and (b) the various neologisms evolved here in the course of our survey's statistical analyses (affiliated Christians, crypto-Christians, radio believers, evangelized non-Christians, etc).

## ENUMERATING THE CHRISTIAN WORLD

*Finding the statistics you want*
Statistics can be useful to the reader in several ways, both specific, general and comparative. Firstly, the reader may want to know the size of one particular figure, for some specific reason (e.g. the number of clergy in the diocese he lives in). Or secondly, he may want a general idea of the size of a particular church (e.g. an overseas denomination he is going to visit). Or thirdly, he may need to compare one church with another, or one set of statistics with another (e.g. which is the largest church in a particular country; or whether the church he supports has more national clergy than expatriate clergy). The statistics in this Encyclopedia attempt to supply these forms of assistance.

*The general order of magnitude*
The main feature of the statistical presentation in this volume is that its primary object is to establish broad areas of magnitude — to give the general order of magnitude of the situation, whether denominational, local, tribal, national, regional, racial, continental or global. From the point of view of the planner, development officer, Bible society executive, broadcaster, journalist or researcher, the important thing is to know (for example) whether Protestants in a particular country number 1,000, or 100,000, or 1 million or 10 million; the exact size to the last digit may be of interest but is of little further use. In the same way, many other totals enumerating approximately the entire Christian enterprise have been computed and presented here, such as radio audiences, unevangelized populations, and so on. The word 'approximately' is the operative word in this survey; absolute precision and accuracy are not to be expected, nor in fact are they necessary for practical working purposes. This means that, although the tables and other statistics may help readers who want specific individual figures, they are mainly designed to give this general-order picture set in the total national and global context. To this end, where detailed local statistics compiled from grass-roots sources have not been available or were incomplete, the tables supply general-order estimates provided by persons familiar with the local statistical situation.

*Comparative statistics*
A second major feature of the statistical presentation is the comparative aspect: statistics of a similar type (e.g. adult membership), if published in a table in a single column, must be comparable from one church to another. Like must be compared with like; and like can only be compared with like. One cannot directly compare Roman Catholic statistics of 'Catholics' with Baptist statistics of 'Baptists', because the former include baptized children and infants and nominal adherents, the latter usually no infants or children but only baptized believing (and usually practising) adults. To present only such statistics as the churches supply in this way would be frustrating and would merely underline the non-comparability of church statistics from one tradition to another. Ideally, we should collect statistics to the same definitions from all the churches, but for historical reasons it is now virtually impossible to get every body to use similar definitions. It is, however, possible to adjust a body's figures to make them comparable with those of others. In this Encyclopedia, therefore, the problem is solved (a) by identifying clearly all statistics as applying to either adults only, or to adults plus children; and (b), in cases where a church only enumerates one of these categories, by computing general-order estimates of the other category. Most churches in fact enumerate each year only one type of membership statistics, either the number of adults or communicants on the rolls or records (as do Baptists, Methodists, Pentecostals and other 'gathered' churches) or the total number on the rolls including children and infants (as do Roman Catholics, Orthodox, Lutherans, Reformed, and other traditions with geographical parishes). Relatively few confessions enumerate both adults and total; these include Anglicans, some Reformed and some Lutherans. To make these data comparable from one tradition to another, therefore, the missing figure (adults or total) has been estimated and added either by the churches themselves or by the editors. These latter general-order estimates can usually be spotted by the reader because they are rounded, or more rounded than the church's main aggregated figure which is often given to the last digit. The major case of this method in this Encyclopedia concerns the Roman Catholic Church. Since Catholic statistics never enumerate adult Catholics, we provide general-order estimates of this category throughout by multiplying total affiliated Catholics (baptized plus catechumens) by the national figure for the percentage of the population over 14 years old. This assumption that the age structure of the Catholic Church is

similar to that in the country as a whole is reasonably true in the Western (developed) world, although somewhat less accurate in Third-World (developing) countries where proportionately larger numbers of children and young people become Catholics than older people. Our assumption does, however, enable direct numerical comparisons to be made between Catholic statistics and Protestant statistics.

In the same way that comparison can only be made if definitions are like, comparisons of different bodies can only be made for the same point in time. One cannot meaningfully compare Catholics in 1930 with Baptists in 1980; they must be compared for the same year. Likewise it is wrong to add up totals of church memberships for different bodies at different dates, although it may be satisfactory if one can assume no change took place between the range of dates.

### Reading percentages correctly
For comparing different quantities we use percentages throughout this survey (e.g. 'Catholics number 70% of the country's population, and Protestants 30%'). However, a single specific religious body or grouping may be quoted in the survey as having several quite different and apparently contradictory percentages attached to it. Thus, in the article on Fiji, we state that Indians who are Roman Catholics form (a) 1.5% of the Indian population of Fiji, (b) 8.9% of all Roman Catholics in Fiji, and (c) 0.8% of the whole population of Fiji. All 3 percentages are correct, and consistent, but refer to 3 different ways of expressing the size of Indian Roman Catholics. Throughout this survey, therefore, the reader interested in a particular percentage, or set of percentages, should take care to ascertain precisely how we define them, what larger population is involved, and hence exactly what the percentages mean.

### Accuracy claimed for particular statistics
Churches and religious bodies do not have at their disposal the vast networks of enumerators and analysts that government censuses and public-opinion polls employ, hence churches' statistics are not able to claim accuracy to the last digit. Similarly, although a government census in 1968 may report the number of Christians to the last digit (e.g. 2,450,793), projections into the future based upon this figure cannot claim complete accuracy but can only be approximations indicating the general order of size of the statistics required. In this Encyclopedia, therefore, the statistics presented fall into 2 categories: general-order estimates, and multi-digit aggregates. General-order estimates can be recognized throughout by their rounded nature, e.g. '5,000', '20,000', '100,000'. Where they occur in Table 2, they usually represent estimates of their own size by the churches themselves; where they occur in Table 1, they represent estimates by persons familiar with the nation, or by the editors. Multi-digit aggregates can be recognized throughout as figures appearing to claim accuracy to several digits, e.g. '5,291', '21,684', '102,735'. In a number of cases in the Encyclopedia's surveys, a church or diocese returned this kind of statistic rather than rounding it to the nearest hundred or thousand as one would do with a general-order estimate. In such cases Table 2 repeats the unrounded number, for 2 reasons: (1) to indicate the church's claim that the statistic is not a rough guess or general-order estimate but is based on some kind of aggregate or grass-roots roll total or head count, and (2) to enable readers familiar with that church's statistics to recognize the particular figure and hence to know its source and the exact date it applies to, in case more up-to-date or reliable figures later become available. It is remarkable how often such a multi-digit aggregate may be quoted for years after its original computation, and how easily recognizable each one is when it turns up again. Preserving the digits in this way is therefore an aid to the proper use of these statistics; but our practice must not be taken to imply bogus precision or any claim to accuracy to this last digit.

### Choice of best data available
Because our survey has attempted to be comprehensive, in certain countries where no hard statistical data or reliable surveys were available, we have had to rely on the informed estimates of experts in the area and subject. In this volume, we have made no detailed attempt at a critique of each nation's censuses and polls or each church's statistical operations. After examining what is available, we have then selected the best data available until such time as better data come into existence.

### Quantifying inaccessible data
There are a number of areas of church or religious life where it is impossible to obtain accurate statistics, usually because of state opposition to Christianity or religions. Thus it will probably never be possible (nor, perhaps, desirable) to get exact head counts of crypto-Christians, or of isolated radio believers, or of annual conversions to underground churches, and the like. Where such information is necessary to our present survey, we have therefore made reasonable and somewhat conservative estimates.

### Totalling figures of varying accuracy
In each table a number of totals are given at the end. When figures which are multi-digit aggregates (e.g. '102,783') are added together with others which are general-order estimates (e.g. '110,000'), the resulting total (212,783) is printed to the last digit in the interests of consistency and exactness of analysis. However, when such a total is quoted or used outside this survey, it should be rounded (to 210,000), to indicate only the general order of accuracy that it is possible to claim. This avoids the quoting and spreading of totals which appear to claim greater accuracy than is justified.

### Totals for churches with dioceses or other sub-divisions
The same applies to totals for a church with dioceses or other jurisdictions. Figures for a church's dioceses or sub-divisions are added and given in Table 2 on its first line to the last digit; but if they are quoted outside this survey they should be rounded.

### Totals and rounding
All our columns of absolute numbers in Tables 1 and 2 always add up exactly to the totals and sub-totals shown. However, as with all large statistical tables, a column of percentages may not always add up to exactly the total or sub-total indicated, due to rounding. Although in most cases throughout this survey component percentages in fact add up exactly to their respective totals, in a small number of cases this is not so because of the rounding feature. As an example we may total: $0.13\% + 0.13\% + 0.13\% = 0.39\%$; when each is rounded to only one place of decimals, the figures become $0.1\% + 0.1\% + 0.1\% = 0.4\%$, which introduces a small discrepancy.

### Dates of statistics
It is important, in changing situations, to know the exact date (year, perhaps also month and sometimes day) to which particular statistics apply. This Encyclopedia compares government statistics of religion with churches' statistics; but in doing so, it must be remembered that a government census (or a public-opinion poll) is almost always taken on a single, known, day; whereas, by contrast, churches' statistics are compiled over a lengthy period that may amount to 3, 4, 5, 6 or even 7 years from the local grass-roots counting of heads to final compilation of totals by a large denomination or church. Denominational totals published in 1975 therefore probably refer to the situation in 1972, 1971 or even 1970 in the case of very large denominations. This point is important in analysing religious change and will be elaborated on below.

### Updating a church's statistics
Many of the largest or best-organized churches publish membership statistics annually. This means that the figures given in our Tables 2 are not always the latest available for those churches, after the year 1976. It would be inaccurate, however, to describe such figures in Tables 2 as 'out-of-date'; they represent accurately the situation for the year 1970. In the case of each such church, the reader wanting the latest available figures should consult the latest edition of that church's yearbook (e.g. *Annuario Pontificio* and *Statistical yearbook of the Church* for the Roman Catholic Church).

### Statistics must be consistent
A major feature of this survey is that care has been taken to make the various statistical categories, the national tables, and the international totals, all fully consistent with each other and without internal statistical discrepancies or contradictions. This means that (1) each statistical category we use has been given a single clear operational definition applicable world-wide and in all countries, churches and religions; and (2) in all complete enumerations in this survey (in Tables 1, 2 et alia), all sub-totals of absolute numbers add up exactly to the relevant total; and all percentages add up to exactly 100% (in practice, such totals are sometimes 0.1% or 0.2% out, due to rounding). In particular, in every country the totals of all religious and non-religious populations add up exactly to the country's population, i.e. to exactly 100%. A number of other consistency checks come readily to mind: e.g. in large paedobaptist (infant-baptizing) state churches with few adult conversions each year, the annual number of infant baptisms should be somewhat smaller than the total number of annual births in the country. Vast numbers of new single facts or items of data can be checked in this way before being inputted to the tables.

**The right to profess one's choice.** Census officials (right, centre) in Iban/Sea Dayak longhouse in Sarawak (Malaysia) in 1960 ask tattooed Iban (left) what religion he professes.

*Conflicting data*
In a few places when data were being collected for this Encyclopedia, different authorities gave, for the same situation, radically divergent data. In most cases the discrepancy was solved and the situation resolved by examining the exact context of the data. It was then found that in almost all cases the differing data referred either to different points in time, or to slightly different geographical areas, or to different definitions of the item in question. As a result this survey is able to give a single figure for every clearly-defined entity at a given point in time. Similarly, where various authorities differ concerning quantifiable matters, we have attempted to present a single statement rather than a series or range of contradictory statements.

## WHO IS A CHRISTIAN?

*Two divergent answers*
There are 2 distinct and different ways in which Christians have been enumerated for well over the last 100 years, and in embryo for very much longer. The first is enumeration from the point of view of the state or society at large or the general public, in which individuals are asked in a government census or public-opinion poll to state publicly what religion they adhere to. The second is enumeration from the point of view of the churches, in which congregations or clergy state the total persons that they know are affiliated with them, i.e. whose names and addresses are on their records. These 2 methods almost always in all countries produce significantly different totals. Until now, the usual explanation has been either that governments are prone to over-enumerate or that churches are prone to under-enumerate, or vice versa. It is much more satisfactory to assume that, given their formidable resources and expertise, both are enumerating substantially correctly but that they are enumerating quite different kinds of person; and this assumption is basic to the present survey.

*Who is a Catholic?*
The difference becomes sharpest over statistics of Roman Catholics. Africa provides a stark contrast. According to governments and polls organizations, there were 52.8 million Roman Catholics in Africa in 1970, rising to 76.8 million by 1980. According to the Vatican, there were only 45.3 million in 1970, rising to 66.2 million by 1980. Why the discrepancy? The answer is that governments were measuring self-identification (persons who call themselves Roman Catholics), and the Vatican was counting only baptized Catholics and catechumens known to its parishes and priests. Both usages must be accepted and must be taken seriously, since neither is likely to be changed; the best procedure therefore is to qualify these usages of 'Roman Catholics' with 2 different adjectives to distinguish the one from the other. This is done here by use of the terms 'professing Roman Catholics' and 'affiliated Roman Catholics' respectively, defining the latter (in mission countries) to mean all baptized Roman Catholics together with any catechumens, i.e. all persons on the books or records of the Roman Catholic Church. The latter term then stands for Roman Catholics as enumerated by that church itself.

*Who is a Pentecostal-charismatic?*
Another illustration comes from the above question. According to the 1980 Christianity Today/Gallup poll, 19% of all adults in the USA identify themselves as Pentecostal-charismatics; yet, according to Gallup, of this 19% only 15% are members affiliated to churches and only 3.5% are regularly active and involved in Pentecostal-charismatic activities. Why the discrepancy? Our answer to all such problems is that all such data are valid and consistent, but that exact definitions must be used in labelling the results: in this case, 19% of the USA are professing Pentecostal-charismatics, 15% are Pentecostal-charismatics affiliated to churches, and 3.5% are regularly-active and involved Pentecostal-charismatics.

*A new methodology*
As a result, this Encyclopedia incorporates a new methodology of enumerating statistics of the Christian world. In the past, certain churches (usually those with a strong link with the state) have quoted, as their membership figures, government census figures of professing adherents; other churches (those with little or no link with the state) have enumerated only those persons regularly or actively participating in church life. These 2 types of statistics are describing quite different entities and therefore cannot properly be compared. Instead, this Encyclopedia divides all membership statistics into 3 basic types: professing Christians, affiliated Christians, and practising Christians. These 3 types will now be elaborated on.

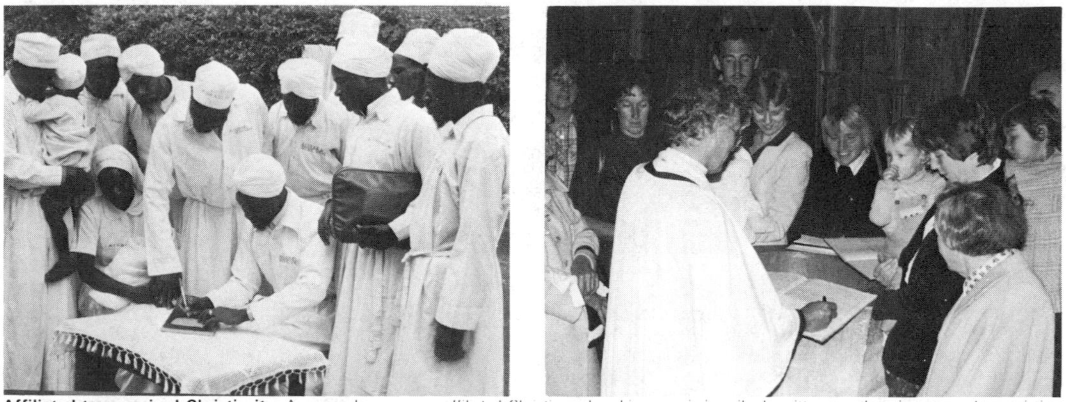

**Affiliated to organized Christianity.** A person becomes an affiliated Christian when his name is inscribed, written or otherwise entered on existing rolls of church members. *Left.* Newly-baptized members of AICN (Kenya) in 1979 have their names written on printed membership cards in presence of witnesses. *Right.* Newly-baptized infants, Luke and Timothy, are entered into 200-year-old parish register in Waterperry, Oxford (England) by Church of England vicar, 1979.

*The right to profess one's choice*
Our new methodology takes as its starting-point the United Nations 1948 *Universal Declaration of Human Rights*, Article 18: 'Everyone has the right to freedom of thought, conscience and religion; this right includes freedom to change his religion or belief, and freedom, either alone or in community with others and in public or private, to manifest his religion or belief in teaching, practice, worship and observance.' Since its promulgation, this group of phrases has been incorporated into the state constitutions of a large number of countries across the world. This fundamental right also includes the right to claim the religion of one's choice, and the right to be called a follower of that religion and to be enumerated as such. The section on religious freedom in the constitutions of very many nations uses the exact words of the Universal Declaration, and many countries instruct their census personnel to observe this principle. The instructions to enumerators in the 8th Census of Canada (1941) are typical in this respect: 'The religion of each person will be entered according as he or she professes'. This Declaration has however been virtually ignored in the churches and by Christians in general. Almost the first interest in it has been a recent action of the Protestant and Roman Catholic churches in Brazil. In 1978 they published and distributed over one million copies of an ecumenical edition of the Declaration, complete with Bible references and official church pronouncements on the subject.

On this definition in the Declaration, then, 'Christians' means all those who profess to be Christians in government censuses or public-opinion polls, i.e. who declare or identify themselves as Christians, who say 'I am a Christian', 'We are Christians', when asked the question 'What is your religion?' From the biblical point of view, there is justification for this definition in passages such as the word of Jesus in Matthew 10.32 (Good News Bible): 'If anyone declares publicly that he belongs to me, I will do the same for him before my Father in heaven'. A parallel passage is Romans 10.9; a person is a saved Christian 'if you confess with your lips that Jesus is Lord' instead of the required obligatory state-worship formula 'Caesar is Lord'. Another term for professing Christians can therefore be confessing Christians.

Public declaration must therefore be taken seriously when endeavouring to survey the extent of Christianity. This definition covers many categories of Christians including the large numbers of groups and individuals who, while striving to follow Christ and being indisputably Christian, nevertheless refuse to identify themselves with any existing organized Christian church or denomination. Statistics of these *professing Christians*, or confessing Christians, or declared Christians, or self-identifying Christians, are widely available, published by governments and polls organizations.

*Affiliated to organized Christianity*
By no means all those who profess to be Christians, however, are affiliated to the organized churches and denominations, and so it is necessary to give here also statistics of *affiliated Christians*. We define these as those known to the churches or known to the clergy (usually by names and addresses) and claimed by them in their statistics, i.e. those enrolled on the churches' books or records, with totals which can be substantiated. This usually means all known baptized Christians and their children, and other adherents; it is sometimes termed the total Christian community (because affiliated Christians are those who are not primarily individual Christians but who primarily belong to the corporate community of Christ), or inclusive membership (because affiliated Christians are church members). This definition of 'Christians' is what the churches usually mean by the term, and statistics of such affiliated Christians are what the churches themselves collect and publish. In all countries, it may be assumed with confidence, the churches know better than the state how many Christians are affiliated to them. This therefore gives us a second measure of the total Christians which is quite independent of the first (government census figures of professing Christians).

*Religious practice*
A third definition of membership relates to those who actually practise their religion, i.e. *practising Christians* who may also be termed active Christians, attending Christians, committed Christians, militant Christians (composing Christ's Church Militant Here on Earth, to quote the Prayer for the Church in the Church of England 1552 Communion Service). Practising Christians are defined here as those who participate in the ongoing institutional and organized life and pattern of the churches. Using the broadest definition, this covers all affiliated church members who attend church services of public worship a minimum of once a year; and it covers all who fulfil the minimum annual obligation of their church, which may be reception of communion at Easter and/or on other occasions annually. Using a more rigorous definition, this category may be sub-divided into monthly attenders (those who attend church at least once a month), or weekly attenders (those who attend regularly every Sunday). Many churches keep such statistics of practice, and in addition many secular polling organizations provide data on church attendance. Where such data exist, statistics of practice for a denomination or diocese are given in Table 2, column 8, using the code P (=% practising); and estimates of practice for the whole country are given in Table 1. Note that the *percentages* for practising and non-practising given in Table 1 refer to percentages of affiliated Christians, not percentages of the whole country's population. To many persons active in the churches, this definition of 'Christians' is the only one they can use; Christians are those who practise the faith regularly within the churches.

## CHILDREN ALSO MUST BE INCLUDED

The place of children in Christian enumeration needs critical examination and radical re-emphasis. All churches would agree that the influence and example of parents are the most powerful of all influences. The family is by far the most important instrumentality through which individuals acquire personal, cultural, and social self-identification. In consequence, children of church members are more likely to remain members than those whose parents are not church members. Children of ardent and practising Christians usually are, to the extent that their years permit, ardent and practising Christians.

**Religious practice.** Palm Sunday in Burundi, with several thousand Catholics and their children (note infants on mothers' backs) in procession.

*Children also can practise their faith*
Many churches however do not enumerate children of under 15 years. One reason is that it has been widely noted that most conversion crises occur in the 13–20 age group in Christian families or in christianized lands. On this view, therefore, children who have not yet reached 15 (known in Protestant circles as 'the age of decision'), cannot reasonably be expected to be practising and believing Christians. We here take the opposite view: children and infants also can properly be called Christians, and can actively and regularly (to the extent of their ability) practise the Christian faith. The photographs of practising Christians shown on this page, and a number of others throughout the Encyclopedia, show children (defined as ages 5–14 years, i.e. the school-age population), infants (defined as under 5 years old, usually termed the pre-school population) and in several cases newborn babies (see infant baptism services portrayed later) who are present and active or in some way participating in Christian worship and witness. To understand the magnitude of this problem, it is advisable at this point to see just how numerous children are in the Christian world.

*How numerous are children?*
Reasonable assumptions on this subject are: (1) in the Christian world the proportions of children and other functional age-groups are (for our own immediate purposes) approximately the same as in their country and in the world at large; (2) children and infants have, in general, the same religion as their parents; and (3) in particular, children and infants of practising Christians usually practise the faith to the extent that they are able and should therefore also be called practising Christians too. We then arrive at the conclusion demonstrated in the table below that in 1980 approximately 372 million children and infants in the world can properly be called practising Christians.

**Children also can practise their faith.** Children and infants who practise the Christian faith (as shown here) number over 350 million, hence deserve proper enumeration. *Above.* Japanese Christian children pray at Ai Kei Gakuen Community Center, Tokyo.

*Enumerate your children and infants*
Since children and infants form in this way over 36% of all professing Christians, and 37% of all practising Christians, it stands to reason that in any statistical survey of world Christianity they must not be ignored, whatever a particular confession's answer may be to the questions 'Can an infant be a Christian?' and 'Can an infant be a practising Christian?'. Churches whose statistical procedures ignore children and infants can now be seen to be seriously under-enumerating their own numerical strengths. On the world scale, this situation has given rise to a serious understatement of the size and numerical strength

of the Christian community in comparison with the total population, a situation which has often then been rationalized theologically by the assertion that the Body of Christ must always be only the little Flock, the Saving Remnant, the Gideon's Band (of only 300 persons), in other words only a tiny minority in a non-Christian world.

For a true assessment of the situation, therefore, children and infants must be enumerated. Those world confessions which are Non-Liturgical, such as Baptists, Methodists, Pentecostals and other Protestants whose present procedures enumerate only adult members (15 years and older, i.e. the working-age and old-age populations in the table below) should therefore note that, in 1980, these adults probably form only around 63% of their true total community, on their own definition of membership. To arrive at a correct estimate of their true strength vis-a-vis the total population around them they should increase their quoted adult membership figures by dividing them by a factor around 0.63 (63%). The exact procedure by which this has been done in the present survey, for all such denominations in all countries of the world, is explained below in the discussion of the methodology of Table 2.

It follows that, to ensure comparability from one confession or church to another, it is important to note whether any statistics that one is examining (or quoting) include children and infants. Baptized listings for the Liturgical world confessions — Catholic, Orthodox, Anglicans and some Protestant churches including Lutherans — and also government census figures, do include children and infants; but communicant rolls and other adult listings exclude children and infants and enumerate only adults. Censuses of church attendance often badly under-represent the true situation because children and infants are not properly included among the total of attenders, who are then divided by the total population (which includes children and infants) to arrive at incorrectly-low percentages. A total of adults cannot properly be compared with another total including children, otherwise misleading conclusions may be drawn. In the same way, all public-opinion polls enquiring about affiliation and religious practice enumerate only the adult population. Since the children and infants of religious parents, and of practising Christians, can also be active attenders, they also must be enumerated to make any accounting complete. In many countries, the religion of children is stated in law to be that of their parents, as in Norway's 1969 law declaring that 'Children born in wedlock belong to the religion of their parents'. It is assumed in this survey therefore that, when such polls data are used, children under 14 have the same characteristics as their parents; i.e. the same religion, and religious practice, as the head of the family; except in rare cases where data to the contrary are available. This means then that the 'Total practising Christians' statistics given in Tables 1 cover the total practising community — men, women and their children and infants.

## DEFINITIONS OF TYPES OF CHRISTIANS

*Operationalizing our definitions*
We can now proceed to relatively exact definitions of the major variables used in our enumeration of all categories of Christians and other religionists. We can also study how they are quantified and how they are operationalized. The latter term has a specific meaning. 'Operationism or operationalism is the insistence upon the use of operational definitions in science wherever the meaning of a term in quantitative discourse is to be understood' (J. Gould & W.L. Kolb, eds, *A dictionary of the social sciences;* London, 1964:475. See also 'The present state of operationalism', chapter 2 in P.G. Frank (ed), *The validation of scientific theories*, New York, 1954). The value of exact definitions is that different observers or analysts

### WORLD POPULATION AND CHRISTIANS BY FUNCTIONAL AGE-GROUPS INCLUDING CHILDREN, 1965-2000

| Functional age groups | Ages | (a) Total population (as % of world) | | | | | (b) Christians | | | (c) Practising Christians | | |
|---|---|---|---|---|---|---|---|---|---|---|---|---|
| | | 1965 | 1970 | 1975 | 1980 | 2000 | 1975 | 1980 | 2000 | 1975 | 1980 | 2000 |
| Pre-school infants | 0–4 | 13.9 | 14.0 | 13.9 | 13.7 | 11.4 | 183,033,000 | 196,278,000 | 230,271,000 | 131,544,000 | 139,515,000 | 151,657,000 |
| School-age children: | 5–14 | 23.4 | 23.0 | 22.8 | 22.9 | 21.4 | 300,226,000 | 328,085,000 | 432,263,000 | 215,771,000 | 233,203,000 | 284,690,000 |
| Junior | 5–9 | 12.4 | 12.0 | 12.1 | 12.1 | 10.9 | 159,330,000 | 173,355,000 | 220,171,000 | 114,510,000 | 123,221,000 | 145,005,000 |
| Senior | 10–14 | 11.0 | 11.0 | 10.7 | 10.8 | 10.5 | 140,896,000 | 154,730,000 | 212,092,000 | 101,261,000 | 109,982,000 | 139,684,000 |
| Working-age population | 15–64 | 57.7 | 57.8 | 57.9 | 57.9 | 61.1 | 762,416,000 | 829,525,000 | 1,234,172,000 | 547,944,000 | 589,628,000 | 812,829,000 |
| Old-age population | over 64 | 5.0 | 5.2 | 5.4 | 5.5 | 6.1 | 71,106,000 | 78,798,000 | 123,215,000 | 51,104,000 | 56,010,000 | 81,150,000 |
| Total population | All ages | 100.0 | 100.0 | 100.0 | 100.0 | 100.0 | 1,316,781,000 | 1,432,687,000 | 2,019,921,000 | 946,362,000 | 1,018,355,000 | 1,330,325,000 |

*Sources.* The world population percentages in (a) above are derived from Table A.4, *World population prospects as assessed in 1968* (United Nations, 1973). The Christian figures in (b) and (c) come from our present survey.

of the same situation should then arrive at similar results. Definitions of simple categories such as 'church personnel', 'institutions', even 'schools', can vary considerably from one user to the next. Our solution here is to formulate definitions which are as precise as possible crossculturally and cross-nationally, and then to apply these standard definitions for all countries and churches.

which may be used by the state against the individual or his family or relatives or associates. Consequently, in countries where Christianity is discriminated against, many rightly choose not to reveal this information to the state. These persons, to whom we give the name crypto-Christians, are so important that we should describe them in detail at this point.

*Crypto-Christians.* This grouping is also called sec-

a good illustration. 'He was born into a party-card-carrying communist family 49 years ago. His father was a militant atheist. His mother was officially an atheist as well, although privately Nikodim said that she had been a secret believer. He apparently discovered this only after he himself joined the Church, during his teens' (*Religion in Communist lands*, 6, 4 (Winter, 1978), 227).

## DEFINITIONS OF TYPES OF CHRISTIANS, WITH 1980 WORLD TOTALS AND PERCENTAGES

| Standpoint | Major categories | | | | | | | | |
|---|---|---|---|---|---|---|---|---|---|
| | WORLD POPULATION 4,374 million 100% | | | | | | | | |
| 1. RELIGION | NON-RELIGIONISTS 911 million 20.8% | RELIGIONISTS 3,463 million 79.2% | | | | | | | |
| 2. CHRISTIANITY (to right of double line) | NON-CHRISTIANS 2,941 million 67.2% | CHRISTIANS 1,433 million 32.8% | | | | | | | |
| 3. PUBLIC PROFESSION | | PROFESSING CHRISTIANS 1,362 million 31.1% | | | | | | CRYPTO-CHRISTIANS 70 million 1.6% | |
| 4. CHURCH AFFILIATION (to right of double dotted line) | NOMINAL CHRISTIANS 109 million 2.5% | Disaffiliated −15 million −0.4% | AFFILIATED CHRISTIANS 1,323 million 30.3% | | | | | Doubly-affiliated −36 million −0.8% | |
| 5. PRACTICE | | NON-PRACTISING CHRISTIANS 305 million 7.0% | PRACTISING CHRISTIANS 1,018 million 23.3% | | | | | | |
| 6. CHURCH ATTENDANCE (mutually exclusive categories) | | Non-attending Christians 305 million | Annual attenders 66 m | Occasional attenders 63 m | Festival attenders 60 m | Radio/TV listeners 58 m | Monthly attenders 132 m | Fortnightly attenders 234 m | Weekly attenders 280 m | Daily attenders 125 m |
| 7. BELIEF | | UNCOMMITTED CHRISTIANS 350 million 8% | PARTIALLY-COMMITTED CHRISTIANS 303 million 7% | | COMMITTED CHRISTIANS 780 million 18% Born-again Christians 420 million | | | | | |

### Enumerating all categories

The key to understanding the enumeration of Christians presented in this Encyclopedia lies therefore in grasping the definitions contained in the diagram above, and in the explanation that follows it. These definitions arise out of 7 different standpoints or ways of looking at the world and its populations. To assist in understanding the definitions, we also add world totals for each of the types of Christians and others in the year 1980. After giving the diagram, we then explain each of the 7 standpoints.

### 1. *Religion*

The world may, to start with, be divided into two according to whether or not persons profess any religion. Those who profess no religion (20.8%) may be called either unbelievers or non-believers, or non-religious (agnostics and atheists); those who profess a religion (79.2%) may be called either believers, or religionists. The term is coming increasingly into use; thus in August 1978 there was held at the Jakko-in Temple Study Centre in Inuyama City, Japan, the Third Conference of Youth Religionists in Japan.

### 2. *Christianity*

Secondly, the world may again be divided into two, into those who are Christians, and those who are non-Christians of all kinds including the non-religious. CHRISTIANS are defined here as all who call themselves followers of Christ, in public or in private, or who regard themselves as followers of Christ or as part of a Christian community or who claim to be such. As has been explained, this is in accordance with the *Universal Declaration of Human Rights*, in which every individual has the right to say to what religion he belongs and to have this accepted by state and society.

### 3. *Public profession*

Christians may first be sub-divided into 2 main categories—professing, and crypto-Christian—depending on whether or not their faith is publicly known, i.e. known and declared to the public and to the state. PROFESSING CHRISTIANS are those who profess (declare, state, confess, identify themselves) publicly to be Christians when asked what their religion is, either in government censuses, or in public-opinion polls, or by social scientists or other researchers conducting surveys. Professing Christians are therefore persons known to state or government, and/or to the public at large, and concerning whom statistical totals are known to the state and government and are often published by them or quoted in their dealings with the churches. However, such census records constitute a formal declaration or statement to the state revealing one's personal religious preference, and one

**Professing Christians.** There are 2 standard methods of enumerating these. *Above.* (1) *Government censuses.* Here, Swaziland government census enumerator (in hat) explains census question 'What is your religion?' to Chief Mbetse and wife (right). The reply 'We are Zionist Christians' is then recorded, tabulated and printed in the government census report. *Right.* (2) *Public-opinion polls.* Here, worker with Gallup International in USA (right) asks question 'What is your religious preference—Protestant, Roman Catholic, Jewish, etc?'.

ret believers, or non-professing Christians, or Christians not publicly baptized, or clandestine or underground believers. They are those who for reasons of family, personal safety, status, employment or other factors do not declare or reveal their commitment to Christ or expose their faith to public or state scrutiny or enquiry but prefer to keep it private. As a result, they are not enumerated as Christians in government censuses or polls but remain unknown and unenumerated in such public enquiries. For various other reasons also, they remain unknown to governments and unregistered with them, or are overlooked or excluded in government census. They are, however, usually known to the churches, or join churches openly, or are known by the churches to have been baptized privately, or in fact constitute their own churches. In almost all cases, churches regard them as affiliated, and include them in their own enumerations of affiliation. The churches count them in their statistics, though they often do not record them by name and they take pains to conceal their identity from the state and from a hostile populace.

A description of the family background of Metropolitan Nikodim of Leningrad (died 1978) provides

Another type of secret believer is found in Islamic countries. There are large numbers of Muslims in these countries who are trying to follow Christ whilst remaining in the Muslim community and not breaking with it.

Secret believers are not necessarily always underground, or persecuted — they are merely unknown to the state or unrecognized by it. Often the state or society at large is completely unaware of the existence of sizeable groups of Christians, especially if they belong to illegal or banned groups (Jehovah's Witnesses, Mormons, New Apostolics, etc). Certain churches in any case prefer to exist clandestinely, deliberately operating unknown to the state.

Underground Christians may be further characterized as crypto-Protestants, crypto-Catholics, crypto-Orthodox, et alii. Another distinction is that a group may be, for instance, crypto-Witnesses (secret Jehovah's Witnesses) but not crypto-Christians because their religion is officially regarded as Roman Catholic or members of some established or state church.

It will be noticed from Tables 1 in certain countries that the 'professing' categories are missing for certain 'affiliated' traditions present there. This means that

# CRYPTO-CHRISTIANS

**CRYPTO-CHRISTIANS.** Secret believers in Christ, including those in 'churches of silence' or undergound churches, totalled 70 millions in 1980. They are defined in this Encyclopedia under the 7 headings given here, for each of which one illustration is given on this page. (1) **Unorganized individuals in legal churches.** Muslim women, including secret believers, leaving Christian Social Centre, Tunis. (2) **Political prisoners or exiles.** Christians being sentenced by people's tribunal, China. In Communist countries, an estimated 8 million Christians are held in prison camps with no fellowship or worship opportunities. (3) **Unregistered Christians.** An underground (illegal) Baptist church near Novosibirsk, Siberia (USSR) : (Above) in winter ; (below) in summer, with congregation of 52 believers. (4) **Deliberately-clandestine Christians.** Worship service in Ukrainian forest near Kharkov. In the USSR, there are over 40 highly-organized totally-clandestine denominations, with over 500,000 members. (5) **Anti-state minority sectarians.** Full Gospel Believers Church (Ethiopia), ex-Orthodox converts viciously persecuted by the state from 1972-75 and hence forced underground. (6) **Anti-church believers.** Prayer meeting before crucifix in Subba Rao Movement, India. Members oppose baptism and denominationalism, and call themselves Hindu believers in Christ. (7) **Isolated radio believers.** Convert in Morocco who has begun a network of house radio churches.

those traditions are in the category of crypto-Christians.

*Safeguarding clandestine Christians.* There is need to preserve the anonymity of crypto-Christians in many countries, due to hostile state apparatus. The data we give in this Encyclopedia are unlikely to harm them because the information usually comes from existing published sources. We mention no persons' names or addresses. In any case, state files on these groups are greatly more detailed, comprehensive and incriminating than anything we publish here. At the same time, it is necessary to urge Christians in Western countries to be on the alert to avoid any possibility of incrimination of secret believers in such countries.

### 4. *Church affiliation*

Professing Christians may be sub-divided into 2 categories — affiliated, and nominal — depending on whether or not they are in any sense attached to or associated with organized or institutional Christianity. AFFILIATED CHRISTIANS are Christians who are known to or in the churches, who have at some time past joined or belonged to one of the churches' categories of membership and affiliation, who hold or have claimed formal membership in a local church, who are known to the churches individually by name and are therefore on the churches' rolls or books at local or grass-roots level. They are therefore Christians with whom the churches are in touch, who are on the records of the institutional churches or organized Christianity, who are not simply individual Christians but are part of the churches' corporate life, community and fellowship, and who are therefore enumerated by the churches as members or adherents in a form which can be substantiated. Statistics of affiliated Christians, as presented in this Encyclopedia, are always those supplied by the churches themselves, although in a handful of public-opinion polls the question 'Are you a member of any church?' has produced similar data (e.g. AIPO 1954 and 1976, in the USA).

In the Western world, affiliated Christians are also professing (known in government censuses), but in Communist countries and in Third-World countries with a dominant non-Christian religion, a sizeable number remain as crypto-Christians. The organized churches, asserting that Jesus is the Christ, are termed by Paul Tillich the manifest church (*Systematic theology*, III, p. 152–382, passim). In cases where 2 churches claim the same people as members (as is widely the case in Latin America with Catholics and Evangelicals), this is shown as a group of doubly-affiliated at the end of Table 2, and in Table 1 on the line immediately after AFFILIATED, with the negative sign to ensure correct enumeration.

NOMINAL CHRISTIANS are defined here as professing Christians who are unaffiliated or unchurched, i.e. not affiliated to churches, nor in contact with them, nor attached to them, nor associated with them, nor known to them nor on their rolls or books. They are therefore Christians who are outside or have rejected the institutional churches or are otherwise not on the records of organized Christianity, who may individually be Christians but who are not part of the corporate life, community or fellowship of the churches, and who therefore from the churches' point of view are regarded as Christians in name only, whilst at the same time often maintaining Christian beliefs and Christian values. Nominal Christians, in other words, are Christians who, for reasons good or bad, do not belong to the visible and organized community of believers. They are sometimes called the latent church as opposed to the manifest church which asserts Jesus as the Christ (Paul Tillich, et alii).

In the Western world (Europe, USA), this term 'nominal' often carries connotations of dishonesty or hypocrisy, and such persons not known to the churches are often regarded as post-Christians forming a penumbra of residual Christianity; though from another point of view they contain large numbers of personally-committed Christians who find themselves indifferent to organized or institutional religion. A full statistical study of this category in one particular nation, the USA, has been undertaken by Gallup International in their poll 'The unchurched

**Affiliated Christians** (on church rolls). With the theme 'Let the Church Stand up', 14,107 duly-accredited 'messengers' representing some 34,000 financially contributing churches here constitute 119th Session of Southern Baptist Convention, June 1976, in Scope Convention Center, Norfolk, VA (USA). Key note speaker was Gerald Ford, 38th President of the USA.

American' (June 1978), whose main finding was: 'A majority of American adults who for one reason or another have rejected the institutional church still adhere to most traditional Christian beliefs and values'. This survey is summarized here in Table 1 for the USA under the footnote NOMINAL CHRISTIANS. Gallup's definition of the category 'unchurched' is more inclusive than ours in this Encyclopedia, as is also explained in the footnote. The situation with regard to being 'nominal' is quite different in regions where Christianity is expanding, especially Africa, where this category covers masses of intending or latent Christians who desire to be Christians and regard themselves as followers of Christ but who have not yet been contacted or initiated (catechumenate and baptism) by the churches, because the latter are quite incapable of handling the huge numbers involved. In many Third-World countries where there is a wide difference between Christianity and the local culture or cultures, there is also the serious problem of existing churches being unsuitable for the reception of new converts. A preliminary article written for the 1978 Asian Leadership Conference on Evangelism explains it thus: 'Many who decide for Christ from non-Christian backgrounds do not become members of the Church in the fellowship of believers... There are several factors hindering the new believers from becoming members of the visible church... In certain cases the new disciples often find it difficult to identify with the existing Christians for social reasons... Uprooting people from their cultures and transposing them into another culture makes it socially difficult for many Asians to become Christians' (George Samuel, 'Nurture the harvest', *Asia's harvest* (ALCOE Newsbulletin), 4 (1978), 1).

Another reason for the existence of large numbers in this category of nominal Christians is that census figures include large numbers of dispersed, or isolated, or scattered Christians, families and groups, including recently-moved or -migrated persons and groups, who are unaffiliated, or not yet affiliated, to churches for a variety of reasons such as a local absence of churches using their own language, or their very recent arrival, and so on.

For all these reasons, the term 'nominal' is therefore used here in its strictly correct or literal sense, i.e. persons who (for whatever reason, good or bad) are at present Christians in name only (viewed from the standpoint of the churches).

Two other variants of affiliation are used in this survey, and will shortly be defined: doubly-affiliated (to 2 denominations at once), and disaffiliated (baptized Christians who have since or recently become professing agnostics or atheists).

'Roll-cleaning' has an important bearing on the size of affiliated membership. Large established or state churches seldom or never 'clean their rolls' (i.e. remove names no longer known to them, or names of members who have left, died, migrated or apostatized). Through not cleaning its rolls regularly and realistically, the Roman Catholic Church in particular has on its rolls vast numbers of names of former Catholics who are now no longer members in any sense. An example of such inflated totals is the so-called 'Red Region' of Emilia-Romagna in Italy. Polls show that its population is heavily communist, 4% being atheists and another 15% agnostics; but *Annuario Pontificio* (1975) reports that this population, roughly coterminous with the Archdiocese of Bologna, is 99.5% Roman Catholics affiliated to the archdiocese. There is of course truth in this, in that the 99.5% in all probability were at one time baptized Catholics; now, however, 20% have disaffiliated themselves. We take care of this phenomenon in our tables with a clearly-defined category which we term 'disaffiliated'. A fuller definition of the latter will shortly be given.

### 5. *Practice*

Affiliated Christians may be sub-divided into 2 categories — practising Christians, and non-practising Christians — depending on whether or not they take any part in the ongoing organized life of the churches. PRACTISING CHRISTIANS are affiliated Christians who are involved in or active in or participate in the institutional or organized life of the churches they are affiliated to; or who are regarded by their churches as practising members because they fulfil their churches' minimum annual attendance obligations or other membership requirements; or who in some way take a recognized part in the churches' ongoing practice of Christianity. Thus in the Church of Scotland, 'active communicants' are defined as persons who communicate (receive communion) at least

once a year. In 1939, this was 76.8% of all communicants on the rolls, 56.7% in 1943, 72.0% in 1946, and 71.3% in 1959. In the Coptic Orthodox Church (Egypt), a 'practising Copt' is one who receives communion at least once every 40 days. Sometimes there is a financial connotation; some denominations only count as practising those adult members who contribute each year to local or central church funds. Certain denominations publish detailed definitions: thus the Christian Church (Disciples of Christ) in the USA explains 'A "participating" member is one who exercises a continuing interest in one or more of the following ways: Attendance, giving, activity, spiritual concern for the fellowship of the congregation regardless of the place of residence; a "non-participating" member is one who exercises no interest in the fellowship of the congregation regardless of place of residence' (Classification of church membership, General Assembly Resolution No. 57, Detroit 1964). The broadest meaning of the term is of annual church attenders, those who attend a service of public worship (within the ordinary pattern of institutional religion) at least once a year regularly; it excludes those who only

attend church on special private family or personal occasions (baptisms, weddings, funerals), or only on civic occasions or state festivals, but it includes all persons who listen to services only over radio and TV (bearing in mind that countless elderly, infirm, sick and handicapped persons who cannot attend church nevertheless listen or view regularly, and that in vast numbers of places where churches are not accessible (e.g. Norway, Africa, oceans) radio/TV services are the only possible form of attendance). In many larger Protestant churches, statistics of affiliated members tend to be close to those of practising members; in other words, their definition of membership is those who partake of communion at least once a year. Similarly, in many smaller Protestant churches, affiliated members means those who attend regularly or even weekly.

NON-PRACTISING CHRISTIANS, in contrast, are affiliated Christians who take no part in their churches' ongoing activities, and who are inactive and non-attending, or who describe themselves as such. They are sometimes termed dormant Christians.

### 6. *Church attendance*

Practising Christians may also be termed active, attending, committed or militant Christians, and may be sub-divided into several mutually-exclusive categories of attending Christians, as shown in the diagram, page 49. This information is often obtainable in part from polls data. It covers the 8 main types of

attenders shown in the diagram, which may be listed as follows in decreasing order of participation: those who attend church services several times a week (daily attenders); those who attend church services every Sunday, or Saturday (weekly or Sunday attenders); those who go only twice a month (fortnightly attenders); those who go only once a month (monthly attenders); those who, for reasons of age, infirmity, sickness or in the absence of local churches, in place of church attendance listen regularly to Sunday radio/TV services every week or once a month (radio/TV service listeners); those who attend church on church festivals only (festival attenders); those who attend from time to time or irregularly, i.e. at most 2 or 3 times a year (occasional attenders); and those who attend or take communion once a year only, often at Christmas or Easter only (annual attenders). As explained above, our definition of practising Christians excludes 2 further categories: civic attenders, i.e. those who attend church services only on civic occasions or state festivals, and private attenders, i.e. those who attend church services only for special private family occasions (baptisms, weddings, funerals). In the Western world, this

**Practising Christians.** One widespread method of counting practising Christians is to know the total seatings (number of seats) in a church building and then to estimate what percent remain unfilled. *Top.* In Full Gospel Central Church in Seoul, Korea, 22,000 people were thus counted at 3 services daily at 1974 missions convention. *Above.* Another method, following Jesus (Mark 6.40), is to make people sit in 50s or 100s, as here with 5,000 at AACJM service, Harare, Zimbabwe. *Left.* A third method of counting crowds is by estimating the number of persons to one square metre; here, 5,000 at Easter 1938 mass in Mugera, Urundi.

latter type of attendance is sometimes irreverently termed '4-wheeler religion' because the main participants enter church only when wheeled in in prams, wedding cars, or hearses. Care should be taken in examining a poll to see whether its categories are intended to be distinct, mutually-exclusive and non-overlapping (this being the usual situation), or whether they overlap in a cumulative manner; 'annual attenders' in a poll may mean either those who attend only once a year, or the aggregate of all who attend once a year (including those who attend monthly, fortnightly, weekly, daily). On average across the world, Christians attending once a month or more are usually well over half the size of the total of practising Christians. In this Encyclopedia, 'practising' percentages always mean % of *affiliated* Christians (as shown in italics in Tables 1; and in Tables 2 column 8, where P = % practising every year, and W = % practising every week, i.e. Sunday attenders); this is because only affiliated Christians can reasonably be expected to practise.

*Attending non-members.* There are 2 further types of church attender that are excluded from our category of practising Christians. The first are attending non-members, i.e. nominal Christians (who by definition are non-church-members) who occasionally or in some cases regularly attend church services. Such individuals are relatively few in number and are sufficiently negligible in aggregate not to be shown specifically in our Tables 1.

*Attending non-Christians.* The second type are attending non-Christians, i.e. persons who attend church services regularly or occasionally, being interested in Christianity, but who are still non-Christians (pagans, Muslims, Hindus, etc). In areas of the world where Christianity is expanding rapidly, large numbers of non-Christians attend church every Sunday as potential converts. This is particularly the case in Black Africa, such as in TEKAN in the Central Belt of Nigeria, in the Tiv Church, and elsewhere in the tropics. All such persons are not included in our category of practising Christians, and in Tables 1 they are included only under their own religions at the times indicated.

## 7. Belief

The foregoing categories of Christians describe the external, visible, observable status of Christianity. However, these categories of themselves can say little or nothing about the inner quality of Christian faith or discipleship, or about faith and belief. For this reason, several Christian traditions go further and are only interested in reporting statistics of 'believing Christians', 'real Christians', 'committed Christians', 'converted Christians', 'nuclear Christians', 'authentic Christians', 'born-again Christians', and so on. Accordingly, we add a last line to the diagram: Christians may be divided into COMMITTED, PARTIALLY-COMMITTED and UNCOMMITTED CHRISTIANS. The term committed can be defined in many different ways; one way, as shown in the diagram, is to regard regular attenders (once a month or more) as the committed nucleus. Unfortunately, all categories of commitment are too subjective to enumerate fairly or scientifically, and so they have to be excluded from Tables 1 and 2. Attempts have been made,

**Belief.** 'Do you believe that Jesus Christ is the Son of God?' Gallup Poll interviewer (left) conducts one of 1,500 detailed interviews on which biennial *Religion in America* (Gallup Opinion Index) is based.

however, to probe deeper and to quantify certain aspects of belief and faith, using public-opinion polls. The most revealingly personal question on belief that has been asked is, perhaps, 'Do you consider that you have been born again (as a Christian)?', 'Do you consider yourself a born-again Christian?', and other variants. The experience of new birth is here defined as a turning point in life when one commits oneself to Christ as Saviour and Lord. To this question in 1976 in Norway, 18% of all Norwegians replied Yes (27% for all young people), and in the USA 34% of all adults (50% of all professing Protestants, 18% of all professing Catholics) (Gallup). Using our definitions of professing, affiliated and practising Christians, and their values for the USA in Tables 1, this means that in the USA 49% of all practising Christians (and 72% of all practising Protestants) define themselves as born-again Christians. What these figures indicate is that, although statistics of belief and commitment on a world scale are unavailable and not likely to become available, existing statistics of profession, affiliation and practice may be taken as a reasonably reliable indicator of the presence of belief and commitment. On the world scale, it is probable that some 40% of all adult practising Christians would claim this experience of new birth. Children and infants, once again, should be enumerated with their parents, so that one can extend this latter sentence to say that 40% of all practising Christians of all ages belong to a self-identifying born-again Christian community. Because this and similar questions have only been asked in a handful of nations, all industrialized, these data are not here systematically documented in Tables 1, but are given in detail in Part 9, Survey Dictionary, under the entry BELIEF.

## Pilgrimages

An important aspect of practising Christianity is religious tourism, travel and pilgrimages. There are

vast numbers of local, national and international shrines and pilgrimage centres across the world, involving huge numbers of persons, and involving Roman Catholic, Orthodox, Anglican, Protestant and indigenous blocs. The total of Christian pilgrims each year is estimated at over 90 million; i.e. 7% of all Christians are on the move as pilgrims every year. A small selection of the major pilgrimage centres described in this Encyclopedia is as follows:

Ankaramalaza (Madagascar),
Aparecida (Brazil; around 1 million a year),
Ars (France),
Bethlehem (Palestine),
Cartago (Costa Rica),
Croagh Patrick (Ireland),
Czestochowa (Poland; 5.5 million a year),
Echmiadzin (USSR),
Einsiedeln (Switzerland; 150,000 a year in the year 1900),

**Pilgrims.** *Above.* Largest church in South America, new Basilica of Our Lady (Archdiocese of Aparecida, Brazil), receives 1.5 million pilgrims a year, with hundreds of busloads arriving every week. Some 7% of the world's Christians (90 millions) are on the move as pilgrims every year. *Below.* Basilica of Our Lady of Ireland, Knock, housing 15,000.

Ekuphakameni (South Africa),
Farihimena (Madagascar; 1 million from 1947–51),
Fatima (Portugal; 400,000 a year, rising to 1 million in 1967),
Goa (India; 1 million a year),
Guadalupe (Mexico; 2 million a year),
Jerusalem (Palestine; over 300,000 a year),
Kiev (USSR; 1.2 million a year in 1886),
Knock (Ireland, since 1879; 1 million a year),
La Salette (France),
Lisieux (France; over 1 million a year),
Lourdes (France; 4.8 million a year, with peak of 8 million in 1958),
Luján (Argentina; 2 million a year),
Luxembourg (40,000 annually),
Meskuiciai (Hill of Crosses, Lithuania),
Montserrat (Spain; 1.3 million a year),
Morija (South Africa),
Nineveh (Kenya),
Nkamba-Jerusalem (Zaire),
Palma Sola (Dominican Republic),

Penha (Brazil),
Rome (first Holy Year in AD 1300, 200,000 pilgrims; 1950, 2.5 million; 1975 Holy Year 8,370,000),
Taizé (France),
Turin (Italy; 3.3 million visiting Holy Shroud from September-October 1978),
Velankanni (India; over 1 million a year),
Walsingham (UK),
Zagorsk (USSR),
Zante (Greece).

### Inclusive and exclusive definitions

From page 49's diagram and definitions, it may be seen that several categories overlap, and several are mutually exclusive. The grand total of all Christians, on this definition, can be counted in 2 ways: (1) from the state's standpoint, as the total of professing and crypto-Christians, or (2) from the churches' standpoint, as the total of nominal and affiliated Christians. Crypto-Christians are always affiliated (never nominal); and nominal Christians are always professing Christians (never crypto-Christians). Similarly, a professing Christian may at the same time be an affiliated Christian and also a practising Christian. But a nominal Christian cannot at the same time be an affiliated Christian, nor a practising Christian; nor indeed can he be a non-practising Christian either. To avoid confusion, therefore, great care must be exercised in the exact choice of the terms one wishes to use.

### Mutually-exclusive adherence

In the same way, this survey uses its terminology for followers of other religions in a mutually-exclusive sense. A person is either a Christian, or a Hindu, or a Muslim, or an atheist, or something else, but he cannot be enumerated here as more than one of these at any given time. We recognize that there are many independent individuals who like to think of themselves as having 2, 3, 4 or even more of these labels simultaneously. However, we would reply that (1) no government census in any country gives such individuals the option of a multiple choice, (2) such individuals are extremely few in number, (3) the vast majority of people in virtually all countries can be clearly described by a single term each, and (4) our survey is a demographic one describing broad populations rather than exceptional individuals. To this extent our use of mutually-exclusive categories is justified.

## QUANTIFYING RELIGIOUS CHANGE

The world religious situation is far from static; change is continual, old religions are waning and new religions are arising. Surges of conversions from one religion to another are constantly taking place; many churches are expanding numerically, others are declining. This survey investigates changes over time in certain quantifiable aspects of church life. It attempts to document this in every country, firstly by compiling statistics for definite years (particularly mid-1970 and mid-1975), and secondly by giving annual rates of increase or decrease for all religions (in Tables 1, as described below) and for numerous individual churches (in Tables 2, column 8, as described below).

Religion, race and society are in fact not dead mosaics or fixed and unchanging patchworks. They are living and active entities constantly changing in a ceaseless flux of action and reaction. We take account of all this in our survey by incorporating into our texts and tables not only religious change but also indicators of societal, demographic and ethnolinguistic change.

### Measuring growth rates

The rates of growth, increase, decrease or decline of membership in many churches can readily be measured from their annually-reported statistics. In this survey this has been done by obtaining the statistics for 2 different years, where possible 5 years apart (to minimize the effects of roll-cleaning and other annual irregularities), usually 1967 and 1972, and working out the average annual growth rate as a percentage. Great care must be taken in such computations to ensure that the statistics used are measuring exactly the same entity (especially geographically) for each of the 2 years concerned. Growth, as per cent increase or decrease per year, must be measured by dividing any annual increase by the identical category of total. Thus a church in a particular country with 500,000 total adherents (including children) in 1967 which grows to 600,000 total adherents (including children) in 1972 shows an increase of 600,000 minus 500,000 = 100,000, which divided by 5 = 20,000 a year, which divided by the mean membership of 550,000 gives an increase rate of 3.64% per year. This is expressed in coded form in Table 2, column 8, as G=3.6%pa; values are given to only one place of decimals because the data in most cases do not permit a greater claim to accuracy. Negative values (e.g. G=–1.0%pa) indicate that a body is decreasing or declining annually. For each country, the nett totals of all such changes in affiliation for the period 1967–72 were then calculated or estimated, then modified to apply to the decade 1970–80. The statistics of Christians in the column 'Total' were then compiled under 'Annual change, 1970–80' in all Tables 1. The same was done for non-Christian religions, in most cases by comparing censuses or polls over 5- or 10-year periods. Where no other data were available, for some countries censuses of 1900 and 1970 were available from which century-long trends could be established.

There are several different ways of measuring the growth of a church or body. Firstly, one can measure either adults only, or total community including children; in Tables 1 and 2 we always use the latter. Secondly, the growth rate of a church or religious grouping can be measured over a single day, or a month, a year, a decade, or 50 years—and all will yield differing results. In this survey we are concerned primarily to measure long-term rates, i.e. rates over 4–5 years in Tables 2, column 8, and rates over the decade 1970–80 in Tables 1. A growth rate measured for a specific church over 1970–73 may not be sustained throughout the decade, which explains differences in rates for the same church obtained at different times.

*Checking for plausibility*
A certain amount of religious change or church growth claimed by some bodies is unlikely, implausible, exaggerated or even physically impossible. Logarithmic graph paper provides a quick method of checking on the plausibility of any time series of figures of church or population growth. One simply plots the claimed figures on a graph against time. The resulting lines will have to be reasonably linear, or slightly curvilinear, to be credible or plausible. In this sense, log paper is a far more valuable analytical tool than ordinary graph paper.

*Demographic inertia*
Before proceeding to analyse annual change into the 2 major component parts utilized in this survey, we should note an important principle affecting the growth and evolution of populations: large populations only change their basic characteristics gradually or slowly. This demographic inertia is a concept from demography, based on the observable fact that changes in the fertility rate take several decades before they have any effect on the growth rate of a population. In fact, any time-series based on large-scale phenomena, particularly populations in the millions, will behave in a relatively stable manner. This has a useful consequence for missiographers constructing tables describing a country's religious evolution over the decades, in that a study of regular series of government censuses of religion in a country (such as Table 9 and its facing page in *1971 Census of Canada: religious denominations*, p. 9-1, for the years 1921-71) leads to an important generalization: The percentage size of a religious community or population in a country does not change appreciably over the years from one census to the next, even when total population is increasing rapidly, unless (a) large-scale conversions are taking place within the community to or from another religion, or (b) its fertility or biological increase rate is markedly different from the national average, or (c) mass emigration or immigration is under way in the community, or (d) an anti-religious revolution takes place in the country, or (e) religious belief within the community is severely eroded by secularism. In the Western world, the percentage figures for particular religions usually remain unchanged from year to year, or change relatively slowly. In the Communist world, percentages change little from one year to the next except as a result of anti-religious revolutions and resulting mass defections or emigrations; and in the Third World, annual increases are gradually taking place in the % Christian of many populations due to mass conversions and long-term missionary activity over the decades.

*Natural change*
The total annual numerical change (growth or decline) of a religious body or grouping in a particular country is composed of 2 quite different types of change which it is important to identify and to separate. The first is (1) *natural change*, which is change as experienced by the whole population of the country concerned, including all religious bodies, and over which religious bodies have, relatively, little or no control. This natural or demographic change is itself composed of 2 parts, (a) biological change (in UN terminology, 'natural' increase or decrease), which is change due to natural causes properly so called, i.e. the annual nett aggregate of births to members of the body minus deaths in it; together with (b) migration change (sometimes termed transfer change), which is the annual nett aggregate of immigration into the body (arrival or transfer of members or co-religionists from other countries) minus emigration out of it

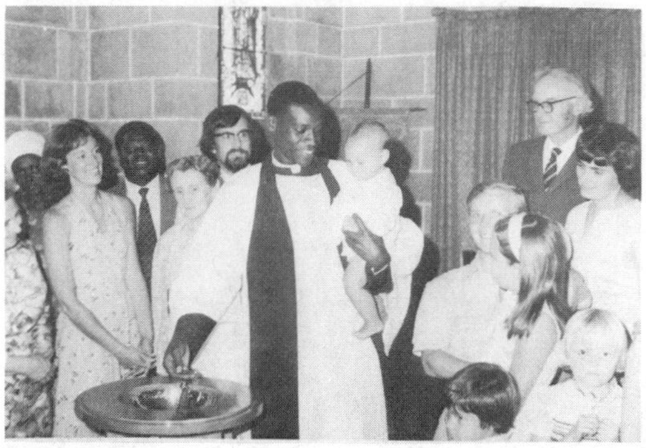

**Natural change.** *Above.* (a) *Biological change.* Claire Elizabeth, infant of 2 Anglican believers, is baptized at All Saints Cathedral, Nairobi in January 1976. All churches experience such biological growth.
**Natural change.** *Right.* (b) *Migration change.* Forest Gate (London) congregation of Holy Order of Cherubim & Seraphim Church, largest African denomination in Britain. The church and its Yoruba members migrated from Nigeria to UK from 1965.

(departure or transfer of members or co-religionists to other countries). Natural change, consisting of these 2 types together, has been calculated for each country in the world in the UN publication, *World population prospects, 1970–2000, as assessed in 1973* (New York: UN, March 1975). In our survey, this rate for the period 1975–80 (UN projection) is given under SECULAR DATA at the head of each country's survey article, broken down into its 3 component parts; the rate may differ slightly from that on the bottom row of Table 1 because the latter is the average for the whole decade 1970–80. All churches in all parts of the world experience biological increase nowadays, though rarely are they aware of it as a cause of their growth. All churches also experience on a small scale the continual ebb and flow of migration, as their members move from one country to another, but in only a few cases is the migration change large enough to warrant comparison with biological change. In all Tables 1, these nett annual changes are shown for all religions as well as countries in the column 'Natural' under 'Annual change, 1970–1980'. When a figure in this column is negative, it means either that deaths are outstripping births, or that nett emigration is outstripping any natural biological increase, or some combination thereof.

*Conversion change*
The natural change just described involves no change in religious allegiance or adherence; from the churches point of view, it is 'natural' because it represents the state of affairs existing before religious conversions take place. There is therefore a second type of change which occurs when changes in religious allegiance or adherence do take place, i.e. when people leave one religion and join another. Depending on the observer's point of view, this can be called unnatural, non-natural or even supranatural or supernatural change. In this survey, we term it (2) *conversion change*, defined here as consisting entirely of changes in religious allegiance, i.e. the annual nett aggregate of conversions to the body of new adherents from other religions or religious bodies, minus defections (sometimes termed apostasies) from it of former adherents leaving to join other religions or religious bodies, or abandoning religion altogether. A large majority of churches in the Third World are experiencing conversion increase nowadays, whilst in the Western world many older denominations are experiencing conversion decrease as former members withdraw from affiliation, usually into non-religion. In all Tables 1, these nett annual changes are shown for all countries and religions in the column 'Conversion' under 'Annual change, 1970–1980'.

It should be carefully noted that our category 'conversions' does not carry here exactly the same theological and evangelistic connotations usually attributed to the term in Christian parlance and scholarship. Rather, our term refers to transfers of allegiance from one religion to another, or from one Christian bloc to another, or from one type of Christian (e.g. 'practising') to another (e.g. 'non-practising'), or from religious to non-religious, and so on. 'Conversion' here includes changes of religious profession due to mixed marriages, one of the commonest causes where Islam and other world religions are involved with Christianity.

*Total=natural+conversion*
By asking, then, how much of the total annual change experienced by any particular religious body

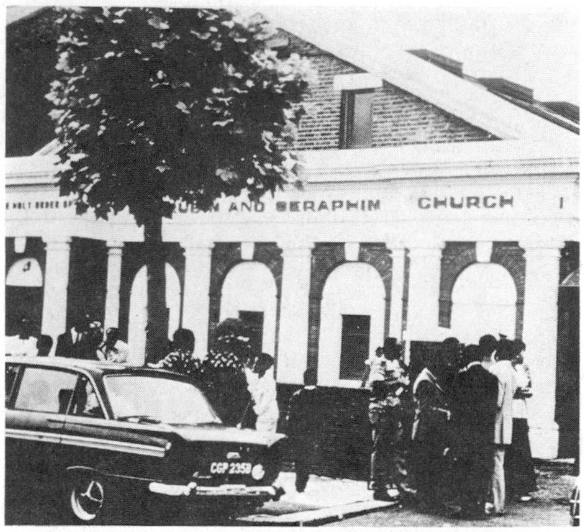


is due to natural biological causes, how much is due to migration, and how much is due to changes of religious allegiance or adherence, we arrive at the formula for annual change in the body:

**Total change=natural change+conversion change.**

In all Tables 1, these 3 types are given for all major religious groupings, giving the totals shown there for all countries and the totals for regions, continents and for the world shown in Parts 1 and 8.

In order therefore to assess whether a church or religious grouping is expanding by conversions or accretions and not simply by natural causes, we must compare its total growth rate with its biological or natural increase rate.

*Differential fertility, mortality and migration*
Because data are rarely available for religious bodies or groupings concerning the actual increase rate due to biological causes (births minus deaths), the assumption has been made in Tables 1 that all groups share the same natural increase rate as the national average, unless evidence to the contrary is available. In fact, certain groups have higher fertility than the average (e.g. Irish Roman Catholics in Britain; Blacks in the USA; Roman Catholics in 20th-century Switzerland and Holland; Muslims across Black Africa); and certain Christian bodies in certain countries in certain eras have experienced markedly-reduced mortality compared to that of the general population, due to the introduction of Western medicine (e.g. churches linked to Western missions in India and other developing nations). In general, however, our assumption is adequate for the tables' main purpose of establishing broad areas of magnitude. In the same way, unless specific information is available concerning the migration rate in religious blocs, this is assumed to parallel that of the nation or country. In several countries, however, for churches or blocs where these rates are vastly different from the national averages, higher fertility or different migration rates for certain religious groups have been included in Tables 1.

*Hidden changes*
An inevitable property of overall compilations of totals such as our Tables 1 and 2 is that many smaller internal increases or decreases are hidden or masked. Rapid growth of one body may be hidden in a government census if combined with rapid decline of another body of the same religion or ecclesiastical tradition,

**Conversion change.** (1) *Non-Christian. Left.* Three Kenya Africans (garlanded) become Hindus at Arya Samaj temple, Nairobi. (2) *To Christianity. Far left.* Emerging from catechumenate class; some of Burundi's 160,000 Catholic catechumens who are in process of being converted from tribal religion to Christianity. *Below.* Mass dance, burning of fetishes and conversion to Christianity by 8,000 West Dani animists in pig fat and headdresses at Pyramid Mountain CMA station, Baliem, West Irian (Indonesia). 1960. 24,000 other Danis held fetish burnings at that time.

or in a different geographical area. Our column 'Annual change' in Tables 1 therefore shows not the entire picture of change but only the nett losses or gains of each religion or religious bloc.

### All totals are nett

As mentioned at various points above, it must again be remembered that all of our totals of change shown in the tables are nett totals, i.e. gains of all kinds (conversions/births/immigrants) minus losses of all kinds (apostasies/deaths/emigrants).

### Massive increases may be spurious

During our analysis of existing compilations of church growth data, we have occasionally found apparently large recorded increase rates for specific churches. On investigation these have proved to be spurious, being the results simply of better and more thorough data collection over the years. Such spurious increases have then been amended and replaced in our tables.

### A general idea of conversion

The whole object of the column 'Conversion' in Tables 1 is to give a very general idea of the broad order of magnitude of the long-term trends in religious change going on in the country during the decade 1970–1980. The figures given here add up to zero for each country, because conversions to one religion or religious grouping must always mean defections or losses from another religion or religious grouping. By examining this column, it is therefore possible to see where converts are coming from. For example, if Protestants are gaining 100,000 converts a year, and tribal religionists are losing 100,000 a year, and all other groups experience few or no conversions a year, then this is a clear case of a mass movement from tribal religion to Protestantism.

As will shortly be explained, the column 'Conversion' was not derived by direct measurement but was derived indirectly by computation. In order to keep the mathematics exact, the figures in the 3 columns under 'Annual change, 1970–1978' are all given to the nearest digit, so that columns and rows add up exactly; however, this must not be taken to imply any claim to bogus precision. A figure such as '1,937' under 'Conversion', therefore, should be taken to mean, and should be quoted to imply, only that something of

the order of 2 thousand people a year are joining that religion or grouping.

### Analysing annual baptisms

Another way of measuring religious change, this time for a single church or denomination, comes from analysing statistics of annual baptisms. For a large number of churches, these data are presented in Tables 2, column 8, and from them it is possible to see to what exent a church or denomination is keeping up with, or exceeding, or falling behind, the natural population increase (in the case of adult baptisms) and/or the birth rate (in the case of infant baptisms). To do this (for churches practising only adult baptism), divide the annual number of adult baptisms (coded Y in column 8) by column 6 (adult members); or (for churches practising infant baptism) divide the annual number of infant baptisms (coded y in column 8) by column 7 (total affiliated). The resulting rate, expressed as a % per year, can then be compared with, respectively, either the national natural population increase rate, or the national birth rate. If a church provides only figures for both adult and infant baptisms combined (as is usually the case with the Roman Catholic Church; coded Yy in column 8), and if this rate is appreciably higher than the birth rate in the country, then it means that substantial adult baptisms are taking place. At the national level, the annual religious change indicated by these data on baptisms for all churches is incorporated here in Tables 1 in the 2 columns 'Natural' and 'Conversion' increase.

### Statistics of new charismatic movements

In many parts of the world, new Christian movements are beginning and growing rapidly, the largest example being the global neo-pentecostal and charismatic movements within the major older denominations. Such groups have little time or opportunity for self-analysis, and usually keep neither statistics nor exact membership lists. Further, many movements exist within the structures of older denominations, value their close relations with them, and oppose the collecting of statistics as tending to artificially crystallize their identity and to appear to divide charismatics from their non-charismatic fellow-Christians. It must be emphasized here, therefore, that such

statistics as we provide in this survey serve merely as an aid to understanding the order of magnitude of the situation and its rapid evolution over the years, and should not be construed as conferring a separate or separatist identity on such movements.

### More elaborate analyses

Our analysis of religious change shown in Tables 1 in the 4 columns 'Annual change' gives an overall general idea of the dynamics of change in any country. In this survey, we have not gone into detail further than this. However, by subdividing the first 2 columns into 15 columns as shown in the suggested table layout below, the reader interested in more detailed analysis of any Christian bloc (Roman Catholic, Anglican, etc) can generate more elaborate tables to indicate even more clearly what is going on. In the expanded format shown below, our 4 basic columns from Tables 1 in this survey are shown as, respectively, the new columns 8, 15, 16 and 17. 'Natural Change' as defined in this survey can be divided into (a) 'Biological change' ('Births' minus 'Deaths') and (b) 'Migration change' or transfer change ('Immigrants' of the same Christian bloc who come into the area or grouping from another country, minus 'Emigrants' who leave the religion or grouping not by defection but by moving or being transferred to another country, these 2 categories encompassing adults, children and infants together). In the same way, Table 1's column 'Conversion change' can be divided into 'Converts' (total all individuals gained from other religions) and 'Defections' (total all individuals lost to other religions or to no religion); and 'Converts' can be subdivided into 'Adults' and 'Children and infants'. It is also possible at this point to introduce, with due care, churches' statistics of annual baptisms (both adult and infant), so that one may compare and correlate annual baptisms or conversion figures with the more generalized church growth figures given in Tables 1. Normally, infant baptisms relate solely to the infants enumerated in 'Births' below; and adult baptisms relate mainly to persons converted from outside. However, there are 2 major exceptions to this.(1) In the case of a paedobaptist or infant-baptizing church which is making many converts from outside, a number of infant baptisms will be of children of these new converts, which we have located below as column

SUGGESTED TABLE LAYOUT FOR FURTHER ANALYSIS OF A CHRISTIAN BLOC.

| Annual change, 1970–1985 | | | | | | | | | | | | | | | | |
|---|---|---|---|---|---|---|---|---|---|---|---|---|---|---|---|---|
| NATURAL CHANGE | | | | | | | | CONVERSION CHANGE | | | | | | | TOTAL CHANGE | RATE % per year |
| Biological change | | | | Migration Change | | | Nett change | Converts | | | | | Defections | Nett change | | |
| Births (New infants) | | Deaths | Increase | Immigrants | Emigrants | Increase | | Adult converts | | | Children and infants | | | | | |
| | | | | | | | | Adult baptisms | | New adults remaining unbaptized | Infant baptisms (children of converts) | Unbaptized | | | | |
| | | | | | | | | Outsiders | Grown church children | | | | | | | |
| Infant baptisms (children of church members) | New infants remaining unbaptized | | | | | | | | | | | | | | | |
| 1 | 2 | 3 | 4 | 5 | 6 | 7 | 8 | 9 | 10 | 11 | 12 | 13 | 14 | 15 | 16 | 17 |

12. Such a church's statistics of infant baptisms must therefore be apportioned between columns 1 and 12. (2) Likewise, in the case of a church which baptizes adults only (not infants) and which is relatively static, i.e. not making converts from outside, all of its baptisms are of existing church children only, i.e. children of long-standing members, who have grown up in the church over the years, but who were not baptized in infancy; these we have located below in column 10. Such a church's statistics of adult baptisms must therefore be apportioned between columns 9 and 10. This can be done by dividing the total of adult baptisms into the 2 further columns 'Outsiders' i.e. baptisms of persons previously completely outside the Christian bloc in question until their baptism this year, and 'Grown church children' (children of long-standing church members in traditions not practising infant baptism, who have now reached the age of adult baptism, usually 10–15 years old). These latter should not strictly speaking be termed 'Converts' but they are included here because 'Adult baptisms' in toto are often so termed.

Other refinements might include investigating differential fertility, mortality and migration, as described above. If these data can be found for each religion and bloc under consideration, the analysis could be made more exact.

In particular countries, the reader may wish to subdivide these columns even further, for instance by sex into males and females, or by age-groups, or by socio-economic groups, or by occupational groups, or by ethnic or linguistic groups, etc. If the data are available, the scope for more elaborate analyses, and therefore for deeper understanding of the whole process, is endless.

## ANALYSING WORLD STATISTICS

Statistics of Christians and of all religions in Part 7 (Tables 1 and 2) are arranged and coded in such a way that the reader can follow any or all of 5 main types of worldwide analysis, and 13 sub-types, depending on whichever are of interest or are valid to him, using the geopolitical and religious typologies and data in Global Table 31. The first 2 types below apply only to affiliated Christians in Tables 2; the rest apply to both Tables 1 and 2. World totals are shown analysed in these ways in Part 1; regional and continental totals are shown analysed in Part 8.

### 1. Ecclesiastical analysis
An important part of any description of a church or denomination is what its ecclesiastical tradition is. This information is given for each country for all denominations in Table 2, column 3 (the last 3 letters). This column lists in coded form 156 different ecclesiastical traditions (detailed in Codebook, Part 6), and world statistics of affiliated Christians are analysed in this way in Global Table 27, in Part 8.

### 2. Conciliar analysis
In Tables 2, column 4, information is given on the membership of the 5 main types of Christian council — confessional, global, continental, regional and national (see Codebook). Christians throughout the world can therefore be analysed according to the involvement or non-involvement of their churches in the different councils existing across the world; this also is done in Global Table 28, in Part 8.

### 3. Geopolitico-religious analysis
A major type of analysis is by groups of countries. There are many possible ways of classifying the 223 countries of the world, using geopolitical, or politico-religious, or purely religious typologies. In this Encyclopedia, we employ 10 sub-types or typologies based on 10 subjects; these will shortly be described. The codes used for them are given in the Codebook, and the information describing each country is given in Global Table 31. Using these typologies, Christians are analysed in the Global Tables in Part 8.

### 4. Ethnolinguistic analysis
In analysing the world's populations, it is important to see people not only as citizens or residents in a particular country, but also to see them as members of the basic homogeneous units to which they belong, and which usually have greater emotional hold over them than the tie of common citizenship. If we can see them thus, they can then more effectively be understood, described, enumerated, approached, reached, known, evangelized and eventually christianized. Such units are people of similar ethnic origin, or of

similar race or colour, or of similar culture, or of similar language, and so on. We do this in this Encyclopedia by employing an ethnolinguistic typology of homogeneous units, or of families or groupings of homogeneous units. Most of the ethnolinguistic units we employ can themselves be broken down further into yet more meaningful homogeneous units. The right place to do this, however, is not in a global survey such as ours but in detailed studies at the national and local level.

In the same way, Christians also may be classified according to their racial, ethnic, cultural and linguistic

**ADULT BAPTISM.** *Top, South Africa.* Baptism in a Zionist indigenous church.
*Left, Papua New Guinea.* Anglican baptism by Bishop Bevan Meredith in New Guinea Highlands river.
*Above, Burma.* Vast mass baptism of 6,215 converts in Irrawaddy river at Naung Nang, Myitkyina, in presence of 100,000 in December 1977 (Kachin Baptist Convention).

as well as national affiliations. This is done in Tables 2, column 8, for many individual churches, denominations and dioceses. It is also done under Tables 2 in the footnotes PEOPLES, for the Christian community as a whole, using the classification and code given in PEOPLES OF THE WORLD, in Part 4. Parallel data on the total secular population are given at the start of each country's survey article under SECULAR DATA. In consequence, the world's populations, and all Christians, can be analysed among the world's major ethnolinguistic homogeneous units, its families and peoples, and this is done in Global Tables 5, 24 and 25.

## SEVEN MAJOR ECCLESIASTICO-CULTURAL BLOCS

A further, fifth, type of description is what we call: 5. *Ecclesiastico-cultural analysis.* This brings us, finally, to a typology of Christians which is the most widely used by observers and scholars but which is also the least clearly defined. As a result we will now describe it in detail at this point, because we will have to coin and justify certain neologisms which will then be used throughout this Encyclopedia.

It has long been considered useful for many purposes to divide the world's Christians into major historico-cultural ecclesiastical blocs, coalitions or ongoing or enduring streams, based on historical, ecclesiastical, cultural and phenomenological con-

siderations. Of such ecclesiastico-cultural major blocs, the most widely recognized and used are the trio (1) *Roman Catholicism,* (2) *Orthodoxy* (both Eastern and Oriental), and (3) *Protestantism.* These are major de facto groupings which have arisen during the course of Christian history among peoples of different cultural areas and nationalities. Although often regarded as worldwide spiritual families, these blocs are not the result of merely religious or theological or spiritual affinities or differences; they incorporate deep nationalistic, ethnic, linguistic and cultural currents as well, as is illustrated from the

early history of the Oriental Orthodox churches: 'Adherence to completely incomprehensible dogmas, like the espousal of the Monophysite doctrine by great masses of people in the Orient and in Egypt, was the expression of an anti-imperial and anti-Hellenic separatist nationalism' (Max Weber, *The sociology of religion,* Boston: Beacon, 1963: 70–1). These 3 blocs are in fact differentiated by many such complex factors.

In any comprehensive survey of how Christians regard themselves, however, it soon becomes apparent that there are many large churches and denominations which do not define themselves under any of these 3 terms, and often reject all three. Since they thus cannot be fitted into the simple 3-fold typology, it means that yet other blocs must exist. Anglicans, for instance, do not regard themselves, as a whole, as either Protestants or Catholics, but regard themselves as forming an intermediate or bridge tradition; Jehovah's Witnesses do not regard themselves as Protestants or as part of main-line Protestantism; and Old Catholics reject any identity with Roman Catholicism. Consequently our survey recognizes the existence of 3 further distinct worldwide blocs or distinct enduring streams of Christianity: (4) *Anglicanism* (mainly the Anglican Communion and its 400 dioceses, originating in Britain around AD 100 and evolving since the 16th century its distinctive 'bridge' position intermediate between the Protestant and Roman Catholic positions), (5) *marginal Protest-*

# MARGINAL PROTESTANTS

This major ecclesiastico-cultural bloc is described on the opposite page, and overleaf.

*Left.* **Christian Scientists.** Christian Science Center, Boston (USA), world headquarters of Church of Christ, Scientist. Small church at upper right of pool: Original Edifice of the Mother Church, built 1894; abutting it, domed 4,000-seat Mother Church Extension, 1905; long colonnaded building to right, Publishing Society (Monitor), 1933; alongside pool, right, 5-storey Church Colonnade (radio/TV etc); top end of pool, 1,100-seat Sunday School, 1971; left, 29-storey Church Administration, 1975.

*Right.* **Unitarians.** Service held by Czechoslovak Unitarian Association, Prague. Unitarians were the earliest marginal Protestants, begun in Hungary in 1566, but have been declining worldwide since 1900. World headquarters are now in Boston (USA).

*Above.* **Jehovah's Witnesses.** Mass baptism of new converts 'accepting Jehovah God as their new owner', in Ruislip Lido, Middlesex (UK) in 1969, in which year 5,563 were baptized in Britain. World headquarters are in Brooklyn, NY (USA).

*Right.* **Mormons.** World headquarters of Church of Jesus Christ of Latter-day Saints, in Salt Lake City, Utah (USA). In foreground, Salt Lake Temple, finished 1893, which is used not for public worship but as school for esoteric teaching, baptism for the dead, and marriage for eternity; centre left, Mormon Tabernacle (1863-67) seating 10,000, with 10,000-pipe organ, home of 375-member Salt Lake Tabernacle Choir, possibly foremost choir on earth.

*antism* (para-Christian, quasi-Christian or tangentially-Christian deviations from mainline Protestantism claiming a second or supplementary or ongoing source of divine revelation in addition to the Bible, either a new revealed Book, or angelic visitations, or visions; these date from 1566 to the present day and include Unitarians, Jehovah's Witnesses, Christian Scientists, Mormons and vast numbers of other more recent movements), and (6) *Catholicism (non-Roman)* (Old Catholic and other autocephalous Catholic churches, and movements out of Protestantism which become sacramentalist and hierarchical churches, originating since 1724). Fuller definitions of these 3 additional blocs are given below under the section 'Table 1'. Between them, these 6 blocs cover almost all varieties of Christianity found in the Middle East, Europe and North America.

### Caucasian-initiated Christianity

Throughout its history, Christianity as represented by these 6 types or blocs or streams has been predominantly the religion of the Caucasian or Caucasoid race of peoples, as defined here in our classification PEOPLES OF THE WORLD, covering the Semitic, European, Indo-Iranian and related races. Caucasians have always exceeded 85% of all Christians until well into the 20th century, as is tabulated here in Part 1. By 1900 they were still 89%. Furthermore, throughout the last millenium Christianity has been predominantly the religion of the White peoples, rising from 61% of all Christians in the year 1000 to 93% in 1500 and only gradually falling to 81% by 1900.

In order to better understand and analyse this 6-fold typology of Christians, it is helpful to consider the evolution of Christianity in terms of its indigeneity, i.e. in terms of the main races and peoples among whom it has arisen as an indigenous religious movement. Indigenous churches are those that are native to a people, belonging naturally to the soil as contrasted with churches originating abroad or in an alien culture (*Little Oxford dictionary*). From this point of view, the history of Christianity and the current phenomenon of world Christianity can be described in terms of 3 distinct phases or groupings of indigenous churches, namely those related to Semitic, White, and Non-White peoples respectively. These will now be described in turn.

### 1. Indigenous Christianity among Semitic peoples

Christianity began in the 1st century among the Semitic peoples of the Middle East (defined here as Caucasians of the Middle Eastern geographical race). Four powerful Semitic indigenous church traditions resulted: Syrian Orthodox (later Arab), Coptic Orthodox (later Arab), Ancient Church of the East (Assyrian, later Nestorian), and in the 4th century AD, Ethiopian Orthodox (Amharic). Although dominant at the end of the 1st century AD (70% of all Christians) and numbering 46 million Christians by AD 500, these Semitic traditions later declined drastically to under 5% of all Christians by 1500 and to only 2% by 1650. Today their influence is relatively small (23 million Christians or 1.8% of the world total) and emanates from headquarters in the Arab world (Damascus, Cairo, Beirut, Baghdad) and in the racially-Caucasian Amharic world (Addis Ababa).

Semitic indigenous churches, as in existence today, may therefore be defined as those original ancient churches among the Semitic peoples dating from the 1st–5th centuries AD which are still in existence today as distinct denominations completely Semitic in membership and leadership (Syrian Orthodox, Coptic Orthodox, Ethiopian Orthodox, Nestorian), excluding those originally Semitic churches which have long since become predominantly White in membership and leadership (Catholic, Eastern Orthodox, etc).

### 2. Indigenous Christianity among White peoples

Europeans, the so-called White peoples, were present on the Day of Pentecost in AD 30 (proselytes from Rome, Cretans and others from Asia Minor — Acts 2.10–11). From then on they numbered about 5% of all Christians, rising by AD 100 to around 30%, and 38% by AD 500. By AD 1000, Whites numbered 61% of all Christians, and the focus and centre of gravity of Christianity's expansion had moved north and northwest into Europe, and it has remained there ever since. As a result, all of the above 6 ecclesiastico-cultural blocs are today predominantly European in origin, history, culture, theology, ideology, psychology, ethos, influence, numerical

**WORLD GROUPINGS OF INDIGENOUS CHURCHES: A 3-FOLD TYPOLOGY.**

*Top.* **Semitic indigenous churches** (begun from AD 30-400; now with only 1.8% of all Christians worldwide). At 1971 Coronation of Coptic Pope Shenouda III (left centre, in crown) in St Mark's Cathedral (Cairo), bishops gather from 4 ancient Middle Eastern Semitic churches begun from AD 30 onwards: Coptic Orthodox, Ethiopian Orthodox, Syrian Orthodox, and Assyrian; as well as from Armenian, Catholic, Eastern Orthodox, Protestant and other churches not or no longer mainly Semitic.

*Centre.* **White indigenous churches** (now 92.0% of all Christians worldwide). Liturgy celebrated by Greek Orthodox Bishop of Elasson in 13th-century Byzantine church in northern Thessaly. The Church of Greece is indigenous to Greeks (a White people) and dates from AD 50.

*Bottom.* **Non-White indigenous churches** (begun since AD 1500; now with 6.2% of all Christians worldwide). Baba Mtakatifu (Holy Father) Simeon Ondeto (right) blesses cardinals and faithful of Maria Legio of Africa (schism ex Rome in 1962), which is 90% Luo, in Western Kenya.

# WHITE—INITIATED CHRISTIANITY

**WHITE-INITIATED CHRISTIANITY (White indigenous churches).** Six of the world's 7 ecclesiastico-cultural major blocs are predominantly European (White) in origin, history, culture, membership and leadership, as is indicated by the cities (given first in capitals) where their world spiritual headquarters are.

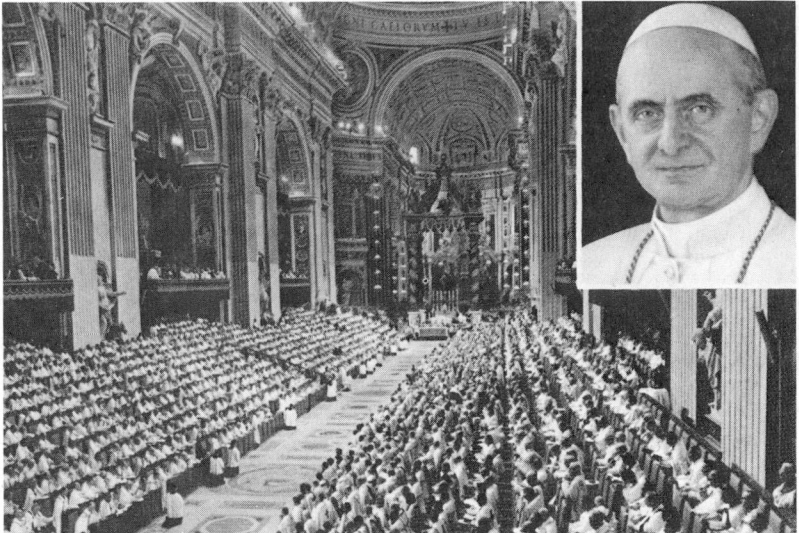

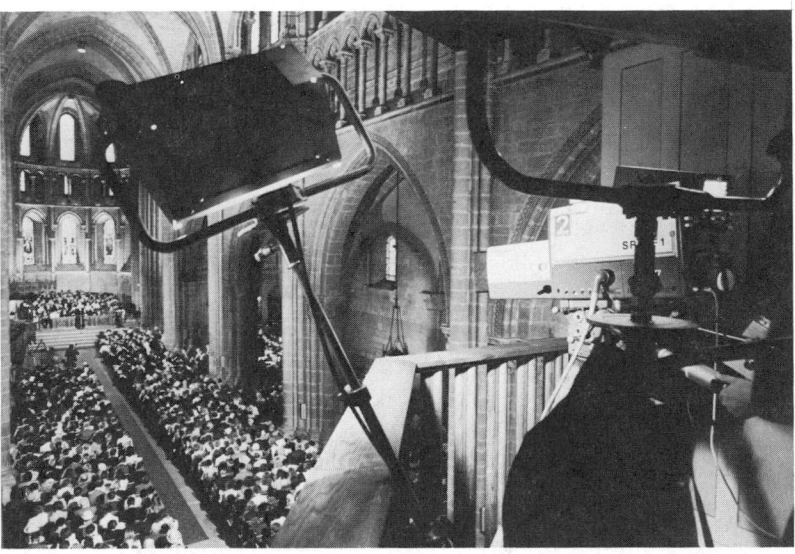

*Left.* **ROME. Roman Catholicism.** Second Vatican Council, 1962-65, attended by 2,200 bishops meets in St Peter's Basilica (Vatican City), presided over by His Holiness Pope Paul VI (inset), an Italian.

*Above.* **GENEVA. Protestantism.** 25th-anniversary celebrations in 1973 of World Council of Churches (whose constituents are 40% Protestants) in St Pierre Cathedral, Geneva (Switzerland), where Protestant reformer John Calvin (a Frenchman) laboured and preached.

*Above.* **CONSTANTINOPLE. Orthodoxy.** Eastern Orthodox liturgy concelebrated by Metropolitans at First Pan-orthodox Pre-conciliar Conference in Chambésy, November 1976. All are Caucasians or Whites, mostly Greeks or Slavs. From left to right: Dorothej of Prague; Archbishop of Cyprus; Stefan of Dalmatia (Yugoslavia); Germanos of Petra (Crete); Archbishop of Great Britain; Meliton of Chalcedon; Patriarch of Antioch; Philaret of Kiev; Patriarch of Romania; Alexandros of Peristerion (Greece); Nikodim of Sliven (Bulgaria); Paavali of Finland.

*Above.* **CANTERBURY. Anglicanism.** 11th Lambeth Conference in 1978 attended by 420 bishops meets in St Augustine's Cathedral, Canterbury (England), presided over by His Grace the Archbishop of Canterbury, an Englishman (centre top, in St Augustine's Chair). *Inset.* Archbishop Runcie of Canterbury.

*Above.* **BOSTON. Marginal Protestantism.** Christian Science Centre, Boston (USA), world HQ of Church of Christ, Scientist, founded by Mary Baker Eddy, a USA White.

*Above.* **DORTMUND. Catholicism (non-Roman)** Apostelversammlung (Council of Apostles) of 1.1 million-member New Apostolic Church meets at world HQ in Dortmund (Germany), with 48 living Apostles presided over by Chief Apostle (a German) with quasi-papal powers regarded as sole successor of Apostle Peter and visible representative or incarnation of Christ on earth.

significance, church organization, membership and leadership. From the point of view of race, their members belong predominantly to the European geographical race (including North America). From the point of view of colour, they are predominantly Whites. From the political point of view, all are predominantly centred either in the Western world or in the Communist world, and have their world spiritual headquarters and centres there. And from the developmental point of view, their main centres are predominantly in the richer and more developed countries.

This European or White Caucasian origin can readily be seen when one considers the origin, and place and date of origin, of each bloc, and the ongoing influence exerted by each. (1) Roman Catholicism worldwide traces its origin to Rome in the 1st century AD (its earliest beginnings being traced in our Tables 2 to AD 30) and is still controlled, guided and inspired from its centre in Vatican City, Rome, in Italy. (2) Eastern Orthodoxy worldwide traces its origin to the Holy Land itself and in our Tables 2 to AD 30 also; it still looks to Constantinople (the Second Rome) in European Turkey and Moscow (the Third Rome) in European Russia. The smaller grouping of Oriental Orthodoxy, which also traces its origin to AD 30 as shown in Tables 2, may be divided into a White part, with the Armenian Apostolic Church having its headquarters in Echmiadzin in Soviet Transcaucasia; and a Non-White although still Caucasian part, as we have seen above, consisting of the Semitic indigenous churches — the Syrian Orthodox, Coptic Orthodox, Ethiopian Orthodox and Assyrian traditions with their headquarters in the racially-Caucasian Semitic world (Damascus, Cairo, Addis Ababa, Baghdad, Beirut). Numerically these Non-White traditions are outnumbered 7 to one by the White Orthodox traditions. (3) Anglicanism worldwide traces its origins (as Tables 2 document) to Britain in AD 61, and to this day it still takes its inspiration from Canterbury and London, in England. (4) Protestantism worldwide is usually dated back to the 16th-century European Reformation in Geneva and Wittenberg, but, as our Tables 2 make clear, its origins in several of the major Protestant churches of Northern Europe go back in unbroken continuity a further 900 years, in fact to at least AD 690; as a bloc it continues to be inspired by German and Scandinavian Lutheranism, by the Dutch and Swiss Reformed traditions, by English Methodism, by the North American Baptist tradition, and a number of other White-initiated traditions. (5) Marginal Protestantism originated in Britain with the Unitarians in 1645, and today it has its major worldwide power centres in the USA (Brooklyn, Boston, Salt Lake City, etc). And lastly, (6) Catholicism (non-Roman) traces its origin to 1724 in the Netherlands and 1863 in Germany, and is still centred (Old Catholics) on Utrecht in Holland and (Catholic Apostolics) on Dortmund in Germany.

Since 1800, and over the last 100 years in particular, these 6 blocs have all demonstrated their vitality and initiative by expanding out from their bases in Europe and North America across the world to the Non-White races; and the churches begun there are still to a greater or lesser extent under their control or influence. The vitality and initiative of this missionary expansion have been, once again, predominantly from among the White races in European and North American churches.

The historical fact of European or White origin, initiative and ongoing influence must not however be equated with, or construed as, White imperialism or White racism. Non-Whites play important roles in these 6 blocs, firstly as members of their churches in Europe and North America, secondly as members and leaders of their daughter churches across the world, and thirdly through initiating new movements which remain within those churches (for example, the East African Revival movement within the Anglican and Protestant churches, or the large numbers of new African religious congregations for priests, brothers and sisters begun by Africans within the Roman Catholic Church). Despite all this, however, the overarching ethos remains both European and White; and the Black and Non-White daughter churches which have resulted, although in the case of almost all the largest churches now completely in the hands of local leadership, are still sufficiently close to their parent bodies (and often closely tied to them or controlled by them or influenced by them in theology, ideology, polity and organization) for it to be correct to call them also, as they call themselves, by the terms Roman Catholic, or Protestant, or Anglican.

In sum, then, the 6 major blocs described above can still be described as predominantly Caucasian initiatives in origin, predominantly European and North American initiatives in origin, predominantly White initiatives indigenous to the White peoples in origin, predominantly found in the richer and more developed countries, and predominantly based in the Western and Communist worlds. They represent expressions of Christianity indigenous originally and primarily to Caucasian, White, European peoples in the Western and Communist worlds of today.

### 3. *Indigenous Christianity among Black & Third-World peoples*

As far back as 1549 (Japan) and 1741 (USA), however, new types of Christianity have emerged that do not fit readily into any of these preceding 6 major blocs, and since 1900 they have rapidly become numerically increasingly significant on the world scale. These consist of denominations, churches and movements that have been initiated, founded, operated, led, controlled and spread not by Caucasian Whites or Europeans from today's Western or Communist worlds but by Black, Non-White or Non-European peoples from most of the major geographical races of what is now termed the Third World — Africans, Afro-Americans, American Indians, Asiatics, Mestizos, Northern Indians, Oceanic Negroes — with no dependence on European or North American White initiative, leadership, control, assistance or ties. In most cases these Black or Non-White bodies have been begun as schisms or secessions from, or have otherwise severed their relations with, White denominations belonging to the 6 Europe-initiated major blocs. Of these schisms the vast majority have broken off from Protestantism, although sizeable numbers have split from Roman Catholicism and Anglicanism, with some from the other 3 blocs also. The main characteristic common to all these bodies, and that which enables us to see in them a single, coherent new major bloc or stream parallel to the other 6, is that all were *begun on Black, Non-White or Non-European initiative, in Third-World countries or among Non-White or Non-European minorities elsewhere*, and since the year 1500. Subsequent to their Black or Third-World origin, they have had their own history; they remain without predominant White or Western control, influence or ties; they have Black or Third-World types of worship, spirituality and organization; in numerous circles they are developing Black or Third-World types of theology; and they have initiated their own foreign missions to many nations. This bloc or stream covers all Christian movements initiated anywhere by Non-Whites or Non-Europeans, without European assistance, mainly in the Third World but also among Black and Non-White minorities in the Western world. It includes the following: the African indigenous churches (African independent churches movement); similar independent or separatist churches in China, India, Indonesia, Japan, Korea, Latin America, the Philippines, and other Third-World countries; indigenous Christian movements in Oceania; American Indian indigenous churches in North America; Black indigenous churches in the Caribbean; and the Black churches of North America.

The Black churches of North America are particularly interesting in this connection because until recently they have always been classified as a part of North American Protestantism, and sometimes as little more than an unorthodox peripheral fringe around it. An examination of the magnitude of their statistics however suggests that this is an unsatisfactory assessment. In 1970, there were 22,580,000 Blacks (Negroes) in the USA; of these, 95% professed to be Christians (62% Baptists, 17% Methodists, 4% Roman Catholics, 1% Episcopalians, 1% Presbyterians, 1% Lutherans, with 9% independents and others), 1% Jews, 1% Muslims, and 3% nonreligious. The total of all Blacks affiliated to churches was about 20,770,000 (92% of the total Black population), of whom only about 8% of all Blacks were in predominantly-White denominations (800,000 Roman Catholics, 500,000 United Methodists, 130,000 SDAs, 95,000 Southern Baptists, 65,000 Episcopalians, etc), and even then were usually found in separate Black parishes or congregations. The rest of this vast body of Christians, 84% of all Blacks (18,929,000 in 1970), were and still are affiliated to independent Black churches and denominations which have separated or split from White churches over the preceding 200 years. These Black-led schisms were originally begun to liberate Black Christians from the effects of Protestant White racism, and today they continue as Black initiatives under Black leadership without dependence on White churches, creating their own distinctive forms of Christianity often related to their African religious heritage. The contrast can be expressed thus: White Protestant churches emphasize the literary tradition, formalized theology, and word-oriented or verbalistic worship; the Black churches emphasize emotion, soul, spontaneous non-literary spirituality, Black oral theology, and Black religious music (Negro Spirituals). Although the oldest of these churches (AMEC, AMEZC, NBCUSA, NBCA) have much in common with their White Protestant counterparts, many newer ones (including all Black pentecostals) have very little in common. Rather than being part of Protestantism, the Black pentecostals of the USA 'belong phenomenologically to the non-literary type of communication of the Third World while living in the literary culture of America' (W.J. Hollenweger, *The Black pentecostals' contribution to the church universal*, Geneva: WCC, 1970:11). So then, rather than to continue labelling these Black churches as Protestant, it would be preferable to regard them as sui generis or a new expression of Christianity and to coin a neologism to describe them. Within this new grouping, the AMEC and other older bodies thus would form a Protestant-type wing closer to Protestantism, and the pentecostals an African-type wing closer to their Third-World parallels.

In the same way, although many other Non-European churches in other countries have arisen out of and broken off from world Protestantism, they cannot properly still be called Protestant, and they themselves usually reject the term. Further bodies have broken off from one or other of the 5 other blocs, and these also cannot now properly still be called 'Roman Catholic', 'Anglican', 'Orthodox', etc. At the same time, the total adherents of all such bodies have by 1980 become numerically so significant (82 million) that they must be taken seriously as a new entity. So far it remains as a somewhat amor-

NON-WHITE INDIGENOUS CHRISTIANITY
(Black/Third-World indigenous Christianity)

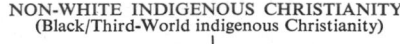

THIRD-WORLD INDIGENOUS

AFRICAN INDIGENOUS
sub-types:
Bantu indigenous
Coloured indigenous
Ethiopian indigenous
Ghanaian indigenous
Kenyan indigenous
Malagasy indigenous
Nigerian indigenous
Tribal indigenous
Yoruba indigenous
Zairian indigenous
(etc)

ASIAN INDIGENOUS
sub-types:
Arab indigenous
Bengali indigenous
Burmese indigenous
Chinese indigenous
Filipino indigenous
Indian indigenous
Indonesian indigenous
Japanese indigenous
Korean indigenous
Nepali indigenous
Pakistani indigenous
Sinhalese indigenous
(etc)

LATIN AMERICAN INDIGENOUS
sub-types:
Amerindian indigenous
Argentinian indigenous
Brazilian indigenous
Chilean indigenous
Colombian indigenous
Guatemalan indigenous
Mexican indigenous
Peruvian indigenous
Salvadorian indigenous
Venezuelan indigenous
(etc)

CARIBBEAN INDIGENOUS
sub-types:
Black indigenous
Cuban indigenous
Guyanan indigenous
Jamaican indigenous
Puerto Rican indigenous
West Indian indigenous
(etc)

PACIFIC INDIGENOUS
sub-types:
Aboriginal indigenous
Melanesian indigenous
Micronesian indigenous
Papuan indigenous
Polynesian indigenous

BLACK INDIGENOUS
(USA)

OTHER NON-WHITE INDIGENOUS
(USA, UK, etc)

Amerindian indigenous
(USA)

# NON-WHITE—INITIATED CHRISTIANITY
## (Non-White indigenous churches)

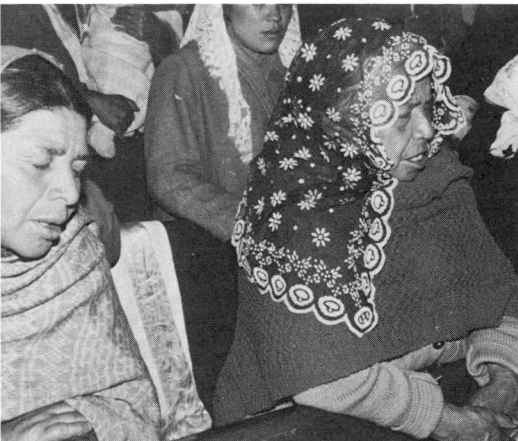

**Amerindian indigenous Christians.** Otomí Indians speaking in tongues in 350,000-strong Independent Pentecostal Christian Church, in Pachuca, Mexico.

**African indigenous Christians.** Pope and cardinals of Maria Legio of Africa (a schism ex Rome) in State House, Nairobi, with Cabinet Minister Hon. Tom Mboya (3rd from left), 1966.

**Latin American indigenous Christians.** Manoel de Mello, founder of 1.5 million-member OBPC (Brazil for Christ), in charismatic blessing of loaves before communion.

**Pacific indigenous Christians.** Member of Ratana Church (also Maori member of parliament) addresses NCCNZ (National Council of Churches in New Zealand) in Maori meeting house in Christchurch.

**Asian indigenous Christians.** World headquarters of True Jesus Church in Taichung (Taiwan), which sends Chinese missionaries across the world.

*Above.* **Caribbean indigenous Christians.** First United Church of Jesus Christ (Apostolic) in Birmingham (UK); members are Jesus-Only pentecostal emigrants from Jamaica's Bethel Apostolic (Shilo) Church.
*Right.* **Black indigenous Christians** (USA). Church of God in Christ (Black pentecostals); District and Field Worker missionaries of Eastern Louisiana (USA) with Supervisor, Mother McGregor Jones, in New Orleans.

phous entity, with as little in common between component parts as is the case with Protestantism itself; and so far there is little awareness of being an entity and no interest as yet in any kind of international meeting together, conferring or organizing. Nevertheless, the fact is that we are faced here with, at least in embryo, an entirely new historico-cultural major Christian bloc.

It is important too to note that this bloc, like the other 6, should not be considered as primarily a racist grouping, although racial in composition. Although Non-White, it is not anti-White. In many ways its churches are open to the White world. A growing number (e.g. the Black churches in Jamaica) send missionaries to White countries, and they and many others (e.g. the South African healing churches) attract sizeable numbers of White members and converts.

The problem arises of what to call this new ecclesiastico-cultural bloc. Whatever new terminology we attempt tentatively to coin and employ, there will always be critics. In the first place, there is no recognized ethnic or cultural term to refer collectively to the peoples outside Europe and North America, or all peoples other than the White peoples, and so the analyst who needs a single term has to resort (as we have had to above) to the somewhat negative terms 'Non-European' and 'Non-White'. Both these terms are unacceptable in many circles, since they define people negatively in terms of what they are not; to overcome this difficulty, we therefore coin, to parallel them, the somewhat cumbrous term Black/Third-World, referring to peoples native to the Third World and to the Black race in particular. We will still have occasionally to use the term Non-White in its technically correct descriptive sense, for example when referring collectively to Black and Chinese and Amerindian churches or peoples; for this reason, therefore, we use it capitalized (Non-White). Secondly, although these movements are often referred to locally as 'independent churches', we cannot name the new bloc 'Independent' because most bodies in the other 6 blocs are ecclesiastically independent also. Thirdly, we cannot use terms like 'Schismatic', 'Separatist' or 'Secessionist' because many of the movements we are analysing began de novo as new revival movements without schism or radical break, and also because such terms cannot be applied exclusively to Non-White movements since sizeable numbers of White schisms and secessions take place every year within the 6 European-initiated blocs. Other terms like Sundkler's South African typology Zionist/Ethiopian/Messianic are not sufficiently general to apply to more than local parts of this bloc.

*Locally-founded indigenous churches.* Another term widely used in the literature describing these movements is 'indigenous'. Correctly used, this word means 'originating or developing or produced naturally in a particular land or region or environment... not introduced directly or indirectly from the outside' (*Webster's third new international dictionary*, 1971). Indigenous churches may be defined as those originating within a country or race or people, or produced naturally by nationals of that country or members of that race or people, as opposed to churches of foreign or alien origin imported from abroad or introduced from outside the group, such as immigrant churches or mission-related churches. As used and defined here, this term says nothing about whether or not the peoples involved are indigenous to, or the original inhabitants of, the country they happen to be in; the term refers only to the production of Christian movements within their midst. The term also refers, further, only to churches of indigenous tradition; thus if the Roman Catholic or Anglican or Lutheran or Methodist church was begun in a particular country by native evangelists of that country (themselves indigenous to that country), we term them in this survey Roman Catholic or Anglican or Protestant, etcetera; their

resulting churches being of foreign rather than indigenous tradition. Indigenous churches are therefore, and are increasingly called today, locally-founded churches. Indigenous churches as defined thus can, strictly speaking, be either European or non-European, White or Black, although in the literature the predominant tendency is, for reasons of historical development, to limit the term to the Black and Non-White races. White secessionist churches in almost all cases regard themselves as having the same tradition as their parent bodies, albeit purified and reformed; by contrast, Third-World schismatic churches sit loosely to the denominational tradition or bloc of their parent bodies; they regard themselves as no longer Catholic, or Protestant, or Anglican, but as part of a new indigenous and independent bloc. All of the groups in this new 7th bloc can properly be called indigenous churches because they were begun in their own countries or among their own peoples by nationals of those countries or members of those peoples. Thus the True Jesus Church is a Chinese indigenous church begun in China by Chinese in 1917; it is strong among Chinese immigrants in Malaysia and in Brazil and in the USA, where it is still correct to call it a Chinese indigenous church. Similarly, the Black churches of the USA, all of which originated in Black-led schisms from White denominations, can properly be called Black indigenous churches in the sense that they were begun among the Black population in the USA by Black people who also happened to be USA nationals. They are indigenous to the Black people of the USA (which has no bearing on the fact that Blacks are not the indigenous peoples or original inhabitants of North America). In particular, USA Black pentecostals represent an indigenous initiative of major significance in that many authorities consider that around the year 1900 they initiated the entire Pentecostal world movement, even though from 1908 onwards in the USA it split into separate Black and White parts. As a result of considerations such as this, we find that we now have 2 adjectives with which to describe this whole new 7th bloc: Black/Third-World-initiated (or Non-White-initiated), and indigenous. Neither adjective by itself is sufficient, but together the 2 are adequate to differentiate the bloc from the preceding 6 blocs.

In this survey, therefore, and until a better or more concise term evolves, we term this new bloc (7) *Non-White or Black/Third-World indigenous Christianity*. On our definition, it consists of Black or Non-White or Non-European churches anywhere in the Third World or among Non-European or Non-White minorities in the Western world. It consists of churches all of which were formed by Non-Europeans since the year 1500, beginning in 1549 in Japan and 1741 in the USA but mostly since 1900, without European assistance or aid and often in the face of European opposition or hostility. It covers and includes African indigenous churches, Amerindian indigenous, Asian indigenous, Black indigenous, Chinese indigenous, Coloured indigenous (in Southern Africa), Filipino indigenous, Indian indigenous (in India), Indonesian indigenous, Japanese indigenous, Korean indigenous, Latin American (Mestizo) indigenous, Oceanic or Pacific indigenous, and other Third-World indigenous churches. It also includes their foreign missions working abroad in other countries. For convenience when discussing these movements in their own contexts we usually refer to them simply as 'indigenous churches' in contrast to the Protestant, Roman Catholic and other Western churches which often appear in those contexts as foreign, foreign-originated or foreign-dominated bodies.

In terms of our ethnolinguistic classification PEOPLES OF THE WORLD (Part 4), this new category of 'indigenous churches' refers to churches formed since AD 1500 and indigenous to any and all peoples and ethnolinguistic groups in any part of the world with

the sole exception of the White peoples, which our definition delineates as the European geographical race together with the Uralian family (Finns, Magyars, etc). The codes for these White peoples as shown in our classification are CEW and MSW.

The links between this large variety of new terms, all coined and used in this Encyclopedia, can best be depicted by means of the family tree on page 60. Almost all these terms are, on our definition, distinct and mutually exclusive categories which do not overlap. However, certain alternative or overlapping terms are sometimes used, such as Bantu indigenous which is part of the wider term African indigenous. Some of this whole range are local ethnic terms, some are geographical, some national, some regional, some continental and one or 2 are global terms. Progressively, these latter terms describe and embrace a range of the former, with at the top our single overall term covering the whole phenomenon.

*Seven major Christian blocs*
To sum up, when attempting to describe and analyse the Christian world in terms of a handful of ecclesiastico-cultural major blocs, the best criterion is to ask from whence the major or predominant initiatives and ongoing impulses came, and continue to come, and where they look to for their major or predominant world spiritual headquarters; who the initiating or dominant peoples are, and what ethnolinguistic families, races and colour, and what types of world, they belong to. We then arrive at the schema below, which is used in this Encyclopedia in Tables 1 and is given in coded form (shown below) for all denominations in Tables 2, column 3, first letter. With its aid we then obtain the analysis of the world's Christians presented in Global Tables 4, 23 et alia.

*World groupings of indigenous churches: a 3-fold typology*
The above schema may be summarized as follows. The world's Christian traditions may be divided into 3 distinct groupings of indigenous churches, respectively Semitic, White and Non-White. (1) Firstly, dating from the 1st century AD, there is the small grouping of Semitic Oriental Orthodox churches, i.e. Semitic (Non-White) initiatives or Middle Eastern indigenous churches. Today they form a minority of the larger ecclesiastico-cultural bloc of Orthodoxy, which is now predominantly White. (2) Secondly, arising over the 1st-20th centuries, there are the 6 ecclesiastico-cultural major blocs, which are predominantly White initiatives, i.e. predominantly White indigenous churches. (3) Thirdly, since the 16th century there has arisen the 7th bloc, Non-White indigenous Christianity, composed of more recent Non-White initiatives, i.e. Non-White indigenous churches begun since AD 1500.

*Description not evaluation*
We should stress again that the object of this survey is primarily descriptive, i.e. to describe as accurately and objectively as possible the actual state of affairs in all significant detail. It is not our purpose, here, to evaluate the authenticity of particular branches of Christianity. Thus the term 'Marginal Protestantism' just coined and defined above contains many movements claiming to be Christian but which, from the standpoint of mainline Catholic, Protestant, Anglican and Orthodox theology, are usually considered to be only pseudo-Christian, or heretical, or even not Christian at all. Examples are the many 'New Age cults' that have attained worldwide expansion in the 1970s. In this particular Encyclopedia we are not concerned either to expound their doctrines or to evaluate their Christian commitment, but only to point out that these movements claim to follow Jesus Christ and hence must be included in any objective world survey of the phenomenon called Christianity.

## DELINEATION OF THE WORLD'S 7 MAJOR ECCLESIASTICO-CULTURAL BLOCS

| BLOC OR STREAM OF CHRISTIANITY | CODE | BEGUN AD | WORLD SPIRITUAL HQS | INITIATING OR DOMINANT PEOPLES Peoples | Family | Race | Colour | PREDOMINANT WORLDS Political | Developed | Missions |
|---|---|---|---|---|---|---|---|---|---|---|
| 1. Roman Catholicism | R | 30 | Rome | Italians | Latin | European | White | Western | More | Sending |
| 2. Orthodoxy | O | 30 | Constantinople, Moscow, &c | Greeks, Slavs | Slavic | European | White | Communist | More | Non-sending |
| 3. Anglicanism | A | 61 | Canterbury, London | English | Germanic | European | White | Western | More | Sending |
| 4. Protestantism | P | 690 | Geneva, New York, &c | Germans, North Americans, &c | Germanic | European | White | Western | More | Sending |
| 5. Marginal Protestantism | M | 1566 | Boston, Brooklyn, Utah, &c | North Americans | Germanic | European | White | Western | More | Sending |
| 6. Catholicism (non-Roman) | C | 1724 | Utrecht, Dortmund | Dutch, Germans | Germanic | European | White | Western | More | Sending |
| 7. Non-White indigenous Christianity | I | 1549 | Africa/Asia/Black USA/&c | Blacks/Asiatics/Mestizos/&c | 44 others | Non-European | Non-White | Third* | Less | Receiving |

(*and Non-White minorities elsewhere)

# POPULAR RELIGION

**POPULAR RELIGION** (see text overleaf). This worldwide phenomenon occurs in 3 varieties. (1) **Non-Christian popular religion.** *Top left.* Figurines to protect fishermen in front of new Hindu temple in Lima village, Ketam island (Malaysia). *Top right.* Islamic popular religion in Jakarta. Indonesia has 300 syncretistic Muslim sects with 55 million adherents. (2) **Popular religiosity** (deviations among Roman Catholics). *Left centre.* Christo-paganism: Mayan shamans at work with crosses and pagan charms by and in lake Chicabal on top of volcano near Xelu (Central America). *(continued below)*

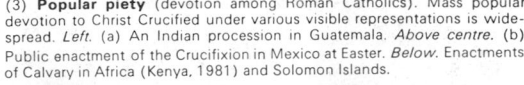

(3) **Popular piety** (devotion among Roman Catholics). Mass popular devotion to Christ Crucified under various visible representations is widespread. *Left.* (a) An Indian procession in Guatemala. *Above centre.* (b) Public enactment of the Crucifixion in Mexico at Easter. *Below.* Enactments of Calvary in Africa (Kenya, 1981) and Solomon Islands.

**NEW CHARISMATIC MOVEMENTS.** Charismatics worldwide have adopted the orant/orante position for prayer (standing upright with raised arms), standard attitude of prayer adopted by early Christians (see Early Christian art, 2nd-6th centuries, especially in Roman catacombs). *Left.* **Neo-pentecostals** (charismatics within non-Pentecostal Protestant denominations) numbered 4,287,000 worldwide by 1980. From very numerous denominations, they often worship with Catholics and Black neo-pentecostals (as here). *Row below.* **Roman Catholic pentecostals** or Catholic charismatics numbered 4,771,000 worldwide by 1980, including *(below)* some 15,000 priests, *(centre)* 50,000 nuns, *(centre left)* 8,000 monks; and several hundred bishops and cardinals. Although expanding phenomenally in numbers, the Renewal's major problem is the enormous turnover in active members. *Bottom.* **Anglican pentecostals,** of whom 3,000 are shown here at 1973 2nd Festival of Praise in Worcester Cathedral (Church of England), numbered 1,090,000 worldwide by 1980. **Orthodox pentecostals** numbered 157,000 worldwide in 1980; *bottom left,* 2nd Annual Orthodox Charismatic Conference, Ann Arbor (USA), July 1974; *inset,* Russian Orthodox charismatic.

# NEW MOVEMENTS

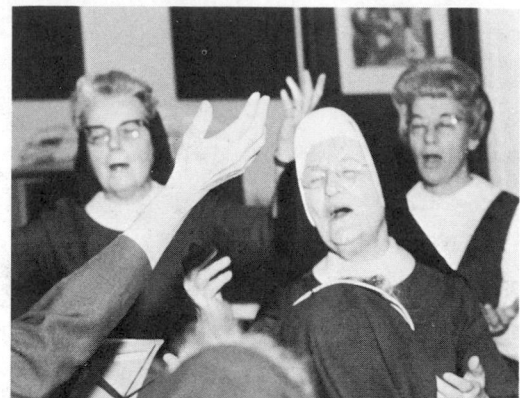

## ECCLESIASTICO-CULTURAL MINOR BLOCS

Within the first 4 of the 7 major ecclesiastico-cultural blocs just described, there are large numbers of Christians who form distinct and clearly-defined sub-blocs or minor blocs, which in consequence are described and often also enumerated in this Encyclopedia. These will now be described under the 3 headings (a) popular religiosity, (b) popular piety, and (c) charismatic and Evangelical renewals. The first 2 of these are here collectively termed popular religion, religion of the masses, or religious manifestations of the people, terms which also cover non-Christian religions. Among christianized manifestations, term (a) refers to deviant versions of popular religion of Christian background, and term (b) refers to more orthodox or recognizably-Christian versions. These various terms will now be described

### Non-Christian popular religion

The term popular religion is generally used to cover the universal phenomenon of widespread or popular expressions or varieties of religion, including both Christian forms and also specifically non-Christian forms such as animism, Chinese folk-religion, Bhakti Hinduism, folk Hinduism, Boddhisattva Buddhism, and so on. These varieties are characterized by a deep sense of the presence of God in everything; belief in the extraordinary power of mediators (whether saints or men), rites and prayers; sacred meanings for all happenings; and the like. In our survey, we describe non-Christian popular religion in the countries where it occurs, but we give more attention to specifically-Christian or christianized forms, using the 2 terms described in the next 2 paragraphs.

### Popular religiosity

In numerous countries of the world, there are within the churches unusual or deviant forms of Christianity widely practised by multitudes who are members of the majority or dominant churches, in particular the Roman Catholic Church in Latin America. This phenomenon includes several varieties of mass syncretistic folk-Christianity, christo-paganism, spiritist Catholicism, cults of miracles and the miraculous and supernatural, cults of the Virgin Mary or of saints, and other manifestations described in this survey under each of the countries concerned.

These popular expressions of religion, faith, thirst for God, and the desire for worship, miracles and healings, on the part of large masses of people and especially of multitudes of the poor, are here collectively termed popular religiosity. On the negative side, this type of popular religion involves distortions of genuine Christianity through the intrusion of superstition, forms of worship without faith in Christ, marginal sects and cults, syncretism, and non-Christian beliefs and values. Great stress is put on images, medals, relics, statuettes, rosaries, shrines, magical practices and taboos, saints' days, litanies, novenas, processions, pilgrimages, associations and the like. Until recently these manifestations have been regarded only as impure or debased versions or caricatures of Christianity, hence have been despised and attacked by theologians, missionaries and churchmen. To quote Paul VI (Evangelii Nuntiandi, section 48), 'Popular religion... is often subject to penetration by many distortions of religion and even superstitions'. Increasingly nowadays, though, they are being revaluated and seen as valid expressions of people's gropings for God and for genuine experience of Christ, although widely infiltrated with non-Christian forms.

Popular religiosity, then, is the term used here to describe deviant forms of Christian or christianized popular religion. Its clearest and most widespread manifestations are found in the Roman Catholic Church in most countries of Latin America. In Tables 1 for those countries, therefore, its followers are enumerated, using the terms Christo-pagans, and Spiritist Catholics.

### Popular piety

The latent Christian values in many types of popular religion are now being discovered by the churches (Roman Catholics in particular), as a result of which they are being seen to be valid expressions of people's search for God, although, again, often falling short of fully-Christian doctrine and practice. Particularly notable is widespread popular devotion to the Crucified Christ under various visible representations (in Brazil, 'Senhor Bom Jesus') and other popular expressions of Catholic faith (devotion to the Madonna, etc) including more definitely-Christian

versions of the list given in the last but one paragraph above. In Evangelii Nuntiandi, Paul VI observed of popular religion: 'It involves an acute awareness of profound attributes of God: fatherhood, providence, loving and constant presence. It engenders interior attitudes rarely observed to the same degree elsewhere: patience, the sense of the Cross in daily life, detachment, openness to others, devotion' (Section 48, 'Popular piety'). A more accurate and positive term for this phenomenon, instead of merely speaking of popular religion, is therefore the title of that section: popular piety. It should also be observed that such manifestations of popular devotion are extremely important in Eastern Europe and other Communist or anti-Christian countries where the churches are under constant repressive pressures from the state. In our survey, these manifestations of popular piety are described for numerous countries, but since they often embrace almost the entire Christian community (in Roman Catholic countries especially), they are not separately enumerated or categorized in Table 1.

### Charismatic renewals

In most countries, there have arisen spiritual renewals which have crystallized out into recognizable and measurable movements today. Among older groupings are the Evangelicals (in the English usage of the term), found among Protestants and Anglicans, dating especially from the 18th-century Evangelical Revival in the Church of England. Followers are enumerated here in Tables 1 for each country under the same term, Evangelicals. Among newer groupings, the best-known is the Charismatic Renewal at present under way since 1960 within (in chronological order of origin) the Anglican, Protestant, Roman Catholic, Catholic (non-Roman), and Orthodox traditions. Followers are enumerated here in Tables 1 for each country under the respective terms Anglican pentecostals, Neo-pentecostals, Catholic pentecostals and Orthodox pentecostals. Only regularly-active and involved participants are here defined as charismatics.

## SECULAR DATA

Before every Table 1 for each country, there is a selection of secular background statistical and other data, in standardized format, concerning items important for evaluating our data that follow on religion, religious change, conversion, church growth and evangelization. Explanatory notes on most of these data now follow. Numerous sources have been utilized, including UN and UNESCO publications, others referred to below, and this Encyclopedia's own field work and original investigations. Unless otherwise dated, all figures refer to the decade 1970-80, and usually to the year 1975 or to the period 1975–80. Where the exact year of the data is important, it is recorded in parentheses; where the year is omitted, the data are known to change little from year to year. Figures absent in a particular country, e.g. TV receivers, or scientific journals, indicate that the item concerned is either zero or negligible in size, or, in a very few cases, of unknown size. Population natural growth rates (totals, births, deaths, migrations) refer to the total de facto (or, present-in-area) resident population for the period 1975–80, and are taken from the UN computerized population projection model given in World population prospects, 1970–2000, as assessed in 1973 (New York: United Nations, 1975). Excluded are tourists, visitors, transients, persons in transit, and other temporary individuals or groups. By definition 'natural growth rate', % per year, is equal to the total of 3 components; crude birth rate expressed as % per year, minus crude death rate as % per year, plus nett immigration as % per year (the latter consisting of all de facto immigrants including those who become illegal residents). Where no migration figure is given in this section, it means that for that country during 1975–80, nett immigration or emigration was small or negligible (under 0.01% per year).

**STATE. Official name:** The full official name in English (as sanctioned by the state for United Nations' usage), followed by that or those in the official language(s) if not English. Main source: UN Terminology Bulletin No. 285/Rev.2 (1977). Members of the UN have official names in each of the 6 UN official languages (Arabic, Chinese, English, French, Russian, Spanish).
**Unofficial name:** Other names in use for the nation, without official status.
**Alternative name:** Other names in use with official

status.
**Earlier name:** Other names still in use unofficially, usually from colonial or pre-Independence days.
**Adjective(s) of nationality:** The officially-sanctioned adjectives, if any (and occasionally a noun or nouns) agreed by the state and the United Nations for all official, correct usage, firstly in English, and secondly (in parentheses) in the official language of the state if not English (French, German, Italian, Portuguese, Spanish only). Note that in Romance languages the adjective is always given with a lower-case first letter. If there is no entry here, there are no officially-approved adjectives, although there may be popular or commonly-used ones. Source: UN Terminology Bulletin No. 285 Rev.2 (1977).
**Flag:** Design officially used as symbol of the nation; verbal description of flag as shown to right of country's name at start of country's survey article.
**Government:** Nature of present government or regime in power (1978–80), with in parentheses brief sketch of historical development.
**Legislature:** Names and sizes of the various legislative chambers.
**Official language(s):** The majority of languages each have an English name that is phonetic or very close to its own self-appellation. In cases where the English name is quite different it is followed by, in italics in parentheses, the name of the language as used by itself. African languages are given here (only) with their prefixes meaning 'the language of'.
**Chief cities and capital:** Anglicized names are used at this point for all countries; spellings in the national language however are used here in our World Atlas of Christianity and Religions (Part 11). Figures for large cities represent the size of the urban agglomeration, where known, and not the size of the city within its official limits. The year shown in parentheses is in most cases a census year and refers to all the subsequent city figures.
**Area:** Varying estimates are given by different sources; some include water areas, others do not; some include disputed territories. We give here official figures in square kilometres and in square miles. In several countries it will be noted that the 2 figures are not exactly compatible in which case each has a slightly different definition.
**Description:** A brief comment on any unusual composition, particularly in the case of numerous islands.
**Agricultural land:** Percentage of total area which is of agricultural use: arable land, land under permanent crops, permanent meadows and pastures. Date: 1974. Source: FAO Production yearbook 1975.
**Political divisions:** The administrative or political sub-divisions into which the country is divided for central and local government purposes.
**Armed forces** (1976): The country's own regular and reserve military forces. Many countries also maintain paramilitary forces as a check on the regular armed forces. Source: The military balance 1976–1977 (London: IISS, 1976).
**Foreign forces** (1973): Resident military forces from outside the country.
**Dependencies:** Territories politically dependent.

**DEMOGRAPHY. Population:** The figure given here is from the latest official census, usually a de facto (present-in-area) census rather than a de jure (legally resident) one. Figures in the bottom row of Table 1 may differ somewhat in cases where the UN Population Division has judged there to have been sizeable under- or overenumeration, or where our definition of population (present-in-area de jure) is different from that of the census.
**Population density** (1975): Rounded to the nearest digit unless under 1.0.
**Under 15 years:** The percentage of the population aged 14 years and under.
**Growth rate** (1975–80): Annual increase in the country's population, divided here into births minus deaths plus the nett balance of migration (immigrants minus emigrants). Main source: World population prospects, 1970–2000, as assessed in 1973 (New York: UN, 1975). Since these figures are projections for 1975–80, they may differ in places from those in our Tables 1, which refer to the whole decade 1970–80.
**Life expectancy** at birth, both sexes (1975–80): Source: World population prospects (1975).
**Household size:** The average size of a household in a country (persons sharing the same unit, whether private or collective or institutional) is not the same as that of the average family, being slightly larger due to inclusion of servants, maids, and lodgers, as well as hospitals, homes and other institutions where people live. Household is usually defined on the basis of the

arrangements made by persons individually or in groups, for providing themselves with food or other essentials for living. The figures given here are based on the UN medium variant for projections. Source: 'Projections of the number of households and families, 1965–1985' (New York: UN Population Division, 1970).

**Major languages:** This listing gives the main distinct or separate or mutually unintelligible languages heard or spoken in the country (excluding dialects or variants), listed approximately in order of significance usually numerically (in most cases down to around 1% of the population) but also culturally, politically, commercially, economically, professionally, academically, religiously, and ecclesiastically, etc. Unlike in 'Official languages' above, African languages are here given without prefixes (with prefixes meaning 'the language of' sometimes added in parentheses). In most cases these major languages are followed by a numerical statement indicating the total of all other distinct and separate languages. Sources: government censuses, our own surveys, *Scriptures of the world* (UBS), and *Ethnologue* (Wycliffe Bible Translators).

**Urban dwellers** (1970): Population living in urban areas, taken from the variable 'urbanization' in *World demographic atlas* (UN, 1973 onwards). The exact definition of urban differs from country to country; in most, it covers cities and towns with a population of over 2,000 or 5,000, or even 20,000, or a density of over 1000/sq.km. (See details of all countries' definitions in *UN Demographic yearbook*). See also Table 161, 'Urban and rural population, 1950–1975', in *World population trends and policies*, Vol. I (1979). In UN statistics, it is usual to tabulate urban population 'as nationally defined', 'corresponding to national concepts', or 'as defined in each country' (ibid).

**Urban growth rate** (1950–70): Annual increase over these 2 decades. Source: *World demographic atlas* (1973).

**Labour force:** Economically active population (both employed and unemployed) as a percentage of total population (excluding students, women at home, retired persons, wholly-dependent persons, et alii). Source: *Year book of labour statistics* (ILO, 1976).

**Refugees** (1977): Officially-classified refugees entering over the last few years, resettled or not, but excluding labour and other migrants and also returnees (forcibly repatriated deportees), together with others not or not yet officially recognized. Source: *World refugee report* (US Committee for Refugees), annual.

**Exiles abroad:** Citizens forced to flee and now temporarily received by the countries of asylum indicated.

**Tourists:** Foreign tourists and visitors from abroad visiting this country during calendar 1974 or earlier years. Source: *UN Statistical yearbook*, 1975.

**ETHNOLINGUISTIC GROUPS:** The percentages refer primarily to the situation in the year 1970, but in most cases are still approximately the same in 1980 (see detailed explanation of derivation in Part 4).

**MONEY** (1977): Currency: name of monetary unit, number of smaller units it comprises, value of US$1 (the operational rate of exchange as used by UN et alia, not the official or free rate) showing symbol used for the local currency.

**National income per person:** The average per capita annual income, usually derived as GNP (gross national product) per capita.

**Average annual family income:** Derived by multiplying the national income per person by the average household size.

**Inflation:** Defined as the annual percentage growth in consumer prices in the country, as measured by the consumer price index.

**Consumer price index:** This index shows changes over time in the price level of goods and services, relative to 1970 prices (=100) in the country concerned. Source: *Monthly bulletin of statistics*, United Nations, June 1976 et seq.

**Cost of living in capital** (1976): This is measured here in the following 2 distinct ways giving figures each of which is directly comparable from one country to another.

**Index:** This is the local index compiled by the US Department of State (source: *Indexes of living costs abroad and quarters allowances*, US Department of Labour, annual), which measures the living costs in the country's capital city for private non-government American citizens, being a basic price comparison of goods and services in the foreign capital with those in Washington, DC, adjusted to reflect modifications in the consumption expenditures made by Americans living in the foreign city.

**Daily cost of living:** This is the daily subsistence allowance rate (in US$ per diem, per employee) used by the United Nations and other international organizations for their employees, to cover food, accommodation and incidentals during their first 60 days in a capital city. After these 60 days, the allowance falls by from 5–25%. These figures, which give the actual living costs per adult for single individuals or for families of foreign citizenship, can be used to indicate what living costs foreign missionaries or other church workers can expect when moving to, or visiting, a capital city, as follows (bearing in mind the differing standards of living of different missionary societies, as reflected in the allowances paid to missionaries). (a) For Protestant and Anglican missionaries from Europe: multiply the figures shown by 0.25 (25%). (b) For Protestant missionaries from North America: multipy the figures shown by 1.20 (120%). (c) Missionaries or church workers from Third-World countries: multiply the figures by 0.10 (10%). For purposes of direct comparison, local citizens in the country as a whole (capital, urban and rural) live at an average daily subsistence level equal to the national income per person divided by 365.

A more exact and detailed direct comparison is given in *Prices and earnings around the globe: a comparison of purchasing power in 41 cities* (Zürich: Union Bank of Switzerland, 1976).

**HEALTH. Hospitals:** General and specialized hospitals and other medical establishments with beds (both government and private). Date: 1969–72. Source: *UN Statistical yearbook 1974*.

**Doctors:** Physicians qualified from a medical school, both in private practice and in state service. Source: *UN Statistical yearbook 1974*.

We next give, in order to delineate serious societal health problems where they exist, statistics of 5 categories of sick or incapacitated or disadvantaged or handicapped persons, or persons who affect the health of society as a whole, with all of whom Christians and churches have long had a history of compassion, aid and concern: lepers, the blind, psychotics, drug addicts, and criminals.

**Lepers.** Prevalence (total number of estimated leprosy patients at any given date) followed in parentheses by the prevalence rate (cases per 1,000 population) in the year 1975. This item is included here because leprosy is still one of the most dreaded diseases, and one with which Christian missions have long been associated. Although nowadays the term 'leper' is not applied to individuals because of the age-long stigma attached to it, it is useful here for statistical purposes in drawing attention to the magnitude of the problem. Leprosy has a special position among diseases because it is the greatest crippler among diseases in the world today, and because of its long duration, relative incurability, high cost of treatment, vast extent (at least 11 million sufferers), and its inexorable persistence (one million new cases every 5 years) as a problem of global magnitude. The figures shown for each country are for estimated cases, registered and unregistered; they date from around 1965–70, but are known to change little from year to year so will still give the general order of magnitude correctly in 1980. The prevalence rate gives a measure of risk of contagion: countries where it is 0.5 per 1,000 or higher are treated as risk areas by WHO; over 10 per 1,000 are high-risk areas. Data are not given for large Western nations with very small numbers of cases (below 100), or for other nations below 30. Sources: 2 articles by L.M. Bechelli & V. Martínez Domínguez: 'The leprosy problem in the world', *Bulletin WHO*, 34 (1966), 811–826, and 'Further information on the leprosy problem in the world', *Bulletin WHO*, 46 (1972), 523–536.

**Blind.** As in most official censuses, these statistics of blind persons refer to the totally blind. The figures come mostly from the most recent WHO global survey, 'Blindness', in *Epidemiological and vital statistics report* (WHO, Geneva), 19 (1966), 433–512, with data updated to 1976 for a number of countries. The next complete global survey of blindness by WHO was underway by 1977–78.

**Psychotics** (the mentally ill). The statistics given represent minimum figures for the total number of sufferers from psychoses or other severe mental disorder or disturbance, in 1975; the mentally ill, or mentally abnormal (which is not the same as mentally retarded or deficient). According to the WHO, 'The per capita incidence of severe or major mental disturbance (psychosis) is much the same in most countries... One percent of the world are, at any one time, incapacitated by severe mental disorder, and 10% are so affected at some period or other of their lives'. Of these sufferers, about one quarter (at least 0.2% of the population) are schizophrenics (sufferers from schizophrenia). Our category here, with its statistics, does not include the much larger category of sufferers from psychoneurosis, estimated at from 15–25% of the world's populations.

**Drug addicts.** The number in 1975 of hard-core drug addicts or drug abusers (opium/cannabis/heroin/cocaine/morphine/psychotropic substances (barbiturates, LSD, hallucinogens)/multiple drug abuse). Source: *Reports*, UN Commission on Narcotic Drugs, 1975–77, et alia. Although statistics are only available for a few countries, drug abuse is serious in many others.

**Criminals.** The total number of distinct criminal offenders detected and identified by the nation's police (but not necessarily arrested or subsequently convicted) during a single year (1972). Source: *International crime statistics* (Saint-Cloud, France: ICPO-Interpol), 12 editions 1950–74. Comparing these figures from one country to another needs caution because a high coefficient of offenders to population may be due to meticulous record-keeping whilst a low one is often due to poor or sporadic record-keeping.

**EDUCATION. Adult literacy:** Percentage of the adult population (15 and over) who can read and write, in any language (years as indicated). Source: *UNESCO Statistical yearbook 1964* (Table 4) and *1977* (Table 1.3). Virtually all the figures given here under SECULAR DATA come from official censuses of the year indicated in parentheses. Readers should be warned that many other divergent figures are widely quoted in literature elsewhere but that they have no basis in fact. In Global Table 31, we interpolate or extrapolate the official figures to give comparative figures for the years 1900, 1950, 1975 and 1980.

**Education rate:** Percentage of the school-age population (aged 5–24) who are enrolled in schools (year, 1973 on average). Source: *UNESCO Statistical yearbook*.

**Schools:** Total institutions at the first and second levels (primary and secondary schools), both public and private. Date: 1970–73 (average 1972), unless an earlier date is given in parentheses. This total includes elementary and secondary schools, but excludes pre-primary, post-secondary, technical, vocational, specialized and special schools.

**Universities:** Number of distinct universities and degree-granting colleges of all kinds.

**LITERATURE. Annual new book titles:** Number of non-periodical commercial publications (books and pamphlets, including new editions and re-editions but not translations, available to the general public, excluding non-public books or reports) produced in 1973, or earlier, including government publications, university theses, and children's books. Source: *UNESCO Statistical yearbook*.

**Periodicals:** Number of publications of periodical issue (appearing at regular intervals, each with 2 or more issues a year, excluding annuals and irregular serials, and in any languages), including scientific journals, but excluding non-daily general-interest newspapers (published 3 times a week or less), and excluding daily general-interest newspapers. Date: 1968–74. Source: *UNESCO Statistical yearbook*.

**Scientific journals:** Period: early 1970s. Source: *UNESCO Statistical yearbook*, et al.

**Newspapers:** General-interest newspapers are defined by UNESCO as publications devoted primarily to recording news of current events in public affairs, international affairs, politics, etc. Daily newspapers are defined as those which are published at least 4 times a week; and non-daily newspapers 3 times or less a week. Source: *UNESCO Statistical yearbook*.

**COMMUNICATION. Phones:** Number of telephones in use, per 1,000 population.

**Radios:** Either estimated number of radio receivers in use (all types including wired receivers), or the number of annual licences issued or sets declared, per 1,000 population.

**TV sets:** Either estimated number of television receivers in use, or the number of annual licences issued, per 1,000 population.

**Daily newspaper circulation:** The total circulation, in copies per 1,000 population, of all general-interest daily newspapers.

## Table: 1
## RELIGIOUS ADHERENTS IN EACH COUNTRY

The population of an area is usually defined as the total of all inhabitants or residents of that area; in technical terms, this is the de jure population. A strict definition of de jure population in a particular government census may include only legal inhabitants, i.e. long-term, legal residents who are citizens, and may exclude aliens, minorities, nomadic groups, armed forces and other groups. Inhabitants are usually defined as persons who dwell or reside permanently in a place or area, and should be distinguished from the term residents which often implies either a temporary or a relatively short-term period of habitation. By contrast with de jure population measuring inhabitants, however, most government censuses measure the present-in-area or de facto population, which includes illegal residents and all other types of residents, and also non-residents, transients, temporary visitors and sometimes even tourists, at the locations where they slept or spent the night. In practice, strict conformity to either the de jure or de facto definition is rarely achieved in national censuses, and so the United Nations produces its own estimates on its own definitions. Statistics of church membership, by contrast, are usually a of modified de jure variety, covering all resident groups but excluding transients, temporary visitors and tourists. In this survey we use the United Nations population definitions, figures and projections, which refer to present-in-area resident populations but excluding non-residents, transients, temporary visitors and tourists, and are therefore more directly comparable with church statistics of membership than either strictly de jure or de facto definitions and figures. In other words, our survey tables here refer to residents rather than to inhabitants.

The term adherents is therefore used in this Encyclopedia as a general term to refer to the whole present-in-area resident population or inhabitants of all varieties at a particular point in time (excluding transients and temporary visitors) belonging to a particular religion or church — men, women, children, infants, nationals and expatriates (citizens and aliens), native and foreign-born, immigrants, immigrant workers, seasonal immigrants, alien minorities, stateless persons, armed forces stationed in the country (national and foreign, together with their dependants), foreign diplomatic personnel, merchant seamen in port or ashore, aborigines, jungle tribes, nomadic groups, alien displaced persons, internees, returnees, refugees, prisoners, prisoners-of-war, slaves, the hospitalized, the sick, the infirm, the disabled, psychotics, vagrants, and any other national or alien groups resident within the country at the time; together with any of the country's residents (armed forces, diplomats, merchant seamen, civilians) who are normally resident but at the exact time in question are very temporarily out of the country. Excluded are tourists, visitors, transients, persons in transit, and all other very temporary individuals or groups, all of whom are enumerated in this survey under their own countries of residence; and also members of the country's armed forces, diplomats, absentee workers, emigrants and other civilians not permanently resident in their own country at the point of time in question. In many countries, as explained above, this definition of ours would be referred to as the de jure population, although in other countries this term means long-term permanent residents or citizens including residents and armed forces abroad but excluding aliens, immigrant workers, etc. In many countries, also, the de facto population includes tourists, transients and all others physically-present on the census day but excludes citizens and residents temporarily abroad. Our definition of both total population and religious populations thus falls in between the strict de facto and de jure definitions. In cases where the available data on a country's population, for example from population censuses, omit any of the groups we wish to include, the data have been modified here to fit our own definition (usually by including all resident alien, minority and underprivileged groups ignored in censuses but known to be present).

*Objects of Table 1*

The object of this table is to show at a glance the overall de facto/de jure religious situation in each country throughout the 20th century, and to assist in analysis of the past, understanding of the present, and planning for the future, by providing the following data:

1. the major significant religious and non-religious blocs and groupings in the country, listed as mutually-exclusive categories, and in order of numerical size in 1970;
2. a standardized demographic base for every country, giving in the last row of every table the country's population statistics at mid-year for the years 1900 (for the area which comprises the country in 1975–80), 1970, 1975, 1980 and 2000, together with annual natural increase in 1975;
3. the religious adherence, or non-adherence, of the entire population (men, women, children and infants);
4. the general order of magnitude of these groupings' adherents, both in absolute numbers and also as percentages of the population, in the years 1970, 1975 and 1980;
5. a direct link with Tables 2 (depicting organized churches and denominations) by incorporating those tables' totals of affiliated Christians in mid-1970, mid-1975 and mid-1980, and the subdivision of these totals into the 7 major ecclesiastical blocs;
6. any contemporary major long-term religious trends in the country, expressed as annual changes in religious profession or affiliation over the decade 1970–1980, due either to natural change (biological change or births minus deaths, plus migration change or immigrants minus emigrants), or to conversion change to or from religions (conversions minus defections);
7. the religious situation in the year 1900 (for the country, within present boundaries, i.e. adjusted to include the territory which in 1975 comprises the country);
8. the probable religious situation in the year AD 2000, projected from current trends;
9. footnotes elaborating the basic census and polls data, and any interesting features and additional data concerning particular categories in the table.

*Summary of the 15 columns*

The columns are not numbered 1–15 in the tables themselves, but are numbered here to assist in identifying particular columns. This describes all Tables 1 in the survey, Part 7; but note that in the Global Tables (Parts 1 and 8), 2 additional columns are added for the year 1985.

1. Major religions and sub-divisions, listed in 1970 order of numerical size
2. Adherents in the year 1900
3. Adherents in 1900 as % total population then
4. Adherents in mid-1970
5. Adherents in mid-1970 as % total population then

6-9. Annual change, 1970–1980; average long-term trend over the decade

6. Annual natural (population) increase among adherents, 1970–1980 (biological increase (births minus deaths) plus nett immigration)
7. Annual conversion (or supranatural) increase (+ or −) to adherents, 1970–80 (measured as col. 8 minus col. 6)
8. Total annual increase (+ or −) of adherents, 1970–80 (= col. 6 plus col. 7) (measured as col. 12 minus col. 4, divided by 10)
9. Rate of change of adherents, 1970–80, as % per year (= col. 8 divided by col. 10)
10. Adherents in mid-1975
11. Adherents in mid-1975 as % total population then
12. Adherents in mid-1980
13. Adherents in mid-1980 as % total population then
14. Adherents in the year 2000
15. Adherents in 2000 as % total population then

*Degrees of non-Christian religiosity*

We have described earlier how the simple category 'Christians' can and should be subdivided in various ways into professing, affiliated, nominal, practising, non-practising, and so on. It is important to realize that in exactly the same way all non-Christian religions, and also atheism and non-religion, also contain the whole range of commitment from deeply-religious mystics and proselytizing zealots (even fanatics) down through the indifferent to the nominally-religious or non-practising doubters. The bulk of the adherents we enumerate in this survey who claim allegiance to Islam, Hinduism, and even to atheism and to no religion, do not practise their profession with any vigour or conviction.

Since this is primarily a survey of the Christian world, our overall statistics of each non-Christian religion are limited to professing adherents only. At the same time the reader should remember throughout that labels like 'Buddhist' include the whole range of degrees of religiosity from devoutly believing and practising Buddhists to non-believing and non-practising Buddhists. Where concise data on these degrees of religiosity, practice and commitment are available for the non-Christian religions, they are given briefly in the footnotes under Tables 1 for the countries concerned.

*Methodology, sources and assumptions*

Each table has been compiled in a standard format, in approximately the order of compilation now to be described, using the types of source data indicated. Our method of compilation has been to move step by step through a whole chain of logical procedures. The method used is similar to solving a jigsaw puzzle or working out a crossword puzzle, one box at a time, using one position to establish another and one set of data to produce the next, i.e. moving from the known to the unknown (from known figures entered in the table to produce the next, unknown, figure or series of figures) through the following 27 stages.

1. *Main religions.* First, an alphabetical listing of the major numerically-significant religions and religious blocs in each country was made.
2. *Population in 1900.* The demographic base line was begun by inserting figures of present-in-area resident population for censuses of the year 1900 published by about 150 countries, summarized in *UN Demographic yearbook* (1948–53, 1955, 1962) for 110 countries (within their present boundaries, i.e. their areas defined by the frontiers of 1980), and supplemented for the remaining countries by extrapolations back to 1900 from Table A 3.8 in *World population prospects* (1966).
3. *Population estimates, 1970–2000.* The rest of the demographic base line was now inserted. The most recent census figure is given for each country in SECULAR DATA at the start of each country's article. In Tables 1, however, we use the standardized and comparative mid-year estimates present-in-area resident population for the years 1970–2000 prepared by the United Nations Population Division in 1973/4 and published later as *World population prospects, 1970–2000, as assessed in 1973* (New York: UN, 1975). This report gives projections prepared in 4 variants based on differing presuppositions: high, medium, and low; and constant fertility trends. For AD 2000, the high variant gives a world population of 6,637 million, and the constant variant 7,151 million. In Tables 1, we have chosen the rather more conservative medium variant projections, which give for AD 2000 a world population of 6,253 million. These UN figures for 1970 and the projections are, for comparative purposes, more reliable and definitive than the actual population census figures themselves as published by countries, because they incorporate the UN's evaluation and, in particular, adjustments when under-enumeration is known to have taken place in a census (as in Mexico 1970), or overenumeration (as in Nigeria 1963), but where the respective governments are reluctant to acknowledge this for internal political reasons. It should be noted in passing that for certain countries (Angola, Colombia, et alia) the Statistical Office of the United Nations still uses church data on baptisms to obtain the estimated number of births and to calculate the crude birth rate (*UN Demographic yearbook* 1974, p. 252).
4. *Annual population increase.* At the start of each country's article, SECULAR DATA includes the 1975 figure for increase, as % per year. This is what we here have called the natural increase, i.e. biological increase plus migration increase, i.e. birth rate minus death rate plus immigration rate minus emigration rate. In Tables 1, a similar figure appears on the last line under the column 'Rate' (rate of increase in 1975), though in this case it is the average value for the years 1970–80 estimated from the UN projections. This figure is obtained by dividing the total natural increase from 1970 to 1980 (obtainable from the last line in Tables 1) by ten and then by the 1975 population, expressing the result as a rate % per year.
5. *Migration.* Migration is usually defined (as in the UK) as a declared intention to reside in or leave a country for at least a year. In a handful of countries, international migration (emigration or immigration, expulsions, refugee movements, etc.) during the period 1970–75 has been significant. Where the numbers involved are large enough to be noticeable in Tables 1, they are

included with biological increase in the column 'Natural increase'. In particular, where migrations of large numbers from a particular religious bloc have been taking place during this period (e.g. Jews emigrating from the USSR), approximate annual figures are included in the columns 'Annual change, 1970–1980' and the situation is described in the footnotes. The data in this Encyclopedia illustrate an often-noted basic principle: migration results in a decline in religious practice, affiliation and even profession. When persons from strongly-religious cultures migrate to distant lands, unless they move into already-established minorities of their own people their religious ties become looser and they tend to become less religious or even non-religious (e.g. Chinese folk-religionists, European Protestants). An estimate of annual nett migration for each country appears under 'Demography' in its section in SECULAR DATA.

6. *Children*. As has been discussed above in the case of Christianity, children and infants must be included in these tables. Our general principle throughout this survey has been that, except in cases where data to the contrary are available, children and infants have the same religious characteristics as their parents. For Tables 1, they are therefore assumed to have their parents' religious profession, or absence of it, unless evidence to the contrary is available. Thus a census showing that 80% of a population are Muslims, or a poll showing 80% of adults are Muslims, also indicates that approximately 80% of all children also are Muslims.

7. *Affiliated Christians*. Figures for Christians affiliated to churches in 1970 were next added, divided into the 7 major ecclesiastical blocs, taken in every case from the figures derived in Table 2 for the country. The absolute numbers were inserted first, in all cases as the exact unrounded totals for 1970 obtained in Tables 2, then the percentages were worked out. Tables 1 and 2 are in fact directly linked numerically at this point, namely the total of all affiliated Christians in mid-1970, and in this total subdivided into the 7 major ecclesiastical blocs.

8. *Double affiliation*. Under certain circumstances, the same persons get counted twice as affiliated members by 2 distinct churches or denominations, and allowance must be made for this when adding up totals from all denominations. In certain countries with a nearly-universal state or majority church, many members of Free churches also get enumerated as members by the majority church. In such cases, totals were estimated and added to Table 1 and then Table 2, as negative quantities (with a minus sign) because they represent a duplication in a series of numbers which when added should give the total number of distinct individuals affiliated to all churches.

9. *Religious profession*. Numbers and percentages of professing adherents in 1970 for each religion were added, based for half the world's countries on the percentages in government censuses of religion or public-opinion polls, updated or backdated to mid-1970 from the last available census or poll during the period 1969–1972. As explained earlier, government census figures do not measure church membership or affiliation but measure what we here call professing Christians. In our presentation here of the results for all censuses, we first of all made the results comparable from one country to another and from one census year to the next by removing from the population figure the small numbers of persons in such categories as 'Not available', 'Unspecified', 'No answer', 'Unknown', 'Object to state', 'No information', which are often present in reports of censuses and polls; the results as percentages were then worked out without them. The accuracy of these census data is high because they are based on a total head count at a single point in time by a vast force of trained enumerators.

10. *Hidden affiliation*. A further phenomenon occurs when persons affiliated to minority or illegal or anti-state or persecuted churches hide this affiliation in government censuses (or whose affiliation is ignored by enumerators) and profess another type of Christianity (usually that of the majority church). Thus, in Latin America, persons affiliated to churches regarded by the state as Evangelical (Evangélica) may profess to be, or be enumerated as, Catholics in the censuses; such persons are therefore termed here Evangelical Catholics. Similarly, in countries where society or the state or the majority church discriminates against or disapproves of a minority denomination (Jehovah's Witnesses, New Apostolics, etc), its members may be put down in the census as professing Roman Catholics or Protestants or whatever the majority church is.

11. *Percentages*. As described in detail earlier under the heading 'Demographic inertia', the percentage size of a religious community in a country does not change appreciably over the years from one census to the next, even when total population is rapidly increasing, unless there are (a) large-scale conversions within the community to or from another religion, (b) fertility or biological increase rates markedly different from the national average, (c) mass emigration or immigration, (d) anti-religious revolutions, or (e) severe erosion of religious belief due to secularism. In the Western world, the percentage figures for particular religions only change slowly from year to year; in the Communist world, percentages decline slowly due to anti-religious revolutions and mass emigrations; whereas in the Third World, the % Christian often increases from year to year due to mass conversions and missionary activity.

12. *Nominal and crypto-Christians*. In all countries where professing Christians outnumber those affiliated (Western countries and others with a Christian majority), the difference results in (by definition) nominal Christians. In countries where affiliated Christians outnumber those professing (countries where Christians are a minority) the difference results in (by definition) crypto-Christians.

13. *Practising Christians*. In the several countries where nation-wide polls of church attendance have been taken, these figures were used. In all other countries, the individual percentages of annual practice from the various denominations were examined, and absolute numbers were computed and totalled, producing the final figures shown in Tables 1. In almost all cases, absolute numbers have been rounded to the nearest 10, greater exactitude being meaningless here. It should be noted that the aggregate of those who attend at least once a year is always greater than the attendance on the major annual festival (Easter or Christmas), because inevitably there are many persons including the sick, infirm, handicapped and radio/TV listeners who are unable to attend on any one specific occasion. This means: (a) for Roman Catholics, the total of all who attend at least once annually is usually around 10% larger than the total of Easter communicants, and may be very much higher in Third-World countries where Catholics face long distances, difficulties of travel, and insufficiency of Easter services; and (b) for Anglicans and Protestants with their far less strict attendance requirements, the total of all who attend at least once annually may be much larger and even up to twice the size of Easter communicants or those who attend on a single major annual festival. This almost universal situation is best documented here in the polls data for the United Kingdom of GB & NI presented under its Table 1.

14. *Sub-groups of professing Catholics*. In a number of countries, mainly Latin or Latin American, analysis of government censuses of religion indicates that there are large numbers of professing Roman Catholics who are mainly oriented to 3 other, non-Catholic, religious systems: Christo-paganism, Evanglicalism (a term used in many Latin government censuses to cover mainly Protestantism, but also including Anglicanism, marginal Protestantism, and indigenous churches), and Spiritism. These sub-groups, where they exist, are shown in Tables 1 under professing Roman Catholics as, respectively, Christo-pagans, Evangelical Catholics, and Spiritist Catholics. It should be noted at this point that the term 'Evangelical' is used throughout this survey in 2 distinct and different senses, firstly as used by states and governments and secondly as used within the churches themselves. These may be described as follows: (1) as understood and used by many non-English-speaking states and governments, notably in their population censuses, the term in the various major languages (Evangelische in German, Evangélique in French, Evangelico in Italian, Evangélico in Spanish and Portuguese) is equivalent to the English term Protestant, or non-Catholic; (2) as understood and used by the churches themselves, especially in the English-speaking world, the term refers to the Evangelical movement within the churches, a sub-division within Protestantism and Anglicanism.

15. *Sub-groups of affiliated Christians*. In most countries of the world, there are sizeable numbers of affiliated Christians who also belong to widely-known worldwide groupings or movements, which form clearly-recognized entities and which therefore may be enumerated without difficulty. Of these, the 2 best-known are (a) Evangelicals (the term as understood and used by and in the churches themselves; sometimes called Conservative Evangelicals) and (b) charismatics; and hence they are enumerated here in Tables 1. The complete list of these sub-groups is as follows, with the related major ecclesiastical bloc of which they are a part: Catholic pentecostals (who are affiliated Roman Catholics); Anglican pentecostals, and Anglican Evangelicals (both being affiliated Anglicans); Neo-pentecostals, and Evangelicals (both being affiliated Protestants); Orthodox pentecostals (being affiliated Orthodox); and Black Evangelicals (a sub-group of affiliated Black indigenous church members, in the USA only).

**Evangelicals.** Seminar on 'The Gospel and Culture', Singapore 1978, sponsored by Asia's 19,257,000 Evangelicals.

16. *Other large religious groupings in 1970*. Where data were available, figures were now inserted for the rest of the larger religious groupings or categories in the listing: Buddhists, Hindus, Muslims, et alii.

17. *Other religionists*. In virtually every country of the world, there are at least a few persons belonging to most of the major world religions, usually diplomats, traders, refugees, military, foreign residents, immigrants and so on. The censuses we report under Tables 1 often show, for instance, 25 Jews in Trinidad, 63 Muslims, 2 Buddhists, etc. In most cases, they number only tens or hundreds and form too negligible a proportion of the population to be included as separate rows for each religion in Tables 1. In the same way, on the fringes of all majority or sizeable religious populations, there is very often a rank growth of ephemeral bodies, exotic sects, transient cults, and so on. In countries where all such groupings are individually small, but in aggregate are not insignificant, they are included at the end of Table 1 in a single row under the blanket term 'Other religionists'.

18. *Quasi-religions*. This term is used by the Protestant theologian Paul Tillich (in ***Christianity and the encounter of the world religions***, New York 1963) to describe those secular pseudo-religious systems which have arisen out of the Judeo-Christian tradition and are now assaulting both Christianity and all other religions. These include Atheism, Marxism, Agnosticism, Humanism, Liberal humanism, scientific materialism, dialectical materialism, nationalism, fascism, Nazism, Communism, Maoism, Leninism, Stalin-

ism, Secularism and similar systems. In this survey, quasi-religionists (adherents of quasi-religions) are enumerated under 2 categories: anti-religious quasi-religionists (atheists) and non-religious quasi-religionists (non-religious agnostics), as will now be explained.

19. *Atheists*. This Encyclopedia provides a first approximation to the problem of quantifying professing atheists throughout the world. Atheists here are defined as either (1) those professing disbelief in God (belief that there is no God and no supernatural), who abstain from religious activities, who have severed all religious affiliation (e.g. by formally withdrawing from state or majority churches), and who are opposed or militantly opposed to all religion, and are often irreligious (hostile to religion) or anti-religious; or (2) dialectical materialists or those professing belief in Marxist-Leninist Communism regarded as a political faith or quasi-religion. Communism is in fact widely regarded as a quasi-religion; Maoism in China, for instance, has been termed a quasi-religion because it can best be understood as the continuation of the humanistic-religious culture of traditional China. Communism elsewhere can be regarded as religious because, like Nazism and Fascism, it is religious in its claims on the ultimate loyalties of men. Marxism-Leninism is a quasi-religion, a secular religion, because it preaches as dogmas the necessity of class warfare, the dictatorship of the proletariat, the abolition of private property and the nationalization of the means of production. The estimates shown in Tables 1 for all countries give the general order of magnitude of the atheistic community, and are based on the following 3 separate kinds of data. (1) Only a few government population censuses have differentiated between atheists (opposed to religion) and agnostics (indifferent to religion); almost all such censuses in the Western world include both under the single category 'No religion'. In many countries, however, public-opinion polls have been taken differentiating between the 2 categories and giving the number of professing atheists as a percentage of the adult population. This percentage is then applied here to the total population of a country to arrive at an approximate figure for the total atheistic community (adults and their children). (2) In countries where no census or polls data are available, a formula was evolved based on a statistical examination of Communist party membership and atheism in several countries where figures are avalable, and derived as follows. In most countries of the world, there is a clear distinction between Christians and communists, based on their ideological commitments; it is regarded as not possible to be both a believer and a materialist, and so a Christian cannot be a communist or vice versa. Hence in all countries of the world, with only 10 exceptions, 'given the clear philosophical bent of Marxism, one may assume members of Communist parties to be overwhelmingly irreligious', which means that around 95% are professing, dedicated or avowed atheists, i.e. anti-religious persons opposed on principle to religion with varying degrees of hostility (N. McInnes, *The Communist parties of Western Europe*, London: OUP, 1975:53). The 10 exceptions are: Italy (where the PCI is a mass party whose members are about 20% atheists, 40% non-religious, and 40% professing Catholics), France (where 60% of the PCF are atheists or non-religious and 40% professing Roman Catholics) and 8 Communist countries with strong religious majorities which are governed by mass Communist parties among which dedicated atheists number only about 15–50% of party members, remaining members being non-religious with a small number of religious members. These are Bulgaria, Czechoslovakia, German DR, Hungary, Poland, Romania, Viet Nam, and Yugoslavia. In all countries as well as adult communists who are avowed atheists, there are often in addition large numbers of youths and children who belong to militantly atheistic or anti-religious movements, such as China's Young Pioneer Corps (Red Scarves; primary schoolchildren), 20 million teenagers aged 14–25 in the Young Communist League (in 1956), and the over 11 million Red Guards in 1967; or the USSR's 14.5 million Octoberists aged 7–9, and 20 million militantly atheistic Pioneers aged 10–15; and there are also many adherents, fellow-travellers, hangers-on, anarchists, criminals and other de facto atheists. Further, in all Western European and most other non-Communist countries, the annual turnover of Communist party membership is extremely high (up to 16% per year), which means that ex-communists are far more numerous than communists, perhaps 3 times as numerous (McInnes, op. cit., p. 36–39). Most ex-communists, who are still presumably atheists, remain part of the Communist electorate; statistics of those who vote Communist are given in the footnotes to Tables 1, but are not used here directly in this quantification of atheists because the majority of those who vote Communist are neither communist, ex-communists nor atheists. All of this means that the total atheistic community in a country is probably at least around 4 times as large as the number of adult atheists in the Communist party (see statistical documentation on the USSR in Table 1, footnote 'Atheists'). (3) Lastly, there are, especially in the Western world, a number of atheistic organizations which are not Communist in ideology and may even be politically rightist; and there are numerous individuals who are atheistic humanists or the like. The formula used in Tables 1 is therefore (where . = multiplied by):

Total atheistic community in a country = 4 . (number of Communist, or other Marxist, party members) . (% of party members who are atheists), plus 4 . (adult membership of any non-Communist atheistic groupings).

20. *Non-religious* (agnostic or indifferent) populations were also added from censuses and polls, usually in the form of persons whose answer to the question 'What is your religion?' is 'None' or 'No religion' or 'Don't know'. Where no government censuses or polls of religion exist, the numbers of adherents were usually estimated first, and the equivalent percentages worked out after, by subtracting all known religious groupings from the total population. This category covers all forms of non-religion from quasi-religions to non-religion proper to complete agnosticism to post-religion (abandonment of all religion or quasi-religion).

21. *Disaffiliated persons* were next calculated for Tables 1 (in 9 countries including France, Italy, Spain and Sweden). These are baptized Roman Catholics and others enumerated as affiliated by the Catholic Church or other majority church, but who have disaffiliated themselves and now profess to be agnostics or atheists, i.e. persons who have recently withdrawn from state or majority churches but who are still regarded as members by those churches.

22. *Christians in 1900*. Figures of Christians in the year 1900 were obtained either from government censuses of that period, or from K. Streit, *Statistische Notizen zum Katholischen Missionsatlas* (1906) for Roman Catholic figures, *Statistical atlas of Christian missions* (World Missionary Conference, 1910) for Protestant and Anglican figures, synod records for the major Orthodox churches, and a variety of other historical records.

23. *Christians in 1975–80*. Projections for the years 1975 and 1980 were derived from the 1970 statistics by estimating the probable changes in percentage size, or by adding the probable annual increase over the period of 5 or 10 years, based on present trends, and checked or augmented or corrected later by later statistics.

24. *Annual religious changes, 1970–80*, were next worked out. As explained above, annual change is composed of 2 elements: natural change (biological increase plus migration increase) and non-natural (or supranatural, i.e. conversion) change. The biological increase rate (births minus deaths, % per year) of religious adherents is assumed to be the same as that in the country in which they are situated, unless evidence to the contrary was available. Migration increase of religious communities can be considerable; in such cases, the annual figures were added to make the natural increase column. Then, for each religious grouping, total annual change of all types and the corresponding rate (% per year) were measured from time series statistics or graphs of the growth of the number of adherents over a period of years; these data were available either from successive church affiliation series or from successive population censuses (documented in the footnotes to Tables 1). In fact, for half of the world's countries, government censuses of religion are available for at least 1950, 1960 and 1970, from which long-term religious trends can be identified. The actual method of calculation used for annual change in Tables 1 was as follows. Starting from the 1970 value, projections were made to 1975 and 1980. Then, the total annual change from 1970–80 was obtained by subtracting the values of 1970 from 1980 and dividing by 10; this figure was then divided by the 1975 figure to obtain the rate, expressed as a percentage per year. By subtracting natural change from this total annual change, we arrive at our figures for conversion change. The figures shown represent nett increase; i.e. for the Christian religion, this means conversions to Christianity from other religions, minus apostasies or defections from Christianity to other religions or to non-religion. These annual changes were usually calculated from available data for the period 1970–75, taking into account probable trends for the period 1975–80; they are therefore presented as average indicators of change for the whole decade 1970–80.

25. *Christians in 2000*. Projections for the year 2000 are necessarily far more tentative, and should be regarded as only a rough guide based on existing long-term trends and the fact that large populations show relative consistency in their growth over years, decades and centuries. The method here was first to examine for each religion and Christian bloc the trend in the percentage size of its followers over the period 1900–1975; to plot this progression on a graph; to determine what new factors were likely to be at work in the period 1975–2000; and then to make a conservative estimate or graphical extrapolation of the probable percentage size of each religion by the year 2000. These percentages were then multiplied by the population in AD 2000 (UN medium variant) to give projected numbers of adherents at the end of the century.

In making these statistical projections for the future, we must emphasize that they should be regarded as only a guide. They are one possible scenario based on current trends. They can in no way invalidate the central Christian principle that only God the Holy Spirit controls the future. It is always possible (though unlikely, bearing in mind the demographic inertia of large populations) that the long-term trends of 1900–1970 may peter out or disappear during the years 1980–2000. At the same time, no-one can foresee whether the trends of 1970–80 may not instead be dramatically accelerated in years to come. As an example, our Tables 1 envisage phenomenal growth in the number of Catholic charismatics (pentecostals) in South America, rising by AD 2000 to 7 million in Brazil alone (but still only 3% of the total population there). This projection is based on present trends; but many observers hold it to be distinctly probable that within the next decade or two the trends may be accelerated and the leadership or even the bulk of the laity in Latin American Catholicism may become predominantly charismatic ('predominantly' means something well over 50%). However, at the same time as we give weight to this element of unpredictability in the future, we must also give due weight to the principle of demographic inertia described above, namely that whole populations (massive populations in particular) can only change and do only change their basic characteristics slowly and over considerable periods of time. The evidence for this in respect of christianization can be seen from (1) Global Table 1 which shows the comparatively slow numerical growth of Christianity over 20 centuries, and (2) Tables 1 and their 1900 and 1970 columns, for most nations of the world.

26. *Missing rows*. It will be noted that in many tables a particular row, which the reader may be looking for, is missing; e.g. the row 'crypto-Christians' is not there for France, the row 'nominal Christians' is absent for Egypt, etc, etc. In our methodology, this means that over the period 1900–2000 these categories are entirely absent, i.e. in size are zero or nil, in those countries.

27. *Religions in order of size*. Lastly, the various religious and non-religious blocs and groupings in each country were then rearranged in order of numerical size in 1970 to form, with their sub-divisions, the final Tables 1 as given in Part 7.

## DEFINITIONS OF RELIGIOUS CATEGORIES AND BLOCS

Summarizing the Christian terms defined above, the following classification defines the major religious groupings in the world as used in Tables 1. Un-indented categories are all mutually exclusive, and their totals always add up to 100%, allowance being made for small rounding discrepancies. Indented categories are sub-divisions of categories less indented: i.e. categories indented 2 spaces after another category are sub-divisions of that category.

Note our 3 basic equations concerning definitions of Christians:
(1) Total 'Christians' = professing + crypto-Christians,
    which also = nominal + affiliated.
(2) Total 'affiliated' = affiliated Roman Catholics + affiliated Protestants + affiliated Orthodox + affiliated Anglicans + affiliated marginal Protestants + affiliated Non-White indigenous + affiliated Catholics (non-Roman), *minus* doubly-affiliated, *minus* disaffiliated.
(3) Total 'affiliated' = total practising + non-practising Christians.

Note also that the first 9 categories below *always* (in Tables 1) refer to aggregate totals for all denominations of Christians (in all 7 major ecclesiastical blocs: Roman Catholic, Protestant, etc) in the whole country.

**Christians** = total of all Christian adherents (professing and crypto-Christians, which is here equal to nominal plus affiliated).

professing = those publicly professing (declaring, stating, confessing, self-identifying) their preference or adherence in a government census or public-opinion poll, hence known to the state or society or the public.

crypto-Christians = secret believers in Christ not professing publicly, nor publicly baptized, nor enumerated or known in government census or public-opinion poll, hence unknown to the state or the public or society (but usually affiliated and known to churches), including those in 'churches of silence' or underground churches, of 7 distinct types: (1) unorganized individuals secretly affiliated to or attending legal churches, including persons who choose to identify themselves publicly as non-Christians (i.e. as Hindus, Muslims, non-religious, etc); (2) individuals or congregations permanently exiled, deported or in prison or labour camps, including political prisoners, treated as non-religious by the state but who remain believing Christians though deprived of worship and fellowship opportunities; (3) organized believers in unregistered denominations, and unregistered congregations in legal denominations, which are forced to operate illegally or underground by the state's refusal to grant registration (sometimes termed churches of silence, or catacomb churches); (4) members of organized deliberately-clandestine networks of illegal underground churches; (5) members of minority churches or marginal bodies or sects in certain countries opposed or hostile to the state hence refusing to divulge their affiliation to census enumerators (Jehovah's Witnesses, New Apostolics, et alii); (6) members of organized movements of believers in Christ who choose not to regard or identify themselves publicly or privately as bodies of Christians (but as Hindus, Muslims, non-religious, etc); and (7) isolated radio believers in non-Christian or anti-Christian areas remote from existing legal churches, initially evangelized through radio programmes or mail or radiophonic correspondence courses, prevented from contacting existing churches, who therefore organize their own small cells or informal house congregations based on radio and/or mails.

nominal = those professing but not affiliated to churches, i.e. not church members; unaffiliated or unchurched (sometimes called residual Christians, latent Christians, anonymous Christians, sometimes post-Christians in industrialized countries); Christians not, no longer, or not yet attached to organized Christianity, or having rejected the institutional churches whilst retaining Christian beliefs and values, who may be Christians individually but are not part of the corporate life, community or fellowship of the churches.

affiliated = church members; all persons belonging to or connected with organized churches; those on the churches' books or records, or with whom the churches are in touch, usually known by name and address to the churches at grass-roots or local parish level; i.e. total of all distinct individuals attached to or claimed by the institutional churches and organized Christianity and hence part of their corporate life, community and fellowship, including children, infants, adherents, catechumens, and members under discipline (totals for 1970–80 are obtained from Tables 2); total church membership, or total church member community, or total Christian community, or inclusive membership; this is the total of affiliated in the 7 major blocs, minus any doubly-affiliated, minus any disaffiliated.

disaffiliated = dechristianized persons: baptized Roman Catholics (or other Christians) enumerated as affiliated by a majority or state-linked Catholic Church (or other majority or state church) but who have recently formally withdrawn or disaffiliated themselves completely from Christianity and now profess to be non-religious (agnostics) or atheists; i.e. recent withdrawals from state or majority churches still however regarded as members by those churches, although in fact now backsliders, lapsed, or apostates; sometimes termed post-Christians; because a duplication, they are shown in the tables as a negative quantity (with a minus sign).

doubly-affiliated = persons affiliated to or claimed by 2 denominations at once (especially Evangelical and Catholic churches in Latin Europe and Latin America); because a duplication, they are shown in the tables as a negative quantity (with a minus sign).

total practising = total affiliated of all denominations who attend public worship at least once a year, or who fulfil their churches' minimum annual attendance requirements, or who are radio/TV-service listeners (% here = % of affiliated, not % of total population); church attenders (daily, weekly, fortnightly, monthly, occasional, on festivals only, or annual), excluding civic attenders, private attenders, attending non-members, and attending non-Christians; active Christians, committed Christians, militant Christians.

non-practising = affiliated but inactive, non-attending (sometimes called dormant Christians) (% = % of affiliated).

Anglicans = persons related to the Anglican Communion, including dissidents in the Western world.

Evangelicals = Anglican Evangelicals (sometimes termed either Conciliar or Conservative Evangelicals, and usually including all whose churchmanship is described as either Evangelical, Conservative Evangelical or Low Church, as distinct from High Church or sacramentalist persuasions, or Central or Broad Church); characterized by commitment to personal religion (including new birth or personal conversion experience), reliance on Scripture as the only basis for faith, preaching and evangelism; enumerated here as the sum of 3 groupings: (1) the total baptized communities (including children) who are affiliated to Anglican dioceses of Evangelical emphasis or persuasion, where the bulk of the parishes also are Evangelical; (2) those who are affiliated to Evangelical parishes in non-Evangelical dioceses; and (3) individual Evangelicals in dioceses and parishes of non-Evangelical or other persuasion, or of mixed persuasions. The most detailed enumeration of the varieties of Anglican Evangelicals in any country, in this Encyclopedia, will be found in the footnote EVANGELICALS in Table 1 for the United Kingdom of GB & NI. The figures were derived by sending questionnaires polling a variety of Evangelical leaders and other influential Anglicans in the General Synod of the Church of England and in the major Evangelical organizations.

Anglican pentecostals = Anglicans regularly active in the organized charismatic renewal (healings, tongues, prophesying).

Catholics (non-Roman) = Old Catholics and others in secessions from the Church of Rome since 1700 in the Western world, and other Catholic-type sacramentalist or hierarchical secessions from Protestantism or Anglicanism.

Marginal Protestants = followers of para-Christian or quasi-Christian Western movements or deviations out of mainline Protestantism (including pseudo-Christian 'New Age' cults), not professing mainstream Protestant christocentric doctrine but claiming a second or supplementary or ongoing source of divine revelation in addition to the Bible (a new Book, angels, visions), but nevertheless centered on Jesus, Christ, the Cross, the Resurrection, and other Christian features.

Non-White indigenous = Black/Third-World indigenous Christians in denominations, churches or movements indigenous to Black or Non-White races originating in the Third World (i.e. all races except the White peoples as defined in Part 4), locally-founded and not foreign-based or Western-imported, begun since AD 1500, Black/Non-White-founded, Black/Non-White-led, forming autonomous bodies independent of Western and Eastern churches, with no Western ties, often schismatic, separatist, anti-establishment, sometimes anti-Western, anti-White or anti-European in reaction to Western influences.

Black Evangelicals = Black Evangelicals, members of Black indigenous churches in the USA (but not elsewhere) who regard themselves as part of the Evangelical/Conservative Evangelical/Fundamentalist movement in the USA.

Black neo-pentecostals = active charismatics (more traditionally, 'sanctified' Black/Negro/Coloured persons) in the non-pentecostal Black denominations of the USA.

Orthodox = Eastern (Chalcedonian), Oriental (Pre-Chalcedonian, Non-Chalcedonian, Monophysite), Nestorian (Assyrian), and non-historical Orthodox.

Orthodox pentecostals = Orthodox active in the organized charismatic renewal (healings, tongues, prophesying).

Protestants = Christians in churches originating in, or reformulated at the time of, or in communion with, the Western world's 16th-century Protestant Reformation; in European languages, usually called Evangéliques (French), Evangelische (German), Evangélicos (Italian, Portuguese, Spanish), though not usually Evangelicals (in English); in Spanish, Portuguese and Italian the term Evangélico in government usage also covers Anglicans, marginal Protestants, and Black/Third-World indigenous Christians.

Evangelicals = a sub-division of affiliated Protestants (Protestants affiliated to churches), namely persons calling themselves Evangelicals as distinct from conciliar ecumenical or non-Evangelical Protestants, or persons belonging to Evangelical congregations, churches or denominations; i.e. Evangelicals properly so called, characterized by commitment to personal religion (including new birth or personal conversion experience), reliance on Holy Scripture as the only basis for faith and Christian living, emphasis on preaching and evangelism, and usually on conservatism in theology; usually divided into the 3 groupings Conservative Evangelicals, Conciliar Evangelicals, and Fundamentalists, defined as follows. (1) Persons calling themselves Conservative Evangelicals (mostly in the USA), or (in Europe) so called by the Ecumenical Movement, are sometimes also called Non-Conciliar Evangelicals, Neo-Evangelicals, or Neo-Fundamentalists, or (in German) Evangelikale as opposed to Evangelische which correctly translated means simply Protestant. The term Conservative Evangelical is not accepted by a large section of this grouping, particularly in the USA, who consider the adjective 'Conservative' superfluous and redundant, and who object to the popularizing of the term by the conciliar movement (led by the WCC) to describe Evangelical groups and individuals outside the Ecumenical Movement. They are enumerated here as (a) the total communities (including children) affiliated to institutionalized Conservative Evangelicalism, i.e. in Protestant denominations affiliated to national evangelical fellowships or alliances themselves affiliated to the World Evangel-

ical Fellowship (WEF), and (b) the total communities affiliated to all other Protestant denominations which regard themselves, or are generally regarded, as Conservative Evangelical in doctrine and emphasis (including Pentecostals) but which are not linked to the WEF or institutionalized Conservative Evangelicalism. (2) Conciliar Evangelicals, sometimes called ecumenical Evangelicals, who usually call themselves simply Evangelicals, are those who remain within and are affiliated to Protestant denominations not regarded as Conservative Evangelical in doctrine or emphasis but which are instead within the Ecumenical Movement affiliated to national ecumenical councils and/or the World Council of Churches (WCC), often called conciliar denominations; enumerated here as (a) the total communities (including children) affiliated to Evangelical congregations or parishes within conciliar denominations, and (b) other individual Evangelicals in non-Evangelical parishes or congregations in those denominations. Lastly (3) Fundamentalists, moderate or extreme, are those who began in the USA in the 1920s to oppose theological Liberalism and Modernism, and who are defined as those stressing either the 5 or the 7 so-called fundamental doctrines (inerrant verbal inspiration of the Bible, Virgin Birth, miracles of Christ, Resurrection, total depravity of man, substitutionary Atonement, premillennial Second Coming); enumerated here as (a) the total communities affiliated to Protestant denominations of Fundamentalist doctrine and emphasis usually affiliated to national Fundamentalist councils and/or the International Council of Christian Churches (ICCC), (b) the total communities affiliated to Fundamentalist congregations in non-Fundamentalist denominations, and (c) individual Fundamentalists in non-Fundamentalist congregations and parishes in those denominations. The most detailed enumeration of all these types of Evangelicals for any country in this Encyclopedia will be found in the footnote EVANGELICALS in Table 1 for the USA. Detailed documentation of other evidence underlying these statistics is given in the prayer survey by P. J. St G. Johnstone, *Operation World* (1978 edition). Note that there is considerable overlap between this category Evangelicals as shown in Tables 1 and the categories Neo-pentecostals and Anglican pentecostals. Note also that, as used in this survey, the English term Evangelicals refers to a sub-division within Protestantism and Anglicanism, and excludes all Black/Third-World indigenous Christians with the exception of those in the USA, where because they are usually termed Black Evangelicals (as e.g. in the National Black Evangelical Association, NBEA) they are given a separate statistical line in Table 1.

Neo-pentecostals = charismatics regularly active in organized renewal groups within non-Pentecostal Protestant denominations (Note: if any such movements subsequently separate from their parent bodies, they are then no longer listed here as Neo-pentecostals but are enumerated in Table 2 as new Pentecostal or indigenous pentecostal denominations. Note also that this category overlaps somewhat with the previous line, Evangelicals, where it occurs).

Roman Catholics = all Christians in communion with the Church of Rome (affiliated Roman Catholics are here defined as baptized Roman Catholics plus catechumens).

Catholic pentecostals = Roman Catholics regularly active and involved in the organized Catholic Charismatic Renewal; Catholic charismatics (healings, tongues, prophesying).

Christo-pagans = Amerindian Roman Catholics in Latin America who syncretize folk-Catholicism with organized traditional Amerindian pagan religion.

Evangelical Catholics = in Latin countries, professing Roman Catholics who also regard themselves as Evangélicos or Evangéliques and are affiliated to churches which the state terms

Evangelical (Protestant, Anglican, indigenous or marginal Protestant); in Latin America, Evangélicos who in a census are still regarded as, or profess to be, Roman Catholics.

Spiritist Catholics = Roman Catholics active in organized high or low spiritism, including syncretistic spirit-possession cults.

**Non-Christians** = all who are not Christian adherents of any kind, including non-believers (agnostics, or atheists).

Afro-American spiritists = followers of Afro-Brazilian, Afro-Cuban and other African religious survivals in the Americas; low spiritists, syncretizing Catholicism with African and Amerindian animistic religions; low spiritists as opposed to high (non-Christian) spiritists; also Afro-American syncretistic cults with Christian elements.

Atheists = those professing atheism, scepticism, impiety, disbelief or irreligion, or Marxist-Leninist Communism regarded as a political faith, or other anti-religious quasi-religions, and who abstain from religious activities and have severed all religious affiliation; and others opposed, hostile or militantly opposed to all religion (anti-religious); dialectical materialists, militant non-believers, anti-religious humanists, sceptics.

Baha'is = followers of the Baha'i World Faith founded by Baha'u'llah (Baha' Allah).

Buddhists = followers of (a) Mahayana (Greater Vehicle) or Northern Buddhism; or (b) Theravada (Teaching of the Elders) or Hinayana Lesser Vehicle) or Southern Buddhism; or (c) Vajrayana (Mantrayana, Guhyamantrayana, Tantrayana (Esoteric Vehicle), Tantrism or Lamaism); or (d) traditional Buddhist sects, but excluding neo-Buddhist new religions or religious movements.

religious Buddhists = Buddhists who profess Buddhism as both a family religion and also a personal religion.

non-religious Buddhists = persons whose family religion is Buddhism but who as individuals profess to have no personal religion.

Chinese folk-religionists = followers of traditional Chinese religion, with 6 elements: local deities including Taoist ones, ancestor veneration, Confucian ethics, Chinese universism, divination and magic, some Buddhist elements.

Confucians = non-Chinese followers of Confucius and Confucianism.

Hindus = followers of the main Hindu traditions: (a) Vaishnavite or Vishnaivite; (b) Saivite or Shivaite; (c) Saktite or Saktist; (d) Arya Samaj and other reformist movements (excluding Jains and Sikhs); and (e) neo-Hindu movements and modern sects arising out of Hinduism.

Jains = followers of Jain reform movement from Hinduism, composed of the Svetambara and Digambara sects.

Jews = followers of the Orthodox, Reformed, or Liberal schools of Judaism; Ashkenazis, Sefardis (Sephardis); also crypto-Jews.

Karaites = Readers of the Scriptures, followers of Qaraism (a Jewish sect).

Samaritans = Children of Israel (Bene-Yisrael) or Shamerim (Observant Ones), a small Jewish sect.

Mandaeans = Gnostics (Mandaiia), followers of 2nd-century AD syncretistic Jewish-Christian fertility religion (Christians of St John, Followers of John the Baptist, Dippers, Sabaeans).

Muslims = followers of Islam, in its 2 main branches (with schools of law, rites or sects): Sunnis or Sunnites (Hanafite, Hanbalite, Malikite, Shafiite), and Shias or Shiites (Ismaili, Ithna-Ashari, Alawite and Zaydi versions), and other orthodox sects; reform movements (Wahhabi, Sanusi, Mahdiya), also heterodox sects (Ahmadiya, Druzes, Kharijites (Ibadites), Yazidis), but excluding syncretistic religions with Muslim elements.

Ahmadis, Druzes, Yazidis = followers of heterodox Muslim sects (allegedly heretical or heterodox bodies; shown indented below the entry 'Muslims', and enumerated also in the total statistics of Muslims).

New-Religionists = followers of the so-called Asiatic 20th-century New Religions, New Religious movements, or radical new crisis religions (new Far Eastern or Asiatic indigenous non-Christian syncretistic mass religions, or new religious movements or sects embodying major innovations and religious systems distinct from those of the traditional world religions, founded since 1800 and mostly since 1945), including the Japanese neo-Buddhist and neo-Shinto new religious movements, and Korean, Chinese, Vietnamese and Indonesian syncretistic religions; et alia.

Non-religious = those professing no religion, or professing unbelief or non-belief, non-believers, doubters, agnostics, freethinkers, liberal thinkers, non-religious humanists, non-religious quasi-religionists, post-religious; indifferent to both religion and atheism, apathetic, opposed on principle neither to religion nor atheism; sometimes termed secularists or materialists; also post-Christian, de-christianized or de-religionized populations.

Parsis (Parsees) = descendants of Zoroastrians.

Shintoists = Japanese who profess, or still profess, Shinto as their first or major religion.

Sikhs = followers of the Sikh reform movement out of Hinduism, who look to the Golden Temple in Amritsar, India (sects: Akali, Khalsa, Nanapanthi, Nirmali, Sewapanthi, Udasi).

Spiritists = non-Christian spiritists or spiritualists, or thaumaturgicalists; high spiritists, as opposed to low spiritists (Afro-American syncretists); followers of medium-religions, medium-religionists.

Tribal religionists = primal or primitive religionists, animists, spirit-worshippers, shamanists, ancestor-venerators, polytheists, pantheists, traditionalists (in Africa), local or tribal folk-religionists (excluding Chinese as a special case); in some government censuses termed 'pagans', 'heathens' (so termed in Solomon Islands census of 9.II.1970, inter alia), 'fetishists', 'without religion'; including adherents of neo-paganism or non-Christian local or tribal syncretistic or nativistic movements, cargo cults, witchcraft eradication cults, possession healing movements, tribal messianic movements; usually confined each to a single tribe or people, hence 'tribal' or local as opposed to 'universal' (open to any or all peoples).

Other religionists = term used here in Tables 1 for total of (a) adherents of other larger non-Christian religions (as listed above) in the country who are however too few for their religions to be individually listed in a particular table (excluding non-religious and atheists), and (b) adherents of all other smaller non-Christian religions, faiths, quasi-religions, pseudo-religions, para-religions, religious systems, religious philosophies, and semi-religious brotherhoods, not included in the above listing (e.g. Gnostic, Occult, Masonic, Mystic religions).

**Country's population** = total present-in-area resident population or inhabitants of country at a given mid-year date.

All columns headed % in Tables 1 refer to percentages of the total population of the country, except for *practising* and *non-practising* Christians which are always given as % of affiliated Christians only (i.e. as a % of only those who are eligible to practise).

# NON-CHRISTIANS: a selection of non-Christian religionists

**Afro-American spiritists.** Woman priest of Macumba (Brazil's major Afro-Brazilian cult) at Sta Barbara centre, whose ceremonies last over 4 hours each.

**Ahmadis.** Large crowd of Ahmadis at prayers in Saltpond (Ghana) led by world leader of Ahmadiya Movement in Islam, Hazrat Hafiz Mirza Nasir Ahmad, Khalifat-ul-Massih III (centre, white turban).

**Atheists.** Militantly anti-religious Red Guards in Peking (August 1966) hold up Mao's Little Red Book prior to destroying churches and temples.

**Baha'is.** Brazilian children at Instituto Baha'i de Gravataí, Rio Grande do Sul.

**Black Muslims.** USA Black women of World Community of Al-Islam in the West/America, formerly Nation of Islam.

**Buddhists.** World's largest Buddhist monument, a stone polyhedron in Borobudur, Central Java (Indonesia), built AD 800, to which come 500,000 visitors a year. Upper circular terraces hold 72 stupas each containing a Buddha. The whole stupa complex with its 500 Buddhas is a mandala (ritual diagram) or allegory of the universe, representing ascending stages of enlightenment towards nirvana (spiritual freedom).

**Hindus.** Spiritual head of Hindu religion worldwide, Swami Satya Mitra Nandgiri, from 1960-74 His Holiness Swami Jagatguru Shankar Acharya, Head of Dandi Sanyasis, Head of Central India Math (Bhanpur, Ujjain).

Hindu festival Vijay Dashmi, celebrated annually (here, in Nairobi, Kenya).

Tamil woman imploring Hindu god Subrahmanya for help during festival procession in Saidapet district, Madras (India). At top left are the god's musicians.

**Chinese folk-religionists.** In See Yeah Temple (Malaysia), Chap Goh Meh (15th Night) is celebrated with glitter, pomp and gaiety, in a blending of Confucianism, Taoism, Buddhism and worship of local deities.

**Jains.** 25-yearly ceremony of anointing colossal 57-ft statue of Digambara saint Bahubali (rain god Gomatesvara) with milk, curds and ghee, at Sravana-Belgola, Mysore (India).

**Jews.** Four UK Jewish leaders are interviewed on BBC-1 television, including Editor of *Jewish Chronicle* (second left) and Chief Rabbi Jakobovits of United Hebrew Congregation of the Commonwealth (right).

**Muslims.** Orthodox (Sunni) Muslims at Great Prayer of Thursday before ancient mud mosque in Mopti (Mali), during which all streets are closed.

Sufi mosque seating 150 in Cape Town, South Africa. The domes represent the various levels of man's conscience.

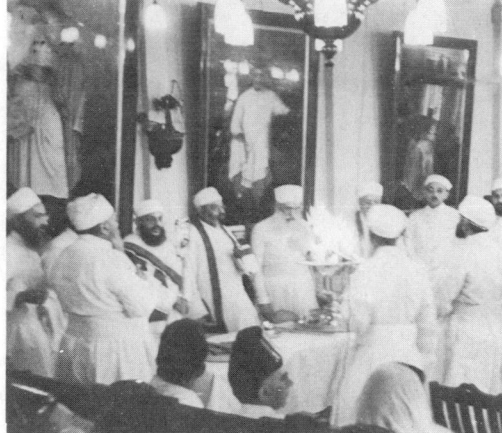

**Parsis.** Zoroastrian or Parsi priests in Fire Temple worship spirit of goodness and light, Ahura Mazda, under form of continually-burning sacred fire. Adherents are declining because no converts are accepted.

**Neo-Hindus.** Largest neo-Hindu movement is the Divine Light Mission. Here, 20% of its 5 million followers attend annual Hans Jayanti celebration in Delhi commemorating Guru's late father's birthday.

Centre of DLM's devotion is Guru Maharaj Ji (born 1958), worshipped as Lord of the Universe, Divine Incarnation, who became Perfect Master in 1966 at age 8.

**Reform Hindus.** Official opening of new centre in Pretoria by Swami Nisreyasananda (left) of the Ramakrishna Mission in Zimbabwe.

**New-Religionists.** 3 modern Asiatic syncretistic religions with Christian elements (and over 90 million adherents). (1) *Above:* Viet Nam: *Cao Daist Missionary Church* (Doctrine of the Third Revelation of God): worshippers facing altar and Divine Eye inside Holy See Great Divine Temple.

(2) Japan: *Rissho-koseikai* (Society for Establishment of Righteousness), with worshippers in Great Sacred Hall, Tokyo, facing 10-foot gold image of Sakyamuni Buddha on main altar.

(3) USA: *Nichiren Shoshu of America*, NSA (True Church of Nichiren/ Soka Gakkai/Value Creation Society): 20,000 NSA conventioneers in Los Angeles in 1972 stage Salute to America.

**Shamanists.** North American Indian shaman of Tlingit tribe (northern British Columbia coast), in spirit helper's headdress, attempts with drum (left) and rattle to effect a cure.

**Shintoists.** In Shinto festival in Japan, young men carry shrines down public street.

**Sikhs.** Five Sikh swordsmen guarding the Granth Sahib (Holy Scriptures) process through Nairobi.

**Tribal religionists.** Fetish post of great power revered by Dogon animists (fetishists) in Mali.

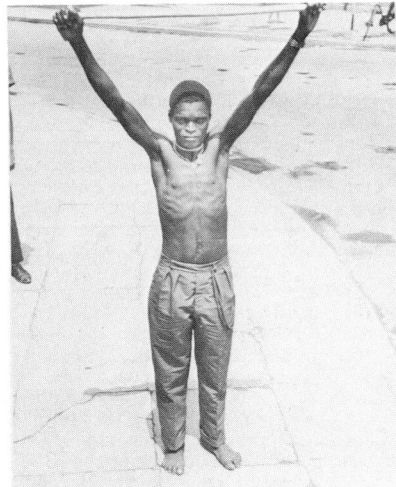

Modern revival of traditional religious practice: Kajiwe (Tsume Washe), renowned Giriama witchcraft eradication leader, in action as a witchfinder along Kenya coast in 1973.

**Other religionists.** This term is used in this Encyclopedia for adherents of smaller non-Christian religions, faiths, quasi-religions, pseudo-religions, para-religions, religious systems, religious philosophies, and semi-religious brotherhoods. Pictured is one example from Ghana.

*Footnotes to Tables 1*

CENSUSES. From its historical usage with regard to population counting, the term census is implicitly reserved for total or complete analysis of a population, although several governments now include partial surveys through sampling procedures. In this Encyclopedia, therefore, the term census always refers only and uniquely to an official government population census (usually complete, 100%, enumeration of the whole population). Footnotes under Tables 1 give details of all censuses which have included a religion question (either complete enumeration or on a sample basis), each shown by the date (day, month, year, in the standard United Nations order) on which it was conducted. Each date is printed in bold type, thus: **9.IV.1961.** Although such data are usually available in published form, in a number of recent cases our survey obtained the data before publication from each country's statistical office or from its annual statistical report to the United Nations on the annual Demographic Yearbook Questionnaire. In a number of other cases, the censuses reported here were official government censuses, but the religion data (and sometimes the entire census results) were never published, or were only made available in duplicated (mimeographed) form. In almost all such cases the editors obtained these unpublished data in visits to government statistical offices or by correspondence with them. It should be noted that in this Encyclopedia we make no detailed attempt at a critique of each nation's censuses, but accept them as the best available data on the subject. Because of the large sizes of the populations enumerated and the need for comparativeness from one census to the next, the results are given here as percentages to the first decimal place (e.g. 65.7%); 2 decimal places are avoided because of their claim to a bogus precision. The major problem faced at this point has been the non-standardized and non-comparable terms and categories used from one census to the next and from one country to another. Thus, many censuses omit certain minorities such as tribal peoples, nomads, aliens, refugees, military, etc. As one example of this, in Australia the legally-defined statistical 'population of Australia' until 1967 was the non-Aboriginal population only. This problem has been solved here by recompiling each census' totals using our standard terminology and methodology. The figures for several censuses as shown in the footnotes have been recomputed and rewritten slightly to incorporate the exact terminology we employ in this survey; thus the category 'Protestants', which in several censuses is used loosely to mean all Christians except Roman Catholics, is here shown divided into our usage of Anglicans, Protestants, Orthodox, Black indigenous, etc. These footnotes contain data from practically all those censuses in all countries in which the religion question has been asked. Consequently, if no census is quoted in a particular country for 1900, or 1960, or 1970, it means that in that year the question on religion was omitted, or not asked, or not processed or never released. It should also be noted that at each decennial census an increasing number of countries abandon the religion question, despite UN prompting, because of the escalating cost of every question in the census schedule and the fact that religion data from past censuses have rarely been of use in government planning.

POLLS. Whereas censuses usually go to and enumerate the entire population, adults plus children, to the last individual, a poll is taken from a very small carefully-constructed sample (usually around 2,500 adults, or 1,500 for Gallup polls) representative of the entire adult population. Because of the additional questions and the care with which they are formulated, accuracy and meaningfulness are often higher than those of censuses. Like censuses, a poll is taken at a single point in time, and if significant this may be indicated in our footnotes thus: 10.IX.1970, or September 1970, or simply: 1970. Because of the small size of samples, however, polls figures are usually given as integers without decimal places. Among specialists their accuracy is regarded as to plus or minus 3% ('Sampling tolerances', *Religion in America 1977-78*, Gallup Opinion Index, p. 116–117).

**NOTES ON RELIGIONS**

CHRISTIANS (etcetera). Next follow further details elaborating certain of the categories in Tables 1, these being listed in alphabetical order. For further details on the composition of Christian totals (e.g. 'Black/Third-World indigenous', 'marginal Protestants'), the reader should turn to the country's Table 2.

ATHEISTS. This footnote summarizes the available source data. Together with secularism, agnosticism (non-religion) et alia, atheism is one of a group of anti-Christian or anti-religious movements collectively known as quasi-religions. Since Communism is widely regarded as a quasi-religion, and since the basic philosophy of Marxists and Marxist regimes is atheistic, the footnote enumerates the Communist phenomenon by giving the name(s) of organized Communist parties, the legal status of each, its attitude vis-a-vis the Sino-Soviet dispute (pro-Soviet, or pro-Chinese, or independent, or split), and statistics of members and of all who voted for Communist parties in any recent elections. Other data on atheism (e.g. polls) are available for certain countries. The method whereby the total of atheists is derived from these data has been described earlier.

*Non-Christian use of 'church'*

The English word 'church' is derived, not directly from the New Testament word *ekklesia*, but from early Christian usage of the Greek word *kyriakon* meaning 'belonging to the Lord'. Historically, the word 'church' has therefore a specifically Christian origin and has always had this exclusively Christian meaning. In recent times, however, with the growth of knowledge concerning community life and values in non-Christian religions, confusion has arisen through the use in English of the word 'church', either in loose or popular or journalistic conversation, or officially in the names of organizations, to describe its non-Christian counterparts, namely for communities of believers in Islam, Buddhism, Hinduism, New Religions, et alia. Examples of the official use of 'church' by non-Christian bodies in this way are:

Cao Daist Missionary Church (Viet Nam)
Church of World Messianity (Sekai Kyusei-kyo)
Church Universal & Triumphant (USA)
First Church of Voodoo (USA)
Heavenly Virtue Holy Church (T'ien Te Sheng Hui, in Hong Kong and Malaysia)
Perfect Liberty Church (PL Kyodan, in Japan)
Satanic Church
True Church of Nichiren (Soka Gakkai of Japan)
Unification Church International (based on Korea)
United Buddhist Churches of Viet Nam
Vedic Church of East Africa (Arya Samaj)
Yellow Church of Tibet (a semi-official term for Yellow Hat Lamaist Buddhism)

In addition, there are a host of other non-Christian bodies, sects and cults calling themselves 'Church', which have arisen on the fringes of Christianity in solidly-Christian lands (especially in the USA) out of Christian roots and retaining some Christian elements. Although we here maintain that 'church' is a specifically Christian term and so should be restricted to Christian usage, we have to recognize that it is becoming increasingly popular as a self-appellation in a number of non-Christian religions.

**Table 2:**
**ORGANIZED CHURCHES AND DENOMINATIONS IN EACH COUNTRY**

After each country's article in Part 7, the second table describes organized denominational Christianity. It lists all Christians organized into bodies, i.e. all Christians affiliated to churches, and gives de facto (not de jure) statistical and other descriptive information about each autonomous church body (denomination, diocese or other jurisdiction) that they belong to, representing the statistical situation for, on average or approximately, the year 1970, and/or the period 1970–1980, with in many cases notes updating statistics to 1978 or 1980, and in all cases totals for the 3 years 1970, 1975 and 1980. In Roman Catholic, Orthodox and Anglican practice, a diocese is an autonomous and self-governing local church, and is therefore regarded here as the proper unit for comparison with a Protestant or indigenous denomination. The practice here then, in order to give a balanced presentation between the world's 2 major Christian blocs (Protestantism and Roman Catholicism), is to include all Roman Catholic, Orthodox and Anglican dioceses (with a very occasional omission in the interests of avoiding undue length), and to include all Protestant denominations, as their counterpart. Some very large Protestant denominations themselves also consist of several dioceses or equivalent sub-divisions, but these are only listed in a few cases for the very largest churches.

*Comparative symbolics*

The table includes the basic descriptive material to enable churches and denominations to be classified and compared with one another, and from one country to another. It thus provides basic or initial material for the science of comparative symbolics. This is the term traditionally applied to that branch of theology or ecclesiology which deals with the various Christian churches and confessions, and their doctrines, creeds, constitutions, ways of worship, devotional life and other distinctive features, studied as a whole.

*Objects of Table 2*

The objects of listing all churches and denominations in a single statistical table are:

1. to provide a complete overview of all organized Christian churches with members and adherents in the country;
2. to show them in comparative ecumenical or interdenominational perspective;
3. to enable information to be located at a glance concerning any particular denomination, or ecclesiastical tradition, or type of church, or confession (world family of churches or denominations), or council of churches (association of different denominations), or missionary society or order;
4. to enable meaningful statistical totals to be compiled for the country, for its region and continent, for world confessions, and for the whole world;
5. to provide a direct and exact numerical link with Table 1 (which enumerates all religions, and over the period 1900–2000) by expanding Table 1's figure of affiliated Christians in mid-1970; and
6. to provide basic or initial classificatory and descriptive material for the science of comparative symbolics.

*One line per denomination or diocese*

This comparative table stretches across the page, a single line being given to a single church body (denomination or diocese). In the case of churches with several dioceses, jurisdictions or other subdivisions, statistics are given on a single line each for each diocese, and the totals for the church are found above them on the first line, occupied by the title of the church itself followed by a colon (e.g. 'Church of England: ').

*Comprehensiveness*

The listing attempts to be comprehensive; it includes all major or significant denominations and dioceses known to exist in the country, together with at the end one or more summary lines covering all other bodies too small to be given a separate line each. In countries with very large numbers of small and relatively insignificant denominations (e.g. USA, Philippines, South Africa), it has been necessary to have a numerical cut-off point, above which all bodies are included, and below which most bodies are not included (e.g. USA, 1,000 adherents). Statistics for these remaining bodies are then summarized at the end of the alphabetical listing under the blanket terms 'Other Protestant denominations... Total 150', 'Other indigenous churches... Total 25', 'Other marginal Protestant bodies... Total 10', and so on.

*Descriptive notes on each body*

Brief notes in Column 8 crystallize the identity of the body concerned, by giving data such as its past and present names, with translation into English where necessary, and brief socio-religious notes of interest to describe the body and to give it a 'personality' that statistics alone cannot confer. Bodies formerly existing in a country, but now defunct or merged or with a new name, may often be found mentioned in column 8.

*Estimating adults and children*

We have already noted above that although a number of denominations produce annual figures of all types of membership, covering and including both adults and children, many other denominations only enumerate one of the 2 standard membership categories we require for this survey (Tables 2, Columns 6 and 7). Either they enumerate adult members only (as do the Non-Liturgical world confessions including most Protestant bodies), or they only enumerate total affiliated community including children and infants (as do the Liturgical world confessions including Roman Catholic, Anglican and Orthodox bodies). To ensure that the statistics in our table are properly comparable from one denomination to another, we have therefore to estimate the missing figure for each such body. The exact procedure for doing this will now be described.

The usual definitions of adults and children, followed in this Encyclopedia, are those employed by the United Nations as shown on page 48 above. 'Adults' refers to the working-age and old-age populations, namely all persons of 15 years and over (over-14s); 'children' refers to under-15s (0–14 years old), who may be subdivided into school-age children (5–14 years) and pre-school children or infants, who are aged 0–4 years (under-5s).

With these definitions, we can draw up another table showing in its first 2 columns, for any countries we are interested in, the relative sizes of (1) the number of children (under-15s) and (2) the number of adults (over-14s) in each country's population. We do this below for a small selection of typical countries across the world. Next we make the assumptions, described earlier, that (a) in any particular denomination the proportions of children and adults are approximately the same as those in its country's total population, and that (b) children and infants have, in general, the same religion and denomination as their parents. We can now derive the last 2 columns in the table; (3) gives the ratio of adults to total affiliated in any denomination, and (4) gives its inverse, namely the ratio of total affiliated to adults. Knowing one of these 2 types of membership figure for a denomination, we can therefore now estimate the other. If a denomination, for example, in the UK has 100,000 total affiliated including children and infants, then we can estimate its adult members at 77,000; if another denomination there reports 100,000 adults, then we can estimate its total affiliated at 130,000.

To estimate the missing figure for a particular body, we must first decide whether its reported membership figure includes, or excludes, children and infants. In general, if infant baptism is practised by the denomination, infants are enumerated in its membership figure; if adult baptism only is practised, the membership figure probably covers adults only. Next, we must establish exactly what age-range is covered by the body's reported figure. For most denominations, the issue will be clearcut: either the age-range will be all ages (0-over 65 years), as with all Roman Catholic and Orthodox dioceses, or it will be only adults over 14, as with most Protestant bodies. Protestant practice here needs to be carefully investigated. In the case of the 2 largest Protestant bodies in the USA, for example, the United Methodist Church's 10,622,173 full members (in 1970) were over-14s (full membership commencing at age 15 on average), whilst the Southern Baptist Convention's 11,629,880 baptized members were over-9s (baptism taking place between the ages of 8 and 10). In the USSR, membership is prohibited by law for persons under 18 years old. These latter 2 cases are unusual, however; and in this survey all Protestant bodies are assumed to define their adult membership as over 14 unless evidence to the contrary is available. We can now proceed to describe our actual estimation procedure, dividing denominations into 5 categories.

1. *Churches with no adult statistics.* Where a body enumerates not adult members but only total affiliated community including children and infants, we can obtain an estimate for adult membership by multiplying this figure by the country's proportion of the total population who are over 14 years of age (column 3 above). This latter information is given in this Encyclopedia for each country in the secular data at the start of its survey article in Part 7. In the USA, for example, of the total population 69% are 15 years or older in age, and so a Roman Catholic or Orthodox diocese there reporting 100,000 total affiliated can be estimated to have a total of adult members of 100,000 x 69% = 69,000.

2. *Churches whose adult statistics refer to over-14s.* Where a body enumerates adults only excluding children under 15 and infants, we follow exactly the reverse procedure, dividing this figure by the proportion of the total population in its country who are adults (or, multiplying by its inverse, given below in column 4). In the USA, a denomination reporting 100,000 adult members over 14 would then be estimated to have a total affiliated community of 100,000 ÷ 69% = 145,000.

3. *Churches whose adult statistics include children over 9.* In some Protestant traditions practising adult baptism and rejecting infant baptism, the minimum age at which adult baptism is permitted has been gradually reduced over the years. In Southern Baptist (USA) churches it takes place between the ages 8–10 years, and sometimes as young as 7 or even 6 years old. For such denominations, the above table cannot be used and instead we have to return to the country's population data to derive a figure for the proportion of the total population who are over 9 years old (10 years and older). For the USA, this figure in 1970 was 81.9%, and so a denomination reporting 100,000 members over 9 would be estimated to have 122,000 total affiliated.

4. *Churches whose adult statistics cover other age-ranges.* If it is known that a denomination's adult statistics cover other ranges of age, such as over-18s only, or over-20s only, or over-12s, then we have to return in the same way to the country's population data again.

5. *Churches whose adult statistics are strictly reduced.* With certain Protestant traditions (Pentecostal, Holiness, independent, smaller Baptist denominations, et alia), a further factor must be taken into account, namely that the figure for adult membership is usually strictly controlled and rolls are regularly 'cleaned' or reduced in size to exclude lapsed or departed members and to include only the church's regularly-attending baptized communicants in good standing. In such cases its figure for total affiliated, which on our definition includes all other kinds of looser affiliation (unbaptized adults, attending sympathizers, irregularly-attending adults, adults under discipline, adherents, catechumens, as well as their children and infants), will often be 2, 3 or even 4 times as large as the adult membership. In such cases, we have evaluated each denomination's situation individually, using the following standard procedure.

For these 5 categories of churches, our procedure when estimating the missing figure for a specific denomination has been as follows. First, we decide in which of the 5 categories it falls. Secondly, if it falls in categories 2–5 we start from whatever adult figure the denomination reports, enter this in Table 2's Column 6, and examine exactly what categories of member it covers. If it falls in category 5, we add an estimate for other types of adult nembership (catechumens, unbaptized attenders, irregular attenders, et alia) multiply this new total by the appropriate Affiliated/Adults factor to incorporate children and infants, and then see if other statistical evidence covering children is available (e.g. Sunday-school attendance) which would justify increasing the total, as a result of all which we arrive at the final estimate of total affiliated which appears in Table 2 as our Column 7.

To sum up, the relationship between our 2 Columns 6 and 7 in Tables 2 is extremely complex, and although we have used the above guiding principles, other evidence in particular cases may modify the procedure we have used.

*Time level of the statistics*

It is important, expecially with rapidly-growing churches, to specify the time level, i.e. the exact date or time to which particular data supplied by the churches refer. Large churches are not able to be very precise about their data, and there is no standardization amongst the denominations with regard to the time of year when numbers are counted. Most statistics vary somewhat during the year. For example, the number of foreign missionaries in a particular country will fluctuate from month to month as some go on furlough, or new replacements arrive; again, church members are added, lost, or die, from day to day in a continuous process. Our statistics were collected from the churches themselves during the period 1965–1980. However, the delays and drawn-out processes involved in the gathering of statistics within most churches mean that most

RATIO OF ADULTS/AFFILIATED, AND AFFILIATED/ADULTS, IN DENOMINATIONS IN SELECTED COUNTRIES

| *Country* | Country's population | | Church membership | |
|---|---|---|---|---|
| | *Children under 15* (1) | *Adults over 14* (2) | *Adults/Affiliated* (3) | *Affiliated/Adults* (4) |
| Austria | 22% | 78% | 0.78 | 1.28 |
| Brazil | 43 | 57 | 0.57 | 1.75 |
| FR Germany | 22 | 78 | 0.78 | 1.28 |
| German DR | 21 | 79 | 0.79 | 1.26 |
| India | 41 | 59 | 0.59 | 1.69 |
| Kenya | 47 | 53 | 0.53 | 1.89 |
| Nigeria | 45 | 55 | 0.55 | 1.82 |
| USSR | 31 | 69 | 0.69 | 1.45 |
| UK | 23 | 77 | 0.77 | 1.30 |
| USA | 31 | 69 | 0.69 | 1.45 |
| **World population** | **37** | **63** | **0.63** | **1.59** |

membership statistics when published reflect in fact the situation several years earlier, though very few large churches acknowledge this and most continue to assume too recent a date. For rough comparative purposes, it may be assumed that taken as a whole the statistics in Tables 2 refer to the situation at mid-1970, updated to mid-1975 and projected to mid-1980. For more exact information in any particular case, the reader should consult annual reports of the churches he is interested in.

*Multiyear time lags*
This time lag or delay in statistical reporting for large churches may be illustrated by considering the annual collecting and publishing of global statistics by the world's biggest church and also statistically its best-organized, namely the Roman Catholic Church. On 9 January 1973 its Central Office of Statistics in Rome published its annual directory *Annuario Pontificio 1973*, containing statistics of Catholics for every jurisdiction in the world. These statistics soon became referred to by interested persons, especially in other churches, as 'the 1973 statistics'. But in fact the statistics referred to the situation at a much earlier date. Working backwards in time from the January 1973 publication date, we find that typesetting began the previous autumn 4 months earlier, and that the manuscript was compiled from questionnaires returned to Rome by the over 2,000 jurisdictions during April-June 1972, having been sent out a couple of months before that. The questionnaire asked all bishops to provide statistical totals describing the situation as at 31 December 1971; the bishops gave their latest available figures, but in fact many of their totals had been obtained or were in circulation several months previously, and a number were repetitions of figures sent in the previous year. These diocesan totals in turn had been compiled from parish returns compiled earlier from actual counts at the parish level done still earlier, in many cases during 1970, or 1969, or in some cases during 1968 or even earlier. In sum, then, *AP 1973* published statistics which described the grass-roots situation at, approximately and on average, at the very latest mid-1970. For this reason in Tables 2 we use Catholic statistics from *AP 1973* to represent the situation as at mid-1970. The only exception is for the nation in which statistical reporting procedures are the most rapid, namely the USA; in this case statistics from *The official Catholic directory* (1972) were assumed to best represent the mid-1970 situation.

It can be shown likewise that similar time lags of 2, 3, 4, 5, 6, 7 or even 8 years accompany the publication of statistics by the other major churches of the world. This being so, it follows that any survey of all churches in the world must be subject to a similar, cumulative and hence even larger, time lag, of at least 6, 7, 8, 9 or even 10 years. In this Encyclopedia we indicate this phenomenon by stating that Tables 2 represent, on average, the situation in the year 1970, projected to 1975 and 1980; Tables 1 then place the figures in the wider religious situation in 1970, 1975, 1980 and projected to 2000.

*Overlapping memberships*
Although in almost all cases the lists of churches and denominations in Tables 2 are mutually exclusive, with each Christian being enumerated once and once only under only one body, in a few cases there is a small amount of overlapping or dual membership of individuals. Sometimes this takes place within a large denomination, as with the Southern Baptist Convention where 'non-resident members' counted in Texas may be the same persons counted as resident members in California whither they have migrated. Sometimes the same individuals belong as members to 2 or more local congregations. Sometimes the overlapping may affect several denominations: in the USA, a number of congregations affiliate themselves to, and pay quotas to, more than one nation-wide

denomination (e.g. Methodist & Presbyterian; or American Baptist & United Church of Christ). Store-front churches among USA Blacks are sometimes claimed by 2 denominations also. Again, there is a certain amount of rebaptism, as when Christians from older denominations baptized in infancy join younger denominations who cause them to be baptized again as adults. Nevertheless, all of these varieties of overlapping are numerically insignificant or even negligible by comparison with the orders of magnitude shown in the tables.

*Double affiliation*
There is however one type of country in the world in which very large numbers of church members are counted twice as affiliated to 2 separate churches. This happens widely in Latin American and European countries with overwhelmingly-large Roman Catholic majorities where sizeable numbers of Catholics have recently (within the previous 10 or 20 years) become Evangelicals (Evangélicos) and joined Protestant, indigenous, Anglican or marginal Protestant churches. They are then counted as affiliated both by their local Roman Catholic church or diocese, because they were baptized as Catholics, and also by their Evangelical church. This state of affairs is most clearly seen in cases where the total of affiliated members claimed by all the churches is greater than the total population of the country. Obviously, in such cases many people are doubly-affiliated, i.e. being counted twice.

In Tables 1 for these countries, the situation is set out clearly so that it is possible to see how double affiliation arises and how it is enumerated. In all such cases, the total of these persons thus doubly-affiliated is taken from Table 1 and inserted as a line at the end of Table 2 immediately before the final totals. In order to keep the mathematics correct, these figures of doubly-affiliated persons are expressed in both tables as negative quantities (with minus signs). The number shown 'affiliated' in Tables 1 and 2 is therefore not the sum of the totals claimed by all churches, but this sum minus the quantity shown as negative, which then gives the total number of distinct individuals affiliated, with each individual counted only once.

*Evangelical Catholics*
A further complication arises during government censuses, when it is clear that many of these new Evangelicals are still regarded as, or are enumerated as, or still profess publicly to be, or still declare themselves as, Roman Catholics. In many Latin American countries it is plain that the total of Evangelicals is much greater than that recorded in the censuses. These persons who are affiliated to Evangelical churches but who are enumerated in the censuses as professing Roman Catholics are termed Evangelical Catholics here in Tables 1. Their number in a country is in almost all cases less than that of the doubly-affiliated, since many of the latter identify themselves clearly in the censuses as Evangelicals.

*Zero and . as information*
The symbol 0 in tables means zero, as for example in a case where the number of Christians in 1900 was nil. This is a definite piece of information, and does not mean 'No information available'. Likewise, in Tables 2, Column 4 (Councils), the symbol . (period, fullstop) means 'Not a member of any council'. The only column in any table where occasionally no information was available is Tables 2, Column 5 (Congregations); in such cases the space has been left blank.

*Totals*
At the end of each Table 2 will be found totals at the average date applicable to the data in the table (mid-1970), and projected totals for mid-1975 and mid-1980, derived from, or in parallel with, Table 1's

analysis of church growth data. Tables 1 and 2 are therefore linked by both giving this one category ('affiliated' Christians) for the years 1970, 1975 and 1980.

*Languages, spellings, and orthography*
In this table, the names of denominations are listed in one of the 6 major European international languages (English, French, German, Italian, Portuguese, Spanish), depending on which one makes the most sense in a global survey; either as the official language, or the dominant one, or the one most widely used; in most cases, it is English. Certain denominations still insist on using for international purposes a minority-language name, untranslated, and occasionally we reproduce them in that language. Certain countries also are bilingual (e.g. Cameroon) or trilingual (e.g. Switzerland); in their cases, church names are given in the churches' own major language.

In Column 1, place names are given in the local spelling and orthography as standardized in the *Oxford world atlas* (1973) (except for its orthography for USSR and China, where we follow Philip's *Concorde world atlas*, 1972), followed in parentheses by the anglicized version, if any. As in the text, place names in column 8 and in the footnotes are anglicized only if widely used (e.g. Rome, Moscow, Copenhagen). It should be noted that different churches in in the same country may differ in their usage for spellings, orthography and transliterations of the same words. If this is the case, we follow each church's usage on its own line. In the same way, in the same country 2 churches may spell an ethnic name in different ways; again, we follow each's usage on its own line.

*Alphabetization*
1. All lists of names throughout this Encyclopedia are alphabetized in the standard order shown below, with 2 additions before Aa–Zz and 9 additions after. A blank space in a name comes first (thus 'Church Society' is listed before 'Churches Society'); then '&', then the alphabet, then all other signs, and lastly numerals.

|  |  |
|---|---|
|  | (blank space) |
| & | (ampersand) |
| Aa–Zz | (letters of alphabet) |
| - | (hyphen) |
| , | (comma) |
| ; | (semicolon) |
| : | (colon) |
| ' | (apostrophe) |
| ( | (parenthesis) |
| ) | (parenthesis) |
| / | (oblique, slash) |
| 0–9 | (numerals) |

2. In the lists of churches in Table 2 for each country, certain frequently-used words (e.g. 'Church', 'Evangelical') are in some cases abbreviated (e.g. to 'Ch', 'Ev') to keep names to a manageable length; these abbreviations are given in the Codebook (Part 6). When alphabetizing, however, the abbreviated forms are alphabetized on their unabbreviated version, to assist the reader to locate them.
3. The abbreviation 'St' (Saint) is likewise alphabetized on the unabbreviated version.
4. A capital letter (A) precedes its lower-case counterpart (a), but only where 2 names are otherwise identical.
5. Letters with accents or subscripts are alphabetized in the following order: a, á, à, â, ã, ä.

In the sections that now follow, we give first the meanings of various columns in the table, and then the various codes employed in Columns 1, 3, 4, and 8.

---

**SUMMARY OF COLUMNS IN TABLES 2**
The first 7 columns give data (names, dates, codes, numbers) that are directly comparable from one line to another in the table, i.e. from one denomination or diocese to another. But in addition, there is a lot of church data available which is not comparable in this way. Some churches enumerate their lay workers, others do not; some are aided by foreign missionary societies, others are not; many operate development projects, many do not; and so on. Column 8 therefore serves as a general space where any further significant data available may be summarized, with the aim of identifying each body clearly, sketching its historical development, and giving it an identity that statistics alone cannot convey. The code used is explained later and is summarized in the Codebook.

After this summary of the 8 columns, detailed explanations and codes are given, but only for Columns 1, 3, 4 and 8.

Column 1    *Name*    = Official name of church, denomination or diocese in the country's major European language in use (or in English in ambiguous cases), including standardized abbreviations for dioceses, jurisdictions or other sub-divisions. Initials of these church names, if widely used (mainly for Protestant and Anglican churches), are added at the beginning of the notes in Column 8.

Column 2 *Begun* = Year (AD) usually given (by historians or officials of the body concerned) as the main or most significant or earliest date of origin of the body in this country, in permanent form, i.e. with subsequent continuity to the present day; i.e. year when body or its predecessors was founded, begun, re-begun, formed, or organized in this country; when evangelization began in this country, or the first evangelists arrived, or the first immigrants of that church came from another country, or the first missionaries arrived from another land (note that in numerous cases a foreign mission society was preceded by nationals or immigrants; or, it built on a previously existing congregation or church); for a diocese or sub-division, year when diocese or sub-division was formally created or formed; for Roman Catholic jurisdictions, date when first created or erected as a distinct and separate jurisdiction; for Roman Catholic local (national) churches (if followed by dioceses and jurisdictions), year when the first specifically Roman Catholic (or Latin or Greek or other Catholic) missionary activity began in the country; for other large churches (followed by several dioceses or sub-divisions), year when first Christian activity began in the country. (Note: c = circa, approximately. For the first 15 centuries AD, a founding date 'in the 5th century' is thus written here 'c 450').

Column 3 *Type* = Ecclesiastical type: ecclesiastico-cultural major bloc (Roman Catholic, Protestant, etc.), followed by ecclesiastical tradition (Latin, Coptic, Reformed, Pentecostal, etc.).

Column 4 *Councils* = Conciliarism: membership in 5 types of council or conciliar body — respectively: confessional, world, continental, regional, national.

Column 5 *Congs* = Congregations or worship centres (all distinct organized groups of worshippers, usually measured by: church buildings, chapels, regular worship premises, worship centres, sites, stations, centres, outposts, preaching points); for the Roman Catholic Church, this column almost always gives the total parishes and quasi-parishes although on a few occasions also with churches and missions (for exact breakdown and meaning in a particular diocese, consult *Annuario Pontificio;* numbers of chapels (often very much greater than number of parishes) are not given in *AP*, but for jurisdictions under Propaganda these are given for 1969 in *Guida delle Missioni Cattoliche 1970*). In many Protestant bodies, 'congregation' is a technical term for an organized self-supporting parish, but the statistics shown here use our wider definition just given. Catholic parishes and quasi-parishes tend to be far larger in size and area than Protestant congregations, but each usually centres on one single parish church building; in addition, a Catholic parish often has numerous mass centres, but these are usually less fixed than Protestant centres and are only rarely enumerated. 'Congregation' here has no reference to the Catholic usage meaning a religious institute, order, community or society; this latter meaning is enumerated in Column 8 (see code 'C' in Codebook).

Column 6 *Adults* = Adult church members (communicants, full members, adult believers, also probationary members, baptized adult non-communicants, sometimes unbaptized attending adults), usually those over 14 years of age, on church's books or rolls (many Protestant bodies enumerate only this adult membership); often termed simply communicants (all those eligible for communion) or full members, although probationary members and baptized adult non-communicants are often also included.

Column 7 *Affiliated* = Total church membership or total church member community or inclusive membership (often called total Christian community) affiliated to a church or on its books or records in a form which can be substantiated (Christians, adult members, their children, their infants, catechumens, registered enquirers, unbaptized adults, non-member supporters, attending sympathizers, non-member attenders, adherents, followers, members under discipline) as defined by the church concerned; sometimes called total constituency. This figure always includes that in the previous column, Adults.

Column 8 *Names, notes* = *Names, notes and other statistics*=Descriptive notes, including some or all of these elements: name of body in local language (if not given in Column 1), initials of name if used, translation of name in Column 1 into English, alternate or former name(s), co-operating foreign missionary societies, brief notes on historical development, ethnic composition of members or adherents, and any other significant statistics that are available.

## COLUMN 1: NAMES OF BODIES

*Churches and denominations*

A strictly alphabetical listing of all churches and denominations is given here, using the full official name of each body. The main advantage of this method is that any body can be located with a minimum of searching. If names are abbreviated in any way, the alphabetization follows the unabbreviated form of these names. Names indented 2 or more spaces are either dioceses or other sub-divisions (see below), or are churches forming part of a larger church or denomination. If a name is followed by a colon alone (:) it indicates that that body is composed of the several smaller bodies shown indented below it, and that its statistics equal the total of their statistics. To assist the reader get an immediate overview of the numerically significant bodies in the nation, we print in boldface type the name of every church with over 10% of the total affiliated Christian population in the country. Most countries have thus from 3 to 6 such names in bold, with a maximum possible number in practice of 9.

The listing gives the names of all denominations existing in the year 1970, with the addition of any further bodies brought into existence during 1970–80 (as may be seen by inspecting Column 2). The statistics, however, refer in all cases to the actual number of persons present in the year 1970. Thus if a denomination suffers a major schism in 1973, the schism is shown with its statistics which are then subtracted from the total the parent body had in 1970 to give the reduced total we show here. With regard to denominations or missions which existed in the country at an earlier period, but which had disappeared, withdrawn or otherwise gone out of existence by 1970, these do not appear in the listing in Column 1. They may be mentioned in the text, if particularly significant, or they may be listed in column 8 of Table 2 if a foreign mission, but in general our survey does not attempt systematically to list all such former bodies no longer present in in 1970.

The languages used for names provide a compromise between (a) the requirements of individual countries, who need the list of churches presented in their own national language, and (b) the requirements of the international community, who need the list presented in an international language. Our practice here is to give weight to the major languages of Christian scholarship and Christian communication rather than either to local languages or to the 6 official languages of the United Nations (Arabic, Chinese, English, French, Russian, Spanish). Our usage therefore is as follows. (1) For countries using as official or first language any of the 6 major European international languages (English, French, German, Italian, Portuguese, Spanish), the listing in Column 1 is in this language. If this first language is not English, translations into English appear at the start of Column 8. It should be noted that the meaning of the official name may often be quite different from the official name used in English or other languages. (2) For countries whose official or first language is not one of the above 6, the listing is given in English, with church names in the national language or vernacular then given in Column 8. (3) For bilingual or trilingual countries using 2 or 3 of the 6 languages, names are in either language.

The definite article 'The', and its equivalents in other languages, form part of the official name of almost all denominations and dioceses. In the interests of brevity, however, we omit it throughout in Column 1 except for a handful of bodies who insist on including 'The' as a part of their title necessary for their full identification (e.g. 'African Church, The' in Nigeria).

It should be noted that in this Encyclopedia we treat names seriously, especially those of smaller denominations and of bodies in developing countries, because they imply a definite identity and often a tenacious self-assertion. A church's official name, however quaint it may appear to others, usually reveals (to the trained observer) its identity, status, origin, affiliation, theological position, ecclesiastical tradition, and also its legitimation. Such names usually imply or involve the existence of a postal address, telephone, premises, bank account, membership rolls, leadership, organization, history, publications, constitution, legal existence, registration, and recognition by government. A church's official name therefore calls for care and respect in its use by outsiders, without misquotation, misspelling or abbreviation.

*Dioceses, jurisdictions and other sub-divisions*

In the table in most countries, the largest churches (especially Roman Catholic, Orthodox and Anglican) are sub-divided into their component dioceses, synods, conferences, or other geographical or ethnic jurisdictions. Being autonomous bodies, these correspond somewhat to Protestant denominations. In the

**OFFICIAL NAMES.** A church's official name reveals its identity, status, origin, affiliation and legitimation, hence should be used by outsiders with care and respect. This selection of noticeboards comes from African indigenous churches, in Togo (Divine Healer's Church of Togo), Nigeria (Eternal Sacred Order of Cherubim & Seraphim) and Zaire (Eglise des Noirs).

However, in those cases where a jurisdiction extends over parts of 2 or more countries, it is shown in the original or base country (that with the see city or the major part of the diocese) without parentheses, but in the other countries (with secondary parts of the jurisdiction) it is shown in Column 1 in parentheses, thus: (D Gibraltar). This means that the statistics of the diocese in the base country will not include figures for the whole diocese but only that part in the base country.

The listing that follows below, of code letters used for jurisdictions and sub-divisions, is given approximately in descending order of size or importance. An alphabetical listing is given in the Codebook.

*Code*

| | |
|---|---|
| EP | ecumenical patriarchate |
| P | patriarchate, patriarchal diocese |
| C | catholicate (catholicossate), diocese of catholicos |
| CR | conciliar region (regione conciliare) |
| R | region (apostolic or conciliar) |
| RE | ecclesiastical region |
| Pro | province |
| EPr | ecclesiastical province |
| M | metropolitan archdiocese (with suffragan dioceses); metropolia (when superior to D) |
| AD | archdiocese |
| UD | united diocese |
| UDs | united dioceses |
| D | diocese, eparchy |
| CP | church province |
| EC | episcopal commissariat |
| Epi | episcopal area |
| PE | patriarchal exarchate |
| EA | exarchate apostolic |
| E | exarchate |
| VP | patriarchal vicariate |
| VA | vicariate apostolic |
| MV | military vicariate or ordinariate |
| V | vicariate |
| PA | prefecture apostolic |
| AA | apostolic administration |
| PN | prelature (prelacy) nullius |
| AN | abbey nullius |
| O | ordinariato |
| J | jurisdiction |
| Co | community (communauté) (used only in Zaire Table 2) |
| Con | conference |
| S | synod |
| CD | church district |
| EM | exarchical monastery |
| RN | priory nullius |
| m | mission (sui juris) |
| : | at end of a name, this indicates a composite body whose statistics are the totals of component bodies indented under it. |
| ( ) | jurisdiction based in another country, of which this body is a part |

*Indenting*
Where one of the titles in this column (or a code letter, or a place name) is found indented one space from the jurisdiction on the line above it, it indicates that it is ecclesiastically dependent on the latter, or subject to it, or a component part of it. Thus almost all Roman Catholic dioceses (coded D) are suffragan dioceses to (i.e. dependent on) a metropolitan archdiocese (coded M), although in practice they are virtually autonomous in the conduct of day-to-day affairs.

*Order for listing Roman Catholic jurisdictions*
The aim of each listing in a country is to show at a glance the structure of the church there, yet at the same time to facilitate the finding of a specific jurisdiction by using a standard amount of alphabetization. Jurisdictions are therefore arranged alphabetically by ecclesiastical province and rank. The order used is as follows:—

*Patriarchates* (P), in alphabetical order irrespective of rite, each followed by its suffragan dioceses and jurisdictions, if any, in alphabetical order and indented 1 space from P.

*Metropolitan archdioceses* (M), in alphabetical order irrespective of rite, each followed by its suffragan dioceses and jurisdictions in alphabetical order and indented 1 space from M.

*Other individual jurisdictions*, not indented, in order of rank (AD, D, EC, EA, VA, PA, AA, PN, AN, O, RN, m), and alphabetized within each rank.

Orthodox world, jurisdictions are often all termed eparchies. The definition of each of these sub-divisions is found in Part 9, Survey Dictionary of World Christianity. The code letters below, when found before a place name in the title of a sub-division, indicate the official title of the jurisdiction concerned, thus: 'D London' (='The Diocese of London'). *Place names* of dioceses are always given in the primary locally-used spelling or transliteration (either the secular name in the national language, or in the language of the particular local church itself). If there is a recognized English or anglicized version, or an alternative spelling, this name follows in brackets, thus: Roma (Rome), Moskva (Moscow), München (Munich), Al Qahirah (Cairo). However, in the case of certain ancient Orthodox and Catholic dioceses, the official name may be an archaic one (e.g. Heliopolis), in which case it is usually given first followed in brackets by the contemporary

secular name. When English is not the national language, the official title in the language is often given also, in Column 8. Thus the Netherlands entry 'D Rotterdam' has in Column 8 '*Bisdom Rotterdam*' as the title in Dutch of the Diocese of Rotterdam. In cases where such a diocese is followed by other similar dioceses, the vernacular titles are given only once and are not repeated. *Eastern-rite Catholics*. These may be identified from the code in Column 3, but also from the name of the rite or sub-rite in italics in parentheses in Column 1 after the name of the jurisdiction, thus: (*Melkite*). Where Latin jurisdictions are in a minority in a country, they themselves are usually identified in the same way: (*Latin*). Elsewhere, Latin jurisdictions, because in the vast majority, are not identified in this manner. *Dioceses extending over more than one country*. Most dioceses (and almost all Roman Catholic jurisdictions) fall completely inside the boundaries of a single country.

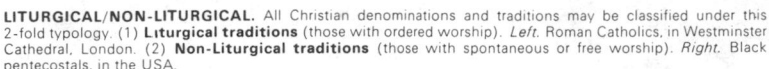

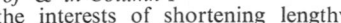

LITURGICAL/NON-LITURGICAL. All Christian denominations and traditions may be classified under this 2-fold typology. (1) **Liturgical traditions** (those with ordered worship). *Left*. Roman Catholics, in Westminster Cathedral, London. (2) **Non-Liturgical traditions** (those with spontaneous or free worship). *Right*. Black pentecostals, in the USA.

### Use of '&' in Column 1

In the interests of shortening lengthy names, the ampersand (&) is used in Column 1 as follows: (1) in all cases instead of the English word 'and', (2) in all names of dioceses and jurisdictions in all languages, (3) to join other geographical names or initials, and (4) in a few other cases where exceptionally lengthy names have to be shortened. For all other cases, i.e. names of denominations in French, German, Italian, Portuguese or Spanish, the ampersand is not used but the words 'et', 'und', 'e', 'y', 'e' are used instead.

### COLUMN 3: ECCLESIASTICAL TYPE
### (4-letter code)

This classification is not based on historical evolution or doctrinal criteria, but, in keeping with the whole of this Encyclopedia, is a contemporary description of the actual situation in world Christianity today. For this purpose, certain necessary neologisms have been created (e.g. Black/Third-World indigenous, marginal Protestant), all of which are fully defined in the Survey Dictionary of World Christianity, in Part 9.

One object of this classification is to facilitate a single world table of all Christians affiliated to churches, divided into major blocs (streams), families or groupings, as shown in Part 1 of this Encyclopedia. The tables there show at a glance the relative strengths of the various kinds of Christians in the world. Also, another object is to facilitate the science of comparative symbolics (comparison of the various Christian churches and confessions).

### Ecclesiastico-cultural major bloc (1-letter code)

The first letter in this column locates the body concerned in the following mutually-exclusive broad classification. The rationale for this 7-fold typology has already been given above, and full definitions have been given in the discussion on Table 1 above. Four of these blocs are usually called Liturgical (R, O, A, C) and the remaining 3 are partly Non-Liturgical (P, M, I). The Liturgical blocs are Pedobaptists (paedobaptists, i.e. practising infant baptism) emphasizing ordered worship, with fixed or written liturgies; the Non-Liturgical blocs are partly Baptist, i.e. they practise adult or believer's baptism only, and ·they emphasize free or spontaneous worship without fixed or written forms. The exceptions to this twofold typology are a few Protestant traditions (Lutheran, Methodist, Reformed) which are not Baptist but are both Liturgical and Pedobaptist; a few marginal Protestant traditions which baptize infants (Mormons,

et alii); and a large number of indigenous churches and bodies which are both Liturgical and Pedobaptist.

### Code

| | |
|---|---|
| R | Roman Catholic |
| O | Orthodox (Eastern, Oriental or Nestorian) |
| P | Protestant (sometimes called Evangelical) |
| A | Anglican (Episcopalian) |
| M | Marginal Protestant (para-Christian of Western origin) |
| C | Catholic (non-Roman) (of Western origin) |
| I | Non-White or Black/Third-World indigenous (independent of the other 6 blocs) |

### Ecclesiastical tradition (3-letter code)

The last 3 letters in Column 3 describe the ecclesiastical tradition or family (rite, liturgical language, confession, denomination, churchmanship, etc) with which each body is most closely connected historically. This does not necessarily imply formal connection with any world confessional family, which is dealt with later under Column 4a, Confessional conciliarism. For the purposes of this classification, an ecclesiastical tradition or family is defined as a number of denominations or churches which share a common heritage (allegiance to a historical tradition), a common thought world (theology, worldview) and a similar life-style (attitudes to money, property, discipline, moral imperatives, etc). It must be emphasized that this coding is purely *descriptive*, and almost always self-descriptive in that this is how the church or diocese described itself on the survey questionnaire. It should be taken to imply the best features of the traditions cited, and must not be taken as a stereotype of any bad connotations of the terms used. The categories as used here are all mutually exclusive; where a given body could be described by more than one of them, the most apt or descriptive has been chosen here for the table.

The following classification by tradition or family was derived from our data on denominations gathered during the present survey. A thorough exposition of this idea of a typology of family groups, with a survey of all other types of classification proposed by sociologists and scholars of religion, is given in J.G. Melton, *A directory of religious bodies in the United States* (New York: Garland, 1977), based on 18 family groups present in the USA. Our typology of 156 families covers many additional groups not found in the USA nor in the Western world. Below, they are set out in systematic fashion, dealing with the 7 blocs in the order in which they have been introduced and discussed above. For a single complete alphabetical listing, see the Codebook.

### ROMAN CATHOLIC

The term Roman Catholic refers to all churches and persons in communion with the Holy See and the Church of Rome. The code here describes the rite or ethnic sub-rite used in each church or jurisdiction. Catholic jurisdictions in communion with Rome use either the Latin rite, or one of 5 major rites known as Oriental or Eastern Catholic rites. These, together with their 22 ethnic sub-divisions, and the liturgical language each uses, are as set out below. Most of these now combine the ancient liturgical languages with their own national language in their liturgies. The Oriental churches are sometimes called Uniate, especially in Eastern Europe. The codes given here to these rites and sub-rites are set out in the left hand column.

| Code | Rite or sub-rite | Liturgical language |
|---|---|---|
| Lat | LATIN RITE | Latin |
| | ORIENTAL (EASTERN) RITES: | |
| | *Alexandrian (Egyptian) rite:* | |
| Cop | Coptic | Coptic & Arabic |
| Eth | Ethiopic | Ge'ez (Old Ethiopian) |
| | *Antiochian (Western Syrian) rite:* | |
| Mal | Malankara (Syro-Malankara) | Malayalam |
| Mar | Maronite | Syriac & Arabic |
| Syr | Syrian | Syriac & Arabic |
| Arm | *Armenian rite* | Old Armenian |
| | *Byzantine (Constantinopolitan) rite:* | |
| Alb | Albanian | Albanian & Old Greek |
| Bul | Bulgarian | Church Slavonic |
| Bye | Byelorussian (White Russian) | Church Slavonic |
| Geo | Georgian | Georgian |
| Gre | Greek | Old Greek (Byzantine) |
| Hun | Hungarian | Church Slavonic |
| IAb | Italo-Albanian | Old Greek & Albanian |
| Mel | Melkite | Old Greek & Arabic |
| Rum | Romanian | Romanian & Church Slavonic |
| Rus | Russian | Church Slavonic (Old Slavic) |
| Rut | Ruthenian | Church Slavonic |
| Slo | Slovak | Church Slavonic |
| Ukr | Ukrainian | Church Slavonic |
| Yug | Yugoslav | Church Slavonic |
| | *Chaldean (Eastern Syrian) rite:* | |
| Cha | Chaldean | Syriac & Arabic |
| SyM | Syro-Malabarese | Malayalam |
| Additional codes used here: | | |
| LEr | jurisdiction for both Latin and Eastern-rite Catholics | Several |
| Ori | jurisdiction for all or several Oriental rites | Several |
| Byz | jurisdiction for all or several Byzantine rites | Several |

### ORTHODOX

The term Orthodox as defined here refers to those churches in Eastern Christendom which claim to hold 'orthodoxy' (right belief, the true faith) as contrasted with heretical beliefs. The code describes the liturgical language used by each church, and/or that traditionally used by its mother church; in addition, there are 5 smaller schismatic traditions. This classification demonstrates the traditional liturgical origins or links of each church.

*Eastern Orthodox* (Chalcedonian, Dyophysite, Byzantine)
The Chalcedonian churches (Eastern churches which accepted the Council of Chalcedon in AD 451, and a total of 7 Ecumenical Councils, and now consider themselves to be in communion (canonical relationship) with the Ecumenical Patriarchate of Constantinople) may be grouped under 2 main families: Greek-speaking (those using Old or Byzantine Greek) and Slavonic-speaking (those using Church Slavonic, sometimes called Old Slavic). A number of churches now use their national language (e.g. Japanese) in their liturgy as well as Greek or Slavonic, even though these national languages (e.g. Japanese) cannot yet be properly called their liturgical languages.

*Code*

| | |
|---|---|
| Alb | Albanian/Greek |
| Ara | Arabic/Greek (arabophone, Arab Greek Orthodox) |
| Cze | Czech/Slavonic |
| Fin | Finnish/Slavonic |
| Geo | Georgian/Slavonic |
| Gre | Greek (New Calendar) |
| Hun | Hungarian/Slavonic |
| Pol | Polish/Slavonic |
| Rum | Romanian |
| Ser | Serbian/Slavonic |
| Sla | Slavonic |

*Oriental Orthodox* (Pre-Chalcedonian, Non-Chalcedonian, Monophysite)
The Oriental churches broke with the Western and Eastern churches at the Council of Chalcedon in AD 451, and only accept 4 of the Ecumenical Councils. Their liturgical languages are as follows (with in parentheses the name of each's church).

*Code*

| | |
|---|---|
| Arm | Armenian (Armenian Apostolic) |
| Cop | Coptic & Arabic (Coptic Orthodox) |
| Eth | Ge'ez/Old Ethiopian (Ethiopian Orthodox) |
| Syr | Syriac & Arabic (Syrian Orthodox, West Syrian, Jacobite) |
| SyM | Syriac & Malayalam (Orthodox Syrian, in India) |

*Nestorian* (Assyrian, East Syrian, Syro-Chaldean; Dyophysite)
The Ancient Church of the East, the original church of Mesopotamia, broke with the Western and Eastern churches at the Council of Ephesus, AD 433. It does not regard itself as part of the Orthodox world, but it is here classified as a third branch of Orthodoxy because its theology, long called Nestorian, was similar to that of the Greek Orthodox patriarch of Constantinople, Nestorius.

*Code*

| | |
|---|---|
| Nes | Assyrian, East Syrian (Messihaye), Chaldean (Syriac)-speaking, Nestorian, Syro-Chaldean. |

*Orthodox schisms*
Relatively recent movements out of historical Orthodoxy, or other schisms from mainstream Othodoxy, which claim to retain full historical Orthodoxy, but which are not recognized as canonical by the bulk of Orthodox churches.

*Code*

| | |
|---|---|
| OBe | Old Believers, Old Ritualists (Russians, using Old Slavonic) |
| OCd | Old Calendarist (or Authentic) Greek Orthodox |
| ReO | Reformed Orthodox (uncanonical reform movement out of Orthodoxy, retaining Orthodox claims) |
| sub | sub-Orthodox Russian sect reflecting Orthodox ritual |
| Tru | True Orthodox (devoutly conservative Russian Orthodox) |

## PROTESTANT

The term Protestant (or Evangelical in French, German, Italian, Portuguese and Spanish: respectively, Évangélique, Evangelische, Evangelico, Evangélico, Evangélico) refers primarily to Western Protestant bodies originating in Europe or North America, which trace their origin or definitive reformulation either to the 16th-century European Protestant Reformation or subsequently (including state churches in Germany and Scandinavia and elsewhere which originated as early as AD 90 (West Germany) but subsequently identified themselves with the Protestant Reformation); and to churches elsewhere throughout the world which are related to them, controlled by them, or in communion with them. The 3-letter code indicates the major denominational, confessional or ecclesiastical tradition followed, evolved, adopted, or claimed, or which best describes objectively the group concerned. Definitions and descriptions of each are given in Part 9, Survey Dictionary of World Christianity. With regard to Pentecostal bodies, note in particular that in this Encyclopedia, proper names of churches excepted, the capitalized terms Pentecostal and Pentecostalism always refer to Classical Pentecostalism among White races and their worldwide related churches and missions, in its varied forms (coded below PeA, Pen, Pe1, Pe2, Pe3, Pe4). By contrast, the non-capitalized forms 'pentecostal' and 'pentecostalism' are reserved for forms of pentecostalism other than White Classical, namely (1) Non-White or Black/Third-World indigenous pentecostalism (and its variants, coded below peA, pen, pe1, pe2, pe3, pe4) and (2) Neo-pentecostal, Catholic pentecostal, Anglican pentecostal and Orthodox pentecostal movements within non-Pentecostal denominations. (In titles or proper names of churches of both kinds, of course, the adjective Pentecostal is always capitalized). This distinction between Pentecostal and pentecostal is made here to make it clear that these are 2 separate ecclesiastical traditions. Non-White or Black/Third-World pentecostalism has arisen, outside the USA, quite independently of Classical Pentecostalism; and within the USA itself, Black pentecostalism has some claim to have preceded White Pentecostalism in time, to be a phenomenon distinct and separate from it, and to itself be regarded as the classical tradition.

These 36 categories as used here are mutually exclusive; where a given body could be described by more than one of them, the most apt or descriptive has been chosen in its Table 2.

In English, as explained above, the term Evangelical has a more specialized meaning than in the other European languages, delineating a sub-group or movement within Protestantism.

*Code*

| | |
|---|---|
| Ade | Christadelphian (Adelphoi, Brothers of Christ) |
| Adv | Adventist (Millerite) |
| Ang | schism from Anglicanism or Episcopalianism, in Protestant direction rejecting Anglicanism (i.e. without claiming or retaining Anglican name, orders, apostolic succession, et alia) |
| Bap | Baptist |
| CBr | Christian Brethren (Plymouth Brethren; Open only, not Exclusive); independent fundamentalist/dispensationalist |
| com | community church or union congregation (formed by 2 or more denominations), open to all denominations and races |
| Con | Congregational, Congregationalist |
| Dis | Disciple, Restorationist, Restorationist Baptist, Christian (Restoration Movement, Campbellites, Disciples, Churches of Christ) |
| Dun | Dunker (Tunker), Dipper, German Baptist, Brethren (baptism by 3-fold immersion) |
| EBr | Exclusive Brethren (Plymouth Brethren, Closed, Strict; Darbyites); exclusive fundamentalist/dispensationalist |
| Hol | Holiness (Conservative Methodist, Wesleyan, Free Methodist, non-Pentecostal Perfectionist) (2-experience: conversion, entire santification); differing from mainline Methodism only in teaching on sanctification |
| ind | independent Evangelical, unrelated to other Protestant or indigenous traditions, usually regarding itself as a denomination |
| int | interdenominational Evangelical Protestant (unaffiliated to any denomination, unrelated to any major tradition, or specifically interdenominational); or, church originating from |

one of the interdenominational Evangelical missionary societies (often called faith missions)

| | |
|---|---|
| Jew | Messianic, Jewish-Christian, or Jewish crypto-Christian |
| LuR | Lutheran/Reformed united church, or joint mission |
| Lut | Lutheran |
| Men | Mennonite, Anabaptist (Left-Wing or Radical Reformation), including other communal Anabaptist sects |
| Met | Methodist (mainline Methodist, United Methodist); English-speaking Pietist |
| Mor | Moravian (Continental Pietist) |
| non | non-denominational (no-church or anti-church groups rejecting being described as a church or denomination, or being classed or linked with other churches or denominations) |
| Ort | schism from Orthodoxy, in Protestant direction (without claiming to retain full historical Orthodoxy) |
| PeA | Apostolic, or Pentecostal Apostolic (differing from other Pentecostals in stress on complex hierarchy of living apostles, prophets and other charismatic officials) |
| Pen | Pentecostal (Classical Pentecostal of unspecified type); charismatic, healing; the 5 sub-types PeA, Pe1, Pe2, Pe3, Pe4, are also termed Classical Pentecostal (as contrasted with Neo-pentecostal, Catholic pentecostal, or Non-White or Black/Third-World pentecostal) |
| Pe1 | Oneness-Pentecostal or Unitarian-Pentecostal: 'Jesus only', sometimes unitarian (Jesus being regarded as the same as the Holy Spirit, also the Father), or non- or anti-trinitarian; baptism in name of Jesus only |
| Pe2 | Baptistic-Pentecostal or Keswick-Pentecostal: 2-crisis-experience (conversion, baptism of the Spirit) |
| Pe3 | Holiness-Pentecostal: 3-crisis-experience (conversion, sanctification, baptism of the Spirit) |
| Pe4 | Perfectionist-Pentecostal, Free Pentecostal, Deliverance-Pentecostal, Radical- or Revivalist-Pentecostal: 4-crisis-experience (recent bodies claiming to revive institutionalized Pentecostalism by reviving, as a 4th experience deliverance/ecstatic confession/ascension/perfectionism/church government through non-rational prophecy and glossolalia, also sometimes the authority/discipling/shepherding emphasis, usually opposing organization or institutionalization) |
| Qua | Friends (Quakers) |
| rad | isolated radio churches, i.e. unorganized isolated house congregations brought into being by radio evangelism, or mail or radiophonic correspondence courses, and unrelated to other denominations; small cells or groups of isolated radio believers |
| Ref | Reformed, Presbyterian (the latter term originates in English-speaking areas, the former in continental Europe) |
| Rom | schism from Roman Catholic Church, in Protestant direction (without claiming to retain full catholicity) |
| Sal | Salvationist (Salvation Army) |
| sin | single congregation(s): one single autonomous congregation, completely independent and unaffiliated to any denomination or grouping, nor claiming to be a denomination; or a de facto unstructured grouping of such congregations |
| tel | TV (television) para-denomination, organized solely around regular worship telecasts |
| uni | united church (voluntary or involuntary (enforced by state) union or merger of bodies of different ecclesiastical traditions) |
| Wal | Waldensian |

## ANGLICAN

The term Anglican refers to churches of the Anglican Communion and their members, whether they call themselves Protestants, Catholics, or Episcopalians, and which trace their origin back to the Church of England in the 6th century and the Celtic Church of the 2nd century AD. These churches accepted the Catholic or Roman tradition up to AD 1540, and thereafter a reformed Anglican tradition. The term also applies to schisms from the Anglican Communion in the Western world, or among European peoples, which claim to remain authentically Anglican, and which retain or claim to retain either apostolic succession of bishops, or Anglican polity, or Anglican orders, or the word Anglican in their title. The code indicates the type of churchmanship recognized by diocesan offices as prevalent in influence or numerically predominant in the church or diocese, or on the part of bishop or clergy, in cases where a clear tradition can be recognized. It is important to realize that this typology should not be related to outmoded party disputes, but is purely descriptive, being a positive and contemporary self-description as viewed from diocesan offices of the actual practice in a church or diocese with regard to liturgy, ritual and churchmanship. In most cases this self-description was returned by diocesan officers on the Encyclopedia's questionnaire to dioceses.

*Code*

ACa Anglo-Catholic (formerly called Tractarian)
Hig High Church (Prayer Book Catholic)
Cen Central or Broad Church (Prayer Book, Liberal, Comprehensive, New Synod Group)
plu no dominant single tradition; plural or mixed traditions across the whole spectrum of churchmanship
Eva Evangelical (Anglican Evangelical, or Conciliar Evangelical, or Evangelical Anglican)
Low Low Church (Conservative Evangelical)

The letter 's' preceding any of the above indicates a schismatic movement not in communion with Canterbury but claiming either Anglican ethos (e.g. using the word Anglican in title) or apostolic succession of bishops. In such cases, 's' is followed by the first 2 letters of the above typology, thus:

*Code*

sEv Anglican schism of Evangelical type, claiming to retain Anglican name, orders, apostolic succession, et alia
sAC Anglican schism of Anglo-Catholic type, claiming to retain Anglican name, orders, apostolic succession, et alia
smi Anglican schism of mixed types of churchmanship, claiming to retain Anglican name, orders, apostolic succession, et alia

Note: Schisms from Anglicanism which do not claim to remain authentically Anglican and which claim neither Anglican ethos nor apostolic succession, but which may nevertheless retain certain Anglican features (e.g. liturgy, polity, vestments), are here classified either under Catholic (non-Roman), or Protestant, or Black/Third-World indigenous, and are given the code Ang or ARo (see below).

## MARGINAL PROTESTANT

Marginal Protestant (para-Christian of Western origin) is a non-judgemental descriptive term coined by this survey and used here to describe those religious systems, churches, bodies, sects or cults, which have arisen out of, or are located on the fringes or margins of, mainline Western Protestant organized Christianity, but which do not fully identify themselves with it, and so represent Protestant deviations, claiming to be Christian and containing major elements derived from Christianity, but not professing mainstream Protestant christocentric doctrine and usually being either non-credal or anti-credal; generally originating in a theophany and affirming a second or supplementary or ongoing source of divine revelation in addition to the Bible. 'Marginal' is therefore used here in contrast to 'mainline', and as such it is widely used in the literature (e.g. I.I. Zaretsky & M.P. Leone, eds, *Religious movements in contemporary America* (1974), which is concerned entirely with marginal religious movements). Subsequent to the origin of these movements on the metaphorical periphery, margin or fringes of Western Protestant Christian orthodoxy, several of these systems have since expanded across the world to many countries.

This category includes only those recognizably Christian bodies among the many which belong to the corpus of the whole vast range of contemporary metaphysical movements. The Christian bodies can be divided into 2 major wings: (a) occult bodies (Christian branches of Spiritualism, Theosophy, psychic movements), and (b) healing bodies (Christian Science, Divine Science, New Thought, Religious Science, Unity School of Christianity).

Most occult metaphysical bodies such as Spiritualism, Theosophy and its offshoot Rosicrucianism are not properly speaking Christian movements at all, although they embody Christian elements. In this survey they are therefore classified as non-Christian religions or cults, and are enumerated in Tables 1 either under 'Other religionists' or under any relevant category such as 'Hindus', 'Spiritists', etc.

*Code*

Apo apocalyptic, eschatological
BrI British-Israelite
Gno Gnostic, esoteric, anthroposophical
Jeh Jehovah's Witnesses (Russellites; self-appellation, Jehovah's Christian witnesses), including Bible Student movement and other schismatics or dissidents
Jew Jewish-Christian (incorporating Jewish teachings or practices); or, Jewish crypto-Christians
LdS Latter-day Saints (Mormons), including schismatics or dissidents
Sci metaphysical science, Divine Science, Religious Science, Christian Science, New Thought, magnetic healing
Spi Spiritualist, Spiritist (thaumaturgical), psychic, psychical, occult, mediumistic, psychedelic of specifically Christian type
Swe Swedenborgian (Church of the New Jerusalem, spiritualistic)
The Theosophist, Theosophical, or synthesist (combining philosophy and religions)
Unt Unitarian, Universalist, Free Christian, Liberal Christian

## CATHOLIC (NON-ROMAN)

The above term as defined in this survey covers a vast range of disparate ecclesiastical phenomena originating in the Western world. These are the mass of over 200 large and small episcopal and non-episcopal autocephalous schismatic churches which exist in the penumbra between Roman Catholicism and Protestantism, and between Roman Catholism and Anglicanism. They have all broken in recent times (since 1500, and almost all since 1800) either from Rome to introduce Protestant features (married priests, lay leadership, women ministers, individual faith, etc), or from Protestantism to introduce Catholic features (sacraments, authority, episcopacy, hierarchy, the historic succession of the episcopate (apostolic succession), apostolic autocracy, ritual, liturgy, etc), or from Anglicanism to introduce Roman features. Numerically, they fall into 2 classes: (1) sizeable schisms, defined here as those which involve over 100 persons each, and (2) miniscule schisms, begun by a single founder (usually a new episcopus vagans, bishop-at-large), with 100 or under others and often with under 10. Ecclesiastically, from the point of view of ecclesiastical tradition, the whole range may be divided into the following 9 types, starting at the Catholic end of the spectrum and moving to the Protestant end. (1) *Old Catholic churches*. These are a number of traditionally Catholic churches in Europe which have separated in recent times from the Church of Rome (especially in 1702, Jansenism; 1724, Church of Utrecht; 1870, Old Catholics; and 1897, Polish National Catholics), opposing recent Roman dogmas including papal infallibility and the immaculate conception and assumption of the Virgin, retaining traditionally conservative Catholic faith and practice and the apostolic succession of bishops, and remaining in communion with and recognized by large parts of historic Christianity (usually Anglicanism and Orthodoxy). (2) *Conservative Catholic churches*. These are other recent sizeable secessions from the Church of Rome in a conservative or reactionary direction protesting against liberal, updating or modernizing trends in Roman Catholicism, retaining episcopacy but without the Old Catholic or other undisputed historic succession of the episcopate. (3) *Miniscule unrecognized autocephalous episcopal churches under bishops-at-large* (episcopi vagantes). These amount to over 130 distinct autocephalous churches schismatic from the Church of Rome or out of communion with it, with 100 or under or even few or no lay members, claiming to be Catholic, Apostolic, Orthodox, and with valid episcopal orders (almost all in the Ferrette, Vilatte or Mathew successions), which, since the movement's origin in Britain in 1866, have proliferated in Europe, North America and Australasia and also to several Third-World countries, and which although not recognized by historic Christianity nevertheless retain traditional Catholic faith and practice and claim to be reviving primitive Christianity and to be inaugurating a new and final reunion of divided Christendom. (4) *Liberal Catholic churches*. These consist of sizeable episcopal churches of unrecognized succession which have formally embraced various liberal or deviant Catholic views including Theosophical, Masonic, Gnostic, magic or occult dogmas and practices. (5) *Marginal Catholic bodies*. These represent other sizeable marginal schisms or movements out of the Church of Rome which have embraced other marginally Christian, non-christocentric or non-Christian dogmas. (6) *Reformed Catholic churches*. These are recent sizeable secessions from the Church of Rome in a distinctively reformed or Protestant direction, radically altering Catholic faith and practice, usually rejecting (initially at least) the apostolic succession of bishops, and usually not in communion with historic Christianity (Anglicanism or Orthodoxy). (7) *Anglo-Roman churches*. These are sizeable schisms out of Anglicanism in a Roman Catholic direction, rejecting Anglican orders and apostolic succession to substitute ones of Roman background (usually Ferrette, Vilatte or Mathew successions). (8) *Ex-Protestant Catholic churches*. These are sizeable schisms out of Protestantism in a Catholic direction, introducing Catholic concepts of ecclesiology, sacramentarianism, ritual, liturgy, authority, and episcopal order, and usually going to considerable lengths to obtain the historic succession of the episcopate. Lastly, (9) *Catholic Apostolic churches*. This is a series of non-episcopal secessions out of Protestantism, beginning in Britain in 1832, introducing the Catholic concepts of the unified church, sacramentarianism, ritual, liturgy, and authority, but rejecting the apostolic succession of bishops and substituting for it a claimed return to Apostolic church government through a hierarchy or college of living apostles, in a successional apostolate headed by a chief apostle with quasi-papal powers regarded as the successor of the Apostle Peter and the visible representative or incarnation of Christ on earth.

These 9 Western types are coded here as shown below. Note that similar movements among Third-World peoples, including schisms from the Church of Rome, are not classified here as in this Catholic (non-Roman) bloc but are classified as in the Non-White indigenous bloc or their ecclesiastical tradition; however, the codes are the same as shown here below. For a tabular listing of all episcopal autocephalous churches with claimed (but disputed) apostolic succession, both in the Western world and in the Third World, including many classified as Anglican, or Orthodox, or Non-White indigenous, see the table 'Episcopal churches with disputed apostolic succession' at the end of Part 9.

*Code*

OCa Old Catholic (recent schism out of Church of Rome retaining recognized Old Catholic apostolic succession of bishops; especially schisms of 1702, 1724, 1870, 1897)
CCa Conservative Catholic (recent schism out of Church of Rome in conservative or reactionary direction, rejecting authority of pope, with or without apostolic succession, protesting against up-dating or liberal trends); Tridentinist, Traditional Catholic
Epi episcopi-vagantes Catholic, in miniscule unrecognized autocephalous episcopal church under bishops-at-large (episcopi vagantes), with disputed apostolic succession; or (in Third World), linked with such Western bodies; with 100 or under members only
Lib Liberal Catholic (church under bishops-at-large holding liberal or deviant Catholic views usually including Theosophical, Masonic, Gnostic, magical or occult dogmas and practices)
mar marginal Catholic (recent schism or movement out of Church of Rome which has embraced marginal, non-christocentric or non-Christian dogmas)
ReC Reformed Catholic (recent schism out of Church of Rome in reformed or Protestant direction)
ARo Anglo-Roman (recent schism out of Anglicanism in a Roman Catholic direction, rejecting Anglican orders for some variant Roman succession)
Pro ex-Protestant Catholic (recent schism out of

# TRADITIONS

**ECCLESIASTICAL TRADITIONS.** On this page and overleaf are illustrated a selection of 23 of the total of 156 distinct Christian traditions analysed in this Encyclopedia. In bold type is given the name of the tradition (as listed here in the Codebook), followed by brief identification of each photograph.

**Anglican Evangelical.** Consecration in Khartoum Cathedral in 1971 of 2 new Sudanese bishops (on either side of Archbishop in Jerusalem (in mitre), with other bishops from Kenya, Iran and Egypt).

**Arab Orthodox.** Arab parish priest in Antioch (Turkey) near border with Syria.

**Armenian Apostolic** (Gregorian). Armenian Catholicos Vasken (left).

**Baptist.** Russian Baptist choir at central church in Moscow.

**Catholic Apostolic.** *Left.* One of many new, ultra-modern, buildings of New Apostolic Church (in Worms, FR Germany). *Right.* Its interior, with NAC symbol of Cross over Rising Sun.

**Chaldean.** Archbishop Youhannan S. Issayi of Tehran (former Nestorians now united to Rome) meets Shah of Iran, 1974.

**Coptic Orthodox.** Pope Shenouda III (left) with his Bishop of Ecumenical Affairs, in Cairo.

**Conservative Catholic.** About 21% of all RCs in Europe and North America are traditionalists who prefer the Tridentine (Latin) mass and support Archbishop M. Lefebvre (pictured), suspended by Pope Paul VI in 1976. Small groups in several countries have formed schismatic churches.

**Episcopi Vagantes** (Bishops-at-large). The Catholicate of the West, a miniscule unrecognized autocephalous church, was begun in Britain in 1944 by (pictured) His Sacred Beatitude Mar Georgius I (H.G. de Willmott Newman), Patriarch of Glastonbury, Apostolic Pontiff of Celtica & of the Indies, Prince-Catholicos of the West, who claimed consecration via 23 lines of apostolic succession.

**Ethiopian Orthodox.** *Left.* Clergy during Timkat (Epiphany) in Addis Ababa. *Right.* Cathedrals new (centre) and old (to right), with obelisks, in Aksum.

**Greek Orthodox.** Greek Patriarch of Alexandria (centre, while serving as Archbishop in East Africa).

**Jehovah's Witnesses** (Russellite). Mass public baptism in Ruislip Lido (UK).

**Liberal Catholic.** Founder (in 1915) and First Presiding Bishop of the Liberal Catholic Church, the Right Rev. J.I. Wedgwood, a leading English Theosophist.

**Lutheran.** Liturgy in Westman Islands, Iceland; first service for population returning after 1973 volcanic eruption disaster.

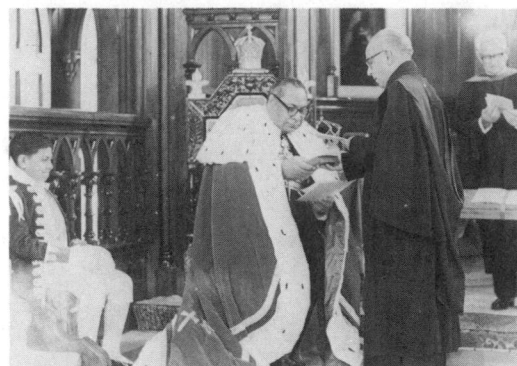

**Methodist.** King of Tonga (a Methodist) receives Bible from Methodist President-General C.F. Gribble during 1967 Coronation.

**Nestorian.** Assyrian world hierarchy led by Catholicos-Patriarch Mar Dinkha IV (centre).

**Non-White pentecostal.** Apostle/Preacher/Evangelist of African Apostolic Church of Johane Maranke, Zimbabwe.

**Old Believer.** Flavian, Old Ritualist (Old Believer) Archbishop of Moscow and All Russia (1879-1960), speaking in Zagorsk in 1952.

**Pentecostal.** Italian Pentecostals in Palermo under text 'We preach Christ the power and wisdom of God'.

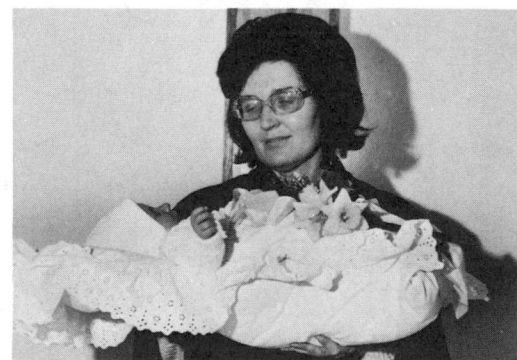

**Reformed Catholic.** Woman minister performs infant baptism in Czechoslovak Hussite Church, Prague.

**Russian Orthodox.** Late Patriarch Alexei during liturgy in Trinity Church, Zagorsk.

**Salvationist.** Jeshi la Wokofu/Salvation Army officers (Captains and Sisters), Kenya Territory, with band.

**Syro-Malabarese.** Liturgy in Diocese of Quilon, Orthodox Syrian Church of the East.

Protestantism in a Roman Catholic direction, embracing episcopacy, apostolic succession)

CAp Catholic Apostolic (1832 Irvingite or Old Apostolic, 1863 New Apostolic, and numerous subsequent schisms), rejecting apostolic succession and substituting government by hierarchy of living apostles

## NON-WHITE OR BLACK/THIRD-WORLD INDIGENOUS

As described at length earlier, this term is used to describe Christian movements and churches originating not among the White races indigenous mainly to the Western or Communist worlds, nor in the Western or Eastern churches which have arisen there, but originating since AD 1500 among the Black or Non-White races indigenous to the Third World, including Black or Non-White minorities in the Western world, i.e. among any race or people other than the European geographical race as defined here in PEOPLES OF THE WORLD, in Part 4. It covers movements indigenous to Black or Non-White peoples without foreign origin (i.e. foreign to them); seceding from or asserting their independence from Western or Eastern bodies, and often rejecting the terms 'Protestant', 'Catholic', 'Anglican' and 'Orthodox'; not related to nor controlled by Western Protestant, Catholic, Anglican or Orthodox bodies, but completely independent of them; indigenous as opposed to foreign, alien, imported or immigrant tradition, with no foreign ties; local, nationalistic, often separatist, schismatic, anti-Western, of contested orthodoxy; founded, led and supported by Blacks or Non-Whites independently of and without assistance from White churches or missionaries, though sometimes subsequently assisted by Western or Eastern church bodies. The code used, which is the same as that for Protestant, Catholic, Anglican and Orthodox above, indicates the main Western or Eastern denominational tradition followed, evolved, adopted, claimed, or from which a schism broke, but only for cases where this tradition is clearcut. The code 'ind' (independent) here indicates that the body follows or parallels no clearcut Western or Eastern tradition. The listing that follows below shows this tradition grouped into the 5 Western or Eastern blocs from which these movements have separated or out of which they have sprung.

*Code*

*CATHOLIC*

CCa Conservative Catholic (recent schism out of Church of Rome in Third-World country, rejecting recent Roman Catholic reforms)

Lib Liberal Catholic (holding liberal or deviant Catholic views)

mar marginal Catholic (recent schism out of Church of Rome embracing marginal or non-Christian dogmas)

ReC Reformed Catholic (recent schism or reform movement out of Church of Rome in Third-World country, claiming to retain full catholicity)

*ORTHODOX*

ReO Reformed Orthodox (recent schism or reform movement out of historical Eastern or Oriental Orthodoxy in Third-World country, claiming full historical Orthodoxy)

*ANGLICAN*

ARo Anglo-Roman (recent schism out of Anglicanism in a Roman Catholic direction)

sAC Anglican schism of Anglo-Catholic type, claiming to retain Anglican name, orders, apostlic succession, et alia

sEv Anglican schism of Evangelical type, claiming to retain Anglican name, orders, apostolic succession, et alia

*PROTESTANT* (a few examples only; see above for the whole range)

Ang schism from Anglicanism, in Protestant direction (without claiming to retain Anglican name, orders, apostolic succession, et alia)

Bap Baptist

Lut Lutheran

Met Methodist

Ort schism from Orthodoxy, in Protestant direction (without claiming to retain full historical Orthodoxy)

pen Black/Third-World indigenous charismatic (pentecostal, Spirit-dominated), or (in Africa) spiritual or zionist or spirit (Roho, uMoya, etc) or aladura (praying) churches; charismatic, enthusiastic, faith-healing (other codes: peA, pe1, pe2, pe3, pe4, with similar meaning to the Protestant codes PeA, Pe1, Pe2, Pe3, Pe4 described above)

*MARGINAL PROTESTANT*

A number of indigenous movements claiming to be Christian are unorthodox or heterodox in christology, usually being non-credal or anti-credal and claiming a second or supplementary source of revelation in addition to the Bible, and are often or generally described as syncretistic, messianic or heretical (or by similar adjectives). They include bodies similar in teaching to those classified above as marginal Protestant. These bodies are here treated as marginal Christian movements, and the following code identifies them as distinct from mainline and mainstream Christian orthodoxy:

mar marginal

*OTHER*

ind independent of any Western or Eastern tradition

rad isolated radio churches among Black or Non-White peoples (isolated house congregations or cells of isolated radio believers or correspondence course students)

## COLUMN 4: CONCILIARISM, COLLEGIALITY, CONSULTATION AND CHURCH ORGANIZATION (5-letter code)

This column describes, in 5 letters, the membership of all denominations in councils and organizations, including the confessional structure of the churches, involvement in the conciliar or interdenominational movement, commitment to the conciliar or consultative principle, involvement in collegiality, consultation and co-responsibility, and formal relationships to national and international councils, conferences, orders, congregations, organizations, and associations of churches.

This classification serves the following purposes: (a) for any particular church, denomination or diocese, to indicate its formal relationships to other churches in its own country and beyond; (b) for Roman Catholic local (nation-wide) churches, to indicate the present extent of the participation of the whole people of God in worldwide collegiality, consultation and co-responsibility; (c) in the case of a missionary jurisdiction of the Roman Catholic Church, to elaborate on this relationship by indicating the personnel, order or congregation responsible for staffing the jurisdiction; (d) for all other denominations, to list each's confessional, international, continental, regional, and national conciliar involvement, including the interconfessional (cross-denominational) councils to which each belongs; (e) to enable the reader to locate at a glance members belonging to a particular council or internal grouping in any particular country; (f) to give the reader an immediate overview of the extent and nature of interdenominationalism, conciliarism, ecumenism, confessionalism, collegiality, consultation and church organization in a given country; and (g) to enable the reader to assess a particular body's attitude to conciliarism and consultation or to involvement in the conciliar movement. The symbol **.** in any of these 5 columns indicates that the body concerned has no such relationships (as known at mid-1980). If subsequently it joins any council, the reader can change the dot (**.**) to the appropriate letter. Bodies with 5 dots (. . . . .) have no interdenominational or conciliar or wider structural ties and so can be termed non-conciliar.

Membership of councils shown in these tables is usually, but not always, all-inclusive; all the member churches present in each country are shown. In a few cases only, a council may have other member churches too small to have been listed in the table, but which are included under the listing 'Other Protestant denominations' or 'Other indigenous churches'.

A further factor is that there exist a number of Christian councils which have individuals or individual congregations as members but not denominations. National councils or alliances or fellowships of this type are listed in the footnotes 'Other national councils' under Tables 2.

The basic problem faced by this column and its coding is that it is extremely difficult to compare Roman Catholicism and Protestantism in detail, because whilst the Roman Catholic Church has a highly centralized structure, Protestantism has either a federal structure or no overall structure at all. Nevertheless, the task is attempted in Column 4.

The Roman Catholic Church is a special case here in that, as a result of the Ecumenical Council of 1962–5 (Vatican II), all local (nation-wide) churches, all dioceses and all other jurisdictions have belonged to, or are represented on, various types of inter-church and inter-jurisdiction Catholic conciliar body: national episcopal conferences, regional and continental conferences, and, at the apex, the Synod of Bishops. (A further type, provincial episcopal councils for all bishops in an ecclesiastical province, existed from the Council of Trent in 1545–63 up to Vatican II but has now disappeared completely, the last being one in Belgium up to 1936). Unlike Protestant conciliarism, however, membership in these Catholic councils is not optional and so all dioceses are part of this structure of councils. The representatives on these councils are always the bishops or ordinaries of the dioceses concerned, and the whole structure represents collegiality — government of the church by the whole college of bishops sitting together. However, an additional obligation since Vatican II has been that all dioceses and jurisdictions begin to involve priests, religious personnel, and laity in the whole process of consultation known as co-responsibility, and in particular that they form both diocesan priests' councils and also diocesan pastoral councils (for the whole people of God — bishops, priests, religious personnel, and laity). This requirement, however, has not been universally implemented although a majority of dioceses now have a priests' council, and a majority also have a pastoral council (at least on paper). In a number of countries, the process of co-responsibility has gone a stage further, and national priests' councils and even national pastoral councils had been set up until in 1973 the Vatican clarified that such national organizations were forbidden and could not be accepted in the official structure of the church. All such bodies have therefore become unofficial pressure groups seeking to assert the involvement of priests, religious and laity in the government of the church.

For dioceses and jurisdictions, Column 4 does not reiterate this participation in nation-wide councils (except in the case of a handful of Protestant federations of which the component parts are virtually the same as autonomous denominations). Instead, the column after the first letter indicates, for Roman Catholics, the extent to which the diocese of jurisdiction is under either local or international influence, by showing whether it is staffed by local diocesan (secular) clergy or (for missionary jurisdictions under Propaganda) by an international missionary order or congregation whose initials are then shown.

Most of the international bodies listed below have official names in 2 or more major international languages. If these are English, French or German they are given below (in that order), followed by their initials if widely used.

### 1st letter: *CONFESSIONAL CONCILIARISM, CONSULTATION & CHURCH ORGANIZATION*

A confession is a large family of distinct or different autonomous churches or denominations around the world which are linked by similar ecclesiastical tradition, history, polity and name, and often by some informal or formal organization. Confessions include: Anglicanism, Greek Orthodoxy, Lutheranism, Methodism, Roman Catholicism, and 40 or so others. Most confessions have councils or permanent organizations and secretariats linking them. Confessional councils as listed here are worldwide in the sense that each is not restricted to any particular part of the world.

The code below indicates either membership in a Protestant confessional body (linking many denominations of similar tradition), or in a confessional consultative body (for consultation or fellowship only), or in a confessional family under an Orthodox patriarchate, or in the internal church organization of the largest confession, the Roman Catholic Church. It thus indicates a body's relationship to its own wider communion or confession.

In addition to the world confessional bodies listed

Ecumenism. In Sydney Town Hall (Australia), 2 December 1970, Pope Paul VI (in white cassock) joins in worship with leaders of 10 denominations including Anglicans, Armenian Apostolic, Orthodox and Salvationists.
Confessional conciliarism. *Below.* Inaugural meeting of Anglican Consultative Council in 1971 at Limuru (Kenya), addressed by Archbishop of Canterbury (A.M. Ramsey). *Right.* First Pan-orthodox Preconciliar Conference, Chambésy (Geneva), 1976 (Eastern Orthodox): concelebration led by (centre) Metropolitan Meliton of Chalcedon.

here, there exist a number of other smaller international bodies (see listing in Codebook). Further, there are a number of continental and regional confessional bodies (e.g. European Baptist Federation, Caribbean Assembly of Reformed Churches). These however are not dealt with or mentioned in column 4 except for a handful of the more significant bodies, which are listed in the Codebook under CONTINENTAL and REGIONAL CONCILIARISM.

*Conference of Secretaries of Christian World Communions/CWCs (until 1979 termed World Confessional Families/WCFs).* The 15 international confessional councils below followed by an asterisk * (making a total of 26 asterisks including duplications) are represented on this Conference, which was begun in 1957. In addition, the following quasi-confessions (non-confessional international denominational bodies, as defined below) are participants: Church of the Brethren, Salvation Army, General Conference of Seventh-day Adventists, World Convention of Churches of Christ (Disciples).

*PROTESTANT* (International confessional families, or world families of churches)

(i) *Membership in world confessional bodies/communions*
The code indicates that the body concerned has formal membership in, and full communion and fellowship with, the world confessional organization named; or, is part of a member based on another country. Notes: (a) in a world confessional body, each member church is autonomous, and can join or leave at will; (b) membership in these bodies is mutually exclusive — no denomination belongs to more than one body (with the exception, shown in the tables, of a handful of united churches which have continued the former affiliations of their component churches; and of a handful of churches which belong to both WARC and RES, or to both WARC and WMC); and (c) confessional bodies of similar tradition (e.g., Reformed) are characterized by differing theological stances.

*Code*

F = member of both WARC (World Alliance of Reformed Churches) and RES (Reformed Ecumenical Synod)*
G = Mennonite World Conference (MWC)*
J = Reformed Ecumenical Synod (RES)*
K = International Federation of Free Evangelical Churches (IFFEC)/Fédération Internationale des Eglises Evangéliques Libres/Internationaler Bund Freier Evangelischer Gemeinden
L = Lutheran World Federation (LWF)/Fédération Luthérienne Mondiale (FLM)/Lutherischer Weltbund (LWB) (member, or congregation formally recognized by LWF)*

l = permanent observer (but not member) relationship to Lutheran World Federation (LWF)*
Q = Friends World Committee for Consultation (FWCC)*
R = World Alliance of Reformed Churches (Presbyterian and Congregational) (WARC) (incorporating former World Presbyterian Alliance, and International Congregational Council)*
r = member of both WARC and IFFEC*
T = Baptist World Alliance (BWA)/Alliance Baptiste Mondiale (ABM)/Baptistischer Weltbund (BWB)*
V = World Methodist Council (WMC)/Conseil Méthodiste Mondial/Methodistischer Weltrat*
W = member of both WMC (World Methodist Council) and WARC (World Alliance of Reformed Churches)*
Z = Pentecostal World Conference (PWC)/Conférence Mondiale des Eglises Pentecôtistes/Weltkonferenz der Pfingstkirchen (triennial, no permanent organization)
. = no international confessional membership

(ii) *Membership in quasi-confessions (non-confessional international denominational bodies)*

x = part of a quasi-confession (non-confessional international denominational body)

A quasi-confession or non-confessional international denominational body is a denomination which does not belong to any of the recognized world confessional bodies as described above, but which functions, or regards itself, or is often regarded, as itself a confessional body or world family of churches with organized branches and churches in a number of nations (3 or more), although in fact it is a single worldwide or international denomination on the definitions used in this Encyclopedia. It is usually in process of worldwide expansion, establishing branches overseas which are usually not completely autonomous but which are in some sense under its central organization (and therefore not usually free of themselves as national bodies to join international or national councils). Examples are: Salvation Army, Seventh-day Adventist Church, Christian Church (Disciples of Christ) with its international arm the World Convention of Churches of Christ, Moravian Church (Unity of the Brethren), and the Alliance World Fellowship (national churches begun by Christian and Missionary Alliance). In addition to these Protestant bodies, there are similar ones which are classified under marginal Protestant below (Church of Christ Scientist, Church of Jesus Christ of Latter-day Saints, Jehovah's Witnesses, Worldwide Church of God, et alia), as well as others which are Anglican, Catholic (non-Roman), Independent or

Indigenous, or Orthodox. Other bodies have the appearance of being world confessional families but are in fact international denominations belonging to larger confessional families (e.g. the World Free Methodist Fellowship, and Wesleyan World Fellowship, whose member churches relate to the Free Methodist Church (USA) and Wesleyan Church (USA) respectively but also belong to the World Methodist Council).

*ANGLICAN*
The code indicates whether any particular Anglican body is in communion with the See of Canterbury, and if so shows its status in the worldwide Anglican Communion. Of the major Anglican councils, the Lambeth Conference has brought together all bishops every 10 years since 1867; the Lambeth Consultative Body until 1970 brought together all primates (archbishops); it has now been replaced by the Anglican Primates Committee (formed 1978), and since 1970 by the Anglican Consultative Council, meeting biennially, with 50 persons (laity, youth and women as well as bishops and clergy) representing the 25 Anglican Churches, 42 Provinces and 400 Dioceses. The code first describes 2 types of Anglican body in communion with Canterbury.

*Code*

A = autonomous body (church, province, quasi-province or diocese), represented on Anglican Consultative Council (ACC)*/Lambeth Conference/Anglican Primates Committee
a = non-autonomous body (missionary diocese under a province or directly under archbishop of Canterbury, assisted diocese, or part of a diocese based in another country)*

Anglican bodies not in communion with the See of Canterbury have in this column one of the following:

x = member of another pan-Anglican body: either (a) Reformed Episcopal Church (Free Church of England), (b) Anglican Orthodox Communion, or (c) Anglican Episcopal Council of Churches (in USA and India); none of which are in communion with Canterbury
. = not in communion with See of Canterbury or any other pan-Anglican body

*ORTHODOX*
If a letter appears in this column, it indicates whether the body concerned is in canonical relationship (full communion) with historical Orthodoxy, either Eastern or Oriental; and the code names the senior historical patriarchate whose primacy it recognizes. Bodies canonically dependent on one of the 4 Greek-speaking Eastern Orthodox patriarchates (Constantinople, Jerusalem, Alexandria, Antioch) are regarded as in canonical relationship with the Ecumenical

Patriarchate of Constantinople and are accepted as Orthodox by all other Eastern Orthodox sister churches, including the Slavonic-speaking churches; they are indicated by the code letter C. Although the Slavonic-speaking Patriarchate of Moscow is also in communion with Constantinople, the long struggle for primacy between the two (Moscow as the 'Third Rome' attempting to replace Constantinople, the Second Rome) has resulted in several Slavonic-speaking churches recognizing or aligning themselves with Moscow rather than with Constantinople; this de facto situation is indicated by the code letter M.

As a confessional family or families, the Orthodox churches are far less organized at the international level than either Protestantism or Roman Catholicism. There are 2 main co-operative councils. (1) Eastern Orthodox churches in communion with Constantinople and Moscow recognize only 7 ecumenical councils, up to Nicea II in AD 787, since when they have neither held nor recognized any further international ecumenical council. The first since the 8th century has been under preparation for several years now, by means of 4 Panorthodox Conferences (Rhodes 1961 up to Chambésy 1968), and Panorthodox Preconciliar Conferences (the first in 1972 and 1976), and is expected to culminate in the Great and Holy Council of the Orthodox Church some time after 1986, and which will be the first Ecumenical Council recognized by Eastern Orthodox since AD 787. (2) Oriental Orthodox churches held their first ecumenical conference since the first 4 centuries in Addis Ababa in 1965, and set up as a continuing body the Oriental Orthodox Churches Conference. A third group is formed by the Ancient Church of the East, which has rival Patriarchates in Baghdad (a minority under Mar Addai as Patriarch) and, in 1979, in Tehran (the majority, recognized by the Vatican, World Council of Churches and the Anglican Communion). In 1979, the latter was still based on Patriarch Mar Dinkha IV's residence in Tehran, but a new Patriarchate was being built for him in Baghdad.

*Senior patriarchate with whom in canonical relationship:*

*Code*

C    =    Ecumenical Patriarchate of Constantinople (hence also Greek Orthodox Patriarchates of Alexandria, Antioch, Jerusalem; and Panorthodox Conferences)*
c    =    relationship with Constantinople claimed on adequate historical grounds, but temporarily disputed or contested by sister churches
M    =    Patriarchate of Moscow recognized, and primacy preferred to Constantinople*
E    =    Armenian Catholicate of Echmiadzin
S    =    Armenian Catholicate of Cilicia (Sis)
D    =    Syrian Orthodox (Jacobite) Patriarchate of Antioch (Damascus)
N    =    Coptic Orthodox Patriarchate of Alexandria
X    =    Ukrainian Orthodox Church of the Free World
Y    =    Ancient Assyrian Church of the East, Patriarchate of the East (Tehran) (Mar Dinkha IV)
y    =    Ancient Assyrian Church of the East, Patriarchate of Baghdad (Mar Addai)
x    =    member or not in canonical relationship with any historical Orthodox patriarchate, but becoming an international communion or denominational body through the establishing of branches on an international scale
.    =    not in canonical relationship with any historical Orthodox patriarchate (though the relationship may be claimed, without adequate historical grounds), nor with international branches

*Pan-Orthodox councils*

C,M    =    members of forthcoming Great and Holy Council of the Orthodox Church (expected to be held after 1986)*
D,E,N,S=    members of Oriental Orthodox Churches Conference

*ROMAN CATHOLIC* (church organization)
Regarding the Roman Catholic Church as a worldwide confession or communion, the code describes the church's worldwide organization or bureaucracy by indicating the congregation or council in the Roman Curia which is responsible for the diocese or jurisdiction concerned. In addition, where relations with other confessions are concerned, Roman Catholics work through their Secretariat for Unity.

*Code*

B    =    Sacred Congregation for Bishops/Sacra Congregazione per i Vescovi/SC pro Episcopis (for most dioceses in Europe, America and other older Roman Catholic areas)*
H    =    Council for the Public Affairs of the Church/ Consiglio per gli Affari Pubblici della Chiesa/ Consilium pro Publicis Ecclesiae Negotiis (for all Portuguese home and overseas territories, up to 1975 when overseas territories were transferred to Propaganda)*
O    =    Sacred Congregation for the Eastern Churches/SC per le Chiese Orientali/SC pro Ecclesiis Orientalibus (for Uniate and Eastern-rite Catholic jurisdictions)*
P    =    Sacred Congregation for the Evangelization of Peoples/SC per l'Evangelizzazione dei Popoli/SC pro Gentium Evangelizatione (formerly Propaganda Fide, for the Propagation of the Faith) (the overseas missionary organization)*
b,h,o,p =    diocese under one of the preceding congregations (B,H,O,P), but immediately subject to the Holy See itself, i.e. not attached to any ecclesiastical province in its own country*

If there is more than one congregation responsible for the dioceses in a country, the code for the line 'Catholic Church in...' indicates which congregation has numerically the major responsibility.

*CATHOLIC (non-Roman)*

*Code*

U    =    Old Catholic churches in the Union of Utrecht (hence represented on International Old Catholic Bishops Conference)*
u    =    member of both Union of Utrecht and also of ACC/Anglican Communion*
x    =    part of a non-confessional international denominational body
.    =    not in communion with any Old Catholic international council

*NON-WHITE OR BLACK/THIRD-WORLD INDIGENOUS*
By 1978, no world confessional organizations of Black, Third-World or Non-White indigenous bodies had been formed.

*MARGINAL PROTESTANT* (para-Christian)
International denominational bodies in the marginal Protestant category include: Church of Christ, Scientist (Christian Science); Church of Jesus Christ of Latter-day Saints (Mormons); Jehovah's Witnesses, et alia. Confessional bodies in the Protestant sense are almost non-existent, the only 2 in this category being: (1) Code i below, begun 1914 to link Christian metaphysical bodies in the USA including Unity School of Christianity (which left in 1922 though links still maintained); and (2) Code I below, begun 1900, which was previously in the Free Christian/ Unitarian tradition but since 1969 has been open to liberal groups in any of the world's religions.

*Code*

I    =    International Association for Liberal Christianity and Religious Freedom (IARF)/ Association Internationale pour la Liberté Religieuse/Weltbund für Religiöse Freiheit
i    =    International New Thought Alliance (INTA)
x    =    non-confessional international denominational body
.    =    no international confessional membership

2nd letter: *WORLD CONCILIARISM, COLLEGIALITY AND CONSULTATION*

The code indicates, for the denomination or diocese concerned, the degree of involvement in, or commitment to, or attitude to, the world interdenominational or ecumenical movement in the widest sense of the term, worldwide consultation between church leaders and clergy and laity, the worldwide conciliar movement (the proliferation of working and planning through councils), and the conciliar principle ('Without counsel plans go wrong; where counsellors are many, plans succeed' — Proverbs 15.22, RSV/ Jerusalem). In Protestantism, this movement began well over a century ago on the mission fields of Asia and Africa; in the Roman Catholic Church, it has only gained momentum since Vatican II. Conciliarism aims to guide church affairs through the co-operation of denominations, dioceses, hierarchies, church leaders, clergy and laity, in councils — whether ecumenical, confessional, inter-denominational, or intra-denominational (i.e. within a large denomination).

There is a difference of emphasis, in this conciliar involvement, between Protestantism and Roman Catholicism. Protestantism consists of large numbers of autonomous national churches and denominations each run more or less on the conciliar principle internally (consultation between clergy and laity at all levels), but relatively out of touch with each other; hence the growth of conciliarism has meant primarily the establishing of national and international interdenominational councils. The Roman Catholic Church, by contrast, is highly centralized and has long had a worldwide administrative structure and bureaucracy, but has lacked both collegiality (government by all bishops together) and also internal consultation between bishops, clergy and laity. Hence Vatican II initiated major internal conciliar reforms by calling for (a) worldwide collegiality (the whole structure of national and regional episcopal conferences, with the Synod of Bishops at the apex), involving all bishops and ordinaries (but not priests, religious or laity); and (b) consultation and co-responsibility, involving priests, religious personnel and laity as well as bishops, by creating, for the first time, diocesan priests' councils or senates, and diocesan pastoral councils (with religious and lay participation). Certain Roman Catholic local (nationwide) churches have gone further in co-responsibility than Vatican II required by establishing national priests' councils and national pastoral councils; but in 1973 the Vatican prohibited their formation as official organs of the church, thus relegating them to unofficial status. Nevertheless, their existence indicates in which countries the movement towards co-responsibility is strongest, liberalism more to the fore than conservatism, and lay and priestly initiatives more pronounced.

Our code here thus portrays how far a denomination or a Roman Catholic local church has progressed along this worldwide road to conciliarism, co-responsibility and consultation.

a. *Protestant, Anglican, Orthodox, Catholic (non-Roman), Indigenous* (world conciliarism, i.e. membership in world councils or international associations). The code indicates membership in, or relation to, an international or world association of denominations of different ecclesiastical traditions. There are 4 categories.

1. *Ecumenical (or conciliar)*

*Code*

W    =    World Council of Churches (WCC)/Conseil Oecuménique des Eglises (COE)/Ökumenischer Rat der Kirchen (ORK)/Consiglio Ecumenico delle Chiese (CEC); this code indicates a member of the WCC in its own right; for a member church spread over several countries, the code W is given to the headquarters branch, and also to all other branches whose countries are listed in the member's official title; other parts or branches are given the code w
u    =    associate member of WCC (small churches, in principle under 10,000 in membership)
w    =    related to WCC; not a member in its own right in its own country, but related (e.g. as a foreign diocese or branch) to some larger WCC member-church or grouping based in a different country; or, part of a member-church but whose country is not listed in the member's official title
v    =    application for membership made to WCC (either formal or preliminary), but either withdrawn, rejected, delayed indefinitely, or not accepted by 1980

*Notes.* (1) In a number of Western nations, foreign missionary societies of denominations in the ecumenical movement are linked in national missionary councils whose scope is international by virtue of their worldwide activities. However, these councils are not used here as indicators of world conciliar membership because both the home denominations and, usually, the national churches they have founded overseas belong to the World Council of Churches. (2) The Roman Catholic Church is not a member of the WCC but has observer status in it.

#### 2. *Conservative Evangelical (sometimes called non-conciliar)*

There is no single world council linking denominations of Conservative Evangelical emphasis. However, although many such denominations and missionary societies reject all interdenominational, ecumenical or formal conciliar links, there are also many which belong to or are related to international missionary

**World conciliarism.** *Left.* Officers of World Council of Churches, 1973: (from left) M.M. Thomas, Chairman of Central Committee; Philip Potter, General Secretary; Patriarch German of Serbia; President; and former General Secretaries W.A. Visser 't Hooft (1948-66) and E. Carson Blake

associations and alliances based on the major Western mission-sending nations (UK, USA, Australia, NZ), and which link the missionary churches they have founded in countries across the world into de facto international Christian consultative bodies or councils. Many of the resulting national churches belong to continental, regional or national Evangelical councils, alliances or fellowships affiliated to the World Evangelical Fellowship (WEF) (before 1951, World Evangelical Alliance, WEA) as described below under NATIONAL CONCILIARISM; however, the WEF itself only accepts national councils as members, and does not accept individual denominations or churches. International conciliarism among Conservative Evangelicals is therefore represented by a church's or denomination's membership in (or relation through its collaborating foreign missionary society to) one of the following associations, which include as members both denominational and non-denominational agencies.

#### Code

F   = church or mission related to Evangelical Foreign Missions Association, USA (EFMA), which is the mission affiliate of the NAE (USA), which is itself a member of WEF; i.e. WEF-linked or WEF-related

G   = church or mission related to Evangelical Missionary Alliance, UK (EMA), related to EAGB but not to EFMA or IFMA, nor directly to WEF

H   = church or mission related to Australian Evangelical Alliance, but not to EFMA or IFMA

q   = church related to EFMA, but which has also applied to WCC for membership

#### 3. *Fundamentalist (or anti-conciliar)*

Western denominations and missionary societies of strongly Evangelical emphasis often describe themselves by the term fundamental or fundamentalist, or non-conciliar, anti-conciliar or anti-ecumenical. A number of such missions in the USA, including several major faith missions, belong to the IFMA which is a de facto world Christian consultative body or council linking only non-denominational (or faith) missions. A more fundamentalist body is the ICCC, which is specifically anti-ecumenical (separated).

#### Code

M   = church or mission related to Interdenominational Foreign Mission Association, USA (IFMA)

N   = church or mission related to both IFMA and EFMA

r   = church related to IFMA, but which has also applied to WCC for membership

T   = International Council of Christian Churches (ICCC)/Conseil Internationale des Eglises Chrétiennes/Internationaler Rat Christlicher Kirchen (IRCK), and The Associated Missions (TAM)

t   = former member of ICCC, or linked with it, but now withdrawn

#### 4. *Non-conciliar*

.   = not a member of or related to any world or international council or association

*(1966-72). Right.* 1979 Conference of Secretaries of Christian World Communions/CWCs (until 1979, World Confessional Families/WCFs) in Athens, Greece; including Anglican, Roman Catholic, and Russian Orthodox leaders.

#### b. *Roman Catholic (worldwide collegiality and consultation)*

All Roman Catholic churches and dioceses are represented at the worldwide Synod of Bishops/Sinodo dei Vescovi/Synodus Episcoporum (every 3 years in Rome, with permanent secretariat) and (in 1962-5) at the worldwide Ecumenical Council (Vatican II). Because all participate, this fact is not here shown in coded form. What is shown in this column in Table 2 requires some explanation of 2 major concepts in Roman Catholic church structure. (1) *Collegiality* is collaboration between the bishops and Rome, and means government through national, regional and continental bishops' conferences, with at the apex the 2 worldwide expressions of collegiality, the Synod of Bishops and the Ecumenical Council. All Catholic local (nation-wide) churches are represented on these 2 bodies by their bishops. This process of worldwide collegiality, however, involves directly only the bishops; it does not involve the rest of the people of God — priests, religious personnel, laity — who do not participate directly. The second concept is (2) *Consultation*, through which the whole people of God — bishops, priests, religious personnel and laity — are involved in the structure and affairs of the church. Officially, consultation by priests, religious personnel and laity must take place only at the diocesan level, through a diocese's pastoral council and its priests' senate; it may also take place at the parish level, though this is not mandatory. At the national level, however, national or nation-wide pastoral councils, and also national priests' councils or senates, have been forbidden by Rome since 1973. Consequently, in many countries priests, religious personnel, laity, and sometimes their bishops, have organized unofficial or unrecognized national priests' organizations and national consultative pastoral bodies.

The code shows where these 2 latter bodies exist in a Catholic local (nation-wide) church, and therefore indicates the extent to which the whole people of God participate in world collegiality and consultation, i.e. the extent to which priests, religious personnel and laity are attempting to participate in the process of worldwide consultation. The data reflect the situation as at 1975-78.

#### Code

x   = church with both a national consultative pastoral body, and also a national priests' organization

y   = church with a national consultative pastoral body, but with no national priests' organization

z   = church with a national priests' organization, but with no national consultative pastoral body

.   = church with neither a national consultative pastoral body nor a national priests' organization (officially)

#### 3rd letter: *CONTINENTAL CONCILIARISM, COLLEGIALITY AND CONSULTATION*

The code indicates membership in a continent-wide association of different denominations and/or dioceses, or of Roman Catholic national episcopal conferences.

The 6 councils marked † below are affiliated to the WCC as regional conferences and hence are often called ecumenical councils. The Pacific Conference of Churches is included here as a continental conference because it represents Oceania, but the smaller Catholic CEPAC (a member of the PCC) is placed under REGIONAL CONCILIARISM below. Similarly, the Caribbean is reckoned here as a quasi-continent and so the Caribbean Conference of Churches is included, whereas its smaller member body the Catholic AEC is placed under REGIONAL CONCILIARISM.

Several continental councils exist which are not coded here because their members are not denominations but are national councils most of whom have members who in turn are not denominations but are local congregations or individuals. These include several in process of formation in 1980, including the South East Asia Evangelical Alliance (related to WEF), and the Latin American Council of Churches in Formation (created 1978; related to WCC).

There are in addition several confessional or denominational councils continent-wide in name which are included not here but below under REGIONAL CONCILIARISM.

Although the Roman Catholic councils here cover each a continent, several are in Catholic usage termed regional conferences because they are each composed of several national episcopal conferences (codes B,F,S).

Corresponding lower-case letters (a,c,e,o,p,u) indicate that a body belongs to the council concerned, not in its own right, but by belonging as a small part (e.g. as a small foreign diocese or branch) to some larger confessional or ecclesiastical grouping based in a different country.

#### Code

A   = All Africa Conference of Churches (AACC)/Conférence des Eglises de Toute l'Afrique (CETA)†

a   = small foreign part of full member of AACC

B   = Consilium Conferentiarum Episcopalium Europae (CCEE) (Council of European Bishops' Conferences)

C   = Conference of European Churches (CEC)/Conférence des Eglises Européennes (CEE)/Konferenz Europäischer Kirchen(KEK)†

c   = observer status in CEC (Armenian, Bulgarian and Serbian Orthodox Churches); or, small foreign part of a full member of CEC

D   = related to European Evangelical Alliance (EEA) through membership in affiliated national fellowship or council or alliance

E   = Christian Conference of Asia (CCA) (until 1972, East Asian Christian Conference, EACC)†

e   = small foreign part of full member of CCA

F   = Federation of Asian Bishops' Conferences (FABC)

G   = related to Association of Evangelicals of Africa and Madagascar (AEAM) (member of WEF) through membership in affiliated national fellowship or council

g   = associate/special member of AEAM (for isolated denominations)

H   = related to Evangelical Association of the Caribbean (EAC) through membership in affiliated national fellowship or council

I   = Organization of African Independent Churches (OAIC), or other continental council of Black/Third-World or Non-White indigenous churches

i   = member of OAIC, also member of AACC

L   = Consejo Episcopal Latinoamericano (CELAM) (Latin American Episcopal Council)

M   = Caribbean Conference of Churches (CCC)†

N   = Caribbean Conference of Churches (CCC) and also member of CELAM

O   = Standing Conference of Canonical Orthodox

**Continental conciliarism.** *Left.* 5th General Assembly of SECAM (Symposium of Episcopal Conferences of Africa and Madagascar), Nairobi, 1978. *Right.* Founding Conference of OAIC (Organization of African Independent Churches), Cairo, November 1978. Front, left to right; Apostle A.A. Abiola, Patriarch Shenouda III, Primate Emmanuel Adejobi (chairman, OAIC), Chef Spirituel N. Diangienda of EJCSK.

Bishops in the Americas (SCOBA)

o = small foreign part of full member of SCOBA

P = Pacific Conference of Churches (PCC)/ Conférence des Eglises du Pacifique†

p = small foreign part of full member of PCC

Q = member of CCC, also related to EAC

S = Symposium of Episcopal Conferences of Africa and Madagascar (SECAM)/Symposium des Conférences Episcopales d'Afrique et de Madagascar (SCEAM)

T = continental council affiliated to ICCC (Latin American Alliance of Christian Churches (LAACC), Far Eastern Council of Christian Churches (FECCC), ICCC European Alliance, Caribbean Council of Christian Churches)

U = Movimiento pro Unidad Evangélica Latino-americana (UNELAM)†, being replaced from 1978 by Latin American Council of Churches (in formation) (CLAI)

u = indirect member of UNELAM/CLAI through membership in a UNELAM/CLAI-affiliated national council

V = Caribbean Conference of Churches (CCC) and also member of UNELAM/CLAI

X = member of CEC, also related to EEA

x = related to EEA, also observer status in CEC

Y = related to both Evangelical Association of the Caribbean (EAC) and ICCC

. = not a member of nor related to any continental council

### 4th letter: *REGIONAL CONCILIARISM, COLLEGIALITY AND CONSULTATION*

The code indicates membership in a council covering a region, which is defined here as a small number of countries (3 or more) within a continent (e.g. Near East, or South Pacific, or Eastern Africa). If not fully named by the code, these regional councils are identified under the country's Table 2. A number are regional councils of churches of a single denominational tradition (Roman Catholic, Anglican, Reformed, Lutheran, Pentecostal, etc); and some are continent-wide in name but in practice are only regional because that denomination's presence is not universal or continent-wide. There are several other smaller confessional or denominational councils not included here (see listing in Codebook). The Middle East Council of Churches is an affiliated regional conference of the WCC. For Roman Catholic councils, it should be noted that using our definition of region this code includes 2 kinds of council: (a) regional councils properly so called as defined by the Catholic Church, each composed of a number of national episcopal conferences (codes B,D,E,F,G below); and (b) multi-national conferences, each composed not of episcopal conferences but directly of bishops of dioceses (H,L,M,Q,S,Y,Z).

*Code*

A = Council of the Church in East Asia (CCEA) (until 1975, CCSEA)

B = Association des Conférences Episcopales du Congo/RCA/Tchad (ACECCT) (formerly ACEACCAM)

C = Consejo Anglicano Sud Americano (CASA)/ Anglican Council for South America (mainly southern region of continent)

D = Secretariado Episcopal de América Central y Panamá (SEDAC) (a regional section of CELAM)

E = Association of Member Episcopal Conferences in Eastern Africa (AMECEA)

F = Conférence Episcopale Régionale de l'Afrique Occidentale Francophone (CERAO) (Regional Episcopal Conference of French-speaking West Africa)

G = Association of Episcopal Conferences of English-speaking West Africa (AECEWA)

H = Conférence Episcopale d'Afrique du Nord/ Episcopal Conference of North Africa

I = regional council of Black/Third-World or Non-White indigenous churches

J = Asociación Regional Episcopal del Norte de Sud América (ARENSA) (Anglican; part of CASA)

K = South Pacific Anglican Council (SPAC)

L = Conférence des Evêques Latins dans les Régions Arabes (CELRA)

M = Antilles Episcopal Conference (AEC)

N = Middle East Council of Churches (MECC/ CEMO) (until 1974, Near East Council of Churches (NECC)/Conseil des Eglises Chrétiennes du Proche-Orient (CEPO)/ Majma' al Kana'is fi al Sharq al Adna)

O = regional council of Orthodox churches

P = attached or partially attached to one of the 6 RC non-Latin Patriarchal Synods (Armenian, Chaldean, Coptic, Maronite, Melkite, Syrian)

Q = Nordic Bishops' Conference (Scandinavian Bishops' Conference/Nordiske Bispekonferanse)

**Regional conciliarism.** Plenary Meeting of AMECEA (Association of Member Episcopal Conferences in Eastern Africa). Nairobi, 1976.

R = Anglican Council of North America and the Caribbean (ACNAC)

S = Interterritorial (Inter-Regional) Meeting of Bishops in Southern Africa (IMBISA) (formerly Southern Africa Catholic Bishops' Conference)

T = regional council affiliated to ICCC (Middle East Bible Council, Central Africa Christian Council, West Africa Council of Christian Churches (WACCC), Australasian Alliance of Bible Believing Christian Churches, Scandinavian Evangelical Council)

U = member of both MECC and CAPA

V = Conference of the Anglican Provinces of Africa (CAPA) (until 1977, Conference of Archbishops of Anglican Provinces in Africa)

W = member of both AMECEA and CELRA

X = Pentecostal Fellowship of North America (PFNA)

Y = Conférence des Evêques du Pacifique (CEPAC)/Episcopal Conference of the Pacific

Z = Regional Conference of Chinese Bishops (Chung Kuo Chu-chiao T'uan)

. = not a member of any regional council

### 5th letter: *NATIONAL OR PLURINATIONAL CONCILIARISM, COLLEGIALITY AND CONSULTATION*

The code indicates the extent to which a church is involved in national (country-wide) interdenominational or ecumenical conciliarism — i.e. membership in national associations of denominations and/or dioceses. In a few cases, such councils cover 2 countries (or very occasionally, 3) and so can be called plurinational. In a number of cases, too, the Roman Catholic Church is a member, or an associate member, of a national council of churches. All national councils are fully identified by name under each country's Table 2. In addition to such national councils, there are a large number of other national councils which do not have denominations as members; they are therefore not coded in Column 4, but they are listed in footnotes 'Other national councils' under Tables 2.

*Code*

a = member of 2 national councils, one WCC-related and one Evangelical (WEF- or AEAM- or EAC-related)

b = member of 2 national councils, one WCC-related and one Black/Third-World or Non-White indigenous

C = national council (Protestant, Western) with no formal external international affiliations

c = associate member of C (preceding line), or related for certain functions

d = member of 2 national councils, one WCC-related and one unaffiliated (Protestant, Western)

E = national Evangelical alliance or council, affiliated to WEF (World Evangelical Fellowship) and also to one of its regional associations or continental counterparts (AEAM, EAC, EEA, et alia) where existing

e = national Evangelical alliance or council, affiliated to EEA (European Evangelical Alliance) but not (in 1978) to WEF

F = national council including Roman Catholic, Protestant, Anglican and Indigenous churches, but with no formal external international affiliations

**National conciliarism.** General secretaries and other officers of national councils of churches in Africa related to WCC and AACC meet in Ho (Ghana), May 1977, representing (left to right, standing): Sierra Leone, Malawi, Mozambique, Botswana, Nigeria, Zimbabwe, Tanzania, Rwanda (1), Zambia, Rwanda (2), Ghana; (squatting) Burundi, Madagascar.

f = formerly in the major national council, but has recently withdrawn

G = national Evangelical council affiliated to AEAM but not (in 1978) to WEF

H = national council of Pentecostal churches (Protestant, Western)

h = member of some other council (incompletely recorded in Table 2, though name and membership are given below it)

I = national council of Black/Third-World or Non-White indigenous churches (run by

them, or predominantly of them)

i = member of I (preceding line) and also of H
J = national council of Black/Third-World or Non-White indigenous churches (different to I)
K = national council of churches, or Christian council, in working relationship with WCC but not affiliated to it
k = associate member of K (preceding line), or affiliated for certain services; or permanent (not occasional) observer or consultative member of K
L = national Evangelical council affiliated to EAC (Evangelical Association of the Caribbean) but not (in 1978) to WEF
l = as L, but also affiliated to ICCC
M = national council of foreign missionary societies (church represented through one or more of its mission bodies)
N = national council of churches, or Christian council, affiliated to CWME of WCC (formerly to IMC)
n = associate member of N (preceding line), or affiliated for certain services; or permanent (not occasional) observer member of N
O = national council or liaison committee of Orthodox churches
P = plurinational Roman Catholic episcopal or bishops' conference (covering 2 or 3 countries included in conference's name)
Q = member of plurinational RC episcopal conference, also full member of national council related to WCC
q = as Q, but only observer or associate member of national council related to WCC
R = national Roman Catholic episcopal or bishops' conference
r = small diocese or church attached to Roman Catholic national episcopal conference in another country (and so not included in conference's name)
S = member of national RC episcopal conference, also full member of national council related to WCC
s = as S, but only observer or associate member of national council related to WCC
T = national council affiliated, or informally related, to ICCC
t = former member of T (preceding line), now withdrawn; or, member of council formerly affiliated to ICCC, now withdrawn
u = member in temporary or once-only co-operative national conference of churches in nation where permanent council prohibited by state
V = member of national RC episcopal conference, also full member of national council not related to WCC
v = as V, but only observer or associate member of national council not related to WCC
W = national (ecumenical) council of churches, or Christian council, formally associated with WCC (these Associate Councils of the WCC have been called ecumenical councils since Davos 1955); in some cases associate councils are also affiliated to CWME of WCC
w = associate member of W (preceding line), or affiliated for certain services; or permanent (not occasional) observer or guest member of W; or member of countrywide council associated with W
x = member of 2 other national councils
y = some other Black/Third-World or Non-White indigenous national council (different to I or J)
Z = member of 3 national councils
z = member of 3 national councils, one WCC-related and one Evangelical
. = not a member of any national council

2nd–5th letters *LOCAL/INTERNATIONAL STAFFING:* for Roman Catholic sub-divisions (dioceses and jurisdictions) only:
The code indicates the extent to which a diocese or jurisdiction is under international, or national, or extra-diocesan, or local control, by describing its staffing. Almost all jurisdictions in the Western world are staffed by secular (diocesan) clergy (with religious clergy for special functions) and can thus be said to be under local control; this is indicated by the code s under the second letter. However, a large number of jurisdictions in mission areas are operated by religious clergy belonging to internationally-organized missionary institutes (orders, congregations and societies). Before 1969, under the system Jus Commissionis, SC Propaganda Fide would formally confide a jurisdiction to the care of a particular institute. This system is still in force for vicariates and prefectures; but since 1969 for dioceses it has been replaced by Propaganda granting a mandate (*mandatum*). This system has proved so tedious that by 1974 mandates had been granted in only 15 dioceses, and both institutes and local bishops have circumvented the procedure by a simple signed contract or agreement between a bishop and an institute concerning the supply of manpower and money. Whichever system is in force in a jurisdiction, in all cases where an institute supplies the major services to a diocese or jurisdiction and its bishop, or is effectively in charge of a diocese or jurisdiction (i.e. furnishing clergy required), these last 4 letters in Column 4 give the initials of the institute concerned.

*Code*

s = local secular or diocesan clergy
s j = served by (formerly confided to) Society of Jesus
All other initials, and their full names, can be identified from the Index of Abbreviations, Acronyms and Initials (Part 14).

2nd–5th letters: STATUS OF DIOCESE IN INTERNAL CONCILIARISM, for dioceses of other large churches. The code describes any relevant and available data providing a differentium from one diocese to another.
*Russian and other Orthodox churches*
The letter indicates the usual rank of the bishop of a diocese, and hence provides an approximate indication of the relative importance attached to the diocese by the church's councils, its hierarchy and the Holy Synod; it is therefore a measure of the influence of a diocese in internal conciliarism, i.e. in the councils of the church.

*Code*

P = patriarch, patriarch-catholicos
m = metropolitan
a = archbishop
e = exarch
b = bishop

## COLUMN 8: NAMES, NOTES AND OTHER STATISTICS

This column serves as a general space where any further data that are available may be summarized. For certain large churches with consistent patterns of gathering statistics for their component dioceses, it has been possible to present data in the form of a sub-table at the end of Column 8, as explained below. The absence of any particular statistic for a church in Column 8 (e.g. no figure for s, seminaries) means, in descending order of probability, either (a) there are none of these items (seminaries) in that particular church, or (b) there is nothing particularly significant to report on that subject, or (c) no information on the subject was available.

The column gives descriptive notes on each denomination and diocese, including a selection of any significant data concerning the church's name (in Column 1) and also the following elements:

initials of body if commonly in use (in italics).
additional parts of name of body, or geographical sub-title of the body itself (in italics), with any wider geographical ecclesiastical jurisdictions or entities (not in italics, but with first letters capitalized).
name of body in major national or local language (if not given in Column 1) (in italics).
translation of names in Column 1 into English (in italics).
alternate name(s) (in italics) or former name(s) not in italics.
co-operating foreign missionary societies (past and/or present).
brief geographical notes (area covered, centres, HQ=headquarters).
brief notes on historical development, e.g., A=year when church became autonomous (if significant).
ethnic or linguistic or national/expatriate (citizen/alien) composition of members or adherents (Christians), as % (ethnic or linguistic groups are always shown here, with or without %s, in descending order of numerical size; a single ethnic name without a % means that all Christians, or almost all, belong to the one group; ethnic names in Column 8 always refer to the Christian population, not to the total population).
and any of the following statistics that are available (Note: Personnel are always the first statistics shown in this column in the table, given in the order C,n,x,m,w,f,pp).

*Code*

B = (at head of a sub-column) location in province or state.
b = parishes (as defined by the church concerned, if different from Column 5).
C = Roman Catholic religious institutes (i.e. orders, congregations and societies) permanently present and officially at work (foreign and local) (the 3 figures given (e.g. C=3+1+15) enumerate the number of distinct institutes of, respectively, *clerics* (priests mainly, occasionally also brothers and seminarians), + *brothers*, + *sisters*).
D = Catholic diocesan councils of post-conciliar (Vatican II) type (reported in Table 2 only for a handful of countries where significant).
Synod = diocesan synod involving whole diocese; either completed, in progress, or being planned (usually a couple of years in duration; such a synod may be regarded as the climax of internal ecumenism).
PC( ) = pastoral council, for laity, religious, and clergy; if followed by 1 number in parentheses ( ), this=total members; if followed by 2 numbers in parentheses, these = priests/religious members, and lay members.
pc( ) = priests' council or senate; if followed by 1 number in parentheses ( ), this=total members; if followed by 3 numbers in parentheses, these=members nominated by bishop, members ex officio, and members elected by all priests.

**Monasteries.** Model of Zagorsk monastery, in Russian Orthodox museum at Zagorsk (USSR).

bc = brothers' council (men religious brothers).
lc = council of laity.
sc = sisters' council (women religious personnel).
d = monasteries (religious houses for men, monks, brothers).

**Schism.** Remains of shattered church in Kano (Kenya) in 1957 after rioting schismatics left the Anglican Diocese of Mombasa to form Church of Christ in Africa.

de = monasteries and convents.
declining=numerical decrease in recent years compared to earlier larger following.

e = convents (religious houses for women, nuns, sisters).

ex = schism (split, secession, break off) from or out of church or mission indicated.

f = foreign missionary personnel (aliens, expatriates), as defined by church or mission (lay and ordained, men and women, often including wives; career missionaries and short-term; usually including only those active on the field, or seconded or on furlough, but not home staff or retired personnel).

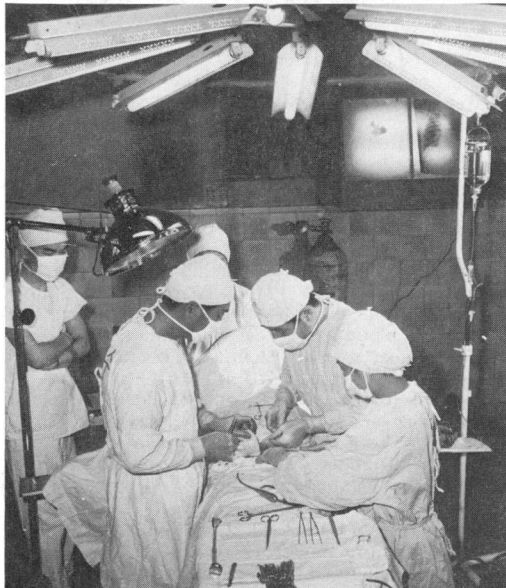

**Hospitals.** Severance Hospital, Seoul, Korea (Methodist).

G = annual growth rate of membership, % pa (% per year), in 1970 or over period 1965–75, where significant (G=0 means virtually zero growth; negative means decrease); the value G is composed of population natural increase plus conversion increase.

H = hospitals operated by church or mission (including leprosaria and sanatoria).

HQ = location of headquarters, see city, episcopal residence, secretariat, denominational offices (usually only given here if not given in, or if not the same as, title in Column 1).

**Printing presses.** Press in Coptic Orthodox monastery El Sourian (Egypt), begun 1950, moved in 1965 to Patriarchate in Cairo.
**Bookshops.** Protestant bookstore in Bangladesh.

h = clinics, dispensaries, maternity centres, hospital outposts, mobile clinics, operated by church or mission.

i = mission stations (of foreign missionary societies).

j = printing presses or publishing houses operated by church or mission.

k = bookshops run by church or mission.

L = (at head of a sub-column) official language used.

M = co-operating foreign missionary societies, past and/or present (listed in full in Index of Abbreviations, Acronyms and Initials, in Part 14), which have a local or national office and administration (and not simply a few individual missionaries) in the country concerned: for Protestant and Anglican missions, the home base's nation usually follows in parentheses (if there are 2 or more nations involved, they are listed in order of the number of missionaries provided); in the case of Roman Catholic jurisdictions, a mission shown in this way in Column 8 is offering some assistance, sometimes in the person of the bishop, but if the jurisdiction has been confided to or is in the charge of a missionary institute, this latter is shown in column 4 (2nd–5th letters).

m = men lay workers, brothers, monks (full-time; nationals plus expatriates; Catholic men religious brothers (members of men's religious institutes, both nationals and expatriates), but not including Catholic lay catechists; Anglican or Orthodox brothers or monks, or Protestants and Anglicans recognized as workers in church pastoral or evangelistic work, e.g. full-time lay preachers; usually nationals but not expatriate missionaries).

mw = total full-time lay workers, men + women (=m+w).

**Priests.** Ethiopian Orthodox clergy.

N = priests prevented by state from functioning (figures in Czechoslovakia only).

n = national (citizen) clergy (ordained ministers, pastors, priests (secular and religious), deacons, including deaconesses and ordained women, also including bishops; either paid or unpaid); active only, excluding retired; resident in area (not visiting only).

nm = total men workers, ordained and lay (=n+m).

nx = total clergy or ministers, both national plus expatriate (=n+x) (1 nx means one of unknown nationality).

P = practising Christians, % (those fulfilling their churches' minimum annual obligations of church attendance, as % of those affiliated and eligible to attend; this usually exceeds Easter communicants) (Roman Catholics: most figures are from 1969 returns to SC Propaganda, modified to exclude non-communicants under 7 years old).

p = Bible schools, catechist training schools: Protestant Bible-training schools or short-term lay training centres, often for lay church workers, often also for ordained workers but of lower entrance standard (primary education) than seminaries (some secondary education); Roman Catholic catechist training schools, of primary or secondary level.

pp = part-time preachers (unsalaried but officially-accredited volunteer spare-time local preachers, lay preachers, lay readers).

q = religious seminaries (not secular or diocesan; Roman Catholic major seminaries for religious clergy).

R = radio letters (normal annual listeners' letters received from this country by all Christian radio stations or agencies, home or foreign).

r = church-related or -operated colleges, teacher-training colleges, major high or secondary schools, academies, technical or industrial schools, or other educational institutions of higher learning.

RE = Catholic ecclesiastical region (USA only).

S = active BCC students (enrolled in Bible correspondence courses).

SS = Sunday-school enrolment (pupils).

s = seminaries for preparation for the ordained ministry (major seminaries, theological colleges with premises, plant and permanent staff; Bible academies, Bible institutes, Bible colleges, officer training schools; usually with entrance requirement of some secondary education; Roman Catholic secular/diocesan major seminaries only (excluding religious/regular seminaries); including university departments of theology only if related to or

**Schools.** St Denys' School and College, Murree, Pakistan (Church of Pakistan).

operated by a church); if a number follows in parentheses, it is of seminarians in training for the ordained ministry.

school = primary or middle schools (not secondary or higher) under church or mission auspices.

ST = state: name or zip code abbreviation for secular or civil state or province coterminous, or nearly so, with diocese.

T = total accumulated BCC enrolments (students who now or in the past have enrolled in Bible correspondence courses).

**Sunday schools.** Anglican class at Pa-an, Burma.

t = Sunday-schools, sabbath schools (often called (in North American usage) church schools, though this term usually means day schools operated by churches) (followed in parentheses by enrolment, which often includes adults).

u = participation in a united seminary (sponsored by 2 or more denominations).

V = BCC conversions (students enrolled in Bible correspondence courses who have professed conversion to Christ as a result).

v = church-related or -operated universities.

W = attending Christians, or weekly church attenders, % (church attenders each Sunday or Saturday or weekend (Roman Catholics: attendance at mass) as % of those affiliated and eligible to attend).

w = women lay workers, sisters, nuns (full-time; nationals plus expatriates; Catholic women religious (members of women's religious institutes) but not including Catholic lay women catechists; Anglican or Orthodox sisters or nuns, Protestants and Anglicans in church pastoral or evangelistic work).

**Sisters (nuns).** Romanian Orthodox nun at prayer.

x    =  expatriate (alien, foreign, non-citizen) clergy (ordained ministers, pastors, priests (secular and religious), deacons, deaconesses, ordained women, bishops, missionaries); active only, excluding retired; resident in area (not simply visiting) (NB: in the Third World, this includes both Western ordained missionaries and also pastors and priests from adjoining or other Third-World countries).

Y,y  =  annual baptisms (new persons baptized in a recent year around 1970–75); Y = adult baptisms (usually over 7 years), y = infant baptisms (under 7), Yy = adults + infants combined. In the case of churches not practising water baptism (Salvation Army, Quakers, EJCSK, etc), Y = new adult members admitted. In the case of the Roman Catholic Church, baptisms of infants are as significant as of adults and so AP always combines the 2 (shown here as Yy); a division into adults and infants for each diocese was however given in AP 1970.

z    =  catechumens, baptismal candidates (these are always included in Column 7; hence for the Roman Catholic Church, the number of baptized Catholics = Column 7 minus catechumens.

( )  =  number of students, monks, nuns, Sunday-school scholars, or pupils in the institutions immediately referred to (e.g. 2s(20) means 2 seminaries with 20 seminarians training for the ordained ministry).

%    =  percentages followed by names are of 2 kinds: (1) % ethnic groups = % of the Christian community who belong to each tribal or ethnic group. (2) % Muslim, % pagan, % Catholic (% RC) = % of the total population in the area or diocese (information only included where significant or unusual compared to other jurisdictions).

*SUB-TABLES IN COLUMN 8.* For the Roman Catholic, Orthodox and Anglican churches, and a few other large churches with several dioceses, Column 8 often ends with a sub-table of up to 8 columns (depending on how much data are available for all dioceses), setting out for each diocese the numbers of national and expatriate clergy, men and women religious personnel, and various other data such as the percentage of practising Christians. For these sub-tables, the identifying codes (n,x,m,w,P, etc) are only given once, with the totals on the first line of the sub-table, and are not repeated on subsequent lines below. It should be noted that these figures of personnel represent usually diocesan workers on diocesan staffs; the actual total of all personnel for a church may be somewhat larger

because of the presence of non-diocesan staff, personnel seconded to ecumenical or secular agencies, and so on.

*SUMMARY TOTALS FOR A CHURCH WITH DIOCESES.* Where a church or denomination has several dioceses indented under it, all statistics on the first line are of grand totals for the whole church, although a full breakdown by dioceses may not be given on the following lines. Thus a church with only one seminary, in one of its dioceses, will show the code '1s' for that diocese, and will also show the total (in this case also '1s') on the line for the whole church. Care must be taken not to construe this repetition as meaning that there are 2 separate seminaries.

*OVERFLOW DATA FROM COLUMN 8.* For certain churches, the amount of significant data available is too large to be included on a single line in Column 8, and is then given in the overflow position at the end of Table 2 after the heading ADDITIONAL DATA ON CHURCHES.

*TOTAL AFFILIATED (1970–75–80).* The first of these 3 rows gives the total of all the preceding denominations' totals, for 1970; the second and third project the totals to 1975 and 1980 (as done in Table 1). The totals of congregations (worship centres) in the bottom 3 rows of Column 5 include estimates for all denominations whose total centres are unreported above in Column 5 because unknown.

*DOUBLY-AFFILIATED.* Persons affiliated to or claimed by 2 denominations at once (as shown, defined and described in Tables 1).

*DISAFFILIATED.* Former Christians recently withdrawn from state or majority churches (as shown, defined and described in Tables 1).

*FOOTNOTES.*
Under Tables 2 is placed additional information on the churches in the form of 4 standardized sections with standardized footnotes, headed as follows and in the following order.

**1. NOTES ON TABLE ABOVE**
  **COLUMNS.** The first note under each table is meant to aid readers who are completely new to the layout employed.
  **NATIONAL COUNCILS.** The last of the 5 letters in Column 4 shows what generic types of national councils of churches exist in the country, and the footnote gives the name of each body in its official language(s), these being separated by slashes, followed by (if English is not official) English translation in parentheses. Also given are the names of any other national councils linking the churches, and totals of any local Christian councils or councils of churches. If this footnote does not appear under a country's Table 2, it indicates that there are no national councils in that country.
  **OTHER PROTESTANT DENOMINATIONS.** In addition to bodies tabulated in Table 2, there is in most countries a number of small or very small bodies too numerous for each to be described. A selection of all such bodies which have congregations and some sort of organization (i.e. not unorganized individual persons) are listed in this footnote, with a summary statistical line at the end of the Table. In parentheses after the names there are often given (1) the year the body began in the nation, (2) the country of origin, (3) the major ethnic group involved, (4) current statistics of membership.
  **OTHER INDIGENOUS CHURCHES.** Additional small Black, Third-World or Non-White indigenous churches are summarized in a line at the end of Tables 2 and a selection of names is given in the footnote, sometimes with in brackets data on year begun, ethnic group, and size of current membership.
  **OTHER CHURCHES.** Likewise, other groupings of small bodies (Orthodox, Catholic/non-Roman, etc) may have a summary line at the end of Table 2 and a footnote elaborating.
  **OTHER MARGINAL PROTESTANT BODIES.** Additional Western marginal Protestant bodies are sometimes summarized in a line at the end of Tables 2 and listed in the footnote.
  **UNITING CHURCHES.** In cases where negotiations for organic union between churches were under way in 1975-80, the names of the churches are given. In some countries 2 or more separate sets of negotiations are under way at the same time.
  *Sources.* Biennial surveys are conducted by the Faith and Order Commission, WCC, and are published in *The ecumenical review* (1954, 1955, 1957, 1960, 1962, 1964, 1966, 1968, 1970, 1972,

1974, 1976, 1978, July 1980). These are usually partial and not globally comprehensive.

**2. PEOPLES** (ethnolinguistic). This footnote gives the ethnolinguistic composition of the total of all affiliated Christians in the country, with peoples or families listed in descending order of size or percentage size (i.e. %s of all affiliated Christians, not %s of total population), down to 0.1%, with smaller groups listed at the end but only where significant numbers are involved. Sometimes the most meaningful breakdown is ethnic, sometimes linguistic, sometimes racial, sometimes national (by nationality or citizenship), sometimes by colour (Black, White, etc). These data are given with one of 3 degrees of accuracy: (1) figures are given to one decimal place when accurate data were available, (2) less accurate data are shown without decimal points, and (3) very approximate estimates are indicated by the use of the word 'about'. The data given in these footnotes were then coded in accordance with the classification and codes given in PEOPLES OF THE WORLD under Culture (Part 4), and the Global Tables in Part 8 prepared. To understand this classification, the explanation there should be read. The figures given here are shown as percentages rather than as absolute numbers, because the latter are growing continuously each year with each country's natural population increase. If the reader requires the absolute number for any particular group in a particular year such as 1980, this may be obtained by multiplying the percentage given here by the country's total of Christians in 1980 (obtainable from either Table 1 or Table 2).

**3. COUNTRY-WIDE TOTALS.** This third section of the footnotes under Tables 2 summarizes other statistics documenting certain aspects of the churches' activities, agencies, plant, personnel, and the international sharing of personnel (foreign missionaries sent and received). If a country has none of the items (e.g. no seminaries, or no missionaries), then the category is omitted in the footnotes; in other words, if any of these headings are omitted in any Table 2, it means that the total for each of those categories in that country is zero (nil).
  **EVANGELIZATION.** This footnote summarizes data on evangelization and evangelism by giving (1) the percentage of the country's population which may be said to have been already demographically evangelized, for the 3 years 1900, 1970 and 1980, with projection to AD 2000. The figures are the same as in Global Table 31, columns 102-104, and their derivation, with our definition of the concept of demographic evangelization, are explained below in Part 5. This footnote further gives: (2) data on recent mass evangelism campaigns in the country, with statistics for attendances and enquirers (the latter often also being termed professions of faith (number of individuals professing new faith at a campaign), conversions, or decisions for Christ); (3) data on recent radio-phonic evangelism, defined here as evangelism using either radio/TV, radiophonic schools or courses (broadcast, with local teachers co-ordinating), radio correspondence courses, or Bible correspondence courses using both radio and postal mails or the mails only; (4) data on annual listeners' letters (in response to radio/TV programmes), on which some of this analysis is based, as will shortly be explained; and (5) data on any mass literature evangelism in the country.
  **FOREIGN MISSIONARIES AND PERSONNEL** (nationals serving abroad) (1973). The footnote documents what each country contributes to the international sharing of personnel, organized and unorganized. The first figure is the total of long-term foreign missionaries or similar personnel of all churches from this country, who are citizens of this country, who were serving abroad in 1973 in, under or through organized missionary societies, boards, institutes or other less-organized agencies, whether based in this country or in another country. These statistics are repeated, for all countries, in Global Table 31, columns 36-43. Our term 'foreign missionaries' refers mainly to persons who would so describe themselves or who are formally sent as such by parent foreign missionary societies; our term 'foreign personnel' refers mainly to similar personnel sent abroad on behalf of their churches but who are not described as, or do not use the term, missionaries. As explained in the

following section, these 2 terms cover a variety of motives and situations. Theologically, however, there is no justification for restricting the term 'missionaries', as has been done in recent history, to White personnel from the Western world who go abroad to serve in Third-World countries. In this survey, therefore, we combine these 2 categories into a single category. The definition of this dual term 'Foreign missionaries and personnel' is almost, but not exactly, the same as that in the next paragraph. The totals given here should be regarded as minimum figures; they are reasonably complete for Protestants, Anglicans and Orthodox, but are not so exact for Roman Catholics because many Third-World nationals serve in Western-based missionary institutes who do not enumerate them by nationality.

**FOREIGN MISSIONARIES AND PERSONNEL** (aliens from abroad) (1973). This footnote (and also Global Table 31 columns 45-55) documents what each country receives through the international sharing of personnel, organized and unorganized. It gives minimum totals of full-time professional (or career) long-term foreign missionaries or similar personnel (men and women) officially or actively at work and resident on the field or abroad in 1973, either in organized and recognized foreign missionary societies, institutes, agencies, boards or sending committees originating in any part of the world, or in less-organized or unorganized bodies or groups. As above, in our usage the term 'foreign missionaries' refers mainly to persons who would so describe themselves or who are formally sent as such by parent foreign missionary societies; our term 'foreign personnel' refers mainly to similar personnel sent abroad on behalf of their churches but who are not described as, or do not use the term, missionaries. The former term covers mainly those sent out consciously and deliberately on the church's task of mission, service and evangelization. The latter term covers a larger variety of motivations and situations, including personnel who voluntarily or involuntarily leave their parent country together with their own ethnic communities when these become emigrants, refugees, or deportees, and who then serve a full-time ministry as civilian or military chaplains, evangelists, religious educators or in some other specialized role in an alien country. Sometimes these personnel are referred to as diaspora missionaries. In this survey we regard these 2 categories as similar and overlapping, and treat them as a single category 'Foreign missionaries and personnel'. The category 'foreign missionary societies' is clearly defined in the Western world; but in Communist and Third-World countries the sending bodies are almost always not missionary societies but the churches and denominations themselves. Consequently, we may say that our survey here defines as foreign missionaries, and includes statistics of, 3 kinds of personnel: (1) those belonging to and sent out by organized societies or churches in the home country, to work either in organized denominations (shown listed in Table 2) or in non-church-planting service agencies; (2) those in less-organized or unorganized groups in their home country, who go abroad on their own initiative but who work in the receiving country in existing denominations or service agencies; and (3) those who go abroad completely independently and who work in the receiving country completely independently. In general, our statistics include (1) and (2) above, but only (3) in those countries where their existence is known. This category is also not coterminous with, and in fact covers more than, the category 'cross-cultural missionaries' (persons of one culture working among those of a different culture). It is a more practical term because it is capable of more exact measurement since its definition is the crossing of, and residence beyond, definite international frontiers. Our definition thus excludes the vast numbers of home missionaries (sent by their church to missionary areas within the same country), but it includes those who (like the Apostles Peter and Paul) cross national frontiers to preach or minister to peoples of their own culture. At the same time, our figures are minimum totals because they list only persons in organized missions, societies, agencies and churches, and exclude many independent individuals and groups who serve abroad, unknown and unheralded, under no organized mission or church but under their own initiative.

In the footnotes under Tables 2, all foreign missionaries and personnel in a country are here first divided, by the nationality of their parent society, into those coming from respectively the Western world, the Communist world, and the Third World. The largest grouping, those from Western countries, are almost all Whites (Europeans, North Americans, Australians and New Zealanders), and remain citizens of those countries. Those who have taken out citizenship in the country of their work are no longer foreign there and so are not enumerated here (unless they have dual citizenship, in which case they are regarded here as expatriates of their other nationality). The totals are next sub-divided, in order of size, into Roman Catholics, Protestants, Anglicans, Orthodox, Catholics (non-Roman), marginal Protestants and Non-White or Black/Third-World indigenous. Then, all except Roman Catholics are in most cases divided (again in order of size) by the nation of origin of their parent society, giving the number of missionaries in those missionary societies, orders, boards or agencies (including branches thereof; all here termed societies) which are based either in (1) the 21 organized-mission-sending and mission-receiving Western nations (Australia, Austria, Belgium, Canada, Denmark, Finland, France, Germany (FRG), Greece, Iceland, Ireland, Italy, Netherlands, New Zealand, Norway, Portugal, Spain, Sweden, Switzerland, UK, USA), (2) the 2 sending but non-receiving Communist nations (Poland, Yugoslavia) and the 5 non-sending non-receiving Communist countries which nevertheless allow limited personnel to go abroad (Bulgaria, Czechoslovakia, Hungary, Romania, USSR), or (3) the 50 mission-sending (as well as mission-receiving) Third-World countries (see survey map in Part 11, World Atlas).

The following 12 points should be noted, to some extent recapitulating and restating the foregoing definition. (a) The exact definition of the term foreign missionaries and personnel usually followed in Tables 2 is as follows, although occasionally a country or council or agency collects its statistics to a slightly different definition which cannot easily be modified to our definition. Foreign missionaries and personnel as enumerated here are defined as all active full-time personnel (either fully-supported career or professional missionaries, or tent-making (self-supporting) missionaries, or chaplains ministering to emigrant communities) sent abroad on a long-term basis by churches or missions to any foreign country (Western, Communist or Third-World), who are aliens or expatriates in the countries they serve in, and who include laymen and ordained personnel, men and women, wives (only if defined as missionaries by the church or mission concerned), who are at present active on the field, including missionary personnel seconded or on loan to or from non-mission agencies. The definition excludes persons who are citizens of the country they serve in; it excludes seasonal assistants (serving under 6 months) and short-service or short-term personnel (serving for a single period of 6 months to under 2 years only); and it also excludes missionaries on furlough in their home countries (usually about 25% of the totals on the field) or those temporarily inactive, retired missionaries, home associates and supporters, candidates and recruits in training, students and missionaries on study courses, and home staffs of missionary societies. (b) Totals of foreign missionaries from abroad (in this footnote) are classified by nationality in a slightly different way to the totals of foreign missionaries sent abroad (in the preceding footnote). The former are classified here by nation of origin of their parent society, agency or branch. However, in several sending countries, a significant number of their citizens serve as missionaries under large or international societies located in other countries (e.g. 100 non-North-Americans serve under the United Methodist Church Board of World Mission, New York, USA; and 500 Canadians serve in societies based in the USA without Canadian offices). Our footnotes of missionaries from abroad do not entirely reveal this latter situation, but the preceding footnotes of missionaries sent abroad do incorporate this information. A further complication, and cause of discrepancy, is that many missionaries are stateless. The Netherlands has 104 stateless persons (mostly sisters) at work, which is 6.3% of all its foreign (non-Dutch) personnel. (c) When comparing our 1973 statistics with statistics from other years, it must be noted that our definition of foreign personnel as those of alien citizenship is complicated by the fact that, over the years, many such personnel take local citizenship, cease to be aliens, and therefore no longer come under our definition. (d) The total Protestant societies reported as coming from a given Western sending country include any national branches of international societies based elsewhere, but only those which have offices located in the country. (e) Missionaries enumerated by Protestant and Anglican societies from Western sending countries are in most cases all nationals of those countries, except for the expatriate personnel in a few large societies referred to in (b) above. These latter, however, are for most societies almost all Whites; very few Protestant societies in the Western world send out non-Western personnel as missionaries. (f) The actual totals of Western missionaries in many countries are somewhat higher than the figures shown in these footnotes, because of the presence of numerous independent missionaries and groupings not related to organized societies. (g) In addition to the societies enumerated in these footnotes, there were in 1973 a number of other Protestant societies claiming to have work in various countries but with no missionaries at work in 1973; they are therefore not enumerated here. (h) These figures of Western missionaries are often not exactly the same as those of expatriates in Column 8 since the latter may include citizens of Communist or Third-World nations. (i) In particular, totals for Roman Catholic missionaries in a number of nations are only approximate (indicated by 'About . . .') because many Western missionary orders and congregations admit non-Western members (Africans, Asians, Latin Americans) and also have numerous members from Communist nations. (j) Roman Catholic totals include the following categories of foreign personnel: bishops, secular priests, religious priests, brothers, sisters, contemplatives, non-diocesan personnel, lay missionaries. (k) Orthodox foreign personnel, for which the totals enumerated here should be regarded as minimum figures because postings from Communist countries are rarely publicized and usually mention only bishops and priests but not monks or nuns or laity, are not usually termed foreign missionaries but are permitted as chaplains to migrant communities abroad or as representatives of their home churches; their work is however missionary in the sense defined in this Encyclopedia. (l) In the 20th century, large numbers of personnel have fled as refugees, exiles or deportees from Eastern Europe, the USSR, China and other Communist countries, as well as from other countries with anti-Christian policies, and also as part of mass population and refugee movements not due to anti-Christian causes. Such personnel are excluded from our definition of foreign personnel if they have renounced or been deprived of their original nationality, or if they have taken out or applied for citizenship in the country of their adoption or otherwise regard themselves as having permanently settled there. They are included in our definition, however, if they remain citizens of their original country and members of their home churches there and intend some day to return, or if they are otherwise legally sent by their home countries.

**INSTITUTIONS** (Christian or church-operated) (1973). The extent to which Christianity is institutionalized, or still institutionalized, in the country is indicated here by giving a total which is a minimal figure for the number of major Christian or church-operated or -related institutions (i.e. fixed centres with premises, plant and permanent staff, excluding church buildings, worship centres, church headquarters or offices) of 10 different kinds. These statistics are derived from the texts on countries in Part 7 together with the listings by subject in the Topical Directory, (Part 13), and also from the unpublished and much fuller directory compiled during this survey. After the total, a partial and selective breakdown is given of sub-totals of main kinds of institution, listed in alphabetical order. Full definitions of each of these types of institution are given in the Survey Dictionary (Part 9), and also (for most) in the Topical Directory (Part 13); we give here abbreviated definitions. This category includes both institutions operated by churches and those operated by independent Christian groups or other Christian organizations. The 10 types are:

(1) *ecumenical centres* (primarily for interdenominational contacts); (2) *higher schools* (junior and senior secondary schools, minor seminaries (secular and religious), technical schools, agricultural schools, vocational schools, teacher-training colleges, non-degree-granting colleges); (3) *lay training centres* (study centres and other specialized training centres); (4) *medical centres* (hospitals, leprosaria, sanatoria, clinics, dispensaries, maternity centres); (5) *presses* (printing presses, publishing houses); (6) *radio and TV stations* (with transmitting plant); (7) major *religious communities* (large monasteries, abbeys, priories, including monasteries in anti-Christian countries where their presence as institutions is significant; mother houses of religious orders and congregations (world headquarters, but not branch houses); ashrams, spiritual life centres; headquarters of local, national or international religious communities, brotherhoods and sisterhoods); (8) *research centres;* (9) *seminaries* (religious and secular major seminaries, theological colleges; preparing persons of secondary or higher education for the ordained ministry; see exact definition in the next paragraph below); and (10) *universities* (degree-granting, including degree colleges; teaching secular subjects). Among lesser, or less important, or smaller types of institution excluded from this enumeration are: Bible schools, bookshops and bookstores, catechist training schools, children's homes, community centres, homes for the aged or handicapped, hostels, minor conference centres, nurseries, orphanages, primary (elementary) schools, radio/TV studios, religious houses (local branches), rest homes, and youth clubs.

*Seminaries: a more detailed definition.* Almost all churches and denominations have a clearly-defined ordained ministry or priesthood, and all train this ministry in one way or another. Smaller denominations usually send their men to seminaries operated by larger denominations, or to seminaries in other countries. Some (especially Third-World or Black indigenous churches) train them as a small group of disciples attached to the denomination's bishop or leader. Most larger denominations, however, prefer to operate in each country at least one small Bible school of their own; and most of the larger denominations have in their own country one or more seminaries or theological colleges (institutions with premises, plant and permanent staff). In some regions and continents (e.g. Latin America), the terms seminary/theological college/Bible school tend to have similar meaning. In others (e.g. Africa), the first 2 accept only persons of some secondary or some higher education, whilst Bible schools are smaller institutions which accept trainees of primary (below secondary) education or less. The statistics in the footnotes to Tables 2 enumerate minimum totals in 1972 of all types of theological colleges and seminaries (restricting the definition to institutions with premises, plant and permanent staff) which train men and women of secondary or higher education for the ordained ministry of the churches. The term covers: (1) Roman Catholic major (but not minor) seminaries (diocesan, interdiocesan, national, international, secular and religious), and (2) Protestant, Anglican, Orthodox, Old Catholic and Third-World or Black indigenous theological colleges and seminaries preparing persons (men and women) of some secondary or higher education for the ordained ministry. This definition and enumeration includes multidenominational, interdenominational, and united theological colleges (all classified as Protestant in the footnotes); it includes Bible schools and colleges which train persons with some secondary education for the ordained ministry; but it excludes Bible schools or colleges training persons of less than secondary education or those training for lay ministries only; it excludes colleges and academies (for example Seventh-day Adventist) primarily teaching secular subjects but with some ministerial courses or training; it excludes training programmes without premises, plant or permanent staff; and it also excludes theological faculties or university departments of theology which have primarily an academic objective without specific preparation for the ordained ministry. Because of widely differing definitions by churches of the terms 'seminary', 'theological college', and 'ordained ministry', these totals should be regarded only as indicators of order of magnitude, useful primarily for comparing the situation in one nation with that in another. The total for a country shown in this footnote is in many cases larger, sometimes much larger, than the total of seminaries shown in Column 8 in the country's Table 2 itself, because of the presence of many non-denominational seminaries which cannot be listed after any one denomination. Lastly it should be noted that many primary-level Bible schools coded in Column 8 as 'p' also train men for the ordained ministry, in Third-World countries.

**PERIODICALS.** This figure gives estimated totals of the number of distinct titles of Christian periodicals (defined here, in contrast to the secular definition of UNESCO, to include newspapers), i.e. church newspapers, journals, magazines, bulletins, house organs and Christian periodicals of all kinds (popular, news, scholarly, professional, academic; daily, semi-weekly, weekly, biweekly, monthly, quarterly, etc; appearing at regular intervals, each with 2 or more issues a year, and excluding annuals and irregular serials), in any languages, that are currently in print and produced and published in this country in printed form (including mimeographed but excluding typed material) by the churches or by other Christian

**Periodicals.** Clergyman in Kenya reads Christian fortnightly newspaper, *Target.*

missions, societies, bodies or individuals, at either the international level, or national, denominational or diocesan levels (but not parish, congregational or local levels), and on the subjects of Christianity, religion, missions, theology, or church affairs. For a number of countries, this total in the footnote is followed by a partial breakdown in parentheses giving any unusual or notable or interesting sub-totals (for particular denominations), which may or may not form a large part of the total for the country. For a few larger countries, the situation is expanded on in a short survey paragraph. These statistics were all collected direct from churches and Christian organizations in each country. One published source giving statistics of professional periodicals in religion and theology is the *UNESCO Statistical yearbook* (e.g. 1974, p.784-806).

**PERSONNEL.** The figure given here refers to the total number, in 1970-73, of officially-recognized, officially-accredited and officially-enumerated active full-time (salaried), or largely full-time, or tent-making (unsalaried but self-supporting), appointed church workers and other recognized and appointed Christian workers residing and working in this country, both men and women, ordained and lay, national (citizen, local) and foreign (alien, expatriate, non-local), including clergy of all kinds, bishops and other hierarchs, priests, pastors, deacons, deaconesses and ordained women, monks, brothers, sisters, nuns, lay ministers, layworkers, parish workers, full-time paid and licensed or self-supporting catechists, evangelists, church officials and administrators, and so on. Excluded are spare-time or part-time, temporary, seasonal, voluntary, volunteer or unpaid workers, unpaid church officers and officials, unpaid spare-time laymen assisting in Sunday church services (lay preachers, lay readers, lay deacons, choirmasters), local (citizen) school teachers, seminarians, short-term missionaries (under 2-year term), unrecognized workers, voluntary part-time (spare-time) unpaid, untrained and unrecognized catechists; etc. Included are Roman Catholic lay catechists, officially so termed and enumerated by the church and its dioceses, both full-time and part-time tent-making (self-supporting), except for catechists specifically termed voluntary, volunteer part-time, spare-time, unpaid or unrecognized. Also included are clergy and workers without, or awaiting, permanent employment or appointment, and other vacancies. The Church of England has, at any one time, around 30 clergy awaiting appointment. Similar vacancies are always occurring, and often take months or sometimes years to fill (as with Russian Orthodox diocesan bishops). The total figure, which is based on the statistics in Table 2, is then usually divided here into 2 categories: (a) nationals

**Religious libraries.** Vatican Library (Rome), which has 900,000 volumes.

**Service agencies.** Oldest and best-known agency serving the churches, British & Foreign Bible Society, showing Warsaw (Poland) HQ in 1970; (centre) Catholicos Ephraim II of Georgia, aged 92.

**Catechists.** Roman Catholic catechist working for his living in ricefields at Mango (Togo).

(i.e. citizens), and (b) foreigners; this latter figure is identical with the total in the footnote above, FOREIGN MISSIONARIES AND PERSONNEL (aliens from abroad). In most churches, particularly in the Third World, the national workers referred to are ordained clergy or pastors only; if there are other types of worker, they are included in our totals and details of their numbers may usually be seen in Column 8 of Table 2 for the denomination concerned. Another important point to note is that in many churches the total of all personnel (workers) is greater than any figures broken down in Column 8; in particular, the total of all Roman Catholic personnel may be somewhat larger than the statistics shown in Column 8 of priests, brothers and sisters working in dioceses, the unrecorded personnel being non-diocesan staff, contemplatives, priests or religious seconded to ecumenical or secular agencies, and so on.

**RELIGIOUS LIBRARIES.** This entry enumerates the major professional theological and religious library collections under church or Christian auspices in the country (libraries specializing primarily in Christianity and religion), at which the enquirer is likely to find detailed literature, published and unpublished, and often research archives, concerning churches and religions in the country. Of these libraries, the vast majority are church-owned and are situated in seminaries, theological colleges, research centres, ecumenical centres, study centres, Christian universities, monasteries, mother houses and other major centres. There are often also valuable specialized and local collections at the headquarters of large denominations or missions or religious orders, at the international headquarters of specialist organizations, and in the offices of information centres and other types of service agency. The total here includes only exclusively-religious libraries, excluding religion sections in large secular libraries; the definition does however include libraries of university faculties of theology or religion if they are held as distinct libraries separate from the main university library. Our definition here excludes small lending libraries at the local or parish level, which are very numerous. Up to 1917, for instance, the Russian Orthodox Church had 34,497 parish libraries; and today almost all Christian schools and most parishes throughout the world have small libraries of a sort. All these are excluded from our total of major libraries. Of the total enumerated here, the largest (those with over 35,000 volumes each in 1966) are listed with their addresses and holdings in the Topical Directory (Part 13). The totals here therefore alert the reader to the presence of large numbers of small but specifically-religious collections of literature and documentation, almost always available for consultation. In all countries there are in addition large secular libraries (national libraries, parliamentary, university and public libraries, research centres, et alia) which often have sizeable holdings on religion; but the smaller religious libraries often have numbers of unpublished documents, reports and records dealing with the local religious situation, and which would not be held in secular libraries.

Partial and incomplete listings for many countries are given in *World guide to libraries/Internationales Bibliotheks-Handbuch* (New York: R.R. Bowker, 4th edition 1974; survey of 36,932 libraries in 157 countries, each with over 30,000 volumes except for new or highly-specialized libraries; total religious or theological libraries listed, 2,100), and in G.M. Ruoss, *World directory of theological libraries* (Metuchen, NJ: Scarecrow, 1968; total libraries listed, 1,778).

**SCRIPTURE DISTRIBUTION** (1975). The totals here are annual figures for 1975 for all types of organized distribution of Bibles and New Testaments (free, subsidized, and commercial) through all agencies including Bible societies and commercial publishers, and also for UBS subsidized distribution of portions (gospels or other complete single books of the Bible) and selections (small seasonal parts of books). A fuller breakdown for each country, and over the period 1900-1975, is given in Global Table 31, columns 63-90. *Translations completed.* This note details the total number of languages indigenous to this country (as listed in *Scriptures of the World*, United Bible Societies, 1974; excluding those more indigenous to other countries, and with each language enumerated only once, under its primary country) into which a portion or book or the New Testament or the complete Bible have been translated, together with the earliest date of completion in each of these 3 categories.

**SERVICE AGENCIES.** An approximate total is given here of service agencies (of 61 varieties) significant at the national or international levels, i.e. the number of major national, international or country-wide bodies, organizations and agencies located or based in the country or with branches or offices there, almost always with full-time staff, which assist or serve the churches but are not themselves denominations or missions directly concerned with the planting or establishing of churches in the country. The greater the number of agencies present in a country, the broader the variety of services offered to the churches there. The total shown here for a country includes Anglican, Catholic, Orthodox, Protestant and independent agencies, both denominational, interdenominational, ecumenical and non-denominational. It includes Bible societies, relief agencies, religious communities, specialized Protestant missionary societies, and 57 other types of service agency which are each detailed as a separate topic in our Topical Directory of World Christianity, i.e. all the Christian topics there except denominations, institutions and church-planting foreign missionary societies. It includes also the Catholic organizations described below under ADDITIONAL DATA ON CHURCHES. It includes all parachurch agencies. It excludes all Christian institutions because these have already been enumerated in a separate footnote above. It also excludes branch offices of all missionary societies and agencies related to direct church or church-planting work, which are already listed or mentioned (in principle, if not in every case) in Column 8 of Tables 2; it does however include the home

headquarters of such societies and agencies, in their home countries only. The total is followed by a brief selective listing of the better-known bodies at work, giving only their initials (identifiable, for international agencies and national Christian councils, from the Index of Abbreviations, Acronyms and Initials (in Part 14); other national agencies are identified and described elsewhere in the country's text or tables).

4. **ADDITIONAL DATA ON CHURCHES.** Each denomination or diocese occupies only one single line in Tables 2. In cases where additional statistical or descriptive data are available and are significant or necessary, this is added in a footnote. This is done for numerous very large churches. For the Roman Catholic Church, it is done in almost all countries. This additional information takes the form of data on some or all of the following, where relevant, in approximately this order: vernacular names, recent pastoral reorganization (if any), dioceses, suppressed dioceses, new dioceses or jurisdictions (created since December 1972), ethnolinguistic composition of membership, diocesan pastoral and priests' councils, historical notes, catechumens, annual baptisms (divided into infants and adults), personnel (bishops, national priests, expatriate priests, brothers, sisters), Catholic charismatics, ordinations, seminaries, seminarians, catechists and training schools, indigenous religious institutes (congregations), main foreign institutes (orders and congregations) including secular institutes and societies; and, lastly, a survey of the main Catholic organizations (in this order: episcopal, religious, presbyteral, lay, diplomatic, international, progressivist and traditionalist, research and social action, theological, missionary, educational, medical, and social service).

### Global Table 31: GEOPOLITICO-RELIGIOUS DATA FOR ALL COUNTRIES

The major table in Part 8, Summary Global, Continental and Confessional Statistical Tables, is Global Table 31 which provides a mass of data for all countries, with totals for continents and the world.

*Object of Global Table 31*
The object of this global table is to present, in comparative format for all 223 countries, with summaries for the world and its 8 continents with their regions, (1) 22 major geopolitical, politico-religious and purely religious typologies of countries, which means 22 different ways of describing and dividing up the world's countries; and (2) columns of religious and statistical data relating to Christian resources and activities, namely organizations; personnel; the international sharing of personnel (foreign missionary personnel); religious books, periodicals and libraries; scripture distribution, Christian broadcasting, and evangelization.

These typologies and national variables can be used for a variety of analyses attempting to correlate them with the secular data and variables given in

Part 7 before each country's descriptive text (or with the 55 secular variables given in C.L. Taylor & M.C. Hudson, *World handbook of political and social indicators*, 2nd edition, 1972).

The full codes used are given in the Codebook (Part 6). Here, we describe only the methodology used in deriving certain of the typologies and other data.

## GEOPOLITICO-RELIGIOUS TYPOLOGIES

### GEOGRAPHY

*Column 1. Country*

This first column identifies all countries, each in alphabetical order (using 1980 names) being assigned a 3-digit number from 001 to 223.

*Columns 2-3. Continent and region*

The simplest and most objective classifications are geographical ones, in which the world's countries are divided up by continents and regions. Unfortunately, 'continent' is too vague a term for our purposes. It usually refers to the larger continuous masses of land, larger than islands such as Greenland; seen thus, the continents are, in order of size: Eurasia, Africa, NAmerica, SAmerica, Antarctica, Australia. According to Webster, a continent is 'a continuous extent or mass of land; one of the great divisions of land on the globe'. The best statement is that there are 7 continents: Europe, Africa, Asia, NAmerica, SAmerica, Australia, and Antarctica. For our more precise enumerative purposes, however, we use here the United Nations standardized classification of countries into 8 'major areas' (continents), sub-divided into 24 'geographic subdivisions' or 'regions' (see Codebook). A world analysis of Christians in this manner is given in Global Table 18, in Part 8.

### POLITICO-ECONOMIC SITUATION

*Column 4. Development, 1980*

Countries are classified by the United Nations as either more developed (the industrialized countries of Europe, Northern America, Australia, New Zealand, Japan, USSR, Temperate South America) or less developed (the rest of the world, usually with a high gross reproduction rate). In 1968, the UN defined more developed countries as ones whose gross reproduction rate per woman was less than 2.0. In 1973, a number of Third-World countries had rates lower than 2.0, but the UN redefined the term 'more developed' to include only the countries listed in the previous sentence but one, which gives the typology used here. A world analysis of Christians by this criterion is given in Global Table 2, in Part 1.

*Column 5. Economy, 1980*

Countries are also classified by the United Nations according to type of economy in 1975: developed market economy (Western Europe, Northern America, Israel, Japan, Australia, New Zealand, South Africa), centrally-planned economy (Eastern Europe, USSR, China, North Korea, Viet Nam, Mongolia), developing market economy (the rest of the world).

*Column 6. Economic system, 1980*

Another classification is into 5 types of economic system: Capitalist, Mixed-economy (combining elements of free-enterprise competition with state ownership or direction of key industries), Third-World Socialist, Social Democratic (term when such parties are in power), and Marxist-Leninist (Communist).

*Columns 7-9. Political alignment, 1970-80*

A widely-used 3-fold typology is that based on political alignment, as seen for example at assemblies of the United Nations. It refers to where countries' cultural, economic and political sympathies lie. It divides the world into the Western (or Capitalist) world (composed of both capitalist and non-Marxist socialist or social democratic countries), the Communist (or Marxist Socialist) world, and the Third World (the latter being non-aligned with either of the former two, though composed of both capitalist and socialist countries). These terms, though in widespread use, are often used loosely and with different meanings. Thus the term 'the Communist bloc' is in disfavour because the Communist world is, since the Sino-Soviet dispute, no longer a monolithic bloc. Similarly, the People's Republic of China regards itself officially as 'a developing socialist country belonging to the Third World'; and somewhat the same with Yugoslavia. We, however, define these 3 worlds as indicated above, and as shown in Global Table 31, columns 7-9, in Part 8. Using this typology, describing political alignment in 1970, 1975, and 1980, we get the analysis of Christians in Global Table 2, in Part 1.

*Column 10. Political freedom, 1980*

This 3-fold typology classifies countries by the extent to which they provide their populations with full individual and corporate freedom in civil and political rights (as assessed by the non-partisan Freedom House organization, New York, USA). The first category, coded 1, covers societies with full civil and political rights; the second, basically-democratic societies but where numbers of political prisoners exist or large segments of society are denied these rights; the third, societies where massive or total suppression of these rights exists. An analysis using this variable is given in Global Table 14.

*Column 11. Political freedom index, 1980*

This index, also developed by Freedom House, is a measure of a nation's respect for liberty, compiled from studies of civil and political rights. The index is scaled up to 100% as the best possible performance (full respect for liberty).

*Column 12. Democratic rule, 1980*

This typology, evolved for this survey, describes the extent to which all de facto political power is in the hands of the populace themselves. The data apply to 1980. The reader can update this column from his daily newspaper to 1981, 1982, etc as required and so build up a time series on this variable. An analysis using this category is given in Global Table 13.

*Column 13. Number of languages, 1980*

The figure shown is the total of all significant languages in use in each country, including all indigenous languages, those originally of foreign origin, and expatriate languages. There is considerable duplication because many languages are spoken (hence counted) each in many different countries.

*Column 14. Official state language*

Countries may also be classified according to their countrywide official language or languages (excluding national languages which are not also official), in 1980. In Global Table 31, these languages are shown in the order usually given (if a country has over 3 official languages, only the first 3 are given). Names are given in the Codebook for all official languages. Using this criterion, Christians are analysed in Global Tables 19 and 20, in Part 8.

### OTHER SECULAR DATA

*Columns 15-16. Urbanization, cinema attendance*

These 2 columns give additional secular data, firstly on the percentage of urban dwellers in each country, and secondly on cinema attendances per year per inhabitant *(UNESCO Statistical yearbook)*.

*Column 17. Quality of life*

The Physical Quality of Life Index (PQLI) is a measure of the effectiveness of social services in a country, recently developed by the Overseas Development Council (Washington, DC, USA). The index includes life expectancy, literacy and infant mortality. The figures are scaled up to 100% as best possible performance.

### RELIGIO-POLITICAL SITUATION (church and state)

*Columns 18-21. State religion or philosophy (de jure), 1900-1980*

This next classification is based on the official religion or philosophy of the state, i.e. on how sovereign or non-sovereign states or ruling regimes or colonial governments officially see themselves (or, saw themselves in 1900, 1970, 1975 and 1980) in their formal relation to religion, religions and the churches (as defined in their state constitutions, party constitutions, manifestos and other definitive legal declarations), to what extent they are formally, officially or explicitly concerned with religion or claim the right to intervene in religious affairs, and to what extent they formally acknowledge or recognize or approve of religions and churches. The following 3-fold typology of state religion or philosophy results. After each definition below, an expanded definition follows in parentheses, and then the type is further defined with statements each of which characterizes the situation in several or many (but not necessarily all) countries of that type. This typology is given, describing the situation in each country as at the 4 years 1900, 1970, 1975 and 1980, in Part 8, and Christians are analysed accordingly in Global Table 15.

| *Code* | *Type* | *Definition, and characteristics* |
|---|---|---|
| R | **Religious** | *State identifies itself with religion and its promotion* (state identified with, or formally linked with, or heavily involved with, or joined in law with, religion or religions or churches and their promotion); state formally proclaims or identifies itself explicitly either as religious (believing in or recognizing the supremacy or existence of God) or as belonging to one particular religion or church; state proclaims or recognizes or favours a state religion or church (legislatively and financially controlled by the state), or an official religion, or a national church or one or more established churches, or recognizes state churches in a majority of the nation's component provinces or parts; state ceremonial and government procedure closely linked with religion or churches; usually no formal or institutional separation of church and state, though separation can co-exist with a state's specifically religious self-identification; a concordat guaranteeing a special or privileged church relationship with the state is in force or in existence; state formally and actively organizes and promotes religion or subsidizes its promotion, or on a formal and permanent basis claims the right of intervention and patronage. |
| S | **Secular** | *State is secular, promoting neither religion nor irreligion* (state separated in law from religion, all religions and all churches and their promotion or suppression, and ignores religion in identifying itself and its role); state neither affirms nor denies any religious, irreligious or philosophical belief, nor shows in its constitution any acknowledgement of the existence of God; state proclaims ideal of complete non-involvement and non-intervention in matters of religion or irreligion, and formally renounces state control over them; separation of religion and politics ordered in constitution. |
| A | **Atheistic** | *State is secular, but formally promotes irreligion* (state identified with Marxist-Leninist atheism, or Marxist (not necessarily Communist) regime almost always with atheistic basic philosophy, formally separated from all religions and churches, but linked for ideological reasons with irreligion and opposed on principle to all religion); de jure freedom of religious belief guaranteed, but right of state claimed to oppose religion by discrimination, obstruction or even suppression; state subsidies or financial aid occasionally given, not for promotion of religion but for purposes of surveillance and control. |

*Expanded code.* Several states regard themselves as religious in general, or as believing in God, without specifying a particular religion. However, many other religious states identify themselves (or did so in the year 1900) with a single religion or church, and so in this table they have a second code letter added, as shown below. The full code is therefore as follows:

| *Code* | |
|---|---|
| R | Religious (unspecified) |
| RA | Anglican |

*Continued on page 100*

# STATE RELIGION OR PHILOSOPHY

On this page and the following two, illustrations are given of the main types of state religion or philosophy as explained and classified opposite.

*Church/state/university proximity.* Senate Square, Helsinki (below) illustrates why Finland is defined here as a Christian state. At the right of the Square can be seen the House of Government (state President's Office, Ministry of Foreign Affairs, et alia) ; at the left, the University with its Faculty of Theology ; in foreground, Police Headquarters, High Court, and City Hall ; all in close proximity to (on far side of Square, up steps) the Cathedral of the state Lutheran Church.

**STATE RELIGION OR PHILOSOPHY.** On this page and opposite are illustrated further aspects of how states officially see themselves, vis-a-vis religion.

**Religious/Christian.** UK (Britain) (a Christian state with 2 established churches): As Head of the Church of England, Her Majesty Queen Elizabeth II (*top*) is crowned by Archbishop of Canterbury in 1953, and (*centre*) opens 1975-1980 General Synod in Church House, Westminster.

**Religious/Non-Christian.** *Right.* Egypt (an Islamic state): During 1978 negotiations between Pope Shenouda III (on right) and President Sadat (left) concerning anti-Christian rioting, noon approached and all agreed to pray, with the Egyptian Cabinet (left, all Muslims) falling to their their knees.

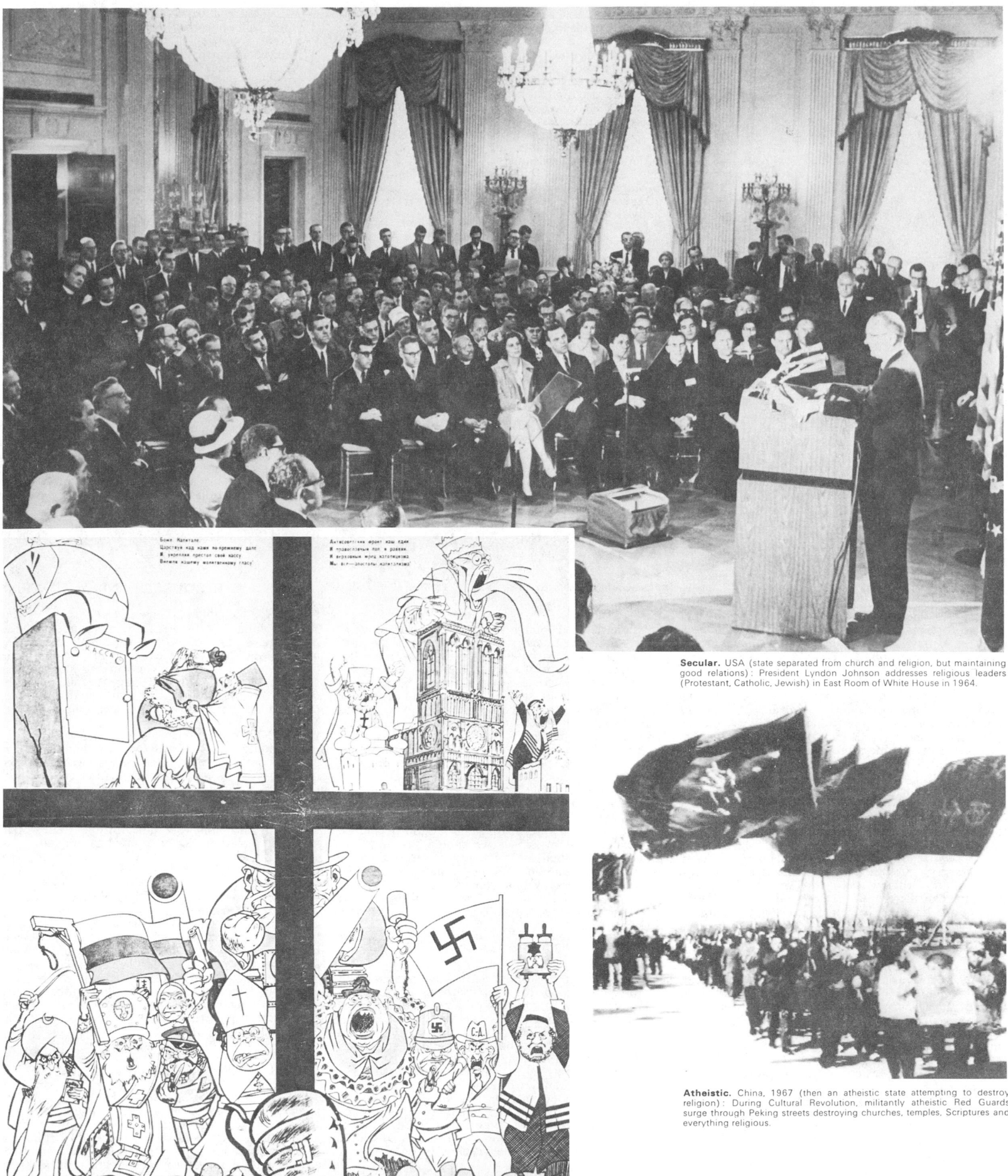

**Secular.** USA (state separated from church and religion, but maintaining good relations): President Lyndon Johnson addresses religious leaders (Protestant, Catholic, Jewish) in East Room of White House in 1964.

**Atheistic.** China, 1967 (then an atheistic state attempting to destroy religion): During Cultural Revolution, militantly atheistic Red Guards surge through Peking streets destroying churches, temples, Scriptures and everything religious.

**Atheistic.** USSR (secular state, but promoting irreligion): Official Soviet anti-religious propaganda attacking pope, patriarchs, bishops, monks, priests, rabbis, mullahs, et alii (dated 1940).

RB    Buddhist
RC    Roman Catholic
RD    Adventist
RG    Confucian
RH    Hindu
RI    Islamic
RJ    Jewish
RL    Lutheran
RM    Methodist
RO    Orthodox
RR    Reformed
RS    Shinto
RT    Tribal religionist
RX    Christian (unspecified)

*Column 22. Religious liberty (de facto), 1980*

The actual or de facto situation in a country with regard to religious freedom as experienced by the churches usually differs considerably from the de jure situation, in which full freedom of religion is guaranteed on paper by the constitution in virtually every country throughout the world except for Albania. An analogous situation exists with regard to all other types of human rights: in 1976, 30 years after the United Nations first began to draft it, an International Bill of Human Rights came into effect, detailing 39 economic, social, cultural, civil and political rights. In practice, however, a majority of all nations continue to ignore many of them. Full freedom or liberty or toleration of religion is defined in this Encyclopedia along somewhat similarly comprehensive lines. It does not mean merely freedom of inner belief and conscience for individuals (as in fact many countries interpret it), but also a whole range of over 30 closely-related other freedoms or rights: freedom of public worship indoors or outdoors, freedom of assembly, freedom of self-government, freedom of association, freedom to organize religious bodies, freedom to organize Bible study circles, freedom to run Christian libraries and bookshops, freedom to collect money and to disburse it, freedom for churches to own buildings or property, freedom to organize credit unions for the benefit of members, freedom to offer medical care where wanted, freedom to engage in mission at home and abroad, freedom to send abroad or receive from abroad foreign missionaries, freedom of Christian political expression, freedom to teach religion and to be taught, freedom for children to join religious associations and to receive Christian instruction, freedom to change one's religion or be converted, freedom of propagation, freedom to travel on religious business within the country and abroad and to return, freedom to listen to radio religious broadcasts from any country, freedom to send and receive religious mail and literature uncensored both inland and abroad; freedom to use national press and broadcasting (radio and TV) facilities; freedom from state interference, surveillance, obstruction, discrimination, harassment, state hostility, persecution, oppression, repression or suppression; and freedom to write, print, publish, mail, broadcast, circulate scriptures, buy and sell literature, distribute, evangelize, proselytize, and baptize. It also includes freedom for minority churches as well as majority churches. Any country which lacks many or most of these freedoms can therefore fairly be said to be deficient in religious liberty. These items can all be arranged as a scale and the status of religious liberty in a country can accordingly be given a numerical value. Countries are here therefore classified by this de facto criterion, describing the situation over the period 1970-80, which varies from substantial state assistance to and genuine promotion (as opposed to control) of Christianity (1-3 below), through complete de facto non-intervention or religious toleration or disinterest (4-5), to ambiguous or ambivalent situations where state interference or obstruction may be accompanied by massive subsidies for purposes of surveillance and control (6-8), and lastly to state hostility or total suppression (9-10). This 10-stage typology, which is based on the documentation given here in our texts on CHURCH AND STATE for each nation, is given in Global Table 31, in Part 8, and Christians are analysed by it in Global Table 16 there.

*Code    Stage of liberty experienced by churches*
1.    state exists solely for promotion of Christanity.
2.    state makes sizeable to massive subsidies to promote (but not control) churches (clergy salaries, new buildings).
3.    state aids churches (without implying control) with special but limited privilege (tax exemption, legal aid, radio/TV times &c).

4.    state makes subsidies not to churches but to church schools and/or church medical/social services.
5.    state non-interference: churches receive no privileges or aid, nor interference or obstruction.
6.    state imposes on all churches limited or occasional restrictions (e.g. on political activity).
7.    state discriminates against or severely obstructs minority churches, or churches of citizens (but not those of expatriates).
8.    state interference, obstruction, discrimination or repression against all churches; proselytism, broadcasting, publishing, all prohibited.
9.    state hostility, antagonism, or harassment: prohibition of evangelism, missionaries, conversion.
10.    state suppression or elimination: no religious activity tolerated.

### MISSION

*Column 23. Foreign mission (country's situation), 1970–1980*

Another way of classifying countries is from the standpoint of the Christian foreign missionary enterprise, namely the sending and receiving of foreign

**Religious liberty or persecution.** In Equatorial Guinea, armed Macias government thugs, shown evicting Spanish missionaries, attempted to wipe out religion from 1969-79.

missionaries and foreign personnel, defined above in detail under the category the INTERNATIONAL SHARING OF PERSONNEL, referring to the situation in 1973. Under this concept of mission, the ultimate ideal for a country is no longer that it should be first and foremost a mission-sending country, but is instead that it should both freely send and freely receive substantial numbers of such personnel. 'Missionaries should flow ever more freely from and to all 6 continents in a spirit of humble service' (*Lausanne Covenant*, 1974, paragraph 9). From the point of view of maximum international co-operation and effectiveness in evangelization, the ideal for countries in the future may well be the seventh category in the typology below, namely sharing in large-scale sending and receiving of foreign missionaries and personnel. To evolve this typology, we should first plot on a graph the total of missionaries received by a country per million of the population, against missionaries sent by that country per million: then we divide the space up into 7 areas, which produces the following 7-fold classification for the world's 223 countries.

*Code*

1.    *Closed countries* (totalling 25), i.e. those closed to foreign mission (but not necessarily closed to internal mission), are defined here as (a) countries which, due to state opposition or societal or communal hostility to Christianity, tolerate neither the sending nor the receiving of foreign missionaries, although in practice up to 8 personnel per million may get in or be sent out without being termed missionaries, usually serving as chaplains or in secular occupations (totalling 16 countries); together with (b) a small number of miniscule territories (totalling 8) down to 90 persons in population which are too tiny to be interested in or concerned with the sending or receiving of foreign personnel.
2.    *Partially-closed countries* (totalling 24) are defined as those which are not fully closed to foreign mission, but in which foreign personnel received exceed 8 per million but are limited in number to under 40 per million, either by means of government control, or by societal or communal pressure, or as a result of other means.

3.    *Restricted countries* (totalling 18) are those in which, although they are not closed or partially-closed countries, the numbers of personnel received number 40 or over per million but are restricted somewhat to under 100 per million, and personnel sent out are restricted to under 40 per million, again either by government control, societal or communal pressure, economic forces, or other factors.
4.    *Receiving countries* (totalling 99) are defined here as those which place no restrictions on numbers of missionaries, and in which 100 or more per million are received whilst those sent out remain under 40 per million.
5.    *Receiving/sending countries* (totalling 35) are defined as those in which missionaries sent out number 40 or more per million, but at the same time missionaries received are always substantially larger in number than those sent out (and usually from quite different churches).
6.    *Sending countries* (totalling 10) are those in which missionaries sent out number 40 or more per million, and greatly outnumber those received which are limited to between 40-99 per million; these are countries which have traditionally concentrated on foreign missions as a sending operation only.
7.    *Sharing countries* (totalling 12) are those which embody the fullest development of the idea of the international sharing of personnel, encouraging both the sending and the receiving of large numbers of personnel among and within the same churches; and are defined here as countries in which large numbers of foreign missionaries and personnel are both sent and received, each being 100 or more per million, although those sent out always at present substantially outnumber those received.

Using this typology, the world's population and the world's Christians are analysed in Global Table 17 in Part 8.

### CHRISTIAN RESOURCES AND ACTIVITIES

ORGANIZATIONS (Columns 24-31)

These columns tabulate, for comparative purposes from one country to another, various items enumerated in and below Tables 2. Three of the items (worship centres, major institutions and service agencies) are also expressed here per million of the country's population (to the nearest digit), in order to get indicators of the extent of evangelization.

PERSONNEL (Columns 32-35)

The number of national (citizen) church workers or full-time Christian personnel is here tabulated (using the data in Tables 2), expressed also per million population (to the nearest digit). There is also the total of all personnel in the country (national and expatriate/foreign/alien), and a derived indicator expressing this somewhat differently as total population per Christian worker of any kind.

INTERNATIONAL SHARING OF PERSONNEL (Columns 36-56)

These columns document the contributions of all countries to the international sending and receiving of full-time long-term Christian workers. The category 'Foreign missionaries and personnel' has already been defined above in great detail, and statistics for all countries are given under Tables 2. This section of Global Table 31 tabulates the same data in order to arrive at regional, continental and global totals, divided up by political worlds of origin (columns 46-48) and ecclesiastico-cultural major blocs (columns 37-43 and 49-55).

BOOKS, PERIODICALS AND LIBRARIES (Columns 57-62)

This is a survey of all new books (titles) published in the one year 1973, or 1974 (on all subjects); new religious books (titles) in the same year, both Christian and from other religions; religious periodicals (Christian only) at international, national, denominational and diocesan (but not parish or local or congregational) levels; major religious libraries (under Christian auspices); and 2 indicators expressed per million population (to the nearest digit).

SCRIPTURE DISTRIBUTION (Columns 63-90)

It should first be noted that, for statistical purposes, the term 'scriptures' covers 4 distinct types of liter-

**Scripture distribution.** Penzotti students sell scriptures in Bogotá, Colombia. In 1975, 87,964 Bibles and 250,586 NTs were distributed in Colombia.

ature: whole Bibles, New Testaments, portions (e.g. gospels), and selections (usually small leaflets reproducing scripture passages).

*Types of distribution*

Present distribution (or circulation, as it is sometimes called) of the Holy Scriptures in the countries of the world is of 2 kinds: unorganized, and organized. Unorganized distribution arises through the uncoordinated efforts of large numbers of individuals and small groups who obtain copies in one country and then mail or otherwise distribute them in another, or who import or print and distribute secretly or illegally. Since no records are kept or compiled centrally, this is impossible to quantify, although the totals probably are small relative to organized activity. Organized distribution arises through the ongoing activities of 3 kinds of major publishers, who through local production and/or imported stock undertake 3 different sub-types of distribution: (1) free distribution (without cost to recipients; Gideons International, PTL, et alia; including the 40 or so 'Bible-smuggling' societies and missions organized to distribute scriptures clandestinely or illegally in Communist or Muslim countries where open distribution is illegal); (2) subsidized distribution (subsidized to local prices that local recipients can afford; UBS and its 64 member societies, also non-UBS Bible societies; the statistics represent total distribution per year out of UBS-related premises; outlets often include commercial bookshops); and (3) commercial distribution (prices fixed on commercial considerations by professional secular or religious publishers; OUP, CUP, Protestant, Catholic and Orthodox commercial publishing houses, etc, without UBS involvement).

*Annual statistics*

In Global Table 31 (Part 8), we give statistics of annual organized distribution of these 3 types, for all countries of the world and over the period 1900-1975, for complete Bibles (all versions), and for New Testaments (all versions). The figures are for distribution during the years shown (e.g. 1970, 1975); they do not record distribution in intermediate years (1971-74), which for free distribution may have been very large in certain countries due to the custom of concentrating on certain countries only for one or 2 years at a time. We also give statistics of annual UBS distribution of portions (gospels or other complete single books of the Bible, averaging over 48 pages in length), and also of UBS scripture selections (small seasonal parts of books; a programme begun by the UBS in 1958 and now including specially-prepared selections for new readers). These 4 types of scriptures are enumerated separately in this Encyclopedia, and are not added to give any such category as 'Total scripture distribution' because the 4 types are far too disparate to be compared with any meaning (a Bible averages 1,300 pages in length, a New Testament 300 pages, a portion only 50 pages, a selection a mere 2 or 3 pages). Neither are they properly comparable from one country to the next or from one year to the next.

The exact meaning of our statistics for the 3 types of distribution is, respectively, (1) placements (copies of scriptures placed in a home or in a recipient's hand), (2) books leaving Bible societies' premises, and (3) retail sales to customers. When compiling and comparing distribution figures from different organizations, care must be taken to understand exactly what definition each organization has used. Gideons International, for instance, publish each year statistics of placements. These however are not annual totals (distribution during the next 12 months) but are instead cumulative totals of all placements since the Gideons began distribution in 1908. In our table we have converted their statistics to annual totals because cumulative totals have little relation to any reality today, given the fact that copies of Gideon Bibles last (in the USA, for example) only about 7 years before they disintegrate or disappear or are otherwise of no more use.

*Exact and estimated totals*

The statistics given in Global Table 31 are of 2 kinds: exact aggregates or totals given by publishers, usually distinguishable by being given to the last digit (e.g. 142,793); and estimated totals, distinguishable by being rounded to end in several zeros (e.g. 140,000). Whereas the former are exact totals actually distributed during the year indicated, the latter have the character of average annual estimates of the general order of magnitude around the period indicated. In particular, where a figure or total is itself zero ('0') it indicates here only that no organized publisher was distributing in that country in that year; however, unorganized distribution on a small scale may well have been going on.

*Saturation point*

The actual totals of scriptures produced by publishers are almost always responses to demand. They are the aggregate demands or requirements of markets, populations, churches and other major agencies. In certain Western countries, however, modern methods of mass production have led to the markets there becoming increasingly saturated. If such saturation could be avoided, undersupplied countries in the Third World could be assisted.

*What does the world need?*

We can attempt to determine how many copies of the scriptures we understand the world and its populations to actually need every year, from the Christian point of view, bearing in mind publishers' limited resources of money, paper, time and distributional personnel and the need to avoid waste, duplication and saturation. What the world needs is not necessarily the printing of a complete Bible by AD 2000 for every person on earth, because vast numbers of people cannot read and at least a quarter of the world are too young to read; also distribution cannot take place in large areas due to religious or irreligious hostility to Christianity. A more reasonable and limited intermediate goal is that proposed by the United Bible Societies at their 1963 Asia Bible Societies Conference in Manila: the provision of 'a Bible for every Christian home, at least a New Testament for every Christian, and at least a scripture portion for all who are literate'. Taking into account the realities of age and illiteracy, we can introduce greater precision and define the immediate goal of distribution to be ownership as follows: a complete Bible for every literate Christian home or family or household, a New Testament for every literate adult Christian individual, and a scripture portion for every literate adult or reader in the population; all of these, ideally, in the individuals' mother tongues. This limited goal does not include, strictly speaking, extension projects such as placement of Bibles in public places or provision of Bibles and Testaments for evangelistic outreach to non-Christians; nevertheless it does give us a useful yardstick by which to measure the actual provision achieved. When provision is lower than this, we can speak of inadequate supply; when it is higher or markedly higher, we can speak of saturation. In many parts of the world, this provision has already been approximately achieved.

## CHRISTIAN BROADCASTING (Columns 91-95)

This section attempts to quantify to some extent the total effect on each country of all Christian religious radio/TV broadcasting (international and national (local radio), shortwave and mediumwave and by all denominations), and in particular to estimate approximately the general order of magnitude of audiences listening regularly (at least monthly) to Christian broadcast programmes, or viewing them. In column 91 we tabulate the number of radio and TV sets per 100 of the population, to the nearest 1%. Column 92 tabulates radio letters (normal annual listeners' letters received from this country by all Christian radio/TV stations or agencies, home or foreign), and in columns 93-95 audience size (Protestant, Catholic, Orthodox, Anglican) as a percentage of the total population of the country. The methodology is as follows.

*Two types of listeners*

Listeners to Christian programmes can be divided into 2 distinct types: (1) those listening to Christian radio or TV stations, situated either within their own country or, in the case of international radio/TV stations, abroad; and (2) those listening to Christian programmes broadcast by state or secular or commercial radio/TV stations, usually within their own country. Naturally, these two overlap to a greater or lesser extent in many countries. In some countries, they represent 2 distinct audiences (differentiated perhaps culturally, or linguistically, or denominationally); in others, they are virtually the same persons. Listeners of type (1) tend to write letters to the stations, whereas those of type (2) only send few to Christian programmes and even fewer to the secular stations themselves. In our Global Table 31, audiences (1) and (2) are given in columns 93 and 94, and are then combined in column 95 to give total demographic audience in each country (including children) for Christian programmes over all stations.

*Potential audience*

In many less developed countries the potential audience (those able to receive and listen to or view Christian broadcasts if they wish to) is considerably smaller than the total population because only a small fraction have radio or TV sets or are exposed to them. Much listening is by households, i.e. an entire family listening to a single set. If therefore there are S radio and TV sets in a country, and n is the average number of persons in a household, the potential audience would be approximately Sn persons. If r = radio and TV sets per 1,000 population, and P = total population able to understand the language used, then $r = (S/P) . 1000$, from which we get Potential audience = Prn/1000.

*Actual audience*

The only scientific way of measuring audience size in a country is to conduct a sample survey there. Often they find surprisingly large audiences for Christian programmes. A survey of radio use in Ghana in 1970 found that 78% of the population in cities and 44% in villages listened to at least one of the 4 weekly religious programmes on the Ghana Broadcasting Corporation. Few if any Christian broadcasting agencies can undertake such surveys, since they are extremely expensive in Western countries, technically difficult in Third-World countries, and impossible for political reasons in Communist countries. Most Christian agencies do, however, maintain detailed statistics of the voluminous correspondence they receive from listeners/viewers (termed hereafter 'listeners'), and most regularly tabulate this incoming listeners' mail by country of origin, language, listener's religion, and subject of letter. In secular broadcasting audience research, listeners' correspondence is regarded as invalid as an indicator of regular (weekly) audience size because listeners who correspond do not form a representative sample of the total audience and are unrepresentative of the silent majority who do not write, and also because of the ease with which letters can be 'pulled', manipulated or stimulated by free offers or by popular personalities or by many varieties of programme. In religious broadcasting, however, listeners' correspondence has a special significance because of the very personal nature of the Christian message to the individual, and its demand to him. As with other types of large-scale Christian ministry (such as mass evangelism) it is reasonable to expect that, all other things being equal, the number of persons responding will bear some relationship to the total persons hearing, and that study of the relevant variables will lead to detection of a basic pattern or basic statistical relationships and probabilities. In the case of radio/TV it is likely therefore that response generated by religious broadcasting can be shown to bear a relation to the total audience. For this Encyclopedia, detailed investigations of the phenomenon of listeners' correspondence in secular and religious broadcasting were

**Christian broadcasting.** *Left.* Britain: The Daily Service, broadcast live every weekday since 1923 by BBC (London). *Right.* Catholic radiophonic school in Sutatenza (Colombia), teaching literacy and other subjects.

undertaken. It was found that it is possible to put forward a tentative method of estimating total monthly audience size for Christian broadcasting, as a first approximation in the absence of any other method. This will now be stated in 2 alternative forms.

(1) In any particular country where one or more well-known and well-established broadcasting agencies or organizations, either internal or external or both, have built up regular and stable Christian programmes or series of programmes in languages understood in the country, then a measure of interest shown in these programmes by all listeners can be obtained from the volume of letters on any subject received from literate listeners to the programmes (individuals, families, DX-ers, churches, organizations). On average in a typical month around 1975, it has been found that, in the normal course of events without letter solicitation or stimulation, something of the order of one person in every 500 listeners, or 0.2% of (or 0.002 times) the total monthly audience (those making a practice of listening to, or those otherwise exposed to, any of the programmes during the course of the month, including children) desire as a result to communicate with the agencies concerned by correspondence (or by telephone, personal visits or other means) on some subject or other, religious or secular. The number who actually do so communicate, and whose communications eventually reach the agencies as listeners' letters, is this number reduced in proportion to the adult literacy rate (L, where L = 100 means 100% adult literacy) in the listeners' country and the mail reliability of the postal systems involved (M, where M = 100 means 100% or complete mail reliability) in both the sending and receiving countries.

(2) Another way of expressing the same relationship is to say that in a particular country, the general order of magnitude of the actual audience for all Christian broadcasting in the course of a month (all agencies, stations, organizations, languages and programmes; both international and national (local radio); both shortwave and mediumwave), can be very approximately estimated from the total regular monthly flow of letters, i.e. the total volume of normal monthly radio listeners' letters and other communications (regular, unsolicited and unstimulated) on any subject (including programme requests, reception reports, and unsolicited requests for Bibles or New Testaments) generated by all Christian programmes heard in the country during the month and received by the broadcasting agencies. Expressed as a formula, this can be put in 2 related forms (with an isolated dot . signifying multiplication, and a slash / signifying division):

**Normal monthly letters = 0.002 . monthly audience . (L/100) . (M/100).**

or, Average monthly audience = 500 . normal monthly letters/(ML/10,000) = 5,000,000 . monthly letters/ML.

This formula is reasonably easy to use in the numerous countries where the number of monthly letters is large and remains approximately constant throughout the year. In many other cases, the monthly total of letters fluctuates widely from January to December, and it is probably more satisfactory to use the normal annual radio listeners' letters (R) and so to express the formula thus:

**Average monthly audience = 40 . normal annual letters/(ML/10,000).**
**= 400,000 R/ML.**

*Mail reliability and censorship*

A key variable in many countries is what we have called mail reliability (M). This is the proportion of Christian mail (i.e. mail to Christian radio stations or programmes), expressed as a percentage, which gets through the postal systems of sending and receiving countries. It stands for the likelihood or probability of Christian mail getting through the postal services, from writer to programme originator, unhindered. It is a composite factor embodying at least 4 distinct elements: the ability of writers to use mail facilities correctly; reliability and efficiency of postal services in the listeners' country, en route and in the originator's country; censorship and interception of mail for political or religious reasons; and the degree to which knowledge of the existence of strict censorship inhibits would-be correspondents. Values of this factor depend on both where the listeners' country is and in which country the programme receives their letters. The value of M to be used in the above formula can be obtained by multiplying together the 2 values of M for the listeners' and programme's countries (for example, 30% × 30% = 9%; or, 5% × 20% = 1%.) This can be done from the following list, which is arranged in descending order of mail reliability.

| | |
|---|---|
| Western world | M = 100% |
| Third World (non-Muslim) | M = 70% |
| Japan | M = 90% |
| India | M = 80% |
| Other non-Muslim countries | M = 70% |
| Algeria | M = 60% |
| Other North African countries | M = 50% |
| Other Muslim countries | M = 25% |
| Communist world: | |
| Yugoslavia | M = 30% |
| Eastern Europe | M = 20% |
| Viet Nam, Laos, Cuba | M = 10% |
| Bulgaria, Mongolia | M = 5% |
| USSR, China, Albania, | |
| NKorea, Kampuchea | M = 1% |

Within the Western world (Europe, Northern America, etc) mail is reliable, uncensored and rarely lost, and virtually 100% gets through. From the Third World, much mail is lost at origin through faulty addressing or stamping, and incoming and outgoing mail services themselves are often unreliable. In Muslim countries, local officials often intercept Christian mail. In Communist countries, political censors intercept most such mail, interception being progressively more thorough and complete in Bulgaria, the USSR, China and Albania. The BBC (London), which has a large audience in the USSR for both secular and religious programmes (several millions

regularly for the latter in 1979), stated in its 1972 annual report that censors had intercepted every single listener's letter posted to them from the USSR the previous year; but with other less well-known agencies and less easily-recognizable addresses, at least 5% of letters from the USSR regularly get through.

*Actual and potential audiences*

Comparing the actual and potential audience figures for each country derived in the above way, we find that there is a very approximate relationship between actual monthly audience size and the number of practising Christians in the country. Expressed as a formula (with . signifying multiplication):

Actual monthly audience = potential audience × (practising Christians) ÷ P × language coverage × national religious interest × technical effectiveness

$$= (Prn/1000) . (C/P) (G/100) (E/100)I$$

$$= (CrnI/1000) (G/100) (E/100)$$

where  P = total population
r = radio and TV sets per 1000
n = persons per household
C = number of practising Christians
G = language coverage, % (proportion of population served by languages broadcast)
E = technical effectiveness of Christian programmes, % (professional standards, signal strength, clarity of reception, competitiveness of times used, language competency; maximum value 100%)
I = religious interest (national interest in religion: in Third World, I=2; in Western world, I=1; in Communist world, I=0.1).

*Quantifying radio churches*

It is also possible to make a first tentative approximation to quantifying another recent phenomenon, namely the large number of individuals across the world who are being converted to faith in Christ through Christian broadcasting and related activities including radiophonic schools, Bible correspondence courses utilizing the mails as well as radio, and the like. The data on which this is based are surveys and correspondence tabulations from the major Christian broadcasting organizations, statistics of correspondence-course agencies, and statistics of mass evangelism organizations. Again, as throughout this Encyclopedia, this is done only to obtain an estimate of the general order of magnitude of this phenomenon. Obviously, exact statistics based on head counts or scientifically-valid samples will remain unobtainable for a long time to come.

The nature of this phenomenon may first be outlined by stating that recently there has been firm evidence of actual conversions of non-Christians, solely through listening to Christian programmes, from Yemen, Morocco, Algeria, Hungary, the USSR, and other countries hostile to Christianity.

In direct mass-evangelistic proclamation (either face-to-face, or broadcast) and also in ordinary non-evangelistic proclamation (either routine church worship and preaching, or routine Christian broadcasting), over a period of time a response, or a desire for commitment, or a decision to become practising Christians, is generated among a small proportion of persons participating. When these forms of proclamation take place regularly, over a long period of time, and on a massive scale demographically across the world (as is the present state of affairs), we can expect to find that this response demonstrates certain clear statistical patterns. The general order of magnitude of this response, on very conservative definitions, may therefore be estimated as follows.

In mass-evangelistic proclamation as exemplified by the 30 years of face-to-face evangelistic campaigns of the Billy Graham Evangelistic Association and many other similar bodies, it has been found that the conversion response rate, i.e. those becoming enquirers or making professions of faith or decisions or commitments for Christ, recorded as a percentage of the total audience present, averages 2% per meeting or campaign in the Western world, and somewhat higher in the Communist world (Yugoslavia 3%) and the Third World (Japan 7%, Tonga 4%, Puerto Rico 4%, Taiwan 6%, Philippines 4%, Argentina 4%, Kenya 3%, India 3%); all these figures are derived from the statistics in the footnotes EVANGELIZATION under Tables 2. Since an average campaign meeting lasts for 2 hours (Western world) to 3 hours (Third World), the conversion response rate can conservatively be expressd as around 1% of the audience per meeting hour.

When either of the 2 mass media, radio and TV, are utilized in conjunction with face-to-face mass-evangelistic campaigns, the proclamation may be extended much wider but the response rate is, understandably, much smaller. Based on the relatively few such campaigns that have taken place by 1975, we can estimate this rate at one hundredth of that in face-to-face campaigns, i.e. 0.01% of the audience per listening/viewing hour.

In ordinary non-evangelistic proclamation, i.e. church worship and preaching that is not specifically evangelistic, a similar conversion response or desire for commitment is also generated but at an even smaller rate which may be estimated at one thousandth of that in evangelistic campaigns, i.e. 0.001% of the audience per meeting hour.

In routine non-evangelistic Christian radio broadcasting, the desire for commitment is again generated but the conversion response rate is naturally even smaller because radio is less personal, more casually listened to, has a less selective audience, has more non-Christians listening, as well as being not specifically evangelistic for more than a fraction of its broadcast time. As a rough and very conservative approximation to the general order of magnitude, it may be estimated that, on average, conversion response is only one two-hundredth of that for radio/TV extension of a face-to-face mass-evangelistic campaign, or one 20-thousandth of that in face-to-face evangelistic campaigns themselves, i.e. 0.00005% of (or, 0.0000005 times) the regular audience for each broadcast hour, which is one convert per hour for every 2 million audience. Hence,

Conversion response per hour = 0.0000005 A,
or, Conversion response per year = 0.000025 Ah,
where A = regular audience, and h = broadcast hours per week (for all Christian programmes received in a country, in all its languages, from all stations, on all wave-lengths). We have already just shown that average audiences are linked with the volume of listeners' letters received, thus:

A = 5,000,000 . monthly letters/ML,
or, A = 400,000 . normal annual letters/ML.

Hence, annual response, measured as the number of converts to Christianity due to broadcasting, is given by

New radio converts per year = 0.000025(400,000 . annual letters . h/ML),
= (10h/LM). annual letters.

Since this situation has been stable in many areas of the world since at least 1960, the total of all such converts 10 years later in 1970 was probably around 10 times this number; thus

Total radio converts = (100h/LM). annual letters.

These are adults; but they are often surrounded by sympathetic families, children, infants, relatives, visitors and other interested persons, at least doubling the total; hence we can estimate

**Total radio convert community**
**= (200h/LM). annual letters.**

In the 1970s, shortwave radio receivers have become widely available in most parts of the world. In many countries, access to them has now become almost universal. In the nature of the case, therefore, radio converts are distributed here and there across the entire country virtually at random. They are in most cases scattered individuals who have begun tuning in, or who have happened to listen, simply as a result of having access to a shortwave receiver and with no contact whatever with existing churches or local Christians. They are mostly young, including many students and large numbers of secondary-school pupils. They are often rural, and from isolated areas as well as in densely-populated zones. Their religious background is that of the country itself: in India most

**Radio churches.** In many areas with no churches, converts worship on Sundays around radio sets; here, listening to noted preacher in Nigeria.

are Hindus; in the Islamic world, Muslim; and in the USSR, China and other Communist lands most have been non-religious. In a majority Christian country, or one with de facto religious liberty (codes 1-5 in our column 22 in Global Table 31), most of these newly-committed radio converts each year eventually find without difficulty, and link up with, a nearby local church in an already existing denomination, Protestant, Catholic, Anglican or Orthodox. For this reason, they do not form separate denominations and so are not shown as such in Tables 2; they appear in Tables 2 only as part of the annual growth of existing rapidly-growing denominations. But in a minority Christian country, or one antagonistic to Christianity, or one without de facto full religious liberty (codes 6-10 in our column 22 in Global Table 31), or one with only very scattered or isolated churches over large areas, or one hostile to persons wanting to find or join existing Christian congregations, or in areas without a single Christian witness, a proportion of these new individual radio converts are completely isolated from existing believers and may remain ignorant of the existence of organized denominations for months or even years. Before long, therefore, they group themselves into new house churches, de facto congregations, cells or nuclei which are neither Protestant nor Catholic nor Orthodox but are simply Christian (though for European countries we classify them in Tables 2 as Protestant since this is the dominant type of Christian broadcasting available to them), and which in Third-World countries are described in this survey as indigenous (because the initiative in their formation is local and not expatriate). Eventually, these new congregations may be heard of by, and approached by, the nearest denominational bodies, and they may then become affiliated to them; but our present concern is with the period before then when they are still isolated from existing organized Christianity. The proportion of all radio converts who find themselves thus isolated from denominations may be estimated, very approximately, as equal to the proportion of non-Christians in the country; i.e. it varies from around zero in the Western world to 64% in the USSR and to around 97% in the Muslim world. Further, it has been found in field visits that these isolated radio churches or cells or congregations average around 20 adult persons each, or 40 including children and infants. In such a country, they form regular on-going aggregates of Christian discipleship somewhat parallel to denominations but without central organization. In this survey, therefore, they are regarded as such and are termed isolated radio churches; and those persons deriving their on-going corporate Christian life primarily from them (adults and their families and children) are here termed isolated radio converts. These latter may be quantified using the above formulae for radio converts, as follows:

Isolated radio convert community = (p/100). total radio convert community = (2ph/LM). annual letters,
where p = per cent non-Christian in country.

The number of new cells or congregations (of, on average, an isolated radio convert community of 40 each) begun each year is given by

New isolated radio churches per year = 0.5 (annual letters) h/LM,

and the total of all such cells or congregations by the formula

**Isolated radio churches = (0.05ph/LM) annual letters.**

There is in these closed or relatively-closed countries a second and parallel phenomenon, namely the proliferation of non-Christian students enrolling for Bible correspondence courses offered by local or foreign Christian organizations, often linked with radio teaching. In the Middle East, by 1969 about 200,000 Muslims, mostly youths, and mostly secondary-school and university students aged from 12 to 25, had enrolled in such courses in Arabic under 18 different agencies; by 1975 this total had risen to 500,000. Of these, all regard themselves as nominally Muslims when applying; but a substantial proportion, on average 4% for all agencies combined, regard themselves as Christians (believers in Jesus Christ) when they finish and in the years subsequently. Living in a non-Christian and often anti-Christian society, they exist as crypto-Christians loosely related to informal and transitory groupings of Christians. This flexibility and the clandestine nature of their Christian profession makes it extremely difficult for hostile secular authorities to trace them, let alone prosecute them. The proportion of these BCC converts varies from organization to organization. The International Correspondence Institute, Belgium (Assemblies of God) in 1975 reported 300,000 students in the Middle East in 20 countries, of whom 18,501 had written in with professions of faith in Christ (6.2%). Radio School of the Bible, Marseilles (North Africa Mission) has experienced a similar response but feels it more realistic to report that 0.6% of its Muslim students have become practising Christians. If we enumerate these aggregate enrolments (also termed inscriptions) as a variable, T, then those among these students who can thus be regarded as crypto-Christians may be quantified for any non-Christian country at, very conservatively, 2% of all enrolments, i.e. 0.02T. However, in any country where all such enrolments, applications and courses are impeded by poor mail reliability or by deliberate anti-Christian mail censorship, these persons represent only the visible tip of the iceberg; many friends and acquantances share the course materials, and so the total of all such would-be students may be estimated by dividing by our mail reliability factor, M%, as follows:

BCC converts = 0.02 (accumulated enrolments) /(M/100),
= 2T/M,

and, including dependants, children and adherents,

BCC convert community = 4T/M.

As with radio converts, many are members of, or join, existing denominations; and the proportion of all BCC students who find themselves isolated from denominations is approximately equal to the proportion of non-Christians in the country (p%); i.e. it varies from around zero in the Western world to over 99% in the Muslim world. Hence we have the formula:

Isolated BCC convert community = (p/100). BCC convert community,
= 0.04pT/M.

Clearly, this phenomenon of isolated BCC converts is parallel to that of isolated radio converts. Both rely on Christian radio programmes for their regular corporate Christian nurture. In this survey, we therefore combine the 2 into a single category, which we term *isolated radio believers*, defining this as the total community of those persons (with their dependants, adults and children, and other adherents) who derive their on-going corporate Christian life primarily from isolated radio churches or isolated BCC student groupings. In certain countries where response to these 2 ministries has been dramatic or even enormous, our 2 categories may overlap considerably; in such cases, therefore, allowance must be made for this overlap by reducing the total of the 2 categories together. Similarly, in countries where BCCs are conducted by radio, BCC letters are often counted as listeners' letters; if they are thus enumerated in our variable R, they should not be counted again by using our second formula above. We then arrive at the following definition and formula, which we use in relatively-closed non-Christian countries to arrive at the somewhat conservative estimates given in Tables 2:

Isolated radio believers = (2ph)/LM. (annual letters) + (0.04p/M) (BCC enrolments), minus any known duplication or overlap of one group with the other, or

Isolated radio believers = $2phR/LM + 0.04pT/M$ minus any duplications.

Another way of expressing this formula is in terms of total regular audience, A. Using the definition of A above, in countries with negligible correspondence course enrolments (e.g. USSR, China), the formula reduces to

**Isolated radio believers = 2phA/400,000.**

Once again, to get the number of isolated groups or radio churches to which these isolated radio believers of both kinds belong, we divide by 20 adults or 40 total community.

In the present survey, isolated radio believers and isolated radio churches have been thus enumerated in 67 countries in which it is difficult for new radio converts to find and join existing denominations. They are then, in each country, given a separate line in each Table 2 as forming a new de facto denomination or grouping there. They also appear in Tables 1 as part of the category of crypto-Christians (believers unknown to the state). The 67 countries fall into 3 groups: (1) Communist countries, (2) Muslim, Buddhist and Hindu countries with a minority Christian presence, and (3) a few other countries with vast undeveloped or inaccessible yet populated regions (such as deserts, forests, jungles) unreached

by missionaries or national churches (in particular the Amazon basin in Bolivia, Brazil, Colombia and Peru). To illustrate our methodology, we will now give one country as an example, and then mention several other countries involved.

Burma is a Third-World country with 94.8% non-Christians, poor mail facilities (M=50%), moderate literacy (L=68%), and Christian radio programmes from abroad (FEBC et alia) totalling about 21 hours a week. Listeners' letters to FEBC, FEBA et alia in 1975 were averaging 330 a month or 3,930 a year. Using our formula, this gives an isolated radio convert community of 4,720. Bible correspondence courses, however, have been difficult to introduce; by 1975 ICI reported only 10 active students or, with other bodies, about 1,000 total enrolments. Using our formula, this gives isolated BCC converts of only 76 or so. The total of isolated radio believers is therefore around 4,800, as shown in Burma's Table 2.

Direct evidence for the existence of this phenomenon of isolated radio believers is becoming increasingly available. The reasons for the rarity of evidence hitherto are their isolation, geographical remoteness, and the desire to keep a low profile and avoid publicity that is natural on the part of crypto-Christians in hostile societies. Nevertheless, there is considerable evidence in Western countries and Western-oriented Third-World countries of whole congregations of believers coming into existence solely through Christian radio programmes. Examples come from Guatemala, through programmes broadcast by station KGEI, and the Philippines through FEBC. In non-Christian or anti-Christian countries, likewise, examples come from Hungary (through IBRA), Kampuchea (FEBC), Morocco (NAM), Poland (SGA) and the USSR (IBRA, SGA). In the same way, whole congregations are known to have come into existence through Bible correspondence courses by mail or through other forms of scripture distribution in many countries including Brazil, India, Indonesia, Japan, Peru, Sri Lanka, Thailand, et alia. For the last 20 years or more, large numbers of these congregations brought into being through the World Literature Crusade (Every Home Crusade) have emerged in isolated areas or towns with no existing churches and are now termed Christ Groups.

One documented case reported by KGEI (FEBC, San Francisco, USA) may be described. In December 1973, an inhabitant named Basilides Caceres in the remote north Peruvian town of Inapari, at the mid-jungle conjunction of Bolivia, Brazil and Peru, tuned in by accident to KGEI. He accepted Christ and then immediately set up a 'listening club'. Two other families accepted Christ. At this stage he wrote a first letter to KGEI, asking for a Bible. While waiting for literature, he picked up the Protestant station in

Lima, Peru, travelled there, contacted the Protestant church (Christian and Missionary Alliance) and was baptized, then after a month's orientation returned to Inapari where he baptized his 'congregation' of 12 adults and 20 children.

A second case is reported by Radio Trans Mundial do Brasil (TWR). On the upper Solimoes (Amazon) river, missionaries in 1978 came across a group of Indians who had never previously been in contact with Christians or Christian literature, but who had been converted to Christ through RTM programmes and had founded their own native Indian church as a result.

In many such ways, Christian radio/TV is having sizeable impact on church growth today.

LITERACY, 1900-80 (columns 96-99)

Four columns of figures here give the adult literacy in each country (persons 15 years or older who can read or write, in any language) for the 4 years 1900, 1950, 1975 and 1980. Figures for the latter 2 years are extrapolated, where necessary, from official census figures reported in *UNESCO Statistical yearbook 1964* (Table 4) and *1977* (Table 1.3). Figures for the year 1900 are taken, in many cases, from C.M. Cipolla, *Literacy and development in the West* (London: Penguin, 1969).

EVANGELIZATION, 1900-2000 (columns 100-107).

The quantification of evangelization is a major subject worked out for the first time in this Encyclopedia. Its methodology is described in Part 5.

*Column 100.* Year evangelization was begun (first resident Christians or missionaries, whether or not subsequently removed). These data can also be used as a typology of countries by dividing the period AD 30-1980 into 2, 3, 4 or more historial periods, as required.

*Extent of evangelization*
*Column 101.* Extent of individual evangelization, e %, in 1970 (Johnstone scale)

Extent of comparative demographic evangelization, E % (Barrett scale):
*Column 102.* in 1900
*Column 103.* in 1970
*Column 104.* in 1980
*Column 105.* in 1985
*Column 106.* in 2000

These data can also be used as an eleven-fold typology of countries from 0-10, by removing the last digit from all numbers in these columns.
*Column 107.* Outreach factor: the total of all evangelized persons in the country divided by the totals of all Christians, in 1980.

# PART 4
# CULTURE
Peoples of the world:
an ethnolinguistic classification

*I saw another angel flying high in the air, with an eternal message of Good News to announce to the peoples of the earth, to every race, tribe, language and nation.*

—Revelation 14.6, Good News Bible.

This section gives the method used to enumerate the ethnolinguistic composition of the world, of global Christianity, and of their component parts, over the period AD 1900–2000. The resulting statistics are given elsewhere, especially in Parts 1, 7 and 8.

# AN ETHNOLINGUISTIC CLASSIFICATION

This Encyclopedia presents an ethnolinguistic descriptive enumeration of each country's (1) total population, and (2) total of affiliated Christians, throughout the 20th century. In this Part we explain the methodology and give the classification itself, with its codes; the statistical tables are later given in Part 8.

Our inclusion of this analysis by races, tribes and cultures is an affirmation of the centrality of indigenous cultures to local expressions of Christianity, of the right to exist of minority tribes and peoples, of their autonomy in their own areas, of their importance from the Christian standpoint vis-a-vis the world's dominant peoples and cultures, and of the need to reduce the imperialistic influence of these latter (especially Western culture) in non-Western local churches and lands. It is also an affirmation of the necessity to view people, not primarily as nationals of a given country, but primarily as members of the natural homogeneous units they belong to, through which they may the most effectively be described, approached, reached, known, evangelized and eventually christianized.

The Bible frequently draws attention to the complex mosaic of peoples who compose the human race. In the Great Commission, the command of Christ is to 'Go and disciple all peoples' (*panta ta ethne*, Matthew 28.19). In attempting to depict this vast diversity of peoples, the Book of Revelation provides descriptive listings at 7 points, each time of 4 entities, as follows (using the RSV text):

1. every tribe and tongue and people and nation (Revelation 5.9);
2. every nation, all tribes and peoples and tongues (7.9);
3. many peoples and nations and tongues and kings (10.11);
4. the peoples and tribes and tongues and nations (11.9);
5. every tribe and people and tongue and nation (13.7);
6. every nation and tribe and tongue and people (14.6);
7. peoples and multitudes and nations and tongues (17.15).

In these 7 listings, we note: (a) 3 of the 4 entities occur in all 7 lists, namely 'nation' (an ethnic term), 'people' (a cultural term), and 'tongue' (a linguistic term); (b) another term, 'tribe' (an ethnocultural term, often with connotations of colour or skin pigmentation) occurs in 5 of the lists; (c) another, 'multitudes' illustrates the demographic aspect; (d) a last term, 'kings' (here used to personify 'kingdoms'), invokes the ideas of nationality, citizenship, subject status, and the like; and (e) in other English versions than the RSV, other synonyms emerge such as 'race' for 'nation' in 10.11 (Good News Bible), 'kindred' for 'tribe' (5.9, AV/KJV), et alia. The Bible can thus be said to be fully aware of the vast ethnolinguistic diversity of the world and of its importance for the Christian world mission.

From a descriptive or anthropological point of view, therefore, a human population (or an individual) has 6 related but distinct characteristics: race, colour, ethnic origin, nationality, culture, and language. Race and colour are inherited (passed from generation to generation), whereas culture and language are learned; and ethnic origin is a less clearly-defined characteristic referring to the main name by which a people is usually known. Ethnic groups are often grouped by anthropologists into primary ethnic culture areas. The sixth term, nationality (citizenship), may be inherited or acquired, and unlike the other 5 characteristics may be changed instantaneously and with ease. Of the 5 which cannot be changed, race and language are the clearest-defined concepts, and their worldwide manifestations have been classified by biologists and linguists respectively as follows.

## Race

From the biological or purely physical or genetic or serological (blood-group) point of view, race (or physical type) is a biological concept referring to the taxonomic (classificatory) unit immediately below the species. Thus, mankind or the human race today consists of a single surviving species, Homo Sapiens, and 5 surviving subspecies or races or racial stocks (many others having long become extinct): Australoid, Capoid, Caucasoid, Mongoloid and Negroid. Between these are various hybrid races, known as clines (Negroid-Caucasoid, Mongoloid-Caucasoid, etc). Race covers such physical features as skin colour, stature, blood group, head shape and hair type. From the point of view of skin colour, all can be given a stylized label each in order to permit approximate numerical analysis. For the 5 races, these are, respectively, (1) Grey (a stylized colour combining the concepts 'early', 'aboriginal', non-White, non-Black, non-Yellow), (2) also Grey, (3) White, (4) Yellow, (5) Black. Government censuses often enumerate populations in this way, especially in the use of White and Black. In Portuguese, in the 1960 and 1970 censuses of Mozambique, Chinese persons were classified as 'Yellows', defined there as persons with 4 Yellow grandparents; and in the Angola censuses, there were 'Whites' (Brancos), 'Blacks' (Pretos), etc. In Spanish, the 1903 census of the Philippines enumerated people as Moreno (Brown), Amarillo (Yellow), Blanco (White), Negro (Black), etc. In our classification, in addition, certain geographical races are labelled Tan, Brown, Red. Tan refers to ochre- or olive- or yellow-brown- or light-brown-skinned peoples. Red is a term traditionally in use for American Indians. The result of all these typologies is a series of possible classifications which vary considerably from scholar to scholar but which approximate to the one we give here entitled PEOPLES OF THE WORLD, especially in the first and third capital letters of each people's coded name.

Where statistics of race are to be gathered, government census and allied bureaux often define their terms with great precision. In the USA, employment regulations define the term 'Indian' exactly as (a) members of any recognized Indian tribe now under Federal jurisdiction, (b) descendants of any such members residing within the present boundaries of any Indian reservation, (c) all others of one-half or more of Indian blood of tribes indigenous to the United States, (d) Eskimos and other Aboriginal people of Alaska, and (e) persons of at least one-quarter degree Indian ancestry. In Viet Nam, 'Chinese' are defined as anyone with a Chinese ancestor 5 generations back.

An important extension of race is the concept of geographical race, as popularized and described by *The new Encyclopædia Britannica* (1975). Geographical race is defined as one of the 13 broad, geographically-delimited races of mankind, a collection of human populations, usually rather similar physically, delimited by some natural boundary, such as an ocean, and tending to have similar heredity, skin colour, hair type, language, and the like.

An important caution needs to be given here. The concept of different races is regarded by many scientists as outdated, for the reasons that the multiple origins of man have not been proven, population movements with resulting interbreeding have been continuous since the origin of man, and that populations today grade into each other to such an extent that no pure stocks exist. There is no such thing as a 'pure' race; instead, there exist almost imperceptible gradations of genetic character from one group of people to the next. Without entering into the pros and cons in detail, we can nevertheless assert that for our purposes this classification is still valuable, it being understood that none of our 5 races and 7

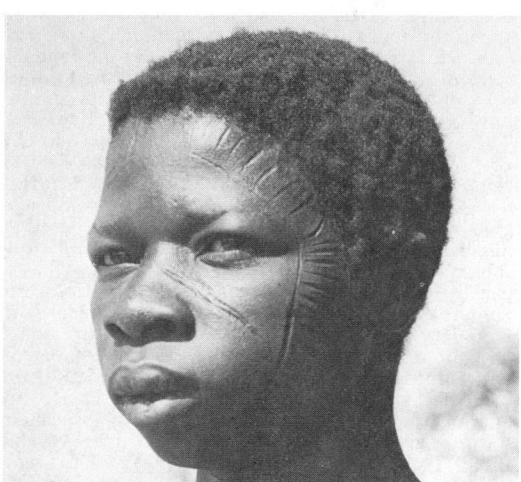

**Race, culture, language.** Three illustrations from Africa of these separate but related characteristics.
*Top.* (1) **Race.** A youth of Negro race, Black skin colour, Central Bantoid family, Mossi tribe, speaking the Moré language. In the old Mossi empire, no person with such facial incisions could be made a slave. Race, skin colour, even identification scars, are inherited and permanent.
*Centre* (2) **Culture.** Bassari singers and dancers in Dakar (Senegal) enact their rich cultural heritage. By individuals, culture is not so much inherited as learned.
*Bottom.* (3) **Language.** Dinka-speaking Nilotic tribesmen in Wau (Sudan) sing and perform traditional tribal dance. Language also is not inherited but learned.

colours are original or pure or isolated stocks and that all overlap to a greater or lesser extent.

## Language

Language is the principal means of communicating culture (a word which itself commonly embraces the entire way of life of a people). From the linguistic point of view, the world's 7,010 distinct living languages (excluding dead languages and those no longer spoken) as shown in our classification can be classified into 10-16 major linguistic families (or 24 major phyla or groupings or superstocks, or from 40-100 families according to some classifications), with several minor ones consisting each of one language isolate. Languages are usually classified in the first instance genetically (evolution from a common ancestral language), in some cases with the superimposing of further classification typologically (grammatical or lexical similarities in language structure). The total of languages according to different scholars varies widely, and is clearly dependent on how one differentiates between language and dialect. The index of languages and alternative names in C.F. & F.M. Voegelin's *Classification and index of the world's languages* (New York: Elsevier, 1977, 658p), lists some 28,300 different names. There is considerable variety also in the classifications proposed by linguists, using techniques such as genetic relationship, glottochronology and lexicostatistics, but they all usually include the following families: Indo-European, Hamito-Semitic, Ural-Altaic, Caucasian (Georgian), Sino-Tibetan, Malayo-Polynesian (Austronesian), Dravidian, Amerindian, Nilotic, Sudanese-Guinean, Hottentot-Bushman, and Bantu. A detailed listing of 5,103 living languages, with all living dialects and alternate spellings, and also Scripture translation status, is given in *Ethnologue*, ed B.F. Grimes (Wycliffe Bible Translators, 9th edition 1978). This work divides living languages into the following 24 phyla: Afro-Asiatic, Austronesian, Austro-Asiatic, Azteco-Tanoan, Australian, Caucasian, Dravidian, Hokan, Indo-European, Indo-European Creole, Kam-Tai, Khoisan, Macro-Algonkian, Macro-Chibchan, Macro-Siouan, Na-Dene, Niger-Kordofanian, Nilo-Saharan, Oto-Manguean, Penutian, Papuan, Paleo-Siberian, Sino-Tibetan, and Ural-Altaic.

There are, therefore, various definitions of language and dialect, some stricter and some looser. For the purposes of this Encyclopedia, we define a distinct language as one which has, or should have, or is agreed to need to have, its own separate and distinct translation of Holy Scripture, instead of its speakers being satisfied with (or being told by missions or translators to be satisfied with) Scriptures already translated into another tongue which is held to be sufficiently close or comprehensible. In many such cases (2 languages using a single translation), the 2 languages may often be correctly regarded as dialects of each other rather than as separate languages.

In our statistical analysis, the category 'Languages' for a given country is enumerated and quantified here as consisting of mother tongues and lingua francas either (a) native to the country, even if miniscule in size (e.g. Bushmen tribes in Southern Africa with a handful of speakers), or (b) in the case of expatriates, with as speakers a community (not just isolated individuals) numbering at least 0.05% of the country's population, or (c) significant enough for them to be officially listed as languages in use in the country by government censuses or schedules or other similar publications.

## Culture

A people is characterized by a distinctive culture based on a distinctive mother tongue. A culture can be described as a group of people who do things together in a patterned way: sharing beliefs and customs with a worldview at the centre, together with values and standards of judgement and conduct, common institutions, a common language, with shared proverbs, myths, folk-tales and arts, a common history, and common land or territory. Classifications of peoples using this criterion usually divide peoples into ethnic culture areas. An example of this may be seen in the chart 'Primary European ethnic culture areas' in *The new Encyclopædia Britannica* (1974: Macropaedia, volume 6, p. 1122), which divides Europe into 4 major culture areas, 22 culture provinces, and 158 distinct peoples. A different aspect of culture is that it can cover a whole range of social strata or socio-religious stratification, such as India's over 26,000 castes in the 4 categories of Vedic theory.

## A single classification

These 3 classifications overlap a good deal, but by no means at all points. There is in fact no precise correlation between race, physical type, colour, language and culture. The world distribution of languages does, however, correspond broadly with that of human races. As we have just noted, the matter is complicated by the fact that, for both race and language, scholars of different nationalities and persuasions have proposed numerous overlapping, often conflicting and even contradictory classifications. For the purposes of this Encyclopedia, however, we need one single stable classification of all living peoples and languages (excluding all now extinct) in which all proper names in use, whether racial, ethnic, national, cultural, linguistic, or pertaining to colour, and whether referring to a single people or language or to a major family or grouping, and all their synonyms and alternate names, can be inserted into a single framework which will show the relationships between all names (in their generally-preferred anglicized versions only, excluding forms in other languages), together with population and other data referring to each name. In the main, members of each ethnic group have a similar mother tongue (first language), whatever country they live in or have migrated to. We have therefore combined the 3 preceding classifications, in their various published versions, and have evolved a single classification (here termed ethnolinguistic) of the peoples of the world at 11 progressively more detailed levels: 5 major races (as detailed above, changing the mainly biological ending -oid for the last 3 races, to obtain Caucasian, Mongolian, and Negro) with 7 skin colours; 13 geographical races and 4 sub-races; 71 ethnolinguistic families (sometimes termed micro-races, sometimes local races); 432 peoples (or sub-families or ethnic culture areas); 8,990 constituent peoples and sub-peoples (7,010 languages); and many thousand additional names ranked in 4 further levels of subdivisions. Our classification is based on the various extant schemes of nearness of language plus nearness of racial, ethnic, cultural, and culture-area characteristics.

The full classification also contains several thousand synonyms, alternative names, variant spellings, and names in other languages than English. It contains Bantu names with ethnic prefixes (Ama-, Ba-, Ma-, Ovi-, Wa-, etc) and linguistic prefixes (Eki-, Ki-, Lo-, Lu-, etc), though we omit these in our present classification. The grand total of all such names with all variant spellings must be over 30,000. Over 12,000 of these tribes, language groups, nations, clans and other social divisions are listed in J.G. Leyburn, *Handbook of ethnography* (New Haven: Yale University Press, 1931); and, as noted above, 28,300 names are listed in Voegelin 1977 in English usage (i.e. in anglicized form), with at least a further 50,000 variations and usages in French, German, Spanish, Portuguese, Italian, Russian and the other major languages of world scholarship. In addition many peoples and languages are named with yet other terms by, and unique to, their surrounding peoples and languages. Altogether, the grand total of all ethnolinguistic names must be over 100,000 distinct terms. A reduced version of our full classification, evolved with special reference to this survey of Christianity, covering the first 6 of the above levels together with codes for the first 5 levels only (races, colours, geographical races, ethnolinguistic families, peoples) is given here in our anglicized listing PEOPLES OF THE WORLD. In it, each ethnolinguistic family, and most of the world's major peoples, are given a code number and are also classified by race, geographical race and colour. Most of the ethnic groups it lists may be seen located geographically in the detailed ethnic maps in *Atlas narodov mira* (Atlas of the peoples of the world, Moscow, 1964). Similar maps, but with a different classification, are found in *Peoples of the earth*: Volume 20, *The future of mankind* (Europa Verlag, 1973).

The reader should note that our classification is neither purely 'ethnic' nor 'racial' nor 'linguistic' nor 'cultural', but is ethnolinguistic; and that on our definition an 'ethnolinguistic people' means an ethnic or ethno-cultural or racial group speaking its own language or mother tongue. In the 20th century, mass international migration has therefore sometimes involved, over a generation or two, a change in the way an ethnic group is classified. For example, in 1972 in the USA, 2.2 million people (1.1% of the population) were of Russian origin (*Statistical abstract of the United States*, 1973, p. 34), but only 334,000 (0.2%) spoke Russian as their mother tongue

(1970 Census of Population). This means that large numbers of persons of Russian origin (0.9% of the USA population) no longer speak Russian as their mother tongue and so (on our classification) have now become USA Whites (English-speaking), leaving only the 0.2% to be classified here as Russian-speaking Russians. In the same way, millions of Europeans have emigrated to South America over the last century, including Russians and Ukrainians, but after the first generation or so they have tended to lose their original mother tongues and have become assimilated to what we call the Latin American White race (Spanish- or Portuguese-speaking). Similarly, in countries such as the USA, Brazil, France, et alia, we distinguish between (e.g.) Polish-speaking Polish immigrants on the one hand, and, on the other, persons of Polish origin who are now assimilated to the dominant race and culture. Likewise, every year millions of individuals and families who migrate to countries of different language and ethnic group are recorded here in those countries by their original mother-tongue ethnic group until such time (usually one generation) as they have changed their mother tongue and become absorbed in the dominant national group (e.g. Italian families who move permanently to Germany and who eventually become Germans linguistically and culturally). A different set of cases concerns peoples who, through emigration, retain a strong identity but change their mother tongue to a local language (e.g. Chinese who now speak only Indonesian, Mexican Indians who are now monolingual in Spanish only, etc); because such peoples still retain their ethnic identity and culture, they are classified here as still members of their original ethnic group.

The term 'ethnolinguistic people' refers to that group which speaks the language shown as its first or primary or cultural or official language. In France, for instance, 82.0% of the population are French-speaking ethnic Frenchmen. Of these, 13 million (24.6%) speak for everyday purposes Occitan (Gascon, Languedoc, Provençal), a Romance language closer to Catalan than to French, although they use French as their official and cultural language. In this classification, therefore, the 13 million are classified under the ethnolinguistic term 'French', the only persons coded under 'Occitan' being the handful for whom Occitan and not French is their primary or cultural or only language.

Our classification includes a number of ethnolinguistic groups whose formal or correct names in the recent past have had, in certain mainly-White circles, unfavourable connotations: Aborigine, Baster, Black, Bush Negro, Chicano, Coloured, Creole, Eurasian, Euronesian, Gypsy, Half-Breed, Half-Caste, Mestizo, Métis, Mulatto, Nomad, Red, Yellow, etc. (The classification excludes their more offensive names such as: Chink, Coolie, Coon, Dago, Darkie, Gook, Kaffir, Nigger, Nip, Pak, Wog, Yid, etc). This is therefore the place to state unequivocally that, from the Christian standpoint, we reject all such bigoted interpretations and instead we affirm the importance of these groups and their cultures in both *Heilsgeschichte* (salvation history) and the contemporary Christian world. It is also noteworthy that most of these names themselves have recently been rehabilitated and are now claimed with pride by the peoples themselves. As a result, we can say that the statistics of these groups presented in this survey are based on what people themselves now claim to be.

In a few cases, it is difficult to be consistent in classification on a global scale because a name has both ethnic, cultural and religious meanings, all closely related, but applied in different countries and their censuses with differing emphases. The major example of this concerns the Jewish people. In most countries and censuses Jews are regarded as an ethnic group as well as a religious group, and they are treated as such in this survey. In the USA, we classify them not in the general 'USA White' category, although they are in fact mostly White and mostly English-speaking, but in our separate category 'Jewish'. The reason is that our main criterion in all such ambiguous situations is their answer to the question: 'What is the first, or main, or primary ethnic or ethnolinguistic term by which persons identify themselves, or are identified by peoples around them?'

Our definition of 'language' in this present classification refers to distinct and separate languages, excluding near variants and dialects except in a handful of special cases. On our definition, for example, there are about 540 Bantu languages in Africa (listed in Voegelin 1977: 56-72). On other, broader, definitions including dialects, the total for this group of languages can be even larger.

*Ethnolinguistic composition of all countries, 1970-80*
In the section SECULAR DATA at the start of each country's survey article in Part 7, under the heading 'ETHNOLINGUISTIC GROUPS', the de facto ethnolingustic composition of the total population is given. These figures were in all cases worked out de novo for the present survey, utilizing population censuses and a host of other sources. Similarly, in the footnotes 'PEOPLES (ethnolinguistic)' under Tables 2, the ethnolinguistic composition of the country's affiliated Christians is given. These 2 sets of data were then prepared in coded form by (a) utilizing the codes given in the classification that here follows, and (b) translating each ethnolinguistic element into an 8- or 9-digit alphanumeric code. For example, '35.0% British' is coded as 350CEW19i, '95.5% Russian' is coded as 955CEW22j, and '1.2% Samoan' is coded as 012MPY55e. The object of this coding is to assist the reader who wishes to make exact numerical comparisons from one country to another, or over a period of time, or to make global or continental analyses using the ethnolinguistic criterion. It also permits our own analysis of the total population of the world, and of all Christians, by ethnolinguistic family and people, whose statistics are given in Part 8.

*How we present the data*
In each country's survey article in Part 7, the ethnolinguistic data for both (a) secular population and (b) Christian population are given in one single standardized and precisely-defined format, concerning which the following 11 points should be carefully noticed. (1) In almost all countries, and in most churches, there are 3 categories of ethnolinguistic groups: (a) dominant groups, (b) other sizeable groups over 0.05% in size, and (c) a mass of smaller groups of yet other ethnic origin, often expatriates, under 0.05% in size and tapering off in size down to a single individual or two. Here, our data in their uncoded form report (a), (b) and where significant the largest of (c) also; in coded form, the data cover (a) and (b) only. For each country, these data therefore give its major races and all numerically-significant ethnolinguistic families and peoples, in the period 1970-80, shown in descending order of size, each as a percentage of total secular or Christian population, to the nearest 0.1, down to 0.1%, with smaller groups (below 0.05% but still numerically significant) in descending order of size at the end. It should thus be remembered that a figure '0.1%' means somewhere in the range 0.05-0.15%. (2) Commas indicate distinct and separate peoples; thus '5% Bantu, Indian' does not imply any relationship between Bantu and Indians but merely refers to the presence of 2 distinct groups, one 5% Bantu and the other (less than 0.05%) Indian. (3) Parentheses and brackets indicate a breakdown, usually only partial, of certain larger categories into their major component peoples. (4) The addition 'et alii' refers to the presence of several other smaller peoples in addition to those listed; the addition '&c' refers to the presence of a large number of other smaller peoples. (5) For some minorities, as well as giving the percentage we give the actual number of persons in 1970 (in parentheses). (6) A slash / indicates a racial mixture between the 2 or more peoples indicated. (7) All percentages given in 'ETHNOLINGUISTIC GROUPS' at the start of a country's article are percentages of the total population of the country; and all percentages given in 'PEOPLES (ethnolinguistic)' under Tables 2 are percentages of the total of all affiliated Christians in the country. (8) The degree of accuracy of these percentages in those 2 locations is indicated by the presence or absence of a decimal point; where this is absent, percentages are more approximate. (9) Note that the percentages for most countries do not reach a total of exactly 100%, the remainder being usually a number of smaller groupings, aliens of many nationalities, refugees, diplomats, traders, students and the like. (10) Under this procedure, the entire population of a country is assigned to one or other of these ethnolinguistic groups; each group thus includes any and all persons of mixed race or tribe who are closer to the group than to any other group. (11) Any discrepancies between these names and percentages and similar listings published by other sources (anthropologists, linguists, government censuses, etc) are due to either (a) differences in the ethnic or linguistic classifications employed, concerning which there is as yet no universal agreement; or (b) alternative possible ways of classifying a people (e.g. Jews can also be Whites, or British, or Spanish-speaking, or aliens, etc); or (c) the fact that many names, and their alternates, can be used by different types of user (anthropologists, linguists, government officials, missionaries, religious officials) in different senses or ways to cover different though overlapping populations.

*Extrapolation to 1900 and 2000*
For the vast majority of countries, the ethnolinguistic composition of either population or Christians has not altered appreciably during the decade 1970-80, and so the figures shown, which describe the situation in 1970 unless otherwise indicated, may be taken to have remained unchanged in 1975 and 1980. In those few countries where the composition has changed markedly since 1970, this is described in situ. In the same way, in most countries the ethnolinguistic composition was much the same in the year 1900, and will doubtless be similar in AD 2000. For this reason our tables in Part 8 give the 1900 and 2000 extrapolations and projections, it being understood that they represent only a first approximation.

*Obtaining absolute numbers*
If the reader wishes to obtain the total number of persons in any particular ethnolinguistic group in 1970, he should multiply its percentage by the country's population in 1970. For countries (the vast majority) whose ethnic composition has remained unchanged from 1970-80, to obtain the total number of persons in any ethnolinguistic group in 1975 or 1980 or 2000, the reader should multiply its percentage by the country's population in 1970 or 1980 or 2000 (given in Tables 1). The resulting figures for the year 2000 will of course only be projected estimates, but they will serve to establish the general order of magnitude of the future situation. It should be noted that the world totals for each people in the year 2000 are likely to be more accurate than national totals because the former will remain unaffected by future migrations across the world. In the same way, world totals for each people in the year 1900, also presented here, are more accurate than national totals based on these percentages because global totals are largely unaffected by the vast migrations of the 20th century.

When calculating sizes of small peoples whose population is shown as '0.2%' or '0.1%', it must again be noted that, because these figures cover the ranges 0.15-0.25%, and 0.05-0.15%, respectively, any totals resulting are only intended to be approximate.

*Ethnolinguistic percentages*
The data given in this survey enable us to present certain clear relationships between the numerical size of peoples and their nations, both total populations and Christian populations. Each ethnolinguistic people, tribe or group in a particular country can be described by 5 main percentage variables (here termed N,n,x,p,a). These are also related to 3 variables describing the group's country (X,P,A), defined below. These 8 variables may be grouped into 3 related formulae, written in 3 ways depending on which data the reader has and which he wishes to compute. In parentheses after each variable are shown the locations in this Encyclopedia where values of the data are presented. The symbols themselves (X,P,A,N,n,x,p,a) are only used at this one point in our survey; elsewhere the symbols have different meanings as shown in the Codebook.

*Variables*
- X = country's total Christians as % of country's total population (Tables 1)
- P = country's professing Christians as % of country's total population (Tables 1)
- A = country's affiliated Christians as % of country's total population (Tables 1)
- N = group's total population as % of country's total population (SECULAR DATA)
- n = group's affiliated Christians as % of country's affiliated Christians (Tables 2, footnotes PEOPLES)
- x = group's total Christians as % of group's total population
- p = group's professing Christians as % of group's total population
- a = group's affiliated Christians as % of group's total population (Part 8)

*Formulae*
(1) $x = nX/N$
(2) $p = nP/N$
(3) $a = nA/N$

When the reader is either checking any of our computed percentages, or taking the analysis further, he needs to remember that a number of these ethnolinguistic terms are enumerated by different users in very different ways (e.g. published statistics for the Yoruba of Nigeria vary from 3 million, referring to the Yoruba proper, to over 11 million Yoruba-speaking persons). A specific name, e.g. Herero, or Mongol, may have different meanings from one denomination to another, from one religion to another, even from one country to another. It may be used to include peripheral sub-tribes in one context, but to exclude them in another. This means that care must be taken to establish exactly what distinct meaning any particular usage has. Having done this, if one is working out a percentage by dividing the total of Yoruba Christians by the total of all Yoruba, both of these 2 totals must use exactly the same definition of the term Yoruba. This principle is observed throughout our own analysis.

*Christian cultures*
The extent to which a people can properly be called a Christian people can be defined in various ways. Firstly, it can be defined in terms of the magnitude of the people's Christian following; secondly, in terms of the years or even centuries of past Christian influence; and thirdly, in terms of the depth of Christian influence upon its language, literature and culture. As a first approximation, for purposes of analysis, we here define a Christian culture as a culture related to a specific ethnolinguistic people or tribe among which affiliated church members number a majority of the total population, i.e. over 50% in number.

## CROSS-CULTURAL FRONTIERS OR BARRIERS

The construction of this classification enables us to quantify a subject that is of prime concern to the Christian world mission. This is the measurement of distance between various cultures, and the number of frontiers or barriers that Christian workers or missionaries have to cross in order to reach peoples of other cultures.

*Cultural distance, C*
This distance is defined here as the number of cultural (ethnic, ethnolinguistic, racial, linguistic) frontiers or barriers that exist between a person or group of one culture (especially a Christian worker, missionary or evangelist, or a group of such) and their target individual, group or people. The distance as defined here can have integer values of 0, 1, 2, 3, 4, 5 or 6; and these 7 distances can be labelled ('C-0', 'C-1', etc), tabulated and explained as follows.

*Measuring cultural distance*
To measure the cultural distance between a particular individual (e.g. a German foreign missionary in Nigeria) and his target population (e.g. the Yoruba people), it is first necessary to compare their codes as given here. These are obtained from the classification below, or can be most rapidly obtained from the Index of Peoples and Languages (in Part 14 of this Encyclopedia). There, German is coded CEW19m; Yoruba is coded NAB59n. Now we compare these 2 codes, answering the 6 questions below with either 0 or 1 or 3 in the end column.

*Measuring distances for countries*
There are a number of possible usages for this index of cultural distance. It can be used to make people aware of the barriers that exist between themselves and other cultures, and therefore of the efforts that must be made in language learning and cultural awareness before good relations and communication can be effected. Distances can also be computed for whole countries; in particular, we can derive measures, for every country in the world, of the average cultural distance of the population from the world's largest Christian culture at 3 points in time: the years 1900, 1980 and 2000.

*Average cultural distance of a country*
The idea of an index of this kind is to obtain an approximation for the number of cultural frontiers or barriers between a country's population and global practising Christianity. As a starting-point in each country, we will now select 4 base cultures

| Distance | Frontiers | Target group | Type of contact |
|---|---|---|---|
| C-0 | No-frontier | Of the same sub-people, language or dialect | Near-neighbour |
| C-1 | One-frontier | Of a different sub-people (but same ethnolinguistic people) | Near-culture |
| C-2 | Two-frontier | Of a different ethnolinguistic people (sub-family) | Cross-populational |
| C-3 | Three-frontier | Of a different ethnolinguistic family (microrace, local race) | Cross-microracial |
| C-4 | Four-frontier | Of a different colour (physical type) | Cross-coloured |
| C-5 | Five-frontier | Of a different geographical race | Cross-geographico-racial |
| C-6 | Six-frontier | Of a different race | Cross-racial |

*A scale for measuring cultural distance between 2 peoples*

Compare the two 6-digit codes of these 2 peoples, and answer the 6 questions below.

| Digit | Frontier | Question | Barriers |
|---|---|---|---|
| 1 | Race | Is the first letter of each different? Yes = 1, No = 0. | |
| 2 | Geographical race | Is the second letter of each different? Yes = 1, No = 0. | |
| 3 | Colour | Is the third letter of each different? Yes = 1, No = 0 | |
| 4-5 | Ethnolinguistic family | Is the 2-digit number of each different? Yes = 3, No = 0. | |
| 6 | People | If each's 2-digit number (4-5) is the same, but if each's 6th letter is different, add 1. | |
| — | Sub-people | If each's 6-digit code is identical, look at the classification PEOPLES OF THE WORLD, last column, opposite this code. Is each people shown there separately, separated from the other by commas? Yes = 1, No = 0. | |

Lastly, add up the numbers in the end column, to get total cultural distance.

Total cultural distance C = _____

---

which represent the largest single Christian peoples in each of the years AD 30, 1900, 1980 and 2000. In AD 30 on the birthday of the Christian church, most Christians were Biblical Jews or Hebrews (shown as CMT30 in our code). At the 3 years 1900, 1980 and 2000, the world's largest single Christian ethnolinguistic peoples were, or will be, as follows: in 1900, Russians (with 59 million Christians; coded here CEW22j); in 1980, USA Whites (with 108 million Christians; coded CEW19s); and in 2000, Latin-American Spanish-speaking Mestizos (with 173 million Christians; coded CLN29). This means that at our 4 base years, the world's largest single missionary-minded culture or people were, or will be, respectively, Biblical Jews, Russians, USA Whites, and Latin-American Mestizos; or (in terms of language) in AD 30 Aramaic/Hebrew, in 1900 Russian, in 1980 USA English, and in 2000 Spanish. Using these 4 cultures as bases or starting-points, we can measure the average cultural distance of each country by multiplying each component ethnolinguistic people in the country at each date by its cultural distance from our 4 cultures. For example, a country in 1980 composed of 90% Chinese and 10% USA Whites has an average cultural distance from USA Whites of $[(90 \times 6) + (10 \times 0)] \div 100$, which is 5.4. This distance provides an idea of the comparative cultural difficulty of the Christian task in all countries.

## CODES FOR ETHNOLINGUISTIC CLASSIFICATION

### A multi-digit code

In the classification that follows below, each ethnolinguistic people is given a 5- or 6-digit alphanumeric code (example: CEW19m) defining its race, geographical race, stylized colour, ethnolinguistic family (microrace or local race), and its own unique code number as a people. These codes are composed as follows:

*Digits*

1  *Race (stock)*
   A = Australoid
   B = Capoid
   C = Caucasian (Caucasoid)
   M = Mongolian (Mongoloid)
   N = Negro (Negroid)

2  *Geographical race*
   A = African
   E = European
   F = Afro-American
   I = American Indian
   L = Latin American
   M = Middle Eastern
   N = Indo-Iranian
   O = Oceanic
   P = Pacific
   R = Arctic Mongoloid
   S = Asian
   U = Austro-Asiatic
   Y = Early African

3  *Colour (stylized)*
   B = Black
   G = Grey
   N = Brown
   R = Red
   T = Tan
   W = White
   Y = Yellow

4-5  *Ethnolinguistic family* (or microrace, or local race)
   A 2-digit code numbered 01 to 71 defines each family uniquely (the 3 preceding letters serve merely to further classify the family by race and colour). The codes for the 71 families are given below in the classification itself.

6  *People* (or sub-family)
   In numerous cases where a family is particularly large or important, especially on the Christian scene, its code has been given here a further digit subdividing the family into its major component peoples, sub-families or other groupings. When this further digit is employed, it is added in the form of lowercase letters (a,b,c,d,e,f, etc), as shown below. The letters x, y and z, when used, refer to other remaining tribes and peoples not covered by the preceding a,b,c... series.
   This classification can be indefinitely extended to encompass all lower levels of subdivisions. The procedure is to add a seventh digit describing subdivisions of each people, where such exist (as shown in the final column in the classification); an eighth to describe each subdivision's components, where such necessitate it; and so on.

### Index of Peoples and Languages

A comprehensive index to all names in this classification is given at the end in Part 14. It enables the reader immediately to locate any name he comes across.

### Statistical analysis

Using the codes above, the ethnolinguistic compositions of each country's population, and of its affiliated Christians, were then quantified. The procedure was to add a 3-digit number in front of each code, this number being the percentage (to the first place of decimals, from 0.1% to 99.9%, omitting decimal points) of the country's total population, or its total of affiliated Christians, who belong to the people that follow it. Thus if the composition of a country's population was '80.0% Chinese, 20% British', this was converted to the 2 coded elements '800MSY42a, 200CEW19i'. When this had been done for all countries, these elements were then added to Tables 1 in the computerized database, whence the ethnolinguistic tables in Part 8 were then computed and produced.

### A ruler is necessary

The classification as shown over the next 4 pages is closely printed in order to provide the reader with as complete an overview as possible, in as compact a space as possible. The reader should use a ruler or straight edge to find his way around as quickly as he requires, both vertically and horizontally.

### Summary description

The following additional points should be noted by way of explanation and summary. (1) Names of the 5 races, 7 colours, 13 geographical races, 71 ethnolinguistic families, 432 major peoples and 8,990 constituent peoples, sub-peoples and additional ethnic groups shown here are given in their usual generally-preferred anglicized form (usually giving the singular form only and not the plural; excluding their forms in other languages; and in almost all cases omitting diacritical marks) in strictly alphabetical order by name (their codes, accordingly, are not fully in alphabetical order throughout). The ethnolinguistic families can then be seen to be numbered 01-71 in numerical sequence. (2) This entire classification gives anglicized (English) names only, together with a handful of non-English terms which have now come into English use also (e.g. Mestizo), or which are necessary here for exact identification or to avoid confusion. Prefixes for Bantu and other peoples (A-, Ama-, Ba-, Ma-, Ovi-, Wa-, &c) are omitted. A large number of all these anglicized names have equivalents in French, German, Italian, Portuguese, Spanish and other international languages, in addition to names in use in their own local languages. These names in other languages are too numerous to be included below, but are stored in our longer computerized version. In the same way, derivations and meanings of these anglicized names are not given here but in the computerized version (many in fact mean simply 'people' or 'man'); for a comprehensive reference to meanings, see the *New Encyclopædia Britannica* (1975). (3) Families (in the second column below, in boldface type) are sub-divided into their component peoples in cases where a family is particularly large or important, especially on the Christian scene. (4) The European geographical race as defined here, and the term European, include Whites who have emigrated outside Europe and the Western world for the first generation (30 years) only, but exclude Whites of the second or more generations in the Third World if they have intermarried or assimilated with Non-Whites, and who are therefore here considered to have become separate Third-World peoples by then. (5) Colour, a term from physical anthropology describing biological race characteristics, is defined here and given (in the third column) as a stylized typology of 7 terms. Where 2 or 3 terms are given (e.g. 'White/Tan/Brown'), it means that the race or family or people concerned is predominantly White but significant numbers are either Tan or Brown; only the predominant colour is included in the code. (6) For each family or people, the last column gives a selection of its major constituent peoples, sub-peoples, tribes, languages (on this classification, 7,010 on the world scene) or dialects, with (in parentheses) synonyms or alternative names in use. Slightly-different alternate spellings are only given occasionally where necessary for easy identification. (7) Names in the last column in roman type are ethnic, or are both ethnic and linguistic. Names in italics are linguistic (mother tongue) only. (8) The addition 'et alii' refers to the presence of several other groupings; the addition '&c' refers to the presence of a large number of other smaller groupings.

### Statistics, 1900-2000

For all ethnolinguistic peoples in our classification, statistics are given here in Global Tables 24 and 25, with world summary statistics in Global Tables 5 and 8. Full statistics, for all peoples, of total populations, total Christians, professing Christians, affiliated Christians, and practising Christians—all given both as absolute numbers, as percentages of their total population, and ranked in various ways—are given in the companion volume to this Encyclopedia (forthcoming).

AUSTR...

Paiwan Aborigine.

New Guinea Papuans.

CAUCASIAN.

Punjabi labourers.

CAPOID

Twa Pygmies.

Kalahari Bushman.

Arusi Galla girl.

English archbishop.

**PEOPLES OF THE WORLD.** A selection illustrating widely-different racial and cultural characteristics. The 5 races are represented here by some 15 peoples, shown in the same order as in the classification overleaf.

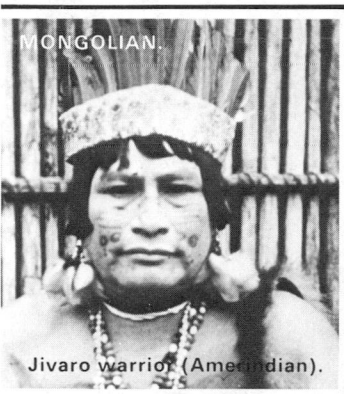

MONGOLIAN.

Jivaro warrior (Amerindian).

Korean girls.

Tibetan (Panchen Lama).

Maori parliamentarian.

NEGRO

Kabre peasant.

Yoruba apostle.

Ruandese (Tutsi king).

Kikuyu witchdoctor.

## PEOPLES OF THE WORLD. AN ETHNOLINGUISTIC CLASSIFICATION

| Code | RACE / GEOGRAPHICAL RACE / Ethnolinguistic family / *People (or sub-family)* | Colour | Main constituent cultures, peoples, additional peoples, sub-peoples, tribes, languages & dialects (in italics), alternative names or synonyms (in parentheses) |
|---|---|---|---|
| | **AUSTRALOID** (Archaic White) | GREY/BROWN | Australoid (Archaic White, Proto-Caucasoid, Classical Australoid) |
| | **AUSTRO-ASIATIC** | GREY | Aboriginals in Australasia, Southeast Asia, India; 140 *Austro-Asiatic* languages, about 360 others |
| AUG01 | **Ainu/Aborigine** | Grey | Ainu; also Ainu-like Formosan Aborigine: *Ami, Atayal, Bunun, Paiwan, Pyuma, Saisiat, Yami*; 22 languages |
| AUG02 | **Australian Aborigine** | Grey | *Arunta, Bidjandjara, Gunwingguan, Kariera, Murngin, Pama-Nyungan, Tiwi, Walbiri, Warramunga*; 260 languages |
| AUG03 | **Mon-Khmer** | Grey/Yellow | Mon-Khmer, Australoid peoples with Mongoloid admixture; over 105 languages |
| AUG03a | Khasi | Grey/Yellow | Khasi (*Standard Khasi*; Lyngngam, Synteng, War) |
| AUG03b | Khmer | Grey/Yellow | Khmer (Cambodian) |
| AUG03c | Mon | Grey/Yellow | Mon (Peguan, Talaing), Niakuol |
| AUG03d | Nicobarese | Grey/Yellow | Central (*Camorta, Katchall, Nancowry, Trinkat*), North (*Bompaka, Car, Chowra, Teressa*), South (*Coastal Great*); *Shompe* |
| AUG03z | other Mon-Khmer | Grey/Yellow | Bahnar, Bo, Boloven, Brao, Cham Re, Katu, Khmu, Ma, Mnong, Oi, Palaung, Pear, Phuteng, Sedang, So, Suai, Wa, &c |
| AUG04 | **Munda-Santal** | Grey | *Munda (Kherwari)*: Northern, Southern, Western; 29 languages |
| AUG04a | Ho | Grey | Ho (*Lankakol*), *Lohara* |
| AUG04b | Mundari | Grey | Birhor, Mundari (Kol, Horo) |
| AUG04c | Santal | Grey | Karmali (Kohle), Mahili (Mahli), Pahariya (Mal Paharia), Santal (*Santali, Satar*) |
| AUG04d | Saora | Grey | Saora (Savara, Sora) |
| AUG04z | other Munda-Santal | Grey | Asuri, Bhumij, Chenchu, Gadaba (Gutob), Geta, Juang, Kharia, Koda, Korku, Korwa, Nahari, Remo, Turi, et alii |
| AUG05 | **Negrito** (Oceanic/Asiatic Pygmoid) | Grey/Black | Aeta, Andamanese, Baluga, Kadar, Malaccan (Aslian), New Guinea Pygmy (Aiome, Ekari (Kapauku), Tapiro), Semang, Senoi |
| AUG06 | **Pre-Dravidian** | Grey | Proto-Australoid (*Pre-Dravidian* Aboriginal); 42 languages |
| AUG06a | Bhil | Grey | Bhil (*Bhili*, with over 20 dialects) |
| AUG06b | Gond | Grey | Gond (*Gondi*): *Adilalad, Betul,* Bisonhorn Maria, *Chhindwara*, Hill Maria, *Koi, Mandla,* Muria |
| AUG06c | Oraon | Grey | Oraon (Kurukh, Kurux, Uraon) |
| AUG06z | other Pre-Dravidian | Grey | Kadir, Kandh, Khond (*Kui*), Kolami, Kolarian, Kurumba, Malto, Naiki, Paniyan, et alii |
| AUG07 | **Vedda** | Grey/Brown | Vedda (Indo-Australoid, Bedda, Veddah, Veddoid, Weddo) |
| | **OCEANIC** | BROWN | Melanesian, Melanesoid, Oceanic Negro, Oceanic Negroid, Papuasian; *Heonesian;* over 1,180 languages |
| AON08 | **Fijian** | Brown | Fijian (*Bauan*), Kadavu, Rotuman |
| AON09 | **Melanesian** | Brown/Black | Melanesian (island, coastal); 380 *Oceanic Austronesian* languages, et alia |
| AON09a | New Caledonian | Brown/Black | New Caledonian: *Houailou (Wailu), Iai, Lifu (Lific), Maré (Nengone), Ponérihouen;* 18 other languages |
| AON09b | New Guinea Melanesian | Brown/Black | *Bwaidoga, Dobu, Graged,* Keopara, *Kiriwina, Motu,* Police Motu, *Tuna, Usiai, Yabem;* over 190 languages |
| AON09c | New Hebridean | Brown/Black | New Hebridean: *Efate, Epi, Malo, Mota, Nguna-Tongoa, Paama,* Tanna; 117 languages |
| AON09d | Solomoni Melanesian | Brown/Black | Solomoni: *Bambatana, Bugotu, Kerebuto, Kwaio, Lau, Maringe, Nggela, Roviana, Saa, To'abaita, Vaturanga;* about 85 languages |
| AON09e | Western Melanesian | Brown/Black | Ambonese, Ceramese, Irianese (Bonggo, Sobei, Tobati, Yamna), other Moluccan and South Moluccan (*Sarmic*); 50 languages |
| AON10 | **Papuan** | Brown | 700 Papuan (*Indo-Pacific, Non-Austronesian*) languages, 450 related to each other, another 50 isolates; Papuasian |
| AON10a | Irianese Papuan | Brown | Asmat, Bentoeni, Damal, Dani, Djabi, Jali, Marind-Anim, Sentani & 340 other tribes |
| AON10b | New Guinea Papuan (Eastern) | Brown | Awa, Chimbu, Enga, Gadsup, Gahuku, Guhu-Samane, Kiwai, New Britain Papuan, Orokaiva, Wabago, & over 450 others |
| AON10c | North Halmaheran | Brown | North Halmaheran: Galelos, Ibu, Kau, Loloda, Makian, Modole, Morotai, Pagu, Tabaru, Ternate, Tidore, Tobelo, Wai |
| AON10d | Solomoni Papuan | Brown | Solomoni Papuan: Bougainvillian, Rendova, Russell Islander, Santa Cruz, Savosavo, Vella Lavella (*Bilua*) |
| AON10e | Timorese Papuan | Brown | Alorese, Kisarese, Timorese Papuan; over 20 languages |
| AON10f | Torres Strait Islander | Brown | Torres Strait Islander: Mabuiag, Mer, Saibai, et alii |
| | **CAPOID** (Archaic African) | GREY/BROWN | Descendants of Early, Paleolithic or Prehistoric Africans |
| | **EARLY AFRICAN** | GREY/BROWN | Aboriginal descendants of Bushmanoid, Sangoan Pygmy, Pygmoid |
| BYG11 | **Khoisan** | Grey | Khoisan (Bushmanoid, *Click*): Central Khoisan (Khoe), North (Zhu), South (Kwi); about 47 languages |
| BYG11a | Bergdama | Grey | Bergdama (Damara, Haukoin, Mountain Damara) |
| BYG11b | East African Bushman | Grey | Boni, Dorobo (Asa, Okiek), Kindiga (Hadzapi, Tindiga), Manjo (Bacha, Fuga), Midgan (Ribi), Sandawe, Sanye, Teuso |
| BYG11c | Hottentot | Grey | Cape Hottentot (Grigriqua), Nama (Namaqua) |
| BYG11d | South African Bushman | Grey | Dukwe, Galikwe, Gwi, Heikum, Hiechware, Hukwe, Korana, Koroca, Kung, Namib, Naron, Nusan, Ohekwe, Tannekwe, Xam |
| BYG12 | **Pygmy** | Grey/Brown | Pygmy (Negrillo, Pygmoid): Binga (Bongo, Koa, Yaga), Central Twa, Gesera (Twa, Zigaba), Mbuti (Aka, Efe, Twides) |
| | **CAUCASIAN** (Causasoid) | WHITE/TAN/BROWN | Caucasian, Caucasoid, *Indo-European;* about 660 languages |
| | **EUROPEAN** | WHITE | European: Alpine, Armenian, Mediterranean, Nordic; about 198 languages |
| CEW13 | **Albanian** | White | Albanian (Shiptar): Gheg (Dukagjin, Malësia), Tosk (Camövia, Labëria, Myzeqe) |
| CEW14 | **Armenian** | White | Armenian (Ashksarhik, Hay, Hayq), Thrace-Phrygian |
| CEW15 | **Baltic** | White | Balt: *East Baltic, Baltic-Slavic* |
| CEW15a | Latvian | White | Latvian (Lett, *Lettish*) |
| CEW15b | Lithuanian | White | Lithuanian, *Samogit* |
| CEW16 | **Basque** | White | Basque (*Euskarian, Navarrese*) |
| CEW17 | **Caucasian** | White | Ibero-Caucasian (Paleocaucasian): about 39 languages |
| CEW17a | Adygo-Abkhazi | White | Abazinian, Abkhazian, Adyghe, Circassian (Cherkess, Karbardian), Ubykh |
| CEW17b | Dagestani | White | Aguly, Andi-Tsezi, Avar, Budukh, Dargin, Dargwa, Khinalug, Kryz, Lakk, Lezgin, Rutul, Tabasaran, Tsakhur, Udi, &c |
| CEW17c | Georgian | White | Georgian (Kartvelian), Laze (Chan, Laz, *Zan*), Mingrelian, Svan |
| CEW17d | Nakh | White | Veinakh: Bat, Chechen (Kokhchi, Shishan), Ingush (Galgai), Kist |
| CEW18 | **Celtic** | White | Celtic: Continental (Gaulish), Insular (*Brythonic*: Breton, Cornish, Welsh; *Goidelic*: Irish, Manx, Scottish) |
| CEW18a | Breton | White | Breton: *Cornouaille, Léon, Tréguier, Vannes* |
| CEW18b | Irish | White | Irish (*Gaelic, Erse*), Irish Traveller (Nomad, *Shelta*) |
| CEW18c | Scottish Gaelic | White | Scottish Gaelic (Gael, Goidel, *Scots Gaelic*) |
| CEW18d | Welsh | White | Welsh (*Cymraeg*) |
| CEW18z | other Celtic | White | Cornish, Manx |
| CEW19 | **Germanic** (Teutonic) | White | *Germanic: North Germanic* (Scandinavian), *West Germanic* (Afrikaans, Dutch, English, Flemish, Frisian, German) |
| CEW19a | Afrikaner | White | Afrikaner (*Afrikaans*, Boer) |
| CEW19b | Alsatian | White | Alsatian, Lotharingian |
| CEW19c | Anglo-Australian | White | Anglo-Australian (*English*) |
| CEW19d | Anglo-Canadian | White | Anglo-Canadian (*English*) |
| CEW19e | Anglo-New Zealander | White | Anglo-New Zealander (*English*), Pakeha |
| CEW19f | Austrian | White | Austrian (*German*), Tirolean |
| CEW19g | Danish | White | Danish (Dane) |
| CEW19h | Dutch | White | Dutch (*Netherlandic*) |
| CEW19i | English (British) | White | British: Briton, English, Scot, Scottish; many regional dialects |
| CEW19j | Faeroese | White | Faeroese (*Faroese*, Faeroe Islander) |
| CEW19k | Flemish | White | Fleming (*Flemish, Netherlandic*) |
| CEW19l | Frisian | White | Frisian: *East, North, West* |
| CEW19m | German | White | German (*East Middle, High, Low, West Middle*): Bavarian, Franconian, German-Swiss, Rhinelander, Saxon, Swabian |
| CEW19n | Icelander | White | Icelander (*Icelandic*) |
| CEW19o | Luxemburger | White | Luxemburger (*Letzeburgesch*) |
| CEW19p | Norwegian | White | Norwegian: *New Norwegian (Nynorsk, Landsmal), Dano-Norwegian (Bokmal), Russonorsk* |
| CEW19q | Swedish | White | Swedish (Swede), Finlander Swede |
| CEW19r | Ulster Irish | White | Ulster Irish (Northern Irish, English-speaking), British Irish |
| CEW19s | USA White | White | English-speaking USA White (of numerous immigrant ethnic backgrounds, but mother tongue now English) |
| CEW20 | **Greek** | White | Hellenic (*Romaic*): *Demotic Greek, Katharevusa;* Cretan, *Old Athenian,* Peloponnesian, *Tsakonian;* Greek Cypriot, Karakachan |
| CEW21 | **Latin** (Romance) | White | Latin (*Romance, Romanic, Italic*), Latin European |
| CEW21a | Catalonian | White | Catalonian (*Catalán*): Andorran, *Balearic, East Catalán, Valencian, West Catalán* |
| CEW21b | French | White | French, Franco-Swiss, metropolitan French, Monégasque; *Bourbonnais, Francien, Gallo, Orléanais,* &c |
| CEW21c | French-Canadian | White | French-Canadian (*French*) |
| CEW21d | Galician | White | Galician (*Northern Portuguese, Gallego*) |
| CEW21e | Italian | White | Italian, Italo-Swiss, Sanmarinese, Sicilian; *Gallo-Italian, Tuscan, Venetan,* &c |
| CEW21f | Moldavian | White | Moldavian (Eastern Daco-Rumanian, Bessarabian) |
| CEW21g | Portuguese | White | Portuguese: *Central, Insular, Northern, Southern* |
| CEW21h | Rhaeto-Romanian | White | Rhaeto-Romanian: Friulian, *Ladin, Rhaetian,* Romansh (Grishun, Rumantsch), Sursilvan, Sutsilvan |
| CEW21i | Romanian | White | Aromanian (Vlach, Volokh), Romanian (Rumanian): Daco-Rumanian, Transylvanian, Wallachian |
| CEW21j | Sardinian | White | Sard (Sardinian, *Sardo*): dialects *Campidanian, Gallurian, Logudorian, Sassarian* |
| CEW21k | Spanish | White | Spaniard, Spanish (*Castellano, Castilian*): Andalusian, Argonese, Asturias, Leonese, &c |
| CEW21l | Walloon | White | Walloon (*French*) |
| CEW21z | other Latin | White | Corsican, *Franco-Provençal, Gibraltarian, Istriot, Latin, Occitan (Gascon, Languedoc, Provençal),* et alii |
| CEW22 | **Slav** | White | Slav (Slavic, *Slavonic*): *East, South, West* |
| CEW22a | Bosnian | White | Bosnian (*Serbo-Croatian*) |
| CEW22b | Bulgar | White | Bulgar (*Bulgarian*), Palityan: *Central, Eastern, Northeastern, Western* |
| CEW22c | Byelorussian | White | Byelorussian (Belorussian, White Russian): *Northeastern, Northwestern, Southwestern* |
| CEW22d | Croatian | White | Croatian (Croat), *Serbo-Croatian;* Cakavian, Kajkavian |
| CEW22e | Czech | White | Czech: Bohemian, Moravian, Silesian; Hanak, Horak, *Yalach,* Zahorak |
| CEW22f | Kashubian | White | Kashubian (Pomeranian), Slovincian |
| CEW22g | Macedonian | White | Macedonian: *Armin* (Macedo-Rumanian), Bulgarian Macedonian |
| CEW22h | Montenegrin | White | Montenegrin (*Serbo-Croatian*) |
| CEW22i | Polish | White | Polish: *Great Polish, Little Polish, Masurich, Mazovian* |
| CEW22j | Russian | White | Russian, *Great Russian: Central, Northern, Southern* |

| | | | |
|---|---|---|---|
| CEW22k | Ruthenian | White | Ruthenian (Carpatho-Russian, Carpatho-Ukrainian, Rusin, Ruthene) |
| CEW22l | Serbian | White | Serbian (Serb, *Serbo-Croatian*, *Shtokavian*); Torlakian |
| CEW22m | Slovak | White | Slovak: *Central*, *Eastern*, *Western* |
| CEW22n | Slovene | White | Slovene (Slovenian): *Northwestern*, *Western* |
| CEW22o | Sorb | White | Sorb (Lusatian, Sorabian, *Sorbian* (*East*, *High*, *Low*), Wendish) |
| CEW22p | Ukrainian | White | Ukrainian: Carpathian, *Little Russian*, *Northern*, *Podolian*, *Ruthenian*, *Southeastern*, *Southwestern*, Volhynian |
| | INDO-IRANIAN | BROWN/TAN/WHITE | Caucasoid peoples from Iran to Indian subcontinent; over 290 *Indo-Aryan* (*Indic*), *Iranian*, *Dravidian* languages |
| CNN23 | **Dravidian** | Brown/Black | Dravidian (Indo-Dravidian, Paleo-Indian): 50 languages |
| CNN23a | Kanarese | Brown/Black | Kanarese (*Kannada*): Badaga |
| CNN23b | Malayali | Brown/Black | Malabari, Malayali (*Malayalam*), Paliyan, Paniyan |
| CNN23c | Tamil | Brown/Black | Tamil: Ceylon Tamil, Indian Tamil, Kling (SE Asia); scripts *Grantha*, *Vattelluttu* |
| CNN23d | Telugu | Brown/Black | Andhra, *Telugu* (Gentoo) |
| CNN23z | other Dravidian | Brown/Black | Brahui (Kur Galli), Ceylon Moor, Coorg, Irula, Koya, Mannan, Parji, Toda, Tulu, Urali, &c |
| CNT24 | **Iranian** | Tan/White | Iranian (*Iranic*): Afghani, Baluchi, Kurdish, Ossetian, Persian, Tadzhik, et alii |
| CNT24a | Afghani | Tan/White | Pathan (Pashtun, *Pushtu*): Afridi, Durrani, Ghilzai, Mahsud, Mangal, Parachi, Shinwari, Waziri, Yusufzai, & 55 other tribes |
| CNT24b | Baluchi | Tan/White | Baluchi (Baluch, Baloch): *Kechi*, *Lotuni*, Makrani, *Rakhshani*, *Sarawani* |
| CNT24c | Kurdish | Tan/White | Kurd (Kurdish): *Akre*, *Amadiyah*, *Dahuk*, *Kermanji*, *Kermanshahi*, Sulaimani (*Mukri*), *Zaza* |
| CNT24d | Nuristani | Tan/White | Nuristani: Ashkun, Kafiri, Kati, Nangalami, Prasun, Tregami, Waigeli, Wai-ala, &c |
| CNT24e | Ossetian | Tan/White | Ossetian (Ossete, Ossetin, *Ossetic: Digor*, *Iron*, *Tagaur*, *Tual*), *Jassic* |
| CNT24f | Persian | Tan/White | Persian (*Dari*, *Farsi*): *Gabri*, *Gazi*, *Khunsari*, *Natanzi*, *Sivandi*, *Soi*, *Tati*, *Vafsi* |
| CNT24g | Tadzhik | Tan/White | Tadzhik: Farsiwan, Mountain Tajik, Pamir Tadzhik (Bartang, Ishkashin, Khuv, Vakhan, Yazgulem), Selekur, Yaghnobi |
| CNT24z | other Iranian | Tan/White | Bakhtiari, Firozkohi, Galesh, Gilaki, Hazara-Berberi, Jamshidi, Luri, Mazanderani, Munji, Shughni, Talysh, Teymur, et alii |
| CNN25 | **North Indian** | Brown/Tan | North Indian (Indic, *Indo-Aryan*); Caribbean East Indian, Indo-Mauritian, Indo-Pakistani; subdivided into 30,000 castes |
| CNN25a | Assamese | Brown/Tan | Assamese Bengali (Eastern, Western) |
| CNN25b | Bengali | Brown/Tan | Bengali (*Calit-Bhasa*, *Sadhu-Bhasa*): caste Bengali (Arzal, Ashraf, &c), outcaste (Namasudra, Paliya, &c); Rajbansi, &c |
| CNN25c | Bihari | Brown/Tan | non-tribal Bihari: *Bhojpuri*, *Magahi*, *Maithili* (*Tirhutia*), *Nagpuri* (*Sadani*) |
| CNN25d | Goanese | Brown/Tan | Goanese (*Konkani*, *Gomantaki; Bankoti*) |
| CNN25e | Gujarati | Brown/Tan | Gujarati: Baria, Gamadia, Gramya Koli (Kohli), Patidar, Patnuli, Tarimuki, &c |
| CNN25f | Gypsy | Brown/Tan | Gypsy (Rom, *Romany*); tribes: Gitano, Kalderash, Lambadi (Banjuri), Lovara, Manush (Sinti), Tschourara |
| CNN25g | Hindi | Brown/Tan | Hindi: *Eastern* (*Awadhi*, *Bagheli*, *Chhattisgarhi*, *Kosadi*, *Kosali*), *Western* (*Braj Bhasa*, *Bundeli*, *Kanauji*) |
| CNN25h | Jat | Brown/Tan | Awan (*Lahnda*), Jat (Jhat, *Jatki*, *Multani*) |
| CNN25i | Kashmiri | Brown/Tan | Dard (*Dardic*): Dogra, *Kafiri* (*Western Dardic*), Kho, *Khowari* (*Central Dardic*), *Kishtwari*, *Kohistani*, *Pashai*, *Poguli*, *Rambani*, *Shina* |
| CNN25j | Marathi | Brown/Tan | Marathi: Dekini, Desi, Kunbi, Maratha, Poona |
| CNN25k | Nepalese | Brown/Tan | Nepalese: Chambiali, *Garhwali*, *Gorkhali*, Khas-kura, Kulu, Nepali, Pahari (Jaunsari, Kumauni, Palpa, Parbate), Tarai, Tharu |
| CNN25l | Oriya | Brown/Tan | Oriya (Odri, Uriya, Utkali): Bhatri, Halbi, Mughalbandi |
| CNN25m | **Parsi** | **Brown/Tan** | Parsi (Parsee) (*Gujarati*) |
| CNN25n | Punjabi | Brown/Tan | Punjabi: *Western* (*Lahnda*), *Gurmukhi*, *Dogri-Kongri*, *Majhi* |
| CNN25o | Rajasthani | Brown/Tan | Rajasthani, Rajput, Thakur: *Ahirwati*, *Harauti*, *Jaipuri*, *Malvi*, *Marwari*, *Mewati*, *Nimadi* |
| CNN25p | Sindhi | Brown/Tan | Sindhi: *Kachchi*, *Lari*, *Lasi*, *Macharia*, *Saraiki*, Sindh, *Thareli*, *Vicholi* |
| CNN25q | Sinhalese | Brown/Tan | Sinhalese (*Cingalese;* Low-Country, Up-Country or Kandyan), Maldivian (Divehi) |
| CNN25r | Urdu | Brown/Tan | Urdu (*Hindustani*, *Khari Boli*): Bangaru, Deccani (*Dakhni*), Deswali, Hariani |
| CNN25z | other North Indian | Brown/Tan/White | Anglo-Indian, Arain, Burusho (*Burushaski*), Ceylon Burgher, Gujar, Julaha, Lamani (Labhani), Lohar, Mussalli, Tarkhan, &c |
| | LATIN AMERICAN | TAN/BROWN/WHITE | Europeans resident in Latin America for over one generation, or partially assimilated, or of mixed race |
| CLT26 | **Latin-American White** (Branco) | Tan/White | Portuguese-speaking White Brazilian of pure Portuguese or other European origin |
| CLT27 | **Latin-American White** (Blanco) | Tan/White | Spanish-speaking White of pure Spanish or other European origin (Argentinian, Costa Rican, Puerto Rican, &c) |
| CLN28 | **Mestiço** (Portuguese) | Brown | Mestiço: mixed Portuguese/Amerindian/African Negro; Caboclo (Portuguese/Amerindian), Mulatto (more White than Black) |
| CLN29 | **Mestizo** (Spanish) | Brown | Chicano, Chilote, Cholo, Ladino, Mestizo, *Pachuco;* mixed Spanish/Amerindian/African Negro, in Latin America and USA |
| | MIDDLE EASTERN | TAN/White | Semito-Hamitic (*Afrasian*, *Afro-Asiatic*, *Erythraic*, *Erythraen*, *Hamito-Semitic*, *Lisramic*) |
| CMT30 | **Arab** (*Arabic*) | Tan/White | Bedouin, Copt, Egyptian, Levantine, Maghreb, Palestinian, Saharan (Baggara, Moor, Shoa), Sudanese, Yemeni, Zanzibari, &c |
| CMT31 | **Assyrian** | Tan/White | Aissor, Aramaean, Chaldean, *Elkoosh: East Aramaic* (*Eastern Neo-Assyrian*, *Syriac*), *Neo-Syriac*, *Targumic*, *West Aramaic* |
| CMT32 | **Berber** | Tan/White | *Berbero-Libyan* (Northern Hamite): Kabyle, Rif, Shawiya, Shluh, Tamazigt, Tuareg, Udalan, Zenati: 38 languages, 110 tribes |
| CMT32a | Arabized Berber | Tan/White | Arabized, Arabic-speaking, detribalized Berber |
| CMT32b | Beraber | Tan/White | Beraber (*Tamazigt*): Idrassen, Ndhir, Seri, Serruchen, Sokhman, Yafelman, Zaer, Zayan, Zemmur |
| CMT32c | Kabyle | Tan/White | Kabyle (Bergus, Sanhajah, *Zouaouah*) |
| CMT32d | Oasis Berber | Tan/White | Oasis Berber: Figig, Filala, Gadames, Jalo, Jofra, Mzab, Siwa, Tuat, Wargla, &c |
| CMT32e | Rif | Tan/White | Rif (Riffian): Metalsa, Znassen, & 17 other tribes |
| CMT32f | Shawiya | Tan/White | Shawiya (*Chaouyah*) |
| CMT32g | Shluh | Tan/White | Shleuh (Shilha, *Masmudah*, *Tashelhayt*): Aghbar, Fruga, Glawa, Hawara, Massat, Susiua, & 30 others |
| CMT32h | Tuareg | Tan/White | Tuareg (*Tamahaq*, *Tamashek*): Ahaggaren, Air, Antessar, Asben, Aulliminden, Azjer, Ifora, Udalan |
| CMT32i | Zenaga | Tan | Zenaga: Allush, Girganke, Mbarek, Meshduf, Nasser, Sirifou, Tichit |
| CMT32z | other Berber | Tan/White | Atta, Drawa, Guanche, Jerba, Menasser, Nefusa, Uregu, Warain, Zekara, et alii |
| CMT33 | **Cushitic** | Tan/Brown | Cushitic (Eastern Hamite, *Hamitic*): *Eastern Cushitic*, *Southern Cushitic*, *West Cushitic* (*Omotic*) |
| CMT33a | Agau | Tan/Brown | Awiya, Awngi, Bilin (Bitin), Bogos, Damot, Falasha (Kaila), Kamta (Hamta), Kemant (Qemant), Khamir (Kamir), Kwara |
| CMT33b | Galla | Tan/Brown | Galla (*Oromo*): Arusi, Bararetta, Boran, Gabbra, Ittu, Kwottu, Macha, Rendille, Salale, Tulama (Shoa Galla), Wallega, Wallo |
| CMT33c | Iraqw | Tan/Brown | Iraqw (Asa, Erokh, Iraku, Mbulu, Ngomwia) |
| CMT33d | Sidamo | Tan/Brown | Bako, Burji, Darasa, Gibe, Gimira, Hadya, Janjero, Kaffa, Kambatta, Konso-Geleba, Maji, Ometo, Reshiat, Walamo, &c |
| CMT33e | Somali | Tan/Brown | Darod, Digil, Dir, Geri, Hawiya, Ishaak, Issa (Esa), Mijertein, Ogaden, Rahanwein, Sab, West Somali |
| CMT33z | other Cushitic | Tan/Brown | Beja (Ababda, Amarar, Amer, Bisharin, Bogo, Hadendowa), Burungi, Danakil (Afar), Goroa, Mbugu, Saho, Wasi, &c |
| CMT34 | **Ethiopic** | Tan/Brown | Ethiopic (*Semitic*, *Ethiosemitic*, *African Semitic*) |
| CMT34a | Amhara | Tan/Brown | Amhara (*Amharic*), Argobba, Harari (Adere); Abyssinian |
| CMT34b | Tigrai | Tan/Brown | Tigrai (*Tigrinya: Habesha*) |
| CMT34c | Tigre | Tan/Brown | Tigre (Hasi, Xassa) |
| CMT34z | other Ethiopic | Tan/Brown | Fuga, Geez (Ethiopic), Gogot (Dobi), Gurage, Maskan, Muher, Soddo, et alii |
| CMT35 | **Jewish** | Tan/White | *Hebrew*: Ashkenazi (American Jew, German Jew, Western, *Yiddish*), Maghreb (Oriental), Sefardi (Judeo-Spanish, Ladino) |
| CMT36 | **Maltese** | Tan/White | Maltese |
| | | | |
| | MONGOLIAN (Mongoloid, Asiatic) | YELLOW/RED | Mongolian (Mongoloid, Asiatic, Oriental) |
| | AMERICAN INDIAN | RED | Amerindian (American Mongoloid, *Amerind*), including mixed-blood (Métis, Half-Breed); about 1,700 languages |
| MIR37 | **Central Amerindian** | Red | Meso-American: *Azteco-Tanoan*, *Mayan*, *Oto-Manguean*, Pueblo Indian, *Uto-Aztecan;* about 270 languages |
| MIR37a | Aztec | Red | Aztec (*Nahuatl*), Nahua (Mexicano, Mexicanero), Pipil |
| MIR37b | Maya | Red | Chol, Chontal, Chorti, Huastec, Lacandón, Mam, Quiché (Cakchiquel, Kekchí, Uspantec), Teco, Tzeltal, Tzotzil, Yucatec |
| MIR37c | Mixtec | Red | Amuzgo, Cuicatec, Mixtec, Trique |
| MIR37d | Otomí | Red | Chichimec (Jonaz), Ixtenco, Matlatzinca, Mazahua, *Mezquital*, North & South Pame, Ocuiltec, Otomí, *Sierra*, *Tenango* |
| MIR37e | Part-Indian | Red | Indian of mixed blood: Half-Indian, Semi-Indian (non-tribal, detribalized) |
| MIR37f | Zapotec | Red | Chatino, Zapotec (Juárez, South Mountain, Valley, Villalta): *Choapán*, *Etla*, *Istmo*, *Mitla*, *Rincon* |
| MIR37z | other Central Amerindian | Red | Chinantecan, Huichol, Lenca, Mazatec, Miskito, Mixé-Zoque, Sumu, Tarahumara, Tarascan, Tepehua, Totonac, Yaqui, &c |
| MIR38 | **Northern Amerindian** | Red | Native Indian (pure Amerindian, registered American Indian); about 195 languages (57 families); also Indian of mixed blood |
| MIR38a | North American Indian | Red | *Algonkian* (Ojibwa), Creek, *Hoka-Siouan* (Cherokee, Sioux), Iroqois, *Na-Dene* (*Athabaskan*: Apache, Navajo), *Penutian*, &c |
| MIR38b | Part-Indian (Métis) | Red/White | Indian/White, Indian/French, Métis (Mixed-Blood, Half-Breed, Half-Caste), unregistered or non-status Indian; *Creole* |
| MIR39 | **Southern Amerindian** | Red | *Andean-Equatorial; Arawakan*, *Cariban*, *Macro-Chibchan*, *Macro-Ge*, *Quechumaran*, *Tucanoan*, *Tupian:* over 1,230 languages |
| MIR39a | Arawak | Red | Arawak (Arowak): Bauré, Campa, Goajiro, Machiguenga, Mojo, Wapishana, Wiriná, & 120 other languages |
| MIR39b | Aymara | Red | Aymara (Oruro), Cauqui (Jaqaru), Lupacca, Ubina |
| MIR39c | Carib | Red | Bakairi, Cannibal, Carib, Cariban, Chocó, Galibi, Guicuru, Island Carib, Makushí, Trio, Waiwai, & 85 others |
| MIR39d | Jungle Amerindian | Red | Auca, Chapacura, Jivaro (Achuale, Murato, &c), Pano, Saparo, Taruma, Tucano, Ve, Witoto; & over 400 others |
| MIR39e | Lowland Amerindian | Red | Bari, Chibcha (Cayapa, Cuna, Guaymí), Chon, Emerillon, Guaraní, Lengua, Mataco, Oyampi, Palikur, Toba, Tupi, Wayana, &c |
| MIR39f | Mapuche | Red | Araucanian, Mapuche: Divihet, Huilliche, Manzanero, Mapudungu, Pehuenche, Picunche, Taluhet |
| MIR39g | Quechua | Red | Quechua: Almaguero, Ancash, Ayacucho, Cajamarca, Huánuco, Junín, Lamano, Ucayali, & 28 others |
| MIR39z | other Southern Amerindian | Red | Over 400 other tribes and languages unrelated to the 7 major language groups; also Half-Indian |
| | ARCTIC MONGOLOID | YELLOW | Arctic, Arctic Mongoloid, Eskimoid |
| MRY40 | **Eskimo-Aleut** | Yellow | Aleut, *Eskaleut*, Eskimo |
| MRY40a | Aleut | Yellow | Aleut (Unangan): *Atka*, *Attuan*, *Unalaskan* |
| MRY40b | Eskimo | Yellow | Eskimo (Inuit): Greenlander (*Greenlandic*), *Inupik* (*Inuk*), Polar Eskimo, Siberian Eskimo (Yuit), *Yupik* (*Yuk*) |
| | ASIAN | YELLOW | Asian, Asiatic (Classical Mongoloid, East Asiatic) |
| MSY41 | **Altaic** | Yellow | Altaic (Altayan): Mongolian, *Tungus-Manchu*, *Turkic* (*Karluk*, *Hunnic*, *Oghuz*); over 60 languages |
| MSY41a | Azerbaijani | Yellow | Azerbaijani (Azerbaijanian, Azeri): *Airym*, *Aynallu*, Karapapakh, *Qasqay*, et alii |
| MSY41b | Bashkir | Yellow | Bashkir: *Burzhan*, *Kuvakan*, *Yurmaty* |
| MSY41c | Chuvash | Yellow | Chuvash (*Anatri*, *Viryal*) |
| MSY41d | Gagauz | Yellow | Gagauz (*Gagauzi*) |
| MSY41e | Kazakh | Yellow | Kazakh (Hasako, Qazag, Qazagi) |
| MSY41f | Khalka-Mongol | Yellow | Mongolian: Bargu, Chakhar, Dariganga, Khalka-Mongol, Kharchin, Meng, Ordos, Ujumuchin, Urat |
| MSY41g | Kirgiz | Yellow | Kirgiz (Kirghiz, Kirghizi, Koerhkossu) |
| MSY41h | Tatar | Yellow | Tatar (Tartar): Central, Mishar (Western), Uralian, Siberian Tatar (Baraba, Ishim, Tara, Tom, Tura), &c |
| MSY41i | Tungus-Manchu | Yellow | Manchu-Tungus: Amur, Even (Lamut), Manchu, Nanai (Gold, Hoche, Olcha), Orochon, Sibo, Tungus (Evenki, Solon) |
| MSY41j | Turkish | Yellow/Tan | Turkish (*Osmanli*): Anatolian Turk (including Yuruk), Asian Turk, Black Sea Turk, Rumelian Turk |
| MSY41k | Turkmen | Yellow | Turkmen (Turkman, Turkoman): Ersari, Kizilbash, Sarak, Tekke |
| MSY41l | Uzbek | Yellow | Uzbek (*Uzbeki*): Kypchak, Lockhay, Oghuz, Qurama, Sart |
| MSY41m | Yakut | Yellow | Yakut (Dolgan, Jeko, Sakha) |
| MSY41y | other Mongolian | Yellow | Bayat, Buryat, Dahur (Dagur), Darkhat, Kalmyk, Mogul, Oyrat (Altai), Paongan, Santa, Tu (Mongour), Tunghsiang, &c |
| MSY41z | other Turkic | Yellow/Tan | Afshar, Kajar, Karaim, Karachay, Kara-Kalpak, Khakas, Khoton, Kumyk, Nogay, Shahseven, Tuvinian, Uighur, &c |
| MSY42 | **Chinese** | Yellow | Chinese (*Sinitic*), including diaspora Chinese (Totok, &c) and overseas non-Chinese-speaking (Peranakan, &c); 68 languages |
| MSY42a | Han Chinese | Yellow | Han: *Mandarin*, Cantonese (Yüeh), Hakka, Hsiang (Hunanese), Kan, Min, Minnan (Amoy-Swatow, Hoklo, Taiwanese), Wu |
| MSY42b | Hui | Yellow | Hui (Dungan) (*Mandarin*-speaking): Ho, Hui-tze, Hwei, Khuei, Panghse, Panthay (Panthe) |
| MSY43 | **Eurasian** | Yellow/White | Asian/European: Anglo-Burmese, Anglo-Chinese, Injerto (Latin American White/Chinese or Japanese), Macanese, *Tay Boi* |
| MSY44 | **Indo-Malay** | Yellow | Indonesian-Malayan (Oceanic & Southern Mongoloid, *Western Austronesian*, *Indonesian*, *Hesperonesian*), Chamic |

| | | | |
|---|---|---|---|
| MSY44a | Balinese | Yellow | Balinese |
| MSY44b | Batak | Yellow | Batak: Angkola, Dairi, Karo, Mandailing, Pakpak, Simalungun, Toba |
| MSY44c | Buginese | Yellow | Buginese (De, Sindjai) |
| MSY44d | Chamorro | Yellow | Chamorro (Guamanian) |
| MSY44e | Iban | Yellow | Iban (Sea Dayak) |
| MSY44f | Ilocan | Yellow | Ilocan (*Ilocano, Iloko*) |
| MSY44g | Javanese | Yellow | Javanese (*Basa Kedatan, Madhya, Ngoko, Pegon*): *Banjuwangi, Cheribon, Indramaju, Tegal, Tengger,* &c |
| MSY44h | Madurese | Yellow | Madurese: *Bangkalan, Bawean, Pamekasan, Sumenep,* &c |
| MSY44i | Makassarese | Yellow | Makassarese (Tawna): Selajar, Tonthian, Turatea |
| MSY44j | Malagasy | Yellow | Antaisaka, Antandroy, Bara, Betsileo, Betsimisaraka, Mahafaly, Merina, Sakalava, Sihanaka, Tanala, Tsimihety |
| MSY44k | Malay | Yellow | *Bahasa Indonesia,* Cham-Malay, Malay: *Baba Malay, Bahasa Malay, Mergui, Pasemah, Pattani, Selung,* &c |
| MSY44l | Minahasan | Yellow | Menadonese, Minahasan (*Ton*): Mongondow, Ratahan, Tombulu, Tomini, Tondano, Tonsawang, Tontemboan: 15 languages |
| MSY44m | Palawan | Yellow | Babuyan, Batah, Palawan (*Palawano*), Tagbanwa |
| MSY44n | Sundanese | Yellow | Sundanese: *Banten, Priangan* |
| MSY44o | Tagalog | Yellow | Tagalog (*Pilipino*) |
| MSY44p | Toraja | Yellow | Toraja (Koro, Palu, Poso, Sadang): 25 languages |
| MSY44q | Visayan | Yellow | Visayan (Bisayan, *Cebuano*): Constantino, Hiligaynon (Ilongo), Kantilan, Samaran (Waray-Waray), Surigaonon |
| MSY44x | other Filipino | Yellow | Bicol, Bontoc (Igorot), Ibanag, Ifugao, Magindanao, Maranao, Pampangan, Pangasinan, Sulu-Samal; & 100 others |
| MSY44y | other Indonesian | Yellow | Achinese, Banjarese, Dayak, Dusun (Kadazan), Kenyah, Lampong, Minangkabau, Nias, Sasak, Timorese; & 250 others |
| MSY44z | other Malaysian | Yellow | Bisaya, Cham, Jarai, Kayan, Kedayan, Kelabit, Melanau, Murut, Orang-Laut (Bajau, Moken, Sea Gypsy, Sekah), Tagal; & 50 others |
| MSY45 | **Japanese** | Yellow | Japanese, Okinawan, Ryukyuan; *Eastern Altaic* |
| MSY45a | Japanese | Yellow | Japanese (Nipponese), Japanese-American (Issei, Kibei, Nisei, Sansei): *Nan-oo, Hoku-oo, Satsuma,* & many other dialects |
| MSY45b | Ryukyuan | Yellow | Ryukyuan: Central (Okinawan, *Luchu*), Northern (Amami), Southern (Miyako, Sakishima), *Hogan* |
| MSY46 | **Korean** | Yellow | Korean (Hangul & Choson Muntcha alphabets); 6 dialects: Central, Cheju-do (Southern), NE, NW, SE, SW |
| MSY47 | **Miao-Yao** | Yellow | Meo-Yao: Kelao, Lakwa, Lati, Miao (Meo, Hmong, Hmu), She (Sho), Yao |
| MSY47 | Miao | Yellow | Chi-lao (Kelao), Miao: Black Meo, Blue Meo, Hwa (Flowered) Meo, Red Meo, Striped Meo, White Meo; 80 different groups |
| MSY47b | Yao | Yellow | Laka, Punu, She (Sho), Yao (Iu Mien, Kim Mien, Lingnan Yao, Man, Yu Mien) |
| MSY48 | **Paleoasiatic** | Yellow | Aboriginal Siberian (Paleosiberian, *Hyperborean*): Chukchi, Gilyak, Itelmen, Kerek, Kett, Koryak, Nivkh, Yukaghir (Odul) |
| MSY49 | **Tai** | Yellow | *Kam-Tai* (*Daic*), Thai-Chuang Tai, Tai-Kadai: *Central, Northern, Southwestern Tai* |
| MSY49a | Chuang | Yellow | *N & C Tai:* Chinese Nung, Chuang (Zhuang), Chungcha, Molao, Thai Nung, Padi, Phula, Tho, Tu, Tudi, Tujen, Tulao, Wuming |
| MSY49b | Lao | Yellow | Lao (Northeastern Thai, Thai Isan, Thai Lao) |
| MSY49c | Shan | Yellow | Shan: Chinese Shan (Tai Dau), Khamti (Ahom), Ngiaw, Shan-Bama (Ngio), Tai Nui, Tai Yai |
| MSY49d | Thai | Yellow | Thai (Central Thai, Khon-Thai, Siamese), Northern Thai (Kammyang), Southern Thai |
| MSY49z | other Tai | Yellow | Be, Black Tai, Giai, Kadai, Kam, Khun, Li, Lu, Neua, Nhang, Phutai, Puyi, Red Tai, Sek, Tay, White Tai, Yuan |
| MSY50 | **Tibeto-Burmese** | Yellow | Tibeto-Burmese (*Tibeto-Burman*), *Gyarung-Mishmi,* Himalayan; over 240 languages |
| MSY50a | Bhotia | Yellow | Bhotia (Bhote, Bhutia, Bhutanese, *Dzongkha*), Sikkimese |
| MSY50b | Burmese | Yellow | Burmese: Arakan, Bama, Burman, Maghi, Tenasserim |
| MSY50c | Chin | Yellow | Asho, Chin, Khumi, Kuki Chin (*Kukish*), Laizo Chin, Mru, Ngawn, Saizang, Siyin, Teizang, Tiddim, Zo, Zomi, Zotung |
| MSY50d | Garo | Yellow | Deori (Chutiya), Garo (Bodo), Hajang, Koch |
| MSY50e | Gurung | Yellow | Gurung, Gurung Gurkha |
| MSY50f | Kachin | Yellow | Kachin: Atzi, Maru, Norra, Nung, Rawang, Singpho (Chingpo, Jinghpaw) |
| MSY50g | Karen | Yellow | Red Karen (Bghai, Bre, Bwe, Geba, Kayah, Padaung, Yinbaw, Zayein), White Karen (Pa-O (Taungthu), Pwo, Sgaw Karen) |
| MSY50h | Kirati | Yellow | Rai, Kirati, Rai Kirati; Athpare, Chamling, Khaling, Saam, Sampange, Thulunge |
| MSY50i | Lahu | Yellow | Hani, Lahu (I, Laku, Mussuh, Nakhi (Moso), No), Lolo (Ho, Kopu, Laka, Nosu, Xa), Piseka, Tuchia, Wu-man |
| MSY50j | Lepcha | Yellow | Lepcha (Rong, Rongke) |
| MSY50k | Limbu | Yellow | Limbu (Chang, Monpa, Subah, Tsong): Fagurai, Fedopia, Tamarkholea |
| MSY50l | Lisu | Yellow | Lisu (Hwa (Yawyin), Lasaw, Lishaw): Black Lisu, Flowery Lisu, Shisham, White Lisu |
| MSY50m | Lushai | Yellow | Lushai (Mizo), Mara (Lakher) |
| MSY50n | Magar | Yellow | Gurkha, Magar |
| MSY50o | Manipuri | Yellow | Manipuri: Meithei, & 25 scheduled hill tribes (Empeo, Kabui, Khoirao, Kwoireng, Maram, et alii) |
| MSY50p | Naga | Yellow | Angami, Ao, Chakesang, Chakru, Chang, Konyak, Lhota, Naga (*Tangsa*), Pochuri, Rengma, Sema, Zemi-Zeliang, Zheza |
| MSY50q | Sherpa | Yellow | Sherpa |
| MSY50r | Tibetan | Yellow | *Bodic*: *Central* (*Lhasa*), *Northern, Southern, Western*; Balti, Bod, Bodpa, Kamba, Ladakhi, Lahuli, Panaka, Tangut, Tsang, Zangskari |
| MSY50s | Tripuri | Yellow | Chakma, Magh, Riang, Tipura (Tipera), Tripuri, Usipi |
| MSY50z | other Tibeto-Burmese | Yellow | Akha, Bawm, Dafla, Hmar, Kachari, Loba, Mung, Nasi, Newari, Nu, Pai, Palaychi, Pyen, Sunwar, Tamang, Yi, &c |
| MSW51 | **Uralian** | White/Yellow | Uralic race (a Caucasoid/Mongoloid cline): *Finno-Ugric,* Neoasiatic, *Uralic;* 3 families: Finnish, Magyar (*Ob-Ugric*), Samoyed |
| MSW51a | Estonian | White | Estonian: *Setu, Tallinn* (*Reval*), *Tartu* (*Dorpat*); *Vod* |
| MSW51b | Finnish | White | Finnish: *Hame, Savo* |
| MSW51c | Karelian | White | Karelian, Ludic, Olonets, Tver |
| MSW51d | Komi | White | Komi (Zyryan): Komi-Permyak, Yazva |
| MSW51e | Lapp | White/Yellow | Lapp (Lopari, Saamian): Inari, Kola, Lule, Pite, Ruija, Skolt, Southern, Ume |
| MSW51f | Livonian | White | Livonian (*Eastern, Western*), Liv, Kurlyad |
| MSW51g | Magyar | White | Magyar (Hungarian), Csango, Siculi |
| MSW51h | Mari | White | Mari (Cheremis): *High Mari, Low Mari* |
| MSW51i | Mordvin | White | Erzya (*Erza*), Moksha, Mordvin (*Mordoff*, Mordovian, Mordva, Mordvinian) |
| MSW51j | Samoyed | White/Yellow | Samoyed: Enets (Yenisei), Kamas, Nenets (Nentsy, Yurak), Nganasan (Tavgi), Selkup (Ostyak-Samoyed) |
| MSW51k | Udmurt | White | Udmurt (*Kalmez, Votyak*) |
| MSW51z | other Finno-Ugric | White/Yellow | Ingrian, Khanti (Ostyak), Mansi (Vogul), Ob Ugrian, Veps, Votic, et alii |
| MSY52 | **Viet-Muong** | Yellow | Muong, Vietnamese (Kinh, Tonkinese) |
| MSY52a | Muong | Yellow | Muong (Viet-Muong): Pi, Thang, Tong, Wang |
| MSY52b | Vietnamese | Yellow | Vietnamese (Annamese, Cochinchinese, Ching, Kinh, *Quoc-ngu,* Tonkinese) |
| MSY52z | other Viet-Muong | Yellow | Arem, Hung Khong Kheng, May, Nguon, Sach, Tay Pong, et alii |
| | PACIFIC | YELLOW/WHITE | Pacific Islander (*Eastern Austronesian, Oceanic*) |
| MPY53 | **Euronesian** | Yellow/White | European/Austronesian: *Bislama,* Filipino Mestizo, *Hawaiian Pidgin, Neo-Melanesian* (*Pidgin*), Part-Samoan, Pitcairner, &c |
| MPY54 | **Micronesian** | Yellow/Black | Micronesian: *Nuclear Micronesian* (Gilbertese, Marshallese, Ponapese, Trukese, Ulithian), Nauruan, Yapese; 18 languages |
| MPY54a | Gilbertese | Yellow/Black | Gilbertese |
| MPY54b | Marshallese | Yellow/Black | Marshallese (*Ebon; Ralik, Ratak*) |
| MPY54c | Nauruan | Yellow/Black | Nauruan |
| MPY54d | Ponapese | Yellow/Black | Ponapese (Ponapean) |
| MPY54e | Trukese | Yellow/Black | Trukese (*Ruk; Faichuk*) |
| MPY54f | Ulithian | Yellow/Black | Ulithian (*Fais, Ngulu, Sonsoral, Sorol*) |
| MPY54g | Yapese | Yellow/Black | Yapese |
| MPY54z | other Micronesian | Yellow/Black | Banaban, Carolinian, Kusaiean, Mortlock, Palauan, Wolean, et alii |
| MPY55 | **Polynesian** | Yellow/White | Polynesian: Hawaiian, Maori, Marquesan, Samoan, Tahitian, Tongan, Uvean; about 34 languages |
| MPY55a | Hawaiian | Yellow/White | Hawaiian, Neo-Hawaiian |
| MPY55b | Maori | Yellow/White | Maori (New Zealand Maori) |
| MPY55c | Marquesan | Yellow/White | Marquesan: Northwest Marquesan, Southeast Marquesan |
| MPY55d | Rarotongan | Yellow/White | Cook Islands Maori (Cook Islander, Rarotongan), Manohiki, Mauke, Mitiaro, Pukapukan, Rakahanga |
| MPY55e | Samoan | Yellow/White | Samoan |
| MPY55f | Tahitian | Yellow/White | Tahitian, *Neo-Tahitian, Rurutu* |
| MPY55g | Tongan | Yellow/White | Tongan (*Tonga-Uvea*): *Niuafo'ou, Niuatoputapu* |
| MPY55h | Tuamotuan | Yellow/White | Tuamotuan (Pa'umotuan), Napukan |
| MPY55i | Uvean | Yellow/White | Uvean (Wallisian) |
| MPY55z | other Polynesian | Yellow/White | Futunan, Niuean, Outlier, Solomoni (Nukuria, Pilheni, Rennellese, Sikaiana, Tikopian), Tokelauan, Tubuaian, Tuvaluan, &c |
| | | | |
| | NEGRO (Negroid, Equatorial) | BLACK | Negro (Negroid, Equatorial, Black) |
| | AFRICAN | BLACK | African: Congoid, Nigritic, *Niger-Congo* (1,450 languages), *Nilo-Saharan Macro-Sudanic* (210 languages); about 1,660 languages |
| NAB56 | **Bantoid** | Black | Bantoid (=Bantu-like) *Broad Bantu, Benue-Congo;* about 380 languages |
| NAB56a | Central Bantoid (*Gur, Voltaic*) | Black | Bariba, Birifor Bobo, Busa, Dagari, Dogon, Grunshi, Gurma, Kabre, Lobi, Moba, Mossi, Senufo, Somba, Tem, Wala; 85 languages |
| NAB56b | Eastern Bantoid (*Benue*) | Black | Anyang, Basakomo, Birom, Ekoi, Ibibio (*Efik*), Jarawa, Jukun, Katab, Tigon, Tiv, Yako, Zumper; *Semi-Bantu;* 240 langauges |
| NAB56c | Western Bantoid (*West Atlantic*) | Black | Balante, Bijogo, Bullom, Diola, Gola, Fulani, Kissi, Limba, Pepel, Serer, Sherbro, Temne, Tenda, Tukulor, Wolof; 56 languages |
| NAB57 | **Bantu** | Black | *Bantu*-speaking (*Benue-Congo*); *Bantu Proper,* Narrow Bantu; about 540 languages |
| NAB57a | Cameroon Highland Bantu | Black | Bamileke, Fia, Fungum, Fut (Bafut), Kom, Li (Bali), Mum (Bamum), Ndob, Nen, Nsaw (Banso), Nsungli, Tikar, Widekum, Wum |
| NAB57b | Central Bantu | Black | Bemba, Chewa, Chokwe, Kimbundu, Kongo, Kuba, Lomwe, Makonde, Makua, Ndembu, Nyanja, Sena, Tumbuka, Vili, Yao |
| NAB57c | Equatorial Bantu | Black | Amba, Babwe, Bangi, Bira, Budu, Dzem, Fang, Kaka, Kota, Kumu, Lokele, Maka, Ngala, Rega, Sanga, Topoke |
| NAB57d | Interlacustrine Bantu | Black | Chiga, Ganda, Gusii, Ha, Haya, Konjo, Luhya, Nkole, Nyoro, Ruanda, Rundi, Shi, Soga, Sonjo, Toro, Zinza |
| NAB57e | Kenya Highland Bantu | Black | Chagga, Embu, Kamba, Kikuyu (Gikuyu), Mbere, Meru, Pare (Asu), Shambala (Sambaa), Taita, Tharaka |
| NAB57f | Luba | Black | Luba (Baluva, Bena Kalundwe, Bena Kanioka), Lulua (Bena Lulua, Lange), Lunda, Mbagani (Kete), Salampasu, Songe, Yeke |
| NAB57g | Middle Zambezi Bantu | Black | East Caprivian, Ila, Koba (Yeye), Lenje, Lozi (Barotse), Lukolwe, Mashasha, Mashi, Mbukushu, Nkoya, Subia, Tonga, Totela |
| NAB57h | Mongo | Black | Bosaka, Ekonda, Kela, Kutshu, Mbole, Mongo, Ngandu, Ngombe, Nkundo, Songomeno, Tetela |
| NAB57i | Nguni | Black | Angoni (Gomani, Mombera, Mpezeni), Fingo, Laka, Manala, Ndebele, Pondo, Swazi, Tembu, Xhosa, Zulu |
| NAB57j | Northeast Coastal Bantu | Black | Bajun, Comorian, Digo, Giriama, Gosha, Hadimu, Nguru, Pemba, Pokomo, Segeju, Shebelle, Shirazi, Swahili, Zaramo, Zigua |
| NAB57k | Northwestern Bantu | Black | Bubi, Duala, Duma, Koko, Kossi, Kpe, Kundu, Lumbo, Mpongwe, Ngumba, Puku, Seke, Shogo, Teke |
| NAB57l | Shona | Black | Kalanga, Karanga (Duma), Korekore (Shangwe), Manyika, Nambya, Ndau (Gova), Tawara (Budjga), Zezuru (Hera, Rozwi) |
| NAB57m | Sotho | Black | Eastern Sotho (Pedi), Northeastern Sotho (Lovedu, Venda), Southern Sotho |
| NAB57n | Southwestern Bantu | Black | Ambo (Ovambo: Kwangali, Ndonga, Okavango), Herero, Mbundu (Ovimbundu), Ndombe, Ngonyelu, Ngumbi, Nyaneka |
| NAB57o | Tanganyika Bantu | Black | Bena, Fipa, Gogo, Hehe, Iramba, Iwa, Kimbu, Nyakyusa, Nyamwezi, Pogoro, Rangi, Safwa, Sagara, Sukuma, Sumbwa, Turu |
| NAB57p | Tsonga | Black | Tsonga (Shangaan): Chopi, Hlengwe, Lenge, Nwanati, Ronga, Tswa, Tsonga (Thonga, Tonga) |
| NAB57q | Tswana | Black | Tswana (Western Sotho): Hurutshe, Kgatla, Kwena, Ngwaketse, Ngwato, Rolong, Tlhaping, Tlharu, Tlokwa |
| NAN58 | **Eurafrican** (Coloured) | Brown/Tan | Afro-European: Aku, Americo-Liberian (Kwi), Baster, Caboverdian, Cape Coloured, Creole, Krio, Mestiço, Mulatto, Wescos |
| NAB59 | **Guinean** (*Kwa*) | Black | Guinean (*Kwa*); about 170 languages |
| NAB59a | Akan | Black | Volta-Comoe: Akim (Akyem), Akwapim, Anyi-Baule, Ashanti, Attie, Brong, Fanti, Gonja, Guan, Kwahu; *Twi* |
| NAB59b | Central Togolese | Black | Adele, Akebu, Akposo, Avatime, Basila, Buem, Kebu, Krachi, Logba, Nyangbo, Tafi, Tribu (Ntrubo) |
| NAB59c | Edo | Black | Edo (Bini): Aakwo, Degema, Engenni, Epie, Eruhwa, Ishan (Esa, Isa), Kukuruku (Afenmai), Uhami: 22 languages |
| NAB59d | Ewe | Black | Anglo, Ewe (Eibe, Ephe, Krepe), Glidyi, Ho |

| | | | |
|---|---|---|---|
| NAB59e | Fon | Black | Fon (Dahomean): Adja, Aizo, Djedj, Fongbe, Hwelanu, Mabi, Wachi, Whydah |
| NAB59f | Ga-Adangbe | Black | Adangbe (Adangme), Anima, Awutu, Ga, Gain, Kpone, Krobo, Ningo, Osuduku, Prampram, Se (Shai) |
| NAB59g | Gun | Black | Gun: Egun, Tofinu, Wemenu |
| NAB59h | Ibo | Black | Ibo (Igbo): Abriba, Adda, Ekpeya, Ika, Izi, Ngwa, Ngwo, Onitsha, Owerri |
| NAB59i | Ijaw | Black | Brass (Nembe), Ibani, Ijaw (Ijo), Ikwere, Kabo, Kalabari, Kumbo, Mein, Nkoro, Okurikan, &c |
| NAB59j | Kru | Black | Bakwe (Krumen), Bassa, Bete, Dida, Grebo, Kran (Krahn), Kru (Crau, Krao, Krawi, Nana), Sapo (Pahn), Wobe |
| NAB59k | Lagoon | Black | Abe, Abure, Ajukru, Alladian (Alagya), Ari, Assini, Avikam, Ebrie, Gwa, Mekyibo, Nzima |
| NAB59l | Popo | Black | Popo (Mina): Anecho, Ge, Mina, Peda, Pla |
| NAB59m | Nupe | Black | Bassange (Nge), Batache, Beni, Dibo, Ebagi, Ebe, Gbedye, Igbira, Kakanda, Kupa, Kusoba, Nupe, Nupe Zam, &c |
| NAB59n | Yoruba | Black | Ana, Bunu, Egba, Ekiti, Ife, Igala, Igbolo, Igbomina, Ijebu, Ikale, Ilaje, Itsekiri, Nago, Ondo, Owo, Oyo, Yoruba |
| NAB59z | other Guinean | Black | Gade, Gbari, Idoma, Isoko, Urhobo (Abraka, Agbon, Ewu, Olomu, Sobo, Ughelli, Uwherun), Yala, &c |
| NAB60 | **Hausa-Chadic** | Black/Brown | Hausa-speaking Chadic peoples, with over 170 of their own languages also |
| NAB60a | Hausa | Black/Brown | Adarawa, Azna, Hausa (*Afuno*), Kanawa, Katsenawa, Kurfei, Maguzawa, Mauri, Tazarawa, Zazzagawa, &c |
| NAB60b | Plateau Chadic | Black | Angas, Bura, Gaberi, Gude, Kapsiki, Kirdi, Kotoko, Mandara, Margi, Masa, Matakam, Musgum, Tangale, Tuburi, Wurkum, &c |
| NAB61 | **Kanuri** (*Saharan*) | Black | Beriberi, Berti, Bideyat, Bornu, Bulgeda, Daza, Kanembu, Kanuri (Saharan Negro), Kawar, Kreda, Manga, Teda, Tubu, Zagawa |
| NAB62 | Nilotic (Para-Nilotic) | Black | *Nilo-Hamitic:* East Nilotic, *Eastern Sudanic*, Niloto-Sudanic, Prenilote, South Nilotic, West Nilotic; about 100 languages |
| NAB62a | Acholi | Black | Acholi (Gan, Gang, Shuli) |
| NAB62b | Alur | Black | Alur (Alua, Lur, Luri) |
| NAB62c | Anuak | Black | Anuak (Yambo), Pari |
| NAB62d | Barea | Black | Barea (Barya, Nera) |
| NAB62e | Bari | Black | Bari: Mondari, Nyambara, Nyepu, Pojulu |
| NAB62f | Dinka | Black | Agar, Bor, Dinka (Denkawi, Jang), Gok, Luaich, Malual, Padang, Raik, Ruweng, Twij |
| NAB62g | Kalenjin | Black | Kalenjin: Elgeyo (Keyo), Kipsigis, Marakwet, Nandi, Tatoga, Tugen |
| NAB62h | Kunama | Black | Kunama (Bazen, Cunama) |
| NAB62i | Lango | Black | Lango (Langi, Leb-Lano, Umiro) |
| NAB62j | Luo | Black | Gaya (Girange, Wageia), Luo (Joluo, *Dholuo*), Nilotic Kavirondo, Nyifwa, Padhola (Dama, JoPadhola) |
| NAB62k | Maasai | Black | Arusha, Elmolo, Kwafi, Lumbwa, Maasai, Njemps, Samburu |
| NAB62l | Mao | Black | Mao (Amam, Anfillo, Mau, Mayo), Busasi |
| NAB62m | Nubian | Black | Nubian: Anag, Barabra (Danagla, Kenuzi, Maha, Nile Nubian, Nubi), Birked, Dair, Dilling, Midobi, Nyimang, Temein |
| NAB62n | Nuer | Black | Atwot, Barr, Gaweir, Jagai, Ji Kany Cien, Lak, Lau, Nuer, Nyuong, Thiang |
| NAB62o | Shilluk | Black | Shilluk: Dembo (Bwodho), Kapango, Shatt (Thuri), Shilluk Luo |
| NAB62p | Suk | Black | Suk (Pokot): Cepleng, Endo, Kimunkon, Upe |
| NAB62q | Teso | Black | Itesyo, Kumam, Teso (Bakedi, Iteso) |
| NAB62r | Turkana | Black | Ngamatak, Nibelai, Nithir, Turkana (Elgume) |
| NAB62y | other Nilotic· | Black | Didinga, Fajulu, Ik, Jie, Jur, Kakwa, Karamojong, Latuka, Murle, Sabei (Sabaot), Suri, Surma (Tirma), Tepeth, Topotha, &c |
| NAB62z | other Prenilote | Black | Berta (Shangalla), Burun, Fung, Gule (Hameg), Gumuz, Ingessana (Tabi), Koma, Meban, Mesongo, Uduk, Ulu, &c |
| NAB63 | **Nuclear Mande** | Black | *Mande:* Bambara, Bozo, Dialonke, Kasonke, Konyanke, Koranko, Malinke, Soninke, Yalunka; about 30 languages |
| NAB63a | Bambara | Black | Bambara (Banmana), Dyangirte, Gan, Kaiongo, Kalongo, Masasi, Nyamosa, Somono, Toro |
| NAB63b | Bozo | Black | Bozo (Sorko, Sorogo) |
| NAB63c | Dialonke | Black | Dialonke (Djalonke, Jallonke) |
| NAB63d | Kagoro | Black | Kagoro (Bagane, Logoro) |
| NAB63e | Kasonke | Black | Kasonke (Kasson, Khasonke, Xasouke) |
| NAB63f | Konyanke | Black | Gyomande, Konyanke (Konianke), Mau |
| NAB63g | Koranko | Black | Koranko (Kuranko), Lele |
| NAB63h | Malinke | Black | Bambugu, Malinke (*Mandingo*, Mandinka, Maninka, Wangara), Mikifore: Komendi, Konya, Manimo, &c |
| NAB63i | Nono | Black | Djennenke, Nono |
| NAB63j | Soninke | Black | Aser, Aswanik, Diawara, Dyakanke, Gadyaga, Marka, Serahuli, Silabe, Soninke (*Sarakole*), Toubakai, Wakore, &c |
| NAB63k | Susu | Black | Susu (Soso) |
| NAB63l | Yalunka | Black | Yalunka |
| NAB63z | other Nuclear Mande | Black | Busansi, Diula (Dyula), Huela, Ligbi, Samo, Sya, et alii |
| NAB64 | **Peripheral Mande** | Black | Mande-fu: Dan, Gagu, Gbande, Guro, Kono, Kpelle, Loko, Loma (Toma), Mende, Ngere, Vai; about 16 languages |
| NAB64a | Dan | Black | Dan (Da), Gio (San, Yafuba, Yakuba), Tura |
| NAB64b | Gagu | Black | Gagu (Gban) |
| NAB64c | Gbande | Black | Belle, Gbande (Bande, Gbassi), Gbundi, Weima |
| NAB64d | Guro | Black | Guro (Gwio, Kwendre, Kweni, Lo), Mwa, Nwan |
| NAB64e | Kono | Black | Kono (Kolo, Kondo, Konnoh) |
| NAB64f | Kpelle | Black | Kpelle (Gbese, Gerse, Guerze, Kpese, Pessy) |
| NAB64g | Loko | Black | Loko (Landro, Landogo) |
| NAB64h | Loma | Black | Loma (Balu, Buzi, Domor, Gisima, Jokoi, Loghoma, Toa, Toma, Wuboma, &c) |
| NAB64i | Mende | Black | Ko (Comende), Kpa, Mende (Boumpe, Hulo, Kossa, Kosso), Sewa |
| NAB64j | Ngere | Black | Mano, Ngere, Niadrubu, Zague, Zahon |
| NAB64k | Vai | Black | Vai (By, Galdinas, Gallina, Karo, Nai, Vei) |
| NAB65 | **Songhai** | Black | Dendi, Songhai, Zerma (Djerma) |
| NAB65a | Dendi | Black | Dendi (Dandawa) |
| NAB65b | Songhai | Black | Gao, Koroboro, Songhai (Sonhrai), Tombmata |
| NAB65c | Zerma | Black | Zerma (Adzerma, Djerma, Dyabarma, Zaberma) |
| NAB66 | **Sudanic** | Black | Sudanic (Central & Eastern Nigritic): *Adamawa-Eastern/Ubangian*, *Surma*, et alii; about 230 languages |
| NAB66a | Azande | Black | Azande (Niam-Niam, Sande, Zande), Bandya, Idio |
| NAB66b | Banda | Black | Banda, Belingo, Dakpwa, Langbwasse, Mbanja, Tagbo, Wada, Wasa, Yakwa |
| NAB66c | Baya | Black | Baya (Baja, Gbaya), Bogoto, Chamba, Duru, Jen, Longuda, Mbum, Mumuye, Vere, Yungur |
| NAB66d | Fur | Black | Baygo, Dagu (Daju), Dalinga, Forenga, Fur, Kimr, Kungara, Mararit, Sila, Sungor, Tama, Temurka |
| NAB66e | Madi | Black | Bongo, Kreish, Logo, Madi, Mittu |
| NAB66f | Mandja | Black | Mandja (Mangia) |
| NAB66g | Moru-Mangbetu | Black | Lendu, Lugbara, Mamvu, Mangbetu, Mayogo, Moru, Okebu, Popoi, Rumbi |
| NAB66h | Nuba | Black | Nuba (*Kordofanian*): Heiban, Kadugli, Katla, Koalib, Krongo, Mesakin, Moro, Otoro, Tagali, Talodi, Tumtum, & 90 others |
| NAB66z | other Sudanic | Black | Bagirmi, Banziri, Bwaka, Kare, Maba, Masalit, Mbai, Mubi, Mundang, Ndogo, Nzakara, Riverine, *Sango*, Sara, Yakoma, &c |
| | AFRO-AMERICAN | BLACK | Black of African or mixed descent: Antillean (Antillese), Black, Cafuso, Coloured, Creole, Mulatto, Negro, Preto, Zambo |
| NFB67 | **Dutch-speaking** | Black | Dutch-speaking Black of African or mixed descent |
| NFB67a | Black | Black | Bush Negro, Dutch-speaking Black, Negro |
| NFB67b | Creole | Black | Antillean, Creole, Mulatto, *Papiamento* (Spanish/Dutch Creole), Sranan (*Taki-Taki*, English/Dutch Creole), Surinam Creole |
| NFB68 | **English-speaking** | Black | English-speaking Black of African or mixed descent including speakers of English-based Pidgin-Creoles |
| NFB68a | Black (African Negro) | Black | African Negro, pure-(full-)blooded Negro, Bush Negro, USA Negro/Black (80% Negro/20% White), West Indian Black |
| NFB68b | Mulatto | Black | Afro-Asian, Afro-Chinese, Black Carib (Garif), Coloured, Creole, Djuka, Guyanese, Maroon, Mulatto, Saramaccan |
| NFB69 | **French-speaking** | Black | French-speaking Black of African or mixed descent |
| NFB69a | Black | Black | Black, Boni, Bush Negro, Noir |
| NFB69b | Creole | Black | Antillean (Antillese), Dominican Creole, French (Black) Creole (*Creole*), French-speaking Mulatto (Mulatre), Haitian Creole |
| NFB70 | **Portuguese-speaking** | Black | Portuguese-speaking Black of African or mixed descent |
| NFB70a | Black | Black | Preto (Black) (African Negro) |
| NFB70b | Mulatto | Black | Cafuso (Negro/Amerindian), Crioulo, Mulato (more Black than Portuguese), Portuguese Creole, Quilombola |
| NFB71 | **Spanish-speaking** | Black | Spanish-speaking Black of African or mixed descent |
| NFB71a | Black | Black | Negro, Spanish Black |
| NFB71b | Mulatto | Black | Chinocholo, Criollo of mixed race, Mulatto, Palenquero, Spanish Creole, Zambo (Negro/Amerindian) |

**TOTALS:**   5 races, 13 geographical races and 4 sub-races, 7 colours, 71 families, 432 major peoples, about 8,990 constituent peoples and cultures, 7,010 distinct languages, 17,000 dialects, 80,000 variant names.

PART 5

# EVANGELIZATION

Quantifying the concept of evangelization

*We wish to remind the entire Church that its first duty is that of evangelization.*
—John Paul I, 1978.

This short section forms the key to a whole new concept evolved in this Encyclopedia. It is the subject of how to measure Christian outreach, the influence of Christ beyond the boundaries of global Christianity. The basic formula is given below, and resulting statistics will be found elsewhere in this volume. Details of method, data and analysis are, however, too extensive for inclusion here and so form the subject of an additional companion volume.

# QUANTIFYING THE CONCEPT OF EVANGELIZATION

The Christian community, that is the church, has long been subjected to quantification and measurement. Since New Testament times, worshippers have been numbered, believers enumerated, and baptism candidates counted. In modern times, major Christian denominations have got into the habit of regularly enumerating their members and their activities, utilizing 70 or 80 different categories of belief, Christian profession, affiliation and practice. Most of these 80 are studied, defined and enumerated in this Encyclopedia, mainly in Parts 3, 6, 7, 8, and 9.

This much is true of the Christian community itself. But when it comes to measuring or enumerating the influence of Christianity and the gospel beyond the bounds of the churches, it is quite another story. No systematic attempt at measuring or quantifying the impact of Christianity on the world's populations as a whole has yet been attempted. We have therefore attempted here a first step in this direction by elaborating on the idea and concept of evangelization. The term is often used incorrectly as if it were synonymous with conversion, or christianization. In fact it has, throughout Christian history, always been used in a broader sense to mean the spreading of the Good News of Jesus Christ and the proclamation of the gospel of the Cross; in other words, to include the impact and influence of Christianity on the non-Christian world as well as on the church and on Christians themselves. We have therefore evolved here a scale which depicts the status of evangelization in any particular country, or region, or ethnolinguistic population.

The scale is, in short, a measure of the overall outreach of the Christian community into the surrounding world.

Using the data compiled for this Encyclopedia, we have utilized the scale to give numerical values to the status of evangelization in all countries and peoples of the world, for the years 1900, 1970, 1980, 1985 and 2000. The values for 223 countries are tabulated in Global Table 31, columns 102-106; and summary totals for 8 continents and for the world are given in Global Tables 11 and 30. A historical overview of numerical evangelization throughout the 20 centuries of Christian history is also given, in Part 2, as 'A Chronology of World Evangelization'. Its data are tabulated in Global Tables 10 and 29.

The reader can utilize the scale himself for any particular country or region or people, by going systematically through its questions and compiling a total score expressed as a percentage. In cases where no hard data are available to answer certain questions, his own considered judgement should produce a reasonable estimate.

A full treatment of this subject necessitates not only historical and sociological analysis, but also a study of semantics and of the theology of evangelization. This is being done by the author in a companion volume to the present Encyclopedia dealing with the history and futurology of world evangelization. This later volume contains the documentation and data necessary for a thorough study and analysis of evangelization, including a bibliography of 1,300 items utilizing the word or its cognates in their titles. It also contains tabulations of all the data needed to quantify evangelization utilizing the scale below, for all countries and peoples of the world.

The scale will now be set forth at this point, on the following 2 facing pages. For a full description of the evolution of this scale, and analysis of each item with illustrative material, the reader is referred to the further volume.

**Evangelization is spreading good news.** *Above.* Youthful followers of Jesus Christ in Paris (France) explain the gospel in word and song to neo-Hindu cultists whilst atheists look on. Evangelization as a concept is quite distinct from conversion, baptism, church growth or christianization. It essentially means spreading the gospel, whether this meets with acceptance or rejection.

## COMPARATIVE DEMOGRAPHIC EVANGELIZATION: A SCALE

This is a scale or check list or inventory or index for measuring the extent or level of evangelization, or the spreading of the gospel through all types of evangelizing activity including the church's evangelism; or, for measuring a country's or people's awareness of Christianity, Christ and the gospel; i.e. for measuring obedience to or fulfilment of the Great Commission, or fulfilment of the Eschatological Sign of missionary proclamation: 'This gospel of the Kingdom will be proclaimed throughout the earth as a testimony to all nations; and then the end will come' (Matthew 24.14, NEB). After question No. 1, the 204 factors listed below are all phrased as dichotomous questions requiring a simple Yes/No answer.

Name of nation, country or people (or other population):
Year concerned:
Size of population in this year:
Main language:
Other major languages (each with over 10% of population):

### A. PRACTISING CHRISTIANS. — Percentage %

1. What percentage of this country's population are practising Christians, of all denominations? (Note: this is not identical with the percentage on the line for 'total practising' in Tables 1, but it may be derived by multiplying that percentage by the proportion of affiliated Christians in the total population for the year concerned)

**B. BACKGROUND CHARACTERISTICS FAVOURING EVANGELIZATION.** The following 22 questions refer to various religious and secular background factors at the national or people-wide level, which do not in themselves constitute direct evangelism or evangelistic activity, but which nevertheless predispose a country to be or to become evangelized. Sixteen are quantifiable; and 15 of these are expressed as percentages or per 1,000 or per million of the country's population. Indicate which assist evangelization here by, where the answer is Yes, giving each a single percentage point (1%) in the end column of its line. Values of these factors for all countries are tabulated in Global Table 31 or given in the section SECULAR DATA at the head of each country's article in Part 7. Question numbers shown followed by an asterisk (*) refer to 20th-century factors non-existent in the year 1900.

2. Have Christians been resident here for 100 years or more?
3.* Radio/TV receivers: are there 200 per 1,000 population or more?
4. Total Bible distribution per year: is it 2,000 per million or more?
5. Total New Testament distribution per year: is it 2,000 per million or more?
6. Worship centres (parishes, churches, congregations): are there 200 per million or more?
7. Local personnel (national workers): are there 200 per million or more?
8. Foreign missionaries and personnel (aliens from abroad): are there 100 per million or more?
9. Christian institutions: are there 40 per million or more?
10. Christian periodicals: do titles number 10 per million or more?
11. Christian service agencies: are there 5 per million or more?
12. Religious libraries: do they number 4 per million or more?
13. Denominations at work: do they number 4 per million or more?
14. Do secular libraries (universities, &c) contain the Bible or Christian literature?
15. Adult literacy: is it 50% or more?
16. Language: is the main language permeated with Christian/biblical phraseology and idiom?
17. Place names: do numerous cities have specifically Christian names?
18. Population density: is it 27/sq.km. (70/sq.mile) or more?
19. Education rate (population aged 5-24 enrolled in schools): is it 50% or over?
20. Is the Bible taught in state schools?
21. Does secular education make pupils aware of Christ in any way?
22. Does the Christian community have blood-ties with 10% or more of all non-Christians?
23. Is there, or has there been in the last 5 years, widespread social disturbance (unrest, upheaval, turmoil, war, disaster, et alia)?

**C. HINDRANCES TO EVANGELIZATION.** The following 21 questions refer to political, religious, cultural and economic background factors which may significantly, markedly, profoundly or severely hinder or obstruct evangelization. Indicate which do so in the country by, where the answer is Yes, giving each a single negative percentage point (−1%) in the end column of its line. Values of these factors for each country may be found from Tables 1, 2 and Global Table 31, or (No. 42) in SECULAR DATA at the head of each country's article. Popular religiosity (No. 34) may often hinder evangelization; if however it is judged in this case to instead favour evangelization (in which case it is better termed 'popular piety'), add +1% in the end column.

24. State religion: is the state either Islamic, Hindu, Buddhist, Jewish, or atheistic?
25. State opposition: does the state officially prohibit conversion, evangelism or proselytism?
26. Religious persecution or harassment: is religious liberty for all denominations severely obstructed or suppressed?
27. Are there systematic state attempts at removing children from Christian parents' influence?
28.* Is there extensive state jamming of Christian radio from abroad?
29. Has the state deliberately dechristianized most Christian-name cities in recent times?
30.* Spread of quasi-religions (secularism, materialism, agnosticism, atheism): are non-religious persons and atheists over 10% of the population?
31. Resurgence among non-Christian religions (Islam, Hinduism, Buddhism, spiritism, et alia): is this occurring?
32. Cultural barriers: is the Christian community culturally or linguistically alien to most non-Christians in this country?
33. Evangelistic distance: are the bulk of Christians separated from non-Christians by more than 5 religious or cultural frontiers?
34. Popular religiosity or piety (mass syncretistic folk-Christianity, christo-paganism, spiritist Catholicism, et alia): are over 10% of the country involved?
35. Nominal Christianity: are nominal and non-practising Christians over 20% of the population?
36. Is there unusual neglect of the Great Commission on the part of the churches?
37. Multiplicity of rival Christian bodies: are there over 30 separate denominations?
38. Have missionary or evangelistic methods/preaching/communication been poor or even bad (e.g. linguistically inadequate)?
39. Is there extreme racial or tribal tension (apartheid, etc) within the churches?
40. Are there other tensions or conflicts within the churches (ideological, political, etc)?
41. Mail reliability and censorship: does less than 50% of all Christian mail (internal and external) get through?
42. Inflation (rising costs): is it 20% per year or more?
43. Is extreme poverty, disease or illiteracy widespread?
44. Is there extreme economic exploitation of the poor by landowners, capitalists, multinationals, military-industrial complexes, etc?

**D. DIRECT CONTRIBUTIONS TO EVANGELIZATION: THE CHURCH'S EVANGELISM AND WITNESS.** Evangelism is the term used for the church's deliberate, planned, organized activities concerned with spreading the gospel; witness is the term used for the more fortuitous, unplanned activity of Christians which results in a spreading of the gospel. On historical grounds, evangelism can be divided into 4 major types using 4 main kinds of media, and into the 14 subtypes shown below.

Which, if any, of the following 114 local, regional or occasionally national items or factors or models of evangelism in factors Nos. 45-158 (means, methods, media, modes, agents and agencies) are making any particularly significant, striking, marked, notable, outstanding, extensive or widespread contribution to the evangelization of this country as a whole at the present time (or over the last 10 years)? List such by giving each a single percentage point (1%) in the end column of its line. Only list items with really significant nationwide effect; e.g. only list Nos. 46, 47 or 48 if these are recognized characteristics of at least 20% of the entire nationwide community of all practising Christians. When an item is phrased as a question (Nos. 57, 85-107, 113-114, and 151 onwards), if the answer is Yes add one point in the end column.

### *THE CHURCH'S EVANGELISM AND WITNESS*

#### *i. Traditional-media evangelism*

PERSONAL EVANGELISM (outreach by individual Christians):

45. active personal witnessing (by word; personal work, small-group evangelism) by adult Christians numbering over 1% of the population
46. Christian witness in the secular worlds of politics, industry, commerce, science, arts, media
47. Christian presence (witness by quality of life)
48. meaningful dialogue with other religions or quasi-religions (atheism, etc)

LOCAL-CHURCH EVANGELISM (corporate outreach by local churches):

49. an evangelistically-attractive church life (*koinonia*, fellowship)
50. an evident 'life for others' (*diakonia*, service), especially to outsiders
51. an evangelistic life-style (markedly simple or sacrificial) on the part of Christians
52. regular Sunday public preaching (*kerygma*) in church
53. liturgical worship: daily or weekly liturgy
54. liturgical preaching (sermons at the Eucharist)
55. other weekly local church activities (services, meetings, special groups)
56. catechesis/baptism instruction, catechumenate, catechetical renewal
57. baptism and other sacraments: do these present any public witness?
58. Sunday schools and local children's ministries
59. corporate witness and involvement of the laity (organized lay ministries, lay apostolate, precinct evangelism, visitation evangelism, house groups, etc)
60. training in discipling, evangelism, local courses, schools of evangelism
61. church open-air activities (local preaching or processions)
62. local parish or congregational evangelistic missions
63.* preaching at weddings and funerals (graveyard evangelism) in post-Christian and atheistic states
64. clandestine (illegal, underground) local church activities

PROFESSIONAL EVANGELISM (outreach by professional personnel):

65. local church workers (clergy, laity, of local citizenship)
66. local evangelists or catechists (related to a single local church congregation)
67. religious orders and personnel (brothers, monks, sisters, nuns), local or foreign
68. foreign missionaries or personnel and their activities
69. foreign chaplains and chaplaincies to alien residents
70. home (domestic) missionary societies and workers
71. chaplains to armed forces, military chaplains and evangelists
72. professional itinerant evangelists
73. clandestine itinerant evangelists, foreign couriers, et alii
74. itinerant musicians, choirs, bands, singing groups, pop groups
75. church music concerts and organ recitals (especially in post-Christian countries)
76. short-term workers, youth teams, youth vacation workers
77. seminarians, theological students (e.g. conducting local missions)

#### *ii. Medieval-media evangelism*

VISUAL-ARTS-MEDIA EVANGELISM (evangelism through art):

78. Christian architecture, churches, cathedrals, buildings, massive statues of Christ
79. religious art with Christian themes: paintings, portraits, murals, icons, sculptures, symbols, popular/mass reproductions, souvenirs
80. Christian exhibitions, displays, tableaux, panoramas

GROUP-MEDIA EVANGELISM (local-media evangelism):

81. folk media evangelism (traditional performing arts, recitation, poetry, mime, song)
82. church-produced drama (live theatre, dance, opera, ballet, mystery plays, passion plays, etc)
83. evangelism using bush telegraph or other traditional media
84. wall newspaper (community-produced) evangelism

PRINT-MEDIA EVANGELISM (literature evangelism):

85. Is a wide range of Christian literature readily available?
86. Are literacy campaigns by churches or missions significant?
87. Are Christian bookshops, or outlets through secular bookshops, widespread?
88. Are Christian periodicals effective in evangelization?
89. Are Christian articles, features, photos or scriptures often printed in secular newspapers?
90. Are Christian tracts (leaflets) being distributed widely?
91. Does clandestine (hand-copied) literature circulate widely?
92. Are there schools or courses for Christian journalists?
93. Is there an extensive literature on dialogue between Christianity and the local majority religion?

SCRIPTURE DISTRIBUTION EVANGELISM:

94. Is the Bible widely available in the main language?
95. Is it widely available in the other major languages?
96. Is the New Testament widely available in the main language?
97. Is it widely available in the other major languages?
98. Are Bible portions (gospels or complete books) widely available?
99.* Are printed scripture selections (leaflets) widely available?
100.* Are scriptures available in Braille for the blind?
101. Are colporteurs and Bible women active in colportage?
102.* Are mailed scriptures widespread (e.g. to all telephone subscribers)?
103. Are daily Bible reading materials in these languages widely available?
104.* Are Bible correspondence courses widespread (mail, or via radio/TV)?
105. Are there scripture free-distribution campaigns?
106. Is clandestine scripture distribution widespread?
107. Are special versions of the Bible available (children, illustrated, media versions, etc)?

#### *iii. Demographic-media evangelism*

INSTITUTIONAL EVANGELISM (outreach by Christian institutions):

108. church-operated schools, colleges, universities, seminaries, centres, monasteries, presses, et alia)
109. ministries of healing through hospitals, clinics, medical services
110. clandestine (illegal) schools, colleges, monasteries, presses, etc

AGENCY EVANGELISM (outreach by professional agencies):

111.* specialized national or international evangelistic associations or agencies
112.* nation-wide clandestine organized evangelistic networks (in atheistic or anti-Christian states)

UNITED EVANGELISM (interdenominational co-operation):

113.* Is there a national Christian council of churches (and/or agencies)?
114. Do all major denominations co-operate in evangelism?

SPECIALIZED-GROUP EVANGELISM:

115. student evangelism, campus evangelism, sectional evangelism, school evangelism
116. evangelistic conferences, seminars, houseparties, conventions
117. family evangelism, family catechesis, family counselling services linked to evangelistic campaigns
118. camp evangelism, camp meetings
119. rural evangelism, village evangelism
120.* occupational evangelism (industrial mission, labour evangelism, factory evangelism, etc)
121. urban mission, urban evangelism, inner-city ministry
122. ship evangelism (visits by evangelistic ships MV Logos, MV Doulos, mission boats, etc)
123. evangelism among the exploited and oppressed: the poor, beggars, refugees, squatters, minorities, et alii
124. evangelism among society's misfits: anarchists, revolutionaries, drug addicts, criminals, delinquents, prisoners, prisoners of war, et alii
125. evangelism among handicapped and incapacitated populations: cripples, lepers, blind, deaf, sick, suffering, bereaved, psychotics, et alii
126.* evangelism for other special groups: children, youth, migrants, athletes, campers, tourists, seamen, gypsies, et alii

MASS EVANGELISM (organized public mass campaigns):

127. national mass marches or processions of witness
128. national days of prayer, Kirchentags, Bible days, Bible weeks, et alia
129.* systematic every-home (house-to-house) visitation campaigns
130. mass evangelistic campaigns (indoor, outdoor, tent campaigns, seaside campaigns, crusades, etc)
131.* total mobilization campaigns (evangelism-in-depth, follow-through evangelism, lordship evangelism)
132.* mass lay- discipleship-/leadership-training programmes, TEE, etc
133.* national congress(es) on evangelism

#### *iv. Modern-media evangelism*

MASS-MEDIA EVANGELISM:

134.* films and audio-visual media (art, photographs, filmstrips, slides, etc)
135.* cassette, tape, videotape, disc (record) and flexidisc evangelism
136.* poster evangelism, professional advertising, billboards, bumper stickers, lapel pins, etc

137.* mediated training packages ..........................................................................
138.* telephone evangelism ................................................................................
139.* postal evangelism (mail evangelism)..............................................................
140.* public media-publicized commercial cinema showings of films on the Bible or life of Christ
141.* public media-publicized commercial theatre plays, musicals, opera, ballet, on the Bible or life of Christ.
142.* multimedia (TV/radio/press/literature) campaigns or crusades with followup..................
143.* multiplication evangelism, saturation evangelism...........................................

RADIOPHONIC EVANGELISM (electronic evangelism):
144.* regular radio evangelism in the main language........................................
145.* regular radio evangelism in the other major languages..................................
146.* regular TV evangelism in the main language...........................................
147.* regular TV evangelism in the other major languages...................................
148.* radiophonic schools (radio/TV plus local classes)....................................
149.* participatory radio/TV (phone-in, talk-back)........................................
150.* clandestine (illegal) Christian radio stations.......................................

*Totals*

TOTALS REACHED BY ORGANIZED EVANGELISM:
151. Local church converts/baptism/confirmations: is the annual aggregate for all churches over 1% of the population?...............................................................................
152. Pupils and students in all types of Christian schools and colleges: do they exceed 1% of the population?...............................................................................
153. Annual medical consultations in Christian hospitals: do they exceed 1% of the population?
154. Pieces of Christian literature (tracts, leaflets, books, scriptures): is the annual number distributed or sold more than 1% of the population?...........................................
155. Campaign attenders or persons reached: is the annual aggregate over 1% of the population?
156. Recorded enquirers or decisions for Christ (all types of campaigns): is the annual aggregate over 1% of the population?.............................................................
157.* Regular audience for Christian radio/TV programmes: is it over 1% of the population?......
158.* Bible correspondence course students: do they exceed 1% of the population?................

E. INDIRECT CONTRIBUTIONS TO EVANGELIZATION: PNEUMATIC EVANGEL-IZATION. The latter term is a neologism referring to any direct or indirect divine evangelizing activity operating upon this population, under the background influence or action of the Holy Spirit, but working through indirect human means rather than through any direct or organized ecclesiastical or human evangelistic activity.
For the following 38 indirect factors, if the answer to the question is Yes, add one point in the end column.

INDIGENIZATION OF CHRISTIANITY:
159. Are there any indigenously-initiated or locally-founded denominations (not imported or foreign-initiated or foreign-related)?.............................................................
160.* Do isolated radio believers number over 0.1% of the population?................................
161. Is there a corpus of indigenous Christian writings?................................................
162. Are there indigenously-composed hymns and songs?.............................................
163. Is there any indigenous Christian theological writing?...........................................
164. Is the country's head of state, or its chief executive, a practising Christian?...................
165. Are personal Christian names frequently reported in the media?................................
166. Are there any indigenous home or foreign mission societies?..................................
167. Does this country send abroad, as foreign missionaries or personnel, more than 40 citizens per million?...............................................................................
RENEWAL MOVEMENTS WITHIN THE CHURCHES:
Is evangelization in this country significantly advanced by:
168.* the Catholic charismatic (pentecostal) renewal?..............................................
169.* the charismatic renewal in the older Protestant, Anglican or Orthodox churches?............
170. widespread and widely-known 'signs following' (healings, deliverances, miracles, tongues, prophecies)?...............................................................................
171.* renewal through basic ecclesial communities (small groups)?.....................................
172. other revival or renewal movements within the churches?......................................
INTERNATIONAL CHRISTIAN/NON-CHRISTIAN CONTACTS:
Is evangelization in this country significantly advanced by these contacts of non-Christians with Christians:
173.* professional contacts with Christian countries (via UN, UNESCO, WHO, UPU, FAO, ILO, commerce, science, diplomacy, journalism, etc)?.........................................
174. mail correspondence with relatives, formerly citizens, who are Christians now living in exile or diaspora?...............................................................................
175. visits from relatives living abroad or in diaspora who have recently become Christians?......
176. returning citizens who have lived abroad in a Christian country (as students, migrant workers, diplomats, military, etc)?...................................................................
LOCAL (INTRANATIONAL) MOBILITY:
Is evangelization here significantly advanced by:
177. internal migration (change of residence) within the country?...................................
178.* internal tourism and travel?.......................................................................
179. internal pilgrimages: do Christian pilgrims annually number over 1% of the population?
INTERNATIONAL MOBILITY (MIGRATION AND TRAVEL):
Is evangelization here significantly advanced by active Christians from abroad among the following categories, or do Christians in each of these categories exceed 1% of the total population?
180. recent diaspora immigrants (minorities from other countries): are Christians among them over 1%?...............................................................................
141.* migrant workers from other countries: are Christians among them over 1%?..................
182. refugees from abroad: are Christians among them over 1%?.....................................
183. expatriate civilians in secular professions (government, industry, commerce): are Christians among them over 1%?...............................................................................
184. foreign armed forces: are Christians among them over 1%?....................................
185. foreign students: are Christians among them over 1%?........................................
186.* tourists (including Bible smugglers, et alii): are Christians among them over 1% annually?
187.* air travellers on business: are Christians among them over 1% annually?......................
188. pilgrims from other countries: are Christians among them over 1% annually?..................
OTHER FACTORS ASSISTING EVANGELIZATION:
Is evangelization in this country significantly advanced by any of the following, whether located or based here or abroad?
189.* modern technology (aviation, helicopters, hovercraft, computers, silicon chips, computerized multilingual hand dictionaries, high-speed presses, telex, satellite TV, etc)?...........
190.* state's official postage stamps and coins: have any recently portrayed the Bible or life of Christ?...............................................................................
191. public auctions of Christian art: are these regular and well-publicized in the media?...........
192. Christian social action, social justice, service, development projects?............................
193. relief, emergency or disaster aid by Christian agencies?...........................................
194. medicine and public health programmes, campaigns, medical workers?............................
195.* conscientization, humanization or liberation programmes?.......................................
196. neighbouring and surrounding countries: are they evangelized?..................................

F. OTHER ASSESSMENTS AND FACTORS.

OVERALL EVANGELISTIC COVERAGE:
Has this country been adequately evangelized from these standpoints:
197. all major geographical areas?.......................................................................
198. all ethnic groups and sub-groups (tribes, languages)?.............................................
199. all minority groups (immigrants, refugees, aliens, etc)?...........................................
200. all socio-economic classes?.........................................................................
201. all age-groups (infants to old people)?...........................................................
202. the worlds of industry, commerce, government?..................................................
203. all non-Christian religious groups?................................................................
204. all other groupings or strata of society?..........................................................
SPECIAL OR UNUSUAL FACTORS:
205. If there are any additional factors either favouring or hindering evangelization in this country, name each, and for each add a percentage point (either plus or minus) in the end column (up to a maximum of plus or minus 10)...............................................

TOTAL OF ALL ABOVE FACTORS 1-205, POSITIVE MINUS NEGATIVE.......................

206. *Closed minorities in evangelized countries.* In otherwise fully-evangelized lands, it is possible for small minority pockets of closely-knit non-Christian groups to exist, closed to all evangelism for linguistic or other reasons (e.g. remote Aboriginal groups, refugees, recent isolated immigrant communities, etc). If such completely non-evangelized groups number x% of the population, and if the population otherwise is fully-evangelized ($E=100\%$), then the closed groups should be subtracted from 100% to give a final value for the country of $E=100-x\%$.

COMPARATIVE DEMOGRAPHIC EVANGELIZATION:
Total extent or level, E% (maximum 100%) ......................................................

# PART 6

# CODEBOOK
Quick-reference codebook for statistical tables

*Les chiffres sont les signes de Dieu—Statistics are signs from God.*
—Prior Roger Schutz of Taizé, 1967.

The 6 pages that follow set out alphabetically or systematically, for quick reference, the meaning of the (mainly mutually-exclusive) classifications, categories, columns, codes and abbreviations used in the 2 statistical tables for every country in Part 7, and in the Global Tables in Parts 1 and 8, including Global Table 31 in Part 8 giving data on all 223 countries. Most of the Global Tables use the same columns and rows as Tables 1 and 2 and hence are not given separate space here. For more detailed explanations at any point, see Methodology (Part 3).

# QUICK-REFERENCE CODEBOOK FOR STATISTICAL TABLES

## TABLES 1 IN PART 7

### TABLE 1: RELIGIOUS ADHERENTS IN EACH COUNTRY

The term adherents refers to the whole de facto (present-in-area) resident population — men, women, children and infants, nationals and expatriates (citizens and aliens), armed services, alien troops, nomadic groups, refugees and so on.

#### BRIEF SUMMARY OF THE 15 COLUMNS
The columns are not numbered 1–15 in the tables themselves, but are numbered below here to assist in identifying particular columns. In the Global Tables (Parts 1 and 8), 2 additional columns are added for the year 1985.
1. Major religions, listed in 1970 order of numerical size, with indented sub-divisions
2. Adherents in the year 1900
3. Adherents in 1900 as % total population then
4. Adherents in mid-1970
5. Adherents in mid-1970 as % total population then
6-9. Annual change, 1970–80; average long-term trend over the decade
6. Annual natural (population) increase among adherents, 1970–80 (biological increase (births minus deaths) plus nett immigration)
7. Annual conversion (or supranatural) increase (+ or −) to adherents, 1970–80 (computed as col. 8 minus col. 6)
8. Total annual increase (+ or −) of adherents, 1970–80 (= col. 6 plus col. 7) (computed as col. 12 minus col. 4, divided by 10)
9. Rate of change of adherents, 1970–80, as % per year (= col. 8 divided by col. 10, times 100%)
10. Adherents in mid-1975
11. Adherents in mid-1975 as % total population then
12. Adherents in mid-1980
13. Adherents in mid-1980 as % total population then
14. Adherents in the year 2000
15. Adherents in 2000 as % total population then

#### DEFINITIONS OF VARIOUS RELIGIOUS CATEGORIES
Indented categories, in the listing below and in the tables, are sub-divisions of categories less indented (see explanation in Part 3).
Note our 3 basic equations concerning definitions of Christians:
(1) Total 'Christians' = professing + crypto-Christians, which also = nominal + affiliated.
(2) Total 'affiliated' = affiliated Roman Catholics + affiliated Protestants + affiliated Orthodox + affiliated Anglicans + affiliated marginal Protestants + affiliated Non-White indigenous + affiliated Catholics (non-Roman), minus doubly-affiliated, minus disaffiliated.
(3) Total 'affiliated' = total practising + non-practising Christians.
Note also that the first 9 categories below always (in Tables 1) refer to aggregate totals for all denominations of Christians (in all 7 major ecclesiastical blocs: Roman Catholic, Protestant, etc) in the whole country.

| | |
|---|---|
| **Christians** | = total of all Christian adherents of all kinds (professing and crypto-Christians, which is by definition equal to nominal plus affiliated). |
| professing | = those publicly professing (declaring, stating, confessing, self-identifying) their preference or adherence in a government census or public-opinion poll, hence known to the state or society or the public. |
| crypto-Christians | = secret believers in Christ not professing publicly nor enumerated or known in government census or public-opinion poll, hence unknown to the state or the public or society (but usually affiliated and known to churches), of the following 7 varieties: (1) unorganized individuals in legal churches, (2) political prisoners or exiles, (3) organized believers in unregistered denominations or congregations, (4) members of deliberately-clandestine illegal under-ground churches, (5) members of anti-state minority churches or sects, (6) organized believers in Christ rejecting the label Christian (anti-church believers), and (7) isolated radio or radiophonic or correspondence-course believers in small groups or cells in non-Christian or anti-Christian areas. |
| nominal | = unaffiliated, unchurched; non-church-members; those professing to be Christians but not affiliated to churches (residual Christians, latent Christians, anonymous Christians, sometimes called post-Christians in industrialized countries); Christians not, or not yet, or no longer, attached to organized Christianity, or who have rejected the institutional churches whilst retaining Christian beliefs and values, who may be Christians individually but are not part of the churches' corporate life, community or fellowship. |
| affiliated | = church members; all persons belonging to or connected with organized churches; those on the churches' books or records, or with whom the churches are in touch, usually known by name and address to the churches at grass-roots or local parish level; i.e. those attached to or claimed by the institutional churches or organized Christianity and hence part of their corporate life, community and fellowship, including children, infants, adherents, catechumens, and members under discipline (totals for 1970–80 are obtained from Table 2); total church membership, or total Christian community or inclusive membership; this is the total of affiliated in the 7 major blocs, minus any doubly-affiliated, minus any disaffiliated. |
| disaffiliated | = dechristianized persons; baptized Roman Catholics (or other Christians) enumerated as affiliated by a majority or state-linked Catholic Church (or other majority or state church) but who have recently formally withdrawn or disaffiliated themselves completely from Christianity and now profess to be non-religious (agnostics) or atheists, i.e. recent withdrawals from state or majority churches still however regarded as members by those churches, although in fact now backsliders, lapsed, or apostates; sometimes termed post-Christians; because a duplication, they are shown in the tables as a negative quantity (with a minus sign). |
| doubly-affiliated | = persons affiliated to or claimed by 2 denominations at once; because a duplication, they are shown in the tables as a negative quantity (with a minus sign). |

| | |
|---|---|
| total practising | = total affiliated of all denominations who attend public worship at least once a year, or who fulfil their churches' minimum annual attendance requirements, or who are radio/TV-service listeners (% here = % of affiliated, not % of total population); church attenders (daily, weekly, fortnightly, monthly, occasional, on festivals only, or annual), excluding civic attenders, private attenders, attending non-members, and attending non-Christians; active Christians, committed Christians, militant Christians. |
| non-practising | = affiliated but inactive, non-attending (dormant Christians) (% = % of affiliated). |
| Anglicans | = those related to the Anglican Communion, Episcopalians, including dissident Anglicans in the Western world. |
| Evangelicals | = Anglican Evangelicals (Conciliar Evangelicals, Conservative Evangelicals, Low Churchmen, and other Evangelicals). |
| Anglican pentecostals | = Anglicans regularly active in the organized charismatic renewal (healings, tongues, prophesying). |
| Catholics (non-Roman) | = Old Catholics and others in secessions from the Church of Rome since 1700 in the Western world, and other Catholic-type sacramentalist or hierarchical secessions from Protestantism or Anglicanism. |
| Marginal Protestants | = followers of para-Christian or quasi-Christian Western movements or deviations out of mainline Protestantism (including pseudo-Christian 'New Age' cults), not professing mainstream Protestant christocentric doctrine but claiming a second or supplementary or ongoing source of divine revelation in addition to the Bible (a new Book, angels, visions), yet nevertheless centered on Jesus, Christ and the Cross. |
| Non-White indigenous | = Black/Third-World indigenous (all categories with 'indigenous') Christians in denominations, churches or movements indigenous to Black or Non-White races originating in the Third World (i.e. to all races except the White peoples as defined in Part 4); locally-founded, Black-founded, Black-led, Non-White founded, Non-White led; begun since AD 1500; forming autonomous bodies independent of White origin or control, often separatist, schismatic, anti-establishment, in reaction to Western influences. (Note: all categories in Tables 1 and 2 with the word 'indigenous' form part of this general category). |
| Black Evangelicals | = Black Evangelicals: Conservative Evangelicals, Conciliar Evangelicals, and Fundamentalists, in the Black churches of the USA. |
| Black neo-pentecostals | = regularly active Black charismatics (more traditionally, 'sanctified') in the non-pentecostal Black denominations in the USA. |
| Orthodox | = Eastern (Chalcedonian), Oriental (Pre-Chalcedonian, Non-Chalcedonian, Monophysite), Nestorian (Assyrian), and non-historical Orthodox. |
| Orthodox pentecostals | = Orthodox active in the organized charismatic renewal (healings, tongues, prophesying). |
| Protestants | = followers of churches originating in, or reformulated at the time of, or in communion with, the Western world's 16th-century Protestant Reformation; called Evangelicals in French, German, Italian, Portuguese and Spanish, although usually more extensive than Evangelicals properly so called. |
| Evangelicals | = Conservative Evangelicals (in denominations outside the Ecumenical Movement), Conciliar Evangelicals (in denominations within the Ecumenical Movement), and Fundamentalists. |
| Neo-pentecostals | = charismatics regularly active in organized groups within non-Pentecostal Protestant denominations (excluding any who secede and form new Pentecostal or indigenous pentecostal denominations). (Note: this category is not distinct from the previous line, Evangelicals, and usually overlaps somewhat with it). |
| Roman Catholics | = all in communion with the Church of Rome (affiliated Roman Catholics are here defined as baptized Roman Catholics plus catechumens). |
| Catholic pentecostals | = Roman Catholics regularly active or involved in the organized Catholic Charismatic Renewal; active Catholic charismatics (healings, tongues, prophesying). |
| Christo-pagans | = Amerindian Roman Catholics syncretizing folk-Catholicism with organized traditional Amerindian pagan religion. |
| Evangelical Catholics | = in Latin countries, professing Roman Catholics (counted in a government census as Roman Catholics) who also regard themselves as Evangélicos or Evangéliques and are affiliated to churches which the state terms Evangelical (Protestant, Anglican, indigenous or marginal Protestant). |
| Spiritist Catholics | = Roman Catholics active in organized high or low spiritism, including syncretistic spirit-possession cults. |

| | |
|---|---|
| **Non-Christians** | = all persons who are not Christian adherents of any kind, including non-believers. |
| Afro-American spiritists | = low spiritists syncretizing Catholicism with African and/or Amerindian animism, also Afro-American syncretistic cults with Christian elements. |
| Atheists | = those professing atheism, scepticism, disbelief or irreligion or other anti-religious quasi-religions, including Marxist-Leninist Communism regarded as a quasi-religion; dialectical materialists and militant non-believers opposed to all religion; sceptics. |
| Baha'is | = followers of the Baha'i World Faith founded by Baha'u'llah (Baha' Allah, Glory of God). |
| Buddhists | = followers of Mahayana (Northern), Theravada (Hinayana or Southern), or Vajrayana (Tantrayana, Tantrism, Lamaism); traditional sects but not neo-Buddhist new religions or religious movements. |
| religious Buddhists | = Buddhists who profess Buddhism as both a family religion and also a personal religion. |
| non-religious Buddhists | = persons whose family religion is Buddhism but who as individuals profess to have no personal religion. |
| Chinese folk-religionists | = followers of traditional Chinese religion; with 6 elements: |

| | |
|---|---|
| | = Taoism and local deities, Confucianism, Buddhist elements, ancestor worship, Chinese universism, divination and magic. |
| Confucians | = non-Chinese followers of Confucius and Confucianism. |
| Hindus | = followers of the main Hindu traditions : (a) Vaishnavites, (b) Saivites, (c) Saktists, (d) Arya Samaj and other reform sectarians, and (e) followers of modern neo-Hindu sects. |
| Jains | = followers of the Svetambara and Digambara sects. |
| Jews | = followers of the Orthodox, Reformed, or Liberal schools of Judaism; Ashkenazis, Sefardis (Sephardis); crypto-Jews. |
| Karaites | = Readers of the Scriptures, followers of Jewish sect Qaraism. |
| Samaritans | = Children of Israel (Bene-Yisrael) or Shamerim (Observant Ones), a small Jewish sect. |
| Mandaeans | = Gnostics (Christians of St John, Followers of John the Baptist, Sabaeans). |
| Muslims | = followers of Islam, in its 2 main branches (Sunnis, Shias) and all other orthodox and heterodox sects and reform movements. |
| Ahmadis, Druzes, Yazidis | = followers of heterodox Muslim sects (enumerated both here and also in total statistics of Muslims in line above). |
| New-Religionists | = followers of the so-called 20th-century New Religions or radical new crisis religions (new Far Eastern or Asiatic indigenous non-Christian syncretistic mass religions embodying major innovations and new religious systems), including Japanese neo-Buddhist and neo-Shinto new religious movements. |
| Non-religious | = those professing no religion, or professing unbelief or non-belief; non-believers, doubters, agnostics, freethinkers, non-religious humanists, non-religious quasi-religionists, post-religious; indifferent to both religion and atheism; secularists, materialists; also post-Christian, dechristianized or de-religionized populations. |
| Parsis (Parsees) | = descendants of Zoroastrians. |
| Shintoists | = Japanese who profess, or still profess, Shinto as their first or major religion. |
| Sikhs | = followers of the Sikh reform movement out of Hinduism. |
| Spiritists | = non-Christian high (as opposed to low) spiritists, spiritualists, thaumaturgicalists, medium-religionists. |
| Tribal religionists | = primal or primitive religionists, animists, spirit-worshippers, shamanists, ancestor-venerators, polytheists, pantheists, traditionalists, local or tribal folk-religionists, including adherents of local or tribal syncretistic or nativistic movements, neo-paganism, cargo cults, witchcraft eradication cults, possession healing movements, tribal messianic movements, et alia. |
| Other religionists | = term used in Tables 1 for total of (a) adherents of remaining non-Christian religions listed above but too few in a particular country for their religions to be individually listed (excluding non-religious and atheists), and (b) adherents of all other smaller non-Christian religions, faiths, quasi-religions, brotherhoods or other religious systems not included in the above listing. |
| **Country's population** | = total present-in-area resident population or inhabitants of country at a given mid-year date. |

PERCENTAGES. All columns headed % in Tables 1 refer to percentages of the total population of the country, except in the rows for *practising* and *non-practising* Christians which are always given as % of affiliated Christians only (i.e. as a % of only those who are eligible to practise).
FOOTNOTES. The notes below Tables 1 consist of (1) a note on columns and rows, (2) source data from any national population censuses of religion or public-opinion polls, and (3) NOTES ON RELIGIONS elaborating on, or giving additional data on, various categories in the table, these being listed in alphabetical order. If no footnote is given for a particular Christian category (e.g. 'Marginal Protestants', 'Black/Third-World indigenous'), details of how the totals are arrived at may be studied in Table 2 for the country.

# TABLES 2 IN PART 7

## TABLE 2: ORGANIZED CHURCHES AND DENOMINATIONS IN EACH COUNTRY

BRIEF SUMMARY OF THE 8 COLUMNS
In all Tables 2, the columns are always numbered 1–8. In the corresponding Global Tables (in Parts 1 and 8), total affiliated membership is expanded to cover the years 1970, 1975, 1980, and 1985.

Column:

| | |
|---|---|
| 1. Name | Official name of church, denomination or diocese; names in boldface (heavy) type are churches each with over 10% of the country's affiliated Christians. |
| 2. Begun | Year when body was begun (or re-begun) permanently in this country (major significant date usually given). |
| 3. Type | Ecclesiastical type: ecclesiastico-cultural major bloc (stream) & ecclesiastical tradition. |
| 4. Councils | Conciliarism: membership in councils (confessional, international, continental, regional, national). |
| 5. Congs | Congregations (places of regular worship). |
| 6. Adults | Adult church members (over 15 years) on rolls (communicants or full members, often with probationary or baptized non-communicant members). |
| 7. Affiliated | Total church membership, or total church member community, or total Christian community, or inclusive membership, or total constituency (adults, children, infants, catechumens, adherents, members under discipline, etc) on the church's books or records, or known to the church (this column always includes those in column 6). |

8. Names, notes and other statistics. Descriptive notes.

The following are the codes and abbreviations used in columns 1, 3, 4 and 8. The codes and statistics used in columns 3–7 are all mutually exclusive (i.e. each body belongs to only the type of council shown, and not to others; and individual congregations and Christians are enumerated only once in each Table 2, under a single body).

### COLUMN 1: NAMES OF BODIES

(1) Abbreviations in names of bodies

In order to reduce names to a manageable length, the following standard abbreviations are used when necessary in the lists; those in bold type below are very widely employed, the others only occasionally. All names are alphabetized in the listings on their unabbreviated versions.

| | |
|---|---|
| Apost | Apostolic, Apostólica |
| Asoc | Asociación |
| Assoc | Association |
| **Ch** | Church (in Italian, Chiesa) |
| **Chr** | Christian, Chrétien(ne), Christliche |
| **Chs** | Churches |
| Conf | Conference |
| Congr | Congregation, Congregación |
| Conv | Convention |
| **E, Egl(s)** | Eglise(s) (=Church(es)) |
| Epis | Episcopal |
| **Ev** | Evangelical, Evangélique(s), Evangelisch(e, -er), Evangélica(s, -o, -os) |
| **Fell** | Fellowship |
| Gem | Gemeinde, Gemeinschaft |
| **Ig, Igl(s)** | Igreja, Iglesia(s) (=Church(es)) |
| Indep | Independent, Independiente(s) |
| Intern(at) | International(e) |
| I(s) | Island(s); occasionally (in Spanish or Portuguese) Iglesia, Igreja |
| JC, J-C, CJ | Jesus Christ, Jésus-Christ, Jesu Cristo, Jesucristo, Cristo Jesús |
| K | Kirche (Church) |
| Luth | Lutheran, Lutherisch(e), Luthérien(ne) |
| Miss, Mis | Mission, Misión |
| Orth | Orthodox(e) |
| Patr | Patriarchate |
| Pente | Pentecostal |
| Presb | Presbyterian, Presbyteriana |
| Soc | Society |
| Syn | Synod |
| Un | Union, Unión |

Other initials in names of bodies refer either to the country concerned (A=Austria, B=Belgium, etc), or to details explained at the end of the church's line in the table or in the notes beneath the table.

(2) Dioceses, jurisdictions and other sub-divisions

| | |
|---|---|
| AA | apostolic administration |
| AD | archdiocese |
| AN | abbey nullius |
| C | catholicate (catholicossate), diocese of catholicos |
| CD | church district |
| Co | community (communauté) (used only in Zaire Table 2) |
| Con | conference |
| CR | conciliar region (regione conciliare) |
| D | diocese, eparchy |
| E | exarchate |
| EA | exarchate apostolic |
| EC | episcopal commissariat |
| EM | exarchical monastery |
| EP | ecumenical patriarchate |
| EPr | ecclesiastical province |
| Epi | episcopal area |
| J | jurisdiction |
| M | metropolitan archdiocese or see; metropolia (when superior to D) |
| MV | military vicariate or ordinariate |
| m | mission (sui juris) |
| O | ordinariate |
| P | patriarchate, patriarchal diocese |
| PA | prefecture apostolic |
| PE | patriarchal exarchate |
| PN | prelature (prelacy) nullius |
| Pro | province |
| R | region (apostolic or conciliar) |
| RN | priory nullius |
| S | synod |
| UD | united diocese |
| UDs | united dioceses |
| V | vicariate |
| VA | vicariate apostolic |
| VP | patriarchal vicariate |
| : | (at end of a name) composite body whose statistics are the total of its components shown below it |
| ( ) | jurisdiction based in another country, of which this body is a part |

### COLUMN 3: ECCLESIASTICAL TYPE (4-letter code)

1st letter: Bloc (Stream) (definitions are given above under Table 1): A, C, O, R=Liturgical, Pedobaptist (infant-baptizing); I, M, P=partly Non-Liturgical, partly Baptist (adult baptism only)

| | |
|---|---|
| A | Anglican (Episcopalian) |
| C | Catholic (non-Roman) (of Western origin) |
| I | Non-White or Black/Third-World indigenous |
| M | Marginal Protestant (para-Christian of Western origin) |
| O | Orthodox (Eastern, Oriental or Nestorian) |
| P | Protestant (sometimes called Evangelical) |
| R | Roman Catholic |

2nd-4th letters (last 3 letters of column): Tradition

| | |
|---|---|
| ACa | Anglo-Catholic |
| Ade | Christadelphian (Adelphoi, Brothers of Christ) |
| Adv | Adventist |
| Alb | Albanian/Greek-speaking (Byzantine or Orthodox) |
| Ang | schism ex Anglicanism or Episcopalianism, in Protestant direction, rejecting Anglicanism |
| Apo | apocalyptic, eschatological |
| Ara | Arabic- or Arabic/Greek-speaking (Orthodox) |
| Arm | Armenian (Orthodox (Gregorian) or Eastern-rite Catholic) |
| ARo | Anglo-Roman (schism ex Anglicanism in Roman direction) |
| Bap | Baptist |
| BrI | British-Israelite |
| Bul | Bulgarian (Byzantine) |
| Bye | Byelorussian/Belorussian (White Russian/White Ruthenian) (Byzantine) |
| Byz | Byzantine-rite (jurisdiction for more than one ethnic group) |
| CAp | Catholic Apostolic (Irvingite) or Old Apostolic, including New Apostolic; sacramentalist, hierarchical |
| CBr | Christian Brethren (Plymouth Brethren; Open only, not Exclusive); independent fundamentalist/dispensationalist |
| CCa | Conservative Catholic (schism ex Rome, protesting liberal or updating trends) |
| Cen | Central or Broad Church Anglican (Prayer Book, Liberal, Comprehensive, New Synod Group) |
| Cha | Chaldean (Eastern Syrian) |
| com | community church or union congregation (formed by 2 or more denominations), open to all denominations and races |
| Con | Congregational, Congregationalist |
| Cop | Coptic (Orthodox or Alexandrian-rite) |
| Cze | Czech/Slavonic-speaking (Orthodox) |
| Dis | Disciple, Restorationist, Restorationist Baptist, Christian (Restoration Movement, Campbellites, Disciples, Churches of Christ) |
| Dun | Dunker (Tunker), Dipper, German Baptist, Brethren (baptism by 3-fold immersion) |
| EBr | Exclusive Brethren (Plymouth Brethren, Closed, Strict; Darbyites); exclusive fundamentalist/dispensationalist |
| Epi | episcopi-vagantes Catholics, i.e. in miniscule unrecognized episcopal church under episcopi vagantes (bishops-at-large) (only those with 100 or under members) |
| Eth | Ethiopic, Ethiopian Orthodox, Ge'ez-speaking |
| Eva | Anglican Evangelical, Evangelical Anglican |
| Fin | Finnish/Slavonic-speaking (Orthodox) |
| Geo | Georgian Orthodox or Byzantine-rite Roman Catholic |
| Gno | Gnostic, esoteric, anthroposophical |
| Gre | Greek (Orthodox or Byzantine, Greek-speaking) (New Calendar) |
| Hig | High Church Anglican (Prayer Book Catholic) |
| Hol | Holiness (Conservative Methodist, Wesleyan, Free Methodist, non-Pentecostal Perfectionist) (2-experience: conversion, entire sanctification); mainly schisms out of mainline Methodism differing chiefly on sanctification |
| Hun | Hungarian/Slavonic-speaking (Byzantine or Orthodox) |
| IAb | Italo-Albanian (Byzantine) |
| ind | independent evangelical, often fundamentalist (dispensationalist), unrelated to other Protestant or other indigenous traditions, usually regarding itself as a denomination |
| int | interdenominational evangelical Protestant (unaffiliated to any denomination, unrelated |

to any major tradition, or specifically interdenominational); faith mission
Ita Italian (Byzantine)
Jeh Jehovah's Witnesses (Jehovah's Christian witnesses; Russellites) including Bible Student movement and other schismatics or dissidents
Jew Messianic, Jewish-Christian, or Jewish crypto-Christian
Lat Latin-rite
LdS Latter-day Saints (Mormons), including Mormon schismatics or dissidents
LEr jurisdiction for both Latin and Eastern-rite Catholics
Lib Liberal Catholic (deviant, Theosophical, Masonic, Gnostic)
Low Low Church Anglican (Conservative Evangelical)
LuR Lutheran/Reformed united church or joint mission
Lut Lutheran
Mal Malankara (Syro-Antiochian, Western Syrian), Syro-Malankarese
Mar Maronite (Syro-Antiochian, Western Syrian)
mar marginal (Black/Third-World indigenous churches, and Catholic schisms, of un-orthodox or syncretistic christology, claiming a second or supplementary source of revelation in addition to the Bible)
Mel Melkite (Byzantine, Greek Catholic; Arabic-speaking)
Men Mennonite, Anabaptist (Left Wing or Radical Reformation), including other communal Anabaptist sects
Met Methodist (mainline Methodist, United Methodist); English-speaking Pietist
Mor Moravian (Continental Pietist)
Nes Assyrian or Nestorian (East Syrian, Messihaye (Christians), Syro-Chaldean; Dyo-physite), including dissidents
non non-denominational (no-church or anti-church groups rejecting being described as a church)
OBe Old Believer, Old Ritualist
OCa Old Catholic
OCd Old Calendarist, Authentic Orthodox
Ori plural Oriental (Roman Catholic jurisdiction for all or several Eastern rites together)
Ort schism from Orthodoxy, in Protestant direction
PeA Apostolic, or Pentecostal Apostolic (stress on complex hierarchy of living apostles, prophets and other charismatic officials)
Pen Pentecostal (Protestant; Classical Pentecostal of unspecified type); charismatic, faith-healing (Classical Pentecostal sub-types include PeA, Pe1, Pe2, Pe3, Pe4)
Pe1 Oneness-Pentecostal or Unitarian-Pentecostal: 'Jesus only', sometimes unitarian, non- or anti-trinitarian
Pe2 Baptistic-Pentecostal or Keswick-Pentecostal: 2-crisis-experience (conversion, baptism of the Spirit)
Pe3 Holiness-Pentecostal: 3-crisis-experience (conversion, sanctification, baptism of the Spirit)
Pe4 Perfectionist-Pentecostal, Free Pentecostal, Deliverance-Pentecostal, Radical-, or Revivalist-Pentecostal: 4-crisis-experience (conversion, sanctification, baptism of the Spirit, deliverance/ecstatic confession/prophecy/perfectionism, also authority/discipling/shepherding)
peA indigenous charismatic pentecostal apostolic (hierarchy of living apostles)
pen indigenous charismatic (pentecostal, spirit-dominated): Black/Third-World indigenous body of pentecostal type (charismatic, enthusiastic, faith-healing); in Africa, spiritual or zionist or spirit or aladura (praying) churches
pe1 indigenous charismatic oneness-pentecostal, unitarian-pentecostal
pe2 indigenous charismatic baptistic-pentecostal (2-crisis-experience)
pe3 indigenous charismatic holiness-pentecostal (3-crisis-experience)
pe4 indigenous charismatic perfectionist, free, radical- or revivalist-pentecostal or deliverance pentecostal (4-crisis-experience)
plu Anglican, of plural or mixed traditions (no single tradition)
Pol Polish/Slavonic-speaking (Orthodox)
Pro ex-Protestant Catholic (movement out of Protestantism in a Catholic direction, receiving episcopacy and apostolic succession)
Qua Friends (Quakers)
rad isolated radio churches (unorganized isolated house congregations or cells of isolated radio believers brought into being by radio, mail and/or radiophonic evangelism)
ReC Reformed Catholic, retaining Roman Catholic claims
Ref Reformed, Presbyterian (the latter originating in English-speaking areas, the former in continental Europe)
ReO Reformed Orthodox (uncanonical reform movement out of Orthodoxy, retaining Orthodox claims)
Rum Romanian (Orthodox or Byzantine)
Rus Russian (Byzantine)
Rut Ruthenian (Byzantine)
sAC Anglican schism of Anglo-Catholic type, retaining Anglicans claims
Sal Salvationist (Salvation Army)
Sci metaphysical science, Divine Science, Religious Science, Christian Science, New Thought, magnetic healing, psychedelic
Ser Serbian/Slavonic-speaking (Orthodox)
sEv Anglican schism of Evangelical type, retaining Anglican claims
sin single congregation(s): one single autonomous congregation, completely independent and unaffiliated to any denomination, nor claiming to be a denomination; or a de facto unstructured grouping of such congregations
Sla Slavonic-speaking (Orthodox)
Slo Slovak (Byzantine)
smi Anglican schism of mixed types of churchmanship, retaining Anglican claims
Spi Spiritualist, Spiritist (thaumaturgical), psychic, psychical, occult, mediumistic, of specifically Christian type
sub sub-Orthodox Russian sect rejecting Orthodox ritual
Swe Swedenborgian (Church of the New Jerusalem; spiritualistic)
SyM Syro-Malabarese (Eastern Syrian), Syriac/Malayalam-speaking, Orthodox Syrian
Syr Syrian, Syriac-speaking (Orthodox or Syro-Antiochian, West Syrian, Jacobite)
tel TV (television) para-denomination, organized around regular worship telecasts
The Theosophist, Theosophical, synthesist (combining philosophy and religions)
Tru True Orthodox (devoutly conservative Russian Orthodox)
Ukr Ukrainian (Byzantine)
uni united church (voluntary or involuntary unions of bodies of different traditions)
Unt Unitarian, Universalist, Free Christian, Liberal Christian
Wal Waldensian
Yug Yugoslav (Byzantine)

## COLUMN 4: CONCILIARISM, COLLEGIALITY, CONSULTATION AND CHURCH ORGANIZATION (5-letter code)

*Note on names.* Most international bodies have official names in 2 or more major international languages. Almost all of these are given in Part 3 and also in the Topical Directory (Part 13), but in the interests of brevity names are given below only once in English (for international bodies with official names in several languages), or in the major European language in use followed by an English translation if widely used. Where a body uses varying sets of initials in its various languages, these are all given below in brackets separated by slashes.

*Conference of Secretaries of Christian World Communions (until 1979 known as World Confessional Families).* The 15 international confessional councils below followed by an asterisk * (making a total of 26 asterisks including duplications) are represented on this Conference, begun in 1957; in addition, the following non-confessional international denominational bodies are participants: Church of the Brethren, Salvation Army, General Conference of Seventh-day Adventists, World Convention of Churches of Christ (Disciples).

**1st letter: Confessional Conciliarism, Consultation and Church Organization (worldwide)**

A = Anglican Consultative Council (ACC)/Lambeth Conference/Anglican Primates Committee: autonomous body (church, province, quasi-province or diocese)*
a = Anglican Consultative Council: non-autonomous body (missionary diocese, assisted diocese, or part of a diocese based in another country)*
B = Sacred Congregation for Bishops*
b = immediately subject to Holy See (under Sacred Congregation for Bishops)*
C = canonical relationship with Ecumenical Patriarchate of Constantinople (also the other 3 Greek-speaking Orthodox patriarchates, and Panorthodox Conference)*
c = claimed but disputed relationship to Ecumenical Patriarchate of Constantinople
D = canonical relationship with Syrian Orthodox (Jacobite) Patriarchate of Antioch (Damascus)
E = canonical relationship with Armenian Catholicate of Echmiadzin
F = member of both WARC and RES (World Alliance of Reformed Churches, and Reformed Ecumenical Synod)*
G = Mennonite World Conference (MWC)*
H = Council for the Public Affairs of the Church (situation up to 1975)*
h = immediately subject to Holy See (under Council for the Public Affairs of the Church)*
I = International Association for Religious Freedom (IARF)
i = International New Thought Alliance (INTA)
J = Reformed Ecumenical Synod (RES)*
K = International Federation of Free Evangelical Churches (IFFEC)
L = Lutheran World Federation (LWF/FLM/LWB) (member, or congregation formally recognized by LWF)*
l = permanent observer (but not member) relationship to Lutheran World Federation (LWF)*
M = canonical relationship with Patriarchate of Moscow (in preference to Constantinople)*
N = canonical relationship with Coptic Orthodox Patriarchate of Alexandria
O = Sacred Congregation for the Eastern Churches*
o = immediately subject to Holy See (under Sacred Congregation for the Eastern Churches)*
P = Sacred Congregation for the Evangelization of Peoples (Propaganda)*
p = immediately subject to Holy See (under Propaganda)*
Q = Friends World Committee for Consultation (FWCC)*
R = World Alliance of Reformed Churches (Presbyterian and Congregational) (WARC)*
r = member of both WARC and IFFEC*
S = canonical relationship with Armenian Catholicate of Cilicia (Sis)
T = Baptist World Alliance (BWA/ABM/BWB)*
U = International Old Catholic Bishops Conference (Union of Utrecht)*
u = member of both Union of Utrecht and ACC/Anglican Communion*
V = World Methodist Council (WMC)*
W = member of both WMC and WARC (World Methodist Council, and World Alliance of Reformed Churches)*
X = Ukrainian Orthodox Church of the Free World
x = quasi-confession (or non-confessional international denominational body), usually with organized branches or world missionary outreach in 3 or more countries; or, non-canonical Orthodox communion with overseas branches; or, pan-Anglican body not in communion with See of Canterbury
Y = canonical relationship with Ancient Assyrian Church of the East, Patriarchate of the East (Tehran) (Mar Dinkha IV)
y = canonical relationship with Ancient Assyrian Church of the East, Patriarchate of Baghdad (Mar Addai)
Z = Pentecostal World Conference (PWC)
C+M = Great and Holy Council of the Orthodox Church (expected to be held around 1986)*
D+E+N+S = Oriental Orthodox Churches Conference
. = not a member of any confessional council, nor in communion with historical Orthodoxy, the Anglican Communion, Old Catholic churches, nor the Roman Catholic Church; not a non-confessional international denominational body; i.e. no international confessional links or membership of any kind.

*Other international confessional councils, not coded here.* Anglican Episcopal Council of Churches, Anglican Orthodox Communion, Confessional Lutheran Synod, Fellowship of French Evangelical and Reformed Churches (CEVAA) (a worldwide body), International Baptist Fellowship, International Evangelical Congregational Union, International League for Apostolic Faith and Order (ILAFO), International Lutheran Conference (ILC), Ligue Oecuménique pour l'Unité Chrétienne.

The codes for the next 4 letters apply to all denominations and churches including Roman Catholic local (nation-wide) churches, but not to dioceses or jurisdictions indented under churches (see code for 2nd-5th letters below).

**2nd letter: World Conciliarism, Collegiality and Consultation**

F = related or linked to World Evangelical Fellowship (WEF): church or mission related to Evangelical Foreign Missions Association (EFMA), hence to NAE (USA), hence to WEF
G = church or mission related to Evangelical Missionary Alliance, UK (EMA), but not to EFMA or IFMA or WEF
H = church or mission related to Australian Evangelical Alliance, but not to EFMA or IFMA or WEF
M = church or mission related to Interdenominational Foreign Mission Association (IFMA), but not to EFMA
N = church or mission related to both IFMA and EFMA
q = church related to EFMA, which has also applied to WCC for membership
r = church related to IFMA, which has also applied to WCC for membership
s = (diocese staffed by secular clergy: see under 2nd-5th letters, below)
T = International Council of Christian Churches (ICCC), and The Associated Missions (TAM)
t = former member of ICCC, or linked with it, but now withdrawn
u = associate member of WCC (small churches in principle under 10,000 in membership)
v = application for membership or enquiry made to WCC, but either withdrawn, rejected, delayed indefinitely, or otherwise not accepted by 1980
W = World Council of Churches (WCC/COE/ORK)
w = not a member of WCC in own right, but participating (e.g. as a foreign diocese or branch) through some larger confessional or ecclesiastical member grouping based in a different country
x = Roman Catholic local (nation-wide) church with both a national consultative pastoral body, and also a national priests' organization
y = Roman Catholic local (nation-wide) church with a national consultative pastoral body, but with no national priests' organization
z = Roman Catholic local (nation-wide) church with a national priests' organization, but with no national consultative pastoral body
. = (Protestant, Anglican, Orthodox) not a member of nor related to any world or international council; or (Roman Catholic) local church with neither a national priests' organization nor a national consultative pastoral body

2nd letter (only for Roman Catholic and Orthodox dioceses and jurisdictions): STATUS AND STAFFING
a = Orthodox diocese under an archbishop
b = Orthodox diocese under a bishop
e = Orthodox diocese under an exarch
m = Orthodox diocese under a metropolitan
p = Orthodox diocese under a patriarch or catholicos
s = Roman Catholic diocese staffed by secular (diocesan) clergy (usually nationals and not expatriates)

2nd-5th letters: LOCAL/INTERNATIONAL STAFFING (only for Roman Catholic dioceses and jurisdictions)
*sj* and all other initials given here indicate the major Catholic religious or secular missionary institute serving a missionary jurisdiction (formerly, confided to the order). All may be identified from the Index of Christian Abbreviations, Acronyms and Initials (Part 14).

**3rd letter: Continental Conciliarism, Collegiality and Consultation**

A = All Africa Conference of Churches (AACC/CETA)
a = small foreign part of full member of AACC
B = Consilium Conferentiarum Episcopalium Europae (CCEE) (Council of European Bishops' Conferences)
C = Conference of European Churches (CEC/CEE/KEK)
c = observer status in CEC; or, small foreign part of full member of CEC
D = related to European Evangelical Alliance (EEA) through membership in affiliated national fellowship or council or alliance
E = Christian Conference of Asia (CCA) (until 1973 East Asian Christian Conference, EACC)
e = small foreign part of full member of CCA
F = Federation of Asian Bishops' Conferences (FABC)
G = related to Association of Evangelicals of Africa and Madagascar (AEAM) through membership in affiliated national fellowship or council
g = associate/special member of AEAM
H = related to Evangelical Association of the Caribbean (EAC) through membership in affiliated national fellowship or council
I = Organization of African Independent Churches (OAIC)
i = member of OAIC, also member of AACC

L = Consejo Episcopal Latinoamericano (CELAM) (Latin American Episcopal Council)
M = Caribbean Conference of Churches (CCC)
N = Caribbean Conference of Churches (CCC) and also member of CELAM
O = Standing Conference of Canonical Orthodox Bishops in the Americas (SCOBA)
o = small foreign part of full member of SCOBA
P = Pacific Conference of Churches (PCC)
p = small foreign part of full member of PCC
Q = member of CCC, also related to EAC
S = Symposium of Episcopal Conferences of Africa and Madagascar (SECAM/SCEAM)
T = continental council affiliated to ICCC (Latin American Alliance of Christian Churches (LAACC), Far Eastern Council of Christian Churches (FECCC), ICCC European Alliance, Caribbean Council of Christian Churches)
U = Movimiento pro Unidad Evangélica Latinoamericana (UNELAM), replaced from 1978 by Latin American Council of Churches (in formation) (CLAI)
u = indirect member of UNELAM/CLAI through membership in a UNELAM/CLAI affiliated national council
V = Caribbean Conference of Churches (CCC) and also member of UNELAM/CLAI
X = member of CEC, also related to EEA
x = related to EEA, also observer status in CEC
Y = related to both Evangelical Association of the Caribbean (EAC) and ICCC
. = not a member of nor related to any continental council

*Other continental councils, not coded here.* There are several other councils which are not coded here either because in formation only or because their members are not denominations but are national councils most of whom have members who in turn are not denominations but are local congregations or individuals. These include: Association of Asian Evangelical Fellowships, and South East Asia Evangelical Alliance (in formation; both related to World Evangelical Fellowship, WEF).

*Lower-case letters* (a, c, e, o, p, u) indicate that a body belongs to the council concerned (A, C, E, O, P, U), not in its own right, but by belonging as a small part (e.g. as a small foreign diocese or branch) to some larger confessional or ecclesiastical grouping based in a different country; or, if listed above, observer status.

**4th letter: Regional Conciliarism, Collegiality and Consultation**

A = Council of the Church in East Asia (CCEA) (until 1975, CCSEA)
B = Association des Conférences Episcopales du Congo/République Centrafricaine/Tchad (ACECCT) (formerly ACEACCAM)
C = Consejo Anglicano Sud Americano (CASA) (Anglican Council for South America)
D = Secretariado Episcopal de América Central y Panamá (SEDAC)
E = Association of Member Episcopal Conferences in Eastern Africa (AMECEA)
F = Conférence Episcopale Régionale de l'Afrique Occidentale Francophone (CERAO) (Regional Episcopal Conference of French-speaking West Africa)
G = Association of Episcopal Conferences of English-speaking West Africa (AECEWA)
H = Conférence Episcopale d'Afrique du Nord
I = regional council of Black/Third-World or Non-White indigenous churches
J = Asociación Regional Episcopal del Norte de Sud América (ARENSA) (Anglican; part of CASA)
K = South Pacific Anglican Council (SPAC)
L = Conférence des Evêques Latins dans les Régions Arabes (CELRA)
M = Antilles Episcopal Conference (AEC)
N = Middle East Council of Churches (MECC/CEMO) (until 1974 Near East Council of Churches, NECC/CEPO)
O = regional council of Orthodox churches
P = attached or partially attached to one of the 6 RC non-Latin Patriarchal Synods (Armenian, Chaldean, Coptic, Maronite, Melkite, Syrian)
Q = Nordic Bishops' Conference (Scandinavian Bishops' Conference) (Nordiske Bispekonferanse)
R = Anglican Council of North America and the Caribbean (ACNAC)
S = Interterritorial (Inter-Regional) Meeting of Bishops in Southern Africa (IMBISA) (formerly Southern Africa Catholic Bishops' Conference)
T = regional council affiliated to ICCC (Middle East Bible Council, Central Africa Christian Council, West Africa Council of Christian Churches (WACCC), Australasian Alliance of Bible Believing Christian Churches, Scandinavian Evangelical Council)
U = member of both MECC and CAPA
V = Conference/Council of the Anglican Provinces of Africa (CAPA)
W = member of both AMECEA and CELRA
X = Pentecostal Fellowship of North America (PFNA)
Y = Conférence des Evêques du Pacifique (CEPAC) (Episcopal Conference of the Pacific)
Z = Regional Conference of Chinese Bishops (Chung Kuo Chu-chiao T'uan)
. = not a member of any regional council

*Other regional councils, not coded here.* These are confessional or denominational councils covering a region, together with a number whose names cover a continent but which in practice are only regional because that denomination's presence is not universal there. These include: Anglican Council of Latin America (CALA), Caribbean Assembly of Reformed Churches, Community of Latin American Evangelical Ministries, Conseil Méthodiste de l'Afrique de l'Ouest/Council of the Methodist Church in West Africa, Council of Evangelical Methodist Churches in Latin America (CIEMAL), Council of Reformed Churches in Central Africa, European Baptist Federation (EBF), European Pentecostal Fellowship (EPF), Federation of Evangelical Lutheran Churches of Southern Africa (FELCSA), Fellowship of Evangelical Baptist Churches in Europe, Methodist Consultative Council of the Pacific (MCCP), North American Presbyterian and Reformed Council (NAPARC).

**5th letter: National or Plurinational Conciliarism, Collegiality and Consultation**

All national (country-wide) councils are identified by name in the footnote under each country's Table 2, which also lists other national councils which do not have denominations as members.

a = member of 2 national councils, one WCC-related and one Evangelical (WEF or AEAM or EAC)
b = member of 2 national councils, one WCC-related and one Black/Third-World or Non-White indigenous
C = national council (Protestant or Western) with no formal external international affiliations
c = associate member of C (preceding line), or related for certain functions
d = member of 2 national councils, one WCC-related and one unaffiliated (Protestant or Western)
E = national Evangelical alliance or council, affiliated to WEF (World Evangelical Fellowship) and also to one of its regional associations or continental counterparts (AEAM, EAC, EEA, et alia) where existing
e = national Evangelical alliance or council, affiliated to EEA (European Evangelical Alliance) but not (in 1978) to WEF
F = national council including Roman Catholic, Protestant, Anglican and Indigenous churches, but with no formal external international affiliations
f = formerly in the major national council, but has recently withdrawn
G = national Evangelical council affiliated to AEAM but not (in 1978) to WEF
H = national council of Pentecostal churches (Protestant)
h = member of some other council (incompletely recorded in Table 2, though name and membership are given below it)
I = national council of Black/Third-World or Non-White indigenous churches (predominantly)
i = member of I (preceding line) and also of H
J = national council of Black/Third-World or Non-White indigenous churches (different to I)
K = national council of churches, or Christian council, in working relationship with WCC but not affiliated to it
k = associate member of K (preceding line), or affiliated for certain services; or permanent observer member of K
L = national Evangelical council affiliated to Evangelical Association of the Caribbean but not (in 1978) to WEF
l = as L, but also affiliated to ICCC
M = national council of foreign missionary societies (church represented through one or more of its mission bodies)
N = national council of churches, or Christian council, affiliated to CWME of WCC (formerly to IMC)
n = associate member of N (preceding line), or affiliated for certain services; or permanent observer member of N
O = national council or liaison committee of Orthodox churches
P = plurinational Roman Catholic episcopal or bishops' conference (covering 2 or 3 countries included in conference's name)
Q = member of plurinational RC episcopal conference, also full member of national council related to WCC
q = as Q, but only observer or associate member of national council related to WCC
R = national Roman Catholic episcopal or bishops' conference
r = small diocese or church attached to RC national episcopal conference in another country (and so not included in conference's name)
S = member of national RC episcopal conference, also full member of national council related to WCC
s = as S, but only observer or associate member of national council related to WCC
T = national council affiliated, or informally related, to ICCC
t = former member of T (preceding line), now withdrawn; or, member of council formerly affiliated to ICCC, now withdrawn
u = member in temporary or once-only national conference of churches in country where permanent council prohibited
V = member of national RC episcopal conference, also full member of national council not related to WCC
v = as V, but only observer or associate member of national council not related to WCC
W = national (ecumenical) council of churches, or Christian council, formally an associate council of WCC
w = associate member of W (preceding line), or affiliated for certain services; or permanent observer member of W; or member of country-wide council associated with W
x = member of 2 other national councils
y = some other Black/Third-World or Non-White indigenous national council (different to I and J)
Z = member of 3 national councils
z = member of 3 national councils (one WCC-related, one Evangelical)
. = not a member of any national council

**COLUMN 8: NAMES, NOTES, AND OTHER STATISTICS**

These descriptive notes include a selection of any significant data concerning some of the following elements (all items in italics are current initials, names, translations or expanded titles of the church's name in column 1): name in major national or local language (in italics), preceded by initials if commonly used (in italics), then geographical sub-title of the body if any (in italics), and wider geographical jurisdictions or entities to which the body belongs (not in italics), translation into English (in italics), alternate name(s) (in italics), former names (not in italics), foreign missionary society(ies) past and/or present, brief geographical or historical notes, ethnic or linguistic or national/expatriate (citizen/alien) composition of members (Christians) as % (in descending order of numerical size, or (single name) dominant ethnic or linguistic group), and other statistics available.

Italicized abbreviations and initials (in italics) in column 8 are either (a) first initial of the country concerned (A for Austria, B for Belgium, etc), or (b) local-language words in titles (e.g. in Indonesia, G=Gereja, Church) identified in the notes under the table. Non-italicized letters are either (c) initials of co-operating missionary societies (listed in full in Index of Abbreviations, Acronyms and Initials),(d) jurisdictions, as listed above under column 1, or (e) abbreviations and codes common to all countries as set out below. In the listings of statistics in this column in the table, personnel are always the first statistics shown, in the order C, n, x, m, w, f, pp.

A = year when church became autonomous (if significant)
B = (at head of a sub-column) location in province or state
b = parishes (as defined by the church concerned, if different from column 5)
bc = Roman Catholic diocesan brothers' council
C = Roman Catholic religious institutes (i.e. orders, congregations and societies) officially at work (foreign and local); the 3 figures given (e.g. C=3+1+15) enumerate the number of distinct institutes of, respectively, *clerics* (priests mainly, occasionally also with some brothers and seminarians), + *brothers*, + *sisters*
D = Roman Catholic diocesan councils of post-conciliar (Vatican II) type (Synod, PC, pc, bc, lc, sc)
d = monasteries (religious houses for men, monks, brothers)
de = monasteries and convents
declining = numerical decrease in recent years compared to earlier larger following
e = convents (religious houses for women, nuns, sisters)
esp = especially
et al = et alia (and other things), et alii (and other people)
ex = schism (split, secession, breakoff) from or out of church or mission indicated
f = foreign missionary personnel (aliens, expatriates), as defined by church or mission (lay and ordained, men and women, usually including only those active on the field, seconded or on furlough)
G = annual growth rate of membership, % pa (% per year), in 1970 or over period 1965–75 (G=0 means zero growth; minus means decline)
H = hospitals operated by church or mission (including leprosaria, sanatoria)
HQ = location of headquarters, see city, episcopal residence, secretariat, denominational offices (usually only given here if not given in, or if not the same as, any location in title in column 1)
h = clinics, dispensaries, maternity centres, mobile clinics, operated by church or mission
i = mission stations (of foreign missionary societies)
j = printing presses or publishing houses operated by church or mission
k = bookshops run by church or mission
L = (at head of a sub-column) official language used
lc = Roman Catholic diocesan council of laity
M = co-operating foreign missionary societies (with a local or national administration) in the past and/or present
MS = Missionary Society (part of title or name)
m = men lay workers, lay preachers, brothers, monks (full-time; nationals plus expatriates; Roman Catholic men religious brothers (members of men's religious institutes, nationals and expatriates) but excluding Roman Catholic lay catechists; Anglican or Orthodox brothers or monks, Protestants and Anglicans in church pastoral or evangelistic work (including nationals but not usually expatriates))
mw = total full-time lay workers, men plus women (=m+w)
N = priests prevented from functioning by atheistic state
n = national (citizen) clergy (ordained ministers, pastors, priests (secular and religious, deacons, deaconesses, ordained women, bishops); active only, excluding retired
nm = total men workers, ordained and lay (=n+m)
nx = total clergy or ministers, national plus expatriate (=n+x)
P = practising Christians, % (those fulfilling their churches' minimum annual obligations of church attendance (e.g. Easter attenders or communicants), as % of affiliated Christians eligible to attend)
PC = Roman Catholic diocesan pastoral council, for laity, religious, and clergy, with total members in parentheses ( ); if followed by 2 numbers in parentheses, these=priests/religious members, and lay members
p = Bible schools, catechist training schools: Protestant Bible-training schools, usually for lay church workers, sometimes also for ordained; Roman Catholic catechist training schools, of primary or secondary level
pc = Roman Catholic diocesan priests' council or senate, with total members in parentheses ( ); if followed by 3 numbers in parentheses, these=members nominated by bishop, members ex officio, and members elected by all priests
pp = part-time preachers (unsalaried but officially-accredited volunteer spare-time local preachers, lay preachers, lay readers)
q = religious seminaries (not secular or diocesan; Roman Catholic major seminaries for religious clergy)
qv = quod vide, which see (i.e. refer elsewhere to the item just mentioned)
R = radio letters (normal annual listeners' letters received from this country by all Christian radio stations or agencies, home or foreign)
r = church-related or -operated colleges, teacher training colleges, major high or secondary schools, academies, technical or industrial schools, or other educational institutions of higher learning
RE = Roman Catholic ecclesiastical region (in the USA only)
S = active BCC students (enrolled in Bible correspondence courses)
s = seminaries for preparation for the ordained ministry (major seminaries, theological colleges, Bible academies, Bible institutes, Bible colleges, officers' training schools, church-operated university faculties of theology; Roman Catholic secular/diocesan (but not religious/regular) major seminaries); sometimes followed in parentheses by number of seminarians (in training for the ordained ministry)
sc = Roman Catholic diocesan sisters' council
school = primary or middle schools (not secondary or higher)

SS = Sunday-school enrolment
ST = state: name or zip code abbreviation for secular or civil state or province co-terminous, or nearly so, with diocese
Synod = Roman Catholic diocesan synod (climax of internal ecumenism)
T = total or accumulated BCC enrolments (students in Bible correspondence courses now or in past)
t = Sunday-schools, sabbath schools
u = participation in a united seminary (sponsored by 2 or more denominations)
V = BCC conversions (students enrolled in Bible correspondence courses who have professed conversion as a result)
v = church-related or -operated universities
W = attending Christians, or weekly church attenders, % (attenders each Sunday or Saturday as % of affiliated Christians eligible to attend)
w = women lay workers, sisters, nuns (full-time; nationals plus expatriates; Roman Catholic women religious (members of women's religious institutes) but excluding Catholic lay women catechists; Anglican or Orthodox sisters or nuns, Protestants and Anglicans in church pastoral or evangelistic work)
x = expatriate (alien, foreign, non-citizen) clergy (ordained ministers, pastors, priests (secular and religious), deacons, deaconesses, ordained women, bishops); active only, not retired
Y,y = annual baptisms (new persons baptized in a recent year around 1970–80; Y=adult baptisms, y=infant baptisms, Yy=adults + infants combined (or, if baptism not practised, Y=new adult members admitted)
z = catechumens, baptismal candidates (these are always included in column 7; hence for the Roman Catholic Church, the number of baptized Catholics = column 7 minus catechumens)
( ) = number of students, monks, nuns, Sunday-school scholars, or pupils in the institutions referred to (e.g. 2s(20) means 2 seminaries with 20 seminarians training for the ordained ministry)
% ethnic group = percentage of Christian population belonging to various ethnic groups
% Catholic (% RC) = percentage of total population in the area of a jurisdiction who are baptized Roman Catholics
% Muslim/pagan/&c = percentage of total population, in the area of a jurisdiction, who are Muslims/pagans/&c

**SUB-TABLES IN COLUMN 8.** For certain large denominations, the Roman Catholic Church in particular, a sub-table for all its dioceses may be given in column 8. The codes for each such table are given on the first line of the table.
**TOTALS FOR A CHURCH WITH DIOCESES.** Statistics in column 8 for the first line of a denomination with indented component dioceses under it always include whatever statistics are shown for the dioceses below. Often the totals on the first line are greater than the totals of those below because the dioceses only show part of the breakdown and do not include non-diocesan staff.
**OVERFLOW DATA.** If the amount of data available here for any denomination is too large for column 8, it will then be found in the overflow position ADDITIONAL DATA ON CHURCHES, below Table 2.
**DOUBLY-AFFILIATED.** Persons affiliated to or claimed by 2 denominations at once (as shown, defined and described in Tables 1).
**DISAFFILIATED.** Former Christians recently withdrawn from state or majority churches (as shown, defined and described in Tables 1).
**FOOTNOTES.** Detailed descriptions and definitions of each of these will be found in Part 3.
**COUNTRY-WIDE TOTALS.** In this footnote under Table 2, there are 9 categories. If any category is omitted under a Table 2, it means that the total for that category is zero (nil).

# GLOBAL TABLES

## GLOBAL TABLE 31: GEOPOLITICO-RELIGIOUS DATA FOR ALL COUNTRIES

Up to this point, the Codebook has dealt with Tables 1 and 2 in Part 7. The same codes apply to many Global Tables in Part 1 and Part 8. The rest of the Codebook now deals with Global Table 31 in Part 8.
Global Table 31 has 107 columns of data for each of the 223 countries. On the left below are given the column numbers which appear at the heads of columns in the table; then the title of each column; then the codes (if any) used in each column. If no code is given, the column reports statistics of the item described in the title. Full explanations of all titles and codes are given in Part 3

### GEOPOLITICO-RELIGIOUS TYPOLOGIES

GEOGRAPHY
Column 1  Country (numbered 001 to 223) (3-digit code)
Column 2  Continent (major area, as defined by UN)
          Code:  1 Africa
                 2 East Asia
                 3 Europe
                 4 Latin America
                 5 Northern America
                 6 Oceania
                 7 South Asia
                 8 USSR
Column 3  Region (UN terminology) (2-digit code)
          Code:  1 China
                 2 Japan
                 3 Other East Asia
                 4 Middle South Asia
                 5 Eastern South Asia
                 6 Western South Asia
                 7 Western Europe
                 8 Southern Europe
                 9 Eastern Europe
                10 Northern Europe
                11 USSR
                12 Western Africa
                13 Eastern Africa
                14 Middle Africa
                15 Northern Africa
                16 Southern Africa
                17 Northern America
                18 Tropical South America
                19 Middle America (mainland)
                20 Temperate South America
                21 Caribbean
                22 Australia & New Zealand
                23 Melanesia
                24 Micronesia & Polynesia

POLITICO-ECONOMIC SITUATION
Column 4  Development, 1980
          Code:  1 more developed (Europe, NAmerica, Aust-NZ, Japan, USSR, Temperate SAmerica)
                 2 less developed (rest of world)
Column 5  Economy, 1980
          Code:  1 developed market economy
                 2 centrally-planned economy
                 3 developing market economy
Column 6  Economic system, 1980
          Code:  1 Capitalist
                 2 Mixed economy (free enterprise plus state ownership)
                 3 Third-World Socialist
                 4 Social Democratic (party in power)
                 5 Marxist-Leninist

Political alignment, 1970-1980:
Column 7  In 1970
Column 8  In 1975
Column 9  In 1980
          Code:  1 Western (or Capitalist) world
                 2 Communist (or Marxist Socialist) world
                 3 Third World (or non-aligned world)
Column 10 Political freedom, 1980
          Code:  1 free (full civil and political rights)
                 2 partially free
                 3 not free
Column 11 Political freedom index, %, 1980 (nation's respect for liberty; 100% = completely free)
Column 12 Democratic rule, 1980 (2-digit code); the extent to which all de facto political power is in the hands of the populace themselves
          Code:  1 *multi-party states* (de facto)
                 a  federal parliamentary republic/state/constitutional monarchy
                 b  parliamentary republic/state/constitutional monarchy
                 c  self-governing parliamentary state in association with another state
                 2 *one-party states* (de jure or de facto)
                 d  ecclesiastical state
                 e  one-party republic/parliamentary state/constitutional monarchy/empire
                 f  one-party socialist or Marxist republic or state
                 g  one-party Communist republic or state
                 3 *no-party countries: dependencies*
                 h  self-governing dependency, colony or territory
                 i  direct-rule dependency, colony or territory
                 j  condominium
                 k  colony under martial law
                 l  occupied territory with regime in exile
                 m  secessionist territory and regime
                 n  forcibly-annexed territory (in last 10 years)
                 4 *no-party countries: military rule*
                 o  republic under martial law
                 p  republic under military rule
                 q  socialist or Marxist military rule
                 r  military junta
                 5 *no-party countries: dictatorships* (autocracies)
                 s  absolute monarchy
                 t  no-party republic under authoritarian rule
                 u  republic under dictatorship
                 v  military dictatorship
                 w  absolute dictatorship, totalitarian rule

LANGUAGES
Column 13 Languages used in country, 1980: total of all significant languages in use, both indigenous, foreign-origin, and expatriate.
Column 14 Official state language(s), 1980:
          (Languages are coded here as one-character variables, and include only those which are countrywide, i.e. official throughout their whole country. These are given in 2 listings: (1) left below, a listing alphabetically by codes, these consisting of firstly (a) capital letters A-Z (in roman type, with 5 in italics: $M', P', R', S', W'$), signifying state languages of populations over 20 million each in 1980, (b) lower-case letters a-z (in roman type, with 5 in italics: $c', g', m', r', u'$), signifying state languages of under 20 million but over one million population each, followed by (c) lowercase letters with diacritical marks (umlauts), signifying state languages of under one million each but over 250,000; followed by (d) numerals 1-9, signifying state languages of under 250,000 each. (2) The second listing, at right below, is given alphabetically by language).

| Code | Language | Language | Code |
|---|---|---|---|
| | (a) *Over 20 million each* | Afrikaans | M |
| A | Arabic | Albanian | a |
| B | Bengali | Amharic | L |
| C | Chinese (Mandarin) | Arabic | A |
| D | Dutch (Flemish) | Bengali | B |
| E | English | Bislama | l |
| F | French | Bulgarian | b |
| G | German | Burmese | W |
| H | Hindi | Catalan | 2 |
| I | Italian | Chewa | $c'$ |
| J | Japanese | Chinese | C |
| K | Korean | Comorian | ä |
| L | Amharic | Czech | c |
| M | Afrikaans | Danish | d |
| $M'$ | Macedonian | Dutch | D |
| N | Persian (Farsi) | Dzongkha | z |
| O | Filipino (Pilipino) | English | E |
| P | Portuguese | Faeroese | 3 |
| $P'$ | Pushtu | Filipino | O |
| Q | Serbo-Croatian | Finnish | f |
| R | Russian | French | F |
| $R'$ | Romanian | German | G |
| S | Spanish | Greek | g |
| $S'$ | Swahili (Kiswahili) | Greenlandic | 4 |
| T | Turkish | Guaraní | $g'$ |
| U | Urdu | Hebrew | e |
| V | Vietnamese | Hindi | H |
| W | Burmese | Hungarian | h |
| $W'$ | Slovenian | Icelandic | 5 |
| X | Indonesian (Bahasa) | Indonesian | X |
| Y | Polish | Irish | i |
| Z | Thai | Italian | I |
| | | Japanese | J |
| | (b) *From 1 to 20 million* | Khmer | k |
| a | Albanian (Tosk) | Korean | K |
| b | Bulgarian | Lao | l |
| c | Czech | Latin | 6 |
| $c'$ | Chewa (Chichewa) | Luxemburgish | ê |
| d | Danish | Macedonian | $M'$ |
| e | Hebrew | Malagasy | m |
| f | Finnish | Malay | $m'$ |
| g | Greek | Maldivian | 7 |
| $g'$ | Guaraní | Maltese | ï |
| h | Hungarian | Mongolian | o |
| i | Irish (Gaelic) | Nepali | n |
| j | Norwegian | Norwegian | j |
| k | Khmer | Persian | N |
| l | Lao | Pijin | p |
| m | Malagasy | Polish | Y |
| $m'$ | Malay | Portuguese | P |
| n | Nepali | Pushtu | $P'$ |
| o | Mongolian | Quechua | q |
| p | Pijin (Neo-Melanesian) | Romanian | $R'$ |
| q | Quechua | Romansh | r |
| r | Romansh | Ruanda | $r'$ |
| $r'$ | Ruanda (Kinyaruanda) | Rundi | y |
| s | Swedish | Russian | R |
| t | Tamil | Samoan | 8 |
| u | Sinhalese | Sango | x |
| $u'$ | Slovak | Serbo-Croatian | Q |
| v | Somali | Sinhalese | u |
| w | Sotho (Sesotho) | | |

*Continued overleaf*

| | | | | |
|---|---|---|---|---|
| x | Sango | Slovak | | |
| y | Rundi (Kirundi) | Slovenian | | $u'$ |
| z | Dzongkha | Somali | | $W'$ |
| | | Sotho | | v |
| (c) *From 250,000 to 1 million* | | Spanish | | w |
| ä | Comorian | Swahili | | S |
| ẽ | Luxemburgish | Swazi | | $S'$ |
| ĩ | Maltese | Swedish | | ö |
| ö | Swazi (isiSwati) | Tamil | | s |
| ü | Tswana (Setswana) | Thai | | t |
| | | Tongan | | Z |
| (d) *Under 250,000* | | Tswana | | 9 |
| 1 | Bislama | Turkish | | ü |
| 2 | Catalan | Urdu | | T |
| 3 | Faeroese | Vietnamese | | U |
| 4 | Greenlandic | | | V |
| 5 | Icelandic | | | |
| 6 | Latin | | | |
| 7 | Maldivian (Divehi) | | | |
| 8 | Samoan | | | |
| 9 | Tongan | | | |

MODERN LIVING, 3 indicators of
Column 15   Urban dwellers, % (to nearest 1%)
Column 16   Cinema attendances per year per member of population
Column 17   Physical quality of life index (PQLI), %, 1978 (effectiveness of social services)

RELIGIO-POLITICAL SITUATION (church and state)
State religion or philosophy (de jure), 1900-1980:
Column 18   in 1900
Column 19   in 1970
Column 20   in 1975
Column 21   in 1980
Code:   R   religious
S   secular (non-religious)
A   atheistic (anti-religious, Marxist)
Expanded codes:
RA   Anglican
RB   Buddhist
RC   Roman Catholic
RD   Adventist
RG   Confucian
RH   Hindu
RI   Islamic
RJ   Jewish
RL   Lutheran
RM   Methodist
RO   Orthodox
RR   Reformed
RS   Shinto
RT   Tribal religionist
RX   Christian (unspecified)
Column 22   Religious liberty (de facto), 1980
Code:   1 state propagates Christianity
2 massive state subsidies to churches
3 limited state subsidies to churches
4 state subsidizes schools only
5 complete state non-interference
6 limited political restrictions
7 minorities discriminated against
8 state interference and obstruction
9 state hostility and prohibition
10 state suppression or eradication

MISSION
Column 23   Foreign mission (country's situation), 1970-1980
(criterion: size of M, missionaries received per million population; and S, missionaries sent out per million)
Code:   1 closed (M and S both less than 8)
2 partially-closed (8 less than M less than 40)
3 restricted (40 less than M less than 100, S less than 40)
4 receiving (M greater than 100, S less than 40)
5 receiving/sending (M greater than S greater than 40)
6 sending (S greater than M, 100 greater than M greater than 40)
7 sharing (S greater than M greater than 100)

## CHURCHES

DENOMINATIONS
Column 24   Denominations, 1975
Column 25   Denominations per million population, 1975
Column 26   Worship centres (church buildings, congregations, sites), 1970
Column 27   Worship centres per million population, 1970

### CHRISTIAN ORGANIZATIONS

INSTITUTIONS
Column 28   Major Christian institutions, 1973-1978
Column 29   Major Christian institutions per million population, 1970

SERVICE AGENCIES
Column 30   Service agencies (parachurch agencies), 1973-1978
Column 31   Service agencies per million population, 1970

### CHRISTIAN PERSONNEL

NATIONALS AND ALIENS
Full-time Christian workers:
Column 32   Total (nationals and foreigners), 1973-1978
Column 33   Population per worker (national and foreign), 1970

NATIONALS
Column 34   National (citizen) personnel only, 1973-1978
Column 35   National personnel per million population, 1970

### INTERNATIONAL SHARING OF PERSONNEL

NATIONALS SENT ABROAD
Foreign missionaries or personnel, 1973-1978:
Column 36   Nationals sent abroad (total)
Column 37   Anglican
Column 38   Black/Third-World indigenous
Column 39   Catholic (non-Roman)
Column 40   Marginal Protestant
Column 41   Orthodox
Column 42   Protestant
Column 43   Roman Catholic
Column 44   Total sent per million population, 1970 (=S)

ALIENS FROM ABROAD
Column 45   Aliens received from abroad (total)
Column 46   (a)   from Western world
Column 47   from Communist world

Column 48   from Third World
Column 49   (b)   Anglican
Column 50   Black/Third World indigenous
Column 51   Catholic (non-Roman)
Column 52   Marginal Protestant
Column 53   Orthodox
Column 54   Protestant
Column 55   Roman Catholic
Column 56   Total received per million population, 1970 (=M)

### CHRISTIAN LITERATURE

BOOKS, PERIODICALS AND LIBRARIES
Column 57   Annual new book titles (all subjects), 1974
Column 58   Annual new religious book titles (all religions), 1974
Column 59   Religious (Christian) periodicals (titles), 1975
Column 60   Periodical titles (Christian) per million population, 1970
Column 61   Major religious libraries (under Christian auspices), 1975
Column 62   Major religious libraries per million population, 1970

#### SCRIPTURE DISTRIBUTION (organized)

Annual organized distribution, 1900-1975

BIBLES PER YEAR
Free distribution:
Column 63   1900
Column 64   1950
Column 65   1960
Column 66   1970
Column 67   1975
Subsidized distribution:
Column 68   1900
Column 69   1950
Column 70   1960
Column 71   1970
Column 72   1975
Column 73   Commercial distribution, 1975
Column 74   Total distribution, 1975
Column 75   Total per million population, 1975

NEW TESTAMENTS PER YEAR
Free distribution:
Column 76   1900
Column 77   1950
Column 78   1960
Column 79   1970
Column 80   1975
Subsidized distribution:
Column 81   1900
Column 82   1950
Column 83   1960
Column 84   1970
Column 85   1975
Column 86   Commercial distribution, 1975
Column 87   Total distribution, 1975
Column 88   Total per million population, 1975

PORTIONS AND SELECTIONS
Column 89   Portions (UBS only), 1975
Column 90   Selections (UBS only), 1975

### CHRISTIAN BROADCASTING

SETS AND LETTERS
Column 91   Radios and TV sets per 100 (hundred) total population (to nearest 1%)
Column 92   Radio letters (annual listeners' letters or other communications received in 1975 by international and national Christian radio and TV stations and programmes).

AUDIENCE
Regular demographic audience for Christian broadcasting, i.e. average monthly radio/TV audience (total regular listening/viewing community, including children, to both worship services and other Christian programmes), as % total population, 1970-78:
Column 93   (a)   listeners to national or international Christian radio/TV stations (Protestant, Catholic, Orthodox, Anglican, et alia);
Column 94   (b)   listeners to Christian programmes over state or other secular stations within the country (or, occasionally, outside);
Column 95   (c)   total demographic audience, i.e. (a) plus (b) minus any duplications.

### LITERACY

ADULT LITERACY RATE, 1900-1980
Adult literacy (15 years and over), i.e. adult literates as % adult population:
Column 96   in 1900
Column 97   in 1950
Column 98   in 1975
Column 99   in 1980

### EVANGELIZATION, 1900-2000

YEAR
Column 100   Year evangelization begun (first resident Christians or missionaries, whether or not subsequently removed); these data can also be used as a typology of countries by dividing the period AD 30-1980 into 2, 3, 4 or more historical periods, as required

EXTENT EVANGELIZED
Column 101   Extent of individual evangelization, e% (1970) (Johnstone scale)

Extent of comparative demographic evangelization, E% (Barrett scale):
Column 102   in 1900
Column 103   in 1970
Column 104   in 1980
Column 105   in 1985
Column 106   in 2000
Code:   0- 9   non-evangelized (untouched)
10-19   sparsely-evangelized
20-29   marginally-evangelized
30-39   slightly-evangelized
40-49   partially-evangelized
50-59   half-evangelized
60-69   moderately-evangelized
70-79   generally-evangelized
80-89   extensively-evangelized
90-99   highly-evangelized
100   fully-evangelized
These data can also be used as an eleven-fold typology of countries from 0 to 10, by removing the last digit from all numbers in these columns.

OUTREACH
Column 107   Outreach factor = total evangelized in country ÷ total Christians, 1980

# PART 7
# SURVEY

A survey of Christianity and religions
in 223 countries

*The Lord spoke to Moses: 'Take a census of the people of Israel. Number the whole community by families. Make a detailed list of them by their tribal hosts.'*
––Numbers 1.1–2, Revised Standard Version and New English Bible.

Information on each country in this survey is set out in a standardized order and format, as follows.

**Secular data** (statistics, description)

**Table 1. Adherents of all religions, AD 1900-2000**
    Footnotes to Table 1

**Non-Christian religions** (narrative)

**Christianity** (narrative)
    Major churches
    Church and State
    Interdenominational organizations
    Broadcasting

**Bibliography** (listing)

**Table 2. Organized Christianity, AD 1970-1980**
    Footnotes to Table 2

Standard categories of data will be found in the same locations under all countries. To locate a standard category, use the Standard and Definitive Locations Index in Part 14.

Note that place names may be spelt in different ways, being anglicized in the text and in most maps in this section, but with local spelling in Tables 2 and in the maps in Part 11.

# AFGHANISTAN

## SECULAR DATA

**STATE. Official name:** The Republic of Afghanistan (Doulati Gamhouriate ye Afghánistán). Adjective of nationality: Afghan.
**Flag** (shown above right): Black, red, and green tricolour, with coat of arms next to hoist.
**Area:** 647,497 sq.km. (250,000 sq.miles). Agricultural land: 22.3%.
**Government:** Marxist republic under military rule, since 1978 (1747 absolute monarchy, 1881 British influence, 1919 Independence declared, 1964 limited constitutional monarchy, 1973 leftist military coup, 1978 Marxist military coup).
**Legislature:** Republican Revolutionary Council.
**Official languages:** Pushtu and Dari (Persian).
**Chief cities:** capital Kabul 534,350 (1973), Kandahar 140,020, Baghlan 110,870, Herat 108,750.
**Political divisions:** 28 Provinces.
**Armed forces** (1976): Total 100,000 regular: army 90,000, air force 10,000 (152 combat aircraft). Reserves: 162,000. Paramilitary forces: 25,000 gendarmerie.
**Foreign forces** (1973): 200 USSR military advisers. (1980) 80,000 USSR military.

**DEMOGRAPHY. Population:** 18,294,000 (official estimate of 1.VII.1973; no censuses yet. For 1970–2000 (UN), see last row of Table 1). Population density (1975): 30/sq.km. (77/sq.mile). Under 15 years: 42%. Growth rate (1975–80): 2.67% per year (births 4.81%, deaths −2.14%). Life expectancy (1975–80): 42.7 years. Household size: 5.4 persons.
**Major languages:** Pushtu, Dari, Tadzhik, Uzbek, Turkoman, Baluchi, Arabic, Brahui, and about 45 smaller languages.
**Urban dwellers** (1970): 7.5%. Urban growth rate (1950–70): 2.8% per year.
**Labour force:** 35%.
**Tourists** (1973): 96,222. (1977) 250,000 (from Canada, UK, USA).

**ETHNOLINGUISTIC GROUPS:** 56.0% Afghani (Pathan, Pashtun: 24% Ghilzai, 16% Durrani), 28.0% Tadzhik, 5.3% Uzbek, 2.7% Hazara, 2.0% Turkmen, 0.7% Nuristani, 0.7% Firozkohi, 0.7% Pashai, 0.6% Baluchi, 0.6% Jamshidi, 0.5% Teymur, 0.3% Persian, 0.2% Afshar, 0.2% Kirgiz, 0.2% Arab, 0.1% Brahui, 0.1% Kurdish, Russian & other European (8,000), USA White (1,300), Indian, Kazakh, Jewish, Chinese, Turkish, other Iranian.

**MONEY** (1977). **Monetary unit:** afgháni (= 100 puls); US$1 = AFS 46.00.
**National income per person:** US$100. Average annual family income: US$540.
**Inflation:** (1970–74) 2.4% per year (1975 consumer price index 135).
**Cost of living in capital** (1976): index 98 (Washington DC=100). Daily cost of living: US$29.

**EDUCATION.** Adult literacy: (1975) 12%. Education rate: 12%. Schools: 3,257. Universities: 2.

**HEALTH.** Hospitals: 55 (2,479 beds). Doctors: 937. Lepers: 7,600 (0.39 per 1,000). Blind: 200,000. Psychotics: 130,000.

**LITERATURE.** Annual new book titles (1973): 33. Periodicals: 24. Newspapers: 18 dailies, 1 non-daily.

**COMMUNICATION** (per 1,000 people). Phones: 1. Radios: 16. Daily newspaper circulation: 6 copies.

### TABLE 1.   RELIGIOUS ADHERENTS IN AFGHANISTAN

| Year | 1900 | | mid-1970 | | Annual change, 1970–1980 | | | | mid-1975 | | mid-1980 | | 2000 | |
|---|---|---|---|---|---|---|---|---|---|---|---|---|---|---|
| Name | Adherents | % | Adherents | % | Natural | Conversion | Total | Rate | Adherents | % | Adherents | % | Adherents | % |
| Muslims | 5,074,200 | 99.5 | 16,856,060 | 99.3 | 502,514 | 408 | 502,922 | 2.63 | 19,143,810 | 99.3 | 21,885,280 | 99.3 | 36,406,840 | 99.3 |
| Hindus | 5,000 | 0.1 | 100,000 | 0.6 | 2,992 | 8 | 3,000 | 2.63 | 114,000 | 0.6 | 130,000 | 0.6 | 216,000 | 0.6 |
| Tribal religionists | 20,000 | 0.4 | 10,000 | 0.1 | 236 | −436 | −200 | −2.22 | 9,000 | 0.0 | 8,000 | 0.0 | 5,000 | 0.0 |
| **Christians** | **300** | 0.0 | **7,740** | 0.0 | **147** | **13** | **160** | **1.89** | **8,470** | 0.0 | **9,340** | 0.0 | **15,730** | 0.0 |
| crypto-Christians | 0 | 0.0 | 200 | 0.0 | 7 | 13 | 20 | 6.67 | 300 | 0.0 | 400 | 0.0 | 2,000 | 0.0 |
| professing | 300 | 0.0 | 7,540 | 0.0 | 140 | 0 | 140 | 1.71 | 8,170 | 0.0 | 8,940 | 0.0 | 13,730 | 0.0 |
| Protestants | 200 | 0.0 | 3,940 | 0.0 | 62 | 0 | 62 | 1.47 | 4,220 | 0.0 | 4,560 | 0.0 | 6,660 | 0.0 |
| Roman Catholics | 100 | 0.0 | 3,400 | 0.0 | 72 | 0 | 72 | 1.94 | 3,720 | 0.0 | 4,120 | 0.0 | 6,600 | 0.0 |
| Anglicans | 0 | 0.0 | 200 | 0.0 | 6 | 0 | 6 | 2.62 | 230 | 0.0 | 260 | 0.0 | 470 | 0.0 |
| nominal | 100 | 0.0 | 4,000 | 0.0 | 35 | 0 | 35 | 0.85 | 4,140 | 0.0 | 4,350 | 0.0 | 6,290 | 0.0 |
| affiliated | 200 | 0.0 | 3,740 | 0.0 | 112 | 13 | 125 | 2.89 | 4,330 | 0.0 | 4,990 | 0.0 | 9,440 | 0.0 |
| total practising | 160 | 80 | 2,620 | 70 | 79 | 8 | 87 | 2.89 | 3,030 | 70 | 3,490 | 70 | 6,140 | 65 |
| non-practising | 40 | 20 | 1,120 | 30 | 33 | 5 | 38 | 2.89 | 1,300 | 30 | 1,500 | 30 | 3,300 | 35 |
| Roman Catholics | 100 | 0.0 | 2,000 | 0.0 | 60 | 0 | 60 | 2.62 | 2,270 | 0.0 | 2,600 | 0.0 | 4,660 | 0.0 |
| Protestants | 100 | 0.0 | 1,620 | 0.0 | 48 | 12 | 60 | 3.12 | 1,920 | 0.0 | 2,220 | 0.0 | 4,500 | 0.0 |
| Evangelicals | 10 | 0.0 | 400 | 0.0 | 12 | 8 | 20 | 4.00 | 500 | 0.0 | 600 | 0.0 | 1,500 | 0.0 |
| Anglicans | 0 | 0.0 | 100 | 0.0 | 3 | 0 | 3 | 2.62 | 110 | 0.0 | 130 | 0.0 | 230 | 0.0 |
| Marginal Protestants | 0 | 0.0 | 20 | 0.0 | 1 | 1 | 2 | 6.67 | 30 | 0.0 | 40 | 0.0 | 50 | 0.0 |
| Sikhs | 0 | 0.0 | 2,000 | 0.0 | 60 | 0 | 60 | 2.62 | 2,300 | 0.0 | 2,600 | 0.0 | 4,300 | 0.0 |
| Atheists | 0 | 0.0 | 1,600 | 0.0 | 48 | 0 | 48 | 2.62 | 1,820 | 0.0 | 2,080 | 0.0 | 3,730 | 0.0 |
| Baha'is | 0 | 0.0 | 400 | 0.0 | 13 | 7 | 20 | 4.00 | 500 | 0.0 | 600 | 0.0 | 2,000 | 0.0 |
| Jews | 500 | 0.0 | 200 | 0.0 | −10 | 0 | −10 | −10.00 | 100 | 0.0 | 100 | 0.0 | 400 | 0.0 |
| **Country's population** | **5,100,000** | 100.0 | **16,978,000** | 100.0 | **506,000** | **0** | **506,000** | **2.62** | **19,280,000** | 100.0 | **22,038,000** | 100.0 | **36,654,000** | 100.0 |

**COLUMNS, ROWS.** For meanings and definitions, see Codebook (Part 6). Note that, by definition, total 'Christians' = professing + crypto-Christians, which also = affiliated + nominal Christians. Percentages may not always total exactly, due to rounding.
**CENSUSES.** No population census has ever been taken.

### NOTES ON RELIGIONS
**ATHEISTS.** Communist Party (fragmented; illegal until 1978): membership (1970) 400. Also 200 USSR military advisers (1973).
**BAHA'IS.** In 4 local spiritual assemblies (1973): mostly Persians.
**CHRISTIANS.** All expatriates (many nominal) except for the handful of crypto-Christians who are nationals. Expatriates are not increasing at the same rate as the general population, due to both nett emigration and lower fertility.
**COUNTRY'S POPULATION.** About 150,000 European youths (and 100,000 other tourists) travel through Afghanistan each year, averaging 3,000 present or resident at any one time. Most are nominal Christians.
**CRYPTO-CHRISTIANS.** Unorganized individual nationals in the recognized churches.
**JEWS.** Rapid decline of traditional resident community 1950–75 due to emigration (leaving only a few families in Kabul and Herat), offset by temporary expatriate personnel.
**MUSLIMS.** 94% Sunnis (mostly of the Hanafite rite), 6% Shias (Twelvers among the Hazara, Kizilbash and other tribes; Neo-Ismailis among the Vokhani and Roshani); and a few Wahhabi reform movement centres in the northeast. There are 15,000 mosques. In 1974 Muslims were observing the feast of Ramadan in large numbers. *Hajj pilgrims to Mecca.* (1969) 9,125; (1970) 13,663; (1971) 10,744; (1972) 17,447; (1973) 6,220; (1974) 6,299; (1975) 5,800; (1976) 8,309.
**NOMINAL CHRISTIANS.** European expatriates who are professing Christians but unaffiliated to churches.
**TRIBAL RELIGIONISTS.** Nuristanis (called Kafirs, unbelievers) retaining ancient animistic religion despite 1890 conversion of tribe to Islam.

**NON-CHRISTIAN RELIGIONS. Islam** is the professed religion of virtually the entire populace, and there are approximately 15,000 mosques in the country. Though Islam has been active in Afghanistan since the 9th century, it did not gain the allegiance of Nooristan until 1890. The majority are Sunnis of the Hanafite rite. Important Shia minorities include the Twelvers among the Hazara, Kizilbash and several other ethnic groups, and Neo-Ismailis in the northwest among the Vokhani and Roshani. During 1974, 6,299 Muslim pilgrims from Afghanistan performed the hajj to Mecca.

**Other religions** include approximately 100,000 Hindu and Sikh Indians, and a small number of Nooristan inhabitants who retain their ancient animistic worship. Several communities of Afghani Jews remain in Kabul and Herat although most have emigrated recently to Israel, Europe and North America.

**CHRISTIANITY.** A bishop of Herat attended the Council of Seleucia in AD 424 and a Nestorian bishop was located at Kabul in the late Middle Ages, but Christian influence was terminated by Timur in the 14th century. A small Armenian church of about a dozen members existed in Kabul until 1898 when the church was destroyed and the group exiled, leaving no national Christians in the country. No missionaries, Catholic or Protestant, have been permitted inside Afghanistan. Since the penalty for apostasy from Islam is death, the few native Afghanis attracted to Christianity have in most cases left the country. The Christian community is therefore composed almost entirely of foreign technicians, diplomats and visitors, who form a growing but fluctuating community.

**CATHOLIC CHURCH.** Catholics do not belong to a diocese but are termed the Work of Spiritual Assistance to Catholics of Afghanistan. Spiritual oversight has been given to Barnabite priests under the Roman Congregation for the Oriental Church, and there has been a priest in Kabul since 1932. A Barnabite priest with official status as chaplain at the Italian

**Christian Community Church of Kabul.** *Top.* First permanent Protestant church building in Afghanistan, completed in 1971, destroyed at government order in 1973. *Bottom.* Its foundation stone.

embassy serves the expatriate community, and a number of religious personnel are engaged in technical assistance within government institutions. Besides several house congregations, there is one public Catholic chapel, located at the Italian embassy in Kabul. Catholics in 1974 were of 32 different nationalities.

OTHER CHURCHES. There are 5 other groups in Kabul: small Assemblies of God and Jehovah's Witnesses communities, a German-speaking primarily Lutheran congregation, an Anglican congregation, and the interdenominational Community Christian Church. The latter was responsible for construction of Afghanistan's first Protestant permanent church building in 1971, but this was demolished by government order in June 1973. The Community Church has also sponsored the creation of 8 other groups which meet in private homes in Herat, Lashkar Gah, Panjau, Yakaolang, Mazar-i-Sharif, Kandahar and Jalalabad.

**CHURCH AND STATE.** Under the monarchy, Islam of the Hanafite rite was the official religion. The king was its protector and was required to belong to this school, although individual Muslims could follow the rite of their choice. Non-Muslims have freedom of worship (constitution of 1964, Articles 2, 7 and 8), but all Christian evangelization among the people of the country was forbidden. In 1933, an agreement between the governments of Afghanistan and Italy created the Work of Spiritual Assistance to Catholics of Afghanistan. In July 1973, the monarchy was overthrown in a military coup, the constitution of 1964 was suspended and numerous decrees enacted, the first beginning as follows: 'Afghanistan is a republican state in accordance with the true spirit of Islam'. This article plus the construction of a new mosque by the new republican government as one of its first acts are generally interpreted as concessionary gestures to appease traditional religious groups which were closely linked to the former monarchy. However, under Afghani law it is still a capital offence for a Muslim to convert to Christianity.

**INTERDENOMINATIONAL ORGANIZATIONS.** There are no ecumenical councils. An interdenominational body, the International Aid (formerly Afghan) Mission begun in 1966, has 70 workers in the country from 10 different countries sponsored by 18 sending agencies. It seeks to serve the people of Afghanistan in the name and spirit of Christ; most of its work is medical assistance under the national government.

**BROADCASTING.** No Christian broadcasting is permitted over the state radio. Programmes are received from outside over several Christian stations.

**BIBLIOGRAPHY**
*Religiöses Volksbrauchtum in Afghanistan: Islamische Heiligenverehrung und Wallfahrtswesen im Raum Kabul.* H. Einzmann. Leiden: Brill. 1977. 480p.

TABLE 2.     ORGANIZED CHURCHES AND DENOMINATIONS IN AFGHANISTAN

| Official name 1 | Begun 2 | Type 3 | Counc 4 | Congs 5 | Adults 6 | Affiliated 7 | Names, notes, and other statistics (see Codebook) 8 |
|---|---|---|---|---|---|---|---|
| Anglican Church | | A Cen | aw... | 1 | 50 | 100 | *St Chrysostom's Church.* Expatriates. Services in Community Church. 1x. |
| Assemblies of God | 1972 | P Pe2 | zf... | 1 | 10 | 20 | M=AoG(USA). Classical Pentecostals. Small medical mission begun. 2f. |
| Catholic Church | 1933 | R Lat | o.... | 3 | 1,200 | 2,000 | *Work of Spiritual Assistance to Catholics of Afghanistan.* 2x,8w,W=25%,15Yy. |
| Community Christian Church of Kabul | 1952 | P com | ..... | 9 | 50 | 800 | *Kalisa baroi Haregis.* Kabul church destroyed 1973. 4x,W=19%,1Y,3y. |
| German-speaking Protestant Church | c1960 | P Lut | ..... | 1 | 190 | 780 | German expatriates, mainly Lutherans. Services in Community Church. |
| Jehovah's Witnesses | 1957 | M Jeh | x.... | 1 | 9 | 20 | First expatriate residents 1957. Restricted activities, completely underground. |
| Seventh-day Adventist Church | | P Adv | x.... | 1 | 10 | 20 | *SDA. Pakistan Union* (HQ Lahore). M=SDA(Philippine Union Mission). 2f. |
| **Total affiliated (mid-1970)** | | | | 17 | 1,519 | 3,740 | Total denominations (1970) . . . 7. |
| **Total affiliated (mid-1975)** | | | | 18 | 1,760 | 4,330 | Total denominations (1975) . . . 8. |
| **Total affiliated (mid-1980)** | | | | 20 | 2,030 | 4,990 | Total denominations (1980) . . . 9. |

**NOTES ON TABLE ABOVE**
COLUMNS: for meanings and CODES (cols. 1, 3, 4, 8), see Codebook (Part 6). Column 1: **Boldface type** = church with over 10% of country's affiliated Christians.

PEOPLES (ethnolinguistic). Christians: about 75% European (German, USA White, UK, Italian), 20% Indian, 5% Afghani.

**COUNTRY-WIDE TOTALS**
EVANGELIZATION (see Part 5). 1900: 3%. 1970: 14%. 1980:

17%. *Mass evangelism.* Visiting teams have had fair receptions, including the 5-member Teen Team (YFCI), 'Music with a message', in Kabul, 1969. *Radiophonic evangelism.* In Pushtu and Farsi, over FEBA (Seychelles).
FOREIGN MISSIONARIES AND PERSONNEL (aliens from abroad) (1973). Total 88. *From Western world.* 82: 71 Protestants (33 in 8 USA societies, 17 in 3 WGermany societies, 13 in 2 Canada societies, 4 in 1 Netherlands society, 3 in 4 Australia societies), about 10 Roman Catholics, 1 Anglican from New

Zealand. *From Third World.* About 6 Protestants from India, Pakistan, Philippines.
PERSONNEL. 88 (all foreign).
SCRIPTURE DISTRIBUTION (1975). Annual totals: 30 Bibles (subsidized), 200 NTs (subsidized). *Translations completed.* 1 language, Pushtu: NT 1818, Bible 1895.
SERVICE AGENCIES. About 12, including BMMF, CB, CT, IAM, MAF, MAP, MCC, NOOR, OM, WVI, YWAM.

# ALBANIA

## SECULAR DATA

**STATE. Official name:** The People's Socialist Republic of Albania (Republika Populllore e Shqipërisë). **Adjective of nationality:** Albanian.
**Flag** (shown above right): Red field, black 2-headed eagle, gold-edged red star.
**Area:** 28,748 sq.km. (11,101 sq.miles). Agricultural land: 43.1%.
**Government:** One-party Communist republic, since 1946 (1478 Turkish rule, 1912 Independence, 1925 republic, 1928 absolute monarchy, 1939 Italian rule).
**Legislature:** National Assembly, 264 members.
**Official language:** Albanian (Tosk) (*Shqip*).
**Capital:** Tiranë 169,300 (1967).
**Political divisions:** 26 Districts (rrethët).
**Armed forces** (1976): Total 47,000 regular (22,500 conscripts): army 36,000, navy 3,000, air force 8,000 (96 combat aircraft). Reserves: 100,000. Paramilitary forces: 26,000.

DEMOGRAPHY. **Population:** 1,626,315 (census of 2.X.1960.

For 1970–2000 (UN), see last row of Table 1). Population density (1975): 86/sq.km. (224/sq.mile). Under 15 years: 41%. Growth rate (1975–80): 2.63% per year (births 3.24%, deaths −0.61%). Life expectancy (1975–80): 69.4 years. Household size: 3.6 persons.
**Major languages:** Albanian (Gheg, Tosk), Greek, Macedonian, Chinese, Romany.
**Urban dwellers** (1970): 37.5%. Urban growth rate (1950–70): 6.0% per year.
**Labour force:** 43%.
**Refugees** (1977): From abroad, none. Recent exiles abroad: about 26,000 Albanians in Yugoslavia. A further 1.5 million Albanians live abroad (1.3 million in Yugoslavia, others in Greece, Italy, USA, Turkey).

**ETHNOLINGUISTIC GROUPS:** 93.1% Albanian, 2.5% Gypsy, 2.4% Greek, 0.6% Aromanian, 0.6% Macedonian, 0.5% Chinese (10,000, falling to 3,000 by 1973 and to 100 by 1977), 0.3% Montenegrin, Jewish, Bulgar, Serb.

**MONEY** (1977). **Monetary unit:** new lek (= 100 quindarka); US$1 = NL 4.10.
**National income per person:** US$650. Average annual family income: US$2,340.
**Inflation:** (1970–74) nil.
**Cost of living in capital** (1976): index 75 (Washington DC=100). Daily cost of living: US$35.

**EDUCATION.** Adult literacy: (1950) 46%, (1955) 71%. Education rate: 60%. Schools: 1,429. Universities: 1.

**HEALTH.** Hospitals: 292 (12,715 beds). Doctors: 14,371. Blind: 2,000. Psychotics: 20,000.

**LITERATURE.** Annual new book titles (1965): 502. Periodicals: 61. Scientific journals: 10. Newspapers: 2 dailies, 20 non-daily.

**COMMUNICATION** (per 1,000 people). Phones: 5. Radios: 73. TV sets: 1.7. Daily newspaper circulation: 50 copies.

TABLE 1.     RELIGIOUS ADHERENTS IN ALBANIA

| Year | 1900 | | mid-1970 | | Annual change, 1970–1980 | | | | mid-1975 | | mid-1980 | | 2000 | |
|---|---|---|---|---|---|---|---|---|---|---|---|---|---|---|
| Name | Adherents | % | Adherents | % | Natural | Conversion | Total | Rate | Adherents | % | Adherents | % | Adherents | % |
| Non-religious | 1,000 | 0.1 | 1,049,370 | 48.4 | 34,436 | 17,497 | 51,933 | 4.02 | 1,291,100 | 52.0 | 1,568,700 | 55.4 | 2,650,240 | 62.2 |
| Muslims | 548,000 | 68.5 | 600,000 | 27.7 | 15,737 | −17,737 | −2,000 | −0.34 | 590,000 | 23.8 | 580,000 | 20.5 | 500,000 | 11.7 |
| Atheists | 0 | 0.0 | 348,000 | 16.0 | 11,682 | 6,318 | 18,000 | 4.11 | 438,000 | 17.6 | 528,000 | 18.7 | 980,260 | 23.0 |
| Christians | 250,000 | 31.2 | 171,430 | 7.9 | 4,340 | −6,073 | −1,733 | −1.07 | 162,700 | 6.5 | 154,100 | 5.4 | 132,500 | 3.1 |
| crypto-Christians | 0 | 0.0 | 171,430 | 7.9 | 4,340 | −6,073 | −1,733 | −1.07 | 162,700 | 6.5 | 154,100 | 5.4 | 132,500 | 3.1 |
| professing | 250,000 | 31.2 | 0 | 0.0 | 0 | 0 | 0 | 0.00 | 0 | 0.0 | 0 | 0.0 | 0 | 0.0 |
| Orthodox | 173,000 | 21.6 | 0 | 0.0 | 0 | 0 | 0 | 0.00 | 0 | 0.0 | 0 | 0.0 | 0 | 0.0 |
| Roman Catholics | 77,000 | 9.6 | 0 | 0.0 | 0 | 0 | 0 | 0.00 | 0 | 0.0 | 0 | 0.0 | 0 | 0.0 |
| nominal | 23,500 | 2.9 | 0 | 0.0 | 0 | 0 | 0 | 0.00 | 0 | 0.0 | 0 | 0.0 | 0 | 0.0 |
| affiliated | 226,500 | 28.3 | 171,430 | 7.9 | 4,340 | −6,073 | −1,733 | −1.07 | 162,700 | 6.5 | 154,100 | 5.4 | 132,500 | 3.1 |
| total practising | 204,000 | 90 | 51,430 | 30 | 1,302 | −1,822 | −520 | −1.07 | 48,810 | 30 | 46,230 | 30 | 53,000 | 40 |
| non-practising | 22,500 | 10 | 120,000 | 70 | 3,038 | −4,251 | −1,213 | −1.07 | 113,890 | 70 | 107,870 | 70 | 79,500 | 60 |
| Orthodox | 160,000 | 20.0 | 101,000 | 4.7 | 2,587 | −3,387 | −800 | −0.83 | 97,000 | 3.9 | 93,000 | 3.3 | 75,000 | 1.8 |
| Roman Catholics | 66,500 | 8.3 | 70,000 | 3.2 | 1,734 | −2,734 | −1,000 | −1.54 | 65,000 | 2.6 | 60,000 | 2.1 | 50,000 | 1.2 |
| Protestants | 0 | 0.0 | 330 | 0.0 | 16 | 51 | 67 | 11.17 | 600 | 0.0 | 1,000 | 0.0 | 7,200 | 0.2 |
| Marginal Protestants | 0 | 0.0 | 100 | 0.0 | 3 | −3 | 0 | 0.00 | 100 | 0.0 | 100 | 0.0 | 300 | 0.0 |
| Jews | 1,000 | 0.1 | 200 | 0.0 | 5 | −5 | 0 | 0.00 | 200 | 0.0 | 200 | 0.0 | 0 | 0.0 |
| **Country's population** | **800,000** | **100.0** | **2,169,000** | **100.0** | **66,200** | **0** | **66,200** | **2.67** | **2,482,000** | **100.0** | **2,831,000** | **100.0** | **4,263,000** | **100.0** |

COLUMNS, ROWS. For meanings and definitions, see Codebook (Part 6). Note that, by definition, total 'Christians' = professing + crypto-Christians, which also = affiliated + nominal Christians. Percentages may not always total exactly, due to rounding.
CENSUSES. **1938:** 69.0% Muslims, 20.7% Orthodox, 10.3%

Roman Catholics, 200 Jews. **1945:** 68.9% Muslims, 19.2% Orthodox, 11.8% Roman Catholics. **1953** (estimate): 66.3% Muslims, 22.4% Orthodox, 11.2% Roman Catholics.

**NOTES ON RELIGIONS**
ATHEISTS. Albania Workers' Party (AWP) (Communist; in

power; pro-Chinese): membership (1970) 86,985 (36% workers, 29% peasants, 34% white-collar), rising rapidly from 66,327 in 1966; Communist voters (election of 20.IX.1970) 1,096,988.
CRYPTO-CHRISTIANS. Since 1967 all Christians have been forced underground. Their numbers are being eroded gradually due to unremitting state pressure, but there is a small but growing

number of organized and unorganized isolated radio believers. MUSLIMS. Mainly Sunnis (80%; Hanafite rite) and 20% Bektashis (dervish monastic order, expelled from Turkey in 1925). Several thousand mosques have been closed and secularized since 1965, and vast numbers of Muslims forced to apostatize. A core of believing Muslims and crypto-Muslims however

remains, and Muslims still observe the fast of Ramadan in large numbers.
NOMINAL CHRISTIANS. Up to 1945 only.
NON-RELIGIOUS. Agnostics, indifferent to religion. In addition to this 48.4% of the population (in 1970), there is a further 7.9% of the population regarded as non-religious by the state but who

remain Christians and so are classified here as crypto-Christians.
PROFESSING CHRISTIANS. These are nil in 1970 onwards, because, since 1967, as an atheistic state Albania has recognized the existence of no Christians.

---

**NON-CHRISTIAN RELIGIONS. Islam** became the majority religion of Albania after a series of mass conversions in the 17th and 18th centuries, and remained the religion of the majority of the population (69%) up to 1945. Until 1967, when all forms of organized religion were abolished, there were 2 principal Muslim groups in Albania, Sunnis and Bektashis. Sunnis of the Hanafite rite were divided into 4 regions each under the authority of a grand mufti: Tirane, Shkoder, Korçe and Gjirokaster. They were found in all parts of the country but were strongest in the central region. The Bektashis were a dervish monastic order derived from the Sunnis, expelled from Turkey in 1925, whose head (baba) resided in Albania.

**CHRISTIANITY.** Albania was successively under the Roman and Byzantine empires, Slavs, Bulgarians, Serbs and the Ottoman Turkish empire until the 20th century. In its early years it was subject to missionary thrusts from both Constantinople (c200 AD) and Rome (c385 AD); but while under the Turks, most of the people became Muslims. During the 19th century, it continually struggled for independence from neighbouring powers and achieved it in 1913. Occupied by foreign forces during World War I, Albania became independent once again in 1918

but was taken over by Italy in 1939, with Communist partisans gaining control of the country at the end of World War II. Prior to World War II, Orthodox numbered 21% of the population and Catholics 11%, with only a few score Protestants. In 1959 there were about 700,000 Muslims, 200,000 Orthodox and 100,000 Catholics out of a total population of 1,556,000.
ORTHODOX CHURCHES. The Orthodox have traditionally been strongest in the south among the Tosk. Prior to 1967 the Albanian Orthodox Church, autocephalous since April 1937, was composed of 4 dioceses: Tirane (the capital), Berat, Gjirokaster and Korçe. Because of the role played by Orthodox Clergy during the Italo-German occupation in World War II, they were not harassed at first by the Communist regime which came to power after resistance fighters had liberated the country in November 1944. However, by 1947 pressure began to build up against them, followed by detention of priests. Between 1949 and 1951, all 4 bishops were arrested and replaced by others more favourable to the regime. After the death of the primate, Paissi, the Holy Synod elected in 1966 the bishop of Gjirokaster, Msgr Damianos Kokonesi, as archbishop of Albania. The Serbian Orthodox Church established a vicariate at Shkoder in the north in 1922 under the Patriarchate of Belgrade, but all relations with the Serbian Holy Synod were cut some years back.
CATHOLIC CHURCH. The Catholic Church has been strongest in the north among the Ghegs. In 1944 there were 2 archdioceses: Durres (founded in the 13th century) and Shkoder (founded in AD 385). Shkoder had 3 suffragan dioceses: Leshe (since the 14th century), Pult (9th century), and Sape (AD 1062). The monastery of St Alexander of Ores was established in 1888, and the Apostolic Administration for Southern Albania in 1939. All these territories were under the supervision of Propaganda in Rome, except the last which was administered by the Congregation for the Oriental Church. Especially because of the ambiguous situation under the Italian occupation and its attitude during this period, the Catholic Church began to experience from December 1944 an increasing number of repressive measures: expulsion of the apostolic delegate and detention of priests in 1945, expulsion of Italian religious priests

and nuns in 1946, and the arrest and execution of 3 bishops in 1948. Since then, over 120 Catholic leaders have been executed or have died in prison: 6 bishops, 60 diocesan priests, 30 Franciscans, 13 Jesuits, 8 sisters and 10 seminarians. The last 3 bishops disappeared without trace in early 1977.

In the spring of 1971, there were only 14 Catholic priests left alive (12 in concentration camps, 2 in hiding), and of these one was executed in 1972 for baptizing a child in a prison camp. Nevertheless, there is considerable underground church activity.

**Catholic Church in Albania.** Priest interned in Lushnje labour camp, Fr Shtjefen Kurtis, who was sentenced to death and executed in 1972 for baptizing an infant at parents' request.

In particular the wearing of white wedding dress, and local celebrations with traditionally religious overtones, are used as deliberate protests.

PROTESTANT CHURCHES. Protestant activity has been very limited in Albania, restricted to the work of Seventh-day Adventists originally related to their Greek Mission, and Methodists part of their Yugoslavia Mission. These organizational contacts have also long since been broken.

**CHURCH AND STATE.** The constitution of 1946 appeared liberal in its attitude towards religion. Article 18 calls for the separation of church and state, freedom of conscience and religion, liberty of internal organization of religions and the material aid of the state to religious organizations. These were realities in the first years of the new republic. In 1949, modified again in 1963, religious communities were obliged to register their statutes with the government. Those of the Albanian Islamic community, the Albanian Bektashi community and the Albanian Orthodox Church were approved in 1950. The Catholic Church did not receive approval until 1951, because the first version of their request was refused by the government who then stipulated the necessity for a complete break of all ties with the Vatican.

A new anti-religious campaign was begun in 1964, followed by the Fifth Communist Party Congress of 1966 which set as its goal the total elimination of religion in Albania. According to the Albanian literary journal *Nendori*, 2,169 mosques, churches and convents were confiscated and secularized in 1967. At the same time the clergy were abolished and priests were assigned to 'productive work'. In October 1967 Radio Tirane proclaimed that Albania was the 'first atheist state of the world', and a few months later the Assembly of the People repealed all earlier decrees concerning religion. Since then, visitors to Albania have found that organized religious life has ceased to exist and all churches have been closed. The last Catholic Church, the cathedral of Tirane, was closed in 1969.

In 1968 under government auspices Albanian youths spread throughout the country destroying places of worship, only a small number of edifices of artistic, cultural or historical value being spared.

**Anti-religion.** View from Shkoder looking towards Buna river. The 5 mosques visible have long been secularized; the famed Camia Plumsi mosque (right) is now used as a cattle barn.

The entire operation lasted a year and a half. Thus at Shkoder in the north, the Catholic cathedral was transformed into a sports hall, the archbishop's house into a hotel for athletes and the Great Mosque was razed to the ground. A museum of atheism was opened in the city, situated in the area where the anti-religious campaign encountered its greatest resistance. Even cemeteries were affected, all crosses and religious inscriptions being removed. In 1972 a 70-year old Catholic priest, Shtjefen Kurti, interned in the work camp of Lushnje, was shot for having baptized an infant. The news of his execution was confirmed by official sources (Radio Tirane, 29 April 1973), although the reason given was that he had engaged in espionage 'to the profit of the Vatican, Great Britain and the United States'. In November 1973, Msgr Damian, head of the Albanian Orthodox Church and archbishop of Tirane, died in prison at the age of 80 where had been interned since 1967, also for alleged espionage. In spite of the draconian measures of 1967–68, religion still survives, as the official publications of the Albanian Communist Party testify. The party ideological organ *Bashkimi* acknowledged in 1973: 'We have by no means achieved complete emancipation from the remnants of religious influences'. It especially deplored the increase in public and private acts of worship and in certain regions public celebration of religious feasts with illegal absence from work. It added that pilgrimages to ancient worship places still continue although the sanctuaries which are central to them have been destroyed, and that visits to parents and friends are used as a pretext to camouflage such manifestations. In 1976 a new clause being drafted for the Albanian constitution clarified the position by stating that Albania 'recognizes no religion and supports and develops atheist propaganda for the purpose of implanting the scientific materialist world outlook'. At the same time the regime ordered a change of all citizens' names that were 'unsuitable... from a political, ideological or moral viewpoint', including all Christian names.

**BROADCASTING.** No religious broadcasting of any kind is permitted within the country. TWR (Monaco) beams programmes to Albania for 30 minutes every Friday.

## BIBLIOGRAPHY


'Albania: an atheist state', B. Tonnes, *Religion in Communist lands*, 3, 1–3 (January–June, 1975), 4–8.

*The fulfilled promise; a documentary account of religious persecution in Albania.* G. Sinishta. Santa Clara, CA (USA), 1976. 250p.

(The twilight of the gods in Albania) *To Lykophos ton Theon stin Alvania.* Chicago: Panepirotic Federation of America and Canada, 1976. 72p.


TABLE 2. ORGANIZED CHURCHES AND DENOMINATIONS IN ALBANIA

| Official name 1 | Begun 2 | Type 3 | Counc 4 | Congs 5 | Adults 6 | Affiliated 7 | Names, notes, and other statistics (see Codebook) 8 |
|---|---|---|---|---|---|---|---|
| **Albanian Orthodox Church** | c 70 | O Alb | M.... | 500 | 60,000 | 100,000 | Suppressed 1967. 4 Eparchies: Tirana, Berat, Gjirokastër, Korçë. Tosks in south. |
| **Catholic Church in Albania** | 385 | R Lat | P.... | 400 | 40,000 | 70,000 | Forced to break with Rome 1951; suppressed 1969. 7 jurisdictions. Ghegs in north. |
| Isolated radio churches | c1960 | P rad | ..... | | 100 | 200 | Isolated radio believers following Protestant programmes (TWR), also Radio Vatican. |
| Jehovah's Witnesses | 1925 | M Jeh | x.... | | 60 | 100 | Active witnessing under way by 1926. Long since forced underground. Many in jail. |
| Methodist Church | c1920 | P Met | ..... | | 60 | 100 | Formerly in Yugoslav Mission, related to USA Methodism through C & S Europe CC. |
| Serbian Orthodox Church: V Shkodër | 1922 | O Ser | Cw... | | 600 | 1,000 | *Srpska Pravoslavna Crkva.* Under P Belgrade, but no contact. Diocese until 1939. |
| Seventh-day Adventist Church | 1903 | P Adv | x.... | | 10 | 30 | *SDA*, formerly part of Greek Mission, Southern European Union Mission. |
| **Total affiliated (mid-1970)** | | | | **1,000** | **100,830** | **171,430** | **Total denominations (1970) . . . 7.** |
| **Total affiliated (mid-1975)** | | | | **900** | **95,700** | **162,700** | **Total denominations (1975) . . . 7.** |
| **Total affiliated (mid-1980)** | | | | **800** | **90,600** | **154,100** | **Total denominations (1980) . . . 6.** |

NOTES ON TABLE ABOVE
COLUMNS: for meanings and CODES (cols. 1, 3, 4, 8), see Codebook (Part 6). Column 1: **Boldface type** = church with over 10% of country's affiliated Christians.

PEOPLES (ethnolinguistic). Christians: about 94% Albanian (Shiptar) (Gheg & Tosk), 2% Gypsy, 2% Greek, 1% Romanian & Macedonian.

COUNTRY-WIDE TOTALS
EVANGELIZATION (see Part 5). 1900: 39%. 1970: 34%. 1980: 35%.

PERSONNEL. About 30 (all nationals).
SCRIPTURE DISTRIBUTION (1975). Annual totals: Nil. *Translations completed.* Portion: 3 languages since 1824. NT: Albanian (Tosk in 1827, Gheg in 1869).

ADDITIONAL DATA ON CHURCHES
ALBANIAN ORTHODOX CHURCH. The church, found mainly in the south among the Tosks, became autocephalous in 1937. From 1949–51, its bishops were replaced by government appointees. In 1944 there were 29 monasteries and convents, and 2 seminaries (Tirana, Korçë). In 1967 all church life was suppressed and clergy secularized.

CATHOLIC CHURCH IN ALBANIA. There are still 7 jurisdictions recognized by the Vatican, 6 of which are Latin-rite in the north among the Ghegs: M Shkodër (Scutari) founded AD 385; D Lesh (Lezhë), begun c1350; D Pult, begun c850; D Sapë, begun 1062; AD Durrës, begun c1250; AN Orosh (Shën Llezhri i Oroshit, St Alexander of Oros), begun 1888; and one Byzantine-rite jurisdiction, AA Southern Albania (1939). The church was forced to break with the Vatican in 1951, and was finally suppressed in 1967–69. *Bishops.* All dead or disappeared by 1977. *Priests.* 14 in 1971; one executed in 1972.

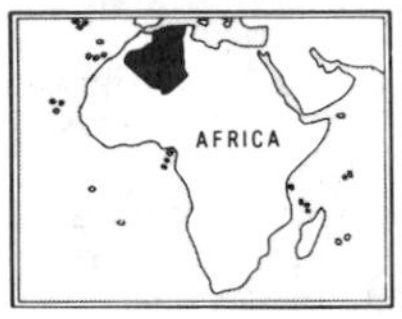


# ALGERIA

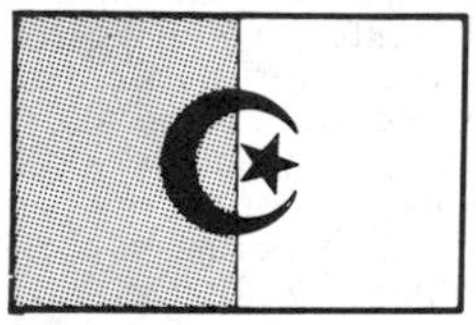

## SECULAR DATA

**STATE. Official name:** The People's Democratic Republic of Algeria (Al-Jumhuriyah al-Jaza'iriya ad-Dimuqratiyah ash-Shabiyah/La République Algérienne Démocratique et Populaire). Adjective of nationality: Algerian (algérien).
**Flag** (shown above right): Green and white bars, centred red crescent enclosing red star.
**Area:** 2,381,741 sq. km. (919,685 sq. miles). Agricultural land: 19.1%.
**Government:** Socialist military junta, since 1965 (c1500 Ottoman rule, 1848 French colony and later department, 1958 French military junta, 1962 Independence as republic).
**Legislature:** National Revolutionary Council, 26 members.
**Official language:** Arabic.
**Chief cities:** capital, Algiers 943,140 (1966), Oran 328,260, Constantine 253,650, Annaba (Bône) 168,790.
**Political divisions:** 15 Departments, 81 Arrondissements, 681 Communes.
**Armed forces** (1976): Total 69,300 regular: army 61,000, navy 3,800, air force 4,500 (182 combat aircraft). Reserves: 100,000. Paramilitary forces: 10,000 gendarmerie.
**Foreign forces** (1973): 1,000 USSR military advisers.

**DEMOGRAPHY. Population:** 11,821,679 (census of 4.IV.1966. For 1970–2000 (UN), see last row of Table 1). Population density (1975): 7/sq. km. (18/sq. mile). Under 15 years: 44%. Growth rate (1975–80): 3.32% per year (births 4.74%, deaths −1.33%, emigrants −0.09%). Life expectancy (1975–80): 55.7 years. Household size: 5.2 persons.
**Major languages:** Arabic, French, Kabyle, Tuareg, Tamahaq, Russian, and 15 other languages.
**Urban dwellers** (1970): 42.9%. Urban growth rate (1950–70): 5.8% per year.
**Labour force:** 24%.
**Refugees** (1977): From abroad 28,200 (20,000 from Spanish Sahara, 8,000 Palestinians. 200 from Chile). In addition, from 1969–74 large numbers of Tuareg nomads fled to Algeria from the drought in Mali. Deportees: 25,000 Moroccan nationals were expelled from Algeria in 1976.
**Tourists:** (1972) 196,700.

**ETHNOLINGUISTIC GROUPS:** 83.0% Algerian Arab, 10.3% Kabyle, 4.2% Shawiya, 1.0% Oasis Berber, 0.6% French, 0.4% Moroccan Arab, 0.1% Tuareg (Tamashek), Russian & Byelorussian (6,000), USSR military (1,000), Maghreb Jewish (1,000), Spaniard, Italian, other European.

**MONEY** (1977). **Monetary unit:** dinar (=100 centimes); US$1 = Ad 4.15.
**National income per person:** US$660. Average annual family income US$3,432.
**Cost of living in capital** (1976): index 137 (Washington DC=100). Daily cost of living: US$52.

**EDUCATION.** Adult literacy: (1948) 18%, (1971) 26%. Education rate: 27%. Schools: 6,990. Universities: 2.

**HEALTH.** Hospitals: 149 (39,053 beds). Doctors: 1,698. Lepers: 22,600 (1.35 per 1,000). Blind: 25,000. Psychotics: 130,000.

**LITERATURE.** Periodicals: 109. Scientific journals: 20. Newspapers: 4 dailies, 15 non-daily.

**COMMUNICATION** (per 1,000 people). Phones: 14. Radios: 46. TV sets: 16. Daily newspapers circulation: 16 copies.

TABLE 1. RELIGIOUS ADHERENTS IN ALGERIA

| Year | 1900 | | mid-1970 | | Annual change, 1970–1980 | | | | mid-1975 | | mid-1980 | | 2000 | |
|---|---|---|---|---|---|---|---|---|---|---|---|---|---|---|
| *Name* | *Adherents* | *%* | *Adherents* | *%* | *Natural* | *Conversion* | *Total* | *Rate* | *Adherents* | *%* | *Adherents* | *%* | *Adherents* | *%* |
| Muslims | 3,983,000 | 86.6 | 14,199,870 | 99.1 | 544,797 | −701 | 544,096 | 3.27 | 16,635,950 | 99.1 | 19,640,830 | 99.1 | 36,157,700 | 98.6 |
| **Christians** | **563,000** | **12.2** | **104,430** | **0.7** | **4,142** | **662** | **4,804** | **3.80** | **126,500** | **0.8** | **152,470** | **0.8** | **382,300** | **1.0** |
| crypto-Christians | 0 | 0.0 | 30,000 | 0.2 | 1,287 | 670 | 1,957 | 4.98 | 39,300 | 0.2 | 49,570 | 0.3 | 126,000 | 0.3 |
| professing | 563,000 | 12.2 | 74,430 | 0.5 | 2,855 | −8 | 2,847 | 3.26 | 87,200 | 0.5 | 102,900 | 0.5 | 256,000 | 0.7 |
| Roman Catholics | 548,700 | 11.9 | 68,830 | 0.5 | 2,642 | −5 | 2,637 | 3.27 | 80,700 | 0.5 | 95,200 | 0.5 | 240,000 | 0.7 |
| Protestants | 14,000 | 0.3 | 2,500 | 0.0 | 95 | 5 | 100 | 3.45 | 2,900 | 0.0 | 3,500 | 0.0 | 7,000 | 0.0 |
| Orthodox | 200 | 0.0 | 2,500 | 0.0 | 95 | −5 | 90 | 3.10 | 2,900 | 0.0 | 3,400 | 0.0 | 7,000 | 0.0 |
| Anglicans | 100 | 0.0 | 600 | 0.0 | 23 | −3 | 20 | 2.86 | 700 | 0.0 | 800 | 0.0 | 2,000 | 0.0 |
| nominal | 5,700 | 0.1 | 0 | 0.0 | 0 | 0 | 0 | 0.00 | 0 | 0.0 | 0 | 0.0 | 0 | 0.0 |
| affiliated | 557,300 | 12.1 | 104,430 | 0.7 | 4,142 | 662 | 4,804 | 3.80 | 126,500 | 0.8 | 152,470 | 0.8 | 382,300 | 1.0 |
| total practising | 445,840 | *80* | 62,660 | *60* | 2,485 | 397 | 2,882 | 3.80 | 75,900 | *60* | 91,480 | *60* | 267,610 | *70* |
| non-practising | 111,460 | *20* | 41,770 | *40* | 1,657 | 265 | 1,922 | 3.80 | 50,600 | *40* | 60,990 | *40* | 114,690 | *30* |
| Roman Catholics | 544,000 | 11.8 | 76,500 | 0.5 | 2,933 | −3 | 2,930 | 3.27 | 89,600 | 0.5 | 105,800 | 0.5 | 257,000 | 0.7 |
| Arab indigenous | 0 | 0.0 | 19,500 | 0.1 | 884 | 666 | 1,500 | 5.74 | 27,000 | 0.2 | 35,000 | 0.2 | 95,000 | 0.3 |
| Protestants | 13,000 | 0.3 | 4,850 | 0.0 | 187 | −2 | 185 | 3.24 | 5,700 | 0.0 | 6,700 | 0.0 | 20,000 | 0.1 |
| Evangelicals | 500 | 0.0 | 2,700 | 0.0 | 105 | 5 | 110 | 3.44 | 3,200 | 0.0 | 3,800 | 0.0 | 12,000 | 0.0 |
| Orthodox | 200 | 0.0 | 2,730 | 0.0 | 105 | 2 | 107 | 3.34 | 3,200 | 0.0 | 3,800 | 0.0 | 8,000 | 0.0 |
| Anglicans | 100 | 0.0 | 800 | 0.0 | 31 | −1 | 30 | 3.19 | 940 | 0.0 | 1,100 | 0.0 | 2,000 | 0.0 |
| Marginal Protestants | 0 | 0.0 | 50 | 0.0 | 2 | 0 | 2 | 3.27 | 60 | 0.0 | 70 | 0.0 | 300 | 0.0 |
| Non-religious | 3,000 | 0.1 | 20,000 | 0.1 | 769 | 31 | 800 | 3.40 | 23,500 | 0.1 | 28,000 | 0.1 | 100,000 | 0.3 |
| Atheists | 1,000 | 0.0 | 4,000 | 0.0 | 154 | 6 | 160 | 3.40 | 4,700 | 0.0 | 5,600 | 0.0 | 20,000 | 0.1 |
| Jews | 50,000 | 1.1 | 1,000 | 0.0 | −90 | 0 | −90 | −18.00 | 500 | 0.0 | 100 | 0.0 | 0 | 0.0 |
| Baha'is | 0 | 0.0 | 700 | 0.0 | 28 | 2 | 30 | 3.53 | 850 | 0.0 | 1,000 | 0.0 | 3,000 | 0.0 |
| **Country's population** | **4,600,000** | **100.0** | **14,330,000** | **100.0** | **549,800** | **0** | **549,800** | **3.27** | **16,792,000** | **100.0** | **19,828,000** | **100.0** | **36,663,000** | **100.0** |

COLUMNS, ROWS. For meanings and definitions, see Codebook (Part 6). Note that, by definition, total 'Christians' = professing + crypto-Christians, which also = affiliated + nominal Christians. Percentages may not always total exactly due to rounding.

CENSUSES. 1856: 92.7% Muslims, 6.3% Christians, 1.0% Jews and others. 1876: 87.7% Muslims, 11.2% Christians, 1.1% Jews 1896: 86.7% Muslims, 12.2% Christians, 1.1% Jews. 1906: 86.8% Muslims, 12.1% Christians, 1.1% Jews. 1921: 86.1% Muslims, 12.7% Christians, 1.2% Jews. 1931: 86.4% Muslims, 12.4% Christians, 1.2% Jews. 1936: 86.8% Muslims, 12.0% Christians, 1.2% Jews. 31.X.1948 (de jure, excluding military): 89.3% Muslims, 9.4% Christians, 1.3% Jews. 31.X.1954 (de jure): 89.6% Muslims, 9.1% Christians, 1.3% Jews. 15.IX.1960: 89.7% Muslims, 9.0% Christians, 1.3% Jews.

NOTES ON RELIGIONS
ARAB INDIGENOUS. Isolated radio believers (see Table 2); mainly Arabs, with some Berbers.

ATHEISTS. Algerian Communist Party (ACP) (proscribed 1962; pro-Soviet), succeeded by the Socialist Vanguard Party (SVP): membership (1970) 400. Also 1,000 USSR military advisers (1973).
BAHA'IS. Expansion has been checked by waves of persecution and the expulsion of 16 Persian missionaries; all activity is still banned (1973).
COUNTRY'S POPULATION. Settlers from France began arriving after 1830, and numbered 7% of the population by 1856, 13% by 1900, and 10% in 1960; of these, 95% (850,000) returned to France in 1962. During the war years 1954–62, an estimated 1 million Algerians and 20,000 French soldiers were killed.
CRYPTO-CHRISTIANS. Arabs and Berbers. Unorganized individual nationals in the recognized churches, with many organized and unorganized isolated radio believers.
JEWS. In 1962, 125,000 of the 140,000 Algerian Jews of French nationality emigrated to France; most of the rest have subsequently left for Israel.
MUSLIMS. 99% Sunnis (of the Malikite rite, with some of

Hanafite rite), 0.6% Ibadi (Kharijite) (in oasis of Mzab). Religious orders: Qadiriya et alia. The Kabyle (Arabic for 'those who after lengthy resistance accepted Islam', 1 million, Berbers) were Christians before the 8th-century Muslim conquest, and are the only tribe in the once-Christian Maghreb to have in any way responded to the Christian faith in the present century; before the Franco-Algerian war and Independence in 1962, there were 200 Kabyle Protestants (mainly Methodists) and 3,000 Catholics. Over the past century the Kabyle have experienced waves of Muslim religious movements called zawiyas (confraternity, prayer house, mutual aid society). *Hajj pilgrims to Mecca.* (1970) 3,960; (1974) 49,028; (1975) 55,010; (1976) 34,150.
NOMINAL CHRISTIANS. Before Independence in 1962, a small proportion of all French settlers were professing Catholics but unaffiliated to the Catholic Church.
PROFESSING CHRISTIANS. Mainly Europeans, both before and after Independence in 1962.
ROMAN CATHOLICS. In the year 1900, all were French except 811 indigenous baptized Catholics and 164 catechumens.

## NON-CHRISTIAN RELIGIONS. Islam

is now the predominant and official religion of Algeria. The overwhelming majority are Sunnis of the Malikite rite, except for a few elderly Turks and Moors, who are Hanafites. A small number (about 80,000) are Kharijite-Ibadites found mostly in the south. They maintain contact with the Kharjite islands of Africa (Djerba in Tunisia, Djebel Nefoussa in Libya) and Oman in Asia, who send their students to study at the Institute al-Haya (Life) of Guerara in Oasis province. For the last 8 centuries, Sunni religious brotherhoods have played an important part in the religious formation and islamization of the countryside. Their influence has been considerably reduced within the last few decades by the efforts of reformers (especially those of the Association of Ulama founded in 1931), the progress of modern education, and changes resulting from the long struggle for nation liberation (1954–1962). These 3 factors helped prepare the way for a renewal of Algerian Islam. Nonetheless, the Tijaniya brotherhood continues its influence in Black Africa. On the level of national orientation, Arab-Muslim culture combined with the socialist and anti-imperialist tendencies of the country, constitutes one of the 2 poles of the Algerian personality. The spread of Muslim religious teaching and Arab-Muslim culture, hindered previously by the French administration, is today advanced by the national press, radio and television, by schools and mosques, by mass meetings, and in general by all national organizations including scouts and women's unions. The family and village nevertheless continue to play an important part in life, a fact which results in the persistence of many superstitions of agrarian origin, especially among Berber women. In 1970, the government secularized 3,000 mosques into 'centres of instruction' for adult literacy work. During 1974, 49,028 Muslim pilgrims from Algeria performed the Haji to Mecca.

**Judaism** had 130,000 followers before 1962, but by 1970 Jews numbered only a few hundred. Most have migrated to Israel.

## CHRISTIANITY.

Christianity spread among the Latin-speaking people of Algeria's northern cities at the end of the 1st and the beginning of the 2nd centuries and subsequently produced some of the church's most eminent theologians: Tertullian, Cyprian and Augustine of Hippo. Later, however, weakened by theological disputes and Berber revolts, the area fell before the Vandals in 429 and became subject to Arab Muslims in 702. The Moors extended their empire into Spain, with Ottoman Islamic forces halting the thrust of Spanish Christians pushing back into Africa in 1556. France entered Algeria in 1830, made northern Algeria a part of France in 1848, and

French settlers rapidly increased in numbers. Open revolt against French rule developed in 1954, and independence was achieved in 1962. During colonial rule, Christianity played an important role in Algeria, but few of the indigenous peoples became Christians. With the exodus of Europeans, Christian influence has been radically reduced.

CATHOLIC CHURCH. In 1838 Algeria became an episcopal see under Aix-en-Provence in France, but the French government forbade all Christian missionary activity among Muslims. Napoleon accepted the principle of religious freedom when Charles Lavigerie, founder of the White Fathers, became archbishop of Algeria in 1867, but missionary efforts achieved little permanent success.

In general one can now distinguish 5 kinds of Catholics: (1) former French colonials who have not yet emigrated (of the 950,000 such Catholics in 1961, about 90% had left the country by 1963); (2) Europeans working in national or foreign enterprises, living in Algeria for a limited period (90% French, with a growing number of other Europeans both Eastern and Western); (3) around 2,500 Europeans who have taken Algerian nationality (technicians, wives of Algerians, and also 5 of the 6 Catholic bishops); (4) several hundred native Algerians (many of the 10,000 who before 1954 emigrated to France); and (5) a growing number of Christians from the Middle East and political refugees from Black Africa and Latin America. Since independence in 1962, the Catholic Church has been drastically reduced numerically, but its new commitment to service in a Muslim milieu with socialist tendencies has been widely noted. The personality and actions of the cardinal archbishop of Algiers, both during the war of

Muslims. Tlemcen Grande Mosquée.

liberation and subsequently, helped greatly towards the establishment of the present good Muslim-Christian relations. Further, in 1970, 20% of Catholic clergy held salaried positions outside church institutions as nurses, engineers, veterinarians, architects and teachers. This emphasis on service to the Algerian community is now the major characteristic of the church in Algeria. In 1974 the diocese of Oran had one-third of its 45 priests serving in a pastoral role, one-third in teaching and one-third in other functions. Diocesan schools all follow the arabization programme of the government. Nuns, who are particularly numerous in relation to the size of the Catholic community, contribute substantially to the involvement of the church in the country's life. In 1974 there were more than 1,000 sisters, half in teaching or the training of women and girls, 200 in medical work, and the rest involved in community and professional tasks.

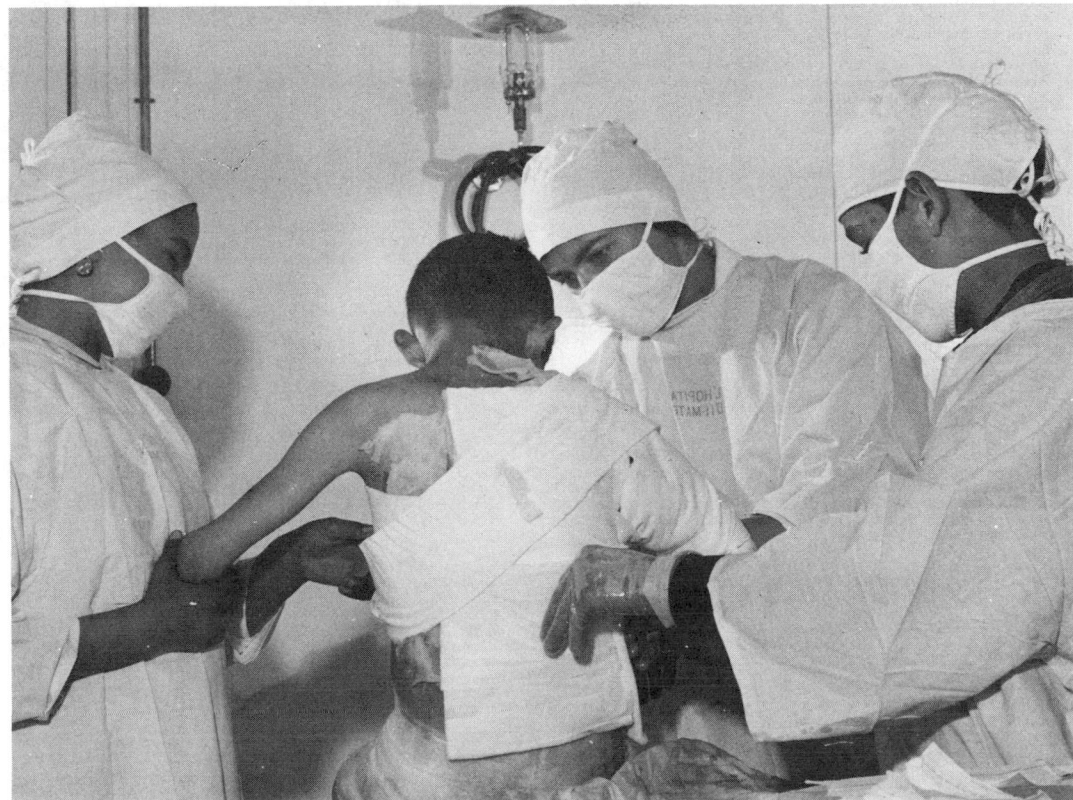

Protestants. Changing dressing of a burn patient at Il-Maten Methodist hospital, begun 1964. Algeria in 1973 had 36 Christian medical centres including hospitals.

PROTESTANT CHURCHES. The first Protestant groups to enter Algeria were the French McCall Mission (1830) and the Basel Mission, but their work did not endure. The North Africa Mission was established in 1881 and has continued to this day. Other early missions include the Open Brethren, Mission Rolland, Seventh-day Adventists and American Methodists.

The Methodists have carried on an effective youth hostel work as well as operating a dispensary at Les Ouaohias and a modern hospital at Il-Maten since 1964. In 1973 they united with the Reformed Church, which had been ministering mainly to French expatriates, to form the Protestant Church in Algeria. The Open Brethren and North Africa Mission have concentrated on Bible correspondence courses for the past decade. A number of independent faith missions have begun in various areas, but their influence remains small.

Protestantism remains small, a presence and witness but little more. Of the few native Algerians to become Christians, most have been Kabyles; and of these the majority have emigrated to France since independence due to local hostility.

ORTHODOX CHURCHES. Although there are no priests, members of 4 different Orthodox churches are found in Algeria, 2 Chalcedonian (Greek and Russian) and 2 in the Oriental Monophysite tradition (Coptic and Jacobite). The Copts form the largest community.

## CHURCH AND STATE.

Article 4 of the constitution of 8 September 1963 states that Islam is the state religion and that the republic 'guarantees to everyone respect for his opinions and beliefs and the free exeicise of worship'. Article 10, defining the fundamental objectives of the Algerian republic, mentions among these 'the struggle against all discrimination, especially that founded on race and religion'.

The Christian churches have no legal status in Algeria. Controversial questions are dealt with amicably by direct contact with the competent civil authorities. Nevertheless, the state has passed legislation of significance for Christians, including: (1) an order of 21 March 1968 concerning the status of private education, followed by a decree of 14 February 1970 defining the authorized categories of private institutions (all categories except those of higher education); (2) a decree of 6 December 1969 giving government allowances to all ministers of any religion who hold Algerian nationality; and (3) an official communiqué declaring Christian festivals as holidays for Christian personnel both Algerian and foreign.

The churches need not register with the government. The ministry charged with religious affairs, previously termed the Ministry of Habous, has become since July 1970 the Ministry of National Education and Religious Affairs (Wizarat al-Ta'alim al-Asli wa al-Su'un al-Dinia).

Freedom of worship exists throughout Algeria, but proselytism is forbidden. The state is particularly vigilant in its efforts to preserve youth from influences considered incompatible with family traditions; national organizations alone may create movements or undertake educational campaigns. Certain Christian groups, notably the Methodist Church and Jehovah's Witnesses, have had leaders and faithful deported, allegedly for having infringed these principles.

## INTERDENOMINATIONAL ORGANIZATIONS.

In 1940 an Evangelical Mission Council was established; but following its re-organization in 1964 as the Association of Protestant Churches and Institutions in Algeria, several members bodies left due to its connections with the World Council of Churches. In 1963 Protestant churches began a significant ecumenical social service project including reafforestation and school lunch programmes, termed the Christian Committee for Service to Refugees (CCSR), which by 1972 had become the Christian Committee for Service in Algeria (CCSA). The present staff of 100 are engaged in a number of development and social service activities, working under government auspices. Another co-operative activity also with Catholic support has been the Christian Centre for Maghrebine Studies in Algiers which had an extensive library. Prior to being closed indefinitely by the government after 1970, the centre provided opportunities for a study of the religions of the Maghreb, offered courses for Christians studying Islam and facilitated Muslim-Christian dialogue. The Catholic Episcopal Conference of North Africa operates a Commission for Ecumenism, and also Coprodev, an ecumenical study centre concerned with the preparation of village development projects.

## BROADCASTING.

The national network Radiodiffusion-Télévision Algérienne permits Catholic and Protestant programmes only on the major church festivals, although a Catholic mass is sometimes televised live from Sainte-Elisabeth church in Algiers. From abroad, Christian radio programmes in Berber, Arabic and French are easily received, coming from TWR (Monaco) and ELWA (Liberia). Since 1960 a large audience has been built up and over 80,000 Muslims have enrolled for Bible correspondence courses.

## BIBLIOGRAPHY

*Baal, Christ and Mohammed: religion and revolution in North Africa*. J.K. Cooley. New York: Holt, Rinehart & Winston, 1965. 369p.

*Missions des Pères Blancs en Tunisie, Algérie, Kabylie, Sahara*. A. Philippe. 1931.

TABLE 2. ORGANIZED CHURCHES AND DENOMINATIONS IN ALGERIA

| Official name 1 | Begun 2 | Type 3 | Counc 4 | Congs 5 | Adults 6 | Affiliated 7 | Names, notes, and other statistics (see Codebook) 8 |
|---|---|---|---|---|---|---|---|
| Armée du Salut | 1934 | P Sal | xwa•C | 5 | 200 | 500 | *Salvation Army*, under France Territory. In 5 cities. French officers until 1970. |
| Assemblées de Dieu | | P Pe2 | Z•••• | 10 | 500 | 1,000 | *Assemblies of God*. M=Assemblées de Dieu (France). Loss by emigration since 1960. |
| Eglise Adventiste du Septième Jour | c1905 | P Adv | x•••• | 4 | 50 | 200 | *Seventh-day Adventists*, NAfrican Miss, Euro-Africa Div. 83% Arab, 17% Berber. 1x. |
| Eglise Anglicane (D Egypt) | | A plu | aw•U• | 1 | 200 | 800 | *Anglican Church*. All expatriates (UK, USA, Arabs). 1 church in Algiers. |
| **Eglise Catholique en Algérie:** | 1625 | R Lat | B•SH• | 114 | 42,800 | 76,500 | *Catholic Ch*. 1% Algerians. C=5+2+34. 37n,W=10%. 345x,60m,1251w,P=22%,232Yy. |
| M El-Djezair (Alger, Algiers) | 1838 | R Lat | Bs | 51 | 28,000 | 50,000 | Mostly transient foreign workers. 500 Kabyles. W=10%. 161 36 711 20 132 |
| D Constantine | 1866 | R Lat | Bs | 13 | 5,500 | 10,000 | Originally a diocese AD 150. Kabyles, Shawia. W=10%. 55 6 200 20 29 |
| D Oran (Ouahran) | 1866 | R Lat | Bs | 35 | 7,300 | 13,000 | Westernmost diocese; coast and Atlas range. W=10%. 75 8 195 20 57 |
| D Laghouat | 1901 | R Lat | pwf | 15 | 2,000 | 3,500 | South, Sahara. Tamahaq area. 35 Algerians. 54 10 145 53 14 |
| Eglise Evangélique Copte | c1970 | P Ref | RWaN• | 1 | 200 | 250 | *Coptic Evangelical Ch*. Immigrant Egyptian workers. No pastors. |
| Eglise Orth Copte: D Afrique du Nord | c1965 | O Cop | NwaN• | 1 | 1,500 | 2,000 | *Coptic Orthodox Ch*. Egyptian immigrant workers. No priests. |
| Eglise Orthodoxe Grecque | | O Ara | Cw•N• | 2 | 200 | 400 | *Greek Orthodox Ch*. 350 under P Antioch. 50 under P Alexandria. No priests. |
| Eglise Orthodoxe Russe | c1922 | O Sla | ••••• | 1 | 20 | 30 | *Russian Orthodox Ch*. White Russian exiles among 6,000 Russians in Algeria. |
| Eglise Orthodoxe Syrienne | | O Syr | Dw•N• | | 200 | 300 | *Syrian Orthodox Ch* (*Jacobites*). Under P Antioch. Syrians. No priests. |
| Eglise Protestante d'Algérie | c1850 | P uni | Wu•NC | 17 | 500 | 1,500 | 1908, M=UMC(USA). 1972 union Eglise Réformée de France. French, 200 Kabyles. 4x. |
| **Eglises radiophoniques isolées** | 1958 | I rad | ••••• | 490 | 9,000 | 19,500 | Isolated radio believers, most aged 12–25. R=2230 (TWR, RSB), T=103000(NAM,GMU,ICI). |
| Frères Larges | c1887 | P CBr | x•••C | 3 | 50 | 100 | *Open Brethren*. M=CMML(UK). Algiers, Kabylia, Bourg. 7f. |
| Mission Baptiste Evangélique | 1950 | P Bap | x•••f | 4 | 50 | 100 | M=Ev Baptist Missions(USA). Missionaries expelled in 1970. |
| Mission Biblique de Ghardaia | 1956 | P ind | ••••C | 1 | 20 | 50 | M=Biblical Mission of Ghardaia (France). Among poor nomadic tribes, Ghardaia oasis. 1h. |
| Mission d'Afrique du Nord | 1881 | P int | xMg•f | 5 | 200 | 300 | M=NAM. 200 Algerians. Bible courses from Marseilles (7000 enrolled). 15f,1Y. |
| Mission Evangélique au Sahara | 1953 | P int | ••••C | 1 | 20 | 50 | M=Sahara Desert Mission(UK,France). At Tamanrasset oasis. Tuareg (Tamahaq). |
| Mission Evangélique de Médéa | | P ind | ••••C | 1 | 10 | 50 | *Ev Mission of Medea*. An independent Swiss mission aided by Action Chrétienne en Orient. |
| Mission Evangélique du Sahara | c1950 | P Hol | ••••C | 1 | 20 | 50 | *Sahara Ev Mission*. M=Emmanuel Holiness Ch(UK). Tamanrasset oasis. |
| Mission Rolland | 1908 | P int | ••••C | 2 | 30 | 200 | M=Rolland Mission (France). In Tizi-Ouzou (Kabylie). Kabyles only. 7f,1h. |
| Témoins de Jéhovah | c1950 | M Jeh | x•••• | 1 | 28 | 50 | *Jehovah's Witnesses*. First reported activity 1952. Missionaries expelled 1970. 4Y. |
| Other Protestant denominations | | P | ••••• | | 200 | 500 | Total about 8 (see list below); 250 Algerians, 100 Arabs. |
| **Total affiliated (mid-1970)** | | | | **675** | **55,998** | **104,430** | **Total denominations (1970) . . . 29.** |
| **Total affiliated (mid-1975)** | | | | **705** | **67,800** | **126,500** | **Total denominations (1975) . . . 30.** |
| **Total affiliated (mid-1980)** | | | | **750** | **81,700** | **152,470** | **Total denominations (1980) . . . 31.** |

NOTES ON TABLE ABOVE
COLUMNS: for meanings and CODES (cols. 1, 3, 4, 8), see Codebook (Part 6). Column 1: **Boldface type** = church with over 10% of country's affiliated Christians.
NATIONAL COUNCILS (Column 4, 5th letter).
C = Association des Eglises et Oeuvres Protestantes en Algérie (ADEOPA) (Association of Protestant Churches and activities in Algeria).
f = formerly member of C, but withdrew about 1964.
OTHER PROTESTANT DENOMINATIONS. These include: Algeria Mennonite Mission (Mennonite Ch of North America), Communauté Evangélique Indépendante, Fellowship of Independent Missions (Morocco Evangelistic Fellowship) (1950), General Association of Regular Baptists (GARB), Southern Baptist Convention.

PEOPLES (ethnolinguistic). Christians: about 81.5% French, 13.5% Arab (Algerian and alien), 2.5% Kabyle, 2.5% Spaniard, Italian and other European, Russian, Byelorussian.

COUNTRY-WIDE TOTALS
EVANGELIZATION (see Part 5). 1900: 15%. 1970: 24%. 1980: 25%. *Radiophonic evangelism*. Annual listeners' letters (1975): 1,870 TWR, 360 RSB. Bible correspondence courses (1975): 103,000 enrolments (90,000 RSB, 8,000 GMU, 5,000 ICI).
FOREIGN MISSIONARIES AND PERSONNEL (nationals serving abroad) (1973). Total about 50 Roman Catholics in France.
FOREIGN MISSIONARIES AND PERSONNEL (aliens from abroad) (1973). Total 1,748. *From Western world*. 1,696: 1,626 Roman Catholics, 70 Protestants (32 in 7 USA societies, 16 in 6 France societies, 12 in 2 UK societies, 7 in 2 Switzerland societies, 2 in 1 WGermany society, 1 in 1 Norway society). *From Communist world*. About 2 Roman Catholics from Yugoslavia. *From Third World*. About 50 Roman Catholics from Egypt, Guadeloupe, India, Lebanon and Palestine, also Coptic Orthodox.
INSTITUTIONS (church-operated) (1973). Total 113, including 64 higher schools (secondary), 36 medical centres (4 hospitals), 6 religious communities (4 monasteries), 4 research centres, 2 study centres.
PERIODICALS. About 15 titles.
PERSONNEL. About 1,816 (68 national, 1,748 foreign).
RELIGIOUS LIBRARIES. About 10.
SCRIPTURE DISTRIBUTION (1975). Annual totals: 400 Bibles (subsidized), 400 NTs (subsidized), 3,600 UBS portions, 2,000 UBS selections. *Translations completed*. Portion: 4 languages since 1872. NT: 2 languages since 1901.
SERVICE AGENCIES. About 26, including ACG, ACI, ACO, ADEOPA, CCSA (100 workers), JOC/F, MCC.

ADDITIONAL DATA ON CHURCHES
EGLISE CATHOLIQUE EN ALGERIE. In Arabic, al-Kanissa al-Katholikia. In 1962, 95% of all Catholics (850,000) left for France. Those who remained were almost all French, but later with many Arab Catholics from Lebanon, Syria and Egypt. *Annual baptisms* (1972). 95.9% infant, 4.1% adult. *Priests, brothers, sisters*. All expatriates, except for 37 priests and 30 sisters who have become Algerian citizens. *Seminaries*. None. *Indigenous religious congregations*. None. *Main foreign congregations*. Priests: WF, CSSp, SJ, CM, Prêtres de Pontigny. Brothers: FSC, PFM. Sisters: White Sisters.
*Catholic organizations*. The Episcopal Conference of North Africa (Conférence Episcopale d'Afrique du Nord), which includes Algeria, Morocco, Tunisia and Libya, has its seat in Algiers. There are no national presbyteral or pastoral councils, but religious personnel are represented in the Union des Supérieures Majeures Diocésaines. The organized lay apostolate (ACI, ACO, ACG and JOC/F) has only about 200 members. More numerous are teams dedicated to study and the development of spiritual life which owe their origin to eucharistic communities and are co-ordinated by the pastoral councils of the 4 dioceses.

The Holy See has diplomatic relations with Algeria and is represented to government and the Catholic hierarchy by a pronuncio based in Algiers.

The Catholic Church carries on an extensive social programme. Through its national secretariat of diocesan schools it provides educational facilities for 41,816 pupils (1969–70), of which 6,869 were in pre-primary; 24,481 in primary; 9,105 in secondary; and 1,361 in technical classes. By 1973 these had declined slightly to 30,496 in 80 primary schools and 9,013 in 64 secondary schools.

Algerian Caritas, representing Medicus Mundi, recruits hospital personnel at the request of the Ministry of Health. The church operates 3 hospitals, one clinic, 2 maternity wards, 8 dispensaries, 20 health care centres, 3 nurseries, and 3 old people's homes, employing in all 108 nurses; also 118 religious nurses work in public institutions and 8 others in private Algerian institutions. The National Union of Religious Personnel in Hospital and Social Action co-ordinates the activities of the church with government programmes.

In the cultural realm the Catholic church operates an Arab Pedogogical Centre, which trains teachers of Arabic and provides courses in literary Arabic for priests and religious personnel; an Interdiocesan Study Centre, specializing in the study of Arabic, Arab dialects, Berber, and Islam; and a Centre of Berber Studies. The social secretariat of Algiers and the social secretariat of Oran serve as study offices for social research at the service of civic authorities, with findings published in the national press. Many Catholic activities are carried on within an ecumenical or governmental framework. Caritas maintains nearly 150 family sewing centres and has contributed to the creation of about 100 Mother and Children centres. The church maintains and staffs a dozen centres for technical training, their programmes being regulated by the Ministry of Works and the Ministry of Education. Literacy centres in school buildings after class hours also exist.

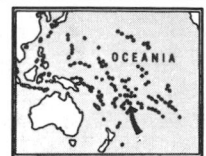

# AMERICAN SAMOA

## SECULAR DATA

**STATE. Official name:** The United States Territory of American Samoa. Unofficial name: Eastern Samoa.
**Flag** (shown above right): Blue field, white triangle bordered with red with apex at midpoint of staff; American eagle at right side of triangle.
**Area:** 197 sq. km. (76 sq. miles). Agricultural land: 40.0%.
**Government:** Unorganized unincorporated territory of the USA administered under US Department of the Interior, since 1900 (1830 chiefdoms, 1889 monarchy).
**Legislature:** Senate, 18 members. House of Representatives, 20 members.
**Official language:** English.
**Chief cities:** capital Pago Pago 2,450 (1970), seat of government Fagatogo.

**Political divisions:** 3 Districts, 14 Counties.

**DEMOGRAPHY. Population:** 27,159 (census of 1.IV.1970. For 1970–2000 (UN), see last row of Table 1). Population density (1975): 162/sq. km. (421/sq. mile). Under 15 years: 48%. Growth rate (1975–80): 3.24% per year (births 4.11%, deaths –0.91%, immigrants 0.04%). Life expectancy (1975–80): 60.3 years. Household size: 6.2 persons.
**Major languages:** English, Samoan.
**Urban dwellers** (1970): 10%.
**Labour force:** 33%.
**Tourists** (1966): 4,400. (1969): 14,000. (1973): about 30,000.

**ETHNOLINGUISTIC GROUPS:** 89.0% Samoan, 10.0% Euronesian (part-Samoan: Samoan/European/Chinese), 1.0% USA White.

**MONEY** (1977). **Monetary unit:** US dollar (= 100 cents).
**National income per person:** US$1,600. Average annual family income: US$9,920.
**Cost of living in capital** (1976): Daily cost of living: US$44.

**EDUCATION.** Adult literacy: 97%. Education rate: 69%. Schools: 32.

**HEALTH.** Hospitals: 1 (177 beds). Doctors: 26. Lepers: 285 (8.9 per 1,000).

**LITERATURE.** Periodicals: 9. Newspapers: 1 daily, 1 non-daily.

**COMMUNICATION** (per 1,000 people). Phones: 14. Radios: 338. TV sets: 1. Daily newspaper circulation: 1 copy.

TABLE 1.    RELIGIOUS ADHERENTS IN AMERICAN SAMOA

| Year | 1900 | | mid-1970 | | Annual change, 1970–1980 | | | | mid-1975 | | mid-1980 | | 2000 | |
|---|---|---|---|---|---|---|---|---|---|---|---|---|---|---|
| Name | Adherents | % | Adherents | % | Natural | Conversion | Total | Rate | Adherents | % | Adherents | % | Adherents | % |
| **Christians** | 5,700 | 100.0 | 26,930 | 99.0 | 1,069 | 0 | 1,069 | 3.37 | 31,680 | 99.0 | 37,620 | 99.0 | 64,990 | 97.0 |
| professing | 5,700 | 100.0 | 26,930 | 99.0 | 1,069 | 0 | 1,069 | 3.37 | 31,680 | 99.0 | 37,620 | 99.0 | 64,990 | 97.0 |
| Protestants | 5,400 | 94.7 | 18,770 | 69.0 | 724 | –131 | 593 | 2.77 | 21,440 | 67.0 | 24,700 | 65.0 | 39,200 | 58.5 |
| Roman Catholics | 300 | 5.3 | 5,060 | 18.6 | 212 | 65 | 277 | 4.42 | 6,270 | 19.6 | 7,830 | 20.6 | 15,410 | 23.0 |
| Marginal Protestants | 0 | 0.0 | 2,450 | 9.0 | 108 | 65 | 173 | 5.41 | 3,200 | 10.0 | 4,180 | 11.0 | 8,710 | 13.0 |
| Polynesian indigenous | 0 | 0.0 | 550 | 2.0 | 21 | 0 | 21 | 3.28 | 640 | 2.0 | 760 | 2.0 | 1,340 | 2.0 |
| Anglicans | 0 | 0.0 | 100 | 0.4 | 4 | 1 | 5 | 3.85 | 130 | 0.4 | 150 | 0.4 | 330 | 0.5 |
| nominal | 60 | 1.0 | 400 | 1.5 | 16 | 1 | 17 | 3.54 | 480 | 1.5 | 570 | 1.5 | 3,350 | 5.0 |
| affiliated | 5,640 | 99.0 | 26,530 | 97.5 | 1,053 | –1 | 1,052 | 3.37 | 31,200 | 97.5 | 37,050 | 97.5 | 61,640 | 92.0 |
| total practising | 5,080 | 90 | 22,550 | 85 | 895 | –1 | 894 | 3.37 | 26,520 | 85 | 31,490 | 85 | 46,230 | 75 |
| non-practising | 560 | 10 | 3,980 | 15 | 158 | 0 | 158 | 3.37 | 4,680 | 15 | 5,560 | 15 | 15,410 | 25 |
| Protestants | 5,340 | 93.7 | 18,435 | 67.8 | 709 | –130 | 579 | 2.75 | 21,020 | 65.7 | 24,220 | 63.7 | 37,190 | 55.5 |
| Evangelicals | 1,000 | 17.5 | 4,200 | 15.4 | 162 | –22 | 140 | 2.92 | 4,800 | 15.0 | 5,600 | 14.7 | 9,000 | 13.4 |
| Roman Catholics | 300 | 5.3 | 5,000 | 18.4 | 210 | 65 | 275 | 4.43 | 6,210 | 19.4 | 7,750 | 20.4 | 14,740 | 22.0 |
| Marginal Protestants | 0 | 0.0 | 2,450 | 9.0 | 108 | 65 | 173 | 5.41 | 3,200 | 10.0 | 4,180 | 11.0 | 8,040 | 12.0 |
| Polynesian indigenous | 0 | 0.0 | 545 | 2.0 | 22 | –2 | 20 | 3.12 | 640 | 2.0 | 750 | 2.0 | 1,340 | 2.0 |
| Anglicans | 0 | 0.0 | 100 | 0.4 | 4 | 1 | 5 | 3.85 | 130 | 0.4 | 150 | 0.4 | 330 | 0.5 |
| **Baha'is** | 0 | 0.0 | 200 | 0.7 | 8 | 0 | 8 | 3.40 | 240 | 0.7 | 280 | 0.7 | 1,500 | 2.2 |
| **Other religionists** | 0 | 0.0 | 70 | 0.3 | 3 | 0 | 3 | 3.75 | 80 | 0.3 | 100 | 0.3 | 510 | 0.8 |
| **Country's population** | 5,700 | 100.0 | 27,200 | 100.0 | 1,080 | 0 | 1,080 | 3.38 | 32,000 | 100.0 | 38,000 | 100.0 | 67,000 | 100.0 |

**COLUMNS, ROWS.** For meanings and definitions, see Codebook (Part 6). Note that, by definition, total 'Christians' = professing + crypto-Christians, which also = affiliated + nominal Christians. Percentages may not always total exactly, due to rounding.
**CENSUSES.** 25.IX.1956: 74.0% Protestants (69.6% Congregationalists, 4.0% Methodists), 15.4% Roman Catholics, 5.7% marginal Protestants, 4.9% other religionists. 1967: 70.1% Protestants (59.0% Congregationalists, 4.7% Methodists, 3.5% Pentecostals, 2.2% Seventh-day Adventists), 18.3% Roman Catholics, 8.5% marginal Protestants (8.4% Mormons, 0.1% Jehovah's Witnesses), 2.1% Polynesian indigenous, 1.0% other religionists.

**NOTES ON RELIGIONS**
BAHA'IS. In 2 local spiritual assemblies (1973).
POLYNESIAN INDIGENOUS. Members of 2 Samoan indigenous churches in 1970 (see Table 2).

---

**NON-CHRISTIAN RELIGIONS.** Two small Baha'i congregations exist on Tutuila Island. Traditional religions have disappeared.

## CHRISTIANITY

PROTESTANT CHURCHES. The history of Christianity in American Samoa is very similar to that in Western Samoa. Congregationalism was implanted in the early 19th century through the activity of the London Missionary Society and of Samoan evangelists, and has been since the beginning the principal denomination. In fact Congregationalists are stronger here than in Western Samoa, largely because Methodists are weaker. Methodists are nearly 16% of the population of Western Samoa whereas they formed only 4.9% in American Samoa in 1967. Although the Congregational Christian Church continues to increase in membership, it has not grown sufficiently to maintain the 69.6% of the population which it had in 1956; and by 1967 it had declined to under 60% through losses to other churches.

Part of the losses of Congregationalists have been due to gains by Seventh-day Adventists, who grew from 0.5% of the population in 1956 to 2.2% a decade later.

Newer denominations include the Assemblies of God, Church of Christ, United Pentecostal Church,

and Church of the Nazarene, which have expanded due to the missionary activity of North American societies since World War II. The fastest growth is being recorded by the Assemblies of God who had attracted 3.5% of the population by 1967.

CATHOLIC CHURCH. Catholic missionaries first arrived in 1845 but made little progress until 1965. American Samoa belongs to the diocese of Apia based in Western Samoa. In 1972 there were 4 parishes and 4 priests, with in each parish numerous catechists serving village communities. Catechists receive an extensive 4-year training course before being placed in village situations, and a number of Samoans are now studying for the priesthood at the

International Seminary in Suva, Fiji. The Samoan Islands are already the most advanced in Catholic indigenous vocations of all the Pacific islands, and it is expected that before long all priests in the islands will be Samoan. The Catholic community increased from 15.4% of the population in 1956 to 18.3% eleven years later.

Church wedding in American Samoa in 1947 between a Samoan nurse (centre) and a Fita Fita guardsman.

MARGINAL CHURCHES. Next to Catholics, Mormons are the fastest-growing church in the islands at the present time, increasing from 5.6% of the population in 1956 to 8.4% a decade later. A small Jehovah's Witness community also exists.

INDIGENOUS CHURCHES. The Congregational Church of Jesus Christ, which was a schism from the

Congregational Christian Church as early as 1846, has followers in both Western and American Samoa and has attracted several hundred adherents. There are scattered adherents of other independent groups also.

**CHURCH AND STATE.** Since the island is a territory of the USA, the separation of church and state is more consciously observed than in many other islands of the Pacific. Private church-related schools are permitted, but they receive no subsidies from the government.

**INTERDENOMINATIONAL ORGANIZATIONS.** An informal council of churches has been established, Interdenominational Committee of American Samoa, linking Congregationalists, Methodists, Anglicans and Roman Catholics. Relations between the churches have recently become greatly improved. These churches jointly observe the Week of Prayer for Christian Unity.

**BROADCASTING.** Television is used for educational purposes in which churches participate.

TABLE 2.     ORGANIZED CHURCHES AND DENOMINATIONS IN AMERICAN SAMOA

| Official name 1 | Begun 2 | Type 3 | Counc 4 | Congs 5 | Adults 6 | Affiliated 7 | Names, notes, and other statistics (see Codebook) 8 |
|---|---|---|---|---|---|---|---|
| Anglican Church (D Polynesia) | | A Hig | awpKC | 1 | 50 | 100 | In D Polynesia, Ch of Province of New Zealand. 60% European, 35% part-Samoan. |
| Assemblies of God in Samoa | 1927 | P Pe2 | ZF... | 22 | 1,000 | 1,500 | M=AoG(USA). Based on Pago Pago. 1970, very rapid growth. 45n,1x,G=2.3%pa,1r,W=67%. |
| Catholic Church (D Samoa & Tokelau) | 1845 | R Lat | PzPYC | 4 | 2,000 | 5,000 | Diocesan HQ Western Samoa. 4 parishes, 2 high schools on Tutuila Is. 4nx,P=78%. |
| Church of Christ | c1965 | P Dis | x.... | 1 | 20 | 35 | M=CC(Non-Instrumental)(USA). Independents. In Pago Pago. 2f. |
| Church of Jesus C of Latter-day Saints | 1888 | M LdS | x.... | | 1,500 | 2,370 | *Mormons.* M=CJCLdS(USA). Many Samoans overseas as missionaries. 50f,G=3.0%pa. |
| Church of the Nazarene | 1960 | P Hol | xF... | 2 | 78 | 150 | M=CoN(USA). Holiness denomination. 143 Sunday-school children. 2n. |
| Community Christian Church | | P com | ..P.. | 1 | 50 | 100 | Union church in Pago Pago. Largely Protestant expatriates, mostly from USA. |
| Congregational Christian Ch in Samoa | c1830 | P Con | RWP.C | | 7,000 | 15,000 | Major part of church is in Western Samoa. M=LMS(UK). |
| Congregational Church of Jesus Christ | 1846 | I Con | ..... | | 300 | 540 | *Ponesi's Ch. Ch of JC in Samoa.* Schism ex Congregational Christian Church. |
| Jehovah's Witnesses | 1938 | M Jeh | x.... | 1 | 63 | 80 | Placed under Australian branch in 1938. First active witnessing 1951. 2Y. |
| Methodist Church in Samoa | 1827 | P Met | VuP.C | | 500 | 1,000 | *Lotu Tonga (Church of Tonga). Tutuila Synod* (4 other synods are in Western Samoa). |
| Samoan Full Gospel Church | c1965 | I pen | ..... | | 50 | 95 | Indigenous pentecostal body. Samoans. Branch also in Western Samoa. |
| Seventh-day Adventist Church | 1895 | P Adv | x...c | | 300 | 600 | *SDA,* Samoa Mission, Central Pacific Union Mission. HQ Pago Pago. |
| United Pentecostal Church | c1965 | P Pel | x.... | 1 | 20 | 50 | *Jesus Only Church.* M=UPC(USA). Unitarian Pentecostals. 2f. |
| **Total affiliated (mid-1970)** | | | | 130 | 12,931 | 26,530 | Total denominations (1970) . . . 14. |
| **Total affiliated (mid-1975)** | | | | 150 | 15,210 | 31,200 | Total denominations (1975) . . . 15. |
| **Total affiliated (mid-1980)** | | | | 180 | 18,100 | 37,050 | Total denominations (1980) . . . 16. |

**NOTES ON TABLE ABOVE**
**COLUMNS:** for meanings and CODES (cols. 1, 3, 4, 8) see Codebook (Part 6). Column 1: **Boldface type** = church with over 10% of country's affiliated Christians.
**NATIONAL COUNCILS (Column 4, 5th letter).**
  C = Interdenominational Committee of American Samoa (ICAS).
  c = related to ICAS.

**PEOPLES** (ethnolinguistic). Christians: 89% Samoan, 10% Euronesian, 1% USA White.

**COUNTRY-WIDE TOTALS**
**EVANGELIZATION** (see Part 5). 1900: 100%. 1970: 100%. 1980: 100%.
**FOREIGN MISSIONARIES AND PERSONNEL** (aliens from abroad) (1973). Total 70. *From Western world.* 50: 40 marginal Protestants (Mormons from USA), 8 Protestants in 4 ·USA societies, 2 Roman Catholics. *From Third World.* 20: about 10 Protestants from Western Samoa, 10 marginal Protestants (Mormons).
**INSTITUTIONS** (church-operated) (1973). Total 3 (secondary schools).
**PERIODICALS.** About 7 titles.

**PERSONNEL.** About 145 (75 national, 70 foreign).
**SCRIPTURE DISTRIBUTION** (1975). Annual totals: 1,100 Bibles (91% subsidized, 9% commercial), 200 NTs (subsidized), 200 UBS portions, 1,600 UBS selections. *Translations completed.* Samoan: Portion 1836, NT 1846, Bible 1855.
**SERVICE AGENCIES.** About 5, including CEF, ICAS.

**ADDITIONAL DATA ON CHURCHES**
**CATHOLIC CHURCH.** Until 1975 the diocese was named Apia. *Catholic organizations.* The church sponsors one primary school in Pago Pago and 2 secondary schools on Tutuila Island. Local Catholics participate in organizations based in Western Samoa.

---

# ANDORRA

## SECULAR DATA

**STATE. Official name:** The Co-Principality of Andorra (Co-Principat d'Andorre/Les Vallés d'Andorre/Valls d'Andorra).
**Flag** (shown above right): Blue, yellow, and red bars, with coat of arms.
**Area:** 453 sq.km. (190 sq.miles). Agricultural land: 57.8%.
**Government:** Autonomous principality, under joint suzerainty of 2 co-princes, the President of the French Republic and the Bishop of Urgel, since 1278.
**Legislature:** General Council of the Valleys, 24 members.
**Official language:** Catalan.

**Capital:** Andorra la Vella, 14,700.
**Armed forces** (1976): None. Paramilitary forces: 25 police.

**DEMOGRAPHY. Population:** 5,664 (census of XI.1954. For 1970–2000 (UN), see last row of Table 1). Population density (1975): 51/sq.km. (131/sq.miles). Under 15 years: 27%. Growth rate (1975–80): 2.34% per year. Household size: 3.6 persons.
**Major languages:** Catalan, Spanish, French.
**Urban dwellers** (1970): 37.0%. Urban growth rate (1950–70): 3.0% per year.
**Tourists** (1974): 3 million (varies, up to 5 million).
**ETHNOLINGUISTIC GROUPS:** 61.3% Spaniard (40% Catalonian), 30.3% Andorran (Catalonian), 5.5% French (1,500), 0.7% English, Jewish, 30 other nationalities.

**MONEY** (1977). **Monetary unit:** French franc, Spanish peseta. **National income per person:** US$5,000. Average annual family income: US$18,000.

**EDUCATION.** Adult literacy: 90%. Education rate: 50%. Schools: 17.

**COMMUNICATION** (per 1,000 people). Phones: 117. Radios: 375. TV sets: 89. Daily newspaper circulation: 250 copies.

TABLE 1.     RELIGIOUS ADHERENTS IN ANDORRA

| Year | 1900 | | mid-1970 | | Annual change, 1970–1980 | | | | mid-1975 | | mid-1980 | | 2000 | |
|---|---|---|---|---|---|---|---|---|---|---|---|---|---|---|
| Name | Adherents | % | Adherents | % | Natural | Conversion | Total | Rate | Adherents | % | Adherents | % | Adherents | % |
| **Christians** | 4,980 | 99.6 | 18,930 | 99.6 | 598 | 0 | 598 | 2.61 | 22,915 | 99.6 | 24,910 | 99.6 | 36,860 | 99.6 |
| professing | 4,980 | 99.6 | 18,930 | 99.6 | 598 | 0 | 598 | 2.61 | 22,915 | 99.6 | 24,910 | 99.6 | 36,860 | 99.6 |
| Roman Catholics | 4,980 | 99.6 | 18,830 | 99.1 | 595 | 0 | 595 | 2.61 | 22,795 | 99.1 | 24,780 | 99.1 | 36,660 | 99.1 |
| Marginal Protestants | 0 | 0.0 | 60 | 0.3 | 2 | 0 | 2 | 2.61 | 70 | 0.3 | 80 | 0.3 | 120 | 0.3 |
| Protestants | 0 | 0.0 | 40 | 0.2 | 1 | 0 | 1 | 2.61 | 50 | 0.2 | 50 | 0.2 | 80 | 0.2 |
| nominal | 480 | 9.6 | 930 | 4.9 | 30 | 0 | 30 | 2.61 | 1,125 | 4.9 | 1,230 | 4.9 | 3,190 | 8.6 |
| affiliated | 4,500 | 90.0 | 18,000 | 94.7 | 568 | 0 | 568 | 2.61 | 21,790 | 94.7 | 23,680 | 94.7 | 33,670 | 91.0 |
| total practising | 4,270 | *95* | 14,400 | *80* | 454 | 0 | 454 | 2.61 | 17,430 | *80* | 18,940 | *80* | 23,570 | *70* |
| non-practising | 230 | *5* | 3,600 | *20* | 114 | 0 | 114 | 2.61 | 4,360 | *20* | 4,740 | *20* | 10,100 | *30* |
| Roman Catholics | 4,500 | 90.0 | 17,900 | 94.2 | 565 | 0 | 565 | 2.61 | 21,670 | 94.2 | 23,550 | 94.2 | 33,470 | 90.5 |
| Marginal Protestants | 0 | 0.0 | 60 | 0.3 | 2 | 0 | 2 | 2.61 | 70 | 0.3 | 80 | 0.3 | 120 | 0.3 |
| Protestants | 0 | 0.0 | 40 | 0.2 | 1 | 0 | 1 | 2.61 | 50 | 0.2 | 50 | 0.2 | 80 | 0.2 |
| Jews | 20 | 0.4 | 70 | 0.4 | 2 | 0 | 2 | 2.61 | 85 | 0.4 | 90 | 0.4 | 140 | 0.4 |
| **Country's population** | 5,000 | 100.0 | 19,000 | 100.0 | 600 | 0 | 600 | 2.61 | 23,000 | 100.0 | 25,000 | 100.0 | 37,000 | 100.0 |

**COLUMNS, ROWS.** For meanings and definitions, see Codebook (Part 6). Note that, by definition, total 'Christians' = professing + crypto-Christians, which also = affiliated + nominal Christians. Percentages may not always total exactly, due to rounding.
**CENSUSES.** The question on religion has not been asked.

**COUNTRY'S POPULATION.** In 1975, 16,000 of the population were foreign residents and only 7,000 were Andorrans.

**NON-CHRISTIAN RELIGIONS.** In 1970 there was a small Jewish community of 70 members in Andorra.

**CHRISTIANITY.** The great majority of the population are Roman Catholics. The church is part of the diocese of Urgel (Spain) with 8 parishes. A Catholic school, the College of St. Ermengol, is administered by the national governing body, the General Council. In 1970 there were also 60 Jehovah's Witnesses in Andorra and 28 Protestants. There are no interdenominational relations or organizations.

**CHURCH AND STATE.** Tradition holds that in the 8th century Charlemagne granted the Andorrans a charter for their support in his war against the Moors. His grandson made the Spanish count of Urgel overlord; and since 1278 the bishop of Urgel has been a co-prince of Andorra with the ruler (now president) of France as co-prince. The bishop of Urgel is in fact, along with the pope in Vatican City, the last Catholic bishop to retain official temporal power. Legislation is enacted by the 24-member General Council of the Valleys, which also names the state's administrators. Political factions include a liberal group leaning to France and a conservative group favouring Spain. France pays for some French-language schools while those near the Spanish border are church-supported.

**BROADCASTING.** Radio Andorra carries Catholic religious programmes every morning.

A quarter of Andorra's postage stamps illustrate churches, Life of Christ scenes, or other Christian topics; here, 3 of the Stations of the Cross.

### TABLE 2.   ORGANIZED CHURCHES AND DENOMINATIONS IN ANDORRA

| Official name 1 | Begun 2 | Type 3 | Counc 4 | Congs 5 | Adults 6 | Affiliated 7 | Names, notes, and other statistics (see Codebook) 8 |
|---|---|---|---|---|---|---|---|
| Iglesia Adventista del Séptimo Día | | P Adv | x.... | 1 | 20 | 40 | *SDA, Seventh-day Adventists*, in Spanish Church, Southern European Union Mission. |
| Iglesia Católica (D Urgel) | c 600 | R Lat | B.B.. | 8 | 13,100 | 17,900 | *Eglesia Católica* (in Catalan). *Catholic Ch.* Part of diocese in Spain. 8n,1r. |
| Testigos de Jehová | c1960 | M Jeh | x.... | 1 | 23 | 60 | *Jehovah's Witnesses. Watch Tower.* Active witnessing first reported in 1963. 4Y. |
| **Total affiliated (mid-1970)** | | | | 10 | 13,143 | 18,000 | Total denominations (1970) . . . 3. |
| **Total affiliated (mid-1975)** | | | | 11 | 15,910 | 21,790 | Total denominations (1975) . . . 3. |
| **Total affiliated (mid-1980)** | | | | 12 | 17,290 | 23,680 | Total denominations (1980) . . . 3. |

**NOTES ON TABLE ABOVE**
COLUMNS: for meanings and CODES (cols. 1, 3, 4, 8), see Codebook (Part 6). Column 1: **Boldface type** = church with over 10% of country's affiliated Christians.

**PEOPLES** (ethnolinguistic). Christians: 61.3% Spaniard (40%

Catalonian), 30.3% Andorran (Catalonian), 5.5% French, 0.7% English.

**COUNTRY-WIDE TOTALS**
EVANGELIZATION (see Part 5). 1900: 100%. 1970: 100%. 1980: 100%.
INSTITUTIONS (church-operated) (1973). Total 1 college.

PERIODICALS. 1 title.
PERSONNEL. About 8 (nationals).
RELIGIOUS LIBRARIES. 1.
SCRIPTURE DISTRIBUTION (1975). Annual totals: 50 NTs (subsidized).
SERVICE AGENCIES. About 2.

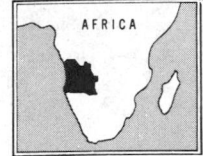

# ANGOLA

## SECULAR DATA

**STATE. Official name:** The People's Republic of Angola (A República Popular de Angola). Adjective of nationality: Angolan.
**Flag** (shown above right): Red and black stripes, yellow symbol of socialism, industry, agriculture.
**Area:** 1,246,700 sq.km. (481,351 sq.miles). Agricultural land: 24.3%.
**Government:** One-party Communist state, since 1975 (14th century kingdom, 1483 Portuguese rule, 1975 Independence).
**Official language:** Portuguese (*Português*).
**Chief cities:** capital Luanda 475,330 (1970), Huambo (Nova Lisboa) 89,000, Lobito 74,000.
**Political divisions:** 15 Regions including Cabinda (detached).
**Armed forces** (1976): Total 30,000 regular army.
**Foreign forces** (1973): 40,000 Portuguese regular troops, 10,000 irregular. (1976) 20,000 Cuban soldiers, with USSR advisers.

**DEMOGRAPHY. Population:** 5,646,166 (census of 15.XII.1970. For 1970–2000 (UN), see last row of Table 1). Population density (1975): 5/sq.km. (13/sq.mile). Under 15 years: 43%. Growth

rate (1975–80): 2.45% per year (births 4.70%, deaths −2.25%). Life expectancy (1975–80): 41.0 years. Household size: 4.9 persons.
**Major languages:** Portuguese, Mbundu, Kimbundu, Kongo (Kikongo), Chokwe, Luchazi, Spanish, and about 30 other tribal languages.
**Urban dwellers** (1970): 14.3%. Urban growth rate (1950–70): 5.0% per year.
**Labour force:** 29%.
**Refugees** (1977): 250,000 from Namibia and Zaire. Internally displaced: 350,000. Exiles abroad: 692,800 Angolans (350,000 in Portugal, 250,000 in Zaire, 60,000 in Zambia, 22,000 in Namibia, 4,700 in South Africa, 1,100 in Botswana).

**ETHNOLINGUISTIC GROUPS:** 33.5% Mbundu, 23.0% Kimbundu, 10.0% Kongo, 8.0% Luchazi, 8.0% Chokwe, 7.0% Portuguese (450,000 in 1973; 50,000 in early 1976, falling to under 5,000 by 1977), 4.0% Nyaneka, 2.0% Ambo, 1.0% Mestiço (Portuguese/African, Caboverdian), 0.9% Lunda, 0.8% Herero, 0.2% Afrikaner (10,000), 0.2% Bushman (7,000), 0.1% Bakwe

Pygmy (5,000), 0.1% British (5,000), Chinese (550). From 1975, 20,000 Cuban military and 4,000 civilians, also.

**MONEY** (1977). Monetary unit: kwanza; US$1 = AK 31.00.
**National income per person:** US$510. Average annual family income: US$2,500.
**Cost of living in capital** (1976): index 141 (Washington DC=100). Daily cost of living: US$56.

**EDUCATION.** Adult literacy: (1950) 3%, (1975) 15%. Education rate: 18%. Schools: 4,966 (4,799 primary, 167 secondary).

**HEALTH.** Hospitals: 669 (15,205 beds). Doctors: 523. Lepers: 56,800 (8.9 per 1,000). Blind: 12,000. Psychotics: 44,000.

**LITERATURE.** Periodicals: 66. Newspapers: 4 dailies, 14 non-daily.

**COMMUNICATION** (per 1,000 people). Phones: 6. Radios: 20. Daily newspaper circulation: 15 copies.

### TABLE 1.   RELIGIOUS ADHERENTS IN ANGOLA

| Year | 1900 | | mid-1970 | | Annual change, 1970–1980 | | | | mid-1975 | | mid-1980 | | 2000 | |
|---|---|---|---|---|---|---|---|---|---|---|---|---|---|---|
| Name | Adherents | % | Adherents | % | Natural | Conversion | Total | Rate | Adherents | % | Adherents | % | Adherents | % |
| Christians | 17,000 | 0.6 | 4,564,350 | 80.5 | 129,946 | 59,909 | 189,855 | 3.47 | 5,463,580 | 86.0 | 6,462,900 | 90.0 | 12,088,100 | 97.0 |
| professing | 17,000 | 0.6 | 4,564,350 | 80.5 | 129,946 | 59,909 | 189,855 | 3.47 | 5,463,580 | 86.0 | 6,462,900 | 90.0 | 12,088,100 | 97.0 |
| Roman Catholics | 15,000 | 0.5 | 3,481,380 | 61.4 | 99,424 | 45,768 | 145,192 | 3.47 | 4,180,270 | 65.8 | 4,933,300 | 68.7 | 9,047,400 | 72.6 |
| Protestants | 2,000 | 0.1 | 1,008,670 | 17.8 | 28,440 | 13,043 | 41,483 | 3.47 | 1,195,760 | 18.8 | 1,423,500 | 19.8 | 2,655,500 | 21.3 |
| African indigenous | 0 | 0.0 | 70,000 | 1.2 | 1,965 | 1,085 | 3,050 | 3.69 | 82,600 | 1.3 | 100,500 | 1.4 | 373,900 | 3.0 |
| Anglicans | 0 | 0.0 | 3,000 | 0.1 | 78 | −18 | 60 | 1.82 | 3,300 | 0.1 | 3,600 | 0.1 | 7,000 | 0.1 |
| Marginal Protestants | 0 | 0.0 | 1,000 | 0.0 | 31 | 29 | 60 | 4.61 | 1,300 | 0.0 | 1,600 | 0.0 | 3,500 | 0.0 |
| Catholics (non-Roman) | 0 | 0.0 | 300 | 0.0 | 8 | 2 | 10 | 2.86 | 350 | 0.0 | 400 | 0.0 | 800 | 0.0 |
| nominal | 4,300 | 0.1 | 1,264,521 | 22.3 | 35,207 | 12,839 | 48,046 | 3.24 | 1,480,280 | 23.3 | 1,744,980 | 24.3 | 3,240,100 | 26.0 |
| affiliated | 12,700 | 0.4 | 3,299,829 | 58.2 | 94,739 | 47,070 | 141,809 | 3.56 | 3,983,300 | 62.7 | 4,717,920 | 65.7 | 8,848,000 | 71.0 |
| total practising | 11,430 | 90 | 2,309,880 | 70 | 66,317 | 32,949 | 99,266 | 3.56 | 2,788,310 | 70 | 3,302,540 | 70 | 5,751,200 | 65 |
| non-practising | 1,270 | 10 | 989,950 | 30 | 28,422 | 14,121 | 42,543 | 3.56 | 1,194,990 | 30 | 1,415,380 | 30 | 3,096,800 | 35 |
| Roman Catholics | 11,700 | 0.4 | 2,824,129 | 49.8 | 80,386 | 32,874 | 113,260 | 3.35 | 3,379,800 | 53.2 | 3,956,730 | 55.1 | 7,128,260 | 57.2 |
| Protestants | 1,000 | 0.0 | 411,500 | 7.3 | 12,450 | 12,735 | 25,185 | 4.81 | 523,480 | 8.2 | 663,350 | 9.2 | 1,360,940 | 10.9 |
| Evangelicals | 1,000 | 0.0 | 397,000 | 7.0 | 12,001 | 12,249 | 24,250 | 4.81 | 504,600 | 7.9 | 639,500 | 8.9 | 1,312,000 | 10.5 |
| African indigenous | 0 | 0.0 | 61,000 | 1.1 | 1,812 | 1,428 | 3,240 | 4.25 | 76,200 | 1.2 | 93,400 | 1.3 | 348,900 | 2.8 |
| Anglicans | 0 | 0.0 | 2,000 | 0.0 | 55 | 5 | 60 | 2.61 | 2,300 | 0.0 | 2,600 | 0.0 | 6,000 | 0.0 |
| Marginal Protestants | 0 | 0.0 | 1,000 | 0.0 | 31 | 29 | 60 | 4.61 | 1,300 | 0.0 | 1,600 | 0.0 | 3,500 | 0.0 |
| Catholics (non-Roman) | 0 | 0.0 | 200 | 0.0 | 5 | −1 | 4 | 1.82 | 220 | 0.0 | 240 | 0.0 | 400 | 0.0 |
| Tribal religionists | 2,953,000 | 99.4 | 1,100,520 | 19.4 | 20,975 | −62,650 | −41,675 | −4.73 | 881,920 | 13.9 | 683,500 | 9.5 | 252,400 | 2.0 |
| Non-religious | 0 | 0.0 | 5,000 | 0.1 | 143 | 2,357 | 2,500 | 41.67 | 6,000 | 0.1 | 30,000 | 0.4 | 100,000 | 0.8 |
| Baha'is | 0 | 0.0 | 400 | 0.0 | 12 | 8 | 20 | 4.00 | 500 | 0.0 | 600 | 0.0 | 1,500 | 0.0 |
| Atheists | 0 | 0.0 | 0 | 0.0 | 24 | 376 | 400 | 40.00 | 1,000 | 0.0 | 4,000 | 0.1 | 20,000 | 0.2 |
| **Country's population** | **2,970,000** | **100.0** | **5,670,000** | **100.0** | **151,100** | **0** | **151,100** | **2.38** | **6,353,000** | **100.0** | **7,181,000** | **100.0** | **12,462,000** | **100.0** |

**COLUMNS, ROWS.** For meanings and definitions see Codebook (Part 6). Note that, by definition, total 'Christians' = professing + crypto-Christians, which also = affiliated + nominal Christians. Percentages may not always total exactly, due to rounding.
**CENSUSES. 1940:** 70.0% tribal religionists, 22.0% Roman Catholics, 7.8% Protestants, 0.1% other religionists. **31.XII.1950:** 50.5% tribal religionists, 36.3% Roman Catholics, 13.1% Protestants, 0.1% non-religious (Whites). **30.XII.1960:** 50.8% Roman Catholics, 32.5% tribal religionists, 16.6% Protestants, 0.1% non-religious (Whites).

**NOTES ON RELIGIONS**
AFRICAN INDIGENOUS. In 13 denominations in 1970 (see Table 2).
ATHEISTS. After Independence in 1975 a Communist party was formed based on the Movimento Popular de Libertação de Angola (MPLA). In 1977 the party was remodelled as a Marxist-Leninist party with membership initially restricted to around 5,000 hand-core revolutionaries. According to president Neto then, 'No party member can be a church member, and no church member can be a member of the party'.
BAHA'IS. In 1 local spiritual assembly (1973).

COUNTRY'S POPULATION. Since 1975, about one million are thought to have been killed or died of starvation.
NON-RELIGIOUS. Up to 1975, mainly Portuguese Whites (Brancos), with a few Macao and other Chinese; after 1975, a growing number of Africans became non-religious and a smaller number atheists.
TRIBAL RELIGIONISTS. Tribes over 60% traditionalist (animist) in 1972: Hukwe Bushmen (95%), Mbukushu (Kusso) (90%), Chokwe (Lunda) (75%), Kwangare (70%), Mbwela (60%). Almost all other tribes have a proportion of residual animists down to under 1% among the Bakongo.

## NON-CHRISTIAN RELIGIONS.

**Traditional religions** have shown a progressive and rapid decline since World War II. In 1940 tribal religionists were 70% of the population, falling to 51% in 1950 and 33% in 1960. By 1972 they were estimated to be only 17%. The Hukwe, a small Bushman tribe on the southern border, are 95% traditionalists; and their Bantu-speaking neighbours to the northeast, the Mbukushu, 90%. Other southeastern peoples with high traditionalist percentages are the Mbwela (60%) and the Kwangare (70%). Of the large tribes, the Chokwe and Lunda of Lunda province (400,000; 75%) have been the most resistant to Christianity. On the other hand, the Bakongo of northern Angola (1.4 million) are only 2% traditionalist and the Mbundu (1.8 million) 10%. The 3 most common vernacular names for God in Angola are Nzambi in the north (Bakongo, Ambundu, Lunda, Chokwe), Suku in the centre (Ovimbundu) and Kalunga in the south (Ambo, Kuanhama). Nevertheless, there is considerable intermixture of names, the term Kalunga also being used among the Ambundu, Lunda and Chokwe and Nzambi or Ndiambi among southern peoples. The cult of ancestral spirits (Mahamba in Chokwe) exists as well as belief in the evil activity of witches (*ndoki* in Kikongo) and the beneficent function of medicine men (*kimbanda* in Kimbundu). During the 20th century a number of spirit possession cults, known by the generic term Mahamba, have arisen among the Luvale, Luchazi, Chokwe, Ovimbundu and Ndembu. The early forms mostly concerned troublesome ancestral spirits, but alien spirits were introduced as new Mahamba in 1925. One of the most important movements of the early 1930s was Tukuka Mahamba which spread eastward among the Ndembu of Northern Rhodesia; and after World War II such other new Mahamba as Ndeke (aircraft) and Sitima (train) made their appearance.

**Baha'i** has been represented in Angola by a small community since the Baha'i World Crusade in Kampala in 1953.

## CHRISTIANITY

CATHOLIC CHURCH. The first Catholic mission to the Congo kingdom, centred on northern Angola's São Salvador, arrived in 1491. The initial group consisted of Franciscans, Dominicans, Canons of St John the Evangelist and secular priests; and a widespread church was formed during the next century under the remarkable Christian king Afonso I. Afonso's son Henrique became the first Black African bishop in Catholic history. After a promising beginning, the ravages of the slave trade caused the disintegration of both kingdom and church. In 1560 Jesuits accompanied the first Portuguese expedition to the Ndongo kingdom inland on the Cuanza river, and in 1576 Luanda was founded. By the end of the century, an episcopal see had been established and 4 monasteries built. Once again the slave trade acted as an impediment to the extension of the church. In spite of the activity of Capuchins, Franciscans and Carmelites at the coast, the 18th and 19th centuries witnessed the decline of Catholic missions. A reversal of this trend did not take place until 1865 when Propaganda was asked to assign Holy Ghost fathers to Angola. By 1890, 4 centres were established at Malange, Caconda, Cassinga and Huíla which served as bases for expansion into the interior. However, many areas were not effectively reached until after World War II.

Catholicism has made remarkable progress in Angola since 1940 as revealed in government census statistics. In 1940, 22.0% of the population professed to be Catholics. By 1950 the figure had risen to 36.3% and to 50.8% in 1960. The estimate for 1972 is over 60%. The church has its greatest strength among the Ovimbundu of central Angola, and is weakest in the east and southeast.

The most serious problem for the Catholic church throughout its history in Angola has been its relationship with the Portuguese government. Portuguese Catholic missions have never played an independent role with regard to the Portuguese colonial system, whether in the realm of social action or in the face

Igreja Católica em Angola. *Above.* Service of infant baptism in Archdiocese of Huambo, among Mbundu tribe. *Below.* Catholic station Radio Ecclesia in Luanda, begun 1954, silenced 1976, seized by regime 1978.

of Angola's principal social problem, forced labour, or in education. The educational system was designed primarily for the indigenous masses with emphasis on rudimentary training rather than on the development of leadership or an elite. The lack of African leadership is also evident in the church hierarchy. The first African bishop of the contemporary era, not only in Angola but for all of Portugal's colonies, was appointed in 1970 as auxiliary bishop of Luanda. In 1973 he was transferred to Malange as ordinary of the diocese. Following the change of regime in Portugal on 25 April 1974, the Holy See in August 1974 named a second African bishop as auxiliary of Luanda.

PROTESTANT CHURCHES. Comity agreements have played a significant role in Angolan church history. Thus the major denominations have tended to restrict themselves to work among specific tribal groups, with very little overlapping even in urban areas.

The first to arrive were British Baptists who opened a mission at São Salvador among the Bakongo of northern Angola in 1878. The Bakongo have in fact become the most christianized people in Angola, in 1960 already 55.8% Catholic and 42.7% Protestant with only 1.5% remaining traditionalist. Two other smaller groups, founded by independent missionaries, have also worked among the Bakongo, the Angola Evangelical Mission (AEM) which arrived in Cabinda and the coastal area south of the Congo estuary in 1897 and the North Angola Mission which entered Uige (Carmona) in 1925. The latter body was founded by a missionary originally recruited by the AEM. The AEM was taken over by Canadian Baptists in 1957 as was the work begun in 1910 in Cabinda by the Christian and Missionary Alliance. The revolution which broke out in 1961 seriously affected the life of the Bakongo church. Following the opening of hostilities, more than 400,000 refugees fled from the area to nearby Zaire where they greatly strengthened local churches. Many churches in northern Angola continued to exist in villages hidden from Portuguese

surveillance. Most missionaries were evacuated in 1961, 2 Canadian Baptist families remaining in Cabinda until 1964. However, since the Portugal coup d'etat of 1974 many of these refugees have returned to northern Angola.

Methodists have worked among the Kimbundu-speaking people east of Luanda since 1885. In 1961 a number of Methodists took refuge in Zaire, and until 1974 many others continued to worship in hidden villages in the Dembos district. There are at present no Methodist missionaries in Angola, and the church has been led by an Angolan bishop since

1972. In 1960–61 Methodists were responsible for 99 schools catering for 5,062 students.

Several missions have been active among the Ovimbundu. The Evangelical Church of Central Angola unites the work originally begun by the American Board in 1880 and the United Church of Canada in 1886. This church is strongest on the Benguela plateau in the area of Nova Lisboa and Silva Porto as well as at Lobito on the coast. In addition to 60 primary and 3 secondary schools, it has the most highly developed medical programme in the territory: 7 hospitals, 20 clinics, 3 leprosaria and an extensive rural public health service.

The region west of the plateau and extending

south to Sá da Bandeira is occupied by the Philafricaine Mission, which was begun in 1897 and since 1908 has been supported by the Swiss Reformed Churches. This church has 20 primary schools, 2 secondary schools, 4 hospitals, 6 clinics and 3 leprosaria. Pentecostals are active in the area of Novo Redondo and Gabela, north of Lobito. Adventists, who first appeared in 1922, are also found among the Ovimbundo although they have extensive work in the Moxico and Lunda of eastern Angola as well. Adventist institutions number 128 primary schools, 2 secondary schools, 1 hospital and 3 clinics. Brethren (CMML) missionaries have worked among the Chokwe and Lunda of the northeast since 1884, but these have shown themselves to be among the most resistant of Angola's peoples to Christian evangelization. The Brethren sponsor 6 primary schools, 2 hospitals and 2 leprosaria.

Southern Angola under comity was assigned to the African Evangelical Fellowship (AEF). Originally called the South African General Mission, the AEF is a faith mission which entered Angola in 1914. Southeastern Angola is virtually devoid of Protestants, and Protestant activity was actually prohibited in the Kwanyama area along the southern border from 1914 to 1960. The AEF is responsible for 2 primary schools, 2 hospitals and a leprosarium.

Although Portuguese (White) congregations exist in Angola's major cities, missionary outreach from metropolitan Portugal to the indigenous peoples has never been extensive. The only active body is a small Portuguese Baptist Mission near Nova Lisboa founded in 1936. Since 1968 Southern Baptist missionaries affiliated with the Portuguese Baptist Convention have been at work with Europeans in Luanda.

INDIGENOUS CHURCHES. Angola is notable for the relative absence of African independent churches, due in part to government suppression of such movements. Kimbanguism, which began among the Bakongo of Zaire in 1921, has had its effect among the people of northern Angola as well. In Angola Kimbanguism has manifested itself as Amicalismo (related to the Congo prophet Matswa André), the Igreja dos Negros (related to the Congo prophet Simon Mpadi) and the Movimento Tonsi (also related to Simon Mpadi); and, more recently, as an organized branch of the EJCSK in Zaire.

Another larger Bakongo group is that formed by the prophet Simão Toco in 1949. Although born in Maquela do Zombo, Toco was 'illuminated by the Holy Spirit' while working as choir leader in a Baptist church in Kinshasa. Toco was expelled to Angola by the Belgian authorities in 1956, and the movement spread rapidly among Toco's own Bombo people. Portuguese attempts to suppress the sect by exiling its leader to other parts of Angola have also contributed to its expansion. Toco himself was exiled to the Azores, but he continues to maintain contact with followers in Angola. As late as 1973 he was known to be seeking Christian literature for them from the Worldwide Evangelization Crusade (UK) and other bodies in Europe.

The Bakongo people of the Cabinda enclave have also had their prophets, the first being an ecstatic named Maiange in 1930. In 1953 an even larger group was gathered together by the Pointe Noire prophet, Simon Zepherin Lassy. Lassyism, also called God of the Candle (Nazambi ya Bougie), continues to exert an important influence in both Cabinda and Congo.

In 1940 a movement called Muvungismo spread among the Yaka across the Kwango river from the Belgian Congo. A strongly anti-White split from the Unevangelized Tribes Mission, it was quickly stamped out by Belgians and Portuguese.

Although very little is known about them, at least 3 distinct independent groups are active in southern Angola: the Olosanto among the Mbundu, the Holy Spirit Group (Grupo do Espirito Santo), and the Bapostola (Apostles) who owe their origin to the Apostolic Church of Johane Maranke in Rhodesia.

**CHURCH AND STATE.** Until Angola's independence in 1975, the Portuguese constitution guaranteed the free exercise of worship and the separation of church and state. Nevertheless, the Catholic Church enjoyed a special relationship with the Portuguese state as stipulated in the concordat, Missionary Agreement and Missionary Statute of 1940 and 1941. The major problem of religious liberty related to the failure of the Portuguese government to provide legal recognition for the Protestant community. The legal basis for this existed since 1921, and de facto recognition was given, but Angolan Protestant organizations were unsuccessful in having their statutes approved. The effect of the Law on Religious Liberty of 22 July 1971, providing for the official recognition of religious associations and organizations other than the Catholic Church, was minimal.

Protestant activity in the Kwanyama area of the south was prohibited between 1914 and 1960, and other restrictions were evident through the years. A Methodist attempt to open a new mission station and secondary school in the Dembos area during the 1950s for example never received government approval. Protestants were generally accused of denationalizing Angolans, and the criticism of existing conditions in 1961 by Baptist and Methodist missionaries contributed to the growing Portuguese distrust of Protestantism. Five Methodist missionaries were imprisoned shortly after the outbreak of hostilities, and numerous Protestant pastors and teachers were killed by Portuguese soldiers and militia in the early days of the civil war. The fact that Protestants were prominent in the revolutionary movement also contributed to Portuguese hostility. The president of MPLA (Popular Movement for the Liberation of Angola), Agostinho Neto, is the son of a Methodist minister, while the president of GRAE (FNLA, National Front for the Liberation of Angola), Holden Roberto, is an active Baptist layman.

Individual Angolan Catholic priests were also imprisoned for alleged involvement in the revolutionary movement. Several were exiled to Portugal, including Msgr Manuel Mendes das Neves, the former vicar general of the Luanda archdiocese, who was arrested in 1961 and died in exile in Portugal in 1967, and Fr Joaquim Pinto de Andrade, former chancellor of the same diocese and brother of the nationalist writer Mario de Andrade, who was exiled to Portugal in 1960 and received a sentence of 3 years imprisonment in 1971 for 'belonging to the MPLA'. The MPLA in fact named him honorary president of the movement.

The long duration of the war and the strengthening of nationalist aspirations among the Angolan population and the African priesthood led some foreign missionaries and a small minority of Portuguese clergy to raise questions regarding the position of the hierarchy and the church vis-a-vis the colonial system and the war. In 1968, Fr Adalberto Postima, professor of philosophy in the interdiocesan seminary of Luanda, was relieved of his functions by the archbishop of Luanda and, returned to his homeland, Italy, for having suggested in an open letter to the archbishop the need of studying the right to self-determination according to the pontifical documents. In the same year, Fr Waldo Garcia, a Spaniard and Professor in the major seminary of Nova Lisboa as well as being a member of the administration of the Catholic Institute, and 2 Portuguese priests, were expelled from Angola by the hierarchy for having organized colloquia dealing with pastoralia and for editing a book on ecumenism. The Catholic Institute for all practical purposes disappeared afterwards. In July 1970, in a letter addressed to the Episcopal Conference and made public a year later, 22 Portuguese Holy Ghost priests protested against the pastoral and indeed administrative role forced onto missionaries. They described the Angolan church as an 'official society intimately associated with the powers that be' and requested of the bishops permission to initiate a new mission experiment which, beginning with a critique of traditional mission, would seek for answers to the concrete situations created by the colonial regime. The Episcopal Conference refused approval and a number of these clergy were forced to leave Angola.

Until April 1974, the Angolan Catholic hierarchy continued unanimous in its support of the Lisbon regime and its colonial policies. On one side, there were declarations condemning African terrorists which were manifestly favourable towards the war carried on by the Portuguese army against the nationalists; and on the other hand, the episcopal documents of recent years dealt with social, moral and spiritual problems as if there were no war in Angola with its attendant repression, massacres and brutality. At a time when the liberation war and Portugal's international isolation put pressure on the government to institute a degree of reform, the Angolan bishops published 2 pastoral letters, one in 1971 and the other in 1972, criticizing the 'social disequilibrium' and 'peace based on the domination of one class by another', without reference to Portuguese colonialism as a cause.

After the military coup in Portugal on 25 April 1974, the Episcopal Conference of Angola published a pastoral note in May and a declaration in June manifesting their embarrassment over their previous position and also expressing somewhat awkwardly their acceptance of the new political orientation of the country. Their condemnation of the injustices of the previous regime was combined with warnings against a repetition of such injustices during the period of transition and by the future government of independent Angola. On the other hand, the pastoral letter published after the agreement of 15 January 1975 guaranteeing the independence of Angola showed a significant change. The bishops there renounced their previous political attitude, based on 'assimilation', in favour of an 'authentically African' church, which is 'derived of necessity by the apostolic requirements of our faith' and not from 'a spirit of calculation or tactics'.

Following the takeover by the Marxist MPLA regime, the new constitution in 1976 proclaimed Angola as a secular state with the right of all to be either religious or non-religious, freedom of conscience, religious belief and the right to worship, with all churches and missions having equal rights. Further, the churches' contribution to the building of the new society in Angola would be welcomed. However, shortly afterwards the regime indicated its true intentions, firstly by silencing the Catholic radio station in Luanda, and secondly by condemning as subversive both Jehovah's Witnesses and also the Bakongo Tokoist movement, the Church of Jesus Christ in the World. In 1978, the regime decreed the final nationalization of Radio Ecclesia and seizure of its property, abolished all religious holidays including Christmas, and began a ceaseless barrage of atheistic propaganda.

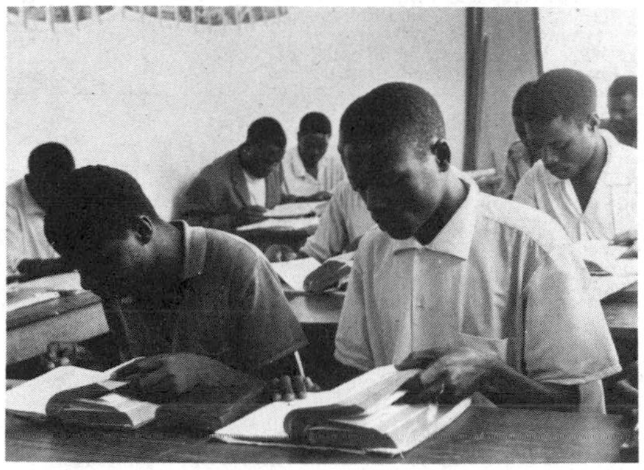

**Igreja Evangélica do Sudoeste de Angola.** Students (60% Mbundu) at SEAM Bible school.

**INTERDENOMINATIONAL ORGANIZATIONS.** The Evangelical Alliance of Angola (Aliança Evangélica de Angola) was formed in 1922 and counts in its membership the main Protestant bodies working in the country, excepting the Adventists. However, the prohibition of annual meetings following the revolution in 1961 severely restricted its effectiveness. In addition to its involvement in regulating comity agreements between the churches, the Alliance helped to co-ordinate the missionary work of the Angolan churches on the island of São Tomé. Another example of Protestant co-operation was the establishment of Emmanuel United Seminary in Dondi in 1957, a joint venture of Methodists and the Evangelical Church of Central Angola. In 1977 an ecumenical council in working relationship with the WCC was formed.

Protestant-Catholic relations have greatly improved since Vatican II, although there are still no formal organizations providing for dialogue or joint action. In July 1966 the first public Protestant-Catholic worship service took place in the College of São José de Cluny in Luanda with the Catholic archbishop and the bishops of the Portuguese Lusitanian and Methodist churches officiating.

**BROADCASTING.** For some years there were 2 Catholic stations, Radio Ecclesia in Luanda (begun 1954) and Radio Nova Lisboa, although the former was seized by the regime in 1978. There are Protestant recording studios at the Emmaus Bible School, Luso, and for the Igreja Evangélica at Sá da Bandeira. In July 1970 the Baptist Convention of Angola began a 15-minute radio programme 'Herald of the Gospel' broadcast by stations in 5 cities. A Bible correspondence course is also offered. From overseas, Vatican Radio has a service in Portuguese beamed to Angola.

## BIBLIOGRAPHY

*Angola: the land of the blacksmith prince*. J. T. Tucker. London: World Dominion Press, 1933. 180p. (Detailed Protestant survey).
*Aspectos dos movimentos associativos na Africa Negra*. J. M. da Silva Cunha. 2 vols. Lisboa: Junta de Investigações do Ultramar, 1958–59. (Lassismo and other cults).
*Atlas missionario português*. A. Rego & E. dos Santos. Lisboa: Junta de Investigações do Ultramar, 1964.
*Boletim eclesiástico de Angola e São Tomé, 1963–64*. Luanda: Missões Católicas Portuguesas, 1963. 239p.
'Do sincretismo mágico e religioso nos fundamentos ideológicos do terrorismo no noroeste de Angola', E. dos Santos, *Garcia de Orta* (Lisboa), X, 1 (1962).
*Liturgia, Cristianismo e sociedade em Angola*. A. F. Santos Neves. Angola: Editorial Coloquios, 1968. 192p.
'L'église toko et le mouvement de libération de l'Angola', *Le mois en Afrique* (mai, 1966), 80–97.
'Nouvelles manifestations du prophétisme en Afrique équatoriale et en Angola', C. Tastevin, *Comptes rendus de l'Académie des Sciences Coloniales* (Paris), XVI, 3 (février, 1956), 149–153.
'O Noroeste angolano e os movimentos profético-salvificos', E. dos Santos, *Ultramar* (Lisboa), 17 (1964), 32–73.
*Religiões de Angola*. E. dos Santos. Lisboa: Junta de Investigações do Ultramar, 1969. 536p.

TABLE 2. ORGANIZED CHURCHES AND DENOMINATIONS IN ANGOLA

| Official name 1 | Begun 2 | Type 3 | Counc 4 | Congs 5 | Adults 6 | Affiliated 7 | Names, notes, and other statistics (see Codebook) 8 |
|---|---|---|---|---|---|---|---|
| Convenção Baptista de Angola | 1936 | P Bap | T...G | 20 | 513 | 1,000 | *Angola Baptist Convention*. M=BCP(Portugal); 1968, SBC(USA). Portuguese. 5n,2f,73Y. |
| Igreja Adventista do Sétimo Dia | 1922 | P Adv | x.... | 42 | 20,810 | 37,000 | 8 Missions in Angola UM. Mbundu. 49n,1H,3h,1j,2r,1s,812t(37515),2775Y. |
| Igreja Anglicana (D Damaraland) | 1924 | A Hig | awaV. | | 1,000 | 2,000 | *Anglican Ch*. Part of D Damaraland (Namibia), CPSA. Ambo. Missionaries forbidden. |
| **Igreja Católica em Angola:** | 1491 | R Lat | H.SSP | 272 | 1,609,700 | 2,824,129 | *Catholic Ch*. C=11+4+25. 12H,128h,5p,1q,2s(214). 141n,519x,121m,652w,116103Yy. |
| M Luanda | 1940 | R Lat | Hs | 84 | 404,700 | 710,000 | Luanda & Cuanza-N (guerrilla areas), Cabinda. 1p, 1s. 21 80 24 215 29000 |
| D Benguela | 1970 | R Lat | Hs | 26 | 213,600 | 374,748 | Lobito port. District of Benguela. Mbundu. 15 31 2 63 16965 |
| D Carmona & São Salvador | 1967 | R Lat | Hs | 14 | 73,200 | 128,388 | Original diocese 1596. War zone. Kongo. 1p. 0 36 12 7 2899 |
| D Luso | 1963 | R Lat | Hosb | 22 | 29 900 | 52,483 | Moxico district, guerrilla area. Lunda, Chokwe. 1p. 21 27 7 17 2394 |
| D Malanje | 1957 | R Lat | Hs | 18 | 125,600 | 220,340 | 81% Kimbundu, 19% Chokwe. Former war area. 8 50 10 67 10018 |
| D Nova Lisboa (1977, M Huambo) | 1940 | R Lat | Hs | 37 | 330,300 | 579,513 | Huambo district. 99% Mbundu. Area 60% Catholic. 1s. 48 168 40 57 28257 |
| D Sá da Bandeira (M Lubango) | 1955 | R Lat | Hs | 40 | 233,100 | 409,044 | 48% Mbundu,17% Ambo,11% Ngangela,7% Ngumbi. 1p. 24 76 9 137 15359 |
| D Silva Porto | 1940 | R Lat | Hs | 31 | 199,300 | 349,613 | Guerrillas. 67% Mbundu,20% Ganguela,10% Chokwe. 1p. 4 51 17 89 11211 |
| Igreja de Deus | 1938 | P Pe3 | ZF... | 21 | 2,015 | 5,000 | *Church of God*. M=CoG(Cleveland)(USA) until expelled 1957. Locally led. 29n. |
| Igreja de Lassy Zepherin | 1953 | I Sal | ..... | | 500 | 1,000 | *Lassismo. Nzambi Bougie* (*God of the Candle*). In Cabinda, from Congo-Brazzaville. |
| Igreja do Nazareno | | P Hol | xF... | | 200 | 500 | *Ch of the Nazarene*. Immigrant Caboverdian farmers from Cape Verde Islands. |
| Igreja do Nosso Senhor Jesus Cristo | 1949 | I pen | ..... | | 10,000 | 20,000 | *Ebundu dia Mfumu eto Yeso Klisto. Red Star Cult*. Ex BMS. Persecuted, expanding. |
| Igreja Evangélica Baptista | 1878 | P Bap | T.A.a | 50 | 5,000 | 10,000 | *Ev Baptist Ch*. M=BMS(UK). Northeast. 99% Kongo. 1961 war, most fled to Zaire. 1s. |
| Igreja Evangélica de Angola | 1897 | P Bap | T...a | | 1,000 | 2,000 | 1897 M=Angola Ev Mission; 1910 CMA; 1957 CBOMB (Canada). Cabinda, NWAngola. Kongo. |
| Igreja Evangélica de Angola Central | 1880 | P uni | .w..K | | 73,000 | 204,000 | *Ev Ch of Central Angola*. M=UCCan,UCC(USA). 98% Mbundu, 1% Kwanyama. 15f,10H,20h,1u. |
| Igreja Evangélica do Norte de Angola | 1925 | P ind | ....a | 2 | 500 | 1,000 | *Ev Ch of Northern A*. Schism by missionary ex Angola Ev Mission. Carmona area. |
| Igreja Evangélica do Sudoeste de A | 1897 | P Bap | ....G | 348 | 8,730 | 45,000 | M=Filafricana(SEAM). 59% Mbundu. 20n,3x,421m,90w,7H,6h,1p,2r,W=40%,712Y,3899z. |
| Igreja Evangélica do Sul de Angola | 1914 | P int | xM..G | 150 | 3,000 | 10,000 | *Ev Ch of South Angola*. M=AEF(SAGM). 50% Chokwe, 45% Ngonyelu. 15f,3H,1p,1s,250Y. |
| Igreja Evangélica dos Irmãos | 1884 | P CBr | x...G | 250 | 10,000 | 20,000 | *Christian Brethren* (Open). M=CMML(UK,USA). Chokwe, Luvale, Lunda. 17f,4H. |
| Igr Ev Pentecostal Assembleia de Deus | c1951 | P Pen | ....G | 10 | 1,000 | 3,000 | *Assemblies of God*. Portuguese. Expelled 1957, returned 1970 Cuanza-Sul. 4n,1p. |
| Igreja Kimbanguista | 1927 | I pen | xwi.K | | 10,000 | 30,000 | *EJCSK* (Zaire). In north among Kongo tribe. Violent persecution until 1974. |
| Igreja Lusitana Católica Apostólica Ev | 1965 | C ReC | uuc.. | 3 | 50 | 200 | *Lusitanian Ch of Portugal*. In communion with Anglican Church. 1n. |
| Igreja Metodista Unida de Angola | 1885 | P Met | Vw..K | 107 | 47,989 | 70,000 | Africa CC, UMC. 97% Kimbundu. 67n,386m,100w,1H,1p,1s,1u,W=70%,1000Y,1800y. |
| Testemunhas de Jeová | c1945 | M Jeh | x.... | 6 | 487 | 1,000 | *Jehovah's Witnesses. Watch Tower*. Active witnessing by 1950. Banned 1976. 91Y. |
| Other African indigenous churches | | I | ..... | | 5,000 | 10,000 | Total about 7 (see list below), including immigrant bodies from Zaire. |
| Other Protestant denominations | | P | ..... | | 2,000 | 3,000 | Including Lutheran Ch of Angola, Christian Ev Ch of Luanda, Ev Pentecostal Mission. |
| **Total affiliated (mid-1970)** | | | | **2,100** | **1,812,494** | **3,299,829** | **Total denominations (1970) . . . 30.** |
| **Total affiliated (mid-1975)** | | | | **2,400** | **2,187,900** | **3,983,300** | **Total denominations (1975) . . . 29.** |
| **Total affiliated (mid-1980)** | | | | **2,700** | **2,591,410** | **4,717,920** | **Total denominations (1980) . . . 28.** |

NOTES ON TABLE ABOVE
COLUMNS: for meanings and CODES (cols. 1, 3, 4, 8), see Codebook (Part 6). Column 1: **Boldface type** = church with over 10% of country's affiliated Christians.
NATIONAL COUNCILS (Column 4, 5th letter).
d = member of AEA and CIAE.
G = Associação de Evangélicos de Angola (AEA) (Association of Evangelicals of Angola) (formed 1922 as Aliança Evangélica de Angola; 1974, attempts to make it a council of churches; 1974, Associação de Evangélicos de Angola formed).
K = Conselho das Igrejas Angolanas Evangélicas (CIAE) (Christian Council of Churches in Angola), formed 1977.
P = Conferência Episcopal de Angola e São Tomé (CEAST) (Episcopal Conference of Angola & São Tomé).
OTHER AFRICAN INDIGENOUS CHURCHES. There are several other unorganized movements, including: Grupo do Espirito Santo (Holy Spirit Group), Igreja Apostólica (Vapostori, Bapostolo; Apostles, from Rhodesia/Zaire), Igreja dos Negros, Olosanto (Holy Ones; Mbundu, 1955). A number of bodies have spread from Zaire into Angola.

PEOPLES (ethnolinguistic). Christians (1970): 86% Bantu, 12% Portuguese, 1.5% Mestiço, 0.3% Afrikaner, 0.1% British, 0.1% Bushman.

COUNTRY-WIDE TOTALS
EVANGELIZATION (see Part 5). 1900: 15%. 1970: 86%. 1980: 95%. *Mass evangelism*. Campaigns by Ev Ch of Southwest Angola in 1966 in 32 villages of Benguela district, with another in the same area in 1970.
FOREIGN MISSIONARIES AND PERSONNEL (nationals serving abroad) (1973). Total 100 (about 54 Roman Catholics, 42 Protestants and 4 African indigenous) in Zaire and São Tomé, mostly as refugees.
FOREIGN MISSIONARIES AND PERSONNEL (aliens from abroad) (1974). Total 1,407. *From Western world*. 1,344: 1,252 Roman Catholics, 92 Protestants (39 in 8 USA societies, 31 in 1 Switzerland society, 13 in 1 Canada society, 9 in 1 UK society). *From Communist world*. 1 Roman Catholic from Czechoslovakia. *From Third World*. 62: 40 Roman Catholics (15 from Brazil, 10 India, 5 Mozambique, 2 Mexico, 2 Cape Verde Is, Zaire et alia), 12 Protestants (5 Methodists from Brazil, 5 Zaire, 2 in 2 South Africa societies), about 10 African indigenous from Zaire.
INSTITUTIONS (church-operated) (1973). Total 290, including 64 higher schools (9 minor seminaries), 204 medical centres (38 hospitals), 2 radio stations, 2 religious communities (monasteries), 8 seminaries (5 Protestant, 3 RC).
PERIODICALS. About 27 titles (including 8 SDA).
PERSONNEL. About 14,036 (12,629 national, 1,407 foreign).
RELIGIOUS LIBRARIES. About 12.
SCRIPTURE DISTRIBUTION (1975). Annual totals: 16,396 Bibles (94% subsidized, 6% commercial), 8,632 NTs (88% subsidized, 12% commercial), 15,763 UBS portions, 110,520 UBS selections. *Translations completed*. Portion: 8 languages since 1888. NT: 5 languages since 1897. Bible: 4 languages since 1955.
SERVICE AGENCIES. About 20, including AEA, BFBS, CEAST.

ADDITIONAL DATA ON CHURCHES
IGREJA CATOLICA EM ANGOLA. The table shows dioceses as existing in 1975. *New dioceses*. Created in 1975: Henrique de Carvalho, Novo Redondo, Pereira de Eça, Serpa Pinto. In 1977, 2 new ecclesiastical provinces were set up, M Huambo (formerly Nova Lisboa) with as suffragans D Benguela, D Silva Porto, D Luso; and M Lubango (formerly Sá da Bandeira) with as suffragans D Pereira de Eça and D Serpa Pinto. *Catechumens*. In 1964, these numbered 208,290; in 1970 the total had increased to 229,787, divided among the 8 dioceses in order as follows (and included in column 7 above): 10000, 24748, 9346, 20825, 50959, 14500, 27621, 71788. *Annual baptisms*. (1972) 72.1% infant, 27.9% adult. *Priests*. Nationals (141) includes both Blacks and those of mixed race. From 1861 to 1961, Luanda seminary produced 57 ordinations of Blacks and Whites. Expatriates (519) indicates Whites (Europeans) born in Angola or elsewhere. *Brothers*. Including 25 Angolans (Black, mixed) and 96 Europeans. *Sisters*. Including 143 Angolans (Black, mixed) and 509 Europeans. *Seminarians*. 214, declining to 175 (1972), all secular. *Catechists*. Total (1964) 10,950. *Indigenous religious congregations*. The 2 congregations of brothers have recently become almost defunct, having in 1972 only 2 members in SPedro Claver and one in Sagrada Familia. Sisters: nil. *Main foreign orders and congregations*. Priests (with 50 or more members): 50 OFMCap. Brothers: PFM, OH. Sisters (with over 50): 188 St-Joseph de Cluny, 140 Ste-Dorothée de Frassinetti, 73 Charité du Bon Pasteur.
*Catholic organizations*. The Episcopal Conference of Angola and São Tomé (Conferência Episcopal de Angola e São Tomé, CEAST), with its headquarters in Luanda, is a member of SECAM. There are no organizations for priests or religious personnel, and only 3 lay associations organized at the national level: St Vincent de Paul Society (Conferências de S Vicente de Paulo) for men and women, Christian Study Courses (Cursos de Cristandade) especially for Europeans and the Legion of Mary (Legião de Maria) which is strongest in the African community.
Until 1975 the Holy See was represented to Angola and its hierarchy by a nuncio in Lisbon. On 11 April 1975 an apostolic delegate was appointed to Luanda.
In 1967 there were 839 Catholic primary schools, 24 secondary schools, 93 nurseries, 11 hospitals, 101 dispensaries, 7 clinics, 20 maternity centres, one leprosarium and 10 homes for the needy. By 1973 educational institutions had increased to 1,641 primary schools (176,709 pupils) and 47 secondary schools (6,399 pupils).
IGREJA DO NOSSO SENHOR JESUS CRISTO. Church of Our Lord Jesus Christ, or Church of Jesus Christ in the World, or Tocoismo; Tokoists. A Bakongo schism from BMS, Jehovah's Witnesses and the Salvation Army, begun by a Kongo prophet Simão Toco, who was alternately imprisoned and released by Portuguese authorities in abortive efforts to prevent its large-scale expansion; and who was eventually banished to Azores as a lighthouse-keeper. 1973, attempt by followers in Angola to get literature aid from M=WEC (UK). 1974, after Independence widespread popularity. 1976, condemned as subversive by MPLA regime; forced underground again. *Membership*. Mainly Kongo, also Mbundu, Kimbundu, Chokwe, and some Songo.
IGREJA EVANGELICA DE ANGOLA CENTRAL. By 1977 also known as the Council of Evangelical Churches in Central Angola (CIEAC).

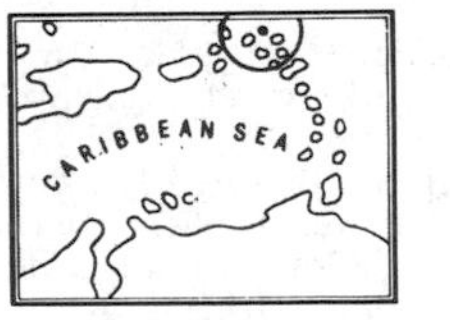


# ANGUILLA

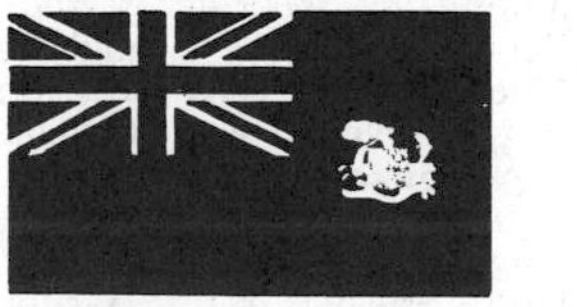

## SECULAR DATA

**STATE. Official name:** The Colony of Anguilla.
**Flag** (shown above right): British Blue Ensign with arms of the Colony in the fly.
**Area:** 91 sq.km. (35 sq.miles). Agricultural land: 42.0%.
**Government:** Self-governing colony or dependency of the United Kingdom (Britain), since 1976 (1650 British colony, ruled from St Kitts until 1967 revolt).
**Official language:** English.
**Capital:** The Valley.

**DEMOGRAPHY. Population:** 5,810 (census of 7.IV.1960. For 1970–2000 (UN), see last row of Table 1). Population density (1975): 68/sq.km. (176/sq.mile). Under 15 years: 43%. Growth rate (1975–80): 0.27% per year (births 2.87%, deaths −0.68%, emigrants −1.92%). Life expectancy (1975–80): 69.1 years. Household size: 4.4 persons.

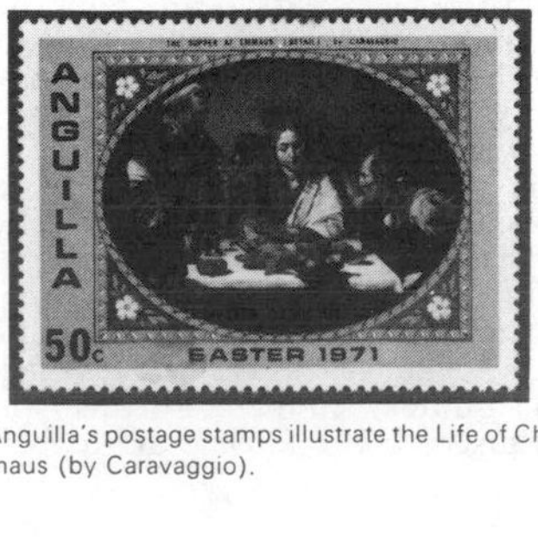


Nearly half of Anguilla's postage stamps illustrate the Life of Christ. *Above*. Supper at Emmaus (by Caravaggio).

**Major language:** English.
**Urban dwellers** (1970): 28.0%. Urban growth rate (1950–70): 2.8% per year.
**Labour force:** 50.0%.

**ETHNOLINGUISTIC GROUPS:** 90% Black (African Negro), 8% Mulatto, White, Indo-Pakistani.

**MONEY** (1977). **Monetary unit:** East Caribbean dollar (= 100 cents); US$1 = EC$2.70.
**National income per person:** US$430. Average annual family income: US$1,892.
**Inflation:** (1970–74) 4.8% per year.
**Cost of living in capital** (1976): Daily cost of living: US$31.

**EDUCATION.** Adult literacy: 80%.

**COMMUNICATION** (per 1,000 people). Phones: 20.

TABLE 1.   RELIGIOUS ADHERENTS IN ANGUILLA

| Year / Name | 1900 Adherents | % | mid-1970 Adherents | % | Annual change, 1970–1980 Natural | Conversion | Total | Rate | mid-1975 Adherents | % | mid-1980 Adherents | % | 2000 Adherents | % |
|---|---|---|---|---|---|---|---|---|---|---|---|---|---|---|
| Christians | 4,200 | 100.0 | 6,050 | 99.2 | 20 | 0 | 20 | 0.32 | 6,150 | 99.2 | 6,250 | 99.2 | 6,550 | 99.2 |
| professing | 4,200 | 100.0 | 6,050 | 99.2 | 20 | 0 | 20 | 0.32 | 6,150 | 99.2 | 6,250 | 99.2 | 6,550 | 99.2 |
| Anglicans | 2,010 | 47.9 | 3,000 | 49.2 | 10 | 0 | 10 | 0.33 | 3,050 | 49.2 | 3,100 | 49.2 | 3,240 | 49.0 |
| Protestants | 2,160 | 51.4 | 2,940 | 48.2 | 10 | −2 | 8 | 0.26 | 2,980 | 48.1 | 3,020 | 47.9 | 3,140 | 47.6 |
| Roman Catholics | 30 | 0.7 | 100 | 1.6 | 0 | 1 | 1 | 0.95 | 105 | 1.7 | 110 | 1.7 | 130 | 2.0 |
| Marginal Protestants | 0 | 0.0 | 10 | 0.2 | 0 | 1 | 1 | 6.67 | 15 | 0.2 | 20 | 0.3 | 40 | 0.6 |
| nominal | 300 | 7.1 | 1,120 | 18.4 | 4 | 0 | 4 | 0.34 | 1,140 | 18.4 | 1,160 | 18.4 | 1,600 | 24.2 |
| affiliated | 3,900 | 92.9 | 4,930 | 80.8 | 16 | 0 | 16 | 0.32 | 5,010 | 80.8 | 5,090 | 80.8 | 4,950 | 75.0 |
| total practising | 3,510 | 90 | 3,700 | 75 | 12 | 0 | 12 | 0.32 | 3,760 | 75 | 3,820 | 75 | 3,220 | 65 |
| non-practising | 390 | 10 | 1,230 | 25 | 4 | 0 | 4 | 0.32 | 1,250 | 25 | 1,270 | 25 | 1,730 | 35 |
| Anglicans | 1,970 | 46.9 | 2,500 | 41.0 | 8 | −1 | 7 | 0.28 | 2,530 | 40.9 | 2,570 | 40.8 | 2,500 | 38.0 |
| Protestants | 1,900 | 45.2 | 2,320 | 38.0 | 8 | −1 | 7 | 0.30 | 2,360 | 38.0 | 2,390 | 37.9 | 2,280 | 34.6 |
| Evangelicals | 1,000 | 23.8 | 800 | 13.1 | 3 | 0 | 3 | 0.37 | 820 | 13.2 | 830 | 13.2 | 800 | 12.1 |
| Roman Catholics | 30 | 0.7 | 100 | 1.6 | 0 | 1 | 1 | 0.95 | 105 | 1.7 | 110 | 1.7 | 130 | 2.0 |
| Marginal Protestants | 0 | 0.0 | 10 | 0.2 | 0 | 1 | 1 | 6.67 | 15 | 0.2 | 20 | 0.3 | 40 | 0.6 |
| Baha'is | 0 | 0.0 | 50 | 0.8 | 0 | 0 | 0 | 0.00 | 50 | 0.8 | 50 | 0.8 | 50 | 0.8 |
| Country's population | 4,200 | 100.0 | 6,100 | 100.0 | 20 | 0 | 20 | 0.32 | 6,200 | 100.0 | 6,300 | 100.0 | 6,600 | 100.0 |

COLUMNS, ROWS. For meanings and definitions, see Codebook (Part 6). Note that, by definition, total 'Christians' = professing + crypto-Christians, which also = affiliated + nominal Christians. Percentages may not always total exactly, due to rounding.
CENSUSES. 4.IV.1881: 51.5% Protestants (51.4% Methodists), 47.9% Anglicans, 0.6% Roman Catholics. 7.IV.1960: 49.2% Protestants (43.4% Methodists, 3.3% SDAs, 1.8% Church of God), 49.2% Anglicans, 1.5% Roman Catholics, 0.1% marginal Protestants (Jehovah's Witnesses).
BAHA'IS. In 1 isolated group (1973).

## NON-CHRISTIAN RELIGIONS.
There is one isolated group of Baha'is.

## CHRISTIANITY
ANGLICAN CHURCH. The largest denomination in Anguilla is Anglicanism which is part of the diocese of Antigua in the Church of the Province of the West Indies. Antigua received its first Anglican priest in 1634, but Anguilla was not reached until later. Originally under the bishop of London, the Leeward Islands were placed in the bishopric of Barbados in 1824, with the diocese of Antigua being established in 1842. The Anglican community is today 95% Black.

PROTESTANT CHURCHES. Methodism is the principal Protestant body, having been brought back to Anguilla in 1813 by John Hodge, a local layman, after his visit to a nearby island. Hodge was ordained in 1822 and was the pioneer in the development of the early work. There are today 4 parishes which form part of the Leeward Islands District, Methodist Church in the Caribbean and the Americas.

Three other small Protestant denominations, each with one congregation, are the Seventh-day

Government stamp portraying The Resurrection of Christ.

Adventists, Church of God (Anderson) and the Brethren.

CATHOLIC CHURCH. Catholicism is weak, consisting of one parish only without a resident priest. Anguilla belongs to the diocese of Saint John's and is served by Redemptorist priests stationed on St Kitts.

CHURCH AND STATE. Anguilla is a secular state which makes provision for complete freedom of religion. Relations between churches and government remain cordial.

INTERDENOMINATIONAL ORGANIZATIONS. The Methodist and Anglican churches are members of the Anguilla Christian Council.

BROADCASTING. Programmes can be heard over neighbouring government stations and over TWR and other international Christian stations.

TABLE 2.   ORGANIZED CHURCHES AND DENOMINATIONS IN ANGUILLA

| Official name 1 | Begun 2 | Type 3 | Counc 4 | Congs 5 | Adults 6 | Affiliated 7 | Names, notes, and other statistics (see Codebook) 8 |
|---|---|---|---|---|---|---|---|
| Anglican Church (D Antigua) | c1650 | A ACa | awMRC | | 1,000 | 2,500 | In CPWI. M=USPG. 95% Blacks. 63% in Central Anguilla, 35% East End. |
| Catholic Church (D Saint John's) | 1861 | R Lat | P.NM. | 1 | 50 | 100 | In D Saint John's (Antigua). M=CSSR. 46% in Central, 42% East End. No priest. |
| Christian Brethren | | P CBr | x.... | 1 | 10 | 20 | One small group of Open Brethren or Plymouth Brethren. M=CMML(UK). |
| Church of God (Anderson) | 1946 | P Hol | x.... | 1 | 30 | 100 | M=CoG(Anderson) (USA). Holiness denomination. 50% in West End, 41% in Central. |
| Jehovah's Witnesses | c1960 | M Jeh | x.... | 1 | 5 | 10 | IBSA. Watch Tower. Small handful of Jehovah's Christian witnesses. |
| Methodist Ch in Caribbean & Americas | 1813 | P Met | VaH.C | 4 | 1,000 | 2,000 | In MCCA(1967 union), Leeward Islands District. M=MMS(UK). 75% in West End. |
| Seventh-day Adventist Church | | P Adv | x.... | 1 | 100 | 200 | SDA, East Caribbean Conference, Caribbean Union Conference. 59% in East End. |
| Total affiliated (mid-1970) | | | | 14 | 2,195 | 4,930 | Total denominations (1970) . . . 7. |
| Total affiliated (mid-1975) | | | | 14 | 2,230 | 5,010 | Total denominations (1975) . . . 7. |
| Total affiliated (mid-1980) | | | | 15 | 2,270 | 5,090 | Total denominations (1980) . . . 7. |

NOTES ON TABLE ABOVE
COLUMNS: for meanings and CODES (cols. 1, 3, 4, 8), see Codebook (Part 6). Column 1: Boldface type = church with over 10% of country's affiliated Christians.
NATIONAL COUNCILS (Column 4, 5th letter).
C = Anguilla Christian Council.

PEOPLES (ethnolinguistic). Christians: 90% Black, 8% Mulatto, 2% White.

COUNTRY-WIDE TOTALS
EVANGELIZATION (see Part 5). 1900: 100%. 1970: 100%. 1980: 100%.
FOREIGN MISSIONARIES AND PERSONNEL (aliens from abroad) (1973). Total 4. From Western world. 4: 3 Protestants, 1 Roman Catholic.
PERIODICALS. About 3 titles.
PERSONNEL. About 10 (4 foreign).
SCRIPTURE DISTRIBUTION (1975). Annual totals: 20 Bibles (subsidized), 20 NTs (subsidized).
SERVICE AGENCIES. About 2.

# ANTIGUA

## SECULAR DATA

STATE. Official name: The State of Antigua.
Flag (shown above right): Red triangles, white and blue bands with yellow sun on black.
Area: 442 sq.km. (170 sq.miles). Agricultural land: 25.0%.
Government: Republic. formerly self-governing state in association with the United Kingdom (Britain), since 1967 (1632 British colony).
Legislature: Bicameral.
Official language: English.
Capital: St John City 21,590 (1960).

DEMOGRAPHY. Population: 65,525 (census of 7.IV.1970. For 1970–2000 (UN), see last row of Table 1). Population density (1975): 165/sq.km. (428/sq.mile). Under 15 years: 43%. Growth rate (1975–80): 0.68% per year (births 2.87%, deaths −0.68%, emigrants −1.51%). Life expectancy (1975–80): 69.1 years.
Household size: 4.4 persons.
Major language: English.
Urban dwellers (1970): 39.8%. Urban growth rate (1950–70): 2.8% per year.

Christian themes occur regularly on the country's official postage stamps.

Labour force: 32%.
Tourists (1973): 72,800.

ETHNOLINGUISTIC GROUPS: 94.4% Black (African Negro), 3.5% Mulatto, 1.3% European, 0.2% Indo-Pakistani.

MONEY (1977). Monetary unit: East Caribbean dollar (= 100 cents); US$1 = EC$2.70.
National income per person: US$540. Average annual family income: US$2,376.
Cost of living in capital (1976): Daily cost of living: US$36.

EDUCATION. Adult literacy: (1946) 81%, (1960) 89%. Schools: 56.

HEALTH. Hospitals: 4 (548 beds). Doctors: 23. Lepers: 200 (2.7 per 1,000). Blind: 120.

LITERATURE. Periodicals: 15. Newspapers: 1 daily, 1 non-daily.

COMMUNICATION (per 1,000 people). Phones: 42. TV sets: 71. Daily newspaper circulation: 55 copies.

## TABLE 1.    RELIGIOUS ADHERENTS IN ANTIGUA

| Year | 1900 | | mid-1970 | | Annual change, 1970–1980 | | | | mid-1975 | | mid-1980 | | 2000 | |
|---|---|---|---|---|---|---|---|---|---|---|---|---|---|---|
| Name | Adherents | % | Adherents | % | Natural | Conversion | Total | Rate | Adherents | % | Adherents | % | Adherents | % |
| Christians | 35,000 | 100.0 | 68,600 | 98.0 | 487 | −79 | 408 | 0.57 | 71,140 | 97.5 | 72,680 | 96.9 | 81,650 | 96.1 |
| professing | 35,000 | 100.0 | 68,600 | 98.0 | 487 | −79 | 408 | 0.57 | 71,140 | 97.5 | 72,680 | 96.9 | 81,650 | 96.1 |
| Anglicans | 18,900 | 54.0 | 31,970 | 45.7 | 225 | −85 | 140 | 0.42 | 32,880 | 45.0 | 33,370 | 44.5 | 37,110 | 43.7 |
| Protestants | 14,700 | 42.0 | 29,470 | 42.1 | 209 | −35 | 174 | 0.57 | 30,590 | 41.9 | 31,210 | 41.6 | 33,490 | 39.4 |
| Roman Catholics | 1,400 | 4.0 | 6,860 | 9.8 | 50 | 29 | 79 | 1.08 | 7,300 | 10.0 | 7,650 | 10.2 | 10,200 | 12.0 |
| Marginal Protestants | 0 | 0.0 | 300 | 0 4 | 3 | 12 | 15 | 4.05 | 370 | 0.5 | 450 | 0.6 | 850 | 1.0 |
| nominal | 4,200 | 12.0 | 18,134 | 25.9 | 128 | −33 | 95 | 0.51 | 18,730 | 25.7 | 19,080 | 25.4 | 21,720 | 25.6 |
| affiliated | 30,800 | 88.0 | 50,466 | 72.1 | 359 | −46 | 313 | 0.60 | 52,410 | 71.8 | 53,600 | 71.5 | 59,930 | 70.5 |
| total practising | 29,260 | 95 | 40,370 | 80 | 287 | −37 | 250 | 0.60 | 41,930 | 80 | 42,880 | 80 | 44,950 | 75 |
| non-practising | 1,540 | 5 | 10,090 | 20 | 72 | −9 | 63 | 0.60 | 10,480 | 20 | 10,720 | 20 | 14,980 | 25 |
| Protestants | 13,300 | 38.0 | 22,166 | 31.7 | 157 | −44 | 113 | 0.49 | 22,920 | 31.4 | 23,300 | 31.1 | 25,080 | 29.5 |
| Evangelicals | 10,000 | 28.6 | 10,500 | 15.0 | 74 | −24 | 50 | 0.46 | 10,800 | 14.8 | 11,000 | 14.7 | 12,000 | 14.1 |
| Anglicans | 16,450 | 47.0 | 22,000 | 31.4 | 155 | −45 | 110 | 0.48 | 22,700 | 31.1 | 23,100 | 30.8 | 24,650 | 29.0 |
| Roman Catholics | 1,050 | 3.0 | 6,000 | 8.6 | 44 | 31 | 75 | 1.17 | 6,420 | 8.8 | 6,750 | 9.0 | 9,350 | 11.0 |
| Marginal Protestants | 0 | 0.0 | 300 | 0.4 | 3 | 12 | 15 | 4.05 | 370 | 0.5 | 450 | 0.6 | 850 | 1.0 |
| Afro-American spiritists | 0 | 0.0 | 700 | 1.0 | 8 | 72 | 80 | 7.27 | 1,100 | 1.5 | 1,500 | 2.0 | 2,000 | 2.3 |
| Baha'is | 0 | 0.0 | 400 | 0.6 | 3 | 7 | 10 | 2.22 | 450 | 0.6 | 500 | 0.7 | 1,000 | 1.2 |
| Muslims | 0 | 0.0 | 300 | 0.4 | 2 | 0 | 2 | 0.65 | 310 | 0.4 | 320 | 0.4 | 350 | 0.4 |
| Ahmadis | 0 | 0.0 | 200 | 0.3 | 2 | 6 | 8 | 3.33 | 240 | 0.3 | 280 | 0.4 | 320 | 0.4 |
| Country's population | 35,000 | 100.0 | 70,000 | 100.0 | 500 | 0 | 500 | 0.68 | 73.000 | 100.0 | 75,000 | 100.0 | 85,000 | 100.0 |

COLUMNS, ROWS. For meanings and definitions, see Codebook (Part 6). Note that, by definition, total 'Christians' = professing + crypto-Christians, which also = affiliated + nominal Christians. Percentages may not always total exactly, due to rounding.
CENSUSES. 7.IV.1960 (de jure): 47.5% Anglicans, 42.9% Protestants, 9.6% Roman Catholics.

**NOTES ON RELIGIONS**
AFRO-AMERICAN SPIRITISTS. Young Blacks, formerly nominal Anglicans or Protestants, who have in increasing numbers joined an Afro-American cult from Jamaica, the Ras Tafari Movement. The movement by 1975 was stressing self-reliance, development projects including literacy, art and handicrafts, thrift schemes, and the training of productive craftsmen living in

community. Recently the government donated an acre of land, and CADEC (an arm of the Caribbean Conference of Churches) made a grant of funds.
BAHA'IS. In 3 local spiritual assemblies (1973).
MUSLIMS. Mainly one Ahmadiya Mission community, since about 1955; Qadianis (world HQ Rabwah, Pakistan).

---

**NON-CHRISTIAN RELIGIONS. Rastafarianism,** an Afro-American cult from Jamaica, has a growing following among unemployed young Blacks, and is now emphasizing development, thrift schemes and the training of craftsmen living in community.

## CHRISTIANITY

ANGLICAN CHURCH. The Church of England has a long history in Antigua dating back to the 17th century, and the population was 47.5% Anglican in 1960. The diocese of Antigua, which covers Anglican work in the Leeward Islands, was formed in

1842 and is part of the Church of the Province of the West Indies. Aid in personnel and finances is received from the Anglican Church of Canada, United Society for the Propagation of the Gospel (UK), and other agencies.
PROTESTANT CHURCHES. The 2 main

Protestant bodies in Antigua are the Moravian Church (21.7% of the population in 1960) and the Methodist Church (14.4% in 1960). Both owe their origin to influences from Europe in the 18th century. Zinzendorf's first Moravian missionaries arrived in the West Indies in 1732 and reached Antigua in 1756. Success was immediate, with a community of 7,000 Christians recorded by 1791. Methodism's beginning in the West Indies was at Antigua through the instrumentality of a local plantation owner, Nathaniel Gilbert, who was converted in 1760 at one of John Wesley's meetings in England. Upon his return, he built up a small congregation, mostly of slaves, which at the time of his death in 1774 numbered 200. The work was carried on by John Baxter, grew to 2,000 members by 1786 and was further strengthened by the visit of Thomas Coke in the same year. Twentieth-century missionary bodies from North America include the Seventh-day Adventist and Wesleyan churches and several other smaller denominations.
CATHOLIC CHURCH. Antigua is only a part of the diocese of Saint John's based in Antigua, for it includes also St Kitts-Nevis, Anguilla, Montserrat and the British Virgin Islands. In 1974 there were in Antigua 2 parishes, 4 stations, 4 priests including the bishop (a West Indian previously bishop in Ghana), 5 FSC brothers and several missionary Sisters of the Immaculate Heart of Mary.

CHURCH AND STATE. Antigua was first settled in 1632. Although the French occupied the island at 2 different periods in the 17th and 18th centuries, their stay was brief which accounts for the relatively small Catholic population. Subsequently there has

been no formal link between any of the churches and the state; there is in fact no established church anywhere in the Leeward Islands.

INTERDENOMINATIONAL ORGANIZATIONS. The Anglican, Catholic, Methodist and Moravian churches and the Salvation Army are members of the Antigua Christian Council.

BROADCASTING. The government Antigua Broadcasting Service gives Protestant programmes 2 hours

**Anglican Church, Diocese of Antigua.** *Far left.* Schoolchildren at St Mary's, Old Road, Antigua. *Above.* USPG missionary priest Fr Wastell talks to villagers at Bolands, Antigua.

daily including Sunday, and Catholic programmes for 15 minutes from Monday to Saturday and one hour on Sunday. Twenty per cent of Protestant programmes are locally produced. A private station 2DK also accepts daily Protestant and Catholic programmes.

## TABLE 2.    ORGANIZED CHURCHES AND DENOMINATIONS IN ANTIGUA

| Official name 1 | Begun 2 | Type 3 | Counc 4 | Congs 5 | Adults 6 | Affiliated 7 | Names, notes, and other statistics (see Codebook) 8 |
|---|---|---|---|---|---|---|---|
| **Anglican Church: D Antigua** | 1634 | A ACa | AwMRK | | 10,000 | 22,000 | Diocese 1842. In CPWI. M=USPG. 95% West Indian (90% Black). 6n,18x,W=58%,1335y. |
| **Catholic Church: D Saint John's** | | R Lat | P.NMK | 7 | 4,000 | 6,000 | Suffragan of M Castries. Includes St Kitts-N. C=1+1+2. 4nx,5m,8w,3r(875),8Y,297y. |
| Christian Brethren | | P CBr | x.... | 3 | 150 | 300 | *Plymouth Brethren. Open Brethren.* 1973, M=CMML(Canada). 2f. |
| Church of God of Prophecy | c1954 | P Pe3 | z.... | 4 | 280 | 500 | M=CGP(USA). Schism in USA ex CoG(Cleveland). Holiness Pentecostals. |
| Church of God (Anderson) | | P Hol | x.... | 10 | 100 | 300 | *General Assembly of the CoG (Antigua).* M=CoG(Anderson)(USA). 8n,W=99%. |
| Churches of Christ in Christian Union | 1962 | P Hol | xF... | | 200 | 500 | *Christian Union Mission.* M=CCCU(USA). Holiness doctrines. HQ St John's. |
| Jehovah's Witnesses | c1940 | M Jeh | x.... | 3 | 144 | 300 | *Watch Tower. IBSA.* Active witnessing under way by 1948. HQ St John's. 16Y. |
| Methodist Ch in Caribbean & Americas | 1760 | P Met | VWM.K | | 2,000 | 4,000 | *MCCA*(1967 union), Leeward Islands District. HQ for MCCA. M=MMS(UK). 3n. |
| **Moravian Church** | 1756 | P Mor | xwM.K | 12 | 3,846 | 8,466 | *Antigua Conference,* Eastern West Indies Province, Unity of Brethren. 2f,W=27%,264Yy. |
| Salvation Army | | P Sal | xwM.K | | 400 | 600 | *Antigua Region,* Caribbean & CAmerica Territory (HQ Jamaica). HQ St John's. |
| Seventh-day Adventist Church | | P Adv | x.... | | 352 | 3,500 | *SDA,* East Caribbean Conference, Caribbean Union Conference. |
| Wesleyan Church | 1911 | P Hol | VF... | 33 | 2,855 | 3,000 | Before 1968, Pilgrim Holiness Ch. M=WC(USA). 15n,G=0.5%pa,1j,1k,W=75%,92Y. |
| Other Protestant denominations | | P | ..... | | 500 | 1,000 | Including: BMAA(USA), Ch of God (Cleveland), Southern Baptist Convention (1968). |
| **Total affiliated (mid-1970)** | | | | 170 | 24,827 | 50,466 | Total denominations (1970) . . . 17. |
| **Total affiliated (mid-1975)** | | | | 175 | 25,800 | 52,410 | Total denominations (1975) . . . 17. |
| **Total affiliated (mid-1980)** | | | | 180 | 26,400 | 53,600 | Total denominations (1980) . . . 18. |

**NOTES ON TABLE ABOVE**
COLUMNS: for meanings and CODES (cols. 1, 3, 4, 8), see Codebook (Part 6). Column 1: **Boldface type** = church with over 10% of country's affiliated Christians.
NATIONAL COUNCILS (Column 4, 5th letter).
K = Antigua Christian Council.

PEOPLES (ethnolinguistic). Christians: 94.6% Black, 3.5% Mulatto, 1.3% British and other European White.

COUNTRY-WIDE TOTALS
EVANGELIZATION (see Part 5). 1900: 100%. 1970: 100%. 1980: 100%. *Mass evangelism.* In 1975 the Evangelistic Association, Pentecostal Assemblies of the West Indies, conducted a large crusade.

FOREIGN MISSIONARIES AND PERSONNEL (aliens from abroad) (1973). Total 31. *From Western world.* 21: 9 Protestants (4 in 4 USA societies, 4 in 1 Canada society, 1 in 1 New Zealand society), about 6 Roman Catholics, 6 Anglicans from UK and Canada. *From Third World.* 10: about 7 Protestants, 3 Anglicans, from Trinidad & Tobago and Jamaica.
INSTITUTIONS (church-operated) (1973). Total 6, including 3 secondary schools.
PERIODICALS. About 7 titles.
PERSONNEL. About 81 (50 national, 31 foreign).
SCRIPTURE DISTRIBUTION (1975). Annual totals: 1,260 Bibles (32% free, 60% subsidized, 8% commercial), 5,000 NTs (80% free, 18% subsidized, 2% commercial), 200 UBS portions, 2,500 UBS selections.
SERVICE AGENCIES. About 9, including AEC, CLC, SPCK,

YMCA, YWCA.

ADDITIONAL DATA ON CHURCHES
CATHOLIC CHURCH. *Catholic organizations.* The diocese is a member of the Antilles Episcopal Conference (AEC), with its headquarters in Kingston, Jamaica, and through it is a member of CELAM. Religious personnel are represented on the Conference of Major Superiors of the Antilles, which belongs to CLAR and also has its seat in Jamaica.
The Holy See has no diplomatic relations with Antigua. It is represented to the Catholic hierarchy by an apostolic delegate based in Port-au-Prince, Haiti.
In 1974 the church sponsored one primary school with 320 pupils and 2 secondary schools with 1,040 students.

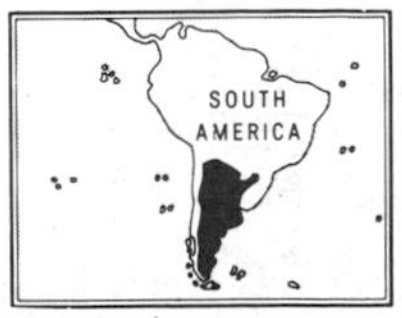


# ARGENTINA

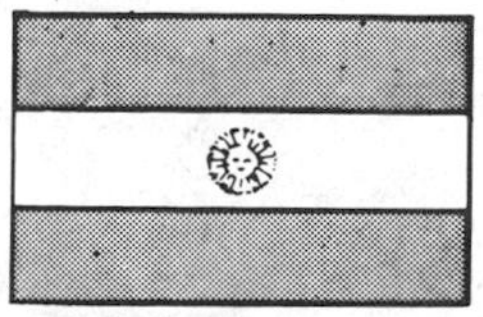

## SECULAR DATA

**STATE. Official name:** The Argentine Republic (La República Argentina). Adjective of nationality: Argentine (argentino).
**Flag** (shown above right). Blue, white, and blue stripes, golden sun.
**Area:** 2,776,889 sq. km. (1,084,120 sq. miles). Agricultural land; 64.2%.
**Government:** Military junta, since 1976 (1516 Spanish rule, 1816 Independence, 1829 onwards a series of dictatorships and republics, 1971 republic, 1976 military rule).
**Official language:** Spanish (*Español/Castellano*).
**Chief cities:** capital Buenos Aires 8,925,000 (urban agglomeration, 1974), Rosario 810,840, Córdoba 798,660, La Plata 506,290, Mendoza 470,900.
**Political divisions:** 22 Provinces, 1 Federal District, National Territories of Tierra del Fuego, Antarctic, South Atlantic Islands.
**Armed forces** (1976): Total 132,800 regular: army 83,500, navy 32,300, air force 17,000 (115 combat aircraft). Reserves: 250,000. Paramilitary forces: 20,000.

**DEMOGRAPHY. Population:** 23,362,204 (census of 30.IX.1970. For 1970–2000 (UN), see last row of Table 1). Population density (1975): 9/sq.km. (24/sq.mile). Under 15 years: 31%. Growth rate (1975–80): 1.28% per year (births 2.14%, deaths −0.89%, immigrants 0.03%). Life expectancy (1975–80): 69.4 years. Household size: 4.1 persons.
**Major languages:** Spanish, Italian, Galician, Quechua, Toba, Mataco, Yiddish, Irish, German, Polish, Ukrainian, Catalan, Portuguese, Arabic, English, Russian, Japanese, et alia.
**Urban dwellers** (1970): 80.4%. Urban growth rate (1950–70); 2.8% per year.
**Labour force:** 38%.
**Refugees** (1977): 37,000 from Chile, Bolivia and Uruguay.
**Tourists** (1974): 795,509.

**ETHNOLINGUISTIC GROUPS:** 76.6% Argentinian White (European origin: 40% Italian, 30% Spaniard, Irish, German, Polish, Ukrainian), 4.7% Italian, 2.5% Paraguayan Mestizo (600,000), 2.5% Bolivian (600,000) (2.0% Indian, 0.5% Mestizo), 2.0% Mestizo, 2.0% Jewish, 1.9% Galician, 1.5% Chilean Mestizo (350,000), 1.4% Spanish, 1.2% Quechua, 0,7% lowland Amerindian (9 Aboriginal tribes including Chiriguano, Mataco, Toba), 0.5% Catalan, 0.5% Polish, 0.4% Uruguayan White (100,000), 0.3% Brazilian (80,000), 0.3% Arab (80,000), 0.1% British (25,000), 0.1% Greek (25,000), 0.1% Russian (20,000), 0.1% Ukrainian (20,000), 0.1% Japanese (19,200), French, Portuguese, Romanian, Czech, Slovak, Serbian, Byelorussian, Croat, Slovene, Bulgar, German, Austrian, USA, Latvian, Lithuanian, Basque, Turkish, Hungarian, Chinese (530), Albanian.

**MONEY** (1977). **Monetary unit:** new peso (= 100 centavos); US$1 = Arg$270.00.
**National income per person:** US$1,900. Average annual family income: US$7,790.
**Inflation:** (1970–74) 43.6% per year, (1975) 183% per year (consumer price index 2920).
**Cost of living in capital** (1976): index 97 (Washington DC = 100). Daily cost of living: US$35.

**EDUCATION.** Adult literacy: (1947) 86%, (1970) 93%. Education rate: 77%. Schools: 20,212. Universities: 33.

**HEALTH.** Hospitals: 2,864 (133,847 beds). Doctors: 49,950. Lepers: 28,500 (1.1 per 1,000). Blind: 14,300. Psychotics: 230,000. Drug addicts: 260,000 (240,000 coca-chewers, 2,600 on cocaine).

**LITERATURE.** Annual new book titles (1972): 4,578. Periodicals: 1,479. Scientific journals: 310. Newspapers: 162 dailies, 63 non-daily.

**COMMUNICATION** (per 1,000 people). Phones: 84. Radios: 370. TV sets: 163. Daily newspaper circulation: 154 copies.

TABLE 1. RELIGIOUS ADHERENTS IN ARGENTINA

| Year | 1900 | | mid-1970 | | Annual change, 1970–1980 | | | | mid-1975 | | mid-1980 | | 2000 | |
|---|---|---|---|---|---|---|---|---|---|---|---|---|---|---|
| *Name* | *Adherents* | *%* | *Adherents* | *%* | *Natural* | *Conversion* | *Total* | *Rate* | *Adherents* | *%* | *Adherents* | *%* | *Adherents* | *%* |
| **Christians** | **4,126,500** | **98.3** | **22,757,300** | **95.8** | **317,344** | **−5,964** | **311,380** | **1.28** | **24,292,700** | **95.7** | **25,871,100** | **95.6** | **31,137,000** | **94.8** |
| professing | 4,126,500 | 98.3 | 22,757,300 | 95.8 | 317,344 | −5,964 | 311,380 | 1.28 | 24,292,700 | 95.7 | 25,871,100 | 95.6 | 31,137,000 | 94.8 |
| Roman Catholics | 4,092,100 | 97.4 | 21,962,300 | 92.5 | 305,271 | −21,241 | 284,030 | 1.21 | 23,368,500 | 92.1 | 24,802,600 | 91.6 | 29,546,200 | 89.9 |
| Evangelical Catholics | 10,600 | 0.3 | 246,381 | 1.0 | 3,322 | 2,060 | 5,382 | 2.12 | 254,300 | 1.0 | 300,200 | 1.1 | 530,100 | 1.6 |
| Christo-pagans | 50,000 | 1.2 | 200,000 | 0.8 | 2,796 | 4 | 2,800 | 1.31 | 214,000 | 0.8 | 228,000 | 0.8 | 197,000 | 0.6 |
| Protestants | 29,400 | 0.7 | 500,000 | 2.1 | 7,626 | 10,034 | 17,600 | 3.03 | 583,800 | 2.3 | 676,600 | 2.5 | 985,800 | 3.0 |
| Argentinian indigenous | 0 | 0.0 | 120,000 | 0.5 | 1,990 | 4,960 | 6,950 | 4.56 | 152,300 | 0.6 | 189,500 | 0.7 | 328,600 | 1.0 |
| Orthodox | 3,000 | 0.1 | 100,000 | 0.4 | 1,398 | 2 | 1,400 | 1.31 | 107,000 | 0.4 | 114,000 | 0.4 | 131,000 | 0.4 |
| Marginal Protestants | 1,000 | 0.0 | 45,000 | 0.2 | 640 | 260 | 900 | 1.84 | 49,000 | 0.2 | 54,000 | 0.2 | 98,600 | 0.3 |
| Catholics (non-Roman) | 0 | 0.0 | 20,000 | 0.1 | 279 | 21 | 300 | 1.40 | 21,400 | 0.1 | 23,000 | 0.1 | 33,000 | 0.1 |
| Anglicans | 1,000 | 0.0 | 10,000 | 0.0 | 140 | 0 | 140 | 1.31 | 10,700 | 0.0 | 11,400 | 0.0 | 13,800 | 0.0 |
| nominal | 21,000 | 0.5 | 337,389 | 1.4 | 4,977 | 4,378 | 9,355 | 2.46 | 380,970 | 1.5 | 430,940 | 1.6 | 576,300 | 1.8 |
| affiliated | 4,105,500 | 97.8 | 22,419,911 | 94.4 | 312,367 | −10,342 | 302,025 | 1.26 | 23,911,730 | 94.2 | 25,440,160 | 94.0 | 30,560,700 | 93.0 |
| doubly-affiliated | −72,300 | −1.7 | −975,000 | −4.1 | −14,450 | −17,188 | −31,638 | 2.86 | −1,106,180 | −4.4 | −1,291,380 | −4.8 | −1,894,320 | −5.8 |
| total practising | 3,694,950 | *90* | 15,693,940 | *70* | 218,657 | −7,240 | 211,417 | 1.26 | 16,738,210 | *70* | 17,808,110 | *70* | 18,336,400 | *60* |
| non-practising | 410,550 | *10* | 6,725,970 | *30* | 93,710 | −3,102 | 90,608 | 1.26 | 7,173,520 | *30* | 7,632,050 | *30* | 12,224,300 | *40* |
| Roman Catholics | 4,132,800 | 98.4 | 22,301,530 | 93.9 | 310,709 | −10,378 | 300,331 | 1.26 | 23,784,810 | 93.7 | 25,304,840 | 93.5 | 30,232,120 | 92.0 |
| Catholic pentecostals | 0 | 0.0 | 500 | 0.0 | 39 | 461 | 500 | 16.67 | 3,000 | 0.0 | 5,500 | 0.0 | 30,000 | 0.1 |
| Protestants | 40,000 | 1.0 | 593,007 | 2.5 | 8,948 | 10,241 | 19,189 | 2.80 | 685,000 | 2.7 | 784,900 | 2.9 | 1,117,300 | 3.4 |
| Evangelicals | 20,000 | 0.5 | 475,000 | 2.0 | 7,168 | 8,212 | 15,380 | 2.80 | 548,700 | 2.2 | 628,800 | 2.3 | 950,000 | 2.9 |
| Neo-pentecostals | 0 | 0.0 | 16,000 | 0.1 | 522 | 5,878 | 6,400 | 16.00 | 40,000 | 0.2 | 80,000 | 0.3 | 150,000 | 0.5 |
| Argentinian indigenous | 0 | 0.0 | 251,400 | 0.9 | 3,645 | 6,395 | 10,040 | 3.60 | 279,000 | 1.1 | 351,800 | 1.3 | 624,400 | 1.9 |
| Orthodox | 3,000 | 0.1 | 122,000 | 0.5 | 1,698 | −98 | 1,600 | 1.23 | 130,000 | 0.5 | 138,000 | 0.5 | 197,000 | 0.6 |
| Marginal Protestants | 1,000 | 0.0 | 63,774 | 0.3 | 941 | 682 | 1,623 | 2.25 | 72,000 | 0.3 | 80,000 | 0.4 | 197,000 | 0.6 |
| Catholics (non-Roman | 0 | 0.0 | 50,000 | 0.2 | 692 | 8 | 700 | 1.32 | 53,000 | 0.2 | 57,000 | 0.2 | 69,000 | 0.2 |
| Anglicans | 1,000 | 0.0 | 13,200 | 0.1 | 184 | −4 | 180 | 1.28 | 14,100 | 0.1 | 15,000 | 0.1 | 18,200 | 0.1 |
| Evangelicals | 1,000 | 0.0 | 13,000 | 0.1 | 182 | −2 | 180 | 1.29 | 13,900 | 0.1 | 14,800 | 0.1 | 17,500 | 0.1 |
| Jews | 6,500 | 0.2 | 475,000 | 2.0 | 6,623 | −123 | 6,500 | 1.28 | 507,000 | 2.0 | 540,000 | 2.0 | 650,000 | 2.0 |
| Non-religious | 5,000 | 0.1 | 210,000 | 0.9 | 3,266 | 4,734 | 8,000 | 3.20 | 250,000 | 1.0 | 290,000 | 1.1 | 500,000 | 1.5 |
| Atheists | 5,000 | 0.1 | 140,000 | 0.6 | 2,025 | 975 | 3,000 | 1.94 | 155,000 | 0.6 | 170,000 | 0.6 | 300,000 | 0.9 |
| Muslims | 4,000 | 0.1 | 50,000 | 0.2 | 699 | 1 | 700 | 1.31 | 53,500 | 0.2 | 57,000 | 0.2 | 70,000 | 0.2 |
| Spiritists | 1,000 | 0.0 | 50,000 | 0.2 | 705 | 95 | 800 | 1.48 | 54,000 | 0.2 | 58,000 | 0.2 | 70,000 | 0.2 |
| Tribal religionists | 50,000 | 1.2 | 30,000 | 0.1 | 327 | −1,327 | −1,000 | −4.00 | 25,000 | 0.1 | 20,000 | 0.1 | 10,000 | 0.0 |
| Buddhists | 1,000 | 0.0 | 10,000 | 0.0 | 137 | −37 | 100 | 0.95 | 10,500 | 0.0 | 11,000 | 0.0 | 13,000 | 0.0 |
| Baha'is | 0 | 0.0 | 5,700 | 0.0 | 82 | 38 | 120 | 1.90 | 6,300 | 0.0 | 6,900 | 0.0 | 11,000 | 0.0 |
| Other religionists | 1,000 | 0.0 | 20,000 | 0.1 | 392 | 1,608 | 2,000 | 6.67 | 30,000 | 0.1 | 40,000 | 0.1 | 100,000 | 0.3 |
| **Country's population** | **4,200,000** | **100.0** | **23,748,000** | **100.0** | **331,600** | **0** | **331,600** | **1.31** | **25,384,000** | **100.0** | **27,064,000** | **100.0** | **32,861,000** | **100.0** |

COLUMNS, ROWS. For meanings and definitions, see Codebook (Part 6). Note that, by definition, total 'Christians' = professing + crypto-Christians, which also = affiliated + nominal Christians. Percentages may not always total exactly, due to rounding.
CENSUSES. 1895 (excluding tribal religionists): 99.0% Roman Catholics, 0.7% Protestants, 0.2% Jews. **10.V.1947** (de jure): 94.3% Roman Catholics, 2.0% Evangelicals, 1.6% Jews, 1.5% non-religious, 0.4% Orthodox, 0.1% Muslims, 0.1% other religionists. 30.**IX.1960**: 93.3% Roman Catholics, 2.7% Evangelicals, 1.7% non-religious and atheists, 1.6% Jews, 0.4% Orthodox, 0.1% Muslims, 0.2% other religionists. After 1960 the religion question was discontinued.

NOTES ON RELIGIONS
ARGENTINIAN INDIGENOUS. In 42 indigenous denominations in 1970 (see Table 2).
ATHEISTS. Partida Comunista Argentina (PCA) (outlawed 1966; pro-Soviet) and several rival parties: membership (1970) 70,000 (50% activists); sympathizers about 70,000. In 1975, the PCA was the largest non-governing Communist party in Latin America.
BAHA'IS Growth from 6 local spiritual assemblies (1964) to 38 (1973). Converts from Indian tribes include Chiriguano, Mapuche, Mataco, Tewelche, Toba.
BUDDHISTS. Japanese immigrants, and about 500 Chinese.
CATHOLIC PENTECOSTALS (or Catholic charismatics). Totals (January 1974): 1,000 involved adults (over 15 years old) in 90 prayer groups; total charismatic community including children, 2,000.
CHRISTO-PAGANS. Amerindians whose syncretistic folk-Catholicism combines 17th-century Spanish Catholicism with their own traditional animism, concepts and world-views.
DOUBLY-AFFILIATED. The term covers those affiliated to, or claimed by, both the Catholic Church and also a church termed Evangélica by the state (Protestan, Argentinian indigenous, Anglican or marginal Protestant) or other church, i.e. baptized Catholics who have recently become Evangelicals or others. Because their statistics represent a duplication, they are shown in the table as a negative quantity (with a minus sign).
EVANGELICAL CATHOLICS. This term is used here to describe persons who are affiliated to churches termed by the state Evangélica (Protestant or Argentinian indigenous, or Anglican or marginal Protestant churches), but who in government censuses are regarded as, or profess to be, Roman Catholics.
JEWS. About 78% Ashkenazi, 22% Sefardi.
MUSLIMS. Including many Palestinian and other Arab immigrants.
NEO-PENTECOSTALS. Charismatics within the non-Pentecostal Protestant denominations, including 20% of adults in the Christian Brethren, also large numbers of Baptists and Mennonites.
OTHER RELIGIONISTS. Adherents of other non-Christian religions and cults, including Japanese New Religions (Soka Gakkai with 2,200 converts by 1975, et alia), Rosicrucians (AMORC, 8 centres), and others. ISKCON (Hare Krishna) also operates 1 centre, the Divine Light Mission and the Ramakrishna Mission others. The Theosophical Society in 1975 had 44 lodges with 883 members.
PRACTISING CHRISTIANS. Urban population, 1966: 15% attend Catholic mass weekly (varying from 7% in central Buenos Aires to 19.5% in small towns), 2% three times a month, 7% twice a month, 6% once a month, 70% only annually or never.
PROTESTANTS. In 1895, Evangelicals were 21% nationals and 79% expatriates.
SPIRITISTS. Organized under the Confederación Espíritista Argentina (CEA). A number of lapsed Catholics and Protestants become spiritists each year, and by 1976 spiritism was recognized as a growing phenomenon.
TRIBAL RELIGIONISTS. Of the 170,000 tribal lowland Amerindians (or Aborigines) in 1970, mostly along the Paraguayan border, a proportion are still shamanists or animists, including a majority of the 20,000 Chiriguano (Guarani) and the other 8 Aboriginal groups: Chane (Guaná), Chorote, Chulupi, Mataco (population 12,000), Mbya, Mocovi, Pilaca and some Toba (17,060). Guaraní shamans in particulars occupy a respected healing role in society, and Guarani mysticism remains the main agent for social cohesion.

**NON-CHRISTIAN RELIGIONS. Judaism** is extremely strong. Argentina's Jewish community is in fact the largest in Latin America and the fifth in importance in the world, after Israel, USA, USSR and France. Of nearly 500,000 Jews in Argentina, about 100,000 are Sefardis, more than 350,000 inhabit Buenos Aires and its suburbs, and others are generally found in such larger centres as Cordoba, Rosario and Santa Fe. The principal national organization of Jews is the Argentina Israelite Mutual Association (Asociación Mutual Israélita Argentina, AMIA) in Buenos Aires. An international Jewish organization with its headquarters in Buenos Aires is the International Council of Jewish Women, founded in Rome in 1912, with national branches in more than 20 countries of the world.

**Islam** is represented by a small community and is served by 3 institutions: the Centre for Islamic

Studies (Centro de Estudios Islamicos) and the Islamic Centre (Centro Islamico), both in Buenos Aires; and the Arab Islamic Society in Mendoza.

**Traditional Indian religions** have largely disappeared although there are still some practitioners among the Chiriguano, as well Guaraní- and Quechua-speaking Bolivians who work as labourers on the northern sugarcane plantations. All Aboriginal groups are over 80% traditionalist.

**Baha'i** has recently grown rapidly, from 6 assemblies in 1964 to 38 by 1973.

## CHRISTIANITY

CATHOLIC CHURCH. Argentina, originally inhabited by nomadic Indians, was first sighted by a Spanish navigator in 1516. Franciscan missionaries arrived in 1539 and the Jesuits in 1586, the latter developing their system of co-operative 'reduction' communities among the Indians in the north until their expulsion in 1767. After Independence in 1816, the new Argentine government, strongly anti-Spanish, attempted to establish a national church. Spanish priests, poorly prepared for missionary work after the expulsion of the Jesuits, soon departed, leaving some 12 priests under 40 years of age to carry the burden of leadership in the face of a strong anti-clerical ruling class and with religious ignorance and supersition rife among the people. Political struggles continued between rural Argentina and the growing urban population, the latter increasingly coming under the influence of northern European countries through growing trade relations and immigration. In 1887 civil marriages were made obligatory, but efforts to legalize divorce did not succeed until the 1950s. Catholicism remains the religion of the majority, although its proportion is gradually declining. In 1895, the population was 99% Catholic, whereas by 1960 this was reduced to 93%. Catamarca still has the highest percentage (98%) because of its highly traditional Spanish culture. Misiones province in the north, on the other hand, where the immigration of Protestant and Orthodox has been relatively important, has the lowest proportion Catholics (82%). Between 1857 and 1950 over 4 million immigrants came to Argentina, 46% being Italian, 31% Spanish, and the rest from Ireland, Germany, Poland and other European countries. Ukrainian immigration to Misiones began about 1897, and there are today about 100,000 Ukrainian-rite Catholics in 3 centres: 50,000 in Buenos Aires, 30,000 in Apostoles (province of Misiones) and 20,000 in Saens Pena (province of Chaco); many are now assimilated Argentinians and no longer speak Ukrainian. For the past century the conservative sector of the upper class and a large portion of the middle class have identified themselves with the church. The middle class has furnished, and continues to furnish, almost all vocations to the priesthood and religious life, as well as contributing much to the effectiveness of lay apostolate movements. If rural Catholicism is the most solid and devotional, it is clearly in a minority position, since in 1960 75% of the population was urban. Sunday attendance reveals a wide range in practice. Only about 7% of those eligible to attend mass actually do so in the 12 parishes of greater Buenos Aires. In the lesser towns, between 8% and 20% attend.

PROTESTANT CHURCHES. Early Protestant expansion in Argentina was due in large part to the immigration of peoples from Germany and Scandinavia at the end of the 19th century and the beginning of the 20th. Also important was the arrival of British executives, accompanied by their pastors, who came to work in the meat industry and on

railroad construction. With a high urban population, Protestantism's literacy rate of 90% is the highest in Latin America. Although Protestants remain a minority of the population, Argentina is an important base for a number of Protestant missions that have spread throughout Latin America. Protestant membership is the fourth largest in Latin America, growing at a rate of 2.8% per year, in contrast to the Argentina population growth of 1.3% per year.

A Bible Society agent James Thompson who was to become the first Protestant missionary in numerous Latin American countries began his work here in 1820. During his brief stay in Buenos Aires, he founded 100 schools. American Methodists arrived in 1836, but confined their work to European immigrants for several decades. The Methodist South American Annual Conference was organized in 1893; the Argentina Conference in 1954; and the church became autonomous in 1968. However, Methodist membership remains small considering the number of years the Church has been at work. The presence of European Lutherans and Reformed in Argentina dates from 1843. In addition to the United La Plata Evangelical Church, there are 6 Lutheran and 6 Reformed bodies, including the Waldensian Evangelical Church. The various Reformed denominations have now joined together to form the Association of Reformed Churches. European Baptists first entered Argentina in 1878, and American Southern Baptists followed in 1903. The Argentina Baptist Convention was organized in 1908. Today it is one of the largest churches in Argentina with most of its congregations self-supporting. Since 1940, 3 other Baptist missions have entered Argentina. Other large constituencies begun at the end of the 19th century are those belonging to the Plymouth Brethren and Seventh-day Adventists.

In spite of initial efforts as early as 1909, Pentecostals registered little growth prior to World War II. Even so, Pentecostalism has not shown a dynamic in Argentina equivalent to that in Brazil or Chile. The principal thrust has come from the USA, but Scandinavian and Canadian Pentecostals have

**Iglesia Católica en la Argentina.** Open-air mass celebrated by several bishops.

also been influential. A charismatic movement, Movimiento de Renovación, appeared among Plymouth Brethren in 1963, extending to over 20% of all members by 1973.

OTHER CHURCHES. Numerous independent pentecostal churches have come into existence in recent years, the most important being the Christian Assemblies among descendants of Italian immigrants. The Evangelical Pentecostal Church of Chile, an indigenous body which has spread to Argentina from neighbouring Chile, is also making a significant impact on the scene. In 1962 the Mennonite work among the Toba Indians experienced a pentecostal outburst which transformed it into the independent Toba United Evangelical Church.

At least 9 different Orthodox churches have arisen,

**Protestants.** Taking offertory (collection) in chapel of Union Theological Seminary, Buenos Aires.

serving Orthodox immigrants from Armenia, Greece, Lebanon, Romania, Russia, Syria, Ukraine and Yugoslavia.

The New Apostolic Church has built up a large following, mostly among German immigrants; and 5 Oriental and Eastern Orthodox traditions are represented in organized communities in the larger cities.

Anglicanism was first brought to Argentina in 1824 through the work of the South American Missionary Society among Patagonia Indians in the extreme south, and Anglicans are now also active among Indians in the northern Chaco and in urban slums.

CHURCH AND STATE. An Agreement between the Holy See and the Argentina republic, reached under the presidency of general Ongania in 1966, put to an end a regime of national patronage which had been incorporated in Articles 67 (paragraphs 19 and 20) and 86 (paragraphs 8 and 9) of the 1853 constitution. The agreement is a direct result of Vatican II, which requested that heads of state renounce their privilege of naming bishops. In the present case, it is nevertheless stipulated that bishops are to be citizens and that their nomination by the Holy See be subject to previous secret consultation with the government. Article 1 of the agreement states that the Argentina government recognizes and guarantees to the Roman Apostolic Catholic Church the freedom and full exercise of its spiritual power, the full public exercise of worship as well as jurisdiction within the limits of its competence to carry out its specific purposes.

This agreement, however, does not disturb the privileged juridical position of the Catholic Church, for it abolishes neither Article 2 of the constitution ('The federal government supports the Roman Apostolic Catholic religion') nor Article 76 which makes belonging to the Catholic community a condition of eligibility to the offices of president and vice-president of the republic. This is resented by non-Catholics as a discriminatory measure.

Freedom of worship is guaranteed for Argentina citizens in the constitution (Article 14) and for foreigners (Article 20). Administrative relations between the churches and the state are handled by the under-secretary of religion, Ministry of Foreign Relations and Religion (Subsecretaria de Culto, Ministerió de Relaciones Exteriores y Culto). Its most important functions include the distribution of subsidies to the Catholic Church (derived from Article 2 of the constitution), and the maintaining of a register of churches, where denominations and religions must be inscribed in order to conduct public activities in the country.

It may be said that the Catholic episcopate in Argentina is dependent on an historical past which made the church a real power, and that it is strongly attached to conserving a maximum of acquired rights, such as indissolubility of marriage, religious education in public schools, and the like. On its side, the state tends to consider the Catholic religion as a pillar of the established order. As a result, in December 1966 the government dedicated the republic 'to the Immaculate Heart of the Virgin Mary' in the presence of 14 of the most conservative bishops of the country, although other bishops declined to participate. Another example is the strong pressures put on the episcopate to control closely the alleged revolutionary activities of certain groups of priests and laymen.

In 1973, a law was passed in Cordoba province establishing a standard procedure for all private schools in the province and requiring that all teaching and administrative posts be filled through a public competitive procedure by which the person with the best qualifications would be hired. The new law was criticized by the Argentine Episcopal Conference, anticipating the possibility that other provinces might pass similar laws.

When general Peron was returned to power on 13 October 1973 the attitude of the Catholic bishops was much more reserved than during his first presidency. The episcopate in fact had played a major role in his fall in 1955. Although (in contrast to many priests) most bishops had never been Peronistas, their reactions were, however, generally favourable. Since Peron's death in July 1974 and the shift to the right of his successors, the bishops have been even more careful to maintain their neutrality, particularly with regard to the Episcopal Conference.

In 1977, the regime banned Jehovah's Witnesses, Hare Krishna and the Divine Light Mission. In 1978, further, it was decreed that all religions except Roman Catholicism must register or re-register with the state, or be pronounced illegal.

## INTERDENOMINATIONAL ORGANIZATIONS.

The Argentina Federation of Evangelical Churches was founded as a separate entity in 1958, having earlier been part of the Confederation of Evangelical Churches of the River Plate (Argentina, Uruguay, Paraguay). It is a large body with 28 churches as full members and several others holding associate

membership, and is affiliated to CWME of the WCC. The Episcopal Commission for Faith and Ecumenism of the Catholic Church has been set up to enter into dialogue with other churches. The Union of Latin American Ecumenical Youth (Unión Latinoamericana de Juventudes Ecuménicas, ULAJE), founded in Lima in 1941 with its headquarters now in Buenos Aires, had 250,000 members in 16 countries in 1973. It sponsors training seminars and publishes pedagogical material with an aim to promoting justice, peace and liberation. The River Plate Christian Study Centre (Centro de Estudios Cristianos del Rio de la Plata), founded in Buenos Aires in 1963, is an international centre for study and dialogue, serving a wide group of churches in the River Plate area of Argentina and Uruguay. Also in Buenos Aires, Union Theological Seminary, considered one of the finest in Latin America, serves several churches.

The Catholic Church has a Jewish-Christian Confraternity and a research bureau on Jewish-Christian relations.

**BROADCASTING.** State radio and television networks both accept religious programmes. In Buenos Aires there are 2 production centres for radio and television. The Instituto Superior de Comunicaciones Sociales (COSAL), founded in 1968, has 3 studios for sound and one for TV, and the Escuela de Televisión has 2 complete studios with equipment for teaching and production. Southern Baptists produce

several effective radio programmes, and have one of the largest Christian film libraries on the continent. Protestants use the studio facilities of CAVEA (Centro Audio Visual Evangélica de Argentina) for radio production. In 1968 CAVEA was producing one weekly TV programme and 3 radio programmes, produced by Brethren and Adventists. In 1976 a new Christian Communications Centre was opened in Buenos Aires. For Catholics, UNDA is represented by a national association.

INCUPO (Instituto de Cultura Popular) in Reconquista has radio schools for northeast Argentina, an area in which 75% are uneducated farmers. Founded in 1968, it has 2 recording studios, where it produces educational programmes which are broadcast by private transmitter.

### BIBLIOGRAPHY
'Argentina', *Pro Mundi Vita* (Brussels), 27 (1969).
*Historia de la Iglesia en la Argentina.* B. Cayetano. 5 vols (1740–1778). Buenos Aires: Editorial Don Bosco, 1966–69. 544p, 584p, 543p, 552p, 552p.
*La Iglesia en Argentina.* E. Amato. Buenos Aires: CIDOR/FERES, 1965. 253p. (Roman Catholic).
*Man, millieu and mission in Argentina.* A. W. Enns. Grand Rapids: Eerdmans, 1971. 258p.
'Migration and church growth in Argentina'. P. A. Larson. Dissertation, Fuller Theological Seminary, Pasadena, CA (USA), 1973. 492p.
*Panorama estadística de la Iglesia Argentina.* N. Rosato. Buenos Aires: CAR y CONFER, 1976. 24p
'Quo Vadis IELU'. J. E. Hennesberger. Thesis, Fuller Theological Seminary, Pasadena, CA (USA), 1968. 401p. (Iglesia Evangélica Luterana Unida).
'Shamanism, illness and power in Toba church life', J. A. Loewen, A. Buckwalter & J. Kratz, *Practical anthropology,* 12, 6 (1965), 250–280.

**Iglesia Anglicana.** A Mataco Indian family at daily family prayers: Evangelicals in Diocese of Northern Argentina. *Above right.* At consecration service in Misión Chaquena in 1976 of Latin America's first Amerindian bishop of any confession, Mario Lorenzo Marino (a Mataco age 43; left), he is greeted by Bishop of Argentina and Eastern South America (right). By contrast, Roman Catholic policy since 1552 Council of Lima has remained almost unchanged: 'Amerindians cannot be ordained'.

TABLE 2.   ORGANIZED CHURCHES AND DENOMINATIONS IN ARGENTINA

| Official name 1 | Begun 2 | Type 3 | Counc 4 | Congs 5 | Adults 6 | Affiliated 7 | Names, notes, and other statistics (see Codebook) 8 |
|---|---|---|---|---|---|---|---|
| Alianza Cristiana y Misionera | 1897 | P Hol | xFu,N | 32 | 1,500 | 4,100 | *Christian & Missionary Alliance.* M=CMA(USA). 1960, big losses. 30n,9f,1s,W=33%,150Y. |
| Asamblea Cristiana Cultural | | I pen | ••••• | 40 | 2,000 | 4,000 | *Cultural Christian Assemblies.* Local indigenous pentecostals. HQ Buenos Aires. |
| Asamblea Cristiana de Argentina | 1916 | P Pe2 | ••u,N | 35 | 3,000 | 10,000 | *Argentinian Christian Assemblies.* HQ Buenos Aires. 25n,7x,G=3.7%pa,W=50%,700Y. |
| Asamblea Cristiana (Italiana) | | I pe2 | ••••• | | 22,000 | 100,000 | *Christian Assemblies (Italian).* Links with M=CCNA(USA). Argentinian pentecostals. |
| Asamblea de Dios | 1941 | I pen | ••••• | 41 | 1,600 | 5,700 | *Assembly of God.* Indigenous pentecostals. HQ Buenos Aires. 16n,2x,W=50%,310Y,100z. |
| Asamblea de Iglesias Cristianas | 1965 | I pen | x•••• | | 1,000 | 2,000 | M=Assembly of Christian Churches, a Puerto Rican mission based on New York. |
| Asambleas Bíblicas | | I pen | ••••• | | 2,000 | 4,000 | *Bible Assemblies.* Indigenous Argentinian pentecostals. |
| Asambleas de Dios | 1910 | P Pe2 | Z•••• | 250 | 25,000 | 50,000 | *Assemblies of God.* M=SFM(Sweden), NPY (Norway), Elim(Denmark). 65n,1500Y,600z. |
| Asociación de Iglesias Reformadas: | | P Ref | ••u,N | 60 | 5,576 | 13,960 | *ADIREIA.* *Association of Reformed Churches.* Scottish, Hungarian, French, Swiss. |
| Igl Cristiana Ev Reformada Húngara | | P Ref | ••u,N | | 1,000 | 2,000 | *Hungarian Reformed Ch.* Refugees from Hungary since 1956. Buenos Aires, Chaco. |
| Iglesia Escocesa Presbiteriana | | P Ref | ••u,N | | 1,600 | 2,000 | *Presbyterian Ch of Scotland.* M=Ch of Scotland(UK). In Buenos Aires. 3f. |
| Iglesia Ev Reformada Francesa | | P Ref | ••u,N | | 100 | 200 | *French Reformed Ch.* Immigrants from Eglise Réformée de France. HQ Buenos Aires. |
| Iglesia Ev Suiza en la Argentina | | P Ref | ••u,N | | 500 | 1,000 | *Swiss Ch.* Immigrants from Eglises Réformées de la Suisse. Buenos Aires, Misiones. |
| Iglesia Evangélica Valdense | 1859 | P Wal | R,u,N | 9 | 1,439 | 6,460 | *Waldensian Ev Ch. Chiesa Ev Valdese.* Italian Protestant immigrants. Santa Fe. |
| Iglesia Reformada en la Argentina | 1962 | P Ref | J,u,N | 15 | 937 | 2,300 | M=DRC(Netherlands). Dutch, Americans. 6n,11x,G=3.0% pa,1s(4),W=75%,60Yy. |
| Congr Cristiana Católica Apostólica | c1960 | I CCa | •v••• | | 100 | 200 | *Catholic Apostolic Christian Congr.* Buenos Aires. 1965, applied to join WCC, rejected. |
| Convención Evangélica Bautista de A | 1878 | P Bap | T,u,n | 450 | 20,440 | 80,000 | 1878 Germans from Russia. 1903, M=SBC(USA). 160n,50x,85f,G=3.5% pa,1s,W=59%,1177Y. |
| Ejército de Salvación | 1889 | P Sal | xwu,N | 60 | 6,000 | 15,000 | *Salvation Army,* in South America East Territory. Division, 4 Districts. 100n,1s. |
| Iglesia Adventista del Séptimo Día | 1894 | P Adv | x•••• | 175 | 20,419 | 60,000 | *Seventh-day Adventists,* Austral UC: 2 Confs. 2x,G=4.6% pa,4H,1j,2p,3r,1s(60),1713Y. |
| Iglesia Anglicana | 1824 | A Eva | AwuCn | 70 | 7,000 | 13,200 | 2 Dioceses. M=SAMS(UK). Mostly Mataco Indians. 32n,18x,61f,W=50%,50Y,300y. |
| Igl Apostólica Armenia: D Argentina | c1880 | O Arm | Ewc•• | 4 | 3,000 | 5,000 | *Armenian Apostolic Ch. Gregorians.* Refugees from USSR. Under C Echmiadzin. 8n. |
| Iglesia Católica Americana Ortodoxa | c1968 | I CCa | ••••• | | 20,000 | 30,000 | Schism ex Rome by RC priests, bishop. M=American Orthodox Catholic Ch(USA Slavs). |
| **Iglesia Católica en la Argentina:** | 1539 | R LEr | B,L,R | 2,657 | 15,388,000 | 22,301,530 | C=60+8+170   5326nx,1277m,12486w,470504Yy. 8 Pastoral Regions (PR) as under: |
| M   Bahía Blanca | 1934 | R Lat | Bs | 53 | 331,000 | 480,000 | PR: Comahue   148   22   406   10011 |
| D   Comodoro Rivadavia | 1957 | R Lat | Bs | 17 | 117,900 | 170,928 | Patagonia   47   9   61   3645   *Buenos Aires.* 7 dioceses. Entirely |
| D   Río Gallegos | 1961 | R Lat | Bs | 15 | 59,000 | 85,000 | Patagonia   40   17   82   3277   urban industrial, 1970 |
| D   Santa Rosa | 1957 | R Lat | Bs | 25 | 114,000 | 165,000 | Comahue   41   2   74   2896   population 8,450,000. Archdiocese |
| D   Viedma | 1934 | R Lat | Bs | 27 | 166,000 | 240,000 | Comahue   77   55   81   5659   has 4 Episcopal Vicariates. |
| M   Buenos Aires | 1582 | R Lat | Bs | 154 | 1,845,900 | 2,675,200 | Buenos Aires   958   375   2958   46342 |
| D   Avellaneda | 1961 | R Lat | Bs | 55 | 626,400 | 907,000 | Buenos Aires   114   8   180   16145   *Centro-Cuyo.* 8 dioceses. |
| D   Lomas de Zamora | 1957 | R Lat | Bs | 63 | 611,000 | 885,000 | Buenos Aires   165   67   530   9380   Industrial centres (Cordoba, |
| D   Morón | 1957 | R Lat | Bs | 51 | 343,200 | 497,419 | Buenos Aires   123   35   270   20399   Mendoza), agricultural areas. |
| D   San Isidro | 1957 | R Lat | Bs | 41 | 581,400 | 842,572 | Buenos Aires   149   63   400   13000   Cordoba: religious and cultural |
| D   San Justo | 1969 | R Lat | Bs | 32 | 435,000 | 630,000 | Buenos Aires   68   16   126   11968   centre, severe social tensions. |
| D   San Martín | 1961 | R Lat | Bs | 75 | 809,000 | 1,173,000 | Buenos Aires   156   15   449   15000   Traditional catholicism. |

*Continued overleaf*

*Table 2–continued*

| Official name 1 | Begun 2 | Type 3 | Counc 4 | Congs 5 | Adults 6 | Affiliated 7 | Names, notes, and other statistics (see Codebook) 8 | | | | | |
|---|---|---|---|---|---|---|---|---|---|---|---|---|
| M Córdoba | 1570 | R Lat | Bs | 84 | 759,000 | 1,100,000 | Centro-Cuyo | 360 | 185 | 970 | 34200 | |
| D Cruz de Eje | 1963 | R Lat | Bs | 18 | 131,000 | 190,000 | Centro-Cuyo | 33 | 0 | 105 | 7650 | *Comahue*. 4 dioceses. A major |
| D Rio Cuarto | 1934 | R Lat | Bs | 45 | 223,100 | 323,270 | Centro-Cuyo | 81 | 8 | 159 | 6804 | industrial area of the future. |
| D San Francisco | 1961 | R Lat | Bs | 31 | 115,000 | 166,600 | Centro-Cuyo | 47 | 11 | 71 | 3103 | Evangelized mainly by Salesians. |
| D Villa Maria | 1957 | R Lat | Bs | 43 | 248,000 | 360,000 | Centro-Cuyo | 63 | 9 | 88 | 5253 | Indian tribes in Andes, including |
| M Corrientes | 1910 | R Lat | Bs | 37 | 214,000 | 310,000 | Nordeste | 84 | 4 | 95 | 11011 | Mapuches from whom came the |
| D Formosa | 1957 | R Lat | Bs | 20 | 145,500 | 210,850 | Nordeste | 31 | 3 | 84 | 5131 | popular saint Ceferino Namuncurá. |
| D Goya | 1961 | R Lat | Bs | 19 | 149,600 | 216,781 | Nordeste | 39 | 2 | 95 | 4834 | |
| D Posadas | 1957 | R Lat | Bs | 556 | 288,500 | 418,082 | Nordeste | 107 | 14 | 198 | 14249 | *La Plata*. 5 dioceses. Urban areas |
| D Presidencia Roque Sáenz Pena | 1963 | R Lat | Bs | 21 | 173,000 | 251,000 | Nordeste | 43 | 5 | 78 | 6183 | becoming industrialized; vast |
| D Resistencia | 1939 | R Lat | Bs | 20 | 157,000 | 227,000 | Nordeste | 61 | 3 | 70 | 5647 | Buenos Aires pampas. Traditional |
| M La Plata | 1887 | R Lat | Bs | 73 | 493,000 | 715,000 | La Plata | 200 | 34 | 585 | 10200 | catholicism. |
| D Azul | 1934 | R Lat | Bs | 41 | 215,100 | 311,757 | La Plata | 83 | 20 | 185 | 6411 | |
| D Mar del Plata | 1957 | R Lat | Bs | 41 | 309,200 | 448,127 | La Plata | 113 | 23 | 285 | 10240 | *Littoral*. 8 dioceses. Urban |
| D Mercedes | 1934 | R Lat | Bs | 134 | 290,000 | 420,000 | La Plata | 109 | 20 | 115 | 14616 | industrial and administrative |
| D Nueve de Julio | 1957 | R Lat | Bs | 39 | 206,600 | 299,377 | La Plata | 66 | 10 | 160 | 6736 | centres in rural areas of |
| M Mendoza | 1934 | R Lat | Bs | 54 | 513,300 | 743,980 | Centro-Cuyo | 173 | 11 | 403 | 16060 | European colonization (pampa |
| D Neuquén | 1961 | R Lat | Bs | 55 | 103,000 | 150,000 | Comahue | 41 | 3 | 30 | 2670 | gringa). Developed, prosperous. |
| D San Rafael | 1961 | R Lat | Bs | 15 | 107,000 | 155,000 | Centro-Cuyo | 23 | 10 | 38 | 4830 | Italian catholicism. Many |
| M Paraná | 1859 | R Lat | Bs | 36 | 241,000 | 350,000 | Littoral | 91 | 16 | 280 | 7805 | religious vocations. In 1969, a major |
| D Concordia | 1961 | R Lat | Bs | 19 | 135,000 | 195,000 | Littoral | 48 | 9 | 93 | 4976 | crisis in D Rosario by resignation |
| D Gualeguaychú | 1957 | R Lat | Bs | 28 | 155,000 | 225,000 | Littoral | 80 | 10 | 94 | 3311 | of 30 priests demanding greater |
| M Rosario | 1934 | R Lat | Bs | 99 | 828,000 | 1,200,000 | Littoral | 269 | 36 | 740 | 15000 | voice in diocesan affairs. |
| D San Nicolás de Los Arroyos | 1947 | R Lat | Bs | 48 | 376,000 | 545,000 | Littoral | 81 | 12 | 181 | 9701 | |
| D Venado Tuerto | 1963 | R Lat | Bs | 29 | 104,000 | 150,000 | Littoral | 30 | 21 | 64 | 2438 | |
| M Salta | 1806 | R Lat | Bs | 37 | 206,000 | 300,000 | Nordoeste | 117 | 11 | 80 | 10050 | *Nordeste*. 7 dioceses. Socially |
| D Catamarca | 1910 | R Lat | Bs | 24 | 128,000 | 186,000 | Nordoeste | 65 | 5 | 95 | 3310 | and economically underdeveloped; |
| D Jujuy | 1934 | R Lat | Bs | 24 | 169,000 | 245,000 | Nordoeste | 50 | 7 | 70 | 7732 | little industry. Catholicism of |
| D Orán | 1961 | R Lat | Bs | 31 | 96,000 | 139,000 | Nordoeste | 14 | 2 | 42 | 3179 | Spanish-Guaraní type with |
| PN Cafayate | 1969 | R Lat | Bs | 7 | 28,100 | 40,800 | Nordoeste | 13 | 0 | 0 | 1039 | European immigrant traditions. |
| PN Humahuaca | 1969 | R Lat | Bs | 6 | 34,300 | 49,700 | Nordoeste | 11 | 4 | 11 | 1572 | |
| M San Juan de Cuyo | 1834 | R Lat | Bs | 26 | 262,200 | 379,974 | Centro-Cuyo | 55 | 3 | 76 | 10961 | *Nordoeste*. Very underdeveloped. |
| D La Rioja | 1934 | R Lat | Bs | 17 | 90,100 | 130,560 | Centro-Cuyo | 38 | 2 | 42 | 2324 | Little European 19th-century |
| D San Luis | 1934 | R Lat | Bs | 21 | 114,800 | 166,398 | Centro-Cuyo | 38 | 1 | 77 | 3989 | immigration. Many Indian groups |
| M Santa Fe | 1897 | R Lat | Bs | 83 | 343,700 | 498,080 | Littoral | 138 | 44 | 404 | 8103 | (in 2 prelatures). Traditional |
| D Rafaela | 1961 | R Lat | Bs | 42 | 124,000 | 180,000 | Littoral | 41 | 12 | 85 | 3348 | Spanish-Indian catholicism. |
| D Reconquista | 1957 | R Lat | Bs | 17 | 105,400 | 152,760 | Nordeste | 33 | 2 | 110 | 3406 | |
| M Tucumán | 1897 | R Lat | Bs | 40 | 276,000 | 400,000 | Nordoeste | 142 | 9 | 288 | 15400 | *Patagonia*. 2 dioceses. Extreme |
| D Añatuya | 1961 | R Lat | Bs | 13 | 99,000 | 144,000 | Nordoeste | 21 | 3 | 30 | 2036 | south and Tierra del Fuego. |
| D Concepción | 1963 | R Lat | Bs | 18 | 175,200 | 253,960 | Nordoeste | 21 | 0 | 37 | 5003 | Recently evangelized, by |
| D Santiago del Estero | 1907 | R Lat | Bs | 32 | 255,500 | 370,355 | Nordoeste | 51 | 6 | 58 | 11508 | Salesians. |
| EA Argentina (*Ukrainian*) | 1968 | R Ukr | Os | 12 | 76,000 | 110,000 | Ukrainian rite. | 19 | 3 | 98 | 453 | Not in any pastoral region. |
| O Argentina | 1959 | R Ori | Os | 12 | 84,000 | 122,000 | Other rites. | 17 | 0 | 0 | 310 | Not in any pastoral region. |
| Iglesia Cristiana Reformada | 1930 | P Ref | JF... | 16 | 1,000 | 1,850 | *Christian Reformed Ch.* Calvinist doctrines. M=CRC(USA). 20f. | | | | | |
| Iglesia de Dios Cristiana Pentecostal | 1954 | I pen | ..u.N | 55 | 5,000 | 7,500 | *Christian Pentecostal Ch of God.* HQ Malaver, Buenos Aires. 30n,2x,G=9.3%pa. | | | | | |
| Iglesia de Dios de la Profecía | 1955 | P Pe3 | Z.... | 11 | 350 | 500 | *Ch of God of Prophecy.* M=CGP(USA). HQ San Jeronimo (Santa Fe). | | | | | |
| Iglesia de Dios en la Argentina | c1930 | P Hol | x.u.N | 22 | 1,260 | 2,000 | *Ch of God.* M=CoG(Anderson) (USA). German immigrants before World War II. 10n,1s. | | | | | |
| Iglesia de Jesucristo de los SUD | 1935 | M LdS | x.... | 50 | 20,000 | 32,774 | *Ch of JC of Latter-day Saints. Mormons.* M=CJCLdS(USA). Rapid growth, 9.4%pa. 400f. | | | | | |
| Iglesia de los Hermanos Libres | 1882 | P CBr | x.u.n | 700 | 26,000 | 100,000 | M=CMML(USA,UK). Many Syrians. 50n,20x,49f,G=4.1%pa,4p,1s(200),W=50%,500Y. | | | | | |
| Iglesia de los Hermanos (Ashland) | 1948 | P Dun | xF... | 17 | 400 | 1,000 | *Brethren Ch.* M=BCMB(Ashland,USA). German Baptist origin. 6f. | | | | | |
| Iglesia de los Hermanos (Grace) | 1909 | P Dun | xF... | 17 | 500 | 1,000 | *Brethren Ch.* M=NFBC(Winona Lake, USA). In USA, 1939 split ex Ashland. 6f. | | | | | |
| Iglesia del Evangelio Cuadrangular | 1959 | P Pe2 | ZFu.N | 63 | 3,370 | 9,000 | *International Ch of the Foursquare Gospel.* M=ICFG(USA). 65nm,2f,3p(51),W=95%,400Y. | | | | | |
| Iglesia Ev Armenia de los Hermanos | | P CBr | x.... | 3 | 96 | 500 | *Armenian Ev Spiritual Brethren.* Split ex Armenian Congregational Ev Ch. In capital. | | | | | |
| Iglesia Ev Congregacionalista Armenia | | P Con | ..u.N | 1 | 100 | 500 | *Armenian Congr. Ev Ch.* Immigrants from Armenia, Turkey, Lebanon. HQ Buenos Aires. | | | | | |
| Igl Ev Congregacionalista en la Rep A | 1924 | P Con | ..u.N | 103 | 8,428 | 20,000 | *Congregational Ch.* Germans from Russia since 1870. 1964,M=UCBWM(USA). 20n,1s. | | | | | |
| Iglesia Evangélica del Nazareno | 1919 | P Hol | xFu.N | 57 | 1,901 | 4,000 | *Ch of the Nazarene.* M=CoN(USA). 18n,12x,13m,23f,G=10.3%pa,1s(70),56t(3556),125Y. | | | | | |
| Iglesia Evangélica del Río de la Plata | 1843 | P LuR | .Wu.N | 95 | 14,875 | 60,000 | *La Plata Ev Ch.* Germans (10% Reformed). 50% nationals. 13n,32x,G=0.6%pa,1s(8). | | | | | |
| Iglesia Ev Discípulos de Cristo | 1906 | P Dis | xuu.N | 10 | 450 | 2,000 | *Disciples of Christ.* M=UCMS(USA). Several institutions. Decline since 1960. 8f. | | | | | |
| Iglesia Evangélica Gracia y Gloria | c1950 | P Pen | ..... | 10 | 350 | 1,000 | *Ev Ch of Grace and Glory.* USA & UK missions. HQ Formosa. Spanish; 2 Toba churches. | | | | | |
| Iglesia Evengélica Luterana Argentina | 1905 | P Lut | x.... | 207 | 14,000 | 22,816 | *Ev Lutheran Ch in Argentina.* M=LC Misiouri S(USA). German-speaking. 56n,1f,G=3%pa,2s. | | | | | |
| Iglesia Evangélica Luterana Unida | 1908 | P Lut | Luu.N | 25 | 3,900 | 5,565 | *United Ev Luth Ch.* 1948, M=LCA(USA). A=1948. Diverse immigrants. 20n,6x,15f,2s. | | | | | |
| Iglesia Evangélica Menonita Argentina | 1917 | P Men | G.u.N | 24 | 837 | 2,000 | *Mennonite Ev Ch in A. Argentina Mennonite Conference.* M=MCNA(USA). 21f. | | | | | |
| Iglesia Evangélica Metodista | 1964 | I Hol | .TT.T | | 1,000 | 2,000 | *Ev Methodist Ch. Bible Methodists.*M=EMC(USA). Koreans. HQ Buenos Aires. 6f. | | | | | |
| Iglesia Evangélica Metodista Argentina | 1836 | P Met | VWu.N | 107 | 9,607 | 40,000 | *Ev Methodist Ch of A.* M=UMC(USA). 58n,14x,32f,G=0%pa,1j,89t,1u,W=32%,244Yy. | | | | | |
| Iglesia Ev Pentecostal Argentina | 1917 | P Pe3 | ZF... | 148 | 9,680 | 20,000 | *Pentecostal Ev Ch.* M=CoG(Cleveland), SFM. Some Toba Indians. 98n,1f, G=10.7%pa,2p. | | | | | |
| Iglesia Ev Pentecostal de Chile | c1940 | I pe2 | x.... | 10 | 17,000 | 30,000 | *Ev Pentecostal Ch of Chile.* Indigenous church from Chile. In all major cities. | | | | | |
| Iglesia Ev Pentecostal Unida | 1967 | P Pe1 | x.... | 10 | 264 | 700 | *United Pentecostal Ch.* M=UPC(USA). Unitarian Pentecostals. 8n,6f,2p(35). | | | | | |
| Iglesia Evangélica Unida Toba | 1943 | I pen | ..... | 62 | 4,000 | 15,000 | Ex Mennonites(M=Chaco Mission). 1962, pentecostal split. 80% of all Toba Indians. 6f. | | | | | |
| Iglesia Galesa | 1865 | P Ref | ..... | 14 | 1,000 | 3,000 | *Welsh Ch.* Welsh immigrants in Patagonia (Chubut Valley). Declining. HQ Trelew. | | | | | |
| Iglesia Luterana Danesa | 1882 | P Lut | ..u.N | 4 | 1,000 | 3,000 | *Danish Lutheran Ch.* Danes from National Ch of Denmark. Begun 1882 in Tandil. | | | | | |
| Iglesia Luterana Noruega | | P Lut | Lw... | 1 | 300 | 825 | *Norwegian Lutheran Ch. Norske Kirke.* Norwegians from national church of Norway. | | | | | |
| Iglesia Nazarena Apostólica Cristiana | 1958 | P Hol | x.... | 20 | 500 | 1,000 | M=Apostolic Christian Ch(Nazarean)(USA). Swiss Mennonite origin. HQ Buenos Aires. | | | | | |
| Iglesia Nueva Apostólica | c1930 | C CAp | x.... | 96 | 25,000 | 50,000 | *NAK. New Apostolic Ch.* German immigrants. World HQ Dortmund(Germany) | | | | | |
| Iglesia Ortodoxa Arabe | c1890 | O Ara | Cwo.. | | 20,000 | 30,000 | *D Buenos Aires.* Under Antiochian Orth Ch(USA) and P Antioch. Syrians, Lebanese. | | | | | |
| Iglesia Ortodoxa Griega | c1870 | O Gre | Cwo.. | 20 | 15,000 | 25,000 | In 10th Archdiocesan District, Greek Orthodox AD N&SAmerica. Greeks. 1 bishop, 16n. | | | | | |
| Iglesia Ortodoxa Romana | c1950 | O Rum | Cwc.. | | 5,000 | 10,000 | *Romanian Orthodox Ch. Biserica Ortodoxa Romana.* Immigrants from Romania. | | | | | |
| Iglesia Ortodoxa Russa | c1880 | O Sla | Mwo.. | 5 | 10,000 | 15,000 | *Russian Orthodox Ch.* In D SAmerica, Orth Ch in America(USA). Russian bishop,2n. | | | | | |
| Iglesia Ortodoxa Russa: D Argentina | c1925 | O Sla | x.... | 9 | 5,000 | 10,000 | *Russian Orthodox Ch Outside of Russia* (HQ New York). Refugees. Ultra-conservative. | | | | | |
| Iglesia Ortodoxa Serba | c1950 | O Ser | Cwc.. | | 3,000 | 7,000 | *Serbian Orthodox Ch. Srpska Pravoslavna Crkva.* Under P Belgrade. Serbs, Albanians. | | | | | |
| Iglesia Ortodoxa Ucrania | c1920 | O Sla | X.... | 5 | 13,000 | 20,000 | *Ukrainian Autocephalous Orthodox Ch in Argentina.* Branch of UOC of the USA. 4n. | | | | | |
| Iglesia Santa Pentecostés | c1930 | P Pe3 | ZF... | 35 | 2,514 | 7,000 | *Pentecostal Holiness Ch.* M=PHC(USA). 3-stage Pentecostals. 37nm,14f. | | | | | |
| Iglesia Sueca | | P Lut | Lw... | 2 | 600 | 2,500 | *Swedish Ch. Svenska Kyrkan.* Swedes from state church of Sweden. HQ Buenos Aires. | | | | | |
| Iglesias Bautistas Ev del Norte A | 1957 | P Bap | xF... | 4 | 75 | 200 | *Baptist Chs of Northern Argentina.* M=BGC(USA). HQ Jujuy. 14f. | | | | | |
| Iglesias de Cristo | 1958 | P Dis | x.... | 5 | 100 | 300 | M=Churches of Christ(Non-Instrumental) (USA). In Buenos Aires, Mendoza. 10f. | | | | | |
| Misión Bautista Conservador | 1946 | P Bap | xF... | 97 | 2,020 | 6,071 | *Gen Assoc of Bapt Chs in N Arg.* M=CBFMS(1900 San Pedro Mission). 3n,43f,W=57%,262Y. | | | | | |
| Misión Evangélica Emmanuel | | P Pe3 | x.... | 3 | 405 | 1,000 | *Emmanuel Holiness Ch.* M=EHC(USA). 3-stage Pentecostals. HQ Formosa. | | | | | |
| Movimiento Cristiano y Misionero | 1958 | I pe2 | ..... | | 3,000 | 6,000 | *Christian & Missionary Movement.* Schism ex Assemblies of God(USA). HQ La Plata. | | | | | |
| Sociedad de la Ciencia Cristiana | | M Sci | x.... | 10 | 500 | 1,000 | *Ch of Christ, Scientist. Christian Science.* M=CCS(Boston,USA). 1m,15w. | | | | | |
| Sociedad Protestante del Sud | | P Lut | ..... | | 2,000 | 3,620 | *Protestant Society in Southern Argentina.* Lutheran immigrants. | | | | | |
| Testigos de Jehová | 1924 | M Jeh | x.... | 361 | 20,750 | 30,000 | *Jehovah's Witnesses. Watch Tower.* 1924, first missionary. 1976, banned. 2481Y. | | | | | |
| Unión Evangélica de Sud America | 1887 | P int | xM... | 50 | 1,000 | 8,000 | First M=RBMU; 1956,EUSA(UK,USA). Primarily evangelistic in interior. 37f. | | | | | |
| Unión Misionera Neotestamentaria | 1904 | P int | x.... | 50 | 2,000 | 4,000 | *New Testament Chs.* M=NTMU(UK). HQ Temperley. Corrientes, Entre Rios, Misiones. 3f. | | | | | |
| Unión Nac de las Asambleas de Dios | 1909 | P Pe2 | ZF..N | 164 | 10,034 | 20,000 | *Assemblies of God.* 1914,M=PAoC,AoG(USA). Slavs. 175n,10x,21f,G=13.0%pa,1j,1s(80),934Y. | | | | | |
| Other indigenous pentecostal churches | | I pen | ..... | | 20,000 | 40,000 | Total about 20 (see list below), begun by Argentinians, also some Chileans. | | | | | |
| Other indigenous churches | | I | ..... | | 2,000 | 5,000 | Total about 10 (see below), including Igreja Católica Apostólica Brasileira. | | | | | |
| Other Protestant denominations | | P | ..... | | 1,500 | 5,000 | Total about 40 (see list below). | | | | | |
| Doubly-affiliated (duplication)(1970) | | | | | –671,401 | –975,000 | Evangelicals who also are or were baptized Roman Catholics. | | | | | |
| **Total affiliated (mid-1970)** | | | | **7,740** | **15,168,900** | **22,419,911** | **Total denominations (1970) . . . 133.** | | | | | |
| **Total affiliated (mid-1975)** | | | | **8,100** | **16,164,300** | **23,911,730** | **Total denominations (1975) . . . 143.** | | | | | |
| **Total affiliated (mid-1980)** | | | | **8,800** | **17,197,500** | **25,440,160** | **Total denominations (1980) . . . 153.** | | | | | |

NOTES ON TABLE ABOVE

COLUMNS: for meanings and CODES (cols. 1, 3, 4, 8): see Codebook (Part 6). Column 1: **Boldface type** = church with over 10% of country's affiliated Christians.

NATIONAL COUNCILS (Column 4, 5th letter).

N = Federación Argentina de Iglesias Evangélicas (FAIE) (Argentina Federation of Evangelical Churches) (also called Concilio Evangélico de Iglesias Argentinas).

n = associate member of FAIE.

R = Conferencia Episcopal Argentina (CEA) (Argentina Episcopal Conference).

T = Argentina Consultative Committee of the ICCC.

OTHER INDIGENOUS CHURCHES. These number at least 20 pentecostal bodies and about 10 non-pentecostal (of which about 5 are members of FAIE), including: Argentina para Cristo, Asociación Cristiana Evangelística, Concilio Ev de Iglesias, Corporación Cooperadores Evangélicos, Iglesia Cristiana Bíblica, Iglesia Cristiana Ev de Mendoza, Iglesia Ev de Mar del Plata, Iglesia Ev Ingenio Ledesma, Iglesia Ev Japonesa, Iglesia Ev Pentecostal Apostólica Argentina, Iglesia Pentecostal de Argentina, Iglesia Pentecostal de la Trinidad (from Chile; 4 pastors), Misión Pentecostal (Indígenas), Testigos Presbiterianas do Brasil, Unión de los Cristianos de la Fe Ev, Unión Ev de la Argentina. There is also a missionary bishop of the Igreja Católica Apostólica Brasileira, from Brazil.

OTHER PROTESTANT DENOMINATIONS. Among the many small Protestant denominations and para-denominations are the following (with names in Spanish or English depending on which is better known): Alianza Cristiana Hebrea Americana, Alianza Misionera Evangélica, Baptist Bible Fellowship International (1959), Ch of Christ (Non-Instrumental), Dutch Reformed Ch of South Africa (NGK; Afrikaans-speaking Boer immigrants after 1918), Eastern Bolivian Mission, Evangelical Alliance Mission, Exclusive Brethren (Kelly-Continental), Friends of Israel Mission, German Mennonite Ch, Gospel Mission of South America (1971), Go-Ye Fellowship, Gypsy Ev Movement (France), Iglesia Presbiteriana de San Andrés, Independent Assemblies of God, Irish Baptist Foreign Mission (Baptist Union of Ireland), Misión Evangélica, Misión Ev a los Judios, Misión Noruega para Marineros, Misión Pentecostal Indios del Norte A, Missionary & Soul-winning Fellowship, New Tribes Mission, Open Bible Standard Chs (1962), Open Way Ch, Religious Society of Friends (Quakers), Seventh-day Adventist Reform Movement, Slavic Gospel Association, Sociedad Bautista Ev, Synod of Ev Lutheran Chs (1941), United World Mission (1965), World Gospel Mission (1969), World Mission Prayer League, World-Wide Missions (1971).

UNITING CHURCHES. In 1974, 2 separate sets of negotiations for organic union were under way, as follows: (1) Iglesia Ev Metodista Argentina, Iglesia Ev Valdense, plus 2 Uruguay bodies (Iglesia Ev Metodista en el Uruguay, Iglesia Ev Valdense del Río de la Plata), plus Iglesia Discípulos de Cristo del Paraguay; (2) Lutheran churches: Iglesia Ev del Río de la Plata, Iglesia Ev Luterana Argentina (Misúri).

PEOPLES (ethnolinguistic). Christians: 78.8% Argentinian White, 4.7% Italian, 2.5% Paraguayan Mestizo, 2.5% Bolivian (2.0% Indian, 0.5% Mestizo), 2.0% Mestizo, 1.9% Galician, 1.5% Chilean Mestizo, 1.4% Spanish, 1.2% Quechua, 0.7% lowland Amerindian, 0.5% Catalan, 0.5% Polish, 0.4% Uruguayan White, 0.3% Brazilian, 0.1% Arab, 0.1% British, 0.1% Greek, 0.1% Russian, 0.1% Ukrainian, Chinese (120), and 17 other nationalities.

COUNTRY-WIDE TOTALS
EVANGELIZATION (see Part 5). 1900: 99%. 1970: 100%. 1980: 100%. *Mass evangelism.* Among recent campaigns: 1956, Oswald Smith campaign (25,000 attenders); Sept-Oct 1962, Billy Graham crusades in Cordoba, Rosario, Buenos Aires (with Brazil, Paraguay, Uruguay, 572,500 attenders, 12,469 enquirers); November 1976, 6-week Luis Palau Crusade in Rosario (with follow-through evangelism techniques, aiming to start 216 new Evangelical congregations within 3 years), with over 5,000 decisions registered; 1978, Here's Life Cordoba (CCCI). *Radiophonic evangelism.* Annual listeners' letters (1975): 13,000 TWR, 2,088 HCJB, 1,581 FEBC. Bible correspondence courses: ICI, et alia. Radiophonic schools (Catholic): 200,000 enrolled.
FOREIGN MISSIONARIES AND PERSONNEL (nationals serving abroad) (1973). Total 991 in 17 countries including Spain, Indonesia, USA: about 915 Roman Catholics, 45 Protestants, 20 marginal Protestants, 6 Argentinian indigenous, 5 Catholics (non-Roman).
FOREIGN MISSIONARIES AND PERSONNEL (aliens from abroad) (1973). Total 8,824. *From Western world.* 7,288: 6,150 Roman Catholics, 607 Protestants (414 in 49 USA societies, 53 in 7 UK societies, 30 in 1 Sweden society, 30 in 5 Canada societies, 28 in 2 Norway societies, 24 in 5 WGermany societies, 8 in 1 Switzerland society, 7 in 1 Denmark society, 7 in 3 Australia societies, 4 in 1 New Zealand society, 2 in 1 Netherlands society), about 450 marginal Protestants (380 Mormons from USA), 61 Anglicans (60 in 3 UK societies, 1 in 1 USA society), about 10 Orthodox from USA, about 10 Catholics (non-Roman) from Germany. *From Communist world.* 146: 141 Roman Catholics (91 from Poland, 50 Yugoslavia), 5 Orthodox (3 USSR, 1 Romania, 1 Yugoslavia). *From Third World.* 1,390: 1,320 Roman Catholics from other Latin American countries (Brazil, Chile, Bolivia, Uruguay, et alia), about 30 Protestants from Chile, Brazil, Japan, Korea and South Africa, about 20 indigenous from Brazil, Chile and Puerto Rico, 18 marginal Protestants (Mormons from Brazil, Chile, Uruguay), 2 Orthodox from Lebanon.
INSTITUTIONS (church-operated) (1973). Total 1,170, including 1,036 higher schools (40 minor seminaries), 8 religious communities (monasteries), 15 research centres, 49 seminaries (25 Protestant, 22 RC, 2 indigenous), 7 universities.
PERIODICALS. About 120 titles.
PERSONNEL. About 21,824 (13,000 national, 8,824 foreign).
RELIGIOUS LIBRARIES. About 90.
SCRIPTURE DISTRIBUTION (1975). Annual totals: 104,159 Bibles (42% subsidized, 58% commercial), 284,033 NTs (24% free, 41% subsidized, 35% commercial), 506,676 UBS portions, 2,066,731 UBS selections. *Translations completed.* Portion: 4 languages since 1881, NT: Mataco in 1962.
SERVICE AGENCIES. About 140, including ACI, AICA, ALER, AMA, ASIT, CACE, CAR, CAVEA, CCAI, CCCI, CEA, CEF, CLC, CMJ, CONFER, CPN, FAIE, MEC, MSTM, MTS, OCMCS, SU, UCADE, UMOFC, WLC(EHC), WSCF, WVI, YMCA, YWCA(ACF).

ADDITIONAL DATA ON CHURCHES
IGLESIA ANGLICANA. Until 1974, 2 missionary dioceses under the jurisdiction of the archbishop of Canterbury (UK): Argentina & Eastern South America & the Falkland Islands (founded 1869 and 1910); and Northern Argentina (1965). In the latter, the Amerindian in history, of any confession, was consecrated bishop in 1976. In 1974, the 2 dioceses became part of the autonomous Anglican province CASA (Consejo Anglicano Sud Americano). In 1977 the Falkland Islands were detached and returned to the metropolitical jurisdiction of the archbishop of Canterbury.
IGLESIA CATOLICA EN LA ARGENTINA. The 53 Latin-rite dioceses are now divided into 8 Pastoral Regions (PR), which are shown above in column 8 on the left, and which are described in the box at the right of column 8. *New dioceses.* In 1976, D Quilmes and D Zárate-Campana were created. *Annual baptisms.* (1972) 98.1% infant, 1.9% adult. *Diocesan priests.* The percentages of nationals (Argentinians) among diocesan (secular) priests in pastoral regions are as follows: Comahue 46%, La Plata 71%, Nordeste 75%, Centro Cuyo 75%, Patagonia 6%. Most bishops also are Argentinians. *Male religious.* Of the 4,625 religious priests and brothers (in 1971), 59% were Argentinians, 3% were from other Latin American countries, and 38% were Europeans (Spain, Italy, Germany, France). *Sisters.* 64% Argentinians (in 1971), 8% other Latin Americans, and 28% Europeans (Italy, Germany, Spain). In addition to those enumerated in the table above, there are other sisters in contemplative congregations. Total all sisters (1970) 14,076. *Catholic charismatics* (January 1974). 1,000 adults including many religious personnel are active in the Charismatic Renewal in 90 prayer groups. *Seminaries.* For secular clergy, the number has been reduced through regrouping from 10 in 1970 to 6 in 1972; for religious clergy the total in 1973 was 16. *Catechist training schools.* Total 5 (2 regional, at elementary level, and 3 at middle level). In addition most dioceses have their own catechist training programmes. *Main religious orders and congregations.* Priests (those with over 100 members): 951 SDB, 307 OFM, 283 SVD, 226 SJ, 120 Hijos de la Divina Providencia, 114 CMF, 104 OFMCap. Brothers (with over 100): 286 PFM, 146 FSC. *Catholic organizations.* The Argentine Episcopal Conference (Conferencia Episcopal Argentina, CEA) is a member of CELAM. There are 2 national associations of religious personnel: the Argentine Conference of Male Religious (Conferencia Argentina de Religiosos, CAR) and the Council of Religious Major Superiors (Consejo de Superioras Mayores Religiosas, COSMARAS) for sisters. Both are members of CLAR. For priests there is a National Pastoral Council (Consejo Pastoral Nacional, CPN) which is a deliberative and consultative body. The CPN had 92 members in 1972, of whom 7 were delegates of regions, 49 of dioceses, and 36 of other sectors (4 brothers, 10 sisters, 10 lay adult, and 12 lay youth). The statutes of the CPN call for 127 members, 61 chosen by the bishops and 66 by the sectors, of whom 39 are to be youth and adult lay representatives. For the armed forces, Argentina forms a military vicariate.

The Sub-Secretariat of the Apostolate of the Laity (Sub-Secretariado de Apostolado de los Laicos) is an executive agency of the Episcopal Commission. The principal movements of the lay apostolate in 1970 were: (1) Argentine Catholic Action (Acción Católica Argentina) including AMAC-AC for women (9,390 members); AHAC-AC for men (5,750); Masculine Youth (Juventud Masculina, JAC) (1,200); Feminine Youth (Juventud Femenina, AJAC) (1,500); JOC/F, JEC and JUC no longer exist. (2) Christian Family Movement (Movimiento Familiar Cristiano), founded in 1948, grew rapidly between 1956 and 1969 and in 1970 existed officially in 48 dioceses with 4,000 homes registered. (3) Legion of Mary (Legión de Maria) founded in 1956, which is implanted in all dioceses and has about 2,000 chapters with 6 members each, grouped in 3 praesidia at Salta, Cordoba and Adrogué.

Lay movements concerned with spirituality and religious training include: (1) Christian Study Courses (Cursillos de Cristiandad) which have played an important civil and religious role since 1966, the number of cursillistes having reached 13,390 in 39 dioceses; (2) Movement for a Better World (Movimiento por un Mundo Mejor) which has been in Argentina since 1958 and reached the height of its influence in 1965–68; (3) Focolare (Movimiento de los Focolares), a movement of lay youth communities begun in Italy after 1945 and which has been in Argentina since 1962, Buenos Aires being the seat of the Latin American secretariat; and (4) Union of Argentine Catholic Scouts (Unión Scouts Católicos Argentinos, USCA), which consists of 200 groups divided in 25 regions with 22,000 members.

The Holy See has diplomatic relations with Argentina and is represented to government and the Catholic hierarchy by a nuncio in Buenos Aires.

Latin American organizations established in Argentina include: (1) the Department of Ecumenism of CELAM, founded in 1968; (2) Organization of Catholic Universities of Latin America (Organización de Universidades Católicas de América Latina, ODUCAL), founded in 1953 and dependent on the Roman Sacred Congregation for Christian Education, whose purpose is to improve relations between the Catholic universities, study their common problems and develop a religious and social conscience among students in the face of the socio-economic problems of Latin America; (3) American Christian Union of Educators (Unión Cristiana Americana de Educadores, UCADE), founded in 1962 with the help of the World Union of Christian Educators (UMEC) in Rome, whose purpose is to unite Christian educators, improve pedagogical methods and disseminate the social doctrine of the church; and (4) Latin American Association for Educational Radio (Asociación Latinoamericana de Educación Radiofónica, ALER), founded in 1972.

Latin American secretariats of international organizations are: (1) Latin American Branch of the World Union of Catholic Feminine Organizations (Organismo Latinoamericano de la Unión Mundial de Organizaciones Femeninas Católicas, UMOFC) with its headquarters in Paris; (2) Latin American Secretariat of the International Catholic Union for Social Service (Secretariado Latinoamericano de la Unión Católica Internacional de Servicio Social, UCISS) with its international headquarters in Brussels; and (3) Latin American Secretariat of the World Federation of Catholic Youth (Secretariado Latinoamericano de la Federación Mundial de Jovenes Católicos, FMJC) also with its international headquarters in Brussels.

Argentine social action groups include the following: (1) Movement of Priests for the Third World (Movimiento de Sacerdotes para el Tercer Mundo, MSTM) which is one of the most influential of Latin American groups declaring itself in favour of revolution, with little support from the bishops and open opposition after 1970 from the government and the army (since the return of Peron and because of the ambiguities of his rule and those who succeeded him, the MSTM has been badly divided); (2) Church and Change Movements in Argentina (Movimiento Iglesia y Cambio en Argentina, MICAR), founded in 1970, which advocates non-violent change in church and state; (3) Argentina Society for the Defence of Tradition, Family and Property (Sociedad Argentina de Defensa de la Tradición, Familia y Propriedad) which is the Argentine Branch of a conservative movement found in other parts of Latin America, especially Brazil; (4) Catholic City (Ciudad Católica) which propagates the social doctrine of the church and trains leaders among unionized workers, teachers and in the armed forces; (5) Twentieth Century Maccabees (Macabeos Siglo XX), founded in 1969, which is a paramilitary secret society seeking 'to initiate again a Maccabean Crusade' against the challenges to the integrity of the faith, and has chosen the Immaculate Virgin as Queen and General; and (6) Argentina Sacerdotal Crusade (Crusada Sacerdotal Argentina), founded in 1970, which is a conservative organization in opposition to the MSTM.

Organizations involved in research are: (1) Centre for Research and Study (Centro de Investigación y Estudio, CIE) attached to the co-ordinating secretariat of COEPAL, and Ecclesiastical Centre for Documentation and Statistics (Centro Ecclesiástico de Documentación y Estadística, CEDE) dependent on the CIE, which are agencies founded in 1969 to serve COEPAL directly and exclusively; (2) Centre for Research and Social Action (Centro de Investigación y Acción Social, CIAS), founded in 1961 by Jesuits, but existing as the Centre for Sociological Information since 1953, to deal with social problems of Argentina and Latin America; (3) Centre for Research and Social Orientation (Centro de Investigación y Orientación Social, CIOS), an independent agency founded in 1966, whose purpose is to provide an objective analysis of national and regional social realities and propose projects leading towards liberation; (4) Institute for Study and Research (Instituto de Estudios y Investigaciones, Fundación FAPES), founded in 1964 and dependent on the Popular Christian Party, whose purpose is to provide an analysis of national realities; (5) Co-ordinating Team for Research concerning Society and Religion (Equipo Coodinator de Investigaciones Sobre Sociedad y Religion, ECOISYR), an independent group founded in 1967 to promote and co-ordinate research on the function of the national pastoralia; and (6) Technical Secretariat of the Archbishopric of Santa Fe (Secretaria Tecnica de Arzobispado de Santa Fe), founded in 1963.

Organizations relating to rural life are: (1) Rural Movement for Catholic Action (Movimiento Rurai de Acción Católica), which provides training for peasants, especially youth (2,000 peasants in 160 groups in 40 rural locations in 1970); and (2) Argentine Rural Missions (Misiones Rurales Argentinas) whose purpose is to improve the spiritual, social, educational and sanitary levels of the rural family, with community development projects at Chubut, Cordoba, and La Rioja.

Theological training is provided in the following institutions: (1) Faculties of Theology at the Argentine Catholic University (Universidad Católica Argentina) in Buenos Aires, which is the best pastoral institute in the country, as well as in the Catholic universities at San Miguel de Tucuman (St Thomas d'Aguin), Cordoba, Buenos Aires (Del Salvador, SJ), Santa Fe, Mar del Plata, and San Miguel (SJ); (2) Superior Institute of Argentine Catechesis (Instituto Superior de Catequesis Argentino, ISCA), founded in Buenos Aires by the Central Catechetical Board, which is the executive arm of the Episcopal Commission for Catechesis; (3) Institute of Sacred Sciences and School of Sacred Sciences (Instituto de Ciencias Sagradas et Escuela de Ciencias Sagradas) in Buenos Aires; (4) Institute of Theology (Instituto de Teologia) in Buenos Aires, with departments for catechesis, diaconate, spirituality and sacred music; (5) Pastoral Institute for Adolescents (Instituto Pastoral de la Adolescencia, IPA), founded in Buenos Aires in 1968 by the FSC, which is concerned with catechesis and specialized pastoralia.

Other Catholic organizations include: (1) Argentine Missionary Action (Acción Misionera Argentina, AMA) a lay movement approved by the episcopate for the evangelization of the underdeveloped interior region (485 missionaries in 31 teams in 16 dioceses in 1970); and (2) Argentine Catholic Information Agency (Agencia Informativa Católica Argentina, AICA).

The Higher Council for Catholic Education (Consejo Superior de Educación Católica) estimates that 70–80% of private instruction is Catholic. Statistics for the entire private educational sector (number of private students, followed by that number as a % of the total number of students at that level) in 1969 were as follows: pre-primary 61,492 (29%); primary 526,740 (15%); secondary 304,833 (33%); superior university 32,133 (13%; of which 18,571 are in Catholic universities); superior extra-university 11,051 (33%); superior studies not forming part of the formal educational system 245,414 (80%). By 1973 schools numbered 1,411 primary (447,286 pupils) and 986 secondary (212,631). Catholic universities are found in Buenos Aires (Pontificia Universidad Católica and Universidad Salvador), Cordoba, Cuyo, La Plata, Mar del Plata, Santa Fe and Santiago del Estero.

Caritas Argentina co-ordinates all Catholic social service activities and in 1950 had committees in 49 of the 51 dioceses. Other organizations concerned with social service are: (1) Argentine Catholic Commission for the Fight against Hunger (Comisión Católica Argentina de la Lucha contra el Hambre) which promotes conscientization concerning hunger in the world; (2) Emaus, founded in 1955, which trains leaders for self-help in social service; (3) League of Family Mothers (Liga de Madres de Familia) with 70,300 participants in 384 sections, which is dedicated to the protection of the family; (4) League of Family Fathers (Liga de Padres de Familia), with 35,000 participants, which places its accent on the problem of housing; (5) Federation of Catholic Workers' Circles (Federación de Círculos Católicos de Obreros) founded in 1892, with 237,019 participants who engage in social work among the working class. There are also Conferencias Vicentinas de Hombres (men), and Conferencias Vicentinas de Mujeres (women).
IGLESIA DE LOS HERMANOS LIBRES. Also known as Plymouth Brethren. *Charismatics.* A Neo-pentecostal renewal, Movimiento de Renovación, begun in Buenos Aires in 1963 and by 1970 had spread to involve 5,000 (20%) of adult members of the Brethren Assemblies. From there the movement has spread to other countries including as far as Costa Rica.
TESTIGOS DE JEHOVA. Known also as Jehovah's Christian witnesses. Growth has been exceptionally rapid, to 486 congregations in 1973 and 604 in 1976; adult members have grown from 1,500 in 1950 to over 31,000 by 1976. In mid-1976 the government ordered all 604 congregations by edict to be closed, thus forcing the movement underground.
UNION NACIONAL DE LAS ASAMBLEAS DE DIOS. Since the 1954 revival in Buenos Aires, congregations have grown from 50 in 1954 to 164 in 1970 and to 260 in 1977.

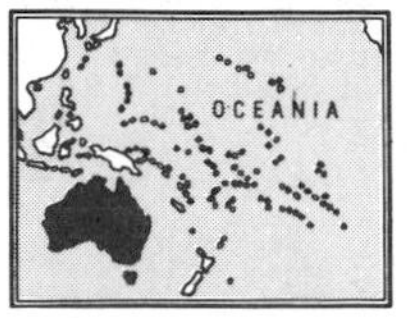


# AUSTRALIA

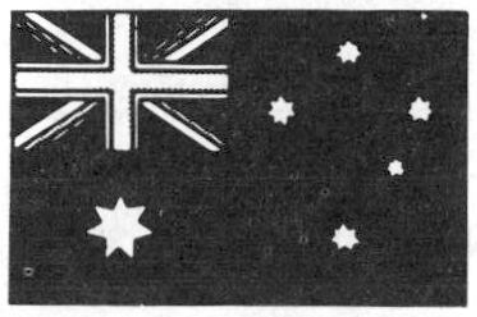

## SECULAR DATA

**STATE. Official name:** The Commonwealth of Australia. Adjective of nationality: Australian.
**Flag** (shown above right): Blue field with Union Jack, white star, five smaller stars.
**Area:** 7,686,848 sq.km. (2,967,909 sq.miles). **Agricultural land:** 64.9%.
**Government:** Federal parliamentary state (also constitutional monarchy), since 1901 (1770 British possession, 1859 six colonies).
**Legislature:** Parliament: Senate, 64 members; House of Representatives, 127 members.
**Official language:** English.
**Chief cities:** capital Canberra 185,000 (1973), Sydney 2,874,380, Melbourne 2,583,900, Brisbane 911,000, Adelaide 868,000.
**Political divisions:** 6 States (New South Wales, Victoria, Queensland, South Australia, Tasmania, Western Australia).
**Armed forces** (1976): Total 69,350 regular: army 31,600, navy 16,200, air force 21,550 (183 combat aircraft). **Reserves:** 26,690.
**Foreign forces** (1973): 1,000 USA troops.
**Dependencies:** Australian Capital Territory (ACT), Northern Territory, Australian Antarctic Territory, Christmas Island, Cocos (Keeling) Islands, Heard & McDonald Islands, Lord Howe Island, Macquarie Island, Norfolk Island.

**DEMOGRAPHY. Population:** 12,755,638 (census of 30.VI.1971. For 1970–2000 (UN), see last row of Table 1). Population density

(1975): 2/sq.km. (5/sq.mile). Under 15 years: 30%. Growth rate (1975–80): 1.84% per year (births 2.14%, deaths −0.80%, immigrants 0.50%). Life expectancy (1975–80): 72.8 years. Household size: 3.3 persons.
**Major languages:** English, Greek, Italian, German, Polish, Irish, Serbo-Croatian, Dutch, Maltese, Arabic, Hungarian, Chinese, Welsh, Russian, Ukrainian, and 260 Aboriginal languages.
**Urban dwellers** (1970): 84.4%. Urban growth rate (1950–70): 2.6% per year.
**Labour force:** 44%.
**Refugees** (1977): From abroad, 62,000 (58.000 from Eastern Europe, about 4,000 from Portuguese Timor, et alia). (1979): A further 20,000, from Viet Nam and Cambodia.
**Tourists** (1972): 426,403. (1973) 472,124.

**ETHNOLINGUISTIC GROUPS:** 82.5% Anglo-Australian (British stock: 50% English, 20% Irish, 10% Scottish, 2% Welsh), 5.2% English, 1.6% Greek, 1.3% Italian, 1.3% Scottish, 1.1% Aborigine (138,000, of whom 106,300 pure-blooded; 260 languages), 1.0% German, 0.6% Polish, 0.5% Jewish, 0.5% Irish, 0.5% New Zealander, 0.5% Serbian, 0.4% Dutch, 0.4% Maltese, 0.3% Austrian, 0.3% Arab, 0.3% Hungarian, 0.3% Chinese (35,000) (Cantonese, Hakka, Mandarin), 0.2% Welsh, 0.2% Latvian, 0.2% Russian, 0.2% Ukrainian, 0.1% Armenian (25,000 by 1978), 0.1% USA, 0.1% Czech, 0.1% Torres Strait Islander (9,700), Macedonian (6,000), Romanian (5,000), Assyrian, (9,000 by 1979), Bulgar, Croat, Slovene, Slovak, Albanian, Hungarian, Finnish, Estonian, Malay, Javanese, Turkish (20,000 by 1977), Basque, Japanese, Gypsy.

**MONEY** (1977). **Monetary unit:** dollar (= 100 cents); US$1 = A$0.94 (operational rate of exchange).
**National income per person:** US$5,460. Average annual family income: US$18,018.
**Inflation:** (1970–74) 9.1% per year, (1975) 15% per year (consumer price index 180), (1977) 9% per year.

**Cost of living in capital** (1976): index 117 (Washington DC = 100). Daily cost of living: US$47.

**EDUCATION.** Adult literacy: 99%. Education rate: 61%. Schools: 8,237. Universities: 15.

**HEALTH.** Hospitals: 2,297 (160,552 beds). Doctors: 16,107. Lepers: 1,500 (0.1 per 1,000). Blind: 18,820. Psychotics: 110,000. Drug addicts: 11,000 (7,644 cannabis, 3,000 opiates). Criminals: 160,000.

**LITERATURE.** Annual new book titles (1972): 3,579. Periodicals: 2,041. Scientific journals: 460. Newspapers: 62 dailies, 538 non-daily.

**COMMUNICATION** (per 1,000 people). Phones: 355. Radios: 213. TV sets: 227. Daily newspaper circulation: 408 copies.

TABLE 1. RELIGIOUS ADHERENTS IN AUSTRALIA

| Year | 1900 | | mid-1970 | | Annual change, 1970–1980 | | | | mid-1975 | | mid-1980 | | 2000 | |
|---|---|---|---|---|---|---|---|---|---|---|---|---|---|---|
| *Name* | *Adherents* | *%* | *Adherents* | *%* | *Natural* | *Conversion* | *Total* | *Rate* | *Adherents* | *%* | *Adherents* | *%* | *Adherents* | *%* |
| **Christians** | **3,640,300** | **96.5** | **11,659,850** | **92.9** | **229,039** | **−121,754** | **107,285** | **0.88** | **12,221,000** | **88.5** | **12,732,700** | **84.1** | **16,540,100** | **81.7** |
| professing | 3,640,300 | 96.5 | 11,659,850 | 92.9 | 229,039 | −121,754 | 107,285 | 0.88 | 12,221,000 | 88.5 | 12,732,700 | 84.1 | 16,540,100 | 81.7 |
| Anglicans | 1,502,200 | 39.8 | 4,242,580 | 33.8 | 79,620 | −82,988 | −3,368 | −0.08 | 4,248,340 | 30.8 | 4,208,900 | 27.8 | 5,054,100 | 25.0 |
| Roman Catholics | 855,800 | 22.7 | 3,589,870 | 28.6 | 75,310 | 13,843 | 89,153 | 2.22 | 4,018,400 | 29.1 | 4,481,400 | 29.6 | 6,478,400 | 32.0 |
| Protestants | 1,274,300 | 33.8 | 3,363,940 | 26.8 | 62,182 | −54,396 | 7,786 | 0.23 | 3,424,600 | 24.8 | 3,441,800 | 22.7 | 4,049,000 | 20.0 |
| Orthodox | 5,000 | 0.1 | 351,460 | 2.8 | 9,505 | 769 | 10,274 | 2.56 | 400,460 | 2.9 | 454,200 | 3.0 | 708,600 | 3.5 |
| Marginal Protestants | 3,000 | 0.1 | 100,000 | 0.8 | 2,174 | 1,026 | 3,200 | 2.76 | 116,000 | 0.8 | 132,000 | 0.8 | 220,000 | 1.1 |
| Catholics (non-Roman) | 0 | 0.0 | 9,000 | 0.1 | 186 | −6 | 180 | 1.82 | 9,900 | 0.1 | 10,800 | 0.1 | 20,000 | 0.1 |
| Non-White indigenous | 0 | 0.0 | 3,000 | 0.0 | 62 | −2 | 60 | 1.82 | 3,300 | 0.0 | 3,600 | 0.0 | 10,000 | 0.0 |
| nominal | 419,200 | 11.1 | 2,073,182 | 16.5 | 45,291 | 27,481 | 72,772 | 3.01 | 2,416,600 | 17.5 | 2,800,900 | 18.5 | 4,656,300 | 23.0 |
| affiliated | 3,221,100 | 85.4 | 9,586,668 | 76.4 | 183,748 | −149,235 | 34,513 | 0.35 | 9,804,400 | 71.0 | 9,931,800 | 65.6 | 11,883,800 | 58.7 |
| total practising | 2,898,990 | *90* | 7,861,070 | *82* | 148,836 | −140,937 | 8,437 | 0.11 | 7,941,560 | *81* | 7,945,440 | *80* | 8,318,700 | *70* |
| non-practising | 322,110 | *10* | 1,725,600 | *18* | 34,912 | −8,836 | 26,076 | 1.40 | 1,862,840 | *19* | 1,986,360 | *20* | 3,565,100 | *30* |
| Anglicans | 1,357,200 | 36.0 | 3,775,628 | 30.1 | 69,909 | −82,472 | −12,563 | −0.34 | 3,730,200 | 27.0 | 3,650,000 | 24.1 | 4,049,000 | 20.0 |
| Evangelicals | 882,000 | 23.4 | 1,548,000 | 12.3 | 28,596 | −33,996 | −5,400 | −0.35 | 1,525,800 | 11.0 | 1,494,000 | 9.9 | 1,660,000 | 8.2 |
| Anglican pentecostals | 0 | 0.0 | 2,000 | 0.0 | 375 | 2,425 | 2,800 | 14.00 | 20,000 | 0.1 | 30,000 | 0.2 | 110,000 | 0.5 |
| Roman Catholics | 840,000 | 22.3 | 3,035,201 | 24.2 | 63,665 | 10,315 | 73,980 | 2.18 | 3,397,000 | 24.6 | 3,775,000 | 24.9 | 5,057,900 | 25.0 |
| Catholic pentecostals | 0 | 0.0 | 1,000 | 0.0 | 225 | 1,975 | 2,200 | 18.33 | 12,000 | 0.1 | 23,000 | 0.2 | 100,000 | 0.5 |
| Protestants | 1,017,900 | 27.0 | 2,340,852 | 18.6 | 41,149 | −78,414 | −37,265 | −1.70 | 2,195,600 | 15.9 | 1,968,200 | 13.0 | 2,004,300 | 9.9 |
| Evangelicals | 680,000 | 18.0 | 750,000 | 6.0 | 13,175 | −24,975 | −11,800 | −1.68 | 703,000 | 5.1 | 632,000 | 4.2 | 640,000 | 3.2 |
| Neo-pentecostals | 0 | 0.0 | 1,000 | 0.0 | 375 | 3,525 | 3,900 | 19.50 | 20,000 | 0.1 | 40,000 | 0.3 | 200,000 | 1.0 |
| Orthodox | 4,000 | 0.1 | 331,600 | 2.6 | 6,857 | 853 | 7,710 | 2.11 | 365,900 | 2.6 | 408,700 | 2.7 | 546,600 | 2.7 |
| Orthodox pentecostals | 0 | 0.0 | 200 | 0.0 | 19 | 161 | 180 | 18.00 | 1,000 | 0.0 | 2,000 | 0.0 | 10,000 | 0.0 |
| Marginal Protestants | 2,000 | 0.1 | 91,887 | 0.7 | 1,930 | 481 | 2,411 | 2.34 | 103,000 | 0.7 | 116,000 | 0.8 | 200,000 | 1.0 |
| Catholics (non-Roman) | 0 | 0.0 | 8,500 | 0.1 | 176 | 4 | 180 | 1.91 | 9,400 | 0.1 | 10,300 | 0.1 | 18,000 | 0.1 |
| Non-White indigenous | 0 | 0.0 | 3,000 | 0.0 | 62 | −2 | 60 | 1.82 | 3,300 | 0.0 | 3,600 | 0.0 | 8,000 | 0.0 |
| Non-religious | 38,000 | 1.0 | 561,750 | 4.5 | 21,604 | 107,901 | 129,505 | 11.23 | 1,152,700 | 8.3 | 1,856,800 | 12.3 | 2,772,100 | 13.7 |
| Atheists | 500 | 0.0 | 200,000 | 1.6 | 5,435 | 13,565 | 19,000 | 6.55 | 290,000 | 2.1 | 390,000 | 2.6 | 640,000 | 3.2 |
| Jews | 15,200 | 0.4 | 62,500 | 0.5 | 1,289 | 1 | 1,290 | 1.88 | 68,800 | 0.5 | 75,400 | 0.5 | 100,000 | 0.5 |
| Muslims | 10,000 | 0.3 | 25,000 | 0.2 | 515 | −15 | 500 | 1.82 | 27,500 | 0.2 | 30,000 | 0.2 | 101,000 | 0.5 |
| Buddhists | 6,000 | 0.2 | 12,000 | 0.1 | 225 | −225 | 0 | 0.00 | 12,000 | 0.1 | 12,000 | 0.1 | 10,000 | 0.0 |
| Baha'is | 0 | 0.0 | 9,100 | 0.1 | 191 | 29 | 220 | 2.16 | 10,200 | 0.1 | 11,300 | 0.1 | 20,000 | 0.1 |
| Tribal religionists | 50,000 | 1.3 | 5,000 | 0.0 | 90 | −130 | −40 | −0.83 | 4,800 | 0.0 | 4,600 | 0.0 | 3,900 | 0.0 |
| Chinese folk-religionists | 10,000 | 0.3 | 5,000 | 0.0 | 94 | −94 | 0 | 0.00 | 5,000 | 0.0 | 5,000 | 0.0 | 5,000 | 0.0 |
| Sikhs | 0 | 0.0 | 1,800 | 0.0 | 37 | 3 | 40 | 2.00 | 2,000 | 0.0 | 2,200 | 0.0 | 2,900 | 0.0 |
| Other religionists | 0 | 0.0 | 10,000 | 0.1 | 281 | 719 | 1,000 | 6.67 | 15,000 | 0.1 | 20,000 | 0.1 | 50,000 | 0.2 |
| **Country's population** | **3,770,000** | **100.0** | **12,552,000** | **100.0** | **258,800** | **0** | **258,800** | **1.87** | **13,809,000** | **100.0** | **15,140,000** | **100.0** | **20,245,000** | **100.0** |

COLUMNS, ROWS. For meanings and definitions, see Codebook (Part 6). Note that, by definition, total 'Christians' = professing + crypto-Christians, which also = affiliated + nominal Christians. Percentages may not always total exactly, due to rounding.
CENSUSES. Most of the official censuses have excluded Aborigines; they have therefore been adjusted to include Aborigines for the table above. **1891:** 39.7% Anglicans, 34.1% Protestants (12.8% Methodists, 11.3% Presbyterians, 2.3% Baptists), 23.0% Roman Catholics, 1.3% non-religious, 0.5% Jews, 0.5% Chinese folk-religionists, 0.4% Muslims, 0.3% Buddhists, 0.2% tribal religionists, 0.1% marginal Protestants. **1901:** 40.3% Anglicans, 34.1% Protestants (13.6% Methodists, 11.5% Presbyterians, 2.4%. Baptists), 23.1% Roman Catholics, 1.0% non-religious, 0.4% Jews, 0.3% Chinese folk-religionists, 0.3% Muslims, 0.2% Buddhists, 0.1% tribal religionists, 0.1% marginal Protestants. **3.IV.1911:** 39.4% Anglicans, 36.5% Protestants (12.9% Presbyterians, 12.6% Methodists, 2.2% Baptists), 21.3% Roman Catholics, 0.6% non-religious, 0.4% Jews, 0.4% Buddhists, Muslims and Chinese folk-religionists. **30.VI.1947** (excluding 47,000 full-blooded Aborigines): 74.5% Anglicans & Protestants, 23.2% Roman Catholics, 0.5% Jews, 0.4% non-religious, 0.3% other religionists, 0.1% Orthodox. **30.VI.1954:** 72.7% Agnlicans & Protestants, 25.4% Roman Catholics, 0.9% Orthodox, 0.6% Jews, 0.3% non-religious, 0.1% other religionists. **30.VI.1961** (excluding full-blooded Aborigines): 39.0% Anglicans, 29.5% Protestants, 27.9% Roman Catholics, 1.6% Orthodox, 0.7% marginal Protestants, 0.7% non-religious, 0.6% Jews. **30.VI.1966** (excluding Aborigines): 36.2% Anglicans, 28.3% Roman Catholics, 27.8% Protestants, 4.0% non-religious, 2.4% Orthodox, 0.7% marginal Protestants, 0.6% Jews. **30.VI.1971:** 33.0% Anglicans. 28.7% Roman Catholics, 26.0% Protestants, 7.4% non-religious and atheists, 2.8% Orthodox, 0.8% marginal Protestants, 0.5% Jews, 0.2% Muslims, 0.1% other religionists.
POLLS. Numerous public-opinion polls of religion have been taken since 1940 (Gallup, Morgan Research Centre, et alia). Some results are given below.

NOTES ON RELIGIONS
ANGLICAN PENTECOSTALS. Anglicans in the charismatic renewal numbered in 1975 about 10,000 adults including 100 clergy in over 200 prayer groups (total charismatic community including children, 20,000, increasing rapidly). This total includes a number of young Jesus People.
ATHEISTS. Communist Party of Australia (CPA) (legal; critical of Soviet Union) and 3 rival parties: membership (1970) 3,900.
BAHA'IS. Entered before 1921. Recent growth from 32 local spiritual assemblies (1964) to 61 (1973; 3 in Tasmania). In Sydney, there is one of the world's 7 Baha'i temples. Large numbers of missionaries have been sent from Australia to Oceania.
BUDDHISTS. Chinese, Japanese, Tibetans and Thais, mainly in cities; including Buddhist Federation of Australia, Chinese Buddhist Society of NSW, Chinese Temple Society, 150 Thai Buddhist students (Sydney).
CATHOLIC PENTECOSTALS (or, Catholic charismatics). Totals (January 1974): 5,000 involved adults (over 15 years old) in 80 prayer groups; total charismatic community including children, 10,000. By 1976, 7,000 adults were involved.
EVANGELICALS. Consisting of 3 groupings: (1) Anglican Evangelicals, (2) Evangelicals, affiliated to Protestant denominations which are Conservative Evangelical in theology, and (3) Evangelicals (sometimes called Conciliar Evangelicals) who are affiliated to non-evangelical Protestant denominations usually within the Ecumenical Movement.
JEWS. Orthodox and Liberal congregations and 1 Sefardi synagogue with 1,000 members.
MUSLIMS. The first Muslims were Afghan camel-drivers in the 1860s. There are now mosques in Canberra, Brisbane, Mareeba, Shepparton, Adelaide, Perth, Melbourne and Sydney; and there is an Australian Federation of Islamic Societies (HQ Victoria). Muslims have immigrated from Lebanon and Yugoslavia, and in recent years over 10,000 Turks have settled in the Sydney-Wollongong region. There are 2 Druze communities (Adelaide, Sydney). There is also a small Ahmadiya Mission in Western Australia. *Haji pilgrims to Mecca* (1976). 22.
NEO-PENTECOSTALS. Charismatics in organized groups within the Methodist, Presbyterian and other non-Pentecostal Protestant denominations, including 10,000 young Jesus People (1973; none before 1969). By 1976, around 30,000 persons were involved.
NON-WHITE INDIGENOUS. In about 7 denominations in 1970 (see Table 2).
ORTHODOX. Numbers have increased rapidly since 1950 by large-scale immigration from Europe and the Middle East.
ORTHODOX PENTECOSTALS (or, Orthodox charismatics). Mainly in the Greek and Russian (ROCOR) churches.
OTHER RELIGIONISTS. There are a large and rapidly-growing number of adherents of other non-Christian religions and syncretistic cults: Hindus (including ISKCON (Hare Krishna) with 3 centres and 470 adherents, Ananda Marga (Path of Bliss) with 14 centres and 250 active members, Eckankar, Ramakrishna Vedanta Society, et alia), Japanese New-Religionists (including 477 adherents of Soka Gakkai, 330 being non-Asians), Rosicrucians (10 AMORC Lodges in 1977, 1 centre (Adelaide) of Lectorium Rosicrucianum, and 2 independent bodies: Rosicrucian Fraternal Society, and Rosicrucian Fellowship, both in Sydney), Subud (300 adherents; a 1925 New Religion from Indonesia), Theosophists (15 Lodges in 1975 with 1,630 members), about 500 Parsis, and numerous others.
PRACTISING CHRISTIANS. *Church attendance*. 1948: weekly, 35% of whole population. 1961–70: 'How long is it since you last went to church, apart from weddings, christenings, funerals, etc?': 1961: 29% 1–7 days ago, 7% 8–14 days ago, 8% 3–4 weeks ago, 23% 2–12 months ago, 33% longer or never. 1970 (same 5 categories): 25%, 6%, 5%, 24%, 40%. 1972 (same 5 categories): 21%, 4%, 6%, 21%, 48%. June 1976: 20% attend weekly (by states: Queensland 19%, NSW 22%, Victoria 20%, Tasmania 9%, SA 26%, WA 14%). *Attendance, by denomination*. 1970: at least once a month: Roman Catholics 61%, Baptists 54%, Presbyterians 32%, Methodists 31%, Anglicans 22%. 1972: regular attendance: Roman Catholics 54%, Baptists 47%, Presbyterians 29%, Methodists 26%, Anglicans 18%. June 1976: 42% of Roman Catholics are weekly attenders, 9% of Anglicans, 11% of Presbyterians, 16% of Methodists. 56% of Baptists. These polls indicate a decline in church attendance at public worship over the period 1961–72, as follows: weekly, from 29% of the population to 21%; monthly or more, from 44% to 31%; and all annual attenders from 67% to 52%. To the latter (1972) figures must be added (about 5%) for radio/TV listeners (sick, infirm, elderly, handicapped).
SIKHS. In 2 organized groups with 1 temple at Woolgoolga (NSW).
TRIBAL RELIGIONISTS. Aborigines declined in number from 300,000 in 1,000 bands in 1770, to 80,000 by 1900, when a majority still retained their traditional religion. By 1970 Aborigines numbered 138,000 (106,300 pure-blooded, though only 40,000 of full descent), and pagans had shrunk to less than 5%. Animistic peoples in 1973: Murngin (Wulamba; population 3,500), Gugu-Yalanji (500), Iwaidja (250), Yanyula (150).

**NON-CHRISTIAN RELIGIONS. Traditional aboriginal religion** is still a significant factor, although a majority of Aborigines now profess to be Christians. The key religious specialist is the medicine man (called *kunki* among the Dieri) who maintains contact with the spirits (Kutchi) and divinities (Mura-muras), the latter being the spirits of the early inhabitants of the region. Appeal with elaborate ceremonies is made to the Mura-muras in time of drought and during rites of passage, especially death. In addition there is a belief in a supreme being known by various tribes as Biamban, Bunjil, Munga-ngama, Nurelli and Nurrundere.

**Other religions** include Judaism (0.5% of the population in 1971) and Islam (0.2%), in addition to small groups of Baha'is (61 local spiritual assemblies) and Buddhists in the larger urban centres. The Jewish community sponsors 10 schools with an enrolment of 3,766 pupils. In 1971, 6.7% of the population stated that they had no religion.

**CHRISTIANITY.** In 1770 captain James Cook took possession of the east coast of Australia for Britain. The slow growth of the churches in the early days can be attributed in part to the fact that Australia was initially used as a penal colony for Britain, the first convicts and soldiers being sent to what is now Sydney in 1788. This practice continued until 1853 in Tasmania and 1868 in Australia itself. Another factor was the early tendency of the population to cluster into urban centres to which the European clergy were unaccustomed. The rest of the population on the other hand went either to sparsely-

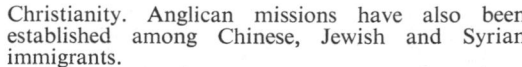

populated and inaccessible ranching areas, or to mining camps with a transient male population unprepared for settled church community life. Churches tended to be strongest in the south.

The discovery of gold in 1851 increased the flow of settlers and 6 colonies including Tasmania had been organized by 1859. These remained independent until a commonwealth was formed in 1901. Following World War II the government encouraged immigration to work in Australia's expanding industries, and 2 million immigrants had arrived by 1970. These recent arrivals have been predominantly from

southern Europe, with a few from Asia, resulting in an increase in the Catholic population in comparison to the early years when settlers were mostly from the British Isles and hence Anglicans or Protestants.

In 1971, 91.7% of the population claimed to be Christian: 33.0% Anglican, 28.7% Roman Catholic, 26.4% Protestant (a third each Methodist and Presbyterian), with the rest belonging to a large number of other churches. Australian Christianity has tended to reproduce the denominational pattern of the British Isles, although more cosmopolitan in membership at the present time. Thus Anglicans are mostly of English origin, Methodists Welsh, Presbyterians Scottish and Catholics Irish. Australian Christianity is further characterized by the relative absence of new groups of local origin, such as are found in the USA or New Zealand. Ties to British churches have been retained for many years through clergy and funds sent from Britian.

ANGLICAN CHURCH. Chaplains arrived in 1788 with the first convicts sent to Australia, and to Tasmania in 1804. Samuel Marsden, arriving in 1793, was responsible for much of the development of the church and accompanying social services throughout Australia and the South Pacific until his death in 1838. In 1823 both Australia and Tasmania were placed under the bishopric of Calcutta; in 1836 a bishop was appointed for Australia, and the country was divided into 5 dioceses by 1847. In 1853 the discovery of gold in Victoria resulted in an increase in state funds which made possible grants to several

denominations, about half going to the Anglican church. Both Victoria and South Australia were settled by non-convict immigrants, and 6 Anglican clergy were sent to South Australia when it became a diocese 11 years after the first settlers arrived. The only minister in Western Australia for many years was the Church of England chaplain at Perth, until the first British missionary arrived in 1836. In 1856 Perth became a separate diocese. Queensland, originally a part of New South Wales, received its first bishop in 1859 while Northern Australia with a large Aborigine population did not have a bishop until 1900.

Of all the denominations, the Anglican Church has carried out the most work among nomadic Aborigines, who were living throughout Australia in some 680 different groups when the first Europeans arrived. As Whites took over their land, Aborigines were pushed back and gradually declined from 300,000 to a third of that number by the end of the 19th century, although they are now increasing again. In Tasmania natives were completely exterminated. The CMS began work among Aborigines in New South Wales in 1826. Today, in addition to 3 CMS stations, the Church of England in Australia through its Australian Board of Missions provides chaplains for 8 government Aborigine centres. The churches have generally found it difficult to build up congregations of baptized members among Aborigines.

In 1891 a mission was opened among the Kanaka labourers imported from the Pacific Islands between 1862 and 1904, who have been very receptive to

Christianity. Anglican missions have also been established among Chinese, Jewish and Syrian immigrants.

Although Anglican membership increased from 1851 to 1971, in proportion to the total population professing Anglicans have steadily declined, from 53% in 1851, to 40% in 1901, to 39% in 1947, and to 33% in 1971. This decrease is due to immigration from Britain being replaced by immigration from southern Europe. In 1966 Tasmania had the highest proportion of Anglicans (45%) and South Australia the lowest (27%). Anglican schools in 1971 numbered 107 with a total enrolment of 49,010.

CATHOLIC CHURCH. Catholics in Australia are predominantly Irish in background, the result of early convicts from Ireland together with Irish immigrants following on the Irish potato famine. The first Catholic priests were appointed in 1803. During the next 10 years a cathedral in Sydney and the first Catholic school were built. In the 1830s a vicar apostolic was appointed for Australia and another for Tasmania. Subsequent highlights in Catholic history include the International Eucharistic Congress of 1929 in Sydney, and the visit of pope Paul VI in 1970.

Professing Catholics as a percentage of the total population have gradually increased over the years, from 21% in 1947, to 27% in 1966, and to 29% in 1971. This increase has been due to the large numbers of recent immigrants from predominantly Catholic countries including Italy, Malta, Croatia (Yugoslavia) and Poland, and also due to the higher Catholic birth-rate than that in other denominations.

Religious care of migrants is the responsibility of the Federal Catholic Immigration Committee, established in 1947. A total of 137 priests from countries sending immigrants are employed as migrant chaplains, and at least 2 orders specialize in this work, namely Capuchin and Scalabrinian priests in South Australia and Victoria.

Among Aborigines, 26% were Catholics in 1966. Many are in process of assimilation in language and eventually socially into White society. The first Aborigine Catholic priest was ordained in 1975.

Religious practice in the states of New South Wales, Victoria and Tasmania is illustrated by Sunday attendance figures for 1966: Catholics 61%, Methodists 26%, Presbyterians 19%, and Anglicans 14%. Over half of all regular churchgoers are Catholics. For the area as a whole the figure was 30%.

The Irish influence in Australian Catholicism has remained dominant until very recently. The Irish bishops who came to Australia were mostly conservative products of Roman seminaries. Even by 1971 all 7 archbishops had trained for the priesthood at the Urban College of Propaganda Fide, Rome. This Irish background is responsible for the pragmatism of Australian Catholicism, as shown in the building of churches, operating social services and comprehensive Catholic primary and secondary school systems, and there has been little interest in theological

Catholic Church in Australia. *Above.* Pope Paul VI arrives at Randwick Racecourse, Sydney, during visit on 1 December 1970. *Below.* Part of crowd of 250,000 as pope celebrated mass.

renewal. At Vatican II it was noteworthy that the Australian bishops refused to be assisted by theologians.

As a minority group, Australian Catholics have developed a ghetto mentality, and the pastoral attitude of the church has been mainly concerned with defending and keeping the faith. The sense of being a beleaguered minority has helped preserve the notable cohesiveness of the Australian Catholic community, although this cohesiveness is now breaking up as Catholics move from being predominantly working-class to being mainly middle-class. The Catholic school system has partially broken down also.

PROTESTANT CHURCHES. In 1809 settlers built a Presbyterian church and their first minister arrived in 1823. A dispute over whether state financial support ought to be accepted led to a division with 2 separate synods established in New South Wales in 1846, later united in 1864. Presbyterian services were also held in Tasmania in 1823. Australian

A flying Presbyterian padre (Australian Inland Mission) prepares navigational plan across Australian desert.

Presbyterians maintain 4 missions for Aborigines in addition to overseas stations in the New Hebrides, Korea and India. Two Chinese Presbyterian churches are located in Sydney and Melbourne. Professing Presbyterians numbered 10% of the population in 1851, 11% in 1901, 10% in 1947 and 8% in 1971. Victoria has the highest proportion (13%) and South Australia the lowest (4%). In 1971 the church sponsored 33 schools (18,645 pupils), 9 hospitals and 7 clinics.

Methodists were among the early settlers in New South Wales, and through their efforts Samuel Leigh arrived from England in 1815 to serve them. He established the British and Foreign Bible Society in Australia and a home for the poor. In 1855 the first Australasian Conference was held in Sydney. With the influx of settlers to Victoria following the discovery of gold, one out of every ten was Methodist by 1886. Methodism began in Tasmania about 1820 and by the 1840s had become self-supporting. In South Australia, Methodists were relatively more numerous in the early years. By 1876 they had nearly 5 times as many churches as Anglicans had and 30 times as many as Presbyterians. In Western Australia, Methodism remained weak, with no clergy appointed until 1840. Queensland was made a Methodist district in 1863. Methodists early became involved in work among Aborigines, and today Methodist Overseas Missions are responsible for 6 stations in Queensland, one in Western Australia and one in Central Australia. In 1851 professing Methodists numbered 6% of the population, 13% in 1901, 12% in 1947 and 9% in 1971. In 1966 South Australia continued to have the highest proportion of Methodists (21%) while New South Wales had the lowest (7.2%). Methodist schools in 1971 numbered 20 with an enrolment of 12,309.

Through the efforts of the London Missionary Society, Congregationalists early had contact with Australia, but their first congregation was not organized until 1829. Since 1963 negotiations have been carried on by the Congregational, Methodist and Presbyterian churches leading towards the

creation in 1977 of the Uniting Church in Australia.

The first Baptist Church in New South Wales was organized in 1813, followed by the Churches of Christ in 1846, Salvation Army in 1881 and Seventh-day Adventists in 1885. The Lutheran Church, whose original missionaries came from Germany and from the USA Missouri Synod, has 3 missions serving Aborigines. The Churches of Christ also have 3 stations among Aboriginal peoples, while Baptists have missionaries at some government stations. Most missions were opened between 1914 and 1937, and several which owe their origin to Christian initiative are now being administered by government. A large number of other smaller Protestant denominations are also at work in Australia. Pentecostals, though growing, are still few in number.

ORTHODOX CHURCHES. In 1901 professing adherents of Orthodox churches numbered 2% of the population, decreasing to 1% in 1947. With the post-war increase in immigration from Southern Europe, they now make up 2.8% of the population,

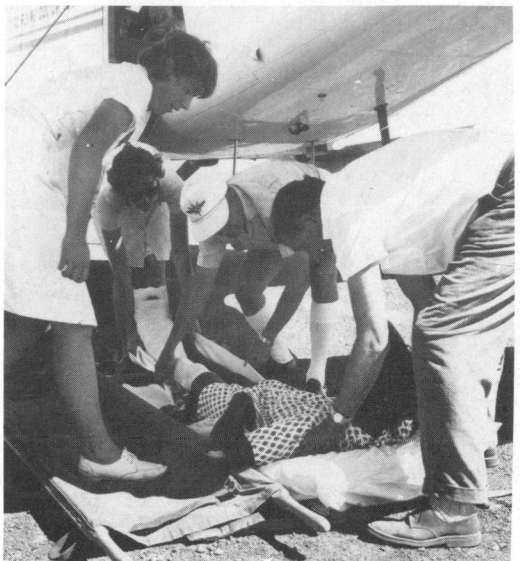

Presbyterian outpost padre and church nursing sister of Australian Inland Mission prepare injured Aboriginal for flight to hospital.

and are divided into 16 distinct communities, the most important being the Greek Orthodox Church.

INDIGENOUS CHURCHES. A variety of pentecostal groups exist among Aborigines, some initiated by trained pastors and some developing spontaneously

CHURCH AND STATE. The Constitution of 9 July 1900, amended 19 December 1946, begins: 'Whereas the people. . ., humbly relying on the blessing of Almighty God, have agreed . . .'

The only legal provision concerning church-state relations in Australia is Scetion 116 of the Australian constitution, modelled on the First Amendment of the constitution of the USA. The section is negative in intent and states simply that there should be no religious test or bar for the holding of public office. It has not been extended by legal interpretation to imply that Australia is formally and officially a secular state, nor that there is a clearly-demarcated wall of separation between the domains of church and state, as the First Amendment has been interpreted in the USA. Some secularists have claimed that Section 116 forbids the giving of financial aid by federal or state governments to such religious organizations as church schools, but this interpretation has not been upheld by the courts. There has been very little legal controversy over Section 116, and except for the question of religious education there has been little church-state conflict in Australia.

Although the Church of England in Australia is numerically the largest religious body, it has no special position nor privileges under the law, nor has any other religious group. Clergy and students for the ministry are however exempt from military service. Members of pacifist Christian bodies including Quakers and Christadelphians are also exempt from military service. Churches receive no direct financial aid from the federal or state governments, and clergy are not paid from government funds. Churches do however receive financial assistance for social services including orphanages, hospitals and family welfare organizations. By virtue of a pro-

gramme to assist Aborigines in the Northern Territory, the Australian government gives a sizeable annual grant to missions run by Anglicans, Catholics and Protestants, which at 5.6 million Australian dollars in 1973 amounted to an increase of 38% over the 1972 grant. Further, church properties and funds are exempt from taxes.

In 1974 for the first time in the history of the country, the Australian government decided to provide subsidies to private schools. One of the required conditions is that interested schools renounce the use of entrance examinations in religion for students who enroll. Education is controlled by federal and state governments, and the syllabus of government schools is non-religious in content, although religious instruction may be given on a voluntary basis from outside. All universities are state institutions and none are operated by churches. There are however denominational colleges within universities which receive governmental subsidies, and facilities are also provided for chaplaincy work. There is no ministry or governmental department in charge of religious or ecclesiastical affairs. Churches are not required to register with either federal or state government.

INTERDENOMINATIONAL ORGANIZATIONS. The Australian Council of Churches (ACC) was begun in 1946 and consists of 12 member and 4 observer churches. In addition there are 7 state councils or committees of churches affiliated with it. Two councils of missions are also active: the National Missionary Council of Australia, which in 1965 became associated with the Australian Council of Churches as its Division of Mission, and the Evangelical Missionary Alliance, an association of mainly non-denominational missionary organizations. Approximately half of Australian Protestant missionaries work in the South Pacific, and one-fifth among Aborigines in Australia.

The Ecumenical Office of the archdiocese of Melbourne is a Catholic body founded in 1933 which presents the Christian message according to the spirit of Vatican II and in co-operation with other churches wherever possible. The Episcopal Conference also sponsors a Committee for Ecumenism.

A Sodepax-type joint secretariat, called Action for World Development, was established in 1970 and is sponsored and supported by the Episcopal Conference and by the Australian Council of Churches. It has embarked on an extensive national programme of development education. Its headquarters is in Brickfield Hill, New South Wales.

Australian Frontier, formerly called the Institute for the Study of Man and Society, is an independent social research institute founded in 1968 which works in co-operation with the churches, government and other institutions. Fields of research are race, development and social concerns.

BROADCASTING. Australia has a national non-commercial system operated by the Australian Broadcasting Commission, which has a Religious Broadcasts Department. There are also numerous licensed commercial radio stations which are required to devote one hour a week to religious material, of which Anglicans and Protestants get 45 minutes and Catholics 15 minutes. Commercial television stations are required to give 1% of their viewing time to the churches' programmes; the Catholic share is 30

Baha'is. First House of Worship (Temple) in Australasia, and one of only 7 in the world, at Ingleside near Sydney, NSW. Known locally as 'The Angel of Sydney', it epitomizes Baha'i claim to unification of all religions under one God.

minutes a week on each TV channel. The tendency in Australia is towards shorter programmes, including 1-minute spots in prime time.

Catholic activity in broadcasting is considerable. In Sydney, the Catholic archdiocese is the major shareholder in the commercial station 2SM, which operates every day 24 hours a day. Catholic production centres include Catholic Radio and TV, in Melbourne, which produces a TV programme each week, and in Sydney a radio and TV centre, founded in 1962, which has production studios assisting Catholic dioceses in mass media work; it has distributed over 500 films. In Homebush, there is the National Catholic Radio & TV Centre established in 1962. UNDA/Australia was formally inaugurated in 1973.

## BIBLIOGRAPHY


'Australia', H. Mol, in *Western religion: a country by country sociological enquiry* (The Hague: Mouton, 1972), p. 27–45.

*Australian Aboriginal religion*. R. M. Berndt. Leiden: Brill, 1974. 151p.

*Australian charismatic directory*. Waverley, NSW: Temple Trust, 1975.

*Australian Evangelical Alliance directory of missions, 1973*. Mont Albert, Victoria: AEA, 1973. 45p.

*Heart of fire: the story of Australian Pentecostalism*. B. Chant. Fullarton, SA: Luke Publications, 1973. 212p.

*Official year book of the Catholic Church in Australia & Papua New Guinea, New Zealand & the Pacific Islands*. Sydney: E. J. Dwyer, 1970. 544p.

*Orthodox and other Eastern churches in Australia*. Townsville, Queensland: Church of England in Australia. n.d. (c 1962). 21p. Second edition 1978.

*Religion in Australia: a sociological investigation*. H. Mol. Melbourne: Nelson, 1971. 380p.

'The Aborigines and the Church'. H. Deakin. Melbourne: Catholic Archdiocese, 1975. 85p.

*The Catholic Church in Australia: a short history, 1788–1967*. P.J.O'Farrell. London: Geoffrey Chapman, 1968. 294p.


TABLE 2. ORGANIZED CHURCHES AND DENOMINATIONS IN AUSTRALIA

| Official name 1 | Begun 2 | Type 3 | Counc 4 | Congs 5 | Adults 6 | Affiliated 7 | Names, notes, and other statistics (see Codebook) 8 |
|---|---|---|---|---|---|---|---|
| Aboriginal pentecostal congregations | 1934 | I pe3 | ••••• | 15 | 1,000 | 2,000 | No White aid. Northeast NSW. Bandjalang tribe and others. 3-stage initiation. |
| Aborigines Inland Mission Fell Ch | 1905 | P ind | •H••E | 152 | 1,400 | 15,000 | *AIM Fellowship Ch.* NSW, NT, Queensland. 8n,113m,G=2.6%pa, 1p,W=80%,550Y,80z. |
| Ancient Assyrian Church of the East | | O Nes | Yw••• | 2 | 3,000 | 4,500 | *Nestorians.* Assyrians. Related to Ch of the East in Iraq and USA. Sydney. 1 priest. |
| Apostolic Church of Australia & NZ | 1928 | P PeA | Z•••• | 35 | 2,008 | 3,100 | Work among Aborigines in west. M=Apostolic Ch(UK). 2s,23n,W=80%,146Y,351z. |
| Apostolic Church of Queensland | c1960 | C CAp | x•••• | 20 | 1,000 | 2,000 | Split ex New Apostolic Ch. In Vereinigung Apostolischer Christen (Switzerland). |
| Armenian Apostolic Church (D India) | c1850 | O Arm | Ewc•W | 2 | 7,000 | 12,000 | *Gregorians.* In D India (Calcutta), under C Echmiadzin. Sydney, Melbourne. 5n. |
| Assemblies of God in Australia | 1922 | P Pe2 | Z•••w | 145 | 5,500 | 12,000 | Slavs, Italians, Finnish; 1,500 Aborigines. M=AoG(USA). 175n,12m,6w,1p,1s,W=88%. |
| Associated Mission Chs of Australia | 1952 | P Pe4 | x•••• | 15 | 400 | 1,000 | *Latter Rain Assemblies.* Radical Pentecostals (government through prophecy, &c). 1p. |
| Australian Aborigines Ev Mission | 1949 | P ind | •H••E | | 1,000 | 2,000 | *AAEM.* In Kundalee, Western Australia. 37 workers. Hostels for working youths. |
| Autocephalic GOC of America & Aust | c1960 | O Gre | ••••• | 10 | 5,000 | 10,000 | Ex Greek OC (AD Australia) by laity opposing hierarchy. In NSW, SA, Victoria. |
| Baptist Union of Australia | 1813 | P Bap | T•••• | 813 | 49,092 | 170,000 | *BUA.* HQ Melbourne. 673n,4x,G=2.4%pa,5p,5s(250),W=85%,2147Y. |
| Bulgarian Orthodox Church | c1950 | O Sla | Mwc•• | 2 | 2,000 | 3,000 | *Balgarskata Pravoslavna Crkva.* In AD N&S America, under P Sofia. Bulgarians. 2nx. |
| Byelorussian Autocephalic Orth Ch | c1950 | Q Sla | x•••• | 4 | 500 | 1,000 | Refugees from White Russian church, suppressed 1922. HQ USA. 1 archbishop. 4n. |
| Catholic Apostolic Church | | C CAp | x•••• | 1 | 200 | 500 | Irvingites from Britain. Declining rapidly from 976 in 1933, and 720 in 1947. |
| **Catholic Church in Australia:** | 1803 | R LEr | B•••s | 1,385 | 2,125,000 | 3,035,201 | From Italy, Poland, Croatia. C=29+8+67.W=61%. 3844nx,2560m,13428w,P=61%,79950Yy. |
| M Adelaide | 1842 | R Lat | Bs | 74 | 135,200 | 193,137 | SAustralia. Metropolitan. Many migrants. 1s. 214 94 670 60 4480 |
| D Darwin | 1847 | R Lat | Bmsc | 6 | 15,000 | 21,000 | Northern Territory. Uninhabitable. Aborigines. 25 12 63 43 639 |
| D Port Pirie | 1887 | R Lat | Bs | 29 | 18,800 | 26,924 | West, north of South Australia, Steel, metals. 40 7 87 60 751 |
| M Brisbane | 1859 | R Lat | Bs | 111 | 191,170 | 273,200 | Tropical agriculture. Charismatics strong. 1s. 292 195 1332 55 6635 |
| D Cairns | 1887 | R Lat | Bs | 23 | 23,200 | 33,210 | Northern Queensland. Aborigines. Agriculture. 32 20 136 46 992 |
| D Rockhampton | 1882 | R Lat | Bs | 37 | 35,000 | 50,000 | North of Brisbane. Mining. Many Aborigines. 76 37 320 71 1659 |
| D Toowoomba | 1929 | R Lat | Bs | 37 | 31,100 | 44,377 | Southwest Queensland. Rich pastoral area. 86 51 188 87 1240 |
| D Townsville | 1930 | R Lat | Bs | 36 | 39,000 | 56,000 | Coastal and back country. Minerals, sugar. 58 47 198 81 1380 |
| M Melbourne | 1847 | R Lat | Bs | 203 | 455,000 | 650,000 | Southern part of Victoria. Commercial. 1s. 825 529 2394 55 18760 |
| D Ballarat | 1874 | R Lat | Bs | 55 | 55,000 | 78,628 | Western part of Victoria. Agriculture, industry. 129 102 449 94 2291 |
| D Sale | 1887 | R Lat | Bs | 27 | 34,000 | 48,537 | EVictoria. Industry, pastoral, agriculture. 43 18 141 99 1881 |
| D Sandhurst | 1874 | R Lat | Bs | 40 | 43,000 | 61,389 | Northern Victoria. Agriculture, light industry. 92 25 316 80 1978 |
| M Perth | 1845 | R Lat | Bs | 105 | 102,100 | 145,800 | SAustralia, desert. Includes Cocos Is. 1s. 224 135 1039 88 5310 |
| D Broome | 1887 | R Lat | Bsac | 8 | 2,700 | 3,800 | Western Australia. Aborigines. 12 9 45 63 253 |
| D Bunbury | 1954 | R Lat | Bs | 26 | 20,000 | 29,000 | Southwest of Western Australia. Agriculture. 39 12 140 47 1510 |
| D Geraldton | 1898 | R Lat | Bs | 15 | 9,200 | 13,200 | WAustralia. Uninhabitable. Mining. Aborigines. 24 24 105 71 413 |
| AN New Norcia | 1867 | R Lat | Bosb | 1 | 300 | 422 | Western Australia, north of M Perth. 22 9 24 99 25 |
| M Sydney | 1842 | R Lat | Bs | 212 | 518,600 | 740,927 | NSW. City of Sydney, suburbs. 3s. 809 832 2952 50 14034 |
| D Armidale | 1869 | R Lat | Bs | 29 | 27,000 | 38,518 | Inland northern NSW. Pastoral, agricultural. 56 23 174 68 1276 |
| D Bathurst | 1865 | R Lat | Bs | 32 | 30,000 | 42,793 | West of Blue Mountains. Agricultural. 64 16 250 95 1382 |
| D Lismore | 1887 | R Lat | Bs | 28 | 31,700 | 45,250 | Northern NSW, coastal. Dairying, agricultural. 63 30 275 83 1214 |
| D Maitland | 1847 | R Lat | Bs | 56 | 61,900 | 88,360 | Coastal NSW. Coal, industry, agriculture. 139 42 554 49 2406 |
| D Wagga Wagga | 1917 | R Lat | Bs | 31 | 30,500 | 43,571 | Southern NSW, along river Murray. Agriculture. 56 30 237 65 1261 |
| D Wilcannia-Forbes | 1887 | R Lat | Bs | 24 | 26,200 | 37,500 | Remote west of NSW. Rural depopulation. 39 19 191 63 1022 |
| D Wollongong | 1951 | R Lat | Bs | 29 | 60,000 | 85,000 | Coastal strip south of Sydney. Steel, mining. 87 50 265 65 2117 |
| AD Canberra | 1862 | R Lat | bs | 57 | 68,000 | 97,000 | Australian Capital Territory. Catholics 32%. 172 149 540 72 2645 |
| AD Hobart | 1842 | R Lat | bs | 47 | 45,200 | 64,618 | State of Tasmania. Major ecumenical activity. 112 42 332 45 2067 |
| EA Australia (*Ukrainian*) | 1958 | R Ukr | Os | 6 | 16,000 | 22,850 | Ukrainians, Ruthenians. Also Oceania,NZ. W=57%. 12 0 8 80 320 |
| m Kalumburu | 1910 | R Lat | Bosb | 1 | 130 | 190 | WAustralia. Drysdale River. Population 235. 2 1 3 98 9 |
| Children of God International | c1969 | P Apo | xv••• | | 500 | 1,000 | From USA. Youth colonies: Melbourne, Sydney. 1973 applied to WCC, ACC (Australia). |
| Christadelphian Ecclesias | | P Ade | x•••• | 109 | 8,000 | 12,000 | *Australian Christadelphian Bible Mission.* 109 ecclesias (churches). Pacifist. |
| Christian & Missionary Alliance | 1969 | P Hol | xF••• | 14 | 138 | 330 | M=CMA(USA). Mostly in NSW, Victoria. HQ Chatswood, NSW. 6n,5x,10f,1s(14),29Y. |
| Christian Brethren | 1870 | P CBr | x•••• | 270 | 14,000 | 30,000 | *Open Brethren.* Strong in Queensland; Aborigines' work. 90m,10f(NZ),1p. |
| Christian Brethren (Exclusive) | | P EBr | x•••• | 122 | 8,300 | 15,000 | *Exclusive* (*Closed*) *Brethren.* Groups; Glanton, Raven Taylor, Kelly-Continental, &c. |
| Christian Israelite Church | | P ind | ••••• | 5 | 500 | 1,000 | Small evangelical body. In Sydney and Strathfield (NSW), also in Indiana (USA). |
| Christian Revival Crusade | 1944 | P Pe2 | x•••h | 59 | 4,000 | 10,000 | *CRC* (NRC till 1952, Commonwealth RC until 1958). 65n,G=20%pa,2s(40),W=88%,300Y. |
| Church of Christ, Scientist | | M Sci | ••••• | 57 | 10,000 | 20,000 | *Christian Science.* M=CCS(Boston, USA). Growth 1933–47: 8,878 to 11,389. 16m,75w. |
| **Church of England in Australia:** | 1788 | A plu | AWEAW | 4,255 | 698,000 | 3,775,628 | Many English clergy. M=USPG,MTS,CA,NZCMS. 131x,35f,9s,W=14%,500Y. 2147n,53400y. |
| Province of New South Wales: | 1847 | A plu | A | 1,538 | 335,000 | 1,564,203 | State of NSW. 3-yearly synod, but all authority rests with dioceses. 890 19500 |
| D Sydney | 1836 | A Low | A | 500 | 200,000 | 1,076,000 | Large urban area. Ministry to instant suburbia. 30x,1s(90),W=15%. 525 10000 |
| D Armidale | 1914 | A Eva | A | 190 | 10,000 | 46,000 | Rural Problems due to sudden collapse of rural industry. W=40%. 50 1170 |
| D Bathurst | 1869 | A ACa | A | 283 | 30,000 | 100,000 | Rural, copper mine. M=Bush Brotherhood. Some Aborigines. W=40%. 67 1510 |
| D Canberra & Goulburn | 1863 | A Cen | A | 52 | 40,000 | 101,203 | Capital, very rapidly expanding. New church buildings appearing. 85 1500 |
| D Grafton | 1914 | A Cen | A | 189 | 25,000 | 70,000 | Rural. Parishes now regrouped into 6 natural regions. 4x,W=20%. 44 1251 |
| D Newcastle | 1847 | A Cen | A | 225 | 20,000 | 130,000 | 80% urban. Coal, steel, 3rd largest port. 1s(30),W=15% 90 3430 |
| D Riverina | 1884 | A Hig | A | 99 | 10,000 | 41,000 | Rural, one zinc mining town. Decline due to rural recession. 29 620 |
| Province of Queensland: | 1905 | A plu | A | 697 | 125,000 | 577,418 | Province covers state and Northern Territory. 346 8435 |
| D Brisbane | 1859 | A ACa | A | 449 | 99,700 | 432,818 | 50% urban. Tractarian tradition. 1s(31),W=12%. 232 6220 |
| D Carpentaria | 1867 | A ACa | a | 33 | 6,000 | 10,000 | Missionary D, in SPAC. Thursday Is. Aerial mission. W=30%. 27 250 |
| D North Queensland | 1878 | A Hig | A | 117 | 8,000 | 78,000 | Rural, 4 urban areas. Home of Bush Brotherhood. 10x,1H,3r. 42 1149 |
| D Rockhampton | 1892 | A Hig | A | 53 | 10,000 | 48,000 | Far West. Aerial Mission at work in remote outback. 26 715 |
| D The Northern Territory | 1968 | A plu | a | 45 | 1,300 | 8,600 | Missionary diocese. M=CMS,BGS,BCAS. Aborigines parishes. 1p,W=35%. 19 101 |
| Province of South Australia: | 1971 | A plu | A | 328 | 28,800 | 258,183 | State of SA. 3-yearly synod, but all authority rests with dioceses. 162 3681 |
| D Adelaide | 1847 | A Hig | A | 129 | 22,036 | 206,527 | 1970, diocese of The Murray separated off. 1s(7). 111 2607 |
| D The Murray | 1970 | A Hig | A | 87 | 4,600 | 43,000 | Formed from D Adelaide. 50% rural. Parishes: 20 rural, 2 urban. 28 589 |
| D Willochra | 1914 | A Eva | A | 112 | 2,164 | 8,656 | 3 rapidly-growing cities. Some Aborigines. 5x,P=37%,W=12%. 23 485 |
| Province of Victoria: | 1905 | A plu | A | 948 | 144,700 | 891,424 | Victoria state. 3-yearly synod, but authority rests with dioceses. 478 12227 |
| D Melbourne | 1847 | A plu | A | 407 | 97,075 | 686,622 | Mainly urban. 1971, divided into 3 Areas of Episcopal Care. 2s(41). 318 8654 |
| D Ballarat | 1875 | A ACa | A | 159 | 20,000 | 55,000 | Rural, with all the problems of rural communities. W=23%. 49 876 |
| D Bendigo | 1901 | A Cen | A | 84 | 7,532 | 34,000 | Rural. 1975, amalgamated with D St Arnaud. W=18%. 25 770 |
| D Gippsland | 1901 | A Cen | A | 124 | 6,993 | 45,000 | 40% urban. 500 Aborigines. Ecumenical experimentation. W=10%. 30 882 |
| D St Arnaud (until 1976) | 1926 | A plu | A | 68 | 4,500 | 26,486 | Rural, fruit industries. 1976, merged with D Bendigo. W=15%. 23 392 |
| D Wangaratta | 1901 | A Hig | A | 106 | 8,600 | 44,316 | Rural diocese adjoining Melbourne and Gippsland. W=15%. 33 653 |
| Province of Western Australia: | 1914 | A plu | A | 429 | 44,500 | 318,400 | State of WA. 3-yearly synod, but all authority rests with dioceses. 184 4566 |
| D Perth | 1856 | A Cen | A | 214 | 30,000 | 234,000 | 75% urban. Rapid urban growth. Some Aborigines. 7r,1s(8),W=40%. 137 3333 |
| D Bunbury | 1904 | A Cen | A | 145 | 12,000 | 67,500 | Rural. Missions to Seamen. 27 English clergy. W=10%. 22 882 |
| D Kalgoorlie (until 1975) | 1913 | A Low | A | 19 | 595 | 5,000 | Rural mining. 1975, merged again with D Perth. W=68%. 6 231 |
| D North West Australia | 1907 | A Cen | A | 51 | 1,905 | 11,900 | Bush diocese with mining areas, new towns. M=BCAS. W=39%. 19 120 |
| D Tasmania | 1842 | A Cen | A | 315 | 20,000 | 166,000 | C of in E Tasmania. Island, 43% Anglican. 74b,2H,1s(7),W=8%. 87 5000 |
| Church of God (Anderson) | 1954 | P Hol | x•••• | 8 | 200 | 500 | M=CoG(Anderson)(USA). Begun by German and USA immigrants. 1 Greek church. 2n. |
| Ch of Jesus C of Latter-day Saints | 1851 | M LdS | x•••• | 100 | 19,000 | 27,087 | *Mormons.* M=CJCLdS(Utah,USA). HQ NSW. Growth: 2,501 (1933), 3,499 (1947). 200f. |
| Church of the Nazarene | 1946 | P Hol | xF••• | 22 | 534 | 2,800 | 3 Churches Greek-speaking. M=CoN(USA). HQ Thornleigh. 25n,1s,SS=2153. |
| Church of the New Jerusalem | | M Swe | x•••• | 1 | 50 | 100 | *Swedenborgian Church.* In Penshurst, NSW. Split in USA ex New Church. |
| Churches of Christ in Australia | 1846 | P Dis | xWE•W | 410 | 42,773 | 94,000 | *Federal Conf.* M=CCCC(Instrumental)(USA). G=–2%pa. 324n,4f,1H,3s(100),W=74%,1393Y. |
| Churches of Christ (Non-Instrumental) | 1949 | P Dis | x•••• | 52 | 1,500 | 3,000 | M=CC(Non-Instrumental)(USA). Across nation. Several churches for the deaf. 28f. |
| Congregational Union of A (Continuing) | 1829 | P Con | RWE•W | 30 | 1,500 | 7,500 | 10% of denomination who refused to enter 1977 Uniting Ch in Australia. W=65%. |
| Cooneyites | c1920 | P ind | x•••• | | 70,000 | 150,000 | *Go-(Tramp-)Preachers.* Irish itinerants, also in UK, USA, South Africa, Ireland. |
| Coptic Orthodox Church (P Alexandria) | c1960 | O Cop | Nwa•W | 4 | 5,000 | 7,000 | Egyptian immigrants since 1947. Churches in Sydney, Melbourne. 2n,2x. |
| Dawn Bible Students Association | | M Jeh | x•••• | 15 | 200 | 500 | Split ex Jehovah's Witnesses. World HQ New Jersey (USA). 15 classes (1 Polish). |
| Estonian Ev Lutheran Church in Exile | 1944 | P Lut | Lwc•• | 1 | 700 | 1,000 | St John's Ch, Sydney. USSR refugees, independent of ELCE (USSR). HQ Stockholm. 1n. |
| Estonian Orthodox Church in Exile | c1940 | O Sla | C•••• | 1 | 1,000 | 2,000 | Estonian refugees after annexation of Estonia by USSR. Bishop in Sweden. |
| Ev Lutheran Congs of the Reformation | | P Lut | ••••• | 5 | 150 | 225 | Independent congregations with office in Kingaroy, Queensland. |
| Evangelical Presbyterian Church of A | c1958 | P Ref | ••••• | 9 | 300 | 700 | 5 Baptist congregations which accepted Westminster Confession. 70% Tasmania. 5n. |
| Fellowship of Evangelical Chs in A | 1956 | P ind | ••••• | 23 | 2,000 | 4,000 | *FECA.* Conservative fellowship of independent congregations. HQ Fitzroy, Victoria. |
| Finnish Evangelical Lutheran Church | 1960 | P Lut | ••••• | 4 | 300 | 475 | *Melbournen Suomalainen.* Finns in Melbourne, Victoria, Tasmania. W=23%,23Yy,11z. |
| Free Reformed Churches of Australia | | P Ref | ••••• | 3 | 500 | 1,500 | Congregations in Launceston and Albany. WA. Calvinistic doctrines. 2n. |
| Free Serbian Orth Ch: D Aus & NZ | c1969 | O Ser | ••••• | 14 | 8,000 | 12,000 | Dissident Yugoslavs rejecting P Belgrade. USA links. One bishop, 9 priests. |

*Continued overleaf*

*Table 2–continued*

| Official name 1 | Begun 2 | Type 3 | Counc 4 | Congs 5 | Adults 6 | Affiliated 7 | Names, notes, and other statistics (see Codebook) 8 |
|---|---|---|---|---|---|---|---|
| Full Gospel Church in Australia | 1962 | P Pen | ..... | 60 | 2,000 | 4,000 | *Associated Full Gospel Chs. Gospel Light Ministry*. Split ex AoG. Many Aborigines. |
| Greater World Chr Spiritualist League | | M Spi | x.... | 2 | 100 | 200 | Chr=Christian. Greater World Sanctuary. In Nowra and Oak Flats, NSW. |
| Greek Orthodox Church: AD Australia | 1896 | O Gre | Cw..W | 95 | 124,400 | 175,100 | All Greeks, recent immigrants. 1959 AD, also E all Oceania. 83nx,W=10%,7000Yy. |
| Independent Greek Orthodox Church | c1950 | O Gre | ..... | 5 | 2,000 | 3,000 | Formed by 10 Greek Orthodox priests looking to Byelorussian AOC archbishop. NSW,SA. |
| Independent Russian Orthodox Church | | O Sla | ..... | 1 | 300 | 500 | One church of Russian emigres, under Greek Orthodox Ch, AD Australia. |
| Internat Ch of the Foursquare Gospel | 1923 | P Pe2 | ZF... | 22 | 596 | 2,000 | *Gospel Lighthouse Chs*. M=ICFG(USA). Finns, Arabs, Swedes, &c. 39nm,2f,1s,W=60%,34Y. |
| Jehovah's Witnesses | 1896 | M Jeh | x.... | 470 | 23,387 | 34,000 | *Watch Tower*. Branch formed 1904. Missions in Pacific. HQ Strathfield, NSW. 1808Y. |
| Latvian Ev Lutheran Church in Exile | 1948 | P Lut | lw... | 19 | 8,943 | 13,503 | *Latvijas Ev Lut Baznica*. Melbourne and District. 11n,G=–3.0%pa,W=50%,126Yy,128z. |
| Liberal Catholic Church | 1916 | C Lib | x.... | 12 | 500 | 2,000 | Theosophist. HQ Ryde. 4 churches in Sydney. 3 bishops. 36n,G=0,1s,W=13%,55Yy,35z. |
| Lutheran Church of Australia | 1838 | P Lut | ....w | 751 | 73,816 | 147,859 | 1966 union: ELCA, United ELCA. 10 languages. 336n,3x,G=2.5%pa,1s(90),W=45%,3442Yy. |
| Macedonian Orth Autocephalous Ch | 1960 | O Sla | cv... | 9 | 4,000 | 6,000 | *Makedonska Pravoslavna Crkva*. Macedonian (Slav) immigrants from Yugoslavia. 7nx. |
| Methodist Ch of Australasia Continuing | 1812 | P Met | VWE.W | 400 | 48,000 | 75,000 | 10% of denomination who refused to enter 1977 Uniting Ch in Australia. |
| National Revival Crusade | 1952 | P Pe2 | Z.... | 30 | 1,000 | 2,000 | Slpit 1952 ex CRC with original name NRC. British Israelite. Rejoining CRC. |
| New Apostolic Church | c1900 | C CAp | x.... | 20 | 1,950 | 3,900 | Schism ex Catholic Apostolic Ch (Irvingites) in Europe. HQ Dortmund(Germany). 16n. |
| New Church in Australia | | M Swe | x.... | 6 | 200 | 500 | *Sydney Society*, and others. Swedenborgians. Originally from UK. |
| Old Believers Russian Orthodox Church | | O OBe | x.... | 4 | 100 | 300 | *Old Ritualist Ch*. Schism in Russia 1667 ex Orth Ch. Russian emigres in Auburn. 1n. |
| Orthodox Catholic Church | | C CCa | ..... | 2 | 50 | 100 | Links with American Catholic Ch (USA), OCC (UK). 2 priests. |
| Orthodox Church in America & Canada | | O Sla | Mw... | 2 | 1,000 | 2,000 | *OCA*. Linked with OCA (USA). Russians, other Slavs. HQ Sydney. 2nx. |
| People's Churches | | P ind | .TTTT | 10 | 1,000 | 2,000 | A number of independent congregations. Best-known: Kew and Reservoir (Victoria). |
| Presbyterian Ch of Australia Continuing | 1809 | P Ref | RWE.W | 519 | 43,000 | 150,000 | *PCA*. 30% of denomination who refused to enter 1977 Uniting Ch in Australia. |
| Presbyterian Ch of Eastern Australia | 1846 | P Ref | J.... | 42 | 1,000 | 2,000 | Schism ex PCA. M=Free Ch of Scotland. 3 Presbyteries. North coast of NSW. 15n. |
| Presbyterian Reformed Church of A | 1968 | P Ref | ..... | 13 | 500 | 1,000 | Schism ex Presbyterian Ch of Australia after Geering heresy trial (in NZ). 13n,1p. |
| Reformed Churches of Australia | 1951 | P Ref | J.... | 39 | 4,012 | 8,358 | Immigrants from Europe, mainly Dutch. 6 Classis. Sydney. 29n,G=2.7%pa,W=13%,15Yy. |
| Reformed Presbyterian Ch of Ireland | | P Ref | J.... | 2 | 100 | 200 | *RPC. Australian Presbytery*. Part of Irish church. HQ MacKinnon, Victoria. 2x. |
| Religious Society of Friends in A | 1832 | P Qua | Qv..W | 12 | 842 | 1,154 | *Australian Yearly Meeting*. A=1964. 7 regional meetings. G=–0.3%pa, 1r,W=50%. |
| Reorganized Ch of JC of L–d Saints | | M LdS | x.... | 36 | 1,500 | 4,270 | Schism ex CJCLdS(Mormons). 5 churches in Sydney. World HQ Independence, MO(USA). |
| Revival Centre | 1958 | P Pe4 | ..... | 14 | 300 | 500 | Schism ex CRC. Teaches both water and Spirit baptism essential for salvation. |
| Romanian Orthodox Church | | O Rum | Cwc.. | 3 | 3,500 | 5,000 | *Biserica Orthodoxa Romana*. Under P Bucharest. Romanian immigrants in Melbourne. 4nx. |
| Russian Orthodox Ch Outside of Russia | c1950 | O Sla | x...w | 81 | 14,000 | 21,000 | *Russkaya Pravoslavnaya Cerkov. D Australia & NZ*. 9 churches in Sydney. 17n,1e,1s. |
| Salvation Army | 1881 | P Sal | xwE.W | 910 | 30,000 | 62,000 | *SA*, Eastern Territory, Southern Terr. 16 Divisions. 110 institutions. 1898n,2s. |
| Self-Independent Macedonian Church | | O Sla | ..... | 1 | 100 | 200 | Macedonian Orthodox immigrants in Fitzroy (Victoria). Slavs. 1 Bulgarian priest. |
| Serbian OC (D WEurope, Australia) | c1960 | O Ser | Cwc.W | 17 | 28,000 | 40,000 | *Srpska Pravoslavna Crkva*. Under P Belgrade. Yugoslav immigrants. Bishop,10nx,1d(4). |
| Seventh-day Adventist Church | 1885 | P Adv | x.... | 356 | 34,100 | 39,000 | *Trans-Tasman/Commonwealth UCs*. 210n,G=2%pa,2H,1j,1s,364t(33884),W=95%,1471Y. |
| SDA Reform Movement of Australia | | P Adv | x.... | 6 | 500 | 1,000 | Schism ex Seventh-day Adventist Church; world HQ West Germany. HQ Auburn, NSW. |
| Sydney City Mission | | P int | ..... | 18 | 1,000 | 2,000 | 18 centres including homes for children, aged, and soup kitchens. |
| Syrian Antiochian Orthodox Church | 1920 | O Ara | Cw.NW | 4 | 3,000 | 5,000 | Under Greek Orthodox P Antioch. Lebanese in NSW, Victoria. Bishop, 5 priests. |
| Ukrainian Autoceph Orth Ch in A & NZ | 1948 | O Sla | X.... | 16 | 8,000 | 15,000 | *AD Aust & NZ, UOCUSA*. Factions: Metropolitan Diocese, United Diocese, Council-led. 14n. |
| Ukrainian OC (Autocephalic) of Aust | | O Sla | X.... | 15 | 2,000 | 4,000 | Ukrainian emigres rejecting USA links of UAOCANZ. Under UGOCC(Canada). 9 priests. |
| Unitarian & Liberal Christian Chs | 1850 | M Unt | I.... | 7 | 1,000 | 2,000 | *Australian Assembly of OLCC*. In UFCC(UK), UUA(USA). Declining. HQ Geelong. |
| United Aborigines Mission of Australia | 1895 | P CBr | .H..E | | 2,000 | 5,000 | *UAM*. White mission to Aborigines. 75% in west, some churches in SA,NSW. 73 workers. |
| United Church in NA & the Territories | | P uni | ..... | | 5,000 | 10,000 | Methodist, Presbyterian and Congregational churches in sparsely-populated NT. 1r. |
| United Pentecostal Church | 1954 | P Pe1 | x.... | 25 | 2,000 | 4,000 | *Jesus Only Church*. M=UPC(USA). Unitarian Pentecostals. 10n,3x,6f,1p,1s,W=50%,100Y. |
| **Uniting Church in Australia** | 1809 | P uni | WWE.W | 4,281 | 560,174 | 1,194,088 | *UCA*. 1977 union of Cong Union of A, Methodist Ch of A, Presbyterian Ch of A. 10H. |
| Universal World Church | | P Pen | x.... | 3 | 200 | 500 | North Queensland and Brisbane. All Torres Strait Islanders. HQ Los Angeles (USA). |
| Welsh Calvinistic Methodist Church | | P Ref | Rw... | 3 | 150 | 300 | Parts of Presbyterian Church of Wales. 3 charges in Victoria. 3n. |
| Wesleyan Church | 1945 | P Hol | VF... | 12 | 250 | 960 | M=WC(USA). Mostly in Victoria. 12n,G=1.7%pa,1p,W=52%,27Yy. |
| Worldwide Church of God | | M BrI | x.... | | 500 | 1,000 | *WCC. Radio Ch of God*. M=WCC(Pasadena,USA). HQ North Sydney. By 1975, 2500 members. |
| Other Protestant denominations | | P | ..... | | 42,350 | 74,300 | Total about 80 (see list below), with numerous independent single congregations. |
| Other Orthodox churches | | O | ..... | | 2,000 | 3,000 | Polish, Russians (P Moscow), Spiritual Christians/Molokans, Syrians (Jacobites). |
| Other marginal Protestant bodies | | M | ..... | | 1,300 | 2,230 | Total over 30 (see list below). |
| Other Non-White indigenous churches | | I | ..... | | 500 | 1,000 | Total over 5 (see below). |
| **Total affiliated (mid-1970)** | | | | **18,900** | **4,187,465** | **9,586,668** | **Total denominations (1970) . . . 210.** |
| **Total affiliated (mid-1975)** | | | | **19,100** | **4,282,600** | **9,804,400** | **Total denominations (1975) . . . 240.** |
| **Total affiliated (mid-1980)** | | | | **19,300** | **4,338,200** | **9,931,800** | **Total denominations (1980) . . . 270.** |

**NOTES ON TABLE ABOVE**

COLUMNS: for meanings and CODES (cols. 1, 3, 4, 8): see Codebook (Part 6). Column 1: **Boldface type** = church with over 10% of country's affiliated Christians.

NATIONAL COUNCILS (Column 4, 5th letter).

- E = Australian Evangelical Alliance (members mostly foreign missionary societies).
- h = Australian Pentecostal Fellowship.
- s = Australian Episcopal Conference, and also observer in ACC.
- T = Australian Consultative Council of the ICCC.
- W = Australian Council of Churches (ACC).
- w = associate member of ACC.

*Other national councils*. Aboriginal and Islander Catholic Council (AICC) (1976, in Queensland only). Australian Assembly of Unitarian Churches (AAUC) (5 small denominations).

*Local councils*. 7 state councils affiliated to ACC.

OTHER PROTESTANT DENOMINATIONS. These include a large number of independent single congregations and independent house groups, as well as the following small denominations or groupings: American Baptist Association, Apostolic Christian Ch (Nazarean) (2 churches), Armenian Ev Spiritual Ch, Armenian Spiritual Brethren, Association of Baptists for World Evangelism (6 churches), Australian Baptist Independent Fellowship, Australian Ev Mission, Baptist Bible Fellowship International (1954) (7 churches), Baptist International Missions (1970), Baptist Mid-Missions (1968), Baptist Missionary Association of America, Bible Christian Ch, Bible Presbyterian Ch (Adelaide), Christian Catholic Ch in Zion (USA; 2 churches), Christian Ch of North America, Christian Reformed Ch. Ch of God of Prophecy (1956; 3 churches, 1 being Greek), Churches of God in the British Isles & Overseas (4 churches, 150 members), City Missions (Hobart, Launceston, et alia), Elim Foursquare Gospel Ch, Ev Baptist Mission, Evangelisation Society of South Australia, Faith Baptist Chs Fellowship of Congregational Chs (NSW; 22 churches), Fellowship of Independent Ev Chs of Australia (WA; 2 churches), Free Presbyterian Ch of Scotland (1 congregation, Grafton, NSW), German Ev Lutheran Ch (5 centres), House of David, Hungarian Reformed Ch (1 church), Independent Congregational Chs (14 churches), Italian Ev Christian Ch (Pentecostal, 300 members), Maranatha Baptist Mission, Melbourne Revival Centre, Missionary Baptist Chs, New Testament Ch of God (3 churches, 5 ministers), Norwegian Seamen's Mission Ch, 'Old Paths' Christadelphians, Reformed Baptists (USA: 4 churches), Reformed Presbyterian Ch (Evangelical Synod), Remnant Ch (Hebrew Christian sabbatarians), Scandinavian Seamen's Missions (3 pastors and churches), Slavic Ev Pentecostal Ch of Australia (3 churches, 400 members), Slavic Gospel Association, Strict & Particular Baptist Chs of Australia (Gospel Standard) (4 churches), United Gospel Mission, United Welsh Ch, Universal Fellowship of Metropolitan Community Churches (from USA; gay/homosexuals), Westminster Presbyterian Ch (4 churches, 200 adherents), World Baptist Fellowship Mission Agency (1969).

OTHER MARGINAL BODIES. These include Anthroposophical Society (Christian Community Ch), Branhamites (End Time Believers; HQ Jeffersonville, IN, USA; Jesus-Only Unitarians), British-Israel Federation, Ch of the Mystic Christ (3 churches), Ch of the New Faith Scientology (banned, and immigrants banned until 1974; rapid growth by 1976 to 30,000 members with 5 centres, 50 full-time ministers and 120 lay workers), Divine Science Federation International (2 churches), Good Samaritan Ch of Truth (1 church in Glen Iris, Victoria), Order of the Cross (3 groups), Seventh Ch, Spiritual Churches. Temple Society in Australia (5 centres; linked with Templegesellschaft in Germany begun 1861; Unitarian), Unity School of Christianity (3 centres, 2 ministers, 250 members); and about 64 spiritualist churches, many independent.

OTHER NON-WHITE INDIGENOUS CHURCHES. Several Third-World indigenous churches have opened branches in Australia, including in 1963 a Korean movement: Holy Spirit Association for the Unification of World Christianity (in 1977: 7 centres, 100 members). The Father Divine Peace Mission Movement (USA Blacks), formerly strong, has 3 remaining churches with under 30 members (HQ Sydney). From India, the Assemblies (Jehova Shammah) of Brother Bakht Singh have a Christian Fellowship Centre in Hurstville (NSW).

PEOPLES (ethnolinguistic). Christians: 83.5% Anglo-Australian, 5.2% English, 1.6% Greek, 1.3% Italian, 1.3% Scottish, 1.0% German, 1.0% Aborigine, 0.6% Polish, 0.5% Irish, 0.5% New Zealander, 0.5% Serbian, 0.4% Dutch, 0.4% Maltese, 0.3% Austrian, 0.3% Hungarian, 0.2% Welsh, 0.2% Latvian, 0.2% Russian, 0.2% Ukrainian, 0.1% Armenian, 0.1% USA, 0.1% Czech, 0.1% Torres Strait Islander, Macedonian, Romanian, Assyrian, Bulgarian, Croat, Slovene, Slovak, Albanian, Gypsy, Finnish, Estonian, Basque, Chinese (4,700).

**COUNTRY-WIDE TOTALS**

EVANGELIZATION (see Part 5). 1900: 100%. 1970: 100%. 1980: 100%. *Mass evangelism*. A few of the many recent campaigns: Billy Graham crusades in 1959 in Melbourne, Sydney Perth, Adelaide, Brisbane and landline relays (3,007,240 attenders, 130,411 enquirers), 1968 in Perth, Brisbane, Adelaide and Sydney, (719,300 attenders, 30,487 enquirers), and in 1969 in Arnhem Land, Darwin, Bundaberg, Devenport, Launceston, Canberra and Melbourne (364,600 attenders, 13,687 enquirers); 1965, Oral Roberts evangelistic crusade; many local campaigns including World Methodist Crusade, Tell Australia, Mission of Reconciliation Evangelism 75; May 1976, Congress on World Missions and Evangelism; October 1977, Leighton Ford crusade in Melbourne (21,000 attenders, 550 decisions); and Tasmania (9,000 attenders, 231 enquirers); 1979 Billy Graham crusade in Sydney. *Radiophonic evangelism*. Annual listeners' letters (1975): 888 HCJB, 312 FEBC, 130 TWR, 48 RVOG, Radio Vatican, et alia. Bible correspondence courses: ICI, SDA/VOP (10,000 active students), et alia.

FOREIGN MISSIONARIES AND PERSONNEL (nationals serving abroad) (1973). Total 3,975: 2,157 Protestants (increase from 1,500 in 1963, and 2,048 in 1966) in over 58 societies, 1,344 Roman Catholics (1,044 foreign missionaries (1966 figures: 259 priests, 130 brothers, 501 sisters, 154 lay) serving in Third-World countries, 300 personnel in Western nations), 444 Anglicans (increase from 352 in 1966) in 4 societies, 30 marginal Protestants (about 20 Jehovah's Witnesses).

FOREIGN MISSIONARIES AND PERSONNEL (aliens from abroad) (1973). Total 2,845. *From Western world*. 2,692: about 1,900 Roman Catholics, 300 Protestants (162 in 32 USA societies, 68 in 9 UK societies, 34 in 14 New Zealand societies, 10 in 1 Finland society, 2 in 1 Canada society), about 250 Anglicans (over 150 clergy from UK, 30 in 3 UK societies, 5 in 1 New Zealand society), about 220 marginal Protestants (200 Mormons) from USA, about 20 Orthodox (10 from USA, 10 Greece), 2 Catholics (non-Roman). *From Communist world*. 58: about 53 Roman Catholics (43 from Poland, 10 Yugoslavia), 5 Orthodox (2 Bulgaria, 2 Yugoslavia). *From Third World*. 95: 40 Roman Catholics (27 India, Brazil, et alia), 29 Protestants (8 Tonga, 8 Fiji, 6 Philippines, PNG, Sri Lanka, Indonesia, New Hebrides, India), about 20 Anglicans (Japan, Hong Kong, Sri Lanka, South Africa), about 5 Asian indigenous (Korea et alia), 1 Orthodox (Egypt).

INSTITUTIONS (church-operated) (1973). Total 885, including 625 higher schools (5 minor seminaries), 140 medical centres (83 hospitals), 4 radio stations, 12 religious communities (5 monasteries), 3 research centres, 80 seminaries (36 Protestant, 34 RC, 9 Anglican, 1 Catholic/non-Roman).

PERIODICALS. About 260 titles (100 Protestant (12 SDA, 6 Pentecostal) (including 65 Protestant missionary periodicals), 60 RC, 40 Anglican).

PERSONNEL. About 35,250 (32,425 national, 2,845 foreign).

RELIGIOUS LIBRARIES. About 110.

SCRIPTURE DISTRIBUTION (1975). Annual totals: 218,683 Bibles (4% free, 78% subsidized, 18% commercial), 456,748 NTs (52% free, 36% subsidized, 11% commercial), 555,337 UBS portions, 1,579,713 UBS selections. *Translations completed*. Portion: 14 languages since 1879. NT: 2 languages since 1897.

SERVICE AGENCIES. About 190, including ACC, AEA, AEC, AEFA, AEM, AICC, AIM, AMS, ARFS, CCCI, CEF, CLC, CMRSWI, CPA, ESA, FCIC, GEM, JEW, MAF, MEL, MTS, NCF, NTM, PTL, SCM, SGM, SIL, SU, WBT, YFC, YLC, YWAM.

**ADDITIONAL DATA ON CHURCHES**

CATHOLIC CHURCH IN AUSTRALIA. *Relation to Roman Curia*. Until 1976, Australia was a mission territory under SC Propaganda in Rome. In March 1976 this ceased when almost all territories were placed instead under the SC for Bishops. *New dioceses*. Created 1973: D St Maron of Sydney, or Maronite rite. *Catholics*. Including (1971) 20,934 Aborigines out of 106,290. *Annual baptisms* (1972). 96.2% infant, 3.8% adult. *Personnel*. About 90% nationals, 10% expatriates (including nearly 700 Irish nuns). *Priests* (1972). 2,471 diocesan, 1,424 religious. *Catholic charismatics* (January 1974). 5,000 adults including religious personnel in 80 prayer groups are active in the Charismatic Renewal. D Brisbane is a major centre. *Seminaries*. There are 2 interdiocesan seminaries in Sydney (one postgraduate), and 5 diocesan seminaries. There are also 26 training houses for religious orders and congregations, mostly in Sydney or Melbourne. *Seminarians* (1972). 497 secular, 495 religious. *Catechists*. Total (1968) 4,925. *Main religious orders and congregations*. Priests (1970): 332 MSCI, 264 CSSR, 249 OFM, 245 SJ, 125 SM2. Sisters (1972): 4,000 Sisters of Mercy, 2,072 Sisters of St Joseph, 684 Good Samaritans, 500 Sisters of Charity, 497 Dominicans.

*Catholic organizations*. In addition to the Australian Episcopal Conference, national bodies include the Association of Major Clerical Religious Superiors, Provincials Conference of Religious Brothers, and the Conference of Major Religious Superiors of Women's Institutes (CMRSWI). No official council of priests exists, nor is there any single co-ordinating body for the lay apostolate. However, the following bodies have national centres: YCW (Melbourne), YCS (Fitzroy), Society of St Vincent de Paul (Sydney), Legion of Mary (Melbourne), Knights of the Southern Cross (Sydney) and National Catholic Rural Movement. Many other associations operate only at the local level. For the armed forces, Australia forms a military vicariate.

The Holy See has diplomatic relations with Australia and is represented to government and the hierarchy by a pro-nuncio, who also serves as apostolic delegate to Papua New Guinea.

There is at present little internal controversy in the Australian Catholic Church, and liberals are more reformist than radical. The main progressivist movements are: (1) groups of Catholic intellectuals centred around *Catholic worker*, an independent journal with a moderate left-wing political and religious stance; (2) a group of Catholic pacifists centred around the journal *Non-violent power*, with a membership of 100; (3) the Catholic Lay Association of Melbourne, a group dedicated to renewal and lay participation at all levels, with a membership of 200; (4) Pax (Catholics for Peace), another Melbourne group with a pacifist orientation and a membership of 150; and (5) a group of progressivist priests centred around the independent reformist journal *Priests' forum* published in Melbourne. On the conservative or traditionalist side, there is a Latin Mass Society.

Missionary action is co-ordinated by the National Missionary Council, founded in 1971, and the main organizations are Pontifical Missionary Works, with offices in each diocese. The principal missionary orders are St Columban's Foreign Missionary Society, Divine Word Missionaries, and Missionaries of the Sacred Heart. There are no Australian-born missionary societies. The main foreign mission fields are in Papua New Guinea, other Pacific islands, Philippines, India, several South American countries and Japan. In 1966, 1,044 Catholic missionary personnel were serving overseas (259 priests, 130 brothers, 501 sisters, 154 lay workers), and 286 were serving in missions to Australian Aborigines (70 priests, 37 brothers, 130 sisters, 49 lay workers).

In 1971 the Federal Catholic Education Office sponsored 1,769 schools with an enrolment of 329,682 pupils on the primary level (18% of primary enrolments), and 165,043 on the secondary level (17%). At this period government schools numbered 7,404, with 1,447,948 primary pupils and 748,364 secondary. Protestant schools numbered about 300, with about 39,000 primary pupils and about 76,000 secondary. In 1973, there were 1,372 Catholic primary schools (308,244 pupils) and 522 secondary schools (187,019). Catholic schools included 8 for Aborigines and 75 other special schools. The Catholic Church has not been directly involved in college education, except through halls of residence and chaplaincies, seminaries, and 8 Catholic teacher-training colleges with 1,576 students. Some 59% of all Catholic children are enrolled in Catholic schools and several thousand catechists teach Catholic children enrolled in non-Catholic schools.

Medical and welfare work in 1971 included 66 hospitals (9,012 beds), 44 homes for the aged (3,438 occupants), 13 schools for handicapped children (678 deaf, blind or retarded), 8 re-education centres for delinquent children (692 places), and 70 homes for orphans and deprived children (3,554 places). Many Catholic hospitals have nursing training schools attached, and a number of homes for the aged have nursing personnel and so qualify as C class hospitals. Commonwealth and state government assistance is provided towards recurrent and capital expenses.

Charitable work in developing countries is co-ordinated by the National Commission for Justice and Peace (1968), which works in close association with Australian Catholic Relief (1964). The National Catholic Welfare Committee was established in 1956 by the Australian Episcopal Conference and represents the church in social action organizations.

CHURCH OF ENGLAND IN AUSTRALIA. *Name.* In 1978 the synod was expected to alter the church's official name to: Anglican Church of Australia. *Charismatics.* A charismatic renewal began after 1970, involving by 1975 over 100 clergy and 2 bishops in several dioceses, especially Melbourne (10% of clergy, 3 archdeacons), North Queensland, Adelaide, Tasmania and Sydney (20 clergy); with around 10,000 involved adults in over 200 prayer groups. As in the Church of England (UK), no exact list or count of such groups is kept or possible, because the renewal remains firmly within existing parish and diocesan structures and the line between charismatic and non-charismatic renewal groups is impossible to determine.

UNITING CHURCH IN AUSTRALIA. Inaugurated in June 1977 as a merger of 3 bodies: Congregational Union of Australia (work begun 1829, autonomous 1960, 1973 joined by an Armenian congregation but still declining at 1.1% per year; 1977, 90% joined union, 10% stayed out), Methodist Church of Australasia (work begun 1812, by 1970 declining at 2.5% per year; 20 colleges; 1977, 90% joined union, 10% stayed out), and Presbyterian Church of Australia (work begun 1809; long history of splits, mergers and unions; 54 Presbyteries; 1977, 70% joined union, 30% stayed out). Congregations rejecting the 1977 union formed 'Continuing' bodies as shown in the table. *Communicants.* After union the total was estimated at 260,000. *Ethnic congregations* (1977). Including 4 Dutch churches, 2 Hungarian, and 1 Assyrian. *Ministers.* About 1,800. In 1972 during union negotiations, 80 dissident Roman Catholic priests applied to join the Uniting Church. *Name.* Originally the name was to have been the 'United' Church. The present name has however been chosen, to indicate the hope that Anglicans, Baptists, Lutherans and others may eventually also join.

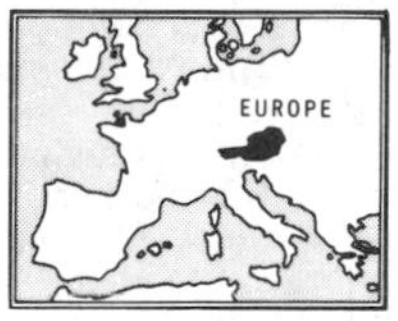


# AUSTRIA

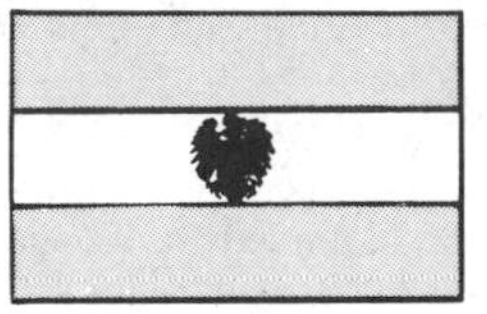

## SECULAR DATA

**STATE. Official name:** The Republic of Austria (Republik Österreich) Adjective of nationality: Austrian.
**Flag** (shown above right): Red, white, and red stripes, black coat of arms.
**Area:** 83,849 sq.km. (32,366 sq.miles). Agricultural land: 45.2%.
**Government:** Federal republic, since 1918 (1282 Hapsburg empire).
**Legislature:** National Assembly: Federal Council (Bundesrat), 54 members; Nationalrat, 183 members.
**Official language:** German (*Deutsch*).
**Chief cities:** capital Vienna 1,614,840 (1971), Graz 248,500, Linz 202,870, Salzburg 128,850, Innsbruck 115,200.
**Political divisions:** 9 Federal States.
**Armed forces** (1976): Total 37,300 regular (25,000 conscripts): army 33,000, air force 4,300 (30 combat aircraft). Reserves: 112,700. Paramilitary forces: 11,250 gendarmerie.

**DEMOGRAPHY Population:** 7,456,403 (census of 12.V.1971. For 1970–2000 (UN). see last row of Table 1). Population density (1975): 90/sq.km. (233/sq.mile). Under 15 years: 22%. Growth rate (1975–80): 0.24% per year (births 1.48%, deaths −1.24%). Life expectancy (1975–80): 72.0 years. Household size: 2.9 persons
**Major languages:** German, Slovenian, Serbo-Croatian, Hungarian, Greek, Russian, Italian, Czech, Turkish, English.

**Urban dwellers** (1970): 53.9%. Urban growth rate (1950–70): 0.8% per year.
**Labour force:** 40%.
**Refugees** (1977): 1,500 Asians from Uganda.
**Tourists** (1974): 10,886,237.

**ETHNOLINGUISTIC GROUPS:** 93.3% Austrian, 3.5% German, 1.1% Slovene, 0.8% Serbo-Croatian, 0.3% Magyar, 0.2% Greek (12,000), 0.2% Russian, 0.1% Italian, 0.1% Czech, 0.1% Jewish, 0.1% Turkish (1971; increasing to 0.3% by 1975), 0.1% USA (4,400), 0.1% British (4,000), Persian (1,800), Egyptian (780), Chinese (500), Estonian, Gypsy (400).

**MONEY** (1977). **Monetary unit:** schilling (= 100 groschen); US$1 = Sch$17.00.
**National income per person:** US$3,917. Average annual family income: US$11,359.
**Inflation:** (1970–74) 7.0% per year, (1975) 8% per year (consumer price index 162).
**Cost of living in capital** (1976): index 145 (Washington DC = 100). Daily cost of living: US$43.

**EDUCATION.** Adult literacy: 99%. Education rate: . 60%. Schools: 3,783. Universities: 17.

**HEALTH.** Hospitals: 317 (81,391 beds). Doctors: 15,888. Blind: 11,000. Psychotics: 75,000. Criminals: 189,670.

**LITERATURE.** Annual new book titles (1973): 5,342. Periodicals: 2,624. Scientific journals: 490. Newspapers: 31 dailies, 126 non-daily.

**COMMUNICATION** (per 1,000 people). Phones: 245. Radios: 287. TV sets: 237. Daily newspaper circulation: 328 copies.

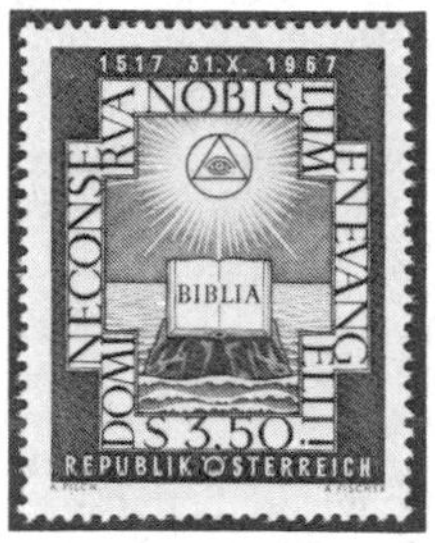


Official state postage stamp commemorating 1517 Reformation, with Bible as Rock, all-seeing Eye, and prayer 'Lord, preserve for us the Light of the Gospel'

TABLE 1. RELIGIOUS ADHERENTS IN AUSTRIA

| Year | 1900 | | mid-1970 | | Annual change, 1970–1980 | | | | mid-1975 | | mid-1980 | | 2000 | |
|---|---|---|---|---|---|---|---|---|---|---|---|---|---|---|
| *Name* | *Adherents* | *%* | *Adherents* | *%* | *Natural* | *Conversion* | *Total* | *Rate* | *Adherents* | *%* | *Adherents* | *%* | *Adherents* | *%* |
| **Christians** | **5,827,780** | **97.1** | **7,220,000** | **97.0** | **17,488** | **−2,850** | **14,638** | **0.20** | **7,283,690** | **96.6** | **7,366,380** | **96.6** | **7,684,000** | **94.6** |
| professing | 5,827,780 | 97.1 | 7,220,000 | 97.0 | 17,488 | −2,850 | 14,638 | 0.20 | 7,283,690 | 96.6 | 7,684,000 | 96.6 | 7,864,000 | 94.6 |
| Roman Catholics | 5,511,780 | 91.8 | 6,640,000 | 89.2 | 16,078 | −2,960 | 13,118 | 0.20 | 6,696,430 | 88.8 | 4,771,180 | 88.8 | 7,007,100 | 86.3 |
| Protestants | 160,000 | 2.7 | 458,000 | 6.2 | 1,113 | 118 | 1,231 | 0.27 | 463,800 | 6.2 | 470,310 | 6.2 | 521,800 | 6.4 |
| Orthodox | 136,000 | 2.3 | 62,000 | 0.8 | 151 | −1 | 150 | 0.24 | 62,760 | 0.8 | 63,500 | 0.8 | 73,000 | 0.9 |
| Catholics (non-Roman) | 20,000 | 0.3 | 34,000 | 0.5 | 83 | −2 | 81 | 0.23 | 34,400 | 0.5 | 34,810 | 0.5 | 40,000 | 0.5 |
| Marginal Protestants | 0 | 0.0 | 24,000 | 0.3 | 58 | −4 | 54 | 0.22 | 24,270 | 0.3 | 24,540 | 0.3 | 40,000 | 0.5 |
| Anglicans | 0 | 0.0 | 2,000 | 0.0 | 5 | −1 | 4 | 0.20 | 2,020 | 0.0 | 2,040 | 0.0 | 2,100 | 0.0 |
| nominal | 9,780 | 0.2 | 36,767 | 0.5 | 336 | 22,146 | 22,482 | 16.08 | 139,780 | 1.8 | 261,590 | 3.4 | 512,640 | 6.3 |
| affiliated | 5,818,000 | 96.9 | 7,183,233 | 96.4 | 17,152 | −24,996 | −7,844 | −0.11 | 7,143,910 | 94.8 | 7,104,790 | 93.1 | 7,171,360 | 88.3 |
| total practising | 5,236,200 | *90* | 5,387,420 | *75* | 12,521 | −46,823 | −34,302 | −0.66 | 5,215,050 | *73* | 5,044,400 | *71* | 4,302,820 | *96* |
| non-practising | 581,800 | *10* | 1,795,810 | *25* | 4,631 | 21,827 | 26,458 | 1.37 | 1,928,860 | *27* | 2,060,390 | *29* | 2,868,540 | *4* |
| Roman Catholics | 5,500,000 | 91.6 | 6,603,148 | 88.7 | 15,743 | −24,958 | −9,215 | −0.14 | 6,557,000 | 87.0 | 6,511,000 | 85.4 | 6,494,400 | 80.0 |
| Catholic pentecostals | 0 | 0.0 | 0 | 0.0 | 2 | 498 | 500 | 50.00 | 1,000 | 0.0 | 5,000 | 0.1 | 40,000 | 0.5 |
| Protestants | 160,000 | 2.7 | 456,210 | 6.1 | 1,108 | −85 | 1,023 | 0.22 | 461,320 | 6.1 | 466,440 | 6.1 | 513,860 | 6.3 |
| Evangelicals | 20,000 | 0.3 | 37,000 | 0.5 | 90 | −10 | 80 | 0.21 | 37,400 | 0.5 | 37,800 | 0.5 | 42,000 | 0.5 |
| Orthodox | 138,000 | 2.3 | 62,000 | 0.8 | 151 | −1 | 150 | 0.24 | 62,760 | 0.8 | 63,500 | 0.8 | 73,000 | 0.9 |
| Catholics (non-Roman) | 20,000 | 0.3 | 36,000 | 0.5 | 87 | −6 | 81 | 0.22 | 36,410 | 0.5 | 36,810 | 0.5 | 40,000 | 0.5 |
| Marginal Protestants | 0 | 0.0 | 23,875 | 0.3 | 58 | 55 | 113 | 0.46 | 24,400 | 0.3 | 25,000 | 0.3 | 48,000 | 0.6 |
| Anglicans | 0 | 0.0 | 2,000 | 0.0 | 5 | −1 | 4 | 0.20 | 2,020 | 0.0 | 2,040 | 0.0 | 2,100 | 0.0 |
| Non-religious | 8,000 | 0.1 | 144,000 | 1.9 | 360 | 336 | 696 | 0.47 | 149,480 | 2.0 | 150,960 | 2.0 | 291,000 | 3.6 |
| Atheists | 2,000 | 0.0 | 50,000 | 0.7 | 121 | −9 | 112 | 0.22 | 50,560 | 0.7 | 51,120 | 0.7 | 77,000 | 0.9 |
| Muslims | 0 | 0.0 | 18,000 | 0.2 | 96 | 2,604 | 2,700 | 6.75 | 40,000 | 0.5 | 45,000 | 0.6 | 50,000 | 0.6 |
| Jews | 166,000 | 2.8 | 10,000 | 0.1 | 23 | −123 | −100 | −1.05 | 9,500 | 0.1 | 9,000 | 0.1 | 7,000 | 0.1 |
| Baha'is | 0 | 0.0 | 2,000 | 0.0 | 5 | 7 | 12 | 0.58 | 2,060 | 0.0 | 2,120 | 0.0 | 3,000 | 0.0 |
| Buddhists | 0 | 0.0 | 1,000 | 0.0 | 2 | 0 | 2 | 0.24 | 1,010 | 0.0 | 1,020 | 0.0 | 2,000 | 0.0 |
| Other religionists | 0 | 0.0 | 2,000 | 0.0 | 5 | 35 | 40 | 1.82 | 2,200 | 0.0 | 2,400 | 0.0 | 4,000 | 0.0 |
| **Country's population** | **6,003,780** | **100.0** | **7,447,000** | **100.0** | **18,100** | **0** | **18,100** | **0.24** | **7,538,500** | **100.0** | **7,628,000** | **100.0** | **8,118,000** | **100.0** |

COLUMNS, ROWS. For meanings and definitions, see Codebook (Part 6). Note that, by definition, total 'Christians' = professing + crypto-Christians, which also = affiliated + nominal Christians. Percentages may not always total exactly, due to rounding.

CENSUSES. **1869**: 96.2% Roman Catholics, 2.4% Protestants, 1.3% Jews. **1900**: 91.8% Roman Catholics (12.0% Greek Catholics), 2.8% Jews, 2.7% Protestants, 2.3% Greek Orthodox, 0.3% Old Catholics. **1923**: 91.1% Roman Catholics, 3.4% Protestants, 3.2% Jews. **1934**: 90.6% Roman Catholics, 4.5% Protestants, 2.8% Jews, 1.6% non-religious, 0.5% Old Catholics. **1939**: 88.7% Roman Catholics, 5.2% Protestants, 1.2% Jews. **1.VI.1951** (de jure): 89.6% Roman Catholics, 6.2% Protestants, 3.8% non-religious, 0.3% other religionists, 0.2% Jews. **21.III.1961** (de jure): 89.0% Roman Catholics, 6.2% Protestants, 3.8% non-religious, 0.4% Old Catholics, 0.1% Jews. **12.V.1971** (adjusted): 89.3% Roman Catholics, 6.2% Protestants, 2.7% non-religious (and atheists), 0.8% Orthodox, 0.4% Old Catholics, 0.2% Muslims, 0.1% Jews.

NOTES ON RELIGIONS

ATHEISTS. Kommunistische Partei Österreichs (KPO) (split between USSR/China) and one small faction: membership (1970, 1974) 25,000; Communist voters (election of XI.1962) 135,482 (3% of all votes), (10.X.1971) 61,756 (1.3% of all votes).

BAHA'IS. Entered before 1921. Growth from 7 local spiritual assemblies (1964) to 11 (1973), and 48 other isolated centres or groups.

BUDDHISTS. Including about 400 Chinese.

CATHOLIC PENTECOSTALS (or, Catholic charismatics). Total involved adults (1975) over 200; total charismatic community including children, around 1,000.

EVANGELICALS. In German, Evangelikale (Conservative Evangelicals).

JEWS. Decline from over 200,000 in 1938 to 4,000 in 1945, rising to 10,000 in 1970, then again declining due to emigration to Israel. 80% Liberal, 20% Orthodox.

MUSLIMS. In 1971, 8,300 Yugoslavs, 7,500 Turks, 1,700 Iranians, 750 Egyptians, rising by 1975 to 40,000 (25,000 being Turkish labourers). All Sunnis, except for a small Ahmadiya mission begun in 1955 under its Swiss mission.

OTHER RELIGIONISTS. Adherents of smaller religions and cults, including Rosicrucians (3 AMORC centres).

PRACTISING CHRISTIANS. 1968: weekly church attenders 38% of population (Gallup). Mass attendance (Catholics), 1976: 3% several times a week, 31% every Sunday and church festivals, 17% at least once a month, 22% on church festivals only, 27% never or almost never.

ROMAN CATHOLICS. Defections of affiliated Catholics each year have gradually increased from 8,368 in 1958 to 23,833 (0.46% per year; mostly urban) in 1972; the former figure was less than the natural population increase among Catholics, but the latter figure (which with children and infants of defectors amounts to 28,000 a year) is nearly twice the natural increase during the period 1970–80 (averaging 15,743 per year), meaning that affiliated Roman Catholics have since about 1965 been gradually decreasing each year in absolute numbers as well as (since about 1955) as a percentage of the population. The analysis 'Annual change, 1970–1980' in the table above is based on an average defection rate of 24,958 affiliated Catholics per year. It should be noted that defection here refers to withdrawal of church affiliation with its legal implications; most defectors however still regard themselves as professing Catholics and are counted as such in the government population census.

## NON-CHRISTIAN RELIGIONS.

**Islam** increased rapidly from 1970–1975 to about 40,000 Muslims, mostly manual labourers from Turkey (25,000) and Yugoslavia, the rest being embassy personnel, students and some 250 immigrants from Bosnia who have taken Austrian citizenship since World War II. Muslim Social Service (Muslimische Sozialdienst), founded in Vienna in 1964, is administered by an imam from Turkey and one from Yugoslavia sponsored by their respective governments. There are 3 Muslim prayer halls in Vienna.

**Judaism** suffered a catastrophic decrease from more than 200,000 Jews in 1938, the year of the Anschluss when Austria was absorbed in Hitler's Third Reich, to 4,000 in 1945. Following World War II, the Jewish community grew initially due to immigration from Hungary (especially in 1956), Romania and Czechoslovakia. There are now approximately 10,000 Jews living in the country, 8,000 of whom are registered in Liberal communities (7,700 in Vienna; 300 in Salzburg, Graz and Innsbruck), while the other 2,000 belong to different Orthodox groups mostly in Vienna. However, the average age of Viennese Jews is 60 years, with high mortality and few replacements, since Jewish youth prefer to emigrate to Israel or to Western countries. Thus the Austrian Hebrew community is at present in decline. Jewish organizations and institutions include: (1) Association of Israelite Religious Communities (Verband der Österreichischen Israelitischen Kultusgemeinden), which sponsors a home in Vienna for 150 residents, with a geriatric department; (2) Youth House (Haus der Jugend) in Vienna, which co-ordinates all Jewish youth organizations; and (3) the Vienna synagogue, which adminsters a kindergarten and 3 Talmud-Torah schools, and organizes religious courses. Orthodox Jews have their own prayer houses. Since 1965 the University of Vienna has maintained an Institute for Judaism (Institut für Judaistik), which sponsors the Austrian Jewish Museum of Eisenstadt Association and provides expositions and annual meetings dedicated to the scientific study of Judaism in Austria.

**Buddhism** is active in Austria although the number of Buddhist groups remains small. Austria is a member of the European Buddhist Community now being organized in France and is strongly influenced from West Germany. Jodoshin-shû (Amidist) has chosen Salzburg as the central headquarters for their work in all German-speaking countries. The Octopus-Versandbuchhandlung in Vienna is an important Buddhist publishing house and also maintains a library. In addition Austrian Buddhists produce a trilingual journal serving the whole of Europe.

## CHRISTIANITY.

The Austrian area of central Europe came under Roman rule at the beginning of the Christian era; Christianity was slowly introduced and earliest evidence of it comes from the year 174. During the next thousand years, central Europe experienced a series of invasions by Ostrogoths, Huns, Lombards, Avars and Slavs, with some unification achieved under Charlemagne. The bishop of Salzburg began sending missionaries eastward, in 955. The duchy of Austria came under the rule of the Bavarian family of Babenberg in 973 and from then onwards gradually gained dominance over other central European duchies. The Hapsburg family was given added powers in 1282 and continued to rule when Austria became an archduchy, from 1438 to 1806. During the Middle Ages the only Christian centres throughout most of the land were the monasteries of different religious orders, and Vienna had no bishop until 1468. In 1519, the houses of Austria, Burgundy,

Aragon and Castile were united through marriage under Charles V, joined later by Bohemia and Hungary. By 1520 there were Protestants in Salzburg and possibly in Vienna. The Lutheran reform movement made progress in Austria and Bohemia prior to the Counter-Reformation which began with the entrance of the Jesuits into Vienna. In 1552 Lutherans were given some recognition, to the exclusion of Calvinists. Following the Thirty Years War, the Hapsburgs accorded no privileges to Protestants but rigidly enforced a united Catholicism in their part of Europe. In 1699 the Turks were defeated at Vienna, Hungary was added to Austria, and the country entered into what has been called Austria's Great Century. Joseph II sought to increase his powers at the expense of the church by destroying monasteries, establishing his own diocesan boundaries, controlling communication between Austria's bishops and Rome, and in 1781 he issued the Edict of Tolerance for Protestants and Orthodox. Following the destruction of Napoleon's advances, Austria became an empire in its own right. Revolutionary movements sought change, with greater religious freedom achieved in the constitution of 1861. Churches of the Augsburg and Helvetic confessions emerged into the open at this time, later to become united as the present Evangelical Church. In 1867 Hungary achieved equal status with Austria in the Austro-Hungarian Empire. In 1918 the defeated empire was dissolved and Austria was reduced in size to its present area, as a republic. While the country continued predominantly Catholic, new churches appeared, and in 1925 the Synods of the Augsburg and Helvetic Confessions began meeting together. In 1934 Austria signed a concordat with Rome to the disadvantage of the Evangelical Church, the latter suffering further by being incorporated into the German Evangelical Church at the time of the Nazi Anschluss.

**Katholische Kirche Österreichs, Diözese Feldkirch.** One of 4 Roman Catholic churches in town of Dornbirn, Vorarlberg.

## CATHOLIC CHURCH.

In Austria there has been a close interrelationship between church and state since the early days of christianization in the time of the Roman empire, but it was the Counter-Reformation which brought about a Catholic pattern of culture simultaneous with the foundation of such new religious congregations as the Jesuits and Capuchins. The establishment of the Catholic Church as the national church in the absolute welfare state of Joseph II was caused by the peculiarly Austrian form that the Enlightenment there took. Catholic doctrine with its values and norms dominated the prevailing culture until the 19th century, and the various competing currents of liberalism, nationalism and socialism had a limited influence on social elites only.

The process of secularization was then initiated by the rise of industrialization and of economic, social and political institutions independent of the church. The middle classes and the social democrats were the first to demand separation of church and state. However, the church maintained an influence in politics and society as a result of both the Christian democratic movement and the ruling Catholic House of Hapsburg. Major ideological controversies between Christian political parties on the one hand and socialists and nationalists on the other raged after the end of the Hapsburg monarchy. The church lost its influence, particularly with the working class, through the failure of the Catholic corporate state experiment of 1934–1938.

Between the 2 world wars a liturgical movement (Pius Parsch) arose which inspired a new conception of the church through its translations of the Bible into the vernacular. A spiritual renewal of the church and a change in its position in state society took place at the time of its persecution by the Nazi regime (1938–1945). During World War II, and thereafter, theological thought was also renewed through the writing of such men as K. Rahner and A. Jungmann, and new pastoral ideas were developed around the pastoral centres founded by K. Rudolf. Catholic organizations also were reshaped for the apostolate along the Italian and French model of Catholic Action, and Catholic priests largely withdrew from party politics to further dialogue with all groups in society.

In 1952, at the first national reunion of Catholics after the war, the Katholikentag, the Catholic Church finally gave up its claim to be the national church and its engagement in party politics, and in its Mariazell manifesto proclaimed a free church in a free society.

At present, most Austrians continue to maintain basic religious convictions. The great majority are baptized Catholics (89% in 1951; 88% in 1971) and practically all Catholic parents continue to have their children baptized. Catholic marriages decreased by 20% between 1955 and 1971, mainly because divorced Catholics may not remarry in the church; but 95% of all first marriages still follow Catholic rites. Almost all Catholics are buried with church rites.

The number of affiliated Catholics leaving the church each year has steadily increased, from 8,368 persons in 1958 to 23,833 in 1972, a process which however only decreased the proportion of professing Catholics in the population by 1% in 20 years; and two-thirds of these persons lived in urban areas.

Regularly-practising Catholics are a minority and are gradually decreasing in number. Major doctrines such as the resurrection are now accepted by only a minority of Catholics (33%), although a large majority (69%) believe in life after death. In 1949, Sunday mass attendance was 39%. In 1974, this had only declined slightly, and mass attendance (Catholics older than 13 years) was: 3% several times a week, 31% every Sunday and on church feast days, 17% at least once a month, 22% on feast days only, and 27% never or almost never. In certain urban areas, however, Sunday attendance has declined much more (Innsbruck: 1950, 51%; 1970, 30%). But even regular churchgoers do not accept all doctrines; the resurrection is believed in by only 50% of Sunday mass attenders. Traditional Catholic religiosity (acceptance of, and compliance with, all church norms) is followed by only 20%.

The number of priests is steadily declining. In 1949 Austrian dioceses had 4,443 secular priests and 1,129 religious priests working in parishes (excluding contemplatives). By 1971 the number of secular priests had decreased (by 11%) to 3,987, whereas the number of religious priests in parishes remained approximately unchanged (1,106 in 1971). In 1945 there was one parish priest for 1,347 Catholics, while in 1971 the average priest had to serve 1,678 Catholics. From 1968 to 1974 ordinations of secular priests averaged 46 per year, whereas from 1961 to 1967 the average had been 93. For religious priests ordinations decreased from 67 to 47 a year. There is therefore now a disproportionate number of older priests. Recently, the church has tried to overcome the shortage by appointing lay theologians to teach religion in public schools and to work as pastoral assistants in parishes. Lastly, nuns in Austria declined from 16,356 in 1950 to 13,574 in 1972. And with regard to the laity, in 1974 5% of all Catholics were members of one of the many Catholic organizations.

Diocesan synods have been held in most of the Austrian dioceses (from October 1968 in Salzburg to October 1972 in Innsbruck), with the exception of Graz-Seckau and Feldkirch, continuing the Aggiornamento of Vatican II. The composition of the synodal councils (50% priests, 50% lay men and women) reflects the new theology of the laity as the People of God. Important decisions have been made concerning the functions of parishes in such areas as preaching, liturgy and charity. This renewal of parish life has led to parish councils being formed to give lay persons a share in decision-making and responsibility. Following the diocesan synods, a National Synod for Austria was held from May 1973 to May 1974 to deal with the problems of shortage of personnel, church and society, education and the mass media.

PROTESTANT CHURCHES. Although Austria is still predominantly Roman Catholic, the Protestant proportion of the population has doubled since the period prior to World War II, to more than 6%. This increase, unique in Europe, is due primarily to migration from Germany during 1938–1945 and the influx of refugees from central, southern and eastern Europe after the war. Some change of affiliation also occurred for political reasons at the time of the Catholic corporate state experiment (1934–1938) and following the absorption of Austria by Nazi Germany in 1938, in addition to other cases motivated by dissatisfaction over the Catholic attitude to divorce.

The principal Protestant body is the Evangelical Church, which is a loose union of the Helvetian (HB) Reformed and Augsburg (AB) Lutheran churches, the latter being by far the most significant in terms of membership. The general synod is the church's supreme authority and carries on its administrative functions through the AB and HB Church Council, with headquarters in Vienna. Protestants are strongest in the Alpine regions of Upper Austria, which were less accessible to suppression at the time of the Counter-Reformation, as well as in Burgenland, which was part of Hungary until 1918. New Protestant groups have been formed among refugees since World War II.

Only 2 other Protestant groups are officially recognized: Moravians, who were given legal status in 1880 but no longer have members or congregations in Austria, and Methodists, who have been active since 1870 and legally recognized since 1951. Austrian Methodists are related to the United Methodist Church in the USA.

A host of smaller Protestant groups continue to function without official recognition, including Adventists, Baptists, Brethren, Friends, Mennonites and Pentecostals.

OTHER CHURCHES. The Old Catholic Church was founded in 1871 as a protest movement against the doctrine of papal infallibility promulgated at Vatican Council I, and was given legal recognition in Austria in 1877. This is now Austria's fourth largest denomination after the Roman Catholic, Lutheran and Orthodox churches. Another Catholic (non-Roman) body, the New Apostolic Church, with headquarters in Dortmund (Germany) has also built up a significant following in Austria.

Eastern Orthodoxy is represented by 6 branches: Armenian, Bulgarian, Greek, Romanian, Russian and Serbian Orthodox Churches. Anglicans serve a small mostly expatriate community in Vienna, in addition to maintaining seasonal chaplaincies in some of the resort areas. Among marginal Protestant groups, only Mormons have been granted legal recognition (in 1955), but Jehovah's Witnesses are much larger.

CHURCH AND STATE. The federal constitution, revised in 1929, contains no stipulation concerning religions. Nevertheless, the Basic Law of 21 December 1867 (RGB1 No 142) dealing with the general rights of nationals, which is considered a constitutional law by Article 149 of the federal constitution, guarantees freedom of conscience and belief (Article 14), the internal autonomy of the churches (Article 15), and freedom of religious instruction (Article 17). The State Treaty for the Re-establishment of an Independent and Democratic Austria (BGB1 No 152), signed in 1955 by the 4 former occupying powers, also guarantees freedom of worship and non-discrimination on the grounds of religious belief (Article 6).

The legal status of religious communities is regulated by a law of 20 May 1874, which continues valid. According to this law, only legally-recognized religious communities may be granted a juridical personality, and their organizations and institutions enjoy a special penal protection.

**Alt-katholische Kirche in Österreich.** Assistant bishop (right) administers priests' communion in Vienna cathedral.

Relations between the Austrian Republic and the Catholic Church are covered by the concordat with the Holy See signed on 5 June 1933. This concordat grants to the church, among other rights, the right to institute, administer and supervise religious instruction for Catholic schools in all branches of the primary and middle educational system. The Catholic Church, its orders and congregations, have the right to open schools which enjoy all benefits of public schools as long as they respect general legal stipulations. The church enjoys full liberty in the administration of its affairs and property as well as in the public celebration of worship. Although the concordat also calls for recognition by the Republic of the civil juridical effects of marriages celebrated according to canon law, this latter stipulation was abolished by the law of 6 July 1938, still in force, concerning the unification of marriage and divorce in Austria and other territories of the German Third Reich, which made civil marriage obligatory.

The concordat has been extended by a series of agreements concluded with the Holy See. These include: (1) the agreements of 23 June 1960 concerning church property, resulting in the restitution to the church of its lands and buildings and commitment by the state to provide it with an annual subsidy of 100 million Austrian shillings, and the apostolic administration of Burgenland, which was raised to the rank of diocese (Eisenstadt); (2) the agreement of 9 July 1962 regarding the educational question, by which the Austrian Republic agreed to subsidize Catholic schools for up to 60% of the cost of its teaching personnel (100% beginning in 1971); and (3) the agreements of 7 July 1964 and 7 October 1968 relating to the creation respectively of the dioceses of Innsbruck and Feldkirch.

Relations between the state and the Evangelical Lutheran and Reformed churches are regulated by the federal law of 6 June 1961. This law explicitly recognizes these churches both as separate entities and as an ecclesiastical federation. They are completely autonomous in their organization. Their parishes are at every echelon in the position of state-recognized corporations, which includes legal assistance by the authorities. Financial contributions from the state to the Old Catholic Church and Jewish religious communities were fixed in October 1960.

Concerning the right to collect ecclesiastical taxes, this was already affirmed for legally recognized churches in Article 15 of the fundamental law of 21 December 1867, but its effective application did not become operative until the promulgation of the German law of 1 May 1939 concerning the collection of ecclesiastical taxes in the 'Land' of Austria.

The Cultural Section of the Federal Ministry for Teaching and Art (Kultursektion des Bundesministeriums für Unterricht und Kunst) is responsible for all matters relating to the churches and religious communities.

INTERDENOMINATIONAL ORGANIZATIONS. The Ecumenical Council of Churches in Austria (Ökumenischer Rat der Kirchen in Österreich), founded in Vienna in 1958, is the principal coordinating body for ecumenical activity in Austria. Members include the Lutheran, Reformed, Old Catholic, Methodist, Anglican and Orthodox churches. Several other denominations and church-related organizations have observer status.

There is no national Catholic commission for ecumenism, but by 1974, 4 diocesan commissions had been created in the dioceses of Vienna, Linz, Salzburg and Graz-Seckau, the latter being itself an interconfessional commission.

Two mixed commissions have been formed: the Joint Catholic/Evangelical Commission of Austria (Gemischte Katholische/Evangelische Kommission Österreichs), founded in Vienna in 1966; and the Old Catholic/Roman Catholic Consultations (Altkatholische/Römisch-Katholische Konsultationen), also in Vienna.

The Society for the Law of the Oriental Churches, founded in Vienna in 1969, is an international interconfessional body, providing for scientific collaboration between specialists in Eastern canon law and civil law concerning the Eastern churches. It unites representatives of Eastern Orthodox, Oriental Orthodox and Eastern-rite Catholic churches, as well as Western specialists. The society organized a congress in Vienna in 1971 and another in Gonia (Crete) in 1973.

Organizations dedicated to practical co-operation include 8 major ones: (1) Austrian Missionary Council (Österreichischer Missionsrat), founded in Vienna in 1963, and affiliated to CWME of the WCC; (2) Ecumenical Youth Council in Austria (Ökumenischer Jugendrat in Österreich), founded in Vienna in 1960–1961, an independent multi-confessional youth organization including Catholics since 1967, which provides for studies and work projects on national and international levels; (3) Theological Work Circle of Vienna (Theologischer Abeitkreis in Wien); (4) Committee for Aid to Serbian Orthodox Immigrant Workers in Austria (Komitee zür Betreuung Serbisch-Orthodoxer Gastarbeiter in Österreich) in Linz, plus another ecumenical group recently formed in Vienna to aid all immigrant workers; (5) Working Group for Voluntary Social Service (Arbeitsgemeinschaft Freiwilliger Sozialer Dienste) in Vienna; (6) Women's Ecumenical Working Group (Ökumenischer Arbeits Kreis der Frauen) in Vienna; (7) International Christian Youth Exchange (Internationaler Christlicher Jugendaustausch), in Vienna; and (8) Telephonic Aid Services, sponsored by Catholics and Evangelicals in Vienna (Telephonseelorge) and Linz (Notrufdienst).

Several ecumenical institutes and centres are active. The Pro Oriente Foundation (Stiftungsfonds Pro Oriente) formed in Vienna in 1964 by the archdiocese of Vienna, promotes understanding of Eastern and Oriental (non-Chalcedonian) Orthodox. In September 1971 it organized the first official meeting between Catholic theologians and representatives of the Oriental Orthodox churches.

Other centres include: (1) Institut für Dogmengeschichte and Ökumenische Theologie, founded in 1966, which is a Catholic institute concerned with the history of dogma and ecumenical theology and is attached to the Faculty of Theology of the University of Graz; (2) Institut für Ökumenische Theologie, a Catholic institute studying ecumenical theology attached to the Faculty of Theology of the University of Salzburg; (3) Catholica Unio, in Salzburg, the Austrian branch of a Catholic ecumenical organization with its international headquarters in Switzerland; (4) Die Offene Tür, in Vienna, which seeks to make available ecumenical information; and (5) Kloster Erlach (Kloster des Allerheiligsten Erlösers), in Niederwaldkirchen, an ecumenical monastic community situated in Upper Austria. The Pastorie für Ökumenische Beziehungen of Vienna was closed in August 1974 but was expected to re-open during 1975 under a new name aiming to deepen contacts with churches in eastern Europe.

Three further groups are dedicated to inter-religious dialogue: (1) Action against Anti-Semitism in Austria (Aktion gegen den Antisemitismus in Österreich), founded in Vienna in 1955, affiliated with the International Council of Christians and Jews in London; (2) Co-ordinating Committee for Collaboration between Christians and Jews (Koordinierungsausschus für Christlich-Jüdische Zusammenarbeit), founded in Vienna in 1965, which promotes conferences, seminars, publications and scientific research; and (3) Information Centre at the Service of Christian-Jewish Understanding (Informationszentrum im Dienste der Christliche-Jüdischen Verstandigung, IDCIV), founded by the Catholic Sisters of Our Lady of Zion in Vienna in 1967, which organizes conferences and makes educational material available.

**BROADCASTING.** The government Österreichischer Rundfunk (ORF), with its Religious Section, broadcasts 140 Catholic programmes a week on radio and TV, including worship, preaching, information and education. Every Sunday, all recognized denominations share in an ecumenical morning celebration over ORF radio. There is a Catholic Centre for Mass Communications (1965). For Catholics, Austria is a member of UNDA.

## BIBLIOGRAPHY


*Alt-katholisches Jahrbuch 1964*. Wien: Alt-katholische Kirche Österreichs, 1964.

'Austria', H. Bogensberger, in H. Mol (ed), *Western religion* (The Hague: Mouton, 1972), p. 47–66.

*Die Katholiken in Österreich: ein religionssoziologischer Uberblick*. E. Bodzenta. Wien: Herder, 1962.

*Jahrbuch für die Kirche von Wien, 1970*. Wien: Erzbischöflischen Pastoralamt im Wiener-Dom Verlag, 1970. (Roman Catholic).

*Kirche in Österreich 1918–1965*. F. Klostermann et al. Wien: Herder, 1966.


TABLE 2. ORGANIZED CHURCHES AND DENOMINATIONS IN AUSTRIA

| Official name 1 | Begun 2 | Type 3 | Counc 4 | Congs 5 | Adults 6 | Affiliated 7 | Names, notes, and other statistics (see Codebook) 8 |
|---|---|---|---|---|---|---|---|
| Alt-katholische Kirche in Österreich | 1871 | C OCa | UWC.W | 66 | 20,000 | 26,000 | *Old Catholic Ch of Austria*. 1925, Diocese of Vienna. 17n,1s,W=9%,178Yy. |
| Anglikanische Kirche (J Fulham) | c1750 | A plu | awc.W | 7 | 1,000 | 2,000 | *Ch of England*. Christ Ch, Vienna; seasonal chaplaincies Innsbruck, Kitzbuhel. 1x. |
| Armenische Apostolische K: V Wien | | O Arm | Ewc.W | 1 | 700 | 1,000 | *Armenian Apostolic Ch (Gregorians)*. Under C Echmiadzin (USSR). 1n. |
| Baptistenkirche | 1967 | P Bap | xF... | 1 | 60 | 100 | *Conservative Baptist Mission*. M=CBFMS(USA). 4f,1t(44),W=95%,2Y. |
| Bulgarisch-Orthodoxe Kirche | | O Sla | Mwc.W | 2 | 1,500 | 2,000 | *Bulgarian Orthodox Ch. Balgarskata Pravoslavna Crkva*. Under P Sofia. |
| Bund der Baptisten-Gemeinden in Ö | 1869 | P Bap | T.D.a | 14 | 800 | 2,000 | *Baptist Union of Austria*. 1965, M=SBC(USA). HQ Vienna. 6n,5f,35Y. |
| Christadelphianer | | P Ade | x.... | 2 | 50 | 100 | *Christadelphian Ecclesias*. HQ Linz: 2 ecclesias (churches). Pacifist, adventist. |
| Christengemeinde/Offene Brüder | 1919 | P CBr | x.D.e | 10 | 500 | 1,000 | *Christian Brethren (Open). Plymouth-Brüder*. 10 missionaries from West Germany. |
| Christliche Wissenschaft | | M Sci | x.... | 2 | 70 | 200 | *Christian Science. Church of Christ, Scientist*. M=CCS(Boston,USA). 1m,3w. |
| Evangelische Kirche AB in Österreich | 1781 | P Lut | LWC.W | 600 | 200,000 | 406,260 | EKAB. *Ev Luth Ch (Augsburg Confession)*. Rapid growth from Catholics, refugees. 200n,1s. |
| Evangelische Kirche HB | 1781 | P Ref | RWC.W | 36 | 13,628 | 20,000 | *Ev Ch of the Helvetic Confession. Reformed Ch of Austria*. Linked to EKAB. 12n. |
| Ev Tschechisch-Brüderische Kirche | | P LuR | Rwc.. | 1 | 2,000 | 3,000 | *Ceskobratrska Cirkev Evangelicka. Ev Ch of Czech Brethren*. Czechs, Slovaks. |
| Evangelische-Methodistenkirche | 1870 | P Met | VwC.W | 12 | 1,093 | 2,000 | *Methodist Ch*. Provisional Annual Conf, C&S Europe Central Conf,UMC(USA). 8n,2f. |
| Freie Christengemeinden in Österreich | 1920 | P Pe2 | ZF..H | 34 | 1,090 | 2,000 | *Free Christians. Philadelphia Ch*. M=SFM(Sweden),AoG(UK,USA). 19n,4f,1s. |
| Gemeinde Christi | 1950 | P Dis | x.... | 7 | 200 | 500 | *Churches of Christ*. M=CC(Non-Instrumental)(USA). Mainly USA expatriates. 22f,1s. |
| Gemeinde Gottes | | P Hol | x.... | | 50 | 100 | M=Ch of God(Anderson)(USA). Small mission of holiness body from USA. |
| Gemeinschaft Evangelisch Taufgesinnter | 1850 | P Hol | x.... | 6 | 30 | 50 | *Apostolic Christian Ch (Nazarean)*. Linked with same USA body. Mennonite origins. |
| Griechisch-Orth Kirche: D Österreich | | O Gre | Cwc.W | 3 | 8,000 | 12,000 | *Greek Orthodox Ch*. Also E Italy, Switzerland & Hungary. Under EP Constantinople. |
| Heilsarmee | 1927 | P Sal | xwx.e | 50 | 4,000 | 10,000 | *Salvation Army, Austria Region*, Switzerland & Austria Territory. HQ Vienna |
| **Katholische Kirche Österreichs:** | 174 | R LEr | BzB.s | 3,048 | 5,214,400 | 6,603,148 | *Cath Ch of Austria*. C=47+3+65. 3q,7s. 6192nx,1084m,13541w,P=41%,W=31%,99760Yy. |
| M Salzburg | c 550 | R Lat | Bs | 205 | 373,400 | 478,667 | Workers: 40% industrial. 1s. 544 146 1062 48 36 8726 |
| D Feldkirch | 1964 | R Lat | Bs | 135 | 190,700 | 244,514 | Vorarlberg. High immigration. Tourism. 280 70 867 45 40 4644 |
| D Graz-Seckau | 1218 | R Lat | Bs | 376 | 826,770 | 1,060,000 | Steiermark. Emigration south, east. 1s. 862 89 1598 40 26 16006 |
| D Gurk | 1071 | R Lat | Bs | 335 | 358,700 | 459,925 | Kärnten/Carinthia. Emigration, tourism. 437 26 599 37 30 7858 |
| D Innsbruck | 1968 | R Lat | Bs | 293 | 298,000 | 382,000 | Workers: 40% industrial, 20% rural. 1s. 485 140 1300 56 49 7500 |
| M Wien (Vienna) | 1469 | R Lat | Bs | 640 | 1,616,600 | 2,072,510 | Capital. Immigration, industries. 1s. 1484 414 4404 30 20 23066 |
| D Eisenstadt | 1922 | R Lat | Bs | 172 | 181,600 | 232,864 | Burgenland. Forests. Emigration. 1s. 180 11 261 53 40 3459 |
| D Linz | 1785 | R Lat | Bs | 463 | 872,800 | 1,037,073 | Oberösterreich. Some industry. 1s. 1151 131 2599 48 42 18434 |
| D Sankt Pölten | 1785 | R Lat | Bs | 421 | 492,900 | 631,895 | Niederösterreich. Rural, emigration. 1s. 727 28 850 54 40 10065 |
| AN Wettingen-Mehrerau | 1227 | R Lat | bsoc | 1 | 30 | 30 | Abbey nullius. In northwest Vorarlberg. 38 29 0 99 99 0 |
| O Österreich (*Byzantine*) | 1945 | R Byz | Os | 7 | 2,900 | 3,670 | For all Catholics of Byzantine rite. 4 0 1 50 30 2 |
| K JC der Heiligen der Letzten Tage | c1922 | M LdS | x.... | | 2,000 | 2,675 | KJC=Kirche Jesu Christi. *Latter-day Saints* (USA). *Mormons*. 60f,G=3.9%pa. |
| Mennonitengemeinde | 1953 | P Men | GF..w | 3 | 400 | 1,000 | 1953, M=Mennonite Brethren Ch of NAmerica. HQ Vienna. 6f. |
| Neuapostolische Kirche | | C CAp | x.... | | 5,000 | 10,000 | *NAK*, Bezirk Schweiz. *New Apostolic Ch*, Switzerland District. HQ Dortmund(Germany). |
| Orthodoxe Kirche von Rumänien | | O Rum | Cwc.W | 1 | 3,000 | 4,000 | *Romanian Orthodox. Ch. Parohia Ortodoxa Romana din Viena*. Under P Bucharest. 1x. |
| Religiöse Gesellschaft der Freunde | 1938 | P Qua | Q.... | 1 | 30 | 100 | *Religious Society of Friends. Quakers*. M=FSC(UK). Work for peace, and refugees. |
| Russisch-Orth K ausserhalb Russlands | c1920 | O Sla | x.... | 45 | 7,000 | 10,000 | 1975: *D Austria, ROC Outside of Russia* (HQ New York). Anti-Moscow. |
| Russisch-Orth Kirche (PE Mitteleuropa) | | O Sla | Mwc.W | 1 | 1,500 | 2,000 | *Russian Orthodox Ch, D Vienna & Austria*. Patriarchal Exarchate of Moscow. 1 bishop. |
| Serbisch-Orthodoxe Kirche | | O Ser | Cwc.W | | 20,000 | 30,000 | In D Western Europe, Serbian Orthodox Ch, P Belgrade. HQ London. Serbian labourers. |
| Siebenten-Tags-Adventisten | 1947 | P Adv | x.... | 45 | 2,586 | 6,000 | *SDA, Austrian Union of Chs*. Decline. 21n,66m,1j,1s,45t(3150),85Y. |
| Vereinigte Pfingstkirche | | P Pel | x.... | 56 | 500 | 1,000 | *United Pentecostal Ch. Jesus Only Ch*. M=UPC(USA). Unitarian Pentecostals. 2x,4f. |
| Zeugen Jehovas | c1910 | M Jeh | x.... | 177 | 10,043 | 20,000 | *Jehovah's Witnesses. Watch Tower*. Active witnessing under way by 1926. 716Y. |
| Other Protestant denominations | | P | ..... | | 500 | 1,000 | Total about 15 (see list below). |
| Other marginal Protestant bodies | | M | ..... | | 300 | 1,000 | Total about 10 (see list below). |
| Other Orthodox churches | | O | ..... | | 700 | 1,000 | Refugees, including Eastern Apostolic Ch in Iraq (applied to join WCC, rejected). |
| **Total affiliated (mid-1970)** | | | | 4,350 | 5,522,730 | 7,183,233 | **Total denominations (1970) . . . 58.** |
| **Total affiliated (mid-1975)** | | | | 4,400 | 5,492,500 | 7,143,910 | **Total denominations (1975) . . . 61.** |
| **Total affiliated (mid-1980)** | | | | 4,450 | 5,462,400 | 7,104,790 | **Total denominations (1980) . . . 64.** |

NOTES ON TABLE ABOVE

COLUMNS: for meanings and CODES (cols. 1, 3, 4, 8): see Codebook (Part 6). Column 1: **Boldface type** = church with over 10% of country's affiliated Christians.

NATIONAL COUNCILS (Column 4, 5th letter).
- a = member of Austrian Evangelical Alliance, and also observer member of ECCA.
- e = Evangelische Allianz Österreichs (Austrian Evangelical Alliance) (affiliated to EEA but not to WEF; members 44 individual congregations, in the major Protestant bodies).
- H = Independent Pentecostal Council of Austria (mostly small groups).
- s = Österreichische Bischofskonferenz (Bishops' Conference of Austria), and also observer in ECCA.
- W = Ökumenischer Rat der Kirchen in Österreich (Ecumenical Council of Churches in Austria, ECCA).
- w = associate member of ECCA.

OTHER PROTESTANT DENOMINATIONS. These include: Baptist Mid-Missions (1967), Bible Christian Union (1962), Christian Brethren (Exclusive), Christian Chs/Chs of Christ (1971; 12 missionaries), Estonian Ev Lutheran Ch in Exile (c1945), Evangelical Alliance Mission (TEAM) (1965), Fellowship of Independent Missions (1971), Gemeinde Bibelglaubiger Christen (Pentecostals), Gospel Missionary Union (1966), Vienna Community Ch (English-language).

OTHER MARGINAL PROTESTANT BODIES. These include: Amis de l'Homme (Sayerce. Freytag), Anthroposophical Society (Christian Community Ch), General Conference of the New Ch (1 church, 42 members), Greater World Christian Spiritualist League (UK; church in Vienna), Reorganized Ch of JC of Latter-day Saints.

**PEOPLES** (ethnolinguistic). Christians: 93.4% Austrian, 3.5% German, 1.1% Slovene, 0.8% Serbo-Croatian, 0.3% Magyar, 0.2% Greek, 0.2% Russian, 0.1% Italian, 0.1% Czech, 0.1% USA, 0.1% British, Estonian.

COUNTRY-WIDE TOTALS

EVANGELIZATION (see Part 5). 1900: 100%. 1970: 100%. 1980: 100%. *Mass evangelism*. 1970, Euro '70 TV Crusade (Billy Graham) in Salzburg, Graz, Vienna, Linz televised from Dortmund (Germany); 1976, campaigns in Vienna, Steiermark, Kärnten; 1976, formation of Association for the Evangelization of Austria. *Radiophonic evangelism*. Annual listeners' letters (1975): about 1,000 Radio Vatican, 311 HCJB, 110 TWR, 18 RVOG, et alia.

FOREIGN MISSIONARIES AND PERSONNEL (nationals serving abroad) (1973). Total 1,856: 1,824 Roman Catholics (920 personnel serving in Western nations, 904 foreign missionaries (234 priests, 39 brothers, 631 sisters) in Third-World nations), about 25 Protestants, 5 marginal Protestants, 2 Catholics (non-Roman).

FOREIGN MISSIONARIES AND PERSONNEL (aliens from abroad) (1973). Total 767. *From Western world*. 751: about 420 Roman Catholics, 257 Protestants (145 in 22 USA societies, 58 in 7 UK societies, 37 in 4 WGermany societies, 10 in 2 Netherlands societies, 5 in 1 Sweden society, 2 in 1 Australia society), about 70 marginal Protestants (55 Mormons from USA), 2 Catholics (non-Roman), 1 Anglican, 1 Orthodox from Greece. *From Communist world*. About 6 Orthodox (2 USSR, 1 Romania, 1 Yugoslavia). *From Third World*. About 10 Roman Catholics from India et alia.

INSTITUTIONS (church-operated) (1973). Total 230, including 151 higher schools (29 minor seminaries), 20 religious communities (11 monasteries), 15 research centres, 15 seminaries (10 RC, 4 Protestant, 1 Catholic/non-Roman), 8 study centres.

PERIODICALS. About 500 titles (400 RC).

PERSONNEL. About 22,267 (21,500 national, 767 foreign).

RELIGIOUS LIBRARIES. About 190.

SCRIPTURE DISTRIBUTION (1975). Annual totals: 165,914 Bibles (2% free, 19% subsidized, 78% commercial), 130,366 NTs (2% free, 17% subsidized, 81% commercial), 39,509 UBS portions, 71,721 UBS selections.

SERVICE AGENCIES. About 195, including ACISJF, AKC, CCCI, CEF, CIDSE, CLC, EAO, ECCA, ESG(SCM), GEM, KAB, KAJ, KHJO, KLJ, KLO, MIR, MIVA, OJRIO, OKB, OM, PTL, SU, VFKO, WLC(EHC).

ADDITIONAL DATA ON CHURCHES

KATHOLISCHE KIRCHE ÖSTERREICHS. *Annual baptisms*. (1972) 99.1% infant, 0.9% adult, *Defections*. Increase from 8,368 a year in 1958 to 23,833 in 1972. *Priests*. The total in the table (6,192) includes 5,093 working in parishes (1971). *Seminaries*. In 1972, 7 secular, 3 religious, declining through amalgamations. *Religious orders and congregations* (1973). Priests (the 5 major ones): OSB, OCist, SJ, SVD, OFM. Brothers: FSC, Barmherzige Brüder, Marianists. Sisters (the 5 major congregations): Kreuzschwestern (1,760 professed), 1,220 Vinzentinerinnen, 725 Schulschwestern vom Hl Franziskus (Vöcklabruck), 692 Barmherzige Schwestern vom Hl Vinzenz v. Paul, 678 Töchter vom Gottl. Heiland. In addition to the 65 congregations of active life, there are 29 monasteries of contemplative sisters (total, 1,000 houses). *Priests' council*. The code used in the table in column 4, second letter, is: z = Arbeitsgemeinschaft Österreichischer Priesterräte (National Priests Council). *Catholic charismatics* (1975). At least 200 adults including religious personnel in over 5 organized prayer groups are active in the Catholic Charismatic Renewal. *Catholic organizations*. Bishops are organized in the Episcopal Conference of Austria (Österreichische Bischofskonferenz), which is a member of CCEE. Religious personnel are represented by 2 organizations: Superiorenkonferenz der Männlichen Ordensgemeinschaften Österreichs, for men, and Vereinigung der Frauenorden und Kongregationen Österreichs, for women. A national presbyteral council (Arbeitsgemeinschaft Österreichischer Priesterräte) has been formed; and although there is as yet no national pastoral council, an Austrian pastoral commission (Pastoralkommission Österreichs) is active. The Austrian Lay Council (Österreichischer Laienrat), founded in Vienna in 1970, co-ordinates the work of the 2 federations of the lay apostolate, namely Arbeitsgemeinschaft der Katholischen Aktion Österreichs, founded in 1945, which in turn co-ordinates all Catholic Action bodies and had 300,000 members in 1970; and Arbeitsgemeinschaft Katholischer Verbände, which co-ordinates 14 organizations outside the jurisdiction of Catholic Action. The principal Catholic Action movements are: Katholische Frauenbewegung Österreichs (adult women); Katholische Männerbewegung Österreichs (adult men); Katholische Arbeitnehmerbewegung Österreichs (adult male and female workers); Katholische Akademierverband Österreichs (intellectuals); Katholische Jungschar Österreichs (children 8–14 years of age; 90,000 members in 1970); Arbeitsgemeinschaft Katholische Jugend Österreichs (adolescents in 4 branches:

workers, students, rural youth, city youth); and Katholische Hochschuljugend Österreichs (students in higher education). The principal movements outside Catholic Action and under the Arbeitsgemeinschaft Katholischer Verbände are: Österreichische Kolpingsfamilie, Kartellverband der Katholischer Österreichischen Studentenverbindungen, Kartellverband Katholischer Nichtfarbentragender Akademischer Vereinigung Österreichs, Österreichische Turn- und Sport-Union, Reichsbund, Katholische Lehrerschaft Österreichs, Mitteschöler-Kartellverband, Marionische Kongregationen, Legio Mariae, Pfadfinder Österreichs (scouts), Katholische Familienverband Österreichs (protection of family rights), Katholische Familienwerk Österreichs (family assistance) and Kanaa-Gemeinschaft. For the armed forces, Austria forms a military vicariate.

The Holy See has diplomatic relations with Austria and is represented to government and the Catholic hierarchy by a nuncio in Vienna.

Two Catholic international bodies have their headquarters in Austria. The International Military Apostolate, founded in Korneuburg in 1967, unites associations and organizations of military personnel based on the Vatican II decree on the apostolate of the laity. Member organizations in 1973 existed in 7 European countries, with associates in other countries of Europe and America. The Cursillo-Europäische Arbeitsgemeinschaft, in Vienna, is the European Working Group of the Cursillos de Cristiandad, with headquarters in Spain. Member branches exist in West Germany, Austria, Spain, Ireland, Italy, Portugal, and the UK.

Unofficial opinion or pressure groups exist representing both progressivist and traditionalist tendencies. There are 3 main organized opinion groups: (1) Committed Christians United (Solidaritätsgemeinschaft Engagiertre Christen, SOG), with about 500 members, half being priests in 1974, which was originally preoccupied with the question of priestly celibacy but is now composed of 2 wings: one centred on intra-ecclesial reforms, especially the professional problems of married ex-priests, and the other oriented increasingly in a political direction; (2) Critical Christianity Work Circle (Arbeitskreis Kritisches Christentum, AKC), founded in 1972, which is the only Christian group openly professing a socialist orientation; and (3) Christian Working Group for Chile (Arbeitsgemeinschaft Christen für Chile), founded in 1974, which gathers information and funds to support concrete projects in Chile. There also exist other groups of moderately progressivist priests who avoid the public eye to avoid reaction from the hierarchy, the most important of these being the Lainzer Kreis in Vienna, with some 40 priests as members. Austrian JOC, with approximately 4,000 members, has also shown an increasingly progressive political stance since 1971; although an official movement of the church, it tends to be compromised by its financial dependence on the hierarchy.

There are 3 main organized traditionalist groups: (1) Una Voce Austria, in Innsbruck, which has its headquarters in Switzerland; (2) Movement for Pope and Church (Bewegung für Papst und Kirche) which is dedicated to undermining intra-ecclesial reforms; and (3) Cartellverbände (CV), which is an association of university professors, assistants and students, who exercise an important influence over the Popular Christian Party through their fight against any advance of Marxism. There exist other organizations, some official, of pronounced conservative tendencies, as well as regional groups of traditionalist priests.

Main organizations for research and social action include: (1) Institut für Kirchliche Sozialforschung (IKS), founded in Vienna in 1962 by the archbishop of Vienna and affiliated to FERES in Belgium, which studies social change and its influence on religious life; (2) Afro-Asiatisches Institut, founded in Vienna in 1959 by the archbishop of Vienna, which sponsors social and economic research, courses and seminars and promotes cultural exchanges between Austria and African and Asian countries; (3) Ungarisches Kirchensoziologischen Institut (UKI), founded in Vienna in 1957, which is a private Hungarian institute for sociology and religion which carries on sociological research concerning the Hungarian Catholic Church and publishes the 'UKI-Berichte'; (4) Katholische Sozialakademie, in Vienna, which organizes courses on the social doctrine of the church; (5) Bundesarbeitsgemeinschaft für Katholische Erwachsenenbildung in Österreich (BAKEB), founded in Vienna in 1963, which is a federation of Catholic organizations concerned with adult education (especially in the social and political realm); (6) Koordinierungstelle für Entwicklungshilfe der Österreichischen Bischofskonferenz, in Vienna, which provides financial support and co-ordinates the activities of the Austrian Catholic Church in aid of international development, and is a member of CIDSE in Belgium; (7) Institut für Internationale Zusammenarbeit (IZA), founded in Vienna, with the aid of Pax Christi, which facilitates university training for Third-World students and sends Austrian technical personnel to developing countries; (8) Katholisches Landjugendwerk für Entwicklungshilfe in Linz, which facilitates the activities of Catholic farming youth in development aid; (9) Katholisches Frauenwerk Österreichenentwicklungshilfe, in Vienna, which provides channels for development aid by women; and (10) Österreicher Entwicklungshilferdienst, in Vienna, which also sponsors development projects. The Austrian Catholic press agency in Vienna is called Katholische Presse-Agentur (Kathpress).

Institutions for pastoral and religious training include: (1) 4 theological faculties at the state universities of Graz (faculty founded in 1586), Innsbruck (1669), Vienna (1384), and Salzburg (1567), the latter with 11 specialized institutes in such areas as liturgy and pastoral theology; (2) Philosophisches Institut, a pontifical institution annexed to the theological faculty of the University of Salzburg; (3) Internationales Forschungszentrum für Grundfragen der Wissenschaften, founded by the Austrian Episcopal Conference in Salzburg in 1961 and directed by the Catholic Academic Foundation of Salzburg, which since its reorganization in 1970 is composed of 4 institutions: Institut für Wissenschaftstheorie (for research in the philosophy of science), Institut für Religionswissenschaft und Theologie (research in language and the methods of religious science, with a section for the theology of the Eastern churches), Institut für Politische Wissenschaft (political science) and Institut für Kirchliche Zeitgeschichte (ecclesiastical history); (4) several institutes for pastoralia and liturgy: Österreichisches Pastoralinstitut (OPI) founded by the Episcopal Conference in Vienna in 1964 as a supra-diocesan centre, Liturgisches Institut (or Institutum Liturgicum) founded by the OSB in Salzburg in 1946 and which serves also as the secretariat of the Austrian Liturgical Commission, Katechisches Institut der Erzdiözese Wien founded in 1922, Katechisches Institut in Graz, Pastoraltheologisches Institut der Universität Innsbruck, and Österreichisches Katholisches Bibelwerk at Klosterneuburg; (5) 2 institutions for lay training: Theologische Kurse für Laien, and Seminar für Kirchliche Berufe, both in Vienna; and (6) a number of intellectual centres: Paulusgesellschaft, a society of university people best known for their 5 international congresses on Christianity and Marxism; Wiener Katholische Akademie, founded in 1945 and especially concerned with questions of science and faith; Katholischer Akademikerverband, which sponsors courses and meetings for Catholic Intellectuals in Vienna; and Salzburger Hochschulwochen, which organizes annual study weeks.

Catholic missionary action is co-ordinated by the Österreichischer Missionsrat, in Vienna. The Missiologisches Institut der Päpstlichen Missionswerke, also in Vienna, serves as a centre for documentation and research for pontifical missionary works. Three agencies for missionary co-operation are: Päpstliche Missionswerke in Österreich, the official organ of the Austrian church for aid to missions; MIVA-Zentrale Österreichs, founded at Stadt-Paura in 1949, which provides transportation for missionaries; and Katholische Jungschar Österreichs, in Vienna, which encourages youth to engage in missionary projects. In 1973 there were 234 Austrian Catholic missionary priests, 39 brothers and 631 sisters, the principal communities being SVD (94 members) and SJ (28) for men, and Servants of the Holy Spirit (176) and Franciscan Missionary Sisters of Maria Hilf (61) for women. Although no male missionary communities have an Austrian origin, 3 female communities do: Missionsschwestern 'Konigin der Apostel' (founded in 1923); Missionsschwestern vom Heiligen Petrus Claver (1894); and Schwestern vom 3 Orden der Heiligen Franziskus (1857).

The Catholic educational programme is co-ordinated by the Kirchliche Zentralstelle für Unterricht und Erziehung im Österreich, in Vienna, which listed the following statistics for 1972: 82 primary schools (13,039 pupils), 61 complementary schools (8,415), 66 regular secondary schools (15,574), 65 domestic science schools (2,938), 7 commercial schools (1,018), 16 teacher training schools (2,388), and 30 special and technical schools (1,950). In all, the Catholic Church maintains 327 schools with 45,322 students, a very small number compared with the state educational system. Most confessional schools were nationalized in 1867.

Social service and medical work are co-ordinated by Österreichische Caritaszentrale, founded in Vienna in 1945, which supervises numerous institutions: 8 nurseries and 403 children's homes (16,000 infants), 6 kindergartens, 3 student homes, 59 homes for mothers and infants, babies and handicapped persons, 7 workshops for handicapped youth, 5 homes for apprentices, plus schools and homes for handicapped infants and vacation camps. Caritas also provides aid to refugees from eastern Europe and migrant workers. Other relief and social service organizations are: Österpriesterhilfe, in Vienna, which provides aid to priests and refugees from eastern Europe; Bauorden, in Vienna, which builds houses and churches; Katholische Jugend Österreichs, an agency of Vienna youth; and SOS Gemeinschaft, also in Vienna.

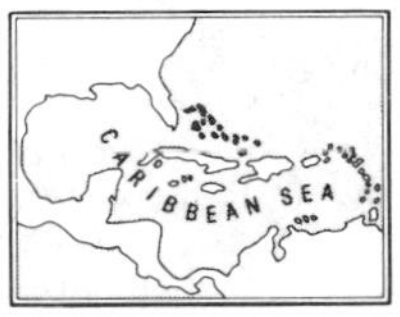


# BAHAMAS

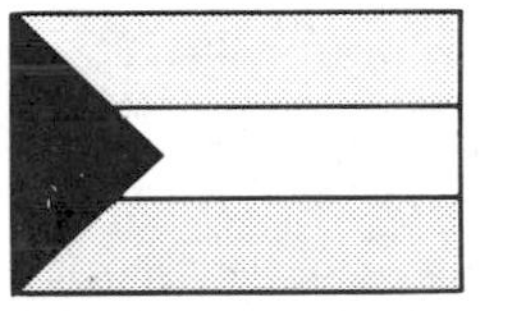

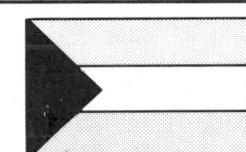

## SECULAR DATA

**STATE. Official name:** The Commonwealth of the Bahama Islands. Adjective of nationality: Bahamian.
**Flag** (shown above right): Black triangle, 2 aquamarine stripes with central gold band.
**Area:** 13,935 sq.km. (5,386 sq.miles). Description: 700 islands (40 inhabited), 1,000 cays, across 90,000 sq. miles of ocean. Agricultural land: 1.2%.
**Government:** Parliamentary state (constitutional monarchy), since 1973 (1626 British colony, 1717 crown colony, 1964 self-government, 1973 Independence).
**Legislature:** House of Assembly, 38 members. Senate, 16 members.
**Official language:** English.
**Capital:** Nassau 101,500 (1970).
**Foreign forces** (1973): 250 USA troops.

**DEMOGRAPHY. Population:** 175,192 (census of 7.IV.1970. For 1970–2000 (UN), see last row of Table 1). Population density (1975): 15/sq.km. (38/sq.mile). Under 15 years: 43%. Growth rate (1975–80): 2.40% per year (births 2.87%, deaths −0.68%, immigrants 0.21%). Life expectancy (1975–80): 69.1 years. Household size: 4.1 persons.
**Major languages:** English, Bahamas Creole (Indo-European Creole), French Creole, Greek, Chinese.
**Urban dwellers** (1970): 71.6%. Urban growth rate (1950–70): 6.3% per year.
**Labour force:** 40%.
**Tourists** (1974): 929,230. (1976) 1.5 million from USA each year.

**ETHNOLINGUISTIC GROUPS:** 72.3% Black (African Negro, including Haitian), 14.2% Mulatto (Black/English), 12.6% White (English, Conchy Joe), 0.3% Greek, 0.3% Jewish, 0.2% Chinese.

**MONEY** (1977). **Monetary unit:** Bahamian dollar (= 100 cents); US$1 = Bah$1.00.

**National income per person:** US$3,000. Average annual family income: US$12,300.
**Inflation:** (1970–74) 7.5% per year, (1975) 10% per year (consumer price index 124).
**Cost of living in capital** (1976): index 130 (Washington DC = 100). Daily cost of living: US$35.

**EDUCATION.** Adult literacy: (1953) 85%, (1963) 90%. Education rate: 62%. Schools: 196.

**HEALTH.** Hospitals: 6 (970 beds). Doctors: 158. Lepers: 35 (0.2 per 1,000). Blind: 110. Criminals: 2,611.

**LITERATURE.** Periodicals: 27. Newspapers: 3 dailies, 5 non-daily.

**COMMUNICATION** (per 1,000 people). Phones: 285. Radios: 440. Daily newspaper circulation: 162 copies.

TABLE 1. RELIGIOUS ADHERENTS IN THE BAHAMAS

| Year | 1900 | | mid-1970 | | Annual change, 1970–1980 | | | | mid-1975 | | mid-1980 | | 2000 | |
|---|---|---|---|---|---|---|---|---|---|---|---|---|---|---|
| *Name* | *Adherents* | *%* | *Adherents* | *%* | *Natural* | *Conversion* | *Total* | *Rate* | *Adherents* | *%* | *Adherents* | *%* | *Adherents* | *%* |
| **Christians** | **51,900** | **97.9** | **171,990** | **97.2** | **5,111** | **−330** | **4,781** | **2.43** | **196,740** | **96.4** | **219,800** | **95.6** | **303,600** | **92.0** |
| professing | 51,900 | 97.9 | 171,990 | 97.2 | 5,111 | −330 | 4,781 | 2.43 | 196,740 | 96.4 | 219,800 | 95.6 | 303,600 | 92.0 |
| Protestants | 21,200 | 40.0 | 87,260 | 49.3 | 2,546 | −543 | 2,003 | 2.04 | 98,030 | 48.0 | 107,290 | 46.6 | 141,900 | 43.0 |
| Anglicans | 25,100 | 47.3 | 40,180 | 22.7 | 1,151 | −409 | 742 | 1.67 | 44,300 | 21.7 | 47,600 | 20.7 | 56,100 | 17.0 |
| Roman Catholics | 5,300 | 10.0 | 39,820 | 22.5 | 1,272 | 611 | 1,883 | 3.85 | 48,960 | 24.0 | 58,650 | 25.5 | 92,400 | 28.0 |
| Black indigenous | 300 | 0.6 | 3,200 | 1.8 | 96 | 4 | 100 | 2.71 | 3,690 | 1.8 | 4,200 | 1.8 | 8,300 | 2.5 |
| Marginal Protestants | 0 | 0.0 | 1,060 | 0.6 | 32 | 7 | 39 | 3.20 | 1,220 | 0.6 | 1,450 | 0.6 | 4,000 | 1.2 |
| Orthodox | 0 | 0.0 | 470 | 0.3 | 14 | 0 | 14 | 2.59 | 540 | 0.3 | 610 | 0.3 | 900 | 0.3 |
| nominal | 2,130 | 4.0 | 18,283 | 10.3 | 601 | 391 | 992 | 4.29 | 23,140 | 11.3 | 28,200 | 12.3 | 51,800 | 15.7 |
| affiliated | 49,770 | 93.9 | 153,707 | 86.8 | 4,510 | −721 | 3,789 | 2.18 | 173,600 | 85.1 | 191,600 | 83.3 | 251,800 | 76.3 |
| total practising | 47,280 | *95* | 126,040 | *82* | 3,698 | −591 | 3,107 | 2.18 | 142,350 | *82* | 157,110 | *82* | 188,800 | *75* |
| non-practising | 2,490 | *5* | 27,670 | *18* | 812 | −130 | 682 | 2.18 | 31,250 | *18* | 34,490 | *18* | 63,000 | *25* |
| Protestants | 20,140 | 38.0 | 86,010 | 48.6 | 2,493 | −637 | 1,856 | 1.93 | 96,000 | 47.0 | 104,580 | 45.5 | 132,150 | 40.0 |
| Evangelicals | 10,600 | 20.0 | 21,200 | 12.0 | 624 | −144 | 480 | 2.00 | 24,000 | 11.8 | 26,000 | 11.3 | 33,000 | 10.0 |
| Roman Catholics | 5,030 | 9.5 | 33,220 | 18.8 | 1,050 | 408 | 1,458 | 3.61 | 40,400 | 19.8 | 47,800 | 20.0 | 75,900 | 23.0 |
| Anglicans | 24,400 | 46.0 | 30,000 | 16.9 | 832 | −502 | 330 | 1.03 | 32,030 | 15.7 | 33,300 | 14.5 | 33,000 | 10.0 |
| Black indigenous | 200 | 0.4 | 3,000 | 1.7 | 90 | 0 | 90 | 2.60 | 3,460 | 1.7 | 3,900 | 1.7 | 6,600 | 2.0 |
| Marginal Protestants | 0 | 0.0 | 1,014 | 0.6 | 31 | 10 | 41 | 3.44 | 1,180 | 0.6 | 1,420 | 0.6 | 3,300 | 1.0 |
| Orthodox | 0 | 0.0 | 463 | 0.3 | 14 | 0 | 14 | 2.64 | 530 | 0.3 | 600 | 0.3 | 850 | 0.3 |
| Non-religious | 0 | 0.0 | 2,600 | 1.5 | 115 | 319 | 434 | 9.82 | 4,420 | 2.2 | 6,940 | 3.0 | 20,800 | 6.3 |
| Afro-American spiritists | 1,000 | 1.9 | 1,700 | 1.0 | 51 | 0 | 51 | 2.60 | 1,960 | 1.0 | 2,210 | 1.0 | 3,200 | 1.0 |
| Jews | 100 | 0.2 | 480 | 0.3 | 14 | 0 | 14 | 2.55 | 550 | 0.3 | 620 | 0.3 | 900 | 0.3 |
| Baha'is | 0 | 0.0 | 230 | 0.1 | 9 | 11 | 20 | 6.06 | 330 | 0.2 | 430 | 0.2 | 1,500 | 0.4 |
| **Country's population** | **53,000** | **100.0** | **177,000** | **100.0** | **5,300** | **0** | **5,300** | **2.60** | **204,000** | **100.0** | **230,000** | **100.0** | **330,000** | **100.0** |

COLUMNS, ROWS. For meanings and definitions, see Code-book (Part 6). Note that, by definition, total 'Christians' = professing + crypto-Christians, which also = affiliated + nominal Christians. Percentages may not always total exactly, due to rounding.
CENSUSES. 6.XII.1953: 55.1% Protestants, 24.1% Anglicans, 15.6% Roman Catholics, 4.7% other religionists, 0.5% non-religious. 15.XI.1963 (de jure): 55.1% Protestants and Black

indigenous, 24.2% Anglicans, 20.3% Roman Catholics, 0.4% marginal Protestants. 7.IV.1970 (de jure): 51.1% Protestants and Black indigenous, 22.7% Anglicans, 22.5% Roman Catholics, 2.5% non-religious, 0.6% marginal Protestants, 0.3% Orthodox, 0.3% Jews.

NOTES ON RELIGIONS
AFRO-AMERICAN SPIRITISTS. Obeah, syncretizing

Christianity with African tribal religions, is practised by many including numerous church members. There are also Rastafarians, from Jamaica.
BAHA'IS. Growth from 1 local spiritual assembly (1964) to 4 (1973).
BLACK INDIGENOUS. In 6 denominations in 1970 (see Table 2).
PROTESTANTS. Including many USA expatriates.

Woman evangelist Rowena Rand featured on postage stamps during International Women's Year 1975.

NON-CHRISTIAN RELIGIONS. Small groups of Jews and Baha'is exist, and a rather larger number claim no religious allegiance.

## CHRISTIANITY

PROTESTANT CHURCHES. The largest denomination is the Bahamas Baptist Union, and in 1970 some 29% of the population professed to be Baptists. The Baptist Missionary Society of Great Britain sent its first missionaries to the Bahamas in the middle of the last century, from which an autonomous church has been developed. New impulses from the USA have come since World War II, especially since the arrival of Southern Baptists in 1951.

Of Protestant groups, the Church of God (Anderson) and the Methodist Church are second in importance. The former has a larger affiliated membership, although a higher percentage of the population claims to be Methodists (7% in 1970). The pioneer Methodist was an ex-slave from the USA, Joseph Paul, who arrived in 1786; and the first British Methodist minister was sent from Barbados in 1800.

Several Pentecostal missions are found in the islands. Both the Church of God (Cleveland) and its splinter body the Church of God of Prophecy made the Bahamas their first overseas field, in 1910 and 1923 respectively, and the Assemblies of God are also active. Other bodies are Adventists, Brethren, Lutherans, Presbyterians and Salvation Army.

ANGLICAN CHURCH. The first English settlement was from Bermuda in the 17th century, served

by Anglican chaplains; and for the next 200 years the Church of England was virtually the only Christian body working in the islands. At the end of the 18th century Anglican membership was increased by the arrival from the USA of many Loyalist settlers who opposed the American Revolution. The Anglican Church is the second largest denomination in the Bahamas.

CATHOLIC CHURCH. Benedictine priests of St John's Abbey, Minnesota (USA) began a mission in the Bahamas in 1891 and continue to support it. A prefecture was erected in 1929, becoming a vicariate in 1941. A major part of the religious personnel and financial support continues to come from the USA and Canada. In 1974 there were parishes on the following islands: New Providence (12), Andros (3), Harbour (1), Eleuthera (4), San Salvador (1), Long

Labour Day Parade in Nassau celebrating 1973 Independence with the words of Martin Luther King: 'Free at last, Great God Almighty, we are free at last'.

Island (2), Inagua (1), Cat (2), Grand Bahama (7), Bimini (1), Exuma (1), and Abaco (1). In addition there are several stations, and Cat Cay is served from Bimini.

CHURCH AND STATE. The Preamble to the constitution states: 'We . . . recognizing the Supremacy of God and believing in the Fundamental Rights and Freedoms of the Individual . . .' In Chapter III, Article 22(1), freedom of religion is defined in detail and is guaranteed.

INTERDENOMINATIONAL ORGANIZATIONS. The Bahamas Christian Council, founded in 1948, is made up of an unusually broad denominational constituency: Adventists, Anglicans, Baptists, Brethren, Greek Orthodox, Lutherans, Methodists, Pentecostals, Roman Catholics and Salvation Army. The Catholic diocese of Nassau also has an Ecumenical Commission.

BROADCASTING. The national Bahamas Broadcasting and Television Commission transmits Protestant programmes daily, 60% of which are locally produced. Catholic groups are heard over the national networks regularly, and the Bahamas Catholic Hour has been featured for nearly 25 years.

### BIBLIOGRAPHY
'Church growth and renewal in the Bahamas'. R. W. Kay. Thesis, Fuller Theological Seminary, Pasadena, CA (USA), 1972. 282p.

TABLE 2.     ORGANIZED CHURCHES AND DENOMINATIONS IN THE BAHAMAS

| Official name 1 | Begun 2 | Type 3 | Counc 4 | Congs 5 | Adults 6 | Affiliated 7 | Names, notes, and other statistics (see Codebook) 8 |
|---|---|---|---|---|---|---|---|
| African Methodist Episcopal Zion Ch | 1877 | I Met | Vw₀₀₀ | 9 | 420 | 1,000 | M=AMEZC(Blacks from USA). 9 pastors and catechists. |
| **Anglican Church: D Nassau & the B** | c1670 | A ACa | AwMRK | 100 | 12,000 | 30,000 | 1861, Diocese in CPWI. Many islands. M=USPG(UK). 95% Black. 5% White. 26n,14x,2r. |
| Assemblies of Brethren | | P CBr | x₀₀₀K | 25 | 2,000 | 4,000 | *Christian Brethren, Plymouth Brethren* (Open). M=CMML(USA). HQ Nassau. 2f. |
| Assemblies of God in the Bahamas | 1928 | P Pe2 | ZF₀₀₀ | 17 | 1,029 | 2,000 | Classical Pentecostals. M=AoG(USA). HQ Nassau. 12n,9x,2f,G=7.0%pa,1p,W=71%,70Y. |
| **Bahamas Baptist Union** | c1830 | P Bap | ₀₀M₀K | 220 | 30,456 | 39,000 | Mainly Bahamians. c1850, M=BMS(UK); since 1951, M=SBC(USA). HQ Nassau. 11f. |
| Christian Brethren (Exclusive) | | P EBr | x₀₀₀₀ | 15 | 1,000 | 2,000 | Exclusive (Closed) Plymouth Brethren. Groups: Booth, Ames, Kelly-Continental. |
| **Catholic Church: D Nassau** | 1885 | R Lat | PxNMK | 86 | 18,900 | 33,220 | Suffragan of M Kingston. M=OSB,SFM,CSSp. C=7+0+11. 51nx,5m,78w,P=80%,3r,2218Yy. |
| Church of Christ, Scientist | | M Sci | x₀₀₀₀ | 2 | 80 | 200 | *Christian Science*. M=CCS(Boston,USA). Nassau, Freeport. 2w. |
| Church of God in Christ | | I pe3 | Z₀₀₀₀ | | 500 | 1,000 | Black pentecostals. M=CoGiC(Black mission from USA). HQ Nassau. 7nx. |
| Church of God in the Bahamas | 1910 | P Pe3 | ZF₀₀K | 60 | 3,000 | 4,000 | *Jumpers*. M=CoG(Cleveland)(USA). Rapid growth. 76n,4f,1p,56Y,902z. |
| Church of God of Prophecy | 1923 | P Pe3 | Z₀₀₀K | 42 | 2,000 | 3,000 | M=CGP(USA), schism ex CoG(Cleveland). Holiness Pentecostals. |
| Church of God (Anderson) | | P Hol | x₀₀₀₀ | | 12,000 | 15,000 | Holiness denomination from USA. M=CoG(Anderson)(USA). |
| Church of the Nazarene | 1971 | P Hol | xF₀₀₀ | 10 | 97 | 200 | Holiness denomination. M=CoN(USA). 1n,2m,3t(125). |
| Churches of Christ | 1952 | P Dis | x₀₀₀K | 2 | 70 | 110 | M=Bahamas Chr M (CCCC Instrumental) (USA). Nassau, Clarence Town. 2n,4f,W=82%,18Y. |
| Greek Orthodox Church | | O Gre | Cwo₀K | 1 | 200 | 463 | Ch of the Annunciation. Nassau. In Greek Orthodox AD North & South America. |
| Jehovah's Witnesses | 1926 | M Jeh | x₀₀₀₀ | 8 | 432 | 814 | *Watch Tower. IBSA*. Active witnessing under way by 1932. HQ Nassau. 70Y. |
| Lutheran Church of Nassau | | P Lut | x₀₀₀K | | 500 | 900 | Small Lutheran community linked with Missouri Synod (USA). |
| Methodist Ch in Caribbean & Americas | 1786 | P Met | VwM₀K | 57 | 4,467 | 6,800 | *MCCA, Bahamas District*. M=MMS(UK). 80% Black. 10n,7x,17f,2r,1s,W=43%,355Yy,162z. |
| Presbyterian Church | | P Ref | Rw₀₀k | | 700 | 1,500 | Scots and British origin. M=Church of Scotland(UK). In Nassau. 2f. |
| Salvation Army | 1931 | P Sal | xwM₀K | | 1,000 | 2,000 | *Bahamas Region*, Carribbean & CAmerica Territory (HQ Jamaica). HQ Nassau. |
| Seventh-day Adventist Church | 1909 | P Adv | x₀₀₀K | 29 | 2,845 | 3,500 | *SDA, Bahamas Conference*. Expanding. 5n,3x,38mw,1r,31t(1980),W=80%,306Y,300z. |
| Other Protestant denominations | | P | ₀₀₀₀₀ | | 1,000 | 2,000 | Total about 10 (see list below). |
| Other Black indigenous churches | | I | ₀₀₀₀₀ | | 500 | 1,000 | Including: AOC(USA), International City Mission, NBCUSA(1942), PAW. |
| **Total affiliated (mid-1970)** | | | | 880 | 95,196 | 153,707 | Total denominations (1970) . . . 36. |
| **Total affiliated (mid-1975)** | | | | 940 | 107,500 | 173,600 | Total denominations (1975) . . . 38. |
| **Total affiliated (mid-1980)** | | | | 980 | 118,700 | 191,600 | Total denominations (1980) . . . 40. |

NOTES ON TABLE ABOVE
COLUMNS: for meanings and CODES (cols. 1, 3, 4, 8), see Codebook (Part 6). Column 1: **Boldface type** = church with over 10% of country's affiliated Christians.
NATIONAL COUNCILS (Column 4, 5th letter).
K = Bahamas Christian Council.
OTHER PROTESTANT DENOMINATIONS. These total about 10, including: American Lutheran Ch (1 church in Freeport), Bahamas United Baptist Mission, Baptist International Missions (1962, 26 missionaries), Baptist Mid-Missions, Bethany

Fellowship Missions (1968), Gospel Missionary Union (1956), West Indies Mission.

PEOPLES (ethnolinguistic). Christians: 72.9% Black, 14.2% Mulatto, 12.5% White (English), 0.3% Greek.

COUNTRY-WIDE TOTALS
EVANGELIZATION (see Part 5). 1900: 100%. 1970: 100%. 1980: 100%. *Mass evangelism*. 1975, first islandwide evangelistic campaign supported by all churches. *Radiophonic evangelism*.

Bible correspondence courses (1975): 92 active ICI students.
FOREIGN MISSIONARIES AND PERSONNEL (aliens from abroad) (1973). Total 223. *From Western world*. 213: about 110 Roman Catholics, 83 Protestants (61 in 13 USA societies, 22 in 2 UK societies), 15 Anglicans in 1 UK society, about 5 Black indigenous from USA. *From Third World*. About 10 (7 Protestants, 3 Anglicans) from Jamaica.
INSTITUTIONS (church-operated) (1973). Total 25, including 7 higher schools, 10 medical centres, 1 religious community, 1 seminary (Protestant).

PERIODICALS. About 12 titles.
PERSONNEL. About 497 (274 national (including 64 RC catechists), 223 foreign)
RELIGIOUS LIBRARIES. About 2.
SCRIPTURE DISTRIBUTION (1975). Annual totals: 7,180 Bibles (56% free, 40% subsidized, 4% commercial), 11,300 NTs (85% free, 12% subsidized, 3% commercial) 1,100 UBS portions, 3,900 UBS selections.
SERVICE AGENCIES. About 22, including OHC, SCM, YWCA.

**ADDITIONAL DATA ON CHURCHES**
CATHOLIC CHURCH. *Catholic organizations.* The diocese of Nassau is a member of the Antilles Episcopal Conference (AEC), itself a member of CELAM. Religious personnel in the Bahamas are part of the Conference of Major Superiors of the Antilles, which is a member of CLAR; and there is both a Senate of Priests and a Diocesan Pastoral Council. A director of Catholic Youth Organizations has been named, and other lay groups include Christian Family Movement. Christian Study Courses (Cursillos de Cristiandad), Confraternity of Christian Doctrine and Legion of Mary.
The Holy See has no diplomatic relations with the Bahamas. It is represented to the Catholic hierarchy by an apostolic delegate based in Port-au-Prince, Haiti.
In 1974 the church sponsored 15 elementary schools (4,120 pupils), 3 secondary schools (1,507 students), 3 pre-natal clinics (217 patients and 815 visits made), 3 general clinics (3,692 patients and 7,152 visits made), a school health programme and home nursing conducted by 3 congregations of sisters.

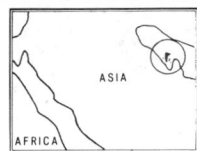

# BAHRAIN

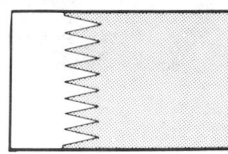

## SECULAR DATA

STATE. **Official name:** The State of Bahrain (Dawlat al-Bhrayn) ('Bahrain' = 'Two Seas'). Adjective of nationality: Bahraini.
**Flag** (shown above right): Scarlet, with white serrated border on hoist.
**Area:** 622 sq.km. (255 sq.miles). Description: 11 islands. Agricultural land: 9.7%.
**Government:** Absolute monarchy, since 1975 (c1550 Portuguese possession, 1820 British protectorate, 1971 Independence, 1973 constitutional monarchy).
**Legislature:** National Assembly, 30 members (dissolved 1975).
**Official language:** Arabic.
**Capital:** Manama 88,790 (1970).
**Armed forces** (1976): Total 1,600 regular army.

DEMOGRAPHY. **Population:** 216,078 (census of 3.IV.1971.

For 1970–2000 (UN), see last row of Table 1). Population density (1975): 404/sq.km. (1,045/sq.mile). Under 15 years: 44%. Growth rate (1975–80): 3.17% per year (births 4.85%, deaths −1.69%, immigrants 0.01%). Life expectancy (1975–80): 49.5 years. Household size: 6.4 persons.
**Major languages:** Arabic, Persian, English, Hindi, Urdu, Punjabi.
**Urban dwellers** (1970): 64.4%. Urban growth rate (1950–70): 3.4% per year.
**Labour force:** 27%.

ETHNOLINGUISTIC GROUPS: 78.0% Bahraini (Arab & Arab/Black), 6.9% Omani & Muscati, 4.0% Iranian, 2.9% Indian, 2.2% Pakistani, 2.2% British, 1.9% other Arab, 1.0% Saudi Arabian, 0.7% USA, 0.1% Jewish, Sudanese.

MONEY (1977). **Monetary unit:** dinar (= 1,000 fils); US$1 = BD 0.395.

**National income per person:** US$2,500. Average annual family income: US$16,000.
**Inflation:** (1970–74) 12.1% per year.
**Cost of living in capital** (1976): index 136 (Washington DC=100). Daily cost of living: US$97.

EDUCATION. Adult literacy: (1950) 13%, (1971) 40%. Education rate: 48%. Schools: 78.

HEALTH. Hospitals: 11 (995 beds). Doctors: 127. Blind: 62. Drug addicts: 300 (on opium). Criminals: 7,200.

LITERATURE. Periodicals: 16. Newspapers: 5.

COMMUNICATION (per 1,000 people). Phones: 77. Radios: 352. TV sets: 78. Daily newspaper circulation: 21 copies.

TABLE 1.    RELIGIOUS ADHERENTS IN BAHRAIN

| Year | 1900 | | mid-1970 | | Annual change, 1970–1980 | | | | mid-1975 | | mid-1980 | | 2000 | |
|------|------|---|----------|---|---------|------------|-------|------|----------|---|----------|---|------|---|
| *Name* | Adherents | % | Adherents | % | Natural | Conversion | Total | Rate | Adherents | % | Adherents | % | Adherents | % |
| Muslims | 64,800 | 99.7 | 204,270 | 95.0 | 7,503 | 1 | 7,504 | 3.15 | 238,390 | 95.0 | 279,310 | 95.0 | 507,600 | 94.7 |
| Christians | 200 | 0.3 | 7,930 | 3.7 | 293 | −4 | 289 | 3.11 | 9,300 | 3.7 | 10,820 | 3.7 | 21,600 | 4.0 |
| crypto-Christians | 100 | 0.1 | 1,480 | 0.7 | 64 | 47 | 111 | 5.50 | 2,020 | 0.8 | 2,590 | 0.9 | 7,100 | 1.3 |
| professing | 100 | 0.1 | 6,450 | 3.0 | 229 | −51 | 178 | 2.44 | 7,280 | 2.9 | 8,230 | 2.8 | 14,500 | 2.7 |
| Anglicans | 50 | 0.0 | 2,500 | 1.2 | 84 | −50 | 34 | 1.27 | 2,680 | 1.1 | 2,840 | 1.0 | 4,800 | 0.9 |
| Protestants | 50 | 0.0 | 1,960 | 0.9 | 72 | 0 | 72 | 3.16 | 2,280 | 0.9 | 2,680 | 0.9 | 4,800 | 0.9 |
| Roman Catholics | 0 | 0.0 | 1,760 | 0.8 | 65 | −1 | 64 | 3.12 | 2,050 | 0.8 | 2,400 | 0.8 | 4,300 | 0.8 |
| Orthodox | 0 | 0.0 | 230 | 0.1 | 8 | 0 | 8 | 2.96 | 270 | 0.1 | 310 | 0.1 | 600 | 0.1 |
| affiliated | 200 | 0.3 | 7,930 | 3.7 | 293 | −4 | 289 | 3.11 | 9,300 | 3.7 | 10,820 | 3.7 | 21,600 | 4.0 |
| total practising | 190 | 95 | 7,530 | 95 | 278 | −3 | 275 | 3.11 | 8,830 | 95 | 10,280 | 95 | 18,360 | 85 |
| non-practising | 10 | 5 | 400 | 5 | 15 | −1 | 14 | 2.98 | 470 | 5 | 540 | 5 | 3,240 | 15 |
| Anglicans | 100 | 0.1 | 2,500 | 1.2 | 88 | −17 | 71 | 2.53 | 2,800 | 1.1 | 3,210 | 1.1 | 5,900 | 1.1 |
| Protestants | 100 | 0.1 | 2,000 | 0.9 | 74 | −4 | 70 | 3.00 | 2,330 | 0.9 | 2,700 | 0.9 | 5,400 | 1.0 |
| Evangelicals | 100 | 0.1 | 1,000 | 0.5 | 38 | 2 | 40 | 3.33 | 1,200 | 0.5 | 1,400 | 0.5 | 2,800 | 0.5 |
| Roman Catholics | 0 | 0.0 | 1,800 | 0.8 | 66 | −6 | 60 | 2.86 | 2,100 | 0.8 | 2,400 | 0.8 | 4,300 | 0.8 |
| Asian indigenous | 0 | 0.0 | 1,400 | 0.7 | 57 | 23 | 80 | 4.44 | 1,800 | 0.7 | 2,200 | 0.7 | 5,400 | 1.0 |
| Orthodox | 0 | 0.0 | 230 | 0.1 | 8 | 0 | 8 | 2.96 | 270 | 0.1 | 310 | 0.1 | 600 | 0.1 |
| Hindus | 0 | 0.0 | 2,350 | 1.1 | 87 | −2 | 85 | 3.09 | 2,750 | 1.1 | 3,200 | 1.1 | 5,400 | 1.0 |
| Baha'is | 0 | 0.0 | 300 | 0.1 | 12 | 8 | 20 | 5.00 | 400 | 0.2 | 500 | 0.2 | 1,200 | 0.2 |
| Jews | 0 | 0.0 | 150 | 0.1 | 5 | −3 | 2 | 1.25 | 160 | 0.1 | 170 | 0.1 | 200 | 0.0 |
| Country's population | 65,000 | 100.0 | 215,000 | 100.0 | 7,900 | 0 | 7,900 | 3.15 | 251,000 | 100.0 | 294,000 | 100.0 | 536,000 | 100.0 |

COLUMNS, ROWS. For meanings and definitions, see Codebook (Part 6). Note that, by definition, 'total 'Christians' = professing + crypto-Christians, which also = affiliated + nominal Christians. Percentages may not always total exactly, due to rounding.
CENSUSES. 3.III.1950: 96.1% Muslims, 2.7% Christians, 0.9% Hindus, 0.3% Jews. 2.V.1959 (excluding foreign military and shipping personnel): 94.8% Muslims, 3.4% Christians, 0.9% Hindus, 0.7% other religionists, 0.2% Jews. 13.II.1965: 95.3% Muslims, 3.2% Christians, 1.4% other religionists,

0.1% Jews. 3.IV.1971 (de jure): 95.7% Muslims, 3.0% Christians, 1.3% other religionists.

NOTES ON RELIGIONS
ASIAN INDIGENOUS. South Indian and Arab indigenous congregations, in 4 denominations or groupings in 1970 (see Table 2).
BAHA'IS. Growth from 1 local spiritual assembly (1964) to 3 (1973).
COUNTRY'S POPULATION. The totals include all categories of resident foreigner, including immigrant workers.
CRYPTO-CHRISTIANS. Local Arab Christians, secret believers in local churches, together with isolated Bahraini radio believers.
HINDUS. Expatriates from India, with a few temples.
MUSLIMS. 50% Sunnis (found in urban areas), 50% Shias (rural areas); Arabs (Bahraini and expatriate), with some Iranians and Pakistanis. *Hajj* pilgrims to Mecca. (1970) 2,418; (1975) 1,928; (1976) 1,989.
PROFESSING CHRISTIANS. Declining slightly in the 1970s due to replacement of expatriate technicians by Bahrainis.

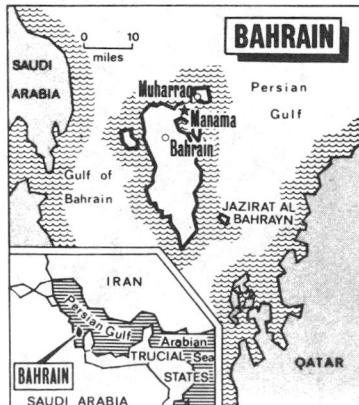

**NON-CHRISTIAN RELIGIONS. Islam** is the religion of virtually all Bahraini citizens and immigrant Arabs. Sunnis predominate in urban centres while Shias are more influential in the rural areas. The 2 communities, which are ancient rivals, are about equal in size and importance.
**Hinduism** exists among the large number of expatriate Indians working in the country.

CHRISTIANITY. In the 3rd century a Christian bishopric was established in the Bahrain Islands. Christian communities existed along the borders of the Arabian peninsula during the 4th and 5th centuries but disappeared at the time of the Islamic invasion. In 1889 the Arabia Mission, sent out by the Reformed Church of America, opened work with an emphasis on schools and hospitals at the head of the Persian Gulf, later spreading out to other areas, including Bahrain. The Catholic vicariate of Arabia, with its see in Aden, was also erected in 1889. Most Christians in Bahrain are expatriates of Indian, British or USA nationality, although there are also some Arab Christians from Jordan, Palestine and Syria. No Bahraini nationals are acknowledged Christians, though secret believers are numerous. All churches are located in Manama except for one at the oil field in Awali which is shared by Anglican, Roman Catholics and Protestants. The great majority of the people at Awali are nominally Christian, although Muslims are now moving into the oil camp.
PROTESTANT CHURCHES. The majority of American and Arab Christians, plus a number of Indians, are members of the National Evangelical Church, which is reformed in tradition. This church sponsors a school and a hospital. Beginning as a dispensary in 1896, the first hospital was built in 1906, and a new installation was completed in 1960. The first predominantly Indian church, the Malayalee

Christian Congregation, has been interdenominational in character since the beginning. Through the years many members have left to form churches of their own home denomination with priests provided from India, although not uncommonly they have maintained an affiliation with the original body and attend services and special programmes.
CATHOLIC CHURCH. Catholics in Bahrain form part of the vicariate apostolic of Arabia erected as a prefecture in 1875. There is one parish, Sacred Heart Church, founded in Manama in 1938. Its 2 Italian Capuchin priests and 12 Verona sisters (in 1975) serve not only the 2,100 Catholics of Bahrain but also the Catholics of Oman.
OTHER CHURCHES. The Anglican community, which is mostly British with some expatriate Arabs, is about equal in size to that of the Roman Catholics and, like the latter, operates its own school. It is part of the Episcopal Church in Jerusalem and the Middle East (formerly the Jerusalem Archbishopric). For many years there was also a Church of England chaplaincy of the Royal Air Force (UK). Syrian Orthodox and Mar Thoma Christians from India are also organized into small communities.
CHURCH AND STATE. As is true of most Muslim countries in the Persian Gulf, there is a strong bias against Christianity. Islam is the official religion of the country, and all Bahraini citizens are counted as

  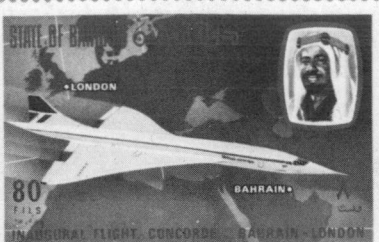 

Unlike many Muslim countries, Bahrain's postage stamps avoid religious themes in favour of secular ones; here, Concorde supersonic airliner (1976)   The ruler portrayed is Shaikh Isa (Jesus, in Arabic).

Muslims. No evangelistic work is allowed among them. Christian churches are permitted as a concession to the expatriate community, which is tending to diminish in size as more Bahrainis are trained in technical skills.

**INTERDENOMINATIONAL ORGANIZATIONS.** Since 1970 the various Christian clergy of Bahrain have met monthly for informal discussion and fellowship.

**BROADCASTING.** Bahrain is a Muslim state with no Christian broadcasting allowed. Christian programmes in Arabic can be easily heard over the stations FEBA (Seychelles) and TWR (Monaco).

TABLE 2.    ORGANIZED CHURCHES AND DENOMINATIONS IN BAHRAIN

| Official name 1 | Begun 2 | Type 3 | Counc 4 | Congs 5 | Adults 6 | Affiliated 7 | Names, notes, and other statistics (see Codebook) 8 |
|---|---|---|---|---|---|---|---|
| **Anglican Church (D Cyprus & the Gulf)** | 1946 | A plu | av... | 2 | 1,500 | 2,500 | In Episcopal Ch in Jerusalem & ME. British. Oil companies' support. 1 school(500),W=5%. |
| Assemblies (Jehova Shammah) | | I CBr | x.... | 1 | 20 | 100 | Missionaries from India (Brother Bakht Singh); HQ Hyderabad, AP. Tamils. |
| **Catholic Church (VA Arabia)** | 1938 | R Lat | P..L. | 1 | 1,000 | 1,800 | *Latini.* Expatriates (Indians, Americans, British). 2x,12w,1r,(954),W=90%. |
| Christian Brethren (Open) | | P CBr | x.... | 1 | 50 | 100 | *Plymouth Brethren.* Expatriates, mostly British and Indians but no Arabs. |
| Church of South India | | P uni | ..... | 1 | 55 | 200 | *CSI.* Former members of Malayalee Christian Congregation. No Arabs. W=65%. |
| Interdenominational Church | | P int | ..... | 1 | 60 | 200 | At Awali oil camp. Mostly USA expatriates. W=60%. |
| Isolated radio churches | c1950 | I rad | ..... | 22 | 400 | 900 | Isolated radio believers, mostly aged 12–25. R=140(FEBA), T=1000(ICI). |
| Malayalee Christian Congregation | | P int | ..... | 1 | 165 | 700 | Serving Malayalam-speaking Indians until own denominations begun. W=80%. |
| Mar Thoma Syrian Ch (D Bahya Kerala) | | I ReO | xwe.. | 1 | 140 | 250 | South Indians from Kerala. Congregation uses Anglican church building. 1x,W=90%. |
| **National Evangelical Ch of Bahrain** | 1889 | P Ref | ..... | 5 | 320 | 700 | Congs: English, Arab, Tamil, Telugu, Urdu. M=RCA(USA),DMS. 50 Arabs. 9f,1H,1k,W=70%. |
| Orthodox Syrian Church of India | | O SyM | Dwe.. | 1 | 130 | 230 | Syrians from Kerala, South India, in D Bahya Keralam (Outside Kerala). W=80%. |
| Pentecostal congregations | | I pen | ..... | 2 | 20 | 100 | House groups for small Indian pentecostal groupings. |
| St Thomas Evangelical Church | c1965 | I ReO | .T... | 1 | 20 | 50 | 1961 schism in Kerala from Mar Thoma Syrian Ch. Home meeting. |
| Other Protestant denominations | 1932 | P | ..... | | | 50 | 100 | Including USA military chaplaincy, Ch of God (1977), and USA Protestant house groups. |
| **Total affiliated (mid-1970)** | | | | 42 | 3,930 | 7,930 | **Total denominations (1970) . . . 15.** |
| **Total affiliated (mid-1975)** | | | | 44 | 4,600 | 9,300 | **Total denominations (1975) . . . 16.** |
| **Total affiliated (mid-1980)** | | | | 46 | 5,360 | 10,820 | **Total denominations (1980) . . . 18.** |

**NOTES ON TABLE ABOVE**
COLUMNS: for meanings and CODES (cols. 1, 3, 4, 8), see Codebook (Part 6). Column 1: **Boldface type** = church with over 10% of country's affiliated Christians.

**PEOPLES** (ethnolinguistic). Christians: 42% British, 32% Indian (Tamil, Telugu, Malayali), 19% USA, 6% Arab.

**COUNTRY-WIDE TOTALS**
EVANGELIZATION (see Part 5). 1900: 9%. 1970: 40%. 1980:

47%. *Mass evangelism.* Ten 5-day evangelistic campaigns yearly held by Malayalee Christian Congregation; 2 or 3 campaigns a year by National Evangelical and Mar Thoma churches. *Radiophonic evangelism.* Broadcasts from FEBA (Seychelles) and other stations. Bible correspondence courses: ICI.
FOREIGN MISSIONARIES AND PERSONNEL (aliens from abroad) (1973). Total 37. *From Western world.* 29: 15 Protestants (9 in 1 USA society, 6 in 1 Denmark society), 14 Roman Catholics. *From Third World.* About 8 (Roman Catholics, Orthodox, Protestants, indigenous) from India.

INSTITUTIONS (church-operated) (1973). Total 3, including 1 secondary school, 1 hospital.
PERIODICALS. About 3 titles.
PERSONNEL. 37 (foreign).

**ADDITIONAL DATA ON CHURCHES**
CATHOLIC CHURCH. *Catholic organizations.* Verona sisters run a school from kindergarten to secondary level, which in 1971–72 enrolled 954 pupils of both sexes including 200 Catholics, 50 other Christians, 550 Muslims and 154 Hindus.

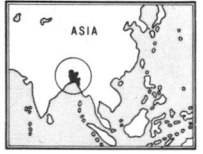

# BANGLADESH

## SECULAR DATA

**STATE. Official name:** The People's Republic of Bangladesh (Gana Prajatantri Bangladesh). Adjective of nationality (unofficial): Bangalee.
**Flag** (shown above right): Orange circle on bottle green field.
**Area:** 142,797 sq.km. (55,126 sq.miles). Agricultural land: 67.4%.
**Government:** Military junta, since 1975 (c1200 Turkish rule, c1750 British rule, 1947 East Pakistan, 1971 Independence as republic, 1975 one-party state).
**Legislature:** Parliament, 300 members.
**Official language:** Bengali.
**Chief cities:** capital Dacca 1,132,370 (1973), Chittagong 492,150, Khulna 467,880, Narayanganj 442,670.
**Armed forces** (1976): Total 63,000 regular: army 59,000, navy 1,000, air force 3,000 (9 combat aircraft). Paramilitary forces: 20,000 Bangladesh Rifles.

**DEMOGRAPHY. Population:** 71,479,071 (census of 1.III.1974. For 1970–2000 (UN), see last row of Table 1). Population density (1975): 516/sq.km. (1,338/sq. mile). Under 15 years: 45%. Growth rate (1975–80): 2.79% per year (births 4.97%, deaths –2.18%). Life expectancy (1975–80): 42.3 years. Household size: 5.4 persons.
**Major languages:** Bengali, English, Urdu, Santali, Garo, Hindi, Lushai, Burmese, and over 30 smaller languages.
**Urban dwellers** (1970): 5.2%. Urban growth rate (1950–70): 4.6% per year.
**Labour force:** 33%.
**Refugees** (1977): Of the up to 10 million who fled in 1971–2, most have been resettled.
**Tourists** (1973): 40,600. (1974) 64,942.

**ETHNOLINGUISTIC GROUPS:** 96.5% Bengali (Muslim Bengali: Ashraf, Ajlaf, Arzal; Hindu Bengali: high-caste, scheduled-caste/outcaste (total 25 including 3.7% Namasudra, also Chamar, Hari, Kochh, Muchi, Paliya, Rajbansil), 1.5% Bihari (Urdu-speaking), 0.9% tribal (0.2% Chakma, 0.2% Santal, 0.1% Magh, 0.1% Garo, 0.1% Tipera, 0.1% Manipuri, 0.1% Khasi, Lushai, Bawm, Oraon, Mahili, Munda, Mru, and over 20 other tribes), 0.6% Urdu, 0.3% Hindi, 0.2% Burmese, Oriya, European, Anglo-Bengali (6,000), Telugu (5,000).

**MONEY** (1977). **Monetary unit:** taka (= 100 paisa); US$1 = Tk 15.00.

**Church of Bangladesh.** Anglican village school in 1962 (right) supervised by CMS missionaries.

**National income per person:** US$70. Average annual family income: US$378.
**Inflation:** (1970–74) 30.4% per year, (1975) 24% per year (consumer price index 279).
**Cost of living in capital** 1976): Daily cost of living: US$22.

**EDUCATION.** Adult literacy: (1961) 22%. Education rate: 30%. Schools: 29,869 (1969). Universities: 1.

**HEALTH.** Hospitals: 11 (10,310 beds). Doctors: 7,663. Lepers: 400,000 (5.4 per 1,000). Blind: 200,000. Psychotics: 440,000.

**LITERATURE.** Periodicals: 120. Scientific journals: 5. Newspapers: 22 dailies.

**COMMUNICATION** (per 1,000 people). Phones: 1. Radios (1969): 8. TV sets: 0.2. Daily newspaper circulation: 2 copies.

TABLE 1. RELIGIOUS ADHERENTS IN BANGLADESH

| Year | 1900 | | mid-1970 | | Annual change, 1970–1980 | | | | mid-1975 | | mid-1980 | | 2000 | |
|---|---|---|---|---|---|---|---|---|---|---|---|---|---|---|
| *Name* | *Adherents* | *%* | *Adherents* | *%* | *Natural* | *Conversion* | *Total* | *Rate* | *Adherents* | *%* | *Adherents* | *%* | *Adherents* | *%* |
| Muslims | 18,807,750 | 65.6 | 55,661,772 | 82.2 | 1,720,856 | –2,169 | 1,718,687 | 2.74 | 62,626,770 | 84.9 | 72,848,640 | 85.9 | 127,628,300 | 88.4 |
| Ahmadis | 0 | 0.0 | 50,000 | 0.1 | 1,346 | 354 | 1,700 | 2.93 | 58,000 | 0.1 | 67,000 | 0.1 | 150,000 | 0.1 |
| Hindus | 9,372,000 | 32.7 | 11,169,000 | 16.5 | –33,400 | –6,500 | –39,900 | –0.40 | 10,100,000 | 13.7 | 10,770,000 | 12.7 | 14,435,000 | 10.0 |
| Buddhists | 157,000 | 0.5 | 450,000 | 0.7 | 11,369 | –3,369 | 8,000 | 1.63 | 490,000 | 0.7 | 530,000 | 0.6 | 722,000 | 0.5 |
| **Christians** | **36,250** | **0.1** | **247,828** | **0.4** | **8,013** | **12,200** | **20,213** | **5.85** | **345,330** | **0.5** | **449,960** | **0.5** | **1,122,400** | **0.8** |
| crypto-Christians | 5,250 | 0.0 | 44,828 | 0.1 | 2,491 | 10,522 | 13,013 | 12.12 | 107,330 | 0.1 | 174,960 | 0.2 | 532,400 | 0.4 |
| professing | 31,000 | 0.1 | 203,000 | 0.3 | 5,522 | 1,678 | 7,200 | 3.03 | 238,000 | 0.3 | 275,000 | 0.3 | 590,000 | 0.4 |
| Roman Catholics | 15,600 | 0.1 | 108,000 | 0.2 | 2,831 | 59 | 2,890 | 2.37 | 122,000 | 0.2 | 136,900 | 0.2 | 280,000 | 0.2 |
| Protestants | 11,600 | 0.0 | 92,900 | 0.1 | 2,633 | 1,577 | 4,210 | 3.71 | 113,400 | 0.2 | 135,000 | 0.2 | 300,000 | 0.2 |
| Bengali indigenous | 0 | 0.0 | 2,000 | 0.0 | 58 | 42 | 100 | 4.00 | 2,500 | 0.0 | 3,000 | 0.0 | 10,000 | 0.0 |
| Orthodox | 100 | 0.0 | 100 | 0.0 | 0 | 0 | 0 | 0.00 | 100 | 0.0 | 100 | 0.0 | 0 | 0.0 |
| Anglicans | 3,700 | 0.0 | 0 | 0.0 | 0 | 0 | 0 | 0.00 | 0 | 0.0 | 0 | 0.0 | 0 | 0.0 |
| affiliated | 36,250 | 0.1 | 247,828 | 0.4 | 8,013 | 12,200 | 20,213 | 5.85 | 345,330 | 0.5 | 449,960 | 0.5 | 1,122,400 | 0.8 |
| total practising | 32,620 | *90* | 185,870 | *75* | 6,009 | 9,151 | 15,160 | 5.85 | 259,000 | *75* | 337,470 | *75* | 785,680 | *70* |
| non-practising | 3,630 | *10* | 61,960 | *25* | 2,004 | 3,049 | 5,053 | 5.85 | 86,330 | *25* | 112,490 | *25* | 336,720 | *30* |
| Roman Catholics | 18,000 | 0.1 | 120,392 | 0.2 | 3,480 | 2,681 | 6,161 | 4.11 | 150,000 | 0.2 | 182,000 | 0.2 | 372,000 | 0.3 |
| Protestants | 13,000 | 0.0 | 99,536 | 0.1 | 3,184 | 4,822 | 8,006 | 5.84 | 137,000 | 0.2 | 179,600 | 0.2 | 450,000 | 0.3 |
| Evangelicals | 10,000 | 0.0 | 85,000 | 0.1 | 2,738 | 4,762 | 7,500 | 6.36 | 118,000 | 0.2 | 160,000 | 0.2 | 420,000 | 0.3 |
| Bengali indigenous | 50 | 0.0 | 27,600 | 0.0 | 1,346 | 4,694 | 6,040 | 10.41 | 58,000 | 0.1 | 88,000 | 0.1 | 300,000 | 0.2 |
| Orthodox | 200 | 0.0 | 200 | 0.0 | 0 | 0 | 0 | 0.00 | 200 | 0.0 | 200 | 0.0 | 0 | 0.0 |
| Marginal Protestants | 0 | 0.0 | 100 | 0.0 | 3 | 3 | 6 | 4.62 | 130 | 0.0 | 160 | 0.0 | 400 | 0.0 |
| Anglicans | 5,000 | 0.0 | 0 | 0.0 | 0 | 0 | 0 | 0.00 | 0 | 0.0 | 0 | 0.0 | 0 | 0.0 |
| Tribal religionists | 300,000 | 1.0 | 100,000 | 0.1 | 2,204 | –3,204 | –1,000 | –1.05 | 95,000 | 0.1 | 90,000 | 0.1 | 70,000 | 0.0 |
| Non-religious | 0 | 0.0 | 50,000 | 0.1 | 1,624 | 2,376 | 4,000 | 5.71 | 70,000 | 0.1 | 90,000 | 0.1 | 300,000 | 0.2 |
| Atheists | 0 | 0.0 | 10,000 | 0.0 | 348 | 652 | 1,000 | 6.67 | 15,000 | 0.0 | 20,000 | 0.0 | 60,000 | 0.0 |
| Baha'is | 0 | 0.0 | 3,200 | 0.0 | 86 | 14 | 100 | 2.70 | 3,700 | 0.0 | 4,200 | 0.0 | 9,000 | 0.0 |
| Parsis | 0 | 0.0 | 200 | 0.0 | 0 | 0 | 0 | 0.00 | 200 | 0.0 | 200 | 0.0 | 300 | 0.0 |
| **Country's population** | **28,673,000** | **100.0** | **67,692,000** | **100.0** | **1,711,100** | **0** | **1,117,100** | **2.32** | **73,746,000** | **100.0** | **84,803,000** | **100.0** | **144,347,000** | **100.0** |

COLUMNS, ROWS. For meanings and definitions, see Codebook (Part 6). Note that, by definition, total 'Christians' = professing + crypto-Christians, which also = affiliated + nominal Christians. Percentages may not always total exactly, due to rounding.
CENSUSES. **1.III.1901** (present-day territory of Bangladesh): 65.7% Muslims, 32.7% Hindus, 1.0% animists, 0.5% Buddhists, 0.11% Christians (0.05% Roman Catholics, 0.04% Protestants, 0.01% Anglicans). **28.II.1951** (East Pakistan; excluding foreigners): 76.8% Muslims, 22.0% Hindus (12.0% scheduled castes), 0.2% Christians, 0.9% other religionists. **1.II.1961** (East Pakistan; excluding foreigners): 80.4% Muslims, 18.4% Hindus (9.8% scheduled castes), 0.7% Buddhists, 0.3% Christians (148,903 persons), 0.1% tribal religionists. **1974**: 85% Muslims.

**NOTES ON RELIGIONS**
AHMADIS. Qadianis; international HQ Rabwah, Pakistan.
ANGLICANS. One of the largest denominations, Anglicans disappeared as a separate entity in 1970 when they merged into the Protestant union, the Church of Bangladesh.
ATHEISTS. Communist Party of Bangladesh (CPBD) (banned 1954, legalized 1971; pro-Soviet) and 4 rival factions: membership (1970) 2,500.
BAHA'IS. In 21 local spiritual assemblies (1973). A number of Baha'is are Persians; new converts are Tipera and Hill Tract tribes.
BENGALI INDIGENOUS. In 3 groupings in 1970 (see Table 2).
BUDDHISTS. Mainly in the Chittagong Hill Tracts, especially the Buddhist tribes Chakma, Chak, Magh and Mru; often syncretized with tribal animism.
CHRISTIANS. In 1975, most Christians were drawn from the Namasudra scheduled-caste Hindus, and the Garo tribe, also Santal, Oraon, Mahili, Tipera, Khasi and other tribes. Between 1961 and 1974 many Christians migrated to India and never returned.
COUNTRY'S POPULATION. In the world's worst natural catastrophe of the 20th century, on 13 November 1970, between 300,000 and 500,000 were killed by a massive cyclone and tidal wave. Thousands more were killed or massacred in the 1971 civil war: first 100,000 non-Bengalis (Urdu-speaking Biharis and others), then over 150,000 killed by the West Pakistan army; and 9 million refugees, mostly Hindus, fled to India, although most returned to Bangladesh within a year or two. In 1973, over 30,000 Biharis again fled.
CRYPTO-CHRISTIANS. Christians affiliated to churches, including isolated radio believers, but unknown as such publicly to state or society.
HINDUS. 48% high-caste (Brahmin, Kshatriya, Vaishya, Sudra), 52% low-caste (formerly depressed classes or outcastes or untouchables, known since 1935 as scheduled castes; over 25 major castes). Hindus include the Tiperas (high-caste Hindus) and Piangs (low-caste). The 8 million who fled to India in 1971 and then lived in refugee camps largely abandoned any Hindu practice, and by 1975 were increasingly open to Christian evangelism. Since 1900 the Hindu community has declined in size relative to the Muslim community due to (1) emigration, (2) mass killings, and (3) lower Hindu fertility due to the prohibition of widow remarriage. The column 'Natural change' above embodies these losses, averaged over the decade 1970–80.
MUSLIMS. Mostly Sunnis of the Hanafite rite, with a number of Wahhabi reform movement centres, and a small Shia minority in towns (descendants of Persian immigrants). Muslim society has 3 social groups: Ashraf (upper-class Muslim) including Mallik, Mughal, Pathan, Saiyed, Sheikh; Ajlaf (lower-class Muslim) with about 20 divisions; and Arzal (degraded-class) with over 7 groups. Another minority, hated and discriminated against are the 4 million Urdu-speaking Bihari Muslims originally from Bihar state (India) with a few from other parts of India. There is also an Ahmadiya Mission (Qadianis; enumerated here as Muslims though declared non-Muslim by Pakistan). *Hajj pilgrims to Mecca.* (1972) 6,595; (1973) 5,187; (1974) 2,921; (1976) 3,490.
PROTESTANTS. Since 1971 there have been large-scale conversions to Christianity in several areas. The most responsive have been the Santalis, among whom in 1972–73, 3,500 former animists were baptized in 20 months in Rajshahi and Dinajpur districts. In 1975, 32 new churches related to BMS (UK) were organized; and 1,200 Garos were baptized. Since 1971 also, about 2,000 Muslims and 2,000 Hindus each year have become Christians (45 Muslims in 1975 through a Bengali evangelist).
TRIBAL RELIGIONISTS. Animists among the Garos, Santals and Chittagong Hill tribes including the Khumi, Koch (population 35,000), Murung (Mru: 20,000), Hajong (15,000), and Banai (2,000).

**NON-CHRISTIAN RELIGIONS. Islam** is the main religion of the country. Muslims are mostly Sunnis with a small Shia minority concentrated in urban areas. The Muslim population increased from 77% in 1950 to 80% in 1960. In 1974, 2,921 Muslim pilgrims from Bangladesh performed the hajj to Mecca.

**Hinduism** is still the principal religious and ethnic minority in spite of a gradual decline from its 22% after partition in 1947, and in spite of severe losses from deaths and refugee movements during the 1971–72 civil war.

**Buddhism** has a very ancient history in the whole of the sub-continent, but the Buddhist population of Bangladesh has never been large and numbers under 1%.

**Traditional tribal religions** are still prevalent among the Garo, Santal and Chittagong Hill tribes.

**CHRISTIANITY.** Bangladesh is one of the most heavily-populated nations in the world. Christians form a very small minority and consist mostly of former low-caste Hindu peasants and a few small tribes including the Garo (now 30% Christian), Santal, Khasi, Tipera and Lushai. The tribes have proved far more receptive to Christianity than the Bengalis, upon whom it has had little influence.

CATHOLIC CHURCH. Although Catholic missionaries were attached to Portuguese trading posts as early as the 16th century, the first of the present 4 dioceses was not erected until 1886. The Catholic Church is strongest in urban areas, notably Dacca, where the church has been able to attract many members of mixed Portuguese descent. Nevertheless, church growth is not keeping pace with the increase in population. Between 1960 and 1969, while the annual population increased at around 4% per year, Catholic membership grew by only 2% per year (90,160 in 1960; 107,030 in 1969), resulting in a gradual decrease in the Catholic proportion of the population from 0.18% to 0.15%. All 4 bishops are local citizens, although 75% of the clergy remain expatriates.

PROTESTANT CHURCHES. Baptists were the first to arrive and remain the strongest of the Protestant traditions. William Carey entered Calcutta in 1793 and within 2 years work was opened at Dinajpur. Dacca was reached by 1816. Mass conversions took place in Mymensingh in the late 19th century, and growth is still considerable among the tribes of the Chittagong Hills. The Baptist Union of Bangladesh is the result of this early British activity, whereas the Bangladesh Baptist Union combines work begun by missionaries from Australia, New Zealand and later Southern Baptists from the USA. The Mymensingh Garo Baptist Convention is an independent body which receives some aid from Australian Baptists.

Anglicans and Presbyterians, the latter owing their origin to English Presbyterian missionary activity, united in 1970 to form one of the dioceses of the Church of Pakistan; but all relations with Pakistan became difficult after the civil war of 1972. For all practical purposes the Church of Bangladesh operates today as an autonomous body.

The Northern Evangelical Lutheran Church grew out of the Santal Mission of the Northern Churches, which was begun in 1867 and has received support from Norwegian, Danish and American Lutheran societies. Before partition in 1947 the church had 40,000 members, but 80% of the church is now in India. The Church of Sylhet was founded by Welsh Presbyterians, and a number of smaller Protestant groups are also active.

Protestant churches sponsor an extensive medical and educational programme and have been heavily involved in relief and rehabilitation following Bangladesh's various natural disasters as well as the civil war of 1971–72.

**CHURCH AND STATE.** Pakistan was created in 1947 when the Punjab and Bengal were partitioned, with the Muslim majority areas forming respectively West and East Pakistan. East Pakistan's substantial Hindu minority acted as a moderating influence against extremist Muslim elements. Nevertheless, the East was dominated by the Punjabi West, which was an increasing source of unrest and ultimately led to civil war. In 1956, largely due to Punjabi pressure, Pakistan was declared an Islamic republic, and there was further erosion of religious liberty during the 1960s. Shortly after independence in 1972, the first president of the republic declared that Bangladesh

**Baptist Union of Bangladesh.** After morning service outside church at Khalishpur. In 1975, 32 new churches related to BMS (UK) were begun.

was a secular socialist state and that its government would commit itself to a policy of complete religious liberty.

Secularism is one of the principles affirmed in the Preamble of the 1972 constitution, promulgated on 4 November 1972. Part II, Article 12, reads: 'The principle of secularism shall be realized by the elimination of: (a) communalism in all its forms; (b) the granting by the state of political status in favour of any religion; (c) the abuse of religion for political purposes; (d) any discrimination against, or persecution of, persons practising a particular religion'. Part III, Article 39, item 1, states: 'Freedom of thought and conscience is guaranteed'. Article 41 states: '(1) Subject to law, public order and morality: (a) every citizen has the right to profess, practise or propagate any religion; (b) every religious community or denomination has the right to establish, maintain and manage its religious institutions; (2) no person attending any educational institution shall be required to receive religious instruction, or to take part in, or to attend any religious ceremony or worship if that instruction, ceremony or worship relates to a religion other than his own'.

Following the first military coup of 1975, the new regime immediately proclaimed Bangladesh to be once again an Islamic state. However, the regime subsequently tended to minimize the significance of that declaration.

By 1978, the future of foreign missionaries was in doubt. One government edict calling for the eviction of all Protestant missionaries during 1978 was only withdrawn under diplomatic pressure.

**INTERDENOMINATIONAL ORGANIZATIONS.** Founded in 1954 as the East Pakistan Christian Council, the Bangladesh National Council of Churches (BNCC) brings together 8 Protestant churches and a number of missions and other agencies. Since the civil war of 1971–72, the council has been preoccupied with the problem of emergency relief, with aid coming from the WCC and Church World Service. In 1972 Bangladesh Ecumenical Relief and Rehabilitation Services was formed, with BNCC, Catholic and government support. A Christian Medical Association helps co-ordinate medical programmes for the churches.

**BROADCASTING.** RVOG (Ethiopia) could easily be heard in Bangladesh until its closure in March 1977. FEBA (Seychelles) broadcasts in Bengali, and a large number of English programmes can be heard.

## BIBLIOGRAPHY

*Catholic directory of Bangladesh, 1973.* Dacca: Catholic Bishops' Conference, 1973.

'Christianity in Bangladesh'. P. Parshall. Dacca, 1974. (Mimeographed).

*Crucial issues in Bangladesh: making missions effective in the mosaic of peoples.* P. McNee. South Pasadena, CA (USA): William Carey Library, 1976. 282p.

*Directory of Christian work in East Pakistan.* Dacca: East Pakistan Christian Council, 1960. 52 + xiip.

'Le syncrétisme religieux d'un village mog du territoire de Chittagong', C. Levi-Strauss, *Revue d'histoire des religions*, 141 (1952), 202–237. (Animist and magico-religious syncretism among a Buddhist tribe, the Mog).

TABLE 2. ORGANIZED CHURCHES AND DENOMINATIONS IN BANGLADESH

| Official name 1 | Begun 2 | Type 3 | Counc 4 | Congs 5 | Adults 6 | Affiliated 7 | Names, notes, and other statistics (see Codebook) 8 |
|---|---|---|---|---|---|---|---|
| All One in Christ Fellowship | 1947 | I Bap | ..... | 60 | 5,000 | 15,000 | *Namasudra Reform Movement*. Ex nominal Baptists. One-caste only. 32m,G=3.8%pa. |
| Armenian Apostolic Church (D India) | c1800 | O Arm | Ewc.. | 1 | 100 | 200 | *Gregorians*. Under C Echmiadzin (USSR). Armenians in Dacca. Declining. |
| Assemblies of God | 1945 | P Pe2 | ZF..n | 22 | 425 | 850 | Begun by Muslim convert. M=AoG(USA). Ex Baptists. All Namasudras. 6n,9f,1p. |
| Assoc of Baptists for World Evangelism | 1956 | P Bap | x.... | 27 | 500 | 1,150 | Regular Baptists. M=ABWE(USA). Bengali, tribal Mru, Tipperah. 7n,35f,1H,2h. |
| Bangladesh Baptist Union | 1882 | P Bap | TH..N | 20 | 782 | 2,276 | *BBU*. M=ABMS(Australia),NZBMS,SBC(USA). Bengalis. 82 schools. 40f,1H,2h,5r,1s. |
| Bangladesh Ev Lutheran Church | 1867 | P Lut | ....N | 123 | 5,000 | 9,000 | *Bangladesh Mission of Northern Chs*. M=SM(Norway),WMPL. Santals. 13f,1h,1p,2100Y. |
| Baptist Union of Bangladesh | 1793 | P Bap | Tu..N | 170 | 6,700 | 22,000 | *BUB*. M=BMS(UK); 1974 Liebenzell Mission. Namasudras, also Mizos. 38f,1H,2h,1s. |
| Bawm Evangelical Christian Church | 1918 | P ind | ....N | 56 | 7,500 | 18,500 | Begun by M=NEIGM(IM). A=1965. Bawm, Mru, Tipperah, Pankho. 20m,1f,1p(20). |
| Bengal Evangelistic Mission | 1833 | I ind | ..... | 3 | 100 | 400 | Indigenous body founded in Gopalganj by an Indian. 2 schools. 1h. |
| **Catholic Church in Bangladesh:** | c1580 | R Lat | P.F.R | 63 | 66,200 | 120,392 | *Katholik Mondoli*. C=3+2+13. 258f,2p. 39n,96x,65m,391w,P=59%,4390Yy. |
| M Dacca | 1886 | R Lat | Pcsc | 31 | 34,000 | 62,000 | Bengali tribal Garos; many of Portuguese origin. 28 32 32 221 49 2393 |
| D Chittagong | 1927 | R Lat | Pcsc | 10 | 9,600 | 17,486 | Urban and rural. Bengali, English spoken. 10 18 23 68 88 522 |
| D Dinajpur | 1927 | R Lat | Ps | 15 | 14,400 | 26,100 | Rural, poor. Santal, Bengali spoken. 1 26 4 22 63 823 |
| D Khulna | 1952 | R Lat | Psx | 7 | 8,200 | 14,806 | *Dharmaprodesh Khulna*. Rural, poor. Bengali. 0 20 6 80 58 652 |
| Christian Brethren | 1961 | P CBr | x.... | 1 | 30 | 50 | *Open Brethren*. Emmaus Bible Courses. M=CMML(UK). In Ramna, Dacca. 2f. |
| Church of Bangladesh | 1805 | P uni | .uE.N | 55 | 6,000 | 17,000 | 1970 union Anglican D Dacca (M=CMS,OMC,PCE(M=CWM). Bengalis. 20n,22f 4H,2h. |
| Church of God (Anderson) | 1969 | P Hol | x...N | 28 | 750 | 1,254 | M=CoG. Remnant of India body. Lalmanirhat, Nilphimari. Khasis, Bengalis. 5n,2f. |
| Church of Sylhet | c1880 | P Ref | ....N | 55 | 2,800 | 5,000 | *Sylhet Christiya Dharmosovar*. M=PCW,SM. Santali, Khasi, Lushai, Garo. 9n,8f. |
| Isolated radio churches | 1952 | I rad | ..... | 300 | 6,000 | 12,200 | Believers mostly aged 12–25. R=250(FEBC,RVOG,HCJB),T=100000(ICF,Emmaus,ICI,VOP). |
| Jehovah's Witnesses | c1932 | M Jeh | x.... | 1 | 30 | 100 | First missionaries about 1932; witnessing reported from 1947. Few converts. |
| Mymensiagh Garo Baptist Union | 1882 | P Bap | .H..N | 88 | 6,972 | 15,000 | Begun by M=BMS, then ABMS. Members 20% of all Garos. 3n,33f,1h,1p(5). |
| Seventh-day Adventist Church | 1906 | P Adv | x.... | 19 | 1,242 | 2,851 | *SDA, Bangladesh Section*, Southern Asia Division. 3nx,88mw,1H,2h,2r,24Y. |
| United Christian Church | 1905 | P Ref | x...N | 18 | 821 | 3,500 | *Sanjukta Christiya Mandali Samuher Sangha*. M=CGNA(USA). Bogra. 6n,5f,1H,1h,92Y. |
| World Missionary Evangelism | c1970 | P ind | x.... | 2 | 50 | 105 | *Mukti Bani Sangsta*. M=American Evangelistic Association. All Namasudras. 35nm. |
| Other Protestant denominations | | P | ..... | | 500 | 1,000 | Total about 5 (see list below). |
| **Total affiliated (mid-1970)** | | | | **1,120** | **117,502** | **247,828** | **Total denominations (1970) . . . 25.** |
| **Total affiliated (mid-1975)** | | | | **1,500** | **163,700** | **345,330** | **Total denominations (1975) . . . 31.** |
| **Total affiliated (mid-1980)** | | | | **2,030** | **213,300** | **449,960** | **Total denominations (1980) . . . 37.** |

### NOTES ON TABLE ABOVE

COLUMNS: for meanings and CODES (cols. 1, 3, 4, 8): see Codebook (Part 6). Column 1: **Boldface type** = church with over 10% of country's affiliated Christians.

NATIONAL COUNCILS (Column 4, 5th letter).
N = Bangladesh National Council of Churches (BNCC) (Jatio Church Parisad, Bangladesh).
n = associate member of BNCC, formerly a full member.
R = Catholic Bishops' Conference of Bangladesh (CBCB).

OTHER PROTESTANT DENOMINATIONS. These include: Indo-Burma Pioneer Mission (Bibles for the World), New Life Center (begun 1972 in Dacca; M=Örebro Mission, 4 missionaries), Salvation Army (1970), World Missions (1972).

PEOPLES (ethnolinguistic). Christians: 59.5% Bengali (45.2% outcaste (40.0% Namasudra, 3.0% Muchi, 1.5% Hari, 0.7% Paliya), 5.0% ex-Muslim), 38.0% tribal [17.5% Garo, 8.5% Santal, 2.5% Oraon, 1.9% Mahili, 1.8% Tipera, 1.8% Bawm (Banjogi), 1.2% Khasi, 0.6% Pahariya, 0.5% Munda, Manipuri, Lushai, Chakma, Mru, Magh], 2.5% Anglo-Bengali, Telugu, European.

### COUNTRY-WIDE TOTALS

EVANGELIZATION (see Part 5). 1900: 15%. 1970: 43%. 1980: 60%. *Mass evangelism.* Among recent campaigns: 1970, New Life in Christ campaign, with many denominations co-operating. At least 10,000 Hindus have requested to become Christians, with their villages, but by 1975 had not been contacted by the churches. 1976, Congress on Evanglism; 1978, Here's Life Dacca (CCCI). *Radiophonic evangelism* (1975). Broadcasts: FEBC (2 hours per week in Bengali). Bible correspondence courses: ICF since 1960 (BBCS) with 45,000 enrolments, Emmaus (1963) with 15,000, Voice of Prophecy (SDA), ICI with 18,118 (13,500 active), EHC (with 5,000 decision cards per month in 1975), et alia. Total enrolments numbered around 100,000 by 1970 and 200,000 by 1976 (about 50% being Hindus and 50% Muslims), with 40,000 papers being marked monthly.

FOREIGN MISSIONARIES AND PERSONNEL (aliens from abroad) (1973). Total 578. *From Western world.* 478: about 240 Roman Catholics, 229 Protestants (70 in 5 UK societies, 66 in 12 USA societies, 40 in 2 Norway societies, 20 in 3 Australia societies, 13 in 4 New Zealand societies, 12 in 1 Denmark society, 4 in 1 Sweden society, 4 in 1 WGermany society), 9 Anglicans in 2 UK societies. By 1975, Protestants had risen to 275, and by 1977 to 300 on the field. *From Third World.* 100 (about 80 Roman Catholics, 15 Protestants (2 Presbyterians from Korea), 5 indigenous) mainly from India, also Burma, Japan, Indonesia, Korea.

INSTITUTIONS (church-operated) (1973). Total 182, including 62 higher schools (2 minor seminaries), 91 medical centres (23 hospitals), 2 religious communities, 1 research centre, 3 seminaries (Protestant).

PERIODICALS. About 20 titles.

PERSONNEL. About 1,759 (1,181 nationals, 578 foreign).

RELIGIOUS LIBRARIES. About 20.

SCRIPTURE DISTRIBUTION (1975). Annual totals: 9,059 Bibles (89% subsidized, 11% commercial), 182,522 NTs (71% free, 24% subsidized, 5% commercial), 271,815 UBS portions, 300,484 UBS selections. *Translations completed.* Portion: 7 languages since 1800. NT: 2 languages since 1801. Bible: Bengali since 1809.

SERVICE AGENCIES. About 40, including BCF (ICF/CEIGM), BERRS, BMMF, BNCC, CBCB, CCCI, CORR, CWS, EHC, LWF, MAP, MCC, OM, RSMT, WLC, WMPL, WVI, YFC.

### ADDITIONAL DATA ON CHURCHES

BAPTIST UNION OF BANGLADESH. Also called, Bangladesh Baptist Sangha. The Union withdrew from pre-1970 church union talks that led to formation of the Church of North India.

CATHOLIC CHURCH IN BANGLADESH. There still remain large groups of Catholics whose origins go back to Portuguese times. The percentage of Muslims is highest in M Dacca, lowest in D Dinajpur. *Catechumens.* (1963) 9,622. *Annual baptisms.* (1972) 84.2% infant, 15.8% adult. *Bishops.* (1974) All 4 are nationals. *Priests.* 8 nationals, 112 expatriates from Italy, USA, Canada. *Brothers.* 10 nationals (14 in 1960), 55 expatriates. In 1975 there were 50 total (11 national, 39 expatriate). *Sisters.* In 1975, 216 nationals (rapid increase from 112 in 1960), rest expatriates (decrease from 196). *Seminarians.* Total (1970) 10, (1973) 24. *Catechists.* Total (1974) 481. *Local congregations.* Sisters: In 1975, were 35 secular priests, and 120 regular priests: Little Handmaids of the Church, Catechist Sisters of the Immaculate Heart of Mary, Associates of Mary Queen of Apostles.

*Catholic organizations.* The Catholic Bishops' Conference of Bangaladesh (CBCB) has its headquarters in Dacca and is a member of FABC in Hong Kong. There are no national presbyteral or pastoral councils.

The Holy See has diplomatic relations with Bangladesh and is represented to government and the Catholic hierarchy by a pro-nuncio in Dacca, who serves also as apostolic delegate to Burma.

Catholic social service and educational organizations include: (1) CORR-BANGLADESH (Christian Organization for Relief and Rehabilitation in Bangladesh), which was founded by the Catholic bishops and has full government recognition; and (2) the Bangladesh Christian Siksha Parishad, an educational body mandated by the bishops which has recently decided to introduce agriculture as a compulsory course in all Catholic mission schools

in the country. In 1975 these numbered 243 primary schools (28,897 pupils), 48 high schools (21,928), 2 colleges (1,300 students) and 3 trade schools (172). Other agencies and institutions include (1975): 34 credit unions (10,740 members), 27 co-operatives (5,329), 27 St Vincent de Paul societies (520), 9 creches, 8 orphanages, 13 hospitals (366 beds), and 48 dispensaries (952,000 patients a year).

CHURCH OF BANGLADESH. The church was formed in 1970 by union of the Anglican Diocese of Dacca with the Rajshahi Church Council (begun by M=PCE (later URC, UK), later M=CWM).
CHURCH OF SYLHET. The first mission was the Presbyterian Church of Wales; in 1966 the Santal Mission took over.

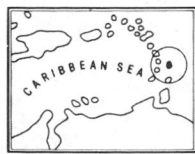

# BARBADOS

## SECULAR DATA

**STATE. Official name:** The Dominion of Barbados. Adjective of nationality: Barbadian.
**Flag** (shown above right): Blue, gold, and blue bars, black trident.
**Area:** 431 sq.km. (166 sq.miles). Agricultural land: 86.0%.
**Government:** Parliamentary state (constitutional monarchy), since 1966 (1625 British possession, 1966 Independence).
**Legislature:** Senate, 21 members. House of Assembly, 24 members.
**Official language:** English.
**Capital:** Bridgetown 8,790 (1970).

**DEMOGRAPHY. Population:** 235,229 (census of 7.IV.1970. For 1970–2000 (UN), see last row of Table 1). Population density (1975): 568/sq.km. (1,472/sq.mile). Under 15 years: 39%. Growth rate (1975–80): 0.58% per year (births 2.20%, deaths −0.88%,

emigrants −0.7%). Life expectancy (1975–80): 70.5 years. Household size: 4.4 persons.
**Major languages:** English, Hindi, Greek.
**Urban dwellers** (1970): 44.0%. Urban growth rate (1950–70): 1.5% per year.
**Labour force:** 35%.
**Tourists** (1973): 220,000.

**ETHNOLINGUISTIC GROUPS:** 89.2% Black (African Negro), 6.0% Mulatto, 4.3% White (English), 0.2% Indo-Pakistani, 0.1% Greek, Chinese, Carib, Jewish.

**MONEY** (1977). Monetary unit: dollar (= 100 cents); US$ 1 = Bar$2.00.
**National income per person:** US$970. Average annual family income: US$4,268.

**Inflation:** (1970–74) 18.2% per year, (1975) 20% per year (consumer price index 235).
**Cost of living in capital** (1976): index 125 (Washington DC = 100). Daily cost of living: US$47.

**EDUCATION. Adult literacy:** (1946) 91%, (1960) 98%. Education rate: 74%. Schools: 156. Universities: 1.

**HEALTH. Hospitals:** 13 (2,216 beds). Doctors: 160. Lepers: 175 (0.7 per 1,000).

**LITERATURE. Annual new book titles** (1971): 23. Periodicals: 130. Newspapers: 1 daily, 2 non-daily.

**COMMUNICATION** (per 1,000 people). Phones: 161. Radios: 458. TV sets: 144. Daily newspaper circulation: 113 copies.

TABLE 1.   RELIGIOUS ADHERENTS IN BARBADOS

| Year | 1900 | | mid-1970 | | Annual change, 1970–1980 | | | | mid-1975 | | mid-1980 | | 2000 | |
|---|---|---|---|---|---|---|---|---|---|---|---|---|---|---|
| Name | Adherents | % | Adherents | % | Natural | Conversion | Total | Rate | Adherents | % | Adherents | % | Adherents | % |
| Christians | 195,500 | 100.0 | 234,770 | 98.2 | 1,250 | −1,037 | 213 | 0.09 | 235,490 | 96.1 | 236,900 | 94.0 | 261,030 | 91.6 |
| professing | 195,500 | 100.0 | 234,770 | 98.2 | 1,250 | −1,037 | 213 | 0.09 | 235,490 | 96.1 | 236,900 | 94.0 | 261,030 | 91.6 |
| Anglicans | 165,000 | 84.4 | 126,900 | 53.1 | 669 | −835 | −166 | −0.13 | 125,930 | 51.4 | 125,240 | 49.7 | 131,100 | 46.0 |
| Protestants | 29,400 | 15.0 | 84,220 | 35.2 | 438 | −746 | −308 | −0.37 | 82,560 | 33.7 | 81,140 | 32.2 | 85,500 | 30.0 |
| Black indigenous | 200 | 0.1 | 12,000 | 5.0 | 66 | 34 | 100 | 0.80 | 12,500 | 5.1 | 13,000 | 5.1 | 15,680 | 5.5 |
| Roman Catholics | 900 | 0.5 | 9,300 | 3.9 | 64 | 493 | 557 | 4.64 | 12,000 | 4.9 | 14,870 | 5.9 | 22,800 | 8.0 |
| Marginal Protestants | 0 | 0.0 | 2,150 | 0.9 | 12 | 18 | 30 | 1.30 | 2,300 | 0.9 | 2,450 | 1.0 | 5,700 | 2.0 |
| Orthodox | 0 | 0.0 | 200 | 0.1 | 1 | −1 | 0 | 0.00 | 200 | 0.1 | 200 | 0.1 | 250 | 0.1 |
| nominal | 31,700 | 16.2 | 74,337 | 31.1 | 411 | 271 | 682 | 0.88 | 77,380 | 31.6 | 81,160 | 32.2 | 98,340 | 34.5 |
| affiliated | 163,800 | 83.8 | 160,433 | 67.1 | 839 | −1,308 | −469 | −0.30 | 158,110 | 64.5 | 155,740 | 61.8 | 162,690 | 57.1 |
| total practising | 155,610 | 95 | 128,350 | 80 | 671 | −1,046 | −375 | −0.30 | 126,490 | 80 | 124,590 | 80 | 113,880 | 70 |
| non-practising | 8,190 | 5 | 32,090 | 20 | 168 | −262 | −94 | −0.30 | 31,620 | 20 | 31,150 | 20 | 48,810 | 30 |
| Anglicans | 146,600 | 75.0 | 90,000 | 37.7 | 464 | −972 | −508 | −0.58 | 87,460 | 35.7 | 84,920 | 33.7 | 85,500 | 30.0 |
| Protestants | 16,280 | 8.3 | 51,333 | 21.5 | 260 | −731 | −471 | −0.96 | 49,000 | 20.0 | 46,620 | 18.5 | 42,750 | 15.0 |
| Evangelicals | 10,000 | 5.1 | 24,000 | 10.0 | 122 | −322 | −200 | −0.87 | 23,000 | 9.4 | 22,000 | 8.7 | 20,000 | 7.0 |
| Roman Catholics | 820 | 0.4 | 9,000 | 3.8 | 59 | 351 | 410 | 3.71 | 11,050 | 4.5 | 13,100 | 5.2 | 18,520 | 6.5 |
| Catholic pentecostals | 0 | 0.0 | 0 | 0.0 | 2 | 78 | 80 | 26.67 | 300 | 0.1 | 800 | 0.3 | 2,000 | 0.7 |
| Black indigenous | 100 | 0.1 | 7,800 | 3.3 | 43 | 37 | 80 | 0.98 | 8,200 | 3.3 | 8,600 | 3.4 | 10,540 | 3.7 |
| Marginal Protestants | 0 | 0.0 | 2,100 | 0.9 | 12 | 8 | 20 | 0.91 | 2,200 | 0.9 | 2,300 | 0.9 | 5,130 | 1.8 |
| Orthodox | 0 | 0.0 | 200 | 0.1 | 1 | −1 | 0 | 0.00 | 200 | 0.1 | 200 | 0.1 | 250 | 0.1 |
| Non-religious | 0 | 0.0 | 2,350 | 1.0 | 41 | 1,025 | 1,066 | 14.16 | 7,530 | 3.1 | 13,010 | 5.2 | 20,820 | 7.3 |
| Baha'is | 0 | 0.0 | 1,300 | 0.5 | 7 | 7 | 14 | 1.02 | 1,370 | 0.6 | 1,440 | 0.6 | 2,000 | 0.7 |
| Muslims | 0 | 0.0 | 400 | 0.2 | 2 | 0 | 2 | 0.49 | 410 | 0.2 | 420 | 0.2 | 500 | 0.2 |
| Hindus | 0 | 0.0 | 100 | 0.0 | 0 | 0 | 0 | 0.00 | 100 | 0.0 | 100 | 0.0 | 100 | 0.0 |
| Jews | 0 | 0.0 | 30 | 0.0 | 0 | 0 | 0 | 0.00 | 30 | 0.0 | 30 | 0.0 | 50 | 0.0 |
| Other religionists | 0 | 0.0 | 50 | 0.0 | 0 | 5 | 5 | 7.14 | 70 | 0.0 | 100 | 0.0 | 500 | 0.2 |
| Country's population | 195,500 | 100.0 | 239,000 | 100.0 | 1,300 | 0 | 1,300 | 0.53 | 245,000 | 100.0 | 252,000 | 100.0 | 285,000 | 100.0 |

**COLUMNS, ROWS.** For meanings and definitions, see Codebook (Part 6). Note that, by definition, total 'Christians' = professing + crypto-Christians, which also = affiliated + nominal Christians. Percentages may not always total exactly, due to rounding.
**CENSUSES. 9.IV.1945:** 58.0% Anglicans, 39.3% Protestants, 1.5% Roman Catholics, 0.5% marginal Protestants, 0.1% Orthodox. **7.IV.1960:** 57.6% Anglicans, 38.6% Protestants (7.9% Methodists, 4.8% Pentecostals, 2.0% SD Adventists), 2.8% Roman Catholics, 0.7% marginal Protestants (Jehovah's Witnesses), 0.1% Muslims. **7.IV.1970:** 53.1% Anglicans, 35.2%

Protestants (8.6% Methodists, 7.2% Pentecostals, 2.6% SD Adventists), 5.0% Black indigenous, 3.9% Roman Catholics, 0.9% marginal Protestants, 0.8% non-religious, 0.7% other religionists.

### NOTES ON RELIGIONS
**BAHA'IS.** Rapid growth of local spiritual assemblies: 1964, none; 1973, 9.
**BLACK INDIGENOUS.** In 10 denominations in 1970 (see Table 2).
**CATHOLIC PENTECOSTALS** (or, Catholic charismatics). Totals (mid-1975): 150 involved adults (over 15 years old) in

4 prayer groups; total charismatic community including children, 300.
**NOMINAL CHRISTIANS.** Since 1950 there has been a rapid decline of professing Anglicans and Protestants, and an even larger decline among affiliated Anglicans and Protestants, resulting in a sharp rise in the number of nominal Christians in these churches.
**OTHER RELIGIONISTS.** Including Rosicrucians (1 AMORC centre).
**ROMAN CATHOLICS.** There has been a rapid increase in professing Catholics by natural increase, immigration and conversion, from 6,429 (1960 census) to 9,219 1970 census.

**NON-CHRISTIAN RELIGIONS.** Muslims make up about 0.2% of the population, and there are also Baha'is and a few East Indian Hindus. In addition there is a larger group which claims no religious allegiance.

## CHRISTIANITY
**ANGLICAN CHURCH.** Anglican clergy accompanied the first British settlers in 1626, and by 1637 the construction of 6 churches and 10 chapels had been completed. The diocese of Barbados, which is part of the Church of the Province of the West Indies, was created in 1824. Today the church has 62 parishes, and professing Anglicans make up 58% of the

population. Church institutions include 39 primary schools, 2 secondary schools, one preparatory school, 2 homes for the aged and one home for handicapped children.
**PROTESTANT CHURCHES.** The Protestant churches of Barbados are a mixture of long-established bodies (Methodists and Moravians) which owe their origin primarily to European efforts in the 18th century and a host of North American missions which have entered during the present century. The 2 largest churches at the present time are the New Testament Church of God, a Pentecostal group dating from World War I, and the older Methodist Church. Other important denominations include the Seventh-day Adventists, Wesleyan Church and Church of the Nazarene.
**CATHOLIC CHURCH.** The diocese of Bridgetown-Kingstown with headquarters in St Michael was erected in 1970 and is responsible for work in the islands of Barbados and St Vincent. Barbados statistics for 1974 include 5 parishes, 4 stations, one diocesan and 10 Dominican priests. Catholicism has been less influential in Barbados than in most of the other islands of the West Indies.
**BLACK INDIGENOUS CHURCHES.** Five Black denominations from the USA are at present at work in Barbados, including one Baptist, 2 Methodist

and 2 pentecostal bodies. The first to arrive was the African Methodist Episcopal Church in 1897. The Church of the First Born, on the other hand, spread to Barbados from Jamaica.

**CHURCH AND STATE.** The Preamble to the constitution of 30 November 1966 states: 'The people of Barbados proclaim that they are a sovereign nation founded upon principles that acknowledge the supremacy of God'. In Article 11, among 'the fundamental rights and freedoms of the individual' is listed 'freedom of conscience and of assembly and association'. The constitutional protection of freedom of conscience is further explained in Article 19, which allows for complete freedom of religious belief and practice and prohibits any hindrance thereof, entitles religious communities to establish and maintain schools at their own expense and to provide for religious instruction in such schools while also exempting those who do not wish to participate and prohibits the administration of oaths contrary to a person's religious convictions.

The Anglican Church has been the established state church from early days. In 1969 an act of parliament (Anglican Church Act, 1969) was passed to repeal the Anglican Church Act, 1911, and to provide eventually for the church's complete dis-

**Anglican Church, Diocese of Barbados.** *Top left.* Anglican theological student at Codrington College. *Above.* After Sunday morning service.

establishment in 1977. Financial grants from the government have been reduced since at the rate of one-sixth annually and terminated entirely in 1977. The 1972 grant was about 35% of the total income of the diocese and almost 50% of the synod's budget.

There is a governmental Ministry of Ecclesiastical Affairs which handles all matters relating to the churches. Churches desiring to perform marriages must be registered. There has been no tension over religious matters between church and state, but in 1975 the prime minister showed resentment over criticisms made by religious leaders.

**INTERDENOMINATIONAL ORGANIZATIONS.** The Barbados Ministerial Fraternal Association has for some time been an informal group of Conservative Evangelical and WCC-oriented clergy representing 16 different church traditions. In 1972, it crystallized out in the formation of the Barbados Council of Evangelical Churches, with 14 member denominations. Five churches also have since begun the process of forming the Barbados Christian Council, in working relationship with the WCC. Christian Action for Development in the Caribbean (CADEC) is a

project initiated through the WCC under Anglican, Methodist, Moravian and Church of God sponsorship and is now an agency of the Caribbean Conference of Churches (CCC), with headquarters in Bridgetown, Barbados. CADEC is a member of CIDSE in Belgium and serves as an affiliate to Sodepax in the Caribbean.

**BROADCASTING.** The government-sponsored Caribbean Broadcasting Corporation accepts Catholic and Protestant programmes.

### TABLE 2.   ORGANIZED CHURCHES AND DENOMINATIONS IN BARBADOS

| Official name 1 | Begun 2 | Type 3 | Counc 4 | Congs 5 | Adults 6 | Affiliated 7 | Names, notes, and other statistics (see Codebook) 8 |
|---|---|---|---|---|---|---|---|
| African Methodist Episcopal Church | 1897 | I Met | VwQ.L | 2 | 70 | 200 | *Windward Is Annual Conf*, 16th Episcopal Dist. M=AMEC. Begun from Bermuda. 5n,14w. |
| Anglican Church: D Barbados | 1626 | A ACa | AwMRK | 62 | 33,800 | 90,000 | *CPWI.* State church, 1626–1969. 96% Black, 4% White. 31n,30x,P=80%,1s,W=46%,2813y. |
| Berean Bible Churches | 1957 | P int | xM... | 10 | 300 | 500 | Interdenominational. M=Berean Mission (USA). HQ Bridgetown. 5f. |
| Bible Missionary Church | 1956 | P Hol | x.... | 4 | 14 | 200 | M=BMC(USA). Members West Indian Blacks. In Strathclyde. 1x,W=20%,6Y. |
| Catholic Ch: D Bridgetown-Kingstown | | R Lat | P.NMK | 5 | 5,500 | 9,000 | 1970, suffragan M Port of Spain. Includes St Vincent. C=3+2+4. 13x,13m,88w,600Yy. |
| Christadelphian Ecclesia | | P Ade | x.... | 1 | 30 | 100 | *Christadelphian Bible Mission (CBM).* 1 ecclesia, linked with Birmingham (UK). |
| Christian Brethren | | P CBr | x.... | 8 | 400 | 1,000 | *Brethren Assemblies.* Open Brethren. 1974, M=CMML(USA). 4f(Blacks). |
| Christian Union Church | 1959 | P Hol | x.H.L | 7 | 400 | 500 | M=Chs of Christ in Christian Union(USA). HQ St Michael. 3n,2x,2f,W=50%,35Y. |
| Church of Christ, Scientist | | M Sci | x.... | 1 | 50 | 100 | *Christian Science.* M=CCS(Boston,USA). First Church, Bridgetown. |
| Church of God of Prophecy | | P Pe3 | z.... | 4 | 180 | 500 | M=CGP(USA). Holiness Pentecostals. Theocratic government. Emigration to UK. |
| Church of God (Anderson) | 1912 | P Hol | x.H.L | 20 | 1,800 | 3,000 | *General Assembly of the CoG (Barbados).* M=CoG(Anderson)(USA). 16n,1x,1k,1r. |
| Church of the First-Born | | I ind | x.... | 4 | 200 | 500 | Indigenous evangelicals from Jamaica (HQ Kingston). Strict ethical standards. |
| Church of the Nazarene | 1926 | P Hol | xFM.L | 34 | 1,610 | 4,000 | *Barbados Dist.* M=CoN(USA). 99% Black. 7n,1x,19m,2f,G=3.4%pa,35t(3023),132Y,115z. |
| Churches of Christ | 1953 | P Dis | x.... | 2 | 50 | 100 | M=CCCC(Instrumental)(USA). Independents. In Bridgetown. 5f. |
| Episcopal Orth Ch (Greek Communion) | c1940 | I Lib | x.... | | 500 | 1,000 | Black. Ex AOC(USA). Begun 1920 in Trinidad, 1921 Cuba, 1939 New York. 20mw,1s. |
| Fundamental Baptist Churches | 1890 | I Bap | ..... | 9 | 1,000 | 3,000 | M=South Atlantic Bapt Mission, NBCUSA(Blacks). Barbados Bapt Academy. 2n,5m,22w. |
| Greek Orthodox Church | | O Gre | Cw... | 1 | 50 | 200 | *Greek Orth Episcopal Church,* Silver Sands, Christ Ch. Greeks, Arabs. One priest. |
| Jehovah's Witnesses | 1932 | M Jeh | x.... | 14 | 841 | 1,900 | *Watch Tower. International Bible Students Association.* HQ Bridgetown. 85Y. |
| Methodist Ch in Caribbean & Americas | 1788 | P Met | xwQ.a | 30 | 4,780 | 9,000 | In *MCCA,* South Caribbean District. 6 Island Circuits. M=MMS. 6n,2x,G=4%pa,514y. |
| Moravian Church | 1765 | P Mor | xwQ.a | 12 | 1,465 | 5,500 | *Barbados Conf,* Eastern WI Prov, Unity of Brethren. 99% Black. 3n,2f,W=48%,80Yy. |
| New Testament Church of God | 1917 | P Pe3 | ZFM.L | 70 | 2,500 | 10,000 | 1935 joined by large Anglican pentecostal group. 1936,M=CoG(Cleveland). 70n,2f,1s. |
| Pentecostal Assemblies of the W Indies | | P Pe2 | Z.H.L | | 300 | 500 | 2-stage Pentecostals. Emigration to UK. Formerly M=PAoC(Canada). |
| Pentecostal Assemblies of the World | | I pel | x.... | | 200 | 500 | M=PAW(USA). Black pentecostal mission from USA. Jesus Only doctrine. 2f. |
| Salvation Army | 1898 | P Sal | xwQ.a | 11 | 1,260 | 3,000 | *Barbados Division,* Caribbean & CAmerica Territory. Many social projects. 19nx. |
| Seventh-day Adventist Church | | P Adv | x.... | | 4,942 | 7,000 | *SDA,* East Caribbean Conference, Caribbean Union Conference. HQ Bridgetown. 1r. |
| United Holy Church of America | 1953 | I pe3 | x.H.L | 14 | 1,000 | 2,500 | *Barbados District.* M=UHCA(USA Blacks). Spread to Trinidad, St Lucia. 10nx,1p. |
| Wesleyan Holiness Church | 1911 | P Hol | VFH.L | 48 | 2,542 | 5,133 | Till 1968, M=Pilgrim Holiness, now WC. 14n,1x,2f,G=0.7%pa,1s(25),W=45%,215Yy,128z. |
| World-Wide Missions of Barbados | c1965 | P ind | x.... | | 150 | 300 | M=World-Wide Missions(USA). Evangelicals linked to Pasadena, CA(USA). |
| Other Protestant denominations | | P | ..... | | 500 | 1,000 | Total about 12 (see list below). |
| Other Black indigenous churches | | I | ..... | 2 | 50 | 100 | Including: AME Zion Ch (1971; Blacks from USA), Antioch Ch, Spiritual Baptists (Shouters). |
| Other marginal Protestant bodies | | M | ..... | | 50 | 100 | Including: Unity School of Christianity (2 churches, 8 associate ministers), from USA. |
| **Total affiliated (mid-1970)** | | | | **400** | **66,534** | **160,433** | Total denominations (1970) . . . 46. |
| **Total affiliated (mid-1975)** | | | | **405** | **65,570** | **158,110** | Total denominations (1975) . . . 49. |
| **Total affiliated (mid-1980)** | | | | **410** | **64,590** | **155,740** | Total denominations (1980) . . . 52. |

### NOTES ON TABLE ABOVE

COLUMNS: for meanings and CODES (cols. 1, 3, 4, 8): see Codebook (Part 6). Column 1: **Boldface type** = church with over 10 % of country's affiliated Christians.
NATIONAL COUNCILS (Column 4, 5th letter).
  a = member of both BCEC and Barbados Christian Council.
  K = Barbados Christian Council (1974, formation begun).
  L = Barbados Council of Evangelical Churches (BCEC).
OTHER PROTESTANT DENOMINATIONS. These include: Apostolic Church, Apostolic Faith, Christian Mission, Exclusive Brethren (groups: Raven-Taylor and Kelly-Continental), International Pentecostal Assemblies (in Black Rock, St Michael), Missionary Ch, Southern Baptist Convention (1972), Streams of Power, West Indies Mission, Worldwide Evangelization Crusade.

PEOPLES (ethnolinguistic). Christians: 89.4% Black, 6.0% Mulatto, 4.3% White (English), 0.1% Greek.

COUNTRY-WIDE TOTALS
EVANGELIZATION (see Part 5). 1900: 100%. 1970: 100%. 1980: 100%. *Mass evangelism.* In the 1960s, several campaigns: Moravian Crusades in parishes of St John, St Thomas and St Michael, with 400 converts (1962–63) Interdenominational

Crusade in St Michael (1964–65), Bob Harrison Crusade in St Michael (1967), first Keswick Convention in St Michael (1969). *Radiophonic evangelism.* HCJB,ICI.
FOREIGN MISSIONARIES AND PERSONNEL (nationals serving abroad) (1973). Total about 6 Anglicans, Roman Catholics and indigenous in Guyana and UK.
FOREIGN MISSIONARIES AND PERSONNEL (aliens from abroad) (1973). Total 171. *From Western world.* 151: about 100 Roman Catholics, 27 Protestants (26 in 13 USA societies, 1 in 1 New Zealand society), 18 Anglicans in 3 UK societies, about 6 Black indigenous from USA. *From Third World.* About 20 (Anglicans, Roman Catholics, Protestants, Black indigenous) mainly from Jamaica.
INSTITUTIONS (church-operated) (1973). Total 18, including 9 higher schools, 1 hospital, 1 research centre, 4 seminaries (2 Protestant, 1 Anglican, 1 indigenous).
PERIODICALS. About 13 titles.
PERSONNEL. About 431 (260 national, 171 foreign).
RELIGIOUS LIBRARIES. About 5.
SCRIPTURE DISTRIBUTION (1975). Annual totals: 4,400 Bibles (98% subsidized, 2% commercial), 11,000 NTs (91% free, 9% subsidized), 2,000 UBS portions, 43,000 UBS selections.
SERVICE AGENCIES. About 25, including CADEC,CCC,

CCW, CEYA, CLC, SCM, SPCK, YMCA, YWCA.

ADDITIONAL DATA ON CHURCHES
CATHOLIC CHURCH. *Religious orders and congregations* (1970). Priests: 7 SFM, 6 OP, SJ. Brothers: 11 Presentation Brothers of Ireland, 5 FSC. Sisters: 56 Franciscan Sisters of the Sorrowful Mother, 16 Ursuline Nuns of the Roman Union, 9 Corpus Christi Carmelites, 7 Sisters of St Joseph of Cluny.
*Catholic organizations.* The diocese is a member of the Antilles Episcopal Conference (AEC), with its headquarters in Kingston, Jamaica, and through it is a member of CELAM. Religious personnel are represented on the Conference of Major Superiors of the Antilles, which belongs to CLAR and also has its seat in Jamaica. There is no presbyteral nor pastoral council. The principal lay movements are Catholic Youth Organization, Society of St Vincent de Paul and Legion of Mary.
The Holy See has no diplomatic relations with Barbados. It is represented to the Catholic hierarchy by an apostolic delegate based in Port-au-Prince, Haiti.
In 1974 the church sponsored 2 primary schools (389 pupils), one all-age school (480 pupils), 2 secondary schools (840 students), one school for mentally-retarded children (67 day pupils) and one hospital (110 beds).

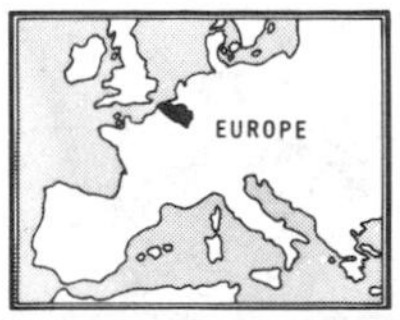


# BELGIUM

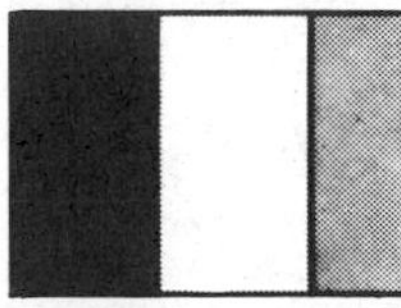

## SECULAR DATA

**STATE. Official name:** The Kingdom of Belgium (Le Royaume de Belgique/Koninkrijk België). Adjective of nationality: Belgian (belge).
**Flag** (shown above right): Bars of black, yellow, and red.
**Area:** 30,513 sq.km. (11,778 sq.miles). Agricultural land: 50.9%.
**Government:** Constitutional monarchy, since 1830 (1555 Spanish rule, 1797 French rule, 1830 Independence).
**Legislature:** Parliament: Senate, 181 members; Chamber of Representatives, 22 members.
**Official languages:** Flemish (*Vlaams*), French (*Français*) and German (*Deutsch*).
**Chief cities:** capital Brussels 1,074,730 (1971), Antwerp 672,700, Liège 440,450, Ghent 224,730.
**Political divisions:** 9 Provinces, 2,359 Communes.
**Armed forces** (1976): Total 88,300 regular (31,050 conscripts): army 64,050, navy 4,350, air force 19,900 (144 combat aircraft). Reserves: 57,600. Paramilitary forces: 15,000 gendarmerie.
**Foreign forces** (1973): 2,000 USA troops.

**DEMOGRAPHY. Population:** 9,650,944 (census of 31.XII.1970. For 1970–2000 (UN), see last row of Table 1). Population density (1975): 323/sq.km. (836/sq.mile). Under 15 years: 24%. Growth rate (1975–80): 0.43% per year (births 1.54%, deaths –1.15%, immigrants 0.04%). Life expectancy (1975–80): 73.4 years. Household size: 2.9 persons.
**Major languages:** 56.3% Flemish, 32.1% French, 0.6% German (along Eastern border), 11.0% bilingual; also Italian, Spanish, Dutch, English, Polish, Yiddish, Arabic, Greek, Russian, Turkish.
**Urban dwellers** (1970): 69.3%. Urban growth rate (1950–70): 1.0% per year.
**Labour force:** 41%.
**Refugees** (1977): 2,347 from Viet Nam.
**Tourists** (1974): 7,477,363.

**ETHNOLINGUISTIC GROUPS:** 58.5% Flemish, 33.6% Walloon (French-speaking), 2.6% Italian (249,500), 0.9% French (86,700), 0.7% Spaniard (67,500), 0.6% Dutch (61,300), 0.6% German-speaking (0.2% German (23,300)), 0.4% Polish, 0.4% Jewish, 0.4% Moroccan Arab (39,300), 0.4% Greek, 0.3% British (30,000), 0.2% Russian, 0.2% Turkish (21,000), 0.1% Luxemburger, 0.1% Zairian (7,600).

**MONEY** (1977). **Monetary unit:** franc (= 100 centimes); US$1 = FB 36.50.
**National income per person:** US$5,044. Average annual family income: US$14,628.
**Inflation:** (1970–74) 7.3% per year, (1975) 13% per year (consumer price index 142).
**Cost of living in capital** (1976): index 132 (Washington DC=100). Daily cost of living: US$58.

**EDUCATION.** Adult literacy: (1947) 97%, (1974) 98%. Education rate: 60%. Schools: 9,754 (8,611 primary, 1,143 middle). Universities: 4.

**HEALTH.** Hospitals: 480 (83,448 beds). Doctors: 15,500. Blind: 4,780. Psychotics: 98,000.

**LITERATURE.** Annual new book titles (1973): 8,953. Periodicals: 5,000. Scientific journals: 1,260. Newspapers: 47 dailies, 2,032 non-daily.

**COMMUNICATION** (per 1,000 people). Phones: 257. Radios: 375. TV sets: 244. Daily newspaper circulation: 258 copies.

TABLE 1. RELIGIOUS ADHERENTS IN BELGIUM

| Year | 1900 | | mid-1970 | | Annual change, 1970–1980 | | | | mid-1975 | | mid-1980 | | 2000 | |
|---|---|---|---|---|---|---|---|---|---|---|---|---|---|---|
| *Name* | *Adherents* | *%* | *Adherents* | *%* | *Natural* | *Conversion* | *Total* | *Rate* | *Adherents* | *%* | *Adherents* | *%* | *Adherents* | *%* |
| **Christians** | **6,623,000** | **99.0** | **8,940,000** | **92.8** | **37,393** | **–17,083** | **20,310** | **0.22** | **9,045,980** | **91.9** | **9,143,100** | **90.9** | **9,117,100** | **84.6** |
| professing | 6,623,000 | 99.0 | 8,940,000 | 92.8 | 37,393 | –17,083 | 20,310 | 0.22 | 9,045,980 | 91.9 | 9,143,100 | 90.9 | 9,117,100 | 84.6 |
| Roman Catholics | 6,612,000 | 98.8 | 8,856,000 | 91.9 | 37,037 | –17,147 | 19,890 | 0.22 | 8,959,900 | 91.0 | 9,054,900 | 90.0 | 9,002,100 | 83.5 |
| Evangelical Catholics | 35,000 | 0.5 | 101,574 | 1.1 | 442 | 594 | 1,036 | 0.97 | 106,790 | 1.1 | 111,930 | 1.1 | 148,000 | 1.4 |
| Protestants | 10,000 | 0.1 | 40,000 | 0.4 | 169 | 31 | 200 | 0.49 | 41,000 | 0.4 | 42,000 | 0.4 | 65,000 | 0.6 |
| Orthodox | 0 | 0.0 | 40,000 | 0.4 | 170 | 33 | 203 | 0.49 | 41,000 | 0.4 | 42,030 | 0.4 | 45,000 | 0.4 |
| Anglicans | 1,000 | 0.0 | 4,000 | 0.0 | 17 | 0 | 17 | 0.42 | 4,080 | 0.0 | 4,170 | 0.0 | 5,000 | 0.0 |
| nominal | 50,000 | 0.7 | 100,524 | 1.0 | 497 | 3,421 | 3,918 | 3.26 | 120,330 | 1.2 | 139,700 | 1.4 | 542,500 | 3.0 |
| affiliated | 6,573,000 | 98.2 | 8,839,476 | 91.7 | 36,896 | –20,504 | 16,392 | 0.18 | 8,925,650 | 90.6 | 9,003,400 | 89.5 | 8,574,600 | 79.5 |
| total practising | 5,915,700 | *90* | 6,806,400 | *77* | 27,672 | –51,064 | –23,392 | –0.35 | 6,694,240 | *75* | 6,572,480 | *73* | 5,573,500 | *65* |
| non-practising | 657,300 | *10* | 2,033,080 | *23* | 9,224 | 30,560 | 39,784 | 1.78 | 2,231,410 | *25* | 2,430,920 | *27* | 3,001,100 | *35* |
| Roman Catholics | 6,518,000 | 97.4 | 8,624,602 | 89.5 | 35,979 | –21,120 | 14,859 | 0.17 | 8,703,900 | 88.4 | 8,773,200 | 87.2 | 8,279,800 | 76.8 |
| Catholic pentecostals | 0 | 0.0 | 200 | 0.0 | 12 | 548 | 560 | 18.67 | 3,000 | 0.0 | 5,800 | 0.0 | 30,000 | 0.3 |
| Protestants | 25,000 | 0.4 | 83,984 | 0.9 | 351 | 11 | 362 | 0.43 | 84,800 | 0.9 | 86,600 | 0.9 | 110,000 | 1.0 |
| Evangelicals | 7,000 | 0.1 | 54,000 | 0.6 | 239 | 81 | 320 | 0.58 | 55,600 | 0.6 | 57,200 | 0.6 | 74,000 | 0.7 |
| Orthodox | 1,000 | 0.0 | 60,000 | 0.6 | 253 | 7 | 260 | 0.42 | 61,300 | 0.6 | 62,600 | 0.6 | 67,000 | 0.6 |
| Marginal Protestants | 20,000 | 0.3 | 50,590 | 0.5 | 223 | 618 | 841 | 1.56 | 54,000 | 0.5 | 59,000 | 0.6 | 95,000 | 0.9 |
| Anglicans | 1,000 | 0.0 | 12,000 | 0.1 | 51 | –1 | 50 | 0.41 | 12,250 | 0.1 | 12,500 | 0.1 | 13,000 | 0.1 |
| Catholics (non-Roman) | 8,000 | 0.1 | 9,300 | 0.1 | 39 | –19 | 20 | 0.21 | 9,400 | 0.1 | 9,500 | 0.1 | 9,800 | 0.1 |
| Non-religious | 50,000 | 0.7 | 460,200 | 4.8 | 2,163 | 11,609 | 13,772 | 2.63 | 523,150 | 5.3 | 597,920 | 5.9 | 1,058,900 | 9.8 |
| Atheists | 10,000 | 0.1 | 100,000 | 1.0 | 529 | 5,471 | 6,000 | 4.69 | 128,000 | 1.3 | 160,000 | 1.6 | 430,000 | 4.0 |
| Muslims | 0 | 0.0 | 90,000 | 0.9 | 2,013 | –13 | 2,000 | 2.00 | 100,000 | 1.0 | 110,000 | 1.1 | 120,000 | 1.1 |
| Jews | 10,000 | 0.1 | 40,000 | 0.4 | 169 | 3 | 172 | 0.42 | 40,840 | 0.4 | 41,720 | 0.4 | 45,000 | 0.4 |
| Buddhists | 0 | 0.0 | 4,000 | 0.0 | 17 | –1 | 16 | 0.39 | 4,080 | 0.0 | 4,160 | 0.0 | 4,000 | 0.0 |
| Baha'is | 0 | 0.0 | 1,800 | 0.0 | 8 | 2 | 10 | 0.54 | 1,850 | 0.0 | 1,900 | 0.0 | 3,000 | 0.0 |
| Other religionists | 0 | 0.0 | 2,000 | 0.0 | 8 | 12 | 20 | 0.95 | 2,100 | 0.0 | 2,200 | 0.0 | 3,000 | 0.0 |
| **Country's population** | **6,693,000** | **100.0** | **9,638,000** | **100.0** | **42,300** | **0** | **42,300** | **0.43** | **9,846,000** | **100.0** | **10,061,000** | **100.0** | **10,781,000** | **100.0** |

COLUMNS, ROWS. For meanings and definitions, see Codebook (Part 6). Note that, by definition, total 'Christians' = professing + crypto-Christians, which also = affiliated + nominal Christians. Percentages may not always total exactly, due to rounding.
CENSUSES. The religion question has not been asked.
POLLS. 1965 estimate: 92.7% Roman Catholics, 6.5% non-religious and atheists, 0.4% Protestants, 0.4% Jews.

NOTES ON RELIGIONS
ATHEISTS. Parti Communiste Belge (PCB) (legal; split over Sino-Soviet dispute) and 2 rival groups: membership (1970) 12,500, (1974) 15,000; Communist voters (election of III.1961) 164,000 (3.1% of all votes), (V.1965) 236,333 (4.6% of all votes), (7.XI.1971) 162,463 (3% of total votes), (III.1974) 169,668 (3.2% of all votes). Communists are 80% French-speaking Walloons, in southern industrial and mining regions. Communists, and also those in the Socialist party, are almost all atheists. There is also the Ligue Humaniste (Humanist League), which is in dialogue with the Protestant Federation of Belgium.
BAHA'IS. Growth from 4 local spiritual assemblies (1964) to 11 (1973).
BUDDHISTS. In 5 separate groups (4 in Brussels, 1 in Liège).
CATHOLIC PENTECOSTALS (or, Catholic charismatics). Totals (January 1974): 1,000 involved adults (over 15 years old) in 30 prayer groups; total charismatic community including children, 2,000. In September 1977, 1,500 met in Brussels.
EVANGELICAL CATHOLICS. This term (the term Protestant Catholics might also be used) is used here to describe persons who are affiliated to churches termed by the state Evangélique (Protestant, marginal Protestant, and Anglican), but who are also baptized or professing Roman Catholics or are regarded by state or government authorities as Roman Catholics. Because no official census question on religion is asked, a large proportion of the Protestant, Anglican, Jehovah's Witnesses and other marginal communities are regarded also by society at large as Roman Catholics.
JEWS. Decline from 85,000 in 1940. Mainly urban, in Brussels (18,000) and Antwerp (12,000); in 12 recognized communities, 10 Ashkenazi and 2 Sefardi. About 45% are religiously practising.
MUSLIMS. Migrants, estimated at 42,200 adult labourers in 1970 (24,600 Moroccans, 12,200 Turks, 3,700 Algerians, and 3,000 Tunisians, Libyans and Egyptians), making with their families a total Muslim community of 90,000, with (by 1974) 20 mosques and 3 imams; almost all Sunnis. In the table above, the figure for 'Natural increase' (2,013) is made up of (1) average immigration of 1,600 a year and (2) natural (biological) increase of 413 a year. *Hajj pilgrims to Mecca.* (1976) 2.
OTHER RELIGIONISTS. Adherents of smaller religions and cults, including Rosicrucians (8 AMORC centres).
PRACTISING CHRISTIANS. Sunday mass attendance: 1964, 44.7% of total population; 1968, 41.7%; 1972, 34.2%; 1974, 32.6%. Annual practice is still relatively high. February 1970: attenders several times a week 6%, once weekly attenders 45%, from time to time 20%, never 14%, non-religious 15%. Weekly mass attendance varies from 90% in some parishes in Limbourg, to 25% in Brussels, and to 2% among workers in heavy industry.

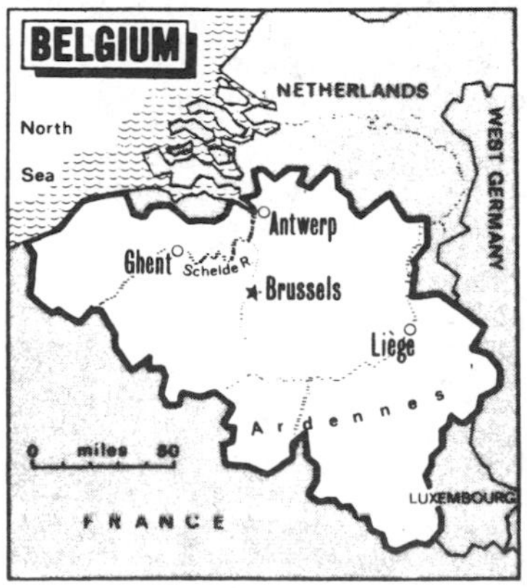


**NON-CHRISTIAN RELIGIONS. Islam** has entered Belgium through the massive immigration of manual workers characterizing many European countries in recent years. From the beginning of the 1960s large numbers of workers have left Muslim Mediterranean countries to live and work in industrial zones of the country, especially in the provinces of Hainault, Liège and Limbourg, and in the Brussels region. In 1970 it was estimated that about 40,000 foreign Muslim workers were living in Belgium: 25,000 Moroccans, 10,000 Turks, 2,000 Algerians and 3,000 Tunisians, Libyans and Egyptians. By 1974 nearly 100,000 nationals of Muslims countries lived in Belgium, including personnel and families of embassies, offices and organizations. The General Council of the Islamic Community, and the Islamic Centre of Muslim Culture, were created in 1963, and in 1969 the Belgian government gave the Islamic Centre a mosque and buildings in Brussels. By the middle of 1974 there were 3 imams and 20 mosques: 9 in Brussels, 4 in Antwerp, 3 in Limbourg and one each in Mons, Charleroi, Liège and Ghent. Official recognition of the Islamic religion by the Belgian parliament in July 1974 has assisted the Muslim community financially, resulting in an increase in the number of imams.

**Judaism** has an ancient history in Belgium, dating back to the 13th century. At the time of Belgian independence in 1830, the Jewish population was 3,000, rising to 10,000 in 1900, 50,000 in 1914 and 85,000 in 1940 at the time of the German invasion. Following the war, however, there were only 30,000 left (1945). In 1970 they numbered 40,000, of whom many originally came from central and eastern Europe, and who were concentrated mostly in urban areas including Brussels (18,000) and Antwerp (12,000). They form a stable population, socially and economically integrated into Belgian society. The number practising their religion is estimated to be about 18,000 (45%). As far as the law is concerned, 12 Jewish communities have received official recognition: 4 in Brussels, 3 in Antwerp, and one each in Liège, Ghent, Charleroi, Ostend and Arlon. Two of these are Sefardi (Latin tradition), and the others are Ashkenazi (central European tradition). Each has proportional representation on the Israelite Central Consistory of Belgium in Brussels, created the day following national independence. There are also a very large number of different Jewish organizations (cultural, philanthropic, political, zionist) which nourish the life of Belgium's Jewish community.

**Buddhism** is represented by a few thousand members

divided into 5 different groups (4 in Brussels and one in Liège), with no attempt at unification.

**CHRISTIANITY.** Christianity came to Belgium at the time of the Roman occupation. By the 4th century the bishoprics of Tongres and Tournai had been established, but these were destroyed during the Frankish invasion. The situation improved during the 6th century, 30 monasteries being built between 530 and 640. A period of consolidation and expansion ensued. The 10th century was characterized by the secularization of the church, but this was followed by the information of new religious institutes, including the Beguines (women living in common and engaging in social service, without religious vows). The 15th century was influenced by the mysticism of John Ruysbroeck, Thomas à Kempis and Denis Chartreus. The University of Louvain was founded in 1425, while the Reformation, led by Guy de Brès in Belgium, made its appearance a century later. The Peace of Westphalia of 1648 divided the Low Countries into religious spheres of influence, Calvinism in northern Holland and Catholicism in Belgium. The Catholic Hapsburgs ruled during 1715–1794 followed by France between 1794 and 1814. The Treaty of Vienna united the Netherlands and Belgium under one crown and in 1830 Belgium was granted independence. Freedom of religion was proclaimed, and 3 religious communities (Catholic, Protestant and Jewish) were officially recognized at independence.

CATHOLIC CHURCH. The Catholic religion is closely related to Belgian history in the sense that it was the common hostility of anti-clerical liberals and Catholics to the Calvinist William I of Holland which led to the creation of the state in 1830. The remarkable progress of Catholicism in Belgium

**Eglise Catholique de Belgique.** *Above.* Cathedral, Diocese of Antwerp *Top right.* Cardinal Primate of Belgium, L.-J. Suenens (centre), world leader of Catholic charismatics, celebrates at a charismatic liturgy.

during the 19th century is related to the fact that the bishops of that time used to the full the liberties offered by the constitution (liberties of teaching, press and association) and the attachment of the majority of the citizens to their religions. Since 1831 there has been a significant restoration of religious orders and a development of parish missions. Charitable institutions of all types have also been established, but primary attention has been given to schools. This blending of initiatives, crowned by the formation of a political party conceived as the defender of church interests, helped to create the strongly institutionalized Catholicism which still characterizes Belgium.

The Catholic Church in Belgium is conceived traditionally as occupying a more important place than in other neighbouring countries. This is due both to its massive presence (90% of the population were baptized Catholics in 1971) and the Catholic bias of many temporal institutions (Catholic trade unions, worker movements, hospitals, schools and universities). Nevertheless, during the past decade, a growing number of Belgian Catholics have begun to question the pastoral conceptions which have prevail-

ed until now and to ask whether the activity of the past has not given way now to passivity. These doubts are shared by a relatively important part of the clergy who through diverse informal groups support the tendency towards the increasing collaboration of Catholics and non-Catholics within pluralistic institutions. This is still a minority movement, but recent trends in Belgian society encourage its growth, such as the weakening of the Christian Social Party (which no longer has a monopoly of Christian votes), the decline in religious practice (from 45% Sunday mass attendance in 1964, to 42% in 1968 and 34% in 1972) and the fall in annual priestly vocations (from 156 in 1964, to 57 in 1973).

The powerful influence of the church and the Catholic world are not spread evenly across the country. A morphological analysis of Belgian Catholicism reveals a clear difference between the Flemish area of the north and the Walloon (Francophone) area of the south. The church thus, like the state, is split by cultural cleavage and experiences the tensions of the communal problem. At least 2 indicators reveal the religious significance of regional differences: Sunday practice and the type of participation of Catholics in the diverse organizations and movements of the church. Concerning the former, in 1968 the total number of Sunday mass attenders was 3.37 million or 41.7% of the Catholic population between 5 and 69 years of age. An analysis by dioceses shows important differences between the various regions, since two-thirds of mass attenders were found in Flemish areas (60% in rural areas, 40% in urban centres), as contrasted with less than 25% in Brussels and the French part of middle Belgium. Flemish-speaking Catholics averaged a Sunday practice of 52% while French-speaking Catholics had only 33%. This reflects the 2 different socio-religious structures characterizing Belgian Catholicism.

Concerning institutional participation, an examination of Catholic Action (youth, adult, family, spirituality and professional movements) reveals once again that involvement is greater among Flemish Catholics than in the French zone. Thus the Germanic cultural context appears to furnish greater possibilities for the development of mass movements and structured organizations than Francophone society. This difference is not always fully evident given the often unified structures of these diverse movements, but the contrast becomes apparent on closer examination.

In reality it is increasingly difficult to speak of a single Catholic Church in Belgium. Although there is one ecclesiastical province and one episcopal conference, the fact is that there are 2 Catholic communities each with their own sensibilities and interests. The clearest proof of this was the 1966 conflict over the Catholic University of Louvain which resulted in the forced removal of the French section of the university to a French-speaking part of the country. Many observers believe that pastoral efficiency will ultimately require a restructuring of

the church to conform to present reality.

Beyond the existence of presbyteral and pastoral councils in each diocese, there is also a Flemish Interdiocesan Pastoral Council (Interdiocesaan Pastoraal Beraad, IPB) which serves in part the function of a permanent synodal assembly for the Flemish part of the country and draws its inspiration from the Netherlands (although, unlike the Netherlands, it has never had to submit its statutes to Rome for approval). No full synod, diocesan or national, has yet been held nor announced.

In 1967 the Episcopal Conference established the Séminaire Cardijn in Jumet, Charleroi, a new type of seminary which permits young workers to remain in their occupations during and after the completion of theological studies. During 1967–71 there were 200 applications, of which 40 (single men, 25 to 50 years of age) were admitted. Training for the priesthood there takes into consideration the particular situation and the human, philosophical and theological needs of each candidate. The first worker priest from Jumet was ordained in 1973. In a parallel manner the diocesan seminary of Brussels is oriented towards the sacerdotal training of employees and teachers. Of note also is the growth of the permanent diaconate in Belgium, with 98 consecrated deacons (out of 1,200 throughout the world at the beginning of 1974).

The presence in Brussels of a large number of foreign officials and their families has led to the creation of a European Catholic centre (Foyer Catholique Européen) concerned to respond to the need for pastoral service of members of the European Economic Community and other international institutions.

PROTESTANT CHURCHES. Though clearly a minority, Protestantism has a long history in Belgium. The country was reached early on by the Reformation and had its own reformer, Guy de Brès, who published in 1561 the Confessio Belgica. However, the political context did not enable Protestantism to survive, other than in a few centres. At the time of independence in 1830, there were only a few thousand Protestants out of Belgium's 3 million inhabitants. At that time Protestants, Catholics and Jews were all officially recognized and accorded the same juridical and material privileges.

The Protestant community in 1975 is about 85,000 affiliated, of which some 20,000 are foreigners living temporarily in Belgium, mostly Africans, British, Germans and Scandinavians. They are distributed unevenly throughout the country, forming 0.9% of the total population, 1.2% of the French area and 0.5% of the Flemish area. They are found principally in Brussels, Charleroi, Antwerp and Borinage. The provinces of Limbourg and Luxembourg, on the other hand, are virtually devoid of Protestants.

The largest and oldest denomination is the Protestant Church of Belgium which is popularly considered by other Protestants to be a national church because of its official recognition and financial support accorded by the state. In 1830, the scattered Protestant congregations then existing joined together to form the Evangelical Protestant Church of Belgium, and in 1969 this body merged with the Methodists to form the present church. All Protestant teachers in state schools must be sponsored by the Protestant Church of Belgium.

Belgium's second Protestant church in both size and age is the Reformed Church of Belgium, formed in 1837 among coal miners through the joint work of the Evangelical Free Church of Switzerland and the British and Foreign Bible Society. Between 1931 and 1969 it was known as the Belgian Christian Missionary Church.

Pentecostalism came to Belgium in 1931 with the arrival of the first missionaries of the Assemblies of God, and this remains the principal Pentecostal community. Five smaller Pentecostal denominations are also present.

Other churches include the Union of Free Evangelical Churches; Reformed Churches of the Netherlands in Belgium; 3 Lutheran, 2 Brethren and 2 Baptist denominations; together with Adventists, Disciples and Mennonites.

ORTHODOX CHURCHES. The Orthodox community in Belgium is composed primarily of Russians and Greeks, with a relatively small number of Belgians, altogether totalling about 60,000. The Russian Orthodox, with about 10,000 practising members, consists for the most part of families in exile since the revolution of 1917. They are divided into 2 groups, those under the Moscow Patriarchate and those belonging to the Russian Orthodox Church Outside of Russia with headquarters in New York. The Greeks, with 20,000 practising members, have grown in recent years through the influx of Greek migrant workers. They are under the Greek archbishop of London, and thus are attached to the Patriarchate of Constantinople, and a Greek bishop serving the Benelux countries (Belgium, Netherlands, Luxembourg) lives in Brussels. For several years the Orthodox community has experienced severe financial difficulties. Lacking the official recognition granted to other traditional denominations in Belgium, Orthodoxy receives no salary support for its ministers nor other financial aid from the state. Recently several Catholic dioceses have put places of worship at the disposal of local Orthodox communities.

MARGINAL CHURCHES. Jehovah's Witnesses, who entered Belgium prior to World War I, have built up a community equal in size to the largest Protestant church. Other marginal bodies include Mormons, Christian Scientists, Unitarians and Apostolic Rosicrucians.

OTHER CHURCHES. The Anglican Church exists mainly for the sizeable English-speaking expatriate community. Nevertheless there are also a few native Belgian members, and the Anglican Church is one of Belgium's 5 officially-recognized religious communities. There are around 10 smaller Catholic (non-Roman) churches: the Belgian Old Catholic Church, which traces its origin to the Jansenist controversy of the early 18th century and is related to the Utrecht-based Old Catholic Church in the Netherlands; the Catholic Apostolic (Irvingite) Church, and its secession the New Apostolic Church; Antoinistes, and several smaller bodies under bishops-at-large.

**CHURCH AND STATE.** The constitution of 1831, still in force, guarantees freedom of religion and worship in its Articles 14 and 15, and the non-intervention of government in the appointment of clergy in Article 16. Although the constitution does not mention specifically the phrase 'recognized churches or religions', 5 churches or denominations or religions are in fact recognized officially, which means that they are accorded juridical personality and receive the benefit of salaries and pensions from the government for heads of churches, bishops, priests and vicars of parishes, as defined in Article 117. At the time of Belgian independence in 1830, official recognition was given to Catholics, Protestants and Jews; this was extended to Anglicans in 1870, and to Muslims in July 1974. The Administrations of Religions of the Ministry of Justice is responsible for relations with these 5 recognized religious bodies, and churches or denominations wishing to benefit from the advantages offered by the Belgian constitution must be affiliated with one of these. Others are not legally registered as churches, although they may be registered as 'non-profit organizations' (in conformity with the law of 21 June 1921), a solution little utilized, or they may receive official recognition as 'establishments for public use'.

The Catholic Church holds a position of unique importance within the Belgian context. Although the government has a definite Catholic stamp to it, there is no concordat with the Holy See, no state religion, nor official collaboration between church and state.

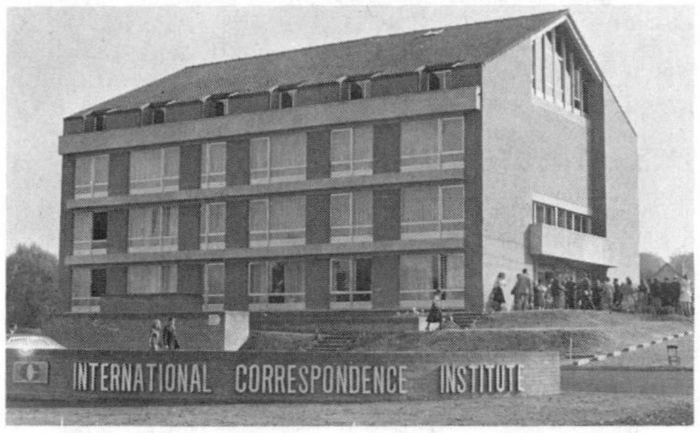


1975 dedication service of Brussels headquarters, Assemblies of God worldwide correspondence college (Pentecostal).

It is a unique system which is neither one of union nor of separation but a reciprocal type of independence in which government recognizes the social usefulness of religion and accords it aid and protection. The constitution affirms the separation of the two, but the administration is practically that of a regime with a concordat, bringing together the advantages of a union with the benefits of independence. In addition to the protection given to private and public exercise of worship and salaries for clergy guaranteed by the constitution, substantial material asistance is also provided for the upkeep of church buildings. The provincial and general laws of 1836 charged the administrative authorities with the responsibility of supplementing the insufficient resources of places of worship and of covering designated necessary expenses. In addition to regular subsidies, churches have also been able to obtain extra subsidies from government in certain cases determined by the law. From the fiscal point of view, churches benefit from other important advantages. Complete freedom of education is maintained, with all impediments removed, according to Article 17 of the constitution. There was nothing to prevent the Catholic Church from establishing a complete educational system, which was accomplished both through generous support from the faithful and large government subsidies. In recent years, this assistance has been increased even more. The laws of 1959 and the 'school pact' concluded between the 3 traditional parties, renewed again in 1973, provide for 3 types of subsidies to denominational academic institutions: (1) subsidies for the salaries of teaching personnel; (2) subsidies for running expenses covering the cost of supplies; and (3) subsidies to cover wholly or partially the expenses of construction and equipment in the schools. Since 1930 the Catholic University of Louvain has received subsidies for the salaries of its scientific staff and equipment; and beginning in 1971 large credits have been made available, aiding in the transfer of its French section to its new site.

There is no doubt that this system of separation with reciprocal consideration has contributed greatly to the strength of the Catholic Church and that it is one of the reasons for the very institutionalized pattern of Catholicism in the country. It is also evident that the protection and assistance which the Catholic Church enjoys in Belgium has negative aspects, even if they do not appear very important at the legal level. These include the obligation to celebrate religious marriages after a civil marriage, and the legal offence involved if a clergyman, while exercising his priestly function, attacks the government or any act of public authority. There exist also certain activities of religious authorities which produce effects within the civil order, and so must first be submitted to government before being put into effect. An example is the creation of new parishes and dioceses whose civil effects, particularly in regard to the payment of salaries and other obligations of the provinces and communities, require that they be undertaken only after arrangements have been made with the civil authorities. But the most significant effect is to be found at another level: the defence and promotion of vast numbers of favours and institutions presupposes the existence of good relations between the church and men of political influence. The coherence of a system in which the church makes use of the government to its own advantage means in turn that it is also made use of through a system of informal ties, binding it to traditional and conservative political forces in the state. This has been in evidence throughout the history of the nation, although less noticeable in recent years. One manifestation of this was the creation and maintenance of a denominational political party, called at first the Catholic Party but since 1944 the Christian Social Party. Its mission was to defend the institutional interests of the church, and for many years it received the open support of the hierarchy. The party likewise identified itself with the cause of king Leopold III during the royal controversy which divided the country between 1944 and 1951. It also identified itself with the school question concerning the financing of Catholic schools between 1950 and 1959. The first evidence of change in the influence of the religious factor on Belgian public life appeared in 1960, when the president of the Confederation of Christian Trade Unions protested publicly against the condemnation by the then cardinal archbishop of Malines of the general strike called at the end of that year. About this time a common front of Christian and Socialist trade unions was created, and the disintegration of the Christian Social Party began. The latter had gained 46.5% of all votes in 1958 but only 30.1% in 1971. Finally in 1966, the intervention of the bishops concerning the maintenance of the French section of the University of Louvain provoked a massive Flemish reaction. With the archbishop's replacement by cardinal Suenens, the pastoral conceptions of the primate of Belgium no longer coincided with the ideas of the Christian Social Party. Even if the change in progress is not without setbacks, it is clear that a new era has begun in the relations of the church to Belgian politics.

**INTERDENOMINATIONAL ORGANIZATIONS.** The Federation of Protestant Churches in Belgium was founded in 1923 and reorganized in 1969. It at present consists of 5 full member churches, and one associate. The main Protestant communities train their pastors in the Protestant Faculty of Theology of Brussels.

For co-ordination of foreign missions, the Protestant Mission of Belgium (Mission Protestante de Belgique), which is affiliated to CWME of the WCC, was founded in 1910 through the efforts of the Reformed churches in Belgium. Originally it was called the Belgian Society of Protestant Missions in the Congo (Société Belge des Missions Protestantes au Congo). At present the mission co-ordinates the activities of churches in Belgium, Switzerland and the Netherlands in their co-operative work with the Evangelical Presbyterian Church in Rwanda.

The Catholic Episcopal Conference maintains a Commission for Ecumenism, and there is also an ecumenical commission attached to each diocese. In the diocese of Antwerp the commision is itself ecumenical in membership, with in 1973 a Protestant president.

Several transconfessional organizations have their headquarters in Belgium. (1) Académie Internationale des Sciences Religieuses, founded in Brussels in 1966, is an independent body consisting of 56 theologians representing different denominations from 11 European countries together with Egypt, Peru and Brazil. Activities include conferences and publications. (2) Secrétariat Européen du Mouvement Chrétien pour la Paix (MCP), founded in Liège in 1923, includes within its membership Catholics, Protestants, Orthodox and Anglicans, although it has no official link with the various church hierarchies. Beginning originally as an organization favouring French-German reconciliation, it now promotes the ideals of peace, justice and development through information services, work projects and international congresses. Branches have been formed in Belgium, Canada, France, Italy, Netherlands, Switzerland, United Kingdom and West Germany, with a branch about to be formed in the USA. (3) Union Internationale Chrétienne des Gérants d'Entreprise (UNIAPAC), founded in Brussels in 1931 as a Catholic organization, has now become interdenominational. Its purpose is to study and promote Christian social teachings. (4) Confédération Mondiale du Travail (CMT), with headquarters in Brussels, also began as a Catholic organization but became interdenominational in 1968. It co-ordinates the activities of 81 worker organizations in 72 countries. The CMT is the smallest of 3 worldwide trade union organizations, the other 2 being the International Confederation of Free Trade Unions (ICFTU), with its headquarters in

Brussels, and the communist-sponsored World Federation of Trade Unions (WFTU) with its headquarters in Prague (Czechoslovakia) and directed from Moscow.

Three ecumenical centres are prominent. (1) The Monastère Bénédictin de Chèvetogne, founded in 1926, is dedicated to the development of spiritual ecumenism, scientific study and dialogue, with special emphasis on relations between Catholics and Orthodox. In addition to an extensive ecumenical library, the centre publishes the journal *Irenikon*. (2) Centre Oecuménique pour Eglise et Société, founded in Brussels in 1965, is recognized, supported and guided by the Churches' Commission to the European Communities. This commission is composed of Christian councils or federations in nearly all the member countries of the European Economic Community (Belgium, France, Italy, Netherlands, West Germany, UK, plus discussions with Denmark). The centre also collaborates with such other pan-European organizations as Ecumenical Research Exchange (Rotterdam), Christian Study Group for Christian Unity (The Hague), Comité des Eglises auprès des Travailleurs Migrants en Europe Occidentale (Geneva), Ökumenischer Leiterkreis der Akademien und Laieninstituten in Europa (Bad Boll, West Germany), and European Contact Group on Church and Industry (Mainz, West Germany). It maintains observers at the WCC and CEC (Conference of European Churches) in Switzerland and OCIPE in Belgium, in addition to publishing an information bulletin. (3) Foyer Oriental Chrétien 'Pro Russia', founded in Brussels in 1954, is a Catholic centre for ecumenical spirituality and dialogue which gives spiritual and material aid to Eastern Christians, especially Russian Orthodox.

The Comité Interecclésial Bruxellois, founded in 1971, groups together the parishes of the major Christian denominations in Brussels. The Carmelite Fathers of Brussels also carry on an important but non-institutionalized ecumenical activity, and plans are now being formulated for the establishment of a centre to assist mixed marriages. The Institut d'Histoire du Christianisme, founded in 1965, is attached to the Faculty of Philosophy and Letters of the Free University of Brussels and offers non-confessional courses, conferences, research and publications.

Centres devoted to inter-religious study, research and dialogue include: (1) Fédération Internationale des Instituts de Recherches Socio-religieuses (FERES), founded in Louvain in 1958, with 40 affiliated centres (26 in Europe, 3 in North America, 4 in Latin America, 5 in Africa, 2 in Asia) and a regional secretariat for Latin America, which promotes socio-religious research on an international, inter-denominational and inter-religious basis and publishes the journal *Social Compass;* (2) Bureau de Documentation sur les Relations Judéo-Chrétiennes, founded in Brussels by the Sisters of Our Lady of Zion, which disseminates information on Jewish-Christian relations; (3) Centre Nationale des Hautes Etudes Juives, founded in 1959 and attached to the Institute of Sociology of the Free University of Brussels, which engages in the scientific study of various aspects of contemporary Judaism, particularly in Belgium; and (4) Institut Belge des Hautes Etudes Bouddhiques, in Brussels, an independent institute engaging in Buddhist studies which works in close co-operation with the University of Louvain.

**BROADCASTING.** Radiodiffusion-Télévision Belge (RTB) and Belgische Radio en Televisie (BRT) transmit religious programmes. The Flemish and French-speaking bodies responsible for Catholic broadcasting are Katholiek Televisie en Radio Centrum (KTRC) and Radio-Télévision Catholique Belge (RTCB). Belgium is a member of UNDA, and Catholics are given a 30-minute radio programme every Sunday evening and a 30-minute TV programme every Friday evening. The Association Protestante de Radio-Télévision (APRT) and its Flemish counterpart are responsible for Protestant broadcasting, which includes a weekly radio programme and 10 TV programmes a year in both languages.

## BIBLIOGRAPHY

'Belgium', F. Houtart, in H. Mol (ed), *Western religion* (The Hague: Mouton, 1972), p. 67–82.
*Histoire de l'Eglise en Belgique*. E. de Moreau. Bruxelles: Editions Universelles, 1949. 2 vols.
*Katholiek Jaarboek voor België/Annuaire Catholique de Belgique, 1971–72*. Bruxelles: Centre Interdiocésain, 1972.
*Sociologische analyse van de katholiciteit*. K. Dobbelaere. Antwerpen: Standard, 1966.

TABLE 2. ORGANIZED CHURCHES AND DENOMINATIONS IN BELGIUM

| Official name 1 | Begun 2 | Type 3 | Counc 4 | Congs 5 | Adults 6 | Affiliated 7 | Names, notes, and other statistics (see Codebook) 8 |
|---|---|---|---|---|---|---|---|
| Armée du Salut | 1889 | P Sal | xwc.. | 12 | 500 | 1,000 | *Leger des Heils. Salvation Army, Belgium Command.* Officers 75, institutions 12. |
| Assemblée Chrétienne Evangélique | | P CBr | ..... | 18 | 1,165 | 2,000 | *Christelijk Evangelische Vergaderingen. Ev Christian Assembly.* 60% Walloon. |
| Assemblée Evangélique Italienne | | P Pen | ....H | 1 | 65 | 130 | *Assemblea Evangelica Italian. Italiana Ev Assembly.* 2p,1s(3),W=88%,6Y,13z. |
| Assemblées de Dieu de Belgique | 1931 | P Pe2 | ZF..H | 40 | 3,750 | 7,000 | *Gemeenten Gods. Assemblies of God.* M=AoG(UK,USA). 70% Walloon. 34n,11x,1s(47). |
| Assemblées des Frères | | P CBr | x.... | 22 | 1,396 | 2,000 | *Vergadering der Broeders. Assembly of Brethren. Open Brethren.* 90% Walloon. 6f. |
| Association des Eglises de Siloam | 1962 | P Pen | ....H | 6 | 200 | 500 | *AES. Association of Churches of Siloam.* Based on Ghent. 1s. |
| Assoc Ev des Egls Baptistes Françaises | 1924 | P Bap | TT... | 2 | 63 | 200 | *AEEB.* French-speaking Baptist Chs. French Bible Mission. Ex FEEBF. 1n,1x,1s,W=33%. |
| Eglise Adventiste du Septième Jour | 1897 | P Adv | x.... | 27 | 1,288 | 1,680 | *SDA, Belgium-Luxembourg Conf.* 9n,1s,G=2.4%pa,1j,1s(5),25t,W=75%,71Y,67z. |
| Eglise Anglicane (J Fulham) | c1650 | A plu | awc.. | 11 | 3,600 | 12,000 | *Anglikaanse Kerk. Anglican Ch.* M=CCCS,PECUSA. Some Belgians. 3x,9f,W=38%,27Yy,40z. |
| Eglise Apostolque | | P PeA | Z.... | 2 | 101 | 200 | *Apostolische Kerk. Apostolic Ch.* Pentecostal body with links to UK and Germany churches. |
| Eglise Catholique Apostolique | c1840 | C CAp | x.... | 3 | 100 | 200 | *Catholic Apostolic Ch. Irvingites.* 3 parishes in Belgium. Rapidly declining. |
| Egl Catholique Apostolique Gallicane | 1870 | C CCa | ..... | | 500 | 1,000 | *Catholic Apostolic Gallican Ch.* Ex Church of Rome. Branch of body in France. |
| **Eglise Catholique de Belgique:** | c 200 | R Lat | B.B.R | 3,919 | 6,554,700 | 8,624,602 | *Katholieke Kerk.* C=41+14+350. 7p,11q,13s(619). 12614nx,4535m,34850w,127189Yy. |
| M Malines-Bruxelles (Brussel) | 1559 | R Lat | Bs | 688 | 1,511,500 | 1,988,835 | Bilingual Flemish/Walloon. 3 Vicariates. 3s. 2057 1644 6800 25075 |
| D Antwerpen (Anvers) | 1559 | R Lat | Bs | 311 | 913,500 | 1,202,000 | Suppressed 1801. Flemish. Port(900,000), rural. 1s. 1803 693 4210 17500 |
| D Brugge (Bruges) | 1559 | R Lat | Bs | 367 | 794,200 | 1,045,000 | Flemish. Rural. Major foreign missions activity. 1707 362 6800 15638 |
| D Gent (Gand)(Ghent) | 1559 | R Lat | Bs | 423 | 912,000 | 1,200,000 | Flemish. Rural, expanding new industry. 1s. 1638 693 6358 19009 |
| D Hasselt | 1967 | R Lat | Bs | 307 | 425,600 | 560,000 | Flemish. 50% rural. Formerly in D Liège. 1s. 1102 321 2417 11750 |
| D Liège | c 350 | R Lat | Bs | 515 | 634,600 | 835,000 | Walloon. Industry declining. Dechristianized. 1s. 1284 66 2394 12100 |
| D Namur (Namen) | 1559 | R Lat | Bs | 728 | 453,000 | 596,057 | Walloon. Namur, Luxembourg, rural areas. 1s. 1535 428 2371 8717 |
| D Tournai (Doornik) | c 550 | R Lat | Bs | 580 | 910,300 | 1,197,710 | Walloon. Rural areas, declining industries. 2s. 1488 328 3500 17400 |
| Eglise de J–C des Saints des DJ | c1860 | M LdS | x.... | | 2,500 | 3,340 | *Kerk van JK Heiligen der Laatste Dagen. Latter-day Saints. Mormons.* 50f,G=1.2%pa. |
| Eglise du Christ, Scientiste | | M Sci | x.... | 2 | 70 | 200 | *Ch of Christ, Christian Scientist. Science.* M=CCS(Boston,USA). 3w. |
| Eglise Ev Allemande en Belgique | | P LuR | ....K | 4 | 3,000 | 5,000 | *Deutschsparachige Ev Kirche in Belgien. German-speaking Ev Ch.* In 4 regions. 4n. |
| Eglise Ev Luthérienne Belge | 1950 | P Lut | Lv... | 1 | 1,000 | 2,600 | *Belgian Ev Luth Ch of Augsburg Confession (BELCAC)*, Holy Trinity Parish. Brussels. Linked EPB. |
| Eglise Evangélique Peniel | 1935 | P Pen | ..... | 12 | 350 | 1,000 | M=Peniel MS(UK). French, German, Dutch sections. 8n,1x,1p,W=86%,22Y,28z. |
| Eglise Ev Protestante Luthérienne de B | 1927 | P Lut | .v... | 1 | 70 | 100 | *Synode de France et de Belgique.* HQ Strasbourg. Ex ERAL. M=LCMS(USA).1n,8z. |
| Eglise Mennonite Belge | 1950 | P Men | G...k | 5 | 101 | 400 | *Belgian Mennonite Mission.* M=MCNA(USA). Notable social work. 2n,3x,W=38%,15Y,12z. |
| Eglise Neo-Apostolique | | C CAp | x.... | | 2,000 | 3,000 | *Nederlandse Bezirk (District), New Apostolic Ch.* Germans. HQ Dortmund (Germany). |
| Eglise Orthodoxe Grecque: D Belgique | 1920 | O Gre | Cwc.. | 12 | 29,000 | 40,000 | *D Belgique, Pays Bas & Luxembourg. Griekse Orthodoxe Kerk.* Cypriots. 6x,W=30%,310y. |
| Egl Orth Russe: D Brussel & België | c1922 | O Sla | Mwc.. | 5 | 9,000 | 15,000 | *Russische Orthodoxe Kerk, PE WEurope. Belgische Orthodoxe Missie.* Russian bishop. |
| Eglise Orthodoxe Russe Hors-Frontières | c1922 | O Sla | x.... | 3 | 3,000 | 5,000 | In *D Western Europe & Austria, Russian Orthodox Ch Outside of Russia.* HQ New York. |
| Eglise Protestante de Belgique | 1830 | P uni | WWC.K | 90 | 17,500 | 30,000 | *Protestantse Kerk van België.* 1969 union Ev Prot Ch, UMC(USA). 48% Walloon. 96n. |
| Eglise Protestante Libérale de Belgique | 1888 | M Unt | I.... | 4 | 5,000 | 16,000 | *Liberal Protestant Ch. Free Christian Ch.* Unitarians. HQ Brussels. Walloons. |
| Eglise Réformée de Belgique | 1837 | P Ref | RWC.K | 48 | 9,936 | 12,000 | *Hervormde Kerk van België.* Formerly BCMC. 93% Walloon. 20n,11x,15p,W=28%,75Yy. |
| Eglise Rosicrucienne Apostolique | | M Epi | .v... | 1 | 30 | 50 | *Apostolic Rosicrucian Ch.* Brussels. Miniscule Gnostic body under episcopi vagantes. |
| Eglise Vieille-Catholique Belge | | C OCa | Uv... | 1 | 50 | 100 | *Belgian Old Catholic Ch.* Brusselles. Related to Old Catholic Ch (Netherlands). |
| Eglises du Christ | 1956 | P Dis | x.... | 11 | 225 | 500 | *Kerk van Kristus. Ch of Christ.* M=CCCC(Instrumental)(USA). USA personnel. 3f. |
| Eglises Pentecôtistes | 1936 | P Pe2 | Z...H | 10 | 475 | 1,000 | *Pentecostal Chs. M*=SFM(Sweden),NPY(Norway). Namur, Brussels. |
| Gereformeerde Kerken in België | | P Ref | Fwc.K | 7 | 811 | 1,874 | *Kring België. Reformed Chs of the Netherlands in Belgium. Flemish Reformed Chs.* 1979, union in UPCB. |
| Société des Antoinistes | 1888 | C mar | x.... | 28 | 3,000 | 4,000 | Begun by RC healer Père Antoine along Meuse. Coal-miners round Liège. In 15 nations. |
| Témoins de Jéhovah | 1901 | M Jeh | x.... | 223 | 14,453 | 30,000 | *Getuigen van Jehovah's Witnesses.* Witnessing under way 1926. 1666Y. |
| Union des Eglises Ev Baptistes de B | 1850 | P Bap | T...K | 12 | 289 | 800 | *UEEBB. Belgian Baptist Union.* 1967, M=SBC(USA). 60% Walloon. 3n,4x,W=42%,21Y. |
| Union des Eglises Ev Libres de Belgique | 1918 | P ind | KM... | 54 | 4,704 | 8,000 | *UEELB. Bond van Vrije Ev Gemeenten.* M=MEB(BGM)(USA). 54% Walloon. 9n,14x,W=60%. |
| Other Protestant denominations | | P | ..... | | 2,000 | 5,000 | Total about 25 (see list below), including USA military chaplaincies. |
| Other marginal Protestant bodies | | M | ..... | | 500 | 1,000 | Total about 6 (see list below). |
| Other Catholic (non-Roman) churches | | C | ..... | | 500 | 1,000 | Liberal Catholic Ch, Mariavite Ch, Vrai Eglise Cath, 5 episcopi vagantes bodies. |
| **Total affiliated (mid-1970)** | | | | **4,740** | **6,676,992** | **8,839,476** | **Total denominations (1970) . . . 77.** |
| **Total affiliated (mid-1975)** | | | | **4,780** | **6,742,100** | **8,925,650** | **Total denominations (1975) . . . 82.** |
| **Total affiliated (mid-1980)** | | | | **4,820** | **6,800,800** | **9,003,400** | **Total denominations (1980) . . . 87.** |

### NOTES ON TABLE ABOVE

COLUMNS: for meanings and CODES (cols. 1, 3, 4, 8), see Codebook (Part 6). Column 1: **Boldface type** = church with over 10% of country's affiliated Christians.

NATIONAL COUNCILS (Column 4, 5th letter).
- H = Union des Eglises Evangéliques de Pentecôte Belge/Vereniging van der Evangelische Pinkster Kerken in België (Union of Belgian Pentecostal Churches); begun 1954.
- K = Fédération des Eglises Protestantes de Belgique (FEPB)/Federatie der Protestantse Kerken van België (Federation of Protestant Churches in Belgium).
- k = associate member of FEPB.
- R = Conférence Episcopale de Belgique/Bisschoppen-conferentie van België (Episcopal Conference of Belgium).

OTHER PROTESTANT DENOMINATIONS. Several state churches in Europe and Scandinavia have one or 2 congregations in Belgium for their expatriate members. In addition, there are a number of independent single congregations. The total includes: Baptist Bible Fellowship International (1962), Ch of Denmark, Ch of God (Cleveland) (USA), Ch of Norway, Eglise Ev Slave (Slavic Missionary Service), Eglise Luthérienne Libre, Elim Foursquare Gospel Alliance, Enfants de Dieu (Children of God), Estonian Ev Lutheran Ch in Exile, European Evangelistic Society, Ev Ch of the Augsburg Confession in Poland in Exile, Ev Lutheran Ch of Finland, Exclusive Brethren (Kelly-Continental, and Continuing Tunbridge Wells), Gospel Missionary Union (1966), Nederlandse Hervormde Kerk, Strict Baptist Mission, United World Mission (1970).

OTHER MARGINAL PROTESTANT BODIES. Including: Amis de l'Homme (Freytag, Sayerce), Eglise Chrétienne Universelle (Témoins du Christ Revenu), General Convention of the New Jerusalem.

UNITING CHURCHES. Negotiations for organic union were under way in 1974 between: Eglise Protestante de Belgique, Eglise Réformée de Belgique, Gereformeerde Kerken. In 1979 they finally united as the United Protestant Church of Belgium (UPCB).

PEOPLES (ethnolinguistic). Christians: 59.0% Flemish, 34.1% Walloon, 2.6% Italian, 0.9% French, 0.7% Spaniard, 0.6% Dutch, 0.6% German, 0.4% Polish, 0.4% Greek, 0.3% British, 0.2% Russian, 0.1% Luxemburger, 0.1% Zairian (Kongo).

COUNTRY-WIDE TOTALS

EVANGELIZATION (see Part 5). 1900: 100%. 1970: 100%. 1980: 100%. *Mass evangelism.* Among recent campaigns: October 1969, at Charleroi, a crusade 'Un Dieu pourquoi faire' sponsored by 35 churches, with 12,000 attenders and 50 enquirers; 1970s Billy Graham Euro '70 TV Crusade in Antwerp and Brussels, televised from Dortmund, Germany; 1973–75, 'Total Evangelization in Belgium and Luxembourg'; July–August 1975, Billy Graham 9-day crusade in Brussels (100,000 attenders, 2,500 enquirers). *Radiophonic evangelism.* Radio Vatican since 1939, HCJB, TWR, ICI.

FOREIGN MISSIONARIES AND PERSONNEL (nationals serving abroad) (1973). Total 9,340: 9,300 Roman Catholics (7,700 foreign missionaries (priests, brothers, sisters, in 49 male and 125 female institutes) serving in Third-World nations, 1,600 personnel in Western nations including 118 in Netherlands), 40 Protestants (decline from 65 in 1963) in 3 societies.

FOREIGN MISSIONARIES AND PERSONNEL (aliens from abroad) (1973). Total 1,278. *From Western world.* 1,170: about 940 Roman Catholics, 147 Protestants (89 in 16 USA societies, 29 in 6 UK societies, 16 in 1 Netherlands society, 6 in 1 Canada society, 4 in 1 Norway society, 3 in 2 Finland societies), about 70 marginal Protestants (45 Mormons from USA), 9 Anglicans (8 in 2 UK societies, 1 in 1 USA society), about 2 Orthodox, 2 Catholics (non-Roman). By 1975, North American missionaries had increased to 145. *From Communist world.* About 2 Orthodox

from USSR. *From Third World.* 106: about 100 Roman Catholics, about 6 Orthodox from Cyprus.
INSTITUTIONS (church-operated) (1973). Total 2,210, including 1,670 higher schools (8 minor seminaries), 280 medical centres (157 hospitals), 180 religious communities (monasteries), 27 research centres, 30 seminaries (24 RC, 6 Protestant), 2 universities.
PERIODICALS. About 220 titles.
PERSONNEL. About 53,078 (51,800 national, 1,278 foreign).
RELIGIOUS LIBRARIES. About 260.
SCRIPTURE DISTRIBUTION (1975). Annual totals: 89,280 Bibles (22% subsidized, 78% commercial), 137,688 NTs (6% free, 21% subsidized, 73% commercial), 32,601 UBS portions, 43,600 UBS selections. *Translations completed.* Portion: Walloon French in 1934.
SERVICE AGENCIES. About 330, including ACISJF, ACWB, ADIC, AFI, AIC, CCCI, CEB, CGAL, CIDSE, CIM, CIPL, CJC, CLAL, CMN, CMT, CSC, EES, EP, FEPB, FGBFI, FIAMC, FIC, FIH, FISCOA, FMJC, FNPF, FNT, GEM, IAD, ICI, IHECS, ISCO, ITECO, JOCI, KJR, KWB, MCP, MOC, MTS, NRGP, OCIC, OCIPE, OIC, OIEC, OM, RTCB, SEUL, SNE, SNEC, SU, UCISS, VF, VKW, WLC(EHC), YMCA.

ADDITIONAL DATA ON CHURCHES
EGLISE CATHOLIQUE DE BELGIQUE. *Annual baptisms.* (1972) 99.9% infant, 0.1% adult. *Male religious personnel* (1973). 10,185 (7,846 priests, 2,339 brothers; 7,378 Flemish-speaking, 2,807 French-speaking; 60% over 60 years old, 6% under 30 years old). *Catholic charismatics* (January 1974). Over 1,000 adults (over 15 years) including many religious personnel in 30 prayer groups are active in the Charismatic Renewal, with active support from the cardinal primate of Belgium. *Seminaries.* 9 diocesan major seminaries, 2 interdiocesan, and 17 study houses of religious orders and congregations (9 Flemish, 8 Walloon). The total is changing due to amalgamations. *Seminarians* (1970). 240 in philosophy, 379 in theology; of these, 364 Flemish, 255 French. *Catechetical schools.* 7 (4 French, 3 Flemish) training primary and lower secondary teachers of religion, also parish catechists. *Main religious orders and congregations* (1972). Priests (with over 400 professed each): 957 SJ, 653 OFM, 578 OPraem, 462 OSB, 410 SDB, 403 OFMCap. Brothers (with over 150 professed each): 795 FSC, 622 Frères de la Charité de Gand, 198 PFM, 187 Frères de N-D de Lourdes. Sisters (with over 500 professed each): 1,877 Franciscaines Missionnaires de Marie, 1,145 Soeurs de la Charité de Jésus et de Marie (Gand), 770 Annonciades de Huldenberg, 505 Soeurs de la Doctrine Chrétienne, 500 Filles de la Charité de St-Vincent de Paul. Sisters' congregations working in Flemish-speaking Belgium number 242, and in French-speaking Belgium 216; many of these work in both language areas.
*Catholic organizations.* The Episcopal Conference of Belgium (Conférence Episcopale de Belgique/Bisschoppenconferentie van België), which is a member of CCEE, serves both French and Flemish parts of the country. Two associations of religious personnel exist: Association des Supérieurs Majeurs de Belgique/ Vereniging der Mannelijke Hogere Oversten van België, for men, and the Union des Supérieures Majeures/Vereniging van de Vrouwelijke Hogere Oversten, for women. A Flemish interdiocesan pastoral council (Interdiocesaan Pastoraal Beraad, IPB) was formed in 1969 with 100 members (40 priests, religious and lay persons representing dioceses; 40 chosen by reason of their functions; and 20 co-opted members, 10 by bishops and 10 by the council itself). There is no similar council for French Belgium. The (Francophone) Conseil Général de l'Apostolat des Laïcs (CGAL), founded in 1956, provides for the co-ordination of the activities of lay organizations with each other and with the episcopate; there is no Flemish equivalent. Youth work is co-ordinated by Conseil de la Jeunesse Catholique (CJC) and Katholieke Jeugdraad (KJR), both formed in 1962. The principal movements of the lay apostolate are: Fédération Nationale des Patros de Jeunes Gens/Chirojeugd-Jongens; Féderation Nationale des Mouvements de Patros de Jeunes Filles/Chirojeugd-Meisjes; Fédération des Scouts Catholiques/Vlaams Verbond der Katholieke Scouts; Guides Catholiques de Belgique/Vlaams Verbond der Katholieke Meisjegidsen; Jeunesse Rurale Catholique/ Katholieke Landelijke Jeugd; MIJARC; JOC/F (Flemish, V/KAJ); JEC/Katholieke Studentenactie, serving boys and girls; Jeunesse Présente/Katholieke Jongeren uit de Middengroep, serving independent youth; Equipes Universitaires d'Action Catholiques, without Flemish equivalent; Action Catholique Générale, serving men and women; Algemene Raad van de Katholieke Vrouwen, serving women only; Equipes Populaires, serving workers, without Flemish equivalent; Vie Féminine Katholieke Arbeiders Vrouwengilden; Action Catholique des Milieux Indépendants, and Action Catholique du Monde Rural, without Flemish equivalents; and Légion de Marie/Legioen van Maria. For the armed forces, Belgium forms a military vicariate.

The Holy See has diplomatic relations with Belgium and is represented to government and the Catholic hierarchy by a nuncio in Brussels. The nuncio also serves as the representative of the Holy See to Luxembourg and the various European communities with headquarters in Brussels (CEE, CECA and EURATOM).

Catholic international organizations with headquarters in Belgium include the following 24 bodies: (1) Conférence des Organisations Internationales Catholiques, founded in 1927 with general secretariat in Switzerland and permanent secretary in Brussels, which unites 31 OICs, 11 of which have their headquarters in Belgium, 7 in Switzerland, 5 in France, 5 in Italy and one each in Ireland and USA (the Commission Eglise-Témoin is a specialized agency whose purpose is to study the possibilities for witness of the OICs in countries where they are still prohibited, especially communist countries); (2) Association Internationale des Charités de St-Vincent de Paul (AIC), founded in France in 1617 and at present existing in 36 countries, which engages in social service and apostolic witness; (3) Association Internationale des Compagnons Batisseurs/Internationale Bouworde (IBO), founded in 1953 at Heverlee near Louvain with national secretariats in 14 countries, which provides scientific and technical assistance by making available funds and personnel to developing countries; (4) Bureau Européen des Délégués des Conseils Presbytéraux, with 12 member countries represented at Brussels, which promotes contacts and dialogue between official presbyteral councils and the episcopate in Europe; (5) Centre International d'Etudes de la Formation Religieuse (Lumen Vitae), founded in Louvain in 1934 and transferred under its present title to Brussels in 1956, which promotes, catechetical study; (6) Comité de Continuité des Conférences Européennes Nationales 'Justice et Paix', in Brussels, which organizes Justice and Peace conferences in Europe; (7) Comité International Catholique des Infirmières et Assistantes Médico-Sociales (CICIAMS), founded in Brussels in 1933, which co-ordinates the activities of 46 affiliated nursing associations throughout the world (1973); (8) Conférence Internationale du Scoutisme Catholique, founded in 1937 in Brussels with its new name adopted in 1948, which unites the Catholic scouting movements of 36 countries; (9) Coopération Internationale pour le Développement Socio-Economique (CIDSE), founded in Rome in 1965 with present headquarters in Brussels, which groups Catholic agencies and associations for development aid (14 members and 2 consultative members) working under the authority of episcopal conferences; (10) Fédération Internationale des Communautés de Jeunesse Catholique Paroissiales (FIMCAP), founded in Rome in 1962 and at present located at Antwerp, with 32 organizations in 18 countries in 1973, which aids development of Christian community life among youth; (11) Fédération Internationale des Mouvements d'Adultes Ruraux Catholiques (FIMARC), founded in Lisbon in 1964 and now located at Brussels, with 13 member movements and 7 associate movements in 19 countries of Africa, Latin America and Europe, which co-ordinates the activities of the rural apostolate among adults; (12) Fédération Mondiale de la Jeunesse Catholique (FMJC), founded in Brussels in 1968 by the fusion of existing male and female federations, with 78 affiliates in 1973, which co-ordinates the worldwide Catholic youth movement; (13) Forum Européen des Comités Nationaux de Laïcs, founded in Switzerland in 1968 and at present located in Antwerp, which unites the lay movements of 25 European countries; (14) Groupe International Femmes et Hommes dans l'Eglise, founded in Brussels in 1970, which promotes the place of women and the collaboration of men and women in the church; (15) Jeunesse Ouvrière Chrétienne Internationale (JOCI), founded in Brussels in 1925 as a national movement and at present found in 109 countries, which seeks to educate young workers concerning their role in society and the church; (16) Mouvement Internationale de la Jeunesse Agricole et Rurale Catholique (MIJARC), founded in Annevoie in 1954 and now located in Louvain, which unites 71 national male and female movements of rural youth; (17) Mouvement Mondial des Travailleurs Chrétiens (MMTC), founded in Rome in 1961 and now located in Brussels, which unites 43 apostolic movements of Christian workers in 36 countries (5 continents) in addition to maintaining relations with corresponding movements in 38 other countries; (18) Office Catholique d'Information sur les Problèmes Européens (OCIPE), founded in 1956, which provides information concerning European societal problems; (19) Office International de l'Enseignement Catholique (OIEC), founded in 1952 in Switzerland and at present located in Brussels, with members in 84 countries and correspondents in 3 others, which disseminates information regarding Catholic education and enlists teachers for service in developing countries; (20) Organisation Catholique Internationale du Cinéma (OCIC), founded in The Hague in 1928 and located at Brussels under its present name and statutes since 1972, with 48 affiliated organizations throughout the world in 1973, which promotes the use of films as an artistic expression of culture and for evangelistic purposes; (21) Pro Mundi Vita Centrum Informationis (PMV), founded in Brussels in 1961, which serves as an international centre for research and the dissemination of information with special emphasis on justice and peace and the future of man; (22) Union Catholique Internationale de Service Social (UCISS), founded in Italy in 1925 and now located in Brussels, which is dedicated to the promotion and training of Christian social service workers; (23) Association Internationale Catholique pour la Radiodiffusion et la Télévision (initials UNDA, the Latin for 'wave'), founded in Fribourg in 1928 with its headquarters in Brussels and regional offices in Uruguay for Latin America and in the Philippines for Asia, which co-ordinates the radio/TV activities of member organizations in 83 countries in co-operation with other international organizations; and (24) Association Internationale des Médicins Catholiques, founded in Rome in 1949 and located in Brussels, which co-ordinates the activities of national Catholic medical associations and generally promotes Christian medical ethics and the development of the medical profession through conferences and publications.

Belgian opinion groups exist representing both progressivist and traditionalist tendencies. In the first category are a large number of organizations, which although active touch only a small proportion of the Catholic community. Among the Flemish-speaking population of Flanders, it is possible to distinguish 2 successive waves. The first (1968–69) was centred on such problems as priestly celibacy and communication with the hierarchy, with the exception of Inspraak (which includes married priests and a few celibate priests); all such groups formed during this period had ceased to exist by 1974. The second wave began in 1971 and continues active through the following organizations: Action Group of the Diocese of Ghent (Aktiegroep Inspraak Bisdom Gent), Informal Group of Priests in Ghent (Informele Priestergroep Gent), Christians for Socialism in Antwerp (Christenen voor het Socialisme), Eliker-Ik Ecclesiastical Alternative (Kerkelijk Alternatief Eliker-Ik) in Ghent, and a group producing the progressive journal *De Nieuwe Maand.* In French-speaking Wallonia and Brussels, there have also been a number of local initiatives including the Assemblée pour une Eglise Servante et Pauvre, in Brussels, Centre Religieux Universitaire, in Louvain, and Centre Communautaire du Cadran, in Liège, in addition to at least 5 better-organized regional movements: (1) Assemblée pour un Concile des Wallons et des Bruxellois (ACWB), founded in 1969 with secretariat in Liège, which advocates the formation of a socialist society and by 1975 was tending to become the French-speaking branch of the Christians for Socialism movement in Belgium; (2) Les Fraternités Jean XXIII, with secretariat at Ottignies, which has abandoned its links with the church in seeking a more political orientation; (3) the group producing the journal *La revue nouvelle*, founded in Brussels in 1945; (4) Présence et Témoignage, founded in 1969 with secretariat in Brussels; and (5) Centre Communautaire International, founded in Brussels in 1965. Most of these are movements of intellectuals, but there is also an evolution in the same direction by youth (JOC).

Traditionalist groups have developed partially in reaction to the pressure of progressivists and partially to minimize the impact of Vatican II, without attacking that council itself. The principal conservative movements are (Francophone) Rassemblement des Silencieux de l'Eglise, in Brussels, and (Flemish) Het Thomas More Genootschap, in Oostaker, both of which are members of Pro Fide et Ecclesia in France. In Wallonia, Amitiés Sacerdotales, founded in Manage-Longsart in 1970, emphasizes the spirituality and celibacy of the priesthood, while in Flanders Christelijk-Vlaams Studie en Documentiecentrum, founded in Ghent in 1971, works through the Christian Social Party (CVP) in defence of Catholic values. Other traditionalist movements include Una Voce Belgica and Mouvement Chrétien d'Opinion, both in Brussels.

Organizations for research and social action include: (1) Centre de Recherches Socio-Religieuses (CRSR), a French centre, with 2 interests (religion and culture, religion and development), which is a member of FERES; (2) Prospective, Centre de Recherche et de Communication pour l'Eglise à Venir, in Brussels, which carries out research under 4 departments (liberation and society, family and population, growth and progress, church and ministries); (3) Centrum voor Socio-Religieus Onderzoek, attached to the Flemish faculty of theology and a member of FERES; (4) Afdeling Godsdienstsociologie aan het Sociologisch Onderzoekinstituut, attached to the Flemish University; (5) Centre de Recherche des Pays en Développement; (6) Centre International de Sexologie 'Cardinal Suenens'; and (7) Centre de Psychologie Religieuse; the latter 3 are attached to the Catholic University of Louvain (UCL).

Organizations for social action include: (1) Mouvement Ouvrier Chrétien (MOC)/Algemeen Christelijk Werkersverbond (ACW) in Brussels, which unites the principal organizations of Christian workers including Confédération des Syndicats Chrétiens (CSC) (one million adherents), Alliance Nationale des Mutualités Chrétiennes, and such training and action movements as Equipes Populaires and Vie Féminine (375,000 members), with corresponding Flemish bodies; (2) Alliance Agricole Belge in Brussels and Boerenbond in Louvain, which are dedicated to defending the economic, social and moral interests of farmers (100,000 members in 1973); (3) the Belgian branch of UNIAPAC; and (4) Mouvement Chrétien des Indépendants et des Cadres (MIC)/Nationaal Christelijk Middenstandsverbond, both in Brussels.

The following agencies furnish aid for the Third World: Entraide et Fraternité/Broederlijk Delen, in Brussels, which provides funds; and ITECO, in Brussels, which provides voluntary workers and technicians and has 15 member organizations, including Amis du Père Damien (to combat leprosy), Coopération des Laïcs en Amérique Latine, Compagnons Bâtisseurs, Medicus Mundi (medical co-operation), Fraternités Terre Nouvelle (for Africa), and Volontaires de l'Enseignement.

Institutions for pastoral and religious training include: (1) 2 faculties of theology (UCL for French Belgium and KUL for Flemish Belgium), plus an international faculty of Canon Law at UCL; (2) 2 catechetical institutes attached to the 2 theological faculties (Institut Supérieur de Sciences Religieuses, and Hoger Instituut voor Godsdienstwetenschappen), in addition to the Ecole Supérieure Catéchétique 'Lumen Vitae' (which is associated with the Faculty of Theology at Louvain, caters for many foreign students and maintains an important centre for documentation) in Brussels and the Commission Interdiocésaine de Pastorale Catéchetique (CIPC), with French and Flemish secretariats; (3) one national liturgical institute, Liturgisch Instituut in Louvain, which is attached to the KUL; several diocesan liturgical centres, the most important being Liturgisch Centrum De Wijngaard in Bruges; and the Commission Interdiocésaine de Pastorale Liturgisque (CIPL), with French secretariat at Mons and Flemish at Brussels; and (4) 2 centres for family pastoralia, Centre d'Education à la Famille et à l'Amour (CEFA) for French Belgium, in Brussels, and Nationaale Raad voor Gezinspastoraal (NRGP) for Flemish Belgium, in Bruges.

Missionary action is co-ordinated by the Conseil Missionnaire National (CMN)/National Missieraad, founded in Brussels in 1968, which is the official organ of the episcopal conference; and the Comité des Instituts Missionnaires (CIM)/Comité van de Missionerende Instituten (CMI), also in Brussels, which is an organization of religious congregations sending missionaries overseas. Missionary studies and training are provided through the following institutions and programmes: (1) Centre de Recherches Missiologiques, in Louvain; (2) Collège pour l'Amérique Latine (COPAL)/College voor Latijns-Amerika, in Louvain; (3) Semaine de Missiologie de Louvain, with secretariat in Heverlee and an annual congress in Namur; (4) CIM Service de Formation, which sponsors a training course for new missionaries; (5) CMN Centre de Documentation; (6) Missionary Information Centre/Wereldkerkcentrum in Bruges; and (7) Pro Mundi Vita. The principal agencies working in aid of missions are AMDAC (Aid to Maternities and Dispensaries of Central Africa), AMAC (Medical Aid to Central Africa), FOMULAC (Medical Foundation of the University of Louvain in Zaire), MIVA (Belgian branch of this West German agency), and FONCABA (Catholic Foundation for Scholarships for Africans).

In 1973 there were about 7,700 Belgian foreign missionaries (priests, brothers and sisters), and in 1970, 71 Fidei Donum missionary priests. A total of 1,641 missionaries were posted to Zaire alone in 1969. More than 49 male and 125 female institutes are involved in missionary activity. Those with the largest Belgian membership include: for men, CICM, which was founded in Belgium in 1862 (with 1,446 members in 1972–73), 503 WF, 500 SJ, 185 OMI, 167 OFM; for women, Missionaries of the Immaculate Heart of Mary (founded in Belgium in 1897, 680 members), Sisters of Charity of Ghent (founded in Belgium in 1803, 161 members), Sisters of Mary of Pittem (founded in Belgium in 1848, 125 members), 177 White Sisters and 155 Missionary Franciscans.

The Catholic educational programme is co-ordinated by the Secrétariat Nationale de l'Enseignement Catholique/Nationaal Secretariaat van het Katholiek Onderwijs, in Brussels. Statistics of schools in 1969–70 (with number of pupils for 1971–72 in parentheses) include 2,736 kindergartens (255,570), 3,436 primary schools (493,721), 651 middle secondary schools (206,182), 76 normal schools (13,055), 885 full-time technical schools (238,393), 236 part-time technical schools (28,347), and 423 special schools (33,473). In 1971–72 the total school population was 1,118,496 in state schools and 1,306,463 in free schools, of which 1,278,741 were in Catholic and 27,722 in non-Catholic schools. In 1973–74 there were 15,332 students in the Université Catholique de Louvain (UCL) and 16,908 in the Katholieke Universiteit te Leuven (KUL). Originally one university, founded in 1425, the disturbances from 1966 caused the French UCL to be moved to Louvain-la-Neuve, 30 kms south of Brussels, and the Faculty of Medicine to Woluwé, a suburb of Brussels beginning in 1972; while the Flemish KUL remained at Louvain. In addition to these 2 complete Catholic universities, there are 3 Flemish and 3 French Catholic faculty centres.

Social service and medical work are co-ordinated through Caritas Catholica Belgica, founded in Brussels in 1938 to serve both French and Flemish communities, which is a member of Caritas Internationalis in Rome. Administered by a central council appointed by the episcopal conference, it co-ordinates the activities of 6 organizations: (1) Fédération des Institutions Hospitalières (FIH), with 157 hospitals, 284 rest houses, 39 psychiatric institutions and 3 sanatoria in 1972; (2) Fédération des Services Médico-Sociaux (FSMS), with 118 health centres, 21 medical inspection centres in schools, 39 crèches and 79 nurseries in 1972; (3) Fédération des Institutions Spécialisées d'Aide à la Jeunesse, with 298 member institutions in 1971 (children's homes, institutions for the handicapped, etc), serving 22,000 infants and youth; (4) Confédération des Institutions d'Aide Sociale, with 18 federations and institutions in 1973 (serving families, single women, the aged, et alii); (5) Secours International de Caritas Catholica, which provides relief aid for refugees, immigrants, foreign students, et alii; and (6) Entraide et Fraternité, which provides development aid for the Third World.
EGLISE REFORMEE DE BELGIQUE. Originally called the Evangelical Society, then the Belgian Christian Missionary Church, BCMC (Eglise Chrétienne Missionnaire Belge), then in 1969 changed to the present name. The church was constituted in 1931 from congregations developed along the line of coal-mines across the country. *Congregations.* Only 2 are Flemish-speaking. *Pastors.* Of 27 French-speaking, 18 are Belgians, 5 Swiss, 3 French, 1 Dutch.

# BELIZE

## SECULAR DATA

**STATE. Official name:** The Colony of Belize. Adjective of nationality: Belizean.
**Flag** (shown above right): Blue with arms of the Colony surrounded by green garland on white disc.
**Area:** 22,963 sq.km. (8,867 sq.miles). Agricultural land: 3.0%.
**Government:** Self-governing colony of United Kingdom (Britain), since 1964 (1862 British colony, known as British Honduras until 1973).
**Legislative:** House of Representatives, 18 members. Senate, 8 members.
**Official language:** English.
**Chief cities:** capital Belmopan 3,000, Belize City 48,420 (1970).
**Foreign forces** (1973): 550 British (UK) troops.

**DEMOGRAPHY. Population:** 119,934 (census of 7.IV.1970.

For 1970–2000 (UN), see last row of Table 1). Population density (1975): 6/sq.km. (16/sq.mile). Under 15 years: 46%. Growth rate (1975–80): 2.90% per year. Household size: 5.7 persons.
**Major languages:** English, Kekchi, Mopan, Yucateco, other Mayan, Spanish, Black Carib.
**Urban dwellers** (1970): 57.4%. Urban growth rate (1950–70): 3.4% per year.
**Labour force:** 28%.

**ETHNOLINGUISTIC GROUPS:** 61.0% Black (Creole), 17.0% Maya Amerindian (2.2% Kekchi, Mopan, Yucateco), 10.0% Black Carib, 5.4% Guatemalan White (Spanish) & Ladino, 5.4% Honduran Mestizo, 1.2% Jewish, British, East Indian, Chinese, Lebanese Arab.

**MONEY** (1977). **Monetary unit:** Belizean dollar (=100 cents); US$1 = Bz$1.98.

**National income per person:** US$800. Average annual family income: US$4,560.
**Cost of living in capital** (1976): index 88 (Washington DC=100). Daily cost of living: US$36.

**EDUCATION.** Adult literacy: (1946) 81%, (1960) 87%. Schools: 218 (199 primary, 19 secondary).

**HEALTH.** Hospitals: 13 (641 beds). Doctors: 41. Blind: 80. Psychotics: 1,000.

**LITERATURE.** Periodicals: 20. Newspapers: 1 daily, 5 non-daily.

**COMMUNICATIONS** (per 1,000 people). Phones: 33. Radios: 515. Daily newspaper circulation: 32 copies.

TABLE 1.    RELIGIOUS ADHERENTS IN BELIZE

| Year | 1900 | | mid-1970 | | Annual change, 1970–1980 | | | | mid-1975 | | mid-1980 | | 2000 | |
|---|---|---|---|---|---|---|---|---|---|---|---|---|---|---|
| Name | Adherents | % | Adherents | % | Natural | Conversion | Total | Rate | Adherents | % | Adherents | % | Adherents | % |
| Christians | 34,950 | 94.5 | 113,100 | 94.3 | 3,964 | 25 | 3,989 | 3.02 | 132,120 | 94.4 | 152,990 | 94.4 | 221,500 | 94.6 |
| professing | 34,950 | 94.5 | 113,100 | 94.3 | 3,964 | 25 | 3,989 | 3.02 | 132,120 | 94.4 | 152,990 | 94.4 | 221,500 | 94.6 |
| Roman Catholics | 14,800 | 40.0 | 77,520 | 64.6 | 2,760 | 308 | 3,068 | 3.21 | 92,000 | 65.7 | 108,200 | 66.8 | 163,800 | 70.0 |
| Christo-pagans | 7,400 | 20.0 | 31,200 | 26.0 | 1,050 | −280 | 770 | 2.20 | 35,000 | 25.0 | 38,900 | 24.0 | 46,800 | 20.0 |
| Anglicans | 10,200 | 27.5 | 17,760 | 14.8 | 597 | −173 | 424 | 2.13 | 19,900 | 14.2 | 22,000 | 13.6 | 26,200 | 11.2 |
| Protestants | 9,950 | 27.0 | 15,820 | 13.2 | 535 | −118 | 417 | 2.34 | 17,820 | 12.7 | 19,990 | 12.3 | 25,420 | 10.9 |
| Black indigenous | 0 | 0.0 | 1,000 | 0.8 | 36 | 4 | 40 | 3.33 | 1,200 | 0.9 | 1,400 | 0.9 | 2,570 | 1.1 |
| Marginal Protestants | 0 | 0.0 | 1,000 | 0.8 | 36 | 4 | 40 | 3.33 | 1,200 | 0.9 | 1,400 | 0.9 | 3,510 | 1.5 |
| nominal | 5,950 | 16.1 | 6,250 | 5.2 | 393 | 881 | 1,274 | 9.72 | 13,100 | 9.4 | 18,990 | 11.7 | 27,300 | 11.7 |
| affiliated | 29,000 | 78.4 | 106,850 | 89.0 | 3,571 | −856 | 2,715 | 2.28 | 119,020 | 85.0 | 134,000 | 82.7 | 194,200 | 83.0 |
| total practising | 23,200 | 80 | 53,430 | 50 | 1,786 | −429 | 1,357 | 2.28 | 59,520 | 50 | 67,000 | 50 | 106,800 | 55 |
| non-practising | 5,800 | 20 | 53,420 | 50 | 1,785 | −427 | 1,358 | 2.28 | 59,500 | 50 | 67,000 | 50 | 87,400 | 45 |
| Roman Catholics | 14,000 | 37.8 | 74,500 | 62.1 | 2,651 | 279 | 2,930 | 3.32 | 88,340 | 63.1 | 103,800 | 64.1 | 156,800 | 67.0 |
| Catholic pentecostals | 0 | 0.0 | 0 | 0.0 | 36 | 264 | 300 | 25.00 | 1,200 | 0.9 | 3,000 | 1.9 | 30,000 | 12.8 |
| Anglicans | 8,000 | 21.6 | 16,000 | 13.3 | 420 | −640 | −220 | −1.57 | 14,000 | 10.0 | 13,800 | 8.5 | 16,400 | 7.0 |
| Protestants | 7,000 | 18.9 | 14,350 | 12.0 | 428 | −503 | −75 | −0.53 | 14,280 | 10.2 | 13,600 | 8.4 | 15,200 | 6.5 |
| Evangelicals | 5,200 | 14.0 | 7,000 | 5.8 | 209 | −239 | −30 | −0.43 | 6,950 | 5.0 | 6,700 | 4.1 | 8,000 | 3.4 |
| Black indigenous | 0 | 0.0 | 1,000 | 0.8 | 36 | 4 | 40 | 3.33 | 1,200 | 0.9 | 1,400 | 0.9 | 2,300 | 1.0 |
| Marginal Protestants | 0 | 0.0 | 1,000 | 0.8 | 36 | 4 | 40 | 3.33 | 1,200 | 0.9 | 1,400 | 0.9 | 3,500 | 1.5 |
| Baha'is | 0 | 0.0 | 2,900 | 2.4 | 103 | 17 | 120 | 3.48 | 3,450 | 2.5 | 4,100 | 2.5 | 6,300 | 2.7 |
| Afro-American spiritists | 750 | 2.0 | 1,500 | 1.2 | 53 | −1 | 52 | 2.97 | 1,750 | 1.2 | 2,020 | 1.2 | 2,500 | 1.1 |
| Jews | 200 | 0.5 | 1,400 | 1.2 | 49 | 0 | 49 | 3.01 | 1,630 | 1.2 | 1,890 | 1.2 | 2,700 | 1.2 |
| Tribal religionists | 1,100 | 3.0 | 1,000 | 0.8 | 27 | −47 | −20 | −2.22 | 900 | 0.6 | 800 | 0.5 | 500 | 0.2 |
| Non-religious | 0 | 0.0 | 100 | 0.1 | 4 | 6 | 10 | 6.67 | 150 | 0.1 | 200 | 0.1 | 500 | 0.2 |
| **Country's population** | **37,000** | **100.0** | **120,000** | **100.0** | **4,200** | **0** | **4,200** | **3.00** | **140,000** | **100.0** | **162,000** | **100.0** | **234,000** | **100.0** |

**COLUMNS, ROWS.** For meanings and definitions, see Codebook (Part 6). Note that, by definitions, total 'Christians' = professing + crypto-Christians, which also = affiliated + nominal Christians. Percentages may not always total exactly, due to rounding.
**CENSUSES. 9.IV.1946:** 99.7% Christians (59.6% Roman Catholics, 21.0% Anglicans, 18.9% Protestants (14.0% Methodists)), 0.3% non-religious. **7.IV.1960** (de jure): 62.3% Roman Catholics, 18.5% Anglicans, 17.4% Protestants (11.9% Methodists, 1.9% SDAs, 0.6% Baptists), 1.2% Jews, 0.5% marginal Protestants (Jehovah's Witnesses). **7.IV.1970:** 64.6%

Roman Catholics, 14.8% Anglicans, 13.2% Protestants (8.9% Methodists, 2.1% SDAs, 0.7% Baptists), 1.2% Jews, 0.8% Black indigenous, 0.8% marginal Protestants.

**NOTES ON RELIGIONS**
**AFRO-AMERICAN SPIRITISTS.** Obeah (a form of magic syncretizing Christianity and African tribal religions) is practised among the Black Caribs.
**BAHA'IS.** Rapid growth from 1 local spiritual assembly (1964) to 33 (1973).

**BLACK INDIGENOUS.** In 2 denominations in 1970 (see Table 2).
**CATHOLIC PENTECOSTALS** (or, Catholic charismatics). Totals (mid-1975): 600 involved adults (over 15 years) in 8 prayer groups, including priests, religious personnel and the bishop. Total charismatic community including children, 1,200.
**CHRISTO-PAGANS.** Maya Amerindians and Black Caribs (Amerindian/Blacks) who syncretize folk-Catholicsm with their own traditional animistic religions.
**TRIBAL RELIGIONISTS.** Amerindians.

---

**NON-CHRISTIAN RELIGIONS. Judaism** has as followers some 1% of the population, and an additional 2% belong to other religions including Amerindians practising traditional Indian religions.

## CHRISTIANITY
**CATHOLIC CHURCH.** The territory's first 7,000 Catholics came from Yucatan, Mexico, following the Indian revolt of 1848. Catholics make up more than 60% of the population and are ethnically for the most part Blacks (African Negroes) and Indians, with a few Whites and natives of the East Indies. The church is served by diocesan and American Jesuit priests.
**ANGLICAN CHURCH.** The Society for the Propagation of the Gospel was the first mission in Belize, coming originally to work with Black labourers from Jamaica. Today Anglicans are second in size to the Catholic Church. The diocese of Belize,

formed in 1891, is part of the Church of the Province of the West Indies.
**PROTESTANT CHURCHES.** British Methodists were the first to open Protestant work in Belize (1825) and along with USA-based Eastern Mennonites are the 2 largest Protestant denominations in the country. Since their arrival in 1959, the Mennonites have had the most numerous expatriate missionary staff, engaged mostly in service and development programmes; but they have also built up a sizeable Christian community. Next in importance are Adventists who entered Belize in 1927, and Nazarenes since 1934.

**CHURCH AND STATE.** The former Spanish sovereignty over Belize was first challenged in 1786, and in 1840 it was formally declared a British colony. Full internal self-government was granted in 1964. Belize is a secular state, and the churches enjoy equal status before the law.

**INTERDENOMINATIONAL ORGANIZATIONS.** The Christian Social Council of Belize was founded in 1957 as the Church World Service Committee, with Methodist, Presbyterian and Salvation Army membership. Adventists, Anglicans, Assemblies of God, Church of God in Christ and Nazarenes joined in 1961, at which time it was reorganized under the name Christian Social Council. More recent changes in membership include the withdrawal of the Assemblies of God in 1968 and the addition of the Catholic Church in 1969. There are no sub-regional or local councils in Belize, but there is a Planning Commission of the Churches (consisting of Anglicans,

CHRISTMAS 1970

The Nativity of Christ, often portrayed on the country's postage stamps.

British Honduras ½ CENT

Methodists and Catholics) which undertakes educational, social and economic projects as well as providing opportunities for ecumenical worship services on specific occasions.

**BROADCASTING.** The government station Radio Belize broadcasts Protestant programmes for 9 hours from Monday to Saturday, with 3 hours on Sunday. Catholic programmes have half an hour each day including Sunday. A quarter of all Protestant programmes are produced locally. The Mennonite mission sponsors 2 radio programmes over Radio Belize. Many Caribs follow the Mennonite programme linked to follow-up Bible correspondence courses.

TABLE 2. ORGANIZED CHURCHES AND DENOMINATIONS IN BELIZE

| Official name 1 | Begun 2 | Type 3 | Counc 4 | Congs 5 | Adults 6 | Affiliated 7 | Names, notes, and other statistics (see Codebook) 8 |
|---|---|---|---|---|---|---|---|
| **Anglican Church: D Belize** | 1776 | A ACa | AwMRK | 45 | 5,500 | 16,000 | In CPWI. 96% Creole, 2% Carib, 1% other Indians. M=USPG. 4n,12x,2r,W=25%,700y. |
| Assemblies of God | 1946 | P Pe2 | ZF..k | 4 | 100 | 350 | Classical Pentecostals (2-stage). M=AoG(USA). 3n,2f,1 day school (250). |
| Baptist Churches in Belize | 1822 | P Bap | xF..C | 7 | 300 | 400 | Begun by BMS(UK); 1960, M=CBHMS(USA). 3 schools. HQ Belize City. 11n,5f,15Y. |
| Belize Mennonite Mission | 1960 | P Men | G.... | 6 | 44 | 100 | Begun by immigrants. M=Mennonite Ch of NAmerica (EMBMC). 24f. |
| **Catholic Church: D Belize** | c1650 | R Lat | P.NMK | 105 | 40,200 | 74,500 | Suffragan, M Kingston. M=SJ. C=1+0+3. 9n,32x,7m,99w,8r,P=35%,135Y,3327y. |
| Christian Brethren | c1952 | P CBr | x.... | 4 | 200 | 400 | *Open Brethren. Plymouth Brethren. Gospel Halls.* Numerous expatriates. |
| Church of God in Christ | | I pe3 | Z...K | | 200 | 500 | M=CoGiC(Black mission from USA). Black pentecostals. |
| Church of God (Cleveland) | 1944 | P Pe3 | ZF... | 7 | 150 | 300 | Holiness Pentecostals. M=CoG(Cleveland)(USA). 4 churches, 3 missions. 6n,2f. |
| Church of the Nazarene | 1934 | P Hol | xF..K | 25 | 534 | 1,000 | Holiness body. M=CoN(USA). 9n,35m,8f,G=4.4%pa,3h,23t(2030),W=61%,36Y,21z. |
| Ev Mennonite Mission Conference | | P Men | G.... | | 50 | 100 | M=Ev Mennonite Mission Conference (HQ Winnipeg, Canada). |
| Gospel Missionary Union | 1955 | P Hol | xM... | 15 | 500 | 800 | Holiness mission from North America. M=GMU(USA). 18f. |
| International City Mission | c1960 | I pen | x.... | | 200 | 500 | From Jamaica (HQ Kingston). Also in Bahamas, Barbados, UK, USA. Women bishops. |
| Jehovah's Witnesses | 1931 | M Jeh | x.... | 11 | 467 | 1,000 | *Watch Tower. IBSA.* Active witnessing under way by 1940. 37Y. |
| Mennonite Church in Belize | 1959 | P Men | G.... | | 3,500 | 4,000 | 2,500 Old Colony Mennonites, 1,000 Kleingemeinde. Amish immigrants in farming. |
| Methodist Ch in Caribbean & Americas | 1825 | P Met | VwM.K | 35 | 2,224 | 3,000 | *MCCA*(1967 union), *Honduras* (*Belize*) *District*. M=MMS(UK). 5n,4x,G=−5%pa,4r,252Yy. |
| Methodist Protestant Church | | P Met | ..T.. | 5 | 100 | 200 | M=MPC(USA). Fundamentalist mission from North America. 2f. |
| Pentecostal Church of God | 1956 | P Pe2 | Z.... | 12 | 100 | 300 | Classical Pentecostals from North America. M=PCG(USA). 4f. |
| Presbyterian Church | c1840 | P Ref | Rw..K | | 100 | 200 | *Church of Scotland.* Small group with Scots and British links in past. |
| Salvation Army | 1915 | P Sal | xwM.K | | 100 | 200 | *Belize Region*, Caribbean & CAmerica Territory (HQ Jamaica). HQ Belize City |
| Seventh-day Adventist Church | 1927 | P Adv | x...K | 20 | 2,077 | 2,500 | *SDA, Belize Mission*, Central America Union Mission. 3nx, 34mw,1r,34t(2088),174Y. |
| Other Protestant denominations | | P | ..... | | 300 | 500 | Total about 10 (see list below). |
| **Total affiliated (mid-1970)** | | | | **340** | **56,946** | **106,850** | **Total denominations (1970) . . . 30.** |
| **Total affiliated (mid-1975)** | | | | **370** | **63,400** | **119,020** | **Total denominations (1975) . . . 32.** |
| **Total affiliated (mid-1980)** | | | | **400** | **71,400** | **134,000** | **Total denominations (1980) . . . 34.** |

NOTES ON TABLE ABOVE
COLUMNS: for meanings and CODES (cols. 1, 3, 4, 8), see Codebook (Part 6). Column 1: **Boldface type** = church with over 10% of country's affiliated Christians.
NATIONAL COUNCILS (Column 4, 5th letter).
C = Evangelical Association.
K = Belize Christian Social Council (BCSC) (note: 1978, renamed Belize Christian Council).
k = associate member of BCSC.
OTHER PROTESTANT DENOMINATIONS. These include: Chs of Christ (Non-Instrumental), Elim Fellowship (1967), Elim Missionary Assemblies, Lutheran Ch, Missionary Ch, Moravian Ch.

**PEOPLES** (ethnolinguistic). Christians: 62.0% Black, 17.0% Mayan, 10.0% Black Carib, 5.4% Guatemalan White and Ladino, 5.4% Honduran Mestizo, British, East Indian.

COUNTRY-WIDE TOTALS
EVANGELIZATION (see Part 5). 1900: 99%. 1970: 100%. 1980: 100%. *Radiophonic evangelism.* HCJB, ICI (1,884 enrolments, 130 conversions).
FOREIGN MISSIONARIES AND PERSONNEL (aliens from abroad) (1973). Total 224. *From Western world.* 204: about 120 Roman Catholics, 72 Protestants in 13USA societies, 12 Anglicans (9 in 1 UK society, 3 in 1 Canada society). *From Third World.* About 20 (Roman Catholics, Anglicans, Protestants, indigenous) from Jamaica.
INSTITUTIONS (church-operated) (1973). Total 27, including 19 higher schools, 6 medical centres (2 hospitals).
PERIODICALS. About 8 titles.
PERSONNEL. About 520 (296 national, 224 foreign).
SCRIPTURE DISTRIBUTION (1975). Annual totals: 520 Bibles (23% free, 58% subsidized, 19% commercial), 7,100 NTs (90% free, 7% subsidized, 3% commercial), 1,000 UBS portions. *Translations completed.* Portion: Garifuna (Carib) in 1847.
SERVICE AGENCIES. About 13, including BCSC, EHC, SPCK, YWCA.

ADDITIONAL DATA ON CHURCHES
CATHOLIC CHURCH. The diocese is a suffragan of M Kingston (in Jamaica). *Annual baptisms.* (1972) 98% infant, 2% adult. *Priests.* 11 diocesan, 27 USA Jesuits, and 2 OSB (USA). 23 are full-time teachers. *Brothers.* SJ brothers. *Sisters.* 60 are full-time teachers. *Catechists.* Total (1969) 156. *Catholic charismatics.* The First Belize National Catholic Charismatic Conference was held in November 1975, with 350 delegates including the bishop. *Foreign religious congregations.* Priests: SJ (Missouri Province). Sisters: Sisters of Mercy (USA), Sisters of the Holy Family (USA), Pallotine Sisters (Germany).
*Catholic organizations.* The diocese is a member of the Antilles Episcopal Conference, with headquarters in Kingston, Jamaica, itself a member of CELAM. Religious personnel are represented by the Major Superiors of the Antilles, a member of CLAR. Lay organizations include Catholic Scouts, Apostleship of Prayer, Legion of Mary and Sodalities.
The Holy See has no diplomatic relations with Belize. It is represented to the Catholic hierarchy by an apostolic delegate based in Port-au-Prince, Haiti.
In 1974 the church sponsored 101 elementary schools (20,310 pupils), 8 high schools (2,476), 2 hospitals (60 beds), several credit unions and co-operatives and an adult training centre.

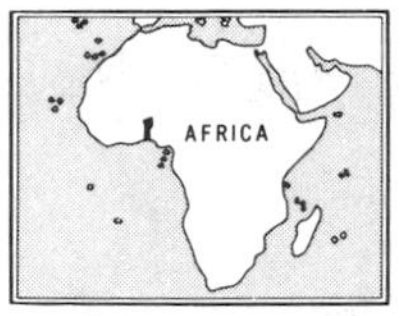


# BENIN

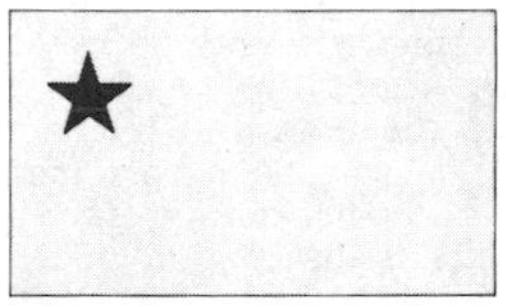

## SECULAR DATA

**STATE. Official name:** The People's Republic of Benin (La République Populaire du Bénin). Earlier name: Dahomey. Adjective of nationality: Beninese (béninois).
**Flag** (shown above right): Green field with red star in upper hoist corner.
**Area:** 112,622 sq.km. (43,483 sq.miles). Agricultural land: 30.1%.
**Government:** One-party Communist state, declared a Marxist-Leninist state in November 1974 (1822 Kingdom, 1851 French rule, 1891 protectorate, 1904 in French West Africa, 1960 Independence as republic of Dahomey, 1963 military rule).
**Official language:** French (*Français*).
**Chief cities:** capital, Porto Novo 74,500 (1965), Cotonou 111,000, Abomey 42,100.
**Armed forces** (1976): Total 1,650 regular: army 1,500, air force 150 (1 combat aircraft). Paramilitary forces: 1,100.

**DEMOGRAPHY. Population:** 2,106,000 (census of 30.IX.1961. For 1970–2000 (UN), see last row of Table 1). Population density (1975): 27/sq.km. (71/sq.mile). Under 15 years: 44%. Growth rate (1975–80): 2.79% per year (births 4.86%, deaths −2.08%). Life expectancy (1975–80): 43.5 years. Household size: 4.9 persons. **Major languages:** Fon, Yoruba, Bariba, Gun, Fulani, Somba, French, Ewe, and about 20 other tribal languages.
**Urban dwellers** (1970): 13.3%. Urban growth rate (1950–70): 6.5% per year.
**Labour force:** 49%.
**Refugees** (1977): About 2,000 from Togo. (1978) 10,000 Beninese, forcibly evicted from the country of their residence Gabon.
**Tourists** (1974): 19,101.

**ETHNOLINGUISTIC GROUPS:** 25.0% Fon, 12.6% Yoruba (Egba, Nago), 12.3% Bariba, 12.0% Gun, 10.8% Adja-Wachi, 5.9% Fulani, 5.7% Somba, 4.5% Aizo, 4.5% Kilinga (Dompago), 2.8% Mina (Popo), 2.0% Dendi (Songhai), 0.9% Tem (Kotokoli), 0.8% Busa, Ewe, Mulatto, & numerous smaller peoples.

**MONEY** (1977). **Monetary unit:** CFA franc (= 100 centimes); US$ = CFAF 250.00.
**National income per person:** US$125. Average annual family income: US$613.
**Cost of living in capital** (1976): index 163 (Washington DC=100). Daily cost of living: US$33. Consumer price index (1975): 142.

**EDUCATION.** Adult literacy: (1962) 8%, (1974) 20%. Education rate: 20%. Schools: 969. Universities: 1.

**HEALTH.** Hospitals: 98 (3,124 beds). Doctors: 95. Lepers: 63,000 (20.5 per 1,000). Psychotics: 18,000.

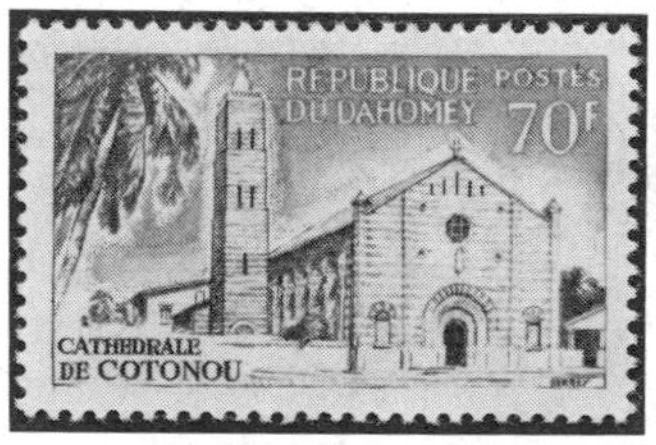


**Eglise Catholique.** Cotonou cathedral.

**LITERATURE.** Periodicals: 20. Newspapers: 2 dailies, 2 non-daily.

**COMMUNICATION** (per 1,000 people). Phones: 3. Radios: 52. TV sets: 1. Daily newspaper circulation: 0.7 copies.

TABLE 1. RELIGIOUS ADHERENTS IN BENIN

| Year | 1900 | | mid-1970 | | Annual change, 1970–1980 | | | | mid-1975 | | mid-1980 | | 2000 | |
|---|---|---|---|---|---|---|---|---|---|---|---|---|---|---|
| *Name* | *Adherents* | *%* | *Adherents* | *%* | *Natural* | *Conversion* | *Total* | *Rate* | *Adherents* | *%* | *Adherents* | *%* | *Adherents* | *%* |
| Tribal religionists | 569,200 | 91.8 | 1,790,000 | 66.6 | 54,329 | −16,279 | 38,050 | 1.93 | 1,969,400 | 64.1 | 2,170,500 | 61.4 | 3,043,200 | 51.4 |
| **Christians** | **7,300** | **1.2** | **515,000** | **19.2** | **17,892** | **12,238** | **30,130** | **4.65** | **648,600** | **21.1** | **816,300** | **23.1** | **1,776,000** | **30.0** |
| professing | 7,300 | 1.2 | 515,000 | 19.2 | 17,892 | 12,238 | 30,130 | 4.65 | 648,600 | 21.1 | 816,300 | 23.1 | 1,776,000 | 30.0 |
| Roman Catholics | 6,000 | 1.0 | 403,000 | 15.0 | 14,171 | 10,999 | 25,170 | 4.90 | 513,700 | 16.7 | 654,700 | 18.5 | 1,416,600 | 23.9 |
| Protestants | 1,200 | 0.2 | 70,000 | 2.6 | 2,204 | −4 | 2,200 | 2.75 | 79,900 | 2.6 | 92,000 | 2.6 | 177,600 | 3.0 |
| African indigenous | 100 | 0.0 | 38,000 | 1.4 | 1,379 | 1,181 | 2,560 | 5.12 | 50,000 | 1.6 | 63,600 | 1.8 | 165,800 | 2.8 |
| Marginal Protestants | 0 | 0.0 | 4,000 | 0.1 | 138 | 62 | 200 | 4.00 | 5,000 | 0.2 | 6,000 | 0.2 | 16,000 | 0.3 |
| nominal | 1,000 | 0.2 | 27,434 | 1.0 | 1,051 | 1,676 | 2,727 | 7.16 | 38,100 | 1.2 | 54,700 | 1.5 | 238,200 | 4.0 |
| affiliated | 6,300 | 1.0 | 487,566 | 18.2 | 16,841 | 10,562 | 27,403 | 4.49 | 610,500 | 19.9 | 761,600 | 21.6 | 1,537,800 | 26.0 |
| total practising | 5,990 | *95* | 438,810 | *90* | 14,820 | 6,797 | 21,617 | 4.02 | 537,240 | *88* | 654,980 | *86* | 1,230,200 | *80* |
| non-practising | 310 | *5* | 48,760 | *10* | 2,021 | 3,765 | 5,786 | 7.90 | 73,260 | *12* | 106,620 | *14* | 307,600 | *20* |
| Roman Catholics | 5,200 | 0.8 | 393,813 | 14.7 | 13,567 | 8,542 | 22,109 | 4.50 | 491,800 | 16.0 | 614,900 | 17.4 | 1,213,800 | 20.5 |
| Protestants | 1,000 | 0.2 | 52,531 | 2.0 | 1,779 | 738 | 2,517 | 3.90 | 65,500 | 2.1 | 77,700 | 2.2 | 148,000 | 2.5 |
| Evangelicals | 1,000 | 0.2 | 26,900 | 1.0 | 919 | 401 | 1,320 | 3.96 | 33,300 | 1.1 | 40,100 | 1.1 | 78,000 | 1.3 |
| African indigenous | 100 | 0.0 | 37,222 | 1.4 | 1,357 | 1,220 | 2,577 | 5.24 | 49,200 | 1.6 | 63,000 | 1.8 | 160,000 | 2.7 |
| Marginal Protestants | 0 | 0.0 | 4,000 | 0.1 | 138 | 62 | 200 | 4.00 | 5,000 | 0.2 | 6,000 | 0.2 | 16,000 | 0.3 |
| Muslims | 43,500 | 7.0 | 376,000 | 14.0 | 12,381 | 3,739 | 16,120 | 3.59 | 448,800 | 14.6 | 357,200 | 15.2 | 1,065,800 | 18.0 |
| Ahmadis | 0 | 0.0 | 200 | 0.0 | 8 | 12 | 20 | 6.67 | 300 | 0.0 | 400 | 0.0 | 2,000 | 0.0 |
| Baha'is | 0 | 0.0 | 3,400 | 0.1 | 121 | 79 | 200 | 4.55 | 4,400 | 0.1 | 5,400 | 0.1 | 18,000 | 0.3 |
| Non-religious | 0 | 0.0 | 600 | 0.0 | 28 | 112 | 140 | 14.00 | 1,000 | 0.0 | 2,000 | 0.1 | 10,000 | 0.2 |
| Atheists | 0 | 0.0 | 0 | 0.0 | 14 | 86 | 100 | 20.00 | 500 | 0.0 | 1,000 | 0.0 | 5,000 | 0.1 |
| Other religionists | 0 | 0.0 | 1,000 | 0.0 | 35 | 25 | 60 | 4.62 | 1,300 | 0.0 | 1,600 | 0.0 | 3,000 | 0.1 |
| **Country's population** | **620,000** | **100.0** | **2,686,000** | **100.0** | **84,800** | **0** | **84,800** | **2.76** | **3,074,000** | **100.0** | **3,534,000** | **100.0** | **5,921,000** | **100.0** |

COLUMNS, ROWS. For meanings and definitions, see Code-book (Part 6). Note that, by definition, total 'Christians' = professing + crypto-Christians, which also = affiliated + nominal Christians. Percentages may not always total exactly, due to rounding.
CENSUSES. 25.V–30.IX.1961 (Africans over 14 years): 70.8% tribal religionists ('fetishists', animists), 13.6% Muslims, 12.3% Roman Catholics, 2.6% Protestants, 0.6% African indigenous.

NOTES ON RELIGIONS
AFRICAN INDIGENOUS. In 20 denominations in 1970 (see Table 2).

AHMADIS. Begun from Nigeria in 1966, the Qadiani mission opened its first mosque, in Porto Novo, in 1974. Largely Yorubas.
ATHEISTS. No communist party; atheists virtually nil, a few intellectuals only, until after 1970.
BAHA'IS. Growth from 1 local spiritual assembly (1964) to 23 (1973). Missionaries from Haiti (West Indies) are at work.
MUSLIMS. All Sunnis (of the Malikite rite). In the south, among the Nago, and spreading also among the Gun; in the north, Fulani, Dendi, Bariba (20% Muslim). The Dendi, long islamized, have helped spread Islam throughout the north, and Dendi is now the lingua franca of Muslims in the north. Orders: Qadiriya; Tijaniya; also Ahmadiya. *Hajj pilgrims to Mecca.* (1970) 468; (1974) 527; (1975) 419; (1976) 545.

OTHER RELIGIONISTS. Including Rosicrucians (6 AMORC centres).
PRACTISING CHRISTIANS. Regular attendance (Catholics): 70% in towns, almost 100% in villages. Easter communicants (Catholics): attendance is much lower than the regular attendance because of distances and difficulties of travel and insufficient Easter services.
TRIBAL RELIGIONISTS. Traditional religion (also termed Vodoun (Voodoo) or fetishism) remains very strong. In Abomey sub-division there are 257 fetishist monasteries. Tribes over 60% traditionalist (animist) in 1972: Dompago (85%), Fon (80%), Boko (80%), Bariba (70%), Egba (Nago) (60%).

## NON-CHRISTIAN RELIGIONS. Traditional African religions

retain the allegiance of over 60% of the population and are active everywhere, especially in rural areas and among women. In spite of their diversity, they have, notably in the south, several common characteristics: a coherent yet mystical view of the universe; a concept of God (Mawu among the Ewe, Mawu-Lisa among the Fon); a desire for communion with the divinities in their various manifestations (Vodoun or Voodoo among the Fon, Orisha among the Yoruba); and a need to know the will of the divinities by consulting the Fa oracles. The Fon, who have been generally resistant to both Islam and Christianity, have traditionalist or fetishist convents in the region of Abomey, and their chief medicine-men play a not inconsiderable part politically in the degree to which they draw their clientele towards active participation in national life. In lower and middle Dahomey, during April and May 1966, they held well-attended conferences to win the protection of the Vodoun, first for the military regime and then for the national quadrennial plan.

**Islam** has been introduced among the Nago of the

served by French and Portuguese priests during the 17th and 18th centuries. By 1830 there were 2,000 Catholics in Dahomey. However, active missionary work in the interior did not begin until 1860, when Dahomey was turned over to the African Missions of Lyons. A prefecture was erected in 1883. By 1900 there were 5,000 Catholics, and a seminary was opened in 1913. The first African priest was ordained in 1928.

The archdiocese of Cotonou was established in 1955 and the first African archbishop appointed in 1960. Strongly represented now in the cities and among the modern elite, Catholicism reaches primarily the populations of the southern half of the country,

**Muslims.** Sunni mosque in Cotonou.

including the Fon, Mina, Adja, and Gun, as well as Mulattoes descended from Portuguese sailors and merchants and repatriated slaves who returned from Brazil during the 19th century.

PROTESTANT CHURCHES. There are 3 principal Protestant churches at work in Dahomey. Methodists, who are associated with the Methodist Church of Great Britain, were the first to enter,

their greatest success among the Logba and Bariba peoples. The extreme northeast and the region west of Djougou are still considered unevangelized areas.

INDIGENOUS CHURCHES. There are a number of small independent churches working in Benin. The most important are the Heavenly Christianity Church begun 1947 and which later spread to Nigeria as the Celestial Church of Christ, Cherubim and Seraphim who entered from Nigeria in 1933, and Eglise Methodiste Africaine (Eledja) which split from the Methodists in 1927.

**CHURCH AND STATE.** According to the constitution of March 1968, the republic is a secular

**Ahmadis.** Two-storey mosque of Ahmadiya Muslim Mission under construction in Porto Novo; later completed after only 6 months' work and opened in 1974.

state (Article 2), but the president takes his oath 'before God and the ancestors' (Article 29). Liberty of conscience and religion is assured.

In practice, the fact that the republic is secular means that the state maintains a neutral stance before all religions, which are considered equal. Legal holidays include the main Christian and Muslim festivals. Official ceremonies are accompanied by libations and offerings to the ancestors and divinities, as well as prayers in churches and mosques. In August 1970, the government organized at Cotonou a colloquium entitled 'The Social Role of the Traditional African Religions'.

Before 1974 the state subsidized education in denominational schools at a rate equivalent to 60% of the gross salary of public school teachers, all other charges being borne by the churches. In public schools, religion classes were normally integrated into the class schedule. On 10 September 1974 all Catholic and Protestant primary schools were taken over by government and state aid to denominational secondary and technical schools abolished.

The historic role played by the Catholic Church in the formation of an elite, by means of its schools, gives it a greater influence than the number of its adherents warrants. In the years 1945–51, such missionary personalities as Fr Aupiais played an important part in the evolution of the colony; but since Independence, the Catholic hierarchy has forbidden priests to interfere in political life or to seek election to political posts.

Since 26 October 1972 Benin has been led by a revolutionary military government (GMR), which stated on 30 November 1974 its choice of the socialist way to development 'on the basis of Marxism-Leninism'. In February 1975, 3 Catholic priests in senior posts were arrested together with a number of influential laymen. One of the priests was condemned to death, an action which provoked widespread attempts and appeals to prevent the application of the sentence. On 12 February 1975 the government warned the Catholic Church against the involvement of priests and laity in opposition to the present regime. Officially the government considers belief or non-belief in religion a personal matter in the face of which the Benin (Dahomean) Revolution maintains

**Tribal religionists.** 80% of the largest tribe, the Fon, are traditionalists (fetishists). *Above.* Pagan temple, with mud walls mixed with blood of sacrificed slaves, in Fon capital of Abomey

Yoruba cluster in the south by the Yoruba and Hausa of Nigeria, and among the Fulani, Dendi and Bariba in the north by the Dendi of Niger. The Qadiriya and Tijaniya orders are active. Largely urban in orientation, many Muslims are merchants. Islam is the religion of 14% of the population of Benin.

**CHRISTIANITY**
CATHOLIC CHURCH. A chapel was built by the Portuguese at Ouidah (Whydah) in 1680 and was

arriving in Abomey in 1843. They are by far the largest Protestant group and have concentrated their attention principally on the Gun of the southern coast. Recently, through the Action Apostolique Commune, a new work begun among the largely unevangelized Fon around Abomey. The Assemblies of God are active in northwest among the Somba and Pilapila tribes, whereas EECOA or ECWA (served by the Sudan Interior Mission), is located in central and northcentral Benin. The latter have had a 'strict neutrality so long as their expressions do not constitute an impediment to the development of the Revolution'. In 1976 all schools were nationalized.

There is no government ministry in charge of religious affairs, but all churches must be registered with the Ministry of the Interior.

**INTERDENOMINATIONAL ORGANIZATIONS.** There are no organizations which co-ordinate the work of Protestants and Catholics, nor is there a Protestant council to further Protestant co-operation; there is however an association of indigenous churches. The Evangelical Pastoral School at Porto Novo trains pastors for the Evangelical Church of Togo and the Methodist Church of Benin-Togo, and the Christian Centre for Lay Training attached to it serves all the churches. In 1965 the Methodists initiated Action Apostolique Commune as a new evangelistic thrust among the Fon. An international, inter-racial and inter-ecclesial team is composed of staff drawn from Cameroon, Togo, Tahiti, Madagascar and France, as well as Benin. Roman Catholic scholars assist with the production of scriptures in Fon.

Regarding Christian and Muslim relations, the Catholic Episcopal Conference has established an Episcopal Commission for Islam and Ecumenism. On an individual basis, dialogue is taking place at Parakou between Catholics and Muslims and at Pobe between Methodists and Muslims.

**BROADCASTING.** The government Radio Benin broadcasts a Catholic mass and a Protestant service every Sunday morning, and a Catholic and Protestant news magazine during the week. From abroad, Christian programmes can be heard over ELWA (Liberia). For Catholics, Benin is registered as a member of UNDA.

**BIBLIOGRAPHY**

'Les sectes au Dahomey', M.C. Merlo, in *Devant les sectes non-chrétiennes* (Luovain: Desclée de Brouwer, 1961), p. 102-119.
'Les société-religieuses en Afrique occidentale', E.G. Parrinder, *Présence africaine*, NS 17-18 (février-mai, 1958), 17-21.

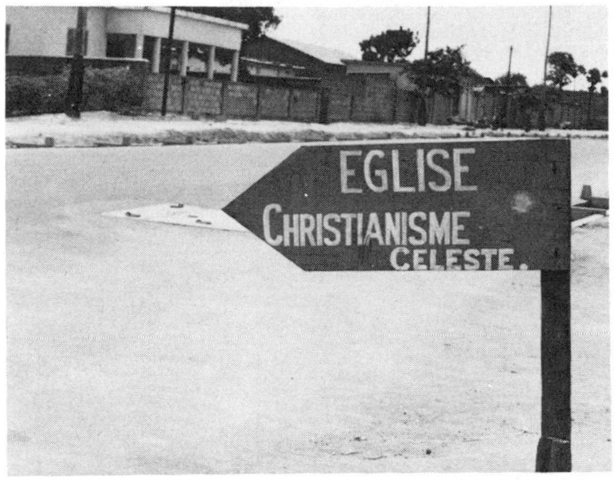


**Eglise du Christianisme Céleste du Bénin.** Signpost to one of this denomination's 100 churches in Benin.

TABLE 2. ORGANIZED CHURCHES AND DENOMINATIONS IN BENIN

| Official name 1 | Begun 2 | Type 3 | Counc 4 | Congs 5 | Adults 6 | Affiliated 7 | Names, notes, and other statistics (see Codebook) 8 |
|---|---|---|---|---|---|---|---|
| Assemblées de Dieu | 1938 | P Pe2 | ZF... | 58 | 2,820 | 6,000 | *Assemblies of God.* M=AoG(USA). Northwest. Sombas. HQ Cotonou. 38n,14f,1s(19). |
| Chérubin et Séraphin | 1933 | I peA | x.I.I | 100 | 3,000 | 6,000 | *Cherubim and Seraphim Society.* Nigerian indigenous pentecostals. Egba, Gun. |
| Eglise Apostolique du Nigérie | 1950 | P PeA | ZG..I | 70 | 3,500 | 7,000 | M=Apost Ch of Nigeria (Lagos). 48 congs in Deve district. Yoruba, Gun, Adja, Mina. |
| Eglise Apostolique du Togo et Bénin | c1960 | I peA | x.I.I | 7 | 1,000 | 2,000 | *Apostolic Ch of T & B. Divine Healer's Temple.* Begun 1951 in Togo. Apostle in Lomé. |
| **Eglise Catholique au Bénin:** | 1680 | R Lat | P.SFR | 161 | 220,500 | 393,813 | *Catholic Ch.* Mainly south. C=2+2+20. 4p,1s(18). 78n,93x,15m,350w,P=23%,13140Yy. |
| M Cotonou | 1883 | R Lat | Ps | 25 | 78,100 | 139,433 | Port, centre of nation. 33% urban. Fon. 27 28 1 121 21 4143 |
| D Abomey | 1963 | R Lat | Ps | 13 | 56,000 | 100,000 | Fon Capital. Strong traditional religion. 22 15 11 71 26 3698 |
| D Lokossa | 1968 | R Lat | Ps | 61 | 13,600 | 24,314 | Rural development, coastal fishing. 9 13 0 35 21 1332 |
| D Natitingou | 1964 | R Lat | Psma | 21 | 3,700 | 6,630 | 15% Somba, 15% Bariba, 15% Kabre, & from south 3 10 1 44 48 764 |
| D Parakou | 1948 | R Lat | Psma | 22 | 6,200 | 11,031 | 41% Muslim. Southerners: 85% Fon, 10% Egba. 2 11 2 33 23 472 |
| D Porto Novo | 1954 | R Lat | Ps | 19 | 62,900 | 112,405 | Densely populated (100/km2). 177 expatriates. 15 16 0 46 21 2731 |
| Eglise du Christianisme Céleste du B | 1947 | I peA | x.I.I | 100 | 14,043 | 20,000 | *Heavenly Christianity Ch.* Schism ex Cherubim. HQ Porto Novo. Gun, Nago, Mina, Ewe. |
| Egl Ev Chrétienne de l'Ouest-Africain | 1946 | P int | xM... | 59 | 782 | 3,335 | *EECOA/ECWA:* M=SIM. 33% Bariba, 32% Logba, 13% Fulani, Nago. 11n,29f,1H,3h,3p(26). |
| Eglise Méthodiste Africaine (Eledja) | 1927 | I Met | x.I.I | 21 | 1,621 | 4,622 | M=United Afr Meth Ch(Fishmongers) (HQ Lagos). 68% Gun, 32% Yoruba. 4n,W=64%,15Y,94y. |
| Eglise Protestante Méthodiste au Bénin | 1843 | P Met | VWA.. | 239 | 16,494 | 35,696 | *Protestant Meth Ch.* M=MMS, PEMS,AAC. 12n,4x,16f,3r,1s(4),W=50%,322Y,1971y,3021z. |
| Eglise Union Africaine | 1895 | I Met | x.I.I | 16 | 700 | 2,000 | *African Union Mission. Boda-Owa*(If it's good, come). In UNAC(Nigeria). Ex MMS. Yoruba. |
| Témoins de Jéhovah | c1935 | M Jeh | x.... | 53 | 1,956 | 4,000 | *Jehovah's Witnesses. Watch Tower.* Active witnessing by 1940s. HQ Cotonou. 154Y. |
| Other African indigenous churches | | I | ..... | | 1,300 | 2,600 | Total 15, including: Christ Apostolic Ch (Nigeria), Eglise Christique Primitive. |
| Other Protestant denominations | | P | ..... | | 200 | 500 | Total 3: Ev Baptist Missions, Southern Baptist Convention, World-Wide Missions. |
| **Total affiliated (mid-1970)** | | | | **905** | **267,916** | **487,566** | **Total denominations (1970) . . . 29.** |
| **Total affiliated (mid-1975)** | | | | **1,050** | **335,500** | **610,500** | **Total denominations (1975) . . . 31.** |
| **Total affiliated (mid-1980)** | | | | **1,200** | **418,500** | **761,600** | **Total denominations (1980) . . . 34.** |

NOTES ON TABLE ABOVE
COLUMNS: for meanings and CODES (cols, 1, 3, 4, 8), see Codebook (Part 6). Column 1: **Boldface type** = church with over 10% of country's affiliated Christians.
NATIONAL COUNCILS (Column 4, 5th letter).
I = Association des Eglises Chrétiennes (Association of Christian Churches).
R = Conférence Episcopale du Bénin/Dahomey (Episcopal Conference of Benin/Dahomey).

PEOPLES (ethnolinguistic). Christians: about 24% Fon, 23% Yoruba (Egba), 21% Gun, 14% Adja, 10% Mina, 4% Bariba, 2% Somba, 1% Dompago (Kilinga, Kabre), Ewe, Mulatto.

COUNTRY-WIDE TOTALS
EVANGELIZATION (see Part 5). 1900: 13%. 1970: 60%. 1980: 70%. *Mass evangelism.* 1966, campaigns at Parakou and Cotonou under Radio ELWA (Liberia). *Radiophonic evangelism.* ELWA, RVOG, ICI (2,500 enrolments, 900 active).
FOREIGN MISSIONARIES AND PERSONNEL (nationals serving abroad) (1973). Total 34 in Nigeria, Togo and Upper Volta: about 20 Roman Catholics, 8 African indigenous, 6 Protestants.
FOREIGN MISSIONARIES AND PERSONNEL (aliens from abroad) (1973). Total 492. *From Western world.* 416: 326 Roman Catholics, 90 Protestants (45 in 6 USA societies, 19 in 2 UK societies, 13 in 1 Canada society, 6 in 1 France society, 3 in 1 Australia society, 2 in 1 Switzerland society, 1 in 1 Netherlands society, 1 in 1 New Zealand society). *From Communist world.* About 2 Roman Catholics from Yugoslavia. *From Third World.* 74: about 40 Roman Catholics, 20 African indigenous from Nigeria, 14 Protestants from Nigeria, Ghana and Togo.
INSTITUTIONS (church-operated) (1973). Total 55, including 12 higher schools (4 minor seminaries), 28 medical centres (9 hospitals), 5 religious communities, 6 seminaries (5 Protestant, 1 RC), 2 study centres.
PERIODICALS. About 15 titles.
PERSONNEL. About 1,382 (890 national, 492 foreign).
RELIGIOUS LIBRARIES. 13.
SCRIPTURE DISTRIBUTION (1975). Annual totals: 2,120 Bibles (24% free, 71% subsidized, 5% commercial), 9,160 NTs (55% free, 44% subsidized, 1% commercial), 3,400 UBS portions, 2,000 UBS selections. *Translations completed.* Portion: 5 languages since 1886. NT: 1 language in 1892. Bible: 1 language in 1923.
SERVICE AGENCIES. About 35, including ACF, CEB, CODIAM, CV/AV, GBUAF, JAC/F, JEC/F, JOC/F, MAP, SBB, UCJG(YMCA), UDAL.

ADDITIONAL DATA ON CHURCHES
EGLISE CATHOLIQUE AU BENIN. *Catechumens.* (1959) 36,266; (1961) 36,907; (1963) 41,879; (1971) 47,403. *Annual baptisms.* (1972) 65.2% infant, 34.8% adult. *Church attendance.* 70% in towns, rising to almost 100% in villages. *Brothers.* Including 3 Dahomeans. *Sisters.* Including 129 Dahomeans. *Seminary.* The major seminary of Ouidah serves Togo also. *Seminarians.* 18, increasing to 26 (1972), all secular. *Catechists.* Total (1970) 600. Training schools: Ouidah, Natitingou, Gogonou. *Indigenous religious congregations.* Sisters: 83 Petites Servantes des Pauvres (begun 1912), 42 Soeurs de St-Augustin (begun 1968). *Main foreign congregations.* Priests: SMA, WF (PB). Sisters: N-D des Apôtres, Petites Servantes du S-C de Menton. *Catholic organizations.* The Episcopal Conference of Benin (Conférence Episcopale du Bénin), is a member of the Inter-Territorial Episcopal Conference of Francophone West Africa, and of SECAM. There are no national presbyteral or pastoral councils, but religious personnel are represented in Anima Una, the Union des Supérieures Majeures des Congrégations Autochtones d'Afrique de l'Ouest Francophone, in Bamako, Mali. The Dahomean Union of the Lay Apostolate (Union Dahoméenne d'Apostolat des Laïcs, UDAL) co-ordinates the activities of CV and AV (2,300 members)' Scouts (1,600), JAC/F (3,600), JOC/F (2,235), Légion de Marie (1,600), as well as Guides, JEC/F, ACF and Teacher Teams.

The Holy See has diplomatic relations with Benin and is represented to government and the Catholic hierarchy by a pro-nuncio, who resides in Abidjan, Ivory Coast.

Under the National Office of Catholic Education, in 1970 there were 220 primary schools (49,823 children) and 5 secondary schools (3,250 pupils). In 1968 Catholic schools accounted for 30% of all children at the primary level and 15% at secondary level. However, in 1974 all Catholic primary schools were taken over by government and subsidies to the 5 secondary schools (2,296 pupils) and technical schools for girls were discontinued.

There are 2 centres for cultural action in Cotonou: Development and Culture Centre, which organizes conferences and a night school; and Inter-African Centre of Training, founded by the Committee for the Development of Intellectual Investments in Africa and Madagascar (CODIAM). The original purpose of the latter was to complete the professional training of Catholic teachers, but it is now open to other cultural and social activities.

In 1969, the Catholic Church sponsored 2 hospitals, 18 dispensaries, 4 leprosariums and 2 maternity hospitals. Further, there are religious personnel working under contract in the public hospitals of Cotonou and Porto Novo.

In the field of social action, Caritas-Benin, which began work in 1958 as Caritas-Dahomey, created in 1967 its own Catholic Dahomean Campaign for Development, including literacy campaigns in local languages, dispensaries, domestic training centres and small farming co-operatives. Catholic Youth, Scouts and Guides are engaged in socio-economic activities including digging wells, farming schools, literacy and educational work at the beginner level, and the creation of model villages for youth. The Social Secretariat, which works in 3 dioceses, provides for classes in economic and social training.
EGLISE EVANGELIQUE CHRETIENNE DE L'OUEST AFRICAIN. Also called Association des Eglises Evangéliques du Bénin/Dahomey (AEED).
EGLISE PROTESTANTE METHODISTE AU BENIN. Part of District Benin-Togo, British Methodist Conference (UK). Work is confined to the southern coastal area. Full membership: 37% Gun, 31% Mina, 28% Nago (Egba), 3% Yoruba. From about 1965 membership because static and even decreased in 1967. Co-operating missions: Methodist Missionary Society, Paris Mission, Action Apostolique Commune (ecumenical).

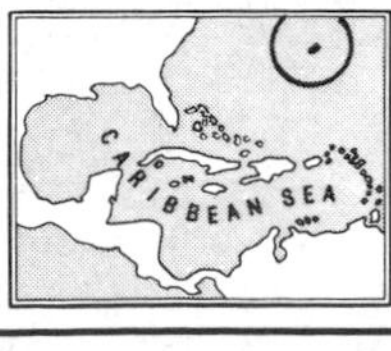

# BERMUDA

## SECULAR DATA

**STATE. Official name:** The Colony of the Bermuda Islands. Alternative name: Somers Islands.
**Flag** (shown above right): That of the UK (Britain).
**Area:** 53.3 sq.km. (20.6 sq.miles). Description: 150 small islands (20 inhabited). Agricultural land: 0.0%.
**Government:** Self-governing dependency of United Kingdom, since 1968 (1684 British crown colony, 1968 internal autonomy).
**Legislature:** Legislative Council, 11 members. House of Assembly, 40.
**Official language:** English.
**Capital:** Hamilton 2,060 (1970).
**Armed forces** (1976): None.
**Foreign forces** (1973): 1,000 USA troops.

**DEMOGRAPHY. Population:** 52,330 (census of 29.X.1970. For 1970–2000 (UN), see last row of Table 1). Population density (1975): 1,051/sq.km. (2,721/sq.mile). Under 15 years: 33%. Growth rate (1975–80): 1.37% per year (1970 births 2.04%, deaths −0.74%). Life expectancy: 69 years. Household size: 3.4 persons.

**Major languages:** English, Portuguese.
**Urban dwellers** (1970): 10.0%. Urban growth rate (1950–70): 3.4% per year.
**Labour force:** 52%.
**Refugees** (1977): About 15,000 from Haiti.
**Tourists** (1971): 412,947.

**ETHNOLINGUISTIC GROUPS:** 56.5% Black (African Negro), 29.0% English, 10.0% Mulatto (White/Black), 4.5% Portuguese, Jewish.

**MONEY** (1977). Monetary unit: Bermuda dollar (= 100 cents); US$1 = Berm$1.00.
**National income per person:** US$4,800. Average annual family income: US$16,320.
**Inflation:** (1970–74) 10.8% per year.
**Cost of living in capital** (1976): index 122 (Washington DC=100).

Daily cost of living: US$49.

**EDUCATION.** Adult literacy: (1950) 97%, (1960) 98%. Schools: 43.

**HEALTH.** Hospitals: 3 (512 beds). Doctors: 65. Blind: 25.

**LITERATURE.** Periodicals: 40. Newspapers: 1 daily, 4 non-daily.

**COMMUNICATION** (per 1,000 people). Phones: 666. Radios: 714. TV sets: 364. Daily newspaper circulation: 250 copies.

TABLE 1.    RELIGIOUS ADHERENTS IN BERMUDA

| Year / Name | 1900 Adherents | % | mid-1970 Adherents | % | Natural | Conversion | Total | Rate | mid-1975 Adherents | % | mid-1980 Adherents | % | 2000 Adherents | % |
|---|---|---|---|---|---|---|---|---|---|---|---|---|---|---|
| **Christians** | **20,260** | **100.0** | **50,810** | **97.7** | 782 | −1 | 781 | 1.43 | 54,710 | 97.7 | 58,620 | 97.7 | 72,580 | 95.5 |
| professing | 20,260 | 100.0 | 50,810 | 97.7 | 782 | −1 | 781 | 1.43 | 54,710 | 97.7 | 58,620 | 97.7 | 72,580 | 95.5 |
| Anglicans | 13,630 | 67.3 | 23,430 | 45.0 | 349 | −166 | 183 | 0.75 | 24,410 | 43.6 | 25,260 | 42.1 | 28,800 | 38.0 |
| Protestants | 2,330 | 11.5 | 13,830 | 26.6 | 209 | −56 | 153 | 1.05 | 14,620 | 26.1 | 15,360 | 25.6 | 6,840 | 9.0 |
| Roman Catholics | 1,260 | 6.2 | 7,590 | 14.6 | 133 | 224 | 357 | 3.83 | 9,300 | 16.6 | 11,160 | 18.6 | 18,240 | 24.0 |
| Black indigenous | 3,040 | 15.0 | 5,440 | 10.5 | 81 | −25 | 56 | 0.98 | 5,710 | 10.2 | 6,000 | 10.0 | 16,420 | 21.6 |
| Marginal Protestants | 0 | 0.0 | 520 | 1.0 | 10 | 22 | 32 | 4.78 | 670 | 1.2 | 840 | 1.4 | 2,200 | 2.9 |
| nominal | 1,230 | 6.1 | 4,585 | 8.8 | 71 | −1 | 70 | 1.41 | 4,920 | 8.8 | 5,280 | 8.8 | 7,680 | 10.1 |
| affiliated | 19,030 | 93.9 | 49,225 | 88.9 | 711 | 0 | 711 | 1.43 | 49,790 | 88.9 | 53,340 | 88.6 | 64,900 | 85.4 |
| total practising | 18,080 | *95* | 41,600 | *90* | 640 | 0 | 640 | 1.43 | 44,810 | *90* | 48,010 | *90* | 51,920 | *80* |
| non-practising | 950 | *5* | 4,620 | *10* | 71 | 0 | 71 | 1.43 | 4,980 | *10* | 5,330 | *10* | 12,980 | *20* |
| Anglicans | 13,000 | 64.2 | 22,200 | 42.7 | 330 | −166 | 164 | 0.71 | 23,090 | 41.2 | 23,840 | 39.7 | 26,600 | 35.0 |
| Protestants | 2,230 | 11.0 | 11,975 | 23.0 | 180 | −58 | 122 | 0.97 | 12,600 | 22.5 | 13,200 | 22.0 | 15,200 | 20.0 |
| Evangelicals | 1,600 | 7.9 | 5,200 | 10.0 | 79 | −19 | 60 | 1.09 | 5,500 | 9.8 | 5,800 | 9.7 | 6,800 | 8.9 |
| Roman Catholics | 1,000 | 4.9 | 7,500 | 14.4 | 131 | 223 | 354 | 3.86 | 9,180 | 16.4 | 11,040 | 18.4 | 15,960 | 21.0 |
| Black indigenous | 2,800 | 13.8 | 4,000 | 7.7 | 60 | −22 | 38 | 0.90 | 4,200 | 7.5 | 4,380 | 7.3 | 4,940 | 6.5 |
| Marginal Protestants | 0 | 0.0 | 450 | 0.9 | 9 | 24 | 33 | 5.32 | 620 | 1.1 | 780 | 1.3 | 2,050 | 2.7 |
| Catholics (non-Roman) | 0 | 0.0 | 100 | 0.2 | 1 | −1 | 0 | 0.00 | 100 | 0.2 | 100 | 0.2 | 150 | 0.2 |
| Non-religious | 0 | 0.0 | 1,000 | 1.9 | 16 | 1 | 17 | 1.56 | 1,090 | 1.9 | 1,170 | 2.0 | 2,960 | 3.9 |
| Baha'is | 0 | 0.0 | 100 | 0.2 | 1 | 1 | 2 | 1.82 | 110 | 0.2 | 120 | 0.2 | 300 | 0.4 |
| Buddhists | 0 | 0.0 | 50 | 0.1 | 1 | −1 | 0 | 0.00 | 50 | 0.1 | 50 | 0.1 | 80 | 0.1 |
| Jews | 0 | 0.0 | 20 | 0.0 | 0 | 0 | 0 | 0.00 | 20 | 0.0 | 10 | 0.0 | 30 | 0.0 |
| Other religionists | 0 | 0.0 | 20 | 0.0 | 0 | 0 | 0 | 0.00 | 20 | 0.0 | 20 | 0.0 | 50 | 0.1 |
| **Country's population** | **20,260** | **100.0** | **52,000** | **100.0** | 800 | 0 | 800 | 1.43 | 56,000 | 100.0 | 60,000 | 100.0 | 76,000 | 100.0 |

**COLUMNS, ROWS.** For meanings and definitions, see Codebook (Part 6). Note that, by definition, total 'Christians' = professing + crypto-Christians, which also = affiliated + nominal Christians. Percentages may not always total exactly, due to rounding.
**CENSUSES. 1901** (Census of the British Empire) (excluding 707 foreign visitors): 67.3% Anglicans, 15.0% Black indigenous (AMEC), 11.5% Protestants (3.5% Presbyterians), 6.2% Roman Catholics. **22.X.1950:** 53.0% Anglicans, 24.4% Protestants (8.1% Methodists & Wesleyans, 3.3% Presbyterians, 2.0% Christian Brethren, 1.9% SDAs, 1.6% Salvation Army, 1.6% Pentecostals), 10.2% Black indigenous (AMEC), 10.0% Roman Catholics, 1.6% non-religious, 0.4% marginal Protestants, 0.3% Buddhists, 0.1% Chinese folk-religionists. **23.X.1960** (excluding tourists and British and USA military and dependants): 48.4% Anglicans, 27.6% Protestants (7.2% Methodists & Wesleyans, 3.1% Presbyterians, 3.0% SDAs, 2.4% Christian Brethren 2.1% Salvation Army, 2.1% Pentecostals), 11.2% Black indigenous (AMEC), 10.4% Roman Catholics, 2.2% non-religious, 0.1% marginal Protestants, 0.1% Buddhists. **25.X.1970:** 45.1% Anglicans, 26.6% Protestants (6.9% Methodists & Wesleyans, 3.6% SDAs, 3.4% Presbyterians, 2.1% Brethren), 14.6% Roman Catholics, 10.5% Black indigenous (AMEC), 2.0% non-religious, 1.0% marginal Protestants, 0.2% other religionists.

**NOTES ON RELIGIONS**
BAHA'IS. In 2 local spiritual assemblies (1973).
BLACK INDIGENOUS. In 2 denominations in 1970 (see Table 2).
OTHER RELIGIONISTS. Small groups of Hindus and Muslims.
PRACTISING CHRISTIANS. Churchgoing is high, about 35% of all affiliated members attending church weekly.

**NON-CHRISTIAN RELIGIONS.** There are small groups of Baha'is, Buddhists, Jews, Hindus and Muslims, and a larger number with no religious profession.

## CHRISTIANITY

ANGLICAN CHURCH. Bermuda was first colonized in 1609, the original settlers being Anglicans from Great Britain. St Peter's Church was built in 1619 and within a few years 9 parishes were established each with a church of its own. Until 1813 Bermuda was under the diocese of London. Between 1813 and 1825 episcopal supervision was provided from Nova Scotia, with the bishop of Newfoundland assuming responsibility from 1825 to 1917. During 1917–1925 the islands were without episcopal oversight, but since 1925 Bermuda has been an extra-provincial diocese under the direct jurisdiction of the archbishop of Canterbury. Anglicanism is the principal denomination, professed by 45% of the population. Two-thirds of Anglicans are Blacks, but by 1973 there was still only one Black priest. Most of the clergy come from Britain.

PROTESTANT CHURCHES. Influences from both the Old World and the New World are responsible for Bermuda's Protestant community. From Europe, British Methodists have built up the most important work, although Scottish Presbyterians, Brethren and Salvation Army also have significant followings. In addition there is a Portuguese Evangelical Church in Hamilton. From North America have come numerous denominations, the largest being Seventh-day Adventists. The majority of these churches are served by expatriate ministers.

CATHOLIC CHURCH. Prior to 1953 Bermuda formed part of the diocese of Halifax (Canada). At that time it was made a prefecture confided to Resurrectionists, was elevated to a vicariate in 1956, and became the diocese of Hamilton in Bermuda in 1967 as a suffragan diocese of Kingston in Jamaica. Professing Catholics grew from 10% of the population in 1960 to 15% in 1970.

BLACK INDIGENOUS CHURCHES. The African Methodist Episcopal Church from the USA has the third largest Christian community in Bermuda, after the Anglican and Catholic churches.

**CHURCH AND STATE.** Until 1974 the Anglican Church was established by law, its legislation coming from the British colonial parliament. In 1693 by act of Parliament the British government initiated payment of clergy stipends which continued to the end of the 19th century. The British Crown held the patronage of all livings until 1882 when after synodical government had been introduced in 1878, this was transferred to the synod. By a 1974 act of parliament and at the request of the diocesan synod, the former name Church of England in Bermuda was changed to Anglican Church of Bermuda, the synod becoming at the same time fully self-governing. The act thus had the effect of disestablishing Anglicanism in Bermuda.

There is no government ministry or department dealing with the churches or religious affairs.

**INTERDENOMINATIONAL ORGANIZATIONS.** The Bermuda Ministerial Association, originally composed of Protestant clergy, and the Anglican Church came together in 1957 to form a co-operative body; since the Catholic Church joined in 1966 this has been known as the Joint Committee of Churches.

3rd Meeting of Lausanne Committee for World Evangelization (LCWE), Willowbank, Bermuda, January 1978.

TABLE 2. ORGANIZED CHURCHES AND DENOMINATIONS IN BERMUDA

| Official name 1 | Begun 2 | Type 3 | Counc 4 | Congs 5 | Adults 6 | Affiliated 7 | Names, notes, and other statistics (see Codebook) 8 |
|---|---|---|---|---|---|---|---|
| African Methodist Episcopal Church | c1870 | I Met | Vw... | 10 | 1,950 | 3,900 | *AMEC*. Black mission from USA. Large work among Blacks, Mulattoes. HQ Harris Bay. |
| **Anglican Ch of Bermuda (D Bermuda)** | 1609 | A Hig | av..C | 17 | 4,462 | 22,000 | Under D Canterbury. 67% Black, 33% White (10% alien). 1n,14x,15pp,W=33%,8Y,475y. |
| Baptist Church | 1956 | P Bap | T.... | 2 | 103 | 175 | *First Baptist Ch*. Devonshire Parish. M=SBC(USA). 1x,4f,W=86%,33Y,3z. |
| Catholic Ch: D Hamilton in Bermuda | 1953 | R Lat | P.NMC | 8 | 5,800 | 7,500 | Suffragan M Kingston. 1,250 Whites. M=CR. C=1+0+1(Canadian). 9nx,11w,1r,13Y,196y. |
| Christian Brethren | | P CBr | x.... | 9 | 500 | 1,000 | *Open (Plymouth) Brethren*. Many British; begun under British influence. Paget. |
| Church of Christ | 1957 | P Dis | x.... | 1 | 30 | 50 | M=CC(Non-Instrumental)(USA). One church in Devonshire. |
| Church of Christ, Scientist | | M Sci | x.... | 1 | 50 | 100 | *Christian Science*. M=CCS(Boston,USA). First Church, Hamilton. 1w. |
| Church of God of Prophecy | 1955 | P Pe3 | Z.... | 1 | 17 | 50 | M=CGP(USA). Schism from CoG(Cleveland). Holiness Pentecostals. HQ Shelly Bay. |
| Church of God (Anderson) | 1905 | P Hol | x.... | 2 | 125 | 300 | *General Assembly of the CoG (Bermuda)*. M=CoG(Anderson)(USA). 2n,2f,250z. |
| Church of Jesus C of Latter-day Saints | | M LdS | x.... | | 30 | 50 | *Mormons*. M=CJCLdS(USA). Mostly North American Whites. |
| Church of the Nazarene | 1961 | P Hol | xF... | 1 | 24 | 150 | Attached to New York District, Ch of the Nazarene. M=CoN(USA). 1n,SS=110,W=50%. |
| Jehovah's Witnesses | 1928 | M Jeh | x.... | 2 | 127 | 300 | *Watch Tower. International Bible Students Assoc*. Active witnessing by 1941. 2Y. |
| Lutheran Church | 1964 | P Lut | Lw... | 2 | 75 | 150 | *Peace Lutheran Ch*. Part of American Lutheran Ch (USA). Paget. 1x,W=63%,7y,15z. |
| Methodist Church | | P Met | Vw... | | 1,000 | 2,000 | Begun by and related to British Methodism from UK. Based in Hamilton. |
| New Testament Church of God | 1921 | P Pe3 | ZF... | 4 | 350 | 500 | *Ch of God*. Holiness Pentecostals. M=CoG(Cleveland) (USA). In Pembroke. 10n. |
| Pentecostal Assemblies of the W Indies | 1938 | P Pe2 | Z.... | | 300 | 500 | Classical Pentecostals (2-stage). In Pentecostal Assemblies of Canada (PAoC). |
| Portuguese Evangelical Church | | P int | ..... | | 100 | 300 | Portuguese-speaking immigrants. In Paget, Hamilton. |
| Presbyterian Church | | P Ref | Rw... | 2 | 300 | 1,000 | Includes M=Ch of Scotland, and Presbyterian Ch in Canada. 1f,8Yy. |
| Reformed Episcopal Church | c1890 | A sEv | x.... | 1 | 100 | 200 | *Reformed Ch of England*. M=REC(USA),FCE(UK). Mainly Black. In 1900, 64 adherents. |
| Salvation Army | 1896 | P Sal | xw... | 10 | 800 | 1,400 | *Bermuda Division*, under Canada & Bermuda Territory. HQ Hamilton. W=57%,25z. |
| Seventh-day Adventist Church | 1900 | P Adv | x.... | 6 | 1,204 | 1,800 | *SDA, Bermuda Mission*, Atlantic UC, NAmerican Division. 5nx,16m,1r,6t(977),48Y. |
| United Church of Canada | | P uni | Ww... | | 100 | 300 | M=UCCanada. Small work related to home body in Canada. In Pembroke Parish. |
| United Holy Church of America | | I pe3 | x.... | 1 | 50 | 100 | Black pentecostals. M=UHCA(USA). |
| World-Wide Missions of Bermuda | 1966 | P ind | x.... | | 140 | 300 | M=World-Wide Missions (USA). Evangelicals from California. |
| Other Protestant denominations | | P | ..... | | 1,000 | 2,000 | Total 40: USA missions, military chaplaincies; Exclusive Brethren (Raven-Taylor). |
| Other Catholic (non-Roman) churches | | C | ..... | | 50 | 100 | Small churches under bishops-at-large, usually visiting from UK or USA. |
| Total affiliated (mid-1970) | | | | 140 | 18,787 | 46,225 | Total denominations (1970) . . . 65. |
| Total affiliated (mid-1975) | | | | 150 | 20,200 | 49,790 | Total denominations (1975) . . . 70. |
| Total affiliated (mid-1980) | | | | 160 | 21,700 | 53,340 | Total denominations (1980) . . . 75. |

**NOTES ON TABLE ABOVE**
COLUMNS: for meanings and CODES (cols. 1, 3, 4, 8), see Codebook (Part 6). Column 1: **Boldface type** = church with over 10% of country's affiliated Christians.
NATIONAL COUNCILS (Column 4, 5th letter).
  C = Joint Committee of Churches.

PEOPLES (ethnolinguistic). Christians: 56.5% Black, 29.0% White (English), 10.0% Mulatto, 4.5% Portuguese.

**COUNTRY-WIDE TOTALS**
EVANGELIZATION (see Part 5). 1900: 100%. 1970: 100%. 1980: 100%. *Mass evangelism*. Several campaigns including one by Billy Graham Evangelistic Association. January 1978: 3rd Meeting of Lausanne Committee for World Evangelization.

*Radiophonic evangelism*. HCJB.
FOREIGN MISSIONARIES AND PERSONNEL (nationals serving abroad) (1973). Total 2 Protestants (Brethren) in St Kitts-Nevis.
FOREIGN MISSIONARIES AND PERSONNEL (aliens from abroad) (1973). Total 41. *From Western world*. 36: about 15 Roman Catholics, about 12 Anglicans from UK, 9 Protestants (8 in 4 USA societies, 1 in 1 UK society). *From Third World*. About 5 Anglicans and Protestants from Jamaica et alia.
INSTITUTIONS (church-operated) (1973). Total 2 secondary schools.
PERIODICALS. About 30 titles.
PERSONNEL. About 141 (100 national (including 50 RC catechists), 41 foreign).

SCRIPTURE DISTRIBUTION (1975). Annual totals: 1,130

Bibles (69% free, 13% subsidized, 18% commercial), 1,750 NTs (86% free, 11% subsidized, 3% commercial), 200 UBS portions, 500 UBS selections.
SERVICE AGENCIES. About 6, including CEF, YLC, YMCA.

**ADDITIONAL DATA ON CHURCHES**
CATHOLIC CHURCH. *Catholic organizations*. The diocese is attached to the Antilles Episcopal Conference (AEC) with its seat in Kingston, Jamaica, which is itself a member of CELAM. Religious personnel belong to the Conference of Major Superiors of the Antilles, also with headquarters in Jamaica.
  The Holy See has no diplomatic relations with Bermuda. It is represented to the Catholic hierarchy by an apostolic delegate based in Port-au-Prince, Haiti.
  In 1974 the church sponsored one primary school (490 pupils) and one secondary school (140 students).

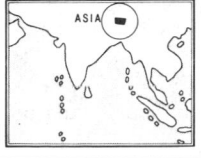

# BHUTAN

## SECULAR DATA

**STATE**. Official name: The Kingdom of Bhutan (Druk-yul). Adjective of nationality: Bhutanese.
**Flag** (shown above right): Yellow triangle above orange one, white dragon in centre.
**Area**: 46,600 sq.km. (18,147 sq.miles). Agricultural land: 3.6%.
**Government**: Constitutional monarchy, since 1969 (1865 British rule, 1907 hereditary absolute monarchy).
**Legislature**: National Assembly (Tsogdu), up to 150 members.
**Official language**: Dzongkha.
**Capital**: Thimbu 8,500.
**Armed forces** (1976): Total 4,000 regular army.

**DEMOGRAPHY**. Population: 1,034,774 (census of XI-XII.1969).

For 1970–2000 (UN), see last row of Table 1). Population density (1975): 25/sq.km. (65/sq.mile). Under 15 years: 42%. Growth rate (1975–80): 2.47% per year (births 4.32%, deaths −1.86%). Life expectancy (1975–80): 46.1 years. Household size: 5.4 persons.
**Major languages**: Dzongkha, Shashap (in east), Nepali, Assamese, Hindi, English, Lepcha, Santali, Kebumtamp(Bhumtam), Tibetan, and numerous others.
**Urban dwellers** (1970): 4.1%. Urban growth rate (1950–70): 3.7% per year.
**Refugees** (1977): 3,000 Tibetans from China.

**ETHNOLINGUISTIC GROUPS**: 57.0% Bhutia (Tibetan), 20.0% Nepali (17.6% Gurung, 1.5% Limba, Rai), 14.0% Assamese, 4.4% Loba, 1.5% Kirati, 1.5% Lepcha, 0.7% Santal, et alii.

**MONEY** (1977). **Monetary unit**: ngultrum (= 100 chetrums); US$1 = Nu 8.70.
**National income per person**: US$60. Average annual family income: US$324.
**Cost of living in capital** (1976): Daily cost of living: US$37.

**EDUCATION**. Adult literacy: 5%. Education rate: 6%. Schools: 89.

**HEALTH**. Hospitals: 1 (2,740 beds). Doctors: 22. Lepers: 5,400 (4.6% per 1,000). Blind: 10,000. Psychotics: 8,000.

**LITERATURE**. Annual new book titles (1973): 25.

**COMMUNICATION** (per 1,000 people). Phones: 1. Radios: 3.

TABLE 1. RELIGIOUS ADHERENTS IN BHUTAN

| Year Name | 1900 Adherents | % | mid-1970 Adherents | % | Annual change, 1970–1980 Natural | Conversion | Total | Rate | mid-1975 Adherents | % | mid-1980 Adherents | % | 2000 Adherents | % |
|---|---|---|---|---|---|---|---|---|---|---|---|---|---|---|
| Buddhists | 241,800 | 79.0 | 719,950 | 68.9 | 19,540 | 850 | 20,390 | 2.51 | 812,800 | 69.3 | 923,850 | 69.6 | 1,532,000 | 71.4 |
| Hindus | 55,900 | 15.0 | 261,500 | 25.0 | 6,994 | −504 | 6,490 | 2.23 | 290,900 | 24.8 | 326,400 | 24.6 | 493,000 | 23.0 |
| Muslims | 3,000 | 1.0 | 52,700 | 5.0 | 1,411 | −41 | 1,370 | 2.33 | 58,700 | 5.0 | 66,400 | 5.0 | 108,000 | 5.0 |
| Tribal religionists | 15,300 | 5.0 | 10,000 | 1.0 | 231 | −311 | −80 | −0.83 | 9,600 | 0.8 | 9,200 | 0.7 | 9,000 | 0.4 |
| **Christians** | **0** | **0.0** | **650** | **0.1** | **18** | **2** | **20** | **2.67** | **750** | **0.1** | **850** | **0.1** | **2,000** | **0.1** |
| crypto-Christians | 0 | 0.0 | 500 | 0.0 | 14 | 4 | 18 | 3.05 | 590 | 0.1 | 680 | 0.1 | 1,600 | 0.1 |
| professing | 0 | 0.0 | 150 | 0.0 | 4 | −2 | 2 | 1.25 | 160 | 0.0 | 170 | 0.0 | 400 | 0.0 |
| Roman Catholics | 0 | 0.0 | 150 | 0.0 | 4 | −2 | 2 | 1.25 | 160 | 0.0 | 170 | 0.0 | 400 | 0.0 |
| affiliated | 0 | 0.0 | 650 | 0.1 | 18 | 2 | 20 | 2.67 | 750 | 0.1 | 850 | 0.1 | 2,000 | 0.1 |
| total practising | 0 | 0 | 585 | 90 | 16 | 2 | 18 | 2.67 | 675 | 90 | 765 | 90 | 1,600 | 80 |
| non-practising | 0 | 0 | 65 | 10 | 2 | 0 | 2 | 2.67 | 75 | 10 | 85 | 10 | 400 | 20 |
| Third-World indigenous | 0 | 0.0 | 300 | 0.0 | 8 | 1 | 9 | 2.61 | 345 | 0.0 | 390 | 0.0 | 900 | 0.0 |
| Roman Catholics | 0 | 0.0 | 250 | 0.0 | 7 | 0 | 7 | 2.46 | 285 | 0.0 | 320 | 0.0 | 700 | 0.0 |
| Protestants | 0 | 0.0 | 100 | 0.0 | 3 | 1 | 4 | 3.33 | 120 | 0.0 | 140 | 0.0 | 400 | 0.0 |
| Baha'is | 0 | 0.0 | 200 | 0.0 | 6 | 4 | 10 | 4.00 | 250 | 0.0 | 300 | 0.0 | 1,000 | 0.0 |
| Country's population | 306,000 | 100.0 | 1,045,000 | 100.0 | 28,200 | 0 | 28,200 | 2.40 | 1,173,000 | 100.0 | 1,327,000 | 100.0 | 2,145,000 | 100.0 |

COLUMNS, ROWS. For meanings and definitions, see Codebook (Part 6). Note that, by definition, total 'Christians' = professing + crypto-Christians, which also = affiliated + nominal Christians. Percentages may not always total exactly, due to rounding.

**NOTES ON RELIGIONS**
BAHA'IS. Mostly Indians; in 1 local spiritual assembly (1973).

BUDDHISTS. The Bhutia (Bhute) ethnic group (of Tibetan extraction) in northern and central Bhutan are Buddhists, followers of Tibetan Lamaism syncretized with pre-Buddhist shamanism (Bon), Taoism and Lepcha traditional animistic beliefs and practices. There are over 6,000 monks. There are less strict Buddhists in eastern Bhutan, who are Bhote, Monpa and Sherdukpen, with fewer monasteries and lamas.
CRYPTO-CHRISTIANS. Unorganized individuals in the recognized churches, also a few isolated radio believers.

HINDUS. Nepali settlers (Rai, Gurung and Limbu ethnic groups, speaking Nepali, but Bhutanese citizens although further immigration has been prohibited since 1959). There are also some Hindu expatriate residents from India in southern and south-western Bhutan.
MUSLIMS. Sunnis, mainly Indians.
TRIBAL RELIGIONISTS. Animists among the hill tribes (Lepcha, et alii).

## NON-CHRISTIAN RELIGIONS.

**NON-CHRISTIAN RELIGIONS. Lamaism** or Tantrayana (Tibetan or Tantric Buddhism) is the religion of the Bhutias, the Tibetan majority of the population. It is an unreformed type of Lamaism which is a mixture of Buddhist ethics and the practice of animistic cults. Bhutan's official Buddhist sect is the Dupka (Red Hat), which is part of Tibetan Lamaism. In Bhutan this also includes an admixture of the pre-Buddhist shamanism known as Bon, also of Taoism and of traditional animistic beliefs and practices of the Lepcha people. There are numerous monasteries (*dzongs*), mainly in central Bhutan, which also serve as administrative centres and storehouses; and the Dzong of Thimbu, the capital, houses the secretariat of the king and his ministers. The Buddhist clergy consists of over 6,000 lamas or bonzes (monks) serving under the authority of the Jey Khempo (chief of monks), whom protocol places on a level of equality with the king.

**Hinduism** is the religion of the Nepali settlers, a fifth of the population, who predominate in southern and southwestern Bhutan. Although now Bhutanese citizens, they are prohibited from settling in central Bhutan, and further immigration of Nepalis has been forbidden since 1959. Hinduism also exists among many Assamese and other Indian residents, who total a sixth of the population.

## CHRISTIANITY

**CATHOLIC CHURCH.** Bhutan comes within the Catholic diocese of Tezpur in India. In 1973 Bhutan had about 250 Catholics, all being Indians working on development projects or in schools. At government invitation, 3 state schools enrolling mainly Buddhist pupils have recently been opened by Catholic religious personnel, and are supervised by them; these are the Don Bosco Technical School begun in 1965 by Salesians (SDB) on the border at Puntsholing, the Sherubtse Public School established in 1968 by Jesuits at Kanglung in eastern Bhutan, and a school conducted by Jesuits in Punakha, the old religious and cultural centre of western Bhutan. Sisters of St Joseph of Cluny are working in the 2 Jesuit schools, having joined the staffs in 1969. In 1970, religious personnel in these schools numbered 3 SDB priests and one SDB brother, 2 SJ priests and 2 SJ brothers, all Canadian-born, and 4 Cluny sisters. The Salesians in Puntsholing are also in charge of the country's only parish, begun in 1965.

**PROTESTANT CHURCHES.** Protestants are found mainly among the large number of Indians engaged in technical assistance to Bhutan, but they are not organized into any recognized church. Because of a prohibition against evangelistic work, Protestant missionary societies have tended to concentrate their attention on Bhutanese living across the border in East Bengal. The Scandinavian Alliance Mission opened its first centre in Baksa Duar in 1892, and 2 other missions were active at an early date: the Santal Mission of the Northern Churches (Ebenezer Lutheran Church), and the Church of Scotland

**Buddhists.** A senior Dupka or Red Hat (Unreformed) lama, one of over 6,000 Tantrayana bonzes (monks) Red Hat Lamaism is the official religion of Bhutan.

Mission later under the United Church of North India (now CNI). The latter body, known also as the Eastern Himalayan Church, is the only Protestant denomination resident and working within Bhutan itself, operating several village schools in the western region. Since 1959 the Free Church of Finland has carried on work among Bhutanese in the border area outside the country itself.

**CHURCH AND STATE.** In 1907 the chief lama or priest-king was replaced as head of state by a maharajah or king as hereditary monarch combining both spiritual and temporal powers. The Dupka sect of Lamaistic Buddhism is the official religion. All evangelistic foreign missionary activity and proselytism are prohibited.

State postage stamp with (right) the Buddha and (left) Christ with Mary (Pieta, by Michelangelo).

TABLE 2.   ORGANIZED CHURCHES AND DENOMINATIONS IN BHUTAN

| Official name 1 | Begun 2 | Type 3 | Counc 4 | Congs 5 | Adults 6 | Affiliated 7 | Names, notes, and other statistics (see Codebook) 8 |
|---|---|---|---|---|---|---|---|
| Assemblies (Jehova Shammah) | | I CBr | x.... | 2 | 40 | 100 | Missionaries from India (Brother Bakht Singh). HQ Hyderabad, AP. |
| Catholic Church (D Tezpur) | 1965 | R Lat | P.F.. | 1 | 200 | 250 | HQ in India. Catholics all Indians in schools or projects. 5x,3m,4w; 3 schools. |
| Church of North India | | P uni | Rwe.. | 3 | 30 | 50 | *Eastern Himalayan Church.* Village schools in western region. M=CSM(UK). |
| Isolated radio churches | c1970 | I rad | ..... | | 120 | 200 | Isolated radio believers, mostly young people, across country. R=30(FEBA). |
| Other Protestant denominations | 1892 | P | ..... | | 30 | 50 | Working from India: Free Ch of Finland, Santal Mission, TEAM, World-Wide Missions. |
| Total affiliated (mid-1970) | | | | 40 | 420 | 650 | Total denominations (1970) . . . 8. |
| Total affiliated (mid-1975) | | | | 45 | 480 | 750 | Total denominations (1975) . . . 8. |
| Total affiliated (mid-1980) | | | | 60 | 550 | 850 | Total denominations (1980) . . . 9. |

**NOTES ON TABLE ABOVE**
**COLUMNS:** for meanings and CODES (cols. 1, 3, 4, 8), see Codebook (Part 6). Column 1: **Boldface type** = church with over 10% of country's affiliated Christians.

**PEOPLES** (ethnolinguistic). Christians: 50% Indian (Assamese, Santal & others), 40% Bhutia, 10% Nepali.

**COUNTRY-WIDE TOTALS**
**EVANGELIZATION** (see Part 5). 1900: 0%. 1970: 12%. 1980: 16%. *Radiophonic evangelism.* FEBA.
**FOREIGN MISSIONARIES AND PERSONNEL** (aliens from abroad) (1973). Total 33. *From Western world.* 17 Protestants (9 in 1 Norway society, 6 in 1 UK society, 2 in 1 Sweden society). *From Third World.* About 16 (10 Roman Catholics, 4 Protestants and indigenous) from India.

**INSTITUTIONS** (church-operated) (1973). Total 3 schools.
**PERSONNEL.** 33 (foreign).
**SCRIPTURE DISTRIBUTION** (1975). Annual totals: 100 NTs (free). *Translations completed.* 1 language, Dzongkha: portion 1970.
**SERVICE AGENCIES.** About 6, including BMMF, MAP, NLL, WME.

---

# BOLIVIA

## SECULAR DATA

**STATE. Official name:** The Republic of Bolivia (La República de Bolivia). Adjective of nationality: Bolivian (boliviano).
**Flag** (shown above right): Stripes of red, gold, and green, coat of arms in centre.
**Area:** 1,098,581 sq.km. (424,160 sq.miles). Agricultural land: 27.7%.
**Government:** Military junta, most of period since 1825 (1200 Inca empire, 1532 Spanish rule, 1825 Independence, many dictatorships).
**Official language:** Spanish (*Español/Castellano*).
**Chief cities:** administrative capital, La Paz 605,200 (1973); legal

capital, Sucre 106,590; Cochabamba 169,930, Oruro 135,010, Santa Cruz 54,020.
**Political divisions:** 9 Departments, 98 Provinces, 1,272 Cantons.
**Armed forces** (1976): Total 22,000 regular: army 17,000, navy 1,000, air force 4,000 (58 combat aircraft). Paramilitary forces: 5,000.

**DEMOGRAPHY. Population:** 2,704,165 (census of 5.IX.1950. For 1970–2000 (UN), see last row of Table 1). Population density (1975): 5/sq.km. (13/sq.mile). Under 15 years: 42%. Growth rate (1975–80): 2.60% per year (births 4.39%, deaths −1.70%, emigrants −0.09%). Life expectancy (1975–80): 48.3 years. Household size: 5.3 persons.

**Major languages:** Spanish, Quechua, Aymara, Guaraní, Japanese, Portuguese, Ryukyuan, and about 45 minor languages.
**Urban dwellers** (1970): 34.3%. Urban growth rate (1950–70): 3.6% per year.
**Labour force:** 32%.

**ETHNOLINGUISTIC GROUPS:** 37.1% Quechua, 30.7% Cholo (Mestizo: Spanish/Amerindian), 23.7% Aymara, 5.0% Bolivian White (Criollo: pure Spanish descent), 2.1% lowland Amerindian (29 tribes, 99,800; Siriono, Tupi-Guaraní, Chiquitano), 0.2% Japanese (8,100), 0.1% Peruvian, 0.1% Brazilian, Jewish, Ryukyuan (Okinawan) (1,000), Chinese (160).

**MONEY** (1977). **Monetary unit:** peso (= 100 centavos); US$1 = $b 20.00.
**National income per person:** US$320. Average annual family income: US$1,696.
**Inflation:** (1970–74) 24.0% per year (1975: consumer price index 321).

**Cost of living in capital** (1976): index 113 (Washington DC = 100). Daily cost of living: US$45.

**EDUCATION.** Adult literacy: (1950) 32%, (1976) 63%. Education rate: 58%. Schools: 6,920 (1965). Universties: 8.

**HEALTH.** Hospitals: 260 (9,451 beds). Doctors: 2,143. Lepers: 4,400 (0.8 per 1,000). Blind: 1,070. Psychotics: 43,000.

**LITERATURE.** Annual new book titles (1973): 586. Periodicals: 80. Scientific journals: 15. Newspapers: 17 dailies.

**COMMUNICATION** (per 1,000 people). Phones: 9. Radios: 288. TV sets: 2. Daily newspaper circulation: 37 copies.

TABLE 1. RELIGIOUS ADHERENTS IN BOLIVIA

| Year | 1900 | | mid-1970 | | Annual change, 1970–1980 | | | | mid-1975 | | mid-1980 | | 2000 | |
|---|---|---|---|---|---|---|---|---|---|---|---|---|---|---|
| *Name* | *Adherents* | *%* | *Adherents* | *%* | *Natural* | *Conversion* | *Total* | *Rate* | *Adherents* | *%* | *Adherents* | *%* | *Adherents* | *%* |
| **Christians** | **1,456,000** | **93.6** | **4,553,000** | **95.3** | **131,278** | **–2,953** | **128,685** | **2.50** | **5,139,030** | **95.0** | **5,839,850** | **94.8** | **9,574,000** | **93.3** |
| professing | 1,456,000 | 93.6 | 4,553,000 | 95.3 | 131,278 | –2,593 | 128,685 | 2.50 | 5,139,030 | 95.0 | 5,839,850 | 94.8 | 9,574,000 | 93.3 |
| Roman Catholics | 1,456,000 | 93.6 | 4,453,000 | 93.2 | 128,213 | –3,528 | 124,685 | 2.48 | 5,019,030 | 92.8 | 5,699,850 | 92.5 | 9,194,000 | 89.5 |
| Christo-pagans | 1,090,000 | 70.0 | 2,300,000 | 48.1 | –63,608 | 22,508 | 41,100 | 1.65 | 2,490,000 | 46.0 | 2,711,000 | 44.0 | 3,700,000 | 36.0 |
| Evangelical Catholics | 1,000 | 0.1 | 96,432 | 2.0 | 3,133 | 3,050 | 6,183 | 5.04 | 122,630 | 2.3 | 158,260 | 2.6 | 239,500 | 2.3 |
| Protestants | 0 | 0.0 | 100,000 | 2.1 | 3,065 | 935 | 4,000 | 3.33 | 120,000 | 2.2 | 140,000 | 2.3 | 380,000 | 3.7 |
| affiliated | 1,456,000 | 93.6 | 4,553,000 | 95.3 | 131,278 | –2,593 | 128,685 | 2.50 | 5,139,030 | 95.0 | 5,839.850 | 94.8 | 9,574,000 | 93.3 |
| doubly-affiliated | –1,000 | –0.1 | –141,415 | –3.0 | –4,011 | 852 | –3,159 | 2.01 | –157,000 | –2.9 | –173,000 | –2.8 | –257,000 | –2.5 |
| total practising | 1,237,600 | *85* | 3,232,630 | *71* | 91,895 | –12,208 | 79,687 | 2.21 | 3,597,320 | *70* | 4,029,500 | *69* | 6,223,100 | *65* |
| non-practising | 218,400 | *15* | 1,320,370 | *29* | 39,383 | 9,615 | 48,998 | 3.18 | 1,541,710 | *30* | 1,810,350 | *31* | 3,350,900 | *35* |
| Roman Catholics | 1,456,000 | 93.6 | 4,495,983 | 94.1 | 129,032 | –7,431 | 121,601 | 2.41 | 5,051,100 | 93.4 | 5,711,990 | 92.7 | 9,206,500 | 89.7 |
| Catholic pentecostals | 0 | 0.1 | 1,000 | 0.0 | 128 | 672 | 800 | 16.00 | 5,000 | 0.1 | 9,000 | 0.1 | 50,000 | 0.5 |
| Protestants | 1,000 | 0.1 | 176,264 | 3.7 | 5,528 | 3,346 | 8,874 | 4.10 | 216,400 | 4.0 | 265,000 | 4.3 | 544,000 | 5.3 |
| Evangelicals | 1,000 | 0.1 | 162,000 | 3.4 | 5,091 | 3,138 | 8,230 | 4.13 | 199,300 | 3.7 | 244,300 | 4.0 | 505,000 | 4.9 |
| Neo-pentecostals | 0 | 0.0 | 500 | 0.0 | 77 | 473 | 550 | 18.33 | 3,000 | 0.1 | 6,000 | 0.1 | 30,000 | 0.3 |
| Bolivian indigenous | 0 | 0.0 | 12,216 | 0.3 | 409 | 369 | 778 | 4.87 | 16,000 | 0.3 | 20,000 | 0.3 | 45,000 | 0.4 |
| Marginal Protestants | 0 | 0.0 | 7,752 | 0.2 | 255 | 270 | 525 | 5.25 | 10,000 | 0.2 | 13,000 | 0.2 | 30,000 | 0.3 |
| Orthodox | 0 | 0.0 | 2,000 | 0.0 | 59 | 1 | 60 | 2.61 | 2,300 | 0.0 | 2,600 | 0.0 | 5,000 | 0.0 |
| Anglicans | 0 | 0.0 | 200 | 0.0 | 6 | 0 | 6 | 2.61 | 230 | 0.0 | 260 | 0.0 | 500 | 0.0 |
| Baha'is | 0 | 0.0 | 94,000 | 0.2 | 3,168 | 3,432 | 6,600 | 5.32 | 124,000 | 2.3 | 160,000 | 2.6 | 360,000 | 3.0 |
| Tribal religionists | 100,000 | 6.4 | 70,000 | 1.5 | 1,796 | –2,016 | –220 | –0.31 | 70,300 | 1.3 | 67,800 | 1.1 | 60,000 | 0.6 |
| Non-religious | 0 | 0.0 | 40,000 | 0.8 | 1,320 | 880 | 2,200 | 4.49 | 49,000 | 0.9 | 62,000 | 1.0 | 205,000 | 2.0 |
| Atheists | 0 | 0.0 | 15,000 | 0.3 | 511 | 489 | 1,000 | 5.00 | 20,000 | 0.4 | 25,000 | 0.4 | 60,000 | 0.0 |
| Buddhists | 0 | 0.0 | 4,000 | 0.1 | 89 | –189 | –100 | –2.86 | 3,500 | 0.1 | 3,000 | 0.0 | 2,000 | 0.0 |
| Jews | 0 | 0.0 | 2,000 | 0.0 | –20 | 0 | –20 | –1.05 | 1,900 | 0.0 | 1,800 | 0.0 | 2,000 | 0.0 |
| Spiritists | 0 | 0.0 | 1,000 | 0.0 | 28 | –8 | 20 | 1.82 | 1,100 | 0.0 | 1,200 | 0.0 | 1,000 | 0.0 |
| New-Religionists | 0 | 0.0 | 500 | 0.0 | 15 | 5 | 20 | 3.33 | 600 | 0.0 | 700 | 0.0 | 2,000 | 0.0 |
| Muslims | 0 | 0.0 | 500 | 0.0 | 15 | 0 | 15 | 2.63 | 570 | 0.0 | 650 | 0.0 | 1,000 | 0.0 |
| **Country's population** | **1,556,000** | **100.0** | **4,780,000** | **100.0** | **138,200** | **0** | **138,200** | **2.55** | **5,410,000** | **100.0** | **6,162,000** | **100.0** | **10,276,000** | **100.0** |

COLUMNS, ROWS. For meanings and definitions, see Codebook (Part 6). Note that, by definition, total 'Christians' = professing + crypto-Christians, which also = affiliated + nominal Christians. Percentages may not always total exactly, due to rounding.
CENSUSES. The religion question has not been asked in government censuses.

NOTES ON RELIGIONS
ATHEISTS. 3 rival parties of Muscovite, Maoist, or Trotskyite emphasis: Communist Party of Bolivia (Soviet-line) (PCB) (1,500 members), Communist Party of Bolivia (Chinese-line) (1,100 members), Revolutionary Workers Party (Trotskyite) (POR) (600 members); all underground, proscribed since 1967. Other factions include Castroites.
BAHA'IS. La Fe Bajay. Since its origin, in 1956 there has been exceptionally rapid response and growth among Amerindians, from 91 local spiritual assemblies (1964) to 625 (1973). From April to August 1970, over 6,000 converts were enrolled.
BOLIVIAN INDIGENOUS. In about 48 denominations or groupings in 1970 (see Table 2).
BUDDHISTS. Several colonies of Japanese immigrants in Santa Cruz district, including 250 families of Ryukyuans (Okinawan-speaking) until the conversion of 60% to Catholicism by 1960.
CATHOLIC PENTECOSTALS (or, Catholic charismatics). Totals (January 1974): 2,000 involved adults (over 15 years old) in 50 prayer groups; total charismatic community including children, 4,000. In June 1977, over 5,000 Catholics active in the Charismatic Renewal held a large public rally in Santa Cruz.
CHRISTO-PAGANS. Amerindians (Guayaru, Aymara, Valley Quechua and others) syncretizing folk-Catholicism with traditional Amerindian pre-Columbian pantheistic animism. In particular, the Aymara have only a thin veneer of Catholicism.
DOUBLY-AFFILIATED. The term covers those affiliated to, or claimed by, both the Catholic Church and also a church termed Evangélical by the state (Protestant, Anglican, Bolivian indigenous, marginal Protestant), i.e. baptized Catholics who have recently become Evangelicals or others. Because their statistics represent a duplication, they are shown in the table as a negative quantity (with a minus sign).
EVANGELICAL CATHOLICS. This term is used here to describe persons who are affiliated to churches termed by the state Evangélica (Protestant, Anglican, Bolivian indigenous or marginal Protestant churches), but who are regarded by state and society as, or profess publicly to be, Roman Catholics.
JEWS. Active in primary and secondary education.
NEO-PENTECOSTALS. Charismatics within the non-Pentecostal Protestant denominations, who meet regularly with Catholic charismatics in the movement called Spiritual Renewal (Renovación Espiritual).
NEW-RELIGIONISTS. Japanese adherents of Soka Gakkai (350 converts) and other New Religions from Japan.
PRACTISING CHRISTIANS. Weekly attenders; 75% of Protestants, 10% of Catholics. Annual attenders: 95% Protestants, 70% Catholics.
SPIRITISTS. Mainly recent adherents among the upper classes.
TRIBAL RELIGIONISTS. Of the total of 99,800 tribal lowland or jungle Amerindians (from 20,000 Chiquitanos down to 7 persons in the Jorá group), a high proportion are still animists. Many Aymara are still openly animist.

**NON-CHRISTIAN RELIGIONS. Baha'i** has experienced in Bolivia one of its greatest missionary expansions. Since its origin in 1956, response among Indians has been phenomenal, and Baha'is have grown from 91 local spiritual assemblies in 1964 to 625 in 1973.

**Traditional Indian religions** continue to hold the allegiance of substantial numbers of the indigenous peoples and are strongest among the Guaraní, Guayaru and Quechua, although many of these (especially the Quechua) are nominally baptized Catholics at the same time. Aymara religion also is a mixture of traditional beliefs with later Inca and Catholic additions. The original name for the supreme being, Viracocha, who was recognized as creator, is no longer used; and Catholic ideas of God now take precedence. However, much more important in daily life is Ekeko, the divinity of good luck, whose carved image in the form of a dwarf is venerated; and Pachamama, old Mother Earth, who plays an important role at the planting and harvesting seasons. For the forgiveness of sins, the blood of llamas and goats is sprinkled on stone altars and wooden crosses commonly found on hillsides, especially in the Carangas area of southwestern Bolivia. Aymaras believe that the earth is peopled by a multitude of spirits (Achachila): guardian spirits; spirits of hills, mountains and lakes; spirits of such natural phenomena as lightning, wind and hail; and a large number of evil spirits (Supaya). The diviner-medicine man continues to play an important role in Aymara society.

**Other religions** include small Jewish groups with synagogues and cemeteries in the major cities, some Buddhists in the newly-formed Japanese colonies, and a renewed interest in spiritism among the upper-classes.

**CHRISTIANITY.** Bolivia became part of the Catholic diocese of Cuzco (Peru) in 1537, when a Christian community was established among the Parias and Charcas. During the 16th and 17th centuries, Franciscans established 17 Indian missions and Jesuits 31 'reductions' (co-operative Indian villages) among the Moxos and Chiquitos before the Society of Jesus was expelled from Spain and its colonies. Bolivia was one of the first Latin American colonies to revolt against Spain and one of the last to achieve independence. During the war for independence bishops generally remained loyal to Spain, while some priests were involved in the rebellion and were later elected to the new legislative assembly. In the years of revolution during the 19th century, church-state relations were in constant turmoil, fluctuating from cordiality to outright hostility. Protestantism did not make its appearance until the end of the 19th century.

CATHOLIC CHURCH. About 94% of the Bolivian population has been baptized in the Catholic Church and are more or less attached to it. Bolivia is no exception to the Latin American phenomenon of popular folk-Catholicism, a mixture of 16th-century Spanish Catholicism and indigenous religions at the time of the Conquest. Regions which remained outside the influence of Christianity or have been abandoned by missionaries retain much of the old religion and show this in syncretistic practices usually termed christo-paganism. At the present time, the church is giving more attention to the creative use of indigenous elements which offer hope for a more vital expression of the faith in the future. An example is the joint pastoral plan for the Aymara-speaking altiplano (high plateau). Also of significance are the over 50 prayer groups of pentecostal Catholics in Santa Cruz, Cochabamba, La Paz and other centres.

Bolivia is one of several Latin American countries which depend heavily on foreign clergy. From 1912 to 1969 the proportion of Bolivians among the total of priests, both secular and religious, continued to decrease. In 1912 there were 641 Bolivians, and by 1960 this had fallen to 215 (29%), in 1964 to 198 (24%), and in 1969 to 197 (22%). During the same period foreign clergy increased correspondingly:

**Baha'is.** Indian Baha'i Community of Hankarachi, Oruro, in the Andean Altiplano. Mass conversions to Baha'i have averaged over 3,000 persons a year since 1965.

to 527 in 1960 (71%), 632 in 1964 (76%), and to 716 in 1969 (78%). Since 1969 there has been a decrease in foreign clergy due in large part to the expulsion or voluntary exile of many following the repression that followed the military coup d'etat of 1971; local clergy have also increased again.

PROTESTANT CHURCHES. Bolivia is unusual in Latin America in the relatively late arrival of Protestant missions. Although a Bible agent travelled through Bolivia in 1827, the first resident missionary, of the Brethren Assemblies, did not appear until 1895. Because of the strict requirements for membership, this church remained small and has not grown rapidly as it has in neighbouring Argentina. Canadian Baptists arrived in 1898, but by 1919 they had enrolled only 63 members, giving most of their attention to the Guatajata farm project and the development of schools. An increased rate of growth has taken place since 1960, although Baptists remain basically an urban middle-class church.

The first permanent Methodist missionary arrived in 1901. Initially Methodists followed the Baptists' early emphasis on schools, both to develop educated leadership and to gain social acceptance, in addition

guarantees as private property (this disposition, although mentioning only the Catholic church, holds true for all religions); (2) Articles 177 and 182, which guarantee freedom of education in general and explicitly freedom of religious education; (3) Article 181 which requires that private schools and colleges must be governed in accordance with official regulations, plans and programmes; (4) Article 188, which authorizes the creation of private universities, without financial obligation to the state, although up to the present time there exists only the Catholic University attached to University of Bolivia; (5) Article 191, which places religious objects of historical or artistic value under the protection of the state and prohibits their exportation.

An agreement concerning Catholic missions was signed in 1957 between the Holy See and the Bolivian government. In general, the agreement gives to vicars apostolic in missionary jurisdictions the power and means of promoting agricultural and industrial development, as well as for the establishment of co-operatives and social services.

The regulation of church-state relations is under the jurisdiction of the Ministry of Religion which is

A number of foreign priests attached to the commission were expelled from Bolivia. In January 1975, during the course of a strike involving 10,000 miners, the government closed and destroyed several radio stations associated with the unions as well as Radio Pio XII in Ouro belonging to the Oblates of Mary Immaculate (OMI). All were accused of subversive propaganda. In spite of these crises, however, a church-state confrontation seems unlikely, because neither of the 2 powers wants it. The military government unceasingly calls itself 'Christian' and has no interest in a test of strength with the Catholic Church, and for its part the ecclesiastical hierarchy does not wish to lose its privileged status as the official religion, with its tax exemptions for the Catholic University, fiscal aid to the daily paper *Presencia* which is sponsored by the episcopal conference, and other benefits.

**INTERDENOMINATIONAL ORGANIZATIONS.** The National Association of Evangelicals in Bolivia (Asociación Nacional de Evangélicos de Bolivia, ANDEB), formed in 1966, has the largest interdenominational membership in the country, but it has experienced tension between its conservative evangelical and ecumenical wings. Other Protestant interdenominational groups include the Bolivian Evangelical Social Action Commission (Comisión Boliviana de Acción Social Evangélica, COMBASE), which offers social and medical assistance, including help to poor children and the Good Shepherd Clinic, in the department of Cochabamba; and the Chepare Team (Equipo Chepare), which is concerned with community development in Chepare. On the part of the Catholic Church, there is no episcopal commission or secretariat charged specifically with ecumenical relations.

Several organizations provide opportunities for co-operation between Catholics and Protestants. Alfalit Boliviano, supported by Protestant churches, works on large-scale literacy campaigns in collaboration with the Catholic and other churches, using parish buildings as literacy centres. A charismatic movement called Spiritual Renewal (Renovación Espiritual) also regularly brings together Protestants and Catholics for Bible study and prayer.

**BROADCASTING.** All commercial stations in Bolivia accept religious programmes. In addition, there are 8 Catholic stations grouped into a national association, Emisoras Culturales Bolivianas with headquarters in La Paz. The Canadian Baptist mission transmits Protestant programmes on Radio La Cruz del Sur.

Radiophonic schools for mass education including systematic tele-education have been widely developed. A number of Catholic schools operate through the national association Escuelas Radiofónicas de Bólivia (ERBOL), founded in La Paz in 1966, which co-ordinates 10 schools related to 8 stations. In 1969 it had 4,375 male students and 13,250 female students. The 10 Catholic radiophonic schools are (with in parentheses the 8 Catholic radio stations over which their programmes are broadcast): Escuelas Radiofónicas San Gabriel (Radio San Gabriel) in La Paz; Escuelas Radiofónicas Fides (Radio Fides) in La Paz; Acción Loyola—ACLO (Radio Loyola) in Suore; Departmento de Investigación y Promoción Social San Rafael (Radio San Rafael) in Cochabamba; Escuelas Radiofónicas San Miguel (Radio San Miguel) in Riberalta; Centro Teórico de Capacitación de Adultos—CETCAR (Emisoras Bolivia) in Oruro; Escuelas Radiofónicas Juan XXIII (Radio Juan XXIII) in San Ignacio-Velasco; Escuelas Radiofónicas Pio XII (Radio Pio XII) in Ouro; Escuelas Radiofónicas 'Montero' in Santa Cruz, and Escuelas Radiofónicas 'Potosi' in Potosi.

For Catholics, Bolivia is a member of UNDA.

**Christo-pagans.** A religious procession of young Aymara boys in tin-mining village of Sicasica. At right, Aymara Indians in traditional dress. 44% of the population follow christo-paganism.

to the establishment of agricultural and medical centres including the Pfeiffer Memorial Hospital in La Paz. More rapid growth has taken place since the early 1960s.

The Evangelical Christian Union, second among Protestants in membership, is the result of a merger of the Andes Evangelical Mission (1903) and the Evangelical Union of South America (1937) in 1959. Both missions were originally organized to reach the Quechua Indians, the older missions being responsible for the Quechua translation of the New Testament and the development of several Bible institutes.

Seventh-day Adventists, now the largest Protestant church in Bolivia, began in 1907 but made little progress until after World War I. At that time the Peruvian and Bolivian Aymaras in the region of Lake Titicaca requested them to provide schools, and the result was a mass movement into the church. Other early Protestant churches which have built up significant followings are the Nazarenes and Friends.

Pentecostals have not been as successful here as in many other Latin American countries, due in part to Bolivia's low degree of urbanization. Nevertheless, the Assemblies of God have grown since 1946 to be the third largest Protestant church. Pentecostals from Sweden, Chile and Brazil have also been active and several indigenous pentecostal groups have been formed.

**CHURCH AND STATE.** The constitution of 2 February 1967 affirms in Article 3 that: (1) the Catholic religion is the official religion of the state, but that public worship on the part of other religions is permitted; (2) relations between the state and the Catholic church are to be regulated by concordats, although in fact none exist, the one concluded on 29 May 1851 never having been put into effect; (3) the state supports the Catholic church, subsidizing the salaries of bishops, canons, military chaplains and charitable works. Other articles in the constitution dealing with church-state relations are: (1) Article 28, which states that church property enjoys the same

part of the Ministry of Foreign Affairs (Ministerio de Relaciones Exteriores y Culto). The Ministry of Religion was created expressly for the Catholic Church, but in actuality it is concerned with all churches and religions, since all are required to be registered.

Numerous legal and customary provisions continue to be applied to the Catholic Church, making it in many cases excessively dependent on the state. Catholic bishops are often considered as public officials, and as a result the other religions enjoy greater freedom of action. Nevertheless, the Catholic Church enjoys certain advantages including economic aid and exemption from taxes. The church renewal of Vatican II and the coup d'etat of the extreme right wing which brought the Banzer regime to power in August, 1971 have created serious tensions between the progressive sector of the church on the one hand, and the government and conservative sector of the church on the other. The repressive measures initiated by the regime, which proclaimed itself 'nationalistic and Christian', have been especially harsh on progressive Catholic circles. Campaigns have been conducted against 'atheistic clergymen', and both Bolivian and foreign priests and religious personnel have been imprisoned or expelled. Catholic militants have been arrested, and police placed in convents and even in bishops' residences for surveillance. This campaign has resulted in weakening of the Catholic Church by the loss of a large number of its most dynamic members. The episcopate was slow to react but finally published a declaration denouncing political repression and the consequent popular misery. However, the abstract tenor and prudence of this document failed to satisfy the Catholic opposition.

During 1974–75 the government came into conflict with 'Catholicism's Justice and Peace Commission which had organized an amnesty campaign for political prisoners and had denounced the killing of 200 peasants in the Cochabamba valley in 1974, of which the government only admitted to 13 killed.

**BIBLIOGRAPHY**
*Animistic Aymaras and church growth.* Q. Nordyke. Newberg, Oregon: Barclay, 1970. 200p.
'Bolivia', *Pro Mundi Vita* (Brussels), 8 (1965).
*Guia de la Iglesia, Bolivia, 1970.* La Paz: SNES, 1970. (Catholic).
*La Iglesia Católica en Bolivia.* J. M. Barnadas. La Paz: Librería Editorial Juventud, 1976. 130p.
*La Iglesia en Perú y Bolivia.* I. Alonso, G. Garrido, J. Dammert & J. Tumiri. Fribourg: FERES, 1962. (Catholic).
*L'univers religieux des Aymaras de Bolivie: observations recueillies dans les carangas: jalons de pastorale.* J. Monast. Sondeos No. 10. Cuernavaca (Mexico): CIDOC, 1966. 300p.
*Mitos, supersticiones y supervivencias populares de Bolivia.* M. R. Paredes. 3rd edition. La Paz: Editorial Isla, 1964. 309p.
'Ritual and cultural lag: the feast of San Isidoro in Tiraque, Bolivia', J. M. Torsa, *Social compass*, XIX, 4 (1972).
'The clergy in Bolivia', *Pro Mundi Vita* (Brussels), Special note 11 (1970). (Catholic).
*The Protestant movement in Bolivia.* C.P. Wagner. South Pasadena: William Carey Library, 1970. 240p.

TABLE 2. ORGANIZED CHURCHES AND DENOMINATIONS IN BOLIVIA

| Official name 1 | Begun 2 | Type 3 | Counc 4 | Congs 5 | Adults 6 | Affiliated 7 | Names, notes, and other statistics (see Codebook) 8 |
|---|---|---|---|---|---|---|---|
| Asambleas de Dios de Bolivia | 1946 | P Pe2 | ZF..C | 208 | 10,400 | 20,000 | *ADB. Ass of God.* M=AoG(USA). 50% Aymara. 151n,10x,14f,G=20%pa,3s(129),W=83%,1100Y. |
| Asambleas de Dios Noruega | | P Pe2 | Z...C | | 100 | 200 | *ADN. Norwegian Assemblies of God.* M=NPY(Norway). In Beni, Pando, Cochabamba. |
| Convención Bautista Boliviana | 1946 | P Bap | T.... | 37 | 650 | 1,000 | *CBB. Bolivian Baptist Convention.* M=Brazilian Bapt Conv. 13n,2x,1s(12),W=75%,40Y. |
| Ejército de Salvación | 1920 | P Sal | xw... | 16 | 2,500 | 4,000 | *Salvation Army, Bolivia Dist.* SAmerica West Territory. Aymaras. 4n,2x,1s,W=79%. |
| Hermanos Libres | 1895 | P CBr | x.... | 50 | 1,500 | 2,500 | *Free (Open) Brethren. Plymouth Brethren.* M=CMML(UK,Australia,NZ,USA). 3m,29f. |
| Iglesia Adventista del Séptimo Día | 1907 | P Adv | x.... | 56 | 23,358 | 50,000 | *Seventh-day Adv. Bolivia Mission*, Inca UM. Aymaras. 1 plane. 18nx,1h,1s,379t(17208),1981Y. |
| Iglesia Anglicana (D Chile & Bolivia) | 1926 | A Low | aw.C. | 1 | 50 | 200 | In CASA. Expatriate English. Student work. M=CMS(Australia). 2x,1Y,1y. |
| Iglesia Asamblea de Dios Boliviana | | I pe2 | ..... | 1 | 50 | 100 | *IADB, Assembly of God Ch in Bolivia.* Cochabamba, Sucre. Brazilian pentecostals. |
| Iglesia Boliviana de Santidad | 1948 | P Hol | x...C | 34 | 1,006 | 2,000 | *IBS. Bolivian Holiness Ch.* M=Holiness Meth Chs(USA). 94% Aymara, 6% Quechua. 1s. |
| **Iglesia Católica en Bolivia:** | 1537 | R Lat | B.L.R | 449 | 2,608,000 | 4,495,983 | *Catholic Ch in Bolivia.* C=30+3+69. 6q,1s(121). 805nx,269m,1340w,124797Yy. |
| M La Paz | 1608 | R Lat | Bs | 95 | 576,000 | 992,000 | Languages: Spanish, Aymara. 3 Pastoral Zones. 197 65 326 30648 |
| D Cochabamba (M from 1975) | 1847 | R Lat | Bs | 51 | 352,000 | 607,442 | Spanish, Quechua. Recent industrialization. 1s. 143 62 287 11963 |
| D Oruro | 1924 | R Lat | Bs | 29 | 157,000 | 270,000 | Spanish, Aymara, Quechua. Mining town and rural area. 56 15 82 6760 |
| PN Corocoro | 1949 | R Lat | Bs | 27 | 158,300 | 272,887 | Aymara, Spanish. Rural altiplano, mining. M=CP. 19 2 18 6905 |
| PN Coroico | 1958 | R Lat | Bs | 17 | 86,000 | 148,000 | Aymara, Spanish. Tropical, rural. M=OFM. 16 10 54 2025 |
| M Sucre | 1551 | R Lat | Bs | 44 | 226,000 | 390,000 | Spanish, Quechua. Old town, growing industrialization. 66 16 112 13000 |
| D Potosí | 1924 | R Lat | Bs | 68 | 509,400 | 878,294 | Spanish, Quechua. Mining population, and rural. 76 4 75 14153 |
| D Santa Cruz de la Sierra | 1605 | R Lat | Bs | 31 | 235,000 | 405,000 | Spanish, Japanese, Guaraní. Prosperous (petrol, gas). 86 38 173 12000 |
| D Tarija | 1924 | R Lat | Bs | 11 | 61,400 | 105,900 | Spanish only. Rural. Close links with Argentina. 21 4 29 6158 |
| PN Aiquile | 1961 | R Lat | Bs | 8 | 52,200 | 89,960 | Quechua, Spanish. Entirely rural. M=OFM. 21 4 8 3820 |
| VA Chiquitos | 1930 | R Lat | Pofm | 16 | 33,400 | 57,500 | Chiquitano, Spanish, Ayoré, Pauserna. Tropical. P=42%. 23 24 71 2642 |
| VA Cuevo | 1919 | R Lat | Pofm | 19 | 39,000 | 67,000 | Spanish, Mataco, Guaraní, Guayaru, Canochana. P=12%. 20 7 28 2701 |
| VA El Beni | 1917 | R Lat | Pofm | 12 | 52,000 | 90,000 | Ignaciano, Trinitario, Bauré, Jora, Moré, Cayuvana. 20 7 20 7160 |
| VA Nuflo de Chávez | 1951 | R Lat | Pofm | 12 | 16,000 | 28,000 | Spanish, Siriono, Guayaru, Ayoré, Chiquitano. P=45%. 12 6 23 1479 |
| VA Pando | 1942 | R Lat | Pmm | 4 | 37,000 | 64,000 | Pacahuara, Aroana, Chama, Spanish. P=15%. 14 2 16 2053 |
| VA Reyes | 1942 | R Lat | Pcssr | 5 | 17,000 | 30,000 | Chama, Tacana, Cavineno, Aroana, Reyasano. P=28%. 15 3 18 1330 |
| Iglesia de Dios | 1960 | P Pe3 | ZF... | 19 | 300 | 500 | *Ch of God.* M=CoG(Cleveland)(USA). 5 churches, 14 missions. HQ Sucre. 10n. |
| Iglesia de Dios Boliviana | 1945 | P Hol | x...C | 28 | 2,100 | 4,000 | *IDB. Bolivian Ch of God.* M=CoGHoliness(Overland Park,USA). Aymaras. 7f,1s. |
| Iglesia de JC de los Santos de los UD | c1961 | M LdS | x.... | | 3,000 | 5,752 | *Ch of JC of LdS. Mormons.* M=CJCLdS(USA). Indians. Rapid growth, 13.8%pa. 70f. |
| Iglesia de la Puerta Abierta | 1955 | I pen | .TT.T | 5 | 100 | 200 | *IPA.* M=Ch of the Open Door(USA). Fundamentalist. HQ Cochabamba. |
| Iglesia del Evangelio Cuadrangular | 1929 | P Pe2 | ZF..C | 34 | 1,130 | 2,000 | M=Internat Ch of Foursquare Gospel(USA). Sirionos. 10nm,2x,1H,1p(8),W=68%,50Y. |
| Iglesia del Nazareno | 1908 | P Hol | xF..C | 116 | 4,066 | 8,000 | M=Ch of the Nazarene (USA). Aymaras. 9n,79m,12f,3h,1s(28),68t(4990),W=63%,161Y. |
| Iglesia Evangélica Boliviana | 1946 | I Ref | .TT.T | 17 | 889 | 1,066 | *Bolivian Ev Ch. Bible Presbyterians.* 90% Aymara. HQ La Paz. 3n,G=3.2%pa,W=20%,89z. |
| Iglesia Evangélica Independiente | | I ind | ..... | 1 | 100 | 200 | *IEI. Independent Ev Ch.* Indigenous Bolivian church in Cochabamba. |
| Iglesia Evangélica Los Amigos | 1919 | P Qua | Q.... | 35 | 1,000 | 1,500 | *IELA. Ev Ch of Friends.* M=BFHM(Central Yearly Meeting,USA). 15n,3x,5f,1p,1s(5). |
| Iglesia Ev Luterana Boliviana | 1938 | P Lut | L...C | 21 | 2,000 | 6,000 | *IELB. Ev Lutheran Ch of B.* M=World Mission Prayer League. Aymaras. 24f,3k,1s. |
| Iglesia Ev Luterana de habla Alemana | 1957 | P Lut | L.... | 5 | 600 | 2,500 | *German-speaking Ev Lutheran Ch in Bolivia.* Recent immigrants, in La Paz. 1x,W=60%. |
| Iglesia Ev Metodista en Bolivia | 1878 | P Met | VuU.. | 47 | 3,480 | 10,000 | *IEMB. Ev Methodist Ch.* M=UMC(USA). A=1969. 36n,40m,37f,5H,4r,1s. Many projects. |
| Iglesia Evangélica Mundial | 1943 | P Hol | xF..C | 45 | 950 | 2,000 | *IEM. World Gospel Church.* M=World Gospel Mission(USA). HQ Santa Cruz. 23f,1s. |
| Iglesia Evangélica Nacional | 1957 | P ind | ....C | 18 | 205 | 1,000 | *National Ev Ch. Assembly of God.* Ex Bethesda Mission. Works with UWM. 2n,W=49%,45Y. |
| Iglesia Ev Pentecostal de Chile | c1935 | I pe2 | x.... | 5 | 2,000 | 4,000 | *IEPC: Ev Pentecostal Ch of Chile.* In Oruro, Chuquisaca, Potosí, Cochabamba, La Paz. |
| Iglesia Luterana Latinoamericana de B | 1967 | P Lut | 1.U.. | 1 | 135 | 489 | *Latin American Lutheran Ch.* Ecumenical split ex WMPL, in La Paz. 2n,W=30%,7y. |
| Iglesia Menonita | 1954 | P Men | G.... | | 2,200 | 5,500 | *Mennonite Ch in Bolivia. Old Colony Mennonites*, from Paraguay. German-speaking. |
| Iglesia Nacional Bethesda | 1950 | P ind | x.... | 17 | 500 | 1,260 | *INB. Bethesda National Ch.* M=Bethesda Mission(USA). 11n,4x,7f,1s(15).W=85%,25z. |
| Iglesia Nacional Ev de Los Amigos | 1924 | P Qua | QF..C | 120 | 4,500 | 7,000 | *INELA. Friends National Ev Ch.* M=Oregon YM(USA). Aymaras. 35n,2x,6f,1s(30),W=99%. |
| Iglesia Ortodoxa Griega | c1970 | O Gre | Cwo.. | 1 | 1,000 | 2,000 | Part of XIth Archidiocesan District, Greek Orthodox AD of N&SAmerica. Greeks. |
| Iglesia Pentecostal Brasilera | | I pen | ..... | 10 | 150 | 300 | *Brazilian Pentecostal Ch.* From Brazil. In Santa Cruz, Cochabamba departments. |
| Iglesia Pentecostal Nacional | | I pen | ....C | 10 | 500 | 1,000 | *National Pentecostal Ch.* Schism ex ICFG. HQ Trinidad. Indigenous pentecostals. |
| Iglesia Pentecostal Sueca | 1920 | P Pe2 | Z...C | 5 | 600 | 1,000 | *Swedish Pentecostal Ch.* M=SFM(Sweden). Cochabamba department. 1H,14mf. |
| Iglesia Unida Mundial | 1936 | P int | xF..C | 5 | 300 | 500 | *United World Ch.* M=UWM(USA). Santa Cruz. Mestizos. 2n,2x,1k,W=20%,20Y,10z. |
| Iglesia radiofónicas solitarias | c1960 | I rad | ..... | 10 | 200 | 350 | Isolated radio believers, mostly young, in remote jungle areas. R=450(HCJB,FEBC). |
| Misión Bautista Internacional | 1967 | P Bap | x.... | 1 | 20 | 50 | M=Baptist International Missions (Tennessee Temple School)(USA).HQ Cochabamba. 6f. |
| Misión Bautista Leta | 1950 | P Bap | ..... | | 100 | 200 | M=Latvian Baptist Mission(Brazil). Latvian colony in jungle. Rincón del Tigre. |
| Misión Bautista Maranata | 1962 | P Bap | x.... | 14 | 300 | 500 | *West Side Baptists.* M=Maranatha Baptist Mission(USA). Cochabamba department. 12f. |
| Misión del Seminario Bíblico | 1919 | P Qua | ....C | 23 | 868 | 1,500 | *MSB.* M=Union Bible Seminary(Westfield, Indiana,USA). Quakers. 1j,1s. |
| Misión Evangélica Bautista | 1956 | P Bap | ..... | 5 | 27 | 50 | *MEB. Ev Baptist Mission.* Independent group from USA. Central region. 1x,W=41%,5z. |
| Misión Llamamiento de Medianoche | 1960 | P ind | x.... | 3 | 100 | 200 | M=Midnight Cry Mission(Switzerland). Beni, Pando departments. Social projects. |
| Misión Neuvas Tribus | 1942 | P int | x...C | 45 | 308 | 1,615 | *MNT.* M=New Tribes Mission(USA). Beni department: 6 Indian jungle tribes. 89f,W=15%,90Y. |
| Misión Sudamericana | 1922 | P ind | .N..C | 16 | 250 | 500 | *Misión de Fe.* M=South America Indian Mission(SAIM)(USA). Ayoré Indians. 19x,20f,15z. |
| Misiones Mundiales de Bolivia | 1961 | P ind | x.... | | 900 | 2,000 | M=World-Wide Missions(USA). Evangelical group from California. |
| Testigos de Jehová | 1932 | M Jeh | x.... | 32 | 1,276 | 2,000 | *Jehovah's Witnesses. Watch Tower.* Witnessing under way by 1932. HQ La Paz. 271Y. |
| Unión Bautista Boliviana | 1898 | P Bap | T.... | 50 | 3,435 | 6,000 | *UBB. BBU. Bolivian Baptist Union.* M=CBOMB(Canada). Cochabamba. 90nm,37f,2r,3s. |
| Unión Bíblica | 1952 | P ind | ..... | 1 | 100 | 200 | M=Seattle Bible Union(USA). Small independent Protestant mission. HQ Camiri. |
| Unión Cristiana Evangélica | 1903 | P int | .M..C | 230 | 13,300 | 28,000 | *UCE. Ev Chr Union.* M=Andes EM, EUSA. A=1950. 148n,15x,76f,1h,3s(250),W=54%,360Yy. |
| Unión Misionera Neotestamentaria | 1926 | P int | x.... | 6 | 200 | 500 | *NT Churches.* M=NTMU(USA,Canada). 1933 split ex SAIM. Puerto Suarez. 2f. |
| Other Bolivian indigenous churches | | I | ..... | | 2,000 | 5,000 | Total about 40 bodies (see below), mainly Aymara independent congregations. |
| Other Protestant denominations | | P | ..... | | 1,000 | 2,000 | Total about 15 smaller bodies (see list below). |
| Doubly-affiliated (duplication) (1970) | | | | | –82,000 | –141,415 | Evangelicals who also are or were baptized Roman Catholics. |
| **Total affiliated (mid-1970)** | | | | **2,010** | **2,621,803** | **4,553,000** | **Total denominations (1970) . . . 104.** |
| **Total affiliated (mid-1975)** | | | | **2,200** | **2,959,000** | **5,139,030** | **Total denominations (1975) . . . 114.** |
| **Total affiliated (mid-1980)** | | | | **2,800** | **3,363,000** | **5,839,850** | **Total denominations (1980) . . . 124.** |

NOTES ON TABLE ABOVE
COLUMNS: for meanings and CODES (cols. 1, 3, 4. 8), see Codebook (Part 6). Column 1: **Boldface type** = church with over 10% of country's affiliated Christians.
NATIONAL COUNCILS (Column 4, 5th letter).

C = Asociación Nacional de Evangélicos de Bolivia (ANDEB) (National Association of Evangelicals of Bolivia).
R = Conferencia Episcopal de Bolivia (CEB) (Episcopal Conference of Bolivia).
T = Confederation of Fundamental Evangelical Churches of Bolivia.

OTHER BOLIVIAN INDIGENOUS CHURCHES. There are scores of Aymara independent congregations, mainly pentecostal, especially in La Paz. Among more organized denominations are: Iglesia Boliviana Los Pelegrinos (member of ICCC), and work (under a missionary bishop from Brazil) of the Igreja Católica Apostólica Brasileira.
OTHER PROTESTANT DENOMINATIONS. These include: Baptist Missionary Association of America, Children of God International (from USA; 1973, 500,000 letters distributed in Bolivia), Church of the Brethren (1942), Chs of Christ in Christian Union, Ev Methodist Ch (1956), Exclusive Brethren (Continuing Tunbridge Wells), United Ev Chs.

PEOPLES (ethnolinguisitic). Christians: 38.2% Quechua, 31.7% Mestizo, 23.0% Aymara, 5.0% Bolivian White, 0.7% lowland Amerindian (including Guaraní), 0.1% Peruvian, 0.1% Brazilian, Japanese, Ryukyuan (Okinawan).

COUNTRY-WIDE TOTALS
EVANGELIZATION (see Part 5). 1900: 96%. 1970: 99%. 1980: 100%. *Mass evangelism.* Campaigns sponsored by the Andes Evangelical Mission: Gideons (1959), Youth for Christ (1961), Pocket Testament League (1963), Evangelization Literature Overseas Workshops (1960, 1964). Other campaigns: 1963, 1970, Fernando Vangioni; 1963, Raimundo Jimenezi; 1965, Evangelism-in-Depth (year-long; 500 participating local churches from 36 denominations, 80,000 homes visited the first day, 4,204 prayer cells, 19,212 professions of faith); 1967, Hermano Pablo 7-day crusade in Cochabamba (5,000 attenders, 1,000 enquirers), Santa Cruz (10,000/1,000), and La Paz (16,000/2,400); 1967, Assemblies of God programme of total evangelism; 1973, crowds up to 60,000 to hear Catholic healing evangelist Julio Cesar Rubial; October 1974, Luis Palau 3-week crusade in Oruro, Santa Cruz and Cochabamba (about 70,000 attenders and 3,000 decisions for Christ); 1978, Luis Palau crusades in La Paz, Santa Cruz, Cochabamba (180,000 attenders, 19,000 enquirers). *Radiophonic evangelism.* In 1970, 18,000 students were enrolled in Catholic radiophonic schools. Protestant broadcasts: HCJB, FEBC.
FOREIGN MISSIONARIES AND PERSONNEL (nationals serving abroad) (1973). Total about 1,610 Roman Catholics in 13 countries including Spain and USA.
FOREIGN MISSIONARIES AND PERSONNEL (aliens from abroad) (1973). Total 2,724. *From Western world.* 2,378: 1,638 Roman Catholics, 658 Protestants (492 in 35 USA societies, 61 in 4 Canada societies, 38 in 5 UK societies, 21 in 4 New Zealand societies, 19 in 1 Norway society, 12 in 4 Australia societies, 6 in 1 WGermany society, 4 in 1 Sweden society, 3 in 2 Netherlands societies, 2 in 1 Switzerland society), about 80 marginal Protestants (70 Mormons from USA), 2 Anglicans from Australia. *From Communist world.* 9 Roman Catholics from Poland. *From Third World.* 337: 253 Roman Catholics from Latin American countries, India, Japan and Philippines, 70 Protestants from Argentina, Brazil, Chile, Colombia, Jamaica, Japan and Uruguay, 14 indigenous from Brazil, Chile, Korea.
INSTITUTIONS (church-operated) (1973). Total 300, including 130 higher schools (14 minor seminaries), 103 medical centres (34 hospitals), 10 radio stations, 1 religious community, 7 research centres, 32 seminaries (25 Protestant, 7 RC), 9 study centres, 1 university.
PERIODICALS. About 50 titles.
PERSONNEL. About 4,224 (1,500 national, 2,724 foreign).
RELIGIOUS LIBRARIES. About 62.
SCRIPTURE DISTRIBUTION (1975). Annual totals: 49,401 Bibles (80% subsidized, 20% commercial), 608,030 NTs (91% free, 7% subsidized, 2% commercial), 84,522 UBS portions, 2,443,465 UBS selections. *Translations completed.* Portion: 17 languages since 1829. NT: 2 languages since 1922.
SERVICE AGENCIES. About 90, including AADET, ACLO, ALFALIT, ANDEB, ANF, CCCI, CEB, COMBASE, CONFER, ERBOL, FBEC, JAC, JAC/F, JARS, MCC, MEC, MOB, SU, WBT (1955; 75 missionaries), WGC, WLC(EHC), YMCA, YWCA(ACF).

ADDITIONAL DATA ON CHURCHES
ASAMBLEAS DE DIOS DE BOLIVIA. *Growth.* Due to 'Each church one church in one year' programme from 1968, by 1977 preaching centres numbered over 600 and members over 27,000.
IGLESIA CATOLICA EN BOLIVIA. *New archdioceses.* Elevated 1975: M Cochabamba, M Santa Cruz de la Sierra. *Annual baptisms.* (1972) 99.5% infant, 0.5% adult. *Priests.* Of the 805 some 238 are nationals (1973: 180 diocesan, 58 religious), and 567 expatriates (56 diocesan, 511 religious). *Brothers.* Of whom 93 are nationals. *Sisters.* Of whom 691 are Bolivians, and 208 other Latin Americans (82 Colombians, 73 Peruvians). Most of the rest are Spanish, Italians, USA, Germans, Austrians, Canadians, with 3 Japanese and 3 from the Philippines. In addition to the sisters enumerated in the table above in 69 congregations, there are 250 sisters of contemplative congregations in 14 monasteries. The total of all sisters was (1970) 1,800. *Catholic charismatics.* (January 1974). 2,000 adults including many religious personnel in 50 prayer groups are active in the Charismatic Renewal. *Catechists.* Total (under Propaganda) about 200. *Indigenous religious congregations.* Sisters: 102 Misioneras Cruzadas de la Iglesia (begun Cochabamba 1925), 21 Hermanas Franciscanas Misioneras Rurales (begun La Paz 1957), 31 Misioneras de Maria Madre de la Iglesia (begun La Paz 1973). *Main foreign religious orders and congregations.* Priests (with over 50): 240 OFM, 173 SJ, 100 SDB, 55 CSSR. Brothers (with over 50): 58 FSC. Sisters (with over 100): 173 Hijas de Santa Ana.
*Catholic organizations.* The Episcopal Conference of Bolivia (Conferencial Episcopal de Bolivia, CEB)is a member of CELAM. Religious personnel are organized into 2 associations: the Conference of Male Religious of Bolivia (Conferencia de Religiosos de Bolivia) and the National Conference of Sisters (Conferencia Nacional de Religiosas), both of which are members of CLAR. There is no official pastoral or presbyteral council although an unofficial National Pastoral Council (Consejo Pastoral Nacional) exists. It is directed by a bishop and is composed of priests and members of the episcopal commissions. Lay movements include the following: Christian Family Movement (Movimiento Familiar Cristiano, MFC), Basic Ecclesiastical Communities (Comunidades Eclesiales de Base, CEB), Christian Study Courses (Cursillos de Cristiandad), Palestra (groups of Christian college youth), Scouts, Women's Association for Catholic Action in Bolivia (Asociación de Mujeres de Acción Católica Boliviana, AMAC), Bolivian Workers' Movement (Movimiento Obrero Boliviano, MOB), and Legion of Mary (Legión de María) with 2,820 members in 1972 in 235 presidia. For the armed forces Bolivia forms a military vicariate.
The Holy See has diplomatic relations with Bolivia and is represented to government and the Catholic hierarchy by a nuncio in La Paz.

There are neither progressivist nor conservative pressure groups in existence in Bolivia.

Several institutions are involved in research and social action. (1) The Centre for Research and Social Action (Centro de Investigación y Acción Social, CIAS) in La Paz is maintained by Jesuits. (2) The Centre for Social Advancement (Centro de Promoción Social), founded in La Paz in 1963 under the name Bolivian Institute for Study and Social Action (IBEAS), was closed in 1970 and re-opened in 1973. Sponsored by Dominicans, it engages in research and trains social workers and technical counsellors, totalling over 20,000 persons from 1967–69. (3) The National Centre for Integral Training (Centro Nacional de Formación Integral, CENAFI), founded in La Paz in 1968 by members of JOC, is an independent institution run by teams of laymen. It provides intensive courses for workers and peasants. Branches are found across the country. (4) The Centre for Research and Rural Advancement (Centro de Investigación y Promoción del Campesinado, CIPCA), founded in La Paz by Jesuits in 1971, is most active in Achacachi, Jesus de Machaca and Coripata and works in close co-operation with the Pastoral Plan for the Aymara Altiplano. It seeks to change existing structures by training leadership and improving the conditions of life of peasants. It also provides training for catechists and deacons. (5) Loyola Cultural Action (Acción Cultural Loyola, ACLO), was founded in Sucre by Jesuits in 1967, and is active in the rural and semi-urban sectors of Chuquisaca and Tarija in southern Bolivia. As with CIPCA, ACLO is a centre for research, study and action which is involved in literacy work, conscientization courses, and community development. It also transmits programmes for several hours daily over Radio Loyola.

in Sucre. (6) The Centre for Socio-Cultural Training of the Aymara Altiplano (Centro de Promoción Socio-Cultural del Altiplano Aymara), founded at Tiwanacu in 1970, offers courses for the diverse communities of the region and enjoys a wide influence. (7) The Institute for Rural Education (Instituto de Educación Rural, IER) founded near Cochabamba in 1961, provides training for peasants, catechists and deacons and engages in rural community development.

Pastoral and theological training is provided at the Advanced Theological Institute (Instituto Superior de Estudios Teológicos, ISET). Founded in Cochabamba in 1969, this is a national institute for training and theological reflection, dependent on the episcopal conference. The Centre for Apostolic Training of Laja (Centro de la Formación Apostólica de Laja) in La Paz trains rural deacons for the relatively new Aymara church. Numerous other training centres have been established in various parts of the country.

The International Language Institute (Instituto Internacional de Idiomas), founded in Cochabamba in 1966, provides training courses for foreign missionaries in Quechua, Aymara, Spanish, anthropology, sociology and culture. With regard to national missionary societies there are 3 Bolivian missionary institutes for sisters: Misioneras Cruzadas de la Iglesia, founded in Cochabamba in 1925, with 700 missionaries in Latin America and Western Europe in 1973; Hermanas Franciscanas Misioneras Rurales, founded in La Paz in 1957, with 21 sisters in La Paz and Cochabamba in 1973; Misioneras de Maria Madre de la Iglesia, founded in La Paz in 1973, with 31 sisters in La Paz and Cochabamba; and Misioneras de la Santísima Trinidad, founded in La Paz in 1960, with 15 sisters in 1974.

In 1970 the Catholic Church sponsored in urban areas 60 pre-primary schools (3,415 infants), 269 primary schools (47,685 pupils), 53 secondary schools (15,873), one teacher-training school (701 students), one advanced technical school (120 students) and one university (Universidad Católica, founded in La Paz in 1965, with 190 students). With the students in 14 literacy schools and 126 adult education schools (6,214 students), there were a total of 74,198 students in Catholic schools, or 15% of all in the country. This contrasts with 79% in state schools, 4% in private secular schools and 2% in Protestant schools. In addition to the above students, there is the Catholic Rural Education Programme (Escuelas de Cristo) which counted in 1969, 25,500 pupils in 567 primary schools, 8 secondary colleges and one rural teacher-training school. By 1973 schools numbered 311 primary (56,328 pupils) and 102 secondary (29,293).

The church maintains 130 medical and social service institutions, some independent of and some in co-operation with the state. These include 26 hospitals, 4 clinics, 60 dispensaries, 28 sanitary posts, 6 health co-operatives, one leprosarium, 10 homes for the aged and 6 children's homes. Caritas Boliviana is involved in the distribution of food, milk and clothing; the creation of parish dispensaries and children's homes; the direction of collective work such as the building of schools; and the foundation of credit unions.

UNION CRISTIANA EVANGELICA. *Membership.* 65% Quechua. In 1970, the conversion rate among them was lower than among the Aymara Indians (from among whom most Evangelicals come).

---

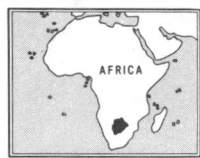

# BOTSWANA

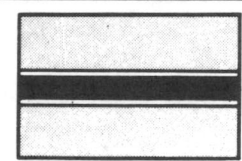

## SECULAR DATA

**STATE. Official name:** The Republic of Botswana.
**Flag** (shown above right): Wide light-blue bands separated by central black band and narrow white stripes.
**Area:** 600,372 sq.km. (231,828 sq.miles). Agricultural land: 69.3%.
**Government:** Republic, since 1966 (chiefdom, 1885 Bechuanaland Protectorate of Britain, 1966 Independence).
**Legislature:** National Assembly, 36 members. House of Chiefs, 12 members.
**Official languages:** English and Setswana.
**Chief cities:** capital Gaborone 17,720 (1971), Selibi-Pikwe 40,000.

**DEMOGRAPHY. Population:** 608,656 (census of 31.VIII.1971. For 1970–2000 (UN), see last row of Table 1. Population density (1975): 1/sq.km. (3/sq.mile). Under 15 years: 42%. Growth rate (1975–80): 2.79% per year (births 4.79%, deaths −2.01%). Life expectancy (1975–80): 46.0 years. Household size: 5.1 persons.

**Major languages:** Tswana, English, Kalanga, Afrikaans, Nguni (Ndebele), Lozi, Pedi, Xhosa, Sotho, Shona, and 10 Bushman languages.
**Urban dwellers** (1970): 4.1%. Urban growth rate (1950–70): 8.6% per year.
**Labour force:** 56%.
**Refugees** (1977): 7,100 (1,100 from Angola, 1,000 from South Africa, Namibia, Zimbabwe).

**ETHNOLINGUISTIC GROUPS:** 70.6% Tswana (27.1% Ngwato, 9.8% Kwena, 9.6% Ngwaketse, 5.7% Tawana, 4.3% Kgatla, 1.9% Malete, 1.4% Rolong, 0.5% Tlokwa), 11.0% Kalanga, 4.8% Bushman, 4.0% Koba (Yeye), 1.7% Ndebele, 1.4% Herero, 1.1% Lozi, 1.0% Shona, 0.9% Subia, 0.9% Pedi, 0.6% Xhosa, 0.6% Sotho, 0.6% European (White) (4,000) (0.3% Afrikaner), 0.6% Coloured (Afro-European) (3,500), Khalagadi, Zulu, Asian (500), Jewish.

**MONEY** (1977). **Monetary unit:** pula (= 100 thebe); US$1 = P 0.867.

**National income per person:** US$340. Average annual family income: US$1,734.
**Inflation:** (1970–74) 12% per year (1975: consumer price index 143).
**Cost of living in capital** (1976): index 86 (Washington DC=100). Daily cost of living: US$32.

**EDUCATION.** Adult literacy: (1946) 21%, (1964) 33%. Education rate: 50%. Schools: 302 (288 primary, 13 secondary). Universities: 1.

**HEALTH.** Hospitals: 13 (1,660 beds). Doctors: 44. Lepers: 2,600 (3 8 per 1,000). Blind: 1,880. Psychotics: 4,000.

**LITERATURE.** Annual new book titles (1973): 52. Periodicals: 30. Newspapers: 2 dailies, 1 non-daily.

**COMMUNICATION** (per 1,000 people). Phones: 9. Radios: 13. Daily newspaper circulation: 21 copies.

TABLE 1.    RELIGIOUS ADHERENTS IN BOTSWANA

| Year | 1900 | | mid-1970 | | Annual change, 1970–1980 | | | | mid-1975 | | mid-1980 | | 2000 | |
|---|---|---|---|---|---|---|---|---|---|---|---|---|---|---|
| Name | Adherents | % | Adherents | % | Natural | Conversion | Total | Rate | Adherents | % | Adherents | % | Adherents | % |
| Tribal religionists | 102,900 | 85.7 | 347,200 | 56.3 | 9,339 | −4,968 | 4,371 | 1.21 | 362,560 | 52.5 | 390,910 | 49.2 | 491,500 | 34.4 |
| Christians | 17,100 | 14.2 | 266,100 | 43.1 | 8,349 | 4,951 | 13,300 | 4.10 | 324,100 | 46.9 | 399,100 | 50.2 | 924,600 | 64.7 |
| professing | 17,100 | 14.2 | 266,100 | 43.1 | 8,349 | 4,951 | 13,300 | 4.10 | 324,100 | 46.9 | 399,100 | 50.2 | 924,600 | 64.7 |
| Protestants | 17,000 | 14.2 | 160,000 | 25.9 | 4,699 | 438 | 5,137 | 2.82 | 182,430 | 26.4 | 211,370 | 26.6 | 424,400 | 29.7 |
| African indigenous | 0 | 0.0 | 50,000 | 8.1 | 1,780 | 2,600 | 4,380 | 6.34 | 69,100 | 10.0 | 93,800 | 11.8 | 242,900 | 17.0 |
| Roman Catholics | 100 | 0.1 | 43,000 | 7.0 | 1,460 | 1,710 | 3,170 | 5.59 | 56,660 | 8.2 | 74,700 | 9.4 | 214,300 | 15.0 |
| Anglicans | 0 | 0.0 | 12,000 | 2.0 | 374 | 176 | 550 | 3.79 | 14,500 | 2.1 | 17,500 | 2.2 | 35,700 | 2.5 |
| Marginal Protestants | 0 | 0.0 | 1,000 | 0.2 | 33 | 27 | 60 | 4.62 | 1,300 | 0.2 | 1,600 | 0.2 | 7,000 | 0.5 |
| Orthodox | 0 | 0.0 | 100 | 0.0 | 3 | 0 | 3 | 2.73 | 110 | 0.0 | 130 | 0.0 | 300 | 0.0 |
| nominal | 4,000 | 3.3 | 111,515 | 18.1 | 3,545 | 2,147 | 5,692 | 4.14 | 137,595 | 19.9 | 168,440 | 21.2 | 353,200 | 24.7 |
| affiliated | 13,100 | 10.9 | 154,585 | 25.0 | 4,804 | 2,804 | 7,608 | 4.08 | 186,505 | 27.0 | 230,660 | 29.0 | 571,400 | 40.0 |
| total practising | 11,790 | 90 | 123,670 | 80 | 3,843 | 2,244 | 6,087 | 4.08 | 149,200 | 80 | 184,530 | 80 | 342,840 | 60 |
| non-practising | 1,310 | 10 | 30,920 | 20 | 961 | 560 | 1,521 | 4.08 | 37,300 | 20 | 46,130 | 20 | 228,560 | 40 |
| Protestants | 13,000 | 10.8 | 93,833 | 15.2 | 2,777 | 560 | 3,337 | 3.09 | 107,800 | 15.6 | 127,200 | 16.0 | 271,500 | 19.0 |
| Evangelicals | 12,500 | 10.4 | 24,000 | 3.9 | 711 | 139 | 850 | 3.08 | 27,600 | 4.0 | 32,500 | 4.1 | 75,000 | 5.2 |
| African indigenous | 0 | 0.0 | 32,000 | 5.2 | 1,102 | 1,418 | 2,520 | 5.89 | 42,800 | 6.2 | 57,200 | 7.2 | 171,500 | 12.0 |
| Roman Catholics | 100 | 0.1 | 21,202 | 3.4 | 711 | 829 | 1,540 | 5.58 | 27,600 | 4.0 | 36,600 | 4.6 | 107,200 | 7.5 |
| Anglicans | 0 | 0.0 | 7,000 | 1.1 | 196 | −16 | 180 | 2.37 | 7,600 | 1.1 | 8,800 | 1.1 | 17,000 | 1.2 |
| Anglican pentecostals | 0 | 0.0 | 0 | 0.0 | 1 | 9 | 10 | 20.00 | 50 | 0.0 | 100 | 0.0 | 400 | 0.0 |
| Marginal Protestants | 0 | 0.0 | 500 | 0.1 | 17 | 13 | 30 | 4.62 | 650 | 0.1 | 800 | 0.1 | 4,000 | 0.3 |
| Orthodox | 0 | 0.0 | 50 | 0.0 | 1 | 0 | 1 | 1.82 | 55 | 0.0 | 60 | 0.0 | 200 | 0.0 |
| Baha'is | 0 | 0.0 | 3,400 | 0.6 | 103 | 17 | 120 | 3.00 | 4,000 | 0.6 | 4,600 | 0.6 | 12,000 | 0.8 |
| Muslims | 0 | 0.0 | 200 | 0.0 | 6 | 0 | 6 | 2.61 | 230 | 0.0 | 260 | 0.0 | 600 | 0.0 |
| Jews | 0 | 0.0 | 100 | 0.0 | 3 | 0 | 3 | 2.73 | 110 | 0.0 | 130 | 0.0 | 300 | 0.0 |
| Country's population | 120,000 | 100.0 | 617,000 | 100.0 | 17,800 | 0 | 17,800 | 2.58 | 691,100 | 100.0 | 795,000 | 100.0 | 1,429,000 | 100.0 |

**COLUMNS, ROWS,** For meanings and definitions, see Codebook (Part 6). Note that, by definition, total 'Christians' = professing + crypto-Christians, which also = affiliated + nominal Christians. Percentages may not always total exactly, due to rounding.
**CENSUS.** 7.V.1946 (Bechuanaland): 73.9% tribal religionists, 23.9% Protestants (16.3% LMS, 4.3% DRC/NGK), 1.5% Anglicans, 0.7% Roman Catholics. No subsequent census has enumerated religion.

### NOTES ON RELIGIONS
**AFRICAN INDIGENOUS.** In about 60 denominations in 1970 (see Table 2).

**ANGLICAN PENTECOSTALS** (or, Anglican charismatics). A small group led in 1977 by the Anglican bishop.
**BAHA'IS.** Growth from 12 isolated groups in 1964 to 23 local spiritual assemblies in 1973. A major effort to convert Kalahari Bushmen had won 9 converts by 1972 and 80 by 1973 in 15 localities (with 2 all-Bushmen assemblies).
**MUSLIMS.** *Hajj pilgrims to Mecca.* (1976) 1.
**NOMINAL CHRISTIANS.** For a hundred years from 1830 the LMS church (UCCSA) was virtually the state church and no other church was allowed (as among the Bamangwato). As a result, large numbers profess to belong to the church still, although the church is only in touch with a small percentage of them. Further, as cattle-raisers many peoples are constantly on

the move to cattle-posts around the Kalahari desert, where the church is unable to maintain contact with them. To a lesser extent, other denominations are out of touch with many of their professing members.
**PROTESTANTS.** In the year 1900, 80% of all Christians belonged to the LMS mission under the Christian chief of the Bamangwato, Khama.
**TRIBAL RELIGIONISTS.** Found among all tribes, with only the 5 Bushmen tribes (60,000) still predominantly traditionalist (90%), in 1972.

**NON-CHRISTIAN RELIGIONS. African traditional religions** continue to exert an influence on Botswana life. The people most resistant to Christian influences are the Bushmen who remain 90% traditionalist. They identify God by various names, the most important being Kaang in the southeast and Huwe in the north and west. Their mythology is richer than that of their Bantu neighbours, with emphasis on the role of certain animals (especially the praying mantis) and celestial bodies (sun, moon, morning star and southern cross) as manifestations of divinity. Among the Tswana the ancestors are called Badimo and God is Modimo. Distinctive Tswana features are the identification of God as mother and extreme reverence for the name Modimo, making its pronunciation taboo for most people. Modimo generally works through the Badimo, who also serve as intermediaries in the approach of men to God.

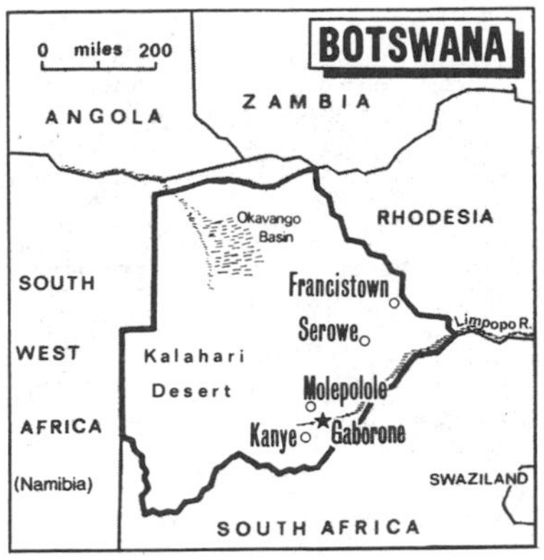


## CHRISTIANITY

PROTESTANT CHURCHES. The Protestant churches have been a significant force in Botswana life since the early part of the 19th century, though very small for many years. The first British resident commissioner in 1885 was a missionary, and since Independence the speakers of the Botswana parliament have been Christian missionaries. The major Protestant denomination is the United Congregational Church, a result of the pioneering efforts of the London Missionary Society. With work in all parts of the country, this has been considered as almost the established church of Botswana; but its growth has been slow in recent years, and there are large numbers of nominal adherents out of touch with it. Although a number of denominations (Methodists, Lutherans, Dutch Reformed) have been in Botswana longer, the Seventh-day Adventists (1921) are the second largest Protestant church. Before Independence all hospital and secondary school facilities were maintained by church organizations, most of which were Protestant prior to World War II; and church involvement in education, medical and social service continues to be extensive.

INDIGENOUS CHURCHES. African independent churches play a significant and increasing role on the Botswana scene, although all remain relatively small. The majority have come from neighbouring South Africa, but since 1960 a number of new indigenous healing groups have arisen in the north.

CATHOLIC CHURCH. The first Catholic mission was founded in 1895, and until 1959 Botswana was divided into 3 different jurisdictions based in South Africa, Namibia and Southern Rhodesia. With the establishment of one national jurisdiction in 1959 came a new sense of identity, and the church has been characterized by rapid growth over the past decade.

**CHURCH AND STATE.** Under the rule of king Khama I (1872–1930), Congregationalism was virtually the state religion. No other church was allowed among the Bamangwato until recently.

Freedom of conscience and religious expression is guaranteed in Articles 11–12 of the 1966 constitution. The same articles give to religious communities the right to establish schools at their own expense and to offer religious instruction to those students wishing to participate. At the present time religious teaching is included in the syllabus of all schools. If a priest or pastor is licensed, he may solemnize marriage which thereby receives legal recognition. There is no governmental register for the churches, nor any separate ministry or department of religion. The Minister of Home Affairs has responsibility for all religious matters affecting government.

**INTERDENOMINATIONAL ORGANIZATIONS.** The Christian Council of Botswana (CCB) was formed in 1966. Seven churches are full members, including Catholics, and 4 others have observer status. It is now an associate council of the World Council of Churches.

The council carries on a significant programme in urban and rural development through its service committee and urban-industrial mission. Another smaller ecumenical body, with 4 members some of whom also belong to the CCB, is the Evangelical Fellowship of Botswana. Further, Lutherans and Catholics sponsor a joint training programme in local crafts.

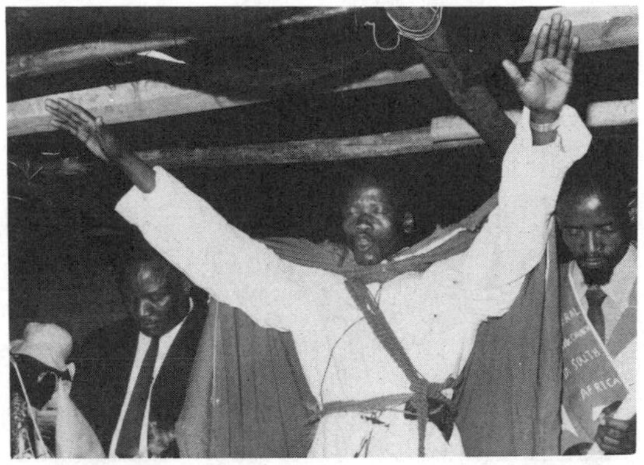
**African indigenous churches.** Service of thanksgiving for religious freedom held by some of the 60 indigenous denominations in Botswana. On left, Botswana minister of local government.

**BROADCASTING.** The state Radio Botswana accepts both Protestant and Catholic regular programmes, all locally produced in Setswana and English. In 1970 the time given to Protestant programming was 26 minutes from Monday to Saturday and one hour 16 minutes on Sundays. For Catholics, Botswana is registered as a member of UNDA.

## BIBLIOGRAPHY


'Bushmen of the Kalahari', E. M. Thomas. *National Geographic magazine*, June 1963, 866–888.

'Farm Bushmen and Mission Bushmen: socio-cultural change in a setting of conflict and pluralism of the San of the Ghanzi District, Republic of Botswana', M. G. Guenther. Dissertation, University of Toronto, 1973.

*Great Lion of Bechuanaland: the life and times of Roger Price, missionary*. E. W. Smith. London: Independent Press, 1957.

*Missionary labours*. R. Moffat. Original edition 1842, many editions including New York 1966.

*Robert Moffat: pioneer in Africa*. C. Northcott. New York: Harper & Row, 1961.


TABLE 2. ORGANIZED CHURCHES AND DENOMINATIONS IN BOTSWANA

| Official name 1 | Begun 2 | Type 3 | Counc 4 | Congs 5 | Adults 6 | Affiliated 7 | Names, notes, and other statistics (see Codebook) 8 |
|---|---|---|---|---|---|---|---|
| African Apost Ch of Johane Maranke | c1960 | I peA | x.... | | 2,000 | 4,000 | *AACJM. VaPostori (Apostles)*. Shona immigrants tinkers from Zimbabwe. |
| African Gospel Church | c1960 | I pen | ..... | | 434 | 1,000 | Schism ex Full Gospel Ch of God(HQ SAfrica). Zulu, Xhosa immigrants; also Tswana. |
| African Methodist Episcopal Church | | I Met | Vw..W | | 190 | 500 | *AMEC*. In 18th Episcopal District, AMEC(USA,SAfrica). USA Black bishop. |
| Anglican Church: D Botswana | 1899 | A Hig | AwaVW | 60 | 2,075 | 7,000 | In CPCA (D 1972). 50% Ngwato, 30% Kwena, 20% White. 5n,2x,1H,3h,P=8%,35Y,130y. |
| Assemblies of God in Botswana | 1963 | P Pe2 | ZFG.a | 28 | 1,023 | 2,000 | Classical Pentecostals. M=AoG(USA). Gaborone, Francistown. 6n,4f,1s(10) |
| **Catholic Church: D Gaborone** | 1880 | R Lat | P.SSW | 10 | 12,300 | 21,202 | First mission 1895. M=CP. C=1+0+3. 2n,21x,2m,33w,P=41%,660Y,1003y,1887z. |
| Christian Brethren | 1968 | P CBr | x.... | 1 | 100 | 200 | *Plymouth Brethren (Open)*. M=CMML(UK). Small group with South Africa links. 2f,1h, |
| Church of God in Christ, Botswana | c1960 | I pe3 | Z...W | 7 | 999 | 1,500 | M=CoGiC(USA Black pentecostals). 2 African bishops (Lobatse, Francistown). 6n. |
| Dutch Reformed Church in Africa | 1869 | P Ref | F.G.a | 10 | 2,000 | 3,000 | M=DRC(SA). Members Black, all Kgatla tribe. HQ Mochudi. 5n,1m,1H,4h. |
| Dutch Reformed Church (Mother Ch) | c1830 | P Ref | F.... | | 1,000 | 2,000 | *NGK. Nederduitse Gereformeerde Kerk (Moederkerk)*. White Afrikaners. |
| Ev Luth Ch in SA (Western Diocese) | 1857 | P Lut | L...W | 6 | 3,000 | 4,433 | *Kereke ya Luthere ya Efangele, Afrika kwa Borwa*. M=HM(Germany). 3n,4m,1H,4h. |
| Full Gospel Ch of God in Southern A | 1968 | P Pe3 | ZF... | 7 | 700 | 1,500 | In rapidly-expanding FGCoGSA. M=CoG(Cleveland)(USA). Holiness Pentecostals. Mochudi. |
| Greek Orthodox Church | | O Gre | Cw... | 1 | 30 | 50 | In D Ioannopolis (Johannesburg), under Patriarchate of Alexandria (Egypt). Greeks. |
| Herero Church | c1960 | I Lut | ..... | | 500 | 1,000 | *Oruuano (Community)*. Mainly immigrant Hereros from Namibia. Several factions. |
| Holiness Union Church of Botswana | c1960 | P Hol | x.G.G | | 300 | 500 | M=Swedish Holiness Union Mission, Swedish Zulu Mission(SAfrica). Begun by immigrant Zulus. |
| Jehovah's Witnesses | c1945 | M Jeh | x.... | 4 | 181 | 500 | *Watch Tower. IBSA*. Active witnessing under way by 1949. 7Y. |
| Methodist Church of South Africa | 1822 | P Met | Vwa.W | | 3,000 | 5,000 | *Botswana Circuit*, Mafeking District, MCSA(SA). In south. Rolong tribe. 2n. |
| Methodist Church, Rhodesia Synod | 1969 | P Met | Vwa.. | | 2,000 | 4,000 | In Plumtree District, Rhodesia Synod, Methodist Ch. White circuit in north. |
| Religious Society of Friends | 1948 | P Qua | Q.... | 1 | 30 | 50 | In Southern Africa YM. M=FSC(UK). 1964–70 in Trinity Ch, Gaborone. 1f. |
| St John's Apost Faith Mission of SA | 1960 | I pen | x.I.. | 8 | 164 | 500 | Branches of indigenous church in South Africa. In Mochudi, Maun, Rasesa. |
| St Paul's Apostolic Faith Mission | 1959 | I pen | ..... | 5 | 200 | 500 | One of many healing bodies. In Serowe, Sikwane, Mochudi, Francistown. |
| St Peter's Apostolic Faith Healing Ch | 1952 | I pen | ..... | 5 | 1,000 | 2,000 | Schism ex St John's Apostolic Faith Mission of SA. HQ Mahalapye. 5Y. |
| Seventh-day Adventist Church | 1921 | P Adv | x...w | 20 | 1,486 | 2,000 | *Botswana Field*. Zambezi Union. 53% Tswana, 47% Lozi. 13nx,1H,6h,93t(6026),547Y. |
| Southern Baptist Mission | 1968 | P Bap | T.G.G | 1 | 37 | 150 | M=Southern Baptist Convention(USA). Francistown. Dental clinic. 8f,8Y. |
| Spiritual Healing Church | c1950 | I pen | ..... | | 3,296 | 5,000 | Begun by, and linked with, MBBRC(Lesotho). Tswana. Bishop and branch in Namibia. |
| Trinity Church, Gaborone | 1964 | P com | ....w | 1 | 600 | 1,000 | Union congregation (Angl,Presb,Congr,Meth), linked to UCCSA. 90% African. |
| United Apostolic Faith Church | 1952 | P Pe2 | x...w | 2 | 500 | 1,000 | M=UAFC(UK). British-Israelite Pentecostals; widespread missions, HQ Pretoria(SA). |
| **United Congr Ch of Southern Africa** | 1816 | P Con | Rwa.W | 190 | 12,045 | 60,000 | *UCCSA Botswana Region*. M=CWM,UCBWM,UMC. 29% Ngwato. 8n,7x,24m,2H,14h,3000Yy. |
| Zion Christian Church of South Africa | 1944 | I pen | x.... | 6 | 500 | 1,000 | Part of ZCC (Lekganyane) in SA. In Mochudi, Maun, Serowe. |
| Other African indigenous churches | | I | ..... | | 7,500 | 15,000 | Total over 50 (see list below), rapidly spreading. |
| Other Protestant denominations | | P | ..... | | 3,000 | 7,000 | Total over 10 (see list below) . |
| **Total affiliated (mid-1970)** | | | | **870** | **61,190** | **154,585** | **Total denominations (1970) . . . 89.** |
| **Total affiliated (mid-1975)** | | | | **970** | **73,800** | **186,505** | **Total denominations (1975) . . . 104.** |
| **Total affiliated (mid-1980)** | | | | **1,100** | **91,300** | **230,660** | **Total denominations (1980) . . . 120.** |

NOTES ON TABLE ABOVE

COLUMNS: for meanings and CODES (cols. 1, 3, 4, 8): see Codebook (Part 6). Column 1: **Boldface type** = church with over 10% of country's affiliated Christians.

NATIONAL COUNCILS (Column 4, 5th letter).

a = member of both CCB and EFB.

G = Evangelical Fellowship of Botswana (EFB) (includes 4 smaller churches: see below).

W = Christian Council of Botswana (Lekgotla la Sekeresete la Botswana) This council is a member of the All Africa Conference of Churches, though none of its member churches are directly.

w = associated observer member of CCB.

*Other national councils*. Botswana Association of Inter-Spiritual Churches (1973 applied to WCC for associate council status; 20 member churches).

*Local councils*. In Francistown and Lobatse.

OTHER AFRICAN INDIGENOUS CHURCHES. Many are branches of bodies centred in the republic of South Africa, with immigrant Shona bodies from Zimbabwe and immigrant Herero bodies from Namibia, but there is also a growing number of zionist and other congregations indigenous to Botswana. These include (with in parentheses date of founding in Botswana, and present headquarters): African Mission Society Ch (member of CCB), Apostolic Ch of Johane Masowe (Shona immigrants), Apostolic Diphapha Ch-in-Zion (1959, Mosung Village, Serowe), Apostolic Sprititual Healing Ch (1969, Gaborone, Mochudi), Bakwena Lutheran Ch, Faith Healing Ch (1966, Francistown, Gaborone), Galatia Apostolic Ch (1961, Serowe, 2 churches), Holy Sarda Apostolic Christian Ch (1961, Serowe), Morians Episcopal Apostolic Ch in Zion (1954, Serowe), National Ch of God in Christ (1960, Mahalapye), Nazirite Baptist Ch (Shembe) (from Zululand), New Apostolic-in-Zion Ch (1966, Tonota), Protestant Unity Ch (Hereros from Namibia), Revelation Healing Ch (1965, Mahalapye), St Apostolic Ch in South Africa (1957, Basimane-Serowe), St Matthew's Apostolic Faith Mission (1958), Serowe), St Philip's Healing Ch (Francistown), Spiritual Apostle Faith Healing Ch (1950, Serowe), United Pentecostal Ch of God in Christ (Molepolole), 11 Apostolic Healing Spirit Ch (1963, Maun), 17 Apostolic Spiritual Healing Ch (1950, Maun).

OTHER PROTESTANT DENOMINATIONS. These include: Apostolic Faith Mission (observer member of EFB), Ch of God of Prophecy (1967), Pentecostal Holiness Ch (member of EFB), Pentecostal Protestant Ch (member of EFB), and other bodies from South Africa.

**PEOPLES** (ethnolinguistic). Christians: 70% Tswana (Ngwato, Kwena, Ngwaketse, Tawana, Kgatla, Malete, Rolong, Tlokwa), 13% Kalanga, 2% Ndebele, 2% Lozi, 2% Herero, 2% Pedi, 2% Xhosa, 2% Koba (Yeye), 1% Sotho, 1% Shona, 1% European (White), 1% Coloured, 1% Bushman, Zulu, Kgalagadi.

COUNTRY-WIDE TOTALS

EVANGELIZATION (see Part 5). 1900: 9%. 1970: 95%. 1980: 98%. *Radiophonic evangelism*. TWR, RVOG (until 1977), ICI (134 active students).

FOREIGN MISSIONARIES AND PERSONNEL (nationals serving abroad) (1973). Total: about 10 Protestants and 5 African indigenous in South Africa and Rhodesia.

FOREIGN MISSIONARIES AND PERSONNEL (aliens from abroad) (1973). Total 237. *From Western world*. 142: 93 Protestants (67 in 9 USA societies, 18 in 3 UK societies, 7 in 1 Sweden society, 1 in 1 Finland society), 47 Roman Catholics, 2 Anglicans in 1 USA society. *From Third World*. 95: about 40 African indigenous from South Africa, 35 Protestants in 8 South Africa societies, about 15 Roman Catholics (10 from South Africa), 5 Anglicans from South Africa (2 Black, 1 Coloured).

INSTITUTIONS (church-operated) (1973). Total 50, including

4 higher schools, 40 medical centres (6 hospitals), 2 religious communities, 1 seminary (Protestant),
PERIODICALS. About 20 titles.
PERSONNEL. About 366 (129 national, 237 foreign).
RELIGIOUS LIBRARIES. 5.
SCRIPTURE DISTRIBUTION (1975: all varieties). Annual totals: 5,100 Bibles (98% subsidized, 2% commercial), 8,000 NTs (subsidized), 10,000 UBS portions, 5,000 UBS selections. *Translations completed.* 1 language, Setswana: portion 1942, NT 1957, Bible 1970.
SERVICE AGENCIES. About 25, including CCB, CWS, EFB, MCC, SACBC, SU, WLC(EHC), YWCA.

**ADDITIONAL DATA ON CHURCHES**
ANGLICAN CHURCH: D BOTSWANA. In the Church of the Province of Central Africa. *Growth.* By 1978 there were 10 parishes, 20 priests, 4 sisters and 33 lay leaders.
CATHOLIC CHURCH. The diocese (PA in 1959, D in 1966) is a suffragan see of M Bloemfontein (South Africa). Mainly desert. *Catholics.* 22% Malete (work begun in 1935), 14% Ngwato, 14% Kwena, 11% Ngwaketse, 10% Kgatla, 10% Rolong, 7% Tlokwa, 2% Tawana. Also, in 1970, 379 Catholics were Europeans and 408 Coloured. *Catechumens.* (1959) 412; (1961) 651; (1963), 1,427; (1970) 1,887. *Annual baptisms.* (1972) 55.8% infant, 44.2% adult. *Priests.* Irish Passionists. *Brothers.* No Africans. *Sisters.* 9 African, 24 European. *Catechists.* Total 29. *Indigenous religious congregations.* Calvary Sisters (begun 1967: 9 in 1970), Handmaids of the Sacred Passion. *Foreign religious congregations.* Priests: CP. Sisters: Sisters of the Cross and Passion. *Catholic organizations.* The diocese is a member of the Southern Africa Catholic Bishops' Conference (SACBC), itself a member of SECAM. There is no national presbyteral nor pastoral council, but religious personnel have representation in the Conference of Clerical Religious Superiors in Southern Africa, and the Association of Women Religious, both with headquarters in South Africa. The principal lay organizations are Guild of St Ann (200 members), Legion of Mary (150 members) and St Vincent de Paul Society (60 members).
The Holy See has diplomatic relations with Botswana and is represented to government and the Catholic hierarchy by a pro-nuncio based in Pretoria, South Africa.
In 1971 the church sponsored 9 primary and 2 secondary schools with a total enrolment of 4,141 pupils, in addition to maintaining 2 dispensaries and 2 hostels. By 1973 the schools had increased slightly to 9 primary (3,646) and 3 secondary (966).
EVANGELICAL LUTHERAN CHURCH IN SOUTHERN AFRICA. A circuit in the Western Diocese of ELCSA. *Growth.* Increasing rapidly among immigrant Lutherans, to 15,000 by 1977.
UNITED CONGREGATIONAL CHURCH OF SOUTHERN AFRICA. Work was begun by LMS (now CWM) in 1816, now assisted by UFCSM among the Kwena and by UMC (USA) at a school in Maun. Other immigrant mission groups work under UCCSA auspices, including the Rhenish Mission from Namibia following up Herero immigrants (1 Herero pastor, several German nursing sisters, at Sehitwa on Lake Ngami). *Membership.* 29% Ngwato, 29% Ngwaketse, 25% Kwena, 17% Tawana. The number of communicants is very small by comparison with total affiliated members and professing members, and the number of nominal members is very high (see note under Table 1, NOMINAL CHRISTIANS). *Growth.* In the 20th century, communicants have increased very slowly, from 3,634 in 1922, to 5,854 in 1935, and to 11,045 around 1970.

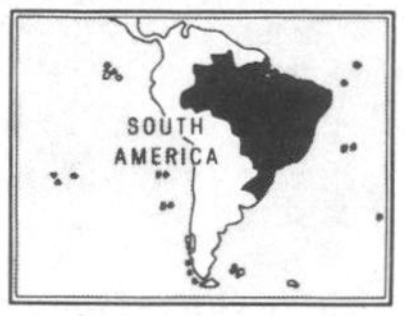


# BRAZIL

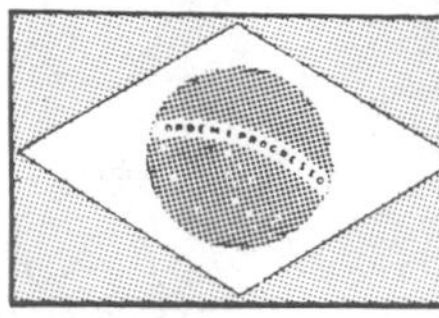

## SECULAR DATA

**STATE. Official name:** The Federative Republic of Brazil (A República Federativa do Brasil). Earlier name: before 1969, United States of Brazil. Adjective of nationality: Brazilian.
**Flag** (shown above right): Green field, centred yellow diamond with blue globe, 22 stars and motto.
**Area:** 8,511,965 sq.km. (3,286,490 sq.miles). Agricultural land: 23.8%.
**Government:** Republic under military rule, since 1964 (1500 Portuguese rule, 1822 Independence as empire, 1889 United States of Brazil, 1964 military junta).
**Legislature:** National Congress: Senate, 66 members; Chamber of Deputies, 310 members.
**Official language:** Portuguese (*Português*).
**Chief cities:** capital Brasília 500,000 (1970), São Paulo 5,869,970, Rio de Janeiro 4,252,000, Belo Horizonte 1,228,300, Recife 1,046,450, Salvador 1,005,220.
**Political divisions:** 22 States, 4 Federal Territories, 1 Federal District.
**Armed forces** (1976): Total 257,200 regular (121,000 conscripts): army 170,000, navy 45,800, air force 41,400 (169 combat aircraft). Paramilitary forces: 250,000.

**DEMOGRAPHY. Population:** 92,341,556 (census of 1.IX.1970. For 1970–2000 (UN), see last row of Table 1). Population density (1975): 13/sq.km. (33/sq.mile). Under 15 years: 43%. Growth rate (1975–80): 2.83% per year (births 3.60%, deaths –0.78%). Life expectancy (1975–80): 63.6 years. Household size: 4.8 persons.
**Major languages:** Portuguese, German, French, English, Italian, Spanish, Japanese, Russian, Arabic, Polish, Chinese, and over 150 smaller languages.
**Urban dwellers** (1970): 56.5%. Urban growth rate (1950–70): 5.2% per year.
**Labour force:** 32%.
**Refugees** (1977): 200,000 from Portugal and Angola.
**Tourists** (1974): 480,267.

**ETHNOLINGUISTIC GROUPS:** 53.0% Brazilian White (15% Portuguese/11% Italian/10% Spanish/3% German), 22.0% Mulatto (White/Negro), 12.0% Mestiço (Mestizo) (Caboclo: White/Amerindian), 11.0% Black (Preto: full-blooded Negro), 0.8% Japanese, 0.4% Portuguese, 0.2% Jewish, 0.1% jungle Amerindian (130,000 in 140 tribes) (0.1% Tupi-Guarani), 0.1% Italian (129,000), 0.1% Spaniard (116,000), 0.1% Russian (70,000), 0.1% Arab (Palestinian, Lebanese, Syrian), 0.1% Polish, Chinese (45,000) (Mandarin, Hakka, Cantonese, Amoy), German (41,000), Armenian (15,000), Ukrainian (15,000), USA White (12,000), Hungarian (10,000), Korean (10,000), Romanian (9,600), Yugoslav (9,400), French (8,000), Greek (4,900), Dutch (4,800), British (3,900), Slovak, Cafuso (Negro/Amerindian), Basque, Turkish, Gypsy, et alii. Total aliens (1970): 1,082,745.

**MONEY** (1977). **Monetary unit:** cruzeiro (= 100 centavos); US$1 = CRS 12.28.
**National income per person:** US$850. Average annual family income: US$4,080.
**Inflation:** (1970–74) 19.1% per year, (1975) 30% per year (consumer price index 641).
**Cost of living in capital** (1976): index 108 (Washington DC = 100). Daily cost of living: US$46.

**EDUCATION.** Adult literacy: (1950) 49%, (1970) 66%. Education rate: 43%. Schools: 188,009 (165,051 primary). Universities 54.

**HEALTH.** Hospitals: 4,067 (367,522 beds). Doctors: 46,051. Lepers: 182,000 (1.7 per 1,000). Blind: 60,700. Psychotics: 770,000.

**LITERATURE.** Annual new book titles (1973): 8,960. Periodicals: 2,000. Scientific journals: 650. Newspapers: 261 dailies, 730 non-daily.

**COMMUNICATION** (per 1,000 people). Phones: 24. Radios: 61. TV sets: 67. Daily newspaper circulation: 37 copies.

**TABLE 1. RELIGIOUS ADHERENTS IN BRAZIL**

| Year | 1900 | | mid-1970 | | Annual change, 1970–1980 | | | | mid-1975 | | mid-1980 | | 2000 | |
|---|---|---|---|---|---|---|---|---|---|---|---|---|---|---|
| *Name* | *Adherents* | *%* | *Adherents* | *%* | *Natural* | *Conversion* | *Total* | *Rate* | *Adherents* | *%* | *Adherents* | *%* | *Adherents* | *%* |
| **Christians** | **17,319,000** | **96.3** | **90,864,000** | **95.4** | **2,952,784** | **–153,584** | **2,799,200** | **2.69** | **103,899,000** | **94.7** | **118,856,000** | **94.0** | **193,708,000** | **91.2** |
| professing | 17,319,000 | 96.3 | 90,864,000 | 95.4 | 2,952,784 | –153,584 | 2,799,200 | 2.69 | 103,899.000 | 94.7 | 118,856,000 | 94.0 | 193,708,000 | 91.2 |
| Roman Catholics | 17,146,900 | 95.3 | 85,904,000 | 90.2 | 2,772,830 | –270,230 | 2,502,600 | 2.56 | 97,567,000 | 88.9 | 110,930,000 | 87.8 | 176,105,000 | 82.9 |
| Spiritist Catholics | 2,010,000 | 11.2 | 13,000,000 | 13.7 | 458,410 | 225,890 | 684,300 | 4.24 | 16,130,000 | 14.7 | 19,843,000 | 15.7 | 40,376,000 | 19.0 |
| Evangelical Catholics | 34,200 | 0.2 | 7,676,401 | 8.1 | 264,710 | 106,100 | 370,810 | 3.98 | 9,314,300 | 8.5 | 11,384,500 | 9.0 | 24,490,000 | 11.5 |
| Protestants | 170,000 | 0.9 | 3,200,000 | 3.4 | 115,384 | 70,216 | 185,600 | 4.57 | 4,060,000 | 3.7 | 5,056,000 | 4.0 | 11,050,000 | 5.2 |
| Brazilian indigenous | 0 | 0.0 | 1,600,000 | 1.7 | 59,255 | 46,145 | 105,400 | 5.06 | 2,085,000 | 1.9 | 2,654,000 | 2.1 | 6,163,000 | 2.9 |
| Orthodox | 2,000 | 0.0 | 100,000 | 0.1 | 3,972 | 3 | 3,300 | 2.84 | 116,000 | 0.1 | 133,000 | 0.1 | 240,000 | 0.1 |
| Marginal Protestants | 0 | 0.0 | 40,000 | 0.0 | 1,364 | 236 | 1,600 | 3.33 | 48,000 | 0.0 | 56,000 | 0.0 | 100,000 | 0.0 |
| Anglicans | 100 | 0.0 | 20,000 | 0.0 | 654 | 46 | 700 | 3.04 | 23,000 | 0.0 | 27,000 | 0.0 | 50,000 | 0.0 |
| affiliated | 17,319,000 | 96.3 | 90,864,000 | 95.4 | 2,952,784 | –153,584 | 2,799,200 | 2.69 | 103,899,000 | 94.7 | 118,856,000 | 94.0 | 193,708,000 | 91.2 |
| doubly-affiliated | –87,300 | –0.5 | –9,144,236 | –9.6 | –314,976 | –110,301 | –425,277 | 3.84 | –11,083,000 | –10.1 | –13,397,000 | –10.6 | –25,501,000 | –12.0 |
| total practising | 13,855,200 | *80* | 56,335,680 | *62* | 1,801,198 | –303,408 | 1,497,790 | 2.36 | 63,378,390 | *61* | 71,313,600 | *60* | 125,910,000 | *65* |
| non-practising | 3,463,800 | *20* | 34,528,320 | *38* | 1,151,586 | 149,824 | 1,301,410 | 3.21 | 40,520,610 | *39* | 47,542,400 | *40* | 67,798,000 | *35* |
| Roman Catholics | 17,200,000 | 95.6 | 87,287,835 | 91.7 | 2,820,255 | –266,488 | 2,553,767 | 2.57 | 99,235,700 | 90.4 | 112,825,500 | 89.3 | 176,936,000 | 83.3 |
| Catholic pentecostals | 0 | 0.0 | 5,000 | 0.0 | 1,705 | 47,795 | 49,500 | 82.50 | 60,000 | 0.1 | 500,000 | 0.4 | 7,000,000 | 3.3 |
| Protestants | 200,000 | 1.1 | 7,277,790 | 7.6 | 255,718 | 128,723 | 384,441 | 4.27 | 8,997,900 | 8.2 | 11,122,200 | 8.8 | 23,801,000 | 11.2 |
| Evangelicals | 180,000 | 1.0 | 5,998,000 | 6.3 | 218,292 | 155,108 | 373,400 | 4.86 | 7,681,000 | 7.0 | 9,732,000 | 7.7 | 22,313,000 | 10.5 |
| Neo-pentecostals | 0 | 0.0 | 50,000 | 0.1 | 5,684 | 24,316 | 30,000 | 15.00 | 200,000 | 0.2 | 350,000 | 0.3 | 1,000,000 | 0.5 |
| Brazilian indigenous | 3,000 | 0.0 | 4,951,000 | 5.2 | 174,750 | 88,480 | 263,230 | 4.28 | 6,148,900 | 5.6 | 7,583,300 | 6.0 | 17,002,000 | 8.0 |
| Marginal Protestants | 1,000 | 0.0 | 262,611 | 0.3 | 9,379 | 5,360 | 14,739 | 4.47 | 330,000 | 0.3 | 410,000 | 0.3 | 950,000 | 0.4 |
| Orthodox | 2,000 | 0.0 | 134,000 | 0.1 | 4,433 | 167 | 4,600 | 2.95 | 156,000 | 0.1 | 180,000 | 0.1 | 300,000 | 0.1 |
| Catholics (non-Roman) | 0 | 0.0 | 50,000 | 0.1 | 1,705 | 295 | 2,000 | 3.33 | 60,000 | 0.1 | 70,000 | 0.1 | 120,000 | 0.1 |
| Anglicans | 300 | 0.0 | 45,000 | 0.0 | 1,520 | 180 | 1,700 | 3.18 | 53,500 | 0.0 | 62,000 | 0.0 | 100,000 | 0.0 |
| Afro-American spiritists | 97,000 | 0.5 | 1,300,000 | 1.4 | 53,003 | 69,797 | 122,800 | 6.58 | 1,865,000 | 1.7 | 2,528,000 | 2.0 | 6,375,000 | 3.0 |
| Spiritists | 40,000 | 0.2 | 1,200,000 | 1.3 | 46,779 | 48,121 | 94,900 | 5.77 | 1,646,000 | 1.5 | 2,149,000 | 1.7 | 5,313,000 | 2.5 |
| Non-religious | 10,000 | 0.1 | 772,000 | 0.8 | 28,050 | 20,750 | 48,800 | 4.90 | 987,000 | 0.9 | 1,260,000 | 1.0 | 3,990,000 | 1.9 |
| Buddhists | 1,000 | 0.0 | 310,000 | 0.3 | 9,947 | –1,947 | 8,000 | 2.28 | 350,000 | 0.3 | 390,000 | 0.3 | 500,000 | 0.2 |
| Atheists | 1,000 | 0.0 | 200,000 | 0.2 | 9,947 | 20,553 | 30,500 | 8.71 | 350,000 | 0.3 | 505,000 | 0.4 | 1,275,000 | 0.6 |
| New-Religionists | 0 | 0.0 | 160,000 | 0.2 | 5,968 | 3,032 | 9,000 | 4.29 | 210,000 | 0.2 | 250,000 | 0.2 | 650,000 | 0.3 |
| Jews | 5,000 | 0.0 | 155,000 | 0.2 | 5,087 | 13 | 5,100 | 2.85 | 179,000 | 0.2 | 206,000 | 0.2 | 346,000 | 0.2 |
| Tribal religionists | 500,000 | 2.8 | 100,000 | 0.1 | 2,274 | –6,274 | –4,000 | –5.00 | 80,000 | 0.1 | 60,000 | 0.0 | 30,000 | 0.0 |
| Muslims | 10,000 | 0.1 | 90,000 | 0.1 | 2,984 | 16 | 3,000 | 2.86 | 105,000 | 0.1 | 120,000 | 0.1 | 210,000 | 0.1 |
| Chinese folk-religionists | 0 | 0.0 | 30,000 | 0.0 | 909 | –509 | 400 | 1.25 | 32,000 | 0.0 | 34,000 | 0.0 | 40,000 | 0.0 |
| Baha'is | 0 | 0.0 | 13,000 | 0.0 | 441 | 59 | 500 | 3.23 | 15,500 | 0.0 | 18,000 | 0.0 | 40,000 | 0.0 |
| Hindus | 0 | 0.0 | 5,000 | 0.0 | 156 | –56 | 100 | 1.82 | 5,500 | 0.0 | 6,000 | 0.0 | 10,000 | 0.0 |
| Other religionists | 1,000 | 0.1 | 5,000 | 0.0 | 171 | 29 | 200 | 3.33 | 6,000 | 0.0 | 7,000 | 0.0 | 20,000 | 0.0 |
| **Country's population** | **17,984,000** | **100.0** | **95,204,000** | **100.0** | **3,118,500** | **0** | **3,118,500** | **2.84** | **109,730,000** | **100.0** | **126,389,000** | **100.0** | **212,507,000** | **100.0** |

COLUMNS, ROWS. For meanings and definitions, see Codebook (Part 6). Note that, by definition, total 'Christians' = professing + crypto-Christians, which also = affiliated + nominal Christians. Percentages may not always total exactly, due to rounding.
CENSUSES. **31.XII.1890** (excluding jungle Indians): 98.9% Roman Catholics (14,179,615 persons), 1.0% Evangelicals (143,743 persons), 7,257 non-religious, 1,327 positivists, 1,673 Orthodox, 300 Muslims. The religion question has been asked during several subsequent national population censuses, as follows. **1940:** 95.0% Roman Catholics, 2.6% Evangelicals (1,074,857 persons), 1.1% spiritists, 0.4% non-religious. **1.VII.1950** (excluding jungle Indians): 93.7% Roman Catholics, 3.4% Evangelicals (1,741,430 persons), 1.6% spiritists, 0.5% non-religious, 0.3% Buddhists, 0.1% Orthodox, 0.1% Jews, 0.3% other religionists. **1.IX.1970:** 91.8% Roman Catholics (including some spiritists), 5.2% Evangelicals (Protestants, Anglicans, marginal Protestants and Brazilian indigenous) (4,814,728 persons), 1.3% spiritists, 1.0% other religionists (including some classified in this survey as Brazilian indigenous), 0.8% non-religious. For many years, also, *Anuário estatístico do Brasil* has published statistics, but of affiliated Christians, i.e. Catholic and Evangelical communicant members gathered direct from municipios and counties, and thence from local churches, but not from church headquarters. Usually these compilations have omitted 10–30% of all Evangelical congregations. For 1933 this government publication listed 149,645 affiliated baptized Evangelical members in 730 local churches, with 13,486 annual baptisms.

**NOTES ON RELIGIONS**
AFFILIATED PROTESTANTS. In addition to communicants and their families, there are large numbers of adult attenders and adherents who cannot become communicants because of irregular marriages. In addition to Protestants and Evangelical Catholics as indicated above, there is also a large number of professing Roman Catholics sympathetic to Protestantism and committed to attendance in varying degrees. *Pentecostals.* Mostly of Mediterranean origin (Italian, Sicilian (half-Arab), Portuguese), and Mestiço; very few Blacks (Negroes) are Pentecostals.
AFFILIATED ROMAN CATHOLICS. The total claimed by the church in 1970 (derived from Table 2) is somewhat higher than the government census of the same year because of double affiliation (see below).
AFRO-AMERICAN SPIRITISTS. The term here is restricted to non-Catholic and non-Christian followers of Umbanda (White Magic), Quimbanda (Black Magic, or Kimbanda invoking Satan and malevolent spirits), and other Afro-Brazilian syncretistic

religions including Batuque (in the south), Xangô (Shango, of Yoruba origin, in Pernambuco), Nago (of Maranhão), Catimbo (northeast), Pajelanca (in Amazonia), Macumba (a more violent form resembling Vodoun, with animal sacrifices), Candomblé (a form of Macumba in Bahia region, also called Afro-Amerindian fetishism), etc, all of which syncretize African and Amerindian traditional religions and animistic concepts with Catholicism, Kardecism, and oriental elements, and which are usually described collectively as low spiritism. In 1969, 302,952 adults were non-Catholic Umbandistas (*Anuário estatístico do Brasil 1970*), with 2,295 meeting places, 99,787 admissions of new members in 1969, and 53,438 losses of members. Umbanda is not controlled centrally although there is a Confederation of Umbandist Spiritism; it is far more widespread throughout Brazil than Kardecism (high spiritism) and since 1973 has been expanding across Uruguay also. In addition to these non-Christian low spiritists, there are very large numbers of Roman Catholics involved, known as spiritist Catholics (see below). Adherents of low spiritism were, originally, African slaves, later mixed Blacks and Mulattoes, but now include large numbers of mixed blood and also Whites. The influence of these religions on the whole population is growing, and Macumba utilizes daily newspapers and radio/TV programmes. Their extraordinary expansion in the 1960s and 1970s is due to (1) opposition to spiritism within the Catholic Church and to the hierarchy's desire since Vatican II to purify Catholicism, as a result of which vast numbers of low spiritists have realized there can be no future for them in the church and now regard themselves as Catholics no longer; and (2) the influential role of medium religions in assisting rootless persons to adapt to urban mass life.

ATHEISTS. Brazilian Communist Party (PCB) (pro-Soviet), 6,000 members; Communist Party of Brazil (CPB) (pro-Chinese), 1,000 members (all communists proscribed 1947). Membership has declined from 30,000 around 1963. In a 1973 poll (Gallup USA) of youths aged 18–24 years, 1% described themselves as atheists and 8% as having no religious affiliation or interest in religion.

BAHA'IS. Entered before 1921. Recent rapid growth from 16 local spiritual assemblies (1964) to 87 (1973). Mainly in Bahia and northeastern states.

BRAZILIAN INDIGENOUS. In about 185 denominations in 1970 (see Table 2).

BUDDHISTS. Mostly Japanese (30% of all Japanese settlers and new immigrants), also Chinese and Koreans.

CATHOLIC PENTECOSTALS (or, Catholic charismatics). Totals (January 1974): 5,000 involved adults (over 15 years old) in 100 prayer groups; total charismatic community including children, 10,000. From these small beginnings the renewal rapidly mushroomed across the country, involving by 1976 hundreds of priests and sisters and a number of bishops. In a number of dioceses (e.g. PN Santarém), charismatics in 1976 totalled over 1% of all Catholics. By 1977 groups exceeded 500.

COUNTRY'S POPULATION. In the year 1800, 2.6 million (800,000 Whites, 1,800,000 Mulatto and Black slaves); 1860, 8.4 million; 1880, 11.7 million.

DOUBLY-AFFILIATED. The term covers those affiliated to, or claimed by, both the Catholic Church and also a church termed Evangélica by the state (Protestant, Brazilian indigenous, Anglican or marginal Protestant), i.e. baptized Catholics who have recently become Evangelicals or others. Because their statistics represent a duplication, they are shown in the table as a negative quantity (with a minus sign).

EVANGELICAL CATHOLICS. This term (in Portuguese, Católicos Evangélicos) is used here to describe persons who are affiliated to churches termed by the state Evangélica (Protestant, or Brazilian indigenous, or Anglican, or marginal Protestant churches), but who in government censuses are regarded as, or profess to be, Roman Catholic. There is evidence that considerable numbers of individuals stay in this category for a time, particularly as pentecostals, but then after a period lapse back to being nominal Catholics again.

EVANGELICALS. This English term, employed here as used and understood within the churches themselves (not as understood by the state), covers 3 main groupings: (1) Conservative Evangelicals, being all persons affiliated to Protestant denominations which are Conservative Evangelical in theology and emphasis; (2) Conciliar Evangelicals, affiliated to non-Evangelical Protestant denominations usually within the Ecumenical Movement; and (3) Fundamentalists, being all persons affiliated to Protestant denominations of fundamentalist emphasis usually affiliated to the ICCC.

HINDUS. A small number of communities, with a Samadhi Hindu Centre (Centro Hinduista Samadhi) in Rio de Janeiro, also 2 centres and a farm run by ISKCON (Hare Krishna), and others run by Ananda Marga. The Theosophical Society in 1975 had 36 Lodges with 1,319 members.

JEWS. Introduced first by immigrants from Germany and Central Europe, now with communities in Rio, São Paulo, Curitiba, Recife, and Belo Horizonte.

MARGINAL PROTESTANTS. As in most other majority-Catholic, Orthodox, Muslim, atheistic and other non-Christian countries, marginal Protestants recorded in government censuses are considerably fewer than members known to those bodies. Thus in Brazil in 1970, Jehovah's Witnesses as recorded by government numbered 18,700, whereas as recorded by the denomination itself they numbered 72,269 adults or 169,835 total community. Similarly the government census in 1970 recorded 17,650 Mormons, whereas Mormon statistics then enumerated 41,776 members.

MUSLIMS. In 1835 there was an unsuccessful revolt by the Muslim Males sect among African Negroes. Since 1948, many Palestinian, Lebanese, Syrian, Egyptian and other Arabs have immigrated from the Middle East. There were also (in 1970) 1,400 Turks, and Yugoslavs, Pakistanis and others.

NEO-PENTECOSTALS. Charismatics within the non-Pentecostal Protestant denominations (excluding those which have seceded or formed new pentecostal denominations as shown in Table 2 below). The movement began among Baptists in 1958.

NEW-RELIGIONISTS. Japanese adherents and Brazilian converts of Soka Gakkai (centres in São Paulo and Rio de Janeiro in 1969; about 35,000 households or 70,000 adherents in 1971), Seicho no Ie (70,000 in Brazil in 1974), Sekai Kyusei Kyo (Church of World Messianity; 40,000 in Brazil in 1974, 70% being Whites), Tenrikyo, and other syncretistic New Religions from Japan.

OTHER RELIGIONISTS. Adherents of other non-Christian religions and cults, including Japanese Shintoists, Rosicrucians (97 AMORC Lodges and centres, 5 centres of Lectorium Rosicrucianum), et alii.

PRACTISING CHRISTIANS. *Roman Catholics.* Sunday mass attendance: in towns and villages, 60–70%; in country areas, as high or higher although services are sporadic due to shortage of clergy; in urban areas, around 15%, and less than 10% in some cities. For the whole country (which is 55.9% urban, 44.1% rural), this gives an average of 45% for weekly attendance, with in consequence around 60% for annual or Easter practice. For Catholic youths aged 18–24 years, a 1973 poll showed 19% weekly church attenders (Gallup). *Protestants.* Weekly attendance averages 65%, annual 80%. *Brazilian indigenous.* Attendance and practice (as %) are higher than for Catholics or Protestants. *Totals.* Combining these figures, we arrive at the total shown in the table of 56 million annually-practising Christians in 1970.

PROFESSING PROTESTANTS. As in almost all other countries where the Roman Catholic Church is a majority church or the established state church, all government-produced statistics of professing Protestants and other Evangelicals are considerably smaller than those churches themselves report to be affiliated to them. Thus in the 1970 census the government reported all Evangelicals as 5.2% of the population, whereas those churches themselves had an affiliated membership totalling 13.1% of the population in 1970, as shown in the table above.

PROTESTANTS. In the year 1860, there were 25,000 Protestants; in 1900, 200,000 in 13 denominations.

SPIRITIST CATHOLICS. This term is here restricted to Roman Catholics who are actively and regularly involved in the practice of the medium religions, high or low spiritism, mainly Afro-American low spiritists (Umbanda, Macumba, etc), as described above. In fact, however, a much larger proportion of all Catholics (around 30%, or 33 million in 1975) can be said to be affiliated to some degree with organized spiritism, and a large majority of all Catholics (over 60 million) defer to spiritist dogmas and participate from time to time.

SPIRITISTS. This term here, when used by itself alone, is restricted to non-Christian and non-Catholic followers of Kardecism or high spiritism (so named because of its emphasis on science, philosophy and religion). In 1969 there were 633,386 adult Kardecistas (*Anuário estatístico do Brasil 1970*, covering only organized non-Christian groups returning census forms). These high spiritists, excluding non-Christian low spiritists (termed Afro-American spiritists in this survey), in 1969 had 3,076 meeting places, 88,234 new members were admitted in 1969, and 99,170 members were lost in 1969. In the census of 1.IX.1970, the number describing themselves as non-Christian spiritists (high or low) was 1.2 million of all ages including children. However, it is estimated that 30% of the nation's population has been affiliated at one time or another with organized spiritist activities, and 15% (14,280,000) were estimated to be regularly and actively engaged in organized spiritism in 1970. Excluding the self-professed spiritists, the remaining 13 million still call themselves Roman Catholics, although they often refer to themselves as Catholic spiritists or spiritist Catholics. Kardecism began in 1857 and became organized in 1884 as the Spiritist Federation of Brazil (Federação Espírita Brasileira, FEB); by 1958 it had 5,000 associations and a wide network of institutions including 31 hospitals, 77 homes and 435 schools. Reincarnationist dogmas are also spread through the related movement of Rosicrucianism (AMORC, Fraternitas Rosa Crucis, Kabbalistic Order of Rosa Cruz, the Igreja Expectante).

TRIBAL RELIGIONISTS. Jungle or lowland Amerindians, estimated at 2 million in the year 1500, had been reduced by massacres and assimilation to 500,000 in 230 tribes in 1900, to 200,000 in 1964, and in 1972 to 130,000 in only 140 tribes (91 in the Amazon basin, 35 in the centre, 10 in the northeast, 4 in the south); of these in 1972, 36% were considered integrated into national life and 27% were marginally so. Many tribes retain traditional animism and have also produced modern reactionary cults.

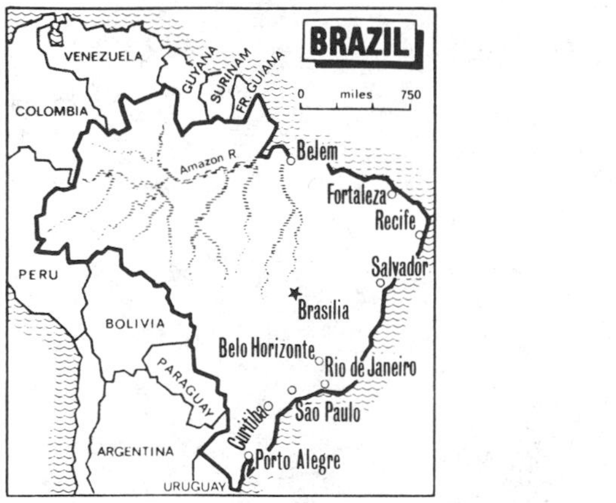


**NON-CHRISTIAN RELIGIONS. Spiritism** is still the principal non-Christian religion in Brazil, and its numerical influence has increased since 1950. The term itself covers 2 distinct kinds of people: non-Christian spiritists, and spiritists who also regard themselves as Roman Catholics. Non-Christian spiritists were 1.8% of the population in 1940, increasing to 2.1% in 1950, then rapidly to 2.7% in 1970. Introduced into Brazil in the middle of the 19th century, the French spiritism of Allan Kardec found a ready response and developed into an organized religion. It absorbed elements of popular Catholicism, in particular devotion to saints and the souls of the dead, as well as specific characteristics of cults of African origin. In addition to those who declare themselves spiritists in censuses, there are numerous others in high positions who regularly or occasionally attend spirit seances but who declare themselves to be Catholics. Not uncommonly the term Catholic spiritists or spiritist Catholics is used to identify them. At present spiritism again may be divided into 2 general categories: a high spiritism *(alto espiritismo)* adhering to Kardecist orthodoxy with a minority of adherents; and secondly, low spiritism, syncretisms of Catholic and African elements including Umbanda with a larger popular following. In its purer form, Kardecism is very active in the social welfare field, developing hospitals, schools, and other social service institutions.

**Afro-American spiritism** is the term used here to describe all forms of low spiritism. Of these the best-known and most active is Umbanda. Under this generic name are included several religious groups derived from the ancient African religions of the Yoruba and Bantu, with a vast number of variations. The product of syncretistic processes still in progress, Umbanda has African, Catholic, Kardecist and oriental elements as well as features from indigenous American Indian religions. The degree to which any of these elements are present in different cults is the basis of their great diversity. Each Umbanda centre is autonomous. Voluntarily created, it recognizes no religious authority, doctrinal or ritual, which accounts for the plurality of its forms. This religious development, appearing within the last 50 years, is remarkable for its growth in adherents who now number over 33 million in Brazil. Similarly to high spiritism, Umbanda sees no contradiction between its own practices and the beliefs of Catholicism. Most of its followers in fact regard themselves as Catholics. Today its members are mostly urban, middle-class, with no racial distinctions. However, occasional members can also be found among the upper classes. Umbanda has resisted a concerted campaign of opposition from the Catholic Church for the past 50 years and today displays great vitality, with centres multiplying throughout the country. There are also several other Afro-Brazilian religions known by different regional names: Candomblé in Bahia, Batuque in Pôrto Alegre, Xangô in Recife and Macumba in Rio de Janeiro; their greatest concentration however is in Bahia. These have all shown a remarkable capacity to adapt traditional African elements to the new conditions of life of modern Brazil.

**Buddhism** was introduced into Brazil by Japanese immigrants. Several temples, pagodas and meditation centres for Buddhism's different denominations are located in the city and province of São Paulo. A Theravada Buddhist Centre (Centro Budista Theravada) was established in Rio de Janeiro in 1968.

**Judaism** was introduced into Brazil by Jewish immigrants from Germany and central Europe as well as by groups from the Near East. Judaism is represented by the Israelite Religious Association (Associação Religiosa Israelita) and councils connected with B'nai B'rith. Jewish communities are found in larger cities including Rio de Janeiro, São Paulo, Curitiba, Belo Horizonte and Recife.

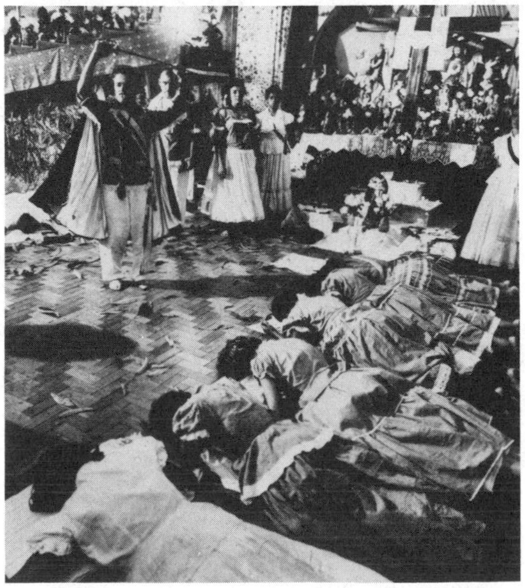

**Afro-American spiritists.** During spiritist service in dishevelled Umbanda temple, girls prostrate themselves before spirit-possessed leader. Note altar, cross, sacred heart of Jesus, and other Christian symbols. Umbanda has some 33 million adherents in Brazil.

**Spiritist Catholics.** A large majority of Brazil's Roman Catholics, over 60 million, defer to spiritist dogmas and from time to time participate in such activities as (above) the Macumba feast of Iemanja, Yoruba goddess of the sea, symbol of fecundity, celebrated on many Brazilian beaches to start the new year, with offerings of flowers, candles et alia.

**Amerindian tribal religions** continue among the indigenous peoples including the Bororo, Nambikuara and Yanomamo. In 1972 the Amerindian population was estimated at 130,000 in 140 tribes, 91 being located in the Amazon basin, 35 in the central region of the country, 10 in the northeast and 4 in the south. Of the total, 35 tribes are considered integrated into the national population, 34 tribes marginally, with the remainder more or less in touch with Whites but still preserving their own traditions. As in other South American countries, Indians have been victims of recent acts of genocide and their numbers are decreasing rapidly. In reaction to this situation a large number of Amerindian nativistic cults and movements have arisen from the 16th century up to the present.

**CHRISTIANITY.** Little resistance was offered by Brazil's Indian tribes when in 1500 Pedro Alvares Cabral claimed the land in the name of Portugal, or later when sugar was introduced, in spite of the fact that large areas of land were allocated to a select number of Portuguese for its production. African slaves were brought in as Brazil became a major world source of sugar in the 17th century and a world supplier of gold and diamonds during the 18th century.

The first organized mission efforts among the Indians began in 1549 when Jesuits were sent to establish schools and churches. During the next century, co-operative Indian villages called reductions were established by the Jesuits in face of opposition by colonists and government. In 1580, 3 additional missionary congregations arrived, followed by 3 congregations of women in 1734 and still later the establishment of the first Brazilian religious congregation. During the first half of the 17th century intermittent warfare took place with the Dutch who were also seeking a foothold on the American continent. The fighting took on religious overtones with the Dutch being Protestants opposing the Catholic religion. Their partial introduction of Protestant worship was completely eliminated, as was true also of an earlier attempt by Huguenots in 1557 to introduce French Calvinism on Villegagnon island.

During the 19th century an increasing number of European immigrants entered Brazil. German Lutherans arrived in 1823 and established the first Protestant church in 1837. American Methodists appeared briefly in 1835 but did not remain. However, they returned again in 1885. The first continuous Protestant mission did not begin until 1855 with the arrival of LMS Scottish Presbyterians. American

Presbyterians entered Brazil in 1859, and by 1888 the Presbyterian Church of Brazil was firmly established. Southern Baptists came in 1881 and in 1907 the Brazilian Baptist Convention was organized. The Anglican Church at first considered that this mission field should be left to Roman Catholics, but American Episcopalians began a mission there in 1889. Seventh-day Adventists came in 1902, and the Assemblies of God opened the first Pentecostal work in 1910. During this period, the Jesuits who had been expelled from Brazil in 1750 returned and new Catholic missions made their appearance. Some governmental reforms and secularization of institutions were initiated as Brazil's economy improved, with the country becoming a major producer of coffee and rubber. During the 1870s the Catholic Church came increasingly under attack. Two bishops were imprisoned and Brazilians were forbidden to enter religious orders. The culmination of this movement was the separation of church and state as part of the inauguration of the republic in 1889. The 20th century has witnessed an extensive development of Catholic seminaries, primary and

Come unto Me : Christ the Redeemer monument (Cristo Redentor no Corcovado), Rio de Janeiro. *Above.* Aerial view with Anglo-French Concorde supersonic airliner. *Below.* The monument at night.

secondary schools, over 40 Brazilian religious congregations, and the appearance of lay religious associations.

**CATHOLIC CHURCH.** While Catholicism continues to be the religion of the majority, its practice is uneven. In small towns Sunday mass attendance ranges from 60% to 70%; in rural areas slightly higher, although the celebration of mass is sporadic due to shortage of priests. In large cities and regions undergoing rapid social change, attendance averages 15%, and sometimes drops to 10%. The Catholicism practised by the majority is a strongly individualistic religion, centred on devotion to saints and ancestral spirits, with the aim of seeking personal protection. For most of the faithful, it is perceived only marginally in relation to the church as an institution. The vast majority remain ignorant of Catholic doctrine. The recognized elements of doctrine in Brazil are derived for the most part from the Council of Trent, namely insistence on participation in the sacraments and persistent anti-Protestantism. Nevertheless, in recent years a new effort at renewal of Christian life has made its appearance, as evidenced by the development of 2 national pastoral plans, the creation of ecclesial basic communities of variable size but localized in rural or poor urban areas, the adoption in 1972 of a 'sister churches' programme whereby dioceses with more resources aid poorer dioceses, and a greater concern for evangelization and social action aimed at humanization.

In terms of structure, the Catholic Church has experienced a rapid growth in the number of juris-

dictions, from 19 in 1900 to 114 in 1950, 154 in 1960, 200 in 1970 and 210 in 1971. The number of parishes increased from 4,455 in 1963 to 5,577 in 1970, with the average number of church members per parish being reduced from 16,775 in 1963 to 16,714 in 1970. Religious clergy administer 37% of all parishes, and more than 100 of the 230 bishops belong to religious orders and congregations. A particularly difficult problem is that of recruitment of new priests and departures from the priesthood by others. By 1974 the total of departures reached 2,000 out of a total of 13,000 priests in Brazil. The Catholic Episcopal Conference (CNBB) would like to retain the services of these secularized priests, giving them specific tasks in pastoralia, which is normally prohibited by the Holy See. In 1973 there were 226 requests for secularization. In 1974 the diocese of São Paulo registered 13 new ordinations and 19 secularizations.

Of special note is the large Japanese community in Brazil, rising to 700,000 by 1975 and to around a million by 1978, of whom some 62% are Christians. There are in fact nearly twice as many Japanese

Catholics in Brazil (630,000 in 1978) as in Japan itself. For these, the CNBB has formed an office for Japan-Brazil Pastoralia (Pastoral Nippo-Brasileira, PANIB), which is served by 318 full-time Japanese priests and religious (33% born in Japan, 67% born in Brazil).

A progressive Catholic minority is active in specialized Catholic Action movements, such as ACO, JOC and JUC, and in the Basic Education Movement at the community level, movements which operate in opposition to a majority of the bishops and which have been nearly destroyed by the military regime

**Igreja Católica no Brasil.** *Above.* Cathedral in Brasília under construction. *Right.* Holy Week procession in Ouro Prêto (Minas Gerais). 1960.

in the 1970s. Chaplains of these movements and priests supporting other allegedly subversive movements have been imprisoned and tortured, as happened to 9 Dominicans of São Paulo imprisoned for participating in the Marighela network in 1969. In contrast, ultra-conservative groups have also been active, such as the Family Rosary Crusade and the Group for the Restoration of the Rosary, which contributed to the success of the Family Marches with God for Liberty which contributed to the fall of the democratic regime in 1964. At present Cursilhos de Cristandade (Christian Study Courses) play a significant role. In 1971 they were introduced into 140 dioceses, mostly in the northeast where are found the most socially militant poor. With their 100,000 cursillistes they form by far the largest and most influential group among Catholic conservatives. By 1972–73, however, its national leadership was being accused of evolving towards Marxism.

PROTESTANT CHURCHES. Protestantism may be classified in 3 categories: (1) traditional mainline denominations owing their origin to the missionary outreach of North American churches beginning in the second half of the 19th century; (2) Pentecostal groups which began with the arrival of the Assemblies of God (USA) in 1910; and (3) Conservative Evangelical bodies from the USA which have proliferated since World War II. Of these three, Pentecostals are the largest and display the greatest growth and vitality. Professing Evangelicals as a whole have increased from 2.6% of the population in 1940 to 5.2% in 1970. In the first category the principal denominations are Baptists, Lutherans, Adventists, Presbyterians and Methodists.

The Brazilian Baptist Convention maintains 30 Bible schools and seminaries and a publishing house which in 1969 produced 200,000 books and 10 million tracts. In addition Brazilians have been sent as missionaries to 4 other countries. A number of other Baptist groups work in Brazil but account for only about 5% of the total Baptist membership. Baptists are second in size only to the Assemblies of God among Protestant denominations, and are one of the fastest growing of the non-Pentecostal churches.

The large Evangelical Church of the Lutheran Confession has its strength among Germans in southern Brazil. It maintains fraternal relations with the American Lutheran Church. A schism in 1890

produced the Lutheran Evangelical Church of Brazil which is related to the Missouri Synod. Seventh-day Adventists have built up a large membership which continues to grow rapidly. Part of their success has been due to their emphasis on radio and correspondence courses. The Presbyterian Church of Brazil's first joint synod was held in 1888, and today two-thirds of its membership is found in the south. In 1903 a schism occurred which resulted in the formation of the Independent Presbyterian Church which is now related to Independent Presbyterians in the USA. Other schisms have produced Conservative Presbyterians in 1940 and Fundamentalist Presbyterians in 1956. Methodists were among the earliest to begin evangelistic outreach in Brazil, but their growth has been slower than that of the other major denominations. The church has been autonomous since 1930. Small Free Methodist and Wesleyan groups also exist.

Although the membership of these churches is large in comparison to other Latin American countries, their growth has not kept pace with the enormous increase in Pentecostalism in recent years. The Pentecostal movement began with the arrival of 2 Swedish ministers from Chicago in 1910. From this early initiative has grown up a complex group of churches, some of which maintain relations with foreign missionary societies while others are completely independent. In the former category are the Assemblies of God which today represent the largest non-Catholic denomination in the country. They have placed emphasis on the training of laymen at large central mother churches, who then go out to plant satellite churches in surrounding areas. In contrast to the historical denominations which have concentrated their attention on the south, the Assemblies of God are found in every state and actually have their greatest membership in the north and northeast.

Many Conservative Evangelical faith missions are now at work in Brazil, a large number of which have

made their appearance since World War II. Most are small with leadership concentrated largely in the hands of foreign missionaries. Several are working exclusively with unevangelized Indian tribes in the interior.

INDIGENOUS CHURCHES. Except for the Brazilian Catholic Apostolic Church which was a schism from Catholicism in 1945 by the former Catholic bishop of Botucatu, the major independent churches are pentecostal in nature. The most important are the Christian Congregation of Brazil which originated in 1910 among Italian immigrants and now is widely spread in the states of São Paulo and Paraná; and the Evangelical Pentecostal Church 'Brazil for Christ', which emerged out of the Assemblies of God in 1955. Most independent pentecostal churches have been formed since 1945.

**CHURCH AND STATE.** Though church and state are separate in law, the state still regards itself as religious, and the constitution of 1967 was promulgated by the National Congress 'invoking the protection of God'. In the introduction it guarantees liberty of conscience and the free exercise of religious worship, on condition that these are not contrary to public order or good morals (Article 150.4). It condemns all interference with personal conscience (Article 150.6) and authorizes religious assistance to armed forces and auxiliary services on condition

that this be offered by Brazilians (Article 150.7). Religious marriage has the same validity as civil marriage if the celebrant or an interested party requests it and on condition that the act be reported to the public registrar. Even if a preliminary request is not made, a religious marriage that has already taken place is equated with a civil marriage if the spouses request it and report the same to a public registrar (Article 167.2, 3).

Until 1889 Brazil was under a regime in which the state and the Catholic Church were united. The proclamation of the republic created a juridical

**Assembleias de Deus.** *Above.* Worship in central church in Madureira, Rio. *Below.* Altar service for baptism in the Holy Spirit during a crusade.

separation which however only gradually brought about an alteration in relations between the two, particularly between the Catholic hierarchy and government leaders. The traditional connection between church and state was re-established in the 1934 constitution but was severed again in 1946. It has only been during the last decade or so that the two have begun to diverge, particularly regarding the social sphere and more recently in relation to individual and public liberties.

In 1963 the episcopate officially pronounced itself in favour of social change and supported the left-of-centre basic reforms of the government. The military coup d'etat of 1964, however, provoked a return to the traditional conservative position on the part of the majority of the bishops. The episcopate for the most part recognized the legitimacy of the new regime on 29 May 1964, which placed the bishops in opposition to the progressive lay minorities in Catholic Action, the Basic Education Movement and the rural trade unions begun in the northeast after 1960. It was not until 1967–68 that the bishops ceased to be silent concerning the increasing number of arrests of priests and Christian militants. Many of the latter had in the meantime left the church and joined the ranks of the Marxists.

The dictatorial regime, made official in December 1968 with the promulgation of Institutional Act No 5, caused the bishops to request the government to begin the work of re-establishing democracy in Brazil. However, the episcopate waited until May 1970 before protesting against violation of human rights such as systematic torture for political prisoners and summary executions by the police 'Death Squadron' (Esquadrão da Morte).

There is no serious conflict between church and state at the constitutional or juridical level. Opposition is rather confined to individuals or groups of Catholics disturbed by the economic situation and present government policies.

A critical study made in 1968 of the Superior Military Academy, from which the highest military

personnel have come since 1964, irritated the regime, and opposition to government by archbishop Helder Câmara of Recife and the bishops of Santo André, Volta Reconda, Crateús and 20 others, provoked a violent repression by the military authorities. In June 1971 the secretary of the episcopate denounced the inequalities produced by the country's rapid economic expansion, and the bishop of São Félix attacked the attitude of the wealthy towards the peasant masses of Mato Grosso. In July 1973 the latter bishop was placed under house arrest along with several of his staff for having come to the defence of P. Jentel, a French priest of his prelature imprisoned for his action on behalf of small-holder peasants of his area. Sentenced on 28 May 1973 to a 10-year prison term, Jentel was released after a year. A survey of the first decade of the military regime in Brazil reveals that more than 500 priests have been victims of a form of repression (imprisonment, torture, expulsion) and that thousands of lay militants of Catholic movements have suffered the same or an even more serious fate.

Nevertheless, the dominant note in church-state relations continues to be a desire for harmony and collaboration made possible by the systematic representation of the Catholic Church at official functions to the virtual exclusion of all other churches. Given this situation, 3 documents are of significance in the disagreement between the two: (1) a manifesto of Catholic Action published in May 1967 under the title 'Development without Justice' which is concerned with the industrial expansion of the northeast and its consequent marginalization of the local population; (2) a document 'I have heard the cry of My people', published in May 1973 by 13 bishops and some religious superiors in the northeast which concerns also the human and social situation of their region; and (3) a public declaration published on 15 March 1973, at the beginning of the Thirteenth General Assembly of the episcopal conference, concerning respect for the rights of man in Brazil. This latter declaration called for the creation of an international court to 'judge, at a moral level, regimes which violate the fundamental rights of individuals' as well as calling for 'simple economic growth' accompanied by 'social integration'. This declaration may be considered the most explicit statement ever adopted by the episcopal conference with regard to the social situation, although it has not yet led to any significant change in the practical attitude of the church vis-a-vis the regime.

On 15 April 1974 for the first time in the history of the 'largest Catholic country in the world', a Protestant, general Ernesto Geisel, became president of the republic. Paradoxically a certain relaxation of tension between the Catholic Church and the state followed, the principal reason being the assumption that the new president would adopt a less rigid political and social policy. Secret contacts were made between Geisel's supporters and the CNBB even before his accession to power, in fact from the time that his predecessor, Medici, had for all practical purposes broken off communication with the episcopal conference. Although the new president has been able to achieve a limited detente in relations with the Catholic Church, this has not impeded police repression, especially of the Christian worker movement and social action in São Paulo.

In 1977 trouble arose for Protestant missions when 84 workers of Wycliffe Bible Translators were ordered out of Indian areas by the end of the year.

By 1978 a crisis had arisen concerning government refusal to grant entry visas for missionaries. Up to May 1977, 500 new missionaries or religious personnel had been admitted each year. Over the following 12 months, however, only 65 Catholic visas and 6 Protestant ones were issued.

## INTERDENOMINATIONAL ORGANIZATIONS.

The Evangelical Federation of Brazil (Confederação Evangélica Brasileira), founded in 1934, is the main co-ordinating body between Protestant churches in Brazil. It is a member of UNELAM and CELADEC, and 4 of its member churches are also members of the WCC. Two associations relating to theological education have been formed: the older Association of Evangelical Theological Seminaries (ASTE), and the Evangelical Theological Association for Extension Training (AETTE). The latter came into existence in 1968 to provide training for the large number of Conservative Evangelical pastors, many being Pentecostals, who have never received any theological training. The Evangelical Institute of Research was created in 1965 as a joint project of ASTE and the Evangelical Federation.

The Catholic Episcopal Conference maintains an Ecumenical Secretariat (Secretaria de Ecumenismo da CNBB e Regionais). Its principal diocesan Commissions for Ecumenical Co-ordination are in Rio de Janeiro, Belo Horizonte, Curitiba, Pôrto Alegre and São Paulo. The commission of Belo Horizonte organizes its ecumenical meetings under the name Informax.

Other ecumenical centres and groups include the following: (1) Ecumenical Centre of Rio de Janeiro (Centro de Ecumenismo do Rio de Janeiro, CERJ) conducted by the Sisters of Notre Dame of Sion, which engages in study and dialogue and sponsors Judeo-Christian meetings; (2) Ecumenical Information Centre (Centro Ecuménico de Informações, CEI) in Copacabana and Rio de Janeiro which conducts research; (3) Interconfessional Counselling Service (Serviço Interconfessional de Aconselhamento, SICA) founded in Pôrto Alegre in 1969, an interdenominational body sponsored by Catholic, Episcopal, Lutheran and Methodist churches which provides advice and aid to anyone in difficulty; (4) Brotherly Team (Equipe Fraterna), founded in Recife in 1969, an interdenominational social and spiritual organization seeking to break down denominational barriers through prayer, dialogue and social service programmes in the most disadvantaged districts; (5) Fraternity of Reconciliation (Fraternidade de Reconciliação), founded in Recife, a monastic community modelled after that of Taizé in France; (6) Christian Association of Youth (Associação Cristã de Moços, ACM), founded in Rio de Janeiro, an interdenominational cultural and recreative centre connected with the WCC; (7) Brazilian Union of Ecumenical Youth Groups (União Brasileira de Juventudes Ecuménicas, UBRAJE) founded in Curitiba, with connections to the WCC; and (8) Women's Association of Rio de Janeiro (Associação Feminina do Rio de Janeiro) also with connections to the WCC. The Centre for Biblical Studies (Centro de Estudos Bíblicos) in Rio de Janeiro, the Episcopal Seminary of São Paulo, and the Theological Institute of Recife, are Catholic study centres for dialogue and ecumenical research.

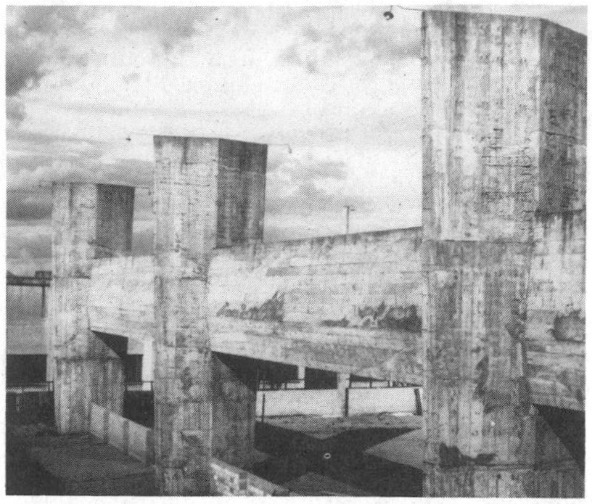

**Igreja Evangélica Pentecostal, OBPC.** Headquarters temple, seating 40,000, of 2nd largest of Brazil's 185 indigenous denominations, under construction in São Paulo in 1969.

On the inter-religious level, there is a council for Judeo-Christian Fellowship (Conselho de Fraternidade Cristão-Judaico, CFCJ), in São Paulo. This is part of the International Council of Christians and Jews with headquarters in London (UK), which seeks to improve Judeo-Christian understanding and to preserve and develop common cultural, spiritual and human values. It organizes meetings, conferences, congresses and seminars. A similar council was active in Rio de Janeiro prior to 1966, the year when it was dissolved to give place to another body working closely with the Israelite Religious Association and a regional council of B'nai B'rith. Throughout the rest of the country (especially at Curitiba, Belo Horizonte and Recife) there are occasional meetings between local councils of B'nai B'rith and Christians interested in Judeo-Christian relations. Apart from the Christian Yoga Centre (Centro Yoga Cristão) in Rio de Janeiro where Christians and Hindus are in contact with one another, Brazil's religious and philosophical groups do not retain permanent and structured relations with each other. There have been personal contacts, however, between members of various Catholic organizations and Umbandist leaders.

**BROADCASTING.** In Brazil there are over 1,200 radio stations, located in every state and territory, of which about 85% are classified as local stations and serve only a limited area. It is these smaller stations that present the greatest opportunity for religious broadcasting. Although the government and larger commercial stations accept religious programmes, it is almost impossible in the large cities to obtain time on these stations at worthwhile hours. In fact, the policy of the larger stations since 1955 has been to decrease the number of hours given to religious broadcasting.

The Catholic Church has been extremely active in the ownership and operation of local radio stations for education on a commercial basis. Most are of low power and spread throughout the interior, although some are found in the industrial area of the coast. In 1974 the important station serving the archdiocese of São Paulo was closed for political reasons by the state governor. In all, Catholics own or control over 250 radio stations (of which 116 sponsor radiophonic schools); this is the largest number of Catholic stations in any nation. They also operate a TV station, Rádio TV Difusora Pôrtoalegrense. This network operates a large mass-education movement through radio schools called Movimento de Educação de Base (MEB), which extends throughout Brazil and fosters community action as well as education. It has founded some 1,000 schools, and in 1969 was operating 1,798 centres with 31,083 participants. A recent project is rural educational broadcasting in the Amazon state run by a network of 16 radio stations, with a central station in Manaus. Catholics also operate many production studios. In São Paulo, the Secretariado Regional Sur I of the CNBB produces programmes for 380 radio stations in the state. For Catholics, Brazil is a member of UNDA. There are also a number of Protestant recording studios in Brazil, often producing imaginative programmes. The most important is the Lutheran-sponsored ISAEC in Pôrto Alegre. A notable Protestant project is the Brazilian Association of Evangelical Radio Stations (ABRE). Under this scheme, affluent Christian businessmen purchase local stations, operate them on a self-supporting commercial basis, and give prime time to Christian programming. In all some 6 radio stations are related to Protestant churches.

## BIBLIOGRAPHY


'Afro-Brazilian religious cults', K. Oberg, *Sociologia*, 21, 2 (May 1959), 134–141.

*A Igreja no Brasil.* A. Gregory. Louvain: FERES, 1965. 227p. (Roman Catholic).

*A mitologia heroica de tribos indígenas do Brasil.* E. Schaden. Ministerio de Educação y Cultura (Brasil), 1946.

*Anuário Católico do Brasil, 1970–71.* Rio de Janeiro: CERIS, 1972. 2,292p.

*A Umbanda no Brasil: orientação para os Católicos.* B. Kloppenburg. Petropolis: Editôra Vozes, 1960. 263p.

*Brazil 1980: the Protestant handbook.* W. R. Read & F. A. Ineson. Monrovia, USA: MARC, 1973. 405p.

'Brazil: the church in process of renewal', *Pro Mundi Vita* (Brussels), 24 (1968).

*Catholic radicals in Brazil.* E. de Kadt. London: Oxford University Press, 1970.

*Católicos, Protestantes, Espíritas.* C. P. Ferreira de Camargo. Petropolis: Editôra Vozes, 1973.

'Essai de typologie du Catholicisme brésilien', C. P. Ferreira de Camargo, *Social compass* (Louvain), XIV, 5–6 (1967), 399–422.

*Il sincretismo religioso afro-cattolico in Brasile.* Bologna, Italia: Nicola Zanichelli, 1955. 2 parts.

*Kardecismo e Umbanda.* C. P. Ferreira de Camargo. São Paulo: Livraria Pioneira Editôra, 1961. 176p.

'La secte musulmane des Males au Brésil et leur revolte en 1835', I. Etienne, *Anthropos*, 4 (1909), 99–105, 405–415. (A liturgical Negro Muslim sect).

*Le Candomblé de Bahia (rite Nagó).* R. Bastide. The Hague: Mouton, 1958. (Full bibliography on African religions in Brazil).

*Les religions africaines au Brésil: vers une sociologie des interpénétrations de civilisations.* R. Bastide. Paris: Presses Universitaires de France, 1960. (Includes long lexicon of terms).

*L'Eglise et la politique au Brésil.* M. Moreira-Alves. Paris: Editions du Cerf, 1974. 263p.

'Messiahs in Brazil', M. I. Pereira de Queiroz, *Past and present*, 31 (July, 1965), 62–86.

*New patterns of church growth in Brazil.* W. R. Read. Grand Rapids, MI: Eerdmans, 1965. 240p.

*O messianismo no Brasil e no mundo.* M. I. Pereira de Queiroz. São Paulo: Dominus Editôra, 1965. 374p.

'Pentecostalismo em São Paulo'. B. Muniz de Souza. Dissertation, Universidade de Campinas, Rio Claro, 1967. 169p.

*Religionen in Brasilien.* M. Gerbert. Berlin: Colloquium Verlag, 1970.

*Roman Catholicism in Brazil: a study of church behavior under stress.* D. E. Mutchler. St Louis, 1965.

'The Catholic Church in Brazil: a sociological perspective', A. Gregory, in *Report of International Conference of Sociology of Religion* (Lille, France, 1973), p. 143–164.

*The political transformation of the Brazilian Catholic Church.* T. C. Bruneau. London: Cambridge University Press, 1974. 270p.

TABLE 2. ORGANIZED CHURCHES AND DENOMINATIONS IN BRAZIL

| Official name 1 | Begun 2 | Type 3 | Counc 4 | Congs 5 | Adults 6 | Affiliated 7 | Names, notes, and other statistics (see Codebook) 8 | | | | | | |
|---|---|---|---|---|---|---|---|---|---|---|---|---|---|
| Aliança Bíblica do Brasil | 1958 | P int | xM... | 13 | 108 | 250 | *Biblical Alliance*. M=Pan-American Mission(WIM) (USA). 1n,4x,14f,1s,W=90%,12Y,93z. | | | | | | |
| Aliança Cristã e Missionária | 1962 | P Hol | xF... | 10 | 80 | 300 | M=Christian & Missionary Alliance(USA). 50% Japanese. 8x,10f,W=97%,13Y. | | | | | | |
| Aliança das Igrejas Cristãs Ev do Brasil | 1931 | P int | xF... | 202 | 10,800 | 20,000 | *Alliance of Christian Ev Chs*. M=UFM(UK,USA). In north. 18m,138f,8h,1s,W=83%,80Y. | | | | | | |
| Assembleias de Deus | 1910 | P Pe2 | ZF..N | 10,576 | 2,783,000 | 4,000,000 | *Assemblies of God*. 1934,M=AoG(USA),SFM,NPY,FFFM. 8221n,1j,3s(494),140000Y,240000z. | | | | | | |
| Assoc das Igs Congregaçionais Bíblicas | c1970 | I Con | .TT.T | 10 | 1,000 | 2,000 | *Association of Congregational Bible Chs of Brazil*. Ex IECC(EUSA). HQ São Paulo. | | | | | | |
| Assoc das Igrejas dos Irmãos Menonitas | 1930 | P Men | GF... | 17 | 2,000 | 5,000 | *AIIM. Mennonite Brethren Ch*. M=MBCNA. German-speaking USSR immigrants. 134f,1p. | | | | | | |
| Ass dos Batistas Evangelismo Mundial | 1942 | P Bap | x.... | | 2,000 | 5,000 | M=Assoc of Baptists for World Evangelism(ABWE)(USA). 74f,2s. | | | | | | |
| Ass Ev de Catequese dos Indios Caiuas | 1928 | P Ref | ..... | 8 | 400 | 900 | *Ev Association for Indian Teaching*. Works in Caiua tribe. 4n,W=50%,105Y,150z. | | | | | | |
| Associação Evangélica Menonita | 1955 | P Men | G.... | 40 | 1,500 | 3,000 | *Ev Mennonite Association*. M=Brazil Mennonite Mission(MCNA); Araguacema. 2f. | | | | | | |
| Assoc Geral das Igs Batistas Regulares | 1939 | P Bap | .TT.T | 40 | 1,600 | 5,000 | *General Assoc of Regular Baptist Chs*. Assisted by USA missionaries. 1n,W=50%. | | | | | | |
| Congregação Cristã do Brasil | 1910 | I pe2 | ..... | 3,500 | 600,000 | 1,000,000 | *Christian Congregation of B*. Italian origins. States: 53% in SPaulo, 30% Paraná. | | | | | | |
| Congregação da Ciéncia Cristã | | M Sci | x.... | 6 | 500 | 1,000 | *Ch of Christ, Scientist. Christian Science*. M=CCS(Boston,USA). 2m,7w. | | | | | | |
| Congregação dos Missionários DSTS | | I ReC | .v... | 2 | 1,000 | 2,000 | DSTS=Discipulos da Santíssima Trindade, Séde. Ex RCC. HQ Caetés. 1970 applied to WCC. | | | | | | |
| Convenção Batista Brasileira | 1881 | P Bap | T.... | 5,389 | 350,294 | 1,050,000 | *Brazilian Baptist Conv*. M=SBC,BMS. Germans, Japanese. 1382n,320f,1H,77h,1j,30p,29690Y. | | | | | | |
| Convenção Batista Nacional | 1967 | I pen | ....I | 95 | 10,000 | 20,000 | *National Baptist Convention. Igreja do Renovaçoã*. Split ex Brazilian Baptist Convention. | | | | | | |
| Conv das Igs Ev Batistas Indep do B | 1912 | P Pe2 | Z.... | 226 | 12,233 | 26,600 | *Indep Bapt Chs*. M=Örebro (Sweden). 55n,44x,G=11%pa,1s,198t(9433),W=80%,928Y,11600z. | | | | | | |
| Cruzada de Evangelização do Acre e Am | 1937 | P Bap | ..... | 12 | 500 | 800 | Am=Amazones. *Missão Ev Amazonica*. M=Acre Gospel Mission(UK). 14f,W=80%,80Y,100z. | | | | | | |
| Cruzada Interamericana do Brasil | 1962 | P int | ..... | | 200 | 500 | *Interamerican Crusade of B*. M=Spanish America Inland Mission(USA). | | | | | | |
| Cruzada Nacional de Evangelização | 1946 | P Pe2 | ZFu.b | 550 | 72,567 | 200,000 | *National Evangelization Crusade*. M.=ICFG(USA). 800nm,7f,2p(81),W=72%,8836Y. | | | | | | |
| Exército de Salvação | 1922 | P Sal | xwu.N | 45 | 3,000 | 6,000 | *Salvation Army, Brazil Territory*. 3 Divisions. Officers 127, institutions 15. 1s. | | | | | | |
| Federação Ev Japonesa do Brasil | | P Dis | x.... | | 3,618 | 5,000 | *Japanese Ev Federation of Brazil*. M=UCMS(USA). Japanese immigrants. | | | | | | |
| Igreja Adventista da Promessa | c1958 | I pen | ....I | 150 | 7,000 | 15,000 | A pent costal split ex SDAs. Meetings changed from Saturdays to Sundays. | | | | | | |
| Igreja Adventista da Reforma | 1947 | P Adv | x.... | 9 | 300 | 600 | *SDA Reform Movement*. Schism from SDAs in Germany 1914, in Brazil since 1947. | | | | | | |
| Igreja Adventista do Sétimo Dia | 1894 | P Adv | x.... | 603 | 173,837 | 300,000 | *SDAs*. E,N,SBrazil. 10 launches, 2 planes. 306nx,56f,4H,6h,1j,8r,2s,2099t(177230),17036Y. | | | | | | |
| Igreja Apostólica Arménia: D Brasil | | O Arm | Ewc.. | 2 | 5,000 | 15,000 | *Armenian Apostolic Ch* (*Gregorians*). Under C Echmiadzin (USSR). Armenians. 2nx. | | | | | | |
| Igreja Batista do Sétimo Dia do Brasil | | P Bap | Tw... | 36 | 1,194 | 3,000 | *Seventh Day Baptist Ch of Brazil*. M=SDBC(USA). Sabbatarians with USA/UK links. | | | | | | |
| Igreja Batista Evangélica Restrita | | P Bap | x.... | 16 | 1,000 | 3,000 | *Strict Baptist Church*. Links with Strict Baptists from England. | | | | | | |
| Igreja Brasileira | 1961 | I CCa | .v... | 10 | 1,000 | 2,000 | *Brazilian Ch*. Schism ex Rome. 6 bishops. Attempt to rejoin RCC as clergy; failed. | | | | | | |
| Igreja Católica Apostólica Brasileira | 1945 | I CCa | ..... | 200 | 1,000,000 | 2,000,000 | *ICAB*. Schism by RC ex-bishop of Botucatu. Nationalistic. 12 Dioceses, 25 bishops. | | | | | | |
| Igreja Católica Livre no Brasil | 1936 | I CCa | ..... | | 1,500 | 3,000 | *Free Catholic Ch*. Ex Rome; 1945, bishop consecrated through ICAB, rejoined RCC 1961. | | | | | | |
| **Igreja Católica no Brasil:** | 1500 | R LEr | B.L.R | 6,568 | 49,754,100 | 87,287,835 | C=101+14+329, 13149nx, 3290m, 40967w, 2394069Yy, | | | | | | Notes on the 14 Pastoral Regions: |
| Centro, Região Pastoral do: | | R Lat | Bs | 82 | 601,400 | 1,055,000 | Centre Pastoral Region. | | | | | 30699 | *Centre*. HQ Brasília. Civil states: |
| M Brasília | 1960 | R Lat | Bs | 44 | 310,600 | 545,000 | DF | FSC | 87 | 42 | 310 | 10300 | Federal District, parts Minas Gerais, |
| D Paracatu | 1929 | R Lat | Bs | 8 | 96,900 | 170,000 | MG | OCar | 11 | 1 | 10 | 6348 | Goiás. Area: 156,023 km2. Population |
| D Uruaçu | 1956 | R Lat | Bs | 12 | 128,400 | 225,000 | GO | CMF | 14 | 1 | 32 | 9336 | 1,079,840, scattered rural. Pastoral |
| PN Formosa | 1956 | R Lat | Bs | 18 | 65,500 | 115,000 | GO | SSCC | 13 | 6 | 51 | 4715 | council only in Uruaçu. |
| Centro-Oeste, Região Pastoral do: | | R Lat | Bs | 227 | 1,431,100 | 2,510,622 | West-Centre Pastoral Region. | | | | | 65904 | *West-Centre*. HQ Goiânia. Civil |
| M Goiânia | 1956 | R Lat | Bs | 34 | 284,300 | 498,700 | GO | CSSR | 118 | 23 | 405 | 11967 | state: most of Goiás. Area: 526,664 |
| D Anapolis | 1966 | R Lat | Bs | 22 | 142,500 | 250,000 | GO | OFM | 16 | 4 | 105 | 5610 | km2. Population: 2,566,700 mostly |
| D Goiàs | 1746 | R Lat | Bs | 82 | 131,100 | 230,000 | GO | OP | 23 | 2 | 52 | 4968 | rural and very scattered. Cities: |
| D Ipameri | 1966 | R Lat | Bs | 12 | 74,200 | 130,261 | GO | OFM | 19 | 2 | 41 | 3341 | Goiánia (390,000). Anápolis, |
| D Itumbiara | 1966 | R Lat | Bs | 10 | 91,200 | 160,000 | GO | OFMConv | 24 | 1 | 29 | 4580 | Itumbiara. Blacks, Indians |
| D Jataí | 1929 | R Lat | Bs | 15 | 128,300 | 225,000 | GO | SA | 29 | 6 | 56 | 5743 | (Caboclos), mixed race. Great |
| D Pôrto Nacional | 1915 | R Lat | Bs | 10 | 101,500 | 178,000 | GO | OP | 12 | 0 | 28 | 5938 | poverty in north and east. Pastoral |
| PN Cristalândia | 1956 | R Lat | Bs | 6 | 52,400 | 92,000 | GO | OFM | 13 | 5 | 19 | 3461 | councils with laity in 4 dioceses: |
| PN Miracema do Norte | 1966 | R Lat | Bs | 6 | 68,400 | 120,000 | GO | CSSR | 7 | 1 | 10 | 3900 | Anápolis, Cristalândia, Jataí, |
| PN Rubiataba | 1966 | R Lat | Bs | 7 | 109,300 | 191,815 | GO | CSSR | 12 | 4 | 32 | 1380 | Goiás. |
| PN São Luís de Montes Belos | 1961 | R Lat | Bs | 11 | 128,200 | 224,846 | GO | CP | 18 | 1 | 21 | 6909 | |
| PN Tocantinópolis | 1954 | R Lat | Bs | 12 | 119,700 | 210,000 | GO | FDP | 18 | 3 | 13 | 8107 | |
| Extremo-Oeste, Região Pastoral do: | | R Lat | Bs | 110 | 960,800 | 1,685,592 | Extreme West Pastoral Region. | | | | | 50230 | *Extreme West*. HQ Campo Grande. |
| M Cuiabá | 1745 | R Lat | Bs | 13 | 102,700 | 180,200 | MT | SDB | 30 | 12 | 102 | 5465 | Civil states: most of Mato Grosso, |
| D Campo Grande | 1957 | R Lat | Bs | 20 | 183,500 | 321,892 | MT | SDB | 65 | 0 | 100 | 13198 | part territory of Rondônia. Area: |
| D Corumbá | 1910 | R Lat | Bs | 14 | 134,000 | 235,000 | MT | SDB | 24 | 1 | 56 | 3887 | 1,228,903 km2. Population: |
| D Dourados | 1957 | R Lat | Bs | 22 | 216,600 | 380,000 | MT | OFM | 37 | 11 | 52 | 12042 | 1,724,600, rural, very scattered. |
| D São Luís de Cáceres | 1910 | R Lat | Bs | 8 | 79,800 | 140,000 | MT | TOR | 9 | 6 | 36 | 5232 | Mixed races, several thousand |
| PN Diamantino | 1929 | R Lat | Bs | 6 | 37,000 | 65,000 | MT | SJ | 23 | 12 | 37 | 423 | Indians. Traditional catholicism. |
| PN Guajará-Mirim | 1929 | R Lat | Bs | 3 | 14,000 | 24,500 | RO,MT | TOR | 6 | 1 | 10 | 552 | Pastoral councils with laity: Corumbá |
| PN Guiratinga | 1914 | R Lat | Bs | 13 | 65,500 | 115,000 | MT | SDB | 31 | 15 | 63 | 5205 | Cuiabá, Dourados, Rondonópolis, |
| PN Rondonópolis | 1940 | R Lat | Bs | 9 | 96,900 | 170,000 | MT | OFM | 11 | 4 | 44 | 3226 | São Félix, São Luís de Cáceres. |
| PN São Félix | 1969 | R Lat | Bs | 2 | 30,800 | 54,000 | MT | CMF | 6 | 0 | 9 | 1000 | |
| Leste I, Região Pastoral do: | | R Lat | Bs | 426 | 3,767,500 | 6,609,674 | East I Pastoral Region. | | | | | 143367 | *East I*. HQ Rio de Janeiro. Civil |
| M Niterói | 1892 | R Lat | Bs | 55 | 552,900 | 970,000 | RJ | SDB | 90 | 12 | 208 | 16847 | states: Guanabara (100%urban, with |
| D Campos | 1922 | R Lat | Bs | 31 | 394,140 | 692,250 | RJ | CSSR | 53 | 2 | 59 | 10287 | City of Rio de Janeiro, 4,316,000), |
| D Nova Friburgo | 1960 | R Lat | Bs | 33 | 200,000 | 350,000 | RJ | SJ | 54 | 8 | 156 | 8832 | Rio de Janeiro (50% rural). Area: |
| D Petrópolis | 1946 | R Lat | Bs | 33 | 530,100 | 930,000 | RJ | OFM | 74 | 145 | 350 | 15331 | 43,334 km2. Population: 9,006,300. |
| M São Sebastião do Rio de J | 1575 | R Lat | Bs | 179 | 1,767,000 | 3,100,000 | GB | SJ | 891 | 103 | 2519 | 62859 | Very industrialized. Cultural, |
| D Barra do Piraí-Volta Redonda | 1922 | R Lat | Bs | 26 | 171,000 | 300,000 | RJ | SVD | 51 | 17 | 89 | 8870 | intellectual, political centre. |
| D Nova Iguaçu | 1960 | R Lat | Bs | 48 | 63,300 | 111,124 | RJ | OFM | 66 | 2 | 80 | 16991 | Pastoral councils with laity in 3 |
| D Valença | 1925 | R Lat | Bs | 20 | 89,000 | 156,230 | RJ | OFM | 30 | 0 | 150 | 3215 | dioceses: Nova Friburgo, Nova Iguaçu, |
| AN Nossa Senhora do Monserrate | 1948 | R Lat | Bs | 1 | 60 | 70 | GB | OSB | 48 | 8 | 0 | 135 | São Sebastião (monthly meetings). |
| Leste II. Região Pastoral do: | | R Lat | Bs | 1,029 | 6,878,900 | 12,068,193 | East II Pastoral Region. | | | | | 351921 | *East II*. HQ Belo Horizonte. Civil |
| M Belo Horizonte | 1921 | R Lat | Bs | 119 | 860,400 | 1,509,497 | MG | SJ | 402 | 111 | 1500 | 37737 | states: most of Minas Gerais, |
| D Divinópolis | 1958 | R Lat | Bs | 32 | 169,900 | 298,000 | MG | OFM | 49 | 8 | 114 | 8440 | Espírito Santo. Area: 573,796 km2. |
| D Luz | 1918 | R Lat | Bs | 36 | 273,600 | 480,000 | MG | CM | 49 | 2 | 90 | 10059 | Population: 12,876,900, mainly |
| D Oliveira | 1941 | R Lat | Bs | 24 | 120,000 | 210,500 | MG | OSC | 30 | 0 | 56 | 5820 | rural, with 3 industrial cities |
| D Sete Lagoas | 1955 | R Lat | Bs | 26 | 115,800 | 203,212 | MG | CSSp | 27 | 0 | 31 | 6570 | (Belo Horizonte 1,255,400, Juíz de |
| M Diamantina | 1854 | R Lat | Bs | 52 | 325,200 | 570,608 | MG | CSSR | 66 | 2 | 33 | 22714 | Fora 200,000, Vitória 136,400). |
| D Arassuaí | 1913 | R Lat | Bs | 26 | 256,500 | 450,000 | MG | OFM | 31 | 0 | 16 | 7808 | Minas Gerais is considered the most |
| D Januária | 1957 | R Lat | Bs | 11 | 154,700 | 271,479 | MG | MSF | 17 | 0 | 10 | 8939 | Catholic state in all Brazil, with |
| D Montes Claros | 1910 | R Lat | Bs | 23 | 342,000 | 600,000 | MG | OPraem | 35 | 6 | 97 | 19180 | both ultra-conservative |
| D Teófilo Otoni | 1960 | R Lat | Bs | 24 | 300,000 | 526,000 | MG | OFM | 41 | 0 | 87 | 13150 | organizations and also groups |
| M Juíz de Fora | 1924 | R Lat | Bs | 68 | 307,800 | 540,000 | MG | SVD | 134 | 33 | 338 | 9890 | fostering Christian revolution. |
| D Leopoldina | 1942 | R Lat | Bs | 41 | 187,400 | 328,835 | MG | AA | 50 | 1 | 135 | 12970 | Pastoral councils with laity in 3 |
| D São João del Rei | 1960 | R Lat | Bs | 30 | 131,600 | 230,901 | MG | SDB | 66 | 47 | 149 | 6818 | dioceses: Belo Horizonte (12 clergy, |
| M Mariana | 1745 | R Lat | Bs | 107 | 473,400 | 830,558 | MG | SDB | 170 | 6 | 309 | 40815 | 32 laity), Diamantina, Mariana. The |
| D Caratinga | 1915 | R Lat | Bs | 42 | 444,900 | 780,560 | MG | SDN | 53 | 9 | 121 | 22695 | bishop of Arassuaí (1975) has been |
| D Governador Valadares | 1956 | R Lat | Bs | 27 | 274,600 | 481,700 | MG | CSSp | 46 | 4 | 73 | 16000 | co-ordinator of the Catholic |
| D Itabira | 1965 | R Lat | Bs | 44 | 228,000 | 400,000 | MG | SDB | 32 | 1 | 106 | 6000 | Charismatic Renewal in Brazil, and |
| M Pouso Alegre | 1900 | R Lat | Bs | 40 | 242,800 | 426,000 | MG | MSC | 79 | 5 | 240 | 11300 | is a leader of ECCLA (Latin American |
| D Campanha | 1907 | R Lat | Bs | 59 | 233,700 | 410,000 | MG | SCJ | 81 | 14 | 335 | 13315 | Catholic Charismatic Leaders |
| D Guaxupé | 1916 | R Lat | Bs | 56 | 246,700 | 432,854 | MG | FSG | 83 | 23 | 245 | 13822 | Conference). Catholic charismatics |
| M Uberaba | 1907 | R Lat | Bs | 22 | 156,900 | 275,293 | MG | FMS | 62 | 22 | 197 | 8348 | are increasing rapidly in numbers. |
| D Patos de Minas | 1955 | R Lat | Bs | 24 | 226,900 | 398,000 | MG | OFMCap | 42 | 10 | 107 | 10893 | |
| D Uberlândia | 1961 | R Lat | Bs | 21 | 114,000 | 200,000 | MG | SSCC | 50 | 2 | 130 | 10000 | |
| AN Claraval | 1968 | R Lat | Bs | 2 | 6,900 | 12,096 | MG | OCist | 6 | 1 | 0 | 322 | |
| M Vitória | 1895 | R Lat | Bs | 37 | 313,500 | 550,000 | ES | FMS | 75 | 41 | 236 | 10000 | |
| D Cachoeiro de Itapemirim | 1958 | R Lat | Bs | 21 | 189,300 | 332,100 | ES | SDB | 42 | 6 | 53 | 11348 | |
| D São Mateus | 1958 | R Lat | Bs | 15 | 182,400 | 320,000 | ES | FSCJ | 35 | 3 | 35 | 6968 | |
| Nordeste I, Região Pastoral do: | | R Lat | Bs | 615 | 5,714,800 | 10,025,936 | Northeast I Pastoral Region. | | | | | 339564 | *Northeast I*. HQ Fortaleza. Civil |
| M Fortaleza | 1854 | R Lat | Bs | 60 | 685,500 | 1,202,650 | CE | OFMCap | 221 | 15 | 234 | 62682 | states: Maranhão, Piauí, Ceará. |
| D Crateús | 1963 | R Lat | Bs | 11 | 173,900 | 305,000 | CE | FC | 11 | 0 | 15 | 10716 | Area: 722,947 km2. Population: |
| D Crato | 1914 | R Lat | Bs | 216 | 316,100 | 554,520 | CE | OFMCap | 69 | 5 | 139 | 24242 | 8,923,150, 25% in towns of over |
| D Iguatú | 1961 | R Lat | Bs | 19 | 237,500 | 416,600 | CE | MSF | 25 | 1 | 35 | 16762 | 50,000 with a gradual |
| D Itapipoca | 1971 | R Lat | Bs | 13 | 155,000 | 271,926 | CE | Nil | 12 | 0 | 29 | 12476 | industrialization except in |
| D Limoeiro do Norte | 1938 | R Lat | Bs | 20 | 191,000 | 335,000 | CE | FMS | 29 | 8 | 50 | 11401 | Fortaleza (872,700); poor area, dry |
| D Quixadá | 1971 | R Lat | Bs | 7 | 140,000 | 245,625 | CE | Nil | 12 | 0 | 47 | 10643 | soil, high illiteracy, traditional |
| D Sobral | 1915 | R Lat | Bs | 21 | 290,700 | 509,966 | CE | OFMCap | 41 | 0 | 200 | 17586 | catholicism. Pastoral councils with |
| D Tianguá | 1971 | R Lat | Bs | 11 | 142,700 | 250,365 | CE | OFMCap | 12 | 0 | | 9182 | laity in 4 dioceses: Crateús, |
| M São Luís do Maranhão | 1677 | R Lat | Bs | 51 | 855,000 | 1,500,000 | MA | OFMCap | 89 | 0 | | 30000 | Pinheiro, Santo Antônio de Balsas |
| D Bacabal | 1968 | R Lat | Bs | 17 | 310,600 | 545,000 | MA | OFM | 21 | 5 | 20 | 7235 | São José do Grajaú. |
| D Brejo | 1971 | R Lat | Bs | 16 | 182,400 | 320,000 | MA | SDS | 8 | 0 | 0 | 6000 | |
| D Caxias do Maranhão | 1939 | R Lat | Bs | 26 | 260,500 | 456,999 | MA | FSCJ | 13 | 0 | 17 | 18560 | |
| D Viana | 1962 | R Lat | Bs | 14 | 333,800 | 585,600 | MA | SCJ | 17 | 1 | 19 | 11700 | |
| PN Cândido Mendes | 1961 | R Lat | Bs | 5 | 35,900 | 63,000 | MA | FSCJ | 9 | 0 | 16 | 2210 | |
| PN Carolina | 1958 | R Lat | Bs | 12 | 101,700 | 178,480 | MA | OFMCap | 18 | 0 | 14 | 4548 | |
| PN Pinheiro | 1939 | R Lat | Bs | 10 | 114,000 | 200,000 | MA | MSC | 27 | 3 | 33 | 9410 | |
| PN Santo Antônio de Balsas | 1954 | R Lat | Bs | 10 | 94,000 | 165,000 | MA | FSCJ | 22 | 5 | 23 | 3621 | |
| PN São José do Grajaú | 1922 | R Lat | Bs | 8 | 131,100 | 230,000 | MA | OFMCap | 19 | 2 | 13 | 7652 | |

*Continued overleaf*

*Table 2 – continued*

| Official name 1 | Begun 2 | Type 3 | Counc 4 | Congs 5 | Adults 6 | Affiliated 7 | Names, notes, and other statistics (see Codebook) 8 | | | | | |
|---|---|---|---|---|---|---|---|---|---|---|---|---|
| M   Teresina | 1902 | R Lat | Ba | 27 | 347,300 | 609,358 | PI | SJ | 47 | 3 | 106 | 22934 |
| D   Oeiras | 1944 | R Lat | Ba | 13 | 243,500 | 427,198 | PI | OFM | 18 | 0 | 19 | 14460 |
| D   Parnaíba | 1944 | R Lat | Ba | 15 | 235,500 | 413,149 | PI | OFMCap | 24 | 3 | 56 | 13294 |
| PN  Bom Jesus do Piauí | 1920 | R Lat | Ba | 8 | 63,000 | 110,500 | PI | OdeM | 9 | 1 | 11 | 5690 |
| PN  São Raimundo Nonato | 1960 | R Lat | Ba | 5 | 74,100 | 130,000 | PI | OdeM | 7 | 0 | 8 | 6560 |
| Nordeste II, Região Pastoral do: | | R Lat | Ba | 471 | 5,678,600 | 9,962,439 | Northeast II Pastoral Region. | | | | | 345536 |
| M   Maceió | 1900 | R Lat | Ba | 30 | 450,300 | 790,096 | AL | SCJ | 53 | 10 | 180 | 20888 |
| D   Palmeira dos Indios | 1962 | R Lat | Ba | 14 | 219,400 | 385,000 | AL | SCJ | 15 | 0 | 35 | 18506 |
| D   Penedo | 1916 | R Lat | Ba | 18 | 248,500 | 436,000 | AL | OFM | 25 | 0 | 20 | 17876 |
| M   Natal | 1909 | R Lat | Ba | 39 | 516,600 | 906,321 | RN | MSF | 62 | 5 | 212 | 28984 |
| D   Caicó | 1939 | R Lat | Ba | 12 | 104,900 | 184,000 | RN | Nil | 12 | 0 | 60 | 6584 |
| D   Mossoró | 1934 | R Lat | Ba | 24 | 221,800 | 389,178 | RN | MSF | 25 | 1 | 48 | 15996 |
| M   Olinda & Recife | 1614 | R Lat | Ba | 71 | 996,100 | 1,742,272 | PE | FMS | 263 | 121 | 1001 | 39570 |
| D   Afogados da Ingàzeira | 1956 | R Lat | Ba | 12 | 156,800 | 275,048 | PE | OFM | 16 | 0 | 40 | 8993 |
| D   Caruaru | 1948 | R Lat | Ba | 21 | 265,300 | 465,473 | PE | OCar | 8 | 0 | 78 | 16823 |
| D   Floresta | 1964 | R Lat | Ba | 9 | 113,700 | 199,500 | PE | MSF | 10 | 0 | 3 | 7705 |
| D   Garanhuns | 1918 | R Lat | Ba | 20 | 313,600 | 550,273 | PE | CSSR | 40 | 2 | 97 | 23385 |
| D   Nazaré | 1918 | R Lat | Ba | 31 | 399,500 | 700,816 | PE | SCJ | 41 | 10 | 184 | 26300 |
| D   Palmares | 1962 | R Lat | Ba | 15 | 159,600 | 280,000 | PE | OFM | 20 | 2 | 59 | 12360 |
| D   Pesqueira | 1910 | R Lat | Ba | 17 | 175,400 | 307,750 | PE | OFM | 22 | 0 | 43 | 15748 |
| D   Petrolina | 1923 | R Lat | Ba | 13 | 178,500 | 313,212 | PE | SDB | 12 | 0 | 73 | 15354 |
| M   Paraíba | 1892 | R Lat | Ba | 41 | 561,200 | 989,500 | PB | OFM | 77 | 12 | 236 | 19500 |
| D   Cajàzeiras | 1914 | R Lat | Ba | 35 | 262,200 | 460,000 | PB | OFMCap | 30 | 1 | 82 | 22600 |
| D   Campina Grande | 1949 | R Lat | Ba | 31 | 210,900 | 370,000 | PB | OFM | 38 | 5 | 50 | 15364 |
| D   Patos | 1959 | R Lat | Ba | 18 | 124,300 | 218,000 | PB | OCar | 24 | 1 | 60 | 13000 |
| Nordeste III, Região Pastoral do: | | R Lat | Ba | 458 | 4,627,000 | 8,117,585 | Northeast III Pastoral Region. | | | | | 218549 |
| M   Aracajú | 1910 | R Lat | Ba | 33 | 230,000 | 403,585 | SE | SDB | 49 | 0 | 179 | 16547 |
| D   Estância | 1960 | R Lat | Ba | 12 | 151,000 | 265,000 | SE | Nil | 14 | 0 | 26 | 9878 |
| D   Propriá | 1960 | R Lat | Ba | 13 | 111,700 | 196,000 | SE | CSSR | 17 | 3 | 20 | 4531 |
| M   São Salvador da Bahia | 1551 | R Lat | Ba | 84 | 1,039,700 | 1,824,000 | BA | OFMCap | 215 | 112 | 696 | 37600 |
| D   Amargosa | 1941 | R Lat | Ba | 21 | 273,600 | 480,000 | BA | OFMCap | 15 | 0 | 43 | 9474 |
| D   Barra (do Rio Grande) | 1913 | R Lat | Ba | 8 | 199,500 | 350,000 | BA | OSB | 18 | 0 | 21 | 6440 |
| D   Bom Jesus da Lapa | 1962 | R Lat | Ba | 14 | 122,000 | 214,000 | BA | CSSR | 8 | 1 | 24 | 7623 |
| D   Bonfim | 1933 | R Lat | Ba | 10 | 159,600 | 280,000 | BA | OFM | 20 | 2 | 40 | 28510 |
| D   Caetité | 1913 | R Lat | Ba | 27 | 228,000 | 400,000 | BA | Nil | 10 | 0 | | 10850 |
| D   Caravelas | 1962 | R Lat | Ba | 16 | 324,900 | 570,000 | BA | OFM | 22 | 3 | 20 | 13619 |
| D   Feira de Santana | 1962 | R Lat | Ba | 30 | 342,000 | 600,000 | BA | OFMCap | 40 | 0 | 32 | 12000 |
| D   Ilhéus | 1913 | R Lat | Ba | 34 | 153,000 | 900,000 | BA | CP | 44 | 0 | 123 | 14230 |
| D   Juàzeiro | 1962 | R Lat | Ba | 10 | 94,000 | 165,000 | BA | CSSR | 15 | 3 | 8 | 8037 |
| D   Livramento de Nossa Senhora | 1967 | R Lat | Ba | 19 | 125,400 | 220,000 | BA | CPS | 11 | 3 | 12 | 4653 |
| D   Paulo Afonso | 1971 | R Lat | Ba | 97 | 171,000 | 300,000 | BA | Nil | | | | 6000 |
| D   Rui Barbosa | 1959 | R Lat | Ba | 15 | 270,800 | 475,000 | BA | OCist | 30 | 4 | 16 | 14304 |
| D   Vitória da Conquista | 1957 | R Lat | Ba | 15 | 270,800 | 475,000 | BA | OFMCap | 25 | 3 | 56 | 14253 |
| Norte I, Região Pastoral do: | | R Lat | Ba | 102 | 814,500 | 1,428,973 | North Pastoral Region. | | | | | 46470 |
| M   Manaus | 1892 | R Lat | Ba | 12 | 185,400 | 325,205 | AM | SDB | 63 | 27 | 174 | 10978 |
| PN  Acre & Purús | 1919 | R Lat | Ba | 9 | 79,800 | 140,000 | AC,AM | OSM | 16 | 1 | 47 | 9628 |
| PN  Alto Solimões | 1910 | R Lat | Ba | 8 | 26,700 | 46,866 | AM | OFMCap | 11 | 3 | 8 | 1592 |
| PN  Borba | 1963 | R Lat | Ba | 4 | 25,600 | 45,000 | AM | TOR | 7 | 1 | 10 | 1326 |
| PN  Coari | 1963 | R Lat | Ba | 4 | 67,300 | 118,000 | AN | CSSR | 8 | 2 | 15 | 3549 |
| PN  Humaitá | 1961 | R Lat | Ba | 4 | 25,600 | 45,200 | AM | SDB | 8 | 1 | 9 | 693 |
| PN  Itacoatiara | 1963 | R Lat | Ba | 4 | 39,900 | 70,000 | AM | SFM | 7 | 0 | 11 | 1308 |
| PN  Juruá | 1931 | R Lat | Ba | 10 | 67,300 | 118,000 | AC,AM | CSSp | 19 | 9 | 31 | 4891 |
| PN  Lábrea | 1925 | R Lat | Ba | 4 | 24,300 | 42,600 | AM | OFM | 9 | 5 | 5 | 1687 |
| PN  Parintins | 1955 | R Lat | Ba | 7 | 51,600 | 90,500 | AM | PIME | 18 | 2 | 16 | 3150 |
| PN  Pôrto Velho | 1925 | R Lat | Ba | 12 | 135,500 | 237,650 | RO,MT | SDB | 17 | 7 | 28 | 2340 |
| PN  Rio Negro | 1925 | R Lat | Ba | 10 | 14,000 | 24,500 | AM | SDB | 20 | 15 | 52 | 786 |
| PN  Roraima | 1944 | R Lat | Ba | 5 | 22,800 | 40,000 | RR | IMC | 14 | 6 | 26 | 1607 |
| PN  Tefé | 1910 | R Lat | Ba | 9 | 48,700 | 85,452 | AM | CSSp | 14 | 4 | 12 | 2935 |
| Norte II, Região Pastoral do: | | R Lat | Ba | 227 | 1,213,300 | 2,128,539 | North II Pastoral Region. | | | | | 66967 |
| M   Belém do Pará | 1719 | R Lat | Ba | 49 | 495,400 | 869,167 | PA | SDB | 130 | 12 | 425 | 25286 |
| PN  Abaeté do Tocantins | 1961 | R Lat | Ba | 6 | 91,200 | 160,000 | PA | SX | 24 | 3 | 18 | 4953 |
| PN  Cametá | 1952 | R Lat | Ba | 7 | 82,400 | 144,546 | PA | CM | 15 | 1 | 24 | 4291 |
| PN  Guamá | 1928 | R Lat | Ba | 12 | 133,400 | 233,857 | PA | B | 21 | 2 | 77 | 10235 |
| PN  Macapá | 1949 | R Lat | Ba | 14 | 61,000 | 107,108 | AP | PIME | 29 | 4 | 29 | 2245 |
| PN  Marabá | 1911 | R Lat | Ba | 2 | 28,500 | 50,000 | PA | OP | 12 | 3 | 36 | 1000 |
| PN  Marajó | 1928 | R Lat | Ba | 10 | 79,800 | 140,000 | PA | OAR | 13 | 0 | 11 | 4779 |
| PN  Obidos | 1957 | R Lat | Ba | 6 | 60,000 | 105,272 | PA | OFM | 14 | 4 | 27 | 3424 |
| PN  Ponta de Pedras | 1963 | R Lat | Ba | 87 | 38,500 | 67,500 | PA | SJ | 6 | 1 | 17 | 1720 |
| PN  Santarém | 1903 | R Lat | Ba | 13 | 120,900 | 212,089 | PA | OFM | 42 | 26 | 75 | 7566 |
| PN  Xingu | 1934 | R Lat | Ba | 21 | 22,200 | 39,000 | PA | CPPS | 7 | 2 | 9 | 1468 |
| Sul I, Região Pastoral do: | | R Lat | Ba | 1,235 | 9,404,700 | 16,499,547 | South I Pastoral Region. | | | | | 360971 |
| M   Aparecida | 1958 | R Lat | Ba | 6 | 55,700 | 97,650 | SP | CSSR | 60 | 46 | 130 | 17527 |
| D   Lorena | 1937 | R Lat | Ba | 12 | 108,300 | 190,000 | SP | SDB | 38 | 74 | 98 | 3639 |
| D   Taubaté | 1908 | R Lat | Ba | 39 | 273,800 | 480,356 | SP | CFP | 81 | 51 | 402 | 22250 |
| M   Botucatu | 1908 | R Lat | Ba | 39 | 216,600 | 380,000 | SP | IMC | 60 | 35 | 320 | 10680 |
| D   Assis | 1928 | R Lat | Ba | 27 | 153,900 | 270,000 | SP | PIME | 47 | 9 | 106 | 5972 |
| D   Bauru | 1964 | R Lat | Ba | 24 | 119,500 | 209,598 | SP | OFM | 42 | 31 | 173 | 4315 |
| D   Lins | 1926 | R Lat | Ba | 49 | 285,000 | 500,000 | SP | OFMCap | 76 | 3 | 280 | 9680 |
| D   Marília | 1952 | R Lat | Ba | 50 | 285,000 | 500,000 | SP | OFMCap | 69 | 23 | 228 | 13124 |
| D   Presidente Prudente | 1960 | R Lat | Ba | 28 | 181,700 | 318,732 | SP | CSSR | 31 | 1 | 51 | 10313 |
| M   Campinas | 1908 | R Lat | Ba | 99 | 541,500 | 950,000 | SP | SJ | 221 | 0 | 850 | 20000 |
| D   Bragança Paulista | 1925 | R Lat | Ba | 21 | 122,600 | 215,000 | SP | OSA | 22 | 0 | 80 | 5904 |
| D   Piracicaba | 1944 | R Lat | Ba | 29 | 181,900 | 319,140 | SP | OFMCap | 29 | 0 | | 6056 |
| D   São Carlos | 1908 | R Lat | Ba | 44 | 262,200 | 460,000 | SP | SVD | 71 | 6 | 195 | 13368 |
| M   Ribeirão Prêto | 1908 | R Lat | Ba | 37 | 213,000 | 373,753 | SP | OAR | 36 | 19 | 236 | 7554 |
| D   Franca | 1971 | R Lat | Ba | 14 | 139,700 | 245,114 | SP | Nil | 29 | 1 | 50 | 6328 |
| D   Jaboticabal | 1929 | R Lat | Ba | 41 | 259,300 | 455,000 | SP | OFM | 47 | 2 | 180 | 10024 |
| D   Jales | 1959 | R Lat | Ba | 25 | 205,200 | 360,000 | SP | AA | 20 | 0 | 25 | 8524 |
| D   Rio Prêto | 1954 | R Lat | Ba | 54 | 253,600 | 445,000 | SP | OSA | 73 | 3 | 125 | 12843 |
| D   São João da Boa Vista | 1960 | R Lat | Ba | 19 | 159,600 | 280,000 | SP | AA | 58 | 10 | 160 | 6453 |
| M   São Paulo | 1745 | R Lat | Ba | 334 | 3,420,000 | 6,000,000 | SP | SJ | 1727 | 231 | 3450 | 85500 |
| D   Itapeva | 1968 | R Lat | Ba | 19 | 145,900 | 256,003 | SP | OCist | 29 | 19 | 71 | 8198 |
| D   Jundiaí | 1966 | R Lat | Ba | 27 | 199,500 | 350,000 | SP | OPraem | 64 | 0 | 186 | 8318 |
| D   Mogi das Cruzes | 1962 | R Lat | Ba | 40 | 302,100 | 530,000 | SP | SSCC | 41 | 5 | 89 | 9313 |
| D   NS do Libano (*Maronite*) | 1971 | R Mar | Os | 3 | 27,400 | 48,000 | SP | Nil | 7 | 0 | 0 | 47 |
| D   NS do Paraíso (*Melkite*) | 1971 | R Mel | Os | 5 | 171,000 | 300,000 | SP | Nil | 7 | 0 | 0 | 485 |
| D   Santo André | 1954 | R Lat | Ba | 67 | 456,000 | 800,000 | SP | OFMConv | 63 | 0 | 0 | 22200 |
| D   Santos | 1924 | R Lat | Ba | 50 | 413,900 | 726,201 | SP | OFMCap | 101 | 16 | 274 | 12266 |
| D   Sorocaba | 1924 | R Lat | Ba | 33 | 250,800 | 440,000 | SP | OFM | 67 | 3 | 100 | 20090 |
| Sul II, Região Pastoral do: | | R Lat | Ba | 478 | 3,785,000 | 6,640,333 | South II Pastoral Region. | | | | | 179316 |
| M   Curitiba | 1892 | R Lat | Ba' | 93 | 483,700 | 840,000 | PR | OFM | 257 | 281 | 1094 | 19320 |
| D   Guarapuava | 1965 | R Lat | Ba | 21 | 22,2900 | 391,000 | PR | OSBM | 43 | 1 | 68 | 10276 |
| D   Palmas | 1933 | R Lat | Ba | 34 | 307,200 | 539,000 | PR | MSC | 59 | 13 | 140 | 17423 |
| D   Paranaguá | 1962 | R Lat | Ba | 11 | 79,600 | 139,707 | PR | CSSR | 25 | 0 | 48 | 4750 |
| D   Ponta Grossa | 1926 | R Lat | Ba | 35 | 265,000 | 465,000 | PR | OFMCap | 126 | 55 | 332 | 9905 |
| D   São João Batista em Curitiba | 1962 | R Ukr | Os | 16 | 73,000 | 128,000 | PR | OSBM | 50 | 30 | 317 | 3228 |
| D   Toledo | 1959 | R Lat | Ba | 38 | 401,300 | 704,000 | PR | SVD | 83 | 21 | 137 | 24237 |
| M   Londrina | 1956 | R Lat | Ba | 43 | 253,200 | 444,275 | PR | SAC | 81 | 0 | 290 | 12744 |
| D   Apucarana | 1964 | R Lat | Ba | 46 | 267,300 | 468,900 | PR | CS | 56 | 7 | 62 | 8607 |
| D   Campo Mourão | 1959 | R Lat | Ba | 43 | 627,000 | 1,100,000 | PR | SCJ | 67 | 0 | 88 | 34368 |
| D   Jacarèzinho | 1926 | R Lat | Ba | 47 | 391,300 | 686,451 | PR | OFMCap | 65 | 4 | 191 | 15477 |
| D   Maringá | 1956 | R Lat | Ba | 30 | 281,600 | 494,000 | PR | FMS | 41 | 11 | 142 | 9687 |
| D   Paranavaí | 1968 | R Lat | Ba | 21 | 136,800 | 240,000 | PR | SST | 33 | 3 | 46 | 9294 |
| Sul III, Região Pastoral do: | | R Lat | Ba | 860 | 3,349,100 | 5,875,699 | South III Pastoral Region. | | | | | 120414 |
| M   Pôrto Alegre | 1848 | R Lat | Ba | 178 | 1,034,000 | 1,814,000 | RS | SJ | 525 | 673 | 2450 | 34169 |
| D   Bagé | 1960 | R Lat | Ba | 15 | 173,900 | 305,000 | RS | SDB | 38 | 8 | 108 | 4500 |
| D   Caxias do Sul | 1934 | R Lat | Ba | 72 | 236,500 | 415,000 | RS | OFMCap | 211 | 120 | 900 | 8665 |
| D   Cruz Alta | 1971 | R Lat | Ba | 308 | 159,600 | 280,000 | RS | Nil | 53 | 0 | 173 | 5600 |
| D   Erexim | 1971 | R Lat | Ba | 25 | 98,300 | 172,412 | RS | Nil | 52 | 16 | 173 | 3143 |

**Names, notes, and other statistics (column 8 descriptions):**

*Northeast II.* HQ Recife. Civil states: Rio Grande do Norte, Paraíba, Pernambuco, Alagoas. Area: 236,801 km2. Population: 10,668,760, 50% rural, 50% urban. Dry area in interior, humid zone along the coast with sugar plantations. Major centres: Recife (1,100,000; major industrial centre in north, vast shanty towns), Natal (270,100), Maceió (249,000), João Pessoa (228,400). Extremes of society, wealth, widespread poverty. Very active Catholic social action under archbishop of Recife. Pastoral councils in 4 dioceses: Paraíba (16 clergy, 11 laity), Floresta, Natal, Penedo.

*Northeast III.* HQ Salvador. Civil states: Sergipe, Bahia. Area: 581,915 km2. Population: 8,408,790. Little industrialization except along the coast (Salvador: 1,020,000, Feira de Santana, Ilhéus, Aracajú). Vast poverty (especially in Salvador *alagados*, lake slums), illiteracy. Blacks and Mulattoes predominant. Traditional catholicism. Pastoral councils with laity in 2 dioceses: Juàzeiro, São Salvador da Bahia.

*North I.* HQ Manaus. Civil states: Acre, Amazonas, part Mato Grosso; also Roraima, part Rondônia. Area: 2,215,099 km2. Population: 1,299,800. Covers half of Amazonia; difficult of access; population very scattered, including several thousand Indians. Trans-Amazon highway will revolutionize life. Church has a missionary structure except in Manaus (population 314,200), Pôrto Velho (86,200), Rio Branco (84,300). Six dioceses have pastoral councils: Borba, Coari, Juruá, Parintins, Roraima, Tefé.

*North II.* HQ Belém do Pará. Civil state: Pará, also territory of Amapá. Area: 1,366,598 km2. Population: 2,222,140. Half population is concentrated in towns: Belém (642,500), Santarém (135,700), Bragança, Cametá, Abactetuba; the other half is scattered across the Amazon basin. Belém has the beginnings of industrialization.

*South I.* HQ São Paulo. Civil state: São Paulo. Area: 244,906 km2. Population: 18,150,200 (73.5 inhabitants/km2), mainly urban. Cities: São Paulo (5,980,000), Santos (320,000), Santo André (290,000), Campinas (252,000), Ribeirão Prêto (170,000). This is the major industrial region in South America. Vast influx from rural areas. Mainly Whites (Blacks and Mulattoes about 18%), with strong Japanese colony of 600,000 (the city of São Paulo has more Japanese Catholics than Tokyo). Strong ultra-conservative organizations and strong Christian revolutionary groups: in M Botucatu in 1969, 90% of all secular priests resigned in opposition to their conservative bishop. The 2 Eastern-rite dioceses extend over the whole of Brazil. Pastoral councils with laity exist in 6 dioceses: Botucatu, Jaboticabal, Jundiaí, Marília, Rio Prêto, Taubaté. The cardinal archbishop of São Paulo (1975) is an open supporter of the Catholic Charismatic Renewal.

*South II.* HQ Curitiba. Civil state: Paraná. Area: 196,541 km2. Population: 6,958,400, 50% rural, 50% urban. Cities: Curitiba (624,000), Londrina (227,000), Ponta Grossa (153,000), Guarapuava (126,000), Maringá (112,000). Mostly Whites. Fervent catholicism among Polish and Italian immigrants. Ukrainian diocese covers all Brazil (HQ Curitiba, spiritual centre Prudentopolis, PR). Pastoral councils with laity: Apucarana, Jacarèzinho.

*South III.* HQ Pôrto Alegre. Civil state: Rio Grande do Sul. Area: 267,528 km2. Population: 6,715,200, 25% in main cities: Pôrto Alegre (903,200), Pelotas (209,000), Canoas (122,000), Santa Maria (142,000), Canoas (122,000).

*Continued opposite*

*Table 2 – continued*

| Official name 1 | Begun 2 | Type 3 | Counc 4 | Congs 5 | Adults 6 | Affiliated 7 | Names, notes, and other statistics (see Codebook) 8 |
|---|---|---|---|---|---|---|---|
| D Frederico Westphalen | 1961 | R Lat | Bs | 34 | 217,700 | 382,000 | RS OSFS 60 4 183 9943 Mostly Whites. Pastoral councils |
| D Passo Fundo | 1951 | R Lat | Bs | 42 | 216,600 | 380,000 | RS FMS 103 56 590 1900 with laity in 5 dioceses: Caxias do |
| D Pelotas | 1910 | R Lat | Bs | 31 | 220,600 | 387,000 | RS FSC 70 0 7000 Sul, Frederico Westphalen, Santa |
| D Rio Grande | 1971 | R Lat | Bs | 14 | 79,800 | 140,000 | RS Nil 30 6 134 2962 Maria, Santo Angelo, Pôrto Alegre |
| D Santa Cruz do Sul | 1959 | R Lat | Bs | 37 | 180,800 | 317,287 | RS MSF 62 9212 (which also has had a Synod of the |
| D Santa Maria | 1910 | R Lat | Bs | 41 | 233,700 | 410,000 | RS SAC 125 126 561 10349 People of God; 4th Assembly |
| D Santo Angelo | 1961 | R Lat | Bs | 28 | 222,300 | 390,000 | RS MSF 75 28 365 5697 April–May 1973). |
| D Uruguaiana | 1910 | R Lat | Bs | 11 | 159,600 | 280,000 | RS FMS 31 0 169 11480 |
| D Vacaria | 1934 | R Lat | Bs | 24 | 115,700 | 203,000 | RS OFMCap 77 9 220 6064 |
| Sul IV, Região Pastoral do: | | R Lat | Bs | 243 | 1,481,800 | 2,599,703 | South IV Pastoral Region. 73931 *South IV*. HQ Florianópolis. Civil |
| M Florianópolis | 1908 | R Lat | Bs | 44 | 297,000 | 528,731 | SC SJ 118 49 388 11795 state: Santa Catarina. Area: 95,483 |
| D Caçador | 1968 | R Lat | Bs | 20 | 142,700 | 248,000 | SC OFM 54 12 156 7108 km2. Population: 2,922,400, rural |
| D Chapecó | 1958 | R Lat | Bs | 32 | 224,700 | 392,000 | SC MSF 83 0 329 7000 with little urban development. Cities: |
| D Joinville | 1927 | R Lat | Bs | 34 | 169,400 | 295,000 | SC SCJ 93 37 388 9787 Florianópolis (143,400), Lages(97,000). |
| D Lages | 1927 | R Lat | Bs | 40 | 229,300 | 400,000 | SC OFM 87 11 318 15990 Traditional catholicism. Pastoral |
| D Rio do Sul | 1968 | R Lat | Bs | 25 | 138,600 | 240,972 | SC CSSp 71 14 343 5575 councils: Florianópolis, Joinville. |
| D Tubarão | 1954 | R Lat | Bs | 48 | 280,100 | 495,000 | SC OFMCap 111 13 478 16676 |
| O Brasil (*Oriental-rite*) | 1951 | R Ori | Os | 5 | 45,600 | 80,000 | HQ Rio de Janeiro 10 0 0 230 *O Brasil* covers whole country. |
| Igreja Cristã Apostólica | 1962 | P Hol | x.... | 18 | 800 | 2,000 | *Corporação Igreja Nazareno. Apostolic Christian Ch.* M=ACC(Nazarean)(USA). |
| Igreja Cristã Batista Bíblica | 1952 | P Bap | xTT.T | 4 | 500 | 1,000 | *Baptist Bible Christian Church.* M=BBFI(USA). HQ São Paulo. 42f,2s. |
| Igreja Cristã Pentecostal da Bíblia | 1958 | I pe2 | ....I | 20 | 2,000 | 4,000 | *Pentecostal Christian Ch of the Bible*. Cruzada Bíblica Sagrada. Schism ex IPI. |
| Igreja Cristã Primitiva | | I ind | ..... | 20 | 1,200 | 2,000 | *Primitive Christian Church*. Small indigenous independent grouping. |
| Igr Cristã Reformada Latinoamericana | 1932 | P Ref | RW... | 18 | 5,000 | 9,000 | *Christian Reformed Ch.* M=Ref Ch of Hungary, CRC(USA). A=1945. Hungarians. 5n,8f. |
| Igreja da Restauração | | I pen | ....I | 70 | 5,000 | 15,000 | *Church of the Restoration*. Schism ex Brazilian Baptist Convention. 15n,40m. |
| Igreja de Cristianismo Decidido | | P int | ..... | 10 | 200 | 500 | *Assoc of Churches of Committed Christians*. M=Marburger Mission(Germany). |
| Igreja de Cristo | 1948 | P Dis | x.... | 60 | 4,000 | 10,000 | *Ch of Christ*. M=Brazil Christian Mission(CCCC Instrumental)(USA). 8n,15x,125f,250Y. |
| Igreja de Cristo Jesus | 1958 | I pe2 | ....I | 12 | 2,000 | 5,000 | *Ch of Jesus Christ*. Schism ex Independent Presbyterian Ch. HQ São Paulo. 8n,20m. |
| Igreja de Cristo Pentecostal do Brasil | 1937 | P Pe3 | x.... | 208 | 6,590 | 30,000 | *Pentecostal Ch of Christ of B*. M=PCC(USA). 27n,1x,G=12.3%pa,W=60%,700Y,500z. |
| Igreja de Deus de Profecia | 1965 | P Pe3 | Z.... | 9 | 2,000 | 5,000 | *Ch of God of Prophecy*. M=CGP(USA), split ex CoG(Cleveland). |
| Igreja de Deus do Brasil | 1923 | P Hol | x.... | 37 | 1,326 | 3,000 | *Ch of God*. M=CoG(Anderson) (USA). 1923, German immigrants to Santa Catarina. 20n. |
| Igreja de Deus do Brasil (Cleveland) | 1935 | P Pe3 | ZF... | 151 | 3,700 | 5,000 | *Ch of God*. M=CoG(Cleveland) (USA). 59 churches, 92 missions. 79n,10f,1p. |
| Igreja de Deus Pentecostal do Brasil | c1955 | P Pe2 | Z.... | 62 | 1,800 | 2,300 | *Pentecostal Ch of God*. Classical Pentecostals. M=PCG(USA). 19n,1x,6f,150Y. |
| Igr de JC dos Santos dos Ultimos Dias | c1925 | M LdS | x.... | 150 | 30,000 | 41,776 | *Mormons*. M=Ch of JC of Latter-day Saints(USA). 70% in South Brazil. 730f,G=7.8%pa. |
| Igreja de Nosso Senhor Jesus Cristo | 1943 | I pe2 | ..... | 22 | 1,000 | 2,000 | *Ch of Our Lord Jesus Christ*. Founded by a Black evangelist in São Paulo. |
| Igreja de Reavivamento Bíblico | c1950 | I pen | ....I | 300 | 30,000 | 50,000 | *Ch of Biblical Revival*. Ex Methodist. Early pentecostal body. HQ São Paulo. |
| Igreja do Nazareno do Brasil | 1934 | P Hol | xFu.N | 32 | 1,184 | 2,500 | *Ch of the Nazarene*. M=CoN(USA). 2n,6x,22m,12f,2s(38),41t(2098),W=80%,158Y. |
| Igreja do Spirito Jesus | | I pe1 | x.... | | 1,000 | 2,000 | *Iesu No Mitama Kyokai. Spirit of Jesus Church*. Indigenous church from Japan. |
| Igreja dos Irmãos | 1949 | P Dun | xF... | 26 | 452 | 800 | M=NFBC(Brethren Ch, Grace) (USA). German Baptist tradition. 6n,6x,17f,G=7.8%pa, 58Y. |
| Igreja dos Wesleyanos | 1960 | P Hol | VF... | 4 | 41 | 382 | M=Wesleyan Church (USA). Holiness denomination. 3x,6f,1p,W=47%,12Yy,20z. |
| Igreja Episcopal do Brasil | 1889 | A Cen | AWuCN | 203 | 20,150 | 45,000 | *Episcopal Ch*. 5 Dioceses. M=PECUSA,SAMS. A=1964. 96n,3x,14m,13f,97pp,1s,W=50%, 2039y. |
| Igreja Evangélica Arabe do Brasil | | P Ref | ..u.N | 3 | 300 | 500 | *Arab Ev Ch of Brazil*. Immigrants from Lebanon and Syria Protestant bodies. |
| Igreja Ev Congregaçional Cristã | 1855 | P Con | Rru.N | 582 | 46,100 | 75,000 | *União das Igr Ev Cong*. M=EUSA,UCC(USA). 119n,3x,35f,G=2.3%pa,1j,2s,W=75%,1000Yy. |
| Igr Ev da Confissão Luterana no Brasil | 1823 | P Lut | LWu.N | 1,599 | 136,917 | 628,690 | *IECLB*. Lutheran Confession, Germans. M=ALC. 183n,106x,34f,G=1.7%pa,1s(90),14012Yy. |
| Igreja Evangélica Holiness do Brasil | 1925 | P Hol | xFu.N | 75 | 1,250 | 4,000 | M=Japan Holiness Ch,OMS(USA). A=1933. Japanese. 5n,9x,20f,1s,W=38%,70Y. |
| Igreja Evangélica Independente | 1958 | P ind | x.... | 4 | 70 | 350 | *Ev Independent Ch*. M=Bethesda Mission(USA). 1x,7f,W=80%. |
| Igreja Evangélica Luterana do Brasil | 1890 | I Lut | x.u.N | 1,112 | 100,000 | 186,200 | *Ev Lutheran Ch of* B. 1890 split ex IECLB. 1899, M=LC Missouri Synod(USA). 394n,6f,1s. |
| Igreja Evangélica Neo-Testamentaria | 1904 | P int | x.... | 20 | 600 | 3,000 | *Ev Ch of the New Testament. NT Churches*. M=NTMU(UK). In interior. 3f. |
| Igreja Evangélica Pentecostal Elim | 1960 | P Pe2 | Z.... | 20 | 980 | 3,000 | *Elim Pentecostal Church*. M=EMS(UK). 2-stage Pentecostals. 4n,G=25.1%pa,W=82%,50z. |
| Igreja Evangélica Pentecostal Unida | 1955 | I pen | ....I | 70 | 10,000 | 30,000 | *United EPC*. Union: IE Cristã Unida, IE de Povo, IP Maravilhas de Jesus. 35n. |
| Igreja Ev Pente 'O Brasil para Cristo' | 1955 | I pe2 | ZWu.b | 4,000 | 250,000 | 1,000,000 | *OBPC. Brazil for Christ*. Ex AoG. Church seating 40,000 in São Paulo. 1H,1s. |
| Igreja Evangélica Reformada do Brasil | 1933 | P Ref | F.... | 15 | 668 | 1,457 | *Ev Reformed Ch*. M=Ref Chs in Netherlands. A=1963. 1n,6x,G=0.4%pa,W=85%,50Yy,803z. |
| Igreja Evangélica Suiça | | P Ref | Rw... | 3 | 200 | 500 | *Swiss Reformed Ch*. 3 parishes only. Mostly immigrants from Switzerland. |
| Igreja Menonita | 1930 | P Men | G.... | 18 | 462 | 1,000 | *Mennonite Ch*. 1954,M=Brazil MM(MCNA). USSR immigrants. 50% German, 50% Portuguese. |
| Igreja Messiánica Mundial do Brasil | | I pen | ..... | 3 | 1,000 | 2,000 | *World Messianic Church of Brazil*, Small Brazilian independent grouping. |
| Igreja Metodista do Brasil | 1835 | P Met | VWu.N | 1,567 | 62,550 | 93,600 | 6 Conferences. M=UMC(USA). A=1935. 300n,30x,83f,G=1.1%pa,1j,3p,1s,W=60%,2843Yy. |
| Igreja Metodista Livre do Brasil | 1928 | P Hol | VFu.N | 68 | 1,795 | 5,000 | M=Free Methodist Ch(USA). Japanese. 12n,12x,10f,G=0.8%pa,1s(65),W=30%,212Y,544z. |
| Igreja Metodista Wesleyana | 1967 | I pen | ..... | 76 | 6,540 | 22,000 | *Wesleyan Meth Ch*. Pentecostal split ex Igreja Metodista. 42n,G=33%pa,W=70%,1914Yy. |
| Igreja Missionária do Brasil | 1962 | P Hol | xF... | 129 | 1,000 | 1,614 | *United Missionary Ch of Brazil*. M=OMS(IAMS),WGM,MC(USA), 11n,5x,G=15.6%pa,228Y. |
| Igreja Nova Apostólica | c1930 | C CAp | x.... | 100 | 25,000 | 50,000 | *NAC. New Apostolic Ch*. Many German immigrants. World HQ Dortmund (Germany). |
| Igreja Ortodoxa Arabe: D São Paulo | | O Ara | Cwo.. | | 10,000 | 20,000 | In Antiochian Orthodox Christian AD New York (USA), & Greek P Antioch. Arabs. 1 bishop. |
| Igreja Ort Grega: AD N&S América | | O Gre | Cwo.. | 6 | 2,500 | 5,000 | In 11th Archdiocesan District, Greek Orthodox Archdiocese of N&S America. Greeks. |
| Igreja Ortodoxa Romana | | O Rum | Cwo.. | 3 | 5,000 | 9,000 | *Parohia Ortodoxa Romana*. Under Romanian Orthodox Missionary Episcopate (USA). 1x. |
| Igreja Ortodoxa Russa | | O Sla | Mwo.. | 10 | 20,000 | 50,000 | Russian Orthodox, with bishop. In D SAmerica, Orthodox Ch in America (USA). |
| Igreja Ortodoxa Russa: D Brasil | | O Sla | x.... | 10 | 10,000 | 15,000 | *Russian Orthodox Ch Outside of Russia*. M=ROCOR(USA). Ultra-conservative Russians. |
| Igreja Ortodoxa Ucrania | | O Sla | X.... | 10 | 5,000 | 10,000 | *Ukrainian Autocephalous Orthodox Ch*. Branch of UOC of USA. Refugees from USSR. 7n. |
| Igreja Pentecostal da Nova Vida | 1960 | P Pe2 | Z.... | 33 | 2,500 | 5,000 | *Cruzada da Nova Vida. New Life Pente Ch*. M=PAoC(Canada). 28n,8f,1p(64),W=53%,285Y. |
| Igreja Pentecostal da Oração | | I pen | ..... | | 1,000 | 2,000 | *Pentecostal Church of Prayer*. Independents. Declined since 1955. |
| Igreja Pentecostal Unida do Brasil | 1952 | P Pe1 | x.... | 80 | 3,300 | 8,000 | *United Pentecostal Ch. Jesus Only*. M=UPC(USA). Unitarian. HQ São Paulo. 50n,11f,2p'(44). |
| Igreja Presb Conservadora do Brasil | 1940 | I Ref | .TT.T | 100 | 1,000 | 2,000 | *Conservative Presbyterian Ch*. Schism ex IPI opposing modernism. 3 Presbyteries. 1s. |
| Igreja Presbiteriana do Brasil | 1859 | P Ref | R.u.N | 2,819 | 124,799 | 623,995 | *IPB, Presbyterian Ch*. 65 Presbyteries. M=UPUSA,PCUS. 574n,155f,2H,2h,2s,2063t(169097). |
| Igreja Presb Fundamentalista do Brasil | 1956 | I Ref | .TT.T | 17 | 400 | 800 | *Fundamental Presbyterian Ch*. Schism ex IPB opposing modernism. HQRecife. G=3.2%pa,1s. |
| Igreja Presb Independente do Brasil | 1903 | I Ref | Rvu.N | 650 | 130,000 | 180,000 | *IPI. Independent Presbyterian Ch*. Schism ex IPB. 1946,M=IBPFM(USA). 235n,1s,W=80%,35Yy. |
| Igrejas de Cristo | 1952 | P Dis | x.... | | 1,000 | 2,000 | M=Chs of Christ(Non-Instrumental)(USA). Independent group of congregations. 52f. |
| Igrejas radiofónicas isoladas | c1950 | I rad | ..... | 50 | 1,000 | 2,000 | Isolated radio believers in remote jungle areas. R=49700(HCJB,TWR,FEBC,Radio Vatican). |
| Irmãos Cristãos | c1905 | P BCr | x.... | 275 | 13,000 | 25,000 | *Christian (Plymouth, Open) Brethren. Gospel Halls*. M=CMML(UK,USA,Australia). 47f. |
| Missão Amazonas | 1949 | P int | ..... | 5 | 300 | 600 | M=Amazon Mission (USA). Pioneer work between Rio Negro and Amazon rivers. |
| Missão Batista Conservadora | 1946 | P Bap | xF... | 40 | 3,251 | 5,494 | *North & South Brazil Missions*. M=CBFMS(USA). 4n,10m,59f,2s,W=39%,178Y. |
| Missão Batista Livre do Brasil | 1958 | P Bap | xF... | 24 | 350 | 658 | *Brazil Free Will Baptist Mission*. M=NAFWB(USA). 3n,12x,22f,G=5%pa,W=88%,33Y,40z. |
| Missão de Evangelização Mundial | 1957 | P int | xF... | 24 | 90 | 500 | M=WEC,WEK(UK,USA,Germany). HQ Belo Horizonte. Declining. 11f,W=75%,40Y,12z. |
| Missão Ev Independente do Brasil | 1965 | P Bap | ..... | 11 | 130 | 550 | M=Evangelical Free Ch(USA). Congregationalist, Baptist. 3n,5x,W=64%,22Y. |
| Missão Interior do Brasil | 1954 | P CBr | ..... | 9 | 262 | 350 | M=Brazil Inland Mission. Open Brethren tradition. 7n,2x,G=21.3%pa,W=99%,38Y,20z. |
| Missão Novas Tribos do Brasil | 1946 | P int | x.... | | 2,000 | 5,000 | M=New Tribes Mission(USA). Work among Amerindian jungle tribes. 181f,2h,1s. |
| Sociedade Betânia do Brasil | 1963 | P ind | xF... | 6 | 496 | 1,000 | M=Bethany Fellowship(USA). Independents. 1n,2x,48f,1H,2s,W=87%,50Y,15z. |
| Sociedade Evangelizadora Bíblica | 1950 | P ind | ..... | 33 | 665 | 2,000 | *Bible Evangelizing Society*. Independents. 1n,17x,G=14.5%pa,1p(14),159Y. |
| Testemunhas de Jeová | 1920 | M Jeh | x.... | 1,202 | 72,269 | 169,835 | *Jehovah's Witnesses*. 70 Korean churches. 2270n,98x,G=11.4%pa,W=56%,7451Y,64921z. |
| União Batista Evangélica | 1957 | P Bap | xF... | | 1,000 | 2,000 | *Ev Baptist Union*. M=Baptist General Conference (USA). HQ São Paulo. 18f,1s. |
| União das Igrejas Ev da América do Sul | 1914 | P int | xN... | 21 | 1,015 | 1,500 | *Union of Ev Chs*. M=SA(Indian)Mission. Tribal Indians. 4n,10x,24f,G=7.1%pa,4h,1s,W=90%. |
| Other indigenous pentecostal churches | | I pen | ..... | | 100,000 | 300,000 | Total over 115 (see list below). |
| Other indigenous churches | | I ind | ..... | | 50,000 | 100,000 | Total over 40 (see list below). |
| Other Protestant denominations | | P | ..... | | 31,072 | 70,000 | Total about 100 (see list below). |
| Other marginal Protestant bodies | | M | ..... | | 20,000 | 50,000 | Total over 50, including New Ch(UK), RCJCLdS(USA). |
| Other Orthodox churches | | O | ..... | | 5,000 | 10,000 | Total about 8 (see list below) |
| Doubly-affiliated (duplication)(1970) | | | | | –5,212,000 | –9,144,236 | Evangelicals who also are or were baptized Roman Catholics. |
| **Total affiliated (mid-1970)** | | | | **47,500** | **50,973,105** | **90,864,000** | **Total denominations (1970) . . . 420.** |
| **Total affiliated (mid-1975)** | | | | **52,500** | **58,285,000** | **103,899,000** | **Total denominations (1975) . . . 460.** |
| **Total affiliated (mid-1980)** | | | | **59,000** | **66,676,000** | **118,856,000** | **Total denominations (1980) . . . 500.** |

NOTES ON TABLE ABOVE

COLUMNS: for meanings and CODES (cols. 1, 3, 4, 8), see Codebook (Part 6). Column 1: **Boldface type** = church with over 10% of country's affiliated Christians.

NATIONAL COUNCILS (Column 4, 5th letter).

- b = member of both CEB and CPB.
- I = Confederação Pentecostal do Brasil (CPB) (Brazil Pentecostal Federation) (an indigenous council begun in 1959, with about 20 members).
- N = Confederação Evangélico Brasileira (CEB) (Evangelical Federation of Brazil).
- R = Conferência Nacional dos Bispos do Brasil (CNBB) (National Bishops' Conference of Brazil).
- T = Confederação das Igrejas Evangélicas Fundamentalistas (CIEF) (Evangelical Federation of Fundamental Churches of Brazil).

*Other national councils*. Federação Evangélica Japonesa do Brasil (Japanese Evangelical Federation of Brazil): members include Igreja Evangélica Holiness do Brasil.

OTHER INDIGENOUS CHURCHES (pentecostal and non-pentecostal). Smaller bodies begun by Brazilians (or other Third-World Christians, e.g. Chinese and Japanese) number at least 155 (115 pentecostal, 40 non-pentecostal), and include the following: Assembleia Cristã, Assembleia de Deus (Missão Batista), Assembly Hall Ch (Chinese), Associação das Igrejas de Cristianismo Decidido, Associação das Igrejas Ev Independentes do Brasil (member of ICCC), Casa de Oração, Cruzada de Fé, Cruzada Ev a Volta de Cristo, Cruzada Ev de Salvação, Gospel of Jesus Ch (Iesu Fukuin Kyodan), Igreja Adventista Apostólica, Igreja Adventista da Reforma Completa, Igreja Apostólica Brasileira, Igreja Apostólica Ev Tenda de Deus pro Salvação e Cura Divina, Igreja Apostólica Pentecostal, Igreja Batista de Parque das Nações, Igreja Batista Revelação, Igreja Cristã Ev Independente, Igreja Cristã Pentecostal do B, Igreja Cristo Jesus, Igreja Ev Apostólica, Igreja Ev de Povo, Igreja Ev do Avivamento Bíblico, Igreja Ev do Espírito Santo, Igreja Ev dos Primogênitos Hebreus, Igreja Ev Maravilhas de Jesus, Igreja Ev Pentecostal, Igreja Ev Pentecostal Livre, Igreja Jesus Fonte de Agua Viva, Igreja Pentecostal Independente, Igreja Pentecostal Jesus Nazareno, Igreja Viva Jesus, Irmandade Metodista Ortodoxa, Korean Presbyterian Ch of São Paulo (member of ICCC), Ordem Católica Apostólica dos Missionários da Santa Cruz (1970 applied to join WCC), Renovação Espiritual, True Jesus Ch (Chinese).

OTHER PROTESTANT DENOMINATIONS. This list includes 53 of the around 100 smaller denominations and recently-arrived foreign Protestant faith missions, most of the latter having under 5 missionaries each (names are given in Portuguese unless the English (or German, or Spanish) name is more used): Acampamento Bíblico Pioneiro (Pioneer Bible Mission), Aliança Missionária do Brasil (Missionary & Soul-Winning Fellowship), Apostolic Ch of Pentecost (Canada, 2 missionaries), Asas (Alas) de Socorro (Mission Aviation Fellowship; several congregations), Associação das Igrejas Luteranas Livres (500 members), Baptist Faith Missions (1923), Baptist International Missions (1965), Baptist Mid-Missions (1936), Baptist Missionary Association of America, Baptist Missionary Society (UK, 1953;

33 missionaries), Berean Mission (1967), Brazil Gospel Fellowship Mission (1939), Brazilian Bible Mission, Children of God International (USA), Christian Bible Mission, Christian Missionary Fellowship (1957), Christian Nationals Evangelism Commission (1969), Congregational Holiness Ch (1972), Convenção Batista do Japão, Darbistas (Exclusive Brethren: Kelly-Continental), Deutsche Indianer Pionier Mission, Emmanuel Association, Federação de Igrejas Batistas do Nordeste do Brasil (member of ICCC), Fellowship of Independent Missions (1964), Gospel Fellowship Missions, Go-Ye Fellowship of Brazil, Iglesia Ev Apostólica, Igreja Batista do Calvário, Igreja Bíblica, Igreja Bíblica Congregaçionalista, Igreja Cristã de São Paulo, Igreja Cristã Presbiteriana do Brasil, Igreja dos Marinheiros (Scandinavian Sailors' Ch), Igreja Eslava Brasileira Pentecostal, Igreja Ev Armenia, Igreja Ev Batista, Independent Bible Baptist Mission (1954), Instituto Apostólico do Brasil (Apostolic Ch of Oklahoma, USA), Japan Ev Mission (1972), Junta Batista Bíblica do Brasil, Missão da Amazónia Ocidental (West Amazon Mission), Missão Evangelística Brasileira (Brazil Evangelistic Mission), Paraná Valley Mission, Slavic Gospel Association, Sociedade Brasileira Amigos de Israel, Sociedade Missionária de Peniel, Sociedade União Cristã (Gnadauer Verband), United Missions, United World Mission (1961), Voz Bíblica Brasileira (Independent Faith Mission), World Gospel Mission (1966), World Missions (1964), World-Wide Missions (1963).
OTHER ORTHODOX CHURCHES. These include: Coptic Orthodox Ch, Old Believers Russian Orthodox Ch (Old Ritualist Ch, Priestless) (1958-61 from China and Turkey), Orthodox Syrian Ch, Serbian Orthodox Ch, Syrian Orthodox Ch.
OTHER CATHOLIC (NON-ROMAN) CHURCHES. Including Antoinists (from Belgium and France), and miniscule episcopal churches under bishops-at-large (episcopi vagantes).

PEOPLES (ethnolinguistic). Christians: 53.3% Brazilian White, 22.2% Mulatto, 12.1% Mestiço (Mestizo), 11.0% Black, 0.6% Japanese, 0.4% Portuguese, 0.1% Italian, 0.1% Spaniard, 0.1% Russian, 0.1% Polish, Armenian, Ukrainian, Hungarian, Korean, USA White, Chinese (10,000), Romanian, Yugoslav, Basque, Greek, Arab (Lebanese, Syrian), Amerindian, French, British, Gypsy, Dutch.

COUNTRY-WIDE TOTALS
EVANGELIZATION (see Part 5). 1900: 98%. 1970: 100%. 1980: 100%. *Mass evangelism.* A few of the vast number of recent campaigns: 1960, Billy Graham rally in Rio de Janeiro (143,000 attenders, 2,193 enquirers), 1962 São Paulo crusade, October 1974 Rio de Janeiro crusade (615,000 attenders, 15,949 enquirers); 1965, simultaneous Protestant crusades in all parts of Brazil; August 1966, Oral Roberts campaign; 1968, New Life in Christ Course prepared by Latin American Evangelical Commission on Christian Education, designed to reach persons with less than 5 years of schooling (80% of the population); launch evangelism in the lower Amazon, carried on by the New Tribes Mission and Unevangelized Fields Mission; December 1971, Morris Cerullo 8-day crusade in upper Amazon jungles (150,000 attenders); 1974–75, Evangelism-in-Depth; 1975, Brazil Congress on Evangelism (Rio de Janeiro). Many denominations have campaigns regularly; one organized by Brazil for Christ (OBPC) in a football stadium drew 152,000 on a single day, with 20,000 converts recorded. *Radiophonic evangelism.* Annual listeners' letters (1975): 21,330 TWR, 15,954 HCJB, 12,000 KGEI, Radio Vatican, et alia. Over 10 million listen to the 80 monthly programmes of Radio Trans Mundial do Brasil (TWR), with 9,000 in its Bible correspondence courses, 1974–77. Bible correspondence courses (1975): for university students, run by University Biblical Alliance of Brazil on 25% of all higher education campuses; also ICI (15,200 active students, 75,000 enrolments). Around 2 million have been enrolled in Catholic radiophonic schools.
FOREIGN MISSIONARIES AND PERSONNEL (nationals serving abroad) (1974). Total 2,456 in over 35 countries: about 2,274 Roman Catholics, 140 Protestants, 25 Brazilian indigenous (including 4 ICAB missionary bishops), 10 marginal Protestants, 5 Catholics (non-Roman), 2 Anglicans.
FOREIGN MISSIONARIES AND PERSONNEL (aliens from abroad) (1973). Total 15,472. *From Western world.* 13,768: about 10,209 Roman Catholics, 2,741 Protestants (2,121 in 107 USA societies, 238 in 12 UK societies, 123 in 12 WGermany societies, 100 in 2 Sweden societies, 76 in 9 Canada societies, 20 in 4 Netherlands societies, 17 in 8 Australia societies, 16 in 4 Norway societies, 9 in 8 New Zealand societies, 5 in 2 Finland societies, 4 in 1 Switzerland society), about 780 marginal Protestants (690 Mormons from USA, 50 Jehovah's Witnesses), about 15 Catholics (non-Roman), 13 Anglicans (7 in 2 UK societies, 6 in 2 USA societies), about 10 Orthodox. *From Communist world.* 284: about 280 Roman Catholics (265 from Poland, others from Yugoslavia, Hungary), 2 Orthodox, 2 Protestants from Hungary. *From Third World.* 1,420: 1,126 Roman Catholics (about 1,000 from other Latin American countries, 120 from Japan, also from Korea, Philippines et alia), about 130 indigenous from Japan, Korea, Taiwan, Hong Kong, Indonesia and Latin American countries, 100 Protestants (35 Japan, Korea, Philippines, Taiwan, Latin American countries), about 60 marginal Protestants (40 Mormons, 10 Jehovah's Witnesses from Korea), 4 Anglicans from Japan.
INSTITUTIONS (church-operated) (1973). Total 2,590, including 1,730 higher schools (231 minor seminaries), 200 medical centres (15 Protestant hospitals and 130 clinics), 280 radio/TV stations, 80 religious communities (72 monasteries), 18 research centres, 145 seminaries (85 Protestant, 54 RC, 5 Brazilian indigenous, 1 Anglican), 27 study centres, 12 universities.
PERIODICALS. About 350 titles (70% RC; 19 SDA, many indigenous).
PERSONNEL. About 78,472 (63,000 national, 15,472 foreign).
RELIGIOUS LIBRARIES. About 450.
SCRIPTURE DISTRIBUTION (1975). Annual totals: 675,980 Bibles (28% subsidized, 72% commercial), 1,971,958 NTs (82% free, 3% subsidized, 15% commercial), 47,945 UBS portions, 14,090,284 UBS selections. *Translations completed.* Portion: 24 languages since 1930.
SERVICE AGENCIES. About 250, including ACF (YWCA), ACISJF, ACM(YMCA), AEC, AETTE, ASTE, CAVE, CCCI, CEB, CEF, CEI, CELADEC, CFCJ, CIC, CIEF, CLC, CNBB, CODEMAS, COMINA, CPB, CRB, CWS, FASE, GISC, IBETE, IDI, JARS, LWR, MAF, MCC, MEB, MFC, MIB, MTS, OC, PTL, SERB, SICA, SIL, SIRE-SEME, SORPE, SU, TFP, UBRAJE, WBT, WLC(EHC), WVI, YFC.

ADDITIONAL DATA ON CHURCHES
ASSEMBLEIAS DE DEUS. *Adult membership.* Since this denomination, operating mainly in north and northeast Brazil, is loosely-organized and does not have a central reporting system for statistics, observers have given widely varying estimates for baptized (communicant) membership. Using 3 differing methodologies, W. R. Read in *New patterns of church growth in Brazil* (1965:120) estimated 950,000 communicants for 1964; in *Latin American church growth* (1969:67) he revised the figure to 1,400,000 for 1967, whereas in *Brazil 1980: the Protestant handbook* (1973:18) he downgraded the total to 746,400 for 1970 to bring it into line with government figures. The denomination itself (in *Annual report 1973*, Assemblies of God Division of Foreign Missions (Springfield, USA), page 10) claimed for 1970–1971 2,057,000 baptized members and 726,000 other (adult) believers, of whom 677,710 had been baptized in the Holy Spirit. Following the methodology employed in the present Encyclopedia, we term the denomination's own figures as 'affiliated' and give them in Table 2 above, and we term government figures as 'professing' and give them in Table 1. *Growth* (1978: reported by church headquarters). Buildings (*templos*) 36,000. Workers (*obreiros*) 55,000. Adult church members (*membros da Igreja*) 3.1 million. Other adherents (*congregados não batizados e crianças*) 2.5 million. Sunday schools 14,000, pupils 900,000. Community (*total de fiéis das Assembleias de Deus*) 5.6 million.
CONGREGACAO CRISTA DO BRASIL. *Adult members.* Of the 600,000 baptized members and other adults in 1970, communicants numbered 357,800. A mission has been established in Portugal.
CONVENCAO DAS IGREJAS EVANGELICAS BATISTAS INDEPENDENTES DO BRASIL. Served by 50 missionaries of the Örebro Mission from Sweden (Sociedade Missionária Batista Independente), and 2 from the Swedish Baptist Union of Finland, the church is also termed Igreja Batista Bethel.
IGREJA CATOLICA APOSTOLICA BRASILEIRA. 12 Dioceses (with 9 auxiliary bishops): Anápolis, Baixada Fluminense, Brasília, Ceará, Natal, Paraná, Recife, Rio de Janeiro, Santa Catarina, Santo Andre, Santos, São Paulo. There are also bishops in Argentina, Bolivia, Panama and Paraguay.
IGREJA CATOLICA NO BRASIL. *Pastoral regions.* In 1954 the country was divided into 7 Pastoral Regions, by 1973 expanded to 14. Each region has its own Secretariado Regional directed by one of its archbishops with a co-ordinator. *Column 8.* The first sub-column gives the postal code of the state(s) in which each diocese is located. (Code: AC Acre, AL Alagoas, AM Amazonas, AP Amapá, BA Bahia, CE Ceará, DF Distrito Federal, ES Espírito Santo, FN Fernando de Noronha, GB Guanabara, GO Goiás, MA Maranhão, MG Minas Gerais, MT Mato Grosso, PA Pará, PB Paraíba, PE Pernambuco, PI Piauí, PR Paraná, RJ Rio de Janeiro, RN Rio Grande do Norte, RO Rondônia, RR Roraima, RS Rio Grande do Sul, SC Santa Catarina, SE Sergipe, SP São Paulo). The second sub-column gives the largest male religious institute (order or congregation with the most priests or brothers serving in the diocese) in 1970. 'Nil' means no religious clergy in 1970. *New dioceses* (created since 1972). Alagoinhas, Barretos, Campo Maior, Cornelio Procopio, Coroatá, Joaçaba, Limeira, Picos, Registro, Umuarama, União da Vitoria. *New prelature.* SS Conceição do Araguaia (1976). *Annual baptisms* (1972; total 2,503,874) 98.8% infant, 1.2% adult. *Priests.* Total 13,149 (7,655 national, 5,396 expatriate, 98 nationality unknown). *National priests* (1970). 3,902 secular, 3,753 regular. *Expatriate priests* (1970). 1,102 secular, 4,294 regular. *Brothers* (1970). 2,421 Brazilians, 859 expatriates. *Sisters* (1970). 36,036 Brazilians, 326 former expatriates now naturalized Brazilians, 4,421 expatriates, 184 of unknown nationality. *Catholic charismatics* (January 1974). 5,000 adults including many religious personnel in 100 prayer groups are active in the Charismatic Renewal. By 1975, the large majority of the over 210 Catholic bishops in Brazil were open to the Charismatic Renewal. In 1976, one of several leaders conferences was held in Santarém, PA, a city where over 1,000 people had been baptized in the Holy Spirit in the previous few years. *Seminaries.* The number of major seminaries for diocesan priests is 26 (1975), and for religious clergy 28 (1973). *Seminarians* (1970). Total 2,467 (1,023 secular, 1,444 regular). *Indigenous religious congregations* (of Brazilian origin). Total 62 for women, including 25 secular institutes. These include: 1,582 Jesus Crucificado, 1,349 Imaculado Coração de Maria, 752 Imaculada Conceição, 502 Catequistas Franciscanas. *Main foreign orders and congregations* (1970). Priests (with over 250 professed each): 1,248 OP, 983 SJ, 929 OFMCap, 915 SDB, 584 CSSR, 287 SVD, 270 CM, 253 FSCJ. Brothers (with over 250 professed each): 889 PFM, 386 FSC. Sisters (with over 500 professed each): 2,396 São Vicente de Paulo, 1,573 São José de Chambéry, 1,432 Salésiennes, 1,249 Divina Providência, 1,089 Franciscanas da Penitência e Caridade Cristã, 725 São Carlos Borromeu, 677 Santa Doroteia de Frassinetti, 590 Sagrado Coração de Jesus, 569 Nossa Senhora.
*Catholic organizations.* The National Conference of the Bishops of Brazil (Conferência Nacional dos Bispos do Brasil, CNBB) was founded in Rio de Janeiro in 1952 and reorganized in 1964 and 1970, and is a member of CELAM. For the armed forces, Brazil forms a single military vicariate.
The Conference of Religious of Brazil (Conferência dos Religiosos do Brasil, CRB), was founded in Rio de Janeiro in 1954 and unites all religious institutes of men and sisters, both Brazilian and foreign. Organized into 14 regional sections corresponding to the pastoral regions of CNBB, and in 3 sectors, the CRB works closely with CNBB. It is a member of CLAR.
The CNBB authorized the formation in 1974 of a National Pastoral Commission (Comissão Pastoral Nacional) consisting of 90 persons, including 26 laymen, brothers, sisters, the titular heads and co-ordinators of the pastoral regions, and 3 bishops from the Pastoral Episcopal Commission. Lacking the status of a true national pastoral council, the commission, which meets twice yearly, serves in an 'advisory capacity to the executive of the episcopal conference'. There is to date no national priests' council or senate.
Lay activities are co-ordinated by the Sector of the Lay Apostolate of the CNBB (CNBB—Sector do Apostolado dos Leigos), and studies are at present being made concerning the creation of a National Council of the Laity. The principal movements of the lay apostolate are Catholic Action (Ação Católica), National Confederation of the Marian Congregations of Brazil (Confederação Nacional das Congregações Marianas do Brasil), Christian Study Courses (Cursilhos de Cristandade), Teams of Our Lady (Equipes de Nossa Senhora), Legion of Mary (Legião de Maria), Christian Family Movement (Movimento Familiar Cristão, MFC), Serra Club, Society of St Vincent de Paul (Sociedade de S Vincente de Paulo), National Union of Family Associations (União Nacional de Associações Familiares), Scouts and Guides.
The Holy See has diplomatic relations with Brazil and is represented to government and the Catholic hierarchy by a nuncio in Brasília.
The headquarters for several continental and international organizations are located in Brazil. The International Catholic Conference of Guides (CICG) was founded in Paris in 1965 and now has its headquarters in Rio de Janeiro. The conference has 22 member bodies in 20 countries, with others corresponding, and co-ordinates Catholic associations of Girl Guides throughout the world and is integrated into the World Association of Guides and Scouts. The Latin American Secretariat for the Christian Family Movement is at Belo Horizonte. The movement defines itself as an apostolate of the family and for the family, dedicated to the growth of conjugal spirituality. There are 4 major sectors: marriage and family life preparation, research into conjugal harmony, parent-child relations, and family education. The movement exists throughout Latin America. The Latin American Secretariat of Caritas (Secretariado Latinoamericano de Caritas, SELAC), located in Rio de Janeiro, is the organization for liasion and information between Latin America and Rome.
There are numerous unofficial opinion groups active in Brazil. Given the political situation in the country, there are no structured, progressivist bodies, but 3 influential conservative groups may be noted. Their common characteristics are their ultra-conservative views regarding politics and their desire to combat 'subversive communism' within the church, namely the minority of the church opposed to the regime. Their tacit alliance with different military governments since 1964 has achieved for them complete freedom of expression although censorship has been severe for others since 1968. These groups are: (1) Brazilian Society for the Defence of Tradition, Family and Property (Sociedade Brasileira de Defensa da Tradição, Família e Propriedade, TFP) is the medium of expression in particular among Catholics who are large property owners. It is found for the most part in the states of São Paulo and Minas Gerais, exists in 15 other states and also in the neighbouring countries of Argentina, Uruguay and Chile. Although reduced to a few hundred militants (for the most part former students of Catholic colleges and universities, with a high proportion of young Japanese descendants), the TFP has succeeded in making an impact on the urban population, due to the publicity generated during its public campaigns. Examples are a 1961–63 campaign against the projected agrarian reform of the Goulart government, a 1966 attack on the projected legalization of divorce in the new constitution, and a 1969 attack on 'subversion within the church' at the 19th assembly of the Brazilian episcopate. (2) Permanence (Permanência), founded in Rio de Janeiro in 1968, is a centre with weekly meetings and its own journal, but its most important influence is through Brazil's large daily newspapers. It is dedicated to the struggle against the return of modernism in the church and has provided support for the regime since 1964. (3) Present Hour (Hora Presente), founded in São Paulo in 1968, is another group with a journal of the same name which promotes explicitly the values of a Christian civilization and advocates the return of the corporative system. The journal opens its columns to corresponding French and Spanish conservatives. The influence of clergy is less apparent here than in the 2 preceding groups.
Several organizations are devoted to research and social action. (1) The Centre for Religious Statistics and Social Investigation (Centro de Estatística Religiosa e Investigações Sociais, CERIS), founded in Rio de Janeiro in 1962, is an organization created by and related to the CNBB. The centre conducts socio-religious and socio-economic research for the benefit of Catholic and other institutions, collects and tabulates statistics on the Catholic Church of Brazil, publishes and updates the Catholic yearbook and offers technical assistance for the analysis and planning of social action and humanitarian projects. It maintains 4 departments: research, statistics, regional agencies (with collaborators in all the CNBB regions) and auxiliary services (library, administration and cartographic operations). (2) The Brazilian Institute of Development (Instituto Brasileiro de Desenvolvimento, IBRADES), founded at Rio de Janeiro by Jesuits in 1969, was created by and is dependent upon the CNBB. It conducts research and contributes to the dissemination of information on development in both its global and national aspects. (3) The Centre for Intercultural Training (Centro de Formação Intercultural, CENFI), was formed in Rio de Janeiro by Ivan Illich in 1961 and passed under the control of CNBB during 1969–70. It conducts research studies on cultural development and change through analysis of the cultural and linguistic situations in Brazil. It provides 2 annual courses of 4 months each. (4) The Federation of Organs for Social and Educational Assistance (Federação de Orgãos para Assistência Social e Educacional, FASE), founded in Rio de Janeiro in 1961, is a working association for the promotion of community development, training of leaders, and basic community education as well as the provision of technical assistance to projects. It also produces and distributes audio-visual materials, and maintains 5 regional bureaux at Belém, Recife, Rio de Janeiro, São Paulo and Pôrto Alegre. (5) The Movement for Basic Education (Movimento de Educação de Base, MEB), founded in Rio de Janeiro in 1961, has been under the CNBB since 1961. Before 1964, the MEB was heavily involved in conscientization, playing an important role in the processes of political socialization of the rural masses. At the height of its activities at the end of 1963, it counted more than 400 permanent staff and 7,000 radiophonic schools, reaching 100,000 students. It utilized for this purpose diocesan transmitters and received financial aid from the federal government. After the 1964 coup, the MEB changed its orientation and at the same time lost its audience at the national level. Its activities were interrupted for financial reasons between 1966 and 1968, but it was revived in 1969. Statistics for that year listed 211 permanent employees, 1,767 assistant teachers and 1,798 centres, with 31,000 students. There are also numerous regional institutions for the promotion of social welfare.
A large number of institutes exist for higher theological studies. The National Institute of Pastoralia (Instituto Nacional de Pastoral, INP), founded in Rio de Janeiro in 1971, was created by and is dependent upon the CNBB. It engages in theological and pastoral study of the problems of the life and mission of the Brazilian church, trains personnel and carries on research. Training for catechists in provided both at the national and regional levels.
Other institutes include the Centre for Biblical and Ecumenical Studies (Centro de Estudos Bíblicos e Ecumênicos), in Rio de Janeiro, and the Latin American Centre for Parapsychology (Centro Latinoamericano de Parapsicologia, CLAP) in São Paulo. The latter is a centre dedicated to research and education, with special concern for combatting superstitions and pseudo-religious interpretations of phenomena which do not accord with scientific and religious truth.
Missionary action is co-ordinated and inspired throughout Brazil by the National Missionary Council (Conselho Missionário Nacional, COMINA), in Rio de Janeiro. Several missionary institutes are also active. (1) The Centre for Missionary Orientation (Centro de Orientação Missionária, COM) founded in Caixas do Sul in 1968, is a diocesan organization dedicated to promoting missionary concern for the diocese and foreign fields. (2) The Anchieta Operation (Operação Anchieta, OPAM), founded in Pôrto Alegre in 1969, is an independent organization which collaborates with official and private bodies engaged in humanitarian projects, particularly with Indians, and sends volunteers to help the marginal population, especially the indigenous peoples of Mato Grosso and the Rondônia. (3) The Indigenous Missionary Council (Conselho Indigenista

Missionário, CIMI), founded in Brasília in 1972, is an official organization of the CNBB, serving Indians and missionaries in Brazil. Its objectives include promotion of pastoral work among Indians, arousing of Brazilians to the problems of Indians, and the establishment of relationships between Catholic Indian missions and the CNBB, governmental organizations (especially the National Foundation for Indians, FUNAI) and non-Catholic missions. Other missionary agencies are CENFI in Rio de Janeiro; Service for International Apostolic Co-operation (Serviço de Cooperação Apostólica Internacional, SCAI) in Rio de Janeiro, dependent on the CNBB; and International and Brazilian Volunteers for the Amazon in Belém.

Missionaries to Brazil serving in jurisdictions under Propaganda (Rome) numbered 1,401 in 1971, 401 being men (38 Brazilians, 363 foreigners), and 1,000 women (525 Brazilians, 475 foreigners). In addition, in 1974, 131 Brazilians were serving as foreign missionaries in 25 countries on 4 continents: 47 in Latin America, 69 in Africa (51 in Portuguese-speaking countries), 9 in Asia and 6 in Oceania. The principal missionary congregations of Brazilian origin are: for men, the Instituto Estrêla Missionária founded in 1967 at Nova Iguaçu, and for women the Congregação das Missionárias Brasileiras, founded in Campinas in 1928, the Congregação das Irmãs Missionárias da Imaculada Conceição da Mãe de Deus, founded in Santarém in 1910, and the Sociedade das Missionárias de Santa Teresinha founded in Praça da Bandeira in 1954.

The National Secretariat for Education and Culture (Sec-retariado Nacional de Educação e Cultura) and the Association for Catholic Education in Brazil (Associação de Educação Católica do Brasil), both of Rio de Janeiro, co-ordinate the Catholic educational programme. In 1969 public schools at the secondary, commercial and teacher-training levels catered for 830,825 students, as contrasted with 1,061,886 in private schools (Catholic and non-Catholic). In 1962, schools numbered 2,184 primary (413,963 pupils) and 2,074 secondary (230,029); in 1973, schools numbered 2,765 primary (534,082 pupils) and 1,431 secondary (347,743). Twelve Catholic universities have been established since 1945: Rio de Janeiro (PUCRJ), São Paulo (PUCSP), Salvador, Rio Grande do Sul (PUCRGS), Campinas, Rio do Sinos (UNISINOS), Minas Gerais (UCMG), Petrópolis, Pernambuco (UCPE), Goiás, Paraná, Pelotas; these 12 universities have 22% of all students. There also exists a series of autonomous establishments for higher Catholic education.

Social action is co-ordinated by Caritas Brasileira, founded in Rio de Janeiro in 1956, which is dependent on the CNBB and is a member of Caritas International in Rome. It consists of 10 regional offices, 192 diocesan offices and 800 associated works. The programme of Caritas consists of food distribution to 2 million, self-help, child and health education and other social services. The Providence Bank (Banco da Providência) promotes a self-help programme of finance for housing construction, trades, hostels and unemployment assistance. Caritas also provides aid to 11 hospitals and 3 clinics for infants.

IGREJA EVANGELICA PENTECOSTAL UNIDA 'O BRASIL PARA CRISTO'. A rapidly-growing free-pentecostal body begun by Manoel de Mello, this church has since 1965 been constructing in São Paulo the largest Evangelical church building in the world, seating 25,000 with standing room for 15,000 more, which aims to be a complete Christian community or New Jerusalem, with attached administrative offices, bookstore, library, bank, crèches, primary and secondary schools, college, clinic, gymnasium, laundry, hotel, restaurant, 300-car garage, et alia. Some assistance and funds are received from Dutch missionaries in Missão Missionária Pentecostal (Holandesa). Its development plan calls for 1,500 farms housing 40 persons each by 1980. *Membership.* Largely mixed race (Mestiços) and Brazilian Whites; mostly urban working class. *Growth.* By 1975 congregations had increased to 5,000 and baptized members to 1.5 million with many more regular attenders; found in all 22 states and in the federal capital. *Radio.* The daily radio programme Voice of OBPC is carried over 150 radio stations across Brazil. *Missions.* OBPC does not believe in propagating itself outside Brazil, hence has no workers or churches abroad.

TESTEMUNHAS DE JEOVA. *Membership.* 54% White, 34% Mestiço (Caboclo (White/Amerindian), Mulatto (White/Negro), Cafuso (Negro/Amerindian)), 10% Negro, 2% Japanese, Korean. Witnesses are found in 75 cities with over 100,000 population each. *Attendance.* At the 1972 Memorial of the death of Christ, 180,866 attended.

---

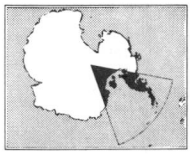

# British Antarctic Territory

## SECULAR DATA

**STATE. Official name:** The Crown Colony of the British Antarctic Territory.
**Flag** (shown above right): That of the UK (Britain).
**Area:** 5,245 sq.km. (2,025 sq.miles) excluding Graham Land (473,000 sq.miles). Agricultural land: 0.0%.
**Government:** Crown colony of the United Kingdom (Britain), formed 1962.
**Official language:** English.

**DEMOGRAPHY. Population:** 79 males (winter 1972. For 1970–2000 (UN), see last row of Table 1). Population density (1975): 0/sq.km. (0/sq.mile). Under 15 years: 0%. Growth rate (1975–80):

0.0% per year (births 0%, deaths 0%). Household size: 2 persons.
**Major language:** English.

**ETHNOLINGUISTIC GROUPS:** 99% European.

**MONEY** (1977). **Monetary unit:** UK£ (= 100 new pence). US$1 = UK£0.55.

**EDUCATION.** Adult literacy: 100%.

*Right.* Postage stamp showing 1953 Coronation oath administered by Archbishop of Canterbury.

TABLE 1.   RELIGIOUS ADHERENTS IN THE BRITISH ANTARCTIC TERRITORY

| Year | 1900 | | mid-1970 | | Annual change, 1970–1980 | | | | mid-1975 | | mid-1980 | | 2000 | |
| Name | Adherents | % | Adherents | % | Natural | Conversion | Total | Rate | Adherents | % | Adherents | % | Adherents | % |
|---|---|---|---|---|---|---|---|---|---|---|---|---|---|---|
| Christians | 0 | 0.0 | 65 | 76.5 | 0 | 0 | 0 | 0.00 | 65 | 76.5 | 65 | 76.5 | 70 | 70.0 |
| professing | 0 | 0.0 | 65 | 76.5 | 0 | 0 | 0 | 0.00 | 65 | 76.5 | 65 | 76.5 | 70 | 70.0 |
| nominal | 0 | 0.0 | 65 | 76.5 | 0 | 0 | 0 | 0.00 | 65 | 76.5 | 65 | 76.5 | 70 | 70.0 |
| Anglicans | 0 | 0.0 | 65 | 76.5 | 0 | 0 | 0 | 0.00 | 65 | 76.5 | 65 | 76.5 | 70 | 70.0 |
| Non-religious | 0 | 0.0 | 20 | 23.5 | 0 | 0 | 0 | 0.00 | 20 | 23.5 | 20 | 23.5 | 30 | 30.0 |
| Country's population | 0 | 100.0 | 85 | 100.0 | 0 | 0 | 0 | 0.00 | 85 | 100.0 | 85 | 100.0 | 100 | 100.0 |

COLUMNS, ROWS. For meanings and definitions, see Codebook (Part 6). Note that, by definition, total 'Christians' = professing + crypto-Christians, which also = affiliated + nominal Christians. Percentages may not always total exactly, due to rounding.
COUNTRY'S POPULATION. In 1972–73, all adult males.

**CHRISTIANITY.** There are no organized churches, since there are no permanent residents and the population consists entirely of scientific personnel on short-term assignments. The territory does not belong to or come under any Anglican, Roman Catholic or Protestant jurisdiction.

---

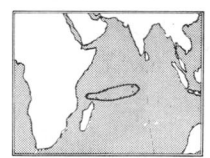

# British Indian Ocean Territory

## SECULAR DATA

**STATE. Official name:** The Crown Colony of the British Indian Ocean Territory (BIOT).
**Flag** (shown above right): That of the UK (Britain).
**Area:** 226 sq.km. (87 sq.miles). Agricultural land: 0.0%.
**Government:** Crown colony of the United Kingdom (Britain), formed 1965.

**Official language:** English.
**Capital:** Administrative HQ, Mahé (Seychelles).
**Foreign forces** (1973): USA naval base at Diego Garcia.

**DEMOGRAPHY. Population:** 2,000, mostly transients (official estimate 31.XII.1965. For 1970–2000 (UN), see last row of Table 1). Population density (1975): 26/sq.km. (66/sq.mile). Under 15 years: 44%. Growth rate (1975–80): 0.0% per year. Household

size: 4.7 persons.
**Major languages:** English, Creole.

**ETHNOLINGUISTIC GROUPS:** 98% Creole (Mauritian, Seychellese), 2.0% British, USA White.

**MONEY** (1977). **Monetary unit:** Seychelles rupee (= 100 cents); US$1 = SR 7.60.

TABLE 1.   RELIGIOUS ADHERENTS IN THE BRITISH INDIAN OCEAN TERRITORY

| Year | 1900 | | mid-1970 | | Annual change, 1970–1980 | | | | mid-1975 | | mid-1980 | | 2000 | |
| Name | Adherents | % | Adherents | % | Natural | Conversion | Total | Rate | Adherents | % | Adherents | % | Adherents | % |
|---|---|---|---|---|---|---|---|---|---|---|---|---|---|---|
| Christians | 200 | 40.0 | 900 | 45.0 | 0 | 0 | 0 | 0.00 | 900 | 45.0 | 900 | 45.0 | 900 | 45.0 |
| professing | 200 | 40.0 | 900 | 45.0 | 0 | 0 | 0 | 0.00 | 900 | 45.0 | 900 | 45.0 | 900 | 45.0 |
| Roman Catholics | 150 | 30.0 | 700 | 35.0 | 0 | 0 | 0 | 0.00 | 700 | 35.0 | 700 | 35.0 | 700 | 35.0 |
| Anglicans | 50 | 10.0 | 200 | 10.0 | 0 | 0 | 0 | 0.00 | 200 | 10.0 | 200 | 10.0 | 200 | 10.0 |
| nominal | 0 | 0.0 | 300 | 15.0 | 0 | 0 | 0 | 0.00 | 300 | 15.0 | 300 | 15.0 | 400 | 20.0 |
| affiliated | 200 | 40.0 | 600 | 30.0 | 0 | 0 | 0 | 0.00 | 600 | 30.0 | 600 | 30.0 | 500 | 25.0 |
| total practising | 140 | 70 | 360 | 60 | 0 | 0 | 0 | 0.00 | 360 | 60 | 360 | 60 | 250 | 50 |
| non-practising | 60 | 30 | 240 | 40 | 0 | 0 | 0 | 0.00 | 240 | 40 | 240 | 40 | 250 | 50 |
| Roman Catholics | 150 | 30.0 | 500 | 25.0 | 0 | 0 | 0 | 0.00 | 500 | 25.0 | 500 | 25.0 | 440 | 22.0 |
| Catholic pentecostals | 0 | 0.0 | 0 | 0.0 | 0 | 16 | 16 | 26.67 | 60 | 3.0 | 160 | 8.0 | 200 | 10.0 |
| Anglicans | 50 | 10.0 | 100 | 5.0 | 0 | 0 | 0 | 0.00 | 100 | 5.0 | 100 | 5.0 | 60 | 3.0 |
| Hindus | 250 | 50.0 | 900 | 45.0 | 0 | 0 | 0 | 0.00 | 900 | 45.0 | 900 | 45.0 | 900 | 45.0 |
| Muslims | 50 | 10.0 | 200 | 10.0 | 0 | 0 | 0 | 0.00 | 200 | 10.0 | 200 | 10.0 | 200 | 10.0 |
| Country's population | 500 | 100.0 | 2,000 | 100.0 | 0 | 0 | 0 | 0.00 | 2,000 | 100.0 | 2,000 | 100.0 | 2,000 | 100.0 |

COLUMNS, ROWS. For meanings and definitions, see Codebook (Part 6). Note that, by definition, total 'Christians' = professing + crypto-Christians, which also = affiliated + nominal Christians. Percentages may not always total exactly, due to rounding.
CENSUSES. No religion question has been asked.
CATHOLIC PENTECOSTALS (or, Catholic charismatics). In 1974, interest in the Catholic Charismatic Renewal was growing among USA servicemen at the Diego Garcia naval base, with about 20 involved adults in a twice-weekly prayer group; total charismatic community including children, 50.

Crucifixion of Christ
(Ethiopic manuscript) on Easter
1973 postage stamp

**NON-CHRISTIAN RELIGIONS.** In 1970 the population was 45% Hindu and 10% Muslim.

## CHRISTIANITY

**CATHOLIC CHURCH.** Catholics on the Chagos Archipelago are under the jurisdiction of the diocese of Port Louis in Mauritius; those of the Aldabra, Farquhar and Des Roches islands are attached to the diocese of Port Victoria in the Seychelles. A priest from the Seychelles visits the islands annually by agreement with the 2 bishops.

**ANGLICAN CHURCH.** Anglicans on the various islands of the territory are attached to the diocese

of Mauritius, in the Church of the Province of the Indian Ocean. Lacking a resident priest, they are visited periodically by Mauritian clergy.

**CHURCH AND STATE.** Freedom of religion is guaranteed as with all territories coming under the jurisdiction of the British Colonial Office.

TABLE 2.    ORGANIZED CHURCHES AND DENOMINATIONS IN THE BRITISH INDIAN OCEAN TERRITORY

| Official name 1 | Begun 2 | Type 3 | Counc 4 | Congs 5 | Adults 6 | Affiliated 7 | Names, notes, and other statistics (see Codebook) 8 |
|---|---|---|---|---|---|---|---|
| **Anglican Church (D Mauritius)** | | A Hig | aw... | 1 | 50 | 100 | Under Diocese of Mauritius, in CPIO. No resident clergy; periodic visits. |
| **Catholic Church** | | R Lat | P.S.. | 1 | 300 | 500 | In D Port Louis (Mauritius), D Port Victoria (Seychelles). Annual visit by priest. |
| Total affiliated (mid-1970) | | | | 2 | 350 | 600 | Total denominations (1970) . . . 2. |
| Total affiliated (mid-1975) | | | | 2 | 350 | 600 | Total denominations (1975) . . . 2. |
| Total affiliated (mid-1980) | | | | 2 | 350 | 600 | Total denominations (1980) . . . 2. |

**NOTES ON TABLE ABOVE**
COLUMNS: for meanings, and CODES (cols. 1, 3, 4, 8), see Codebook (Part 6). Column 1: **Boldface type** = church with over

10% of country's affiliated Christians.

PEOPLES (ethnolinguistic). Christians: 96% Creole (Mauritian, Seychellese), 4% British, USA White.

COUNTRY-WIDE TOTALS
EVANGELIZATION (see Part 5). 1900: 50%. 1970: 90%. 1980: 95%.

---

# BRITISH VIRGIN ISLANDS

## SECULAR DATA

**STATE. Official name:** The Colony of the British Virgin Islands.
**Flag** (shown above right): British Blue Ensign with arms of the Colony in the fly.
**Area:** 153 sq.km. (59 sq.miles). Description: 36 islands (16 inhabited). Agricultural land: 53.3%.
**Government:** British colony, since 1956 (1666 British colony of Leeward Islands, 1956 separate colony).
**Legislature:** Executive Council, 6 members. Legislative Council, 10 members.
**Official language:** English.
**Capital:** Road Town 2,260.

**DEMOGRAPHY. Population:** 9,672 (census of 7.IV.1970. For 1970–2000 (UN), see last row of Table 1). Population density (1975): 74/sq.km. (192/sq.miles). Under 15 years: 43%. Growth rate (1975–80): 2.80% per year (births 2.87%, deaths −0.68%, immigrants 0.61%). Life expectancy (1975–80): 69.1 years. Household size: 4.4 persons.
**Major languages:** English, Portuguese, Hindi, Arabic.
**Labour force:** 41%.
**Tourists** (1973): 57,839.

**ETHNOLINGUISTIC GROUPS:** 90.0% Black (African Negro), 7.3% White (Germanic European, USA, 0.3% Portuguese), 1.6% Mulatto, 0.7% Indo-Pakistani, 0.1% Arab (Syro-Lebanese).

**MONEY** (1977). **Monetary unit:** US dollar (= 100 cents).
**National income per person:** US$1,700. Average annual family income: US$7,480.
**Cost of living in capital** (1976): Daily cost of living: US$51.

**EDUCATION.** Literacy: (1946) 84%, (1960) 93%. Schools: 22.

**HEALTH** (1970). Hospitals: 1 (43 beds). Doctors: 7. Lepers: 20 (1.8 per 1,000).

**LITERATURE.** Periodicals: 3. Newspapers: 1 non-daily.

**COMMUNICATION** (per 1,000 people). Phones: 200. Radios: 600.

TABLE 1.    RELIGIOUS ADHERENTS IN THE BRITISH VIRGIN ISLANDS

| Year | 1900 | | mid-1970 | | Annual change, 1970–1980 | | | | mid-1975 | | mid-1980 | | 2000 | |
|---|---|---|---|---|---|---|---|---|---|---|---|---|---|---|
| Name | Adherents | % | Adherents | % | Natural | Conversion | Total | Rate | Adherents | % | Adherents | % | Adherents | % |
| Christians | 4,900 | 100.0 | 9,490 | 98.1 | 327 | −50 | 277 | 2.54 | 10,925 | 96.1 | 12,260 | 93.8 | 17,100 | 90.0 |
| professing | 4,900 | 100.0 | 9,490 | 98.1 | 327 | −50 | 277 | 2.54 | 10,925 | 96.1 | 12,260 | 93.8 | 17,100 | 90.0 |
| Protestants | 4,390 | 89.6 | 6,730 | 69.6 | 220 | −114 | 106 | 1.44 | 7,345 | 64.6 | 7,790 | 59.6 | 9,080 | 47.8 |
| Anglicans | 490 | 10.0 | 2,070 | 21.4 | 74 | 4 | 78 | 3.17 | 2,460 | 21.6 | 2,850 | 21.8 | 4,370 | 23.0 |
| Roman Catholics | 20 | 0.4 | 590 | 6.1 | 27 | 46 | 73 | 7.93 | 920 | 8.1 | 1,320 | 10.1 | 2,850 | 15.0 |
| Marginal Protestants | 0 | 0.0 | 100 | 1.0 | 6 | 14 | 20 | 10.00 | 200 | 1.8 | 300 | 2.3 | 800 | 4.2 |
| nominal | 490 | 10.0 | 2,120 | 21.9 | 82 | 33 | 115 | 4.21 | 2,730 | 24.0 | 3,270 | 25.0 | 5,320 | 28.0 |
| affiliated | 4,410 | 90.0 | 7,370 | 76.2 | 245 | −83 | 162 | 1.98 | 8,195 | 72.1 | 8,990 | 68.8 | 11,780 | 62.0 |
| total practising | 3,970 | 90 | 5,900 | 80 | 196 | −67 | 129 | 1.97 | 6,560 | 80 | 7,190 | 80 | 8,830 | 75 |
| non-practising | 440 | 10 | 1,470 | 20 | 49 | −16 | 33 | 2.01 | 1,640 | 20 | 1,800 | 20 | 2,950 | 25 |
| Protestants | 3,960 | 80.8 | 5,270 | 54.5 | 166 | −118 | 48 | 0.87 | 5,540 | 48.7 | 5,750 | 44.0 | 6,420 | 33.8 |
| Evangelicals | 2,500 | 51.0 | 1,600 | 16.5 | 51 | −35 | 16 | 0.94 | 1,700 | 15.0 | 1,760 | 13.5 | 2,000 | 10.5 |
| Anglicans | 440 | 9.0 | 1,500 | 15.5 | 52 | −2 | 50 | 2.86 | 1,750 | 15.4 | 2,000 | 15.3 | 2,660 | 14.0 |
| Roman Catholics | 10 | 0.2 | 500 | 5.2 | 21 | 23 | 44 | 6.24 | 705 | 6.2 | 940 | 7.2 | 1,900 | 10.0 |
| Marginal Protestants | 0 | 0.0 | 100 | 1.0 | 6 | 14 | 20 | 10.00 | 200 | 1.8 | 300 | 2.3 | 800 | 4.2 |
| Baha'is | 0 | 0.0 | 60 | 0.6 | 2 | 1 | 3 | 4.00 | 75 | 0.7 | 90 | 0.7 | 190 | 1.0 |
| Non-religious | 0 | 0.0 | 50 | 0.5 | 9 | 49 | 58 | 20.00 | 290 | 2.6 | 630 | 4.8 | 1,590 | 8.4 |
| Hindus | 0 | 0.0 | 40 | 0.4 | 1 | 0 | 1 | 2.00 | 45 | 0.4 | 50 | 0.4 | 60 | 0.3 |
| Muslims | 0 | 0.0 | 30 | 0.3 | 1 | 0 | 1 | 2.86 | 33.5 | 0.3 | 40 | 0.3 | 60 | 0.3 |
| Country's population | 4,900 | 100.0 | 9,670 | 100.0 | 340 | 0 | 340 | 2,99 | 11,370 | 100.0 | 13,070 | 100.0 | 19,000 | 100.0 |

**COLUMNS, ROWS.** For meanings and definitions, see Codebook (Part 6). Note that, by definition, total 'Christians' = professing + crypto-Christians, which also = affiliated + nominal Christians. Percentages may not always total exactly, due to rounding.

**CENSUSES. 7.IV.1960** (de jure): 81.5% Protestants (73.2% Methodists), 16.2% Anglicans, 1.0% Roman Catholics, 0.3% non-religious, 1.0% other religionists. **7.IV.1970:** 69.6% Protestants (51.9% Methodists, 4.6% SDAs, 2.5% Baptists), 21.4% Anglicans, 6.1% Roman Catholics, 1.0% marginal Protestants,

0.5% non-religious.

**NOTES ON RELIGIONS**
HINDUS. Indians.
MUSLIMS. Indo-Pakistanis, some Arabs.

Christian themes are common on postage stamps. *Left*, Virgin and Child, by Pintoricchio. *Right*, Holy Bible, presented (*far right*) to Queen at 1953 Coronation.

## CHRISTIANITY

PROTESTANT CHURCHES. Methodism, which owes its origin to British missionary activity at the end of the 18th century, is the dominant Christian influence in the islands. Although many are not active members, the population in 1960 was 73% Methodist, the largest percentage for Methodism in many of the islands of the West Indies. By 1970 this had dropped to 52% due to non-Methodist immigration. Other Protestant denominations are Seventh-day Adventists and the Church of God (Cleveland).

ANGLICAN CHURCH. Anglicans made up 16%

of the population in 1960 and 21% in 1970, and are the principal denomination on Virgin Gorda. Since 1916 the islands have been served by the Protestant Episcopal Church in the USA. The diocese of the Virgin Islands, which is part of PECUSA and includes both the British and US Virgin Islands, was formed in 1947.

CATHOLIC CHURCH. This British territory has the smallest Catholic population of any of the islands of the West Indies. Originally part of the prelature of the Virgin Islands, a suffragan of the archdiocese of Washington DC (USA), in February 1971 it was transferred to the diocese of St John's

in Antigua. In 1974 there was one parish served by one SVD priest, with no Catholic institutions. The number of professing Catholics increased largely by immigration, from 80 in 1960 to 590 in 1970.

CHURCH AND STATE. The islands have been a British possession since 1666. Freedom of religion has been the norm. There is no established church in the territory.

INTERDENOMINATIONAL ORGANIZATIONS. Anglicans, Catholics and Methodists co-operate in the Tortola Inter-Church Council.

TABLE 2.   ORGANIZED CHURCHES AND DENOMINATIONS IN THE BRITISH VIRGIN ISLANDS

| Official name 1 | Begun 2 | Type 3 | Counc 4 | Congs 5 | Adults 6 | Affiliated 7 | Names, notes, and other statistics (see Codebook) 8 |
|---|---|---|---|---|---|---|---|
| **Anglican Church (D Virgin Islands)** | c1700 | A ACa | avMRC | 3 | 500 | 1,500 | Begun under Ch of England. 1963, in PECUSA. Major body on Virgin Gorda. School. 1f. |
| Baptist Church | | P Bap | x.... | 1 | 100 | 230 | M=Baptist Missionary Association of America. Fundamentalist Baptists. |
| Catholic Church (D Saint John's) | 1960 | R Lat | B.NMC | 1 | 200 | 500 | In D Saint John's (Antigua). One SVD priest. No institutions. |
| Church of God | | P Pe3 | ZF... | 1 | 100 | 300 | Holiness Pentecostals. M=CoG(Cleveland)(USA). 1 church on Tortola. 1n. |
| Jehovah's Witnesses | c1940 | M Jeh | x.... | 1 | 62 | 100 | *Watch Tower. IBSA.* Active witnessing under way by 1947. 1Y. |
| Methodist Ch in Caribbean & Americas | 1789 | P Met | VsM.C | | 2,000 | 4,000 | In MCCA (1967 union), Leeward Islands District. M=MMS(UK). 2 schools. 2n,1x,1w,1f. |
| Seventh-day Adventist Church | | P Adv | x.... | | 340 | 440 | *SDA,* East Caribbean Conference, Caribbean Union Conference. |
| Other Protestant denominations | | P | ..... | | 100 | 300 | Including: Ch of the Nazarene (1961; 4 churches), Moravian Church (80 adherents). |
| **Total affiliated (mid-1970)** | | | | 30 | 3,402 | 7,370 | Total denominations (1970) . . . 9. |
| **Total affiliated (mid-1975)** | | | | 32 | 3,780 | 8,195 | Total denominations (1975) . . . 9. |
| **Total affiliated (mid-1980)** | | | | 34 | 4,150 | 8,990 | Total denominations (1980) . . . 10. |

### NOTES ON TABLE ABOVE

COLUMNS: for meanings, and CODES (cols. 1, 3, 4, 8), see Codebook (Part 6). Column 1: Boldface type = church with over 10% of country's affiliated Christians.
NATIONAL COUNCILS (Column 4, 5th letter).
   C = Tortola Inter-Church Council.

PEOPLES (ethnolinguistic). Christians: 90.8% Black, 7.3%

White (UK, USA, Portuguese), 1.6% Mulatto.

COUNTRY-WIDE TOTALS
EVANGELIZATION (see Part 5). 1900: 100%. 1970: 100%. 1980: 100%.
FOREIGN MISSIONARIES AND PERSONNEL (aliens from abroad) (1973). Total 7. *From Western world.* 3: 1 Anglican in

1 USA society, 1 Protestant in 1 UK society, 1 Roman Catholic. *From Third World.* 4 (Anglicans, Methodists) from Jamaica.
PERIODICALS. 2 titles.
PERSONNEL. About 17 (10 national, 7 foreign).
SCRIPTURE DISTRIBUTION (1975). Annual totals: 100 Bibles (subsidized).
SERVICE AGENCIES. About 3.

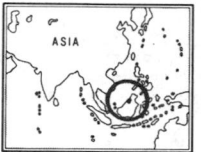

# BRUNEI

## SECULAR DATA

**STATE.** Official name: The Sultanate of Brunei (Negeri Brunei/The State of Brunei).
**Flag** (shown above right): Yellow field, diagonal white and black stripes, with coat of arms in centre.
**Area:** 5,765 sq.km. (2,226 sq.miles). Agricultural land: 3.3%.
**Government:** Self-governing British-protected constitutional monarchy, since 1971 (16th century sultanate, 1888 British protectorate, 1963 opted not to join Malaysia).
**Legislature:** Legislative Council, 21 members.
**Official languages:** Malay and English.
**Capital:** Bandar Seri Begawan 37,000 (1971).
**Foreign forces** (1973): 1,000 British (UK) troops.

**DEMOGRAPHY. Population:** 136,256 (census of 10.VIII.1971. For 1970–2000 (UN), see last row of Table 1). Population density (1975): 25/sq.km. (66/sq.miles). Under 15 years: 45%. Growth rate (1975–80): 1.80% per year. Household size: 5.1 persons.
**Major languages:** Malay, Chinese (Fukienese), English, Kedayan, Dusun, Melanau, Iban.
**Urban dwellers** (1970): 46.4%. Urban growth rate (1950–70): 5.2% per year.
**Labour force:** 30%.

**ETHNOLINGUISTIC GROUPS:** 40.0% Malay, 26.7% Chinese (Fukienese), 13.8% Kedayan, 6.9% Dusun (Kadazan), 5.7% Melanau, 2.3% English, 2.3% Iban (Sea Dayak), 1.6% Indo-Pakistani & Sinhalese.

**MONEY** (1977). **Monetary unit:** Brunei dollar (= 100 sen); US$1 = Br$2.45.
**National income per person:** US$2,000. Average annual family income: US$10,200.
**Cost of living in capital** (1976): Daily cost of living: US$34.

**EDUCATION.** Literacy: (1947) 37%, (1971) 64%. Schools: 134.

**HEALTH.** Hospitals: 4 (483 beds). Doctors: 40.

**LITERATURE.** Annual new book titles (1973): 16. Periodicals: 17. Newspapers: 1 daily, 3 non-daily.

**COMMUNICATION** (per 1,000 people). Phones: 56. Radios: 152. Daily newspaper circulation: 60 copies.

TABLE 1.   RELIGIOUS ADHERENTS IN BRUNEI

| Year Name | 1900 Adherents | % | mid-1970 Adherents | % | Annual change, 1970–1980 Natural | Conversion | Total | Rate | mid-1975 Adherents | % | mid-1980 Adherents | % | 2000 Adherents | % |
|---|---|---|---|---|---|---|---|---|---|---|---|---|---|---|---|
| Muslims | 11,580 | 60.9 | 82,700 | 62.2 | 1,706 | 296 | 2,002 | 2.16 | 92,900 | 63.2 | 102,720 | 64.2 | 146,900 | 68.0 |
| Buddhists | 1,330 | 7.0 | 17,960 | 13.5 | 358 | −54 | 304 | 1.56 | 19,500 | 13.3 | 21,000 | 13.1 | 25,000 | 11.6 |
| Christians | 100 | 0.5 | 10,670 | 8.0 | 216 | 1 | 217 | 1.85 | 11,750 | 8.0 | 12,840 | 8.0 | 25,000 | 11.6 |
| crypto-Christians | 0 | 0.0 | 570 | 0.4 | 16 | 59 | 75 | 8.62 | 870 | 0.6 | 1,320 | 0.8 | 17,920 | 8.3 |
| professing | 100 | 0.5 | 10,100 | 7.6 | 200 | −58 | 142 | 1.31 | 10,880 | 7.4 | 11,520 | 7.2 | 3,450 | 1.6 |
| Roman Catholics | 60 | 0.3 | 4,300 | 3.2 | 88 | −6 | 82 | 1.71 | 4,780 | 3.2 | 5,120 | 3.2 | 14,470 | 6.7 |
| Anglicans | 40 | 0.2 | 3,800 | 2.9 | 72 | −52 | 20 | 0.51 | 3,900 | 2.7 | 4,000 | 2.5 | 6,900 | 3.2 |
| Protestants | 0 | 0.0 | 1,500 | 1.1 | 29 | −9 | 20 | 1.25 | 1,600 | 1.1 | 1,700 | 1.1 | 3,970 | 1.8 |
| Asian indigenous | 0 | 0.0 | 500 | 0.4 | 11 | 9 | 20 | 3.33 | 600 | 0.4 | 700 | 0.4 | 2,600 | 1.2 |
| affiliated | 100 | 0.5 | 10,670 | 8.0 | 216 | 1 | 217 | 1.85 | 11,750 | 8.0 | 12,840 | 8.0 | 1,000 | 0.5 |
| total practising | 70 | *70* | 7,470 | *70* | 151 | 1 | 152 | 1.85 | 8,220 | *70* | 8,990 | *70* | 17,920 | 8.3 |
| non-practising | 30 | *30* | 3,200 | *30* | 65 | 0 | 65 | 1.84 | 3,530 | *30* | 3,850 | *30* | 10,750 | 60 |
| Roman Catholics | 60 | 0.3 | 4,520 | 3.4 | 91 | −6 | 85 | 1.72 | 4,940 | 3.4 | 5,370 | 3.3 | 7,170 | 40 |
| Anglicans | 40 | 0.2 | 4,000 | 3.0 | 81 | −1 | 80 | 1.82 | 4,400 | 3.0 | 4,800 | 3.0 | 7,100 | 3.3 |
| Protestants | 0 | 0.0 | 1,600 | 1.2 | 32 | 0 | 32 | 1.82 | 1,760 | 1.2 | 1,920 | 1.2 | 6,300 | 2.9 |
| Evangelicals | 0 | 0.0 | 1,100 | 0.8 | 22 | 3 | 25 | 2.08 | 1,200 | 0.8 | 1,350 | 0.8 | 3,020 | 1.4 |
| Asian indigenous | 0 | 0.0 | 550 | 0.4 | 12 | 8 | 20 | 3.08 | 650 | 0.4 | 750 | 0.5 | 2,200 | 1.0 |
| Chinese folk-religionists | 1,140 | 6.0 | 9,980 | 7.5 | 193 | −91 | 102 | 0.97 | 10,500 | 7.1 | 11,000 | 6.9 | 1,500 | 0.7 |
| Tribal religionists | 4,750 | 25.0 | 9,860 | 7.4 | 190 | −153 | 37 | 0.36 | 10,330 | 7.0 | 10,230 | 6.4 | 13,000 | 6.0 |
| Hindus | 100 | 0.5 | 1,300 | 1.0 | 26 | −6 | 20 | 1.43 | 1,400 | 1.0 | 1,500 | 0.9 | 10,080 | 4.7 |
| Baha'is | 0 | 0.0 | 530 | 0.4 | 11 | 7 | 18 | 2.90 | 620 | 0.4 | 710 | 0.4 | 2,000 | 0.9 |
| | | | | | | | | | | | | | 1,100 | 0.5 |
| **Country's population** | 19,000 | 100.0 | 133,000 | 100.0 | 2,700 | 0 | 2,700 | 1.84 | 147,000 | 100.0 | 160,000 | 100.0 | 216,000 | 100.0 |

COLUMNS, ROWS. For meanings and definitions, see Codebook (Part 6). Note that, by definition, total 'Christians' = professing + crypto-Christians, which also = affiliated + nominal Christians. Percentages may not always total exactly, due to rounding.
CENSUSES. 21.XI.1947: 67.1% Muslims, 17.2% Chinese folk-religionists and Buddhists, 10.9% tribal religionists, 4.3% Christians (2.3% Anglicans, 1.7% Roman Catholics, 0.3% Protestants), 0.5% other religionists. 9.VIII.1960: 60.2% Muslims, 31.7% Chinese folk-religionists and Buddhists and tribal religion-

ists, 8.1% Christians (6,796 persons). 1.IX.1971: 62.2% Muslims, 13.5% Buddhists, 7.6% Christians, 7.5% Chinese folk-religionists, 8.8% other religionists.

NOTES ON RELIGIONS
ASIAN INDIGENOUS. In 2 groupings in 1970 (see Table 2): Chinese indigenous Christians, and isolated radio believers.
BAHA'IS. In 2 local spiritual assemblies and 27 isolated groups (1964, 1973). Growth has been far slower than was planned and anticipated by Baha'i leaders in 1964.

BUDDHISTS. Chinese (Mahayana), with a few Sinhalese (Theravada) from Sri Lanka.
HINDUS. Indians.
MUSLIMS. All the Malays (Shafiite Sunnis), and all Tutongs (Melanau), are Muslims; also about 70% of Kedayans, Dusuns and Belaits; and a few Indo-Pakistanis. *Hajj pilgrims to Mecca.* (1975) 431; (1976) 11.
TRIBAL RELIGIONISTS. Most of the Sea Dayaks, and also some Kedayans, Dusuns and Belaits, are animists or spirit-worshippers.

## NON-CHRISTIAN RELIGIONS.

**Islam** is the official religion of Brunei; and 63% of the population, mostly Malays, are professing Muslims. Following a visit in AD 1425 to sultan Muhammed Shah

(Parameswara) of Malacca, the Hindu ruler of Brunei, Awang Alak Betatar, became a Muslim. Arab scholars were later invited to carry on missionary work in the country which resulted in the conversion

of the majority of the population to Islam.

**Other religions** include Buddhism, Confucianism and Taoism among the Chinese, traditional animism among the Aboriginal peoples, and Baha'i.

## CHRISTIANITY

**CATHOLIC CHURCH.** Brunei is part of the Catholic diocese of Miri, the other half of the diocese being formed by 2 of the 5 administrative divisions of Sarawak in eastern Malaysia. In 1970 there were 4,500 baptized members, mostly native Chinese, with Indian and European expatriates, 20 catechumens, 5 Chinese and 2 European priests, the latter being Mill Hill missionaries, 6 nuns of the Franciscan Missionary Sisters of St Joseph and Little Sisters of St Francis, and 3 primary and 3 secondary schools.

**OTHER CHURCHES.** Anglicans form the strongest of the non-Catholic churches. Their membership is approximately 60% Chinese and 10% Iban, with 13% Indian and 13% European. About 40% are expatriates working for the Shell petroleum enterprise or for the government. The Anglican diocese of Kuching includes Brunei and a portion of Sarawak, and belongs to the Council of the Church

**Muslims.** *Above.* Omar Ali Saifuddin Mosque, Brunei. *Top right.* Protestant evangelistic ship MVLogos visits Brunei in May 1975.

in East Asia (Anglican).

The Borneo Evangelical Mission is an Australian interdenominational faith mission working with Aboriginal peoples in the interior.

Methodism owes its origin to British missionary influence and is organized as part of the Sarawak Chinese and Iban Conferences of the Methodist Church in Malaysia and Singapore. Seventh-day Adventists are also active.

The True Jesus Church was founded in mainland China in 1917 as a result of an indigenous revival movement. Entirely Chinese in membership, it has spread to a number of countries in the China diaspora since the Communist accession to power on the mainland in 1949.

**CHURCH AND STATE.** According to the constitution of 1959, which was amended in 1965, Islam is the state religion and the sultan is its head (Article 3, paragraphs 1 and 2); but the free practice of all other religions is guaranteed (paragraph 1). The sultan is assisted in his duties by a counsellor for religious affairs (paragraph 3).

TABLE 2.    ORGANIZED CHURCHES AND DENOMINATIONS IN BRUNEI

| Official name 1 | Begun 2 | Type 3 | Counc 4 | Congs 5 | Adults 6 | Affiliated 7 | Names, notes, and other statistics (see Codebook) 8 |
|---|---|---|---|---|---|---|---|
| **Anglican Church (D Kuching)** | | A Hig | aweA. | 3 | 2,340 | 4,000 | 60% Chinese, 13% Indian, 13% English, 10% Iban. M=USPG,ABM. 1n,2x,W=25%,31Y,27y. |
| **Catholic Church (VA Miri)** | c1600 | R Lat | P.F.. | 3 | 2,500 | 4,520 | Mainly Chinese; also Indians, some Europeans in petrol industry. 3n,2x,6w,20z. |
| **Evangelical Church of Borneo** | 1928 | P int | .H... | 2 | 500 | 1,000 | *Sidang Injil Borneo.* M=BEM(Australia). HQ Lawas, Sarawak. Converts from animism. |
| **Isolated radio churches** | 1952 | I rad | ..... | | 20 | 50 | Isolated radio believers (FEBC), mostly young people, across country. S=4(ICI). |
| **Methodist Church** | | P Met | Vwe.. | 1 | 50 | 100 | Part of *Chinese and Iban Conferences,* Methodist Ch, Malaysia & Singapore. |
| **Seventh-day Adventist Church** | 1961 | P Adv | x.... | 1 | 200 | 500 | *SDAs.* In Sarawak Mission (SDA Ch of Sarawak), Southeast Asia Union Mission. |
| **True Jesus Church** | c1940 | I peI | x.... | 3 | 300 | 500 | Chinese indigenous church begun on mainland China. Strong in Sabah (Malaysia). |
| **Total affiliated (mid-1970)** | | | | 17 | 5,910 | 10,670 | Total denominations (1970) . . . 7. |
| **Total affiliated (mid-1975)** | | | | 18 | 6,500 | 11,750 | Total denominations (1975) . . . 7. |
| **Total affiliated (mid-1980)** | | | | 19 | 7,100 | 12,840 | Total denominations (1980) . . . 7. |

**NOTES ON TABLE ABOVE**
**COLUMNS:** for meanings and CODES (cols. 1, 3, 4, 8), see Codebook (Part 6). Column 1: **Boldface type** = church with over 10% of country's affiliated Christians.

**PEOPLES** (ethnolinguistic). Christians: about 75% Chinese, 10% tribal (interior tribes: 4% Iban (Sea Dayak), Land Dayak, Kenyah, Kayan), 7% Indian, 6% British, 2% Malay.

**COUNTRY-WIDE TOTALS**
**EVANGELIZATION** (see Part 5). 1900: 6%. 1970: 45%. 1980: 55%. *Radiophonic evangelism.* FEBC, ICI (4 active students).
**FOREIGN MISSIONARIES AND PERSONNEL** (aliens from abroad) (1973). Total 11. *From Western world.* 7: 5 Roman Catholics, 2 Anglicans. *From Third World.* About 4 (Roman Catholics, Protestants), from Korea, Taiwan, Hong Kong.
**INSTITUTIONS** (church-operated) (1973). Total 3 schools.
**PERIODICALS.** 2 titles.
**PERSONNEL.** About 21 (10 national, 11 foreign).

**SCRIPTURE DISTRIBUTION** (1975). Annual totals: 190 Bibles (53% free, 47% subsidized), 4,610 NTs (free), 20 UBS portions, 30 UBS selections. *Translations completed.* In 1 language, Lun Bawang (Murut): portion 1947, NT 1962.

**ADDITIONAL DATA ON CHURCHES**
**CATHOLIC CHURCH.** Part of vicariate based in Sarawak (Malaysia). *Priests.* 3 Chinese, 2 European (MHM). *Sisters.* Franciscan Missionary Sisters of St Joseph, Little Sisters of St Francis. There are 3 Catholic primary and 3 secondary schools.

---

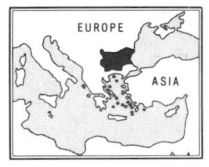

# BULGARIA

## SECULAR DATA

**STATE. Official name:** The People's Republic of Bulgaria (Narodna Republika · Bulgarija). Adjective of nationality: Bulgarian.
**Flag** (shown above right): Stripes of white, green, and red, national coat of arms in top left corner.
**Area:** 110,912 sq.km. (42,823 sq.miles). Agricultural land: 54.0%.
**Government:** One-party Communist state, since 1945 (1396 Ottoman rule, 1908 Independence as empire).
**Legislature:** National Assembly, 400 members.
**Offical language:** Bulgarian (*Bulgarski*).
**Chief cities:** capital Sofia 937,070 (1973), Plovdiv 274,740, Varna 255,860, Ruse 164,990.
**Political divisions:** 28 Provinces (okruzi); 188 urban and 973 rural Communes.
**Armed forces** (1976): Total 164,500 regular (100,000 conscripts): army 131,000, navy 8,500, air force 25,000 (253 combat aircraft). Reserves: 285,000. Paramilitary forces: 166,000 (150,000 People's Militia).

**DEMOGRAPHY. Population:** 8,227,866 (census of 1.XII.1965. For 1970–2000 (UN), see last row of Table 1). Population density (1975): 79/sq.km. (205/sq.mile). Under 15 years: 26%. Growth rate (1975–80): 0.63% per year (births 1.59%, deaths −0.96%). Life expectancy (1975–80): 72.5 years. Household size: 3.2 persons.
**Major languages:** Bulgarian, Turkish, Romany, Russian, Armenian, Yiddish, Greek, Macedonian, Gagauzi, and several others.
**Urban dwellers** (1970): 51.5%. Urban growth rate (1950–70):

3.9% per year.
**Labour force:** 53%.
**Tourists** (1974): 3,818,026.

**ETHNOLINGUISTIC GROUPS:** 82.5% Bulgar, 9.0% Turkish, 5.0% Gypsy, 2.5% Macedonian, 0.3% Armenian, 0.2% Russian, 0.1% Jewish, 0.1% Greek, 0.1% Gagauz, 0.1% Tatar, Romanian, Karakachan.

**MONEY** (1977). **Monetary unit:** lev (= 100 stótinki); US$1 = Lv 0.972.
**National income per person:** US$1,650. Average annual family income: US$5,280.
**Inflation:** (1970–74) 0.0% per year (1973: consumer price index 100).
**Cost of living in capital** (1976): index 118 (Washington DC=100). Daily cost of living: US$46.

**EDUCATION.** Adult literacy: (1946) 76%, (1965) 91%. Education rate: 60%. Schools: 3,622 (304 secondary). Universities: 3.

**HEALTH.** Hospitals: 4,453 (69,139 beds). Doctors: 17,023. Blind: 3,312. Psychotics: 88,000.

**LITERATURE.** Annual new book titles (1973): 3,963. Periodicals: 1,708. Scientific journals: 150. Newspapers: 13 dailies, 33 non-daily.

**COMMUNICATION** (per 1,000 people). Phones: 74. Radios: 263. TV sets: 160. Daily newspaper circulation: 206 copies.

TABLE 1. RELIGIOUS ADHERENTS IN BULGARIA

| Year | 1900 | | mid-1970 | | Annual change, 1970–1980 | | | | mid-1975 | | mid-1980 | | 2000 | |
|---|---|---|---|---|---|---|---|---|---|---|---|---|---|---|
| *Name* | *Adherents* | *%* | *Adherents* | *%* | *Natural* | *Conversion* | *Total* | *Rate* | *Adherents* | *%* | *Adherents* | *%* | *Adherents* | *%* |
| **Christians** | **3,065,780** | **81.9** | **5,641,130** | **66.4** | **38,317** | **–17,100** | **21,217** | **0.37** | **5,759,300** | **65.5** | **5,853,300** | **64.5** | **6,080,900** | **60.6** |
| crypto-Christians | 0 | 0.0 | 3,358,430 | 39.5 | 22,698 | –13,698 | 9,000 | 0.26 | 3,411,570 | 38.8 | 3,448,430 | 38.0 | 3,481,580 | 34.7 |
| professing | 3,065,780 | 81.9 | 2,282,700 | 26.9 | 15,619 | –3,402 | 12,217 | 0.52 | 2,347,730 | 26.7 | 2,404,870 | 26.5 | 2,599,320 | 25.9 |
| Orthodox | 3,032,690 | 81.0 | 2,207,700 | 26.0 | 15,095 | –3,511 | 11,584 | 0.51 | 2,268,910 | 25.8 | 2,323,540 | 25.6 | 2,510,000 | 25.0 |
| Roman Catholics | 28,570 | 0.8 | 40,000 | 0.5 | 279 | 121 | 400 | 0.95 | 42,000 | 0.5 | 44,000 | 0.5 | 50,180 | 0.5 |
| Protestants | 4,520 | 0.1 | 35,000 | 0.4 | 245 | –12 | 233 | 0.63 | 36,820 | 0.4 | 37,330 | 0.4 | 39,140 | 0.4 |
| nominal | 186,430 | 5.0 | 0 | 0.0 | 0 | 0 | 0 | 0.00 | 0 | 0.0 | 0 | 0.0 | 0 | 0.0 |
| affiliated | 2,879,350 | 76.9 | 5,641,130 | 66.4 | 38,317 | –17,100 | 21,217 | 0.37 | 5,759,300 | 65.5 | 5,853,300 | 64.5 | 6,080,900 | 60.6 |
| total practising | 2,591,410 | *90* | 3,441,090 | *61* | 22,990 | –21,754 | 1,236 | 0.03 | 3,455,580 | *60* | 3,453,450 | *59* | 3,344,500 | *55* |
| non-practising | 287,940 | *10* | 2,200,040 | *39* | 15,327 | 4,654 | 19,981 | 0.87 | 2,303,720 | *40* | 2,399,850 | *41* | 2,736,400 | *45* |
| Orthodox | 2,848,050 | 76.1 | 5,534,000 | 65.2 | 37,575 | –17,218 | 20,357 | 0.36 | 5,647,670 | 64.2 | 5,737,570 | 63.2 | 5,948,520 | 59.3 |
| Roman Catholics | 27,000 | 0.7 | 57,000 | 0.7 | 392 | 8 | 400 | 0.68 | 59,000 | 0.7 | 61,000 | 0.7 | 70,250 | 0.7 |
| Protestants | 4,300 | 0.1 | 48,600 | 0.6 | 339 | 101 | 440 | 0.86 | 51,000 | 0.6 | 53,000 | 0.6 | 60,000 | 0.6 |
| Evangelicals | 4,000 | 0.1 | 40,000 | 0.5 | 279 | 101 | 380 | 0.90 | 42,000 | 0.5 | 43,800 | 0.5 | 50,000 | 0.5 |
| Marginal Protestants | 0 | 0.0 | 1,500 | 0.0 | 11 | 9 | 20 | 1.25 | 1,600 | 0.0 | 1,700 | 0.0 | 2,100 | 0.0 |
| Catholics (non-Roman) | 0 | 0.0 | 30 | 0.0 | 0 | 0 | 0 | 0.00 | 30 | 0.0 | 30 | 0.0 | 30 | 0.0 |
| Non-religious | 3,000 | 0.1 | 1,205,870 | 14.2 | 8,951 | 17,482 | 26,433 | 1.98 | 1,336,500 | 15.2 | 1,470,200 | 16.2 | 2,007,200 | 20.0 |
| Muslims | 642,500 | 17.2 | 934,000 | 11.0 | 6,318 | –3,518 | 2,800 | 0.29 | 949,600 | 10.8 | 962,000 | 10.6 | 983,500 | 9.8 |
| Atheists | 1,000 | 0.0 | 700,000 | 8.2 | 4,914 | 3,136 | 8,050 | 1.09 | 738,600 | 8.4 | 780,500 | 8.6 | 953,400 | 9.5 |
| Jews | 32,000 | 0.9 | 7,000 | 0.1 | 0 | 0 | 0 | 0.00 | 7,000 | 0.1 | 7,000 | 0.1 | 8,000 | 0.1 |
| Other religionists | 0 | 0.0 | 2,000 | 0.0 | 0 | 0 | 0 | 0.00 | 2,000 | 0.0 | 2,000 | 0.0 | 3,000 | 0.0 |
| **Country's population** | **3,744,280** | **100.0** | **8,490,000** | **100.0** | **58,500** | **0** | **58,500** | **0.67** | **8,793,000** | **100.0** | **9,075,000** | **100.0** | **10,036,000** | **100.0** |

COLUMNS, ROWS. For meanings and definitions, see Codebook (Part 6). Note that, by definition, total 'Christians' = professing + crypto-Christians, which also = affiliated + nominal Christians. Percentages may not always total exactly, due to rounding.

CENSUSES. **1887** (Kingdom of Bulgaria): 77.1% Orthodox (76.9% Bulgarian Orthodox, 0.2% Armenian Apostolic), 21.4% Muslims, 0.8% Jews, 0.6% Roman Catholics, 0.0% Protestants. **1892:** 78.9% Orthodox (78.7% Bulgarian, 0.2% Armenian), 19.4% Muslims, 0.9% Jews, 0.7% Roman Catholics, 0.1% Protestants. **1900:** 81.0% Orthodox (80.66% Bulgarian, 0.37% Armenian), 17.2% Muslims, 0.9% Jews, 0.8% Roman Catholics, 0.1% Protestants. **1905:** 83.1% Orthodox (82.90% Bulgarian, 0.31% Armenian), 15.0% Muslims, 0.9% Jews, 0.7% Roman Catholics, 0.1% Protestants. **1910:** 84.0% Orthodox, 13.9% Muslims, 2.1% other Christians and other religionists. **1934:** 84.8% Orthodox (84.4% Bulgarian, 0.4% Armenian), 13.5% Muslims, 0.9% Jews, 0.8% Roman Catholics, 0.1% Protestants. **31.XII.1946:** 85.2% Orthodox (84.9% Bulgarian Orthodox, 0.3% Armenian Apostolic), 13.3% Muslims, 0.6% Jews, 0.6% Roman Catholics, 0.2% non-religious, 0.1% Protestants. No subsequent census has included religion.

POLLS. Several polls have been conducted by Bulgarian social scientists. One in 1962 by J. Ochavkov (published in H. Mol, *Western religion*, 1972) obtained the following results: persons with an individual active religion 35.5% of the population (of whom 26.7% Orthodox, 6.5% Muslims, 0.5% Roman Catholics, 0.8% Protestants and Jews), persons with no active religion 64.4%; who have had children baptized about 50% of the population, persons regularly attending church 21.6% (60.8% of all defined as religious), 36.1% married by religious ceremony, 91.9% persons who have had relations buried in a religious ceremony since 1945; and since 1945, 80% of all burials in Bulgaria have taken place after a religious ceremony.

**NOTES ON RELIGIONS**

ATHEISTS. Bulgarian Communist Party (BCP) (in power; pro-Soviet): membership (1970) 700,000; Communist voters (election of 27.VI.1971) 6,154,082 (99.9% of all votes). Of Communist party members, about 25% are estimated to be militant atheists, the other 75% being non-religious, with few or no Christians. Other Communist organizations: Dimitrov Young Communist League (15–17 years old) 1,161,000 members; Pioneers (primary school children); Fatherland Front (all priests are members) 3,762,537 members.

CRYPTO-CHRISTIANS. Persons not professing to be Christians in polls, but who are affiliated to churches; mainly unorganized individuals including government officials who attend Orthodox activities irregularly or clandestinely; also members of illegal or underground churches.

JEWS. 3 synagogues, 7 rabbis.

MUSLIMS. Turks, 120,000 Gypsies, some 200,000 southeastern Bulgarians (Pomaks), and 5,000 Tatars; almost all Sunnis (of the Hanafite rite). In 1950, 250,000 Bulgarian Turks were forcibly returned to Turkey. Active Muslims numbered only 6.5% in 1962, but many others practise privately unknown to the state. In 1966, there were 1,180 mosques and 460 imams under a grand mufti. Muslims have been severely repressed by the state since 1950. By 1974, only 600 mosques were open.

NOMINAL CHRISTIANS. Only before 1946.

NON-RELIGIOUS. Agnostics, indifferent to religion. In addition, there is a further 39.5% (in 1970) of the population regarded as non-religious by the state but who are affiliated to churches and hence are classified here as crypto-Christians.

OTHER RELIGIONISTS. Including about 100 Baha'is in 2 isolated centres.

PRACTISING CHRISTIANS. Most Orthodox attend church only on great feasts and for weddings or other family services; regular weekly attendance averaged 13% of affiliated Orthodox in 1962.

PROFESSING CHRISTIANS. Persons known to the state through social scientists' surveys.

**NON-CHRISTIAN RELIGIONS. Islam** has the major non-Christian religious community in the country, with 1,180 mosques, 460 imams and over half a million Muslims in 1966. There are 3 groups of Muslims: (1) Turks, by far the most numerous, living in enclosed communities in the districts of Schumen, Razgrad, Kerdschali and Haskovo; (2) Gypsies (Tziganes) scattered in small groups, especially in towns; and (3) Bulgarians (known as Pomaks) in the southeast of the country near Mount Rhodopes, who have about 120 mosques and 100 imams. Muslims along with Catholics are the religious communities most oppressed by the regime and most under attack from official atheistic propaganda, as a result of which large numbers no longer profess to be Muslims. Because many of the Muslims are Turks, there is a tendency to consider all Muslims as being under the influence of Turkey.

**Atheism** is widely professed in Bulgaria, though with little fervour compared with former years. Some 28% of the population are atheists or agnostics without religion.

**Judaism** is nominally the religion of about 7,000 ethnic Jews, but very few practise their religion. The civil authorities have shown a certain tolerance towards the Jewish community. In 1967, authorization was granted for the first time to publish a religious yearbook, *Godichnik*. There are 3 synagogues and 7 rabbis.

**CHRISTIANITY.** By the 2nd century, churches had been founded at Anchialus and Debeltum near Burgas. During the first centuries of the Christian era, Goths, Huns, Slavs, Bulgars, Avars and other barbarian tribes from the north surged into the Roman and Byzantine empires through the Balkan peninsula; yet throughout these invasions Christian communities and diocesan structures continued to exist. The large number of Slavs entering in the 6th and 7th centuries adopted the language and culture of the land in which, under the rule of Constantinople, Christianity had become an intrinsic part. The Bulgars of Turkish origin next seized the peninsula and were in turn assimilated. The Latin church sent missionaries to the Slavs and Bulgars from the northwest, and Byzantine rulers from the southeast. The Bulgarian king Boris was first baptized by Greek clergy, then turned to Rome, then returned again to Constantinople. In 870 he achieved his goal when a Bulgar was consecrated archbishop of Bulgaria. Bulgarian leaders began to send their sons to Constantinople to be educated; and the Greek missionaries Methodius and Constantine (Cyril) translated existing Christian literature into Slavonic as well as training Slav missionaries. In 889 Boris abdicated to enter a monastery, while his son Simeon left life as a monk to continue his father's ideal of substituting Slavonic for Greek in the church of the Bulgars. Under his leadership the Bulgarian bishops declared the church autocephalous with a patriarch at its head, over Constantinople's opposition. Thus by Simeon's death in 927 Bulgaria had become an independent Christian nation with its own autonomous church. With Bulgarian support, the Serbs to the west also adopted the Eastern Orthodox faith, then obtained the right to choose their own patriarch and became autocephalous.

**Bulgarian Orthodox Church.** Patriarch Cyril leads worship in Sofia cathedral on occasion of WCC executive committee, 1971.

In 1018 the Bulgarian kingdom fell to the Byzantine rulers and the Bulgarian patriarchate was suppressed. Bulgaria regained its independence in 1186 and the partriarchate was re-established in 1235 following an ephemeral 30-year union with Rome. Finally in 1396 Bulgaria fell before a third wave of Muslim invaders, the Ottoman Turks.

For almost 500 years including the period when the Protestant Reformation was taking place from western Europe eastwards to Hungary, the Turks controlled Bulgaria and the Greek Orthodox controlled its church. In the Bulgarian revolt of 1876, Russia lent its support and brought about a treaty which gave Bulgaria independence. Other European nations, apprehensive of Russia's influence in the Balkans, revised the original treaty and divided Bulgaria into 3 parts under Turkish control. In 1908 Bulgaria was finally able to proclaim its full independence. In siding with Germany in World War I Bulgaria lost much territory, which it attempted to regain by joining with Germany once again in World War II. At the end of the war the country was occupied by the USSR.

ORTHODOX CHURCHES. In 1870 the Turkish sultan permitted the re-establishment of a national Bulgarian church which was promptly excommunicated by a Greek Orthodox council in 1872. After some efforts at reunion with Rome, reconciliation with the ecumenical patriarchate in Constantinople was effected in 1945.

The Bulgarian Orthodox Church has 11 dioceses under the authority of a patriarch and 11 diocesan bishops. For Bulgarians living in the USA, Canada and Australia, there are 3 other dioceses with seats in New York, Akron (Ohio) and Detroit. The Bulgarian church has priests and officials in both Constantinople and Moscow, and there are also churches and priests in Romania and Hungary. The Bulgarian monastery of St George on Mount Athos (Greece) is however under the authority of the patriarch of Constantinople.

Prior to World War II, Orthodox made up 85% of the population. A sociological survey conducted in 1962 estimated them to have declined to 27% of the population, although the church itself claimed an affiliated community of over 5 million (65%) in 1970.

Much property and many institutions were lost in 1945 following the war. All monasteries were expropriated; but after the church officially and formally pledged its loyalty to the Communist regime in 1953, these were returned to church control. Since 1953 the church has received financial aid from the government but remains relatively poor. Two institutions, Tcherepich Seminary near Vraca and the Sofia Theological Academy, remain open and cater for some 270 students. The church has a press and produces a weekly *Official gazette of the Bulgarian Orthodox Church*, a monthly *Spiritual culture* dealing with religion, philosophy, science and art, and an annual scholarly journal, *Yearbook of the Theological Academy*.

The Armenian Apostolic Church has 12 congregations in Bulgaria served by 10 priests. Armenians first came to Bulgaria in the 5th century. The first church was built in Sofia in the 11th century and in Plovdiv a century later. Armenians and their churches today are found principally in the cities of Sofia, Plovdiv, Varna, Ruse, Haskovo and Sliven.

Sofia. In 1971 for the first time in many years there was an ordination to the priesthood. In the same year the Latin-rite church had an apostolic vicar residing at Plovdiv and at least 44 priests. Only 3 Latin priests have been ordained since 1945. These studied in other countries, France in particular, and were recently permitted re-entry into Bulgaria. This situation, which would have been impossible in the 1950s, indicates the gradual amelioration of relations.

Until the visit of the Bulgarian president Zhivkov to the pope in Rome in 1975, the 2 Latin-rite jurisdictions had been without bishops since the execution of the bishop of Nicopoli in 1952. During his visit Zhivkov agreed to let the Vatican fill these vacancies, and subsequently there has been a marked thaw in state relations with the Catholic Church.

PROTESTANT CHURCHES. Protestantism was introduced by American Congregationalist missionaries in 1856, American Methodists in 1857, and

prevented from carrying out any special pastoral activity; and religious communities may not engage in the education of children or youth, nor supervise hospitals, orphanages or other similar establishments (Articles 20 and 21).

The legal status of the Bulgarian Orthodox Church was established in 1953 on the basis of Article 3 of the Law concerning Religious Faiths. It enjoys a special status in comparison with other religious communities. Since the Roman Catholic churches do not wish to become national churches, they do not benefit from this type of juridical status.

There also exists under the Ministry of Foreign Affairs a Committee for Questions concerning the Bulgarian Orthodox Church and Religious Denominations (Komitet pri Ministerstvoto na Vunschnite Raboti po Vuprosite na Bulgarskata Pravoslavna Curkov i na Religioznite Kultove).

In actual fact as in most other Communist countries

**Bulgarian Orthodox Church.** *Left.* A parish priest and 2 nuns. *Right.* Rila monastery, one of 123 still operated by Orthodox Church.

CATHOLIC CHURCH. From the 9th century to the 14th century, the Catholic Church of the Latin rite repeatedly sent missionaries into the Balkans, first from Germany and its other strongholds in northern Europe, and then through the Crusaders and the new Dominican and Franciscan missionary orders. The majority of Bulgarian Catholics today are descendants of Bogomils converted to Catholicism by Franciscans in the 17th century. In 1758 the vicariate of Sofia was established and in 1789 the diocese of Nicopoli. From 1870 onwards some Uniate groups were recognized by Rome, and in 1926 an exarchate of Sofia was created for Catholics of the Byzantine rite.

Catholics are widely dispersed across Bulgaria. Those of the Byzantine rite numbered about 7,000 in 1970 and are to be found in Sofia, Plovdiv and along the Greek border. Those of the Latin rite are about 50,000 and are divided into different groups of which the most important is established in the small town of Rakovski near Plovdiv, with 15,000 Catholics. Nikolaievo is one of the few towns which is entirely Catholic, numbering 7,000 with 2 priests. A few other similar towns are found along the length of the Danube. The Catholic church in Sofia is attended by foreign diplomats and their families.

Until the end of World War II, the church in Bulgaria was under Propaganda, now the Congregation for the Evangelization of Peoples. As a result it had no legal status and there were only missions established by religious orders (OFM, OFMCap, AA, CP, SJ). Over the period 1946–48 the church lost all its institutions and, apart from a few churches, all of its possessions, buildings, schools (including 9 colleges in 1944), hospitals (of which there were 2 in 1944), and orphanages. Foreign religious personnel and priests were expelled in 1948. Most of the others were arrested and sentenced and many died in prison.

At present, however, the Catholic Church has survived despite such difficulties as the material poverty of priests, the ageing of the faithful, and continuous pressures to prevent baptism of infants or church attendance. The Eastern-rite Catholics or Uniates include many Latin elements; and in contrast to what took place in Romania, they have not been forcibly reunited with the Orthodox Church, no doubt because of their small numbers. In 1971 the Catholic Church of the Byzantine rite had an apostolic exarch, with about 20 priests; there were also 2 religious communities, an order of Bulgarian origin the Eucharistines, and 7 cloistered Carmelites in

Baptists from Russia in 1865. Seventh-day Adventists arrived in 1891 as emigrants from the Russian Crimea and settled in northern Dobruja. Pentecostalism was established in 1921 by Russian Pentecostals at Burgas. Pentecostals are at present divided into 2 denominations, the Bulgarian Pentecostal Evangelical Church and the Free Pentecostal Churches, which together serve a Christian community greater than all other Protestants.

CHURCH AND STATE. A new constitution promulgated in May 1971 stipulates in Article 53: '(1) Freedom of conscience and of religion is guaranteed to all citizens. They have the right to engage in both religious rites and anti-religious propaganda. (2) The church is separated from the state. (3) The juridical status of religious communities and questions concerning their maintenance and right to be internally organized and administered are regulated by law. (4) Abusive acts which tend to place the church and religion at the service of political organizations of a religious background are forbidden. (5) Religion may not be used to justify refusal to carry out duties imposed by the constitution or the law'. Educational establishments belong to the state (Article 45, item 2), and the education of youth must be carried out in a communist spirit (Article 39, item 1). All citizens are equal before the law (Article 35, items 1 and 2) and 'hating and humiliating a man' on account of his religious belief is forbidden (Article 35, item 4).

The law regulating the juridical status and internal organization of religious communities which went into effect in March 1949 is based on the stipulations of the constitution of 1947 and is called the Law concerning Religious Faiths (Official Journal, No. 48/1949). It declares: 'The Bulgarian Orthodox Church is the traditional faith of the Bulgarian people. It is bound up with their history and as such, by its structure, its nature and its spirit can be considered a church of the popular democracy' (Article 3). All churches are free to manage their organizational structure, rites and religious buildings (Article 5). A church becomes legal and receives juridical status at the time it is ratified by the Ministry of Foreign Affairs (Article 6). The churches may receive revenue as provided for by their own statutes; and 'When it appears necessary, the state may subsidize the support of ecclesiastical institutions' (Article 13). Freedom of conscience and religion are guaranteed (Article 1), but there are some restrictions; lay religious organizations are for all practical purposes

churches are only barely tolerated by the state. The law of 1949 is strictly applied, in particular concerning Articles 13 and 26, and the material situation of the churches is difficult. The Bulgarian Orthodox Church is more fortunate than others in that it has been authorized to maintain its rural property, and receives from the state an annual subsidy of 700,000 levas (about US$400,000) for the construction and support of churches and for the salaries of its personnel. The state thus provides 17% of the church's financial requirements. Orthodox priests are also paid at the rate of teachers and bishops at the rate of academicians. However, any religious activity undertaken by churches outside the walls of their property is liable to prosecution and punishment. The majority of churches in Bulgaria are considered as organizations dependent on foreign resources. Clergy other than Orthodox are not paid by the state and live from contributions of the faithful.

The Catholic Church suffered the most from the persecutions of the 1950s. Its last imprisoned priests were not freed until 1964 and some have not yet been granted residence or work permits.

In their struggle for survival, the churches have had to find a modus vivendi with the state. This has included a formal declaration of loyalty to the state on the part of church dignitaries, their participation in the peace movement, and their celebrations of state holidays. As one result the major national holiday has been recognized as the major festival of the Bulgarian Orthodox Church.

INTERDENOMINATIONAL ORGANIZATIONS. None have been encouraged or permitted.

BROADCASTING. No religious broadcasting of any kind is permitted within the country. From abroad, Trans World Radio (Monaco) in 1974 broadcast in Bulgarian for 15 minutes each on Fridays and Saturdays and for 30 minutes on Sundays; and Radio Vatican for 15 minutes daily in Bulgarian.

BIBLIOGRAPHY
'Bulgaria', J. Ochavkov, in H. Mol (ed), *Western religion* (The Hague: Mouton, 1972), p. 83–99.
*Churches and religions in the People's Republic of Bulgaria.* Sofia: Holy Synod, 1975 (revised edition).
*Die bulgarische orthodoxe Kirche, 1944–1956.* D. Slijepcevic. München, 1957.
'Kirche und Staat in Bulgarien', G. Podskalsky, *Stimmen der Zeit*, 97 (1972), 122–4.
'Sotsiologichesko izsledvane na religioznostta na pulnoletnoto naselenie v Bulgaria' (Sociological survey of religiosity of the adult population of Bulgaria), J. Ochavkov, *Novo Vreme*, 5 (1964).

TABLE 2. ORGANIZED CHURCHES AND DENOMINATIONS IN BULGARIA

| Official name 1 | Begun 2 | Type 3 | Counc 4 | Congs 5 | Adults 6 | Affiliated 7 | Names, notes, and other statistics (see Codebook) 8 |
|---|---|---|---|---|---|---|---|
| Armenian Apostolic Ch: D Sofija | c1050 | O Arm | Evc.. | 12 | 16,000 | 22,000 | *Gregorians.* Under C Echmiadzin. First Armenians in 5th century. In cities. 10n. |
| Baptist Union of Bulgaria | 1865 | P Bap | T.... | 23 | 800 | 2,000 | *Baptistka Crkve.* Begun 1865 in Lom through Baptists from Russia. HQ Sofia. 23n. |
| **Bulgarian Orthodox Church:** | c 150 | O Sla | MWc.. | 3,720 | 4,070,000 | 5,500,000 | *Balgarskata Pravoslavna Crkva.* 1785n,123de(200m,360w),1j,P=61%,2s(330),W=13%. |
| P Sofija (Sofia) | 870 | O Sla | Mp | 730 | 803,000 | 1,085,200 | Diocese of patriarch, in capital city. 1s(70 in theological academy). |
| D Dorostola Cerven | | O Sla | Mm | 290 | 316,400 | 427,600 | *Eparchija (Metropolia).* HQ Ruse. Political districts: Razgrad, Ruse, Silistra. |
| D Lovec | | O Sla | Mm | 100 | 106,400 | 143,800 | HQ (Seat) at Lovec. All dioceses are autonomous though loosely under Sofia. |
| D Nevrokope | | O Sla | Mm | 140 | 149,400 | 201,900 | HQ Blagoevgrad. Boundaries of dioceses are not exactly defined. Macedonians. |
| D Plovdiv | | O Sla | Mm | 760 | 830,600 | 1,122,400 | HQ Plovdiv. Largest diocese. Political districts: Smolyan, Haskovo, Plovdiv et alia. |
| D Sliven | | O Sla | Mm | 370 | 411,000 | 555,400 | HQ Sliven. Dioceses do not follow political divisions exactly. |
| D Stara Zagora | | O Sla | Mm | 160 | 179,700 | 242,800 | HQ Stara Zagora. Covers political district of Stara Zagora. |
| D Varna & Preslav | | O Sla | Mm | 470 | 510,400 | 689,700 | HQ Varna. Covers political districts of Tolboukhin and Turgovishte. |
| D Veliko Tarnovo | 1186 | O Sla | Mm | 310 | 335,000 | 452,700 | HQ Veliko Tarnovo. Covers part of Pleven political district. |
| D Vidin | | O Sla | Mm | 180 | 198,300 | 268,000 | HQ Vidin, in extreme northwestern tip of country. |
| D Vraca (Vratza) | | O Sla | Mm | 210 | 229,800 | 310,500 | HQ Vraca. 1s(St John of Rila, Cherepich Monastery; 200 students). |
| Bulgarian Pentecostal Ev Church | c1910 | P Pe2 | Z.... | 160 | 9,500 | 20,000 | *Petdesetna Evangelska Crkva.* Links with AoG(USA), EES(UK). Mostly registered. 70n,600Y. |
| Catholic Apostolic Church | c1900 | C CAp | x.... | 1 | 20 | 30 | One small congregation of Irvingites (begun 1832 in Britain) in Sofia. |
| Catholic Church in Bulgaria: | 1565 | R LEr | O,B,R | 52 | 42,000 | 57,000 | *Rimo-Katoliceskata Crkva.* Bogomil descendants. Diaspora. Seminary prohibited. 64n. |
| D Nicopoli | 1789 | R Lat | os | 12 | 15,000 | 20,000 | *Eparchija Nicopoli.* Bishop arrested and executed in 1952. 11n,4m,113w. |
| VA Sofija & Plovdiv | 1758 | R Lat | Os | 15 | 22,000 | 30,000 | *Apostolski Vikarijat Sofija.* 22,000 in 2 towns. Violent persecutions from 1952. 33n. |
| EA Sofija (*Bulgarian*) | 1926 | R Bul | Os | 25 | 5,000 | 7,000 | Uniates. Work began 1860. 1945, not forced into Orthodox Ch. 20n,2e(21). |
| Christian Brethren | | P CBr | x.... | 118 | 3,000 | 5,000 | *Plymouth (Open) Brethren.* Not legally recognized; meetings in homes. |
| Congregational Church in Bulgaria | 1856 | P Con | .v... | 20 | 4,500 | 5,000 | *Soborna Congrezanska Crkva.* South. 32 congregations lost (12 to Pentecostals). 14n. |
| Free Pentecostal Churches | c1950 | P Pe4 | ..... | 50 | 4,000 | 8,000 | *Petdesatnik Crkva.* Dissidents rejecting registration with state. |
| Isolated radio churches | c1954 | P rad | ..... | | 50 | 100 | Isolated radio believers, mostly students and youths. R=92(TWR,HCJB, Radio Vatican). |
| Jehovah's Witnesses | 1922 | M Jeh | x.... | 10 | 500 | 1,000 | Active witnessing under way by 1926. 1 pastor. Suppressed; completely underground. |
| Methodist Church | 1857 | P Met | Vwc.. | 15 | 632 | 2,500 | *Methodistka Crkva.* Bulgaria Provisional Conf. C&S Europe CC, UMC(USA). North. |
| Romanian Orthodox Church | | O Rum | Cwc.. | 1 | 1,000 | 2,000 | *Parohia Ortodoxa Romana din Sofia.* Romanians. Decline from 75,000 in 1900. 1x. |
| Seventh-day Adventist Church | 1891 | P Adv | x.... | 70 | 2,803 | 5,000 | *Adventisti. SDA, Bulgarian Church,* Euro-Africa Division. 9n,14mw,70t(2940). |
| Unitarian Church | | M Unt | I.... | 1 | 200 | 500 | Decline from 862 in 1946. Links with Unitarians in Romania, Hungary, Czechoslovakia. |
| Other Orthodox churches | | O | ..... | | 7,000 | 10,000 | Including: Greek OC, Old Ritualists (Old Believers), Russian OC, Serbian OC. |
| Other Protestant denominations | | P | ..... | | 500 | 1,000 | Including: Ch of Christ (Non-Instrumental), Reformed Ch. |
| Total affiliated (mid-1970) | | | | 4,310 | 4,162,500 | 5,641,130 | Total denominations (1970) . . . 21. |
| Total affiliated (mid-1975) | | | | 4,350 | 4,249,700 | 5,759,300 | Total denominations (1975) . . . 21. |
| Total affiliated (mid-1980) | | | | 4,390 | 4,319,000 | 5,853,300 | Total denominations (1980) . . . 22. |

**NOTES ON TABLE ABOVE**
**COLUMNS:** for meanings and CODES (cols. 1, 3, 4, 8), see Codebook (Part 6). Column 1: **Boldface type** = church with over 10% of country's affiliated Christians.
NATIONAL COUNCILS (Column 4, 5th letter).
 R = Bulgarian Catholic Bishops' Conference (unofficial).

**PEOPLES** (ethnolinguistic). Christians: 91.7% Bulgar, 5.0% Gypsy, 2.5% Macedonian, 0.4% Armenian, 0.2% Russian, 0.1% Greek, 0.1% Gagauz, Romanian.

**COUNTRY-WIDE TOTALS**
EVANGELIZATION (see Part 5). 1900: 96%. 1970: 75%. 1980: 80%. *Radiophonic evangelism.* Radio Vatican, TWR, HCJB.
FOREIGN MISSIONARIES AND PERSONNEL (nationals serving abroad) (1973). Total 35 Orthodox (mainly priests but

with several monks) in 10 countries.
FOREIGN MISSIONARIES AND PERSONNEL (aliens from abroad) (1973). Total 4. *From Western world.* 2: 1 Orthodox, 1 Protestant in 1 USA society. *From Communist world.* 2 Orthodox from Romania, USSR.
INSTITUTIONS (church-operated) (1973). Total 130, including 125 monasteries, 1 press (Orthodox), 1 research centre, 2 seminaries (Orthodox).
PERIODICALS. About 10 titles (6 Orthodox).
PERSONNEL. About 2,604 (2,600 national, 4 foreign).
RELIGIOUS LIBRARIES. About 135.
SCRIPTURE DISTRIBUTION (1975). Annual totals: 100 Bibles (free), 1,000 NTs (free). *Translations completed.* Portion: 6 languages since 1665. NT: 2 languages since 1840. Bible: Bulgarian in 1864.
SERVICE AGENCIES. About 10.

**ADDITIONAL DATA ON CHURCHES**
BULGARIAN ORTHODOX CHURCH. Although the BOC is itself an independent patriarchate in communion with both EP Constantinople and P Moscow, it tends more to recognition of the latter patriarchate than the former. In addition to the 11 dioceses in Bulgaria, there are 3 others (New York, Akron, Detroit) for the faithful in the USA, Canada and Australia. *Membership.* In the 1946 census the number of professing Orthodox was 5,967,992, most baptized. Subsequent to the Communist assumption of power, the number has been continuously eroded; a 1962 poll (Ochavkov) found about 50% of the population admitting to having been baptized as Orthodox (about 4,100,000). *Priests.* The number has declined from 2,381 in 1940 to 1,910 in 1961, and to 1,785 in 1965, due to lack of vocations. *Ordinations.* About 10 new priests are ordained each year (1972).

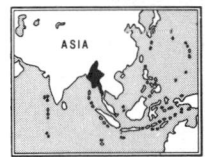

# BURMA

**SECULAR DATA**

**STATE. Official name:** The Socialist Republic of the Union of Burma (Pyi-Daung-Su Socialist Thammada Myanma-Nainggnan-Daw. Shortened form: Myanma). Adjective of nationality: Burmese.
**Flag** (shown above right): Red field, blue rectangle with 14 white stars.
**Area:** 678,033 sq.km. (261,789 sq.miles). Agricultural land: 15.9%.
**Government:** One-party socialist republic, since 1974 (1826 British possession, 1885 province of British India, 1948 Independence as Union of Burma, 1962 socialist military dictatorship, 1974 socialist republic).
**Legislature:** National Assembly, 451 members.
**Official language:** Burmese, with use of English permitted.
**Chief cities:** capital Rangoon 2,055,360 (1973), Mandalay 920,000.
**Political divisions:** 4 States, 8 Divisions (taing), 1 Special Division.
**Armed forces** (1976): Total 169,500 regular: army 153,000, navy 9,000, air force 7,500 (10 combat aircraft). Paramilitary forces: 35,000 People's Police Force.

**DEMOGRAPHY. Population:** 28,885,867 (census of 31.III.1973. For 1970–2000 (UN), see last row of Table 1). Population density (1975): 46/sq.km. (119/sq.mile). Under 15 years: 38%. Growth rate (1975–80): 2.38% per year (births 3.80%, deaths −1.42%). Immigration: −0.17% per year for 1964–68, zero for 1975–80. Life expectancy (1975–80): 52.5 years. Household size: 5.1 persons.
**Major languages:** Burmese, Shan, Karen, Kuki-Chin, English, Chinese, and over 100 smaller tribal languages.
**Urban dwellers** (1970): 18.5%. Urban growth rate (1950–70): 3.1% per year.
**Labour force:** 44%.
**Refugees** (1977): None. Exiles abroad: 30,000 refugees from Burma in Thailand.
**Tourists** (1973): 16,400.

**ETHNOLINGUISTIC GROUPS:** 71.3% Burmese, 10.5% Karen, 7.0% Shan, 2.2% Chinese (610,000) (Mandarin, Amoy, Cantonese), 1.9% Mon, 1.5% Chin, 1.9% Kachin, 1.3% Indo-Pakistani (350,000) (Tamil, Telugu, Hindustani, Pakistani, Bengali, Oriya, Punjabi), 0.7% Palaung, 0.5% Kayah, 0.3% Lahu, 0.3% Lisu, 0.2% Lushai (Mizo), 0.1% Naga, 0.1% Eurasian, Manipuri, Lu, Khon-Thai, Lao, Malay, Jewish, & around 100 other tribes.

**MONEY** (1977). **Monetary unit:** kyat (= 100 pyas); US$1 = K 6.80.
**National income per person:** US$100. Average annual family income US$510.

**Inflation:** (1970–74) 14.5% per year, (1975) 39% per year (consumer price index 240).
**Cost of living in capital** (1976): index 70 (Washington DC = 100). Daily cost of living: US$22.

**HEALTH. Hospitals:** 385 (24,074 beds). Doctors: 4,414. Lepers: 591,600 (18.9 per 1,000). Blind: 210,000. Psychotics: 220,000. Drug addicts: over 300,000. Criminals: 261,491.

**EDUCATION.** Adult literacy: (1953) 56%, (1962) 60%, (1975) 68%. Education rate: 31%. Schools: 19,856. Universities: 2.

**LITERATURE.** Annual new book titles (1973): 1,506. Periodicals: 133. Scientific journals: 30. Newspapers: 7 dailies.

**COMMUNICATION** (per 1,000 people). Phones: 1. Radios: 22. Daily newspaper circulation: 10 copies.

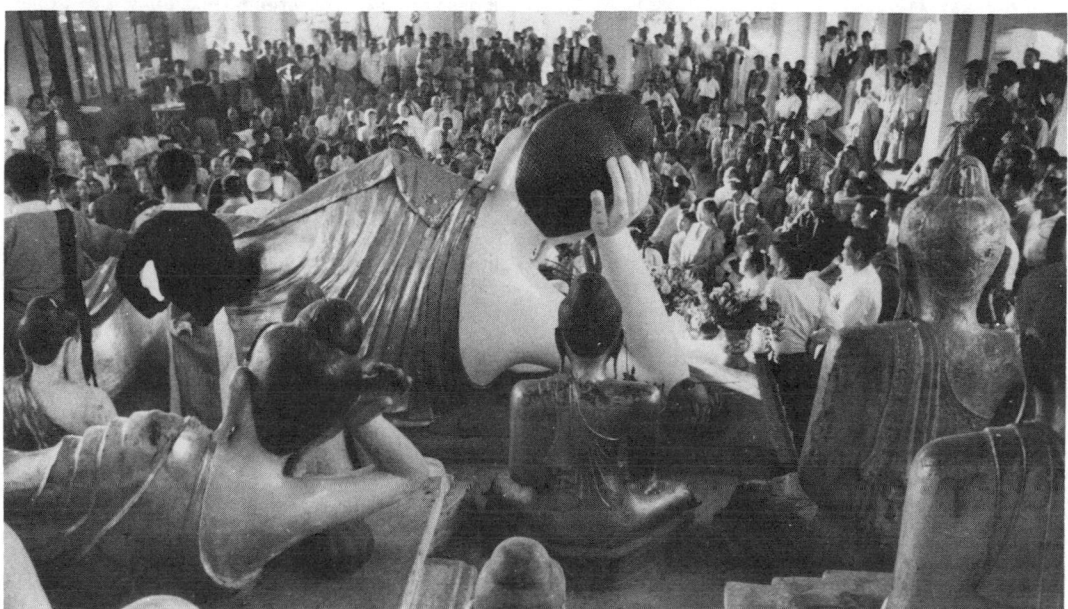

**Buddhists.** Inside a Buddhist temple, with several large reclining Buddhas.

TABLE 1. RELIGIOUS ADHERENTS IN BURMA

| Year | 1900 | | mid-1970 | | Annual change, 1970–1980 | | | | mid-1975 | | mid-1980 | | 2000 | |
|---|---|---|---|---|---|---|---|---|---|---|---|---|---|---|
| *Name* | *Adherents* | *%* | *Adherents* | *%* | *Natural* | *Conversion* | *Total* | *Rate* | *Adherents* | *%* | *Adherents* | *%* | *Adherents* | *%* |
| Buddhists | 9,055,280 | 86.7 | 24,377,000 | 87.8 | 652,192 | –21,092 | 631,100 | 2.31 | 27,335,210 | 87.5 | 30,688,000 | 87.2 | 47,187,500 | 85.9 |
| **Christians** | **232,500** | **2.2** | **1,337,349** | **4.8** | **38,725** | **24,630** | **63,355** | **3.90** | **1,624,500** | **5.2** | **1,970,900** | **5.6** | **4,009,000** | **7.3** |
| crypto-Christians | 85,500 | 0.8 | 255,149 | 0.9 | 8,897 | 15,802 | 24,699 | 6.62 | 373,220 | 1.2 | 502,140 | 1.4 | 1,389,000 | 2.5 |
| professing | 147,000 | 1.4 | 1,082,200 | 3.9 | 29,828 | 8,828 | 38,656 | 3.09 | 1,251,280 | 4.0 | 1,468,760 | 4.2 | 2,620,000 | 4.8 |
| Protestants | 89,000 | 0.9 | 842,000 | 3.0 | 23,093 | 5,327 | 28,420 | 2.93 | 968,400 | 3.1 | 1,126,200 | 3.2 | 1,976,000 | 3.6 |
| Roman Catholics | 36,200 | 0.3 | 220,000 | 0.8 | 6,198 | 3,502 | 9,700 | 3.73 | 260,000 | 0.8 | 317,000 | 0.9 | 604,000 | 1.1 |
| Anglicans | 21,500 | 0.2 | 20,000 | 0.1 | 541 | –1 | 540 | 2.38 | 22,700 | 0.1 | 25,400 | 0.1 | 40,000 | 0.1 |
| Orthodox | 300 | 0.0 | 200 | 0.0 | –4 | 0 | –4 | –2.22 | 180 | 0.0 | 160 | 0.0 | 0 | 0.0 |
| affiliated | 232,500 | 2.2 | 1,337,349 | 4.8 | 38,725 | 24,630 | 63,355 | 3.90 | 1,624,500 | 5.2 | 1,970,900 | 5.6 | 4,009,000 | 7.3 |
| total practising | 209,250 | *90* | 1,069,880 | *80* | 30,980 | 19,704 | 50,684 | 3.90 | 1,299,600 | *80* | 1,576,720 | *80* | 3,006,750 | *75* |
| non-practising | 23,250 | *10* | 267,470 | *20* | 7,745 | 4,926 | 12,671 | 3.90 | 324,900 | *20* | 394,180 | *20* | 1,002,250 | *25* |
| Protestants | 132,000 | 1.3 | 969,736 | 3.5 | 27,780 | 16,806 | 44,586 | 3.83 | 1,165,400 | 3.7 | 1,415,600 | 4.0 | 2,800,000 | 5.1 |
| Evangelicals | 115,000 | 1.1 | 694,000 | 2.5 | 19,928 | 12,272 | 32,200 | 3.85 | 836,000 | 2.7 | 1,016,000 | 2.9 | 2,020,000 | 3.7 |
| Roman Catholics | 70,000 | 0.7 | 267,513 | 1.0 | 8,191 | 7,288 | 15,479 | 4.50 | 343,600 | 1.1 | 422,300 | 1.2 | 878,000 | 1.6 |
| Burmese indigenous | 0 | 0.0 | 71,100 | 0.2 | 1,955 | 435 | 2,390 | 2.91 | 82,000 | 0.3 | 95,000 | 0.3 | 270,000 | 0.5 |
| Anglicans | 30,000 | 0.3 | 27,000 | 0.1 | 739 | 61 | 800 | 2.58 | 31,000 | 0.1 | 35,000 | 0.1 | 55,000 | 0.1 |
| Evangelicals | 0 | 0.0 | 4,000 | 0.0 | 110 | 10 | 120 | 2.61 | 4,600 | 0.0 | 5,200 | 0.0 | 8,500 | 0.0 |
| Marginal Protestants | 0 | 0.0 | 2,000 | 0.0 | 60 | 40 | 100 | 4.00 | 2,500 | 0.0 | 3,000 | 0.0 | 6,000 | 0.0 |
| Orthodox | 500 | 0.0 | 0 | 0.0 | 0 | 0 | 0 | 0.00 | 0 | 0.0 | 0 | 0.0 | 0 | 0.0 |
| Muslims | 338,000 | 3.2 | 1,000,000 | 3.6 | 27,032 | –232 | 26,800 | 2.36 | 1,134,000 | 3.6 | 1,268,000 | 3.6 | 1,976,000 | 3.6 |
| Ahmadis | 0 | 0.0 | 500 | 0.0 | 18 | 32 | 50 | 6.67 | 750 | 0.0 | 1,000 | 0.0 | 2,000 | 0.0 |
| Tribal religionists | 522,500 | 5.0 | 590,000 | 2.1 | 14,894 | –7,024 | 7,870 | 1.26 | 624,800 | 2.0 | 668,700 | 1.9 | 823,000 | 1.5 |
| Hindus | 284,000 | 2.7 | 250,000 | 1.0 | 6,100 | –100 | 6,000 | 2.14 | 280,000 | 0.9 | 310,000 | 0.9 | 384,000 | 0.7 |
| Chinese folk-religionists | 10,000 | 0.1 | 100,000 | 0.4 | 2,694 | –94 | 2,600 | 2.30 | 113,000 | 0.4 | 126,000 | 0.4 | 110,000 | 0.2 |
| Non-religious | 0 | 0.0 | 50,000 | 0.2 | 1,669 | 2,331 | 4,000 | 5.71 | 70,000 | 0.2 | 90,000 | 0.3 | 270,000 | 0.5 |
| Atheists | 0 | 0.0 | 26,000 | 0.1 | 906 | 1,494 | 2,400 | 6.32 | 38,000 | 0.1 | 50,000 | 0.1 | 100,000 | 0.2 |
| Baha'is | 100 | 0.0 | 11,200 | 0.0 | 312 | 68 | 380 | 2.90 | 13,100 | 0.0 | 15,000 | 0.0 | 30,000 | 0.1 |
| Sikhs | 6,600 | 0.1 | 5,000 | 0.0 | 135 | –5 | 130 | 2.30 | 5,650 | 0.0 | 6,300 | 0.0 | 9,000 | 0.0 |
| Parsis | 240 | 0.0 | 200 | 0.0 | 5 | 0 | 5 | 2.27 | 220 | 0.0 | 250 | 0.0 | 200 | 0.0 |
| Jews | 680 | 0.0 | 200 | 0.0 | 5 | 0 | 5 | 2.27 | 220 | 0.0 | 250 | 0.0 | 300 | 0.0 |
| Other religionists | 100 | 0.0 | 1,051 | 0.0 | 31 | 24 | 55 | 4.22 | 1,300 | 0.0 | 1,600 | 0.0 | 3,000 | 0.0 |
| **Country's population** | **10,450,000** | **100.0** | **27,748,000** | **100.0** | **744,700** | **0** | **744,700** | **2.38** | **31,240,000** | **100.0** | **35,195,000** | **100.0** | **54,902,000** | **100.0** |

COLUMNS, ROWS. For meanings and definitions, see Codebook (Part 6). Note that, by definition, total 'Christians' = professing + crypto-Christians, which also = affiliated + nominal Christians. Percentages may not always total exactly, due to rounding.

CENSUSES. **1.III.1901:** 87.5% Buddhists, 5.0% tribal religionists, 3.2% Muslims, 2.7% Hindus, 1.4% Christians (0.8% Baptists, 0.3% Roman Catholics, 0.2% Anglicans), 0.1% Sikhs. **24.II.1931:** 84.3% Buddhists, 5.2% tribal religionists, 4.0% Muslims, 3.9% Hindus, 2.3% Christians. **1.II.1953** (de jure; urban areas of nation only): 82.6% Buddhists, 8.0% Muslims, 5.0% Hindus, 2.4% Christians, 1.5% tribal religionists, 0.4% Chinese folk-religionists. **1953–54:** 88.5% Buddhists, 5.5% Muslims, 3.1% Hindus, 1.8% Christians, 0.9% tribal religionists, 0.2% Chinese folk-religionists. **31.XII.1969** (government registration, but not a census): 89.4% Buddhists, 3.9% Christians, 3.6% Muslims, 2.1% tribal religionists, 1.0% Hindus.

NOTES ON RELIGIONS

AHMADIS. Qadianis from Pakistan since 1938, with a mission established in 1952. There are 2 mosques.

ATHEISTS. 2 parties, both illegal and underground since 1964: Burma Communist Party (White Flag) (Chinese-supported): membership 6,000 men under arms in north, mainly in the Shan and Kachin states; and Communist Party of Burma (Red Flag) (Trotskyist), about 500 scattered members.

BAHA'IS. Begun from India in 1878; recent rapid growth from 11 local spiritual assemblies (1964) to 75 (1973). Converts include Chin, Karen and Shan.

BUDDHISTS. Most ethnic Burmese and Shan are Theravada (or Hinayana, Little Vehicle) Buddhists. Sects: Thudhamma, Shewgyin, Dwara. The Chinese practise Mahayana (Great Vehicle) Buddhism; the Sino-Burmese practise Theravada. The centre of Burmese Buddhism is Mandalay.

BURMESE INDIGENOUS. In over 31 denominations in 1970 (see Table 2), including isolated radio believers.

CRYPTO-CHRISTIANS. Christians affiliated to churches but not known as such in censuses or to society or the state, of 3 kinds: (1) persons in the recognized churches who prefer not to reveal their commitment publicly, (2) members of clandestine churches, and (3) isolated radio and correspondence course believers.

HINDUS. South Indians, mainly Tamil and Telugu. Numbers decreased rapidly by forced emigration in the 1960s.

JEWS. With one synagogue in Rangoon.

MUSLIMS. Sunnis (of the Hanafite rite). Islam is practised by half of the Arakan peoples, by Bengalis, and by Yunnan immigrants. There is also a small Ahmadiya mission based on Rangoon.

ORTHODOX. In the 1901 census, there were 240 Armenian Apostolics and 67 Greek Orthodox, all Europeans. With the repatriation of Indians, their Orthodox churches in Burma were closed, although a handful of them still remain.

**OTHER RELIGIONISTS. In the year 1900, there were 100 Jains. In 1970 there were adherents also of several other non-Christian religions and cults.**

PARSIS. Zoroastrians; originally Indians from Bombay or Persians.

PRACTISING CHRISTIANS. Protestants: about 75% of all Baptists attend church one or more times a year, and about 90% for other Protestants.

PROFESSING CHRISTIANS. In the census of 1931, the ethnic composition of Christians was as follows: 66.1% Karen, 9.3% European and Anglo-Indian, 9.1% Indian (Tamil, Telugu), 4.7% Kachin, 4.4% Burmese, 2.4% Kuki Chin, 0.7% Shan, 0.4% Chinese, 3.6% others.

PROTESTANTS. In 1900, Baptist members (adults) numbered 42,000. In 1970, about 95% of all Baptists were from animistic backgrounds, and only 5% were from Buddhism.

SIKHS. Punjabis from India; decreasing by repatriation.

TRIBAL RELIGIONISTS. Animists, known as *nat*(spirit)-worshippers, among over 100 ethnic groups. Animism is widely practised among Montagnard groups (Moken, Naga); also, the larger northern tribes (including Karen, Chin-Lushai, Kachin-Lisu) still have large numbers of traditionalists, as do the Shan, Mon and Arakanese.

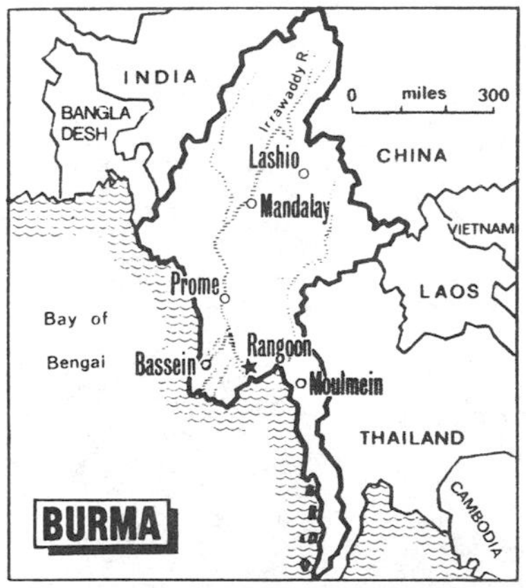


**NON-CHRISTIAN RELIGIONS. Theravada Buddhism,** also called Hinayana or Little Vehicle, entered Burma in the first centuries of the Christian era. During subsequent centuries it absorbed a number of elements from Burmese traditional religions. It has been the dominant religion since the 9th century and has exerted great influence on the development of Burmese culture. Today over 87% of the population is Buddhist, including the overwhelming majority of ethnic Burmese and Shan peoples. In most villages there is a monastery *(kyaung)* occupied by monks *(pongyi)*. The principal sect is the Thudhamma; others include the Shewgyin and Dwara sects. The Buddhist University of Pali, established in 1950 with state support, sets as one of its goals the training of Buddhist missionaries. The fifth world synod in the history of Buddhism took place in 1871, and the sixth synod was held in Burma during 1954–56. Its purpose was to revise the official edition of the Dhamma, the teaching of the Buddha. The Shwe Dagon pagoda in Rangoon is one of the most important sanctuaries of all Buddhism and is believed to contain authentic relics of the Buddha himself.

**Mahayana Buddhism,** or Great Vehicle, is practised by a part of the Chinese community, but the Sino-Burmese, now assimilated into the local population, are adherents of Theravada Buddhism.

**Islam** is the religion of approximately half the Arakan peoples who inhabit the southwest near the border with Bangladesh; it is also practised by Bengali communities south of Prome and the Panthay immigrants from Yunnan province in China.

**Traditional religions** are still widely practised among Montagnard groups (including the Moken and Naga) and continue to influence Buddhism. Wooden statues serving as the abode of spirits (Nats) play an important role in family worship. Traditional beliefs and practices also remain significant for the Karens, of whom 80% have not become Christians. The success of Christianity among the 20% has been due in part to an ancient Karen prophecy that the Golden Book of Y'wa, their supreme being, would be returned to them by a White man. Karens also manifest a strong tendency toward syncretism, as seen in several cults beginning with that of Hpo Pai San in 1866.

**Hinduism, Taoism** and **Confucianism** are largely confined to the Indian and Chinese communities.

**Judaism** is followed by a few expatriates; there is one synagogue in Rangoon.

**CHRISTIANITY.** There were Nestorians in Pegu by the 10th century, Roman Catholics by 1544, and Protestants by 1813. Response to the Christian faith has varied widely in the different ethnic groups. Several tribes, notably the Karen, Chin and Kachin peoples, have embraced Christianity for many years and have built up strong indigenous Christian communities. Others have ignored or rejected the Christian message. There are very few Bhama (ethnic Burmese) converted to Christianity. Christians in fact represent no more than a small minority who are found largely in the Irrawaddy delta region and in the border areas. Baptists and Catholics are the 2 principal Christian groups. Prior to the nationalization of private schools in 1965–66, numerous secondary schools were run by churches.

**Buddhists.** The Kaba E (World Peace) Pagoda, dedicated to cause of world peace; 7 miles from Rangoon, it was completed in 1952 near Great Sacred Cave where 6th Great Buddhist Synod was held from 1954-56.

PROTESTANT CHURCHES. The largest Christian force in Burma is the Burma Baptist Convention, which owes its origin to the pioneering activity of the American Baptist missionary, Adoniram Judson, in 1813. Beginning in Rangoon, church headquarters was transferred to Moulmein in 1826, from where it spread out to the borders of

Burma in every direction. The Karen tribe was the first reached in 1827, followed by Chins in 1845 and Kachins in 1876, and these 3 ethnic groups continue to make up the bulk of Baptist membership. Of the 16 member bodies of the Convention, 3 represent more than 75 per cent of the Baptist community: Kachin Baptist Convention, Karen Baptist Convention (Sgaw), and Zomi (Chin) Baptist Convention.

retain a limited network of charitable institutions, which are concentrated mostly in the diocese of Kengtung. In 1969, these included 3 leprosaria with 1,361 lepers, 24 orphanages with 959 children, 8 homes for 281 infants, 7 homes for the aged with 424 persons, and one home for the infirm with 13 patients. Six priests have pastoral charge of 3,537 Chinese Catholics (1969) out of a total of 700,000

development of national leadership. The Independent Church of India was thus formed in 1930 dissociating itself from the mission, though subsequently supported by it, and later followers over the border began the Independent Church of Burma.

**CHURCH AND STATE.** The relationship between the Burmese state and the religions, particularly Buddhism, has been strongly influenced by the political evolution of the country since Independence, especially by the governments of U Nu (1948–58, 1960–62) and Ne Win (1958–60, 1962 to the 1970s). Throughout its existence, the U Nu regime followed a policy of giving increasing support to Buddhism which it considered compatible with the process of Burmese modernization. During its reign, the following parliamentary acts were successively adopted: (1) the Vinasaya Act (1949), establishing a system of ecclesiastical courts and requiring all members of the Sangha (community of monks) to register, a measure which was meant to improve governmental financial assistance to the Sangha and to draw attention to those who were not members; (2) the Dhammacuriya Act (1950), establishing the University of Pali; and (3) the Union Buddha Sasana Council Act (1950), creating the governmental organization for Buddhist affairs (UBSC). Finally in 1961 Buddhism was declared the state religion, although the rights of minority religions were guaranteed. The U Nu government consistently supported the Buddhist Council, which groups together laymen and monks, and favoured the creation in the suburbs of Rangoon of a vast complex including an Institute of Higher Buddhist Studies and a large institution for the production of Buddhist religious literature.

In contrast, the military regime of Ne Win (still in power in 1979) has shown considerable reluctance to involve the government in religious affairs. Working for the establishment of a 'Burmese way towards socialism', the regime in 1962 withdrew from Buddhism recognition as the state religion and decreed that all religions would be equally respected. In 1964–65 it abolished all previous parliamentary acts concerning Buddhism, and reorganized and then finally suppressed the UBSC in favour of a new and unique Organization of the Council for the Buddhist Community, embracing all Buddhist sects. After an initial attempt at resistance, the Sangha gave in and has adopted a position of patient waiting. The establishment of a one-party state in 1964 forced on all groups, including religious organizations, the

**Methodist Church, Burma.** Minister and family outside Tahan Methodist Church.

The Burma Baptist Convention (BBC) was organized in 1865 and has met annually since, except for a brief period during World War II. After 1945, responsibility for the convention's work was transferred from the American mission to indigenous leadership. Subsequently this work has grown to number nearly 3,000 congregations with a Christian community of 900,000. Prior to the nationalization of Christian institutions in 1965–66, there were 12 hospitals and dispensaries and more than 600 schools with 45,000 pupils.

The next Protestant group to arrive were Lutherans and Methodists. American Methodist missionaries first came to Burma from India in 1879 and settled in the south. They were followed 7 years later by British Methodists who concentrated their attention on northern Burma. Both churches are autonomous today.

Twentieth-century efforts include the work of the Salvation Army begun in 1915, Seventh-day Adventists in 1919, Assemblies of God in 1930, Church of Christ in 1949 and Presbyterianism in 1954. Whereas the first 3 groups were begun by Western missionaries, the Presbyterian Church of Burma was formed by immigrant Lushais from Assam, India, who migrated to Burma after World War II and brought their church with them, and the Church of Christ is composed primarily of Chinese immigrants from the north. The Assemblies of God are perhaps the fastest-growing denomination in Burma today, registering large increases in the number of congregations during a 3-year period at the end of the last decade.

CATHOLIC CHURCH. The first Catholic contacts with Burma were established by the Portuguese in the 16th century. The Bayingyi, a group of ancient Eurasian origin, descendants of Portuguese and Burmese, are the oldest Catholic community, but 90% of the faithful are Karen, Kachin, Chin, Shan and Kaw. The lack of priests is compensated for by the large number of seminary students, catechists and nuns, all of whom teach catechism and are involved in liturgical and sacramental functions. The Ne Win government has allowed Catholics to

Chinese in Burma.

ANGLICAN CHURCH. Although there were Anglican chaplains in Burma as early as 1825 and an increased number after British annexation of the territory in 1853, the first USPG missionaries did not begin at Moulmein until 1859. Nevertheless Anglicans usually date the founding of the church in Burma to 1877 when the first bishop of Rangoon was appointed. The USPG began its work among ethnic Burmese and later extended it to Karens and Chins. In 1924 a second Anglican mission arrived, the BCMS, who directed their attention to upper Burma and the Khumis of west Burma. The church formed part of the Church of India, Pakistan, Burma and Ceylon (CIPBC) until the India and Pakistan dioceses were incorporated into united churches in 1970; since the corresponding Burma union negotiations were not so advanced, an autonomous Church of the Union of Burma was then formed.

INDIGENOUS CHURCHES. Independent churches begun by Burmese nationals have been formed from many of the major traditions working in Burma. The first was the Self-Supporting Karen Baptist Missionary Society, a split in 1912 from the Karen Baptist Convention. Other Baptist schisms have produced the People's Church Movement and the Brethren; the latter has developed new relationships with several overseas Brethren groups. In 1962 disturbances were caused among Baptist Zomi Chins by the Dancing Christian Movement (Hlimsang). Two independent Anglican churches have been St Gabriel's Church Union, a large Tamil-speaking congregation in Rangoon, and the Independent Anglican Church which broke from BCMS work among the Kachins of upper Burma. The Independent Methodist Church of Burma is a recent schism from the Methodists of lower Burma historically related to American Methodism.

The largest indigenous church in the nation is the Independent Church of Burma, a schism from the Indo-Burma Pioneer Mission which first opened work in India in 1910. The immediate cause was a conflict in 1929 between the missionary founder and the home board in the USA over his insistence upon the

**Kachin Baptist Convention.** Baptism of 6,215 converts in Irrawaddy river on single occasion in December 1977, during centennial celebration at Naung Nang, Myitkyina, in presence of 100,000.

obligation to register with the authorities. In a move more nationalist and socialist than anti-Christian, Christian schools and hospitals were nationalized in 1965–66, with the exception of seminaries and a few homes and medical institutions. Lastly in 1966, again for the same nationalistic reasons, the government refused to renew the residence permits of all foreign missionaries who had not worked in the country before Independence, which resulted in the expulsion of 234 Catholic missionaries (priests, brothers and sisters), 56 American Baptists, 29 BCMS and USPG Anglicans, 18 American Methodists, 15 British Methodists, 8 Salvation Army and 7 Assemblies of God workers. In all, nearly 375 missionaries were evicted by this decree.

Subsequently, the churches have not been interfered with by the state. In 1976, the president in fact agreed to authorize the government printing press to provide paper for and to print 10,000 Bibles in Burmese, and a similar request concerning Kachin was under consideration.

**INTERDENOMINATIONAL ORGANIZATIONS.** In 1914, a Regional Council for Burma was formed under the National Christian Council of India, which in 1949 became the independent Burma Christian Council, and by 1975 the Burma Council of Churches. This is an associate council of the WCC and is also affiliated to its Commission on World Mission and Evangelism, as well as being a member of the Christian Conference of Asia (formerly EACC). Several of Burma's churches are also members of the WCC and the CCA. Local councils of churches are being formed in towns where there are 2 or more denominations. Of the 15 regional councils, the Rangoon Council of Churches is the largest.

**BROADCASTING.** Government radio stations operate only for short periods and no religious broadcasts are allowed. A recording studio in Mandalay operated by the American Baptist Mission did at one stage prepare programmes for the Burma Broadcasting Service, BBC (15 minutes every Sunday) and for 30 minutes daily over FEBC (Manila). Later they prepared programmes for release over SEARV and FEBC (both Manila). Because of government restrictions on the import and export of tapes, scripts are sent to the CCA (formerly EACC) studio in Bangkok, where they are made into programmes. Studio Rangoon operated by the Assemblies of God with limited facilities prepares programmes for release over FEBC (Manila). International stations from Manila have been easily received in Burma: FEBC, South East Asia Radio Voice (SEARV), and Radio Veritas (Catholic). Languages used include English, Burmese, Chinese, tribal languages and Thai.

## BIBLIOGRAPHY


'A messianic Buddhist association in Upper Burma', E.M. Mendelson, *Bulletin of the School of Oriental & African Studies*, 24, 4 (1961), 560–580.

*Buddhist backgrounds of the Burmese revolution.* E. Sarkisyanz. The Hague: Nijhoff, 1966.

*Burma Baptist chronicle: Judson Sesquicentennial edition.* Maung Shwe Wa, et al. Rangoon: Burma Baptist Convention, 1963. 448p. (42 historical essays).

'Catholic directory of Burma, 1969'. Rangoon: Catholic Archdiocese, 1969. (Duplicated).

*Christian progress in Burma.* A. McLeish. London: World Dominion Press, c1932.

*Religion and nationalism in Southeast Asia: Burma, Indonesia, the Philippines.* F. R. Von der Mehden. Madison, WI: University of Wisconsin Press, 1963. 253p.

'The Kachin Baptist Church of Burma'. H. G. Tegenfeldt. Thesis, Fuller Theological Seminary, Pasadena, CA (USA), 1973. 496p.


TABLE 2. ORGANIZED CHURCHES AND DENOMINATIONS IN BURMA

| Official name 1 | Begun 2 | Type 3 | Counc 4 | Congs 5 | Adults 6 | Affiliated 7 | Names, notes, and other statistics (see Codebook) 8 |
|---|---|---|---|---|---|---|---|
| Assemblies of God | 1930 | P Pe2 | ..... | 250 | 28,000 | 50,000 | Begun by Lisu. Kachin State. Fusion with Tibet Border Mission (China). 112n,2s. |
| **Burma Baptist Convention:** | 1813 | P Bap | TWE.W | 2,427 | 248,966 | 798,560 | *BBC*, organized 1865. M=ABFMS. 19p(827),P=75%,4s,1300t. 640n, 2274mw, 9680Y. |
| Asho Chin Baptist Conference | 1856 | P Bap | T | 30 | 3,923 | 12,600 | Asho Chin language group (Lower Burma Chin). 1p(9). 17 50 70 |
| Burma Baptist Churches Union | 1819 | P Bap | T | 73 | 8,714 | 28,000 | Burmese-speaking. 9 Associations. All urban. 2p(91),1s. 48 55 12 |
| Burma Baptist Indian Convention | 1829 | P Bap | T | 11 | 643 | 2,100 | Tamils and Telugus from South India, most now returning. 5 20 25 |
| Immanuel Baptist Church | 1855 | P Bap | T | 1 | 440 | 1,400 | English-speaking and Chinese-speaking, Rangoon. 1 6 20 |
| Judson Baptist Church | 1932 | P Bap | T | 1 | 50 | 160 | English-speaking congregation for University of Rangoon. 1 4 4 |
| Kachin Baptist Convention | 1876 | P Bap | T | 180 | 34,669 | 111,000 | Kachins (Jinghpaw); north and northeast. 2p(88). 90 149 1930 |
| Karen Baptist Convention (Sgaw) | 1828 | P Bap | T | 985 | 105,833 | 340,000 | Sgaw Karens, Paku, Bwe, Padaung, Red Karens. 7p(448),1s. 249 1273 2126 |
| Kengtung Lahu Baptist Association | 1901 | P Bap | T | 41 | 4,566 | 14,700 | Lahu (Muhso) (Black, Gold). 15,000 more Lahu Baptists in Yunnan. 4 45 180 |
| Kengtung Shan Baptist Association | 1904 | P Bap | T | 19 | 1,512 | 4,900 | Eastern Shan. Borders on China, Laos, Thailand. Literacy 30%. 1 26 165 |
| Mon Baptist Churches Union | 1827 | P Bap | T | 11 | 1,100 | 3,500 | Mon people (Talaing, Peguan). Union registered in 1952. 3 9 40 |
| Northern Lahu Wa Mission | 1935 | P Bap | T | 139 | 9,342 | 30,000 | HQ Lashio. 20,000 more Lahu and Wa Christians live in China. 19 182 1173 |
| Pangwai Baptist Conference | 1925 | P Bap | T | 142 | 9,785 | 31,000 | Lahu, Akha, Wa, Kachin, in east and northeast. 1p(15). 23 154 564 |
| Pwo Karen Baptist Conference | 1836 | P Bap | T | 174 | 14,677 | 47,000 | 5 Associations. Pwo Karens (15% Christians). 4p(115),1s. 56 161 362 |
| Shan States Home Mission Society | 1838 | P Bap | T | 15 | 3,079 | 9,900 | Shan, Pa-O Karen, Lisu, Kayah. 1962 first woman ordained. 1p. 12 45 113 |
| Shweli Valley Baptist Association | 1902 | P Bap | T | 4 | 1,035 | 3,300 | Shan, Palaung, Chinese. Largest group of Shan Baptists. 3 6 36 |
| Zomi Baptist Convention | 1899 | P Bap | T | 601 | 49,599 | 159,000 | Zomi Chins. 1962, Dancing Christian Movement. 1p(36),1s. 108 89 2860 |
| **Catholic Church in Burma:** | 1544 | R Lat | P.F.R | 492 | 165,900 | 267,513 | *Catholic Athindaw*. 55% Karen. C=5+5+8.G=2.1%pa,1s. 175nx,60m,475w,P=63%,14013Yy. |
| M Mandalay | 1866 | R Lat | Ps | 131 | 24,600 | 39,744 | Chins. Rapid growth from 23,410 in 1960: G=5.4%pa. 36 16 78 87 1868 |
| D Kengtung | 1927 | R Lat | Ppime | 17 | 18,000 | 29,035 | *Thathana Kengtung*. Kachins. 7,000 converts a year. 14 5 80 40 2274 |
| D Myitkyina | 1939 | R Lat | Ps | 19 | 22,400 | 36,089 | *Thathana Myitkyina*. Kaws, Lahus Many converts. 1p. 16 0 31 58 2259 |
| M Rangoon | 1866 | R Lat | Ps | 32 | 30,300 | 48,868 | *Thathanabaing Rangoon*. Capital. M=MEP. 2p,1s. 37 21 117 52 2090 |
| D Bassein | 1955 | R Lat | Ps | 12 | 23,400 | 37,778 | Extreme southwest. Karens, Indians, Chinese. 1p. 15 17 65 59 1525 |
| D Prome | 1940 | R Lat | Ps | 4 | 5,900 | 9,468 | Formerly PA Akyab. Central west. Mainly Chins. M=MS. 11 0 19 50 304 |
| D Taunggyi | 1961 | R Lat | Ps | 265 | 25,700 | 41,373 | East of M Mandalay. Karens. Formerly M=PIME. 26 0 5 70 2672 |
| D Toungoo | 1870 | R Lat | Ps | 12 | 15,600 | 25,158 | Adjoining Rangoon. Catholics almost entirely Karens. 20 1 80 75 1021 |
| Christian Brethren | | I CBr | x.... | 1 | 100 | 300 | Small schisms ex Burma Baptist Convention, with overseas Open Brethren links. |
| Church of Christ | c1949 | P int | ....w | | 25,000 | 50,000 | M=OMF(formerly CIM). Refugees from China: Chinese, Wa, Lahu, Lisu, Rawang. 80n. |
| Church of God | | I ind | ..... | 1 | 100 | 300 | Small indigenous group at Insein, a few kilometres north of Rangoon. |
| Church of the Province of Burma: | 1825 | A plu | AWEAW | 150 | 13,200 | 27,000 | In CIPBC until 1970. M=SPG,BCMS, until 1965. 100n,48m,5w,98pp,2s(20),2000y. |
| D Rangoon | 1877 | A Cen | A | 66 | 5,500 | 10,500 | 33% Khumi Chin, 31% Pwo Karen, 11% Asho Chin, 6% Burmese. 38n,1s(4),W=40%,1600Yy. |
| D Akyab | 1971 | A Eva | A | 25 | 1,700 | 3,500 | Extreme west. Rural. 100% Khumi Chins (Kumi). Rapid growth. 12n,W=40%,40Y,30y. |
| D Mandalay | 1970 | A Cen | A | | 4,000 | 8,000 | Northern half of country. Majority Kachins; some Burmese, Shans, Chins. 30n. |
| D Pa'an | 1970 | A Cen | A | | 2,000 | 5,000 | Long southern strip of Burma. 95% Sgaw Karens and Pwo Karens. 20n. |
| Independent Anglican Church | 1958 | I Ang | ..... | 2 | 800 | 1,500 | Split from Anglicans (BCMS mission). Kachins. HQ Mohnyin, Upper Burma. 1n. |
| Independent Church of Burma | 1938 | I ind | ....w | | 8,500 | 20,000 | Lushai split ex Indo-Burma Pioneer Mission, now in 3 factions. HQ Tahan. 82m. |
| Independent Methodist Church of Burma | 1967 | I Met | ..... | 7 | 350 | 500 | *Free Methodist Ch.* Split ex Methodist Ch of Union of Burma. 2n,G=8.0%pa,W=80%,17Y. |
| Indian Lutheran Church (Bethlehem) | 1878 | P Lut | Lwe.W | | 100 | 300 | Union of 2 Indian churches: Andhra ELC (Telugus), Tamil ELC (Tamils). Emigrating. |
| Isolated radio churches | 1952 | I rad | ..... | 400 | 2,400 | 4,800 | Isolated radio believers, mostly aged 12–25. R=3930(FEBC,FEBA),S=10(ICI). |
| Jehovah's Witnesses | 1910 | M Jeh | x.... | 19 | 584 | 2,000 | *Watch Tower. IBSA.* Active witnessing under way by 1926. Re-established 1946. 63Y. |
| Lakher Independent Evangelical Church | 1907 | P ind | ..... | 10 | 1,000 | 3,000 | Members are 95% of whole Lakher headhunting tribe, mostly in India. M=LPM(UK). |
| Lisu Christian Church | | I ind | ....W | | 8,000 | 20,000 | Lisu Christians from China, often migrating in order to obtain Lisu Bibles. |
| Mara Christian Church | | P Con | ..... | 10 | 2,000 | 4,000 | Strong across border in Assam as Mara Independent Ev Ch. Manipuris. |
| Methodist Church of the Union of Burma | 1879 | P Met | VwE.W | 21 | 2,819 | 5,000 | *Methodist Ch. Lower Burma.* M=UMC(USA). Many Chinese, including bishop. 15n,21t. |
| Methodist Church, Burma | 1886 | P Met | V.E.W | | 9,000 | 18,771 | *Methodist Ch, Upper Burma.* M=MMS(UK). 80% Lushai, 17% Khongsai (Kuki Chins). 140n. |
| People's Church Movement | | I Bap | ..... | | 600 | 2,000 | In Chin Hills, ex Zomi Baptists; led by Chin prophet. Catholic features. |
| Presbyterian Church of Burma | 1954 | P Ref | R...W | 93 | 5,126 | 14,605 | Lushai migrants from Mizo Presb Ch, Assam. 15n,19m,G=10.2%pa,1s(5),W=60%,646Yy. |
| St Gabriel's Church Union, CIB | 1925 | I Ang | ....W | 1 | 50 | 200 | CIB=Ch of India & Burma. Rangoon Anglican split. Tamils, returning to India. |
| Salvation Army | 1915 | P Sal | xwE.W | 23 | 300 | 500 | *Ke-tin-gyin Tut. SA, Burma Command.* 2 Districts. Officers 12, institutions 4. |
| Self-Supporting Karen Baptist Miss Soc | 1912 | I Bap | ....W | | 5,000 | 10,000 | *SSKBS.* Split from Karen work of BBC. Sgaw and Pwo Karen. HQ Rangoon. 40n. |
| Seventh Day Baptist Church | 1965 | I Bap | ..... | 8 | 479 | 1,500 | Chins who affiliated with SDB Ch (USA) through correspondence courses. HQ Tahan. |
| Seventh-day Adventist Church | 1919 | *P Adv | x.... | 91 | 5,430 | 15,000 | *SDA, Burma Union* (4 Sections). HQ Rangoon. 34n,132mw,1j,1s,142t(6927),507Y. |
| United Pentecostal Church | | P Pel | x.... | 37 | 4,000 | 10,000 | *Jesus Only Church.* M=UPC(USA). Unitarian Pentecostals. 35n,1p(10). |
| Other Burmese indigenous churches | | I | ..... | | 5,700 | 10,000 | Numerous small independent groups (over 20), especially among Karens. 50n. |
| **Total affiliated (mid-1970)** | | | | **4,970** | **543,504** | **1,337,349** | **Total denominations (1970) . . . 46.** |
| **Total affiliated (mid-1975)** | | | | **6,050** | **660,200** | **1,624,500** | **Total denominations (1975) . . . 48.** |
| **Total affiliated (mid-1980)** | | | | **7,300** | **800,970** | **1,970,900** | **Total denominations (1980) . . . 50.** |

### NOTES ON TABLE ABOVE

COLUMNS: for meanings and CODES (cols. 1, 3, 4, 8), see Codebook (Part 6). Column 1: **Boldface type** = church with over 10% of country's affiliated Christians.

NATIONAL COUNCILS (Column 4, 5th letter).
R = Burma Catholic Bishops' Conference.
W = Burma Council of Churches (BCC).
w = associate member of BCC.
*Local councils.* 15 councils are affiliated to the BCC.

UNITING CHURCHES. Negotiations (begun in 1967) for organic union were under way in 1974 between the Methodist Churches of Upper and Lower Burma.

PEOPLES (ethnolinguistic). Christians: 46.3% Karen, 18.6% Chin, 11.5% Kachin, 6.0% Lahu, 5.4% Lisu, 3.8% Mizo (Lushai), 2.2% Burmese, 2.0% Eurasian, 0.9% Shan, 0.8% Naga, 0.7% Chinese, 0.3% Manipuri, 0.3% Mon (Talaing, Peguan), 0.2% Lakher, 0.2% South Indian (Tamil, Telugu).

### COUNTRY-WIDE TOTALS

EVANGELIZATION (see Part 5). 1900: 20%. 1970: 40%. 1980: 48%. *Mass evangelism.* Widespread local campaigns, especially led by Baptists, but unpublicized outside local areas. 1978, Here's Life Rangoon (CCCI). *Radiophonic evangelism.* FEBC, FEBA, ICI.

FOREIGN MISSIONARIES AND PERSONNEL (nationals serving abroad) (1973). Total 55 in 5 countries: 30 Protestants, 25 Roman Catholics. Since 1883 scores of Karen Baptists have worked as missionaries in neighbouring countries.

FOREIGN MISSIONARIES AND PERSONNEL (aliens from abroad) (1973). Total 79. *From Western world.* 50 Roman Catholics; no Anglicans or Protestants since 1966. *From Communist world.* 1 Roman Catholic from Poland. *From Third World.* 28: about 20 Roman Catholics, 8 Protestants, from India, Thailand, Hong Kong.

INSTITUTIONS (church-operated) (1973). Total 41, including 4 higher schools (minor seminaries), 3 medical centres (leprosaria), 2 religious communities, 25 seminaries (21 Protestant, 2 RC, 2 Anglican), 5 study centres.

PERIODICALS. About 20 titles (5 SDA).

PERSONNEL. About 4,804 (4,725 national, 79 foreign).

RELIGIOUS LIBRARIES. About 33.

SCRIPTURE CIRCULATION (1975). Annual totals: 2,378 Bibles (15% free, 85% subsidized), 31,236 NTs (90% free, 10% subsidized), 37,979 UBS portions, 29,771 UBS selections. *Translations completed.* Portion: 27 languages since 1815. NT: 16 languages since 1832. Bible: 7 languages since 1835.

SERVICE AGENCIES. About 20, including AYPA, BCBC, BCC, CAVE, CCCI, CRSB, MU, UIM, WVI, YMCA, YWCA.

### ADDITIONAL DATA ON CHURCHES

BURMA BAPTIST CONVENTION. *Growth.* (1958) 188,719 baptized adults; (1962) 2,172 churches, 204,805 baptized adults; (1972) 2,500 organized local congregations, 270,000 baptized adults (active); (1977) 321,525 baptized adults. Growth of Kachin Baptist Convention: (1968) 34,669 baptized; (1977) 57,000 baptized, 170,000 total Christian community. The statistics in the table above are from the 1968 church census, except for affiliated which are 1970 estimates. *Conversions.* 95% of members are converts from animism, and only 5% from Buddhism. *Members abroad.* Several of the BBC's conventions border on neighbouring countries and have members across the border. In particular, in addition to Lahu Baptists in the Kengtung Association, there are about 15,000 more Lahu Baptists living in Yunnan (China).

CATHOLIC CHURCH IN BURMA. *New jurisdiction.* Created in 1975: PA Lashio. *Catholics.* Including 3,537 Chinese. *Catechumens.* (1959) 22,510; (1961) 23,201; (1963) 28,218. *Growth.* In 1949 there were 130,832 Catholics; by 1977, 331,530 Catholics. *Annual baptisms.* (1972) 68.1% infant, 31.9% adult. *Bishops.* In 1971, 5 of the 8 bishops were Burmese; in 1978, all but one of the 9. The first indigenous bishop was consecrated in 1954. *Priests.* In 1949, out of 225 priests, 77 were Burmese. In 1971, out of 175 priests 125 were Burmese (or other Asians). The first Chin priest was ordained in 1960, and the first Kachin in 1965. In 1977, there were 169 local diocesan priests and 46 religious priests (11 Burmese, 35 foreign). *Brothers.* (1977) 62, in 5 congregations. *Sisters.* (1977) 605, in 9 congregations. *Seminaries* (1973). 1 secular, 1 religious. *Seminarians.* (1972) 81, (1977) 110. *Catechists.* Total (1970) 372, (1973) 653 (247 full-time). *Indigenous religious congregations* (1969). 28 Brothers of St Francis Xavier, 133 Sisters of St Francis Xavier. *Foreign congregations* (1969). Priests: 25 PIME, 18 MEP, 17 SSC, 8 MS, 7 SDB. Brothers: 35 FSC (declining to 31 by 1973), 16 Brothers of St Joseph. Sisters: 235 Sisters of Charity and Sisters of Reparation, 60 Sisters of St Joseph, 54 Franciscan Missionaries of Mary, 24 Sisters of the Seven Sorrows, 23 Sisters of Mary, 10 Sisters of St Aloysius. *Catholic organizations.* The Burma Catholic Bishops' Conference has its headquarters in Rangoon. There are no national presbyteral or pastoral councils. Religious personnel are represented in the Conference of Religious Sisters of Burma (CRSB).

The Holy See has no diplomatic relations with Burma. It is represented to the Catholic hierarchy by an apostolic delegate based in Dacca, Bangladesh.

All Catholic schools and hospitals were nationalized in April 1965. Because of past links, however, 248 schools with 8,389 pupils are still regarded as in some sense of Catholic influence. The church continues to run some leprosaria, nursery schools and homes for the aged.

CHURCH OF THE PROVINCE OF BURMA. Name in Burmese: Myanmanainggan Karityan Athindaw.

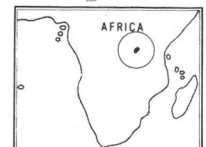

# BURUNDI

## SECULAR DATA

**STATE. Official name:** The Republic of Burundi (La République du Burundi/Republika y'u Kirundi). Adjective of nationality: Burundian (burundais).
**Flag** (shown above right): White diagonal cross, red quarters above and below, green quarters at sides, centred white circle with 3 red stars.
**Area:** 27,834 sq. km. (10,747 sq.miles). Agricultural land: 60.7%.
**Government:** Military junta, since 1966 (17th century Tutsi absolute monarchy, 1898 German rule, 1919 Belgian mandated territory, 1962 Independence as monarchy, 1966 military rule).
**Official languages:** Kirundi and French (Français).
**Chief cities:** capital Bujumbura 78,810 (1970), Kitega 10,000.
**Political divisions:** 8 Provinces, 18 Arrondissements, 181 Communes.
**Armed forces** (1973): Total 3,500 regular army.

**DEMOGRAPHY. Population:** 3,350,000 (census of 1970–71. For 1970–2000 (UN), see last row of Table 1). Population density

(1975): 135/sq.km. (350/sq.mile). Under 15 years: 43%. Growth rate (1975–80): 2.60% per year (births 4.73%, deaths −2.13%). Life expectancy (1975–80): 43.0 years. Household size: 4.9 persons.
**Major languages:** Rundi (Kirundi), Ruanda (Kinyarwanda), French, Swahili.
**Urban dwellers** (1970): 2.6%.
**Labour force:** 55%.
**Refugees** (1977): 48,500 from Rwanda. Exiles abroad: 141,900 Burundians (110,500 in Tanzania, 24,000 in Zaire, 7,400 in Rwanda).
**Tourists** (1974): 14,467.

**ETHNOLINGUISTIC GROUPS:** 96.1% Rundi (83.3% Hutu, 14.0% Tutsi), 1.6% Ruanda (54,000), 1.2% Zairian (40,000), 1.0% Twa Pygmy, 0.1% Swahili (Arab), European (French, Belgian), Asian.

**MONEY** (1977). **Monetary unit:** franc (= 100 centimes); US$1 = BuFr 89.55.

**National income per person:** US$90. Average annual family income: US$441.
**Inflation:** (1970–74) 17% per year (1975: consumer price index 160).
**Cost of living in capital** (1976): index 137 (Washington DC=100). Daily cost of living: US$32.

**EDUCATION.** Adult literacy: (1962) 14%. Education rate: 18%. Schools: 970. Universities: 1.

**HEALTH.** Hospitals: 136 (4,221 beds). Doctors: 74. Lepers: 40,000 (10.6 per 1,000). Blind: 11,000. Psychotics: 24,000.

**LITERATURE.** Annual new book titles (1966): 17. Periodicals: 15. Newspapers: 1 daily, 2 non-daily.

**COMMUNICATION** (per 1,000 people). Phones: 1. Radios: 25. Daily newspaper circulation: 0.1 copies.

### TABLE 1. RELIGIOUS ADHERENTS IN BURUNDI

| Year / Name | 1900 Adherents | % | mid-1970 Adherents | % | Annual change, 1970–1980 Natural | Conversion | Total | Rate | mid-1975 Adherents | % | mid-1980 Adherents | % | 2000 Adherents | % |
|---|---|---|---|---|---|---|---|---|---|---|---|---|---|---|
| **Christians** | 100 | 0.0 | 2,479,000 | 74.0 | 75,040 | 43,660 | 118,700 | 3.94 | 3,012,000 | 80.0 | 3,666,000 | 85.5 | 6,950,000 | 95.5 |
| professing | 100 | 0.0 | 2,479,000 | 74.0 | 75,040 | 43,660 | 118,700 | 3.94 | 3,012,000 | 80.0 | 3,666,000 | 85.5 | 6,950,000 | 95.5 |
| Roman Catholics | 40 | 0.0 | 2,265,800 | 67.6 | 68,664 | 40,497 | 109,161 | 3.96 | 2,756,090 | 73.2 | 3,357,090 | 78.3 | 6,299,800 | 86.5 |
| Protestants | 0 | 0.0 | 150,000 | 4.5 | 4,409 | 1,602 | 6,011 | 3.40 | 176,960 | 4.7 | 210,110 | 4.9 | 422,200 | 5.8 |
| Anglicans | 60 | 0.0 | 60,000 | 1.8 | 1,876 | 1,558 | 3,434 | 4.56 | 75,300 | 2.0 | 94,340 | 2.2 | 218,400 | 3.0 |
| African indigenous | 0 | 0.0 | 2,000 | 0.1 | 57 | 3 | 60 | 2.61 | 2,300 | 0.1 | 2,600 | 0.1 | 7,000 | 0.1 |
| Orthodox | 0 | 0.0 | 1,200 | 0.0 | 34 | 0 | 34 | 2.52 | 1,350 | 0.0 | 1,540 | 0.0 | 2,600 | 0.0 |
| nominal | 66 | 0.0 | 188,900 | 5.6 | 5,440 | 1,398 | 6,838 | 3.13 | 218,370 | 5.8 | 257,280 | 6.0 | 582,400 | 8.0 |
| affiliated | 34 | 0.0 | 2,290,100 | 64.8 | 69,600 | 42,262 | 111,862 | 4.00 | 2,793,630 | 74.2 | 3,408,720 | 79.5 | 6,367,600 | 87.5 |
| total practising | 34 | *100* | 2,015,290 | *88* | 61,248 | 37,190 | 98,438 | 4.00 | 2,458,390 | *88* | 2,999,670 | *88* | 5,094,080 | *80* |
| non-practising | 0 | *0* | 274,810 | *12* | 8,352 | 5,072 | 13,424 | 4.00 | 335,240 | *12* | 409,050 | *12* | 1,273,520 | *20* |
| Roman Catholics | 34 | 0.0 | 2,107,500 | 62.9 | 64,182 | 39,402 | 103,584 | 4.02 | 2,576,160 | 68.4 | 3,143,340 | 73.3 | 5,804,100 | 79.7 |
| Protestants | 0 | 0.0 | 135,000 | 4.0 | 3,936 | 1,464 | 5,400 | 3.42 | 158,000 | 4.2 | 189,000 | 4.4 | 378,600 | 5.2 |
| Evangelicals | 0 | 0.0 | 112,000 | 3.3 | 3,289 | 1,311 | 4,600 | 3.48 | 132,000 | 3.5 | 158,000 | 3.7 | 318,000 | 4.4 |
| Anglicans | 0 | 0.0 | 45,000 | 1.3 | 1,408 | 1,382 | 2,790 | 4.94 | 56,500 | 1.5 | 72,900 | 1.7 | 174,700 | 2.4 |
| Evangelicals | 0 | 0.0 | 45,000 | 1.3 | 1,408 | 1,382 | 2,790 | 4.94 | 56,500 | 1.5 | 72,900 | 1.7 | 174,700 | 2.4 |
| African indigenous | 0 | 0.0 | 1,500 | 0.0 | 42 | 8 | 50 | 2.94 | 1,700 | 0.0 | 2,000 | 0.0 | 6,000 | 0.1 |
| Orthodox | 0 | 0.0 | 1,000 | 0.0 | 28 | 0 | 28 | 2.50 | 1,120 | 0.0 | 1,280 | 0.0 | 2,200 | 0.0 |
| Marginal Protestants | 0 | 0.0 | 100 | 0.0 | 4 | 6 | 10 | 6.67 | 150 | 0.0 | 200 | 0.0 | 2,000 | 0.0 |
| **Tribal religionists** | 1,007,900 | 99.8 | 839,400 | 25.1 | 17,861 | −43,761 | −25,900 | −3.61 | 716,900 | 19.0 | 580,400 | 13.5 | 252,000 | 3.5 |
| **Muslims** | 2,000 | 0.2 | 30,000 | 0.9 | 852 | 88 | 940 | 2.75 | 34,200 | 0.9 | 39,400 | 0.9 | 73,000 | 1.0 |
| **Baha'is** | 0 | 0.0 | 1,600 | 0.0 | 47 | 13 | 60 | 3.16 | 1,900 | 0.0 | 2,200 | 0.1 | 5,000 | 0.1 |
| **Country's population** | 1,010,000 | 100.0 | 3,350,000 | 100.0 | 93,800 | 0 | 93,800 | 2.49 | 3,765,000 | 100.0 | 4,288,000 | 100.0 | 7,280,000 | 100.0 |

**COLUMNS, ROWS.** For meanings and definitions, see Codebook (Part 6). Note that, by definition, total 'Christians' = professing + crypto-Christians, which also = affiliated + nominal Christians. Percentages may not always total exactly, due to rounding.

**NOTES ON RELIGIONS**
AFRICAN INDIGENOUS. In 2 groups in 1970 (see Table 2).
BAHA'IS. In 1964, 3 local spiritual assemblies; 1973, 47 isolated groups.

**COUNTRY'S POPULATION.** In 1972–73, about 4,000 Tutsis and later 150,000 Hutus were massacred.

**MUSLIMS.** Africans are Sunnis (of the Malakite rite), with 400 Asian Shias (Ismailis) and Bohora, Ithna-Ashari and Kharijite minorities. The largest number in a Catholic diocese in 1970 was 17,000 in the diocese of Bujumbura. Islam is growing gradually; many Rundi are converted to Islam in Bujumbura.
**PRACTISING CHRISTIANS.** Of all Catholics 'tenus aux

Pâques' (under obligation to attend Easter communion), 73.5% made their Easter communion in 1967, and 74.5% in 1968. In addition there were other regularly practising Catholics who were unable to attend at Easter for various reasons.
**TRIBAL RELIGIONISTS.** Only the Twa pygmies (Gesera; 30,000) remain predominantly traditionalist or animist (90%). There are however still many Rundi animists; the Catholic diocese with the highest percentage in 1968 was Bururi, 46.3% of whose population were animists.

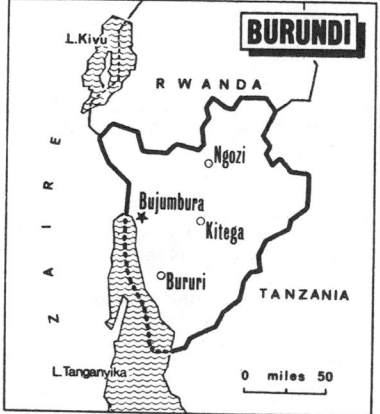

**NON-CHRISTIAN RELIGIONS. Traditional religions** are followed by one fifth of the population. The Twa pygmies, however, remain 90% traditionalist. The Barundi name for the creator God is Imana. He is normally invisible but sometimes visits his people in the form of a white lamb. Few prayers are addressed to Imana, Barundi attention being focused on the cult of a former human being Kiranga which originated in Rwanda where he is known as Ryangombe. The highly-organized Kiranga cult is attended by initiates of varying rank known as Abana b'Imana (children of Imana). Kiranga periodically possesses his highest-ranked initiate, to whom special honour is accorded. Although not himself God, Kiranga is able to enhance or prevent

**Eglise Catholique au Burundi.** A packed pontifical mass celebrated at Mugera in 1938 at height of mass movement into church in Urundi, when 1,000 a week were being baptized.

Imana's aid and thus serves as intermediary between God and man.

**Islam** accounts for less than 1% of the population. There are about 30,000 Muslims, most of whom work as merchants, fishermen and artisans in centres on Lake Tanganyika. In Bujumbura there are 16,000 including 13,000 Africans and 3,000 Asians; at Rumange 5,000, and 1,000 at Nyanza-Lac. Africans are Sunnis and Asians Ismailis, with Bohora, Ithna-Asheri and Kharijite minorities. Since they speak Swahili, they have difficulty in obtaining access to education although there are some Quranic schools. They maintain relations with Muslims in neighbouring countries.

**CHRISTIANITY.** In the 15th century, tall pastoral Tutsi warriors migrated from Ethiopia to the Ruanda-Urundi area and established a feudal system over the Hutu and Twa pygmies. The Hutu, 85% of population, became the serfs of the cattle-owning

and prayer huts (without Sunday services and with incomplete catechetical instruction). The lack of priests has necessitated that certain parishes be placed under lay responsibility. A variety of catechetical training centres have been developed, with catechists carrying much of the responsibility for the instruction of new converts.

The life of the church was deeply affected by the violence of the Hutu rebellion of 29 April 1972 in the Bururi region of southern Burundi and the Tutsi repression throughout the country which followed. Violence continued during 1973, provoked particularly by armed incursions of Hutu refugees from bordering countries. The initial rebellion cost 3,000 to 4,000 dead, mostly Tutsis but also some Hutus who tried to protect them or refused to join the rebels. The 100,000 killed (mostly Hutus, plus a few Tutsis favourable to the Hutu cause) in the Tutsi repression of 1972 accounted for 2.7% of the total population and 3.2% of the Hutu population of Burundi. Of

American Free Methodists took over the fifth Neukirchener station in 1935 and later added 3 more. The Swedish Free Mission, a Pentecostal body, also began in 1935 in the region of Bururi; and they are now the largest Protestant community in Burundi, with 38 missionaries in the field. The World Gospel Mission entered in 1938.

Protestants are heavily involved in education, medical and social service. In 1970 Protestants and Anglicans were responsible for 275 primary schools (40,058 pupils, 22.2% of the total), 3 secondary schools (323 students, 9% of the total) and 3 teacher-training schools (395 students) in addition to technical, trade, agricultural and domestic science institutions.

ANGLICAN CHURCH. The Rwanda General and Medical Mission (CMS) entered Burundi in 1934. The East African Revival which began in Rwanda in 1927 swept through Burundi in the 1930s, having its greatest influence in Anglican churches. Most members were Tutsi, many of whom were later killed in tribal fighting. CMS medical facilities were particularly hard-pressed when 120,000 Tutsi refugees poured into Burundi with the first Hutu uprisings in Rwanda following its independence. The Anglican Church shares in sponsoring 2 teacher-training colleges in addition to Warner Theological College which provides training for priests and for other full-time workers. The first African bishop was consecrated in Burundi in 1965, and Burundi became an independent diocese within the Church of Uganda, Rwanda and Burundi in 1966. During the Hutu uprising of 1972 and the massacres which followed, the clergy were reduced by half. Approximately 100 catechists lost their lives, leaving 350 untrained and badly-paid men to help the remaining pastors in the out-churches. Only 2 of the 17 clergy in 1974 had had secondary education, and the annual income of the church was reduced by half as a result of the country's internal troubles. In 1973 there were 535 congregations grouped in 28 parishes.

INDIGENOUS CHURCHES. In 1962 two-thirds of all Anglicans in southern Burundi seceded to form the Eglise de Dieu (Church of God), Although at one time numbering 20,000 members, it was accused of subversion in 1965 and suppressed. An earlier schismatic group broke away from the Friends in 1959, but it has also largely disappeared. There is one immigrant Kimbanguist congregation from Zaire.

**CHURCH AND STATE.** Although the country became independent in 1962, it continued to be ruled by the Mwami (king), who governed with the assistance of Ganwa (princes). The Ganwa each administered a different province, each had his own court and army, and frequently quarrelled among themselves. In 1966 the monarchy and Ganwa system were overthrown by an army colonel Micombero who set up a military regime with himself as president. In 1969 discussions were held between the chief of state and representatives of the Catholic and Anglican churches, which were followed by a joint pastoral letter whose aim was to lessen ethnic tensions. Later that year 25 alleged conspirators against the government were executed, and the number of Tutsi from the south within the government were increased. These events were then followed by the Hutu rebellion and Tutsi repression of 1972.

The churches in general play an important role in social action and education. The Catholic Church in particular is sufficiently strong for its declarations to be listened to with seriousness. As with the former Belgian colonial administration and private enterprise, the church has since the beginning tended to place more confidence in Tutsis than Hutus, the former being considered more open and dynamic; and thus the church also contributed to the social and political cleavage of the country and to the fact that at Independence the intellectual and political elite were for the most part Tutsis while the majority of the population were Hutus. The failure of the Catholic hierarchy to take a clear and vigorous position in the face of the evolving situation was evident both before and after the 1972 rebellion. During 1972–73 the Tutsi bishops were the only ones who could express themselves without constraint. Many Hutus and missionaries have complained about the failure of episcopal declarations to condemn the massacres and especially the failure to make any comment on the social and ethnic causes for the 1972 Hutu rebellion, although everyone is in agreement that the situation is extremely complex. A number of missionaries were expelled from Burundi in 1972 and 1973.

The constitution of 11 July 1974 states that 'Burundi is a unitary, indivisible, secular and democratic

**Eglise Catholique au Burundi, Archdiocèse de Gitega.** Leaving cathedral of Archdiocese of Gitega after Sunday mass. About 70% of all Catholics in Burundi are Easter communicants.

Tutsi and both tribes came to speak the same language. Europeans were late in arriving, the first being Speke and Burton in 1858 seeking the source of the Nile. Livingstone and Stanley also shared in this search in the 1870s. The White Fathers established their first mission in Burundi in 1879. In 1881, 2 priests and a lay helper were murdered, and they were not replaced until 1899. Burundi became part of German East Africa at the Berlin Conference in 1884, and in 1907 Bethel Lutherans sought to establish themselves in this area. Belgian troops from the Congo occupied the country in 1916 and German missions were forced to close. In 1923 Belgium received a mandate to administer Ruanda-Urundi. Belgian Protestant missions were too few in number to meet the request to take over German missions, and so other Protestant missions were allowed to enter.

CATHOLIC CHURCH. In 1922 Burundi was made a vicariate apostolic, having at that time 5 stations, 18 missionaries and 14,356 Catholics. The first Murundi priest was ordained in 1925. In 1930 a mass movement into the church began to take place, with an average of 1,000 baptisms a week by 1935. By 1937 the Catholic population had risen to 250,000 baptized and 230,000 cathechumens. In 1959 the first African bishop in Burundi was appointed, to a new diocese, and the country became an ecclesiastical province. At that time the number of baptized Catholics was 1,200,000 or 55% of the population. At territorial independence 3 years later, the number of baptized was 1,445,000 with 127,000 catechumens, and a fourth diocese was created. In 1971 there were 90 parishes averaging in size over 23,400 baptized and catechumens, each divided into central branches (with Sunday services and a complete cycle of catechetical instruction for adults and children), semi-central branches (with Sunday services and an incomplete cycle of catechetical instruction)

these, 18 were priests (17 Hutus and one Tutsi), 7 male and female religious personnel, 2,100 catechists and teachers in Catholic schools (out of 4,580), a large number of nurses and Hutu medical assistants and in general the major portion of the Hutu intelligentsia. Some 100,000 Hutus (including some seminary students) became refugees: 50,000 in Tanzania, 40,000 in Rwanda and 10,000 in Zaire.

For the most part, the unity of the local Tutsi and Hutu clergy was not seriously threatened by these trials, although some Tutsi priests found themselves in opposition to missionary clergy who were often outspokenly critical of the repression. A number of missionaries were expelled from the country. In May and June 1972, a difference of opinion arose between the missionary religious superiors (both male and female) and the president of the episcopal conference concerning the attitude of the hierarchy to the situation. A confidential note from the superiors to the bishops, dated 24 May 1972, stated: 'We desire that the hierarchy take a firm and unambiguous position concerning these events.' At the time 2 of the bishops, including the archbishop of Gitega who also presided over the episcopal conference, were Tutsis, 2 were Hutus and one was Belgian, although the latter withdrew in September 1973 and was replaced by an open-minded Tutsi.

PROTESTANT CHURCHES. The Neukirchener Mission followed the Bethel Lutherans into Ruanda-Urundi and established 5 stations before being forced to leave at the time of the first World War. Seventh-day Adventists entered in 1921 and now operate 2 fields, West Burundi and East Burundi, which were organized respectively in 1936 and 1964. In 1928 Danish Baptist missionaries took over the work of 3 Neukirchener stations evacuated in 1916. A fourth Neukirchener mission was occupied by the Kansas Yearly Meeting of Friends in 1932, and the Friends have since developed 4 additional centres.

Republic' (Article 1); and that 'All Barundi have equal rights and responsibilities without distinction of sex, origin, race, religion and opinion' (Article 4). Article 9 reads: 'Freedom of thought and the practice of religion are guaranteed to all. Within the limits and conditions fixed by law, the State protects the free exercise of worship without intervening in its practice.'

In Burundi, clergy and religious congregations have been exempted from taxes, and both Protestant and Catholic schools and dispensaries receive large government subsidies. The state university of Bujumbura was originally founded under Jesuit initiative and both the rector and faculty members are for the most part Catholic priests. Catholic religious personnel are employed in numerous state medical institutions.

In April 1977, the government expelled without warning or explanation 15 Catholic missionaries in the diocese of Bujumbura (14 Italians, one Mexican; mostly Verona priests).

**INTERDENOMINATIONAL ORGANIZATIONS.** The Alliance of Protestant Churches of Burundi, founded in 1935 as the Protestant Alliance, includes Baptists, Free Methodists, Anglicans, Friends, and World Gospel Mission, with Plymouth Brethren and Swedish Pentecostals maintaining a co-operative relationship. One division, Secours Protestant, has provided material assistance through contributions from overseas agencies. A series of ecumenical seminars providing opportunity for dialogue between

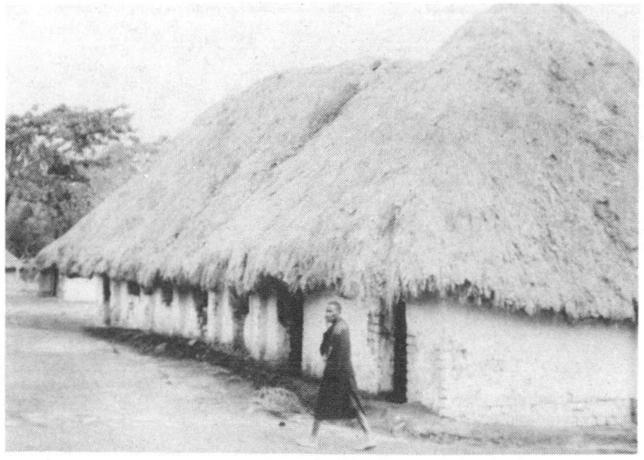

**Eglise de Dieu au Burundi.** Headquarters building of a small breakoff from the Protestant Episcopal Church in 1962.

Protestants and Catholics was begun by CERAS of Bujumbura in 1967.

**BROADCASTING.** The state radio La Voix de la Révolution accepts both Protestant and Catholic programmes. For Catholics, Burundi is registered as a member of UNDA. Catholics produce a 40-minute broadcast on Saturdays at 7 pm, alternately in French and Kirundi; and a sung mass is broadcast every week from Regina Mundi Cathedral. For Protestants, the Central Africa Broadcasting Company (Quaker) operated the medium-wave station Radio CORDAC (Corporation Radiodiffusion de l'Afrique Centrale) as an interdenominational faith radio ministry, which began in 1963 as the first missionary radio station in Central Africa. With 3 transmitters and a radius of 1,500 miles, it broadcast in Kirundi, Swahili, French, English and Ebembe, and devoted 75% of its time to the presentation of the gospel. There was also a radio school with night classes in both English language and radio work, together with a 4-year course in technical radio and programming at the secondary-level Cordac Institute of the Arts and Sciences of Radio Electronics. In April 1977, however, the government, acting under pressure from Libya, ordered Radio CORDAC to close and to dismantle its equipment. From abroad, French programmes from RVOG (Ethiopia) were easily received until its closure in 1977.

**BIBLIOGRAPHY**

*Annuaire ecclésiastique, Burundi et Rwanda, 1970-1971.* Bujumbura: SECOREB, 1970. (Roman Catholic).
'Burundi', *Pro Mundi Vita* (Brussels), 9 (1965).
*Burundi et Rwanda, 1964-1968: plan quinquennal de développement.* Usumbura: COREB, 1963. 160p.
*Church growth in Burundi.* D. Hohensee. South Pasadena (CA): William Carey Library, 1978. 153p.
'Conflict in Burundi', *Pro Mundi Vita,* Special note 25 (1973), 1–28.
*Naissance d'une église: histoire du Burundi chrétien.* J. Perraudin. Usumbura: Presses Lavigerie, 1963. 228p.
*Road to revival: the story of the Ruanda Mission.* A. C. Stanley Smith. London: Church Missionary Society, 1946. 116p.
*Théologie et pastorale au Rwanda et au Burundi,* VII, 1 (January, 1967), 1–60.

TABLE 2. ORGANIZED CHURCHES AND DENOMINATIONS IN BURUNDI

| Official name 1 | Begun 2 | Type 3 | Counc 4 | Congs 5 | Adults 6 | Affiliated 7 | Names, notes, and other statistics (see Codebook) 8 |
|---|---|---|---|---|---|---|---|
| Assemblées des Frères | 1938 | P CBr | x...k | 22 | 1,500 | 2,000 | *Open Brethren.* From Zaire; M=WGT,CMML(USA,UK), Immanuel Mission (Zaire). 5m,5f,1h. |
| Eglise Adventiste du Septième Jour | 1921 | P Adv | x.... | 61 | 8,395 | 20,000 | *Seventh-day Adventists, E&W Burundi Fields.* 21n,4x,6f,1s,88t(18847),W=90%,1229Y. |
| **Eglise Catholique au Burundi:** | 1879 | R Lat | P.S.P | 440 | 1,201,600 | 2,107,500 | *Catholic Ch.* C=9+6+30. 3p,1s(51). 135n,290x,141m,606w,P=74%,79328Yy. |
| M Gitega (Kitega) | 1912 | R Lat | Ps | 172 | 330,500 | 579,200 | 84% Hutu. Rwandan refugee camp at Mugera. 40 73 50 179 81 20892 |
| D Bujumbura | 1959 | R Lat | Ps | 145 | 294,700 | 517,000 | Northwest. Only urban centre in nation. 1p,1s. 47 92 48 215 73 18193 |
| D Bururi | 1961 | R Lat | Pwf | 13 | 111,700 | 196,000 | Extreme south. Rundi, 1% Bembe and Fulero. 7 45 12 51 68 8679 |
| D Muyinga | 1968 | R Lat | Ps | 13 | 164,300 | 288,200 | Formed out of D Ngozi. Impoverished. 18 31 8 42 74 12979 |
| D Ngozi | 1949 | R Lat | Ps | 97 | 300,400 | 527,100 | North centre. Highest population density. 2p. 23 49 23 119 68 18585 |
| Eglise de Dieu au Burundi | 1962 | I Ang | ..... | 10 | 500 | 1,000 | *Ch of God. Kinamaites.* Schism of 20,000 ex EAB(RCMS). 1966, suppressed. |
| Eglise Evangélique des Amis | 1932 | P Qua | QF..K | 37 | 2,700 | 4,000 | *Burundi Quarterly Mtg.* M=Friends Africa Gospel Mission(Kansas YM). 20f,1H,3h,1s,225Y. |
| Eglise Evangélique Mondiale | 1938 | P Hol | xF..K | 73 | 1,000 | 2,000 | *EEM.* M=World Gospel Mission(USA). East and southeast. Hutu. 30f,1H,3h,1j,1k,1p. |
| Eglise Kimbanguiste | c1968 | I pen | xwi.. | 1 | 300 | 500 | *Ch of Christ on Earth through the Prophet Simon Kimbangu.* M=EJCSK(Zaire). Zairians. |
| Eglise Libre Méthodiste au Burundi | 1935 | P Hol | VFA.K | 127 | 6,915 | 10,000 | *ELMB.* M=Free Methodist Ch(USA). 92% Rundi, 7% Bembe. 25n,4x,160m,17f,1H,3h,2s. |
| Eglise Orthodoxe: AD Afrique Centrale | 1958 | O Gre | Cw... | 5 | 500 | 1,000 | *Orthodox Ch.* Under Greek P Alexandria (Egypt). Greek traders. 1 school. 2x. |
| Egl Protestante Episcopale du Burundi | 1934 | A Low | AwAVK | 535 | 15,497 | 45,000 | *EAB. Protestant Episcopal Ch.* M=RCMS(UK). 30n,3x,31f,3H,6p,3r,1s(15),W=60%,3421Yy. |
| Eglises de Pentecôte | 1935 | P Pe2 | Z...k | 600 | 45,000 | 90,000 | *ADEEP. Chs of Pentecost.* M=SFM. 13n,1x,428m,38f,5h,1k,1p(44),1s(23),W=80%,1585Y. |
| Témoins de Jéhovah | c1960 | M Jeh | x.... | 1 | 56 | 100 | *Jehovah's Witnesses. Watch Tower. IBSA.* First activity reported 1964. 3Y. |
| Union des Eglises Baptistes du Burundi | 1911 | P Bap | T.A.K | 77 | 3,307 | 6,000 | *UEBB/Baptist Union.* 1911, Germans; 1928, M=DBM. 95% Hutu. 5n,670m,18f,1H,4h,1r,223Y |
| Other Protestant denominations | | P | ..... | | 500 | 1,000 | Total about 5 small denominations from neighbouring countries. |
| **Total affiliated (mid-1970)** | | | | **2,010** | **1,287,770** | **2,290,100** | **Total denominations (1970) . . 18.** |
| **Total affiliated (mid-1975)** | | | | **2,230** | **1,570,800** | **2,793,630** | **Total denominations (1975) . . . 21.** |
| **Total affiliated (mid-1980)** | | | | **2,480** | **1,916,600** | **3,408,720** | **Total denominations (1990) . . . 24.** |

NOTES ON TABLE ABOVE
COLUMNS: for meanings and CODES (cols. 1, 3, 4, 8): see Codebook (Part 6). Column 1: **Boldface type** = churches with over 10% of country's affiliated Christians.
NATIONAL COUNCILS (Column 4, 5th letter).
K = Alliance des Eglises Protestantes du Burundi (AEPB) (Alliance of Protestant Churches of Burundi).
k = associated with AEPB for educational matters.
P = Conférence des Ordinaires du Rwanda et du Burundi (COREB) (Bishops' Conference of Rwanda & Burundi).

PEOPLES (ethnolinguistic). Christians: 97.1% Rundi (84.2% Hutu, 14.1% Tutsi), 1.6% Ruanda, 1.2% Zairian, 0.1% Twa Pygmy, European (French, Belgian).

COUNTRY-WIDE TOTALS
EVANGELIZATION (see Part 5). 1900: 1%. 1970: 100%. 1980: 100%. *Mass evangelism.* 1960, Billy Graham 7-day crusade in Bujumbura (26,650 attenders, 1,551 enquirers); 1971, New Life for All campaign. *Radiophonic evangelism.* Radio Cordac, RVOG, ELWA. Bible correspondence courses: ICI, Roman Catholics (INADES).
FOREIGN MISSIONARIES AND PERSONNEL (nationals serving abroad) (1973). Total about 30 Roman Catholics in Zaire.
FOREIGN MISSIONARIES AND PERSONNEL (aliens from abroad) (1973). Total 818. *From Western world.* 770: 598 Roman Catholics, 139 Protestants (87 in 11 USA societies, 38 in 1 Sweden society, 12 in 1 Denmark society, 2 in 1 Finland society), 31 Anglicans in 2 UK societies, 2 Orthodox. *From Communist world.* 24 Roman Catholics (17 from Poland, also Yugoslavia). *From Third World.* 24: 20 Roman Catholics from Rwanda and Zaire, 2 Anglicans from Uganda.
INSTITUTIONS (church-operated) (1973). Total 140, including 40 higher schools (5 minor seminaries), 68 medical centres (10 hospitals), 1 press, 1 radio station, 5 religious communities, 3 research centres, 7 seminaries (5 Protestant, 1 RC, 1 Anglican).
PERIODICALS. About 13 titles.
PERSONNEL. About 5,957 (5,139 national, 818 foreign).
RELIGIOUS LIBRARIES. 17.
SCRIPTURE DISTRIBUTION (1975). Annual totals: 6,000 Bibles (67% subsidized, 33% commercial), 5,420 NTs (6% free, 92% subsidized, 2% commercial), 20,000 UBS portions, 4,000 UBS selections. *Translations completed.* 1 language, Kirundi: portion 1920, NT 1951, Bible 1967.
SERVICE AGENCIES. About 40, including AEPB, CEF, COREB, COSUMA, GBUAF, JEC/F, JOC/F, NLFA, SNEC, SU, UACPB.

ADDITIONAL DATA ON CHURCHES
EGLISE CATHOLIQUE AU BURUNDI. With the rapid reduction in the percentage of traditionalists (pagans), the number of catechumens as a percentage of baptized Catholics fell from 16% in 1959 to 8% in 1968. Totals were: (1959) 193,892, (1961) 148,003, (1963) 134,581, (1967) 147,684, (1968) 169,065, (1969) 171,084. Column 7 therefore includes 160,000 catechumens, divided among the 5 dioceses in order as follows: 40,000, 34,000, 35,000, 20,000, 40,000. *New diocese* (created 1973). Ruyigi, formed out of D Bururi and M Gitega. *Annual baptisms* (1972). 67.7% infant, 32.3% adult. *Priests.* The first Rundi priests were ordained in 1925. *Brothers.* Of whom 66 Rundi. *Sisters.* Of whom 373 Rundi. *Seminarians.* 51, increasing to 63 (1972), all secular. *Catechists.* Total (1970) 3,129, of whom 157 had diplomas. *Indigenous religious congregations.* Brothers: 56 Bene Yosefu (Sons of Joseph, begun 1944), 5 Bene Paulo (begun 1962). Sisters: 351 Bene Tereziya (Daughters of Teresa, begun 1931), 59 Bene Mariya (begun 1956), 9 Bene Umukama (Daughters of the King, begun 1970). *Main foreign congregations.* Priests: WF, SJ, SX, CR, FSCJ, SSS. Brothers: Frères de la Charité, FICP, N-D de la Miséricorde, PFM. Sisters: White Sisters, Dames de Marie, Coeur Immaculé de Marie.
*Catholic organizations.* The Bishops' Conference of Rwanda and Burundi (Conférence des Ordinaires du Rwanda et du Burundi, COREB) is a member of SECAM. Its general secretariat is responsible for the common services of the 2 countries and has its headquarters in Bujumbura. It sponsors also a centre for socio-religious research and a department of relief service (Service d'Entraide). The conference normally meets in full assembly twice yearly but during 1972–73 it did not meet at all due to fighting within the country. At its session in December 1973, it called upon the faithful to effect 'an authentic reconciliation based on justice and compassion.'

Religious personnel are served by 2 organizations: the Conference of Male Major Superiors (Conférence des Supérieurs Majeurs) for men, and the Union of Female Major Superiors (Union des Supérieures Majeures) for sisters. There is no council of priests, but an association has been formed called the Apostolic and Cultural Union of Burundi Priests (Union Apostolique et Culturelle des Prêtres Burundais, UACPB) which serves as a permanent secretariat for the clergy. Several movements of the lay apostolate are active. The numbers of members in 1970 in lay groups were as follows: Chiro (28,000), JOC/F (9,000), Xaveri (1,600), JEC/F (1,000), Eucharistic Crusade (Croisade Eucharistique; 2,591), Legion of Mary (Légion de Marie; 32,400), in addition to the Family Movement (Mouvement Familial), Teacher Teams (Equipes Enseignantes) and Sacred Heart League (Ligue du SC).

The Holy See has diplomatic relations with Burundi and is represented to government and the Catholic hierarchy by a nuncio in Bujumbura.

In 1970 the national secretariat for Catholic education sponsored 686 primary schools (128,156 pupils, 71% of the total), 12 secondary schools (2,008 students, 55% of the total), 14 teacher-training schools (1,768 students) in addition to other technical, trade, agricultural and domestic science institutions. By 1973, there were 559 primary schools (109,634) and 29 secondary (4,802). Medical and social service activities in 1971 included the following: one maternity hospital at Ngozi; 37 dispensaries, maternity centres or health centres; 2 leprosaria; 5 out-patient services for lepers; 29 nutritional centres; 4 orphanages; one home for the aged; 2 institutes for the handicapped; 3 homes for girls; 60 social centres for training girls and women; 2 centres for agricultural training; 6 sewing workshops; 7 co-operatives; and a literacy programme for 309,681 (85,877 catechumens and 223,804 baptized) non-school children providing reading, writing, arithmetic, basic education and catechesis. The INADES correspondence courses follow the pattern developed in Ivory Coast. Two Bujumbura-based co-ordinating agencies in the field of social service are Caritas-Burundi, affiliated to Caritas Internationale, and the Centre d'Entraide et de Développement (CED), which is involved in the promotion of cultural, sanitary, human and social development.
EGLISE EVANGELIQUE MONDIALE. The WGM serves as the official missionary society (in Burundi, as elsewhere) for missionaries from 3 USA denominations: Churches of Christ in Christian Union, Congregational Methodist Church, and Evangelical Methodist Church.
EGLISE PROTESTANTE EPISCOPALE DU BURUNDI. Also known as the Eglise Anglicane du Burundi (EAB), the church up to 1976 formed the Diocese of Burundi in the Church of Uganda, Rwanda, Burundi and Boga-Zaire (CURBZ). From 1976 it divided into two, D Buye and D Bujumbura, prior to the formation of a new French-speaking Anglican province covering Burundi, Rwanda and Zaire. The church has the largest percentage of Tutsi members of all churches in Burundi (about 20%). *Growth.* By 1977 membership had grown to 57,000 (D Buye 40,000, D Bujumbura 17,000). *Parishes* (1977). D Buye 19, D Bujumbura 15. *Clergy* (1977). D Buye 21, D Bujumbura 24. *Missionaries* (1977). 17. *Catechists* (1977). 200 in D Bujumbura.

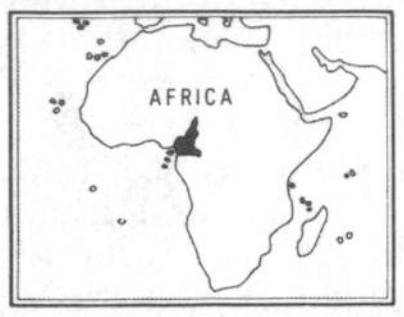
AFRICA

# CAMEROON

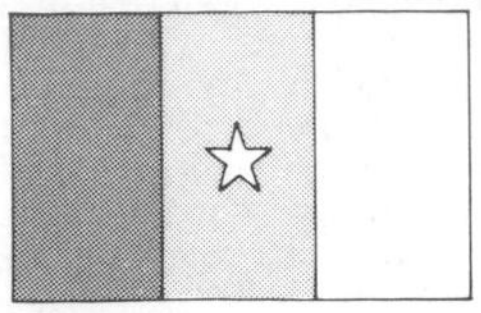

## SECULAR DATA

**STATE. Official name:** The United Republic of Cameroon (La République Unie du Cameroun). Adjective of nationality: Cameroonian (camerounais).
**Flag** (shown above right): Tricolour of green, red, and yellow bars, centred yellow star.
**Area:** 475,442 sq.km. (183,569 sq.miles). Agricultural land: 32.9%.
**Government:** One-party republic, since 1960 (1884 German protectorate, 1918 under French and British, 1946 UN trust territory, 1960 Independence).
**Legislature:** National Federal Assembly, 50 members; and a provincial assembly each for East and West Cameroon.
**Official languages:** French (*Français*) and English.
**Chief cities:** capital Yaoundé 250,000, Douala 350,000, Nkongsamba 100,000.
**Political divisions:** 2 Provinces, East and West.
**Armed forces** (1976): Total 5,600 regular: army 5,000, navy 300, air force 300 (9 combat aircraft). Paramilitary forces: 7,000.

**DEMOGRAPHY. Population:** 5,017,000 (censuses of 1960–65. For 1970–2000 (UN), see last row of Table 1). Population density (1975): 13/sq.km. (35/sq.mile). Under 15 years: 40%. Growth rate (1975–80): 2.05% per year (births 4.09%, deaths −2.04%). Life expectancy (1975–80): 43.5 years. Household size: 4.9 persons.
**Major languages:** Bulu Fang, Bamileke, French, English, Douala, Pidgin English, Fulani, Hausa, and in addition over 180 other tribal languages.
**Urban dwellers** (1970): 20.5%. Urban growth rate (1950–70): 5. 9% per year.
**Labour force:** 48%.
**Refugees** (1977): From abroad, 35,000 (30,000 from Equatorial Guinea).
**Tourists** (1974): 96.060.
**ETHNOLINGUISTIC GROUPS:** 27% Cameroon Highland Bantu (Bamileke, Tikar, Widekum, Bamenda, Bamum, Banen), 25% Equatorial Bantu (Beti-Pahouin) (Ewondo, Eton, Bane, Fond, Bulu, Fang, Maka, Djem), 15% Kirdi (Masa, Tuburi, Matakam, Musgum, Gisiga, Fali, Kapsigi, Mundang), 9.5% Fulani (Peul), 8% Northwestern Bantu (Bassa-Koko, Duala, Mbo, Kpe (Bakwiri), Kossi, 8% Hausa, 6% Baya-Mbum (with Duru, Chamba), 1.0% Nigerian (Ibo, Ibibio, Jukun), Shuwa Arab, Kanuri, Hausa, Mandara, Kotoko, Pygmy, French, & numerous smaller peoples.

**MONEY** (1977). **Monetary unit:** CFA franc (= 100 centimes); US$1 = CFAF 250.00.
**National income per person:** US$260. Average annual family income: US$1,274.
**Inflation:** (1970–74) 8.2% per year (1975: consumer price index 163).
**Cost of living in capital** (1976): index 175 (Washington DC = 100). Daily cost of living: US$44.

**EDUCATION.** Adult literacy: (1962) 19%. Education rate: 25%. Schools: 4,275. Universities: 1.

**HEALTH.** Hospitals: 80 (19,141 beds). Doctors: 225. Lepers: 115,000 (18.0 per 1,000). Blind: 15,630. Psychotics: 45,000.

**LITERATURE.** Annual new book titles (1966): 30. Periodicals: 45. Newspapers: 2 dailies, 4 non-daily.

**COMMUNICATION** (per 1,000 people). Phones: 4. Radios: 36. Daily newspaper circulation: 3 copies.

TABLE 1. RELIGIOUS ADHERENTS IN CAMEROON

| Year | 1900 | | mid-1970 | | Annual change, 1970–1980 | | | | mid-1975 | | mid-1980 | | 2000 | |
|---|---|---|---|---|---|---|---|---|---|---|---|---|---|---|
| *Name* | *Adherents* | *%* | *Adherents* | *%* | *Natural* | *Conversion* | *Total* | *Rate* | *Adherents* | *%* | *Adherents* | *%* | *Adherents* | *%* |
| **Christians** | **9,500** | **0.4** | **2,768,600** | **47.4** | **64,604** | **52,126** | **116,730** | **3.53** | **3,301,400** | **51.6** | **3,935,900** | **55.5** | **7,348,000** | **63.4** |
| professing | 9,500 | 0.4 | 2,768,600 | 47.4 | 64,604 | 52,126 | 116,730 | 3.53 | 3,301,400 | 51.6 | 3,935,900 | 55.5 | 7,348,000 | 63.4 |
| Roman Catholics | 3,000 | 0.1 | 1,750,000 | 30.0 | 40,689 | 32,411 | 73,100 | 3.51 | 2,079,300 | 32.5 | 2,481,000 | 35.0 | 4,633,000 | 40.0 |
| Protestants | 5,000 | 0.2 | 875,000 | 15.0 | 20,408 | 16,842 | 37,250 | 3.57 | 1,042,900 | 16.3 | 1,247,500 | 17.6 | 2,201,000 | 19.0 |
| African indigenous | 1,500 | 0.1 | 116,700 | 2.0 | 2,878 | 2,462 | 5,340 | 3.63 | 147,100 | 2.3 | 170,100 | 2.4 | 394,000 | 3.4 |
| Marginal Protestants | 0 | 0.0 | 25,000 | 0.4 | 587 | 413 | 1,000 | 3.33 | 30,000 | 0.5 | 35,000 | 0.5 | 116,000 | 1.0 |
| Orthodox | 0 | 0.0 | 1,000 | 0.0 | 22 | −2 | 20 | 1.82 | 1,100 | 0.0 | 1,200 | 0.0 | 2,000 | 0.0 |
| Catholics (non-Roman) | 0 | 0.0 | 900 | 0.0 | 20 | 0 | 20 | 1.96 | 1,000 | 0.0 | 1,100 | 0.0 | 2,000 | 0.0 |
| nominal | 1,780 | 0.1 | 391,574 | 6.7 | 8,735 | 1,978 | 10,713 | 2.40 | 446,390 | 7.0 | 498,700 | 7.0 | 997,300 | 8.6 |
| affiliated | 7,720 | 0.3 | 2,377,026 | 40.7 | 55,869 | 50,148 | 106,017 | 3.71 | 2,855,010 | 44.6 | 3,437,200 | 48.5 | 6,350,700 | 54.8 |
| total practising | 7,410 | *96* | 1,687,690 | *71* | 39,667 | 35,605 | 75,272 | 3.71 | 2,027,060 | *71* | 2,440,410 | *71* | 4,128,000 | *65* |
| non-practising | 310 | *4* | 689,340 | *29* | 16,202 | 14,543 | 30,745 | 3.71 | 827,950 | *29* | 996,790 | *29* | 2,222,700 | *35* |
| Roman Catholics | 2,720 | 0.1 | 1,528,760 | 26.2 | 35,808 | 31,316 | 67,124 | 3.67 | 1,829,830 | 28.6 | 2,200,000 | 31.0 | 4,054,000 | 35.0 |
| Catholic pentecostals | 0 | 0.0 | 0 | 0.0 | 10 | 190 | 200 | 40.00 | 500 | 0.0 | 2,000 | 0.0 | 50,000 | 0.4 |
| Protestants | 4,000 | 0.2 | 721,866 | 12.4 | 17,027 | 15,686 | 32,713 | 3.76 | 870,130 | 13.6 | 1,049,000 | 14.8 | 1,853,000 | 16.0 |
| Evangelicals | 3,000 | 0.1 | 532,000 | 9.1 | 12,524 | 11,576 | 24,100 | 3.77 | 640,000 | 10.0 | 773,000 | 10.9 | 1,390,000 | 12.0 |
| African indigenous | 1,000 | 0.0 | 104,500 | 1.8 | 2,504 | 2,636 | 5,140 | 4.02 | 127,960 | 2.0 | 155,900 | 2.2 | 347,500 | 3.0 |
| Marginal Protestants | 0 | 0.0 | 20,000 | 0.3 | 489 | 511 | 1,000 | 4.00 | 25,000 | 0.4 | 30,000 | 0.4 | 92,700 | 0.8 |
| Orthodox | 0 | 0.0 | 1,000 | 0.0 | 22 | −1 | 21 | 1.91 | 1,100 | 0.0 | 1,210 | 0.0 | 1,800 | 0.0 |
| Catholics (non-Roman) | 0 | 0.0 | 900 | 0.0 | 19 | 0 | 19 | 1.96 | 990 | 0.0 | 1,090 | 0.0 | 1,700 | 0.0 |
| Tribal religionists | 2,479,500 | 94.6 | 1,864,000 | 31.9 | 33,046 | −66,356 | −33,310 | −1.97 | 1,688,700 | 26.4 | 1,530,900 | 21.6 | 1,229,800 | 10.6 |
| Muslims | 131,000 | 5.0 | 1,167,200 | 20.0 | 26,613 | 12,597 | 39,210 | 2.88 | 1,360,000 | 21.3 | 1,559,300 | 22.0 | 2,780,000 | 24.0 |
| Baha'is | 0 | 0.0 | 29,500 | 0.5 | 751 | 1,259 | 2,010 | 5.23 | 38,400 | 0.6 | 49,600 | 0.7 | 162,200 | 1.4 |
| Non-religious | 0 | 0.0 | 5,000 | 0.1 | 137 | 263 | 400 | 5.71 | 7,000 | 0.1 | 9,000 | 0.1 | 50,000 | 0.4 |
| Atheists | 0 | 0.0 | 1,000 | 0.0 | 29 | 71 | 100 | 6.67 | 1,500 | 0.0 | 2,000 | 0.0 | 10,000 | 0.1 |
| Other religionists | 0 | 0.0 | 700 | 0.0 | 20 | 40 | 60 | 6.00 | 1,000 | 0.0 | 1,300 | 0.0 | 3,000 | 0.0 |
| **Country's population** | **2,620,000** | **100.0** | **5,836,000** | **100.0** | **125,200** | **0** | **125,200** | **1.96** | **6,398,000** | **100.0** | **7,088,000** | **100.0** | **11,583,000** | **100.0** |

COLUMNS, ROWS. For meanings and definitions, see Codebook (Part 6). Note that, by definition, total 'Christians' = professing + crypto-Christians, which also = affiliated + nominal Christians. Percentages may not always total exactly, due to rounding.
CENSUSES. No census question on religion has been asked for the whole country. West Cameroon only, 1964: 43.9% Protestants, 28.7% tribal religionists (termed 'animists', 'pagans'), 25.1% Roman Catholics, 2.3% Muslims.

NOTES ON RELIGIONS
AFRICAN INDIGENOUS. In about 28 denominations in 1970 (see Table 2).
ATHEISTS. No communist party; mainly intellectuals and expatriates.
BAHA'IS. One of the first pioneers was an African Baha'i from Uganda. Growth from 63 local spiritual assemblies (1964) to 197 (1973). Particularly strong in Mamfe division, West Cameroon, attracting disaffected Presbyterians.
CATHOLIC PENTECOSTALS (or, Catholic charismatics). In 1976, 45 persons active in the Catholic Charismatic Renewal attended a conference at the Cistercian monastery in Bamenda.
MUSLIMS. All Sunnis (of the Malikite rite). Muslim tribes: Fulani, Bamum, Tikar, Kotoko, Mandara, and Shoa (Shuwa or Black Arabs). Under the German and French regimes, forced conversions to Islam lasted until the end of the 1930s. Since the 1930s, Islam has spread rapidly among the Kirdi (pagans of the north), especially the Mbum (now 60% Muslims), Duru (5%), Lakka, Kutin, Giddar, Fali (50,000; became 80% islamized in 2 generations), Mofu, Matakam (5%), Mundang (5%), Musgu (5%). *Sects.* Qadiriya (the oldest; HQ Garoua; declining), Tijaniya (introduced 1840; HQ Yola), Mahdism (strong among Fulani, producing a new mahdi every decade or so). The north is now 50% Muslim, 5% Christian. *Hajj pilgrims to Mecca.* (1970) 808; (1974) 4,422; (1975) 1,005; (1976) 779.
OTHER RELIGIONISTS. Including Rosicrucians (11 AMORC centres).
PRACTISING CHRISTIANS. Sunday attenders (Protestants): about 40% in urban areas, 65% in rural areas; Catholics under 40%.
PROTESTANTS. In 1886, the Basel Mission had 203 converts, rising to 8,913 by 1926 and 20,307 by 1936. In 1913, Baptists had 3,000 converts and 3,000 pupils.
ROMAN CATHOLICS. In 1900, 2,457 baptized Catholics and 263 catechumens.
TRIBAL RELIGIONISTS. Over 24 tribes were in 1972 still over 60% traditionalist (animist), and 11 were 90% or more: Gisiga (99%), Gude (99%), Laka (99%), Matakam (95%), Budugum (90%), Duru (90%), Gisei (90%), Kotopo (90%), Musei (90%), Podokwo (90%), Tigon (90%). Although large numbers of traditionalists are being converted to Islam, there is also a steady trickle returning from Islam. In 1962, a large number of Mundang who had been Muslim converts abandoned Islam and returned to their traditional agrarian rites and ancestor worship; and there are similar more recent cases.

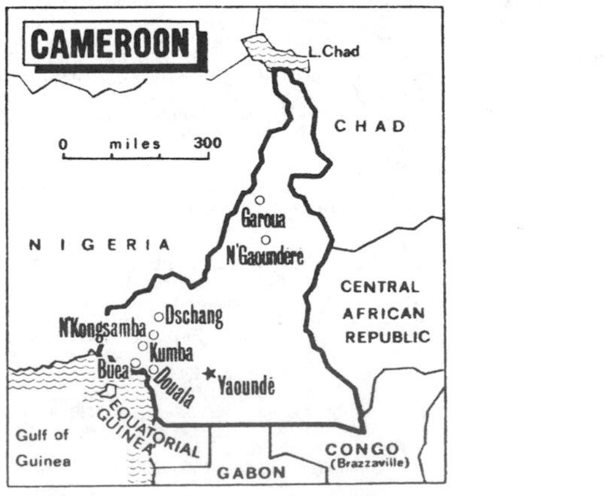
CAMEROON
L.Chad
CHAD
0 miles 300
NIGERIA
Garoua
N'Gaoundere
CENTRAL
AFRICAN
REPUBLIC
Dschang
N'Kongsamba
Kumba
Buea
Douala
Yaoundé
EQUATORIAL GUINEA
Gulf of
Guinea
GABON
CONGO
(Brazzaville)

**NON-CHRISTIAN RELIGIONS. Traditional religions** are followed by around a quarter of the population. Those peoples who are more than 90% traditionalist include the following: Budugum, Duru, Gisei, Gisiga, Gude, Kotopo, Laka, Matakam, Musei, Podokwo, and Tigon. Others who are at least 60% traditionalist are the Adamawa, Fungom, Kapsiki, Kundu, Li, Mambila, Mundang, Namshi, Nen, Tuburi, Utange and Wute. The traditional blacksmith, who serves equally as a diviner among several peoples, plays a significant role at birth and death, as well as during illness, pottery-making and iron-smelting. The importance of sacrifices, especially of cattle, is also widely emphasized. Traditional names for the supreme being among Cameroonian peoples are Si (for the Bamileke), Njinyi (Bamum), Hoel (Banen), Mebee (Bulu), Loba (Duala), Osawa (Ekoi), Nzame (Fang), Lova (Kpe), Nyooiy (Tikar), Buimulvong (Gisiga), Masing (Mundang), Bah (Tupuri), Zigile (Matakam) and Zigta (Mukulehe).

**Islam** was introduced in the 18th century by the Fulani (Peul) who entered northern Cameroon from Mali and Nigeria. At the beginning of the 19th century, the Fulani chiefs in the north began to impose their authority on the pagan peoples, and in this way formed the Fulani kingdoms, in which the temporal and religious leader is known as the lamido. Some local peoples submitted and adopted Islam, but the majority took refuge in the mountains and retained their traditional religions. The Fulani then set up a feudalistic system which has subsequently impeded economic and social development.

Apart from the Fulani, the principal islamized ethnic groups are the Bamum and the arabized Shoa. Islam is now the religion of 20% of the population, and in 1969 there were 25 Quranic schools with 2,755 pupils. The Qadiriya is the principal Muslim brotherhood. In 1974, 4,422 Muslim pilgrims from Cameroon performed the hajj to Mecca.

**Baha'i** has grown rapidly from 63 local spiritual assemblies in 1964 to 197 by 1973, and is particularly strong in West Cameroon.

**CHRISTIANITY.** The churches are strongest in southern Cameroon. In the central and northern parts of the country Christians have faced stiff resistance from Islam, and their progress has been slower. In the region north of Ngaoundere and also in Bankim and Galim in central Cameroon, churches have experienced severe persecution. Chapels have been destroyed and authorization to open new work has often been refused. In the Rey Bouba area, there has been a recent exodus of Christians due to Muslim

**Muslims.** Sultan of Meiganga with bodyguards and entourage armed with rifles, bows and arrows. Since the 1930s, Islam has spread rapidly in Northern Cameroon.

harassment. Catholic membership in the nation is nearly twice that of Protestants, although in West Cameroon Catholics number less than Protestants. Catholicism is strongest in urban areas whereas Protestant churches are more rural.

CATHOLIC CHURCH. Catholic missions were permanently introduced in 1890 in the south by German Pallotins, and by 1934 a mass movement into the Catholic Church was taking place. The population in the archdiocese of Yaoundé has now passed 74% Catholic. In the north, Catholic evangelization did not begin until after World War II. The church has had its greatest success among the younger generation due to its extensive involvement in education. Easter communicants are high, rising from 37% in Yaoundé to over 70% or more in some rural dioceses.

A major effort has been made recently to adapt the liturgy and religious teaching to the cultural and religious milieu of the country. In 1969, 2 associations of African priests were formed: Interdiocesan Association of Indigenous Priests (Association Interdiocésaine des Prêtres Indigènes, AIPI) in the dioceses of Nkongsamba and Bafoussam, which in spite of its small numbers exerts a significant influence in Bamileke country; and a group called Serve and Liberate (Servir et Libérer) in the diocese of Douala with 15 members in 1972. Aiming to promote the interests of priests and dioceses generally, these associations testify to uneasiness about existing Western structures in pastoral work and indicate the desire of clergy to indigenize the church. In 1970, the Episcopal Conference attempted to create a National Liaison Committee for Cameroonian Priests (Comité National de Liaison pour les Prêtres Camerounais), but because of its imposition from the top nothing came of the attempt. The 2 English-speaking dioceses (Bamenda and Buea) have organized a Catholic Convention, a kind of synod, beginning in 1967 and whose third and final session was held at Bamenda in 1972. Membership consisted of 150 delegates elected by the laity, priests, and male and female religious personnel.

PROTESTANT CHURCHES. The largest Protestant churches are the Evangelical Church of Cameroon (EEC), Presbyterian Church of Cameroon (EPC), and Presbyterian Church in West Cameroon. They have extensive educational programmes, an increasing evangelistic outreach and large numbers of national workers.

The Evangelical Church of Cameroon and the Union of Baptist Churches (UEBC) both owe their origin to the Baptist Missionary Society (UK) from 1845 onwards. With the German occupation in 1884, part of the work was ceded to the Basel Mission and part to the Baptist Mission of Berlin. Although

following World War I both were turned over to the Paris Mission, separate organizations were maintained and they remain in fact autonomous denominations. In 1957 the EEC joined with the UEBC to form the Council of Baptist and Evangelical Churches of Cameroon, with united efforts in the medical, social, educational and evangelistic fields.

In 1879 the French-speaking Presbyterian Church of Cameroon was begun in the south through the instrumentality of Presbyteran missionaries from the USA, eventually leading to a first general assembly of the autonomous EPC organized in 1957.

The English-speaking Presbyterian Church in West Cameroon originated with Basel missionaries in 1884 and has now grown to be the largest church in West Cameroon. It became autonomous in 1957 although it continues to receive support from the Basel Mission.

In 1891 a missionary of the North American Baptist General Conference was sent to Cameroon under the auspices of the Baptist Mission of Berlin. Today this work is organized separately from UEBC and since 1954 has been called the Cameroon Baptist Convention. The church's strength is concentrated in the western region.

There are 2 Lutheran denominations in Cameroon. The Evangelical Lutheran Church of Cameroon is the union of 2 missions, the Sudan Mission supported by the American Lutheran Church and the Norwegian Mission Society which arrived in 1925. The church became autonomous in 1960. The second group, the Church of the Lutheran Brethren in North Cameroon (Eglise Fraternelle Luthérienne au Cameroun), originated with the American mission of the same name in 1918, and became autonomous in 1964.

The Sudan United Mission (Swiss Branch) works in the extreme north where Swiss missionaries appeared in 1938. Other groups include the European Baptist Mission which entered the north in 1954,

A series of postage stamps showing (from top, left to right) Buea RC Cathedral, Yaoundé RC Cathedral, Garoua Mosque, Greek Orthodox Church in Yaoundé.

and Seventh-day Adventists who have been in Cameroon since 1928.

INDIGENOUS CHURCHES. As a reaction to foreign missionary influence, secessions led by African Baptists began in Cameroon in 1864 and again in 1888, when Duala Baptists left the Basel Mission to form ultimately the Native Baptist Church and the Eglise Baptiste Camerounaise, the latter being Cameroon's largest indigenous body. The first Presbyterian schism, the African Protestant Church, occurred in 1934 and includes half the entire Ngumba tribe. Numerous other secessions have taken place since then.

CHURCH AND STATE. The constitution of the united republic (1972) proclaims a secular state, assures the equality of all citizens before the law and affirms its acceptance of the fundamental liberties inscribed in the Universal Declaration of Human Rights (Preamble and Article 1). Law 67–LF–19 of 12 June 1967, which deals with 'freedom of association', stipulates that all religious and confessional associations and congregations must obtain legal recognition. This was decreed by the president of the republic after being proposed by the minister charged with territorial administration.

Before Independence in 1960, the opening of new missions or catechetical posts required prior authorization. This measure is no longer applied in the south but continues in vigour in the Muslim north, where such authorization is difficult to obtain. Religious youth movements have not been permitted since 1963 except for those which have accepted

integration in government-controlled youth federations. Confessional trade unions have also been suppressed.

By Law 64–LF–11 of 26 June 1964, the state recognizes private denominational instruction and subsidizes it by providing a portion of teachers' salaries. The whole confessional system of education may however soon be taken over by the state. This transfer has the support of government and for financial reasons is also desired by some Catholic

**Eglise Baptiste Camerounaise.** EBC, begun 1884, largest of Cameroon's 28 indigenous denominations. The pastor of one of the largest of the 239 EBC congregations is shown.

bishops. On the other hand such action is feared by other bishops and by a number of priests, some of whom are found within the associations of Cameroonian priests as well as by progressive missionaries who see confessional schools and associations as an obstacle to political totalitarianism. This tendency towards state control is also evident in medical institutions and indeed in a general way in all areas where the churches exercise a function parallel to or in place of that of the state.

The head of state since Independence in 1960 has been a Muslim, and the northern peoples exercise an important influence at the centre of government. In spite of the often unjustified fears of Christians, especially Catholics, the problems of relations between the Christian churches and the state have been political rather than religious. Although the ideology of the regime, sometimes called 'the ethics of unity', implies a minimal and even restrictive definition of the role of religion, religious authorities at all levels do not hesitate to make personal interventions to protect the population from arbitrary measures and to call the attention of the government to the problems of disadvantaged ethnic and social groups. The exercise of the churches' prophetic ministry has created tensions and conflicts, but their gravity is limited by the fact that ecclesiastical authorities have never called in question the established political system.

The Catholic Church has strenuously opposed activities of the revolutionary movement Union of the Peoples of Cameroon (Union des Populations Camerounaises, UPC), which was very active among the Bamileke between 1955 and 1965, accusing it of being communist. In retaliation UPC followers systematically destroyed Catholic missions. An added complication occurred when the Catholic bishop of Nkongsamba was implicated in a plot against the head of state with the UPC leader and both were sentenced to death, the latter being executed and the bishop's sentence eventually commuted to life imprisonment. On 17 May 1975 the bishop and 49 other persons imprisoned with him were pardoned by the president of the republic. Many UPC militants have had Protestant education and the movement itself has some support in Protestant circles, especially among the Presbyterian and Evangelical churches. This has resulted from an increasing lack of understanding between Protestant leaders and civil authorities. Likewise relations between the state and the Catholic Church, which has traditionally been more conservative than the Protestants and some of whose bishops have actively supported a major political rival of the head of state, have also deteriorated.

Considering that in a developing country the number of public holidays should be limited, the Catholic hierarchy of Cameroon requested and obtained from Rome at the end of 1973 authorization to celebrate those feast days which fall during the week on the following Sunday, Christmas being the only exception.

**INTERDENOMINATIONAL ORGANIZATIONS.** The Federation of Protestant Churches and Missions in Cameroon (Fédération des Eglises et Missions Evangéliques du Cameroun, FEMEC), was established in 1970, replacing a wider regional federation including Rio Muni, Gabon and Congo-Brazzaville formed in 1943. The Ecumenical Study Circle (Cercle d'Etudes Oecuméniques, CEO) is an independent organization not officially recognized by the churches but which receives support from the Catholic episcopal conference and FEMEC. Founded in 1964, it consisted in 1972 of 100 members (40 active, 60 sympathizers), including priests, pastors, religious personnel and laymen, most being Europeans. Its activities include monthly meetings, organization of conferences, and other forms of ecumenical dialogue.

**BROADCASTING.** The government station Radiodiffusion du Cameroun carries several Christian programmes (mainly in French and English) on its national network, totalling about 2 hours per week each for Catholics and Protestants. Such regional government stations as Buea, Douala and Garoua also have regular Catholic and Protestant programmes. Catholics own several recording studios (Douala, Garoua). Cameroon is registered as a member of UNDA. On the Protestant side, the FEMEC studio in Yaoundé produces programmes for the national station as well as (until 1977) for RVOG (Ethiopia) in the French language, and is also involved in training. In Ngaoundéré, the studio Sawtu Linjiila produces a 30-minute daily programme in Fulani.

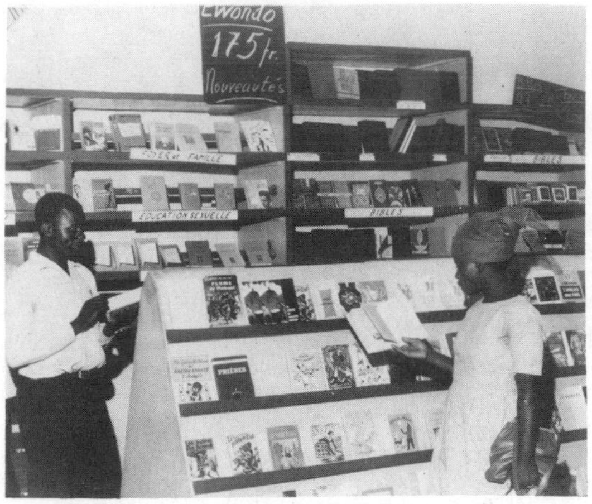

Christian bookshop in Eastern Cameroon.

## BIBLIOGRAPHY

*Conquérants du Golfe de Guinée*. H. Nicod. Lausanne: Secrétariat Romand de la Mission de Bâle, 1947. 306p.
*Ethno-sociologie religieuse des Duala et apparentés*. R. Bureau. Yaoundé: IRCAM, 1962. 380p.
*Histoire de l'Eglise en Afrique* (Cameroun). J. van Slageren. Yaoundé: Editions Clé, 1969. 149p.
*Le Catholicisme au Nord-Cameroun*. D. Veillette-Santerre. Québec: Université Laval, 1979.
*Les origines de l'Eglise Evangélique du Cameroun: missions européennes et christianisme autochtone*. J. van Slageren. Leiden: Brill, 1972. 298p.
'Origine et développement d'une église indépendante africaine: l'Eglise Baptiste Camerounaise', L.R. Brutsch, *Le monde non-chrétien* (Paris), NS 12 (Oct–Dec, 1949), 408–424.
*Presbyterian Church in West Cameroon, Forest District: a survey, 1961*. (Also Grassfield District, 1962).
'Protestant Christianity in West Cameroon, 1841–1886'. L.E. Kwast. Thesis, Fuller Theological Seminary, Pasadena, CA (USA), 1972. 406p.
*The discipling of West Cameroon: a study of Baptist growth*. L.E. Kwast. Grand Rapids, MI: Eerdmans, 1971. 205p.
'The Evangelical Lutheran Church of East Cameroun'. C. S. Michelsen. Thesis, Fuller Theological Seminary, Pasadena, CA (USA), 1969. 226p.

TABLE 2. ORGANIZED CHURCHES AND DENOMINATIONS IN CAMEROON

| Official name 1 | Begun 2 | Type 3 | Coun 4 | Congcs 5 | Adults 6 | Affiliated 7 | Names, notes, and other statistics (see Codebook) 8 |
|---|---|---|---|---|---|---|---|
| Cameroon Baptist Convention | 1891 | P Bap | TF... | 558 | 35,482 | 55,000 | *CBC*. M=NABGMS(USA). 11 Fields. 53n,373m,76f,3H,5h,1s(104),W=75%,1390Y,4557z. |
| Cherubim and Seraphim | | I peA | x.... | | 2,000 | 5,000 | Nigerian pentecostals. M=C&S(Nigeria). In many villages from Loum to Douala. |
| Confédération Baptiste du Cameroun | 1864 | I Bap | .v... | | 2,500 | 5,000 | Ex first Baptists (now UEBC). HQ Bali, Duala. 1964, applied to join WCC; rejected. |
| Congrégation Baptiste du Cameroun | 1963 | I Bap | .T... | 2 | 1,000 | 2,000 | *CBC. Baptist Congregation*. Schism ex EBC and EEC. Pentecostal. Duala. HQ Deido. |
| Eglise Adventiste du Septième Jour | 1928 | P Adv | x.... | 55 | 13,319 | 25,000 | *SDA*. Equatorial Africa UM. 56% Bulu. 19nx,6f,1H,6h,1j,1r,1s,283t(22564),1456Y. |
| Eglise Baptiste Camerounaise | 1884 | I Bap | .vA.K | 239 | 18,000 | 35,000 | *EBC. Cameroon Baptist Ch*. Schism ex BM. Duala tribe, spreading across nation. 49n. |
| Eglise Baptiste Suédoise | | P Pe2 | Z.... | 13 | 12,736 | 20,000 | Baptist Pentecostals. M=Örebro Mission(from Örebro town, Sweden). |
| **Eglise Catholique au Cameroun:** | 1883 | R Lat | P.S.R | 1,150 | 917,300 | 1,528,760 | *Catholic Ch*. C=14+8+65. 5p,2s(92). 198n, 523x, 268m, 972w, P = 48%, 65282Yy. |
| M Yaoundé | 1890 | R Lat | Ps | 260 | 243,700 | 406,129 | 87% Fang(Ewondo, Eton), 4% Bamileke. 1s. 53 99 85 269 37 16684 |
| D Bafia | 1965 | R Lat | Pcssp | 23 | 35,700 | 59,480 | Savannah. Christianized only in south. 1p. 3 26 7 43 37 1766 |
| D Bafoussam | 1970 | R Lat | Ps | 250 | 81,000 | 135,055 | Prosperous Bamileke farmers. 4 monasteries. 15 28 8 48 41 6247 |
| D Bamenda | 1970 | R Lat | Ps | 23 | 77,800 | 129,714 | In west. English-speaking. 7 tribes. 1s. 7 47 26 96 55 8381 |
| D Buea | 1923 | R Lat | Pmhm | 19 | 58,400 | 97,265 | 40 tribes: Kossi, Nsaw, Widekum, Kpe, Fut. 1p. 10 33 9 23 55 6465 |
| D Douala | 1931 | R Lat | Ps | 37 | 139,500 | 232,420 | 42% Koko, 32% Bamileke, 12% Fang, 8% Duala. 47 49 53 141 54 8008 |
| D Doumé | 1949 | R Lat | Pcssp | 22 | 46,400 | 77,384 | 43% Maka, 31% Dzem. Mission among Pygmies. 5 46 30 74 45 3455 |
| D Garoua | 1947 | R Lat | Pomi | 413 | 14,700 | 24,483 | 36% Muslim (Fulani). 6 tribes. 1p. 0 59 9 57 59 1605 |
| D Mbalmayo | 1961 | R Lat | Ps | 21 | 61,000 | 101,751 | Southeast of Yaoundé. Rural. Beti tribe. 1p. 24 16 1 41 55 2421 |
| D Nkongsamba | 1914 | R Lat | Ps | 27 | 88,200 | 146,997 | 20% urban. Bamileke, Mbo. 1965, bishop jailed. 24 23 27 49 41 7425 |
| D Sangmélima | 1963 | R Lat | Ps | 25 | 53,600 | 89,300 | Rural. High % Protestant, 750 Orthodox. 1d. 9 39 13 51 87 1680 |
| PA Maroua-Mokolo (D, from 1973) | 1968 | R Lat | Pomi | 14 | 5,800 | 9,628 | Dense pastoral Fulani. Hill tribes. 1 28 7 44 68 506 |
| PA Yagoua (D, from 1973) | 1968 | R Lat | Pomi | 16 | 11,500 | 19,154 | 5 tribes. New area. 1973: elevated to diocese. 0 30 3 36 57 639 |
| Eglise de Dieu | 1970 | P Pe3 | ZF... | 101 | 7,218 | 15,000 | Holiness Pentecostals (3-stage). M=Church of God(Cleveland) (USA). 35n,1p. |
| Eglise du Christ | 1957 | P Dis | x.... | 40 | 1,400 | 3,000 | *Ch of Christ*. M=CC(Non-Instrumental) (USA). Missionaries in Kumba. 11f,1h,1s. |
| Eglise Evangélique du Cameroun | 1845 | P Ref | .WA.K | 653 | 136,637 | 215,000 | *EEC*. M=PEMS. 33% Bamileke. 91n,9x,911m,62w,67f,1s,1u,W=57%,8944Y,11832y,11098z. |
| Eglise Ev Luthérienne du Cameroun | 1915 | P Lut | L...K | 823 | 13,368 | 63,398 | *EEL*. M=NMS,SM(ALC). A=1960. 28n,21x,57f,2H,1h,2p,1s(25),W=60%,1971Y,1557y,7471z. |
| Eglise Fraternelle Luthérienne au C | 1918 | P Lut | x...K | 359 | 4,304 | 22,325 | M=CLB. 58% Mundang, 23% Masana. 20n,4x,15f,G=13.9%pa,1H,2h,15p,1s(22),1001Yy,2592z. |
| Eglise Orthodoxe Grecque (D Accra) | | O Gre | Cw... | 1 | 500 | 1,000 | Under Greek P Alexandria, Egypt. 8 parishes in West Africa, 3 priests. HQ Yaoundé. |
| Eglise Pentecostale Unie | | P Pel | x.... | 2 | 265 | 700 | *United Pentecostal Ch, Jesus Only Church*. M=UPC(USA). 5n,2f,1p(12) |
| Eglise Presbytérienne Camerounaise | 1879 | P Ref | RWA.K | 1,745 | 73.500 | 112,815 | M=UPUSA. 26% Bulu. 136n,7x,37f,G=−2%pa,5H,24h,1p,1s(33),W=80%,5011Y,5713y,15208z. |
| Eglise Presb Camerounaise Orthodoxe | 1967 | I Ref | .T... | 300 | 15,000 | 20,000 | *Continuing Presbysterian Ch*. Schism ex EPC by 13 pastors. Bulu. 1967, M=IBPFM(USA). |
| Eglise Protestante Africaine | 1934 | I Ref | .uA.K | 36 | 6,800 | 11,000 | *EPA. African Protestant Ch*. Schism ex EPC(American M) over language policy. Ngumba tribe. 11n. |
| Eglises Chrétiennes | | P Dis | x.... | 20 | 600 | 2,000 | *Christian Churches*. Independent congregations. M=CCCC(Instrumental) (USA). 2f. |
| Free Prot Episcopal Ch (D West Africa) | 1970 | C ARo | x.... | 6 | 750 | 900 | M=FPEC(UK). Douala. 84% nationals, 16% Nigerians. 1n,6m,2w,1r,W=99%,70Y,175z. |
| Global Frontier Church | c1960 | P Pe4 | x.... | | 2,000 | 5,000 | All over Forest in West. M=Wings of Healing(USA). Revival and healing campaigns. |
| Mission Baptiste Européenne | 1954 | P Bap | x...K | 42 | 460 | 1,060 | *MBE*. M=EBMS. Link with UEBC. 26% Kola, 19% Gisiga, 11% Mofou. 2n,3x,19m,15f. |
| Mission Unie du Soudan | 1938 | P int | x...K | 65 | 8,000 | 12,000 | *Union des Eglises Ev au Nord-C*. M=SUM(Swiss). Far north. Matakam, Kirdi. 56m,25f. |
| Native Baptist Church | 1888 | I Bap | ..... | 5 | 200 | 500 | Schisms among Kpe (Bakwiri) in 1888, 1898, 1917, 1960 opposing mission prohibitions. |
| Presbyterian Church in Cameroon | 1884 | P Ref | RWA.K | 861 | 79,549 | 127,068 | M=Basel M. 30% Widekum. 67n,16x,337m,40f,3H,7r,1s(12),W=90%,2866Y,10330y,5140z. |
| Témoins de Jéhovah | c1935 | M Jeh | x.... | 277 | 10,054 | 20,000 | *Jehovah's Witnesses*. Strong in West. Banned 1970, but active underground. 592Y. |
| Union Baptiste Camerounaise | 1931 | I Bap | ..... | | 500 | 1,000 | *Cameroon Baptist Union*. Schism ex UEBC. M=Coopération Ev Mondiale (Switzerland). |
| Union des Eglises Baptistes du Cameroun | 1845 | P Bap | TWA.K | 165 | 21 000 | 40,000 | *UEBC. Union of Baptist Chs*. M=PEMS(France), BEFG. 27% in Douala. 40n,42f,1u. |
| World-Wide Missions of Cameroon | 1961 | P ind | x.... | | 1,200 | 2,000 | M=World-Wide Missions(USA). Evangelicals from California. |
| Other African indigenous churches | | I | ..... | | 12,000 | 25,000 | Total about 20 (see below). |
| Other Protestant denominations | | P | ..... | | 200 | 500 | Total about 5 small missions, including Exclusive Brethren (Kelly-Continental). |
| **Total affiliated (mid-1970)** | | | | **7,730** | **1,397,842** | **2,377,026** | **Total denominations (1970) . . . 54.** |
| **Total affiliated (mid-1975)** | | | | **8,700** | **1,678,900** | **2,855,010** | **Total denominations (1975) . . . 59.** |
| **Total affiliated (mid-1980)** | | | | **9,800** | **2,021,300** | **3,437,200** | **Total denominations (1980) . . . 64.** |

**NOTES ON TABLE ABOVE**
COLUMNS: for meanings and CODES (cols. 1, 3, 4, 8): see Codebook (Part 6). Column 1: **Boldface type** = church with over 10% of country's affiliated Christians. *Language*. Names in column 1 are given in either French or English, depending on which is in major usage; the former work mainly in East Cameroon, the latter in West Cameroon.
NATIONAL COUNCILS (Column 4, 5th letter).
K = Fédération des Eglises et Missions Evangéliques du Cameroun (FEMEC)/Federation of Protestant Churches & Missions in Cameroon.
R = Conférence Episcopale du Cameroun/Episcopal Conference of Cameroon.
*Other national councils*. Conseil des Eglises Baptistes et Evangéliques du Cameroun (CEBC) (1957; members EEC and UEBC).
OTHER AFRICAN INDIGENOUS CHURCHES. There are many pentecostal and other immigrant groups from Nigeria, particularly in the west. Others include: Apostolic Ch, Eglise Chrétienne, Spiritual Holiness Ch of Cameroon (archbishop, in West Cameroon).
UNITING CHURCHES. Negotiations for organic union were under way in 1977 between: Eglise Ev du Cameroun, Eglise Presbytérienne Camerounaise, Eglise Protestante Africaine, Presbyterian Ch in West Cameroon. In 1976, the first 2 of these and the last formally agreed to unite on 19 August 1978.

**PEOPLES** (ethnolinguistic). Christians: 46% Cameroon Highland Bantu (Bamileke, Tikar, Widekum, Bamenda), 31% Equatorial Bantu (Ewondo, Eton, Bulu, Fang, Maka, Dzem), 14% Northwestern Bantu (Bassa-Koko, Duala, Mbo, Kpe (Bakwiri), Kossi), 4% Baya, 2% Kirdi, 2% Nigerian (Ibo, Ibibio), French.

**COUNTRY-WIDE TOTALS**
EVANGELIZATION (see Part 5). 1900: 16%. 1970: 88%. 1980: 92%. *Mass evangelism*. 1970–72, New Life for All 2-year campaign sponsored by evangelism department of FEMEC. *Radiophonic evangelism*. RVOG, ICI. As a result of programmes produced in Ngaoundere and broadcast by RVOG (Ethiopia), there are many Fulani secret believers.
FOREIGN MISSIONARIES AND PERSONNEL (nationals serving abroad) (1973). Total 177 in 6 countries: about 162 Roman Catholics (2 Jesuits in USA), 15 Protestants.
FOREIGN MISSIONARIES AND PERSONNEL (aliens from abroad) (1973). Total 1,901. *From Western world*. 1,834: 1,363 Roman Catholics, 470 Protestants (191 in 16 USA societies, 111 in 2 Norway societies, 68 in 4 WGermany societies, 51 in 2 Switzerland societies, 23 in 2 France societies, 18 in 2 Netherlands societies, 5 in 1 Canada society, 3 in 1 Finland society), 1 Orthodox. *From Communist world*. 27 Roman Catholics (23 from Poland, also Yugoslavia). *From Third World*. 40: about 20 indigenous from Nigeria and Ghana, about 10 Roman Catholics from Colombia, Haiti and Zaire, about 10 Protestants from Nigeria.
INSTITUTIONS (church-operated) (1973). Total 290, including 128 higher schools (13 minor seminaries), 130 medical centres (26 hospitals), 9 religious communities (5 monasteries), 10 seminaries (9 Protestant, 1 RC), 2 study centres.
PERIODICALS. About 30 titles.
PERSONNEL. About 11,714 (9,813 national, 1,901 foreign).
RELIGIOUS LIBRARIES. 21.
SCRIPTURE DISTRIBUTION (1975). Annual totals: 15,000 Bibles (80% subsidized, 20% commercial), 22,490 NTs (95% subsidized, 5% commercial), 22,000 UBS portions, 162,306 UBS selections. *Translations completed*. Portion: 18 languages since 1843. NT: 12 languages since 1861. Bible: 5 languages since 1872.
SERVICE AGENCIES. About 57, including ACE, ACF, AIPI, ATSFA, CEC, CENTAVEP, CETA(AACC), CV/AV, FEMEC, FUACE(WSCF), GBUAF, JAC/F, JARS, JEC/F, JOC/F, LWR, MIJARC, NLFA, SECDD, SU, UCEC, UCJG(YMCA), USMDC, WBT.

**ADDITIONAL DATA ON CHURCHES**
CAMEROON BAPTIST CONVENTION. English-speaking. Work was begun in 1891 by the Baptist Mission Society of Germany, and was eventually taken over by NABGMS (USA) after 1935. *Membership*. 30% Nsungli, 25% Kom, 20% Nsaw, 15% Mambila.
EGLISE BAPTISTE CAMEROUNAISE. Baptist Church in Cameroon. By 1975 the EBC had 25,070 adult members, 124 parishes in 67 districts, with 12 primary schools.
EGLISE CATHOLIQUE AU CAMEROUN. All dioceses are French-speaking except the 2 in English-speaking West Cameroon, Buea and Bamenda. *Catechumens*. (1959) 103,008; (1961) 107,368; (1963) 106,920; (1971) 125,000; divided among the 13 dioceses as follows, in the order shown (and included in column 7): 8043, 4037, 12220, 17323, 16781, 7726, 9963, 8731, 5500, 8640, 6200, 7253, 12583. *Annual baptisms* (1972). 61.4% infant, 35.9% adult. *National priests*. Including 176 secular and 17 regular. The first ordination of a Cameroon priest was in 1935. *Brothers*. Including 75 nationals. *Sisters*. Including 325 nationals. *Seminarians*. The 92 seminarians are not all studying in Cameroon. 56 are from French-speaking Cameroon studying at Yaoundé, and 32 are from English-speaking Cameroon studying at Bodija (Ibadan, Nigeria). *Catechists*. Total (1970) 6,833. The 5 schools have a 2-year course each. *Indigenous religious congregations*. Sisters: 115 Filles de Marie (M Yaoundé, 8 houses), 67 Servantes de Marie (D Douala, 10 houses), 50 Soeurs des Sacrés-Coeurs (D Nkongsamba, 7 houses), Soeurs Damianites (D Douala,

3 houses). *Main foreign orders and congregations.* Priests: CSSp, OMI, MHM, SCJ, SJ, OP, CICM, SAC, PIME, FMI, SSS, OCSO, Mission de France, Pères des Saints-Apôtres. Brothers: FSC, PFM, SC, Petits Frères de Jésus. Sisters: Filles du St-Esprit, Filles de Jésus, Soeurs Missionnaires du St-Esprit, Soeurs Franciscaines du Tyrol, Rosary Sisters (Ireland), Présentation de Marie, Filles de N-D du S-C.
*Catholic organizations.* The Episcopal Conference of Cameroon (Conférence Episcopale du Cameroun) is a member of ACECCT and SECAM. Two organizations cater for religious personnel: the Conference of Major Superiors of Cameroon (Conférence des Supérieurs Majeurs du Cameroun) and the Union of Major Superiors and Deputies of Cameroon (Union des Supérieures Majeures et Déléguées du Cameroun, USMDC); but there is no official council of priests. The National Council for the Lay Apostolate was formed in 1972 and exercises co-ordinating leadership for several organizations. The following youth movements are active: JAC/F especially in the south and east; CV/AV in 7 dioceses; JEC/F; JOC/F; Scouts and Guides; Xaveri and ACE in 2 dioceses. Adult organizations are the Legion of Mary (Légion de Marie) and the Christian Home Association (Association Chrétienne des Foyers).

The Holy See has diplomatic relations with Cameroon and is represented to government and the Catholic hierarchy by a pro-nuncio.

Under the National Board for Catholic Education, in 1970 there were 1,078 primary schools with 202,000 pupils (29% of the total number of pupils at this level), 43 secondary schools with 12,401 pupils (37%), and 22 technical schools with 2,767 students (24%). By 1973 schools numbered 1,085 primary (284,401 pupils), and 100 secondary (22,148). There were also 9 hospitals, 63 dispensaries and maternity centres, 2 specialist maternity centres, 5 nurseries, 2 orphanages and 88 health service projects. Most Catholic medical institutions are administered either by Ad Lucem, a lay organization independent of the hierarchy, or by dioceses themselves as employers of sisters.

In 1971 a Social Welfare Department was created as part of the secretariat of the Episcopal Conference, whose task is to co-ordinate all the activities of the Catholic Church in the field of socio-economic development. It collaborates with the Commission for Development (Commission pour le Développement) of FEMEC and with the state; and its projects, especially the activities of JAC/F, form part of the government's five-year plan. The economic role of the Catholic Church, as also that of the Protestant, is extensive, especially so among the northern traditionalist peoples where professional training, farm schools and co-operatives have been established. Caritas-Cameroon is also active, and Yaoundé serves as the centre for the pan-African secretariat of MIJARC (International Movement of Catholic Rural and Agricultural Youth), whose headquarters is in Belgium.
EGLISE EVANGELIQUE DU CAMEROUN. Work was founded by LMS (UK) in 1845, taken over by the Basel Mission in 1886, by the Paris Mission in 1918, and the church became autonomous in 1957. At present, foreign missions assisting are PEMS and the Oegeest Mission (Netherlands). A special feature of the EEC is its regular mass evangelistic campaigns in which the entire church membership participates, as among the Bamileke people during the civil war of the 1960s. *Membership.* 33% Bamileke, 26% Koko, 26% Duala, 12% Mum.
EGLISE EVANGELIQUE LUTHERIENNE DU CAMEROUN. Autonomous 1960. *Membership.* 64% Baya, 6% Duru, 6% Mbum, 5% Tikar.
EGLISE FRATERNELLE LUTHERIENNE AU CAMEROUN. *Membership.* 58% Mundang, 23% Masana, 10% Gude, 8% Tubiri. *1975 situation.* 223 parishes, 206 annexes, 28 ordained pastors, 399 catechists, 6,235 communicants, 9,035 non-communicant adult members, 3,181 catechumens, 801 adult baptisms (in 1975) and 1,124 infant baptisms, 84 confirmations, 27,832 Sunday attenders (over 15 years), 465 Sunday-school teachers and 6,456 pupils. Growth of communicants from 1969 to 1976: 69%.
EGLISE ORTHODOXE GRECQUE. The Greek bishop, a Greek citizen, lives in Athens (Greece) and visits West Africa only for the Christmas and Easter celebrations.
EGLISE PRESBYTERIENNE CAMEROUNAISE (Cameroon Presbyterian Church). In Bulu, = Kirk Presbiterian ya Cameroun. The church has 3 Synods: Municam (104 Parishes, Bulu and Beti tribes), Bassa-Cameroun (60 Parishes, Bassa tribe), Est-Cameroun (117 Parishes; Beti, Bulu, Bafia, Maka and other tribes). *Membership.* 26% Bulu, 24% Beti, 23% Bassa, 13% Maka, 10% Bafia, 2% Ngumba, 2% Batanga. *Schism.* A major anti-ecumenical schism took place in 1967 when 13 pastors left with about 20% of the membership, mainly in Municam Synod with a few parishes in East Cameroon Synod. *Practice.* Numbers have long vastly exceeded those affiliated or on the rolls. Sunday church attenders: 1967, 279,942; 1968 (after schism), 179,765; 1969, 142,840. The number of Sunday-school children in 1964 was 169,479.
FREE PROTESTANT EPISCOPAL CHURCH, also known as the Ecumenical Church Foundation, Diocese of West Africa (HQ Monrovia, Liberia); world headquarters St Leonards-on-Sea (UK).
PRESBYTERIAN CHURCH IN CAMEROON. English-speaking. Begun by BMS (UK) in 1885, then in 1886 by the Basel Mission, the church became autonomous in 1957 and in 1968 took over all mission institutions. After 1970 the church's name was officially changed from the former Presbyterian Church in West Cameroon. *Membership.* From many of the 50 small tribes: 30% Widekum, 13% Kom, 13% Kundu, 9% Fut, 9% Kpe, et alia; together with 5,000 Nigerians. *Languages.* 55% of members speak Mungaka, in Grassfield area; 36% speak Duala, in Forest area; and 9% speak English. In addition, Pidgin English is the lingua franca over all West Cameroon. *Growth.* By 1976 pastors had increased in numbers to 230, Sunday-school children to 73,094 and total community to 157,328. Among active members, women outnumbered men by a ratio of 5:1.

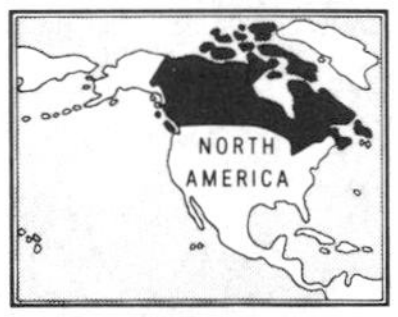


# CANADA

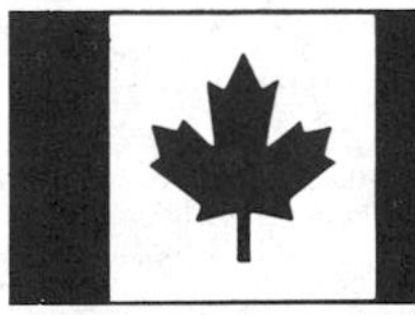

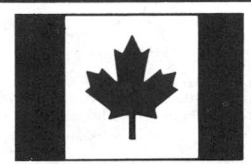

## SECULAR DATA

**STATE. Official name:** The Dominion of Canada (Le Dominion du Canada). (Since 1949 the term Dominion has fallen into disuse). Adjective of nationality: Canadian (canadien).
**Flag** (shown above right): Red maple leaf on white field, with red bars at each side.
**Area:** 9,976,139 sq.km. (3,851,807 sq. miles). Agricultural land: 6.8%.
**Government:** Federal parliamentary state (also constitutional monarchy), since 1867 (1534 French rule, 1763 British rule, 1867 Dominion of Canada).
**Legislature:** Parliament: Senate, 102 members; House of Commons, 264 members.
**Official languages:** English and French (*Français*). In Quebec, French only (since 1974).
**Chief cities:** capital Ottawa 619,000 (1973), Montreal 2,775,000, Toronto 2,692,000, Vancouver 1,116,000.
**Political divisions:** 10 Provinces.
**Armed forces** (1976): Total 77,900 (2,700 women) regular: land forces 28,500, maritime forces 13,400, air forces 36,000 (210 combat aircraft). Reserves: 19,100.
**Foreign forces** (1973): 2,000 USA troops.

**DEMOGRAPHY. Population:** 21,568,310 (census of 1.VI.1971. For 1970–2000 (UN), see last row of Table 1). Population density (1975): 2/sq.km. (6/sq.mile). Under 15 years: 34%. Growth rate (1975-80): 1.50% per year (births 2.04%, deaths −0.79%, immigrants 0.25%). Life expectancy (1975–80): 72.5 years. Household size: 3.5 persons.
**Major languages:** English, French, German, Italian, Ukrainian, Dutch, Polish, Yiddish, Norwegian, Greek, Hungarian, Chinese, Swedish, Serbo-Croatian, Danish, Portuguese, Eskimo, and over 70 others.
**Urban dwellers** (1970): 76.3%. Urban growth rate (1950–70): 3.4% per year.
**Labour force:** 43%.
**Refugees** (1977): 29,450 (17,000 from Eastern Europe, 6,275 from Viet-Nam (50,000 by 1980), 6,175 Asians from Uganda).
**Tourists** (1974): 13,758,700. Arrivals at borders, including excursionists (1970): 38 million.

**ETHNOLINGUISTIC GROUPS:** 37.7% Anglo-Canadian, 28.7% French Canadian (& French), 6.2% German, 3.4% Italian, 3.3% English, 2.7% Ukrainian, 2.0% Dutch, 1.8% part-Indian (Métis, Half-Breed) & non-status Indian (400,000), 1.8% USA White, 1.5% Polish, 1.4% Jewish, 1.4% Amerindian (registered Native Indian) (295,200), 0.8% Norwegian, 0.6% Greek, 0.6% Hungarian, 0.6% Chinese (118,800), 0.5% Swedish, 0.5% Yugoslav, 0.4% Danish, 0.4% Portuguese, 0.3% Czech, 0.3% Russian, 0.3% Finnish, 0.2% Austrian, 0.2% Belgian, 0.2% North American Black (34,400), 0.2% Japanese (37,200), 0.2% Indo-Pakistani, 0.1% Slovak, 0.1% Spaniard, 0.1% Arab (Syrian, Lebanese, Palestinian), 0.1% West Indian Black (28,000), 0.1% Eskimo (17,500), 0.1% Egyptian, 0.1% Armenian, 0.1% Romanian, 0.1% Estonian, 0.1% Icelander (27,900), 0.1% Latvian, 0.1% Lithuanian, Bulgarian, Macedonian, Byelorussian, Korean (10,000), Vietnamese, & 50 smaller peoples.

**MONEY** (1977). **Monetary unit:** dollar (= 100 cents); US$1 = C$1.10.
**National income per person:** US$5,672. Average annual family income: US$19,852.
**Inflation:** (1970–74) 6.5% per year, (1975) 11% per year (consumer price index 150).
**Cost of living in capital** (1976): index 105 (Washington DC = 100). Daily cost of living: US$40.

**EDUCATION.** Adult literacy: 100%. Education rate: 60%. Schools: 16,608. Universities: 67.

**HEALTH.** Hospitals: 1,407 (211,109 beds). Doctors: 34,509. Blind: 27,184. Psychotics: 230,000. Drug addicts (1976): 190,000 (163,279 on cannabis or hashish, 19,000 on heroin). Criminals: 3,200,000.

**LITERATURE.** Annual new book titles (1973): 4,083. Periodicals: 3,000. Scientific journals: 540. Newspapers: 121 dailies, 1,031 non-daily.

**COMMUNICATION** (per 1,000 people): Phones: 527. Radios: 865. TV sets: 348. Daily newspaper circulation: 230 copies.

TABLE 1. RELIGIOUS ADHERENTS IN CANADA

| Year | 1900 | | mid-1970 | | Annual change, 1970–1980 | | | | mid-1975 | | mid-1980 | | 2000 | |
|---|---|---|---|---|---|---|---|---|---|---|---|---|---|---|
| *Name* | *Adherents* | *%* | *Adherents* | *%* | *Natural* | *Conversion* | *Total* | *Rate* | *Adherents* | *%* | *Adherents* | *%* | *Adherents* | *%* |
| **Christians** | **5,504,320** | **98.4** | **20,217,000** | **94.4** | **288,715** | **−73,995** | **214,720** | **1.01** | **21,136,500** | **92.7** | **22,364,200** | **91.0** | **26,871,000** | **85.0** |
| professing | 5,504,320 | 98.4 | 20,217,000 | 94.4 | 288,715 | −73,995 | 214,720 | 1.01 | 21,136,500 | 92.7 | 22,364,200 | 91.0 | 26,871,000 | 85.0 |
| Roman Catholics | 2,304,000 | 41.2 | 9,889,600 | 46.2 | 144,514 | 11,766 | 156,280 | 1.48 | 10,579,700 | 46.4 | 11,452,400 | 46.6 | 14,858,000 | 47.0 |
| Protestants | 2,414,620 | 43.2 | 6,644,100 | 31.0 | 91,808 | −68,768 | 23,040 | 0.34 | 6,721,100 | 29.5 | 6,874,500 | 28.0 | 7,238,000 | 22.9 |
| Anglicans | 755,000 | 13.5 | 2,547,300 | 11.9 | 34,882 | −31,562 | 3,320 | 0.13 | 2,553,700 | 11.2 | 2,580,500 | 10.5 | 2,687,000 | 8.5 |
| Orthodox | 15,700 | 0.3 | 599,000 | 2.8 | 8,715 | 185 | 8,900 | 1.39 | 638,000 | 2.8 | 688,000 | 2.8 | 948,000 | 3.0 |
| Marginal Protestants | 10,000 | 0.2 | 257,000 | 1.2 | 4,357 | 9,263 | 13,620 | 4.27 | 319,000 | 1.4 | 393,200 | 1.6 | 632,000 | 2.0 |
| Catholics (non-Roman) | 5,000 | 0.1 | 220,000 | 1.0 | 3,196 | 64 | 3,260 | 1.39 | 234,000 | 1.0 | 252,600 | 1.0 | 318,000 | 1.0 |
| Non-White indigenous | 0 | 0.0 | 60,000 | 0.3 | 1,243 | 5,057 | 6,300 | 6.92 | 91,000 | 0.4 | 123,000 | 0.5 | 190,000 | 0.6 |
| nominal | 393,320 | 7.0 | 4,257,411 | 19.9 | 59,432 | −36,003 | 23,429 | 0.54 | 4,350,900 | 19.1 | 4,491,700 | 18.3 | 4,933,000 | 15.6 |
| affiliated | 5,111,000 | 91.4 | 15,959,589 | 74.5 | 229,283 | −37,992 | 191,291 | 1.14 | 16,785,600 | 73.6 | 17,872,500 | 72.7 | 21,938,000 | 69.4 |
| total practising | 4,855,450 | *95* | 14,363,630 | *90* | 204,062 | −67,645 | 136,417 | 0.91 | 14,939,180 | *89* | 15,727,800 | *88* | 17,550,000 | *80* |
| non-practising | 225,550 | *5* | 1,595,960 | *10* | 25,221 | 29,653 | 54,874 | 2.97 | 1,846,420 | *11* | 2,144,700 | *12* | 4,388,000 | *20* |
| Roman Catholics | 2,230,000 | 39.9 | 9,074,959 | 42.4 | 132,678 | 11,676 | 144,354 | 1.49 | 9,713,200 | 42.6 | 10,518,500 | 42.8 | 13,593,000 | 43.0 |
| Catholic pentecostals | 0 | 0.0 | 2,000 | 0.0 | 695 | 10,105 | 10,800 | 21.60 | 50,000 | 0.2 | 110,000 | 0.4 | 700,000 | 2.2 |
| Protestants | 2,288,000 | 40.9 | 4,508,348 | 21.1 | 62,601 | −44,036 | 18,565 | 0.41 | 4,583,000 | 20.1 | 4,694,000 | 19.1 | 5,058,000 | 16.0 |
| Evangelicals | 1,321,000 | 23.6 | 1,500,000 | 7.0 | 20.899 | −14,899 | 6,000 | 0.39 | 1,530,000 | 6.7 | 1,560,000 | 6.3 | 1,750,000 | 5.5 |
| Neo-pentecostals | 0 | 0.0 | 5,000 | 0.0 | 410 | 3,590 | 4,000 | 13.33 | 30,000 | 0.1 | 45,000 | 0.2 | 150,000 | 0.5 |
| Anglicans | 559,000 | 10.0 | 1,177,414 | 5.5 | 16,195 | −13,516 | 2,679 | 0.22 | 1,185,600 | 5.2 | 1,204,200 | 4.9 | 1,264,000 | 4.0 |
| Evangelicals | 84,000 | 1.5 | 90,000 | 0.4 | 1,261 | −1,101 | 160 | 0.18 | 90,700 | 0.4 | 91,600 | 0.4 | 96,600 | 0.3 |
| Anglican pentecostals | 0 | 0.0 | 1,000 | 0.0 | 41 | 359 | 400 | 13.33 | 3,000 | 0.0 | 5,000 | 0.0 | 25,000 | 0.1 |
| Orthodox | 15,000 | 0.3 | 583,300 | 2.7 | 8,482 | 188 | 8,670 | 1.40 | 621,000 | 2.7 | 670,000 | 2.7 | 885,000 | 2.8 |
| Orthodox pentecostals | 0 | 0.0 | 0 | 0.0 | 14 | 286 | 300 | 30.00 | 1,000 | 0.0 | 3,000 | 0.0 | 20,000 | 0.1 |
| Marginal Protestants | 15,000 | 0.3 | 327,568 | 1.5 | 4,983 | 4,040 | 9,023 | 2.47 | 364,800 | 1.6 | 417,800 | 1.7 | 632,000 | 2.0 |
| Catholics (non-Roman) | 4,000 | 0.1 | 213,000 | 1.0 | 3,101 | 99 | 3,200 | 1.41 | 227,000 | 1.0 | 245,000 | 1.0 | 316,000 | 1.0 |
| Non-White indigenous | 0 | 0.0 | 75,000 | 0.3 | 1,243 | 3,557 | 4,800 | 5.27 | 91,000 | 0.4 | 123,000 | 0.5 | 190,000 | 0.6 |
| Non-religious | 10,000 | 0.2 | 632,000 | 3.0 | 7,593 | 47,597 | 55,190 | 6.33 | 872,000 | 3.8 | 1,183,900 | 4.8 | 2,746,000 | 8.7 |
| Jews | 16,400 | 0.3 | 294,000 | 1.4 | 4,275 | 75 | 4,350 | 1.39 | 313,000 | 1.4 | 337,500 | 1.4 | 379,000 | 1.2 |
| Atheists | 1,000 | 0.0 | 100,000 | 0.5 | 3,114 | 23,786 | 26,900 | 11.80 | 228,000 | 1.0 | 369,000 | 1.5 | 948,000 | 3.0 |
| Muslims | 50 | 0.0 | 42,000 | 0.2 | 9,290 | 2,010 | 11,300 | 11.30 | 100,000 | 0.4 | 155,000 | 0.6 | 464,000 | 1.5 |
| Chinese folk-religionists | 5,120 | 0.1 | 30,000 | 0.1 | 382 | −782 | −400 | −1.43 | 28,000 | 0.1 | 26,000 | 0.1 | 20,000 | 0.1 |
| Baha'is | 0 | 0.0 | 24,000 | 0.1 | 437 | 1,163 | 1,600 | 5.00 | 32,000 | 0.1 | 40,000 | 0.2 | 60,000 | 0.2 |
| Hindus | 0 | 0.0 | 20,000 | 0.1 | 2,490 | 10 | 2,500 | 6.25 | 40,000 | 0.2 | 45,000 | 0.2 | 53,000 | 0.2 |
| Buddhists | 10,410 | 0.2 | 16,000 | 0.1 | 232 | 8 | 240 | 1.41 | 17,000 | 0.1 | 18,400 | 0.1 | 23,000 | 0.1 |
| Tribal religionists | 44,000 | 0.8 | 12,000 | 0.1 | 150 | −350 | −200 | −1.82 | 11,000 | 0.1 | 10,000 | 0.0 | 8,000 | 0.0 |
| Sikhs | 0 | 0.0 | 7,000 | 0.0 | 102 | −2 | 100 | 1.33 | 7,500 | 0.0 | 8,000 | 0.0 | 11,000 | 0.0 |
| New-Religionists | 0 | 0.0 | 2,000 | 0.0 | 56 | 244 | 300 | 7.50 | 4,000 | 0.0 | 5,000 | 0.0 | 10,000 | 0.0 |
| Other religionists | 1,000 | 0.0 | 10,000 | 0.0 | 164 | 236 | 400 | 3.33 | 12,000 | 0.1 | 14,000 | 0.1 | 20,000 | 0.1 |
| **Country's population** | **5,592,300** | **100.0** | **21,406,000** | **100.0** | **317,000** | **0** | **317,000** | **1.39** | **22,801,000** | **100.0** | **24,576,000** | **100.0** | **31,613,000** | **100.0** |

COLUMNS, ROWS. For meanings and definitions, see Codebook (Part 6). Note that, by definition, total 'Christians' = professing + crypto-Christians, which also = affiliated + nominal Christians. Percentages may not always total exactly, due to rounding.

CENSUSES. **1871** (Dominion of Canada only): 43.6% Protestants (16.3% Methodists, 16.2% Presbyterians, 6.8% Baptists), 41.7% Roman Catholics, 13.7% Anglicans, 1% Buddhists/Confucians/pagans, 0.0% Jews. **1901** (Dominion only): 44.0% Protestants, 41.7% Roman Catholics, 12.8% Anglicans, 1.2% Buddhists/Confucians/pagans, 0.3% Jews. Note: the 1900 column above is based on the separate 1901 censuses for the Dominion of Canada (5,371,315) plus Newfoundland & Labrador (220,984). **1911:** 43.9% Protestants, 39.4% Roman Catholics, 14.5% Anglicans, 1.2% Buddhists/Confucians/pagans, 1.0% Jews. **1921:** 41.3% Protestants, 38.7% Roman Catholics, 16.1% Anglicans, 1.9% Orthodox, 1.4% Jews, 0.3% marginal Protestants, 0.2% non-religious, 0.1% Buddhists. **1931:** 39.8% Protestants (19.5% United Ch of Canada), 39.5% Roman Catholics, 15.8% Anglicans, 2.6% Orthodox, 1.5% Jews, 0.3% marginal Protestants, 0.2% non-religious, 0.1% Buddhists. **1941**: 41.8% Roman Catholics, 38.1% Protestants (19.2% United Ch of Canada), 15.2% Anglicans, 2.6% Orthodox, 1.5% Jews, 0.3% marginal Protestants, 0.2% non-religious, 0.1% Buddhists. **1.VI.1951** (de jure): 43.3% Roman Catholics, 36.9% Protestants (20.5% United Ch of Canada), 14.7% Anglicans, 2.6% Orthodox, 1.5% Jews, 0.5% marginal Protestants, 0.4% non-religious, 0.1% Buddhists. **1.VI.1961** (de jure): 45.7% Roman Catholics, 35.5% Protestants (20.1% United Ch of Canada), 13.2% Anglicans, 2.7% Orthodox, 1.4% Jews, 0.8% marginal Protestants (0.4% Jehovah's Witnesses), 0.5% non-religious, 0.1% Buddhists, 0.1% tribal religionists. **1.VI.1971** (de jure): 46.2% Roman Catholics, 32.0% Protestants (17.5% United Ch of Canada), 11.8% Anglicans, 4.3% non-religious and atheists, 2.8% Orthodox, 1.3% Jews, 1.2% marginal Protestants (0.8% Jehovah's Witnesses), 0.1% Buddhists, 0.3% other religionists. The detailed census statistics of religion every decade from 1921–71 given in *Religious denominations, 1971 Census of Canada* (1973), p. 9–1, permit clear comparisons for all confessions except the Orthodox, whose census labels ('Greek Orthodox' and 'Ukrainian Catholic') are too imprecise to clearly enumerate the complex Catholic/Orthodox/Greek/Russian/Ukrainian/etc situation, as has here been done in our Table 2 below.

POLLS. Numerous polls of profession, attendance (see below) and belief have been taken since 1940 (Gallup Poll of Canada, et alia).

NOTES ON RELIGIONS

ANGLICAN PENTECOSTALS (or, Anglican charismatics). In the Diocese of Toronto, out of 300 Anglican clergy at the beginning of 1974, 40 (13%) were actively involved in the charismatic renewal.

ATHEISTS. 2 parties: Communist Party of Canada (CPC) (legal; pro-Soviet); membership (1970) 1,500, and Communist Party of Canada Marxist-Leninist (CPCM/L) (legal; pro-Chinese); membership (1970) 300; Communist voters (election of 30.X.1972) 9,339 for CPCM/L, 5,962 for CPC (total, 0.2% of all votes).

BAHA'IS. Entered before 1921. Recent growth from 68 local spiritual assemblies (1964) to 160 (1973), including several on Indian reservations.

BUDDHISTS. Japanese and Chinese followers of Mahayana Buddhism, with some White converts.

CATHOLIC PENTECOSTALS (or, Catholic charismatics). Totals (January 1974): about 10,000 involved adults (over 15 years old) in 500 prayer groups; total charismatic community including children, 20,000. (Mid-1976) In Quebec alone, 35,000 involved adults including 10,000 in the movement's youth wing Youth Testimony; total community including children for all Canada, about 100,000. In June 1977, 50,000 attended a French-speaking renewal conference in Montreal.

CHINESE FOLK-RELIGIONISTS. In 1900, these numbered 5,120 (called Confucians) out of a total of 17,300 Chinese. A blend of Confucianism, Taoism and Buddhism, folk religion is practised by over a third of all Chinese in Canada.

HINDUS. Immigrants from India and (1972) Uganda Asians; also Canadian converts to new sects including Sri Chinmoy Centre (1,000 adherents, 200 committed disciples), Ananda Marga, and 90,000 members of various religions who are also followers of a movement with Hindu origins which claims to be a philosophy but not a religion: the Science of Creative Intelligence (SCI) or Transcendental Meditation (TM). ISKCON (Hare Krishna) operates 4 centres and a farm. The Theosophical Society in 1975 had 13 Lodges with 312 members.

JEWS. 170 Orthodox, 25 Conservative and 5 Reform congregations. The total 'Natural change' above includes immigration of about 2,000 a year.

MUSLIMS. In 1965 mostly Canadian-born, with immigrants after 1965 from Pakistan, India, Guyana, Uganda (20,000 Ismaili Asians), Malaysia, Indonesia, Iran, Turkey, Albania, Lebanon, Egypt and other Arab countries. Muslims live throughout Canada in urban and rural areas, and also in the isolated northern settled areas. Mosques: Ottawa, Edmonton. There is also a small Ahmadiya Mission based in Toronto. The total 'Natural change' above includes over 6,000 immigrants a year. *Hajj pilgrims to Mecca.* (1976) 22.

NEO-PENTECOSTALS. Charismatics in the non-Pentecostal Protestant denominations, including Jesus Movement followers. In January 1975, in the Toronto Conference of the United Church of Canada, out of the 257 ministers in pastoral charges, 72 (28%) were actively involved in the charismatic renewal.

NEW-RELIGIONISTS. Adherents of various Asian syncretistic New Religions including 2,500 converts to Nichiren Shoshu (Soka Gakkai) from Japan.

NON-RELIGIOUS. Mainly Whites; also about 50,000 of the 120,000 Chinese claim no religion.

NON-WHITE INDIGENOUS. In over 25 denominations in 1970 (see Table 2).

ORTHODOX PENTECOSTALS (or, Orthodox charismatics). Mainly in Ukrainian Orthodox communities in Saskatchewan and Manitoba.

OTHER RELIGIONISTS. Adherents of a variety of other non-Christian religions, including 1,200 Rastafarians (Blacks from Jamaica and other West Indies islands; 800 in Toronto; 600 allegedly with criminal records), and a host of syncretistic cults from the USA including Rosicrucians (27 AMORC centres), and I Am Religious Movement (in Calgary and Edmonton) and its offshoot the Church Universal and Triumphant (in BC, Ontario and Quebec).

PRACTISING CHRISTIANS. Weekly church attendance has declined from 67% of the population in 1946 (Roman Catholics 83%), to 55% in 1965, to 44% in 1970 (Roman Catholics 65%, Protestants including Anglicans 28%), to 39% in 1974 (Roman Catholics 59%, Protestants 27%), and to 38% in 1977 (Roman Catholics 53%, Protestants 28%) (CIPO). Winter 1965–66: 45% of population attend at least weekly, 10% 2 or 3 times a month, 7% once a month, 27% a few times a year, 6% never, 5% non-Christians. 1973 (CIPO): 'Is organized religion a relevant part of your life at the present time or not?'—50% Yes (18–29 years 37%, 30–39 years 39%, 40–49 years 52%, 50 years and over 63%), 50% No. Despite this assertion, 88% of the population attended church at least once a year in 1965; excluding about 20% who attended only for family occasions (weddings etc), this leaves about 68% of the entire population as practising Christians attending public worship at least once a year. Dividing this figure by the number of affiliated Christians in the nation, this gives our figure of 90% for practising Christians in the table above in 1970.

SIKHS. First immigrants settled in Vancouver early in the 20th century.

TRIBAL RELIGIONISTS. Shamanists. In 1900, 44,000 out of a total of 108,000 Canadian Indians followed their tribal religion (the rest: 32% RCs, 14% Anglicans, 13% Protestants). After declining from 200,000 in the 16th century, the Indian population began to increase again in the 20th. By 1970 about 96% of all Indians were members of Christian churches.

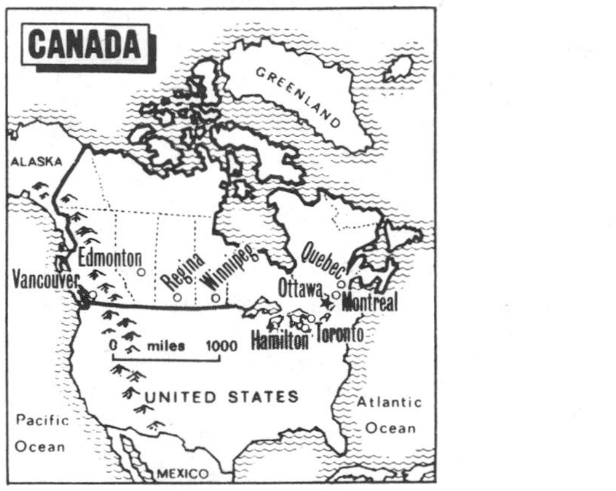


**NON-CHRISTIAN RELIGIONS.** **Judaism** is the largest non-Christian religious community in Canada. There are at present 170 Orthodox, 25 Conservative and 5 Reform congregations. Some 25 national organizations exist including: for Orthodox Judaism, the Rabbinical Council of America (Canadian section) and the Union of Orthodox Jewish Congregations; for Conservative Judaism, the Rabbinical Assembly (Canada Division); and for Reform Judaism, the Council of Reform Synagogues. In addition, there is the Canadian Jewish Congress, founded in Montreal in 1919, which represents Canadian Jewry as a whole. Each synagogue is autonomous, choosing its own rabbi and administering its affairs. Many synagogues have schools for teaching Hebrew and the history of Judaism.

**Islam** is rapidly growing with the continuous arrival of immigrants from Pakistan, India, Guyana, Uganda (Asians) and some Arab countries. The Ottawa Muslim Association was founded in 1962, and funds have recently been collected for the construction of the first Canadian mosque in the capital. There is also a mosque in Edmonton, Alberta. Muslims often meet in rented halls, and university students in their campus student union. The principal co-ordinating body since 1952 has been the Federation of Islamic Associations of the United States and Canada (FIA) with headquarters in the USA, and in 1973 a national organization was formed in Toronto, the Council of Muslim Communities of Canada. Various provincial Islamic associations and city chapters are affiliated with the council. The Muslim Students Association of US and Canada is centred in Gary, Indiana (USA). The non-confessional Institute of Islamic Studies was founded in 1952 at McGill University, Montreal, for research and the teaching of Islamics.

**Baha'i** is organized under the National Spiritual Assembly of the Baha'is of Canada with its headquarters in Willowdale, Ontario. A part of the Baha'i World Community centred in Haifa, Israel, there are 160 local spiritual assemblies, or a total of 800 Baha'i centres throughout the country, several of which are found on Indian reservations. Baha'i schools include the National Teaching Institute in Fort Qu'Appelle, Saskatchewan, and summer schools in Ontario, British Columbia and Quebec.

**Hinduism** has continued to increase due to the influx of Asians from the Indian sub-continent and most recently from Uganda. Two Hindu organizations exist in Montreal: the Yoga Vedanta Sivananda Center and the Sound of India.

**Buddhism** has many adherents organized into 18 groupings called churches, and organized under a national office in Toronto into 4 districts (Eastern, with 3 churches, Manitoba with one church, Alberta with 7 churches and British Columbia with 7 churches). The Buddhist Churches of Canada belong to the Jodo Shin sect of Mahayana Buddhism. Buddhist strength is concentrated in the Japanese-Canadian community in western Canada. There is a Buddhist Centre in Montreal.

**Shamanism** continues to influence the Eskimo peoples in spite of the formal conversion of most to Christianity. In the Yukon, sickness is believed to be caused by evil spirits (Aguiqtuq) who originate when the names of dead persons are not passed on to the new-born children of succeeding generations. Shamans or medicine men use 'helping' spirits in their role as intermediaries between the natural and supernatural worlds.

**CHRISTIANITY.** The first Catholic missionary, a French secular priest, arrived in 1608, and began work among the Micmac Indians; and he was followed shortly afterwards by a Jesuit party, and 3 Récollet priests in 1615. Huguenot merchants from France and Anglican explorers and traders from Great Britain were early on the scene, but opposition to Protestantism in French Canada was strong. Regular Anglican services were not begun until 1700 in Newfoundland and a decade later in Nova Scotia. SPG missionaries arrived in Halifax in 1749, and the first Anglican bishop was named for Nova Scotia in 1787. Sometime after 1750 began the

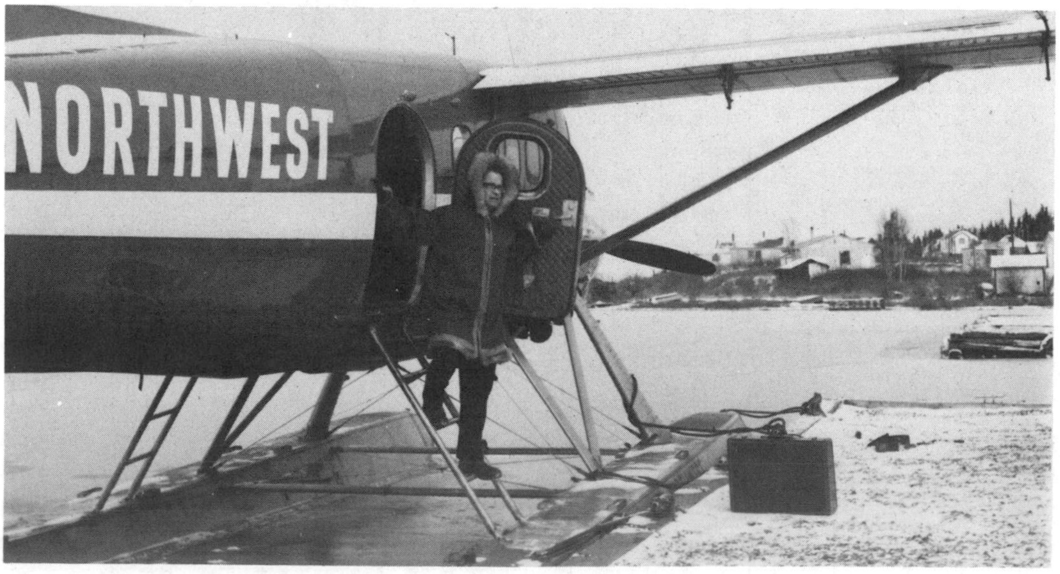


**United Church of Canada.** Pastoral visit by floatplane on part of UCC minister from Yellowknife in far North.

immigration of New England Congregationalists into Nova Scotia, and within the next decade Ulster Irish Presbyterians (1763) and New England Baptists had also settled there.

Methodism came to Newfoundland from Great Britain in 1765. Yorkshire Methodists entered Nova Scotia in 1772, and the Bay of Quinte was reached by 1785. Anglicanism grew more rapidly following the American war of independence due to the influx of American Loyalists as well as through British immigration after the Napoleonic wars in Europe. These early patterns have continued to dominate the Canadian religious scene. While French Canada has remained overwhelmingly Catholic, English Canada has been influenced mostly by Anglican and Protestant groups from Britain and the USA.

CATHOLIC CHURCH. From the time of the British victory in Canada until the beginning of the 1960s, the Catholic Church was closely allied with French Canadian society and made a profound contribution to the development of Quebec identity. Beginning about 1960 a rapid and often violent movement for the deconfessionalization of Catholic institutions has gained force and contributed to the disintegration of existing Catholic ecclesial structures. According to the report of the episcopal conference's Dumont Study Commission concerning laity and the church, this manifests itself in a decline in religious practice, a decrease in vocations (from 2,000 new priestly vocations in 1946 to 100 in 1970), the indifference of youth and the collapse of lay organization. A survey carried out during 1968–70 by CRSR (Laval University, Quebec) estimated the total number of Canadian priests to be 15,546, of which 1,541 were resident outside the country. The majority are French-speaking, 70.3% of the diocesan clergy and 74.1% of the regular clergy, while English-speaking clergy were respectively 27.8% and 20.5% and those with other mother tongues were 1.8% and 5.4%. A major finding was that every year since 1963 the number of young priests has diminished significantly in all categories, religious and secular as well as French- and English-speaking.

Ecclesial activity now manifests itself through new grass-roots communities, marginal groups and post-conciliar institutions. In recent years Quebec has witnessed the creation of numerous religious life entities outside the formal structures of the church, some of which are informally related to the official church while others are not. Several different types of groups may be distinguished such as parish communities, marginal communities and extra-ecclesial religious groups. Parish communities consist of groups of faithful within a parish or regional grouping of several parishes. They are usually organized by parish clergy and are dedicated to experimenting with new liturgical forms and missionary ventures. Although often of progressivist tendencies, they define their role in relationship to the universal church. Primarily an urban phenomenon, their principal problems revolve around their functional relationship to official parish structures. Their numerical importance is considerable since they numbered at least 150 communities by 1970.

In addition, marginal communities exist without ties to any official structures of the church. They express a similar intensity of Christian conviction as that evident in parish communities, but their participation is more limited. They are strongest in the urban milieu and manifest sectarian tendencies in some cases. Not uncommonly they present themselves as study groups including non-Catholics, without the participation of clergy. Among these are extra-ecclesial religious bodies generally belonging to the Canadian revival movement, and often influenced by pentecostal and marginal groups including Mormons and Jehovah's Witnesses. They are found exclusively in urban areas among the younger elements in the population. All of these new movements are found in the English-speaking as well as French-speaking Catholic areas.

Several post-conciliar institutions have also come into prominence since Vatican II. Some parish pastoral councils (conseils de pastorale) play a role which is not only consultative but often determinative in the material administration of the parish and the selection of the parish priests. Two diocesan synods are active. One, in the archdiocese of Rimouski, has been meeting since 1969. It consists of 120 elected members, each with one vote, including the archbishop. By 1973 it had studied 13 themes and consulted 25,000 persons. The other, in the archdiocese of Trois-Rivières under the official name of Pastoral Council of Trois-Rivières, was initiated in 1970 and held its first synodal assembly in March 1973. It consists of 170 members (120 lay, 50 priests and religious, elected by their respective groups). It has studied 16 themes and consulted 40,000 persons.

PROTESTANT CHURCHES. The largest Protestant denomination is the United Church of Canada which came into being in 1925 uniting the work of the Methodist, Congregational and nearly half the Presbyterian churches. In 1968 the Canadian Conference of the Evangelical United Brethren joined as well and church union discussions with the Anglican Church are continuing. The UCC is organized into 11 geographical conferences which are further sub-divided into 93 presbyteries. The chief

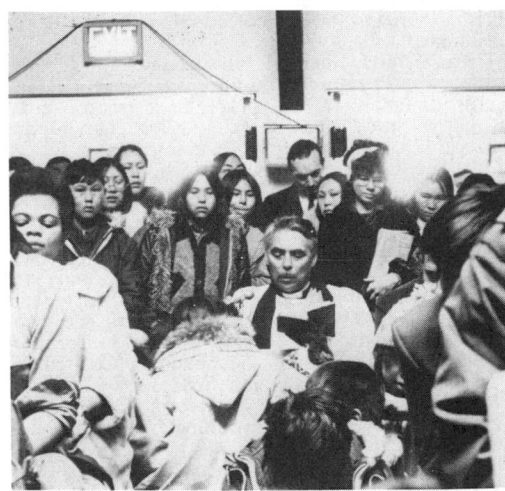

Anglican Church of Canada. Members include: *top*, 80% of all Eskimos (shown at 1974 consecration of Bishop of The Arctic); *bottom*, Athabascan/Haida and Tsimshian Amerindians (at Aiyansh, BC); *right*, Anglo-Canadians and Blacks (at 1969 General Synod, Sudbury).

policy-making body is the General Council which meets every 2 years. United Church service agencies are organized into 5 divisions dealing with Communication; Finance; Ministry, Personnel and Education; Mission in Canada; and World Outreach.

The Presbyterian Church in Canada, the second largest Protestant body, was formed from those Presbyterian congregations which refused to go into union in 1925. National agencies include the Boards of World Missions, Christian Education, Stewardship and Budget, Evangelism and Social Action and the Women's Missionary Society.

Canadian Baptists are found principally in the Baptist Federation of Canada whose member bodies are the Baptist Convention of Ontario and Quebec, Baptist Union of Western Canada, French Baptist Union and United Baptist Convention of the Atlantic Provinces. The federation carries on its work through 4 departments dealing with Canadian Missions, Christian Education, Ministry, and Overseas Missions. Of other bodies not forming part of the federation, the most important is the Fellowship of Evangelical Baptist Churches. Other smaller groups include the Baptist General Conference, which was established through the efforts of Swedish Missionaries from the USA; Canadian Baptist Conference, which is related to the Southern Baptist Convention of the USA; Convention of Regular Baptists; North American Baptist General Conference; and Primitive Baptist Conference of New Brunswick.

Over 15 distinct Pentecostal churches have been organized. Most are small and many have direct connections with similar groups in the USA. By far the largest is the Pentecostal Assemblies of Canada which is the fourth largest Protestant denomination in Canada, is the Canadian counterpart to the USA Assemblies of God, and which has widespread overseas missionary work.

Several Lutheran denominations are active, the most important being the Lutheran Church in America—Canada Section, which consists of the 3 Canadian synods of the American church; the Lutheran Church—Canada, which has been autonomous since 1959 but retains fraternal ties with its parent body, the Lutheran Church—Missouri Synod in the USA; and the Evangelical Lutheran Church in Canada, which until 1967 was the Canada District of the American Lutheran Church. In addition there is the small Latvian Evangelical Lutheran Church, which consists exclusively of refugees from eastern Europe.

Mennonites are widely dispersed across Canada. Of 14 distinct bodies, the Conference of Mennonites of Canada, General Conference Mennonite Church and the Mennonite Brethren Churches of North America are the largest.

Other significant Protestant groups are the Salvation Army, Christian Reformed Churches in Canada and the Seventh-day Adventist Church.

ANGLICAN CHURCH. The Anglican Church of Canada is organized into 28 dioceses in 4 provinces

(British Columbia, Canada, Ontario and Rupert's Land), each under a metropolitan or archbishop, the head of the general synod bearing the title of primate. Service agencies of the church include 5 divisions (National and World Program, Parish and Diocesan Services, Communication, Planning, Pensions) in addition to the Missionary Society and the Department of Administration and Finance. Canadian Anglicanism has been autonomous for more than a century.

ORTHODOX CHURCHES. Immigration patterns have helped to create a wide variety of Orthodox churches of different traditions: Arab, Armenian, Bulgarian, Byelorussian, Coptic, Estonian, Greek, Macedonian, Old Believer, Romanian, Serbian, Syrian, Russian and Ukrainian. The largest body is the Ninth Archidiocesan District of the Greek Orthodox Archdiocese of North and South America, which is under the jurisdiction of the Ecumenical Patriarchate of Constantinople and whose primate resides in the USA.

CHURCH AND STATE. The churches have been separated from the state since 1852, the year when the Anglican Church, the official church at the time, become a voluntary association similar to Canada's other denominations. Freedom of religion was proclaimed at the same time which today is expressed in the following terms in the Law Digest of Quebec: 'The enjoyment and free exercise of worship of every religious profession without distinction or preference are permitted by the constitution and laws of this province, but in a manner which does not serve as an excuse for licence neither authorizes practices which are incompatible with the peace and security of the province'. A similar situation exists in other provinces of Canada. Religious questions are not handled primarily by either provincial or federal authorities, but may come under the jurisdiction of either depending upon the issue in question. No public organization deals specifically with religious or ecclesiastical affairs.

Canadian public law is not specifically Christian, but throughout its history it has accorded a place of honour to all forms of Christianity, particularly Catholicism in Quebec. Religious groups have often enjoyed privileges, notably tax exemptions. In some provinces, including Quebec, education is organized according to religious preference. However, for some years now there has been an accelerated secularization of state institutions; and the separation of church and state, already a legal fact, has tended to become an increasing reality in practice. This evolution is especially evident in Quebec, which up to the early 1960s displayed under the Duplessis regime all the characteristics of a clerical state.

Pan-Indian Ecumenical Association of the USA & Canada, at their 1971 annual conference in Stoney Reserve, Alberta.

**INTERDENOMINATIONAL ORGANIZATIONS.** The Canadian Council of Churches (CCC) was founded in 1944, building on the foundations of many other prior organizations: Moral and Social Reform Council of Canada in 1907, Social Service Council of Canada in 1914, Religious Education Council of Canada in 1917, Committee on Evangelism in 1930, World Council of Churches Canadian Committee in 1938, Christian Social Council of Canada in 1939, University Christian Mission Committee in 1940, Inter-Church Committee on Missionary Education in 1941, Conference of Secretaries of Foreign Mission Boards in 1942 and Canadian Overseas Mission Council in 1944. Twenty-four regional and local ecumenical bodies work in co-operation with CCC. One such body which includes Catholic participation is the Joint Working Group of the Montreal Churches/Groupe de Travail des Eglises de Montréal, a bilingual body formed in 1970, consisting of 26 members officially appointed by the Catholic, United, Anglican, Presbyterian, Orthodox, Lutheran and Baptist churches. The Group is open to all denominations and serves as an authentic Council of Churches for Montreal.

The Office National d'Oecuménisme (French sector), founded in 1963, and the National Secretariat for Ecumenism (English sector), founded in 1966, are executive bodies of 2 ad hoc Catholic episcopal commissions charged with the organization and co-ordination of ecumenical activity in Catholic dioceses. The Council of Ecumenism, consisting of 10 members, assists them in a consultative capacity.

The Joint Working Group CCC-CCC (Canadian Council of Churches and Canadian Catholic Conference) was founded in 1968 on the model of the Joint Working Group of the Roman Secretariat for Unity and the World Council of Churches. Consisting of 7 members from each organization, it inspires and co-ordinates the activities of the Canadian churches. The Joint CCC-CCC Steering Committee on Poverty Strategy has a similar composition, but its aims and objectives are more limited. The 2 CCCs have also together created the Canadian Coalition for Development, a bilingual body grouping together some 20 Christian and non-Christian organizations interested in all aspects of development.

There are a number of other ecumenical centres and bodies. The Canadian Liturgical Society is an interdenominational English-speaking group which engages in study and research for the churches in collaboration with the Joint Working Group CCC-CCC. The Centre Oecuménique Diocésain of the Catholic archdiocese of Montreal, founded in 1960, handles information, dialogue and teaching on ecumenism. The Catholic Information Centre, founded in Toronto in 1958 and directed by Paulists (CSP) and laymen, engages in adult training in theology with an ecumenical orientation, including preparation of couples for mixed marriages. The Ecumenical Institute of Canada, founded in Toronto in 1963, and directed by the Canadian Council of Churches and the Canadian School of Missions, gives courses for theology students. The Centre d'Information et d'Oecuménisme, in Montreal, is sponsored jointly by the Consistory of Montreal and the United Church of Canada and gives special attention to youth.

Of ecumenical significance also is the fact that the Catholic Church has 6 members on the bilingual and interdenominational Faith and Constitution Commission and is involved in official dialogue bilingually with Anglicans and in English with Lutherans.

Centres devoted to interreligious dialogue are: (1) Centre Mi-ca-el, until 1965 known as the Centre Ratisbonne, a Catholic institution run by Notre-Dame de Sion sisters in collaboration with the National Office of Ecumenism, where study and dialogue between Judaism and Catholicism are carried on; (2) Centre Monchanin, founded in 1963, a non-confessional body which engages in research and organizes encounters between representatives of the major religions and cultures; (3) Institute of Islamic Studies, founded in 1952 at McGill University in Montreal, which has no religious affiliation but is devoted to research and the teaching of Islamics; (4) Canadian Council of Christians and Jews, in Toronto, which is a member of the International Council of Christians and Jews in London; and (5) Service Incroyance et Foi, a Catholic office in Montreal dedicated to dialogue with non-believers.

**BROADCASTING.** Virtually all networks in Canada accept religious programmes. The government Canadian Broadcasting Corporation does not allow outside-produced religious programmes, and broadcasts very few devotional-type programmes.

Religious programmes vary greatly from area to area. On radio, formats are generally short with religious messages ranging from one to 5 minutes in length. The Telephone-In Programme, and special seasonal programmes have longer time periods. On television, programmes are usually 30 minutes in length, though great use is made of one-minute announcements as well. In 1972 the CBC was producing 2 weekly half-hour programmes, 'Man Alive' and 'Hymn Sing'.

There are many Catholic production centres. In Cap-de-la-Madeleine, there is a Catholic station, Radio Marie, which also has a studio where programmes are produced for numerous radio stations throughout the country. In Montreal, there is Emissions Témoignage which sends out programmes on 50 Canadian stations; and the Commission de la Radio et de la TV. In Toronto, Interchurch Broadcasting works in collaboration with other churches and the National Catholic Communication Centre. This centre has a recording studio which co-operates with national radio and TV networks. For Catholics. Canada is a member of UNDA. Two Protestant stations in St John's, Newfoundland, are VOAR, owned by the Seventh-day Adventists, and VOWR, owned by Wesley United Church.

## BIBLIOGRAPHY


*A history of the churches in the United States and Canada.* R. T. Handy. Oxford History of the Christian Church. Oxford: Oxford University Press, 1977. 486p.

*Anglican year book, 1972.* Toronto: Anglican Church of Canada, 1972. 206p.

*Annuaire/Directory, 1969–1970.* Ottawa: Canadian Catholic Conference, 1970. (Roman Catholic).

*Church and sect in Canada.* S. D. Clark. Toronto: University of Toronto Press, 1965.

*Le Canada ecclésiastique/Catholic directory of Canada, 1971-72.* Montreal: Librairie Beauchemin, 1971.

*Religion in Canadian society.* Ed S. Crysdale & L. Wheatcroft. Toronto: Macmillan & MacLean Hunter, 1976.

*Religious denominations, 1971 Census of Canada.* Ottawa: Statistics Canada, 1973. (Detailed tables, maps).

*The Anglican Church in Canada: a history.* P. Carrington. Toronto: Collins, 1963. 320p.

*The changing church in Canada: beliefs and social attitudes of United Church people.* S. Crysdale. Toronto: United Church of Canada, 1965. 125p.

*The Christian church in Canada.* H. H. Walsh. Toronto: Ryerson Press, 1956, 1968. 355p.

*The church grows in Canada.* D Wilson. Toronto: Canadian Council of Churches, 1966. 224p.

'The Church in Canada' (map). P. Furse. Toronto: Canadian Council of Churches, 1966. (A detailed historical map).

*The churches and the Canadian experience: a Faith and Order study of the Christian tradition.* Ed J. W. Grant. Toronto: Ryerson Press, 1963.

*United Church of Canada year book, 1974.* 2 vols (volume I, Statistics). Toronto: UCC, 1974.

*Yearbook of American and Canadian churches, 1976.* Ed C. H. Jacquet, Jr. New York: NCCCUSA & Abingdon Press, 1976. 280p. (Annual for Canada since 1973 edition).


TABLE 2. ORGANIZED CHURCHES AND DENOMINATIONS IN CANADA

| Official name 1 | Begun 2 | Type 3 | Counc 4 | Congs 5 | Adults 6 | Affiliated 7 | Names, notes, and other statistics (see Codebook) 8 |
|---|---|---|---|---|---|---|---|
| African Methodist Episcopal Church | | I Met | Vw... | 3 | 1,000 | 3,000 | M=AMEC(USA). US Blacks. Canadian HQ Toronto, USA HQ New York. |
| African Orthodox Church | 1921 | I ARo | x.... | 1 | 500 | 1,000 | *AOC*. Begun 1919 in New York. Large Black community on east coast of Canada. |
| Anglican Church of Canada: | 1700 | A plu | AW,RW | 3,614 | 672,103 | 1,176,914 | 95% English-speaking. 27f,2H,25r,10s,2197t(150776),5v. 2095n, P=61%, 1600Y, 2,7967y. |
| Province of British Columbia: | 1914 | A plu | A | 377 | 61,332 | 114,434 | Extreme west and northwest. English-speaking. 240 95 3022 |
| D British Columbia | 1859 | A Cen | A | 75 | 15,186 | 27,733 | Only Vancouver Island. Decline in membership. W=19%. 64 72 66 732 |
| D Caledonia | 1879 | A plu | a | 45 | 3,476 | 9,153 | Assisted diocese. Rural, towns. 55% Indians. W=18%. 19 45 18 205 |
| D Cariboo | 1914 | A Cen | a | 49 | 2,919 | 7,598 | Assisted. 75% English, 21% Indian, 4% Asian. W=26%. 10 47 0 205 |
| D Kootenay | 1904 | A Cen | A | 77 | 8,722 | 15,970 | No Anglican Indians, Shared ministries with UCC. W=35%. 32 60 10 261 |
| D New Westminster | 1879 | A Cen | A | 101 | 30,229 | 48,813 | Vancouver, 25,000 sailors. Rapid urbanization. 1s,W=35%. 103 64 0 1605 |
| D Yukon | 1891 | A Cen | a | 30 | 800 | 5,167 | Assisted diocese. Mining boom. Many Indians. W=85%. 12 66 1 14 |
| Province of Canada: | 1862 | A plu | A | 1,180 | 182,676 | 332,405 | Extreme east of Canada; Anglicans 3%. French-speaking. 490 253 8242 |
| D Fredericton | 1845 | A Cen | A | 202 | 19,194 | 46,713 | 50% urban. 25% increase in members, 1965–69. W=46%. 83 82 123 929 |
| D Montreal | 1852 | A Cen | A | 151 | 42,113 | 69,890 | 99% English-speaking, 150 French-speaking. W=50%. 136 58 39 1677 |
| D Newfoundland (1976, 3 dioceses) | 1839 | A plu | A | 400 | 71,883 | 126,982 | 95% English. 1976, 3 dioceses: Central Eastern,Western. 98 38 55 3457 |
| D Nova Scotia | 1787 | A plu | A | 300 | 37,986 | 69,820 | First diocese in Canada. Urban, rural. English. W=54%. 123 68 26 1864 |
| D Quebec | 1793 | A Cen | A | 127 | 11,500 | 19,000 | 50% urban. All congregations English-speaking. W=35%. 50 59 10 315 |
| Province of Ontario: | 1912 | A plu | A | 1,189 | 323,864 | 526,931 | North of the Great Lakes. Anglicans English-speaking. 942 770 12292 |
| D Algoma | 1873 | A Hig | A | 169 | 17,190 | 30,932 | Rural, urban, English, French, Indians. Decline. W=34%. 67 68 86 722 |
| D Huron | 1857 | A Cen | A | 285 | 62,254 | 109,000 | English-speaking. Steady growth of members. W=41%. 180 65 0 2627 |
| D Moosonee | 1872 | A plu | a | 51 | 6,410 | 13,555 | Assisted diocese. 90% rural. 3,400 Indians. W=66%. 26 74 14 475 |
| D Niagara | 1875 | A Hig | A | 126 | 55,150 | 93,985 | Largely urban, with rural parishes. W=32%. 112 55 178 1770 |
| D Ontario | 1862 | A Hig | A | 114 | 16,751 | 34,251 | Urban, rural. Ministry to tourists. 53b,68t(4029),W=25%. 64 81 61 711 |
| D Ottawa | 1896 | A Cen | A | 150 | 34,970 | 53,333 | Mainly English-speaking. Capital city of Canada. 78b. 115 74 37 1097 |
| D Toronto | 1839 | A plu | A | 294 | 131,139 | 191,875 | Two-thirds urban. English, 1 Japanese church. W=34%. 378 61 394 4890 |
| Province of Rupert's Land: | 1875 | A plu | A | 868 | 104,231 | 203,144 | Vast area in centre and centre west of Canada. 423 482 4411 |
| D Athabasca | 1914 | A Cen | a | 60 | 2,661 | 8,261 | Assisted. Includes Episcopal District of Mackenzie. W=46%. 21 54 150 27 |
| D Brandon | 1924 | A plu | a | 77 | 7,601 | 17,080 | Assisted. Rural, mining. Some Indians. Decline. 28 62 0 424 |
| D Calgary | 1888 | A plu | A | 113 | 18,230 | 33,992 | Half rural. 90% English, 9% Indian, 1% Japanese. W=32%. 74 63 0 892 |
| D Edmonton | 1913 | A Hig | A | 77 | 12,500 | 22,930 | Rural, continual migration to towns. Central Alberta. 65 60 41 593 |
| D Keewatin | 1902 | A plu | a | 67 | 9,000 | 13,492 | Assisted diocese. 4,200 Indians. 2 aircraft. W=39%. 23 76 37 109 |
| D Qu'Appelle | 1884 | A Hig | a | 183 | 11,666 | 21,010 | Assisted diocese. Some Ukrainians, Indians. 1s,W=52%. 54 60 44 417 |
| D Rupert's Land | 1849 | A Low | A | 88 | 19,103 | 35,437 | Urban, rural fringe. All English. W=39%. 72 69 196 848 |
| D Saskatchewan | 1932 | A Eva | a | 77 | 6,500 | 14,404 | Assisted diocese. Rural. 25 Indian missions. W=40%. 27 55 0 300 |
| D Saskatoon | 1874 | A Cen | A | 90 | 6,970 | 13,538 | Rural. 93% English, 7% Cree Indians. 1s. 41 61 14 301 |
| D The Arctic | 1933 | A Low | a | 36 | 10,000 | 23,000 | Assisted diocese. 43% Eskimo (=80% all Eskimos). W=68%. 18 32 0 500 |
| Antiochian Orth Archdiocese of Toledo | c1940 | O Ara | ..... | 1 | 200 | 500 | In communion with Greek P Antioch. HQ Toledo, Ohio (USA). Arabs. 1nx. |

*Continued opposite*

*Table 2 – continued*

| Official name 1 | Begun 2 | Type 3 | Counc 4 | Congs 5 | Adults 6 | Affiliated 7 | Names, notes, and other statistics (see Codebook) 8 | | | | |
|---|---|---|---|---|---|---|---|---|---|---|---|
| Antiochian Orth Christian AD New York | | O Ara | Cwo.f | 8 | 16,000 | 25,000 | Formerly Syrian Antiochian Orth Ch. HQ Montreal. Under Greek P Antioch. Arabs. 6n. | | | | |
| Apostolic Christian Church (Nazarean) | | P Hol | x.... | 11 | 533 | 715 | Swiss immigrants related to Mennonites. In 17 nations. 32n,31t(320). | | | | |
| Apostolic Church in Canada | 1924 | P PeA | Z..X. | 20 | 1,000 | 2,000 | Related to Apostolic Church (UK). HQ Toronto. Missions in West Africa. | | | | |
| Apostolic Ch of Pentecost in Canada | 1921 | P Pe1 | x.... | 100 | 12,000 | 30,000 | Schism ex PAoC over Jesus-only teaching. Ukrainians, Germans, Scandinavians. 3s. | | | | |
| Apostolic Faith Mission of Canada | 1910 | P Pe3 | x.... | 8 | 700 | 1,000 | HQ Portland, Oregon (USA). Strongest in Alberta. 8n,G=2.1%pa,W=75%,50Y. | | | | |
| Armenian Apostolic Church: D Canada | 1930 | O Arm | Ewc.W | 4 | 10,000 | 15,000 | *Armenian Ch of N America. Gregorians.* Under jurisdiction C Echmiadzin (USSR). 4n. | | | | |
| Armenian Evangelical Union of Chs | | P Con | RW... | 3 | 200 | 500 | Linked with unions in Middle East, France, USA. Armenian World War I refugees. | | | | |
| Associated Gospel Churches | 1922 | P CBr | ..... | 104 | 7,000 | 20,000 | Founded as Christian Workers Church of Canada. Plymouth Brethren. 167n,101t. | | | | |
| Assoc of Independent Holiness Churches | 1958 | P Hol | ..... | 17 | 350 | 650 | Small denomination in holiness tradition. 10n,1s(2),W=75%. | | | | |
| Assoc of Regular Baptist Churches of C | 1926 | P Bap | .T..T | | 5,000 | 7,000 | Association of local congregations. Schism ex Baptist Conv of Ontario & Quebec. | | | | |
| Baptist Federation of Canada: | 1944 | P Bap | Tv..W | 1,131 | 134,245 | 250,800 | *Federation Baptists.* Supports M=CBOMB. 874n,G=−1.2%pa,973t(54899),2899Y. | | | | |
| Baptist Conv of Ontario & Quebec | | P Bap | .v... | 380 | 48,372 | 100,000 | *Convention Baptists.* 18 Associations. Declining. 389n,380t(17644),1011Y. | | | | |
| Baptist Union of Western Canada | 1873 | P Bap | Tv... | 145 | 17,265 | 50,000 | HQ Edmonton, Alberta. 159n,G=−0.7%pa,1p(12),132t(14522),W=30%,387Y. | | | | |
| French Baptist Union | 1855 | P Bap | ..... | 10 | 400 | 800 | *Union d'Eglises Baptistes Françaises.* Grand Ligne Mission. 14n,G=0,W=56%,21Y. | | | | |
| United Baptist Conv of Atlantic Prov | 1848 | P Bap | ..... | 596 | 68,208 | 100,000 | Prov=Provinces. Convention Baptists. 312n,1p,1s(30),461t(22683),1390Y. | | | | |
| Baptist General Conference | | P Bap | TF... | 110 | 12,432 | 20,000 | *BGC.* In west, Swedes from USA. 3 conferences: Central, Alberta, Columbia. 30Y. | | | | |
| Bible Holiness Movement | 1949 | P Hol | x.... | 7 | 103 | 300 | HQ Vancouver. Work in USA, India, Nigeria, Philippines. 5n,G=28%pa,W=49%. | | | | |
| Brethren in Christ Church | 1788 | P Men | GF..E | 27 | 1,466 | 12,000 | *Canadian Conference. Tunkers.* Ontario, Saskatchewan. HQ Sherkston. 47n,27t(2806). | | | | |
| Bulgarian Orthodox Church | | O Sla | MwO.. | 2 | 3,000 | 7,000 | Bulgarian immigrants. Under P Sofia. Parish and cathedral in Toronto. | | | | |
| Byelorussian Autocephalic Orth Ch in C | 1948 | O Sla | x.... | 1 | 500 | 1,000 | White Russians. 1922 attempt at autonomy in USSR crushed. 1 bishop, HQ USA. | | | | |
| Canadian Baptist Conference | 1959 | P Bap | ..... | 25 | 1,688 | 5,000 | In BC despite SBC(USA) agreement not to work in Canada. 23n,25t(2633).111Y. | | | | |
| **Catholic Church of Canada:** | 1534 | R LEr | Bz..R | 4,890 | 5,989,500 | 9,074,959 | L, B. *Eglise Catholique.* C=63+17+196. 11q,15s. | 13749nx, | 5946m, | 44364w, | 179085Yy. |
| M Edmonton | 1871 | R Lat | Bs | 94 | 91,900 | 139,237 | Eng Alb English-French, Polish, German. | 200 | 39 | 728 | 3548 |
| D Calgary | 1912 | R Lat | Bs | 73 | 74,600 | 113,000 | Eng Alb English-speaking. | 152 | 23 | 202 | 2774 |
| D St Paul in Alberta | 1948 | R Lat | Bs | 66 | 13,900 | 21,049 | Fre Alb French-speaking. | 35 | 1 | 135 | 641 |
| M Grouard-McLennan | 1862 | R Lat | Pomi | 42 | 20,300 | 30,789 | Fre Alb Very extended. 40% Indians, mixed. P=86%. | 60 | 12 | 126 | 967 |
| D Mackenzie-Fort Smith | 1901 | R Lat | Pomi | 46 | 12,500 | 18,927 | Fre NWT Missionary diocese, 5 towns. P=50%. | 48 | 29 | 101 | 613 |
| D Prince George | 1944 | R Lat | Pomi | 92 | 17,200 | 26,000 | Eng BC Missionary diocese. P=68%. | 30 | 14 | 49 | 754 |
| D Whitehorse | 1944 | R Lat | Pomi | 2 | 3,900 | 5,910 | Eng Yuk Mining area, consmopolitan influx. P=56%. | 23 | 4 | 13 | 197 |
| M Halifax | 1842 | R Lat | Bs | 50 | 79,200 | 120,000 | Eng NS Many charismatics, including archbishop. 1s. | 127 | 1 | 460 | 2426 |
| D Antigonish | 1844 | R Lat | Bs | 92 | 82,300 | 124,684 | Eng NS 8-parish industrial mission. D=pc,Synod. | 199 | 16 | 664 | 2946 |
| D Charlottetown | 1829 | R Lat | Bs | 61 | 30,100 | 45,677 | Eng PEI 1976: 1,000 charismatics (15 priests). | 86 | 0 | 270 | 1037 |
| D Yarmouth | 1953 | R Lat | Bs | 25 | 20,700 | 31,392 | Fre NS Relative poverty and emigration. D=pc,sc. | 49 | 1 | 93 | 562 |
| M Keewatin–Le Pas | 1910 | R Lat | Pomi | 34 | 15,200 | 23,000 | Fre Man Missionary diocese, many Indians. P=79%. | 54 | 28 | 140 | 720 |
| D Churchill-Baie d'Hudson | 1925 | R Lat | Pomi | 16 | 2,400 | 3,589 | Fre Man Mainly Indians. P=49%. | 23 | 6 | 14 | 139 |
| D Labrador-Schefferville | 1945 | R Lat | Pomi | 20 | 12,100 | 18,366 | Fre Que 1,600 Indians and Eskimos. P=99%. | 26 | 8 | 34 | 597 |
| D Moosonee | 1938 | R Lat | Pomi | 14 | 2,300 | 3,500 | Fre Ont Indian work. P=44%. | 15 | 21 | 25 | 255 |
| M Kingston | 1826 | R Lat | Bs | 52 | 35,900 | 54,337 | Eng Ont English-speaking. D=PC. | 95 | 1 | 305 | 1454 |
| D Alexandria-Cornwall | 1890 | R Lat | Bs | 33 | 35,600 | 54,000 | Fre Ont English-French. D=pc. | 57 | 14 | 170 | 910 |
| D Peterborough | 1882 | R Lat | Bs | 33 | 24,200 | 36,730 | Eng Ont English-speaking. | 57 | 1 | 193 | 961 |
| D Sault Sainte-Marie | 1904 | R Lat | Bs | 98 | 105,600 | 160,000 | Eng Ont 60% English-, 40% French-speaking. | 243 | 6 | 550 | 4727 |
| M Moncton | 1936 | R Lat | Bs | 48 | 46,900 | 71,048 | Fre NB 75% French, 25% English. D=pc,PC. | 145 | 20 | 463 | 1534 |
| D Bathurst in Canada | 1860 | R Lat | Bs | 70 | 66,400 | 100,687 | Fre NB All French-speaking. | 121 | 31 | 455 | 2116 |
| D Edmundston | 1944 | R Lat | Bs | 31 | 32,700 | 49,569 | Fre NB 92% French-speaking. D=pc. | 80 | 30 | 284 | 938 |
| D St John, New Brunswick | 1842 | R Lat | Bs | 51 | 44,700 | 67,762 | Eng NB All English-speaking. D=pc. | 111 | 3 | 269 | 1896 |
| M Montréal | 1836 | R Lat | Bs | 275 | 1,099,000 | 1,665,000 | Fre Que Parishes: 212 French, 34 English. D=pc,1s. | 2201 | 1175 | 9590 | 24402 |
| D Joliette | 1904 | R Lat | Bs | 166 | 77,900 | 118,006 | Fre Que French-speaking. 98% Catholic. D=pc. | 235 | 141 | 793 | 1578 |
| D Saint-Jean de Québec | 1933 | R Lat | Bs | 88 | 204,600 | 310,032 | Fre Que French. Urban. 84% RC. D=pc,PC bc,sc. | 296 | 195 | 853 | 5084 |
| D Saint-Jérôme | 1951 | R Lat | Bs | 62 | 115,700 | 175,290 | Fre Que French. 29% RC. D=pc,PC; Synod abandoned. | 238 | 261 | 418 | 2905 |
| D Valleyfield | 1892 | R Lat | Bs | 63 | 82,000 | 124,168 | Fre Que French-speaking, with bilingual zones. | 185 | 117 | 523 | 2247 |
| M Ottawa | 1847 | R Lat | Bs | 108 | 173,700 | 263,113 | Fre Ont Parishes: 63 French, 29 English. 1s. | 515 | 333 | 1600 | 4118 |
| D Hearst | 1938 | R Lat | Bs | 47 | 21,100 | 31,914 | Fre Ont French-speaking half rural. D=pc,PC. | 44 | 6 | 83 | 640 |
| D Hull | 1963 | R Lat | Bs | 63 | 92,100 | 139,497 | Fre Que 95% French-speaking. 91% RC. D=PC. | 181 | 27 | 422 | 2927 |
| D Mont-Laurier | 1913 | R Lat | Bs | 62 | 45,200 | 68,525 | Fre Que French-speaking. Tourism ministry. 98% RC. | 131 | 21 | 354 | 1036 |
| D Pembroke | 1898 | R Lat | Bs | 52 | 34,800 | 52,779 | Eng Que Parishes: 65% English, 35% French. | 92 | 2 | 345 | 1270 |
| D Timmins | 1915 | R Lat | Bs | 79 | 62,500 | 94,722 | Fre Que 90% English, 10% French | 127 | 45 | 359 | 3125 |
| M Québec | 1674 | R Lat | Bs | 276 | 526,500 | 797,814 | Fre Que French, urban. 99% RC. D=pc,PC,bc,1c. 1s. | 1533 | 949 | 6884 | 11791 |
| D Amos | 1938 | R Lat | Bs | 79 | 63,200 | 95,719 | Fre Que French-speaking, rural. 95% RC. D=pc. | 118 | 52 | 415 | 1906 |
| D Chicoutimi | 1878 | R Lat | Bs | 95 | 168,000 | 254,568 | Fre Que French. 99% RC. D=pc,PC,bc,sc,1c. 1s. | 450 | 186 | 1250 | 4102 |
| D Sainte Anne de-la-Pocatière | 1951 | R Lat | Bs | 54 | 59,600 | 90,252 | Fre Que French, rural. 100% RC. D=pc,PC,bc,1c. | 200 | 32 | 564 | 1454 |
| D Trois-Rivières | 1852 | R Lat | Bs | 100 | 154,100 | 233,469 | Fre Que French, urban. 98% RC. D=pc, Synod. 1s. | 402 | 323 | 1546 | 2988 |
| M Regina | 1910 | R Lat | Bs | 101 | 62,700 | 95,000 | Eng Sas English-speaking. D=pc. | 167 | 20 | 350 | 2465 |
| D Gravelbourg | 1930 | R Lat | Bs | 27 | 10,700 | 16,275 | Fre Sas French-speaking, rural. D=pc. | 41 | 8 | 142 | 330 |
| D Prince Albert | 1907 | R Lat | Bs | 53 | 27,000 | 40,988 | Fre Sas Immigrants from Europe and eastern Canada. | 101 | 9 | 258 | 946 |
| D Saskatoon | 1933 | R Lat | Bs | 42 | 26,000 | 39,336 | Eng Sas 75% English, 5% French, 20% others. | 79 | 7 | 238 | 1090 |
| **AN Saint Peter-Muenster** | 1921 | R Lat | Bs | 26 | 8,500 | 12,900 | Eng Sas English-speaking, rural. | 36 | 11 | 85 | 225 |
| M Rimouski | 1867 | R Lat | Bs | 118 | 109,100 | 165,305 | Fre Que French, half urban. 90% RC. D=Synod. 1s. | 319 | 104 | 1327 | 2515 |
| D Gaspé | 1922 | R Lat | Bs | 66 | 66,400 | 100,606 | Fre Que 90% French, rural. 89% RC. D=pc. | 131 | 20 | 490 | 1722 |
| D Hauterive | 1905 | R Lat | Bs | 48 | 59,200 | 89,770 | Fre Que French. 50% urban. Charismatics strong. | 104 | 29 | 331 | 1832 |
| M Saint-Boniface | 1847 | R Lat | Bs | 70 | 48,900 | 74,125 | Fre Man Half urban. D=pc. 1s. | 157 | 40 | 647 | 1665 |
| M Saint John's, Newfoundland | 1847 | R Lat | Bs | 39 | 56,000 | 84,840 | Eng New English, half in capital. D=pc. | 74 | 62 | 386 | 2582 |
| D Grand Falls | 1856 | R Lat | Bs | 27 | 21,800 | 33,000 | Eng New English-speaking. | 36 | 14 | 68 | 1285 |
| D Saint George's | 1904 | R Lat | Bs | 20 | 26,900 | 40,723 | Eng New English-speaking, half urban. | 30 | 13 | 79 | 1308 |
| M Sherbrooke | 1874 | R Lat | Bs | 133 | 129,400 | 196,038 | Fre Que French-speaking. D=pc,PC. 93% RC. 1st,1v. | 492 | 307 | 1790 | 3623 |
| D Nicolet | 1885 | R Lat | Bs | 85 | 101,900 | 154,388 | Fre Que French. D=pc,PC. 99% RC. | 292 | 199 | 1005 | 2455 |
| D Saint-Hyacinthe | 1852 | R Lat | Bs | 112 | 169,300 | 256,513 | Fre Que French-speaking. D=pc. 94% RC. 1s. | 398 | 371 | 1747 | 4367 |
| M Toronto | 1841 | R Lat | Bs | 170 | 432,300 | 655,000 | Eng Ont English, urban. Italian, Portuguese. 1s. | 728 | 350 | 601 | 18008 |
| D Hamilton | 1856 | R Lat | Bs | 106 | 147,700 | 223,769 | Eng Ont English-speaking. D=pc. | 286 | 60 | 651 | 6491 |
| D London | 1855 | R Lat | Bs | 143 | 183,700 | 278,286 | Eng Ont English, French minority. D=pc,PC.1s. | 380 | 43 | 959 | 6413 |
| D Saint Catharines | 1958 | R Lat | Bs | 47 | 62,000 | 93,893 | Eng Ont English-speaking. | 102 | 6 | 137 | 2353 |
| D Thunder Bay | 1952 | R Lat | Bs | 89 | 36,300 | 55,000 | Eng Ont Missionary diocese. English. | 71 | 6 | 103 | 1478 |
| M Vancouver | 1890 | R Lat | Bs | 69 | 99,000 | 150,000 | Eng BC Urban. English, with minorities. D=pc. 1s. | 179 | 30 | 410 | 3485 |
| D Kamloops | 1945 | R Lat | Bs | 21 | 12,400 | 18,800 | Eng BC English-speaking, half rural. | 27 | 4 | 44 | 667 |
| D Nelson | 1936 | R Lat | Bs | 37 | 22,300 | 33,798 | Eng BC English-speaking, rural. | 48 | 2 | 57 | 571 |
| D Victoria | 1846 | R Lat | Bs | 52 | 21,800 | 33,000 | Eng BC English. Virtually a missionary diocese. | 52 | 8 | 175 | 788 |
| AD Winnipeg | 1915 | R Lat | bs | 74 | 64,300 | 97,500 | Eng Man English-speaking. | 162 | 0 | 385 | 2441 |
| M Winnipeg (*Ukrainian*) | 1912 | R Ukr | Os | 41 | 39,600 | 60,000 | Eng Man Widespread use of Ukrainian in churches. | 60 | 2 | 25 | 1045 |
| D Edmonton (*Ukrainian*) | 1948 | R Ukr | Os | 154 | 34,300 | 51,985 | Eng Alberta, BC, Yukon, western NWT. | 64 | 22 | 35 | 1000 |
| D Saskatoon (*Ukrainian*) | 1951 | R Ukr | Os | 38 | 23,100 | 35,000 | Eng Sas French- and Ukrainian-speaking. | 39 | 5 | 40 | 1000 |
| D Toronto (*Ukrainian*) | 1948 | R Ukr | Os | 70 | 36,300 | 55,000 | Eng Ontario, Quebec, NS, NB, Newfoundland. | 101 | 20 | 57 | 650 |
| Christadelphian Ecclesias in Canada | | P Adv | x.... | 29 | 1,500 | 2,000 | Loose relationship with Birmingham HQ (UK). 29 ecclesias (churches). Pacifist. | | | | |
| Christian & Missionary Alliance in C | 1889 | P Hol | xF..E | 188 | 10,937 | 21,355 | *CMA.* HQ Nyack(USA). Members mostly in Alberta. 200n,G=1.7%pa,1s,178t(25951). | | | | |
| Christian Brethren | | P CBr | x.... | 380 | 10,000 | 20,000 | *Open Brethren.* Mainly Ontario, BC, Quebec. 150 missionaries abroad. 185m. | | | | |
| Christian Brethren (Exclusive) | | P EBr | x.... | | 3,000 | 5,000 | Groups: Booth, Ames, Continuing Tumbridge Wells, Raven-Taylor, Kelly-Continental. | | | | |
| Christian Church (Disciples of Christ) | 1813 | P Dis | xW..W | 41 | 2,916 | 8,039 | *All Canada Committee.* Related to USA denomination. HQ Toronto. 47n,41t(2554). | | | | |
| Christian Churches & Chs of Christ | 1820 | P Dis | x.... | 115 | 5,036 | 10,000 | *Churches of Christ* (*Non-Instrumental*). No central organization. 56n,77t(3265). | | | | |
| Christian Congregation | | P Hol | ..... | 9 | 1,434 | 2,000 | From rural mountainous USA; HQ Monroe, North Carolina. Holiness body. 9n,9t(928). | | | | |
| Christian Reformed Churches in Canada | | P Ref | .F... | 175 | 34,826 | 70,747 | Dutch immigrants from Holland. Schism in USA ex Reformed Ch in America. 149n. | | | | |
| Church of Christ, Scientist | | M Sci | x.... | 87 | 10,000 | 25,000 | *Christian Science.* M=CCS(Boston, USA). 41 churches in Ontario, 25 in BC. 24m,96w. | | | | |
| Church of God in Canada | | P Pe3 | ZF... | 25 | 1,000 | 3,000 | M=CoG(Cleveland) (USA). 2 Divisions: Eastern, Western. Holiness Pentecostals. | | | | |
| Church of God in Christ, Mennonite | c1880 | P Men | G.... | 12 | 2,183 | 4,000 | Branch of USA Mennonite body. Immigrants over the years. 25n. | | | | |
| Church of God of Prophecy in Canada | 1937 | P Pe3 | Z.... | 30 | 650 | 1,150 | Ex CoG(Cleveland). BC,Man,Alberta,Sask,Ont,Quebec. 42n,G=22%pa,29t(1287),W=70%. | | | | |
| Church of God (Anderson) | c1920 | P Hol | x.... | 46 | 2,122 | 4,000 | HQ Anderson, USA. Holiness denomination. Mainly in Alberta. 1s,46t(3515),W=80%. | | | | |
| Church of Jesus C of Latter-day Saints | 1832 | M LdS | x.... | 214 | 30,000 | 67,890 | *Mormons.* 11 Stakes. Temple: Cardston. 1239n,740f,G=4%pa,214t(29400),12000Y. | | | | |
| Church of the First-Born | c1960 | I ind | x.... | 10 | 500 | 1,000 | Blacks from Barbados & Jamaica (HQ Kingston). Branches in UK, USA. Strict ethics. | | | | |
| Church of the Lutheran Brethren | | P Lut | x.... | | 200 | 500 | Based on USA. HQ Fergus Falls, Manitoba. | | | | |
| Church of the Nazarene | 1911 | P Hol | xF... | 160 | 7,394 | 20,000 | Mainly in Alberta. HQ Calgary. World HQ in USA. 200n,1s. | | | | |
| Church of the New Jerusalem | | M Swe | x.... | 6 | 200 | 500 | *Swedenborgian Ch.* USA-related. 2 Societies (Toronto, Kitchener), 2 Circles. 2n. | | | | |
| Chs of God in the British I & Overseas | | P EBr | x.... | 6 | 300 | 600 | I=Isles. *Chs of God in the Fellowship of the Son of God.* Ex Open Brethren in UK. | | | | |
| Convention of Regular Baptists of BC | | P Bap | ..... | | 500 | 1,000 | Independent groupings of Regular Baptists. HQ Vancouver (British Columbia). | | | | |
| Cooneyites | | P ind | x.... | | 7,000 | 10,000 | *Go-Preachers.* 1,500 in Alberta. Itinerants. 300,000 others in UK, USA, Australia. | | | | |
| Coptic Orthodox Church in Canada | 1961 | O Cop | NwaNw | 4 | 16,000 | 25,000 | Egyptian immigrants since 1965 in Montreal, Toronto, Ottawa. Rapid growth. | | | | |
| Estonian Evangelical Alliance Church | | P ind | ..... | | 200 | 500 | Estonian refugees from USSR. HQ Vancouver, BC. | | | | |
| Estonian Orthodox Church | c1940 | O Sla | C.... | 3 | 500 | 1,000 | Refugees from USSR. Parishes: Toronto, Montreal, Vancouver. HQ Los Angeles (USA). | | | | |
| Evangelical Church in Canada | c1850 | P Hol | ....E | 50 | 3,736 | 10,000 | *Northwest Canada Conference.* EUB members rejecting 1968 UCC merger. 62n,50t. | | | | |
| Evangelical Covenant Ch of Canada | 1904 | P Con | K.... | 23 | 1,044 | 2,000 | Branch of USA body. Ethnic Scandinavians. HQ Edmonton. 13n,21t(1751). | | | | |
| Evangelical Free Church of Canada | | P Con | KF..E | 80 | 300 | 500 | Branch of Ev Free Ch of America. Especially in Western Canada. HQ Vancouver. | | | | |
| Evangelical Lutheran Church of Canada | 1880 | P Lut | LW... | 337 | 52,768 | 83,274 | *ELCC.* Formerly in American LC. 242n,G=2.5%pa,2p,1s(19),285t(23746),W=21%,1895Yy. | | | | |
| Ev Mennonite Brethren Conference | c1880 | P Men | G.... | 16 | 1,645 | 3,000 | *Defenseless Mennonites.* Branch of USA body. Immigrants from Russia. 25n. | | | | |
| Evangelical Mennonite Conference | 1874 | P Men | GF... | 38 | 4,000 | 6,000 | *Kleingemeinde.* Branches in Mexico, Nicaragua, Paraguay. 70n,G=1.7%pa,1p,144Y. | | | | |
| Ev Mennonite Mission Conference | 1874 | P Men | G.... | 23 | 1,850 | 3,000 | *Rudnerweide.* Dutch-German. Branch in Belize, CAmerica. 58n,G=1.1%pa,2p,40Y. | | | | |
| Fellowship of Ev Baptist Churches in C | c1925 | P Bap | ..... | 350 | 34,000 | 110,000 | Ex BCOQ; 1953 union Regular Baptists. Aided by CBHMS(USA). 335n,G=1.5%pa,2s. | | | | |

*Continued overleaf*

*Table 2–continued*

| Official name 1 | Begun 2 | Type 3 | Counc 4 | Congs 5 | Adults 6 | Affiliated 7 | Names, notes, and other statistics (see Codebook) 8 |
|---|---|---|---|---|---|---|---|
| Free Methodist Church in Canada | 1876 | P Hol | VF..E | 175 | 5,379 | 15,000 | Strong in Alberta, West, Ontario. Schism, United Holiness Ch. G=0.9%pa,W=71%,466z. |
| Free Reformed Ch of North America | | P Ref | ..... | 10 | 2,525 | 3,000 | In independent Reformed traditions. 2 churches also in USA. |
| General Conference Mennonite Church | c1880 | P Men | G.... | 151 | 20,553 | 30,000 | *Conference of Mennonites in Canada*. (HQ USA). HQ Winnipeg. 300n,4s. |
| Glad Tidings Churches | | P Pe2 | x.... | | 1,000 | 2,000 | HQ Vancouver. Missions in 7 nations, especially Uganda and China (Taiwan.). |
| Gospel Missionary Association | | P Bap | ..... | 20 | 1,500 | 3,000 | Fundamentalist churches. Mainly in Alberta. HQ Calgary. |
| Greek Ch of True Orthodox Christians | | O Gre | ..... | 2 | 2,000 | 3,000 | Ex GOC, claiming restoration of authentic Orthodoxy. Parishes: Montreal, Toronto. |
| Greek Orthodox AD of N & S America | | O Gre | CwO.W | 34 | 140,000 | 210,000 | *9th Archdiocesan District* (*Canada*). Under EP Constantinople. 124,000 Greeks. 28n. |
| Holy Cath Apost & Roman Renewed Ch | 1960 | C CCa | ..... | 2 | 1,000 | 2,000 | *Eglise du Christ-Roi Rénovée*. HQ Clémery (France). Papal claimant Clement XV. |
| Hutterian Brethren | 1918 | P Men | x.... | 130 | 4,613 | 14,100 | *Hutterites*. Descendants of Swiss Brethren. Pacifists. Alberta, Manitoba, Saskatchewan. |
| Independent Assemblies of God, Canada | c1945 | P Pe4 | ..... | 105 | 2,500 | 5,500 | Links with Pentecostal movement in Sweden. 165n,1s(Temple Bible College),50t. |
| Independent Holiness Church | 1938 | P Hol | ..... | 12 | 400 | 800 | *Holiness Movement of Canada*, rejecting 1958 merger in Free Methodist Ch. 13n. |
| Internat Ch of the Foursquare Gospel | 1934 | P Pe2 | ZF.X. | 26 | 4,600 | 15,000 | Branch of ICFG (Los Angeles, USA). In Western Canada. HQ Burnaby, Vancouver. 1s. |
| Italian Pentecostal Church of Canada | 1913 | P Pe2 | ...X. | 14 | 1,300 | 3,000 | Ex Italian Presbyterian Ch. Links with PAoC. Missions to Italy. 12n,10t(1402). |
| Jehovah's Witnesses | 1880 | M Jeh | x.... | 821 | 50,105 | 175,000 | *Témoins de Jéhovah. IBSA*. 31 congregations on Newfoundland (begun 1910). 3907Y. |
| Latter Rain Assemblies | 1947 | P Pe4 | x.... | | 200 | 500 | Schism ex PAoC in Saskatoon, as a Pentecostal renewal. HQ North Battleford. 1s. |
| Latvian Ev Lutheran Ch Outside Latvia | 1948 | P Lut | LW... | 24 | 5,654 | 8,000 | *Latvijas Evangeliské Luteriské Baznica*. From USSR. 15n,G=−1.2%pa,W=30%,57y,150z. |
| Liberal Catholic Church | 1925 | C Lib | xv... | 5 | 250 | 1,000 | Branch of LCC of the USA. Ex ORCC. Theosophical. World HQ London (UK). 7n. |
| Lutheran Ch in America, Canada Section | 1763 | P Lut | Lw..W | 347 | 81,945 | 121,202 | Synods: Central, Eastern,Western. A=1962. 314n,G=0.3%pa,2s(25),300t(28906),3050Yy. |
| Lutheran Church—Canada | 1854 | P Lut | x.... | 375 | 65,459 | 98,097 | *LC-C*. In LCMS(Missouri Synod) (St Louis, MO, USA). HQ Edmonton. 287n,337t(29037). |
| Macedonian Orthodox Church | | O Sla | cv... | | 500 | 1,000 | Yugoslavs from Macedonia; canonical orthodoxy disputed. Overlea, Toronto. |
| Mennonite Brethren Chs of NAmerica | c1880 | P Men | GF..E | 135 | 17,982 | 30,000 | *Canadian Conference*. Branches: USA, 14 nations. Russians. 252n,1j,4s,130t(18293). |
| Mennonite Church in Canada | | P Men | G.... | | 9,793 | 14,000 | Old Colony, Bergthaler, Chortitz, Reinland and Sommerfelder congregations. |
| Mennonite Church (Canada) | 1898 | P Men | G.... | 90 | 8,984 | 13,000 | *Region I* of MCNAmerica (HQ USA). HQ Kitchener, Ontario. 81n,67t(10004). |
| Missionary Church—Canada | 1883 | P Hol | xF... | 77 | 4,121 | 6,000 | Districts Canada West,Ontario. Formerly Mennonite. 91n,G=4.3%pa,2s,52t(6600),551Y. |
| Moravian Church in America | 1771 | P Mor | xw..f | 15 | 1,005 | 1,583 | *Canadian District*, American Province North, Labrador Province, Unity of Brethren. 11n. |
| Native American Church | c1900 | I mar | x...I | | 20,000 | 40,000 | *NAC*. From USA, among all American Indian tribes. Strict ethics; peyote eating. |
| Native Evangelical Fellowship of Canada | 1967 | I ind | ....I | 23 | 3,000 | 5,000 | *NEF*. Founded as Indigenous Indian Fellowship within Northern Canada Ev Mission. |
| New Apostolic Church | c1880 | C CAp | x.... | 1,000 | 130,000 | 200,000 | *Canada Church Bezirk*(also UK, Asia, SAmerica). HQ Dortmund (Germany). Germans. |
| New Testament Church of God | c1940 | P Pe3 | ZF.X. | 21 | 800 | 2,000 | *Ch of God* (*Cleveland*). HQ USA. Includes many Jamaicans and other West Indians. 2s. |
| North American Baptist General Conf | 1865 | P Bap | xF... | 102 | 18,000 | 50,000 | German Baptist immigrants. USA body. HQ Winnipeg. 102n,G=1.4%pa,92t(12570),413Y. |
| Old Believers Russian Orthodox Church | | O OBe | x.... | | 200 | 500 | *Old Ritualist Ancient Orthodox Christians;* 1667 schism in Russia. USSR refugees. |
| Old Calendar Greek Orth Ch in NAmer | c1950 | O OCd | c.... | | 2,000 | 3,000 | 1924 schism in Greece ex GOC rejecting New Calendar. 1974, D Montreal formed. |
| Old Order & Wisler Mennonite Chs | 1886 | P Men | G.... | 70 | 2,100 | 3,000 | Branch of USA Mennonite body (Ohio). Schism ex Mennonite Church. 15n. |
| Old Roman Catholic Church | c1960 | C CCa | .v... | 2 | 500 | 1,000 | *ORCC, Orthodox Orders*. HQ Havelock, Ontario. 1967 applied to join WCC and CCC. |
| Orthodox Ch in America: AD Canada | | O Sla | MwO.f | 52 | 30,000 | 50,000 | *OCA*. Russian refugees. 1970, given autocephalous status by P Moscow. 18n,3x(USA). |
| Pentecostal Assemblies of Canada | 1910 | P Pe2 | ZF.XE | 810 | 110,000 | 170,000 | *PAoC*.80% English, 8% Amerindian, 5% German. 4% Slav,2% French. 1150n,1H,5r,7s,831t(100000). |
| Pentecostal Assemblies of Newfoundland | 1925 | P Pe2 | ZF.X. | 139 | 12,000 | 24,000 | Close co-operation with Pentecostal Assemblies of Canada. 50 schools. 287n,1j,2k. |
| Pentecostal Holiness Church of Canada | 1943 | P Pe3 | ZF.X. | 27 | 755 | 2,000 | Holiness Pentecostals. HQ Toronto. World HQ USA. 53n. |
| People's Church, Toronto | | P ind | ..... | 2 | 3,500 | 6,000 | Largest Protestant congregation and SS. Colour TV services. 410 missionaries abroad. 1r(300). |
| Polish National Catholic Ch of Canada | 1904 | C OCa | Uw... | 11 | 4,000 | 8,000 | 1967, *Canadian Diocese*, *PNCC*(USA). Poles; schism ex RCC. 8n,G=0,10t,W=19%,150y. |
| Presbyterian Church in Canada | 1875 | P Ref | RW..W | 1,890 | 186,584 | 530,000 | Congregations (over 50%) rejecting 1925 merger in UCCanada. 866n,G=−1.5%pa,5868Yy. |
| Primitive Baptist Conf of N Brunswick | 1874 | P Bap | ..... | 20 | 5,595 | 10,000 | Schism from Baptist group over offerings. Arminian, fundamentalist. 21n,15t(900). |
| Process Church of Final Judgement | 1971 | M Apo | xv... | | 500 | 1,000 | From UK. HQ Toronto. Ministry to drug addicts. Black robes. 1972 applied to WCC. |
| Reformed Church in America | | P Ref | Rw..W | 20 | 2,542 | 11,990 | *RCA*, *Classis of Ontario*. Part of USA denomination. HQ Woodstock. 24n,18t(1588). |
| Reformed Episcopal Church | 1873 | A sEv | x...f | 3 | 100 | 300 | Anti-sacramentarian. M=REC(Maryland, USA), Free Ch of England. HQ Victoria. |
| Reformed Mennonite Church | c1850 | P Men | G.... | 1 | 193 | 400 | Branch of USA body. Nonresistant, pacifist, anti-political. Foot-washing. |
| Reformed Presb Ch, Evangelical Synod | | P Ref | x.... | | 200 | 500 | Part of RPCES(USA). HQ Calgary (Alberta). Calvinist doctrines. |
| Reorganized Ch of JC of L-d Saints | 1833 | M LdS | xv... | 88 | 5,000 | 11,178 | Schism in USA ex CJCLdS(Utah). Decline. HQ Guelph, Ontario. 942n,G=0.2%pa,244Yy. |
| Religious Society of Friends | c1790 | P Qua | QW..W | 32 | 972 | 2,000 | *Canadian Yearly Meeting*. *Quakers*. M=FUM,FGC(USA). No clergy. 13t(215),W=60%. |
| Revival Fellowship Assemblies | | P ind | ..... | | 200 | 500 | Independent revivalist congregations. Faith Temple, Toronto. |
| Romanian Orthodox Church in America | 1902 | O Rum | CwO.. | 18 | 10,000 | 15,000 | *Missionary Episcopate*, HQ USA. Romanians. A=1950. HQ Windsor. 12n,8t(373). |
| Romanian Orth Episcopate of America | 1929 | O Rum | Mwo.. | 14 | 6,000 | 10,000 | 1951 broke ex Orthodox Ch in Romania; under Orthodox Ch in America. 9n,10t(530). |
| Russian Orthodox Church in Canada | 1897 | O Sla | MwO.. | 23 | 3,000 | 4,500 | Patriarchal Exarchate, under P Moscow. Russians. Bishop, 15 clergy. HQ Edmonton. |
| Russian Orthodox Ch Outside of Russia | c1950 | O Sla | x.... | 26 | 20,000 | 30,000 | *D Canada*, Refugese from USSR since World War II. HQ New York. Ultra-conservative. |
| Salvation Army in Canada | 1882 | P Sal | xw..W | 526 | 99,200 | 123,600 | *Armée du Salut*. *SA*, *Canada & Bermuda Territory*. 1735n,G=1.1%pa,10H,40p,2s,W=41%. |
| Serbian Orth Ch(D East USA&Canada) | 1963 | O Ser | CwO.. | 10 | 5,000 | 10,000 | Immigrants from Yuglosavia. Under jurisdiction of P Belgrade. HQ Toronto. 10nx. |
| Seventh-day Adventist Church | 1853 | P Adv | x.... | 188 | 20,190 | 28,000 | *SDA*, *Canada Union Conf*. NAmerica Division. 137n,1552mw,2H,1j,4r,219t(19451),1149Y. |
| Standard Churches of America | 1916 | P Pe2 | ZF.X. | 65 | 5,000 | 10,000 | *Canadian Section*. Branch of Open Bible Standard Chs(USA). HQ Brockville, Ont. 1p. |
| Syrian Orthodox Church of Antioch | | O Syr | Dw... | 1 | 200 | 500 | Under Syrian P Antioch, HQ Hackensack, NJ (USA). Parish in Sherbrooke, Quebec. |
| Ukrainian Greek-Orthodox Ch of Canada | 1918 | O Sla | X.... | 288 | 100,000 | 140,000 | Uniates, schism ex RCC in Canada. Largest UOC outside Ukraine. 3 Dioceses. 95n,1s. |
| Ukrainian Orthodox Church of America | c1930 | O Sla | C.O.. | 8 | 1,000 | 2,000 | *UOCA* (*Ecumenical Patriarchate*) (HQ Jamaica, LI, USA). HQ Winnipeg. 10n. |
| Union of Spiritual Communities of Christ | 1899 | C sub | ..... | 25 | 5,100 | 21,300 | *Orthodox Doukhobors* (*Spirit-Wrestlers*). Russian refugees. Many factions. 8t(632). |
| Unitarian Universalist Association | 1842 | M Unt | I.... | 55 | 6,035 | 15,000 | *Canadian Unitarian Council*, 3 of the 22 UUA districts (HQ Boston, USA). 23n. |
| United Brethren in Christ | 1850 | P Hol | xF... | 12 | 773 | 1,500 | *Ontario Conference*. Part of United Brethren in Christ (USA). 14n,10t(875). |
| United Conf of Icelandic Chs in NA | | M Unt | I.... | 20 | 2,000 | 5,000 | Unitarians, Liberal Christians. From Iceland. In Manitoba and Saskatchewan. |
| **United Church of Canada:** | 1765 | P uni | WW..W | 4,442 | 1,016,706 | 2,277,446 | 1925 union, declining since 1960. 4p,6s,W=35%. 2079n,3800t(327801),2539Y,33103y. |
| Alberta Conference | 1925 | P uni | W | 390 | 73,735 | 237,186 | Marked rural decline. 10 Presbyteries. 2H,1s. 180 324 30231 262 3362 |
| Bay of Quinte Conference | 1925 | P uni | W | 351 | 91,477 | 181,361 | English, along the St Lawrence. 7 Presbyteries. 162 315 27873 155 2541 |
| British Columbia Conference | 1925 | P uni | W | 304 | 66,708 | 222,054 | Rural. 10 Presbyteries. 1 aircraft. 5H,1s. 175 253 23859 165 2417 |
| Hamilton Conference | 1925 | P uni | W | 403 | 130,794 | 252,198 | Steel industry. 7 Presbyteries. 242 376 40911 350 3557 |
| London Conference | 1925 | P uni | W | 407 | 121,488 | 212,185 | 8 Presbyteries based on London (Ontario). 221 397 37363 254 3167 |
| Manitoba Conference | 1925 | P uni | W | 324 | 75,947 | 193,320 | Rural. 9 Presbyteries. 1H,1s. 162 293 25063 329 3202 |
| Maritime Conference | 1925 | P uni | W | 717 | 117,050 | 230,577 | NB,NS,PEI. Some French. 14 Presbyteries. 1s,1v. 243 561 40440 311 3478 |
| Montreal & Ottawa Conference | 1925 | P uni | W | 336 | 93,429 | 165,992 | English, some French churches. 4 Presbyteries. 170 286 23418 161 2571 |
| Newfoundland Conference | 1925 | P uni | W | 275 | 18,466 | 87,962 | Once Methodist. 3 Presbyteries. 1H,600 schools. 66 176 12366 39 1959 |
| Saskatchewan Conference | 1925 | P uni | W | 497 | 79,192 | 201,061 | Marked decline in rural areas. 11 Presbyteries. 168 411 24817 232 2489 |
| Toronto Conference | 1925 | P uni | W | 438 | 148,420 | 293,550 | Very large area. HQ of UCC. 10 Presbyteries. 290 408 41469 281 4360 |
| United Pentecostal Church in Canada | | P Pel | x.... | 85 | 5,000 | 15,000 | Linked with UPC(USA). HQ Picton, Ont. 1972, 30 churches in process of seceding. |
| Wesleyan Methodist Ch of America in C | 1889 | P Hol | VF... | 75 | 3,000 | 8,000 | 1968 union Wesleyan Methodist Ch, Pilgrim Holiness Ch; called Wesleyan Ch in USA. |
| Worldwide Church of God | | M BrI | x.... | 51 | 4,000 | 7,000 | *WCG*. Radio Ch of God. Radio, TV. Non-trinitarian. HQ Pasadena, CA (USA). 103nx. |
| Other Protestant denominations | | P | ..... | 1,000 | 47,475 | 97,000 | Total over 100 (see list below). |
| Other Non-White indigenous churches | | I | ..... | | 12,000 | 25,000 | Total over 20 (USA Blacks, West Indians, Amerindians, Koreans; see list below) |
| Other marginal Protestant bodies | | M | ..... | | 10,000 | 20,000 | Total over 20 smaller groups (see list below). |
| Other Orthodox churches | | O | ..... | | 3,000 | 8,000 | Total over 10, including: Armenian Apostolic Ch (C Sis), Sons of Freedom Doukhobors. |
| Other Catholic (non-Roman) churches | | C | ..... | | 500 | 1,000 | About 10: Antoinists, NAORCC, ORCC(English Rite), and bodies under bishops-at-large. |
| Other Anglican denominations | | A | ..... | | 100 | 200 | Small schisms, rapidly expanding after 1975, including Anglican Catholic Ch in NAmerica (1977). |
| **Total affiliated (mid-1970)** | | | | **26,900** | **9,474,649** | **15,959,589** | **Total denominations (1970) . . . 280.** |
| **Total affiliated (mid-1975)** | | | | **28,100** | **9,965,000** | **16,785,600** | **Total denominations (1975) . . . 300.** |
| **Total affiliated (mid-1980)** | | | | **29,300** | **10,610,000** | **17,872,500** | **Total denominations (1980) . . . 330.** |

**NOTES ON TABLE ABOVE**

COLUMNS: for meanings and CODES (cols. 1, 3, 4, 8): see Codebook (Part 6). Column 1: **Boldface type** = church with over 10% of country's affiliated Christians.

NATIONAL COUNCILS (Column 4, 5th letter).

- E = Evangelical Fellowship of Canada (EFC).
- f = former member of Canadian Council of Churches, now withdrawn (Moravian Church was in friendly association).
- I = Pan-Indian Ecumenical Association of the USA and Canada.
- R = Canadian Catholic Conference (CCC)/Conférence Catholique Canadienne (CCC).
- T = Canadian Council of Evangelical Protestant Churches.
- W = Canadian Council of Churches (CCC)/Conseil Canadien des Eglises.
- w = associate member of Canadian Council of Churches.

*Other national councils.* The 3 largest Lutheran churches co-operate in the Lutheran Council in Canada (LCIC). Canadian Holiness Federation (members include Free Methodist Church in Canada). National Catholic Federation of Canada (Old Roman Catholic bodies).

*Local councils.* 22 local and 3 regional ecumenical councils co-operate with the Canadian Council of Churches.

OTHER PROTESTANT DENOMINATIONS. The number is very large because many USA denominations, and a number of European and Third-World denominations also, have small branches in Canada. Among these others are: American Baptist Association, Baptist Bible Fellowship International, Beachy Amish Mennonite Ch, Canadian Reformed Chs, Children of God International, Christ Assemblies, Christian Community in Canada, Christian Congregational Churches, Ch of God (Pentecostal), Community Ch of Canada, Deeper Walk, Ev Lutheran Synod, Fundamental Baptists (Maritimes), Gospel Missionary Association, Independent Baptist Fellowship, Lutheran Free Ch, Manifested Sons of God (perfectionist Pentecostals), Members in Christ Assemblies (Toronto), Northern Canada Ev Mission, Old German Baptist Brethren in Canada, Old Mennonite Conference, Overcomers Ch, Pentecostal Missionary Fellowship (by 1976 a de facto schism ex United Pentecostal Ch), Reformed Baptists (USA), Reformed Presbyterian Ch of NA, The Way International, Ukrainian Baptist Chs, United Holiness Ch (schism ex Free Methodist Ch), Universal Christian Apostolic Ch, Waldensian Ch, Wisconsin Ev Lutheran Synod, Worldwide Christian Ev Mission of Canada. There are also several very large independent single congregations in Winnipeg, Toronto, et alia.

OTHER NON-WHITE INDIGENOUS CHURCHES. USA Black churches (including AME Zion Ch, Christian Union, Coloured Zion Ch, Father Divine Peace Mission), West Indian bodies, Unification Ch of Korea (1963), Amerindian groups, et alia.

OTHER MARGINAL PROTESTANT BODIES. The many small groups include: Branhamites (End Time Believers, Local Believers; HQ Edmonton; Jesus-Only Unitarians), Ch of Our Lord Jesus Christ (Bickertonites), Ch of Scientology (6,000 members), Divine Science Federation International, Eglise Humanitaire, Greater World Christian Spiritualist League (Hamilton, Ontario), United Ch of Religious Science (1 church), Unity Ch of Truth, Unity School of Christianity (9 churches, 8 ministers).

UNITING CHURCHES. Negotiations for organic union were under way in 1974 between: (1) Anglican Ch of Canada, Christian Church (Disciples of Christ), United Ch of Canada. (2) Ev Lutheran Ch of Canada, Lutheran Ch in America (Canada Section), Lutheran Ch—Canada (Missouri Synod), Synod of Ev Lutheran Churches.

**PEOPLES** (ethnolinguistic). Christians: 39.2% Anglo-Canadian, 29.8% French-Canadian (& French), 6.2% German, 3.4% Italian, 3.3% English, 2.7% Ukrainian, 2.0% Dutch, 1.8% part-Indian (Métis, Half-Breed) and non-status Indian, 1.8% USA White, 1.5% Polish, 1.3% Amerindian, 0.8% Norwegian, 0.6% Greek, 0.6% Hungarian, 0.5% Swedish, 0.4% Danish, 0.4% Portuguese, 0.3% Russian, 0.3% Finnish, 0.3% Czech, 0.3% Croatian, 0.2% North American Black, 0.2% Austrian, 0.2% Belgian, 0.2% Serbian, 0.1% Eskimo, 0.1% Egyptian, 0.1% Armenian, 0.1% Romanian, 0.1% Estonian, 0.1% Icelander, 0.1% Latvian, 0.1% Lithuanian, 0.1% Slovak, 0.1% Spaniard, 0.1% Syro-Lebanese Arab (including Palestinian), 0.1% West Indian Black, 0.1% Chinese (18,000), Bulgarian, Macedonian, Byelorussian, Japanese, Indo-Pakistani, et alii.

**COUNTRY-WIDE TOTALS**

EVANGELIZATION (see Part 5). 1900: 99%. 1970: 100%. 1980: 100%. *Mass evangelism.* Among the large number of recent campaigns: Oral Roberts (1961 Vancouver, 1963 Toronto, 1967 Edmonton); Billy Graham in 1955 for 3-week Toronto crusade (356,000 attenders, 7,438 enquirers), 1965 Vancouver for 3 days (77,800/1,751), 1967 Winnipeg for 8 days (126,300/3,470), June 1978 Toronto crusade (209,000 attenders, 9,305 decisions); 1969, 100 children's crusades (Canadian Sunday School Mission) with 24,000 attenders; 1970, Canada Congress on Evangelism; 1976, Vancouver Reachout (Leighton Ford) (200 churches, 75,000 homes contacted, 24,000 attenders, 450 enquirers); 1977, Here's Life Canada (CCCI) in 20 cities; 1979, Canadian Congress on World Evangelization. *Radiophonic evangelism.* Many radio and TV programmes; HCJB (1,852 annual letters), many BCC programmes.

FOREIGN MISSIONARIES AND PERSONNEL (nationals serving abroad) (1974). Total 10,173: 7,250 Roman Catholics (4,850 foreign missionaries (decline from 5,256 in 1970) (16 bishops, 1,294 religious priests, 91 diocesan priests, 809 brothers, 2,424 sisters, 120 lay, in over 175 societies) serving in Third-World countries, 2,400 personnel in Western nations), 2,726 Protestants (decline from 3,221 in 1960) in 70 societies in 85 countries, about 140 marginal Protestants (110 Jehovah's Witnesses, 20 Mormons), 30 Catholics (non-Roman), 27 Anglicans (decline from 59 in 1960) in 14 countries.

FOREIGN MISSIONARIES AND PERSONNEL (aliens from abroad) (1973). Total 5,027. *From Western world.* 4,420: about 3,000 Roman Catholics, about 800 marginal Protestants (740 Mormons, 30 Jehovah's Witnesses) from USA, about 400 Protestants (mostly in USA societies, with a number from Europe including 16 in 5 UK societies, 2 in 1 WGermany society, 1 in 1 Switzerland society), 180 Anglicans (many clergy from UK; also 13 in 4 UK societies, 5 in 1 USA society), about 42 Catholics (non-Roman), about 30 Orthodox. *From Communist world.* 128: 108 Roman Catholics (102 from Poland, also Yugoslavia and Hungary), about 20 Orthodox from Bulgaria, USSR and Yugoslavia. In 1975 there were 24 Jesuits from Eastern Europe serving in Canada, but most had adopted, or applied for, Canadian citizenship. *From Third World.* 479: about 400 Roman Catholics (including 6 Jesuits), about 40 Protestants from Hong Kong, Japan, Korea, Philippines, Taiwan, Zambia et alia, about 20 indigenous from Jamaica, Japan, Korea et alia, about 6 Orthodox from Egypt and Syria, 13 Anglicans from South Africa et alia.

INSTITUTIONS (church-operated) (1973). Total 750, including 5 ecumenical centres, 430 higher schools (25 minor seminaries), 100 medical centres (40 hospitals), 2 radio stations, 30 religious communities (10 monasteries), 27 research centres, 88 seminaries (50 Protestant, 26 RC, 10 Anglican, 1 Orthodox, 1 Catholic/non-Roman), 20 study centres, 15 universities.

PERIODICALS. About 500 titles (200 RC including 6 diocesan newspapers with 1977 circulation of 121,000 and 1 national newspaper with 13,800).

PERSONNEL. About 84,607 (79,580 national, 5,027 foreign).

RELIGIOUS LIBRARIES. About 250.

SCRIPTURE DISTRIBUTION (1975). Annual totals: 508,799 Bibles (9% free, 22% subsidized, 69% commercial), 1,297,250 NTs (43% free, 24% subsidized, 33% commercial), 586,942 UBS portions, 2,612,872 UBS selections. *Translations completed.* Portion: 25 languages since 1787. NT: 9 languages since 1826. Bible: 3 languages since 1862.

SERVICE AGENCIES. About 350, including ACPC, AEQ, BMFF, CCC/CCC, CCC/CWC, CCF, CCODP, CEF, CEQ, CIS, CNM, CSSM, CUF, ECUSAT, EFC, IFES, IVCF, JEC, JIC, JOC, JOCI, LCIC, MTC, MTS, NCFC, NMC, OCU, ONCS, POEM, PTL, SAVI, SCM, SGM, VICS, WBT, WRMF, WVI, YFC, YLC, YMCA, YWCA.

**ADDITIONAL DATA ON CHURCHES**

ANGLICAN CHURCH OF CANADA. Title in French: Eglise Episcopale du Canada. There are 10 missionary dioceses known as assisted dioceses, which are not yet self-supporting but receive grants annually from central church funds. *New dioceses* (1975). D Newfoundland is now divided into 3 dioceses. *Priests* (1977). Including 15 women. *Deaconesses* (1977). 16. *Lay readers* (1977). 1,537. *Seminarians* (1977). 200.

CATHOLIC CHURCH OF CANADA. The relatively large number of dioceses (68 for 9 million Catholics) is explained by the vast distances and the large variety of rites and ethnic groups. *New dioceses* (created since 1973). New Westminster of the Ukrainians, Rouyn-Noranda. *Catholics* (column 7). Ethnic or linguistic breakdown (1968): French-speaking 5,737,652 (Quebec 4,891,579, Ontario 377,054, New Brunswick 218,809, Manitoba 97,426, Alberta 63,983, Saskatchewan 57,687, Nova Scotia 31,114); English-speaking 2,728,329 (Ontario 1,554,200, Alberta 247,000, British Columbia 222,056, Newfoundland 155,207, Saskatchewan 151,000, Manitoba 97,500, New Brunswick 66,000, Prince Edward Isle 45,813); Ukrainians 185,117 (Manitoba 58,200, Alberta 51,917, Ontario 50,000, Saskatchwan, 25,000). The proportions of baptized Catholics to total population by provinces in 1968 were: Quebec 82.5%, New Brunswick 45.6%, Prince Edward Isle 41.6%, Newfoundland 30.5%, Nova Scotia 30.3%, Ontario 27%, Manitoba 26%, Saskatchewan 24.3%, Alberta 23.7%, British Columbia 11%. *Indians, Eskimos and mixed-race.* Total Catholics (1971) 143,994 (36,922 in the north, 80,926 in the west, 26,146 in the east). There are also 4,200 Chinese Catholics. *Column* 8. The first sub-column, headed L (language), indicates which linguistic sector (French or English) of the Canadian Catholic Conference the diocese has been officially assigned to. The second sub-column, headed B, gives the civil province in which the diocese is situated. Code, similar to postal codes: Alb (Alta)=Alberta, BC=British Columbia, Man=Manitoba, NB=New Brunswick, New (Nfld)=Newfoundland, NS=Nova Scotia, NWT=North West Territories, Ont=Ontario, PEI=Prince Edward Island, Que(PQ)=Quebec, Sas (Sask)=Saskatchewan, Yuk=Yukon. Also noted are dioceses where almost the whole population are Catholics (e.g. 90% Catholic, 90% RC). *Annual baptisms.* (1972) 97.4% infant, 2.6% adult. *Personnel.* About 90% nationals, 10% expatriates. *Religious priests.* In 1975, 5,947 (289 in Canadian home missions). *Catholic charismatics* (January 1974). 10,000 adults including many religious personnel and 2 bishops are active in 500 prayer groups in the Charismatic Renewal. Dioceses with particularly strong groups: Halifax (NS), London. By 1976, Quebec province had 20,000 French-speaking Catholics in the Renewal, in 535 prayer groups, spreading exceptionally fast. M Montreal alone has 70 prayer groups. *Seminaries.* 9 for the French-speaking sector, 4 English-speaking (Halifax, London, Toronto, Vancouver); all are interdiocesan except Chicoutimi, Saint-Hyacinthe, Sherbrooke, Toronto, Trois-Rivières. *Seminarians.* French-speaking sector: annual entrants dropped from 156 (1968) to 75 (1971), and annual ordinations of priests from 124 (1967) to 44 (1970). *Catechists.* There are only about 80 left, in the jurisdictions under Propaganda.

*Catholic organizations.* The Canadian Catholic Conference (CCC), founded in 1943 and reorganized in 1973, is an assembly of all the Catholic bishops divided into French and English sectors. Each diocese regardless of geographical location is attached to one of these sectors, each sector in turn having 5 or 6 specialized offices dealing with missions, social affairs, liturgy and the like. The general secretariat of the episcopal conference is assisted by a mixed French-English 'pastoral team for study and action'. At the regional level there are 4 episcopal conferences: (1) Assemblée des Evêques du Québec (AEQ), with its permanent secretariat in Montreal since 1971, which is the oldest permanent regional assembly; (2) Atlantic Episcopal Assembly, with its secretariat at Halifax, Nova Scotia; (3) Catholic Conference of Ontario, in Toronto; and (4) Western Catholic Conference, in McLennan, Alberta. The first is entirely French-speaking, the other 3 are bilingual. The Ukrainian bishops also have a Ukrainian Catholic Metropolitan Conference. For the armed forces, Canada forms a single military vicariate.

The Canadian Religious Conference, founded in 1954, is an association of major superiors of religious personnel composed of 2 bilingual sections (masculine and feminine) and 4 regions: Atlantic, Quebec, Ontario and West. Its general secretariat and departments are also bilingual. The National Federation of Senates of Priests unites the presbyteral councils of the English sector, although there is nothing comparable for the French sector. English-speaking lay movements are co-ordinated by the Office of Lay Apostolate. There is no similar body in the French sector, but Catholic associations and apostolates which are very numerous are united to diocesan structures. In general they are of 4 different types: (1) pious associations such as Femmes Chrétiennes, Chrétiens d'Aujourd'hui, Union St-Joseph and Congrégation Mariâle; (2) philanthropic and educational associations such as those dealing with poverty (Conférences St-Vincent-de-Paul) and for education (Lacordaire, Parents Chrétiens, Unions de Famille and Association Parents-Maîtres); (3) movements for specialized Catholic action including Mouvement des Travailleurs Chrétiens, JOC, JEC and JIC (membership in these groups in Quebec dropped from 28,000 in 1961 to 3,000 in 1971); and (4) parish structures for stimulating the Christian life dealing with pastoralia, liturgy, home life and preparation for marriage.

The Holy See has diplomatic relations with Canada and is represented to government and the Catholic hierarchy by a nuncio in Ottawa, who serves also as apostolic delegate for St Pierre and Miquelon.

Two international organizations are the Non-Confessional Association for Religious Studies and the Sociology of Religion section of the International Association of Sociology, with headquarters in Toronto.

Of the few structured opinion groups existing in Canada mention may be made of the progressivist Chrétiens pour le Socialisme in Quebec and the traditionalist Catholics United for the Faith (CUF), which is affiliated to a similar organization in the USA. Non-structured basic communities and marginal groups are also active.

Research and social action bodies include the following: (1) Centre de Recherche en Sociologie Religieuse (CRSR), founded in 1958 and attached to the Faculty of Theology of Laval University, which attempts to make available the results of studies in religious sociology for the teaching of theology and pastoralia; (2) Office National des Affaires Sociales (French sector) and Social Affairs Office (English sector), which are co-ordinating bodies of the CCC founded in 1948, and which constitute the provisional secretariat for the Commission Justice et Paix in collaboration with the Conseil National d'Action Sociale; (3) Canadian Catholic Organization for Development and Peace, a bilingual organization in aid of development outside Canada, which is a member of CIDSE in Belgium; and (4) Conseil de Développement Social du Montréal Métropolitain, a French group working for the improvement of the life of the disadvantaged by studying their problems, stimulating agencies to help and marshalling community resources.

Pastoral and religious training is provided by a number of institutions. Ten faculties and departments of theology are found at the following universities: Laval, Montreal, Sherbrooke, Quebec at Rimouski, Quebec at Trois-Rivières, St Paul, Mount St Vincent, St Mary's, St Francis Xavier and St Michael's College. Advanced institutes of catechesis include, for the French sector, the Institut Supérieur de Sciences Religieuses founded in 1954 and attached to the Faculty of Theology of the University of Montreal, and the Institut de Catéchèse founded in 1961 and attached to the Faculty of Theology of Laval University; and for the English sector, the Divine Word International Centre of Religious Education, founded at London, Ontario in 1965. The Institut de Pastorale, founded by OP in Montreal in 1960 and affiliated with the Dominican College of Philosophy and Theology in Ottawa, has since 1967 given university diplomas in pastoralia. Since 1920 it has included also the Centre de Pastorale en Milieu Ouvrier (CPMO). The English-language Institute of Mediaeval Studies was founded in Toronto in 1939.

Several bodies are involved in the co-ordination of missionary action. (1) The Conseil National Missionnaire (CNM) for the French sector and the National Missionary Council (NMC) for the English sector are official organs for consultation and action related to the Office d'Entraide Apostolique et Missionnaire, having as their aim the promotion of unity and co-ordination of Canada's diverse missionary activities, stimulation of the missionary spirit and awakening of vocations to the missionary life. (2) The bilingual Office des Missions de la CCC assists the churches of different overseas countries in their programme of evangelization, provides help aimed at resolving their economic and social problems and co-ordinates Canadian Catholic aid in personnel and finances. (3) The bilingual Missions Department of the Canadian Religious Conference assists major superiors as a liaison agency between Canadian religious, and civil authorities, engages in research into missionary problems and provides a service of information and documentation. (4) The Office Canadien Catholique de l'Amérique Latine serves as an intermediary between the CCC and the Latin American church, assisting the latter in its programme of evangelization and development. (5) Entr'aide Missionnaire provides co-operative services, contacts and information with and for missionaries. The bilingual Institute of Missions Studies at the University of St Paul in Ottawa trains personnel in missiology, and Volunteer International Christian Service (VICS), founded by Spiritans (CSSp) in Toronto in 1971, is an ecumenical and missionary agency which recruits, trains and sends lay missionaries to Third-World countries.

In 1971 there were 6,141 Canadian Catholic missionary personnel, of whom 1,826 were priests, 1,038 brothers, 2,989 sisters, 92 members of secular institutes, and 167 lay. Geographically there were 2,245 in Africa, 1,894 in Latin America, 981 in Asia, 136 in Oceania, and 885 in Canadian missions among Indians and Eskimos. The principal missionary communities of Canadian origin in 1971 were the Scarboro Foreign Mission Society (SFM), an English male society founded in 1918, with 101 missionaries; Société des Missions Etrangères du Québec (PME), a French male society with 151 missionaries; Société des Saints-Apôtres (SSSA), a male diocesan society with 16 missionaries; Soeurs Missionnaires de l'Immaculée Conception, founded in 1902, with 415 missionaries; Soeurs Grises de Montréal, founded in 1737, with 159 missionaries; Soeurs de la Charité d'Ottawa, founded in 1845, with 107 missionaries; Socurs Missionnaires de Notre-Dame des Anges, founded in 1919, with 94 missionaries; Oblates Missionnaires de Marie-Immaculée, founded in 1952, with 84 missionaries; Soeurs Missionnaires du Christ-Roi, founded in 1928, with 77 missionaries; Soeurs de la Charité de la Providence, founded in 1843, with 75 missionaries.

Catholic educational statistics for 1968 included 140,692 children in nursery schools, 1,536,920 in primary schools and 551,305 in secondary schools. In Quebec there were 1,342,981 pupils in Catholic schools. By 1973 these had fallen to 379,770 pupils in 1,400 primary schools and 157,927 in 327 secondary. Each Canadian province had 2 educational systems, one being state and the other Catholic, except Quebec and Newfoundland which each had Catholic and Protestant systems. Beginning in 1972, especially in Quebec, major changes have taken place in the direction of secularization. The Catholic system is no longer described in terms of the 'structures of Catholic education' but the concept now is of the 'pastoralia of Christian education'. At the university level only the theological faculties and institutes of catechesis remain confessional. Laval University and the University of Montreal now have civil charters.

Concerning medical and social service, the Office National du Bien-être et de la Santé co-ordinates the relief, health and development activities of the French sector of the CCC, and is a member of Caritas International. The National Office for Social Action and Family Life Bureau assumes the same responsibilities for the English sector. The Catholic Charities Council of Canada also serves the English-speaking community. The bilingual Catholic Hospital Association of Canada is one of the first medical and hospital associations formed in Canada and as such plays an important role in the professional domain. The bilingual Catholic Immigrant Services is given responsibility by the CCC for all questions relating to immigrants into Canada, who numbered 161,531 in 1969. In Montreal 3 Catholic or ecumenical organizations are involved in helping immigrants: the Service d'Accueil aux Voyageurs et aux Immigrants (SAVI); the Comité d'Accueil Interconfessionnel; and the Office des Néo-Canadiens. The Société de Service Social aux Familles in Montreal provides assistance for needy families, alcoholics and others, and the Conseil des Oeuvres et du Bien-être du Diocèse de Québec studies the needs of the population of Quebec and co-ordinates charitable activities among them.

PENTECOSTAL ASSEMBLIES OF CANADA. *Origin.* The first Pentecostal church was organized in Calgary in 1910. The denomination was organized in 1919. *Indians.* Of the 850 mainland assemblies in 1977, 125 were composed of Canadian Indians (Amerindians and Métis). *Growth* (1977). 851 churches, 2,200 ministers, 225 missionaries, 5 colleges (also 160 churches in Newfoundland).

UNITED CHURCH OF CANADA (UCC). Formed by union in 1925 of Methodist, Presbyterian and Congregational churches, and later (1968) Evangelical United Brethren. At the time of union, Methodists made up 69% of the membership. The UCC is a member of the World Methodist Council; but since the other 31% were Presbyterian and Congregational, the UCC also belongs to WARC, World Alliance of Reformed Churches (Presbyterian and Congregational). *Membership* (1970). 99% White (86% British or British origin, 10% other European). *Column 8.* The first sub-column here gives the number of ministers serving charges. In addition, there are about 1,500 other ordained ministers (assistants, teachers, et al). *Growth.* The church has been declining since 1960 at a rate (in 1970) of −0.6% pa. *Closed churches.* The number of preaching places open declined from 5,741 in 1961 to 4,442 in 1971.

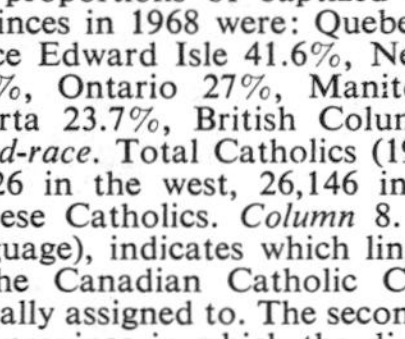

# Canton & Enderbury Islands

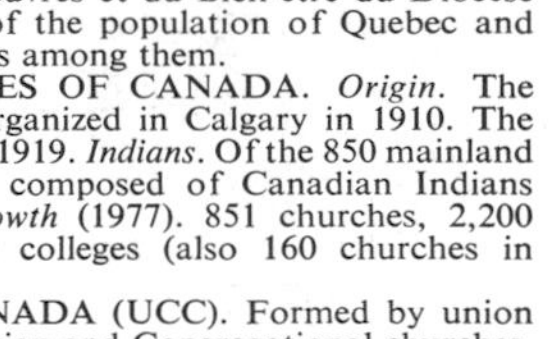

## SECULAR DATA

**STATE. Official name:** The Anglo-American Condominium of the Canton and Enderbury Islands.
**Flag** (shown above right): Those of UK and USA.
**Area:** 70 sq.km. (27 sq.miles). Agricultural land: 0.0%.
**Government:** Anglo-American condominium or joint administration, since 1939.

**Official language:** English.

**DEMOGRAPHY. Population:** uninhabited (census of 1.IV.1970. For 1970–2000 (UN), see last row of Table 1). Population density (transients, 1975): 3/sq.km. (7/sq.mile). Under 15 years: 44%. Growth rate (1975–80): 1.31% per year (births 3.49%, deaths −0.79%, emigrants −1.39%). Life expectancy (1975–80): 63.8 years. Household size: 4 persons.
**Major languages:** English, Samoan, Gilbertese.

**ETHNOLINGUISTIC GROUPS:** 90% USA military, 10% Samoan, Gilbertese.

**MONEY** (1977). **Monetary unit:** USA dollar (= 100 cents).

TABLE 1.    RELIGIOUS ADHERENTS IN THE CANTON & ENDERBURY ISLANDS

| Year | 1900 | | mid-1970 | | Annual change, 1970–1980 | | | | mid-1975 | | mid-1980 | | 2000 | |
|---|---|---|---|---|---|---|---|---|---|---|---|---|---|---|
| Name | Adherents | % | Adherents | % | Natural | Conversion | Total | Rate | Adherents | % | Adherents | % | Adherents | % |
| **Christians** | 0 | 0.0 | 160 | 80.0 | 0 | 0 | 0 | 0.00 | 160 | 80.0 | 160 | 80.0 | 160 | 80.0 |
| professing | 0 | 0.0 | 160 | 80.0 | 0 | 0 | 0 | 0.00 | 160 | 80.0 | 160 | 80.0 | 160 | 80.0 |
| Protestants | 0 | 0.0 | 120 | 60.0 | 0 | 0 | 0 | 0.00 | 120 | 60.0 | 120 | 60.0 | 120 | 60.0 |
| Roman Catholics | 0 | 0.0 | 40 | 20.0 | 0 | 0 | 0 | 0.00 | 40 | 20.0 | 40 | 20.0 | 40 | 20.0 |
| nominal | 0 | 0.0 | 130 | 65.0 | 0 | 0 | 0 | 0.00 | 130 | 65.0 | 130 | 65.0 | 130 | 65.0 |
| affiliated | 0 | 0.0 | 30 | 15.0 | 0 | 0 | 0 | 0.00 | 30 | 15.0 | 30 | 15.0 | 30 | 15.0 |
| total practising | 0 | 0 | 27 | 90 | 0 | 0 | 0 | 0.00 | 27 | 90 | 27 | 90 | 30 | 15.0 |
| non-practising | 0 | 0 | 3 | 10 | 0 | 0 | 0 | 0.00 | 3 | 10 | 3 | 10 | 21 | 70 |
| Roman Catholics | 0 | 0.0 | 30 | 15.0 | 0 | 0 | 0 | 0.00 | 30 | 15.0 | 30 | 15.0 | 9 | 30 |
| Non-religious | 0 | 0.0 | 40 | 20.0 | 0 | 0 | 0 | 0.00 | 40 | 20.0 | 40 | 20.0 | 30 | 15.0 |
| | | | | | | | | | | | | | 40 | 20.0 |
| **Country's population** | 0 | 100.0 | 200 | 100.0 | 0 | 0 | 0 | 0.00 | 200 | 100.0 | 200 | 100.0 | 200 | 100.0 |

COLUMNS, ROWS. For meanings and definitions, see Codebook (Part 6). Note that, by definition, total 'Christians' =

professing + crypto-Christians, which also = affiliated + nominal Christians. Percentages may not always total exactly, due to rounding.

CHRISTIANS. Expatriate USA and Samoan military personnel.
COUNTRY'S POPULATION. The islands are uninhabited for part of the year.

**CHRISTIANITY.** Enderbury was discovered in 1823 and Canton in 1854, both being uninhabited at the time. During the latter part of the 19th century various American and British companies worked the large guano deposits on the islands. Britain annexed Canton in 1889, but this was disputed in 1937. In April 1939, Canton and Enderbury were placed under joint British and American control.

Although there is only one Catholic group, the small population is made up of Christians of various denominations. Until 1968 most came from the nearby Gilbert and Ellice Islands; after they were withdrawn by the British, USA military with Samoan personnel were installed. The islands are part of the Catholic diocese of Tarawa.

**CHURCH AND STATE.** Religion has never been an issue in the administration of the islands.

TABLE 2.    ORGANIZED CHURCHES AND DENOMINATIONS IN THE CANTON & ENDERBURY ISLANDS

| Official name 1 | Begun 2 | Type 3 | Counc 4 | Congs 5 | Adults 6 | Affiliated 7 | Names, notes, and other statistics (see Codebook) 8 |
|---|---|---|---|---|---|---|---|
| **Catholic Church (D Tarawa)** | | R Lat | P.PY. | 1 | 10 | 30 | Under Diocese of Tarawa (Gilbert Is). All USA expatriates. |
| **Total affiliated (mid-1970)** | | | | 1 | 10 | 30 | Total denominations (1970) . . . 1. |
| **Total affiliated (mid-1975)** | | | | 1 | 10 | 30 | Total denominations (1975) . . . 1. |
| **Total affiliated (mid-1980)** | | | | 1 | 10 | 30 | Total denominations (1980) . . . 2. |

**NOTES ON TABLE ABOVE**
COLUMNS: for meanings and CODES (cols. 1, 3, 4, 8): see Codebook (Part 6). Column 1: **Boldface type** = church with

over 10% of country's affiliated Christians.

PEOPLES (ethnolinguistic). Christians: 90% USA military (81% White, 9% Black), 10% Samoan, Gilbertese.

**COUNTRY-WIDE TOTALS**
EVANGELIZATION (see Part 5). 1900: 0%. 1970: 100%. 1980: 100%.

---

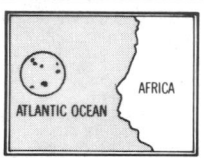

# CAPE VERDE

## SECULAR DATA

**STATE. Official name:** The Republic of Cape Verde (A República de Cabo Verde). Adjective of nationality: Cape Verdean.
**Flag** (shown above right): Red vertical bar at hoist with black star and green corn stalks and yellow sea shell, 2 horizontal stripes yellow over green.
**Area:** 4,033 sq.km. (1,557 sq.miles). Description: 15 islands. Agricultural land: 12.4%.
**Government:** One-party state, since 1975 (c1450 Portuguese rule, 1951 province of Portugal, 1975 Independence).
**Legislature:** National Assembly, 56 members.
**Official language:** Portuguese (*Português*).
**Capital:** Praia 13,142 (1960).
**Political divisions** (1974): 13 Counties (concelhos), 31 Parishes (freguesias).

**DEMOGRAPHY. Population:** 272,071 (census of 15.XII.1970. For 1970–2000 (UN), see last row of Table 1). Population density (1975): 73/sq.km. (189/sq.mile). Under 15 years: 35%. Growth rate (1975–80): 1.79% per year (births 2.98%, deaths −1.18%). Life expectancy (1975–80): 52.5 years. Household size: 4.9 persons.
**Major languages:** Portuguese, Portuguese Creole, Brava Island Creole, Fulani, Balante, Manjaco.
**Urban dwellers** (1970): 8.0%. Urban growth rate (1950–70): 3.5% per year.
**Labour force:** 53%.

**ETHNOLINGUISTIC GROUPS:** 69.6% Caboverdian Mestiço (Portuguese/Black), 28.4% Black (14.6% Balante & Manjaco, 12.2% Fulani), 2.0% White (Portuguese).

**MONEY** (1977). **Monetary unit:** escudo (= 100 centavos); US$1 = CVEsc 25.4.
**National income per person:** US$250. Average annual family income: US$1,225.
**Inflation:** (1970–74) 20% per year (1975: consumer price index 238).
**Cost of living in capital** (1976): Daily cost of living: US$21.

**EDUCATION.** Literacy: (1950) 21%, (1970) 37%. Schools: 420.

**HEALTH.** Hospitals: 15 (376 beds). Doctors: 13. Lepers: 2,000 (6.8 per 1,000).

**LITERATURE.** Periodicals: 6. Newspapers: 3 non-daily.

**COMMUNICATION** (per 1,000 people). Phones: 5. Radios: 19.

TABLE 1.    RELIGIOUS ADHERENTS IN CAPE VERDE

| Year | 1900 | | mid-1970 | | Annual change, 1970–1980 | | | | mid-1975 | | mid-1980 | | 2000 | |
|---|---|---|---|---|---|---|---|---|---|---|---|---|---|---|
| Name | Adherents | % | Adherents | % | Natural | Conversion | Total | Rate | Adherents | % | Adherents | % | Adherents | % |
| **Christians** | 69,300 | 99.0 | 266,000 | 99.5 | 5,453 | −173 | 5,280 | 1.80 | 292,500 | 99.2 | 319,400 | 98.9 | 414,000 | 95.8 |
| professing | 69,300 | 99.0 | 266,000 | 99.5 | 5,453 | −173 | 5,280 | 1.80 | 292,500 | 99.2 | 319,400 | 98.9 | 414,000 | 95.8 |
| Roman Catholics | 69,300 | 99.0 | 261,200 | 97.5 | 5,315 | −465 | 4,850 | 1.70 | 285,100 | 96.6 | 309,700 | 95.9 | 396,700 | 91.8 |
| Evangelical Catholics | 0 | 0.0 | 3,350 | 1.3 | 67 | −3 | 64 | 1.79 | 3,570 | 1.2 | 3,990 | 1.2 | 9,000 | 2.1 |
| Protestants | 0 | 0.0 | 5,400 | 2.0 | 138 | 292 | 430 | 5.81 | 7,400 | 2.5 | 9,700 | 3.0 | 17,300 | 4.0 |
| nominal | 700 | 1.0 | 6,456 | 2.4 | 155 | 250 | 405 | 4.87 | 8,330 | 2.8 | 10,510 | 3.3 | 20,900 | 4.8 |
| affiliated | 68,600 | 98.0 | 260,144 | 97.1 | 5,298 | −423 | 4,875 | 1.71 | 284,170 | 96.3 | 308,890 | 95.6 | 393,100 | 91.0 |
| total practising | 61,740 | 90 | 208,110 | 80 | 3,974 | −3,163 | 811 | 0.38 | 213,130 | 75 | 216,220 | 70 | 255,500 | 65 |
| non-practising | 6,860 | 10 | 52,030 | 20 | 1,324 | 2,740 | 4,064 | 5.72 | 71,040 | 25 | 92,670 | 30 | 137,600 | 35 |
| Roman Catholics | 68,600 | 98.0 | 251,394 | 93.8 | 5,094 | −713 | 4,381 | 1.60 | 273,200 | 92.6 | 295,200 | 91.4 | 366,800 | 84.9 |
| Protestants | 0 | 0.0 | 8,700 | 3.2 | 203 | 287 | 490 | 4.50 | 10,900 | 3.7 | 13,600 | 4.2 | 25,900 | 6.0 |
| Evangelicals | 0 | 0.0 | 8,000 | 3.0 | 186 | 264 | 450 | 4.50 | 10,000 | 3.4 | 12,500 | 3.9 | 24,000 | 5.6 |
| Marginal Protestants | 0 | 0.0 | 50 | 0.0 | 1 | 3 | 4 | 5.71 | 70 | 0.0 | 90 | 0.0 | 400 | 0.1 |
| Non-religious | 0 | 0.0 | 1,000 | 0.4 | 37 | 163 | 200 | 10.00 | 2,000 | 0.7 | 3,000 | 0.9 | 15,000 | 3.5 |
| Baha'is | 0 | 0.0 | 100 | 0.0 | 3 | 7 | 10 | 6.67 | 150 | 0.0 | 200 | 0.1 | 1,000 | 0.2 |
| Other religionists | 700 | 1.0 | 300 | 0.1 | 7 | 3 | 10 | 2.86 | 350 | 0.1 | 400 | 0.1 | 2,000 | 0.5 |
| **Country's population** | 70,000 | 100.0 | 268,000 | 100.0 | 5,500 | 0 | 5,500 | 1.86 | 295,000 | 100.0 | 323,000 | 100.0 | 432,000 | 100.0 |

COLUMNS, ROWS. For meanings and definitions, see Codebook (Part 6). Note that, by definition, total 'Christians' = professing + crypto-Christians, which also = affiliated + nominal Christians. Percentages may not always total exactly, due to rounding.
CENSUSES. 15.XII.1950: 98.2% Roman Catholics, 1.0% Protestants, 0.2% other religionists.

**NOTES ON RELIGIONS**
BAHA'IS. Begun 1957.
COUNTRY'S POPULATION. In 1947–48 severe drought killed 30,000 persons. Since Independence there has been a major population exodus to Europe and North America; in particular, there is a large Cape Verdean population in southeastern New England (USA).

EVANGELICAL CATHOLICS. This term is used here to describe persons who are affiliated to churches termed by the state Evangélica (Protestant or marginal churches), but who profess publicly to be, or are regarded as, Roman Catholics.
OTHER RELIGIONISTS. In 1900, Muslims and tribal religionists; in 1970, Muslims, a few Jews, and others.

**NON-CHRISTIAN RELIGIONS.** Traditional African religions have now ceased to have adherents. Some Cape Verdeans have become Baha'is.

**CHRISTIANITY**
CATHOLIC CHURCH. The Cape Verde Islands were discovered by the Portuguese explorer Diogo Gomes in 1460, and within 2 years Catholic clergy had arrived. Franciscan missionaries appeared in 1466, and in 1532 a diocese was erected which in-

Port of São Vincente, Cape Verde, with parish church in distance.

Postage stamp commemorating 1951 Exposition of Sacred Missionary Art.

cluded the African coast between Gambia and Cape Palmas. Jesuits were at work between 1604 and 1642, and the first Capuchins arrived in 1656. At present the diocese is served by Holy Ghost and Capuchin priests and 2 congregations of sisters (Holy Ghost, Love of God). Although there are no local religious congregations, half the clergy are natives of the islands, many of the rest coming from Goa (India). In recent years a process of marked dechristianization has been noticeable.

PROTESTANT CHURCHES. Protestants are a small minority. Most are Nazarenes, who opened their first station on the islands in 1903. Seventh-day Adventists, with 8 congregations now, established

the Cape Verde Islands Mission in 1935.

CHURCH AND STATE. Until 1975 relations between church and state were governed by the 1940 concordat between Portugal and the Holy See. After Independence from Portugal, a move towards secularization of the state was begun.

BIBLIOGRAPHY
'Descobrimento povoamento evangelização do Archipélago de Cabo Verde', A. Brásio, *Cabo Verde*, NS 14 (1963), 4–17.

TABLE 2.   ORGANIZED CHURCHES AND DENOMINATIONS IN CAPE VERDE

| Official name 1 | Begun 2 | Type 3 | Counc 4 | Congs 5 | Adults 6 | Affiliated 7 | Names, notes, and other statistics (see Codebook) 8 |
|---|---|---|---|---|---|---|---|
| Igreja Adventista do Sétimo Dia | 1935 | P Adv | x•••• | 8 | 418 | 1,000 | *Seventh-day Adventists*, Portugal Mission. 1n,7mw,G=4.2%pa,4t(417),W=80%,46Y,66z. |
| Igreja Católica: D Santiago de Cabo V | 1462 | R Lat | H,B,r | 30 | 163,400 | 251,394 | *Catholic Ch.* Suffragan of P Lisbon. C=3+0+2. 52nx,2m,23w,411Y,10030y,433z. |
| Igreja do Nazareno | 1903 | P Hol | xF••• | 52 | 1,578 | 7,500 | *Nazarenes.* M=CoN(USA). 9n,2x,21m,6f,G=2.5%pa,1j,1s(7),100t(6982),W=83%,73Y,224z. |
| Testemunhas de Jeová | c1955 | M Jeh | x•••• | 1 | 10 | 50 | *Jehovah's Witnesses. Watch Tower. IBSA.* Active witnessing under way by 1962. |
| Other Protestant denominations | | P | ••••• | | | 100 | 200 | Including: Baptist Missionary Association of America (from USA). |
| **Total affiliated (mid-1970)** | | | | 95 | 165,506 | 260,144 | **Total denominations (1970) . . . 6.** |
| **Total affiliated (mid-1975)** | | | | 100 | 180,800 | 284,170 | **Total denominations (1975) . . . 6.** |
| **Total affiliated (mid-1980)** | | | | 105 | 196,500 | 308,890 | **Total denominations (1980) . . . 7.** |

NOTES ON TABLE ABOVE
COLUMNS: for meanings and CODES (cols. 1, 3, 4, 8), see Codebook (Part 6). Column 1: **Boldface type** = church with over 10% of country's affiliated Christians.
NATIONAL COUNCILS (Column 4, 5th letter).
   r = attached to Conferência Episcopal Portuguesa da Metrópole (CEPM) (Portuguese Metropolitan Episcopal Conference).

PEOPLES (ethnolinguistic). Christians: 69.6% Caboverdian (Cape Verdean) Mestiço, 28.4% Black (14.6% Balante & Manjaco, 12.2% Fulani), 2.0% Portuguese (White).

COUNTRY-WIDE TOTALS
EVANGELIZATION (see Part 5). 1900: 100%. 1970: 100%. 1980: 100%.
FOREIGN MISSIONARIES AND PERSONNEL (nationals serving abroad) (1973). Total about 4 Roman Catholics (2 in

Angola).
FOREIGN MISSIONARIES AND PERSONNEL (aliens from abroad) (1973). Total 28. *From Western world.* 28: about 20 Roman Catholics, 8 Protestants in 2 USA societies.
INSTITUTIONS (church-operated) (1973). Total 7, including 1 higher school (minor seminary), 2 hospitals, 1 press, 2 seminaries (1 RC, 1 Protestant).
PERIODICALS. 4 titles.
PERSONNEL. About 128 (100 national, 28 foreign).
RELIGIOUS LIBRARIES. 3.
SCRIPTURE DISTRIBUTION (1975). Annual totals: 300 Bibles (commercial), 19,820 NTs (92% free, 5% subsidized, 3% commercial).
SERVICE AGENCIES. About 8, including CNIR, FNIRF.

ADDITIONAL DATA ON CHURCHES
IGREJA CATOLICA. *Priests.* 17 diocesan. Half of all clergy are indigenous, and many of the rest come from Goa, India.

*Seminarians.* 17, studying in Portugal. The major seminary was closed some years ago. *Indigenous religious congregations.* None. *Foreign orders and congregations.* Priests: CSSp, OFMCap (Piedmont, Rome), SDB. Sisters: Holy Spirit, Love of God. *Catholic organizations.* The Cape Verde Islands are included in the Portuguese Metropolitan Episcopal Conference, the National Conference of Religious Institutes (CNIR) for male religious personnel and the National Federation of Female Religious Institutes (FNIRF) for sisters. There is no presbyteral nor pastoral council. The Legion of Mary and Catholic Action are well organized.
   The Holy See had diplomatic relations with Portugal, and through it with the Cape Verde Islands, and was represented to government and the Catholic hierarchy by a nuncio residing in Lisbon. In 1976 the Holy See set up diplomatic relations with the new republic.
   In 1970 there were 99 church primary schools (4,740 pupils) and 2 medical institutions; in 1973, 53 primary schools (5,166).

---

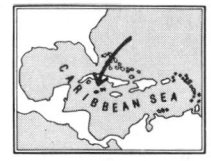

# CAYMAN ISLANDS

## SECULAR DATA

STATE. Official name: The Crown Colony of the Cayman Islands.
Flag (shown above right): British Blue Ensign with arms of the Colony in the fly.
Area: 259 sq.km. (100 sq.miles). Description: 3 islands. Agricultural land: 7.7%.
Government: Crown colony of the United Kingdom (Britain), since 1959 (before 1959 ruled from Jamaica as a dependency).
Legislature: Legislative Assembly, Executive Council.
Official language: English.
Capital: Georgetown 3,975 (1970).

DEMOGRAPHY. Population: 10,460 (census of 7.IV.1970).

For 1970–2000 (UN), see last row of Table 1). Population density (1975): 44/sq.km. (113/sq. mile). Under 15 years: 43%. Growth rate (1975–80): 0.70% per year (births 2.87%, deaths −0.68%, emigrants −1.49%). Life expectancy (1975–80): 69.1 years. Household size: 4.4 persons.
Major languages: English, Hindi.
Labour force: 37%.
Tourists (1973): 45,750.

ETHNOLINGUISTIC GROUPS: 52.5% Mulatto (White/Black), 25.8% Black (African Negro), 19.3% White (European), 1.9% Jewish, 0.3% Indo-Pakistani.

MONEY (1977). Monetary unit: Cayman Islands dollar (= 100

cents; US$1 = Cay$0.833.
National income per person: US$2,600. Average annual family income: US$11,400.
Cost of living in capital (1976): index 122 (Washington DC=100). Daily cost of living: US$35.

EDUCATION. Adult literacy: (1960) 93%. Schools: 13.

HEALTH. Hospitals: 1 (34 beds). Doctors: 2. Blind: 10.

LITERATURE. Periodicals: 3. Newspapers: 2 non-daily.

COMMUNICATION (per 1,000 people). Phones: 260. Radios: 550. TV sets: 400.

TABLE 1.   RELIGIOUS ADHERENTS IN THE CAYMAN ISLANDS

| Year / Name | 1900 Adherents | % | mid-1970 Adherents | % | Annual change, 1970–1980 Natural | Conversion | Total | Rate | mid-1975 Adherents | % | mid-1980 Adherents | % | 2000 Adherents | % |
|---|---|---|---|---|---|---|---|---|---|---|---|---|---|---|
| **Christians** | 4,800 | 100.0 | 10,340 | 96.6 | 125 | −7 | 118 | 1.08 | 10,930 | 96.3 | 11,520 | 96.0 | 12,220 | 94.0 |
| professing | 4,800 | 100.0 | 10,340 | 96.6 | 125 | −7 | 118 | 1.08 | 10,930 | 96.3 | 11,520 | 96.0 | 12,220 | 94.0 |
| Protestants | 4,740 | 98.7 | 9,840 | 92.0 | 119 | −11 | 108 | 1.04 | 10,390 | 91.5 | 10,920 | 91.0 | 11,440 | 88.0 |
| Roman Catholics | 50 | 1.0 | 260 | 2.4 | 3 | 2 | 5 | 1.79 | 280 | 2.5 | 310 | 2.6 | 390 | 3.0 |
| Marginal Protestants | 0 | 0.0 | 130 | 1.2 | 2 | 2 | 4 | 2.67 | 150 | 1.3 | 170 | 1.4 | 260 | 2.0 |
| Anglicans | 10 | 0.2 | 110 | 1.0 | 1 | 0 | 1 | 1.15 | 110 | 1.0 | 120 | 1.0 | 130 | 1.0 |
| nominal | 480 | 10.0 | 2,060 | 19.2 | 26 | 22 | 48 | 2.09 | 2,300 | 20.3 | 2,540 | 21.2 | 3,260 | 25.1 |
| affiliated | 4,320 | 90.0 | 8,280 | 77.4 | 99 | −29 | 70 | 0.81 | 8,630 | 76.0 | 8,980 | 74.8 | 8,960 | 68.9 |
| total practising | 3,890 | *90* | 6,620 | *80* | 79 | −23 | 56 | 0.81 | 6,900 | *80* | 7,180 | *80* | 6,720 | *75* |
| non-practising | 430 | *10* | 1,660 | *20* | 20 | −6 | 14 | 0.81 | 1,730 | *20* | 1,800 | *20* | 2,240 | *25* |
| Protestants | 4,280 | 89.2 | 7,800 | 72.9 | 93 | −33 | 60 | 0.74 | 8,110 | 71.5 | 8,400 | 70.0 | 8,240 | 63.4 |
| Evangelicals | 3,360 | 70.0 | 4,400 | 41.1 | 53 | −13 | 40 | 0.87 | 4,600 | 40.5 | 4,800 | 40.0 | 4,700 | 36.2 |
| Roman Catholics | 40 | 0.8 | 250 | 2.3 | 3 | 2 | 5 | 1.85 | 270 | 2.4 | 300 | 2.5 | 360 | 2.8 |
| Marginal Protestants | 0 | 0.0 | 130 | 1.2 | 2 | 2 | 4 | 2.67 | 150 | 1.3 | 170 | 1.4 | 260 | 2.0 |
| Anglicans | 0 | 0.0 | 100 | 0.9 | 1 | 0 | 1 | 1.15 | 100 | 0.9 | 110 | 0.9 | 100 | 0.8 |
| **Jews** | 0 | 0.0 | 200 | 1.9 | 2 | 1 | 3 | 1.43 | 210 | 1.9 | 230 | 1.9 | 250 | 1.9 |
| **Non-religious** | 0 | 0.0 | 110 | 1.0 | 2 | 4 | 6 | 4.29 | 140 | 1.2 | 170 | 1.4 | 400 | 3.1 |
| **Baha'is** | 0 | 0.0 | 50 | 0.5 | 1 | 2 | 3 | 4.29 | 70 | 0.6 | 80 | 0.7 | 130 | 1.0 |
| **Country's population** | 4,800 | 100.0 | 10,700 | 100.0 | 130 | 0 | 130 | 1.15 | 11,350 | 100.0 | 12,000 | 100.0 | 13,000 | 100.0 |

COLUMNS, ROWS. For meanings and definitions, see Codebook (Part 6). Note that, by definition, total 'Christians' = professing + crypto-Christians, which also = affiliated +

nominal Christians. Percentages may not always total exactly, due to rounding.
CENSUSES. 7.IV.1960 (de jure): 95.9% Protestants (37.4% Presbyterians, 26.4% Ch of God, 11.5% Pilgrim Holiness Ch),

2.2% Roman Catholics, 0.9% non-religious, 0.7% Anglicans, 0.3% marginal Protestants. 7.IV.1970: results invalidated because 16% were returned 'Not stated'.

**NON-CHRISTIAN RELIGIONS.** A small Jewish community exists, as well as isolated followers of other religions including the Ras Tafari cult (Jamaica), and a small number without religion.

**CHRISTIANITY.** The Cayman Islands are unique among former British possessions in the West Indies in that the traditionally strong Catholic, Anglican and Methodist churches have had little impact on the scene.

**PROTESTANT CHURCHES.** Presbyterianism, which owes its origin to Church of Scotland influences as early as 1800, is the most important tradition with more than one-third of the population. The Cayman Islands have been closely associated with Jamaica from earliest days, and so were included in the union negotiations of Jamaican Presbyterians and Congregationists which resulted in 1965 in the United Church of Jamaica and Grand Cayman. On the Caymans there is also a small community related to the Reformed Presbyterian Church, Evangelical Synod (USA). The Baptist Church, with nearly 10% of the population, is another Old-

The Resurrection of Christ, one of many Christian themes on the islands' postage stamps; here, 'Noli me tangere' (Do not touch me) by Titian, and a stained-glass window.

World Christian community whose origin dates back to the last century. Protestant missions from the

USA have made considerable progress in the present century. The Church of God (Anderson) and Church of God (Holiness), both of which began work in the 1930s, claimed the allegiance of more than 25% of the population in 1960. The Pilgrim Holiness Church opened its first worship centre in 1911, and the Adventist Cayman Islands Mission was organized in 1944.

**CATHOLIC CHURCH.** The Cayman Islands are a part of the diocese of Kingston in Jamaica. In 1972 the islands had 62 Catholic families, about two-thirds being Europeans, South Americans or Central Americans, the other third being of African or mixed-African descent. There is one parish in Grand Cayman, with one Jesuit priest who periodically visits Little Cayman and Cayman Brac.

**CHURCH AND STATE.** The Cayman Islands were discovered in 1503 by Columbus but were never colonized by Spain. They were ruled from Jamaica as a British dependency until 1959 when they became a separate colony. There has never been an established church in the islands.

TABLE 2.   ORGANIZED CHURCHES AND DENOMINATIONS IN THE CAYMAN ISLANDS

| Official name 1 | Begun 2 | Type 3 | Counc 4 | Congs 5 | Adults 6 | Affiliated 7 | Names, notes, and other statistics (see Codebook) 8 |
|---|---|---|---|---|---|---|---|
| Anglican Church (D Jamaica) | | A Cen | awMR. | 1 | 50 | 100 | *CPWI.* In Ch of the Province of the West Indies. Growing; support from Jamaica. |
| Baptist Church | c1870 | P Bap | ..... | | 400 | 800 | Baptists related to Jamaica Baptist Union. |
| Catholic Church (M Kingston) | | R Lat | P.NM. | 1 | 150 | 250 | Under M Kingston (Jamaica). On Cayman Brac. 60% White, 40% Black. 1x(SJ),3w. |
| Christian Churches & Chs of Christ | | P Dis | x.... | 2 | 50 | 100 | Independent Churches of Christ missionaries. M=CCCC(Instrumental)(USA). 2f. |
| Church of God Holiness | 1933 | P Hol | x.... | 3 | 200 | 500 | M=CoG Holiness(Overland Park, Kansas,USA). Wesleyan doctrines. 2f. |
| Church of God (Anderson) | 1930 | P Hol | x.... | 5 | 500 | 2,000 | Holiness denomination. M=CoG(Anderson) (USA). 3n,1x,W=12%. |
| Jehovah's Witnesses | c1950 | M Jeh | x.... | 1 | 17 | 30 | *Watch Tower. IBSA.* Active witnessing under way by 1956. |
| Reformed Presb Ch, Evangelical Synod | | P Ref | x.... | | 100 | 200 | Reformed mission from North America. Calvinists. M=WPM(RPCES)(USA). |
| Reorganized Ch of Jesus Christ of LdS | | M LdS | x.... | | 30 | 100 | LdS=Latter-day Saints. Schism in USA ex Mormons claiming legal succession. |
| Seventh-day Adventist Church | 1944 | P Adv | x.... | 6 | 520 | 700 | *Cayman Islands Mission,* West Indies Union Conference. 2nx,11mw,1r,5t(484),129Y. |
| United Ch of Jamaica & Grand Cayman | c1800 | P uni | RWM.. | | 2,000 | 3,000 | Formerly Presb Ch of J & Grand Cayman; 1965 union Congreg Union of Jamaica. |
| Wesleyan Church | 1911 | P Hol | VP... | 3 | 71 | 400 | Formerly Pilgrim Holiness Ch. Declining (977 in 1960). 2n,1x,2f,G=−7%pa,W=90%,13Y. |
| Other Protestant denominations | | P | ..... | | 50 | 100 | Total about 3, including: Ch of God(Cleveland), Disciples of Christ. |
| Total affiliated (mid-1970) | | | | 45 | 4,138 | 8,280 | Total denominations (1970) . . . 15. |
| Total affiliated (mid-1975) | | | | 47 | 4,310 | 8,630 | Total denominations (1975) . . . 16. |
| Total affiliated (mid-1980) | | | | 49 | 4,490 | 8,980 | Total denominations (1980) . . . 17. |

**NOTES ON TABLE ABOVE**
COLUMNS: for meanings and CODES (cols. 1, 3, 4, 8): see Codebook (Part 6). Column 1: **Boldface type** = church with over 10% of country's affiliated Christians.
OTHER MARGINAL BODIES. Church of Christ, Scientist (1 woman practitioner).

**PEOPLES** (ethnolinguistic). Christians: 53.7% Mulatto, 25.9% Black, 19.3% White (European), Indian.

**COUNTRY-WIDE TOTALS**
EVANGELIZATION (see Part 5). 1900: 100%. 1970: 100%. 1980: 100%.
FOREIGN MISSIONARIES AND PERSONNEL (aliens from abroad) (1973). Total 14. *From Western world.* 10: 6 Protestants in 3 USA societies, 2 Black indigenous from USA, about 2 Roman Catholics. *From Third World.* About 4 Protestants from Jamaica.
INSTITUTIONS (church-operated) (1973). Total 1 secondary school.
PERIODICALS. 3 titles.

PERSONNEL. About 39 (25 national, 14 foreign).
SCRIPTURE DISTRIBUTION (1975). Annual totals: 30 Bibles (subsidized), 40 NTs (subsidized), 100 UBS portions, 200 UBS selections.

**ADDITIONAL DATA ON CHURCHES**
CATHOLIC CHURCH. *Catholic organizations.* The church sponsors one primary school with 4 grades and 120 pupils, conducted by 3 Franciscan missionary sisters from Jamaica and one lay teacher.

---

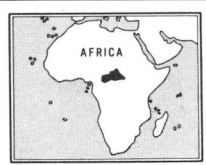

# CENTRAL AFRICAN REPUBLIC

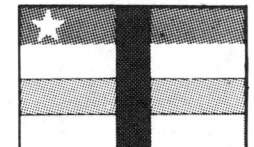

## SECULAR DATA

**STATE. Official name:** The Central African Republic (La République Centrafricaine); before 1976, Central African Republic, the Empire until 1979. Adjective of nationality: centrafricain.
**Flag** (shown above right): Blue, white, green, and yellow stripes crossed by vertical red bar: gold star in upper hoist corner.
**Area:** 622,984 sq.km. (240,535 sq.miles). Agricultural land: 9.6%.
**Government:** Republic since 1979 (1894 French territory, 1905

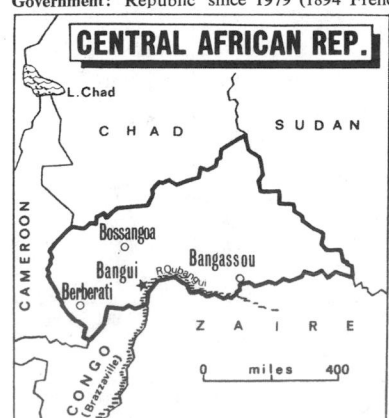

colony in French Equatorial Africa, 1960 Independence as republic 1966 military dictatorship and empire).
**Official language:** French (*Français*). National language: Sango.
**Chief cities:** capital Bangui 187,000 (1971), Berbérati 93,000.
**Armed forces** (1976): Total 1,000 regular: army, air force (about 6 combat aircraft).

**DEMOGRAPHY. Population:** 2,255,536 (census of 1968, not accepted by UN. For 1970–2000 (UN), see last row of Table 1).
Population density (1975): 3/sq.km. (7/sq.mile). Under 15 years: 42%. Growth rate (1975–80): 2.27% per year (births 4.30%, deaths −2.03%). Life expectancy (1975–80): 43.5 years. Household size: 4.9 persons.
**Major languages:** Banda, Baya, French, Sango, Mandja, Mbum, and over 45 other tribal languages.
**Urban dwellers** (1970): 25.4%. Urban growth rate (1950–70): 5.4% per year.
**Labour force:** 36%.
**Refugees** (1977): About 2,000 from Zaire and Chad.
**Tourists** (1974): 4,077.

**ETHNOLINGUISTIC GROUPS:** 34.2% Banda (Linda, Kreich, Langba), 26.7% Baya, 7.2% Mandja, 6.9% Sara, 6.7% Mbum, 6.5% Mbaka (Bwaka), 4.0% Riverine (Yakoma, Sango, Banziri), 4.0% Nzakara, 2.0% Kare, 0.5% Azande, Binga Pygmy, Rounga, Gula, Youla, French, Sudan Arab, Hausa, Camerounais, Zairois, et alii.

**MONEY** (1977). **Monetary unit:** CFA franc (= 100 centimes); US$1 = CFAF 250.00.
**National income per person:** US$110. Average annual family income: US$539.
**Inflation:** (1970–74) 7.8% per year, (1975) 16% per year (consumer price index 157).
**Cost of living in capital** (1976): index 172 (Washington DC=100). Daily cost of living: US$41.

**EDUCATION.** Adult literacy: (1962) 7%, (1975) 18%. Education rate: 36%. Schools: 717. Universities: 1.

**HEALTH.** Hospitals: 52 (3,161 beds). Doctors: 59. Lepers: 117,000 (65.4 per 1,000). Blind: 27,000. Psychotics: 13,000.

**LITERATURE.** Annual new book titles (1967): 23, Periodicals: 15. Newspapers: 1 daily, 1 non-daily.

**COMMUNICATION** (per 1,000 people). Phones: 3. Radios: 38. Daily newspaper circulation: 0.3 copies.

**Eglise Catholique à la RCA, Diocèse de Berbérati.** Postage stamp of 1971 consecration of Berbérati Cathedral.

TABLE 1. RELIGIOUS ADHERENTS IN THE CENTRAL AFRICAN REPUBLIC

| Year / Name | 1900 Adherents | % | mid-1970 Adherents | % | Annual change, 1970–1980 Natural | Conversion | Total | Rate | mid-1975 Adherents | % | mid-1980 Adherents | % | 2000 Adherents | % |
|---|---|---|---|---|---|---|---|---|---|---|---|---|---|---|
| **Christians** | 50 | 0.0 | 1,233,200 | 76.5 | 31,594 | 14,426 | 46,020 | 3.19 | 1,442,700 | 80.6 | 1,693,400 | 84.5 | 3,057,600 | 91.0 |
| professing | 50 | 0.0 | 1,233,200 | 76.5 | 31,594 | 14,426 | 46,020 | 3.19 | 1,442,700 | 80.6 | 1,693,400 | 84.5 | 3,057,600 | 91.0 |
|   Protestants | 0 | 0.0 | 725,500 | 45.0 | 18,503 | 7,747 | 26,250 | 3.11 | 844,900 | 47.2 | 988,000 | 49.3 | 1,747,200 | 52.0 |
|   Roman Catholics | 50 | 0.0 | 483,600 | 30.0 | 12,386 | 5,584 | 17,970 | 3.18 | 565,600 | 31.6 | 663,300 | 33.1 | 1,199,500 | 35.7 |
|   African indigenous | 0 | 0.0 | 16,100 | 1.0 | 471 | 729 | 1,200 | 5.58 | 21,500 | 1.2 | 28,100 | 1.4 | 60,500 | 1.8 |
|   Marginal Protestants | 0 | 0.0 | 8,000 | 0.5 | 234 | 366 | 600 | 5.61 | 10,700 | 0.6 | 14,000 | 0.7 | 50,400 | 1.5 |
| nominal | 0 | 0.0 | 543,714 | 33.7 | 12,791 | −4,422 | 8,369 | 1.43 | 584,100 | 32.6 | 627,400 | 31.3 | 705,600 | 21.0 |
| affiliated | 50 | 0.0 | 689,486 | 42.8 | 18,803 | 18,848 | 37,651 | 4.38 | 858,600 | 48.0 | 1,066,000 | 53.2 | 2,352,000 | 70.0 |
|   total practising | 47 | 95 | 517,110 | 75 | 14,102 | 14,136 | 28,238 | 4.38 | 643,950 | 75 | 799,500 | 75 | 1,646,400 | 70 |
|   non-practising | 3 | 5 | 172,370 | 25 | 4,701 | 4,712 | 9,413 | 4.38 | 214,650 | 25 | 266,500 | 25 | 705,600 | 30 |
|   Protestants | 0 | 0.0 | 397,960 | 24.7 | 10,742 | 9,772 | 20,514 | 4.18 | 490,500 | 27.4 | 603,100 | 30.1 | 1,290,200 | 38.4 |
|   Evangelicals | 0 | 0.0 | 396,000 | 24.6 | 10,665 | 9,635 | 20,300 | 4.17 | 487,000 | 27.2 | 599,000 | 29.9 | 1,280,000 | 38.1 |
|   Roman Catholics | 50 | 0.0 | 277,926 | 17.2 | 7,682 | 8,615 | 16,297 | 4.64 | 350,800 | 19.6 | 440,900 | 22.0 | 1,008,000 | 30.0 |
|   African indigenous | 0 | 0.0 | 8,500 | 0.5 | 234 | 316 | 550 | 5.14 | 10,700 | 0.6 | 14,000 | 0.7 | 33,600 | 1.0 |
|   Marginal Protestants | 0 | 0.0 | 5,100 | 0.3 | 145 | 145 | 290 | 4.39 | 6,600 | 0.4 | 8,000 | 0.4 | 20,200 | 0.6 |
| **Tribal religionists** | 766,950 | 99.6 | 327,300 | 20.3 | 6,282 | −15,012 | −8,730 | −3.04 | 286,800 | 16.0 | 240,000 | 12.0 | 169,400 | 5.0 |
| **Muslims** | 3,000 | 0.4 | 48,000 | 3.0 | 1,215 | 395 | 1,610 | 2.90 | 55,500 | 3.1 | 64,100 | 3.2 | 121,000 | 3.6 |
| **Baha'is** | 0 | 0.0 | 3,500 | 0.2 | 109 | 191 | 300 | 6.00 | 5,000 | 0.3 | 6,500 | 0.3 | 12,000 | 0.4 |
| **Country's population** | 770,000 | 100.0 | 1,612,000 | 100.0 | 39,200 | 0 | 39,200 | 2.19 | 1,790,000 | 100.0 | 2,004,000 | 100.0 | 3,360,000 | 100.0 |

**COLUMNS, ROWS.** For meanings and definitions, see Codebook (Part 6). Note that, by definition, total 'Christians' = professing + crypto-Christians, which also = affiliated + nominal Christians. Percentages may not always total exactly, due to rounding.
**CENSUSES. X.1960–IV.1961** (persons over 13 years): 41.8% Protestants, 28.1% Roman Catholics, 27.6% tribal religionists, 2.5% Muslims.

**NOTES ON RELIGIONS**
**AFFILIATED.** The column 'Conversion' above shows a nett annual total (conversions minus defections) of 18,848 persons. Most of these converts receive adult baptism in the churches, as can be seen from baptism figures in column 8 in Table 2 below.
**AFRICAN INDIGENOUS.** In about 6 denominations in 1970 (see Table 2).
**BAHA'IS.** Growth from 1 local spiritual assembly (1964) to 21 (1973). Radio broadcasts over government radio began in 1973. Missionaries from Haiti (West Indies) are at work.
**MUSLIMS.** Strongest in towns among non-Africans (31%); also among Hausa and Bororo nomads in north. Mostly Sunnis (of the Malikite rite). There has been lengthy infiltration among the Gbaya (Baya), who are now somewhat islamized in some areas. *Hajj pilgrims to Mecca.* (1975) 390; (1976) 361.
**NOMINAL CHRISTIANS.** The very large proportion of Christians who are nominal (professing in censuses, but not known to the churches) and who form a nominal fringe of nearly 600,000 around affiliated Christians, reflects a situation typical of rapid mass conversions of societies: vastly more persons regard themselves as having broken with non-Christian society, and having become believers, than the churches are capable of contacting, initiating by baptism, and discipling. Many have attended Christian-originated schools and regard themselves as Christians as a result.
**TRIBAL RELIGIONISTS.** Tribes over 60% traditionalist (animist) in 1972: Binga Pygmies, Mbimou (60%). Among several movements covered by this category is Nzapa ti Azande which is government-recognized as an authentic African religion.

**NON-CHRISTIAN RELIGIONS. Traditional religions** are still professed by a small minority of each of the main tribes, as well as by 99% of the Binga Pygmies. In 1960, 28% of the population was recorded as traditionalist with the following tribal breakdown: Banda 27%, Baya 35%, Mandja 25%, Sara 21%, Mbaka 23%, Mbum 17%, Nzakara 22% and Azande 13%. All these figures have since been substantially reduced, to 16% for the nation by 1975. The most common Baya name for God is So, although Zambi is also used. Meanwhile, the government has granted recognition as an authentic African religion to the Nzapa ti Azande movement.
**Islam** is strongest among the non-African population which in 1960 was 31% Muslim. The Banda then were only 0.4% Muslim, Baya 1.6%, and Mandja 2.6%, making 2.5% for the whole population. Except for some Hausa and Bororo nomads in the north, Islam has had little impact on rural peoples and is primarily an urban phenomenon. In 1976 president Bokassa announced his conversion to Islam after a visit by president Gaddaffi of Libya.

**CHRISTIANITY.** Since territorial independence in 1959, the number of professing Christians rose dramatically from 42% Protestant and 28% Catholic (1960) to 47% Protestant and 32% Catholic (1975), making this mass influx one of the most dramatic in Africa.
**PROTESTANT CHURCHES.** The 2 largest Protestant denominations are the Baptist and Brethren churches, both of which were started by North American missionary societies following World War I. The first to arrive was Baptist Mid-Missions, coming in 1920 from Congo-Kinshasa and building their first centre at Rafai among the Azande. They now have 12 stations concentrated primarily among the Banda, Mandja and Nzakara. A year later followed the Church of the Brethren mission, which in addition to a large number of self-supporting congregations sponsors a hospital, 16 dispensaries, several Bible schools and a school of theology. Other denominations include those begun by Swedish and Swiss Pentecostals. Lutheran work was begun by the Sudan Mission in 1923, assisted later by the American Lutheran Church and the Church of Norway; its work extends over the border into Cameroon.
**CATHOLIC CHURCH.** The first Catholic mission was opened at Bangui in 1894. A prefecture was erected in 1909, elevated to a vicariate in 1937. The Catholic Church is now organized into 5 dioceses under an African archbishop.
**INDIGENOUS CHURCHES.** A schism by Mandja tribesmen out of Baptist Mid-Missions in 1956 resulted in the Comité Baptiste, which has since received missionaries from Coopération Évangélique Mondiale (France, Switzerland); and a split from the Church of the Brethren by a Banda pastor at Bouca in 1960 resulted in the formation of the Eglise Centrafricaine. In addition, numerous

**Union des Eglises Baptistes.** *Above.* Baya-speaking Pentecostal church elders sweep up after service, with pastor and wife at far left. *Below,* their church building at Bossemptele.

white-robed adherents of independent churches from Zaire including Kimbanguists now live and work in Bangui and other centres.

**CHURCH AND STATE.** The constitution was suspended in January 1966, and the country subsequently governed by decree; there are therefore no juridical provisions for relations between church and state. There are however de facto agreements recognized: (1) the Ministry of Social Affairs subsidizes church rural development projects and sometimes even the construction of church buildings; (2) all primary, secondary, and technical schools are run by government, although religious orders are allowed to operate schools in Bangui (Lyceum of The Rapids, by Marist brothers, and Lyceum Pius XII, by Sisters of the Holy Spirit) as well as a number of primary schools outside the capital, and missions operate 2 recognized private schools (Protestants at Crampel, and Catholics in the diocese of Bangui run by Sisters of the Holy Spirit); (3) although chaplains of lyceums have no legal status, religious instruction is permitted outside school hours; and (4) a small nominal tax is paid by clergy and religious personnel, at the same rate as villagers. There is no government ministry in charge of religious affairs, but churches are required to keep the Ministry of the Interior informed about their activities in the country.
Catholic bishops have over the last few years tended to withdraw from their earlier close connections with the political authorities. In 1977 they, and the Vatican, refused to perform the coronation ceremony requested by the emperor.
In June 1977 the Central African Evangelical Baptist Church was decreed dissolved because it 'constitutes a danger to public order.'

**INTERDENOMINATIONAL ORGANIZATIONS.** There is no ecumenical council nor other organization. Most Protestants co-operate in the Association of Central African Evangelical Churches, organized in 1974 and a member of AEAM. Relations between all denominations are limited and are confined largely to Bible translation work. The AEAM however has sponsored, and in 1976 opened, the interdenominational Bangui Evangelical School of Theology (BEST), offering higher degrees in biblical theology and serving Protestants throughout francophone Africa.

**BROADCASTING.** The state Radiodiffusion Nationale Centrafricaine accepts both Protestant and Catholic programmes, and they are broadcast every Sunday morning. There is a Protestant recording studio in Bangui. Christian programmes in French are easily received from international stations in Liberia (ELWA), and until 1977 Ethiopia (RVOG). For Catholics, the CAR is registered as a member of UNDA.

**BIBLIOGRAPHY**
'The christianization of the Central African Republic'. R. W. Hill. Thesis, Fuller Theological Seminary, Pasadena, CA (USA), 1969. 301p.

Graduate-level Bangui Evangelical School of Theology (BEST) under construction.

TABLE 2. ORGANIZED CHURCHES AND DENOMINATIONS IN THE CENTRAL AFRICAN REPUBLIC

| Official name 1 | Begun 2 | Type 3 | Counc 4 | Congs 5 | Adults 6 | Affiliated 7 | Names, notes, and other statistics (see Codebook) 8 |
|---|---|---|---|---|---|---|---|
| Christianisme Prophétique en Afrique | c1970 | I pen | .v... | 2 | 100 | 300 | *Prophetic Christianity in Africa*. Healings. HQ Bangui. 1973 applied to join WCC. |
| Comité Baptiste | 1956 | I pen | ..... | 10 | 3,000 | 7,000 | *Baptist Committee*. Schism ex BMM among Mandja. M=Coopération Ev Mondiale(Switz). |
| Eglise Adventiste du Septième Jour | 1960 | P Adv | x.... | 35 | 467 | 1,800 | *Seventh-day Adv, CAR Mission*. 60% Mbougou, 15% Baguiro, 15% Baya. 1x,1h,1s,123Y. |
| **Eglise Catholique à la RCA:** | 1894 | R Lat | P.SBR | 549 | 161,200 | 277,926 | *Catholic Ch in the CAR*. C=4+1+25. 8p. 12n, 180x, 53m,271w,P=41%, 12300Yy. |
| M Bangui | 1909 | R Lat | Ps | 26 | 67,000 | 115,618 | 45% Banda, 30% Baya, 8% Banziri. 5 65 18 104 35 3318 |
| D Bambari | 1965 | R Lat | Pcssp | 10 | 23,900 | 41,150 | Banda, Banziri. Formed out of M Bangui. 1p. 0 20 1 36 35 2269 |
| D Bangassou | 1954 | R Lat | Pcssp | 272 | 28,100 | 48,414 | 1964–73, 25,000 Sudanese refugees. 1p. 5 24 13 51 36 3127 |
| D Berbérati | 1940 | R Lat | Pofmc | 228 | 23,100 | 39,800 | 72% Baya, 19% Mbimou,6% Pana,3%Kare. 3p. 1 40 15 56 55 990 |
| D Bossangoa | 1959 | R Lat | Pofmc | 13 | 19,100 | 32,944 | Baya, Banda, Banziri. In northwest. 3p. 1 31 6 24 58 2596 |
| Eglise Centrafricaine | 1960 | I ind | ..... |  | 100 | 200 | *Central African Ch*. Schism ex EEF by Banda pastor at Bouca. Dying out. |
| Eglise Evangélique Centrafricaine | 1924 | P int | xMG.G | 100 | 1,000 | 5,000 | M=AIM(USA). 90% Azande, 5% Kare. 1964–73, many Sudanese refugees. 18f,4h, |
| **Eglise Evangélique des Frères** | 1921 | P Dun | xFG.G | 450 | 63,000 | 150,000 | *EEF. Brethren Ch.* M=NFBC(USA). 70% Baya, 20% Mandja, 10% Karre. 56f,1H,16h,1r,2s, |
| Eglise Evangélique du Réveil | 1927 | P Pe2 | Z.G.G | 150 | 6,500 | 20,000 | M=Elim MA,SPM(Switzerland). 99% Banda. HQ Alindao. 59n,8x,1h,1s(33),W=65%,646Y. |
| Eglise Ev Luthérienne de la RCA | 1923 | P Lut | L.... | 154 | 6,151 | 15,960 | M=Sudan M,NMS,ALC(USA). 99% Baya. 3n,2x,65m,G=9.0%pa,1p,600Y,447y,603z. |
| Eglise Protestante du Bangui |  | P Ref | ..... | 1 | 100 | 200 | *Protestant Ch in Bangui*. Christ-Roi. Union church. Largely expatriates. |
| **Eglises Baptistes de la RCA** | 1920 | P Bap | xT... | 375 | 60,000 | 150,000 | *Baptist Chs of CAR*. M=BMM(USA). 70% Banda, 20% Mandja. 80f,1H,6h,12i,1j,2p,1s. |
| Mission Evangélique (Américaine) | 1937 | P ind | ..... |  | 3,000 | 5,000 | *Ev Mission (American)*. M=Central Africa Pioneer Mission (USA). HQ Carnot. |
| Témoins de Jéhovah | c1945 | M Jeh | x.... | 28 | 1,243 | 5,100 | *Jehovah's Witnesses. Watch Tower*. Active witnessing under way by 1948. 10f,103Y. |
| Union des Eglises Baptistes | 1923 | P Pe2 | Z.G.G | 29 | 26,595 | 50,000 | M=Örebro M(Sweden). 90% Baya, 10% Mpimo. 38n,65f,1H,7h,2p(26),1s(12),3563Y,10446z. |
| Other African indigenous churches |  | I | ..... |  | 500 | 1,000 | Several small prophet groups from Zaire (see list below). |
| **Total affiliated (mid-1970)** |  |  |  | **1,920** | **332,956** | **689,486** | **Total denominations (1970) . . . 18.** |
| **Total affiliated (mid-1975)** |  |  |  | **2,100** | **414,600** | **858,600** | **Total denominations (1975) . . . 20.** |
| **Total affiliated (mid-1980)** |  |  |  | **2,300** | **514,800** | **1,066,000** | **Total denominations (1970) . . . 22.** |

**NOTES ON TABLE ABOVE**
COLUMNS: for meanings and CODES (cols. 1, 3, 4, 8): see Codebook (Part 6). Column 1: **Boldface type** = church with over 10% of country's affiliated Christians.
NATIONAL COUNCILS (Column 4, 5th letter).
G = Association des Eglises Evangéliques Centrafricaines (AEEC) (Association of Central African Evangelical Churches).
R = Conférence des Evêques de la RCA (CERCA) (Bishops' Conference of the CAR).
OTHER AFRICAN INDIGENOUS CHURCHES. These groups have come mostly from Zaire, including the EJCSK (Kimbanguist Church), Kanda Dia Kinzinga (People for Eternal Life; since 1945), Kitawala and Kolinga.

**PEOPLES** (ethnolinguistic). Christians: 33% Banda, 27% Baya, 8% Mandja, 8% Mbum, 8% Sara, 7% Mbaka, 4% Nzakara, 2% Banziri, 2% Kare, 0.7% Azande, French, et alii.

**COUNTRY-WIDE TOTALS**
EVANGELIZATION (see Part 5). 1900: 0%. 1970: 99%. 1980: 100%. *Mass evangelism*. 1970–71, New Life for All campaign; 1975, Bangui churches' campaign (25,000 decisions over 18 months).
FOREIGN MISSIONARIES AND PERSONNEL (nationals serving abroad) (1973). Total about 3 Roman Catholics.
FOREIGN MISSIONARIES AND PERSONNEL (aliens from abroad) (1973). Total 743. *From Western world*. 720: 473 Roman Catholics, 236 Protestants (160 in 4 USA societies, 65 in 1 Sweden society, 4 in 1 Canada society, 3 in 1 UK society, 2 in 1 Switzerland society, 2 in 1 France society), 10 marginal Protestants (Jehovah's Witnesses), 1 Anglican in 1 UK society. *From Third World*. 23: 21 Roman Catholics from Brazil, Sudan and Zaire, 2 indigenous from Zaire.
INSTITUTIONS (church-operated) (1973). Total 90, including 7 higher schools (4 minor seminaries), 70 medical centres (11 hospitals), 1 press, 6 seminaries (Protestant), 1 study centre.
PERIODICALS. About 12 titles.
PERSONNEL. About 3,029 (2,286 national, 743 foreign).
RELIGIOUS LIBRARIES. 8.
SCRIPTURE DISTRIBUTION (1975). Annual totals: 6,100 Bibles (98% subsidized, 2% commercial), 25,000 NTs (subsidized), 7,100 UBS portions, 5,600 UBS selections. *Translations completed*. Portion: 7 languages since 1927. NT: 4 languages since 1935. Bible: 1 language in 1966.
SERVICE AGENCIES. About 28, including AEEC, ARF, BNEC, CERCA, CV/AV, GBUAF, JAC/F, JEC/F, JOC/F, NLFA, WVI.

**ADDITIONAL DATA ON CHURCHES**
EGLISE CATHOLIQUE A LA RCA. *New diocese*. (1978) D Bouar (26,250 Catholics, 4,700 catechumens), formed out of D Berbérati. *Catechumens*. (1959) 44,054; (1961) 51,450; (1963) 51,148; (1971) 52,343. *Annual baptisms*. (1972) 35.1% infant, 64.9% adult. *Brothers*. Including 1 national. *Sisters*. Including 30 nationals. *Catechists*. Total (1970) 1,886, of whom 15 were full-time. In addition to the 8 training schools, 3 new ones are being set up (2 in M Bangui, one in D Bangassou). *Indigenous religious congregations*. None. *Main foreign orders and congregations*. Priests: OFMCap, CSSp, FSCJ, OP. Brothers: Marists. Sisters: Missionnaires du St-Esprit, St-Paul de Chartres, Franciscaines de l'Immaculée Conception. In 1972 there were also 2 congregations of sisters temporarily refugees from the Sudan. *Catholic organizations*. The Conference of Bishops of the Central African Repulic (Conférence des Evêques de la République Centrafricaine, CERCA) is a member of ACECCT (and formerly of ACEACCAM) and SECAM. There are no national presbyteral or pastoral councils, nor associations of religious personnel. The General Bureau of Works (Direction Générale des Oeuvres) co-ordinates the activities of Légion de Marie, JOC/F (especially at Bangui), JAC/F (90 teams), JEC/F, CV/AV, Scouts and Guides (26 groups).

The Holy See has diplomatic relations with the Central African Republic and is represented to government and the Catholic hierarchy by a pro-nuncio in Bangui.

The Catholic Church is heavily involved in rural development. A programme known as Women's Rural Animation (ARF) was registered with the Ministry of the Interior in 1963; with 34 centres and 9,400 participants. It provides courses in literacy, agricultural production, nutrition, hygiene, housekeeping and sewing. Medical activity includes 23 dispensaries, 7 maternity hospitals, one leprosarium and a rest home. Educational facilities in 1973 included 19 primary schools (10,413 pupils) and 1 secondary school (430).

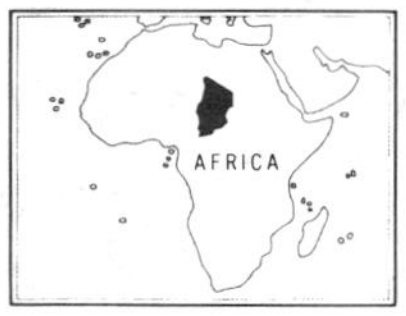


# CHAD

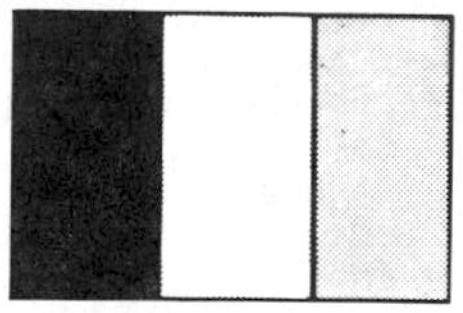

## SECULAR DATA

**STATE. Official name:** The Republic of Chad (La République du Tchad). Adjective of nationality: tchadien.
**Flag** (shown above right): Blue, yellow, red bars.
**Area:** 1,284,000 sq.km. (495,750 sq.miles). Agricultural land: 40.5%.
**Government:** Military junta, since 1975 (1900 French military territory, 1910 colony in French Equatorial Africa, 1960 Independence as republic).
**Official language** (also proclaimed National Language): French (*Français*).
**Capital:** N'djamena 179,000 (1972), formerly named Fort-Lamy.
**Armed forces** (1976): Total 4,700 regular: army 4,500, air force 200 (5 combat aircraft). Paramilitary forces: 6,000.
**Foreign forces** (1971): 2,500 French troops; (1978) 1,800.

**DEMOGRAPHY. Population:** 3,254,000 (census of XII.1963–VIII.1964. For 1970–2000 (UN), see last row of Table 1). Population density (1975): 3/sq.km. (8/sq.mile). Under 15 years: 45%. Growth rate (1975–80): 2.12% per year (births 4.40%, deaths −2.28%). Life expectancy (1975–80): 40.0 years. Household size: 4.9 persons.
**Major languages:** Sara, Sango, Arabic, French, Hausa, Fur, Kanuri, Berber, and about 100 other tribal languages.
**Urban dwellers** (1970): 6.9%. Urban growth rate (1950–70): 4.9% per year.
**Labour force:** 36%.
**Tourists** (1973): 16,691.

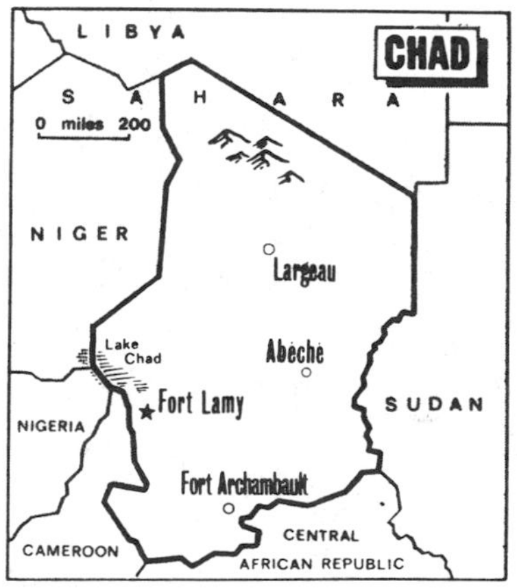


**ETHNOLINGUISTIC GROUPS:** 30% Sudan Arab (Shuwa; 19% nomadic), 33% Sudanic (7% Mbum, 5% Bagirmi, Sara, Mbai, Dai, Gula, Kare, Kim, Nduka, Tuburi, Mundang, Baya, Banda), 11% Kanuri (Saharan Negro) (7.5% Tubu (Teda), 2.3% Kanembu, 0.7% Zagawa), 10% Fur (6.3% Tama, 2.4% Dagu, 0.1% Fur), 9.5% Nilotic Saharan Sudanic (5.5% Maba/Masalit, 4.0% Mubi, Lisi), 4% Plateau Chadic (Gaberi, 2.2% Masa/Musgum, &c), 2.2% Hausa, 0.2% French (3,500), Kotoko, Somrai, Fulani.

**MONEY** (1977). **Monetary unit:** CFA franc (= 100 centimes); US$1 = CFAF 250.00.
**National income per person:** US$94. Average annual family income: US$461.
**Inflation:** (1970–74) 16% per year (1975: consumer price index 154).
**Cost of living in capital** (1976): index 168 (Washington DC=100). Daily cost of living: US$42.

**EDUCATION.** Adult literacy: (1963) 6% (1975) 10%. Education rate: 17%. Schools: 761.

**HEALTH.** Hospitals: 47 (3,551 beds). Doctors: 60. Lepers: 103,000 (25.6 per 1,000). Blind: 175,000. Psychotics: 24,000.

**LITERATURE.** Periodicals: 16. Newspapers: 1 daily, 1 non-daily.

**COMMUNICATION** (per 1,000 people). Phones: 1. Radios: 16. Daily newspaper circulation: 0.2 copies.

TABLE 1. RELIGIOUS ADHERENTS IN CHAD

| Year | 1900 | | mid-1970 | | Annual change, 1970–1980 | | | | mid-1975 | | mid-1980 | | 2000 | |
|---|---|---|---|---|---|---|---|---|---|---|---|---|---|---|
| *Name* | *Adherents* | *%* | *Adherents* | *%* | *Natural* | *Conversion* | *Total* | *Rate* | *Adherents* | *%* | *Adherents* | *%* | *Adherents* | *%* |
| Muslims | 612,000 | 36.0 | 1,528,000 | 42.0 | 35,822 | 8,178 | 44,000 | 2.54 | 1,730,000 | 43.0 | 1,968,000 | 44.0 | 3,249,000 | 47.0 |
| **Christians** | **0** | **0.0** | **1,128,000** | **31.0** | **26,648** | **8,152** | **34,800** | **2.70** | **1,287,000** | **32.0** | **1,476,000** | **33.0** | **2,419,000** | **35.0** |
| professing | 0 | 0.0 | 1,128,000 | 31.0 | 26,648 | 8,152 | 34,800 | 2.70 | 1,287,000 | 32.0 | 1,476,000 | 33.0 | 2,419,000 | 35.0 |
| Roman Catholics | 0 | 0.0 | 728,000 | 20.0 | 17,082 | 4,018 | 21,100 | 2.56 | 825,000 | 20.5 | 939,000 | 21.0 | 1,451,000 | 21.0 |
| Protestants | 0 | 0.0 | 393,000 | 10.8 | 9,318 | 3,382 | 12,700 | 2.82 | 450,000 | 11.2 | 520,000 | 11.6 | 899,000 | 13.0 |
| African indigenous | 0 | 0.0 | 7,000 | 0.2 | 248 | 752 | 1,000 | 8.33 | 12,000 | 0.3 | 17,000 | 0.4 | 69,000 | 1.0 |
| nominal | 0 | 0.0 | 650,455 | 17.9 | 13,910 | −9,486 | 4,424 | 0.66 | 671,800 | 16.7 | 694,700 | 15.5 | 672,000 | 9.7 |
| affiliated | 0 | 0.0 | 477,545 | 13.1 | 12,738 | 17,638 | 30,376 | 4.94 | 615,200 | 15.3 | 781,300 | 17.5 | 1,747,000 | 25.3 |
| total practising | 0 | *0* | 420,240 | *88* | 11,210 | 15,520 | 26,730 | 4.94 | 541,380 | *88* | 687,540 | *88* | 1,397,600 | *80* |
| non-practising | 0 | *0* | 57,300 | *12* | 1,528 | 2,118 | 3,646 | 4.94 | 73,820 | *12* | 93,760 | *12* | 349,400 | *20* |
| Protestants | 0 | 0.0 | 239,634 | 6.6 | 6,419 | 9,018 | 15,437 | 4.98 | 310,000 | 7.7 | 394,000 | 8.8 | 829,000 | 12.0 |
| Evangelicals | 0 | 0.0 | 239,300 | 6.6 | 6,411 | 8,859 | 15,270 | 4.93 | 309,600 | 7.7 | 392,000 | 8.8 | 825,000 | 11.9 |
| Roman Catholics | 0 | 0.0 | 231,111 | 6.3 | 6,087 | 7,902 | 13,989 | 4.76 | 294,000 | 7.3 | 371,000 | 8.3 | 850,000 | 12.3 |
| African indigenous | 0 | 0.0 | 6,700 | 0.2 | 228 | 702 | 930 | 8.45 | 11,000 | 0.3 | 16,000 | 0.4 | 66,000 | 1.0 |
| Marginal Protestants | 0 | 0.0 | 100 | 0.0 | 4 | 16 | 20 | 10.00 | 200 | 0.0 | 300 | 0.0 | 2,000 | 0.0 |
| Tribal religionists | 1,088,000 | 64.0 | 978,000 | 26.9 | 20,679 | −16,439 | 4,240 | 0.42 | 998,700 | 24.8 | 1,020,400 | 22.8 | 1,218,000 | 17.6 |
| Baha'is | 0 | 0.0 | 5,000 | 0.1 | 124 | 76 | 200 | 3,33 | 6,000 | 0.1 | 7,000 | 0.2 | 20,000 | 0.3 |
| Non-religious | 0 | 0.0 | 1,000 | 0.0 | 27 | 33 | 60 | 4.62 | 1,300 | 0.0 | 1,600 | 0.0 | 6,000 | 0.1 |
| **Country's population** | **1,700,000** | **100.0** | **3,640,000** | **100.0** | **83,300** | **0** | **83,300** | **2.07** | **4,023,000** | **100.0** | **4,473,000** | **100.0** | **6,912,000** | **100.0** |

COLUMNS, ROWS. For meanings and definitions, see Codebook (Part 6). Note that, by definition, total 'Christians' = professing + crypto-Christians, which also = affiliated + nominal Christians. Percentages may not always total exactly, due to rounding.
CENSUSES. XII.1963–VIII.1964 (de jure): 41.0% Muslims, 29.8% tribal religionists, 19.6% Roman Catholics (494,970 persons), 9.6% Protestants (241,370 persons). (North): 95% Muslims, 4% tribal religionists, 4,260 Roman Catholics, 2,270 Protestants. (South): 47% tribal religionists, 32% Roman Catholics (490,710 persons), 16% Protestants (239,100 persons), 5% Muslims. (Urban centres): 39% Muslims, 29% Roman Catholics, 20% Protestants, 12% tribal religionists.

NOTES ON RELIGIONS
AFRICAN INDIGENOUS. In about 6 groupings in 1970 (see Table 2).
BAHA'IS. Rapid expansion to 50 local spiritual assemblies by 1973, with 3,500 active members and a school at Gassi.
CHRISTIANS. By the time the first generation of Christian children had grown up (about 1960), a massive people movement began in southern Chad, which by 1970 had become about 16.5% Protestant.
MUSLIMS. Islamization began in the 11th century with major waves in the 16th and 17th centuries; it is almost complete (over 95%) in the northern and eastern regions. Most are Sunnis (Shafiite and Malikite rites). Orders: Hamalliya (50% of all Muslims), Tijaniya (20% of all Muslims), Sanusiya, Qadiriya, Mahdiya, et alia. In the south, Islam is weak (5%), confined to the Fulani (Léré region) and the urban Bornu. *Hajj pilgrims to Mecca.* (1970) 2,034; (1974) 4,921; (1975) 965; (1976) 1,392.
NOMINAL CHRISTIANS. The very large nominal fringe around the churches (a phenomenon larger in Chad than in any other African country), i.e. unaffiliated Christians not on the churches' records, is due to the exceptionally rapid influx into the churches from 1945–70 (an average growth rate of 17% per year) and widespread popularity of confessional schools. The fringe is made up of (1) intending Christians, who have broken with pagan society and regard themselves as followers of Christ but have not as yet been contacted or initiated by the churches, (2) others influenced by the large Christian (especially Catholic) social programmes, and (3) many thousands of schoolchildren in Christian (especially Catholic) schools, with their relatives and friends. After 1970 the fringe began proportionately to decrease in size as the churches began to catch up with and initiate (catechumenate and baptism) the vast numbers of professing Christians.
PRACTISING CHRISTIANS. In southern Chad in 1969, about 5% of the 2.5 million population (and in some areas 10%), i.e. 78% of all affiliated Protestants, attended Protestant churches regularly every Sunday. Annual church attenders: Catholics 82%, Protestants 95%.
TRIBAL RELIGIONISTS. Tribes over 60% traditionalist (animist) in 1972: Banana Marba (Masa) (85%), Bua (80%), Mbai (68%), Gaberi (60%), Sara (60%).

**NON-CHRISTIAN RELIGIONS. Islam** first penetrated Chad in the 11th century; then in successive waves in the 16th and 17th centuries it spread throughout the country. Chad is now about 43% Muslim. Islamization is almost complete in the northern and eastern regions which are geographically immense but sparsely populated with only 3 to 4 inhabitants per square kilometre. Islamic influence on the southern Black peoples is a more recent 20th-century phenomenon. In Chad one finds many different Islamic schools and brotherhoods, including Tijaniya, Sanusiya, Qadiriya and Madhism. The number of Muslims from Chad who perform the hajj to Mecca each year has risen rapidly from 2,034 in 1970 to 4,921 in 1974, after which it declined.

**Traditional African religions** are still significant south of the Chari river and are more generally found among the Black population living by agriculture and fishing. Tribes resistant to both Islam and Christianity include the Banana Marba (Masa), Bui, Gaberi, Mbai and Sara.

## CHRISTIANITY

CATHOLIC CHURCH. Although an attempt was made to open work in Chad by Capuchins in 1663, the first permanent mission was not founded until 1929, when Holy Ghost priests from Bangui built a station at Kou. Nevertheless, it is only since 1947 that Catholic activity has become extensive and organized. It reaches the younger levels of the population but its effectiveness with urban adults is limited, especially those of the middle and upper classes. It is relatively strong in the southern territories but sporadic in the Muslim zones, except in the urban centres among Catholics who have emigrated from the south.

PROTESTANT CHURCHES. The work of the Sudan United Mission has been joined to that of the French Mennonites and the Worldwide Evangelization Crusade to form the largest Protestant church in the country, Eglises Evangéliques du Tchad. Its youth movement called Flambeau (Little Flame) is particularly effective in its evangelistic outreach. The total Protestant community is slightly larger than that of Roman Catholicism. Protestant service projects include a secondary school, hospital and orphanage; 6 clinics; several adult literacy projects; and a rural development programme Société Chrétienne Rurale.

INDIGENOUS CHURCHES. Christian independency has not been a significant factor in Chad. Although a few groups have emerged from time to time, the majority have returned to the mission churches, including a group encouraged by the Tombalbaye regime in 1974 in its attempt to force traditional customs back on the churches.

**CHURCH AND STATE.** The constitution of 14 April 1962 states in the Preamble that Chad is a secular republic which assures for all equality before the law without distinction of origin or religion (Article 3). Nevertheless a strong sense of religion permeates political life; thus in 1972 the Bureau Politique National (BPN) proclaimed that on 28 November every year all Chadians must pray to God on behalf of Chad, in the manner prescribed by their own religion.

Religious associations such as denominations and dioceses must be registered with government, thereby becoming legal entities with the rights which follow from it. Catholic and Protestant private education is recognized, controlled by the state, and subsidized usually by about 50%.

The imam of the mosque in N'djamena, the Catholic archbishop, and a Protestant representative have been members of the Economic and Social Council and commonly invited to official receptions. The president of the republic and members of government also attend important religious ceremonies.

*Above.* **Eglise Fraternelle Luthérienne.** Theological college.
*Below.* 'Missionaire' prototype hovercraft developed by Missionary Aviation Fellowship for use on Lake Chad before latter began to dry up. Range: 150 miles. Cruising speed: 35 mph.

Because of its developed organization, number of places of worship, and the role of its educational and social work, the Catholic Church receives more consideration than its numbers warrant.

In November 1973 president Ngarta Tombalbaye launched an 'authenticity' or *chaditude* programme requiring that all Chadians undergo the traditional Yondo initiation rites of his own Sara tribe, and prohibiting the use of foreign names. At the same time, 18 Baptist missionaries were expelled, 13 Chadian pastors imprisoned and all Baptist churches and schools serving the Sara people were closed. Some Christians who opposed the government decrees were forcibly initiated, others were harassed, and still others killed. In the 12 months from November 1973, at least 130 Protestant African pastors were put to death, including the 13 leading Chadian Baptist pastors. Also during 1974 the government was instrumental in helping to establish an independent church among dissident Sara Baptists. In February 1975, 9 Swedish Pentecostal missionaries (SFM) were expelled. On 13 April 1975 Tombalbaye was assassinated, and the new military regime later assured Christians that no-one would thereafter be required to participate in any rites against his wishes. Both the new head of state and the chairman of the Supreme Council in 1975 were committed Protestants. On 3 May 1975 the government announced that all laws restricting religious freedom were repealed, affirmed once again that the Chadian state was secular, and reinstated as public holidays the major Christian and Muslim festivals.

**BROADCASTING.** The government Radio Chad broadcasts Catholic and Protestant programmes, 15 minutes every Sunday in French for both and 30 minutes in local languages alternating between the two. International stations can be heard, especially (until 1977) programmes of RVOG (Ethiopia) in French and Fulani. UNDA in Chad is represented by a national association. Correspondence courses linked to radio programmes, especially those of the North Africa Mission (Marseilles, France), have wide followings.

**BIBLIOGRAPHY**
'The Lutheran Brethren Church in Chad and Cameroun'. R.W. Venberg. Thesis, Fuller Theological Seminary, Pasadena, CA (USA), 1970. 178p.

**Eglises Evangéliques au Tchad.** WEC missionary distributes vitaminized foods to unevangelized Masalit children during drought in Ouaddai province.

TABLE 2. ORGANIZED CHURCHES AND DENOMINATIONS IN CHAD

| Official name 1 | Begun 2 | Type 3 | Counc 4 | Congs 5 | Adults 6 | Affiliated 7 | Names, notes, and other statistics (see Codebook) 8 |
|---|---|---|---|---|---|---|---|
| **Assemblées Chrétiennes du Tchad** | 1921 | P CBr | x...C | 250 | 20,000 | 60,000 | *Open Br.* M=CMML. 63% Mbai, 12% Dai, 12% Kim, 6% Kado. 300m,150w,20f,W=90%,200Y. |
| Assemblées de Dieu | c1960 | P Pe2 | Z.... | 10 | 200 | 400 | *Assemblies of God.* M=AdD(France). Formed ex EEF in Baibokoum. Medical work. |
| Eglise Adventiste du Septième Jour | c1962 | P Adv | x.... | 3 | 114 | 300 | *SDA, Chad Mission.* Equatorial African Union Mission. 10nxm,7t(225),27Y. |
| **Eglise Catholique au Tchad:** | 1929 | R Lat | P.SBR | 91 | 127,100 | 231,111 | *Catholic Ch.* C=3+0+24. 6p. 1n,152x,40m,177w,P=72%,12337Yy. |
| M N'djamena (Fort-Lamy) | 1947 | R Lat | Psj | 24 | 13,100 | 23,876 | Capital (50% Muslim, 50% pagan). 33% White. 1p. 0 27 13 46 65 940 |
| D Moundou | 1951 | R Lat | Pofmc | 22 | 84,900 | 154,348 | Oldest RC work (1928). Ngambais. 63% pagan. 3p. 1 52 13 49 70 8806 |
| D Pala | 1956 | R Lat | Pomi | 29 | 13,700 | 24,887 | 87% pagan. Farmers, cattlemen, fishermen. 1p. 0 34 5 46 88 1141 |
| D Sarh (Fort-Archambault) | 1961 | R Lat | Psj | 16 | 15,400 | 28,000 | Pagan farmers, Muslim cattlemen. 1p. 0 39 9 36 73 1450 |
| Eglise de Dieu | c1960 | P Pe3 | ZF... | 36 | 1,842 | 4,000 | *Ch of God.* M=CoG(Cleveland)(USA). Between Ft-Lamy and Bongor. Orphanage. 16n,1p. |
| Eglise Dissidente du Tchad | 1951 | I pen | ..... | | 500 | 1,000 | *Independent Ch of Chad.* Schism ex BMM. M=La Porte Ouverte(France). Ngama, Sara. |
| Eglise Evangélique des Frères | 1928 | P Dun | xF... | 30 | 5,000 | 15,000 | *EEF. Ev Ch of the Brethren.* M=NFBC(USA); begun from Central African Republic. 2f. |
| Eglise Evangélique du Tchad | 1974 | I int | ..... | 20 | 2,000 | 5,000 | *Ev Ch of Chad.* State church set up by government. Sara Protestants forced to join. |
| Egl Fraternelle Luthérienne au Tchad | 1920 | P Lut | x...C | 361 | 7,568 | 27,434 | M=CLB(USA). 40% Mundang. 24n,3x,6f,G=16%pa,20p,(1645),1s(22) 646Y,793y,2932z. |
| Eglises Baptistes du Tchad | 1925 | P Bap | xT..C | 150 | 20,000 | 30,000 | *Chad Baptist Chs.* M=BMM(USA). 1973 mission expelled. 25n,10x,57m,25f,1H,2h,2p,1r. |
| **Eglises Evangéliques au Tchad** | 1926 | P int | xM..C | 372 | 20,000 | 100,000 | *Ev Chs of Chad.* M=TEAM,SUM,WEC,EMEK. 47n,291mw,37f,1H,3h,1r,7s,W=80%,1626Y,1159z. |
| Eglises radiophoniques isolées | 1960 | I rad | ..... | | 100 | 200 | Isolated radio believers, mostly aged 12–25 in north. S=1397(RSB Arabic courses). |
| Témoins de Jéhovah | c1945 | M Jeh | x.... | 2 | 49 | 100 | *Jehovah's Witnesses. Watch Tower.* Active witnessing under way by 1948. 4f,5Y. |
| Other Protestant denominations | | P | ..... | | 1,200 | 2,500 | Total 6, including: Coopération Ev Mondiale (Mission Ev du Plein Evangile), SFM. |
| Other African indigenous churches | | I | ..... | | 200 | 500 | Several small schisms ex CMML, SUM, CLB. |
| **Total affiliated (mid-1970)** | | | | **1,350** | **205,873** | **477,545** | **Total denominations (1970) . . . 22.** |
| **Total affiliated (mid-1975)** | | | | **1,600** | **265,200** | **615,200** | **Total denominations (1975) . . . 23.** |
| **Total affiliated (mid-1980)** | | | | **1,950** | **336,800** | **781,300** | **Total denominations (1980) . . . 24.** |

NOTES ON TABLE ABOVE
COLUMNS: for meanings and CODES (cols. 1, 3, 4, 8): see Codebook (Part 6). Column 1: **Boldface type** = church with over 10% of country's affiliated Christians.
NATIONAL COUNCILS (Column 4, 5th letter).
C = Fédération des Eglises Evangéliques du Tchad (FEET) (Federation of Evangelical Churches of Chad), a loose grouping of missions and some national churches.
R = Conférence Episcopale du Tchad (CET) (Chad Episcopal Conference).

PEOPLES (ethnolinguistic). Christians: about 93% Sudanic (about 50% Ngambai, Sara, Ngama, Nduka, Gula, Mbai, Mundang, Baya, Banda, Mbum), 5% Gaberi, Musgum & other

COUNTRY-WIDE TOTALS
EVANGELIZATION (see Part 5). 1900: 0%. 1970: 54%. 1980: 64%. By 1975 the whole of southern Chad had been highly-evangelized; in tribes such as the Mesmé, everybody had heard of the name Jesus. *Mass evangelism.* 1970–71, New Life for All campaign. The SUM has initiated a rural evangelism project through farm aid called Faith on the Farm. *Radiophonic evangelism.* RVOG, Radio School of the Bible (Marseilles) with 1,397 students for Arabic courses. As a result of programmes in Fulani produced at the Ngaoundere studio (Cameroon) and broadcast over RVOG (Ethiopia), there are many Fulani believers in Muslim areas.
FOREIGN MISSIONARIES AND PERSONNEL (nationals serving abroad) (1973). Total about 2 Roman Catholics.
FOREIGN MISSIONARIES AND PERSONNEL (aliens from abroad) (1973). Total 541. *From Western world.* 507: 366 Roman Catholics, 137 Protestants (50 in 6 USA societies, 27 in 2 Canada societies, 23 in 3 WGermany societies, 12 in 3 Australia societies, 10 in 2 France societies, 7 in 3 UK societies, 6 in 1 Netherlands society, 2 in 1 New Zealand society), 4 marginal Protestants (Jehovah's Witnesses). *From Communist world.* About 2 Roman Catholics from Yugoslavia. *From Third World.* 32: about 20 Protestants from Nigeria and CAR, about 12 Roman Catholics (7 from Lebanon, also CAR and Zaire).
INSTITUTIONS (church-operated) (1973). Total 55, including 10 higher schools (2 minor seminaries), 30 medical centres (5 hospitals), 8 seminaries (Protestant).
PERIODICALS. About 10 titles.
PERSONNEL. About 4,031 (3,490 national, 541 foreign).
RELIGIOUS LIBRARIES. 8.
SCRIPTURE DISTRIBUTION (1975). Annual totals: 1,500 Bibles (subsidized), 16,000 NTs (subsidized), 20 UBS portions. *Translations completed.* Portion: 11 languages since 1932. NT: 6 languages since 1943.
SERVICE AGENCIES. About 26, inrcluding CET, CV/AV, FEET, GBUAF, JAC/F, JEC/F, JOC/F, MAF.

ADDITIONAL DATA ON CHURCHES
EGLISE CATHOLIQUE AU TCHAD. *Catechumens.* (1959) 50,195; (1961) 46,392; (1963) 53,713; (1970) 55,102, divided among the 4 dioceses (and included in column 7) as follows: 3,687; 28,000; 13,415; 10,000. *Annual baptisms.* (1972) 45.9% infant, 54.1% adult. *National priests.* The first was ordained in 1958. In addition to the 1 shown above (1970), 4 others were ordained from 1971–3. *Brothers.* All expatriates. *Sisters.* Including 3 nationals. *Seminarians.* Total 7, studying at the major seminary in Yaoundé, Cameroon. *Catechists.* Total (1970) 2,500 part-time and 900 assistant catechists. Fort-Lamy and Moundou have each a diocesan training school; the other schools are centres for married catechists in rural work. *Indigenous religious congregations.* None. *Main foreign orders and congregations.* Priests: SJ, OFMCap, OMI. Sisters: N–D des Apôtres.
*Catholic organizations.* The Episcopal Conference of Chad (Conférence Episcopale du Tchad) is a member of ACECCT (formerly ACEACCAM) and of SECAM. There are no national presbyteral or pastoral councils, nor associations of religious personnel. The principal lay movements are JAC/F (381 teams), JEC/F (74 teams), JOC/F (42 teams), Scouts (2,000 boys), Guides (1,580 girls), CV/AV (about 7,500 children), 386 house groups and Teacher Teams.

The Holy See has no diplomatic relations with Chad. In 1973 it was represented to the Catholic hierarchy by an apostolic delegate residing in Bangui, Central African Republic.

The Catholic educational programme in 1970 included 43 primary and 5 secondary schools, 8% and 7% respectively of the total in the country, in addition to 8 nursery schools and numerous bush-type catechist schools. By 1973 there were 54 primary (14,024 pupils) and 6 secondary schools (814 pupils). The medical sector has 14 dispensaries and 3 leprosariums, and religious sisters also work in government hospitals and social centres. Community development is furthered through the training facilities of the Centre of Study and Formation for Development (CEFOD, begun 1971) in N'djamena (Fort-Lamy), plus numerous domestic science and farming youth workshops on the local level. The weaving and embroidery work done by Catholic women at Baro, N'djamena and Dony furnishes an important part of the artisanal work for Chad's exports.
EGLISE FRATERNELLE LUTHERIENNE AU TCHAD. By 1975, these statistics had increased to: 219 parishes, 186 annexes, 35 ordained pastors, 388 catechists, 9,082 communicants, 12,471 non-communicant adult members, 3,885 catechumens, 612 adult baptisms (in 1975) and 1,185 infant baptisms, 277 confirmations, 29,179 Sunday attenders (over 15 years), 450 Sunday-school teachers and 6,959 pupils (aged 7–13). Growth of communicants from 1969 to 1976: 51%.
EGLISES EVANGELIQUES AU TCHAD, Membership: 77% Ngambai, 14% Nangdjere, 8% Lele. Served by the Mission Evangélique Unie, with 5 branches: (1) TEAM (USA), formerly SUM Canadian Branch, HQ Moundou; (2) Mission Franco-Suisse du Tchad (SUM, French Branch at Abeché, Swiss Branch at Massena); (3) WEC (UK), working under SUM French Branch in Abeché and Adré; (4) EMEK (French Mennonites), working under SUM French Branch in Fort-Lamy; and (5) Pentecostal congregations resulting from the work of the Mission Evangélique au Guéra (begun in 1946 as Burckhardt Mission) round Mongo. *Growth.* By 1975, places of worship had increased to 570, with 80,000 average weekly attendance.

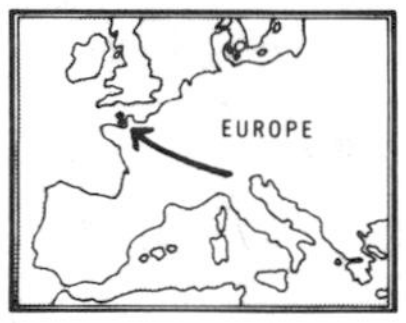


# CHANNEL ISLANDS

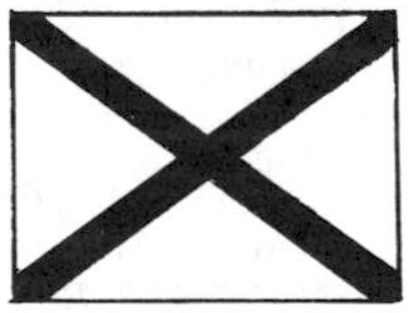

## SECULAR DATA

**STATE. Official name:** The Channel Islands (Les Iles Anglo-Normandes).
**Flag:** Jersey (shown above right): White with a red saltire. Guernsey: White with a red cross.
**Area:** 195 sq.km. (75 sq.miles). Agricultural land: 52.6%.
**Government:** Self-governing British crown dependency, since 1066.
**Legislature:** Assemblies of the States: The States of Jersey, 57 members: The States of Deliberation (Guernsey), 60 members; and States of Election.
**Official languages:** English and French (*Français*). Jersey: French.
**Chief cities:** capital St Helier (Jersey) 26,460 (1971), St Peter Port (Guernsey) 16,800.
**Political divisions:** 4 States: Bailiwick of Jersey; Bailiwick of Guernsey; Alderney; Sark.
**Armed forces** (1976): British.

**DEMOGRAPHY. Population:** 123,063 (census of 4/25.IV.1971. For 1970–2000 (UN), see last row of Table 1). Population density (1975): 656/sq.km. (1,700/sq.mile). Under 15 years: 23%. Growth rate (1975–80): 0.80% per year. Household size: 2.7 persons.
**Major languages:** English, French.
**Urban dwellers** (1970): 44.4%. Urban growth rate (1950–70): 1.2% per year.
**Labour force:** 50%.
**Tourists** (1974): 1,400,000.

**ETHNOLINGUISTIC GROUPS:** 99.4% European (British, some French), 0.3% non-European (Indo-Pakistani, et alii), 0.1% Jewish.

**MONEY** (1977). **Monetary unit:** Jersey pound, Guernsey pound (= 100 new pence); US$1 = £0.585.
**National income per person:** Jersey US$5,000, Guernsey US$2,500.
Average annual family income: US$10,100.

**EDUCATION.** Adult literacy: 100%.

**HEALTH.** Hospitals: 11 (1,342 beds). Doctors: 144. Blind: 120. Psychotics: 1,000.

**COMMUNICATION** (per 1,000 people). Phones: 313. Radios: 366. TV sets: 362.

TABLE 1. RELIGIOUS ADHERENTS IN THE CHANNEL ISLANDS

| Year | 1900 | | mid-1970 | | Annual change, 1970–1980 | | | | mid-1975 | | mid-1980 | | 2000 | |
|---|---|---|---|---|---|---|---|---|---|---|---|---|---|---|
| *Name* | *Adherents* | *%* | *Adherents* | *%* | *Natural* | *Conversion* | *Total* | *Rate* | *Adherents* | *%* | *Adherents* | *%* | *Adherents* | *%* |
| **Christians** | **82,170** | **99.0** | **115,900** | **95.0** | **1,045** | **0** | **1,045** | **0.86** | **121,600** | **95.0** | **126,350** | **95.0** | **136,800** | **90.0** |
| professing | 82,170 | 99.0 | 115,900 | 95.0 | 1,045 | 0 | 1,045 | 0.86 | 121,600 | 95.0 | 126,350 | 95.0 | 136,800 | 90.0 |
| Anglicans | 59,350 | 71.5 | 77,270 | 63.3 | 697 | 1 | 698 | 0.86 | 81,080 | 63.3 | 84,250 | 63.3 | 91,000 | 59.9 |
| Roman Catholics | 8,710 | 10.5 | 21,350 | 17.5 | 192 | 1 | 193 | 0.86 | 22,400 | 17.5 | 23,280 | 17.5 | 28,880 | 19.0 |
| Protestants | 14,110 | 17.0 | 16,880 | 13.8 | 152 | 0 | 152 | 0.86 | 17,710 | 13.8 | 18,400 | 13.8 | 16,470 | 10.8 |
| Orthodox | 0 | 0.0 | 200 | 0.2 | 2 | 0 | 2 | 0.86 | 210 | 0.2 | 220 | 0.2 | 250 | 0.2 |
| Marginal Protestants | 0 | 0.0 | 200 | 0.2 | 2 | –2 | 0 | 0.00 | 200 | 0.2 | 200 | 0.2 | 200 | 1.0 |
| nominal | 1,660 | 2.0 | 12,120 | 9.9 | 109 | –1 | 108 | 0.85 | 12,710 | 9.9 | 13,200 | 9.9 | 22,680 | 14.9 |
| affiliated | 80,510 | 97.0 | 103,780 | 85.1 | 936 | 1 | 937 | 0.86 | 108,890 | 85.1 | 113,150 | 85.1 | 114,120 | 75.1 |
| total practising | 72,460 | *90* | 72,650 | *70* | 655 | 0 | 655 | 0.86 | 76,220 | *70* | 79,200 | *70* | 68,470 | *60* |
| non-practising | 8,050 | *10* | 31,130 | *30* | 281 | 1 | 282 | 0.86 | 32,670 | *30* | 33,950 | *30* | 45,650 | *40* |
| Anglicans | 58,930 | 71.0 | 69,250 | 56.8 | 625 | 1 | 626 | 0.86 | 72,700 | 56.8 | 75,510 | 56.8 | 76,000 | 50.0 |
| Evangelicals | 21,000 | 25.3 | 18,300 | 15.0 | 165 | 5 | 170 | 0.89 | 19,200 | 15.0 | 20,000 | 15.0 | 20,000 | 13.1 |
| Roman Catholics | 8,300 | 10.0 | 20,500 | 16.8 | 185 | 2 | 187 | 0.87 | 21,500 | 16.8 | 22,370 | 16.8 | 25,840 | 17.0 |
| Protestants | 13,280 | 16.0 | 13,600 | 11.1 | 122 | –2 | 120 | 0.84 | 14,240 | 11.1 | 14,800 | 11.1 | 11,760 | 7.7 |
| Evangelicals | 7,000 | 8.4 | 3,500 | 2.9 | 32 | –2 | 30 | 0.81 | 3,700 | 2.9 | 3,800 | 2.9 | 3,000 | 2.0 |
| Marginal Protestants | 0 | 0.0 | 230 | 0.2 | 2 | 0 | 2 | 0.86 | 240 | 0.2 | 250 | 0.2 | 270 | 0.2 |
| Orthodox | 0 | 0.0 | 200 | 0.2 | 2 | 0 | 2 | 0.86 | 210 | 0.2 | 220 | 0.2 | 250 | 0.2 |
| Non-religious | 780 | 0.9 | 5,700 | 4.7 | 51 | –8 | 43 | 0.72 | 5,940 | 4.6 | 6,130 | 4.6 | 14,350 | 9.4 |
| Baha'is | 0 | 0.0 | 200 | 0.2 | 2 | 8 | 10 | 4.00 | 250 | 0.2 | 300 | 0.2 | 600 | 0.4 |
| Other religionists | 50 | 0.1 | 200 | 0.2 | 2 | 0 | 2 | 0.86 | 210 | 0.2 | 220 | 0.2 | 250 | 0.2 |
| **Country's population** | **83,000** | **100.0** | **122,000** | **100.0** | **1,100** | **0** | **1,100** | **0.86** | **128,000** | **100.0** | **133,00** | **100.0** | **152,000** | **100.0** |

COLUMNS ROWS. For meanings and definitions, see Codebook (Part 6). Note that, by definition, total 'Christians' = professing + crypto-Christians, which also = affiliated + nominal Christians. Percentages may not always total exactly, due to rounding.

CENSUSES. The religion question has not been asked.

NOTES ON RELIGIONS
BAHA'IS. In 1 local spiritual assembly and 1 other centre (1973).

OTHER RELIGIONISTS. There are a few Jewish, Muslim, Buddhist and Hindu families resident (1975), with one Jewish congregation (70 members), and one Buddhist congregation on Alderney.

Ecumenical procession, under auspices of Jersey Council of Churches, from St Helier to Elizabeth Castle. *Left.* Crossing the causeway. *Right.* Constable (Mayor) of St Helier at Chapel and Shrine of St Helier.

**NON-CHRISTIAN RELIGIONS.** Several Asian families live on Jersey, of Muslim, Buddhist and Hindu background. A few families of Jews live on Jersey and have recently opened a synagogue in the countryside. There are also 2 Baha'i centres. Those claiming to be without religion increased from 1% of the population in 1900 to 5% in 1970.

**CHRISTIANITY.** The Christian faith came to the Channel Islands with the Breton migration of the 6th century and was strongly influenced by the missionary activity of St Helier (martyred c550) and St Sampson. Administratively the islands were included in the Norman diocese of Coutances, and a large portion of their land was owned by Norman monasteries.

Calvinist refugees from France brought the 16th-century Reformation to the islands, organizing the first Presbyterian synod in 1564, and Presbyterianism dominated the islands during subsequent years.

Anglicanism was first organized in Jersey in 1623 and in Guernsey in 1663, but made little progress prior to the 19th century. Forming part of the diocese of Winchester of the Church of England, the islands are now predominantly Anglican. There are 2 deaneries, one for Jersey with 21 parishes and the other for Guernsey with 15 parishes. Their deans exercise authority similar to but greater than that of archdeacons in England, including delegated episcopal authority to institute clergy to parish livings.

Catholic responsibility for the Channel Islands is invested in the diocese of Portsmouth of the

Catholic Church in England and Wales. The church's strength is concentrated in Jersey which maintains its French language and traditions. Catholics are divided into 17 parishes served by 3 institutes: OMI, FSC and FICP. The Catholic Church sponsors 10 schools.

The islands were strongly influenced by Wesleyan Methodism in the 18th and 19th centuries, and the Methodist Church of Great Britain continues to play an important role. Its Channel Islands District consists of 3 circuits, with 30 congregations served by 22 ministers. Other Protestant groups include the Baptist Union, Elim Pentecostals, Friends (Quakers), United Reformed Church (formerly Congregationalists), and a Presbyterian church which did not join the URC at union.

**CHURCH AND STATE.** The Channel Islands are under the British Crown and are ecclesiastically part of the diocese of Winchester of the established Church of England, and so the Church of England is the established or state church in the islands. The Anglican dean of Jersey is an ex officio member without vote of the legislative council known as the States of Jersey; a similar provision is however not made for the dean of Guernsey in Guernsey's States of Deliberation. The fabric of parish churches is maintained out of public funds, for which secular local authorities are responsible. There are therefore, in contrast to England, no parochial church councils (PCCs). Measures passed by the Church Assembly and the British parliament in London and still in force as legislation in the Channel Islands are:

Channel Islands (Representation) Measure, 1931; Channel Islands (Church Legislation) Measure, 1931, and its (Amendment) Measure, 1957.

**INTERDENOMINATIONAL ORGANIZATIONS.** Two local church councils are active, the Guernsey Council of Churches and the Jersey Council of Churches. Both are associate members of the British Council of Churches. Ecumenism is comparatively strong in the islands.

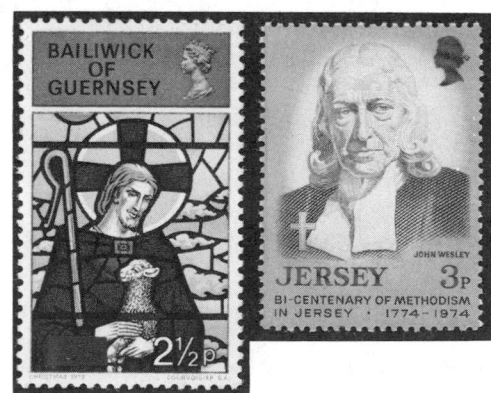

The Islands' postage stamps often illustrate Christian topics: *left,* Christ the Good Shepherd (in St-Michel du Valle); *right,* evangelist John Wesley.

TABLE 2.    ORGANIZED CHURCHES AND DENOMINATIONS IN THE CHANNEL ISLANDS

| Official name 1 | Begun 2 | Type 3 | Counc 4 | Congs 5 | Adults 6 | Affiliated 7 | Names, notes, and other statistics (see Codebook) 8 |
|---|---|---|---|---|---|---|---|
| Baptist Union of GB & Ireland | 1864 | P Bap | Twc.w | 4 | 300 | 800 | 3 Baptist churches on Guernsey, 1 on Jersey. Independent congregations. |
| Catholic Ch in E & W (D Portsmouth) | 1802 | R Lat | B.B.s | 17 | 15,800 | 20,500 | E&W=England & Wales. 75% on Jersey. M=OMI(English & French), SJ,FSC,FICP.C=2+2+6. |
| Church of Christ, Scientist | | M Sci | x.... | 2 | 30 | 50 | *Christian Science.* M=CCS(Boston, USA). Congregation in St Helier. |
| Church of England (D Winchester) | 1111 | A Cen | awc.w | 38 | 25,000 | 69,250 | 2 Deaneries: Jersey (21 parishes), Guernsey (15 parishes). Also Alderney and Sark. |
| Church of Jesus C of Latter-day Saints | | M LdS | x.... | 1 | 20 | 30 | *Mormons.* M=CJCLdS(Utah, USA). On Jersey. |
| Elim Pentecostal Church | | P Pe2 | z...h | 4 | 200 | 600 | *Channel Islands Presbytery.* 3 on Guernsey, 1 on Jersey. |
| Greater World Christian Spiritualist C | | M Spi | x.... | 1 | 30 | 100 | C=Church, *Greater World Sanctuary.* Specifically Christian spiritualists. St Helier. |
| Greek Orthodox Ch (AD Thyateira & GB) | | O Gre | Cwc.w | 1 | 100 | 200 | *Orthodox Community of St Andrew,* St Helier, Visiting priest from Bristol (UK). |
| Methodist Church of Great Britain | 1774 | P Met | Vwc.w | 30 | 3,710 | 10,000 | *Channel Islands District.* 3 Circuits: on all 4 islands. 22nx. |
| New Church | | M Swe | xv..w | 1 | 30 | 50 | *Jersey Society, General Conf of the New Ch* (Swedenborgian). St Helier. 1n. |
| United Reformed Church | 1800 | P Ref | Rwc.w | 4 | 200 | 400 | Formerly Congregationalists. 2 churches on Guernsey, 2 on Jersey. |
| Other Protestant denominations | | P | ..... | 13 | 900 | 1,800 | Total about 10, including: Open Brethren, Presbyterian Ch, Quakers, Salvation Army. |
| | | | | | | | |
| Total affiliated (mid-1970) | | | | 116 | 46,310 | 103,780 | Total denominations (1970) . . . 21. |
| Total affiliated (mid-1975) | | | | 122 | 48,590 | 108,890 | Total denominations (1975) . . . 22. |
| Total affiliated (mid-1980) | | | | 130 | 50,490 | 113,150 | Total denominations (1980) . . . 23. |

NOTES ON TABLE ABOVE
COLUMNS: for meanings and CODES (cols. 1, 3, 4, 8): see Codebook (Part 6). Column 1: **Boldface type** = church with over 10% of country's affiliated Christians.
NATIONAL COUNCILS (Column 4, 5th letter).
h = British Pentecostal Fellowship.
s = in Bishops' Conference of England & Wales, also JCC, GCC.
w = Jersey Council of Churches (JCC), & Guernsey Council of Churches (GCC) (associated councils of the British Council of Churches, BCC).
*Other councils.* Jersey Free Church Federal Council (dissolved).

PEOPLES (ethnolinguistic). Christians: 97.4% British, 2.0% French.

COUNTRY-WIDE TOTALS
EVANGELIZATION (see Part 5). 1900: 100%. 1970: 100%. 1980: 100%. *Mass evangelism.* In 1972, a 15-day campaign Crusade 72 took place in Jersey based on Corbière and St Helier and sponsored by the Movement for World Evangelization.
FOREIGN MISSIONARIES AND PERSONNEL (nationals serving abroad) (1973). Total about 10, mostly Anglicans.
FOREIGN MISSIONARIES AND PERSONNEL (aliens from abroad) (1973). Total 8. *From Western world.* About 8 Roman Catholics and Anglicans.
INSTITUTIONS (church-operated) (1973). Total 4, including 2 higher schools, 1 religious community.
PERIODICALS. About 10 titles.
PERSONNEL. About 48 (40 national, 8 foreign).
RELIGIOUS LIBRARIES. About 5.
SCRIPTURE DISTRIBUTION (1975). Annual totals: 3,900 Bibles (15% subsidized, 85% commercial), 1,950 NTs (18% subsidized, 82% commercial), 2,000 UBS portions, 4,000 UBS selections. *Translations completed.* Portion: French/Norman/Guernsey in 1863.
SERVICE AGENCIES. About 12, including BFBS, CCCS.

# CHILE

## SECULAR DATA

**STATE. Official name:** The Republic of Chile (La República de Chile). Adjective of nationality: Chilean (chileno).
**Flag** (shown above right): Stripes of white and red, blue square with white star.
**Area:** 756,945 sq.km. (292,258 sq.miles). Agricultural land: 22.9%.
**Government:** Military junta, since 1973 (1541 Spanish rule, 1810 Independence from Spain, military juntas, 1942 constitutional democracy, 1970 Marxist regime, 1973 military rule).
**Legislature:** National Congress (in abeyance).
**Official language:** Spanish (*Español/Castellano*).
**Chief cities:** capital Santiago 3,068,650 (1971), Valparaíso 250,000, Concepción 161,000.
**Political divisions:** 25 Provinces.
**Armed forces** (1976): Total 79,600 regular (21,600 conscripts): army 45,000, navy 23,800, air force 10,800 (67 combat aircraft). Reserves: 160,000. Paramilitary forces: 30,000.
**Dependencies:** Chilean Antarctic Territory, Diego Ramírez Islands, Easter Island, Juan Fernández, Salay Gomez and other uninhabited Pacific islands.

**DEMOGRAPHY. Population:** 8,834,820 (census of 22.IV.1970. For 1970–2000 (UN), see last row of Table 1). Population density (1975): 14/sq.km. (35/sq.mile). Under 15 years: 40%. Growth rate (1975–80): 1.83% per year (births 2.72%, deaths −0.86%, emigrants −0.03%). Life expectancy (1975–80): 64.4 years. Household size: 5.1 persons.
**Major languages:** Spanish, German, Mapuche, Italian, Quechua, Aymara, Greek, and over 10 other languages.
**Urban dwellers** (1970): 72.9%. Urban growth rate (1950–70): 3.8% per year.
**Labour force:** 27%.
**Refugees** (1977): From abroad, 3,000. Exiles abroad: 63,000 Chileans (37,000 in Argentina, 10,000 in Venezuela, 5,000 in Ecuador, 4,000 in France, 2,000 in Mexico, 1,600 in USA, 1,000 in Costa Rica, et alia).
**Tourists** (1968): 261,214. (1973) 168,741.

**ETHNOLINGUISTIC GROUPS:** 72.5% Mestizo, 20.0% Chilean White (Spanish, 0.3% German), 5.0% Amerindian (3.5% Mapuche (320,000), 0.7% Quechua, 0.5% Aymara, Huilliche, Ranquelche, Fuegian), 1.5% alien (Argentinian, English, German, Spanish, Italian, Yugoslav), 0.3% Jewish (30,000), 0.1% Greek, Chango, Arab, Basque, Chinese (560), Turkish, Armenian.

**MONEY** (1977). **Monetary unit:** peso (= 100 centésimos); US$1 = Ch$17.96.
**National income per person:** US$896. Average annual family income: US$4,570.
**Inflation:** (1970–74) 175.9% per year, (1975) 375% per year (consumer price index 68,188).
**Cost of living in capital** (1976): index 89 (Washington DC = 100). Daily cost of living: US$36.

**EDUCATION.** Adult literacy: (1952) 80%, (1970) 88%. Education rate: 60%. Schools: 8,072. Universities: 8.

**HEALTH.** Hospitals: 231 (36,700 beds). Doctors: 5,572. Blind: 2,910. Psychotics: 92,000.

**LITERATURE.** Annual new book titles (1973): 652. Periodicals: 600. Scientific journals: 150. Newspapers: 128 dailies.

**COMMUNICATION** (per 1,000 people). Phones: 44. Radios: 149. TV sets: 50. Daily newspaper circulation: 89 copies.

TABLE 1. RELIGIOUS ADHERENTS IN CHILE

| Year | 1900 | | mid-1970 | | Annual change, 1970–1980 | | | | mid-1975 | | mid-1980 | | 2000 | |
|---|---|---|---|---|---|---|---|---|---|---|---|---|---|---|
| *Name* | *Adherents* | % | *Adherents* | % | *Natural* | *Conversion* | *Total* | *Rate* | *Adherents* | % | *Adherents* | % | *Adherents* | % |
| **Christians** | **2,863,000** | **96.8** | **8,666,300** | **92.5** | **174,613** | −4,289 | **170,324** | **1.80** | **9,474,340** | **92.4** | **10,369,540** | **92.3** | **13,923,110** | **90.7** |
| professing | 2,863,000 | 96.8 | 8,666,300 | 92.5 | 174,613 | −4,289 | 170,324 | 1.80 | 9,474,340 | 92.4 | 10,369,540 | 92.3 | 13,923,110 | 90.7 |
| Roman Catholics | 2,841,700 | 96.0 | 7,899,800 | 84.3 | 157,243 | −24,973 | 132,270 | 1.55 | 8,531,380 | 83.2 | 9,222,500 | 82.1 | 11,892,030 | 77.4 |
| Evangelical Catholics | 10,000 | 0.3 | 821,090 | 8.8 | 16,852 | 3,161 | 20,013 | 2.19 | 914,370 | 8.9 | 1,021,220 | 9.1 | 1,765,820 | 11.5 |
| Christo-pagans | 50,000 | 1.7 | 230,000 | 2.5 | 4,604 | −4 | 4,600 | 1.82 | 253,000 | 2.5 | 276,000 | 2.5 | 350,000 | 2.3 |
| Chilean indigenous | 0 | 0.0 | 562,000 | 6.0 | 13,227 | 20,453 | 33,680 | 4.69 | 717,710 | 7.0 | 898,800 | 8.0 | 1,535,500 | 10.0 |
| Protestants | 20,000 | 0.7 | 140,500 | 1.5 | 2,838 | −36 | 2,802 | 1.82 | 154,000 | 1.5 | 168,520 | 1.5 | 307,100 | 2.0 |
| Marginal Protestants | 0 | 0.0 | 35,000 | 0.4 | 719 | 275 | 994 | 2.55 | 39,000 | 0.4 | 44,940 | 0.4 | 107,480 | 0.7 |
| Orthodox | 300 | 0.0 | 25,500 | 0.3 | 516 | −8 | 508 | 1.81 | 28,000 | 0.3 | 30,580 | 0.3 | 75,000 | 0.5 |
| Anglicans | 1,000 | 0.0 | 3,500 | 0.0 | 70 | 0 | 70 | 1.84 | 3,800 | 0.0 | 4,200 | 0.0 | 6,000 | 0.0 |
| nominal | 29,590 | 1.0 | 421,300 | 4.5 | 8,692 | 1,982 | 10,674 | 2.26 | 471,640 | 4.6 | 528,040 | 4.7 | 844,520 | 5.5 |
| affiliated | 2,833,410 | 95.8 | 8,245,000 | 88.0 | 165,921 | −6,271 | 159,650 | 1.77 | 9,002,700 | 87.8 | 9,841,500 | 87.6 | 13,078,590 | 85.2 |
| doubly-affiliated | −10,000 | −0.3 | −1,036,549 | −11.1 | −23,063 | −23,857 | −46,920 | 3.75 | −1,251,390 | −12.2 | −1,505,750 | −13.4 | −2,234,560 | −14.6 |
| total practising | 2,266,730 | *80* | 6,183,750 | *75* | 116,144 | −94,822 | 21,322 | 0.34 | 6,301,890 | *70* | 6,396,970 | *65* | 7,847,150 | *60* |
| non-practising | 566,680 | *20* | 2,061,250 | *25* | 49,777 | 88,551 | 138,328 | 5.12 | 2,700,810 | *30* | 3,444,530 | *35* | 5,231,440 | *40* |
| Roman Catholics | 2,812,110 | 95.0 | 7,693,958 | 82.1 | 154,762 | −6,259 | 148,503 | 1.77 | 8,397,210 | 81.9 | 9,178,990 | 81.7 | 11,516,250 | 75.0 |
| Catholic pentecostals | 0 | 0.0 | 1,000 | 0.0 | 110 | 890 | 1,000 | 16.67 | 6,000 | 0.1 | 11,000 | 0.1 | 40,000 | 0.3 |
| Chilean indigenous | 0 | 0.0 | 1,325,300 | 14.1 | 28,911 | 23,937 | 52,848 | 3.37 | 1,568,710 | 15.3 | 1,853,780 | 16.5 | 3,224,550 | 21.0 |
| Protestants | 30,000 | 1.0 | 192,053 | 2.0 | 3,889 | −64 | 3,825 | 1.81 | 211,000 | 2.0 | 230,300 | 2.0 | 383,870 | 2.5 |
| Evangelicals | 28,000 | 0.9 | 104,000 | 1.1 | 2,105 | −35 | 2,070 | 1.81 | 114,200 | 1.1 | 124,700 | 1.1 | 210,000 | 1.4 |
| Marginal Protestants | 0 | 0.0 | 40,738 | 0.4 | 825 | −19 | 806 | 1.80 | 44,770 | 0.4 | 48,800 | 0.4 | 107,480 | 0.7 |
| Orthodox | 300 | 0.0 | 25,500 | 0.3 | 516 | −8 | 508 | 1.81 | 28,000 | 0.3 | 30,580 | 0.3 | 75,000 | 0.5 |
| Anglicans | 1,000 | 0.0 | 4,000 | 0.0 | 81 | −1 | 80 | 1.82 | 4,400 | 0.0 | 4,800 | 0.0 | 6,000 | 0.0 |
| Evangelicals | 1,000 | 0.0 | 4,000 | 0.0 | 81 | −1 | 80 | 1.82 | 4,400 | 0.0 | 4,800 | 0.0 | 6,000 | 0.0 |
| Non-religious | 2,000 | 0.1 | 321,200 | 3.4 | 6,808 | 3,765 | 10,573 | 2.86 | 369,110 | 3.6 | 426,930 | 3.8 | 818,530 | 5.3 |
| Atheists | 1,900 | 0.1 | 240,000 | 2.6 | 5,102 | 2,356 | 7,458 | 2.69 | 276,830 | 2.7 | 314,580 | 2.8 | 491,360 | 3.2 |
| Tribal religionists | 90,000 | 3.0 | 100,000 | 1.1 | 1,843 | 0 | 0 | 0.00 | 100,000 | 1.0 | 100,000 | 0.9 | 80,000 | 0.5 |
| Jews | 1,000 | 0.0 | 30,000 | 0.3 | −2,000 | 0 | −2,000 | −10.00 | 20,000 | 0.2 | 10,000 | 0.1 | 10,000 | 0.1 |
| Baha'is | 0 | 0.0 | 7,800 | 0.1 | 160 | 20 | 180 | 2.07 | 8,700 | 0.1 | 9,600 | 0.1 | 16,000 | 0.1 |
| Muslims | 100 | 0.0 | 2,000 | 0.0 | 40 | −4 | 36 | 1.65 | 2,180 | 0.0 | 2,360 | 0.0 | 5,000 | 0.0 |
| Buddhists | 0 | 0.0 | 500 | 0.0 | 10 | −1 | 9 | 1.67 | 540 | 0.0 | 590 | 0.0 | 1,000 | 0.0 |
| Other religionists | 1,000 | 0.0 | 1,200 | 0.0 | 24 | −4 | 20 | 1.54 | 1,300 | 0.0 | 1,400 | 0.0 | 10,000 | 0.1 |
| **Country's population** | **2,959,000** | **100.0** | **9,369,000** | **100.0** | **186,600** | **0** | **186,600** | **1.82** | **10,253,000** | **100.0** | **11,235,000** | **100.0** | **15,355,000** | **100.0** |

COLUMNS, ROWS. For meanings and definitions, see Codebook (Part 6). Note that, by definition, total 'Christians' = professing + crypto-Christians, which also = affiliated + nominal Christians. Percentages may not always total exactly, due to rounding.
CENSUSES. **1907** (excluding Indians): 98.8% Roman Catholics, 1.1% Evangelicals, 0.1% non-religious. **1920:** 95.8% Roman Catholics, 2.6% non-religious, atheists and tribal religionists, 1.4% Evangelicals, 0.1% Jews. **1930:** 97.7% Roman Catholics, 1.5% Evangelicals, 0.7% non-religious, atheists, and tribal religionists, 0.1% Jews. **1940:** 93.7% Roman Catholics, 3.5% non-religious, atheists and tribal religionists, 2.5% Evangelicals, 0.2% Jews, 0.1% Orthodox. **24.IV.1952:** 92.3% Roman Catholics, 4.2% Evangelicals (Protestants, Anglicans, marginal Protestants, and Chilean indigenous), 3.2% non-religious, atheists and tribal religionists, 0.2% Jews, 0.1% Orthodox. **29.XI.1960:** 89.2% Roman Catholics, 5.7% Evangelicals (Protestants, Anglicans, marginal Protestants and Chilean indigenous), 4.7% non-religious, atheists and tribal religionists, 0.1% Orthodox, 0.1% Jews, 0.1% other religionists (Hindus, Buddhists).
POLLS. Surveys in the archdiocese of Santiago from 1956–65 showed higher proportions of non-believers than in the country as a whole: 1956, 7.5% non-religious; 1958, 9.8%; 1965, 6.6%.

NOTES ON RELIGIONS
ATHEISTS. Partido Comunista de Chile (PCCh) (in government until 1973 coup; pro-Soviet): membership (1965) 30,000, rising to (1970) 120,000, halved by 1974; Communist voters (election of 4.IX.1970) 1,070,334 (36.2% of all votes). A certain proportion of communists are practising Evangelicals, pentecostals and Catholics.
BAHA'IS. Growth from 8 local spiritual assemblies (1964) to 51 (1973). Converts include Mapuche Indians.
BUDDHISTS. Chinese.
CATHOLIC PENTECOSTALS (or, Catholic charismatics). Totals (January 1974): 2,500 involved adults (over 15 years old) in 60 prayer groups; total charismatic community including children, 5,000. Numbers of Machi and Mapuche Indians are involved. By December 1976, there were over 60 prayer groups in the capital alone, endorsed by the cardinal archbishop.
CHILEAN INDIGENOUS. In over 170 indigenous denominations in 1970 (see Table 2). Leadership in the 2 major indigenous pentecostal bodies is mainly White (Italian, Spanish, especially former railway drivers or instructors) or Mestizo, but there are several Indian-speaking congregations with many Indian members.
CHRISTO-PAGANS. Aymara, Quechua and Mapuche Indians who syncretize folk-Catholicism with their traditional religions.
DOUBLY-AFFILIATED. The term covers those affiliated to, or claimed by, both the Catholic Church and also a church termed Evangélica by the state (Protestant, Chilean indigenous, Anglican or marginal Protestant), i.e. baptized Catholics who have recently become Evangelicals or others. Because their statistics represent a duplication, they are shown in the table as a negative quantity (with a minus sign).
EVANGELICAL CATHOLICS. This term (in Spanish, Católicos Evangélicos) is used here to describe persons who are affiliated to churches termed by the state Evangélica (Protestant, or Chilean indigenous, or Anglican or marginal Protestant churches), but who in government censuses are regarded as, or profess to be, Roman Catholics.
EVANGELICALS. This English term is used in the sense understood within the churches (not as understood by the state) to mean: (a) Conservative Evangelicals, namely all persons affiliated to Protestant denominations of Conservative Evangelical theology, (b) Conciliar Evangelicals, affiliated to non-Evangelical Protestant denominations usually within the Ecumenical Movement, (c) Fundamentalists, namely all persons affiliated to Protestant denominations themselves affiliated to the ICCC or other fundamentalist councils, and (d) Anglican Evangelicals. The definition as used here excludes Chilean indigenous pentecostals, because they are not part of Protestantism or Anglicanism.
OTHER RELIGIONISTS. Including spiritists, 56 Theosophists in 9 lodges (1975), Rosicrucians (2 AMORC centres), et alii.
PRACTISING CHRISTIANS. Roman Catholics: about 15% weekly (12.9% in archdiocese of Santiago), 64% less frequently, 15% hardly ever, 6% never; total practising, 75%. Protestants: about 80%. Catholic weekly practice declined by over 40% from 1960 to 1970.
PROTESTANTS. In 1907, 34% nationals and 66% expatriates; in 1920, 69% nationals, 31% expatriates.
TRIBAL RELIGIONISTS. Of the 468,000 Amerindians in 1970 (Araucanian Indians, especially Mapuche, also Aymara and Quechua in the north), about 21% were non-Catholics still practising animism, ancestor-veneration, polytheism and shamanism.

**NON-CHRISTIAN RELIGIONS. Agnosticism** has grown considerably over the last 25 years, and the non-religious form over 3% of the population, increasing annually in number.

**Traditional Indian religions** still account for a substantial 1% of the population. Arauca (Mapuche), Quechua and Aymara Indians make up about 5% of the population. The Mapuche (People of the Land), who number 360,000, are polytheists who retain belief in a supreme being Nenechen who is head of a pantheon of divinities (sun, moon, thunder, stars, earth, sea), although there are no Mapuche temples. The divinity of thunder or volcanoes is called Pillan. Medicine men or shamans are active and fear of sorcerer-witches is prevalent, but the main focus of Mapuche religion is the ancestor cult.

**Judaism** is the religion of 0.2% of the population, though the number is declining rapidly due to emigration. The University of Chile in Santiago has a Department of Jewish Culture which is part of its Pedagogical Institute, and there are several other centres for Jewish culture and studies in the country.

## CHRISTIANITY

**CATHOLIC CHURCH.** The first priest arrived in 1541, and in 1561 the diocese of Santiago was erected as a suffragan of Lima. A seminary was built in Santiago in 1584. Catholicism was recognized as the state religion when Chile became independent in 1810, but relations became increasingly strained after 1878, resulting finally in the separation of church and state in 1925.

Since 1960, the Catholic Church has experienced a significant renewal, of which there are 5 principal elements. (1) A carefully prepared national plan was launched in 1962, before the Second Vatican Council, to mobilize the various potential apostolates in the Catholic community. The plan included liturgical reform and reorganization of pastoral work to meet needs more adequately at diocesan, parish and sub-parish levels. (2) Greater involvement of women's religious communities in diocesan pastoral work was obtained by abandoning a number of traditional activities (schools, clinics, homes for the aged) and concentrating instead on evangelization through small groups. (3) Synods were held in most dioceses throughout the country. The synod of the archdiocese of Santiago (1966–69) was the first post-conciliar synod both in Chile and anywhere in the world, and has been one of the most open. It brought together some 500 persons, most of them elected at grassroots level. Members at the first session included 98 secular priests, 87 religious brothers, 5 seminarians, 9 lay brothers, 85 nuns and 209 lay persons. The themes of the synod were priority for evangelization, involvement of the church in the world, ecclesiastical institutions, the church and non-believers, ecumenism, and Judeo-Christian dialogue. (4) Socio-religious surveys were widely conducted concerning religious attitudes and Sunday observance, especially in Santiago, Talca and Concepción. Sunday mass attendance in Santiago was found to be 13% of those eligible. A comparison of the results of surveys made in 1960 and 1970 indicated a drop in Sunday observance of 50% during the decade for the age group 11–20 years. (5) Lastly, there has been a new understanding of the social and economic problems facing the country, as evidenced by pastoral letters and actions concerning agrarian reform. In Chile, Catholicism has had a longer tradition of social concern and involvement than anywhere else in Latin America, dating back to 1910. Msgr Larrain, bishop of Talca and the first president of CELAM, was the first Latin American prelate to distribute church agricultural land to workers who farmed it; and at Vatican II the progressive role of the Chilean church was pronounced. Chile was also one of the first countries in the world to organize a Christians for Socialism movement (1971). In April 1972 the first Latin American meeting of Christians for Socialism was held in Santiago, with 170 priests, 40 Protestant pastors, 30 religious personnel and 160 lay persons in attendance. The coming to power in 1970 of the Allende government from the communist and non-communist left did not provoke the kind of disturbance among churchmen that would have occurred in other parts of the continent. In 1971 the Bellarmino Institute conducted a survey on attitudes held by clergy concerning Marxism. The sample consisted of 60% of all priests in Chile, both national and foreign. Results indicated that 53% believed the practical attitude of Christians should express itself through 'friendly collaboration' without ignoring ideological differences; 37% were opposed to Marxism but

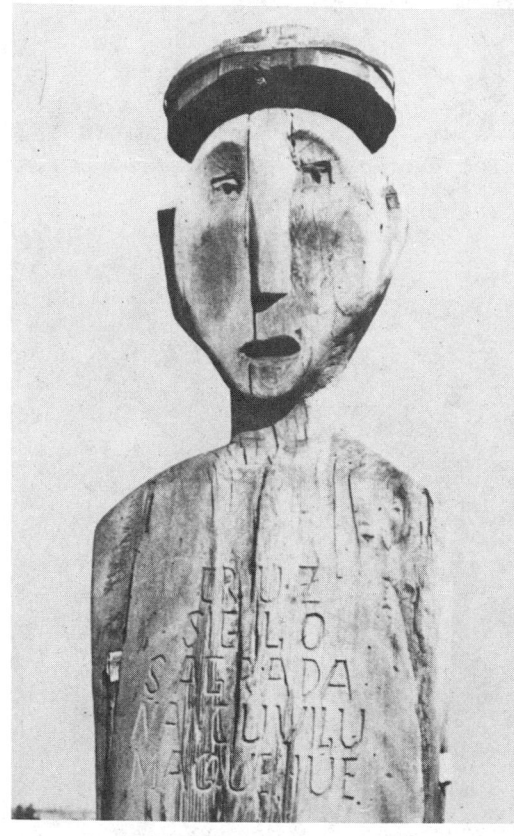

**Tribal religionists.** An ancient Amerindian wooden image from Araucania.

wanted to maintain dialogue with Marxists; 3% believed Christians and Marxists should work closely together; 1% wanted to avoid all contact with them; and the remaining 5% indicated that it was necessary to fight Marxist doctrine as 'intrinsically perverse'.

**INDIGENOUS CHURCHES.** Local pentecostal groups have grown very rapidly in Chile as in Brazil. The movement in Chile can be dated to 1909 when a Methodist missionary, W. C. Hoover, received baptism in the Holy Spirit. Repudiated by his own church, he helped form the Methodist Pentecostal Church (IMP), which is distinguished by its retention of many Wesleyan traditions, including infant baptism, semi-authoritarian government, elected bishops, and a belief that the gift of tongues is not essential to baptism in the Spirit. Its rapid expansion has been influenced by centralized organization, freedom from foreign control, and consequent ability to adapt to local conditions. In 1933 a schism in this church produced the Evangelical Pentecostal Church (IEP), which has also expanded enormously. The IMP and the IEP are now by far the largest non-Catholic churches in Chile. A large number of similar bodies also exist, though smaller in size. Taken together there were over 1.3 million indigenous pentecostals affiliated to churches in Chile in 1970 (1.5 million in 1975) compared to only 200,000 persons in Protestant churches. The world's largest Evangelical congregation is the Jotabeche Pentecostal Church (IMP) in Santiago, which has 80,000 regular members. Of particular significance is that all of this pentecostal growth has been achieved with no financial support from outside.

**PROTESTANT CHURCHES.** The first Protestant missionary was an agent of the British and Foreign Bible Society, who established several schools in 1821 at the invitation of Chile's new president. The first resident missionary was David Trumbull in 1845, with a group of Christians from several traditions which became the nucleus for the work of the Presbyterian Church USA in 1873. Efforts to train a national clergy met with misunderstandings almost from the beginning, which has greatly hindered Presbyterian expansion. More successful have been the Lutherans, who came in 1846, but they remain primarily German in membership.

In 1877 a Methodist, William Taylor, established self-supporting schools in that part of Bolivia which later was ceded to Chile. Emphasis on self-support, development of a lay ministry, and the relatively low salaries of American missionaries, contributed to the very rapid growth of Methodism between 1893 and 1907. However, Methodists were badly divided by a schism in 1910 over pentecostalism from which they never fully recovered.

Seventh-day Adventists arrived in 1890 and are now the largest Protestant church in Chile.

German immigrants founded the first Baptist church in 1892 followed by the organization of the Chilean Baptist Convention in 1908. In 1917 Southern Baptists sent their first missionaries from the USA to work with this developing church. Baptist history has been characterized by numerous schisms, but overall growth has not been significantly impaired. In some cases membership has actually increased as a result of divisions. Of the major denominations, Baptists have been least affected by the expansion of pentecostalism, largely due to the freedom and flexibility of Christian expression which is given to each local congregation. The church has maintained a steady growth of about 5% per year over the past decade.

Several foreign Pentecostal missions have recently entered Chile with the object of helping the rapidly-growing indigenous pentecostal churches, but disagreements concerning doctrine have discouraged co-operation. The largest of these bodies is the Church of God (Cleveland).

**CHURCH AND STATE.** The constitution of 1925, modified in 1970, guarantees freedom of conscience, and freedom of expression and practice for all religions. The text in Article 10 specifies that 'Places of worship and related buildings are exempt from taxation'. The 1925 constitution put an end to the *patronato* or close relation between the Catholic Church and the state as defined in the 1833 constitution. Henceforth no governmental ministry was responsible for religious or ecclesiastical affairs, and the government no longer officially subsidized churches, although it continued to aid their social and educational work. Numerous denominational

**Ejercito de Salvación.** Salvation Army officer in front of his church.

colleges still receive government grants of up to 50% of the cost per pupil. In 1972 the Chilean congress granted to officials of all churches (priests, religious, rabbis and pastors) the status of 'workers', thus procuring for them social security benefits for illness or retirement. Foreign priests who have worked at least 5 years in Chile are also beneficiaries. Churches and denominations enjoy a large measure of independence and are not required to register with government.

During and after the electoral campaign in 1970

**Iglesia Metodista Pentecostal de Chile.** *Above.* Earliest (1909) and largest of 170 Chilean indigenous churches. IMP's members in procession through Santiago, culminating (*below*) in mass rally

whom are known to have been tortured and killed. About 10 Chilean priests fled the country and 100 foreign priests were expelled: at least 40 Dutch, 20 Canadians, 20 Spanish, 15 French and others from various countries.

In 1974 the prolongation of repression and the deterioration of the social situation provoked the episcopal conference, also the cardinal and several individual bishops, to take a strong position concerning the rights of man. On 23 August 1974, the leaders of 4 of Chile's religious communities (Catholic cardinal, secretary of the Catholic episcopal conference, Lutheran bishop, Methodist bishop, and Jewish chief rabbi) addressed a letter to general Pinochet, head of state, in which they pleaded for reconciliation and peace. On the other hand, on 19 December 1974 the representatives of 32 Evangelical churches, in a full-page advertisement in the magazine *El Mercurio*, published a declaration of unreserved support for the junta. A few months later, Pinochet with other government leaders officially opened the new IMP cathedral (Jotabeche Pentecostal Church) in Santiago in the presence of 100,000 Chilean pentecostals. Evangelicals and pentecostals are thus reasserting the right of Christians to political expression long left to Catholics alone.

## INTERDENOMINATIONAL ORGANIZATIONS.

The Evangelical Council of Chile, with 10 members, was begun in 1941 building on an earlier committee founded in 1916, but has in recent years split into 2 factions over relations with the World Council of Churches. The more conservative Confederation of Evangelical Fundamentalist Churches has 5 member bodies. The Evangelical Theological Community is an ecumenical training centre sponsored by Methodists, Anglicans and some pentecostal groups. The interdenominational Evangelical Audio-Visual Centre, founded in 1967 by the Lutheran and pentecostal churches, has developed programmes of education and communications based on the psycho-social methods of Paulo Freire, and engages in community development work with pentecostal churches. Caritas and Evangelical Aid work together in the distribution of food in areas of need.

**BROADCASTING.** All the numerous commercial radio stations accept religious programmes. Catholics operate 3 radio stations, and for TV operate through national TV channels. The Catholic University (Pontificio Universidad Católica de Chile) transmits on channel 13 in Santiago, and channel 4 in Valparaiso; in 1970 it had 12,000 students following classes in basic education. In Santiago, INAP (Instituto Nacional de Acción Poblacional) prepares programmes for channel 13 on the national TV network. And in Osorno, Radio La Voz de la Costa operates a radio school, Escuelas Radiofónicas Santa-Clara. For Catholics, Chile is a member of UNDA. Protestants have a few production studios, including CAVE (Evangelical Audio-Visual Centre) in Santiago, and there are many denominational radio programmes.

which brought Allende to power, the Catholic episcopate maintained complete neutrality in spite of heavy pressures on them to take issue. In November 1970, the cardinal archbishop of Santiago was present at the installation of the government, which was considered to be a gesture of recognition of the leftist government by the church. In 1971 and 1972 the episcopate, following the cardinal's lead, continued this policy of providing practical support for government measures concerning the changing of social structures as well as support for constitutional legality and political pluralism. In July 1971 the cardinal explicitly approved nationalization of the big copper mines and later received in audience the Cuban leader Fidel Castro during his official visit to Chile. At the end of 1972 and in 1973, in spite of the crises and political conflicts which became increasingly serious, the episcopate held firmly to the need of respect for legality, opposing all violence which would risk the threat of civil war. With the agreement and sometimes at the request of the government, it also played a role as mediator between government and the forces of the political right. Nevertheless, during 1973 the bishops began to separate themselves increasingly from Allende's regime. They criticized the proposals for educational reform, which were never put into effect, and did not participate in the 1973 May Day celebration.

The military coup d'etat of 11 November 1973 presented itself as a crusade to 'remove the Marxist cancer'. In this sense it was applauded by the Christian Democratic party and a certain number of bishops. About 10 of the latter provided the military junta with a religious justification for their action, 2 or 3 others explicitly refused to do the same, while another 10 or so (including the cardinal of Santiago) tacitly legitimized the new regime in the name of the non-involvement of the church in politics, ignoring the illegality of the new regime. The first declaration of the permanent committee of the Chilean episcopate was neither complete condemnation nor unreserved approval, but the same day the committee visited the junta to 'express its sentiments of respect and esteem' as well as its 'thanks for the signs of deference that the new authorities have shown to bishops throughout the country'.

Cardinal Silva Henriquez has found himself increasingly isolated. Although he did not condemn the coup, the government and the forces of the right have suspected him because of his sympathetic attitude toward the Allende government. Moreover, he has been involved trying to help political prisoners and other victims of the regime. Among these are included Christians of the left and priests, some of

## BIBLIOGRAPHY

*A study of the older Protestant missions and churches in Peru and Chile.* J. B. A. Kessler. Goes, Netherlands: Oosterbaan & le Cointre, 1967. 369p.

'Chile', *Pro Mundi Vita* (Brussels), 49 (1974), 1–40.

*El Protestantismo en Chile.* I. Vergara. Santiago: Editorial del Pacífico, 1962. 261p.

*Followers of the new faith: culture change and the rise of Protestantism in Brazil and Chile.* E. Willems. Nashville, TN: Vanderbilt University Press, 1967. 290p.

*Guia eclesiástica y parroquial de Chile, 1972.* Santiago: Arzobispado de Santiago, 1973. (Roman Catholic).

*Haven of the masses: a study of the Pentecostal movement in Chile.* C. L. d'Epinay. London: Lutterworth Press, 1969. 263p.

*Historia del Avivamiento pentecostal en Chile.* W. C. Hoover. Santiago: Imprenta El Esfuerzo, 1931. 125p. (By the leader of the 1909 revival).

*La Iglesia en Chile.* I. Alonso, R. Robert & G. Garrido. Fribourg: FERES, 1962. 223p. (Roman Catholic).

'Les religions au Chili entre l'aliénation et la prise de conscience', C. L. d'Epinay & J. Zylberberg, *Social compass*, XXI, 1 (1974), 85–100.

*Sociología religiosa de Chile.* H. Muñoz Ramirez. Santiago: Ediciones Paulinas, 1957.

'The Chilean hierarchy and the political events of 1973–1975', *Pro Mundi Vita* (Brussels), Special note 42 (1975), 1–20.

TABLE 2. ORGANIZED CHURCHES AND DENOMINATIONS IN CHILE

| Official name 1 | Begun 2 | Type 3 | Counc 4 | Congs 5 | Adults 6 | Affiliated 7 | Names, notes, and other statistics (see Codebook) 8 |
|---|---|---|---|---|---|---|---|
| Asambleas de Dios | 1941 | P Pe2 | ZF... | 154 | 4,201 | 10,000 | *Assemblies of God.* M=AoG(USA). No aid to indigenous pentecostals. 74n,10f,3s(81). |
| Asambleas de Dios Autónomas | 1925 | P Pe2 | Z.... | 22 | 4,500 | 10,000 | *Misión Sueca. Autonomous Assemblies of God.* 1937, M=SFM(Sweden). 3n,156Y,113z. |
| Asoc Bautista para la Ev del Mondo | 1952 | P Bap | x.... | | 500 | 1,000 | M=Association of Baptists for World Evangelism(USA). HQ Santiago. 22f,1h,1s. |
| Congr Ev de la Fe Apostólica del SD | 1936 | I pen | ..... | 24 | 10,000 | 15,000 | SD=Séptimo Día. *Ev Congr of the Apostolic Faith Seventh-day.* G=7.4%pa,W=60%,300Y. |
| Convención Ev Bautista de Chile | 1892 | P Bap | T.... | 268 | 10,792 | 30,000 | *Ev Baptist Convention of Chile.* 1917, M=SBC(USA). SS=12,334. 74n,53f,1h,1s,860Y. |
| Corporación Evangélica de Vitacura | 1933 | I pe2 | ..u.N | 42 | 3,000 | 10,000 | *Ev Corporation of Vitacura* (Santiago). Ex IMP. M=AFM(Portland,USA). Mestizos. |
| Corporación Evangélica Pentecostal | 1956 | I pen | ..... | | 15,000 | 20,000 | *Coronel. Ev Pentecostal Corporation.* Schism ex IEP, in Concepción province. |
| Corporación Iglesia del Señor | | I pen | ..... | | 8,000 | 15,000 | *Ch of the Lord Corporation.* Schism ex Iglesia del Señor. Round Puerto Montt. |
| Ejército de Salvación | 1909 | P Sal | xw... | 37 | 3,235 | 5,451 | *Salvation Army.* in South America West Territory. 47n,19x,G=2.7%pa,1s,W=71%,161z. |
| Ejército Evangélico de Chile | 1937 | I pen | ..... | 100 | 9,000 | 15,000 | *Ev Army of Chile.* Schism ex IMP. Until 1942, Ejército Ev Uniformado. Mestizos. |
| Ejército Evangélico Nacional | 1942 | I pe4 | ..u.I | 23 | 600 | 1,000 | *National Evangelical Army.* Schism ex Ejército Ev de Chile. Mestizos. |
| Hermanos Libres Nacionales | 1928 | P CBr | x.... | 12 | 210 | 500 | *Christian Brethren. Plymouth (Open) Brethren.* M=CMML(USA). 10f. |
| Iglesia Adventista del Séptimo Día | 1890 | P Adv | x.... | 97 | 18,469 | 30,000 | *Seventh-day Adventists, Chile UM* (2 Confs). 37nx,10f,1h,1r,1s,186t(10826),1612Y. |
| Igl Adventista, Movimiento de Reforma | 1929 | P Adv | x.... | 8 | 150 | 500 | *SDA Movement of Reform.* Schism ex SDA church. World HQ Charlottenlund, Denmark. |
| Igl Aliancista Nacional de Sostén y GP | 1929 | I Hol | .TT.T | 50 | 2,500 | 5,000 | GP=Gobierno Propio. *Self-support Self-governing Alliance Ch.* Schism ex CMA. |
| Iglesia Alianza Cristiana y Misionera | 1897 | P Hol | xFu.N | 202 | 8,911 | 12,000 | *Christian & Missionary Alliance Ch.* M=CMA(USA). Over 4 schisms. 50n,19f,1j,1s. |
| Iglesia Anglicana: D Chile & Bolivia | 1837 | A Low | Aw.C. | 73 | 2,300 | 4,000 | M=SAMS(UK). 69% Araucanian, 22% UK, 9% Chilean. 16n,12x,36f,1s,1u,W=50%,30Y,40y. |
| Iglesia Apostólica Armenia | | O Arm | Ew... | | 3,000 | 5,000 | *Armenian Apostolic Ch, D South America. Gregorians.* Refugees from USSR. |
| Iglesia Bautista Nacional | 1940 | I Bap | .TT.T | 25 | 500 | 1,000 | *Misión Chilena. National Baptist Ch.* Anti-mission schism ex Baptist Convention. |
| **Iglesia Católica en Chile:** | 1541 | R Lat | BxL.R | 1,123 | 4,616,000 | 7,693,958 | *Catholic Ch in Chile.* C=49+4+136. 1090x,12p,3s. 2190nx,758m,5884w,171372Yy. |
| M Antofagasta | 1928 | R Lat | Bs | 27 | 127,500 | 212,500 | Most northerly province. Pampa, desert, mining. 1p. 33 2 67 2631 |
| D Iquique | 1929 | R Lat | Bs | 16 | 54,000 | 90,000 | In extreme north, south of PN Arica. 24 2 33 1745 |
| PN Arica | 1959 | R Lat | Bs | 11 | 54,000 | 90,000 | In extreme north adjoining Peru and Bolivia. M=SJ. 17 1 18 2296 |
| PN Calama | 1965 | R Lat | Bs | 28 | 60,000 | 100,000 | In northeast, adjoining Argentina and Bolivia. 11 0 10 2195 |
| M Concepción | 1563 | R Lat | Bs | 52 | 412,800 | 688,000 | Central coastal diocese. 1p,1s. 135 2 379 8010 |
| D Chillén | 1925 | R Lat | Bs | 30 | 160,200 | 266,963 | Central, bordering Argentina; Nuble province. 1p. 52 6 112 6917 |
| D Los Angeles | 1959 | R Lat | Bs | 17 | 119,200 | 198,604 | In Bio-Bio civil province. 33 3 49 6755 |
| D Temuco | 1925 | R Lat | Bs | 176 | 200,000 | 333,500 | Protestant stronghold. Malleco, Cautin provinces. 1p. 74 10 251 7212 |
| D Valdivia | 1944 | R Lat | Bs | 18 | 115,000 | 191,720 | Covers part of Valdivia civil province. 1p. 39 3 69 3639 |
| M La Serena | 1840 | R Lat | Bs | 25 | 173,900 | 289,776 | Northern. In civil province of Coquimbo. 1p. 61 11 143 7554 |
| D Copiapó | 1954 | R Lat | Bs | 16 | 82,100 | 136,800 | In Atacama civil province. 1p. 26 2 78 3880 |
| PN Illapel | 1960 | R Lat | Bs | 11 | 41,000 | 69,000 | Southernmost area of ecclesiastical province. M=OFM. 13 3 31 1482 |
| M Puerto Montt | 1939 | R Lat | Bs | 26 | 108,000 | 180,000 | Most southerly province, including Tierra del Fuego. 45 6 141 3010 |
| D Osorno | 1955 | R Lat | Bs | 16 | 93,400 | 155,705 | Northernmost diocese in ecclesiastical province. 37 11 51 4007 |
| D Punta Arenas | 1916 | R Lat | Bs | 9 | 56,000 | 93,000 | In extreme south, including half Tierra del Fuego. 44 15 69 1815 |
| D San Carlos de Ancud | 1840 | R Lat | Bs | 183 | 60,000 | 100,000 | Chiloé and other southern islands, 29 2 33 2270 |
| M Santiago de Chile | 1561 | R Lat | Bs | 203 | 1,380,000 | 2,300,000 | Decline from W=13%(1964) to 7%(1973). P=79%,1p,2s. 922 528 2815 43372 |
| D Linares | 1925 | R Lat | Bs | 30 | 150,000 | 251,300 | Covers Linares and Maule civil provinces. 1p. 61 17 136 7307 |
| D Rancagua | 1925 | R Lat | Bs | 58 | 297,000 | 495,000 | In O'Higgins and Colchagua civil provinces. 1p. 92 30 176 19050 |
| D San Felipe | 1925 | R Lat | Bs | 27 | 93,700 | 156,104 | Covers Aconcagua civil province. 45 20 142 3048 |
| D Talca | 1925 | R Lat | Bs | 42 | 234,000 | 390,000 | Covers Curico and Talca civil provinces. 76 46 262 12625 |
| D Valparaíso | 1925 | R Lat | Bs | 65 | 312,000 | 520,000 | Covers Valparaíso civil province 1p. 240 10 510 10717 |
| VA Araucanía | 1901 | R Lat | Pofmc | 32 | 203,400 | 338,986 | Indians; also Easter Island (3500km west). P=18%,1.p 63 24 278 7619 |
| VA Aysén | 1940 | R Lat | Posm | 5 | 28,000 | 47,000 | HQ Puerto Aisén. Very low practice: P=4%. Declining. 18 4 31 1226 |
| Iglesia Cristiana Apostólica | 1929 | I pe4 | ..u.I | 5 | 450 | 1,000 | *Apostolic Christian Ch.* Schism ex Methodist Church. Mestizos. HQ Santiago. |
| Iglesia Cristiana de la Fe Apostólica | 1933 | I pen | x.... | 1 | 60 | 200 | *Christian Ch of the Apostolic Faith.* Schism ex IEP. M=AFM(Portland,Oregon,USA). |
| Iglesia de Cristo Evangélica Nacional | 1946 | I pen | ..... | 3 | 100 | 200 | *National Ev Church of Christ.* Schism ex Iglesia Metodista Pentecostal. Mestizos. |
| Iglesia de Dios de la Profecía | 1975 | P Pe3 | Z.... | 2 | 45 | 100 | *Ch of God of Prophecy.* M=CGP(USA), a split in USA ex CoG(Cleveland). |
| Iglesia de Dios en Chile | 1951 | P Pe3 | ZF... | 118 | 8,644 | 15.000 | *Ch of God.* M=CoG(Cleveland)(USA). Opossed to indigenous pentecostals. 78n,1p,1s. |
| Iglesia de Dios Pentecostal | 1951 | I pe2 | Z.... | 170 | 65,000 | 100,000 | *Pentecostal Ch of God.* Split ex Iglesia Ev Pentecostal. M=PCG(USA). Mestizos. |
| Iglesia de JC de los Santos de los UD | 1956 | M LdS | x.... | | 10,000 | 20,238 | *Latter-day Saints. Mormons.* M=CJCLdS(USA). Rapid growth, 11.9%pa. 300f. |
| Iglesia del Evangelio Cuadrangular | 1940 | P Pe2 | ZF... | 92 | 2,476 | 8,000 | M=Int Ch Foursquare Gospel(USA). To 1959, Igl Cr Apost. 44nm,2f,1p(31),W=79%,203Y. |
| Iglesia del Nazareno | 1962 | P Hol | xF... | 13 | 198 | 1,500 | *Ch of the Nazarene.* M=CoN(USA). HQ Santiago. 4n,10x,8f,1s(8),7t(1066). |
| Iglesia del Señor | 1913 | I pen | ..u.N | 11 | 8,000 | 15,000 | *Church of the Lord.* Indigenous pentecostals. Schism ex IMP. Mestizos. |
| Iglesia Evangélica Cristiana | 1936 | I pe4 | ..u.I | 28 | 1,000 | 2,000 | *Ev Christian Church.* Schism ex IMP. Especially strong in Santiago. Mestizos. |
| Iglesia Evangélica del Emanuel | 1945 | I pen | ..... | 1 | 100 | 200 | *Ev Ch of Emmanuel.* 1945 split ex Pentecostal Methodists. Mestizos. |
| Igl Ev el Pesebre Humilde de Cristo | 1943 | I pen | ..... | 2 | 200 | 400 | *Humble Manger of Christ Church.* 1943 split ex IMP. Mestizos. |
| Iglesia Ev Israelita del Nuevo Pacto | 1948 | I Adv | ..... | 3 | 100 | 300 | *Ev Israelite Ch of New Covenant. Cabañistas (Tabernaclers)* Old Testament rituals. |
| Iglesia Evangélica Luterana en Chile | 1846 | P Lut | LW... | 53 | 10,432 | 25,687 | Germans, Swiss. A=1937. 1962, M=LCA. 1974, schism. 3n,12x,G=−0.7%pa,1u,W=15%,167Yy. |
| IEvMP Reunida en el Nombre de Jesús | 1950 | I pen | ..... | 200 | 60,000 | 100,000 | *Ev Meth Pentecostal Ch Re-united in Name of Jesus.* Split ex IMP; O'Higgins province. |
| Iglesia Evangélica Pentecostal de C | 1933 | I pe2 | x.u.N | 1,109 | 200,000 | 400,000 | *IEP. Ev Pentecostal Ch.* Split ex IMP. Many schisms. Missions in 5 nations. 109n,1j. |
| Iglesia Evangélica Universal | 1940 | I pe4 | ..u.I | 7 | 1,000 | 2,000 | *Universal Ev Ch.* Split ex CMA, in Concepción province. HQ Coronel. Mestizos. |
| Iglesia Evangélica Universal de Cristo | | I Hol | ..... | 2 | 120 | 300 | *Universal Ev Church of Christ.* Split ex Iglesia Evangélica Universal. Mestizos. |
| Iglesia Luterana (Misurí) | 1953 | P Lut | x.... | 1 | 50 | 115 | M=Lutheran Ch, Missouri Synod(USA). Work begun at Valparaíso. |
| Iglesia Metodista Independiente | 1950 | I Met | .TT.T | 5 | 500 | 1,000 | *Independent Methodist Ch.* Schism ex Methodists. Mestizos. |
| Iglesia Metodista Nacional de Chile | 1877 | P Met | VuV.. | 98 | 7,676 | 20,000 | *Methodist Ch of Chile.* A=1969. M=UMC(USA). Many pentecostal splits. 44n,25f,4r,1u. |
| Iglesia Metodista Pentecostal de Chile | 1909 | I pen | ..U.N | 900 | 150,000 | 400,000 | *IMP. Pentecostal Meth Ch.* Split ex Methodists; 20 schisms since. 1967, M=PHC. 120n,1u. |
| Iglesia Misión San Pablo | 1942 | I pen | ..... | 15 | 400 | 1,000 | *Church of St Paul's Mission.* Schism ex Iglesia Wesleyana Nacional. Mestizos. |
| Iglesia Misionera de Cristo | 1947 | I pen | ..... | 3 | 700 | 1,500 | *Missionary Ch of Christ.* Schism ex Ejército Ev Nacional. Mestizos. Santiago area. |
| Iglesia Ortodoxa Griega | | O Gre | Cwo.. | 6 | 5,000 | 15,000 | Part of 10th Archdiocesan District, Greek Orthodox AD of N&S America. Greeks. |
| Iglesia Ortodoxa Russa | | O Sla | Mw... | | 200 | 500 | *Russian Orthodox Ch.* Under Moscow Patriarchate. Russian immigrants. One bishop. |
| Iglesia Ortodoxa Russa: D Chile | | O Sla | x.... | 6 | 1,000 | 2,000 | *Russian Orthodox Ch Outside of Russia* (HQ New York). Refugees. Ultra-conservative. 1e. |
| Iglesia Ortodoxa: D Santiago de Chile | | O Ara | Cwo.. | | 2,000 | 3,000 | Under Antiochian Orthodox Ch(USA), & Greek P Antioch. Arabs (Lebanese). |
| Iglesia Pentecostal Apostólica | 1938 | I pen | ..u.N | 15 | 11,000 | 20,000 | *IPA. Apostolic Pentecostal Ch.* Schism ex IMP. Has itself suffered several splits. |
| Iglesia Pentecostal Apostólica Libre | 1943 | I pe4 | ..u.I | | 1,000 | 2,000 | *Free Apostolic Pentecostal Ch.* Schism ex Iglesia Pentecostal Apostólica. |
| Iglesia Pentecostal de Chile | 1946 | I pen | ZWu.N | 766 | 76,165 | 100,000 | *IPC. Pentecostal Ch of Chile.* Schism ex IMP. 1961, joined WCC. 83n,G=2.1%pa,2s,2459Y. |
| Iglesia Pentecostal de Chile Austral | 1950 | I pen | ..... | | 13,500 | 20,000 | *Pentecostal Ch of Southern Chile.* Schism ex IMP. Works with Iglesia Pentecostal de Chile. |
| Iglesia Pentecostal de la Trinidad | 1965 | I pen | .v... | 35 | 14,000 | 20,000 | *Pentecostal Ch of the Trinity.* Schism ex IPA. N&S Chile; also Argentina. HQ Temuco. |
| Iglesia Pentecostal Unida de Chile | 1964 | P Pe1 | x.... | 18 | 818 | 2,000 | *United Pentecostal Ch. Jesus Only Church.* M=UPC(USA). HQ Santiago. 9n,2f. |
| Iglesia Presbiteriana en Chile | 1845 | P Ref | Rv... | 25 | 3,000 | 10,000 | *IPC. Presbyterian Ch of Chile.* M=UPUSA. A=1964. 1966 applied to join WCC. 18n,1u. |
| Iglesia Presbiteriana Fundamentalista | c1960 | I Ref | .TT.T | | 200 | 500 | *Fundamentalist Presbyterian Ch.* Schism ex IPC. Mestizos. HQ Chillán. |
| Iglesia Presbiteriana Nacional | 1943 | P Ref | xTT.T | 35 | 700 | 1,500 | *National Presbyterian Ch.* Schism ex IPC. M=WPM(RPCES)(USA). HQ Quillota. 15f,1s. |
| Iglesia Sionista | 1945 | I Adv | ..... | 17 | 500 | 1,000 | *Zionist Church. Cabañistas (Tabernaclers).* Ex SDA church. Old Testament customs. |
| Iglesia Unión de Centros Bíblicos | 1923 | P ind | .M... | 81 | 1,200 | 3,000 | *Union of Bible Centres.* M=Gospel Mission SA. 14n,45f,G=10.7%pa,2h,1p,1s,W=75%,162Y. |
| Iglesia Universal de Cristo | 1938 | I pen | ..... | 12 | 500 | 1,000 | *Universal Ch of Christ.* Ex Christian & Missionary Alliance Ch. HQ Curanilahue. |
| Iglesia Wesleyana Nacional | 1928 | I pen | ..u.N | 100 | 3,000 | 15,000 | *National Wesleyan Ch.* Members must be in trade unions and leftist politics. 1H. |
| Iglesias Cristianas | 1949 | P Dis | x.... | | 200 | 500 | *Christian Chs & Chs of Christ.* M=CCCC(Instrumental) (USA). 10f. |
| Misión Cristiana Apostólica | 1938 | I pen | ..u.N | 6 | 200 | 500 | *Apostolic Christian Mission.* Schism ex IMP. Mestizos. HQ Santiago. |
| Misión Cristiana, Igl Ev Pentecostal | 1951 | I pen | ..... | 2 | 100 | 200 | *Christian Mission, Ev Pentecostal Ch.* Schism ex Methodists. Mestizos. |
| Misión Iglesia Pentecostal | 1952 | I pen | .Wu.N | 60 | 15,000 | 25,000 | *Misión Ev Pentecostal Chileana.* Ex IEP. Internal split 1971. In WCC 1961. 36n,1h,1p. |
| Sociedad de la Ciencia Cristiana | 1937 | M Sci | x.... | 5 | 200 | 500 | *Ch of Christ, Scientist. Christian Science.* M=CCS(Boston,USA). In Santiago. 2w. |
| Sociedad Noruega de Evangelización | 1948 | P Pe2 | Z.... | 2 | 100 | 200 | *Norwegian Society for Evangelism in Chile.* M=NPY(Norway). Radio ministry. 3n,2x. |
| Testigos de Jehová | 1929 | M Jeh | x.... | 127 | 8,231 | 20,000 | *Jehovah's Witnesses.* Begun 1929 by Argentina witnesses with own literature. 1141Y. |
| Other indigenous pentecostal churches | | I pen | ..... | | 5,000 | 10,000 | Total over 100 (see list below). |
| Other Protestant denominations | | P | ..... | | 2,000 | 5,000 | Total about 20 (see list below). |
| Other indigenous churches | | I ind | ..... | | 1,000 | 3,000 | Total about 30 (see list below). |
| Doubly-affiliated (duplication) (1970) | | | | | −600,000 | −1,036,549 | Evangelicals who also are or were baptized Roman Catholics. |
| **Total affiliated (mid-1970)** | | | | **6,950** | **4,813,933** | **8,245,000** | **Total denominations (1970) . . . 220.** |
| **Total affiliated (mid-1975)** | | | | **7,200** | **5,256,300** | **9,002,700** | **Total denominations (1975) . . . 240.** |
| **Total affiliated (mid-1890)** | | | | **7,900** | **5,746,100** | **9,841,500** | **Total denominations (1980) . . . 260.** |

NOTES ON TABLE ABOVE

COLUMNS: for meanings and CODES (cols. 1, 3, 4, 8): see Codebook (Part 6). Column 1: **Boldface type** = church with over 10% of country's affiliated Christians.

NATIONAL COUNCILS (Column 4, 5th letter).

- I = Unión de Misiones Pentecostales Libres (UMPL) (Union of Free Pentecostal Missions and Churches) (35 member smaller denominations, in 1975; affiliated to UNELAM and CWME/WCC).
- N = Concilio Evangélico de Chile (CEC) (Evangelical Council of Chile) (since 1961 split into 2 factions).
- R = Conferencia Episcopal de Chile (CECH) (Episcopal Conference of Chile).
- T = Confederación Fundamentalista de Iglesias Evangélicas de Chile (CFEC or CIEF or CCIEF) (Confederation of Evangelical Fundamentalist Churches of Chile).

*Other national councils.* Nuevo Concilio Evangélico Nacional (New National Evangelical Council) (Holiness churches; pro-communist in 1972). Also, Concilio Evangélico Independiente (inactive).

OTHER INDIGENOUS PENTECOSTAL CHURCHES. The total of over 100 other distinct denominations begun by Chileans (mostly Mestizos, with some Indians), of which over 70 are legally registered, includes the following: Asociación Ev Metodista Pentecostal, Corporación Ev Pentecostal 'Nuevo Amanecer', Corporación Ev Universal de Cristo, Corporación Iglesia Ev Nacional Belén (1952), Corporación Iglesia Ev Pentecostal (1956), Corporación Iglesia Metodista Pentecostal, Corporación Iglesia Unida Metodista Pentecostal, Ejército Ev Pentecostal, Iglesia Apostólica Cristiana, Iglesia Apostólica Pentecostal (member of UMPL), Iglesia Cristiana, Iglesia Cristiana Ganada con su Sangre (1936), Iglesia Cristiana Pentecostal (1942), Iglesia Cristiana Universal, Iglesia de Dios en Cristo Jesús, Iglesia de Dios Mensajeros de Jesús, Iglesia del Señor Apostólica (1930), Iglesia del Se or de la Fe Apostólica (1953), Iglesia del Señor Jesús, Iglesia de Señor la cual El ganó con su Sangre (1941), Iglesia Embajadores de Cristo (1959), Iglesia Ev de la Nuevo Jerusalem (1957), Iglesia Ev de los Hermanos (1925), Iglesia Ev de los Hermanos Pentecostales, Iglesia La Voz de Cristo, Iglesia Misión Apostólica Universal, Iglesia Misionera Pentecostal, Iglesia Obreros de Cristo, Iglesia Pentecostal de Cristo (member of UMPL), Iglesia Pentecostal el Pesebre Luz del Mundo, Iglesia Pentecostal Ev de Cristo, Iglesia Pentecostal Indus, Iglesia Pentecostal Somos de Cristo, Iglesia Wesleyana Pentecostal, Misión Cristiana Ev Pentecostal (1953), Misión Cristiana Pente-

costal (1942), Misión Ev Misionera, Misión Iglesia de Señor, Movimiento Evangélico Nacional (1960), Templo de la Fe Apostólica del 7 Día (1946).
OTHER PROTESTANT DENOMINATIONS. These include: Baptist Bible Fellowship International (1955), Bible Methodist Missions, Ch of Christ (Non-Instrumental), Ch of Scotland, Ev Methodist Ch (1960), Exclusive Brethren (Kelly-Continental), Friends Ch (Oregon), Gospel Fellowship Missions, Hermanos de Dos en Dos (1936), Iglesia de Cristo (Kansas), Maranatha Baptist Mission (1963), World Baptist Fellowship Mission, World-Wide Missions (1970), Worldwide Evangelization Crusade (UK, USA, Germany). In 1975, 2 parishes seceded from the Evangelical Lutheran Ch in Chile and remain independent (2,100 members; Valparaiso, Puerto Montt).
OTHER INDIGENOUS NON-PENTECOSTAL CHURCHES. These include: Alianza Cristiana Nacional (1935), Asamblea Bíblica Bautista, Asamblea Bíblica Misión Mundial (1965), Asamblea Cristiana (1950), Corporación Ev El Redentor Cristo, Iglesia Aliancista Nacional (1940), Iglesia Alianza Ev, Iglesia Bautista Libre, Iglesia Bautista Rural, Iglesia de Cristo, Iglesia de Oración Cristiana, Iglesia de Santidad, Iglesia Hebrea Cristiana, Iglesia Libre, Iglesia Presbiteriana Independiente (1962), Misión Comunidad del Señor, Sociedad Ev de Chile, Tabernaculo Bautista, Unión Cristiana Ev.

**PEOPLES** (ethnolinguistic). Christians: 73.8% Mestizo, 20.0% Chilean White, 4.0% Amerindian (2.8% Mapuche, 0.6% Quechua, 0.4% Aymara), 1.5% alien (Argentinian, English, German, Yugoslav, Spaniard, Italian), 0.1% Greek, Basque, Arab, Armenian.

**COUNTRY-WIDE TOTALS**
EVANGELIZATION (see Part 5). 1900: 99%. 1970: 100%. 1980: 100%. *Mass evangelism.* A few of the recent campaigns: 1962, Billy Graham 8-day crusade, Santiago; 1967, Oral Roberts 1-week campaign; 1967, Baptist campaign and 6-month Pentecostal urban campaign; 1972–73, Evangelism-in-Depth in southern Chile, and 1973–75 in Santiago. *Radiophonic evangelism.* HCJB, FEBC, ICI (797 enrolments).
FOREIGN MISSIONARIES AND PERSONNEL (nationals serving abroad) (1973). Total 649 in over 15 countries including Mexico and Kenya: about 550 Roman Catholics, 53 Chilean indigenous, 32 Protestants, 14 marginal Protestants.
FOREIGN MISSIONARIES AND PERSONNEL (aliens from abroad) (1973). Total 5,534. *From Western world.* 5,011: 4,350 Roman Catholics, about 320 marginal Protestants (280 Mormons from USA), 303 Protestants (253 in 27 USA societies, 20 in 1 Sweden society, 11 in 2 UK societies, 7 in 1 Canada society, 5 in 1 Norway society, 3 in 1 WGermany society, 3 in 2 Australia societies, 1 in 1 Finland society), 36 Anglicans in 2 UK societies, about 2 Orthodox. *From Communist world.* 18: 17 Roman Catholics from Poland, 1 Orthodox. *From Third World.* 505: 480 Roman Catholics from other Latin American countries, about 15 Protestants and 10 indigenous from Argentina and Brazil.
INSTITUTIONS (church-operated) (1973). Total 820, including 330 higher schools (26 minor seminaries), 430 medical centres (22 hospitals), 3 presses, 6 radio stations, 5 religious communities (4 monasteries), 4 research centres, 21 seminaries (14 Protestant, 3 RC, 3 Chilean indigenous, 1 Anglican), 6 study centres, 2 universities.
PERIODICALS. About 100 titles.
PERSONNEL. About 10,634 (5,100 national, 5,534 foreign).
RELIGIOUS LIBRARIES. About 50.
SCRIPTURE DISTRIBUTION (1975). Annual totals: 68,736 Bibles (42% subsidized, 58% commercial), 185,328 NTs (49% free, 29% subsidized, 22% commercial), 92,524 UBS portions, 2,502,368 UBS selections. *Translations completed.* Portion: Mapuche (Mapudungu) in 1901.
SERVICE AGENCIES. About 95, including ACF(YWCA), ACJ(YMCA), ACR, CAVE-CHILE, CAVISAT, CCCI, CEC, CECH, CEF, CFEC/CIEF, CLC, CONFERRE, DESAL, DOPAS, FEDAP, INAP, INCAMI, INVICA, LWR, MEC, MOAC, MOPAC, MTS, OCEC, SEDECOS, SU, UMPL, WLC(EHC), WVI.

**ADDITIONAL DATA ON CHURCHES**
IGLESIA CATOLICA EN CHILE. *Membership.* Statistics of Catholics in M Santiago de Chile from *Annuario Pontificio* have shown extremely large increases (*AP 1970*, 2,089,021; *AP 1972*, 3,078,000; *AP 1974*, 3,358,130). Our table above (which is for the year 1970) uses a mean figure of 2,300,000. *Annual baptisms.* (1972) 99.0% infant, 1.0% adult. *Priests.* 1,090 expatriates (1972). Total including non-diocesan and contemplatives 2,483, made up of 842 secular (580 Chileans), 1,641 religious (677 Chileans). *Brothers.* About 200 Chileans. *Male religious personnel.* Out of 2,343 men religious (priests and brothers) in 1971, 45% were Chileans, 2% were from other Latin American countries, and 53% were from other continents (Europe, USA). *Sisters.* Out of 5,884 sisters in 1971, 45% were Chileans, 7% were from other Latin American countries, and 47% were from other continents. *Catechists.* These are very numerous: AD Santiago alone has 30,000 catechists assisted by catechist-guides, for catechesis in parishes, small groups, and in the state school system. Their organization is decentralized and split into 4 zones covering the entire country: North, Centre, South, Extreme South. *Catholic charismatics* (January 1974). 2,500 adults including many religious personnel were active in 1974 in 60 prayer groups in the Charismatic Renewal; by 1976 there were over 60 prayer groups in Santiago city alone. In particular, the renewal is strong in VA Aysén. *Religious congregations.* Priests (with over 100 members): SJ, SDB. Brothers (with over 100 members): FSC. *Catholic organizations.* The Episcopal Conference of Chile (Conferencia Episcopal de Chile, CECH) is a member of CELAM. The Conference of Religious Major Superiors (Conferencia de Superiores Mayores Religiosos), for men and women, is a member of CLAR. A National Pastoral Council (Consejo Pastoral Nacional) was founded in 1961 under the name Oficina Técnica de Planificación Pastoral. Composed of priests and laity, sociologists and theologians, the council is in fact a technical agency of the episcopate in the service of pastoral planning. It does not function on a permanent basis and is giving way in importance to the Pastoral Committee (Comité Pastoral) formed by 3 bishops which relies heavily on the advice of specialists in various aspects of pastoral work. The National Secretariat for Specialized Catholic Action (Secretariado Nacional de Acción Católica Especializada) co-ordinates lay activities, the principal movements being JOC, Movimiento Obrero de Acción Católica, Acción Católica Independiente, Movimiento Familiar Cristiano and Asociación de Mujeres de Acción Católica (AMAC). For the armed forces, Chile forms a military vicariate.
The Holy See has diplomatic relations with Chile and is represented to government and the Catholic hierarchy by a nuncio based in Santiago.
Two Latin American agencies based in Chile are the Departamento de Educación Sección Planeamiento which belongs to CELAM, and the Instituto Superior de Pastoral de Juventud, which is dependent on the Latin American Federation of Religious Personnel (CLAR). Founded in 1971, the latter trains pastors and youth workers and engages in research.
The Secretariado de Cristianos por el Socialismo, also called the Grupo de los Ochenta, was formed by a group of 80 priests in April 1971 who declared themselves in favour of the installation of socialism even by revolutionary means if necessary. Laymen and a few Protestant pastors also joined, making 200 members by April 1972 when they organized the first Latin American Encounter of Christians for Socialism. The group has been dispersed since the military coup of 1973.
The Sociedad para la Defensa de la Tradición, de la Familia y de la Propriedad (also called *Fiducia* from the name of its publication) is a traditionalist group established in Chile in 1961–64 when the bishops began the distribution of land to peasants and wrote pastoral letters dealing with social problems. Following the election of S. Allende as president of the republic, most members left the country voluntarily, the remainder abstaining from public activity. The group has become active again since the 1973 coup.
Research and social action centres include: (1) Centro Bellarmino (CIAS), founded in 1957 by Jesuits with a religious sociology section, which studies social change in terms of social justice and applies the result of sociological studies to pastoral work; (2) Oficina de Sociología Religiosa de la Conferencia Episcopal, founded in 1957, which relates socio-religious studies to pastoral problems; (3) CIDE, founded in 1965, which is a centre for applied research and the distribution of teaching and educational material with special concern for youth and marginalized peoples; (4) Instituto de Viviendas Populares (INVICA), and Hogar de Cristo Viviendas, which are Catholic organizations involved in the construction of low-cost housing; (5) Instituto Indígena, in Temuco, which is dedicated to improving the spiritual, economic and cultural life of the 125,000 Mapuche Indians living in the diocese of Temuco and helping to co-ordinate work among them; (6) Instituto Católico Chileno de Migración (INCAMI), which is a member of CCIM and provides aid to migrants; and (7) Centro para el Desarrollo Económico y Social de América Latina (DESAL), in Santiago which is related to DESAL in Bogotá, Colombia.
Pastoral and religious training is provided by several institutions. (1) The Facultad de Teología, Universidad Católica de Chile (Santiago) offers courses in theology, religious culture and catechesis. Associated with it is the Hogar Catequístico Juanita Ossa de Valdés, which trains teachers of religion recognized by the Ministry of Education, offers training courses in religion for mothers, develops religious programmes and prepares catechetical material. (2) The Instituto Nacional de Pastoral carries on research concerning pastoral orientation in relation to secularization, Marxism and evangelization. (3) The Centro de Educación Pastoral is under the direction of the Department of Catechesis of the Archdiocese of Santiago.
The Catholic educational programme in 1971 included 1,200 Catholic schools with 322,272 pupils distributed as follows: 259,204 in primary schools, 66,454 in secondary schools and 16,614 at the professional level. Catholic education is part of a system of private schools (Sistema Particular) which in 1969 consisted of 556,270 pupils (24% of the school population) while the state system (Sistema Fiscal) grouped 1,717,886 pupils (76%). Catholic universities are 2 in number; in addition to the Universidad Católica de Chile in Santiago, there is the Universidad Católica de Valparaíso.
Caritas Chile, founded in 1955, is the co-ordinating body for Catholic relief and development work and is recognized as such by the government. Its activities include health (21 hospitals; 400 clinics, dispensaries and rural posts in 1971), social action (training 500 voluntary assistants yearly for work in youth clubs, kindergartens and vacation programmes), social assistance (catering for the interests of immigrants and youth), and relief and development (food distribution in co-operation with CRS-USCC/USA and economic and community development on the basis of self-help principles).
IGLESIA EVANGELICA LUTERANA EN CHILE. In 1974 a serious schism began, opposing its bishop's political involvement. By 1976 the church was reduced to 1,500 members in 5 congregations, most of the rest forming a new Lutheran Church of Chile (Iglesia Luterana en Chile; HQ Osorno; 23,000 members).
IGLESIA EVANGELICA PENTECOSTAL DE CHILE. *Membership.* Estimates vary from 200,000 to 600,000 adults. *Worship.* No musica linstruments are permitted in church services. *Missions.* Widespread foreign work in Argentina, Bolivia, Peru, Uruguay, also a mission in New York (USA).
IGLESIA METODISTA PENTECOSTAL DE CHILE. *Membership* (1971). Estimates vary from 300,000 to 500,000 (1970), and (1975) 650,000. Its Jotabeche congregation in Santiago has 80,000 members (1975), the largest Evangelical congregation in the world. *Members' employment.* 47% working-class, 23% white-collar, 25% self-employed. Voters in election of 4.IX.1970: 14% voted Communist, 36% Socialist, 13% Christian Democrat, 30% non-voters. Of all members, 15% are trade-unionists; 5% belong to a political party; 79% supported Marxist-revolutionary Allende regime; 76% considered it not wrong to vote communist; 50% of adult pentecostals were converted during previous 10 years. *Growth.* Annual growth before 1935 was around 2%; subsequently it has averaged 6%. There are however a large number of lapsed members, including many children of members. *Baptism.* Infants are baptized. *Church polity.* Wesleyan church discipline, with episcopacy. *Foreign missionary aid.* Since 1967, the church has had affiliation with the Pentecostal Holiness Church (PHC), USA. *Foreign missionaries sent.* Extensive mission work is undertaken in Argentina, Bolivia and Peru.

# CHINA

## SECULAR DATA

**STATE. Official name:** The People's Republic of China (Chung-Hua Jen-Min Kung-Ho Kuo; modernized form, Zhongguo). Adjective of nationality: Chinese.
**Flag** (shown above right): Red field, 5 gold stars.
**Area:** 9,596,961 sq.km. (3,691,523 sq.miles.) Agricultural land: 35.7% (12% cultivated).
**Government:** One-party Communist state, since 1949 (1644 Manchu dynasty, 1912 Republic of China, 1917 Nationalist China).
**Legislature:** National People's Congress, 3,040 members.
**Official language:** Chinese (*Kuo yu*). (Uighur is official in Chinese Turkestan).
**Chief cities:** capital Peking (Beijing) 7,570,000 (1970), Shanghai 10,820,000, Tientsin 4,280,000.
**Political divisions:** 22 Provinces (including Taiwan), 5 Autonomous Regions, 3 Municipalities (Peking, Shanghai, Tientsin).
**Armed forces** (1976): Total 3,525,000 regular: army 3 million (37 armies), navy 275,000, air force 250,000 (4,250 combat aircraft). Paramilitary forces: 14 million (5 million Armed Militia, Urban Militia, et alia).

**DEMOGRAPHY. Population:** 590,194,715 (census of 30.VI.1953. For 1970–2000 (UN), see last row of Table 1). Population density (1975): 86/sq.km. (222/sq.mile). Under 15 years: 39%. Growth rate (1975–80): 1.58% per year (births 2.52%, deaths −0.95%). Life expectancy (1975–80): 63.6 years. Household size: 4.8 persons.
**Major languages:** Chinese (Mandarin, Northern, Western, Southern, and numerous other dialects), English, Tibetan, Uighur, Mongolian, Manchu, Korean, Japanese, Russian. In addition there are over 170 other languages.
**Urban dwellers** (1970): 25.5%. Urban growth rate (1950–70): 5.7% per year.
**Labour force:** 46%.
**Refugees** (1979): From abroad, 230,000 from Viet Nam. Exiles abroad: 280,730 Chinese (114,730 in Hong Kong, 70,000 Tibetans in India, 60,000 in USSR, 25,000 in Macao, 10,000 Tibetans in Nepal, 1,000 Tibetans in Switzerland). Two million other Chinese are thought to have escaped to Hong Kong in recent years.
**Tourists** (1978): 530,000.

**ETHNOLINGUISTIC GROUPS:** 94.0% Han Chinese [dialect: 62.0% Mandarin (Modern Standard Chinese; Northern (Peking), Western, Southern), 8.5% Wu (Kiangsu Chekiang), 5.0% Cantonese (Yüeh), 5.0% Hsiang (Hunanese), 4.0% Hakka (Ke-chia), 4.0% Min (Fuchow, North Fukienese), 2.6% Minnan (Amoy-Swatow, South Fukienese, Hokkienese, Hoklo), 2.5% Kan (Kiangsi), Hweichow, et alia], 1.1% Chuang, 0.6% Dungan (Hui), 0.6% Uighur, 0.6% Yi, 0.5% Tibetan, 0.4% Manchurian, 0.4% Miao, 0.3% Mongolian, 0.2% Korean, 0.2% Puyi, 0.1% Yao, 0.1% Kazakh; & 45 other peoples.

**MONEY** (1977). **Monetary unit:** yuan (= 10 chiao = 100 fen); for foreign currency, jen min pi (YRMB), US$ 1 = YRMB 1.90.
**National income per person:** US$200. Average annual family income: US$960.
**Inflation:** Nil.
**Cost of living in capital** (1976): Daily cost of living: US$21.

**EDUCATION.** Adult literacy: 55%. Education rate: 50%. Schools: (1958) 660,000. Universities: 28 (61 in 1961).

**HEALTH.** Hospitals: 15,000 (800,000 beds). Doctors: 170,000 (also about 500,000 traditional-style doctors). Lepers: 2,279,000 (2.8 per 1,000). Blind: 2,000,000. Psychotics: 4,000,000.

**LITERATURE.** Periodicals: 2,000. Scientific journals: 660. Newspapers (1955): 392 dailies.

**COMMUNICATION** (per 1,000 people). Phones: 28. Radios: 16 shortwave (local sets 122). TV sets: 0.5. Daily newspaper circulation: 19 copies.

TABLE 1. RELIGIOUS ADHERENTS IN THE PEOPLE'S REPUBLIC OF CHINA

| Year | 1900 | | mid-1970 | | Annual change, 1970–1980 | | | | mid-1975 | | mid-1980 | | 2000 | |
|---|---|---|---|---|---|---|---|---|---|---|---|---|---|---|
| *Name* | *Adherents* | % | *Adherents* | % | *Natural* | *Conversion* | *Total* | *Rate* | *Adherents* | % | *Adherents* | % | *Adherents* | % |
| Non-religious | 30,000 | 0.0 | 398,805,500 | 52.6 | 7,390,009 | 5,416,458 | 12,806,467 | 2.78 | 460,140,830 | 56.0 | 526,869,670 | 59.2 | 765,504,900 | 67.9 |
| Chinese folk-religionists | 376,299,000 | 79.7 | 198,000,000 | 26.1 | 3,050,586 | −4,964,299 | −1,913,713 | −1.01 | 189,945,520 | 23.1 | 178,862,870 | 20.1 | 135,275,400 | 12.0 |
| Atheists | 1,000 | 0.0 | 88,000,000 | 11.6 | 1,558,308 | 320,072 | 1,878,380 | 1.94 | 97,028,450 | 11.8 | 106,783,800 | 12.0 | 146,050,000 | 13.0 |
| Buddhists | 60,000,000 | 12.7 | 50,000,000 | 6.6 | 831,978 | −492,788 | 339,190 | 0.66 | 51,803,320 | 6.3 | 53,391,900 | 6.0 | 56,364,700 | 5.0 |
| Muslims | 24,000,000 | 5.1 | 20,000,000 | 2.6 | 330,150 | −194,150 | 135,676 | 0.66 | 20,556,880 | 2.5 | 21,356,760 | 2.4 | 22,100,000 | 2.0 |
| **Christians** | **1,670,000** | **0.4** | **2,000,000** | **0.3** | **30,515** | **−50,515** | **−20,000** | **−1.05** | **1,900,000** | **0.2** | **1,800,000** | **0.2** | **1,500,000** | **0.1** |
| crypto-Christians | 0 | 0.0 | 1,900,000 | 0.3 | 28,909 | −66,909 | −38,000 | −2.11 | 1,800,000 | 0.2 | 1,610,000 | 0.2 | 1,100,000 | 0.1 |
| professing | 1,670,000 | 0.4 | 10,000 | 0.0 | 1,606 | 16,394 | 18,000 | 18.00 | 100,000 | 0.0 | 190,000 | 0.0 | 400,000 | 0.0 |
| Roman Catholics | 1,200,000 | 0.3 | 6,000 | 0.0 | 964 | 9,836 | 10,800 | 18.00 | 60,000 | 0.0 | 114,000 | 0.0 | 240,000 | 0.0 |
| Protestants | 400,000 | 0.1 | 2,700 | 0.0 | 433 | 4,427 | 4,860 | 18.00 | 27,000 | 0.0 | 51,300 | 0.0 | 108,000 | 0.0 |
| Chinese indigenous | 1,000 | 0.0 | 1,000 | 0.0 | 161 | 1,639 | 1,800 | 18.00 | 10,000 | 0.0 | 19,000 | 0.0 | 40,000 | 0.0 |
| Anglicans | 35,000 | 0.0 | 0 | 0.0 | 0 | 0 | 0 | 0.00 | 0 | 0.0 | 0 | 0.0 | 0 | 0.0 |
| Orthodox | 34,000 | 0.0 | 300 | 0.0 | 48 | 492 | 540 | 18.00 | 3,000 | 0.0 | 5,700 | 0.0 | 12,000 | 0.0 |
| nominal | 160,000 | 0.0 | 0 | 0.0 | 0 | 0 | 0 | 0.00 | 0 | 0.0 | 0 | 0.0 | 0 | 0.0 |
| affiliated | 1,510,000 | 0.3 | 2,000,000 | 0.3 | 30,515 | −50,515 | −20,000 | −1.05 | 1,900,000 | 0.2 | 1,800,000 | 0.2 | 1,500,000 | 0.1 |
| total practising | 1,208,000 | *80* | 200,000 | *10* | 3,051 | −5,051 | −2,000 | −1.05 | 190,000 | *10* | 180,000 | *10* | 450,000 | *30* |
| non-practising | 302,000 | *20* | 1,800,000 | *90* | 27,464 | −45,464 | −18,000 | −1.05 | 1,710,000 | *90* | 1,620,000 | *90* | 1,050,000 | *70* |
| Roman Catholics | 1,100,000 | 0.2 | 1,200,000 | 0.2 | 18,309 | −30,309 | −12,000 | −1.05 | 1,140,000 | 0.0 | 1,080,000 | 0.0 | 900,000 | 0.0 |
| Catholic pentecostals | 0 | 0.0 | 1,000 | 0.0 | 48 | 452 | 500 | 16.67 | 3,000 | 0.0 | 6,000 | 0.0 | 30,000 | 0.0 |
| Protestants | 350,000 | 0.1 | 550,000 | 0.1 | 8,391 | −13,891 | −5,500 | −1.05 | 522,500 | 0.0 | 495,000 | 0.0 | 412,500 | 0.0 |
| Evangelicals | 270,000 | 0.1 | 330,000 | 0.0 | 5,620 | −1,620 | 4,000 | 1.14 | 350,000 | 0.0 | 370,000 | 0.0 | 380,000 | 0.0 |
| Chinese indigenous | 1,000 | 0.0 | 200,000 | 0.0 | 3,052 | −5,052 | −2,000 | −1.05 | 190,000 | 0.0 | 180,000 | 0.0 | 150,000 | 0.0 |
| Anglicans | 30,000 | 0.0 | 40,000 | 0.0 | 610 | −1,010 | −400 | −1.05 | 38,000 | 0.0 | 36,000 | 0.0 | 30,000 | 0.0 |
| Orthodox | 29,000 | 0.0 | 10,000 | 0.0 | 153 | −253 | −100 | −1.05 | 9,500 | 0.0 | 9,000 | 0.0 | 7,500 | 0.0 |
| Tribal religionists | 10,000,000 | 2.1 | 1,000,000 | 0.1 | 14,454 | −34,454 | −20,000 | −2.22 | 900,000 | 0.1 | 800,000 | 0.1 | 500,000 | 0.0 |
| **Country's population** | **472,000,000** | **100.0** | **757,805,000** | **100.0** | **13,206,000** | **0** | **13,206,000** | **1.61** | **822,275,000** | **100.0** | **889,865,000** | **100.0** | **1,127,295,000** | **100.0** |

COLUMNS, ROWS. For meanings and definitions, see Codebook (Part 6). Note that, by definition, total 'Christians' = professing + crypto-Christians, which also = affiliated + nominal Christians. Percentages may not always total exactly, due to rounding. The statistics given here for 1970–2000 are rough estimates only, assessing very approximately the general order of magnitude of the situation.
CENSUSES. No question on religion has been asked in recent censuses.

NOTES ON RELIGIONS
AFFILIATED CHRISTIANS. From 1900, the membership of all churches rose rapidly. In 1949, churches' statistics of affiliation were: 3,266,000 Roman Catholics, 1,295,000 Protestants (600,000 being communicants) of whom 100,000 were Pentecostals, 440,000 Chinese indigenous (246,000 being communicants), 300,000 Orthodox (90% Russians, with some Chinese converts), and 76,741 baptized Anglicans. Under Communist rule after 1949, numbers were drastically and continuously eroded, although most of the decline had tapered off by 1970.
ANGLICANS. After 1950 the Anglican Church continued to exist only in its own eyes, but not in the eyes of the state for whom it had ceased to exist as a separate entity and operated only through the Three-Self Reform Movement.
ATHEISTS. Chinese Communist Party (CCP) (Chung-kuo Kung Ch'an Tang) (in power since 1949): membership rose from 4.5 million (1949) to 10,750,000 (1956), to 17 million (1961) and to 35 million by 1977. Youth membership: many million Little Red Guards (aged 7–12), several million in the Young Pioneer Corps (Red Scarves; primary schoolchildren), 20 million teenagers aged 14–25 in the Young Communist League (in 1956), and (1967) over 11 million militantly anti-religious Red Guards. More than in other Communist countries, in China atheism, Communism and the cult of Mao have been developed into a secular quasi-religion. By 1968, more than 1,000 million copies of Mao's writings had been distributed.
BUDDHISTS. In 1900, most of the 60 million Buddhists (Mahayana, with 2 million Tibetan Lamaists) also accepted Chinese folk religion to a large extent. Since 1949, large numbers of Buddhists have become non-religious, although it is thought that at least 40 million conscientious devotees still remain, as well as numerous seasonal or occasional supporters. The one million Buddhists in Tibet (introduced AD 640) follow Lamaism (Tantrayana) and have been more ruthlessly secularized than other Buddhists; by 1976 less than a dozen of Tibet's former 5,000 monasteries were functioning, no new monks were being recruited, and the practice of Buddhism had virtually disappeared. In 1978 there were only 300 practising monks in Tibet compared to over 100,000 in 1950.
CATHOLIC PENTECOSTALS (or, Catholic charismatics). A flourishing Catholic lay movement of pentecostal type exists in Fukien province. There are reports also of pentecostal youth groups elsewhere.
CHINESE FOLK-RELIGIONISTS. In 1900, four-fifths of the population adhered to Chinese folk religion, a mixture of Confucian ethics, ancestor veneration, local divinities and deified heroes (some Taoist), popular religious beliefs and practices, and some Buddhist elements; also, about 10% of folk-religionists regarded themselves as Taoists. After 1949, militant communist teaching and action resulted in most village temples being secularized, and vast numbers of rural folk-religionists became non-religious (estimated above at almost 5 million a year since 1970).
CHINESE INDIGENOUS. From 1906 onwards a number of new indigenous denominations were begun by Chinese, sometimes as secessions from Western mission churches. In 1949 the 440,000 total community were found in over 30 indigenous denominations. They were subsequently persecuted and suppressed far more than were Western churches; but in 1968 they were observed to be still constituting a more effective Christian witness than the Western-originated denominations. In 1976, 5,000 adult baptisms were reported from an area associated with Assembly Hall Churches.
COUNTRY'S POPULATION. During the purges from 1949 to the present day, an estimated 15 million persons were killed and 40 million others imprisoned in labour camps, including a sizeable proportion of all Christians. In 1976, vast numbers were killed in earthquakes, 655,237 alone in the northern city of Tangshan. *Population estimates.* The last official census was in 1953 (602 million Chinese, 12 million living abroad). Estimates for the 1980 population vary from 800 to 1,000 million.
CRYPTO-CHRISTIANS. Although there is no highly-organized underground church, most Christians remain invisible keeping their faith and activities private. Only very occasional glimpses of this activity have been evident. In 1955 authorities discovered 200 physically-underground Catholic churches in the province of Hopei; and 20 years later, mass baptisms of up to 100 youths at a time were being reported from remote areas. Some observers believe that Evangelical Christianity on the mainland has more than doubled in size since 1949, instancing Shanghai where 2 house congregations of around the year 1955 are known to have grown to over 40 such groups in 20 years. Nevertheless the total of all Christians continues to shrink by erosion under the continuous pressure of state and society, particularly due to the dying off of older pre-1949 Christians and the secularizing of their children and succeeding generations.
MUSLIMS. Primarily Sunnis (of the Hanafite rite), with some Shias (Tadzhiks). Mainly-Muslim peoples: Hui (Dungan), Uighurs, Kazakhs, Kirgiz, Uzbeks, Tatars, Tunghsiang, Paoans, Salars. In June 1975, an attempt to suppress Islam among the Hui met with violent resistance and troops arrested 500 Hui.
NOMINAL CHRISTIANS. Before 1949 only.
NON-RELIGIOUS. As a result of a massive anti-religious programme of secularization from 1949–1970, something over half of the population have become indifferent to religion. However, the initial momentum had slowed considerably by 1970, and resistance on the part of remaining religionists of all kinds was increasing perceptibly.
PRACTISING CHRISTIANS. Most believers were able to attend church until the Cultural Revolution of 1966–69, when all churches were closed and all Christians were prevented from practising. In 1972, 2 church buildings were opened in Peking (with 6,000 local Roman Catholics and 500 Protestants); this did not prove to be the beginning of any widespread movement, although in Nanking (population 1,800,000) 500 Christians were meeting regularly in 1973 in 4 areas of the city; and in Chekiang, one county had as many Christian services in 1973 as it did before 1949, with the former Anglican bishop of Chekiang (K. H. Ting) speaking of churches there once again 'filled with people'. Elsewhere, public worship and observance of Christian ceremonies remained suspended, and practice was only possible in small irregular groups meeting in different places in rotation. The Christian community now shows marked opposition to the reopening, use and upkeep of church buildings as a holdover from the days of Western domination.
PROFESSING CHRISTIANS. As known to the state, the only Christians in China are expatriates (diplomats, technicians, etc.) and handfuls of Chinese scattered across the country. By 1975 the latter however were growing rapidly in numbers as crypto-Christians emerged and became publicly visible, acknowledging their faith but at the same time stressing their patriotism, communism, loyalty to the state, and the right to their own private beliefs.
TRIBAL RELIGIONISTS. A number of hill tribes on the southern borders of China remain mainly animists; these include the Lisu and Yao. The Lolo in southern Yunnan have shamanistic practices; also the Moso or Na-khi (Tibeto-Burmese in southwest China) and the Monguor or T'u-jen of Sining (northwest China). Since 1960 extensive efforts to secularize them all through schools and party structure have been under way.

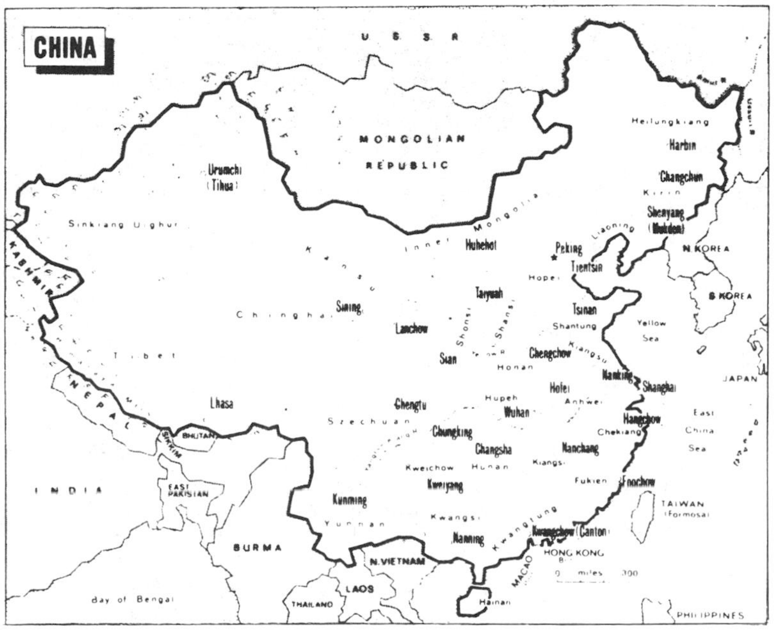


**Orthography.** The Pin-yin system of romanization for the Chinese language, based on Northern Mandarin/Peking dialect, was adopted in 1958 to aid the spread of modern standard Chinese across China. The map at left uses the older, anglicized spelling; whereas Map 5, in Part II (Atlas) uses Pin-yin.

**NON-CHRISTIAN RELIGIONS. Atheism** and **agnosticism** are now the majority philosophies of modern Chinese. The former Chinese folk religion has been drastically undermined since 1949 as a result of massive anti-religious programmes of secularization and indoctrination.

**Chinese folk religion** is a complex amalgam of 6 elements: ancestor veneration, which is accorded a place in Confucian tradition; Confucian ethics; devotion to local divinities and deified heroes, some of which are Taoist; Chinese universism; some Buddhist elements; and a whole series of practices related to fortune-telling, divination, magic and sorcery. The government labels this amalgam 'superstition', and a serious effort has been made to rid the masses of their folk rituals. Since the Cultural Revolution from 1966–69 most local shrines have been closed and such traditional worship paraphernalia as joss sticks can no longer be purchased. Attempts have also been made to alter traditional religious practices relating to marriage, burial and the celebration of national festivals. Folk religion is the most elusive of all China's religions. Although its communal elements have been suppressed, its individual and family aspects continue to hold wide sway over the masses.

**Taoism** is a system so closely interwoven with folk religion that it is difficult to distinguish one from the other. Some 10% of folk-religionists in the past professed to be also Taoists. Since 1949 they have been accused of being counter-revolutionaries fostering feudalistic and superstitious ideas among the population, but Taoism's lack of centralized organization makes it almost as difficult to suppress as folk religion. In an effort to gain control of the movement, in 1953 the government formed the Chinese Taoist Association. Its purpose was to encourage Taoists 'to continue and develop the beautiful tradition of Taoism so that under the direction of the popular government they might love their nation and actively support the building of socialism in the country'. However, the association

was invited to an official banquet given in honour of personalities visiting Peking from nearby Buddhist countries, including Japan and Sri Lanka.

**Islam** came to China during the Tang dynasty through the silk trade and southeastern ports, but it did not grow extensively until the founding of the Yuan dynasty in 1260. Statistical estimates of adherents range from 48 million, claimed by Muslim sources, to 10 million, as stated by a Chinese Communist source in 1953; a probable figure for 1970

apostolic exarchate of the Byzantine rite) and a large number of educational and medical institutions (1,849 primary schools, 202 secondary schools, 3 universities, 194 hospitals and hostels, 6 leprosariums, 257 orphanages and 864 dispensaries, together with 29 presses and 55 periodicals). There were then 2,542 Chinese and 3,046 foreign priests, 803 major seminarians, 663 Chinese and 414 foreign brothers, 4,717 Chinese and 2,036 foreign religious women. Chinese clergy, 45% of the total, directed 35 ecclesiastical jurisdictions (25% of the total); the rest were confided to 27 European and North American missionary orders. Between 3 November 1949 and 20 September 1955, the Holy See nominated 50 bishops, Chinese and foreign. In 1951 the government closed the Catholic Central Bureau, expelled the nuncio and nationalized all medical and educational institutions with the exception of a school for diplomats' children in Peking run by 14 Franciscan Missionaries of Mary until 1966, when they also were expelled. At the end of 1951, remaining foreign missionaries were arrested or expelled; several Chinese priests also were arrested. The Vatican several times condemned the government-created Three Autonomies corresponding to the Protestant Three-Self Movement (self-support, self-government, self-propagation). By 1952 Taiwan had been recognized by the Holy See and the expelled nuncio designated pro-nuncio in Taipei, and so the rupture between Rome and Peking had become total. In July 1957, the National Patriotic Catholic Association was created on the mainland, directed by the Catholic archbishop of Shenyang (Mukden). Between 1957 and 1963 a Constitutional Church was developed, followed by the election and consecration of 45 Chinese bishops. These are considered by Rome to be valid but illicit and therefore unacceptable. During the Cultural Revolution all traces of the visible church, including the Constitutional Church, were obliterated. By 1975, the number of Chinese clergy had been reduced to between 450 and 650, due to emigration, deaths, numerous arrests, sentencing of clergy to forced labour, and also the small number of new ordinations. In 1975, however, it was reported that there were still 123 known Jesuit priests in China.

**Maoism as a quasi-religion.** Six members of 11 million militantly anti-religious Red Guards (1966-69 Cultural Revolution) pause near Canton to read from Chairman Mao's *Thoughts* before moving into action against churches and Christians. These 6 are from Mao's birthplace.

has never played an important role, and has not been heard of since 1966. Like other religions, Taoism suffered through the closure of shrines and destruction of religious objects during the Cultural Revolution.

**Confucianism** is not properly speaking a separate religion but is an ethical system which makes its influence felt on all religion and also on those who claim no religious allegiance. Confucius' teachings have been labelled feudalistic by the Party and stated to be contrary to the doctrines of Mao Tse-tung. In 1966 Red Guards initiated a campaign to condemn and burn the writings of Confucius, and destroyed a temple built in his honour at his birthplace in Shantung province. An even wider anti-Confucian campaign was launched in August 1973.

**Mahayana Buddhism** was introduced into China from central Asia in the 1st century AD under the dynasty of Han. Its principal expansion took place during the Tang dynasty, from 618–906. Although there were around 60 million Buddhists in 1900, the number had fallen to about 50 million by 1970 through large numbers abandoning religion and religious profession. In Tibet, the form of Buddhism known as Lamaism or Tantrism (Tantrayana) was held by its one million people until Chinese armies occupied Tibet in 1950; thereafter, religion was virtually exterminated, over 1,000 monasteries were destroyed, many priests killed, and 90% of all lamas were secularized. However, under Communist rule, a Chinese Buddhist Association was started in 1953; among its honorary presidents originally were the Dalai Lama and the Panchen Lama; and its president was Shirob Jaltso, a Tibetan, who was then vice-governor of the province of Tsinghai. All its former leaders have been in disgrace since the beginning of the Cultural Revolution and Red Guard activities. At the end of 1972 the association was revived, although Buddhism as a cultural expression has nearly disappeared. A certain number of monasteries remain active in various parts of China, but many others have been taken over for secular purposes or made into museums. In general those still functioning seem to be more or less cut off from the people, in spite of the attempt by monks to combine their monastic life with productive work outside the monasteries. The existing Buddhist presence in Peking is due at least in part to the desire of the government to create and maintain good contacts with friendly Buddhist nations and foreign delegations visiting the Chinese capital. In 1974 the director of the Buddhist Association of China, Chao Pu-chu,

is 20 million. Islam is the predominant religion of 10 ethnic minorities: Hui (3.9 million in 1961), found in all the provinces but dominant in the Nigshia region; Uighurs (3.9 million in 1961), concentrated in the Uighur region of Sinkiang (Chinese Turkestan); Kazakhs (533,000 in 1961), who are located especially northeast of Sinkiang; and 7 other groups of less importance (Kirgiz, Tadzhiks, Uzbeks, Tatars, Tunghsiang, Paoans and Salars). Chinese Muslims are primarily Sunnis, but the Tadzhiks are Shias. Of all the organized regions, Islam seems to have suffered the least under the Cultural Revolution. It is true that imams and practising Muslims were imprisoned, most of their centres were closed and a Revolutionary Group for the Abolition of Islam was organized. But of greater significance was the reopening of a mosque to serve diplomats in Peking in January 1967. In 1968, 2 other mosques were opened, in Peking and Shanghai. At the end of 1969 the Hui were again allowed to celebrate Islamic events in several areas. On 17 February 1970, Corban (Eid el Seghir) was solemnly celebrated at the Tan Szu mosque in Peking. The Chinese Islamic Association created in 1953 was revived in 1969, but its former president Burhan Shahidi has not been heard of since 1964. By 1975 mosques had been opened in several other large cities.

**Animism** is still the predominant belief of the Lisu, Yao and other minority tribal groups inhabiting the mountainous areas of southwest China, despite extensive secularization campaigns among them.

## CHRISTIANITY

The first Christian missionary known to have entered China was the Nestorian Alopen from Syria who arrived in Sian the Tang capital in AD 635. A Nestorian monument erected outside Sian in AD 781 was excavated in 1625. However, the so-called Luminous Religion faded and was finally wiped out in 845. Nestorian missionaries returned in the 13th century but with no lasting result.

CATHOLIC CHURCH. The first Franciscan missionary visited Peking in 1294 and later claimed 6,000 converts, but Catholicism did not take root until the arrival of the pioneer missionary Matteo Ricci at the end of the 16th century. When Mao Tse-tung came to power in 1949, the Catholic Church had 3,251,347 baptized faithful and 190,850 catechumens, 144 ecclesiastical jurisdictions (20 archdioceses, 90 dioceses, 33 prefectures and an

Since 1970 the government has shown signs of a relaxation in its attitude towards the church. In July 1970 it released bishop Walsh, the last foreign bishop still imprisoned in China, and authorized the recommencing of religious services at the Church of the Immaculate Conception (also called Church of the South or Nan Tang) in Peking, a church which has been attended by foreign travellers since November 1971 and which has provided an opportunity for Westerners to meet a handful of priests in Peking. Catholic services in Peking are held only in the Nan Tang Church, where they are led by 4 priests including bishop Wang Ki-ting (who is not recognized by the Vatican) and the vice-president of the Patriotic Committee of the Catholic Church in Peking, Tien Sun. Mass is said in Latin according to the pre-Vatican II liturgy. Those in attendance are for the most part foreigners: diplomats, African students and visitors. The first public religious marriage, of a French couple, was celebrated in September 1974. By June 1975 no visitors had yet been invited to participate in Catholic services outside Peking. Since November 1971 several interviews with foreign travellers have been given by the bishop of Peking and also by a group consisting of 3 priests. From these interviews it has been learned that the last ordination in People's China took place in 1963, which confirms the testimony of a Mexican priest as early as 1965 that he had met this new priest. The last 2 major seminaries, Peking and Shanghai, were closed in 1954 and 1955 respectively. These interviews have also revealed that the number of Catholics affiliated to the National Patriotic Catholic Association is estimated by them to be about 2 million; sources outside China tend to estimate a more drastic erosion by two-thirds since 1949 to 1.2 million by 1970. The number of Chinese Catholics in Peking is likewise stated to be between 5,000 and 6,000, with 20 priests, 30 sisters and 20 seminary students who are following a 15-year training programme under the direction of 5 or 6 full-time priests. Younger sisters work in hospitals while older ones have dedicated themselves to prayer in a retirement home. Information has also been obtained that there is a bishop for every region in China, each 'democratically elected', although none has yet been seen by foreigners.

PROTESTANT AND ANGLICAN CHURCHES. Protestant missionary work in China began with the arrival of Robert Morrison of the London Missionary Society in 1807. Under difficult, often hostile, conditions, his major contribution was in the field of Bible translation. The American Board of Commissioners for Foreign Missions next sent the first medical missionary to China. Over the years medicine became one of the major areas of service by the churches. Mission work received an impetus following the Opium War, when in 1842 China was forced to open its doors to both opium and foreign residents including missionaries. Anglican missions began with separate work by 4 English, one Canadian, one American, and one Australian, missionary bodies. Shanghai soon became the headquarters of missionary societies from all over the world. Baptist, Methodist, Presbyterian and Lutheran missions from the USA were at work, in addition to numerous European societies. The China Inland Mission under Hudson Taylor, beginning in 1865, grew to be the largest mission in China (with over 1,000 missionaries in 1914) and became a model for the faith missions approach. Its missionaries adopted Chinese dress and customs, concentrated on small inland cities and towns, constructed 330 mission stations and thousands of out-stations, and eventually built up a self-supporting church of 85,000 members.

New missions continued to enter and by 1907 there were 94 Protestant mission societies with 3,445 missionaries at 632 stations, 166 hospitals and 389 post-primary schools. Anti-foreigner agitation gradually increased, and the Boxer (League of Righteous Fists) rebellion of 1900, which resulted in the death of 189 Protestant missionaries and their families, was the largest of such demonstrations. During the following decade, more numerical progress was made than in the previous half-century. In 1914 there were 543 Protestant high schools, 33 colleges, 265 hospitals, 386 dispensaries, 411 medical doctors, and over 6 million scriptures were distributed annually. In 1911 the Manchu dynasty fell, and a Christian, Sun Yat-sen, became the leader of the new republic. At the climax of the missionary era (1926) there were 160 Protestant missionary societies in China, with over 8,000 missionaries. Pentecostal missions began in China with the entry of British Assemblies of God into Yunnan in 1911. Various marginal Protestant missions also arrived; Jehovah's Witnesses were begun in Shanghai in 1929 by a Japanese, and a branch office was opened in 1932. Although the number of Protestant Christians never rose above 0.2% of the population, in the 1930s 35% of the Chinese elite had received Christian education, 90% of all nurses were Christians and 70% of all hospitals were mission institutions. The vast amount of mission property and money attracted roaming bandits, and 29 Protestant missionaries were killed and 80 kidnapped between 1924 and 1935.

In 1922 the National Christian Council of China was created, including a home missionary society controlled and supported by Chinese churches. Church union discussions made a certain amount of progress. In 1927 the Church of Christ in China was formed and held its first assembly in Shanghai, uniting 7 denominations.

In the 1930s Japan was invading China; many missionaries remained during the Japanese occupation, but after the Japanese attack on Pearl Harbour in 1941 they were imprisoned or fled. After World War II four thousand Protestant missionaries returned to China, but they were not to remain long. At the time of the Communist victory in 1949, Protestants numbered 1,295,000 adherents in about 270 denominations, and Anglicans 76,741 in 14 dioceses, with 13 universities and many secondary schools. The Christian Manifesto was published, signed by 1,527 church leaders and eventually by 400,000 Christians. It recognized the contributions of missionaries but attacked their association with imperialism. It was announced that Article 88 of China's constitution guaranteeing freedom of religion would not be honoured until the church had freed itself of all signs of imperialism. During the next year almost all missionaries were expelled from China. The Three-Self Reform Movement followed in 1951, led by the YMCA executive Y.T. Wu, which set itself the task of helping churches to rid themselves of imperialism, feudalism and bourgeois thinking. This was carried out through denunciation meetings, with attacks on both former missionaries and Chinese church leaders, and through study sessions concerning communist doctrine. Many churches succeeded in meeting these requirements and were permitted to continue Sunday morning services.

In the period prior to 1966, Christians were relatively free to worship, but national denominational structures were bypassed and fell into disuse as the Three-Self Reform Movement (or Chinese Christian Three-Self Patriotic Church) and the National Patriotic Catholic Association were organized under the government's Bureau of Religious Affairs. While official government policy tolerated freedom of religious belief, the activities of the churches were increasingly curtailed. The numerous seminaries were consolidated until there was only one, at Nanking, which was itself closed in 1966. Many local churches were closed in a consolidation movement beginning in 1958; in Peking where there had been 65 Protestant churches the previous year, only 4 remained open by the end of the year. In rural areas, village churches disappeared throughout the land. Members of widely disparate denominations were forced either to worship together or not at all. In 1964 it became illegal to teach religion to children under 18 years of age.

With the outbreak of the Great Proletarian Cultural Revolution in August 1966, a spontaneous attack led by Red Guard youth groups was directed against all visible forms of religion, as part of their assault on the 'Four olds' (old habits, old customs, old ideas, old culture). Buddhist temples and Muslim mosques were closed, sacked or converted to secular use. Individual believers lost Bibles and all religious

literature. No communications from church leaders were received by the outside world during 1966–69, neither was any official pronouncement made for or against the attack on religion, nor was Article 88 of the constitution revoked.

Reports in 1971 indicated that clandestine Christian practice was continuing in Kwangtung province and a number of other regions as well. In late 1971 permission was given for one Protestant church and one Catholic church to reopen in Peking. The first known Protestant worship service in the capital since 1966 was at Easter 1972, and regular services have been held since then. The principal participants at these services were European diplomats and young Africans from Tanzania and Zambia in China for courses in railway engineering. In February 1972 and again in 1973, the Anglican bishop K. H. Ting stated in interviews that there were 500 Christians in Nanking and considerable Christian activity in Chekiang and Fukien. He also affirmed that plans were being made to recruit new students for Nanking Seminary in 1974. Bishop Ting noted that Christians were reluctant to use their former church buildings, usually preferring to meet in private homes as families or in small groups in halls or other meeting places after work. In some cases, such as in Szechuan province, church buildings are rented out to the government and the rents used to care for the needs of religious people, Buddhists and Taoists as well as Christians. Conversations with representatives of the Three-Self Movement in 1973 revealed that the Protestant adult community of Peking is estimated to be about 500.

INDIGENOUS CHURCHES. The first major indigenous quasi-Christian movement was the God Worshippers Society (Pai Shang-ti Hui) begun in 1847 under a visionary, Hung Hsiu-ch'uan, among impoverished peasants in Kwangsi. In 1851 Hung proclaimed a new dynasty, the Heavenly Kingdom of Great Peace (T'ai P'ing T'ien Kuo). Originally

religious and non-violent, it eventually became militant with one million zealous soldiers, and syncretistic with the addition of Confucian, Buddhist and Taoist elements. Land reforms were included in its programme and tens of thousands of peasants joined the march of the Taipings to establish their kingdom. Some 35 million were killed during the 17 years before it was finally suppressed in 1868.

From the 1880s attempts began to found a Chinese church separate from Western missionary control. The missions gave little ground, and so from 1906 onwards, groups of Chinese Christians began to break off from Western foreign missions and found indigenous self-supporting churches, developing their own highly-successful evangelistic outreach. Their numbers increased rapidly, and by 1949 there were 440,000 adherents in 30 or more denominations, including (in order of size) True Jesus Church (125,000; begun 1917 by separation from the Apostolic Faith Movement), Little Flock or Assembly Hall Churches (70,000; begun 1926 by Watchman Nee), China Jesus Independent Church (30,000; begun 1906), China Christian Independent Church (begun 1912), Jesus Family (6,000 adults in 141 communal societies; begun 1921). Although such churches were completely Chinese in leadership and outlook, they were among the first to be persecuted and suppressed after 1949. Watchman Nee himself was sentenced to 15 years in prison; and at least one body, the Jesus Family, is thought to have been wiped out completely by 1955. Nevertheless, there is evidence that indigenous churches are continuing to exist and even expanding underground.

ORTHODOX CHURCH. Russian Orthodox chaplains accompanied cossacks to Peking in 1686, and an Othodox mission was set up there in 1715. Large-scale missionary work began about 1900, and by 1914 there were 5,000 Chinese converts, with Chinese priests and a seminary. This activity increased considerably after the Russian revolution of 1917, with many Russian clergy fleeing from Siberia to China. By 1939 there were 200,000 Orthodox in China and Manchuria (mostly Russians) with 5 bishops and an Orthodox university at Harbin. In 1949 the diocese in Manchuria had 100,000 faithful, mainly White Russian refugees, 60 parishes, 200 priests, 2 monasteries and a seminary; the rest of China had 150 parishes and 200,000 parishioners. But with the coming of the Chinese Communists to power, Orthodoxy fared no better than the rest of the churches, and Russian bishops, clergy and laity were expelled; in 1955 there were only 30 Russian priests left. By 1957 the Orthodox Church had become entirely Chinese, an autonomous church loosely related to the Moscow Patriarchate, with 20,000 faithful and 2 bishops (Shanghai, Peking).

MARGINAL CHURCHES. These have had virtually no impact on China. Jehovah's Witnesses began in 1883 with a former Presbyterian missionary, had their first baptism of 2 Chinese in 1931, had only 13 members in 1939, and were finally completely suppressed in 1958.

CHURCH AND STATE. The constitution of 17 January 1975, which contains only 30 articles, stipulates in Article 28 'Citizens . . . have the freedom to practise a religion, the freedom to not practise a religion and to propagate atheism'. The earlier constitution of 1954, in Article 88, limited itself to affirming freedom of religious belief: 'Citizens of the People's Republic of China enjoy freedom of religious belief'. The addition of freedom to propagate atheism is a direct consequence of the Cultural Revolution of 1966–69. In fact the Party always interpreted the 1954 Article 88 to mean also freedom to oppose religion. Article 87 of the 1954 constitution provided for freedom of speech, press, assembly, association, procession and demonstrations; but whereas these freedoms are applied to religious bodies only within church and temple buildings, atheism has the right to propagate its doctrines throughout society's public domain. The government's position is that all religion has its basis in class oppression and fear of natural forces. Socialism will thus automatically undermine its appeal. As if by a natural law of development, freedom of religious belief, combined with education, will result ultimately in the destruction of religion. Religious associations formed under government pressure in the early 1950s are considered 'organizations of the masses' and are regulated by the Bureau of Religious Affairs under the Central Committee of the Party. The government's objective has been to exercise direct Party control over all activities of religious bodies, cutting them off from their corresponding foreign communities and utilizing them for political purposes in both internal and external affairs. The imprisonment of clergy, closure of churches and the like have always been interpreted officially not as anti-religious acts but as political acts against feudalists and counter-revolutionaries. However, the argument loses much of its force in the light of the regime's avowed atheism and especially the attacks suffered by religious groups during the Cultural Revolution. The violently anti-religious campaign unleashed through the Red Guards during 1966–69 resulted in the closure of virtually all places of worship and the suspension of religious associations. Since the 19th Party Congress of April, 1969, which marked the end of the Cultural Revolution, there has been a more tolerant attitude towards churches and religions. Many church buildings continue to belong to Christian communities although few are now used for worship services. Such churches, along with Buddhist and Taoist temples and the Three-Self theological school in Nanking, are exempt from property taxes. Nevertheless, the negative attitude of the regime towards religion continues unaltered. Indeed, the anti-Confucian campaign inaugurated in August 1973 manifests traces of the earlier anti-religious and anti-Christian violence.

**Situation since 1977.** Since the death of Mao Tse-tung in 1976, the Four Modernizations programme has resulted in a new openness in China towards the Western world. This has been accompanied by a lifting of repressive restrictions on Christians in China. Some Western mission societies, Catholic as well as Protestant, have entertained the prospect of returning soon to the Mainland. Others, however, have sought to restrain any such premature attempt to reintroduce foreign missions.

To 'handle the problem of religion' correctly, the regime has recently convened 2 major study conferences: the China Atheistic Seminar (Nanking, December 1978) calling for scholarly research on atheism, and the National Planning Conference on Religious Studies (Kunning, February 1979) calling for scholarly research on religions from the Marxist standpoint. The China Society for Religious Studies was then founded. On 15 March 1979, the regime promulgated a new policy statement entitled 'Religion and Superstition', re-establishing the pre-1966 religious policy as 'correct'. The Religious Affairs Bureau in Peking formally resumed operation the next day. Open persecution of believers is now expected to decline, but authentic legal toleration remains unlikely. In fact, the widely-heralded state toleration of religion after 1978 is interpreted by many observers as a tactic to allow the church to surface in order to assess its strength.

In July 1979, a new Catholic bishop, Michael Fu Tieshan, was appointed from within China, although the Vatican made it clear that he and his church were still formally excommunicated from Rome.

By 1981, evidence was increasing of very rapid church growth in many areas of China, including among tribal peoples; with large numbers of young people present everywhere. Reports have been received indicating that many hundreds of thousands of new believers are pouring into the churches. However, this is numerically offset by the rapid dying off of the older generations of Christians, and by the continuous erosion of numbers due to relentless state harassment. The nett picture is therefore that of gradual overall decline shown in Table 1.

**INTERDENOMINATIONAL ORGANIZATIONS.** Protestant and Anglican denominations as separate entities have disappeared, the only existing national structure being the Three-Self Patriotic Movement. In general, Catholics and Protestants work separately from each other and rarely meet.

**BROADCASTING.** Christian broadcasting has a long history. In 1933 the Shanghai Christian Broadcasting Association was organized (Station XMHD), covering the entire Far East including Australia with daily services and other broadcasts in Chinese (several dialects), French, Russian and English. In 1935, the North China Christian Broadcasting Association (Station XLKA) was begun from Peking; and others were formed in Hankow (Wuhan), Shaohing, Tsinan, Ch'engtu, Chang-sha and Nanking, as well as in Hong Kong. From 1949 all such broadcasting from within China ceased, but beginning with FEBC in 1949 external Christian broadcasts have become increasingly frequent up to the present day. No religious broadcasting of any kind is permitted within the country; however, there is extensive coverage from foreign stations. Each week in 1976 about 150 hours of Christian programmes reached mainland China from all Christian stations including the Voice of Free China, Radio Singapore, FEBC (Manila), KSBU (Okinawa), and RVOG (Ethiopia), the latter until 1977 beaming to China in Mandarin, TWR (Monaco) broadcasting to China for 15 minutes on Mondays, Vatican Radio which beamed in Catholic programmes totalling by 1977 30 minutes daily in Chinese, and the Catholic Radio Veritas (Manila) for an hour every day in Chinese. One group of programmes, produced in co-operation with the United Bible Societies in Hong Kong, broadcasts for 30 minutes every day selected Bible portions read at dictation speed. The amount and variety of programmes from abroad increases markedly every year. Although evidence of listening comes only from the occasional letter or refugee, it is known that a sizeable audience exists.

In a major development, in 1975 FEBC began broadcasting into China not only over shortwave (potentially reaching China's 12 million sets), but also with AM (amplitude modulation) transmissions, audible over China's 100 million local radio receivers and hence potentially reaching 90% of China's total population for (in 1978) 19 hours of broadcasting every day.

**BIBLIOGRAPHY**


*A bibliography of the history of Christianity in China.* Jonathan Chao, 1970.

'China and the Churches in the making of one world', *Pro Mundi Vita* (Brussels), 55 (1975), 1–39. (Best concise history and analysis of the subject).

*Chinese religions from 1000 BC to the present day.* D. H. Smith. New York: Holt, Rinehart & Winston, 1968. 222p.

*Christian faith and the Chinese experience.* Bastad, Sweden, Vol. II. Lutheran World Federation & Pro Mundi Vita. Geneva & Brussels, 1974.

*Le St-Siège et la Chine, de Pie XI à nos jours.* L. Wei Tsing-Sing. Paris: Allais, 1968.

*Religion in Chinese society: a study of contemporary social functions of religion and some of their historical factors.* C. K. Yang. Berkeley: University of California Press, 1961. 473p.

*Religion in Communist China.* R. C. Bush. New York: Abingdon, 1970. 432p (Fully-documented).

*Religious policy and practice in Communist China: a documentary history.* D. E. MacInnis. London: Hodder & Stoughton, 1972. (392 pages; 117 documents).

*Sectarianism and religious persecution in China.* J. J. M. de Groot. Taipei, Taiwan: Literature House, 1963. 2 vols, 595p.

*The Buddhist revival in China.* H. Welch. Cambridge, MA: Harvard University Press, 1968.

*The Louvain consultation on China: essential documents. Pro Mundi Vita* (Brussels), 54 (1975), 1–38.

*The practice of Chinese Buddhism.* H. Welch. Cambridge, MA: Harvard University Press, 1967. (Lay and monastic Buddhism from 1911–49).

*The religion of China: Confucianism and Taoism.* Max Weber. Glencoe, IL: Free Press, 1951. 308p.

*Theological implications of the New China.* Bastad, Sweden, Vol I. Lutheran World Federation & Pro Mundi Vita. Geneva & Brussels, 1974. 200p.


TABLE 2. ORGANIZED CHURCHES AND DENOMINATIONS IN THE PEOPLE'S REPUBLIC OF CHINA

| Official name 1 | Begun 2 | Type 3 | Counc 4 | Congs 5 | Adults 6 | Affiliated 7 | Names, notes, and other statistics (see Codebook) 8 |
|---|---|---|---|---|---|---|---|
| Assembly Hall Churches | 1926 | I EBr | x...N | 1,500 | 15,000 | 30,000 | *Chu Hui So. Little Flock.* 1949: 636 congregations, 70,000 members. 1960: still growing. |
| **Catholic Church in China** | 1298 | R Lat | ....R | 30,000 | 600,000 | 1,200,000 | *Tien Chu Chiao Hui.* 1949: 2542n,3046x. 1972: 650n(123 Jesuits), 70 jurisdictions. |
| Holy Catholic Church in China | 1844 | A plu | AW..N | 2,000 | 15,000 | 40,000 | *Chung Hua Sheng Kung Hui.* 14 Anglican dioceses, with Chinese bishops. |
| Isolated radio churches | 1933 | I rad | ..... | 4,000 | 40,000 | 80,000 | Isolated radio believers, mostly students and youths. R=1000(FEBC,Radio Vatican, et alia). |
| Jesus Family | 1921 | I ind | ..... | 200 | 2,000 | 5,000 | *Ye-su Chia T'ing.* 1949: 141 communal societies in 8 provinces, 6,000 adults. |
| Orthodox Church of China | 1686 | O Sla | M.... | 500 | 5,000 | 10,000 | *Tung Cheng Hui.* 280,000 Russians left 1949–53. Autonomous. D Peking, D Shanghai. |
| **Three-Self Reform Movement** | 1807 | P uni | ....N | 10,000 | 195,000 | 550,000 | Protestants. All forced to unite. In 1949, 6204f, 1s(Nanking). |
| True Jesus Church | 1917 | I pel | x...N | 1,700 | 15,000 | 35,000 | *Chen Ye-su Chiao Hui.* 1949: 1,000 congregations, 125,000 members. |
| Other Chinese indigenous churches | 1906 | I ind | ..... | 2,500 | 25,000 | 50,000 | 1949: 225,000 adherents, in China Jesus Independent Ch, Spiritual Food Ch, &c. |
| **Total affiliated (mid-1970)** | | | | **52,400** | **912,000** | **2,000,000** | **Total denominations (1970) . . . 14.** |
| **Total affiliated (mid-1975)** | | | | **51,000** | **860,000** | **1,900,000** | **Total denominations (1975) . . . 14.** |
| **Total affiliated (mid-1980)** | | | | **50,000** | **810,000** | **1,800,000** | **Total denominations (1980) . . . 14.** |

**NOTES ON TABLE ABOVE**

COLUMNS: for meanings and CODES (cols. 1, 3, 4, 8): see Codebook (Part 6). Column 1: **Boldface type** = church with over 10% of country's affiliated Christians. The statistics given here are rough estimates only estimating the general order of magnitude of persons with some Christian affiliation. They include sizeable numbers of expatriate Christians, and also resident non-Chinese groups including about 10,000 Koreans.

SURVEYS. The last detailed statistical survey of Christian bodies was undertaken in 1949 and is published in the *World Christian handbook 1952*, p. 141–2, 267. Statistics of affiliation for the major Christian blocs in 1949 are given above in the notes under Table 1.

CONCILIARISM (Column 4). The Church of Christ in China (largest body in the Three-Self Reform Movement) is still a member of WARC (World Alliance of Reformed Churches) and WCC (World Council of Churches).

NATIONAL COUNCILS (Column 4, 5th letter).

N = Three-Self Reform Movement (which replaced the pre-1949 National Christian Council of China).

R = National Patriotic Catholic Association.

**PEOPLES** (ethnolinguistic). Christians: about 90% Han Chinese, 9% hill tribe and other minority tribe, 0.5% Korean, a few European and Asian expatriates.

COUNTRY-WIDE TOTALS

EVANGELIZATION (see Part 5). 1900: 28%. 1970: 19%. 1980: 29%. *Mass evangelism.* There has been a long history of co-operative evangelism. In 1930 the bulk of the churches launched the Five Year Movement, and in 1935 the National Christian Council of China decided to continue the Movement for a further 5 years. All such organized evangelism ceased from 1949. *Radiophonic evangelism.* Many stations and agencies beam into China each day since FEBC began in 1950. By 1975 total broadcast hours per week in Chinese were around 150 (FEBC, 103 hours per week). Listeners' letters: after averaging 18 letters a year since 1970, they numbered 58 in 1978, then increased vastly to 5,644 (to FEBC) in the first 4 months of 1979, 90% being from non-Christians. *Literature evangelism.* Large quantities of literature enter China through returning residents and others. World Literature Crusade (EHC) alone has sent over 2 million booklets into China since 1950.

FOREIGN MISSIONARIES AND PERSONNEL (aliens from abroad) (1973). Nil, since about 1960. *Rise and decline.* Protestants and Anglicans: (1876) 473, (1889) 1,296, (1906) 3,833, (1920) 6,204, (a peak in 1926) 8,518, (1947) 3,943 (899 ordained, 1,362 laymen, 1,682 women; including 198 Anglicans), (1957) nil. Roman Catholics: (1939) 5,800, (1948) 5,496 (3,046 priests, 414 brothers, 2,036 sisters), (1956) 27 (13 in prison).

INSTITUTIONS (church-operated) (1973). 1 seminary (Protestant/Anglican; Nanking, reopened 1973).

PERIODICALS. 10 (clandestine).

PERSONNEL. About 1,100 (national).

RELIGIOUS LIBRARIES. 10 (1 in Nanking).

SCRIPTURE DISTRIBUTION (1975). Annual totals: 63,000 NTs (clandestine free distribution). Since 1949 a small number of Bibles have been printed in China by the churches themselves. *Translations completed.* Portion: 45 languages since 1810. NT: 24 languages since 1814. Bible: 14 languages since 1822.

ADDITIONAL DATA ON CHURCHES

HOLY CATHOLIC CHURCH IN CHINA. The Anglican Church, with 14 dioceses in 1949 and 76,741 baptized members, was originally part of the Three-Self Reform Movement, then managed to retain its identity in its own eyes for a time, but by 1970 had disappeared as a separate entity so far as the state was concerned and existed only through the Three-Self Reform Movement.

THREE-SELF REFORM MOVEMENT. The name refers to the ideal of a church that is self-supporting, self-governing, and self-propagating. Before 1951, Protestantism consisted of about 270 distinct denominations with 1,295,000 adherents (major ones: Church of Christ in China (Chung Hua Chi Tuh Chiao Hui) 176,983; Methodist Church (Chung Hua Chi Tuh Chiao Wei Li Kung Hui) 102,693; China Inland Mission (Nei Ti Hui) 85,345; and many Pentecostal groups such as China Assemblies of God (Chung Kuo Shen Chao Hui) 30,000). The Anglican Church also became part of the Three-Self Reform Movement, eventually lost its identity, and by 1965 had ceased to exist as an organized body in the eyes of the state.

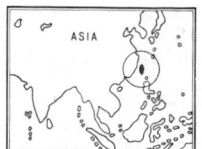

# CHINA (Taiwan)

## SECULAR DATA

**STATE. Official name:** The Republic of China (Chung-Hua Min-Kuo). **Unofficial names:** Taiwan, Formosa. **Adjectives of nationality:** Chinese, Taiwanese.
**Flag** (shown above right): Red field bearing blue rectangle, upper left, containing 12-pointed white sun.
**Area:** 35,961 sq.km. (13,885 sq.miles). Agricultural land: 25.9%.
**Government:** One-party parliamentary republic (1895 part of Japan, 1945 return to China, 1949 Independence).
**Legislature:** National Assembly: Control (Executive) Yuan, 70 members; Legislative Yuan, 442 members.
**Official language:** Chinese (Peking dialect) (*Kuo yu*).
**Chief cities:** capital Taipei 2,022,080, Kaohsiung 828,190 (1970), Tainan 474,840, Taichung 448,140.
**Political divisions:** 16 Counties (hsien), 4 Municipalities, 1 Special Municipality (Taipei).
**Armed forces** (1976): Total 470,000 regular: army 330,000, navy 35,000, marines 35,000, air force 70,000 (268 combat aircraft). Reserves: 1,170,000. Paramilitary forces: 100,000 militia.
**Foreign forces** (1973): 9,000 USA troops (plus 40,000 US Navy and marines afloat in area).

**DEMOGRAPHY. Population:** 15,290,000 (estimate of 31.XII. 1972. For 1970–2000 (UN), see last row of Table 1). Population density (1975): 435/sq.km. (1,127/sq.mile). Under 15 years: 45%. Growth rate (1975–80): 1.95% per year (births 2.42%, deaths −0.47%). Life expectancy (1975–80): 68.0 years. Household size: 5.1 persons.
**Major languages:** Mandarin Chinese, Taiwanese, Hokkien, Hakka, English, Kaoshan, with over 20 smaller languages.
**Urban dwellers** (1970): 62.0%.
**Labour force:** 39%.
**Refugees** (1977): The formerly vast numbers from mainland China after 1949 (in 1949, 1.8 million soldiers and their dependants) have now been integrated into life in Taiwan.

**ETHNOLINGUISTIC GROUPS:** 77% Taiwanese (Han Chinese) (67% Minnan Hoklo (South Fukienese), 10% Hakka, Hokkien Fukienese), 20.9% Mainland Chinese (Mandarin), 2.0% Aborigine (Kaoshan, Highlander) (300,000) (0.7% Ami, 0.5% Atayal, 0.4% Paiwan, Bunun, Kanabu, Rutkai, Saisiat, Saroa, Seepeg, Yami), 0.1% USA White, European, Jewish, Japanese, Malay.

**MONEY** (1977). **Monetary unit:** New Taiwan dollar (= 100

cents); US$1 = NT$38.
**National income per person:** US$700. Average annual family income: US$3,570.
**Inflation:** (1970–74) 14.0% per year (1975: consumer price index 183), 40% per year in 1975, falling to 2.8% per year by 1977.
**Cost of living in capital** (1976): index 106 (Washington DC=100). Daily cost of living: US$36.

**EDUCATION. Adult literacy:** (1950) 50%, (1975) 85%. Education rate: 78%. Schools: 3,235 (2,295 primary, 940 secondary). Universities: 8.

**HEALTH.** Hospitals: 216 (12,365 beds). Doctors: 11,708. Lepers: 41,000 (2.6 per 1,000). Blind: 18,510. Psychotics: 125,000. Criminals: 30,000.

**LITERATURE.** Annual new book titles (1967): 2,252. Periodicals: 1,135. Scientific journals: 200. Newspapers: 31 dailies.

**COMMUNICATION** (per 1,000 people). Phones: 49. Radios: 103. TV sets: 79. Daily newspaper circulation: 99 copies.

TABLE 1.    RELIGIOUS ADHERENTS IN CHINA (TAIWAN)

| Year | 1900 | | mid-1970 | | Annual change, 1970–1980 | | | | mid-1975 | | mid-1980 | | 2000 | |
|---|---|---|---|---|---|---|---|---|---|---|---|---|---|---|
| Name | Adherents | % | Adherents | % | Natural | Conversion | Total | Rate | Adherents | % | Adherents | % | Adherents | % |
| Chinese folk-religionists | 2,193,000 | 75.6 | 7,208,900 | 51.4 | 169,093 | −44,159 | 124,934 | 1.60 | 7,806,330 | 49.9 | 8,458,240 | 48.5 | 10,016,000 | 40.6 |
| Buddhists | 580,000 | 20.0 | 5,750,000 | 41.0 | 142,291 | 31,909 | 174,200 | 2.65 | 6,569,000 | 42.0 | 7,492,000 | 43.0 | 11,592,600 | 47.0 |
| Christians | 9,000 | 0.3 | 943,000 | 6.7 | 24,032 | 10,482 | 34,514 | 3.11 | 1,109,460 | 7.1 | 1,288,140 | 7.4 | 2,491,200 | 10.1 |
| professing | 9,000 | 0.3 | 943,000 | 6.7 | 24,032 | 10,482 | 34,514 | 3.11 | 1,109,460 | 7.1 | 1,288,140 | 7.4 | 2,491,200 | 10.1 |
| Protestants | 6,000 | 0.2 | 360,000 | 2.6 | 9,147 | 3,633 | 12,780 | 3.03 | 422,300 | 2.7 | 487,800 | 2.8 | 807,000 | 3.3 |
| Roman Catholics | 3,000 | 0.1 | 350,000 | 2.5 | 8,809 | 3,231 | 12,040 | 2.96 | 406,700 | 2.6 | 470,400 | 2.7 | 838,600 | 3.4 |
| Chinese indigenous | 0 | 0.0 | 220,000 | 1.6 | 5,760 | 3,600 | 9,360 | 3.52 | 265,900 | 1.7 | 313,600 | 1.8 | 764,600 | 3.1 |
| Marginal Protestants | 0 | 0.0 | 10,000 | 0.1 | 243 | 17 | 260 | 2.32 | 11,200 | 0.1 | 12,600 | 0.1 | 75,000 | 0.3 |
| Anglicans | 0 | 0.0 | 3,000 | 0.0 | 73 | 1 | 74 | 2.20 | 3,360 | 0.0 | 3,740 | 0.0 | 6,000 | 0.0 |
| nominal | 1,850 | 0.1 | 122,827 | 0.9 | 3,103 | 578 | 3,681 | 2.57 | 143,260 | 0.9 | 159,640 | 0.9 | 172,700 | 0.7 |
| affiliated | 7,150 | 0.2 | 820,173 | 5.8 | 20,929 | 9,904 | 30,833 | 3.19 | 966,200 | 6.2 | 1,128,500 | 6.5 | 2,318,500 | 9.4 |
| total practising | 6,440 | 90 | 656,140 | 80 | 16,743 | 7,923 | 24,666 | 3.19 | 772,960 | 80 | 902,800 | 80 | 1,738,900 | 75 |
| non-practising | 710 | 10 | 164,030 | 20 | 4,186 | 1,981 | 6,167 | 3.19 | 193,240 | 20 | 225,700 | 20 | 579,600 | 25 |
| Roman Catholics | 2,650 | 0.1 | 304,877 | 2.2 | 7,791 | 3,531 | 11,322 | 3.15 | 359,700 | 2.3 | 418,100 | 2.4 | 764,600 | 3.1 |
| Catholic pentecostals | 0 | 0.0 | 0 | 0.0 | 22 | 178 | 200 | 20.00 | 1,000 | 0.0 | 2,000 | 0.0 | 20,000 | 0.1 |
| Protestants | 4,500 | 0.1 | 299,808 | 2.1 | 7,454 | 2,635 | 10,089 | 2.93 | 344,100 | 2.2 | 400,700 | 2.3 | 738,900 | 3.0 |
| Evangelicals | 4,000 | 0.1 | 238,600 | 1.7 | 5,929 | 2,101 | 8,030 | 2.93 | 273,700 | 1.7 | 318,900 | 1.8 | 595,000 | 2.4 |
| Chinese indigenous | 0 | 0.0 | 204,800 | 1.5 | 5,420 | 3,720 | 9,140 | 3.65 | 250,200 | 1.6 | 296,200 | 1.7 | 740,000 | 3.0 |
| Marginal Protestants | 0 | 0.0 | 8,623 | 0.1 | 212 | 6 | 218 | 2.22 | 9,800 | 0.1 | 10,800 | 0.1 | 70,000 | 0.3 |
| Anglicans | 0 | 0.0 | 2,065 | 0.0 | 52 | 12 | 64 | 2.65 | 2,400 | 0.0 | 2,700 | 0.0 | 5,000 | 0.0 |
| Muslims | 6,000 | 0.2 | 60,000 | 0.4 | 1,556 | 894 | 2,450 | 3.41 | 71,800 | 0.5 | 84,500 | 0.5 | 150,000 | 0.6 |
| Tribal religionists | 110,000 | 3.8 | 20,000 | 0.1 | 390 | −790 | −400 | −2.22 | 18,000 | 0.1 | 16,000 | 0.1 | 10,000 | 0.0 |
| Non-religious | 0 | 0.0 | 20,000 | 0.1 | 563 | 837 | 1,400 | 5.38 | 26,000 | 0.2 | 34,000 | 0.2 | 220,000 | 0.9 |
| Atheists | 0 | 0.0 | 10,000 | 0.1 | 303 | 697 | 1,000 | 7.14 | 14,000 | 0.1 | 20,000 | 0.1 | 100,000 | 0.4 |
| Baha'is | 0 | 0.0 | 3,000 | 0.0 | 87 | 113 | 200 | 5.00 | 4,000 | 0.0 | 5,000 | 0.0 | 10,000 | 0.0 |
| Jews | 0 | 0.0 | 100 | 0.0 | 2 | 0 | 2 | 2.17 | 110 | 0.0 | 120 | 0.0 | 200 | 0.0 |
| Other religionists | 2,000 | 0.1 | 20,000 | 0.1 | 483 | 17 | 500 | 2.24 | 22,300 | 0.1 | 25,000 | 0.1 | 75,000 | 0.3 |
| Country's population | 2,900,000 | 100.0 | 14,035,000 | 100.0 | 338,800 | 0 | 338,800 | 2.17 | 15,641,000 | 100.0 | 17,423,000 | 100.0 | 24,665,000 | 100.0 |

COLUMNS, ROWS. For meanings and definitions, see Codebook (Part 6). Note that, by definition, total 'Christians' = professing + crypto-Christians, which also = affiliated + nominal Christians. Percentages may not always total exactly, due to rounding.
CENSUSES. The religion question has not been asked in government censuses.
POLLS. *Religious preference.* Survey of July 1969: 52% Chinese folk-religionists (28% ancestor-worshippers, 24% virtually non-religious except in name), 38% Buddhists, 10% Christians and others.

## NOTES ON RELIGIONS
ATHEISTS. No communists or Communist party are tolerated, but there are underground groups, also non-communist humanists.
BAHA'IS. Rapid growth from 2 local spiritual assemblies (1964) to 17 (1973).
BUDDHISTS. Mostly of the Pure Land school, with the Contemplative school influential among intellectuals. In 1959 there

were 354 monks and 482 nuns in 881 monasteries and nunneries; in 1964, 365 monks and 1,355 nuns; but by 1976 these had risen to 7,750 religious personnel in 2,250 temples and monasteries. Only around 3 million are in any way active Buddhists. The Buddhist Association of the Republic of China had (in 1968) 1,900 organizations and 48,493 individual members, with 13 academies. There are also a few Mongolian and Tibetan Lamaists, with a worship centre in Taipei.
CATHOLIC PENTECOSTALS (or, Catholic charismatics). Totals (January 1974): 300 involved adults (over 15 years old) in 20 organized prayer groups; total charismatic community including children, 600.
CHINESE FOLK-RELIGIONISTS. Mainly followers of Taiwanese popular religion (with some mainland Chinese), which is an amalgam of Buddhism, Taoism, Confucianism, animism and local elements; including 21,000 orthodox Taoist devotees with 2,800 Taoist temples, and 100,000 prohibited but underground Taoists in the powerful I-Kuan-Tao sect. There are

also other underground sects.
CHINESE INDIGENOUS. In over 60 denominations in 1970 (see Table 2); Chinese, with a few Korean indigenous Christians.
MUSLIMS. 50% are refugees from mainland China since 1950 (Sunnis of the Hanafite rite). In 1964, there were 6 mosques, rising to 12 by 1974. Since 1960, Muslim missionaries from Saudi Arabia have been at work and now claim 40,000 as their converts. *Hajj pilgrims to Mecca.* (1976) 100.
NON-RELIGIOUS. Mainly young Chinese abandoning their family religions.
OTHER RELIGIONISTS. Including followers of syncretistic New Religions not enumerated above as either Buddhist sects or Taiwanese folk religion; also of the Hindu sect Ananda Marga.
PRACTISING CHRISTIANS. Protestants: weekly attenders about 60%.
TRIBAL RELIGIONISTS. Aboriginal tribes in the mountains; animists.

## NON-CHRISTIAN RELIGIONS. Chinese folk religion,
known here as Taiwanese popular religion, is practised by the Taiwanese who were immigrants

from China in the 6th and 7th centuries AD. It consists of a combination of magic, ancestor-veneration and devotion to divinities, with influences from Taoism, Buddhism and Confucianism as well as traditional animistic beliefs and practices. The proportion of each varies between different localities depending upon the socio-religious group which constitutes it. Among the divinities worshipped in Taiwan are Kuan-yin, goddess of mercy, and Thi-Kong, Jade Emperor and Supreme Ruler of Heaven who is generally believed to be superior to Buddhist and Taoist deities. Popular religion is still influential in rural areas and small towns, where new temples continue to be built. However, in large cities, apart from religious festivals and processions it is confined to observances in the home. Young educated people do not normally participate in temple ceremonies, but those who are expected to take part in practices related to ancestor-veneration. In 1966, only 1% of college youths claimed to hold these beliefs.

**Buddhism** is a strong force in Taiwan, but those who practice it strictly are few. The majority of Taiwan's Buddhists belong to the Pure Land school, although the Contemplative school is more influential among

**Chinese folk-religionists.** The Confucius Temple in Taipei. Taiwanese folk religion worships 250 deities.

intellectuals. Several Buddhist groups are collectively known as Vegetarians (Chai-chiao), having adopted elements from Confucianism and Taoism. They are treated by orthodox Buddhists as heretics on account of their alleged syncretism. Buddhism shows evidence of revival, with a number of new temples being built

**Buddhists.** Mammoth statue of the Buddha at Changh.

recently and new magazines published. Especially among youth there is a concern that Buddhism be purified from superstitious influences and become involved in social action. There are over 7 million Buddhists in Taiwan. In 1959 there were 354 monks and 482 nuns, rapidly rising by 1976 to 7,750 religious personnel.

**Islam** is primarily confined to the Chinese community, one-half of all Muslims being refugees from the mainland since 1950. In 1964 there were 6 mosques in Taiwan, 2 more than existed in 1963. There are 2 important Muslim organizations: (1) the Chinese Muslim Association, founded in 1937 on the mainland, with the entire Muslim population of 60,000 counted as members in 1969, which is active in promoting friendship and cultural exchange with Muslim countries; and (2) the Chinese Muslim Youth League, with 500 members, whose purpose is to study Islamic culture and to promote conversions to Islam.

**Taoism** exists in 2 forms: as a formal orthodox organization, and as part of the syncretistic popular religion which has wide currency in Taiwan. Orthodox Taoism concentrates on a higher level of worship, the Tao itself, and is represented by the National Taoist Association of the Republic of China with 21,000 members. There is also a powerful sect of Taoism operating underground, called I-Kuan-Tao, which has strict rules and is said to have attracted up to 100,000 members from the common people.

**Tribal religions** are still practised by remnants of the 10 Aboriginal tribes in the mountains who until recently were all head-hunting animists. Since 1945 they have experienced mass conversion to Christianity.

## CHRISTIANITY

CATHOLIC CHURCH. Dominicans from the Philippines began work on Taiwan in 1621, but their work was not sustained after the Dutch gained control during 1624–62. Taiwan was later administered as part of China with ports closed until 1858; Catholics then returned the following year. Japan gained possession of the island from 1895 to 1945. Taiwan became a Catholic prefecture in 1913 when there were over 3,000 Catholics, with the number increasing to 8,000 in 1945. Refugees from mainland China and work among the Aborigines raised the total to 48,400 by 1955 and more than 300,000 by 1970. As with the total Christian population, Catholics in Taiwan are divided into 3 more or less equal groups: about 100,000 Aborigines, 100,000 Taiwan islanders and 100,000 China mainlanders. The fast-developing industrialization of the country, with its rapid shifts in population, has had detrimental effects on church growth. However, steps are now being taken to identify and aid rural parishioners when they

migrate to Taiwan's cities. Lay cell groups are increasingly effective in providing informal meeting-places for fostering spiritual nurture. The Legion of Mary is also active in missionary outreach.

Religious personnel have been decreasing in number since 1973, after having increased regularly in preceding years; and it appears that this tendency will continue. In 1974 only 12% of clergy were less than 40 years of age, and among Chinese priests 9%. Since Vatican II, 5 diocesan synods have been held: Tainan in February 1966, Taipei in May 1967, Chiai in October 1971 and Kaohsiung in 1975; but only the latter 2 have been markedly innovative in following the conciliar spirit.

PROTESTANT CHURCHES. During the Dutch occupation from 1624–62, about 6,000 conversions among the tribal peoples were recorded by the Dutch Reformed Church; but all missionaries and Christians were killed when a Chinese pirate later took control of the island. The first Protestant missionaries of the present era were English Presbyterians who arrived in the south in 1865. Canadian Presbyterians followed 7 years later in the north. When the Japanese occupied Taiwan in 1895 and attempted to suppress Christianity, membership increased two-fold during the first 10 years. Forty years later a similar resistance to Japan's anti-Christian campaign became evident when hundreds were brought to Christ during World War II through the instrumentality of Chi-oang, a Sediq (Atayal) tribeswoman. Missionaries returned after the war to find 4,000 Atayals meeting in churches which they had built themselves. A Presbyterian Double-the-Church movement succeeded in more than doubling the number of churches and members during the decade 1955–65. Today all 10 mountain tribes are rapidly turning to Christianity. Five Presbyterian missions co-operate with the Presbyterian Church in Taiwan, the largest Protestant denomination. By 1977 the church had completed a 5-year plan for planting 500 new churches.

When mainland China was evacuated by missionaries in 1949, many followed the Nationalist Chinese to Taiwan. These and new groups attracted to the island at that time have resulted in a vast increase in the number of Protestant missions, the majority being from North America. The most successful of these new missions has been the Southern Baptist Convention, USA. Christianity has achieved some prestige due to the fact that the former president, Chiang Kai-chek, was a practising Christian. Churches are becoming self-supporting, but church growth is beginning to decline.

INDIGENOUS CHURCHES. The Little Flock, or Assembly Hall Churches, the third largest church

**Chinese indigenous churches.** In 1975 these numbered 280,000 Christians affiliated to 70 denominations. *Above.* Largest body: Assembly Hall Churches (Little Flock), showing new building seating 2,000 in Taichung. *Below.* Second largest body: True Jesus Church in Taiwan, showing a packed congregation.

in Taiwan (after Catholics and Presbyterians), was begun on the mainland in 1926 under the notable leadership of Watchman Nee. Similar in the looseness of its structure to the Plymouth Brethren, but denying any relationship to Protestant churches, it was brought to Taiwan in 1948, growing to 40,000 adult members and a Christian community of 80,000 by 1970. Stress is placed on small house churches and personal evangelism as well as prayer, preaching, tract distribution, parades, and home visitation. The True Jesus Church, fourth in size, is a pentecostal group founded by Paul Wei in Peking in 1917. Spreading to Taiwan in 1926, it grew to 5,000 adherents by the end of World War II, and has since multiplied to embrace a Christian community of 50,000. In contrast to the Assembly Hall Churches, it has a sophisticated organization which, without diminishing the importance of the local congregation, involves one national and 5 regional councils. Most of its new members are tribal converts. Both of these indigenous denominations stress church-planting and also lay training. A number of other small independent churches have been formed since 1950.

CHURCH AND STATE. The constitution of 1947 guarantees freedom of religious belief (Article 13) and of assembly and association (Article 14). This freedom is not to be restricted by law 'except by such as may be necessary to prevent infringement upon the freedom of other persons, to avert imminent crisis, to maintain social order or to advance public welfare' (Article 23).

Churches and adjacent buildings are legally considered as being available for service to the public, although churches are not obliged to register officially. The Bureau of Social Affairs of the Ministry of the Interior is in charge of religious matters.

Church developments are closely watched for their socio-political significance, especially by the government which, strongly anti-communist, has viewed with growing irritation the entry of Communist-world churches into the ecumenical movement. Recent events in international Christian affairs, particularly the WCC coming out in favour of admission to the UN for the People's Republic of China, the satisfaction shown by the Vatican after that admission in 1971, and the choice of Hong Kong instead of Taipei as a stopping-place during Paul VI's 1970 Asian journey, have all placed the Presbyterian and Catholic churches in an embarrassing situation vis-a-vis government. Some members of the Catholic hierarchy, especially cardinal Yupin, are closely associated with the governmental anti-communist crusade. For its part the Presbyterian Church withdrew from the WCC in 1970 because of its position regarding the People's Republic of China. In similar vein, in 1975 the government refused to allow the Episcopalian bishop, a Chinese, to attend the 5th WCC Assembly in Nairobi, Kenya. On the other hand, the confiscation of 2,000 Taiwanese Bibles by the government in early 1975 has provoked a conflict between Christians (especially Presbyterians) and the state. Their action was justified by the authorities as an attempt to 'unify the language and culture of the island', mainly by promoting Mandarin at the expense of Taiwanese, but Christians saw it as a violation of human rights and a suppression of religious freedom.

INTERDENOMINATIONAL ORGANIZATIONS. There is no ecumenical council of churches in Taiwan, but several organizations co-ordinate Protestant activities. In 1966 the Association of Christian Churches of the Republic of China was organized with membership open to all denominations, local churches and individuals; its organization is loose, serving primarily as a link between the Christian community and government. The Catholic Church has formed a Committee for Christian Unity within its Episcopal Commission for Social Action and the Lay Apostolate. Another body, the Taiwan Missionary Fellowship, has more than 800 foreign missionaries as members from 78 societies and agencies. An Ecumenical Co-operative Committee has also come into existence composed of 8 churches and Christian organizations. Taiwan Christian Service co-ordinates relief activities sponsored by Church World Service and Lutheran World Relief, and for Catholics the Taiwan Ecumenical Industrial Ministry (TEIM) works in close co-operation with other churches.

The Association of Friends for the Study of Chinese Culture is a small group composed of Taoists, Buddhists, Muslims, Catholics and Protestants who meet regularly for dialogue and discussion concerning beliefs and practices of the various religions in Taiwan.

**BROADCASTING.** All of the major cities have radio and TV stations and Christian broadcasts can be heard on these daily, even in remote areas, and (TV) even in Mountain areas as well. Programmes are very numerous and varied. On radio, these include the Voice of Righteousness (service to the mainland in Mandarin, Tibetan and Cantonese), Voice of Salvation (6 hours a day in English, Mandarin and Taiwanese), Gospel program (3.5 hours a week), and Our Church (Mondays to Saturdays). On TV, they include Heavenly Melody (since 1962, by Overseas Radio and TV), Weekly Theatre (Lutheran), and Voice of Signs (Seventh-day Adventist). There is also Studio Classroom, produced by ORTV and transmitted over all main radio stations, which has 20,000 members and has great influence. Programmes are produced in over 8 Protestant studios. In 1977 the China Lutheran Hour began a 30-minute TV broadcast every Sunday afternoon, reaching 2 million (12% of the population).

Catholics have 2 radio stations (Chungsheng, and Yi-shih). There are several Catholic production centres. At Taipei, the Kuangchi Programme Service for Radio and TV has a vast tape library with over 4,500 radio programmes in Mandarin, Amoy and Hakka. Two theatrical programmes in Mandarin and 4 in Taiwanese are produced each month for TV. They also produce educational programmes with 45 radio stations in Taiwan, transmitting over 400 programmes a week. These programmes are used also in Hong Kong, the Philippines, Mauritius and South East Asia. For Catholics, Taiwan is a member of UNDA.

From 1976–78 a Catholic TV programme 'The Most Unforgettable Story' has had large-scale success, being viewed each Saturday by 1.2 million persons.

## BIBLIOGRAPHY


*An introduction to Taiwanese folk religions.* G. P. Kramer & G. Wu. Taipei, 1970. 71p.

'Christianity and animism: China and Taiwan'. A. F. Gates. Dissertation, Fuller Theological Seminary, Pasadena, CA (USA), 1971. 262p.

*Church directory of the Republic of China, 1969.* Taipei: China Evangelical Fellowship, 1969. 94p. (In Chinese).

*Faith that moves mountains: a study of the Tribal Church in Taiwan.* G. Vicedom. Taipei: China Post, 1967. 145p.

*Joint action for mission in Formosa: a call for advance into a new era.* C. H. Hwang. New York: CWME & Friendship Press, 1967. 127p.

*Taiwan Catholic directory 1970.* Taipei: Catholic Central Bureau, 1970.

*Taiwan Christian yearbook 1968: a survey of the Christian movement in Taiwan, 1965–1968.* Taipei: Taiwan Missionary Fellowship, 1968. 198p.

***Taiwan Missionary Fellowship directory 1972.* Taipei: Dixon Press, 1972. 159p.**

*Taiwan: mainline versus independent church growth: a study in contrasts.* A. J. Swanson. South Pasadena: William Carey Library, 1970. 299p.

'The Chinese of the diaspora in South East Asia', *Pro Mundi Vita* (Brussels), 23 (1968).

*The description of the True Jesus Church.* Taipei: General Assembly of the True Jesus Church in Taiwan, 1967. 41p.


TABLE 2. ORGANIZED CHURCHES AND DENOMINATIONS IN CHINA (TAIWAN)

| Official name 1 | Begun 2 | Type 3 | Counc 4 | Congs 5 | Adults 6 | Affiliated 7 | Names, notes, and other statistics (see Codebook) 8 |
|---|---|---|---|---|---|---|---|
| Assembly Hall Churches | 1948 | I EBr | x.... | 50 | 40,000 | 80,000 | *Chu Hui So. Little Flock.* Begun on mainland 1926 by Watchman Nee. Mandarin. 70n. |
| Baptist Bible Fellowship | 1950 | P Bap | x.... | 15 | 1,440 | 3,000 | M=BBFI(USA). Fundamentalists. HQ Taichung. 6n,5m,11f,14t(950). |
| **Catholic Church in Taiwan:** | 1621 | R Lat | P.FZK | 523 | 167,700 | 304,877 | *T'ien Chu Chiao.* C=16+2+50. 3p,2q,2s(135). 390n, 447x, 93m, 1035w, P=51%, 2346Y, 4499y. |
| M T'aipe (Taipeh) | 1949 | R Lat | Ps | 125 | 28,400 | 51,586 | *Taipei Tsung Chiao-ch'u.* Trilingual. 182 132 35 334 50 645 571 |
| D Chiai (Kiayi) | 1952 | R Lat | Ps | 49 | 11,300 | 20,562 | *Chiayi Chiao-ch'u.* Rural. 80% Minnan. 58 21 4 73 50 180 287 |
| D Hsinchu | 1961 | R Lat | Ps | 166 | 34,400 | 62,484 | Rural, industry in north. Quadrilingual. 31 96 18 193 58 409 622 |
| D Hualien (Hwalien) | 1952 | R Lat | Pmep | 44 | 33,100 | 60,166 | Multilingual. 70% Amis (Aborigines). 7 66 5 60 41 414 1434 |
| D Kaohsiung | 1949 | R Lat | Ps | 54 | 27,500 | 50,058 | Multilingual. Rapid new industrialization. 37 49 8 115 58 306 883 |
| D Taichung | 1950 | R Lat | Pmm | 42 | 22,000 | 40,018 | 44% Taiwanese, 39% Mainlander, 17% Aborig. 21 64 13 159 50 188 523 |
| D T'ainan | 1961 | R Lat | Ps | 43 | 11,000 | 20,003 | 90% Minnan. Also Pescadores Islands. 54 19 10 101 40 204 179 |
| Central Taiwan Lutheran Church | | P Lut | ..... | 12 | 195 | 400 | M=Norwegian Evangelical Lutheran Free Chucrh Mission. 2n,5m,13f,9t(395),1u. |
| China Assemblies of God | 1948 | P Pe2 | ZF... | 52 | 3,472 | 6,000 | *Taiwan District.* M=AoG(USA). 7,052 in mail courses. 54n,17f,1s(59),50t(587),W=64%. |
| China Christian Lutheran Church | 1951 | P Lut | l.... | 20 | 1,145 | 2,000 | *Chung-Hua.* M=CLB. In Taiwan Lutheran Ch till 1957. 7n,4x,7f,G=−1.0%pa,23t,1u,57Yy. |
| China Evangelical Lutheran Church | 1951 | P Lut | l.... | 25 | 1,040 | 3,000 | Western cities. M=LC Missouri Synod(USA). 18n,4x,24f,G=17%pa,1s,25t(1344),109Yy. |
| China Free Methodist Church | 1952 | P Hol | VF... | 44 | 1,914 | 3,000 | M=FMC(USA). In southwest and Taipei. 35n,10f,G=4.8%pa,1s(22),39t(1749),138z. |
| China Holiness Church | 1953 | P Hol | x.... | 18 | 500 | 2,000 | M=Swedish Holiness Mission. Northwest. 2n,4x,7m,8f,15t(750),W=33%,15Y,20z. |
| China Peniel Church | 1946 | P Hol | x.... | 7 | 320 | 500 | M=VOCA(Voice of China & Asia MS)(USA).HQ Mushan, Taipei. 7n,2m,2f,7t(435). |
| China Presbyterian Church of Christ | 1934 | P Ref | .TT.T | 4 | 225 | 400 | M=IBPFM(USA). Mandarin, some Taiwanese. 1966, 40% secede. 6n,5m,3f,5t(200). |
| China (Chung-Kuo) Lutheran Church | 1953 | P Lut | ..... | 14 | 914 | 2,000 | M=Norwegian Lutheran Mission. 3n,8m,10f,12t(570),1u. |
| Christian & Missionary Alliance | 1952 | P Hol | xF..E | 9 | 382 | 1,000 | *Union of Taiwan.* M=CMA(USA). Mandarin. 5n,15f,G=6.9%pa,10t(625),W=60%,42Y,58z. |
| Christian Assemblies | | P CBr | x.... | 18 | 1,000 | 3,000 | *Christian (Plymouth, Open) Brethren.* M=CMML(USA,Australia,UK). 18m,14f,14t(800). |
| Christian Church of Salvation | 1958 | I ind | .TT.T | 6 | 650 | 2,000 | Formerly Shou Shan Christian Ch. Independent of foreign missions. 2n,8m,6t(200). |
| Chr Nationals Evangelism Commission | 1959 | P int | xF... | 4 | 243 | 500 | *CNEC.* Begun China 1942, Mission now based on San José, CA(USA). 5n,4t(300). |
| Christian Revival Fellowship | 1953 | P Pe2 | Z.... | 5 | 300 | 500 | M=Independent AoG(USA) (Scandinavian Pentecostals). 4n,4f,5t(160). |
| Christianity Bible Church | 1956 | I ind | ..... | 4 | 100 | 200 | Small indigenous body begun by Chinese. 1n,3m. |
| Church of Jesus C of Latter-day Saints | 1950 | M LdS | x.... | | 3,000 | 4,623 | *Mormons.* M=CJCLdS(Utah,USA). Many USA expatriates and military. 120f,G=27.2%pa. |
| Church of the Nazarene | 1956 | P Hol | xF... | 24 | 598 | 3,000 | M=CoN. Mandarin,Taiwanese,Paiwanese. 6n,5x,23m,10f,G=27%pa,1s(24),25t,W=65%,150Y. |
| Churches of Christ | 1960 | P Dis | x.... | 19 | 240 | 600 | M=CCCC(Instrumental)(USA). Taichung, Taipei. Many USA personnel. 11f. |
| Conservative Baptist Association | 1952 | P Bap | xF... | 17 | 527 | 2,000 | M=CBFMS(USA). Mandarin. 6n,5x,8m,41f,G=1.5%pa,1k,1s(21),21t(900),W=45%,45Y,243z. |
| Covenant Church of China | 1952 | P Con | K.... | 13 | 736 | 2,000 | M=Free Mission Covenant Ch (Finland), ECCA(USA). Mostly Mandarin. 9m,10f,12t(500). |
| Elim Foursquare Gospel Alliance | 1963 | P Pe2 | ZF... | 17 | 2,200 | 5,000 | M=Elim FGA(UK), PAoC(Canada). HQ Taipei. 15n,6f. |
| Evangelical Alliance Mission | 1951 | P int | xM... | 26 | 1,117 | 3,000 | M=TEAM,FEGC(USA). Began in Hualien area. Radio work. 18m,81f,1H,2h,31t(1500). |
| Evangelize China Fellowship | 1947 | I int | x.... | 6 | 1,800 | 4,000 | Begun in China by a Chinese. M=ECF(HQ,USA). Some Aborigines, 12n,10m,7t(500). |
| Formosa Christian Mission | 1955 | I ind | ..... | 10 | 320 | 1,000 | Indigenous, entirely Chinese, 2n,16m,5t(114),450z. |
| Full Gospel Assemblies | 1953 | P Pe2 | Z.... | 24 | 925 | 3,000 | M=FFFM(Finland). Counties: Miaoli, Taichung, Hualien. 8n,11m,14f,32t(1000). |
| Glad Tidings Church | 1952 | P Pe2 | x.... | 16 | 440 | 600 | M=Glad Tidings Missionary Soc(Canada). HQ Taichung. 8n,8m,13f,1p(120),13t(600). |
| Gospel Baptist Church | 1953 | P Bap | x.... | 6 | 375 | 800 | M=Baptist Missionary Association of America. 3n,2f,6t(150). |
| Gospelaires Missionary Church | 1955 | P int | .TT.T | 3 | 741 | 2,000 | M=Gospelaires Missionary Association. HQ Taipei, 3n,8m,3t(200). |
| Independent Mandarin churches | 1952 | P int | xM... | 35 | 3,000 | 7,000 | M=Overseas Missionary Fellowship (former CIM, Nei Ti Hui). 44f,1j. |
| Independent Presbyterian Ch of Taiwan | 1952 | I Ref | ..... | 7 | 243 | 500 | Split from China Presbyterian Church of Christ. 4n,7t(220),259z. |
| Internat Ch of the Foursquare Gospel | | P Pe2 | ZF... | | 200 | 500 | M=ICFG(USA). Classical Pentecostals; world HQ Los Angeles, USA, HQ Taipei. |
| International Gospel League | 1958 | P int | ..T.T | 3 | 55 | 200 | *Jesus Christ's Gospel Hall,* et al. M=IGL(USA). Declining. 4n,3t(40). |
| Jehovah's Witnesses | 1928 | M Jeh | x.... | 37 | 1,150 | 4,000 | *Watch Tower.* First lectures 1928, public witnessing 1932. Many Ami tribals. 63Y. |
| Korean Church in Taiwan | 1949 | P Ref | ..... | 3 | 105 | 215 | Migrant Presbyterians from Korea, maintaining own separate organization. 1n,5m. |
| Liebenzelle Church | 1953 | P int | xM... | 6 | 97 | 200 | M=LM(USA), from Bad Liebenzell (Germany). HQ Puli (Nantou). 7f,4t(80). |
| Living Way Presbyterian Church | | I Ref | .TT.T | 5 | 128 | 400 | Formerly Tao-Seng Mission. Split ex China Presb Ch of Christ. 5n,10m,5t(188),105z. |
| Local Mandarin-speaking Churches | | I ind | ..... | 14 | 2,840 | 7,000 | Indigenous independent congregations loosely related to preacher Wu Yung. 15n. |
| Lutheran Church of South Taiwan | 1956 | P Lut | ..... | 18 | 436 | 1,000 | M=Finnish Missionary Society. Hengchun(extreme south). 2n,24f,1h,50t(2300),1u. |
| Mandarin Christian Church | 1963 | P Pe2 | ZF... | 24 | 2,000 | 5,000 | Classical (2-stage) Pentecostals. M=PAoC(Canada). 3n,12m,3f,30t(3000). |
| Mennonite Church in Taiwan | 1948 | P Men | G...K | 14 | 654 | 1,600 | M=General Conference MC(USA). 11n,7m,34f,G=6.6%pa,1H,1p(5),11t(394),W=49%,87Y,80z. |
| Methodist Ch of the Republic of China | 1952 | P Met | VwE.K | 20 | 4,227 | 10,000 | *Taiwan Annual Conference, UMC*(USA); A=1972. 13n,16f,2H,2s,21t(1683),1u,1v,554z. |
| Norwegian Missionary Alliance | 1945 | P int | ..... | 6 | 150 | 300 | M=NMA(Norske Misjonsallianse), begun China 1901. HQ Puli. 1n,6m,17f,2H,10t(310). |
| Norwegian Pentecostal Mission | c1960 | P Pe2 | Z.... | 3 | 3,000 | 5,000 | M=Norske Pinsevenners Ytremisjon. Begun unintentionally by itinerant Chinese. |
| **Presbyterian Church in Taiwan** | 1865 | P Ref | R.E.K | 927 | 65,443 | 154,680 | 70% Taiwanese, 30% Aborigine. 373n,12x,76f,2H,4s(548),929t(58221),W=35%,8697Yy. |
| Quemoy Christian Church of Christ | | I ind | .TT.T | | 500 | 1,000 | *Quemoy Huo Pu Christian Ch.* Fundamentalists on island 5 miles from mainland China. |
| Salvation Army | 1928 | P Sal | xwE.E | 12 | 180 | 400 | *Kuei Sai Kuen. SA, Taiwan Region.* Pioneers Japanese. 10n,4x,1s,4t(270),W=88%,50z. |
| Seventh-day Adventist Church | 1912 | P Adv | x.... | 104 | 5,252 | 15,000 | *SChina Island UM.* Mountain tribes. 32n,122m,33f,1H,1j,1r,2s(82),113t(8342),151Y. |
| Spiritual Food Church | c1965 | I int | x.... | 1 | 200 | 700 | *Ling Liang Worldwide Evangelistic Mission* (from Hong Kong). 1n,1t(80),50z. |
| Taiwan Assembly of God | 1953 | I ind | ..... | 22 | 1,359 | 3,000 | Indigenous local assemblies begun by Chinese. 5n,33m. |
| Taiwan Baptist Convention | 1948 | P Bap | T...K | 102 | 10,175 | 25,000 | M=SBC. Mandarin; few Taiwanese. 49n,71f,G=2.1%pa,1s(23),95t(7420),W=50%,696Y,1500z. |
| Taiwan Congregational Association | | P Con | .TT.T | 8 | 120 | 200 | M=Congregational Christian Churches(USA). Fundamentalists. 2n,7t(350). |
| Taiwan Episcopal Church (D Taiwan) | c1940 | A Hig | awEAK | 14 | 1,023 | 2,065 | 1960 missionary Diocese of PECUSA, Province VIII. Static. 16n,2x,9f,2h,1r,7t(321),1u,4Y,30y. |
| Taiwan Fellowship Deaconry Mission | 1952 | P int | ..... | 10 | 245 | 500 | M=Marburger Mission (Germany). Former Yunnan Mission in China. 3n,11m,13f,6t(500). |
| Taiwan Friends Church | 1953 | P Qua | QF... | 28 | 1,400 | 3,000 | M=Taiwan Friends Mission (Ohio,USA). Mostly in Chiayi. 13n,10f,1s,26t(1000). |
| Taiwan Gospel Church | | P int | ..... | 4 | 500 | 1,000 | M=Taiwan Gospel Mission. Independent congregations. Declining. 4n,4t(200). |
| Taiwan Holiness Church | 1928 | P Hol | xF... | 61 | 2,858 | 5,000 | Begun 1929 by Japanese. 1951, M=OMS(USA). 55n,16f,1s(38),53t(2911),201Y,1103z. |
| Taiwan Lutheran Church | 1951 | P Lut | L...K | 45 | 2,284 | 5,913 | Begun by mainland refugees. 8 missions. Declining. 23n,23f,1H,1s,44t(2280). |
| Taiwan Reformed Presbyterian Church | 1950 | P Ref | xF... | 19 | 481 | 800 | M=CRC,OPC,EPC(all USA),RC(New Zealand). 5n,11m,18f,1s,18t(785),256z. |
| True Jesus Church in Taiwan | 1926 | I pel | x...K | 187 | 25,000 | 50,000 | *Chen Ye-su Chiao Hui.* Rapid growth. Taiwanese. 43n,43m,1s(12),132t(9352),1000Yy. |
| Other indigenous congregations | | I sin | ..... | 150 | 15,000 | 50,000 | In over 30 groupings. Mostly single congregations unrelated to others. 200nm. |
| Other Protestant denominations | | P | ..... | | 1,000 | 8,000 | About 15 bodies (see list below), including USA military chaplaincies. |
| Other indigenous churches | | I | ..... | | 2,000 | 5,000 | Total about 15 bodies (see below). |
| **Total affiliated (mid-1970)** | | | | **3,200** | **387,864** | **820,173** | **Total denominations (1970) . . . 120.** |
| **Total affiliated (mid-1975)** | | | | **3,600** | **456,900** | **966,200** | **Total denominations (1975) . . . 135.** |
| **Total affiliated (mid-1980)** | | | | **4,300** | **533,600** | **1,128,500** | **Total denominations (1980) . . . 150.** |

NOTES ON TABLE ABOVE
COLUMNS: for meanings and CODES (cols. 1, 3, 4, 8): see Codebook (Part 6). Column 1: **Boldface type** = church with over 10% of country's affiliated Christians.
NATIONAL COUNCILS (Column 4, 5th letter).
- E = Evangelical Fellowship of Taiwan (begun 1952 as China Evangelical Fellowship; mostly individuals).
- K = Ecumenical Co-operative Committee (K = co-operating bodies, not formal membership).
- T = Republic of China Council of Christian Churches.

*Other national councils.* Taiwan Missionary Fellowship (composed of all Protestant missionaries). Association of Christian Churches of the Republic of China (for all Protestant groups to obtain representation before government). Taiwan Christian Service (co-operating with almost all Christian bodies except Little Flock, Mormons, Jehovah's Witnesses).
OTHER PROTESTANT DENOMINATIONS. About 15 smaller bodies, including: Apostolic Church of Pentecost (Canada), Baptist Mid-Missions (1972), Ch of Christ, Emmanuel Baptist Mission, Ev Wesleyan Mission, Go-Ye Fellowship, Hundred Nations Crusade (member of ICCC), International Missions (1946), Swedish Free Mission, Taiwan Ev Presbyterian Church, Wesleyan Ch, Worldwide Evangelization Crusade, World-Wide Missions (1961). There are also USA military chaplaincies among the 9,000 USA troops (1970).
OTHER INDIGENOUS CHURCHES. These include: China Ch of Christ (member of ICCC), Conservative Congregational Ch (member of ICCC), Holy Spirit Association for Unification of World Christianity (from Korea), Taipei Chunking Christian Ch (member of ICCC).

**PEOPLES** (ethnolinguistic). Christians: about 35% Taiwanese (Minnan Hoklo, Hakka), 34% Aborigine (Kaoshan, Highlander), 30% Mainland Chinese (Mandarin), 0.5% USA, European & other alien.

**COUNTRY-WIDE TOTALS**
EVANGELIZATION (see Part 5). 1900: 13%. 1970: 78%. 1980: 89%. *Mass evangelism.* Among recent campaigns: 1955–65,

'Double-the-Church Movement' by Presbyterian Church; Billy Graham crusades in 1956 and in 1963 in Taipei and Kaohsiung (100,000 attenders, 6,000 enquirers); 1960, Oral Roberts in Taipei; March-May 1965, Taiwan Christianity Centennial Campaigns in 40 cities and towns; 1965–70, Five-Year Campaign by Taiwan Baptist Convention; 1969, Assemblies of God healing campaign (12,000-seat indoor stadium); 1971, Taiwan Congress on Evangelism; October–November 1975, Billy Graham 5-day crusade in Taipei (250,000 attenders, 11,595 enquirers); 1976, Knowing Jesus campaign, then 1977 Tell the Good News multi-media movement (supported by 2,000 churches), with estimated 10 million persons exposed to the gospel. *Radiophonic evangelism.* Numerous radio and TV programmes. 1976–78, Catholic TV programme 'The Most Unforgettable Story, (1.2 million viewers every week for over a year). Bible correspondence courses (1975): over 40,000 enrolments (ICI 25,212, Roman Catholics 4,070, et alia).

FOREIGN MISSIONARIES AND PERSONNEL (nationals serving abroad) (1973). Total 203 in 25 countries: over 73 Chinese indigenous, 70 Protestants, about 60 Roman Catholics.

FOREIGN MISSIONARIES AND PERSONNEL (aliens from abroad) (1973). Total 1,857. *From Western world.* 1,742: about 810 Roman Catholics, 788 Protestants (535 in 69 USA societies, 68 in 5 Norway societies, 45 in 6 UK societies, 41 in 4 Canada societies, 40 in 4 Finland societies, 26 in 5 WGermany societies, 13 in 7 New Zealand societies, 8 in 1 Sweden society, 8 in 6 Australia societies, 3 in 1 Denmark society, 1 in 1 Netherlands society), about 135 marginal Protestants (115 Mormons) from USA, 9 Anglicans (6 in 1 USA society, 3 in 1 UK society). *From Communist world.* About 15 Roman Catholics (13 from Poland, also Yugoslavia). *From Third World.* 100: 48 indigenous from Hong Kong, Japan and Korea, 32 Protestants from Hong Kong, Japan, Korea, Philippines and South Africa, about 10 Roman Catholics, about 10 marginal Protestants (Mormons) from Hong Kong and Japan.

INSTITUTIONS (church-operated) (1973). Total 275, including 53 higher schools (13 minor seminaries), 150 medical centres (38 hospitals), 2 radio stations, 13 religious communities, 1 research centre, 35 seminaries (30 Protestant, 4 RC, 1 Chinese indigenous), 5 study centres, 1 university.

PERIODICALS. About 56 titles.

PERSONNEL. About 5,742 (3,885 national, 1,857 foreign).

RELIGIOUS LIBRARIES. About 60.

SCRIPTURE DISTRIBUTION (1975). Annual totals: 60,031 Bibles (83% subsidized, 17% commercial), 457,518 NTs (52% free, 42% subsidized, 6% commercial), 723,152 UBS portions, 4,968,482 UBS selections. *Translations completed.* Portion: 8 languages since 1661. NT: 5 languages since 1873. Bible: Taiwanese in 1884.

SERVICE AGENCIES. About 90, including ASEDROC, CCCI, CCF, CEF, COTE, CULC, CWS, FABC, ISAC, MSP, OC, PTL, SU, TCF, TEIM, TMF, WLC(EHC), WVI, YCW.

ADDITIONAL DATA ON CHURCHES

ASSEMBLY HALL CHURCHES. *Foreign missions.* In 1975 there were about 22 missionaries and wives serving in Brazil, Hong Kong, Indonesia, Japan, Korea, Philippines, Singapore, Thailand, and the USA; also others emigrate and carry on evangelistic work.

CATHOLIC CHURCH IN TAIWAN. Trilingual = speaking Mandarin, Minnan, Atayal. Quadrilingual = Mandarin, Minnan, Hakka, Atayal. *Pescadores Islands.* 1,267 Catholics. *M Taipeh:* excluding the military strongholds of Quemoy and Matsu, still officially in mainland China (D Amoy and M Foochow respectively) and since 1968 placed by SC Propaganda under an apostolic administrator (1971 statistics: 68 Catholics, 3 parishes, 4 CICM priests, 2 sisters, 1 hospital). *Catechumens.* (1959) 49,238; (1961) 45,611; (1963) 53,388. After 1963 the numbers of both catechumens and adult converts decreased rapidly, until by 1973 D Tainan had only 165 catechumens and D Kiayi 520. *Growth.* The fastest-growing diocese is D Hsinchu, whose membership is 60% Hakka. *Baptisms.* During 1955–58, there was a mass movement into the church; of the 69,000 baptisms then, 87.4% were of Taiwanese, 10.0% Mainlanders, and 2.4% Aborigines. *Annual baptisms.* (1972) 65.5% infant, 34.5% adult. *Priests.* 272 diocesan, 545 religious. Nationals: all Chinese except one Aboriginal priest ordained in 1970. *Brothers.* 32 Chinese. *Sisters.* 678 Chinese. *Catholic charismatics* (January 1974). 300 adults including many religious personnel are active in 20 organized prayer groups in the Charismatic Renewal. *Seminarians* (1972). 92 secular, 43 religious. *Catechists.* Total (1971) 785 full-time. *Indigenous religious congregations.* Priests: 23 Congregatio Discipulorum Domini (CDD). Brothers: 7 St John the Baptist. Sisters (all orders begun in mainland China before 1949): 88 Sisters of the Sacred Heart of Mary, 48 Missionary Sisters Oblates of the Holy Family, 33 Sisters of Our Lady of China, 26 Dominican Sisters of Funing, 25 Theresian Sisters, 16 Providence Sisters Catechists, and 2 others. *Major foreign orders and congregations.* Priests: CICM, OFM, MM, MEP, OP, SJ, SVD, SDB, CM. Sisters: Dominican Catechists Sisters of St Joseph, Franciscan Missionary Sisters of the Immaculate Conception of the Mother of God, Maryknoll Sisters, Sisters of the Sacred Heart of Jesus. *Catholic organizations.* The Regional Conference of Chinese Bishops (Chung Kuo Chu-chiao T'uan) consists of the ordinaries of Taiwan and other bishops residing in the territory and is a member of the Federation of Asian Bishops' Conferences (FABC) in Hong Kong. In 1971, there were 15 members. There are no national presbyteral or pastoral councils. Religious personnel are represented on the Association of Major Superiors of Religious Men in Taiwan, and the Association of Major Superiors of Religious Women in Taiwan. Lay activities are co-ordinated by the National Council of the Lay Apostolate, founded in 1971. The principal lay movements in 1970 were Legion of Mary (1,200 members), Cursillos de Cristiandad (1,120), Pax Romana Catholic Students (5,000), YCW (500) and Christian Life Movement (400).

The Holy See has diplomatic relations with Taiwan and is supposed to be represented to government and the Catholic hierarchy by a pro-nuncio in Taipei. However, since 1971 the pro-nuncio has been indefinitely withdrawn and is in fact serving in Bangladesh. In 1972 he was replaced by a chargè d'affaires which is generally interpreted as a diplomatic move on the part of the Holy See in the direction of mainland China.

Two FABC organizations are located in Taiwan: the Office of Ecumenical and Inter-Religious Affairs and the Institute for the Study of East Asian Christian Spirituality. The latter was founded in April 1975.

The principal organization for social action is the Association for Socio-Economic Development in the Republic of China (ASEDROC), with headquarters in Taipei, which trains local leaders in socio-economic fields as well as providing a legal umbrella for 4 independent social-action groups which operate as ASEDROC committees: the Institute for Social Action in China (ISAC), which was founded in 1968 and sponsors many community development projects; Credit Union League of China (CULC); Taiwan Ecumenical Industrial Ministry (TEIM); and Mountain Service Programme (MSP). ASEDROC is a member of ICRA in Italy. The St Anthony Sociological Institute, founded by the OFM, is located in Taipei.

There is in Taiwan one single school system in which all private schools run by Catholics are included. Catholic statistics for 1972 list 401 kindergartens (52,431 children), 8 primary schools (5,208), 26 middle schools (25,797), 9 technical schools (1,791 students), 7 language schools (968), 3 colleges and universities (7,936). Fujen Catholic University plays an important role in higher education, with its Faculty of Theology, College of Liberal Arts, College of Law and Business, and College of Natural Science and Languages, including a Chinese Language Institute. The Tien Educational Center and the Ricci Institute for Chinese Studies, both belonging to Jesuits, engage in cultural activities, and Kuangchi Program Service in the field of radio and television. Nearly 200 Catholic institutions were listed under medical action and welfare in 1972: 24 hospitals (1,400 beds), 94 dispensaries (387,203 out-patients), one home for the aged (200 people), 3 orphanages (70 orphans) and 63 hostels (5,901 students). In addition, there are several social or service centres involved in rehabilitation and providing assistance to Aborigines. The Catholic Hospital Association of China has its headquarters in Taipei.

PRESBYTERIAN CHURCH IN TAIWAN. Tai-oan Ki-tok Tiu-lo Kau-hoe. Begun 1865 by Presbyterian Church of England, now 6 co-operating missions (UK, USA, Canada) under a Mission Council. Two areas: Plains Churches (473 churches), Mountain Churches (413). 1955–65, communicants rose from 32,000 to 67,000 as result of Double-the-Church movement. Main sub-culture: Taiwanese. The church joined the World Council of Churches in 1951 withdrew in 1970 in protest against WCC policy then rejoined later. *Growth.* In 1970 the church was experiencing numerical decline at a rate of —0.8% pa. *Foreign missions.* In 1976 the church supported 44 of its Chinese pastors and wives as foreign missionaries in Brazil, Canada, Hong Kong, Japan, Korea, Mauritius, Singapore, Thailand and the USA; and through the Burning Bush Missionary Society (Mustard Seed), 8 mountain-tribe pastors and wives in Indonesia and Sarawak (Malaysia).

TRUE JESUS CHURCH IN TAIWAN. The church began in mainland China in 1917. *Congregations.* In Taiwan, these grew from 182 in 1970 to 210 in 1975. *Membership* (including baptized infants). These have grown uniformly from 29,300 in 1970 to 34,000 in 1975 (a growth rate of 3.2% per year). In addition, there are many unbaptized adherents. *Foreign missions.* In 1975 there were about 20 missionaries serving in Hong Kong, India, Indonesia, Japan, Korea, Malaysia (Sabah), Singapore and the USA.

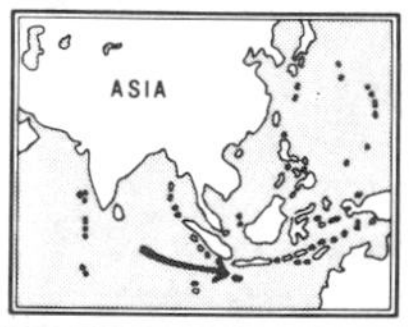


# CHRISTMAS ISLAND

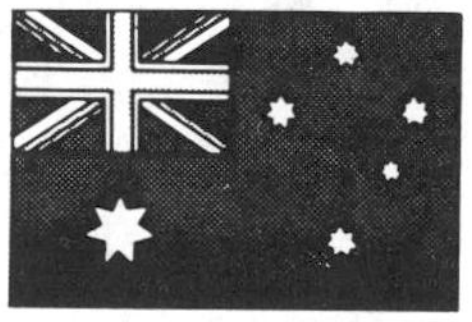

## SECULAR DATA

**STATE. Official name:** The Territory of Christmas Island. (Note: This territory should not be confused with Christmas Island, part of the Line Islands in the Gilbert Islands).
**Flag** (shown above right): That of Australia.
**Area:** 135 sq.km. (52 sq.miles). Agricultural land: 0.0%.
**Government:** External territory (dependency) of Australia, since 1958 (1888 British territory).
**Official language:** English.
**Capital:** Flying Fish Cove.

**DEMOGRAPHY. Population:** 2,691 (census of 30.VI.1971. For 1970–2000 (UN), see last row of Table 1). Population density (1975): 24/sq.km. (63/sq.mile). Under 15 years: 44%. Growth rate (1975–80): 1.31% per year (births 3.49%, deaths −0.79%, emigrants −1.39%). Life expectancy (1975–80): 63.8 years.
Household size: 3.7 persons.
**Major languages:** English, Chinese, Malay, Javanese.
**Labour force:** 51%.

**ETHNOLINGUISTIC GROUPS:** 50.4% Chinese, 18.7% Malay, 16.4% Cocos Islander, 9.9% European, 2.7% Javanese, 1.0% Eurasian, 0.6% Indo-Pakistani.

**MONEY** (1977). **Monetary unit:** Australian dollar (= 100 cents). **National income per person:** US$1,400. Average annual family income: US$5,180.

**EDUCATION.** Adult literacy: (1957) 63%. Schools: 4.

**HEALTH** (1975). Hospitals: 1.

**COMMUNICATION** (per 1,000 people). Phones: 100.

TABLE 1. RELIGIOUS ADHERENTS IN CHRISTMAS ISLAND

| Year | 1900 | | mid-1970 | | Annual change, 1970–1980 | | | | mid-1975 | | mid-1980 | | 2000 | |
|---|---|---|---|---|---|---|---|---|---|---|---|---|---|---|
| *Name* | *Adherents* | *%* | *Adherents* | *%* | *Natural* | *Conversion* | *Total* | *Rate* | *Adherents* | *%* | *Adherents* | *%* | *Adherents* | *%* |
| Chinese folk-religionists | 460 | 66.0 | 1,465 | 44.4 | 0 | 0 | 0 | 0.00 | 1,465 | 44.4 | 1,465 | 44.4 | 1,440 | 40.0 |
| Muslims | 210 | 30.0 | 695 | 21.1 | 0 | 0 | 0 | 0.00 | 695 | 21.1 | 695 | 21.1 | 720 | 20.0 |
| Non-religious | 0 | 0.0 | 625 | 18.9 | 0 | 0 | 0 | 0.00 | 625 | 18.9 | 625 | 18.9 | 900 | 25.0 |
| **Christians** | **30** | **4.0** | **515** | **15.6** | **0** | **0** | **0** | **0.00** | **515** | **15.6** | **515** | **15.6** | **540** | **15.0** |
| professing | 30 | 4.0 | 515 | 15.6 | 0 | 0 | 0 | 0.00 | 515 | 15.6 | 515 | 15.6 | 540 | 15.0 |
| Roman Catholics | 20 | 3.0 | 230 | 6.9 | 0 | 0 | 0 | 0.00 | 230 | 6.9 | 230 | 6.9 | 250 | 7.0 |
| Protestants | 0 | 0.0 | 175 | 5.3 | 0 | 0 | 0 | 0.00 | 175 | 5.3 | 175 | 5.3 | 180 | 5.0 |
| Anglicans | 10 | 1.0 | 110 | 3.3 | 0 | 0 | 0 | 0.00 | 110 | 3.3 | 110 | 3.3 | 110 | 3.0 |
| nominal | 0 | 0.0 | 185 | 5.6 | 0 | 0 | 0 | 0.00 | 185 | 5.6 | 185 | 5.6 | 290 | 8.0 |
| affiliated | 30 | 4.0 | 330 | 10.0 | 0 | 0 | 0 | 0.00 | 330 | 10.0 | 330 | 10.0 | 250 | 7.0 |
| total practising | 20 | *70* | 200 | *60* | 0 | 0 | 0 | 0.00 | 200 | *60* | 200 | *60* | 120 | *50* |
| non-practising | 10 | *30* | 130 | *40* | 0 | 0 | 0 | 0.00 | 130 | *40* | 130 | *40* | 120 | *50* |
| Roman Catholics | 20 | 3.0 | 150 | 4.5 | 0 | 0 | 0 | 0.00 | 150 | 4.5 | 150 | 4.5 | 140 | 4.0 |
| Protestants | 0 | 0.0 | 100 | 3.0 | 0 | 0 | 0 | 0.00 | 100 | 3.0 | 100 | 3.0 | 70 | 2.0 |
| Anglicans | 10 | 1.0 | 80 | 2.4 | 0 | 0 | 0 | 0.00 | 80 | 2.4 | 80 | 2.4 | 40 | 1.0 |
| **Country's population** | **700** | **100.0** | **3,300** | **100.0** | **0** | **0** | **0** | **0.00** | **3,300** | **100.0** | **3,300** | **100.0** | **3,600** | **100.0** |

COLUMNS, ROWS. For meanings and definitions, see Codebook (Part 6). Note that, by definition, total 'Christians' = professing + crypto-Christians, which also = affiliated + nominal Christians. Percentages may not always total exactly, due to rounding.

CENSUSES. **30.VI.1961:** 84.6% Chinese folk-religionists and Muslims, 5.9% Roman Catholics, 4.8% Anglicans, 4.3% Protestants, 0.5% non-religious, 0.4% Orthodox (7 persons only). **30.VI.1966:** 58.1% Chinese folk-religionists and Muslims, 14.0% non-religious, 12.3% Roman Catholics, 8.2% Anglicans, 7.3% Protestants. **30.VI.1971:** 44.4% Chinese folk-religionists, 21.1% Muslims, 18.9% non-religious, 6.9% Roman Catholics, 5.4% Protestants, 3.3% Anglicans.

COUNTRY'S POPULATION. With such small numbers, the various percentages of religious groups can fluctuate greatly depending on what religion new immigrants have. For the purposes of this table, it is assumed that the 1971 census percentages remain unchanged during the decade 1970–80, and thereafter vary only slightly.

MUSLIMS. 91% Malays, 9% Javanese and other Indonesians.

NON-RELIGIOUS. Mainly former Buddhist Chinese, mostly young persons who have abandoned family religion.

**NON-CHRISTIAN RELIGIONS. Chinese folk religion** is predominant in Christmas Island whose population was 50% Chinese in 1970. This is a mixture of Buddhist, Taoist and Confucian ideas and practices, together with ancestor veneration.

**Islam** is second in importance, among the Malay population, and those professing to be without religion (mainly Chinese) have increased substantially in the last decade or two.

**CHRISTIANITY.** Christians formed 16% of the population in 1971 and are divided into Catholic, Protestant and Anglican congregations. Catholic work is part of the diocese of Singapore, while

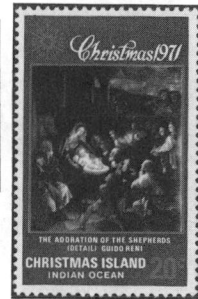

Over half of all the Island's postage stamps have celebrated the birth of Christ, including The Flight into Egypt (1975).

Anglicans belong to the Church of England in Australia, diocese of Perth.

**CHURCH AND STATE.** Christmas Island is administered by an official representative appointed by the Ministry of Territories of the Australian government. Freedom of religion is guaranteed under the Australian constitution.

TABLE 2.    ORGANIZED CHURCHES AND DENOMINATIONS IN CHRISTMAS ISLAND

| Official name 1 | Begun 2 | Type 3 | Counc 4 | Congs 5 | Adults 6 | Affiliated 7 | Names, notes, and other statistics (see Codebook) 8 |
|---|---|---|---|---|---|---|---|
| Catholic Church (AD Singapore) | | R Lat | p,F.. | 1 | 100 | 150 | Part of AD Singapore. Australians; including many Chinese, some Eurasians. |
| Ch of England in Australia (D Perth) | 1888 | A Cen | awe.. | 1 | 50 | 80 | Included in Diocese of Perth. Australians, a few Eurasians and Chinese. |
| Other Protestant denominations | | P | ..... | 3 | 50 | 100 | Informal groups serving Congregationalists, Methodists, Presbyterians. |
| Total affiliated (mid-1970) | | | | 5 | 200 | 330 | Total denominations (1970) . . . 5. |
| Total affiliated (mid-1975) | | | | 5 | 200 | 330 | Total denominations (1975) . . . 5. |
| Total affiliated (mid-1980) | | | | 5 | 200 | 330 | Total denominations (1980) . . . 5. |

**NOTES ON TABLE ABOVE**
COLUMNS: for meanings and CODES (cols. 1, 3, 4, 8): see Codebook (Part 6). Column 1: **Boldface type** = church with

over 10% of country's affiliated Christians.
**PEOPLES** (ethnolinguistic). Christians: 68% European (Anglo-Australian, British), 25% Chinese, 7% Eurasian.

**COUNTRY-WIDE TOTALS**
EVANGELIZATION (see Part 5). 1900: 8%. 1970: 60%. 1980: 70%.

---

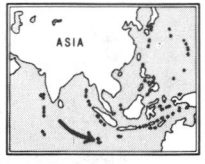

# Cocos (Keeling) Islands

## SECULAR DATA

**STATE. Official name:** The Territory of Cocos (Keeling) Islands.
**Flag** (shown above right): That of Australia.
**Area:** 14 sq.km. (5.4 sq.miles). **Description:** 27 small coral islands.
Agricultural land: 0.0%.
**Government:** Australian dependency, since 1955 (1857 British colony).
**Official language:** English.

**DEMOGRAPHY. Population:** 618 (census of 30.VI.1971. For 1970–2000 (UN), see last row of Table 1). Population density (1975): 50/sq.km. (130/sq.mile). Under 15 years: 44%. Growth rate (1975–80): 1.31% per year (births 3.49%, deaths −0.79%, emigrants −1.39%). Life expectancy (1975–80): 63.8 years. Household size: 6.3 persons.
**Major languages:** Malay, English, Chinese.
**Labour force:** 41%.

**ETHNOLINGUISTIC GROUPS:** 66.0% Malay, 29.0% English & Anglo-Australian, 4.0% Chinese.

**MONEY** (1977). **Monetary unit:** Australian dollar (= 100 cents). **National income per person:** US$1,400. Average annual family income: US$8,820.

**COMMUNICATION** (per 1,000 people). Phones: 120.

TABLE 1.    RELIGIOUS ADHERENTS IN THE COCOS (KEELING) ISLANDS

| Year | 1900 | | mid-1970 | | Annual change, 1970–1980 | | | | mid-1975 | | mid-1980 | | 2000 | |
|---|---|---|---|---|---|---|---|---|---|---|---|---|---|---|
| Name | Adherents | % | Adherents | % | Natural | Conversion | Total | Rate | Adherents | % | Adherents | % | Adherents | % |
| Muslims | 522 | 87.0 | 452 | 64.6 | 0 | −5 | −5 | −1.37 | 424 | 60.6 | 394 | 56.3 | 410 | 51.3 |
| Christians | 60 | 10.0 | 210 | 30.0 | 0 | 4 | 4 | 1.90 | 231 | 33.0 | 254 | 36.3 | 296 | 37.0 |
| professing | 60 | 10.0 | 210 | 30.0 | 0 | 4 | 4 | 1.90 | 231 | 33.0 | 254 | 36.3 | 296 | 37.0 |
| Anglicans | 48 | 8.0 | 127 | 18.1 | 0 | 4 | 4 | 2.52 | 147 | 21.0 | 164 | 23.5 | 192 | 24.0 |
| Roman Catholics | 6 | 1.0 | 53 | 7.6 | 0 | 1 | 1 | 2.62 | 61 | 8.7 | 69 | 9.8 | 80 | 10.0 |
| Protestants | 6 | 1.0 | 30 | 4.3 | 0 | −1 | −1 | −3.91 | 23 | 3.3 | 21 | 3.0 | 24 | 3.0 |
| nominal | 6 | 1.0 | 100 | 14.3 | 0 | 3 | 3 | 2.57 | 113 | 16.1 | 129 | 18.4 | 144 | 18.0 |
| affiliated | 54 | 9.0 | 110 | 15.7 | 0 | 1 | 1 | 1.27 | 118 | 16.8 | 125 | 17.9 | 152 | 19.0 |
| total practising | 43 | 80 | 66 | 60 | 0 | 1 | 1 | 1.27 | 71 | 60 | 75 | 60 | 76 | 50 |
| non-practising | 11 | 20 | 44 | 40 | 0 | 0 | 0 | 1.27 | 47 | 40 | 50 | 40 | 76 | 50 |
| Anglicans | 48 | 8.0 | 70 | 10.0 | 0 | 1 | 1 | 1.82 | 77 | 11.0 | 84 | 12.0 | 104 | 13.0 |
| Roman Catholics | 6 | 1.0 | 40 | 5.7 | 0 | 0 | 0 | 0.24 | 41 | 5.8 | 41 | 5.9 | 48 | 6.0 |
| Chinese folk-religionists | 18 | 3.0 | 21 | 3.0 | 0 | 0 | 0 | 0.00 | 21 | 3.0 | 21 | 3.0 | 24 | 3.0 |
| Baha'is | 0 | 0.0 | 10 | 1.4 | 0 | 0 | 0 | 0.00 | 10 | 1.4 | 10 | 1.4 | 30 | 3.7 |
| Non-religious | 0 | 0.0 | 7 | 1.0 | 0 | 1 | 1 | 10.00 | 14 | 2.0 | 21 | 3.0 | 40 | 5.0 |
| Country's population | 600 | 100.0 | 700 | 100.0 | 0 | 0 | 0 | 0.00 | 700 | 100.0 | 700 | 100.0 | 800 | 100.0 |

COLUMNS, ROWS. For meanings and definitions, see Codebook (Part 6). Note that, by definition, total 'Christians' = professing + crypto-Christians, which also = affiliated + nominal Christians. Percentages may not always total exactly, due to rounding.
CENSUSES. **30.VI.1961:** 73.2% Muslims and Chinese folk-religionists, 13.5% Anglicans, 6.8% Protestants, 5.8% Roman

Catholics, 0.5% non-religious. **30.VI.1966:** 71.2% Muslims and Chinese folk-religionists, 16.3% Anglicans, 6.9% Roman Catholics, 5.4% Protestants, 0.2% non-religious.

**NOTES ON RELIGIONS**
BAHA'IS. A first spiritual assembly was begun in 1960 on West

Island, but has not grown appreciably.
CHRISTIANS. Europeans, Anglo-Australians, and some Chinese.
MUSLIMS. Descendants of Malays, among whom there are still animistic practices.
NON-RELIGIOUS. Europeans and Anglo-Australians.

---

**NON-CHRISTIAN RELIGIONS. Islam** is the main religion of the Malays who make up 69% of the population. There are also a few Chinese folk-religionists.

**CHRISTIANITY.** Christians are largely Europeans and Australians, with some Chinese. For Anglicans, the Cocos Islands are part of the Church of England in Australia. For Catholics, the territory is under the archdiocese of Perth. The number of Catholics

varies according to the work force on the island. There are no resident religious personnel, but a priest visits the island yearly. Protestants numbered 5% of the population in 1966, mostly Presbyterians and Methodists from Australia.

**CHURCH AND STATE.** As a private and commercial property, then later a British and Australian territory, the islands have never made religion a factor of importance. Uninhabited until 1826, the islands were

first discovered by William Keeling of the East India Company in 1609. John Clunies-Ross arrived in 1827 and developed extensive coconut plantations, virtually ruling the area as his private possession after 1831. Britain annexed the islands in 1878, but the Clunies-Ross family was left in control until 1955 when they became an Australian Commonwealth territory. The Australian constitution makes provision for free profession and practice of religion in all its territories.

TABLE 2.    ORGANIZED CHURCHES AND DENOMINATIONS IN THE COCOS (KEELING) ISLANDS

| Official name 1 | Begun 2 | Type 3 | Counc 4 | Congs 5 | Adults 6 | Affiliated 7 | Names, notes, and other statistics (see Codebook) 8 |
|---|---|---|---|---|---|---|---|
| Catholic Church (M Perth) | | R Lat | P.... | 1 | 30 | 40 | Expatriate labourers. No resident personnel; annual visit from Perth (Australia). |
| Ch of England in Australia (D Perth) | | A Cen | awe.. | 1 | 30 | 70 | Included in Diocese of Perth. Expatriates; services in English. |
| Total affiliated (mid-1970) | | | | 2 | 60 | 110 | Total denominations (1970) . . . 2. |
| Total affiliated (mid-1975) | | | | 2 | 65 | 118 | Total denominations (1975) . . . 2. |
| Total affiliated (mid-1980) | | | | 2 | 70 | 125 | Total denominations (1980) . . . 2. |

**NOTES ON TABLE ABOVE**
COLUMNS: for meanings and CODES (cols. 1, 3, 4, 8): see Codebook (Part 6). Column 1: **Boldface type** = church with

over 10% of country's affiliated Christians.
**PEOPLES** (ethnolinguistic). Christians: 99% English, 1% Chinese, some Anglo-Australian.

**COUNTRY-WIDE TOTALS**
EVANGELIZATION (see Part 5). 1900: 20%. 1970: 70%. 1980: 80%.

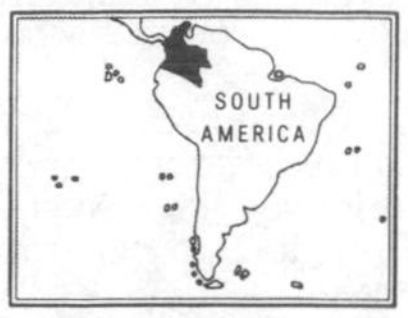


# COLOMBIA

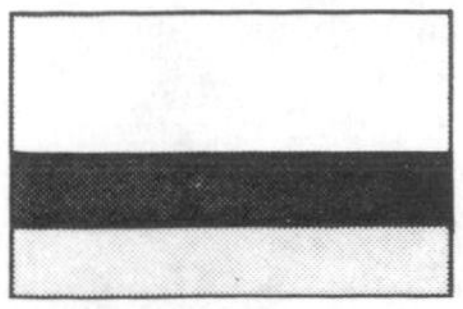

## SECULAR DATA

**STATE. Official name:** The Republic of Colombia (La República de Colombia). Adjective of nationality: Colombian (colombiano).
**Flag** (shown above right): Tricolour with wide yellow stripe atop narrower blue and red stripes.
**Area:** 1,138,914 sq.km. (456,535 sq.miles). Agricultural land: 19.7%.
**Government:** Parliamentary republic, since 1974 (1514 Spanish colony, 1819 Independence from Spain as New Granada, 1863 renamed United States of Colombia, 1974 2-party republic).
**Legislature:** Congress: Senate, 118 members; House of Representatives, 210 members.
**Official language:** Spanish (*Español/Castellano*).
**Chief cities:** capital Bogotá 2,850,000 (1973), Medellín 1,207,800, Cali 1,022,200.
**Political divisions:** 23 Departments, 4 Intendencies, 4 Commissaries.
**Armed forces** (1976): Total 54,300 regular: army 40,000, navy 8,000, air force 6,300 (28 combat aircraft). Reserves: 250,000. Paramilitary forces: 5,000.

**DEMOGRAPHY. Population:** 20,727,328 (census of 24.X.1973. For 1970–2000 (UN), see last row of Table 1). Population density (1975): 23/sq.km. (59/sq.mile). Under 15 years: 47%. Growth rate (1975–80): 3.09% per year (births 3.83%, deaths −0.75%). Life expectancy (1975–80): 63.4 years. Household size: 5.8 persons.
**Major languages:** Spanish, English, German, Chibcha, Guajiro, and about 90 other tribal languages.
**Urban dwellers** (1970): 59.6%. Urban growth rate (1950–70): 5.6% per year.
**Labour force:** 29%.
**Tourists** (1971): 197,503. (1974) 362,917.

**ETHNOLINGUISTIC GROUPS:** 47.8% Mestizo, 23.0% Mulatto (Mestizo/Black/White), 20.0% Colombian White, 6.0% Black (African Negro), 1.6% jungle Amerindian (80 tribes; 360,000) (1.0% Chibcha group, 0.5% Guajiro, Choco, Carib), 1.0% Zambo (Amerindian/Negro), German, Jewish (10,000), Arab (Palestinian, Syro-Lebanese), USA, Chinese (5,000).

**MONEY** (1977). **Monetary unit:** peso (= 100 centavos); US$1 = Col$35.90.
**National income per person:** US$460. Average annual family income: US$2,668.
**Inflation:** (1970–74) 17.5% per year, (1975) 26% per year (consumer price index 263).
**Cost of living in capital** (1976): index 71 (Washington DC = 100). Daily cost of living: US$29.

**EDUCATION.** Adult literacy: (1951) 62%, (1973) 81%. Education rate: 58%. Schools: 26,598. Universities: 29.

**HEALTH.** Hospitals: 747 (44,762 beds). Doctors: 10,317. Lepers: 36,000 (1.4 per 1,000). Blind: 30,000. Psychotics: 210,000. Drug addicts: about 130,000.

**LITERATURE.** Annual new book titles (1972): 848. Periodicals: 300. Scientific journals: 75. Newspapers: 36 dailies, 16 non-daily.

**COMMUNICATION** (per 1,000 people). Phones: 47. Radios: 120. TV sets: 53. Daily newspaper circulation: 109 copies.

TABLE 1. RELIGIOUS ADHERENTS IN COLOMBIA

| Year | 1900 | | mid-1970 | | Annual change, 1970–1980 | | | | mid-1975 | | mid-1980 | | 2000 | % |
|---|---|---|---|---|---|---|---|---|---|---|---|---|---|---|
| *Name* | *Adherents* | *%* | *Adherents* | *%* | *Natural* | *Conversion* | *Total* | *Rate* | *Adherents* | *%* | *Adherents* | *%* | *Adherents* | |
| **Christians** | **3,055,000** | **79.9** | **21,554,700** | **97.6** | **794,252** | **−2,242** | **792,010** | **3.13** | **25,261,900** | **97.6** | **29,474,800** | **97.6** | **49,632,500** | **96.4** |
| professing | 3,055,000 | 79.9 | 21,554,700 | 97.6 | 794,252 | −2,242 | 792,010 | 3.13 | 25,261,900 | 97.6 | 29,474,800 | 97.6 | 49,632,500 | 96.4 |
| Roman Catholics | 3,054,000 | 79.8 | 21,354,700 | 96.7 | 786,706 | −2,696 | 784,010 | 3.13 | 25,021,900 | 96.6 | 29,194,800 | 96.6 | 49,112,500 | 95.4 |
| Evangelical Catholics | 1,000 | 0.0 | 209,651 | 0.9 | 8,957 | 11,348 | 20,305 | 7.13 | 284,900 | 1.1 | 412,700 | 1.4 | 1,080,000 | 2.1 |
| Christo-pagans | 115,000 | 3.0 | 80,000 | 0.4 | 2,955 | −55 | 2,900 | 3.08 | 94,000 | 0.4 | 109,000 | 0.4 | 154,000 | 0.3 |
| Protestants | 1,000 | 0.0 | 200,000 | 0.9 | 7,546 | 454 | 8,000 | 3.33 | 240,000 | 0.9 | 280,000 | 0.9 | 520,000 | 1.0 |
| affiliated | 3,055,000 | 79.9 | 21,554,700 | 97.6 | 794,252 | −2,242 | 792,010 | 3.13 | 25,261,900 | 97.6 | 29,474,800 | 97.6 | 49,632,500 | 96.4 |
| disaffiliated | −4,000 | −0.1 | −203,000 | −0.9 | −7,860 | −1,840 | −9,700 | 3.88 | −250,000 | −1.0 | −300,000 | −1.0 | −500,000 | −1.0 |
| doubly-affiliated | −2,000 | −0.1 | −414,631 | −1.9 | −16,368 | −7,809 | −24,177 | 4.64 | −520,600 | −2.0 | −656,400 | −2.2 | −1,397,500 | −2.7 |
| total practising | 2,932,800 | *96* | 19,830,320 | *92* | 730,712 | −2,062 | 738,650 | 3.13 | 23,240,950 | *92* | 27,116,820 | *92* | 42,187,600 | *85* |
| non-practising | 122,200 | *4* | 1,724,380 | *8* | 63,540 | −180 | 63,360 | 3.13 | 2,020,950 | *8* | 2,357,980 | *8* | 7,444,900 | *15* |
| Roman Catholics | 3,058,980 | 80.0 | 21,757,580 | 98.6 | 801,788 | −4,386 | 797,402 | 3.13 | 25,501,600 | 98.5 | 29,731,600 | 98.4 | 49,920,000 | 97.0 |
| Catholic pentecostals | 0 | 0.0 | 3,000 | 0.0 | 2,200 | 17,500 | 19,700 | 28.14 | 70,000 | 0.3 | 200,000 | 0.7 | 900,000 | 1.7 |
| Protestants | 2,000 | 0.1 | 275,827 | 1.2 | 10,583 | 4,834 | 15,417 | 4.58 | 336,600 | 1.3 | 430,000 | 1.4 | 926,000 | 1.8 |
| Evangelicals | 2,000 | 0.1 | 210,000 | 1.0 | 8,112 | 3,988 | 12,100 | 4.69 | 258,000 | 1.0 | 331,000 | 1.1 | 720,000 | 1.4 |
| Neo-pentecostals | 0 | 0.0 | 200 | 0.0 | 31 | 149 | 180 | 18.00 | 1,000 | 0.0 | 2,000 | 0.0 | 10,000 | 0.0 |
| Colombian indigenous | 0 | 0.0 | 108,180 | 0.5 | 4,873 | 6,309 | 11,182 | 7.21 | 155,000 | 0.6 | 220,000 | 0.7 | 580,000 | 1.1 |
| Marginal Protestants | 20 | 0.0 | 23,644 | 0.1 | 975 | 661 | 1,636 | 5.28 | 31,000 | 0.1 | 40,000 | 0.1 | 90,000 | 0.2 |
| Orthodox | 0 | 0.0 | 4,000 | 0.0 | 148 | −8 | 140 | 2.98 | 4,700 | 0.0 | 5,400 | 0.0 | 8,000 | 0.0 |
| Anglicans | 0 | 0.0 | 2,000 | 0.0 | 72 | −2 | 70 | 3.04 | 2,300 | 0.0 | 2,700 | 0.0 | 4,000 | 0.0 |
| Catholics (non-Roman) | 0 | 0.0 | 1,100 | 0.0 | 41 | −1 | 40 | 3.08 | 1,300 | 0.0 | 1,500 | 0.0 | 2,000 | 0.0 |
| Tribal religionists | 765,000 | 20.0 | 280,000 | 1.3 | 9,778 | −4,578 | 5,200 | 1.67 | 311,000 | 1.2 | 332,000 | 1.1 | 360,000 | 0.7 |
| Non-religious | 3,000 | 0.1 | 99,000 | 0.4 | 4,465 | 5,305 | 9,770 | 6.88 | 142,000 | 0.5 | 196,700 | 0.7 | 1,003,000 | 1.9 |
| Muslims | 0 | 0.0 | 50,000 | 0.2 | 1,842 | −24 | 1,800 | 3.10 | 58,000 | 0.2 | 68,000 | 0.2 | 120,000 | 0.2 |
| Atheists | 1,000 | 0.0 | 44,000 | 0.2 | 1,792 | 808 | 2,600 | 4.56 | 57,000 | 0.2 | 70,000 | 0.2 | 200,000 | 0.4 |
| Baha'is | 0 | 0.0 | 24,300 | 0.1 | 975 | 395 | 1,370 | 4.42 | 31,000 | 0.1 | 38,000 | 0.1 | 90,000 | 0.2 |
| Spiritists | 1,000 | 0.0 | 10,000 | 0.0 | 346 | −146 | 200 | 1.82 | 11,000 | 0.0 | 12,000 | 0.0 | 20,000 | 0.0 |
| Jews | 0 | 0.0 | 10,000 | 0.0 | 368 | 2 | 370 | 3.16 | 11,700 | 0.0 | 13,700 | 0.0 | 23,000 | 0.0 |
| Buddhists | 0 | 0.0 | 1,000 | 0.0 | 35 | −15 | 20 | 1.82 | 1,100 | 0.0 | 1,200 | 0.0 | 1,500 | 0.0 |
| Chinese folk-religionists | 0 | 0.0 | 1,000 | 0.0 | 31 | −31 | 0 | 0.00 | 1,000 | 0.0 | 1,000 | 0.0 | 0 | 0.0 |
| Hindus | 0 | 0.0 | 0 | 0.0 | 94 | 506 | 600 | 20.00 | 3,000 | 0.0 | 6,000 | 0.0 | 10,000 | 0.0 |
| Other religionists | 0 | 0.0 | 1,000 | 0.0 | 40 | 20 | 60 | 4.62 | 1,300 | 0.0 | 1,600 | 0.0 | 4,000 | 0.0 |
| **Country's population** | **3,825,000** | **100.0** | **22,075,000** | **100.0** | **814,000** | **0** | **814,000** | **3.14** | **25,890,000** | **100.0** | **30,215,000** | **100.0** | **51,464,000** | **100.0** |

COLUMNS, ROWS. For meanings and definitions, see Codebook (Part 6). Note that, by definition, total 'Christians' = professing + crypto-Christians, which also = affiliated + nominal Christians. Percentages may not always total exactly, due to rounding.
CENSUSES. The religion question has not been asked in government censuses.

### NOTES ON RELIGIONS

ATHEISTS. 2 parties: Communist Party of Colombia (PCC) (legal; pro-Soviet): membership (1970) 10,000, with 1.4% of total popular vote in 1970; and Communist Party of Colombia Marxist-Leninist (pro-Chinese), membership 1,000.
BAHA'IS. Very rapid growth from 11 local spiritual assemblies (1964) to 161 (1973). Mass conversions have occurred in the Guajira in the extreme north.
BUDDHISTS. Chinese.
CATHOLIC PENTECOSTALS (or, Catholic charismatics). Totals (January 1974): 10,000 involved adults (over 15 years old). (1980) Over 10,000 charismatic prayer groups, 100,000 adults, total charismatic community including children, 200,000.
CHRISTO-PAGANS. Nominally-Catholic Amerindians who syncretize folk-Catholicism with traditional animism, including the Guanano (population 1,000).
COLOMBIAN INDIGENOUS. In about 40 denominations or groupings in 1970 (see Table 2).
COUNTRY'S POPULATION. During the undeclared civil war La Violencia of 1940–52, over 100,000 persons were killed including many Protestants.
DISAFFILIATED. This term is used here to describe persons who, although baptized Roman Catholics and therefore regarded by the Catholic Church as still affiliated to it (and hence enumerated as such), have recently withdrawn or disaffiliated themselves completely from Christianity and now profess publicly to be either non-religious (agnostics) or atheists. Because their statistics represent a duplication, they are shown in the table above as a negative quantity (with a minus sign).
DOUBLY-AFFILIATED. The term covers those affiliated to, or claimed by, both the Catholic Church and also a church termed Evangélica by the state (Protestant, Colombian indigenous, marginal Protestant or Anglican), i.e. baptized Catholics who have recently become Evangelicals or others. Because their statistics represent a duplication, they are shown in the table as a negative quantity (with a minus sign).
EVANGELICAL CATHOLICS. This term is used here to describe persons who are affiliated to churches termed by the state Evangélica (Protestant, or Colombian indigenous, or marginal Protestant, or Anglican churches), but who are regarded by state and society as, or who profess publicly to be, Roman Catholics.
HINDUS. Converts since 1972 to the Divine Light Mission from India and the USA (led by Guru Maharaj Ji); young people in Cali and other cities. ISKCON (Hare Krishna) also operates a centre, and in 1975 the Theosophical Society had 9 Lodges with 138 members.
JEWS. Greeks, Turks, Germans and other Europeans since 1918; in large cities; 4 synagogues and 3 communities (Ashkenazi, Sefardi, Eastern).
MUSLIMS. Arab immigrants from the Middle East, including numerous Palestinians.
NEO-PENTECOSTALS. Charismatics within the non-Pentecostal Protestant denominations, especially the Interamerican Churches (OMS), Presbyterian Church (UPUSA), and those linked with LAM, WEC and CMA.
OTHER RELIGIONISTS. Adherents of smaller religions and cults including Rosicrucians (4 AMORC centres).
PRACTISING CHRISTIANS. 1970 (ICODES): 63% of Catholics attend mass at least once weekly; 67% pray to God daily, 24% never pray.
TRIBAL RELIGIONISTS. In 1850, Amerindians numbered over a million (almost all then being tribal religionists) and made up 50% of the entire nation, falling to 2.5% (390,000) by 1950 and 1.6% by 1970. Of the 360,000 lowland or jungle Amerindians in over 50 tribes left in the interior in 1970, a high proportion were still animists. The largest tribe today, the Guajiro (100,000), remains 80% traditionalist. Others include the Arhuaco (4,000), Coreguaje, Cuna, Macu, Barasano and Tatuyo.

**NON-CHRISTIAN RELIGIONS. Amerindian tribal religions** are practised by a number of unevangelized lowland and jungle tribes in the interior, including the Arhuaco, Coreguaje, Cuna, Guajiro, Macu, Barasano and Tatuyo.

**Baha'i** has grown very rapidly since 1964, to 161 local spiritual assemblies by 1973.

**Judaism,** with about 10,000 adherents, is present in the larger urban centres of Bogotá, Medellín, Cali and Barranquilla. There are 4 Jewish synagogues and 3 communities (Ashkenazi, Sefardi and Eastern), with members of Greek, Turkish, German and Central European origin who arrived after World War I. Of university students 2% are Jewish. Several Jewish sports and social clubs are active, as well as the organizations B'nai B'rith and WIZO.

**Other religions** include Islam, Hinduism (the Divine Light Mission since 1972) and spiritism. In 1975 a first World Congress of Sorcery was held in Bogotá.

## CHRISTIANITY

CATHOLIC CHURCH. Spanish explorers touched northwestern South America in 1499, and it became known as New Granada with headquarters at Bogotá. The first Catholic diocese was established in 1534 and the first seminary in 1582. Encomiendas (commissions) were established and made responsible for organizing the material welfare of the Indians, and peaceful relations with them, but because of their abuses missionaries often found themselves in conflict with the encomienda system. A severe decline in the number of clergy took place with the declaration of Independence in 1819 and the dissolution of the patronage system with Spain. Six episcopal sees were vacant by 1813. The government's usurpation of the right of patronage was rejected by Rome, and religious persecution increased during the next decades. By 1853 separation of church and state was established and civil marriage and divorce introduced. In 1861 all church property was appropriated by the government and church officials continued to be exiled; and 2 years later a new constitution was promulgated which disregarded the juridical personality of the church. Negotiations were renewed with the Holy See in 1878 and a concordat eventually completed in 1887.

In Colombia where the church is reputed to be

the most uniformly conservative of all Roman Catholic churches in Latin America, the specific action of the church is carried on in good measure by the need to conserve, defend and extend what is frequently called the Catholic 'fact', that is the existence of a Colombian people who are considered to be almost 100% Catholic. Thus episcopal documents do not speak of the faith as being the free and conscious response of a person but insist on a collective understanding of 'customs', 'traditions' and the 'Christian heritage'. Another criterion of church action is protection of the people's faith against errors and deviations from religious conduct, and the importance given to large meetings and massive concentrations of the faithful, for motives which are detached from the concerns of the People of God themselves.

Several concrete examples of this situation can be given. The first concerns the International Eucharistic Congress of 1965. Shortly beforehand in April 1965, the metropolitan archbishops published a declaration listing alleged evils of the country against which the forthcoming Congress should serve as a protection; this list varied from 'comic programmes on the radio' to the advance of Communism identified as 'the most serious peril for religion and the country'. Secondly, in 1958 Marian congresses were organized in every parish in Colombia specifically to combat crime, violence and guerrilla warfare. The same objects had earlier been the case also in the National Marian Congress of 1954, the procession of the statue of the Virgin of Fatima in 1950, and the National Eucharistic Congress of 1949.

On the other hand, it was at Medellín in Colombia that the Second General Conference of CELAM took place in 1968, which made a major impact on the Catholic Church in Latin America and provided the basis for change in its life and attitudes. At Medellín the Latin American bishops affirmed their intention of involving the church in the life of the people and seeking their full liberation. It was decided there that the church's preaching, catechesis and liturgy should reflect the communal nature of Christianity, and should denounce class conflicts, colonialism and repression as affronts to the gospel. A few years later, however, the Colombian bishops provided active support for those opposed to a theology of liberation and rejected a catechetical plan patterned after the directives of Medellín. The archbishop of Bogotá even prevented Dom Helder Câmara, a radical fellow-prelate from Recife in Brazil, from speaking in Colombia. This situation resulted in the creation of several opposition movements within the church, the most renowned being Golconda, founded in Buenaventura in 1968 by about 50 priests, which had drawn in numerous laity also before going out of existence in 1970 to be succeeded by other smaller less-structured bodies. All of these groups have in common a socialist orientation and opposition to privilege in the church and to its pre-conciliar structures.

A majority of the institutions of CELAM are located in Medellín, including its general secretariat, its only pastoral institute and a large number of its departments. The same is true for CLAR, which serves a similar function for religious personnel in Latin America.

With regard to individual faith and practice, a 1970 survey found that 63% of all Catholics claim to attend mass at least once a week, 67% pray to God daily, and 66% pray to the Virgin Mary; only 24% do not pray at all. This is in marked contrast to the situation in 1951 when only 10% of the Colombian people were said to fulfil the minimum requirements of Catholicism. Since then there has been a resurgence of conservative Catholic practice.

Colombia is characterized by a severe scarcity of priests. In 1969, 2,873 diocesan priests (68% of the total) worked in the 9 archdioceses and 29 dioceses which cover 35% of the country and 92% of the population; 1,363 religious priests (32%) were responsible for the remaining 18 mission vicariates and prefectures.

Most priests and religious are native Colombians, although the first Indian priest, of the Paez people, was not ordained until 1973. In 1970–71, 55 of the prelates were from Colombia and 7 from other countries.

PROTESTANT CHURCHES. The first Protestant missionary arrived in Colombia in 1825, an agent of the British and Foreign Bible Society, and by the second half of the century the society had published the first New Testament in South America. In 1856 the Presbyterian Church, USA sent its first missionary to Bogotá. For many years Presbyterians were the only Protestant workers in Colombia and achieved renown through their well-developed schools and medical centres. However, church membership has remained small compared with more recent arrivals. The Evangelical Alliance Mission (TEAM) opened work in 1906 in both Venezuela and then eastern Colombia, while the Gospel Missionary Union extended its work from neighbouring Ecuador to Colombia in 1908, beginning a printing press and a monthly publication. The Christian and Missionary Alliance entered Colombia from Ecuador in 1923. Its bookstore in Cali supplies 80% of all literature sold in Colombia's Evangelical bookshops.

With the exception of Cumberland Presbyterians (1925), Adventists (1921) and Salvation Army (1929),

the remaining Protestant churches all appeared after 1930. The United Pentecostal Church had the largest membership until 1970, followed by the International Church of the Foursquare Gospel, which is also Pentecostal, and the Seventh-day Adventists. Protestantism is especially strong among the large Negro population on the islands of San Andres and Providencia, which are located near Nicaragua, 400 miles from Colombia.

With the close alliance at times between the Catholic Church and the Colombian government, Protestantism has been as suspect as Communism, and Protestant missions consistently met with frequent harassment until recent years. Only when the Liberal party came to power in 1930 did Protestant missions receive government recognition. The influx of Protestant missionaries during the period of the Liberal Party, particularly during World War II, was immediately followed by the undeclared civil war La Violencia during 1948–52 when the Conservative Party returned to power. More than 100,000 persons were killed, including many Protestants, and in addition 270 Protestant schools were closed and 60 churches destroyed including three-quarters of all churches of the Gospel Missionary Union. During this period, however, Protestantism grew rapidly from 7,908 baptized believers in 1948 to 11,958 in 1953 and to 33,156 in 1960. In recent years the atmosphere has improved markedly, and Evangelicals are given increasing freedom to hold open-air meetings, street parades, city-wide campaigns and radio broadcasts. As one result, Protestant growth today is rapid, with a multiplication of small churches and out-stations by conservative and Pentecostal churches, which are particularly successful in the large shanty town areas of urban centres.

INDIGENOUS CHURCHES. A number of independent, mostly pentecostal, churches have been formed in Colombia since World War II, but all remain small except for a massive schism in 1970 of Colombian pentecostals rejecting centralized control from the USA headquarters of the United Pentecostal Church. The new body has developed extensive overseas mission work by Colombians.

CHURCH AND STATE. Two juridical tests provide the foundation for defining the relationship between church and state in Colombia: the constitution of 1886, frequently revised; and the new concordat signed on 12 July 1973 between the government and the Holy See replacing the concordat of 31 December 1887 and all other conventions later signed by the 2 parties, notably the Convention concerning Missions of 29 January 1953 intended to last for 25 years.

**Iglesia Católica en Colombia.** *Below.* An Andean Amerindian funeral procession near Guambia township, Cauca region. Many customs are characterized by christo-paganism. *Above.* Wedding reception at La Campana community house in Guambia township.

Argentinian evangelist Luis Palau addresses 3,000 believers in Capital Plaza, Bogotá, before 19 October 1977 Presidential 'Banquet of Hope' that day.

communists, Torres ultimately requested lay status for himself. He was killed in February 1966 by Colombian forces fighting a Castroite guerrilla organization the Army of National Liberation (ELN). He had joined the movement 4 months earlier, convinced that armed revolt was the only hope for social change.

Torres was influential in leading other priests and laymen to enter the ranks of the ELN. Several of these have been captured by the Colombian army. Domingo Lain, a Spanish priest expelled from Colombia in 1969 who later returned clandestinely to a position of leadership within the ELN, was killed in February 1974 during a clash between the army and the ELN.

In 1975 increasingly frequent accusations were made by progressivist Catholic groups of priests and religious personnel to the effect that certain North American Protestant missions, the Evangelical Confederation of Colombia and various sectors of the Catholic Church, especially the papal nuncio, were linked to the CIA (Central Intelligence Agency, USA). The nunciature was burned to the ground during student demonstrations in April 1975.

**INTERDENOMINATIONAL ORGANIZATIONS.** Twenty Protestant churches belong to the Evangelical Confederation of Colombia (Confederación Evangélica de Colombia) begun in 1950, with a Presbyterian as secretary. The Ministerial Association of Bogotá, composed of both Protestant and Catholic clergy, was founded in 1970 for the purpose of dialogue and prayer.

**BROADCASTING.** The many commercial stations all accept religious programmes. There were also 42 Catholic radio stations in 1975 as contrasted with 6 in 1970. A Catholic national institution called Acción Cultural Popular (ACPO) promotes basic education, as well as conventional news and entertainment programmes. ACPO's radio schools have a national network, Escuelas Radiofónicas de Sutatenza, with 4 radio stations, dedicated to the education of farming communities. In Bogotá there is a production centre for these stations, Técnicas de Comunicación para el Desarrollo, which produces radio programmes for education, culture and entertainment. ACPO, which is a member of ICRA in Rome, also publishes a magazine, *El Campesino*, and maintains an important publishing house. For Catholics, Colombia is a member of UNDA. Protestants have a rather large number of radio programmes on different stations and one theologically-conservative radio station, Nuevo Continente, in Bogotá.

The constitution (Article 53) guarantees freedom of conscience, declares that 'No-one will be disturbed because of his religious opinions nor obliged to profess belief nor to observe practices contrary to his conscience', and ensures also 'freedom to all religions which are not contrary to Christian morals or to the law'.

The new concordat, of 32 articles, continues to accord the Catholic Church a privileged status, although this is formulated in language more adapted to the modern era. Certain former privileges have been removed. Whereas Article 1 of the former concordat stated that 'The Roman Catholic Apostolic Religion is the religion of Colombia', Article 1 of the new concordat expresses it in these terms: 'The State, in view of the traditional Catholic sentiment of the Colombian nation, considers the Roman Catholic Apostolic Religion as an essential element of the common welfare and of the integral development of the national community. The State guarantees to the Catholic Church and to those who belong to it the full enjoyment of their religious rights without prejudice to the just religious liberty of other confessions and their members, as well as those of every citizen.' The most significant change of the new agreement is the ending of the 1953 missions treaty which gave to religious orders exclusive rights in evangelization and education in mission territories, ignoring the rights of Protestant and other missionaries.

Article 7 recognizes the validity of marriages within the church, although it is understood that these marriages must be recorded also in a civil registry. A more controversial subject is dealt with in Article 9 which provides an opening for legislation making civil marriage possible for Catholics without their having to renounce their faith. Thus Article 9 opens the way to divorce for Colombians who are not married in religious ceremonies. Among other provisions, the Catholic Church is guaranteed 'full freedom and independence' (Article 2); the government is to make available public funds for the

support of Catholic educational institutions (Article 11); Catholic instruction is to be offered in all public schools (Article 12); canonical law, although independent of civil law, is to be 'respected by the authorities of the Republic'; the Catholic Church is to be the beneficiary of a juridical personality, as are dioceses, religious communities and other entities permitted such by canon law; and the exemption from taxes on all property, which the Catholic Church previously profited from, is to be removed, except in the case of worship places, diocesan curias, dwellings of bishops and priests, and seminaries.

The signing of the concordat provoked considerable controversy among the public and impassioned debate in parliament, the House of Representatives finally approving it at the end of 1974 by 111 votes to 39. The opponents of the new concordat, especially the Evangelical Confederation of Colombia, were especially critical of the articles concerning marriage and generally all matters that they considered constituted an 'infringement of religious liberty'. Many Catholics are also sceptical concerning the real changes brought by the new text and hold that a concordat is no longer necessary. In January 1975 tax exemption was extended to Protestant churches and Jewish synagogues.

There is no government ministry of religious affairs in Colombia, nor obligation for churches or religions to be registered.

In recent years, an increasing number of Catholic priests and militant laymen, especially trade union members, have clashed with the dominant oligarchy and that part of the Catholic hierarchy closely linked with it. The most celebrated of these figures was Camilo Torres, chaplain of students at the University of Bogotá in 1958. Trying various non-political movements of social action, he decided to enter the political arena as the only sphere offering possibilities for fundamental social change. Disavowed by cardinal Concha for having founded the United Front, a movement aiming to regroup all forces on the left, including

**BIBLIOGRAPHY**
*Camilo Torres.* Sondeos No. 5. Cuernavaca (Mexico): CIDOC, 1966. 377p.
*Directorio de la Iglesia en Colombia, 1969.* Bogotá: Departamento de Sociología, 1969. (Roman Catholic).
*Directorio Evangélico y Calendario de Oración de Colombia, 1975–76.* Medellín: Tipografía Unión, 1975. (Annual).
*Explosion of people evangelism.* D. C. Palmer. Wheaton, IL: Moody, 1977. 91p. (Pentecostal growth).
*Guia de las Iglesias Evangélicas de Colombia.* Medellín: Retiro Nacional de Pastores, 1971.
*Historia del Cristianismo Evangélico en Colombia.* F. Ordoñez. Medellín: Tipografía Unión, 1956.
*La Iglesia en Colombia: estructuras eclesiásticas.* G. Pérez & I. Wust. Bogotá: Centro de Investigaciones Sociales, 1961. 194p.
'The Catholic Church and political development in Colombia'. S. J. Brzezinski. Dissertation, University of Illinois (USA), 1973. 241p.
*The Colombian concordat: in the light of recent trends in Catholic thought concerning church-state relations and religious liberty.* G. Castillo Cardenas. Sondeos No. 22. Cuernavaca (Mexico): CIDOC, 1968. 140p.
'The growth of the Pentecostal churches in Colombia'. D. C. Palmer. Thesis, Trinity Evangelical Divinity School (USA), 1972. 196p.
*The persecution of Protestant Christians in Colombia, 1948–58, with an investigation of its background and causes.* J. E. Goff. Sondeos No. 23. Cuernavaca (Mexico): CIDOC, 1968. 492p.

TABLE 2.   ORGANIZED CHURCHES AND DENOMINATIONS IN COLOMBIA

| Official name 1 | Begun 2 | Type 3 | Counc 4 | Congs 5 | Adults 6 | Affiliated 7 | Names, notes, and other statistics (see Codebook) 8 |
|---|---|---|---|---|---|---|---|
| Alianza Cristiana y Misionera | 1923 | P Hol | xF..C | 99 | 5,731 | 10,000 | *ACM. M=*CMA,MC(USA). 1969, pentecostal movement. 23 schools. 2k,34f,G=13%pa,2s. |
| Asambleas de Dios de Colombia | 1930 | P Pe2 | ZP..C | 221 | 8,756 | 20,500 | *Assemblies of God.* M=AoG(USA). Since 1961, G=30%. 198m,10x,18f,3s(181),500Y,1059z. |
| Asoc de Iglesias Ev de C del Oriente | 1906 | P int | xM... | 99 | 1,207 | 2,400 | *Association of Chs of Eastern C.* Alianza Ev. 1923,M=TEAM. 10n,9x,33f,G=10.8%pa,1s(75),157Y. |
| Asociación de Iglesias Ev del Caribe | 1937 | P ind | xN..C | 390 | 3,100 | 12,000 | *Federation of Ev Ministries.* M=LAM(USA). 7n,1x,23f,G=20.9%pa,1p,2s,W=50%,734Y. |
| Asoc de Iglesias Ev del Magdalena | 1941 | P int | xM..C | 79 | 600 | 2,000 | *Assoc of Chs of Magdalena.* M=EUSA(UK,USA). 4n,2x,30f,G=11%pa,1p(10),W=28%,107Y. |
| Asoc de Iglesias Ev Interamericanas | 1943 | P Hol | xF..C | 120 | 2,215 | 11,215 | *Assoc of Interamerican Chs.* M=OMS(Interamerican M) (USA). 8n,40f,G=19%pa,1s,311Y,158z. |
| Asoc Nacional de Iglesias Cristianas | c1965 | I ind | ..... | 4 | 119 | 300 | *National Association of Christian Churches.* Small Colombian indigenous grouping. |
| Congregaciones Luteranas | 1949 | P Lut | L.... | 10 | 530 | 1,507 | *Congregación San Mateo,* Bogotá (Germans, 957); San Martín, Cali(550). 1x,11Yy,85z. |
| Convención Bautista Colombiana | 1941 | P Bap | T...h | 118 | 5,791 | 10,000 | *Colombian Baptist Conv.* M=SBC(USA). SS=11,095. 61n,62f,G=5.5%pa,1H,7h,1s,900Y. |
| Corporación Pro-Cultural | | P ind | ..... | 1 | 30 | 50 | *CPC. Corporation for Culture.* Small independent foreign mission, Bucaramanga. 1k. |
| Cruzada Hispanoamericana | 1937 | P int | x.... | | 350 | 1,000 | M=Spanish America Inland Mission(USA). Decline since 1966. |
| Ejército de Salvación | 1929 | P Sal | xw... | 1 | 50 | 100 | *Salvation Army.* Work began 1929, later discontinued officially. |

*Continued opposite*

*Table 2 – continued*

| Official name 1 | Begun 2 | Type 3 | Counc 4 | Congs 5 | Adults 6 | Affiliated 7 | Names, notes, and other statistics (see Codebook) 8 | | | | |
|---|---|---|---|---|---|---|---|---|---|---|---|
| Embajadores Cristianos de Colombia | c1950 | I pe2 | ..... | 22 | 140 | 500 | *Christian Ambassadors of Colombia. Asambleas de Jesucristo. Assemblies of JC.* 5m. | | | | |
| Hermanos | | P EBr | x.... | 40 | 2,000 | 4,000 | *Exclusive (Plymouth) Brethren.* Group: Kelly-Continental (links with UK, USA, NZ). | | | | |
| Hermanos en Cristo | c1933 | P CBr | x...C | 15 | 268 | 1,000 | *Christian Brethren, Plymouth (Open) Brethren.* M=CMML(USA,UK,NZ). HQ Pasto. 43f. | | | | |
| Hermanos Menonitas | 1943 | P Men | GF..C | | 538 | 1,500 | *Conferencia de los HM.* M=Mennonite Brethren Ch(USA). HQ Cali. 10f,1h,1k,1p. | | | | |
| Iglesia Adventista del Séptimo Día | 1921 | P Adv | x.... | 131 | 30,654 | 60,000 | *Seventh-day Adventists, Colombia-Venezuela UM.* 35nx,20f,165mw,6r,427t,2347Y. | | | | |
| Iglesia Anglicana Ortodoxa | 1972 | I Ang | xT... | 1 | 100 | 130 | *Anglican Orthodox Church.* Schism ex Episcopal Church. M=AOC(USA). 2n. | | | | |
| Iglesia Bautista Independiente | 1939 | P Bap | x.... | 1 | 23 | 100 | *Independent Baptist Ch.* M=ABWE(USA), In Leticia, Amazones. 2f,1h. | | | | |
| **Iglesia Católica en Colombia:** | 1512 | R Lat | B.L.R | 2,031 | 11,530,400 | 21,757,580 | *Catholic Ch.* C=46+2+128. 5p,38q,15s(1378),W=63%. | 5030nx, | 1250m, | 17285w, | 673635Yy. |
| M Barranquilla | 1932 | R Lat | Bs | 54 | 413,000 | 780,000 | 90% urban, highly industrialized. 1s. | 126 | 55 | 580 | 28800 |
| D Santa Marta | 1534 | R Lat | Bs | 33 | 273,000 | 515,000 | 20% urban, 50% industrialized. Tourism. | 54 | 4 | 147 | 20537 |
| D Valledupar | 1952 | R Lat | Bs | 22 | 165,000 | 312,000 | Very low priest/people ratio, 1:12000. P=14%. | 26 | 4 | 92 | 11422 |
| M Bogotá | 1564 | R Lat | Bs | 176 | 1,166,000 | 2,200,000 | Ecclesiastical centre for Latin America. 1s. | 921 | 275 | 4074 | 52914 |
| D Espinal | 1957 | R Lat | Bs | 38 | 212,000 | 400,000 | Rural, poor, Very traditional religiosity. | 55 | 4 | 80 | 4335 |
| D Facatativá | 1962 | R Lat | Bs | 33 | 185,000 | 350,000 | Rural, impoverished, traditional religiosity. | 68 | 21 | 190 | 10287 |
| D Girardot | 1956 | R Lat | Bs | 42 | 239,300 | 451,482 | Rural, poor, Priest/people 1:7000. | 47 | 5 | 304 | 8801 |
| D Ibagué (M from 1974) | 1900 | R Lat | Bs | 49 | 395,000 | 745,000 | 20% urban, industrial. Priest/people 1:7000, 1s. | 105 | 20 | 279 | 16502 |
| D Villavicencio | 1904 | R Lat | Bs | 24 | 136,100 | 256,760 | Mission zone. Very poor. High % Black. | 43 | 8 | 82 | 11265 |
| D Zipaquirá | 1951 | R Lat | Bs | 47 | 184,700 | 348,467 | Rural, with industrialization beginning. | 81 | 14 | 237 | 9920 |
| M Cali | 1910 | R Lat | Bs | 64 | 516,400 | 974,385 | 90% urban, industrialized, Mass immigration. W=10%. | 219 | 47 | 991 | 36186 |
| D Buga | 1966 | R Lat | Bs | 29 | 345,000 | 650,000 | 20% urban, half industrialized. | 82 | 12 | 250 | 10830 |
| D Cartago | 1962 | R Lat | Bs | 34 | 228,000 | 430,000 | Rural, poor, traditional religiosity. | 54 | 0 | 163 | 9418 |
| D Palmira | 1952 | R Lat | Bs | 28 | 149,000 | 281,000 | Half industrialized. Adjacent to Cali. | 56 | 23 | 152 | 10214 |
| M Cartagena | 1534 | R Lat | Bs | 49 | 297,000 | 560,000 | 20% urban, half industrialized; touristic center. | 67 | 14 | 320 | 16250 |
| D Magangué | 1969 | R Lat | Bs | 20 | 155,000 | 292,000 | Mission zone, high % Black. | 27 | 2 | 91 | 23250 |
| D Montería | 1954 | R Lat | Bs | 30 | 348,000 | 657,000 | Mission zone, Many Blacks. | 53 | 8 | 238 | 19541 |
| D Sincelejo | 1969 | R Lat | Bs | 22 | 182,000 | 343,000 | Mission zone, Very poor. High % Black. 1:13000. | 26 | 0 | 169 | 9893 |
| PN Alto Sinú | 1969 | R Lat | Bs | 7 | 62,000 | 117,000 | Mission zone. Poor. High % Black. 1:12000. M=CMP. | 10 | 1 | 25 | 2492 |
| M Manizales | 1900 | R Lat | Bs | 65 | 289,000 | 545,000 | 20% urban, half industrialized. 1s. | 224 | 47 | 625 | 21020 |
| D Armenia | 1952 | R Lat | Bs | 22 | 237,000 | 448,000 | 20% urban. Small dense diocese. | 64 | 22 | 269 | 11034 |
| D Pereira | 1952 | R Lat | Bs | 47 | 318,000 | 600,000 | 20% urban. Densely populated. | 126 | 10 | 251 | 15266 |
| M Medellín | 1868 | R Lat | Bs | 168 | 851,800 | 1,607,183 | 90% urban. Site of 1968 CELAM 'Vatican II'. 2s. | 615 | 335 | 2898 | 54775 |
| D Antioquia | 1804 | R Lat | Bs | 32 | 183,000 | 346,000 | Rural, impoverished, traditional religiosity. | 60 | 0 | 160 | 13430 |
| D Jericó | 1915 | R Lat | Bs | 28 | 127,000 | 240,000 | Rural, poor. Sufficient clergy. | 76 | 4 | 240 | 7839 |
| D Santa Rosa de Osos | 1917 | R Lat | Bs | 74 | 224,600 | 423,775 | Rural, impoverished, traditional religiosity. 1s. | 162 | 39 | 352 | 15153 |
| D Sonsón-Rionegro | 1957 | R Lat | Bs | 33 | 211,000 | 398,110 | Rural. Industry growing. Bishop a charismatic. | 137 | 69 | 423 | 12788 |
| M Nueva Pamplona | 1835 | R Lat | Bs | 25 | 85,000 | 159,500 | Rural, very poor. Traditional religiosity. 1p,1s. | 69 | 0 | 62 | 5228 |
| D Barrancabermeja | 1928 | R Lat | Bs | 28 | 173,000 | 327,000 | 20% urban, half industrialized. | 45 | 5 | 153 | 10945 |
| D Bucaramanga (M from 1974) | 1952 | R Lat | Bs | 64 | 306,900 | 579,118 | 20% urban, half industrialized. 1p,1s. | 152 | 11 | 447 | 19954 |
| D Cúcuta | 1956 | R Lat | Bs | 26 | 178,000 | 335,000 | 20% urban, half industrialized. 10. | 62 | 22 | 260 | 8115 |
| D Ocaña | 1962 | R Lat | Bs | 33 | 145,000 | 274,000 | Rural, impoverished. Traditional religiosity. | 48 | 0 | 73 | 10520 |
| PN Bertrania en el Catatumbo | 1951 | R Lat | Bs | 7 | 51,000 | 96,000 | Mission zone. Poor. White settlers, Indians. M=OP. | 7 | 0 | 11 | 1636 |
| M Popayán | 1546 | R Lat | Bs | 57 | 323,000 | 610,000 | Rural, poor, very traditional religiosity. 1p,1s. | 99 | 23 | 350 | 28470 |
| D Garzón | 1900 | R Lat | Bs | 52 | 258,000 | 486,820 | Rural, impoverished. 1s. | 89 | 4 | 212 | 16624 |
| D Ipiales | 1964 | R Lat | Bs | 39 | 170,000 | 320,000 | Rural, very poor area, on Ecuador border. | 61 | 14 | 100 | 15309 |
| D Pasto | 1859 | R Lat | Bs | 48 | 194,000 | 366,024 | Rural, impoverished, traditional religiosity. 1s. | 111 | 36 | 394 | 11274 |
| M Tunja | 1880 | R Lat | Bs | 92 | 322,000 | 608,000 | Rural, poor, traditional religiosity. 1p, 1s. | 210 | 11 | 280 | 3184 |
| D Duitama | 1955 | R Lat | Bs | 47 | 223,000 | 420,000 | Rural, with beginnings of industrialization. | 93 | 5 | 183 | 13840 |
| D Socorro & San Gil | 1895 | R Lat | Bs | 71 | 221,200 | 417,356 | Mission zone. Extremely impoverished. 1s. | 104 | 1 | 352 | 13514 |
| VA Arauca | 1915 | R Lat | Pmxy | 13 | 77,000 | 145,000 | Orinoco. White settlers, bilingual Indians. P=9%. | 25 | 2 | 35 | 3585 |
| VA Buenaventura | 1952 | R Lat | Pmxy | 8 | 74,000 | 140,000 | Humid, unhealthy, along Pacific. High % Black. P=27%. | 19 | 2 | 49 | 3530 |
| VA Casanare | 1893 | R Lat | Porsa | 14 | 52,000 | 98,000 | Orinoco. White settlers, bilingual Indians. P=16%. | 21 | 1 | 55 | 2927 |
| VA Florencia | 1951 | R Lat | Pimc | 22 | 102,000 | 193,000 | Amazon. White settlers, bilingual Indians. P=46%. | 36 | 6 | 82 | 7291 |
| VA Istmina | 1908 | R Lat | Pmxy | 16 | 78,700 | 148,500 | Humid, unhealthy. Pacific coast. High % Black. P=8%. | 25 | 4 | 112 | 2968 |
| VA Quibdó | 1928 | R Lat | Pcmf | 11 | 52,700 | 99,500 | Humid, unhealthy, coastal. High % Black. P=58%. | 27 | 3 | 52 | 3895 |
| VA Riohacha | 1905 | R Lat | Pofmc | 7 | 42,000 | 80,000 | Atlantic littoral in northeast. High % Black. P=17%. | 18 | 3 | 55 | 5880 |
| VA Sibundoy | 1904 | R Lat | Pcssr | 10 | 41,600 | 78,500 | Amazon basin. 1969, OFM accused of 'theocracy'. | 18 | 9 | 49 | 4508 |
| VA Tumaco | 1927 | R Lat | Pocd | 9 | 105,800 | 199,600 | Ecuador frontier, coastal. High % Black. 1:10500. | 19 | 0 | 49 | 7172 |
| PA Ariari | 1964 | R Lat | Psdb | 22 | 61,000 | 115,000 | Arid. 8% Protestants. 1,500 spiritists. P=10%. | 16 | 5 | 14 | 4623 |
| PA Guapí | 1954 | R Lat | Pofm | 4 | 36,000 | 67,000 | Humid, unhealthy, Pacific coast. High % Black. P=27%. | 11 | 6 | 24 | 544 |
| PA Leticia | 1951 | R Lat | Pofmc | 3 | 10,000 | 18,000 | Virgin forest, Amazon basin. Southeast. P=58%. | 11 | 3 | 37 | 972 |
| PA Mitú | 1949 | R Lat | Pmxy | 11 | 18,000 | 35,000 | Largest diocese (167,785 km2). Area 73% Catholic. | 16 | 7 | 38 | 480 |
| PA San Andrés & Providencia | 1912 | R Lat | Pofmc | 7 | 7,000 | 14,000 | Caribbean isles. 67% Catholic, 30% Protestant, P=27%. | 10 | 18 | 32 | 452 |
| PA Tierradentro | 1921 | R Lat | Pcm | 6 | 23,600 | 44,500 | Dry region in the interior. P=29%. | 12 | 1 | 46 | 1434 |
| PA Vichada | 1956 | R Lat | Psmm | 9 | 6,000 | 12,000 | Orinoco. White settlers, Indians. 44% RC. P=10%. | 12 | 5 | 24 | 635 |
| Iglesia Católica Liberal | | C Lib | x.... | 2 | 50 | 100 | *Liberal Catholic Ch.* Split ex Swedenborgians. Province of M=LCC(USA). 1 bishop, 2n. | | | | |
| Iglesia Cristiana del Norte | c1950 | I pen | ..... | | 395 | 1,000 | *ICN. Christian Ch. of the North.* Indigenous pentecostals. HQ Bogotá. | | | | |
| Iglesia Cristiana Elim | 1964 | P Pe2 | Z.... | 1 | 81 | 200 | *Elim Christian Ch.* M=EMA(USA). One congregation in Bogotá. 7f. | | | | |
| Iglesia Cristiana Pentecostés | c1965 | I pen | ..... | 9 | 457 | 1,000 | *Pentecost Christian Ch.* 9 churches in Cundinamarca, Meta, Santanders. | | | | |
| Iglesia Cruzada Evangélica Colombiana | 1933 | P Pen | xF..C | 144 | 1,717 | 3,600 | Pentecostal. M=WEC,CHC,CoN. 45% Indian. 40n,30x,G=8%pa,1H,1j,1p,1s(40),W=53%,277Y. | | | | |
| Iglesia de Cristo Pentecostal | c1965 | I pen | x.... | 9 | 270 | 700 | *Pentecostal Ch of Christ.* Indigenous. 9 congregations in Cundinamarca. | | | | |
| Iglesia de Dios en Colombia | 1954 | P Pe3 | ZF... | 34 | 1,239 | 2,500 | *Ch of God in Colombia.* M=CoG(Cleveland)(USA). 24n,G=17.7%pa,1s(4),W=95%,31Y,50z. | | | | |
| Iglesia de Dios Pentecostal | | P Pe2 | Z.... | | 410 | 1,000 | *Pentecostal Ch of God.* M=PCG(Puerto Rico, also USA). Classical Pentecostals. | | | | |
| Iglesia de JC de los Santos de los UD | c1967 | M LdS | x.... | | 1,500 | 3,394 | *Latter-day Saints. Mormons.* M=CJCLdS(USA). Indians. Rapid growth, 11.8%pa. 50f. | | | | |
| Iglesia del Evangelio Cuadrangular | 1942 | P Pe2 | ZF..C | 353 | 23,459 | 70,000 | *Int Ch of the Foursquare Gospel.* M=ICFG(USA). 250nm,7f,G=14%pa,9'p(239),W=29%,742Y | | | | |
| Iglesia Episcopal; D Colombia | 1963 | A Cen | aw.JC | 12 | 1,200 | 2,000 | *Episcopal Ch. In* PECUSA, Province IX. 50% local, 50% USA. 4n,4x,W=36%,25Yy. | | | | |
| Iglesia Ev Cristiana Casa de Oración | c1963 | I pen | ..... | | 134 | 300 | *House of Prayer Mission.* Indigenous Colombain pentecostals. | | | | |
| Iglesia Ev Cristiana Independiente | | I ind | ..... | 7 | 50 | 150 | *Independent Ev Christian Ch. Assoc of Ev Christian Chs.* HQ Bucaramanga. | | | | |
| Iglesia Evangélica La Hermosa | | I ind | ..... | 1 | 25 | 100 | *The Beautiful Evangelical Church.* Small local indigenous congregation. | | | | |
| Iglesia Ev Luterana, Sinodo de Colombia | 1936 | P Lut | L...C | 12 | 800 | 1,055 | *Lutheran Ch.* 1944, M=ALC(USA). 1948–57 severe persecution. 5n,7x,8f,G=4.5%pa,lu,18Yy. | | | | |
| Iglesia Ev Menonita de Colombia | 1943 | P Men | G...C | 8 | 300 | 850 | *Mennonite Ch.* M=General Conf MC(USA). 2n,3x,13f,G=7.5%pa,1h,1p(2),W=41%,29Y,20z. | | | | |
| Iglesia Evangélica Nacional Colombiana | c1965 | I pen | ..... | 4 | 165 | 400 | *Colombian National Ev Ch.* Indigenous body in Cundinamarca and Caldas. | | | | |
| Iglesia Evangélica Pentecostal | | I pe2 | x.... | 1 | 135 | 300 | *Ev Pentecostal Ch.* Related to IEP from Chile. HQ Bogotá. 6f. | | | | |
| Iglesia Metodista Wesleyana de C | 1940 | P Hol | VF..C | 51 | 450 | 2,250 | M=Wesleyan Ch(USA). Medellín. 6n,2x,7f,G=4.6%pa,1h,1j,1k,1p(11),W=50%,66Yy,125z. | | | | |
| Iglesia Nueva Apostólica | | C CAp | x.... | | 500 | 1,000 | *Nwe Apostolic Ch.* In Canada Bezirk (District). Germans. HQ Dortmund (Germany). | | | | |
| Iglesia Ortodoxa Griega | | O Gre | Cwo.. | 1 | 2,000 | 4,000 | In 12th Archdiocesan District, Greek Orthodox AD N&S America. Greeks, Arabs. | | | | |
| Iglesia Pentecostal Unida (Colombia) | 1970 | I pel | ..... | 570 | 47,000 | 95,000 | 95% split ex UPC rejecting USA control. Many Arhuacos. 14 missionaries in Spain. | | | | |
| Iglesia Pentecostal Unida (USA) | 1936 | P Pel | x.... | 30 | 3,000 | 5,000 | M=UPC(Canada, USA). Remnant after 95% split rejecting control from St Louis (USA). | | | | |
| Iglesia Presbiteriana Cumberland | 1925 | P Ref | ....C | 10 | 1,218 | 3,000 | M=Cumberland Presbyterian Ch(USA Whites). 3 schools. HQ Cali. 10f,G=4%pa. | | | | |
| Iglesia Presbiteriana de Colombia | 1856 | P Ref | R...C | 170 | 2,915 | 21,200 | M=UPUSA. 1967, pentecostalism. 18n,3x,29f,G=5.9%pa,6h,87t(3600),1u,W=10%,15Yy. | | | | |
| Iglesia Swedenborgiana | | M Swe | x.... | | 100 | 200 | *Swedenborgian Ch. Ch of the New Jerusalem.* Links with USA, UK. 2d. | | | | |
| Iglesia Unión de Bogotá | | P com | ..... | 1 | 217 | 1,000 | *Union Church of Bogotá.* Interdenominational. English-speaking expatriates. | | | | |
| Iglesias de Cristo | 1962 | P Dis | x.... | 2 | 50 | 100 | *Churches of Christ.* M=CCCC(Instrumental)(USA). In Medellín, Bogotá. 8f. | | | | |
| Iglesias radiofónicas solitarias | c1940 | I rad | ..... | 100 | 1,000 | 2,000 | Isolated radio believers in jungles &c. R=18500(TWR,HCJB,FEBC, Radio Vatican). | | | | |
| Miembros del Cuerpo de Cristo | c1965 | I pen | ..... | 4 | 481 | 1,000 | *Members of the Body of Christ.* Indigenous pentecostals. In Cundinamarca. | | | | |
| Misión Bíblica Cristadelfiana | | P Adv | x.... | 1 | 30 | 50 | M=Christadelphian Bible Mission(USA). 1 ecclesia (church). Pacifist. Growing. | | | | |
| Misión Cristiana La Fe | c1962 | I pen | ..... | 3 | 115 | 300 | *Faith Christian Mission.* Indigenous Colombian pentecostals. | | | | |
| Misión Evangélica de Colombia | 1946 | P ind | ..... | 5 | 2,000 | 10,000 | *MEC, CEM.* M=Colombia Evangelistic Mission(Canada). HQ Sincelejo, Bolivar. | | | | |
| Misión Indígena de Sur América | 1934 | P int | xM..C | | 185 | 500 | M=South America Indian Mission(SAIM)(USA). In far north, Guajira peninsula. 20f,2h. | | | | |
| Misión Nuevas Tribus de Colombia | 1944 | P int | x...C | 200 | 3,600 | 10,000 | *MNT.* M=New Tribes Mission. In 6 main Indian tribes in eastern region. 30x,59f,1h. | | | | |
| Misión Panamericana de Colombia | 1956 | I peA | x.... | 40 | 1,400 | 2,000 | *Panamerican Mission.* Run by Colombians. Rapid growth. Medellín, Bogotá. | | | | |
| Misiones Mundiales de Colombia | 1964 | P ind | x.... | | 300 | 600 | Evangelicals from Pasadena, CA (USA). M=World-Wide Missions(USA). | | | | |
| Sociedad de Amigos | | P Qua | Q.... | 1 | 26 | 50 | *Religious Society of Friends. Quakers.* | | | | |
| Sociedad de la Ciencia Cristiana | | M Sci | x.... | 1 | 20 | 50 | *Ch of Christ, Scientist. Christian Science.* M=CCS(Boston,USA). Bogotá Society. 1w. | | | | |
| Testigos de Jehová | c1895 | M Jeh | x.... | 149 | 8,275 | 20,000 | *Jehovah's Witnesses. Watch Tower.* Active witnessing under way by 1929. 1277Y. | | | | |
| Unión Misionera Evangélica | 1908 | P Hol | xM..C | 182 | 1,579 | 3,500 | M=Gospel Missionary Union(USA). 63n,15x,21f,G=9.2%pa,1H,1j,3k,1u,W=91%,173Y,225z. | | | | |
| Other Protestant denominations | | P | ..... | | 1,000 | 2,000 | Total about 10 (see list below). | | | | |
| Other indigenous pentecostal churches | | I pen | ..... | | 1,000 | 2,000 | Total about 20 (see list below), including among West Indian Blacks. | | | | |
| Other Colombian indigenous churches | | I ind | ..... | | 500 | 1,000 | A small number of transitory independent congregations (see below). | | | | |
| Doubly-affiliated (duplication) (1970) | | | | | –219,800 | –414,631 | Evangelicals who also are or were baptized Roman Catholics. | | | | |
| Disaffiliated (duplication) (1970) | | | | | –107,600 | –203,000 | Baptized Catholics now completely disaffiliated agnostics or atheists. | | | | |
| **Total affiliated (mid-1970)** | | | | **5,610** | **11,376,550** | **21,554,700** | **Total denominations (1970) . . . 95.** | | | | |
| **Total affiliated (mid-1975)** | | | | **6,200** | **13,333,200** | **25,261,900** | **Total denominations (1975) . . . 105.** | | | | |
| **Total affiliated (mid-1980)** | | | | **7,200** | **15,556,800** | **29,474,800** | **Total denominations (1980) . . . 115.** | | | | |

NOTES ON TABLE ABOVE

COLUMNS: for meanings and CODES (cols. 1, 3, 4, 8): see Codebook (Part 6). Column 1: **Boldface type** = church with over 10% of country's affiliated Christians.

NATIONAL COUNCILS (Column 4, 5th letter).

C = Confederación Evangélica de Colombia (CEDEC) (Evangelical Confederation of Colombia).

h = Asociación Pro-Indígenas de Colombia (Association for the Indians of Colombia), which also has as members the Episcopal Ch, Lutheran Ch, Presbyterian Ch, CMA, GMU, and others.

R = Conferencia Episcopal de Colombia (Episcopal Conference of Colombia).

OTHER PROTESTANT DENOMINATIONS. These, mostly missions from the USA, include: Baptist Bible Fellowship International (1972), Brethren in Christ, Chs of Christ, Ev Covenant Ch of America (1968), Ev Methodist Ch (1948), Fellowship of Ev Baptist Chs (Canada: 1969), Fundamental

Baptist Mission of Canada (mainly correspondence courses), Missionary Ch, United Ev Chs, World Baptist Fellowship Mission Agency (1967).

OTHER INDIGENOUS PENTECOSTAL CHURCHES. Among these are: Independent Pentecostal Ch of Luruaco (31 communicants), Independent Pentecostal Chs of Barranquilla (50), and bodies among West Indian Blacks.

OTHER COLOMBIAN INDIGENOUS CHURCHES. A handful of smaller West Indian Black or Mestizo bodies come into existence as independent congregations and tend shortly thereafter to disappear or merge with other churches. These include: Iglesia Fundamental Trinitaria.

**PEOPLES** (ethnolinguistic). Christians: 48.9% Mestizo, 23.0% Mulatto, 20.0% Colombian White, 6.0% Black, 1.0% Zambo, 0.4% jungle Amerindian, German, USA, Chinese (2,500), Arab.

**COUNTRY-WIDE TOTALS**

EVANGELIZATION (see Part 5). 1900: 83%. 1970: 99%. 1980: 99%. *Mass evangelism.* Among recent campaigns: 1962 Billy Graham crusade in Cali; 1966, campaigns in 10 cities sponsored by CEDEC (42,000 attenders in Campaña Evangélica (Luis Palau) in Bogotá, televised 7 times; 865 enquirers); 1968, Evangelism-in-Depth (19 regional crusades, 3 mass meetings in Barranquilla, Cali, Medellín; 20,000 enquirers, 7,000 prayer cells formed); 1976, 4-week campaign in Bogota by Puerto Rican Pentecostalist Yiye Aila (23,000 decisions); 1978, Here's Life Cali (CCCI; 200,000 decisions during 500,000-pilgrim Easter climb up Hill of the Three Crosses, Cali). *Radiophonic evangelism.* Annual listeners' letters (1975): 13,000 TWR, 5,034 HCJB, 404 FEBC, Radio Vatican, et alia. Radiophonic schools: growth from 250,000 in 1954 to 300,000 in 1973 in 4,700 Catholic schools.

FOREIGN MISSIONARIES AND PERSONNEL (nationals serving abroad) (1970). Total 1,497 in about 23 countries: over 1,452 Roman Catholics, 25 Protestants, 20 indigenous.

FOREIGN MISSIONARIES AND PERSONNEL (aliens from abroad) (1973). Total 4,288. *From Western world.* 3,316: 2,400 Roman Catholics, 848 Protestants (760 in 48 USA societies, 52 in 4 Canada societies, 11 in 2 UK societies, 9 in 2 WGermany societies, 9 in 7 New Zealand societies, 5 in 5 Australia societies, 2 in 1 Netherlands society), about 60 marginal Protestants (50 Mormons from USA, Jehovah's Witnesses, Swedenborgians), 5 Anglicans in 1 USA society, 2 Catholics (non-Roman), 1 Orthodox. *From Communist world.* About 11 Roman Catholics (10 from Yugoslavia, 1 from Poland). *From Third World.* 961: about 900 Roman Catholics from Latin American countries, about 35 indigenous from Chile, Jamaica, Trinidad & Tobago, et alia, 26 Protestants from Costa Rica, Ecuador, Puerto Rico, et alia.

INSTITUTIONS (church-operated) (1973). Total 2,090, including 1,246 higher schools (66 minor seminaries), 660 medical centres (415 hospitals), 48 radio stations, 4 religious communities (3 monasteries), 5 research centres, 89 seminaries (53 RC, 35 Protestant, 1 Colombian indigenous), 4 study centres, 4 universities.

PERIODICALS. About 80 titles.

PERSONNEL. About 29,288 (25,000 national, 4,288 foreign).

RELIGIOUS LIBRARIES. About 120.

SCRIPTURE DISTRIBUTION (1975). Annual totals: 87,964 Bibles (43% subsidized, 57% commercial), 215,586 NTs (51% free, 21% subsidized, 28% commercial), 433,500 UBS portions, 3,122,500 UBS selections. *Translations completed.* Portion: 19 languages since 1944. NT: 3 languages since 1964.

SERVICE AGENCIES. About 140, including ACF(YWCA), ACJ(YMCA), ACPO, ALISTE, CALA, CAVE-COLOMBIA, CCCC, CCCI, CEC, CEDEC, CEF, CEHILA, CELAM, CENPRO, CIEC, CLAF, CLAR, CRC, DEMECOS, DMC, ICODES, IDES, ILP, IPLAJ, ISAV, JAC, JACF, JARS, JOC, JTC, MAF, MEC, MFC, MXY, OC, OSAL, SETRAC, SNPS, SU, TFP, UNICO, WBT (1962: 192 missionaries), WLC(EHC), WVI.

**ADDITIONAL DATA ON CHURCHES**

IGLESIA CATOLICA EN COLOMBIA. In 1966, dioceses (M, D and PN) covered 34.5% of the country's territory and 92% of the total population (43 persons/km2), whereas the missionary jurisdictions (VA and PA) covered 65.5% of the country's territory and only 8.3% of the population (2 persons/km2). *New archdioceses.* Elevated in 1974: M Bucaramanga, M Ibagué. *New dioceses.* In 1977: Chiquinquirá, Garagoa. *Catholics.* The number of Catholics reported by dioceses in the past has sometimes exceeded the total populations of those dioceses as estimated by secular sources. In addition, the population of urban centres like Bogotá and Cali are expanding rapidly each year. As one result, the population reported for M Bogotá has fluctuated considerably, and the number of Catholics reported has grown from 2,000,000 (*Annuario Pontificio 1970*) to 3,073,915 (*AP 1973*). The figures for Catholics in the table above have therefore been selected to represent the situation in all dioceses as at, approximately, mid-1970. *Ethnic groups.* The total includes 2,500 Chinese Catholics (1975). *Annual baptisms.* (1972) 99.2% infant, 0.8% adult. *Priests.* 68% secular, 32% religious. *Male religious personnel* (priests and brothers). 82% Colombians, 1% other Latin Americans, 17% from other continents (mainly Spanish and Italians). The total including non-diocesan and contemplatives was 4,725 in 1970. *Bishops.* In 1970, 55 Colombians, 7 expatriates. *Sisters.* 89% Colombians, 4% other Latin Americans, 7% others (mainly Spanish and Italians). In addition to those enumerated in the table, there are also many contemplatives. Total all sisters (1970): 20,780. *Catholic charismatics* (January 1974). Over 10,000 adults including many religious personnel are active in well over 200 prayer groups in the Charismatic Renewal. One parish in Cali has 40 such groups in a poor barrio. *Seminaries.* 8 are interdiocesan. There are, further, 24 seminaries for religious congregations. *Seminarians.* 873 secular, 505 religious. *Catechists.* Total (under Propaganda) about 2,000. *Catholic organizations.* The Episcopal Conference of Colombia (Conferencia Episcopal de Colombia) is a member of CELAM. There is no unified pastoral organization for all dioceses but 22 of them have been regrouped into 3 pastoral regions: 9 rural dioceses in the centre of the country, 9 in the southwest and 4 rural dioceses in the department of Antioquia. The Conference of Religious Personnel of Colombia (Conferencia de Religiosos de Colombia, CRC) is a member of CLAR. There are no national presbyteral or pastoral councils. Colombia Catholic Action (Acción Católica Colombiana) included the following specialized movements in 1970: Acción Católica Femenina (4,000 members); Juventud Obrera Católica, JOC (2,000); Equipos Universitarios (150); Movimiento Familiar Cristiano (3,000). Other important lay movements included: Antiguas Alumnas del Sagrado Corazón (2,000); Congregaciones Marianas (20,000); Cruzada Social (1,500); Cursillos de Cristiandad (4,540); Hermandades del Trabajo (200 militants); Legión de Maria (20,000); Movimiento Apostólico Socializante (120); and the newly-formed and dynamic Selección de Trabajadores Católicos, SETRAC (500 militants). For the armed forces, Colombia forms a single military vicariate.

The Holy See has diplomatic relations with Colombia and is represented to government and the Catholic hierarchy by a nuncio based in Bogotá.

Latin American organizations in Colombia include CELAM (Consejo del Episcopado Latino-Americano), which is the general secretariat for all the episcopal conferences of Latin America, and which has the following 7 departments: (1) Departamento de Educación (DEC) which aims to co-ordinate Catholic education throughout Latin America; (2) Departamento de Liturgia, which promotes and co-ordinates liturgics, co-operates in the translation of liturgical books and trains both experts and the clergy in general; (3) Departamento de Ministerios Jerárquicos, Secretariado General, Secretaria del Clero, Secretaria del Diaconado; (4) Departamento de Misiones (DMC), which co-ordinates pastoral work and provides training and information regarding missionary work in Latin America; (5) Departamento de Pastoral de Conjunto, which provides theological thought and technical assistance concerning pastoral work in its totality including the training of priests, religious and laity; (6) Comité Latinoamericano de la Fe, Sección Catequística, which is related to CLAP in Paraguay; and (7) Instituto Pastoral Latinoamericano (IPLA), founded in Medellín in 1974, which joins together 5 catechetical, liturgical and pastoral institutes in Colombia, Ecuador and Chile and serves also as the headquarters for the Comisión de Estudios de Historia Religiosa Latinoamericana (CEHILA).

Other Latin American organizations established in Colombia are: (1) Confederación Latinoamericana de Religiosos (CLAR) founded in 1958, which co-ordinates the national conferences of religious personnel (numbering 28 in 1971) throughout Latin America, and which is dedicated to the renewal, adaptation and promotion of the religious life; (2) Equipos Docentes de América Latina, a lay apostolate association of Christian teachers in public education, which serves as the Latin American branch of the international Lay Apostolate Association of Christian Teachers in Public Education, located in France; and (3) Confederación Interamericana de Educación Católica (CIEC), founded in 1945 as a branch of the International Organization of Catholic Instruction (OIEC), which co-ordinates the work of all national federations of Catholic instruction in North and South America.

Two progressivist opinion groups are Sacerdotes para América Latina (SAL) and Servicio Colombiano de Comunicación Social in Bogotá, while conservative groups include Juventud de Colombia Pro-Civilización Cristiana, Sociedad Colombiana de Defensa de la Tradición, Familia y Propriedad, in Bogotá and Grupo Tradicionalista de Jovenes Cristianos de Colombia, in Medellín. Conservative group members are opposed to agrarian reform 'in the name of tradition, the family and private property' and regularly cite extracts from pontifical documents and the Bible to support their position.

Several centres for research have been established, including: (1) Centro de Investigación y Acción Social, founded in Bogotá by Jesuits; (2) Instituto de Doctrina y Estudios Sociales (IDES), in Bogotá, which engages in socio-religious studies, statistics and pastoral planning for the whole of Colombia; (3) Instituto Colombiano de Desarollo Social (ICODES), in Bogotá, which carries on studies relating to the problem of development in Colombia; (4) Instituto Campesino de Buga, which provides a general training for peasant leaders; (5) Juventud Trabajadora Colombiana (JTC), a non-confessional but principally Catholic movement founded in 1962 by splitting from JOC because of JOC'S close relationship with hierarchy and political parties, which by 1972 had become stronger than JOC, being well-established in the 6 most industrialized cities of Colombia; and (6) Study Centre for the Development and Interpretation of Latin America (CEDIAL), founded by a Jesuit in Bogotá, which has an anti-revolutionary orientation and is especially opposed to the 'theology of liberation'.

Theological training is provided in the theological faculties of the Javeriana University (under Jesuits), La Salle University (FSC), Santo Tomas University, Bolivariana University, and San Buenaventura College (OFM).

The Instituto de Misiones Extranjeras de Yarumal (IMEY, or MXY) is a society for foreign missions, founded by Xavier priests in 1927, which operates in Bolivia, Ecuador and Venezuela in addition to its major responsibility for 4 missionary jurisdictions within Colombia itself. In 1970 it numbered 124 priests (89 in Colombia) and 21 brothers (18 in Colombia), and in 1977, 158 members (115 priests). In 1977 it ventured outside Latin America to open work in Angola. Ethnographic studies and training are available at the Centro Antropológico de Misiones (ETHNIA) in Bogotá.

The Federación Nacional de Centros Docentes (National Federation of Teaching Centres) and the Conferencia Nacional de Colegios Católicos (National Conference of Catholic Colleges) co-ordinate educational work. In 1968 there were 1,022 pre-primary schools (38,117 infants, i.e. 95% of the school population at this level); 1,839 primary schools (234,293 pupils; 8%); 998 secondary schools (147,513; 42%); 49 institutions of higher learning (8,534 students; 53%) including the Universidad Pontificia Javeriana at Bogotá, Universidad Pontificia Bolivariana (Medellín), Universidad San Buenaventura (Bogotá and Medellín), Universidad La Salle (Bogotá), Colegio Nuestra Señora (Manizales). By 1973, primary schools numbered 2,693 (416,424 pupils), and secondary schools 1,158 (267,492 pupils).

Caritas Colombiana is linked to the national secretariat for social pastoralia of the Colombian episcopate, with headquarters at Bogotá, and has subsidiary departments in all dioceses, which are especially involved in free distribution of food. Its social service programme in 1960 included 408 hospitals, 213 dispensaries, 67 homes, 254 institutions for children and 53 other institutions.

Other societies caring for orphans and the needy are Sociedad de San Vicente de Paul, Amparo de Niños (Bogotá), Ciudades del Niño (Medellín), Minuto de Dios (Bogotá), and Granjas del Padre Luna (Bogotá).

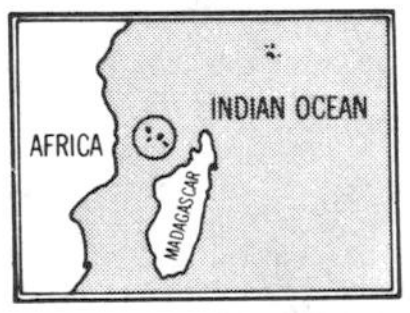


# COMOROS

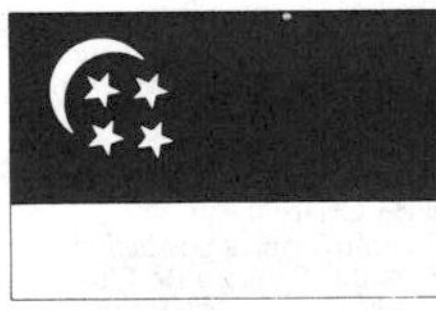

## SECULAR DATA

**STATE. Official name:** The Republic of the Comoros (La République des Comores/Etat Comorien). Adjective of nationality: Comorian (comorien).
**Flag** (shown above right): Red stripe over green stripe; white crescent and 4 white stars.
**Area:** 1,862 sq.km. (719 sq.miles). Agricultural land: 53.0%.
**Government:** Republic under revolutionary council, since 1975 coup (1843 French colony, 1947 French overseas territory, 1975 Independence. In 1976 Mayotte voted to secede as a dependency of France).
**Official language:** Comorian.
**Capital:** Moroni 12,000 (1974).
**Political divisions:** 3 Prefectures.
**Foreign forces:** Before Independence in 1975, around 2,000 French troops (French and Reunionese); after, none.

**DEMOGRAPHY. Population:** 243,948 (census of VII-IX.1966, for all 4 Comoro islands. For 1970–2000 (UN), see last row of Table 1). Population density (1975): 141/sq.km. (366/sq. mile). Under 15 years: 45%. Growth rate (1975–80): 2.51% per year (births 4.45%, deaths –1.95%). Life expectancy (1975–80): 45.0 years. Household size: 4.9 persons.

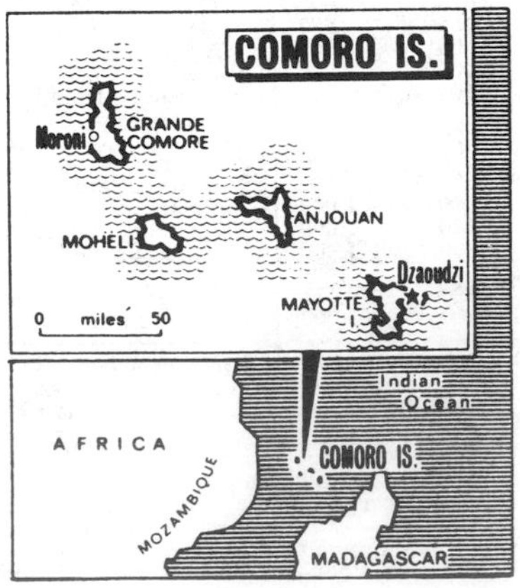


**Major languages:** Comorian, Swahili, French, Kikomozo (Kingazidja), Malagasy, Makua, French Creole, Arabic.
**Urban dwellers** (1970): 3.0%.

**ETHNOLINGUISTIC GROUPS:** 96.9% Comorian (Swahili), 1.6% Makua, 0.4% European (French), 0.1% Malagasy (Sakalava), 0.1% Reunionese Creole, Arab, Malay.

**MONEY** (1977). **Monetary unit:** CFA franc (= 100 centimes); US$1 = CFAF 250.00.
**National income per person:** US$150. Average annual family income: US$735.
**Cost of living in capital** (1976): Daily cost of living: US$46.

**EDUCATION.** Adult literacy: (1966) 58%. Education rate: 70%. Schools: 114.

**HEALTH.** Hospitals: 10 (559 beds). Doctors: 21. Lepers: 1,500 (5.7 per 1,000).

**LITERATURE.** Periodicals: 3.

**COMMUNICATION** (per 1,000 peoples). Phones: 4. Radios: 120.

**TABLE 1. RELIGIOUS ADHERENTS IN THE COMOROS**

| Year | 1900 | | mid-1970 | | Annual change, 1970–1980 | | | | mid-1975 | | mid-1980 | | 2000 | |
|---|---|---|---|---|---|---|---|---|---|---|---|---|---|---|
| Name | Adherents | % | Adherents | % | Natural | Conversion | Total | Rate | Adherents | % | Adherents | % | Adherents | % |
| Muslims | 69,900 | 99.9 | 230,709 | 99.2 | 6,688 | −3 | 6,685 | 2.56 | 261,210 | 99.3 | 297,560 | 99.7 | 396,550 | 99.6 |
| Christians | 100 | 0.1 | 1,491 | 0.6 | −96 | 2 | −94 | −6.53 | 1,440 | 0.5 | 550 | 0.2 | 900 | 0.2 |
| crypto-Christians | 0 | 0.0 | 31 | 0.0 | 1 | 1 | 2 | 4.75 | 40 | 0.0 | 50 | 0.0 | 300 | 0.1 |
| professing | 100 | 0.1 | 1,460 | 0.6 | −97 | 1 | −96 | −6.86 | 1,400 | 0.5 | 500 | 0.2 | 600 | 0.2 |
| Roman Catholics | 100 | 0.1 | 1,090 | 0.5 | −90 | 1 | −89 | −8.90 | 1,000 | 0.4 | 200 | 0.1 | 300 | 0.1 |
| Protestants | 0 | 0.0 | 370 | 0.1 | −7 | 0 | −7 | −1.75 | 400 | 0.1 | 300 | 0.1 | 300 | 0.1 |
| affiliated | 100 | 0.1 | 1,491 | 0.6 | −96 | 2 | −94 | −6.53 | 1,440 | 0.5 | 550 | 0.2 | 900 | 0.2 |
| total practising | 90 | 90 | 1,040 | 70 | −67 | 1 | −66 | −6.53 | 1,010 | 70 | 380 | 70 | 540 | 60 |
| non-practising | 10 | 10 | 450 | 30 | −29 | 1 | −28 | −6.53 | 430 | 30 | 170 | 30 | 360 | 40 |
| Roman Catholics | 100 | 0.1 | 1,091 | 0.5 | −90 | 1 | −89 | −8.90 | 1,000 | 0.4 | 200 | 0.1 | 300 | 0.1 |
| Protestants | 0 | 0.0 | 370 | 0.1 | −7 | 0 | −7 | −1.75 | 400 | 0.1 | 300 | 0.1 | 400 | 0.1 |
| Evangelicals | 0 | 0.0 | 150 | 0.1 | 0 | 1 | 1 | 0.56 | 180 | 0.1 | 160 | 0.1 | 250 | 0.1 |
| African indigenous | 0 | 0.0 | 30 | 0.0 | 1 | 1 | 2 | 5.00 | 40 | 0.0 | 50 | 0.0 | 200 | 0.0 |
| Baha'is | 0 | 0.0 | 300 | 0.1 | 8 | 1 | 9 | 2.57 | 350 | 0.1 | 390 | 0.1 | 550 | 0.1 |
| Country's population | 70,000 | 100.0 | 232,500 | 100.0 | 6,600 | 0 | 6,600 | 2.51 | 263,000 | 100.0 | 298,500 | 100.0 | 398,000 | 100.0 |

COLUMNS, ROWS. For meanings and definitions, see Codebook (Part 6). Note that, by definition, total 'Christians' = professing + crypto-Christians, which also = affiliated + nominal Christians. Percentages may not always total exactly, due to rounding.
CENSUSES. No question on religion has ever been asked.

**NOTES ON RELIGIONS**
AFRICAN INDIGENOUS. Isolated radio believers across the islands (see Table 2).
BAHA'IS. In 1973, 2 local spiritual assemblies and 3 other centres.
CHRISTIANS. All were expatriate French, Réunionais and Malagasy, until the first 2 Comorian converts in 1975.
COUNTRY'S POPULATION. In 1976, the government agreed to receive back the 60,000 Comorian citizens resident in Madagascar, all of whom were Muslims.

MUSLIMS. Sunnis (of the Shafiite rite). 780 mosques, numerous Quranic schools. The Comoros were islamized in the 15th century. A grand mufti resides in the capital. *Hajj pilgrims to Mecca.* (1976) 131.
ROMAN CATHOLICS. At Independence in August 1975, there was a sudden drop from 1,000 Catholics to 200, with the mass departure of the French.

**NON-CHRISTIAN RELIGIONS. Islam,** the predominant religion of the islands, dates from the settlement of Arabs in the 14th century, and the Comoros were islamized in the following century. Muslims are Sunnis of the Shafiite rite, with 780 mosques and numerous Quranic schools.

**CHRISTIANITY**
CATHOLIC CHURCH. Catholics are composed mostly of those of mixed race from Reunion, or metropolitan French, and were attached to the diocese of Ambanja in Madagascar until a separate apostolic administration was set up in 1975. There are 4 chapels organized into 2 parishes, one for Grande Comore and Mohéli and the other for Anjouan also covering Mayotte.
PROTESTANT CHURCH. There is a loosely-structured community consisting of a small number of Malagasy Protestants of various denominations, some of whom are seasonal workers in the islands. There is also one congregation of Adventists. The Africa Inland Mission sent several missionaries from 1975 onwards, but in 1978 the 18 Protestant missionaries were expelled.

**Eglise de Jésus-Christ aux Comores.** Christians of Moroni parish bid farewell to their Malagasy pastor (centre, dark suit) at Moroni airport.

**CHURCH AND STATE.** The Portuguese first sighted the islands in 1503, and the French arrived in 1517. The Comoros were placed under a French protectorate in 1886, granted internal autonomy in 1961, and eventually declared independence from France in 1975. Freedom of religion has been guaranteed under the French and subsequently, but special deference is made to Islam in the legal system. Islamic courts are given responsibility for questions of marriage and divorce and other personal matters relating to Muslims; and although basic education is provided for Muslim students in French in the morning, the afternoons are reserved for Quranic schools.

**BROADCASTING.** RVOG (Ethiopia) could easily be heard in the Comoro Islands until its closure in 1977.

**TABLE 2. ORGANIZED CHURCHES AND DENOMINATIONS IN THE COMOROS, 1970–75 (Grande Comore, Mohéli, Anjouan)**

| Official name 1 | Begun 2 | Type 3 | Counc 4 | Congs 5 | Adults 6 | Affiliated 7 | Names, notes, and other statistics (see Codebook) 8 |
|---|---|---|---|---|---|---|---|
| Eglise Adventiste du Septième Jour | | P Adv | x,.... | 1 | 10 | 30 | *SDA. Seventh-day Adventists.* In Indian Ocean Union Mission (HQ Tananarive). |
| Eglise Catholique: AA Comoro Islands | 1517 | R Lat | P,S,r | 3 | 600 | 1,091 | Till 1975 in D Ambanja, Madagascar. French, Reunionese. C=1+0+1. 2x,4w,2b,1h,1r. |
| Eglise de Jésus-Christ aux Comores | | P Ref | ..... | 2 | 150 | 300 | *EJCC.* Malagasy Protestants (seasonal workers, officials), French military. 1x. |
| Eglise de l'Africa Inland Mission | 1975 | P int | xMC,.. | 1 | 20 | 40 | Linked to EJCC. M=AIM(USA,UK;doctors, teachers). 2 converts training as pastors. |
| Eglises radiophoniques isolées | 1970 | I rad | ..... | | 10 | 30 | Isolated radio believers (through FEBA, RVOG), mainly young people aged 12–25. |
| Total affiliated (mid-1970) | | | | 10 | 790 | 1,491 | Total denominations (1970) . . . 5. |
| Total affiliated (mid-1975) | | | | 11 | 760 | 1,440 | Total denominations (1975) . . . 5. |
| Total affiliated (mid-1980) | | | | 12 | 300 | 550 | Total denominations (1980) . . . 6. |

**NOTES ON TABLE ABOVE**
COLUMNS: for meanings and CODES (cols. 1, 3, 4, 8): see Codebook (Part 6). Column 1: **Boldface type** = church with over 10% of country's affiliated Christians.
NATIONAL COUNCILS (Column 4, 5th letter).
r = Conférence Episcopale de Madagascar (Episcopal Conference of Madagascar).

PEOPLES (ethnolinguistic). Christians: (mid-1975) about 68% expatriate (metropolitan) French, 15% Reunionese Creole, 15% Malagasy. (1976) 50% Reunionese Creole, 50% Malagasy.

**COUNTRY-WIDE TOTALS**
EVANGELIZATION (see Part 5). 1900: 1%. 1970: 30%. 1980: 40%.
FOREIGN MISSIONARIES AND PERSONNEL (aliens from abroad) (1973). Total 7. *From Western world.* 6 Roman Catholics. *From Third World.* 1 Protestant. (1977) 18 Protestants; expelled 1978.
INSTITUTIONS. Total 2: 1 higher school, 1 dispensary.
PERSONNEL. 7 (foreign).
SERVICE AGENCIES. About 8.

**ADDITIONAL DATA ON CHURCHES**
EGLISE CATHOLIQUE. The parish of Moroni on Grande Comore was begun in 1939. Before 1975 the church was part of the diocese of Ambanja (Madagascar), then was formed into a separate apostolic administration; there are also 2 chapels, 2 French priests (OFMCap, Strasbourg province), 4 Soeurs de Notre-Dame de Grace, 1 primary and secondary school (500 pupils, three-quarters Muslims), one dispensary. *Catholics.* Before Independence (1 August 1975), metropolitan French,

Creoles and Malagasy; immediately after, sharply reduced (in Moroni, from 1,000 to 50), with departure of French, to 200 Catholics.
*Catholic organizations.* The jurisdiction is attached to the Episcopal Conference of Madagascar, which is a member of SECAM. There is no presbyteral nor pastoral council. Religious personnel are represented in 2 associations: the Union of Major Superiors of Madagascar (Union des Supérieurs Majeurs de Madagascar) for men, and the Union of Religious Sisters of Madagascar (Union des Religieuses de Madagascar). The principal lay movements are the National Catholic Youth Council, JAC/F, JEC/F, MIJARC, Prayer and Life, Scouts and Guides.
The Holy See has no diplomatic relations with the Comoros. It is represented to the Catholic hierarchy by an apostolic delegate based in Tananarive, Madagascar.

# CONGO

**SECULAR DATA**

STATE. Official name. The People's Republic of the Congo (La République Populaire du Congo). Adjective of nationality: Congolese (congolais).
**Flag** (shown above right): Red field with green wreath, yellow star, hammer and hoe.
**Area:** 342,000 sq.km. (132,047 sq.miles). Agricultural land: 43.7%.
**Government:** One-party Marxist state, since 1970 (1785 French influence, 1885 French rule, 1910 colony in French Equatorial Africa, 1960 Independence as republic).
**Legislature:** Council of State.
**Official language:** French (*Français*).
**Chief cities:** capital Brazzaville 250,000, Pointe-Noire 150,000.
**Armed forces** (1976): Total 7,000 regular: army 6,500, navy 200, air force 300 (no combat aircraft). Paramilitary forces: 2,900.

DEMOGRAPHY. **Population:** 1,300,106 (census of 7.II.1974. For 1970–2000 (UN), see last row of Table 1). Population density (1975): 4/sq.km. (10/sq.mile). Under 15 years: 42%. Growth rate (1975–80): 2.60% per year (births 4.49%, deaths −1.89%).

Life expectancy (1975–80): 46.0 years. Household size: 4.9 persons.
Major languages: Kongo (Kikongo), French, Lingala, Munokotoba, Kibougo, Teke, and about 30 other tribal languages. Urban dwellers (1970): 29.7%. Urban growth rate (1950–70): 4.9% per year.
Labour force: 28%.
Refugees (1977): About 5,000 from Angola.

ETHNOLINGUISTIC GROUPS: 46.5% Kongo (21% Lari, Sundi, Vili, Yombe), 20% Teke, 11% Mbochi (Bangi, Kuyu,

Maku, Furu, Ngiri), 7% Mbete, 5% Sanga (Mbimu, Bombo, Besom), 4% Eshira, 3% Maka, 1.4% French, 1.0% Binga Pygmy (12,000), 1% Kota, Greek, Japanese, Chinese, Portuguese, expatriate African, Cuban (1977: 300 military, 150 civilian).

**MONEY** (1977). **Monetary unit:** CFA franc (= 100 centimes); US$1 = CFAF 250.00.
**National income per person:** US$350. Average annual family income: US$1,715.
**Inflation:** (1970–74) 5.7% per year, (1975) 17% per year (consumer price index 149).
**Cost of living in capital** (1976): Daily cost of living: US$51.

**EDUCATION.** Adult literacy: (1961) 16%, (1976) 20%. Education rate: 73%. Schools: 940.

**HEALTH.** Hospitals: 110 (5,541 beds). Doctors: 162. Lepers: 30,500 (22.7 per 1,000). Blind: 4,000. Psychotics: 9,000.

**LITERATURE.** Periodicals: 10. Newspapers: 3 dailies, 7 non-daily.

**COMMUNICATION** (per 1,000 people). Phones: 10. Radios: 75. TV sets: 4. Daily newspaper circulation: 1 copy.

TABLE 1. RELIGIOUS ADHERENTS IN THE CONGO (BRAZZAVILLE)

| Year | 1900 | | mid-1970 | | Annual change, 1970–1980 | | | | mid-1975 | | mid-1980 | | 2000 | |
|---|---|---|---|---|---|---|---|---|---|---|---|---|---|---|
| *Name* | *Adherents* | *%* | *Adherents* | *%* | *Natural* | *Conversion* | *Total* | *Rate* | *Adherents* | *%* | *Adherents* | *%* | *Adherents* | *%* |
| **Christians** | **13,500** | **2.5** | **1,095,720** | **92.0** | **31,542** | **1,366** | **32,908** | **2.65** | **1,244,100** | **92.5** | **1,424,800** | **93.0** | **2,543,200** | **93.5** |
| professing | 13,500 | 2.5 | 1,095,720 | 92.0 | 31,542 | 1,366 | 32,908 | 2.65 | 1,244,100 | 92.5 | 1,424,800 | 93.0 | 2,543,200 | 93.5 |
| Roman Catholics | 13,500 | 2.5 | 634,800 | 53.3 | 18,278 | 817 | 19,095 | 2.65 | 720,900 | 53.6 | 825,750 | 53.9 | 1,471,500 | 54.1 |
| Protestants | 0 | 0.0 | 288,320 | 24.2 | 8,279 | 234 | 8,513 | 2.61 | 326,550 | 24.3 | 373,450 | 24.4 | 662,900 | 24.4 |
| African indigenous | 0 | 0.0 | 166,700 | 14.0 | 4,807 | 273 | 5,080 | 2.68 | 189,600 | 14.1 | 217,500 | 14.2 | 391,700 | 14.4 |
| Marginal Protestants | 0 | 0.0 | 5,500 | 0.5 | 167 | 43 | 210 | 3.18 | 6,600 | 0.5 | 7,600 | 0.5 | 16,300 | 0.6 |
| Orthodox | 0 | 0.0 | 400 | 0.0 | 11 | −1 | 10 | 2.22 | 450 | 0.0 | 500 | 0.0 | 800 | 0.0 |
| nominal | 5,000 | 0.9 | 407,255 | 34.2 | 11,563 | −797 | 10,766 | 2.36 | 456,060 | 33.9 | 514,920 | 33.6 | 760,900 | 28.0 |
| affiliated | 8,500 | 1.6 | 688,465 | 57.8 | 19,979 | 2,163 | 22,142 | 2.81 | 788,040 | 58.6 | 909,880 | 59.4 | 1,782,300 | 65.5 |
| total practising | 8,080 | *95* | 550,770 | *80* | 15,983 | 1,730 | 17,713 | 2.81 | 630,430 | *80* | 727,900 | *80* | 1,069,400 | *60* |
| non-practising | 420 | *5* | 137,690 | *20* | 3,996 | 433 | 4,429 | 2.81 | 157,610 | *20* | 181,980 | *20* | 712,900 | *40* |
| Roman Catholics | 8,500 | 1.6 | 399,165 | 33.5 | 11,594 | 1,340 | 12,934 | 2.83 | 457,300 | 34.0 | 528,500 | 34.5 | 1,033,600 | 38.0 |
| Protestants | 0 | 0.0 | 167,000 | 14.0 | 4,807 | 243 | 5,050 | 2.66 | 189,600 | 14.1 | 217,500 | 14.2 | 405,300 | 14.9 |
| Evangelicals | 0 | 0.0 | 143,000 | 12.0 | 4,117 | 233 | 4,350 | 2.68 | 162,400 | 12.1 | 186,500 | 12.2 | 351,000 | 12.9 |
| African indigenous | 0 | 0.0 | 119,000 | 10.0 | 3,478 | 552 | 4,030 | 2.94 | 137,200 | 10.2 | 159,300 | 10.4 | 326,400 | 12.0 |
| Marginal Protestants | 0 | 0.0 | 3,000 | 0.3 | 91 | 29 | 120 | 3.33 | 3,600 | 0.3 | 4,200 | 0.3 | 16,300 | 0.6 |
| Orthodox | 0 | 0.0 | 300 | 0.0 | 9 | −1 | 8 | 2.35 | 340 | 0.0 | 380 | 0.0 | 700 | 0.0 |
| Tribal religionists | 526,500 | 97.5 | 79,580 | 6.7 | 1,933 | −2,567 | −634 | −0.83 | 76,240 | 5.7 | 73,240 | 4.8 | 75,800 | 2.8 |
| Non-religious | 0 | 0.0 | 5,900 | 0.5 | 274 | 826 | 1,100 | 10.19 | 10,800 | 0.8 | 16,900 | 1.1 | 49,000 | 1.8 |
| Muslims | 0 | 0.0 | 5,100 | 0.4 | 146 | 0 | 146 | 2.53 | 5,760 | 0.4 | 6,560 | 0.4 | 19,000 | 0.7 |
| Baha'is | 0 | 0.0 | 3,100 | 0.3 | 137 | 173 | 310 | 5.74 | 5,400 | 0.4 | 6,200 | 0.4 | 19,000 | 0.7 |
| New-Religionists | 0 | 0.0 | 500 | 0.0 | 25 | 125 | 150 | 15.00 | 1,000 | 0.1 | 2,000 | 0.1 | 6,000 | 0.2 |
| Atheists | 0 | 0.0 | 500 | 0.0 | 20 | 40 | 60 | 7.50 | 800 | 0.1 | 1,100 | 0.1 | 4,000 | 0.2 |
| Other religionists | 0 | 0.0 | 600 | 0.1 | 23 | 37 | 60 | 6.67 | 900 | 0.1 | 1,200 | 0.1 | 3,000 | 0.1 |
| **Country's population** | **540,000** | **100.0** | **1,191,000** | **100.0** | **34,100** | **0** | **34,100** | **2.53** | **1,345,000** | **100.0** | **1,532,000** | **100.0** | **2,720,000** | **100.0** |

COLUMNS, ROWS. For meanings and definitions, see Codebook (Part 6). Note that, by definition, total 'Christians' = professing + crypto-Christians, which also = affiliated + nominal Christians. Percentages may not always total exactly, due to rounding.
CENSUSES. **IX.1960–II.1961** (Africans): 52.8% Roman Catholics, 27.0% Protestants, 11.1% tribal religionists, 8.9% African indigenous, 0.3% Muslims.

NOTES ON RELIGIONS
AFRICAN INDIGENOUS. In 21 denominations in 1970 (see Table 2).
ATHEISTS. The Parti Congolais du Travail (PCT), although Marxist in ideology, has few avowed atheists among its members.
BAHA'IS. Rapid growth to 21 local spiritual assemblies by 1973.
MUSLIMS. 4,500 non-Congolese expatriate traders (Sunnis of the Malikite rite) from francophone North and Western African states, living in the cities and towns; and 600 Congolese in Pointe Noire and Brazzaville.
NEW-RELIGIONISTS (followers of new East Asian religions). Tenrikyo, a Shinto sect from Japan, began in Brazzaville in 1966. In 1971 there were 200 adult followers, 4 stations and a medical dispensary.
NOMINAL CHRISTIANS. The expansion of Christianity in the Congo has been so rapid that there has been a large number of nominal Christians (professing but not affiliated). In 1970 this nominal fringe numbered 34% of the population, or 59% the size of all affiliated Christians. As the expansion of Christianity slowed down after 1970, the nominal fringe began to decrease in proportion to affiliated Christians, indicating that the churches had begun to catch up with the expansion and to initiate and disciple the large number of nominal Christians.
NON-RELIGIOUS. Including many French expatriates.
OTHER RELIGIONISTS. Including Rosicrucians (5 AMORC centres).
PRACTISING CHRISTIANS. Regular Sunday attendance: Protestants about 80%, Catholics about 50%. Catholic Easter communicants are very low (26%) because of difficulties of travel and insufficient Easter services in all localities.
ROMAN CATHOLICS. In 1900 there were 4,492 baptized Catholics and about 4,000 catechumens.
TRIBAL RELIGIONISTS. Tribes over 60% traditionalist (animist) in 1972: Bakwili (60%), Ngwili (60%). Though professed animists are now few in number, festishism is increasing.

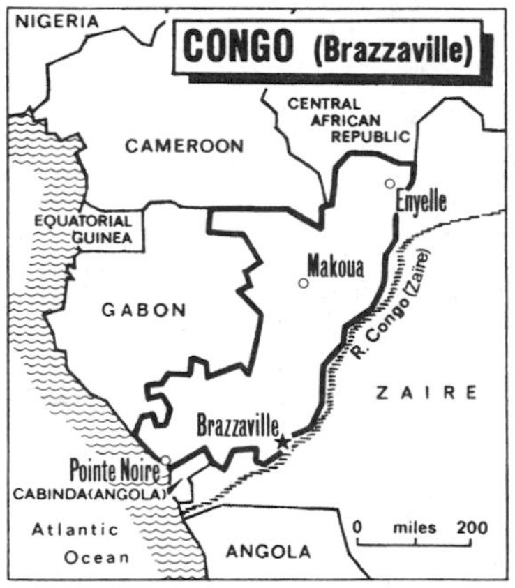
NIGERIA
CONGO (Brazzaville)
CENTRAL AFRICAN REPUBLIC
CAMEROON
EQUATORIAL GUINEA
Enyelle
Makoua
GABON
R. Congo (Zaire)
ZAIRE
Brazzaville
Pointe Noire
CABINDA (ANGOLA)
Atlantic Ocean
ANGOLA
0 miles 200

**NON-CHRISTIAN RELIGIONS. Traditional religions** were still followed by 11.1% of the population in 1961 although by 1972 most of these professed to be Christians. Two small tribes (Bakwili and Ngwili) have been more resistant to evangelization and remain 60% traditionalist. Traditional beliefs continue to manifest themselves within Christianity. Most of the country's peoples share a common name for God: Nzambi (among Kongo-Sundi, Dondo, Ndasa), Nzama (Teke) and Nziame (Kuta). Nzambi is the all-powerful creator of the sky, earth and man. He is conceived of in 2 aspects: Nzambi Watanda (above) who is good and Nzambi Wamutsele (below) who is wicked. The double-sided nature of God thus explains the reality of life itself with its alternating periods of good and bad fortune. Two classes of ancestral spirits widely believed in are the Binyumba who inhabit the kingdom of the dead and the Bakuyu who have not yet been admitted to the abode of deceased spirits. These latter wander restlessly about and are much feared and propitiated through offerings. Fetishism, which was widely practised prior to the prophetic activity of Simon Kimbangu in 1921, is now once again reviving.

**Islam** has made little impact in Congo-Brazzaville and makes up no more than 0.4% of the population. Most of these are expatriate Muslims from northern Muslim countries.

**Tenrikyo,** one of the Japanese so-called New Religions, is a Shinto sect founded in Japan in 1838; in 1966 it established a centre in Brazzaville. In 1971 the mission consisted of 200 followers, 4 stations and a dispensary with a doctor and 5 nurses. Tenrikyo doctrine gives special emphasis to health care and healing of the sick.

## CHRISTIANITY

CATHOLIC CHURCH. Portuguese explorers discovered the Congo river in 1482 and the first missionary expedition was sent to the Kingdom of the Congo in 1491. The result was a flourishing Christian community during the 16th century under Afonso I, one of the major Christian figures of African history. Afonso's son, Henrique, was the first Catholic bishop of African descent. Ravaged by the slave trade, both the kingdom and its church disintegrated during the 17th and 18th centuries. However, the church was never as influential in the area now in Congo-Brazzaville as it was in Zaire and northern Angola to the south.

A new era for Catholic missions began in 1883 with the arrival of the first Holy Ghost priests at the coast, and a vicariate of the French Congo was begun in 1886. A mission was sent to the upper Congo in 1889, and the following year a second vicariate was erected for that area. The first Congolese priest of modern times was ordained in 1895. Since World War II further progress has been made in the organization of the church. The archdiocese of Brazzaville, with 2 suffragan dioceses, was established in 1955 and a Congolese bishop consecrated in 1961. Catholic growth has been steady since the beginning, as these figures of baptized Catholics indicate: 1,850 in 1895; 4,492 in 1900; 120,668 in 1940; 175,512 in 1950; 257,866 in 1960 and 376,000 in 1970.

PROTESTANT CHURCHES. Protestant work was not begun until 1909 and was the result of the expansion of the Swedish Evangelical Mission (Svenska Missionsförbundet) from neighbouring Belgian Congo. The growth of this church has been strongly affected by fluctuating indigenous movements which have come and gone in the area over the past half century. The prophetic activity of Simon Kimbangu in 1921 created a revival in the church, characterized by spirit possession (*ngunza*) and the burning of fetishes. In 1941 there was a movement away from the church and a drop in baptisms due to a widespread belief that the newly-arrived Salvation Army provided protection from sorcery *(kindoki)* and that its flag was efficacious in healing the sick and raising the dead. Similar decreases were noted in 1946 and 1952 when other Ngunzist movements made their appearance. Nevertheless these periods of decline were often followed by renewal, as in the revival of 1947. The Evangelical Church became autonomous in 1961. Today it is by far the largest Protestant church. The majority of its centres are located in the densely-populated southern region.

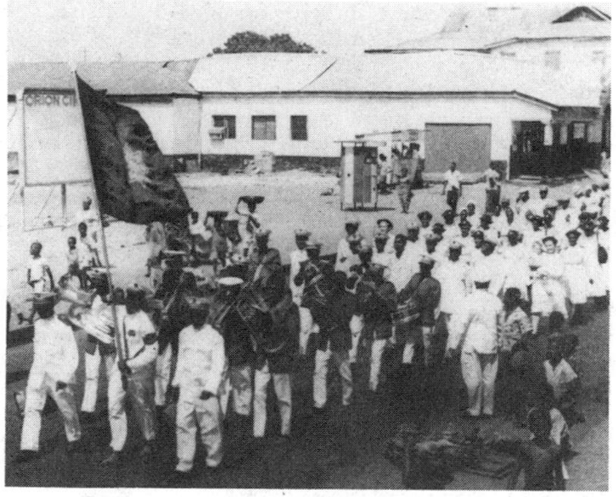

**Armée du Salut.** Begun in 1935, the Salvation Army has provided several Congolese indigenous churches with an archetype for uniforms, processions, discipline and music.

The Salvation Army entered Brazzaville in 1935 and has also concentrated its attention in the south. With a heavy emphasis on church planting in addition to its traditional concern for social service, the increase in its membership has been significant. The Baptist Church, which is aided by the Swedish Pentecostal-Baptist Örebro Mission, has been at work in the sparsely-populated northeast since 1921.

INDIGENOUS CHURCHES. The Kimbanguist Church (Eglise de Jésus-Christ sur la terre par le Prophète Simon Kimbangu, EJCSK), which is the largest independent church in Africa, has a large following in Congo-Brazzaville, although only a fraction of the parent church in neighbouring Zaire. After a long history of persecution as an underground church until 1960, Kimbanguists have now become part of the ecumenical movement, being members of the WCC, AACC and the newly-formed Federation of Christian Churches in the Congo.

Other groups of a more syncretistic nature include the Eglise Matsouaniste, Eglise Dieudonné au Congo, and Lassyism or Nzambi ya Bougie (God of the Candle). Begun by the Vili prophet Zepherin Lassy in 1953, the Bougists numbered 8.7% of the population in 1961. Their membership and influence have however subsequently declined.

Another more recent religious movement has been the notable campaign against witchcraft, magic and sorcery known as the Mouvement Croix-Koma (Nailed to the Cross) begun in 1964 by a Roman Catholic layman of the Lari tribe, Ta (Father) Malanda. By 1966, 30,000 persons a year (50% pagans, 30% Catholics, 20% Protestants) were coming to spend a structured 7-day period at his Kankata headquarters, surrendering their *nkisi* (fetishes) for public and permanent exhibition. Individuals were allowed to visit Kankata for the ceremonies only once, and the founder always regarded his movement as not a church but as a movement within the Roman Catholic Church. In 1967, the JMNR (Jeunesse du Mouvement National Revolutionnaire) under president Massamba-Débat proposed that Croix-Koma become the Congo's 'église officielle', but Malanda refused. By the end of 1970, a total of 184,789 pilgrims had visited Kankata; by the end of 1971, 20% of the entire population of the Congo had taken part, including virtually the entire Kongo, Lari and Sundi populace. After Malanda's death in 1971, the movement was carried on by his nephew. In 1976 it was still a highly-influential movement, but had abandoned all links with the Roman Catholic Church and operated as an independent religious movement or institution.

**CHURCH AND STATE.** Since Independence the country has had 3 constitutions, namely those of the first republic under abbé Fulbert Youlou, 1960–63; the second republic under Massamba-Débat, 1963–68; and the third republic since December 1968, under commandant Marien Ngouabi. According to the latest constitution of 30 December 1969, 'The Congo is a popular republic, one, indivisible and secular' (Article 1). 'Citizens enjoy freedom of speech, of the press, of association, of processions and demonstrations under conditions determined by the law' (Article 17). 'Freedom of conscience and religion are guaranteed to all citizens'. 'Religious communities are free in all questions relating to their beliefs and their external practices. It is forbidden to misuse religion or the church for political ends. Political organizations based on religion are forbidden' (Article 19).

Since 1964, the government has become progressively more socialist, defining its socialism as first scientific and then Marxist. In 1964 a single national party, trade union and youth movement were established, resulting in the prohibition of religious trade unions and the de facto suppression of various Christian movements for youth and adults. At the end of 1964 and during 1965, a number of priests and lay missionaries were expelled or imprisoned, and in August 1965 a decree nationalized all Evangelical, Salvation Army and Catholic private schools with the exception of those training 'servants of God' (major and minor seminaries, religious

**Mouvement Croix-Koma.** The Nailed-to-the-Cross movement was begun in 1964 by a Roman Catholic layman, Ta Malanda, with massive followings. *Above.* Malanda and the Cross. *Below.* Malanda reads Croix-koma's unique liturgy.

novitiates and theological colleges). At the time of the decree, half of all primary pupils were in Catholic schools.

The third republic, which has subsequently proclaimed itself to be Marxist-Leninist, has not changed the preceding legislation, and the position of the churches remains ambiguous. On the one hand, the government is developing at intermediate levels, including schools, army, and trade unions, an intense programme of ideological indoctrination emphasizing the incompatibility of being at the same time a militant revolutionary and a professing Christian; and at the level of political leadership anti-religious propaganda is evident here and there. On the other hand, at the level of government and law the authorities do everything possible to prevent disturbances and they retain courteous relationships with the leaders of the principal Christian denom-

inations, including Catholics, Evangelicals, Salvationists and Kimbanguists. Seminaries for clergy and schools for catechists operate normally.

Medical personnel at the numerous church-related dispensaries (11 Catholic, 14 Evangelical, 7 Salvation Army) are paid by the state, which also itself employs 11 Catholic sisters in state hospitals, as well as 11 other sisters and 2 priests in state schools. The Catholic weekly *La semaine* continues to appear without hindrance, and through prudent self-censorship enjoys a freedom and independence rare in French-speaking Africa.

In March 1977 the Catholic cardinal Biayenda was murdered soon after the assassination of the head of state.

In February 1978, the regime banned over 30 Christian and non-Christian religious bodies, including the Assemblies of God, Baha'i, Jehovah's Witnesses, Rosicrucians, Seventh-day Adventists, and all religious youth organizations; and confiscated all their buildings, furniture and other property. Only 7 groups were allowed to continue in legal existence: the Roman Catholic Church, Evangelical Church of the Congo, Salvation Army, Muslim Committee of the Congo, 2 indigenous churches (Kimbanguist Church, and Church of Zepherin Lassy), and Tenrikyo. However, even these 7 were forbidden to teach religion to young people.

**INTERDENOMINATIONAL ORGANIZATIONS.** The Federation of Evangelical Churches and Missions of Cameroon and Equatorial Guinea was established in 1943 to serve churches and missions in Cameroon, Rio Muni, Gabon and Congo-Brazzaville, but the organization disintegrated during the 1960s due to new political realities after independence in those countries. In the Congo, a desire for closer contacts at the local level brought together 4 denominations in a new ecumenical venture in September 1970: the Federation of Christian Churches in the Congo (Fédération des Eglises Chrétiennes du Congo-Brazzaville). Member bodies are the Salvation Army, Kimbanguist, Baptist, and Evangelical churches, and much later the Catholic Church also. The Salvation Army, Evangelical Church and Kimbanguist Church are all members both of the AACC and the WCC.

Concerning Catholic-Protestant relations, an interconfessional committee without official title has functioned since 1969. It has been responsible for organizing the Week of Prayer for Christian Unity, mutual invitations to church festivals and other events, and represents a significant step in the direction of wider ecumenical dialogue.

**BROADCASTING.** The state radio and TV Voix de la Révolution Congolaise formerly broadcast 15 to 20-minute programmes produced by the main confessions: Catholics, Protestants and Kimbanguists. This has now been reduced to 5-minute programmes, on radio only, for each denomination. French programmes were easily received from RVOG in Ethiopia until 1977. For Catholics, the Congo is registered as a member of UNDA.

**BIBLIOGRAPHY**
*Churches at the grass-roots: a study in Congo-Brazzaville.* E. Andersson. London: Lutterworth, 1968. 296p.
'La Mission Evangélique Suédoise et la naissance de l'Eglise Evangélique du Congo'. H. N'Kounkou. Thesis, Faculté Libre de Théologie Protestante, Montpellier (France), 1961.
*Le Matsouanisme.* F. Youlou. Brazzaville: Imprimerie Centrale, 1955.
'Le mouvement Croix-Koma: une nouvelle forme de lutte contre la sorcellerie en pays Kongo', J.-F. Vincent, *Cahiers d'études africaines*, 24 (1966), 527–563.

TABLE 2. ORGANIZED CHURCHES AND DENOMINATIONS IN THE CONGO (BRAZZAVILLE)

| Official name 1 | Begun 2 | Type 3 | Counc 4 | Congs 5 | Adults 6 | Affiliated 7 | Names, notes, and other statistics (see Codebook) 8 |
|---|---|---|---|---|---|---|---|
| Armée du Salut | 1935 | P Sal | xwA.C | 335 | 14,000 | 40,000 | *Salvation Army, Congo Territory.* Nkangu a Luvulusu. 96n,10x,7h,1j,1k,1s,W=50%. |
| Eglise Apostolique Unie en Afrique | 1971 | I pen | .v... | 12 | 1,500 | 3,000 | *EAUA. United Apostolic Ch (Zaire).* HQ Brazzaville. 1973 applied to WCC. 3n,23m. |
| Eglise Baptiste du Congo Populaire | 1921 | P Pe2 | Zvg.C | 61 | 2,197 | 4,000 | M=Örebro M(Sweden). 40% Bonguili, 40% Dzem. 7n,4x,G=1.1%pa,1p(7),W=50%,62Y,553z. |
| Eglise Catholique au Congo: | 1883 | R Lat | P,SBV | 83 | 231,500 | 399,165 | *Catholic Ch in Congo.* C=5+4+16. 3p,1s(19). 34n,131x,43m, 197w,P=26%,5004Y,6380y. |
| M  Brazzaville | 1890 | R Lat | Pa | 39 | 95,800 | 165,215 | Capital, 50% urban. Mainly Balali tribe. 18  56  21  101  25  3023  3667 |
| D  Fort-Rousset | 1950 | R Lat | Pa | 24 | 44,900 | 77,400 | Many tribes; evangelization in Lingala. 10  19  3  30  17  424  264 |
| D  Pointe-Noire | 1886 | R Lat | Pa | 20 | 90,800 | 156,550 | Diocese with most Protestants. M=CSSp. 6  56  19  66  31  1557  2449 |
| EdeJC sur la Terre par le Prophète SK | 1921 | I pen | xwi.C | | 18,000 | 30,000 | *EJCSK. Eglise Kimbanguiste.* M=Kimbanguist Ch (Zaire). Mostly Bakongo. |
| Eglise des Noirs en Afrique Centrale | 1941 | I Sal | ..... | | 1,000 | 2,000 | *ENAC. Ch of the Black Race.* Kaki Ch. Founder patriarch Simon Mpadi, Zaire. Ex SA. |
| Eglise Evangélique de la Likouala | 1946 | P int | xF... | 9 | 1,000 | 3,000 | *Mission d'Impfondo.* M=UWM(USA). Rain-forest along river. Bondjo, Bondongo. 9f,1h. |
| Eglise Evangélique du Congo | 1909 | P Con | .WA.C | 90 | 68,800 | 120,000 | *EEC.* M=SMF,MCCN. A=1961. 1947 revival. Kongo. 67n,3988m,14th,12i,1k,1s,W=80%,3190Y. |
| Eglise Matsouaniste | 1930 | I mar | ..... | | 500 | 1,000 | *Amical Balali.* Remnants of politico-messianic movement begun by André Matswa. |
| Eglise Orthodoxe: AD Afrique Centrale | | O Gre | Cw... | 1 | 200 | 300 | Under P Alexandria (Egypt). HQ Burundi. Lebanese, Greeks. Parish in Pointe-Noire. |
| Mission de Dieu du Bougie | 1953 | I Sal | ..... | | 20,000 | 50,000 | *Ch of God of the Candle.* Vili messiah Zepherin Lassy. Ex SA. Declining. |
| Mouvement Croix-Koma | 1964 | I ReC | ..... | 1 | 10,000 | 30,000 | *Dibundu dia Croix-Koma (Nailed to the Cross).* Ex RCC; renouncing witchcraft. |
| Témoins de Jéhovah | c1945 | M Jeh | x.... | 31 | 1,761 | 3,000 | *Jehovah's Witnesses.* Active witnessing by 1948. Severe persecution. 151Y. |
| Other African indigenous churches | | I | ..... | | 2,000 | 3,000 | Total about 15, including Eglise Dieudonné au Congo; all banned in 1978. |
| Total affiliated (mid-1970) | | | | 760 | 372,458 | 688,465 | Total denominations (1970) . . . 26. |
| Total affiliated (mid-1975) | | | | 820 | 426,300 | 788,040 | Total denominations (1975) . . . 27. |
| Total affiliated (mid-1980) | | | | 880 | 492,200 | 909,880 | Total denominations (1980) . . . 28. |

## NOTES ON TABLE ABOVE

COLUMNS: for meanings and CODES (cols. 1, 3, 4, 8), see Codebook (Part 6). Column 1: **Boldface type** = church with over 10% of country's affiliated Christians.
NATIONAL COUNCILS (Column 4, 5th letter).
C = Fédération des Eglises Chrétiennes du Congo (FECC) (Federation of Christian Churches in the Congo), or Conseil Oecuménique du Congo (Ecumenical Council of the Congo).
V = Conférence Episcopale du Congo (CEC) (Episcopal Conference of the Congo), also member of Ecumenical Council of the Congo.

PEOPLES (ethnolinguistic). Christians: 47% Kongo (21% Lari, Sundi, Vili, Yombe), 20% Teke, 11% Mbochi (Bangi, Kuyu, Maku, Furu, Ngiri), 7% Mbete, 5% Sanga (Mbimu, Bombo, Besom), 4% Eshira, 3% Maka, 1.4% French, 1% Kota, Greek, Portuguese, expatriate African, Pygmy.

## COUNTRY-WIDE TOTALS

EVANGELIZATION (see Part 5). 1900: 14%. 1970: 99%. 1980: 99%. *Mass evangelism.* Since 1960, extensive campaigns and large meetings (up to 15,000 attenders) under a team led by pastor Daniel N'Doundou of the Evangelical Church of the Congo.
FOREIGN MISSIONARIES AND PERSONNEL (nationals serving abroad) (1973). Total about 8 in Zaire: 6 Roman Catholics and 2 African indigenous.
FOREIGN MISSIONARIES AND PERSONNEL (aliens from abroad) (1973). Total 466. *From Western world.* 423: 300 Roman Catholics, 123 Protestants (62 in 2 Sweden societies, 32 in 1 Norway society, 9 in 1 Switzerland society, 9 in 2 USA societies, 6 in 1 Finland society, 3 in 2 UK societies, 2 in 1 Denmark society). *From Communist world.* 13 Roman Catholics from Poland. *From Third World.* 30: about 15 Roman Catholics and 15 indigenous from Zaire.
INSTITUTIONS (church-operated) (1973). Total 50, including 5 higher schools (minor seminaries), 32 medical centres, 4 religious communities (2 monasteries), 3 seminaries (2 Protestant, 1 RC).
PERIODICALS. About 9 titles.
PERSONNEL. About 6,166 (5,700 national, 466 foreign).
RELIGIOUS LIBRARIES. 7.
SCRIPTURE DISTRIBUTION (1975). Annual totals: 2,600 Bibles (23% subsidized, 77% commercial), 1,700 NTs (94% subsidized, 6% commercial). *Translations completed.* Portion: 5 languages since 1885. NT: 2 languages since 1891. Bible: 1 language in 1905.
SERVICE AGENCIES. About 13, including CEC, FECC, GBUAF, JEP(SCM), and others banned in 1978.

## ADDITIONAL DATA ON CHURCHES

ARMEE DU SALUT. In Kikongo, = Nkangu a Luvulusu. The Congo Territory has 5 Divisions. *Adult members.* Declined from 15,000 in 1966 to 14,000 in 1971, partly due to strict membership requirements (monogamy, rejection of alcohol and tobacco). *Membership.* 27% Kongo, 27% Bassangi, 20% Lari, 13% Vili, 13% Badondo.
EGLISE BAPTISTE DU CONGO POPULAIRE. Formerly known as Eglises Baptistes de la Sangha.
EGLISE CATHOLIQUE AU CONGO. *Catechumens.* (1959) 24,275; (1961) 27,639; (1963) 33,872. In 1972 they numbered 22,650, divided as follows among the 3 dioceses in the order shown (and included in column 7): 7800, 5150, 9700. *Priests.* The first Congolese was ordained in 1895. *Brothers.* Including 17 Congolese. *Sisters.* Including 54 Congolese. *Catechists.* Total (1970) 1,300, and also many part-time volunteers; (1973) 903 (404 full-time). *Indigenous religious congregations* (including novices). Brothers: 35 Frères de St-Joseph, 2 Frères de St-Pierre Claver. Sisters: 51 Religieuses du Rosaire (begun 1970). *Main foreign orders and congregations.* Priests (with over 10 members): 114 CSSp, 14 OSB (8 being Africans). Brothers (with over 10): 12 Frères de St-Gabriel (6 being Congolese). Sisters (with over 20): 44 St-Joseph de Cluny, 27 Spiritaines, 26 Franciscaines Missionnaires de Marie.
*Catholic organizations.* The Episcopal Conference of the Congo (Conférence Episcopale du Congo) is a member of SECAM and formerly in the Association of the Episcopal Conferences of Central Africa and Cameroon (ACEACCAM). There are no councils of priests or religious personnel, and youth and Catholic Action movements have been suppressed since 1964. Nevertheless the Legion of Mary (Légion de Marie) is active, especially in Brazzaville and Pointe-Noire, and a group called Scholas Populaires is oriented towards spiritual renewal at the parish level.
The Holy See had no diplomatic relations with Congo-Brazzaville until they were set up in 1977.

# COOK ISLANDS

## SECULAR DATA

**STATE. Official name:** The Territory Overseas of the Cook Islands.
**Flag** (shown above right): That of New Zealand.
**Area:** 234 sq.km. (93 sq.miles). Description: 15 islands (inhabited).
Agricultural land: 47.8%.
**Government:** Self-governing territory overseas of New Zealand, since 1965 (1888 British protectorate, 1901 annexed to New Zealand).
**Official language:** English.
**Capital:** Avarua, on Rarotongo.
**Armed forces** (1976): New Zealand forces.

**DEMOGRAPHY. Population:** 21,317 (census of 1.XII.1971. For 1970–2000 (UN), see last row of Table 1). Population density (1975): 107/sq.km. (277/sq.mile). Under 15 years: 48%. Growth rate (1975–80): 3.19% per year (births 4.11%, deaths −0.91%, emigrants −0.01%). Life expectancy (1975–80): 60.3 years Household size: 5.8 persons.
**Major languages:** English, Maori (Rarotongan), Manohiki, Pukapukan, Rakahanga.
**Labour force:** 30%.
**Tourists** (1975): About 35,000.

**ETHNOLINGUISTIC GROUPS:** 81.3% Cook Islands Maori, 15.4% Euronesian (part-Maori), 2.4% European (460), 0.6% other Pacific islander.

**MONEY** (1977). **Monetary unit:** NZ dollar (= 100 cents).
**National income per person:** US$700. Average annual family income: US$4,060.
**Cost of living in capital** (1976): Daily cost of living: US$30.

**EDUCATION. Adult literacy:** (1951) 92%. Schools: 33.

**HEALTH.** Hospitals: 8 (173 beds). Doctors: 3. Lepers: 900 (36 per 1,000).

**LITERATURE.** Newspapers: 1 daily.

**COMMUNICATION** (per 1,000 people). Phones: 43. Radios: 105. Daily newspaper circulation: 48 copies.

TABLE 1.    RELIGIOUS ADHERENTS IN THE COOK ISLANDS

| Year | 1900 | | mid-1970 | | Annual change, 1970–1980 | | | | mid-1975 | | mid-1980 | | 2000 | |
| --- | --- | --- | --- | --- | --- | --- | --- | --- | --- | --- | --- | --- | --- | --- |
| Name | Adherents | % | Adherents | % | Natural | Conversion | Total | Rate | Adherents | % | Adherents | % | Adherents | % |
| **Christians** | 8,200 | 100.0 | 21,160 | 99.3 | 764 | −8 | 756 | 3.05 | 24,790 | 99.2 | 28,720 | 99.0 | 50,960 | 98.0 |
| professing | 8,200 | 100.0 | 21.160 | 99.3 | 764 | −8 | 756 | 3.05 | 24,790 | 99.2 | 28,720 | 99.0 | 50,960 | 98.0 |
| Protestants | 8,140 | 99.3 | 17,310 | 81.3 | 622 | −35 | 587 | 2.91 | 20,150 | 80.6 | 23,180 | 79.9 | 39,680 | 76.3 |
| Roman Catholics | 60 | 0.7 | 2,680 | 12.6 | 99 | 16 | 115 | 3.57 | 3,220 | 12.9 | 3,830 | 13.2 | 7,280 | 14.0 |
| Marginal Protestants | 0 | 0.0 | 850 | 4.0 | 32 | 11 | 43 | 4.10 | 1,050 | 4.2 | 1,280 | 4.4 | 3,120 | 6.0 |
| Polynesian indigenous | 0 | 0.0 | 170 | 0.8 | 6 | 0 | 6 | 3.08 | 200 | 0.8 | 230 | 0.8 | 520 | 1.0 |
| Anglicans | 0 | 0.0 | 150 | 0.7 | 5 | 0 | 5 | 3.08 | 170 | 0.7 | 200 | 0.7 | 360 | 0.7 |
| nominal | 160 | 2.0 | 1,374 | 6.4 | 51 | 8 | 59 | 3.55 | 1,650 | 6.6 | 1,960 | 6.7 | 3,640 | 7.0 |
| affiliated | 8,040 | 98.0 | 19,786 | 92.9 | 713 | −16 | 697 | 3.01 | 23,140 | 92.6 | 26,760 | 92.3 | 47,320 | 91.0 |
| total practising | 7,640 | 95 | 15,830 | 80 | 570 | −12 | 558 | 3.01 | 18,510 | 80 | 21,410 | 80 | 33,120 | 70 |
| non-practising | 400 | 5 | 3,960 | 20 | 143 | −4 | 139 | 3.00 | 4,630 | 20 | 5,350 | 20 | 14,200 | 30 |
| Protestants | 7,990 | 97.4 | 16,146 | 75.8 | 578 | −35 | 543 | 2.90 | 18,770 | 75.1 | 21,580 | 74.4 | 37,230 | 71.6 |
| Evangelicals | 5,000 | 61.0 | 3,000 | 14.1 | 108 | −8 | 100 | 2.86 | 3,500 | 14.0 | 4,000 | 13.8 | 7,200 | 13.8 |
| Roman Catholics | 50 | 0.6 | 2,260 | 10.6 | 83 | 10 | 93 | 3.44 | 2,700 | 10.8 | 3,190 | 11.0 | 5,980 | 11.5 |
| Marginal Protestants | 0 | 0.0 | 1,140 | 5.4 | 43 | 11 | 54 | 3.86 | 1,400 | 5.6 | 1,680 | 5.8 | 3,430 | 6.6 |
| Polynesian indigenous | 0 | 0.0 | 140 | 0.6 | 5 | −2 | 3 | 2.00 | 150 | 0.6 | 170 | 0.6 | 420 | 0.8 |
| Anglicans | 0 | 0.0 | 100 | 0.5 | 4 | 0 | 4 | 3.08 | 120 | 0.5 | 140 | 0.5 | 260 | 0.5 |
| Baha'is | 0 | 0.0 | 100 | 0.5 | 4 | 2 | 6 | 4.62 | 130 | 0.5 | 160 | 0.6 | 500 | 1.0 |
| Non-religious | 0 | 0.0 | 40 | 0.2 | 2 | 6 | 8 | 10.00 | 80 | 0.3 | 120 | 0.4 | 540 | 1.0 |
| **Country's population** | 8,200 | 100.0 | 21,300 | 100.0 | 770 | 0 | 770 | 3.08 | 25,000 | 100.0 | 29,000 | 100.0 | 52,000 | 100.0 |

COLUMNS, ROWS. For meanings and definitions, see Codebook (Part 6). Note that, by definition, total 'Christians' = professing + crypto-Christians, which also = affiliated + nominal Christians. Percentages may not always total exactly, due to rounding.
CENSUSES. **25.IX.1945:** 89.1% Protestants, 9.8% Roman Catholics, 1.0% other religionists, 0.1% non-religious. **25.IX.1956:** 99.5% Christians, 0.2% other religionists, 0.1% Baha'is, 0.1% non-religious. **1.IX.1966:** 82.7% Protestants (76.2% Cook Islands Christian Ch., 6.1% SD Adventists), 12.3% Roman Catholics, 3.3% marginal Protestants, 0.8% Polynesian indigenous (Free Ch), 0.7% Anglicans, 0.2% non-religious, 0.1% Baha'is.

## NOTES ON RELIGIONS
BAHA'IS. Begun about 1950. In 1973, there was 1 local spiritual assembly, and 2 other centres.
POLYNESIAN INDIGENOUS. In 1 small group in 1970 (see Table 2).

The Islands' postage stamps often carry Christian themes, here The Resurrection of Christ by Raphael.

**NON-CHRISTIAN RELIGIONS.** Since almost the entire population was converted to Christianity during the 19th century, traditional religions have long ceased to exist as separate entities although they continue to manifest themselves in indigenous expressions of the Christian faith. A small Baha'i community has been formed.

### CHRISTIANITY
PROTESTANT CHURCHES. The principal denomination in the territory is the Cook Islands Christian Church which owes its origin to LMS missionary activity beginning in 1823. The church played a prominent role in the early expansion of Christianity in the Pacific; from 1872–96 it sent 70 of its own missionaries to evangelize Papua. Despite the encroachments of Catholicism, Mormonism and Seventh-day Adventists in the 20th century, two-thirds of the population are still members of the CICC. In addition, 12,000 other members have emigrated to or are temporarily working in New Zealand, where they come loosely under the care of the Presbyterian Church of New Zealand.

Rev. L.I. Sio (right), a Cook Islander now chairman of Congregational Union of New Zealand, inducts a Samoan pastor, Rev. Kenape Faletoese (left) in Christchurch, New Zealand, where some 14,000 Cook Islanders have emigrated.

Seventh-day Adventists arrived in 1892 and have built up a sizeable community. The SDA Cook Islands Mission is part of the Central Pacific Union Mission. A small Assemblies of God work was begun from New Zealand in 1963.

In 1971 there were 112 primary schools operated by Protestants (mainly the CICC), as well as several secondary and technical schools.

CATHOLIC CHURCH. Catholics first reached the islands in 1894, and in 1922 a prefecture was established. The diocese of Rarotonga is now a suffragan of the archdiocese of Suva in Fiji.

OTHER CHURCHES. Mormons were extremely active in the latter half of the 1960s and are now the second largest church of the islands. Many Maori missionaries from New Zealand have worked here, and growth is rapid, largely at the expense of losses from the CICC.

One small indigenous church is known to exist, the Amuri Free Church, which came into being on Aitutaki island through a schism from the Cook Islands Christian Church at the beginning of World War II.

An Anglican church has been built to serve the expatriate community. The church is administratively part of the diocese of Polynesia, in the Church of the Province of New Zealand.

CHURCH AND STATE. There is no established church and no government ministry or department handling religious affairs. The churches receive no direct financial aid from government although they are exempt from certain taxes and their educational and charitable institutions receive some subsidy. Clergy may obtain recognition as officiating ministers for the purpose of conducting weddings.

INTERDENOMINATIONAL ORGANIZATIONS. The Cook Islands Christian Church is a member of the National Council of Churches in New Zealand, founded in 1941.

BROADCASTING. The government Radio Cook Islands accepts religious programmes, with time rotated among the 4 leading churches. Each evening there are 5-minute prayers, and programmes on both Sunday mornings and afternoons. Special religious services are occasionally broadcast live. For Catholics, an association grouping the Cook Islands with Samoa, Tonga and Wallis & Futuna is a member of UNDA.

BIBLIOGRAPHY
'A modern Polynesian cargo cult', R. G. Crocombe, *Man*, LXI, 28 (1961), 40–41. (On Atiu Island among LMS Christians in 1947 led by woman healer and prophetess Kapuvai).

TABLE 2.     ORGANIZED CHURCHES AND DENOMINATIONS IN THE COOK ISLANDS

| Official name 1 | Begun 2 | Type 3 | Counc 4 | Congs 5 | Adults 6 | Affiliated 7 | Names, notes, and other statistics (see Codebook) 8 |
|---|---|---|---|---|---|---|---|
| Amuri Free Church | c1940 | I Con | ..... | | 80 | 140 | Schism ex LMS. On Aitutaki island. 50% decline from 296 adherents in 1951. |
| Anglican Church (D Polynesia) | | A Hig | avpK. | | 50 | 100 | In Diocese of Polynesia, Ch of the Province of New Zealand. Expatriates. |
| Assemblies of God | 1963 | P Pen | ..... | 1 | 50 | 100 | M=AoG(New Zealand). Classical Pentecostals (2-stage). |
| Catholic Church: D Rarotonga | 1894 | R Lat | P.PY. | 11 | 1,100 | 2,260 | Suffragan, M Suva (Fiji). Includes Niue Is. M=SSCC. C=2+0+1. 13x,7w,P=44%,15Y,98y. |
| Ch of Jesus C of Latter-day Saints | c1952 | M LdS | x.... | | 700 | 1,100 | *Mormons*. M=CJCLdS(USA). Rapid growth, G=7.2%pa. 20f. |
| Cook Islands Christian Church | 1823 | P Con | .WP.W | 95 | 3,031 | 14,746 | *CICC*. M=LMS(UK). 12,000 other members are emigres in New Zealand. 23n,1x,1s,481Yy. |
| Jehovah's Witnesses | 1961 | M Jeh | x.... | | 18 | 40 | Active witnessing reported 1962, lapse, then since 1968 new activity. |
| Seventy-day Adventist Church | 1892 | P Adv | x.... | 19 | 631 | 1,300 | *CI Mission*. Mass emigration to New Zealand. 2n,2x,G=−6.8%pa,1s,12t(1228),W=90%,211Y. |
| Total affiliated (mid-1970) | | | | 135 | 5,660 | 19,786 | Total denominations (1970) . . . 8. |
| Total affiliated (mid-1975) | | | | 145 | 6,620 | 23,140 | Total denominations (1975) . . . 9. |
| Total affiliated (mid-1980) | | | | 155 | 7,650 | 26,760 | Total denominations (1980) . . . 10. |

NOTES ON TABLE ABOVE
COLUMNS: for meanings and CODES (cols. 1, 3, 4, 8), see Codebook (Part 6). Column 1: Boldface type = church with over 10% of country's affiliated Christians.
NATIONAL COUNCILS (Column 4, 5th letter).
    W = National Council of Churches in New Zealand (NCCNZ).

PEOPLES (ethnolinguistic). Christians: 81.3% Cook Islands Maori, 15.4% Euronesian (part-Maori), 2.4% European (White), 0.6% other Pacific islander.

COUNTRY-WIDE TOTALS
EVANGELIZATION (see Part 5). 1900: 100%. 1970: 100%. 1980: 100%.

FOREIGN MISSIONARIES AND PERSONNEL (nationals serving abroad) (1973). Total about 3 Protestants in New Zealand. Over the years since 1830, over 200 Cook Islander Congregationalists have served overseas as foreign missionaries.
FOREIGN MISSIONARIES AND PERSONNEL (aliens from abroad) (1973). Total 49. *From Western world*. 24: about 10 Roman Catholics, about 10 marginal Protestants (Mormons from USA, New Zealand), 4 Protestants in 2 New Zealand societies. *From Third World*. 25 (about 10 marginal Protestants (Mormons), 10 Roman Catholics, 5 Protestants) from Fiji, Western Samoa et alia.
INSTITUTIONS (church-operated) (1973). Total 2 seminaries (Protestant).
PERIODICALS. 3 titles.
PERSONNEL. About 79 (30 national, 49 foreign).

RELIGIOUS LIBRARIES. 2.
SCRIPTURE DISTRIBUTION (1975). Annual totals: 850 Bibles (subsidized), 150 NTs (subsidized), 200 UBS portions, 70 UBS selections. *Translations completed*. Rarotonga: Portion 1828, NT 1836, Bible 1851.

ADDITIONAL DATA ON CHURCHES
CATHOLIC CHURCH. *Catholic organizations*. The bishop of Rarotonga is a member of the Episcopal Conference of the Pacific (CEPAC) with its seat in Fiji. The Holy See is represented to the Catholic hierarchy by the Apostolic Delegation to New Zealand and the Islands of the Pacific based in Wellington, New Zealand. The Catholic Church sponsors 2 schools (320 pupils) and one kindergarten.

---

# COSTA RICA

## SECULAR DATA

STATE. Official name: The Republic of Costa Rica (La República de Costa Rica). (Costa Rica = The Rich Coast). Adjective of nationality: Costa Rican (costarricense).
Flag (shown above right): Stripes top to bottom of blue, white, red, white, blue; national crest in white oval.
Area: 50,700 sq.km. (19,575 sq.miles). Agricultural land: 40.8%.
Government: Parliamentary republic, since 1838 (1502 Spanish colony, 1838 Independence, 3 dictatorships since).
Legislature: Legislative Assembly, 57 members.
Official language: Spanish (*Español/Castellano*).
Capital: San José 395,400 (1973).
Political divisions: 7 Provinces.
Armed forces (1976): No regular army. Paramilitary forces: 5,000.

DEMOGRAPHY. Population: 1,871,780 (census of 14.V.1973. For 1970–2000 (UN), see last row of Table 1). Population density (1975): 39/sq.km. (102/sq.mile). Under 15 years: 47%. Growth rate (1975–80): 2.73% per year (births 3.24%, deaths −0.51%). Life expectancy (1975–80): 70.2 years. Household size: 5.8 persons.
Major languages: Spanish, English, Chinese.
Urban dwellers (1970): 36.5%. Urban growth rate (1950–70): 4.5% per year.
Labour force: 31%.
Refugees (1977): From abroad, 2,000 (1,000 from Cuba, 1,000 from Chile).
Tourists (1971): 170,396. (1973) 246,825.

ETHNOLINGUISTIC GROUPS: 86.8% Costa Rican White, 7.0% Mestizo (Spanish/Indian), 1.9% Chinese (30,000) (Cantonese, Mandarin), 1.6% Nicaraguan, 1.0% Black (African Negro) (Jamaican, Caribbean), 1.0% Mulatto, 0.5% Amerindian (8,000) (0.2% Cabecar, 0.1% Boruca, 0.1% Bribrí, Half-Indian), 0.1% Jewish, Slav, British.

MONEY (1977). Monetary unit: colón (= 100 céntimos); US$1 = CRC8.57.
National income per person: US$802. Average annual family income: US$4,652.
Inflation: (1970–74) 12.8% per year, (1975) 17% per year (consumer price index 203).
Cost of living in capital (1976): index 94 (Washington DC=100). Daily cost of living: US$39.

EDUCATION. Adult literacy: (1950) 79%, (1973) 88%. Education rate: 51%. Schools: 2,865 (2,706 primary, 159 secondary). Universities: 1.

HEALTH. Hospitals: 48 (7,356 beds). Doctors: 1,323. Lepers: 1,600 (0.8 per 1,000). Blind: 2,000. Psychotics: 18,000.

LITERATURE. Annual new book titles (1971): 327. Periodicals: 50. Scientific journals: 15. Newspapers: 8 dailies.

COMMUNICATION (per 1,000 people). Phones: 47. Radios: 74. TV sets: 65. Daily newspaper circulation: 93 copies.

Catholicism is the state religion. *Above*. Inside the metropolitan cathedral, Archdiocese of San José.

TABLE 1. RELIGIOUS ADHERENTS IN COSTA RICA

| Year | 1900 | | mid-1970 | | Annual change, 1970–1980 | | | | mid-1975 | | mid-1980 | | 2000 | |
|---|---|---|---|---|---|---|---|---|---|---|---|---|---|---|
| *Name* | *Adherents* | *%* | *Adherents* | *%* | *Natural* | *Conversion* | *Total* | *Rate* | *Adherents* | *%* | *Adherents* | *%* | *Adherents* | *%* |
| **Christians** | **318,800** | **99.6** | **1,703,600** | **98.1** | **53,830** | **−58** | **53,772** | **2.75** | **1,955,150** | **98.0** | **2,241,320** | **98.0** | **3,538,600** | **95.8** |
| professing | 318,800 | 99.6 | 1,703,600 | 98.1 | 53,830 | −58 | 53,772 | 2.75 | 1,955,150 | 98.0 | 2,241,320 | 98.0 | 3,538,600 | 95.8 |
| Roman Catholics | 315,300 | 98.5 | 1,580,600 | 91.0 | 49,797 | −975 | 48,822 | 2.70 | 1,808,650 | 90.7 | 2,068,820 | 90.5 | 3,206,400 | 86.8 |
| Spiritist Catholics | 3,200 | 1.0 | 40,000 | 2.3 | 1,321 | 379 | 1,700 | 3.54 | 48,000 | 2.4 | 57,000 | 2.5 | 111,000 | 3.0 |
| Christo-pagans | 6,500 | 2.0 | 7,000 | 0.4 | 193 | −193 | 0 | 0.00 | 7,000 | 0.4 | 7,000 | 0.3 | 6,000 | 0.2 |
| Protestants | 3,000 | 0.9 | 90,000 | 5.2 | 2,910 | 430 | 3,340 | 3.16 | 105,700 | 5.3 | 123,400 | 5.4 | 221,700 | 6.0 |
| Marginal Protestants | 0 | 0.0 | 20,000 | 1.2 | 713 | 487 | 1,200 | 4.63 | 25,900 | 1.3 | 32,000 | 1.4 | 73,900 | 2.0 |
| Non-White indigenous | 0 | 0.0 | 9,000 | 0.5 | 283 | −3 | 280 | 2.72 | 10,300 | 0.5 | 11,800 | 0.5 | 29,600 | 0.8 |
| Anglicans | 500 | 0.2 | 4,000 | 0.2 | 127 | 3 | 130 | 2.83 | 4,600 | 0.2 | 5,300 | 0.2 | 7,000 | 0.2 |
| nominal | 1,000 | 0.3 | 3,840 | 0.2 | 243 | 810 | 1,053 | 11.94 | 8,820 | 0.4 | 14,370 | 0.6 | 16,300 | 0.4 |
| affiliated | 317,800 | 99.3 | 1,699,760 | 97.8 | 53,587 | −868 | 52,719 | 2.71 | 1,946,330 | 97.6 | 2,226,950 | 97.4 | 3,522,300 | 95.3 |
| doubly-affiliated | −1,000 | −0.3 | −60,000 | −3.5 | −2,032 | −884 | −2,916 | 3.95 | −73,800 | −3.7 | −89,150 | −3.9 | −210,000 | −5.7 |
| total practising | 301,910 | *95* | 1,444,800 | *85* | 45,549 | −738 | 44,811 | 2.71 | 1,654,380 | *85* | 1,892,910 | *85* | 2,641,700 | *75* |
| non-practising | 15,890 | *5* | 254,960 | *15* | 8,038 | −130 | 7,908 | 2.71 | 291,950 | *15* | 334,040 | *15* | 880,600 | *25* |
| Roman Catholics | 316,600 | 98.9 | 1,688,471 | 97.2 | 53,253 | −820 | 52,433 | 2.71 | 1,934,180 | 97.0 | 2,212,800 | 96.8 | 3,510,000 | 95.0 |
| Catholic pentecostals | 0 | 0.0 | 0 | 0.0 | 36 | 264 | 300 | 23.08 | 1,300 | 0.1 | 3,000 | 0.1 | 40,000 | 1.1 |
| Protestants | 2,000 | 0.6 | 49,621 | 2.9 | 1,646 | 482 | 2,128 | 3.56 | 59,800 | 3.0 | 70,900 | 3.1 | 129,300 | 3.5 |
| Evangelicals | 2,000 | 0.6 | 48,000 | 2.8 | 1,591 | 469 | 2,060 | 3.56 | 57,800 | 2.9 | 68,600 | 3.0 | 125,000 | 3.4 |
| Neo-pentecostals | 0 | 0.0 | 100 | 0.0 | 28 | 262 | 290 | 29.00 | 1,000 | 0.1 | 3,000 | 0.1 | 20,000 | 0.5 |
| Marginal Protestants | 0 | 0.0 | 14,524 | 0.8 | 493 | 345 | 838 | 4.68 | 17,900 | 0.9 | 22,900 | 1.0 | 66,500 | 1.8 |
| Non-White indigenous | 0 | 0.0 | 5,280 | 0.3 | 168 | 4 | 172 | 2.82 | 6,100 | 0.3 | 7,000 | 0.3 | 22,000 | 0.6 |
| Anglicans | 200 | 0.1 | 1,864 | 0.1 | 59 | 5 | 64 | 2.96 | 2,150 | 0.1 | 2,500 | 0.1 | 4,500 | 0.1 |
| Non-religious | 0 | 0.0 | 9,300 | 0.5 | 303 | 67 | 370 | 3.36 | 11,000 | 0.6 | 13,000 | 0.6 | 103,000 | 2.8 |
| Baha'is | 0 | 0.0 | 5,600 | 0.3 | 193 | 87 | 280 | 4.00 | 7,000 | 0.4 | 8,400 | 0.4 | 15,000 | 0.4 |
| Chinese folk-religionists | 400 | 0.1 | 5,000 | 0.3 | 146 | −86 | 60 | 1.13 | 5,300 | 0.3 | 5,600 | 0.2 | 6,000 | 0.2 |
| Atheists | 0 | 0.0 | 5,000 | 0.3 | 165 | 35 | 200 | 3.33 | 6,000 | 0.3 | 7,000 | 0.3 | 15,000 | 0.4 |
| Buddhists | 200 | 0.1 | 2,000 | 0.1 | 61 | −21 | 40 | 1.82 | 2,200 | 0.1 | 2,400 | 0.1 | 3,500 | 0.1 |
| Jews | 100 | 0.0 | 1,500 | 0.1 | 47 | 1 | 48 | 2.82 | 1,700 | 0.1 | 1,980 | 0.1 | 3,200 | 0.1 |
| Tribal religionists | 500 | 0.2 | 1,000 | 0.1 | 26 | −36 | −10 | −1.05 | 950 | 0.0 | 900 | 0.0 | 700 | 0.0 |
| Other religionists | 0 | 0.0 | 4,000 | 0.2 | 129 | 11 | 140 | 2.98 | 4,700 | 0.2 | 5,400 | 0.2 | 10,000 | 0.3 |
| **Country's population** | **320,000** | **100.0** | **1,737,000** | **100.0** | **54,900** | **0** | **54,900** | **2.75** | **1,994,000** | **100.0** | **2,286,000** | **100.0** | **3,695,000** | **100.0** |

COLUMNS, ROWS. For meanings and definitions, see Codebook (Part 6). Note that, by definition, total 'Christians' = professing + crypto-Christians, which also = affiliated + nominal Christians. Percentages may not always total exactly, due to rounding.
CENSUSES. **27.XI.1864:** 99.75% Roman Catholics, 0.24% Evangelicals (286 persons), 0.01% Hindus. No subsequent census has included a question on religion, but in 1972 an official estimate was published by the Civil Registry of the Republic, as follows: 90.0% Roman Catholics, 7.0% Protestants (128,912 persons), 2.5% others (46,390 persons) including Jews, Masons, Rosicrucians, Theosophists, Baha'is, Spiritists, Mormons, and Aquarians (*Registro Civil de la Republica,1972*). After adjusting these categories to fit the definitions in this Encyclopedia, we arrive at the percentages given in the table above for professing Christians and non-Christian religions in 1970.

NOTES ON RELIGIONS
ATHEISTS. Popular Vanguard Party (PVP) (Communist, proscribed; pro-Soviet): membership (1970) 1,000; best-organized and most sophisticated Communist party in Central America.
BAHA'IS. Growth from 22 local spiritual assemblies (1964) to 56 (1973).
CATHOLIC PENTECOSTALS (or, Catholic charismatics). Totals (January 1974): 400 involved adults in 22 prayer groups; total charismatic community including children, 800.
CHRISTO-PAGANS. Amerindians whose syncretistic folk-Catholicism combines 17th-century Spanish Catholicism with their own traditional animism, concepts and world-views.
DOUBLY-AFFILIATED. The term covers those affiliated to, or claimed by, both the Catholic Church and also an Evangelical church (Protestant, marginal Protestant, Anglican or Non-White indigenous), i.e. baptized Catholics who have recently become Evangelicals. Because their statistics represent a duplication, they are shown in the table as a negative quantity (with a minus sign).
JEWS. Only a small proportion are practising Jews.
NEO-PENTECOSTALS. Charismatics within the non-Pentecostal Protestant denominations, beginning with the spread from Argentina of the charismatic renewal in 1969 known as the Renovación Josefina (renewal in the Iglesia Josefina, i.e. Evangelical churches in the area of greater San José). Denominations involved: Asociación de Iglesias Bíblicas, Asociación de Iglesias Ev Centroamericanas, Iglesia Metodista. The headquarters is the Templo Bíblico, San José (before 1972 a non-Pentecostal church in the Asociación de Iglesias Bíblicas).
NON-RELIGIOUS. Costa Rican Whites, but also many Chinese especially youths rejecting family religion.
NON-WHITE INDIGENOUS. In about 14 denominations in 1970 (see Table 2).
OTHER RELIGIONISTS. Including non-Christian Spiritists, Theosophists, a few Hindus, Rosicrucians (AMORC, 1 centre), Aquarians, et alii. ISKCON (Hare Krishna) also operates a centre.
PRACTISING CHRISTIANS. Weekly attendance at Catholic mass: 15% of whole urban population, 25% of rural population. Annual attendance: 83% of population (85% of all affiliated Christians).
TRIBAL RELIGIONISTS. Of the 8,000 Amerindians (1970), a proportion are still animists, mainly on the Caribbean side in the southern Talamanca district; tribes include the Bribrí, Cabecar, Boruca, Guatuso and Oritiña.

**NON-CHRISTIAN RELIGIONS.** According to an estimate of the Civil Registry of the republic, in 1972 about 2.5% of the population belonged to numerous marginal Protestant and quasi-Christian bodies: Rosicrucians, Theosophists, Spiritists, Mormons, Aquarians, Masons; there were also Jews and followers of Baha'i. During the last century, Freemasonry made some impact in intellectual circles, contributing towards a degree of anti-clericalism among government officials.

**Judaism** is only practised by a small part of the Jewish population, living mostly in San José and consisting mainly of descendants of immigrant Jews.

**Traditional religions** have virtually disappeared due to the decline of the indigenous Indian population. These latter were estimated in the year 1502 to number 27,000; in 1569 they were 17,166, decreasing to 9,000 in 1741 and to 8,000 in 1970.

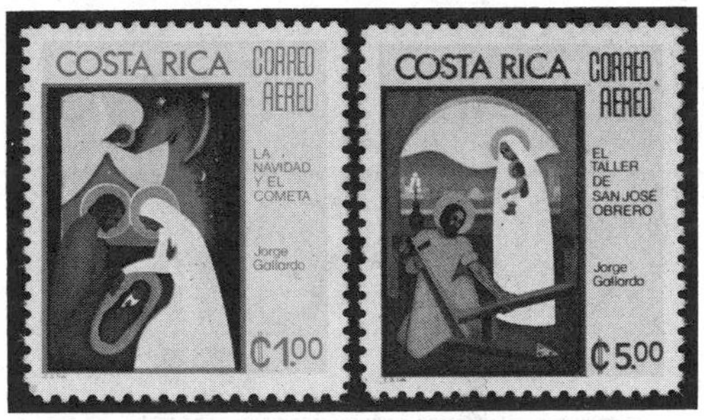


Christianity is often represented on postage stamps: here (1975), *left* The Nativity and the Comet, *right* Joseph in his workshop, both by Jorge Gallardo.

## CHRISTIANITY

CATHOLIC CHURCH. Columbus arrived off Costa Rica in 1502, and the first Catholic missionaries disembarked in 1514. Originally a province under the viceroy of Guatemala (1569), the rugged terrain and inadequate labour supply contributed to the development of small farms in contrast to the more common latifundia (landed aristocracy) pattern of most Latin American countries. This in turn resulted in the growth of an independent, individualistic character among the people. In spite of early mass baptisms among the Chorotega Indians (6,000 being baptized in 1522 with their chief) and Costa Rica's inclusion in the diocese of Leon (Nicaragua) in 1531, little effective pastoral attention was given to the area. In 1711, a visiting bishop noted the spiritual poverty of the people and ordered the building of chapels in all parishes and the fulfilment of church obligations by all families; but nothing came of this.

Spain's negative reaction to the Protestant Reformation resulted in Central America being closed to the influence of all other European nations, thus limiting economic as well as religious development. Upon achieving independence from Spain in 1821, Costa Rica invited Europeans and Americans to help develop its resources. Expatriate businessmen in turn contributed to the coffee and banana trade and helped initiate the first Protestant services in a private home in 1848.

The Catholic Church continued to be the only recognized religious body after Independence, but the constitution was liberalized in 1848, and even greater religious liberty was granted in 1860. A concordat with the Holy See was concluded in 1852. Jesuits entered in 1875 but were suppressed in 1884, and the church was forbidden to interfere in the affairs of the state. Throughout its history, however, Costa Rica has experienced little political turmoil, in part the result of the general absence of a landed aristocracy.

Religious practice among Catholics is largely confined to Sunday observance, about 15% of the faithful participating in Sunday mass in large cities and up to 25% in rural areas. For the majority, religion is individualistic, centred in the veneration of saints and often mixed with superstition.

OTHER CHURCHES. In 1865, when the first non-denominational church was built in San José, there were only 286 Protestants known in the country. The church was served intermittently by Congregationalist and Methodist clergy prior to being taken over by Anglicans in 1896. Negro immigrants from the West Indies began to flood into the country in the latter part of the 19th century, and several West Indies churches sent missionaries to serve them: the Jamaica Baptist Missionary Society in 1887, the Methodist Missionary Society (UK) in 1894 and the Anglican SPG in 1896. The Baptist Convention was later aided by the BMS (UK) and since 1949 by Southern Baptists from the USA. The Methodist Church maintains ties with British Methodism and American Episcopalians have assumed responsibility for the early SPG work.

The first North American missionary society was the Central American Mission, in 1891. This was followed by American Methodists in 1917 and the Latin America Mission in 1921. Pentecostals made their initial appearance in 1930–32, with the arrival of missionaries from the Assemblies of God and the Church of God of Prophecy. These were followed by others from the Church of God (Cleveland) in 1935, and the International Church of the Foursquare Gospel in 1953. The latter is the largest Protestant denomination in Costa Rica at the present time.

Some 14 other new missions have established themselves in various parts of the country since World War II. However, none has yet achieved a significant following.

**CHURCH AND STATE.** The constitution of 1949 invokes the 'name of God', in its preamble. Article 76 declares that the Catholic religion 'is that of the State'; the latter therefore contributes to its support while guaranteeing freedom of conscience and practice to all other religions. Article 28 in its last paragraph prohibits priests from engaging in any political propaganda based on religious beliefs or motivations.

The only church marriages which have civil validity are those celebrated in the Catholic Church, to the exclusion of other churches. Priests must register marriages with the state, in addition to providing proper information concerning the civil state of the contracting parties, failure to provide which may lead to legal prosecution. The Catholic religion is taught in the public schools and the Catholic Church is exempt from property taxes. In 1973 a law was proposed in parliament extending these privileges to all churches, but it had not yet been acted upon by 1974. Concerning episcopal appointments, beginning in 1952 the state no longer presents to the apostolic nuncio a list of 3 candidates when a new archbishop is to be chosen, as had formerly been the custom in virtue of the Spanish system of patronage.

Since the expulsion of religious orders at the end of the 19th century, which was repealed in 1942, there have been no serious conflicts between church and state. In 1943 the Catholic Church played an important role in the implementation of a number of major social reforms, including promulgation of a code of employment, creation of a social security fund for medical assistance to workers, and the founding of a national university. At the political level, these endeavours have obliged the church to support publicly a coalition government consisting of reformists and communists.

**INTERDENOMINATIONAL ORGANIZATIONS.** The Costa Rican Evangelical Alliance (Alianza Evangélica Costarricense), formed in 1951 to represent the cause of Evangelical Christians before government, has a constituency of 14 member churches. Adventists, Baptists and Episcopalians are not members. In 1962 the Alliance initiated Good Will Caravans to provide medical, nutritional, literacy and agricultural assistance to areas affected by floods, and by 1968 75 caravans had visited 37 isolated rural communities. The programme is now administered separately from the Alliance with Episcopalian co-operation.

The Spanish Language Institute, begun in Colombia in 1942 by United Presbyterians (USA) for training their missionary personnel, was transferred to San José in 1950 and serves all Christian groups. By 1967, 3,325 missionary students representing well over 100 different societies had studied at the institute. The average annual enrolment is 320.

The Catholic Church has no official ecumenical organizations, but there are in Costa Rica several small interconfessional movements. The various progressivist youth groups including Movimiento Iglesia Joven, Juventud Obrera Cristiana and Juventud Universitaria Cristiana, although principally composed of Catholics, also have Protestant members. Another progressivist interdenominational group Exodo, founded in 1971 in San José, publishes a critical weekly paper entitled *Pueblo* which is dedicated to the systematic conscientization of the oppressed classes. Exodo is related to ISAL in Uruguay. The Asociación Latinoamericana de Escuelas Teológicas (ALET), in San José, sponsors a SODEPAX programme for Costa Rica, in co-operation with SODEPAX headquarters in Switzerland.

**BROADCASTING.** The numerous commercial radio stations all accept religious programmes, also the national TV network. The Latin American Mission has since 1945 had its own radio station in San José, TIFC (Lighthouse of the Caribbean), and broadcasts Protestant programmes for 15 minutes daily from Monday to Saturday. Difusiones Interamericanas (DIA, Interamerican Gospel Communications) is an outgrowth of the Pan-American Christian network begun in 1951 with headquarters in San José. DIA communicates the gospel throughout the Spanish-speaking world by means of over 800 tape-recorded programmes distributed monthly. In Costa Rica, the Catholic church's 3 stations and radiophonic schools act as purely commercial bodies and only rarely broadcast cultural or educational programmes, and then only ones produced in North America or Europe. For Catholics, Costa Rica is a member of UNDA. International stations over which Protestant programmes can be easily heard are FEBC (California), TWR (Netherlands Antilles) and HCJB (Ecuador).

**BIBLIOGRAPHY**

*A history of Protestantism in Costa Rica*. W. M. Nelson. Lucknow, India: Lucknow Publishing House, 1963. 258p.
*Estado del Clero de la Provincia de Costa Rica*. San José: Exodo, 1972.

TABLE 2. ORGANIZED CHURCHES AND DENOMINATIONS IN COSTA RICA

| Official name 1 | Begun 2 | Type 3 | Counc 4 | Congs 5 | Adults 6 | Affiliated 7 | Names, notes, and other statistics (see Codebook) 8 |
|---|---|---|---|---|---|---|---|
| Asambleas de Dios | 1930 | P Pe2 | ZF..C | 56 | 2,841 | 7,500 | *Conferencia Ev de la AdD*. M=AoG(USA). 74n,3x,14f,G=17%pa,2s(72),W=33%,345Y,1245z. |
| Asociación Bautista Costarricense | 1940 | P Bap | x...C | 7 | 109 | 300 | *Costa Rican Baptist Association*. M=American Baptist Association(USA). HQ San José. |
| Asoc de Igls Bíblicas Costarricenses | 1921 | P int | xN..C | 40 | 1,574 | 3,000 | *Association of CR Bible Chs*. M=LAM(USA). Rural. Radio station. 7n,88f,1H,1j,1k,1s. |
| Asoc de Igls Ev Centroamericanas | 1891 | P int | xM... | 33 | 1,050 | 2,000 | *Assoc of Central American Chs*. M=CAM(USA). 1937, major schism. A=1948. 9n,18m,16f. |
| Compañerismo Bautista Mundial | 1963 | P Bap | xT... | 2 | 50 | 100 | M=World Baptist Fellowship Mission Agency(USA). Fundamentalists. |
| Consejo de Igls Luteranas en CA & P | 1962 | P Lut | x...C | 2 | 23 | 52 | *Sinodo de Misuri. Lutheran Ch*. M=LC Missouri Synod(USA). HQ San José. 1n,1x,5Yy. |
| Convención Bautista de Costa Rica | 1887 | P Bap | T.... | 44 | 1,268 | 2,419 | 1887, M=JBMS(Jamaica); 1949,SBC(USA). 10% Jamaicans. 26n,8x,16f,G=5.1%pa,1s(6),222Y. |
| Ejército de Salvación | 1907 | R Sal | xwM.. | 2 | 100 | 300 | *Salvation Army*. In Caribbean & CA Territory. After 1969 eruption, Mercy Caravan. 2f. |
| Iglesia Adventista del Séptimo Día | 1903 | P Adv | x.... | 28 | 2,507 | 5,000 | *Seventh-day Adventists, CR Mission*, CAmerican UM. Declining, 2nx,2f,1r,35t,194Y. |
| Iglesia Bautista Nacional | c1950 | I Bap | ..... | 2 | 30 | 50 | *National Baptist Ch*. Small local indigenous Costa Rican body. |
| **Iglesia Católica en Costa Rica:** | 1514 | R Lat | B.LDR | 154 | 894,900 | 1,688,471 | *Catholic Ch in CR*. C=8+5+23. 225n,1p,1q,1s. 370nx,71m,898w,53043Yy. |
| M San José de Costa Rica | 1850 | R Lat | Bs | 68 | 407,000 | 767,898 | Urban, suburban, industrial. Descendants of Spaniards. 231 63 702 23907 |
| D Alajuela | 1921 | R Lat | Bs | 31 | 168,200 | 317,464 | Rural. Descendants of original Spanish settlers. 70 8 87 8537 |
| D San Isidro de El General | 1954 | R Lat | Bs | 12 | 95,400 | 180,000 | Rural. Large banana plantation with expatriate labour. 14 0 35 6830 |
| D Tilarán | 1961 | R Lat | Bs | 19 | 165,400 | 312,000 | Rural. Mestizos. Vast latifundia (landlordist) estates 35 0 50 8828 |
| VA Limón | 1921 | R Lat | Pcm | 24 | 58,900 | 111,109 | Rural. Bananas. Slave descendants, Jamaica Blacks. P=65%. 20 0 20 4941 |
| Iglesia de Dios de CR (Anderson) | 1935 | P Hol | x...C | 5 | 140 | 400 | M=CoG(Anderson)(USA). San José, Siquirres, Limón, Cimarrones. 2x,4f,W=95%. |
| Iglesia de Dios de CR (Cleveland) | 1935 | P Pe3 | ZF..C | 60 | 1,731 | 3,300 | M=CoG(Cleveland) (USA). 10% English-speaking Blacks. Several splits. 40n,2f,1p. |
| Iglesia de Dios de la Profecía | 1932 | P Pe3 | Z.... | 4 | 250 | 500 | *Ch of God of Prophecy*. M=CGP(USA). Split ex CoG(Cleveland) in USA. HQ San José. |
| Iglesia de Dios (Universal) | c1962 | I pe3 | ..... | 2 | 36 | 80 | *Ch of God (Universal)*. Schism ex CoG(Cleveland) (USA). 1n. |
| Iglesia de JC de los Santos de los UD | c1953 | M LdS | x.... | | 1,300 | 2,524 | *Latter-day Saints. Mormons*. M=CJCLdS(USA). HQ San José. 40f,G=3.6%pa. |
| Iglesia del Evangelio Cuadrangular | 1953 | P Pe2 | ZF..C | 49 | 2,511 | 8,000 | *International Ch of the Foursquare Gospel*. M=ICFG(USA). 53nm,3f,1s(15),W=63%,212Y. |
| Iglesia del Nazareno | 1948 | P Hol | xF..C | 6 | 62 | 300 | *Ch of the Nazarene*. M=CoN(USA). 1n,15m,5f,G=22%pa,1s(32),7t(242),W=71%,12Y,16z. |
| Iglesia Episcopal: D Costa Rica | 1896 | A Hig | aw.R. | 15 | 1,173 | 1,864 | *PECUSA, Province IX*. 90% English-speaking Blacks in banana trade. 9n,2x,1s,11Y,91y. |
| Iglesia Ev Luterana de Costa Rica | c1946 | P Lut | L.... | 1 | 500 | 750 | *Ev Luth Ch in CR, El Sal,Hond,Nic,Panama*. Germans, Scandinavians. 1x,W=5%,7y,65z. |
| Iglesia Ev Metodista de Costa Rica | 1917 | P Met | Vu..C | 24 | 1,538 | 2,500 | *CR annual Conference, United Methodist Ch*(USA). 1 school (1120). 23n,17f,1k,1s,25t. |
| Iglesia Evangélica Nacional | c1960 | I ind | ..... | 2 | 20 | 50 | *National Ev Ch*. Local Costa Rican indigenous body. |
| Iglesia La Luz del Mundo (Aaronistas) | | I pel | x.... | 2 | 50 | 100 | *Light of the World Ch*, from Guadalajara (Mexico). Unitarian pentecostals. |
| Iglesia Metodista | 1894 | P Met | VwV.C | 5 | 700 | 1,500 | In *MCCA* (HQ Antigua). M=MMS(UK). Declining. Coast Blacks. 1n,3f,G=−10%pa,11Yy. |
| Iglesia Santa Pentecostés | 1930 | P Pe3 | ZF... | 13 | 415 | 1,000 | *Pentecostal Holiness Ch*. M=PHC(USA). HQ San José. 3n,1x,7f,1s. |
| Iglesia Union de San José | | P com | ....C | 1 | 300 | 1,000 | *Union Ch of San José*. English-speaking, mainly expatriates. 1x. |
| Iglesias de Cristo | 1967 | P Dis | x...C | 8 | 200 | 500 | *Chs of Christ*. M=CC(Non-Instrumental) (USA). San José, Limón, Buffalo, et al. 1p. |
| Misión Evangélica Menonita | 1962 | P Men | G...C | 9 | 98 | 200 | *Ev Mennonite Ch*. M=Conservative Mennonite BMC(USA). Some Amish from USA. 3x,22f. |
| Testigos de Jehová | c1915 | M Jeh | x.... | 78 | 3,271 | 7,000 | *Jehovah's Witnesses, Watch Tower. IBSA*. Active witnessing since 1920s. 190Y. |
| Other Protestant denominations | | P | ..... | | 5,000 | 9,000 | Total about 20 (see list below). |
| Other Black indigenous churches | | I | ..... | | 3,000 | 5,000 | Total about 10, including NBCUSA(1961; USA Blacks). |
| Other marginal Protestant bodies | | M | ..... | | 2,500 | 5,000 | Several fringe cults, including Christian Spiritists. |
| Doubly-affiliated (duplication) (1970) | | | | | −31,800 | −60.000 | Evangelicals who also are or were baptized Roman Catholics. |
| **Total affiliated (mid-1970)** | | | | **770** | **897,447** | **1,699,760** | **Total denominations (1970) . . . 59.** |
| **Total affiliated (mid-1975)** | | | | **820** | **1,027,600** | **1,946,330** | **Total denominations (1975) . . . 66.** |
| **Total affiliated (mid-1980)** | | | | **870** | **1,175,800** | **2,226,950** | **Total denominations (1980) . . . 73.** |

NOTES ON TABLE ABOVE

COLUMNS: for meanings and CODES (cols. 1, 3, 4, 8), see Codebook (Part 6). Column 1: **Boldface type** = church with over 10% of country's affiliated Christians.

NATIONAL COUNCILS (Column 4, 5th letter).
- C = Alianza Evangélica Costarricense (AEC) (Costa Rican Evangelical Alliance).
- R = Conferencia Episcopal de Costa Rica (CECOR) (Episcopal Conference of Costa Rica).

*Other national councils*. There is also an Alianza Evangélica de Costa Rica, whose constitution forbids it to enter into foreign correspondence.

OTHER PROTESTANT DENOMINATIONS. These smaller bodies, mostly denominations from the USA, include: Baptist Bible Fellowship International (1968), Baptist International Missions (1968), Baptist Missionary Association of America (1961), Bethel Temple World Missionary Assistance Plan, Children of God International (in Guadalupe), Christadelphian Ecclesias, Christian Brethren (Open), Congregational Holiness Ch (1967), Conservative Baptist Home Mission Society (1955; 2 churches), Elim Missionary Assemblies (1964), Ev Lutheran Synod (1972), Pentecostal Ch of God, Religious Society of Friends (1946 immigrant community from USA), World-Wide Missions (1965). There are also a few independent congregations.

UNITING CHURCHES. Negotiations for organic union were under way in 1974 between: Iglesia Ev Metodista de Costa Rica (Unida) and the Methodist Ch of the Caribbean & the Americas.

PEOPLES (ethnolinguistic). Christians: 88.0% Costa Rican White, 7.1% Mestizo, 1.6% Nicaraguan, 1.0% Black, 1.0% Mulatto, 0.7% Chinese, 0.4% Amerindian, Slav, British.

COUNTRY-WIDE TOTALS

EVANGELIZATION (see Part 5). 1900: 100%. 1970: 100%. 1980: 100%. *Mass evangelism*. Among recent campaigns: 1961 nation-wide Evangelism-in-Depth campaign (192 participating local churches from 11 denominations, 50,757 homes visited, 3,153 professions of faith, 1,000 prayer cells); 1963, 1966 Costa Rica host to international workshops on Evangelism-in-Depth; 1967, Hermano Pablo 15-day crusade in San José (30,000 attenders, 1,121 enquirers). *Radiophonic evangelism*. HCJB, FEBC, Radio Vatican, et al. Radiophonic schools (Catholic): 50,000 enrolled. Bible correspondence courses (1975): ICI (3,092 enrolments, 800 active,-80 conversions).

FOREIGN MISSIONARIES AND PERSONNEL (nationals serving abroad) (1973). Total 197 in 6 countries: about 190 Roman Catholics, 7 Protestants.

FOREIGN MISSIONARIES AND PERSONNEL (aliens from abroad) (1973). Total 1,004. *From Western world*. 522: 246 Protestants (226 in 32 USA societies, 12 in 2 Canada societies, 7 in 3 UK societies, 1 in 1 New Zealand society), 234 Roman Catholics, about 40 marginal Protestants (Mormons) from USA, 2 Anglicans in 1 USA society. *From Third World*. 482 (467 Roman Catholics, 10 Protestants, 5 indigenous) from Mexico, Jamaica and other Latin American and Caribbean countries.

INSTITUTIONS (church-operated) (1973). Total 65, including 37 higher schools (2 minor seminaries), 1 hospital, 3 radio stations, 2 research centres, 11 seminaries (8 Protestant, 2 RC, 1 Anglican), 3 study centres.

PERIODICALS. About 25 titles.

PERSONNEL. About 2,244 (1,240 national, 1,004 foreign).

RELIGIOUS LIBRARIES. About 20.

SCRIPTURE DISTRIBUTION (1975). Annual totals: 34,222 Bibles (42% subsidized, 58% commercial), 78,288 NTs (38% free, 37% subsidized, 25% commercial), 426,542 UBS portions, 916,645 UBS selections. *Translations completed*. Portion: 2 languages since 1905.

SERVICE AGENCIES. About 76, including ACISJF, AEC, AEPE, ALET, CCCI, CECOR, CEF, CLAME, COCC, DIA, FECOR, FEREC, JEC, JOC, JUC, MEC, MFC, MJC, SEDAC, SU, WRMF, YLC.

ADDITIONAL DATA ON CHURCHES

IGLESIA CATOLICA EN COSTA RICA. *Catholics*. Including 10,000 Chinese (1966). *Annual baptisms*. (1972) 99.8% infant, 0.2% adult. *Male religious*. Total (1970) 220, of whom 35% nationals, 65% expatriates (4% from other Latin American countries, 61% from other continents). *Brothers*. Many others are not reported by dioceses. Total (1973) 77 nationals, 143 expatriates. *Sisters*. Contemplatives and others are not reported by dioceses. Total all sisters (1973) 1,068: 575 nationals, 493 expatriates. *Catholic charismatics* (January 1974). 400 adults in 22 organized prayer groups are active in the Catholic Charismatic Renewal. *Catechists*. Total (1974) 250 (under Propaganda). *Main religious orders and congregations*. Priests: CM, OFMConv. Sisters: Sisters of Zion, Good Shepherd Sisters, Sisters of St Anne (the largest congregation, with 150 professed), Sisters of Mary Help of Christians, Oblates of the Divine Love.

*Catholic organizations*. The Episcopal Conference of Costa Rica (Conferencia Episcopal de Costa Rica, CECOR) has its headquarters in San José and is a member of CELAM and SEDAC. Associations of religious personnel, which are members of CLAR and SERCAP, are the Federación Costarricense de Religiosos (FECOR) and Federación de Religiosas de Costa Rica (FEREC). The Comisión Arquidiocesana de Pastoral, founded in 1970 to serve the archdiocese of San José, is the only co-ordinating body for lay movements in Costa Rica. In 1973 the principal groups were: Movimiento Familiar Cristiano (Christian Family Movement), founded in 1958 with about 150 groups; Movimiento Hermandades del Trabajo, founded in 1958, with more than 400 workers; Juventud Estudiantil Católica, founded in 1965 with over 300 students; Acción Cristiana Universitaria, founded in 1967 but in decline with only 40 members; Legión de María, consisting of small groups mostly in rural areas; Ligos Espirituales de Obreros Católicos, begun in 1943; Liga de Damas Católicas, begun in 1945; Club Serra, an elitist group; and Pálestia.

The Holy See has diplomatic relations with Costa Rica and is represented to government and the Catholic hierarchy by a nuncio in San José.

The international headquarters for the Federación Centro-Americana de Centros de Integración Familiar is located in San José. The Federation acts as a co-ordinating body for activities of Christian Family Movement type in Latin America. The Secretariado Episcopal de América Central y Panamá (SEDAC), which is the regional secretariat of CELAM, is also based in Costa Rica.

Non-official opinion groups include the following: (1) Movimiento Iglesia Joven, founded in San José in 1971, which is a group of Christians for Socialism composed of about 50 Catholic and Protestant students, dedicated to the study of national realities, the diffusion of liberation theology and political action in support of workers and peasants; (2) Juventud Obrera Cristiana (JOC), with some 50 workers in San José, which engages in political action and the promotion of liberation theology and has been repudiated by the episcopate; (3) Juventud Universitaria Cristiana (JUC), in S Pedro de Montes de Oca, which was also repudiated by the episcopate for its promotion of liberation theology; (4) Movimiento Estudiantil Cristiano, with about 50 Christians for Socialism, which has achieved an important place in the country's student movement; (5) Movimiento Juvenil Cristiano, founded in Heredia in 1970, with more than 450 mostly secondary pupils as members, which is less fixed in its political orientation but has demonstrated its solidarity with workers and peasants.

Research and social action are carried on in the Escuela Social Juan XXIII, founded in Curridabat in 1963, which is a diocesan centre 'for teaching, defending and disseminating the social doctrine of the Church and for co-ordinating, promoting and initiating all diocesan endeavours of Catholic Social Action'. The centre provides training courses for community leaders and trade unionists and social action seminars for priests and students.

Theological training is provided by the Instituto de Teología para Seglares, founded in San José in 1970, which offers a 5-year theological course for laymen at the university level; and the Instituto Pedagógico de Religión, in San José, which is dependent on the Junta Nacional de Catequesis and trains parish leaders and teachers of religion in schools.

The Catholic school programme in 1969 operated in 74 schools (15,423 pupils) of which 18 were pre-primary (1,381), 23 primary (5,242) and 33 on the secondary level (8,800). By 1973 there were 29 primary schools (7,313 pupils) and the 33 secondary had 10,909 pupils. Because of their high fees, most of these schools serve the upper classes of society only.

All of Costa Rica's medical and social service institutions are maintained by the state, although some employ Catholic sisters. Caritas de Costa Rica, which is affiliated to Caritas International in Rome, was created in 1963 to aid in the promotion of the USA's Alliance for Progress programme with the support of CRS-USCC.

**IGLESIA EPISCOPAL.** In 1977 the diocese was granted extra-provincial status, by the General Convention of the Episcopal Church in the USA, conferring ecclesiastical autonomy but with the diocese remaining an associated diocese of the Province of the Caribbean (Province IX) of ECUSA.

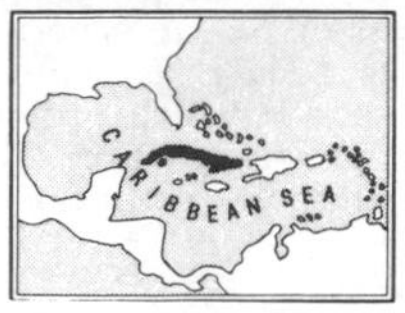


# CUBA

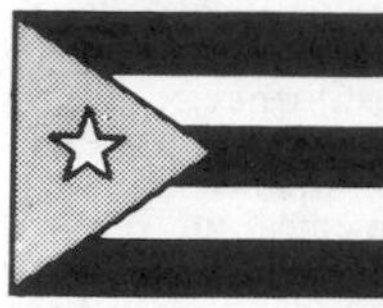

## SECULAR DATA

**STATE. Official name:** The Republic of Cuba (La República de Cuba). Adjective of nationality: Cuban (cubano).
**Flag** (shown above right): Alternate blue and white stripes, red triangle with white star.
**Area:** 114,524 sq.km. (44,206 sq.miles). Agricultural land: 56.1%.
**Government:** One-party Communist state, since 1959 (1492 Spanish possession, 1898 Independence).
**Legislature:** Council of Ministers, 23 members.
**Official language:** Spanish (*Español/Castellano*).
**Chief cities:** capital Havana 1,751,220 (1970), Santiago de Cuba 277,600, Camagüey 197,720.
**Political divisions:** 6 Provinces and 126 Municipalities.
**Armed forces** (1976): Total 175,000 regular: army 146,000, navy 9,000, air force 20,000 (195 combat aircraft). Reserves: 90,000. Paramilitary forces: 113,000 (100,000 People's Militia).
**Foreign forces** (1973): 3,000 USA troops and 3,000 USA civilians at Guantánamo naval base.

**DEMOGRAPHY. Population:** 8,569,121 (census of 6.IX.1970. For 1970–2000 (UN), see last row of Table 1). Population density (1975): 83/sq.km. (214/sq.mile). Under 15 years: 36%. Growth rate (1975–80): 2.10% per year (births 2.78%, deaths –0.67%). Life expectancy (1975–80): 70.4 years. Household size: 4.4 persons.
**Major languages:** Spanish, Russian, Chinese, English.
**Urban dwellers** (1970): 55.5%. Urban growth rate (1950–70): 2.5% per year.
**Labour force:** 31%.
**Refugees** (1977): From abroad, none. Exiles abroad: 670,370 (655,980 in USA, 14,390 in Spain, Costa Rica et alia).
**Tourists** (1974): 15,000. (1976) 65,000, mostly from Canada.

**ETHNOLINGUISTIC GROUPS:** 72% Cuban White (Spanish origin), 15% Mulatto (White/Black), 12% Black (African Negro), 1% Asiatic (0.4% Chinese (34,000)), Greek, Basque, Russian, Jewish. By 1977, Russians had increased to 19,000 (8,000 being technicians).

**MONEY** (1977). **Monetary unit:** peso (= 100 centavos); US$1 = Cub$0.825.
**National income per person:** US$570. Average annual family income: US$2,508.
**Cost of living in capital** (1976): Daily cost of living: US$54.

**EDUCATION.** Adult literacy: (1953) 78%, (1975) 97%. Education rate: 90%. Schools: 15,474. Universities: 3.

**HEALTH.** Hospitals: 242 (37,276 beds). Doctors: 7,000. Lepers: 11,500 (1.2 per 1,000). Blind: 4,600. Psychotics: 76,000.

**LITERATURE.** Annual new book titles (1972): 942. Periodicals: 300. Scientific journals: 100. Newspapers: 10 dailies, 6 non-daily.

**COMMUNICATION** (per 1,000 people). Phones: 32. Radios: 171. TV sets: 71. Daily newspaper circulation: 95 copies.

TABLE 1. RELIGIOUS ADHERENTS IN CUBA

| Year | 1900 | | mid-1970 | | Annual change, 1970–1980 | | | | mid-1975 | | mid-1980 | | 2000 | |
|---|---|---|---|---|---|---|---|---|---|---|---|---|---|---|
| *Name* | *Adherents* | *%* | *Adherents* | *%* | *Natural* | *Conversion* | *Total* | *Rate* | *Adherents* | *%* | *Adherents* | *%* | *Adherents* | *%* |
| **Christians** | **1,796.000** | **97.1** | **4,016,808** | **46.9** | **87,575** | **–45,856** | **41,719** | **0.99** | **4,219,000** | **44.5** | **4,434,000** | **42.1** | **5,305,000** | **34.7** |
| crypto-Christians | 0 | 0.0 | 496,808 | 5.8 | 14,800 | 32,719 | 47,519 | 6.66 | 713,000 | 7.5 | 972,000 | 9.2 | 1,391,000 | 9.1 |
| professing | 1,796,000 | 97.1 | 3,520,000 | 41.1 | 72,775 | –78,575 | –5,800 | –0.17 | 3,506,000 | 37.0 | 3,462,000 | 32.9 | 3,914,000 | 25.6 |
| Roman Catholics | 1,792,000 | 96.9 | 3,426,000 | 40.0 | 70,845 | –76,345 | –5,500 | –0.16 | 3,413,000 | 36.0 | 3,371,000 | 32.0 | 3,817,000 | 25.0 |
| Spiritist Catholics | 555,000 | 30.0 | 857,000 | 10.0 | 17,706 | –19,106 | –1,400 | –0.16 | 853,000 | 9.0 | 843,000 | 8.0 | 763,000 | 5.0 |
| Protestants | 3,000 | 0.2 | 85,000 | 1.0 | 1,764 | –1,864 | –100 | –0.12 | 85,000 | 0.9 | 84,000 | 0.8 | 92,000 | 0.6 |
| Anglicans | 1,000 | 0.1 | 9,000 | 0.1 | 166 | –366 | –200 | –2.50 | 8,000 | 0.1 | 7,000 | 0.1 | 5,000 | 0.0 |
| nominal | 148,000 | 8.0 | 0 | 0.0 | 0 | 0 | 0 | 0.00 | 0 | 0.0 | 0 | 0.0 | 0 | 0.0 |
| affiliated | 1,648,000 | 89.1 | 4,016,808 | 46.9 | 87,575 | –45,856 | 41,719 | 0.99 | 4,219,000 | 44.5 | 4,434,000 | 42.1 | 5,305,000 | 34.7 |
| total practising | 1,483,200 | *90* | 1,606,720 | *40* | 35,030 | –18,342 | 16,688 | 0.99 | 1,687,600 | *40* | 1,773,600 | *40* | 2,652,500 | *50* |
| non-practising | 164,800 | *10* | 2,410,090 | *60* | 52,545 | –27,514 | 25,031 | 0.99 | 2,531,400 | *60* | 2,660,400 | *60* | 2,652,500 | *50* |
| Roman Catholics | 1,644,000 | 88.9 | 3,819,229 | 44.6 | 82,895 | –47,718 | 35,177 | 0.88 | 3,991,500 | 42.1 | 4,171,000 | 39.6 | 4,885,000 | 32.0 |
| Protestants | 3,000 | 0.2 | 121,779 | 1.4 | 2,802 | 20 | 2,822 | 2.09 | 135,000 | 1.4 | 150,000 | 1.4 | 198,000 | 1.3 |
| Evangelicals | 2,500 | 0.1 | 80,000 | 0.9 | 1,839 | 1 | 1,840 | 2.08 | 88,600 | 0.9 | 98,400 | 0.9 | 142,000 | 0.9 |
| Cuban indigenous | 0 | 0.0 | 51,700 | 0.6 | 1,370 | 1,860 | 3,230 | 4.89 | 66,000 | 0.7 | 84,000 | 0.8 | 183,000 | 1.2 |
| Anglicans | 1,000 | 0.1 | 12,000 | 0.1 | 259 | –159 | 100 | 0.80 | 12,500 | 0.1 | 13,000 | 0.1 | 15,000 | 0.1 |
| Marginal Protestants | 0 | 0.0 | 10,100 | 0.1 | 249 | 141 | 390 | 3.25 | 12,000 | 0.1 | 14,000 | 0.1 | 23,000 | 0.2 |
| Orthodox | 0 | 0.0 | 2,000 | 0.0 | 0 | 0 | 0 | 0.00 | 2,000 | 0.0 | 2,000 | 0.0 | 1,000 | 0.0 |
| Non-religious | 2,000 | 0.1 | 3,790,892 | 44.3 | 91,409 | 42,080 | 133,489 | 3.03 | 4,403,740 | 46.4 | 5,125,780 | 48.7 | 8,456,000 | 55.4 |
| Atheists | 0 | 0.0 | 500,000 | 5.8 | 11,998 | 5,402 | 17,400 | 3.01 | 578,000 | 6.1 | 674,000 | 6.4 | 1,160,000 | 7.6 |
| Afro-American spiritists | 37,000 | 2.0 | 150,000 | 1.8 | 3,342 | –1,542 | 1,800 | 1.12 | 161,000 | 1.7 | 168,000 | 1.6 | 199,000 | 1.3 |
| Spiritists | 5,000 | 0.3 | 90,000 | 1.0 | 2,076 | –76 | 2,000 | 2.00 | 100,000 | 1.1 | 110,000 | 1.0 | 120,000 | 0.8 |
| Buddhists | 0 | 0.0 | 5,000 | 0.1 | 114 | –14 | 100 | 1.82 | 5,500 | 0.1 | 6,000 | 0.1 | 6,000 | 0.0 |
| Jews | 9,000 | 0.5 | 1,800 | 0.0 | 42 | –2 | 40 | 2.00 | 2,000 | 0.0 | 2,200 | 0.0 | 3,000 | 0.0 |
| Baha'is | 0 | 0.0 | 500 | 0.0 | 12 | 0 | 12 | 2.14 | 560 | 0.0 | 620 | 0.0 | 1,000 | 0.0 |
| Other religionists | 1,000 | 0.1 | 10,000 | 0.1 | 232 | 8 | 240 | 2.14 | 11,200 | 0.1 | 12,400 | 0.1 | 17,000 | 0.1 |
| **Country's population** | **1,850,000** | **100.0** | **8,565,000** | **100.0** | **196,800** | **0** | **196,800** | **2.08** | **9,481,000** | **100.0** | **10,533,000** | **100.0** | **15,267,000** | **100.0** |

COLUMNS, ROWS. For meanings and definitions, see Codebook (Part 6). Note that, by definition, total 'Christians' = professing + crypto-Christians, which also = affiliated + nominal Christians. Percentages may not always total exactly, due to rounding.
POLLS. *Religious preference.* 1957 (sample survey by Agrupación Católica Universitaria): 72.5% of Cubans professed to be Catholics, 19.0% non-religious, 6.0% Protestants and Anglicans, 1.0% Spiritists, 0.5% Afro-American spiritists (Afro-Cuban cultists), 0.5% Jews, 0.5% Freemasons. *Practice.* 1957 (same survey): 65% of the population had at some time or other made their first communion; about 27% attended mass every Sunday. 1970 and 1972: about 1.5% of the population attend mass every Sunday.

NOTES ON RELIGIONS
AFRO-AMERICAN SPIRITISTS. Negroes and Mulattoes belonging to numerous Afro-Cuban syncretistic cults, including: Santería (Lucumis or Yoruban, based on Yoruba rites), Nañiguismo or Nañagismo (from Calabar, Nigeria), Arará (o-Dahomean origin), Mayombe (based on Congolese religion), and Ganga (Bantu).
ANGLICANS. Growth and decline of affiliated Episcopalians: 2,029 (1925), 12,278 (1938), 35,284 (1948), 48,800 (1951), 62,100 (1956), and 74,400 (1960); after this the mass exodus of Cubans and North Americans to the USA reduced the total to 12,000 by 1970.
ATHEISTS. Communist Party of Cuba (PCC) (in power since 1959; pro-Soviet): membership (1970) 125,000.
BAHA'IS. In 4 local spiritual assemblies (1964, 1973).
BUDDHISTS. Chinese.
COUNTRY'S POPULATION. After the 1959 revolution, a total of 650,000 Cubans had, by 1974, either fled or been expelled, mostly to the USA, including a large proportion of the business and middle classes, the great majority of all Protestants and Anglicans, and a substantial Catholic minority.
CRYPTO-CHRISTIANS. Christians affiliated to churches but not known as such to the state, of 3 kinds: (1) unorganized individuals in the recognized churches, who remain practising Catholics or Protestants but keep it private; (2) members of unrecognized, banned, underground or persecuted denominations (Jehovah's Witnesses, Batiblancos, Seventh-day Adventists); and (3) isolated radio believers.
CUBAN INDIGENOUS. In about 18 denominations in 1970 (see Table 2).
NOMINAL CHRISTIANS. Before 1959 only.
NON-RELIGIOUS. Agnostics, indifferent to religion. In 1957 before the Communist revolution, they already numbered 19% of the population; after 10 years of Communist rule, they numbered 44%. In addition, there are another 7.5% of the population (in 1975) whom the state (through polls and surveys) regards as non-religious but who are affiliated to churches and so are classified here as crypto-Christians.
OTHER RELIGIONISTS. Including Muslims (mostly immigrants), Hindus, Rosicrucians (AMORC, 4 centres), and adherents of other non-Christian religions or cults. In 1975 the Theosophical Society had 19 Lodges with 413 members.
PRACTISING CHRISTIANS. Weekly practice for Roman Catholics fell from 27% of the whole population in 1957 to the very low figure of 1.5% in 1972 (varying from 0.7% to 2.0% in the various dioceses). Marriage practice among Catholics (1968): 4.8% celebrated in church. In 1970, the majority of Protestant churches in Cuba, especially Baptist, were well-attended and filled with young people. Total attendance, for all churches is therefore about 8% weekly, and around 40% of all affiliated Christians annually.
PROTESTANTS. The total has fallen drastically, due to the mass exodus of Cubans and North Americans to the USA, from 6.0% Protestants (with Anglicans) in 1957 to 1.6% by 1970. Throughout this latter period the USA maintained a naval base at Guantánamo with 6,000 USA expatriates (half military, half civilian), and their dependants, about 50% of whom were Protestants and so are included in the totals above.
SPIRITIST CATHOLICS. Roman Catholics involved in organized Afro-Cuban spiritism (Santería, Nañiguismo, Arará, Mayombe, Ganga).
SPIRITISTS. Followers of organized high spiritism.

**NON-CHRISTIAN RELIGIONS. Agnosticism** and **atheism** have increased markedly in numbers since 1959.

**Afro-Cuban cults,** whose followers are principally Negroes and Mulattoes, represented 0.5% of the population in 1957. These sects can be divided into 3 categories: (1) Santería, also called Lucumis or Yoruban after the Yoruba slaves originally brought to Cuba, is a syncretistic movement which borrows images and ceremonies from the cult of Catholic saints, and which usually conducts its services during the celebration of Catholic feasts. (2) Nañiguismo, the society of the Nañigos or the Abakua cult, which originated in Calabar (Nigeria) and was brought to Cuba in 1834–36, is made up of Naguerian secret societies who have kept their African characteristics and continue to include traditional occult practices. (3) Bantu religions have in several cases evolved into magical cults, such as the Mayombe sect embodying the Yoruba and Congolese world-view, and the Ganga sect which organizes funeral rites for its members. Most followers of Afro-Cuban cults call themselves either Catholics, or revolutionaries and communists, but the Cuban government has not assisted them and has taken measures to control their expansion. Sociological and ethnographic studies of them undertaken by the Institute of

Ethnology and Folklore have increased considerably since the revolution.

## CHRISTIANITY

**CATHOLIC CHURCH.** Dominican missionaries came to Cuba in 1512 soon after Columbus' arrival in 1492. The first jurisdiction was established in 1517 and Franciscans arrived a few years later. Owing to the absence of gold on the island and the decimation of most of the original population, both church and government remained stagnated for the next two and a half centuries. Towards the end of the 18th century more liberal Spanish policies were set in motion, the island began to flourish economically, and a progressive bishop for the first 30 years of the 19th century contributed much to the expansion of church institutions. During the remainder of the century, however, the church again went into decline due to the identification of the hierarchy with the Spanish government and the arrival of conservative Spanish clergy from newly-independent Latin American countries. Strongly anti-clerical feeling arose resulting in the separation of church and state after Cuban independence in 1898. The church took on new life in the 20th century largely due to the influence of Catholic lay movements from abroad, new institutions for education and social services, and an increase in Cuban clergy including a cardinal, 2 archbishops and 5 bishops. Nevertheless, the continued use of conservative Spanish priests and the close relationship with |the| Batista | government after 1930 left the church unprepared for the radical changes in political and economic policies that followed the 1959 revolution.

Church attendance for Catholics has declined catastrophically since 1959. In 1957 a survey found that 72.5% of the population professed to be Catholics, 65% had at some time made their first communion, and about 27% attended mass every Sunday. A further survey in 1970, organized by the episcopate and carried out by parish priests, reported that only 1% of the population attended Sunday mass in the diocese of Matanzas and 0.73% in Camagüey. Attenders in other dioceses ranged from 0.7% to 1.5%. A third survey was made in 1972 in which the laity counted those present at mass in 62 churches throughout the island, yielding an average attendance of about 1.5% of the population. In 1968, 4.8% of all weddings took place in church.

Church-state conflicts since the beginning of Fidel Castro's regime in 1959 have had severe repercussions on religious vocations. At the end of 1958, the Cuban church had 725 diocesan and religious priests, 461 brothers, 2,407 sisters and 81 seminarians. In July 1962, there remained no more than 231 priests, under 200 sisters and very few brothers. This drastic decrease was due in large part to a massive exodus from the island, at times on the orders of religious superiors. Fear of the new regime was the major factor, but there was as well inability to adapt to other work following the nationalization of Catholic schools. In 1953 the city of Havana with a population of one million had 16 parishes with on average 2 priests each, but there were 200 priests working in Catholic secondary schools in the city. Among the priests who emigrated were the bishops of Cienfuegos and Camagüey. All seminarians, both diocesan and religious, left Cuba in 1961 on the orders of superiors. In 1961 there were further losses due to expulsion by government of 136 priests, including 46 Cubans and the auxiliary bishop of Havana; at that time however no brothers or sisters were expelled. Of the 136 exiled priests, 18 later returned including the present

archbishop of Havana. From 1962 to 1967, 79 new priests entered Cuba, whereas from 1963 to 1967, 7 more priests were expelled including 2 Cubans. There have been no further expulsions. Early in 1971 there were held the first ordinations in Cuba since 1961, all 15 ordinands having received their complete training in Cuba. All of Cuba's 8 active residential bishops at the present time including 2 auxiliaries have been appointed since the revolution without any state interference. The small number of priests (one to every 39,175 people in 1969) and the exclusively religious character of their activities (only one Cuban priest was doing secular work in 1972) have restricted the life of faith entirely to the sacramental level.

**OTHER CHURCHES.** In 1957, 6% of the population professed to be Protestants or Anglicans. The largest single tradition is Pentecostalism which owes its origin to the missionary activity of the Assemblies of God from the USA in 1920. Today there are many different pentecostal groups, the largest being the indigenous Iglesia Evangélica Pentecostal. In fact, except for Catholicism this independent church is the largest denomination in Cuba at present.

The first non-Catholic services were held in Cuba in 1741 by British Anglicans, and in 1871 the first permanent pastor was sent by the Episcopal Church of the USA to serve the increasing number of Americans and British in the country. Anglicanism developed most rapidly among Cubans who fled the country for the USA during the revolutionary fervour of the latter part of the 19th century. Several Episcopal laymen returned to Cuba for evangelistic work, but this was halted during the Spanish-American war. The first resident bishop was appointed in 1906 and the first Cuban bishop in 1967, and now all clergy are Cubans. The Anglican Church is strongest in the cities and towns.

In 1873 Southern Methodists began working in Florida among exiles who flooded into the USA prior to Cuban independence in 1898. Ten years later 2 Cubans returned as missionaries to Havana. Following the war of 1898, Methodists built some of the best schools and dispensaries in the country, concentrating on rural areas. Continued work among Cuban exiles in the USA since 1959 has resulted in their membership equalling that in Cuba itself. The Methodist Church in Cuba became autonomous in 1964.

The Baptist Convention of Cuba grew out of the early efforts of a Cuban exile who returned in 1883 as a Bible colporteur, developing a small group of believers who later amalgamated with the USA Southern Baptist Convention. The work of this original group centres in the west and south. North American Baptist missionaries (ABHMS) have been active in eastern Cuba. The Baptist Convention of Cuba unites these 2 groups and is the largest non-Catholic non-Pentecostal denomination in the country. In 1965, 30 Baptist preachers were imprisoned as alleged American spies, but most were

subsequently released.

In 1884 a Cuban organized small churches which served as the nucleus for the Presbyterian Church in Cuba, and after 1898 Presbyterian missionaries from the USA made their appearance. When Congregationalists left Cuba in 1909 and Disciples in 1918, their work was passed on to the Presbyterians. The church became independent of the New Jersey Synod in 1967.

The Salvation Army, Friends, Nazarenes, Church of God and many others are active in Cuba. Greek Orthodox also have one congregation in Havana. Following the 1959 revolution all churches experienced leadership losses with the departure of more than 500,000 Cubans to the USA. Compulsory military training further reduced the number of clergy and theological students. However, the churches have recuperated markedly and are now stronger than before the revolution. Reports in 1975 indicated that many Protestant church services are full to overflowing every Sunday, with young people prominent.

**CHURCH AND STATE.** After Independence in 1898, the constitution of 1901 declared that church and state were to be absolutely separated and that there was to be freedom of worship. Before the eventual promulgation of the socialist constitution announced in 1965, to be voted on in a national citizens referendum in 1976, the theoretical juridical status of churches and other religious organizations continues to be regulated by Article 35 of the constitution of 1940, as was reaffirmed in the basic laws of the republic of Cuba of 7 February 1959. This article proclaims and guarantees 'free profession of all religions', freedom of worship, separation of church and state, and prohibits the state from granting subsidies to any religious body. The official position of the revolution in regard to religious activities has moreover been clearly stated in a declaration adopted by delegates at the first national congress of education and culture held at Havana in April 1971 (Declaración del Primer Congreso Nacional de Educación y Cultura). This policy rests on 7 basic principles, as follows. (1) Priority is given to the construction of a socialist society, the 'religious phenomenon' being only a subsidiary matter. (2) There is absolute separation between church and state, and between church and education, in all areas. (3) There can be no support nor aid for any kind of religious group; and in return, nothing can be asked of them. (4) There is no official adherence nor support for either religious beliefs or worship. (5) Respect will be given to the religious belief and practice of each individual and no-one is to be persecuted for his beliefs. (6) Freedom is accorded to all independent of their religious or philosophical beliefs to participate in 'the work of transformation of the Revolution'. (7) There must be vigilance against 'obscurantist and counter-revolutionary sects'. The whole declaration also embodies a short analysis of the situation of 3 sects and of the Catholic Church, no other groups being cited by name. Jehovah's Witnesses, Bando

Cuban President Fidel Castro (centre) is presented with Jerusalem Bible in 1971 by (left) Cardinal Raul Silva Henriquez, Archbishop of Santiago in Chile, and his auxiliary bishop.

Evangelistico Gedeón or Batiblancos, and Seventh-day Adventists are described as 'the major sects in their position of confrontation with regard to the Revolution'. They are particularly reproached as vehicles of counter-revolutionary ideology, and for 'infiltrating the culturally poorest sectors of the population'. Concerning the Catholic Church, it is stated that the situation in Cuba needs to be analysed in the light of that church's worldwide reform movement, the attitude of the hierarchy to revolutionary process, and the role played today in Latin America by Catholic revolutionary groups relating their activity to the Cuban model. The declaration adds that the separation of socio-economic problems from philosophical problems has opened the door to the individual participation of Catholics in the economic and social construction of the revolution.

To enter the Communist Party, it is necessary to suppress one's religious ideas, if such are held. As far as the churches are concerned, they have complete internal freedom of administration. Religious instruction, prohibited in public schools since 1902, continues to be given in places of worship and adjoining buildings. All private schools and universities were nationalized in 1961. All external religious manifestations, such as processions or public meetings, have been banned since the Catholic processions of 1960–61 which took a counter-revolutionary turn. Because of the Law of Urban Reform of 14 October 1960 abolishing rental property, the churches have lost a large number of their properties. Nevertheless, government provides an indemnity to former owners, which in the case of the Catholic archdiocese of Havana constitutes one of its principal financial resources. The celebration of Christmas and other religious feasts falling during the week is implicitly prohibited by a 1972 law which established the number of legal holidays. Prior to that Christmas vacations were moved to July so as not to interfere with the sugar-cane harvest which is most pressing during December.

The recent history of the Catholic Church in Cuba can be interpreted in terms of its unpreparedness for confronting a revolutionary situation. When in January 1959 Castro declared that 'The Catholics of Cuba have provided decisive collaboration with the cause of freedom', he was referring to priests, chaplains to guerrillas, and militant laymen who took arms against the Batista regime. But both hierarchy and laity were too closely linked to the ideology of preceding regimes to be able to adjust to the progressive socialization of Cuban life and its economy. Relations between the Catholic Church and the new regime rapidly deteriorated during the first years of the revolution. The episcopate protested in 1960 against the establishment of diplomatic relations with the USSR. The policy of nationalization was also criticized as 'excessive state control' in social and economic life. The USA forces invading the Bay of Pigs in April 1961 included a group of Catholics accompanied by 3 Spanish priests who claimed they had come 'in the name of God' to fight 'against atheists'. The holding of politico-religious demonstrations further exacerbated tensions. In September 1961 a procession of several thousand faithful in Havana turned into a protest against the regime as a result of which the government expelled the auxiliary bishop and 135 priests. At the beginning of 1963, the new papal chargé d'affaires, who later in 1974 became nuncio, adopted a conciliatory attitude towards the regime and cultivated good personal relations. The situation however remained strained until 1969 when the Cuban episcopate made a step in the direction of the revolution by publishing 2 collective pastoral letters. The letter of 20 April called on Catholics to reconsider their conception of social morality and to play a role in the development of society. It also condemned the economic blockade against Cuba, without making any pronouncement regarding its origin. The letter of 3 September listed the conditions necessary for Christians to conserve and develop their faith in the context of Cuban society. Symbolic gestures of voluntary agricultural work were made by priests and seminarians in 1968 and 1971, and in 1970 an ecumenical group of priests and pastors participated in the harvest of sugar cane. In 1973 the general of the Society of Jesus visited Jesuits in Cuba; and between 27 March and 7 April 1974, Msgr Casaroli, secretary of the Council for Public Affairs of the Church, of the Holy See, also visited the Cuban church, carrying on at the same time important discussions with the political authorities. The amelioration of relations is also explained by the ideological flexibility of Fidel Castro. Attacking 'dogmatism' in 1968, he affirmed that Christians should be shown the possibility of their being true revolutionaries. There have also been ideological shifts in the church in Latin America, the death of the guerrilla priest Camilo Torres in Colombia, and the political and social evolution of progressivist sectors of the church on the continent. Thus the period of open conflict between church and state seems to have ended in Cuba. This does not however mean than the Cuban church has yet fully accepted a new mode of existence within the framework of a socialist society, nor has it yet been clarified what the role of the church will be.

**INTERDENOMINATIONAL ORGANIZATIONS.** The Cuban Council of Protestant Churches (Consejo de Iglesias Evangélicas de Cuba) was begun in 1941, and in 1977 was renamed the Ecumenical Council of Cuba. It has 14 member churches, including representatives of the Protestant, Anglican and Orthodox traditions. It works through 6 commissions: Christian Education, Ecumenical Education, Church and Society, Laity, Promotion of Bible Reading, and Youth. In 1947 a Union Theological Seminary was founded in Matanzas, attended by Presbyterian, Methodist and Episcopalian seminarians.

The Catholic episcopate sponsors the National Episcopal Commission of Ecumenism (Comisión Episcopal Nacional de Ecumenismo), and the Episcopal Conference has created at the major seminary of Havana a Centre for Ecumenical Studies (Centro de Estudios Ecuménicos, CENDESEC) with a Catholic as president and staff of various confessions. Another similar study centre was created by Protestants at Camagüey in collaboration with priests and lay Catholics.

**BROADCASTING.** No religious broadcasting is permitted on state radio or TV. Chinese Gospel Crusade, an evangelistic organization aiming to reach the Chinese of the world by radio, uses station 4VEH in Haiti to beam religious programmes into Cuba, and also broadcasts daily to Cuba from Trans World Radio (Bonaire, Netherlands Antilles). Spanish-World Gospel Broadcasting buys time on Christian and commercial radio stations abroad for reception in Cuba.

## BIBLIOGRAPHY


*Christianity and revolution: the lesson of Cuba*. L. Dewart. New York: Herder & Herder, 1963.

'Cuba', chapter VIII in J. L. Gonzalez, *The development of Christianity in the Latin Caribbean* (Grand Rapids, Michigan: Eerdmans, 1969), p. 83–98.

*Cuba, church and crisis*. L. Dewart. London: Sheed & Ward, 1963.

'Cuba: la chiesa in una società rivoluzionaria', L. Muratori, *Humanitas*, XXV, 6 (1970), 625–635.

'Cuban spiritism'. M. Daley. Thesis, Union Theological Seminary, New York (USA). (Based on a strong Efik (Nigeria) culture, revived from 1890 onwards).

*Directorio eclesiástico de Cuba, 1971*. La Habana: Conferencia Episcopal de Cuba, 1971. (Roman Catholic).

*Ecué, Changó y Yemayá*. J. L. Martín. La Habana, 1930. 164p. (Essays on Afro-Cuban religion).

*Historia eclesiástica de Cuba*. I. Teste. Burgos: Editorial El Monte Carmelo, 1969. 527p.

*Religion in Cuba today: a new church in a new society*. Eds A. L. Hageman & P. E. Wheaton. New York: Association Press, 1971. 317p.

'The focus of Cuban Santería', W. R. Bascom, *Southwestern journal of anthropology* (Spring, 1950), 64–68.


TABLE 2. ORGANIZED CHURCHES AND DENOMINATIONS IN CUBA

| Official name 1 | Begun 2 | Type 3 | Counc 4 | Congs 5 | Adults 6 | Affiliated 7 | Names, notes, and other statistics (see Codebook) 8 |
|---|---|---|---|---|---|---|---|
| Asambleas de Dios | 1920 | P Pe2 | ZF... | 290 | 4,205 | 10,000 | *Assemblies of God*. M=AoG(USA). Vast campaigns 1950s; decline 1960. 121n,1k,1s. |
| Asociación Evangélica de Cuba | 1928 | P int | xMu.N | 60 | 6,000 | 10,000 | *Evangelical Association*. Formerly, M=West Indies Mission(USA). 2f,2s. |
| Convención Bautista de Cuba Occidental | 1883 | P Bap | T.... | 98 | 7,000 | 12,000 | *Baptist Convention of Western Cuba*. M=SBC(USA). 1965, 30 pastors jailed. 1s,319Y. |
| Convención Bautista de Cuba Oriental | 1899 | P Bap | T.... | 110 | 9,000 | 15,000 | *Baptist Convention of Eastern Cuba*. Formerly M=ABHMS(USA), left 1961. 1s. |
| Convención Bautista Libre de Cuba | 1941 | P Bap | x.u.N | 14 | 1,800 | 3,000 | *Free Baptist Convention of Cuba*. Formerly M=NAFWB(USA). Missions abroad. 8n. |
| Ejército de Salvación | 1918 | P Sal | xwV.N | | 1,000 | 2,000 | *Salvation Army, Cuba Division*, Caribbean & CAmerica Territory (HQ Jamaica). 1s. |
| Hermanos Libres | | P CBr | x.... | 15 | 500 | 1,000 | *Open Brethren. Plymouth Brethren*. Decline from 20 congregations in 1959. |
| Iglesia Adventista del Séptimo Día | 1905 | P Adv | x.... | 108 | 7,550 | 20,000 | *SDA. Seventh-day Adventist Ch in Cuba*. HQ Santiago de las Vegas. |
| Iglesia Apostólica de Jesucristo | | I pel | x.... | 2 | 1,000 | 2,000 | *Apostolic Ch of Jesus Christ*. Related to Mexican indigenous body IAFCJ. HQ Havana. |
| **Iglesia Católica en Cuba:** | 1512 | R Lat | B.L.R | 472 | 2,444,000 | 3,819,229 | *Catholic Ch*. C=13+1+15. Low practice: W=2%. 1s(58). 91n, 117x, 29m, 236w, 51172Yy. |
| M San Cristóbal de la Habana | 1787 | R Lat | Bs | 153 | 678,500 | 1,060,000 | Havana, the capital. 90% urban. 45% Catholic. 1s. 43 59 23 188 16068 |
| D Matanzas | 1912 | R Lat | Bs | 32 | 176,000 | 275,000 | Half urban industrial. 55% Catholic. W=2%. 8 8 0 12 5706 |
| D Pinar del Río | 1903 | R Lat | Bs | 27 | 256,000 | 400,000 | Extreme west of island. 70% rural. 63% Catholic. 5 7 0 4 8640 |
| M Santiago de Cuba | 1522 | R Lat | Bs | 119 | 607,500 | 949,229 | 60% rural; sugar, cattle. 32% Catholic. 18 17 2 17 19910 |
| D Camagüey | 1912 | R Lat | Bs | 17 | 320,000 | 500,000 | Half urban; sugar, cattle. 59% Catholic. W=1.5%. 9 9 0 3 3730 |
| D Cienfuegos-Santa Clara | 1903 | R Lat | Bs | 124 | 406,000 | 635,000 | 60% rural, rapid urbanization. 46% Catholic. 8 17 4 12 17118 |
| Iglesia Congregacional Pentecostal | 1955 | P Pe3 | x.u.n | 34 | 3,000 | 5,000 | *Congregational Holiness Ch*. Formerly M=CHC(USA). Holiness Pentecostals. |
| Iglesia Cristiana Pentecostal de Cuba | 1956 | I pen | ..u.N | | 4,000 | 10,000 | *Christian Pentecostal Ch*. Schism 1956 ex AoG. 1976, M=CC(Disciples) (USA). HQ Camagüey. |
| Iglesia de Dios | 1910 | P Pe3 | ZF... | 10 | 136 | 500 | *Ch of God*. Formerly M=CoG(Cleveland) (USA). HQ Santiago de Cuba. |
| Iglesia de Dios de la Profecía | | P Pe3 | Z.u.N | 11 | 951 | 3,000 | Formerly M=CoG of Prophecy(USA). Split in USA ex Cleveland. HQ Güines, Havana. |
| Iglesia de Dios en Cuba | | P Hol | x.u.N | 10 | 500 | 1,000 | *Ch of God in Cuba*. Formerly M=CoG(Anderon) (USA). Holiness denomination. |
| Iglesia de Dios Pentecostal | | I pe2 | Z.... | 9 | 500 | 1,000 | *Pentecostal Ch of God*. Formerly mission from Puerto Rico, and USA. |
| Iglesia de los Amigos | 1900 | P Qua | Q.u.N | 8 | 500 | 2,000 | *Iglesia de los Cuaqueros* (*Quakers, Friends*). M=FUM(USA). HQ Banes (Oriente). |
| Iglesia del Evangelio Cuadrangular | | P Pe2 | ZF... | 30 | 1,000 | 2,000 | *Internat Ch of the Foursquare Gospel*. M=ICFG(USA), until workers expelled 1960. |
| Iglesia del Nazareno | 1902 | P Hol | xFu.N | 35 | 1,456 | 2,000 | *Ch of the Nazarene*. Formerly M=CoN(USA). HQ Marianao, Havana. 1s. |
| Iglesia Episcopal de Cuba | 1741 | A Hig | AwuRN | 46 | 2,286 | 12,000 | Under a Metropolitan Council. A=1966. Decline from 74,400(1960). 15n,1u,65Y,910y. |
| Iglesia Evangélica Pentecostal de Cuba | | I pen | ..... | 80 | 15,000 | 30,000 | *Evangelical Pentecostal Ch*. Largest Cuban independent pentecostal church. |
| Iglesia Luterana de Cuba (Misurí) | 1912 | P Lut | x.... | 6 | 100 | 207 | *Lutheran Ch*. 1947, M=LC Missouri Synod(USA). HQ Nueva Gerona, Isla de Pinos. |
| Iglesia Metodista en Cuba | 1883 | P Met | Vuu.N | 120 | 2,934 | 10,000 | *Methodist Ch in Cuba*. Begun by Cubans. A=1964. Affiliated to UMC(USA). 23n,1u. |
| Iglesia Orthodoxa Africana | c1920 | I ARo | x.... | 5 | 500 | 1,000 | *African Orthodox Ch*. M=AOC(USA) Blacks. West Indian Blacks. 1 bishop. |
| Iglesia Ortodoxa de Cuba | | O Gre | Cwu.n | 1 | 1,000 | 2,000 | *Orthodox Ch*. 12th Archdiocesan District, Greek Orthodox AD N&S America. Havana. |
| Iglesia Presbiteriana Reformada en C | 1884 | P Ref | Ruu.N | 56 | 1,913 | 8,872 | *Presbyterian Reformed Ch*. Formerly M=UPUSA. A=1967. Decline since 1960. 21n,23t,1u. |
| Iglesia Santa Pentecostés | 1952 | P Pe3 | ZFu.N | 16 | 412 | 1,000 | *Pentecostal Holiness Church*. Formerly M=PHC(USA). HQ Bayamo (Oriente). 34nm. |
| Iglesia Biblicas | 1937 | P Pe2 | Z.... | 12 | 2,500 | 5,000 | *Open Bible Standard Chs*. Until 1960, M=OBSC(USA), a schism in USA ex ICFG. 1p. |
| Iglesias de la Fe Apostólica | | P Pe3 | x.... | 2 | 100 | 200 | *Churches of the Apostolic Faith*. Formerly M=AFM(Portland, Oregon, USA). HQ Havana. |
| Iglesias Elim | | P Pe2 | Z.... | 14 | 500 | 1,000 | Formerly M=Elim Missionary Churches(USA). HQ Matanzas. |
| Iglesias radiofónicas solitarias | 1959 | I rad | ..... | 170 | 3,300 | 6,700 | Isolated radio believers (students, &c). R=480(279 HCJB, 92 FEBC, TWR, Radio Vatican). |
| Sociedad de la Ciencia Cristiana | | M Sci | x.... | 1 | 50 | 100 | *Ch of Christ, Scientist. Christian Science*. M=CCS(USA). First Church, Havana. 1w. |
| Testigos de Jehová | c1925 | M Jeh | x.... | 153 | 5,485 | 10,000 | *Jehovah's Witnesses*. Active witnessing under way by 1929. Largely underground. |
| Other Protestant denominations | | P | ..... | | 3,000 | 7,000 | Total about 15 (see list below); also 5,000 USA Protestants at military base. |
| Other indigenous pentecostal churches | | I pen | ..... | | 500 | 1,000 | Total about 12 (see list below). |
| **Total affiliated (mid-1970)** | | | | 2,170 | 2,533,678 | 4,016,808 | **Total denominations (1970) . . . 60.** |
| **Total affiliated (mid-1975)** | | | | 2,240 | 2,661,200 | 4,219,000 | **Total denominations (1975) . . . 60.** |
| **Total affiliated (mid-1980)** | | | | 2,310 | 2,796,800 | 4,434,000 | **Total denominations (1980) . . . 59.** |

NOTES ON TABLE ABOVE
COLUMNS: for meanings and CODES (cols. 1, 3, 4, 8), see Codebook (Part 6). Column 1: **Boldface type** = church with over 10% of country's affiliated Christians.
NATIONAL COUNCILS (Column 4, 5th letter).
N = Consejo Ecuménico de Cuba (Ecumenical Council of Cuba) (until 1977, Consejo de Iglesias Evangélicas de Cuba/Cuban Council of Protestant Churches).
n = observer member of Ecumenical Council of Cuba.
R = Conferencia Episcopal de Cuba (CEC) (Episcopal Conference of Cuba).
OTHER PROTESTANT DENOMINATIONS. There were about 15 other Protestant missions, mostly from the USA, at work in 1960; although all foreign personnel were subsequently expelled or left, the work of many bodies still continues, sometimes under different names. These bodies include: Berean Mission (c1950), Brethren in Christ (1953–60), Christian Reformed Ch (c1957), Chs of Christ, International Pentecostal Assemblies, Misión Evangélica al Interior, United World Mission (1946). There are also USA military chaplaincies, Churches of Christ, et alia among the 5,000 USA Protestants (half military, half civilian) at Guantánamo US naval base.
OTHER INDIGENOUS PENTECOSTAL CHURCHES. There are a small number of other Black or Cuban smaller indigenous bodies, including: African Methodist Episcopal Ch (USA), Bando Evangelistico Gedeón (Batiblancos), Ch of God (former mission of USA Black pentecostals), Damascus Christian Ch (Puerto Ricans), Iglesia Bethel, Iglesia de Cristo, Iglesia de Los Pinos (split ex Presbyterian Ch; rural). There are also remnants of earlier Black churches, including the Episcopal Orthodox Church (Greek Communion) begun in Cuba in 1921.

PEOPLES (ethnolinguistic). Christians: about 74.7% Cuban White, 15% Mulatto, 10% Black, 0.3% Chinese, Greek.

COUNTRY-WIDE TOTALS
EVANGELIZATION (see Part 5). 1900: 100%. 1970: 65%. 1980: 60%. *Mass evangelism.* May 1975, Congress on Evangelism. *Radiophonic evangelism.* HCJB, FEBC, ICI, et alia.
FOREIGN MISSIONARIES AND PERSONNEL (nationals serving abroad) (1973). Total about 5, mostly Cuban indigenous in USA. There is also a large number of Cuban Roman Catholic personnel who fled or were expelled from 1959–67, but these have now settled in the USA or Latin American countries and most have become citizens there.
FOREIGN MISSIONARIES AND PERSONNEL (aliens from abroad) (1973). Total 222. *From Western world.* 205: 201 Roman Catholics from Spain, Canada, Italy and France, 4 Protestants in 3 USA societies. *From Third World.* 17: about 10 Roman Catholics and 2 Protestants from Mexico and Puerto Rico, about 5 indigenous from Jamaica.
INSTITUTIONS (church-operated) (1973). Total 13, including 1 higher school (minor seminary), 2 research centres, 9 seminaries (8 Protestant, 1 RC).
PERIODICALS. About 15 titles.
PERSONNEL. About 872 (650 national, 222 foreign).
RELIGIOUS LIBRARIES. 11.
SCRIPTURE DISTRIBUTION (1975). Annual totals: 2,000 Bibles (subsidized), 1,000 NTs (subsidized).
SERVICE AGENCIES. About 20, including ASO, CCOC, CEC, CIEC, CONCUR, MEC.

ADDITIONAL DATA ON CHURCHES
IGLESIA CATOLICA EN CUBA. *Catholics.* Including 12,000 Chinese (1966), declining to 5,400 by 1975. *Annual baptisms.* (1972) 95.0% infant, 5.0% adult. *Priests.* 44% diocesan (secular), 56% religious. Expatriates: 83 Spanish, 20 Canadians, 4 Italians, 3 French. *Sisters.* 75% Cubans, 25% Spanish, Canadians and other Europeans. *Seminarians.* Decline from 88 (1966) to 58 (1972) to 45 (1976). *Main religious orders and congregations.* Priests: 21 SJ, 18 PME, 15 OFM. Sisters: 76 Soeurs des Vieux Abandonnés & Servants of Mary; 35 Cloistered of St Catherine, Carmelites & Adorers of the Precious Blood; also 4 Canadian congregations.
*Catholic organizations.* The Episcopal Conference of Cuba (Conferencia Episcopal de Cuba, CEC) is a member of CELAM. There are 2 national organizations of religious personnel, the Cuban Federation of Male Religious (Federación Cubana de Religiosos, CONCUR) and the Cuban Federation of Sisters (Federación Cubana de Religiosas); but there are no national councils for priests or laity. There are however several lay organizations: the Organized Secular Apostolate (Apostolado Segla Organizado, ASO) in 1972 in process of formation under the Episcopal Commission; and at the local level, Marian congregations and groups of the Third Order.
The Holy See has diplomatic relations with Cuba, and is represented to government and the Catholic hierarchy by the Apostolic Nunciature of Cuba, administered after 1963 by a chargé d'affaires who became nuncio in 1974.
The Catholic church administers 4 institutions: 2 hospitals conducted by the Brothers of St John of God (a psychiatric hospital and a children's orthopaedic hospital); and 2 homes for the aged. Catholic sisters also work in a leprosarium, a children's home and a child clinic operated by the state.
IGLESIA EPISCOPAL DE CUBA. Membership: 97% citizens, 3% expatriates; 72.5% White, 27% Black, 0.5% Yellow (Chinese).

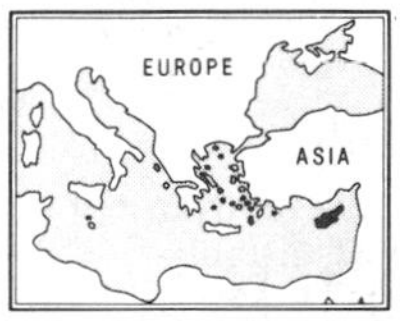


# CYPRUS

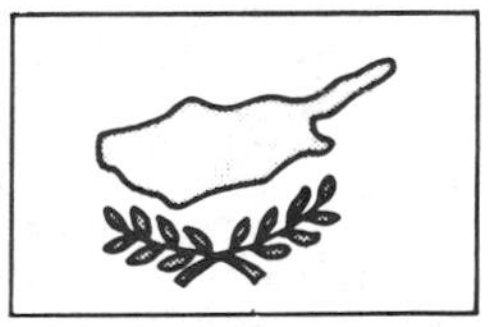

## SECULAR DATA

**STATE. Official name:** The Republic of Cyprus (Kypriaki Dimokratia/Kibris Cumhuriyeti). Adjective of nationality: Cypriot. In 1975, Turkish Cypriots proclaimed their own Turkish Federated State of Cyprus.
**Flag** (shown above right): White field, map of Cyprus in gold, crossed green olive branches.
**Area:** 9,251 sq.km. (3,572 sq.miles). Agricultural land: 56.8%.
**Government:** Republic; since 1974 divided into de facto Greek and Turkish states, the latter declared autonomous in 1975 (1925 British crown colony, 1960 Independence).
**Legislature:** House of Representatives, 50 members.
**Official languages:** Greek (*Ellinika*) and Turkish (*Türkçe*).
**Capital:** Nicosia 116,120 (1973).
**Political divisions:** 6 Administrative Districts.
**Armed forces** (1976): National Guard (set up 1964), Cyprus Police Force.
**Foreign forces** (1973): 9,000 British (UK) troops and Royal Air Force (plus 7,000 dependants), 1,000 USA troops; others from Denmark, Austria, Finland, Sweden (1976); about 20,000 Turkish troops.

**DEMOGRAPHY. Population:** 631,778 (census of 1.IV.1973. For 1970–2000 (UN), see last row of Table 1). Population density (1975): 73/sq.km. (188/sq.mile). Under 15 years: 37%. Growth rate (1975–80): 1.19% per year (births 2.19%, deaths −0.71%, emigrants −0.29%). Life expectancy (1975–80): 72.3 years. Household size: 5.2 persons.
**Major languages:** Greek, Turkish, English, Armenian, Arabic.
**Urban dwellers** (1970): 44.4%. Urban growth rate (1950–70): 3.6% per year.
**Labour force:** 44%.
**Refugees** (1977): From abroad 3,000 (from Lebanon). Internally displaced: 200,000 (55,000 Turkish).
**Tourists** (1972): 405,908. (1974) 150,478.

**ETHNOLINGUISTIC GROUPS:** 78.1% Greek, 18.2% Turkish, 1.7% British & USA, 0.9% Armenian, 0.3% Arab, Jewish, Assyrian.

**MONEY** (1977). **Monetary unit:** pound (= 1,000 mils); US$1 = C£0.417.
**National income per person:** US$1,340. Average annual family income: US$6,968.
**Inflation:** (1970–74) 5.6% per year, (1975) 14% per year (consumer price index 149).
**Cost of living in capital** (1976): index 107 (Washington DC = 100). Daily cost of living: US$23.

**EDUCATION.** Adult literacy: (1946) 61%, (1960) 76%. Education rate: 69%. Schools 564.

**HEALTH.** Hospitals: 129 (3,488 beds). Doctors: 482. Lepers: 800 (1.2 per 1,000). Blind: 1,209. Psychotics: 5,000. Criminals: 1,823.

**LITERATURE.** Annual new book titles (1973): 484. Periodicals: 36. Scientific journals: 10. Newspapers: 12 dailies, 21 non-daily.

**COMMUNICATION** (per 1,000 people). Phones: 99. Radios: 265. TV sets: 102. Daily newspaper circulation: 124 copies.

TABLE 1. RELIGIOUS ADHERENTS IN CYPRUS

| Year | 1900 | | mid-1970 | | Annual change, 1970–1980 | | | | mid-1975 | | mid-1980 | | 2000 | |
|---|---|---|---|---|---|---|---|---|---|---|---|---|---|---|
| *Name* | *Adherents* | *%* | *Adherents* | *%* | *Natural* | *Conversion* | *Total* | *Rate* | *Adherents* | *%* | *Adherents* | *%* | *Adherents* | *%* |
| **Christians** | **185,720** | **78.3** | **503,770** | **79.6** | **6,428** | −308 | **6,120** | **1.15** | **534,070** | **79.4** | **564,970** | **79.1** | **655,100** | **77.4** |
| professing | 185,720 | 78.3 | 503,770 | 79.6 | 6,428 | −308 | 6,120 | 1.15 | 534,070 | 79.4 | 564,970 | 79.1 | 655,100 | 77.4 |
| Orthodox | 183,230 | 77.3 | 482,770 | 76.3 | 6,464 | −324 | 6,140 | 1.20 | 513,170 | 76.3 | 544,170 | 76.2 | 630,600 | 74.5 |
| Anglicans | 310 | 0.1 | 9,000 | 1.4 | −190 | 0 | −190 | −2.35 | 8,080 | 1.2 | 7,100 | 1.0 | 5,100 | 0.6 |
| Roman Catholics | 1,980 | 0.8 | 8,200 | 1.3 | 105 | 5 | 110 | 1.26 | 8,720 | 1.3 | 9,300 | 1.3 | 11,800 | 1.4 |
| Protestants | 200 | 0.1 | 3,800 | 0.6 | 49 | 11 | 60 | 1.46 | 4,100 | 0.6 | 4,400 | 0.6 | 7,600 | 0.9 |
| nominal | 700 | 0.3 | 3,830 | 0.6 | 65 | 262 | 327 | 6.06 | 5,400 | 0.8 | 7,100 | 1.0 | 16,900 | 2.0 |
| affiliated | 185,020 | 78.0 | 499,940 | 79.0 | 6,363 | −570 | 5,793 | 1.09 | 528,670 | 78.6 | 557,870 | 78.1 | 638,200 | 75.4 |
| total practising | 179,470 | *97* | 469,940 | *94* | 5,981 | −535 | 5,446 | 1.09 | 496,950 | *94* | 524,400 | *94* | 542,500 | *85* |
| non-practising | 5,550 | *3* | 30,000 | *6* | 382 | −35 | 347 | 1.09 | 31,720 | *6* | 33,470 | *6* | 95,700 | *15* |
| Orthodox | 182,820 | 77.1 | 482,400 | 76.2 | 6,309 | −710 | 5,599 | 1.10 | 510,410 | 75.8 | 538,390 | 75.4 | 612,000 | 72.3 |
| Roman Catholics | 1,900 | 0.8 | 6,400 | 1.0 | 82 | 8 | 90 | 1.32 | 6,800 | 1.0 | 7,300 | 1.0 | 9,300 | 1.1 |
| Anglicans | 200 | 0.1 | 6,000 | 0.9 | −100 | 0 | −100 | −1.85 | 5,400 | 0.8 | 5,000 | 0.7 | 4,200 | 0.5 |
| Protestants | 100 | 0.0 | 3,140 | 0.5 | 40 | 4 | 44 | 1.31 | 3,360 | 0.5 | 3,580 | 0.5 | 5,900 | 0.7 |
| Evangelicals | 100 | 0.0 | 2,400 | 0.4 | 31 | 9 | 40 | 1.54 | 2,600 | 0.4 | 2,800 | 0.4 | 4,500 | 0.5 |
| Marginal Protestants | 0 | 0.0 | 2,000 | 0.3 | 32 | 128 | 160 | 5.93 | 2,700 | 0.4 | 3,600 | 0.5 | 6,800 | 0.8 |
| Muslims | 51,310 | 21.6 | 117,000 | 18.5 | 1,499 | 11 | 1,510 | 1.21 | 124,500 | 18.5 | 132,100 | 18.5 | 160,700 | 19.0 |
| Non-religious | 0 | 0.0 | 10,000 | 1.6 | 137 | 153 | 290 | 2.54 | 11,400 | 1.7 | 12,900 | 1.8 | 21,100 | 2.5 |
| Atheists | 0 | 0.0 | 2,000 | 0.3 | 32 | 128 | 160 | 5.93 | 2,700 | 0.4 | 3,600 | 0.5 | 7,000 | 0.8 |
| Baha'is | 0 | 0.0 | 200 | 0.0 | 4 | 16 | 20 | 6.67 | 300 | 0.0 | 400 | 0.1 | 2,000 | 0.2 |
| Jews | 120 | 0.1 | 30 | 0.0 | 0 | 0 | 0 | 0.00 | 30 | 0.0 | 30 | 0.0 | 100 | 0.0 |
| **Country's population** | **237,150** | **100.0** | **633,000** | **100.0** | **8,100** | **0** | **8,100** | **1.20** | **673,000** | **100.0** | **714,000** | **100.0** | **846,000** | **100.0** |

COLUMNS, ROWS. For meanings and definitions, see Codebook (Part 6). Note that, by definition, total 'Christians' = professing + crypto-Christians, which also = affiliated + nominal Christians. Percentages may not always total exactly, due to rounding.
CENSUSES. **1881**: 73.9% Greek Orthodox, 24.4% Muslims, 1.1% Roman Catholics, 0.1% Armenian Apostolic. **1891**: 75.8% Greek Orthodox, 22.9% Muslims, 1.0% Roman Catholics, 0.1% Armenian Apostolic, 0.1% Anglicans, 0.1% Protestants, 0.1% Jews. **1.IV.1901**: 77.1% Greek Orthodox, 21.6% Muslims, 0.8% Roman Catholics, 0.2% Armenian Apostolic, 0.1% Anglicans, 0.1% Protestants. **2.IV.1911**: 78.2% Greek Orthodox, 20.6% Muslims, 0.7% Roman Catholics, 0.2% Armenian Apostolic, 0.1% Anglicans, 0.1% Protestants. **1921**: 78.8% Greek Orthodox, 19.8% Muslims, 0.7% Roman Catholics, 0.4% Armenian Apostolic. **1931**: 79.5% Greek Orthodox, 18.5% Muslims, 1.0% Armenian Apostolic, 0.7% Roman Catholics. **10.XI.1946** (excluding 12,422 UK military): 80.2% Greek Orthodox, 17.9% Muslims, 0.8% Armenian Apostolic, 0.7% Roman Catholics, 0.3% Protestants. **11.XII.1960** (excluding 4,049 UK military and tourists): 77.6% Orthodox (77.0% Greek, 0.6% Armenian), 18.3% Muslims, 1.3% Roman Catholics.

NOTES ON RELIGIONS
ANGLICANS. Mostly expatriate UK military, dependants and civilians. The column 'Natural change' above includes annual emigrants of about 287 professing Anglicans, or 165 affiliated Anglicans (mostly all military personnel).
ATHEISTS. Communist Party of Cyprus (Anorthotikon Komma Ergazomenou Laou, AKEL) (legal; pro-Soviet): membership (1970) 14,000, (1974) 12,000; Communist voters (election of 5.VII.1970) 79,280 (39.7% of all votes). Communists are all Greek Cypriots (no Turkish), and most are practising Orthodox Christians.
MUSLIMS. All Turkish except for 0.3% Arabs; mostly Sunnis (of the Hanafite rite) under the mufti of Cyprus, with some Shias in dervish orders (Ticani, Mevlevi or Whirling Dervishes, Bektasi, Fufai or Howling Dervishes). *Hajj pilgrims to Mecca.* (1976) 1.
ORTHODOX. Among the many groups within Orthodoxy are a small number of crypto-Orthodox known as Linobambakoi (linsey-woolseys), who throughout the Ottoman period concealed their faith by taking Muslim names and keeping Muslim ceremonies externally while practising the Orthodox faith in secret.
PRACTISING CHRISTIANS. Among the Orthodox, weekly practice is low, but the great majority attend at church festivals each year.

**NON-CHRISTIAN RELIGIONS. Islam** is the religion of 18% of the island, virtually the entire Turkish population being Muslim. Most Muslims are Sunnis of the Hanafite rite under the mufti of Cyprus. The few Shias belong for the most part to dervish orders, particularly the Ticani, Mevlevi and Bektasi. Turkish Cypriots tend to be more conservative than those in mainland Turkey, but they are increasingly influenced by recent reforms instituted by the Turkish government.

**CHRISTIANITY.** The apostles Paul and Barnabas visited Salamis, Barnabas' birthplace, in AD 46, and Barnabas later became the first bishop of Cyprus. In 441 the third ecumenical council at Ephesus discussed the separation of the Church of Cyprus

from the Church of Antioch, and during the reign of the eastern emperor Zeno (474–491) the Cypriot church received autocephalous status along with the patriarchates of Antioch, Jerusalem, Alexandria and Constantinople. From the 8th to the 10th centuries, Cyprus was subjected to a series of Arab raids, after which a considerable number of monasteries were built. In 1054, the schism between the Eastern and Western churches became a reality. At the invitation of the Latin king Gui de Lusignan, the initial immigration of Maronites from Lebanon to Cyprus occurred during the Crusades at the end of the 12th century. Their number ultimately reached 80,000, divided into 60 villages. The Maronite archdiocese of Cyprus was founded in 1352. From the 12th to the 15th centuries Cyprus was ruled by followers of the Latin rite, the Franks and then the Genoese, who placed a Latin hierarchy over both the Latin and Orthodox churches. When Venice gained control of Cyprus in 1489, it relaxed many of the former restrictions on the Eastern church, but antagonism between the 2 churches continued. Many Gothic churches and cathedrals were built during this period of domination by the Latin church. When the Turks invaded the island in 1572, they restored the Orthodox church to its former position in recognition of its help in the war against Venice. The Latin church was banished. The Maronites were also persecuted because of their alliances with the Lusignan dynasty and later the Venetians. Some returned to Lebanon, including the Maronite bishop, while others converted to the Orthodox Church or Islam. Only a small minority of Maronites remained in Cyprus. Franciscans, who had first come to Cyprus in 1226 during the lifetime of Francis of Assisi, were later given permission to re-establish the Latin rite at Nicosia and Larnaca. Through the Muslim policy of using the religious leader of a conquered people as their political leader, the archbishop (ethnarch) of the Orthodox church increased in

power, being given responsibility for collecting taxes and maintaining law and order. By the beginning of the 19th century both Greeks and Turks were restive under his growing domination, and in 1821 following the Greek war of independence the ethnarch and several of his closest collaborators were executed. In 1878 Cyprus came under British influence, formal annexation following in 1914. Agitation for union with Greece (*enosis*) gradually increased among the Greeks under British rule, with church leaders playing an active part; and in 1956 the ethnarch, archbishop Makarios, was banished from the island. He was later allowed to return and was elected president in 1959. Formal independence was declared in August 1960.

ORTHODOX CHURCHES. Three-quarters of the population, and 96% of all Christians, are members of the Orthodox Church of Cyprus. The Orthodox constitution of 1909 states that the church is governed by the Holy Synod, consisting of its 3 diocesan bishops under the presidency of the archbishop.

There are 11 major Orthodox monasteries active at present in Cyprus, with most of the remaining 67 disused and in ruins. Income from these lands is an important source of finance for the church. Only a small percentage of the people attend liturgical services regularly, but feast days are widely observed. Traditional fasting is now seldom practised, but the Great Week leading up to Easter is considered a highly important religious holiday. Orthodox religion in Cyprus centres on the home, each of which has its own honoured icon. Church weddings and funerals are also widely observed. Cypriot village priests have little theological training but are adept in the exact performance of Orthodox ritual. They have a close relationship with the people and are proud upholders of the national culture. The Theological Seminary of the Apostle Barnabas became in 1972 a major seminary providing a full training for the priesthood. Cyprus has no university, but some, mostly lay theologians who become teachers, go on for further studies at the University of Athens.

The Armenian Apostolic Church has 3,500 members in Cyprus. Armenians have lived on the island since the 11th century, but a large number of immigrants fled there from Turkey during and after World War I. Cyprus forms a diocese under the Catholicate of Cilicia, located in Lebanon.

CATHOLIC CHURCH. There are 6,400 faithful divided among 4 rites, including 200 Armenian Catholics, 200 Greek Catholics, 1,000 Latin-rite Catholics and 5,000 Maronites, but only the latter two have organized communities in Cyprus. The Maronite archdiocese of Cyprus includes both the island of Cyprus and a part of Lebanon. The Cypriot part is the more extensive geographically but less important numerically, with only 5,000 faithful out of a total of 83,000 baptized members in the archdiocese. They live in 4 exclusively Maronite

villages, and in a few towns. In all there are 10 parishes served by clergy, with 150 baptisms and 70 marriages annually. On the island, there are 12 Maronite secular priests, 3 monks in the Monastery of the Prophet Elijah and about 40 Maronite sisters enrolled in Latin congregations, mostly Franciscan missionaries. Outside Cyprus these are 7 Cypriot nuns in Lebanon, 10 monks and 4 seminarians at the Jesuit seminary in Athens. The Maronite community in Cyprus is led by a Cypriot vicar-general.

Latin-rite Catholics are mostly expatriates. Cyprus forms part of the Latin patriarchate of Jerusalem, the present head being a Franciscan patriarchal vicar-general. Ecclesiastical personnel include 10 Franciscan priests, 39 Franciscan Sisters of the Sacred Heart and 24 St Joseph Sisters.

OTHER CHURCHES. Anglicans are mostly expatriates served by 3 British clergy. There are 10 congregations, the largest being in Nicosia. The island forms a diocese in the Episcopal Church in Jerusalem and the Middle East, formerly called the Jerusalem Archbishopric. Protestants are divided into a number of small groups, the largest of which is the Greek Evangelical Church. The Reformed Presbyterian Church sponsors 2 secondary schools, one for girls in Nicosia and the other for boys in Larnaca, and Seventh-day Adventists administer a physiotherapy clinic and a Bible correspondence course. Jehovah's Witnesses also have an active community in Cyprus.

CHURCH AND STATE. The constitution of 16 August 1960 was the result of a joint effort on the part of Britain, Greece and Turkey to stabilize a political situation endangering the security of the Western world. The constitution united Greeks and Turks in the same state, while clearly maintaining their separation. With the exception of foreigners, the population was divided into 2 communities, Greek and Turkish, with all citizens having to choose either one or the other. In general, citizens belonging to the Greek Orthodox Church, or those of Greek origin, culture and language, were officially part of the Greek community. The same was true for Muslims, or those of Turkish origin, culture and language, who were considered to belong to the Turkish community (Article 2, items 1 and 2). Any Greek or Turkish citizen, however, could individually choose to be part of the other community (Article 2, items 5 and 6). Nationals not belonging to either of the 2 communities still had to choose one or the other. If they belonged to a religious group, the religious body made the choice, but the right of each individual to decide otherwise was guaranteed (Article 2, item 3). There were 1,000 such persons in Cyprus at the time the constitution went into force, at least 500 of whom became citizens of the new republic on that date. Each community had its own communal chamber (Article 86), and each religious group elected representatives to its chamber

**Orthodox Church of Cyprus.** *Left.* A priest at home, dressed similarly to his portrait of the Apostle Barnabas, by tradition first Bishop of Cyprus.

*Above.* Former President and Archbishop Makarios on 1971 visit to Kenya when he baptized 5,000 Africans.

(Article 109). The communal chambers were given authority to levy taxes and to safeguard the right of members of their community. They were also authorized to handle all religious and cultural questions, and they had full jurisdiction in matrimonial matters (Article 87). The autonomous Greek Orthodox Church of Cyprus was given the sole right of regulating and administering its internal affairs and properties according to its holy canons and its charter (Article 110, item 1). Moreover, the constitution recognized the institution of Waqfs (Muslim religious trusts), all questions concerning them being regulated solely by the Laws or Principles of Waqfs *(ahkamul evkaf)* as well as by the laws and regulations promulgated by the Turkish communal chamber (Article 110, item 2). For other religious groups, the former colonial legislation remained basically unchanged under the republic. If at any time the Greek or Turkish communities determined that the number of teachers or ministers of religion *(din adami)* was insufficient for the operation of their institutions, they could ask the Greek or Turkish governments to supply additional personnel, but only that 'strictly necessary to meet their needs' (Article 108, item 2).

In December 1959, the ethnarch of the Church of Cyprus, archbishop Makarios, became president of the republic. He had been a firm supporter of independence from colonial rule, with the ultimate aim of union with Greece (enosis). However, he later withdrew his support of enosis and also rejected the demand of the church's Holy Synod in March 1972 that he resign from his secular duties. Opposition on the part of bishops to his dual role increased, and in mid-1973 Makarios, with the support of heads of other Eastern Orthodox churches, deposed the 3 diocesan bishops who had been calling for his resignation.

On 15 July 1974 archbishop Makarios was forcibly evicted from power by a coup d'etat engineered from Athens, which provoked Turkey's armed forces to invade the island 5 days later. Although Makarios returned as president on 7 December 1974, he was unable to heal the de facto division of the island between Turks and Greeks. On 13 February 1975 an autonomous Turkish Cypriot state was proclaimed in the north and a referendum to accept a new constitution for the Turkish zone voted on 8 June 1975. However, Greek Cypriots in the south have refused to accept the validity of these decisions. Makarios died in mid-1977.

**INTERDENOMINATIONAL ORGANIZATIONS.** Prior to the coup d'etat in 1974, an informal organization of Cypriot church leaders met monthly in Nicosia including the Armenian Orthodox vicar, Latin-rite vicar, Anglican priest, pastor of the Nicosia Community Church, with the Maronite vicar as secretary, and with occasional participation by Greek Orthodox priests.

**BROADCASTING.** In view of the strained relations between Muslims and Orthodox, internal religious programmes are carefully scrutinized and controlled. The government Radio Cyprus does however broadcast Greek Orthodox programmes. Other Christian programmes can be heard over the British Forces broadcasting stations, produced by local clergy for British military and RAF personnel on the island. The Middle East Communication Fellowship in Beirut has recently arranged for a daily 15-minute religious programme in Arabic to be broadcast from Radio Cyprus to Arabic-speaking countries. In May 1974, Trans World Radio began transmitting nightly programmes from Cyprus in co-operation with TWR Monaco. The primary focus is on broadcasts in Arabic to the Middle East, especially Lebanon, Syria, Israel, Jordan, Egypt, Libya, Saudi Arabia and Iraq.

## BIBLIOGRAPHY


*Thriskeutiki kai Ithiki Egyklopaidia* (Religious and ethical encyclopedia). Athens: A. Martinos, 1962–68. 12 vols. (Articles on dioceses and church history).

'Religion', chapter 8 in *US Army area handbook for Cyprus* (Dept of the Army Pamphlet, Washington, DC: US Government Printing Officer, 1964), p. 139–165.


TABLE 2. ORGANIZED CHURCHES AND DENOMINATIONS IN CYPRUS

| Official name 1 | Begun 2 | Type 3 | Counc 4 | Congs 5 | Adults 6 | Affiliated 7 | Names, notes, and other statistics (see Codebook) 8 |
|---|---|---|---|---|---|---|---|
| Anglican Church: D Cyprus & the Gulf | | A Cen | Aw.N. | 10 | 2,000 | 6,000 | In Episcopal Ch in Jerusalem & the ME. 95% UK military and civilians. 3x. |
| Armenian Apostolic Church: D Cyprus | c1050 | O Arm | Sw.N. | 3 | 2,200 | 3,500 | Under jurisdiction of C Sis (Lebanon). Cathedral in Muslim hands. 4 schools. 1r. |
| Catholic Church in Cyprus: | 1099 | R LEr | O.... | 16 | 4,000 | 6,400 | *Katholici Eklissia.* Maronite, Latin, Armenian, Melkite. Baptisms: 99.3% infant. |
| P Jerusalem (V Cyprus) | 1099 | R Lat | Os | 6 | 900 | 1,400 | 2% of P Jerusalem. Latin-rite, in 6 towns. M=OFM. Also 200 Armenians. 10x,63w. |
| AD Cyprus (*Maronite*) | 1353 | R Mar | Os | 10 | 3,100 | 5,000 | 95% of AD is in Lebanon. In 4 Greek-speaking villages. 12n,3m,40w,2d(3),150Yy. |
| Christian Brethren | | P CBr | x.... | 3 | 150 | 300 | *Plymouth (Open) Brethren.* M=CMML(UK). Mainly English, some Cypriots. 2f. |
| Church of God of Prophecy | 1935 | P Pe3 | Z.... | 3 | 104 | 300 | *Pentecostal Church.* M=CGP(USA). No schools or institutions. HQ Neapolis, Nicosia. |
| Church of God Pentecostal | 1947 | P Pe3 | ZF... | | 45 | 200 | M=CoG(Cleveland) (USA). Holiness Pentecostals (3-stage). |
| Greek Evangelical Church | | P Ref | Rwc.. | | 200 | 500 | *Hellenike Evangelike Ekkesia.* Greeks. HQ Athens (Greece). |
| Jehovah's Witnesses | c1925 | M Jeh | x.... | 12 | 662 | 2,000 | *Watch Tower. IBSA.* Active witnessing under way by 1940. 1k(Nicosia),63Y. |
| Nicosia Community Church | | P com | ..... | 1 | 50 | 100 | Small English-speaking union church in capital. British, American expatriates. |
| **Orthodox Church of Cyprus:** | 46 | O Gre | CWCN. | 570 | 265,000 | 478,900 | Autocephalous. 67 disused monasteries. 2s(60). 685n,8d(89),3e(75). |
| AD Nicosia (New Justiniana) | | O Gre | Ca | 195 | 100,000 | 218,000 | *AD Levkósia.* Kykkos monastery (business, agriculture). 275 4 57 1 10 |
| D Paphos (Néa Páfos) | | O Gre | Cm | 120 | 50,000 | 80,000 | Western part of island. HQ Néa Páfos. 150 2 15 0 0 |
| D Kition | | O Gre | Cm | 135 | 65,000 | 100,000 | Larnaca and Limassol. Southern parts. HQ Larnaca. 150 1 15 2 65 |
| D Kyrenia (Kirínia) | | O Gre | Cm | 120 | 50,000 | 80,000 | Northern coast of island. HQ Kirínia. 110 1 2 0 0 |
| Reformed Presbyterian Church | 1887 | P Ref | xF... | 1 | 20 | 40 | *Covenanters.* M=RPCNA(USA). Armenians, Cypriots. 2 schools (Nicosia, Larnaca). 14f. |
| Seventh-day Adventist Church | 1932 | P Adv | x.... | 1 | 30 | 100 | *Cyprus Station*, East Mediterranean Field. Correspondence courses. Nicosia. 2f,1h. |
| Union of Armenian Ev Chs in Near East | | P Con | Rw.N. | 1 | 100 | 300 | Armenian refugees from 1915–16 Turkey massacres. Main body in Lebanon, Syria, USA. |
| Other Protestant denominations | | P | ..... | | 800 | 1,300 | About 8: Chs of Christ, Missionary Ch (USA), USA & UK military chaplaincies. |
| **Total affiliated (mid-1970)** | | | | **635** | **275,361** | **499,940** | **Total denominations (1970) . . . 21.** |
| **Total affiliated (mid-1975)** | | | | **637** | **291,200** | **528,670** | **Total denominations (1975) . . . 21.** |
| **Total affiliated (mid-1980)** | | | | **639** | **307,300** | **557,870** | **Total denominations (1980) . . . 21.** |

NOTES ON TABLE ABOVE
COLUMNS: for meanings and CODES (cols. 1, 3, 4, 8): see Codebook (Part 6). Column 1: **Boldface type** = church with over 10% of country's affiliated Christians.

PEOPLES (ethnolinguistic). Christians: 95.9% Greek, 2.1% British & USA, 1.1% Armenian, 0.1% Arab, Assyrian.

COUNTRY-WIDE TOTALS
EVANGELIZATION (see Part 5). 1900: 94%. 1970: 94%. 1980: 97%. *Radiophonic evangelism.* TWR, ICI (1,000 enrolments).
FOREIGN MISSIONARIES AND PERSONNEL (nationals serving abroad) (1972). Total 77 Orthodox priests in 6 countries.
FOREIGN MISSIONARIES AND PERSONNEL (aliens from abroad) (1973). Total 119. *From Western world.* 114: about 70 Roman Catholics, 31 Protestants (18 in 5 USA societies, 11 in 3 UK societies, 2 in 1 Canada society), about 10 Orthodox, 3 Anglicans. *From Third World.* 5 Roman Catholics from Israel, Lebanon and Syria.
INSTITUTIONS (church-operated) (1973). Total 22, including 3 higher schools, 2 medical centres, 1 radio station, 13 religious communities (monasteries), 2 seminaries (Orthodox).
PERIODICALS. About 6 titles.
PERSONNEL. About 1,089 (970 national, 119 foreign).
RELIGIOUS LIBRARIES. 16.
SCRIPTURE DISTRIBUTION (1975). Annual totals: 1,462 Bibles (21% free, 32% subsidized, 47% commercial), 11,840 NTs (13% free, 86% subsidized, 1% commercial), 1,653 UBS portions.
SERVICE AGENCIES. About 10, including CEF, CLC, SASRA, TWR, YWCA.

ADDITIONAL DATA ON CHURCHES
CATHOLIC CHURCH IN CYPRUS. *Catholic organizations.* Since the beginning of 1973 the Holy See has had diplomatic relations with Cyprus and is represented to government and the Catholic hierarchy by a pro-nuncio, who resides in Jerusalem and serves also as apostolic delegate for Jerusalem and Palestine.
Latin-rite Catholics sponsor 4 schools for girls (2,378 pupils) and one for boys (555 pupils), but very few pupils are Catholics. These are private schools, where instruction is given in foreign languages. A government school in the Maronite village of Kormakit and a home for the aged at Larnaca are also directed by religious personnel.
ORTHODOX CHURCH OF CYPRUS. In Greek, Ekklesia tes Kyprou.

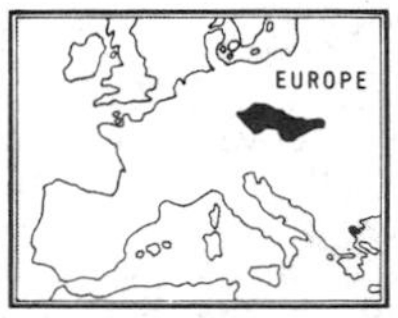


# CZECHOSLOVAKIA

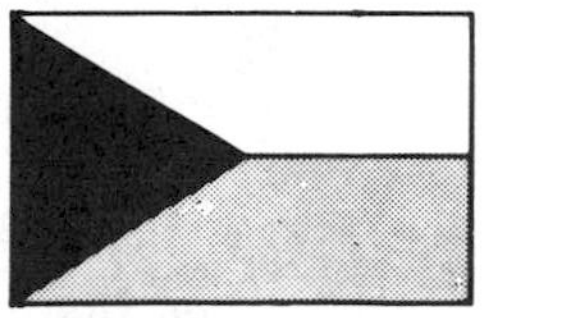

## SECULAR DATA

**STATE. Official name:** The Czechoslovak Socialist Republic, CSR (Ceskoslovenská Socialistická Republika, CSSR). Adjective of nationality: Czechoslovak.
**Flag** (shown above right): White over red stripe with blue triangle at hoist.
**Area:** 127,869 sq.km. (49,371 sq.miles). Agricultural land: 55.1%.
**Government:** One-party Communist state, since 1946 (1918 republic created).
**Legislature:** Federal Assembly; Chamber of the Nations, 75 Czechs and 75 Slovaks; Chamber of the People, 200 members.
**Official languages:** Czech (*Cesky*) and Slovak (*Slovensky*).
**Chief cities:** federal capital Prague 1,095,600 (1974), Brno 343,860, Bratislava 328,760.
**Political divisions:** 2 Socialist Republics (Czech and Slovak), with 12 Administrative Regions, including the 2 republican capitals Prague and Bratislava.
**Armed forces** (1976): Total 180,000 regular (110,000 conscripts): army 135,000, air force 45,000 (458 combat aircraft). Reserves: 350,000. Paramilitary forces: 20,000 (10,000 People's Militia).
**Foreign forces** (1973): 48,000 USSR troops (5 divisions).

**DEMOGRAPHY. Population:** 14,344,986 (census of 1.XII.1970. For 1970–2000 (UN), see last row of Table 1). Population density (1975): 115/sq.km. (299/sq.mile). Under 15 years: 27%. Growth rate (1975–80): 0.58% per year (births 1.74%, deaths −1.16%). Life expectancy (1975–80): 70.0 years. Household size: 3.3 persons.
**Major languages:** Czech, Slovak, Hungarian, Romany, Russian, German, Polish, Ukrainian.
**Urban dwellers** (1970): 52.1%. Urban growth rate (1950–70): 1.9% per year.
**Labour force:** 50%.
**Tourists** (1974): 11,785,733.

**ETHNOLINGUISTIC GROUPS:** 62.5% Czech, 29.0% Slovak, 4.0% Hungarian (Magyar) (565,000), 2.5% Gypsy, 0.6% German, 0.5% Polish (72,000), 0.4% Ukrainian (59,000), 0.3% USSR military (48,000), 0.1% Jewish.

**MONEY** (1977). **Monetary unit:** koruna (= 100 haler); US$1 = Kcs 11.46.
**National income per person:** US$3,000. Average annual family income: US$9,900.
**Inflation:** (1970–74) 0.0% per year, (1975) 0.6% per year (consumer price index 101).
**Cost of living in capital** (1976): index 108 (Washington DC = 100). Daily cost of living : US$43.

**EDUCATION.** Adult literacy: 100%. Education rate: 52%. Schools: 10,247. Universities: 6.

**HEALTH.** Hospitals: 413 (147,012 beds). Doctors: 31,426. Blind: 10,000. Psychotics: 150,000.

**LITERATURE.** Annual new book titles (1973): 8,567. Periodicals: 1,081. Scientific journals: 420. Newspapers: 27 dailies, 105 non-daily.

**COMMUNICATION** (per 1,000 people). Phones: 162. Radios: 260. TV sets: 234. Daily newspaper circulation: 279 copies.

TABLE 1. RELIGIOUS ADHERENTS IN CZECHOSLOVAKIA

| Year | 1900 | | mid-1970 | | Annual change, 1970–1980 | | | | mid-1975 | | mid-1980 | | 2000 | |
|---|---|---|---|---|---|---|---|---|---|---|---|---|---|---|
| *Name* | *Adherents* | *%* | *Adherents* | *%* | *Natural* | *Conversion* | *Total* | *Rate* | *Adherents* | *%* | *Adherents* | *%* | *Adherents* | *%* |
| **Christians** | **11,798,840** | **97.0** | **11,598,712** | **80.9** | **68,198** | **–18,189** | **50,009** | **0.42** | **11,839,900** | **80.2** | **12,098,800** | **79.7** | **12,724,000** | **75.7** |
| crypto-Christians | 0 | 0.0 | 2,421,612 | 16.9 | 14,677 | 10,652 | 25,329 | 0.99 | 2,548,100 | 17.3 | 2,674,900 | 17.6 | 3,013,700 | 17.9 |
| professing | 11,798,840 | 97.0 | 9,177,100 | 64.0 | 53,521 | –28,841 | 24,680 | 0.26 | 9,291,800 | 63.0 | 9,423,900 | 62.0 | 9,710,300 | 57.8 |
| Roman Catholics | 10,959,100 | 90.1 | 7,398,900 | 51.6 | 43,351 | –17,711 | 25,640 | 0.34 | 7,526,100 | 51.0 | 7,655,300 | 50.4 | 7,967,000 | 47.4 |
| Protestants | 826,740 | 6.8 | 1,061,100 | 7.4 | 6,121 | –4,391 | 1,730 | 0.16 | 1,062,500 | 7.2 | 1,078,400 | 7.1 | 1,109,000 | 6.6 |
| Catholics (non-Roman) | 1,000 | 0.0 | 630,900 | 4.4 | 3,542 | –6,632 | –3,090 | –0.50 | 615,000 | 4.3 | 600,000 | 4.2 | 550,000 | 3.3 |
| Orthodox | 12,000 | 0.1 | 86,000 | 0.6 | 507 | –107 | 400 | 0.45 | 88,000 | 0.6 | 90,000 | 0.6 | 84,000 | 0.5 |
| Anglicans | 0 | 0.0 | 200 | 0.0 | 0 | 0 | 0 | 0.00 | 200 | 0.0 | 200 | 0.0 | 300 | 0.0 |
| nominal | 608,000 | 5.0 | 0 | 0.0 | 0 | 0 | 0 | 0.00 | 0 | 0.0 | 0 | 0.0 | 0 | 0.0 |
| affiliated | 11,190,840 | 92.0 | 11,598,712 | 80.9 | 68,198 | –18,189 | 50,009 | 0.42 | 11,839,900 | 80.2 | 12,098,800 | 79.7 | 12,724,000 | 75.7 |
| total practising | 10,071,760 | *90* | 8,119,100 | *70* | 47,738 | –12,732 | 35,006 | 0.42 | 8,287,930 | *70* | 8,469,160 | *70* | 9,543,000 | *75* |
| non-practising | 1,119,080 | *10* | 3,479,610 | *30* | 20,460 | –5,457 | 15,003 | 0.42 | 3,551,970 | *30* | 3,629,640 | *30* | 3,181,000 | *25* |
| Roman Catholics | 10,429,000 | 85.8 | 9,610,058 | 67.0 | 56,593 | –13,459 | 43,134 | 0.44 | 9,825,200 | 66.6 | 10,041,400 | 66.1 | 10,647,700 | 63.4 |
| Protestants | 750,000 | 6.2 | 1,112,954 | 7.8 | 6,461 | –3,836 | 2,625 | 0.23 | 1,121,500 | 7.6 | 1,139,200 | 7.5 | 1,176,000 | 7.0 |
| Evangelicals | 150,000 | 1.2 | 216,000 | 1.5 | 1,254 | –754 | 500 | 0.23 | 217,600 | 1.5 | 221,000 | 1.5 | 228,000 | 1.4 |
| Catholics (non-Roman) | 840 | 0.0 | 656,000 | 4.6 | 3,825 | –1,425 | 2,400 | 0.36 | 664,000 | 4.5 | 680,000 | 4.4 | 630,000 | 3.7 |
| Orthodox | 11,000 | 0.1 | 200,000 | 1.4 | 1,175 | –375 | 800 | 0.39 | 204,000 | 1.4 | 208,000 | 1.4 | 202,000 | 1.2 |
| Marginal Protestants | 0 | 0.0 | 19,500 | 0.1 | 144 | 906 | 1,050 | 4.20 | 25,000 | 0.2 | 30,000 | 0.2 | 68,000 | 0.4 |
| Anglicans | 0 | 0.0 | 200 | 0.0 | 0 | 0 | 0 | 0.00 | 200 | 0.0 | 200 | 0.0 | 300 | 0.0 |
| Non-religious | 31,160 | 0.3 | 1,526,288 | 10.6 | 10,281 | 11,790 | 22,071 | 1.35 | 1,638,000 | 11.1 | 1,747,000 | 11.5 | 2,395,000 | 14.2 |
| Atheists | 10,000 | 0.1 | 1,200,000 | 8.4 | 7,309 | 6,391 | 13,700 | 1.08 | 1,269,000 | 8.6 | 1,337,000 | 8.8 | 1,681,000 | 10.0 |
| Jews | 328,000 | 2.7 | 12,000 | 0.1 | –800 | 0 | –800 | –10.00 | 8,000 | 0.1 | 4,000 | 0.0 | 2,000 | 0.0 |
| Other religionists | 0 | 0.0 | 2,000 | 0.0 | 12 | 8 | 20 | 0.95 | 2,100 | 0.0 | 2,200 | 0.0 | 5,000 | 0.0 |
| **Country's population** | **12,168,000** | **100.0** | **14,339,000** | **100.0** | **85,000** | **0** | **85,000** | **0.58** | **14,757,000** | **100.0** | **15,189,000** | **100.0** | **16,807,000** | **100.0** |

COLUMNS, ROWS. For meanings and definitions, see Codebook (Part 6). Note that, by definition, total 'Christians' = professing + crypto-Christians, which also = affiliated + nominal Christians. Percentages may not always total exactly, due to rounding.
CENSUSES. **31.XII.1910** (adjusted to 1921 boundaries): 90.2% Roman Catholics (4.4% Greek Catholics), 6.8% Protestants (4.3% Lutherans, 2.5% Reformed), 2.7% Jews, 0.3% non-religious. **1930**: 77.5% Roman Catholics (including 4.0% Greek Catholics), 7.7% Protestants, 5.8% non-religious, 5.3% Catholics (non-Roman) (Czechoslovak Church), 2.7% Jews, 1.0% Orthodox.
POLLS. Southern Moravia (1963): 81% get married in church, 83% get their children baptized, 49% attend church festivals, 34% attend church from time to time, 13% attend regularly (similar poll in 1946 showed 20% regular attenders). 1967 sample survey, all Czechoslovakia: 50.5% Roman Catholics (Latin only), 36.0% non-religious and atheists, 7.4% Protestants, 4.4% Catholics (non-Roman) (Hussite Ch), 1.1% Greek Catholics (disputed with Orthodox), 0.6% Orthodox. Czech lands only: 46.4% non-religious, 44.1% Roman Catholics, 6.1% Catholics (non-Roman) (Czechoslovak Church), 2.6% Protestants, 0.8% Greek Catholics. Slovakia: 65.5% Roman Catholics, 18.8% Protestants, 11.9% non-religious, 1.9% Orthodox, 1.7% Greek Catholics (disputed with Orthodox), 0.2% Catholics (non-Roman).

NOTES ON RELIGIONS
ATHEISTS. Czechoslovak Communist Party (in power since 1948; pro-Soviet): membership (1970) 1,200,000, declining from 1,699,677 in 1968; Communist voters (election of 26.XI.1971) 10,197,234 (99.8% of all votes). There is also the Communist-directed Czechoslovak Youth Federation with 46,000 groups and over 1,518,000 members in 1963. About 25% of Communist party members are estimated to be committed atheists, the rest being non-religious with a very few professing Christians. In 1975–76, a new wave of militant atheism was inaugurated by the authorities.
CRYPTO-CHRISTIANS. Christians affiliated to churches but not known as such to the state, of 3 kinds: (1) unorganized individuals in the legal churches, (2) members of illegal or underground churches, and (3) isolated radio believers.
JEWS. Decline from 360,000 in 1938 by over 85% as a result of massacres during Nazi holocaust, and subsequent emigration. During the disturbances of 1968, 4,500 Jews escaped the country. They have since been rapidly declining by emigration, averaging 1,000 emigrants a year from 1970. Now they remain only in cities (1,200 in Prague with 2 synagogues) and in the sub-Carpathian Ukraine.
NOMINAL CHRISTIANS. Before 1949 only.
NON-RELIGIOUS. Agnostics, indifferent to religion, including most Communist party members. In addition, there are another 17% of the population whom the polls record as non-religious but who are affiliated to churches and so are classified here as crypto-Christians.
OTHER RELIGIONISTS. Including Muslims, and Baha'is in 2 centres.

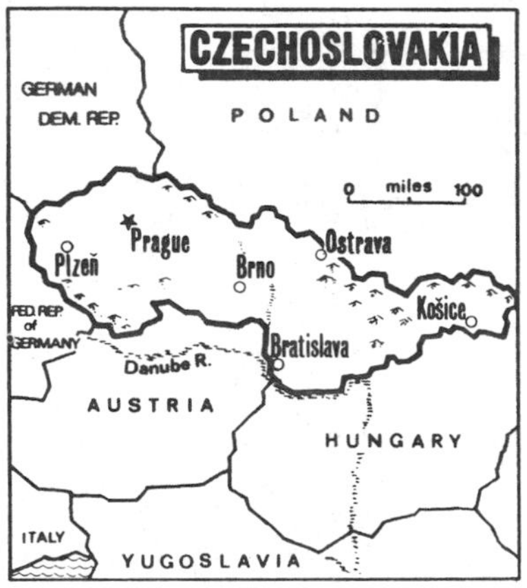


**NON-CHRISTIAN RELIGIONS. Atheism** and **agnosticism** are significant forces in Czech life, representing as they do the official ideology of the government in power. Communist Party membership has however decreased markedly since 1948, when 20% of the population were members, to 12% in the 1960s and 8% in the 1970s. Membership in fact fell to 1.2 million members in 1971 as contrasted with 1.7 million in 1968, a half million resigning or being purged after the overthrow of the Dubcek regime.

**Judaism** decreased in number by more than 85% as a result of the Nazi massacres of the 1930s and 1940s. However there still exists an historic community in Prague and in the large cities, as well as a Jewish folk-community in the sub-Carpathian Ukraine. The Jewish Museum of the State of Prague conducts scientific research into the history of the Jewish people, particularly in Czechoslovakia, and publishes a journal in French and German.

**CHRISTIANITY.** The history of Czechoslovakia has been influenced by its central European position, the country being subject between AD 600 and 1000 to Franco-Teutonic pressures from the north and west, and Magyar and Slavic pressures from the south and east. Early German missionaries originally propagated the Roman faith, while the growing rift between Rome and Constantinople resulted in Slavic-speaking people to the south coming increasingly under the influence of the Byzantine church, particularly because of its acceptance of the vernacular for liturgical purposes. Moravia, the central portion of present-day Czechoslovakia, achieved its greatest glory in the 9th and 10th centuries, largely through the missionary efforts of Cyril and Methodius. The Kingdom of Bohemia under king Wenceslas also became Catholic in the 10th century. Bohemia flourished during the 14th century when the Holy Roman Emperor who was also king of Bohemia, Charles IV, established Prague as an archdiocese in 1344, and introduced the first university of central Europe there in 1348. Religious congregations grew, monasteries were built, and many priests ordained; but their extravagant living drew condemnation. The influence of John Wycliffe of England was augmented when the English king married Anne of Bohemia; and John Huss, the Bohemian Protestant martyr, emerged as one of the first pre-Reformation figures, combining Bohemian nationalist feelings against the domination of Germans within their population as well as against worldliness of the clergy and the authority of the pope.

A second movement within Czech Protestantism developed when a number of Christians left Prague in 1457 to establish a village of their own based on early Christian principles. These became known as the Unitas Fratrum (Unity of Brethren), later called the Moravian Brethren when they had become dispersed in other lands. A third movement was Lutheranism, which developed more fully the ideas promulgated by Huss; and in 1573 these 3 movements adopted a joint declaration of faith. The Czech Reformation reached its height at this time, with sympathetic Hussite and Calvinist kings in power. However, this came to an end in 1621 when the Austrian Catholic Hapsburgs gained control of Bohemia and Moravia, and Protestantism was suppressed. In 1781 an Edict of Toleration was issued, but only the Lutheran Augsburg Confession and the Calvinist Helvetic Confession were permitted, approximately one-third of the Protestants choosing to affiliate with the former, and two-thirds with the latter. In 1848 another edict permitted the use of local languages, and Protestants were granted equal rights with Catholics.

World War I created a new political entity when Slovakia was removed from the Hungarian empire, necessitating new ecclesiastical alignments; and World War II was followed by the rise of Communism with even more drastic repercussions on the life of the churches.

CATHOLIC CHURCH. Catholicism remains the majority religion of Czechoslovakia in spite of the impediments imposed on it by the present Communist regime. Of the Latin-rite dioceses, 7 were without residential bishops in 1973. Four of these were in the Czech part of the country and 3 in Slovakia. The archdiocese of Prague was under an apostolic administrator who was also archbishop but only in name. The bishop named by the Holy See to the diocese of Hradek Kralove in 1950 was never allowed to carry out his functions. Three of the residential bishops belonged to or were connected with either the Pacem in Terris Association, an official movement sanctioned and controlled by the Communist Party, or its predecessor the Priests for Peace Movement, as were the capitular vicars (appointed directly by the government) for the 4 dioceses without residential bishops. The jurisdictions of Trnava and the Tesin zone were both under apostolic administrators equally bound to Pacem in Terris. The jurisdiction of Szatmar had no administrator. The chancellors of several dioceses and jurisdictions also belonged to Pacem in Terris.

Religious orders and congregations were dissolved in 1950 and were able to reconstitute themselves somewhat only in 1968. This included the creation of Czech and Slovak committees of religious congregations. However, since the fall of the Dubcek regime, they have again been suppressed. They have not been forcibly dissolved, but their activities are closely watched and held in check. According to a confidential report of a meeting of the Communist Party of Slovakia, the situation in that republic in 1970 was as follows. There were 16 male orders and congregations, 2 being Greek Catholic, with 581 members, 372 being priests and 209 brothers. Of the 372 priests, 170 were active in the pastoral ministry, 129 'occupied in other matters' and 73 had reached the age of retirement. Women's congregations were 22 in number, 2 being Greek Catholic, with 3,080 members including those formerly at work in Bohemia but now deported. Among these were 2,124 still at work and 956 in retirement. Some 664 were over 60 years of age, and 591 were aged 55–60. The total number of sisters including those without employment is at least 7,247 for all Czechoslovakia. The Ministry of Culture's 'Plan for limiting the activity of the Churches in Slovakia' severely limits the field of action of religious personnel to pastoral work by brothers, and to social welfare for sisters, that is to the degree that they have not been deprived of all activity. This is in marked contrast to the situation in 1968 when the majority of sisters had become parish assistants. For both, it is now forbidden to admit novices or to erect new communities. It appears, nevertheless, that the policy adopted in the Czech Republic is less rigorous. According to the Austrian Catholic agency Kipa, the Office of Ecclesiastical Affairs in Prague did not give in to the demand of its counterpart in Bratislava to terminate all activities of Slovakian sisters in hospitals and sanitoria in areas under its competence. Even in Slovakia sisters often succeed in asserting their rights to have work contracts conforming to the law, and in asserting that no legal disposition prevents them from exercising their religious vocation.

Only 2 seminaries or faculties of theology are tolerated. The administration and academic staff of both were appointed and controlled by government administration before the liberalization of 1968, and have continued to exist since then under the same conditions. These are the Faculty of St Cyril and St Methodius of Prague with its seat at Litomerice (Rímskokatolická Cyrilometodejská Bohoslovecká Fakulta v Praze se sídlem v Litomericich) for the Czech regions; and the Faculty of St Cyril and St Methodius of Bratislava for Slovakia. In 1968 direct interference on the part of the civil powers ceased, and the numerus clausus imposed until then limiting the number of new candidates accepted each year to 20 was no longer enforced. Seminaries at the time received many applications from those who had been systematically rejected in preceding years but who still wished to enter the priesthood. Another faculty was opened in 1968 at Olomouc in the Czech sector. Between 1963–64 and 1965–66 the number of seminarians had risen from 130 to 149 at Litomerice and Bratislava; but between 1968–69 and 1970–71 the number rose from 414 to 561 at Litomerice, Olomouc and Bratislava. A numerus clausus was then re-established at the beginning of the 1971–72 year, with only 98 candidates admitted out of the 205 who had applied. After April 1970 no candidate was accepted at Olomouc, and the seminary was finally closed in June 1973. Conditions of administration at the Bratislava seminary for the year 1972–73, imposed by the Slovak government, excluded candidates studying or having completed advanced or technical studies. In practice, the more brilliant students were also eliminated. At Bratislava the church authorities had been trying at length to secure authorization to open an annexe to the seminary in an episcopal residence at Spisske Podhradie where priests for the Greek Catholic Church could be trained, but this has been consistently rejected by the Ministry of Culture.

The age pyramid of the clergy in Czechoslovakia is disturbing. In 1968 the journal *Via* gave the following statistics for the dioceses of Prague, Hradek Kralove, Litomerice and Ceske-Budejovice: 84% of active parish priests were over 40 years of age, with 38% between 50 and 60 years old. This situation will not soon be altered as a result of the large number of candidates entering in 1968–70. The average ages of men ordained in various dioceses in July 1972 were: Prague 36 years, Olomouc 42 years, Brno 41 years and Tesin 33 years. Altogether, of the 55 priests ordained for Bohemia-Moravia in July 1972,

27 were between 23 and 40 years, while 28 were between 41 and 60. To this must be added the fact that numerous priests are prevented from exercising their ministry and many parishes are vacant.

Since 1950 it has not been possible to speak of genuinely free Catholic associations or movements, apart from a few ephemeral efforts during the first half of 1968. During this period (May 1968) there was begun the Work of Conciliar Renovation (Dilo Kocilové Obnovy, or Dielo Koncilovej Obnovy, DKO). Made up of hierarchy, clergy and laity meeting for renewal of the Church in Czechoslovakia under the inspiration of Vatican II, the DKO was without doubt the only free Catholic movement which has existed under the Czechoslovakian Communist regime. Accused of desiring to · restore 'political Catholicism', this movement failed to secure approval as a recognized association even from the Dubcek regime, and it was dissolved in October 1968 soon after the Russian invasion.

The Pacem in Terris Association for Catholic Priests in the CSR (Sdruzeni Katolickych Duchovnich Pacem in Terris CSSR) is strictly subordinate to the regime and has been the instrument through which the latter directly interferes in the internal affairs of the Catholic Church. Officially founded in November 1971 in the presence of 400 priests from all parts of the country as well as representatives of the federal government, it is an effort to reconstitute the former Movement for Peace of Catholic Clergy (Mirové Hnuti Katolicheho Duchovenska, MHKD). The MHKD was created in 1951 and was directed by a former priest, abbé Plojhar, a deputy and minister of health under several governments. Discredited, the MHKD was dissolved during the first half of 1968. By the end of August 1971 and prior to its official foundation, the new association Pacem in Terris established 2 sections, one Czech and the other Slovakian. Czech and Slovak Caritas (Ceska Katolicka Charita, and Ustredna Charita na Slovensku) are also directly under the control of the regime, particularly through Priests for Peace. The activities of Caritas have been reduced to directing homes for retired priests and sisters, in addition to a few institutions run by sisters for the aged, infirm and mentally retarded. Caritas controls the Catholic press and produces liturgical articles; it is not affiliated with Caritas International. The Society of St Adalbert (Spolok Svätého Vojdecha) is a cultural association and publishing centre for the Catholic Church in Slovakia which resumed its activities in 1968. Today it is responsible to Slovak Caritas which severely limits its activities prohibiting all co-operation with foreign publishers. The Catholic press is in the hands of priests belonging to Pacem in Terris and produces various journals. Several new journals begun in 1968 have since disappeared. Of note also is the activity of the Czech Religious Centre of Velehrad, which was founded in Rome by cardinal Beran, the former archbishop of Prague who was freed

in 1963 and who died in Rome in 1969, together with other Czech ecclesiastical refugees. The centre is regularly and violently attacked by the Czech government.

The Greek Catholic (Uniate) Church (Grecko-Katolicka Církev), of the Byzantine rite, is virtually limited to the diocese of Presov in Slovakia. Its future is bound to that of its counterpart in Romania as well as its tenuous relationship with the Orthodox Church. On 28 April 1950 some irregularly-authorized delegates of the Greek Catholic clergy and laity in Czechoslovakia were brought to Presov by the Orthodox metropolitan Eleutheros and there proclaimed the reunion of their church with the Orthodox Church. On the following 27 May a decree of the government in Prague recognized the legitimacy of this transfer and ipso facto endorsed the disappearance of the Greek Catholic Church of Czechoslovakia. The Orthodox Church inherited its parishes, churches and all its pastoral properties. Some 320,000 faithful were thus officially and forcibly reintegrated into Orthodoxy. Of the 311 Greek Catholic priests at the time, 28 accepted the new situation; the rest were imprisoned. The bishop and his auxiliary were both deported. During the liberalization of 1968, a government decree of 13 June (which had among its signatories G. Husak who succeeded Dubcek as chief of government in 1969) authorized the reconstitution of the Greek Catholic Church, recognizing that its liquidation had been a political act of assimilation which had trampled on its rights. A referendum in each parish was then organized, based on a simple majority vote of the faithful. In March 1969, of the 246 Greek Catholic parishes in existence in 1950, 200 voted to rejoin the Roman Catholic Church and only 2 to remain in the Orthodox Church, with 40 others not yet reported; and in addition 69 priests asked to be received by the Roman Catholic Church. At the end of 1973, however, the existence of the Greek Catholic Church was again threatened. The official position of the Slovak Socialist Republic, as revealed in the 'Plan for limiting the activity of the Churches in Slovakia' is stated as: 'The Minister of Culture recalls that the authorization accorded the Greek Catholic Church to resume its activity in virtue of governmental decree 205 of the Czechoslovakian Republic of 13 June 1968 did not receive the approval of the Central Committee of the Communist Party of Bohemia and Slovakia'. As a result, 'Eventually. . . the existence of the Greek Catholic Church could be called in question' if the conflicts between Orthodox and Greek Catholics could not be resolved 'due to bad will on the part of the Greek Catholic Church'. In the meantime, the Minister of Culture 'shall propose changes in the leadership of the Greek Catholic Church'. In fact since 1968 this church has been the target of a concerted attack which could presage its demise. It has been prevented from opening a theological seminary of its own, while at the same

**Czechoslovak Hussite Church.** One of the world's largest denominations in the Reformed Catholic tradition, founded in 1920 by secession of 20% of the Roman Catholic Church. *Above.* Divine service on July 6 (Magister John Huss Day) in Rabi castle ruins. *Right.* The Patriarch, Dr Miroslav Novak, presiding at the service.

time being refused permission to send candidates to the Latin seminary at Bratislava. Undoubtedly their conflict with the Orthodox is of major proportions, and real, as was evident from numerous tragic incidents during the parish referendum of 1968–69. Nevertheless, these problems were being resolved following a joint appeal launched on 24 November 1968 by the Greek Catholic bishop and the Orthodox metropolitan, calling for mutual reconciliation. The whole rapprochement has now been placed in jeopardy by governmental intervention 'to protect socialist public order and political security'. Since 1968, the diocese of Presov has been directed by an ad interim ordinary with residential episcopal powers. The auxiliary bishop in office before 1950 has been prevented from returning to his diocese. In 1974–75 the regime removed from Greek Catholics control over their own worship places and required that they be used jointly with the Orthodox, an action which could provoke conflicts among the 2 churches and bring discredit on Christianity in general.

PROTESTANT CHURCHES. Lutheranism is the predominant Protestant tradition in Czechoslovakia. The largest body is the Slovak Evangelical Church of the Augsburg Confession, established in 1530, which except for 2 congregations in the Czech lands is confined to Slovakia. The unit of church organization is the congregation, and neighbouring congregations are grouped into seniorates. There are 2 districts, the Eastern District consisting of 6 seniorates, with 9 in the Western District. The 15 seniorates constitute what is termed the General Church. The membership is largely of conservative peasant extraction, urban dwellers being few. A second body, the Silesian Evangelical Church of the Augsburg Confession, is a Polish-speaking Lutheran denomination found in the Tesin, Karvina and Ostrava border areas of Moravia and Slovakia. Two-thirds of its membership are in the Beskyd valleys of Tesin where most are iron-workers. Coal-miners and steel-workers also predominate among the Lutherans of the Ostrava-Karvina region. The principal administrative organ is the Church Council which is elected by the Synod for a 6-year period, the synod itself meeting every 3 years.

The Evangelical Church of Czech Brethren is the result of a union in 1918 of the former Lutheran and Czech Reformed churches; it traces its origin to the Hussite and Brethren reformation beginning in the 14th century. Today there are 670 congregations in 13 seniorates. The chief legislative body is the Synod, which meets every 3 years, while administration is lodged in the Synodical Council. The Comenius Theological Faculty has had an important influence on the church in large part due to the activities of J.L. Hromádka, who played an important role in trying to initiate Christian-Communist dialogue in Czechoslovakia.

The Reformed Christian Church in Slovakia was created in 1918 after Slovakia was severed from the Hungarian empire, and the Hungarian and Slovak languages are accorded equal status in the liturgical and administrative life of the church. There are 7 seniorates making up the General Church, the supreme legislative and executive organs being the Synod and the Synodal Presidium.

Other smaller denominations include Moravians, Methodists, Adventists, Baptists and Pentecostals.

CATHOLIC (NON-ROMAN) CHURCHES. At the conclusion of World War I, the refusal of Rome to respond to the request of Czech Catholic priests and laymen for the use of the vernacular in the liturgy, married priests, and greater participation of laity in the administration of the church, resulted in Los von Rom, a massive exodus of Catholics who then formed the Czechoslovak Church, which was renamed the Czechoslovak Hussite Church in 1972. Leaving behind an earlier trend towards unitarianism, the church reintroduced the apostolic succession of bishops in 1935 and has tended towards greater orthodoxy in recent years. While adopting Hussite emphases, it has retained also many Catholic features and considers itself to be a Reformed Catholic rather than a Protestant church. It remains the largest denomination in Czechoslovakia today after the Catholic Church itself.

ORTHODOX CHURCH. The first Orthodox communities were established in Prague in 1863. Suppressed during World War I, they were re-established after peace was restored. Over the years the Orthodox Church, which is strongest in eastern Slovakia, has functioned under the jurisdictions of the patriarchs of Serbia, Constantinople and Moscow. Suffering persecution again during World War II, Prague was reconstituted as a metropolitan see under Moscow in 1949. In 1950 the conflict with Catholicism erupted over the status of the Greek Catholic (Uniate) Church, which conflict has not yet been resolved. In 1951 the church was declared autocephalous.

CHURCH AND STATE. The constitutional law of the Czechoslovakian Federation promulgated on 27 October 1968 and put into effect on 1 January 1969 includes no reference to religious questions. In principle, these remain regulated by the constitution of 11 July 1960 (the first socialist constitution in the world after that of the USSR), which will remain valid until the adoption of a new federal constitution by each of the Federation's 2 republics. Article 32 of the 1960 constitution takes up the article of the same number in the preceding constitution of 1948, as follows: 'Freedom of religion is guaranteed. One may profess any religion or no religion. Religious practices may be observed inasmuch as they do not transgress the law' (Paragraph 1). 'Religious faith or convictions cannot be used as a pretext for refusing to carry out individual civil responsibilities fixed by law' (Paragraph 2).

The Federal Office of State for Ecclesiastical Affairs within the Ministry of Culture (Ministerstvo Kultury, Urad Predsednictva Vlády, Sekretariát pro Veci Církevní) is authorized to handle all religious questions. Created by Parliament in 1949, it was given the task of 'watching over ecclesiastical and religious life to see that it develops in harmony with the constitution and the principles of the Popular Democratic Regime, assuring thus that each citizen has the freedom of religion guaranteed by the constitution, on the basis of religious tolerance and juridical equality for all denominations'. All churches and religious communities require official recognition. According to a report published in 1972 by the Central Committee of the Czechoslovak Communist Party, the state recognizes 18 religious communities. After 1968 the Office was divided into Czech (Církevne Urad v Praze) and Slovak (Církevne Urad v Bratislava) sections, which in turn, were further decentralized into districts. In actuality, it is an organ for control and opens the door for the state to enter into the internal affairs of the churches.

It is possible to distinguish 3 periods in the development of relations between churches and the state since the Prague Coup of February 1948 which carried a Communist government into power. The period from 1948 to 1968 was characterized by violence, exemplified by restrictive laws, arrests and confiscations. Most of these concerned directly the Catholic Church, as the Christian majority in Czechoslovakia, but other churches were also affected.

At the start of the first period, from early 1948 to the beginning of 1949 the following 7 actions were taken in rapid succession: (1) suppression or control of the press and religious publishing houses (February 1948); (2) nationalization of all landed properties of the church, the state guaranteeing the restoration of worship places of artistic value (21 March 1948); (3) nationalization and secularization of all church schools (11 June 1948); (4) nationalization of hospitals (19 July 1948); (5) suppression of all Catholic organizations, including Catholic Action, and imprisonment of their lay leaders, some (particularly in Slovakia) serving up to 17 years in prison (1948); (6) the attempt to create a new Catholic Action group controlled by the government, which however failed to materialize (1949); and finally (1949) (7) rupture of diplomatic relations with the Holy See.

Certain decrees of that period made stipulations which still regulate church-state affairs. Decree 118/49 of 14 October 1949 dealt with financial and personnel matters. 'Activities of a sacred character, proper to churches and to religious societies, can only be exercised by those who have received permission from the state'. Decree 219/49 of 18 October 1949, which is applied specifically to the Catholic Church, states that 'Priests must be persons loyal to the demands of the state, not laying themselves open to criticism and responding to the general conditions required for entering into the service of the state' (Article 18, Paragraph 1). Failure to arrive at agreement with the state causes any post requiring a priest to be 'considered as vacant' (Article 18, Paragraph 2). On the other hand, the state pays a salary to recognized priests. In April 1950 came the de facto suppression of religious orders and congregations following a police order requiring the 'concentration' of religious personnel in 'central convents'. They were later ejected back into secular life as workers, with only a few receiving permission to engage in parish work or serve in homes for the aged or mentally retarded.

Decree 112/50 of 14 July 1950 concerns the suppression of Catholic theological faculties and seminaries which were replaced by 2 state seminary faculties for all Czechoslovakia and the imposition of the numerus clausus restricting the number of seminarians. From 1950 to 1960 the various levels of church leadership were decimated by a series of deportations, house arrests and refusals to permit episcopal vacancies to be filled. Moreover, before priests, pastors or bishops could begin work, they had first to swear allegiance to the state. In addition to having to secure this authorization their work was limited to controlled religious activities in designated parishes or in a single specified job of a non-parochial nature. Religious instruction was permitted only in state primary schools (the only schools existing) for one hour a week after normal school hours. Parents were required to request this in writing. Courses could only be given by priests or pastors authorized to do so by government. Because of the insufficient number of priests, laymen could also

**Orthodox Church of Czechoslovakia.** *Above.* Parish church of St Cyril & St Methodius at Stropkov. *Right.* Metropolitan Dorotheos of Prague & All Czechoslovakia celebrates divine liturgy in Teplice, 1974.

obtain authorization from the local Communist National Council of the district; but because of the pressures and difficulties, the religious education programme became compromised, ineffective and unimplemented.

A second period began in January 1968 until July 1969 when a new breath of air swept through both nation and churches. In a very concrete fashion, church affairs were returned to church control. The Federal Office of Ecclesiastical Affairs was directed by Mme Kadlecova, who initiated a dialogue with a quite new tolerance. The rights of the church, which had previously been ignored, were recognized and the rehabilitation of clergy and laymen unjustly condemned took place. The numerus clausus was lifted from the seminaries and government control loosened. This period saw a rebirth of pastoral initiatives, religious education of youth, liberation of religious personnel and the resurrection of a free religious press.

The third period began in April 1969, with the replacement of A. Dubcek by G. Husak as head of government. However, the churches were not directly affected until July 1969 when the former head of the Office of Ecclesiastical Affairs, Hruza, was reinstated in his old post. He at once inaugurated a new campaign against church life and activity throughout Czechoslovakia, resulting in a rapid return to the previous state of affairs. Once again there was an attempt to reduce the influence of the churches and a concerted effort to oppose all Christian action of post-conciliar type. Thus the development of the aggiornamento of the Catholic Church following Vatican II was made impossible. In various ways the Evangelical Church of Czech Brethren was repressed following the holding of its Seventeenth Synod which resulted in a critical revision of its understanding of the mission of the church in a society now called both 'socialist' and 'normalized'. This renewed state policy accompanied the persecution of the nonconformist Marxist intelligentsia, as well as other figures in the worlds of culture, sport and the press. Moreover, government has once again limited the field of action of churches by exercising strict control over them and by placing government appointees in positions of authority within the churches. In similar fashion the religious education programme for youth again fell on hard times decreasing from 62% of the school population in 1969–70 to 48% in Slovakia and 22% in Bohemia-Moravia for the year 1971–72. Moreover, institutes and courses for teachers and catechists created in 1968 have all been suppressed, and the meetings, retreats and youth camps which had burst forth in 1968–69 have now been prohibited.

In 1969 came the 'Plan for limiting the activity of the Churches in Slovakia', prepared by the Republic's Ministry of Culture, which although limited geographically to the Slovak Republic well illustrates the government's policy towards religion. It was the subject of consultation in October and November 1969 among representatives of the Czech and Slovak Offices of Ecclesiastical Affairs and corresponding Soviet and Hungarian offices, consultations which were labelled as being 'progressively extended to other socialist countries'. As a whole, this document indicates the will of the state in relation to the churches following the liberalization of 1968, especially a return to a stricter application of the laws of 1948–50 which were created for the purpose of forcing an exclusively religious character on the churches. The longest part is centred on the Latin-rite Catholic Church, recommending that

**Czechoslovak Unitarian Association.** Children sing at service. Begun 1921 as Free Brotherhood Association, this body now belongs to International Association for Religious Freedom, and Christian Peace Conference.

vacant episcopal seats, 6 out of 7 at the time, be left vacant and that plans be made 'to prepare the foundation of a new movement of Catholic clergy to take the place of the old Priests for Peace group'. The role assigned to this movement is 'to paralyse the irritating influence of the Vatican... as well as the regrettable attitudes of the hierarchy of our country'. Actions envisaged call for reducing as much as possible the role and influence of the Society of St Adalbert (religious publishers) and Caritas, restricting entrance to seminaries, and strictly limiting the field of activities of sisters as well as religious education in state schools. The existence of the Greek Catholic Church, authorized in 1968, is again 'called in question'; while waiting for a decision on the matter, measures are to be enacted for the 'consolidation' of its 'relations with the Orthodox Church'. Concerning the Lutheran Church, surveillance is to be maintained regarding meetings of 'extremist' elements and pressure groups within it. For 'other religious groups, sects and Jewish communities' the Ministry of Culture should create before the end of June 1970 a National (Slovak) Ecclesiastical Administrative Centre, regrouping them all in terms of the federalization of the state since 1 January 1969, and should 'require that these groups develop their own constitutions and statutes'. Finally, the domain of ecumenical activities is to be severely controlled. The Ministry of Culture must undertake 'an examination of the activities of the Ecumenical Council of Churches in the Czechoslovak Socialist Republic during the past year' (1968), giving 'its point of view on the activity of the Christian Peace Conference' and elaborating on 'its projects for future activity'. This must also include an examination of the participation of churches in foreign ecumenical organizations.

On 27 February 1973, after negotiations since October 1970, the Vatican formally announced the conclusion of a partial settlement with the Czech government, providing for the naming of 4 new bishops who were all members of the Pacem in Terris Czechoslovak Association of Priests, on the condition nevertheless that one of them, Msgr Vrana, named apostolic administrator and nutum Sanctae Sedis (i.e. the Holy See being free to transfer him whenever it wishes) of the archdiocese of Olomouc, renounce all participation in Pacem in Terris of which he had been federal president. Just before that, Pacem in Terris had chosen a new federal president in the person of another ordinary, Msgr Vesely, apostolic administrator of Tesin.

In March 1978, cardinal Frantisek Tomasek was appointed archbishop of Prague after that post had been vacant for 30 years. A new Catholic province of Slovakia was also set up.

**INTERDENOMINATIONAL ORGANIZATIONS.** Since the beginning of 1971 there have been 2 church councils authorized for Czechoslovakia, one for the Slovak Republic and the other for the Czech Socialist Republic. The division was required by government due to the strength of the former Czech Ecumenical Council, which was founded in 1970 building on the Ecumenical Council of Churches in Czechoslovakia in 1956. However, by 1974 there was still no council in Slovakia due to Lutheran/Reformed rivalry and government determination to deal directly with individual denominations.

The Christian Peace Conference (CPC) (Krest'anská Mírovà Konference) grew out of consultations between the 2 Protestant theological faculties (Slovak Faculty in Bratislava and Comenius Faculty in Prague) in 1957. The first conference sessions were held in 1958 and the first All-Christian Peace Assembly in 1961. Its headquarters are in Prague.

Several Catholic dioceses have commissions for ecumenism, including the diocese of Prague. The Ecumenical Institute (Ekumenicky Institut) of the Comenius Evangelical Faculty of Theology in Prague is undoubtedly the most advanced centre for ecumenical studies in Czechoslovakia. Conferences, dialogue and research are carried on in co-operation with a wide range of Czech denominations, including the Catholic Church.

The Ecumenical Section of the Huss Theological Faculty (Joannis Hus Facultas Theologica Pragae, Sectio Oecumenica), founded in Prague in 1969, is a university research institute which involves the collaboration of several Protestant, Orthodox and Old Catholic bodies, in addition to its sponsor, the Czechoslovak Hussite Church. Special attention is given to ecclesiology, ecumenical relations and the Czech Reformation. In addition to a large annual conference for clergy, smaller conferences and special courses are offered periodically at the theological school.

In 1968, on the initiative of the Paulus Gesellschaft from Austria, a Marxist-Christian dialogue was begun in Prague, with the participation of several well-known Western visitors. Nothing further has happened in this area since 1969.

**BROADCASTING.** No religious broadcasting of any kind is permitted within the country. From outside (1974), Protestant programmes are beamed in over Radio Luxembourg for 15 minutes in Czech on Sundays, by Trans World Radio (Monaco) for 5.5 hours every week in Czech and 30 minutes on Thursdays in Slovak. Catholic programmes transmitted by Radio Vatican in Czech and Slovak total 3.5 hours a week in each language.

**BIBLIOGRAPHY**
'Czechoslovakia', E. Kadlecová, in H. Mol (ed), *Western religion* (The Hague: Mouton, 1972), p. 117–134.
*Fellowship of service: life and work of Protestant churches in Czechoslovakia.* Ed D. Capek. Prague: Ecumenical Council of Churches, 1961. 152p.
'Panorama historique du protestantisme tchèque', A. Molnar, *Christianisme social*, 73 (1965), 229–247.
*Stimmen aus der Kirche der CSSR: Dokumente und Zeugnisse.* B. Ruys & J. Smolik. München: Kaiser, 1968. 208p.
*The Evangelical Church of Czech Brethren (Presbyterian).* Edinburgh, UK: Saint Andrew Press, 1970.
'The forced liquidation of the Union of Uzhorod. Part II: The destruction of the diocese of Presov', M. Lacko, *Slovak studies* (Rome), I (1961), 145–185.
'The Orthodox Church in Czechoslovakia', G. Novak, *Orthodoxy* (Athens, 1964), 240–252.
'The position of the church in Czechoslovakia', *Pro Mundi Vita* (Brussels), Special note 28 (1973).
'The religious situation in Czechoslovakia', M. Kalinovska, *Religion in Communist lands*, 5, 3 (Autumn, 1977), 148–157.
'The re-establishment of the Greek-Catholic Church in Czechoslovakia', M. Lacko, *Slovak studies* (Rome), XI (1971), 159–189.
*The witness of Czech Protestantism.* J. Otter. Prague: Evangelical Church of Czech Brethren, 1970.
*Yesterday and today: a survey of Czechoslovak Protestantism.* Prague: Preparatory Committee, Ecumenical Council of Churches in Czechoslovakia, 1955. 56p.

Despite state repression of religion, Christian topics recur on the state's postage stamps. Here, Slovak icons on stamps issued in 1970: (*left*) 'Adam and Eve with Archangel Michael' (16th century); (*centre*) 'Mandylion' (Icon of Christ) (16th century); (*right*) 'Archangel Michael' (18th century).

TABLE 2. ORGANIZED CHURCHES AND DENOMINATIONS IN CZECHOSLOVAKIA

| Official name<br>1 | Begun<br>2 | Type<br>3 | Counc<br>4 | Congs<br>5 | Adults<br>6 | Affiliated<br>7 | Names, notes, and other statistics (see Codebook)<br>8 |
|---|---|---|---|---|---|---|---|
| Anglican Ch (J North Central Europe) | c1850 | A plu | awc.. | 2 | 100 | 200 | *Anglican Ch in Europe, J Fulham*. Chaplaincies, begun in Prague and Marienbad. |
| Apostolic Faith | 1918 | P Pe3 | x.... | | 1,000 | 2,000 | *Apostolská Víra*. Linked AFM(Portland,Oregon,USA). Holiness Pentecostals. Banned. |
| Baptist Unity of Brethren | 1885 | P Bap | Tv..W | 27 | 4,152 | 10,000 | *Ustredi Bratrske-Jednoty-Baptistu*. 50% Slovak. 1948, applied to WCC. 21n,110m. |
| **Catholic Church in Czechoslovakia:** | 828 | R Lat | B.... | 4,690 | 7,015,300 | 9,610,058 | *Katolicka Církev*. 1,621 unstaffed parishes. 332de. 3752n(510N),7258w,151209Yy. |
| M Olomouc | 1063 | R Lat | Bs | 652 | 1,095,000 | 1,500,000 | North Moravia. Population traditionally Catholic. 550 45 1472 26511 |
| D Brno | 1777 | R Lat | Bs | 451 | 715,000 | 980,000 | *Dieceze Brno*. Moravia capital. Vigorous Catholicism. 401 55 756 15566 |
| M Praha (Prague) | 973 | R Lat | Bs | 825 | 1,095,000 | 1,500,000 | *Arcidiecéze Praha*. Province covers Bohemia. 530 20 478 11409 |
| D Ceské Budejovice | 1785 | R Lat | Bs | 430 | 411,000 | 563,000 | South Bohemia. Before 1945, Catholics mostly Germans. 210 37 290 9041 |
| D Hradec Králové | 1664 | R Lat | Bs | 477 | 584,000 | 800,000 | NE Bohemia (N Sudeten). Before 1945, half Germans. 274 64 955 10607 |
| D Litomerice | 1655 | R Lat | Bs | 433 | 292,000 | 400,000 | 1972, 3 Silesian deaneries lost to D Gorzów (Poland). 169 32 811 5874 |
| M Trnava | 1922 | R Lat | Bs | 439 | 1,033,600 | 1,415,910 | Small villages, traditionally Catholic; Hungarians. 524 59 791 23524 |
| D Banská Bystrica | 1776 | R Lat | bs | 120 | 238,900 | 327,224 | Traditional Catholicism, declining. 130 25 236 6575 |
| D Kosice | 1804 | R Lat | Bs | 174 | 410,200 | 561,900 | Eastern Slovakia. Population half Hungarians. 195 28 45 12928 |
| D Nitra | 880 | R Lat | bs | 151 | 464,500 | 636,309 | Northwest Slovakia. Small villages, mountains. 196 26 320 12022 |
| D Roznava | 1776 | R Lat | Bs | 87 | 155,100 | 212,437 | Until 1978 suffragan of D Eger (Hungary). SE Slovakia. 95 7 170 3849 |
| D Spis | 1776 | R Lat | bs | 156 | 270,000 | 369,278 | N Slovakia. Slovak, German, Ruthenian, Hungarian. 182 28 152 8275 |
| D Presov (Byzantine) | 1818 | R Byz | os | 201 | 128,000 | 176,000 | Remains of 'Church of Silence', liquidated 1945–50. 197 65 78 2728 |
| AA Ceský Tesín | 1972 | R Lat | Bs | 81 | 110,000 | 150,000 | Remnant of Polish diocese after 1972 reorganization. 79 16 700 2000 |
| AA Satu Mare (Szatmár) | 1939 | R Lat | Bs | 13 | 13,000 | 18,000 | *Apostolska Administratura*. Slovak part of Romanian D. 20 3 4 300 |
| Christian Communities (Closed) | | P EBr | ..... | 10 | 400 | 1,000 | *Exclusive Brethren* (Kelly-Continental). Ex Open Brethren, rejecting state recognition. |
| Christian Communities (Open) | c1905 | P CBr | x.... | 140 | 5,000 | 10,000 | *Krestanské Sbory*. *Christian Brethren*. German Bohemia. Not recognized by state. 2f. |
| Church of Brethren (Congregational Ch) | 1868 | P Con | r...W | 215 | 5,000 | 10,000 | *Církev Braská*. Formerly Unity of Czech Brethren. Workers, farmers. 56n. |
| Czechoslovak Hussite Church | 1920 | C ReC | IWC.W | 1,500 | 475,000 | 650,000 | *Ceskoslovenská Církev Husitská*. *Los von Rom* (20%RCC split). 5 Dioceses. 347n,lu(57). |
| Czechoslovak Unitarian Association | 1921 | M Unt | I.... | 6 | 2,000 | 4,000 | *Religious Society of Unitarians in Czechoslovakia*. Linked UUA(USA). Prague. 3b. |
| Evangelical Church of Czech Brethren | c1370 | P LuR | RWC.W | 670 | 81,110 | 295,354 | *Ceskobratrská Církev Evangelická* (1918). 70% urban. Slovaks, Poles. 293n,G = −1.5%pa. |
| Isolated radio churches | c1950 | P rad | ..... | 38 | 700 | 1,500 | Isolated radio believers (students, youths). R = 2000(790 TWR,107 HCJB, Radio Vatican, &c). |
| Jehovah's Witnesses | 1912 | M Jeh | x.... | 237 | 7,680 | 15,000 | 1948, suppressed; undergound, but rapid growth. Many Gypsies. G = 5.6%pa. |
| New Apostolic Church Community | | C CAp | x.... | | 500 | 1,000 | *Bezirk Schweiz*. World HQ Dortmund (Germany). Leader jailed 1965. |
| Old Catholic Church in Czechoslovakia | 1898 | C OCa | U...W | 17 | 3,000 | 4,000 | *Starokatolicka Církev, D Warnsdorf*. 1945, 50,000; then all Germans deported. 11n. |
| Orthodox Church of Czechoslovakia: | 1863 | O Cze | MWC.W | 141 | 147,000 | 200,000 | *Církev Pravoslavná v Ceskoslovenská*. Mainly Slovaks in east. A = 1951. 137n,1s. |
| M Praha (Prague) | 1921 | O Cze | Mm | 34 | 29,000 | 40,000 | Seat of metropolitan. West. Remnants of Czech Orthodox Ch liquidated 1942. 28n. |
| D Mikhailov | 1950 | O Cze | Mb | 17 | 30,000 | 40,000 | East Slovakia. Large gains from former Catholic Uniates. 21n. |
| D Olomouc-Brno | 1945 | O Cze | Mb | 20 | 15,000 | 20,000 | East Slovakia. Slovaks, Hungarians, some Ukrainians. Gains from Uniates. 11n. |
| D Presov | 1949 | O Cze | Mb | 70 | 73,000 | 100,000 | East. 1950, Greek Catholic D Presov forcibly annexed to Orthodoxy. 77n,1s(20). |
| Pentecostal Movement | | P Pe2 | ZF... | 84 | 2,000 | 3,000 | *Letnicní Hnuti*. Formerly prohibited. Links with M = AoG(USA). Mainly Slovakia. 60n. |
| Reformed Christian Church in Slovakia | 1918 | P Ref | RWC.f | 396 | 120,000 | 165,000 | Until 1918 in Reformed Ch of Hungary. 80% Hungarian, 15% Slovak. Mostly farmers. 182n. |
| Seventh-day Adventist Church | 1919 | P Adv | x.... | 127 | 7,212 | 15,000 | *SDA, Czechoslovakian Union Conference*. HQ Prague. 48nx,42mw,1s,190t(10200),334Y. |
| Silesian Ev Ch of Augsburg Confession | 1528 | P Lut | LWC.W | 19 | 36,000 | 50,100 | *Slezká Církev Evangelická Augsburského Vyznáni y CSSR*. Polish speaking. 26n. |
| Slovak Ev Ch of Augsburg Confession | 1530 | P Lut | LWC.f | 384 | 370,000 | 510,000 | *Slovenská Evanjelická AV Církev*. Diaspora church, violent history. HQ Bratislava. 1s. |
| United Methodist Ch in Czechoslovakia | 1922 | P Met | VwC.W | 42 | 10,000 | 20,000 | *Ev Církev Metodistická*. Autonomous. M = C&S Europe CC,UMC(USA). HQ Prague. 16n,10t. |
| Unity of Brethren (Unitas Fratrum) | 1457 | P Mor | xv..W | 17 | 9,800 | 20,000 | *Jednota Bratrská*. *Moravian Ch, Czechoslovak Province*. 1949 applied to WCC. 17n. |
| Other Catholic (non-Roman) churches | | C | ..... | | 500 | 1,000 | Including: New Catholic Ch (1925, ex RCC, HQ Roudnice/Elbe). |
| Other marginal Protestant bodies | | M | ..... | | 200 | 500 | Including: Anthroposophical Society, CJCLdS(Mormons) (began 1929), New Church. |
| **Total affiliated (mid-1970)** | | | | **8,840** | **8,303,654** | **11,598,712** | **Total denominations (1970) . . . 26.** |
| **Total affiliated (mid-1975)** | | | | **8,830** | **8,476,300** | **11,839,900** | **Total denominations (1975) . . . 26.** |
| **Total affiliated (mid-1980)** | | | | **8,820** | **8,661,700** | **12,098,800** | **Total denominations (1980) . . . 26.** |

NOTES ON TABLE ABOVE
COLUMNS: for meanings and CODES (cols. 1, 3, 4, 8): see Codebook (Part 6). Column 1: **Boldface type** = church with over 10% of country's affiliated Christians.
NATIONAL COUNCILS (Column 4, 5th letter).
f = member of ECCC until withdrew in 1971.
W = Ecumenical Council of Churches in the CSR (ECC-CSR) (Ekumenická Rada Církví v Ceské Socialistické Republice); this council works only in Bohemia and Moravia; by 1974 there was still no council in Slovakia due to Lutheran/Reformed rivalry and the government's preference for dealing directly with individual denominations.

PEOPLES (ethnolinguistic). Christians: 62.5% Czech, 29.4% Slovak, 4.0% Hungarian, 2.5% Gypsy, 0.6% German, 0.5% Polish, 0.4% Ukrainian, USSR military.

COUNTRY-WIDE TOTALS
EVANGELIZATION (see Part 5). 1900: 100%. 1970: 95%. 1980: 98%. *Mass evangelism.* Although no mass rallies were permitted, during the Euro '70 TV Crusade in Europe, associates of the Billy Graham team took part in meetings in Prague and Bratislava. *Radiophonic evangelism.* TWR, HCJB, RVOG, ICI.
FOREIGN MISSIONARIES AND PERSONNEL (nationals serving abroad) (1973). Total 13: about 12 Roman Catholics (6 priests in Switzerland, 2 priests in the Netherlands, 1 in Angola), 1 Orthodox priest working in GDR. The Ev Ch of Czech Brethren has attempted unsuccessfully to send persons and money abroad. In addition, excluded here, there are a number of former Czechoslovak personnel exiled or deported, who have now become citizens elsewhere.
FOREIGN MISSIONARIES AND PERSONNEL (aliens from abroad) (1973). Total 10. *From Western world.* About 10 Protestants (2 in 1 USA society).
INSTITUTIONS (church-operated) (1973). Total 14, including 1 press, 3 religious communities, 2 research centres, 8 seminaries (3 RC, 3 Protestant, 1 Orthodox, 1 Catholic/non-Roman).
PERIODICALS. About 45 titles (8 SDA, 3 LdS).
PERSONNEL. About 12,460 (12,450 national, 10 foreign).
RELIGIOUS LIBRARIES. 14.
SCRIPTURE DISTRIBUTION (1975). Annual totals: 51,000 Bibles (subsidized), 21,000 NTs (5% free, 95% subsidized), 50,000 UBS portions. *Translations completed.* Portion: Moravian Romani in 1936. NT: Czech in 1475. Bible: Czech in 1488, Slovak in 1832.
SERVICE AGENCIES. About 20, including CPC, ECCC, SSV.

ADDITIONAL DATA ON CHURCHES
CATHOLIC CHURCH IN CZECHOSLOVAKIA. In both Czech and Slovak, Katolicka Církev. Statistics from *AP 1973* and *Miteinander* (Canisinswerk, Vienna, 1972). *New province.* In January 1978, the Vatican created a new province in Slovakia: M Trnava, with as suffragans D Banska Bystrica, D Kosice, D Nitra, D Roznava, and D Spis. *Catholics.* Slovak Catholics of the Byzantine rite in D Presov (356,000 including 50,000 Ruthenian Ukrainians and 6,000 Hungarians) are claimed both by the Roman Catholic Church (under the name Grecko-Katolicka Cirkev) and also by the Orthodox Church; before 1968 the latter, aided by the state, had the better claim, but after 1968 its hold became more tenuous. *Parishes.* Of the 4,690 parishes, those without priests in 1971 numbered 1,621, divided as follows among the 15 dioceses in order: 174, 117, 533, 196, 223, 287, 18, 16, 9, 5, 10, 2, 14, 17, 0. *Annual baptisms.* (1972) 98.4% infant, 1.6% adult. *Priests.* The second column in column 8, (510N), gives the numbers of priests prevented from exercising their ministry. Out of 3,752 priests in 1971, 510 were thus inactive. *Sisters.* Most are not free to choose their place of residence or to exercise their apostolate. *Religious houses.* In 1970 there were 332 monasteries, convents and religious houses, divided as follows among the 15 dioceses in order: 53, 32, 41, 21, 46, 50, 18, 12, 11, 10, 8, 15, 5, 10, 0. *Seminaries.* 3; in 1973 one was suppressed. *Catholic organizations.* There is no episcopal conference, nor are there any associations of religious personnel, pastoral or presbyteral councils or organizations of the lay apostolate.
The Holy See has no diplomatic relations with Czechoslovakia.
CZECHOSLOVAK UNITARIAN ASSOCIATION. Nábozenská Spolecnost Unitáru Ceskoslovenskych.
EVANGELICAL CHURCH OF CZECH BRETHREN. The original Hussite (or Utraquist) Church, embracing 90% of Czech Protestants over the centuries, the church was inaugurated in 1918 as a union of 126,000 Czech Reformed and 34,000 Czech Lutherans, joined by 90,000 Roman Catholics from the Los von Rom (Away from Rome) movement. *Renewal.* In 1974 a renewal group, New Orientation, pledged to work for 'socialism with a human face', was active among pastors and theologians, though subjected to state harassment.
JEHOVAH'S WITNESSES. The first converts were made in 1912 by Witnesses from Hungary.
REFORMED CHRISTIAN CHURCH IN SLOVAKIA. Reformovaná Krestanská Církev na Slovensku.

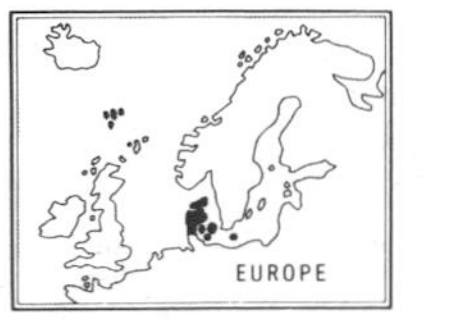


# DENMARK

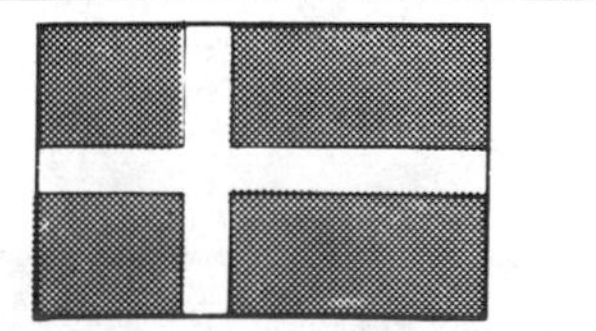

## SECULAR DATA

**STATE. Official name:** The Kingdom of Denmark (Kongeriget Danmark). Adjective of nationality: Danish, a Dane.
**Flag** (shown above right): White Latin cross on red field.
**Area:** 43,069 sq.km. (16,629 sq.miles). Agricultural land: 68.5%.
**Government:** Constitutional monarchy, since 1849 (1660 absolute monarchy).
**Legislature:** Folketing, 179 members.
**Official language:** Danish (*Dansk*).
**Chief cities:** capital Copenhagen 1,342,670 (1970), Aarhus 245,210, Odense 167,790.
**Political divisions:** 16 Administrative Divisions (14 Counties), 227 Municipalities (Kommuner).
**Armed forces** (1976): Total 34,700 regular (12,270 conscripts): army 21,800, navy 5,800, air force 7,100 (116 combat aircraft). Reserves: 153,200.
**Dependencies:** Overseas Areas: Faeroe Islands, Greenland.

**DEMOGRAPHY. Population:** 4,937,579 (census of 9.XI.1970. For 1970–2000 (UN), see last row of Table 1). Population density (1975): 117/sq.km. (302/sq.mile). Under 15 years: 25%. Growth rate (1975–80): 0.31% per year (births 1.37%, deaths −1.06%). Life expectancy (1975–80): 74.2 years. Household size: 2.8 persons.
**Major languages:** Danish, German, Swedish, English, Norwegian, Polish, Turkish, Faroese, and several others.
**Urban dwellers** (1970): 80.3%. Urban growth rate (1950–70): 1.6% per year.
**Labour force:** 49%.
**Refugees** (1977): About 2,000 from Eastern Europe.
**Tourists** (1972): 14,600,000. (1974) 13,800,000.

**ETHNOLINGUISTIC GROUPS:** 97.5% Danish, 1.1% German, 0.4% Swedish, 0.2% Norwegian, 0.2% Jewish, 0.2% British (10,000), 0.1% Polish, 0.1% USA (4,000), 0.1% Turkish (4,800), Greenlander, Icelander, Pakistani, Moroccan, Yugoslav (Serbian, Croatian), Algerian, Faroese, Portuguese, French, Russian.

**MONEY** (1977). **Monetary unit:** krone (= 100 ore); US$1 = DKr 5.80.

**National income per person:** US$5,403. Average annual family income: US$15,128.
**Inflation:** (1970–74) 9.2% per year, (1975) 10% per year (consumer price index 160).
**Cost of living in capital** (1976): index 148 (Washington DC = 100). Daily cost of living: US$48.

**EDUCATION.** Adult literacy: 100%. Education rate: 58%. Schools: 2,221. Universities: 3.

**HEALTH.** Hospitals: 184 (44,525 beds). Doctors: 8,000. Blind: 9,350. Psychotics: 50,000. Criminals: 14,351.

**LITERATURE.** Annual new book titles (1973): 6,500. Periodicals: 4,978. Scientific journals: 400. Newspapers: 53 dailies, 14 non-daily.

**COMMUNICATION** (per 1,000 people). Phones: 408. Radios: 327. TV sets: 282. Daily newspaper circulation: 361 copies.

## TABLE 1. RELIGIOUS ADHERENTS IN DENMARK

| Year | 1900 | | mid-1970 | | Annual change, 1970–1980 | | | | mid-1975 | | mid-1980 | | 2000 | |
|---|---|---|---|---|---|---|---|---|---|---|---|---|---|---|
| Name | Adherents | % | Adherents | % | Natural | Conversion | Total | Rate | Adherents | % | Adherents | % | Adherents | % |
| Christians | 2,439,480 | 99.6 | 4,763,200 | 96.6 | 16,841 | −3,561 | 13,280 | 0.27 | 4,836,820 | 96.2 | 4,896,000 | 95.9 | 5,079,900 | 94.8 |
| professing | 2,439,480 | 99.6 | 4,763,200 | 96.6 | 16,841 | −3,561 | 13,280 | 0.27 | 4,836,820 | 96.2 | 4,896,000 | 95.9 | 5,079,900 | 94.8 |
| Protestants | 2,429,210 | 99.2 | 4,719,400 | 95.7 | 16,686 | −3,560 | 13,126 | 0.27 | 4,792,240 | 95.3 | 4,850,660 | 95.0 | 5,029,800 | 93.8 |
| Roman Catholics | 5,480 | 0.2 | 28,000 | 0.6 | 99 | 1 | 100 | 0.35 | 28,500 | 0.6 | 29,000 | 0.6 | 32,000 | 0.6 |
| Marginal Protestants | 800 | 0.0 | 10,000 | 0.2 | 36 | 4 | 40 | 0.39 | 10,200 | 0.2 | 10,400 | 0.2 | 11,000 | 0.2 |
| Anglicans | 180 | 0.0 | 4,000 | 0.1 | 14 | 0 | 14 | 0.35 | 4,080 | 0.1 | 4,140 | 0.1 | 5,500 | 0.1 |
| Catholics (non-Roman) | 3,810 | 0.2 | 1,600 | 0.0 | 5 | −5 | 0 | 0.00 | 1,600 | 0.0 | 1,600 | 0.0 | 1,400 | 0.0 |
| Orthodox | 0 | 0.0 | 200 | 0.0 | 1 | −1 | 0 | 0.00 | 200 | 0.0 | 200 | 0.0 | 200 | 0.0 |
| nominal | 2,000 | 0.1 | 24,803 | 0.5 | 129 | 2,876 | 3,005 | 8.07 | 37,220 | 0.7 | 54,850 | 1.1 | 151,000 | 2.8 |
| affiliated | 2,437,480 | 99.5 | 4,738,397 | 96.1 | 16,712 | −6,437 | 10,275 | 0.21 | 4,799,600 | 95.5 | 4,841,150 | 94.8 | 4,928,900 | 91.9 |
| doubly-affiliated | −10,000 | −0.4 | −109,000 | −2.2 | −404 | −896 | −1,300 | 1.12 | −116,000 | −2.3 | −122,000 | −2.4 | −139,000 | −2.6 |
| total practising | 1,706,240 | 70 | 3,174,730 | 67 | 11,030 | −13,828 | −2,798 | −0.09 | 3,167,740 | 66 | 3,146,750 | 65 | 2,957,300 | 60 |
| non-practising | 731,240 | 30 | 1,563,670 | 33 | 5,682 | 7,391 | 13,073 | 0.80 | 1,631,860 | 34 | 1,694,400 | 35 | 1,971,600 | 40 |
| Protestants | 2,437,280 | 99.5 | 4,784,350 | 97.1 | 16,888 | −5,824 | 11,064 | 0.23 | 4,850,000 | 96.5 | 4,895,000 | 95.9 | 4,986,000 | 93.0 |
| Evangelicals | 367,000 | 15.0 | 345,000 | 7.0 | 1,242 | 1,008 | 2,250 | 0.63 | 356,800 | 7.1 | 367,500 | 7.2 | 402,000 | 7.5 |
| Neo-pentecostals | 0 | 0.0 | 0 | 0.0 | 17 | 1,183 | 1,200 | 24.00 | 5,000 | 0.1 | 12,000 | 0.2 | 50,000 | 0.9 |
| Marginal Protestants | 2,000 | 0.1 | 28,093 | 0.6 | 104 | 287 | 391 | 1.30 | 30,000 | 0.6 | 32,000 | 0.6 | 43,000 | 0.8 |
| Roman Catholics | 5,000 | 0.2 | 27,254 | 0.6 | 97 | 3 | 100 | 0.36 | 27,800 | 0.6 | 28,250 | 0.6 | 31,000 | 0.6 |
| Anglicans | 200 | 0.0 | 6,000 | 0.1 | 21 | −1 | 20 | 0.33 | 6,100 | 0.1 | 6,200 | 0.1 | 6,500 | 0.1 |
| Catholics (non-Roman) | 3,000 | 0.1 | 1,500 | 0.0 | 5 | −5 | 0 | 0.00 | 1,500 | 0.0 | 1,500 | 0.0 | 1,200 | 0.0 |
| Orthodox | 0 | 0.0 | 200 | 0.0 | 1 | −1 | 0 | 0.00 | 200 | 0.0 | 200 | 0.0 | 200 | 0.0 |
| Non-religious | 3,640 | 0.1 | 96,500 | 2.0 | 385 | 2,215 | 2,600 | 2.35 | 110,600 | 2.2 | 122,500 | 2.4 | 171,600 | 3.2 |
| Atheists | 2,000 | 0.1 | 47,000 | 1.0 | 193 | 1,232 | 1,425 | 2.58 | 55,300 | 1.1 | 61,250 | 1.2 | 80,400 | 1.5 |
| Muslims | 0 | 0.0 | 12,000 | 0.2 | 44 | 56 | 100 | 0.80 | 12,500 | 0.2 | 13,000 | 0.2 | 16,000 | 0.3 |
| Ahmadis | 0 | 0.0 | 600 | 0.0 | 2 | 18 | 20 | 2.86 | 700 | 0.0 | 800 | 0.0 | 1,100 | 0.0 |
| Jews | 3,480 | 0.1 | 7,000 | 0.1 | 25 | 0 | 25 | 0.35 | 7,130 | 0.1 | 7,250 | 0.1 | 8,000 | 0.1 |
| Baha'is | 0 | 0.0 | 1,300 | 0.0 | 5 | 5 | 10 | 0.74 | 1,350 | 0.0 | 1,400 | 0.0 | 1,600 | 0.0 |
| Buddhists | 0 | 0.0 | 1,000 | 0.0 | 3 | −3 | 0 | 0.00 | 1,000 | 0.0 | 1,000 | 0.0 | 1,600 | 0.0 |
| Other religionists | 900 | 0.0 | 1,000 | 0.0 | 4 | 56 | 60 | 4.62 | 1,300 | 0.0 | 1,600 | 0.0 | 2,600 | 0.0 |
| Country's population | 2,449,500 | 100.0 | 4,929,000 | 100.0 | 17,500 | 0 | 17,500 | 0.35 | 5,026,000 | 100.0 | 5,104,000 | 100.0 | 5,361,000 | 100.0 |

COLUMNS, ROWS. For meanings and definitions, see Codebook (Part 6). Note that, by definition, total 'Christians' = professing + crypto-Christians, which also = affiliated + nominal Christians. Percentages may not always total exactly, due to rounding.

CENSUSES. 1901: 99.3% Protestants (98.7% state church), 0.2% Roman Catholics, 0.2% Catholics (non-Roman) (3,810 Irvingites). 1921: 97.2% state church. 1966 (estimate): 97.0% Protestants, 2.4% non-religious and atheists, 0.6% Roman Catholics.

POLLS. February 1970: 96% Protestants, 3% non-religious and atheists, 1% Roman Catholics.

### NOTES ON RELIGIONS

AHMADIS. Begun 1956; about 600 Ahmadis (Qadianis), including 100 Pakistanis and 200 Danish converts, and their children, with since 1967 their own mosque in Copenhagen.
ATHEISTS. Danish Communist Party (Danmarks Kommunistiske Parti, DKP) (legal; pro-Soviet): membership (1970, 1974) 7,000; Communist voters (election of X.1945) 225,536 (12.5%

of all votes), (21.IX.1971) 39,344 (1% of all votes), (XII.1973) 110,809 (3.6% of all votes).
BAHA'IS. Growth from 5 local spiritual assemblies (1964) to 9 (1973).
BUDDHISTS. With headquarters for Scandinavia in Copenhagen; Tibetans, and sympathizers.
DOUBLY-AFFILIATED. A large majority of members of Protestant free churches (including Salvation Army, Evangelical Church of Germany, also marginal Protestant bodies) are also regarded as members of the state church which therefore enumerates them all as such.
JEWS. In Denmark since 1600; mostly in Copenhagen, with 2 synagogues.
MUSLIMS. Mostly migrant labourers from the Balkans and Turkey, with a vigorous Ahmadiya Mission (enumerated here as Muslims although declared non-Muslim by Pakistan). Legal immigrants with permission to work in 1972 numbered 8,500 (4,800 Turks, 2,000 Pakistanis, 1,300 from the North African Maghreb, about 400 Yugoslavs); however, there are many clandestine and illegal immigrants.
NEO-PENTECOSTALS. The total in 1975 included 800 lay

charismatics and 10 clergy within the state church in 30 organized prayer groups, and also about 1,500 in other non-Pentecostal Protestant denominations, including many young people; total charismatic community including children, 5,000. In 1975 over 2,000 adults were attending meetings and activities. By the end of 1976, about 80 clergy in the state church had become involved.
OTHER RELIGIONISTS. Including, in 1975, 355 members of the Theosophical Society in 15 Lodges, also Rosicrucians (AMORC, 2 centres).
PRACTISING CHRISTIANS. Weekly church attendance in the state church is 5% of the population (1970); nearly 40% of Roman Catholics attend church weekly in Copenhagen, and 30% for the whole country, but this is declining gradually. 1966: 2.8% attend church once or more a week, 5.3% twice a month, 25.0% now and then, 30.5% on the major church festivals, 31.4% never. Christmas attenders: 40% of the population. Others unable to attend through sickness, old age, etc, listen to radio/TV services; listeners to the broadcast daily morning devotional vary from 16% (urban) to 44% (rural); listeners to Sunday morning broadcast service, 13% (urban), 44% (rural).

NON-CHRISTIAN RELIGIONS. Islam has entered Denmark through the recent immigration of foreign workers; in 1972 those from Muslim countries legally present numbered 8,500 adult workers (4,800 Turks; 2,000 Pakistanis; and 1,300 from North Africa). In addition there are the families of such workers, and other clandestine workers from Muslim countries, also 400 or so Muslim immigrants from Yugoslavia.

**Judaism** is represented by a small community of about 7,000, centred primarily in Copenhagen. Jews have been in Denmark since the beginning of the 17th century, although they were not legally recognized by the state until 1849.

**Buddhism** in Scandinavia has its headquarters in Copenhagen, where are located the Centre for Tibetan Buddhism and the Kagyudpa-Karmapa Tibetan School, with extensive facilities for individual and collective meditation. Local centres have also been established in Stockholm, Göteborg and Oslo.

CHRISTIANITY. Anskar, apostle of the north, visited Denmark as early as AD 826, and the first church was built in 850. Lutheranism was officially adopted by king Christian III in 1536 and all Roman Catholic activity forbidden after 1569. In 1648 Catholics made a new attempt at work through the auspices of the Spanish ambassador, followed by

French Huguenots during the latter part of the 17th century and Moravians in the 18th century.

PROTESTANT CHURCHES. The foremost church of Denmark, as has been true since the Reformation, is the Evangelical Lutheran People's Church of Denmark, which includes in its membership over 95% of the total population of the country. Since its final legislative and financial authority is the Danish Parliament, it is sometimes referred to as the State Church, but its leaders prefer the term National Church of Denmark.

The juridical character of the regular assembly of bishops, under the presidency of the bishop of Copenhagen, remains ambiguous. Bishops are appointed by the king, in each case on presentation of a candidate elected by priests and delegates of parish councils (menighedsrad) which are themselves elected by universal suffrage in order to choose the priests for the king's nomination. Clergy are trained at the theological faculties of the Universities of Copenhagen and Aarhus. Numbers of new ordinations have shown a steady decline in recent years: from 1930–39, there were 620; 1940–49, 564; 1950–59, 462; and 1960–69, 320. Ordination of laymen lacking full theological education is now beginning, and women are also admitted to the pastoral ministry. There were 35 ordained women in 1970 and 90 in 1975.

Theoretically the National Church is limited to the frontiers of the kingdom, which includes Greenland and the Faeroe Islands, but in practice it includes work among Danes in other parts of the world. Danish Church Abroad was founded in 1919 to care for such communities, the largest of which is composed of 52 congregations in south Schleswig, an ancient Danish territory taken over by Germany in 1864. An important work is also carried on among Danish sailors in foreign ports. Missionary activities in Africa and Asia have originated with missionary societies which are independent of the Danish church. The National Church has strongly influenced the total life of the country. The parish minister was until recently invariably the president of the commune's school commission, and the church was largely responsible for the formation of People's Upper Schools. Today, a significant programme of social service is carried on by the church's National Church Aid (Folkekirkens Nodhjaelp).

Although the number of convinced and practising adherents is limited, the Evangelical Lutheran Church remains a national institution which one rarely withdraws from. In Copenhagen and surroundings, official acts of departure or withdrawals from the National Church rose from 2,967 in 1968 to 4,564 in 1969; and names of new-born babies declared to the state by civil action without baptism rose from

**National Church of Denmark.** *Left.* Aagerup church, a typical medieval Danish village church. *Right.* Dedication service of new church in Islev, suburb of Copenhagen.

12% in 1968 to 23% in 1972. In Denmark, a new-born child is declared simply as boy or girl and must then, within a year, receive a name communicated to the state either after baptism or by a simple declaration.

Free church movements in Denmark have been generally much less successful in winning adherents than their counterparts in other Scandinavian countries. The largest of the free churches is the Baptist Union.

CATHOLIC CHURCH. The modern era of the Catholic Church in Denmark dates from 1849 when a new constitution proclaiming freedom of religion was adopted. In its early years there was a strong foreign element in its congregations, but today most of the faithful are Danes. The Catholic community is largely urban, about 40% living in or near Copenhagen and forming the greatest density of Catholics in any Nordic country. An exception to this is found in the rural parishes of southern Denmark, especially South Jutland and the southern islands, where Polish immigrants settled during World War I. In 1956 those born in Slavic countries represented 25% of the total Catholic population in the southern islands. Moreover, the number of new immigrant Catholic workers including Croats from Yugoslavia and Portuguese is constantly growing. Mixed marriages (with a Protestant partner) are common among Catholics; in 1965 the figure was 81%. A study made in 1969 of 9,212 Catholics married for more than 16 years showed that 4,860 were married to Catholics and 4,352 were partners in mixed marriages.

Weekly attendance at mass is 30%, declining gradually. About the same proportion participate in parish elections and donations to the freely-organized church tax. To understand this relatively low percentage, one must consider the large number of baptized Catholics not known to or affiliated with parishes, the number of those not eligible or fit to attend (children and the aged), and the relatively large distances between parishes outside Copenhagen, which are on average 30 kilometres. In Copenhagen itself Sunday attendance in 1969 was nearly 40%, although regular practice has been decreasing since then.

The post-conciliar organization of the church in Denmark was established by a Diocesan Synod in 1969 composed of 65 priests, 25 religious personnel and 110 lay persons, three-fourths of whom were chosen by universal suffrage. Since 1970 the following elected councils have begun to function: parish councils, exercising pastoral responsibilities in all parishes; 6 regional councils, namely 3 for Copenhagen and outskirts, one for North Jutland, one for South Jutland and Fionia and one for the other islands; pastoral and presbyteral councils; and a council of religious personnel. In 1977 Denmark was transferred from the jurisdiction of Propaganda to that of the Congregation for Bishops.

CHURCH AND STATE. Article 4 of the constitution of 1953 recognizes the Evangelical Lutheran Church as the National Church, or People's Church (Danske Folkekirke), for which the state is responsible. The king must be a member (Article 6), but liberty of worship is guaranteed to all by Articles 67 to 70. In reality, the term Danske Folkekirke, which is purely descriptive, means that this is the church of almost all the Danish people. Article 66 of the constitution states that the church's status is subject to regulation by law, but no general legislation has ever been developed. The church is under the general control of Parliament and the government's Ministry for the Church (Kirkeministeriet) which exercise their authority with tact and tolerance. The state's support of the church is evident in its respect for Christian festivals, its provision for religious instruction at all levels in schools (although students who are not members of the National Church are exempt) and its financial support from the general budget. In addition, the state levies directly an ecclesiastical tax (Kirkeskat) on all except those members of recognized confessions who prove that they contribute an equivalent amount to their own religious bodies.

No special restrictions are placed on the activities of other churches or religious communities. Many of them have received official recognition, including Anglicans, Baptists, Catholics, Norwegian and Swedish Lutherans, French and German Reformed and Russian Orthodox, as well as the Jewish community. Among these groups, religious acts such as baptism, marriage and burial, and their corresponding certificates, have legal validity.

Experimental 'manna-mass' at 1974 Ecumenical Church Festival in Haslev.

In 1975 Parliament passed a law stipulating that henceforth members of all religious confessions could be interred in cemeteries belonging to the National Church, following ceremonies led by their own ministers in their own places of worship.

INTERDENOMINATIONAL ORGANIZATIONS. The Ecumenical Council of Denmark (Okumeniske Faellesrad i Danmark) was founded in 1939 and adopted a new constitution in 1971. Present membership includes the Evangelical Lutheran, Catholic, Baptist, Salvation Army, Mission Covenant, Apostolic, Methodist, Reformed, Anglican and Russian Orthodox churches. Affiliated organizations include the Ecumenical Institute annexed to the theological faculty of the University of Copenhagen, and the Ecumenical Centre, a private institution created by students of the University of Aarhus which provides facilities for meetings of youth and international students. The Institute of Ecumenical Theology and Missiology, with its library, is attached to the centre. In 1973 another Ecumenical Centre (Okumeniske Centre) was founded in Copenhagen, including an ecumenical hostel, to which numerous Catholic organizations are attached. A Sodepax Committee was in process of formation in 1975.

BROADCASTING. In Denmark all radio and TV is government-owned and state-controlled; there are no privately-owned stations. The Lutheran state church is given 2 broadcast services each Sunday, and a devotional service from the cathedral in Copenhagen on week-days. At regular intervals the Free Churches also are given these times. A Catholic liturgy or preaching service is broadcast every 2 months. From abroad, Trans World Radio (Monaco) broadcasts in Danish for 15 minutes each on Mondays and Saturdays. For Catholics, Denmark is a member of UNDA.

BIBLIOGRAPHY
'Denmark', J. Thorgaard, in H. Mol (ed), *Western religion* (The Hague: Mouton, 1972), p. 135–141.
*History of the Church of Denmark*. J. C. Kjaer. Blair, Nebr, 1945.
*The Danish Church*. Ed P. Hartling. Copenhagen: Danske Selskab, 1964. 164p.

TABLE 2.    ORGANIZED CHURCHES AND DENOMINATIONS IN DENMARK

| Official name 1 | Begun 2 | Type 3 | Counc 4 | Congs 5 | Adults 6 | Affiliated 7 | Names, notes, and other statistics (see Codebook) 8 |
|---|---|---|---|---|---|---|---|
| Apostolic Church in Denmark | 1923 | P PeA | Z,D,z | 77 | 9,000 | 15,000 | *Apostolske Kirke i Danmark.* Begun through Apostolic Ch (UK), Elim(UK). 1j,1s. |
| Apostolic Faith Mission | 1943 | P Pe3 | x,... | 2 | 100 | 200 | *Apostolisk Tro's Mission.* M=AFM(Portland,Oregon,USA). Holiness Pentecostals. |
| Baptist Union of Denmark | 1839 | P Bap | TWX,z | 149 | 6,828 | 20,000 | *Danske Baptistsamfund.* Begun by Danes. Declining. 43n,G= −1.1%pa,1s,55Y,284z. |
| Catholic Apostolic Church | c1850 | C CAp | x,... | 29 | 300 | 500 | *Katolsk-Apostolske Kirke. Irvingites.* In 1900, 3,812 adherents. No clergy left. |
| Catholic Church: D Kobenhavn | 1648 | R Lat | bxBQW | 51 | 20,000 | 27,254 | *Katolske Kirke.* 95% urban. C=10+0+14. D=Synod. 40n,84x,11m,642w,W=30%,543Yy. |
| Christian Brethren | | P CBr | x,... | 3 | 150 | 300 | *Plymouth Brethren.* Open Brethren. 3 gospel halls. |
| Church of Christ, Scientist | | M Sci | x,... | 3 | 100 | 200 | *Christian Science.* M=CCS. 2 churches (Aarhus, Copenhagen), 1 society (Odense). 6w. |
| Church of England (J Fulham) | 1887 | A plu | avc,W | 3 | 2,000 | 6,000 | St Alban's, Copenhagen. English chaplaincy. In 1900, 176 Anglicans. 1x. |
| Church of God | | P Pe3 | x,... | 2 | 32 | 100 | Holiness (3-stage) Classical Pentecostals, links with USA body. 3n. |
| Church of God (Anderson) | | P Hol | x,... | 9 | 120 | 300 | M=CoG(Anderson) (USA). No longer any missionaries from USA. 4n,W=71%. |
| Ch of Jesus C of Latter-day Saints | 1850 | M LdS | x,... | 25 | 2,700 | 4,193 | *Mormons.* M=CJCLdS(USA). HQ Copenhagen. In 1900, 717 adherents. 190f,G=2.4%pa. |
| Church of Sweden | | P Lut | Lwc,. | 1 | 1,000 | 2,500 | *Svenska Kyrkan.* Swedish immigrants and residents, with own church organization. |
| Church of the Nazarene | 1959 | P Hol | xF... | 2 | 26 | 50 | *Nazaraeerens Kirke.* Holiness denomination. M=CoN(USA). HQ Rodovre. 2n,1x. |
| Churches of Christ | | P Dis | x,... | 4 | 100 | 200 | *Kristi Kirke.* M=CC(Non-Instrumental) (USA). In Copenhagen, Aarhus, Odense. |
| Congregation of God | | P Lut | ...C | | 500 | 1,000 | *Guds Menighed.* Danish/Norwegian Old Lutherans; old Bible versions used. |
| Danish Moravian Church | 1727 | P Mor | xwc,. | 1 | 300 | 500 | Continental Province, Unity of the Brethren. Danish Moravian Missionary Association. |
| Elim Church | 1918 | P Pe2 | Z,... | 50 | 5,000 | 10,000 | *Elimforsamlingen.* M=AoG(UK). Widespread missions overseas. HQ Copenhagen. 22n,1j. |
| Free Church Union | 1928 | M Unt | x,... | 5 | 300 | 500 | *Fri Kirkesamfund.* Unitarian. M=UUA(USA). Missions abroad. In 1900, 62 adherents. |
| Free Lutheran Congregations | | P Lut | ..... | 10 | 500 | 1,000 | Congregations separated from national church, retaining Lutheran tradition. |
| Jehovah's Witnesses | 1891 | M Jeh | x,... | 214 | 13,620 | 23,200 | *Watch Tower. IBSA.* Active witnessing under way before 1926. HQ Virum. 947Y. |
| Methodist Church in Denmark | 1853 | P Met | Vvx,z | 87 | 3,196 | 5,000 | *Denmark Annual Conf, UMC*(USA). 1900: 3,895 adherents. 22n,G= −0.2%pa,1s,W=36%,60Yy. |
| Mission Covenant Church of Denmark | 1888 | P Con | K,D,z | 132 | 2,917 | 6,000 | *Danske Missionsforbund.* 19th-century revival in state church. 18n,G=0.5%pa,W=90%. |

*Continued opposite*

*Table 2 – continued*

| Official name 1 | Begun 2 | Type 3 | Counc 4 | Congs 5 | Adults 6 | Affiliated 7 | Names, notes, and other statistics (see Codebook) 8 |
|---|---|---|---|---|---|---|---|
| **National Church of Denmark:** | 826 | P Lut | LWX.a | 2,313 | 3,500,000 | 4,700,000 | *Evangelisk-lutherske Folkekirke i Danmark*. 99 Deaneries. 1824n,P=40%,2s. W=4%. |
| D Kobenhavn (Copenhagen) | 1923 | P Lut | L | 700 | 1,050,000 | 1,400,000 | *Kobenhavns Stift*. Capital; also includes Faeroe Is, Greenland. 2 |
| D Alborg (Aalborg) | 1060 | P Lut | L | 230 | 370,000 | 500,000 | North Jutland. Decline in weekly church attendance: 1927,W=11%;1970,W=5%. 5 |
| D Arhus (Aarhus) | 1060 | P Lut | L | 330 | 520,000 | 700,000 | Mideastern part of Jutland. Includes Aarhus city (250,000). 4 |
| D Fyn | c1020 | P Lut | L | 250 | 370,000 | 500,000 | Island of Fyn: Odense (170,000), Svendborg. 3 |
| D Haderslev | 1923 | P Lut | L | 103 | 150,000 | 200,000 | Covers southeastern part of Jutland. 4 |
| D Helsingor (Elsinore) | 1961 | P Lut | L | 150 | 220,000 | 300,000 | Frederiksborg province, extreme northeast Sjaelland. Very low attendance. 2 |
| D Lolland-Falster | 1803 | P Lut | L | 100 | 150,000 | 200,000 | Southeastern islands of Lolland and Falster. Low church attendance. 3 |
| D Ribe | 948 | P Lut | L | 100 | 150,000 | 200,000 | Oldest diocese. Covers southwestern part of Jutland. High attendance. 6 |
| D Roskilde | c1020 | P Lut | L | 150 | 220,000 | 300,000 | West of capital, part of Copenhagen province; covers western Sjaelland. 4 |
| D Viborg | 1060 | P Lut | L | 200 | 300,000 | 400,000 | Midwestern part of Jutland. Highest church attendance of all dioceses. 7 |
| New Apostolic Church | | C CAp | x.... | | 500 | 1,000 | *NAC*, in Hamburg Bezirk (District). Germans. World HQ Dortmund (Germany). |
| Pentecostal Movement in Denmark | 1907 | P Pe2 | ..D.x | 29 | 4,000 | 7,000 | *Pinsebevaegelsen. Tabor Meningheden*. Smallest Scandinavian Pentecostal movement. |
| Reformed Church Synod in Denmark | 1685 | P Ref | R.D.a | 4 | 1,100 | 1,500 | French, German, Dutch. Huguenot refugees from France. 1900: 1,112 adherents. 3n,20Yy. |
| Religious Society of Friends | 1875 | P Qua | Q.... | 2 | 53 | 100 | *Vennernes Samfund* (*Kvaekerne*). *Quakers*. In 1900, 66 adherents. Copenhagen. G=0%pa. |
| Russian Orthodox Church | | O Sla | ....W | 1 | 100 | 200 | Russian refugees from USSR. One congregation in Copenhagen. |
| Salvation Army | 1887 | P Sal | xwx.z | 64 | 3,900 | 5,000 | *Frelsens Haer. Denmark Territory. Eastern, Western Divs*. 26 institutions. 210n,1s. |
| Seamen's Churches | | P Lut | ..... | 3 | 200 | 500 | Swedish, Norwegian and Icelandic seamen's congregations. |
| Seventh-day Adventist Church | 1872 | P Adv | x.... | 62 | 3,964 | 7,000 | *Syvende Dags Adventister. E,W Denmark Confs*. 21nx,G=–0.6%pa,1H,1j,1r,W=60%,137Y. |
| United Pentecostal Church | c1960 | P Pe1 | x.... | 2 | 50 | 100 | *Jesus Only Church*. M=UPC(USA). Unitarian Pentecostals. |
| Other Protestant denominations | | P | ..... | | 500 | 1,000 | Total about 15 (see list below). |
| Doubly-affiliated (duplication) (1970) | | | | | –81,700 | –109,000 | Salvation Army and free church members also counted as state church members. |
| **Total affiliated (mid-1970)** | | | | **3,370** | **3,501,456** | **4,738,397** | **Total denominations (1970) . . . 47.** |
| **Total affiliated (mid-1975)** | | | | **3,390** | **3,546,700** | **4,799,600** | **Total denominations (1975) . . . 51.** |
| **Total affiliated (mid-1980)** | | | | **3,410** | **3,577,400** | **4,841,150** | **Total denominations (1980) . . . 56.** |

NOTES ON TABLE ABOVE
COLUMNS: for meanings and CODES (cols. 1, 3, 4, 8): see Codebook (Part 6). Column 1: **Boldface type** = church with over 10% of country's affiliated Christians.
NATIONAL COUNCILS (Column 4, 5th letter).
a = member of both ECD and EAD.
C = Council of Free Churches (CFC) (Evangelisk Frikirkerad).
E = Evangelical Alliance of Denmark (EAD) (Evangelisk Alliance i Danmark) (members: National Church and 7 free churches).
W = Ecumenical Council of Denmark (ECD) (Okumeniske Faellesrad i Danmark).
x = member of both CFC and EAD.
z = member of ECD, CFC and EAD.
OTHER PROTESTANT DENOMINATIONS. There are over 10 other small denominations, including: Children of God (from USA), Ch of Norway, Ev Ch of Germany (EKD), Lutheran Ch of Greenland, Norwegian Reformed Parishes, Old Reformed Ch (Tysk-Reformerte Kirke), Reformed Ch of France, Seventh-day Adventist Reform Movement (HQ Charlottenlund), Swedish Reformed Parishes.
OTHER MARGINAL BODIES. The General Ch of the New Jerusalem has a Circle in Copenhagen.

PEOPLES (ethnolinguistic). Christians: 97.8% Danish, 1.1% German, 0.4% Swedish, 0.2% Norwegian, 0.2% British, 0.1% Polish, 0.1% USA, Yugoslav (Serbian, Croatian), Portuguese, French, Russian.

COUNTRY-WIDE TOTALS
EVANGELIZATION (see Part 5). 1900: 100%. 1970: 100%. 1980: 100%. *Mass evangelism*. Among recent campaigns: Billy Graham rally in 1955 at Aarhus (10,000 attenders, 200 enquirers), in 1965 Copenhagen 8-day crusade (65,700 attenders, 681 enquirers), and in 1970 Euro '70 TV Crusade in Copenhagen televised from Dortmund, Germany; 1979, Here's Life Roskilde (CCCI).
FOREIGN MISSIONARIES AND PERSONNEL (nationals serving abroad) (1974). Total 366: 330 Protestants (decrease from 345 in 1969, and from 333 in 1963) in 28 societies in 30 countries, about 20 marginal Protestants (mainly Jehovah's Witnesses), about 16 Roman Catholics (5 in Sweden).
FOREIGN MISSIONARIES AND PERSONNEL (aliens from abroad) (1973). Total 890. *From Western world*. 814: 601 Roman Catholics including lay missionaries, about 200 marginal Protestants (180 Mormons from USA), 10 Protestants (8 in 5 USA societies, 2 in 2 UK societies), about 2 Catholics (non-Roman), 1 Anglican. *From Communist world*. About 76 Roman Catholics from Poland (4 priests, 72 sisters).
INSTITUTIONS (church-operated) (1973). Total 100, including 60 higher schools (including folk high schools), 12 medical centres, 1 monastery, 6 research centres, 7 seminaries (Protestant), 5 study centres.
PERIODICALS. About 180 titles (majority Lutheran).
PERSONNEL. About 3,340 (2,450 national, 890 foreign).
RELIGIOUS LIBRARIES. About 30.
SCRIPTURE DISTRIBUTION (1975). Annual totals: 31,088 Bibles (2% free, 92% subsidized, 6% commercial), 178,503 NTs (16% free, 80% subsidized, 4% commercial), 6,585 UBS portions, 26,232 UBS selections. *Translations completed*. Danish: NT 1524, Bible 1550.
SERVICE AGENCIES. About 90, including CEF, CFC, DKK, DMS, DUK, EAD, ECD, KSF, NEC, NMC, SU, YMCA, YWAM, YWCA.

ADDITIONAL DATA ON CHURCHES
CATHOLIC CHURCH. Diocese of Copenhagen = Bispedømmet Kobenhavn. Catholics are 70% Danes, 25% Slavs (mostly Poles), with many Croat and other immigrants recently. *Annual baptisms*. (1972) 99.0% infant, 1.0% adult. *Priests*. Employment: 80 in pastoral work, 5 university, 8 primary school. Nationals: 26 secular, 14 religious. Expatriates: 12 secular, 72 religious; nationality (1970) 29 Dutch, 19 German, 9 Austrian, 7 Belgian. Numbers (nationals + expatriates): 1860, 0 + 3; 1886, 7+ 19; 1934, 16 + 59; 1955, 30 + 73. *Brothers*: All expatriates. *Sisters*. 136 Danish, 506 expatriates (306 German, 72 Polish, 46 Belgian, 25 Dutch). Numerical decline from 775 in 1960 due to disappearance of once numerous Danish vocations. 45% of all sisters are over 60 years, 15% under 40. *Catholic charismatics* (January 1974). 100 adults including religious personnel are active in 5 organized prayer groups in the Charismatic Renewal. *Seminarians*. 2 Danish, 6 expatriate. *Foreign religious congregations*. Priests: SJ (German), CSSR (Dutch), OMI (American), and 7 others. Sisters: 45% St Joseph de Chambéry, and 13 other congregations.
*Catholic organizations*. The Nordic or Scandinavian Episcopal Conference (Nordiske Bispekonferense, also called Conferentia Episcopalis Scandiae) based in Copenhagen is a member of CCEE. The Union of Superiors of the Female Religious Congregations of Denmark was founded in 1960 as a Council of Sisters and was reorganized in 1970. A Presbyteral Council, consisting of elected members, was formed in 1968, followed by the creation of a Pastoral Council in 1970. The latter body is composed of 26 lay members, 10 priests and 6 sisters, all elected by universal suffrage of the entire Catholic community. Denmark's principal lay movements are Danmarks unge Katolikker (DUK) for youth, Danmarks Katolske Kvindeforbund for women, Academicum Catholicum for intellectuals and Bifrost for students.
The Holy See has no diplomatic relations with Denmark. It is represented to the Catholic hierarchy by an apostolic delegate to Scandinavia based in Copenhagen.
In the church's educational and social programme in 1972 were 11 kindergartens with 532 children of whom 8% were Catholics; 16 primary schools, of which 9 Realskole prepared for elementary certificate with 5,738 pupils (32% Catholics); one Jesuit college or secondary school with 236 pupils (42% Catholics); 13 homes for the aged or convalescents with 300 boarders (35% Catholics) and 10 hospitals and clinics. In addition, aid is provided to refugees, immigrant workers and developing countries through Caritas-Danmark in close collaboration with the Lutheran Folkekirkens Nodhjaelp and government services. The Nordisk Katolsk Udvicklingshjaelp, founded in Copenhagen in 1969 as the development aid organ of the Nordic Episcopal Conference, is a member of CIDSE in Belgium.

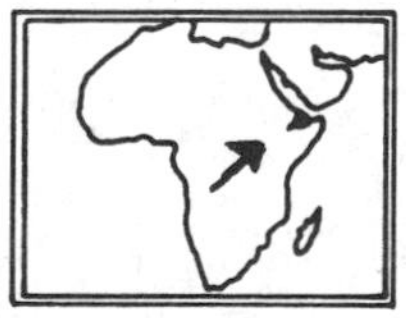

# DJIBOUTI

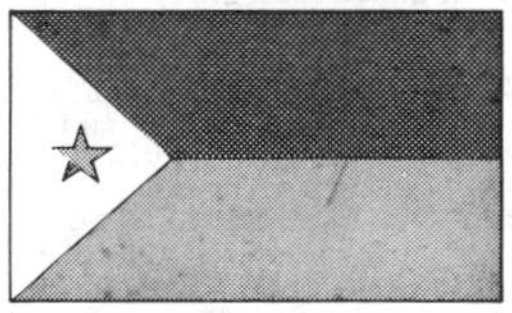

## SECULAR DATA

**STATE. Official name:** The Republic of Djibouti (La République de Djibouti). Earlier name: The French Territory of the Afars and Issas (Le Territoire Français des Afars et des Issas).
**Flag** (shown above right): Blue and green stripes with red star in white triangle on left.
**Area:** 22,000 sq.km. (8,494 sq.miles). Agricultural land: 11.1%.
**Government:** Republic, since 1977 (1862 French protectorate, 1888 French colony, 1958 French overseas territory, 1977 Independence).
**Legislature** (1977): Assembly, 40 deputies.
**Official language:** French (*Français*.)
**Capital:** Djibouti 62,000 (1970).
**Armed forces** (1976): Total 5,100 French regular: army 4,400, navy 150, air force 550; (1978) total 4,500.

**DEMOGRAPHY. Population:** 81,200 (census of 1960–61. For 1970–2000 (UN), see last row of Table 1). Population density (1975): 5/sq.km. (12/sq.mile). Under 15 years: 44%. Growth rate (1975–80): 2.31% per year. Household size: 4.9 persons.
**Major languages:** French, Somali, Afar, Arabic.
**Urban dwellers** (1970): 65%. Urban growth rate (1950–70): 3.7% per year.
**Refugees** (1977): About 10,000. (1978): 11,000.

**ETHNOLINGUISTIC GROUPS:** 35.1% Afar (Danakil), 28.2% alien (12% Yemeni Arab, 0.6% Ethiopian, 0.4% Greek, Sudanese, other Arab, alien Somali, Indian, et alii), 21.9% Issa & other citizen Somali, 12.2% French (& other European, & mixed race), 2.5% French Arab.

**MONEY** (1977). **Monetary unit:** Djibouti franc (= 100 centimes); US$1 = DFr 177.00.
**National income per person:** US$980. Average annual family income: US$4,802.
**Cost of living in capital** (1976): Daily cost of living: US$49.

**HEALTH.** Hospitals: 11 (943 beds). Doctors: 44. Lepers: 1,500 (14.2 per 1,000). Blind: 300. Psychotics: 700. Drug addicts: over 80% of the population chew khat (cocaine).

**EDUCATION.** Schools: 32.

**LITERATURE.** Periodicals: 3. Newspapers: 1 non-daily.

**COMMUNICATION** (per 1,000 people). Phones: 29. Radios: 70. TV sets: 18.

TABLE 1. RELIGIOUS ADHERENTS IN DJIBOUTI

| Year | 1900 | | mid-1970 | | Annual change, 1970–1980 | | | | mid-1975 | | mid-1980 | | 2000 | |
|---|---|---|---|---|---|---|---|---|---|---|---|---|---|---|
| *Name* | *Adherents* | *%* | *Adherents* | *%* | *Natural* | *Conversion* | *Total* | *Rate* | *Adherents* | *%* | *Adherents* | *%* | *Adherents* | *%* |
| Muslims | 19,900 | 99.5 | 82,400 | 86.7 | 2,563 | –27 | 2,536 | 2.70 | 94,080 | 88.7 | 107,760 | 90.6 | 171,800 | 91.9 |
| Ahmadis | 0 | 0.0 | 100 | 0.1 | 3 | 1 | 4 | 3.33 | 120 | 0.1 | 140 | 0.1 | 400 | 0.2 |
| **Christians** | **100** | **0.5** | **12,000** | **12.6** | **–173** | **13** | **–160** | **–1.43** | **11,200** | **10.6** | **10,400** | **8.7** | **12,500** | **6.7** |
| crypto-Christians | 0 | 0.0 | 1,000 | 1.0 | 27 | 13 | 40 | 3.33 | 1,200 | 1.1 | 1,400 | 1.2 | 3,000 | 1.6 |
| professing | 100 | 0.5 | 11,000 | 11.6 | –200 | 0 | –200 | –2.00 | 10,000 | 9.4 | 9,000 | 7.6 | 9,500 | 5.1 |
| Roman Catholics | 100 | 0.5 | 10,000 | 10.5 | –200 | 0 | –200 | –2.22 | 9,000 | 8.5 | 8,000 | 6.7 | 8,000 | 4.3 |
| Orthodox | 0 | 0.0 | 800 | 0.8 | 0 | 0 | 0 | 0.00 | 800 | 0.8 | 800 | 0.7 | 1,000 | 0.5 |
| Protestants | 0 | 0.0 | 200 | 0.2 | 0 | 0 | 0 | 0.00 | 200 | 0.2 | 200 | 0.2 | 500 | 0.3 |
| affiliated | 100 | 0.5 | 12,000 | 12.6 | –173 | 13 | –160 | –1.43 | 11,200 | 10.6 | 10,400 | 8.7 | 12,500 | 6.7 |
| total practising | 80 | *80* | 7,680 | *64* | –152 | 8 | –144 | –2.07 | 6,940 | *62* | 6,240 | *60* | 7,500 | *60* |
| non-practising | 20 | *20* | 4,320 | *36* | –21 | 5 | –16 | –0.38 | 4,260 | *38* | 4,160 | *40* | 5,000 | *40* |
| Roman Catholics | 100 | 0.5 | 11,000 | 11.6 | –173 | 13 | –160 | –1.57 | 10,200 | 9.6 | 9,400 | 7.9 | 11,000 | 5.9 |
| Orthodox | 0 | 0.0 | 800 | 0.8 | 0 | 0 | 0 | 0.00 | 800 | 0.8 | 800 | 0.7 | 1,000 | 0.5 |
| Protestants | 0 | 0.0 | 200 | 0.2 | 0 | 0 | 0 | 0.00 | 200 | 0.2 | 200 | 0.2 | 500 | 0.3 |
| Hindus | 0 | 0.0 | 300 | 0.3 | 0 | 0 | 0 | 0.00 | 300 | 0.3 | 300 | 0.3 | 400 | 0.2 |
| Non-religious | 0 | 0.0 | 200 | 0.2 | 7 | 13 | 20 | 6.67 | 300 | 0.3 | 400 | 0.3 | 2,000 | 1.1 |
| Baha'is | 0 | 0.0 | 100 | 0.1 | 3 | 1 | 4 | 3.33 | 120 | 0.1 | 140 | 0.1 | 300 | 0.2 |
| **Country's population** | **20,000** | **100.0** | **95,000** | **100.0** | **2,400** | **0** | **2,400** | **2.26** | **106,000** | **100.0** | **119,000** | **100.0** | **187,000** | **100.0** |

COLUMNS, ROWS. For meanings and definitions, see Codebook (Part 6). Note that, by definition, total 'Christians' = professing + crypto-Christians, which also = affiliated + nominal Christians. Percentages may not always total exactly, due to rounding.

## NOTES ON RELIGIONS
BAHA'IS. In one local spiritual assembly (1973), begun in 1955. In 1972 extensive missionary activity from Ethiopia began.

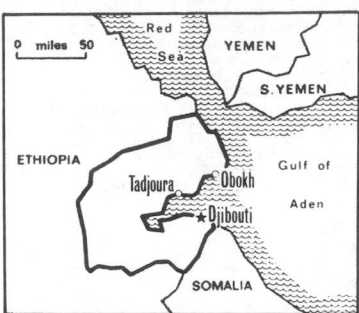

**NON-CHRISTIAN RELIGIONS. Islam** was definitively planted in the 12th century and today accounts for about 90% of the population. Most are Sunnis of the Hanafite and Shafiite rites except for a few Indian Shias. The principal religious brotherhoods are Qadiriya, Salihiya and Rifaiya; Ahmadiya from Pakistan is also present.

**Hinduism** is the religion of a small community of 300 Indians.

## CHRISTIANITY
CATHOLIC CHURCH. The French bought an area on the coast from Danakil chiefs in 1862, extending their protectorate in 1884 and building the port of Djibouti in 1888. Catholic priests from the vicariate of Arabia arrived in 1883. A prefecture was erected in 1914 and attached to the vicariate apostolic of Gallas. In 1955 the diocese of Djibouti was created, directly subject to the Holy See.

The Catholic Church is the most active of the

CHRISTIANS. Up to 1975, mostly (87%) expatriate French military and civilians. The decline after 1975 is due largely to emigration and withdrawal of French personnel. Figures under the column 'Natural change' are negative due to this emigration.
CRYPTO-CHRISTIANS. Roman Catholics, almost all Somalis (including Issas), many from former Italian Somaliland; with only one or 2 Afars (Danakils).
HINDUS. Indians.
MUSLIMS. Islam was planted definitively in the 12th century.

4 Christian denominations in the country, and is the only church that has made converts from the local population. Of 11,000 members in 1970, 10,400 were metropolitan French on temporary contracts and 600 were native Catholics, mostly middle-class Somalis. The church has 5 parishes and is served by Capuchin priests, FSC brothers and 3 congregations of sisters.

ORTHODOX CHURCHES. The Orthodox community is composed of 2 groups: Greek Orthodox (Europeans) and Ethiopians. The latter use or attend the Greek Orthodox church in Djibouti.

PROTESTANT CHURCHES. There is only one Protestant body in the territory, the Protestant Church of Djibouti, which dates from World War II and is related to the Reformed Church of France. Its small membership consists entirely of Europeans, principally French and German nationals.

**CHURCH AND STATE.** As a French overseas territory until 1976, its legal statutes relating to freedom of religion were the same as in metropolitan France. Catholic schools receive subsidies from the government, and an official convention between the Catholic diocese and the local government allows 9 nursing sisters to work in government hospitals.

**BROADCASTING.** The government Radio-Télévision Djibouti transmits a religious programme every Sunday at noon, alternately Catholic and Protestant. For Catholics, the territory is registered as a member of UNDA. Protestant programmes were heard over Radio Voice of the Gospel (RVOG) from Ethiopia until its closure in 1977.

Muslims are Sunnis (Hanafite and Shafiite rites), with a few Shias (Indians). Brotherhoods: Qadiriya, Salihiya, Rifaiya, and Ahmadiya (enumerated here under Muslims, though declared non-Muslim by Pakistan). *Hajj pilgrims to Mecca.* (1975) 124; (1976) 483.
NON-RELIGIOUS. In 1970–75, French.
ROMAN CATHOLICS. In 1947, there were 2,200 European Catholics (1,000 being French) and 300 indigenous.

**Muslims.** The Afar (Danakil) people, as this warrior outside Tadjoura, have long been completely islamized.

## BIBLIOGRAPHY
'Côte Français des Somalis', special issue of *Vivante Afrique* (Namur), 250 (mai-juin, 1967).

TABLE 2.   ORGANIZED CHURCHES AND DENOMINATIONS IN DJIBOUTI

| Official name 1 | Begun 2 | Type 3 | Counc 4 | Congs 5 | Adults 6 | Affiliated 7 | Names, notes, and other statistics (see Codebook) 8 |
|---|---|---|---|---|---|---|---|
| **Eglise Catholique: D Djibouti** | 1883 | R Lat | p.SLr | 6 | 6,000 | 11,000 | *Catholic Ch.* 94% French, 5% Somali. M=OFMCap. C=1+1+3. 12x,14m,37w,P=54%,2r,41Yy. |
| Eglise Orthodoxe Ethiopienne | | O Eth | Nwa.. | 1 | 300 | 500 | *Ethiopian Orthodox Ch.* Amharas from Ethiopia working in Djibouti; using Greek church. |
| Eglise Orthodoxe Grecque | | O Gre | Cw... | 1 | 200 | 300 | *Greek Orthodox Ch.* Europeans (Greeks). 1 church building in Djibouti. |
| Eglise Protestante de Djibouti | c1940 | P Ref | ..A.. | 1 | 100 | 200 | *Protestant Ch of Djibouti.* Related to Reformed Church of France. French, Germans. |
| **Total affiliated (mid-1970)** | | | | 9 | 6,000 | 12,000 | Total denominations (1970) . . . 4. |
| **Total affiliated (mid-1975)** | | | | 9 | 6,160 | 11,200 | Total denominations (1975) . . . 4. |
| **Total affiliated (mid-1980)** | | | | 9 | 5,720 | 10,400 | Total denominations (1980) . . . 4. |

## NOTES ON TABLE ABOVE
COLUMNS: for meanings and CODES (cols. 1, 3, 4, 8): see Codebook (Part 6). Column 1: **Boldface type** = church with over 10% of country's affiliated Christians.
NATIONAL COUNCILS (Column 4, 5th letter).
  r = consultative member, Conférence Episcopale de France (Episcopal Conference of France).

**PEOPLES** (ethnolinguistic). Christians: 87.5% French (White) & mixed race & other European, 4.6% Somali, 4.2% Ethiopian, 2.5% Greek.

## COUNTRY-WIDE TOTALS
EVANGELIZATION (see Part 5). 1900: 5%. 1970: 65%. 1980: 70%.
FOREIGN MISSIONARIES AND PERSONNEL (aliens from abroad) (1973). Total 63. *From Western world.* 62: 59 Roman Catholics, 2 Protestants, 1 Orthodox. *From Third World.* 1 Orthodox.

INSTITUTIONS (church-operated) (1973). Total 2 secondary schools.
PERSONNEL. 118 (55 national, 63 foreign).
SERVICE AGENCIES. About 10, including ACI, AV, RSMT (2 missionaries; bookshop).

## ADDITIONAL DATA ON CHURCHES
EGLISE CATHOLIQUE. *Catholics.* All expatriates (French, Ethiopians, part-Europeans) except (in 1969) 600 indigenous, all Somalis (with a few Issas) and (in 1970) only 2 Danakil (Afar). A lot of the Somalis came from former Italian Somaliland. One brother is indigenous (1970), and 3 sisters. *Annual baptisms.* (1972) 94.3% infant, 5.7% adult. *Catechists.* Total (1973) 51. *Indigenous religious congregations.* Formerly Soeurs Oblates Franciscaines de Marie Immaculée, now part of FMND. *Foreign religious orders and congregations.* Priests: OFMCap. Brothers: FSC. Sisters: Franciscaines Missionnaires de Notre-Dame (FMND), Ste-Catherine de Metz, Petites Soeurs de Jésus de Charles de Foucauld.

*Catholic organizations.* The diocese is attached, with consultative voice, to the Episcopal Conference of France (Conférence Episcopale de France) and to the Conference of Latin Bishops of the Arab Regions (CELRA) with headquarters in East Jerusalem. There are no presbyteral or pastoral councils, nor associations of religious personnel. The principal lay movements are AV, Foyers de Jeunes, Légion de Marie and ACI.

The Holy See in 1976 had no diplomatic relations with the territory. It is represented to the Catholic hierarchy by an apostolic delegate in Khartoum, Sudan.

In 1976 the church operated 5 primary schools with 1,831 pupils, 2 secondary schools with 744 pupils, and 10 domestic science or technical schools with 557 pupils; also 3 orphanages with 119 children. Under Caritas, 9 sisters work in hospitals and dispensaries.

---

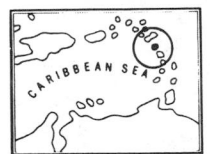

# DOMINICA

## SECULAR DATA

**STATE. Official name:** The Commonwealth of Dominica.
**Flag** (shown above right): Multicoloured background with green Sisserou parrot.
**Area:** 751 sq.km. (290 sq.miles). Agricultural land: 25.3%.
**Government:** Republic since 1978, formerly self-governing state in association with the United Kingdom (Britain), since 1967 (c1600 French colony, 1759 British colony, 1978 Independence).
**Legislature:** House of Assembly, 14 members.
**Official language:** English.
**Capital:** Roseau 10,420 (1960).

**DEMOGRAPHY. Population:** 70,300 (census of 7.IV.1970. For 1970–2000 (UN), see last row of Table 1). Population density (1975): 100/sq.km. (259/sq.mile). Under 15 years: 47%. Growth

rate (1975–80): 1.37% per year (births 3.35%, deaths −0.77%, emigrants −1.21%). Life expectancy (1975–80): 67.4 years.
Household size: 4.4 persons.
**Major languages:** English, Dominican Creole (French patois), Carib, Hindi.
**Urban dwellers** (1970): 26.9%. Urban growth rate (1950–70): 2.8% per year.
**Labour force:** 37%.
**Tourists** (1973): 17,560.

**ETHNOLINGUISTIC GROUPS:** 89.0% Black (African Negro), 7.3% Mulatto, 1.7% Carib remnants (1,200), 1.0% Indo-Pakistani, 1.0% White, Syro-Lebanese, Chinese, Japanese.

**MONEY** (1977). **Monetary unit:** East Caribbean dollar (= 100 cents); US$1 = EC$2.70.

**National income per person:** US$370. Average annual family income: US$1,628.
**Inflation:** (1970–74) 13.2% per year, (1975) 18% per year (consumer price index 194).
**Cost of living in capital** (1976): Daily cost of living: US$41.

**EDUCATION.** Adult literacy: (1946) 59%, (1975) 80%. Schools: 54 (1965).

**HEALTH.** Hospitals: 7 (305 beds). Doctors: 13.

**LITERATURE.** Periodicals: 7. Newspapers: 3 non-daily.

**COMMUNICATION** (per 1,000 people). Phones: 37.

## TABLE 1. RELIGIOUS ADHERENTS IN DOMINICA

| Year | 1900 | | mid-1970 | | Annual change, 1970–1980 | | | | mid-1975 | | mid-1980 | | 2000 | |
|---|---|---|---|---|---|---|---|---|---|---|---|---|---|---|
| *Name* | *Adherents* | *%* | *Adherents* | *%* | *Natural* | *Conversion* | *Total* | *Rate* | *Adherents* | *%* | *Adherents* | *%* | *Adherents* | *%* |
| Christians | 28,800 | 100.0 | 70,180 | 99.8 | 968 | −2 | 966 | 1.29 | 74,860 | 99.8 | 79,840 | 99.8 | 90,650 | 99.6 |
| professing | 28,800 | 100.0 | 70,180 | 99.8 | 968 | −2 | 966 | 1.29 | 74,860 | 99.8 | 79,840 | 99.8 | 90,650 | 99.6 |
| Roman Catholics | 27,070 | 94.0 | 63,130 | 89.8 | 871 | 0 | 871 | 1.29 | 67,360 | 89.8 | 71,840 | 89.8 | 81,550 | 89.6 |
| Protestants | 1,440 | 5.0 | 5,550 | 7.9 | 76 | −15 | 61 | 1.04 | 5,840 | 7.8 | 6,160 | 7.7 | 6,820 | 7.5 |
| Anglicans | 290 | 1.0 | 1,200 | 1.7 | 16 | 0 | 16 | 1.25 | 1,280 | 1.7 | 1,360 | 1.7 | 1,370 | 1.5 |
| Marginal Protestants | 0 | 0.0 | 300 | 0.4 | 5 | 13 | 18 | 4.86 | 370 | 0.5 | 480 | 0.6 | 910 | 1.0 |
| nominal | 590 | 2.0 | 2,180 | 3.1 | 39 | 143 | 182 | 6.03 | 3,020 | 4.0 | 4,000 | 5.0 | 7,300 | 8.0 |
| affiliated | 28,210 | 98.0 | 68,000 | 96.7 | 929 | −145 | 784 | 1.09 | 71,840 | 95.8 | 75,840 | 94.8 | 83,350 | 91.6 |
| total practising | 25,390 | 90 | 47,600 | 70 | 650 | −101 | 549 | 1.09 | 50,290 | 70 | 53,090 | 70 | 54,180 | 65 |
| non-practising | 2,820 | 10 | 20,400 | 30 | 279 | −44 | 235 | 1.09 | 21,550 | 30 | 22,750 | 30 | 29,170 | 35 |
| Roman Catholics | 26,780 | 93.0 | 62,500 | 88.9 | 853 | −143 | 710 | 1.08 | 66,000 | 88.0 | 69,600 | 87.0 | 76,350 | 83.9 |
| Catholic pentecostals | 0 | 0.0 | 0 | 0.0 | 0 | 10 | 10 | 25.00 | 40 | 0.0 | 100 | 0.1 | 800 | 0.9 |
| Protestants | 1,150 | 4.0 | 4,200 | 6.0 | 57 | −13 | 44 | 1.00 | 4,420 | 5.9 | 4,640 | 5.8 | 5,000 | 5.5 |
| Evangelicals | 900 | 3.1 | 2,000 | 2.8 | 27 | −7 | 20 | 0.95 | 2,100 | 2.8 | 2,200 | 2.7 | 2,400 | 2.6 |
| Anglicans | 280 | 1.0 | 1,000 | 1.4 | 14 | −2 | 12 | 1.14 | 1,050 | 1.4 | 1,120 | 1.4 | 1,090 | 1.2 |
| Marginal Protestants | 0 | 0.0 | 300 | 0.4 | 5 | 13 | 18 | 4.86 | 370 | 0.5 | 480 | 0.6 | 910 | 1.0 |
| Baha'is | 0 | 0.0 | 50 | 0.1 | 1 | 1 | 2 | 3.33 | 60 | 0.1 | 70 | 0.1 | 150 | 0.2 |
| Other religionists | 0 | 0.0 | 70 | 0.1 | 1 | 1 | 2 | 2.50 | 80 | 0.1 | 90 | 0.1 | 200 | 0.2 |
| Country's population | 28,800 | 100.0 | 70,300 | 100.0 | 970 | 0 | 970 | 1.29 | 75,000 | 100.0 | 80,000 | 100.0 | 91,000 | 100.0 |

COLUMNS, ROWS. For meanings and definitions, see Codebook (Part 6). Note that, by definition, total 'Christians' = professing + crypto-Christians, which also = affiliated + nominal Christians. Percentages may not always total exactly, due to rounding.
CENSUSES. 7.IV.1960: 90.0% Roman Catholics, 8.1% Protestants (6.1% Methodists), 1.7% Anglicans, 0.2% marginal Protestants.

### NOTES ON RELIGIONS
CATHOLIC PENTECOSTALS (or, Catholic charismatics). In mid-1975 there were 20 involved adults (over 15 years) in 2 prayer groups; total charismatic community including children, 40.
OTHER RELIGIONISTS. Mainly a few Muslims, Afro-American spiritists including Dreads or Rastafarians (Ras Tafari cult) from Jamaica, also converts to Nichiren Shoshu (Soka Gakkai) from Japan.

## CHRISTIANITY

CATHOLIC CHURCH. Dominican priests (OP) began work in 1642, but from 1702 to 1730 there was no priest on the island. French Franciscans arrived in 1747 but were expelled when the British assumed control in 1782. Roseau became a diocese in 1850. Dominica is predominantly Catholic, and the island now makes up the entire diocese of Roseau. In 1974 there were in Dominica 16 parishes, 31 stations, 28 religious and 3 diocesan priests, and 35 Missionary Sisters of the Immaculate Heart of Mary.

OTHER CHURCHES. Methodism, which first came to Dominica in 1787, is the principal non-Catholic faith. Adventists are next followed by Anglicans. In the 4 Windward Islands, Anglicans are strong in Grenada and St Vincent and weak in St Lucia and Dominica, the latter 2 being more than 90% Catholic. Several other small missionary societies are also active in Dominica. Since 1975, Pentecostals have become increasingly influential.

CHURCH AND STATE. In 1967 Dominica became a state in association with Britain, with full responsibility for internal affairs. Catholics, Anglicans and Protestants had equal status before the law, and freedom of religion was as in other Britain-related territories of the Caribbean. After Independence in 1978 the same situation prevailed.

INTERDENOMINATIONAL ORGANIZATIONS. The Anglican, Catholic and Methodist churches co-operate in the Dominica Christian Council.

BROADCASTING. Over Windward Islands Broadcasting Service, shared with Grenada, St Lucia and St Vincent, Catholic programmes were in 1974 allowed a total of one hour from Monday to Saturday and half an hour on Sunday; and Protestants 3 hours from Monday to Saturday and half an hour on Sunday. A station in Roseau, Radio Dominica, also accepts Protestant and Catholic programmes.

Dominica has many postage stamps with Christian themes: here, (*above*) Adoration of the Kings (Bruegel), and (*left*) Christ and the Pilgrims of Emmaus (Velasquez).

## TABLE 2. ORGANIZED CHURCHES AND DENOMINATIONS IN DOMINICA

| Official name 1 | Begun 2 | Type 3 | Counc 4 | Congs 5 | Adults 6 | Affiliated 7 | Names, notes, and other statistics (see Codebook) 8 |
|---|---|---|---|---|---|---|---|
| Anglican Church (D Antigua) | | A ACa | a·wMRC | | 500 | 1,000 | *CPWI.* In Ch of Province of West Indies. M=USPG. 90% West Indian (Black). |
| **Catholic Church: D Roseau** | 1642 | R Lat | P,NMC | 47 | 33,100 | 62,500 | Suffragan of M Castries. 500 Whites. C=2+1+2. 31nx,7m,37w,P=47%,2r,2000Yy. |
| Church of God of Prophecy | c1963 | P Pe3 | Z.... | 2 | 65 | 200 | M=CGP(USA). Split in USA ex CoG(Cleveland). Holiness Pentecostals. |
| Church of God (Cleveland) | c1963 | P Pe3 | ZP... | 1 | 50 | 100 | M=CoG(Cleveland) (USA). Holiness Pentecostals (3-stage). Large 1975 open-air crusade. |
| Churches of Christ in Christian Union | 1943 | P Hol | xF.... | | 100 | 200 | M=CCCU(USA). Holiness denomination with Wesleyan doctrine. 1 school. 5f,1p. |
| Jehovah's Witnesses | | M Jeh | x.... | 7 | 189 | 300 | *Watch Tower. IBSA.* Rapid growth since 135 adherents in 1960. 6Y. |
| Methodist Ch in Caribbean & Americas | 1787 | P Met | V·M.C | | 1,000 | 2,000 | In *MCCA* (1967 union), Leeward Islands District. M=MMS(UK). Blacks. 4n. |
| Seventh-day Adventist Church | | P Adv | x.... | | 889 | 1,200 | *SDA,* East Caribbean Conf, Caribbean Union Conference (HQ Bridgetown, Barbados). |
| Other Protestant denominations | | P | ..... | 5 | 200 | 500 | Including: Berean Mission, Christian Brethren, Maranatha Baptists, PAoWI, WEC. |
| **Total affiliated (mid-1970)** | | | | 85 | 36,093 | 68,000 | Total denominations (1970) . . . 13. |
| **Total affiliated (mid-1975)** | | | | 88 | 38,130 | 71,840 | Total denominations (1975) . . . 13. |
| **Total affiliated (mid-1980)** | | | | 91 | 40,250 | 75,840 | Total denominations (1980) . . . 14. |

### NOTES ON TABLE ABOVE
COLUMNS: for meanings and CODES (cols. 1, 3, 4, 8): see Codebook (Part 6). Column 1: Boldface type = church with over 10% of country's affiliated Christians.
NATIONAL COUNCILS (Column 4, 5th letter).
 C = Dominica Christian Council.

PEOPLES (ethnolinguistic). Christians: 90% Black, 7.3% Mulatto, 1.7% Carib, 1% White.

COUNTRY-WIDE TOTALS
EVANGELIZATION (see Part 5). 1900: 100%. 1970: 100%. 1980: 100%. *Mass evangelism.* In 1975 the Evangelistic Association, Pentecostal Assemblies of the West Indies, conducted a large open-air crusade, with 10,000 attenders and 2,000 enquirers.
FOREIGN MISSIONARIES AND PERSONNEL (aliens from abroad) (1973). Total 67. *From Western world.* 57: about 40 Roman Catholics, 17 Protestants (14 in 5 USA societies, 3 in 1 Canada society). *From Third World.* About 10 Roman Catholics,

Protestants and indigenous from Caribbean countries.
INSTITUTIONS (church-operated) (1973). Total 4, including 3 higher schools, 1 study centre.
PERIODICALS, 6 titles (4 RC).
PERSONNEL. About 207 (140 national, 67 foreign).
RELIGIOUS LIBRARIES. 1.
SCRIPTURE DISTRIBUTION (1975). Annual totals: 900 Bibles (subsidized), 1,100 NTs (subsidized), 250 UBS portions, 5,600 UBS selections. *Translations completed.* Dominican Creole: portion 1894.
SERVICE AGENCIES. About 14, including CLC, DCC, SPCK, YCW.

ADDITIONAL DATA ON CHURCHES
CATHOLIC CHURCH. The diocese is a suffragan of M Castries (St Lucia) since 1974 (and previously of M Port of Spain, Trinidad). *Annual baptisms.* (1972) 100% infants, no adults. *Catechists.* Total (1974) 120. *Foreign religious congregations.* Priests: 15 FMI, 13 CSSR. Brothers: FSC. Sisters: Missionary Sisters of the Immaculate Heart of Mary, Daughters of Jesus.
*Catholic organizations.* The diocese is a member of the Antilles Episcopal Conference (AEC), with its headquarters in Kingston, Jamaica, and through it is a member of CELAM. Religious personnel are represented on the Conference of Major Superiors of the Antilles, which belongs to CLAR and also has its seat in Jamaica. There is no presbyteral nor pastoral council. The principal lay movements are Confraternity of Christian Doctrine, Legion of Mary, Social League and YCW.
The Holy See has no diplomatic relations with Dominica. It is represented to the Catholic hierarchy by an apostolic delegate based in Port-au-Prince, Haiti.
In 1974 the church maintained 21 pre-schools, 4 primary schools (2,957 pupils) and 2 secondary schools (1,062). In addition there is a social centre in Roseau with handicrafts, a sewing industry, health department, food programme and other housing and co-operative projects. The centre sponsors a social league with branches in 44 villages.

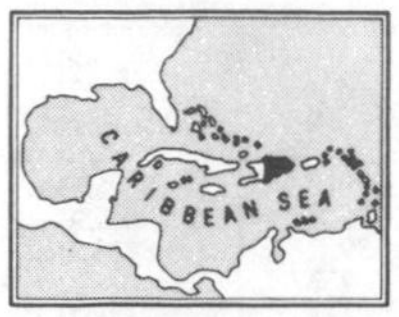


# DOMINICAN REPUBLIC

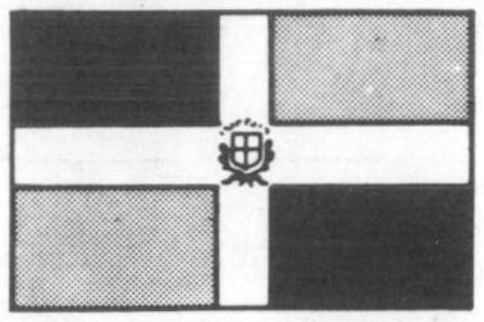

## SECULAR DATA

**STATE. Official name:** The Dominican Republic (La República Dominicana). Adjective of nationality: Dominican (dominicano). **Flag** (shown above right): White cross with national coat of arms; 2 red and 2 blue quarters.
**Area:** 48,734 sq.km. (18,816 sq.miles). Agricultural land: 50.2%.
**Government:** Republic, since 1962 (1492 Spanish colony, 1844 Independence from Spain and Haiti, 1930 military dictatorship).
**Legislature:** National Congress: Senate, 27 members; Chamber of Deputies, 91 members.
**Official language:** Spanish (*Español/Castellano*).
**Chief cities:** capital Santo Domingo 671,400 (1970), Santiago de los Caballeros 155,150.
**Political divisions:** 25 Provinces.
**Armed forces** (1976): Total 18,000 regular: army 11,000, navy 3,500, air force 3,500 (32 combat aircraft). Paramilitary forces: 10,000 gendarmerie.

**DEMOGRAPHY. Population:** 4,006,405 (census of 9.I.1970. For 1970–2000 (UN), see last row of Table 1). Population density (1975): 105/sq.km. (272/sq.mile). Under 15 years: 47%. Growth rate (1975–80): 3.35% per year (births 4.47%, deaths −0.95%, emigrants −0.17%). Life expectancy (1975–80): 60.2 years. Household size: 4.4 persons.
**Major languages:** Spanish, English, French Creole, French.
**Urban dwellers** (1970): 38.4%. Urban growth rate (1950–70): 5.9% per year.
**Labour force:** 31%.
**Refugees** (1977): 300,000 from Haiti.
**Tourists** (1972): 133,036. (1975): 200,000.

**ETHNOLINGUISTIC GROUPS:** 70.9% Mulatto (Spanish/Black), 16.1% Dominican White (Spanish), 10.7% Black (African Negro) (including 1.0% Haitian, 0.3% Jamaican), 1.0% White (European) (Spanish, German Jewish), 0.1% Chinese, Japanese, Lebanese.

**MONEY** (1977). **Monetary unit:** peso (= 100 centavos); US$1 = RD$1.00.

**National income per person:** US$550. Average annual family income: US$2,420.
**Inflation:** (1970–74) 10.0% per year, (1975) 15% per year (consumer price index 181).
**Cost of living in capital** (1976): index 113 (Washington DC = 100). Daily cost of living: US$46.

**EDUCATION.** Adult literacy: (1950) 43%, (1970) 67%. Education rate: 46%. Schools: 5,245. Universities: 3.

**HEALTH.** Hospitals: 306 (11,975 beds). Doctors: 2,220. Lepers: 350 (0.1 per 1,000). Blind: 2,850. Psychotics: 41,000. Drug addicts: numerous (cannabis).

**LITERATURE.** Annual new book titles (1973): 32. Periodicals: 40. Scientific journals: 10. Newspapers: 7 dailies.

**COMMUNICATION** (per 1,000 people). Phones: 19. Radios: 40. TV sets: 35. Daily newspaper circulation: 38 copies.

TABLE 1. RELIGIOUS ADHERENTS IN THE DOMINICAN REPUBLIC

| Year | 1900 | | mid-1970 | | Annual change, 1970–1980 | | | | mid-1975 | | mid-1980 | | 2000 | |
|---|---|---|---|---|---|---|---|---|---|---|---|---|---|---|
| *Name* | *Adherents* | *%* | *Adherents* | *%* | *Natural* | *Conversion* | *Total* | *Rate* | *Adherents* | *%* | *Adherents* | *%* | *Adherents* | *%* |
| **Christians** | **588,000** | **98.0** | **4,276,650** | **98.5** | **168,005** | **−1,838** | **166,167** | **3.30** | **5,031,300** | **98.3** | **5,938,320** | **98.1** | **11,341,400** | **96.4** |
| professing | 588,000 | 98.0 | 4,276,650 | 98.5 | 168,005 | −1,838 | 166,167 | 3.30 | 5,031,300 | 98.3 | 5,938,320 | 98.1 | 11,341,400 | 96.4 |
| Roman Catholics | 586,800 | 97.8 | 4,220,150 | 97.2 | 165,639 | −2,792 | 162,847 | 3.28 | 4,960,450 | 96.9 | 5,848,620 | 96.6 | 11,102,400 | 94.4 |
| Spiritist Catholics | 180,000 | 30.0 | 2,170,000 | 50.0 | 85,483 | 17 | 85,500 | 3.34 | 2,560,000 | 50.0 | 3,025,000 | 50.0 | 4,700,000 | 40.0 |
| Evangelical Catholics | 1,000 | 0.2 | 52,944 | 1.2 | 2,329 | 1,357 | 3,686 | 5.28 | 69,750 | 1.4 | 89,800 | 1.5 | 287,000 | 2.4 |
| Protestants | 1,000 | 0.2 | 45,000 | 1.0 | 1,880 | 820 | 2,700 | 4.80 | 56,300 | 1.1 | 72,000 | 1.2 | 176,000 | 1.5 |
| Marginal Protestants | 0 | 0.0 | 6,000 | 0.1 | 267 | 133 | 400 | 5.00 | 8,000 | 0.2 | 10,000 | 0.2 | 47,000 | 0.4 |
| Non-White indigenous | 100 | 0.0 | 3,000 | 0.1 | 120 | 0 | 120 | 3.34 | 3,600 | 0.1 | 4,200 | 0.1 | 9,000 | 0.1 |
| Anglicans | 100 | 0.0 | 2,500 | 0.1 | 99 | 1 | 100 | 3.39 | 2,950 | 0.1 | 3,500 | 0.1 | 7,000 | 0.1 |
| nominal | 30,000 | 5.0 | 446,060 | 10.3 | 19,301 | 10,493 | 29,794 | 5.15 | 578,000 | 11.3 | 744,000 | 12.3 | 1,764,000 | 15.0 |
| affiliated | 558,000 | 93.0 | 3,830,590 | 88.2 | 148,704 | −12,331 | 136,373 | 3.06 | 4,453,300 | 87.0 | 5,194,320 | 85.8 | 9,577,400 | 81.4 |
| total practising | 502,200 | *90* | 2,681,410 | *70* | 104,093 | −8,632 | 95,461 | 3.06 | 3,117,310 | *70* | 3,636,020 | *70* | 5,746,400 | *60* |
| non-practising | 55,800 | *10* | 1,149,180 | *30* | 44,611 | −3,699 | 40,912 | 3.06 | 1,335,990 | *30* | 1,558,300 | *30* | 3,831,000 | *40* |
| Roman Catholics | 555,800 | 92.6 | 3,721,146 | 85.7 | 144,009 | −14,642 | 129,367 | 3.00 | 4,312,700 | 84.3 | 5,014,820 | 82.9 | 9,051,400 | 76.9 |
| Catholic pentecostals | 0 | 0.0 | 1,000 | 0.0 | 668 | 6,232 | 6,900 | 34.50 | 20,000 | 0.4 | 70,000 | 1.2 | 300,000 | 2.6 |
| Protestants | 2,000 | 0.3 | 92,005 | 2.1 | 3,930 | 1,970 | 5,900 | 5.01 | 117,700 | 2.3 | 151,000 | 2.5 | 412,000 | 3.5 |
| Evangelicals | 2,000 | 0.3 | 78,200 | 1.8 | 3,336 | 1,674 | 5,010 | 5.02 | 99,900 | 2.0 | 128,300 | 2.1 | 352,000 | 3.0 |
| Marginal Protestants | 0 | 0.0 | 10,000 | 0.2 | 467 | 333 | 800 | 5.71 | 14,000 | 0.3 | 18,000 | 0.3 | 70,000 | 0.6 |
| Non-White indigenous | 100 | 0.0 | 4,300 | 0.1 | 174 | 6 | 180 | 3.46 | 5,200 | 0.1 | 6,100 | 0.1 | 35,000 | 0.3 |
| Anglicans | 100 | 0.0 | 3,139 | 0.1 | 124 | 2 | 126 | 3.41 | 3,700 | 0.1 | 4,400 | 0.1 | 9,000 | 0.1 |
| Afro-American spiritists | 12,000 | 2.0 | 43,000 | 1.0 | 1,686 | −86 | 1,600 | 3.17 | 50,500 | 1.0 | 59,000 | 1.0 | 94,000 | 0.8 |
| Non-religious | 0 | 0.0 | 11,000 | 0.3 | 598 | 992 | 1,590 | 8.86 | 17,940 | 0.4 | 26,900 | 0.4 | 231,000 | 2.0 |
| Atheists | 0 | 0.0 | 5,600 | 0.1 | 334 | 906 | 1,240 | 12.40 | 10,000 | 0.2 | 18,000 | 0.3 | 70,000 | 0.6 |
| Baha'is | 0 | 0.0 | 3,900 | 0.1 | 157 | 3 | 160 | 3.41 | 4,700 | 0.1 | 5,500 | 0.1 | 20,000 | 0.2 |
| Buddhists | 0 | 0.0 | 1,500 | 0.0 | 58 | −8 | 50 | 2.86 | 1,750 | 0.0 | 2,000 | 0.0 | 2,000 | 0.0 |
| Jews | 0 | 0.0 | 350 | 0.0 | 14 | −1 | 13 | 3.17 | 410 | 0.0 | 480 | 0.0 | 600 | 0.0 |
| Other religionists | 0 | 0.0 | 1,000 | 0.0 | 48 | 32 | 80 | 5.71 | 1,400 | 0.0 | 1,800 | 0.0 | 3,000 | 0.0 |
| **Country's population** | **600,000** | **100.0** | **4,343,000** | **100.0** | **170,900** | **0** | **170,900** | **3.34** | **5,118,000** | **100.0** | **6,052,000** | **100.0** | **11,762,000** | **100.0** |

COLUMNS, ROWS. For meanings and definitions, see Codebook (Part 6). Note that, by definition, total 'Christians' = professing + crypto-Christians, which also = affiliated + nominal Christians. Percentages may not always total exactly, due to rounding.
CENSUSES. **6.VIII.1950: 98.3% Roman Catholics, 1.5% Evangelicals (0.1% SD Adventists), 0.1% Anglicans, 0.1%** non-religious, 0.2% other religionists. **7.VIII.1960: 98.1% Roman Catholics, 1.3% Evangelicals (0.2% SD Adventists),** 0.1% Anglicans, 0.1% non-religious, 0.4% other religionists. Evangelicals (including Adventists and Anglicans) enumerated in these censuses increased slightly in numbers from 33,440 in 1950 to 35,070 in 1960. Excluding the rapid increase in Adventists (from 2,902 to 5,380), the rest decreased from 30,538 to 29,690 during this 10-year period. Subsequent to 1970 Evangelicals were increasing again with the growth of Pentecostal bodies.

NOTES ON RELIGIONS
AFRO-AMERICAN SPIRITISTS. The term here is restricted to non-Catholic and non-Christian followers of spiritism and Voodoo. Spiritism is strong in the republic; and the many immigrants from Haiti as well as numerous Dominicanos follow Voodoo (Vodoun). In addition, there are many adherents of the Liborismo cult, a syncretistic movement which is a recent revival of a cult begun about 1900 by Liborio. There are also a few Rastafarians (from Jamaica).
ATHEISTS. 6 rival Communist factions, totalling 1,400 members; illegal since 1947.
BAHA'IS. Growth from 7 local spiritual assemblies (1964) to 26 (1973). In 1972, 1,700 new believers were enrolled in 6 areas, but there have been many defections.
BUDDHISTS. Chinese, and a small Japanese farming community in the Constanza Valley.
CATHOLIC PENTECOSTALS (or, Catholic charismatics). Totals (January 1974): about 4,000 involved adults in 150 prayer groups; total charismatic community including children, 8,000. In 1976 a regular weekly crowd of 3,000 was attending healing charismatic meetings in the towns of Nagua and Pimentel, with 42,000 at the latter on one occasion. By November 1977, there were 990 organized prayer groups in the country, increasing rapidly. In January 1978, over 25,000 persons attended the first National Conference of the Catholic Charismatic Renewal, in Santo Domingo.
EVANGELICAL CATHOLICS. This term is used here to describe persons who are affiliated to churches termed by the state Evangélica (Protestant, marginal Protestant, Anglican or indigenous churches), but who in government censuses are regarded as, or profess to be, Roman Catholics.
JEWS. A small colony of German Jews.
NON-WHITE INDIGENOUS. In 13 denominations in 1970 (see Table 2).
OTHER RELIGIONISTS. Including Rosicrucians (1 AMORC centre).
PRACTISING CHRISTIANS. Weekly mass attenders (Catholics, 1967): 11.5% for urban areas; 16.1% for youths aged 7–21 years; 14.5% for sugar-cane cutters.
SPIRITIST CATHOLICS. Roman Catholics active in the Liborismo cult, or in Vodoun, or in spiritism.

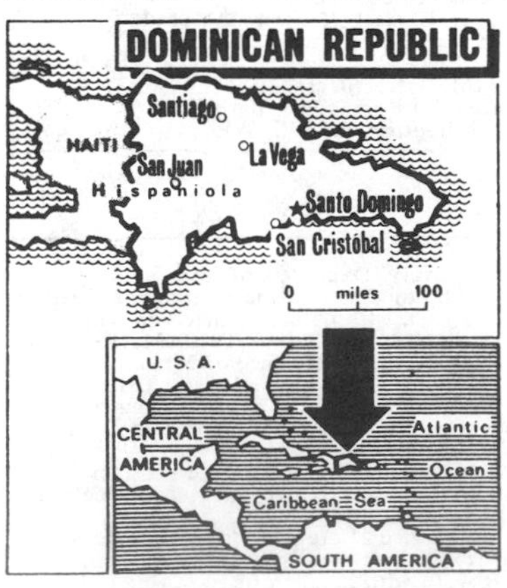


NON-CHRISTIAN RELIGIONS. Voodooism (Vodoun), a syncretistic mixture of Catholic practices with traditional African rites, is strong in the republic, particularly through immigrants from neighbouring Haiti. In addition, the Liborismo cult, which originally began around 1900 and has recently been revived, has many followers. Although the majority of these are Catholics, a number have no Catholic affiliation or profession.

## CHRISTIANITY

CATHOLIC CHURCH. From the nation's origins the Catholic Church has been intimately bound up with the culture and history of the people. The first bishopric west of the Atlantic was established here in 1511 and St Thomas University in 1538. Recently, there has been a marked decline in its influence on people's lives. There has been a continual decrease in the proportion of church marriages; in 1960, 68% of all marriages were canonical (in church), decreasing to 59% in 1956 and to 54% by 1968. In 1967, weekly attendance at Sunday mass was 11.5% in urban centres across the country. Among sugar-cane cutters, attendance then was 14.5%.

The attention of the church in recent years has centred on 3 developments: (1) a pastoral assembly, at national and diocesan levels, which created the Institute of Pastoral Adaptation with courses for both foreign and local priests and religious personnel; (2) small rural communities with voluntary assembly presidents serving with the approval of the bishop in preaching, distributing communion and presiding at marriages, which provide for closer involvement with the popular culture as well as counter-balancing the shortage of priests; and (3) presbyteral councils, largely consultative in nature, erected in each diocese between 1968 and 1970.

OTHER CHURCHES. Protestantism entered the Dominican Republic during the Haitian occupation when North American Negroes were encouraged to populate the island. Requests for religious leadership resulted in the arrival of the first Methodist pastor from England in 1834, followed by a North American from the African Methodist Episcopal Church.

The Dominican Republic was, however, the last of the Latin American countries to receive sustained Protestant missionary activity. In 1907 the Free

**Spiritist Catholics.** Followers of Liborismo cult kneel before movement's shrine, 3 crosses in village of Palma Sola. Pilgrims, mostly Catholics, come from all over the Republic.

Methodist Church (USA) entered the country, building on the foundations laid by an independent missionary in 1889. Further missionary work was initiated through Puerto Rican churches in 1911. Appeals to various mission boards in the USA resulted in the formation of the Board for Christian Work in 1920, with the participation of North American Methodists, Presbyterians and Evangelical United Brethren, joined in later years by Moravians. The resulting church (Iglesia Evangélica Dominicana), became autonomous in 1953. In addition to evangelistic work, medical services, rural reconstruction and education, its bookstore and publishing house have printed and distributed a wide variety of Christian and secular books, many by local authors. The relatively slow growth of this church has been attributed in part to this emphasis on institutional concerns.

In 1941 the Assemblies of God (USA) took over responsibility for several churches which had been established by a Puerto Rican evangelist as early as 1933. Its total community is now the largest non-Catholic body in the republic, followed by Seventh-day Adventists who entered in 1908.

Protestantism has thus made relatively small numerical inroads in the Dominican Republic, though its cultural and social contributions have been significant. For a long time Dominican Protestantism has had the smallest number of national pastors and the lowest membership relative to the total population of any country in the Latin Caribbean.

**CHURCH AND STATE.** Relations between church and state are delineated in the constitution of November 1966, in which Article 8 guarantees 'freedom of conscience and of religion, subject to public order and good morals', and in the concordat of June 1954 negotiated by the Trujillo regime and the apostolic nuncio at that time. The principal dispositions of the latter are as follows: (1) the government recognizes Catholicism as the religion of the Dominican nation and accepts the prerogatives of canon law; (2) Catholic dioceses, institutions and associations are given legal status; (3) government finances diocesan administration and the construction of cathedrals; (4) priests, religious personnel and seminarians are exempt from military service, and clergy and church property are exempt from taxation; (5) civil recognition is given to canonical marriages as well as marriage annulments pronounced by ecclesiastical tribunals; Catholic married couples however may not be divorced; (6) government public schools must orient their teaching to the religious and moral principles of Catholicism and must also offer courses in the Catholic religion, subject to inspection by the ordinary; and (7) provision is made for religious chaplaincies to the armed forces.

The Secretary of State for Education, Fine Arts and Religion is in charge of religious affairs, but there is no special register for churches. Protestant denominations are customarily established juridically as non-profit civil organizations.

The Catholic Church enjoys wide respect among the middle class and government officials, but not among nonconformists. Since the 1965 civil war 8 priests have identified themselves openly with opposition constitutionalists, who are considered communist by Catholic conservatives; and in 1965 also the nuncio and the bishop of Santiago exerted pressure on the Episcopal Conference to issue a communique disassociating itself from the forces of the right. The nuncio also played a role in preventing the crushing of the constitutionalists. Some clergy have denounced social injustices and the crimes of the Banda, a paramilitary group acting for some sections of the army. Among the population, however, especially among youth and students, disillusionment towards the church grows with each indication of ecclesiastical identification with the established political power. This identification inevitably appears when patriotic and liturgical elements are mixed in cathedral and other functions.

**INTERDENOMINATIONAL ORGANIZATIONS.** There is no national council of churches. Presbyterians, United Methodists, and Moravians work in the united Dominican Evangelical Church, which co-operates also with the Episcopal Church. In 1962 the Social Service of Dominican Churches (Servicio Social de Iglesias Dominicanas) was started, with stimulus and substantial help from Church World Service in the USA. About 20 churches participate, distributing USA surplus food through various organizations and handling a number of agricultural projects. A Centre for Ecumenical Planning and Action (CEPAE) attempts to create a sense of community among the churches.

**BROADCASTING.** Commercial stations accept religious programmes on both radio and TV, and there are also 3 Catholic radio stations. In Santo Cerro, there is a Catholic radio station La Voz de Santa Maria with radiophonic schools which since 1964 have instructed about 9,000 people a year. In Santo Domingo, Radio ABC is a commercial station with radiophonic schools and 150,000 students which work in conjunction with Universidad Popular. For Catholics, the Dominican Republic is a member of UNDA.

**BIBLIOGRAPHY**
*Directorio de la Iglesia Católica en República Dominicana, 1972.* Santo Domingo: Conferencia del Episcopado Dominicano, 1972.
*The Church and the crisis in the Dominican Republic.* J. A. Clark, 1966. (Catholic).
*The Churches of the Dominican Republic in the light of history: a study of the root causes of current problems.* W. L. Wipfler. Sondeos No. 11. Cuernavaca (Mexico): CIDOC, 1966. 300p.
'The Dominican Republic', in J. L. Gonzalez, *The development of Christianity in the Latin Caribbean* (Grand Rapids: Eerdmans, 1969), p. 73–82.

**Catholic pentecostals.** *Above.* Crowd of over 42,000 at charismatic renewal meeting in Pimentel, July 1975, with numerous healings reported. *Above centre.* Charismatic leader Fr Emiliano Tardif leads in prayer in Pimentel meeting.

TABLE 2. ORGANIZED CHURCHES AND DENOMINATIONS IN THE DOMINICAN REPUBLIC

| Official name 1 | Begun | Type 3 | Counc 4 | Congs 5 | Adults 6 | Affiliated 7 | Names, notes, and other statistics (see Codebook) 8 |
|---|---|---|---|---|---|---|---|
| Asamblea de Iglesias Cristianas | 1939 | I pen | x...k | | 200 | 500 | *Assembly of Christian Chs.* M=ACC(Puerto Ricans from USA). 1p. |
| Asambleas de Dios | 1933 | P Pe2 | ZF..k | 551 | 19,024 | 27,000 | *Igl Ev AdD. Assemblies of God.* M=AoG(USA). 132n,4x,6f,G=12%pa,1s(49),685Y,2472z. |
| Associación Adventista del Séptimo Día | 1908 | P Adv | x...k | 77 | 13,539 | 20,000 | *Seventh-day Adv, Central Dominican Conf.* 16nx,6f,98mw,1h,1r,208t(23591),1313Y. |
| Associación de Templos Evangélicos | 1938 | P int | xM..K | 44 | 2,000 | 3,545 | *Association of Ev Churches.* M=West Indies Mission(USA). HQ La Vega. 3n,19f,1p. |
| Convención Bautista Dominicana | 1962 | P Bap | T.... | 13 | 223 | 1,000 | *Dominican Baptist Convention.* M=SBC(USA). 2 schools. 5n,15f,7h,1s,37Y. |
| Hermanos Libres | c1925 | P CBr | x.... | 60 | 500 | 1,400 | *Christian (Plymouth, Open) Brethren. Brethren Assemblies.* M=CMML(USA). 15f. |
| Iglesia Africana Metodista Episcopal | c1840 | I Met | VwM.k | | 500 | 1,800 | *Dominican Rep Annual Conference*, 16th Episcopal District. M=AMEC (USA Blacks). |
| **Iglesia Católica en la Rep Dominicana:** | 1494 | R Lat | B.L.R | 297 | 1,972,200 | 3,721,146 | *Catholic Ch.* C=19+1+32. 5p,2q,2s(55). 107n, 349x, 109m, 1225w, 124020Yy. |
| M Santo Domingo | 1511 | R Lat | Bs | 76 | 655,800 | 1,237,445 | 50% urban. Many Haitian sugar workers. 1s,W=16%. 38 183 65 732 43834 |
| D La Vega | 1953 | R Lat | Bs | 36 | 341,100 | 643,583 | Rural. Many smallholders. In north centre. 27 55 8 138 25235 |
| D NS de la Altagracia en Higüey | 1959 | R Lat | Bs | 123 | 135,000 | 254,000 | NS=Nuestra Señora. Rural. 1971 shrine controversy. 10 8 4 33 7567 |
| D San Juan de la Maguana | 1953 | R Lat | Bs | 19 | 289,000 | 545,000 | Rural. Impoverished soil due to rain scarcity. 0 34 0 52 10776 |
| D Santiago de los Caballeros | 1953 | R Lat | Bs | 43 | 551,300 | 1,041,118 | Rural. Most progressive diocesan structure. 1s. 32 69 32 270 36608 |
| Iglesia Cristiana Bíblica | 1949 | P int | xM... | 13 | 150 | 300 | *Alianza Bíblica Cristiana.* M=UFM(USA). HQ San Pedro de Macorís. 14f,1p. |
| Iglesia de Dios de la Profecía | 1940 | P Pe3 | Z...k | 21 | 2,000 | 3,000 | *Ch of God of Prophecy.* M=CGP(USA), ex CoG(Cleveland). HQ San Pedro de Macorís. |
| Iglesia de Dios en Cristo | | I pe3 | Z.... | 25 | 200 | 500 | *Church of God in Christ.* M=CoGiC (Black mission from USA). Strong in Haiti. |
| Iglesia de Dios (Anderson) | | P Hol | x...k | 18 | 1,300 | 2,000 | *Ch of God.* M=CoG(Anderson) (USA). Holiness deonmination. |
| Iglesia de Dios (Cleveland) | 1939 | P Pe3 | ZF..k | 149 | 3,791 | 6,000 | *Pentecostal Ch of God.* M=CoG(Cleveland) (USA). 72 churches, 77 missions. 70n,2f,1p. |
| Iglesia del Evangelio Cuadrangular | | P Pe2 | ZF... | | 58 | 100 | *Internat Ch of the Foursquare Gospel.* M=ICFG(USA). Classical Pentecostals. |
| Iglesia Episcopal Dominicana | 1898 | A Cen | aw.RK | 15 | 1,509 | 3,139 | *Episcopal Ch.* Diocese, PECUSA IX. 94% citizens (10% Black). 5n,5x,16Y,136y. |
| Iglesia Evangélica Dominicana | 1834 | P uni | V.U.K | 82 | 5,197 | 12,000 | *Dominican Ev Ch.* 1920 union, M=Board for Christian Work. A=1953. 19n,8h,1j,1k,39t. |
| Iglesia Evangélica Menonita | 1945 | P Men | GF..K | | 625 | 1,500 | M=Ev Mennonite Ch (Defenseless Mennonite Ch) (USA). 10f,2h,1s. |
| Iglesia Metodista Libre Dominicana | 1889 | P Hol | VF..K | 337 | 4,473 | 10,000 | 1907, M=FMC(USA). North coast. 13n,8f,G=12.2%pa,6h,1k,1r,1s(20),1716z. |
| Iglesia Misionera | 1945 | P Hol | xF... | | 202 | 1,000 | *Missionary Church.* M=MCA, since 1969 Missionary Ch(USA). 17f. |
| Iglesia Pentecostal Unida | 1962 | P Pe1 | x.... | 9 | 500 | 1,000 | *United Pentecostal Ch.* M=UPC(USA). Unitarian Pentecostals. 7n. |
| Iglesias de Cristo | | P Dis | x.... | 4 | 100 | 200 | *Churches of Christ.* M=CC(Non-Instrumental) (USA). In Santo Domingo. |
| Iglesias de la Fe Apostólica | | P Pe3 | x.... | | 50 | 100 | *Chs of the Apostolic Faith.* M=AFM(Portland,Oregon,USA). Holiness Pentecostals. |
| Misión Bautista | 1950 | P Bap | x.... | | 118 | 360 | M=Baptist Mid-Missions(USA). Fundamentalist Baptists. 10f. |
| Testigos de Jehová | 1945 | M Jeh | x.... | 73 | 3,906 | 9,500 | *Jehovah's Witnesses. Watch Tower. IBSA.* First missionaries 1945. 464Y. |
| Other Non-White indigenous churches | | I | ..... | | 500 | 2,000 | Total about 10 (see below), mostly from Puerto Rico, Jamaica, Trinidad et alia. |
| Other Protestant denominations | | P | ..... | | 600 | 1,500 | Total about 10 (see list below). |
| Other marginal Protestant bodies | | M | ..... | | 200 | 500 | Including: Unity School of Christianity (from USA; 2 ministers). |
| **Total affiliated (mid-1970)** | | | | **1,870** | **2,033,465** | **3,830,590** | **Total denominations (1970) . . . 42.** |
| **Total affiliated (mid-1975)** | | | | **1,920** | **2,364,000** | **4,453,300** | **Total denominations (1975) . . . 44.** |
| **Total affiliated (mid-1980)** | | | | **2,040** | **2,757,400** | **5,194,320** | **Total denominations (1980) . . . 46.** |

NOTES ON TABLE ABOVE
COLUMNS: for meanings and CODES (cols. 1, 3, 4, 8): see Codebook (Part 6). Column 1: **Boldface type** = church with over 10% of country's affiliated Christians.
NATIONAL COUNCILS (Column 4, 5th letter).
There is no national council of churches, but there is a service organization, SSID.

K = Servicio Social de Iglesias Dominicanas (SSID) (Social Organization of the Dominican Churches).
k = associate member of SSID.
R = Conferencia del Episcopado Dominicano (CED) (Conference of the Dominican Episcopate).

OTHER NON-WHITE INDIGENOUS CHURCHES. These, mostly of pentecostal background from Puerto Rico, Jamaica, Trinidad and elsewhere, include the following: Ch of Our Lord Jesus Christ of the Apostolic Faith (1950) (USA Black pentecostals), Iglesia Bautista Bethel, Iglesia Defensores de la Fe (begun 1947 by Puerto Ricans), Iglesia del Dios Vivo, Iglesia Monte Zión, Iglesia Pentecostal de JC, Primer Concilio Evangélico Pentecostés Dominicano.
OTHER PROTESTANT DENOMINATIONS. Baptist International Missions (1970), Exclusive Brethren (Continuing Tunbridge Wells), International Gospel League (1970), Maranatha Baptist Mission, Moravian Ch (1907), Salvation Army (1971), Union Ch of Santo Domingo, Worldwide Evangelization Crusade (Cruzada Evangelistica Mundial) (1941).

**PEOPLES** (ethnolinguistic). Christians: 71.0% Mulatto, 16.1% Dominican White, 10.7% Black (1.0% Haitian, 0.3% Jamaican), 1.0% European (White, Spanish), Chinese (1,000), Lebanese.

COUNTRY-WIDE TOTALS
EVANGELIZATION (see Part 5). 1900: 100%. 1970: 100%. 1980: 100%. *Mass evangelism.* Among recent campaigns: 1962, Billy Graham South American tour; 1965–66, Evangelism-in-Depth (over 300,000 homes visited, 175,000 scripture portions and 200,000 tracts distributed, Goodwill Caravans in rural areas), terminating in intensive 3-week crusade in Santo Domingo (12,000 enquirers); 1969, Hermano Pablo crusades in Santo Domingo (80,050 attenders, 1,150 enquirers) and Santiago (28,500 attenders, 850 enquirers); 1973, 2-week Luis Palau crusade in Santo Domingo (5,000 attenders nightly, 2,600 decisions) plus nightly TV talk show; 1977, Luis Palau crusade in Santo Domingo (104,000 attenders, 4,000 enquirers); 1978 Here's Life Santo Domingo (CCCI). *Radiophonic evangelism.* Annual listeners' letters (1975): 6,300 (TWR, HCJB, FEBC, et alia). Bible correspondence courses: ICI (661 enrolments).
FOREIGN MISSIONARIES AND PERSONNEL (nationals serving abroad) (1973). Total about 60 Roman Catholics in Costa Rica, Haiti et alia.
FOREIGN MISSIONARIES AND PERSONNEL (aliens from abroad) (1973). Total 1,748. *From Western world.* 1,647: about 1,500 Roman Catholics, 141 Protestants (124 in 22 USA societies, 17 in 2 Canada societies), 6 Anglicans (4 in 1 USA society, 2 in 1 Canada society). *From Communist world.* 1 Roman Catholic from Poland. *From Third World.* 100: 60 Roman Catholics from other Latin American and Caribbean countries, about 30 indigenous from Puerto Rico, Jamaica and other islands, 10 Protestants from Caribbean countries.
INSTITUTIONS (church-operated) (1973). Total 180, including 110 higher schools (5 minor seminaries), 50 medical centres (17 hospitals), 1 radio station, 1 research centre, 9 seminaries (5 Protestant, 4 RC), 1 study centre.
PERIODICALS. About 16 titles.
PERSONNEL. About 2,498 (750 national, 1,748 foreign).
RELIGIOUS LIBRARIES. 12.
SCRIPTURE DISTRIBUTION (1975). Annual totals: 32,324 Bibles (1% free, 68% subsidized, 31% commercial), 55,258 NTs (59% free, 32% subsidized, 9% commercial), 276,169 UBS portions, 2,820,893 UBS selections.
SERVICE AGENCIES. About 40, including CASC, CCOC, CED, CEF, CENICOS, CONDOR, CWS, JEC, JOC/F, MFC, MTC, SSID, SU, UNCC.

ADDITIONAL DATA ON CHURCHES
IGLESIA CATOLICA EN LA REPUBLICA DOMINICANA. The 5 dioceses (and D Barahona, created in 1976) vary considerably with regard to liberal and conservative trends. D Santiago has updated its structure the most, with now a permanent diaconate, presidents of assemblies, and the like. At the other pole, D Higüey, which covers an impoverished population subject to latifundia (landlordism), inaugurated in 1971 a national shrine to the Virgin, a vast basilica-sanctuary which has become a centre of controversy both because of its cost (over 4 million US dollars) and also because of the political implications of its appellation 'an achievement of the national government'. *Catholics.* Including 1,000 Chinese (1975). *Annual baptisms.* (1972) 96.2% infant, 3.8% adult. *National priests.* In addition to the 107 Dominican priests at work in 1971, there were 10 other Dominicans working in Puerto Rico and the USA. *Priests* (total). 113 secular + 343 religious, divided among the dioceses as follows: Santo Domingo 40 + 181; La Vega 24 + 58; Higüey 11 + 7; San Juan 3 + 31; Santiago 35 + 66. The total in 1960 was 99 + 184. The large influx of religious clergy subsequently followed on the mass expulsion of foreign priests from Cuba under Castro. *Male religious.* 486. *Brothers.* 36 nationals, 73 expatriates (1971). *Sisters.* 615 nationals, 610 expatriates (1971). Total including contemplatives and non-diocesan (1970): 1,285. In 1960, sisters numbered 825; subsequently there was a large influx from Cuba. *Catholic charismatics* (January 1974). Around 4,000 adults including many priests and sisters are active in 150 prayer groups in the Catholic Charismatic Renewal. *Catechists.* Voluntary catechists are very numerous, e.g. 2,000 in D La Vega. Candidates are chosen by parishes, and trained for one or 2 weeks at 5 catechetical centres (one in each diocese). *Main religious orders and congregations.* Priests: 132 SJ, 80 SDB, 41 MSC1, 23 OFMCap, 22 SFM, 21 CICM. Brothers: 22 FSC. Sisters: 208 Sisters of Charity of Cardinal Sancha, 152 Sisters of Charity of St Vincent de Paul, 165 Mercédaires de la Charité, 110 Daughters of Marie Auxiliaire, 88 Sisters of Perpetual Help, 62 Franciscan Tertiaries.
*Catholic organizations.* The Dominican Episcopal Conference (Conferencia del Episcopado Dominicano) is a member of CELAM. The Dominican Confederation of Religious Personnel (Confederación Dominicana de Religiosos, CONDOR) is a member of CLAR. There are no national presbyteral or pastoral councils. The principal lay movements are Christian Study Courses (Cursillos de Cristiandad), which by 1971 had held 495 sessions with 17,325 participants; Legión de Maria; Franciscan Tertiaries with 119 fraternities and 12,500 members; Christian Family Movement (Movimiento Familia Cristiano) with 200 teams; JOC/F; and JEC. For the armed forces, the republic forms a single military vicariate.
The Holy See has diplomatic relations with the Dominican Republic and is represented to government and the Catholic hierarchy by a nuncio in Santo Domingo.
In 1970 Catholic schools accounted for 79,700 primary and secondary pupils (10.2% of the total) and 1,491 (8.5%) at university level, in addition to an extensive technical school programme (2,700 students). In 1973 there were 136 primary schools (44,850 pupils) and 101 secondary (21,865). The church maintains one university, Universidad Católica Madre y Maestra.
In the medical sector, there are 16 hospitals and one leprosarium. In the category of social service activities, there are centres for training farmers on the practical level and grass-roots community development with the support of Dominican Caritas. In 1970 the latter sponsored 913 different projects including the construction of back roads, schools, community centres, dispensaries and education in the operation of co-operatives. Other social service organizations include the Federation of Christian Land Leagues; Centro de Investigación y Acción Social, founded by Jesuits; and Centro de Orientación Juvenil 'Casa Abierta', which attempts to provide help to youth with drug, alcohol and sex problems.
IGLESIA EVANGELICA DOMINICANA. Formed in 1920 to be an ecumenical denomination from its origins, supported by major USA foreign missions, i.e. Methodist Episcopal, Presbyterian and Evangelical United Brethren. From the First Evangelical Church thus founded had grown by 1970 8 other churches in Santo Domingo, and over 30 in the whole republic. The Moravian Church and its 2 congregations later joined also. The co-operating missions work through the Board for Christian Work in Santo Domingo, based on New York, USA.

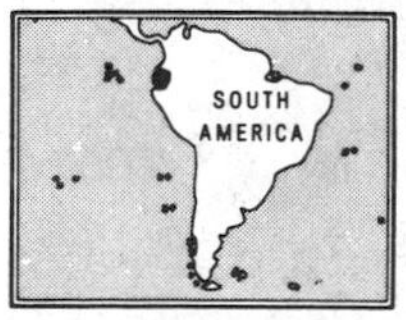


# ECUADOR

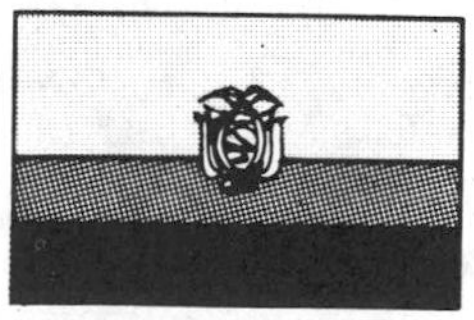

## SECULAR DATA

**STATE. Official name:** The Republic of Ecuador (La República del Ecuador). Adjective of nationality: Ecuadorian (ecuatoriano).
**Flag** (shown above right): Yellow, blue, and red stripes, national coat of arms at centre.
**Area:** 283,561 sq.km. (109,484 sq.miles). Agricultural land: 23.0%.
**Government:** Military junta, since 1972 (1534 Spanish conquest, 1830 Independence, several dictatorships).
**Official language:** Spanish (*Español/Castellano*).
**Chief cities:** capital Quito 564,900 (1972), Guayaquil 860,600.
**Political divisions:** 20 Provinces, 97 Cantons, 169 Urban Parishes, 626 Rural Parishes.
**Armed forces** (1976): Total 23,550 regular: army 17,500, navy 3,450, air force 2,600 (27 combat aircraft). Paramilitary forces: 5,800.
**Dependencies:** Galapagos Archipelago.

**DEMOGRAPHY. Population:** 6,500,845 (census of 8.VI.1974. For 1970–2000 (UN), see last row of Table 1). Population density (1975): 25/sq.km. (65/sq.mile). Under 15 years: 45%. Growth rate (1975–80): 3.16% per year (births 3.97%, deaths −0.82%). Life expectancy (1975–80): 62.1 years. Household size: 5.1 persons.
**Major languages:** Spanish, Quechua, English, German, Jivaro, Norwegian, Chinese, and about 15 other languages.
**Urban dwellers** (1970): 39.1%. Urban growth rate (1950–70): 4.9% per year.
**Labour force:** 30%.
**Refugees** (1977): About 5,000 from Chile.
**Tourists** (1974): 148,071.

**ETHNOLINGUISTIC GROUPS:** 41.3% Quechua, 40.0% Mestizo, 10.0% Ecuadorian White, 5.0% Black (African Negro), 1.0% jungle Amerindian (61,750) (10 major tribes including 0.5% Andoa, 0.5% Achuale, 0.2% Cofán, 0.2% Orejon, Jivaro), 1.0% Mulatto (White/Black), 1.0% European (White) (German, Norwegian, USA), 0.1% Chinese (6,500), Jewish, Syro-Lebanese Arab.

**MONEY** (1977). **Monetary unit:** sucre (= 100 centavos); US$1 = Su 27.80.
**National income per person:** US$474. Average annual family income: US$2,417.
**Inflation:** (1970–74) 13.0% per year, (1975) 15% per year (consumer price index 199).
**Cost of living in capital** (1976): index 86 (Washington DC=100). Daily cost of living: US$40.

**EDUCATION.** Adult literacy: (1950) 56%, (1974) 74%. Education rate: 40%. Schools: 7912. Universities: 6.

HEALTH. Hospitals: 214 (13,357 beds). Doctors: 2,080. Lepers: 3,500 (0.5 per 1,000). Blind: 10,000. Psychotics: 50,000.

LITERATURE. Annual new book titles (1972): 32. Periodicals: 110. Scientific journals: 30. Newspapers: 22 dailies, 18 non-daily.

COMMUNICATION (per 1,000 people). Phones: 19. Radios: 279. TV sets: 25. Daily newspaper circulation: 47 copies.

TABLE 1. RELIGIOUS ADHERENTS IN ECUADOR

| Year | 1900 | | mid-1970 | | Annual change, 1970–1980 | | | | mid-1975 | | mid-1980 | | 2000 | |
|---|---|---|---|---|---|---|---|---|---|---|---|---|---|---|
| *Name* | *Adherents* | *%* | *Adherents* | *%* | *Natural* | *Conversion* | *Total* | *Rate* | *Adherents* | *%* | *Adherents* | *%* | *Adherents* | *%* |
| **Christians** | **1,430,000** | **87.7** | **5,930,600** | **98.3** | **223,489** | **31** | **223,520** | **3.20** | **6,974,200** | **98.4** | **8,165,800** | **98.3** | **14,395,000** | **97.4** |
| professing | 1,430,000 | 87.7 | 5,930,600 | 98.3 | 223,489 | 31 | 223,520 | 3.20 | 6,974,200 | 98.4 | 8,165,800 | 98.3 | 14,395,000 | 97.4 |
| Roman Catholics | 1,430,000 | 87.7 | 5,830,600 | 96.7 | 219,387 | −1,667 | 217,720 | 3.18 | 6,846,200 | 96.6 | 8,007,800 | 96.4 | 14,026,000 | 94.9 |
| Christo-pagans | 652,000 | 40.0 | 1,300,000 | 21.6 | 45,440 | −25,940 | 19,500 | 1.37 | 1,418,000 | 20.0 | 1,495,000 | 18.0 | 1,773,000 | 12.0 |
| Evangelical Catholics | 100 | 0.0 | 79,108 | 1.3 | 3,320 | 2,639 | 6,059 | 5.85 | 103,600 | 1.5 | 139,700 | 1.7 | 358,000 | 2.4 |
| Protestants | 0 | 0.0 | 100,000 | 1.7 | 4,102 | 1,698 | 5,800 | 4.53 | 128,000 | 1.8 | 158,000 | 1.9 | 369,000 | 2.5 |
| affiliated | 1,430,000 | 87.7 | 5,930,600 | 98.3 | 223,489 | 31 | 223,520 | 3.20 | 6,974,200 | 98.4 | 8,165,800 | 98.3 | 14,395,000 | 97.4 |
| doubly-affiliated | −100 | 0.0 | −93,064 | −1.5 | −3,845 | −2,648 | −6,493 | 5.41 | −120,000 | −1.7 | −158,000 | −1.9 | −414,000 | −2.8 |
| total practising | 1,287,000 | *90* | 4,744,480 | *80* | 178,791 | 25 | 178,816 | 3.20 | 5,579,360 | *80* | 6,532,640 | *80* | 10,076,500 | *70* |
| non-practising | 143,000 | *10* | 1,186,120 | *20* | 44,698 | 6 | 44,704 | 3.20 | 1,394,840 | *20* | 1,633,160 | *20* | 4,318,500 | *30* |
| Roman Catholics | 1,430,000 | 87.7 | 5,843,556 | 96.9 | 219,874 | −1,758 | 218,116 | 3.18 | 6,861,400 | 96.8 | 8,024,720 | 96.6 | 14,079,000 | 95.3 |
| Catholic pentecostals | 0 | 0.0 | 0 | 0.0 | 32 | 168 | 200 | 20.00 | 1,000 | 0.0 | 2,000 | 0.0 | 30,000 | 0.2 |
| Protestants | 100 | 0.0 | 140,550 | 2.3 | 5,672 | 2,673 | 8,345 | 4.71 | 117,000 | 2.5 | 224,000 | 2.7 | 517,000 | 3.5 |
| Evangelicals | 100 | 0.0 | 130,000 | 2.2 | 5,287 | 2,713 | 8,000 | 4.85 | 165,000 | 2.3 | 210,000 | 2.5 | 498,000 | 3.4 |
| Ecuadorian indigenous | 0 | 0.0 | 23,380 | 0.4 | 1,122 | 1,540 | 2,662 | 7.61 | 35,000 | 0.5 | 50,000 | 0.6 | 148,000 | 1.0 |
| Marginal Protestants | 0 | 0.0 | 14,668 | 0.2 | 609 | 224 | 833 | 4.39 | 19,000 | 0.3 | 23,000 | 0.3 | 60.000 | 0.4 |
| Orthodox | 0 | 0.0 | 1,000 | 0.0 | 38 | 0 | 38 | 3.17 | 1,200 | 0.0 | 1,380 | 0.0 | 3,000 | 0.0 |
| Anglicans | 0 | 0.0 | 510 | 0.0 | 19 | 0 | 19 | 3.17 | 600 | 0.0 | 700 | 0.0 | 2,000 | 0.0 |
| Tribal religionists | 200,000 | 12.3 | 50,000 | 0.8 | 1,589 | −1,609 | −20 | −0.04 | 49,600 | 0.7 | 49,800 | 0.6 | 60.000 | 0.4 |
| Non-religious | 0 | 0.0 | 19,000 | 0.3 | 853 | 1,287 | 2,140 | 8.01 | 26,700 | 0.4 | 40,400 | 0.5 | 219,000 | 1.5 |
| Baha'is | 0 | 0.0 | 16,400 | 0.3 | 705 | 355 | 1,060 | 4.82 | 22,000 | 0.3 | 27,000 | 0.3 | 60,000 | 0.4 |
| Atheists | 0 | 0.0 | 6,000 | 0.1 | 256 | 144 | 400 | 5.00 | 8,000 | 0.1 | 10,000 | 0.1 | 30,000 | 0.2 |
| Chinese folk-religionists | 0 | 0.0 | 4,000 | 0.1 | 122 | −162 | −40 | −1.05 | 3,800 | 0.1 | 3,600 | 0.0 | 1,000 | 0.0 |
| Buddhists | 0 | 0.0 | 2,000 | 0.0 | 64 | −64 | 0 | 0.00 | 2,000 | 0.0 | 2,000 | 0.0 | 1,000 | 0.0 |
| Jews | 0 | 0.0 | 2,000 | 0.0 | 80 | 0 | 80 | 3.33 | 2,400 | 0.0 | 2,800 | 0.0 | 4,000 | 0.0 |
| Other religionists | 0 | 0.0 | 1,000 | 0.0 | 42 | 18 | 60 | 4.62 | 1,300 | 0.0 | 1,600 | 0.0 | 3,000 | 0.0 |
| **Country's population** | **1,630,000** | **100.0** | **6,031,000** | **100.0** | **227,200** | **0** | **227,200** | **3.20** | **7,090,000** | **100.0** | **8,303,000** | **100.0** | **14,773,000** | **100.0** |

COLUMNS, ROWS. For meanings and definitions, see Codebook (Part 6). Note that, by definition, total 'Christians' = professing + crypto-Christians, which also = affiliated + nominal Christians. Percentages may not always total exactly, due to rounding.
CENSUSES. The religion question has not been asked in government censuses.

NOTES ON RELIGIONS
ATHEISTS. 3 rival Communist parties, total members 1,200 (1970), about 4,000 sympathizers.
BAHA'IS. Very rapid growth from 5 local spiritual assemblies (1964) to 164 (1973); 2 centres on Galapagos Island. Mainly Indians and Blacks, with a school in Esmeraldas (1,000 children). Radio and TV are widely used.
BUDDHISTS. Chinese.
CHRISTO-PAGANS. Amerindians syncretizing 17th-century Spanish Catholicism with their traditional pre-Columbian religion to produce their own distinctive folk-Catholicism.
DOUBLY-AFFILIATED. The term covers those affiliated to, or claimed by, both the Catholic Church and also a church termed Evangélica by the state (Protestant, Anglican, Ecuadorian indigenous, marginal Protestant), i.e. baptized Catholics who have recently become Evangelicals or others. Because their statistics represent a duplication, they are shown in the table as a negative quantity (with a minus sign).
ECUADORIAN INDIGENOUS. In about 68 denominations or groupings in 1970 (see Table 2).
EVANGELICAL CATHOLICS. This term is used here to describe persons who are affiliated to churches termed by the state Evangélica (Protestant, Ecuadorian indigenous, Anglican or marginal Protestant churches), but who are regarded by state and society as, or profess publicly to be, Roman Catholics.
OTHER RELIGIONISTS. Including Rosicrucians (2 AMORC centres).
TRIBAL RELIGIONISTS. Of the 61,750 jungle or lowland or pure tribal Amerindians (Araguro, Auca, Cayapa, Cofán, Colorado, Jivaro, Salasaca, Secoyas, et alii) in 1970, a very high proportion are still animists.

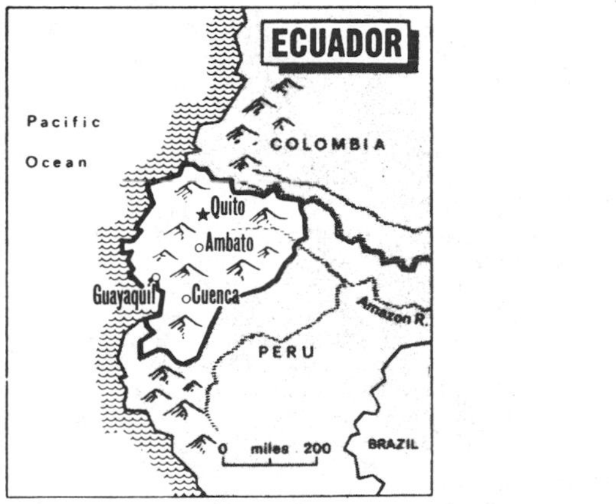


**NON-CHRISTIAN RELIGIONS. Traditional religions** are practised by several jungle and lowland Indian tribes in the eastern headwaters of the Amazon, among whom are the Araguro, Auca, Cayapa, Cofán, Colorado, Jivaro, Salasaca, and Secoyas.
**Baha'i** has built up a strong following since 1960.

## CHRISTIANITY

CATHOLIC CHURCH. By the time the Spanish founded Quito in 1534, the Inca race had gained supremacy over other Indians. Quito then became part of the viceregency of Peru, later of New Grenada (Colombia). The diocese of Quito was established in 1545, the first hospital built in 1565 and the first diocesan synod held in 1594; and the evangelization of the Amazon region was begun in 1599. During the next 200 years an increasing number of schools and colleges were built. By 1780 there were 896 priests and religious personnel in Quito, whose population then was 28,500. Independence from Spain in 1822 resulted in a rapid decline in the number of priests. The 19th century was a period of conflict as liberals and conservatives alternated in their control of government, while Ecuador lost increasing amounts of territory in conflicts with neighbouring countries. A concordat with Rome was signed in 1862 but was revoked by the anti-clerical government of 1895. Divorce was legalized in 1906 and church lands appropriated in 1908.

Catholic rituals today are taken most seriously by people living in the Andes, and many travel long distances to observe them. Catholicism in the mountains is of a popular type, cosmological and closely linked to ancestral beliefs; the usual term describing it is christo-paganism. In the coastal regions, where both urban and rural populations are more middle class and have received Catholic secondary school education, religious observance is of a formal and socially conservative nature. Here rates of baptism, confirmation and Sunday mass attendance are the lowest in the country; not more than 25% of marriages are performed in church in contrast to 80% in the mountains.

There are 3 Catholic archdioceses, 10 dioceses and 9 apostolic vicariates, prefectures, and prelatures.

For several years now attention has been focused on the diocese of Riobamba and its bishop who is an avowed defender of Indian rights and an instigator of profound pastoral reforms. He has been responsible for numerous conscientization movements, especially radiophonic schools for peasants, and an institute for training rural community directors. A group of conservative Catholics linked to the political and social establishment has attempted to divide the bishop from his diocese or to obtain his dismissal, and in 1973 prevailed upon the Holy See to send an apostolic visitor to examine the administrative and pastoral situation in his diocese. The visitor eventually concluded his investigation by reporting strongly in favour of the bishop, without however succeeding in reconciling him with the other Ecuadorian bishops, who have continued to exclude him from meetings of the episcopal conference. The bishop of Riobamba played a key role in the creation of the Latin American Pastoral Institute (IPLA) at Quito in 1968, which of the 4 such institutes of CELAM has been the most involved in conciliar renewal. However, when CELAM decided in 1973 to reorganize its institutes, IPLA along with the other 3 went out of existence, being replaced by a single institute located in Medellín, Colombia.

PROTESTANT CHURCHES. An agent of the British and Foreign Bible Society, who was also the first Protestant missionary to Colombia and Venezuela, entered Ecuador to initiate the sale of Bibles in 1824. However, no permanent mission was established until 1896 when 3 missionaries of the Gospel Missionary Union took up work in the country. Their arrival coincided with the promulgation of the liberal constitution of Eloy Alfae and the repudiation of the concordat signed with the Holy See. The GMU has been active among the Mestizos of the coastal lowlands and Jivaro Indians in the Amazon area, but its strength is among the Quechua in the Andes, among whom a mass movement has been taking place. The Evangelical Missionary Union Church is now the largest Protestant denomination in Ecuador. The Christian and Missionary Alliance, beginning in 1897, also works in the coastal, mountain and eastern areas. Its large missionary staff is concentrated primarily in the Alliance Academy, which serves 18 missionary societies, and in its numerous Bible school programmes. Seventh-day Adventists arrived in 1905 although they have not been as successful among the Indians here as in other nearby countries. In 1945, 4 major USA denominations (Evangelical and Reformed Church, (later part of the USA's UCC), Presbyterian Church US, United Presbyterian Church USA and the Evangelical United Brethren which later joined the UMC) formed the United Andean Indian Mission to evangelize Andean Indians in Ecuador, Peru and Bolivia. Thus far Ecuador remains its only field. Although it is engaged in agricultural, educational, medical and evangelistic programmes, its growth has been very small. The second largest Protestant group in Ecuador at the present time, the International Church of the Foursquare Gospel, did not appear on the scene until 1953. In 1962 there were only 2 churches and 70 members; but following widely-publicized miraculous healings during a Roberto Espinoza evangelistic and healing campaign in 1964, 2,300 converts were reported with 15 new churches and 19 meeting places opened.

Missionary work in Ecuador received worldwide attention in 1956 when Auca Indians killed 5 missionaries from 3 different societies. The wife and sister of 2 of those killed later returned, and today 30 Aucas have been baptized, including the original killers. Numerous other small denominations also exist, the majority having entered Ecuador since World War II.

**CHURCH AND STATE.** According to the constitution of 1945, which was abolished in 1946 but revived again in 1972 by the military government of Guillerma Rodrigues Lara, 'The State recognizes no official religion, each person being free to profess the religion of his choice' (Article 141, item 11). However, the state regards itself as religious, as is evident from the Preamble to the constitution: 'The people of Ecuador. . . invoke the protection of God'. The constitution guarantees freedom of opinion, expression, propagation and conscience (Article 141: 10–11). Public education is lay and free at all levels. There is a Ministry of Government and Religions but no obligatory registration of churches.

Relations between the state and the Catholic

*Above.* Market day in Santo Domingo de los Colorados, small cattle town near Guayaquil. About 75% of the population shown here are practising Catholics
*Right.* Headquarters of world's first missionary broadcasting station, Radio HCJB (Voice of the Andes) in Quito. Its first broadcast was on Christmas Day, 1931

ment. In the name of the 9 dioceses holding the greatest amounts of land, the Episcopal Conference has asked the Interamerican Bank for Development to furnish it with the funds necessary to carry out major agrarian reform. The dioceses of Quito, Riobamba, Ibarra and Cuenca then began the reform in 1971, entrusting its implementation to the Ecuadorian Centre for Agricultural Services (CESA).

By 1976 these reforms had irritated the right-wing government to the point where the Riobamba co-operative was denounced as subversive; and in August, 17 Catholic bishops from Mexico, Brazil and other Latin American countries who were meeting for a pastoral conference at Riobamba were suddenly arrested and deported.

**INTERDENOMINATIONAL ORGANIZATIONS.** The Inter-Mission Fellowship embracing all Protestant missions was discontinued in 1965 and replaced by the Ecuador Evangelical Fellowship. Churches as well as missions are included in the latter, with churches encouraged to assume the greater leadership. A number of study seminars have been sponsored, but the Fellowship continues to experience tensions between its conservative and ecumenical members. In 1967, in co-operation with Lutherans and Roman Catholics, the Episcopal Church established in Quito an ecumenical library.

**BROADCASTING.** There are 5 Protestant and 21 Catholic radio stations in Ecuador (out of a total of 200). One of the largest Christian broadcasting projects in the world is the Protestant station Voice of the Andes (HCJB), in Quito, owned by the World Radio Missionary Fellowship (USA). This station broadcasts programmes across the world in 15 languages. In addition to its international operation, HCJB is also operating a local station in Guayaquil. In 1977, it was strengthening its transmitter facilities by 500,000 watts to increase its world coverage. Similarly, the Gospel Missionary Union operates 3 stations, HCGM-7, HCUE-6 and HCUE-5. All commercial radio and TV stations accept religious programmes, and several Protestant missions, including Southern Baptists, have recording studios for programmes and spots on commercial stations.

Catholic broadcasting emphasizes mass education. In 1962, Escuelas Radiofónicas Populares began regular educational radio work in Riobamba, which later developed on a nation-wide scale with lessons and educational programmes in Indian languages including Quechua and Shuar (Jivaro). In Sucua, the Radio Federación de Centros Shuaras de Morona Santiago has 14,000 members who work for moral, social and economic development, through educational programmes on radio schools. These are broadcast in Shuar and Spanish. There are also radio schools in Pichincha. For Catholics, Ecuador is a member of UNDA.

**BIBLIOGRAPHY**
'A componential analysis of the Ecuadorian Protestant church'. J. F. Reed. Dissertation, Fuller Theological Seminary, Pasadena, CA (USA), 1974.
'An Ecuadorian impasse'. W. C. Weld. Thesis, Fuller Theological Seminary, Pasadena, CA (USA), 1968.
'Ecuador', *Pro Mundi Vita* (Brussels), 31 (1970).
*La Iglesia en Venezuela y Ecuador.* I. Alonso et al. Fribourg: FERES, 1962.
'The evangelization of the Quichuas of Ecuador'. D. R. Dilworth. Thesis, Fuller Theological Seminary, Pasadena, CA (USA), 1967. 124p.
*Through gates of splendour: the martyrdom of 5 missionaries in the Ecuador jungle.* E. Elliot. London: Hodder & Stoughton, 1957. 192p. (Among the Auca Indians).

Church are subject to the modus vivendi signed in July 1937 by the government and the Holy See. It is an agreement consisting of 10 points, which guarantees to the Catholic Church the free exercise of its proper activities (Article 1) and the right to establish and manage schools (Article 2). Other articles provide for missionary work in the eastern Amazon forests (Article 3), prohibition of clergy from taking part in partisan or political activities (Article 4), recognition of the juridical personality of dioceses as well as other Catholic organizations and institutions (Article 5), and the right of government to oppose for political reasons the nomination of bishops (Article 7). An additional convention of 5 articles regulates the church's freedom to preach and publish, as well as the nationalization of church property. This 1937 agreement has been generally respected by both parties over the subsequent years.

In 1965 the Catholic episcopate of Ecuador decided to proceed with agrarian reform for lands owned by the church. At that time the church was considered second only to the state in the size of its holdings. After converting its property into investments, the church now finds itself in a transition stage between latifundism and capitalism in its economic involve-

TABLE 2.   ORGANIZED CHURCHES AND DENOMINATIONS IN ECUADOR

| Official name 1 | Begun 2 | Type 3 | Counc 4 | Congs 5 | Adults 6 | Affiliated 7 | Names, notes, and other statistics (see Codebook) 8 | | | | |
|---|---|---|---|---|---|---|---|---|---|---|---|
| Asamblea del Señor | | I pen | ••••• | 1 | 50 | 100 | *Assembly of the Lord.* One indigenous pentecostal congregation. | | | | |
| Asambleas de Dios en el Ecuador | 1962 | P Pe2 | ZF... | 38 | 2,269 | 5,000 | *Assemblies of God in E.* M=AoG(USA). 25n,3x,10f,G=32%pa,1k,1s(56),W=56%,112Y,125z. | | | | |
| Asoc de Iglesia Ev Interamericanas | 1952 | P Hol | xF... | 37 | 841 | 2,000 | *Ass of Interamerican Ev Chs.* M=OMS(USA). Coast.19n,4x,19f,G=17%pa,1h,1s(30),131Y. | | | | |
| Asociación del Iglesias Misioneras | 1945 | P Hol | xF... | 17 | 650 | 1,000 | *Association of Missionary Chs.* M=Missionary Church(USA). 11n,10f,1h,1k,1s. | | | | |
| Hermanos Libres | c1935 | P CBr | x.... | 6 | 365 | 800 | *Brethren Assemblies. Christian Brethren (Open).* M=CMML(USA,UK,NZ). Quito. 20f,1p. | | | | |
| Iglesia Adventista del Séptimo Día | 1905 | P Adv | x.... | 27 | 3,850 | 10,000 | *Seventh-day Adventists, Ecuador Mission,* Inca UM. 9nx,8f,63mw,1H,2h,1r,44t(3640),420Y. | | | | |
| Iglesia Alianza Cristiana y Misionera | 1897 | P Hol | xF... | 56 | 4,924 | 8,000 | *Christian & Missionary Alliance Ch.* M=CMA(USA). 24n,60f,G=7.1%pa,7h,1j,2k,1p,1s. | | | | |
| Iglesia Bautista | 1950 | P Bap | T.... | 53 | 1,281 | 4,000 | *Baptist Ch.* M=SBC(USA). 3,145 in Sunday schools. 40n,32f,G=20%pa,1h,2k,2s,269Y. | | | | |
| Iglesia Católica en el Ecuador: | 1534 | R Lat | BxL,R | 629 | 3,214,500 | 5,843,556 | *Catholic Ch in E.* C=20+2+37. 1q,2s(217). | 1429nx,452m,3165w,166000Yy. | | | |
| M   Cuenca | 1786 | R Lat | Bs | 57 | 264,400 | 480,685 | 10% Indian. 31% urban, increasing rapidly. | 128 | 21 | 299 | 8594 |
| D   Azogues | 1968 | R Lat | Bs | 21 | 79,100 | 143,750 | 50% Indian. 7% urban. In southwest. | 31 | 5 | 96 | 4980 |
| D   Loja | 1862 | R Lat | Bs | 43 | 212,800 | 386,909 | 10% Indian. 10% urban. South, on Peru border. | 80 | 31 | 171 | 15000 |
| D   Machala | 1954 | R Lat | Bs | 20 | 111,000 | 202,000 | 24% urban. Export industry in bananas. | 22 | 4 | 83 | 9712 |
| M   Guayaquil | 1838 | R Lat | Bs | 64 | 666,000 | 1,210,000 | Urban diocese. Major port and commercial centre. | 194 | 17 | 495 | 41500 |
| D   Portoviejo | 1871 | R Lat | Bs | 34 | 330,000 | 600,000 | 80% Mestizo. Banana industry. 6% urban. | 73 | 19 | 155 | 10000 |
| PN Los Ríos | 1948 | R Lat | Bs | 19 | 190,000 | 345,000 | 80% Mestizo. Banana industry. 6% urban. HQ Babahoyo. | 21 | 2 | 12 | 11750 |
| M   Quito | 1545 | R Lat | Bs | 88 | 393,000 | 715,000 | Mainly urban (Quito 565,000). Rural areas Indian. 1s. | 423 | 226 | 1040 | 15000 |
| D   Ambato | 1948 | R Lat | Bs | 42 | 176,600 | 321,090 | 40% Indian. 30% urban: industrialization growing. | 74 | 23 | 142 | 5988 |
| D   Guaranda | 1957 | R Lat | Bs | 19 | 103,000 | 187,000 | 5% Indian. 7% urban. Very small area. | 27 | 0 | 50 | 5400 |
| D   Ibarra | 1862 | R Lat | Bs | 40 | 113,000 | 205,000 | 30% Indian. 5% Black. 17% urban. North. | 72 | 18 | 70 | 7153 |
| D   Latacunga | 1963 | R Lat | Bs | 30 | 129,700 | 235,844 | 35% Indian. 7% urban. Industrialization beginning. | 45 | 3 | 65 | 5660 |
| D   Riobamba | 1863 | R Lat | Bs | 35 | 203,000 | 370,000 | 55% Indian. 14% urban. Major diocesan reforms. | 70 | 9 | 165 | 11005 |
| D   Tulcán | 1965 | R Lat | Bs | 19 | 66,800 | 121,500 | Very few Indians. High literacy. 17% urban. | 29 | 6 | 79 | 3810 |

*Continued opposite*

*Table 2 – continued*

| Official name 1 | Begun 2 | Type 3 | Counc 4 | Congs 5 | Adults 6 | Affiliated 7 | Names, notes, and other statistics (see Codebook) 8 |
|---|---|---|---|---|---|---|---|
| VA Canelos (1976 renamed Puyo) | 1893 | R Lat | Pop | 8 | 8,500 | 15,500 | Amazon (selva oriental; total 200,000 Indians). P=34%. 9 12 15 614 |
| VA Esmeraldas | 1945 | R Lat | Pfscj | 21 | 95,700 | 173,933 | 80% Black; some Cayapas. 30% urban. Bananas. P=13%. 35 9 46 5084 |
| VA Méndez | 1893 | R Lat | Psdb | 11 | 23,000 | 41,000 | Amazon forest. Southeast. On Peru border. P=56%. 34 18 57 1735 |
| VA Napo | 1871 | R Lat | Pcsj | 23 | 19,000 | 35,000 | Amazon. 76% Indian, 24% Mestizo. P=41%. 29 7 67 1320 |
| VA Zamora | 1893 | R Lat | Pofm | 10 | 12,500 | 22,700 | Amazon. Extreme south border. 94% settlers. P=55%. 12 4 19 1395 |
| PA Aguarico | 1953 | R Lat | Pofmc | 5 | 6,400 | 11,745 | Amazon. 70% Indian, rest Mestizo; 18 expatriates. 10 10 15 144 |
| PA Galapagos | 1950 | R Lat | Pofm | 12 | 2,500 | 4,500 | Population 5,000 on 13 islands 600 miles west. P=23%. 4 4 12 69 |
| PA San Miguel de Sucumbíos | 1924 | R Lat | Pocd | 10 | 8,500 | 15,400 | Amazon forest. 69% Indian tribes, 26% Mestizo. P=80%. 7 4 12 75 |
| Iglesia de Cristo Jesús, Misión Ev | 1960 | I pen | ..... | 6 | 125 | 380 | *Ch of Christ Jesus, Ev Mission.* HQ Guayaquil. 4n,G=12%pa,1p(7),W=58%,24Y,16z. |
| Iglesia de JC de los Santos de los UD | 1966 | M LdS | x.... | | 1,000 | 1,668 | *Ch of JC of Latter-day Saints. Mormons.* M=CJCLdS(USA). 30f. |
| Iglesia del Espíritu Santo | 1967 | I pen | ..... | | 254 | 1,000 | *Church of the Holy Spirit.* Small grouping of indigenous pentecostals. |
| Iglesia del Evangelio Cuadrangular | 1953 | P Pe2 | ZF... | 180 | 6,000 | 20,000 | *Int Ch of the Foursquare Gospel.* M=ICFG(USA). 116nm,4f,G=12%pa,1s(90),W=33%,1800Y. |
| Iglesia del Pacto Evangélico en el E | 1947 | P Con | K...C | 17 | 657 | 1,500 | *Ev Covenant Ch.* M=SMCC(Sweden), ECCA(USA). Quito. 6n,2x,27f,G=18%pa,W=30%,78Yy,50z. |
| Iglesia Episcopal: D Ecuador | | A ACa | aw.JC | 6 | 358 | 510 | *Episcopal Ch.* 1966, missionary diocese, PECUSA, Province IX. 1n,3x,W=60%,3Y,10y. |
| Iglesia Evangélica Bereana | 1958 | P int | xM... | 8 | 146 | 400 | *Berean Ev Ch.* M=Berean Mission(USA). Only in Guaranda. Quechuas, 2n,6x,4f,1p,15Y. |
| Iglesia Evangélica Cristo Rey | 1958 | I pen | ..... | 7 | 90 | 5,000 | *Evangelical Ch of Christ the King.* West of Quito. G=10.3%pa,55Y,30z. |
| Iglesia Evangélica del Nazareno | 1972 | P Hol | xF... | 4 | 100 | 400 | *Ch of the Nazarene.* M=CoN(USA). Holiness denomination. 2f. |
| Iglesia Evangélica Luterana | 1953 | P Lut | L...C | 5 | 1,600 | 2,000 | *Ev Lutheran Ch.* Germans, Norwegians, in Quito, Guayaquil, Cuenca. 1x,12f,1p,5Yy. |
| Iglesia Evangélica Unida del Ecuador | 1945 | P uni | ..U.. | 30 | 1,500 | 2,000 | 1965 union UPUSA,PCUS,EUB,UCC,CoB. Indians. 3n,3x,24f,1p(4),1s,105Yy,500z. |
| Iglesia Independiente Nacional | | I pen | ..... | 35 | 3,000 | 6,000 | *National Independent Churches.* Loose grouping of many indigenous congregations. |
| Igl Independiente Universal de Cristo | 1970 | I pen | ..... | | 536 | 1,500 | *Universal Independent Church of Christ.* Large group of indigenous pentecostals. |
| Iglesia La Voz de Jesucristo | | I pen | ..... | 1 | 50 | 100 | *Voice of Jesus Christ Church.* One indigenous pentecostal congregation. |
| Iglesia Ortodoxa | | O Ara | Cwo.. | 1 | 500 | 1,000 | Under Antiochian Orthodox Ch (USA) and Greek P Antioch. Arab Lebanese and Syrians. |
| Iglesia Pentecostal Unida del Ecuador | 1959 | P Pe1 | x.... | 37 | 8,510 | 20,000 | *United Pentecostal Ch. Jesús Solo.* M=UPC(Colombia,USA). 1 school. 25n,4f,1p(35). |
| Iglesia Unión Misionera Ev en el E | 1896 | P Hol | xM... | 200 | 8,000 | 56,000 | M=GMU(USA). Mass movement, 98% Quechua. In Chimburazo. 6n,76f,G=21%pa,2h,1k,1p. |
| Iglesias de Cristo | 1959 | P Dis | x.... | 35 | 1,000 | 2,000 | *Chs of Christ.* 1966, M=CC(Non-Instrumental) (USA). Quito, Guayaquil. 2n,15f,45Y,20z. |
| Iglesias radiofónicas solitarias | 1931 | I rad | ..... | 60 | 1,100 | 2,300 | Isolated radio believers (jungle &c). R=25600(25332 HCJB,Radio Vatican,&c),S=355(ICI). |
| Misión Evangélica Luterana | 1951 | P Lut | l.... | 6 | 92 | 200 | *Ev Lutheran Mission.* M=WMPL(USA). Andean Indians. 1n,1x,1s(5),W=40%,10Yy,14z. |
| Misión Lut Sudamericana de Noruega | 1968 | P Lut | ..... | 6 | 20 | 250 | Lut=Luterana. M=Norwegian Lutheran South American Mission. 3x,W=36%,4Y. |
| Testigos de Jehová | c1930 | M Jeh | x.... | 50 | 3,023 | 12,000 | *Jehovah's Witnesses.* Missionaries began 1947. Use own scriptures. 124m,39f,671Y. |
| Voz de Aclamación | 1971 | M Pe1 | x.... | | 300 | 1,000 | *Branhamites.* M=William Branham Evangelistic Assoc(USA). Jesus-Only Unitarians. |
| World Radio Missionary Fellowship | 1931 | P int | .M... | 14 | 500 | 2,000 | Radio/TV HCJB, Voice of the Andes. 14 churches. M=WRMF(USA,UK). 168f,2H,1h,2r. |
| Other independent indigenous churches | | I sin | ..... | 60 | 2,000 | 4,000 | Total about 30, mostly independent single congregations (non-pentecostal). |
| Other indigenous pentecostal churches | | I pen | ..... | 50 | 1,500 | 3,000 | Total about 30 (see list below), including many single congregations. |
| Other Protestant denominations | | P | ..... | | 1,300 | 3,000 | Total about 20 (see list below). |
| Doubly-affiliated (duplication) (1970) | | | | | –51,200 | –93,064 | Evangelicals who also are or were baptized Roman Catholics. |
| **Total affiliated (mid-1970)** | | | | **1,790** | **3,220,791** | **5,930,600** | **Total denominations (1970) . . . 110.** |
| **Total affiliated (mid-1975)** | | | | **1,990** | **3,787,500** | **6,974,200** | **Total denominations (1975) . . . 120.** |
| **Total affiliated (mid-1980)** | | | | **2,440** | **4,434,700** | **8,165,800** | **Total denominations (1980) . . . 130.** |

NOTES ON TABLE ABOVE
COLUMNS: for meanings and CODES (cols. 1, 3, 4, 8): see Codebook (Part 6). Column 1: **Boldface type** = church with over 10% of country's affiliated Christians.
NATIONAL COUNCILS (Column 4, 5th letter).
C = Confraternidad Evangélica Ecuatoriana (CEE) (Ecuador Evangelical Fellowship).
R = Conferencia Episcopal Ecuatoriana (Ecuador Episcopal Conference).
*Other national councils.* Consejo Evangélico Luterano del Ecuador (CELE), in 1974 renamed Federación de Iglesias Evangélicas Luteranas del Ecuador (FIEL).
OTHER INDIGENOUS PENTECOSTAL CHURCHES. In addition to numerous independent pentecostal single congregations, these include: Iglesia Apostólica del Nombre de Jesús, Iglesia de Dios Pentecostal Trinitaria, Iglesia de Dios (Misión Mundial).
OTHER PROTESTANT DENOMINATIONS. These smaller bodies with congregations include: Alas de Socorro (Missionary Aviation Fellowship), Asambleas de Dios (M=AdD, Brazil), Bethesda Missions, Ch of God (Cleveland) (USA), Ch of the Brethren (1942), Elim Missionary Assemblies (1966), English Fellowship, Ev Methodist Ch (1962), Fellowship of Independent Missions (1967), Free Will Baptist Mission, Iglesia Ev Luterana (Misúri), Mennonite Brethren Ch of NAmerica (1953), Mennonite Ch (1969), Pentecostal Ch of God of America, Slavic Gospel Association (1942), World Baptist Fellowship Mission Agency (1972).

PEOPLES (ethnolinguistic). Christians: 41.8% Quechua, 40.4% Mestizo, 10.0% Ecuadorian White, 5.0% Black, 1.0% Mulatto, 1.0% European (German, Norwegian, USA), 0.1% jungle Amerindian, Syro-Lebanese Arab, Chinese (270).

COUNTRY-WIDE TOTALS
EVANGELIZATION (see Part 5). 1900: 90%. 1970: 100%. 1980: 100%. *Mass evangelism.* Among recent campaigns: 1962, Billy Graham crusade in Quito; 1969–70, Evangelism-in-Depth; 1969, Cruzada de las Américas (Luis Palau) in Quito (10 sponsoring churches, 19,000 attenders, 581 decisions for Christ); 1970, 6-day Hermano Pablo Cruzada Unida (promoted by EAF/EID) in Quito (30,000 attenders, 2,000 enquirers) and Cuenca (6,000 attenders, 2,500 enquirers); 1972, Crusade of the Americas; 1974 Luis Palau 3-week crusade in Quito (3,100 decisions for Christ), beamed live by Radio HCJB throughout South and Central America; 1978, Here's Life Quito (CCCI). *Radiophonic evangelism.* Annual listeners' letters (1975): 25,332 HCJB, 94 FEBC, Radio Vatican, et alia. Radiophonic schools (Catholic): 50,000 enrolled. Bible correspondence courses: ICI (355 active), et alia.
FOREIGN MISSIONARIES AND PERSONNEL (nationals serving abroad) (1973). Total 150 in Colombia and Peru: about 120 Roman Catholics, 20 Protestants and 10 Ecuadorian indigenous.
FOREIGN MISSIONARIES AND PERSONNEL (aliens from abroad) (1973). Total 1,911. *From Western world.* 1,658: 950 Roman Catholics, 636 Protestants (540 in 31 USA societies, 39 in 3 Canada societies, 30 in 1 Norway society, 15 in 1 Sweden society, 8 in 3 UK societies, 2 in 2 Australia societies, 2 in 1 New Zealand society), 69 marginal Protestants (39 Jehovah's Witnesses, 30 Mormons from USA), 3 Anglicans in 1 USA society. By 1975 North American missionaries had increased to 672. *From Communist world.* About 6 Roman Catholics (4 from Yugoslavia, 2 Poland). *From Third World.* 247: 230 Roman Catholics from other Latin American countries, 17 Protestants from Argentina, Brazil, Chile, Colombia, Japan, Korea, Mexico.
INSTITUTIONS (church-operated) (1973). Total 330, including 230 higher schools (11 minor seminaries), 40 medical centres (3 hospitals), 26 radio stations, 5 religious communities (monasteries), 2 research centres, 13 seminaries (10 Protestant, 3 RC), 2 study centres, 2 universities.
PERIODICALS. About 50 titles.
PERSONNEL. About 6,921 (5,010 national, 1,911 foreign).
RELIGIOUS LIBRARIES. About 45.
SCRIPTURE DISTRIBUTION (1975). Annual totals: 51,878 Bibles (42% subsidized, 58% commercial), 142,950 NTs (50% free, 29% subsidized, 21% commercial), 357,642 UBS portions, 1,424,737 UBS selections. *Translations completed.* Portion: 10 languages since 1917. NT: 3 languages since 1954.
SERVICE AGENCIES. About 58, including ACJ, CCCI, CEDOC, CEDUCI, CEE, CEF, CELE, CER, CESA, COC, INVICA, JARS, JUC, MAF, MFC, OMICO, UMAC, WBT (1953,83 missionaries), WGC, WLC(EHC), WRMF(HCJB).

ADDITIONAL DATA ON CHURCHES
IGLESIA CATOLICA EN EL ECUADOR. *Annual baptisms.* (1972) 99.6% infant, 0.4% adult. *Priests.* Nationals: approximately 43% diocesan, 57% religious. Expatriates: approximately 11% diocesan, 89% religious. *Male religious.* 1,564 (76% nationals, 23% from Europe and North America, 0.2% from other Latin American countries). *Brothers.* Approximately 71% nationals, 29% expatriates. *Sisters.* Approximately 82% nationals, 18% expatriates. In addition to those shown in the table, there are numerous contemplative sisters. Total all sisters (1970) 4,145. *Catechists.* Total about 360 (in jurisdictions under Propaganda). *Religious orders and congregations.* Priests (with over 50 members); 170 SDB, 160 SJ, 97 OFM, 64 CSSR, 63 OP, 60 MJ. Brothers (with over 50 professed): 140 FSC. Sisters (with over 150 professed): 668 Hermanas de la Caridad, 302 Marianistas, 296 Dominicanas de Maria Inmaculada, 280 Salesianas, 252 Providencia, 235 Misioneras Franciscanas de la Inmaculada de San Diego, 220 Misioneras Lauritas, 200 Oblatas, 180 Sagrados Corazones. *Catholic organizations.* The Ecuador Episcopal Conference (Conferencia Episcopal Ecuatoriana) is a member of CELAM. The Ecuadorian Conference of Religious Personnel (Conferencia Ecuatoriana de Religiosos, CER), a member of CLAR, caters for both male and female religious. There are no official national pastoral or presbyteral organizations, but a non-official national presbyteral council (Consejo Nacional de Presbíteros del Ecuador) was formed in Quito in 1970 following the first National Convention of Priests of Ecuador, supported by 99 priests and 3 bishops.
Lay movements include the Union of Women for Catholic Action (Unión de Mujeres de Acción Católica); Catholic Action for Girls (Juventud Femenina de AC); Catholic Action for Men (Hombres de Acción Católica); Christian Family Movement (Movimiento Familiar Cristiano); and Legion of Mary (Legión de Maria).
The Holy See has diplomatic relations with Ecuador and is represented to government and the Catholic hierarchy by a nuncio in Quito.
Several non-official progressivist movements are active: 4 groups of priests at Quito (called Equipo de Reflexión), Cuenca, Ambato and Ibarra; a university group at Quito; about 210 small widely-scattered youth groups; and a group of Riobamba priests who have been in open rebellion against their bishop.
Research and social action are carried on by the Centro de Investigación y Acción Social (CIAS), founded by Jesuits in 1962; and by rural co-operatives in the dioceses of Ambato, Guaranda, Ibarra and Riobamba.
Theological training is provided at the Instituto de Ciencias Sagradas, which is part of the Catholic University of Ecuador at Quito; and since 1972 the university, through its School of Philosophy and Pedagogy, has offered specialized courses in catechesis.
The Catholic educational programme in 1970 included 61 kindergartens (2,909 pupils); 944 primary schools (161,724); 369 secondary schools (60,708); and 2 universities (3,200), namely the Pontificia Universidad Católica del Ecuador, founded at Quito in 1946, and another Catholic university at Guayaquil. A third Catholic university, as yet unrecognized by the hierarchy, is being formed at Cuenca. Catholic education accounted for 228,541 of Ecuador's 1,096,275 pupils in 1970. All hospitals belong to government but the Andes mission has recently built some dispensaries.
Caritas del Ecuador is involved in the construction of medium-rental housing through the Instituto Vivienda Cáritas (INVICA). CEDOC is an organization of Christian trade unions, created in opposition to trade unions of Marxist inspiration. The Society of St Vincent de Paul is also active in social work.
IGLESIA EVANGELICA UNIDA DEL ECUADOR. Formerly United Andean Indian Mission (UAIM) from 1945 to 1965, when it united with the Church of the Brethren to form the present church.

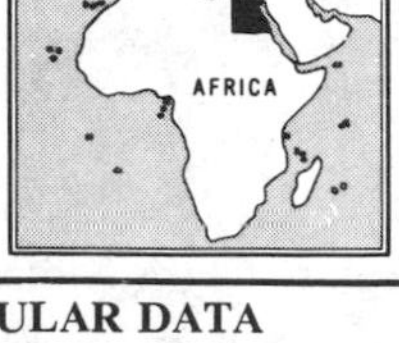


# EGYPT

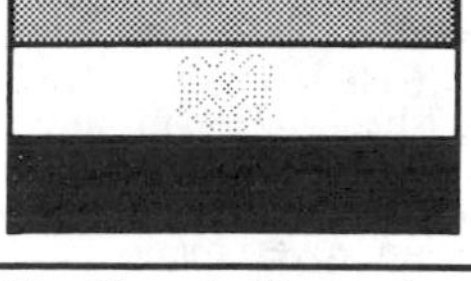

## SECULAR DATA

**STATE. Official name:** The Arab Republic of Egypt (Jumhuriya Misr al-Arabiyah). Adjective of nationality: Egyptian.
**Flag** (shown above right): Red, white, and black stripes, with gold hawk emblem.
**Area:** 1,001,449 sq.km. (386,662 sq.miles). Agricultural land: 2.9%.
**Government:** One-party socialist state, since 1953 (c1200 Turkish rule, 1914 British protectorate, 1922 Independence as constitutional monarchy, 1953 republic, 1958 United Arab Republic, United Arab States).
**Legislature:** National Assembly, 360 members.
**Official language:** Arabic.
**Chief cities:** capital Cairo 8,000,130 (1976), Alexandria 2,318,660, Giza City 1,246,050, Suez 315,000, Port Said 313,000.
**Political divisions:** 2 Districts: Wagh-el-Bahari (Lower Egypt), El-Said (Upper Egypt); 25 Governorates (Muhafazah).
**Armed forces** (1976): Total 342,500 regular: army 295,000, navy 17,500, air force 30,000 (488 combat aircraft). Reserves: 515,000. Paramilitary forces: 120,000.
**Foreign forces** (1973): 20,000 USSR troops and advisers (expelled soon after). (1976) Small detachments of troops from several nations in UNEF.

**DEMOGRAPHY. Population:** 30,075,858 (census of 30.V.1966. For 1970–2000 (UN), see last row of Table 1). Population density (1975): 37/sq.km. (97/sq.mile). Under 15 years: 42%. Growth rate (1975–80): 2.31% per year (births 3.55%, deaths –1.24%). Life expectancy (1975–80): 54.9 years. Household size: 5.2 persons.
**Major languages:** Arabic, English, French, Greek, Russian, Armenian, Nile Nubian (Fiadija, Kenuzi), Siwa and several others.
**Urban dwellers** (1970): 43.5%. Urban growth rate (1950–70): 4.0% per year.
**Labour force:** 28%.
**Refugees** (1977): 12,000 from Lebanon, 4,000 from Ethiopia.
**Tourists** (1971): 428,000 (1974) 679,476.

**ETHNOLINGUISTIC GROUPS:** 86.5% Egyptian Arab, 6.1% other Arab (0.2% Sudanese, 0.2% Yemeni, 0.1% Palestinian (33,000)), 2.0% Arabized Berber, 2.0% Hamitic nomad, 2.0% Muslim Gypsy, 0.8% Nubian, 0.1% Greek, 0.1% Armenian, USSR military (20,000 in 1972), Amhara, Oasis Berber (Siwa), Beja, Indo-Pakistani (2,000), Galla, Italian, French, British, USA, Jewish. Total aliens (1976): 95,300 (0.26%). Total Egyptians resident abroad (1976): 1,425,000 (3.7%).

**MONEY** (1977). **Monetary unit:** pound (= 100 piastres = 1,000 milliemes): US$1 = £E 0.391.
**National income per person:** US$270. Average annual family income: US$1,404.
**Inflation:** (1970–74) 5.0% per year, (1975) 10% per year (consumer price index 139), (1979) 30% per year.
**Cost of living in capital** (1976): index 124 (Washington DC=100).
Daily cost of living: US$39.

**EDUCATION.** Adult literacy: (1947) 20%, (1976) 43%. Education rate: 52%. Schools: 8,838. Universities: 6.

**HEALTH.** Hospitals: 1,418 (73,943 beds). Doctors: 23,501. Lepers: 65,000 (1.7 per 1,000). Blind: 75,000. Psychotics: 260,000.
Drug addicts: numerous (cannabis/hashish). Criminals: 150,000.

**LITERATURE.** Annual new book titles (1972): 2,055. Periodicals: 194. Scientific journals: 70. Newspapers: 14 dailies, 26 non-daily.

**COMMUNICATION** (per 1,000 people). Phones: 13. Radios: 143. TV sets: 16. Daily newspaper circulation: 22 copies.

TABLE 1. RELIGIOUS ADHERENTS IN EGYPT

| Year | 1900 | | mid-1970 | | Annual change, 1970–1980 | | | | mid-1975 | | mid-1980 | | 2000 | |
|---|---|---|---|---|---|---|---|---|---|---|---|---|---|---|
| *Name* | *Adherents* | *%* | *Adherents* | *%* | *Natural* | *Conversion* | *Total* | *Rate* | *Adherents* | *%* | *Adherents* | *%* | *Adherents* | *%* |
| Muslims | 8,514,900 | 81.1 | 27,003,572 | 81.0 | 738,005 | 8,474 | 746,479 | 2.44 | 30,551,310 | 81.4 | 34,468,360 | 81.8 | 53,273,300 | 82.5 |
| Ahmadis | 0 | 0.0 | 1,000 | 0.0 | 28 | 12 | 40 | 3.33 | 1,200 | 0.0 | 1,400 | 0.0 | 3,000 | 0.0 |
| **Christians** | **1,954,000** | **18.6** | **6,193,628** | **18.6** | **140,100** | **–8,079** | **132,021** | **1.93** | **6,844,890** | **18.2** | **7,513,840** | **17.8** | **10,489,700** | **16.2** |
| crypto-Christians | 1,169,000 | 11.1 | 4,000,628 | 12.0 | 94,000 | –2,279 | 91,721 | 2.06 | 4,457,190 | 11.9 | 4,917,840 | 11.7 | 7,129,700 | 11.0 |
| professing | 785,000 | 7.5 | 2,193,000 | 6.6 | 46,100 | –5,800 | 40,300 | 1.69 | 2,387,700 | 6.4 | 2,596,000 | 6.2 | 3,360,000 | 5.2 |
| Orthodox | 690,000 | 6.6 | 2,063,400 | 6.2 | 44,005 | –6,825 | 37,180 | 1.66 | 2,243,000 | 6.0 | 2,435,200 | 5.8 | 3,128,800 | 4.8 |
| Protestants | 19,000 | 0.2 | 62,000 | 0.2 | 1,004 | 596 | 1,600 | 2.30 | 69,500 | 0.2 | 78,000 | 0.2 | 110,000 | 0.2 |
| Roman Catholics | 65,000 | 0.6 | 54,000 | 0.2 | 867 | 333 | 1,200 | 2.00 | 60,000 | 0.2 | 66,000 | 0.2 | 100,000 | 0.2 |
| Arab indigenous | 1,000 | 0.0 | 13,000 | 0.0 | 210 | 90 | 300 | 2.07 | 14,500 | 0.0 | 16,000 | 0.0 | 20,000 | 0.0 |
| Anglicans | 10,000 | 0.1 | 400 | 0.0 | 10 | 0 | 10 | 2.22 | 450 | 0.0 | 500 | 0.0 | 700 | 0.0 |
| Marginal Protestants | 0 | 0.0 | 200 | 0.0 | 4 | 6 | 10 | 4.00 | 250 | 0.0 | 300 | 0.0 | 500 | 0.0 |
| affiliated | 1,954,000 | 18.6 | 6,193,628 | 18.6 | 140,100 | –8,079 | 132,021 | 1.93 | 6,844,890 | 18.2 | 7,513,840 | 17.8 | 10,489,700 | 16.2 |
| total practising | 1,758,600 | *90* | 5,264,580 | *85* | 119,085 | –6,867 | 112,218 | 1.93 | 5,818,160 | *85* | 6,386,760 | *85* | 8,391,760 | *80* |
| non-practising | 195,400 | *10* | 929,050 | *15* | 21,015 | –1,212 | 19,803 | 1.93 | 1,026,730 | *15* | 1,127,080 | *15* | 2,097,940 | *20* |
| Orthodox | 1,800,000 | 17.1 | 5,851,500 | 17.6 | 132,382 | –9,512 | 122,870 | 1.90 | 6,457,400 | 17.2 | 7,080,200 | 16.8 | 9,817,400 | 15.2 |
| Protestants | 40,000 | 0.4 | 158,750 | 0.5 | 3,359 | –234 | 3,125 | 1.80 | 174,000 | 0.5 | 190,000 | 0.5 | 280,000 | 0.4 |
| Evangelicals | 35,000 | 0.3 | 120,000 | 0.4 | 2,539 | –169 | 2,370 | 1.80 | 131,500 | 0.4 | 143,700 | 0.3 | 220,000 | 0.3 |
| Roman Catholics | 100,000 | 1.0 | 139,328 | 0.4 | 2,992 | 75 | 3,067 | 1.98 | 155,000 | 0.4 | 170,000 | 0.4 | 250,000 | 0.4 |
| Arab indigenous | 2,000 | 0.0 | 42,700 | 0.1 | 1,338 | 1,592 | 2,930 | 5.14 | 57,000 | 0.2 | 72,000 | 0.2 | 140,000 | 0.2 |
| Anglicans | 12,000 | 0.1 | 1,000 | 0.0 | 21 | –1 | 20 | 1.82 | 1,100 | 0.0 | 1,200 | 0.0 | 1.700 | 0.0 |
| Marginal Protestants | 0 | 0.0 | 350 | 0.0 | 8 | 1 | 9 | 2.31 | 390 | 0.0 | 440 | 0.0 | 600 | 0.0 |
| Non-religious | 1,000 | 0.0 | 100,000 | 0.3 | 2,583 | –583 | 2,000 | 1.82 | 110,000 | 0.3 | 120,000 | 0.3 | 700,000 | 1.1 |
| Atheists | 0 | 0.0 | 30,000 | 0.1 | 822 | 178 | 1,000 | 2.86 | 35,000 | 0.1 | 40,000 | 0.1 | 120,000 | 0.2 |
| Baha'is | 100 | 0.0 | 1,100 | 0.0 | 30 | 10 | 40 | 3.08 | 1,300 | 0.0 | 1,500 | 0.0 | 5,000 | 0.0 |
| Jews | 30,000 | 0.3 | 700 | 0.0 | –40 | 0 | –40 | –8.00 | 500 | 0.0 | 300 | 0.0 | 0 | 0.0 |
| **Country's population** | **10,500,000** | **100.0** | **33,329,000** | **100.0** | **881,500** | **0** | **881,500** | **2.35** | **37,543,000** | **100.0** | **42,144,000** | **100.0** | **64,588,000** | **100.0** |

COLUMNS, ROWS. For meanings and definitions, see Codebook (Part 6). Note that, by definition, total 'Christians' = professing + crypto-Christians, which also = affiliated + nominal Christians. Percentages may not always total exactly, due to rounding.
CENSUSES. **I.VI.1897:** 92.2% Muslims, 6.09% Coptic Orthodox, 0.6% Roman Catholics (0.05% Coptic), 0.5% other Orthodox (Greek, Oriental), 0.26% Jews, 0.25% Protestants (0.13% Coptic). **29.IV.1907:** 91.8% Muslims, 5.96% Coptic Orthodox, 0.69% Greek Orthodox, 0.65% Roman Catholics (0.13% Coptic), 0.35% Jews, 0.33% Protestants (0.22% Coptic), 0.25% Oriental Orthodox. **1.III.1917:** 91.4% Muslims, 6.74% Orthodox (Coptic, Greek, Oriental), 0.8% Roman Catholics, 0.5% Jews, 0.4% Protestants, 0.1% other Christians. **18.II.1927:** 91.2% Muslims, 6.1% Coptic Orthodox, 0.9% other Orthodox (Greek, Oriental), 0.8% Roman Catholics (0.2% Coptic), 0.5% Protestants, 0.4% Jews. **26.III.1937:** 91.4% Muslims, 8.2% Christians (6.2% Coptic Orthodox, 0.8% Roman Catholics (0.2% Coptic), 0.7% other Orthodox (Greek, Oriental), 0.5% Protestants), 0.4% Jews. **26.III.1947:** 91.7% Muslims, 7.9% Christians (7.1% Coptic Orthodox), 0.3% Jews. **20.IX.1960:** 92.6% Muslims, 7.4% Christians, 0.0% Jews. **31.V.1966:** 93.3% Muslims, 6.7% Christians, 0.0% Jews. **22.XI.1976:** 93.7% Muslims, 6.3% Christians.

NOTES ON RELIGIONS
AFFILIATED CHRISTIANS. The column 'Natural' includes some 21,000 Christian emigrants a year during 1970–80. The column 'Conversion' shows losses to Islam; in the Nile Delta, around 750 baptized Coptic Orthodox are converted to Islam every month.
AHMADIS. Qadianis (world HQ Rabwah, Pakistan), based in Cairo; severely persecuted as heretical; enumerated here under Muslims, although proclaimed non-Muslim by Pakistan.
ANGLICANS. In 1900, almost entirely expatriate British; in 1970, 95% Egyptian Arabs.
ARAB INDIGENOUS. This term describes churches begun by Arabs within the last hundred years, including since 1950 isolated radio believers in radio churches; in 12 denominations in 1970 (see Table 2).
ATHEISTS. No legal or organized communist party, but numerous intellectuals are atheists, as well as expatriates, USSR military, et alii.
BAHA'IS. Reached Egypt before 1892. Banned by decree 1960, severe persecution; in 1964, only 13 local spiritual assemblies.
CRYPTO-CHRISTIANS. Affiliated Christians claimed by the churches have always been over twice the size of Christians as enumerated in government censuses. The reason advanced in this survey is that due to Muslim pressure on the Christian minority many Christians are recorded, or record themselves, in censuses as Muslims; in this survey we term them crypto-Christians.
JEWS. Rapid emigration since 1957 has almost completely removed the Jewish community, which in 1950 numbered 75,000 (of whom 5,000 were Egyptian citizens, 30,000 aliens from France, Italy, UK or Germany, and 40,000 stateless).
MUSLIMS. The numbers in the table above are lower than those in the censuses; the difference is due to crypto-Christians, namely persons considered as Muslims by the state but who are at the same time affiliated to churches. Muslims in Egypt are all Sunnis (of the Shafiite and Malikite rites in Upper Egypt, or the Hanafite rite in Lower Egypt). There are also about 2,000 Asians (Indo-Pakistanis and others), and a very small persecuted Ahmadiya minority based in Cairo. *Hajj pilgrims to Mecca.* (1968) 7,134; (1969) 10,875; (1970) 11,490; (1971) 29,171; (1972) 39,606; (1973) 36,452; (1974) 89,617; (1975) 51,230; (1976) 28,045.
NON-RELIGIOUS. In 1900, all expatriate Europeans; in 1970–75, French, British and other European expatriates, and USSR military.
ORTHODOX. From a few thousand in 1900, Greek Orthodox increased rapidly in 2 waves of immigration to 100,000 by 1915, almost all retaining Greek nationality. After 1955, ten of thousands of Orthodox of Lebanese or Syrian origin emigrated to Lebanon; Greek Orthodox were reduced from 150,000 in 1930 to 80,000 in 1953 and to 30,000 by 1970.
PRACTISING CHRISTIANS. A sociological survey in 1960 under the auspices of the Coptic Orthodox Church found the following attendances in Cairo (among the 1 million Orthodox there) at liturgical services (excluding all other ancillary services and activities): 10% of all adults attended weekly, about 30% (total) monthly, and 80% (total) attend from time to time during the year, especially on festivals. In Upper Egypt, especially around Luxor, the figures are higher: about 85% attend from time to time. These percentages have risen slightly since 1960 with the relaxing of pressures against Christians.
PROFESSING CHRISTIANS. In AD 640, Christianity was the religion of Egypt, and Coptic Christians were estimated at about 3 million in 100 dioceses in Egypt, with 200,000 Chalcedonians (Greek Orthodox). After the rise of Islam these numbers were continuously eroded to 10% of the population by 1400, until professing Christians numbered only 160,000 in 1800, and 100,000 in 1820, Thereafter, as active persecution receded, the numbers of professing Christians increased rapidly to 785,000 in 1900. *Annual increase.* In 1975, biological increase (births minus deaths) among professing Christians was about 56,100; but since around 10,000 professing Christians were emigrating each year (3,000 a year to Australia in 1969), the nett increase in the 'Natural' column was only 46,100 a year. In addition, about 5,800 professing Christians a year were being converted to Islam, mostly through mixed marriages or the need for divorce, or the need to obtain employment or government posts.

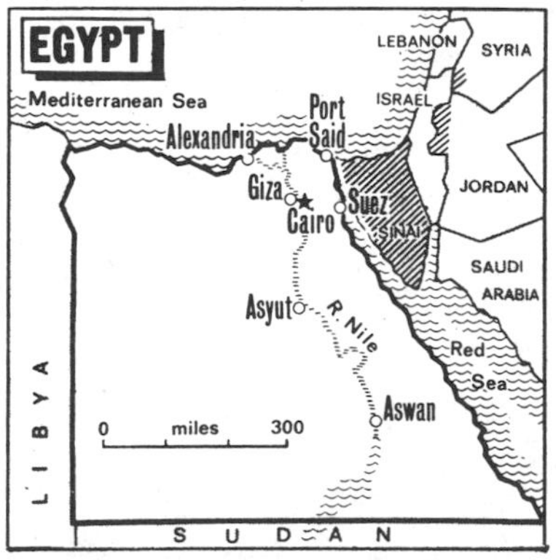


**NON-CHRISTIAN RELIGIONS. Islam** was established in Egypt in the 7th century. Egyptian Muslims are Sunnis of the Shafiite, Hanafite and Malikite rites. Since the revolution of 1952, successive Egyptian governments have contributed significantly to the renewal of Islam both internally and internationally, making Egypt the major world centre for modern Islam. Several important Islamic institutions have been created or reformed, among them the following. (1) The Supreme Council for Islamic Affairs (Al-Majlis al-Ala li al-Shu'un al-Islamiya) was founded in 1960, with the purpose of extending Islamic culture in Egypt and overseas. Between 1960 and 1970, the council has edited and distributed, often gratuitously, 8 million copies of works on Islamic culture in 14 languages, mostly African and Asian. It also edits a journal and a large number of pamphlets dealing with the Quran and the call to prayer. It makes financial grants for the construction of mosques and Islamic institutes throughout the world as well as scholarships for foreign students studying in Egypt. (2) The Council for Islamic Studies, founded in 1961, aims 'to re-activate Islamic culture, to purify it of all sectarian or political fanaticism, and to offer advice and counsel regarding religious and social problems in conformity with Islamic doctrine'. (3) The University of Al-Azhar was founded in AD 973, and, after a complete reorganization by the government in 1961, has become a vast complex consisting of: (a) the Supreme Council of Azhar; (b) the Academy for Islamic Research (Majma' al-Buhuth al-Islamiya), administered jointly with the Council for Islamic Studies; (c) a Department of Culture and Islamic Missions; (d) a number of other Azharian institutes; and (e) the university itself. In addition to its traditional faculties of religion, there are now secular faculties and a faculty for Muslim young women. Azhar also administers a large complex dedicated to Muslim missions (Madinat al-Buhuth al-Islamiya), consisting of facilities for training 5,000 foreign students and from which numerous missionaries are sent to various countries of Africa, Asia and, more recently, Latin America. (4) Other institutions include Quran House (Dar al-Qur'an) which distributes the Quran; Radio Cairo, which broadcasts daily Muslim religious programmes to listeners in many foreign countries; the Halabi Press which publishes the Quran and other religious books in Arabic, French, English and several African languages; and such international journals as *Liwa al-Islam* (Islamic Standard) and *Minbar*

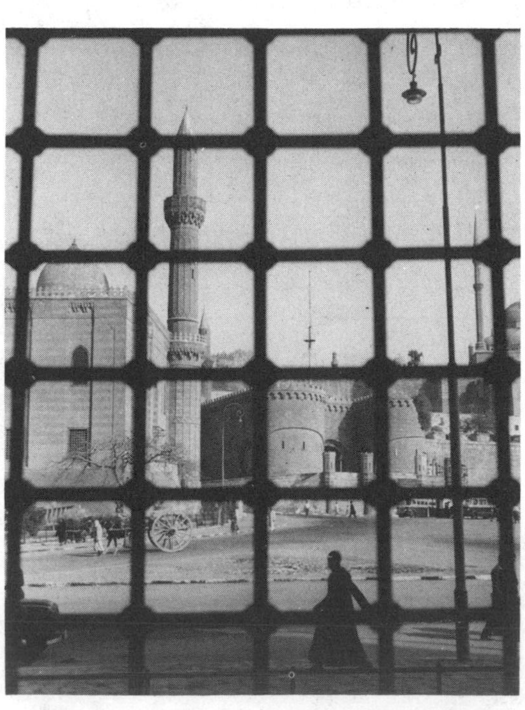

**Muslims.** Citadel, Cairo, with minarets of mosques, seen through window of Medersah of Sultan Hassan.

*al-Islam* (Islamic Tribune), the Muslim cultural journal published by the Supreme Council for Islamic Affairs; and, finally, the Egyptian Institute of Islamic Studies in Madrid, Spain, which is supported financially by the Egyptian government.

**Baha'i** has had a long history in Egypt going back to 1892, but has been subject to both governmental ban and severe popular persecution.

**Judaism** has been reduced to less than 500 persons, since the exodus of 75,000 Jews from 1950 onwards.

**CHRISTIANITY.** Christianity came to Egypt during the 1st century AD, when tradition states that St Mark was the founder of the church of Alexandria. In the following centuries many important Christian movements were begun there: the catechetical school of Pantaenus and Origen (2nd and 3rd centuries), monasticism under the anchorite Anthony (4th century), the Arian-Athanasian controversy (4th century), Cyril's opposition to Nestorianism (5th century) and the controversy over the nature of Christ which came to a head at the Council of Chalcedon in 451. Monophysitism grew in strength in Egypt, with the term Melkite being given to those Christians who accepted the dogmatic decisions of Chalcedon. By 639 the overwhelming majority of Christians had accepted the Monophysite position, and this remains the official stance of the Coptic Orthodox Church. Massive conversions to Islam took place during the following 5 centuries, in part the result of opposition to the Byzantine administration. During the 17th century Capuchins and Jesuits opened Catholic work in Egypt, followed later by the formation of several Uniate Catholic churches. The first Protestant missionaries, Presbyterians from the USA, began work in 1854.

The Christian churches today are faced with 2 major problems: conversions to Islam, and emigration. The conversion of Christians to Islam is most evident among Coptic Orthodox, who lose 7,000 professing members every year. The principal reasons for these conversions are the difficulties encountered by non-Muslims in finding employment, the desire to obtain posts in the administration, problems associated with mixed marriages (a Muslim woman is not allowed to marry a non-Muslim man), and the possibility of obtaining a divorce in cases where the churches will not give permission. The second problem is emigration, which has until recently affected mostly the other churches but is now a major factor for Coptic Orthodox also, as evidenced by the formation of new Coptic Orthodox parishes in Lebanon, Canada, the USA, and Australia. Some Christian communities have lost more than half their members and some, such as the Greek Orthodox, Armenian Catholics, Chaldeans and Syrians are rapidly disappearing. Among Catholics, information supplied by bishops lists the following estimated losses: Syrians, 3,000 in 7 years (1963–70); Armenians, more than 2,000 in 10 years (1960–70); Copts, 2,000 in the last years of the 1960s, largely through emigration to Canada; Latins, 4,780 (mostly Europeans) in the diocese of Heliopolis alone between 1960 and 1970. All Catholic parishes in the region of the Suez Canal were abandoned following the Arab-Israeli war of 1967, although by 1974 these had been re-occupied.

The Christian community of Egypt remains by far the most important numerically in the entire Arab world. Egyptian Christians emphasize the fact that they are the purest descendants of the Egyptians of Pharaonic times, the term Copt being an Arabic deformation of the Greek world for Egyptian.

Although coexistence between Christians and Muslims in terms of domicile and work seems to function reasonably well in the cities, in villages the 2 groups live in separate residential quarters and have few contacts with one another. Christians display considerable fear of being absorbed by the Muslim masses.

ORTHODOX CHURCHES. The Coptic Orthodox Church is numerically the most important national church in the Near East. According to tradition the church was founded through the preaching of St Mark in AD 42. The Copts have always contested government statistics of their membership, which were listed as only 2.3 million in 1976, the last year that official statistics were published. Coptic Orthodox estimates for 1975, based on carefully-kept membership lists, were about 6.6 million. As Table 1 indicates, this implies a large crypto-Christian community of over 4 million.

The Coptic Orthodox Church is characterized by a strong monastic trait. All its bishops are former

**Coptic Orthodox Church.** *Above.* Deir El-Sourian monastery in Western desert.
**Church of Sinai: AD Mount Sinai.** *Inset.* State postage stamp (1966) commemorating 14th centenary of St Catherine's Monastery.

monks, and its laity are also influenced by monasticism. Cases of Coptic university students losing their faith are rare. The church has experienced a marked renaissance over the past few years, due principally to lay initiatives. Evidences of renewal are as follows. (1) Church schools have arisen offering courses in the catechism on Fridays (the Egyptian day of rest) to pre-school children and those frequenting government schools deficient in religious instruction. (2) Large numbers of new monastic vocations to the desert monasteries have occurred among young people; these have been especially numerous for Wadi El-Natroun (Nitrie Valley). Monastic life has also been re-established for the first time in 1,300 years in Wadi El-Bayyan, 40 kilometres from Fayyum. (3) There has been a marked flowering of religious literature, dealing especially with spirituality. Of particular significance, and illustrative of these various tendencies, is the existence in Cairo of the House of Consecration for the Service of Preaching of St Mark (Bait al-Takris li Khidmat al-Kiraza al-Marqusiya), where laymen, some dedicated to celibacy, live in common and engage in the work of the apostolate, at the same time supporting themselves. It is also a centre for religious literature. This initiative and many others are due largely to Matta El-Meskin, a lay monk who has exercised a profound influence on Coptic youth. Parish clergy are for the most part married and are recruited according to local needs. Priests are often deficient in educational background, but the Holy Synod decided in 1959 that in future only seminary graduates would be ordained. Coptic seminaries train both priests and preachers, the latter either retaining their lay status or becoming deacons. During recent years, a number of university graduates have become priests. In August 1970, a professor of Cairo University faculty of sciences was ordained, which provoked unfavourable comment in the Egyptian press and forced him to offer his resignation. This the university refused to accept, and thus for the first time in its history Cairo University had on its teaching staff a Coptic Orthodox priest.

The Greek Orthodox Church has never been a properly indigenous movement, and the Greek population has declined markedly in recent years. Nevertheless, the Alexandrian Patriarchate enjoys a prestige in the world-wide Byzantine community second only to that of the Ecumenical Patriarchate. Armenian Orthodox are administratively related to the Catholicate of Echmiadzin (in Soviet Armenia) and not to that of Sis (Antelias in Lebanon). There were at one time 3 times as many Armenians in Egypt as now, but their numbers have been drastically reduced by emigration in recent years. Syrian Orthodox once composed a flourishing community in Egypt with a bishop in Cairo until recently, but they also have been reduced by emigration to 50 families most of whom reside in Cairo.

CATHOLIC CHURCH. Catholicism in Egypt is the most liturgically diverse of any country in the world; it is divided into 7 communities, each of which worships according to its own rite and serves its own ethnic group, as follows. (1) Coptic Catholics are native Egyptians and form the largest community. United with Rome since the 18th century, their principal centres are the Faggalah quarter of Cairo, the suburbs of Heliopolis and the cities of Minia, Tahta and Luzor in Upper Egypt. They also operate a number of schools in the south and in Cairo, as well as seminaries in Maadi and Giza. They are the only Egyptian Catholic community which is expanding numerically at the present time. (2) Greek Catholic Melkites are a small community whose original background was Syrian, Lebanese or Palestinian. There are several schools and colleges in Cairo, Heliopolis and Alexandria. (3) Maronites are from a background in Lebanon, where the Maronite patriarch now resides. Churches are found in Shubra, Daher and Heliopolis, and schools in the 2 latter cities. (4) Syrian Catholics have churches and schools in Daher and Heliopolis. (5) Armenian-rite Catholics are of Armenian extraction, the remnants of a once sizeable community. (6) Chaldeans form the smallest Catholic community and are centred in Heliopolis. They are of distant Iraqi origin. (7) Latin-rite Catholics are mostly foreign, especially Italians. They have very few parishes but their missionary service through education, study, research, and medical and social services is noteworthy, some of it dating back more than a century. The existence of these 7 communities makes Egypt the only country in the world where most major Catholic rites and sub-rites coexist. A large number of these Catholics are Egyptians by birth or nationality which nevertheless does not prevent the Catholic Church from being considered a foreign body.

The church has 260 worship places, of which over 70 are in Cairo spread in 26 different quarters of which Shubra and Heliopolis have the most dense population. Half are Coptic centres in 98 cities and villages in Upper Egypt.

OTHER CHURCHES. Moravians from Europe undertook a mission to Copts in the 18th century but later withdrew. The Church Missionary Society arrived in 1818, also attempting to work with the Coptic Orthodox Church, but had little success. Anglicans have been a separate denomination since 1882, part of the former Jerusalem Archbishopric.

The strongest Protestant Church in the Middle East is the Coptic Evangelical Church, which was begun by 3 American Presbyterian missionaries in 1854. Drawing its membership mostly from nominally Orthodox Copts, the church has grown rapidly. By 1899 there were 4 presbyteries, and 7 by 1972. Originally part of the United Presbyterian Church of North America, the church has been autonomous since 1957. It continues to carry on extensive medical and educational programmes.

The Christian Brethren are a large independent body which split from the Coptic Evangelical Church in 1869 and since that time have been entirely under

Egyptian leadership. Several Holiness missions entered Egypt before the turn of the century and are responsible for the establishment of 2 churches, Faith Church and the larger Free Methodist Church. Adventist and Pentecostal communities also owe their origin to this period. Small Greek and Armenian Protestant denominations exist as well but are declining rapidly due to emigration.

official report of 28 November, the commission, without placing the responsibility for the incident on one or the other party, mentioned among the various causes of unrest the 1934 law dealing with the construction of churches, which it considered unconstitutional. This law imposed 10 conditions for obtaining permission to construct a Christian church, one of which required that no mosque exist in the

religion is often taught by teachers who lack competence and, although nominally Christians, are indifferent to religion. In public and private schools, beginning with the 5th year of primary education, all teachers of Arabic must be Muslims.

There exists at the Ministry of Waqfs (religious trusts) a section which is responsible for religious and ecclesiastical affairs. Church representatives related to this ministry are: for the Oriental churches (Catholic and Orthodox) their respective patriarchs, for Latin Catholics the apostolic pro-nuncio, for Egyptian Protestants the community council (Majlis Milli). Churches are required to register with government, which sometimes refuses such requests, as has been the case with Jehovah's Witnesses. Churches do not pay taxes; neither do priests or nuns whether nationals or expatriates, for although religious workers require work permits they are not classed as salaried workers.

In early 1977 there occurred a nation-wide buildup of anti-Coptic incidents, attacks on priests and stonings of bishops, at least some of which appear to have been organized with the knowledge of Al Azhar University. After a visit by pope Shenouda to president Sadat and a televised confrontation with Muslim leaders, Shenouda won widespread support for a policy of coexistence towards the Christian minority. By mid-year, however, the situation had worsened with the government's determination, under pressure from militant Islamic nations, to introduce harsh Islamic law including amputation of hands for theft and the death penalty for apostasy from Islam.

A more conciliatory note was struck in November 1977 by the 13th Islamic World Congress, held in Cairo, which resolved to stop all attempts at converting Christians living in Muslim countries, largely as a result of the better relationships of Western European countries towards their Muslim immigrant communities.

Coptic Orthodox Church. *Left.* Bishops, priests, nuns, laity and guests at 1965 foundation stone ceremony for new St Mark's cathedral in Cairo. *Centre.* St Mark's Cathedral, Cairo, after completion, with (right) the Parish Church of SS Peter & Paul. *Top, inset.* Bishop Yohannes of Al Gharbiyah-Tanta (rear centre) leaves Cairo cathedral after service, preceded (foreground) by priests (in black) and deacons (in white).

**CHURCH AND STATE.** The constitution of the Arab Republic of Egypt promulgated in September 1971 displays a more pronounced religious and Islamic character than the constitution of 1956. Numerous references to religion are made in the 'Act of Proclamation of the Constitution' (preamble). Article 2 of the new constitution declares that 'Islam is the religion of the State and Arabic its official language; the principles of Islamic law constitute a major source for legislation'. Article 46 stipulates that 'The State guarantees freedom of belief and religious practice'. Moreover, religion is, along with ethics and patriotism, one of the foundations of the family (Article 9). Society 'should assure the maintenance of a high level of religious education' (Article 12), this latter being a 'principal element in programmes of general education' (Article 19).

Although the constitution declares that 'All citizens are equal before the law. . . without distinction of race, origin, language, religion or belief' (Article 40), it is the case that Egyptian Christians are victims of non-official discrimination in numerous sectors of social and political life. Hardly any high government functionaries are Christians; in the army, Coptic officers never go beyond the grade of captain or commandant and are often retired prematurely. This situation is not so much due to government policy as to the Muslim mentality, which without being hostile to non-Muslims is unable to place them on the same level of equality with Muslims.

It is strictly forbidden to all churches to proselytize among Muslims, but under certain conditions it is possible for Muslims to become Christians as well as for Christians to become Muslims. Concerning worship itself, freedom is in general assured, although Copts have sometimes encountered difficulties in obtaining the necessary permission from the president of the republic for the construction of churches. Between 1971 and the end of 1972 a number of incidents of conflict occurred between Copts and Muslims. On 13 November 1972, the day following the burning of the Coptic Orthodox Church of Khanka (a suburb of Cairo), president Sadat appointed a parliamentary commission of investigation composed of 3 Muslims and 3 Copts. In its

Assemblies of God in Egypt. Men's side of assembly during Good News Crusade in Cairo, 1974; women's side at left. About 90% are former Copts.

neighbourhood. The result is that advantage is often taken of administrative delays and a mosque is rapidly constructed near the terrain chosen for the construction of a church, which in turn encourages Copts to open worship centres without prior authorization.

The policy of president Sadat which systematically favours elements of traditional and religious law tends to encourage rightist forces which are difficult to control. Among the principal beneficiaries of this political reorientation are the Muslim Brotherhood who were kept in check by the Nasser regime but have since reorganized themselves in semi-clandestine groups for the purpose of combatting leftist forces, notably those in university circles. However, since 1973 the Coptic Orthodox Church has had an agreement with president Sadat on the procedure for opening new churches. The church prepares each year a list of up to 50 new church buildings needed and presents it to the minister of the interior, who then approves. By 1975, 50 a year were in fact being opened.

Religious teaching, Muslim or Christian, is provided for in all government and private schools. Between the 4th year of primary and the 2nd year of secondary education, students must obtain a grade of 55% in this subject. In government schools, the Christian

**INTERDENOMINATIONAL ORGANIZATIONS.** Ecumenical relationships in Egypt are complex and are promoted by a number of diverse organizations. Before the 1956 Suez war, almost all Protestant missions co-operated through the Egypt Inter-Mission Council, but with the expulsion of many missionaries this ceased to function. There is no national council of churches, but there is a de facto council for practical co-operation, the Ecumenical Advisory Council for Church Service in Egypt (EACCSE), with representation from Orthodox, Catholic and Protestant churches. The council deals primarily with the distribution of inter-church aid and scholarships. It works in close co-operation with government through the Joint Committee for the Co-ordination of Services and Aid to Displaced Persons and Victims of Aggression, with 5 government members and 5 representatives from the churches; and the Commission on Christian Religious Tourism which handles the visits of Christians to the republic and furnishes information to visitors regarding Christian worship services. Protestants and Anglicans, and Coptic, Greek and Syrian Orthodox co-operate in the Middle East Council of Churches which was founded in 1927 as the NECC and renamed MECC in 1974; it has its headquarters in Beirut, Lebanon. It carries on a variety of services, with an especially fine film library and audio-visual programmes which are widely used by all the churches including Catholics. A more conservative Protestant organization is the Evangelical Fellowship of Egypt which was formed in 1966 and now has 7 members, some very small in size. The Association for Theological Education in the Near East (ATENE) has since 1967 attempted to provide opportunities for contacts between the various theological faculties of the region. In Cairo the Coptic Orthodox, Coptic Evangelical, and Coptic and Franciscan Catholic seminaries are members. Although the Upper Egypt Christian Association for Schools and Social Services was founded by Catholics in 1941, 4 Coptic Orthodox were added to its administrative council in 1972; and this is now a fully interdenominational organization. There are also local inter-confessional pastoral committees (such as the Council of Churches in Alexandria) which sponsor the Week of Prayer for Christian Unity annually in January.

**BROADCASTING.** The state Broadcasting and TV Corporation permits a regular 45-minute Orthodox (or Evangelical) church service every Sunday, and longer broadcasts at Christmas. From abroad, Christian programmes in Arabic are beamed in by Radio Vatican (3 hours 30 minutes a week), Trans

World Radio (Monaco and Cyprus) for 4 hours a week, RVOG (Ethiopia) for 90 minutes daily (until 1977), FEBA (Seychelles) and ELWA (Liberia). For 15 years prior to the military coup in Ethiopia in 1974, the Coptic Orthodox Church was allowed a one-hour broadcast in Arabic every Sunday over the state radio. After this was banned by the new regime, the Church changed to broadcasts over RVOG, until it in turn was seized. Listeners' letters have been received for years from Yemen, Saudi Arabia, and other closed Muslim lands.

## BIBLIOGRAPHY


*A lonely minority: the modern stage of Egypt's Copts.* E. Waker. New York: Moscow, 1963.

*Annuaire Catholique d'Egypte, 1973.* Cairo: Nonciature Apostolique, 1973.

*Christian Egypt, ancient and modern.* O. F. A. Meinardus. Cairo: American University Press, 1965. 2nd edition, 1976. 680p.

*Christian Egypt, faith and life.* O. F. A. Meinardus. Cairo: American University Press, 1970. 513p.

*Christianity in Egypt: a cultural history to 1171 AD.* C. C. Walters. London: Brill, 1978.

*Histoire de l'Eglise Copte.* M. Roncaglia. Beirut: Dar Al-Kalima, 1966— (to 6 vols).

*Pagan and Christian Egypt: Egyptian art from the 1st to the 10th century AD.* J. D. Cooney. London: Brill, 1969 (first edition 1941). 200p.

*Saint and Sufi in modern Egypt.* M. Gilsenan. New York: Oxford University Press, 1973.

*St Mark and the Coptic Church.* Cairo: Coptic Orthodox Patriarchate, 1968. 164p.

'The Coptic Church and social change in Egypt', M. M. Assad, *International review of mission*, LXI, 242 (April, 1972), 117–129.

*The Copts through the ages.* Bishop Athanasius of Beni-Suef and Bahnasa. Cairo: State Information Service, 1973 (3rd edition).

*The story of the Coptic Church of Egypt, established by St Mark.* I. Habib el-Masry. Cairo: Coptic Orthodox Patriarchate, 1978. 400p. (Translation from 4-volume Arabic version. History, up to 1970).


TABLE 2. ORGANIZED CHURCHES AND DENOMINATIONS IN EGYPT

| Official name 1 | Begun 2 | Type 3 | Counc 4 | Congs 5 | Adults 6 | Affiliated 7 | Names, notes, and other statistics (see Codebook) 8 |
|---|---|---|---|---|---|---|---|
| Armenian Apostolic Church: AD Cairo | 553 | O Arm | Ew..K | 5 | 10,000 | 20,000 | Begun 1250 with 70,000 Armenian slaves at Sohag. Rapid emigration. 1j. |
| Armenian Evangelical Church | 1896 | P Con | .T... | 1 | 200 | 500 | Congregation in Alexandria. Split ex Union of AEC. Armenians. |
| Assemblies of God in Egypt | 1907 | P Pe2 | ZF..C | 144 | 11,784 | 20,000 | 1910, Asyut work; 1,100 orphans. M=AoG(USA). 90% former Copts. 65n,5f,1h,1s(20). |
| Catholic Church in Egypt: | 1219 | R LEr | O.S.S | 260 | 80,800 | 139,328 | *Al-Kanissa al-Katholikia.* C=10+1+31,162x,1h,2q,1s(17). 398nx,121m,1453w,1952Yy. |
| P Al Iskandariya (Alexandria) | 1895 | R Cop | Os | 30 | 23,500 | 40,000 | Egyptians of Coptic rite. Patriarch lives in Cairo. 2s. 54 0 74 65 |
| D Al Minya (Ermopoli Maggoire) | 1896 | R Cop | Os | 36 | 10,400 | 18,000 | Egyptians (Copts). 19 schools, 7 institutes. 33 2 68 366 |
| D Asyut (Lycopolis) | 1947 | R Cop | Os | 44 | 15,700 | 27,000 | Coptic dioceses are the only expanding Catholic ones. 38 1 45 961 |
| D Thebes (Luxor) (Tahta) | 1895 | R Cop | Os | 65 | 12,800 | 22,000 | Egyptians (Copts). 30 schools (6,905 pupils). 5H,13h. 40 5 165 350 |
| P Al Iskandariya (Alexandria) | 1772 | R Mel | Os | 15 | 4,700 | 8,200 | Egyptians of Melkite rite under VP Egypt & Sudan. 21 0 11 94 |
| D Al Iskandariya | 1885 | R Arm | Os | 3 | 1,000 | 1,750 | Armenians in P Cilicia (Lebanon). Rapid emigration. 1r. 4 0 6 3 |
| D Al Qahirah (Cairo) | 1946 | R Mar | Os | 13 | 4,600 | 8,000 | Egyptian Lebanese of Maronite rite (P Antioch). 12x,2r. 14 0 28 32 |
| VP Al Qahirah (Cairo) | 1970 | R Cha | Os | 3 | 300 | 525 | Egyptian Chaldean-rite Iraqis under P Babylon. Bishop. 1 0 0 0 |
| VP Al Qahirah (Egypt & Sudan) | 1965 | R Syr | Os | 4 | 1,600 | 2,700 | Egyptians of Syrian rite. Under P Antioch (Lebanon). 5 0 4 20 |
| VA Al Iskandariya of Egypt (*Latin*) | 1839 | R Lat | Oofm | 35 | 5,300 | 9,115 | Europeans of Latin rite, mostly Italians. 1n. 117 84 639 32 |
| VA Bur Sa'id (Port Said) (*Latin*) | 1926 | R Lat | Oofm | 6 | 50 | 80 | Lost all members 1967; administered by VA Alexandria. 3 0 17 0 |
| VA Heliopolis of Egypt (*Latin*) | 1886 | R Lat | Osma | 6 | 1,100 | 1,958 | Latins. 24 parish clergy, 48 in schools. 3n. 68 29 396 29 |
| Christian Brethren (Exclusive) | 1869 | I EBr | x.... | 165 | 10,000 | 20,000 | Schism ex American M (Coptic Ev Ch), now large Egyptian-run denomination. |
| Christian Brethren (Open) | 1878 | P CBr | x.... | 40 | 1,500 | 2,500 | *Open Brethren. Plymouth Brethren.* M=CMML(UK). 20 assemblies in Upper Egypt. 5m. |
| Church of Christ, Scientist | | M Sci | x.... | 1 | 30 | 50 | *Christian Science.* M=CCS(Boston,USA). In Cairo. |
| Church of God | 1907 | P Hol | x...d | 15 | 300 | 800 | In Asyut; Cairo, Alexandria. Linked with Faith Ch. M=CoG(Anderson) (USA). 7n,W=99%. |
| Church of Sinai: AD Mount Sinai | c 200 | O Ara | Cw... | 1 | 250 | 900 | *St Catherine's Monastery*, begun 537. Autonomous, under Greek P Jerusalem. 28 monks. |
| Coptic Evangelical Church | 1854 | P Ref | RWANK | 270 | 30,000 | 100,000 | 7 Presbyteries. M=UPUSA. A=1958. 95% former Coptic Orthodox. 200n,98m,19f,2H,10r,1s. |
| **Coptic Orthodox Church:** | 30 | O Cop | NWANK | 1,933 | 3,367,000 | 5,800,000 | *Al-Kanisah al-Kebtiah al-Orthodoxiah.* 9d(380),5e(200),1500n,P=85%,5s(200),W=20%. |
| P Al Iskandariya (Alexandria) | 42 | O Cop | Np | 180 | 290,000 | 500,000 | Traditional base of pope/patriarch of Alexandria, though HQ in Cairo. 27 churches. |
| D Al Qahirah (Cairo) | 356 | O Cop | Np | 320 | 522,000 | 900,000 | Under patriarch as bishop. Many Coptic institutions. 2e,P=82%,4s(Cairo),W=10%. |
| D Abu Tig, Tima & Tahta | c 330 | O Cop | Nb | 35 | 70,000 | 120,000 | *Iparshia Abu Tij.* Upper Egypt. Bishop lives in Abu Tig, 10 km south of Asyut. |
| D Akhmim & Saqulta | c 350 | O Cop | Nb | 4 | 9,000 | 16,000 | *Iparshia Akhmim wa Saqulta.* Smallest diocese, also one of poorest financially. |
| D Al Balyana | c 850 | O Cop | Nb | 5 | 12,000 | 20,000 | Bishop in Al Balyana, Upper Egypt; small diocese, south of Girga. |
| D Al Fayyum (Fayoum) | c 320 | O Cop | Nb | 35 | 70,000 | 120,000 | Upper Egypt. Noted for ancient pilgrimage church, Al Azab. Rich diocese. |
| D Al Gharbiyah | c 270 | O Cop | Nb | 20 | 35,000 | 60,000 | Bishop in Tanta, between 2 branches of Nile. Extensive textile industries. |
| D Al Jizah (Giza) | c 350 | O Cop | Nb | 180 | 350,000 | 600,000 | Area of Pyramids, Sphinx. 15 new parish churches built since 1960. Rich diocese. |
| D Al Minufiyah (Menoufia) | 1150 | O Cop | Nb | 35 | 70,000 | 120,000 | Bishop in Shibinel-Kom. Province of Al Manufiyah, north of Cairo between Nile. |
| D Al Minya & Ashmunayn | c 850 | O Cop | Nb | 250 | 406,000 | 700,000 | Upper Egypt. Largest diocese in area, many Coptic activities. 1976, divided into 3. |
| D Al Uqsur (Luxor), Isna, Aswan | c 350 | O Cop | Nb | 35 | 72,000 | 124,000 | Upper Egypt: pharaohs' tombs, Aswan high dam, steel industry. 1975, divided into 2. |
| D Asyut (Assyout) | c 230 | O Cop | Nb | 150 | 290,000 | 500,000 | Upper Egypt. Youth work in University of Asyut. Many Protestant activities. |
| D Bani Suwayf & Bahnasa | c 340 | O Cop | Nb | 120 | 232,000 | 400,000 | Bani Suwayf, in Upper Egypt. Youth work, home industries. 2 retreat houses. Rich. |
| D Buhayrah (Behera, The Lake) | c 270 | O Cop | Nb | 50 | 64,000 | 110,000 | Includes Mudiriyat Al-Tahrir (Liberation Province reclaimed from desert), and North Africa. |
| D Dairut & Sanabu | c 350 | O Cop | Nb | 25 | 46,000 | 80,000 | Upper Egypt. Small diocese north of Manfalut. One small monastery. |
| D Daqahliya (Dakahlia) | 1925 | O Cop | Nb | 35 | 70,000 | 120,000 | Bishop in Mensurah, on Nile near sea. Noted healing pilgrimage centre Meitdemsis. |
| D Dumyat (Damietta) & Kafr El S | c 450 | O Cop | Nb | 4 | 12,000 | 20,000 | Damietta & Kafr El Sheikh. 4 parishes only; Christians very small minority. |
| D Girga | c1650 | O Cop | Nb | 25 | 46,000 | 80,000 | Relatively poor diocese, south of Sohag. Girga, Naga Hamadi & Bahgourah. |
| D Hulwan (Helwan) | 1967 | O Cop | Nb | 35 | 58,000 | 100,000 | Area for new heavy industry and military base, 20km south of Cairo on east bank. |
| D Manfalut & Abnub | c1450 | O Cop | Nb | 25 | 46,000 | 80,000 | Upper Egypt. Small diocese between Asyut to the south and Al Minya to north. |
| D Qalyub (Kalyubia) | 1965 | O Cop | Nb | 40 | 87,000 | 150,000 | HQ Benha, north of Cairo. Districts of Quweisna, Qalyub, Shibin al-Qanatir, Benha. |
| D Qena (Kena) & Qus | 969 | O Cop | Nb | 125 | 162,000 | 280,000 | Upper Egypt: area of tombs of pharaohs, immediately north of Luxor. |
| D Sharqiyah & Mohafazat | 1925 | O Cop | Nb | 30 | 58,000 | 100,000 | In Delta. 1976–7, 3 new Dioceses divided off: Zagazig; Port Said; Suez & Ismailia. |
| D Sohag (Sawhaj) | c1952 | O Cop | Nb | 170 | 290,000 | 500,000 | Sohag & Menshah. Upper Egypt, boundary of Southern Desert province. Monastery. |
| Episcopal Ch in Jerus & ME: D Egypt | 1847 | A Cen | Aw.UK | 10 | 500 | 1,000 | *Al Kanisa el Usqufiya.* ME=Middle East. M=MCS,JEM,CMJ. 95% Egyptians. 5n,2x,6f,1h. |
| Faith Church | 1895 | P Hol | xF..C | 23 | 540 | 1,500 | *Kenisa el Eeman.* 1905, M=EFM(USA),CHM(Canada). 13n,6m,2f,1s,W=90%,72Y,26y,43z. |
| Free Methodist Church | 1895 | P Hol | VF..C | 92 | 4,250 | 15,250 | *Holiness Ch.* M=Peniel Missionary Soc, FMC(USA). Many new converts and churches. 6f,1s. |
| Gospel Preaching Church | 1960 | P ind | x.... | | 2,600 | 4,000 | M=World-Wide Missions(USA). Evangelicals based in Pasadena, California. |
| Greek Evangelical Church | 1920 | P Ref | Rwc.. | | 200 | 500 | Greek Protestants. Remnant among rapidly-emigrating Greek community. |
| Greek Orth Patriarchate of Alexandria | 30 | O Ara | CW.NK | 55 | 7,000 | 30,000 | Broke with Copts at Chalcedon, AD 451. Rapid emigration. 4d,P=85%,W=15%,495y. |
| P Alexandria | | O Ara | Cp | 28 | 3,500 | 15,000 | Alexandria, Cairo. 13,000 Greeks plus many Arab Orthodox (since 1832). 16nx. |
| D Hermopolis (Tanta) | | O Ara | Cm | 9 | 1,200 | 5,000 | HQ Tanta. Remnants of once large Greek community. 2 priests only left. |
| D Leontopolis (Isma'iliya) | | O Ara | Cm | 12 | 1,600 | 7,000 | Az-Zaqaziq and Al Isma'iliyah. Greeks. HQ Ismailia. 4nx. |
| D Pelusium (Bur Sa'id & Kantara) | | O Ara | Cm | 6 | 700 | 3,000 | Port Said area. HQ Port Said. Only handful of Greeks left, with 3 priests. |
| Isolated radio churches | c1950 | I rad | ..... | 490 | 10,000 | 19,700 | Isolated radio believers; youths. R=3800(TWR,ELWA,RV),T=72000(ICI,GMU,RSB). |
| Jehovah's Witnesses | c1925 | M Jeh | x.... | 8 | 134 | 300 | *Watch Tower. IBSA.* Underground. 1970: severe persecution, many deportations. |
| Pentecost Faith Mission | | P Pen | ..... | 12 | 2,200 | 4,000 | Mission from Indiana, USA. Classical Pentecostals. |
| Pentecostal Church of God | 1910 | P Pe3 | ZF... | 24 | 1,635 | 5,000 | *Apostolic Church of God.* M=CoG(Cleveland) (USA). 18 churches, 6 missions. 13n,5m. |
| Russian Orthodox Church | | O Sla | Mw... | 1 | 60 | 100 | *Russkaya Pravoslavnaya Tserkov.* Under P Moscow. Russian officials, technicians. |
| Russian Orthodox Ch Outside of Russia | | O Sla | x.... | 1 | 50 | 100 | M=ROCOR(HQ New York, USA). Conservative Russians in exile. |
| Seventh-day Adventist Church | 1879 | P Adv | x.... | 14 | 2,329 | 3,000 | *SDA, Egypt Field*, Middle East Union. HQ Heliopolis. 5nx,39mw,1f,1r,25t(1674),155Y. |
| Syrian Orthodox Church (P Antioch) | c 600 | O Syr | Dw.NK | | 300 | 400 | *Jacobites.* Long history; bishop still in Cairo, only 50 families left. |
| Union of Armenian Ev Chs in Near East | 1896 | P Con | Rw.N. | 5 | 30 | 200 | Armenian Protestants. Declining. Losses to Armenian Spiritual Brethren. HQ Cairo. |
| Other Egyptian indigenous churches | 1948 | I | ..... | | 1,500 | 3,000 | Total about 10 (see list below). |
| Other Protestant denominations | | P | ..... | | 1,000 | 1,500 | Total about 20 (see list below). |
| **Total affiliated (mid-1970)** | | | | **3,910** | **3,546,192** | **6,193,628** | **Total denominations (1970) . . . 55.** |
| **Total affiliated (mid-1975)** | | | | **4,260** | **3,919,000** | **6,844,890** | **Total denominations (1975) . . . 58.** |
| **Total affiliated (mid-1980)** | | | | **4,630** | **4,302,000** | **7,513,840** | **Total denominations (1980) . . . 61.** |

NOTES ON TABLE ABOVE

COLUMNS: for meanings and CODES (cols. 1, 3, 4, 8), see Codebook (Part 6). Column 1: **Boldface type** = church with over 10% of country's affiliated Christians.

NATIONAL COUNCILS (Column 4, 5th letter).
- C = Evangelical Fellowship of Egypt (EFE).
- d = member of EFE and also associate member of EACCSE.
- K = Ecumenical Advisory Council for Church Service in Egypt (EACCSE).
- S = Bishops' Assembly of Egypt (for all rites), also member of EACCSE.

OTHER EGYPTIAN INDIGENOUS CHURCHES. These smaller bodies begun by Egyptians include: Baptist Ev Ch (1955), Baptist Evangelistic Mission (1932), Ch of Christ (1948), Ch of Grace (1940), First Baptist Biblical Ch (1961), Holiness Ev Coptic Ch. A USA Black pentecostal mission is also at work: Pentecostal Assemblies of the World.

OTHER PROTESTANT DENOMINATIONS. These smaller bodies include: Armenian Brotherhood, Armenian Ev Spiritual Brethren, Baptist Chs, Children of God International (USA), Ch of Christ (Non-Instrumental), Ch of God of Prophecy (1950), Ch of God (General Conference) (1972), Day of Pentecost Ch, Eglise de Langue Française (Cairo), Middle East General Mission (previously Egypt Mission Band, then Egypt General Mission), Egypt Salaam Mission, German Ev Mission, Ma'adi Community Ch, Missionary Ch, North Africa Mission, Pentecostal Grace Ch, Salvation Army (1936), Unevangelized Fields Mission (1964), World Gospel Mission (1949).

PEOPLES (ethnolinguistic). Christians: 98.2% Egyptian Arab (Copt), 0.6% Greek, 0.5% Armenian, 0.2% other Arab (Lebanese, Syrian, Iraqi, Palestinian), 0.2% Italian, French, British, USA, Amhara, et alii.

COUNTRY-WIDE TOTALS

EVANGELIZATION (see Part 5). 1900: 34%. 1970: 48%. 1980: 58%. *Mass evangelism.* 1960, Billy Graham one-day rally in Cairo (7,000 attenders, 453 enquirers). The Christian Centre for Audio-Visual Services in Cairo uses microbuses with audiovisuals in villages along the Nile. 1975, pastors' Conference on Evangelism. Since the 1960s several Coptic Orthodox monasteries have become evangelistic centres reaching all surrounding areas. 1978, African Evangelistic Enterprise (Alexandria, Cairo, Asyut; 23,000 attenders, 1,100 first-time decisions); Here's Life Alexandria (CCCI). *Radiophonic evangelism.* Annual listeners' letters (1975): 3,470 TWR, 100 ELWA, 62 RSB et alia. Bible correspondence courses: RSB, ICI (about 70,000 enrolments). *Literature evangelism.* The Coptic Orthodox patriarch's weekly *Megalet el-Kiraza* (Evangelizing Journal), linked to his weekly 7,000-attendance Bible studies in St Mark's Cathedral, Cairo, has a circulation of 30,000 of which a large proportion are purchased by Muslims.

FOREIGN MISSIONARIES AND PERSONNEL (nationals serving abroad) (1973). Total 200 in 18 countries: 113 Orthodox, 75 Roman Catholics, about 12 Protestants.

FOREIGN MISSIONARIES AND PERSONNEL (aliens from abroad) (1973). Total 1,203. *From Western world.* 1,162: about 1,100 Roman Catholics, 53 Protestants(41 in 17 USA societies, 9 in 1 WGermany society, 2 in 1 Switzerland society, 1 in 1 Netherlands society), 6 Anglicans in 2 UK societies, about 2 Orthodox, 1 Black indigenous from USA. *From Communist world.* About 5 Roman Catholics (3 from Poland, 2 Yugoslavia). *From Third World.* 36: about 30 Roman Catholics from Brazil, India and Lebanon, 4 Orthodox, 2 Protestants.

INSTITUTIONS (church-operated) (1973). Total 200, including 73 higher schools (3 minor seminaries), 65 medical centres (8 hospitals), 30 religious communities (21 active monasteries), 7 research centres, 12 seminaries (5 Orthodox, 4 Protestant, 3 RC).

PERIODICALS. About 30 titles (9 Orthodox).

PERSONNEL. About 5,303 (4,100 national, 1,203 foreign).

RELIGIOUS LIBRARIES. About 52.

SCRIPTURE DISTRIBUTION (1975). Annual totals: 21,193 Bibles (11% free, 84% subsidized, 5% commercial), 54,976 NTs (2% free, 96% subsidized, 2% commercial), 171,634 UBS portions, 229,435 UBS selections. *Translations completed.* Portion: 3 languages since 1860. NT: 3 languages since 1716. Bible: ecumenical translation in Egyptian Arabic in progress. The Coptic Orthodox Church has published 2 New Testaments around 1945, both long out of print: one in Coptic, the other Coptic & Arabic diglot.

SERVICE AGENCIES. About 60, including CCCI, CEOSS, CRSUSCC, EACCSE, EFE, ICMC, OM, SPCK, UECASSS, WSCF, YMCA, YWAM, YWCA.

ADDITIONAL DATA ON CHURCHES
CATHOLIC CHURCH IN EGYPT. *Annual baptisms.* (1972) 99.4% infant, 0.6% adult. *Sisters.* 446 Egyptians, 1,007 expatriates from 32 different countries including Italy (541), France (157), Lebanon (128). Over half (777) live and work in Cairo; 344 in Alexandria, 267 in Upper Egypt, 73 in Lower Egypt and the Canal Zone. Of all sisters, 29% work as teachers and 25% in socio-medical work. *Catechists.* Total around 300 (lay). *Coptic religious congregations* (founded in Egypt). Priests: 40 Franciscans of the Egyptian Vicariate (begun 1928), 3 Brothers of the Preaching of St Mark (priests; begun 1959). Sisters: 90 Egyptian Sacred Heart Sisters (begun 1913). *Other oriental congregations.* Sisters: 7 Our Lady of Perpetual Help Sisters (Greek Melkite). *Main foreign orders and congregations* (1972). Priests: 44 SDB, 41 OFM Custody (including 11 brothers), 35 SJ, 16 SMA, 8 OP. Brothers: 45 FSC. Sisters: 284 Pie Madri della Nigrizia, 198 Franciscans of the Immaculate Heart of Mary, 139 Our Lady of the Apostles, 87 Charité du Bon Pasteur d'Angers, 85 Daughters of Charity of St Vincent de Paul. *Catholic organizations.* Each oriental rite is attached to its corresponding patriarchate. The Latin vicariates are part of the Conference of Latin Bishops of the Arab Regions (CELRA), with its seat in East Jerusalem. There is also an Inter-Rite Catholic Assembly in Egypt. There are no national presbyteral or pastoral councils, but religious personnel are represented on the Assembly of Major Superiors of Religious Men, and the Union of Major Superiors of Religious Women. Catholic Action, an inter-rite organization, co-ordinates the work of the Legion of Mary (730 members in Cairo and 300 elsewhere in 1970); Society of St Vincent de Paul (83 conferences with 688 active members in 1970); Children's Apostolate Movement (33 groups throughout the country, with 17 in Cairo); Youth Witnesses of Christ; and house groups in Cairo.

The Holy See has diplomatic relations with Egypt and is represented to government and the Catholic hierarchy by a pro-nuncio in Cairo.

An international organization having its headquarters in Egypt is The Grail, an association of lay women of 23 countries on all continents, founded in 1921.

Several Catholic organizations are engaged in research and contribute to social and ecumenical action. The Dar el-Salam Study Centre, founded in 1940, sets as its goal witnessing 'by means of conferences, publications and periodicals' to 'a double fidelity to Christianity in its doctrinal purity and to the Arab culture in its classic perfection'. Although its immediate aim is neither ecumenism nor Christian-Muslim dialogue, it has contributed considerably to both. In 1970 it began publication of a bi-monthly bulletin entitled *Christian interconfessional information.* The Franciscan Centre for Oriental Christian Studies (Centro Francescano di Studi Orientali Cristiani) was opened in 1954 and devotes itself especially to studies of the pre-Chalcedonian churches. In addition to maintaining a library of 25,000 volumes, it publishes a journal, *Studia Christiana Orientalia.* The Dominican Institute for Oriental Studies (IDEO) is the only Christian organization in Egypt specializing in dialogue with Islam. It promotes Islamic studies and cultural exchanges with Muslim intellectuals, maintains a library and produces a journal with contributions from both Christian and Muslim scholars. The Centre for Arab Studies (CEA), founded in Cairo in 1970, offers courses in the Arab language and civilization.

Training in catechetics is provided at the Catechetical Institute, founded in Cairo in 1970, with branches in Alexandria and Asyut, the latter serving Upper Egypt. In 1971–72 there were 150 students, half of whom were lay persons and the rest sisters.

The Catholic school programme is co-ordinated by the General Secretariat of Catholic Schools, founded in Cairo in 1950, which is a member of OIEC in Belgium and aims to defend the interest of Egypt's Catholic schools. The administration of the schools is divided into 4 parts respectively under the authority of the patriarchs, feminine and masculine religious congregations, and the Upper Egypt Christian Association for Schools and Social Service (UECASSS). In 1973 there were 191 primary and 51 secondary Catholic schools with 81,133 pupils (59% girls, 41% boys) of all confessions, Christian and Muslim. More than 64% of these pupils are in schools in Cairo and Alexandria, with 27% in Upper Egypt and 8% in various towns in the Delta. UECASSS was founded as a Catholic school association in 1941 but was transformed into an interdenominational organization, with a social service concern in addition, in 1972. In 1973 it was responsible for 39 free primary schools, 3 kindergartens, about 40 catechetical centres (teaching catechism to pupils in government schools and others not in school), 62 dispensaries, 64 sanitary posts (open 2 or 3 times weekly) and 31 social centres with hygiene, literacy and trades apprenticeship programmes.

In 1970, 221 sisters worked in 18 government hospitals, and 191 others in Catholic medical and charitable institutions: one hospital, one clinic, 62 dispensaries and 7 homes for the aged. Caritas-Egypt, which is affiliated to Caritas-Internationalis in Rome, was founded in 1967 following the Arab-Israeli war of 1967 and is fully recognized by government. Other important social service organizations include the As-Sanabel Association founded in Cairo in 1950, which sponsors creches, homes, infants clubs and social centres in the Koubbeh gardens quarter of Cairo; and Catholic Relief Services (CRS-USCC) in Cairo and Alexandria.

CHURCH OF SINAI. St Catherine's Monastery has around it 1,200 Bedouin nomads living there, who are considered as 'brothers' and receive medical aid from it. *Monks.* By 1975 the number had declined to 23. *Visitors.* In 1975, 55,000 (1,000 a week), 35% of whom are scholars.

COPTIC ORTHODOX CHURCH. *Membership.* The totals of baptized (affiliated) members are based on the church's own private censuses and lists of membership compiled and checked carefully over the years. *Older dioceses.* Many dioceses date from the time of pope Athanasius (328–373). For the first 200 years after Christ, the only diocese was Alexandria, but by 350 there were 100 dioceses (bishoprics) during the zenith of Coptic Christianity. Under Islam the number of bishoprics shrank to 12 during the church's darkest period, the 10th–17th centuries. *Diocese of Cairo.* Originally founded in AD 356 as Diocese of Babylon, with its own bishop; AD 640 renamed D Fostat; AD 969 renamed D Misr (Egypt, or Cairo); AD 1240–1854, under patriarch as bishop; 1854–69, own bishop; since 1869, under patriarch as bishop. *New dioceses.* The table represents those dioceses in existence at the accession of pope Shenouda III in 1971. Diocesan boundaries have since been realigned with political boundaries, and dioceses reduced in size by division. In 1975, D Luxor was divided into D Aswan, and D Luxor & Isna. In 1976, D Al Minya was divided into 3: D Malawwi (which was itself an early diocese, begun c250, joined to Minya c1650), D Samalout, with D Al Minya continuing. The new bishops were formerly professional men (doctors, engineers). In 1976 also, parts of D Sharqiyah were divided off to form D Zagazig, and D Port Said, with a further new diocese of Suez & Ismailia in 1977. Also in 1977, D Nagh Hamadi was formed from D Qena. *Churches.* By 1975 about 50 new churches every year were being opened. *Renewal movements.* There have been several such movements, including the Sunday school movement (with 1 million children in Sunday schools by 1976). Many people including young persons have been influenced by the Coptic Revival Movement within the church (Khalasul-Nafoos). In 1978 a new renewal movement, including tongues, healings and other charismatic phenomena, emerged at St Mark's Church, Heliopolis, under the leadership of a priest, Father Zacharia Botros, attracting weekly crowds of 3,000 and baptizing 200 converts from Islam before being banned by the patriarch. *Bishops.* Before 1971, all jurisdictions were called metropolitanates, by both church and state, and their heads were consecrated as metropolitans. Since 1971, the canonically more correct term bishoprics has been used, with heads consecrated as bishops. At Pentecost 1977, 7 new bishops were consecrated, including 2 in the new grade of sub-bishop. The Holy Synod now comprised 40 metropolitans and bishops headed by the pope of Alexandria, together with 5 abbots and the vicars of Alexandria and Cairo. In addition to diocesan and assistant bishops, there are bishops for each of these 4 special functions: Public, Ecumenical & Social Relations; Theological and Educational Institutions; Higher Studies and Coptic Culture; and (since 1976) African Affairs (HQ Nairobi, Kenya; specializing in liaison with African indigenous churches). *Catechists.* 22 full-time. *Sub-deacons.* Very numerous.

ISOLATED RADIO CHURCHES. Small house groups of isolated radio believers (mostly youths and students aged 12–25) in solidly Muslim areas.

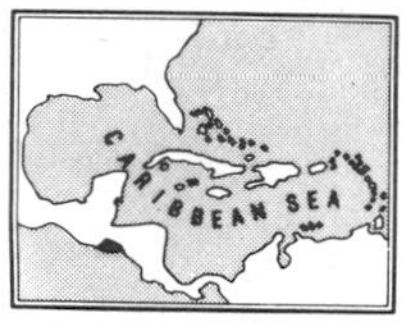

# EL SALVADOR

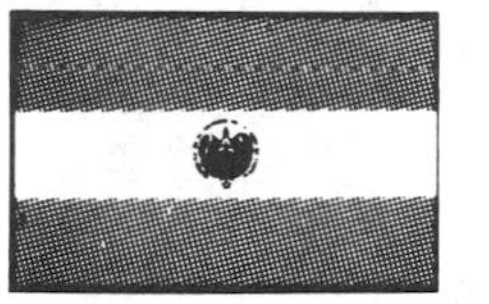

## SECULAR DATA

**STATE. Official name:** The Republic of El Salvador (La República de El Salvador). Adjective of nationality: Salvadorian (salvadoreño).
**Flag** (shown above right): Blue, white, and blue stripes, with national coat of arms in centre.
**Area:** 21,393 sq.km. (8,260 sq.miles). Agricultural land: 63.8%.
**Government:** Republic under military control, since 1961 (1525 Spanish rule, 1841 Independence from Spain, many dictatorships).
**Legislature:** Legislative Assembly, 52 members.
**Official language:** Spanish (*Español/Castellano*).
**Capital:** San Salvador 337,170 (1971).
**Political divisions:** 14 Departments.
**Armed forces** (1976): Total 7,155 regular: army 6,000, navy 155, air force 1,000 (18 combat aircraft). Paramilitary forces: 3,000.

**DEMOGRAPHY. Population:** 3,554,648 (census of 28.VI.1971. For 1970–2000 (UN), see last row of Table 1). Population density (1975): 192/sq.km. (497/sq.mile). Under 15 years: 45%. Growth rate (1975–80): 3.16% per year (births 4.11%, deaths −0.95%). Life expectancy (1975–80): 60.7 years. Household size: 5.2 persons.
**Major languages:** Spanish, English, Pipil, Lenca.
**Urban dwellers** (1970): 40.9%. Urban growth rate (1950–70): 3.7% per year.
**Labour force:** 36%.
**Refugees** (1977): In 1969, 140,000 Salvadorians resident in Honduras were forcibly repatriated.
**Tourists** (1974): 285,415.

**ETHNOLINGUISTIC GROUPS:** 92.3% Mestizo, 5.0% Amerindian (176,000) (3.2% Pipil, 0.6% Lenca, 0.2% Kekchi, Pokomam, Chorotega, Half-Indian), 1.7% Salvadorian White, 0.4% Honduran Mestizo, Guatemalan, German, Scandinavian, Mexican, Chinese (700), Jewish, Arab (Palestinian, Syrian, Lebanese), Turkish, Swiss.

**MONEY** (1977). **Monetary unit:** colón (= 100 centavos); US$1 = ESC 2.50.

**National income per person:** US$373. Average annual family income: US$1,940.
**Inflation:** (1970–74) 6.1% per year, (1975) 19% per year (consumer price index 160).
**Cost of living in capital** (1976): index 98 (Washington DC = 100). Daily cost of living: US$35.

**EDUCATION.** Adult literacy: (1950) 40%, (1975) 62%. Education rate: 52%. Schools: 3,193. Universities: 2.

**HEALTH.** Hospitals: 75 (6,398 beds). Doctors: 952. Lepers: 520 (0.1 per 1,000). Blind: 660. Psychotics: 37,000.

**LITERATURE.** Annual new book titles (1967): 27. Periodicals: 46. Scientific journals: 15. Newspapers: 12 dailies, 12 non-daily.

**COMMUNICATION** (per 1,000 people). Phones: 12. Radios: 85. TV sets: 26. Daily newspaper circulation: 74 copies.

TABLE 1. RELIGIOUS ADHERENTS IN EL SALVADOR

| Year | 1900 | | mid-1970 | | Annual change, 1970–1980 | | | | mid-1975 | | mid-1980 | | 2000 | |
|---|---|---|---|---|---|---|---|---|---|---|---|---|---|---|
| *Name* | *Adherents* | *%* | *Adherents* | *%* | *Natural* | *Conversion* | *Total* | *Rate* | *Adherents* | *%* | *Adherents* | *%* | *Adherents* | *%* |
| **Christians** | **1,029,000** | **98.0** | **3,497,000** | **99.5** | **128,852** | **−1,143** | **127,709** | **3.13** | **4,081,150** | **99.3** | **4,774,090** | **99.2** | **8,647,200** | **98.2** |
| professing | 1,029,000 | 98.0 | 3,497,000 | 99.5 | 128,852 | −1,143 | 127,709 | 3.13 | 4,081,150 | 99.3 | 4,774,090 | 99.2 | 8,647,200 | 98.2 |
| Roman Catholics | 1,029,000 | 98.0 | 3,401,900 | 96.8 | 125,266 | −2,231 | 123,035 | 3.10 | 3,967,540 | 96.6 | 4,632,250 | 96.2 | 8,347,200 | 94.8 |
| Christo-pagans | 31,000 | 3.0 | 120,000 | 3.4 | 4,420 | −20 | 4,400 | 3.14 | 140,000 | 3.4 | 164,000 | 3.4 | 264,000 | 3.0 |
| Evangelical Catholics | 100 | 0.0 | 96,968 | 2.8 | 3,844 | 746 | 4,590 | 3.77 | 121,770 | 3.0 | 142,870 | 3.0 | 290,100 | 3.3 |
| Protestants | 0 | 0.0 | 80,000 | 2.3 | 2,949 | 601 | 3,550 | 3.80 | 93,400 | 2.3 | 115,500 | 2.4 | 228,900 | 2.6 |
| Marginal Protestants | 0 | 0.0 | 10,000 | 0.3 | 451 | 469 | 920 | 6.43 | 14,300 | 0.3 | 19,200 | 0.4 | 52,800 | 0.6 |
| Non-White indigenous | 0 | 0.0 | 5,000 | 0.1 | 183 | 17 | 200 | 3.45 | 5,800 | 0.1 | 7,000 | 0.1 | 18,000 | 0.2 |
| Anglicans | 0 | 0.0 | 100 | 0.0 | 3 | 1 | 4 | 3.64 | 110 | 0.0 | 140 | 0.0 | 300 | 0.0 |
| nominal | 31,500 | 3.0 | 141,846 | 4.0 | 5,508 | 1,446 | 6,954 | 3.99 | 174,450 | 4.2 | 211,390 | 4.4 | 486,800 | 5.5 |
| affiliated | 997,500 | 95.0 | 3,355,154 | 95.4 | 123,344 | −2,589 | 120,755 | 3.09 | 3,906,700 | 95.1 | 4,562,700 | 94.8 | 8,160,400 | 92.7 |
| doubly-affiliated | −100 | 0.0 | −140,000 | −4.0 | −5,463 | −737 | −6,200 | 3.58 | −173,000 | −4.2 | −202,000 | −4.2 | −396,000 | −4.5 |
| total practising | 947,620 | *95* | 2,851,880 | *85* | 104,843 | −2,201 | 102,642 | 3.09 | 3,320,700 | *85* | 3,878,300 | *85* | 6,120,300 | *75* |
| non-practising | 49,880 | *5* | 503,270 | *15* | 18,501 | −388 | 18,113 | 3.09 | 586,000 | *15* | 684,400 | *15* | 2,040,100 | *25* |
| Roman Catholics | 997,400 | 95.0 | 3,303,086 | 93.9 | 121,375 | −3,685 | 117,690 | 3.06 | 3,844,320 | 93.6 | 4,479,990 | 93.1 | 7,966,300 | 90.5 |
| Catholic pentecostals | 0 | 0.0 | 0 | 0.0 | 3 | 7 | 10 | 50.00 | 20 | 0.0 | 100 | 0.0 | 5,000 | 0.1 |
| Protestants | 100 | 0.0 | 146,352 | 4.2 | 5,576 | 969 | 6,545 | 3.71 | 176,600 | 4.3 | 211,800 | 4.4 | 422,500 | 4.8 |
| Evangelicals | 100 | 0.0 | 127,000 | 3.6 | 4,837 | 843 | 5,680 | 3.71 | 153,200 | 3.7 | 183,800 | 3.8 | 370,000 | 4.2 |
| Non-White indigenous | 0 | 0.0 | 28,500 | 0.8 | 1,073 | −23 | 1,050 | 3.09 | 34,000 | 0.8 | 39,000 | 0.8 | 79,200 | 0.9 |
| Marginal Protestants | 0 | 0.0 | 17,061 | 0.5 | 777 | 887 | 1,664 | 6.76 | 24,600 | 0.6 | 33,700 | 0.7 | 88,000 | 1.0 |
| Anglicans | 0 | 0.0 | 155 | 0.0 | 6 | 0 | 6 | 3.16 | 180 | 0.0 | 210 | 0.0 | 400 | 0.0 |
| Tribal religionists | 21,000 | 2.0 | 9,500 | 0.3 | 278 | −418 | −140 | −1.59 | 8,800 | 0.2 | 8,100 | 0.2 | 7,000 | 0.1 |
| Baha'is | 0 | 0.0 | 5,100 | 0.1 | 284 | 706 | 990 | 11.00 | 9,000 | 0.2 | 15,000 | 0.3 | 51,000 | 0.6 |
| Non-religious | 0 | 0.0 | 2,400 | 0.1 | 199 | 781 | 980 | 15.55 | 6,300 | 0.2 | 12,200 | 0.3 | 89,000 | 1.0 |
| Buddhists | 0 | 0.0 | 600 | 0.0 | 22 | −2 | 20 | 2.86 | 700 | 0.0 | 800 | 0.0 | 1,000 | 0.0 |
| Atheists | 0 | 0.0 | 600 | 0.0 | 32 | 58 | 90 | 9.00 | 1,000 | 0.0 | 1,500 | 0.0 | 5,000 | 0.1 |
| Jews | 0 | 0.0 | 300 | 0.0 | 11 | 0 | 11 | 3.16 | 350 | 0.0 | 410 | 0.0 | 800 | 0.0 |
| Other religionists | 0 | 0.0 | 500 | 0.0 | 22 | 18 | 40 | 5.71 | 700 | 0.0 | 900 | 0.0 | 2,000 | 0.0 |
| **Country's population** | **1,050,000** | **100.0** | **3,516,000** | **100.0** | **129,700** | **0** | **129,700** | **3.16** | **4,108,000** | **100.0** | **4,813,000** | **100.0** | **8,803,000** | **100.0** |

COLUMNS, ROWS. For meanings and definitions, see Code-book (Part 6). Note that, by definition, total 'Christians' = professing + crypto-Christians, which also = affiliated + nominal Christians. Percentages may not always total exactly, due to rounding.

CENSUSES. The religion question has not been asked in government censuses.

NOTES ON RELIGIONS

ATHEISTS. Communist Party of El Salvador (PCES) (illegal; pro-Soviet): membership (1970) 150.

BAHA'IS. Rapid growth from 3 local spiritual assemblies (1964) to 54 (1973). In 1968, 37,000 leaflets were distributed, in 1970, 71,000, and in 1972, 108,000 leaflets and 490 radio announcements.

BUDDHISTS. Chinese.

CATHOLIC PENTECOSTALS (or, Catholic charismatics). In 1977 renewal began among the Franciscan order.

CHRISTO-PAGANS. Amerindians whose syncretistic folk-Catholicism combines 17th-century Spanish Catholicism with their own traditional animism, concepts and world-views.

DOUBLY-AFFILIATED. The term covers those affiliated to, or claimed by, both the Catholic Church and also a church termed Evangélica by the state (Protestant, marginal Protestant, Anglican or Non-White indigenous), i.e. baptized Catholics who have recently become Evangelicals or others. Because their statistics represent a duplication, they are shown in the table as a negative quantity (with a minus sign).

EVANGELICAL CATHOLICS. This term is used here to describe persons who are affiliated to churches termed by the state Evangélica (Protestant, marginal Protestant, Anglican or Non-White indigenous churches), but who are regarded by state and society as, or who profess publicly to be, Roman Catholics.

NON-WHITE INDIGENOUS. In about 13 denominations in 1970 (see Table 2).

OTHER RELIGIONISTS. Including Rosicrucians (1 AMORC centre) and a few Muslims (Palestinian Arabs).

TRIBAL RELIGIONISTS. Of the 176,000 Amerindians in 1970, a proportion remain animists among the Pipil, Lenca and others.

**NON-CHRISTIAN RELIGIONS. Traditional religions** exist among the Pipil and Lenca Indians, although the majority are baptized Catholics.

**Baha'i** has grown rapidly from 3 local spiritual assemblies in 1964 to 54 by 1973.

**CHRISTIANITY.** Spanish Catholic priests first came to El Salvador in 1525 when it was conquered by Spain, but Spanish indifference to the territory because of its lack of precious metals resulted in a slower rate of christianization than in surrounding countries. When Central America separated from Spain in 1821, it claimed to inherit the right of patronage and established the diocese of San Salvador, but this was not officially recognized by Rome until 1842. El Salvador in the meantime (1838) had gained its independence from Guatemala. During the next 40 years, successive governments alternated in accepting and rejecting Catholicism as the official religion. In 1886, the 8th constitution established freedom of religion and secular education, in addition to prohibiting religious orders; but the systematic religious persecution of the early years gradually abated with passage of time.

CATHOLIC CHURCH. The number of Catholic baptisms decreased considerably in urban districts between 1965–69. Infant baptisms in relation to births in the city of San Salvador fell from 90% in 1965 to 85% in 1969. This has been a result of the development, after 1950, of Pentecostal churches and other bodies from North America.

Religious behaviour among the Catholic population can be classified according to a 3-fold typology born in the colonial period: (1) bourgeois Catholicism, representing about 4% of the total population, is composed of the upper classes largely of Spanish descent who send their children to Catholic schools and help in social work; (2) popular Catholicism, about 30%, is held by those who have little religious education but who participate in popular religious festivals; and (3) mayanized Catholicism, a mixture of Catholicism and traditional Mayan Indian beliefs and customs, is accepted by 60% of the population although pure-blooded Indians practising christo-paganism number under 4%. A number of Catholics, principally in the archdiocese of San Salvador, are involved in Catholic action under the influence of the 1968 Medellín conference in Colombia. The tensions in the Salvadorian church can be seen in the fact that the conclusions of a National Pastoral Week in June 1970 calling for a 'revolutionary attitude with regard to the problem of sin and oppression' were condemned by the Episcopal Conference, although 2 of its members defended these views. However, even if the conclusions of the Week have not led to institutional change, the pastoral action of the church has taken on an orientation which favours concrete proposals for change.

PROTESTANT CHURCHES. Protestant work began in El Salvador in 1896 with the arrival of the Central American Mission, followed by the Church of God (Cleveland), Seventh-day Adventists and American Baptists before World War I. All of these churches have made progress, but the most spectacular gains have come in recent years among the Assemblies of God, who have built up a large following since their arrival in 1922. Pentecostalism represents the principal alternative to Catholic dominance in El Salvador at the present time.

**CHURCH AND STATE.** The constitution of January 1962 states in its Preamble: 'The Constituent Assembly, in the name of the Salvadorian people, with trust in God and the high destiny of the country...'. It guarantees the free exercise of religion and forbids clergy from engaging in 'all forms of political propaganda calling on religious motivations'. It also forbids criticism of laws of the state and government during religious acts in Protestant churches (Article 157). The Catholic Church, which is the official state religion, has a juridical personality and other churches may obtain it in accordance with the law (Article 161). Protestant churches and their dependencies are exempt from land tax (Article 119).

Church and state maintain an attitude of mutual recognition and try to avoid conflict. Government does not allow itself to be pressured by the Catholic Church, and the Catholic hierarchy shows concern for the wishes of government. However, the archbishop of San Salvador is widely known for his courageous stand on social issues and his statements sometimes provoke strong reactions in economic, political and military circles.

In the election of 1972, the Christian Democratic Party joined with the Socialist Party to form a unified front (UNO); but although results by provinces were never published, the conservative party was declared the winner.

In 1977 serious trouble erupted between leftist terrorists and rightist landowners. Conflict had been building up for some time between the Catholic Church and the regime of A. Molina, primarily on the issue of land reform as a result of the Church's calls for a more equitable distribution of wealth. A number of priests, especially Jesuits, encouraged peasants to take over unused lands belonging to large landowners. From January 1977 over 15 priests, mainly Jesuits, were expelled; in May the country's foreign minister was assassinated by the Popular Forces of Liberation, and in June the clandestine rightist White Warriors Union threatened to kill 50 Jesuit priests unless they left the country.

**INTERDENOMINATIONAL ORGANIZATIONS.** El Salvador has no council of churches. The Baptist

Iglesia Católica en El Salvador, Diócesis de Santa Ana. *Above right.* Cathedral of St Anne, Santa Ana, in main coffee-producing area. *Above.* Parish church in town of Izalco. In the background is the still-active Izalco volcano which for centuries erupted every hour and was known as the Lighthouse of America, and is still a focus for Amerindian christo-paganism.

Association is an affiliate member of UNELAM founded in 1965 at Campinas, Brazil. The Catholic Episcopal Conference sponsors a Commission for Ecumenism and Non-believers (Comisión de Ecumenismo y No Creyentes).

**BROADCASTING.** Government and commercial stations accept religious broadcasting. The government Radio Nacional de El Salvador has Protestant and Catholic programming each for 15 minutes daily. There is one Protestant station, Radio Progreso, which broadcasts 2 hours daily, and 2 Catholic stations Radio Popular and La Voz Pan-americana. Escuelas Radiofónicas de El Salvador is a department of the Catholic Interdiocesan Social Secretariat which groups 512 radiophonic schools in a religious, cultural, literacy and agricultural development programme for the rural population, with 13,000 registered students in 1974. Christian programmes from abroad can be easily heard on the international stations FEBC (California), TWR (Netherlands Antilles) and HCJB (Ecuador). For Catholics, El Salvador is a member of UNDA.

## BIBLIOGRAPHY

*Anuario eclesiástico de El Salvador, 1970*. San Salvador: Secretariado Social Interdiocesano, 1970.

TABLE 2. ORGANIZED CHURCHES AND DENOMINATIONS IN EL SALVADOR

| Official name 1 | Begun 2 | Type 3 | Counc 4 | Congs 5 | Adults 6 | Affiliated 7 | Names, notes, and other statistics (see Codebook) 8 |
|---|---|---|---|---|---|---|---|
| Asambleas de Dios | 1922 | P Pe2 | ZF... | 352 | 81,600 | 100,000 | *Assemblies of God*. M=AoG(USA). 12,100 baptized. Radio LARE. 408n,7f,1k,1s(95). |
| Associación Bautista de El Salvador | 1911 | P Bap | TvU.. | 40 | 2,995 | 6,000 | *Baptist Association of ES*. M=ABCIM(USA). 1966, applied to join WCC. 4f. |
| Consejo de Igls Luteranas en CA & P | 1947 | P Lut | x.... | 14 | 295 | 476 | *Lutheran Ch (Missouri Synod)*. 1952, M=LCMS(USA). German-speaking. 9t,W=29%,5Yy,7z. |
| Convención Bautista Nacional | 1965 | I Bap | T.... | | 1,200 | 1,500 | *National Baptist Convention*. M=NBCUSA (USA Black missionaries). |
| Hermanos Libres | | P CBr | x.... | 4 | 200 | 400 | *Christian Brethren. Plymouth (Open) Brethren*. M=CMML(USA,NZ). 4f. |
| Iglesia Adventista del Séptimo Día | 1915 | P Adv | x.... | 71 | 4,194 | 15,000 | *SDA. Seventh-day Adventists, ES Mission*, CAmerican UM. 12n,2x,G=2.6%pa,W=60%,724Y. |
| Igl Apostólica de la Fe en Cristo Jesus | 1950 | I pe1 | x.... | 64 | 700 | 2,000 | *Apostolic Ch of the Faith in CJ*. Mexicans; with UPC(USA). Mestizos. 38nx,160z. |
| **Iglesia Católica en El Salvador:** | 1525 | R Lat | B.LDR | 227 | 1,816,700 | 3,303,086 | *Catholic Ch*. C=18+1+29. 1s(122) (closed in 1973). 224n,213x,65m,641w,103509Yy. |
| M San Salvador | 1842 | R Lat | Bs | 96 | 613,300 | 1,115,603 | 50% urban, 50% rural. Only diocese with D=pc(1969). 113 140 43 423 44562 |
| D San Miguel | 1913 | R Lat | Bs | 37 | 303,300 | 551,433 | Main zone for cotton production. Extreme east. 27 20 10 26 17443 |
| D San Vicente | 1943 | R Lat | Bs | 35 | 243,000 | 441,800 | Agricultural area; from coast to Honduras border. 28 16 2 66 13018 |
| D Santa Ana | 1913 | R Lat | Bs | 40 | 388,000 | 705,000 | Main zone for coffee production. Extreme west. 41 24 10 115 13486 |
| D Santiago de Maria | 1954 | R Lat | Bs | 19 | 269,100 | 489,250 | Coffee, cotton, grain. Strip adjoining D San Miguel. 15 13 0 11 15000 |
| Iglesia Centroamericana | 1896 | P int | xM... | 100 | 2,540 | 6,500 | *Central American Church*. M=CAM(USA). Interdenominational in emphasis. 13f,1k. |
| Iglesia de Dios de la Profecía | 1954 | P Pe3 | Z.... | 13 | 300 | 600 | *Ch of God of Prophecy*. M=CGP(USA). Split in USA ex CoG(Cleveland). 2f. |
| Iglesia de Dios (Anderson) | | P Hol | x.... | 15 | 500 | 1,000 | *Ch of God*. M=CoG(Anderson) (USA). Holiness denomination. 10n. |
| Iglesia de Dios (Cleveland) | 1904 | P Pe3 | ZF... | 343 | 5,144 | 13,000 | M=CoG(Cleveland)(USA). 140 churches, 203 missions. 1 brickery, 1 dairy, 140n,1p. |
| Igl de JC de los Santos de los UD | c1952 | M LdS | x.... | | 9,000 | 12,061 | *Ch of JC of Latter-day Saints. Mormons*. M=CJCLdS(USA). 200f,G=19.1%pa. |
| Iglesia de los Amigos | 1915 | P Qua | Q.... | 4 | 63 | 186 | *Central America Yearly Meeting of Ev Friends Ch. Quakers*. G=7%pa,W=51%,10Y. |
| Iglesia del Nazareno | 1964 | P Hol | xF... | 8 | 237 | 800 | M=Ch of the Nazarene(USA). Holiness body. 1n,3x,10m,6f,15t(712),W=85%,74Y,80z. |
| Iglesia del Príncipe de Paz | | I pe2 | x.... | | 2,000 | 5,000 | *Ch of the Prince of Peace*. Indigenous pentecostals from Guatemala. |
| Iglesia Episcopal: D El Salvador | | A Cen | aw.R. | 1 | 73 | 155 | *Episcopal Ch*. 1968, missionary diocese, PECUSA, Province IX. 1x,W=55%,3y. |
| Iglesia Ev Luterana de CR,ES,H,N,P | 1954 | P Lut | 1.... | 1 | 260 | 390 | *ELC in Costa Rica, ES, Hond, Nic, Panama*. Germans, Scandinavians. 1x,W=10%,6Yy. |
| Iglesias de Cristo | | P Dis | x.... | 25 | 500 | 1,000 | *Churches of Christ*. M=CC(Non-Instrumental)(USA). Radio work. 2f. |
| Testigos de Jehová | c1930 | M Jeh | x.... | 34 | 2,181 | 5,000 | *Jehovah's Witnesses. Watch Tower. IBSA*. Active witnessing under way by 1932. 329Y. |
| Other indigenous pentecostal churches | | I pen | ..... | | 10,000 | 20,000 | Total about 10, including: Asamblea Espiritual Nacional, Iglesia Santa Sion. |
| Other Protestant denominations | | P | ..... | | 500 | 1,000 | Total about 10 (see list below). |
| Doubly-affiliated (duplication) (1970) | | | | | –77,000 | –140,000 | Evangelicals who also are or were baptized Roman Catholics. |
| **Total affiliated (mid-1970)** | | | | **1,440** | **1,864,182** | **3,355,154** | **Total denominations (1970) . . . 40.** |
| **Total affiliated (mid-1975)** | | | | **1,590** | **2,170,600** | **3,906,700** | **Total denominations (1975) . . . 43.** |
| **Total affiliated (mid-1980)** | | | | **1,760** | **2,535,100** | **4,562,700** | **Total denominations (1980) . . . 46.** |

**NOTES ON TABLE ABOVE**
COLUMNS: for meanings and CODES (cols. 1, 3, 4, 8), see Codebook (Part 6). Column 1: **Boldface type** = church with over 10% of country's affiliated Christians.
NATIONAL COUNCILS (Column 4, 5th letter).
R = Conferencia Episcopal de El Salvador (CEDES) (Episcopal Conference of El Salvador).
OTHER PROTESTANT DENOMINATIONS. These smaller bodies include: Baptist International Missions (1967), Evangelistic Faith Missions (1963), Iglesia Menonita (48 adherents), union congregations (in cities), World-Wide Missions (1955).

**PEOPLES** (ethnolinguistic). Christians: 92.6% Mestizo, 4.7% Amerindian (Pipil, Lenca, Kekchi, Half-Indian), 1.7% Salvadorian White, 0.4% Honduran Mestizo, Guatemalan, German, Scandinavian, Mexican, Palestinian & other Arab.

**COUNTRY-WIDE TOTALS**
EVANGELIZATION (see Part 5). 1900: 100%. 1970: 100%. 1980: 100%. *Mass evangelism*. Among recent campaigns: November 1969, Elmer Good campaign at Cathedral del Aire (800 professions of faith); March 1970, Luis Palau 4-week San Salvador Crusade (12 sponsoring churches, 17,000 attenders, 1,550 enquirers); 1978, Here's Life San Salvador (CCCI). *Radiophonic evangelism*. FEBC, HCJB, CAM, ICI (1,100 active students). Escuelas Radiofónicas de El Salvador (Catholic): 512 radiophonic schools, 13,000 enrolled.
FOREIGN MISSIONARIES AND PERSONNEL (nationals serving abroad) (1973). Total about 80 Roman Catholics in Mexico, Panama et alia.
FOREIGN MISSIONARIES AND PERSONNEL (aliens from abroad) (1973). Total 1,092. *From Western world*. 591: 342 Roman Catholics, about 200 marginal Protestants (190 Mormons) from USA, 48 Protestants (46 in 14 USA societies, 2 in 1 New Zealand society), 1 Anglican in 1 USA society. *From Communist world*. 1 Roman Catholic from Poland. *From Third World*. 500: 486 Roman Catholics from other Latin American countries, about 10 indigenous from Mexico and Guatemala, about 4 Protestants.
INSTITUTIONS (church-operated) (1973). Total 70, including 35 higher schools (8 minor seminaries), 20 medical centres (4 hospitals), 3 radio stations, 3 religious communities (monasteries), 1 research centre, 4 seminaries (3 Protestant, 1 RC), 1 university.
**PERIODICALS.** About 20 titles.
PERSONNEL. About 2,062 (970 national, 1,092 foreign).
RELIGIOUS LIBRARIES. 12.
SCRIPTURE DISTRIBUTION (1975). Annual totals: 36,513 Bibles (45% subsidized, 55% commercial), 37,620 NTs (22% free, 51% subsidized, 27% commercial), 60,674 UBS portions, 1,305,134 UBS selections.
SERVICE AGENCIES. About 39, including ACUS, CCCI, CEDES, CONFRES, JAC, JEC, JOC, MEC, MFC, MIIC, SEDAC, SERCAP.

**ADDITIONAL DATA ON CHURCHES**
IGLESIA CATOLICA EN EL SALVADOR. *Annual baptisms*. (1972) 99.9% infant, 0.1% adult. *Priests*. Nationals: 189 diocesan, 35 religious. Expatriates: 30 diocesan and 183 religious (origin: 85 Spain, 46 Italy, 24 USA, 11 Guatemala, 10 Costa Rica, 8 Mexico). *Male religious*. Total (1970) 369. *Brothers*. The total including contemplatives is 130. *Sisters*. Total including contemplatives (1970): 818 (19% nationals, 59% from other Latin American countries, 22% from other continents). *Seminarians*. In addition to the 122 Salvadorian seminarians shown, the national seminary has others from Nicaragua and Guatemala. *Main religious orders and congregations*. Priests: SDB, SJ, OFM, OAR, OP, MJ. Brothers: PFM. Sisters: Daughters of Charity of St Vincent de Paul, Salesians, Daughters of the Divine Saviour (indigenous), Carmelites of San José (indigenous), Good Shepherd of Angers, Ascension of Our Saviour, Dominicans of the Annunciation, Franciscans of the Immaculate Conception. *Catholic organizations*. The Episcopal Conference of El Salvador (Conferencia Episcopal de El Salvador, CEDES) is a member of CELAM and SEDAC. There are no national presbyteral or pastoral councils. Male and female religious personnel are represented on the Confederation of Religious Personnel of El Salvador (Confederación de Religiosos de El Salvador, CONFRES) which is a member of SERCAP and CLAR. The Commission for the Lay Apostolate of CEDES (Comisión de Apostolado Seglar de la CEDES) co-ordinates the following specialized movements of Catholic Action: ACU, JAC, JEC, JOC, MFC, Cursillos de Cristiandad, MIIC-Pax Romana, Jornadas de Vida Cristiana, Comunidades de Vida Cristiana, Club Serra and Legión de Maria. For the armed forces, El Salvador forms a military vicariate.

The Holy See has diplomatic relations with El Salvador and is represented to government and the Catholic hierarchy by a nuncio in San Salvador.

El Salvador serves as the headquarters of 3 co-ordinating agencies for Latin America: (1) Secretariado para Religiosos de Centroamérica y Panamá (SERCAP), a regional organization of religious personnel corresponding to SEDAC for CELAM; (2) Coordinación Centroamericana de Centros Campesinos Cristianos, formed in 1974, which serves as liaison for rural development centres in Guatemala, Honduras, El Salvador, Nicaragua and Costa Rica; and (3) Coordinación de las Comisiones Nacionales de Justicia y Paz para México, Centroamérica y Panamá, founded in 1970, for justice and peace commissions. The Centro de Animación Misionera was founded in Apulo in 1972 to stimulate missionary interest within Central America and Panama.

The Secretariado Social Interdiocesano co-ordinates a programme of social action through 5 departments dealing with radiophonic schools, information, rural development, publications and the creation of basic communities. It engages in conscientization using the methods of Paulo Freire under teams of priests and sisters in Suchitoto, Chalatenango and Cojutepeque and under JEC with help from JAC. Moreover, each diocese has at least one centre for rural development, there being 6 for 5 dioceses in 1975, and other basic communities. The Fundación Promotora de Cooperativas unites 11,500 families in 64 savings and credit co-operatives, of which 58 are in poor rural areas, and 9 consumer co-operatives.

Parish schools are supervised through the Secretariado Nacional de Educación while boarding schools are under the Federación de Colegios Católicos. In 1969, 14,164 pupils were enrolled in parish primary schools and 20,119 in boarding primary schools, with more than 3,000 students in 87 secondary and technical colleges. By 1973 schools numbered 117 primary (36,005 pupils) and 25 junior and secondary (5,144 pupils). The Universidad José Simeón Cañas, with 2,470 students in 1974, is one of the 4 sections of the Universidad Católica Centro-Americana, which includes also Guatemala, Nicaragua and Panama.

In 1969 the Catholic Church was responsible for 4 hospitals, 14 dispensaries and 2 homes for the aged. Caritás de El Salvador also is active.

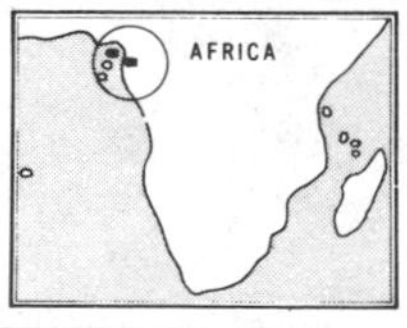


# EQUATORIAL GUINEA

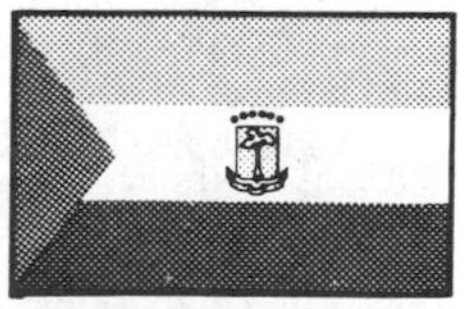

## SECULAR DATA

**STATE. Official name:** The Republic of Equatorial Guinea (La República de Guinea Ecuatorial). Adjectives of nationality: guineano, guineo.
**Flag** (shown above right): Green, white, and red stripes, blue triangle at hoist: centred coat of arms.
**Area:** 28,051 sq.km. (10,831 sq.miles). Agricultural land: 11.9%.
**Government:** Dictatorship, since 1969 (1471 Portuguese possession, 1778 ceded to Spain, 1968 Independence as republic).
**Legislature:** National Assembly, 35 members (in abeyance).
**Official language:** Spanish (*Español*).
**Capital:** Malabo (formerly Santa Isabel) 37,240 (1960).
**Political divisions:** 2 Provinces: Rio Muni, and Fernando Poo Island.
**Armed forces** (1976): Total 1,000 in Guardia Nacional.

**DEMOGRAPHY. Population:** 245,989 (census of 31.XII.1960. For 1970–2000 (UN), see last row of Table 1). Population density (1975): 11/sq.km. (29/sq.mile). Under 15 years: 33%. Growth rate (1975–80): 1.76% per year (births 3.55%, deaths –1.79%). Life expectancy (1975–80): 46.0 years. Household size: 4.9 persons.
**Major languages:** Spanish, Bulu Fang, Yoruba, French, Bubi, Pidgin English, Portuguese patois, and 10 others.
**Urban dwellers** (1970): 30.0%. Urban growth rate (1950–70): 5.3% per year.
**Labour force:** 36%.
**Refugees** (1977): None from abroad. Exiles abroad: 90,000 Equatorial Guineans in Cameroon, Gabon, Congo, Nigeria, other African countries and Spain; in 1975–76, 45,000 Nigerian contract labourers on Fernando Poo were evacuated by Nigeria.
**ETHNOLINGUISTIC GROUPS:** (1970) 65.0% Fang (Ntumu, Okak, Bulu), 14.5% Nigerian (Yoruba, Ibo, Ibibio, Hausa), 5.3% Bubi, 4.0% Puku (Batanga, Benga, Kombe), 2.8% Spaniard, 2.5% Seke (Lengi), 2.4% Eurafrican (Crioulo, Fernandino), 2.0% Ngumba (Mabea), 0.7% Bayele (Binga Pygmy), 0.4% Maka, 0.1% Indo-Pakistani, Sierra Leonian, other Cameroonian, Cuban. By 1976, most Nigerians and Spaniards had left, and Cubans numbered 450.

**MONEY (1977). Monetary unit:** ekuele (ekpwele) (= 100 centimos); US$1 = EK 68.00.
**National income per person:** US$350. Average annual family income: US$1,715.
**Cost of living in capital** (1976): Daily cost of living: US$30.

**EDUCATION.** Adult literacy: 20%. Education rate: 76%. Schools: 133.

HEALTH. Hospitals: 16 (1,637 beds). Doctors: 25. Lepers: 11,500 (37.1 per 1,000). Blind: 800. Psychotics: 2,500.

LITERATURE. Periodicals: 10. Scientific journals: 1. Newspapers: 2 dailies.

COMMUNICATION (per 1,000 people). Phones: 5. Radios: 230. TV sets: 2. Daily newspaper circulation: 4 copies.

TABLE 1. RELIGIOUS ADHERENTS IN EQUATORIAL GUINEA

| Year | 1900 | | mid-1970 | | Annual change, 1970–1980 | | | | mid-1975 | | mid-1980 | | 2000 | |
|---|---|---|---|---|---|---|---|---|---|---|---|---|---|---|
| Name | Adherents | % | Adherents | % | Natural | Conversion | Total | Rate | Adherents | % | Adherents | % | Adherents | % |
| Christians | 6,500 | 5.4 | 251,387 | 88.2 | 4,778 | 178 | 4,956 | 1.81 | 274,290 | 88.5 | 300,950 | 88.8 | 437,000 | 87.9 |
| crypto-Christians | 0 | 0.0 | 33,987 | 11.9 | 648 | 78 | 726 | 1.95 | 37,190 | 12.0 | 41,250 | 12.2 | 59,800 | 12.0 |
| professing | 6,500 | 5.4 | 217,400 | 76.3 | 4,130 | 100 | 4,230 | 1.78 | 237,100 | 76.5 | 259,700 | 76.6 | 377,200 | 75.9 |
| Roman Catholics | 6,000 | 5.0 | 202,300 | 71.0 | 3,843 | 104 | 3,947 | 1.79 | 220,600 | 71.2 | 241,770 | 71.3 | 349,800 | 70.4 |
| Protestants | 500 | 0.4 | 12,800 | 4.5 | 244 | −4 | 240 | 1.71 | 14,000 | 4.5 | 15,200 | 4.5 | 22,900 | 4.6 |
| Catholics (non-Roman) | 0 | 0.0 | 2,300 | 0.8 | 43 | 0 | 43 | 1.72 | 2,500 | 0.8 | 2,730 | 0.8 | 4,500 | 0.9 |
| affiliated | 6,500 | 5.4 | 251,387 | 88.2 | 4,778 | 178 | 4,956 | 1.81 | 274,290 | 88.5 | 300,950 | 88.8 | 437,000 | 87.9 |
| total practising | 6,170 | 95 | 208,650 | 83 | 3,918 | −406 | 3,512 | 1.56 | 224,920 | 82 | 243,770 | 81 | 327,700 | 75 |
| non-practising | 330 | 5 | 42,740 | 17 | 860 | 584 | 1,444 | 2.92 | 49,370 | 18 | 57,180 | 19 | 109,300 | 25 |
| Roman Catholics | 6,000 | 5.0 | 230,712 | 80.9 | 4,384 | 144 | 4,528 | 1.80 | 251,710 | 81.2 | 275,990 | 81.4 | 397,200 | 79.9 |
| Protestants | 500 | 0.4 | 14,300 | 5.0 | 272 | 18 | 290 | 1.86 | 15,600 | 5.0 | 17,200 | 5.1 | 26,300 | 5.3 |
| Evangelicals | 500 | 0.4 | 10,000 | 3.5 | 190 | −10 | 180 | 1.65 | 10,900 | 3.5 | 11,800 | 3.5 | 17,500 | 3.5 |
| African indigenous | 0 | 0.0 | 3,300 | 1.2 | 63 | 7 | 70 | 1.94 | 3,600 | 1.2 | 4,000 | 1.2 | 6,500 | 1.3 |
| Catholics (non-Roman) | 0 | 0.0 | 2,575 | 0.9 | 49 | −1 | 48 | 1.73 | 2,800 | 0.9 | 3,060 | 0.9 | 5,000 | 1.0 |
| Marginal Protestants | 0 | 0.0 | 500 | 0.2 | 10 | 10 | 20 | 3.45 | 580 | 0.2 | 700 | 0.2 | 2,000 | 0.4 |
| Tribal religionists | 113,500 | 94.6 | 18,813 | 6.6 | 303 | −624 | −321 | −1.85 | 17,400 | 5.6 | 15,600 | 4.6 | 10,000 | 2.0 |
| Non-religious | 0 | 0.0 | 10,000 | 3.5 | 216 | 314 | 530 | 4.27 | 12,400 | 4.0 | 15,300 | 4.5 | 30,000 | 6.0 |
| Atheists | 0 | 0.0 | 2,800 | 1.0 | 64 | 126 | 190 | 5.14 | 3,700 | 1.2 | 4,700 | 1.4 | 15,000 | 3.0 |
| Muslims | 0 | 0.0 | 1,300 | 0.5 | 25 | 0 | 25 | 1.77 | 1,401 | 0.5 | 1,550 | 0.5 | 2,500 | 0.5 |
| Baha'is | 0 | 0.0 | 700 | 0.2 | 14 | 6 | 20 | 2.50 | 800 | 0.3 | 900 | 0.3 | 2,500 | 0.5 |
| Country's population | 120,000 | 100.0 | 285,000 | 100.0 | 5,400 | 0 | 5,400 | 1.74 | 310,000 | 100.0 | 339,000 | 800.0 | 497,000 | 100.0 |

COLUMNS, ROWS. For meanings and definitions, see Codebook (Part 6). Note that, by definition, total 'Christians' = professing + crypto-Christians, which also = affiliated + nominal Christians. Percentages may not always total exactly, due to rounding.
CENSUSES. The religion question has not been asked.

NOTES ON RELIGIONS
AFRICAN INDIGENOUS. In 3 groupings in 1970 (see Table 2).
ATHEISTS. Party militants, mostly Fang.
BAHA'IS. Growth from nothing in 1964 to 5 local spiritual assemblies (4 on Fernando Poo) in 1973.
COUNTRY'S POPULATION. Since Independence in 1968 and the subsequent reign of full-scale terror, tens of thousands have been murdered and about 95,000 including Nigerians and other expatriates have fled as refugees to Cameroon, Gabon, Europe or their own countries. In 1978, a further 50,000 were reported murdered.
MUSLIMS. Sunnis of the Malikite rite, mainly Hausa expatriate traders and labourers from Nigeria, with some Indo-Pakistani traders.
TRIBAL RELIGIONISTS. Mostly among Fang sub-tribes (Okak, Ntumu, Bulu), with some Nigerians also.

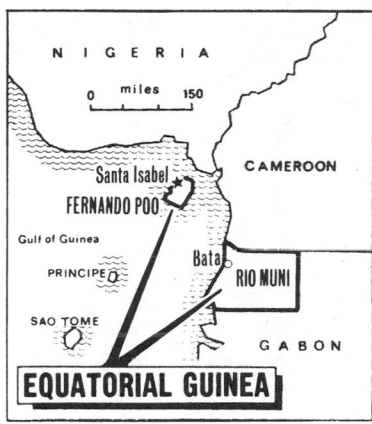

EQUATORIAL GUINEA

NON-CHRISTIAN RELIGIONS. Traditional religions are followed by under 5% of the population, mostly among the interior sub-tribes of the Fang: Okak, Ntumu and Bulu. The Fang word for God is Nzame, while the ancestral spirits are known as Bekon and the medicine man as uganga or ngang. The principal secret society is Bwiti which entered from neighbouring Gabon after 1927. It is dedicated to the remembrance of the great Fang ancestors and includes as initiates both men and women. A certain part of this society has been sufficiently christianized to be regarded as an indigenous church (Iglesia de los Banzie).

Atheism has spread as a result of the regime's militantly atheistic policies since 1968.

Islam has not taken root in Equatorial Guinea due largely to Catholicism's strong influence on society. Muslims are less than 1% of the population.

CHRISTIANITY

CATHOLIC CHURCH. Equatorial Guinea has had a long association with Catholicism dating from the 15th century, and it existed for lengthy periods under Portuguese, Spanish and French colonial administration prior to Independence in 1968. A prefecture was erected at Fernando Poo in 1855 which was elevated to a vicariate in 1904. In 1965 a second vicariate was formed for work in Río Muni. At present the diocese of Bata is responsible for the mainland and the diocese of Malabo (Santa Isabel) for the islands. Both dioceses are under the supervision of Spanish CMF priests.

Equatorial Guinea has a higher proportion of baptized Catholics (81%) than any other country of continental Africa. Because of the political situation, most Spanish priests were expelled a few months prior to Independence. The Spanish bishop of Malabo was expelled in 1970, and the Guinean bishop of Bata has been unable to return from Rome due to illness. Both bishops resigned their posts in 1974. In their place the Holy See appointed 2 Guinean apostolic administrators, although the one assigned to Bata and his secretary are now under house arrest. In 1973 the government expelled numerous Spanish sisters, Oblates of Mary Immaculate, who had refused to enrol their pupils in the notorious 'Forward with Macias' Youth Movement. Many Guinean priests have been imprisoned and only about 20 priests were actively in service in 1973. Nevertheless, the country's first major seminary was opened in October 1973 at Niefang, in the diocese of Bata.

PROTESTANT CHURCHES. Baptist missionaries from the West Indies arrived in Fernando Poo as early as 1841 but were expelled by the Spanish authorities in 1858. In 1870 an appeal from the local Protestant community via a ship's captain was received favourably by the Primitive Methodist Church in England, and missionaries were sent to the island. Methodism is still the major Protestant body on Fernando Poo. The Evangelical Church, which is autonomous but receives support from the United Presbyterian Church in the USA and since 1970 the Worldwide Evangelization Crusade (WEC) of UK, is the principal denomination in Río Muni. Beginning in 1850 on the island of Corisco, the Presbyterian mission reached the mainland in 1865. The first African pastor was ordained in 1870, and within 10 years an African missionary had been sent to open work at Batanga in Cameroon. Although evangelistic activity was impeded by the Spanish government, progress has been made. The church's strongest congregations today are found inland on the borders with Cameroon and Gabon. The WEC entered Río Muni in 1933, during a period of religious freedom, and has had some success among the Okak people. In 1970 it merged its work with that of the Presbyterians to form the Evangelical Church.

INDIGENOUS CHURCHES. The Bwiti movement, also called the Church of the Initiates (Iglesia de los Banzie), originated among the Fang in Gabon at the turn of the century and spread from there into Equatorial Guinea. Highly syncretistic in its early years, Bwiti has become progressively more Christian with increasing emphasis on Jesus as divine Saviour. A more orthodox denomination is the Assembly of Brethren (Asamblea de los Hermanos) which split from the Kombe Presbyterians in 1937.

OTHER CHURCHES. The most recent group to establish itself in the nation is the Free Protestant Episcopal Church, which is a Catholic (non-Roman) body from the UK and USA under African leadership and based in Liberia and Nigeria. In Equatorial Guinea it is composed mostly of expatriate English-speaking Africans from Nigeria and Sierra Leone.

CHURCH AND STATE. Portugal ceded Fernando Poo to Spain in 1778, but Río Muni did not become a Spanish territory until after the Berlin conference of 1885. Except for a brief period following the founding of the Spanish Republic (1932–36), Protestant activity under Spanish rule was severely restricted. Baptists had been expelled in 1858 and Methodists were only allowed to remain in 1870 through the intervention of the British consul. In Río Muni, the Catholic Church was declared the 'only' and 'official' church, and Presbyterians were not recognized until 1906. Protestant missionaries were withdrawn between 1924 and 1932 due to government opposition. The Spanish constitution of 1948 stated that 'No one will be molested because of his religious belief'; but the 1853 concordat with the Holy See, which identified Catholicism as the state religion and provided for its legal protection from 'competing' faiths, seemed to take precedence. All Protestant chapels were closed in 1952, but those established prior to Franco's assumption of power in 1939 were later allowed to re-open. The close relationship between the Catholic Church and the

Voters (81% Roman Catholics) in 1968 Independence election await presidential candidate Bonifacio Ondo Edu, later defeated and then murdered by Francisco Macias Nguema.

Atheists. Anti-religious guards of notorious 'Forward with Macias' Youth Movement search evicted Spanish Catholic refugees at Bata airport, 1969. In 1978 Nguema had 2 men publicly crucified and others killed in enforced re-enactment of the Way of the Cross.

Spanish state also had its influence on the educational system, instruction being founded on the 'principles of dogma and Catholic morals'. Protestant schools were not permitted during the period of Spanish rule.

With the granting of internal self-government in 1963 and full independence in 1968, numerous difficulties have arisen between the government and Catholic clergy. The constitution of 1968 provided for the full exercise of religious liberty, and the constitution of 1973 prohibits, in Article 24, all discrimination based on race, ethnic origin, religion, sex or social condition. Article 35 stipulates: 'The exercise of any religion is free provided that it respects the law and public order. It is illegal and punishable to place faith and religious belief in opposition to the principles and purposes of the state'.

However, since its accession to power at Independence, the regime of president Macias Nguema has subjected the country to despotic rule and an unprecedented reign of terror. The constitutions of 1968 and 1973 have been completely ignored, and anti-Christian propaganda has been openly encouraged and promoted by the regime, whose de facto philosophy has become one of militant atheism. At Malabo, Protestant buildings were confiscated; one Catholic church building was converted into an arms depot and the Catholic cathedral of Bata closed. By 1975, almost all foreign missionaries had been expelled, and local clergy have suffered increasing pressures, including imprisonment and torture. Thousands of Guineans in all walks of life have been victims of political assassination. In June 1974, 150 prisoners were killed in Bata prison, the official explanation being that they had formed a religious group called Christ Liberation

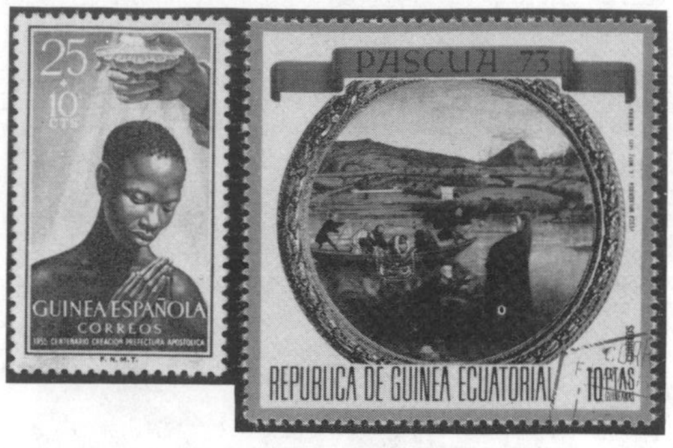


Numerous postage stamps have had Christian themes. *Left.* Baptism of an African convert (1955). *Right.* The Risen Christ by the Lakeside,' by K. Witz (1973).

Crusade but committed collective suicide when discovered. Guineans studying abroad have been unable to return, and church leaders have been refused permission to leave the country. In the attempt to suppress political intrigue all meetings of more than 10 persons have been banned, which has limited the activity of the church to personal contacts and officially recognized worship services. Group activity is no longer possible, and religious education is also prohibited. In 1974 a presidential decree was announced requiring priests and pastors to read at each worship service a message of praise to president Macias, as follows: 'Never without Macias, all for Macias. Down with colonialism and those who are ambitious'.

Harsher measures began in 1975. In July, the 3 seminaries were closed. In October, the pastoral vicar and acting bishop of Bata was executed with 22 others after torture. New anti-religious laws in February 1976 prohibited religious meetings, funerals, giving money to churches, baptism without government supervision, and the giving of Christian names to children by parents.

In 1978 anti-church measures instigated by the president included live burials in gaols, torture, a mock Way of the Cross in Bata gaol, and at least 2 public crucifixions of political prisoners.

In 1979, Macias was overthrown and executed.

**INTERDENOMINATIONAL ORGANIZATIONS.** There is no national council of churches. From 1943–70 the Evangelical Church was a member of the Federation of Evangelical Churches of Cameroon and Equatorial Africa based at Yaoundé, Cameroon. It is now a member of the All Africa Council of Churches.

**BROADCASTING.** No religious broadcasts are permitted over the state radio system. Christian programmes from outside can occasionally be heard over Radio Vatican and various Protestant stations.

### BIBLIOGRAPHY

'El Mbueti y sus doctrinas', G. de Pablo, *Cuadernos de estudios africanos* (Madrid), 2 (1946), 69–92.
*Equatorial Guinea, Macias country: the forgotten refugees.* R. A. Klintenberg. Geneva: International University Exchange Fund, 1978. 87p.
*La Iglesia en la Guinea Ecuatorial.* T. L. Pujadas. Madrid: Editorial Iris de Paz, 1968. 528p.
*La Secta del Bwiti en la Guinea Española.* A. de V. Vilaldach. Madrid: Instituto de Estudios Africanos, 1958. 63p.
'Terror grips Equatorial Guinea', *One world* (Geneva, WCC), 1 (November, 1974), 7–9.

TABLE 2. ORGANIZED CHURCHES AND DENOMINATIONS IN EQUATORIAL GUINEA

| Official name 1 | Begun 2 | Type 3 | Counc 4 | Congs 5 | Adults 6 | Affiliated 7 | Names, notes, and other statistics (see Codebook) 8 |
|---|---|---|---|---|---|---|---|
| Asamblea de los Hermanos | 1937 | I EBr | ••••• | 3 | 100 | 300 | *Assembly of Brethren.* Schism ex Kombe Presbyterians. M=Swiss Brethren (Closed). |
| Iglesia Adventista del Séptimo Día | 1961 | P Adv | x•••• | 2 | 132 | 300 | *SDA. Seventh-day Adventists, EG Mission District.* On Fernando Poo. 1nx,2mw,30Y. |
| **Igl Católica en la Guinea Ecuatorial:** | 1484 | R Lat | p•S•• | 58 | 154,600 | 230,712 | *Catholic Ch in EG.* C=2+0+2. 1s(in D Bata). 18n, 13x, 6m,42w,7965Yy. |
| D Bata | 1965 | R Lat | pcmf | 16 | 115,400 | 172,200 | Río Muni, Corisco, Elobeys. 90% Fang. 2,700 Whites. 1500z. 10 4 1 30 5010 |
| D Malabo (Santa Isabel) | 1904 | R Lat | pcmf | 42 | 39,200 | 58,512 | Fernando Poo and Annobón. 2,300 Whites. P=73%,2844z. 8 9 5 12 2955 |
| Iglesia de los Banzie (Bwiti) | c1910 | I mar | ••••• | 50 | 1,000 | 2,700 | *Ch of the Initiates. Mbueti. Religion d'Eboga* (a drug). Fang syncretistic body. |
| Iglesia Evangélica en la Guinea E | 1850 | P Ref | RuA•• | 100 | 4,000 | 12,000 | *Ev Ch in EG.* M=UPUSA,WEC(UK). A=1960. 90% Fang, 6% Kombe. 5n,2f,60Y,150y. |
| Iglesia Evangélica Episcopal Libre | 1968 | C ARo | xv••• | 208 | 850 | 2,575 | *Free Protestant Episcopal Ch, D West Africa.* Nigerians. 4n,6x,2p,2r,W=71%,500Y,275y. |
| Iglesia Metodista | 1870 | P Met | Vwa•• | | 600 | 2,000 | 1870, Primitive Methodists(UK) on Fernando Poo. Circuit of Methodist Ch, Nigeria. |
| Iglesias radiofónicas solitarias | c1968 | I rad | ••••• | | 200 | 300 | Isolated radio believers; scattered. R=250(ELWA,RVOG,Radio Vatican,et alia). |
| Testigos de Jehová | c1945 | M Jeh | x•••• | 9 | 221 | 500 | *Jehovah's Witnesses.* First witnessing reported 1949 Fernando Poo, 1964 Río Muni. |
| **Total affiliated (mid-1970)** | | | | **470** | **160,703** | **251,387** | **Total denominations (1970) . . . 9.** |
| **Total affiliated (mid-1975)** | | | | **480** | **176,400** | **274,290** | **Total denominations (1975) . . . 9.** |
| **Total affiliated (mid-1980)** | | | | **490** | **193,600** | **300,950** | **Total denominations (1980) . . . 9.** |

**NOTES ON TABLE ABOVE**

COLUMNS: for meanings and CODES (cols. 1, 3, 4, 8), see Codebook (Part 6). Column 1: **Boldface type** = church with over 10% of country's affiliated Christians.

**PEOPLES** (ethnolinguistic). Christians: (1970) 65.8% Fang (Ntumu, Okak, Bulu), 12.0% Nigerian (Ibo, Ibibio, Yoruba), 6.0% Bubi, 4.5% Puku (Batanga, Benga, Kombe), 3.1% Spaniard, 2.8% Seke, 2.7% Eurafrican, 2.2% Ngumba, 0.4% Maka, 0.3% Binga Pygmy (Bayele), Sierra Leonian.

COUNTRY-WIDE TOTALS

EVANGELIZATION (see Part 5). 1900: 17%. 1970: 100%. 1980: 100%. *Mass evangelism.* The Evangelical Church sponsors itinerant evangelistic teams on annual one-week village campaigns. There are a few Bible correspondence course students (ICI).

FOREIGN MISSIONARIES AND PERSONNEL (nationals serving abroad) (1973). Total about 10 Roman Catholics in Spain et alia (refugees).

FOREIGN MISSIONARIES AND PERSONNEL (aliens from abroad) (1973). Total 40. *From Western world.* 26: 24 Roman Catholics, 2 Protestants in 1 USA society. *From Third World.* 14: 10 Catholics (non-Roman) from Nigeria and Liberia, 2 Protestants from Nigeria, 2 Roman Catholics.

INSTITUTIONS (church-operated) (1973). Total 60, including 16 higher schools (2 minor seminaries), 35 medical centres (7 hospitals), 2 religious communities (monasteries), 1 seminary (RC), 3 study centres.

PERIODICALS. About 6 titles.

PERSONNEL. About 455 (415 national, 40 foreign).

RELIGIOUS LIBRARIES. About 6.

SCRIPTURE DISTRIBUTION (1975). Annual totals: nil. *Translations completed.* Portion: 3 languages since 1849. NT: 1 language in 1871.

SERVICE AGENCIES. About 4.

ADDITIONAL DATA ON CHURCHES

IGLESIA CATOLICA EN LA GUINEA ECUATORIAL. *Annual baptisms.* (1972) 93.5% infant, 6.5% adult. *Brothers.* All expatriates (1972). *Sisters.* 37 nationals, 5 expatriates (1972). *Seminarians.* 8 secular and 7 Clarétins (CMF), studying in Cameroon, Spain and Rome. *Catechists.* Total (1974) 340. *Indigenous religious congregations.* Sisters: Oblatas de Maria Inmaculada (begun 1936). *Main foreign congregations.* Priests: CMF, Scolopes. Sisters: Conceptionist Sisters. *Catholic organizations.* There is no episcopal conference, nor association of religious personnel, nor presbyteral or pastoral council.

The Holy See has no diplomatic relations with Equatorial Guinea. It is represented to the Catholic hierarchy by an apostolic delegate based in Yaoundé, Cameroon.

Of the 25 schools (6,200 students) operated by the Catholic Church in 1970, only 13 remained open in 1973. They are operated for the most part by Guinean sisters or more advanced students. In 1970 there were 2 orphanages, a leprosarium and a home for the aged.

IGLESIA EVANGELICA EN LA GUINEA ECUATORIAL. Work was begun in 1850 by American Presbyterians, which later became the West Africa Mission of the UPUSA, then the Iglesia Evangélica Presbiteriana en Río Muni. In 1970 it united with the work of the Misión Evangélica Cruzada (Worldwide Evangelization Crusade), with 4,000 adherents among the Okak, and assumed its present name. The membership is 90% Fang (60% Ntumu, 30% Okak), 6% Kombe (sub-tribe of Puku), 3% Oné, 1% Benga.

IGLESIA EVANGELICA EPISCOPAL LIBRE. The Free Protestant Episcopal Church in Guinea is part of the church's Diocese of West Africa, based on Lagos, Nigeria, with 5 Pastoral Districts in Santa Isabel and 6 Pastoral Districts in Río Muni, organized in 1970. This Nigerian church, also known as the Ecumenical Church Foundation, is the African branch of a Catholic (non-Roman) body from the UK and USA. Its members are largely immigrant labourers on Fernando Poo, as follows (1970): 1,600 Nigerians, 200 Sierra Leonians (now naturalized citizens), 700 Guineans, and 75 Cameroonians.

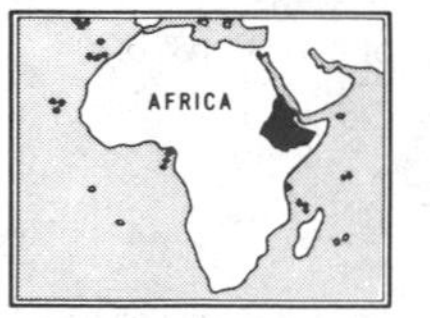


# ETHIOPIA

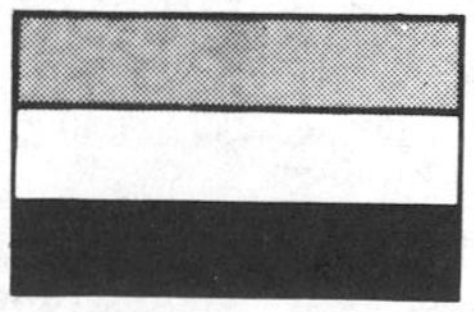

## SECULAR DATA

**STATE. Official name:** The Socialist Republic of Ethiopia (Ityopya). Alternative name: Socialist Ethiopia. Earlier name: The Empire of Ethiopia (Ye Ityopya Neguse Neguest Menguist). Adjective of nationality: Ethiopian.

**Flag** (shown above right): Green, yellow, and red stripes.

**Area:** 1,221,900 sq.km. (471,778 sq.miles). Agricultural land: 64.4%.

**Government:** Socialist military junta (leading to a People's Democratic Republic), since 1974 coup (3rd century empire (absolute monarchy), 1936–41 Italian rule, 1966–75 constitutional monarchy).

**Legislature:** Dergue (Administration), 120-man military committee; Provisional Military Administrative Council (PMAC).

**Official language:** Amharic (*Amharinya*).

**Chief cities:** capital Addis Ababa 1,083,420 (1974), Asmara 296,040.

**Political divisions:** 14 Provinces (Kifle-Hager).

**Armed forces** (1976): Total 50,800 regular: army 47,000, navy 1,500, air force 2,300 (36 combat aircraft). Reserves: 28,000. Paramilitary forces: 11,200.

**Foreign forces** (1973): 1,000 USA troops. (1978): 19,000 Cuban troops with USSR advisers.

**DEMOGRAPHY. Population:** 27,946,000 (estimate of 1.VII.1975; no censuses yet. For 1970–2000 (UN), see last row of Table 1). Population density (1975): 23/sq.km. (59/sq.mile). Under 15 years: 41%. Growth rate (1975–80): 2.39% per year (births 4.87%, deaths −2.48%). Life expectancy (1975–80): 39.0 years. Household size: 4.9 persons.

**Major languages:** Amharic, Gallinya, Tigrinya, Tigre, Arabic, Somali, Afar, Italian, English, French, Sidamo, Nilotic, and about 90 other smaller languages.

**Urban dwellers** (1970): 8.7%. Urban growth rate (1950–70): 5.0% per year.

**Labour force:** 46%.

**Refugees** (1977): 11,000 from Sudan, making a total of around 500,000 including Sudanese and Somalis after the Ogaden war. Exiles abroad: 95,000 Ethiopians (91,000 in Sudan, others in Kenya et alia).

**Tourists** (1974): 50,220.

**ETHNOLINGUISTIC GROUPS:** 40.0% Galla (Oromo) (9.7% Wallo, 5.0% Wallega, 3.4% Arusi, Boran, Jima, Kosa, Gera, Raya, Yaju, &c), 36.0% Amhara cluster (25.0% Amhara proper, 6.0% Tigrai, 2.5% Gurage, 2.0% Tigre, 0.2% Harari), 9% Kafa-Sidamo (4.5% Ometo, 1.3% Kambatta, 1.1% Darasa,

0.7% Kafa-Mocha, 0.4% Hadya, 0.3% Konso, 0.1% Bako, 0.1% Burji, 0.1% Maji, Gibe, Gimira, Janjero, &c), 6% Somali, 6% Nilotic (4.5% Shangalla, 0.3% Barea, 0.3% Nuer, 0.3% Kunama, 0.2% Anuak, 0.1% Berta, 0.1% Mesongo, Koma, Mao, &c), 0.9% Afar (Danakil), 0.5% Saho, 0.5% Agau (Awiya, Falasha, Kemant, et alii), 0.3% Beja, 0.2% Arab (Yemeni, Sudanese), 0.1% Italian, Greek, British & USA, French, Turkana, Asian (Indo-Pakistani) (2,500), Cuban (700, increasing to 19,000 military in 1978), Armenian & numerous smaller peoples.

**MONEY** (1977). **Monetary unit**: birr (dollar) (= 100 cents); US$1 = Eth$2.05.
**National income per person**: US$105. Average annual family income: US$515.
**Inflation**: (1970–74) 2.8% per year, (1975) 7% per year (consumer price index 130).
**Cost of living in capital** (1976): index 120 (Washington DC = 100). Daily cost of living: US$28.

**EDUCATION.** Adult literacy: (1965) 6%. Education rate: 8%. Schools: 2,603. Universities: 2.

**HEALTH.** Hospitals: 85 (8,415 beds). Doctors: 350. Lepers: 200,000 (7.1 per 1,000). Blind: 90,000. Psychotics: 220,000.

**LITERATURE.** Periodicals: 45. Newspapers: 9 dailies, 3 non-daily.

**COMMUNICATION** (per 1,000 people). Phones: 2. Radios: 7. TV sets: 1. Daily newspaper circulation: 2 copies.

TABLE 1. RELIGIOUS ADHERENTS IN ETHIOPIA

| Year | 1900 | | mid-1970 | | Annual change, 1970–1980 | | | | mid-1975 | | mid-1980 | | 2000 | |
|---|---|---|---|---|---|---|---|---|---|---|---|---|---|---|
| *Name* | *Adherents* | *%* | *Adherents* | *%* | *Natural* | *Conversion* | *Total* | *Rate* | *Adherents* | *%* | *Adherents* | *%* | *Adherents* | *%* |
| **Christians** | **2,941,000** | **36.8** | **13,573,000** | **54.6** | **372,017** | **67,383** | **439,400** | **2.81** | **15,610,000** | **55.8** | **17,967,000** | **57.0** | **32,199,000** | **60.0** |
| professing | 2,941,000 | 36.8 | 13,573,000 | 54.6 | 372,017 | 67,383 | 439,400 | 2.81 | 15,610,000 | 55.8 | 17,967,000 | 57.0 | 32,199,000 | 60.0 |
| Orthodox | 2,900,000 | 36.3 | 12,500,000 | 50.3 | 342,625 | 61,805 | 404,430 | 2.81 | 14,376,700 | 51.4 | 16,544,300 | 52.5 | 29,457,000 | 54.9 |
| Protestants | 1,000 | 0.0 | 900,000 | 3.6 | 24,666 | 5,134 | 29,800 | 2.88 | 1,035,000 | 3.7 | 1,198,000 | 3.8 | 2,254,000 | 4.2 |
| Roman Catholics | 40,000 | 0.5 | 170,000 | 0.7 | 4,647 | 453 | 5,100 | 2.62 | 195,000 | 0.7 | 221,000 | 0.7 | 483,000 | 0.9 |
| Anglicans | 0 | 0.0 | 3,000 | 0.0 | 79 | –9 | 70 | 2.12 | 3,300 | 0.0 | 3,700 | 0.0 | 5,000 | 0.0 |
| nominal | 100,000 | 1.3 | 581,435 | 2.3 | 18,660 | 27,197 | 45,857 | 5.86 | 783,000 | 2.8 | 1,040,000 | 3.3 | 2,952,000 | 5.5 |
| affiliated | 2,841,000 | 35.5 | 12,991,565 | 52.3 | 353,357 | 40,186 | 393,543 | 2.65 | 14,827,000 | 53.0 | 16,927,000 | 53.7 | 29,247,000 | 54.5 |
| total practising | 2,556,900 | *90* | 9,094,100 | *70* | 247,350 | 28,130 | 275,480 | 2.65 | 10,378,900 | *70* | 11,848,900 | *70* | 20,472,900 | *70* |
| non-practising | 284,100 | *10* | 3,897,460 | *30* | 106,007 | 12,056 | 118,063 | 2.65 | 4,448,100 | *30* | 5,078,100 | *30* | 8,774,100 | *30* |
| Orthodox | 2,796,500 | 35.0 | 11,903,800 | 47.9 | 322,865 | 28,755 | 351,620 | 2.60 | 13,547,500 | 48.4 | 15,420,000 | 48.9 | 26,125,000 | 48.7 |
| Protestants | 1,000 | 0.0 | 816,866 | 3.3 | 22,664 | 5,949 | 28,613 | 3.01 | 951,000 | 3.4 | 1,103,000 | 3.5 | 2,147,000 | 4.0 |
| Evangelicals | 1,000 | 0.0 | 720,000 | 2.9 | 19,969 | 5,231 | 25,200 | 3.01 | 837,900 | 3.0 | 972,000 | 3.1 | 1,895,000 | 3.5 |
| Neo-pentecostals | 0 | 0.0 | 1,000 | 0.0 | 119 | 1,781 | 1,900 | 38.00 | 5,000 | 0.0 | 20,000 | 0.1 | 100,000 | 0.2 |
| Roman Catholics | 43,500 | 0.5 | 161,849 | 0.6 | 4,385 | 430 | 4,815 | 2.62 | 184,000 | 0.7 | 210,000 | 0.7 | 429,000 | 0.8 |
| Ethiopian indigenous | 0 | 0.0 | 105,000 | 0.4 | 3,336 | 5,064 | 8,400 | 6.00 | 140,000 | 0.5 | 189,000 | 0.6 | 537,000 | 1.0 |
| Anglicans | 0 | 0.0 | 3,000 | 0.0 | 76 | –36 | 40 | 1.25 | 3,200 | 0.0 | 3,400 | 0.0 | 4,000 | 0.0 |
| Marginal Protestants | 0 | 0.0 | 1,050 | 0.0 | 31 | 24 | 55 | 4.23 | 1,300 | 0.0 | 1,600 | 0.0 | 5,000 | 0.0 |
| Muslims | 2,080,000 | 26.0 | 7,705,000 | 31.0 | 208,006 | 11,294 | 219,300 | 2.51 | 8,728,000 | 31.2 | 9,898,000 | 31.4 | 17,280,000 | 32.2 |
| Tribal religionists | 2,969,000 | 37.1 | 3,541,000 | 14.2 | 85,626 | –79,226 | 6,400 | 0.18 | 3,592,900 | 12.8 | 3,605,000 | 11.4 | 4,061,000 | 7.6 |
| Jews | 10,000 | 0.1 | 28,500 | 0.1 | 739 | –189 | 550 | 1.77 | 31,000 | 0.1 | 34,000 | 0.1 | 50,000 | 0.1 |
| Baha'is | 0 | 0.0 | 7,500 | 0.0 | 217 | 133 | 350 | 3.85 | 9,100 | 0.0 | 11,000 | 0.0 | 25,000 | 0.0 |
| Non-religious | 0 | 0.0 | 0 | 0.0 | 71 | 429 | 500 | 16.67 | 3,000 | 0.0 | 5,000 | 0.0 | 40,000 | 0.1 |
| Atheists | 0 | 0.0 | 0 | 0.0 | 24 | 176 | 200 | 20.00 | 1,000 | 0.0 | 2,000 | 0.0 | 10,000 | 0.0 |
| **Country's population** | **8,000,000** | **100.0** | **24,855,000** | **100.0** | **666,700** | **0** | **666,700** | **2.38** | **27,975,000** | **100.0** | **31,522,000** | **100.0** | **53,665,000** | **100.0** |

COLUMNS, ROWS. For meanings and definitions, see Codebook (Part 6). Note that, by definition, total 'Christians' = professing + crypto-Christians, which also = affiliated + nominal Christians. Percentages may not always total exactly, due to rounding.
CENSUSES. No censuses of population have been taken for the whole of Ethiopia. A city census of Addis Ababa dated 10–11.IX.1961 gave: 86.9% Ethiopian Orthodox, 9.8% Muslims, 2.5% other Christians, 0.9% other religionists. The 1970 figures above of religious profession for the whole nation are based on a number of estimates over the years.

NOTES ON RELIGIONS
ATHEISTS. The first Communist activity began in 1975 and within a year 2 clandestine Marxist-Leninist parties were operating underground: the Ethiopian Communist Party, and the People's Ethiopian Revolutionary Party.
BAHA'IS. Growth from 3 local spiritual assemblies in 1964 (2 in Eritrea) to 51 in 1973. In 1970, over 1,000 converts were enrolled.
COUNTRY'S POPULATION. In the 1973 famine at least 150,000 died.
ETHIOPIAN INDIGENOUS. These groups of former Orthodox and crypto-Orthodox, who have seceded to form pentecostal bodies, have had to operate largely underground since their formation and have been subjected to severe police harassment, persecution and imprisonments. In 1970 they formed 7 separate groups including immigrant bodies from Black Africa (see Table 2).
JEWS. Archaic Judaism is practised by the Falashas (Felashas) or Black Jews (28,000 population; language Amharic), who accept the Old Testament but not the Talmud. Since 1860, about 120 Falashas each year have been baptized by the Anglican CMJ and the Ethiopian Orthodox Church. There are also 500 foreign (expatriate) Jews in the country.
MUSLIMS. Mainly Sunnis (of the Shafiite rite). Eritrea is about 42% Muslim, 55% Christian. There are also 2,500 Asian Muslims. Among pagan tribes, the Shangalla are gradually being islamized. *Hajj pilgrims to Mecca*. (1970) 2,955; (1974) 3,473; (1975) 1,889; (1976) 2,246. *Pilgrimages in Ethiopia*. The most renowned among a number of centres are Sheikh Hussein north of Goba in the Galla province of Bale, where 100,000 pilgrims gather twice a year; Abred, in Gurage land, where 10,000 pilgrims gather on festivals; and Ja'a between Begi and Asosa near the Sudan border, also with 10,000. *Quranic schools*. There are over 10,000 local schools, 100 advanced, and a small number of higher schools. *Missionaries*. A large number of Egyptian missionaries sent by Al-Azhar University (Cairo) have begun work in the recent past, especially Eritrea.
NEO-PENTECOSTALS. Charismatics within the non-Pentecostal Protestant denominations, in particular the ECMY and the Bethel Evangelical Church, and among UPUSA and SIM missionaries.
ORTHODOX. Conversions to the Ethiopian Orthodox Church (in the table above, 28,755 a year) come from pagan tribes in the south and west, and come via 2 agencies: (1) the 2 Orthodox home mission societies, and (2) Protestant missions permitted to evangelize in certain areas on the understanding that converts are passed to the Orthodox Church for baptism.
PRACTISING CHRISTIANS. After the overthrow of the emperor in 1974, weekly churchgoing increased markedly, and by 1976 packed churches were being reported from all over the country.
PROTESTANTS. Although most conversions are from tribal religion, Muslims are becoming Protestants in some areas. In 1970 among the Kambatta, 100 Muslims became Lutherans and were baptized.
ROMAN CATHOLICS. In 1900, 41,089 indigenous baptized Catholics (including 14,000 in Eritrea), 2,072 catechumens, and a few Europeans.
TRIBAL RELIGIONISTS. Tribes over 60% traditionalist (animist) in 1972 numbered 14: Reshiat (99% animist), Mesongo (99%), Gimira (98%), Anuak (95%), Bako (90%), Suri (90%), Nuer (90%). Maji (90%), Darasa (80%), Konso (80%), Ometo (80%), Kafa (70%), Wallega Galla (70%), Berta (Shangalla) (60%).

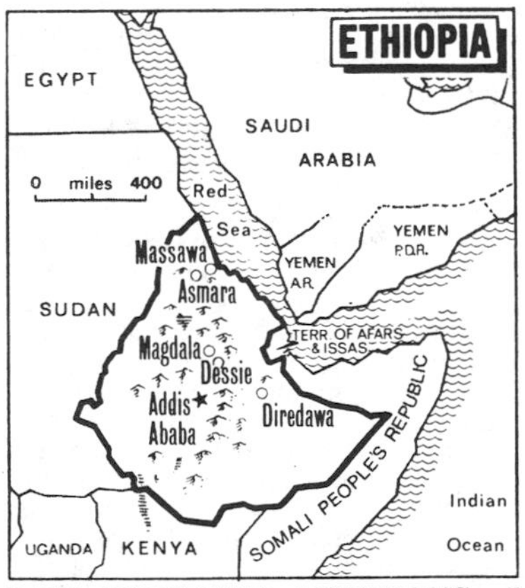


**NON-CHRISTIAN RELIGIONS. Islam** has an ancient history in Ethiopia, Muhammed having sent a group of his followers there prior to the Hegira in AD 622. The islands of the Dahlak archipelago, off Massawa, were occupied by Muslims in 705 as a bridgehead for contacts with East Africa, and this was followed by trade and conversions to Islam, especially in the coastal region. In 1506 Ahmed Granj of Harar succeeded in establishing Islam in the Amhara highlands, although he was later defeated by the Orthodox Christians with the help of the Portuguese. Nevertheless, Islam continues to play an important role in the country and is strongest in Eritrea, in the east and southeast of the country (principally among the Danakil, Somali and Harari peoples) and on the northwestern border with Sudan. Muslims in Ethiopia are mostly Sunnis of the Shafiite rite. The principal centres of learning are located in rural areas: at Dana on the western edge of the Danakil desert, Abred southwest of Addis Ababa, and Kolito near Sodo in southern Ethiopia. The principal shrine is that of Sheikh Hussein near Ginir to the east of Goba, where up to 100,000 pilgrims gather on Muslim feast days; another shrine is found at Ja'a near Asosa on the Sudan border.

**Traditional religions** retain the allegiance of a number of ethnic groups in the southwestern part of the country. The largest tribes, each with traditionalists over 60%, are the Darasa, Ometo, and Wallega Galla. Smaller tribes (all with over 90%) include the Anuak, Bako, Gimira, Mesongo, Nuer, Reshiat and Suri. The idea of a supreme being is prevalent under various names, the principal ones being Waka, Tosa and Tuma, or their derivatives: Waka or Wakaio (among the Boran, Wallega Galla, Mesongo), Wak (Guleb), Wa'a (Hadya); Tosa (Kullo, Tishena, Walamo), Tsosa (Zala), Tsuossa (Gofa), Tosso (Kuca); Tuma (Mekan, Suri-Surma, Tishena), Tummu (Murle). Other names are Tel (Ingessana), Yaro (Kafa), Sosi (Male), Yere (Mao), Magano (Sidamo) and Arumgimis (Udhuk). Among the Wallega Galla the obda tree is the centre of village worship, prayers of thanksgiving and offerings being made to the spirit which resides in the tree. The kolo rites performed by men at the obda tree involve the offering of sacrifices to placate the spirits of mountains and springs. Two female spirit-possession cults are Atete and Maram, both for aid in child-bearing.

**Judaism** is found in an archaic form among some 28,000 Falasha (Black Jews) in the region of Gondar, north of Lake Tana, as well as in isolated communities near Addis Ababa. There is no unanimity of opinion regarding the origin of the Falasha although it has been well established that they date back some 20 centuries and were probably converted to Judaism by the large number of Jews who emigrated to Ethiopia between the 1st and 7th centuries AD. They have resisted assimilation in a remarkable way and still scrupulously observe the sabbath and the Mosaic rituals. Their liturgical language is Ge'ez, but they also use many Hebrew words in their

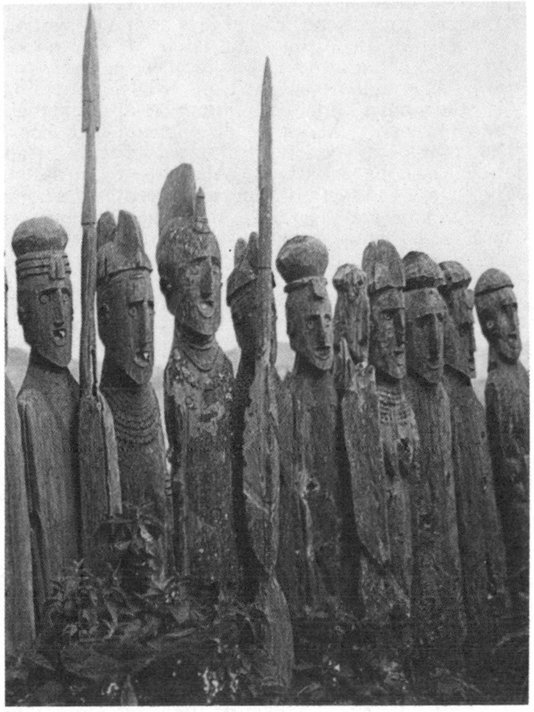

**Tribal religionists.** Sculptured wooden representations of tribal ancestors, serving as tombstones in Gemu Gefa province.

prayers. Prior to the creation of the state of Israel, the Jews of Palestine built dispensaries for them and 13 primary schools, training their headmasters in Palestine. Nevertheless, it was not until 1972 that the 2 chief rabbis of Israel recognized them officially as Jews and descendants of the tribe of Dan. At the same time it was suggested that they needed to be 'converted' since they do not observe all the rites of present-day Judaism. The state of Israel does not extend to the Falasha the benefits of its Law of Return in the same way as it does to other Jews throughout the world, and only about 250 Falasha have succeeded in emigrating to Israel since 1967. In addition to the Falasha, there are also about 500 foreign Jews in Ethiopia.

## CHRISTIANITY.

A shipwrecked youth from Tyre, north of Palestine, Frumentius, brought Christianity to Ethiopia in the early part of the 4th century, and Athanasius patriarch of Alexandria later appointed Frumentius bishop. The Ethiopian Orthodox Church dates its foundation to AD 332. In spite of constant pressure from Islam after the 7th century, Ethiopia remained officially Orthodox. A new Muslim threat in the early part of the 16th century was met with the aid of Portugal, and this was followed in 1555 by the arrival of the first Jesuit missionary. Although well received initially their attempt to propagate Roman Catholicism provoked lasting resentment and produced few fruits. The first Protestants, Swedish Lutherans, arrived in 1866, but neither Protestants nor Catholics made much impact on the scene prior to the present century.

ORTHODOX CHURCHES. The Ethiopian Orthodox Church is both the largest denomination in Ethiopia and also the largest non-Chalcedonian Orthodox church in the world. It continues to be the established church although its relationship to the new revolutionary government since 1974 has been increasingly tenuous. From earliest times the abuna (archbishop) had always been an Egyptian appointed by the Coptic patriarch of Alexandria, but in 1959 agreement was reached between the patriarch and the emperor Haile Selassie providing that the abuna should in future be an Ethiopian national bearing the title of patriarch-catholicos. The abuna has ecclesiastical precedence over all Coptic bishops except the Alexandrian patriarch. The church's strength is found almost entirely among the Amhara and Tigrai rural population, but its quasi-feudal conservative attachment to the past and its lack of trained priests have contributed to a weakening of its position in the cities and among youth. Reforms regarding the training of a more adequate priesthood have resulted from the establishment of Holy Trinity Seminary, a secondary school, and Holy Trinity Theological College (a faculty of Haile Selassie University), as well as the Lake Zwai Training Centre aided by the World Council of Churches. A total of 1,463 traditional schools are under the direct supervision of the church. Two Anglican societies (Church's Ministry among the Jews (CMJ) since 1855, and Bible Churchmen's Missionary Society (BCMS) from 1933 withdrawing in 1975) have worked within the Orthodox Church, teaching in convents and seminaries and helping in literature production and Bible translation work. Renewal of spiritual life within the Orthodox Church has been largely due to lay organizations, mainly the following: Society for Preaching of the Gospel (Sewasewa Berhan/Spreading of the Light), College Students Association (Haimanote Abew/Faith of Our Fathers), Apostolic Society (Mahbere Hawariat), Apostles of the Gospel Society (Yewengel Malak-tennoch Mahber), Holy Trinity Society (Mahbere

**Ethiopian Orthodox Church.** *Left.* Young deacons. *Right.* Mural of a parish church. *Above.* Priest with gospel during liturgy, in Gondar.

Sellassie), Dissemination of Light (Fenote Berhan) Society, and Fruit of the Faith (Fere Haimanot) Society.

Two other Orthodox churches have communities in Ethiopia. The Armenian Apostolic Church has a priest in Addis Ababa, and the Greek Orthodox Patriarchate of Alexandria has an archbishop and 2 priests in the Greek diocese of Aksum (Axum).

PROTESTANT CHURCHES. With a Christian community of about half a million, the Word of Life Evangelical Church related to the Sudan Interior Mission is the largest Protestant denomination. It supports 433 schools, 6 hospitals and leprosaria, 25 clinics, several orphanages, a literature publication centre and its own national missionary society. The church is active in 35 different areas and is strongest among the Wallamo (Ometo).

Lutheran bodies include the Evangelical Church Mekane Yesus (Dwelling-place of Jesus, in Amharic), second in size to the Word of Life Church, and the Evangelical Church of Eritrea. The Mekane Yesus Church has its strength in the western part of the country, but there is also an important nucleus in Addis Ababa and some congregations in the north. It is supported by Lutheran missions from the USA, Germany, Norway, Sweden, Denmark and Iceland. The church's extensive social service programme includes 9 secondary schools, 3 teacher-training colleges, 4 hospitals and 24 dispensaries. The Evangelical Church of Eritrea was founded in 1866 by the Swedish Lutheran EFS mission and has a large secondary school at Asmara.

Other Protestant bodies are Seventh-day Adventists (1907) in southern and western areas, the Meserete Kristos Church which receives help from American Mennonites, 3 Baptist denominations and several small Pentecostal groups.

**Catholic Church in Ethiopia.** Seminarians using Ethiopian music and drums in liturgy.

CATHOLIC CHURCH. Although there are no uniate churches, Ethiopic-rite and Latin-rite congregations exist together within an ecclesiastically unified church. A vicar apostolic in Asmara has primary responsibility for Latin-rite Catholics, and an eparch in Addis Ababa for those of the Ethiopic-rite. More than half of Ethiopia's Catholic membership is found in Eritrea province because of the long Italian influence there. The church has suffered extensively as a result of mistakes made by its missionaries in the 16th century and more recently by its identification with the Italian occupation during 1936–41. Nevertheless, the Catholic Church has made substantial contributions to the development of education and social service.

INDIGENOUS CHURCHES. Ethiopia's largest indigenous denomination is the Full Gospel Church which has sprung from an extensive pentecostal revival since the beginning of the 1960s, mainly among nominally Orthodox populations, with assistance from Swedish and Finnish Pentecostal missionaries. The church has undergone severe persecution since 1972 and for a long time was forced to operate underground. Another indigenous body, the Kambatta Evangelical Church, split in 1955 from the Word of Life Church opposing SIM control. In 1965 it applied to join the Lutheran Mekane Yesus Church, and after lengthy preparation was admitted as a synod of that church. Another pentecostal body beginning in 1966 has been the God's All Times Association (also called Yesemaye Berhan, Light of Heaven), formed by a group of young Orthodox and Protestant students after participation in revival meetings held at several colleges and the university in Addis Ababa beginning in 1964. All leaders and elders were youths, but again it has suffered persecution since 1970. Lastly, by 1975 immigrant bodies were beginning to arrive, including in Addis Ababa a colony of Vapostori (Apostles) from Zimbabwe (Rhodesia).

CHURCH AND STATE. According to Article 126 of the revised constitution of 4 November 1955, the Ethiopian Orthodox Church, which bases itself on the teaching of St Mark of Alexandria, was recognized as the established church of the empire and as such was supported by the state. Article 127 stated that the organization and secular administration of the established church was to be governed by law. The archbishop and bishops were elected by the Ecclesiastical Electoral College composed of representatives of clergy and laity. These elections were approved by the emperor, who also had the right to promulgate decrees, edicts and public regulations concerning the church, except on matters concerning monastic life and spiritual ministrations. In addition to these 2 articles, the constitution contained references to the emperor as 'elected by God', to the archbishop and his membership in the Council of Regency and the Crown Council (Articles 10 and 70) and to the 'Ethiopian Orthodox Faith' to which all members of the imperial family must belong (Article 16). The terms Coptic (Egyptian) and Monophysite did not appear in the constitution, and indeed the latter word is repudiated by the Orthodox Church. Finally, Article 40 introduced into Ethiopia for the first time the constitutional principle of religious toleration, with the free exercise of rites of any religion or creed provided that such religious practices were not utilized for political purposes. In Ethiopian usage, the appellation 'established church' meant that the church was spiritually independent, did not owe its origin to the state, yet was nevertheless supported and protected by the state. The government later withdrew certain privileges previously enjoyed by the Orthodox Church, including exemption from taxation, and affirmed its jurisdiction over temporal matters. The emperor took particular interest in pressing the established church to evolve and adapt to the modern world. A governmental office, the General Administration of the Ethiopian Orthodox Church (Ye-Biete Kehnet wanna Sera askeaje), handled relations between church and state.

With regard to foreign missionary societies, under Decree 3 of 1944 'Regulations governing the activities of missions', the emperor established a Committee of Missions under the presidency of the Ministers of Education, the Interior and Foreign Affairs, with the Ministry of Education bearing primary responsibility for the execution of its decisions. The committee considered applications of non-Orthodox groups and assigned them areas where they could operate. Such areas were inhabited predominantly by non-Christians and were known as 'open areas', as contrasted with 'Ethiopian Church areas' where the majority of the population were Orthodox. Permission was also on occasion granted to non-Orthodox missions to establish hospitals and non-denominational schools in closed areas provided that no proselytizing was carried on. The capital city itself was declared to be an open area.

In the late 1930s, the Italian dictator Mussolini expelled all non-Italian missionaries from Ethiopia, but at the end of World War II Italian missionaries suffered the same fate. In 1971, the newly inaugurated Ethiopian patriarch, Abuna Thewophlos, publicly stated that he would 'exert all my energy against every teaching and movement that may battle against the Ethiopian Church', a fact which has led some observers to blame the Orthodox Church for the recent persecution of indigenous pentecostals in the country. In mid-1972 nearly 300 members of the Full Gospel Church were imprisoned on charges of treason and immorality.

In the early months of 1974 the army began progressively to take control of the country. In March a petition was circulated among Orthodox lower clergy, protesting against the general social and economic situation and particularly the wealth and mode of life of the Orthodox hierarchy. On 20 April a demonstration was organized by Muslims in Addis Ababa advocating an equality with Coptic Orthodox Christians, and a mammoth Coptic counter-demonstration took place 2 days later. On 22 August the national synod of the Orthodox Church published a memorandum proclaiming its hostility to the proposed constitution, which would involve an alleged disestablishment of their church. According to this memorandum, clergy should continue to sit in parliament and the patriarch preside at the coronation ceremonies of emperors. However, on 11 September 1974 the patriarch affirmed that 'God blessed the great revolutionary movement directed by the armed forces with the support of the people'. This action appeared to be due to pressure exercised by the military on the Orthodox hierarchy, the latter being criticized for indifference concerning the famine in Wallo and Tigre and threatened with the loss of church wealth and imprisonment. The following day the military co-ordination committee (DEURG) deposed emperor Haile Selassie, who had been in power since 1928 and whose titles included the following: Conquering Lion of Judah, Elect of God, 225th Descendant of the Queen of Sheba and King Solomon, and Emperor of Ethiopia.

Ethiopia is now moving in the direction of a multi-confessional secular state. The proposed constitution prepared by the army stipulates that 'Religion is an individual matter' and that no religious differences may exist in the country. In December 1974 to gain the support of Muslims, the DEURG proclaimed Id El Adeha (Aid el Kabir) a national holiday, which has had the effect of equalizing even more the religious factor, although the Orthodox Church by 1976 had still not been disestablished.

In Eritrea, the guerrilla war begun in 1960 by Muslims of the Front for the Liberation of Eritrea (FLE), was reinforced in May 1971 by a new group called the Popular Liberation Force (PLF). The PLF is composed of leftist Christians who are much more radical ideologically than the leaders of the FLE. In the beginning the PLF formed a united front with the more progressive wing of the FLE, but the front collapsed in April 1972 with religious divisions playing a major role.

On 4 March 1975 the provisional military council proclaimed an agrarian reform throughout the country. All land was nationalized and became the collective property of the Ethiopian people, the

state promising nevertheless to redistribute 10-hectare lots to peasants. Because of its extensive properties the Ethiopian Orthodox Church is bound to be seriously affected. The same decree also abolished the rights of spiritual and customary chiefs. Also during 1975, the Orthodox bishop of Hosanna was murdered and his successor detained by the military, who then gave the entire Orthodox Church one year to put their financial and personnel affairs in order. Finally, in 1976 the regime arrested patriarch Thewophols and declared him deposed for corrupt practices, and later announced the election as patriarch (with the title Abuna Tikle Haimanot) of Malaku Wolde Mikael, an evangelistic monk credited with converting 300,000 animists and building over 100 churches and schools in Wallo province since 1934. However, the Coptic Orthodox pope in Cairo refused to recognize the deposition and prevailed on all other WCC member churches, and also the Church of Rome, to boycott the enthronement of the new patriarch on 29 August.

In February 1977 a further military coup brought to power a regime more Marxist-Leninist than its predecessor, which the following month seized the radio station RVOG and announced its national-

ization under the new name 'Radio Voice of the Revolution'. In 1978 a wave of local persecution of Protestant churches was reported; and the regime forcibly retired 8 Orthodox bishops and attempted to force its own candidates to replace them.

Ethiopian Christianity's traditional confrontation with Islam has created political problems with such neighbouring Muslim countries as Somalia, Sudan, Egypt and Libya. A central question remains the future of Eritrea with its large Muslim population.

## INTERDENOMINATIONAL ORGANIZATIONS.
The Ethiopian Inter-Mission Council, founded in 1943 with 15 member bodies, was the only ecumenical council in the country until 1978, although not officially recognized. Regarding the Orthodox Church, Anglican BCMS and CMJ missions have worked within it; and there have been signs recently of co-operation in specific projects between Orthodox and Protestant groups, most notably with Presbyterians. The Ethiopian Orthodox Church is a member of both the AACC and the WCC. At Sabbata near Addis Ababa is located a Christian community composed of 2 Ethiopian Orthodox, 2 English Protestants and 2 Catholic Combonian of Verona sisters. The sisters live together and jointly operate a dispensary. Capuchins have also founded an ecumenical centre at Adi Ugri, called the St Frumentius Ecumenical Centre. In 1973 an ecumenical committee for development aid, the Christian Relief and Development Association, was formed by

Catholics and other churches and voluntary agencies.

In 1978, 9 of the largest churches in Ethiopia, after some years' discussions, founded the Council for Co-operation of Churches in Ethiopia (CCCE), to co-operate in developmental and welfare work.

## BROADCASTING.
The state controlled Radio Addis Ababa in 1975 was giving a 30-minute daily programme to the Ethiopian Orthodox Church, which has its own radio production studio in the capital and was also accepting Protestant (but not Roman Catholic) programmes. From abroad, Radio Vatican beams in programmes in Amharic and Tigrinya for one hour 45 minutes a week. The Sudan Interior Mission is also starting a studio to prepare programmes for release over FEBA in the Seychelles.

Until March 1977, Addis Ababa was the site of one of the world's largest Christian broadcasting services, the international station Radio Voice of the Gospel (RVOG), owned and operated by the Lutheran World Federation in co-operation with the World Association of Christian Communication (WACC). RVOG employed about 180 people in Ethiopia and was allied with 14 local studios, from Nigeria to Hong Kong, which were sponsored by churches in

*Above.* Radio Voice of the Gospel (RVOG). Addis Ababa; begun 1963, seized by regime March 1977.
**Full Gospel Believers Church.** *Above left.* Speaking in tongues at worship service. Members, mostly converts from Orthodoxy, were severely persecuted from 1972-75 and hence went underground.
**Neo-pentecostals.** *Left.* All-night prayer meeting by Lutheran youths at charismatic youth conference in Nakamte, 1975 (Evangelical Church Mekane Yesu, Central Synod). In 1974 this group seceded from ECMY but later rejoined.

their areas. They produced programmes which were sent to Addis Ababa to be transmitted back to the target areas during 20 hours of daily short-wave broadcasting in 13 languages: Amharic, Arabic, Chinese, English, Farsi, French, Fulani, Hausa, Hindi, Malagasy, Swahili, Tamil and Telugu. RVOG covered much of Africa, the Middle East and south-east Asia. Programmes were 30% evangelistic and 70% information and education. RVOG also had 7 hours of daily transmissions on medium wave for the Addis Ababa area in Amharic, English and French, with daily programmes produced by the Ethiopian Evangelical and Orthodox churches. Following the seizure of RVOG by the regime, many of the international programmes were transferred to Christian stations elsewhere.

## BIBLIOGRAPHY
'An annotated and classified bibliography of English literature pertaining to the Ethiopian Orthodox Church'. J. J. Bonk. Thesis, Trinity Evangelical Divinity School (USA), 1972. 177p. (466 items, covering AD 330–1959).
'An ethnohistory of Ethiopia'. E. J. Elliston. Thesis, Fuller Theological Seminary, Pasadena, CA (USA), 1968. 177p.
*Born at midnight.* P. Cotterell. Addis Ababa: SIM, 1972. (On the SIM revival).
*Catholic directory of Ethiopia, 1968.* Addis Ababa: Conference of Catholic Bishops. 1968.
*Die Kirche Athiopiens.* F. Heyer. Berlin: Walter de Gruyter, 1971. 360p.
*Ethiopia Tikdem—Ethiopia First: the shades of things past and the shape of things to come for Roman Catholic Christianity in Southern Ethiopia.* M. Singleton. Brussels: Pro Mundi Vita, 1977. 232p.

*Fire on the mountain: the story of a miracle—the Church in Ethiopia.* New York: Sudan Interior Mission, 1966. 253p. (SIM work in Wallamo province).
*General survey concerning Christian literature in Ethiopia.* J. R. H. Conacher. Addis Ababa: Christian Literature Development Project, 1970. 384p.
*Islam in Ethiopia.* J. S. Trimingham. London: Oxford University Press, 1952.
'L'Eglise Catholique en Ethiopie', G. Van Winsen, *Nouvelle revue des sciences missiologiques*, XXI (1965), 118–131.
'Planting the church among nomads'. G. Kjaerland. Thesis, Fuller Theological Seminary, Pasadena, CA (USA), 1971. 309p. (Borana nomads).
*Priests and politicians: Protestant and Catholic missions in Orthodox Ethiopia, 1830–1868.* D. Crummey. Oxford: Clarendon, 1972. 188p.
'Religion', chapter 7 in G. A. Lipsky, *Ethiopia: its people, its society, its culture* (New Haven: HRAF, 1962), p. 100–120.
*The Church of Ethiopia: a panorama of history and spiritual life.* Ed S. Selassie. Addis Ababa: Ethiopian Orthodox Church, 1970. 97p.
'The Church's Ministry among the Jews in Ethiopia'. F. G. Payne. London: CMJ, 1972. Manuscript.
*The Ethiopian Orthodox Church.* Eds A. Wondmagegnehu & J. Motovu. Addis Ababa: Ethiopian Orthodox Mission, 1970. 181p.
*The Oriental Orthodox Churches, Addis Ababa Conference, January 1965.* Addis Ababa: Interim Secretariat, Oriental Orthodox Conference, 1965. 142p.
*The Qemant: a pagan-hebraic peasantry of Ethiopia.* F. C. Gamst. New York: Holt, Rinehart & Winston, c1963. (On the Falasha Jews).

TABLE 2. ORGANIZED CHURCHES AND DENOMINATIONS IN ETHIOPIA

| Official name 1 | Begun 2 | Type 3 | Counc 4 | Congs 5 | Adults 6 | Affiliated 7 | Names, notes, and other statistics (see Codebook) 8 |
|---|---|---|---|---|---|---|---|
| Anglican Church (D Egypt) | 1926 | A Cen | aw.U. | 15 | 400 | 3,000 | M=USPG(UK). Expatriates. Other Anglican work (1855 CMJ, 1934 BCMS) is within EOC. |
| Armenian Apostolic Ch: V Addis Abeba | 1887 | O Arm | Ewc.. | 5 | 500 | 1,200 | Armenian residents. 1 priest, 1 primary school (Addis Ababa). Under C Echmiadzin. |
| Baptist Evangelical Church | 1950 | P Bap | TF..K | 27 | 661 | 2,000 | M=BGC(USA). 80% Shoa Galla, 20% Amhara. South-central. 2 schools. 36f,3H,3h,1s. |
| Baptist Mission of Ethiopia | 1967 | P Bap | T...K | 3 | 20 | 50 | M=SBC(USA). Home meetings. Rural development in Amhara closed (EOC) area. 22f,9h. |
| Bethel Evangelical Church of Ethiopia | 1919 | P Ref | R.A.K | 146 | 20,000 | 42,000 | M=UPUSA,RCA. 1975, merger with ECMY. 86% Galla, 10% Anuak. 23n,68f,2H,18h,1p,2r. |
| Catholic Church in Ethiopia: | 1555 | R LEr | O.SES | 167 | 95,500 | 161,849 | *Katolikawit Bete-Cristian.* C=10+1+20. 5q,3s(117). 211n, 147x, 291m, 1013w, 6180Yy. |
| M Addis Abeba (Addis Ababa) | 1951 | R Eth | Os | 23 | 16,900 | 28,700 | Includes 10,000 Latins (foreigners) in Addis. 1H,1s. 30 43 27 61 1055 |
| D Adigrat | 1937 | T Eth | Os | 16 | 5,200 | 8,639 | *Bete-Papas Katolikawi.* 60% Irob, 40% Tigrina. 1s. 39 3 0 39 290 |
| D Asmera (Asmara) | 1930 | R Eth | Os | 85 | 29,500 | 50,000 | *Katolikawi Membre Pepesenna.* Tigrai, Mensa. 1s. 92 0 155 401 1765 |
| VA Asmera of the Latins | 1894 | R Lat | Oofmc | 10 | 24,200 | 41,000 | 80% Kunama, 20% Italians & Europeans. 1v. 35 29 93 397 657 |
| VA Gimma (Jimma) (*Latin*) | 1913 | R Lat | Pcm | 14 | 4,900 | 8,300 | *Hawariawi Enderrasié Gimma.* Galla, Kaffa. 1s,P=74%. 6 20 1 18 388 |
| VA Harer (Harar) (*Latin*) | 1846 | R Lat | Pofmc | 2 | 5,300 | 9,030 | 48% Kambatta, 32% Galla, 20% Wallamo. P=64%. 8 15 10 70 284 |
| PA Awasa (Neghelli) (*Latin*) | 1937 | R Lat | Pfscj | 6 | 1,000 | 1,780 | *Mision Katolic.* Dry southern desert. 70 expatriates. 0 20 4 21 698 |
| PA Hosanna (*Latin*) | 1940 | R Lat | Pofmc | 11 | 8,500 | 14,400 | Fast-expanding church among responsive Hosanna tribe. 1 17 1 6 1043 |
| Chrischona Mission in Ethiopia | 1854 | P ind | x.... | 2 | 30 | 100 | M=Chrischona Mission(Switzerland). Falashas, also SW of Addis. HQ Addis Ababa. 8f,2i,1r. |
| Christ Foundation Church | 1948 | P Men | G.A.K | 9 | 817 | 2,000 | *Meserete Kristos Ch.* M=EMBMC. 60% Galla, 30% Amhara. 4n,5x,42f,2H,2h,1r,1s,50Y. |
| Christian Brethren | 1952 | P CBr | x.... | 3 | 40 | 210 | *Open.* M=CMML(UK). Among Galla and Danakil Muslims. 50% Galla, 50% Amhara. 9f,6Y. |
| Ch of Jesus C of Latter-day Saints | | M LdS | x.... | 1 | 30 | 50 | *Mormons.* M=CJCLdS(Utah,USA). Mainly USA expatriates. |
| Churches of Christ | 1963 | P Dis | x.... | 130 | 10,000 | 15,000 | M=CMF,CCCC(Instrumental)(USA). Southwest. 1n,3x,26f,G=15%pa,W=80%,200Y,300z. |
| Emmanuel Baptist Church | 1960 | P Bap | x...K | 23 | 1,300 | 3,000 | M=BBFI(USA). Mainly in east (Bale, Harar). HQ Addis Ababa. 36f,1s. |
| **Ethiopian Orthodox Church:** | 332 | O Eth | NWA.K | 15,000 | 7,020,000 | 11,897,600 | *EOC. Ethiopia Tewahido Bete-Cristian.* 30f. 1463r,6s. 75839n, 67082m, 795d. |
| P Shewa (Shoa, Addis Ababa) | 332 | O Eth | Np | 2,251 | 1,324,200 | 2,244,500 | Capital. 18% urban. 55% Orthodox, 45% Muslim. 317r,1s. 8816 11012 104 |
| D Arusi | 1955 | O Eth | Na | 265 | 349,600 | 592,500 | 97% rural. 50% Orthodox, 40% Muslim, 10% pagan. 20r. 1056 1256 1 |
| D Bale | 1960 | O Eth | Na | 61 | 10,000 | 17,000 | 12% urban. 60% Muslim, 30% pagan, 10% Orthodox. 18r. 180 279 0 |
| D Begemdir | 1928 | O Eth | Na | 2,024 | 806,200 | 1,366,500 | 96% rural. 95% Orthodox (Amhara), 5% pagan. 148r. 14306 10470 274 |
| D Eritrea | 1955 | O Eth | Na | 687 | 490,700 | 831,700 | 9% urban. 50% Orthodox (Tigre & others), 50% Muslim. 10076 6938 24 |
| D Gemu Gefa | 1955 | O Eth | Na | 102 | 53,000 | 90,000 | 97% rural. 80% pagan, 10% Orthodox, 10% Muslim. 7r. 229 287 4 |
| D Gojam (Gojjam) | 1928 | O Eth | Na | 2,441 | 944,000 | 1,597,100 | 95% rural. 95% Orthodox, 3% pagan, 2% Muslim. 322r. 15000 10500 166 |
| D Harer (Harar, Harage) | 1955 | O Eth | Na | 97 | 421,300 | 714,100 | 95% rural. 80% Muslim, 20% Orthodox. 34r. 425 642 1 |
| D Ilubabor | 1955 | O Eth | Na | 138 | 41,000 | 70,000 | 96% rural. 60% pagan, 30% Muslim, 10% Orthodox. 11r. 409 553 0 |
| D Kefa (Kaffa) | 1955 | O Eth | Na | 187 | 107,400 | 182,100 | 7% urban. 70% Muslim, 25% Orthodox, 5% pagan. 31r. 933 1125 1 |
| D Sidamo | 1955 | O Eth | Na | 161 | 48,000 | 82,000 | 95% rural. 85% pagan, 5% Orthodox, 5% Muslim. 31r. 302 456 0 |
| D Tigre | 1928 | O Eth | Na | 1,897 | 1,379,000 | 2,338,000 | 96% rural. 95% Orthodox (Tigrai, Amhara), 5% Muslim. 253r. 17917 17142 169 |
| D Welega (Wallega) | c1935 | O Eth | Na | 361 | 358,400 | 607,400 | 97% rural. 40% Orthodox (Galla), 25% Muslim, 25% pagan. 19r. 827 1281 2 |
| D Welo (Wallo) | c1935 | O Eth | Na | 1,445 | 687,200 | 1,164,700 | 97% rural. 65% Muslim, 35% Orthodox (Amhara). 252r. 5452 5110 49 |
| Evangelical Church Mekane Yesus | c1880 | P Lut | LWA.K | 1,203 | 46,502 | 177,000 | *ECMY. Dwelling of Jesus.* A=1958. 91n,61x,558m,239f,4H,24h,15p,13r,2s(41),2872Y,5871y. |
| Evangelical Church of Eritrea | 1866 | P Lut | L.... | 83 | 2,480 | 7,138 | *Wangelawit Bete Kristian Ertra.* M=EFS. 82% Tigrinya, 12% Mensa. 7n,8x,5h,13Y,148y. |
| Faith Church of Christ | 1950 | P Hol | xF... | 30 | 123 | 3,000 | Western Eritrea. M=Evangelistic Faith Missions(USA). 19n,10x,5m,8f,1s,73Y,484z. |
| Full Gospel Believers Church | c1960 | I pe3 | ....K | | 50,000 | 100,000 | Indigenous; Swedish & Finnish aid. 1972–75 persecution, 300 imprisoned. 200n. |
| God's All Times Association | 1966 | I pen | ..... | | 1,500 | 4,000 | *Mulu Wangel* (*Full Gospel*), *Yesemaye Berhan* (*Light of Heaven*). Students; banned 1968. |
| Greek Orth P Alexandria: D Aksum | c1900 | O Ara | Cw... | 5 | 2,000 | 5,000 | Mostly Greeks and Arabs; 3,000 in Addis Ababa. Archbishop, 2 expatriate priests. |
| Jehovah's Witnesses | c1950 | M Jeh | x.... | 8 | 596 | 1,000 | *Watch Tower. IBSA.* Active witnessing under way by 1951. Underground. 50Y. |
| Light of Life Church | 1959 | P Pe2 | Z...K | 86 | 4,000 | 8,000 | M=Philadelphia Church Mission(SFM,Sweden). South. Darasa. 34x,27f,G=10%pa,8i,3p,470Y. |
| Lutheran Ch of Bible-true Friends in E | 1921 | P Lut | l.... | 40 | 2,000 | 3,500 | M=SLM(BVM,Bible True Friends) (Sweden). Low-church Lutherans. HQ Addis Ababa. |
| Lutheran Church of Eritrea | 1911 | P Lut | l.... | 20 | 500 | 1,168 | 1911 split from EFS. M=SLM(BVM,Bible True Friends) (Sweden). HQ Asmara. 14f,1i. |
| Middle East General Mission | c1957 | P int | .G... | 4 | 50 | 100 | Was Egypt General Mission. Aids EC of Eritrea; Kunama, Barea. 50m,49f,1H,1h,7i. |
| Orthodox Presbyterian Church | 1944 | P Ref | Jt... | 5 | 50 | 100 | Eritrea. M=OPC(USA). HQ Mekele (Tigre). 12f,1H. |
| Seventh-day Adventist Church | 1907 | P Adv | x.... | 304 | 15,968 | 45,000 | *Ethiopia UM.* 39% Galla, 20% Wallamo, 15% Amhara. 4n,20x,81f,4H,3h,1j,3r,226t(39888),3124Y. |
| United Pentecostal Church of Ethiopia | 1967 | P Pe1 | x.... | 19 | 2,500 | 6,000 | *Jesus Only Church.* M=UPC(USA). Unitarian Pentecostals. HQ Addis Ababa. 6n,3p(24). |
| Word of Life Evangelical Church | 1927 | P Bap | xM..K | 2,051 | 181,463 | 500,000 | *WLEC.* M=SIM. 1438n,100x,600m,332f,G=10%pa,6H,25h,50p,2s(25),W=85%,10000Y,40000z. |
| Other Protestant denominations | | P | ..... | | 500 | 1,500 | Total about 14 (see list below). |
| Other African indigenous churches | | I | ..... | | 500 | 1,000 | Total 5: Apostolic Ch of Johane Masowe (Zimbabwe), Holy Ghost Fire Ch (Nigeria; 2 congs in Addis). |
| **Total affiliated (mid-1970)** | | | | **19,950** | **7,460,030** | **12,991,565** | **Total denominations (1970) . . . 47.** |
| **Total affiliated (mid-1975)** | | | | **20,900** | **8,514,000** | **14,827,000** | **Total denominations (1975) . . . 50.** |
| **Total affiliated (mid-1980)** | | | | **21,950** | **9,720,000** | **16,927,000** | **Total denominations (1980) . . . 53.** |

NOTES ON TABLE ABOVE
COLUMNS: for meanings and CODES (cols. 1, 3, 4, 8), see Codebook (Part 6). Column 1: **Boldface type** = church with over 10% of country's affiliated Christians.
NATIONAL COUNCILS (Column 4, 5th letter).
K = Council for Co-operation of Churches in Ethiopia (CCCE).
S = Conference of the Catholic Bishops of Ethiopia, also full member of CCCE.
*Other national councils.* Ethiopian Inter-Mission Council (Protestant missions).
OTHER PROTESTANT DENOMINATIONS. These smaller bodies include: Assemblies of God (USA; 1975), Christian Union (1951), Eglise Francophone d'Addis Ababa, Elim Fellowship (1956), German-speaking Ev Lutheran Ch in Ethiopia (1952), Mennonite Brethren Chs, Red Sea Mission Team (1951, 16 missionaries among the Afar), Sefere Guenet Ch (Village of Heaven Ch, in Addis Ababa Market area; M=FFFM; member of CCCE), Southern Methodist Ch, World-Wide Missions (1966); also USA military chaplaincies until 1974.
UNITING CHURCHES. (1) The Baptist Bible Fellowship and Baptist Evangelical Church are now associated with the Word of Life Evangelical Church. (2) The Bethel Ev Ch of Ethiopia has attempted a merger with the Ev Ch Mekane Yesus.

PEOPLES (ethnolinguistic). Christians: 58.5% Amhara cluster (45.5% Amhara proper, 9.9% Tigrai, 2.0% Gurage, Tigre), 25.0% Galla (Oromo, with Arusi, Wallega, Wallo), 12.2% Kafa-Sidamo (Kambatta, Maji, Ometo, Wallamo, Darasa, Konso), 3.5% Nilotic (Kunama, Barea, Berta, Koma, Anuak, Nuer, Shangalla), 0.2% Italian, 0.1% Agau, 0.1% Saho (Irob, Minifere), French, British, USA, Greek, Arab, Armenian.

COUNTRY-WIDE TOTALS
EVANGELIZATION (see Part 5). 1900: 51%. 1970: 86%. 1980: 88%. *Mass evangelism.* Among recent campaigns: 1960, Billy Graham 2-day rally in Addis Ababa (18,000 attenders, 739 enquirers); May 1973, Kaffa province 15-month campaign led by 8 Wallamo evangelists (400 family conversions); 1975–76, New Life for All (NLFA) campaign. *Radiophonic evangelism.* Annual listeners' letters (1975): 14,541 RVOG, TWR, FEBA et alia. Bible correspondence courses: ICI, LCMS.
FOREIGN MISSIONARIES AND PERSONNEL (nationals serving abroad) (1973). Total 54 Orthodox (priests, with some religious personnel) in 8 countries.
FOREIGN MISSIONARIES AND PERSONNEL (aliens from abroad) (1973). Total 1,733. *From Western world.* 1,708: 1,418 Protestants (540 in 25 USA societies, 321 in 3 Norway societies, 133 in 4 Sweden societies, 78 in 6 UK societies, 73 in 8 WGermany societies, 67 in 3 Canada societies, 59 in 3 Finland societies, 52 in 5 Australia societies, 44 in 4 Denmark societies, 23 in 4 New Zealand societies, 14 in 1 Switzerland society, 10 in 2 Iceland societies, 4 in 1 Netherlands society), 257 Roman Catholics, 31 Anglicans (30 in 2 UK societies, 1 in 1 USA society), 2 Orthodox. *From Communist world.* About 4 Roman Catholics from Yugoslavia. *From Third World.* 21: about 10 Orthodox from Egypt, 6 Roman Catholics from India, 5 Protestants from Korea, Philippines and Japan.
INSTITUTIONS (church-operated) (1973). Total 2,610, including 1,560 higher schools (1,463 Orthodox, 10 RC minor seminaries), 200 medical centres (30 hospitals), 1 radio/TV station, 800 religious communities (797 monasteries), 2 research centres, 20 seminaries (8 RC, 6 Orthodox, 6 Protestant), 1 university.
PERIODICALS. About 30 titles.
PERSONNEL. About 161,130 (159,397 national, 1,733 foreign).
RELIGIOUS LIBRARIES. About 60.
SCRIPTURE DISTRIBUTION (1975). Annual totals: 36,865 Bibles (3% free, 89% subsidized, 8% commercial), 219,535 NTs (19% free, 80% subsidized, 1% commercial), 203,395 UBS portions, 523,434 UBS selections. *Translations completed.* Portion: 17 languages since 1513. NT: 7 languages since 1549. Bible: 4 languages since 1840.
SERVICE AGENCIES. About 69, including ALERT, BCMS (1933; 16 missionaries; withdrew 1975), CMJ (1855; 20 missionaries), GMF, HAESA, HANSEA(SCM), LWR, MAF (5 aircraft), NLFA, RVOG(LWF), SENM, SU, WGC, WVI, YCS, YCW, YMCA, YWCA.

ADDITIONAL DATA ON CHURCHES
BAPTIST EVANGELICAL CHURCH. In Amharic, Berhane Wongel (Light of the Gospel) Church.
BETHEL EVANGELICAL CHURCH OF ETHIOPIA. Autonomous since 1938, the church in 1975 merged, as a synod, with the Evangelical Church Mekane Yesus. Since 1966 it has developed a missionary relationship with the Ethiopian Orthodox Church which has baptized and received its converts.
CATHOLIC CHURCH IN ETHIOPIA. Full name in Amharic: Katolikawit Romawit Bete-Cristian. M Addis Abeba = Biete-Like Papasat Zekatolikawian; VA Harar = Hawariawi Enderrasié Harar. *Annual baptisms.* (1972) 77.2% infant, 22.8% adult. *Priests.* The first Ethiopians were ordained in 1846. By 1972 there were over 40 Ethiopian Capuchins. Expatriates: all religious. *Brothers.* 254 Ethiopians, 37 expatriates. *Sisters.* 940 Ethiopians, 73 expatriates. *Seminarians.* All religious. *Catechists.* Total (1972) 197. *Indigenous religious congregations.* None, except 2 Ethiopian branches of Cistercians and Consolata. *Main foreign orders and congregations.* Priests: OFMCap (provinces of Malta, Lombardy, Paris), Cistercians, CM, FSCJ, SJ. Brothers: FSC. Sisters: 220 Verona Sisters (Pie Madri della Nigrizia, of whom 60 belonged in 1970 to the Ethiopian rite), Daughters of St Anne, Ursulines of Gandino.
*Catholic organizations.* The Conference of the Catholic Bishops of Ethiopia has its headquarters in Addis Ababa. It is a member of SECAM, and since February 1977 of AMECEA also. There are no national presbyteral or pastoral councils, but 2 associations of religious personnel are active: the Conference of Religious Personnel in Southern Ethiopia, and the Conference of Major Religious Superiors in Northern Ethiopia. The principal lay movements are Catholic Action for Men (500 members), Catholic Action for Women (350 members), YCS (150 members), Pax Romana (100 university students), YCW, Legion of Mary and Crusaders.
The Holy See has diplomatic relations with Ethiopia and is represented to government and the Catholic hierarchy by a pro-nuncio based in Addis Ababa.
In 1968 the Catholic Church sponsored 170 primary and secondary schools, with 31,000 students, and also played an important role in the establishment of 2 universities: Haile Selassie University in Addis Ababa, and the Catholic University of Asmara. The latter institution was founded by Combonian sisters (Pie Madre della Nigrizia) in 1958 and was fully recognized in 1968. A faculty of theology exists in Addis Ababa, and an interdiocesan catechetical centre has been created by the episcopal conference at Dongora, Sidamo province, in the prefecture apostolic of Awasa. By 1973 schools had increased to 212 primary (37,906 pupils) and 32 secondary (4,280 pupils).
The church was responsible for 88 medical and charitable centres in 1968. Co-ordinating organizations for development and social service include the Ethiopian Catholic Welfare Organization, which is a member of Caritas Internationalis, and Agri-Service-Ethiopia, which offers correspondence courses in agricultural development.
ETHIOPIAN ORTHODOX CHURCH. *Dioceses.* These follow political boundaries. Diocese of Shoa = Shewa Hageresibket. *Column 5* above gives numbers of parishes. *Column 8.* The 3 columns of the sub-table show (n) number of Ethiopian priests, (m) number of deacons (aged 12–20 years), and (d) number of monasteries (which have sections for both men and women, with on average 15 monks per monastery). *Schools.* The code 'r' here designates traditional ecclesiastical higher schools for church studies (total 1,463, with 57,635 pupils). In addition, there are 15,000 church elementary schools (*nebab bet*). *Membership.* The EOC has as members about 95% of the Amhara, 80% Tigrinya-speakers, and substantial followings among the Darasa, Kambatta, Falasha (7%), Kafa (25%), Ometo (20%), Teshenna (70%) and Wallega Galla (30%). *Foreign missions.* Two Anglican societies work within the EOC: the CMJ (20 missionaries), and the BCMS (10 missionaries, until 1975).
EVANGELICAL CHURCH MEKANE YESUS. In Amharic, = Wangelawit Betekristian Mekane Yesus Beitiopia. The church was constituted in 1958, and is assisted by the following 8 foreign missionary societies: ALC (USA), DEM (Denmark), FMS (Finland), HM (Germany, 44 missionaries), Iceland MS, NLM,

NMS (Norway), SEM (EFS, Sweden). *Synods*. These number 5: Central (formerly Shoa & East Wallega; mostly in capital); Kambatta (a 25,000-strong part of the SIM which in 1952 seceded and appealed to ECMY, who finally accepted them as a synod in 1963; M = FMS); North Ethiopia (formerly Wallo-Tigre; M = ALC, EFS; Galla, among whom about 500 Muslims a year are being baptized); South Ethiopia (formerly Sidamo-Gamugoffa; Sidamo, Guji; M = NMS, Iceland MS); and Western (formerly Western Wallega; M = GHM, EFS, NMS; Galla, some Shangalla). *Membership*. 50% Wallega (Galla), 30% Kambatta, 13% Sidamo, 2% Tigrinya. *Growth*. Annual growth rate (1970–73): Gemu Gefa 14%, Sidamo 14%, Shoa (Kambatta) 22%. By 1975 total membership had risen to 210,000;

and by 1977, to 283,000 (including Bethel Evangelical Church). *Schools*. 86 primary, 11 secondary, 1 teacher-training, 675 basic, 465 literacy, 10 vocational, 5 home economics. *Neo-pentecostals*. A charismatic movement mainly among young people began in Nakamte ECMY congregation in 1973. After a temporary schismatic existence it reunited with the church in 1975.
FULL GOSPEL BELIEVERS CHURCH. Earlier called Full Gospel Church; in Amharic, Mulu Wangel.
LIGHT OF LIFE CHURCH. In Amharic, Yehiwot Berhane Church· also earlier termed Sidamo Free Churches.
WORD OF LIFE EVANGELICAL CHURCH. In Amharic, Kale Heywot Beta-Kristiyanat. Also known, nationally, as Fellowship of Evangelical Believers (Yewengel Amanyoch

Undinet Mahaba) (which includes the Baptist General Conference). The missionary body SIM (Sudan Interior Mission) is registered in Ethiopia as the Society of International Missionaries. *Congregations*. Total: (1958) 688, (1964) 988, (1971) 1,794. *Membership*. 60% Wallamo, 13% Kambatta, 12% Darasa, 10% Sidamo, 2% Burji, 1% Arusi, 1% Bako, 1% Amhara; other tribes include Janjero, Ara, Malli, Gujee, Shangalla, Bunna. *Growth*. Annual growth rate (1970–73): Arusi 33%, Gema Gefa 6%, Sidamo (Wallamo) 9%, Shoa (Kambatta) 8%. In 4 months from September 1975, the SIM's 240 Darasa churches gained over 24,000 adult converts during the NLFA campaign. In 5 months from September 1977, there were 17,500 adult baptisms in Woltayo district (Durami and Darasa). *Schools*. Total 422.

---

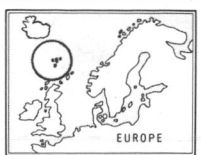

# FAEROE ISLANDS

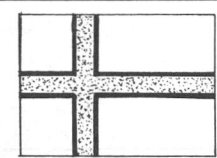

## SECULAR DATA

STATE. Official name: The Faeroe Islands (Foroyar; in Danish, Faeroerne).
Flag (shown above right): White with red blue-edged Scandinavian cross.
Area: 1,399 sq.km. (540 sq.miles). Description: 21 islands (17 inhabited). Agricultural land: 2.1%.
Government: Self-governing overseas area of the Kingdom of Denmark, since 1948 (1380 Danish crown possession, 1948 home rule granted).
Legislature: Lagting (Parliament), 26 members.
Official language: Faeroese.

Capital: Tórshavn 9,738 (1966); in Danish orthography, Thorshavn.
Armed forces (1976): Danish.

DEMOGRAPHY. Population: 38,612 (census of 16.II.1970. For 1970–2000 (UN), see last row of Table 1). Population density (1975): 29/sq.km. (74/sq.mile). Under 15 years: 35%. Growth rate (1975–80): 0.69% per year. Household size: 3.0 persons.
Major languages: Faeroese, Danish.
Urban dwellers (1970): 25%.
Labour force: 39%.

ETHNOLINGUISTIC GROUPS: 97% Faeroe Islander (Scandinavian), 2.5% Danish, Swedish, Norwegian, other European.

MONEY (1977). Monetary unit: Faeroese krona (= 100 ore); US$1 = FKr 6.1.
National income per person: US$4,100. Average annual family income: US$12,300.

EDUCATION. Adult literacy: 100%.

HEALTH. Hospitals: 3 (240 beds). Doctors: 32. Blind: 20.

LITERATURE. Periodicals: 42. Newspapers: 7 non-daily.

COMMUNICATION (per 1,000 people). Radios: 390.

### TABLE 1. RELIGIOUS ADHERENTS IN THE FAEROE ISLANDS

| Year / Name | 1900 Adherents | % | mid-1970 Adherents | % | Annual change, 1970–1980 Natural | Conversion | Total | Rate | mid-1975 Adherents | % | mid-1980 Adherents | % | 2000 Adherents | % |
|---|---|---|---|---|---|---|---|---|---|---|---|---|---|---|
| Christians | 15,000 | 100.0 | 38,960 | 99.9 | 200 | −1 | 199 | 0.50 | 39,960 | 99.9 | 40,950 | 99.9 | 44,550 | 94.8 |
| professing | 15,000 | 100.0 | 38,960 | 99.9 | 200 | −1 | 199 | 0.50 | 39,960 | 99.9 | 40,950 | 99.9 | 44,550 | 94.8 |
| Protestants | 15,000 | 100.0 | 38,810 | 99.5 | 199 | −1 | 198 | 0.50 | 39,810 | 99.5 | 40,790 | 99.5 | 44,370 | 94.4 |
| Marginal Protestants | 0 | 0.0 | 100 | 0.3 | 1 | 0 | 1 | 0.50 | 100 | 0.3 | 105 | 0.3 | 120 | 0.3 |
| Roman Catholics | 0 | 0.0 | 50 | 0.1 | 0 | 0 | 0 | 0.50 | 50 | 0.1 | 55 | 0.1 | 60 | 0.1 |
| nominal | 0 | 0.0 | 610 | 1.6 | 3 | −1 | 2 | 0.32 | 625 | 1.6 | 630 | 1.5 | 2,250 | 4.8 |
| affiliated | 15,000 | 100.0 | 38,350 | 98.3 | 197 | 0 | 197 | 0.50 | 39,335 | 98.3 | 40,320 | 98.3 | 42,300 | 90.0 |
| total practising | 14,300 | 95 | 34,510 | 90 | 177 | 1 | 178 | 0.50 | 35,400 | 90 | 36,290 | 90 | 29,610 | 70 |
| non-practising | 700 | 5 | 3,840 | 10 | 20 | −1 | 19 | 0.48 | 3,930 | 10 | 4,030 | 10 | 12,690 | 30 |
| Protestants | 15,000 | 100.0 | 38,200 | 97.9 | 196 | 0 | 196 | 0.50 | 39,185 | 97.9 | 40,160 | 97.9 | 42,120 | 89.6 |
| Evangelicals | 7,500 | 50.0 | 10,000 | 25.6 | 51 | −1 | 50 | 0.49 | 10,250 | 25.6 | 10,500 | 25.6 | 11,000 | 23.4 |
| Marginal Protestants | 0 | 0.0 | 100 | 0.3 | 1 | 0 | 1 | 0.50 | 100 | 0.3 | 105 | 0.3 | 120 | 0.3 |
| Roman Catholics | 0 | 0.0 | 50 | 0.1 | 0 | 0 | 0 | 0.50 | 50 | 0.1 | 55 | 0.1 | 60 | 0.1 |
| Baha'is | 0 | 0.0 | 40 | 0.1 | 0 | 1 | 1 | 2.50 | 40 | 0.1 | 50 | 0.1 | 100 | 0.2 |
| Non-religious | 0 | 0.0 | 0 | 0.0 | 0 | 0 | 0 | 0.00 | 0 | 0.0 | 0 | 0.0 | 2,350 | 5.0 |
| Country's population | 15,000 | 100.0 | 39,000 | 100.0 | 200 | 0 | 200 | 0.50 | 40,000 | 100.0 | 41,000 | 100.0 | 47,000 | 100.0 |

COLUMNS, ROWS. For meanings and definitions, see Codebook (Part 6). Note that, by definition, total 'Christians' = professing + crypto-Christians, which also = affiliated + nominal Christians. Percentages may not always total exactly, due to rounding.

CENSUSES. The religion question has not been asked.
BAHA'IS. In 1 isolated group.

## CHRISTIANITY

PROTESTANT CHURCHES. The principal denomination in the islands, as in Denmark itself, is the Evangelical Lutheran Church, often referred to as the Danish National Church. In the Faeroes, the church is dependent on the Lutheran bishop of Copenhagen, but in recent years the dean of Tórshavn has been elevated to the rank of assistant bishop and now enjoys considerable autonomy. The country is divided into 11 clerical districts with 57 churches and 17 priests, the majority of whom are native Faeroese, trained in Danish universities. Because of difficulties of travel between the islands, a priest can hold services in only one church within his district on any Sunday. In his absence in his other churches, lay parish-clerks conduct worship services. The Old and New Testaments and the Danish hymnal are in use translated into Faeroese, which is the church-language of the people. In the Faeroes the Lutheran Church generally receives rather more enthusiastic support than in Denmark.

Other Protestant denominations include the Christian Brethren who began work in 1865 and have developed a significant following in the northern islands; in percentage terms, Brethren are stronger in the Faeroes than in any other country in the world. There are also small Adventist and Salvation Army communities.

CATHOLIC CHURCH. Roman Catholic worship, suppressed after the 16th-century Reformation, began again in 1931 with the arrival of 2 priests and 5 sisters. The territory is under the jurisdiction of the Catholic diocese of Copenhagen. There is a parish at Tórshavn with 50 members, most of whom are natives of the isles and reside in the capital. A parish council was created in 1970. Personnel include one OMI North American priest, who served earlier in Greenland, and 20 Franciscan Missionaries of Mary.

**Lutheran Church.** Ruins of unfinished Magnus Cathedral at Kirkebo (7 miles from Torshavn), oldest cultural centre in Islands. At left, ancient bishop's residence, of logs with thatched roof.

**CHURCH AND STATE.** Legal statutes and relationships between church and state are the same as in Denmark.

**INTERDENOMINATIONAL ORGANIZATIONS.** Relations between Lutherans and Catholics have improved over recent years. During the Week of Prayer for Christian Unity (each January), joint worship services are held in Tórshavn.

**BROADCASTING.** From overseas, Trans World Radio (Monaco) beams in a weekly 15-minute programme in Faeroese on Monday evenings.

TABLE 2.  ORGANIZED CHURCHES AND DENOMINATIONS IN THE FAEROE ISLANDS

| Official name 1 | Begun 2 | Type 3 | Counc 4 | Congs 5 | Adults 6 | Affiliated 7 | Names, notes, and other statistics (see Codebook) 8 |
|---|---|---|---|---|---|---|---|
| Catholic Church (D Kobenhavn) | 1931 | R Lat | bxBQ. | 1 | 30 | 50 | In Bispedømment Kobenhavn, Katolske Kirke. Closed from Reformation to 1931. 1x,20w. |
| Christian Brethren | 1865 | P CBr | x.... | 26 | 4,000 | 8,000 | *Plymouth (Open) Brethren.* M=CMML(UK). Begun by Scots. Strongest in northern isles. |
| Jehovah's Witnesses | c1950 | M Jeh | x.... | 3 | 61 | 100 | *Watch Tower. IBSA.* First activity reported 1954. 8Y. |
| Lutheran Ch of Denmark (D Kobenhavn) | c 750 | P Lut | Lwc.. | 57 | 19,500 | 30,000 | In Evangelisk-lutherske Folkekirke i Danmark. 11 Districts. Active laity. 16n,1x. |
| Salvation Army | 1924 | P Sal | xwc.. | 1 | 50 | 100 | *Frelsunarherurin* (in Faeroese). *Iceland & Faeroes Div.* Norway & Iceland Territory. |
| Seventh-day Adventist Church | | P Adv | x.... | 1 | 50 | 100 | *Syvende Dags Adventist. SDAs,* East Denmark Conference. |
| Total affiliated (mid-1970) | | | | 89 | 23,691 | 38,350 | Total denominations (1970) . . . 6. |
| Total affiliated (mid-1975) | | | | 91 | 24,310 | 39,335 | Total denominations (1975) . . . 6. |
| Total affiliated (mid-1980) | | | | 93 | 24,920 | 40,320 | Total denominations (1980) . . . 6. |

**NOTES ON TABLE ABOVE**
COLUMNS: for meanings and CODES (cols. 1, 3, 4, 8), see Codebook (Part 6). Column 1: **Boldface type** = church with over 10% of country's affiliated Christians.

**PEOPLES** (ethnolinguistic). Christians: 97.0% Faeroe Islander (Scandinavian), 2.5% Danish, Swedish, Norwegian, other European.

**COUNTRY-WIDE TOTALS**
EVANGELIZATION (see Part 5). 1900: 100%. 1970: 100%. 1980: 100%.

FOREIGN MISSIONARIES AND PERSONNEL (nationals serving abroad) (1973). Total 4 Protestants (Brethren) in Greenland and Iceland.
FOREIGN MISSIONARIES AND PERSONNEL (aliens from abroad) (1973). Total 22. *From Western world.* 22: 20 Roman Catholics, 2 Protestants (1 in 1 Denmark society, 1 in 1 Norway society).
PERIODICALS. 6 titles.
PERSONNEL. About 46 (24 national, 22 foreign).
SCRIPTURE DISTRIBUTION (1975). Annual totals: 597 Bibles (subsidized), 794 NTs (subsidized). *Translations completed.* Faeroese: portion 1823, NT 1931, Bible 1948.

SERVICE AGENCIES. About 4.

**ADDITIONAL DATA ON CHURCHES**
CATHOLIC CHURCH. *Catholic organizations.* The church sponsors one nursery school with 50 children; one kindergarten of 90 children; and one primary school with 350 children, of whom only 3% are Catholics. Apostolatus Maris has also been established.

---

# FALKLAND ISLANDS

## SECULAR DATA

**STATE.** Official name: The Crown Colony of the Falkland Islands and Dependencies. Alternative name (used by Argentina): Malvinas.
**Flag** (shown above right): British Blue Ensign with arms of the Colony on white disc in the fly.
**Area:** 11,961 sq.km. (4,618 sq.miles). Description: 2 islands, 200 islets. Agricultural land: 98.6%.
**Government:** Crown colony of the United Kingdom (1765 British settlement).
**Legislature:** Legislative Council, 11 members.
**Official language:** English.

**Capital:** Stanley 1,098 (1970).
**Armed forces** (1976): British.
**Dependencies:** South Georgia, South Sandwich groups.

**DEMOGRAPHY. Population:** 1,957 (census of 3.XII.1972. For 1970–2000 (UN), see last row of Table 1). Population density (1975): 0.2/sq.km. (0.4/sq. mile). Under 15 years: 30%. Growth rate (1975–80): 0.0% per year. Household size: 4.0 persons.
**Major languages:** English, Spanish.
**Labour force:** 51%.

**ETHNOLINGUISTIC GROUPS:** 97.8% British, 1.4% Argentinian, 0.5% Chilean, Norwegian.

**MONEY** (1977). **Monetary unit:** Falkland Islands pound (= 100 new pence); US$1 = FI£ 0.43.
**National income per person:** US$2,000. Average annual family income: US$8,000.

**EDUCATION.** Adult literacy: 98%. Schools: 31.

**HEALTH.** Hospitals: 1 (27 beds). Doctors: 4.

**LITERATURE.** Periodicals: 10. Newspapers: 2 non-daily.

**COMMUNICATION** (per 1,000 people). Phones: 240. Radios: 520.

TABLE 1.  RELIGIOUS ADHERENTS IN THE FALKLAND ISLANDS

| Year / Name | 1900 Adherents | % | mid-1970 Adherents | % | Natural | Conversion | Total | Rate | mid-1975 Adherents | % | mid-1980 Adherents | % | 2000 Adherents | % |
|---|---|---|---|---|---|---|---|---|---|---|---|---|---|---|---|
| **Christians** | **2,205** | **98.0** | **1,820** | **92.9** | 0 | −14 | −14 | −0.80 | **1,750** | **89.3** | **1,680** | **85.7** | **1,580** | **79.0** |
| professing | 2,205 | 98.0 | 1,820 | 92.9 | 0 | −14 | −14 | −0.80 | 1,750 | 89.3 | 1,680 | 85.7 | 1,580 | 79.0 |
| Anglicans | 1,552 | 69.0 | 1,060 | 54.1 | 0 | −14 | −14 | −1.41 | 990 | 50.5 | 920 | 46.9 | 740 | 42.0 |
| Protestants | 293 | 13.0 | 530 | 27.0 | 0 | 0 | 0 | 0.00 | 530 | 27.0 | 530 | 27.0 | 500 | 25.0 |
| Roman Catholics | 360 | 16.0 | 220 | 11.2 | 0 | 0 | 0 | 0.00 | 220 | 11.2 | 220 | 11.2 | 220 | 11.0 |
| Marginal Protestants | 0 | 0.0 | 10 | 0.5 | 0 | 0 | 0 | 0.00 | 10 | 0.5 | 10 | 0.5 | 20 | 1.0 |
| nominal | 105 | 4.7 | 100 | 5.1 | 0 | 6 | 6 | 4.62 | 130 | 6.6 | 160 | 8.2 | 180 | 9.0 |
| affiliated | 2,100 | 93.3 | 1,720 | 87.3 | 0 | −20 | −20 | −1.23 | 1,620 | 82.7 | 1,520 | 77.5 | 1,400 | 70.0 |
| total practising | 1,470 | 70 | 860 | 50 | 0 | −10 | −10 | −1.23 | 810 | 50 | 760 | 50 | 560 | 40 |
| non-practising | 630 | 30 | 860 | 50 | 0 | −10 | −10 | −1.23 | 810 | 50 | 760 | 50 | 840 | 60 |
| Anglicans | 1,460 | 64.8 | 1,000 | 51.0 | 0 | −26 | −26 | −2.99 | 870 | 44.4 | 740 | 37.8 | 590 | 29.5 |
| Protestants | 290 | 12.9 | 500 | 25.5 | 0 | 6 | 6 | 1.13 | 530 | 27.0 | 560 | 28.5 | 590 | 29.5 |
| Roman Catholics | 350 | 15.5 | 210 | 10.7 | 0 | 0 | 0 | 0.00 | 210 | 10.7 | 210 | 10.7 | 200 | 10.0 |
| Marginal Protestants | 0 | 0.0 | 10 | 0.5 | 0 | 0 | 0 | 0.00 | 10 | 0.5 | 10 | 0.5 | 20 | 1.0 |
| Non-religious | 0 | 0.0 | 70 | 3.6 | 0 | 13 | 13 | 9.63 | 135 | 6.9 | 200 | 10.2 | 300 | 15.0 |
| Baha'is | 0 | 0.0 | 40 | 2.0 | 0 | 1 | 1 | 2.22 | 45 | 2.3 | 50 | 2.6 | 80 | 4.0 |
| Other religionists | 45 | 2.0 | 30 | 1.5 | 0 | 0 | 0 | 0.00 | 30 | 1.5 | 30 | 1.5 | 40 | 2.0 |
| **Country's population** | **2,250** | **100.0** | **1,960** | **100.0** | **0** | **0** | **0** | **0.00** | **1,960** | **100.0** | **1,960** | **100.0** | **2,000** | **100.0** |

COLUMNS, ROWS. For meanings and definitions, see Codebook (Part 6). Note that, by definition, total 'Christians' = professing + crypto-Christians, which also = affiliated + nominal Christians. Percentages may not always total exactly, due to rounding.

CENSUSES. 1901 census of the British Empire (as in 1900 column above, adjusted). 28.III.1953: 86.1% Anglicans and Protestants, 10.6% Roman Catholics, 3.4% other religionists. 18.III.1962: 64.7% Anglicans, 24.2% Protestants, 10.9% Roman Catholics, 0.2% marginal Protestants. 3.XII.1972: 54.2% Angli-

cans, 27.6% Protestants, 11.0% Roman Catholics, 4.8% non-religious, 1.9% other religionists, 0.5% marginal Protestants.
BAHA'IS. In 1 local spiritual assembly (1973).

**Church of England in the Falkland Islands.** *Right,* Anglican cathedral in Port Stanley, with in foreground whalebone monument commemorating British occupancy. *Left.* Postage stamp set commemorating centenary of Bishop Stirling's 1869 consecration (1969).

**CHRISTIANITY.** The population is almost entirely Christian and is primarily Anglican in denomination. The first colonial chaplain was J. L. Moody who arrived in Stanley in 1845, but the great builder of the Anglican Church was L. Ξ. Brandon during 1877–1907. Missionaries of the South American Missionary Society established their first station in the Falklands in 1854. Smaller Catholic and Scottish Presbyterian communities also exist in the islands. The first Catholic church was built in 1857 and the first Presbyterian minister settled at Darwin in 1872.

In 1869 the Anglican diocese of the Falkland Islands was founded, with its cathedral in Port Stanley, serving the islands and also British expatriates throughout all South America except British Guiana.

In 1910 the diocese of Argentina and Eastern South America was separated off, and the diocese of the Falkland Islands became particularly responsible for Anglicans in Chile, Bolivia and Peru. In 1946 the 2 dioceses were reunited in a single diocese of Argentina, Eastern South America & the Falkland Islands; in 1964 the diocese of Paraguay was separated off, and in 1965 the diocese of Northern Argentina.

In 1976 long-standing anti-Spanish resentment on the part of the Anglican population, largely of British origin, came to a head and they wrote to the British sovereign protesting against being increasingly incorporated within and overwhelmed by the rapidly-expanding Spanish-speaking Anglicaism, and by CASA (Anglican Council for South America) in particular. As a result, in 1977 the Falkland Islands were detached from the diocese of Argentina and from the autonomous Anglican province (CASA), and were returned once more to the metropolitical jurisdiction of the archbishop of Canterbury.

**CHURCH AND STATE.** Since the Falkland Islands are a British crown colony, freedom of religion is guaranteed. There is no established church.

**INTERDENOMINATIONAL ORGANIZATIONS.** Ecumenical relations between the 3 churches are informal but cordial; no formal organization exists.

TABLE 2.     ORGANIZED CHURCHES AND DENOMINATIONS IN THE FALKLAND ISLANDS

| Official name 1 | Begun 2 | Type 3 | Counc 4 | Congs 5 | Adults 6 | Affiliated 7 | Names, notes, and other statistics (see Codebook) 8 |
|---|---|---|---|---|---|---|---|
| **Catholic Church: PA Falkland Islands** | 1857 | R Lat | P.... | 1 | 200 | 210 | M=MHM. Not in CELAM. 39% expatriates. C=1+0+0. 3x,1m(expatriate),P=63%,1Y,1y. |
| **Church of England in the Falkland Is** | 1765 | A Eva | aw,... | 11 | 150 | 1,000 | Until 1977, in D Argentina (CASA). 1854, M=SAMS(UK). 99% British. 1n,W=27%. |
| Jehovah's Witnesses | c1960 | M Jeh | x.... | 1 | 6 | 10 | *Watch Tower. IBSA.* Very little growth since 1962 total of 5 adherents. |
| **United Free Church of the Falkland Is** | 1872 | P Ref | ..... | 5 | 200 | 500 | Includes Lutherans and some Baptists. M=Ch of Scotland Overseas Council(UK).1f. |
| **Total affiliated (mid-1970)** | | | | 18 | 556 | 1,720 | Total denominations (1970) . . . 4. |
| **Total affiliated (mid-1975)** | | | | 18 | 520 | 1,620 | Total denominations (1975) . . . 4. |
| **Total affiliated (mid-1980)** | | | | 18 | 490 | 1,520 | Total denominations (1980) . . . 4. |

**NOTES ON TABLE ABOVE**
COLUMNS: for meanings and CODES (cols. 1, 3, 4, 8): see Codebook (Part 6). Column 1: **Boldface type** = church with over 10% of country's affiliated Christians.

**PEOPLES** (ethnolinguistic). Christians: 97.8% British, 1.4% Argentinian, 0.5% Chilean, Norwegian.

**COUNTRY-WIDE TOTALS**
EVANGELIZATION (see Part 5). 1900: 100%. 1970: 100%.

1980: 100%. *Literature evangelism.* By 1975, every house had been evangelized by the Every Home Crusade.
FOREIGN MISSIONARIES AND PERSONNEL. (aliens from abroad) (1973). Total 6. *From Western world.* 6: 4 Roman Catholics, 1 Protestant in 1 UK society, 1 Anglican.
PERSONNEL. About 8 (2 national, 6 foreign).
SCRIPTURE DISTRIBUTION (1975). Annual totals: 5 Bibles (subsidized), 10 NTs (subsidized).

**ADDITIONAL DATA ON CHURCHES**
CATHOLIC CHURCH. *Catholic organizations.* There is no episcopal conference, nor association of religious personnel, presbyteral or pastoral councils or lay organizations. Catholics in the Falkland Islands are dependent on the Apostolic Delegation to the UK, based in London.
CHURCH OF ENGLAND IN THE FALKLAND ISLANDS. Until 1977, in the Diocese of Argentina, Eastern South America & the Falkland Islands (in CASA); in 1977, detached and returned to the metropolitical jurisdiction of the archbishop of Canterbury.

---

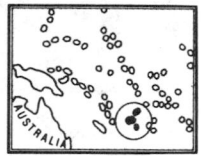

# FIJI

## SECULAR DATA

**STATE.** Official name: The Dominion of Fiji (Viti).
**Flag** (shown above right): Azure blue with Fiji shield centred on right; Union Jack in upper hoist quarter.
**Area:** 18,272 sq.km. (7,055 sq.miles). Description: 844 islands and islets (106 inhabited). Agricultural land: 16.1%.
**Government:** Parliamentary state (constitutional monarchy), since 1970 (c1800 chiefdoms, 1874 British crown colony, 1970 Independence).
**Legislature:** Parliament: Senate, 22 members; House of Representatives, 52 members. Also the Great Council of Chiefs (advisory).
**Official language:** English.
**Capital:** Suva 80,428 (1966).
**Political divisions:** 14 Provinces.
**Armed forces** (1976): small regular force, territorial and reserve; paramilitary Royal Fiji Police, 896 men.

**DEMOGRAPHY. Population:** 476,727 (census of 12.IX.1966. For 1970–2000 (UN), see last row of Table 1). Population density (1975): 32/sq.km. (82/sq.mile). Under 15 years: 48%. Growth rate (1975–80): 1.91% per year (births 2.32%, deaths −0.41%). Life expectancy (1975–80): 71.4 years. Household size: 6.3 persons.
**Major languages:** English, Fijian, Hindustani, Tongan, Tamil, Bihari, Telugu, Chinese, Rotuman, Kadavu, Lauan, Nadroga, and several others.
**Urban dwellers** (1970): 18.3%. Urban growth rate (1950–70): 4.5% per year.
**Labour force:** 28%.
**Tourists** (1970): 110,042. (1971): 152,200. (1975): about 250,000.

**ETHNOLINGUISTIC GROUPS:** 50.6% Indian (29.5% Hindustani, 8.6% Tamil, 3.7% Bihari, 3.7% Telugu, 2.5% Bengali, 1.0% Punjabi), 42.9% Fijian (Bauan), 1.8% Euronesian, 1.3% other Pacific islander (Solomoni, Samoan), 1.2% Rotuman, 1.2% Chinese, 1.0% European (0.8% Anglo-Australian), Gilbertese, Ellice Islander.

**MONEY** (1977). Monetary unit: dollar (= 100 cents); US$1 = F$ 0.97.
**National income per person:** US$650. Average annual family income: US$4,095.
**Inflation:** (1970–74) 10.2% per year, (1975) 13% per year (consumer price index 185).
**Cost of living in capital** (1976): index 112 (Washington DC=100). Daily cost of living: US$37.

**EDUCATION.** Adult literacy: (1946) 64%, (1975) 85%. Education rate: 65%. Schools: 700. Universities: 1.

**HEALTH.** Hospitals: 26 (1,513 beds). Doctors: 256. Lepers: 6,000 (10.4 per 1,000). Blind: 4,000. Psychotics: 4,000. Criminals: 17,967.

**LITERATURE.** Newspapers: 1 daily.

**COMMUNICATION** (per 1,000 people). Phones: 53. Radios: 97. Daily newspaper circulation: 35 copies.

TABLE 1.     RELIGIOUS ADHERENTS IN FIJI

| Year / Name | 1900 Adherents | % | mid-1970 Adherents | % | Annual change, 1970–1980 Natural | Conversion | Total | Rate | mid-1975 Adherents | % | mid-1980 Adherents | % | 2000 Adherents | % |
|---|---|---|---|---|---|---|---|---|---|---|---|---|---|---|---|
| Christians | 103,800 | 86.5 | 262,540 | 50.5 | 5,453 | −151 | 5,302 | 1.84 | 288,630 | 50.0 | 315,560 | 49.7 | 403,800 | 47.7 |
| professing | 103,800 | 86.5 | 262,540 | 50.5 | 5,453 | −151 | 5,302 | 1.84 | 288,630 | 50.0 | 315,560 | 49.7 | 403,800 | 47.7 |
| Protestants | 97,500 | 81.2 | 207,920 | 40.0 | 4,285 | −463 | 3,822 | 1.68 | 226,830 | 39.3 | 246,140 | 38.8 | 307,200 | 36.3 |
| Roman Catholics | 6,000 | 5.0 | 44,720 | 8.6 | 960 | 278 | 1,238 | 2.44 | 50,800 | 8.8 | 57,100 | 9.0 | 77,900 | 9.2 |
| Anglicans | 300 | 0.3 | 7,300 | 1.4 | 153 | 17 | 170 | 2.10 | 8,100 | 1.4 | 9,000 | 1.4 | 13,000 | 1.5 |
| Marginal Protestants | 0 | 0.0 | 1,600 | 0.3 | 34 | 16 | 50 | 2.78 | 1,800 | 0.3 | 2,100 | 0.3 | 4,000 | 0.5 |
| Melanesian indigenous | 0 | 0.0 | 1,000 | 0.2 | 21 | 1 | 22 | 1.99 | 1,100 | 0.2 | 1,220 | 0.2 | 1,700 | 0.2 |
| nominal | 12,000 | 10.0 | 19,089 | 3.7 | 417 | 150 | 567 | 2.57 | 22,030 | 3.8 | 24,760 | 3.9 | 39,800 | 4.7 |
| affiliated | 91,800 | 76.3 | 243,451 | 46.8 | 5,036 | −301 | 4,735 | 1.78 | 266,600 | 46.2 | 290,800 | 45.8 | 364,000 | 43.0 |
| total practising | 87,210 | 95 | 206,930 | 85 | 4,281 | −256 | 4,025 | 1.78 | 226,610 | 85 | 247,180 | 85 | 291,200 | 80 |
| non-practising | 4,590 | 5 | 36,520 | 15 | 755 | −45 | 710 | 1.78 | 39,990 | 15 | 43,620 | 15 | 72,800 | 20 |
| Protestants | 86,800 | 72.3 | 189,662 | 36.5 | 3,884 | −620 | 3,264 | 1.59 | 205,610 | 35.6 | 222,300 | 35.0 | 267,600 | 31.6 |
| Evangelicals | 72,000 | 60.0 | 104,000 | 20.0 | 2,246 | −456 | 1,790 | 1.59 | 112,700 | 19.5 | 121,900 | 19.2 | 147,000 | 17.4 |
| Neo-pentecostals | 0 | 0.0 | 100 | 0.0 | 19 | 171 | 190 | 19.00 | 1,000 | 0.2 | 2,000 | 0.3 | 10,000 | 1.2 |
| Roman Catholics | 4,800 | 4.0 | 43,515 | 8.4 | 935 | 283 | 1,218 | 2.46 | 49,500 | 8.6 | 55,700 | 8.8 | 76,200 | 9.0 |
| Catholic pentecostals | 0 | 0.0 | 0 | 0.0 | 9 | 91 | 100 | 20.00 | 500 | 0.1 | 1,000 | 0.2 | 5,000 | 0.6 |
| Anglicans | 200 | 0.2 | 6,500 | 1.2 | 137 | 13 | 150 | 2.07 | 7,250 | 1.3 | 8,000 | 1.3 | 12,000 | 1.4 |
| Marginal Protestants | 0 | 0.0 | 2,474 | 0.5 | 53 | 20 | 73 | 2.59 | 2,800 | 0.5 | 3,200 | 0.5 | 6,000 | 0.7 |
| Melanesian indigenous | 0 | 0.0 | 1,300 | 0.2 | 27 | 3 | 30 | 2.08 | 1,440 | 0.2 | 1,600 | 0.2 | 2,200 | 0.3 |
| Hindus | 13,400 | 11.2 | 210,000 | 40.4 | 4,979 | −9 | 4,970 | 2.12 | 234,800 | 40.7 | 259,700 | 40.9 | 355,700 | 42.0 |
| Muslims | 2,600 | 2.2 | 40,500 | 7.8 | 895 | −5 | 890 | 1.98 | 44,900 | 7.8 | 49,400 | 7.8 | 66,000 | 7.8 |
| Ahmadis | 0 | 0.0 | 3,000 | 0.6 | 80 | 130 | 210 | 5.25 | 4,000 | 0.7 | 5,100 | 0.8 | 9,300 | 1.1 |
| Sikhs | 200 | 0.2 | 3,200 | 0.6 | 71 | −1 | 70 | 1.97 | 3,550 | 0.6 | 3,900 | 0.6 | 5,200 | 0.6 |
| Non-religious | 0 | 0.0 | 2,560 | 0.5 | 70 | 114 | 184 | 5.26 | 3,500 | 0.6 | 4,400 | 0.7 | 12,700 | 1.5 |
| Baha'is | 0 | 0.0 | 1,000 | 0.2 | 28 | 52 | 80 | 5.71 | 1,400 | 0.2 | 1,800 | 0.3 | 3,400 | 0.4 |
| Chinese folk-religionists | 0 | 0.0 | 200 | 0.0 | 4 | 0 | 4 | 1.99 | 220 | 0.0 | 240 | 0.0 | 200 | 0.0 |
| **Country's population** | **120,000** | **100.0** | **520,000** | **100.0** | **11,500** | **0** | **11,500** | **1.99** | **577,000** | **100.0** | **635,000** | **100.0** | **847,000** | **100.0** |

**COLUMNS, ROWS.** For meanings and definitions, see Codebook (Part 6). Note that, by definition, total 'Christians' = professing + crypto-Christians, which also = affiliated + nominal Christians. Percentages may not always total exactly, due to rounding.
CENSUSES. **21.X.1946:** 46.5% Protestants and Anglicans, 38.8% Hindus, 7.4% Roman Catholics, 6.6% Muslims, 0.4% Sikhs, 0.1% Chinese folk-religionists, 0.1% non-religious. **27.IX.1956:**

42.2% Protestants (40.1% Methodists), 39.8% Hindus, 8.0% Roman Catholics, 7.4% Muslims, 1.5% Anglicans, 0.5% Sikhs, 0.5% non-religious, 0.1% Chinese folk-religionists. **12.IX.1966:** 41.1% Protestants (38.3% Methodists), 40.3% Hindus, 8.4% Roman Catholics, 7.8% Muslims, 1.4% Anglicans, 0.6% Sikhs, 0.3% non-religious.

**NOTES ON RELIGIONS**
AHMADIS. Qadianis, with 5 mosques and HQ in Samabula, Suva.
BAHA'IS. Growth of local spiritual assemblies: 1964, none; 1973, 17.
CATHOLIC PENTECOSTALS (or, Catholic charismatics). Totals (January 1975): about 100 including priests and sisters; the archbishop of Suva also is a charismatic leader.

COUNTRY'S POPULATION. Indians came as indentured labourers from 1879–1916; of the 60,000 who came to Fiji, only 60 were Christians. In the 1901 census, of the 120,124 population, 94,937 were Fijians and 17,105 (14.2%) Indians. HINDUS. South Indians originally from Kerala and Madras. As indicated by the last 30 years' population censuses, the fertility of the Hindu community is higher than the national average; this means that their natural increase used in the table above (2.12%) is higher than the average (1.99%). Among Hindu

sects, ISKCON (Hare Krishna) has 1 centre, the Ramakrishna Mission others.
MELANESIAN INDIGENOUS. In 2 bodies in 1970 (see Table 2).
MUSLIMS. Sunnis. There is also an Ahmadiya Mission (enumerated here under Muslims though declared non-Muslim by Pakistan). *Hajj pilgrims to Mecca.* (1976) 36.
NON-RELIGIOUS. Europeans, and young Chinese who are abandoning family folk religion.

PRACTISING CHRISTIANS. Attenders: about 60% weekly, 85% annually.
PROTESTANTS. All Fijians had become Christians, at least nominally, by 1885. By 1900 there were no traditional religionists left. In 1900 a large number of Methodists were children in Methodist schools; in 1909, there were 1,019 Methodist schools in Fiji and 22 in Rotuma.
SIKHS. Indians (Punjabis).

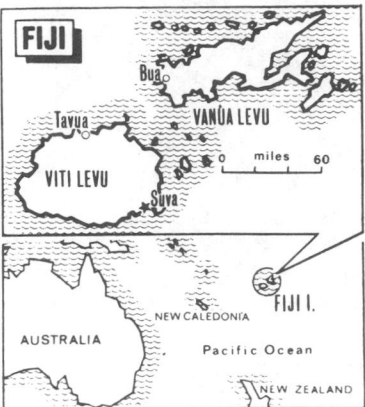

## NON-CHRISTIAN RELIGIONS. Hinduism is the largest religion of the islands after Christianity, 40% of the population being Hindus in 1966. Indians, who are 80% Hindu, first came to Fiji mostly from Kerala and Madras as plantation workers after 1879; and many of their descendants are now successful farmers. They make up the largest single ethnic group in the country.

**Islam** is also confined to the Indian population. In 1966, 7.8% of the population were Muslims.

**Sikhism** was represented by 3,000 persons (0.6%) in 1966. Sikhs are all of Indian background.

**Chinese folk religion** still plays a part in Chinese life, although the proportion of Chinese who state that they have no religion is higher than for any other group (18.6% in 1966); most are young persons who are in process of abandoning their family religion.

**Traditional religion** has virtually disappeared as a distinct religious category, and almost all ethnic Fijians today profess to be Christians. Nevertheless, the heritage of traditional religion continues to manifest itself both in indigenous expressions of Christianity and also in periodic movements such as the Tuka cult founded by the prophet Ndungumoi in 1885, which was an anti-Christian revival of ritual cannibalism. Witchcraft still remains widespread; most practising witchdoctors now are Christians.

## CHRISTIANITY

PROTESTANT CHURCHES. Two Tahitian teachers of the LMS arrived in 1830. Later through comity agreements the islands were assigned to Methodists who sent 2 missionaries and a team of Tongan teachers to Fiji in 1835. Little progress was made prior to the baptism of the principal chief, Thakombau, in 1854. Fijians have since become missionaries to many other parts of the South Pacific. The Methodist Church continues to be the principal denomination. It has its strength among the ethnic Fijian population, 83% of whom claim to be Methodists, as well as among the Rotumans (62%), part-Europeans (39%) and other Pacific islanders (38%). Work among Indians began in 1897 and a separate Indian synod had developed by 1945. The Methodist Church has also been heavily involved in education, more than one thousand village schools being established by 1876. At the present time the church is responsible for 19 primary schools, 8 secondary schools, one hospital, the Navuso Agricultural School, a handicraft and farming scheme for girl school-leavers, and the Methodist Leadership Training Centre with an expanding programme of vocational work.

The Assemblies of God came to Fiji in 1926 but made little impact prior to 1965. They have since grown from less than 3,000 in 1966 to 20,000 by 1970. Seventh-day Adventists have been active since 1889. There are also small groups of Brethren, Congregationalists and Presbyterians, the latter being almost entirely European.

CATHOLIC CHURCH. The first Catholic missionaries arrived in 1844. The islands became a vicariate apostolic in 1887, and the first Fijian priest was ordained in 1955. In 1966 the various races had the following Catholic proportions: Europeans

16.8%, Fijians 12.8%, Indians 1.3%, part-Europeans 44.3%, Rotumans 34.4%, and other Pacific islanders 23.6%. In 1969 there were 1,670 Catholics among the Chinese minority of 5,980, served by 2 Chinese priests. In recent years, the church has made a special effort to establish contact with the Indian majority, and by 1974 1.5% of the Indian population were Catholics. Attention has been given to language study and the development of contacts through the bishops of India, and on the invitation of the government a group of Gabriel Brothers arrived from India in 1973 to set up a boys' town in Fiji.

ANGLICAN CHURCH. Anglicans are mostly Europeans, 45.4% of the European population being identified as Anglican in 1966. Fiji belongs to the diocese of Polynesia and is part of the Church of the Province of New Zealand. Anglicans sponsor 6 primary schools and one secondary school.

INDIGENOUS CHURCHES. In 1942 a prophet named Kelevi Nawai, who was termed the Vessel of Christ, established himself at Kadavu-Levu. His emphasis on magical healing, communication with the dead and the raising of dead persons, and immortality, had a strong appeal among Methodists prior to the suppression of the movement by government.

Another schism from Methodism, begun by Ratu Emosi after World War II and still active, is the Church of Time, which lays great stress on the right use of time by members. Still a third split is the Messiah Club of Sairusi Nabogibogi who has modelled his services on those of the Methodists and whose members are still encouraged to attend the Methodist Church. A cargo-cult emphasis is given to the higher standard of living which the messiah is expected to bring about in the future. Also stressed are the Ten Commandments and exposition of the Bible.

CHURCH AND STATE. Early Methodist opposition to Catholicism had government backing and sanction. Catholic conversions were actually forbidden by the governor in 1888; but freedom of religion was restored in 1897.

There is no government ministry or department dealing with religion, the churches or religious affairs. The Religious Bodies Registration Ordinance requires that all religious groups be registered and have trustees appointed for holding property. The Marriage Ordinance provides for the registration of the names of marriage officers.

All denominational schools must also be registered and church medical institutions receive government subsidies. The Methodist Church is involved in a

Postage stamp set (1973) illustrating festivals of major religions: Chinese folk religion (New Year), Islam (Id-ul-Fitar), Hinduism (Diwali) and Christianity (Christmas)

**Methodist Church in Fiji.** *Above.* Sunday family service. *Above right.* Fijian preacher.

government-sponsored adult rural education programme, and Catholic sisters work in the government's anti-leprosy campaign.

The phrases 'dedication to God' and 'reverence for God' appear in the Preamble to the constitution of 1970, with the words: 'Whereas all the peoples of Fiji have... acknowledged... their reverence for God....' Freedom of religion is guaranteed in Article 11, the first section of which reads as follows: 'Except with his own consent, no person shall be hindered in the enjoyment of his freedom of conscience, and for the purposes of this section the said freedom includes freedom of thought and of religion, freedom to change his religion or belief and freedom, either alone or in community with others, and both in public and in private, to manifest and propagate his religion or belief in worship, teaching, practice and observance'. Sections 2–4 give religious communities the right to open schools and teach religious education, provided that no person is forced to participate against his will; while section 5 prohibits the use of oaths which are contrary to a person's religion or belief. All of these freedoms are assured provided that they do not conflict with the rights of others or the interests of public safety, order, morality, health and defence (Article 11, section 6).

**INTERDENOMINATIONAL ORGANIZATIONS.** The Fiji Council of Churches was founded in 1964 with 4 members: the Methodist, Anglican, Congregational and Presbyterian churches. The Catholic Church joined in 1968. Activities include the Week of Prayer for Christian Unity, Bible Week, a chaplaincy programme (hospital, prison and university) and joint service projects such as HART (Housing and Relief Trust) and a low-cost housing scheme in Suva.

The Pacific Conference of Churches, founded in 1969, has its headquarters in Suva, Fiji. It began originally as a regional Protestant body, but the Catholic Episcopal Conference of the Pacific (CEPAC) joined as a full member in January 1976 after applying for membership a few years earlier.

In 1966 the interdenominational Pacific Theological School was opened at Suva. Sponsored by the Anglican, Congregational, Methodist and Presbyterian churches, the school serves Fiji and a number of other Pacific islands.

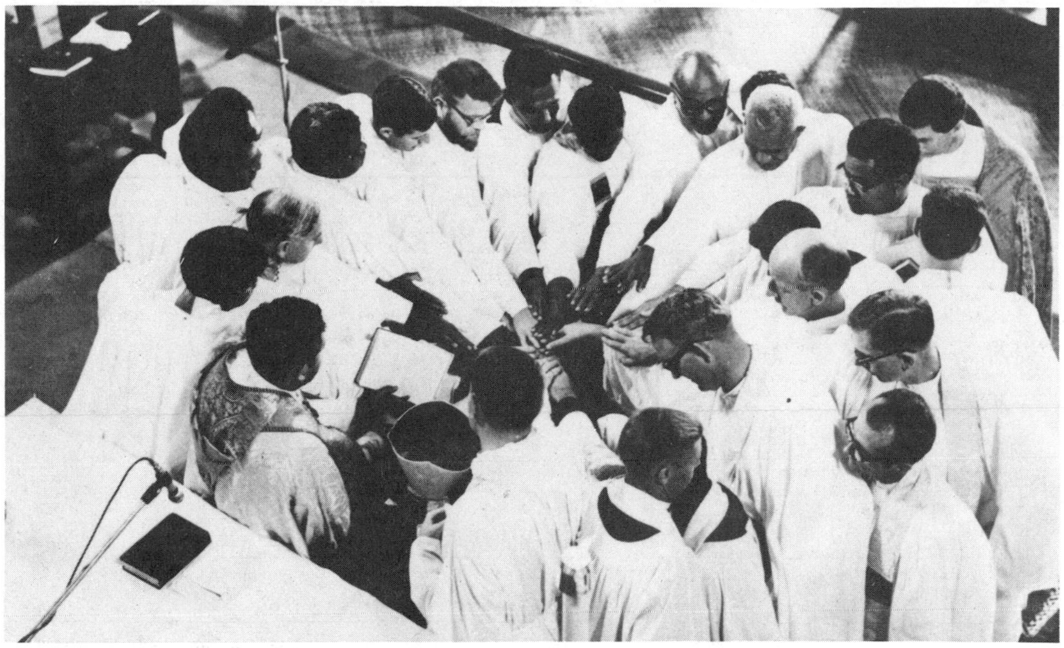

**Anglican Church, Diocese of Polynesia.** Ordination of a priest by laying on of hands, Holy Trinity Cathedral, Suva, in 1968.

**BROADCASTING.** The government Fiji Broadcasting Commission donates time for religious broadcasts, allocated among the various denominations by a Religious Advisory Committee. Catholics receive about 25% of the available air time. There are daily morning devotionals, worship on Sunday mornings, and Wednesday evening news and interview programmes, conducted in both English and Fijian. Separate programmes are made for the English-language and Fijian/Hindustani stations. Programmes for the latter are prepared in Fijian by Fijian pastors and churchmen. For Catholics, an association grouping Fiji with the Gilbert and Ellice Islands is a member of UNDA.

## BIBLIOGRAPHY


'A new religious cult in Fiji', A. C. Cato, *Oceania*, 18 (1947), 145–156.

*Directory, Archdiocese of Suva, Fiji, 1973.* Suva: Catholic Supply Store, 1973.

'Disintegration, syncretization and change in Fijian religion', A. C. Cato, *Mankind*, 5, 3 (September, 1956), 101–106.

'Institutions religieuses et messianismes modernes à Fiji', J. Guiart, *Archives de sociologie des religions*, 4 (1957), 3–30.

'Religion and symbolism in Fiji', W. C. Mann, *Journal of general psychology*, 23 (1940), 169–184.

*The growth of the Indian church in Fiji.* A. H. Blackett. South Australia (privately printed), 1960.


TABLE 2. ORGANIZED CHURCHES AND DENOMINATIONS IN FIJI

| Official name 1 | Begun 2 | Type ·3 | Counc 4 | Congs 5 | Adults 6 | Affiliated 7 | Names, notes, and other statistics (see Codebook) 8 |
|---|---|---|---|---|---|---|---|
| Anglican Church. D Polynesia | 1860 | A Hig | awPKK | 54 | 4,000 | 6,500 | *Lotu Jiaji*. CPNZ. 34% Indian, 26% Solomoni, 19% White. 16n,13x,1u,W=27%,97Y,217y. |
| Assemblies of God of Fiji | 1926 | P Pe2 | ZF••• | 766 | 10,440 | 20,000 | Rapid growth since 1957. M=AoG(USA). 65% Fijian, 35% Indian. 292n,4f,1s(56),W=75%. |
| **Catholic Church: M Suva** | 1844 | R Lat | PxPYK | 35 | 22,600 | 43,515 | 9.1% Indian, 3.8% Chinese. C=5+4+5. 15n,68x,42m,264w,P=88%,1s(8),W=75%,2199Yy. |
| Christian Brethren | 1934 | P CBr | x•••• | 7 | 250 | 427 | *Samabula Gospel Chapel. Open Brethren.* M=CMML(NZ). 2n,1x,16f,G=15%pa,W=80%,6Y,8z. |
| Church of Christ | 1968 | P Dis | x•••• | 5 | 500 | 1,000 | M=CC(Non-Instrumental) (USA). Churches in Suva. Rapid growth. |
| Ch of Jesus C of Latter-day Saints | 1954 | M LdS | x•••• | 21 | 800 | 1,424 | *Mormons*. M=CJCLdS(USA). Rapid growth. 50% Fijian, 50% Indian. 1x,10f,W=30%,200Yy. |
| Church of Time (Daku Community) | c1945 | I Met | ••••• | 4 | 100 | 300 | *Lotu ni Gauna*. Founder red-robed Ratu Emosi, ex Methodist. Stress on use of time. |
| Congregational Christian Church | | P Con | Rwp•K | 1 | 500 | 1,000 | *LMS Church in Fiji*. M=London Missionary Society (UK). Expatriate Samoans. 1u. |
| Jehovah's Witnesses | 1930 | M Jeh | x•••• | 9 | 478 | 1,000 | *Watch Tower. IBSA*. First limited witnessing began in 1930. 88Y. |
| Messiah Club | c1965 | I Met | ••••• | 20 | 500 | 1,000 | Ex Methodists, young messiah Sairusi. HQ Ra. Only Fijians and Solomonis may join. |
| **Methodist Church in Fiji** | 1835 | P Met | VWP•K | 1,354 | 35,084 | 157,635 | M=MCA(Austr). 94% Fijian, 4% Indian. 205n,7x,G=2.7%pa,1H,9p,1s,1u,W=50%,73Y,4687y. |
| Presbyterian Church | 1876 | P Ref | ••••K | | 500 | 1,000 | *St Andrew's Ch.* All Whites (Australian, NZ, British), from scattered areas. W=8%. |
| Seventh-day Adventist Church in Fiji | 1889 | P Adv | x•••• | 87 | 5,469 | 8,000 | In CPacific UM. Fijians, 150 Indians. 16n,2x,G=6%pa,1r,1s(8),80t(7041),W=90%,502Y. |
| Other Protestant denominations | | P | ••••• | | 300 | 600 | Total 6 (see list below). |
| Other marginal Protestant bodies | | M | ••••• | 1 | 20 | 50 | Including: Church of Christ, Scientist; Reorganized Ch of JC of Latter-day Saints. |
| **Total affiliated (mid-1970)** | | | | **2,370** | **84,541** | **243,451** | **Total denominations (1970) . . . 21.** |
| **Total affiliated (mid-1975)** | | | | **2,480** | **92,580** | **266,600** | **Total denominations (1975) . . . 22.** |
| **Total affiliated (mid-1980)** | | | | **2,590** | **101,000** | **290,800** | **Total denominations (1980) . . . 23.** |

NOTES ON TABLE ABOVE

COLUMNS: for meanings and CODES (cols. 1, 3, 4, 8), see Codebook (Part 6). Column 1: **Boldface type** = church with over 10% of country's affiliated Christians.

NATIONAL COUNCILS (Column 4, 5th letter).
K = Fiji Council of Churches (FCC).

OTHER PROTESTANT DENOMINATIONS. These include: Baptist Ch, Christadelphian Ecclesias, Lutheran Ch in America, Pentecostal (Vakapenitiko) Ch, World-Wide Missions (1968). In Fijian, Protestant = Porotesitedi.

PEOPLES (ethnolinguistic). Christians: 80.7% Fijian (including Rotuman), 8.5% Indian, 3.6% Euronesian, 2.6% other Pacific islander (Solomoni, Samoan, Gilbertese, Ellice Islander), 2.5% Chinese, 2.0% European (Anglo-Australian).

COUNTRY-WIDE TOTALS
EVANGELIZATION (see Part 5). 1900: 95%. 1970: 95%. 1980: 97%. *Mass evangelism.* 1962, Allan Walker one-week 'Mission to Fiji' in Suva (31,000 attenders, 2,445 enquirers); 1968, A. A. Haqq of Billy Graham Evangelistic Association, 2 days in Lautoka and 4 days in Suva (475 enquirers); 1972, 6-week Methodist campaign (5,640 decisions for Christ). *Radiophonic evangelism.* ICI (3,007 enrolments, 1,331 active, 300 conversions).

FOREIGN MISSIONARIES AND PERSONNEL (nationals serving abroad) (1973). Total 55 in 10 countries: 45 Protestants, 5 Roman Catholics, 4 marginal Protestants, 1 Anglican. Over the years since 1840, over 270 Fijian Methodists have served overseas as foreign missionaries to other islands.

FOREIGN MISSIONARIES AND PERSONNEL (aliens from abroad) (1973). Total 343. *From Western world.* 308: 230 Roman Catholics, 65 Protestants (42 in 2 Australia societies, 16 in 2 New Zealand societies, 6 in 3 USA societies, 1 in 1 UK society), about 10 marginal Protestants (Mormons from USA), 3 Anglicans in 1 USA society. *From Third World.* 35: 20 Roman Catholics mainly from India, 10 Anglicans mostly from Solomon Islands, 5 Protestants from New Caledonia, Western Samoa et alia.

INSTITUTIONS (church-operated) (1973). Total 25, including 11 higher schools, 4 medical centres (hospitals), 3 religious communities, 5 seminaries (4 Protestant, 1 RC).

PERIODICALS. About 15 titles (3 SDA).

PERSONNEL. About 1,171 (828 national, 343 foreign).

RELIGIOUS LIBRARIES. 8.

SCRIPTURE DISTRIBUTION (1975). Annual totals: 8,200 Bibles (18% free, 79% subsidized, 2% commercial), 21,000 NTs (67% free, 33% subsidized), 49,000 UBS portions, 160,000 UBS selections. *Translations completed.* Portion: 2 languages since 1839. NT: 2 languages since 1847. Bible: Fijian in 1864.

SERVICE AGENCIES. About 34, including CCCI, CEF, CEPAC, FCC, HART, PCC, PICEC, SCM, SPATS, SU, UNDA, YCW, YMCA, YWCA.

ADDITIONAL DATA ON CHURCHES

CATHOLIC CHURCH. In Fijian, Catholic = Katolika vaka-Roma. *Catholics.* Including 12% aliens (1,670 Chinese in 1975). *Mission.* Mainly SM2. *Annual baptisms.* (1972) 86.1% infant, 13.9% adult. *Priests.* Including 2 Chinese priests and 1 Indian. All expatriates are religious priests. *Brothers.* 12 indigenous, 30 expatriates. *Sisters.* 127 indigenous, 137 expatriates. *Catholic charismatics.* In 1975 there were many Catholics involved in the Charismatic Renewal, including priests, sisters and the archbishop. *Seminary.* Pacific Regional Seminary (Suva) mainly for English-speaking dioceses in CEPAC. *Catechists.* Total (1970) 128. *Indigenous religious congregations.* Brothers: 6 Ai Vukevuke Ni Bete, Brothers of St Joseph. Sisters: 107 Sisters of Our Lady of Nazareth. *Foreign orders and congregations.* Priests: SM2, CM, SSC, OFMCap, Indian Missionary Society. Brothers: PFM, Gabriel Brothers (Indian Province). Sisters: Missionary Sisters of the Society of Mary, Sisters of St Joseph of Cluny, Marists Sisters, Sisters of Our Lady of Compassion.

*Catholic organizations.* Fiji is a member of the Episcopal Conference of the Pacific (CEPAC), which has its headquarters in Suva. Created in 1968 to break the traditional isolation of the church in these islands, the principal accomplishments of CEPAC have been the creation of: (1) a regional Catholic seminary for the Pacific; (2) a Commission on Justice and Peace which has devoted itself to the problems of development, social injustice and racialism; and (3) UNDA-Oceanic for the development of mass media in the Pacific. A senate of priests was founded in 1969 and National Pastoral Council in 1973. Lay organizations are the YCW, St Vincent de Paul Society, Legion of Mary and the Catholic Women's League.

The Holy See has no diplomatic relations with Fiji, and is represented to the hierarchy by the Apostolic Delegation to New Zealand and the Islands of the Pacific, based in Wellington, New Zealand.

In 1968 the church was responsible for 35 primary schools (9,326 pupils), 6 secondary schools (1,526) and one teacher training college (79 students). By 1973 these had become 39 primary schools (9,818) pupils and 10 secondary schools (2,640 pupils). Other institutions include a diocesan hospital, a home for the handicapped, a boys' town and a home for the aged. There has also been a remarkable development of credit unions, 340 groups with 45,000 members having been founded by 1974.

METHODIST CHURCH IN FIJI. *Members.* In addition to the 38,084 full members shown in the table, there are about 9,000 preparatory members. In 1966, 71,320 (and in 1969, 91,054) were members under nurture or under preparation for confirmation.

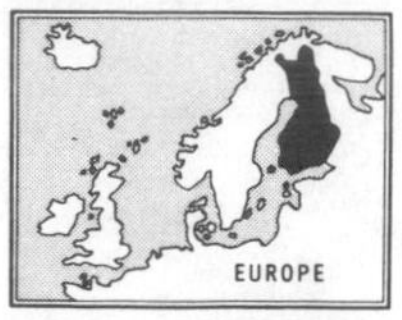


# FINLAND

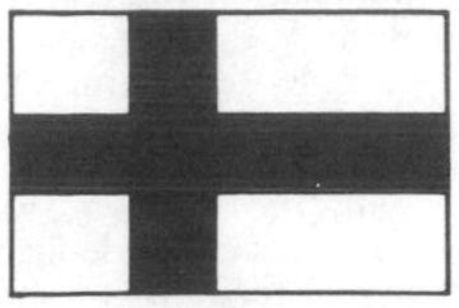

## SECULAR DATA

**STATE. Official name**: The Republic of Finland (Suomen Tasavalta/Republiken Finland). Adjectives of nationality: Finnish, a Finn.
**Flag** (shown above right): Light blue cross on a white field.
**Area**: 337,009 sq.km. (130,120 sq.miles). Agricultural land: 8.3%.
**Government**: Parliamentary republic, since 1917 (1809 Russian grand duchy, 1917 Independence declared).
**Legislature**: Parliament, 200 members.
**Official languages**: Finnish (*Suomi*) and Swedish (*Svensk*).
**Chief cities**: capital Helsinki 837,550 (1973), Tampere 231,760, Turku 227,240.
**Political divisions**: 12 Provinces (lääni/län).
**Armed forces** (1976): Total 35,800 regular (28,000 conscripts): army 30,300, navy 2,500, air force 3,000 (80 combat aircraft). Reserves: 690,000. Paramilitary forces: 4,000.

**DEMOGRAPHY. Population**: 4,598,336 (census of 31.XII.1970. For 1970–2000 (UN), see last row of Table 1). Population density (1975): 14/sq.km. (36/sq.mile). Under 15 years: 30%. Growth rate (1975–80): 0.16% per year (births 1.30%, deaths −1.01%, emigrants −0.13%). Life expectancy (1975–80): 70.9 years. Household size: 3.0 persons.
**Major languages**: Finnish, Swedish, Russian, Lapp, Romany.
**Urban dwellers** (1970): 60.7%. Urban growth rate (1950–70): 2.8% per year.
**Labour force**: 47%.
**Tourists** (1974): 4,865,000.

**ETHNOLINGUISTIC GROUPS**: 92.0% Finnish, 7.4% Swedish, 0.1% Russian, 0.1% Gypsy (4,000), 0.1% Lapp (3,500), Turkish, USA, Jewish, Estonian.

**MONEY** (1977). **Monetary unit**: markka (= 100 penni); US$1 = MK 3.80.
**National income per person**: US$4,184. Average annual family income: US$12,552.
**Inflation**: (1970–74) 10.1% per year, (1975) 18% per year (consumer price index 196).
**Cost of living in capital** (1976): index 134 (Washington DC=100). Daily cost of living: US$43.

**EDUCATION**. Adult literacy: 100%. Education rate: 40%. Schools: 4,236. Universities: 7.

**HEALTH**. Hospitals: 746 (60,606 beds). Doctors: 5,475. Blind: 3,345. Psychotics: 46,000. Criminals: 187,918.

**LITERATURE**. Annual new book titles (1973): 3,594. Periodicals: 2,029. Scientific journals: 280. Newspapers: 60 dailies, 202 non-daily.

**COMMUNICATION** (per 1,000 people). Phones: 329. Radios: 418. TV sets: 263. Daily newspaper circulation: 425 copies.

TABLE 1. RELIGIOUS ADHERENTS IN FINLAND

| Year | 1900 | | mid-1970 | | Annual change, 1970–1980 | | | | mid-1975 | | mid-1980 | | 2000 | |
|---|---|---|---|---|---|---|---|---|---|---|---|---|---|---|
| *Name* | *Adherents* | *%* | *Adherents* | *%* | *Natural* | *Conversion* | *Total* | *Rate* | *Adherents* | *%* | *Adherents* | *%* | *Adherents* | *%* |
| **Christians** | **2,713,000** | **100.0** | **4,439,320** | **96.4** | **7,823** | **−9,205** | **−1,382** | **−0.03** | **4,438,000** | **95.4** | **4,425,500** | **94.4** | **4,272,300** | **90.0** |
| professing | 2,712,000 | 100.0 | 4,439,300 | 96.4 | ,823 | −9,205 | −1,382 | −0.03 | 4,438,000 | 95.4 | 4,425,500 | 94.4 | 4,272,300 | 90.0 |
| Protestants | 2,665,000 | 98.3 | 4,358,000 | 94.6 | 7,674 | −9,906 | −2,232 | −0.05 | 4,353,130 | 93.6 | 4,335,680 | 92.5 | 4,160,700 | 87.6 |
| Orthodox | 46,100 | 1.7 | 57,300 | 1.2 | 100 | −150 | −50 | −0.09 | 57,050 | 1.2 | 56,800 | 1.2 | 52,000 | 1.1 |
| Marginal Protestants | 100 | 0.0 | 20,000 | 0.4 | 41 | 759 | 800 | 3.43 | 23,300 | 0.5 | 28,000 | 0.6 | 50,000 | 1.0 |
| Roman Catholics | 800 | 0.0 | 3,600 | 0.1 | 7 | 93 | 100 | 2.44 | 4,100 | 0.1 | 4,600 | 0.1 | 9,000 | 0.2 |
| Anglicans | 0 | 0.0 | 300 | 0.0 | 1 | −1 | 0 | 0.00 | 300 | 0.0 | 300 | 0.0 | 400 | 0.0 |
| Catholics (non-Roman) | 0 | 0.0 | 120 | 0.0 | 0 | 0 | 0 | 0.00 | 120 | 0.0 | 120 | 0.0 | 200 | 0.0 |
| nominal | 35,500 | 1.3 | 12,864 | 0.3 | 293 | 28,812 | 29,105 | 17.51 | 166,200 | 3.6 | 303,910 | 6.5 | 846,800 | 17.8 |
| affiliated | 2,676,500 | 98.7 | 4,426,456 | 96.1 | 7,530 | −38,017 | −30,487 | −0.71 | 4,271,800 | 91.8 | 4,121,590 | 87.9 | 3,425,500 | 72.2 |
| doubly-affiliated | −5,000 | −0.2 | −140,000 | −3.0 | −270 | −1,200 | −1,470 | 0.96 | −153,540 | −3.3 | −154,700 | −3.3 | −190,000 | −4.0 |
| total practising | 2,408,850 | *90* | 3,452,640 | *78* | 5,798 | −37,821 | −32,023 | −0.97 | 3,289,290 | *77* | 3,132,410 | *76* | 2,397,800 | *70* |
| non-practising | 267,650 | *10* | 973,820 | *22* | 1,732 | −196 | 1,536 | 0.16 | 982,510 | *23* | 989,180 | *24* | 1,027,700 | *30* |
| Protestants | 2,635,600 | 97.2 | 4,488,207 | 97.4 | 7,659 | −37,370 | −29,711 | −0.68 | 4,345,000 | 93.4 | 4,191,100 | 89.4 | 3,513,000 | 74.0 |
| Evangelicals | 550,000 | 20.3 | 1,336,000 | 29.0 | 2,461 | 9,239 | 11,700 | 0.84 | 1,396,000 | 30.0 | 1,453,000 | 31.0 | 1,661,000 | 35.0 |
| Neo-pentecostals | 0 | 0.0 | 1,000 | 0.0 | 14 | 1,886 | 1,900 | 23.75 | 8,000 | 0.2 | 20,000 | 0.4 | 50,000 | 1.1 |
| Orthodox | 45,000 | 1.7 | 56,774 | 1.2 | 98 | −230 | −132 | −0.24 | 55,850 | 1.2 | 55,450 | 1.2 | 47,000 | 1.0 |
| Marginal Protestants | 100 | 0.0 | 18,219 | 0.4 | 37 | 741 | 778 | 3.71 | 21,000 | 0.5 | 26,000 | 0.6 | 47,000 | 1.0 |
| Roman Catholics | 800 | 0.0 | 2,868 | 0.1 | 6 | 42 | 48 | 1.55 | 3,100 | 0.1 | 3,350 | 0.1 | 8,000 | 0.2 |
| Anglicans | 0 | 0.0 | 269 | 0.0 | 0 | 0 | 0 | 0.00 | 270 | 0.0 | 270 | 0.0 | 300 | 0.0 |
| Catholics (non-Roman) | 0 | 0.0 | 119 | 0.0 | 0 | 0 | 0 | 0.00 | 120 | 0.0 | 120 | 0.0 | 200 | 0.0 |
| Non-religious | 0 | 0.0 | 112,800 | 2.4 | 261 | 7,076 | 7,337 | 4.94 | 148,600 | 3.2 | 186,170 | 4.0 | 313,700 | 6.6 |
| Atheists | 0 | 0.0 | 49,000 | 1.1 | 105 | 1,995 | 2,100 | 3.51 | 59,800 | 1.3 | 70,000 | 1.5 | 150,000 | 3.2 |
| Baha'is | 0 | 0.0 | 1,500 | 0.0 | 3 | 97 | 100 | 5.00 | 2,000 | 0.0 | 2,500 | 0.1 | 5,000 | 0.1 |
| Jews | 0 | 0.0 | 1,460 | 0.0 | 3 | 0 | 3 | 0.18 | 1,470 | 0.0 | 1,490 | 0.0 | 2,000 | 0.0 |
| Muslims | 0 | 0.0 | 920 | 0.0 | 2 | 0 | 2 | 0.18 | 930 | 0.0 | 940 | 0.0 | 2,000 | 0.0 |
| Other religionists | 0 | 0.0 | 1,000 | 0.0 | 3 | 37 | 40 | 3.33 | 1,200 | 0.0 | 1,400 | 0.0 | 2,000 | 0.0 |
| **Country's population** | **41,000** | **100.0** | **4,606,000** | **100.0** | **8,200** | **0** | **8,200** | **0.18** | **4,652,000** | **100.0** | **4,688,000** | **100.0** | **4,747,000** | **100.0** |

COLUMNS, ROWS. For meanings and definitions, see Codebook (Part 6). Note that, by definition, total 'Christians' = professing + crypto-Christians, which also = affiliated + nominal Christians. Percentages may not always total exactly, due to rounding.
CENSUSES. **1860**: 97.7% Lutherans, 2.3% Greek Orthodox. **1880**: 98.0% Lutherans, 1.9% Greek Orthodox, 0.1% Roman Catholics. **1900**: 98.1% Lutherans, 1.7% Greek Orthodox, 1.0% Baptists, 0.03% Roman Catholics. Since 1917 there has been in censuses a civil register for those not wishing to belong to any recognized religion or denomination. Those on it are mostly men, mostly urban, workers and intellectuals, former Christians now withdrawn from the Lutheran church, atheists, and communists; but there is also a sizeable proportion in unrecognized new denominations (Pentecostals and others). **1920**: 99.9% registered Christians, 0.0% civil register. **1940**: 98.0% registered Christians, 1.9% civil register. **31.XII.1950**: 95.0% registered Protestants, 3.0% civil register, 1.8% Orthodox. **31.XII.1960** (de jure): 92.8% registered Protestants (not on civil register) (92.5% Lutherans), 5.5% civil register (non-religious, and unregistered Protestants), 1.4% Orthodox, 0.2% non-Christians, 0.05% Roman Catholics. **31.XII.1970** (including returns from church bodies): 92.7% registered Protestants (not on civil register) (92.4% Lutherans), 5.2% civil register (3.3% non-religious and atheists, 1.9% unregistered Protestants), 1.3% Orthodox, 0.4% marginal Protestants, 0.1% Catholics.
POLLS. Numerous polls of religion and belief have been taken (Gallup, et alia). Religious preference, February 1970: 95% Protestants, 3% non-religious, 1% Orthodox. Figures for practice are given below.

### NOTES ON RELIGIONS

ATHEISTS. Finnish Communist Party (Suomen Kommunistinen Puolue, SKP) (legal; pro-Soviet): membership (1970) 49,000, (1974) 48,000; Communist voters (election of III.1945) 398,618 (23.5% of all votes), (2.I.1972) 438,414 (17.1% of all votes). Although most communists are atheists, many others belong to the Lutheran church; and the SKP has as members several theological students and clergy in Helsinki.
BAHA'IS. Finnish Baha'i Association (Suomen Baha'i-yhdyskunta). Growth from 4 local spiritual assemblies (1964) to 9 (1973). Converts include Gypsies and Lapps.
DOUBLY-AFFILIATED. The term describes the large number of individuals who are members of Free churches (including Salvation Army and also marginal cults) who are also still regarded as members of the state Lutheran Church which therefore enumerates them all as such.
JEWS. Mostly in Helsinki, with synagogues in Helsinki and Turku.
MUSLIMS. Including Turkish labourers.
NEO-PENTECOSTALS. The total (1975) includes 1,500 lay charismatics and 25 clergy within the Lutheran state church in 75 organized prayer groups, and also about 2,000 in other non-Pentecostal Protestant denominations; total charismatic community including children, about 8,000.
NON-RELIGIOUS. Mostly persons on the civil register in censuses, who register their protest by withdrawal from the state Lutheran Church. These are mainly urban male workers and intellectuals. The size of the civil register is 4 times as large in the cities as in rural areas.
OTHER RELIGIONISTS. Adherents of smaller religions and cults, including Rosicrucians (1 AMORC centre).
PRACTISING CHRISTIANS. Weekly church attenders fell from 25% of the whole population (1948) to 5% (1968) and to 4% (1970); annual communicants 55% of population in 1912, declining to 33% in 1923, 23% in 1937, 22% in 1951, and 20% in 1970. Attenders twice a year 43% of population. Regular radio/TV service listeners 42% of population. Occasional radio/TV service listeners 71% of population. Altogether these indicate that practising Christians, as defined in this Encyclopedia, numbered in 1970 about 75% of the population, or 78% of all affiliated Christians.
ROMAN CATHOLICS. Growth is higher than the country's natural increase, with a number of conversions annually.

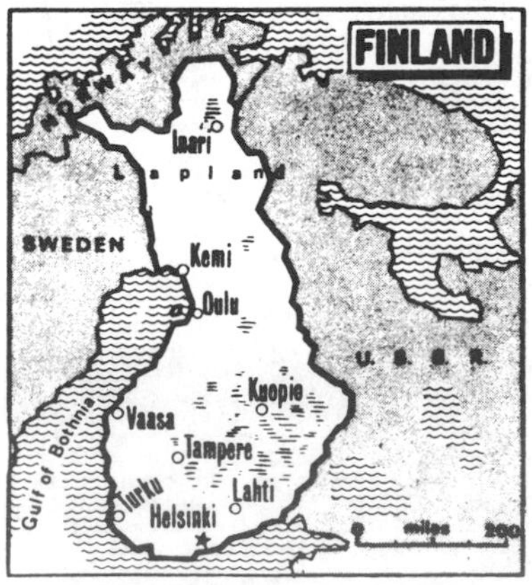


**NON-CHRISTIAN RELIGIONS.** Small communities of Jews (about 1,160 in synagogues in Turku and Helsinki, mostly the latter), Muslims (920 in 2 congregations) and Baha'i (9 local spiritual assemblies) exist in Finland. While Jews and Muslims have decreased since 1966, Baha'i doubled in number from 1964 to 1973.

**CHRISTIANITY.** In spite of some penetration through seamen and merchants touching its ports, Finland remained largely pagan prior to the crusade launched by Eric IX of Sweden in AD 1155. A Catholic bishop, Henry of Uppsala, accompanied the Swedish forces and was later martyred; he is now looked on as the founder of Christianity in Finland. Orthodoxy was introduced into eastern Finland from neighbouring Russia in the middle of the 12th century. Dominicans entered in 1249 and an important step forward was taken in 1291 when a Finn, Magnus, was appointed bishop of Abo. Finland was attached to Sweden at the time of the 16th-century Reformation and gradually followed king Gustavus Adolphus into accepting Lutheranism, particularly through the efforts of a Finn, Michael

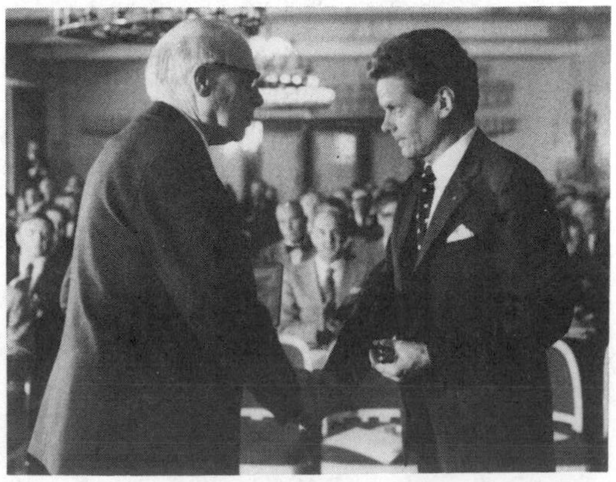

**Evangelical Lutheran Church of Finland.** Finnish Primate, Archbishop Simojoki of Turku (left), receives 1974 award for promoting freedom of press.

Agricola. Catholicism did not return until the middle of the 19th century, a period which also saw the introduction of Free churches into the country.

PROTESTANT CHURCHES. Although there are 2 national churches in Finland, Lutheran and Orthodox, the Evangelical Lutheran Church is by far the largest and most influential body. This church has numerical strength in all parts of the country and all strata of society, although over the past decade it has suffered a gradual decline in membership.

Regular Sunday attendance is low, averaging about 4% of the population above 15 years of age, with the figure in parishes varying from 1% to 15%. In Helsinki where the population is 83% Lutheran only 55% of all church attenders go to Lutheran services. Nevertheless, participation in evening prayers and religious radio and TV programmes is more common, and the proportion being confirmed remains high (94%).

The Lutheran Church is composed of 8 dioceses, one of which (Borga) unites the Swedish-speaking congregations of the west and south. The highest administrative and legislative organ of the church is the Church Assembly which meets every 5 years. Interim matters are handled by the Enlarged Bishops' Meeting (with 39 lay, ministerial and episcopal members) and the Administrative Board with 8 members. The archbishop of Finland is chairman of all these bodies.

The Free church movement came to Finland from Sweden after the middle of the last century. The first was a Baptist congregation formed among Swedish-speakers in Föglö in 1856, and by 1870 Baptist work had also begun among Finnish-speaking peoples. Today these are separate churches. Methodism, which was brought to Finland by a sailor in the 1860s and which organized its first congregation in 1881, also has Finnish-speaking and Swedish-speaking conferences. A similar pattern is evident in churches of the Congregationalist tradition, which came from Sweden in 1878 and are represented

**Evangelical Lutheran Church of Finland.** Part of vast crowd in prayer at revivalist movement's meeting. Revival members number 200,000 Laestadians, 19,900 LEAF Evangelicals, 13,800 Pietists, 5,000 Praying Movement members, and 8,000 Neo-Pentecostals (1975).

Procession in Helsinki protesting against persecution of Christians in Soviet Union's underground churches.

in the Finnish-speaking Free Church of Finland and the Swedish-speaking Free Mission Covenant Church. Other free churches established at the end of the 1880s were the Salvation Army and Seventh-day Adventist, and a number of Pentecostal groups during the present century. The Pentecostal movement expanded rapidly until 1965 when it began to decline numerically. Unlike Catholicism, Jehovah's Witnesses and Mormons, all of which are growing rapidly, all Protestant denominations are declining in numbers today relative to the country's population and its natural increase.

ORTHODOX CHURCH. Members of the Orthodox Church of Finland, originally in large part farmers from the eastern region, have now spread throughout the country, this dispersion having arisen from the USSR's annexation of Karelia after

World War II. Their number is slowly diminishing because of mixed marriages with Lutherans. Although autonomous, the church is under the authority of the ecumenical patriarch of Constantinople.

CATHOLIC CHURCH. Now largely Finnish in leadership, the Catholic Church is growing faster than the general population growth, with births and conversions outnumbering deaths and defections. The diocese of Helsinki, which has the smallest membership of any Catholic diocese in Europe, consists of 5 parishes, 2 in Helsinki and one each in Turku, Tampere and Jyväskylä. Although there are influential Catholics among both intellectuals and workers, most of the faithful belong to the middle class. In 1977 Finland was transferred from the jurisdiction of Propaganda to that of the Congregation for Bishops.

**CHURCH AND STATE.** Article 8 of the constitution of 1919 guarantees freedom of conscience and worship, and this is further clarified by the earlier Law of the Church (Kirkkelaki, 1869) and the Religious Liberty Law of 1922. The parish registers of the 2 national churches, Lutheran and Orthodox, replace civil state registers, and marriages celebrated by them are valid as civil marriages. Religious instruction is given in all state and private schools.

As for the Lutheran Church, the principal state church, the Law of the Church stipulates that 'Its supreme government in the whole of the country is the concern of the Finnish government' (paragraph 14). The fact is that the church makes its laws freely but must submit them to Parliament which may approve or reject but not modify them. The president of the republic convokes the synod, when the archbishop so proposes. He also nominates bishops, choosing them from the first 3 names on the list from episcopal elections in vacant dioceses. He has in fact always chosen the candidate first on the list, with the exception of 4 cases between 1940 and 1975, when the second candidate was chosen. The state imposes on the faithful and on church societies a church tax which is then administered by the church without external constraint. The state also provides funds for various subsidies and salaries. The Orthodox Church of Finland receives similar treatment.

Other churches and religious groups may either obtain legal recognition at their own request, under certain conditions, or allow themselves to come under the general laws covering societies and groups. The following churches have been recognized since 1929: Free Church of Finland, Church of Sweden, Catholic Church, Seventh-day Adventists, Baptists, Methodists and Jehovah's Witnesses. Their marriages receive civil recognition, and they are given permission to tax their own members. Since 1971, the official register kept by each of these churches has been replaced by a central register. Citizens belonging to no religious confession have been registered since 1917 in a special civil register. The Ministry of Public Education (Opetusministeriö) is charged with religious questions which must be submitted to Parliament or to the head of state. Jews and Muslims are also officially recognized.

In 1966, the Lutheran bishops set up a study commission for the reform of church-state relations. The report, published in 1970, states among other things that the supreme adminstration of the church should not be under the control of the state but under the enlarged episcopal conference of an analogous body chosen by the church, with the government retaining responsibility only for questions or church activities involving the political domain. In September 1971, the main political party of the country, the Social Democrats, presented a detailed programme for the eventual separation of church and state, although nothing further has happened since then. By the end of 1975, the Finnish government had not yet taken the initiative in a study of the problem.

**INTERDENOMINATIONAL ORGANIZATIONS.** Ecumenical work in Finland is co-ordinated through the Ecumenical Council of Finland (Suomen Ekumeeninen Neuvosto), founded in 1950, in which the Catholic Church is a member. Two institutes are active: the Ecumenical Institute of the University of Helsinki (Helsingin Yliopiston Ekumeeninen Arkisto) is annexed to the Lutheran faculty which also possesses an Orthodox Institute (Ortodoksinen Laitos). The Institute for Ecumenism and Social Ethics of the University of Turku (Institut for Ekumenik och Socialetik vid Turku Akademi) is non-confessional, its main orientation being sociology of religion. Centres for dialogue and co-operation include the following. (1) The Ecumenical Society of Finland (Suomen Ekumeeninen Seura) is interconfessional and includes in its membership Lutherans, Orthodox, Catholics, Methodists and Salvationists; it seeks to increase mutual understanding and co-operation among churches; (2) The Dominican Culture Centre (Studium Catholicum, Dominikaainien Kulttuurikeskus) is the seat of the Ecumenical Secretariat of the Catholic diocese of Helsinki (Helsingin Hiippakunnan Ekumeeninen Sihteeristö); (3) The Ecumenical Centre of Myllyjärvi (Myllyjärven Ekumeeninen Keskus) is a Catholic Oriental-rite centre specializing in youth meetings.

**BROADCASTING.** Finland radio is government-owned and -controlled, and has 3 programmes, A, B, and C. Programme A carries religious broadcasting for 40 minutes from Mondays to Saturdays, and 85 minutes on Sundays. Programme B carries no religious broadcasting. Programme C, limited to Swedish-speaking areas (Helsinki, Turku, Vaasa, Mariehamn), broadcasts 2 religious programmes of 20 minutes each during the week and 70 minutes on Sundays. There are also local programmes in various areas, and these have their own religious services of around 60 minutes on Sundays. Time is rotated amongst the various churches, Lutherans having the largest share. Television programme I has 5 minutes per week of religious broadcasting and 10 Sunday worship services per year of about an hour each; Lutherans again have most of this time. From abroad, Trans World Radio (Monaco) beams in a 15-minute programme in Finnish on Tuesdays and Thursdays.

## BIBLIOGRAPHY


*Die Kirche Finnlands*. G. Sentzke. 3rd edition. Helsinki: Pohjois-Karjalan Kirjapaino Oy, 1968. 283p.

*Ecclesiastical trends in Finland in the late Sixties*. P. Niemelä. Tampere: Research Institute of the Lutheran Church, 1977.

'Finland', P. Seppänen, in H. Mol (ed), *Western religion* (The Hague: Mouton, 1972), p. 143–173.

*Suomen Evankelisluterilainen Kirkko, vuosina 1962–1966*. Kuopio, 1968. 196p.

*Suomen uskonnolliset liikkeet* (Religious movements in Finland). A. Haavio. Helsinki: WSOY, 1955.

*The challenge for Evangelical missions to Europe: a Scandinavian case study*. H. Mäläskä. South Pasadena: William Carey Library, 1970. 178p.

*The Church in Finland*. M. Sinnemaki. Otava, 1973.

*The Church of Finland*. Ed M. Ojala. Helsinki: Inner Mission Society of the Church of Finland, 1963. 48p.

'The Orthodox Church in Finland', E. Piiroinen, *International review of mission*, LXII, 245 (January, 1973), 51–6.


TABLE 2. ORGANIZED CHURCHES AND DENOMINATIONS IN FINLAND

| Official name 1 | Begun 2 | Type 3 | Counc 4 | Congs 5 | Adults 6 | Affiliated 7 | Names, notes, and other statistics (see Codebook) 8 |
|---|---|---|---|---|---|---|---|
| Baptist Union of Finland | 1854 | P Bap | T...C | 25 | 1,767 | 3,000 | *Suomen Baptistiyhadyskunta*. Finnish-speaking, 70% Finns. 15n,G=−1.2%pa,2s,W=50%,20Y. |
| Catholic Ch in Finland: D Helsinki | 1860 | R Lat | bzBQW | 5 | 2,000 | 2,868 | *Katolinen Kirkko Suomessa*. M=SCJ. C=2+0+3. 1n,21x,4m,36w,G=1.4%pa,P=48%,2Y,71y. |
| Christian Community in Finland | | P ind | ..... | | 130 | 200 | Small independent Protestant group of believers. |
| Church of Christ, Scientist | | M Sci | x.... | 1 | 20 | 50 | *Christian Science*. M=CCS(Boston, USA). *Helsinki Society*. |
| Church of England (J Fulham) | c1850 | A plu | awc.. | 1 | 190 | 269 | *Englantilainen Kirkkokunta*. English chaplaincy. Cathedral chapel. Senaatintori. 1x. |
| Ch of Jesus C of Latter-day Saints | c1880 | M LdS | x.... | 18 | 2,000 | 3,169 | *Myöhempien Aikojen Pyhien Jeesuksen Kristuksen Kirkko/Mormoonit*. Mormons. 100f,G=3.2%pa. |
| Church of Sweden | | P Lut | Lwc.. | 1 | 1,500 | 2,188 | *Olaus Petri. Ruotsinmaalainen Seurakunta*. Parish of Sweden state church. |
| Churches of Christ | | P Dis | x.... | 2 | 50 | 100 | *Kristuksen Seurakunta*. M=CC(Non-Instrumental)(USA). In Helsinki, Tampere. |
| Confessional Lutheran Ch of Finland | 1929 | P Lut | ..... | 12 | 290 | 431 | *Suomen Tunnustuksellinen Lutherilainen Kirkko*. Pure Lutheran. 4n,G=0.6%pa,W=45%,7Yy. |
| **Evangelical Lutheran Ch of Finland:** | c1100 | P Lut | LWC.W | 820 | 2,907,059 | 4,360,588 | *Suomen Evankelis-Luterilainen Kirkko*. 1818n,G=0.7%pa,17p,2s(1400),W=3%,71575Yy. |
| AD Turku (Abo) | 1276 | P Lut | L | 95 | 387,712 | 581,568 | In AD Uppsala till 1817. Southwest. Centre of Praying Movement revivalists. |
| D Helsinki | 1959 | P Lut | L | 59 | 514,875 | 772,312 | Capital city (527,000). Urbanized, industrialized, secularized. W=4.7%. |
| D Kuopio | 1939 | P Lut | L | 69 | 352,851 | 529,277 | In northeast. City, 52,000. North Savo. Pietists strong, Laestadians in west. |
| D Lapua | 1956 | P Lut | L | 64 | 312,392 | 468,587 | West central. Town, 16,000. Strongest area of Evangelical Movement revival. |
| D Mikkeli | 1895 | P Lut | L | 67 | 356,225 | 534,338 | In southeast. South Savo province, strong past Revival influence. Pietists strong. |
| D Oulu (Uleaborg) | 1851 | P Lut | L | 81 | 356,209 | 534,313 | Northern third of country. Sparsely-populated. Strongest Laestadian revival area. |
| D Porvoo (Borga) | 1923 | P Lut | L | 84 | 206,648 | 309,972 | Diocese for all Swedish-speaking parishes, and 2 German-speaking. Pietists strong. |
| D Tampere (Tammerfors) | 1554 | P Lut | L | 72 | 420,147 | 630,221 | D Viipuri until 1923. South; centre of Finnish industry. Revivals insignificant. |
| Filadelfia Assemblies | | P Pe2 | Z...C | | 500 | 1,000 | *Filadelfiaforsamlingen*. Swedish-speaking, linked to Swedish Filadelfia. M=SFM. |
| Finnish Mission Congregation | | P Pen | ..... | | 200 | 500 | *Suomen Lähetysseurakunta*. Small independent Finnish-speaking Pentecostal body. |
| Free Assoc of Ev Luth Congregations | | P Lut | ..... | 12 | 500 | 1,100 | *Suomen Vapaat Evankelis-Luterilainen Seurakuntalüto*. Decline. M=LCMS. HQ Lahti. |
| Free Catholic Church of Finland | | C Lib | x.... | 2 | 80 | 119 | *Suomen Vapaa Katolinen Kirkko*. Small conservative Liberal Catholic group. Declining. |
| Free Church of Finland | 1878 | P Con | Kv..C | 64 | 5,886 | 8,100 | *Suomen Vapaakirkko*. 1879 revival. Finnish-speaking. 49n,G=0.4%pa,1s,W=60%,95Yy. |
| Free Mission Covenant Church | 1921 | P Con | K...W | 30 | 1,500 | 2,500 | *Fria Missionsförbundet. Assoc of Free Ev Congs*. Swedish-speaking, ex FCF. 30n. |
| Free Pentecostal Revival of Finland | | P Pe4 | ..... | | 2,000 | 4,000 | *Suomen Vapaa-Helluntailähetys*. Free Pentecostals (renewal). HQ Helsinki. |
| Jehovah's Witnesses | 1909 | M Jeh | x.... | 282 | 10,836 | 15,000 | *Jehovan Todistajat*. Active witnessing under way by 1926. G=3.1%pa,W=75%,771Y. |
| Maranatha Pentecostal Church | 1959 | P Pe4 | x.... | | 2,000 | 5,000 | *Maranata Helluntailaiset*. Schism in Sweden ex Filadelfia Churches. |
| Methodist Church in Finland | 1866 | P Met | Vwc.d | 33 | 2,194 | 3,000 | *Metodistikirkko*. 2 Confs(Swedish, Finnish),NEurope CConf,UMC(USA). 28n,G=−1.4%pa. |
| Orthodox Church of Finland: | c1150 | O Fin | CwC.W | 68 | 38,000 | 54,000 | *Suomen Ortodoksinen Kirkko*. Autonomous 1923. Karelians. 54n,3d,1e,G=−0.9%pa,1s. |
| D Helsinki | 1925 | O Fin | Cb | | 18,000 | 25,000 | 40% in capital; urban influx. 93% intermarriage losses to Lutherans. 28n,W=4%. |
| D Karelia (Kuopio) | 1925 | O Fin | Ca | | 20,000 | 29,000 | Heavy losses in World War II. Diaspora farmers. Liturgy in Finnish only. 24n,1s, |
| Pentecostal Friends | 1923 | P Pe4 | ..... | 25 | 3,600 | 5,000 | Schism ex Pentecostal Revival, opposing organization. 10n,G=−3.6%pa,W=85%. |
| Pentecostal Revival of Finland | 1911 | P Pe2 | Z...C | 250 | 40,000 | 50,000 | *Helluntal-Ystävät*. Finnish- and Swedish-speaking congregations. G=0,1j,1s. |
| Private Greek Catholic Church | | O Sla | Mwc.. | 2 | 1,000 | 1,412 | *Yksityinen Kreikkalaiskatolienn Kirkkolinen Yhdyskunta*. Russians under D Leningrad. |
| Russian Orthodox Church | | O Sla | Mwc.. | | 950 | 1,362 | *Private Russian Orthodox Congregations*. Under jurisdiction of P Moscow. |
| Salvation Army, Finland Territory | 1889 | P Sal | xwc.W | 237 | 18,288 | 30,000 | *Pelastursameija* (Finnish), *Frälsningsarmén* (Swedish). 234n,G=−1%pa,1s. |
| Seventh-day Adventist Ch of Finland | 1892 | P Adv | xv..w | 64 | 5,787 | 7,500 | *Suomen Adventtikirkko*. Finl UC; Swedish C. 25n,1x,G=0.4%pa,2H,1h,1j,1r,W=59%,303Y. |
| Swedish Baptist Church of Finland | 1856 | P Bap | T...C | 36 | 1,832 | 3,000 | *Finlands Svenska Baptistmission*. Swedish-speaking. 20n,G=−1.0%pa,W=50%,35Y. |
| Other Protestant denominations | | P | ..... | | 500 | 1,000 | Total over 5 (see list below). |
| Doubly-affiliated (duplication)(1970) | | | | | −98,000 | −140,000 | Free church members (Salvation Army, &c) also in state Lutheran church. |
| **Total affiliated (mid-1970)** | | | | **2,060** | **2,952,659** | **4,426,456** | **Total denominations (1970) . . . 34.** |
| **Total affiliated (mid-1975)** | | | | **2,065** | **2,849,500** | **4,271,800** | **Total denominations (1975) . . . 36.** |
| **Total affiliated (mid-1980)** | | | | **2,070** | **2,749,300** | **4,121,590** | **Total denominations (1980) . . . 38.** |

### NOTES ON TABLE ABOVE

COLUMNS: for meanings and CODES (cols. 1, 3, 4, 8): see Codebook (Part 6). Column 1: **Boldface type** = church with over 10% of country's affiliated Christians.

NATIONAL COUNCILS (Column 4, 5th letter).

- C = Council of Free Christians and Churches in Finland (CFCCF) (Suomen Vapaitten Kristittyjen ja Kirkkokuntien Neuvosto) (2 branches: Finnish- and Swedish-speaking).
- d = member of both ECF and CFCCF.
- W = Ecumenical Council of Finland (ECF) (Soumen Ekumeeninen Neuvosto; in Swedish, Ekumeniska Radet i Finland).
- w = observer member of ECF.

OTHER PROTESTANT DENOMINATIONS. These include: American Advent Mission Society (1967), Friends of Truth (Totuuden Ystävät), Gypsy Evangelical Movement (France, Switzerland).

**PEOPLES** (ethnolinguistic). Christians: 92.0% Finnish, 7.4% Swedish, 0.1% Russian, 0.1% Gypsy, 0.1% Lapp, USA, Estonian.

### COUNTRY-WIDE TOTALS

EVANGELIZATION (see Part 5). 1900: 100%. 1970: 100%. 1980: 100%. *Mass evangelism*. Among recent campaigns: 1961, Oral Roberts campaign in Helsinki; 1967, formation of Evangelical Lutheran People's Mission, for regular evangelistic activity; 1973, Finland Congress on Evangelism; 1978, Here's Life Tampere (CCCI). *Radiophonic evangelism*. Annual listeners' letters (1975): 550 TWR, 438 HCJB, 111 RVOG, 50 FEBC, et alia.

FOREIGN MISSIONARIES AND PERSONNEL (nationals serving abroad) (1973). Total 547: 522 Protestants (increase from 250 in 1963) in 51 countries (including 211 Pentecostals), about 20 marginal Protestants (mainly Jehovah's Witnesses), about 5 Roman Catholics in Scandinavia.

FOREIGN MISSIONARIES AND PERSONNEL (aliens from abroad) (1973). Total 224. *From Western world*. 221: about 100 marginal Protestants (90 Mormons from USA), 58 Roman Catholics, 60 Protestants (mostly from Scandinavia; 6 in 6 USA societies, 3 from Sweden, 1 in 1 UK society), about 2 Orthodox, 1 Anglican. *From Communist world*. About 3 Orthodox.

INSTITUTIONS (church-operated) (1973). Total 130, including 2 ecumenical centres, 95 higher schools (90 folk high schools), 5 medical centres (hospitals), 4 religious communities (monasteries), 3 research centres, 8 seminaries (7 Protestant, 1 Orthodox).

PERIODICALS. About 105 titles (8 SDA).

PERSONNEL. About 2,574 (2,350 national, 224 foreign).

RELIGIOUS LIBRARIES. About 60.

SCRIPTURE DISTRIBUTION (1975). Annual totals: 82,228 Bibles (1% free, 93% subsidized, 6% commercial), 96,572 NTs (2% free, 88% subsidized, 10% commercial), 6,709 UBS portions. *Translations completed*. Portion: 2 languages since 1903. NT: Finnish in 1548, Bible in 1642.

SERVICE AGENCIES. About 55, including CCCI, CEF, CFCCF, ECF, FFFM, KATT, PBS, SU, WLC(EHC), YMCA, YWAM, YWCA.

### ADDITIONAL DATA ON CHURCHES

CATHOLIC CHURCH. Over half of all Catholics live in 2 parishes in Helsinki (Helsingfors). All parishes have post-conciliar-type parish councils. *Growth*. By 1974, the diocese had 4,000 faithful. *Priests*. One Finnish OP. Since the Reformation, only 2 other Finns have become priests. Expatriates are Dutch and French; 2 are Byzantine-rite. *Brothers*. All Dutch. *Sisters*. 3 Finns, the rest Dutch and American. *Catholic charismatics* (January 1974). 25 adults including some religious personnel were active in an organized prayer group in the Charismatic Renewal. *Foreign religious orders and congregations*. Priests: SCJ (Dutch province), OP (French province). Sisters: Sisters of the Sacred Heart of Jesus, Most Precious Blood, Little Sisters of Jesus of Charles de Foucauld.

*Catholic organizations*. The Nordic or Scandinavian Episcopal Conference (Nordiske Bispekonferense, or Conferentia Episcopalis Scandiae), based in Copenhagen, Denmark, is a member of CCEE. All of Finland's priests are members of the Presbyteral Council founded in 1967. The principal lay movements are Katolinen Opiskelijayhdistis (Circle of Catholic Students), Academicum Catholicum for intellectuals and Juventus Catholica for youth.

The Holy See has diplomatic relations with Finland and is represented to government and the Catholic hierarchy by a pro-nuncio residing in 1973 in Copenhagen, Denmark.

Catholic social work is minimal; there are 4 kindergartens, the sole confessional primary school in the country, Caritas welfare aid for the aged, and work among alcoholics by the community of Emmaus.

EVANGELICAL LUTHERAN CHURCH OF FINLAND. The church, founded about AD 1100, was reformed in 1593. *Attendance*. Although Sunday attenders are only 2.6% of the population, there is widespread weekday activity, especially in the revivalist and old pietist movements. *Revivals*. Membership in the 4 early movements (begun 1830–40): 200,000 Laestadians, 19,893 Evangelicals (Lutheran Evangelical Association of Finland), 13,800 Pietists, 5,000 Praying Movement members (1963). Movements begun after 1945: People's Bible Society, Inner Mission Foundation, Bible School of Helsinki, People's Mission. *Baptisms*. 92.3% of the population still receive infant baptism in the state church. *Sunday schools*. Total 15,000 in the state church, with 300,000 children. *Confirmation*. Persons confirmed (at 15 years of age) number 94% of the population. *Parish personnel*. 1,205 parish clergy (46% urban, 54% rural), 140 lectors (female pastors), 689 church musicians, 780 deacons, 925 parish administrators; total including youth and children's workers 8,730, most being voluntary and unpaid. Total clergy of all kinds including retired: over 2,000.

ORTHODOX CHURCH OF FINLAND. Members are 84% Finnish, 10% Russians, 5% Swedes, with 500 Lapps. The church suffered very heavy losses during World War II.

PRIVATE GREEK CATHOLIC CHURCH. Declining at 2.2% per year.

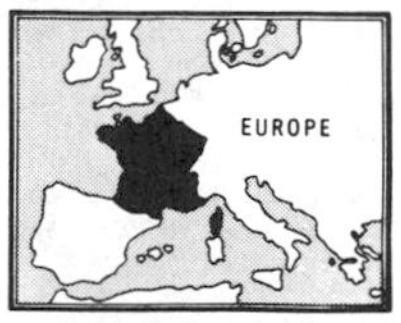


# FRANCE

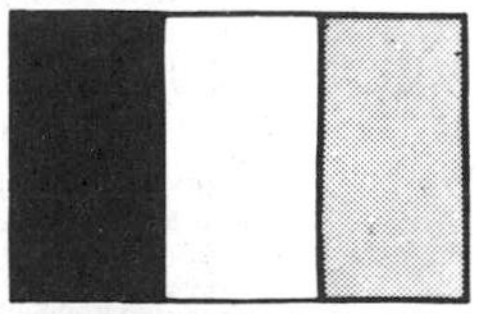

## SECULAR DATA

**STATE. Official name:** The French Republic (La République Française). Adjectives of nationality: French, a Frenchman, the French (français).
**Flag** (shown above right): Tricolour of blue, white, and red bars.
**Area:** 547,026 sq.km. (211,208 sq.miles). Agricultural land: 59.3%.
**Government:** Parliamentary republic, since 1871 (c1500 kingdom and empire, 1789 revolutionary republic, 1799 military dictatorship, 1821 monarchy, 1848 Second Republic).
**Legislature:** Parliament: Senate, 283 members; National Assembly, 490 members.
**Official language:** French (*Français*).
**Chief cities:** capital Paris 8,196,750 (1968), Lyons 1,074,820, Marseilles 964,410, Lille 881,440.
**Political divisions:** 95 Departments, 37,708 Communes.
**Armed forces** (1976): Total 512,900 regular (279,300 conscripts): army 338,500, navy 70,000, air force 104,400 (470 combat aircraft). Reserves: 450,000. Paramilitary forces: 73,000 gendarmerie.
**Dependencies:** French Guiana, French Polynesia, Guadeloupe, Martinique, Mayotte, New Caledonia, New Hebrides, Reunion, St Pierre and Miquelon, French Southern and Antarctic Territories, Wallis and Futuna.

**DEMOGRAPHY. Population:** 52,544,400 (census of 20.II.1975). For 1970–2000 (UN), see last row of Table 1). Population density (1975): 97/sq.km. (251/sq.mile). Under 15 years: 26%. Growth rate (1975–80): 0.81% per year (births 1.70%, deaths −1.03%, immigrants 0.14%). Life expectancy (1975–80): 73.5 years. Household size: 3.1 persons.
**Major languages:** French, Occitan (Provençal, Languedoc), Yiddish, Flemish, English, German, Armenian, Russian, Polish, Romany, Arabic, Portuguese, Spanish, Italian, Vietnamese, Breton, Catalan, Basque. In addition there are over 20 other languages.
**Urban dwellers** (1970): 69.9%. Urban growth rate (1950–70): 2.2% per year.
**Labour force:** 42%.
**Refugees** (1977): From abroad 132,000 (56,000 from Spain, 27,000 from Eastern Europe (Poland, Hungary, Romania, Czechoslovakia), 17,000 from USSR, 15,000 from Lebanon, 13,000 from Viet Nam, 4,000 from Chile.
**Tourists** (1960): 8,200,000. (1970) 13,700,000. (1974) 16,573,000.

**ETHNOLINGUISTIC GROUPS:** 92.0% citizen [82% French (24.6% also speaking Occitan), 2.7% Alsatian, 2.4% Breton, 1.1% Jewish, 0.7% Flemish, 0.5% Corsican, 0.4% Catalan, 0.4% Antillean Creole (Martiniquan, Guadeloupan), 0.4% German, 0.4% Armenian, 0.3% Gypsy (150,000), 0.2% Russian, 0.2% Polish (100,000), et alii], 8.0% alien [1.6% Algerian (800,000), 1.5% Portuguese (750,000), 1.2% Spaniard (600,000), 1.1% Italian (580,000), 0.8% Vietnamese (400,000; by 1972, 500,000), 0.4% Moroccan (190,000), 0.4% African & Malagasy, 0.3% Basque, 0.2% Tunisian (100,000), 0.1% Greek, 0.1% Walloon, 0.1% Chinese (50,000), 0.1% British (30,000), 0.1% Cambodian (50,000 by 1978), Serbian, Franco-Swiss, USA, Czech, Turkish, Central Asian; a small number of all these groups have become citizens].
**MONEY** (1977). **Monetary unit:** franc (= 100 centimes); US$1 = Fr 5.00.
**National income per person:** US$4,486. Average annual family income: US$13,907.
**Inflation:** (1970–74) 8.0% per year, (1975) 12% per year (consumer price index 161), (1977) 6.2% per year.
**Cost of living in capital** (1976): index 168 (Washington DC = 100). Daily cost of living: US$49.

**EDUCATION.** Adult literacy: (1964) 96%, (1975) 99%. Education rate: 37%. Schools: 59,081. Universities: 54.

**HEALTH.** Hospitals: 3,602 (539,700 beds). Doctors: 71,039. Lepers: 400. Blind: 43,000. Psychotics: 580,000. Drug addicts: 100,000. Criminals: 727,154.

**LITERATURE.** Annual new book titles (1973): 27,186. Periodicals: 13,969. Scientific journals: 2,780. Newspapers: 105 dailies, 1,007 non-daily.

**COMMUNICATION** (per 1,000 people). Phones: 217. Radios: 329. TV sets: 237. Daily newspaper circulation: 237 copies.

TABLE 1. RELIGIOUS ADHERENTS IN FRANCE

| Year | 1900 | | mid-1970 | | Annual change, 1970–1980 | | | | mid-1975 | | mid-1980 | | 2000 | |
|---|---|---|---|---|---|---|---|---|---|---|---|---|---|---|
| *Name* | *Adherents* | *%* | *Adherents* | *%* | *Natural* | *Conversion* | *Total* | *Rate* | *Adherents* | *%* | *Adherents* | *%* | *Adherents* | *%* |
| **Christians** | **40,731,100** | **99.3** | **42,559,900** | **84.0** | **349,256** | **−194,166** | **155,090** | **0.36** | **43,351,700** | **81.9** | **44,110,800** | **80.1** | **44,775,000** | **72.1** |
| professing | 40,731,100 | 99.3 | 42,559,900 | 84.0 | 349,256 | −194,166 | 155,090 | 0.36 | 43,351,700 | 81.9 | 44,110,800 | 80.1 | 44,775,000 | 72.1 |
| Roman Catholics | 39,807,600 | 97.1 | 40,704,900 | 80.3 | 333,726 | −192,166 | 141,560 | 0.34 | 41,424,000 | 78.3 | 42,120,500 | 76.4 | 42,567,000 | 68.5 |
| Protestants | 910,000 | 2.2 | 1,030,000 | 2.0 | 8,540 | −2,540 | 6,000 | 0.57 | 1,060,000 | 2.0 | 1,090,000 | 2.0 | 1,200,000 | 1.9 |
| Orthodox | 10,000 | 0.0 | 400,000 | 0.8 | 3,367 | −367 | 3,000 | 0.72 | 418,000 | 0.8 | 430,000 | 0.8 | 490,000 | 0.8 |
| Marginal Protestants | 0 | 0.0 | 210,000 | 0.4 | 1,813 | 1,187 | 3,000 | 1.33 | 225,000 | 0.4 | 240,000 | 0.4 | 300,000 | 0.5 |
| Catholics (non-Roman) | 3,000 | 0.0 | 200,000 | 0.4 | 1,684 | −284 | 1,400 | 0.67 | 209,000 | 0.4 | 214,000 | 0.4 | 200,000 | 0.3 |
| Anglicans | 500 | 0.0 | 15,000 | 0.0 | 126 | 4 | 130 | 0.83 | 15,700 | 0.0 | 16,300 | 0.0 | 18,000 | 0.0 |
| affiliated | 40,731,100 | 99.3 | 42,559,900 | 84.0 | 349,256 | −194,166 | 155,090 | 0.36 | 43,351,700 | 81.9 | 44,110,800 | 80.1 | 44,775,000 | 72.1 |
| disaffiliated | −129,400 | −0.3 | −2,677,538 | −5.3 | −23,872 | −33,474 | −57,346 | 1.94 | −2,963,000 | −5.6 | −3,251,000 | −5.9 | −4,349,000 | −7.0 |
| doubly-affiliated | −400,000 | −1.0 | −850,000 | −1.7 | −7,668 | −12,032 | −19,700 | 2.07 | −952,000 | −1.8 | −1,047,000 | −1.9 | −1,367,000 | −2.2 |
| total practising | 34,621,400 | *85* | 31,919,920 | *75* | 258,450 | −230,354 | 28,096 | 0.09 | 32,080,260 | *74* | 32,200,880 | *73* | 29,103,700 | *65* |
| non-practising | 6,109,700 | *15* | 10,639,980 | *25* | 90,806 | 36,188 | 126,994 | 1.13 | 11,271,440 | *26* | 11,909,920 | *27* | 15,671,300 | *35* |
| Roman Catholics | 40,344,000 | 98.4 | 44,405,899 | 87.6 | 366,604 | −150,994 | 215,610 | 0.47 | 45,505,000 | 86.0 | 46,562,000 | 84.5 | 48,462,000 | 78.0 |
| Catholic pentecostals | 0 | 0.0 | 4,000 | 0.0 | 700 | 28,900 | 29,600 | 32.88 | 90,000 | 0.2 | 300,000 | 0.5 | 1,200,000 | 1.9 |
| Protestants | 902,000 | 2.2 | 951,449 | 1.9 | 7,976 | −621 | 7,355 | 0.74 | 990,000 | 1.9 | 1,025,000 | 1.9 | 1,100,000 | 1.8 |
| Evangelicals | 120,000 | 0.3 | 260,000 | 0.5 | 2,179 | −179 | 2,000 | 0.74 | 270,500 | 0.5 | 280,000 | 0.5 | 302,000 | 0.5 |
| Neo-pentecostals | 0 | 0.0 | 1,000 | 0.0 | 80 | 1,820 | 1,900 | 19.00 | 10,000 | 0.0 | 20,000 | 0.0 | 70,000 | 0.1 |
| Orthodox | 10,000 | 0.0 | 376,500 | 0.7 | 3,166 | 184 | 3,350 | 0.85 | 393,000 | 0.7 | 410,000 | 0.7 | 465,000 | 0.7 |
| Catholics (non-Roman) | 3,000 | 0.0 | 178,700 | 0.4 | 1,450 | −1,120 | 330 | 0.18 | 180,000 | 0.4 | 182,000 | 0.3 | 150,000 | 0.2 |
| Marginal Protestants | 1,000 | 0.0 | 157,390 | 0.3 | 1,450 | 3,811 | 5,261 | 2.92 | 180,000 | 0.3 | 210,000 | 0.4 | 290,000 | 0.5 |
| Anglicans | 500 | 0.0 | 15,000 | 0.0 | 126 | 4 | 130 | 0.83 | 15,700 | 0.0 | 16,300 | 0.0 | 18,000 | 0.0 |
| Third-World indigenous | 0 | 0.0 | 2,500 | 0.0 | 24 | 76 | 100 | 3.33 | 3,000 | 0.0 | 3,500 | 0.0 | 6,000 | 0.0 |
| Non-religious | 92,000 | 0.2 | 4,560,000 | 9.0 | 45,128 | 170,132 | 215,260 | 3.84 | 5,601,400 | 10.6 | 6,712,600 | 12.2 | 11,432,000 | 18.4 |
| Atheists | 30,000 | 0.1 | 1,520,000 | 3.0 | 13,639 | 21,661 | 35,300 | 2.09 | 1,693,000 | 3.2 | 1,873,000 | 3.4 | 2,796,000 | 4.5 |
| Muslims | 50,000 | 0.1 | 1,350,000 | 2.7 | 29,503 | 797 | 30,300 | 1.95 | 1,550,000 | 2.9 | 1,653,000 | 3.0 | 2,175,000 | 3.5 |
| Jews | 86,900 | 0.2 | 550,000 | 1.1 | 4,624 | 176 | 4,800 | 0.84 | 574,000 | 1.1 | 598,000 | 1.1 | 674,000 | 1.1 |
| New-Religionists | 0 | 0.0 | 30,000 | 0.1 | 252 | 8 | 260 | 0.83 | 31,300 | 0.1 | 32,600 | 0.1 | 40,000 | 0.1 |
| Chinese folk-religionists | 0 | 0.0 | 30,000 | 0.1 | 243 | −443 | −200 | −0.69 | 29,000 | 0.1 | 28,000 | 0.1 | 20,000 | 0.0 |
| Buddhists | 0 | 0.0 | 27,000 | 0.1 | 227 | 3 | 230 | 0.82 | 28,200 | 0.1 | 29,300 | 0.1 | 33,000 | 0.1 |
| Baha'is | 0 | 0.0 | 3,100 | 0.0 | 27 | 33 | 60 | 1.76 | 3,400 | 0.0 | 3,700 | 0.0 | 6,000 | 0.0 |
| Other religionists | 10,000 | 0.0 | 40,000 | 0.1 | 401 | 1,799 | 2,200 | 4.31 | 51,000 | 0.1 | 62,000 | 0.1 | 180,000 | 0.3 |
| **Country's population** | **41,000,000** | **100.0** | **50,670,000** | **100.0** | **443,300** | **0** | **443,300** | **0.84** | **52,913,000** | **100.0** | **55,103,000** | **100.0** | **62,131,000** | **100.0** |

COLUMNS, ROWS. For meanings and definitions, see Codebook (Part 6). Note that, by definition, total 'Christians' = professing + crypto-Christians, which also = affiliated + nominal Christians. Percentages may not always total exactly, due to rounding.
CENSUSES. The religion question has not been asked in government censuses, except for Alsace-Lorraine as follows. **1954:** 77.5% Roman Catholics, 21.7% Protestants, 0.6% Jews, 0.2% Muslims: and **1962:** 78.0% Roman Catholics, 20.7% Protestants, 0.7% Jews, 0.6% Muslims.
POLLS. Many public-opinion polls of religion have been taken since 1940 (IFOP, SOFRES, Gallup, et alia), including several commissioned or encouraged by the Catholic Church since Vatican II. In 1960, 91.5% of all children were being baptized in the Catholic Church. 1966 (IFOP): 'Have you been baptized?': 96% Yes, 3% No. 'Were you married in church?': 87% Yes, 13% No. 'Did you make your first communion (i.e. at 12 years old)?': 87% Yes. After first communion, 34% never attend church again, 33% only for a few years, but 32% attend regularly thereafter. 'Do you belong to a Catholic family?': 90% Yes. 'What is your religion at present?': 79% Catholic, 10% none, 2% Protestant, 2% other, 7% no answer. 1967 (IFOP): 80% Catholics (22% regularly-practising, 37% seasonally-practising, 21% non-practising), 12% non-religious and atheists, 3% Protestants, 1% Jews, 1% other religionists. 'What is or was the religion of your parents?': 90% Catholic, 4% none, 3% Protestant, 2% other religion. Some results for practice are given below. Almost all polls up to 1975 have ignored the presence of Muslims, hence these figures have been modified in the table above to include the 3% of the de facto population who are Muslims.

## NOTES ON RELIGIONS

ATHEISTS. Parti Communiste Français (PCF) (legal; neutral re Sino-Soviet split): estimated membership (1930) 38,000, (1946) 1,000,000 (plus 93,000 in youth organizations), (1970) 295,000, (1974) 250,000, also small Trotskyite and pro-Chinese factions; Communist voters (election of 1936) 15.3% of all votes, (X.1945) 5,005,336 (26% of all votes), (23.VI.1968) 4,435,357 (20% of all votes), (III.1973) 5,156,619 (21.2% of votes). In France there is no Christian or Catholic socialist party, hence many Christians vote Communist. Of party members, 40% profess to be Roman Catholics also; of Communist voters, 24% are practising Catholics. Communist militants in the PCF had fallen by 1966 to under 40,000. Among Communist voters, in 1966, 77% were non-practising Catholics or non-religious, falling to 71% by 1972; in 1966, 15% occasionally practised a religious rite, rising to 28% in 1972 who were occasional churchgoers. Several polls have been taken. 1952: 17% of all ages declared themselves without religion (i.e. not affiliated to any church, also non-religious, also atheists). In 1959 and 1961, 8% of all youths declared themselves without religion and 9% atheist (IFOP). 1966: 10% without religion (non-affiliated, non-religious, and atheists), 7% uncertain. Among youths aged 18–24, in 1974 10% professed to be atheists (Gallup).
BAHA'IS. Entered before 1921. Growth from 8 local spiritual assemblies (1964) to 16 (1973)
BUDDHISTS. Mahayana. 1970: 15,000 Vietnamese, Laotian, Cambodian and Chinese immigrants since 1950, and 12,000 French Buddhists. In 1975 a further wave arrived from Viet Nam.
CATHOLIC PENTECOSTALS (or, Catholic charismatics). Totals (January 1974): 10,000 involved adults (over 15 years old) in over 120 prayer groups; total charismatic community including children, 20,000. (1980) Total charismatic community, 300,000.
DISAFFILIATED. This term is used here to describe dechristianized persons who, although baptized Roman Catholics and therefore regarded by the Catholic Church as still affiliated to it (and hence enumerated in Table 2 as such), have recently withdrawn or disaffiliated themselves completely from Christianity and now profess to be either non-religious (agnostics) or atheists. Because their statistics represent a duplication, they are shown in the table above as a negative quantity (with a minus sign). The vast majority of these dechristianized persons are in the Paris region. In 1970, the archdiocese of Paris reported (in *AP 1973*) a total population of 2,573,732, of whom baptized Catholics numbered 2,316,388 (90.0%); in 1972, the archdiocese was still reporting Catholics as 80.7% of the population (*AP 1975:* 2,090,000 Catholics out of 2,590,770). However, in 1966 (IFOP), non-religious and atheists in Paris amounted to 32%, gradually increasing in size with each subsequent year. It is clear therefore that a large number of baptized Catholics on the archdiocese's records have in fact recently become agnostics or atheists. The table above incorporates all of these data and interpretations.
DOUBLY-AFFILIATED. The term covers those affiliated to, or claimed by, both the Catholic Church and also a church termed Evangélique by state or society (Protestant, Anglican, marginal Protestant) or other church, i.e. baptized Catholics who have recently become Evangelicals or others. Because their statistics represent a duplication, they are shown in the table as a negative quantity (with a minus sign).
JEWS. Increasing due to immigration from North Africa (100,000 from Egypt); now throughout France. Since 1960, Sefardis outnumber Ashkenazis for the first time in France. City populations: Paris 300,000, Marseilles 80,000, Nice 30,000, Lyons 16,000, Strasbourg 15,000.
MUSLIMS. There has been a rapid increase in numbers from 0.7% of the population (350,000) in 1966. By 1970, about 25% were naturalized immigrants, 75% migrant workers; including (in 1971) 798,700 Algerians, 194,300 Moroccans, 106,800 Tunisians, 50,000 Black West Africans (rising to 150,000 by 1973; from Senegal, Mali, Mauritania), 18,300 Turkish, 200 Pakistanis; also Yugoslavs, 150,000 French Muslims (former Algerians, now of French nationality), and at least 100,000 clandestine (illegal) immigrants from Algeria, Tunisia and West Africa. Almost all are Sunnis. *Hajj pilgrims to Mecca*. (1970) 372; (1974) 556; (1975) 795; (1976) 563. *Immigration*. The column 'Natural change' above includes 16,500 annual immigrants as well as about 13,000 biological increase. *Conversions*. Each year a number of former Muslims who had lapsed are won back to Islam.
NEO-PENTECOSTALS. Charismatics in organized groups within the non-Pentecostal Protestant denominations, including many youth in the Jesus Movement. The movement began within the Reformed Church of France in 1932, with a new surge from 1972 onwards. In the east of France, the renewal in the Lutheran and Reformed state churches of Alsace-Lorraine is developing a pronounced ecumenical cross-fertilization between Protestants and Catholics.
NEW-RELIGIONISTS. Mainly Cao Daists among the 500,000 Vietnamese (1972) in France; and a Soka Gakkai mission headquarters for Europe in Paris, with in 1971, 4,000 households in Europe (8,000 adherents), and in 1975, 5,300 adherents in France alone.
NON-RELIGIOUS. Of these persons, about 90% were once baptized Catholics; 72% once made their first communion (at 12 years old) but then ceased all church attendance, 19% at one time belonged to a Christian youth movement, 4% have parents who were practising Christians. In Paris, a very high proportion were non-religious in 1966: 32%. Of all non-religious, 32% in 1966 voted Communist, 17% socialist, 11% radical.
OTHER RELIGIONISTS. Including Hindus (with one ISKCON

Hare Krishna centre, also Ananda Marga, and Ramakrishna Mission), and adherents of numerous esoteric religions including Rosicrucians (98 AMORC Lodges and centres; also Lectorium Rosicrucianum). The Theosophical Society in 1975 had 44 Lodges with 1,377 members. There are also in France some 10,000 Freemasons, often considered a quasi-religion.

PRACTISING CHRISTIANS. 1948: weekly church attenders 37% of the whole population. 1960: 26% weekly mass attenders, 32.5% annual Easter communicants. 1961 (IFOP): 37% weekly, 42% from time to time, 20% never. 1964 (VC): 'Are you a practising religious believer?': 33% believe and practise, 42% believe but not practise, 14% not believe but some private practice (weddings), 7% neither believe nor practise, 4% opposed to all religions. 1966 (IFOP): of all professing Catholics and Protestants. 9% are very regularly practising (attending mass every Sunday or more often, and communion at least once a month), 15% regularly practising (mass every Sunday, communion several times a year), 36% seasonally-practising (several Sundays a year, communion once a year), 26% indifferent (professing Catholics, but never attending church). 1966 (IFOP): of all professing Catholics and Protestants, 3% attend church several times a week, 27% every Sunday, 45% several times a year, 25% never. 1966 (IFOP): of all professing Catholics and Protestants, 2% take communion several times a week, 5% once weekly, 13% once monthly, 28% once a year, 27% never. 1968: weekly attenders 25% of the population. 1970: 90% of the population are baptized Catholics, 20% attend mass weekly. February 1970: 4% of population attend several times a week, 20% once a week, 39% from time to time, 26% never, 11% non-affiliated or non-religious. 1971: Easter communicants 35%. 1971: 18% attend every Sunday, 42% several times a year, 29% never, 10% not Catholics. 1972: Easter communicants 32%; church marriages and funerals, over 80%. Christmas attenders 41% (17% taking communion). 1974: of youths aged 18–24, 8% attend church weekly (Gallup). Sunday attendance varies greatly with area: in rural Brittany 80%, in urban Marseilles 11%. 1975: 16% attend every Sunday, 22% on important occasions, 40% once or twice a year (35% on family feast days), 20% never. *Pilgrims*. Around 2 million pilgrims a year visit the Shrine of the Virgin at Lourdes, with a peak of 8 million during the centenary year of 1958. Over a million pilgrims a year, also, visit the basilica of Ste-Thérèse in Lisieux, Normandy. Other pilgrimage centres include Ars and La Salette.

THIRD-WORLD INDIGENOUS. In about 4 denominations in 1970 (see Table 2), rising to 8 by 1975.

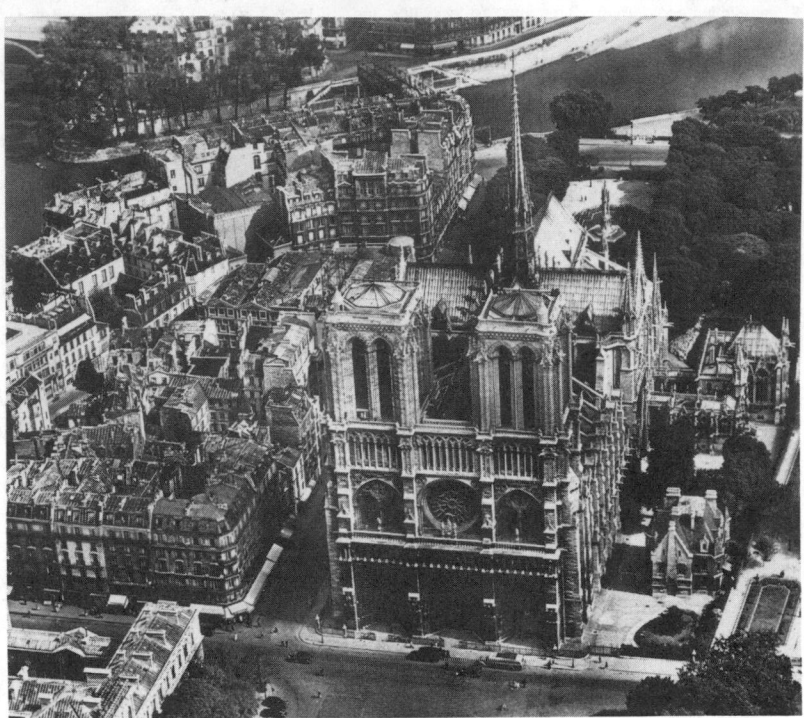

**Eglise Catholique de France, Archidiocèse de Paris.** Gothic Cathedral of Notre-Dame de Paris, on Ile Saint-Louis, built AD 1163-1240.

**NON-CHRISTIAN RELIGIONS. Islam** forms the second largest religious community in France, after the Catholic Church, France having in 1975 more Muslims than any other West European country. Muslim immigration began in the early part of the present century, with the arrival of Algerian male workers, followed later by a broad spectrum of North African workers with their families. During the early 1960s other Muslims entered from Yugoslavia, Turkey and former French Black Africa; and by 1973, over 1.3 million persons from Muslim countries or regions had settled legally in France. The largest communities of legal immigrants by 1973 were those from Algeria (798,690), Morocco (226,496), Tunisia (133,315), Turkey (25,066) and such Black African countries as Senegal, Mali and Mauritania (more than 150,000). These figures do not include clandestine immigration, which is significant among Algerians, Tunisians and Black Africans and which is only partially compensated by the number of registered aliens leaving the country after the expiration of their residence permits. There are also at least 150,000 French Muslims (of French citizenship), mostly Algerians who were officially recognized as French prior to Algerian independence in 1962.

Although Muslim immigrants are dispersed throughout France, they are especially numerous in the southeast (Provence; Côte d'Azur) and in the regions of Paris and Lyons. Their living conditions are often difficult. Mosques (without imams) exist in Marseilles, Montpellier, Draguignan, Lyons, Le Mans and other cities. Most offer literacy courses and Quranic lectures, and all except the mosque at Lille are directed by representatives of the great mosque of Paris. The latter is the headquarters of the Muslim Institute of Paris, the only national Muslim religious organization, and the International Muslim Union, the latter being founded in 1968 to provide aid for the needy, defend the Muslim community, make known Islamic thought and organize Muslim worship where needed. The Paris mosque was founded between 1921–26 and is subsidized by the city of Paris and the French Ministry of the Interior. A serious conflict exists between the leaders of the Muslim Institute and both the Algerian authorities and many North African Muslims in France, a conflict related to the political orientation of the institute given the fact that many of its leaders were partisans of the 'Algérie française' faction at the time of the war for independence.

**Judaism** is widespread and extensive, the Jewish community of France being the largest in Europe (with the exception of the Soviet Union) and the fourth largest in the world, after the USA, USSR and Israel. In 1971 there were 580,000 Jews in France, of which about half were from North Africa. Of the 270,000 French Jews at the beginning of World War II, 120,000 were deported during the Nazi occupation. The rapid increase in the Jewish population after the war has been due for the most part to immigration: first displaced persons from other parts of Western Europe; then Jews from Poland, Romania and Hungary; 100,000 from Egypt between 1954 and 1961; others from Morocco and Tunisia after their independence in 1956 (a movement which continues to this day); and 120,000 from Algeria since 1962.

The massive immigration from North Africa has introduced important changes in Jewish life. For the first time in French history Sefardis (who originate in the eastern Mediterranean and North Africa) outnumber Ashkenazis (from central Europe), a fact which has created material, cultural and religious problems of adjustment as well as causing considerable strains on existing Jewish organizations. The extensive multiplication of Jewish communities, from 128 in 1957 to 600 in 1970, has also created new problems of adjustment relating to the integration of Judaism into French society as a whole. Many cities now have Jewish communities for the first time. In 1970 the principal urban concentrations of Jews were found in Paris and its suburbs (300,000), Marseilles (65,000), Lyons (25,000), Toulouse (25,000), Nice (18,000) and Strasbourg (13,500).

Communities of Orthodox Judaism, Liberal or Reformed Judaism, and Consistorial Judaism (the later being similar to conservative Judaism in the USA), are also found in France, although most Jews are not attached to any of these traditions. The Orthodox have only a few hundred adherents and Liberal Judaism not more than 3,000 while even the third group, the largest, counts no more than 70 consistorial rabbis in the whole of France.

An international Jewish organization based in France is the Universal Israelite Alliance, founded in Paris in 1860. The principal national organizations are: (1) Consistoire Israélite de France, founded in the 19th century, which is concerned primarily with worship and administers the Israelite Seminary of France in Paris; (2) Conseil Représentatif des Israélites de France (CRIF), founded in Paris in 1944, which is dedicated to the defence of Jewish interests; and (3) Fonds Social Juif Unifié (FSJU) founded in Paris after World War II, which is especially influential in the reconstruction of the Jewish community after the war and continues to provide aid in the areas of education and social service. During 1955–71 the FSJU was responsible for the construction of 60 community centres throughout the country. Jewish primary and secondary schools exist in Paris and Strasbourg, with 3,000 students, and there are other centres for religious instruction, including 7 Yeshiva schools offering rabbinic studies.

**Buddhism** exists both among aliens from southeast Asia (15,000 from Viet-Nam, Cambodia and Laos) and native French citizens (12,000). Vietnamese are found in relatively large numbers and have built a Buddhist temple at Fréjus (Var). Their principal associations are: Fédération des Bouddhistes Vietnamiens d'Outre-Mer and Eglise Unifiée du Vietnam. The French Buddhist movement, on the other hand, is being developed largely through the activity of the Communauté Bouddhique de France, in Paris, which groups together representatives of the major Buddhist organizations, facilitates the dissemination of information regarding Buddhism through public meetings and provides support for the creation of the Buddhist Community of Europe, in process of formation. Buddhist monasteries are found at Gretz (Mahayana Zen), Fort-les-Bancs (Lamaism) and Mougins (Zen Soto); and a large Buddhist temple is at present being built in Paris to serve foreigners and citizens of all traditions.

**Other religions,** including Vietnamese New-Religionists (Cao Daist Missionary Church), Confucianism and Baha'i, have small communities. In addition about 14% of the population is without religion. The French Communist party has 250,000 members, but of these 40% profess to be Catholics as well.

**CHRISTIANITY.** The first Christians entered France at an early date from Italy, and a strong Christian community had been established in Lyons by AD 150. There were 10 bishops by AD 250, and the first general council of the West was held at Arles in France in 314. The mass baptism of the Frank king, Clovis, with his warriors in 496 was a major milestone in the development of French Christianity. The Middle Ages were characterized by the missionary activity of Columban and Boniface from Ireland and Britain, the theological studies of Thomas Aquinas in Paris, the Crusades, and the monastic reforms of Benedict of Cluny and Bernard of Clairvaux, followed by the 14th-century schism which produced rival popes at both Avignon and Rome. France was also affected by the Reformation. The influence of Luther and Zwingli was strongest in Alsace while Calvinism gained many followers in other parts of the country. Calvin's Huguenots established 2,000 churches prior to holding their first National Synod of Reformed Churches in 1559. The Counter-Reformation resulted in serious religious conflict and persecution of Protestants; and it was not until the proclamation of the Edict of Nantes in 1598 that a degree of religious freedom was restored. The revocation of that edict by Louis XIV in 1685 resulted in a new wave of persecution which drove thousands into exile. Protestants were to remain a persecuted minority until the French Revolution of 1794. Napoleon negotiated a concordat with Rome in 1801 recognizing Catholicism as the religion of the majority, and in the following year the Lutheran and Reformed churches were also officially recognized. A number of new Protestant bodies entered France during the 19th century and this influx has increased during the present century. During this century also, French Catholics became predominant in the Catholic missionary world.

CATHOLIC CHURCH. The period since World War II has been marked by profound structural and pastoral changes in the French church. In 1964, the old Plenary Assembly of Cardinals and Archbishops gave place to the present French Episcopal Conference which, according to its new statutes adopted in 1973, includes a permanent council of 13 members and a Bureau of Doctrinal Studies. The conciliar period has witnessed an acceleration of this transformation of structures while at the same time the lay organization Catholic Action has developed and been reorganized and has had a great influence on pastoral life and on ecclesiastical appointments including those of bishops. The orientation of the Church of France towards the working classes is perhaps its most marked characteristic. The worker-priest movement began in France in 1943–45, but there were confrontations and arrests involving priests in 1954 and 1959 which resulted in the demise of the movement. Official sanction to begin again was given in 1966, after an unanimous decision by the plenary assembly of the French episcopate, with papal agreement, during the last session of Vatican II. However, more difficulties appeared, and in 1969 the administrative council of the Mission de France was dismissed. Nevertheless, this group remains an important influence in the church. In May 1975, for the first time a worker-priest was appointed a bishop. At that time there were in France 600 full-time worker-priests (prêtres-ouvriers), and another 150 priests were engaged in full-time employment outside the church (prêtres-employés). As in other European countries, the uneasiness of the French clergy concerning the church's relationship to society has been increasingly apparent since 1968.

Concerning membership, a census of baptized Catholics took place in 1958, showing that 91.5% of the French population had been baptized in the Catholic Church. By 1971 the figure had dropped to 88.7%. This national figure however shows important regional variations: 27% of Paris' population are not baptized Catholics, and 21% of that of Marseilles. In 1968 about 85% of baptized Catholics over 15 years of age had made their first communion, which is 75% of the population. The proportion of religious marriages is harder to establish. In urban areas, about 80% of marriages and virtually all funerals are religious.

Concerning religious practice, it is estimated that 23% of the total population (25% of those baptized) attend Sunday mass every week (1975). Rural practice is by no means always higher than urban practice. In districts where church attendance by the rural population is strong, in the local towns it is relatively weak; whereas in areas where the level of practice is weak, it is higher in the towns than in the countryside. The main factor affecting town practice is the general level of practice in any given socio-cultural region, and not (as is often widely thought) the percentage of working-class persons in the population. Age also affects practice: 28% of those from 15–19 years of age attend Sunday mass, falling to 13% for those from 20–24 years, 8% for ages 25–34, 2% for ages 35–44, rising again to 11% for ages 45–64. In some regions 50% of all young persons abandon church attendance immediately following their first communion. Practice among various professions is as follows: liberal professions and elites (men and women) 31%; middle-class employees 19% (men 13%, women 22%); labourers 5% (men 4%, women 8%).

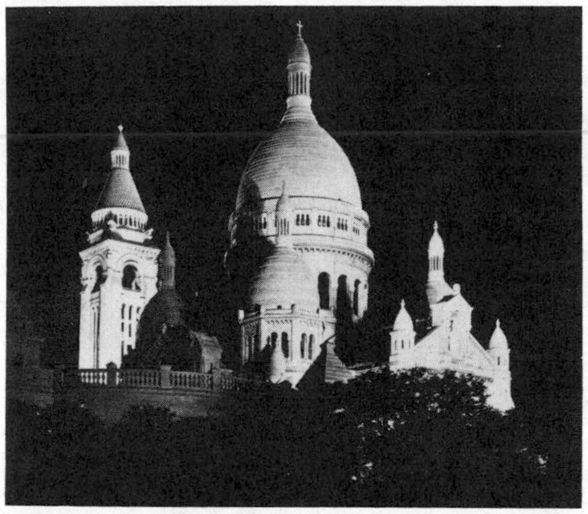

**Eglise Catholique de France.** Basilica of the National Vow to the Sacred Heart (Sacré Coeur), in Montmartre, Paris, built 1876-1919.

In January 1965 there were 40,994 secular and 3,414 religious priests serving with dioceses (as well as numerous contemplatives and others not in parish work). Vocations have progressively decreased since 1948 when there were 779 ordinations to the priesthood, to 338 in 1969, 284 in 1970, 237 in 1971, and to only 99 in 1977. Moreover, departures from the priesthood have increased: 80 in 1967, 90 in 1968 and 150 in 1969. The national average of 962 inhabitants per priest in 1948 increased to 1,316 in 1965. At the beginning of 1973, there were 469 Fidei Donum priests, mostly working in Africa (279) and South America (154). In 1970 there were 24,000 French male religious personnel of whom 13,000 were priests (8,600 French priests in France and 4,400 in foreign missions), 2,000 novices and 2,600 lay. Teaching brothers number 6,000 (5,000 in France and 1,000 overseas). Brothers occupy an important place in Catholic education at all levels, and in pastoral work they play a significant role in liturgical, scriptural and theological renewal. Recent statistics show a marked increase in interest in contemplation on the part of both men and women, a third of all religious candidates in 1972 choosing the contemplative life.

In 1973 there were in France 105,800 female religious personnel including contemplatives (as contrasted with 114,420 in 1969), about 10,000 of whom were expatriates most belonging to French congregations; there were also 8,450 French sisters (excluding contemplatives) in foreign fields. Of all sisters 9,220 are contemplatives. The drop in vocations is not a recent phenomenon but has become more serious since 1960: 4,440 novices in 1945; 4,000 in 1955; 3,720 in 1960; 2,620 in 1965; 1,660 in 1969 and 750 in 1973. The largest proportion of sisters is consecrated to social or medical work (29%) and to teaching (23%), with only 21% undertaking the purely religious functions. The tendency now is to leave traditional occupations and institutions for new activities. Departures of sisters remained relatively stable at about 150 per year between World War II and 1969, but they doubled to 300 a year between 1969 and 1973. Demographic projections for the clergy are not optimistic. Estimates for 1975 give only 31,825 priests in parish work and 91,000 sisters.

With regard to the laity, over the past 40 years specialized Catholic Action programmes for youth and adults have been developed to serve the 3 major categories of French society: workers, independents (middle, bourgeois and aristocratic classes) and rural inhabitants. Education and childhood are also influenced by Catholic Action with the most noticeable effects taking place among school populations. Catholic Action also influences almost all parishes, enlisting in its programmes about 8% of all practising Catholics. Other movements are active and well-developed, but the episcopate gives priority to Catholic Action. Movements of dissent, traditionalist and progressivist, have also developed considerably since 1968.

Two diocesan synods have been held in France. The first was at Rouen, consisting of two 5-day sessions (January 1968 and April 1969), with 104 priests and brothers, 24 sisters and 87 lay delegates (30% being members by right, the others elected) which studied the significance of the Vatican II texts for the diocese of Rouen. The other was in the diocese of Saint-Brieuc, which also met in 2 sessions (February 1969 and February 1970), with 134 priests, 51 sisters and 126 lay delegates (appointed and elected); it studied 2 themes: 'A missionary diocesan church' and 'A community diocesan church'.

PROTESTANT CHURCHES. Most of the French Protestant population are of either the Reformed or Lutheran traditions. The Reformed Church of France, the product of a merger in 1938 of Congregationalists, Methodists and 2 Reformed bodies, is the largest denomination in France after the Catholic Church. Since World War II, attention has been centred on rebuilding churches, liturgical renewal (especially that relating to the Holy Communion), exploring the possibilities of a more complete regional community life, and evangelization of industrial areas. The latter activity has been promoted by the Central Society for Evangelization and Evangelical Popular Mission. An important body which rejected the 1938 merger is the National Union of Independent Evangelical Reformed Churches, and even more significant is the localized Reformed Church of Alsace-Lorraine.

The 2 principal Lutheran groups are the Church of the Augsburg Confession of Alsace and Lorraine, which is the main Protestant church of Alsace, and the Evangelical Lutheran Church of France, which is divided into 2 sections (inspections): one for Paris and the other for Montbéliard. Since 1950 their efforts have been co-ordinated in the National Alliance of the Lutheran Churches of France. The Lutheran Interior Mission of Paris and worker-pastors are active in urban areas where Christian influence is marginal. Lutherans have also been involved in liturgical renewal.

The Assemblies of God have built up a strong following since their arrival in 1929 and, with its autonomous Gypsy counterpart (Eglises Tziganes), it is now the fifth largest Protestant denomination in France. Other Pentecostal groups exist, but most have had little impact on the scene.

Smaller churches begun during the 19th century include the Federation of Evangelical Baptist Churches in 1832, Darbyites (Plymouth Brethren) in 1844 and Seventh-day Adventists in 1874. The former is a member of the Protestant Federation of France and has a special relationship with the Southern Baptist Convention in the USA, although numerically there are less than 2,500 adult Baptists.

Although Protestants are found in all parts of the country, their strength varies considerably from one area to another. They are most numerous in Alsace and the Rhone valley. The following 8 departments, arranged in order of the most Protestants, each report them as more than 5% of the population: Bas-Rhin, Gard, Doubs, Ardéche, Haut-Rhin, Drôme, Lozere and Deux-Sèvres.

ORTHODOX CHURCHES. Greeks, Armenians and Russians form the bulk of Orthodoxy in France, the latter two owing their origin principally to emigres and refugees since the 1917 revolution in the USSR. The Russians are divided ecclesiastically into 3 groups: the Russian Orthodox Church belonging to the Exarchate for Western Europe (with headquarters in Germany) under the Moscow Patriarchate; the Russian Orthodox Church Outside of Russia with its headquarters in New York, which is opposed to Moscow; and, by far the largest, the Orthodox Church, Archdiocese of France and Western Europe, since 1971 under the jurisdiction of the Ecumenical Patriarchate in Constantinople. The Armenian Apostolic Church is under the Catholicate of

**Enfants de Dieu.** Children of God witness along Rue Saint Severin, Paris.

Echmiadzin in Russia (with a small faction under Sis in Lebanon); while the Greek Orthodox Church of France, which is in the Greek tradition, is under the Ecumenical Patriarchate through the archbishop of London. Smaller groups of Romanian, Serbian, Ukrainian and Georgian Orthodox are also found in France.

MARGINAL CHURCHES. A number of marginal Protestant bodies have been active in France since the last century. The first to arrive were American Mormons, who continue to maintain 600 missionaries in France although their work has been singularly unsuccessful, numerically. A major schism around 1900 from Jehovah's Witnesses produced the Aurore (Dawn) Association of the Students of the Bible which moved its headquarters from Lille to Nice in 1953. Shortly after the turn of the century, the Lay Interior Missionary Movement (Mouvement Missionnaire Intérieur Laïque), a schism from Aurore and Jehovah's Witnesses in the USA, set up headquarters in Denain. However, they have lost membership to the Witnesses since World War II. Their name was changed in 1959 to the French Association of Free Students of the Bible.

Two other bodies owing their origin to the Witnesses are the Freytag and Sayerce branches of the Friends of Man, which came from Switzerland in, respectively, 1934 and 1947. Jehovah's Witnesses themselves entered France also around 1900, but they were not officially installed in Paris until 1930. Since then they have grown rapidly and now rank fourth in size among non-Catholic groups.

CATHOLIC (NON-ROMAN) CHURCHES. At least 75 distinct bodies have split from the Church of Rome in the last hundred years, usually over faith-healing, ecclesiastical authority, gallicanism, or insistence on Latin or Celtic rites. Most remain small and localized in influence. The largest are the Antoinistes (Religious Association of Antoine) begun by a Belgian Catholic healer, and the Old Roman Catholic Church which has grown rapidly since 1960.

**CHURCH AND STATE.** For centuries the established church, the Catholic Church was finally separated from the state in 1905.

The juridical status of the churches in France at present is governed by the principle that the state is secular, as promulgated by the law of 9 December 1905, 'The separation of the churches and state' (Article 1 and 2), and repeated in the constitutions of 1946 (4th Republic) and 1958 (5th Republic: Article 2). The result is that the state gives no preference to any religion and refuses to intervene in religious and spiritual matters. Public services and public education must be completely secular in

character, including their locations, programmes and personnel. Clergy may not teach in primary schools in virtue of the law of 30 October 1886, Article 17, nor in secondary schools since the decision of the council of state of 10 May 1912. The secular nature of the state excludes subsidies to denominations for specifically religious work, although this does not extend to secular activities of religious inspiration such as cultural, welfare and social work. An exception regarding clergy is made for chaplains of such public institutions as schools, prisons, hospitals, hostels and the army, which then pay clergy delegated to them, although in actuality not all receive remuneration from government sources. Primary schools are required to set aside a day each week for the religious instruction of those children whose parents request it.

Church property must receive a juridical basis conforming to law, the churches having the status of 'moral personalities'. Diocesan associations, created in 1924, have handled this problem for the Catholic Church, while Protestants and Jews have organized themselves since 1905 into 'religious associations' as defined in the law of that year.

Religious congregations are regulated by the law of 1 June 1901, Title III, which has subsequently been modified several times. They only have legal existence if they have been officially recognized, but in practice this is only the case for congregations which had received this status prior to the law of 1901. Subsequently there has been only a handful of recognitions, including the Chartreux recognized in 1940, and the Cistercians of the Strict Observance of Melleray in Brittany recognized in 1973. The property of congregations without this recognition is placed under the legal care of 'parallel' institutions, associations or civil societies, which along with its disadvantages serves the useful purpose of removing them from the rather strict control which the state exercises over recognized congregations.

Private denominational instruction may be freely conducted, with only a few somewhat liberal juridical conditions. Subsidies from public funds for this are subject to different regulations depending on the educational level: forbidden at the primary level, permitted under certain conditions in secondary schools, largely authorized for technical instruction, and free for higher education (for want of regulations). The old pattern of 'concurrence' has disappeared and is today replaced by a policy of 'collaboration' with public education. State involvement in the support of private educational institutions began in 1919 with the passage of the law on technical education, and continued progressively until 1959 when a series of 'contracts' between the state and private technical schools came into effect. At that

time the state assumed almost complete financial responsibility, at the same time increasing its control over them.

The principle of secularity imposes on the state the need to respect the religious freedom of its citizens and the right to manifest both individually and collectively their convictions, including private and public worship, except where public order is endangered. Certain special dispositions, however, govern the separation of church and state. The Holy See is obliged to consult with the government before the appointment of bishops. Clergy may not officiate at marriages or funerals before first completing the required civil formalities. Moreover, clergy, seminarians and religious novices are subject to military conscription.

There is one striking exception to this separation of church and state. Alsace and Lorraine, consisting of the 3 departments of Haut-Rhin, Bas-Rhin, and Moselle which were annexed by the Germans in 1870 and returned to France in 1918, enjoy a unique status since the 1905 law of church-state separation does not apply there. The legislation however is not the same for all denominations. The Napoleonic Concordat of 1801 remains valid for the Catholic Church with the state officially naming new bishops (in actuality only after negotiations with the Vatican); state agreement is also necessary before the appointment of parish priests. Protestant churches operate under the Organic Articles of 1801–2, completed in 1852. The Reformed Church is governed by its own synod, but the Lutheran Church has structures which are more administrative than ecclesiastical, and its president is named by government without in principle any consultation with members of the church. The Jewish community, recognized in 1808, must also receive government approval for the election of members to its consistories. All clergy are ranked as civil servants and receive salary from the state.

In recent years, 3 new factors have emerged to modify relations between the Catholic Church and the state in France: the rise of political issues on the part of Catholic movements, a desire on the part of the hierarchy to retreat from its traditional semi-official role alongside state authorities, and the firm stand taken by the churches in 1973 on the sale of arms and atomic weapons. This change of climate, seen by some observers as the beginning of a 'second separation' of church and state, suggests that significant developments may take place in church-state relations in the coming years.

**INTERDENOMINATIONAL ORGANIZATIONS.** The major Protestant co-ordinating body is the Protestant Federation of France (Fédération Protestante de France, FPF), founded in 1913 and composed of 8 Reformed, Lutheran, Baptist and other churches representing the majority of French Protestants. Outside the Federation, the major Reformed and Lutheran churches also maintain a joint office, have a common ordination service and in some instances hold joint synod meetings. Catholic ecumenical questions are handled by the French Secretariat for the Unity of Christians (Secrétariat Français pour l'Unité des Chrétiens), founded in 1967 as an organ of the Catholic Episcopal Committee for Unity.

The interdenominational Paris Evangelical Missionary Society (Société des Missions Evangélique de Paris) was founded in 1822 and has recently been playing an important role in establishing autonomous churches in various parts of Africa and the South Pacific. It ceased to exist as the PEMS in 1972, and has been replaced by the Communauté Evangélique d'Action Apostolique (CEVAA), which is international, multiracial and interconfessional, and groups 23 churches in France, Switzerland, Italy and overseas; and the Département Evangélique Français d'Action Apostolique (DEFAP) which deals with the French churches' participation in CEVAA.

Certain joint commissions exist. The Comité Mixte Catholique-Protestant was formed in 1968 by the FPF and the Catholic Episcopal Committee for Unity. It is a technical committee which engages in theological study, prepares theological and pastoral documents and makes joint declarations. The Groupe Mixte Anglican-Catholique Romain was formed in 1969 by the Catholic Episcopal Committee and the Anglican bishops having jurisdiction in France. Its interests are theological and pastoral and it provides support for the isolated Anglican community in France. Since 1964 meetings have been held between official representatives of the Catholic Episcopal Committee and the FPF's Commission on Relations with Catholicism; and since 1966 similar encounters have taken place between representatives of the Catholic Episcopal and Orthodox Interepiscopal Committees.

Four international ecumenical bodies have their base in France. Entraide Missionnaire Internationale (EMI) was founded in Geneva in 1965 by Catholic religious personnel and Protestant pastors but now has its headquarters at Levallois, near Paris. It provides economic and social assistance to religious institutes, dioceses, associations and movements with special emphasis on the needs of Christian groups in the Third World. Some 376 member organizations, plus 66 associated overseas newer dioceses, exist throughout the world. Assistance is organized into 3 departments dealing with sickness (19,500 beneficiaries in 1972), death-disability insurance, and old age assistance. Secondly, the Conférence Mondiale des Chrétiens pour la Palestine (CMCP), founded in Paris in 1969, united in 1973 Anglicans, Catholics, Orthodox and Protestants of 57 countries in informing Christians concerning the Arab Palestinian question, builiding bridges between Arab Christians on one side and Western and African Christians on the other and affirming solidarity with the Palestinian victims of the partition of Palestine in 1947. The CMCP has organized 2 international conferences, one at Beirut in 1970, and the other at Canterbury, England in 1972. Thirdly, the Assemblée Internationale des Chrétiens Solidaires des Peuples Vietnamien, Laotien et Cambodgien, which provided an outlet for the expression of Christian concern for the peoples of Indochina during the Vietnam war, has had its headquarters in Paris. Finally, the Comité Oecuménique de Liaison Internationale (COELI), founded in Paris in 1974, serves as the liaison organization for Chrétiens pour le Socialisme groups throughout the world, especially in Belgium, Canada (Quebec), France, Italy, Portugal, as well as clandestine groups in Spain and most countries of Latin America.

There are numerous ecumenical institutes and centres; 13 may be mentioned here. (1) The Centre d'Etudes Oecuméniques, founded in Strasbourg in 1965, is related to the Lutheran World Federation. Through research, conferences, seminars and courses, its purpose is to make the various Lutheran bodies aware of ecumenical theology. (2) The Institut Supérieur d'Etudes Oecuméniques, founded in Paris in 1967, is attached to the faculty of theology of the Catholic Institute of Paris and works in co-operation with other Protestant and Orthodox theological faculties in France and the Ecumenical Institute of Bossey in Switzerland. Apart from its role in teaching and ecumenical research, it possesses an important ecumenical library (13,000 volumes) which it established jointly with the Catholic Institute, the Protestant Federation and the Catholic Association for the Study of the Bible. It also promotes knowledge concerning Judaism. (3) The Centre d'Etudes Istina, founded in Paris by the OP in 1924, engages in theological and historical research concerning current ecumenical problems with special emphasis on Eastern Christianity and Judeo-Christian relations. It works in close co-operation with other ecumenical centres, especially the Institut St Serge of Paris. (4) The Centre St-Irénée, founded in Lyons by the OP in 1953, is especially concerned with the promotion of pastoral ecumenism and works in close collaboration with the Centre Istina. (5) The Institut Français d'Etudes Byzantines, founded in Paris by the AA in 1897, is dedicated to research concerning the Eastern churches, especially the Greek and Slavic bodies. Its library of 45,000 volumes specializes in the Byzantine church. (6) The Groupe Interconfessionnel des Dombes, founded in 1937 with a Catholic secretary in Paris and a Protestant secretary in Lyons, is a private organization without official affiliation composed of 36 theologians (half Catholic, half Reformed) whose purpose is to study the possibility of establishing an ecumenical theology between the Catholic and Reformed churches. Meetings have been held alternatively at Trappe des Dombes and Taizé. The group reached agreement regarding the eucharist in 1971 and is now at work on the question of the mutual recognition of ministries. A similar body is the Groupe Oecuménique des Bords de la Rance. (7) The Centre de Recherche et de Documentation des Institutions Chrétiennes (CERDIC), founded in Strasbourg in 1968, is an associate of the Centre National de la Recherche Scientifique (CNRS). A multi-disciplinary interconfessional research centre, it conducts seminars and colloquia and publishes studies (especially RIC, an annual world bibliography

**Protestants.** Protestant Community of Taizé, Burgundy. *Right.* Noticeboard outside Church of Reconciliation. *Above.* Inside, at Morning Prayer.

of Christianity). (8) The Centre Oecuménique Unité Chrétienne, founded in Lyons in 1954, is interconfessional although predominantly Catholic. Through conferences, retreats and pilgrimages, it provides ecumenical training for all varieties of Christians, and along with the WCC prepares the French text of the Week of Prayer for Christian Unity. (9) The Centre de Recherche de Villemétrie, founded at Orgemont near Paris in 1954, is a Protestant centre for study and dialogue which attempts to study the relationship of the Christian faith to the modern world. (10) The Communauté de Taizé, founded in Bourgogne in 1940, is a strongly ecumenical Protestant body which sponsors international meetings for youth, including the Council of Youth which met in August 1974 after 4 years' preparation. (11) The Centre Oecuménique Enotikon, founded in Paris in 1951, is an inter-Orthodox institute for dialogue and ecumenical encounters. (12) Two Orthodox university institutes are also engaged in ecumenical activities, the Institut de Théologie Orthodoxe St-Serge (Russian), founded in Paris in 1925, and the Institut Orthodoxe Saint-Denys founded in Paris in 1944, which is dependent on the Orthodox Catholic Church. (13) Two Benedictine (OSB) abbeys are dedicated to the promotion of spirituality and ecumenical dialogue, the Abbaye Notre-Dame du Bec, founded in 1948 at Le Bec Helluin, which has special responsibility from the Catholic episcopate for relations with Anglicanism, and the Abbaye St Martin, founded at Ligugé in 1959, which is especially concerned with such pastoral matters as providing ecumenical preparation for mixed marriages.

Among interchurch aid agencies is CIMADE (Comité Inter-Mouvements auprès des Evacués), established by the Reformed churches during World War II to provide aid to refugees and migrants as well as other disadvantaged persons in French society. The Orthodox later joined CIMADE and more recently but unofficially the Catholics. It works in close co-operation with the Protestant Federation of France and the WCC.

Ecumenical information centres include the Centre d'Information sur le Développement (CIDEV), founded in Paris in 1970, which attempts to inform the public concerning the Third World, the causes of underdevelopment and the questions that this poses for developed countries. There is also BIP-SNOP in Paris, which is jointly sponsored by the Catholic National Secretariat of Public Opinion and the Protestant Information Bureau, and which has published a weekly information bulletin since 1971.

**BROADCASTING.** The national radio and TV companies (formerly ORTF) have regular Christian programmes on Sunday mornings: a Catholic mass and a Protestant service on the radio station France-Culture: and on TV, 90 minutes for the Catholics (magazine and mass), 30 minutes for Protestants and 30 minutes fortnightly for Orthodox. The Catholic body responsible for radio and TV production is Office Catholique Français de Radio-Télévision (OCFTR), and the Protestant one is Service Radio-Télévision of the Fédération Protestante de France. Some government regional stations, especially Radio Strasbourg, also have regular Christian programmes.

There are several Catholic publications on broadcasting, including the weekly *Telerama*, and France is a member of UNDA. Catholic programmes in French are beamed in by Radio Vatican for 5 hours 15 minutes a week; and several Protestant Evangelical groups also buy time on the so-called stations periphériques (stations located outside French territory), such as Radio Luxembourg, Europe Number 1 and Trans World Radio (Monaco), to broadcast programmes which are easily heard in France. Radio Evangile (French branch of TWR) has 3 programmes at good listening hours. Six other groups offer 11 other programmes also over TWR a total of 16 hours weekly. Other evangelistic broadcasting groups, including Radio Réveil, La Voix de l'Evangile, La Voix du Christ aux Nations, Ecole Radio Biblique and Christ Vous Appelle, are heard over Europe Number 1 and Radio Luxembourg. Their weekly total is 5 hours.

**BIBLIOGRAPHY**

*Annuaire catholique de France 1973.* Paris: Publicat, 1973.
*Annuaire des Eglises, associations et institutions orthodoxes.* Paris: CIMADE, 1966.
*Annuaire évangélique, 1970.* Grenoble: DEFI, 1970.
*Destin du Catholicisme français.* A. Dansette. Paris: Flammarion, 1967.
*Eglises et évêques catholiques non romains.* I. D. de la Thibauderie. Paris: Dervy-Livres, 1962. 134p.
'France', F. A. Isambert, in H. Mol (ed), *Western religion* (The Hague: Mouton, 1972), p. 175–187.
*Guide juif de France.* Eds R. Berg, C. Chémouny & F. Didi. Paris: Editions Migdal, 1971 (2nd edition). 507p.
*La France protestante, Annuaire 1974.* Paris: Fédération Protestante de France, 1974. 504p.
*Le monde spirituel des sectaires.* K. Hutten. Neuchâtel: Delachaux et Niestlé, 1965. 110p.
*Les Chrétiens en France.* R. Solé. Coll. Dossier Thémis, No. 43. Paris: Presses Universitaires de France, 1972. 95p.
*Les forces religieuses dans la société française.* A. Coutrot et al. Paris: Librairie Armand Colin, 1965.
*Les sectes protestantes dans la France contemporaine.* J. Séguy. Paris: Beauchesne et fils, 1956.
*L'offensive des sectes.* H.–Ch. Chéry. 3rd edition. Paris: Cerf, 1961. 520p.
*Petites églises de France.* G. Dagon. Anneville: Armand, 1971.
*Petites églises et grandes sectes.* G. Dagon. Paris: S.C.E., 1951, 1963. 128p.
*Renouveau charismatique chez les Catholiques: essai bibliographique de langue française.* M. Lambert. Bruxelles: Bureau de Documentation Pastorale, 6 Jan 1975. 32p. (327 items).
*Traité de sociologie du Protestantisme.* R. Mehl. Neuchâtel: Editions Delachaux et Niestlé, 1965.
*Visage du Protestantisme français.* P. Lestringant. Tournai: Les Cahiers de Réveil, 1959. 214p.

TABLE 2. ORGANIZED CHURCHES AND DENOMINATIONS IN FRANCE

| Official name 1 | Begun 2 | Type 3 | Counc 4 | Congs 5 | Adults 6 | Affiliated 7 | Names, notes, and other statistics (see Codebook) 8 |
|---|---|---|---|---|---|---|---|
| Action Biblique | 1906 | P ind | ..... | 6 | 400 | 1,000 | *Maisons de la Bible* (*Bible Houses*). *Alexandrists* (after founder H. E. Alexander). |
| Alliance Chrétienne Missionnaire de F | | P Hol | xF..C | 5 | 120 | 250 | *ACM*. M=Christian & Missionary Alliance(USA). Many Vietnamese. 2n,2x,W=60%,15Y. |
| Alliance des Egls Ev Indépendantes | | P ind | ....C | 13 | 500 | 1,000 | *AEEI. Alliance of Independent Ev Chs*. HQ Orsay (Seine-et-Oise). 7n. |
| Alliance Spirituelle et Fraternelle | | P Pen | ..... | 27 | 1,000 | 2,000 | *ASF. Spiritual & Fraternal Alliance*. Widespread Pentecostal grouping. |
| Amis de l'Homme (Freytag) | 1934 | M Jeh | x.... | | 3,900 | 5,000 | *Friends of Man*. Split by A. Freytag ex Jehovah's Witnesses. Many in Switzerland. |
| Amis de l'Homme (Sayerce) | 1947 | M Jeh | x.... | | 9,700 | 15,000 | *Friends of Man*. Schism by former Catholic B. Sayerce ex Freytag. Philanthropic. |
| Armée du Salut | 1881 | P Sal | xwx.E | 96 | 4,000 | 6,000 | *Salvation Army*, *France Territory*. 5 million free meals yearly. HQ Paris. 208n,1s. |
| Assemblée des Béguins | 1789 | C CCa | ..... | | 300 | 400 | *Assembly of Hooded Brotherhood*. Rigid morality, closed services. In Loire area. |
| Assemblées de Dieu en France | 1929 | P Pe2 | ZF... | 454 | 30,000 | 60,000 | *Assemblies of God*. 90% former RCs. Mainly Normandy. 252n,7f,1s(29). |
| Assemblées des Frères | 1857 | P CBr | x.... | 160 | 5,800 | 10,000 | *Brethren Assemblies*. *Open Brethren*. 1857 broke with Darbyites. HQ Lyons. |
| Assemblées des Frères Alexandre | | P ind | ..... | 7 | 250 | 500 | *Assemblies of the Brothers Alexandre*. In Lille, Dunkerque, HQ St-Michel (Aisne). |
| Association Culturelle Antoiniste | 1910 | C mar | x.... | 120 | 10,000 | 50,000 | *Religious Assoc of Antoine* (a Belgian Catholic faith-healer). HQ Paris. 1n 15 nations. |
| Assoc des Etudiants de la Bible Aurore | c1900 | M Jeh | ..... | | 6,000 | 10,000 | *Dawn Association of Bible Students*. Schism ex Jehovah's Witnesses. In north. |
| Assoc Evangélique des Egls Baptistes | 1850 | P Bap | TT... | 19 | 726 | 2,000 | *AEEB. French Bapt Chs. French Bible Mission*. Ex FEEBF. 12n,1x,G=2%pa,1s,W=35%,23Y. |
| AF des Libres Etudiants de la Bible | c1905 | M Jeh | ..... | | 1,000 | 2,000 | AF=Assoc Française. *French Assoc of Free Bible Students*. Schism ex Association Aurore. |
| Aumônerie Générale Indép Mixte | | C Epi | .v... | 2 | 50 | 100 | *Orient-Occident*, *Abbaye Missionnaire de Behême*. 1968, applied to WCC, rejected. |
| Communauté des Chrétiens | c1925 | P ind | ..... | | 115 | 300 | *Community of Christians*. Centred on eucharistic worship. Across Europe. HQ Paris. |
| Communautés Ev Nazaréennes | 1845 | P Hol | x.... | 8 | 220 | 400 | *Nazarene Ev Communities*. Alsace-Lorraine. M=ACC(N)(USA). HQ Strasbourgh-Neudorf. |
| Communautés Judéo-Chrétiennes | | M Jew | ..... | | 500 | 1,000 | *Jewish-Christian Communities*. Jewish converts unwilling to join public churches. |
| Eglise Adventiste du Septième Jour | 1874 | P Adv | x.... | 90 | 5,162 | 10,000 | *SDA. Seventh-day Adventists*, *N&S French Confs*. 35n,G=2.3%pa,1j,1s(25),W=80%,245Y. |
| Eglise Adv du SJ Mouv de Réforme | | P Adv | x.... | 5 | 100 | 200 | *Seventh-day Adventist Ch*, *Movement of Reform*. HQ Colmar. World HQ Denmark. |
| Eglise Anglicane (J Fulham) | c1580 | A plu | awc.. | 43 | 5,000 | 15,000 | *Church of England*. M=CCCS(UK). English chaplaincies, several seasonal. 12x. |
| Eglise Apostolique | 1924 | P PeA | ZG... | 40 | 1,000 | 3,000 | *Apostolic Ch*. Linked with Apostolic Ch (UK). HQ Sanvic. Mainly in Normandy. 2f. |
| Egl Apostolique Arménienne: D France | 1956 | O Arm | Sw.N. | 30 | 20,000 | 30,000 | *Gregorians*. Under C Cilicia (Sis)(Lebanon). 1956 schism ex C Echmiadzin (USSR). |
| Egl Apost Arménienne: D WEurope | 1917 | O Arm | Ewc.. | 100 | 80,000 | 150,000 | *Gregorians*. Under C Echmiadzin (USSR); 1917, Armenian refugees from Turkey. |
| Eglise Catholique Apostolique | c1840 | C CAp | x.... | 3 | 100 | 200 | *Irvingites*. Adventist schism ex ConfS(UK). No clergy left; dying out. |
| Egl Catholique Apostolique Gallicane | 1935 | C CCa | .v... | | 27,000 | 40,000 | *Cath Apostolic Gallican Ch*. Schism ex Rome. 1975, large synod held in Bordeaux. |
| Egl Cath Apost Primitive d'Antioche | 1956 | C CCa | .v... | | 600 | 1,000 | *Eglise Catholique Ancienne*. Syrian (Jacobite) succession. In 19 nations. |
| **Eglise Catholique de France** | c 80 | R LEr | B.B.R | 38,233 | 32,859,800 | 44,405,899 | *Catholic Ch in F*. C=71+9+397. 4p,11q,39s. 44551nx,5778m,96585w,661897Yy. |
| Région Centre: | 1961 | R Lat | Bs | 2,922 | 1,950,600 | 2,636,026 | *Central Apostolic Region*. One of 9 Apostolic Regions covering France. HQ Nevers. |
| D Blois | 1697 | R Lat | Bs | 295 | 196,100 | 265,000 | Population 273,500. 46% urban. Growth 1.1%pa. D=PC. 194 0 320 4425 |
| M Bourges | c 250 | R Lat | Bs | 507 | 370,000 | 500,000 | Cher 53% urban, Indre 56% rural. Pop 563,500 343 162 710 7820 |
| D Chartres | c 250 | R Lat | Bs | 389 | 219,000 | 269,000 | 56% urban, 44% rural. Annual students' pilgrimage. 281 14 670 4880 |
| D Moulins | 1817 | R Lat | Bs | 319 | 277,500 | 375,000 | Population 386,530. 56% urban. G=0.3%pa. 247 74 382 3890 |
| D Nevers | c 550 | R Lat | Bs | 311 | 177,600 | 240,000 | Population 247,700. 48% urban. G=1.4%pa. 179 5 331 3253 |
| D Orléans | 346 | R Lat | Bs | 294 | 292,700 | 395,500 | Population 430,500. 64% urban. G=1.7%pa. 1s. 360 42 670 6412 |
| M Sens | c 200 | R Lat | Bs | 511 | 158,700 | 214,526 | HQ Auxerre. 60% rural, 40% urban. D=PC. 272 3 320 3600 |
| M Tours | c 250 | R Lat | Bs | 296 | 259,000 | 350,000 | Population 437,870. 61% urban. G=1.7%pa. 1s. 316 26 926 4000 |
| Région Centre-Est: | 1961 | R Lat | Bs | 4,342 | 3,778,500 | 5,106,073 | *East Central Apostolic Region*. HQ Chambéry. |
| D Annecy | 1822 | R Lat | Bs | 319 | 270,600 | 365,620 | Savoie, Haute Savoie. 65% urban. 622 44 1038 6181 |
| D Autun | 313 | R Lat | Bs | 545 | 384,800 | 520,000 | Population 550,400. 55% urban. G=0.5%pa. 487 22 974 8210 |
| D Belley | c 450 | R Lat | Bs | 362 | 214,600 | 290,000 | Pop 366,400. 51% urban. Ars pilgrimage centre. 384 79 829 5786 |
| M Chambéry | 1779 | R Lat | Bs | 357 | 190,200 | 256,973 | Includes old D Tarentaise, D St-Jean-de-Maurienne. 502 22 600 4280 |
| D Clermont | c 250 | R Lat | Bs | 521 | 388,500 | 525,000 | Clermont-Ferrand. 60% urban. G=1.2%pa. 1s. 445 84 896 5875 |
| D Grenoble | c 350 | R Lat | Bs | 569 | 518,000 | 700,000 | Population 849,700. 76% urban. G=2.2%pa. 632 30 1200 8000 |
| D Le Puy-en-Velay (Velais) | c 250 | R Lat | Bs | 304 | 148,300 | 200,480 | Population 208,300. 41% urban. G=−0.2%pa. 1s. 401 165 1228 2616 |
| M Lyon | c 150 | R Lat | Bs | 522 | 865,800 | 1,170,000 | Rhône, 1,325,600. 90% urban. G=2%pa. 1p,2s. 1428 470 3950 14123 |
| D Saint-Etienne | 1971 | R Lat | Bs | 221 | 399,600 | 540,000 | Loire, 722,880. 79% urban. G=0.6%pa. 465 150 960 9018 |
| D Valence | 374 | R Lat | Bs | 250 | 229,400 | 310,000 | Population 341,950. 64% urban. G=2.0%pa. 385 91 760 4153 |
| D Viviers | c 350 | R Lat | Bs | 372 | 168,700 | 228,000 | Population 257,900. 47% urban. G=0.6%pa. 366 0 1700 3807 |
| Région Est: | 1961 | R Lat | Bs | 4,968 | 3,463,200 | 4,680,089 | *Eastern Apostolic Region*. HQ Metz. |
| M Besançon | 346 | R Lat | Bs | 895 | 547,600 | 740,000 | Haute-Saône, Doubs, Belfort. About 70% urban. 1s. 928 73 1713 11852 |
| D Dijon | 1731 | R Lat | Bs | 527 | 318,400 | 430,290 | Population 432,300. 62% urban. G=1.4%pa. 1s. 349 71 647 5407 |
| D Metz | c 250 | R Lat | bs | 684 | 640,100 | 865,000 | Moselle, 994,100. 74% urban. G=0.3%pa. 1s. 949 131 1998 15000 |
| D Nancy | 1717 | R Lat | Bs | 650 | 497,000 | 671,600 | Population 723,600. 78% urban. G=−0.4%pa. 1s. 670 54 1100 11216 |
| D Saint-Claude | 1742 | R Lat | Bs | 392 | 162,800 | 220,000 | Population 233,550. 45% urban. G=0.6%pa. 1s. 342 28 610 3229 |
| D Saint-Dié | 1777 | R Lat | Bs | 464 | 281,200 | 380,000 | Population 388,200. 64% urban. G=0.3%pa. 465 11 920 6552 |
| D Strasbourg | 346 | R Lat | bs | 786 | 865,900 | 1,170,199 | Bas & Haut-Rhin, 1,412,400. 70% urban. D=PC. 2x. 1679 90 4000 25769 |
| D Verdun | 346 | R Lat | Bs | 570 | 150,000 | 203,000 | Population 209,500. 44% urban. G=−0.6%pa. 270 8 216 3367 |
| Région Midi-Pyrénées: | 1961 | R Lat | Bs | 4,791 | 1,983,700 | 2,680,668 | *Mid-Pyrenees Apostolic Region*. HQ Rodez. |
| M Albi | c 250 | R Lat | Bs | 509 | 222,000 | 300,000 | Population 332,000. 62% urban. G=0.7%pa. 349 29 932 4015 |
| M Auch | c 450 | R Lat | Bs | 507 | 133,200 | 180,000 | Population 181,580. 32% urban. G=0. 217 10 320 1775 |
| D Cahors | c 300 | R Lat | Bs | 405 | 100,700 | 136,078 | Population 151,000. 30% urban. G=0.2%pa. 185 4 334 2237 |
| D Carcassonne | 589 | R Lat | Bs | 339 | 155,400 | 210,000 | 48% urban, with towns all under 50,000. 255 9 610 2846 |
| D Mende | 314 | R Lat | Bs | 133 | 47,400 | 64,000 | Population 76,180. 30% urban. Towns under 50,000. 292 50 600 1029 |
| D Montauban | 1317 | R Lat | Bs | 295 | 131,000 | 177,000 | Population 183,600. 46% urban. G=0.7%pa. 215 0 463 2642 |
| D Pamiers | 1295 | R Lat | Bs | 336 | 96,200 | 130,000 | Population 138,500. 48% urban. G=0.2%pa. 131 0 110 1820 |
| D Perpignan | 571 | R Lat | Bs | 251 | 198,900 | 268,797 | Population 281,980. 69% urban. G=1.9%pa. 173 23 314 3288 |
| D Rodez | c 450 | R Lat | Bs | 643 | 207,000 | 279,793 | Population 281,600. 39% urban. G=−0.3%pa. 689 116 2113 3808 |
| D Saint-Flour | 1317 | R Lat | Bs | 227 | 122,100 | 165,000 | Population 168,800. 2% urban. D=PC. 272 8 417 2609 |
| D Tarbes & Lourdes | 506 | R Lat | Bs | 522 | 125,800 | 170,000 | Lourdes shrine: 3 million pilgrims a year. 314 37 907 3139 |
| M Toulouse | c 250 | R Lat | Bs | 624 | 444,000 | 600,000 | Population 690,700. 74% urban. G=2.6%pa. 3s. 585 172 1283 8366 |
| Région Nord: | 1961 | R Lat | Bs | 7,453 | 5,461,500 | 7,381,195 | *Northern Apostolic Region*. HQ Evreux. |
| D Amiens | 346 | R Lat | Bs | 835 | 351,500 | 475,000 | Population 512,113. 54% urban. Growing 0.8%pa. 362 37 465 7948 |
| D Arras | c 550 | R Lat | Bs | 1,020 | 814,000 | 1,100,000 | Population 1,397,200. 86% urban. G=0.7%pa. 1025 33 1541 23239 |
| D Beauvais | c 250 | R Lat | Bs | 712 | 360,300 | 486,900 | Population 541,000. 58% urban. G=2%pa. 355 27 460 6232 |
| M Cambrai | 346 | R Lat | Bs | 452 | 753,300 | 1,017,986 | Département du Nord. 89% urban. G=0.9%pa. 606 25 1075 15037 |
| D Châlons | c 300 | R Lat | Bs | 475 | 177,600 | 240,000 | HQ Châlons-sur-Marne. Population 250,600. 231 14 355 4155 |
| D Evreux | c 250 | R Lat | Bs | 587 | 244,200 | 330,000 | Population 383,400. 47% urban. G=0.9%pa. 289 27 585 5460 |
| D Langres | c 250 | R Lat | Bs | 444 | 151,700 | 205,000 | Population 214,300. 46% urban. G=0.5%pa. 206 13 218 3212 |
| D Lille | 1913 | R Lat | Bs | 396 | 936,100 | 1,265,000 | City of Lille: 1,410,674 people. 90% urban. 1p,2s. 1443 170 1180 23900 |
| M Reims | c 250 | R Lat | Bs | 718 | 397,800 | 537,598 | Ardennes and Reims (550,000). 1s. 426 14 696 10395 |
| M Rouen | c 150 | R Lat | Bs | 811 | 777,000 | 1,050,000 | Population 1,114,000. 69% urban. G=1.2%pa. D=PC. 652 25 630 15930 |
| D Soissons | c 300 | R Lat | Bs | 578 | 350,000 | 473,711 | Population 526,300. 54% urban. G=0.4%pa. 373 13 456 6747 |
| D Troyes | 313 | R Lat | Bs | 425 | 148,000 | 200,000 | Population 270,300. 57% urban. G=1%pa. 213 43 497 3500 |
| Région Ouest: | 1961 | R Lat | Bs | 5,070 | 4,445,500 | 6,007,171 | *Western Apostolic Region*. HQ Nantes. |
| D Angers | c 350 | R Lat | Bs | 420 | 370,000 | 500,000 | Population 584,700. 53% urban. G=0.9%pa. 3s. 869 153 3416 11432 |
| D Bayeux & Lisieux | c 150 | R Lat | Bs | 722 | 362,600 | 490,000 | Pilgrimage centre, Ste Thérèse de Lisieux. 2s. 523 34 1700 9286 |
| D Coutances | c 450 | R Lat | Bs | 671 | 331,500 | 448,000 | Population 451,900. 41% urban. G=0.2%pa. 561 35 1026 7791 |
| D Laval | 1855 | R Lat | Bs | 295 | 168,300 | 227,485 | Population 252,800. 33% urban. G=0.5%pa. 441 27 961 3799 |
| D Le Mans | 453 | R Lat | Bs | 402 | 313,100 | 423,117 | Population 461,800. 52% urban. G=0.7%pa. 427 56 1449 8151 |
| D Luçon | 1317 | R Lat | Bs | 305 | 296,000 | 400,000 | Population 421,250. 39% urban. G=0.5%pa. 1s. 740 239 1918 8142 |
| D Nantes | c 350 | R Lat | Bs | 299 | 592,000 | 800,000 | 69% urban (59% in urban areas of over 50,000). 2s. 1050 320 3150 14500 |
| D Quimper | c 450 | R Lat | Bs | 338 | 565,000 | 763,500 | Population 768,900. 59% urban. G=0.4%pa. 956 357 2411 13608 |
| M Rennes | c 250 | R Lat | Bs | 401 | 481,000 | 650,000 | Population 652,700. 52% urban. G=1%pa. 2s. 1062 240 3550 12239 |
| D Saint-Brieuc | c 450 | R Lat | Bs | 416 | 370,000 | 500,000 | Population 506,100. 37% urban. G=0.1%pa. D=PC 758 64 2519 8898 |
| D Sées | c 250 | R Lat | Bs | 501 | 200,000 | 270,000 | Population 280,550. 40% urban. G=0.5%pa. 454 0 1250 5123 |
| D Vannes | c 450 | R Lat | Bs | 300 | 396,000 | 535,069 | Population 540,470. 43% urban. G=0.3%pa. 851 350 2930 8840 |
| Région Parisienne: | 1966 | R Lat | Bs | 1,579 | 5,642,900 | 7,625,680 | *Paris Apostolic Region*. HQ Paris. Population 9,250,700. 96% urban. G=1.5%pa. |
| D Corbeil | 1966 | R Lat | Bs | 206 | 569,800 | 770,000 | Corbeil-Essonnes. About 95% urban. 313 70 1000 11012 |
| D Créteil | 1966 | R Lat | Bs | 79 | 546,000 | 737,892 | 95% urban. Central area, pan-diocesan services. 268 0 900 4500 |
| D Meaux | c 250 | R Lat | Bs | 542 | 388,500 | 525,000 | 95% urban. Ecclesiastical, civil boundaries same. 377 51 700 6677 |
| D Nanterre | 1966 | R Lat | Bs | 118 | 962,000 | 1,300,000 | 96% urban. Central metropolitan area. 411 15 1482 10001 |
| M Paris | c 250 | R Lat | Bs | 93 | 1,714,100 | 2,316,388 | Urban diocese, growing at 1.5% per year. 1p,3s. 2159 372 4752 12626 |
| D Pontoise | 1966 | R Lat | Bs | 202 | 370,000 | 500,000 | Northwest of Paris area. 95% urban. 280 0 486 7260 |
| D Saint-Denis | 1966 | R Lat | Bs | 83 | 648,500 | 876,400 | 96% urban. Many services common to all dioceses. 266 17 515 11306 |
| D Versailles | 1801 | R Lat | Bs | 256 | 444,000 | 600,000 | Area southwest of Paris. 96% urban. 418 0 950 12700 |
| Région Provence-Méditerranée: | 1961 | R Lat | Bs | 2,389 | 2,978,100 | 4,024,417 | *Provence-Mediterranean Apostolic Region*. HQ Marseilles. |
| M Aix | c 408 | R Lat | Bs | 124 | 291,100 | 393,417 | Aix. Arles & Embrun. HQ Aix. D=PC. 264 2 514 6260 |
| D Ajaccio | c 250 | R Lat | Bs | 438 | 132,500 | 179,000 | Covers Corsica. Population 275,600. 45% urban. 174 11 194 1787 |
| M Avignon | 439 | R Lat | Bs | 175 | 251,600 | 340,000 | Population 354,000. 70% urban. G=2.6%pa.1s. 235 20 476 5678 |
| D Digne | c 370 | R Lat | Bs | 192 | 74,000 | 100,000 | Population 103,900. 51% urban. G=2.2%pa. 104 0 285 1326 |
| M Fréjus & Toulon | 374 | R Lat | Bs | 194 | 370,000 | 500,000 | Southern coast. HQ Fréjus. 70% urban. G=3.0%pa. 269 25 426 7076 |
| D Gap | 517 | R Lat | Bs | 194 | 60,700 | 82,000 | Population 92,000. 51% urban. G=0.8%pa. 138 0 250 500 |
| M Marseille | 314 | R Lat | bs | 121 | 666,000 | 900,000 | Port, 950,000 people. 94% urban. G=2.8%pa. 1p,2s. 545 58 1435 11374 |
| D Montpellier | c 250 | R Lat | Bs | 423 | 370,000 | 500,000 | Population 591,400. 73% urban. G=2.3%pa. 1s. 483 95 1024 7610 |
| D Nice | 314 | R Lat | Bs | 240 | 481,000 | 650,000 | Population 722,070. 93% urban. G=2.6%pa. 498 16 996 7381 |
| D Nîmes | 396 | R Lat | Bs | 288 | 281,200 | 380,000 | Protestants strong. Population 478,500. 71% urban. 343 80 666 5259 |

*Continued opposite*

*Table 2 – continued*

| Official name 1 | Begun 2 | Type 3 | Counc 4 | Congs 5 | Adults 6 | Affiliated 7 | Names, notes, and other statistics (see Codebook) 8 | | | | |
|---|---|---|---|---|---|---|---|---|---|---|---|
| Région Sud-Ouest: | 1961 | R Lat | Bs | 4,684 | 3,126,400 | 4,224,805 | *Southwestern Apostolic Region*. HQ Tulle. | | | | |
| D Agen | 357 | R Lat | Bs | 429 | 199,600 | 269,755 | Population 289,800. 51% urban. G=0.9%pa. D=PC. | 237 | 10 | 287 | 4505 |
| D Aire | 506 | R Lat | Bs | 326 | 181,300 | 245,000 | HQ Dax. Population 277,380. 42% urban. D=PC. 1s. | 349 | 23 | 323 | 3817 |
| D Angoulême | c 250 | R Lat | Bs | 363 | 242,800 | 328,050 | Population 331,000. 45% urban. G=0.2%pa. | 247 | 6 | 507 | 4553 |
| D Bayonne | c 500 | R Lat | Bs | 527 | 373,700 | 505,000 | Population 508,700. 65% urban. G=1.4%pa. 1s. | 917 | 40 | 1768 | 6978 |
| M Bordeaux | 314 | R Lat | Bs | 624 | 592,000 | 800,000 | Population 1,009,400. 70% urban. D=PC. 2s. | 597 | 18 | 1275 | 13089 |
| D La Rochelle | 1317 | R Lat | Bs | 496 | 325,600 | 440,000 | Population 496,340. 50% urban. D=PC. | 283 | 13 | 520 | 6267 |
| D Limoges | c 200 | R Lat | Bs | 481 | 310,000 | 420,000 | Haute-Vienne; Creuse (81% rural, declining –0.7%pa). | 352 | 10 | 610 | 5840 |
| D Périgueux | 361 | R Lat | Bs | 538 | 266,400 | 360,000 | Population 374,070. 39% urban. G=0. D=PC. | 249 | 33 | 464 | 5300 |
| D Poitiers | c 300 | R Lat | Bs | 605 | 467,700 | 632,000 | Vienne (43% urban), Deux-Sèvres (34% urban). 1s. | 621 | 56 | 1000 | 10371 |
| D Tulle | 1317 | R Lat | Bs | 295 | 166,500 | 225,000 | Pop 237,900. 41% urban. Towns all under 50,000. | 209 | 11 | 198 | 2874 |
| Extra-regional jurisdictions: | 1961 | R LEr | Os | 35 | 29,400 | 39,775 | 4 jurisdictions not in Apostolic Regions. | | | | |
| PN Mission de France (Pontigny) | 1954 | R Lat | Bs | 1 | 500 | 774 | 43 priest-teams in 30 dioceses; 11 in 10 dioceses overseas. | 361 | 3 | 0 | 15 |
| O France (*Oriental rites*) | 1954 | R Ori | Os | 13 | 5,200 | 7,000 | For all Oriental-rite Catholics without a bishop. | 51 | 0 | 58 | 23 |
| EA France (*Armenian*) | 1960 | R Arm | Os | 8 | 11,100 | 15,000 | Suffragan ad instar of M Paris. Armenian emigres. | 9 | 0 | 7 | 43 |
| EA France (*Ukrainian*) | 1960 | R Ukr | Os | 13 | 12,600 | 17,000 | Suffragan ad instar of M Paris. Ukrainian refugees. | 13 | 0 | 8 | 30 |
| Eglise Catholique des Mariavites | 1906 | C CCa | Uv... | 5 | 100 | 200 | *Mariavite Catholic Ch. Imitators of Mary*. Founded in Poland by nun. 1 bishop,4n. | | | | |
| Eglise Catholique Française | 1883 | C CCa | ..... | 12 | 700 | 1,000 | *Eglise Gallicane*. 1907, restored by Vilatte. Gnostic, occult, faith-healing, magic. | | | | |
| Egl Catholique Gallicane Autocéphale | 1959 | C Lib | .v... | 6 | 1,000 | 2,000 | *D Normandie, Egl Vieille-Cath Libérale. Succession Apostolique Oecuménique*. 4 bishops. | | | | |
| Eglise Catholique Libérale | 1923 | C Lib | x.... | 9 | 400 | 600 | *Liberal Catholic Ch*. Branches UK, USA, Netherlands. Theosophical. 16n,W=50%,3Yy. | | | | |
| Eglise Cath Orthodoxe Ev de France | 1924 | C Lib | C.... | 20 | 2,000 | 4,000 | Ex LCC(UK). 1937, joined P Moscow, later ROCOR, then P Bucharest. 15n,1s(St Denys). | | | | |
| Eglise Chrétienne Universelle | 1950 | M Lib | ..... | 10 | 4,500 | 5,000 | *Universal Chr Ch. Témoins du Christ Revenu* (*Witnesses*). Messiah Georges Roux. | | | | |
| Eglise Christique Primitive | 1938 | C ReC | ..... | | 500 | 1,000 | *Primitive Christian Ch*. Begun by Catholic faith-healer. Also Germany, Switzerland. | | | | |
| Eglise de Dieu en France | 1960 | P Pe3 | ZF... | 8 | 83 | 250 | *Church of God in France*. M=CoG(Cleveland)(USA). 7n,1x,G=10%pa,W=48%,17Y. | | | | |
| Eglise de J-C des Saints des DJ | 1850 | M LdS | x.... | 23 | 5,000 | 8,190 | *Ch of JC of Latter-day Saints. Mormons*. 600 USA missionaries. HQ Paris. G=3.3%pa. | | | | |
| Eglise de la CA d'Alsace et de Lorraine | 1521 | P Lut | LWC.K | 370 | 140,000 | 233,366 | *ECAAL*. CA=Augsburg Confession. 7 Inspectorates (districts). 245n,2x,1s(60),3552Yy. | | | | |
| Eglise du Christ-Roi Rénovée | 1951 | C CCa | ..... | 2 | 2,000 | 4,000 | *Holy Cath Ap & Roman Renewed Ch*. Ex RC D Nancy. Papal claimant Clement XV, died 1974. | | | | |
| Eglise du Christ, Scientiste | c1890 | M Sci | x.... | 18 | 520 | 1,000 | *Ch of Christ, Scientist. Christian Science*. M=CCS(Boston,USA). HQ Paris. 5m,18w. | | | | |
| Eglise Evangélique Hinschiste | 1831 | P ind | ..... | 1 | 160 | 300 | Founded by Coraly Hinsch. In Nîmes. Bible studies, no sacraments. One girls' home. | | | | |
| Egl Evangélique Luthérienne de France | 1871 | P Lut | LWC.K | 125 | 25,000 | 60,000 | *EELF*. Ev Lutheran Ch. ECAAL. 2 Inspectorates: Paris. Montbéliard. 59n,55b,2s(6). | | | | |
| Eglise Evangélique Luthérienne Libre | 1921 | P Lut | x.... | 16 | 1,950 | 3,100 | *Synode de France et Belgique. Free Ev Luth Ch*. Ex ECAAL. M=LCMS(USA). 13n,W=56%,32Yy. | | | | |
| Eglise Gnostique Apostolique | 1953 | C Lib | ..... | | 1,000 | 2,000 | *Apostolic Gnostic Ch*. Closed group protecting Gospel from world. Belgium, Brazi!, Italy. | | | | |
| Eglise Néo-Apostolique | 1900 | C CAp | x.... | 100 | 14,300 | 20,000 | *New Apostolic Ch* (HQ Dortmund). Almost all in Alsace-Lorraine. HQ Vanves (Seine). | | | | |
| Eglise Orthodoxe Copte (P Alexandria) | c1970 | O Cop | NwaN. | 3 | 500 | 1,000 | Led by 2 bishops formerly French Catholic bishops. In Paris, Toulon, Marseilles. | | | | |
| Eglise Orthodoxe Grecque en France | 1963 | O Gre | Cwc.O | 18 | 30,000 | 40,000 | *D France*, and E Spain. Under EP Constantinople. Greeks, Cypriots, Levantines. 1d. | | | | |
| Eglise Orth Roumaine en Europe Occ | 1948 | O Rum | x.... | 10 | 4,000 | 7,000 | *Romanian OC*. Under ROCOR (New York). 1973, split over rejoining P Bucharest. 15x. | | | | |
| Eglise Orthodoxe Russe Hors-Frontières | 1920 | O Sla | x.... | 20 | 5,000 | 9,000 | *D Western Europe, ROC Outside of Russia*. HQ New York. Russian influx 1920–30. | | | | |
| Egl Orth Russe (PE Europe Occidentale) | 1922 | O Sla | Mwc.O | 10 | 10,000 | 5,000 | *Russian Orthodox Ch*. In Patriarchal Exarchate of Moscow (HQ London). Russians. 3d. | | | | |
| Eglise Orthodoxe Serbe | | O Ser | Cwc.O | 10 | 10,000 | 15,000 | *Serbian Orthodox Ch*. Under P Belgrade. Migrant workers. Paris, L'Hôpital/Moselle. | | | | |
| Eglise Orthodoxe Syrienne | | O Syr | Dw.N. | | 200 | 500 | *Syrian Orthodox Ch, P Antioch*. 100 Syrian families in Marseilles, Lyons, Paris. | | | | |
| Eglise Orth: AD France & Europe Occ | 1922 | O Sla | Cwc.O | 70 | 70,000 | 100,000 | Under EP Constantinople 1931–65 and since 1971. 90% Russians, Romanians. 1s. | | | | |
| Eglise Primitive Cath et Apostolique | 1937 | C CCa | .v... | 10 | 100 | 300 | *Eglise Catholique Primitive*. Ex LCC(UK). Based on first Antioch Christian rites. HQ Paris. | | | | |
| Eglise Protestante Evangélique | 1945 | P Pen | ..... | | 2,850 | 3,000 | *Ev Protestant Ch*. Pentecostals around Lyons. Begun by faith-healer Soeur Gaillard. | | | | |
| Eglise Réformée de France | 1520 | P Ref | RWC.K | 1,263 | 200,000 | 328,700 | *ERF. Reformed Ch of F*. 1938 union (Congr, Meth, 2 Reformed chs). 563n,3s(119). | | | | |
| Egl Réformée d'Alsace et de Lorraine | 1528 | P Ref | RWC.K | 141 | 40,173 | 50,368 | *ERAL. Reformed Ch of A-L*. French, German. 68n,1x,G=1.2%pa,1s(12),W=80%,705Yy. | | | | |
| Eglise Ukrainienne Orth Autocéphale | | O Sla | X.... | 4 | 3,000 | 5,000 | *Ukrainian Orthodox Autocephalic Ch*. Linked to UOC of USA. 1 parish in Paris. | | | | |
| Eglise Vieille-Catholique de France | 1870 | C OCa | Uv... | 2 | 300 | 700 | *Old Catholic Church of France*. Uses borrowed buildings. 3n,W=10%,4Yy,10z. | | | | |
| Eglise Vieille-Catholique Romaine en F | 1960 | C CCa | ..... | 2 | 20,000 | 30,000 | *Old Roman Catholic Ch*. Rapid expansion claimed since 1960. 7n,1p,1s(5),W=12%,280Yy. | | | | |
| Eglise Vieille-Cath (Branche Française) | | O Sla | .v... | | 200 | 500 | Part of American Orthodox Catholic Ch (USA). Russians. Work in Nigeria, Zaire. | | | | |
| Eglises Baptistes Indépendantes | 1948 | P Bap | x.... | 7 | 60 | 100 | *Independent Baptist Churches*. M=Baptist Mid-Missions(USA). HQ Paris. 13f. | | | | |
| Eglise Cath Apost Orth d'Occident | c1940 | C Epi | .v... | | 50 | 100 | *Cath Apostolic Orth Chs of the West*. HQ Alouette-Pessac (Gironde). 1947, rejected by WCC. | | | | |
| Eglises du Christ | c1910 | P Dis | x.... | 10 | 400 | 1,000 | *Chs of Christ*. M=CC(Non-Instrumental)(USA). Paris, Lille, Reims. USA civilians. | | | | |
| Eglises Evangéliques Mennonites de F | | P Men | G.... | 28 | 2,000 | 3,000 | *Association des EEMF. Ev Mennonite Chs*. German-speaking; Alsace-Lorrine. | | | | |
| Eglises Evangéliques Méthodistes de F | 1852 | P Met | ..... | 37 | 340 | 1,000 | Methodists refusing 1938 ERF merger. Paris, SE France. 8n,G=–0.9%pa,1H,W=60%,10Yy. | | | | |
| Eglises Mennonites de Langue Française | | P Men | G.... | 10 | 500 | 1,000 | *French-speaking Mennonite Churches*. HQ Montbéliard (Doubs). | | | | |
| Egls Réformées Ev Indéqendantes de F | 1872 | P Ref | Jt..K | 108 | 20,000 | 30,000 | *EREI. National Union of Indep Ev Ref Chs*. Rejected 1938 ERF merger. 35n,1s(4). | | | | |
| Eglises Tziganes | 1950 | P Pe2 | x...K | 500 | 15,000 | 40,000 | *Gypsy Ev Movement*. Nomadic caravan churches. M=GGMS,AoG(USA). 200m,G=4%pa,1p. | | | | |
| Enfants de Dieu | c1968 | P Apo | xv... | | 1,000 | 2,000 | *Children of God International*. Jesus People. Communes. HQ Montgeron, Paris. | | | | |
| Fédération des Assemblées de Réveil | | P Pe2 | ..... | 18 | 3,000 | 5,000 | *Federation of Assemblies of Revival*. Schism ex Assemblies of God. HQ in Rouen. | | | | |
| Fédération des Egls Ev Baptistes de F | 1832 | P Bap | T...K | 115 | 2,347 | 5,000 | *FEEBF. French Baptist Federation*. 1960, M=SBC(USA). HQ Paris. 53n,4f,1p(7),114Y. | | | | |
| Frères Exclusifs (Darbystes) | 1844 | P EBr | x.... | 128 | 9,700 | 20,000 | *Frères Etroits* (Closed). *Momiers* (Bigots). Raven-Taylor, Kelly-Continental. | | | | |
| Frères Larges Pentecôtisants | | P Pen | ..... | | 200 | 500 | *Pentecostal Christian Brethren*. Grouping of former Plymouth Brethren. | | | | |
| La Porte Ouverte et Associés | c1958 | P Pen | ..... | 11 | 100 | 300 | *The Open Door*. HQ Châlon-sur-Saône. Foreign missions in Chad, CARepublic, et alia. | | | | |
| La Première Pentecôte | 1949 | I pe2 | ..... | | 150 | 500 | *The First Pentecost*. Begun by Ceylon Pentecostal Mission. HQ Dieppe. | | | | |
| Mission Alliance Evangélique | 1952 | P int | xM... | 10 | 500 | 1,000 | M=TEAM(USA). Paris suburbs, southern France. Emphasis on youth, camps. 33f. | | | | |
| Mission de l'Evangile | | P Pen | ..... | 20 | 200 | 500 | *Mission of the Gospel*. Pentecostals. From Basel, Switzerland. Mainly Alasce. | | | | |
| Mission Evangélique Baptiste en France | 1962 | P Bap | xF... | 4 | 51 | 225 | *EBC. Eglise Baptiste Conservateur*. M=CBFMS(USA). 7x,19f,W=13%,13Y. | | | | |
| Mission Ev des Alpes Françaises | c1910 | P int | xM... | 4 | 93 | 200 | *French Alps/Mission Ev de Thonon*. 1962, M=UFM(UK,USA). 1n,4x,25f,W=60%,1Y. | | | | |
| Mission Populaire Evangelique de France | 1872 | P Ref | ....K | 15 | 1,000 | 3,000 | *French Protestant Industrial Mission* (*McAll M*). 20 settlements. Immigrants. 27nm. | | | | |
| Mission Suisse de Pentecôte | | P Pe2 | Z.... | 8 | 300 | 1,000 | *SPM. Schweizerische Pfingstmission. Swiss Pentecostal Mission*. Classical. | | | | |
| Nouvelle Eglise (Swedenborgiens) | | M Swe | x.... | 10 | 100 | 200 | *New Church, Swedenborgian Ch*. French HQ in Paris. | | | | |
| Pentecôtistes des Eaux Vives | | P Pe4 | ..... | | 400 | 600 | *The Living Waters*. Schism ex Assemblies of God. Based on Marseilles. | | | | |
| Petite Eglise (Vendéenne) | 1801 | C CCa | ..... | 20 | 3,500 | 5,000 | *Little Ch*. Schism of 38 bishops ex RCC rejecting 1801 concordat. Dying; no clergy. | | | | |
| Ravinistes | | P EBr | ..... | 14 | 200 | 500 | *Closed Brethren*. Schism ex Taylor Brethren (Exclusive). | | | | |
| Sainte Eglise Apostolique | 1955 | C Lib | ..... | | 500 | 1,500 | *Holy Apostolic Ch*. Uniate Armenian succession. Gallican. Healing, exorcism. HQ Colombes. | | | | |
| Ste Egl Ap Orth Celtique en Brétagne | 1956 | C CCa | ..... | | 500 | 1,500 | *Celtic Apostolic Orthodox Ch in Brittany*. 300 Celtic-rite Breton families. 10 bishops, 20n. | | | | |
| Société Religieuse des Amis | 1785 | P Qua | Q.... | 5 | 150 | 300 | *Religious Society of Friends. Quakers*. M=FSC(UK). HQ Paris. No sacraments. 4f. | | | | |
| Témoins de Jéhovah | 1900 | M Jeh | x.... | 636 | 41,203 | 100,000 | *Jehovah's Witnesses. Watch Tower*. HQ Boulogne-Billancourt. 4977Y. | | | | |
| Union de l'Eglise Evangélique | | P Ref | ..... | 32 | 500 | 1,100 | *Union of the Ev Ch*. Pietist schism ex ERAL in Alsace-Lorraine, through USA influence. | | | | |
| Union des Chrétiens Apostoliques | 1954 | C CAp | x.... | | 1,000 | 2,000 | *Union of Apostolic Christians*. Schism ex New Apostolic Ch. 60,000 in world. | | | | |
| Union des Egls Chrétiennes Bibliques | 1946 | P ind | .M..C | 13 | 300 | 640 | *Union of Bible Christian Chs*. HQ Courbevoie (Seine). 5n,9x,G=8%pa,W=47%,18Y,17z. | | | | |
| Union des Eglises Ev Libres de France | 1849 | P Ref | K...C | 35 | 2,200 | 3,000 | *Union of Free Ev Chs of France*. Calvinist origin. Mainly of Marseilles. 9n. | | | | |
| Union des Sociétés Evangéliques | 1840 | P ind | x.... | 55 | 520 | 1,000 | *St-Chrischona* (near Basel). *Union of Ev Socs*. Europe, Ethiopia. HQ Colmar. 12n. | | | | |
| Union d'Eglise Ev Méthodiste | 1868 | P Met | Vwc.K | 3 | 105 | 250 | *United Methodist Ch*(USA). 60% French-speaking, 40% German. 2n,1x,W=40%,5Yy. | | | | |
| Union Nat des Eg Ev Arméniennes de F | c1930 | P Con | Rw... | 24 | 850 | 2,500 | *Armenian Evangelical Union of Churches of France*. HQ Beirut. 1918 refugees. | | | | |
| Union pour le Réveil | | P Pe2 | ..... | 7 | 550 | 1,000 | *Union for Revival*. Founded by George Jeffreys (Elim Church). Pentecostals. | | | | |
| Vrai Eglise Catholique | 1964 | C CCa | ..... | | 500 | 1,000 | *True Catholic Ch*. In Lorraine and Belgium, begun by excommunicated RC priest. | | | | |
| Other Protestant denominations | | P | ..... | 200 | 25,000 | 50,000 | Total over 100 (see list below). Includes many independent single congregations. | | | | |
| Other Catholic (non-Roman) churches | | C | ..... | | 3,000 | 10,100 | Total about 50, including over 30 led by bishops-at-large with few lay adherents. | | | | |
| Other marginal Protestant bodies | | M | ..... | | 5,000 | 10,000 | Many small groups and cults (see list below). | | | | |
| Other Orthodox churches | | O | ..... | | 4,800 | 8,500 | Several bodies including Eglise Orthodoxe Géorgienne (refugees from USSR). | | | | |
| Other Third-World indigenous churches | | I | ..... | | 1,000 | 2,000 | Total about 7 bodies (see below), including EJCSK, HSAUWC. | | | | |
| Doubly-affiliated (duplication)(1970) | | | | | –629,000 | –850,000 | Evangelicals who also are or were baptized Roman Catholics. | | | | |
| Disaffiliated (duplication)(1970) | | | | | –1,981,400 | –2,677,538 | Baptized Catholics now completely disaffiliated agnostics or atheists. | | | | |
| **Total affiliated (mid-1970)** | | | | **44,600** | **31,202,348** | **42,559,900** | **Total denominations (1970) . . . 274.** | | | | |
| **Total affiliated (mid-1975)** | | | | **44,900** | **31,782,900** | **43,351,700** | **Total denominations (1975) . . . 294.** | | | | |
| **Total affiliated (mid-1980)** | | | | **45,200** | **32,339,400** | **44,110,800** | **Total denominations (1980) . . . 315.** | | | | |

NOTES ON TABLE ABOVE

COLUMNS: for meanings and CODES (cols. 1, 3, 4, 8), see Codebook (Part 6), Column 1: **Boldface type** = church with over 10% of country's affiliated Christians.

NATIONAL COUNCILS (Column 4, 5th letter).

- C = Fédération Evangélique de France (Evangelical Federation of France) (a few denominations, and over 25 single congregations); formerly Union des Eglises et Associations Evangéliques Françaises, founded 1967.
- E = Alliance Evangélique Française (AEF) (French Evangelical Alliance) (members: Salvation Army; one college; and individuals).
- K = Fédération Protestante de France (FPF) (Protestant Federation of France).
- O = Comité Interépiscopal Orthodoxe de France (Orthodox Interepiscopal Liaison Committee of France).
- R = Conférence Episcopale de France (CEF) (Episcopal Conference of France).

*Other national councils*. National Alliance of the Lutheran Churches of France.

OTHER PROTESTANT DENOMINATIONS. The total is over 100, many of which are small independent groups, large single congregations, or chaplaincies of a number of large national churches in other countries throughout the world. These include (with names in French or English according to which is better known): American Baptist Association, American Ch (Paris), Association Ev de Générargues, Baptistes Pentecôtisants, Christian Ch of North America, Ch of Scotland, Eglise Allemande Luthérienne, Eglise Danoise de Paris, Eglise de Pentecôte Primitive, Eglise de Pentecôte 'Latter Rain', Eglise Elim, Eglise Espagnole, Eglise Ev des Frères, Eglise Ev Russe, Eglise Ev Vietnamienne (CMA/ACM), Eglise Protestante Malgache de France, Eglise Réformée Hongroise en France, Eglise Réformée Néerlandaise, Eglise Roumaine Ev Baptiste, Eglise Suédoise Luthérienne, Eglise Suisse-Allemande, Eglises Baptistes de la Mission Ev de France, Eglises Vaudoises d'Italie en France (Waldensians), Emmanuel Baptist Ch, European Christian Mission (17 missionaries), France Mission, Gospel Missionary Union (1960), Greater Europe Mission (1949), Mission Alpine, Mission Chrétienne Européenne, Mission Chrétienne Française, Mission de Réveil, Mission du Tabernacle, Mission Ev Baptiste, Mission Ev de France, Mission Ev en Brétagne, Mission Foi Evangile, Mission Internationale aux Mineurs, Mission Libre Suédoise (SFM), Mission Norvégienne des Marins, Mouvement Ev Russe, National Association of Free Will Baptists (1966), National Fellowship of Brethren Chs, North Africa Mission (1963, 43 missionaries), Pentecôtistes Libres, Reformed Baptists (USA), Slavic Gospel Association, Strict Baptist Mission, Union Chrétienne Baptiste, Union Chrétienne Ev de Pentecôte, Union Missionnaire d'Auvergne, Worldwide Evangelization Crusade (11 missionaries).

OTHER MARGINAL PROTESTANT BODIES. Among the many bodies are: Eglise Réformée du Foyer de l'Ame (Unitarians), Eglise Rosicrucienne Apostolique, Order of the Cross, Reorganized Ch of Jesus Christ of Latter-day Saints (USA), Unitarian Universalist Association (3 churches), Unité Métaphysique Chrétienne (Unité Universelle) (from USA), United Ch of Religious Science (from USA; 1 church).

OTHER THIRD-WORLD INDIGENOUS CHURCHES. These include small groups from francophone Africa (EJCSK from Zaire, in Paris; &c), Hong Kong, also the Unification Ch of France (from Korea; 1,000 members by 1976), also the Father Divine Peace Mission Movement (USA Blacks).

**PEOPLES** (ethnolinguistic). Christians: 86.0% French, 2.7% Alsatian, 2.4% Breton, 1.5% Portuguese, 1.2% Spaniard, 1.1% Italian, 0.7% Flemish, 0.5% Corsican, 0.4% Catalan, 0.4% German, 0.4% Antillean Creole (Martiniquan, Guadeloupan), 0.4% Armenian, 0.3% Basque, 0.3% Gypsy, 0.2% Russian, 0.2% Polish, 0.2% Vietnamese, 0.2% African & Malagasy, 0.1% Greek, 0.1% Walloon, 0.1% British, Serbian, Franco-Swiss, USA, Czech, Jewish, et alii.

**COUNTRY-WIDE TOTALS**

EVANGELIZATION (see Part 5). 1900: 100%. 1970: 100%. 1980: 100%. *Mass evangelism.* Among the large number of recent campaigns: 1955, Billy Graham 5-day crusade in Paris (43,619 attenders, 2,153 enquirers), also 1963 in Paris, Lyons, Mulhouse, Toulouse, Montaubon, Nancy and Douai (95,800 attenders, 2,698 enquirers) and in 1970 Euro '70 TV crusade televised from Dortmund, Germany; 1964, Oral Roberts campaign; 1969, team of Africans sponsored by PEMS for 3-month tour; 1970, Alain Choiguierand 'Reims for Christ' crusade; 1978, nationwide evangelistic campaign IMPACT 78 (under AEF). Among Gypsies, large Pentecostal conventions were attracting 1,500 Gypsy caravans by 1975. *Radiophonic evangelism.* Annual listeners' letters (1975): 16,550 TWR, about 2,000 Radio Vatican, 549 HCJB, RVOG, RSB. Bible correspondence courses: many, including ICI (467 active students), RSB (324 Arabs). *Literature evangelism.* From 1972–75, Every Home Crusade delivered 16,777,830 leaflets to homes; July 1977, Operation Village 77.

FOREIGN MISSIONARIES AND PERSONNEL (nationals serving abroad) (1973). Total 22,921: 22,719 Roman Catholics (16,719 foreign missionaries (4,869 priests, 1,500 brothers, 9,550 sisters, 800 lay) serving in Third-World countries, about 6,000 other personnel in Western nations), 160 Protestants in 30 countries, 40 marginal Protestants (about 30 Jehovah's Witnesses), about 2 Catholics (non-Roman).

FOREIGN MISSIONARIES AND PERSONNEL (aliens from abroad) (1973). Total 13,772. *From Western world.* 11,799: 10,500 Roman Catholics, about 700 marginal Protestants (600 Mormons from USA), 561 Protestants (384 in 49 USA societies, 142 in 23 UK societies, 12 in 2 Sweden societies, 10 in 4 Canada societies, 3 in 2 Netherlands societies, 3 in 3 Australia societies, 3 in 1 Switzerland society, 2 in 1 Finland society, 1 in 1 Denmark society, 1 in 1 WGermany society), about 20 Orthodox, 12 Anglicans (8 in 2 UK societies, 4 in 1 USA society), about 6 Catholics (non-Roman). *From Communist world.* 212: about 190 Roman Catholics, about 22 Orthodox. *From Third World.* 1,761: about 1,719 Roman Catholics from Africa, India, Madagascar, Viet Nam, West Indies (45 from Guadeloupe) et alia, about 20 Protestants from Africa, Korea and Viet Nam, about 12 Orthodox from Cyprus, Lebanon and Syria, about 10 indigenous from Hong Kong, Ivory Coast, Sri Lanka et alia.

INSTITUTIONS (church-operated) (1973). Total 4,340, including 15 ecumenical centres, 2,865 higher schools (64 minor seminaries), 750 medical centres, 500 religious communities (430 monasteries), 58 research centres, 71 seminaries (50 RC, 17 Protestant, 3 Orthodox, 1 Catholic/non-Roman), 17 study centres, 6 universities.

PERIODICALS. About 1,200 titles (170 Protestant (10 Pentecostal), 15 Orthodox; including many periodicals of religious orders and congregations).

PERSONNEL. About 154,772 (141,000 national, 13,772 foreign).

RELIGIOUS LIBRARIES. About 670.

SCRIPTURE DISTRIBUTION (1975). Annual totals: 352,972 Bibles (5% free, 10% subsidized, 85% commercial), 583,016 NTs (6% free, 17% subsidized, 77% commercial), 612,320 UBS portions, 313,327 UBS selections. *Translations completed.* Portion: 15 languages or dialects since 1820. NT: 5 languages since 1474. Bible: 4 languages since 1530.

SERVICE AGENCIES. About 610, including ACFEB, ACMEC, ACNAV, ACO, AEF, AFAR, AFP, AFVP, AJCF, AMA, ANPCP, APF, BCEOM, BIM, BIP, CARP, CCCI, CEDIMA, CEEEFE, CEF, CEME, CEVAA, CFTC, CICD, CIMADE, CIOF, CISR, CLC, CREC, CTIC, DEFAP, DIAL, EMI, EPIS, FAGEC, FEF, FIAC, FIPC, FOCS, FOI, FPF, GBU, ICYWE, JECI, MCP, MIDADE, MIR, MRJC, MTS, OCD, OCES, OCM, OCIC, OCIPE, OCL, OM, PTL, SDF, SEAR, SHPF, SIF, SNEC, STE, SU, UCIP, UCJG(YMCA), UFFMS, WLC (EHC), YFC, YLC, YWAM, YWCA.

**ADDITIONAL DATA ON CHURCHES**

EGLISE CATHOLIQUE DE FRANCE. *Apostolic regions.* Since 1961 the church in metropolitan France has been divided into 9 Régions Apostoliques with the object of planning the pastoral task at a regional level. Each region has full autonomy of organization. The ecclesiastical provinces have not been suppressed because they still constitute the only canonical divisions, but they no longer are of anything but historical interest. The new organization, moreover, has permitted the integration into the pastoral task of the 3 dioceses still immediately subject to the Holy See (Marseilles, Metz, Strasbourg). *Dioceses.* In most cases each diocese corresponds to a civil administrative department. *New diocese* (created 1974). Le Havre. *Annual baptisms.* (1972) 99.5% infant, 0.5% adult. *Personnel.* About 94% nationals, 6% expatriates. *Priests.* The total has declined gradually for the last 20 years. *Diocesan priests' councils.* A presbyteral council exists in almost every diocese. *Diocesan pastoral councils.* In mid-1971, 13 dioceses had pastoral councils (as shown above by PC in column 8). The territory of Lourdes also had a Conseil de Pastorale des Sanctuaires de Lourdes. *Sisters.* In addition to those shown in the table, there were 9,220 contemplatives in 1973, making a total then of 105,800. *Catholic charismatics* (January 1974). 10,000 adults including many religious personnel are active in over 120 prayer groups in the Charismatic Renewal. *Seminaries.* The tendency has been to regroup and consolidate previous seminaries. In 1973, there were 40 training schools for secular priests: 5 diocesan, 35 interdiocesan (of the latter, 5 are university seminaries; Angers, Lyons, Paris, Strasbourg, Toulouse). In addition to residential seminaries, in 1973 there were 85 young men in training groups in the world of industry and 139 in the university world, all doing the first 2 of the 6 years' training for the priesthood. In 1973 there were 11 seminaries for religious priests. *Congregations.* 397 for sisters, regrouped and consolidated from 540 in 1962. There are also 319 monasteries for contemplatives. *Main religious orders and congregations.* Priests (1973: with over 500 professed each): 1,300 SJ, 830 OCSO, 780 OSB, 656 OP, 577 OFM, 536 OFMCap. Brothers (1973: major ones): 2,004 FCS, 665 PFM, 631 FICP. Sisters of active life (with over 1,000 professed each in 1972): Divine Providence de Ribeauvillé, Filles de la Charité de Jésus, Filles de la Charité de St-Vincent de Paul, Filles de Jésus (Kermaria), Filles de la Sagesse, Filles du Coeur de Marie, Filles du St-Esprit, Instruction Chrétienne, N-D de la Charité du Bon Pasteur d'Angers, Petites Soeurs de l'Assomption, Petites Soeurs des Pauvres, Sacrés Coeurs de Jésus et Marie, Très Saint Sauveur. Sisters of contemplative life: 3,000 Carmélites, 1,945 Bénédictines, 1,632 Visitandines, 1,343 Clarisses. *Traditionalist opposition.* In 1976 a traditionalist, archbishop Marcel Lefebvre, was suspended by the pope but continued to attack both him and the reforms of Vatican II, and to operate a seminary at Ecône in Switzerland, ordaining 30 deacons and 2 priests. In 1976 Lefebvre had 25,000 followers in France, and (according to polls) was supported by 20% of all France's Catholics (and opposed by 24%), and supported by 24% of all Switzerland's Catholics (and opposed by 39%). By 1977 the movement was spreading to Germany and the USA. In June 1977, Lefebvre ordained 40 more clergy at Ecône in the presence of a crowd of 4,000, and excommunication and open schism seemed likely.

*Catholic organizations.* The French Episcopal Conference (Conférence Episcopale Française), which is member of the CCEE includes the bishops of French overseas departments and territories, the former with deliberative voice and the latter consultative only. Two organizations of religious personnel are active: Union des Supérieurs Majeurs de France (priests and brothers) and Union des Supérieures Majeures de France (sisters). For the armed forces, France forms a military vicariate. There are no pastoral or presbyteral councils. A first national priests-bishops assembly, uniting all bishops and a hundred delegate priests, took place in Issy-les-Moulineaux (Paris) at Pentecost in 1969. A continuation committee was established which prepared a second meeting at Lourdes in November 1969. Although the committee (3 bishops and 9 priests) continues to exist, there have been no further meetings.

For lay organizations, the Secrétariat Général pour l'Apostolat des Laïcs provides liaison with each other and with the episcopate. The Equipe de Liaison des Laïcs (ELL), created in 1970 without formal links to the hierarchy, unites a large number of lay bodies through meetings, exchanges, and the like. Official movements of the lay apostolate specializing in adult work are the ACI (33,000 members in 1973), ACO (workers, with 25,000 militants in 1973), and CMR (rural Christians, with 35,000 militants in 1973). Those specializing in youth work are JIC/F (independents), JOC/F (workers), JEC/F (students), ACU (university students), Mission Etudiante, Mouvement Chrétien en Grande Ecole, Jeunesse Maritime Chrétienne (JMC), and Mouvement Rural de la Jeunesse Chrétienne (MRJC) with 10,000 teams. Those specializing in children's work are the Coeurs Vaillants and Ames Vaillantes. General organizations of the lay apostolate include ACGH for men, ACGF for women (80,000 members in 1973) and ACG Foyers. In addition there are 14 professional movements of which 4 belong to the lay apostolate, special communities such as university parishes, educational movements (Scouts, Guides, Vie Nouvelle, Fédération Sportive et Culturelle de France), philanthropic movements (Secours Catholique, Société de St Vincent de Paul/Louise de Marillac, Equipes St Vincent), movements for social action (UNCEAS), 11 movements dedicated to the advancement of spirituality (Légion de Marie, Vie Evangélique, et alia), movements dealing with the sick, and movements concerned with co-operation and mission (Foi et Cultures, Cercle St Jean Baptiste).

The Holy See has diplomatic relations with France and is represented to government and the Catholic hierarchy by a nuncio in Paris.

Catholic international organizations with their headquarters in France include the following 18 bodies: (1) Académie Internationale des Ecrivains Catholiques, in Puylaurens, Pyrénées, which unites 3,000 Catholic writers across the world, of traditionalist tendencies; (2) Comité Internationale de Liaison des Facultés Catholiques de Théologie, founded in Salamanca, Spain in 1973 with headquarters now in Paris, with 60 members, which deals with pedagogical and administrative rather than theological questions; (3) Croisade des Aveugles, founded in Paris in 1957, which co-ordinates associations for Christian action by blind Christians in 20 countries of Africa, America, Asia and Europe; (4) Dialogue et Coopération/Equipes Enseignantes, founded in Paris in 1963, which organizes exchanges between the Christian teachers of the world, with 800 teams in France in addition to others in Spain, Portugal, Italy, French-speaking Africa, Latin America and Asia; (5) Equipes Notre-Dame, founded in Paris in 1937, which is a movement for spiritual commitment with 20,000 member homes in 37 countries; (6) Fédération Internationale Catholique d'Education Physique et Sportive (FICEP), founded in Paris in 1911 and renamed in 1957, which unites national federations for physical education and sport in Europe, Africa, Latin America, Oceania and among refugees and is a member of the Conseil International pour l'Education Physique et le Sport (UNESCO); (7) Fédération Internationale des Associations d'Enfants de Marie-Immaculée, founded in Paris in 1847, which unites Marian associations on 5 continents; (8) Fédération Internationale des Pharmaciens Catholiques (FIPC), founded in Le Vésinet in 1954, which studies the problems of Catholic pharmacists; (9) Fédération Internationale des Universités Catholiques (FIUC), founded in Paris in 1949, for co-operation between Catholic universities and with other international universities through its 80 member bodies in 21 countries; (10) Fraternité Catholique des Malades et Infirmes, founded in Verdun in 1942, for the development of Christian commitment of and to the sick and handicapped in 12 countries; (11) Groupe International Laïcat et Communauté Chrétienne, founded in Algiers in 1966, with teams in 19 countries of Africa, America and Europe, which is dedicated to the advancement of universal brotherhood and conscientization regarding human values, as part of the Christian task of witness and evangelization; (12) Jeunesse Etudiante Catholique Internationale (JECI), founded in Fribourg in 1946 and renamed in 1954 with its present headquarters in Paris, which unites 69 member Catholic student movements and 20 collaborating movements representing every continent; (13) Mouvement International d'Apostolat des Enfants (MIDADE), founded in Paris in 1929 and restructured under its present name in 1966, which promotes the apostolate of children in 32 countries, 15 being African; (14) Office Catholique d'Information sur les Problemes Européens (OCIPE), with its juridical headquarters in France and its principal secretariat in Belgium, which is basically an information agency; (15) Organisation Mondiale des Anciens et Anciennes Elèves de l'Enseignement Catholique, founded in Rome in 1967 but now located in Paris, which co-ordinates the work of 10 international and 5 national organizations of Catholic teachers with a special concern for academic freedom; (16) Société de St-Vincent de Paul, founded in Paris in 1833, with a membership of men only, which through its member bodies in 108 countries seeks to provide moral and material aid for the needy; (17) Pro Fide et Ecclesia, founded in Paris in 1972, which is a European federation uniting national committees of traditionalist or conservative Catholics (including Rassemblement des Silencieux de l'Eglise, Thomas Moregenootschap, Der Fels, Pro Fide (in UK), Rots, Credo-groep); (18) Union Mondiale des Organisations Féminines Catholiques (UMOFC), founded in Brussels in 1910 but now located under its new name in Paris, which is a federation of 134 Catholic women's organizations in 78 countries on all continents, dedicated to the development of Christian women.

Certain Catholic international organizations with their general secretariats elsewhere have sections in France. The Organisation Catholique Internationale du Cinéma (OCIC) (HQ Belgium), has a Centre Audio-Visuel in Ste-Foy-lez-Lyon and Service Scolaire in St-Etienne. Pax Romana (HQ Fribourg, Switzerland) has a Secrétariat International des Ingénieurs, des Agronomes et des Cadres Economiques Catholiques (SIIAEC) in Paris, with 15 national associations in 1970, and a Secrétariat International des Questions Scientifiques (SIQS) in Paris (both of which are attached to MIEC); and also a Secrétariat International des Elèves Ingénieurs Catholiques (SIEIC) in Paris (attached to MIEC). Although it is not strictly speaking an international organization, Aide à l'Implantation Monastique (AIM), founded in Vanves in 1966, is recognized officially as the missionary secretariat of the Benedictine order. It promotes the establishment of contemplative monasteries in the Third World and has organized international monastic meetings at Bouaké (Ivory Coast) in 1964, Rome in 1966, Bangkok (Thailand) in 1968, and Bangalore (India) in 1973.

Opinion groups exist representing both progressivist and traditionalist tendencies. In the first category, there is the recent formation of Basic Communities (Communautés de Base) which are anti- or extra-institutional bodies concerned with social change and urbanization. Their number has grown since the student crisis of 1968, and some 5,000 are now known to exist. In 1972, 1,800 persons met at Rennes as the Rassemblement National des Communautés de Base. Organized progressivist groups include: (1) Concertation, founded in 1969 with 4,000 members in 1970, which is an informal confederation aiming to further contacts between basic communities in the Rhône valley and Val de Loire; (2) Le Lien, founded in 1968, which unites basic communities in Paris and the other large cities; (3) Chrétiens Critiques, founded in Paris in 1975 after the dissolution of a similar body (Echanges et Dialogue), a well-organized movement of dissident priests and lay persons without episcopal recognition, working for the married priesthood as well as justice in the church and in the world; (4) Chrétiens pour le Socialisme, founded in 1974, a group consisting mostly of Catholics, with a few Protestants also; and (5) Chrétiens Marxistes, founded in 1974, an extreme-leftist organization politically. These and many other progressivist groups publish a considerable number of newspapers and journals with large circulations.

Organized traditionalist groups include: (1) Rassemblement des Silencieux de l'Eglise, founded in Paris in 1969 under the name Comité Française pour l'Unité de l'Eglise with 15,000 adherents in 1975, which accepts Vatican II in a restricted manner, is critical of the pastoral action of the French episcopate, serves as the French branch of Pro Fide et Ecclesia, and which created in 1971 a women's branch called Action Féminine pour une Pastorale de l'Enfance et de la Jeunesse and in 1975 a Fédération Missionnaire Foi-Eglise; (2) Credo, founded in Paris in 1974 as a more conservative group than Rassemblement des Silencieux, which declares itself to be in complete agreement with the pope and aims to propagate and defend the truths contained in the Nicene Creed; (3) Ligue de la Contre-Réforme Catholique, founded in 1970 at St Parres-les-Vandes, whose purpose is to 'demystify the Reform' of Vatican II; (4) Le Combat de la Foi, founded at Bléré in 1968, with 12,000 member families in 1971, which also interprets Vatican II conservatively; (5) Una Voce, founded in Paris in 1964 with 25,000 members in 1970, which seeks to defend the use of Latin, Gregorian chant and sacred polyphony and is affiliated with the international federation of the same name in Switzerland; (6) Opus Sacerdotale, L'Oeuvre Sacerdotale placée sous le Patronage de Marie, Mère de l'Eglise, founded in Angers in 1964 with 400 priests in 1971, which claims to accept Vatican II but also in a limited manner; (7) Office Internationale des Oeuvres de Formation Civique et d'Action Culturelle selon le Droit Naturel et Chrétien, founded in Paris in 1963, which organizes congresses within and outside France; and (8) L'Armée Bleue de Notre-Dame de Fatima, which has its international headquarters in Switzerland and its regional secretariat in Paris. These and other traditionalist bodies publish numerous newspapers and journals. Lastly, there are in addition several paramilitary groups, including Alliance St-Michel, and Action contre l'Auto-Destruction dans l'Eglise, which organize 'commandos' to disrupt by violence liturgical ceremonies they consider subversive.

Organizations for research and social action include: Centre Régional d'Etudes Socio-Religieuses, founded in Lille in 1959; Semaines Sociales de France, founded in Paris in 1904, which organizes national and regional colloquia on social action in various French cities; Centre L. J. Lebret/Foi et Développement, founded in Paris in 1971, for theological studies in relation to development and politics; Action Populaire/Centre d'Etudes, de Recherches et d'Action Sociales (CERAS), founded by Jesuits in Vanves in 1903, which studies the moral implications involved in the evolution of modern society and which has a specialized library of 90,000 volumes; Economie et Humanisme, founded at Caluire, Rhône in 1941, which is dedicated to the promotion of a more humane society and an economy in the service of man; Institut Oecuménique au Service du Développement des Peuples (INODEP), in Paris, which is concerned for intercultural training; Union Nationale des Centres d'Etudes et d'Action Sociale (UNCEAS), in Paris, which co-ordinates the activies of 140 centres for study and social action; Comité Catholique contre la Faim et pour le Développement (CCFD), in Paris, which is a member of CIDSE in Brussels and provides financial aid for the Third World; Délégation Catholique pour la Coopération (DCC), in Paris, which provides aid in personnel for the Third World in co-operation with several regional bodies including: Service et Développement (Lyons), Entraide pour le Développement Intégral (Lyons), Centre de Formation pour le Développement (Strasbourg), Fraternités 'Terre nouvelle' (Clichy), Medicus Mundi (Paris), Centre de Formation et d'Echanges Internationaux (Nogent), Jeunes Travailleurs en Service (Troyes), Centre de Formation pour la Coopération Internationale (St-Ilan, Yffiniac), and Auxiliaires Missions Assomption (Paris).

Institutions for pastoral and religious training include: (1) 5 theological institutes founded in 1875–77 with 25,000 students in 1972, with faculties of theology, philosophy and canon law (2 in Paris, one each in Angers, Lille and Toulouse); (2) lay theological training ,which is given through the Institut Catholique de Paris founded in 1969, Centre pour l'Intelligence de la Foi (CIF) founded in Paris in 1971, Centre d'Enseignement Théologique à Distance (CETAD) founded in Paris in 1973 for theological education by extension, Ecole Théologique du Soir in Strasbourg, and Institut de Sciences Religieuses de Nancy; (3) several advanced catechetical institutes including the Institut Supérieur de Pastorale Catéchétique (ISPC), founded in Paris in 1950; Institut de Pastorale Catéchétique de Strasbourg (CSPR), founded in 1962; Centre National de l'Enseignement Religieux in Paris, which promotes and co-ordinates catechesis; CIDAL, in L'Hôtellerie near Lisieux, which places audio-visuals at the service of catechesis; and the Association Catéchétique Nationale pour l'Audio-Visuel (ACNAV), founded in Paris in 1974; (4) advanced liturgical institutes including the Institut Supérieur de Liturgie founded in Paris in 1956, Institut de Musique Liturgique in Paris and the Centre National de Pastorale Liturgique in Paris which works for liturgical reform and co-ordinates work in liturgics in co-operation with Union Fédérale Française de Musique Sacrée (UFFMS); (5) institutions for the study of philosophy and world religions, including the Centre d'Etudes et de Recherches Philosophiques (CERP) founded by Jesuits in Paris; Centre Thomas More founded in Arbresle near Lyons in 1970 by the OP; and Institut de Sciences Sociales des Religions; (6) other institutions for research and reflection, including the Centre St-Dominique at the Convent of Arbresle near Lyons; Les Fontaines in Chantilly; Centre International d'Echanges Religieux, Culturels et Sociaux (CIDERCS) in Paris; Association Culturelle de Boquen; Centre de Plougrescant in Côtes-du-Nord; Centre International de la Ste-Baume near Marseilles; Centre Jean-Bark in Paris; Centre Philippe-Néri in Paris; and Centre Catholique des Intellectuels Français (CCIF) in Paris.

Missionary action is co-ordinated by the Comité Episcopal des Missions à l'Extérieur (CEME) in Paris, assisted by the Conseil Missionnaire National (CMN) and the Secrétariat du Comité Episcopal France-Amérique Latine. Studies and services are provided by: the Centre de Recherche Théologique Missionnaire (CRTM), founded in Paris in 1970, which is a member of the ecumenical International Association for Mission Studies based on Oslo and Aberdeen; Institut de Science et de Théologie des Religions (ISTR) in Paris; Bureau d'Information Missionnaire (BIM) in Paris; Centre de Documentation Latino-Américaine, founded in Paris in 1973; Faculté Catholique de Médecine de Lille, which provides medical orientation for missionaries; and Centre de Formation Missionnaire, founded in Versailles in 1974. The principal agencies providing aid to missions are Pontifical Missionary Works, Institut de Presse Missionnaire, Aide aux Missions d'Afrique, Oeuvre Apostolique, and Groupe d'Organismes de Coopération Missionnaire (OCM). French missionary personnel in 1970–71 included 4,869 priests, 1,500 brothers, 9,550 sisters and 800 lay persons. The principal French missionary congregations are: for men, Missions Etrangères de Paris (MEP) founded in 1658, Pères du St-Esprit (Holy Ghost fathers, CSSp) founded in 1703, Missionnaires du S-C de Jésus d'Issoudun founded in 1854, Société des Missions Africaines (SMA) founded in 1856, and Missionnaires d'Afrique or White Fathers (PB, WF) founded in 1868; and for women, Missionnaires de N-D d'Afrique or White Sisters founded in 1869, Missionnaires de N-D des Apôtres founded in 1876, Franciscaines Missionnaires de Marie founded in 1877, Missionnaires du St-Esprit founded in 1921, and St-Joseph de Cluny founded in 1798.

The Catholic educational programme is co-ordinated by the Secrétariat Général de l'Enseignement Catholique. In 1971–72 there were 7,814 Catholic primary schools, 1,011 complementary courses, 1,026 secondary schools and 642 technical schools catering for a total of 1,787,665 pupils, or 15.3% of the nation's school population. Between 10% and 15% of all students study religion outside school hours. At university level may be mentioned the Institut Catholique de Paris, Facultés Catholiques de Lyon, Université Catholique de l'Ouest in Angers, Institut Catholique de Toulouse, and Facultés Catholiques de Lille.

Social service and medical work are co-ordinated through Secours Catholique, which is a member of Caritas Internationalis in Rome and is represented in each diocese. Other agencies include the Secrétariat National des Oeuvres Catholiques Sanitaires et Sociales, and the Union Nationale Interfédérale des Oeuvres et Organismes Privés Sanitaires et Sociaux (UNIOPSS). In 1971 it was estimated that there were 668 Catholic hospitals and clinics, 32 psychiatric hospitals, 3 physiotherapy clinics, 70 preventoria, sanatoria and aeriums, 1,286 rest and convalescent homes for the sick, handicapped and aged, 54 hostels for the chronically ill, 9 rest homes for priests, 25 nursing schools, 9 schools providing specialized teaching training, 372 orphanages and children's homes, 187 establishments for retarded schoolchildren, 99 institutions for delinquents and pre-delinquents, 4 post-penal homes, 577 hostels, and 174 rest and vacation homes.

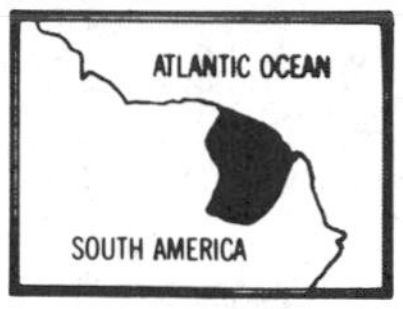


# FRENCH GUIANA

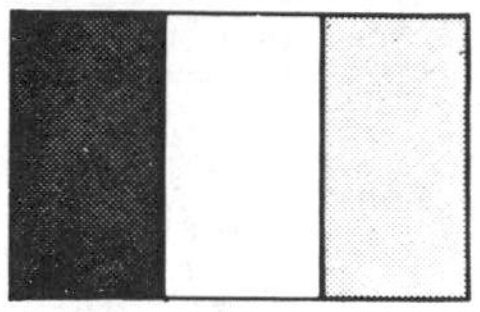

## SECULAR DATA

**STATE. Official name:** The Department of French Guiana (Le Département de la Guyane Française).
**Flag** (shown above right): That of France.
**Area:** 91,000 sq.km. (35,135 sq.miles). Agricultural land: 0.1%.
**Government:** Overseas department of France, since 1946 (1677 French possession).
**Legislature:** Council-General, 16 members.
**Official language:** French (*Français*).
**Capital:** Cayenne 24,520 (1967).
**Political divisions:** 2 Arrondissements.
**Armed forces** (1976): French.

**DEMOGRAPHY. Population:** 44,392 (census of 16.X.1967. For 1970–2000 (UN), see last row of Table 1). Population density (1975): 0.7/sq.km. (1.7/sq.mile). Under 15 years: 47%. Growth rate (1975–80): 3.27% per year. Household size: 3.4 persons.
**Major languages:** French, French Creole, Arawak, Portuguese, English, Chinese, Javanese.
**Urban dwellers** (1970): 56.0%. Urban growth rate (1950–70): 2.5% per year.
**Labour force:** 27%.

**ETHNOLINGUISTIC GROUPS:** 54.0% Creole (Mulatto) (White/Black/Asian), 16.0% Guianan White (French), 9% metropolitan French, 7.8% Black (4,000) (Bush Negro, Boni, Saramaccaner), 3.9% Brazilian (2,000) 3.3% Chinese (1,700), 3.2% Amerindian (Oyampi, Roucouyenne, Galibi, Emerillon, Arawak, Wayana, Palikur), 1.0% Indonesian (Javanese), 1.0% Lebanese, French military, Jewish.

**MONEY** (1977). **Monetary unit:** French franc (= 100 centimes); US$1 = Fr 5.00.
**National income per person:** US$1,500. Average annual family income: US$5,100.
**Inflation:** (1970–74) 6.3% per year, (1975) 14% per year (consumer price index 160).
**Cost of living in capital** (1976): Daily cost of living: US$38.

**EDUCATION.** Adult literacy: (1961) 72%, (1967) 74%. Schools: 36.

**HEALTH.** Hospitals: 4 (553 beds). Doctors: 39. Lepers: 2,900 (48.3 per 1,000).

**LITERATURE.** Periodicals: 6. Newspapers: 1 daily, 2 non-daily.

**COMMUNICATION** (per 1,000 people). Phones: 119. Radios: 96. TV sets: 59. Daily newspaper circulation: 36 copies.

TABLE 1. RELIGIOUS ADHERENTS IN FRENCH GUIANA

| Year | 1900 | | mid-1970 | | Annual change, 1970–1980 | | | | mid-1975 | | mid-1980 | | 2000 | |
|---|---|---|---|---|---|---|---|---|---|---|---|---|---|---|
| *Name* | *Adherents* | *%* | *Adherents* | *%* | *Natural* | *Conversion* | *Total* | *Rate* | *Adherents* | *%* | *Adherents* | *%* | *Adherents* | *%* |
| **Christians** | **19,500** | **92.8** | **46,680** | **91.5** | **1,830** | **–41** | **1,789** | **3.26** | **54,910** | **91.5** | **64,570** | **90.9** | **106,250** | **90.0** |
| professing | 19,500 | 92.8 | 46,680 | 91.5 | 1,830 | –41 | 1,789 | 3.26 | 54,910 | 91.5 | 64,570 | 90.9 | 106,250 | 90.0 |
| Roman Catholics | 19,500 | 92.8 | 44,680 | 87.6 | 1,750 | –41 | 1,709 | 3.25 | 52,510 | 87.5 | 61,770 | 87.0 | 101,250 | 85.8 |
| Evangelical Catholics | 0 | 0.0 | 1,350 | 2.6 | 53 | 3 | 56 | 3.54 | 1,580 | 2.6 | 1,910 | 2.7 | 3,100 | 2.6 |
| Protestants | 0 | 0.0 | 2,000 | 3.9 | 80 | 0 | 80 | 3.33 | 2,400 | 4.0 | 2,800 | 3.9 | 5,000 | 4.2 |
| nominal | 0 | 0.0 | 830 | 1.6 | 40 | 47 | 87 | 7.25 | 1,200 | 2.0 | 1,700 | 2.4 | 5,900 | 5.0 |
| affiliated | 19,500 | 92.8 | 45,850 | 89.9 | 1,790 | –88 | 1,702 | 3.17 | 53,710 | 89.5 | 62,870 | 88.5 | 100,350 | 85.0 |
| total practising | 15,600 | *80* | 27,510 | *60* | 1,074 | –53 | 1,021 | 3.17 | 32,230 | *60* | 37,720 | *60* | 55,200 | *55* |
| non-practising | 3,900 | *20* | 18,340 | *40* | 716 | –35 | 681 | 3.17 | 21,480 | *40* | 25,150 | *40* | 45,150 | *45* |
| Roman Catholics | 19,500 | 92.8 | 42,500 | 83.3 | 1,658 | –92 | 1,566 | 3.15 | 49,730 | 82.9 | 58,160 | 81.9 | 92,250 | 78.2 |
| Protestants | 0 | 0.0 | 3,000 | 5.9 | 118 | 2 | 120 | 3.38 | 3,550 | 5.9 | 4,200 | 5.9 | 7,000 | 5.9 |
| Evangelicals | 0 | 0.0 | 1,000 | 2.0 | 40 | 0 | 40 | 3.33 | 1,200 | 2.0 | 1,400 | 2.0 | 2,300 | 1.9 |
| Marginal Protestants | 0 | 0.0 | 300 | 0.6 | 12 | 2 | 14 | 3.78 | 370 | 0.6 | 440 | 0.6 | 1,000 | 0.8 |
| Anglicans | 0 | 0.0 | 50 | 0.1 | 2 | 0 | 2 | 3.33 | 60 | 0.1 | 70 | 0.1 | 100 | 0.1 |
| Tribal religionists | 1,000 | 4.8 | 1,250 | 2.5 | 40 | –60 | –20 | –1.74 | 1,150 | 1.9 | 1,050 | 1.5 | 700 | 0.6 |
| Afro-American spiritists | 400 | 2.0 | 1,000 | 2.0 | 39 | 1 | 40 | 3.39 | 1,180 | 2.0 | 1,400 | 2.0 | 2,000 | 1.7 |
| Chinese folk-religionists | 0 | 0.0 | 700 | 1.4 | 27 | –7 | 20 | 2.50 | 800 | 1.3 | 900 | 1.3 | 1,000 | 0.8 |
| Muslims | 100 | 0.5 | 500 | 1.0 | 20 | 0 | 20 | 3.33 | 590 | 1.0 | 700 | 1.0 | 1,000 | 0.8 |
| Non-religious | 0 | 0.0 | 500 | 1.0 | 30 | 100 | 130 | 14.44 | 900 | 1.5 | 1,800 | 2.5 | 5,900 | 5.0 |
| Baha'is | 0 | 0.0 | 300 | 0.6 | 13 | 7 | 20 | 5.00 | 400 | 0.7 | 500 | 0.7 | 1,000 | 0.8 |
| Jews | 0 | 0.0 | 20 | 0.0 | 1 | 0 | 1 | 3.33 | 20 | 0.0 | 30 | 0.0 | 50 | 0.0 |
| Other religionists | 0 | 0.0 | 50 | 0.1 | 0 | 0 | 0 | 0.00 | 50 | 0.1 | 50 | 0.1 | 100 | 0.1 |
| **Country's population** | **21,000** | **100.0** | **51,000** | **100.0** | **2,000** | **0** | **2,000** | **3.33** | **60,000** | **100.0** | **71,000** | **100.0** | **118,000** | **100.0** |

COLUMNS, ROWS. For meanings and definitions, see Codebook (Part 6). Note that, by definition, total 'Christians' = professing + crypto-Christians, which also = affiliated + nominal Christians. Percentages may not always total exactly, due to rounding.

NOTES ON RELIGIONS
AFRO-AMERICAN SPIRITISTS. Black and Mulatto followers of Vodoun, Obeah, Boni and Bush Negro syncretistic cults, including Brazilians. Since around the year 1800 there have been isolated Negro spirit-possession cults in the interior.
BAHA'IS. In 2 local spiritual assemblies (1973).
COUNTRY'S POPULATION. In 1976 the government of France began a massive immigration and colonization scheme designed to bring in at least 30,000 new French colonists from France (farmers, forestry workers, investors et alii).
EVANGELICAL CATHOLICS. This term is used here to describe persons who are affiliated to churches termed by the state Evangélique (Protestant, marginal Protestant or Anglican churches), but who are regarded by state and society as, or who profess publicly to be, Roman Catholics.
MUSLIMS. Javanese and Lebanese Arabs.
NON-RELIGIOUS. French.
OTHER RELIGIONISTS. Including Rosicrucians (1 AMORC centre).
TRIBAL RELIGIONISTS. Of the 1,650 lowland or jungle Amerindians in the interior, a large proportion are animists, especially among the Oyampi, Cussaris and Emerillon.

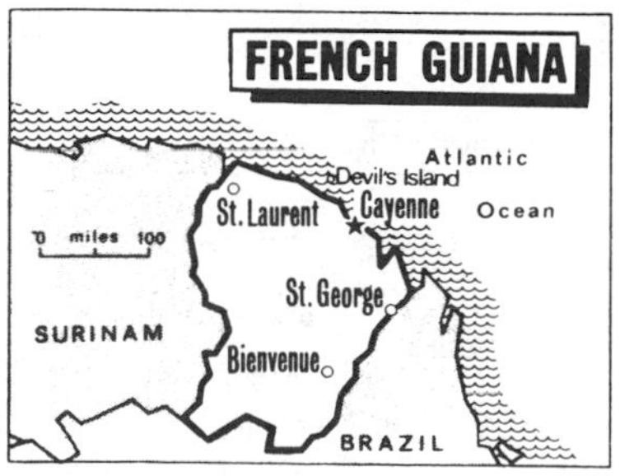


**NON-CHRISTIAN RELIGIONS.** Although the population of French Guiana is overwhelmingly Catholic, there is a residue of adherents to traditional religions among the Oyampi, Cussaris and Emerillon Indians, in addition to a few small communities from other world religions.

## CHRISTIANITY

CATHOLIC CHURCH. France began to colonize Guiana in 1635, and the Catholic Church gained an early foothold which it has never relinquished. The great majority of Catholics are either people born in Guiana (Whites, Mulattoes, and Amerindians), or immigrant technicians and labourers from France, the Antilles and Brazil, primarily for work at the space base of Kourou. There are 24 parishes served by Holy Ghost priests and 3 congregations of sisters. No Guianian had been ordained priest until 1971.

OTHER CHURCHES. Protestant work has never been strong in Guiana. The Protestant Church (Eglise Evangélique) consists of chaplaincies to the military

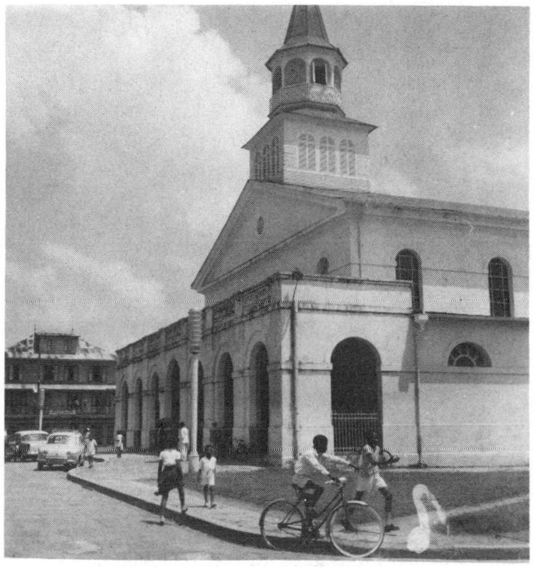

**Eglise Catholique, Diocèse de Cayenne.** Cathedral in Cayenne, with Chinese shops to left.

and civilian French communities. Adventists have a similar constituency, followed by the Assemblies of God and Brethren, the latter concentrating its attention on radio and literature distribution. The Anglican Church serves primarily the European community.

**CHURCH AND STATE.** Since French Guiana is an overseas province of France, its laws relating to religious freedom are the same as those for metropolitan France.

**BROADCASTING.** The national network Radio Cayenne has a Catholic religious programme every Friday.

TABLE 2. ORGANIZED CHURCHES AND DENOMINATIONS IN FRENCH GUIANA

| Official name 1 | Begun 2 | Type 3 | Counc 4 | Congs 5 | Adults 6 | Affiliated 7 | Names, notes, and other statistics (see Codebook) 8 |
|---|---|---|---|---|---|---|---|
| Assemblées de Dieu | 1968 | P Pe2 | ZF... | 5 | 240 | 500 | *Assemblies of God.* Classical Pentecostals (2-stage). M=AoG(USA). 5n,2f. |
| Courants de Puissance | | P Pe4 | x.... | | 100 | 200 | *Currents of Power.* Led by Dutch missionaries. HQ Saint-Laurent-du-Maroni. |
| Eglise Adventiste du Septième Jour | 1940 | P Adv | x.... | 10 | 464 | 1,000 | *SDA. Seventh-day Adventists. FG Mission.* 1n,13mw,G=10.5%pa,8t(477),W=80%,33Y,20z. |
| Eglise Anglicane (D Guyana) | | A ACa | awMR. | 1 | 30 | 50 | In Ch of the Province of the West Indies. Europeans, some Blacks. |
| **Eglise Catholique: D Cayenne** | 1604 | R Lat | PzNMr | 24 | 22,500 | 42,500 | M=CSSp. 18% White. C=1+0+3. 1n,29x,1m,89w,P=28%,1400Yy,240z. |
| Eglise Evangélique | | P Ref | ..... | 5 | 500 | 1,000 | French military and civilian chaplaincies especially to Kourou space base. 1x. |
| Frères Larges Mission Evangélique | c1905 | P CBr | x.... | 6 | 150 | 300 | *Open Brethren.* Begun by a Barbadian. M=CMML(UK,USA,Switz). Radio, literature. 5f. |
| Témoins de Jéhovah | c1945 | M Jeh | x.... | 1 | 149 | 300 | *Jehovah's Witnesses.* Active witnessing under way by 1947. 24Y. |
| **Total affiliated (mid-1970)** | | | | **54** | **24,133** | **45,850** | **Total denominations (1970) . . . 8.** |
| **Total affiliated (mid-1975)** | | | | **59** | **28,270** | **54,710** | **Total denominations (1975) . . . 8.** |
| **Total affiliated (mid-1980)** | | | | **67** | **33,090** | **62,870** | **Total denominations (1980) . . . 9.** |

NOTES ON TABLE ABOVE
COLUMNS: for meanings and CODES (cols. 1, 3, 4, 8): see Codebook (Part 6). Column 1: **Boldface type** = church with over 10% of country's affiliated Christians.
NATIONAL COUNCILS (Column 4, 5th letter).
r = member, Conférence Episcopale de France (Episcopal Conference of France).

PEOPLES (ethnolinguistic). Christians: 59.0% Creole (Mulatto), 27.3% French (17.6% Guianan White, 9.7% metropolitan French (civilian and military)), 7.8% Black, 3.9% Brazilian, 1.0% Chinese, 0.2% Amerindian.

COUNTRY-WIDE TOTALS
EVANGELIZATION (see Part 5). 1900: 97%. 1970: 99%. 1980: 100%.
FOREIGN MISSIONARIES AND PERSONNEL (aliens from abroad) (1973). Total 142. *From Western world.* 126: 118 Roman Catholics, 8 Protestants (4 in 2 USA societies, 3 in 1 Switzerland society, 1 in 1 Netherlands society). *From Third World.* 16: about 9 Roman Catholics from Guadeloupe and Martinique, about 7 Protestants from Jamaica.
INSTITUTIONS (church-operated) (1973). Total 10, including 2 higher schools, 7 medical centres (hospitals).
PERIODICALS. 2 titles.
PERSONNEL. About 211 (69 national, 142 foreign).
SCRIPTURE DISTRIBUTION (1975). Annual totals: 400 Bibles (subsidized), 150 NTs (subsidized), 2,800 UBS portions, 16,000 UBS selections.
SERVICE AGENCIES. About 12, including AHIG, CLC, CTCG, CV/AV.

ADDITIONAL DATA ON CHURCHES
EGLISE CATHOLIQUE. Catholic Church. The diocese is a suffragan of M Fort-de-France & St-Pierre (Martinique). Most Catholics live in Cayenne. *Annual baptisms.* (1972) 97.1% infant, 2.9% adult. *Priests.* The first Guianan priest was ordained in 1971. Expatriate priests are all from metropolitan France. *Brothers.* One indigenous. *Sisters.* 6 born in Guiana, the rest in France (expatriates). *Seminarians* (1972). 2, studying in France. *Catechists.* Total (1969) 52. *Indigenous religious congregations.* None. *Foreign religious congregations.* Priests: CSSp. Sisters: St-Joseph de Cluny, St-Paul de Chartres, Franciscaines de Marie. *Catholic organizations.* The diocese is a member of the Episcopal Conference of France (Conférence Episcopale de France). The ecclesiastical province of Martinique-Guadeloupe-French Guiana has been a member with consultative voice of the Antilles Episcopal Conference since February 1971. There is a Presbyteral Council, but no organizations of religious personnel. The principal lay movements, founded mostly at Cayenne, are CV/AV, Scoutisme, Action Catholique, and Légion de Marie.
The Holy See has no diplomatic relations with French Guiana. It is represented to the Catholic hierarchy by an apostolic delegate based in Port-au-Prince, Haiti.
In addition to 6 primary schools and one technical school, the church's Association of Indian Men of Guiana sponsors 8 hostels for young Amerindians of both sexes aimed at facilitating their integration into school and social life. The church also administers 2 hospitals, 3 dispensaries, one sanatorium, one maternity hospital and 3 orphanages.

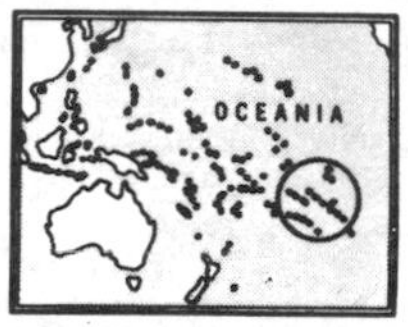


# FRENCH POLYNESIA

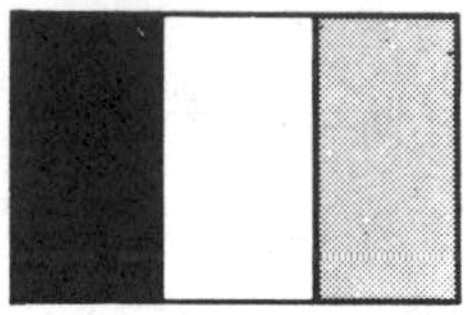

## SECULAR DATA

**STATE. Official name:** The Territory of French Polynesia (Le Territoire de la Polynésie Française).
**Flag** (shown above right): That of France.
**Area:** 4,000 sq.km. (1,544 sq.miles). Description: Nearly 130 islands. Agricultural land: 23.5%.
**Government:** Overseas territory of France, since 1946 (1842 French protectorate, 1880 French colony).
**Legislature:** Government Council, 5 members. Territorial Assembly, 30 members.
**Official language:** French (*Français*).
**Capital:** Papeete 36,780 (1971).
**Political divisions:** 5 Circonscriptions.
**Armed forces** (1976): French.

**DEMOGRAPHY. Population:** 119,168 (census of 8.II.1971. For 1970–2000 (UN), see last row of Table 1). Population density (1975): 32/sq.km. (83/sq.mile). Under 15 years: 48%. Growth rate (1975–80): 3.27% per year (births 4.11%, deaths −0.91%, immigrants 0.07%). Life expectancy (1975–80): 60.3 years. Household size: 5.0 persons.
**Major languages:** Tahitian, French, Chinese.
**Urban dwellers** (1970): 28.2%. Urban growth rate (1950–70): 4.0% per year.
**Labour force:** 33%.
**Tourists** (1970): 48,803. (1972) 111,300.

**ETHNOLINGUISTIC GROUPS:** 43.0% Tahitian, 20.0% Euronesian (European/Polynesian), 12.0% Chinese (Hakka), 9.0% Tuamotuan, 5.0% French, 5.0% Marquesan, 5.0% Tubuaian, 1.0% Mangarevan.

**MONEY** (1977). **Monetary unit:** CFP franc (= 100 centimes); US$1 = CFPF 91.00.
**National income per person:** US$3,000. Average annual family income: US$15,000.
**Inflation:** (1970–74) 8.5% per year, (1975) 19% per year (consumer price index 165).
**Cost of living in capital** (1976): Daily cost of living: US$41.

**EDUCATION.** Adult literacy: (1962) 95%. Schools: 174 (160 primary, 14 secondary).

**HEALTH.** Hospitals: 31 (961 beds). Doctors: 62. Lepers: 1,170 (9.1 per 1,000). Blind: 96. Psychotics: 800.

**LITERATURE.** Periodicals: 14. Newspapers: 3 dailies.

**COMMUNICATION** (per 1,000 people). Phones: 98. Radios: 360. TV sets: 130. Daily newspaper circulation: 94 copies.

TABLE 1. RELIGIOUS ADHERENTS IN FRENCH POLYNESIA

| Year | 1900 | | mid-1970 | | Annual change, 1970–1980 | | | | mid-1975 | | mid-1980 | | 2000 | |
|---|---|---|---|---|---|---|---|---|---|---|---|---|---|---|
| *Name* | *Adherents* | *%* | *Adherents* | *%* | *Natural* | *Conversion* | *Total* | *Rate* | *Adherents* | *%* | *Adherents* | *%* | *Adherents* | *%* |
| **Christians** | **36,700** | **99.2** | **103,200** | **94.7** | **3,967** | **−67** | **3,900** | **3.23** | **120,900** | **94.5** | **142,200** | **94.2** | **250,200** | **93.0** |
| professing | 36,700 | 99.2 | 103,200 | 94.7 | 3,967 | −67 | 3,900 | 3.23 | 120,900 | 94.5 | 142,200 | 94.2 | 250,200 | 93.0 |
| Protestants | 28,550 | 77.2 | 57,650 | 52.9 | 2,089 | −824 | 1,265 | 1.99 | 63,680 | 49.8 | 70,300 | 46.6 | 107,100 | 34.8 |
| Roman Catholics | 7,400 | 20.0 | 37,700 | 34.6 | 1,554 | 626 | 2,180 | 4.60 | 47,360 | 37.0 | 59,500 | 39.4 | 115,700 | 39.0 |
| Marginal Protestants | 750 | 2.0 | 7,200 | 6.6 | 294 | 106 | 400 | 4.46 | 8,960 | 7.0 | 11,200 | 7.4 | 24,200 | 9.0 |
| Polynesian indigenous | 0 | 0.0 | 650 | 0.6 | 30 | 25 | 55 | 6.11 | 900 | 0.7 | 1,200 | 0.8 | 3,200 | 1.2 |
| nominal | 2,200 | 6.0 | 10,406 | 9.5 | 411 | 58 | 469 | 3.75 | 12,520 | 9.8 | 15,100 | 10.0 | 31,800 | 11.8 |
| affiliated | 34,500 | 93.2 | 92,794 | 85.1 | 3,556 | −125 | 3,431 | 3.17 | 108,380 | 84.7 | 127,100 | 84.2 | 218,400 | 81.2 |
| total practising | 27,600 | *80* | 60,320 | *65* | 2,312 | −83 | 2,229 | 3.16 | 70,450 | *65* | 82,610 | *65* | 131,000 | *60* |
| non-practising | 6,900 | *20* | 32,480 | *35* | 1,244 | −42 | 1,202 | 3.17 | 37,930 | *35* | 44,490 | *35* | 87,400 | *40* |
| Protestants | 26,650 | 72.0 | 47,000 | 43.1 | 1,671 | −871 | 800 | 1.57 | 50,900 | 39.8 | 55,000 | 36.4 | 75,300 | 28.0 |
| Evangelicals | 23,000 | 62.2 | 12,400 | 11.4 | 463 | −103 | 360 | 2.55 | 14,100 | 11.0 | 16,000 | 10.6 | 25,500 | 9.5 |
| Roman Catholics | 7,000 | 19.0 | 36,058 | 33.1 | 1,486 | 599 | 2,085 | 4.60 | 45,300 | 35.4 | 56,900 | 37.7 | 110,300 | 41.0 |
| Marginal Protestants | 850 | 2.3 | 7,936 | 7.3 | 327 | 129 | 456 | 4.57 | 9,980 | 7.8 | 12,500 | 8.3 | 26,900 | 10.0 |
| Polynesian indigenous | 0 | 0.0 | 1,800 | 1.6 | 72 | 18 | 90 | 4.09 | 2,200 | 1.7 | 2,700 | 1.8 | 5,900 | 2.2 |
| Non-religious | 0 | 0.0 | 4,800 | 4.4 | 196 | 78 | 274 | 4.59 | 5,970 | 4.7 | 7,540 | 5.0 | 17,200 | 6.4 |
| Chinese folk-religionists | 200 | 0.6 | 400 | 0.4 | 13 | −13 | 0 | 0.00 | 400 | 0.3 | 400 | 0.3 | 200 | 0.1 |
| Buddhists | 100 | 0.3 | 300 | 0.3 | 11 | −7 | 4 | 1.25 | 320 | 0.2 | 340 | 0.2 | 300 | 0.1 |
| Baha'is | 0 | 0.0 | 200 | 0.2 | 9 | 7 | 16 | 5.71 | 280 | 0.2 | 360 | 0.2 | 800 | 0.3 |
| Other religionists | 0 | 0.0 | 100 | 0.1 | 4 | 2 | 6 | 4.62 | 130 | 0.1 | 160 | 0.1 | 300 | 0.1 |
| **Country's population** | **37,000** | **100.0** | **109,000** | **100.0** | **4,200** | **0** | **4,200** | **3.28** | **128,000** | **100.0** | **151,000** | **100.0** | **269,000** | **100.0** |

COLUMNS, ROWS. For meanings and definitions, see Codebook (Part 6). Note that, by definition, total 'Christians' = professing + crypto-Christians, which also = affiliated + nominal Christians. Percentages may not always total exactly, due to rounding.
CENSUSES. **10.VI.1946:** 57.7% Protestants, 24.0% Roman Catholics, 12.4% Chinese non-religious and folk-religionists, 5.3% marginal Protestants, 0.6% Buddhists. **17.IX.1951:** 55.9% Protestants, 24.2% Roman Catholics, 14.1% Chinese non-religious, folk-religionists and Buddhists, 5.1% marginal Protestants, 0.5% other religionists. **9.XI.1962:** 56.5% Protestants, 29.7% Roman Catholics, 6.3% non-religious, 6.3% marginal Protestants, 0.6% Polynesian/Chinese indigenous, 0.3% Chinese folk-religionists, 0.3% Buddhists. **8.II.1971:** 52.9% Protestants, 34.6% Roman Catholics, 6.6% marginal Protestants (3.2% Mormons, 2.9% Sanitos, 0.4% Jehovah's Witnesses), 4.6% non-religious, 0.7% Chinese folk-religionists and Buddhists, 0.6% Polynesian/Chinese indigenous.

NOTES ON RELIGIONS
BAHA'IS. Begun in 1955. In 2 local spiritual assemblies (1973).
BUDDHISTS. Chinese. The first Chinese workers arrived in 1865. Most are Hakkas from southern China.
NON-RELIGIOUS. Mainly Chinese youth who have abandoned their family religion, also French.
OTHER RELIGIONISTS. Including Rosicrucians (1 AMORC centre on Tahiti).
POLYNESIAN INDIGENOUS. In 3 denominations in 1970 (see Table 2).

**NON-CHRISTIAN RELIGIONS. Tribal religion,** now virtually without followers, includes belief in a supreme being, Ta'aroa, who is recognized as creator, and an extensive pantheon of divinities (Oro, Tane, Ro'o, Tu) who preside over local cults, occupational pursuits and such natural phenomena as the sea, thunder and wind. The most important of these is Oro, who is the divinity of war and patron of the Ariori society, a religious cult group noted for its erotic dances and songs. Other elements include ancestral veneration, divination, spirit possession and belief in the evil activity of sorcerers.

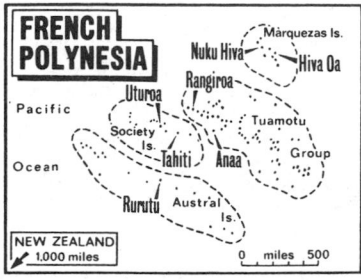

Traditional religion has largely disappeared as a separate entity although traditional concepts continue to influence the Polynesian expression of Christianity.

**Chinese folk religion,** including Buddhism and Confucianism, exists among the Chinese inhabiting Papeete. A growing number of Chinese youth however have abandoned their family religion.

**Eglise Evangélique de Polynésie Française.** *Left.* Service in Siloama parish led by Malagasy secretary-general of CEVAA. *Right.* Christmas 1974 baptism service in Siloama parish.

# CHRISTIANITY.
Originally discovered by the British and Spanish, these islands alternated under their control during the 17th and 18th centuries, finally coming under French rule during the 19th century. Protestant and Catholic dominance shifted accordingly with the colonial power.

PROTESTANT CHURCHES. The Evangelical Church of Polynesia owes its origin to the missionary activity of 3 societies (London Mission, Basel Mission, Paris Mission) from as early as 1797, and became autonomous in 1963. It is still the largest denomination although others are growing more rapidly at the present time. Following a schism in 1968, the Chinese community within the Evangelical Church was reduced to about 200. Theological training has been provided for students at both Montpelier, France, and Yaoundé, Cameroon, in Africa.

Seventh-day Adventists first came to Tahiti in 1892. The French Polynesia Mission, organized in 1916, is part of the Central Pacific Union Mission. The Adventist community grew from 1,686 in 1962 to 2,000 in 1970.

Protestantism is strongest in the Society and Austral Islands. In 1971, 2,000 pupils were enrolled in Protestant schools.

CATHOLIC CHURCH. The first Catholic efforts to evangelize the islands began during 1659–1667. An attempt was made in 1772 by Franciscans from Peru, followed by French priests in the Gambier Islands in 1831, the Marquesas in 1838, Tahiti in 1842 and Tuamotu in 1849.

Catholicism has grown rapidly in recent years, having its greatest strength in the Gambier and Marquesas Islands. The Rotatoria Movement (Living Rosary) of Pauline Jaricot is very strong having enlisted the majority of the Catholic population in its membership. The Catholic Church has 84 parishes and is served by SSCC priests, FICP brothers and 3 congregations of sisters.

The church has recently held a synod which held 2 important sessions: in July 1970 (with 70% of its members laity) and September 1973.

MARGINAL CHURCHES. The Mormon church is increasing rapidly, having grown from 2,330 professing adherents in the 1962 census to 4,800 affiliated in 1970. During the same period Jehovah's Witnesses expanded their membership from 152 to 464. A large schism from the Mormons is the Reorganized Church of Jesus Christ of Latter-day Saints, known as Kanito or Sanito (Saints); beginning in the Tuamotu archipelago in 1884, it later spread throughout the territory. It has nativistic tendencies, giving prominence to the magical powers of its priests and the evocation of the dead.

INDIGENOUS CHURCHES. There has been a history of independent movements. From 1823–35 the Mamaia sect flourished, begun by an LMS deacon (elder) who announced he was Jesus Christ or his immediate representative, come to evict all Whites. Three groups have split from the Evangelical Church since World War II: Keretitiano in 1950, the Autonomous Church in 1954 and the Polynesian Pentecostal Churches in 1968. The latter group is entirely Chinese.

**Eglises Pentecostales Polynésiennes.** Opening service of Chinese congregation.

**CHURCH AND STATE.** Relations between church and state in French Polynesia are similar to those in metropolitan France. However, the separation of church and state does not prevent government from providing funds for specific projects, including their recent financial grant towards the building of a girls' hostel belonging to the Evangelical Church in Papeete.

**INTERDENOMINATIONAL ORGANIZATIONS.** There is no Christian council, but the Evangelical Church is represented on the continuation committee of the Pacific Conference of Churches as well as being a member of the WCC. Relations between the Evangelical and Catholic churches are improving as evidenced by their current joint participation in ceremonies related to the Week of Prayer for Christian Unity.

**BROADCASTING.** A half-hour is allocated weekly by Radio-Tahiti for religious broadcasts, 15 minutes each in French and Tahitian, and a 15-minute religious TV Special is presented on Sunday evenings. For Catholics, no UNDA-related association has yet been formed.

**BIBLIOGRAPHY**
*Le Tahiti catholique.* P. O'Reilly. Paris: Nouvelles Editions Latines, 1970. 32p.
*Protestant church at Tahiti.* D. Mauer. Paris: Nouvelles Editions Latines, 1970. 35p.
'The Tahitian web', chapter 1 in A. R. Tippett, *People movements in Southern Polynesia* (Chicago: Moody Press, 1971), p. 9–39.

18th-century wooden representation of Tahitian deity Tangaroa, in act of creating other gods and man. Traditional religion now has no organization or followers, but its influence remains.

TABLE 2.    ORGANIZED CHURCHES AND DENOMINATIONS IN FRENCH POLYNESIA

| Official name 1 | Begun 2 | Type 3 | Counc 4 | Congs 5 | Adults 6 | Affiliated 7 | Names, notes, and other statistics (see Codebook) 8 |
|---|---|---|---|---|---|---|---|
| Christianisme | 1950 | I Ref | •••• | 1 | 100 | 300 | *Keretitiano. Christianity.* Schism of EEPF pastor and his parish. Declining. |
| Eglise Adventiste du Septième Jour | 1892 | P Adv | x•••• | 9 | 1,147 | 2,000 | *SDA. Seventh-day Adventists. FP Mission.* Central Pacific UM. 7nx,29t(1616),92Y. |
| Eglise Autonome | 1954 | I Ref | •••• | | 300 | 500 | *Autonomous Church.* Founded by pastor expelled from EEPF. Now very active. |
| Eglise Catholique de Polynésie Française | 1659 | R Lat | P.PY. | 84 | 18,700 | 36,058 | On Gambier, Marquesas. 10% Chinese. C=1+1+3. 200z    4n,38x,37m,59w,1417Yy. |
| M   Papeete | 1848 | R Lat | Psscc | 72 | 16,100 | 31,000 | Excludes Marquesas. 2,000 Catholics are Chinese. P=23%.    4    31    35    52    1226 |
| D   Taiohae (Tefenuaenata) | 1848 | R Lat | Psscc | 12 | 2,600 | 5,058 | Covers Marquesas Islands in extreme north. P=60%.    0    7    2    7    191 |
| E de JC des Saints des Derniers Jours | 1844 | M LdS | x•••• | | 3,000 | 4,836 | *Latter-day Saints. Mormons.* M=CJCLdS(USA). Only in Papeete. 70f,G=2.4%pa. |
| Eglise Evangélique de Polynésie Française | 1797 | P Ref | .WP.. | 79 | 23,000 | 45,000 | *EEPF.* M=LMS,Basel M,PEMS(CEVAA)(France). A=1963. 200 Chinese. 50n,5x,20f,1s. |
| Eglise Sanito (Saints) | 1884 | M LdS | x•••• | | 1,400 | 2,800 | *Sanitos, Kanitos (Saints).* M=Reorganized Ch of JC of LdS(USA). On Tuamotu. |
| Eglises Pentecostales Polynésiennes | 1968 | I pen | •••• | | 600 | 1,000 | *Polynesian Pentecostal Chs.* Schism of all EEPF Tahitians of Chinese descent. |
| Témoins de Jéhovah | 1932 | M Jeh | x•••• | 2 | 165 | 300 | *Jehovah's Witnesses. Watch Tower.* 1970, international assembly held. 17Y. |
| | | | | | | | |
| Total affiliated (mid-1970) | | | | 220 | 48,412 | 92,794 | Total denominations (1970) . . .    9. |
| Total affiliated (mid-1975) | | | | 230 | 56,540 | 108,380 | Total denominations (1975) . . .    9. |
| Total affiliated (mid-1980) | | | | 240 | 66,300 | 127,100 | Total denominations (1980) . . .    10. |

**NOTES ON TABLE ABOVE**
COLUMNS: for meanings and CODES (cols. 1, 3, 4, 8): see Codebook (Part 6). Column 1: **Boldface type** = church with over 10% of country's affiliated Christians.

**PEOPLES** (ethnolinguistic). Christians: 47.5% Tahitian, 23.3% Euronesian, 9.0% Tuamotuan, 5.0% French, 5.0% Marquesan, 5.0% Tubuaian, 3.5% Chinese (Hakka), 1.0% Mangarevan.

**COUNTRY-WIDE TOTALS**
EVANGELIZATION (see Part 5). 1900: 100%. 1970: 100%. 1980: 100%.
FOREIGN MISSIONARIES AND PERSONNEL (aliens from

abroad) (1973). Total 205. *From Western world.* 181: about 100 Roman Catholics, about 60 marginal Protestants (Mormons from USA, New Zealand), 21 Protestants (12 in 1 France society, 9 in 1 Switzerland society). *From Communist world.* About 3 Roman Catholics (2 from Yugoslavia, 1 Poland). *From Third World.* 21: about 10 marginal Protestants (Mormons from Samoa et alia), 10 Roman Catholics, 1 Protestant.
INSTITUTIONS (church-operated) (1973). Total 18, including 15 higher schools, 1 seminary (Protestant), 1 study centre.
PERIODICALS. About 10 titles (6 SDA, 1 LdS).
PERSONNEL. About 322 (117 national, 205 foreign).
RELIGIOUS LIBRARIES. 2.
SCRIPTURE DISTRIBUTION (1975). Annual totals: 2,600 Bibles (62% subsidized, 38% commercial), 2,000 NTs (subsidized), 4,000 UBS portions, 5,000 UBS selections. *Translations completed.*

Portion: 2 languages since 1818. NT: Tahitian in 1829, Bible in 1838.
SERVICE AGENCIES. About 12, including CV/AV, UCJG (YMCA).

### ADDITIONAL DATA ON CHURCHES
EGLISE CATHOLIQUE. *Annual baptisms.* (1972) 90.0% infant, 10.0% adult. *Catechists.* In 1975, 28, with 105 voluntary catechists. *Local religious congregations.* Sisters: Filles de Jésus-Sauveur (2 professed, in 1974). *Foreign religious congregations.* Priests: SSCC. Brothers: FICP. Sisters: St-Joseph de Cluny, Notre-Dame des Anges (Canada), Bon Pasteur d'Angers.
*Catholic organizations.* The bishops of French Polynesia are members of the Bishops' Conference of the Pacific (Conférence des Evêques du Pacifique, CEPAC). There are no organizations

of priests or religious personnel, but several lay groups are active: Scouts and Guides, CV/AV, Eucharistic Movement of Youth (Mouvement Eucharistique des Jeunes) and Legion of Mary (Légion de Marie).
The territory has no diplomatic relations with the Holy See, but the latter is represented to the hierarchy by the Apostolic Delegation to New Zealand and the Islands of the Pacific, based in Wellington, New Zealand.
In 1973 the Catholic Church was responsible for 11 primary schools with 6,700 pupils, and 10 higher schools with 3,689 pupils. Children of the influential Chinese minority in Papeete also frequent Catholic schools, and a Polynesian priest of Chinese background provides pastoral care for them.

---

# French Southern & Antarctic Territories

## SECULAR DATA

**STATE. Official name:** French Southern and Antarctic Territories (Les Terres Australes et Antarctiques Françaises, TAAF).
**Flag** (shown above right): That of France.
**Area:** 7,557 sq.km. (2,918 sq.miles). **Description:** 2 islands, 2 archipelagos, 1 continental area (Terre Adélie). Agricultural land: 0.0%.

**Government:** Overseas territories of France, created 1955.
**Official language:** French (*Français*).
**Capital:** Port aux Français, Kerguélen.
**Armed forces** (1976): French military camp on Kerguélen.

**DEMOGRAPHY. Population:** 183 (census of 1.VII.1975. For 1970–2000 (UN), see last row of Table 1). Population density (1975): 0/sq.km. Under 15 years: 0%. Growth rate (1975–80): 0% per year. Household size: 2 persons.

**Major language:** French.

**ETHNOLINGUISTIC GROUPS:** 90% French, 9% other European.

**MONEY** (1977). **Monetary unit:** French franc (= 100 centimes).

**EDUCATION.** Adult literacy: 100%.

TABLE 1.    RELIGIOUS ADHERENTS IN THE FRENCH SOUTHERN & ANTARCTIC TERRITORIES

| Year | 1900 | | mid-1970 | | Annual change, 1970–1980 | | | | mid-1975 | | mid-1980 | | 2000 | |
|------|---------|-----|----------|------|---------|------------|-------|------|----------|------|----------|------|----------|-------|
| *Name* | Adherents | % | Adherents | % | Natural | Conversion | Total | Rate | Adherents | % | Adherents | % | Adherents | % |
| **Christians** | 0 | 0.0 | 100 | 58.8 | 0 | 0 | 0 | 0.00 | 100 | 58.8 | 100 | 58.8 | 100 | 33.3 |
| professing | 0 | 0.0 | 100 | 58.8 | 0 | 0 | 0 | 0.00 | 100 | 58.8 | 100 | 58.8 | 100 | 33.3 |
| nominal | 0 | 0.0 | 100 | 58.8 | 0 | 0 | 0 | 0.00 | 100 | 58.8 | 100 | 58.8 | 100 | 33.3 |
| Roman Catholics | 0 | 0.0 | 100 | 58.8 | 0 | 0 | 0 | 0.00 | 100 | 58.8 | 100 | 58.8 | 100 | 33.3 |
| **Non-religious** | 0 | 0.0 | 70 | 41.2 | 0 | 0 | 0 | 0.00 | 70 | 41.2 | 70 | 41.2 | 200 | 66.7 |
| **Country's population** | 0 | 100.0 | 170 | 100.0 | 0 | 0 | 0 | 0.00 | 170 | 100.0 | 170 | 100.0 | 300 | 100.0 |

COLUMNS, ROWS. For meanings and definitions, see Codebook (Part 6). Note that, by definition, total 'Christians' =

professing + crypto-Christians, which also = affiliated + nominal Christians. Percentages may not always total exactly,

due to rounding.
CHRISTIANS. Mostly Roman Catholics.

The TAAF consists of 2 archipelagos (Kerguelen and Crozet), 2 islands (St Paul and New Amsterdam) and an area situated on the Antarctic continent (Terre Adélie). All are located in the South Indian Ocean. Kerguelen Archipelago was discovered in 1772 and the territory was created as an administrative unit in 1955. Activities include research and meteorological stations, 2 hospitals and a military camp.

**CHRISTIANITY.** The population consists entirely of male French scientific and military personnel (185 in 1974) serving one-year terms in 3 permanent sub-antarctic bases. The majority are Roman Catholics, and the TAAF is, in principle, dependent on the archdiocese of Paris. However, there are no organized churches in the territories.

**CHURCH AND STATE.** The state guarantee of freedom of religion is the same as in metropolitan France.

30th anniversary stamp commemorating 1947-48 French Polar Expeditions. Inhabitants are entirely French and other scientists.

---

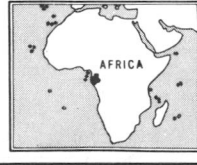

# GABON

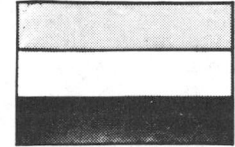

## SECULAR DATA

**STATE. Official name:** The Gabonese Republic (La République Gabonaise). Adjective of nationality: Gabonese (gabonais).
**Flag** (shown above right): Stripes of green (top), yellow, and blue (bottom).
**Area:** 267,667 sq.km. (103,347 sq.miles). Agricultural land: 18.5%.
**Government:** One-party state, since 1968 (1850 French colony, 1910 in French Equatorial Africa, 1960 Independence as republic).
**Legislature:** National Assembly, 47 members.
**Official language:** French (*Français*).
**Capital:** Libreville 110,000 (1974).
**Armed forces** (1976): Total 1,050 regular: army 900, air force 150.
**Foreign forces** (1978): 500 French troops.

**DEMOGRAPHY. Population:** 448,564 (census of 8.X.1960–V.1961. For 1970–2000 (UN), see last row of Table 1). Population density (1975): 2/sq.km. (5/sq.mile). Under 15 years: 34%. Growth rate (1975–80): 0.76% per year (births 2.79%, deaths −2.02%). Life expectancy (1975–80): 43.5 years. Household size: 4.9 persons.
**Major languages:** Bulu Fang, French, Eshira, Bandjabi, Kota, and over 40 tribal languages.
**Urban dwellers** (1970): 19.2%. Urban growth rate (1950–70): 5.6% per year.
**Labour force:** 47%.
**Refugees** (1977): About 60,000 from Equatorial Guinea. In 1978, 10,000 Beninese nationals living in Gabon were forcibly repatriated.

**Tourists** (1973): 52,453.

**ETHNOLINGUISTIC GROUPS:** 29% Fang (Ntumu, Mvae, Okak), 19% Eshira (with Bapounou, Bavoungou, Balumbu), 15% M'Bete (Bandjabi), 11% Kota, 6% French (30,000), 5% Omyene (Mpongwe), 4% Bakele, 4% Okande (Bapindji, Mitsogo, Okande), 4% Seke (with Benga), 2.0% Beninese (10,000) (Dahomean), 1.0% other expatriate African (Hausa, Senegalese, other African), Bakwe Pygmy.

**MONEY** (1977). **Monetary unit:** CFA franc (= 100 centimes); US$1 = CFAF 250.00.
**National income per person:** US$1,500. Average annual family income: US$7,350.
**Inflation:** (1970–74) 6.3% per year (1976: consumer price index 185).
**Cost of living in capital** (1976): index 177 (Washington DC=100). Daily cost of living: US$46.

**EDUCATION.** Adult literacy: (1960) 12%, (1975) 20%. Education rate: 78%. Schools: 688.

**HEALTH.** Hospitals· 44 (4,995 beds). Doctors: 96. Lepers: 18,000 (34.2 per 1,000). Blind: 1,300. Psychotics: 4,000.

**LITERATURE.** Annual new book titles (1965): 10.

**COMMUNICATION** (per 1,000 people). Phones:·21. Radios: 124. TV sets: 3.

TABLE 1. RELIGIOUS ADHERENTS IN GABON

| Year | 1900 | | mid-1970 | | Annual change, 1970–1980 | | | | mid-1975 | | mid-1980 | | 2000 | |
| --- | --- | --- | --- | --- | --- | --- | --- | --- | --- | --- | --- | --- | --- | --- |
| *Name* | *Adherents* | *%* | *Adherents* | *%* | *Natural* | *Conversion* | *Total* | *Rate* | *Adherents* | *%* | *Adherents* | *%* | *Adherents* | *%* |
| Christians | 20,900 | 7.5 | 478,500 | 95.7 | 4,416 | 234 | 4,650 | 0.92 | 505,000 | 96.0 | 525,000 | 96.2 | 640,200 | 97.0 |
| professing | 20,900 | 7.5 | 478,500 | 95.7 | 4,416 | 234 | 4,650 | 0.92 | 505,000 | 96.0 | 525,000 | 96.2 | 640,200 | 97.0 |
| Roman Catholics | 15,000 | 5.4 | 325,000 | 65.0 | 2,999 | 121 | 3,120 | 0.91 | 342,900 | 65.2 | 356,200 | 65.2 | 447,500 | 67.8 |
| Protestants | 3,100 | 1.1 | 93,000 | 18.6 | 860 | 100 | 960 | 0.98 | 98,400 | 18.7 | 102,600 | 18.8 | 126,700 | 19.2 |
| African indigenous | 2,800 | 1.0 | 60,500 | 12.1 | 557 | 13 | 570 | 0.89 | 63,700 | 12.1 | 66,200 | 12.1 | 66,000 | 10.0 |
| nominal | 2,650 | 0.9 | 5,387 | 1.1 | 65 | 296 | 361 | 4.88 | 7,400 | 1.4 | 9,000 | 1.6 | 19,800 | 3.0 |
| affiliated | 18,250 | 6.5 | 473,113 | 94.6 | 4,351 | −62 | 4,289 | 0.86 | 497,600 | 94.6 | 516,000 | 94.5 | 620,400 | 94.0 |
| total practising | 16,420 | *90* | 354,830 | *75* | 3,264 | −47 | 3,217 | 0.86 | 373,200 | *75* | 387,000 | *75* | 434,300 | *70* |
| non-practising | 1,830 | *10* | 118,280 | *25* | 1,087 | −15 | 1,072 | 0.86 | 124,400 | *25* | 129,000 | *25* | 186,100 | *30* |
| Roman Catholics | 12,500 | 4.5 | 321,113 | 64.2 | 2,947 | −198 | 2,749 | 0.82 | 337,000 | 64.1 | 348,600 | 63.8 | 428,800 | 65.0 |
| Protestants | 2,950 | 1.1 | 91,000 | 18.2 | 842 | 108 | 950 | 0.99 | 96,300 | 18.3 | 100,500 | 18.4 | 124,100 | 18.8 |
| Evangelicals | 2,500 | 0.9 | 21,000 | 4.2 | 194 | 26 | 220 | 0.99 | 22,200 | 4.2 | 23,200 | 4.2 | 29,000 | 4.4 |
| African indigenous | 2,800 | 1.0 | 60,500 | 12.1 | 557 | 13 | 570 | 0.89 | 63,700 | 12.1 | 66,200 | 12.1 | 66,000 | 10.0 |
| Marginal Protestants | 0 | 0.0 | 500 | 0.1 | 5 | 15 | 20 | 3.33 | 600 | 0.1 | 700 | 0.1 | 1,500 | 0.2 |
| Tribal religionists | 259,100 | 92.5 | 17,000 | 3.4 | 142 | −262 | −120 | −0.74 | 16,140 | 3.1 | 15,800 | 2.9 | 12,900 | 2.0 |
| Muslims | 0 | 0.0 | 4,000 | 0.8 | 37 | 3 | 40 | 0.95 | 4,210 | 0.8 | 4,400 | 0.8 | 5,300 | 0.8 |
| Baha'is | 0 | 0.0 | 200 | 0.0 | 2 | 8 | 10 | 4.00 | 250 | 0.0 | 300 | 0.1 | 600 | 0.1 |
| Other religionists | 0 | 0.0 | 300 | 0.1 | 3 | 17 | 20 | 5.00 | 400 | 0.1 | 500 | 0.1 | 1,000 | 0.2 |
| Country's population | 280,000 | 100.0 | 500,000 | 100.0 | 4,600 | 0 | 4,600 | 0.87 | 526,000 | 100.0 | 546,000 | 100.0 | 660,000 | 100.0 |

COLUMNS, ROWS. For meanings and definitions, see Code-book (Part 6). Note that, by definition, total 'Christians' = professing + crypto-Christians, which also = affiliated + nominal Christians. Percentages may not always total exactly, due to rounding.

**NOTES ON RELIGIONS**
AFFILIATED PROTESTANTS. In 1902, the Paris Mission reported 900 members and 2,200 catechumens in 4 stations with 40 annexes, 58 African evangelists and 13 French missionaries.
AFRICAN INDIGENOUS. In 2 denominations in 1970 (see Table 2).
BAHA'IS. In 8 isolated groups (1973).

MUSLIMS. Hausa and Senegalese traders in the north (Sunnis of the Malikite rite). *Hajj pilgrims to Mecca.* (1976) 21.
OTHER RELIGIONISTS. Including Rosicrucians (3 AMORC centres).
TRIBAL RELIGIONISTS. Fetishism remains very powerful among the Kota and others.

## NON-CHRISTIAN RELIGIONS.

**Traditional religions** have reduced in influence to a following of less than 4% of the population, although traditional ideas continue to influence the African expression of Christianity. All of Gabon's peoples have a belief in God, who is called Anambye (among the Omyene), Ndjambe (Seke), Nyambi (Eshira), Manambi (Okande), Nzambye (Bakele), Nzame (Fang) and Nzambe (Bakota). The veneration of ancestral spirits (Malumbi among Eshira, Mabambe among Bakele, Bekon among Fang) is also widely practised. Three important secret societies with elaborate ceremonies are Bwiti, a male group dedicated to the remembrance of the great ancestors; Mwiri, a male group concerned for the protection of nature and maintenance of public places as well as the punishment of those who desecrate them; and Njembe, a female society. Among the Fang, Bwiti initiates women as well as men and includes anti-Catholic elements. Although part of the Bwiti movement remains predominantly traditionalist, another part has developed sufficiently in a Christian direction to be listed as an indigenous church.

**Islam** has not played an important role in Gabon. There are a few thousand Muslims in the north, including Hausa and Senegalese traders, who represent less than 1% of the population. In 1973 president Bongo announced his conversion to Islam.

## CHRISTIANITY

CATHOLIC CHURCH. Italian Capuchins began work in Gabon in the 17th century but were expelled by the Portuguese in 1777. The Congregation of the Sacred Heart of Mary came in 1841 and was later

strengthened by its amalgamation with the Holy Ghost (CSSp) mission in 1848. The vicariate apostolic of Senegambia and the Two Guineas was established soon after, with the vicar residing in Gabon. This was a large area comprising the western half of Africa between the Senegal prefecture and the Orange river with no clear boundaries in the interior.

By 1863 the area was divided and separate vicariates came into existence. In 1958 the diocese of Mouila and archdiocese of Libreville were formed. Growth in the number of Catholics has been steady since the end of the last century: 1,100 in 1850, 16,000 in 1910, 120,300 (including catechumens) in 1940, 280,000 in 1967, and well over 300,000 by 1972.

PROTESTANT CHURCHES. There are 3 Protestant churches, the largest being the Evangelical Church of Gabon. Begun by the American Board (ABCFM) in the lower region of the Gabon river in 1842, the mission was turned over to American Presbyterians in 1870. The latter left in 1892 when French was made a requirement in mission schools, and the work was then transferred to the Paris Mission (PEMS). After a slow beginning, the church grew rapidly and became autonomous in 1961. Gabon's best-known missionary was Albert Schweitzer who worked at Lambarene until his death in 1965.

In 1934 the Christian and Missionary Alliance in Congo was asked by the Paris Mission to undertake evangelistic activity in the southern part of the country. The result was the formation of the Evangelical Church of South Gabon in 1956. A revival in 1968 increased the membership of this church by 20% in a single year.

A third much smaller group is the Evangelical Church of Pentecost, which was formed in 1936 by a dissident PEMS missionary.

INDIGENOUS CHURCHES. The Church of the Initiates (Eglise des Banzie), also known as the Religion d'Eboga (after the drug *eboga* it employs) or the Bwiti movement, began originally at the end

Grave of missionary pioneer, at Lambaréné.

**Eglise Evangélique du Gabon.** Open-air service outside church. Members are Fang, and 80% are women.

Postage stamps commemorating (*below*) Protestant pioneer Albert Schweitzer, and (*above*) Roman Catholic pioneer Msgr J.R. Bessieux.

of the last century as a secret society with syncretistic elements, attempting to express in more relevant terms the traditional concerns of the Fang ancestral cult in the face of challenges from Christianity and the Western secular world. With the passage of time, however, some Bwiti groups have become increasingly Christian, with a significant new impulse towards the adoption of Christian symbolism after 1945. The present emphasis on Jesus as divine Saviour has changed the movement into a more specifically Christian one, although ambiguities remain. Bwiti is not a separatist church since no schism from an existing church or mission body has been involved. Since Independence it has become increasingly active, virile and aggressive, and aspires to be the national church of Gabon. It has over 20 churches in Libreville. There is no ecclesiastical organization and no hierarchy, and initiation with eboga replaces baptism.

**CHURCH AND STATE.** The constitution of 21 February 1961, revised in 1967, begins in its Preamble: 'The Gabonese people, conscious of their responsibility before God...'. It then recognizes 'the freedom of conscience, the free practice of religion' (Article 1, paragraph 1) as well as the right 'to form religious communities' (Article 1, paragraph 8). The republic of Gabon 'respects all beliefs' (Article 2). Public education is organized on the basis of 'religious neutrality' and religious instruction is provided to students at the request of their parents (Article 1, paragraph 12).

Private education, which is also authorized by the constitution (Article 1, paragraph 12), is regulated by the law of 15 June 1963 which provides for the payment of salaries by government to national and foreign teaching personnel. Nevertheless, funds for the functioning of these schools have been reduced in recent years, which has created increasing difficulties for private schools.

In 1972, numerous government ministers and officials were Protestants; but in 1973, the president of the republic, A. Bongo, who had never been baptized as a Christian, converted to Islam, and the following year Gabon became a member of the Islamic Conference (centred in Saudi Arabia), although there are only about 4,000 Muslims in the country. On 15 January 1974 an official communiqué reaffirming the freedom of religion was published following a meeting of the council of ministers, which was given over especially to 'a broad exchange of views on confessional questions'.

**INTERDENOMINATIONAL ORGANIZATIONS.** There are no local ecumenical organizations. The Evangelical Church of Gabon is a member of the All Africa Conference of Churches and also of the World Council of Churches.

**BROADCASTING.** The government network Radio-diffusion Télévision Nationale Gabonaise broadcasts both Catholic and Protestant programmes, all in French. Both Catholics and Protestants are given a 30-minute devotional every Sunday and a fortnightly news magazine on radio. A 30-minute Sunday morning TV programme is also made available to the churches, followed by a Catholic mass. Both Catholics and Protestants have recording studios. For Catholics, Gabon is registered as a member of UNDA. From abroad, RVOG (Ethiopia) was easily heard until its closure in 1977.

**BIBLIOGRAPHY**


'Christian acculturation and Fang witchcraft', J. W. Fernandez & P. Bekale, *Cahiers d'études africaines*, II, 6 (Fall, 1961), 224–270.
*L'Eglise Evangélique du Gabon, 1842–1961*. P. Stoecklin et al. Alençon: Imprimerie Corbière et Jugain, 1962. 52p.
*Rites et croyances des peuples du Gabon: essai sur les pratiques religieuses d'autrefois et d'aujourd'hui*. A. Raponda-Walker & R. Sillans. Paris: Présence Africaine, 1962. 377p.
'The idea and symbol of the Saviour in a Gabon syncretistic cult: basic factors in the mythology of messianism', J. W. Fernandez, *International review of missions*, LIII, 211 (July, 1964), 281–9.


TABLE 2. ORGANIZED CHURCHES AND DENOMINATIONS IN GABON

| Official name 1 | Begun 2 | Type 3 | Counc 4 | Congs 5 | Adults 6 | Affiliated 7 | Names, notes, and other statistics (see Codebook) 8 |
|---|---|---|---|---|---|---|---|
| **Eglise Catholique au Gabon:** | 1673 | R Lat | P.S.R | 54 | 211,900 | 321,113 | *Catholic Ch in Gabon*. C=2+3+12, 3p,1q. 35n,70x,58m,160w,P=33%,9333Yy,31630z. |
| M Libreville | 1863 | R Lat | Ps | 23 | 90,600 | 137,261 | Capital. 4,500 expatriates. 40% Fang. 20 26 39 87 34 2789 7946 |
| D Mouila | 1958 | R Lat | Pcssp | 19 | 68,000 | 103,000 | 42% Bandjabi, 32% Bapounou, 8% Eshira. 9 30 15 52 31 4259 15000 |
| D Oyem | 1969 | R Lat | Ps | 12 | 53,300 | 80,852 | Formed out of M Libreville. Iron mining. 6 14 4 21 34 2285 8684 |
| **Eglise des Banzie (Bwiti)** | c1890 | I mar | ..... | 1,000 | 10,000 | 60,000 | *Ch of the Initiates. Religion d'Eboga* (a drug). *Eglise du Gabon*. Fang syncretism. |
| Eglise Evangélique de Pentecôte | 1936 | P Pe2 | ..... | 2 | 200 | 1,000 | *Ev Ch of Pentecost*. Begun by PEMS missionary. M=MFSP,AdD(French,Swiss). Static. |
| **Eglise Evangélique du Gabon** | 1842 | P Ref | .WA.. | 310 | 17,850 | 75,000 | *EEG. Ev Ch of Gabon*. M=PEMS(France). 96% Fang (80% women). 22n,5x,195m,18f,2p. |
| Eglise Evangélique du Sud Gabon | 1934 | P Hol | xF... | 188 | 6,854 | 15,000 | South. A=1956. M=CMA(USA). 1968, revivals. 17n,9x,55mw,31f,3h,2p,W=73%,264Y. |
| Eglise Kimbanguiste | c1955 | I pen | xwi.. | 2 | 200 | 500 | *Ch of Christ on Earth through Prophet Simon Kimbangu*. M=EJCSK(Zaire). In Libreville. |
| Témoins de Jéhovah | c1945 | M Jeh | x.... | 6 | 251 | 500 | *Jehovah's Witnesses*. Active by 1948; 1970, suppressed. Canada missionaries. 35Y. |
| **Total affiliated (mid-1970)** | | | | **1,562** | **247,255** | **473,113** | **Total denominations (1970) . . . 7.** |
| **Total affiliated (mid-1975)** | | | | **1,580** | **260,050** | **497,600** | **Total denominations (1975) . . . 7.** |
| **Total affiliated (mid-1980)** | | | | **1,600** | **270,000** | **516,000** | **Total denominations (1980) . . . 8.** |

**NOTES ON TABLE ABOVE**
COLUMNS: for meanings and CODES (cols. 1, 3, 4, 8): see Codebook (Part 6). Column 1: **Boldface type** = church with over 10% of country's affiliated Christians.
NATIONAL COUNCILS (Column 4, 5th letter).
R = Conférence Episcopale du Gabon (CEG) (Episcopal Conference of Gabon).

**PEOPLES** (ethnolinguistic). Christians: 30% Fang (Ntumu, Mvae, Okak), 21% Eshira (with Bapounou, Bavoungou, Balumbu), 15% M'Bete (Bandjabi), 9% Kota, 6% French, 5% Omyene (Mpongwe), 4% Bakele, 4% Okande, 4% Seke, 1% Beninese, 0.2% other expatriate African, Bakwe Pygmy.

**COUNTRY-WIDE TOTALS**
EVANGELIZATION (see Part 5). 1900: 23%. 1970: 100%. 1980: 100%. *Mass evangelism*. New Life for All movement.
FOREIGN MISSIONARIES AND PERSONNEL (nationals serving abroad) (1973). Total about 10 Roman Catholics.
FOREIGN MISSIONARIES AND PERSONNEL (aliens from abroad) (1973). Total 261. *From Western world*. 239: 190 Roman Catholics, 49 Protestants (31 in 1 USA society, 8 in 1 France society, 8 in 1 Netherlands society, 2 in 1 Switzerland society). *From Third World*. 22: about 10 Roman Catholics, about 10 Protestants, 2 indigenous.
INSTITUTIONS (church-operated) (1973). Total 50, including 28 higher schools (3 minor seminaries), 16 medical centres, 1 religious community, 1 seminary (RC), 2 study centres.
PERIODICALS. 4 titles.
PERSONNEL. About 1,758 (1,497 national, 261 foreign).
RELIGIOUS LIBRARIES. 4,
SCRIPTURE DISTRIBUTION (1975). Annual totals: 1,050 Bibles (61% subsidized, 39% commercial), 2,000 NTs (commercial), 1,700 UBS portions. *Translations completed*. Portion: 12 languages since 1850. NT: 4 languages since 1869. Bible: 3 languages since 1927.
SERVICE AGENCIES. About 20, including CEG, CV/AV, GBUAF, JAC, JAC/F, JEC/F, JOC/F.

**ADDITIONAL DATA ON CHURCHES**
EGLISE CATHOLIQUE AU GABON. *Catechumens*. (1959) 31,467; (1961) 29,185; (1963) 28,999; (1969) 31,630, as shown in column 8, and included in column 7. *New diocese* (created 1974). Franceville, formed out of D Mouila. *Annual baptisms*. (1972) 54.5% infant, 45.5% adult. *Priests*. The first Gabonese was ordained in 1889. *Brothers*. In M Libreville: 13 nationals, 26 expatriates. *Sisters*. In M Libreville: 41 nationals, 46 expatriates. *Catechists*. Total (1970) 1,037. One national catechetical school in Libreville, one each in the other 2 dioceses. *Indigenous religious congregations*. Soeurs de Sainte-Marie du Gabon (begun 1917 as Petites Soeurs de Ste-Marie; 49 professed in 1971). *Main foreign congregations*. Priests: CSSp, SDB. Brothers: 27 Frères de Saint-Gabriel. Sisters: 40 Immaculée-Conception de Castres, 12 St-Rosaire de Pont-de-Beauvoisin.
*Catholic organizations*. The Episcopal Conference of Gabon is a member of SECAM. There are no national councils of priests nor religious personnel, but several lay organizations are active: JOC/F JAC/F, JEC/F, CV/AV, Catholic Guides and Scouts, and the Legion of Mary.
The Holy See has diplomatic relations with Gabon, and is represented to government and the Catholic hierarchy by a pro-nuncio with residence in Yaoundé, Cameroon.
In 1970 the Catholic educational programme included 10 nursery schools (937 infants), 249 primary schools (39,751 pupils), 19 secondary schools (3,213 pupils) and 2 technical schools. By 1973 these were 196 primary schools (37,514 pupils) and 23 secondary (4,122). Catholic education is responsible for 42% of all school pupils, as contrasted with 9% for Protestants and 46% for the state.
In 1970 the church also sponsored 9 hospitals and dispensaries (50 beds), 2 leprosaria, 9 girls' hostels, 4 homes for the aged, 3 day care centres, 9 sewing rooms, one rural centre and 6 medical aid programmes of service to non-Catholic hospitals by nursing sisters.

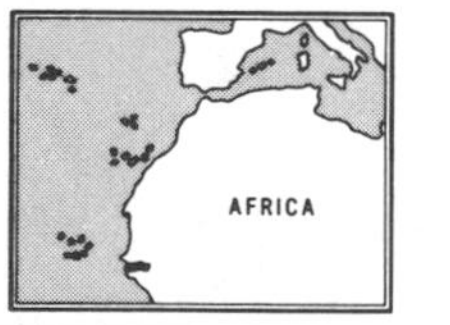


# GAMBIA

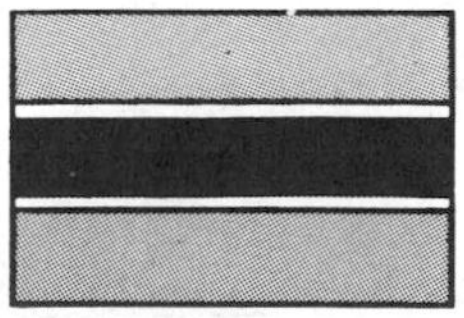

## SECULAR DATA

**STATE. Official name:** The Republic of the Gambia. Adjective of nationality: Gambian.
**Flag** (shown above right): Red (top), white, blue, white, and green stripes.
**Area:** 11,295 sq.km. (4,361 sq.miles). Agricultural land: 54.9%.
**Government:** Parliamentary republic, since 1970 (1843 British crown colony, 1965 Independence).
**Legislature:** House of Representatives, 37 members.
**Official language:** English.
**Capital:** Banjul 41,047 (1974).
**Political divisions:** 35 Districts.

**DEMOGRAPHY. Population:** 493,197 (census of 21.IV.1973. For 1970–2000 (UN), see last row of Table 1). Population density (1975): 45/sq.km. (117/sq.mile). Under 15 years: 40%. Growth rate (1975–80): 2.01% per year (births 4.30%, deaths −2.29%). Life expectancy (1975–80): 41.0 years. Household size: 4.9 persons.
**Major languages:** Mandingo, Fulani, English, Wolof, Diola, Soninke, and about 8 other languages.
**Urban dwellers** (1970): 10.0%. Urban growth rate (1950–70): 3.3% per year.
**Labour force:** 41%.
**Tourists** (1975): About 30,000 (mostly Scandinavians).

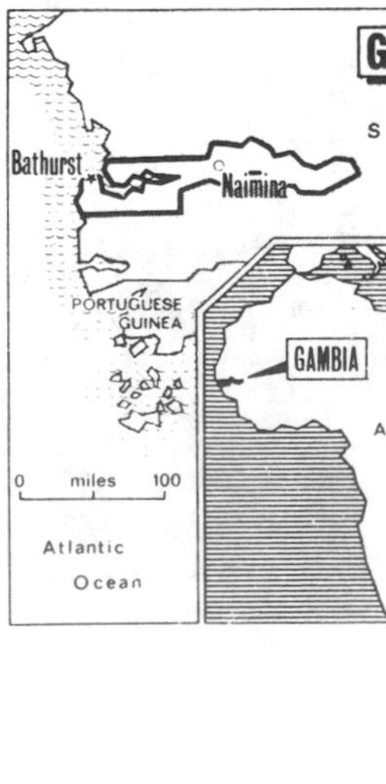


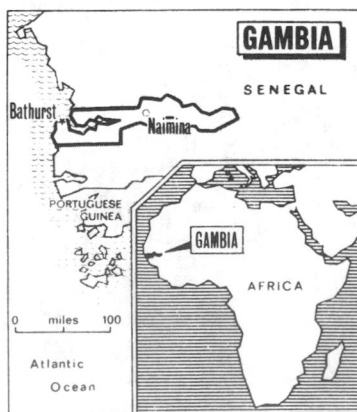

**ETHNOLINGUISTIC GROUPS:** 45% Mandingo (Malinke), 19.5% Fulani (Peul), 14.5% Wolof, 7% Diola (Jola), 6.5% Soninke (Sarakole), 3.2% Manjak, 1.3% Serer, 1.3% Susu, 0.6% Aku (Acko, Creole), 0.1% Nigerian, Senegalese, British, Greek, Arab.

**MONEY** (1977). **Monetary unit:** dalasi (= 100 bututs); US$1 = D 2.42.
**National income per person:** US$120. Average annual family income: US$588.
**Inflation:** (1970–74) 26% per year (1975: consumer price index 184).
**Cost of living in capital** (1976): index 128 (Washington DC=100). Daily cost of living: US$27.

**EDUCATION.** Adult literacy: (1962) 6%, (1975) 10%. Education rate: 19%. Schools: 117 (95 primary, 22 secondary).

**HEALTH.** Hospitals: 5 (488 beds). Doctors: 19. Lepers: 14,000 (27.5 per 1,000). Blind: 2,700. Psychotics: 3,000.

**LITERATURE.** Periodicals: 6. Newspapers: 11 non-daily.

**COMMUNICATION** (per 1,000 people). Phones: 4. Radios: 157. Daily newspaper circulation: 21 copies.

TABLE 1. RELIGIOUS ADHERENTS IN THE GAMBIA

| Year | 1900 | | mid-1970 | | Annual change, 1970–1980 | | | | mid-1975 | | mid-1980 | | 2000 | |
|---|---|---|---|---|---|---|---|---|---|---|---|---|---|---|
| Name | Adherents | % | Adherents | % | Natural | Conversion | Total | Rate | Adherents | % | Adherents | % | Adherents | % |
| Muslims | 72,120 | 81.0 | 389,884 | 84.2 | 8,449 | 283 | 8,732 | 2.03 | 430,000 | 84.5 | 477,200 | 84.8 | 729,600 | 85.7 |
| Ahmadis | 0 | 0.0 | 200 | 0.0 | 6 | 14 | 20 | 6.67 | 300 | 0.1 | 400 | 0.1 | 2,000 | 0.2 |
| Tribal religionists | 13,100 | 14.7 | 55,560 | 12.0 | 1,149 | −515 | 634 | 1.08 | 58,500 | 11.5 | 61,900 | 11.0 | 76,700 | 9.0 |
| Christians | 3,700 | 4.2 | 13,356 | 2.9 | 310 | 224 | 534 | 3.38 | 15,800 | 3.1 | 18,700 | 3.3 | 36,000 | 4.2 |
| crypto-Christians | 100 | 0.1 | 856 | 0.2 | 39 | 215 | 254 | 12.59 | 2,020 | 0.4 | 3,400 | 0.6 | 8,800 | 1.0 |
| professing | 3,600 | 4.0 | 12,500 | 2.7 | 271 | 9 | 280 | 2.03 | 13,780 | 2.7 | 15,300 | 2.7 | 27,200 | 3.2 |
| Roman Catholics | 1,850 | 2.1 | 8,790 | 1.9 | 191 | −3 | 188 | 1.94 | 9,680 | 1.9 | 10,670 | 1.9 | 18,500 | 2.2 |
| Protestants | 850 | 1.0 | 1,800 | 0.4 | 39 | 11 | 50 | 2.50 | 2,000 | 0.4 | 2,300 | 0.4 | 4,300 | 0.5 |
| Anglicans | 900 | 1.0 | 1,800 | 0.4 | 39 | 1 | 40 | 2.02 | 1,980 | 0.4 | 2,200 | 0.4 | 4,200 | 0.5 |
| Orthodox | 0 | 0.0 | 110 | 0.0 | 2 | 0 | 2 | 1.96 | 120 | 0.0 | 130 | 0.0 | 200 | 0.0 |
| affiliated | 3,700 | 4.2 | 13,356 | 2.9 | 310 | 224 | 534 | 3.38 | 15,800 | 3.1 | 18,700 | 3.3 | 36,000 | 4.2 |
| total practising | 3,510 | 95 | 12,020 | 90 | 279 | 202 | 481 | 3.38 | 14,220 | 90 | 16,830 | 90 | 28,800 | 80 |
| non-practising | 190 | 5 | 1,340 | 10 | 31 | 22 | 53 | 3.35 | 1,580 | 10 | 1,870 | 10 | 7,200 | 20 |
| Roman Catholics | 1,800 | 2.0 | 9,328 | 2.0 | 220 | 197 | 417 | 3.73 | 11,200 | 2.2 | 13,500 | 2.4 | 25,600 | 3.0 |
| Protestants | 900 | 1.0 | 2,028 | 0.4 | 47 | 30 | 77 | 3.22 | 2,400 | 0.5 | 2,800 | 0.5 | 6,000 | 0.7 |
| Evangelicals | 900 | 1.0 | 1,900 | 0.4 | 45 | 35 | 80 | 3.48 | 2,300 | 0.4 | 2,700 | 0.5 | 5,700 | 0.7 |
| Anglicans | 1,000 | 1.1 | 2,000 | 0.4 | 43 | −3 | 40 | 1.82 | 2,200 | 0.4 | 2,400 | 0.4 | 4,400 | 0.5 |
| Baha'is | 0 | 0.0 | 4,100 | 0.9 | 90 | 10 | 100 | 2.17 | 4,600 | 0.9 | 5,100 | 0.9 | 9,500 | 1.1 |
| Hindus | 80 | 0.1 | 100 | 0.0 | 2 | −2 | 0 | 0.00 | 100 | 0.0 | 100 | 0.0 | 200 | 0.0 |
| Country's population | 89,000 | 100.0 | 463,000 | 100.0 | 10,000 | 0 | 10,000 | 1.96 | 509,000 | 100.0 | 563,000 | 100.0 | 852,000 | 100.0 |

COLUMNS, ROWS. For meanings and definitions, see Codebook (Part 6). Note that, by definition, total 'Christians' = professing + crypto-Christians, which also = affiliated + nominal Christians. Percentages may not always total exactly due to rounding.

CENSUSES. 1901 Census of the British Empire: (Colony only): 57.3% Muslims, 26.3% Christians, 16.4% tribal religionists. In this 1901 census, 3,540 Christians were recorded in the Colony (including 200 Whites mostly British, 910 Aku, 350 Ibos, 145 Popos and 20 Goans); also 81 Hindus. 1911 (Colony): 51.4% Muslims, 42.7% Christians, 5.9% tribal religionists. 1911 (Protectorate): 84.6% Muslims, 14.8% tribal religionists, 0.6% Christians. 1911 (Colony and Protectorate): 82.9% Muslims, 14.3% tribal religionists, 2.8% Christians. 1921: 78.2% Muslims, 18.9% tribal religionists, 2.9% Christians. 1931: 84.5% Muslims, 12.7% tribal religionists, 2.7% Christians (1.2% Roman Catholics,

0.9% Protestants, 0.6% Anglicans). 1945: 82.8% Muslims, 14.3% tribal religionists, 2.9% Christians; (Colony: Bathurst and Kombo St Mary): 57.5% Muslims, 32.5% Christians, 10.0% tribal religionists; (Protectorate): 85.1% Muslims, 14.7% tribal religionists, 0.2% Christians.

### NOTES ON RELIGIONS
AHMADIS. Begun 1960; Qadianis from Pakistan.
BAHA'IS. Growth from 7 local spiritual assemblies (1964) to 27 (1973). Most Baha'is are Diola (Jola), and expansion among them is continuing.
CRYPTO-CHRISTIANS. Since the expansion of Christian ministries among Muslims, and in particular the growth of Bible correspondence courses and radiophonic evangelism for Muslims, the number of secret believers (non-professing Christians) rose markedly during the 1970s.
MUSLIMS. Sunnis (of the Malikite rite). Mainly among the

Mandingo, Fula (Fulani), Wolof and Sarakole. Several professional castes (drummers, tanners, praise-singers) have been partially islamized. Orders include Tariqiya and Muridiya from Senegal. There is also a small Ahmadiya mission (Qadianis; enumerated here as Muslims though declared non-Muslim by Pakistan). Hajj pilgrims to Mecca. (1969) 250; (1970) 347; (1974) 597; (1975) 590; (1976) 667.
ORTHODOX. In 1969 there were 105 professing Greek Orthodox in the Gambia, almost all in the capital, but without regular organized church life.
PRACTISING CHRISTIANS. Regular church attendance (2 or more times a month): 80% for Methodists, 65% Anglicans, 80% Roman Catholics.
TRIBAL RELIGIONISTS. Mainly Serer, Diola (Jola), Pacari, Bassari. Animists among the Fulbe (Fulani) and Wolof, and some professional castes (including the Mangsuanka palmwine tappers), are still untouched by Islam.

## NON-CHRISTIAN RELIGIONS.
**Islam** has its strongest concentration among the Mandingo, Fula (Fulani, Peul), Wolof and Sarakole peoples. The Gambia is largely a Muslim country (85%) with mosques found in the majority of its towns and villages.
•**African traditional religions** are strongest among the Serer, Diola (Jola) and Bassari peoples. The total population is still about 11% traditionalist. The Serer know God as Rog (Creator). Prayers are not common, but appeal is made to Rog when the Serer are threatened with war. Close contact is maintained with departed ancestral spirits, especially in the period following a funeral when they are believed to hover temporarily about the homes of the living. The Serer also believe in the transmigration of souls, the living dead taking abode in both animate and inanimate objects.

## CHRISTIANITY.
Although Catholicism touched the Gambia through Portuguese mariners and merchants as early as 1445, the first permanent Catholic mission was not founded until 1849. An Anglican chaplain arrived in 1816 and was followed later by missionaries of the SPG, while the first British Methodist entered in 1821. The Worldwide Evangelization Crusade has had missionaries since 1966. None of these, which are still the only churches at work in the Gambia, has been particularly successful in attracting members. Christianity is now the professed religion of only about 3% of the people, being strongest in urban areas among the detribalized Aku Creoles who are descendants of freed slaves. Among the indigenous peoples, some Mandingo and recently larger numbers of Wolof tribesmen have come into the churches. All the denominations are active in Banjul; in addition Catholics work in the Kombo region, Anglicans in Fatoto and Methodists in Mausa Konko, Georgetown and south of Brikama. The churches are also engaged in educational, medical

and agricultural ministries. Although there are still no indigenous Catholic priests or major seminaries, there were 24 minor seminaries in 1973. Catholic missionary work is run by Irish Holy Ghost priests, assisted by Gambian and expatriate sisters and a large number of local catechists. The Anglican and Methodist churches have both indigenous and expatriate clergy.

## CHURCH AND STATE.
The constitution of 24 April 1970 guarantees freedom of conscience for all, including freedom of thought and religion and their public manifestation and propagation (Article 21, paragraph 1). 'Every religious community shall be entitled, at its own expense, to establish and maintain places of education and to manage any place of education which it wholly maintains' (Article 21, paragraph 3). There is no ministry for religious affairs.

## INTERDENOMINATIONAL ORGANIZATIONS.
The Gambia Christian Council was established in 1963 and includes Catholics, Anglicans and Methodists in its membership. These 3 churches also co-operate in the production and distribution of scriptures and other Christian literature as well as joint services of worship and witness.

## BROADCASTING.
Radio Gambia (Ministry of Information) broadcasts an epilogue each Sunday, rotated among the Catholic, Anglican and Methodist churches. Christian programmes from abroad can be easily heard over ELWA (Liberia). For Catholics, the Gambia is registered as a member of UNDA.

## BIBLIOGRAPHY
Island base: a history of the Methodist Church in the Gambia, 1821–1969. B. Prickett. Bo, Sierra Leone: Bunumbu Press, 1969. 246p.

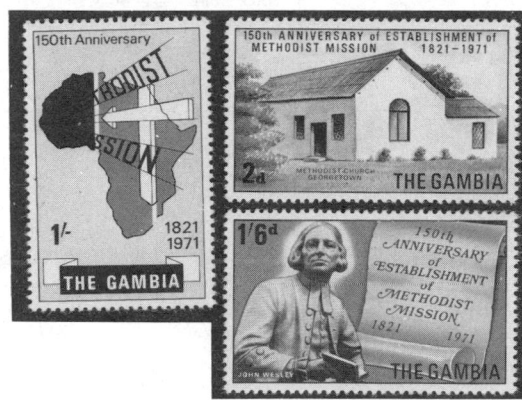

**Methodist Church in the Gambia.** Above. Gambia postage stamps commemorating 150th Anniversary. Below. Rally in Macarthy Square, 1971, on 150th Anniversary of Methodism in the Gambia: (Front, from left) Lady Jarawa and her husband, President of the Gambia, both Muslims; Chairman of Methodist District; Roman Catholic Bishop; Secretary of Conference, Methodist Church Nigeria.

TABLE 2. ORGANIZED CHURCHES AND DENOMINATIONS IN THE GAMBIA

| Official name 1 | Begun 2 | Type 3 | Counc 4 | Congs 5 | Adults 6 | Affiliated 7 | Names, notes, and other statistics (see Codebook) 8 |
|---|---|---|---|---|---|---|---|
| Anglican Ch: D Gambia & Rio Pongas | 1816 | A ACa | AwAVK | 15 | 700 | 2,000 | Begun for British troops. 1935, D in CPWA. Bishop from Haiti. 4n,2x,W=60%. |
| Catholic Church: D Banjul (Bathurst) | 1849 | R Lat | pxSGQ | 3 | 5,600 | 9,328 | M=CSSp. 54% Wolof, 16% Serer, 15% Diola. C=1+0+2. 17x,2m,16w,W=80%,624Yy,1500z. |
| Churches of Christ | c1968 | P Dis | x•••• | 3 | 100 | 300 | M=Churches of Christ(Non-Instrumental)(USA). Gambia Bible Seminar, Banjul. 4f. |
| Gambian Evangelical Fellowship | 1966 | P Int | xFg•• | 3 | 50 | 200 | M=WEC(UK),WEK(Germany). Formerly within Methodist Church, now separate. 12f. |
| Methodist Church in the Gambia | 1821 | P Met | VwA•K | 13 | 1,197 | 1,528 | Gambia District. M=MMS. 88% Aku, 6% Manjak. 1n,2x,3w,4f,3h,W=75%,33Yy. |
| Total affiliated (mid-1970) | | | | 37 | 7,647 | 13,356 | Total denominations (1970) . . . 5. |
| Total affiliated (mid-1975) | | | | 39 | 9,050 | 15,800 | Total denominations (1975) . . . 5. |
| Total affiliated (mid-1980) | | | | 41 | 10,700 | 18,700 | Total denominations (1980) . . . 5. |

### NOTES ON TABLE ABOVE
COLUMNS: for meanings and CODES (cols. 1, 3, 4, 8), see Codebook (Part 6). Column 1: Boldface type = church with over 10% of country's affiliated Christians.
NATIONAL COUNCILS (Column 4, 5th letter).
K = Gambia Christian Council (GCC).
Q = Inter-Territorial Episcopal Conference of the Gambia, Liberia & Sierra Leone, also member of GCC.

PEOPLES (ethnolinguistic). Christians: about 48% Wolof, 18% Aku (Creole), 17% Serer, 11% Diola, 4% Nigerian, 1% Manjak, British, Ghanaian, Senegalese.

COUNTRY-WIDE TOTALS
EVANGELIZATION (see Part 5). 1900: 17%. 1970: 69%. 1980:

75%. Mass evangelism. 1970, 2,000 Catholics, Anglicans and Methodists in procession of witness at Bathurst; 1970, 1971 Methodist youth crusades in Bathurst.
FOREIGN MISSIONARIES AND PERSONNEL (aliens from abroad) (1973). Total 57. From Western world. 50: about 30 Roman Catholics, 20 Protestants (7 in 2 UK societies, 6 in 1

WGermany society, 5 in 2 USA societies, 2 in 1 Australia society). *From Third World.* 7: about 3 Roman Catholics, 3 Anglicans from Haiti, Ghana and Bahamas, 1 Protestant from Ghana.
INSTITUTIONS (church-operated) (1973). Total 15, including 10 higher schools, 3 medical centres.
PERIODICALS. 2 titles.
PERSONNEL. About 273 (216 national, 57 foreign).
SCRIPTURE DISTRIBUTION (1975). Annual totals: 100 Bibles (subsidized), 150 NTs (subsidized). *Translations completed.* Portion: 2 languages in 1837 and 1882.
SERVICE AGENCIES. About 17, including CPA, CRS-USCC, GCC, SU.

ADDITIONAL DATA ON CHURCHES
CATHOLIC CHURCH. *Catechumens.* (1959) 625; (1961) 980; (1963) 1,231; (1969) 1,500; (1971) 1,103. *Annual baptisms.* (1972) 64.9% infant, 35.1% adult. *Priests.* All expatriate. *Brothers.* Both expatriate. *Sisters.* 2 Gambian, 14 expatriate. *Catechists.* Total (1971) 93 full-time, 111 part-time. 3 schools include training of catechists. *Seminarians.* No Gambians are major seminarians, but in 1973 there were 24 minor seminarians. *Foreign religious congregations.* Priests: CSSp (Irish province). Sisters: St Joseph of Cluny, Presentation of Mary (American and Canadian province). *Catholic organizations.* The Inter-Territorial Episcopal Conference of Liberia, Sierra Leone, the Gambia, with its headquarters in Freetown, Sierra Leone, is a member of SECAM and also of the Regional Episcopal Conference of Ghana, Liberia, Sierra Leone and the Gambia. The latter also has its seat in Freetown. A Pastoral Council has been formed, but there are no organizations of religious personnel. Lay activities are co-ordinated by the Lay Apostolate Council, the main movements being the Catholic People's Association, for youth, and Legion of Mary (with 6 praesidia) for adults.
The Holy See had no diplomatic relations with the Gambia until 1978 when they were set up with a pro-nuncio in Banjul.
In 1971 the Catholic Education Secretariat was responsible for 41 schools with 3,748 students. Of the 4 secondary schools then, 2 were confessional, one being run by 8 St Joseph of Cluny sisters, who also manage schools at Serrekunda and Basse. By 1973 these had become 31 primary schools (2,976 pupils) and 8 secondary (1,637). Catholic Relief Services of the USA provide a school-lunch programme for all schools.

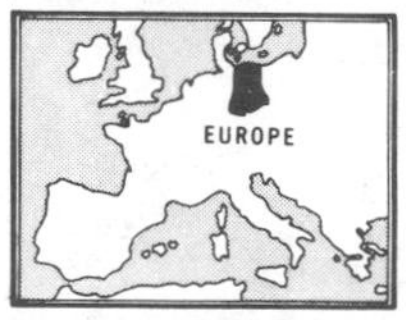


# GERMAN DEMOCRATIC REPUBLIC

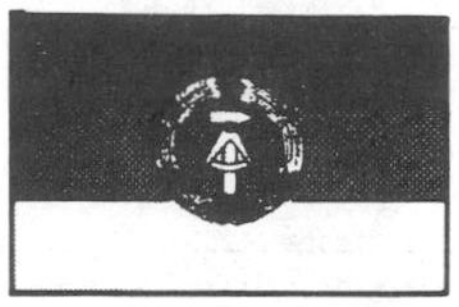

## SECULAR DATA

**STATE. Official name:** The German Democratic Republic, GDR (Deutsche Demokratische Republik, DDR). Unofficial name: East Germany.
**Flag** (shown above right): Black, red, and gold stripes, with centred coat of arms.
**Area:** 107,771 sq.km. (41,768 sq.miles). Agricultural land: 58.1%.
**Government:** One-party Communist state, created 1949 (1871 empire, 1919 republic, 1933 Nazi dictatorship).
**Legislature:** Volkskammer (People's Chamber), 500 members.
**Official language:** German (*Deutsch*). In east regions of Cottbus and Dresden, Sorabian is also official.
**Chief cities:** capital East Berlin 1,088,830 (1973), Leipzig 575,910, Dresden 505,410, Karl-Marx-Stadt 301,830.
**Political divisions:** 15 Bezirke, 218 Districts (27 Urban, 191 Rural), 8,404 Divisions.
**Armed forces** (1976): Total 157,000 regular (92,000 conscripts): army 105,000, navy 16,000, air force 36,000 (441 combat aircraft). Reserves: 405,000. Paramilitary forces: 419,000 (350,000 Workers' Militia).
**Foreign forces** (1973): 500,000 USSR troops (22 divisions).

**DEMOGRAPHY. Population:** 17,068,318 (census of 1.1.1971. For 1970–2000 (UN), see last row of Table 1). Population density (1975): 160/sq.km. (413/sq.mile). Under 15 years: 21%. Growth rate (1975–80): 0.19% per year (births 1.46%, deaths −1.27%). Life expectancy (1975–80): 73.3 years. Household size: 2.6 persons.
**Major languages:** German, Russian, Sorabian.
**Urban dwellers** (1970): 81.2%. Urban growth rate (1950–70): 0.4% per year.
**Labour force:** 48%.
**Refugees** (1977): From abroad, none. Exiles abroad: 16,286 citizens left in 1975 for the FRG (10,275 legal, 6,011 escapees). Since World War II, 14.5 million have moved as refugees to West Germany. From 1949–61, 2.7 million escaped to West Germany. Since 1961, 200,000 have left legally and 107,027 have escaped.
**Tourists** (1974): 15,229,400.

**ETHNOLINGUISTIC GROUPS:** 95.4% German, 2.9% USSR military (500,000), 1.5% Sorb (Sorabian, Slav, Lusatian, Wendish), 0.1% Greek, Russian (civilian), Jewish.

**MONEY** (1977). **Monetary unit:** mark (= 100 pfennig); US$1 = VM 2.40.
**National income per person:** US$3,300. Average annual family income: US$8,580.
**Inflation:** (1970–74) −0.3% per year (1973: consumer price index 99).
**Cost of living in capital** (1976): Daily cost of living: US$46.

**EDUCATION.** Adult literacy: 99%. Education rate: 55%. Schools: 5,042. Universities: 6.

**HEALTH.** Hospitals: 608 (186,075 beds). Doctors: 28,590. Blind: 15,000. Psychotics: 190,000.

**LITERATURE.** Annual new book titles (1973): 5,224. Periodicals: 2,000. Scientific journals: 550. Newspapers: 40 dailies, 612 non-daily.

**COMMUNICATION** (per 1,000 people). Phones: 137. Radios: 358. TV sets: 292. Daily newspaper circulation: 425 copies.

TABLE 1. RELIGIOUS ADHERENTS IN THE GERMAN DEMOCRATIC REPUBLIC

| Year | 1900 | | mid-1970 | | Annual change, 1970–1980 | | | | mid-1975 | | mid-1980 | | 2000 | |
|---|---|---|---|---|---|---|---|---|---|---|---|---|---|---|
| *Name* | *Adherents* | % | *Adherents* | % | *Natural* | *Conversion* | *Total* | *Rate* | *Adherents* | % | *Adherents* | % | *Adherents* | % |
| **Christians** | **12,210,000** | **99.3** | **11,876,107** | **69.6** | **19,806** | **−107,577** | **−87,771** | **−0.78** | **11,324,400** | **65.9** | **10,998,400** | **63.4** | **10,950,000** | **60.0** |
| crypto-Christians | 0 | 0.0 | 1,799,907 | 10.5 | 3,759 | 67,940 | 71,699 | 3.34 | 2,149,100 | 12.5 | 2,516,900 | 14.5 | 3,647,000 | 20.0 |
| professing | 12,210,000 | 99.3 | 10,706,200 | 59.1 | 16,047 | −175,517 | −159,470 | −1.74 | 9,175,300 | 53.4 | 8,481,500 | 48.9 | 7,303,000 | 40.0 |
| Protestants | 11,008,000 | 89.5 | 8,870,200 | 52.0 | 14,133 | −154,763 | −140,630 | −1.74 | 8,080,700 | 47.0 | 7,463,900 | 43.0 | 6,382,000 | 35.0 |
| Roman Catholics | 1,200,000 | 9.8 | 1,194,000 | 7.0 | 1,894 | −20,614 | −18,720 | −1.73 | 1,083,200 | 6.3 | 1,006,000 | 5.8 | 912,000 | 5.0 |
| Orthodox | 1,000 | 0.0 | 10,000 | 0.1 | 17 | −117 | −100 | −1.05 | 9,500 | 0.1 | 9,000 | 0.1 | 8,000 | 0.0 |
| Catholics (non-Roman) | 1,000 | 0.0 | 2,000 | 0.0 | 3 | −23 | −20 | −1.05 | 1,900 | 0.0 | 1,800 | 0.0 | 1,000 | 0.0 |
| nominal | 610,000 | 5.0 | 0 | 0.0 | 0 | 0 | 0 | 0.00 | 0 | 0.0 | 0 | 0.0 | 0 | 0.0 |
| affiliated | 11,600,000 | 94.3 | 11,876,107 | 69.6 | 19,806 | −107,577 | −87,771 | −0.78 | 11,324,400 | 65.9 | 10,998,400 | 63.4 | 10,950,000 | 60.0 |
| total practising | 10,440,000 | *90* | 7,125,660 | *60* | 11,884 | −64,546 | −52,662 | −0.78 | 6,794,640 | *60* | 6,599,040 | *60* | 6,570,000 | *60* |
| non-practising | 1,160,000 | *10* | 4,750,450 | *40* | 7,922 | −43,031 | −35,109 | −0.78 | 4,529,760 | *40* | 4,399,360 | *40* | 4,380,000 | *40* |
| Protestants | 10,478,000 | 85.2 | 10,317,841 | 60.5 | 17,161 | −95,415 | −78,254 | −0.80 | 9,812,200 | 57.1 | 9,535,300 | 54.9 | 9,679,000 | 53.1 |
| Evangelicals | 1,476,000 | 12.0 | 2,559,000 | 15.0 | 4,510 | −10 | 4,500 | 0.17 | 2,579,000 | 15.0 | 2,604,000 | 15.0 | 2,735,000 | 15.0 |
| Neo-pentecostals | 0 | 0.0 | 0 | 0.0 | 5 | 595 | 600 | 20.00 | 3,000 | 0.0 | 6,000 | 0.0 | 30,000 | 0.2 |
| Roman Catholics | 1,100,000 | 8.9 | 1,344,266 | 7.9 | 2,285 | −10,002 | −7,717 | −0.59 | 1,306,700 | 7.6 | 1,267,100 | 7.3 | 1,094,000 | 6.0 |
| Catholics (non-Roman) | 20,000 | 0.2 | 144,000 | 0.8 | 236 | −2,136 | −1,900 | −1.41 | 135,000 | 0.8 | 125,000 | 0.7 | 100,000 | 0.5 |
| Marginal Protestants | 1,000 | 0.0 | 52,000 | 0.3 | 94 | 206 | 300 | 0.56 | 53,500 | 0.3 | 55,000 | 0.3 | 62,000 | 0.3 |
| Orthodox | 1,000 | 0.0 | 18,000 | 0.1 | 30 | −230 | −200 | −1.18 | 17,000 | 0.1 | 16,000 | 0.1 | 15,000 | 0.1 |
| Non-religious | 20,000 | 0.2 | 3,646,793 | 21.4 | 7,196 | 65,535 | 72,713 | 1.77 | 4,107,800 | 23.9 | 4,374,100 | 25.2 | 4,922,700 | 27.0 |
| Atheists | 10,000 | 0.1 | 1,527,900 | 9.0 | 3,068 | 42,042 | 45,110 | 2.57 | 1,754,000 | 10.2 | 1,979,000 | 11.4 | 2,355,000 | 12.9 |
| Jews | 60,000 | 0.5 | 1,200 | 0.0 | −70 | 0 | −70 | −8.75 | 800 | 0.0 | 500 | 0.0 | 300 | 0.0 |
| Other religionists | 0 | 0.0 | 6,000 | 0.0 | 0 | 0 | 0 | 0.00 | 6,000 | 0.0 | 6,000 | 0.0 | 5,000 | 0.0 |
| **Country's population** | **12,300,000** | **100.0** | **17,058,000** | **100.0** | **30,000** | **0** | **30,000** | **0.17** | **17,193,000** | **100.0** | **17,358,000** | **100.0** | **18,233,000** | **100.0** |

COLUMNS, ROWS. For meanings and definitions, see Codebook (Part 6). Note that, by definition, total 'Christians' = professing + crypto-Christians, which also = affiliated + nominal Christians. Percentages may not always total exactly, due to rounding.
CENSUSES. (a) *Undivided German Empire in 1900:* 62.5% Protestants, 36.1% Roman Catholics, 1.0% Jews (586,948): 0.4% other Christians. (b) *GDR* (1970 territory). **29.X.1946** (de jure, including 133,327 refugees, internees, prisoners of war): 82.2% Protestants, 12.2% Roman Catholics, 5.5% non-religious, 0.1% other religionists. **31.VIII.1950** (de jure): 82.1% Protestants, 11.1% Roman Catholics, 6.8% non-religious. **31.XII.1964:** 68.0% Christians (59.4% Protestants, 8.1% Roman Catholics), 31.9% non-religious and atheists.

NOTES ON RELIGIONS
ATHEISTS: Socialist Unity Party (SED) (in power; pro-Soviet): membership (1970) 1,845,280 full, 64,579 candidate members; Communist voters (election of 14.XI.1971) 11,207,388 (99.9% of all votes). Of Communist party members, about 20% are estimated to be committed atheists, the other 80% being non-religious with a small number being professing Christians.
COUNTRY'S POPULATION. Since World War II, some 14.5 million East Germans, including a high proportion of practising Christians, have moved as refugees to West Germany.
CRYPTO-CHRISTIANS. Christians affiliated to churches but not know as such to the state, of 3 kinds: (1) unorganized individuals in the legal churches, (2) members of illegal or underground churches, and (3) isolated radio believers.
NEO-PENTECOSTALS. In 1971 a spontaneous charismatic youth movement began independently of the Protestant churches. By 1976 it was still spreading though still unrelated to the structures and officials of the churches.
NOMINAL CHRISTIANS. Before 1948 only.
NON-RELIGIOUS. Agnostics, indifferent to religion, including most Communist party members. In addition, there are another 12.5% of the population (in 1970) whom polls record as non-religious but who are affiliated to churches and so are classified here as crypto-Christians. For many years the state has applied pressure for all types of leaders, military as well as civil, to renounce religion before registrars and so to withdraw formally from the churches.
OTHER RELIGIONISTS. Adherents of several smaller non-Christian religions and cults.
PRACTISING CHRISTIANS. Regular (weekly or fortnightly) attendance (1970–75): Protestants 5%, Roman Catholics 20% (regular attenders as Sunday mass), Free Churches 90%; total persons 1,010,000, i.e. 8.5% of all affiliated Christians. Annual practice: about 60%. East Berlin: Catholic weekly mass attenders 25%, Easter communicants 30% (figures for whole country are slightly lower because East Berlin has a sizeable Polish minority resident).
PROFESSING CHRISTIANS. The causes of the rapid and ongoing decline (from 93.2% in the 1950 census to 68.0% in the 1964 census) have been: (1) about a quarter is due to direct emigration of Christians to West Germany; (2) under a tenth is due to atheistic propaganda; and (3) the rest is due to the process of secularization and the resulting secularism, enforced by the government, leading to continuous withdrawals from the churches.

**NON-CHRISTIAN RELIGIONS. Judaism** faces the same problems in East Germany as in the Federal Republic, namely the growing age of the Jewish population and the lack of replacements for their loss in membership, except that in the GDR the problem is even more serious. The number of Jews belonging to communities was reduced from 5,000 at the beginning of the 1960s to about 1,100 at the end of 1973. The East Berlin community lost more than half its members between 1962 and 1973, having at the end of 1973 only 445 members of whom 11 were children, 24 youths, 96 adults under 60 years of age, and 314 adults over 60 years of age. There are in all 8 Jewish communities: in Berlin, Schwerin, Magdeburg, Halle, Erfurt, Leipzig, Dresden and Karl-Marx-Stadt. All are juridically autonomous but are members of the Association of Jewish Communities in the GDR (Verband der Jüdischen Gemeinden in der DDR) in Dresden. The state subsidizes for the most part their current financial expenses as well as all costs involved in the construction, reconstruction and upkeep of the 9 synagogues and Jewish cemeteries in the GDR. Jewish communities also maintain several homes for the aged and horticultural establishments.

**CHRISTIANITY.** As early as the 3rd century, Christianity established itself in western Germany; but the conversion of the eastern German peoples, especially those of the northeast, was a slow process. Charlemagne attempted to use force in spreading the faith among the Saxons in the 9th century, and this was repeated by the Order of Templars in the 13th century. The 16th-century Protestant Reformation had its greatest appeal in the northeast, and this has continued to the present day.
Church membership has decreased markedly since World War II. In 1950, 82% of the population were professing Protestants, 11% Catholics and 7% without religious affiliation, falling by 1964 to 59% Protestants and 8% Catholics, with 32% in the non-religious category.

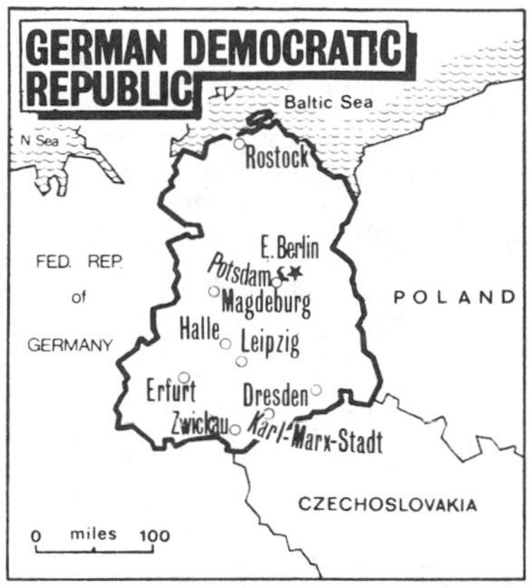


PROTESTANT CHURCHES. The population of East Germany is overwhelmingly Protestant and is mostly found in 8 territorial churches which are all members of the Federation of Evangelical Churches in the GDR. Four are United Lutheran-Reformed Churches (Berlin-Brandenburg, Greifswald, Görlitz, Saxony); 3 are Lutheran (Saxony, Thuringia, Mecklenburg); and the eighth is the Evangelical Church of the Union which serves Anhalt and is also Lutheran-Reformed in tradition. Prior to 1968, all these churches were members of the all-Germany Evangelical Church of Germany (EKD), while the 3 Lutheran churches belonged to the United Evangelical Lutheran Church of Germany (VELKD) and the 4 united churches along with the Church of the Union of Anhalt were part of the Evangelical Church of the Union (EKU). Meetings then were held in West Germany, and it was often difficult for East German church representatives to obtain travel visas to participate. In 1968, under pressure from the government, the East German churches withdrew from the all-German organizations. Another important group urging independence for the East German churches from West German influence has been the Association of Protestant Clergy in the GDR (Bund Evangelischer Pfarrer in der DDR) established in 1958 with active state support; the group now has a membership of about 300 pastors and exerts an influence far greater than its numbers suggest.

Although the 8 regional churches are all part of one federation, they are characterized more by division than unity. They have neither a unified leadership nor a common liturgy and continue to perpetuate with little change the religious traditions which arose during the Reformation period. The expectation that greater unity might result from the churches' present situation in an anti-religious state has not been realized. Rather the opposite has occurred, with new divisions based on intellectual and ideological concerns coming to the fore. A major problem facing the regional churches is a shortage of pastors and a decreasing number of divinity students offering for ordination. A survey made in the late 1960s in Saxony revealed that 740 out of 1,800 parishes were without minister or pastoral visitation; and in 1966 in Anhalt 37 out of 133 parishes also lacked a pastor. Although by no means the only reason, this decline in pastoral supervision has contributed to a general weakening of religious practice and lay participation. Comparative studies in Leipzig show a decline in annual baptisms from 5,700 in 1949 to 1,400 in 1960, while annual confirmations dropped during the period 1949–1959 from 6,200 to 840. Between 1954 and 1963 in Anhalt, yearly church wedding totals declined from 2,100 to 860, and annual baptisms from 5,700 to 2,400. Part of this decrease is due to a general fall in church membership caused by the exodus to West Germany but it is clear that the forces of secularization have also taken their toll. Not only is church membership decreasing, but a significant and disproportionate reduction in church practice is also evident. The concept of the People's church (Volkskirche) is clearly undergoing radical revision.

Apart from the large territorial churches of the Federation, a number of smaller Protestant groups are also active. The largest of these denominations are the Baptist and Methodist churches both of which were introduced into East Germany during the first half of the 19th century. Several underground Pentecostal groups have associated themselves with the Baptist Union, while the Methodist church was greatly strengthened by the merger in 1968 of the Methodists and Evangelical United Brethren in both Germany and the USA. Until recently a part of the Germany Central Conference with headquarters in West Germany, the present Evangelical Methodist Church in the GDR is now a separate central conference of the United Methodist Church based in the USA.

Other Protestant churches in East Germany are the Seventh-day Adventists, who first arrived in 1909, Conference of Reformed Congregations in the GDR, Old Lutherans and Moravian Brethren. Although the latter have only a small community today, their centre at Herrnhut (founded by count Zinzendorf in 1722) continues to serve as the Moravian world headquarters. Small groups of Congregationalists, Friends, Plymouth Brethren, Mennonites and others are also present.

The Protestant churches are still heavily involved in medical and social service, with in 1974 over 2,200 institutions including 49 hospitals and clinics with 7,100 beds.

CATHOLIC CHURCH. The organization of the East German Catholic dioceses has constituted since 1945 a major problem for the Holy See. Until recently the latter had always refused to accept the fact of 2 German states and the changes in the German-Polish frontier, since peace treaties had not yet been signed. Therefore with the exception of the bishoprics of Berlin (which includes also West Berlin) and Meissen, the rest of the territory, more than half of the GDR, was dependent on Polish and West German bishoprics.

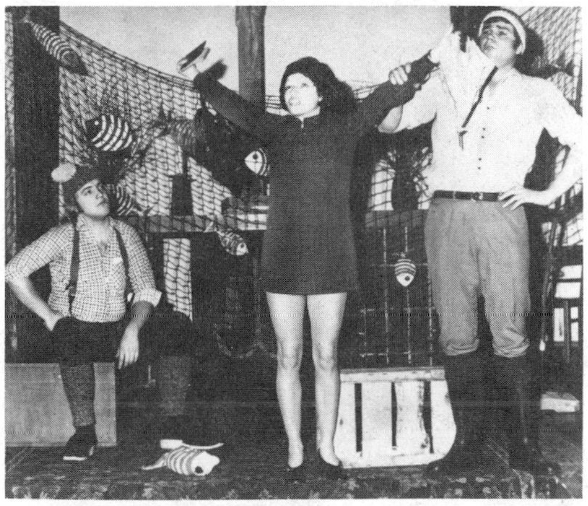

**Bund der Evangelischen Kirchen in der DDR.** Parable of Net full of Fishes (John 21) performed by lay group touring Protestant parishes.

Following the signing of the treaty of 7 December 1970 between the Federal Republic of Germany and Poland, by which the FRG government recognized the Oder-Neisse frontier, the Holy See proceeded in 1972 to modify the borders of Polish dioceses, thus regularizing 2 anomalies in the GDR. The ancient 'archiepiscopal office' of Görlitz attached until then to the Polish archdiocese of Wroclaw (ex-Breslau) was made an independent apostolic administration, and the diocese of Berlin until then suffragan to Wroclaw was made directly dependent on the Holy See. The situation of the episcopal commissariats attached to West German dioceses is also moving towards normalization. On 23 July 1973, after the signing of the Basic Treaty between the 2 Germanys (2 December 1972) and its ratification by the Bonn parliament, the pope appointed 3 apostolic administrators for the territories of Erfurt-Meiningen, Magdeburg and Schwerin. While these territories continue to be attached to West Germany dioceses, their administrators are directly responsible to the Holy See, not to West German bishops.

The German political drama has since World War II strongly influenced the internal situation of East German Catholicism as well as Protestantism, caused by many factors: the massive flight of Christians to the FRG, the need of financial support from the church in the FRG for that in the GDR (especially for the building of new churches, in spite of the aid provided by the GDR government for reconstruction of some) and the impossibility for East German bishops of participating in meetings of the German Bishops' Conference (in West Germany) of which they were theoretically a part. The ordinaries of the GDR have now formed their own Conference of Ordinaries of Berlin (Berliner Ordinarienkonferenz), although it does not have the status of a national episcopal conference since the GDR is not recognized by the Holy See. West Berlin is administered by a vicar-general dependent on a bishop who resides in East Berlin and is authorized to pass 3 days per month in West Berlin.

The pastoral situation is difficult to review because of the absence of precise statistics. At the beginning of 1975, a diocesan newspaper edited in East Berlin estimated that 20% of East German Catholics were regular attenders at Sunday mass. In East Berlin itself the estimate for weekly mass attendance is 25%, and 30% for Easter communicants, but these figures are higher than the national average partly due to the presence of a significant Polish colony in the city. In 1968, there were 1,174 secular and regular priests active. The advancing age of the clergy is a serious problem, and appeals have been made since 1956 to lay helpers (non-ordained auxiliary deacons who retain their secular professions) to meet the pastoral needs of the parishes. At the end of 1973, the number of auxiliaries in the GDR was about 700, among whom about 40, mostly married, expected to receive diaconal ordination; and 9 were in fact ordained deacons on 31 December 1974.

It is important to note the role, especially in the ecumenical field, of the Oratory of Leipzig, to which belongs the bishop of Meissen who initiated the pastoral synod. This synod has involved all 7 ecclesiastical jurisdictions in the GDR and is the first Catholic national synod in a Communist state. In the planning stage since 1971, its first session was held at Dresden in 1973 in the presence of foreign Catholic observers from the episcopates of the FRG, Austria, Switzerland, Poland, Hungary, Yugoslavia and Luxembourg, as well as Protestant and Orthodox observers from the GDR. According to cardinal Bengsch, its president, the synod is a purely internal activity of the Catholic Church, avoiding all questions relating to the political consequences of Christian involvement in a socialist society. The synod thus reflects the attitude of resignation and introversion of the great majority of East German Catholics in relation to the existing socio-political situation.

OTHER CHURCHES. Apart from the 8 territorial churches and the Roman Catholic Church, the largest Christian community in the GDR is that of the New Apostolic Church with its world headquarters in Dortmund, West Germany. Other Catholic non-Roman churches include the Reformed Apostolic Community, a split from the New Apostolic Church in 1921, and the Old Catholic Church.

Orthodoxy is represented by 2 groups, the Greek Orthodox Church, which is part of the diocese of Germany and East Middle Europe under the Ecumenical Patriarchate of Constantinople, and the Russian Orthodox Church under the Patriarchate of Moscow.

Marginal bodies include the Horpenites, Anthroposophical Society, St John the Divine Church and a number of Mormons. Jehovah's Witnesses, banned since 1949, have a zealous underground following.

**CHURCH AND STATE.** The constitution of 8 April 1968, completed and amended on 7 October 1974, is of importance for the churches because of 3 of its articles: (1) Article 39, paragraph 1: 'Every citizen of the GDR has the right to freedom of conscience and to the free practice of the religion of his choice'; paragraph 2: 'The churches and other religious communities regulate their affairs and exercise their activities within the structure of the constitutional and legal regulations of the GDR. The regulations in detail may be defined in special conventions'; (2) Article 20, paragraph 1: 'All citizens of the GDR have the same rights and the same duties, without regard to nationality, race, ideology or confession, origin or social position. Freedom of conscience and religious opinion is guaranteed. All citizens are equal before the law'; and (3) Article 6, paragraph 5: 'Manifestations of hate against creeds, races and peoples are crimes and are punishable as such'. This latter paragraph places in the same category 'militaristic propaganda' and 'incitement to war'. The formulation of Article 39 has been criticized by the representatives of both the Evangelical and Catholic churches for its imprecision and especially for its suppression of the juridical personality of the churches which removes from them all legal assistance before courts of law. The previous constitution of 1949 consisted of 9 articles concerning religion and gave explicit recognition to the rights of the churches, although it must be admitted these were often more of theoretical than of practical significance. While Ulbricht was still chief of state, he insisted that the 1968 text would not change anything in this state of affairs (*Neues Deutschland*, 3 February 1968).

35,000 East and West German Protestants hold 6th open-air rally, 1954, in Leipzig.

While it is true that pastoral work, liturgy and religious instruction are unobstructed, all church activities organized outside ecclesiastical edifices require prior authorization from the local authorities. The principal religious ceremonies (baptism, confirmation, marriage) are rivalled by parallel rites with ceremonies termed socialist. In this domain, the efforts of the state are especially concentrated on the consecration of youth in the Jugendweihe, a secular form of confirmation instituted in 1955, which has come into wide usage due to the system of rewards and pressures attached to it. The fulfilment of military service, or civil service for conscientious objectors, is accompanied by a pledge of allegiance to the socialist state. Finally, all non-conformist positions relative to social or political questions create severe problems because they are interpreted as a mark of defiance vis-a-vis the state. Up to the present, this has only been safe for bishops who have expressed their opinions on such questions as marriage and the family, abortion, socialist consecration of youth and other matters by means of pastoral letters and requests addressed to the state. Thus the Catholic bishops disseminated in all their churches on 17 November 1974 a pastoral letter opposing monopolization of education by the state and the ethical training of youth. Similarly, in May 1975, the synod of the Evangelical Church of Berlin-Brandenburg requested the competent authorities to terminate their 'discrimination against practising Christian youth' in schools and professional training.

In the eyes of the East German government, the most important question is whether the churches of the GDR are ready to accept the consequences of the existence of 2 separate German states (Article 39, paragraph 2 of the constitution of 1968). In this, it needs to be stressed that the Evangelical Church in the GDR is, in its totality, less reluctant than the Catholic Church to participate in the building of a new socialist society. For the former the situation became even clearer when, on 30 September 1969, it broke its last institutional links with the West German EKD. In the same direction, the Catholic Church made an important first step in 1973 when the Vatican appointed apostolic administrators independent of FRG bishops. Rome interpreted this officially to be a recognition of the existence of the GDR, but the East German government wishes the Vatican to go further in creating new bishoprics whose boundaries would coincide with those of the GDR. That this will ultimately take place is only a question of time.

In March 1978 a major agreement took place between Erich Honecker, leader of the Socialist Unity Party (SED) and the presiding bishop of the Federation of Evangelical Churches in the GDR, which offered the prospect of a major transformation in church-state relationships. Although during 1958–78 only 10 new Protestant church buildings had been permitted, the agreement allowed 55 more to be built over the following 2 years. Discrimination against Christian children and youths would also end, church congresses (Kirchentagen) would be permitted, and both Protestant and Catholic churches would now be given weekly radio time and TV time on festivals.

**INTERDENOMINATIONAL ORGANIZATIONS.** The Council of Christian Churches in the GDR (Arbeitsgemeinschaft Christlicher Kirchen in der DDR) was founded in 1970 with, as members, the 8 territorial Protestant churches, plus the Baptists, Reformed, Mennonites, Methodists, Moravians, Congregationalists, Old Catholics and Old Lutherans. In addition the Friends are a guest member and the Catholic Church an observer. It is an associate council of the WCC. Of its member churches, 11 are also members of the WCC, and 12 are members of the Conference of European Churches.

The Conference of Ordinaries of Catholic Dioceses and Episcopal Commissariats has appointed a representative for ecumenical questions, residing in Leipzig. A Catholic-Lutheran Mixed Commission is active, and 4 ecumenical institutes and centres are functioning. (1) The Ökumenisches Institut beim Ökumenisch Missionarischen Amt, founded in East Berlin by the Evangelical Church in 1962, is an institute of university rank and a study centre for all ecclesiastical disciplines. It gathers information on Protestant ecumenical activities and holds consultations involving all churches in the GDR, except the Catholic Church. (2) The Konfessionskundliches Arbeitwerk der Evangelischen Kirche in der DDR, founded in Potsdam in 1964, is a centre for infor-

All religious matters come under the State Secretariat for Religious Questions (Staatssekretariat für Kirchenfragen). In contrast to the FRG, the GDR does not recognize the validity of the concordat of 1933 with the Holy See and so has no diplomatic relations with the Vatican.

Although real, the difficulties experienced by the churches since the assumption of control by the Communist regime following World War II are not as severe as those in other East European countries (with the exception of Poland), nor are the persecutions suffered more serious than those at the time of the 19th-century kulturkampf in Germany. Indeed they are part of the general problem of re-organization after 1945. Neither the agrarian reform nor the creation of agricultural co-operatives in 1960 have seriously affected church property. According to a recent CDU brochure entitled 'Christians and Churches in the GDR', the Evangelical churches alone still possess more than 200,000 hectares of arable land. Educational and social service institutions, as well as confessional hospitals, still retain their place in the mixed economy of the country, and there is effectual freedom of worship. Without being recognized legally, Evangelical and Catholic churches receive regular state subsidies which are used mostly for their charitable institutions. The state has also provided materials for the reconstruction of old churches destroyed during the War and more rarely for the construction of new ones. Protestant and Catholic seminarians are exempt from military service, and the universities of Berlin, Leipzig, Halle,

Jena, Rostock and Greifswald each retain a faculty of Protestant theology. Since state and churches are separate, the faithful make their financial contributions directly to their churches, and not through the state as in the FRG. Moreover, the Christian Democratic Union (Christlich Demokratische Union, CDU), which has nothing to do with the West German party of the same name although both include Protestants and Catholics, is one of the 5 legal political parties in the GDR. The East German CDU was founded on 26 June 1945 in the Soviet zone of occupation; and as with all other political parties of the GDR, it supports the socialist policy of the government and is a member of the National Front of Democratic Germany. The CDU is represented in parliament (50 delegates out of 500 in 1973, including some ecclesiastics and theologians) and in the government (one minister in 1973), but it has only a secondary influence over the population because its position among the workers is very weak. Nevertheless, some members of the party play an important role in the state apparatus.

No less true is the fact that social pressure limits this freedom. It is difficult to obtain a post of real responsibility without holding a membership card of the Socialist Unity Party (SED), which is a coalition of Social Democrats and Communists but dominated by the latter; and it is impossible for a Christian known to be deeply-committed to obtain a professional post in higher education. Marxism-Leninism is an obligatory university course and it is necessary to pass it well to receive a doctorate.

mation, instruction, ecumenical study and research, dependent on the Evangelical Church. It encourages studies and dialogue with the Catholic Church and other Christian denominations. (3) The Ökumenische Arbeitstelle der Diözese Meissen, founded in Leipzig in 1967, is a Catholic ecumenical centre which promotes dialogue and training and serves as a source for information. (4) The Institut für Konfessionskunde der Orthodoxie an der Ev-Theologische Fakultät, founded at the Universität Halle-Wittenberg in 1952, offers seminar courses and other studies and maintains an important library, with emphasis on Orthodoxy.

An organization dedicated to improving relations between Protestants and Jews is Action of Expiation in the Service of Peace (Aktion Sühnezeichen Friedensdienste) founded in West Berlin in 1958, with its East Berlin centre established in 1961. It is a branch of the Inner Mission and Service of Inter-church Aid of the Evangelical Churches of the GDR.

**BROADCASTING.** No religious programmes were permitted over the Staatliches Komitee für Rundfunk until the 1978 agreement permitted weekly Protestant and Catholic radio programmes and TV services on festivals. From abroad, Protestant programmes in German are beamed in by Trans World Radio (Monaco) for 15 hours 55 minutes a week, and by Radio Luxembourg for 9 hours 30 minutes; and Catholic programmes in German by Radio Vatican for 5 hours 15 minutes a week.

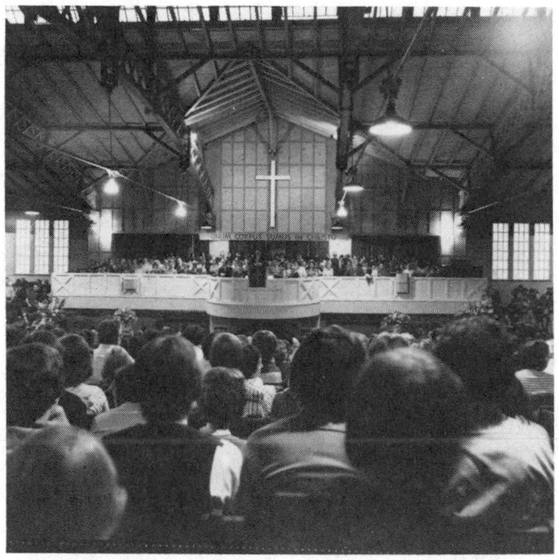

*Left.* 2,500 youth delegates at 79th Alliance Conference, Bad Blankenburg, 1977.

## BIBLIOGRAPHY


*Christ in der DDR.* J. Hamel. Berlin: Käthe Vogt, 1957. 51p.
'Die Evangelischen Kirchen in der DDR: ein Überblick', I. Roitsch, *Informationsdienst des Katholischen Arbeitskreises für Zitgeschichtliche Fragen* (Bonn-Bad Godesberg), No. 83, 1977.
'German Democratic Republic', B. Wilhelm, in H. Mol (ed), *Western religion* (The Hague: Mouton, 1972), p. 213–228.
'Katholische Kirche in der DDR', K. Richter, *Jahrbuch für christliche Sozialwissenschaften*, XIII (1972), 215–245.
*Neue Erde ohne Himmel: der Kampf des Atheismus gegen das Christentum in der DDR: Modell einer Weltweiten Auseinandersetzung.* H.-G. Koch. Stuttgart: Quell-Verlag, 1963. 591p.
*Stimmen aus der Kirche in der DDR.* B Ruys. Zürich: EVZ-Verlag, 1965. 210p.
*Zwischen Gestern und Morgen: Evangelische Gemeinden in der DDR.* L. Borgmann. Berlin: Evangelische Verlagsanstalt, 1969.


TABLE 2. ORGANIZED CHURCHES AND DENOMINATIONS IN THE GERMAN DEMOCRATIC REPUBLIC

| Official name 1 | Begun 2 | Type 3 | Counc 4 | Congs 5 | Adults 6 | Affiliated 7 | Names, notes, and other statistics (see Codebook) 8 |
|---|---|---|---|---|---|---|---|
| Alt-Katholische Kirche in der DDR | c1875 | C OCa | UW..W | | 1,200 | 2,000 | *Gemeindeverband der A-KK. Old Catholic Ch.* 3 priests, 2 deacons. HQ Leipzig. |
| Apostelamt Jesu Christi | 1923 | C CAp | ..... | 163 | 4,000 | 10,000 | *Apostolate of Jesus Christ.* Ex Apostelamt Juda. Churches across to Oder. |
| Apostelamt Juda | 1902 | C CAp | ..... | | 3,000 | 5,000 | *Apostolate of Judah. Gemeinschaft des Gottlichen Sozialismus.* Ex NAK. HQ Berlin. |
| **Bund der Ev Kirchen in der DDR:** | 1946 | P LuR | 1WC.W | 5,103 | 7,975,800 | 10,096,077 | *Federation of Ev Chs in the GDR* (1967 broke ex EKD in WGermany). 4220n,G=−4.4%pa. |
| Anhalt: Ev Landeskirche Anhalts | | P LuR | .wC.x | 133 | 217,200 | 275,000 | *Evangelical Ch of Anhalt.* Parts of Halle and Magdeburg districts. 100n. |
| Berlin-Brandenburg, Ev Kirche in | 1528 | P LuR | .wC.x | 400 | 1,501,000 | 1,900,000 | *Evangelical Ch in Berlin-Brandenburg, Eastern Region.* 860n,3s(90+80+40). |
| Görlitz: EKGörlitzer Kirchengebietes | | P LuR | .wC.x | 70 | 142,200 | 180,000 | *Ev Ch of Görlitz Region* (until 1968, Silesia). Parts of Dresden, Cottbus. 80n. |
| Greifswald, Ev Landeskirche | | P LuR | LwC.x | 300 | 434,500 | 550,000 | *Ev Ch of Greifswald* (Pomerania). Part Rostock, Neubrandenburg. 190n,1s(55),2790Yy. |
| Kirchenprovinz Sachsen, EK der | 1517 | P LuR | .wC.x | 2,000 | 1,896,000 | 2,400,000 | *Ev Ch of Province of Saxony.* Halle, Magdeburg, Erfurt. 930n,3s(80+90+30). |
| Mecklenberg, Ev-Luth Landeskirche | 1523 | P Lut | LwC.d | 400 | 671,500 | 850,000 | *Ev Luth Ch of Mecklenberg.* Schwerin, Rostock, Mecklenberg. 340n,1s(40). |
| Sachsen: Ev-L Landeskirche Sachsens | 1517 | P Lut | LwC.d | 900 | 2,165,400 | 2,741,077 | *Ev Luth Ch of Saxony.* Dresden, Leipzig, Karl-Marx-Stadt. 1100n,2s(110+150). |
| Thuringen, Ev-Lutherische Kirche in | 1527 | P Lut | LwC.d | 900 | 948,000 | 1,200,000 | *Ev Luth Ch in Thuringia.* Reformation heartland: Erfurt, Gera, Suhl. 620n,1s(95). |
| Bund der Kämpfer für Glaube & W | 1918 | M Spi | x.... | | 3,000 | 5,000 | *W=Wahrheit. Warriors for Faith & Truth. Horpenites.* In Saxony, FRG, Spain, USA, SW Africa. |
| Bund Ev-Freikirchlicher Gemeinden | 1834 | P Bap | T.C.W | 224 | 23,648 | 100,000 | *Baptist Union.* Includes Elim and underground Pentecostals. 125n,G=−2%pa,1s(16). |
| Bund Freier Ev Gemeinden in der DDR | | P Con | K...W | 52 | 1,350 | 4,000 | *Federation of Free Evangelical Congregations.* Declining. HQ Falkensee. 13n. |
| Christengemeinschaft | 1922 | M Gno | x.... | 30 | 5,000 | 7,000 | *Sonnenwesen (Sun-Being). Anthroposophical Society.* 7 sacraments. HQ Erfurt. |
| Christliche Gemeinschaft Hirt & Herde | 1894 | P Hol | ..... | | 5,000 | 10,000 | *Christian Society of Shepherd & Flock.* Holiness doctrines. Legal recognition 1951. |
| Chr G der Deutschen Pfingstbewegung | | P Pen | Z.... | 10 | 1,000 | 2,000 | Chr G=*Christlichen Gemeinschaftsverband. Mulheimer Bewegung.* Banned 1951. |
| Evangelische Brüder-Unität | 1722 | P Mor | xWC.W | 10 | 3,200 | 5,000 | *District Herrnhut* (in GDR). European Continental Province. Unity of Brethren. 20n. |
| Evangelische Johannische Kirche | 1926 | M Spi | x.... | 60 | 6,000 | 10,000 | *Ev Ch of the Revelation of St John the Divine.* Decline from 120,000 in 1929. |
| Ev-Luth (Altlutherische) Kirche | 1830 | P Lut | ..C.W | 40 | 7,800 | 9,864 | *Ev Lutheran (Old Lutheran) Ch in the GDR* (formerly Prussia). HQ Berlin 102. 25n. |
| Ev-Methodistische Kirche in der DDR | 1849 | P Met | VwC.W | 348 | 28,588 | 40,000 | 1968 merger with Ev Gemeinschaft/EUB. M=UMC(USA). HQ Dresden. 139n,7f,1s(12),207t. |
| Freier Brüderkreis | c1870 | P CBr | x.... | 30 | 1,000 | 2,000 | *Free Brethren. Christliche Versammlung. Plymouth-Brüder. Open Brethren.* |
| Griechisch-Orthodoxe Kirche | | O Gre | Cwc.. | | 7,000 | 10,000 | *Greek Orthodox Ch.* In D Germany & East Middle Europe, under EP Constantinople. |
| Isolated radio churches | 1939 | P rad | ..... | 440 | 9,000 | 17,600 | Isolated radio believers. R=5200(Radio Vatican since 1939;TWR,HCJB,RVOG,&c). |
| **Katholische Kirche Deutschlands:** | 772 | R Lat | ..B.s | 653 | 1,062,100 | 1,344,266 | *Catholic Ch in Germany.* C=15+0+14. 3s. 1336n,71m,2443w,9811Yy. |
| D Berlin | 1930 | R Lat | bs | 110 | 192,000 | 243,000 | *Bistum Berlin.* East Berlin (D also covers W Berlin). 240 30 600 1800 |
| D Meissen | 968 | R Lat | bs | 128 | 243,000 | 307,540 | Saxonia. Only diocese with a priests' council. 312 4 470 2275 |
| EC Erfurt | 1973 | R Lat | bs | 150 | 197,500 | 250,000 | *Bischofliches Kommissariat Erfurt.* Part of D Fulda. 1s. 260 0 500 1800 |
| EC Magdeburg | 1973 | R Lat | bs | 109 | 258,900 | 327,696 | Part of M Paderborn (West Germany)(12 Deaneries). 317 22 377 2400 |
| EC Meiningen | 1973 | R Lat | bs | 30 | 31,600 | 40,000 | Part of D Würzburg, but directly under Holy See. 30 0 100 300 |
| EC Schwerin | 1973 | R Lat | bs | 67 | 80,600 | 102,000 | Part of D Osnabrück; directly under Holy See. 86 11 127 700 |
| AA Görlitz | 1972 | R Lat | bs | 59 | 58,500 | 74,030 | In southeast. In east there are Slav Catholics. 91 4 269 536 |
| K JC der Heiligen der Letzten Tage | 1845 | M LdS | x.... | | 6,000 | 10,000 | *Latter-day Saints.* Pre 1945, most German Mormons lived in east. HQ Dresden. 50f. |
| Kirchenbund Ev-reformierter G | 1949 | P Ref | R...W | 21 | 5,000 | 8,100 | *G=Gemeinden. Conference of Rreformed Congregations in the GDR.* 5 Districts, 3·parishes. 20n. |
| Mennonitengemeinde in der DDR | | P Men | G...W | | 350 | 1,000 | *Mennonite Congregations in the GDR.* Mennonite remnants with FRG links. HQ Berlin. 1n. |
| Neuapostolische Kirche | c1863 | C CAp | x.... | 500 | 80,000 | 120,000 | *NAK. New Apostolic Ch.* Ex Irvingites. World HQ Dortmund (FRGermany). 5 Apostles. |
| Reformiert-Apost Gemeindebund | 1921 | C CAp | x.... | | 3,000 | 7,000 | *Reformed Apostolic Community.* In VAC (Switzerland). Ex NAK. HQ Dresden. Declining. |
| Religiöse Gesellschaft der Freunde | | P Qua | Q...w | | 50 | 200 | *Religious Society of Friends (Quakers).* Small private house groups. HQ Werdau. |
| Russisch-Orth K (PE Mitteleuropa) | | O Sla | Mwc.. | 4 | 2,000 | 3,000 | *Russian OC, Patriarchal Exarchate of Moscow, D Berlin & Tegel.* Russian bishop,2x. |
| Siebenten-Tags-Adventisten in der DDR | 1909 | P Adv | x.... | 334 | 12,062 | 20,000 | *Gemeinschaft der STA. Seventh-day Adventists.* Declining 2% pa. 112n,1r,1316t,298Y. |
| USSR military groups | 1945 | O Sla | ..... | | 3,000 | 5,000 | Small private groups among mainly Orthodox believers in USSR armed forces. |
| Zeugen Jehovas | c1900 | M Jeh | x.... | | 10,000 | 20,000 | *Jehovah's Witnesses.* Strong before 1945; banned 1949, but now strong underground. |
| Other Protestant denominations | | P | ..... | | 1,000 | 2,000 | Total about 5, including Exclusive Brethren (Raven-Taylor, Kelly-Continental). |
| **Total affiliated (mid-1970)** | | | | **8,410** | **9,270,148** | **11,876,107** | **Total denominations (1970) . . .** 32. |
| **Total affiliated (mid-1975)** | | | | **8,350** | **8,839,500** | **11,324,400** | **Total denominations (1975) . . .** 32. |
| **Total affiliated (mid-1980)** | | | | **8,300** | **8,585,000** | **10,998,400** | **Total denominations (1980) . . .** 32. |

NOTES ON TABLE ABOVE
COLUMNS: for meanings and CODES (cols. 1, 3, 4, 8), see Codebook (Part 6). Column 1: **Boldface type** = church with over 10% of country's affiliated Christians.
NATIONAL COUNCILS (Column 4, 5th letter).
d = Vereinigte Evangelisch-Lutherische Kirche DDR (VELKDDR) (United Evangelical Church of GDR), a 1969 federation; members also belong to ACKDDR.
s = Berliner Ordinarienkonferenz (Berlin Episcopal Conference), also observer member of ACKDDR.
W = Arbeitsgemeinschaft Christlicher Kirchen in der DDR (ACKDDR) (Council/Association of Christian Churches in the GDR).
w = associate (guest) member of ACKDDR.
x = Evangelische Kirche der Union (EKU) (Ev Ch of the Union; also 3 members in FRG); members also belong to ACKDDR.
*Other national councils.* Evangelical Alliance in the GDR (affiliated to EEA but not to WEF; over 2,000 local groups).

PEOPLES (ethnolinguistic). Christians: 98.2% German, 1.5% Sorb (Slav, Lusatian, Wendish), 0.1% Greek, 0.1% Russian (military and civilian).

COUNTRY-WIDE TOTALS
EVANGELIZATION (see Part 5). 1900: 100%. 1970: 97%. 1980: 98%. Although mass evangelism is difficult to organize, religious music concerts and organ recitals regularly attract large audiences expecially of young people. *Radiophonic evangelism.* TWR, HCJB, RVOG, Radio Vatican (since 1939), et alia. Annual listeners' letters (1972): 973 HCJB.
FOREIGN MISSIONARIES AND PERSONNEL (nationals serving abroad) (1973). Nil. None are permitted out, but a few have obtained West German citizenship in order to serve overseas.
FOREIGN MISSIONARIES AND PERSONNEL (aliens from abroad) (1973). Total 135. *From Western world.* 132: about 100 marginal Protestants (Mormons et alii) mainly from FR Germany, 20 Roman Catholics, 10 Protestants in 2 USA societies, about 2 Orthodox. *From Communist world.* About 3 Orthodox from USSR, Czechoslovakia.
INSTITUTIONS (church-operated) (1973). Total 315, including 2 ecumenical centres, 7 higher schools (2 minor seminaries), 245 medical centres (45 hospitals), 5 publishing houses, 2 research centres, 19 seminaries (16 Protestant, 3 RC), 25 study and specialized training centres.
PERIODICALS. About 50 titles. The 5 regional newspapers of the Evangelical Church have a combined circulation of 150,000.
PERSONNEL. About 9,035 (8,900 national, 135 foreign).
RELIGIOUS LIBRARIES. About 60.
SCRIPTURE DISTRIBUTION (1975). Annual totals: 19,873 Bibles (subsidized), 51,786 NTs (subsidized), 24,189 UBS portions, 183,749 UBS selections. *Translations completed.* Portion: 7 languages since 1475. NT: 4 languages since 1706. Bible: 5 languages since 1466.
SERVICE AGENCIES. About 35, including ACKDDR, BK, EKU, ENA, KAG, OMR, VELKDDR.

ADDITIONAL DATA ON CHURCHES
BUND DER EV KIRCHEN IN DER DDR (BEK). *Seminarians.* The first group of theological students (in brackets) listed for Berlin-Brandenburg, Greifswald, Kirchenprovinz Sachsen, Mecklenberg, Sachsen, Thüringen, are in university departments of theology. *Membership decline.* The church's official figures show a decline of total affiliated members from 10,096,077 (1970) to 9,070,000 (1 January 1973) and to 8,470,000 (mid-1974), i.e. a decline of 400,000 a year (−4.4% per year). *Institutions.* Social institutions of all kinds including minor centres number over 2,200.
BUND EV-FREIKIRCHLICHER GEMEINDEN. There has been a 30% decline in membership since 1953.
EVANGELISCH-LUTHERISCHE (ALTLUTHERISCHE) KIRCHE. In 1976 this church was joined by the Evangelical Lutheran Free Church in the GDR, with the joint name Union of Independent Evangelical Lutheran Churches in the GDR; with 43 pastors. *Co-operating foreign body.* Lutheran Church—Missouri Synod (USA).
KATHOLISCHE KIRCHE DEUTSCHLANDS. *Annual baptisms.* (1972) 99.0% infant, 1.0% adult. *Personnel.* All nationals. *Religious orders and congregations.* In 1961, 2,764 religious personnel in 120 convents and monasteries. Men religious: 15 congregations (1969) including Dominicans, Franciscans and secular priests' communities. Sisters: 14 congregations, including: Benedictines, Ursulines, Cistercians, Franciscans, Grey Sisters of St Elizabeth, St Charles Borromeo.
*Catholic organizations.* The Conference of Ordinaries of Berlin (Berliner Ordinarienkonferenz), although lacking the status of a national episcopal conference, plays a role similar to that of episcopal conferences in other countries. There are no associations for religious personnel, nor pastoral or presbyteral councils. The Bonifatius Hilfswerk für die Katholische Deutsche Diaspora, in Magdeburg, which caters for the reception and training of Catholics in heavily-Protestant areas, is the only lay apostolate institution remaining in the GDR.

The Holy See has no diplomatic relations with the GDR.

Concerning opinion groups, the existence of 2 minority tendencies should be noted. The first involves Catholics, especially in university circles, who recognize the GDR as the place where they have to live and work and who accept the limitations their society imposes on them. The second tendency is grouped around the Berlin Conference of Catholic Christians from European States (Berliner Konferenz Katholischer Christen aus Europäischen Staaten, BK). This was founded in 1964 by the Catholic section of the East German CDU, and serves as a permanent forum of Catholics for peace (detente in Europe and justice in the world) to which renowned Catholics from 26 West and East European countries belong. The conference, which has contacts with Justitia et Pax in the Holy See and the ecclesiastical movement Pax Christi in the Netherlands, sponsors study groups as well as bilateral and international meetings of various kinds. This group also has close relations with the progressivist Catholic journal *Begegnung, Zeitschrift progressiver Katholiken*, founded in Berlin in 1961.

The training of clergy takes place at the major seminary of Erfurt. Clergy for West Berlin are trained in the FRG. Religious instruction for children is organized by the Catechetical Working Community (Katechetischen Arbeitsgemeinschaft). In 1974 there were 13 spiritual retreat houses, plus centres for the training of catechists, parish helpers, specialists in church music, an institution for young singers at Dresden and 2 publishing houses: St Benno Verlag at Leipzig, the most important, and its associate, Verlag FW Cardier at Heilbad Heiligenstadt. There are 2 diocesan newspapers, for Berlin and Meissen.

Medical and social service is co-ordinated by Deutscher Caritasverband, with headquarters in Berlin and local branches in each ecclesiastical jurisdiction. In 1974, Catholic confessional institutions included 34 hospitals (5,438 beds), 11 nursing homes, 107 homes for the aged, 137 nursing stations, 14 homes for the handicapped, 30 homes for children and infants, 39 recreation and health resort homes and 82 welfare centres. In addition the church maintains training centres for nurses (7), welfare workers (1), workers with children (2), youth (11) and the elderly (2), and educational workers (2). All of these involved as workers a total of 7,347 Catholic personnel, including 1,498 religious sisters.
KIRCHENBUND EV-REFORMIERTER GEMEINDEN. In addition, there are a further 17,000 Reformed members in congregations within the Bund der Ev Kirchen in der DDR.

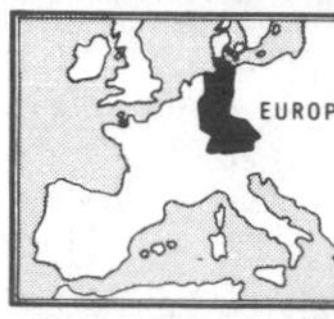


# GERMANY, West

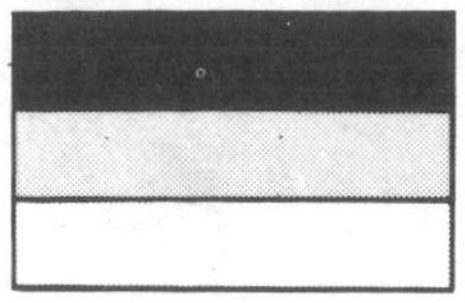

## SECULAR DATA

**STATE. Official name:** The Federal Republic of Germany, FRG (Bundesrepublik Deutschland, BRD). Unofficial name: West Germany.
**Flag** (shown above right): Black, red, and gold stripes.
**Area:** 247,973 sq.km. (95,976 sq.miles). Agricultural land: 54.0%.
**Government:** Federal republic, created 1948, sovereign independent country 1955 (1871 unified constitutional empire, 1919 Weimar republic, 1933 Nazi dictatorship).
**Legislature:** Bundesrat, 41 members. Bundestag (Federal Diet), 496 members.
**Official language:** German (*Deutsch*).
**Chief cities:** capital Bonn 283,260 (1974), West Berlin 2,047,950, Hamburg 1,751,620, Munich 1,336,580, Cologne 832,400, Essen 674,000, Frankfurt 663,420.
**Political divisions:** 10 Länder (States) and West Berlin (special status).
**Armed forces** (1976): Total 495,000 regular (227,000 conscripts): army 345,000, navy 39,000, air force 111,000 (462 combat aircraft). Reserves: 1,181,000. Paramilitary forces: 20,000.
**Foreign forces** (1973): 228,000 USA troops, 55,000 British (UK) troops. (1976) 193,400 USA troops plus 50,000 US Air Force, 58,000 British (UK) troops plus 8,600 Royal Air Force, 32,000 Belgian troops, others from Canada, Netherlands, et alia.

**DEMOGRAPHY. Population:** 60,650,599 (census of 27.V.1970. For 1970–2000 (UN), see last row of Table 1). Population density (1975): 249/sq.km. (644/sq.mile). Under 15 years: 22%. Growth rate (1975–80): 0.11% per year (births 1.16%, deaths −1.24%, immigrants 0.19%). Life expectancy (1975–80): 71.2 years. Household size: 2.7 persons.
**Major languages:** German, Turkish, Serbo-Croatian, Italian, Greek, Spanish, English, Arabic, French, Frisian, Danish.
**Urban dwellers** (1970): 81.9%. Urban growth rate (1950–70): 1.7% per year.
**Labour force: 44%.**
**Refugees** (1977): 52,286 (24,000 from Poland, 16,286 from GDR during 1975 (10,275 legal, 6,011 escapees), 12,000 from USSR). Since 1961, 200,000 have left the GDR legally and 107,027 have escaped to the FRG.
**Tourists** (1974): 6,950,627.

**ETHNOLINGUISTIC GROUPS:** 93.6% German, 1.5% Turkish, 1.1% Serbian, 1.0% Italian, 0.7% Greek, 0.5% Spaniard, 0.3% Austrian, 0.2% Dutch, 0.2% Portuguese, 0.1% Polish, 0.1% Danish, 0.1% Estonian, 0.1% Russian, 0.1% USA (68,000), 0.1% French (55,400), 0.1% British (47,000), 0.1% Jewish, Gypsy (30,000), Swiss (25,000), Moroccan (22,300), Frisian (20,000), Persian (18,500), Tunisian (15,800), Palestinian Arab (15,000), Armenian, Latvian, Lithuanian, Romanian, Korean, Ukrainian, Czech, Chinese (5,000), et alii. Total aliens (1973): 3,966,200 (2,595,000 foreign workers excluding dependants, falling by 1977 to 1.9 million with 2 million dependants).

**MONEY** (1977). **Monetary unit:** Deutsche mark (= 100 pfennig); US$1 = DM 2.37.
**National income per person:** US$5,462. Average annual family income: US$14,747.
**Inflation:** (1970–74) 6.2% per year (1975: consumer price index 140); (1977) 3.9% per year; (1978) 3.1% per year.
**Cost of living in capital** (1976): index 165 (Washington DC=100). Daily cost of living: US$49.

**EDUCATION.** Adult literacy: 100%. Education rate: 55%. Schools: 19,590. Universites: 50.

**HEALTH.** Hospitals: 3,519 (701,263 beds). Doctors: 113,561. Blind: 60,000. Psychotics: 680,000. Drug addicts: 40,000. Criminals: 967,799.

**LITERATURE.** Annual new book titles (1971): 40,354. Periodicals: 9,000. Scientific journals: 2,560. Newspapers: 1,223 dailies, 58 non-daily.

**COMMUNICATION** (per 1,000 people): Phones: 287. Radios: 332. TV sets: 298. Daily newspaper circulation: 294 copies.

TABLE 1. RELIGIOUS ADHERENTS IN THE FEDERAL REPUBLIC OF GERMANY

| Year | 1900 | | mid-1970 | | Annual change, 1970–1980 | | | | mid-1975 | | mid-1980 | | 2000 | |
|---|---|---|---|---|---|---|---|---|---|---|---|---|---|---|
| *Name* | *Adherents* | *%* | *Adherents* | *%* | *Natural* | *Conversion* | *Total* | *Rate* | *Adherents* | *%* | *Adherents* | *%* | *Adherents* | *%* |
| **Christians** | **29,323,000** | **98.3** | **57,830,000** | **95.3** | **27,425** | **−54,695** | **−27,270** | **−0.05** | **57,734,300** | **93.6** | **57,557,300** | **92.8** | **54,252,000** | **81.9** |
| professing | 29,323,000 | 98.3 | 57,830,000 | 95.3 | 27,425 | −54,695 | −27,270 | −0.05 | 57,734,300 | 93.6 | 57,557,300 | 92.8 | 54,252,000 | 81.9 |
| Protestants | 15,301,800 | 51.3 | 29,420,000 | 48.5 | 8,963 | −55,433 | −46,470 | −0.16 | 29,199,800 | 47.3 | 28,955,300 | 46.7 | 25,758,000 | 38.9 |
| Roman Catholics | 13,980,000 | 46.9 | 27,080,000 | 44.6 | 13,068 | −4,468 | 8,600 | 0.03 | 27,140,000 | 44.0 | 27,166,000 | 43.8 | 26,563,000 | 40.1 |
| Orthodox | 1,000 | 0.0 | 597,000 | 1.0 | 5,000 | 300 | 5,300 | 0.84 | 630,000 | 1.0 | 650,000 | 1.0 | 750,000 | 1.1 |
| Catholics (non-Roman) | 40,000 | 0.1 | 400,000 | 0.7 | 193 | 7 | 200 | 0.05 | 401,000 | 0.7 | 402,000 | 0.6 | 470,000 | 0.7 |
| Marginal Protestants | 0 | 0.0 | 300,000 | 0.5 | 176 | 4,824 | 5,000 | 1.52 | 330,000 | 0.5 | 350,000 | 0.6 | 660,000 | 1.0 |
| Anglicans | 200 | 0.0 | 30,000 | 0.0 | 14 | −14 | 0 | 0.00 | 30,000 | 0.0 | 30,000 | 0.0 | 35,000 | 0.0 |
| Third-World indigenous | 0 | 0.0 | 3,000 | 0.0 | 11 | 89 | 100 | 2.86 | 3,500 | 0.0 | 4,000 | 0.0 | 16,000 | 0.0 |
| nominal | 130,000 | 0.4 | 332,626 | 0.5 | 252 | 85,175 | 85,427 | 11.93 | 716,200 | 1.2 | 1,186,900 | 1.9 | 3,993,500 | 6.0 |
| affiliated | 29,193,000 | 97.8 | 57,497,374 | 94.7 | 27,173 | −139,870 | −112,697 | −0.20 | 57,018,100 | 92.4 | 56,370,400 | 90.9 | 50,258,500 | 75.9 |
| doubly-affiliated | −100,000 | −0.3 | −1,050,000 | −1.7 | −500 | 24,500 | 24,000 | −2.61 | −920,000 | −1.5 | −810,000 | −1.3 | −530,000 | −0.8 |
| total practising | 26,273,700 | *90* | 45,422,920 | *79* | 21,195 | −222,966 | −201,771 | −0.45 | 44,474,120 | *78* | 43,405,210 | *77* | 35,180,900 | *70* |
| non-practising | 2,919,300 | *10* | 12,074,450 | *21* | 5,978 | 83,096 | 89,074 | 0.71 | 12,543,980 | *22* | 12,965,190 | *23* | 15,077,600 | *30* |
| Protestants | 15,276,000 | 51.2 | 29,412,213 | 48.4 | 8,836 | −129,017 | −120,181 | −0.42 | 28,929,600 | 46.9 | 28,210,400 | 45.5 | 22,853,500 | 34.5 |
| Evangelicals | 2,387,000 | 8.0 | 6,070,000 | 10.0 | 1,922 | 36,078 | 38,000 | 0.60 | 6,292,000 | 10.2 | 6,450,000 | 10.4 | 7,949,000 | 12.0 |
| Neo-pentecostals | 0 | 0.0 | 5,000 | 0.0 | 10 | 9,490 | 9,500 | 47.50 | 20,000 | 0.0 | 100,000 | 0.2 | 500,000 | 0.8 |
| Roman Catholics | 13,950,000 | 46.8 | 27,610,000 | 45.5 | 13,390 | −43,390 | −30,000 | −0.11 | 27,400,000 | 44.4 | 27,310,000 | 44.0 | 25,834,000 | 39.0 |
| Catholic pentecostals | 0 | 0.0 | 5,000 | 0.0 | 24 | 24,476 | 24,500 | 49.00 | 50,000 | 0.1 | 250,000 | 0.4 | 800,000 | 1.2 |
| Orthodox | 3,000 | 0.0 | 596,500 | 1.0 | 4,950 | 400 | 5,350 | 0.85 | 630,000 | 1.0 | 650,000 | 1.0 | 750,000 | 1.1 |
| Catholics (non-Roman) | 60,000 | 0.2 | 551,000 | 0.9 | 271 | 2,729 | 3,000 | 0.53 | 570,000 | 0.9 | 581,000 | 0.9 | 650,000 | 1.0 |
| Marginal Protestants | 3,000 | 0.0 | 354,661 | 0.6 | 213 | 4,321 | 4,534 | 1.18 | 383,000 | 0.6 | 400,000 | 0.6 | 650,000 | 1.0 |
| Anglicans | 1,000 | 0.0 | 20,000 | 0.0 | 10 | −10 | 0 | 0.00 | 20,000 | 0.0 | 20,000 | 0.0 | 25,000 | 0.0 |
| Third-World indigenous | 0 | 0.0 | 3,000 | 0.0 | 3 | 597 | 600 | 10.91 | 5,500 | 0.0 | 9,000 | 0.0 | 26,000 | 0.0 |
| Non-religious | 60,000 | 0.2 | 1,913,900 | 3.1 | 994 | 37,656 | 38,650 | 1.85 | 2,092,200 | 3.4 | 2,300,400 | 3.7 | 6,635,500 | 10.0 |
| Muslims | 0 | 0.0 | 450,000 | 0.7 | 103,549 | 301 | 103,850 | 8.31 | 1,250,000 | 2.0 | 1,488,500 | 2.4 | 1,788,500 | 2.7 |
| Ahmadis | 0 | 0.0 | 600 | 0.0 | 100 | 40 | 140 | 11.67 | 1,200 | 0.0 | 2,000 | 0.0 | 10,000 | 0.0 |
| Atheists | 30,000 | 0.1 | 400,000 | 0.7 | 234 | 15,566 | 15,800 | 3.20 | 493,000 | 0.8 | 558,000 | 0.9 | 3,312,000 | 5.0 |
| Jews | 420,000 | 1.4 | 31,700 | 0.1 | 60 | 0 | 60 | 0.19 | 32,000 | 0.1 | 32,300 | 0.1 | 35,000 | 0.1 |
| Baha'is | 0 | 0.0 | 9,400 | 0.0 | 5 | 205 | 210 | 2.00 | 10,500 | 0.0 | 11,500 | 0.0 | 25,000 | 0.0 |
| Buddhists | 0 | 0.0 | 5,000 | 0.0 | 2 | −2 | 0 | 0.00 | 5,000 | 0.0 | 5,000 | 0.0 | 4,000 | 0.0 |
| Other religionists | 5,000 | 0.0 | 60,000 | 0.1 | 31 | 969 | 1,000 | 1.54 | 65,000 | 0.1 | 70,000 | 0.1 | 190,000 | 0.3 |
| **Country's population** | **29,838,000** | **100.0** | **60,700,000** | **100.0** | **132,300** | **0** | **132,300** | **0.21** | **61,682,000** | **100.0** | **62,023,000** | **100.0** | **66,242,000** | **100.0** |

COLUMNS, ROWS. For meanings and definitions, see Codebook (Part 6). Note that, by definition, total 'Christians' = professing + crypto-Christians, which also = affiliated + nominal Christians. Percentages may not always total exactly, due to rounding.
CENSUSES. (a) *Undivided German empire in 1900:* 62.5% Protestants, 36.1% Roman Catholics, 1.0% Jews, 0.4% other Christians. (b) *Area covered by FRG (BRD) in 1970.* **1871:** 51.1% Protestants, 47.5% Roman Catholics. **1890:** 51.7% Protestants, 46.9% Roman Catholics. **1910:** 51.4% Protestants, 46.9% Roman Catholics. **1925:** 50.8% Protestants, 46.6% Roman Catholics. **1933:** 50.0% Protestants, 46.4% Roman Catholics. **1939:** 48.6% Protestants, 46.4% Roman Catholics. (c) *Federal Republic of Germany* (1970 territory, including West Berlin). **29.X.1946** (including 931,971 refugees, internees, prisoners of war): 49.7% Protestants, 45.9% Roman Catholics, 3.0% non-religious, 1.1% other religionists, 0.3% Jews. **13.IX.1950** (de jure): 51.2% Protestants (50.2% Ev Ch of Germany), 45.4% Roman Catholics, 3.2% non-religious, 0.1% Orthodox, 0.1% Catholics (non-Roman). **6.VI.1961** (de jure): 52.3% Protestants (50.8% Ev Ch of Germany), 44.4% Roman Catholics, 3.0% non-religious, 0.1% Orthodox, 0.1% other religionists (Muslims, Jews, Buddhists, Hindus). **27.V.1970:** 48.5% Protestants (47.0% Ev Ch of Germany), 44.6% Roman Catholics, 3.9% non-religious and atheists, 1.0% Orthodox, 0.7% other Christians, 0.7% Muslims, 0.5% marginal Protestants, 0.1% Jews.

### NOTES ON RELIGIONS

AHMADIS. Begun 1926. There are 2 Ahmadiya (Qadiani) mosques, in Hamburg (1957) and Frankfurt (1959), with a few hundred German Ahmadis as well as Pakistanis.
ATHEISTS. Deutsche Kommunistische Partei, DKP (formerly KPD, banned 1956; split on Sino-Soviet dispute) and rival factions: membership (1930: all Germany) 124,000, (1970) 35,000, (1974) 39,344; Communist voters (election of 1949) 1,362,000 (5.75% of all votes), (19.XI.1972) 113,891 (0.3% of all votes). West Berlin: Sozialistische Einheitspartei Westberlins (SEW) (legal; pro-Soviet): membership (1970, 1974) 8,000; Communist voters (election of 14.III.1971) 33,500 (2.3% of all votes). Although most communists are atheists, in 1972 the DKP had as members 50 Evangelical clergy, mainly in Hesse. Among youths aged 18–24 in West Germany in 1974, 6% professed to be atheists (Gallup).
BAHA'IS. Entered before 1921. Recent growth from 31 local spiritual assemblies (1964) to 59 (1973), with 392 other isolated centres or groups. One of the 7 Baha'i temples in the world is at Langenhain/Hofheim, Frankfurt.
BUDDHISTS. Mostly Theraveda, from the intellectual classes in Germany, served by the German Buddhist Union (1958); also about 1,500 Chinese.
CATHOLIC PENTECOSTALS (or, Catholic charismatics). Totals (1975): about 25,000 involved adults (over 15 years old); total charismatic community including children, 50,000. Observers in 1975 expected the movement to grow exceptionally rapidly from 1976 at perhaps the fastest rate for the charismatic renewal in any country in the world.
CHRISTIANS. Since 1968, defections from affiliation with the EKD and the Catholic Church (detailed under Table 2) have rapidly increased. From 1968–73 an estimated 750,000 Germans (150,000 a year on average) formally (legally) renounced Christianity and so became exempt from the obligation to pay church taxes. A majority of them however still continued to regard themselves as Christians and were so enumerated in the 1970 census.
COUNTRY'S POPULATION. Until its government-ordered restriction on labour immigrants in 1973, West Germany was receiving up to 600,000 new workers each year. Most of the annual population increase after 1970 was due to Muslim immigration of about 100,000 a year, with many Greek and Serbian Orthodox also.
DOUBLY-AFFILIATED. This term describes Free Church members, Jehovah's Witnesses, New Apostolic Church members, aliens (including refugees and members of USA and UK military chaplaincies) and members of other churches who are also enumerated as affiliated by either the EKD or the Catholic Church.
EVANGELICALS. The English term as used here is equivalent to Conservative Evangelicals (in German, Evangelikale, as distinct from Evangelische which is usually translated as 'Protestant'), and refers to (1) all persons affiliated to Protestant denominations which are Conservative Evangelical in theology and emphasis, and (2) individual Evangelicals within the non-Evangelical or conciliar Protestant churches affiliated to the Ecumenical Movement.
JEWS. 564,000 (1.4% of population) in 1925, declining to 27,000 by 1945 due to Nazi pogroms. In 1973, there were 68 congregations, 53 synagogues, 12 rabbis, and 26,772 practising Jews.
MUSLIMS. The total increased very rapidly from 1970 to 1975 due to massive labour immigration. In 1974 Muslims had risen to 1,200,000, composed of 1 million labourers from Turkey and 65,000 from Yugoslavia, 15,000 from Morocco, 11,000 from Tunisia, and 12,000 from other countries; there were also 500 diplomats (from 29 Muslim states), 10,000 merchants (Iranians), 8,000 students, a colony of 3,500 refugees from Turkestan, 300 Germany converts, also around 250,000 illegal immigrants. Schools of law (1973): 1,189,000 Sunnis, 10,000 Shias, 990 Ahmadis (enumerated here under Muslims although declared non-Muslim by Pakistan). By 1973 there were 6 new mosques in Germany (including one in the Munich area for 30,000 Muslims there). *Hajj pilgrims to Mecca.* (1976) 7.
NEO-PENTECOSTALS. First stirrings of the charismatic movement in the Lutheran churches date from 1910. In 1975, Neo-pentecostals were mostly in the EKD, and mainly in south and southeast West Germany. As in other national or state churches in other countries, the charismatic movement organizes

its activities firmly within the established structures of the church. There are also large numbers of youth in the Jesus Movement.
NOMINAL CHRISTIANS. As defined in this Encyclopedia, nominal Christians are very few in West Germany because both the EKD and the Catholic Church have statistics of affiliated Christians either (EKD) exactly the same as professing EKD Christians in the government census of 27.V.1970, or (Catholic Church) very similar. They are thus able to account for all professing members of these 2 churches, and even have detailed statistics of baptisms and of annual influx and exodus of members, based on the census figures.
ORTHODOX. The large natural increase around and after 1970 was due to heavy immigration of Greek and Serbian Orthodox foreign workers.
OTHER RELIGIONISTS. There is a large variety of followers of smaller bodies, including Hindus, Hindu sectarians (Ananda Marga, et alia), Theosophists (Theosophical Society, with in 1975 13 Lodges with 310 members), Rosicrucians (19 AMORC Lodges and centres), Sikhs, about 2,000 Chinese folk-religionists, and Soka Gakkai from Japan (one mission hall in Dusseldorf in 1969, 600 adherents by 1975). Although the number of committed occultists is only a few thousand, it is estimated that 3 million West Germans subscribe to some form of the occult, and perhaps 7 million more sympathize with the occult sciences. In addition, there were in 1975 about 54,000 members of various religions who are also followers of a movement with Hindu origins which claims to be a philosophy but not a religion: the Science of Creative Intelligence (SCI) or Transcendental Meditation (TM). There are also many Freemasons, members of a worldwide quasi-religious secret brotherhood, some of whom practise it as a non-Christian religion although in Germany most are either Protestants or non-religious.
PRACTISING CHRISTIANS. Regular church attendance by Roman Catholics declined steadily from 56.3% in 1935, to 50.6% in 1950, to 48.3% in 1951, to 44.9% in 1961, and to 40.4% in 1967 (another 20% attending every 2 or 3 weeks only); and to 32.4% in 1972 and 1975; and Roman Catholic Easter communicants similarly from 57.5% in 1915, to 51.2% in 1933, to 50.7% in 1961, and to 47.4% in 1967. In the EKD, weekly attendance fell from 7.3% (1963) to 5.6% (1971). For the country as a whole, regular attendance (once a month or more, mostly weekly) was 27% in 1956 and remained at 27% in 1968 also (youths aged 18–24 years, 9%) (Gallup). June 1959: 32% attend at least weekly, 31% once in a while, 20% only on major festivals, 10% never, 4% non-religious. May–June 1968 (Emnid): 27% weekly, 9% fortnightly, 18% monthly, 19% once every 2 months, 27% less than yearly, or never. February 1970: 3% of population attend several times a week, 26% once a week, 46% from time to time, 21% never, 4% non-religious. 1977: 24% attend worship regularly. *Kirchentagen.* Every year massive public meetings are held known as the Ecumenical Whitsun Assembly (Kirchentag), when crowds of 500,000 including many young people gather. Numbers have been reduced since 1970 due to TV coverage. *Percentage practising.* The percentages in the table above give practising Christians as a percentage of affiliated Christians. The polls above show practising Christians as 75% of the total population in 1970, which is 79% of affiliated Christians at that time. *Students of theology.* An indicator of the growth of interest in religion among the young is the recent increase in lay students of theology: (1964) 1,310; (1970) 2,880; (1974) 3,500; (1976) 6,000.
PROTESTANTS. The totals included, in 1970, 167,300 Protestant aliens (mostly from Europe), rising to 250,000 by 1973. From 1975–76, 125,000 Lutherans and Reformed of German origin were allowed to immigrate from Poland after the Helsinki Accord.
ROMAN CATHOLICS. Although large numbers of affiliated Catholics deregistered themselves from 1962–76 (see figures under Table 2), and many professing Catholics abandoned any Christian profession, this decline has been offset by large-scale immigration of Catholics from Southern Europe. As a result, Catholic profession has been declining far slower than has been the case with Protestants.
THIRD-WORLD INDIGENOUS. In 2 denominations in 1970 (see Table 2), with several others entering or attempting to enter. In particular, the Unification Church of Germany (world HQ in Korea) has had rapid expansion to 6,000 by 1976.

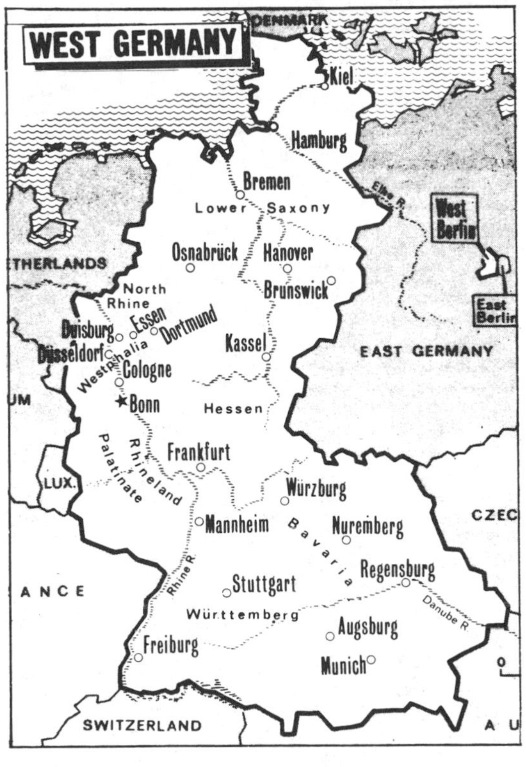


**NON-CHRISTIAN RELIGIONS. Islam** has recently become significant in West Germany. According to the Federal Office of Statistics in Wiesbaden and the Federal Bureau for Work in Nuremberg, there were resident in the FRG and West Berlin in 1973 about 1.2 million Muslims (1,189,000 Sunnis, 10,000 Shias, 990 Ahmadis). These included diplomats from 29 Muslims states (a few hundred persons), merchants mostly Shia Iranians in Hamburg and Frankfurt (10,000), students (8,000), trainees (6,000), Germans converted to Islam (300), and workers in various industrial centres (Berlin, the Ruhr, Cologne, Bielefeld, Hannover, Frankfurt, Stuttgart, Munich) from Turkey (1 million), Yugoslavia (65,000), Morocco (15,000), Tunisia (11,000), and other countries (12,000). To these figures must be added a fluctuating but important number of illegal immigrants (between 75,000 and 250,000), as well as 3,500 Muslims from Turkestan and the Soviet Caucasus who took refuge around Munich and Bamberg after World War II.

In addition to meeting places and other facilities made available to Muslims by Christian institutions, factories, railways and universities (Münster, Cologne, Bonn, Gressen, Heidelberg (Union of Islamic Students), Stuttgart (Association of Islamic Students) and Munich), Sunnis maintain the following mosques and centres: an Islamic centre and mosque at Aix-la-Chapelle (Aachen, 1967); mosques for workers at Allendorf (1970), Hamm (1973) and Bielefeld (1973); a mosque and centre belonging to the Muslim Community of South Germany in Munich; small communities of converted Germans at Bremen (36 persons), Hamburg (40), Mannheim and Berlin (130), the latter having close relations with the Pakistani Ahmadiya community which built a mosque in Berlin as early as 1926. Ahmadis are also found in Hamburg, Frankfurt, Hannover and Nuremberg. In addition Shias have a mosque and centre in Hamburg.

**Judaism** continues to decrease in numbers and significance. In 1925, the Jewish population of Germany was 564,379. Between 1933 and 1939 some 295,000 Jews emigrated. Of those remaining 30,000 died natural deaths, 25,000 escaped during World War II (mostly through Russia and Japan or through Portugal) and 160,000 were murdered in Nazi concentration camps. At the end of the war, 8,000 Jews returned from exile to join 19,000 who had survived illegally through marriage to non-Jews. In addition, a few thousand displaced persons, while in transit across the FRG after the war, decided to remain there. At the beginning of the 1960s, some 6,000 more German Jews returned and 2,000 others took up residence in Germany, making a total Jewish population of about 40,000 (30,000 affiliated to communities, and 10,000 others). However, their numbers have decreased since then because of the unfavourable age pyramid, deaths exceeding both births and new immigrants. At the end of 1973 Jewish members of communities numbered only 26,906. Most of these communities are small, with no more than 100 to 200 members. Only 6 have more than a thousand members: West Berlin (5,277 in 1973 as contrasted with 5,965 in 1966), Frankfurt (4,168 in 1966), Munich (3,345 in 1966), Dusseldorf (1,579 in 1966), Hamburg (1,500 in 1966), and Cologne (1,304 in 1966). Because of the advanced age of their members, the smaller communities are likely to die out soon. Thus the future of Judaism in the FRG is linked to the more important communities. The small size of communities also explains the large number of mixed marriages. In spite of these unfavourable circumstances, Jewish life in Germany has undergone a certain development. At present there are some 20 Jewish associations of which the most important are: the Central Council of Jews in Germany, founded in Dusseldorf in 1950; the Provident Society for Jews in Germany, in Frankfurt; and the Conference of Rabbis in the FRG, in Cologne. Since there is no rabbinical seminary in Germany, all rabbis are trained elsewhere and most are foreigners. The federal law of 1965 concerning damaged property has made possible the restoration of many synagogues. Moreover, a Jewish school has been reopened in Frankfurt and an academy in Heidelberg.

**CHRISTIANITY.** Three Catholic episcopal sees were erected in Germany during the 3rd century, but Christianity did not become dominant until after the conversion of the Frankish king, Clovis, in 496. Scottish-Irish missionary monks, including Columba, were active during the 6th century, and Charles Martel protected the efforts of Boniface, who became archbishop without a fixed see in 722 and gave himself to the conversion of the German people. Charlemagne enforced christianization with the sword during the 9th century, arousing the enmity of Saxons; but his son Louis the Pious encouraged the peaceful means of Anskar, who carried the Christian faith to Scandinavia. Power conflicts between papacy and German emperors over the mutual responsibilities of church and state were largely resolved by the Concordat of Worms in 1122. By the end of the 12th century Saxony, the last independent duchy, was subdued; and through the military campaigns of the Order of Teutonic Knights, Christianity was extended to the northeast. In 1415 John Huss was burned at the stake because of his critical attitude towards the abuses of the clergy; and a century later, in 1517, Martin Luther issued his 95 theses at Wittenberg, signalling the start of the Protestant Reformation. The Schmalkaldic League was formed in 1531 primarily among northern princes following the Lutheran position; and intermittent fighting took place with the emperor Charles V and Catholic princes to the south. Sparked in part by the presence of Turks at Vienna, the Peace of Augsburg of 1555 provided for agreement that the faith of a principality would be either Lutheran or Catholic as determined by its leader. The Council of Trent (1545–1563) consolidated the position of the Catholic Church and brought on the Counter-Reformation, led by Jesuits, Benedictines and Capuchins. Another direct though delayed result was the Thirty Years' War (1618–1648) between Catholic and Protestant princes. Germany was devastated, its population being reduced from 16 to 6 million; and its commerce and intellectual life were destroyed. The Protestant cause was ultimately saved by the military genius of Gustavus Adolphus, king of Sweden. The Peace of Westphalia (1648) again accorded the princes the right to determine the religion of their subjects, with the Reformed tradition of Calvin and Zwingli also added as an accepted religion. The religious unity of the German territorial states remained largely unaltered until the time of Napoleon when numerous small states were amalgamated into larger political units characterized by greater religious heterogeneity. Following World War I and the fall of the monarchy, the Protestant territorial churches lost their political supremacy although they continued to count as their membership a majority of the population. At the time of the Third Reich an attempt was made to create a united Protestant church under government control, but the move was unsuccessful.

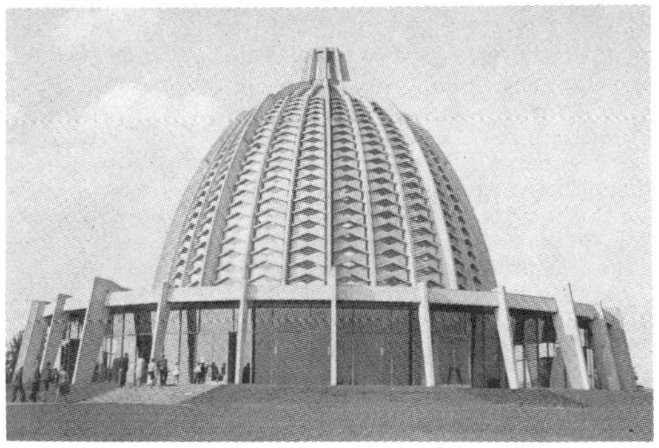
**Baha'is.** First Baha'i House of Worship (Temple) on European continent, and one of only 7 in the world, in Langenhain/Hofheim west of Frankfurt.

PROTESTANT CHURCHES. The population of the FRG is slightly under 50% Protestant, the great majority of whom are found in 20 territorial people's churches (Landeskirchen), reduced to 17 from 1977. All are members of the Evangelical Church in Germany (Evangelische Kirche in Deutschland, EKD) formed after World War II with the object of creating a strong Protestant church out of the confused divisions resulting from the groupings and regroupings of the preceding 400 years. This hope has not been realized, and the EKD remains much more a federation of autonomous churches than a single church.

The EKD originally included the 8 regional churches of East Germany (GDR); but under pressure from the East German regime in 1968, these churches were forced to drop their EKD affiliation. In terms of tradition, of the present 17 member churches, 7 are Lutheran (Bavaria, Brunswick, Hannover, Nordelbische (Eutin, Hamburg, Lübeck, Schleswig-Holstein), Oldenburg, Schaumburg-Lippe, Württemberg); 8 are united Lutheran and Reformed (Baden, Berlin-Brandenberg, Bremen, Hessen & Nassau, Kurhessen-Waldeck, Pfalz, Rhineland, Westphalia); and 2 are Reformed (Lippe, Northwest Germany). While retaining their membership in the EKD, 5 of the 7 Lutheran territorial churches (excepting only Oldenburg and Württemberg) have also formed their own church federation, called the United Evangelical Lutheran Church of Germany (Vereinigte Evangelisch-Lutherischen Kirche in Deutschland, VELKD). Another federation, the Evangelical Church of the Union (Evangelische Kirche der Union, EKU), groups together 3 of the united churches (Berlin-Brandenburg, Rhineland, Westphalia). Prior to 1968, the united churches of the GDR were also members of the EKU, and the East German Lutheran churches were members of the VELKD, but this is no longer the case. The evangelical churches of the FRG have not experienced the large loss in membership which has characterized the situation in the GDR and a number of other Western countries, although the 10% church tax deducted automatically by the government for all registered church members has provoked an increase in the withdrawal rate since 1970. Polls indicate that 27% of the total population claims to go regularly to church (which German Protestants define as monthly attendance), while 20% say that they never attend. Baptisms and church funerals are still observed for nearly all members, while church weddings account for about 85% of all marriages.

The territorial churches of the EKD are heavily involved in development and social service. Although most schools in the FRG are now under direct state control, some secondary schools sponsored by churches (Gymnasien) have been in existence since the time of the Reformation. There are at present 59 church-sponsored primary schools (including 52 special schools for handicapped children), 190 secondary schools (including 49 Gymnasien), 9 professional high schools and 4 theological schools, in addition to 12 Protestant theological faculties at Germany's various state universities.

Medical and social service is co-ordinated by the Diaconal Work of the Evangelical Church in Germany (Diakonisches Werk der EKD), founded in 1957, which carries on the responsibilities of Evangelical Relief (Evangelisches Hilfswerk) begun in 1945 and the Inner Mission (1948). At present there are 130,000 full members of staff, of which 34,000 are deaconesses and 5,200 deacons. Diakonisches Werk co-ordinates the activities of 319 medical institutions (hospitals, clinics, dispensaries) and 18,157 other institutions (homes for orphans, youth, aged, alcoholics, ex-convicts, et alia). In order to provide for joint collaboration in the various activities of the churches in development aid, the Joint Committee for Church Development Service (Arbeitsgemeinschaft Kirchlicher Entwicklungsdienst, KED) was founded in 1969. Participating agencies are: (1) several church development committees and boards of the EKD (Ausschuss Kirchliche Mittel für Entwicklungsdienst, Kammer für Entwicklungsdienst, Kirchliches Aussenamt, et alia); (2) Bread for the World (Brot für die Welt), which makes appeal to both the EKD and free churches and by 1971 had provided 250 million Deutschmarks (DM) for 900 projects throughout the world; (3) Joint Committee for Overseas Service (Arbeitsgemeinschaft Dienste in Ubersee), which has since 1960 sent 421 specialists to 34 countries, plus 129 other persons in short-term emergency programmes; (4) Evangelical Joint Committee for World Mission (Evangelische Arbeitsgemeinschaft für Weltmission), which was formed in 1963 for the purpose of integrating church and mission in Germany and supports, through its annual budget of 10 million DM, ecumenical missionary ventures abroad; and (5) Protestant Central Agency for Development Aid (Evangelische Zentralstelle für Entwicklungshilfe) which has since 1963 provided about 332 million DM for 475 educational, social and health assistance projects in developing countries. Since its founding in 1969, the KED itself has made available (largely from the funds of the church tax put at the disposal of member churches of the EKD) some 170 million DM for 293 development projects in various Third-World countries.

Apart from the territorial churches, a number of other Lutheran and Reformed denominations are also active. The largest is the Independent Evangelical Lutheran Church which was created in 1972 by the merger of the Evangelical Lutheran Free Church with the Old Lutherans, the latter tracing their history back to 1830. There is also a separate Evangelical Lutheran Church in Baden and a small Confessional Evangelical Lutheran Church related to Missouri and Wisconsin Synod Lutherans in the USA. Several other Lutheran churches have also been established to cater for refugees from Eastern Europe, namely the Estonian, Hungarian, Latvian and Lithuanian Evangelical Lutheran Churches in Exile. The Church of Denmark and the Church of Sweden minister to the needs of Scandinavian Lutherans living in the FRG. Two small Reformed churches serving refugees and expatriates are the Reformed Church of Hungary and the Reformed Church of the Netherlands, while the Old Reformed churches continue their work in the northwest.

Mennonites trace their history to the 16th century and Moravians to the 18th century, while several other Protestant traditions have been represented in Germany since the early part of the 19th century. At present the Baptists (1834) are strongest and work in co-operation with Southern Baptists from the USA. The Evangelical Methodist Church (1830) was greatly strengthened by the merger in 1968 of the former Methodist and Evangelical United Brethren churches both in the USA and Germany, and this church retains its status as a central conference affiliated to the United Methodist Church with headquarters in the USA. Since 1968 the Methodists of the GDR have had their own separate central conference. Other important groups originating in the last century are the Plymouth Brethren (1847), Congregationalists (1854) and Salvation Army (1886). Other earlier groups include Seventh-day Adventists (1875), Assemblies of God (1907), and the Association of Christian Assemblies (1909); and some 10 other small Pentecostal denominations have been formed.

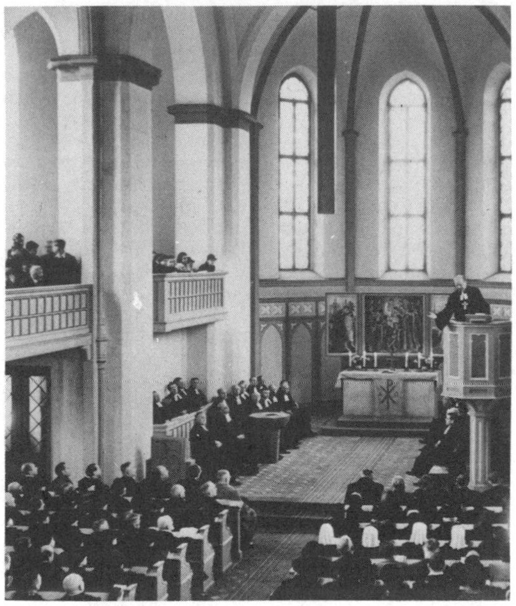

**Evangelische Kirche in Berlin-Brandenburg.** 'Thus says the Lord'. Late Bishop Otto Dibelius, whose Lutheran/Reformed church covers East and West Berlin, preaches in West Berlin.

CATHOLIC CHURCH. The situation of the Catholic Church in the FRG can be explained only in terms of the profound disorders that followed World War II. The creation of the 2 states of East and West Germany brought about not only differing developments in Catholicism within each state but it also imposed political boundaries that no longer coincided with ecclesiastical jurisdictions. In 1975, the dioceses of Berlin, Fulda, Hildesheim, Osnabrück, Paderborn and Würzburg still overlapped both countries. In addition, the vast migration of over 15,000,000 refugees since 1945 from East Germany and Eastern Europe has already brought about 2 fundamental and permanent changes in the churches of the FRG, particularly for the Catholic Church. These include: (1) the loss of the minority character of the latter, and this for the first time since 1871 (First Reich); by 1970, 44.6% of the total population declared themselves to be Catholic; and (2) a reduced denominational homogeneity in the regions, present since the Reformation and Counter-Reformation, each having been formerly dominated by a single church. Following the influx of refugees, the Catholic proportion rapidly increased in all regions of the north, as the following increases from 1939 to 1970 indicate: Schleswig-Holstein, an increase from 4.3% to 6.0%; Hamburg, 5.9% to 9.1%; Bremen, 8.9% to 10.2%; Lower Saxony, 16.6% to 19.6%; Hesse, 26.0% to 32.8%. In 1970, West Berlin was 12.5% Catholic. Catholicism has generally declined numerically in the south and west, as the figures also for 1939 and 1970 indicate: Rhineland (North Westphalia), from 56.8% to 52.5%; Palatinate Rhineland, from 58.0% to 55.7%; Bavaria, from 73.2% to 69.9%. In 2 southern provinces, however, Catholics have increased: Baden-Württemberg, from 45.1% to 47.4%, and the Saar, from 71.5% to 73.8%.

One of the consequences of the decline of denominational homogeneity in these regions has been the growth of contacts between Protestants and Catholics, changing the image each community had of the other. Other factors have been the diminution of internal cohesiveness within Catholicism coinciding with the end of the minority character of this church, the betterment of the economic situation of Catholics ending earlier feelings of inferiority, and the new political constellation which took place after 1945 when the 3 Western allies assigned to the Catholic and Protestant churches a definite role in the reorganization of the new Germany. One result was the establishment of the Christian Democrats (CDU/CSU), an accomplishment of both Catholics and Protestants. This party played an important role in the political development of the FRG and governed the country without interruption until 1969. Catholics formed 75% of its party membership, as well as the majority of its electorate. This link with the government party also reinforced the institutional and juridical position of the church, notably in the areas of education, family, youth, public health, social security, property and social participation. Moreover, the revenue from ecclesiastical tax, 2.5 billion DM in 1972, plus government grants for public institutions operated by the church, assured for the church both economic prosperity and freedom of action.

As external political threats ceased to trouble the church, internal problems became more grave, which explains why the processes of intra-ecclesial identification are at present in the forefront of all debates. In the FRG, church membership is to a large extent taken for granted. In 1970, only 3.9% of the population belonged to no religious community, and the annual exodus of Catholics from the church, while increasing from 23,089 in 1962 to 53,772 in 1972, does not constitute a significant change. Almost all children of Catholics are baptized and most marriages are celebrated in church. Despite this large and relatively constant increase in membership, however, other factors are in decline. Thus, weekly attendance at Sunday mass fell from 50.6% in 1950 to 32.4% in 1972, the most significant decrease being in urban areas among workers. Between 1965 and 1972, the number of secular priests decreased by 5%, while the number of lay Catholics increased. In 1972 there was one priest in pastoral service for every 2,073 Catholics, in contrast to one for 1,780 in 1964. About half of all priests are 60 years of age or over. The number of religious priests has remained relatively constant since 1964, but the number of theological students in religious orders has fallen during this same period, from 1,799 to 565, as is true also of annual ordinations which fell from 166 in 1964 to 63 in 1971. Ordinations of secular clergy declined from 506 in 1964 to 251 in 1971 and candidates to the priesthood fell from 3,484 in 1964 to 1,895 in 1972. Between 1962 and 1972, the number of religious brothers also decreased from 4,595 to 3,692, while that of sisters fell from 89,452 to 78,245.

In contrast, one notes a definite increase in the number of lay theologians. In 1972 they were almost twice as numerous as candidates for the priesthood. Moreover, there has been a significant increase in the involvement of the laity in ecclesiastical service. In social work, while religious personnel decreased from 60,447 in 1950 to 54,546 in 1970, lay workers increased during the same period from 45,611 to 173,938. This indicates clearly that what is happening is that willingness to tie oneself to the church is being called into question. Identification with the church binding one to irreversible decisions seems to receive less and less acceptance. This is underlined by the fact that 6% of all priests abandoned their ministry during the first 4 years of service. It is also within this context that one must understand the debates on divorce and remarriage. The creation of inflexible norms of behaviour, linked to the requirement of obedience, seems to leave too little space for individual initiative and thus becomes increasingly unacceptable. One notes rather a desire for norms permitting action more adaptable to situations and alternative behaviour. Creativity and spontaneity have become in actuality the central values in society, and this cannot fail to have repercussions on the church.

These changes in relations between the Catholic and Protestant churches, one evidence of which is the increasing number of mixed marriages, have resulted in sharp confrontations within the church. The post-conciliar age has seen a decrease in uniformity and a diversifying of opinions within Catholicism. Communities of work and action among priests and laity have developed which openly defend their opinions in partial opposition to the ecclesiastical hierarchy. The church has tried to recuperate structurally from this differentiation by an enlargement of its bureaucracy, always important in Germany, as well as by the revitalization of its synodal structures. This extension of bureaucratization has only been possible because of the vast revenue available from ecclesiastical taxes. Thus the diocese of Essen, which with 1.3 million Catholics is a medium-sized diocese for the FRG, employed about 300 persons in its curia in 1973. On the other hand, in establishing councils at diocesan and parish levels, as well as sanctioning the Joint Synod of the dioceses of the FRG (Gemeinsame Synode, GS) during 1971–75, the hierarchy tried to overcome the contradiction emphasized by a section of the laity and minor clergy concerning the relative importance of laity and priests and their ability to influence ecclesiastical decisions. These attempts at reorganization, however, have not developed without friction. The powers of the new councils have not been clearly defined, and their relationships with other existing institutions have not been sufficiently clarified. A conflict exists between the role of the Central Committee of German Catholics (Zentralkomitee der Deutschen Katholiken, ZDK) whose origin goes back over a hundred years, and that assigned to the Joint Synod of implementing the decrees of Vatican II and of moulding Christian life in conformity with the faith of the church. Similar power conflicts are manifest when one considers the distribution of the various commissions of the Synod, as well as the nominating body of the members of the Central Committee and the Joint Synod. For the latter, 7 delegates represent each diocesan council, of whom 3 are priests; 40 delegates are elected by the Central Committee to represent the church's various organizations; all bishops are members; as well as 40 other persons designated by the bishops.

The interdiocesan Joint Synod was requested in the beginning by the Critical Catholicism (Kritischer Katholizismus) group at the time of the Katholikentag in Essen in 1968; it was convoked by the Episcopal Conference in 1969 and was approved the following year by the Holy See. Synod sessions were preceded by a mammoth survey of almost 21 million German Catholics 16 years of age and over. It constitutes an important event in the Catholic life of the FRG because it provides for the opening of dialogues within the body of a church which is strongly hierarchical and highly structured. For all that, it is very different from the Netherlands Pastoral Council as far as the composition of its assembly and its powers are concerned. In the FRG there are 314 members, of whom 50% are bishops and priests and 50% lay persons, whose powers are strictly limited. The German bishops retain the right of veto which allows them to prevent the submission of any resolution for vote, and any modification of their statutes or terms of reference must have the approval of the Holy See. The 10 commissions of the Synod as set up in 1971 at the time of the first session deal with the following subjects: faith and preaching; liturgy, sacraments and spirituality; Christian service; marriage and the family; social tasks of the church; education, training, information; gifts, services and ministries; forms of co-responsibility within the church; regulation of pastoral structures; co-operation at the level of the universal church and ecumenism. All the assemblies have been held in Würzburg, and in principle the Synod was expected to finish its work in 1975. The caution exhibited at the time of the establishment of the commissions, as well as that exercised in the choice of themes for discussion, with subjects considered too controversial being put aside, has not prevented the Synod from adopting

a moderate line of openness and renewal. This is manifest by the adoption during the third session (January 1973) of a report concerning the 'participation of the laity in the homily of the mass'. The decisions taken on this occasion created serious tensions with the Congregation for the Clergy in Rome, which maintained that they were in opposition to the conclusions of the interpretative commission of Vatican II. The firm position of the German episcopate, however, made possible a softening of the Roman decision to invalidate this schema.

Beyond strictly intra-ecclesial concerns, the problems of foreign workers in the FRG and also in the Third World have pre-occupied the Catholic

**Neuapostolische Kirche.** Third largest church in Germany, the New Apostolic Church co-operates with no other churches. It has 1.1 million members worldwide. *Inset.* Its 2,900 church buildings are distinctive, with symbol of cross over rising sun. *Above.* Government is through a hierarchy of 48 living Apostles presided over by a Chief Apostle regarded as sole representative of Christ on earth. *Below.* Sunday services are usually packed.

Church; and pastoral assistance to Catholics of foreign cultures, who numbered between 1.3 and 1.8 million in 1973, has been the object of considerable concern. In 1973 the Katholisches Auslandssekretariat employed 504 specialized chaplains, of whom 451 were engaged uniquely in this form of pastoral work. Also in 1973, the third session of the Joint Synod adopted a vigorous report on the 'social and ecclesial situation of the foreign worker' which included passages strongly critical of governmental policy in the matter as well as of the attitude of German Catholics. As for the problems of the Third World, this has held the attention of the Catholic Church since the end of the 1950s. Already-existing aid organizations have been enlarged, and others have been created. These are either organiz-

ations of inter-church aid or those oriented to socio-economic development. Considerable financial resources have thus been disbursed.

ORTHODOX CHURCHES. Seven Orthodox bodies are present in West Germany, the largest being Greek Orthodox who are part of the diocese of Germany and East Middle Europe under the Ecumenical Patriarchate. Russian Orthodox are divided into 2 groups, a small community under the Patriarchate of Moscow with headquarters in East Berlin, and a much larger exile body, the Russian Orthodox Church Outside of Russia, with headquarters in New York. Other communities of refugees in exile from Russia and Eastern Europe are the Armenian, Romanian, Serbian and Ukrainian Orthodox churches.

CATHOLIC (NON-ROMAN) CHURCHES. Several bodies exist intermediate between Protestantism and Roman Catholicism. The Old Catholic Church, the result of a split from the Catholic Church following the promulgation of the dogma of papal infallibility at Vatican I, was formed in 1874. A quite different body is the Catholic Apostolic Church, which began in England in 1830 and made its first German converts in 1840. In 1863 a dispute over leadership produced a schism resulting in the creation of the New Apostolic Church, a sacramentalist and hierarchical body stressing the Catholic concepts of the unified church, ritual, liturgy and authority, and governed by a college of 48 living apostles in a successional apostolate with at its head a Chief Apostle with quasi-papal powers regarded as the successor of the Apostle Peter and visible representative or incarnation of Christ on earth. The NAC has expanded widely outside Germany, has over a million members worldwide, and maintains its world headquarters in Dortmund. Displaying an extraordinary vitality, this is now Germany's largest Christian community outside the Roman Catholic and territorial churches. A number of splits from the New Apostolic Church have taken place including the small Apostolic Community in 1921; but there has also been an attempt to unite these schisms. In 1954 the Union of Apostolic Christians was formed in Switzerland for this purpose, and its work was extended 2 years later to Germany with the formation of the Apostolic Fellowship.

MARGINAL CHURCHES. Jehovah's Witnesses first came to Germany at the end of the last century and continue to expand. Over the years schisms from the Witnesses have produced the Kingdom of God Church and the Free Bible Congregation. Mormons have been on the scene since the 1840s, as have the Unitarians. Other marginal Protestant groups include Christian Science (1907), Anthroposophical Society (1922), Nature Philosophy Union (1927), Evangelical Church of the Revelation of St John the Divine (1926) and Free Christian People's Church (1945).

CHURCH AND STATE. The Preamble to the Basic Law (Grundgesetz) of the FRG of 8 May 1949, as amended to 1 January 1966, reads: 'The German People... conscious of their responsibility before God and men...'. The constitution then guarantees a 'free Church in a free State'. While retaining effectively the freedom of religion both from an individual and the collective standpoints, allowances are made for co-operative arrangements between the state and the religious communities, especially the 2 largest, the Evangelical Church in Germany (EKD) and the Catholic Church.

In regard to constitutional law, the fundamental norms regulating the relationship between church and state in the FRG are found in the Basic Law. These norms include the fundamental right to religious liberty (Article 4), the institutional guarantee concerning the teaching of religion (Article 7, paragraph 3), as well as Article 140 on the church which reproduces the principal dispositions concerning ecclesiastical law of the Weimar constitution of 1919. According to that constitution (Article 137, paragraph 1), no state church exists, there being neither an ecclesiastical state regime nor an ecclesiastical jurisdiction with special official status; but on the other hand, separation between church and state is not total. This situation is manifest in the involvement of the churches in education, social service and military chaplaincies to the armed forces.

Article 137, paragraph 3, of the Weimar constitution guarantees to all religious and philosophical communities the right to regulate and administer their affairs without interference and within the limits of general legislation valid for all. Each religious community assumes responsibility for itself, without the intervention of the state or public authorities.

Article 137, paragraph 5, of the same constitution is concerned with the status of religious communities. They remain entities in public law in the same way that they have always been. The same rights will be accorded to other religious societies on their request if, because of their constitution and membership, they show signs of permanence. Their organic status however is only 'formal'; it does not signify any integration with the state but merely the capacity to retain certain rights and legal dispositions. By virtue of Article 141, and to the extent that there is a need to provide for worship and a pastoral ministry in the army, hospitals, penal institutions and other public establishments, religious communities are free to exercise their religious functions.

Other regulations concerning ecclesiastical questions in the cultural realm are left to the competence of the provinces. The provincial constitutions contain numerous dispositions relative to these questions. Further, Article 137, paragraph 8, of the Weimar constitution adds to the list of religious communities 'associations which have the purpose of serving in common a specified conception of the universe'.

There have been several concordats and treaties involving the churches. Between World Wars I and II, concordats were signed between the Roman Catholic Church and the provinces of Bavaria (1924), Prussia (1929), and Baden (1932). These concordats remained valid until after 1945. In addition, the concordat

concluded on 20 July 1933 between the Holy See and the Third Reich was declared valid by a decision of the Constitutional Court on 26 March 1957.

The concordat of the Reich includes conventions concerning the juridical rights of ecclesial communities, bishoprics and their establishments, the right of the Roman Catholic Church to administer its own affairs, exchange of ambassadors, the guarantee of independence for the church by the state, authorization for Catholic theological faculties and the possibility of creating confessional schools. Regarding schools, however, since the provinces retain sovereignty in cultural matters, they are not legally obligated to follow federal treaty agreements in educational matters. Moreover, the concordat of the Reich determines the special content of state legislation relative to civil marriage as well as the suppression of ecclesiastical jurisdiction over temporal affairs.

Since World War II, agreements have been signed with several other provinces, including: the convention of 1 January 1958 with the Rhineland of North Westphalia, concerning the erection of the diocese of Essen; the concordat of 26 February 1965 with Lower Saxony; the convention of 15 May 1973 with the Palatinate Rhineland dealing with educational establishments and the permanent training of teaching staff; and the convention of 21 February 1975 with the Saar over educational questions.

On 22 February 1957 the Federal Republic concluded a convention with the Evangelical Church in Germany (EKD) concerning organization of the Protestant chaplaincy to the armed forces. There are also ecclesiastical conventions between the EKD and the following provinces; Baden (9 December 1932), Hesse, Lower Saxony, Palatinate Rhineland and Schleswig-Holstein.

Five special issues are important for an understanding of church-state relations in the FRG. The first is the religious education of children. According to the law of the Reich of 15 July 1921, it is the free agreement of parents which prevails in this domain. After the age of 12, no child's confession can be changed without his consent, and after 14 each individual is free to decide which confession he belongs to.

Secondly, with regard to religious instruction, private schools and theological faculties, Article 7, paragraph 3, of the Basic Law clarifies that religious instruction is a regular part of the curriculum of public schools, with the exception of nonconfessional schools. Article 141 permits the solution adopted by the province of Bremen, namely that religious instruction is assured by the church outside school. Although the state retains the right of supervision, religious instruction is offered in agreement with the principles of the religious communities. The right to establish private schools is guaranteed by Article 7, paragraph 4, of the Basic Law. Private schools which replace public schools must have state approval and must conform to the laws of the province. Theological faculties are state institutions and are in part under the constitutional protection of the provinces (as in Hesse and in Palatinate Rhineland). The most recent ecclesiastical conventions envisage the church's right of intervention in appointments to professorial chairs in theology, and sometimes also in philosophy.

A third special issue relates to the military chaplaincy. The juridical base of the Protestant military chaplaincy is the convention of 1957 between the FRG and the EKD. The legal dispositions are also analogous for Catholic military chaplains although the juridical basis for the Catholic chaplaincy rests on Article 27 of the concordat of the Reich (1933). The ecclesiastical direction of these 2 chaplaincies rests with a bishop appointed by each church (by the Vatican for the Catholic Church) after consultation with the federal government. The central administrative tasks are assured by 2 ecclesiastical offices for the federal army, one directed by a Protestant military general dean and the other by a Catholic general vicar, who depend directly on the Ministry of Defence.

Fourthly, concerning ecclesiastical taxes (Kirchensteuer) and direct financial contributions by the state, as entities in public law the churches have the right to collect taxes according to the official lists of each province. To this effect they utilize the provinces' administrative channel for finances, and it is the task of the provinces to arrange the details by appropriate laws. In 1975 the church tax represented 8 to 9% of all revenue in the provinces. All persons are subject to this tax except those whose

income is not taxable (their number varies between 30% and 40% depending on the province) and those who expressly request to be excluded from their religious community and so are exempt. In 1972 the ecclesiastical tax raised 7 billion DM for the Catholic and Protestant churches. They have recently declared themselves in favour of retaining the tax, as have the 2 principal political parties, Christian Democrats and Social Democrats. However, a growing if small number of persons are formally declaring before the state that they belong to no church in order to obtain exemption from paying. In 1973, the Liberal Party, the third largest political force in the country, openly went on record for the suppression of the Kirchensteuer. In addition to the ecclesiastical tax, state and church are linked by numerous other dispositions, some involving financial obligations including paying salaries of Protestant church authorities, Catholic bishops and cathedral deans. The federal authorities pay the expenses of the military chaplaincy and the cost of the federal border police chaplaincy. The provinces assume responsibility for the police chaplaincy, the salaries of teachers of religion and catechists, and they also subsidize the salaries of pastors.

Fifthly, there also exists close co-operation between church and state in the domain of social assistance. From the public budget, contributions are made for specific aid projects and are administered by a 'working group of central associations for private aid in Germany'. Six private organizations are members, of which 3 are confessional (Protestant, Catholic, Jewish). Government assistance to Catholic development projects reached 44 million DM by 1974. In addition, the churches are represented on governing boards of radio and TV stations and similarly in other areas.

There is no federal ministry for ecclesiastical affairs. Questions concerning the churches are mostly handled by provincial ministries of religion as responsible for cultural matters. Problems arising at the federal level are handled by the Ministries of the Interior and Foreign Affairs. The Evangelical Church is represented to the legislative organs of the federal government and other federal agencies by a member of the council of the EKD, with an office in Bonn. The corresponding Catholic organ is the Commissariat of the German Bishops (Katholisches Büro) in Bonn. There also exist analogous Catholic offices for the regional governments of Palatinate Rhineland, Lower Saxony, Rhineland of North Westphalia and the Saar. In foreign relations, an exchange of ambassadors exists between Bonn and the Vatican.

In general, all churches are well satisfied with their relations with the state. Nevertheless, the Protestant churches find themselves in a more difficult situation in church-state relations than the Catholic Church, because of both their doctrine concerning the state and their unique historical experience. This does not, however, impede them from participating in political life even at the level of parliament and active participation in all parties. This is not true of the Catholic Church, which continues to retain its special allegiance to the Christian Democrats. Catholics have abandoned their original aim of keeping equidistant from all parties, and now justify their position by various theories. Only sporadically do reform groups engage in self-criticism of the Catholic political stance. On the other hand, the political forces of youth, liberalism, humanism and socialism are pressing inexorably towards a clear separation between the state and the churches.

INTERDENOMINATIONAL ORGANIZATIONS. The principal co-ordinating body for the ecumenical activity of the churches is the Council of Christian Churches in the FRG and West Berlin (Arbeitsgemeinschaft Christlicher Kirchen in der BRD und Berlin-West), founded in 1948 with headquarters in Frankfurt. Since the addition of Catholics and Greek Orthodox in 1973, there are now 10 member churches, the others being the EKD with its territorial churches, Baptists, Mennonites, Methodists, Moravians, Old Catholics, Old Reformed and Salvation Army. Several others are observers including Congregationalists, Quakers and Mülheim-Ruhr Pentecostals. Conceived as a platform for dialogue leading to mutual understanding and joint action, the council promotes theological study, research and ecumenical co-operation on the local, national and international level and is an associate council of the WCC.

The Commission for Ecumenical Questions of the

Conference of German Catholic Bishops (Kommission für Ökumenische Fragen der Konferenz der Katholischen Bischöfe Deutschlands) co-ordinates ecumenical affairs through 4 sections dealing with the Reformed (including Lutheran), Orthodox, Anglican and Old Catholic churches.

Two joint commissions involving direct ecumenical dialogue are those dealing with relations between the Catholic Church and the EKD (Gemeinsame Kommission des Rates der EKD und der Konferenz der Katholischen Bischöfe Deutschlands) and between Catholics and Old Catholics (Gemeinsame Kommission der Konferenz der Katholischen Bischöfe Deutschlands und der Alt-Katholischen Kirche in Deutschland). There are numerous other co-operative

Other institutes of an ecumenical nature include: (1) Konfessionskundlichen Institut des Evangelischen Bundes, founded at Bensheim in 1947, an evangelical institute dedicated to research on Catholic life and doctrine; (2) Johann Adam Möhler-Institut für Ökumenik (Paderborn, 1957), a Catholic institute for the scientific study of ecumenical questions, especially on Luther and the Reformation; (3) Ökumenisches Institut der Abtei Niederaltaich (1962), a Benedictine community promoting research and ecumenical action with special concern for mixed marriages; (4) Ostkirchliches Institut der Augustiner (Würzburg, 1947), an Augustinian institute studying the Greek and Slavic Orthodox churches; (5) Anglikanisches Institut der Abtei St

non-Christian religions, in the promotion of religious liberty; (4) Action 365, Ökumenische Laienbewegung (Frankfurt); (5) Evangelischer-Katholischer Ökumenischer Abeitkreis (Munich, 1946) which is composed of 20 Catholics and 20 Protestants (EKD) and studies a fixed theme each year; (6) Bund für Evangelisch-Katholische Wedervereinigung (Dalherda, 1960), an independent organization dedicated to prayer, action and study for union between Protestant and Catholic dioceses; (7) Evangelische Arbeitsgruppe für die Ökumenische Gebetswoche, and Katholischer Arbeitskreis für die Weltgebetswoche, the Protestant and Catholic organizations for the Week of Prayer for Christian Unity; (8) Frankfurter Gesprach (1964), which unites 14 Protestant fundamentalist groups seeking renewal of the church through worship, liturgy, teaching and prayer; (9) Lebenszentrum für die Einheit der Christen (Wetzhausen, 1968), which groups Christians of different confessions in living the common life as well as through retreats and study sessions, with emphasis on family life; (10) Ökumenisches Lebenszentrum Ottmaring (ÖLZ) (Ottmaring, 1968), an interdenominational centre for ecumenical spirituality with stress on creating a common community life between Catholics and Lutherans; (11) Jesus-Brüderschaft (Gnadenthal), a centre dedicated to spirituality and ecumenical action, including retreats and construction of chapels; (12) Societas Christi Regis (Meitingen and Augsburg), a secular institute of the Sisters of Christ the King promoting peace and the unity of Christians; (13) Ökumenischer Arbeitskreis der Evangelischen Michaelsbrüderschaft (Soest), which organizes annual meetings of Anglican, Protestant, Catholic and Orthodox theologians; (14) Ökumenische Jugenddienste (ÖJD) (Stuttgart), which organizes interdenominational work camps for youth; (15) Ökumenischer Brüderdienst (Niederaltaich), for youth social service projects; (16) Catholica Unio (Würzburg), the German branch of Catholica Unio Internationalis, based in Switzerland; (17) Deutsche Sektion, Internationale Ökumenische Gesellschaft (Trier), centred in the UK; and (18) Ökumenisches Archiv der EKD (Berlin). In addition there are regional ecumenical working communities in the church circles (Kirchenkreise) of Baden-Baden, Braunfels and Wetzlar, Bremen, Cologne, Dortmund, Dusseldorf (2), Flensburg, Frankfurt, Freiburg, Hagen, Hannover, Hildesheim, Hof, Hofheim, Hornberg and Villingen, Karlsruhe, Kiel, Kleve,

**Kirchentag** Huge open-air Ecumenical Whitsun Assemblies or church congresses or rallies have been held approximately every 2 years since 1945; they last 4-7 days, and at one time involved 600,000 persons though now reduced to 20-50,000 due to TV coverage. Above, 600,000 (with 25,000 from East Germany) at closing service of 1956 Frankfurt Kirchentag. Below, A working-group session at 15th German Protestant Kirchentag in Dusseldorf, 1973, on theme 'Not by Bread Alone', which for first time included Catholics, Orthodox, Anglicans and Free Protestants.

agencies, co-ordinating Catholic and EKD work at all levels. A complete list is reproduced in the brochure 'Ökumenische Kontakte in der BRD'.

The main interconfessional body dealing with foreign missions is the German Missionary Council (Deutscher Evangelischer Missions-Rat), founded in 1934, building on the foundations laid by the Standing Committee of German Protestant Missions (Ausschuss der Deutschen Evangelischen Missionsgesellschaften) in 1885 and the German Protestant Missionary Alliance (Deutsche Evangelische Missionsbund) in 1922. At the present time the council has 36 regular and 15 special member bodies and is affiliated with the CWME/WCC. Some of the more Evangelical missionary societies belong to this council but others belong either to Deutscher Evangelischer Missions-Tag (DEMT), or to Arbeitsgemeinschaft Evangelikaler Missionen, or to both.

International interconfessional associations and societies active in the FRG include: (1) International Society for Liturgical Study and Renewal (Societas Liturgica), founded at Driebergen in the Netherlands in 1967, with German headquarters at Trier, which unites teachers, researchers and those responsible for liturgical renewal in 20 countries; (2) Ecumenical Association of Directors of Academies and Laity Training Centres in Europe (EDA) (Ökumenischer Leiterkreis der Akademien und Laieninstitute in Europa), founded in 1958 in Bad Boll über Göppingen, an independent association uniting groups involved in social and international justice and changes of lifestyle; (3) International Association for Religious Freedom (Weltbund für Religiöse Freiheit), founded in Frankfurt in 1900, with member churches and groups in 20 countries on 5 continents (1973), which is dedicated to the promotion of liberal elements in the churches and religious freedom; and (4) European Contact Groups on Church and Industry, in Mainz.

Government-sponsored ecumenical institutes are attached to 11 universities in Bochum, Bonn, Erlangen-Nuremberg, Hamburg, Heidelberg, Marburg, Mainz, Munich, Münster, Tübingen, and Würzburg.

Matthias (Trier, 1964), a Catholic institute for the study of Anglicanism; (6) Byzantinisches Institut der Abtei Scheyern (1938), a Catholic institute affiliated with the Patristic Commission of the West German Academy of Sciences in Munich, giving particular attention to Greek Patristics; and (7) Byzantinisches Institut Ettal (1951) which studies the history and theology of the Byzantine churches.

The following 18 centres for action, co-operation and study are functioning: (1) Ökumenische Zentrale (Frankfurt, 1948), a study and action centre of the Council of Christian Churches in Germany, co-ordinating ecumenical activities in the FRG; (2) Arbeitsgemeinshaft Ökumenischer Kreise in der BRD und West-Berlin (AÖK) (Frankfurt, 1969), which promotes ecumenism on the local, regional and national levels; (3) Arbeitsgemeinschaft der Kirchen und Religionsgesellschaften in Berlin (1947), an independent association working in liaison with some 30 churches and religious associations, including

Limburg, Mannheim, Münster, Nuremberg (2), Pforzheim, Soest, Wiesbaden (2) and Wuppertal.

An organization dedicated to the improvement of Jewish, Christian and Muslim relations is the Ständige Konferenz Europaïscher Juden, Christen und Muslims, which is a local branch of the Permanent Conference of Jews, Christians and Muslims in Europe, with headquarters in the UK. Two centres are located in the FRG, one at Bendorf and the other in West Berlin (Evangelische Akademie Berlin).

Nine different organizations cater for Jewish-Christian dialogue: (1) Deutscher Koordinierungsrat der Gesellschaften für Christlich-Jüdische Zusammenarbeit (DKR) (Frankfurt, 1949), which has 45 member societies (1974), representing Catholics, Protestants and Jews, and is a member of the International Council of Christians and Jews, with headquarters in London; (2) Ständiger Gesprächskreis 'Juden und Christen' beim Zentralkomitee der Deutschen Katholiken (1971), composed equally of

Jews and Catholics; (3) Freiburger Rundbrief (FR), Arbeitskreis für Christlich-Jüdische Begegnung (Freiburg, 1948), which promotes spiritual relations between the 2 communities; (4) Arbeitsgruppe Juden und Christen beim Deutschen Evangelischen Kirchentag (Fulda, 1961), which promotes joint conferences, public discussions, Bible studies and celebrations; (5) Evangelisch-Lutherischer Zentralverein für Mission unter Israël (Leipzig, 1871, reorganized Nuremberg 1945, with branches in Schwabuch, Stuttgart and Löhne), which provides for the teaching of the gospel to Israel and spiritual support for Christian Jews; (6) Institutum Judaicum Delitzschianum (Leipzig, 1886, reorganized Münster, 1948), which has been related since 1973 to the University of Münster, although it continues to be supported by the Evangelical Lutheran Central Union, and which promotes mutual recognition and knowledge of the 2 religions through research and scientific publications; (7) Institutum Judaicum der Universität Tübingen (1957) related to the Department of Evangelical Theology of the University of Tübingen, which engages in research concerning 1st-century Judaism; (8) Institut Kirche und Judentum (Berlin-Zehlendorf, 1960) an agency of the Evangelical Church of West Berlin and related to the Theological School of Berlin; and (9) Action of Expiation in the Service of Peace (Aktion Sühnezeichen Friedensdienste), founded in 1958 during the EKD Synod at Berlin-Spandau, which sponsors concrete actions for reconciliation with the Jews as the principal victims of Nazism.

A number of non-confessional associations and institutes of religious studies are active. The International Association for the Psychology of Religion (Internationale Gesellschaft für Religionspsychologie), founded in Nuremberg in 1914 and now located in Munich, is an international organization of specialists in religious psychology from 11 different countries (1974) with its headquarters in the FRG. Three national associations are: Gesellschaft für Geistesgeschichte, founded in Erlangen in 1958, a society dedicated to the study of the history of ideas; Jahrbuch für Religions- und Wissens-Soziologie, in Freiburg, concerned with religious sociology; and Germania Judaica, founded in Cologne in 1958, which maintains a library on the history of the Jews in Germany. Non-confessional institutes of religious studies are for the most part joined to theological faculties. These and their institutes are largely governmental bodies and are not linked institutionally to any church. Nevertheless, they often present a denominational character from the fact that they are either Protestant or Catholic in background. The more important are located at the following universities: (1) for the history of religions, Erlangen-Nuremberg, Freiburg, Göttingen, Heidelberg, Mainz, and Marburg; (2) for general questions related to Christianity, Frankfurt, Freiburg, and Marburg; (3) for religious sociology, Freiburg, Marburg, Munich, Münster, Tübingen, and Würzburg; and (4) for religious sciences, Berlin, Bonn, Mainz, Marburg, Munich, and Münster.

**BROADCASTING.** There are no church-operated radio stations, but all 10 West German government radio stations have a churches' department (Kirchenfunk) responsible for Christian broadcasting. There are numerous Catholic and Protestant studios, commissions and organizations. Catholic and Protestant programmes are also broadcast over Germany's 2 TV stations, ZDF and ARD. There is thus a very large number of Christian broadcasts of every variety every week.

From abroad, Radio Vatican beams in German programmes for 5 hours 15 minutes a week; and Protestant programmes in German are broadcast by Trans World Radio (Monaco) for 15 hours 55 minutes a week, and by Radio Luxembourg for 9 hours 30 minutes a week. For Catholics, West Germany is a member of UNDA.

## BIBLIOGRAPHY


*Adressbuch für das katholische Deutschland.* Bonn: Zentralkomitee der Deutschen Katholiken, 1972.

*Freikirchen in Deutschland: Geschichte, Lehre, Ordnung.* W. Bartz. Trier: Spee-Buchverlag, 1973. 180p.

*Handbuch zu Freikirchen und Sekten.* 2 vols. Hannover: Lutherischer Kirchenamt, 1966.

*Kirche und Katholiken in der Bundesrepublik: Daten und Analysen.* E. Golomb. Coll. Der Christ in der Welt (Eine Enzyklopädie). Aschaffenburg: Paul Pattloch Verlag, 1974. 142p.

*Kirchliches Handbuch: Amtliches statistisches Jahrbuch der katholischen Kirche Deutschlands, 1968.* Köln: Amtlichen Zentralstelle für kirchliche statistik des katholischen Deutschlands 1968.

*Seher Grübler Enthusiasten: Sekten und Religiöse Sondergemeinschaften der Gegenwart.* K. Hutten. Stuttgart: Quell-Velag, 1958. 751p.

*Sonderdruck aus Kirchliches Jahrbuch für die Evangelische Kirche in Deutschland* (Gütersloh: Verlagshaus Gerd Mohn, 1972), p. 425–485. (Part of a regularly-updated statistical documentation).

*Taschenbuch der Evangelischen Kirchen in Deutschland, 1974.* Stuttgart: Evangelisches Verlagswerk, 1974. 924p.

*Wie Stabil ist die Kirche?* H. Hild. Gelnhauser-Berlin: Burckhardthaus-Verlag, 1974.


TABLE 2. ORGANIZED CHURCHES AND DENOMINATIONS IN THE FEDERAL REPUBLIC OF GERMANY

| Official name 1 | Begun 2 | Type 3 | Counc 4 | Congs 5 | Adults 6 | Affiliated 7 | Names, notes, and other statistics (see Codebook) 8 |
|---|---|---|---|---|---|---|---|
| Altreformierte Kirchen in Deutschland | 1834 | P Ref | ....W | 24 | 6,100 | 8,000 | *Old Reformed/Christian Reformed Chs in WGermany.* Northwest. 12n,G=1.7%pa,W=50%. |
| Alt-Katholische Kirche in Deutschland | 1874 | C OCa | UWC.W | 212 | 15,000 | 20,000 | *Old Catholic Ch, D Bonn.* Schism ex Ch of Rome over papal infallibility. 62n,1s. |
| Anglikanische Kirche (J Fulham) | 1630 | A plu | awc.. | 100 | 10,000 | 20,000 | *Ch of England.* English-speaking chaplaincies, some seasonal, some military. 10x. |
| Apostolische Gemeinschaft | 1956 | C CAp | x.... | 60 | 10,000 | 15,000 | Belongs to VAC (Switzerland). Union of splits ex New Apostolic Ch. In 6 nations. |
| Apostolische Kirche in Deutschland | 1946 | P PeA | Z.... | 6 | 500 | 1,000 | *Urchristliche Mission. Apostolic Ch in G.* Begun by UK and Danish churches. 1j. |
| Arbeitsgem der Christengemeinden in D | 1907 | P Pe2 | ZF... | 253 | 14,000 | 40,000 | *Assemblies of God.* 1953 union. M=AoG(USA,UK). Some Korean churches. 233n,11f,1s(80). |
| Armenische Apostolische Kirche | | O Arm | Ewc.. | | 10,000 | 20,000 | *Armenian Apostolic Ch, C* Echmiadzin. *Gregorian.* Refugees from USSR and Turkey. |
| Bund Ev-Freikirchlicher Gemein in D | 1834 | P Bap | T.C.W· | 695 | 66,672 | 250,000 | *Baptist Union of Germany.* 1961, M=SBC(USA). 404n,4x,10f,G=−0.3%pa,1s,W=30%,1312Y. |
| Bund Freier Ev Gemeinden in D | 1854 | P Con | KF..w | 477 | 19,817 | 45,048 | *Fed of Free Ev Congs in G. Congregational Union.* 130n,G=−0.3%pa,1p(2),W=50%,750Y. |
| Bund Freireligiöser Gem Deutschlands | c1845 | M Unt | I.... | 50 | 1,000 | 3,000 | Gem=Gemeinden. *Free Religious Congregations.* Unitarians. 7 groups. HQ Hannover. |
| Christadelphianer | | P Ade | x.... | 10 | 10,200 | 15,300 | *Christadelphian Bible Mission (CBM).* 10 ecclesias (churches). Pacifist, adventist. |
| Christengemeinschaft | 1922 | M Gno | x.... | 70 | 7,000 | 30,000 | *Sonnenwesen/Being. Anthroposophical Society.* 7 sacraments. HQ Stuttgart. 150n. |
| Christliche Missionsunternehmen | c1945 | P Pe2 | ..... | 20 | 1,000 | 3,000 | *Freie Volksmission. Free People's Mission.* Classical Pentecostals (2-stage). |
| Christliche Wissenschaft | 1907 | M Sc† | x.... | 114 | 5,500 | 10,000 | *Ch of Christ, Scientist. Christian Science.* M=CCS(Boston,USA). Declining. 13m,75w. |
| Christlicher Gemeinschaftsverband | 1909 | P Pen | Zv..w | | 14,000 | 40,000 | *Mülheim-Ruhr Bewegung. Assoc of Chr Assemblies.* Declining. 1967 applied to WCC. 1j. |
| Deutschen Spätregen Gemeinden | c1930 | P Pe4 | x.... | 17 | 900 | 2,000 | *Latter Rain Mission.* Pentecostal renewal. Missionaries from and to South Africa. |
| Evangelische Brüder-Unität in D | c1730 | P Mor | xWC.W | 7 | 3,200 | 8,600 | *Herrnhuter Brüdergemeine, Distrikt Bad Boll,* European Continental Province. 3r,1s. |
| **Evangelische Kirche in Deutschland:** | 1946 | P uni | 1WC.W | 19,601 | 22,215,000 | 28,480,000 | *EKD.* 20 Landeskirchen. 300p,39s,P=26%,W=6%. 13819n,G=−0.6%pa,5836Y,441674y. |
| Baden, Evangelische Landeskirche in | 1520 | P LuR | .wc.. | 1,224 | 1,070,000 | 1,372,000 | *Ev Ch in Baden.* Territorial ch. HQ Karlsruhe. 1s. 856 0.2 145 21243 |
| Bayern, Ev-Lutherische Kirche in | 1530 | P Lut | LWc.d | 2,995 | 1,993,000 | 2,555,000 | Bavaria. Disestablished 1919. Conservative. Munich. 1s. 1627 0.5 148 38703 |
| Berlin-Brandenburg, Ev Kirche in | 1528 | P LuR | .wc.x | 282 | 1,108,000 | 1,421,000 | Covers West Berlin. HQ Berlin. 518 −4.9 763 14399 |
| Braunschweig, Ev-l Landeskirche in | 1528 | P Lut | LWc.d | 493 | 485,000 | 622,000 | *ELC Brunswick.* Kirchentags. HQ Wolfenbüttel. 1s. 291 −0.8 181 9734 |
| Bremen: Bremische Ev Kirche | 1522 | P LuR | .wc.. | 86 | 380,000 | 487,000 | *Ev Ch of Bremen.* FRG's second largest port. 146 −1.8 339 7492 |
| Eutin, Ev-Lutherische Landeskirche | 1535 | P Lut | LWc.d | 21 | 68,000 | 87,000 | *ELC of Eutin.* 1919 autonomy from ELC Oldenburg. 27 1.9 10 1449 |
| Hamburg: ElK im Hamburgischen S | 1529 | P Lut | LWc.d | 170 | 466,000 | 598,000 | *S=Staate. ELC in State of Hamburg.* Disestablished 1918. 231 −4.7 723 7688 |
| Hannover, Ev-luth Landeskirche | 1533 | P Lut | LWc.d | 2,002 | 3,046,000 | 3,905,000 | Organized 1866, disestablished 1918. 1s,W=5%. 1711 −0.2 559 66814 |
| Hessen und Nassau, Ev Kirche in | 1523 | P LuR | .wc.. | 1,707 | 1,785,000 | 2,289,000 | *EC in Hessen & Nassau.* HQ Darmstadt. 2s(380),W=5%. 1104 −0.5 182 34198 |
| Kurhessen-Waldeck, Ev Kirche von | 1934 | P LuR | .wc.. | 1,310 | 863,000 | 1,106,000 | *United Ch of K-W.* HQ Kassel-Wilhelmshöhe. 1s. 599 0.0 57 18066 |
| Lippe: Lippische Landeskirche | | P Ref | Rwc.h | 140 | 194,000 | 249,000 | 82% Reformed, 18% Lutheran in 6 classes. HQ Detmold. 114 −0.2 15 4147 |
| Lübeck, Ev-lutherische Kirche in | 1529 | P Lut | LWc.d | 53 | 155,000 | 199,000 | *ELC in Lübeck.* 1933–45 Confessing Church strong. 90 −1.4 69 3185 |
| Nordwestdeutschlands, Ev-ref K in | 1882 | P Ref | Rwc.h | 209 | 158,000 | 202,000 | *Ev Reformed Ch in Germany.* HQ Leer. 1s, W=8%. 119 0.3 23 3529 |
| Oldenburg, Ev-Lutherische Kirche in | 1523 | P Lut | Lwc.. | 229 | 420,000 | 539,000 | *Ev Lutheran Ch in Oldenburg.* 1919 disestablished. 235 −0.2 131 10351 |
| Pfalz, Vereinigte Prot-Ev-Chr K der | | P LuR | .wc.. | 651 | 565,000 | 724,000 | *United Prot Ev Chr Church of Palatinate.* HQ Speyer. 387 −0.5 34 10812 |
| Rheinland, Ev Kirche im | 1520 | P LuR | .wc.x | 2,063 | 2,930,000 | 3,756,000 | *EC in Rhineland.* HQ Dusseldorf. 4p,1s(540),W=6%. 1625 −0.7 673 54220 |
| Schaumburg-Lippe, E-L Landeskirche | 1559 | P Lut | LWc.d | 41 | 59,000 | 75,000 | Synodical structure under council of 7. W=9%. 29 0.8 1 1157 |
| Schleswig-Holstein, E-Landeskirche | 1542 | P Lut | LWc.d | 2,276 | 1,853,000 | 2,375,000 | Disestab 1918. 1933–45 Kirchenkampf. Kiel. W=2%. 870 −0.4 992 39839 |
| Westfalen, Ev Kirche von | 1817 | P LuR | .wc.x | 1,576 | 2,646,000 | 3,392,000 | *EC of Westphalia.* HQ Bielefeld. 3p,1s(585),W=10%. 1525 −0.6 587 52956 |
| Württemberg, Ev Landeskirche in | 1534 | P Lut | Lwc.. | 2,073 | 1,971,000 | 2,527,000 | 1918 disestablished. Swabians. 1s,W=10%. 1715 −0.1 204 41692 |
| Evangelisch-Johannische Kirche | 1926 | M Spi | x.... | 15 | 2,000 | 4,000 | *Ev Ch of Revelation of St John the Divine.* HQ Dusseldorf. Mainly in GDR. Growing. |
| Ev-lutherische Bekenntniskirche | | P Lut | ..... | | 1,000 | 1,500 | *Confessional ELC.* Pure Lutheranism. M=Missouri, Wisconsin Synods(USA). HQ Bremen. |
| Ev-Lutherische Kirche Estlands in Exil | 1944 | P Lut | LwC.. | 53 | 2,000 | 2,500 | *Estonian Ev Lutheran Ch in Exile.* Refugees from Estonia (USSR). HQ Stockholm. |
| Ev-lutherische Kirche in Baden | | P Lut | Lw... | | 3,800 | 4,886 | *Ev Lutheran Ch in Baden.* Lutheran minority in United church area. |
| Ev-luth Kirche Lettlands im Exil | 1944 | R Lut | LwC.. | 53 | 5,351 | 11,400 | *Latvian ELC in Exile.* Refugees from USSR, HQ Esslingen. 9n,G=−6.7%pa,W=35%,28Yy. |
| Ev-Lutherische Kirche von Dänemark | 1864 | P Lut | Lwc.. | 52 | 2,000 | 3,000 | *Church of Denmark.* Parishes of state church of Denmark, in south Schleswig. Danes. 20nx. |
| Evangelisch-methodistische Kirche in D | 1830 | P Met | VwC.W | 1,242 | 59,049 | 100,000 | 1968 merger Ev Gemeinschaft D/EUB in UMC(USA). 398n,G=−1.3%pa,14H,1s,W=65%,654Yy. |
| Freie Bibelgemeinde | 1931 | M Jeh | ..... | | 2,000 | 4,000 | *Free Bible Congregation.* Schism ex Jehovah's Witnesses. HQ Bünde (Westphalia). |
| Freie Christliche Volkskirche in D | 1945 | M Unt | ..... | | 7,000 | 20,000 | *Free Christian People's Church.* HQ Stuttgart. Expanding. Liberal theology. |
| Freier Brüderkreis | 1847 | P CBr | x.... | 200 | 35,000 | 80,000 | *Free Brethren. Plymouth-Brüder.* 3 Open groups. Unions with Baptists. HQ Betzdorf. |
| Gemeinde Christi | 1947 | P Dis | x.... | 40 | 3,000 | 5,000 | *Chs of Christ.* M=CC(Non-Instrumental) (USA). 70% USA military personnel. 29f. |
| Gemeinde Christi | 1956 | P Dis | x.... | 30 | 2,000 | 4,000 | *Christian Chs/Chs of Christ.* M=CCCC(Instrumental). USA military personnel. 21f. |
| Gemeinde der Christen Ecclesia | 1944 | P Pe2 | ..... | 192 | 7,000 | 15,000 | *Community of Christians Ch.* Begun by industrialist. Healing ministry. Declining. |
| Gemeinde Gottes (Anderson) | 1901 | P Hol | x.... | 80 | 3,500 | 6,000 | M=Ch of God(Anderson)(USA). HQ Essen. Mainly in rural areas. 40n,1s. |
| Gemeinde Gottes (Cleveland) | 1936 | P Pe3 | ZF... | 63 | 4,500 | 7,000 | M=Ch of God(Cleveland)(USA). HQ near Stuttgart. Some Black members. 57n,2f,2s. |
| Gemeinde Jesu Christi in Deutschland | 1943 | P Pe2 | ..... | 15 | 500 | 1,000 | Small Pentecostal body founded in Stammheim by a German-American. 1p. |
| Gemeinschaft Entschiedener Christen | | P Pe2 | ..... | 3 | 400 | 1,000 | *Society of Definite Christians.* In Karlsruhe (HQ), Lörrach, Scharzwald. |
| Gesellschaft zur Vereinigung des WC | c1965 | I mar | x.... | | 500 | 1,000 | WC=Weltchristentums. *Unification Ch of Germany.* M=HSAUWC(Korea). 6,000 by 1976. |
| Gralsbewegung | 1927 | M The | x.... | 40 | 1,400 | 2,000 | *Nature Philosophy Union.* Theocratic, messianic. HQ Vomperberg/Tyrol. In 8 nations. |
| Griechisch-Orth Metropolie von D | | O Gre | Cwc.W | 50 | 249,000 | 358,000 | *Greek Orthodox Diocese,* & E Middle Europe, under EP Constantinople. Greek labourers. |
| Heilsarmee | 1886 | P Sal | xwc.W | 78 | 10,000 | 15,000 | *Salvation Army, Germany Territory.* 3 Divisions. 33 institutions. Officers 162, 1s. |
| Katholische Apostolische Kirche | c1840 | C CAp | xv... | 170 | 11,000 | 20,000 | *Urkirche. Catholic Apostolic Ch (Original Ch).* Declining. 1948, applied to WCC. |
| **Katholische Kirche Deutschlands:** | c 90 | R LEr | B.B.S | 11,911 | 21,537,000 | 27,610,000 | *Catholic Ch in G.* C=44+15+302. 10q,20s(1895). 23866nx,4340m,75530w,341421Yy. |
| M Bamberg | 1007 | R Lat | Bs | 350 | 625,000 | 801,000 | *Erzbistum Bamberg.* Northern Bavaria. 685 136 1880 10293 |
| D Eichstätt | 745 | R Lat | Bs | 254 | 309,000 | 396,000 | *Bistum Eichstätt.* Central Bavaria. 505 58 1365 4796 |
| D Speyer | c 350 | R Lat | Bs | 330 | 537,000 | 688,000 | South of Rhineland Palatinate and east Saar. 510 32 2104 8547 |
| D Würzburg | 741 | R Lat | Bs | 609 | 700,000 | 898,000 | NW Bavaria. Small part in GDR (EC Meiningen). 1017 303 4300 12485 |
| M Freiburg im Breisgau | 1821 | R Lat | Bs | 1,081 | 1,732,000 | 2,220,000 | Northwest and west Baden-Württemberg. 1879 201 6510 30025 |
| D Mainz | c 350 | R Lat | Bs | 342 | 687,000 | 881,000 | Part Baden-Württemberg/Hesse/Rhineland-Palatinate. 634 92 1497 10643 |
| D Rottenburg | 1821 | R Lat | Bs | 1,020 | 1,620,000 | 1,970,000 | Centre and east of Baden-Württemberg. 1476 154 4707 27819 |
| M Köln (Cologne) | c 150 | R Lat | Bs | 813 | 2,103,000 | 2,696,000 | North Rhineland-Westphalia including Bonn. 2333 438 6401 28661 |
| D Aachen | 1801 | R Lat | Bs | 555 | 1,113,000 | 1,427,000 | N Rhineland-Westphalia (Belgian/Dutch frontiers). 1180 209 3604 16639 |
| D Essen | 1957 | R Lat | Bs | 312 | 1,006,000 | 1,290,000 | Centre of North Rhineland-Westphalia. 990 38 1845 13633 |
| D Limburg | 1821 | R Lat | Bs | 327 | 686,000 | 880,000 | Western Hesse, eastern Rhineland-Palatinate. 828 353 2200 9378 |
| D Münster | 800 | R Lat | Bs | 684 | 1,618,000 | 2,074,000 | 2 areas apart: Lower Saxony, Rhineland-Münster. 1621 312 6882 30379 |

*Continued opposite*

*Table 2 – continued*

| Official name 1 | Begun 2 | Type 3 | Counc 4 | Congs 5 | Adults 6 | Affiliated 7 | Names, notes, and other statistics (see Codebook) 8 | | | | |
|---|---|---|---|---|---|---|---|---|---|---|---|
| D Osnabrück | 772 | R Lat | Bs | 359 | 640,000 | 820,000 | 13% RC. Part in GDR (EC Schwerin); 2 parts in FRG. | 711 | 59 | 2333 | 10800 |
| D Trier | c 90 | R Lat | Bs | 971 | 1,412,000 | 1,810,000 | Rhineland-Palatinate, most of Saar. 75% RC. | 1726 | 445 | 4035 | 22230 |
| M München (Munich) & Freising | 739 | R Lat | Bs | 647 | 1,728,000 | 2,215,000 | Southeast Bavaria. HQ Munich. 79% RC. | 2020 | 420 | 7300 | 22198 |
| D Augsburg | c 550 | R Lat | Bs | 1,036 | 1,140,000 | 1,462,000 | Also called D Augusta. Southwest Bavaria. 79% RC. | 1012 | 410 | 4990 | 19935 |
| D Passau | 737 | R Lat | Bs | 307 | 385,000 | 493,000 | Also called D Passavia. Eastern Bavaria. 93% RC. | 656 | 166 | 1920 | 7757 |
| D Regensburg | 739 | R Lat | Bs | 776 | 986,000 | 1,264,000 | Ratisbon. Northeastern Bavaria. 86% RC. | 1262 | 263 | 4277 | 18641 |
| M Paderborn | 805 | R Lat | Bs | 541 | 1,485,000 | 1,904,000 | 33% RC. Rhineland. Part in GDR (EC Magdeburg). | 1790 | 129 | 5610 | 22300 |
| D Fulda | 1752 | R Lat | Bs | 101 | 335,000 | 429,000 | Half in GDR (EC Erfurt). In FRG, in Hesse. | 180 | 73 | 359 | 3900 |
| D Hildesheim | 800 | R Lat | Bs | 356 | 548,000 | 703,000 | Lower Saxony. 13% RC. 4 parishes of 7,000 in GDR. | 588 | 19 | 797 | 8520 |
| D Berlin | 1930 | R Lat | bs | 120 | 198,000 | 254,000 | West Berlin; part of D Berlin (HQ in GDR). | 240 | 30 | 600 | 1800 |
| EA Deutschland (*Ukrainian*) | 1959 | R Ukr | Os | 20 | 25,000 | 32,000 | For Ukrainians of Byzantine rite. HQ Munich 27. | 23 | 0 | 14 | 42 |
| Kirche des Nazareners | 1958 | P Hol | xF... | 12 | 433 | 1,000 | *Ch of the Nazarene*. Holiness body. M=CoN(USA). HQ Frankfurt. Expanding. 15n,1s. | | | | |
| K des Reiches Gott/Menschenfreunde | 1950 | M Jeh | x.... | | 15,000 | 50,000 | *Kingdom of God/Friends of Man*(Sayerce). Ex Jehovah's Witnesses. In 12 nations. | | | | |
| Kirche Gottes in Christus | | I pe3 | Z.... | 10 | 1,000 | 2,000 | M=CoG in Christ(Memphis,TN,USA). Blacks in US armed forces. Non-combatants. | | | | |
| K JC der Heiligen der Letzten Tage | 1845 | M LdS | x.... | 200 | 10,000 | 21,161 | *KJC=Kirche Jesus Christi. Ch of JC of Latter-day Saints. Mormons*. 950f,G=1.9%pa. | | | | |
| Kirche Schwedens | | P Lut | Lwc.. | 1 | 200 | 350 | *Church of Sveden. Svenska Kyrkan*. Chaplaincy of state church. Swedes. 1x. | | | | |
| Litauische Ev-Lutherische Exilkirche | 1945 | P Lut | LvC.. | | 9,000 | 12,000 | *Lietuviu Evangeliku Liuteronu Baznycia. Lithuanian ELC in Exile*. USSR refugees. | | | | |
| Neuapostolische Kirche | 1863 | C CAp | x.... | 2,900 | 335,000 | 490,000 | *New Apostolic Ch*. Ex Catholic Apostolic Ch. World HQ Dortmund. 16 Apostles. 1j. | | | | |
| Neue Kirche in Deutschland | 1824 | M Swe | xv... | 3 | 300 | 500 | *New Church in Germany*. Swedenborgian. HQ Essen-Werden. 1968, applied to join WCC. | | | | |
| Orthodoxe Kirche von Rumänien | | O Rum | Cwc.. | 3 | 5,000 | 7,500 | *Biserica Ortodoxa Romana din Baden-Baden. Romanian Orthodox Ch*. Under P Bucharest. | | | | |
| Philadelphia-Verein | 1946 | P Pe2 | ..... | | 5,000 | 7,000 | *Philadelphia Community*. In Württemberg. School of prophets, unction, visions. 1j. | | | | |
| Reformierte Kirche von Niederlande | | P Ref | Rwc.. | 16 | 3,000 | 4,937 | *Netherlands Reformed Church*. Congregations of Dutch residents. | | | | |
| Reformiert-Apostolische Gemeindebund | 1921 | C CAp | ..... | | 500 | 1,000 | *Reformed Apostolic Community*. Schism ex New Apostolic Church. HQ Dresden (GDR). | | | | |
| Religiöse Gesellschaft der Freunde | 1830 | P Qua | Q...w | 28 | 533 | 800 | *Quäker. Religious Society of Friends* (*Quakers*). Links with Quakers in UK, USA. | | | | |
| Russisch-Orth K ausserhalb Russlands | 1920 | O Sla | x.... | 70 | 20,000 | 30,000 | *D Germany, ROC Outside of Russia* (HQ New York). Conservative. 3 bishops. 33b. | | | | |
| Russisch-Orth K (PE Mitteleuropa) | | O Sla | Mwc.. | 9 | 1,000 | 2,000 | *Russian Orth Ch*. 2 Dioceses: Dusseldorf & NW Deutschland, Baden-Baden & Bayern. | | | | |
| Selbständige Ev-Lutherische Kirche | 1830 | P Lut | ..C.w | 247 | 36,000 | 48,192 | *Indep ELC*. 1972 merged with Altluth K(1830), EL Freikirche. 105n,1s,W=35%,500Yy. | | | | |
| Serbische Orthodoxe Kirche | | O Ser | Cwc.. | | 80,000 | 160,000 | *D Western Europe, Serbian Orthodox Ch*. Under P Belgrade. Serbian migrant workers. | | | | |
| Siebenten-Tags-Adventisten | 1875 | P Adv | x.... | 436 | 26,016 | 50,000 | *Seventh-day Adventists, S&W German UCs*. 10 Confs. 201n,1H,1j,1r,886t(30599),650Y. | | | | |
| Syrisch-Orthodoxe Kirche (P Antioch) | | O Syr | Dw.N. | | 1,000 | 2,000 | *Syrian Orthodox Ch, P Antioch*. By 1975, 600 immigrant families. Arabs. | | | | |
| Ukrainische Autokephale Orthodoxe K | | O Sla | X.... | 30 | 10,000 | 15,000 | *Ukrainian Autocephalic Orthodox Ch in Exile*. Links with UOC of USA. 19nx. | | | | |
| Ukrainische Ev-Baptistische Kirche | | P Bap | .v... | | 500 | 1,000 | *Ukrainian Ev Baptist Chs in Germany*. HQ Augsburg. 1948, applied to join WCC. | | | | |
| Ungarisch-Lutherische Exilkirche | c1945 | P Lut | ..... | 13 | 700 | 1,000 | *Hungarian Lutheran Ch in Exile*. Refugees from Hungary, especially since 1956. | | | | |
| Ungarisch-Reformierte Kirche | c1945 | P Ref | ..... | | 2,000 | 3,500 | *Reformed Church of Hungary*. Refugees, especially since 1956 uprising in Hungary. | | | | |
| Verband B-W-B Mennonitengemeinden | | P Men | G.... | 24 | 1,300 | 3,000 | *B-W-B=Badisch-Württembergisch-Bayrischer. Union of Mennonite Congs*. Declining. | | | | |
| Vereinigte Pfingstkirche | c1950 | P Pe1 | x.... | 2 | 60 | 200 | *United Pentecostal Ch. Jesus Only Church*. M=UPC(USA). 1 school. 5f. | | | | |
| V der Deutschen Mennonitengemeinden | 1525 | P Men | GWC.W | 35 | 7,500 | 14,000 | *V=Vereinigung. Assoc of German Mennonite Congs* (1886). Saar, Rhineland. 15n. | | | | |
| Volksmission Entschiedener Christen | 1934 | P Pe2 | ..... | 200 | 5,000 | 10,000 | *People's Mission of Definite Christians*. HQ Stuttgart. Overseas missions. 1j. | | | | |
| Zeugen Jehovas | 1897 | M Jeh | x.... | 1,157 | 95,207 | 160,000 | *Jehovah's Witnesses*. 150,313 at 1973 Memorial. HQ Wiesbaden. G=4%pa,1j,5438Y. | | | | |
| Other Protestant denominations | | P | ..... | | 60,000 | 105,000 | Total over 115 (see list below), including USA military chaplaincies. | | | | |
| Other marginal Protestant bodies | | M | ..... | | 15,000 | 50,000 | Total over 20 (see list below). | | | | |
| Other Catholic (non-Roman) churches | | C | ..... | | 3,000 | 5,000 | Total 39: Antoinists, Apostelamt Juda, Liberal Cath Ch, Mariavite Ch, 20 episcopi vagantes, &c. | | | | |
| Other Orthodox churches | | O | ..... | | 1,000 | 2,000 | Total over 5 (see below): Byelorussian, Coptic, Estonian, and Serbian Orthdox. | | | | |
| Doubly-affiliated (duplication)(1970) | | | | | –819,000 | –1,050,000 | Free Protestants and others enumerated also by EKD or Roman Catholic dioceses. | | | | |
| **Total affiliated (mid-1970)** | | | | **43,100** | **44,290,138** | **57,497,374** | **Total denominations (1970) . . . 243.** | | | | |
| **Total affiliated (mid-1975)** | | | | **43,300** | **43,920,800** | **57,018,100** | **Total denominations (1975) . . . 250.** | | | | |
| **Total affiliated (mid-1980)** | | | | **43,500** | **43,422,000** | **56,370,400** | **Total denominations (1980) . . . 260.** | | | | |

NOTES ON TABLE ABOVE
COLUMNS: for meanings and CODES (cols. 1, 3, 4, 8), see Codebook (Part 6). Column 1: **Boldface type** = church with over 10% of country's affiliated Christians.
NATIONAL COUNCILS (Column 14, 5th letter).
- d = Vereinigte Evangelisch-Lutherische Kirche Deutschlands (VELKD) (United Evangelical Lutheran Church in Germany), a 1948 federation of Lutheran Landeskirchen (members also belong to the CCCG).
- h = Reformierte Bund (Federation of Reformed Churches), representing the over 1,000 Reformed congregations and churches in Germany, with 2 million members and 1,000 ministers, mostly in Lutheran-Reformed United churches.
- S = Plenarkonferenz der Bischözesen Deutschlands (Plenary Conference of Bishops of German Dioceses), a member of ACKD (CCCG).
- W = Arbeitsgemeinschaft Christlicher Kirchen in der BRD und Berlin-West (ACKD) (Council/Association of Christian Churches in the FRG and West Berlin, CCCG). EKD churches are members of this through the EKD.
- w = associate (guest) member of ACKD (CCCG).
- x = Evangelische Kirche der Union (EKU) (Evangelical Church of the Union) (a confederation of United churches, with 5 more in GDR); members also belong to the CCCG.

*Other national councils*. Deutsche Evangelische Allianz (DEA) (German Evangelical Alliance) (members individuals, not denominations; affiliated to EEA and WEF). Arbeitsgemeinschaft der Christengemeinden (Working Fellowship of Christian Churches), a Pentecostal council. Vereinigung Evangelischer Freikirchen in Deutschland (Association of Free Churches in Germany): members = Bund Ev-Freikirchlicher Gemeinden in D, Bund Freier Ev Gemeinden in D, and Ev-methodistische Kirche in D. Konferenz Bekennender Gemeinschaften in den Evangelischen Kirchen Deutschlands (anti-ecumenical). *Local councils*. 10 sub-regional councils and 150 local councils, affiliated with ACKD.
OTHER PROTESTANT DENOMINATIONS. The over 100 more smaller bodies include (with names given in the language they are best known in): American Baptist Association (1957; 2 churches; Korean pastor), Apostolic Christian Ch (Nazarean) (31 churches), Apostolische Glaubensgemeinde, Baptist Mid-Missions (1949), Bible Christian Union (20 missionaries), Biblische Glaubensgemeinde, Brüderhand, Bruderschaft 'Der König kommt!', Children of God (from USA), Chrischona Mission, Christen-gemeinden Elim, Christian Ch of North America, Ch of God of Prophecy, Communauté des Chrétiens, Conservative Mennonite Conference, Cooneyites (Ireland), Exclusive Brethren (Raven-Taylor, and Kelly-Continental), Freie Ev Lukasgemeinde Guissen, Freie Innere Mission, Glaubenshaus Bethanien, Glaubenshaus in Warngau, Gospel Missionary Union (1961), Greater Europe Mission, Greek Evangelical Ch (3 congregations, HQ Darmstadt), Gypsy Evangelical Movement (France), Hungarian Free Protestant Ch in Western Europe, International Ch of the Foursquare Gospel, Jugendhilfswerk Brüderliebe, Mennonite Brethren Ch, Mission zum Dienst am Vollem Evangelium, National Fellowship of Brethren Chs, Remonstrantse Broederschap, Seventh-day Adventist Reform Movement (with world HQ), Seventh Day Baptist Churches in Germany, Slavic Gospel Association, Tabernakelbewegung, The Way International (USA), Urgemeinde Gottes, Verband Christlicher Glaubensgemeinschaften, Worldwide Evangelization Crusade (1969), World-Wide Missions (1960). In addition, there are large numbers in USA and UK military chaplaincies not already listed in the table above.
OTHER MARGINAL PROTESTANT BODIES. These include: Arbeitsgemeinschaft Freier Religion (Offenbach-aM), Branhamites (End Time Believers; HQ Jeffersonville, IN, USA; Jesus-Only Unitarians), Deutscher Bund für Freies Christentum (Frankfurt), Eglise Chrétienne Universelle (Témoins du Christ Revenu), Reichs-Israel-Gemeinde, Reorganized Ch of Jesus Christ of Latter-day Saints (1,200), Tempelgesellschaft (begun 1861; 800 adherents, most near Stuttgart; Unitarian), Unity School of Christianity. Other Unitarian groups, with over 40,000 members, include: Free Religious Community, German Unitarian Religious Community, German Unitarian Union, Union of Free Communities, Unitarian Religious Community (Free Protestant).
OTHER ORTHODOX CHURCHES. Refugees and immigrants, including: Byelorussian Autocephalic Orthodox Ch, Coptic Orthodox Ch (Frankfurt), Estonian Orthodox Ch, Serbian Orthodox Ch (Independent).
UNITING CHURCHES. Negotiations for organic union were under way in 1974 between the Landeskirchen of Eutin, Hamburg, Lübeck and Schleswig-Holstein, with the Harburg district of the Ev-luth Landeskirche Hannovers, to become the Evangelisch-lutherische Kirche Nordelbien (or Nordelbische Ev-Luth Kirche).

PEOPLES (ethnolinguistic). Christians: 96.0% German, 1.0% Italian, 0.7% Greek, 0.5% Spaniard, 0.3% Serbian, 0.3% Austrian, 0.2% Dutch, 0.2% Portuguese, 0.1% Polish, 0.1% Danish, 0.1% Estonian, 0.1% Russian, 0.1% USA (military & civilian), 0.1% French, 0.1% British, Swiss, Armenian, Latvian, Lithuanian, Romanian, Gypsy, Ukrainian, Czech, Frisian, Chinese (300), Korean, Japanese, Indonesian, et alii.

COUNTRY-WIDE TOTALS
EVANGELIZATION (see Part 5). 1900: 100%. 1970: 100%. 1980: 100%. *Mass evangelism*. Among the large number of recent campaigns: Billy Graham campaigns in 1955 in 5 cities (235,000 attenders, 10,200 enquirers), in 1960 in Essen, Hamburg and Berlin (649,000 attenders, 16,636 enquirers), in 1963 in Nuremberg and Stuttgart (255,000 attenders, 6,578 enquirers), in 1966 in Berlin (90,000 attenders, 2,400 enquirers), and in 1970 in Dortmund for the Euro '70 Crusade (largest evangelistic campaign ever held in Europe; 8-language simultaneous translation, closed-circuit TV to 36 cities in Europe and British Isles (13 cities in Germany); total 839,075 attenders, 15,813 enquirers; in Dortmund itself there were 123,500 attenders and 2,905 enquirers); other events include Oral Roberts in 1961 Frankfurt campaign; 1966, World Congress on Evangelism (Berlin); 1977, yearlong campaign Missio Berlin 77, in conjunction with 17th German Protestant Kirchentag; 1980, All Germany Crusade (DEA). *Radiophonic evangelism*. Annual listeners' letters (1975): 89,600 TWR, about 6,000 Radio Vatican, 5,370 HCJB, 196 RVOG, RSB, FEBC, et alia. Bible correspondence courses: many, including ICI (10,200 enrolments).
FOREIGN MISSIONARIES AND PERSONNEL (nationals serving abroad) (1975). Total 16,857: 14,614 Roman Catholics (8,414 foreign missionaries (2,205 religious priests, 177 secular priests, 731 brothers, 5,236 sisters, 65 lay) in Africa, Asia and Latin America, about 6,200 other personnel serving in Western nations including 1,293 in Netherlands, 325 in Denmark, 250 in Norway, et alia), 1,770 Protestants in 82 societies in over 80 countries (1,358 through DEMT, 200 through KEM, over 150 other independents), 350 marginal Protestants (about 200 Jehovah's Witnesses, also Mormons et al), about 123 Catholics (non-Roman) (mainly New Apostolics).
FOREIGN MISSIONARIES AND PERSONNEL (aliens from abroad) (1973). Total 6,077. *From Western world*. 5,508: about 4,000 Roman Catholics, about 1,000 marginal Protestants (900 Mormons from USA), 458 Protestants (341 in 57 USA societies, 54 in 2 Canada societies, 43 in 8 UK societies, about 20 from Denmark, Norway and Sweden), about 40 Orthodox from Greece, 10 Anglicans (8 in 1 UK society, 2 in 1 USA society). *From Communist world*. 134: about 106 Roman Catholics, about 28 Orthodox from Romania, USSR, Yugoslavia. *From Third World*. 435: 400 Roman Catholics, about 15 Protestants from Indonesia, Japan, Korea, South Africa et alia, 10 Orthodox from Cyprus, 10 indigenous from Korea, Indonesia et alia. After 1973 the number of Koreans working in Germany increased rapidly.
INSTITUTIONS (church-operated) (1973). Total 6,280, including 1,140 higher schools (33 minor seminaries), 4,820 medical centres, 55 religious communities (30 monasteries), 95 research centres, 82 seminaries (50 Protestant, 30 RC, 2 Catholic/non-Roman), 30 study centres.
PERIODICALS. About 2,850 titles.
PERSONNEL. About 127,077 (121,000 national, 6,077 foreign).
RELIGIOUS LIBRARIES. About 850.
SCRIPTURE DISTRIBUTION (1975). Annual totals: 967,116 Bibles (3% free, 46% subsidized, 51% commercial), 736,496 NTs (22% free, 38% subsidized, 40% commercial), 117,237 UBS portions, 1,351,114 UBS selections. *Translations completed*. Portion: 7 languages since 1475. NT: 4 languages since 1706. Bible: 5 languages since 1466.
SERVICE AGENCIES. About 750, including ACKD(CCCG), AGEH, AKID, AKP, BDKJ, BKED, CAJ, CCCI, CEF, CFD, CGBD, CLC, CMC, CVJM(YMCA), DEA, EAB, EAGWM, EAL, EKU, EWJD(YWCA), FR, IAML, IMHEKD, JBGA, KAB, KDSE, KFD, KLJB, KNA, KSZ, MFSC, OJD, OSCO, PKE, PTL, SASRA, SERPAL, SIL, SOG, SU, TWR, VBE, VDO, VELKD, VHOD, VKDL, WCFBA, WLC(EHC), YFC, YWAM, ZDK.

ADDITIONAL DATA ON CHURCHES
EVANGELISCHE KIRCHE IN DEUTSCHLAND (EKD). The table shows the 20 territorial churches as existing up to 1976. *New territorial church*. In 1977, the churches of Eutin, Hamburg, Lübeck and Schleswig-Holstein united as the Nordelbische Evangelisch-Lutherische Kirche (North Elbian ELC). *EKD*. The EKD is a federation of 17 (previously 20) Landeskirchen (territorial churches) of which 7 (previously 10) are Lutheran, 2 Reformed, and 8 United (Lutheran/Reformed) in tradition. Their 10,671 legally independent church congregations are joined together in 511 areas (Kirchenkreis, Dekanat, Propstei) and into 42 larger regions (Sprengel, Prälaturen, General- and Landessuperintendenturen), forming the 17 (20) Landeskirchen. These latter were completely independent legislatively and organizationally until federation in 1946. *Membership*. This has gradually fallen despite the population growth of the country, from 28,376,000 in 1961, to 28,480,000 (1970), and to 28,210,000 (1972), which is an average annual decrease of 0.6% (in 1971). As shown in column 8 above, in 1971, 13 Landeskirchen were experiencing numerical decline, one zero growth and 6 numerical increase. *Other data*. Statistics in the table for congregations and in the sub-table are those reported for the years 1968–71. *Baptisms*. 99% of all annual baptisms are of children, and 92% are of children under one year old. Annual totals have declined steadily from 475,843 in 1966 (a baptism rate of 1.6% per year) to 462,931 in 1967, to 441,674 in 1968, and to 283,103 in 1970. *Confirmations*. These have also declined, from 424,527 in 1967 to 379,723 in 1969. *Communicants*. EKD statistics enumerate not communicant persons but the total communion breads distributed on the 4 Sundays in the year when communion is celebrated. These declined from 7,868,478 breads (in 269,949 celebrations) in 1967, to 7,604,969 (265,347) in 1968, to 6,994,542 (255,841) in 1969. The figures for adult members in column 6 of the table are editorial estimates of the number of eligible communicants bearing in mind that virtually all German Protestant children receive confirmation. If practising communicants attend on average twice a year, in 1969 they would have numbered 3.5 million or 15% of eligible communicants. *Conversions*. New adult members from outside each year (converts from Catholicism and other bodies) declined from 36,128 (1963) to 33,773 (1966) to 28,939 (1967; 14,009 being converts from Catholicism and 12,844 being unbelievers), to 26,154 (1968) and to 15,000 (1972). *Defections*. Adult losses each year (converts to Catholicism or departures to non-religious status) increased from 40,272 (1966) to 42,270 (1967; probably about 14,000 being converts to Catholicism and 28,000 to no religion), to 58,547 (1968) to 111,576 (1969) to 202,823 (1970) to 159,980 (1971) to 135,000 (1972), to 215,000 (1974). *Church attendance*. Weekly church-goers in the EKD have dropped from 1,168,000 adults and 561,000 Sunday-school children (1963) to 942,000 adults and 379,000 children (1971). These

totals are based on counts on 4 average Sundays each year (1st Sunday in Lent, 4th Sunday after Easter, 16th or 17th Sunday after Trinity, 1st Sunday in Advent). Expressed as a % of EKD membership, weekly attendance declined each year for the period 1963–71 as follows: 7.3% (1963), 7.2%, 6.9%, 7.0%, 6.8%, 6.1%, 5.9%, 5.6% (1971), and then to 5.4% by 1974. *Seminaries.* 12 university faculties of theology, 4 Kirchliche Hochschulen (church-sponsored), 23 preacher-seminaries. *Lay training schools.* About 300.

KATHOLISCHE KIRCHE DEUTSCHLANDS. *Parishes.* (1971) 10,291. *Annual baptisms.* (1972) 99.6% infant, 0.4% adult. *Personnel.* About 96% nationals, 4% expatriates. *Priests in parish work* (1971). 12,680 secular, 1,778 religious. *Church attendance.* (1950) 50.6%, (1968) 41.6% of all Catholics, (1969) 39.4%, (1970) 37.6%, (1971) 35.6%, (1972) 32.4%. *Easter communicants.* (1968) 49.3%, (1969) 47.0%, (1970) 45.5%, (1971) 43.1%. *Defections* (from Catholic Church). (1962) 23,089, (1968) 27,995, (1969) 38,712, (1970) 69,455, (1971) 58,361, (1972) 53,772, (1974) 83,000. *Admissions or returns* (from non-Catholic bodies). (1968) 9,355, (1969) 7,308, (1970) 5,857, (1971) 5,514. *Catholic charismatics* ((January 1974). Nearly 1,000 adults including many religious personnel are active in 30 prayer groups in the Charismatic Renewal. *Seminaries.* Each diocese has its own major seminary. *Seminarians* (theological students). The numbers have fallen rapidly: (secular) 3,484 in 1964, 2,926 in 1968, 2,636 in 1969, 2,343 in 1970, 2,078 in 1971, 1,895 in 1972; (religious) 1,799 in 1964, 1,234 in 1968, 1,023 in 1969, 843 in 1970, 703 in 1971, 565 in 1972. *Main religious orders and congregations* (1973). Priests (with over 600 professed): 1,500 OSB, 1,167 OFM, 860 SJ, 648 SAC, 620 SVD. Brothers (with over 100 professed): 180 Ordre Hospitalier, 135 Barmherzige Brüder v. Maria-Hilf, 125 PFM. Sisters (the 3 largest congregations): Arme Schulschwestern uLFr, Franziskanerinnen, Vinzentinerinnen. The total of female congregations shown (302) is that of provinces and monasteries, and includes: 76 provinces whose generalates are in other countries, 30 provinces whose generalates are in the FRG, 47 monasteries and orders of contemplatives, and 64 other isolated cloisters.

*Catholic organizations.* The German Bishops' Conference (Deutsche Bischofskonferenz), which is a member of CCEE, has its headquarters in Bonn. Although in principle it unites the bishops of both East and West Germany, in fact only the latter participate. A vicar-general of the diocese of Berlin (GDR) resides in West Berlin and represents the bishop of Berlin in the West German episcopal conference. Regional episcopal conferences also cover all of the FRG except 2 dioceses in the north (Osnabrück, Hildersheim); however, except for the Bavarian Conference (Bayerische Bischofskonferenz) in Munich, none has a secretariat. Associations of religious personnel include the Association of Major Superiors of Germany (Vereinigung Deutscher Ordensoberen, VDO), Association of Major Superiors of Orders and Congregations of Brothers in Germany (Vereinigung Höherer Ordensoberen der Brüderordern und -kongregationen Deutschlands, VHOB) and Association of Female Major Superiors of Germany (Vereinigung der Ordensoberinnen Deutschlands, VHOD). For the armed forces, the federal republic forms a military vicariate.

There is no national pastoral council, but for priests there exists a National Presbyteral Council (Arbeitsgemeinschaft der Priesterräten der Diözesen der BRD und West Berlins, AGPR) in the Rhineland, which works in liaison and collaboration with the Bishops' Conference for matters relating to priests. Lay movements are co-ordinated in Bonn by the Central Committee of German Catholics (ZDK), founded in 1868, which was suppressed by the Nazis but restored again in 1952. The Central Committee is composed of about 160 members from the following groups: 60 representatives of organizations of Catholic laity, 44 delegates of diocesan councils, 30 directors of institutions created by the episcopate (Misereor, Adveniat, et alia) and 25 personalities from the world of science, economics, politics, trade unions and culture. The principal movements are Bund der Katholische Jugend (16 youth organizations), Deutsche Kolpingsfamilie (about 400,000 members), Junge Christlichen Arbeitnehmern (CAJ) (youth workers), Bundesverband der Katholische Arbeiter-Bewegung (KAB) (Christian workers, 250,000, Bund Katholischer Unternehmer (Catholic employers) and Deutscher Caritasverband (2 million members).

The Holy See has diplomatic relations with the Federal Republic and is represented to government and the Catholic hierarchy by a nuncio in Bonn.

International organizations having their headquarters in West Germany include the following ten. (1) The Catholic Media Council—Publicity Media Planning for Developing Countries (Publizistische Medienplanung für Entwicklungsländer), founded in Aachen in 1969, brings together representatives of OCIC (Belgium), UCIP (Switzerland) and UNDA (Belgium with representatives of the principal Catholic agencies providing aid to the Third World for use of mass media in developing countries. (2) The European Federation for Catholic Adult Education (Europaische Föderation für Katholische Erwashsenenbilding), founded in Lucerne, Switzerland, in 1963 and now located in Bonn, co-ordinates the work of 8 national groups (1973) concerned with adult education. (3) The International Centre for the Diaconate (Internationales Diakonatszentrum), founded in Freiburg in 1965, had relations with groups in 35 countries in 1974. (4) International Catholic Youth Work for East and Middle Europe (Internationales Katholisches Jugendwerk für Ost- und Mitteleuropa), founded in Madrid in 1958 and now located in Munich, helps to resettle and train refugee youth and facilitates contacts between various national refugee groups. (5) The International Federation of Catholic Popular Rural High Schools (Internationale Föderation Katholische Ländlicher Heimvolkshochschulen), founded in Bonn-Oberkassel in 1963, provides for contacts between the schools of 5 countries (FRG, Austria, Holland, Switzerland and Italy) and is a member of ICRA in Italy. (6) International Kolping Society (Kolpingwerk International), founded in 1849 by A. Kolping to aid young artisans both socially and religiously, has been extended to include the question of the renewal of society. The organization exists in 17 countries with a total of 300,000 members (1974). (7) Sobrietas International Catholic League (Liga Catholica Internationalis Sobrietas), founded in Brussels in 1897 and now located in Freiburg, is concerned with the problems of alcoholism and drug addiction. (8) Medicus Mundi International, in Aachen, is an association open to physicians, pharmacists and para-medical personnel whose purpose is to make medicine available to the rural poor in developing countries. In 1974 it had active national branches in 6 European countries: Belgium, France, Holland, Spain, Switzerland and West Germany. (9) The International Union of Laity in the Service of the Church (Unio Internationalis Laicorum in Servitio Ecclesiae), founded in Cologne in 1965, is a grouping of national lay associations in 8 European countries (1973). (10) The World Catholic Federation for the Biblical Apostolate (WCFBA) (Katholische Bibelföderation), founded in Rome in 1969 and now located in Stuttgart, has 18 member biblical associations (1973), working for the promotion of Bible-reading in the Catholic Church.

Progressivist organizations include the Association of German Catholic Youth (Bund der Deutschen Katholischen Jugend, BDKJ) and its numerous sub-groups of young workers (Junge Christlichen Arbeitnerhmern, CAJ) and young peasants (Katholische Landjugend Bewegung, KLJB); groups belonging to the German section of Pax Christi; as well as student communities united in the Association of German Catholic Students Catholische Deutsche Studenten-Einigung, KDSE), in Bonn, from which the Bishops' Conference withdrew its recognition and financial support in March 1973 because of its socialist sympathies. New spontaneous groups have arisen at the local level, especially the Family Circles (Familienkreise). In preparation for the Joint Synod, synod working groups (Synoden-Arbeitkreise) were created in 1970 but have greatly reduced their activities since, in part due to disappointment regarding the development of the synod. A series of Third-World Work Circles (Arbeitkreise Dritte Welt) orginated among Catholic students but are now largely divorced from confessional orientation. Critical Catholicism also was formed by students and continues to produce a journal of the same name with a socialist orientation. Among other spontaneous groups may be mentioned: (1) Action 365, in Frankfurt, a social and ecumenical group advocating intercommunion; and (2) Bensberger Circle (Bensberger Kreis), which meets in various cities, uniting 200 Catholic intellectuals and journalists for discussion regarding social questions as they relate to the church.

In 1968 and 1969, groups of priests (Priester- and Solidaritätsgruppen, SOG) critical of present ecclesial structures were formed in most dioceses. In some dioceses they number 10% of the clergy, the most important being those in Aix-la-Chapelle, Munich, Münster, Paderborn, Rottenburg and Trier. In most cases the laity and even laicized priests are also involved as participants. In 1969 the various local groups came together in Frankfurt to form an association of United Priests Groups (Arbeitsgemeinschaft von Priester- und Solidaritätsgruppen in der BRD, AGP), which in 1973 had 1,500 priests and 400 lay persons as members. Relations with the bishops vary but are generally poor whereas support among progressivist lay persons and theologians is generally good.

In 1970, Action 365, Synod Working Groups, Bensberger Circle, KDSE, SOG and others of like mind joined together to form the Synod Association (Arbeitsgemeinschaft Synode) which nevertheless was unable to influence the course of the synod. Since then the progressivist group has been reorganized under the name Open Church (Offene Kirche) but is no longer oriented towards the synod. The group Initiative of Readers of *Publik* (Leserinitiative Publik) with local branches owes its origin to the banning in 1971 by the German bishops of a Catholic journal. The group now contributes to the publication of the journal *Public-Forum.*

In opposition to these progressivist initiatives, conservative priests have formed organizations in many dioceses called Circles of Priests for Conciliar Renewal (Priesterkreise für Konziliare Erneverung, PKE) which had about 2,000 members in 1973. There are differences among them, some belonging to the ultra-conservative Movement for Pope and Church (Bewegung für Papst und Kirche) which is a member of Pro Fide et Ecclesia in France. Another important group of traditionalists is attached to Una Voce in Deutschland, in Rheinhausen, which is affiliated to Una Voce Internationale in Switzerland.

A number of organizations are engaged in research and social action. (1) The Amtliche Zentralstelle für Kirchliche Statistik des Katholischen Deutschlands, founded in Cologne in 1915, is the central bureau for Catholic statistics in the FRG and publishes the *Kirchliches Handbuch.* (2) The Institut für Kirchliche Sozialforschung des Bistums Essen (IKSE), founded in Essen in 1958 and attached to the diocese of Essen, is virtually the only institute of this type in the FRG and is affiliated with FERES in Belgium. (3) Sozialteam, located in Augsburg-Steppach, is involved in research and social work, in addition to pastoral projects. (4) The Katholische Sozialwissenschaftliche Zentralstelle (KSZ), founded in Mönchengladbach in 1962, is dependent on the Bishops' Conference and is concerned with the study of political, social and economic development from the standpoint of Catholic social doctrine. (5) The Institut für Gesellschaftspolitik, founded by Jesuits in 1971, works in the field of theological and philosophical anthropology, with special emphasis on conscientization regarding social justice and international relations. (6) The Institut für Gesellschaftswissenschaft, founded at Bornheim-Walberberg by Dominicans, is dedicated to the study of social and economic ethics. (7) The Katholisches Sozialinstitut Honnet is involved in studies relating to workers.

In adult education, there are certain central organizations: Arbeitsgemeinschaft Katholische-Sozialer Bildungswerke in der BRD (in Bonn), Bundesarbeitsgemeinschaft für Katholische Erwaschenenbildung (Bonn), Görres-Gesellschaft zur Pflege der Wissenschaft (Cologne) and Verband Katholische Landvolkhochschulen Deutschlands (Wernau).

Socio-professional groups in the FRG are: Bundesverband des Katholischen Arbeitnehmerbewegung Deutschlands (KAB) (serving salaried workers; in Cologne), Kolpingwerk-Deutscher Zentralverband (for young artisans and salaried workers; in Cologne), Katholische Landvolkbewegung Deutschlands (KLB) (serving the rural world; in Bonn), Verband der Katholiken in Wirtschaft und Verwaltung (KKV) (for merchants and functionaries; in Essen), and Bund Katholischer Unternehmer (for employers; in Cologne). In addition there were, in 1972, 21 Catholic academies, mostly attached to dioceses, which provide for avenues of exchange between the Catholic intelligentsia and contemporary currents of thought.

Pastoral and religious training is provided by several institutions. There are 11 Catholic theological faculties attached to state universities: Augsburg (1970), Bamberg (1973), Bochum (1965), Bonn (1818), Freiburg (1657), Mainz (1946), Munich (1472), Münster (1780), Regensburg (1962), Tübingen (1477) and Würzburg (1402). Theological faculties are also found at Eichstätt, Paderborn, Trier, Frankfurt, Fulda, Königstein and Passau. Specialized training institutions include: (1) Institut für Staatskirchenrecht der Diözesen Deutschlands, founded in Bonn in 1971, which specializes in canon law; (2) 3 liturgical institutions: Liturgisches Institut at Trier, Abt-Herwegen-Institut für Liturgische und Monastische Forschung, at the Abbey of Maria Laach, and Allgemeiner Cäciliern-Verband für die Länder der Deutschen Sprache in Bonn; (3) 2 institutions for catechesis: Institut für Katechetik und Homiletik, founded in Munich in 1964; and Deutscher Katechete Verein, also founded in Munich in 1887; (4) 2 pastoral institutions: Institut der Orden für Missionarische Seelsorge und Spiritualität (IMS), founded in Frankfurt in 1960 to serve missionary orders and congregations; and Katholisches Zentralinstitut für Ehe- und Familienfragen, in Cologne, which caters especially for marriage and family problems; (5) 2 organizations providing pastoral training for Catholics in predominantly Protestant areas: Bonifatiuswerk der Deutschen Katholiken and Diaspora-Kommissariat der Deutschen Bischöfe, both centred in Paderborn. Other institutes and societies involved in pastoral training are the Albertus-Magnus Institut in Bonn and the Paulus Gesellschaft.

The principal organization for the co-ordination of missionary action is the Deutscher Katholischer Missionsrat, founded in Cologne in 1953. Missiological studies are provided by the Catholic theological faculties of the universities of Münster (Internationales Institut für Missionswissenschaftliche Forschungen, founded in 1911), Munich (Institute of Missionary Research) and Würzburg (Seminar für Missionswissenschaft, founded in 1959). The latter specializes in research in the history of missions in China, Japan and India. Organizations involved in raising funds, personnel and other services and publicizing the cause of missions include: (1) MISSIO-Internationales Katholisches Missionswerk, at Aachen and Munich, which in 1972 raised 63.6 million DM for missions in Africa, Asia and Oceania; (2) pontifical missionary works for priests (Priester-Missionsbund, at Aachen and Munich), children (Päpstliches Missionswerk der Kinder in Deutschland, at Aachen), women and girls (Päpstliches Werk der Missionsvereinigung Katholisches Frauen und Jungfrauen, in Koblenz); (3) ADVENIAT, founded in Essen in 1961, whose principal concern is Latin America; (4) Missionsärztliches Institut, founded in Würzburg in 1922, which provides medical personnel for Third-World countries; (5) MIVA, which helps to arrange transportation for missionaries; and (6) Servicio Radiofónico para Latinoamérica (SERPAL), in Munich, which prepares radio programmes and aids Catholic radio stations in Latin America in co-operation with ACPO in Bogotá, Colombia.

The principal German missionary congregations are: for men, Benediktiner-Missionare (St Ottilien, founded in 1884), Steyler Missionare (SVD, 1875) and Arme Brüder vom Heiligen Franziskus Seraphikus (Aachen, 1857); and for women, Dienerienneu des Heiligen Geistes (Wimbern, 1889), Franziskanerinnen von Aiterhofen (Aiterhofen, 1946), Franziskanerinnen von der Unbefleckten Empfängnis (Bonlanden, 1854), Missionsbenediktinerinnen von Tutzing (Tutzing, 1885), Missionsschwestern vom Heiligsten Herzen Jesu (Hiltrup, 1899), Schwestern der Christlichen Liebe (Paderborn, 1849) and Solanus-Schwestern (Landshut/Bavaria, 1925).

The Catholic educational programme in the FRG is co-ordinated by the Central Bureau of the Episcopate for Schools and Education (Bischöfliche Haupstelle für Schule und Erziehung) in Cologne; Central Office of the Church for Catholic Free and Boarding Schools (Kirchliche Zentrale für Katholische Freie Schulen und Internate) in Cologne; Central Association for Catholic Kindergartens (Zentralverband Katholischer Kindergärten) in Cologne; and Katholisches Schulkommissariat Bayern I und Bayern II, in Munich for Bavaria. Education in the FRG varies from one province to another. Most provinces provide for both confessional and state systems, except Hesse where there are only state schools and the Saar where there are only confessional schools. Religion courses are provided in all state schools. Statistics for Catholic confessional schools in 1971-72 were: 1,027 schools and 199,625 pupils (respectively 2.7% and 1.9% of the total figures for education in the FRG), divided into 77 primary schools (16,220 pupils), 386 secondary and non-university higher schools (149,101), 494 professional schools (28,161), and 70 specialized schools for the blind, deaf and dumb, et alia (6,143). In 1970 the number of infants in Catholic kindergartens totalled 517,344.

Three organizations are involved in the co-ordination of Catholic medical and social service: (1) Deutscher Caritasverband, founded in Freiburg in 1887, which works through 22 diocesan sections; (2) Arbeitsstelle für Soziale Arbeit in Übersee, which caters for overseas aid to the Third World; and (3) Not- und Katastrophenhilfe, which provides emergency aid to disaster areas in co-operation with other national and international agencies. Caritas in 1970 sponsored 4,487 hospitals and homes (387,632 places or beds), 9,601 day institutions (586,104 places or beds) and 20,726 other institutions, plus 716 places of instruction serving 26,782 persons, making a total of 35,530 institutions with 1,000,518 places or beds, served by 54,546 religious and 137,938 lay persons. The principal national agencies involved in social service in the parishes are: Caritas-Konferenzen Deutschlands (Freiburg) and Gemeinschaft der Vinzenzkonferenzen Deutschlands (Cologne) for juveniles, Sozialdienst Katholischer Frauen (Dortmund) for women, Sozialdienst Katholischer Männer (Düsseldorf) for youths, Deutscher Verband Katholischer Mädchensozialarbeit (Freiburg) for girls, Arbeitsgemeinschaft Katholischer Lagerdienst (Freiburg and Munich) for Sudeten refugees, Katholische Arbeitsgemeinschaft gegen die Suchtgefahren (Hamm) for drug addicts, and Malteser-Hilfsdienst (Rodenkirchen) for the sick and accident cases.

NEUAPOSTOLISCHE KIRCHE. *Congregations.* These have grown from 80 in 1895, to 488 in 1905, 1,200 in 1928, 2,922 in 1952, and 2,900 in 1970. *Membership.* The church's own statistics enumerate *versiegelte* or sealed (baptized) members, a ceremony in or after early childhood. In 1910, these numbered 100,000, in 1925, 138,000 and in 1952, 312,832. In 1971 sealed members in Germany numbered 335,000. Together with adult sympathizers and adherents, but not infants or young children, the total was 420,000. Since infants and children under 8 form 14% of the population in Germany, this gives a total church community of 490,000. *Growth.* The period of most rapid growth of this church in Germany was in the 1950s; after the death of the Chief Apostle in 1960, large numbers defected to the state churches, and by 1973 numerical decline had set in inside Germany, although large-scale expansion overseas was still under way. *World membership.* In 1971, there were 900,000 sealed members, including in Germany, or about 1,300,000 total community across the world. Of these, the majority were either German, German-speaking or of German origin. *Apostles.* From 8 in 1895, these have increased to 20 in 1928, 34 in 1952, and to 48 (worldwide) in 1964. *Missionaries.* The church does not have a category of foreign missionaries as such. However, in addition to the sending out of Apostles, numbers of helpers (over 100) go abroad to assist branch churches.

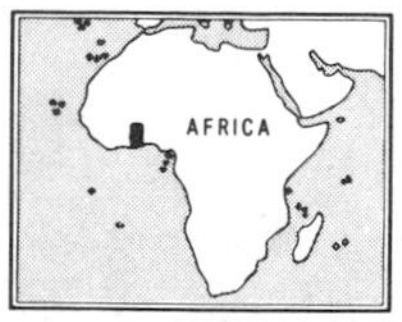


# GHANA

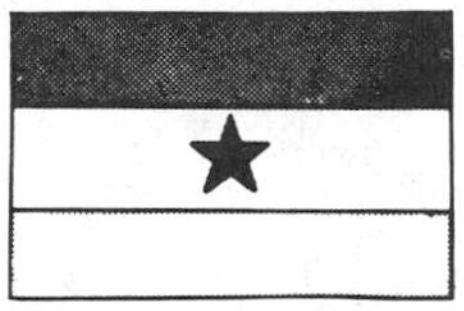

## SECULAR DATA

**STATE. Official name:** The Republic of Ghana. Adjective of nationality: Ghanaian.
**Flag** (shown above right): Red, gold, and green stripes, with centred black star.
**Area:** 238,537 sq.km. (92,100 sq.miles). Agricultural land: 56.6%.
**Government:** Military junta, since 1972 (1874 Gold Coast colony (British), 1957 Independence, 1960 republic).
**Official language:** English.
**Chief cities:** capital Accra 738,500 (1970), Kumasi 345,120, Sekondi-Takoradi 160,870.
**Political divisions:** 9 Regions.
**Armed forces** (1976): Total 17,600 regular: army 15,000, navy 1,200, air force 1,400 (6 combat aircraft). Paramilitary forces: 3,000.

**DEMOGRAPHY. Population:** 8,559,313 (census of 1.III.1970. For 1970–2000 (UN), see last row of Table 1). Population density (1975): 41/sq.km. (107/sq.mile). Under 15 years: 47%. Growth rate (1975–80): 2.96% per year (births 4.86%, deaths −1.91%). Life expectancy (1975–80): 46.0 years. Household size: 4.9 persons.
**Major languages:** Twi (Akan), Ewe, Ga, English, Hausa, Mole. There are over 100 other tribal languages.
**Urban dwellers** (1970): 31.2%. Urban growth rate (1950–70): 6.0% per year.
**Labour force:** 40%.
**Refugees** (1977): About 5,000 from Togo.
**Tourists** (1974): 30,151.

**ETHNOLINGUISTIC GROUPS:** 46.1% Akan (13.3% Ashanti, 11.3% Fante, 4.8% Brong, 3.0% Akyem, 2.6% Nzima, 2.2% Akwapim, 2.0% Kwahu, 1.5% Anyi-Baule), 17.0% Mole-Dagbani (3.2% Dagomba, 3.0% Dagati, 2.1% Frafra, 1.8% Kusasi, 1.6% Mossi, 0.9% Lobi, Mamprusi, Nankansi, Talensi), 13.0% Ewe, 8.3% Ga-Adangbe, 3.7% Guan, 3.5% Gurma, 2.2% Grusi, 2% alien African (Nigerian, Togolese), 1.4% Mande, 0.9% Hausa, 0.7% Tem, 0.2% European (British), 0.2% Fulani, Asian (Indo-Pakistani) (4,000), Songhai, Kru, Chinese, & numerous smaller tribes.

**MONEY** (1977). **Monetary unit:** cedi (= 100 pesewas); US$1 = C 1.15.
**National income per person:** US$340. Average annual family income: US$1,666.
**Inflation:** (1970–74) 12.4% per year, (1975) 41% per year (consumer price index 275).
**Cost of living in capital** (1976): index 138 (Washington DC = 100). Daily cost of living: US$48.

**EDUCATION.** Adult literacy: (1970) 30%. Education rate: 52%. Schools: 10,323. Universities: 1.

**HEALTH.** Hospitals: 203 (11,374 beds). Doctors: 951. Lepers; 63,000 (6.4 per 1,000). Blind: 65,000. Psychotics: 80,000. Criminals : 190,000.

**LITERATURE.** Annual new book titles (1971): 136. Periodicals: 140. Newspapers: 7 dailies, 9 non-daily.

**COMMUNICATION** (per 1,000 people). Phones: 6. Radios: 85. TV sets: 3. Daily newspaper circulation: 46 copies.

TABLE 1. RELIGIOUS ADHERENTS IN GHANA

| Year | 1900 | | mid-1970 | | Annual change, 1970–1980 | | | | mid-1975 | | mid-1980 | | 2000 | |
|---|---|---|---|---|---|---|---|---|---|---|---|---|---|---|
| *Name* | *Adherents* | *%* | *Adherents* | *%* | *Natural* | *Conversion* | *Total* | *Rate* | *Adherents* | *%* | *Adherents* | *%* | *Adherents* | *%* |
| **Christians** | **103,000** | **4.7** | **4,546,900** | **52.7** | **162,598** | **99,232** | **261,830** | **4.60** | **5,696,700** | **57.7** | **7,165,200** | **62.6** | **15,873,000** | **75.0** |
| professing | 103,000 | 4.7 | 4,546,900 | 52.7 | 162,598 | 99,232 | 261,830 | 4.60 | 5,696,700 | 57.7 | 7,165,200 | 62.6 | 15,873,000 | 75.0 |
| Protestants | 90,000 | 4.1 | 2,053,200 | 23.8 | 68,998 | 11,642 | 80,640 | 3.34 | 2,417,350 | 24.5 | 2,859,600 | 25.0 | 3,974,800 | 18.8 |
| Roman Catholics | 9,000 | 0.4 | 1,360,600 | 15.8 | 48,471 | 29,509 | 77,980 | 4.59 | 1,698,200 | 17.2 | 2,140,400 | 18.7 | 5,291,000 | 25.0 |
| African indigenous | 1,000 | 0.0 | 880,000 | 10.2 | 36,917 | 58,223 | 95,140 | 7.36 | 1,293,400 | 13.1 | 1,831,400 | 16.0 | 5,925,900 | 28.0 |
| Anglicans | 3,000 | 0.1 | 195,800 | 2.3 | 6,199 | −1,779 | 4,420 | 2.03 | 217,200 | 2.2 | 240,000 | 2.1 | 423,300 | 2.0 |
| Marginal Protestants | 0 | 0.0 | 56,000 | 0.6 | 1,969 | 1,631 | 3,600 | 5.22 | 69,000 | 0.7 | 92,000 | 0.8 | 254,000 | 1.2 |
| Orthodox | 0 | 0.0 | 1,000 | 0.0 | 34 | 6 | 40 | 3.33 | 1,200 | 0.0 | 1,400 | 0.0 | 3,000 | 0.0 |
| Catholics (non-Roman) | 0 | 0.0 | 300 | 0.0 | 10 | 0 | 10 | 2.86 | 350 | 0.0 | 400 | 0.0 | 1,000 | 0.0 |
| nominal | 23,000 | 1.0 | 1,320,106 | 15.3 | 47,906 | 34,123 | 82,029 | 4.89 | 1,678,400 | 17.0 | 2,140,400 | 18.7 | 4,867,700 | 23.0 |
| affiliated | 80,000 | 3.6 | 3,226,794 | 37.4 | 114,692 | 65,109 | 179,801 | 4.47 | 4,018,300 | 40.7 | 5,024,800 | 43.9 | 11,005,300 | 52.0 |
| total practising | 76,000 | *95* | 2,581,430 | *80* | 91,754 | 52,087 | 143,841 | 4.47 | 3,214,640 | *80* | 4,019,840 | *80* | 7,703,710 | *70* |
| non-practising | 4,000 | *5* | 645,360 | *20* | 22,938 | 13,022 | 35,960 | 4.47 | 803,660 | *20* | 1,004,960 | *20* | 3,301,590 | *30* |
| Roman Catholics | 7,500 | 0.3 | 1,167,312 | 13.5 | 41,424 | 23,835 | 65,259 | 4.50 | 1,451,300 | 14.7 | 1,819,900 | 15.9 | 3,703,700 | 17.5 |
| Catholic pentecostals | 0 | 0.0 | 0 | 0.0 | 57 | 943 | 1,000 | 50.00 | 2,000 | 0.0 | 10,000 | 0.1 | 50,000 | 0.2 |
| Protestants | 70,000 | 3.2 | 1,038,565 | 12.0 | 31,600 | −18,296 | 13,304 | 1.20 | 1,107,150 | 11.2 | 1,171,600 | 10.2 | 1,689,000 | 8.0 |
| Evangelicals | 55,000 | 2.5 | 655,700 | 7.6 | 22,542 | 6,888 | 29,430 | 3.73 | 789,800 | 8.0 | 950,000 | 8.3 | 1,672,000 | 7.9 |
| Neo-pentecostals | 0 | 0.0 | 2,000 | 0.0 | 228 | 2,572 | 2,800 | 35.00 | 8,000 | 0.1 | 30,000 | 0.3 | 150,000 | 0.7 |
| African indigenous | 500 | 0.0 | 862,691 | 10.0 | 36,352 | 58,229 | 94,581 | 7.43 | 1,273,600 | 12.9 | 1,808,500 | 15.8 | 5,100,500 | 24.1 |
| Anglicans | 2,000 | 0.1 | 100,000 | 1.2 | 3,311 | −111 | 3,200 | 2.76 | 116,000 | 1.2 | 132,000 | 1.2 | 275,100 | 1.3 |
| Marginal Protestants | 0 | 0.0 | 56,826 | 0.7 | 1,958 | 1,449 | 3,407 | 4.97 | 68,600 | 0.7 | 90,900 | 0.8 | 233,000 | 1.1 |
| Orthodox | 0 | 0.0 | 1,000 | 0.0 | 34 | 6 | 40 | 3.33 | 1,200 | 0.0 | 1,400 | 0.0 | 3,000 | 0.0 |
| Catholics (non-Roman) | 0 | 0.0 | 400 | 0.0 | 13 | −3 | 10 | 2.22 | 450 | 0.0 | 500 | 0.0 | 1,000 | 0.0 |
| Tribal religionists | 1,987,000 | 90.3 | 2,864,000 | 33.2 | 76,794 | −118,054 | −41,260 | −1.53 | 2,690,600 | 27.3 | 2,451,400 | 21.4 | 1,177,500 | 5.6 |
| Muslims | 110,000 | 5.0 | 1,199,000 | 13.9 | 41,698 | 18,072 | 59,770 | 4.09 | 1,460,900 | 14.8 | 1,796,700 | 15.7 | 3,809,000 | 18.0 |
| Ahmadis | 0 | 0.0 | 543,600 | 6.3 | 20,008 | 16,052 | 36,060 | 5.14 | 701,000 | 7.1 | 904,200 | 7.9 | 2,330,000 | 11.0 |
| Non-religious | 0 | 0.0 | 9,000 | 0.1 | 337 | 183 | 520 | 4.48 | 11,600 | 0.1 | 14,200 | 0.1 | 215,000 | 1.0 |
| Baha'is | 0 | 0.0 | 6,600 | 0.1 | 237 | 103 | 340 | 4.10 | 8,300 | 0.1 | 10,000 | 0.1 | 60,000 | 0.3 |
| Hindus | 0 | 0.0 | 1,000 | 0.0 | 34 | 46 | 80 | 5.71 | 1,400 | 0.0 | 1,800 | 0.0 | 5,000 | 0.0 |
| Buddhists | 0 | 0.0 | 300 | 0.0 | 8 | −8 | 0 | 0.00 | 300 | 0.0 | 300 | 0.0 | 500 | 0.0 |
| New-Religionists | 0 | 0.0 | 200 | 0.0 | 60 | 420 | 480 | 24.00 | 2,000 | 0.0 | 5,000 | 0.0 | 20,000 | 0.1 |
| Other religionists | 0 | 0.0 | 1,000 | 0.0 | 34 | 6 | 40 | 3.33 | 1,200 | 0.0 | 1,400 | 0.0 | 4,000 | 0.0 |
| **Country's population** | **2,200,000** | **100.0** | **8,628,000** | **100.0** | **281,800** | **0** | **281,800** | **2.85** | **9,873,000** | **100.0** | **11,446,000** | **100.0** | **21,164,000** | **100.0** |

COLUMNS, ROWS. For meanings and definitions, see Codebook (Part 6). Note that, by definition, total 'Christians' = professing + crypto-Christians, which also = affiliated + nominal Christians. Percentages may not always total exactly, due to rounding.
CENSUSES. Before 1960, all censuses (especially 1891, 1901, 1931 and 1948) collected religion data supplied direct from the churches, hence reported affiliated members only, and that incompletely, as follows. **1891**: 25,000 total Christians. **1901**: 40,305. **1911**: 100,000 total Christians, 63,491 total Muslims. **1931**: 89.5% tribal religionists, 8.6% Christians, 1.8% Ahmadis. **1.II.1948** (Gold Coast, including Togoland): 84.1% tribal religionists, 15.9% Christians (7.7% Roman Catholics, 7.2% Protestants, 0.9% Anglicans), 0.6% Ahmadis. **20.III.1960** (national sample, adults aged 15 and over): 45.2% tribal religionists, 42.8% Christians (13.4% Roman Catholics, 10.3% Methodists, 9.9% Presbyterians, 5.0% African indigenous, 2.6% Anglicans, 1.6% other Christians), 12.0% Muslims (6.8% Malikites, 4.7% Ahmadis, 0.5% Shafiites and others). **1.III.1970** (national sample, over 15 years old): 52.7% Christians (15.8% Roman Catholics, 12.0% Presbyterians, 11.4% Methodists, 10.2% African indigenous, 2.3% Anglicans, 0.6% marginal Protestants, 0.4% other Christians), 33.3% tribal religionists, 13.9% Muslims (6.4% Malikites, 6.3% Ahmadis, 1.2% Shafiites and others), 0.1% Baha'is.

NOTES ON RELIGIONS
AFFILIATED ROMAN CATHOLICS. In 1900, 7,000 indigenous baptized Catholics and 500 catechumens.
AFRICAN INDIGENOUS. In over 420 denominations in 1970 (see Table 2).
AHMADIS. The Ahmadiya Movement (HQ Pakistan) has its largest mission in the world in Ghana, begun in 1921. Many of its adherents are present or past schoolchildren or others influenced by its institutions. Of the around 16,000 annual conversions to Ahmadiya, the vast majority are converts from other Islamic schools (81%) or from Christianity (15%) rather than from paganism (4%). In 1970, there were 260 mosques, 30 Ghanaian missionaries, 5 expatriate missionaries, a missionary training college, 4 hospitals, 19 primary and 8 middle and secondary schools. About 10% of adherents are in the north, 25% in the Kumasi area, and 65% in Fante country in the south.
BAHA'IS. Growth from 10 local spiritual assemblies (1964) to 39 (1973).
BUDDHISTS. Chinese.
COUNTRY'S POPULATION. In 1969–70 the government deported 2 million alien African (1 million Nigerians, 196,000 Togolese, 186,000 Upper Voltans, et alii).
HINDUS. Until the 1970s, only a handful of Indian traders. In 1975, an Indian missionary (the Black Monk of Africa) established in Accra the first Hindu monastery in Africa, headed by a Ghanaian, with 24 other African monks (sanyasis). They are opening branches in other parts of Ghana and of West Africa, with emphasis on clinics and social welfare organizations. A Hindu sect also at work is Ananda Marga.
MUSLIMS. The first Muslims date from about 1380. In 1900, 1% of the South were Muslims, and far more in the North. Muslims are mostly Sunnis of the Malikite rite (6.8% of the population in 1960, dropping to 6.4% in 1970), and Shafiite rite; also Ahmadiya (4.7% in 1960 rising to 6.3% in 1970; enumerated here under Muslims, though declared non-Muslim by Pakistan). Islam is strongest in the north, among the Wala (90%), Dagomba (60%), Mamprusi (35%), Moba (30%), Chakossi (30%), Konkomba (25%), and Vagala (20%), among all of whom conversions of pagans are still taking place. There are also about 4,000 Asian Muslims. In 1969 the Aliens Act resulted in the expulsion of some 200,000 immigrant Muslims and the closure of many small Quranic schools. As a result, the conservative alien-dominated Ghana Muslim Community gave way to the rival and progressivist southern-dominated Ghana Muslim Mission. *Missionaries*. A number of Egyptian missionaries sent by Al-Azhar University (Cairo) are at work. *Hajj pilgrims to Mecca*. (1970) 402; (1974) 1,105; (1975) 2,703; (1976) 3,107.
NEO-PENTECOSTALS. Mostly in the Methodist and Presbyterian churches.
NEW-RELIGIONISTS. By 1975, 2,000 converts to the Japanese movement Nichiren Shoshu (Soka Gakkai).
NOMINAL CHRISTIANS. In 1970, these were mainly nominal Protestants (Methodists and Presbyterians) and nominal Anglicans, and can be seen from the table to be slightly greater in number than those actually affiliated to these churches. It is from this huge nominal fringe around the older denominations that a majority of new converts to the African indigenous (spiritual) churches were coming in the period 1960–1975.
OTHER RELIGIONISTS. Adherents of smaller religions and cults, including Rosicrucians (5 AMORC centres), and the Church Universal & Triumphant (Summit; from USA).
PRACTISING CHRISTIANS. Weekly church attendance: Roman Catholics 35%, Protestants 50%, African indigenous 80%. Annual practice (all churches together): about 80%. Catholic Easter communicants are much lower (37%) because of difficulties of travel and distance and insufficiency of services.
TRIBAL RELIGIONISTS. Mainly in the north, among the Gurensi (90% traditionalist in 1972), Grunshi (75%), Dagari (LoDagaa) (40%), and (all over 60% traditionalist) Builsa, Chakossi, Konkomba, Mamprusi, Moba, Vagala.

**NON-CHRISTIAN RELIGIONS. Traditional religions** are followed by 27% of the population (1975), through this proportion is rapidly shrinking (from 45% in 1960) due to conversions to Christianity. The heaviest concentration of traditionalists is among the northern peoples. Tribes more than 60% traditionalist include the Builsa, Chakossi, Konkomba, Mamprusi and Moba, while the proportions of traditionalists among the Dagari, Grunshi and Gurensi are even higher (70%, 75% and 90% respectively). Names for God include Nyame and Nyankopon (among the Akan, Ashanti, Fanti), Onyankopon (Twi), We (Birifor, Grunshi, Tallensi), Mawu (Ewe), Dzemawon (Ga), Omborr (Konkomba) and Na'angmin (LoDagaa). Among the Ashanti, prior to 1930, altars (called Nyame Dua, God's tree) for daily offerings to God were found in most compounds, but they are now rare. In addition to the worship of God, there is a belief in Asase Yaa, old mother earth; an elaborate pantheon of divinities (Abosom) who are remembered in annual festivals, the most important being the river spirits Tano, Bea and Bosomtwe; a continuing relationship between the living and their ancestral spirits (Ntoro) involving food offerings and libations; and dynamistic practices which express themselves positively in the form of charms or amulets *(suman)* or negatively through the work of witches *(abayifo)*.

**Islam** has its strength in northern Ghana although Muslim penetration is not as extensive as is commonly thought. Most northern tribes are about 30% Muslim, as shown in these figures: Chakossi 30%, Dagari 30%, Konkomba 25%, Mamprusi 35%, Moba

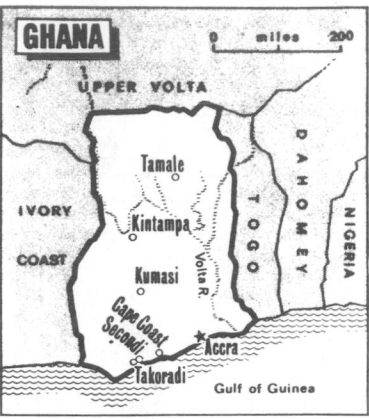

30% and Vagala 20%. Islam is stronger among the Dagomba (60%), and the Wala are almost entirely Muslim. In the south, Islam has been confined largely to Hausa immigrants from Nigeria and Cameroon. However, the Aliens' Compliance Order of December 1969 resulted in the expulsion from Ghana of nearly two-thirds of all Hausas during 1970. Muslims are mostly of the Malikite rite (6.4% of the population in 1970) or Ahmadis (6.3%). Only 1.2% belong to the Shafiite rite or other Muslim sects.

## CHRISTIANITY

PROTESTANT CHURCHES. The 3 largest Protestant denominations in Ghana are the Methodist, Presbyterian and Evangelical Presbyterian churches, all members of the Christian Council founded in 1929. The population of Ghana in 1970 professed to be 12% Presbyterian and 11% Methodist. The Presbyterian Church was the first Protestant denomination in the Gold Coast, resulting from the activity of the Swiss Basel Mission. Beginning at Christiansborg in 1828, the work was greatly strenthened by Moravian Christians from Jamaica after 1843. During World War I, the Basel Mission had to withdraw and the church became autonomous, but aid was later provided by the United Free Church of Scotland and the Netherlands Reformed Church. The first missionary from the British Wesleyan Methodist Church came to Cape Coast in 1835, followed 3 years later by a missionary pioneer of mixed race, Thomas Birch Freeman, who remained for 52 years during which time the Methodist mission expanded greatly. The formation of an African clergy has always been a major concern, and in 1961 the church became automous.

The Evangelical Presbyterian Church grew out of the Bremen Mission from northern Germany. The mission opened work among the Ewe tribe of Togoland beginning at Peki in 1847. This area, formerly a German colony and later the Trusteeship Territory of British Togoland, is now the Volta region

of Ghana. When the mission was expelled in 1914 the church gained its autonomy.

In 1970, these 3 churches sponsored 1,832 primary schools, 10 secondary schools, 15 teacher-training colleges, 5 hospitals, 2 dispensaries and 4 mobile clinics. They have also been involved in agricultural and community development projects.

Adventists, Baptists, Salvation Army and several Pentecostal missionary bodies are also present.

CATHOLIC CHURCH. The first Catholics to reach the Gold Coast were Portuguese in 1471 who built a fort at Mina off the coast in 1482. Although occasional preaching forays were made into the interior, extensive missionary work was not begun until the arrival of Lyons missionaries in 1880, aided by White Fathers after World War I. Following the establishment of the hierarchy in 1950, the first Ghanaian bishop was consecrated in 1957 and became archbishop in 1960. The number of affiliated Catholics grew from 8,716 in 1906 to 51,842 in 1924 and to well over a million by 1970. In 1970, 15.8% of the population professed to be Catholics.

Christians made up 32% of the entire affiliated Christian community in Ghana.

ANGLICAN CHURCH. Anglican missionaries arrived as early as 1752, but work was for many years confined to Cape Coast. The Society for the Propagation of the Gospel (UK) has been active; and by 1960, 2.6% of the population claimed to be Anglicans, falling to 2.3% by 1970. The diocese of Accra, formed in 1909, is part of the Church of the Province of West Africa. Since 1970, plans for sub-division into the 3 dioceses of Accra, Cape Coast and Kumasi have been making slow progress.

CHURCH AND STATE. In the preamble to the constitution of the Second Republic dated 22 August 1969, later suspended by the National Redemption Council in 1972, the following phrase was found: 'In the name of Almighty God, from whom all authority is derived and to whom all actions of both men and states should be referred'. One of the purposes of the constitution was stated to be that of guaranteeing 'freedom of thought, expression and

Catholic Church in Ghana, Diocese of Wa. 'Rejoice in the Lord'. Sunday mass at Nandom in extreme northwest, among Dagari and Grunshi traditionalists.

Traditional religionists. 25% of population (mostly in north: Gurensi, Grunshi, Dagari, et alii) still adhere to tribal religions, with veneration given to tribal ancestors (the 'living dead'), their graves, and fetish objects as here in north.

INDIGENOUS CHURCHES. The first independent church in the Gold Coast was the short-lived Methodist Society, a Fante schism from the Wesleyan Methodists in Cape Coast in 1862. In 1896, the AME Zion Church was begun by a Fante named Pinanko, supported later by American Negro missionaries. At present there are 2 conferences, the East Conference centered in Keta and the West Conference at Cape Coast. Two other similar Methodist denominations owing their origin to American Negro missionary influence are the AME and CME churches. Prior to World War I, the Church of the Twelve Apostles arose as the first of Ghana's many spiritual churches; it was formed through the preaching of John Nackabah, a disciple of Prophet William Wadé Harris. Other early churches include the Army of the Cross of Christ Church in 1922, and Prophet Wovenu's Apostles Revelation Society in 1939. Nigerian independent churches have also spread to Ghana in recent years, the most important being Christ Apostolic Church. The largest at the present time is the Divine Healer's Church. The Eden Revival Church, with a Christian community of 50,000, is as yet the only one of the locally-founded indigenous churches to be accepted into membership in the Christian Council of Ghana.

The growth of the spiritual churches in Ghana has been phenomenal. By 1970, over 420 indigenous denominations were active, and many more have subsequently been begun. By 1975, indigenous

religion' (Preamble). Article 21 also speaks of 'freedom of conscience'. No new constitution has since been promulgated, and this religious emphasis has not been revoked.

Denominational schools have not been nationalized except in the Volta region during 1959–60 under the Nkrumah regime. An incident occurred there which led to a take-over by government of Protestant schools, followed a short time later by Catholic schools. However, in the course of 1960 the matter was resolved and the schools were returned to their respective owners. In 1974, Ghana's Director of Pedagogical Service declared that the government envisaged the nationalization of some 80 private schools.

INTERDENOMINATIONAL ORGANIZATIONS. The Christian Council of the Gold Coast was founded in 1929 and changed its name in 1957 to Christian Council of Ghana. It provides member churches with an opportunity to participate in a united ministry of service and outreach. Areas of common action include literature production, family planning clinics, preparation of religious education material, united theological education, and a Christian Service Committee conducting relief, agricultural and development programmes. Seven member denominations of the council are engaged in negotiations towards church union, with 3 others as observers. Local Christian councils have been formed in Accra,

**African indigenous churches.** *Left* and *right*. The National Council of Spiritual Churches of Ghana, shown in procession in 1973, is one of 4 nationwide councils uniting Ghana's 420 indigenous denominations.

Akwatia, Cape Coast, Ho, Koforidua, Kumasi, Northern Region, Sekondi, Tema and Winneba.

The Ghana Evangelical Fellowship, founded in 1969, has 5 member denominations including the indigenous Christ Apostolic Church.

Ecumenical relations between the Catholic Church and the Christian Council of Ghana have improved greatly since Vatican II. In 1966 a Committee of Co-operation was established to co-ordinate the activities of the Christian Council and the National Catholic Secretariat. Other organizations include the Joint Committee on Christian Marriage and Family Life, Christian Medical Workers Fellowship (CMWF) and Christian Hospital Association of Ghana (CHAG). An ecumenical committee is now operating in Tema, and a fraternal group of Catholic priests and ministers of various denominations was established in Kumasi in 1972.

**BROADCASTING.** The state-owned Ghana Broadcasting Corporation transmits fortnightly both Catholic and Protestant programmes, and on television monthly religious services in addition to morning and evening prayer and meditation. The Christian Council of Ghana has an active communication committee which produces regular programmes for the GBC. There is a Protestant recording studio at the Oti River leprosarium in Kpandai. Christian programmes from abroad can be easily heard on ELWA (Liberia), and until 1977 on RVOG (Ethiopia). For Catholics, Ghana is registered as member of UNDA.

**BIBLIOGRAPHY**

*A history of Christianity in Ghana.* H. W. Debrunner. Accra: Waterville Publishing House, 1967. 375p.
*Akan doctrine of God.* J. B. Danquah. London: Lutterworth, 1966.
*Akan religion and the Christian faith: a comparative study of the impact of two religions.* S. G. Williamson. Accra: Ghana University Press, 1965. 186.
'Aspects of religion', C. G. Baëta, chapter VII in W. Birmingham et al, *A study of contemporary Ghana,* vol. II, *Some aspects of social structure* (Evanston, IL: Northwestern University Press, 1967), p. 240–250.
'Church and state in Ghana, 1949–1966', J. S. Pobee, in Pobee (ed), *Religion in a pluralistic society* (Leiden: Brill, 1976).
*Eden Revival: spiritual churches in Ghana.* D. M. Beckmann. St Louis: Concordia Publishing House, 1975. 144p.
*Five hundred churches: a brief survey of Christianity in Ghana.* Ed P. Barker. Accra: Christian Council of Ghana, 1978. 210p.
*Ghana Catholic diary, 1970.* Accra: Catholic Press, 1970. (Annual).
*Prophetism in Ghana: a study of some 'spiritual' churches.* C. G. Baëta. London: SCM Press, 1962.
*The churches and Ghana society, 1918–55.* R. T. Parsons. Leiden: Brill, 1963.
*The roots of Ghana Methodism.* F. L. Bartels. Cambridge: Cambridge University Press, 1965. 368p.
*Witchcraft in Ghana: a study on the belief in destructive witches and its effect on the Akan tribes.* H. W. Debrunner. Accra: Presbyterian Book Depot, 1959; 2nd edition 1961. 213p.

TABLE 2.    ORGANIZED CHURCHES AND DENOMINATIONS IN GHANA

| Official name 1 | Begun 2 | Type 3 | Counc 4 | Congs 5 | Adults 6 | Affiliated 7 | Names, notes, and other statistics (see Codebook) 8 |
|---|---|---|---|---|---|---|---|
| African Faith Tabernacle Church | 1919 | I pen | ....I | 370 | 40,000 | 50,000 | Link with Faith Tabernacle Ch(USA). Medicine allowed. Missions in 3 nations. 500n. |
| African Methodist Episcopal Church | 1933 | I Met | Vw..W | 65 | 3,000 | 12,400 | M=AMEC(USA). Ex AMECZ. 65% Ashanti, 25% Fante, 8% Akim. 27n,W=58%,1500Y,500y. |
| African Methodist Episcopal Zion Ch | 1896 | I Met | Vw..W | 101 | 18,196 | 36,250 | M=AMEZC(USA). 60% Fante, 29% Ewe. 118 schools. 51n,15m,5w,2H,2h,5r,1s,475Y,838y. |
| African Orthodox Church | 1931 | I ARo | x.... | 6 | 800 | 2,000 | Diocese of Accra. Link with M=AOC(USA Blacks). Akwapim and Kwahu tribes. 3n,1x. |
| Anglican Church of Ghana: | 1752 | A ACa | AwAVW | 300 | 50,000 | 100,000 | In *CPWA.* 1904, M=USPG. 69n,1x,500m,100w,23f,300pp, 1H,5r,1u,W=45%,4795Y,8156y. |
| D   Accra | 1909 | A ACa | A | 150 | 30,530 | 60,000 | Members urban Ga-Adangbe. 1909, formed from D Sierra Leone; sub-divided 1974. |
| D   Cape Coast | 1978 | A ACa | A | 80 | 12,000 | 25,000 | Mainly Fante. Many aliens including Nigerians until 1969 deportations. |
| D   Kumasi | 1974 | A ACa | A | 70 | 8,000 | 15,000 | Mainly Ashanti. Archdeaconry of Kumasi till subdivision from D Accra. |
| Apostles Revelation Society | 1939 | I pen | x...I | 350 | 30,000 | 60,000 | *ARS. Apostolowo be Dedefia Habobo.* Founder prophet CKN Wovenu. 90% Ewe. 101n,1s. |
| Apostolic Church, Ghana | 1936 | P PeA | ZG..C | 400 | 18,384 | 50,000 | M=ACMM(UK). 1953, missionary founder splits, forms Ch of Pentecost. 50n,2x,4f. |
| Apostolic Divine Church of Ghana | 1957 | I peA | ....I | 33 | 12,000 | 15,000 | Schism ex Methodists. Indigenous pentecostals. HQ Accra. 7n. |
| Apostolic Reformed Church of Ghana | 1958 | I pen | ..... | 23 | 1,151 | 1,601 | Schism ex Presbyterian Ch of Ghana. Indigenous pentecostals. 2n. |
| Army of the Cross of Christ Church | 1922 | I pen | .v..I | 483 | 15,472 | 55,542 | *MDCC. Musama Disco Christo Ch.* Fante. 1958, applied to WCC. 60n,1s,2208Y,4417y. |
| Assemblies of God in Ghana | 1916 | P Pe2 | ZF..C | 350 | 14,150 | 30,000 | M=AoG(USA). 44% Ashanti, 15% Kusasi, 8% Ga, 8% Dagomba. 25n,45f,2h,1j,2s(46). |
| Baptist Mid-Missions | 1946 | P Bap | x.... | 15 | 188 | 238 | M=BMM(USA). Work in northwest among Dagati and Sissala. HQ Tumu. 11n,17m,24f,1s. |
| Bethany Church Mission | 1962 | I pen | ....I | | 1,000 | 2,000 | *Bethany Chapel.* Split ex Holy Trinity Healing Ch, by founder's son. 85% women. Ashanti. |
| Bethel Church of Christ | 1967 | I pen | ....I | 4 | 800 | 1,350 | *Bible Ch of Christ.* 56% Akan, 33% Ga, 11% Ewe. 3n,13m,10w,W=81%,100Y. |
| Bethesda Church Mission | 1965 | I pen | ..... | 18 | 8,000 | 11,000 | Ex Divine Healer's Ch. Kumasi. 66% Ashanti, 27% Ga, 5% Fante, 2% Ewe. 8n,W=70%. |
| Bethlehem Revival Church | 1951 | I pen | ..... | 1 | 3,500 | 5,000 | Ex Apostolic Ch. 27% Ga, 26% Akan, 21% Ewe, 14% Frafra, 11% Hausa. 6n,5m,1w,500Y. |
| Buem-Krachi Presbyterian Church | 1954 | I Ref | ..... | 20 | 500 | 1,000 | Schism ex EPC over polygamy; 1964, part rejoined EPC. Buem and Krachi tribes. 2n. |
| Catholic Church in Ghana: | 1481 | R Lat | P,SGR | 427 | 618,800 | 1,167,312 | C=4+7+20. 4p,1q,2s(94),W=35%.   113n,237x,93m,363w,P=37%,35682Yy. |
| M   Cape Coast | 1879 | R Lat | Ps | 10 | 86,400 | 163,000 | Central Region. 10% Protestant, 1.5% Muslim.   15   24   6   41   25   5048 |
| D   Accra | 1943 | R Lat | Psvd | 319 | 77,400 | 146,041 | 35% Twi, 30% Ewe, 20% Krobo, 12% Ga-Adangbe.   12   62   33   96   33   8265 |
| D   Keta-Ho | 1923 | R Lat | Ps | 23 | 130,000 | 245,200 | 82% Ewe, 10% Buem, 8% Akyem. 5% Muslim. M=SMA.   24   25   0   16   52   8167 |
| D   Kumasi | 1932 | R Lat | Ps | 27 | 161,600 | 304,712 | Area 24% Muslim. 90% Ashanti, 10% Fante.   19   36   2   50   25   4019 |
| D   Navrongo-Bolgatanga | 1956 | R Lat | Pwf | 18 | 10,300 | 19,467 | Kasena, Frafra, Talensi, Kusasi, Bulsa.   12   25   6   18   46   820 |
| D   Sekondi-Takoradi | 1969 | R Lat | Ps | 14 | 97,500 | 184,000 | Western Region. 11% Protestant. 1.5% Muslim.   16   6   12   23   25   5924 |
| D   Tamale (1977, M) | 1926 | R Lat | Pwf | 7 | 8,400 | 15,862 | 7% Dagomba, 3% Chakossi; rest from south.   0   37   7   18   38   365 |
| D   Wa | 1959 | R Lat | Ps | 9 | 47,200 | 89,030 | 99% Dagari, 1% Sissala (neglected by RCs).   15   22   27   101   88   3074 |
| Christ Apostolic Church | 1921 | I peA | x,I,C | 330 | 85,000 | 100,000 | M=CAC(Nigeria). 9 Regional Apostles in Ghana. 32% ex Methodist. 150n,19x,1s,3000Y. |
| Christ Revival Church | 1960 | I pen | .v..I | 7 | 1,000 | 2,000 | Ex Apostolic Ch. Healing ministry. Twi-speaking. 1971 applied to join WCC. 3n,4m. |
| Christian Assembly | 1947 | I mar | ....I | 35 | 4,318 | 6,318 | Use of occult. Mechanized farm, commercial school, carpet firm. 20n,15m,4w,1500Y. |
| Christian Divine Church | 1960 | I pen | ....I | 70 | 4,672 | 6,000 | Ex Methodists. Healings of incurables, mental cases. 20n,28m,1p,W=80%,200Y. |
| Christian Methodist Episcopal Church | c1950 | I Met | Vw..W | | 1,160 | 2,200 | *Ghana-Togoland Conference.* Ex AMEC. 1959, invited in M=CMEC(USA Blacks). 5n,1r. |
| Church of Christ (Spiritual Movement) | 1958 | I peA | ..... | 34 | 16,000 | 20,000 | Split ex Ghana Apostolic Ch. 50% Ashanti, 30% Ga, 8% Fante, 3% Ewe. 30n,W=70%. |
| Church of Gethsemane | 1969 | I pen | ....I | 11 | 935 | 1,354 | Team of 12 evangelists and bandsmen. Converts join any pentecostal church. 3n,12m. |
| Church of God | 1963 | P Pe3 | ZF... | 32 | 1,225 | 4,000 | 1966, M=CoG(Cleveland)(USA). Holiness Pentecostals. 12n,2x,12m,1s,W=76%,29Y. |
| Church of Grace | 1949 | I pen | ....I | 13 | 2,000 | 3,500 | Begun by healing prophetess evicted ex Methodists. W=90%,100Y. |
| Church of Messiah | 1965 | I pen | ....I | 9 | 1,315 | 2,000 | Begun by prophetess. HQ Kumasi. Healings. Mostly Twi. 9n,3m,W=78%,250Y. |
| Church of Pentecost | 1937 | P PeA | ZG..C | 1,387 | 56,859 | 100,000 | 1953, ex Apostolic Ch. M=EMS(UK). 60% Akan,15% Ewe, 12% Ga. 118n,3x,4f,6998Y,4864y. |
| Church of the Lord (Aladura) | 1953 | I pen | xwT,I | 82 | 40,000 | 60,000 | *Aladura = Praying.* M—CLA(Nigeria). Healings, oils, incense. 40n,8x,W=50%,1000Y. |
| Church of the Lord (Ghana) | 1953 | I pen | ..I,I | 46 | 5,000 | 7,000 | Ex CLA(Nigeria). 1971, 10 more CLA churches joined. 60% Akan, 16% Ga. 46n,5m,4w. |
| Church of the Messiah | 1967 | I pen | ....I | 6 | 2,050 | 4,000 | Split ex Ransomed Ch. HQ Accra. 78% Ga, 15% Akan, 7% Ewe. 3n,12m,13w,W=65%,400Y. |
| Church of the Twelve Apostles | 1914 | I pen | ....I | 107 | 8,983 | 14,030 | Founder Prophet Harris' disciple John Nackabah; now under John Nackabah III. |
| Churches of Christ | 1961 | P D1s | x.... | 70 | 1,500 | 4,200 | M=CCCC(Instrumental)(USA). 90% Ashanti, 10% Kwahu. 40n,4x,254m,9f,2p,W=85%,750Y. |
| Divine Fellowship | 1962 | I pen | ..... | 10 | 3,500 | 5,500 | *Twer Nyame Ch.* Ex CLA. Healings, incense. 98% Akan. 2n,15m,3w,120Y. |
| Divine Healer's Church | 1954 | I pe3 | ..I... | 160 | 50,000 | 150,000 | *The Lord is There Temple,* Accra. Brother GA Lawson. Strong % Ga. 76n,W=40%,2400Y. |
| Divine Healing Church of Christ | 1950 | I pen | ..... | 25 | 1,911 | 2,517 | Founded by prophetess. Indigenous pentecostals. Midnight vigils. 10n,8m,4w,80Y. |
| Eden Revival Church | 1963 | I pen | xvI,W | 20 | 30,000 | 50,000 | *F'Eden Church.* Akan, Ga. 1971 applied to WCC, blocked. Accra. 31n,40m,4r,1s. |
| Emissaries of Divine Light | 1954 | I pen | ....I | 13 | 2,500 | 5,000 | Link with Emissaries Ch(USA). Ashanti, Ga, Akwapim. HQ Sekondi. 19n,W=12%,200Y. |

*Continued overleaf*

*Table 2 – continued*

| Official name 1 | Begun 2 | Type 3 | Counc 4 | Congs 5 | Adults 6 | Affiliated 7 | Names, notes, and other statistics (see Codebook) 8 |
|---|---|---|---|---|---|---|---|
| Epis Holy Temple & Tabernacle Mission | 1920 | I pen | .T..I | 4 | 1,400 | 2,000 | 1920, National Ch of Christ; name changed 1953. Ashanti. 6n,1p,1s,W=60%,50Y. |
| Evangelical Churches of West Africa | 1956 | P int | xM... | 2 | 100 | 300 | M=ECWA(Nigeria); 1956, SIM(USA), in schools and literature. 14f,1s. |
| Evangelical Lutheran Church of Ghana | c1950 | P Lut | l...W | 17 | 116 | 422 | M=LCM(USA). Fante, Ashanti, Kusasi. Nigerian Efiks deported 1969. 1n,5x,9t,W=90%. |
| Evangelical Presbyterian Church | 1847 | P Ref | RWA.W | 521 | 40,372 | 122,292 | *EPC*.Formerly Ewe Presb Ch.M=BrM,CSM,UCBWM. 55% Ewe. 76n,3x,1s,W=65%,2060Y,10300y. |
| Evangelical Presbyterian Reformed Ch | 1964 | I Ref | ..... | 12 | 1,800 | 3,000 | HQ Accra New Town. Mainly Ewe, also Ga, Akan. One school. 4n,9m,2w,W=17%,40Y. |
| First Miracle Healing Church | 1959 | I pen | ..... | 11 | 3,960 | 5,000 | Healing by oil, water, incense, handkerchiefs. 80% Ga. Declining. 4n,18m,3w,325Y. |
| Free Prot Episcopal Ch: D West Africa | c1960 | C ARo | xv... | | 200 | 300 | *Ecumenical Church Foundation*. M=FPEC(UK,USA). HQ Monrovia (Liberia). |
| Ghana Baptist Convention | 1920 | P Bap | T...W | 80 | 1,200 | 2,000 | M=NBC(Nigeria); 1947, SBC(USA). Yorubas, deported 1969. 23n,8x,51f,1H,1h,2s,104Y. |
| Ghana Mennonite Church | 1956 | P Men | G...W | 14 | 481 | 700 | Begun by a Ghanaian. M=MCNA. In south. HQ Accra. 45% Ga. 1x,11m,12f,W=70%,25Y. |
| Greek Orth P Alexandria: D Accra | | O Gre | Cw... | 2 | 500 | 1,000 | Under P Alexandria (Egypt). HQ Yaoundé, Cameroon. Bishop lives in Greece. |
| Harris Church | c1940 | I ind | ..... | 40 | 2,490 | 3,770 | Harris movement in Ivory Coast, 1913. Organized in Ghana 1964, under bishop. 40n. |
| Holy Trinity Healing Church | 1954 | I pen | ....I | 8 | 1,000 | 2,419 | Ex RCs. HQ Kumasi. 1962. founder's son broke off, formed Bethany Church Mission. |
| Inner Temple of Christ | 1964 | I pen | ....I | 9 | 5,600 | 7,000 | Ex Divine Healer's Ch. 40% decline since 1966. 50% Ashanti, 30% Ga. 7n,W=70%,600Y. |
| Jehovah's Witnesses | 1924 | M Jeh | x.... | 366 | 17,156 | 55,826 | *Watch Tower*. First lectures given 1924, converts made. HQ Accra. 898mw,1j,1700Y. |
| Jesus Divine Healing Church | 1952 | I pen | ..... | 6 | 1,325 | 1,600 | Ex RCC. Epileptics healed with crucifix, oils. Akan, Ewe, Ga. 2n,3m,1w,120Y. |
| Liberal Catholic Church in Ghana | | C Lib | x.... | 1 | 50 | 100 | Split in UK ex Old Roman Catholic Ch. Theosophical. M=LCC(UK,USA) HQ Accra. |
| Methodist Church, Ghana | 1835 | P Met | VWA.W | 1,757 | 122,861 | 257,649 | 40% Akan, 35% Ga-Adangbe, 12% Nzima, 10% Ewe. 133n,7x,21f,1H,5r,1s,1u,3250Y,12796y. |
| Nazarene Healing Church | 1939 | I pen | ..... | 8 | 7,000 | 14,000 | Ex Methodists. Healing herbs, shea-butter, soap. Akan, Ga, Ewe. 9n,3m,600Y. |
| Nigritian Episcopal Church | 1907 | I pen | ....I | 56 | 3,511 | 7,924 | Ex Methodists. 46% Fante, 28% Ga, 22% Ashanti. 31n,19m,25w,1p,1s,W=95%,200Y,100y. |
| Pentecostal Holy Church of Ghana | 1954 | I pen | ..... | 21 | 800 | 2,000 | Ex AoG. M=CGC(USA). Ashanti. Declining; schism in 1970. 6n,W=80%,20Y,20z. |
| Presbyterian Church of Ghana | 1828 | P Ref | RWA.W | 868 | 60,041 | 279,104 | M=BM,UFCSM. 48% Akyem, 20% Ashanti, 17% Adangbe. 116n,5x,3H,3h,2s,1u,2426Y,20444y. |
| Religious Society of Friends | 1927 | P Qua | Q...W | 2 | 24 | 60 | Began by expatriate British at Achimota. Decline since 1961. M=FSC(UK). 2f. |
| Sacred Cherubim & Seraphim Ch of G | 1952 | I peA | x.I.I | 36 | 2,000 | 4,000 | M=C&S(Nigeria). Members Akan, Ewe, Ga; Nigerians deported 1969. 25n,100m,150w. |
| Sacred Order of the Silent Brotherhood | 1961 | I pen | ..... | 11 | 1,449 | 2,500 | *Divine Healing Crusade*. HQ Ho. 3 Temples, 8 rented halls. W=83%,194Y. |
| Salvation Army | 1922 | P Sal | xwA.W | 106 | 8,351 | 15,000 | *Nkwagye Don No* (in Twi). *SA, Ghana Command*. 75% Akan. 64n,14f,6h,1s,W=73%,390Y. |
| Saviour Church of Ghana | 1924 | I ind | ..... | 150 | 7,000 | 10,000 | *Memeneda Gyidifo. Saturday Believers*. 14 Districts. Ex Methodist. Akyem/Twi. 500Y. |
| Seventh-day Adventist Church | 1894 | P Adv | x.... | 81 | 17,073 | 50,000 | *Ghana Conf*. 53% Ashanti, 29% Akyem, 9% Dagomba. 25n,3x,43f,1H,1j,4r,W=93%,1615Y. |
| Supreme Healing Home | 1963 | I pen | ..... | 1 | 1,291 | 2,000 | One of many healing homes; Accra. 23% Akan, 23% Guan, 23% Fanti, 19% Ga, 12% Ewe. |
| True Church of Christ (New Bethlehem) | 1957 | I pen | ....I | 25 | 5,050 | 6,000 | Founder Lucy Kudjo. Incurables healed; power handkerchiefs. Ashanti. 25n,600Y. |
| True Faith Church | 1921 | I pen | ..... | 96 | 11,635 | 15,000 | One of earliest indigenous pentecostal bodies, ex Methodists. 6 Districts. 45n. |
| United Christians Church | 1940 | I pen | ..... | 10 | 650 | 2,000 | Begun by 85-yrs-old prophetess Salome Mamle Odum; 1963, evicted ex Presb Ch. Krobos. |
| United Pentecostal Church of Ghana | 1968 | P Pel | x.... | 80 | 7,200 | 20,000 | *Jesus Only Ch*. Unitarian Pentecostals. M=UPC(USA). 40n,3x,5f,1p(30),W=70%,1000Y. |
| Universal Prayer Group | 1932 | I pen | ..... | 60 | 4,500 | 12,500 | Ex Presbyterians; led by prophetesses since 1932. Akan, Ewe, Ga. 150n,1500Y. |
| White Cross Society | 1941 | I pen | ..... | 20 | 3,000 | 5,370 | *Atitso Gaxie Habobo. EP Healing Group*, expelled by EPC. 76% Ewe, 15% Kabre. 123Y. |
| Worldwide Evangelization Crusade | 1940 | P int | xF..C | 56 | 850 | 2,600 | M=WEC(UK). North. 56% Konkomba, 32% Birifor, 12% Bassari. 7n,22x,3h,2p,W=90%,12Y. |
| World-Wide Missions of Ghana | 1961 | P ind | x.... | | 65,000 | 90,000 | M=World-Wide Missions (USA). Evangelicals based in Pasadena, CA (USA). |
| Other African indigenous churches | | I | ..... | | 30,000 | 60,000 | Total over 370 (see list below). |
| Other Protestant denominations | | P | ..... | | 5,000 | 10,000 | Total about 20 (see list below). |
| Other marginal Protestant bodies | | M | ..... | | 500 | 1,000 | Total over 10 Western spiritist and other bodies (see below). |
| **Total affiliated (mid-1970)** | | | | **11,300** | **1,598,935** | **3,226,794** | **Total denominations (1970) . . . 480.** |
| **Total affiliated (mid-1975)** | | | | **13,400** | **1,991,200** | **4,018,300** | **Total denominations (1975) . . . 520.** |
| **Total affiliated (mid-1980)** | | | | **15,500** | **2,489,900** | **5,024,800** | **Total denominations (1980) . . . 570.** |

NOTES ON TABLE ABOVE

COLUMNS: for meanings and CODES (cols. 1, 3, 4, 8), see Codebook (Part 6). Column 1: **Boldface type** = church with over 10% of country's affiliated Christians.

NATIONAL COUNCILS (Column 4, 5th letter).
- C = Ghana Evangelical Fellowship (GEF).
- I = Pentecostal Association of Ghana (89 member spiritual churches in 1972).
- R = Ghana Bishops' Conference (GBC).
- W = Christian Council of Ghana (CCG).

*Other national councils*. National Council of Pentecostal (Spiritual) Churches of Ghana (NCPC/NCSC) (begun 1966; until 1971, Ghana Council for Liberal Churches (GCLC); affiliated members are not denominations but over 500 smaller spiritual churches and evangelistic organizations, with 110,000 total members; 1971, applied to join AACC, 1974 applied to join WCC). International Council of Christian Churches of Ghana (ICCC). Christian Brotherhood Council. Ghana Council of United Churches (indigenous).

*Local councils*. 10 local councils affiliated to CCG.

OTHER AFRICAN INDIGENOUS CHURCHES. There are over 370 other bodies, almost all known in Ghana as 'spiritual churches' (indigenous charismatics or pentecostals), as well as various immigrant bodies from Nigeria although most were deported after the 1969 Aliens Compliance Order. A complete survey was done by the Christian Council of Ghana from 1969–73. Most have between 50 and 1,000 adherents, and about 35% of all members are converts from tribal religion. Among the larger bodies are the following (with, in brackets, date of founding and number of adherents in 1970–2): Apostolic Gospel Ch (1957: 3,694), Bethel Divine Ch (1959: 1,500), Christ Deliverance Ch (1964: 1,354), Christ Divine Healing Ch (1962: 1,020), Christ Evangel Ch (1968: 1,600), Christ Followers Divine Ch (1958), Ch of the Holy Saints (Brotherhood of the Essens; 1953: 1,145), Ch of Light Mission (1956: 5,000), Ch of the Living God (1975 application to WCC), Divine Prayer Society 1944 (Ch of the Family of God & of Jesus Christ; mission in UK), Ev Ch of God (1966: 655), Faith Brotherhood Praying Circle (1967: 2,453), Ghana Christian Ch (1963: 2,095), God is Our Light Ch, Healing Hand of God Mission (1952: 3,000), Holy Ch of Messiah (1965: 1,000), Holy Ghostal Ch (1955: 1,100 adherents), Holy Healing Ch (1967: 1,500), Lord's Healing Ch of Ghana (1957: 4,000), Lord's Peace Healing Ch (1971: 3,000), Nuba Divine Healing Ch (1957), Pan-African (Spiritual) Ch, Reformed Ch Mission-Ghana (1964: 261), Salvation in Christ Ch (1962: 2,250), Sanctuary Christian Methodist Episcopal Ch (1949: 800 adherents). In addition, there are 2 USA Black missions: National Baptist Convention USA (1950), Pentecostal Assemblies of the World.

OTHER PROTESTANT DENOMINATIONS. These smaller bodies include: Apostolic Christian Ch (Nazarean), Children of God International (from USA), Ch of God (Abrahamic Faith) (1970), Ev Protestant Mission in Ghana (1965), Ghana Association of Regular Baptist Chs, Mennonite Brethren Chs (1971), Pentecostal Holiness Ch. There are also small immigrant bodies from neighbouring countries and Nigeria.

OTHER MARGINAL PROTESTANT BODIES. These Western bodies include: Church of Christ, Scientist (one society in Accra), Ch of Jesus Christ of Latter-day Saints (Mormons; Accra), Unity School of Christianity (USA; many Ghanaians receive mail courses).

UNITING CHURCHES. Negotiations for organic union were begun in 1957 under the name Ghana Church Union Committee (United Church), between: AME Church, CPWA (Anglican Ch; withdrew in 1976), Ev Lutheran Ch of Ghana, Ev Presbyterian Ch, Ghana Mennonite Ch, Methodist Ch Ghana, Presbyterian Ch of Ghana; with as observer churches: AME Zion Ch, Eden Revival Ch, Ghana Baptist Convention. By 1980, the Church of Christ in Ghana was scheduled to be formed in 1981, uniting the Methodist, Presbyterian, and Evangelical Presbyterian Churches.

PEOPLES (ethnolinguistic). Christians: 64.2% Akan (18.2% Ashanti, 17.1% Fante, 5.4% Akyem, 4.9% Brong, 4.9% Nzima, 3.5% Akwapim, 2.8% Kwahu, 1.9% Anyi-Baule), 14.7% Ewe, 10.5% Ga-Adangbe (5.6% Ga, 3.5% Adangbe), 3.7% Guan, 3.5% Mole-Dagbani (2.8% Dagati, 0.3% Dagomba, 0.2% Frafra, 0.2% Kusasi), 1.4% Central Togolese, 1.2% Yoruba, 0.4% European (British), 0.2% Grusi, Kru, et alii.

COUNTRY-WIDE TOTALS

EVANGELIZATION (see Part 5). 1900: 23%. 1970: 94%. 1980: 96%. *Mass evangelism*. Among recent campaigns: January 1960, Billy Graham crusades in Accra and Kumasi (45,000 attenders, 3,280 enquirers); 1970–71, New Life for All campaign (renewed 1977–79); July 1977, Ghana Congress on Evangelism; 1978, Here's Life Africa (CCI) in Kumasi. *Radiophonic evangelism*. ELWA, RVOG, HCJB, ICI (6,324 enrolments), et alia.

FOREIGN MISSIONARIES AND PERSONNEL (nationals serving abroad) (1973). Total 210 in 15 countries: about 102 Ghanaian indigenous (sent out by over 30 spiritual churches to organized branches in Cameroon, Ivory Coast, Liberia, Nigeria, Sierra Leone, Togo, Uganda, UK, Upper Volta), 60 Roman Catholics, 45 Protestants, 3 Anglicans.

FOREIGN MISSIONARIES AND PERSONNEL (aliens from abroad) (1973). Total 1,057. *From Western world*. 890: about 470 Roman Catholics, 393 Protestants (248 in 26 USA societies, 88 in 10 UK societies, 14 in 3 Australia societies, 14 in 3 W Germany societies, 12 in 1 Switzerland society, 10 in 3 Netherlands societies, 6 in 4 New Zealand societies, 1 in 1 Finland society), 23 Anglicans (22 in 3 UK societies, 1 in 1 Canada society), 3 Black indigenous from USA, 1 Orthodox. *From Communist world*. About 17 Roman Catholics (13 from Poland, 4 Yugoslavia). *From Third World*. 150: about 80 indigenous from Nigeria, Togo and Ivory Coast, about 50 Roman Catholics from Nigeria, Brazil, Philippines et alia, about 20 Protestants.

INSTITUTIONS (church-operated) (1973). Total 250, including 80 higher schools (8 minor seminaries), 100 medical centres (35 hospitals), 5 religious communities, 29 seminaries (16 Protestants, 10 African indigenous, 3 RC).

PERIODICALS. About 80 titles.

PERSONNEL. About 9,797 (8,740 national, 1,057 foreign).

RELIGIOUS LIBRARIES. About 35.

SCRIPTURE DISTRIBUTION (1975). Annual totals: 122,594 Bibles (2% free, 73% subsidized, 24% commercial), 123,520 NTs (42% free, 50% subsidized, 8% commercial), 236,001 UBS portions, 421,043 UBS selections. *Translations completed*. Portion: 18 languages since 1843. NT: 5 languages since 1859. Bible: 5 languages since 1866.

SERVICE AGENCIES. About 65, including ACP, BRAVS, CCCI, CCG, CHAG, CMWF, COF, CWS, GBC, GEF, GHAFES(IVF), NLFA, SCM, SECAM, SED, SU, WBT, YCS, YCW, YMCA, YWCA.

ADDITIONAL DATA ON CHURCHES

ANGLICAN CHURCH OF GHANA. By 1977 the proposed diocese of Cape Coast had still not been formally organized. In 1980, D Accra was being divided into 5: Cape Coast, Takoradi, Tamale-Bolgatanga, Koforidua, Accra. *Personnel* (1977). 600 lay workers (100 women), 300 licensed lay readers (50 women). *Seminarians* (1977). 20.

CATHOLIC CHURCH IN GHANA. *New diocese* (created 1973). Sunyani, formed out of D Kumasi. *New province* (erected 1977). Tamale, with as suffragans D Navrongo-Bolgatanga and D Wa. *Church growth*. There has recently been a mass movement to Catholicism in the Diocese of Wa, from 50,000 Catholics in 1965 to 294,342 by 1976 (72% of the total population). The tribes involved are the Dagaaba, Sisaala and numerous others. Table 2 above reflects the 1970 situation; Table 1 includes the mass movement. *Catechumens*. Totals: (1959) 93,805; (1961) 105,379; (1963) 136,571; (1969) 106,400, divided as follows among the 8 dioceses in the order shown (and included in column 7 above): 10000, 18545, 5000, 41073, 2242, 10000, 2562, 17000. *Annual baptisms*. (1972) 65.7% infant, 34.3% adult. *Priests*. 33% diocesan, 67% religious. *Brothers*. About a third Ghanaians. *Sisters*. Including 184 Ghanaians. *Catechists*. Total (1972) 274 full-time, 1,966 part-time. *Indigenous religious congregations*. Brothers: Holy Cross Brothers, Immaculate Conception Brothers, Divine Word Brothers. Sisters: 93 Sisters of Mary Immaculate (begun 1947), Franciscan Missionary Sisters of Mary (begun 1954), Servants of the Divine Redeemer (begun 1956), 4 Congregation of the Infant Jesus (begun 1961), Handmaids of the Holy Child. *Main foreign congregations*. Priests: SVD, WF, SMA. Brothers: St John of God, Immaculate Conception, Holy Cross. Sisters: Our Lady of Apostles, Holy Child (Handmaids), Franciscan Missionary Sisters of Mary, White Sisters, Medical Mission Sisters. *Catholic organizations*. The Ghana Bishops' Conference, with headquarters in Accra, is a member of SECAM (Symposium of Episcopal Conferences of Africa and Madagascar) and also of the Regional Episcopal Conference of Ghana, Liberia, Sierra Leone and the Gambia, the latter having its general secretariat in Sierra Leone. SECAM, whose headquarters are in Accra, has held 5 general assemblies: at Kampala in 1968, Abidjan in 1970, Kampala in 1972, Rome (because of the Holy Year) in 1975, and Nairobi in 1978. Two organizations of religious personnel are active: the Conference of Major Superiors of Religious Personnel, for men, and the Conference of Major Superiors of Religious Women. There are no pastoral or presbyteral councils. The Department of Pastoral and Social Action of the National Catholic Secretariat co-ordinates lay activities, the principal national organizations being: Legion of Mary, Catholic Youth Organization, YCW, YCS, Pax Romana, Knights of St John, Knights of Marshall (1,000 members), Ladies of Marshall (500 members) and Catholic Women's Federation.

The Holy See had no diplomatic relations with Ghana until 1976 when they were set up with a pro-nuncio in Accra.

The Catholic Church has been heavily involved in education and social services. In 1969, within the public sector the Catholic Education Unit managed 1,657 primary and middle schools out of a total of 10,494 schools (15.8%). This included some local authority schools under temporary church control. Enrolment was 225,137 in Catholic schools out of a total of 1,398,026 in all primary and middle schools (16.1%). There were also 16 Catholic secondary schools (14.8%) with an enrolment of 6,880 (14.8%) and 10 teacher-training colleges (12%) with an enrolment of 2,800 (14.4%). In the private sector, in 1969 there were 240 Catholic private schools not supported by government. Among these were one kindergarten and 3 international primary schools with an enrolment of 1,000, one secondary school, 6 minor seminaries, 4 of which were open to other students, 2 technical schools with 500 students and 4 vocational schools. By 1973, schools numbered 1,613 primary (250,253 pupils) and 42 secondary (11,406). In the medical field, in 1972 there were 25 Catholic hospitals; 13 clinics, maternity homes and orphanages; one home for the handicapped; and various other dispensaries and welfare facilities. The Department of Socio-Economic Development (SED) of the National Catholic Secretariat co-ordinates and stimulates all Catholic efforts in the field of development.

CHURCH OF PENTECOST. Beginning in 1937, this large church became a clearcut denomination when in 1953 a majority of the members of the Apostolic Church (UK-related) broke off under that church's British missionary founder. It took the name Gold Coast Apostolic Church (1958, Ghana Apostolic Church; then 1960, Church of Pentecost). It is now supported by Elim Pentecostal Church (UK). *Membership*. 60% Akan, 15% Ewe, 12% Ga-Adangbe, 8% Nzima, 5% Dagomba-Wala. The recent rapid rises in membership are due to mass open-air evangelistic rallies. *Growth*. In 1976, 68 new assemblies were opened.

METHODIST CHURCH, GHANA. Founded and still assisted by the Methodist Missionary Society (UK).

# GIBRALTAR

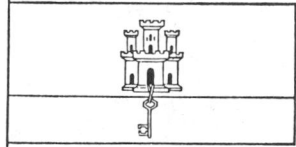

## SECULAR DATA

**STATE. Official name:** The Colony of Gibraltar.
**Flag** (shown above right): White with red stripe along bottom, red triple-towered castle with gold key depending from gateway.
**Area:** 6.5 sq.km. (2.5 sq.miles). Agricultural land: 0.0%.
**Government:** Self-governing British colony (1704 British possession).
**Legislature:** Gibraltar House of Assembly, 18 members.
**Official language:** English.
**Capital:** Gibraltar Town 24,880 (1965).
**Foreign forces** (1973): 1,000 British (UK) troops.

**DEMOGRAPHY. Population:** 26,833 (census of 6.X.1970. For 1970–2000 (UN), see last row of Table 1). Population density (1975): 4,154/sq.km. (10,758/sq.mile). Under 15 years: 26%. Growth rate (1975–80): 0.65% per year. Household size: 3.6 persons.
**Major languages:** English, Spanish, Italian, Maltese, Arabic, Yiddish.
**Urban dwellers** (1970): 93%.
**Labour force:** 35%.
**Tourists** (1974): 139,924.

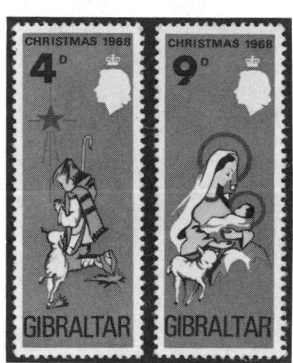

Many postage stamps portray the Nativity of Christ.

**ETHNOLINGUISTIC GROUPS:** 66.2% Gibraltarian (Spanish/Italian (Genoese)/Portuguese/Maltese), 11.0% British, 10.0% Spaniard, 9.5% Moroccan Arab, 2.3% Jewish, 1.0% Indian,

**MONEY** (1977). **Monetary unit:** Gibraltar pound (= 100 new pence); US$1 = Gib£ 0.43.
**National income per person:** US$1,500. Average annual family income: US$5,400.
**Inflation:** (1970–74) 12.0% per year, (1975) 19% per year (consumer price index 188).

**EDUCATION.** Adult literacy: 94%. Education rate: 95%. Schools: 13.

**HEALTH.** Hospitals: 3 (252 beds). Doctors: 19. Lepers: 20 (0.7 per 1,000). Blind: 140.

**LITERATURE.** Newspapers: 2 dailies, 2 non-daily.

**COMMUNICATION** (per 1,000 people). Phones: 250. Radios: 220. TV sets: 204. Daily newspaper circulation: 211 copies.

### TABLE 1.    RELIGIOUS ADHERENTS IN GIBRALTAR

| Year | 1900 | | mid-1970 | | Annual change, 1970–1980 | | | | mid-1975 | | mid-1980 | | 2000 | |
|---|---|---|---|---|---|---|---|---|---|---|---|---|---|---|
| *Name* | *Adherents* | *%* | *Adherents* | *%* | *Natural* | *Conversion* | *Total* | *Rate* | *Adherents* | *%* | *Adherents* | *%* | *Adherents* | *%* |
| Christians | 19,480 | 96.4 | 22,970 | 88.3 | 176 | −9 | 167 | 0.70 | 23,790 | 88.1 | 24,640 | 88.0 | 26,880 | 86.7 |
| professing | 19,480 | 96.4 | 22,970 | 88.3 | 176 | −9 | 167 | 0.70 | 23,790 | 88.1 | 24,640 | 88.0 | 26,800 | 86.7 |
| Roman Catholics | 18,170 | 89.9 | 20,420 | 78.5 | 156 | −23 | 133 | 0.63 | 21,080 | 78.1 | 21,750 | 77.7 | 23,370 | 75.4 |
| Anglicans | 1,210 | 6.0 | 2,080 | 8.0 | 16 | 6 | 22 | 1.00 | 2,190 | 8.1 | 2,300 | 8.2 | 2,700 | 8.7 |
| Protestants | 100 | 0.5 | 390 | 1.5 | 3 | 6 | 9 | 2.09 | 430 | 1.6 | 480 | 1.7 | 620 | 2.0 |
| Marginal Protestants | 0 | 0.0 | 80 | 0.3 | 1 | 2 | 3 | 3.33 | 90 | 0.3 | 110 | 0.4 | 190 | 0.6 |
| nominal | 600 | 3.0 | 1,540 | 5.9 | 12 | 14 | 26 | 1.59 | 1,640 | 6.1 | 1,800 | 6.4 | 2,270 | 7.3 |
| affiliated | 18,880 | 93.5 | 21,430 | 82.4 | 164 | −23 | 141 | 0.64 | 22,150 | 82.0 | 22,840 | 81.6 | 24,610 | 79.4 |
| total practising | 15,100 | 80 | 10,720 | 50 | 82 | −12 | 70 | 0.63 | 11,080 | 50 | 11,420 | 50 | 14,770 | 60 |
| non-practising | 3,780 | 20 | 10,710 | 50 | 82 | −11 | 71 | 0.64 | 11,070 | 50 | 11,420 | 50 | 9,840 | 40 |
| Roman Catholics | 17,780 | 88.0 | 19,130 | 73.6 | 145 | −31 | 114 | 0.58 | 19,710 | 73.0 | 20,270 | 72.4 | 21,540 | 69.5 |
| Anglicans | 1,000 | 5.0 | 1,900 | 7.3 | 15 | −1 | 14 | 0.71 | 1,970 | 7.3 | 2,040 | 7.3 | 2,290 | 7.4 |
| Protestants | 100 | 0.5 | 300 | 1.2 | 3 | 6 | 9 | 2.57 | 350 | 1.3 | 390 | 1.4 | 530 | 1.7 |
| Marginal Protestants | 0 | 0.0 | 100 | 0.4 | 1 | 3 | 4 | 3.33 | 120 | 0.4 | 140 | 0.5 | 250 | 0.8 |
| Muslims | 0 | 0.0 | 2,120 | 8.2 | 18 | 16 | 34 | 1.48 | 2,300 | 8.5 | 2,460 | 8.8 | 3,100 | 10.0 |
| Jews | 700 | 3.5 | 590 | 2.3 | 4 | −15 | −11 | −2.04 | 540 | 2.0 | 480 | 1.7 | 370 | 1.2 |
| Hindus | 20 | 0.1 | 260 | 1.0 | 2 | 6 | 8 | 2.67 | 300 | 1.1 | 340 | 1.2 | 400 | 1.3 |
| Baha'is | 0 | 0.0 | 30 | 0.1 | 0 | 2 | 2 | 5.00 | 40 | 0.1 | 50 | 0.2 | 100 | 0.3 |
| Non-religious | 0 | 0.0 | 30 | 0.1 | 0 | 0 | 0 | 0.00 | 30 | 0.1 | 30 | 0.1 | 150 | 0.5 |
| Country's population | 20,000 | 100.0 | 26,000 | 100.0 | 200 | 0 | 200 | 0.74 | 27,000 | 100.0 | 28,000 | 100.0 | 31,000 | 100.0 |

**COLUMNS, ROWS.** For meanings and definitions, see Codebook (Part 6). Note that, by definition, total 'Christians' = professing + crypto-Christians, which also = affiliated + nominal Christians. Percentages may not always total exactly, due to rounding.
**CENSUSES. 3.VII.1951:** 87.9% Roman Catholics, 8.3% Anglicans & Protestants, 3.0% Jews, 0.5% Hindus, 0.2% other religion-

ists, 0.1% non-religious. **3.X.1961** (excluding 2,717 military and shipping personnel): 87.5% Roman Catholics, 7.5% Anglicans, 3.0% Jews, 1.2% Protestants, 0.6% Hindus, 0.2% marginal Protestants, 0.1% non-religious. **6.X.1970** (excluding families of servicemen): 78.6% Roman Catholics, 8.2% Muslims 8.0% Anglicans, 2.3% Jews, 1.5% Protestants, 1.0% Hindus, 0.3% marginal Protestants, 0.1% non-religious.

**NOTES ON RELIGIONS**
ANGLICANS. Including a number of expatriate British military, dependants and civilians.
BAHA'IS. In 1 isolated centre.
HINDUS. Indians.
JEWS. With 4 synagogues.
MUSLIMS. Almost all Moroccans, immigrants since 1961.

**NON-CHRISTIAN RELIGIONS.** In 1970 Gibraltar was 2.3% Jewish, 1.0% Hindu, and 0.1% professed no religion. There are 4 synagogues in the colony.
**Islam** has entered since 1961 in the persons of over 2,000 immigrant Moroccan Arabs.

## CHRISTIANITY
CATHOLIC CHURCH. Catholics were active in Gibraltar in 1492, but the church was suppressed by the British when they took possession in 1704. In 1806 a Catholic priest was appointed for Italian immigrants. Gibraltar became a vicariate apostolic in 1817 and a diocese in 1910, now under Propaganda in Rome and immediately subject to the Holy See. Most of the civilian population is Catholic (87.5% in 1961, declining to 78.5% by 1970), the principal ethnic groups being of Italian (Genoese), Maltese, Portuguese and Spanish descent.
OTHER CHURCHES. Anglicans are the principal non-Catholic denomination. Their proportion has fluctuated from 8.8% in 1921, to 7.5% in 1961, and to 8.0% in 1970. The diocese of Gibraltar was established in 1842 and co-ordinates the activities of

Anglican chaplaincies throughout southern and eastern Europe including Turkey. It is a missionary diocese of the Church of England under the jurisdiction of the archbishop of Canterbury, and forms part of the Anglican Church in Europe.
The services of the Scottish Presbyterian church are attended by a wide variety of Christians, the majority being Presbyterians and Methodists; and there is also a small Adventist community. Protestants formed 1.5% of the population in 1970.

**CHURCH AND STATE.** There is no established church or state religion, and freedom of religion is guaranteed to all. Each communion (Catholic, Anglican, Presbyterian) receives an annual subsidy of £500 from the government.

**Catholic Church, Diocese of Gibraltar.** *Right.* Church of Our Lady of Dolours, in Catalan Bay (La Caleta), where first settlers arrived from Genoa in 17th century.

### TABLE 2.    ORGANIZED CHURCHES AND DENOMINATIONS IN GIBRALTAR

| Official name 1 | Begun 2 | Type 3 | Counc 4 | Congs 5 | Adults 6 | Affiliated 7 | Names, notes, and other statistics (see Codebook) 8 |
|---|---|---|---|---|---|---|---|
| Catholic Church: D Gibraltar | 1492 | R Lat | p.B.. | 6 | 12,000 | 19,130 | Nationals (Genoese, Portuguese, Maltese, Spanish). 8n,2x,10m,22w,P=30%,11Y,330y. |
| Church of England: D Gibraltar | 1704 | A plu | awc.. | 3 | 1,000 | 1,900 | Missionary diocese under D Canterbury, for SE Europe to Turkey. 70% aliens. 5x. |
| Jehovah's Witnesses | c1955 | M Jeh | x.... | 1 | 48 | 100 | *Watch Tower, IBSA.* Active witnessing under way by 1959. 7Y. |
| Methodist Church | | P Met | Vwc.. | 1 | 40 | 100 | Related to Methodist Ch of Great Britain. Mainly English-speaking expatriates. |
| Presbyterian Church | | P Ref | Rv... | 1 | 100 | 140 | Scottish and other Presbyterians. M=Church of Scotland(UK). 1f. |
| Seventh-day Adventist Church | | P Adv | x.... | 1 | 40 | 60 | *SDA*, part of Spanish Church (Iglesia Española), Southern European Union Mission. |
| Total affiliated (mid-1970) | | | | 13 | 13,228 | 21,430 | Total denominations (1970) . . . 6. |
| Total affiliated (mid-1975) | | | | 13 | 13,670 | 22,150 | Total denominations (1975) . . . 6. |
| Total affiliated (mid-1890) | | | | 14 | 14,100 | 22,840 | Total denominations (1980) . . . 6. |

NOTES ON TABLE ABOVE
COLUMNS: for meanings and CODES (cols. 1, 3, 4, 8), see Codebook (Part 6). Column 1: **Boldface type** = church with over 10% of country's affiliated Christians.

PEOPLES (ethnolinguistic). Christians: 76.5% Gibraltarian, 12.2% British, 11.3% Spaniard, a few Moroccan.

COUNTRY-WIDE TOTALS
EVANGELIZATION (see Part 5). 1900: 100%. 1970: 100%. 1980: 100%.

FOREIGN MISSIONARIES AND PERSONNEL (aliens from abroad) (1973). Total 32. *From Western world.* 32: about 25 Roman Catholics, 5 Anglicans from UK, 2 Protestants from UK.
INSTITUTIONS (church-operated) (1973). Total 1 middle school.
PERIODICALS. About 4 titles.
PERSONNEL. About 49 (17 national, 32 foreign).
SCRIPTURE DISTRIBUTION (1975). Annual totals: 20 Bibles (50% subsidized, 50% commercial), 60 NTs (16% subsidized, 84% commercial), 20 UBS portions.
SERVICE AGENCIES. About 3, including CLC.

ADDITIONAL DATA ON CHURCHES
CATHOLIC CHURCH. *Catholic organizations.* In 1970 the church sponsored 2 primary schools (500 pupils), one middle school (70 pupils) and one orphanage (125 orphans).
CHURCH OF ENGLAND. The Diocese of Gibraltar was founded in 1842.

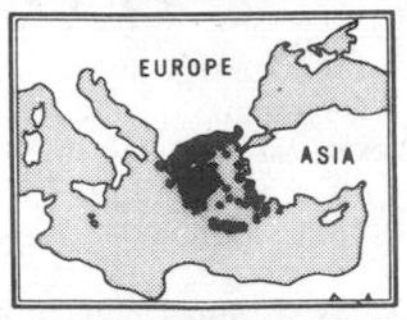


# GREECE

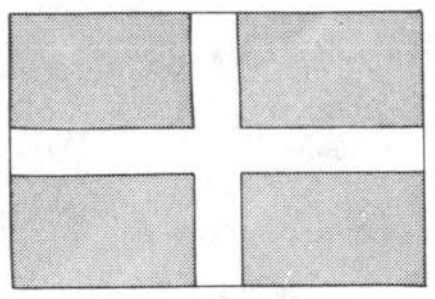

## SECULAR DATA

**STATE. Official name:** The Hellenic Republic (Ellenike Dimokratía). Adjective of nationality: Greek.
**Flag** (shown above right): Blue field with large white cross.
**Area:** 131,944 sq.km. (50,944 sq.miles). Agricultural land: 69.4%.
**Government:** Parliamentary republic, since 1974 (1830–1973 monarchy, 1967 military junta).
**Legislature:** Parliament, 300 members.
**Official language:** Greek (*Ellinika*).
**Chief cities:** capital Athens 2,101,100 (1971), Salonika 557,360 Piraeus 439,140.
**Political divisions:** 53 Prefectures (Nomoi).
**Armed forces** (1976): Total 199,500 regular (148,000 conscripts): army 160,000, navy 17,500, air force 22,000 (247 combat aircraft). Reserves: 240,000. Paramilitary forces: 103,500.
**Foreign forces** (1973): 3,000 USA troops. (1976) 800 USA troops.

**DEMOGRAPHY. Population:** 8,768,640 (census of 14.III.1971. For 1970–2000 (UN), see last row of Table 1). Population density (1975): 68/sq.km. (175/sq.mile). Under 15 years: 27%. Growth rate (1975–80): 0.33% per year (births 1.54%, deaths −1.00%, emigrants −0.21%). Life expectancy (1975–80): 72.3 years. Household size: 3.6 persons.
**Major languages:** Greek, Turkish, Albanian, Macedonian, English, Bulgarian, Armenian, Romany, Ladino.
**Urban dwellers** (1970): 48.5%. Urban growth rate (1950–70): 2.1% per year.
**Labour force:** 37%.
**Refugees** (1977): 7,000 from Lebanon.
**Tourists** (1971): 2,813,925. (1974) 1,956,414.

**ETHNOLINGUISTIC GROUPS:** 94.9% Greek, 1.8% Macedonian, 1.4% Turkish, 0.6% Albanian, 0.6% Aromanian (Vlach), 0.2% Bulgar, 0.1% Armenian, 0.1% Gypsy, 0.1% USA (4,000 military, 6,000 dependants), 0.1% British (7,000), 0.1% Jewish (5,000), et alii. By 1978, there were also 35,000 Coloured (Arab, African), mostly illegal migrant workers.

**MONEY** (1977). **Monetary unit:** drachma (= 100 lepta); US$1 = Dr 36.90.

**National income per person:** US$2,090. Average annual family income: US$7,524.
**Inflation:** (1970–74) 12.0% per year (1975: consumer price index 191).
**Cost of living in capital** (1976): index 115 (Washington DC = 100). Daily cost of living: US$30.

**EDUCATION.** Adult literacy: (1951) 74%, (1971) 84%. Education rate: 52%. Schools: 9,750. Universities: 4.

**HEALTH.** Hospitals: 798 (55,958 beds). Doctors: 15,351. Lepers: 2,700 (0.3 per 1,000). Blind: 13,000. Pyschotics: 80,000. Criminals: 102,276.

**LITERATURE.** Annual new book titles (1973): 2,007. Periodicals: 853. Scientific journals: 60. Newspapers: 104 dailies, 557 non-daily.

**COMMUNICATION** (per 1,000 people). Phones: 207. Radios: 146. TV sets: 106. Daily newspaper circulation: 77 copies.

TABLE 1. RELIGIOUS ADHERENTS IN GREECE

| Year | 1900 | | mid-1970 | | Annual change, 1970–1980 | | | | mid-1975 | | mid-1980 | | 2000 | |
|---|---|---|---|---|---|---|---|---|---|---|---|---|---|---|
| *Name* | *Adherents* | *%* | *Adherents* | *%* | *Natural* | *Conversion* | *Total* | *Rate* | *Adherents* | *%* | *Adherents* | *%* | *Adherents* | *%* |
| **Christians** | **2,599,000** | **85.2** | **8,643,000** | **98.3** | **28,188** | **−1,348** | **26,840** | **0.31** | **8,770,790** | **98.2** | **8,911,400** | **98.1** | **9,358,300** | **97.3** |
| professing | 2,599,000 | 85.2 | 8,643,000 | 98.3 | 28,188 | −1,348 | 26,840 | 0.31 | 8,770,790 | 98.2 | 8,911,400 | 98.1 | 9,358,300 | 97.3 |
| Orthodox | 2,540,800 | 83.3 | 8,592,000 | 97.7 | 28,021 | −1,341 | 26,680 | 0.30 | 8,718,990 | 97.6 | 8,858,800 | 97.6 | 9,299,300 | 96.7 |
| Roman Catholics | 55,000 | 1.8 | 37,000 | 0.4 | 121 | −1 | 120 | 0.32 | 37,600 | 0.4 | 38,200 | 0.4 | 41,000 | 0.4 |
| Protestants | 3,000 | 0.1 | 11,000 | 0.1 | 36 | 4 | 40 | 0.36 | 11,200 | 0.1 | 11,400 | 0.1 | 14,000 | 0.1 |
| Anglicans | 200 | 0.0 | 3,000 | 0.0 | 10 | −10 | 0 | 0.00 | 3,000 | 0.0 | 3,000 | 0.0 | 4,000 | 0.0 |
| nominal | 10,000 | 0.3 | 53,482 | 0.6 | 229 | 3,503 | 3,732 | 5.23 | 71,400 | 0.8 | 90,800 | 1.0 | 289,000 | 3.0 |
| affiliated | 2,589,000 | 84.9 | 8,589,518 | 97.7 | 27,959 | −4,851 | 23,108 | 0.26 | 8,699,390 | 97.4 | 8,820,600 | 97.1 | 9,069,300 | 94.3 |
| doubly-affiliated | −50,000 | −1.6 | −110,000 | −1.2 | −373 | −1,327 | −1,700 | 1.47 | −116,000 | −1.3 | −127,000 | −1.4 | −144,000 | −1.5 |
| total practising | 2,511,330 | *97* | 7,902,360 | *92* | 25,443 | 21,825 | 3,618 | 0.04 | 7,916,440 | *91* | 7,938,500 | *90* | 7,255,400 | *80* |
| non-practising | 77,670 | *3* | 687,160 | *8* | 2,516 | 16,974 | 19,490 | 2.49 | 782,950 | *9* | 882,060 | *10* | 1,813,900 | *20* |
| Orthodox | 2,573,800 | 84.4 | 8,566,519 | 97.4 | 27,882 | −4,354 | 23,528 | 0.27 | 8,675,490 | 97.1 | 8,801,800 | 96.9 | 9,038,700 | 93.9 |
| Orthodox pentecostals | 0 | 0.0 | 3,000 | 0.0 | 32 | 2,668 | 2,700 | 27.00 | 10,000 | 0.1 | 30,000 | 0.3 | 100,000 | 1.0 |
| Marginal Protestants | 0 | 0.0 | 50,226 | 0.6 | 177 | 800 | 977 | 1.77 | 55,100 | 0.6 | 60,000 | 0.7 | 80,000 | 0.8 |
| Roman Catholics | 60,000 | 2.0 | 45,723 | 0.5 | 151 | 7 | 158 | 0.34 | 47,000 | 0.5 | 47,300 | 0.5 | 51,000 | 0.5 |
| Protestants | 5,000 | 0.2 | 33,050 | 0.4 | 108 | 17 | 125 | 0.37 | 33,700 | 0.4 | 34,300 | 0.4 | 38,000 | 0.4 |
| Evangelicals | 4,000 | 0.1 | 17,000 | 0.2 | 57 | 3 | 60 | 0.34 | 17,900 | 0.2 | 18,200 | 0.2 | 19,200 | 0.2 |
| Anglicans | 200 | 0.0 | 3,000 | 0.0 | 10 | −10 | 0 | 0.00 | 3,000 | 0.0 | 3,000 | 0.0 | 4,000 | 0.0 |
| Catholics (non-Roman) | 0 | 0.0 | 1,000 | 0.0 | 4 | 16 | 20 | 1.82 | 1,100 | 0.0 | 1,200 | 0.0 | 1,600 | 0.0 |
| Muslims | 390,000 | 12.8 | 130,000 | 1.5 | 425 | −25 | 400 | 0.30 | 131,900 | 1.5 | 134,000 | 1.5 | 135,000 | 1.4 |
| Non-religious | 1,000 | 0.0 | 10,000 | 0.1 | 48 | 952 | 1,000 | 6.67 | 15,000 | 0.2 | 20,000 | 0.2 | 100,000 | 1.0 |
| Atheists | 0 | 0.0 | 5,000 | 0.1 | 22 | 378 | 400 | 5.71 | 7,000 | 0.1 | 9,000 | 0.1 | 20,000 | 0.2 |
| Jews | 60,000 | 2.0 | 3,800 | 0.0 | 12 | −2 | 10 | 0.26 | 3,860 | 0.0 | 3,900 | 0.0 | 4,000 | 0.0 |
| Baha'is | 0 | 0.0 | 200 | 0.0 | 1 | 9 | 10 | 4.00 | 250 | 0.0 | 300 | 0.0 | 700 | 0.0 |
| Other religionists | 0 | 0.0 | 1,000 | 0.0 | 4 | 36 | 40 | 3.33 | 1,200 | 0.0 | 1,400 | 0.0 | 3,000 | 0.0 |
| **Country's population** | **3,050,000** | **100.0** | **8,793,000** | **100.0** | **28,700** | **0** | **28,700** | **0.32** | **8,930,000** | **100.0** | **9,080,000** | **100.0** | **9,621,000** | **100.0** |

COLUMNS, ROWS. For meanings and definitions, see Codebook (Part 6). Note that, by definition, total 'Christians' = professing + crypto-Christians, which also = affiliated + nominal Christians. Percentages may not always total exactly, due to rounding.
CENSUSES. The first census was taken in 1828 (giving a population of 938,765) and thereafter at least once a decade. From 1870 to 1947, however, new territories were being annexed every 2 decades, hence the censuses cannot be compared without considerable adjustment, as has been done in the 1900 column above. **1928:** 96.1% Orthodox, 2.0% Muslims, 1.2% Jews, 0.6% Roman Catholics, 0.1% Protestants. **1940:** 96.7% Orthodox, 1.9% Muslims, 0.9% Jews, 0.4% Roman Catholics, 0.1% Protestants. **7.IV.1951** (excluding foreign military personnel, but including Greek military overseas): 97.9% Greek Orthodox, 1.5% Muslims, 0.4% Roman Catholics, 0.1% Protestants, 0.1% other Christians, 0.1% Jews. **1961:** 97.8% Greek Orthodox, 1.3% Muslims, 0.4% Roman Catholics, 0.2% Protestants, 0.1% marginal Protestants, 0.1% Jews.

NOTES ON RELIGIONS
ATHEISTS. Greek Communist Party (Kommonistikon Komma Elladas, KKE) (proscribed 1947, illegal 1967–74, pro-Soviet): membership (1970–74) 28,000; also, a total of 82,000 have subscribed to KKE objectives; Communist voters (election of XI.1974) 464,331 (9.4% of all votes). A large number of party members regard themselves as Orthodox Christians and many still attend church on festivals.
BAHA'IS. In 1 local spiritual assembly and 4 other centres.
COUNTRY'S POPULATION. In 1923, 1,500,000 Greek Orthodox resident in Turkey, including the 50,000 Karamanlis (Turkish-language Orthodox) were forcibly repatriated to Greece in exchange for 400,000 Muslim Turks resident in Greece.
DOUBLY-AFFILIATED. The term covers those affiliated to or claimed both by minority churches (Protestant, Roman Catholic, marginal Protestant, Catholic (non-Roman), Anglican) and also by the state church; this includes baptized members of the Church of Greece who have recently become Protestants or Jehovah's Witnesses but are still enumerated as Orthodox by the Church of Greece and its dioceses.
JEWS. Decrease from 75,000 in 1943 due to Nazi massacres. Now mostly in Thessalonika, and mostly Ladino-speaking.
MUSLIMS. In 1923, 400,000 Muslims (Turks) in Greece were forcibly repatriated to Turkey in exchange for 1,500,000 Greeks from Turkey. Muslims today are Sunnis (of the Hanafite rite) in eastern Thrace, with 300 mosques. They are 82% Turkish, 17% Pomak (Bulgarian-speaking Muslims), with a small number of Chamurians (Albanians) adjacent to Albania. Almost all Pomaks are Muslims, but about 100,000 Turkish-speakers are Orthodox. *Hajj pilgrims to Mecca.* (1970) 223; (1974) 175; (1975) 487; (1976) 144.
NON-RELIGIOUS. Many expatriates from France, Germany, UK, USA, et alia.
ORTHODOX PENTECOSTALS (or, Orthodox charismatics). The first strictly Orthodox charismatic organization in Greece began in 1945, but operated underground until 1975 when it had prayer groups in all major cities in the country. Other organizations include the Brotherhood of Christian Renewal (Athens). Charismatic renewal within the Church of Greece became noticeable in 1959, and by mid-1974 numbered around 5,000 adults (including 400 on Crete) in 200 prayer groups including laity, lay theologians, priests, monks and Old Calendrists; total charismatic community including children among all Orthodox bodies, about 10,000 in 1975. A Crusade for Christ in Athens was planned for 1977.
OTHER RELIGIONISTS. Including the Spiritual Association of Athens (denied legal registration in 1970), and the Theosophical Society (in 1975 with 5 Lodges and 228 members).
PRACTISING CHRISTIANS. Poll of 21 Sept 1963 (taken in Athens by newspaper *Nea*): 31% attend church every Sunday, 32% attend 2 or 3 times a month, 15% once a month, 14% only on festivals, 3% only 'when I have time'. 13 Dec 1970 (a Sunday): 14% attenders in a town in D Kavalla (Philippi), 21% in countryside: 13% in D Florina. In the countryside, ordinary Sunday attendance averages 5–10%, but virtually everybody attends at festivals. In 1971, the Church of Greece stated that on average 20% of all members attended each Sunday; and almost 100% took communion at Easter and other festivals 'except communists and atheists'. 1970: weekly attenders 26% (Gallup).
PROTESTANTS. Including many expatriates (USA civilian, USA military, et alii).

**NON-CHRISTIAN RELIGIONS. Islam** is the religion of 1.5% of the population, most being Turks in eastern Thrace, the area of Greece adjoining the small part of Turkish territory in Europe. According to Law 2345 concerning minorities, the Great Mufti of Greece is the recognized head of the Muslim community. Muslims in Greece have about 300 mosques and several Quranic schools.

**Judaism** has greatly decreased in influence since World War II. The present total of 3,800 Jews contrasts vividly with the 75,000 living there in 1943 before the Nazi deportations and massacres. The Central Board of the Jewish Communities in Greece, founded in Athens in 1945, is their officially-recognized governing body.

**CHRISTIANITY.** The Apostle Paul brought the gospel to Greece in the first century, and in spite of periods of persecution Christianity found fertile soil in the Greco-Roman world. In 312 Constantine became the first Roman emperor to embrace the Christian faith; and in 330 he built a new capital at Byzantium, which he renamed Constantinople. After his death, the Roman empire was divided, the western capital being at Rome while the east continued to have its centre in Constantinople. Barbarian invasions from the north radically altered the situation in the western part of the empire, producing further estrangement between east and west. The crowning of Charlemagne as emperor of the Holy Roman Empire by the pope in 800 was interpreted by the Byzantine emperor as an act of schism.

These political events were accompanied also by theological controversy, the main issues being the growth of papal claims and the filioque conflict over

the procession of the Holy Spirit in the Nicene creed. Matters came to a head when in 1054 the Catholic cardinal Humbert placed a bull of excommunication on the altar of Santa Sophia cathedral in Constantinople, an event which is generally recognized as the beginning of the Great Schism. In subsequent centuries various attempts were made to heal the wounds of division between the Catholic and Orthodox churches, but without success.

ORTHODOX CHURCHES. The proclamation of the Greek war of independence against the Turks in 1821 resulted in the immediate rupture of relations between the Church of Greece and the Ecumenical Patriarchate in Constantinople, with the administration of the church placed in the hands of regional committees for eastern and western Greece and for the Peloponnese. The demand for self-determination was welcomed by most Greeks and was expressed by the government of the time in the following manner: 'Greece is autonomous and independent, and her Church is autocephalous'. In 1833 bishops and government published jointly the first constitutional charter of the Church of the Kingdom, by which the church proclaimed itself to be the Autocephalous Church of Greece. This charter was submitted to the patriarch of Constantinople for his approval; and after much discussion and many objections, autocephality was finally recognized in 1850.

Originally the church was called simply the 'Greek Church' to correspond to the political appellation 'Greek State', and its jurisdiction covered the regions of the Hellenic kingdom, continental Greece and the Peloponnese. In 1864 the Ionian islands were added and in 1881 Thessalia. Together these are known today as the Ancient Regions (Palaiai Chorai) with 37 dioceses. Following the liberation from the Turks in 1912–13 of Macedonia, Epirus and the islands of the Aegean Sea, these also were annexed by the Church of Greece, although this was not recognized by the ecumenical patriarch until 1928. These are now known as the New Regions (Neai Chorai) with 33 dioceses.

The Monastic Republic of Mount Athos, the Church of the Dodecanese, the Patriarchal Exarchate of Patmos and the Church of Crete have all subsequently developed independently of the state church. The Church of Crete with 8 dioceses is semi-autonomous but is still dependent upon the patriarch of Constantinople. Its supreme administration is the Holy Synod at Iraklion, consisting of the bishops of the island together with, as president, the archbishop of Crete. The Church of the Dodecanese with 4 dioceses, by contrast, is under the direct jurisdiction of the ecumenical patriarch. Mount Athos and the Patriarchal Exarchate of Patmos are also directly dependent on Constantinople, although their regions do not constitute dioceses. Mount Athos is a sovereign self-administering region of the Greek state, governed by a Holy Community consisting of a representative from each of its 20 monasteries (11 conservative, 9 liberal). These representatives are in turn divided into 4 groups of five, each group serving as the region's Holy Administration (Iera Epistasia) for a year. Recent years have witnessed a radical decline in the number of monks serving on Mount Athos; from 40,000 in earlier days the total fell to 7,970 by 1913, to 3,000 by 1954, to 1,350 in 1969 and to 1,145 in 1971. A further problem is that whereas this was a centre for theological scholarship in Byzantine times, most of its monks now come from peasant families, with little education.

Greece remains the only country in the world which is officially Eastern Orthodox and in which the state church is Orthodox, in spite of the periodic shifts in governmental structure of the Greek nation in recent times. The church's dioceses remain very small and in consequence Greek bishops are able to maintain close contact with their people, delegating less responsibility to parish priests than is the case in the Western churches. Married parish priests usually do not preach sermons, which is due in part to their having received relatively little education. Being natives of the villages where they serve, after ordination they frequently return to their previous trades, such as carpentry. The universities at Athens and Salonika maintain schools of theology in which the majority of the teaching staff are laymen, many of whom have studied in Western Europe, Germany in particular. Greek theology today is thus characterized more by this Western academic influence than by the mysticism that once characterized Greek theology when its centre was on Mount Athos. Male monastic communities throughout Greece have been declining in membership, whereas the number of nuns has been increasing, many belonging to communities founded in the 20th century.

The major recent innovation within the Greek church has been the home missionary movements concerned with evangelistic and educational work. Apostolic Service, the church's official organization for home missions, was created in 1930. Parallel privately-begun movements include Zoe (Life), Sotir (Saviour) and the Orthodox Christian Unions, with at least 30 related organizations for men, women, youth, publishing and other activities. The oldest, largest and most controversial is Zoe which was begun in 1907. Semi-monastic, its members remain unmarried but take no formal vows and are free to leave at any time. One-fourth of the Zoe membership of 50 (a decline from 135 in 1959) consists of monks, although they do not live regularly in community; the rest are laymen. The home missionary movements stress Bible study and frequent communion, and publish numerous periodicals and books. Approximately 9,500 catechetical schools now exist, and a wide programme of youth work has been established.

In addition to these Greek churches in communion with Greek Orthodoxy, a number of other Orthodox bodies have small communities: the Ancient Church of the East, Armenian Apostolic Church, Bulgarian Orthodox Church, Russian Orthodox Church, and the Authentic Old Calendar Orthodox Church. The latter, also called Paleohemerologites (Old Calendar Orthodox), consists of a large number of laity, clergy and bishops who split from the state church in 1924 rejecting the church's change in that year from the Old (Julian) Calendar to the New (Gregorian) Calendar. They still have a widespread structure of parishes and dioceses with a hierarchy, 250 priests,

81 monasteries and convents, and nearly a quarter of a million faithful.

MARGINAL CHURCHES. Jehovah's Witnesses have made extraordinary progress since their entry in 1900. They are strong in Athens but are also found in many of Greece's smaller towns and villages. At present there are over 400 congregations with a total Christian community greater than that of any other non-Orthodox body including the Catholic Church.

CATHOLIC CHURCH. Roman Catholicism is represented in Greece by 3 rites (Latin, Byzantine, and Armenian), of which the Latin is the most important. There are 9 Latin ecclesiastical divisions and one each for the Byzantine and Armenian rites. There have been Latin Catholics in Greek territories since the time of the Crusades, especially on the Ionian Islands and the islands of the Aegean Sea where Genoan and Venetian merchants lived. Under Turkish occupation in the years following the Crusades, ancient Catholic episcopal sees fell into disuse. After the 19th-century Greek struggle for independence, the Catholic archdiocese of Athens was restored in 1875. The vicariate of Salonica (Thessaloniki) was created in 1926 following the annexation of Turkish territories in eastern Thrace, and today a majority of Latin Catholics are again scattered among the islands.

The establishment of Catholic parishes and the apostolic exarchate of the Byzantine rite dates from

**Church of Crete, Diocese of Kissamos & Selinos.** *Above.* 'Christ is risen!'. In 1972, Bishop Ireneos (an active protagonist of lay renewal) with 6 priests celebrates Easter liturgy in small monastery outside Orthodox academy. *Above right.* Bishop baptizes an infant. On left, present Metropolitan of Kydonia & Apocoronos (Chania).

the arrival in Greece of Greeks formerly living in Turkey, particularly in that part of Europe in dispute during the Greco-Turkish war of 1922. The total number of refugee Greeks was 1.5 million among whom Catholics of the Byzantine rite constituted only a small minority of 2,000, including a few priests and a bishop. In 1972 its 2 parishes and one quasi-parish (2 in Athens, and one at Yannitsa in Macedonia) were responsible for serving members widely dispersed throughout the whole country. Nine chapels are in use, most of which are located in the houses of Pammakaristos sisters and Little Sisters of Jesus under the jurisdiction of the Greek Catholic exarch. The exarchate has played an important role in moving Latin Catholics in the direction of ecumenism. It has also developed a network of institutions for philanthropic works, publications and news services out of all proportion to its very modest membership of lay and religious personnel.

Armenian-rite Catholics also came to live in Greece after the Greco-Turkish war of 1922. The 2 Armenian parishes are located in Athens but serve dispersed families across the entire country.

Of the 45,000 Catholics living in Greece, about 80% belong to the worker and peasant classes. Little by little the number of Catholic students, intellectuals and businessmen is increasing, which presents the church with a novel challenge.

PROTESTANT CHURCHES. The 2 main Protestant denominations are the Greek Evangelical Church and the Free Evangelical Churches of Greece, founded respectively in 1858 and 1908. The former is Presbyterian in structure while the latter is more congregational in polity. A number of smaller evangelical bodies exist, some being of Greek origin while others are of foreign background. Greek-Americans have also had an impact on the development of Protestantism. The Armenian Evangelical Church entered Greece following the Greco-Turkish war of 1922 and is now divided into 3 parishes. Eight different Greek and foreign Pentecostal bodies, the first being the Church of God of Prophecy in 1927, make up a Pentecostal community of slightly over 7,000. Seventh-day Adventists were the first foreign missionaries to work in Greece, but as with most Protestant groups, their progress has been slow. Rules regarding proselytism are very strict in Greece, and Protestants have been imprisoned for attempting to share their faith with Greek Orthodox. Protestant clergy, both foreign and Greek, are permitted to minister only to their own faithful.

**CHURCH AND STATE.** The national constitution of 1 January 1952 began: 'In the name of the Holy, Consubstantial and Indivisible Trinity.... The established religion in Greece is that of the Eastern Orthodox Church of Christ...'. That of 15 November 1968, amended by the constitutional Act of 1 June 1973 which installed the presidential Republic, stipulates that 'The dominant religion is that of the Eastern Orthodox Church of Christ' (Article 1, paragraph 1) and that this church 'is indissolubly united, as to dogma, to the Great Church of Christ at Constantinople and to every other *homodoxe* (of the same faith) Church of Christ. She observes immutably, as do they, the sacred apostolic and synodal canons concerning dogma and worship as well as the holy traditions. She is autocephalous, exercises her sovereign rights independently of every other Church and is administered by a Holy Synod of Bishops' (Article 1, paragraph 2).

The constitutional guarantee of the administrative independence of the Orthodox Church contains an essential recognition of its sanctifying spiritual acts, in which any state intervention would be inadmissable. The constitutional recognition of the Eastern Orthodox Church as 'dominant' does not signify the sovereignty of this church over other confessions or religions, but rather the fact that this is the religion of the majority of Greece's citizens. Nevertheless, this 'dominant' character of the Orthodox Church gives it a special significance, implying on the one hand obligatory stipulations concerning the person of the head of state and on the other the granting by the state to the Orthodox Church of a series of privileges guaranteed by the constitution and by legislation promulgated later in the same vein.

The president and vice-president of the Greek republic must profess the religion of the Orthodox Church (Article 33), and their own oaths are taken according to the rites of this church (Article 36, paragraphs 2–3). Moreover, the calendar of state holidays and their official ceremonies are fixed to correspond with the feast days of this same church.

In the chapter dealing with the privileges granted to the Orthodox Church are mentioned the following: (1) the prohibition of proselytism and anything else detrimental to the official religion (Article 1, paragraph 1) which implies a certain right of surveillance over the activities of other confessions; (2) the unchanging conservation of the Greek text of the Holy Scriptures (Article 1, paragraph 4); (3) the recognition of the Orthodox Church of Greece as autocephalous (Article 1, paragraph 2); and (4) the

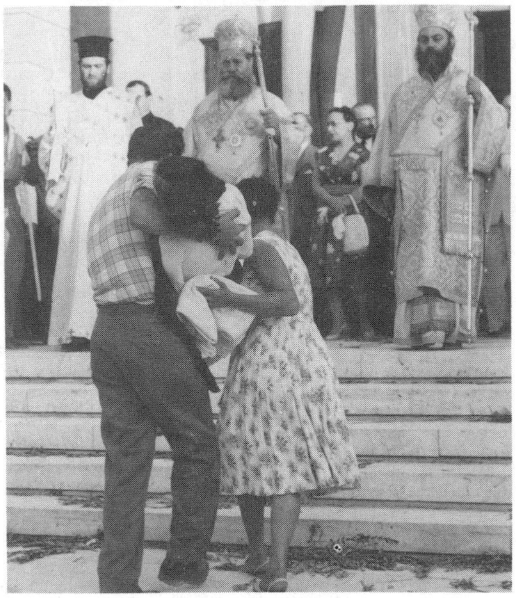

**Church of Greece, Diocese of Zakinthos (Zante).** Paralyzed woman is carried by relatives to bishop in search of miraculous healing. Every 24 August the well-preserved body of patron saint Dyonisios, a 17th-century abbot, is paraded on the island, and sick and crippled persons come from all over Greece to lie in the streets. Many cures are attested; but in 1979 a major scandal erupted across Greece involving alleged commercialism.

requirement that the permanent Holy Synod be consulted regarding any proposed law concerning the organizations or administration of the church (Article 1, paragraph 5). This last stipulation was introduced for the first time in the constitution of 1968.

Beyond these special privileges, the Greek government provides the Orthodox Church with other forms of aid: direct material assistance to parish clergy (Law 536 of 1945, 'Concerning the organization of salary payments of the Orthodox parish clergy of Greece'), and indirect assistance by various levies of contributions and taxes for ecclesiastical purposes, tax exemptions for the church, the requirement that religious education be obligatory in elementary and middle schools, and support of faculties of theology in the universities of Athens and Salonica, as well as of schools and seminaries for the training of clergy and candidates for the priesthood (Law 671 of 1943, Article 6, paragraph 6; Law 540 of 1945 'Concerning ecclesiastical education'; Law 876 of 1971 'Concerning the responsibility of the Church of Greece for public religious education').

The recognition of the autocephalous nature of the Church of Greece signifies the proclamation by the state of the ecclesiastical and administrative independence of the Church of Greece relative to other Orthodox churches and especially to the Phanar, the Ecumenical Patriarchate of Constantinople. Nevertheless, it is necessary to note that, both by right and practice, this autonomy is not complete. The ecumenical patriarch's Tomos of 1850 recognized the detachment from his jurisdiction of the church of southern Greece whose autonomy had been proclaimed in 1833. This was effected by the Greek government which was anxious to separate the Greek clergy from the administrative jurisdiction of the Phanar since the latter had long been under pressure from the Ottoman government. The patriarchal Act of 4 September 1928 proclaimed the temporary transfer 'by procuration' *(epitropikôs)* of the dioceses of northern Greece to the Church of Greece. In this Act, which was considered by the Phanar to be a tripartite contract between itself, the Church of Greece and the Greek government, the ecumenical patriarch retained a long list of rights expressed in 10 points, imposing certain obligations on the Church of Greece. From an ecclesiastical point of view, parts of Greek territory continue to depend directly on the Phanar. This is the case of the Church of Crete, although it is governed by a special constitutional charter (Law 4149 of 1961) giving it a semi-autonomous administration and its own Holy Synod composed of the archbishop of Iraklion and 7 metropolitans. The 4 metropolitans of the Dodecanese, as well as the exarchate of Patmos with its monastery, are directly dependent upon the Phanar which also has under its spiritual jurisdiction the monastic state of the Holy Mountain of Athos. Athos is governed by a charter approved by the Greek government in 1926 and is dependent from a civil point of view on the Greek Ministry of Foreign Affairs. More recently the archbishop of Athens and All Greece, with support from the Greek government, has attempted to become even more independent of the Phanar, as have other autocephalous churches. The ecumenical patriarch has protested against this attempt to reduce his rights yet further, and the Greek civil authorities, especially the Council of State, have given heed, in part at least, to his protests.

In March 1969 the then head of state, G. Papadopoulos, placed before archbishop Hieronymos and the hierarchical synod in Athens a constitutional charter of the Church of Greece (Law 126 of 1969). The government had earlier expressed the desire that the church's hierarchy should accept a more pyramidical structure similar to that of the government and the army. The charter, described as very democratic by the archbishop, placed the responsibility for the administration of the church in the hands of both clergy and laymen. The permanent Holy Synod was constituted by the archbishop of Athens as its president, and by 10 metropolitans who were presidents of the 10 permanent synodal commissions. This synod was assisted by 20 other metropolitans (2 for each commission) and 60 specialists, mostly laymen, who were also members of the 10 commissions. Each permanent synodal commission consisted of 3 metropolitans and 4 or 6 scholars or university professors. For the first time in the history of the Church of Greece, this charter conferred on the hierarchy and on the permanent Holy Synod the power to legislate: 'Within the limits of law and according to the authority attributed to it by its holy canons, the hierarchical synod shall publish decrees and decisions of validity for the entire Church of Greece concerning questions of faith, divine worship, ecclesiastical discipline, organization and the internal government of the Church' (Articles 6, paragraph D; 10, paragraph 2 and 51, paragraph 3). Because of this, the archbishop and Holy Synod were in possession of the state seal which allowed them to promulgate and publish in the state gazette. Between 1969 and 1973, the church passed 47 regulations (Kanonismoi) having the validity of law before the courts and 46 canonical decrees (Kanonistikai Diataxeis) being equivalent to royal or presidential decrees. The texts have relevance especially for the functioning of the diverse organs of the church, its administration and its property. The charter was rescinded in September 1975.

By Law 876 of May 1971, the state placed under the jurisdiction of the Church of Greece the direction, administration and property of ecclesiastical schools, which train clergy, monks, nuns, choristers, deaconesses, nursing sisters and foreign missionaries.

Beyond the constitutional privileges of the Orthodox Church the state exercises ultimate supervision over it through the Ministry of Foreign Affairs for that which concerns the Ecumenical Patriarchate, Mount Athos, and Greek clergy in foreign lands: and especially through the Ministry of National Instruction and Religions (Hypourgeion Ethnikis Paideias kai Thriskevmaton). This latter consists of an Office for Religions (Geniki Dievthynsis Thriskevmaton), with 3 sub-offices and 3 councils: (1) Office of Ecclesiastical Government, with one section for the Church of Greece and another for the Churches of Crete and the Dodecanese; (2) Office for Ecclesiastical Instruction and Religious Education, with a section corresponding to each of its domains; (3) Office for Non-Orthodox Religions (Heterothriskon) with sections for Christians and for other religions; (4) Legal Council (Nomimophro Synis); (5) Council of Personnel for Ecclesiastical Instruction; and (6) Council for Control of Ecclesiastical Instruction.

The Minister of National Instruction and Religions represents the state during the election of an archbishop of Athens. He publishes the presidential decree by which one of the 3 candidates proposed by the Holy Synod is chosen as metropolitan of any vacant see. By virtue of Article 11 of the constitutional charter of the Church of Greece, he may participate (either personally or through the Director General for Religions), but without the right of vote, at the regular and special meetings of the hierarchical Synod and the Permanent Holy Synod. He must be invited in writing, with a list of the questions to be discussed; but the omission of the prior invitation does not make null and void the decisions taken at these meetings. Between 1972 and 1974 this minister required all bishops to ordain only priests holding a 'certificate of civics' given by the Ministry of Public Order after a security check.

On 25 November 1973 a second military coup d'état removed general Papadopoulos from power and installed in his place general Ghizikis. Three weeks later (15 December), archbishop Hieronymos of Athens resigned because of his close association with the preceding regime. The metropolitan of Ioannina, Seraphim, succeeded to the title of archbishop of Athens and primate of Greece, it being before Seraphim that Ghizikis had taken the oath of office on the day of the coup.

Following the country's return to democratic government in August 1974, a law was passed on 27 September formally annulling the charter giving the Orthodox Church of Greece the power to legislate, which had been granted in March 1969. Moreover, the Caramanlis government returned to a partial observance of the constitution of 1952; and in May 1975 a proposed new constitution was debated in parliament. This stipulates that freedom of conscience is inviolable although the dominant religion remains that of the Eastern Orthodox Church.

An analysis of the previous 7 years of military dictatorship (1967–74) makes clear that for the first time in the history of the Greek Church the episcopate became completely politicized and divided into 2 camps: one headed by Hieronymos collaborating openly with Papadopoulos; and the other centred in Seraphim. Archbishop Seraphim has not been harassed by the Caramanlis government; rather, his position has been consolidated by laws ratifying his attempt to undo what his predecessor had enforced relative to the reorganization of the church.

Other churches and confessions may seek recognition from the Office for Non-Orthodox Religions, and their clergy act as officers of the civil state. Article 1, paragraph 1, which forbids proselytism gives the Church of Greece the right of surveillance over other confessions in the following areas: a permit from the local Orthodox bishop must be obtained before construction of any non-Orthodox church; under pain of nullity, mixed marriages must be celebrated before an Orthodox priest; and special permission must be obtained from the Orthodox bishop, as well as from the Ministry of National Instruction and Religions, for the residence in Greece of foreign priests and their appointments. The Catholic Church benefits from a special situation due to the fact that the Western powers in 1821 imposed on Greece the recognition of existing Catholic dioceses. The bishops of these dioceses remain official personages and enjoy certain privileges, such as the right to hold processions of the sacraments, which are not shared by Catholic dioceses created after 1821.

In daily life the question of church-state relations is extremely complex due both to the Byzantine heritage and also to the development of Hellenic nationalism over the past century and a half. The intervention of the state in the affairs of the Orthodox Church is continual and considered natural even when not desired. These interventions are especially evidenced during church crises and are frequently accompanied by appeals from clergy and laity, especially those involved in government. Such crises have become almost endemic, particularly in recent decades, and they have been little affected by changes in government. At times the internal conflicts have been so severe that solutions are possible only by resort to the politicization of the issue and the passage of government laws.

Ultimately, therefore, the Greek state proclaims itself the guardian of the Orthodox Faith and traditions. Bishops and theologians occasionally call for the separation of church and state, but such a divorce would be extremely difficult to affect. The church meanwhile continues to experience the difficulty of trying to retain its Byzantine heritage in a modern state.

**INTERDENOMINATIONAL ORGANIZATIONS.** Relations between the Church of Greece and the Church of Rome, bad during the days of Catholic proselytism, have remained frigid since Vatican II, with periodic denunciations of Roman Catholicism by Orthodox bishops and officials. To this day, no official ecumenical organizations exist; but an Orthodox-Catholic discussion group, consisting of priests and laymen from both sides, has been meeting in Athens since 1964. The Byzantine Institute in Athens also engages in ecumenical projects of a co-operative nature. The Catholic episcopal conference does not have a special commission for ecumenism, and Protestantism is also lacking in interdenominational councils. Since 1972 all Catholics in Greece celebrate Easter on the same day as the Orthodox.

**BROADCASTING.** The National Hellenic Broadcasting Institute has regular Greek Orthodox programmes, and also accepts Roman Catholic programmes. From abroad, Trans World Radio (Monaco) broadcasts in Greek for 15 minutes daily and 30 minutes on Sundays; the Pentecostal station IBRA is also widely heard. In 1976 the Church of Greece was building its own radio station with transmitter on Mount Pendelikon east of Athens, to provide initially 3 hours daily covering Attica, Central Greece, the Peloponnese and Cyclades; a television transmitter is to follow shortly.

## BIBLIOGRAPHY


*Anatomy of a church: Greek Orthodoxy today.* M. Rinvolucri. London: Burns & Oates, 1966. 192p.

'Between partnership and separation: relations between church and state in Greece under the constitution of 9 June 1975', A. Basdekis, *Ecumenical review* (Geneva), 29, 1 (January, 1977), 52–61.

*Hemerologion tes Ekklesias tes Hellados* (Yearbook of the Church of Greece). Athens: Apostolic Service, 1977. 540p. (Annual).

'Rapports des recherches sur la sociologie religieuse en Grèce'. Athènes: EKKE, 1971. (5 papers).

'Sociology of Greek Orthodoxy', *Social compass*, XXII, 1 (1975), 1–147. (7 articles).

*Thriskeutiki kai ithiki egyklopaidia* (Religious and ethical encyclopedia). 12 vols. Athens: A. Martinos, 1962–68. (Articles on all Greek dioceses, church events, festivals, bishops, theologians, movements).


TABLE 2. ORGANIZED CHURCHES AND DENOMINATIONS IN GREECE

| Official name 1 | Begun 2 | Type 3 | Counc 4 | Congs 5 | Adults 6 | Affiliated 7 | Names, notes, and other statistics (see Codebook) 8 |
|---|---|---|---|---|---|---|---|
| Ancient Church of the East | | O Nes | Yw... | 1 | 50 | 100 | *Nestorians.* Assyrian refugees from massacres in Middle East since 1850. |
| Armenian Apostolic Church: D Athínai | 1922 | O Arm | Sw.N. | 11 | 5,000 | 11,000 | *Gregorians.* Under C Cilicia (Lebanon). 1956 schism ex C Echmiadzin. 6n,W=30%,41y. |
| Assemblies of God | 1931 | P Pe2 | ZF... | 11 | 1,150 | 2,000 | *Ekklesia tes Pentecostes.* Greek origin. M=AoG(USA). Katerini, Athens. 20n,5f,1s. |
| Authentic Old Calendar Orthodox Ch | 1924 | O OCd | c.... | 170 | 100,000 | 200,000 | *Paleohemerologites. Old Calendar Greek OC.* Ex Ch of G. In USA, Canada, 250n,81de,1100w. |
| Bulgarian Orthodox Church | | O Sla | Mwc.. | | 2,000 | 5,000 | *Balgarskata Pravoslavna Crkva.* Under P Sofia. Bulgarian residents. |
| Catholic Church in Greece: | c 300 | R LEr | OzB.R | 51 | 33,500 | 45,723 | *Katholiki Eklissia.* Declining. No proselytism. C=4+2+12. 114nx,53m,199w,435y. |
| M Corfú, Zante & Cefalonia | 1212 | R Lat | Oaa | 9 | 2,000 | 2,700 | Kérkira/Zákinthos/Kefallinía. United 1919. Ionians, Epirus. 8 0 11 16 |
| M Náxos, Andros, Tínos & Míkonos | c 850 | R Lat | Os | 2 | 2,300 | 3,135 | Tinos, c850. 3 dioceses united 1919. Cyclades isles. 7% RC. 14 0 27 26 |
| D Khíos (Chios)(Diikissis) | c1250 | R Lat | Os | 3 | 30 | 47 | On Tinos island. Northern Cyclades next to Turkey. 0 0 5 0 |
| D Santorino (Thíra) | 1204 | R Lat | Osj | 1 | 100 | 140 | Under bishop of Syra. Southern Cyclades. HQ Syra. 1 0 7 1 |
| D Síros & Mílos (Syra & Milo) | c1250 | R Lat | Osj | 11 | 5,300 | 7,235 | Covers the western Cyclades. HQ Syros. Area 36% RC. 22 4 11 97 |
| AD Athínai (Athens) | 1205 | R Lat | os | 10 | 19,000 | 26,000 | Central and south Greece, Euboea and isles. Restored 1875. 37 34 78 252 |
| AD Ródhos (Rhodes) | c 350 | R Lat | os | 4 | 300 | 421 | Archdiocese was united with Malta from 1797–1928. 2 5 2 1 |
| D Candia (Iráklion) | 1213 | R Lat | Os | 2 | 300 | 420 | Crete. Suffragan diocese of Izmir (Turkey). Under D Síros. 2 0 6 1 |
| VA Salonica (Thessaloniki) | 1926 | R Lat | Osj | 4 | 1,500 | 2,000 | Northern Greece to Turkish border. HQ Thessaloniki. 8 10 22 21 |
| EA Greece (Hellas)(*Byzantine*) | 1923 | R Byz | Os | 3 | 2,200 | 3,000 | Byzantine-rite Catholics resident in Greece. HQ Athens. 18 0 30 18 |
| O Greece (Hellas) (*Armenian*) | 1925 | R Arm | Os | 2 | 470 | 625 | Armenian-rite Catholics resident in Greece. HQ Athens. 2 0 0 1 |
| Church of Christ in Greece | 1962 | P Dis | x.... | 2 | 70 | 200 | *Ekklesia tou Kristou.* M=CC(Non-Instrumental) (USA). USA civilians, military. 5x. |
| Church of Christ, Scientist | | M Sci | x.... | 1 | 50 | 100 | *Christian Science.* M=CCS(Boston, USA). First Church, Athens. 1w. |
| Church of Crete | c 50 | O Gre | Cwc.. | 3,365 | 333,000 | 456,246 | Under EP Constantinople. A=1967. 1s(278). 766n,720b,33d(181m),11e(252w). |
| AD Kríti (Archiepiscopi Kristis) | 1967 | O Gre | Ca | 670 | 102,000 | 140,000 | Covers north central Crete. HQ Iráklion. 192 170 5 67 4 135 |
| D Gortuni & Arcadia | 1962 | O Gre | Cm | 533 | 44,000 | 60,000 | South central Crete. HQ Mirai. 83 83 4 38 1 55 |
| D Ierápetra & Sitía | 1962 | O Gre | Cm | 417 | 29,000 | 40,000 | Eastern extremity of Crete. HQ Ierápetra. 72 72 4 8 1 2 |
| D Kissamos & Selinos | 1962 | O Gre | Cm | 578 | 22,000 | 30,000 | Numerous social projects. HQ Kastelli. 81 78 1 10 2 10 |
| D Kydonia & Apocoronos | 1962 | O Gre | Cm | 480 | 66,000 | 90,000 | HQ Chania (Khaniá). Lay academy. 110 80 3 19 1 43 |
| D Labi & Sfekíon | 1962 | O Gre | Cm | 157 | 13,000 | 17,666 | West south central area. HQ Spilion. 59 75 2 9 0 0 |
| D Petra (Petras) | 1962 | O Gre | Cm | 276 | 24,000 | 33,024 | East central Crete. HQ Neapolis. 79 76 6 11 0 0 |
| D Réthimnon & Avlopotamos | 1962 | O Gre | Cm | 254 | 33,000 | 45,556 | North west centre of island. HQ Réthimnon. 90 86 8 19 2 7 |
| Church of England (D Gibraltar) | 1804 | A plu | awc.. | 3 | 1,000 | 3,000 | Chaplaincies 1836 at Athens (St Paul), 1816 Corfu (seasonal), Patras (St Andrews). 1x. |
| Church of God of Pentecost | 1952 | P Pe3 | ZF... | 3 | 108 | 300 | *Ekklesia tou Theou tou Plerous Evangelion.* M=CoG(Cleveland). 2n,W=99%,5Y,8z. |
| Church of God of Prophecy | 1927 | P Pe3 | Z.... | 3 | 120 | 300 | *Ekklesia Theou Pentecostes.* M=CGP(USA). Holiness Pentecostals (3-stage). 3n. |
| Church of God (Anderson) | 1947 | P Hol | x.... | 4 | 100 | 300 | *Ekklesia tou Theou.* M=CoG(Anderson,USA). No missionaries now. 1n,W=25%. |
| **Church of Greece:** | 50 | O Gre | CWC.. | 24,995 | 5,668,000 | 7,769,723 | *Ekklesia tes Hellados.* P=95%,11s(1297),W=26%. 7530n,7184b,144d(891m),163e(1709w). |
| Old regions (Palaiai Chorai): | 1881 | O Gre | C | 17,339 | 3,822,000 | 5,236,349 | Regions annexed to Greek state and church from Turks over period 1833–1881. |
| AD Athínai (Athens) | 50 | O Gre | Ca | 260 | 1,278,000 | 1,750,000 | *Archiepiscopi Athinon.* HQ Athens. 2s,1v. 481 185 2 150 6 59 |
| D Aitolia & Acarnania | 1922 | O Gre | Cm | 786 | 147,000 | 201,313 | Bishop's residence (HQ) Messologion. 198 210 4 4 2 14 |
| D Argolis (Argolidos) | 1189 | O Gre | Cm | 452 | 56,000 | 76,823 | Northeast Peloponnese. HQ Nafplion. 74 75 0 0 5 64 |
| D Arta (Artis) | 1922 | O Gre | Cm | 201 | 41,000 | 56,885 | West centre of Greece. HQ Arta. 81 80 2 10 2 18 |
| D Attica & Megaridos (Attikis) | 1936 | O Gre | Cm | 648 | 147,000 | 201,460 | Area all around Athens city. HQ Kifissia. 189 118 1 25 13 155 |
| D Dimitriados (Demetrias) | 1922 | O Gre | Cm | 349 | 117,000 | 160,000 | Southeastern part of Thessaly. HQ Volos. 138 130 2 10 2 22 |
| D Gortynos & Megalópolis | 1922 | O Gre | Cm | 143 | 44,000 | 60,000 | Central Peloponnese. HQ Megalópolis. 112 106 1 12 5 36 |
| D Idhra, Spetson & Egines | 1936 | O Gre | Cm | 789 | 26,000 | 35,000 | Extreme east Peloponnese. HQ Idhra (Hydra). 45 47 2 145 5 195 |
| D Ilia (Ilias) | 1899 | O Gre | Cm | 300 | 120,000 | 164,860 | Northwest Peloponnese. HQ Pyrgos. 211 203 3 20 14 90 |
| D Kalávrita & Egialia | 1923 | O Gre | Cm | 562 | 58,000 | 80,000 | In northern Peloponnese. HQ Egion. 135 150 6 70 3 30 |
| D Káristos & Skíros | 1923 | O Gre | Cm | 200 | 35,000 | 47,995 | Eastern Evvoia and Skíros island. HQ Kymi. 86 98 1 1 2 11 |
| D Kafallinía (Kefallinías) | 1790 | O Gre | Cm | 185 | 27,000 | 36,657 | Extreme western island. HQ Argostalion. 59 165 5 8 4 44 |
| D Kérkira (Corfu) & Paxoi | 1824 | O Gre | Cm | 577 | 67,000 | 92,300 | Extreme northwestern island. HQ Kerkyra. 140 148 4 18 2 16 |
| D Khalkís (Khalkidos) | 1922 | O Gre | Cm | 644 | 93,000 | 126,769 | Seminary in Khalkís monastery. HQ Khalkís. 131 129 3 25 8 52 |
| D Kíthira (Kithiron) | 1922 | O Gre | Cm | 229 | 3,000 | 4,083 | Smallest diocese (one island). HQ Chora. 14 34 0 0 0 0 |
| D Kórinthos (Kórinthias) | c 350 | O Gre | Cm | 803 | 81,000 | 111,000 | NE Peloponnese. HQ Kórinthos (Corinth). 1s. 164 149 2 4 6 76 |
| D Lárisa & Platamonos | c 650 | O Gre | Cm | 235 | 98,000 | 134,520 | In central Thessaly. HQ Lárisa. 103 105 1 6 0 0 |
| D Levkás & Itháki | 1922 | O Gre | Cm | 105 | 18,000 | 24,559 | Ithaca and western islands. HQ Levkás. 49 66 2 1 1 1 |
| D Mantinia & Kynouria | 1924 | O Gre | Cm | 576 | 51,000 | 69,397 | Centre west of Peloponnese. HQ Tripolis. 124 147 5 13 7 50 |
| D Messíni (Messinias) | 1922 | O Gre | Cm | 588 | 88,000 | 119,876 | South of Peloponnese. HQ Kalamata. 192 226 1 3 7 72 |
| D Monemvasía & Spárti | 1920 | O Gre | Cm | 896 | 44,000 | 60,000 | Southeastern part of Peloponnese. HQ Spárti. 119 141 1 8 2 20 |
| D Návpaktos & Evrytania | 1933 | O Gre | Cm | 674 | 42,000 | 57,813 | In centre of country. HQ Návpaktos. 142 181 3 3 2 11 |
| D Neas Pelagonias & ED | 1968 | O Gre | Cm | 125 | 36,000 | 50,000 | *ED=Enoplon Dynameon.* New diocese. Athens. 24 0 0 0 0 0 |
| D Nikaia (Nikeas) | 1966 | O Gre | Cm | 46 | 248,000 | 340,276 | HQ Níkaia (western suburb of Athens). 113 31 0 0 0 0 |

*Continued overleaf*

*Table 2 – continued*

| Official name 1 | Begun 2 | Type 3 | Counc 4 | Congs 5 | Adults 6 | Affiliated 7 | Names, notes, and other statistics (see Codebook) 8 |
|---|---|---|---|---|---|---|---|
| D Páronaxia (Páronaxias) | 1083 | O Gre | Cm | 538 | 17,000 | 23,000 | 2 islands. 14 vacant monasteries. HQ Naxos. 32 38 3 25 3 46 |
| D Pátrai (Pátron) | c 750 | O Gre | Cm | 264 | 110,000 | 150,000 | In north of Peloponnese. HQ Pátrai. 194 152 5 47 1 21 |
| D Phokidos | 1923 | O Gre | Cm | 198 | 30,000 | 41,310 | North of Gulf of Corinth. HQ Amphissa. 90 106 3 8 0 0 |
| D Phthiotidos | 1922 | O Gre | Cm | 775 | 113,000 | 154,720 | In southern Thessaly. HQ Lamia. 247 224 1 3 3 22 |
| D Piraiéus (Pireos) | 1962 | O Gre | Cm | 36 | 159,000 | 218,270 | New diocese. HQ Piraiéus (port of Athens). 73 27 0 0 0 0 |
| D Síros, Tínos, Andros & Kéa | 1922 | O Gre | Cm | 1,687 | 36,000 | 50,000 | HQ Ermoupolis. Population 30% Catholics. 99 125 5 14 4 97 |
| D Thessaliotis&Phanariophersala | 1921 | O Gre | Cm | 418 | 96,000 | 131,756 | In southern Thessaly. HQ Kardista. 210 203 5 4 2 7 |
| D Thíra, Amorgós & Nissa | 1814 | O Gre | Cm | 453 | 15,000 | 20,000 | Many scattered islands. HQ Thíra. 33 33 2 5 1 5 |
| D Thívai (Thebes) & Levádheia | 1922 | O Gre | Cm | 323 | 80,000 | 110,000 | In north of Attica. HQ Levadia. 99 93 3 19 5 38 |
| D Trika & Stagon | 1910 | O Gre | Cm | 527 | 91,000 | 125,300 | In west centre of country. HQ Tricala. 186 189 6 25 5 57 |
| D Triphylia & Olympia | 1922 | O Gre | Cm | 980 | 73,000 | 100,000 | In west Peloponnese. HQ Kyparissia. 127 145 1 4 4 15 |
| D Yítheion & Itylos | 1922 | O Gre | Cm | 601 | 15,000 | 20,251 | Extreme southern promontory. HQ Gythion. 74 106 1 1 1 2 |
| D Zákinthos (Zákinthou, Zante) | 1824 | O Gre | Cm | 166 | 22,000 | 30,156 | One of Ionian islands in west. HQ Zákinthos. 51 48 4 8 0 0 |
| New regions (Neai Chorai): | 1928 | O Gre | C | 7,656 | 1,846,000 | 2,533,374 | Assigned 1928 to Ch of Greece by EP Constantinople after Macedonia liberated. |
| D Alexandroúpolis | 1885 | O Gre | Cm | 69 | 40,000 | 55,366 | Thrace, also Samothrace. Many Muslims. 60 49 0 0 0 0 |
| D Dhidhimóteikhon & Orestiás | 1387 | O Gre | Cm | 112 | 59,000 | 80,800 | Extreme northeast. HQ Dhidhimóteikhon. 107 102 1 2 0 0 |
| D Dráma (Drámas) | 1359 | O Gre | Cm | 124 | 66,000 | 91,015 | In northeast along Bulgaria border. HQ Dráma. 101 100 1 11 1 9 |
| D Dryinopolis, Pogonianí, K | 1834 | O Gre | Cm | 448 | 14,000 | 19,140 | K=*Kónitsa*. Extreme NW. HQ Delrinakion. 64 98 3 6 0 0 |
| D Edhessa. Pélla & Almopia | 1922 | O Gre | Cm | 344 | 92,000 | 126,201 | Edge of Macedonia. HQ Edhessa. 129 129 2 6 2 12 |
| D Elasson (Elassonos) | 1814 | O Gre | Cm | 133 | 36,000 | 49,528 | In northern Thessaly. HQ Elasson. 47 55 1 6 0 0 |
| D Elevtheroupolis | 1889 | O Gre | Cm | 75 | 25,000 | 35,000 | East of Salonica. HQ Elevtheroupolis. 35 37 0 0 0 0 |
| D Flórina, Prespa & Eordea | 1925 | O Gre | Cm | 142 | 62,000 | 85,253 | In 1967, 200 Muslims baptized. HQ Flórina. 125 112 2 8 0 0 |
| D Grevená (Grevenon) | c1450 | O Gre | Cm | 271 | 26,000 | 35,385 | On southern edge of Macedonia. HQ Grevená. 83 101 1 4 0 0 |
| D Ierissós, Agion Oros, & A | 1932 | O Gre | Cm | 119 | 28,000 | 37,756 | *A=Ardamerios*. Mount Athos. HQ Arnea. 44 46 1 5 0 0 |
| D Ioánnina (Ioánninon) | 1319 | O Gre | Cm | 245 | 98,000 | 134,356 | Greece's richest diocese. HQ Ioánnina. 216 202 7 9 1 2 |
| D Kassándra (Kassándrias) | 1932 | O Gre | Cm | 284 | 48,000 | 65,112 | Covers Khalkidhiki. HQ Polygyros. 72 72 0 0 1 15 |
| D Kastoría (Kastorías) | 1384 | O Gre | Cm | 253 | 39,000 | 54,075 | Edge of Macedonia. HQ Kastoría. 112 106 3 5 1 14 |
| D Kateríni (Kitrous) | 1924 | O Gre | Cm | 173 | 73,000 | 100,000 | HQ Kateríni. Many Greek Evangelicals in area. 79 75 1 10 0 0 |
| D Khíos (Chios), Psará & I | 1571 | O Gre | Cm | 755 | 39,000 | 53,929 | *I=Inoussos*. 14 vacant monasteries. HQ Chios. 105 108 4 21 15 197 |
| D Langadhás | 1967 | O Gre | Cm | 55 | 37,000 | 50,100 | Orthodox fire-walking sect, Anastenarides. 44 42 0 0 0 0 |
| D Límnos & Agios Evstrátios | 1450 | O Gre | Cm | 377 | 17,000 | 23,000 | North Aegean Sea. HQ Myrina, Limnos. 28 37 0 0 0 0 |
| D Maronia (Maronias) | 1365 | O Gre | Cm | 135 | 44,000 | 60,000 | Thrace, Thasos. HQ Komotini. Many Muslims. 76 65 1 7 0 0 |
| D Mithimna (Mithimnis) | c1250 | O Gre | Cm | 108 | 19,000 | 25,996 | Northern half island of Lesbos. HQ Kalloni. 28 33 1 6 2 14 |
| D Mitilíni, Eresós & Plomárion | c 950 | O Gre | Cm | 701 | 51,000 | 70,189 | Southern half of Lesbos. HQ Mytilene. 68 61 2 11 1 15 |
| D Nicopolis & Préveza | 1881 | O Gre | Cm | 292 | 63,000 | 86,616 | Mid-western coast of Greece. HQ Préveza. 98 116 1 6 1 4 |
| D Paramithiá, Philiaton & Gir | 1895 | O Gre | Cm | 513 | 37,000 | 51,284 | In Ipeiros, in northwest. HQ Paramithiá. 121 147 2 3 0 0 |
| D Philippi, Neapolis & Thásos | 1924 | O Gre | Cm | 100 | 89,000 | 121,491 | Also called D Kavalla. HQ Kavalla. 89 75 1 9 2 23 |
| D Poliana & Kilkís | 1924 | O Gre | Cm | 156 | 68,000 | 93,500 | In Macedonia. HQ Kilkís. 149 146 1 2 0 0 |
| D Sámos & Ikaría | 1841 | O Gre | Cm | 397 | 30,000 | 41,687 | Off Turkey mainland. 11 vacant monasteries. 108 90 3 10 2 4 |
| D Sérrai & Nigríta | c1050 | O Gre | Cm | 141 | 148,000 | 202,771 | In north near Bulgaria border. HQ Sérrai. 115 111 1 17 1 4 |
| D Sérvia & Kozáni | 1882 | O Gre | Cm | 136 | 51,000 | 70,000 | In northern Thessaly. HQ Kozáni. 85 86 2 2 0 0 |
| D Sidhirókastron (Sidirokastrou) | 1913 | O Gre | Cm | 113 | 37,000 | 51,000 | Along Bulgaria border. HQ Sidhirókastron. 61 57 1 1 2 20 |
| D Sissanios & Siátista | 1855 | O Gre | Cm | 391 | 36,000 | 50,000 | Northwest, near Albania border. HQ Siátista. 59 92 3 5 0 0 |
| D Thessaloniki (Thessalonikis) | 796 | O Gre | Cm | 96 | 219,000 | 300,000 | Major city. Strong seminary and university. 131 78 2 4 1 3 |
| D Véroia & Náousa | c1350 | O Gre | Cm | 212 | 91,000 | 125,000 | Area west of Salonica. HQ Véroia. 99 94 4 12 1 6 |
| D Zánthi & Peritheorios | 1284 | O Gre | Cm | 113 | 32,000 | 43,824 | Thrace. Many Muslims in area. HQ Xáanthi. 1s. 78 79 1 1 1 6 |
| D Zichnon & Nevrokopis | 1924 | O Gre | Cm | 73 | 32,000 | 44,000 | Northeast, near Bulgaria. HQ Nea Zichni. 75 70 7 4 2 15 |
| Ch of Jesus C of Latter-day Saints | | M LdS | x.... | | 100 | 126 | *Mormons*. M=CJCLdS(USA). Mostly USA expatriates and military personnel. |
| Church of the Dodecanese: | c 60 | O Gre | Cwc.. | 788 | 85,800 | 117,517 | Under EP Constantinople. Off Turkey mainland. 159n,138b,4d(9m),6e(80w),1s(12). |
| D Kárpathos & Kásos | 1948 | O Gre | Cm | 48 | 5,800 | 8,000 | 3 islands SW of Rhodes. 2 disused monasteries. 18 18 0 0 0 0 1 |
| D Kos (Cos) | 1838 | O Gre | Cm | 142 | 12,100 | 16,561 | Single island 5 km from Turkey. HQ Kos. 25 17 0 0 1 5 3 |
| D Léros, Kálimnos & Astipalea | 1888 | O Gre | Cm | 100 | 16,100 | 22,000 | HQ (winter) Léros. (summer) Kálimnos. 29 26 2 4 5 75 1 |
| D Ródhos (Rhodes) | c 450 | O Gre | Cm | 498 | 51,800 | 70,956 | 22 monasteries (20 disused). Many Muslims. 87 77 2 5 0 0 7 |
| Free Apostolic Church of Pentecost | 1965 | P Pen | ..... | 6 | 400 | 1,500 | *Eleuthera Apostolike Ekklesia Pentecostes*. Greek origin. 1n(Athens). |
| Free Evangelical Churches of Greece | 1908 | P CBr | K.... | 40 | 1,000 | 3,000 | *Eleuthera Evangelike Ekklesia*. *Brethren*. Ex state church. 10n,2f,1p.W=70%, 40Y. |
| German Evangelical Church | 1837 | P LuR | ..... | 7 | 400 | 700 | Serving German-speaking community, mostly expatriates. 1x,G=6%pa, W=12%,34Yy,20z. |
| Greek Bible Centre | 1964 | P ind | ..... | 2 | 60 | 200 | *Hellenikon Kentron Biblou*. Greek origin, few expatriate links. 2n(Athens). |
| Greek Evangelical Church | 1858 | P Ref | RWC.. | 32 | 3,000 | 9,000 | *Hellenike Evangelike Ekklesia*. HQ Athens. 18n,G=4%pa,1p(Katerini),W=80%,50Yy,250z. |
| Gypsy Evangelical Movement | | P Pe2 | x.... | 5 | 500 | 1,500 | Nomadic caravan communities. Large meetings round Thessalonica. M=GGMS(Switzerland). |
| Internat Ch of the Foursquare Gospel | 1946 | P Pe2 | ZF... | 16 | 148 | 500 | M=ICFG(USA). Classical Pentecostals (2-stage). 11 national workers, 2f,W=41%,8Y. |
| Jehovah's Witnesses | 1900 | M Jeh | x.... | 409 | 15,753 | 50,000 | Many in Athens, also throughout country. State hostility: banned till 1972. 545Y. |
| Monastic Republic of Mount Athos | c 350 | O Gre | Cwc.. | 20 | 1,233 | 2,687 | *Agion Oros*. Under Ecumenical Partriarchate. 20d(1,233 monks; once 40,000; u,970 in 1913),1. |
| New Apostolic Church | | C CAp | x.... | | 500 | 1,000 | *NAC*. In Wiesbaden Bezirk (District); world HQ Dortmund (Germany). Germans. |
| Oriental Apostolic Church | 1947 | P Hol | xF... | 5 | 30 | 50 | *Anatolike Apostolike Ekklesia*. Foreign origin. M=Oriental MS(USA). 5n. |
| Patriarchal Exarchate of Pátmos | 1088 | O Gre | Cwc.. | 62 | 2,400 | 3,246 | Under EP Constantinople. 11n,7b,1d(St John the Divine: 28m),3e(64w),1s(10). |
| Seventh-day Adventist Ch, Greek Mission | 1903 | P Adv | x.... | 10 | 296 | 500 | *Adventistai tes Evdomes Hemeras*. 5n, 1x,G=2%pa,1j,1p,16t(314),W=80%,18Y. |
| Union of Armenian Ev Chs in Near East | 1923 | P Con | Rw.N. | 3 | 300 | 1,000 | *Armenike Evangelike Ekklesia*. Armenian residents. 1n (in Piraeus). 2 schools. |
| Other Protestant denominations | | P | ..... | 10 | 6,000 | 12,000 | Total about 20 (see list below), including USA military chaplaincies. |
| Other Orthodox churches | | O | ..... | | 500 | 1,000 | Including: Russian Orthodox Ch (16 monks on Mount Athos). |
| Doubly-affiliated (duplication) (1970) | | | | | –80,300 | –110,000 | Minority church members still enumerated as baptized Orthodox in state church. |
| **Total affiliated (mid-1970)** | | | | **30,040** | **6,182,268** | **8,589,518** | **Total denominations (1970) . . . 51.** |
| **Total affiliated (mid-1975)** | | | | **30,150** | **6,261,300** | **8,699,390** | **Total denominations (1975) . . . 53.** |
| **Total affiliated (mid-1980)** | | | | **30,300** | **6,348,600** | **8,820,600** | **Total denominations (1980) . . . 56.** |

NOTES ON TABLE ABOVE
COLUMNS: for meanings and CODES (cols. 1, 3, 4, 8), see Codebook (Part 6). Column 1: **Boldface type** = church with over 10% of country's affiliated Christians.
SOURCES AND DATES OF STATISTICS. Churches of Crete, Greece, Dodecanese. Survey for year 1971 by E. Loupassakis, EKKE, Athens.
NATIONAL COUNCILS (Column 4, 5th letter).
R = Catholic Episcopal Conference of Greece (Synodos Katholikis Ierarchias Ellados).
*Other national councils*. Panhellenic (Greek) Evangelical Alliance.
OTHER PROTESTANT DENOMINATIONS. There are a large number of bodies catering for USA civilians, also USA military chaplaincies. Foreign chaplaincies include Christus Kirche, Kifissia Protestant Chapel, St Andrew's American Ch. Other groups with some Greek membership include: American Mission to Greeks (1942), Bible Christian Union, Children of God International (discotheque in Athens), Christadelphian Ecclesias, Ch of the Brethren (1951), Corfu Evangelistic Association, Exclusive Brethren (Kelly-Continental), Gospel Missionary Union (1959), Greek Ev Mission (1920)/Greater Europe Mission (Greek Bible Institute/Society of Biblical Studies), Independent Pentecostal Ch, Southern Baptist Convention (1972), Swedish Free Mission, Trinity Baptist Ch, United Pentecostal Ch (1975).

**PEOPLES** (ethnolinguistic). Christians: 96.7% Greek (1.2% Turkish-speaking), 1.8% Macedonian, 0.6% Aromanian (Vlach), 0.4% Albanian, 0.1% Armenian, 0.1% Bulgar, 0.1% Gypsy, 0.1% USA (military and dependants), 0.1% British, Russian, Assyrian, et alii.

COUNTRY-WIDE TOTALS
EVANGELIZATION (see Part 5). 1900: 96%. 1970: 100%. 1980: 100%. *Mass evangelism*. 1977: a campaign organized by Orthodox charismatics, Crusade for Christ in Athens. *Radiophonic evangelism*. Radio IBRA (Pentecostal) is widely heard, and large numbers of tracts and scriptures are mailed in response to listeners' requests.
FOREIGN MISSIONARIES AND PERSONNEL (nationals serving abroad) (1973). Total 196 Orthodox (mostly bishops and priests) in 37 countries.
FOREIGN MISSIONARIES AND PERSONNEL (aliens from abroad) (1973). Total 377. *From Western world*. 253: about 180 Roman Catholics, 51 Protestants (40 in 20 USA societies, 5 in 2 UK societies, 3 in 1 WGermany society, 2 in 1 Denmark society, 1 in 1 Canada society), about 20 Orthodox, 1 Anglican, 1 Catholic (non-Roman). *From Communist world*. 118 Orthodox (108 monks, 10 priests; 61 from Romania, 26 Yugoslavia, 16 USSR, 9 Bulgaria). *From Third World*. 6: 5 Orthodox mainly from Cyprus, 1 Protestant.
INSTITUTIONS (church-operated) (1973). Total 540, including 23 higher schools (3 minor seminaries), 3 medical centres (2 hospitals), 470 monasteries, 1 radio station, 8 research centres, 15 seminaries (14 Orthodox, 1 Protestant).
PERIODICALS. About 90 titles.
PERSONNEL. About 14,007 (13,630 national, 377 foreign).
RELIGIOUS LIBRARIES. About 500, mostly small.
SCRIPTURE DISTRIBUTION (1975). Annual totals: 24,492 Bibles (9% free, 50% subsidized, 41% commercial), 87,283 NTs (77% subsidized, 23% commercial), 58,784 UBS portions, 27,486 UBS selections.
SERVICE AGENCIES. About 60, including CEF, CRS, CWS, EEM, LWR, OC, OCIC, SCA, SU, URG, YMCA, YWAM, YWCA.

ADDITIONAL DATA ON CHURCHES
AUTHENTIC OLD CALENDAR ORTHODOX CHURCH. In Greek, Palaioimerologitai; or Ekklesia Gnesion Orthodoxon Cristianon tes Ellados. Although schismatic from the Church of Greece, these Orthodox are in relation with the other Old Calendar patriarchates (Jerusalem, Moscow, Sofia, Belgrade). Numbers have declined in recent years; in 1955 some 1.5 million were claimed. They maintain a widespread hierarchy of bishops, and number among their monasteries the Old Calendarist Convent of Our Lady at Keratea in Attica, founded in 1925, with about 280 nuns. Total monks 230, nuns 1,100.
CATHOLIC CHURCH IN GREECE. The church has declined from 200,000 in 1850 to 46,000 in 1970. Its former active proselytizing finally ceased in 1945. *Annual baptisms*. (1972) 100% infants, no adults. *Personnel*. About half nationals, half expatriates. *Priests* (1972). 35 diocesan, 66 religious. *Seminary*. The Greek College in Rome, Italy. *Religious orders and congregations* (1973). Priests: 18 SJ, 12 OFMCap, 8 AA, 6 CM. Brothers: 31 FSC, 22 PFM. Sisters: 33 Ursulines, 29 Pammakaristos (Byzantine-rite), 27 St-Joseph de Marseille, 23 St-Vincent de Paul, 8 Dominicans, 8 Carmelites, 5 Petites Soeurs de Jésus (Byzantine-rite), and 24 sisters in several other congregations. *Catholic organizations*. The Catholic Episcopal Conference of Greece (Synodos Katholikis Ierarchias Ellados) is a member of CCEE (Council of European Bishops' Conferences). For religious communities, the Union of Religious Personnel of Greece (URG) was formed in 1974. Although no pastoral or presbyteral councils exist, there is a Pastoral Commission (Pimantiki Epitropi), composed of 7 priests (2 being religious) and one bishop, which meets twice yearly. In addition, informal joint meetings of hierarchy and clergy are held. The only organization of the lay apostolate active in Greece is Pax Romana. Inter-rite Catholic institutions include 8 elementary and 8 secondary schools.

The Holy See had no diplomatic relations with Greece until 1977 when a concordat was being drawn up to establish relations for the first time in history.

Latin Catholic institutions in 1972 included one hospital at Salonica with 160 beds, one home for girls in Athens and another in preparation at Kiphissia near Athens, an orphanage for boys at Maroussi near Athens, a domestic science school on the island of Tinos, a rug factory to provide work for poor Catholic girls on the island of Santorini, and 2 homes for the elderly. Jesuits direct a centre for the study of culture called Dionysius the Areopagite Scientific Conference Centre (Kentron Epistimonikon Omilion Dionysios Areopagitis), which since January 197073as published a Greek scientific review *Problems of theology*. In l)s19 Catholics retained links with 19 primary schools (3,487 ph upi and 18 secondary schools (6,928).

Byzantine Catholics sponsor Caritas Greece which is affiliated with Caritas Internationalis in Rome and is responsible for a hospital with 190 beds to which is attached a school of mercy, a hostel for university students, 2 hostels for 180 students and young workers, an orphanage joined to a small seminary, a hostel for refugee girls, a boarding school for girls, a home for the aged and some holiday camps. All these works are located in Athens or its vicinity except the last which are at Vourla. For the most part they are open to anyone without distinction of religion. The Office of the Good Press (Bureau de la Bonne Presse), the only Catholic publishing house in Greece, has published 250 books and pamphlets since its founding in 1936, as well as an international religious information weekly, *Katholiki*, which is the only Catholic news journal in Greece. It maintains 2 bookshops in Athens and Salonica.
CHURCH OF GREECE. *Column 1*. Names of dioceses in modern orthography are followed in parentheses by the often-used Greek genitive form 'of . . .'. Boundaries of dioceses do not correspond exactly with political boundaries. *New dioceses*. In 1974, 2 new dioceses were formed in the New Territories: Néa Krini & Kalamaria, and Néapolis & Stavropolis. After 1974: D Kaisariane, Vyron & Hymettos; D Mégara & Salamis; D Mesogaia & Laureotica; D Néa Ionia & Néa Philadelphia; D Néa Smyrna; D Peristérion. *Column 5*. For the 3 Churches of Crete, Greece and the Dodecanese, the grand total of 29,148 includes 8,049 parish churches and 20,063 chapels. *Column 8*. Of the 7,530 active priests, 6,865 were married, 665 celibate; 504

were category A (university theology graduates), 2,261 were B (graduates of major seminary), 3,267 were C (2 years in minor seminary), and 1,498 were D (primary school education only); there were also 1,019 retired priests. In addition to the 1,297 seminarians, there were 312 theological students in the University of Athens and 311 in the University of Thessaloniki. *Brotherhoods.*

(1) Zoe (Adelphotes Theologon He Zoe, begun 1907); members fell from 135 in 1959 to 50 by 1970; periodical with 100,000 circulation. (2) Sotir (Adelphotes Theologon Ho Soter, a 1960 split from Zoe by 3 brothers); members 70 in 1968; 2 periodicals with 170,000 circulation. *Bishops.* In addition to active bishops, in 1970 a further 16 (23%) were in retirement.

CHURCH OF CRETE. In Greek, Ekklesia tes Kretes. Of the 766 priests, 676 were married, 90 celibate; 40 were category A (see above), 488 B, 119 C, 119 D.
CHURCH OF THE DODECANESE. Of the 159 priests, 152 were married, 7 celibate; 8 were category A (see above), 25 B, 58 C, 68 D.

# GREENLAND

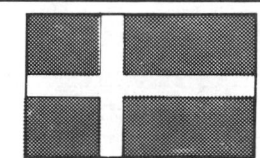

## SECULAR DATA

**STATE. Official name:** Greenland (Gronland).
**Flag** (shown above right): That of Denmark.
**Area:** 2,175,600 sq.km. (840,000 sq.miles). Agricultural land: 0.01%.
**Government:** Self-governing overseas area of the Kingdom of Denmark, since 1953.
**Legislature:** Landsrad (Provincial Council).
**Official languages:** Greenlandic, Danish (*Dansk*).
**Capital:** Godthaab 3,585 (1965).

**Foreign forces** (1973): 1,000 USA troops.

**DEMOGRAPHY. Population:** 46,531 (census of 31.XII.1970. For 1970–2000 (UN), see last row of Table 1). Population density (1975): 0/sq.km. Under 15 years: 46%. Growth rate (1975–80): 1.78% per year. Household size: 5.0 persons.
**Major languages:** Greenlandic, Danish, English.
**Labour force:** 40%.

**ETHNOLINGUISTIC GROUPS:** 79.1% Greenlander (Eskimo, with some Eskimo/Danish), 13.6% Danish, 6.0% USA military (3,000) (White, Black).

**MONEY** (1977). **Monetary unit:** Danish krone (= 100 ore); US$1 = DKr 6.1.
**National income per person:** US$3,000. Average annual family income: US$15,000.
**HEALTH.** Hospitals: 18 (666 beds). Doctors: 42.

**LITERATURE.** Periodicals: 2. Newspapers: 22 non-daily.

**COMMUNICATION** (per 1,000 people). Radios: 157.

### TABLE 1. RELIGIOUS ADHERENTS IN GREENLAND

| Year | 1900 | | mid-1970 | | Annual change, 1970–1980 | | | | mid-1975 | | mid-1980 | | 2000 | |
|---|---|---|---|---|---|---|---|---|---|---|---|---|---|---|
| Name | Adherents | % | Adherents | % | Natural | Conversion | Total | Rate | Adherents | % | Adherents | % | Adherents | % |
| Christians | 10,530 | 90.0 | 49,200 | 98.4 | 1,183 | 17 | 1,200 | 2.14 | 56,180 | 98.6 | 61,200 | 98.7 | 76,970 | 98.7 |
| professing | 10,530 | 90.0 | 49,200 | 98.4 | 1,183 | 17 | 1,200 | 2.14 | 56,180 | 98.6 | 61,200 | 98.7 | 76,970 | 98.7 |
| Protestants | 10,530 | 90.0 | 49,050 | 98.1 | 1,179 | 13 | 1,192 | 2.13 | 55,990 | 98.2 | 60,970 | 98.3 | 76,560 | 98.2 |
| Marginal Protestants | 0 | 0.0 | 100 | 0.2 | 3 | 3 | 6 | 4.62 | 130 | 0.2 | 160 | 0.3 | 300 | 0.4 |
| Roman Catholics | 0 | 0.0 | 50 | 0.1 | 1 | 1 | 2 | 3.33 | 60 | 0.1 | 70 | 0.1 | 110 | 0.1 |
| nominal | 1,170 | 10.0 | 14,120 | 28.2 | 342 | 31 | 373 | 2.30 | 16,240 | 28.5 | 17,850 | 28.8 | 23,400 | 30.0 |
| affiliated | 9,360 | 80.0 | 35,080 | 70.2 | 841 | −14 | 827 | 2.07 | 39,940 | 70.1 | 43,350 | 69.9 | 53,570 | 68.7 |
| total practising | 8,420 | *90* | 24,560 | *70* | 589 | −11 | 578 | 2.07 | 27,960 | *70* | 30,340 | *70* | 32,140 | *60* |
| non-practising | 940 | *10* | 10,520 | *30* | 252 | −3 | 249 | 2.08 | 11,980 | *30* | 13,010 | *30* | 21,430 | *40* |
| Protestants | 9,360 | 80.0 | 34,930 | 69.9 | 837 | −18 | 819 | 2.06 | 39,750 | 69.7 | 43,120 | 69.5 | 53,160 | 68.2 |
| Evangelicals | 4,700 | 40.2 | 4,000 | 8.0 | 95 | −10 | 85 | 1.89 | 4,500 | 7.9 | 4,850 | 7.8 | 5,850 | 7.5 |
| Marginal Protestants | 0 | 0.0 | 100 | 0.2 | 3 | 3 | 6 | 4.62 | 130 | 0.2 | 160 | 0.3 | 300 | 0.4 |
| Roman Catholics | 0 | 0.0 | 50 | 0.1 | 1 | 1 | 2 | 3.33 | 60 | 0.1 | 70 | 0.1 | 110 | 0.1 |
| Shamanists | 1,170 | 10.0 | 500 | 1.0 | 10 | −23 | −13 | −2.83 | 460 | 0.8 | 370 | 0.6 | 230 | 0.3 |
| Baha'is | 0 | 0.0 | 200 | 0.4 | 5 | 3 | 8 | 3.33 | 240 | 0.4 | 280 | 0.5 | 400 | 0.5 |
| Non-religious | 0 | 0.0 | 100 | 0.2 | 2 | 3 | 5 | 4.17 | 120 | 0.2 | 150 | 0.2 | 400 | 0.5 |
| Country's population | 11,700 | 100.0 | 50,000 | 100.0 | 1,200 | 0 | 1,200 | 2.11 | 57,000 | 100.0 | 62,000 | 100.0 | 78,000 | 100.0 |

**COLUMNS, ROWS.** For meanings and definitions, see Codebook (Part 6). Note that, by definition, total 'Christians' = professing + crypto-Christians, which also = affiliated + nominal Christians. Percentages may not always total exactly, due to rounding.
**CENSUSES.** The religion question has not been asked.

**NOTES ON RELIGIONS**
**CHRISTIANS.** Virtually all Greenlanders are baptized Christians, the last known adult baptism of a heathen Eskimo having taken place in Thule in 1934. Only a small residue of traditional religion remains in the remote north.
**COUNTRY'S POPULATION.** The totals, being of de facto population, include 3,000 USA troops from 1970 onwards.
**NON-RELIGIOUS.** Danish and North Americans.
**PROTESTANTS.** Including a number of expatriate USA military and civilians.
**SHAMANISTS.** Non-Christian Eskimos still following traditional Eskimo religion are few in number, mainly in the remote north.

**NON-CHRISTIAN RELIGIONS.** Although most native Greenlanders have become Christians, a residue of traditional Eskimo religion remains. This includes a vague belief in a supreme being, Tornarsuk (the Great Tornak). However, the principal place in popular devotion is held by a female divinity, the Old Woman of the Sea, variously called Nerrivik or Sedna.

## CHRISTIANITY

PROTESTANT CHURCHES. The first Christians were brought by the Norse leader Lief Ericson around AD 990. The Lutheran Church of Greenland, organized in 1721, is an integral part of the Evangelical Lutheran Church of Denmark and retains the allegiance and fidelity of the majority of the population. Church services are popular and festive occasions and enjoy considerable community support. The church is divided into 18 clerical districts with 26 priests and 174 lay catechists. Because of the difficulties of travel, catechists assume important clerical responsibility. The administrative head of the church is the dean of Greenland who lives at Godthab and works under the bishop of Copenhagen.

In view of the special conditions of the country, the dean's authority is great and corresponds to that of a bishop. Regular synods consisting of all pastors make recommendations which carry considerable weight. Committees of lay representatives have consultative voice in dealing with their local pastors and with the dean. Secularization is growing with the increase in higher education in Danish, but at present it has much less influence than in Denmark.

Pentecostals, Adventists, Brethren and others have begun work in Greenland, but their influence at present is small.

CATHOLIC CHURCH. Roman Catholicism came to Greenland in 1960. Its work consists of a single parish (the largest in the world in area, with one of the smallest memberships), confided to the Oblates of Mary Immaculate, forming part of the diocese of Copenhagen. There is one church at Godthab with a total membership of 50 Catholics in 1970 (60 in 1975) of whom half are at Godthab and the others widely dispersed. Most are Danish, plus a few foreigners and 2 foreign priests. The community also includes 3 Greenlanders, 2 of whom were converted outside the country, and a priest converted in Denmark during studies and ordained in 1963. The latter was appointed director of Radio Greenland in 1974. The Catholic clergy co-operate in existing cultural and social activities following the traditions of the Protestant pastors of Greenland. The first mass in the Greenlandic language was celebrated in May 1973.

CHURCH AND STATE. With the exception of the activity of Moravian missionaries between 1732 and 1900, the Lutheran Church had a monopoly on Christian work during the colonial period. With

**Pentecostal Churches.** *Above.* Zionsborg, a mission station at Holsteinsborg built by Swedish missionaries in 1965. On steps, *Centre,* a 70-year-old

woman Greenlander converted in 1956, and now mission administrator.

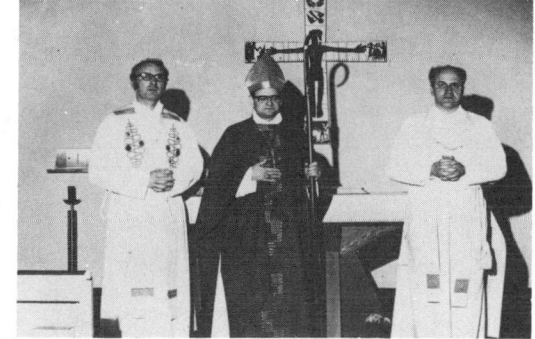

**Catholic Church.** Blessing of parish church of Greenland in 1972 by Catholic Bishop of Copenhagen, a Danish Jesuit.

the promulgation of the Danish constitution in 1953, Greenland obtained the freedom of religion prevailing in the rest of the Danish kingdom. Nevertheless, certain special regulations indicate a continuing close relation between the Danish Folkekirke and the state, in Greenland, although there are no taxes and thus no church tax. Administrative questions come under the jurisdiction of the Ecclesiastical

Commission of Greenland (Gronlandskei Kirkenaeun), including the governor and the dean, which is responsible to the Danish Ministry of Ecclesiastical Affairs (Kirkeministeriet). The church's final legislative and financial authority is parliament and its highest administrative authority is thus a political minister.

### INTERDENOMINATIONAL ORGANIZATIONS.
There are no ecumenical organizations in Greenland, but the good relations between Catholics and Lutherans in Denmark (both being members of the Ecumenical Council of Denmark) have had an important influence on the ecumenical climate in Greenland.

#### TABLE 2.    ORGANIZED CHURCHES AND DENOMINATIONS IN GREENLAND

| Official name 1 | Begun 2 | Type 3 | Counc 4 | Congs 5 | Adults 6 | Affiliated 7 | Names, notes, and other statistics (see Codebook) 8 |
|---|---|---|---|---|---|---|---|
| Catholic Church (D Kobenhavn) | 1960 | R Lat | b.BQ. | 1 | 30 | 50 | *Katolske Kirke.* Godthab. Part of Bispedommet Kobenhavn. M=OMI. Danish. 1n,2x. |
| Jehovah's Witnesses | c1950 | M Jeh | x.... | 2 | 39 | 100 | *Watch Tower. International Bible Students Association.* First witnessing 1955. |
| Lutheran Church of Greenland | 1721 | P Lut | Lwc.. | 91 | 25,000 | 34,000 | *Ilagit Kalatdlit Luterikussut.* D Kobenhavn. Eskimos. 26n,174m,G=0,1s,W=50%,1485Yy. |
| Pentecostal Churches | c1952 | P Pe2 | z.... | 3 | 100 | 500 | *Zionmenigheden.* M=Elim(Denmark),SFM(Sweden),NPY(Norway). HQ Julianehab. |
| Seventh-day Adventist Church | 1953 | P Adv | x.... | 1 | 1 | 30 | *SDA, Greenland Mission.* West Nordic Union Conf. HQ Godthab. 1m,1h,W=99%,2Y,8z. |
| Other Protestant denominations | | P | ..... | 3 | 250 | 400 | Total 4; Apostolic Ch, Brethren (1970), from Faeroe Is), USA military chaplaincy. |
| **Total affiliated (mid-1970)** | | | | **101** | **25,429** | **35,080** | Total denominations (1970) . . . 9. |
| **Total affiliated (mid-1975)** | | | | **103** | **28,950** | **39,940** | Total denominations (1975) . . . 9. |
| **Total affiliated (mid-1980)** | | | | **105** | **31,420** | **43,350** | Total denominations (1980) . . . 9. |

**NOTES ON TABLE ABOVE**
**COLUMNS:** for meanings and CODES (cols. 1, 3, 4, 8), see Codebook (Part 6). Column 1: **Boldface type** = church with over 10% of country's affiliated Christians.

**PEOPLES** (ethnolinguistic). Christians: 79.1% Greenlander (Eskimo), 13.6% Danish, 6.0% USA military (White, Black).

**COUNTRY-WIDE TOTALS**
EVANGELIZATION (see Part 5). 1900: 97%. 1970: 100%. 1980: 100%.

FOREIGN MISSIONARIES AND PERSONNEL (aliens from abroad) (1973). Total 17. *From Western world.* 17: 15 Protestants (7 in 2 Denmark societies, 5 in 1 Norway society, 2 in 1 Faeroes society, 1 in 1 USA society), 2 Roman Catholics.
INSTITUTIONS (church-operated) (1973). Total 2, including 1 medical centre, 1 seminary (Protestant).
PERIODICALS. 2 titles.
PERSONNEL. About 227 (210 national, 17 foreign).
RELIGIOUS LIBRARIES. 1.
SCRIPTURE DISTRIBUTION (1975). Annual totals: 170 Bibles (subsidized), 300 NTs (subsidized), 500 UBS portions,

1,000 UBS selections. *Translations completed.* Eskimo: portion in 1744, NT 1766, Bible 1900.
SERVICE AGENCIES. About 3, including YMCA.

**ADDITIONAL DATA ON CHURCHES**
LUTHERAN CHURCH OF GREENLAND. From being a Danish mission, in 1905 it became formally a church. The church is part of the Diocese of Kobenhavn, National Church of Denmark. There are 18 clerical districts, with 174 first-class catechists who are all Eskimos.

---

# GRENADA

## SECULAR DATA

**STATE. Official name:** The Dominion of Grenada. Adjective of nationality: Grenadian.
**Flag** (shown above right): Red border with yellow stars above and below green and yellow triangles; red circle with yellow star in centre; nutmeg on green triangle.
**Area:** 344 sq.km. (133 sq.miles). Description: Islands of Grenada, Carriacou and Petit Martinique. Agricultural land: 50.0%.
**Government:** Parliamentary state (constitutional monarchy), since 1974 (1815 British colony, 1967 self-governing state in association with the UK, 1974 Independence).
**Legislature:** House of Assembly, 15 members. Senate, 13 members.
**Official language:** English.
**Capital:** St George's 7,300 (1970).
**Armed forces** (1976): British.

**DEMOGRAPHY. Population:** 94,500 (census of 7.IV.1970. For 1970–2000 (UN), see last row of Table 1). Population density (1975): 280/sq.km. (727/sq mile.). Under 15 years: 47%. Growth rate (1975–80): 0.41% per year (births 3.35%, deaths −0.77%, emigrants −2.17%). Life expectancy (1975–80): 67.4 years. Household size: 4.4 persons.
**Major languages:** English, French patois.
**Urban dwellers** (1970): 14.8%. Urban growth rate (1950–70): 2.8%/per year.
**Labour force:** 27%.
**Tourists** (1969) 29,627. (1972) 37,900.

**ETHNOLINGUISTIC GROUPS:** 52.7% Black (African Negro), 42.2% Mulatto, 4.2% Indo-Pakistani (East Indian), 0.8% White (700), a few Carib (9 only 1960).

**MONEY** (1977). **Monetary unit:** EC dollar (= 100 cents); US$1 = EC$2.70.
**National income per person:** US$390. Average annual family income: US$1,716.
**Cost of living in capital** (1976): Daily cost of living: US$31.

**EDUCATION.** Adult literacy: (1946) 76%, (1975) 93%.

**HEALTH.** Hospitals: 8 (692 beds). Doctors: 21. Blind: 90. Psychotics: 800.

**LITERATURE.** Newspapers: 2 dailies.

**COMMUNICATION** (per 1,000 people). Phones: 41. Radios: 210. Daily newspaper circulation: 31 copies.

#### TABLE 1.    RELIGIOUS ADHERENTS IN GRENADA

| Year / Name | 1900 Adherents | % | mid-1970 Adherents | % | Natural | Conversion | Total | Rate | mid-1975 Adherents | % | mid-1980 Adherents | % | 2000 Adherents | % |
|---|---|---|---|---|---|---|---|---|---|---|---|---|---|---|
| Christians | 63,190 | 99.6 | 93,560 | 99.0 | 396 | −5 | 391 | 0.41 | 95,520 | 99.0 | 97,470 | 99.0 | 104,710 | 98.8 |
| professing | 63,190 | 99.6 | 93,560 | 99.0 | 396 | −5 | 391 | 0.41 | 95,520 | 99.0 | 97,470 | 99.0 | 104,710 | 98.8 |
| Roman Catholics | 36,440 | 57.4 | 60,100 | 63.6 | 256 | 77 | 333 | 0.54 | 61,760 | 64.0 | 63,430 | 64.4 | 69,540 | 65.6 |
| Anglicans | 22,480 | 35.4 | 21,390 | 22.6 | 87 | −187 | −100 | −0.48 | 20,940 | 21.7 | 20,390 | 20.7 | 20,140 | 19.0 |
| Protestants | 4,270 | 6.7 | 11,170 | 11.8 | 49 | 79 | 128 | 1.09 | 11,770 | 12.2 | 12,450 | 12.6 | 13,230 | 12.5 |
| Black indigenous | 0 | 0.0 | 500 | 0.5 | 2 | 8 | 10 | 1.82 | 550 | 0.6 | 600 | 0.6 | 800 | 0.8 |
| Marginal Protestants | 0 | 0.0 | 400 | 0.4 | 2 | 18 | 20 | 4.00 | 500 | 0.5 | 600 | 0.6 | 1,000 | 0.9 |
| nominal | 630 | 1.0 | 2,060 | 2.2 | 11 | 121 | 132 | 4.89 | 2,700 | 2.8 | 3,380 | 3.4 | 5,090 | 4.8 |
| affiliated | 62,560 | 98.6 | 91,500 | 96.8 | 385 | −126 | 259 | 0.28 | 92,820 | 96.2 | 94,090 | 95.5 | 99,620 | 94.0 |
| total practising | 56,300 | 90 | 73,200 | 80 | 308 | −101 | 207 | 0.28 | 74,260 | 80 | 75,270 | 80 | 69,730 | 70 |
| non-practising | 6,260 | 10 | 18,300 | 20 | 77 | −25 | 52 | 0.28 | 18,560 | 20 | 18,820 | 20 | 29,890 | 30 |
| Roman Catholics | 36,240 | 57.1 | 60,000 | 63.5 | 256 | 38 | 294 | 0.48 | 61,470 | 63.7 | 62,940 | 63.9 | 67,840 | 64.0 |
| Catholic pentecostals | 0 | 0.0 | 0 | 0.0 | 8 | 392 | 400 | 20.00 | 2,000 | 2.1 | 4,000 | 4.1 | 15,000 | 14.2 |
| Anglicans | 22,200 | 35.0 | 20,000 | 21.2 | 80 | −228 | −148 | −0.77 | 19,300 | 20.0 | 18,520 | 18.8 | 16,960 | 16.0 |
| Protestants | 4,120 | 6.5 | 10,300 | 10.9 | 44 | 39 | 83 | 0.78 | 10,700 | 11.1 | 11,130 | 11.3 | 12,720 | 12.0 |
| Evangelicals | 2,540 | 4.0 | 5,600 | 5.9 | 24 | 16 | 40 | 0.69 | 5,800 | 6.0 | 6,000 | 6.1 | 6,900 | 6.5 |
| Black indigenous | 0 | 0.0 | 700 | 0.7 | 3 | 7 | 10 | 1.33 | 750 | 0.8 | 800 | 0.8 | 1,000 | 0.9 |
| Marginal Protestants | 0 | 0.0 | 500 | 0.5 | 2 | 18 | 20 | 3.33 | 600 | 0.6 | 700 | 0.7 | 1,100 | 1.0 |
| Afro-American spiritists | 120 | 0.2 | 400 | 0.4 | 2 | −2 | 0 | 0.00 | 400 | 0.4 | 400 | 0.4 | 400 | 0.4 |
| Muslims | 40 | 0.1 | 220 | 0.2 | 1 | 0 | 1 | 0.41 | 220 | 0.2 | 230 | 0.2 | 340 | 0.3 |
| Ahmadis | 0 | 0.0 | 200 | 0.2 | 1 | 1 | 2 | 0.95 | 210 | 0.2 | 220 | 0.2 | 300 | 0.3 |
| Baha'is | 0 | 0.0 | 120 | 0.1 | 1 | 3 | 4 | 2.86 | 140 | 0.1 | 160 | 0.2 | 150 | 0.1 |
| Non-religious | 0 | 0.0 | 100 | 0.1 | 0 | 4 | 4 | 3.33 | 120 | 0.1 | 140 | 0.1 | 200 | 0.2 |
| Hindus | 90 | 0.1 | 50 | 0.1 | 0 | 0 | 0 | 0.00 | 50 | 0.1 | 50 | 0.1 | 100 | 0.1 |
| Other religionists | 0 | 0.0 | 50 | 0.1 | 0 | 0 | 0 | 0.00 | 50 | 0.1 | 50 | 0.1 | 100 | 0.1 |
| **Country's population** | **63,440** | **100.0** | **94,500** | **100.0** | **400** | **0** | **400** | **0.41** | **96,500** | **100.0** | **98,500** | **100.0** | **106,000** | **100.0** |

**COLUMNS, ROWS.** For meanings and definitions, see Codebook (Part 6). Note that, by definition, total 'Christians' = professing + crypto-Christians, which also = affiliated + nominal Christians. Percentages may not always total exactly, due to rounding.
**CENSUSES. 1901** Census of the British Empire (as in 1900 column above). **7.IV.1960:** 63.1% Roman Catholics, 24.7% Anglicans, 11.6% Protestants (4.0% Methodists, 3.0% SDAs, 1.7% Presbyterians, 0.9% Pentecostals), 0.4% marginal Protestants (Jehovah's Witnesses), 0.2% non-religious and other religionists.

**NOTES ON RELIGIONS**
AFRO-AMERICAN SPIRITISTS. There are numerous centres of Shango (Yoruba syncretism). Unlike in Trinidad, women predominate in its leadership. There are also a few Rastafarians (from Jamaica), Big Drum, et alia.
BAHA'IS. Growth from 1 local spiritual assembly (1964) to 6 (1973).
BLACK INDIGENOUS. In about 7 denominations in 1970 (see Table 2).
CATHOLIC PENTECOSTALS (or, Catholic charismatics). Begun 1971. Totals (mid-1975): 1,000 involved adults (over 15

years) in 25 prayer groups; total charismatic community including children, 2,000.
MUSLIMS. Of whom about 200 are Ahmadis, begun around 1955, in 1 community (world HQ Rabwah, Pakistan). Though proclaimed non-Muslim and heretical by Pakistan, Ahmadis are enumerated in this survey as Muslims and are included in totals of Muslims.
OTHER RELIGIONISTS. Including Rosicrucians (1 AMORC centre).

## NON-CHRISTIAN RELIGIONS. Afro-American

**spiritism** is widespread, with numerous centres of Shango (Yoruba syncretism), in whose leadership women play the major role.

**Baha'i** has grown somewhat in recent years to 6 local spiritual assemblies by 1973.

### CHRISTIANITY

CATHOLIC CHURCH. As the island of Grenada was settled in the mid-17th century by the French before being finally ceded to Britain in 1783, the majority of the people are Catholics. All 19 parishes are situated on Grenada island except for one parish and 4 stations in Carriacou and a station in Petit Martinique served from Carriacou. In 1956 the diocese of St George's in Grenada was erected as a suffragan of the archdiocese of Port-of-Spain (Trinidad); in 1974, it became a suffragan of Castries (St Lucia).

ANGLICAN CHURCH. The Church of England began work in 1784 shortly after the island came under British control. The diocese of the Windward Islands was formed in 1878 and is part of the Church of the Province of the West Indies. During the 20th century, Anglicans have declined gradually as a proportion of the population, from 35% in 1900 to 22% by 1975.

PROTESTANT CHURCHES. The 2 principal Protestant bodies are Methodists and Seventh-day Adventists. The Methodist Church, historically related to British Methodism, opened work in Grenada in 1789, and Adventists arrived in 1903, later initiating the South Caribbean Conference of which Grenada is a part. Small groups of Baptists, Brethren,

The capital, St George's, showing cathedral and some of the other 130 churches.

Pentecostals, Presbyterians and Salvation Army have also established congregations in Grenada. Two additional American societies have been active since 1957, the West Indies Mission and the Berean Mission.

CHURCH AND STATE. Discovered by Columbus, the Windward Islands were first under Spanish rule and Catholic influence, passing later to the French and then to the British. Grenada was granted home rule by Britain in 1967 and became independent in

1974 as a state with acknowledged religious foundations.

The constitution of 7 February 1974 declares (Schedule 3): 'Whereas the people of Grenada have affirmed that their nation is founded upon principles that acknowledge the fatherhood and supremacy of God and man's duties toward his fellow man . . .' and that they 'firmly believe that all men are endowed by the Creator with equal rights'. In Article 1 of chapter I, among the fundamental rights and freedoms enjoyed by every person in Grenada is listed 'freedom of conscience, of expression and of assembly and association'. The constitutional protection of freedom of conscience is further explained in Article 9, which allows for complete freedom of religious belief and practice and prohibits any hindrance thereof, entitles religious communities to establish and maintain schools at their own expense and to provide for religious instruction in such schools while also exempting those who do not wish to participate and prohibits the administration of oaths contrary to a person's religious convictions.

In practice, all private schools are grant-aided by the state.

INTERDENOMINATIONAL ORGANIZATIONS. The Grenada Inter-Church Council for Social Welfare includes in its membership 9 churches including Anglican and Catholic. In 1974 the formation began of a Grenada Christian Council.

The Life of Christ is often portrayed on Grenada's postage stamps: here, The Adoration of the Shepherds (Roberti), Christ crowned with Thorns (Van Dyck), and the Risen Christ (Bellini).

### TABLE 2. ORGANIZED CHURCHES AND DENOMINATIONS IN GRENADA

| Official name 1 | Begun 2 | Type 3 | Counc 4 | Congs 5 | Adults 6 | Affiliated 7 | Names, notes, and other statistics (see Codebook) 8 |
|---|---|---|---|---|---|---|---|
| Anglican Church (D Windward Isles) | 1784 | A ACa | awMRC | 30 | 7,000 | 20,000 | In CPWI, based on St Vincent. 95% West Indians (90% Black). HQ St George's. W=20%. |
| Berean Bible Church | 1957 | P int | xM... | 10 | 300 | 500 | M=BM(USA). 9 Districts. Mass campaigns in Queen's Park. 8f,1k(St George's). |
| Catholic Ch: D St George's in Grenada | c1650 | R Lat | PxNMC | 19 | 32,000 | 60,000 | 1974, suffragan of M Castries (St Lucia). C=2+1+5. 23nx,7m,26w,5r,1879Yy. |
| Christian Brethren | | P CBr | x,,,C | 7 | 350 | 700 | *Gospel Hall. Plymouth Brethren. Open Brethren.* M=CMML (USA). HQ St George's. 2f. |
| Church of God (Cleveland) | 1958 | P Pe3 | ZF,.C | 6 | 106 | 300 | Founded from Trinidad. M=CoG(Cleveland)(USA). 4 churches, 2 missions. 4n. |
| Evangelical Church of the West Indies | 1957 | P int | xM... | 5 | 200 | 500 | M=West Indies Mission(USA). Evangelical faith mission. 3f. |
| Jehovah's Witnesses | 1931 | M Jeh | x,,,, | 6 | 205 | 450 | *Watch Tower.* Including on Carriacou Island. Witnessing reported since 1932. 17Y. |
| Methodist Ch in Caribbean & Americas | 1789 | P Met | VwM,C | 10 | 1,097 | 2,000 | *MCCA.* SCaribbean Dist. M=MMS(UK). Decline from 3,600 in 1900. 2n,19m,G=−1%pa,70y. |
| Pentecostal Assemblies of the W Indies | | P Pe2 | ZF,,C | | 400 | 800 | M=PAoC(Canada). Many emigrants to UK, forming Shilo Pentecostal Fellowship. |
| Presbyterian Ch in Trinidad & Grenada | 1800 | P Ref | RWM,C | 4 | 300 | 1,000 | Black; many East Indians. In 1900, 580 adherents. HQ St George's. 1n,G=6.0%pa. |
| Salvation Army | | P Sal | xwM,C | | 200 | 500 | In Caribbean & CAmerica Territory (HQ Jamaica). HQ St George's. |
| Seventh-day Adventist Church | 1903 | P Adv | x,,,C | | 1,500 | 3,000 | *SDA.* South Caribbean Conference. Caribbean Union Conference. HQ St George's. 1r. |
| Spiritual Baptist Churches | c1900 | I pen | ,,,,, | | 200 | 400 | *Shouters, Shakers.* White robes, vestments, birettas, RC ritual, Obeah practised. |
| Other Protestant denominations | | P | ,,,,, | | 500 | 1,000 | Total about 8 (see list below). |
| Other Black indigenous churches | | I | ,,,,, | | 200 | 300 | Including: AMEC (USA), Ch of God Fellowship, New Testament Assembly, PAoW(USA). |
| Other marginal Protestant bodies | | M | ,,,,, | | 20 | 50 | Including: Unity School of Christianity (from USA; 2 churches). |
| **Total affiliated (mid-1970)** | | | | **126** | **44,578** | **91,500** | Total denominations (1970) . . . 26. |
| **Total affiliated (mid-1975)** | | | | **129** | **45,220** | **92,820** | Total denominations (1975) . . . 27. |
| **Total affiliated (mid-1980)** | | | | **132** | **45,840** | **94,090** | Total denominations (1980) . . . 28. |

**NOTES ON TABLE ABOVE**
COLUMNS: for meanings and CODES (cols. 1, 3, 4, 8), see Codebook (Part 6). Column 1: Boldface type = church with over 10% of country's affiliated Christians.
NATIONAL COUNCILS (Column 4, 5th letter).
C = Grenada Inter-Church Council for Social Welfare. *Other national councils.* Grenada Christian Council (1974, information).
OTHER PROTESTANT DENOMINATIONS. These include: Bethany Fellowship Missions (1968), Ch of Christ (Non-Instrumental), Ch of God (Anderson), Ch of Scotland, Holiness Ch, Southern Baptist Convention (1972).

PEOPLES (ethnolinguistic). Christians: 53.4% Black, 42.1% Mulatto, 3.7% East Indian, 0.8% White.

**COUNTRY-WIDE TOTALS**
EVANGELIZATION (see Part 5). 1900: 100%. 1970: 100%. 1980: 100%. *Mass evangelism.* In 1975 the Evangelistic Association, Pentecostal Assemblies of the West Indies, conducted a large crusade.
FOREIGN MISSIONARIES AND PERSONNEL (nationals serving abroad) (1973). Total 2 Black indigenous in UK.
FOREIGN MISSIONARIES AND PERSONNEL (aliens from abroad) (1973). Total 61. *From Western world.* 53: about 40

Roman Catholics, 13 Protestants in 5 USA societies. *From Third World.* 8: 5 Roman Catholics and 3 Protestants from Trinidad & Tobago.
INSTITUTIONS (church-operated) (1973). Total 9, including 7 higher schools.
PERIODICALS. About 12 titles.
PERSONNEL. About 121 (60 national, 61 foreign).
SCRIPTURE DISTRIBUTION (1975). Annual totals: 1,250 Bibles (24% free, 76% subsidized), 500 NTs (subsidized), 300 UBS portions, 1,500 UBS selections.
SERVICE AGENCIES. About 21, including CWS, GCC, HCA, SPCK, UCM, YMCA, YWCA.

**ADDITIONAL DATA ON CHURCHES**
CATHOLIC CHURCH. From 1956–74, the diocese was a suffragan of M Port of Spain (Trinidad); from 1974, of M Castries (St Lucia). *Annual baptisms.* (1972) 98.7% infant, 1.3% adult. *Priests.* In 1968, one quarter were either nationals or from the Antilles. In 1970, 4 were secular, 17 religious. *Foreign religious orders and congregations.* Priests: 13 OP (English province), 7 SPS. Brothers: 4 Presentation Brothers of Ireland. Sisters: 13 St Joseph of Cluny, 5 Corpus Christi Carmelites, 5 Sisters of the Sorrowful Mother, 4 Sisters of the Immaculate Heart of Mary, 4 Benedictine Sisters (Cloistered).

*Catholic organizations.* The diocese is a member of the Antilles Episcopal Conference (AEC), with its headquarters in Kingston, Jamaica, and through it is a member of CELAM. Religious personnel are represented on the Conference of Major Superiors of the Antilles, which belongs to CLAR and also has its seat in Jamaica. Both a pastoral council and a senate of priests have been formed. The principal lay movements are Catholic Scouts and Guides, Catholic Youth Organization, Holy Childhood Association, Legion of Mary, Society of St Vincent de Paul, Children of Mary and Union of Catholic Mothers.
The Holy See has no diplomatic relations with Grenada. It is

represented to the Catholic hierarchy by an apostolic delegate based in Port-au-Prince, Haiti.
Total institutions in 1974 were 30 primary schools with 15,470 pupils, including one each on Carriacou and Petit Martinique, 6 secondary schools with 1,112 pupils, one other school, 6 nurseries, one house for social and charitable work in Carriacou called Madonna House, one home economics training centre and a home for the sick and aged.
SPIRITUAL BAPTIST CHURCHES. Also found in St Vincent, and Trinidad & Tobago.

---

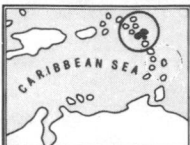

# GUADELOUPE

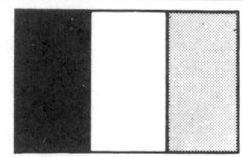

## SECULAR DATA

**STATE. Official name:** The Department of Guadeloupe and Dependencies (Le Département de la Guadeloupe et Dépendances).
**Flag** (shown above right): That of France.
**Area:** 1,779 sq.km. (687 sq.miles). **Description** (Guadeloupe): 2 islands. Agricultural land: 41.6%. |

**Government:** Overseas department of France, since 1946 (1635 French colony).
**Official language:** French (*Français*).
**Chief cities:** seat of government, Basse-Terre 15,690; economic capital, Point-à-Pitre 29,520.
**Dependencies:** Marie Galante, Les Saintes, Désirade, St Barthélemy, St Martin.

**DEMOGRAPHY. Population:** 312,724 (census of 16.X.1967. For 1970–2000 (UN), see last row of Table 1). Population density (1975): 199/sq.km. (515/sq.mile). Under 15 years: 43%. Growth rate (1975–80): 1.51% per year (births 2.80%, deaths −0.61%, emigrants −0.68%). Life expectancy (1975–80): 70.7 years. Household size: 4.4 persons.
**Major languages:** French, French Creole, Tamil.
**Urban dwellers** (1970): 47.6%. Urban growth rate (1950–70): 3.2% per year.
**Labour force:** 34%.
**Tourists:** Over 100,000 annually.

**ETHNOLINGUISTIC GROUPS:** 77% Creole (Mulatto; Black/French), 10% Black (African Negro), 10% Guadeloupe Mestizo (French/Amerindian), 2% White (French), 1% East Indian (Tamil), Syrian.

**MONEY** (1977). **Monetary unit:** French franc (= 100 centimes); US$1 = Fr 5.00.
**National income per person:** US$1,100. Average annual family income: US$4,840.
**Inflation:** (1970–74) 9.2% per year.
**Cost of living in capital** (1976): Daily cost of living: US$43.

**EDUCATION.** Adult literacy: (1954) 65%, (1967) 83%. Schools: 380 (337 primary, 43 secondary).

**HEALTH.** Hospitals: 25 (3,566 beds). Doctors: 174. Lepers: 2,150 (6.1 per 1,000). Blind: 90. Psychotics: 2,800.

**LITERATURE.** Newspapers: 2 dailies.

**COMMUNICATION** (per 1,000 people). Phones: 56. Radios: 80. TV sets: 32. Daily newspaper circulation: 144 copies.

---

TABLE 1.　RELIGIOUS ADHERENTS IN GUADELOUPE

| Year / Name | 1900 Adherents | % | mid-1970 Adherents | % | Annual change, 1970–1980 Natural | Conversion | Total | Rate | mid-1975 Adherents | % | mid-1980 Adherents | % | 2000 Adherents | % |
|---|---|---|---|---|---|---|---|---|---|---|---|---|---|---|---|
| **Christians** | 180,000 | 98.9 | 319,500 | 97.4 | 5,251 | −135 | 5,116 | 1.49 | 344,230 | 97.2 | 370,660 | 97.0 | 464,900 | 94.3 |
| professing | 180,000 | 98.9 | 319,500 | 97.4 | 5,251 | −135 | 5,116 | 1.49 | 344,230 | 97.2 | 370,660 | 97.0 | 464,900 | 94.3 |
| Roman Catholics | 180,000 | 98.9 | 314,000 | 95.7 | 5,153 | −207 | 4,946 | 1.46 | 337,830 | 95.4 | 363,460 | 95.1 | 453,600 | 92.0 |
| Evangelical Catholics | 0 | 0.0 | 10,900 | 3.3 | 193 | 207 | 400 | 3.15 | 12,700 | 3.6 | 14,900 | 3.9 | 25,100 | 5.1 |
| Spiritist Catholics | 1,800 | 1.0 | 3,000 | 0.9 | 49 | 1 | 50 | 1.56 | 3,200 | 0.9 | 3,500 | 0.9 | 4,000 | 0.8 |
| Protestants | 0 | 0.0 | 5,500 | 1.7 | 98 | 72 | 170 | 2.66 | 6,400 | 1.8 | 7,200 | 1.9 | 11,300 | 2.3 |
| nominal | 900 | 0.5 | 3,500 | 1.1 | 72 | 164 | 236 | 4.99 | 4,730 | 1.3 | 5,860 | 1.5 | 14,800 | 3.0 |
| affiliated | 179,100 | 98.4 | 316,000 | 96.3 | 5,179 | −299 | 4,880 | 1.44 | 339,500 | 95.9 | 364,800 | 95.5 | 450,100 | 91.3 |
| doubly-affiliated | 0 | 0.0 | −12,400 | −3.8 | −221 | −219 | −440 | 3.03 | −14,500 | −4.1 | −16,800 | −4.4 | −30,000 | −6.1 |
| total practising | 152,230 | 85 | 221,200 | 70 | 3,625 | −209 | 3,416 | 1.44 | 237,650 | 70 | 255,360 | 70 | 292,560 | 65 |
| non-practising | 26,870 | 15 | 94,800 | 30 | 1,554 | −90 | 1,464 | 1.44 | 101,850 | 30 | 109,440 | 30 | 157,540 | 35 |
| Roman Catholics | 179,100 | 98.4 | 312,000 | 95.1 | 5,109 | −359 | 4,750 | 1.42 | 334,900 | 94.6 | 359,500 | 94.1 | 443,700 | 90.0 |
| Protestants | 0 | 0.0 | 11,400 | 3.5 | 200 | 150 | 350 | 2.67 | 13,100 | 3.7 | 14,900 | 3.9 | 23,100 | 4.7 |
| Evangelicals | 0 | 0.0 | 4,600 | 1.4 | 78 | 32 | 110 | 2.16 | 5,100 | 1.4 | 5,700 | 1.5 | 7,400 | 1.5 |
| Marginal Protestants | 0 | 0.0 | 5,000 | 1.5 | 91 | 129 | 220 | 3.67 | 6,000 | 1.7 | 7,200 | 1.9 | 13,300 | 2.7 |
| Non-religious | 0 | 0.0 | 2,900 | 0.9 | 51 | 67 | 118 | 3.48 | 3,390 | 1.0 | 4,080 | 1.1 | 14,600 | 3.0 |
| Muslims | 2,000 | 1.1 | 3,000 | 0.9 | 49 | 1 | 50 | 1.56 | 3,200 | 0.9 | 3,500 | 0.9 | 4,400 | 0.9 |
| Atheists | 0 | 0.0 | 2,000 | 0.6 | 38 | 62 | 100 | 4.00 | 2,500 | 0.7 | 3,000 | 0.8 | 7,400 | 1.5 |
| Baha'is | 0 | 0.0 | 500 | 0.2 | 9 | 5 | 14 | 2.46 | 570 | 0.2 | 640 | 0.2 | 1,500 | 0.3 |
| Other religionists | 0 | 0.0 | 100 | 0.0 | 2 | 0 | 2 | 1.82 | 110 | 0.0 | 120 | 0.0 | 200 | 0.0 |
| **Country's population** | 182,000 | 100.0 | 328,000 | 100.0 | 5,400 | 0 | 5,400 | 1.53 | 354,000 | 100.0 | 382,000 | 100.0 | 493,000 | 100.0 |

---

**COLUMNS, ROWS.** For meanings and definitions, see Codebook (Part 6). Note that, by definition, total 'Christians' = professing + crypto-Christians, which also = affiliated + nominal Christians. Percentages may not always total exactly due to rounding.
**CENSUSES.** The religion question has not been asked.

**NOTES ON RELIGIONS**
ATHEISTS. Communist Party of Guadeloupe (legal; pro-Soviet): membership (1970) 3,000; Communist voters (election of 23.VI.1968) 21,100 (39% of all votes). Many party members are also practising or professing Catholics.

BAHA'IS. In 5 local spiritual assemblies (1973). Missionaries from Haiti are at work.
DOUBLY-AFFILIATED. The term covers those affiliated to, or claimed by, both the Catholic Church and also a Protestant or marginal Protestant church, i.e. baptized Catholics who have recently joined other churches. Because their statistics represent a duplication, they are shown in the table as a negative quantity (with a minus sign).
EVANGELICAL CATHOLICS. This term is used here to describe persons who are affiliated to churches termed by the state Evangélique (Protestant or marginal Protestant churches), but who are regarded by state and society as, or profess publicly

to be, Roman Catholics.
MUSLIMS. Immigrants from other islands, and Syrians.
NON-RELIGIOUS. Largely metropolitan French and French Creoles.
OTHER RELIGIONISTS. Including Rosicrucians (1 AMORC centre).
SPIRITIST CATHOLICS. This term describes the East Indian community, who are Roman Catholics but who follow a hybrid Hindu-Catholic spirit-possession cult whose chief deity is Malieman (the Virgin Mary, and also Mari-amma the Tamil goddess of disease from South India).

---

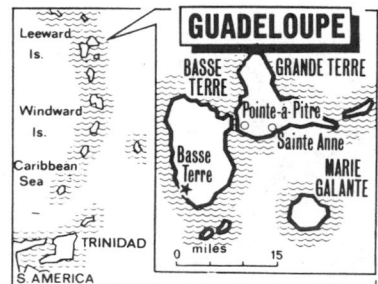

## CHRISTIANITY

CATHOLIC CHURCH. Colombus discovered Guadeloupe in 1493, opening the way for Catholic penetration of the island. In 1523 the first missionaries were killed by Carib Indians but their place was taken by Dominicans, Capuchins, Jesuits and Carmelites during the 17th century. A prefecture apostolic for Guadeloupe and Martinique was formed in 1816, and in 1850 the island became a suffragan diocese of Bordeaux in France. Almost the whole of the population are baptized Catholics,

**Eglise Catholique, Diocèse de Basse-Terre.** Centenary of consecration and dedication of Basilica of Our Lady of Guadeloupe, in Place St François, 11 December 1977. *Right.* Vast crowd outside during service. (See opposite, top).

but magical and superstitious practices continue. In 1960, 37% of women and 15% of men in the territory actively practised the Catholic religion. Anti-clericalism and atheism have subsequently continued to spread, especially among youth, intellectuals and in the liberal professions.

The first indigenous priests were ordained in 1925 and now number 40 of which 10 are serving outside Guadeloupe. There are also 189 local sisters, of whom 102 work in other countries: Martinique (44), France (45), French Guiana (6), Algeria, Haiti and Ecuador.

PROTESTANT CHURCHES. The oldest Protestant Church in Guadeloupe is that of the Moravians who began Protestant missionary work in the Antilles. Since World War II a number of new North American-based missionary societies have entered, including the Church of God (Cleveland), Pentecostal Assemblies of Canada, Seventh-day Adventists and West Indies Mission. Of these the most successful have been the latter two.

CHURCH AND STATE. The official laws of Guadeloupe relating to church and state are the same as those of metropolitan France. In the context of its general policy of departmentalization and to deal with the demand for autonomy which is very strong in Guadeloupe, the French government has long insisted on the maintenance of a Catholic hierarchy of French metropolitan origin. However, since August 1970 the diocese has been under a native bishop who made notable public statements of a liberal nature at the time of the strike of agricultural workers in 1971. The Presbyteral Council also intervened in similar fashion, thus reflecting the development of a more independent attitude on the part of the Catholic Church with regard to state patronage.

During a recent visit by French president Giscard

**Eglise Catholique.** Concelebration of liturgy in Basilica on Centenary (centre, Bishop Oualli of Guadeloupe).

d'Estaing, the bishop submitted to him a document prepared by the Justice and Peace Commission, which called attention to the difficulties of the people of Guadeloupe. For having made allusion to this document during the 15-minute weekly Catholic radio programme, Catholic officials were later publicly rebuked by the station administration, and the government later put this radio and TV time in the hands of known Catholic traditionalists.

BROADCASTING. The only network Radiodiffusion Télévision Française allows religious programmes. Protestant and Catholic programmes are each broadcast for half an hour every Sunday.

TABLE 2.    ORGANIZED CHURCHES AND DENOMINATIONS IN GUADELOUPE

| Official name 1 | Begun 2 | Type 3 | Counc 4 | Congs 5 | Adults 6 | Affiliated 7 | Names, notes, and other statistics (see Codebook) 8 |
|---|---|---|---|---|---|---|---|
| Assemblées de Dieu | | P Pe2 | ZF... | | 200 | 500 | M=PAoC(Canada), Assemblées de Dieu(France). Radio work. 2f(1x). |
| Association des Egls de la Guadeloupe | 1947 | P int | xM... | 9 | 1,500 | 3,000 | *Association of Churches in Guadeloupe.* M=West Indies Mission(USA). 14f,1s. |
| Eglise Adventiste du Septième Jour | 1965 | P Adv | x.... | 23 | 3,277 | 5,000 | *Seventh-day Adventists.* In Franco-Haitian UM. 6nx,43mw,1r,42t(4444),182Y. |
| **Eglise Catholique: D Basse-Terre** | 1635 | R Lat | PxRMr | 75 | 178,000 | 312,000 | *Catholic Ch.* Suffragan M Fort-de-France. C=1+1+10. 33n,80x,25m,224w,W=30%,8794Yy. |
| Eglise de Dieu | 1946 | P Pe3 | ZF... | 5 | 102 | 200 | M=Ch of God (Cleveland)(USA). Guadeloupe: 2 congs; St Martin: 3 congs. 4n. |
| Eglise Evangélique de la Guadeloupe | | P Ref | ....C | 18 | 700 | 2,000 | *Protestant Ch.* French missionaries and military chaplains to French personnel. 12nx,9m. |
| Eglise Morave | | P Mor | xwM.. | | 100 | 200 | *Moravian Ch.* Immigrants from other Moravian areas in Caribbean. |
| Témoins de Jéhovah | c1935 | M Jeh | x.... | 20 | 1,705 | 5,000 | *Jehovah's Witnesses. Watch Tower. IBSA.* Active witnessing under way by 1940. 210Y. |
| Other Protestant denominations | | P | ..... | | 200 | 500 | Including: Ch of the Nazarene, Southern Baptist Convention (1964), Streams of Power. |
| Doubly-affiliated (duplication)(1970) | | | | | −7,070 | −12,400 | Evangelicals who also are or were baptized Roman Catholics. |
| Total affiliated (mid-1970) | | | | 167 | 178,714 | 316,000 | Total denominations (1970) . . . 12. |
| Total affiliated (mid-1975) | | | | 170 | 192,000 | 339,500 | Total denominations (1975) . . . 13. |
| Total affiliated (mid-1980) | | | | 173 | 206,300 | 364,800 | Total denominations (1980) . . . 14. |

NOTES ON TABLE ABOVE
COLUMNS: for meanings and CODES (cols. 1, 3, 4, 8), see Codebook (Part 6). Column 1: **Boldface type** = church with over 10% of country's affiliated Christians.
NATIONAL COUNCILS (Column 4, 5th letter).
   C = member of Fédération Evangélique de France (Evangelical Federation of France).
   r = member of Conférence Episcopale de France (Episcopal Conference of France).

PEOPLES (ethnolinguistic). Christians: 77.1% Mulatto (Creole), 10% Black, 10% Guadeloupe Mestizo (French/Amerindian), 2% White (French), 0.9% East Indian (Tamil).

COUNTRY-WIDE TOTALS
EVANGELIZATION (see Part 5). 1900: 100%. 1970: 100%. 1980: 100%. *Radiophonic evangelism.* HCJB, RVOG, Christ Vous Appelle (Assemblées de Dieu, France).
FOREIGN MISSIONARIES AND PERSONNEL (nationals serving abroad) (1973). Total 112 Roman Catholics (10 priests, 102 sisters) (50 in France, 48 Martinique, 6 French Guiana, Algeria, Haiti, Ecuador).
FOREIGN MISSIONARIES AND PERSONNEL (aliens from abroad) (1973). Total 281. *From Western world.* 270: 246 Roman Catholics, 24 Protestants (20 in 3 USA societies, 2 in 1 France society, 2 in 1 Canada society). *From Communist world.* 1 Roman Catholic from Poland. *From Third World.* About 10 Roman Catholics, mainly from Martinique.

INSTITUTIONS (church-operated) (1973). Total 21, including 16 higher schools (1 minor seminary), 1 research centre, 2 seminaries (Protestant), 1 study centre.
PERIODICALS. About 10 titles.
PERSONNEL. About 1,671 (1,390 national, 281 foreign).
RELIGIOUS LIBRARIES. 4.
SCRIPTURE DISTRIBUTION (1975). Annual totals: 10,000 Bibles (90% subsidized, 10% commercial), 1,200 NTs (17% subsidized, 83% commercial), 3,700 UBS portions, 18,000 UBS selections.
SERVICE AGENCIES. About 15, including CDTCG, CEF, JEC, JOC, MRJC.

ADDITIONAL DATA ON CHURCHES
EGLISE CATHOLIQUE. The diocese, also called D Basse-Terre & Pointe-à-Pitre, or D Guadeloupe, was erected in 1850. *Annual baptisms.* (1972) 99.9% infant, 0.1% adult. *Priests.* Nationals are in majority Mulattoes, mixed Black/French, and Blacks or Whites born in Guadeloupe. In addition to nationals shown here, 10 others work abroad. Expatriate priests are mostly from France (CSSp). *Brothers.* Including 1 national and 1 Martinique national. *Sisters.* 81 nationals, mostly Black or mixed. In 1971 there were 89 other national sisters serving in other countries including France; by 1974, the total of local sisters serving abroad had risen to 102 (45 in France, 44 Martinique, 6 Guyana, Algeria, Haiti, Ecuador). *Seminarians.* 8 studying in France. *Catechists.* Total (1970) 1,200. Training: Centre Diocésain d'Enseignement Religieux (Pointe-à-Pitre). *Indigenous religious*

*congregations.* None. *Main foreign congregations.* Priests: CSSp. Brothers: FSC. Sisters: St-Paul de Chartres, St-Joseph de Cluny, Tiers-Ordre de St-Dominique de Ste-Catherine de Sienne à Albi (Dominicaines d'Albi).
*Catholic organizations.* The diocese is a member of the Episcopal Conference of France (Conférence Episcopale de France), and the ecclesiastical province of Martinique-Guadeloupe-French Guiana has been a member with consultative voice of the Antilles Episcopal Conference since February 1971. There are no associations of religious personnel, although a Commission de la Pastorale des Religieuses does exist. A Pastoral Council was created in 1964 composed of appointed priests, followed by the formation of a Presbyteral Council in 1966, the majority of whose members are elected. The National Bureau of Works and Movements (Direction Nationale des Oeuvres et des Mouvements) co-ordinates lay activities, the most active being such youth groups as Scouts, JEC, JOC and MRJC.

The Holy See has no diplomatic relations with Guadeloupe. It is represented to the Catholic hierarchy by an apostolic delegate based in Port-au-Prince, Haiti.

The Catholic Church supervises 15 primary schools, 4 secondary, 4 technical, 3 domestic science and 2 trades schools containing in all 5,510 students. Religious sisters work in 5 hospitals and in other government medical institutions. The Centre for Study and Social Action (CEAS) is a research institution devoted to economic, political and social affairs.

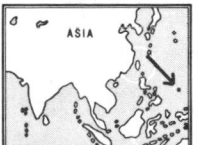

# GUAM

## SECULAR DATA

STATE. Official name: The United States Territory of Guam.
Flag (shown above right): Territorial seal on blue field bordered in red.
Area: 549 sq.km. (212 sq.miles). Agricultural land: 36.4%.
Government: Self-governing unincorporated territory of the USA, since 1950 (1668 Spanish colony, 1898 US colony).
Legislature: Unicameral, 21 seats.

Official language: English.
Capital: Agaña 2,119 (1970).
Foreign forces (1973): 17,000 USA troops.

DEMOGRAPHY. Population: 84,996 (census of 1.IV.1970. For 1970–2000 (UN), see last row of Table 1). Population density (1975): 180/sq.km. (467/sq.mile). Under 15 years: 44%. Growth rate (1975–80): 2.69% per year (births 3.49%, deaths −0.79%).

Life expectancy (1975–80): 63.8 years. Household size: 5.8 persons.
Major languages: English, Chamorro, Filipino, Korean.
Urban dwellers (1970): 8.0%. Urban growth rate (1950–70): 10.9% per year.
Labour force: 38%.
Refugees: 1975, vast influx from Viet Nam.
Tourists (1969): 34,745. (1970): 50,000. (1973): 213,960.

**ETHNOLINGUISTIC GROUPS:** 44% Guamanian (Chamorro/Spanish/Mexican/Filipino), 33% USA military (31% White, 2% Black), 13% Filipino (Ilocan), 10% foreign worker (9,000, mostly Korean), Chinese.

**MONEY** (1977). **Monetary unit:** US dollar (= 100 cents). **National income per person:** US$4,200. Average annual family

income: US$24,360.
**Cost of living in capital** (1976): Daily cost of living: US$44.

**EDUCATION.** Adult literacy: 90%. Education rate: 95%. Schools: 33.

**HEALTH.** Hospitals: 1 (242 beds). Doctors: 37. Lepers: 500

(5.0 per 1,000). Blind: 150.

**LITERATURE.** Periodicals: 14. Newspapers: 2 dailies, 5 non-daily.

**COMMUNICATION** (per 1,000 people). Phones: 402. Radios: 1,100. TV sets: 110. Daily newspaper circulation: 240 copies.

### TABLE 1.    RELIGIOUS ADHERENTS IN GUAM

| Year | 1900 | | mid-1970 | | Annual change, 1970–1980 | | | | mid-1975 | | mid-1980 | | 2000 | |
|---|---|---|---|---|---|---|---|---|---|---|---|---|---|---|
| Name | Adherents | % | Adherents | % | Natural | Conversion | Total | Rate | Adherents | % | Adherents | % | Adherents | % |
| Christians | 9,610 | 99.8 | 84,800 | 96.4 | 2,415 | 45 | 2,460 | 2.57 | 95,650 | 96.6 | 109,400 | 96.8 | 176,600 | 96.0 |
| professing | 9,610 | 99.8 | 84,800 | 96.4 | 2,415 | 45 | 2,460 | 2.57 | 95,650 | 96.6 | 109,400 | 96.8 | 176,600 | 96.0 |
| Roman Catholics | 9,610 | 99.8 | 70,000 | 79.5 | 1,988 | −4 | 1,984 | 2.52 | 78,740 | 79.5 | 89,840 | 79.5 | 142,140 | 77.3 |
| Protestants | 0 | 0.0 | 13,500 | 15.3 | 388 | 36 | 424 | 2.76 | 15,350 | 15.5 | 17,740 | 15.7 | 30,360 | 16.5 |
| Marginal Protestants | 0 | 0.0 | 500 | 0.6 | 16 | 14 | 30 | 4.62 | 650 | 0.7 | 800 | 0.7 | 2,200 | 1.2 |
| Anglicans | 0 | 0.0 | 500 | 0.6 | 14 | −2 | 12 | 2.14 | 560 | 0.6 | 620 | 0.5 | 1,000 | 0.5 |
| Filipino indigenous | 0 | 0.0 | 300 | 0.3 | 9 | 1 | 10 | 2.86 | 350 | 0.4 | 400 | 0.4 | 900 | 0.5 |
| nominal | 0 | 0.0 | 257 | 0.3 | 12 | 42 | 54 | 10.86 | 500 | 0.5 | 800 | 0.7 | 3,700 | 2.0 |
| affiliated | 9,610 | 99.8 | 84,543 | 96.1 | 2,403 | 3 | 2,406 | 2.53 | 95,150 | 96.1 | 108,600 | 96.1 | 172,900 | 94.0 |
| total practising | 9,130 | 95 | 68,480 | 81 | 1,946 | 3 | 1,949 | 2.53 | 77,070 | 81 | 87,970 | 81 | 129,680 | 75 |
| non-practising | 480 | 5 | 16,060 | 19 | 457 | 0 | 457 | 2.53 | 18,080 | 19 | 20,630 | 19 | 43,220 | 25 |
| Roman Catholics | 9,610 | 99.8 | 70,000 | 79.5 | 1,983 | −56 | 1,927 | 2.45 | 78,500 | 79.3 | 89,270 | 79.0 | 138,760 | 75.4 |
| Protestants | 0 | 0.0 | 13,000 | 14.8 | 375 | 43 | 418 | 2.81 | 14,850 | 15.0 | 17,180 | 15.2 | 29,440 | 16.0 |
| Evangelicals | 0 | 0.0 | 6,070 | 6.9 | 174 | 19 | 193 | 2.80 | 6,900 | 7.0 | 8,000 | 7.1 | 13,800 | 7.5 |
| Marginal Protestants | 0 | 0.0 | 743 | 0.8 | 22 | 17 | 39 | 4.35 | 890 | 0.9 | 1,130 | 1.0 | 2,800 | 1.5 |
| Anglicans | 0 | 0.0 | 500 | 0.6 | 14 | −2 | 12 | 2.14 | 560 | 0.6 | 620 | 0.5 | 1,000 | 0.5 |
| Filipino indigenous | 0 | 0.0 | 300 | 0.3 | 9 | 1 | 10 | 2.86 | 350 | 0.4 | 400 | 0.4 | 900 | 0.5 |
| Shamanists | 0 | 0.0 | 1,000 | 1.1 | 18 | −68 | −50 | −7.14 | 700 | 0.7 | 500 | 0.4 | 400 | 0.2 |
| Non-religious | 0 | 0.0 | 700 | 0.8 | 20 | 0 | 20 | 2.53 | 800 | 0.8 | 900 | 0.8 | 2,000 | 1.1 |
| Baha'is | 0 | 0.0 | 500 | 0.6 | 16 | 14 | 30 | 4.62 | 650 | 0.7 | 800 | 0.7 | 2,000 | 1.1 |
| Other religionists | 20 | 0.2 | 1,000 | 1.1 | 31 | 9 | 40 | 3.33 | 1,200 | 1.2 | 1,400 | 1.2 | 3,000 | 1.6 |
| Country's population | 9,630 | 100.0 | 88,000 | 100.0 | 2,500 | 0 | 2,500 | 2.53 | 99,000 | 100.0 | 113,000 | 100.0 | 184,000 | 100.0 |

**COLUMNS, ROWS.** For meanings and definitions, see Codebook (Part 6). Note that, by definition, total 'Christians' = professing + crypto-Christians, which also = affiliated + nominal Christians. Percentages may not always total exactly, due to rounding.

**NOTES ON RELIGIONS**
**BAHA'IS.** Growth of local spiritual assemblies: 1964, none; 1973, 6.
**FILIPINO INDIGENOUS.** One denomination from the Philippines (see Table 2).

**NON-RELIGIOUS.** North Americans.
**OTHER RELIGIONISTS.** Mostly Korean Buddhists and Confucians, and some New-Religionists.
**SHAMANISTS.** Korean workers adhering to Korean traditional religion.

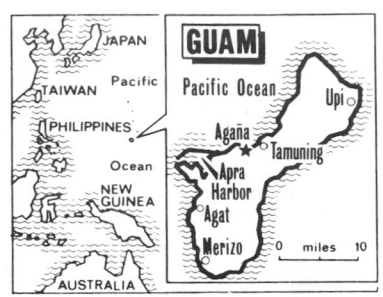

**NON-CHRISTIAN RELIGIONS. Traditional religions** have disappeared among the Guamanian indigenous population, but shamanism has been introduced through the large community of Korean immigrant workers.

**Buddhism, Confucianism** and the Korean **New Religions** all have followers among the Korean population.

**Baha'i** has a small following with 6 local spiritual assemblies.

### CHRISTIANITY

**CATHOLIC CHURCH.** The first Spanish priests arrived in 1668, and today the large majority of Guamanians are Catholics. The diocese of Agaña is a suffragan of the archdiocese of San Francisco (USA). The church's attention has recently been turned to the growing Chinese community, many

of whom have immigrated from the Ryukyu Islands since these were returned to Japan in 1972.

**OTHER CHURCHES.** Although General Baptists have been at work in Guam since 1911, no other Protestant groups entered until after World War II. The largest denominations today are Seventh-day Adventists and Southern Baptists. Two American Pentecostal groups are active, Assemblies of God and the Church of God (Cleveland), in addition to a number of small conservative and holiness groups. The Anglican mission is part of the diocese of Hawaii of the Episcopal Church in the USA.

**CHURCH AND STATE.** Guam was first discovered by Magellan in 1521, and Spain took possession of the island in 1565. Early Catholic work was closely associated with Spanish colonial conquest. Following the Spanish-American War in 1898, Guam was ceded to the USA and became a US naval base. As in all its possessions, American policy has attempted to maintain a clear line of separation between church and state. However, Protestant and Catholic chaplains serving with the armed forces are recruited and paid by government.

**BROADCASTING.** The local commercial network, KUAM Radio-TV, broadcasts a 30-minute Catholic radio news programme every Sunday morning and 2 Catholic TV broadcasts: a 30-minute religious education programme on Saturdays and a 15-minute recitation of the rosary on Sundays. Trans World Radio, with its headquarters in Monaco, has built

a superpower shortwave station on Guam, which went into operation in 1976 as TWR Pacific (KTWG/KTWR), beaming Evangelical programmes to eastern Russia, mainland China, Japan, southeast Asia, India, Australia and New Zealand. For Catholics, an association grouping Guam with the Northern Marianas is a member of UNDA.

**Catholic Church, Diocese of Agaña.** Faithful enter cathedral in Agaña for Sunday mass.

### TABLE 2.    ORGANIZED CHURCHES AND DENOMINATIONS IN GUAM

| Official name 1 | Begun 2 | Type 3 | Counc 4 | Congs 5 | Adults 6 | Affiliated 7 | Names, notes, and other statistics (see Codebook) 8 |
|---|---|---|---|---|---|---|---|
| Assemblies of God | 1960 | P Pe2 | ZF... | 3 | 300 | 1,000 | M=AoG(USA). Classical Pentecostals (2-stage). HQ Agaña. 2f. |
| **Catholic Church: D Agaña** | 1668 | R Lat | P.... | 20 | 40,000 | 70,000 | Suffragan of M San Francisco. 13% White. C=2+0+5. 55nx,6m,153w,1h,P=68%,1s,2736Yy. |
| Christian Reformed Church | 1962 | P Ref | JF... | 2 | 100 | 200 | M=CRC(USA). Small mission run by body from Grand Rapids MI (USA). 6f. |
| Church of Christ | 1969 | I ind | x.... | | 100 | 300 | M=Iglesia ni Cristo (Manalista). HQ Quezon (Philippines). Filipinos. 2f. |
| Church of Christ, Scientist | | M Sci | x.... | 1 | 25 | 50 | *Christian Science.* M=CCS(Boston,USA). Agaña Heights Society. 1w. |
| Church of God (Anderson) | 1956 | P Hol | x.... | 3 | 100 | 300 | M=CoG(Anderson) (USA). Begun by USA government teachers. Holiness body. 1t(100). |
| Church of God (Cleveland) | 1956 | P Pe3 | ZF... | 5 | 60 | 200 | M=CoG(Cleveland) (USA). Members mostly Filipino-Americans; Holiness Pentecostals. |
| Ch of Jesus C of Latter-day Saints | c1932 | M LdS | x.... | | 300 | 493 | *Mormons.* M=CJClLdS(Utah,USA). USA personnel and military. 20f,G=3.9%pa. |
| Churches of Christ | | P Dis | x.... | 3 | 300 | 500 | M=CC(Non-Instrumental)(USA). In Agaña. USA servicemen and personnel. |
| Conservative Baptist Mission | 1956 | P Bap | xF... | 1 | 120 | 200 | M=Conservative Baptist Home Mission Society(USA). 4f,22Y. |
| Episcopal Church in the USA | 1960 | A Cen | aw... | 2 | 300 | 500 | Part of Diocese of Hawaii, PECUSA. Many USA expatriates, military. W=80%. |
| General Baptist Mission | 1911 | P Bap | TF... | | 450 | 1,000 | M=GBFMS(General Association of General Baptists,USA). 6n,4f. |
| Jehovah's Witnesses | c1950 | M Jeh | x.... | 1 | 121 | 200 | *Watch Tower. International Bible Students Association.* First witnessing 1952. 14Y. |
| Pacific Ocean Mission | 1956 | P Hol | ..... | 5 | 60 | 100 | Mission from USA. Members expatriate Americans, Filipinos, Koreans. 1n,W=80%,2Y. |
| Seventh-day Adventist Church | 1948 | P Adv | x.... | 10 | 891 | 2,000 | *Far Eastern Island Mission,* Far Eastern Div. 7n,G=12%pa,2h,1r,8t(950),W=80%,89Y. |
| Southern Baptist Mission | 1961 | P Bap | T.... | 3 | 899 | 2,000 | M=SBC(USA). Sunday school enrolment 560. 10f,41Y. |
| Other Protestant denominations | | P | ..... | | 2,200 | 5,500 | Total about 6 (see list below), including USA military chaplaincies. |
| **Total affiliated (mid-1970)** | | | | 115 | 46,229 | 84,543 | Total denominations (1970) . . . 22. |
| **Total affiliated (mid-1975)** | | | | 120 | 52,030 | 95,150 | Total denominations (1975) . . . 23. |
| **Total affiliated (mid-1980)** | | | | 125 | 59,380 | 108,600 | Total denominations (1980) . . . 24. |

**NOTES ON TABLE ABOVE**
**COLUMNS:** for meanings and CODES (cols. 1, 3, 4, 8), see Codebook (Part 6). Column 1: **Boldface type** = church with over 10% of country's affiliated Christians.

**OTHER PROTESTANT DENOMINATIONS.** Including Baptist Bible Fellowship International (1975), Ch of the Nazarene (1946), Guam National Ch (Liebenzell Mission), and USA military chaplaincies.

**PEOPLES** (ethnolinguistic). Christians: 45% Guamanian, 34% USA military (32% White, 2% Black), 13% Filipino (Ilocan), 8% Korean, Chinese.

COUNTRY-WIDE TOTALS
EVANGELIZATION (see Part 5). 1900: 100%. 1970: 100%. 1980: 100%.
FOREIGN MISSIONARIES AND PERSONNEL (aliens from abroad) (1973). Total 278. *From Western world.* 245: about 200 Roman Catholics, 29 Protestants (27 in 6 USA societies, 2 in 1 WGermany society), about 15 marginal Protestants (Mormons from USA), 1 Anglican in 1 USA society. *From Third World.* 33 (about 20 Roman Catholics, 6 Protestants, about 5 marginal Protestants (Mormons), 2 indigenous) mostly from Philippines, also Korea.
INSTITUTIONS (church-operated) (1973). Total 15, including 9 higher schools (1 minor seminary), 3 medical centres, 1 radio station, 1 seminary (RC).
PERIODICALS. About 9 titles.
PERSONNEL. About 346 (68 national, 278 foreign).
RELIGIOUS LIBRARIES. 2.
SCRIPTURE DISTRIBUTION (1975). Annual totals: 300 Bibles (commercial), 12,000 NTs (87% free, 8% subsidized, 4% commercial).
SERVICE AGENCIES. About 15, including CCD, CEF, TWR, WVI, YWAM.

ADDITIONAL DATA ON CHURCHES
CATHOLIC CHURCH. The diocese, a suffragan of M San Francisco (USA), also covers the Mariana Islands and Wake Island. *Catholics.* Many are Filipinos. *Annual baptisms.* (1972) 98.9% infant, 1.1% adult. *Priests.* The first Guamanian priest was ordained in 1938 (but died in 1944). *Catechists.* Total (1969) 48. *Religious orders and congregations.* Priests: 30 SJ, 10 OFMCap. Sisters: OCD Carmelite Nuns, Franciscan Sisters of Perpetual Adoration, Religious Sisters of Mercy, Mercedarian Missionaries of Berriz, and School Sisters of Notre Dame.
*Catholic organizations.* Since D Agaña is a suffragan of M San Francisco (USA), such USA organizations as the episcopal conference, associations of religious personnel, pastoral and presbyteral bodies, and the apostolic delegation, all have jurisdiction in Guam. Catholic lay organizations include Third Order Fraternities, Holy Name Societies, Sodalities of Mary, Christian Mothers, Apostleship of Prayer, Boy and Girl Scouts of America, Confraternity of Christian Doctrine and the Cursillo Movement (Cursillos de Cristiandad). Catholic institutions include 5 elementary schools, 3 junior and 3 senior high schools, with a total enrolment of 5,079 pupils (compared with 21,000 pupils in state schools). One medical centre treats 45,500 out-patients yearly.

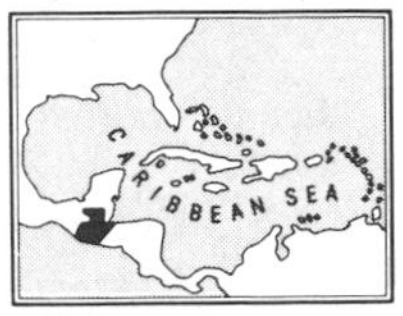


# GUATEMALA

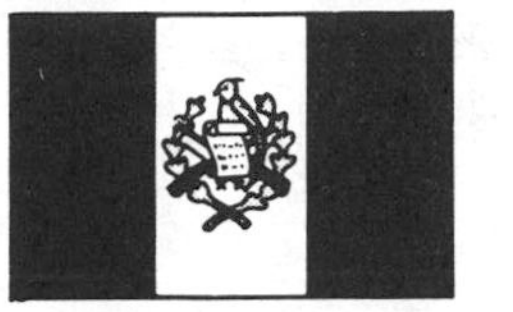

## SECULAR DATA

**STATE. Official name:** The Republic of Guatemala (La República de Guatemala). Adjective of nationality: Guatemalan (guatemalteco).
**Flag** (shown above right): Blue, white, and blue bars, national coat of arms in centre.
**Area:** 108,889 sq.km. (42,042 sq.miles). Agricultural land: 23.9%.
**Government:** Republic, since 1944 (1524 Spanish possession, 1821 Independence, many military dictatorships).
**Legislature:** National Congress, 61 members.
**Official language:** Spanish (*Español/Castellano*).
**Chief cities:** capital Guatemala City 706,920 (1973), Quezaltenango 54,500.
**Political divisions:** 22 Departments.
**Armed forces** (1976): Total 10,870 regular: army 10,000, navy 500, air force 370 (10 combat aircraft). Paramilitary forces: 3,000.

**DEMOGRAPHY. Population:** 5,175,400 (census of 26.III.1973. For 1970–2000 (UN), see last row of Table 1). Population density (1975): 56/sq.km. (146/sq.mile). Under 15 years: 46%. Growth rate (1975–80): 2.94% per year (births 4.13%, deaths −1.20%). Life expectancy (1975–80): 55.7 years. Household size: 5.2 persons.
**Major languages:** Spanish, Quiché, Cakchiquel, Mam, Kekchi, English, and 40 smaller languages.
**Urban dwellers** (1970): 31.0%. Urban growth rate (1950–70): 4.1% per year.
**Labour force:** 28%.
**Tourists** (1973): 420,000.

**ETHNOLINGUISTIC GROUPS:** 55.2% Ladino (Mestizo) (Spanish/Indian), 41.8% Maya Amerindian (13.9% Quiché, 8.5% Cakchiquel, 7.2% Mam, 5.9% Kekchi, 1.3% Pocomchi, 1.3% Tojolabali, 1.0% Ixil, 0.6% Tzutuhil, 0.5% Uspantec), 2.0% Black (African Negro), 0.9% Guatemalan White (Spanish), 0.1% Chinese (7,500), 1,500 Black Carib (Amerindian/Black), Carib, Jewish, Palestinian Arab.

**MONEY** (1977). **Monetary unit:** quetzal (= 100 centavos); US$1 = Q 1.00.
**National income per person:** US$490. Average annual family income: US$2,548.
**Inflation:** (1970–74) 7.3% per year (1975: consumer price index 168).
**Cost of living in capital** (1976): index 95 (Washington DC = 100). Daily cost of living: US$41.

**EDUCATION.** Adult literacy: (1950) 29%, (1973) 46% (3% in Indian areas). Education rate: 25%. Schools: 5,912. Universities: 4.

**HEALTH.** Hospitals: 101 (12,732 beds). Doctors: 1,208. Lepers: 600 (0.1 per 1,000). Blind: 6,000. Psychotics: 55,000.

**LITERATURE.** Annual new book titles (1973): 166. Periodicals: 93. Scientific journals: 15. Newspapers: 8 dailies, 13 non-daily.

**COMMUNICATION** (per 1,000 people). Phones: 10. Radios: 115. TV sets: 16. Daily newspaper circulation: 39 copies.

TABLE 1. RELIGIOUS ADHERENTS IN GUATEMALA

| Year | 1900 | | mid-1970 | | Annual change, 1970–1980 | | | | mid-1975 | | mid-1980 | | 2000 | |
|---|---|---|---|---|---|---|---|---|---|---|---|---|---|---|
| *Name* | *Adherents* | *%* | *Adherents* | *%* | *Natural* | *Conversion* | *Total* | *Rate* | *Adherents* | *%* | *Adherents* | *%* | *Adherents* | *%* |
| **Christians** | **1,689,700** | **99.4** | **5,262,600** | **99.3** | **178,574** | **−2,564** | **176,010** | **2.90** | **6,073,700** | **99.1** | **7,022,700** | **98.9** | **12,131,500** | **98.0** |
| professing | 1,689,700 | 99.4 | 5,262,600 | 91.9 | 178,574 | −2,564 | 176,090 | 2.90 | 6,073,700 | 99.1 | 7,022,700 | 98.9 | 12,131,500 | 98.0 |
| Roman Catholics | 1,689,200 | 99.4 | 5,032,600 | 95.0 | 170,286 | −6,066 | 164,220 | 2.83 | 5,791,800 | 94.5 | 6,674,800 | 94.0 | 11,376,500 | 91.9 |
| Christo-pagans | 1,020,000 | 60.0 | 1,430,460 | 27.0 | 46,865 | −12,411 | 34,454 | 2.16 | 1,594,000 | 26.0 | 1,775,000 | 25.0 | 2,598,000 | 21.0 |
| Evangelical Catholics | 400 | 0.0 | 103,775 | 2.0 | 4,531 | 6,492 | 11,023 | 7.15 | 154,070 | 2.5 | 214,000 | 3.0 | 621,000 | 5.0 |
| Protestants | 500 | 0.0 | 230,000 | 4.3 | 8,288 | 3,502 | 11,790 | 4.18 | 281,900 | 4.6 | 347,900 | 4.9 | 755,000 | 6.1 |
| nominal | 128,800 | 7.6 | 582,376 | 11.0 | 20,722 | 6,240 | 26,962 | 3.83 | 704,800 | 11.5 | 852,000 | 12.0 | 1,732,400 | 14.0 |
| affiliated | 1,560,900 | 91.8 | 4,680,224 | 88.3 | 157,852 | −8,804 | 149,048 | 2.78 | 5,368,900 | 87.6 | 6,170,700 | 86.9 | 10,399,100 | 84.0 |
| total practising | 1,404,810 | *90* | 3,510,170 | *75* | 118,389 | −6,604 | 111,785 | 2.78 | 4,026,670 | *75* | 4,628,020 | *75* | 7,279,400 | *70* |
| non-practising | 156,090 | *10* | 1,170,050 | *25* | 39,463 | −2,200 | 37,263 | 2.78 | 1,342,230 | *25* | 1,542,680 | *25* | 3,119,700 | *30* |
| Roman Catholics | 1,560,000 | 91.8 | 4,346,449 | 82.0 | 145,033 | −18,798 | 126,235 | 2.56 | 4,932,930 | 80.5 | 5,608,800 | 79.0 | 9,023,100 | 72.9 |
| Catholic pentecostals | 0 | 0.0 | 0 | 0.0 | 29 | 471 | 500 | 50.00 | 1,000 | 0.0 | 5,000 | 0.1 | 50,000 | 0.4 |
| Protestants | 800 | 0.0 | 266,254 | 5.0 | 9,911 | 6,064 | 15,975 | 4.74 | 337,100 | 5.5 | 426,000 | 6.0 | 990,000 | 8.0 |
| Evangelicals | 800 | 0.0 | 266,000 | 5.0 | 9,902 | 6,048 | 15,950 | 4.74 | 336,800 | 5.5 | 425,500 | 6.0 | 989,000 | 8.0 |
| Guatemalan indigenous | 0 | 0.0 | 45,950 | 0.9 | 1,982 | 2,653 | 4,635 | 6.88 | 67,400 | 1.1 | 92,300 | 1.3 | 260,000 | 2.1 |
| Marginal Protestants | 0 | 0.0 | 20,821 | 0.4 | 900 | 1,278 | 2,178 | 7.12 | 30,600 | 0.5 | 42,600 | 0.6 | 124,000 | 1.0 |
| Anglicans | 100 | 0.0 | 750 | 0.0 | 26 | −1 | 25 | 2.87 | 870 | 0.0 | 1,000 | 0.0 | 2,000 | 0.0 |
| Afro-American spiritists | 1,700 | 0.1 | 10,000 | 0.2 | 353 | 47 | 400 | 3.33 | 12,000 | 0.2 | 14,000 | 0.2 | 25,000 | 0.2 |
| Non-religious | 0 | 0.0 | 9,000 | 0.2 | 515 | 1,225 | 1,740 | 10.42 | 16,700 | 0.3 | 26,400 | 0.4 | 121,000 | 1.0 |
| Tribal religionists | 8,500 | 0.5 | 5,000 | 0.1 | 147 | −147 | 0 | 0.00 | 5,000 | 0.1 | 5,000 | 0.1 | 2,000 | 0.0 |
| Baha'is | 0 | 0.0 | 4,400 | 0.1 | 168 | 92 | 260 | 4.56 | 5,700 | 0.1 | 7,000 | 0.1 | 16,000 | 0.1 |
| Atheists | 0 | 0.0 | 3,000 | 0.1 | 400 | 1,400 | 1,800 | 15.00 | 12,000 | 0.2 | 21,000 | 0.3 | 74,000 | 0.6 |
| Jews | 100 | 0.0 | 1,000 | 0.0 | −50 | 0 | −50 | −7.14 | 700 | 0.0 | 500 | 0.0 | 500 | 0.0 |
| Buddhists | 0 | 0.0 | 1,000 | 0.0 | 29 | −29 | 0 | 0.00 | 1,000 | 0.0 | 1,000 | 0.0 | 1,000 | 0.0 |
| Chinese folk-religionists | 0 | 0.0 | 1,000 | 0.0 | 26 | −46 | −20 | −2.22 | 900 | 0.0 | 800 | 0.0 | 0 | 0.0 |
| Other religionists | 0 | 0.0 | 1,000 | 0.0 | 38 | 22 | 60 | 4.62 | 1,300 | 0.0 | 1,600 | 0.0 | 3,000 | 0.0 |
| **Country's population** | **1,700,000** | **100.0** | **5,298,000** | **100.0** | **180,200** | **0** | **180,200** | **2.94** | **6,129,000** | **100.0** | **7,100,000** | **100.0** | **12,374,000** | **100.0** |

COLUMNS, ROWS. For meanings and definitions, see Codebook (Part 6). Note that, by definition, total 'Christians' = professing + crypto-Christians, which also = affiliated + nominal Christians. Percentages may not always total exactly, due to rounding.

CENSUSES. **1940:** 98.1% Roman Catholics, 1.5% Evangelicals. **18.IV.1950:** 96.9% Roman Catholics, 2.8% Evangelicals, 0.3% other religionists. In this census, Evangelicals were 29% Indians, 71% Ladinos. In 1964 an unofficial sample survey was taken which proved to be unreliable and unusable, which gave the total population of the country as only 1,820,960. This survey gave the total of Evangelicals as 8.2% of the total population, and in the Department of Huehuetenango as 33.6% of all Indians, which can only be described as grossly inflated. The above table gives more probable estimated figures for 1970.

NOTES ON RELIGIONS
AFRO-AMERICAN SPIRITISTS. Non-Christian adherents of Afro-Caribbean spirit-possession cults syncretizing Christianity with African religion; mostly Jamaicans and other Blacks.
ATHEISTS. Guatemalan Labor Party (PGT) (proscribed since 1954; pro-Soviet): membership (1970) 750. There have also long been communist guerrillas in remote parts of the country.
BAHA'IS. Growth from 8 local spiritual assemblies (1964) to 29 (1973), mainly among Indian areas in the west, with from 1971 many coastal Blacks.
BUDDHISTS. Chinese.
CATHOLIC PENTECOSTALS. In 1976, including 2 bishops (one auxiliary of Guatemala City) and many priests and sisters.
CHRISTO-PAGANS. Maya Amerindians (including 1,500 Black Caribs) syncretizing 17th-century Spanish Catholicism with their traditional pre-Columbian religion to produce their own distinctive folk-Catholicism or *costumbre* (pagan religion and ritual) incorporating patron saints, fiestas, Christ as the sun god, the cult of the cross, sacrifices, prayer-makers (*rezadores*) and shamans.
EVANGELICAL CATHOLICS. This term is used to describe persons who are affiliated to churches termed by the state Evangélica (Protestant, Anglican, Guatemalan indigenous, marginal Protestant), but who are regarded by state and society as, or who profess publicly in censuses to be, Roman Catholics.
GUATEMALAN INDIGENOUS. In about 30 denominations in 1970 (see Table 2).
OTHER RELIGIONISTS. Including Rosicrucians (2 AMORC centres), and small Muslim communities (immigrant Palestinian Arabs).
PROTESTANTS. Growth of Protestants among the various Maya peoples, from 1969 to 1974 (total Evangelical community): Quiché from 25,000 to 35,000; Cakchiquel from 22,000 to 33,000; Kekchi from 5,000 to 10,000; Tzutuhil from 5,000 to 6,000; Chuj from 3,700 to 4,600; Mam from 3,000 to 4,100; Kanjobal from 2,600 to 3,500; Aguacatec from 1,400 to 1,600; Chorti from 900 to 1,000; Jacaltec from 100 to 150; Achi from 55 to 80.
TRIBAL RELIGIONISTS. A small number of monolingual Amerindians have resisted both Catholicism, christo-paganism and also Protestant missions.

**NON-CHRISTIAN RELIGIONS.** Although Guatemalans are nearly all professing Christians, many Mayan Indians, especially the Quiché, continue to accommodate their traditional rites and beliefs to those of Catholicism. The resulting christo-paganism of 26% of the population is most notable at Chichicastenango and at many similar Indian centres. Less than 1% of the population denies any association with Christianity. This includes a small Jewish community of about 1,000, resident for the most part in the capital. The principal Jewish organization is the Consejo Central de la Comunidad Israelita de Guatemala.

**CHRISTIANITY**
CATHOLIC CHURCH. In their 16th-century conquest of Guatemala, the Spanish found in the Quiché-speaking Maya Indians a deeply religious people, whose worship included the recognition of a supreme being named Qabovil, with Tikal in the north being their great cultural centre. The socio-religious organization of these people did not survive Spanish colonization. Regrouped into Spanish-type villages, Indians were forced to study Catholic doctrine in the churches, which they then accommodated to their own religious ethos. Four centuries later popular Catholicism still strongly manifests this mixture, in some areas revealing many Indian and Spanish cultural elements existing side-by-side without blending, with little or no religious acculturation. From 1524 to 1821 Guatemala was the centre of the Spanish government in Central America, with which the Catholic Church was closely associated. Little change took place after Guatemala's independence. In 1871 the church was separated from the state and its property confiscated; and in 1874 the religious orders were dissolved. Free to operate without impediment since 1954, the church in Guatemala continues to suffer from a shortage of priests, in large measure due to the absence of any interest

in the priesthood on the part of the over 2 million Indians, since baptism is in fact the only sacrament widely accepted by them.

The vast gulf that exists between on the one hand the clergy and bishops, who are almost all foreigners with close ties to the Ladinos (Mestizos), and on the other hand the Indian population, has generated considerable tension between local and foreign clergy and poses serious problems in the area of pastoral action. In addition, a large number of foreign religious personnel are absorbed in functions not directly pastoral. Thus in Guatemala City many are involved in administration or teaching in schools for children of the middle classes. There do exist, however, especially in dioceses outside Guatemala City, a number of important institutions for social development, although their relations with the hierarchy are frequently tenuous.

PROTESTANT CHURCHES. Protestantism has grown steadily since 1940 at the expense of Catholicism, as the following figures of professing Christians indicate: 1940, 98.5% Catholics, 1.5% Evangelicals (Protestants); 1950, 96.9% Catholics, 2.8% Evangelicals; 1970, 95.0% Catholics, 4.3% Evangelicals. The size of the Protestant population varies among the states, from around 15% in the northwest state of Huehuetenango (next to the strongly Protestant Mexican state of Chiapas) to 2% in the north central state of Alta Verapaz. The religio-ethnic composition also varies from state to state, Indians forming over 90% of Protestants in Huehuetenango, and Ladinos over 90% in El Progreso. The Protestant population includes many converts and evidences a somewhat higher education than the general population. Among the Maya Indians, the Evangelical community grew rapidly from 68,800 in 1969 to 99,100 in 1974.

American Presbyterians entered Guatemala in 1882 upon the invitation of president Barrios who believed Protestants could make a contribution to the progress and development of the country. The National Presbyterian Church of Guatemala became fully autonomous in 1962, and is today the second largest of the non-Pentecostal Protestant churches. Presbyterians have developed a new method of theological education in which men and women study at home, as well as in regional centres which receive weekly visits from seminary teachers. This church in fact originated the method of theological education by extension (TEE) which in 10 years has now become a worldwide movement. The Quiché Bible Institute in San Cristobal, established especially to serve the needs of the Quiché Indians, is conducted jointly with the Primitive Methodists, the latter being a denomination from the USA with foreign missionaries only in Guatemala. The Central American Church, autonomous since 1927, owes its origin to the pioneer work of the Central American Mission in 1899. Its Robinson Bible Institute has been preparing pastors for work among Indians since 1923, and another Bible institute in Guatemala City trains leaders for all Central American countries. Other early arrivals who have made considerable progress are the Friends who came in 1902, Nazarenes in 1904, Adventists in 1908 and Brethren in 1925. Of groups coming after World War II, Baptists have recorded the most significant growth.

As is true of most Latin American countries, Pentecostals, who first entered in 1916, have made a significant impact on Guatemala. Guatemala's largest single Protestant denomination is the Assemblies of God which began in 1937, and another important Pentecostal group is the Full Gospel Church of God.

As with Catholics, Protestants have been heavily involved in education and social service. The Presbyterian Church sponsors 6 secondary schools, 5 clinics, a cultural and recreational centre and an agricultural extension programme. In addition, Protestants maintain their own university, Universidad Mariano Galvez, the first of its kind to be established in Latin America (1966).

INDIGENOUS CHURCHES. The formation of independent churches in Guatemala is a recent phenomenon dating from the end of World War II. The majority are pentecostal, the largest being the Church of the Prince of Peace.

CHURCH AND STATE. Although church and state were legally separated in 1871, the latest constitution (15 September 1965) still states: 'The Catholic Apostolic Roman religion is that of the State which contributes to its maintenance without preventing the free exercise of other faiths'. After invoking 'the protection of God' in its preamble, the constitution, which became law on 6 May 1966, stipulates in Article 66: 'Freedom of religion is guaranteed. Everyone has the right to practise his religion or belief, both publicly and privately, through education, worship and observance, with no limitations except that public order, morals and peace be observed and respect given to national symbols. Religious associations or groups may not intervene in party political activity nor may clergy engage in political action within such parties.' Article 67 states: 'The Catholic Church and other denominations are recognized as juridical personalities. They can acquire and dispose of property to be used for religious purposes, for social service or education. Such property is exempt from taxation.' Religious manifestations taking place outside of church buildings are permitted and regulated by law (Article 63). Religious education is declared to be of 'national interest' with the same rights as civil and moral education; it is optional in state schools and may be included in the ordinary curriculum in all schools in the country (Article 92). Clergy are ineligible as deputies or as president of the republic; to become eligible they must withdraw from the ministry (Articles 164:7, 184:5, 200:5).

In 1954, under the military regime which overthrew president Arbenz, the Catholic Church recovered the juridical personality it had lost following the liberal revolution of 1879. Since 1954 there has resulted a large influx of foreign missionaries and the birth of a new relationship between church and state.

In September 1971 a declaration was signed in common by representatives of the different churches in the country requesting an end to the state of emergency that had been in effect since November 1970 and to the wave of terror which resulted from it. In response to this ecumenical document without precedent in Guatemala, the government immediately deported all foreigners who had signed it, including Catholic priests, Protestant clergy and the Episcopalian bishop. The apostolic administrator of Izabal, a Guatemalan national, was the only Catholic bishop to sign the declaration; he was then publicly repudiated by another bishop acting for the absent cardinal, who soon after reaffirmed the support of the Catholic Church for the regime in power.

During the presidential election of 8 March 1974, the organizations of the democratic Left regrouped themselves around the Christian Democratic Party in an unsuccessful attempt to defeat the candidate of the extreme Right. Two days before the election, a group of 28 priests and lay persons, Catholics and Protestants, published a statement condemning the

*Above.* **Iglesia Católica en Guatemala, Diócesis de Santa Cruz del Quiché.** St Thomas parish church in Indian town of Chichicastenango. *Top.* **Christo-pagans.** Traditional prayers with incense by shamans and prayer-makers on steps of St Thomas, Chichicastenango. Over 1.5 million Mayan Indians syncretize 17th-century Spanish Catholicism with their traditional pre-Columbian religion to produce *costumbre,* their own christo-pagan religion and ritual.

manoeuvres of the powers that be and expressing surprise at the silence of the hierarchies of the various churches in the face of this infringement of their civil rights. The president of the Catholic Episcopal Conference later protested against the arrest of foreign priests accused of subversive activities and the expulsion of 2 Maryknoll missionaries. As for the Christian Democratic Party, several of its leaders were assassinated following the election.

By 1977 a serious feud had developed between the Catholic Church and the officialist political party, previously its staunchest ally. The Bishops' Conference had released a document calling for greater social justice. In reply, the country's vice-president claimed that the Church was becoming a vehicle for Communism by its actions in the name of renewal.

**INTERDENOMINATIONAL ORGANIZATIONS.** Although there is no national council of churches, the Evangelical Alliance of Guatemala (Alianza Evangélica de Guatemala, AEG), founded in 1953, provides a united forum for its 17 member churches. A non-official Association of Evangelical Ministers of Guatemala (Associación de Pastores Evangélicos de Guatemala) meets periodically in Guatemala City to discuss co-operative ventures. In 1976, Central America's worst earthquake devastated many areas of Guatemala, killing 24,000, injuring 77,000, leaving 1.2 million homeless, and destroying 254,000 homes and over 500 Protestant churches alone. Amongst other Christian responses, the AEG-sponsored CEPA (Comité Evangélica Permanente Ayuda), begun in 1974 representing 45% of all Protestants, administered massive relief aid. In 1977 it was reorganized as CEDI (Evangelical Committee for Integral Development).

The Evangelical Committee for Social and Cultural Service (Junta Evangélica de Servicio Social y Cultural, JESSYC) was formed in 1963 and is responsible for an extensive programme of health care, literacy and leadership training in co-operation with Church World Service. There are no Catholic ecumenical organizations.

**BROADCASTING.** Guatemala has many radio stations, all accepting religious programmes. In Guatemala City there are 2 Protestant stations. The Central American Benevolent Mission broadcasts on Radio Cultural; and the missionary La Voz Evangélica de América transmits 18 hours of Protestant programming from Monday to Saturday and 3 hours on Sunday. They also accept Catholic programmes. The Central American Mission owns TGNA, which began broadcasting in 1950 and covers Guatemala and southern Mexico, and also a low-power tropical-band station Radio Maya which broadcasts in 7 Indian languages. There is also a Pentecostal station. In Santa Cruz Barillas, a Protestant pastor broadcasts on Radio Maya de Barillas in Spanish and Indian dialects. Several hundred Evangelical programmes can also be heard over commercial stations.

From abroad, Christian programmes can be easily heard on the international stations KGEI (FEBC, California), TWR (Bonaire, Netherlands Antilles) and HCJB (Ecuador). There are 10 Catholic radio stations. The Guatemala Federation of Radiophonic Schools, founded in Guatemala City in 1966, is a Catholic body with 7 stations which develops rural communities and marginal urban zones by teaching Spanish, literacy and primary education.

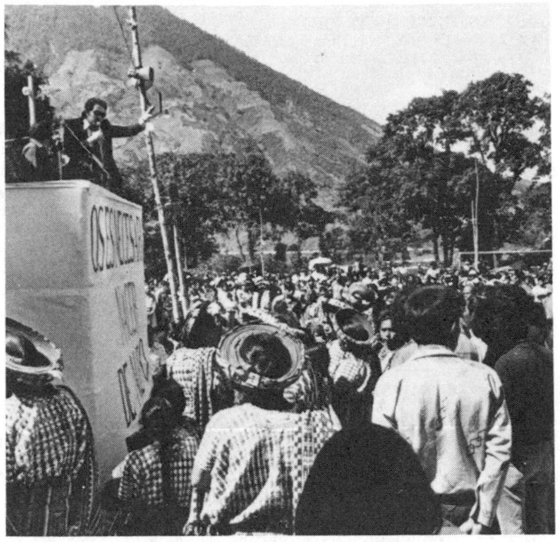
Guatemala City Crusade, December 1977, led by Argentinian evangelist Luis Palau: here in Santiago Atitlan, 1,000 decisions for Christ were recorded.

**BIBLIOGRAPHY**

*Chichicastenango: a Guatemalan village.* R. Bunzel. Seattle: University of Washington Press, 1952. (Christo-paganism: Quiché syncretism with Catholicism).
*Directorio de la Arquidiócesis de Guatemala, 1971.* Guatemala Ciudad: Palacio Arzobispal, 1972.
*Estadistica de la obra religioso-cristiana en Guatemala.* L. E. Stahlke. Guatemala City: Iglesia Luterana, 1966. 235p.
'Maya paganism and Christianity: a history of the fusion of two religions'. D. E. Thompson, in M. S. Edmonson, *op. cit.*, p. 1–35.
'Maya peasant evangelism'. H. Weerstra. Thesis, Fuller Theological Seminary, Pasadena (CA), 1972. 393p.
*Nativism and syncretism.* M. S. Edmonson et al. Publication 19, Middle American Research Institute. New Orleans: Tulane University, 1960. 203p. (Several papers on christo-paganism).
*Protestantism in Guatemala: its influence on the bicultural situation, with reference to the Roman Catholic background.* G. M. Emery. Sondeos No. 65. Cuernavaca (Mexico): CIDOC, 1970. 242p.
'Religion and world-view in a Guatemalan village'. E. M. Mendelson. Microfilm Collection of Manuscripts on Middle American Cultural Anthropology, No. 52. University of Chicago Libraries, 1957.
'The king, the traitor and the Cross: an interpretation of a highland Maya religious conflict', E. M. Mendelson, *Diogenes*, 21 (Spring, 1958), 1–10. (Mayan Judas-Iscariot worship).
*Santa Eulalia: the religion of a Cuchumatán Indian town.* O. La Farge. Chicago: Chicago University Press, 1947.
'The social and religious life of a Guatemalan village'. C. Wagley. Memoirs of the American Anthropological Association, No. 71, 1949.
*The two crosses of Todos Santos: survivals of Mayan religious ritual.* M. Oakes. Bollingen series XXVII. New York: Pantheon, 1951. (Mam shamans).
*Unidos en la esperanza: presencia de la Iglesia en la reconstrucción de Guatemala.* Episcopado de Guatemala. Guatemala: Libreria Loyala, 1976. 58p.

TABLE 2. ORGANIZED CHURCHES AND DENOMINATIONS IN GUATEMALA

| Official name 1 | Begun 2 | Type 3 | Counc 4 | Congs 5 | Adults 6 | Affiliated 7 | Names, notes, and other statistics (see Codebook) 8 |
|---|---|---|---|---|---|---|---|
| Assembleas de Dios | 1937 | P Pe2 | ZF... | 875 | 32,731 | 60,000 | *Assemblies of God.* M=AoG(USA). 501n,14x,G=6%pa,1j,1k,2s(148),W=77%,1373Y,2096z. |
| Asambleas de Hermanos | 1925 | P CBr | x.... | 102 | 4,000 | 8,000 | *Assemblies of Brethren. Open Brethren.* M=CMML(USA,UK,NZ). South coast. 11f. |
| Asoc de Igls Ev Hispanoamericanas de G | 1947 | P int | x...C | 65 | 5,000 | 10,000 | *Assoc of Spanish American Chs. Cruzada Hispanoamericana.* M=SAIM(USA). W=80%. |
| Asociación Emanual (Guatemala) | 1937 | P Hol | ..... | 15 | 1,000 | 2,000 | Linked with M=Emmanuel Association(USA), 2 schools. 7f,1p(10),W=80%. |
| Consejo Nacional de Iglesias Luteranas | c1935 | P Lut | x...C | 23 | 912 | 2,583 | *National Council of Lutheran Chs.* 1947, M=LCMS. Germans. 1n,5x,2h,W=30%,78Yy,65z. |
| Convención Bautista de Guatemala | 1946 | P Bap | T...C | 89 | 3,123 | 16,000 | *Baptist Convention of G.* 1948, M=SBC(USA). 32n,7x,26f,4p,2s(26).W=70%,386Y,450z. |
| Iglesia Adventista del Séptimo Día | 1908 | P Adv | x.... | 150 | 8,792 | 25,000 | *Seventh-day Adventists, Guatemala Mission*, CAmerican UM. 6nx.12f,1h,1r,148t,758Y. |
| Igl Apostólica de la Fe en Cristo Jesus | 1952 | I pel | x.... | 24 | 350 | 1,000 | *IAFCJ. Apostolic Ch of the Faith in CJ.* Mexicans. Mestizos. 14m,2f,1s,47z. |
| **Iglesia Católica en Guatemala:** | 1524 | R Lat | B.LDR | 317 | 2,347,100 | 4,346,449 | *Catholic Ch in Guatemala.* C=14+2+27. 5q.1s. 114n,490x,220m,946w,148703Yy. |
| M Guatemala | 1534 | R Lat | Bs | 88 | 479,000 | 886,972 | *Arquidiócesis de Guatemala.* City to south coast. 72 212 173 492 31796 |
| D Huehuetenango | 1961 | R Lat | Bs | 20 | 173,000 | 320,000 | In west. Extensive social action programme. 4 32 10 63 9967 |
| D Jalapa en Guatemala | 1951 | R Lat | Bs | 26 | 227,100 | 420,527 | *Diócesis de Jalapa.* Southeast, near El Salvador. 14 15 0 20 10186 |
| D Quezaltenango | 1921 | R Lat | Bs | 29 | 316,000 | 585,000 | In southwest. Strong Mayan christo-paganism. 6 46 8 110 14055 |
| D San Marcos | 1951 | R Lat | Bs | 25 | 170,000 | 315,000 | In extreme southwest, bordering on Mexico. 5 19 3 58 12244 |
| D Santa Cruz del Quiché | 1967 | R Lat | Bs | 20 | 130,000 | 240,000 | Maya christo-pagan stronghold at Chichicastenango. 1 24 0 25 12547 |
| D Sololá | 1951 | R Lat | Bs | 35 | 275,500 | 510,128 | Christo-paganism widespread. 5 42 2 63 21296 |
| D Vera Paz (Cobán) | 1921 | R Lat | Bs | 20 | 174,600 | 323,400 | Tropical rain-forest in north of diocese. 3 35 5 33 12858 |
| D Zacapa | 1951 | R Lat | Bs | 16 | 126,100 | 233,500 | East centre, bordering Honduras. 2 21 10 36 6435 |
| PN Escuintla | 1969 | R Lat | Bs | 11 | 108,000 | 200,000 | *Prelatura Nullius de Escuintla.* South of capital. 1 16 0 16 6725 |
| PN Santo Cristo de Esquipulas | 1956 | R Lat | Bs | 6 | 11,800 | 21,922 | Famed pilgrimage centre (Black Christ). 0 5 6 5 877 |
| AA El Petén | 1951 | R Lat | Bs | 12 | 59,000 | 110,000 | Tropical rain-forest. M=OP. Bishop a charismatic. 0 13 1 9 2403 |
| AA Izabal | 1968 | R Lat | Bs | 9 | 97,000 | 180,000 | Tropical rain-forest, bordering on sea. Many Blacks. 1 10 2 16 7314 |
| Iglesia Católica Nacional Guatemalteca | 1978 | I ReC | ..... | 10 | 2,000 | 5,000 | *Guatemalan National Catholic Ch.* Split ex RCC by ultraliberal RC priest Padre Chemita. 8n. |
| Iglesia Centroamericana en Guatemala | 1899 | P int | xM..C | 170 | 12,000 | 30,000 | M=CAM(USA). A=1927. West. Indians: Cakchiquel, Conob, Chuj. 70n,93f,1h,1k,3p,1s. |
| Iglesia de Dios de la Profecía | 1923 | P Pe3 | Z.... | 38 | 3,000 | 5,000 | *CoG of Prophecy.* M=CGP(USA). 1942 outbreak of mass glossolalia (prophecy). 30n. |
| Iglesia de Dios del Evangelio Completo | 1916 | P Pe3 | ZF... | 651 | 12,663 | 30,000 | *Full Gospel CoG. IdD Pentecostal.* M=CoG(Cleveland)(USA). 391n,8f,1s(44). |
| Iglesia de Dios Galilea | 1954 | I Hol | ..... | 17 | 580 | 2,500 | *Ch of God* (*Galilee*). Indigenous holiness body. 12n,G=18%pa,165Y,90z. |
| Iglesia de Dios Misionera | 1954 | I pe3 | ..... | 32 | 1,000 | 3,000 | Schism ex CGP. Link with M=Missionary Ch of God(Houston,USA). Escuintla. 114nm. |
| Iglesia de Dios (Anderson) | c1950 | P Hol | x...C | 10 | 1,500 | 3,000 | *Ch of God.* M=CoG(Anderson)(USA). Some work in Cakchiquel. No missionaries. 8n,1s. |
| Iglesia de JC de los Santos de los UD | c1952 | M LdS | x.... |  | 8,500 | 15,721 | *Latter-day Saints. Mormons.* M=CJCLdS(USA). Maya Indians. 290f,G=7.9%pa. |
| Iglesia Defensores de la Fe | 1956 | I pen | ..... | 9 | 1,500 | 2,000 | *Defenders of the Faith Ch.* Loose affiliation with Mexico, and DFM(USA). 9n. |
| Iglesia del Evangelio Cuadrangular | 1945 | P Pe2 | ZF... | 32 | 2,000 | 5,000 | *Internation Ch of the Foursquare Gospel.* M=ICFG(USA). 23nm,2f,1p(8),W=43%,97Y. |
| Iglesia del Príncipe de Paz | 1945 | I pe2 | x.... | 111 | 13,000 | 20,000 | *Ch of the Prince of Peace.* Many Indians. Strong in Petén. Exorcism, healing. 1p. |
| Iglesia Episcopal: D Guatemala | c1870 | A Hig | aw.R. | 15 | 500 | 750 | In *PECUSA Province IX.* 80% Ladino, 10% UK, 7% Black, 3% Kekchi. 3n,4x,1s,W=33%,15y. |
| Iglesia Ev del Nazareno de Guatemala | 1904 | P Hol | xF..C | 98 | 3,305 | 15,000 | *Nazarenes.* M=CoN(USA). 25n,2x,48m,6f,G=6%pa,4h,2p,2s(108),98t(9697),W=39%,469Y. |
| Iglesia Gethsemane | 1928 | I ind | .T..C | 24 | 1,500 | 2,000 | *Misión Ev Independiente.* Long history of litigation, schisms. 8n,2x,W=42%,21Y. |
| Iglesia Metodista Primitiva | 1921 | P Hol | VF..C | 30 | 1,800 | 2,100 | *IMP.* Main field of M=Primitive Methodist Ch(USA). 95% Quiché. 15n,14f,1H,4h,lu. |
| Iglesia Monte Sinaí |  | I ind | ..... | 10 | 200 | 400 | *Mount Sinai Church.* Indigenous body in capital and El Progreso department. |
| Iglesia Nacional Presbiteriana de G | 1882 | P Ref | R...C | 214 | 11,500 | 25,000 | *National Presbyterian Ch.* M=UPUSA. A=1962. Many Quiché, Mam. 45n,18f,5h,6r,1s,1u. |
| Iglesia Presbiteriana Bíblica de G | 1962 | I Ref | .TT.. | 31 | 800 | 1,350 | *Presbiterio Bíblico Fundamentalista.* 1964, M=IBPFM. 9n,G=6%pa,1s,W=70%,104Yy. |
| Iglesias de Cristo | 1959 | P Dis | x.... | 75 | 1,000 | 2,000 | *Chs of Christ.* M=CC(Non-Instrumental) (USA). Has a colony in Petén. 10m,12f,1h. |
| Iglesias Ev Amigos de Centroamérica | 1902 | P Qua | QF..C | 221 | 1,963 | 7,489 | *CA YM of Friends.* M=California YM. Northeast. 29n,6x,11f,G=6%pa,1p,1s,W=56%,175Y. |
| Iglesias radiofónicas solitarias | c1950 | I rad | ..... |  | 300 | 700 | Isolated radio believers. R=4400(TGNA,HCJB,FEBC,Radio Vatican),T=1150(ICI). |
| Misión Emanuel (Jalapa) | 1945 | P Hol | xF... | 18 | 400 | 1,000 | *Emmanuel Mission, Jalapa.* 1960, M=Evangelistic Faith Missions. 16n,8f,1k,1p(25). |
| Misión Evangélica Interdenominacional | 1938 | P ind | .T... | 30 | 600 | 1,500 | *Ev Interdenominational Mission.* Split by missionary ex CAM(USA). In capital. |
| Misión Menonita | 1968 | P Men | G...C | 3 | 33 | 82 | *Mennonite Mission.* M=EMBMC(USA). Non-German origin. HQ Chimaltenango. 10f,1h. |
| Misión Mundo Unido | 1953 | P int | xF..C | 10 | 200 | 500 | *United World Mission.* 1953, M=UWM(USA). HQ Guatemala City. 6n,1m,6f,1s. |
| Misiones Mundiales de Guatemala | 1962 | P ind | x.... |  | 1,500 | 3,000 | M=World-Wide Missions(USA). Linked with Evangelicals from Pasadena, CA (USA). |
| Templo Espiritualista |  | M Spi | ..... | 1 | 50 | 100 | *Spiritualist Temple.* One congregation in Guatemala City. |
| Testigos de Jehová | 1920 | M Jeh | x.... | 38 | 2,604 | 5,000 | *Jehovah's Witnesses.* First English-speaking convert 1920, Spanish 1923. 283Y. |
| Unificación Evangélica de Pentecostés |  | I pen | ....C | 10 | 300 | 1,000 | *Ev Pentecostal Union.* Loose federation in Escuintla and Guatemala City. 3n. |
| Other Protestant denominations |  | P | ..... |  | 6,000 | 12,000 | Total about 20 (see list below). |
| Other indigenous churches |  | I | ..... |  | 3,500 | 7,000 | Total about 20 (see list below). |
| **Total affiliated (mid-1970)** |  |  |  | **3,790** | **2,498,806** | **4,680,224** | **Total denominations (1970) . . . 72.** |
| **Total affiliated (mid-1975)** |  |  |  | **4,900** | **2,866,500** | **5,368,900** | **Total denominations (1975) . . . 77.** |
| **Total affiliated (mid-1980)** |  |  |  | **6,350** | **3,294,600** | **6,170,700** | **Total denominations (1980) . . . 82.** |

NOTES ON TABLE ABOVE
COLUMNS: for meanings and CODES (cols. 1, 3, 4, 8), see Codebook (Part 6). Column 1: **Boldface type** = church with over 10% of country's affiliated Christians.
NATIONAL COUNCILS (Column 4, 5th letter).
C = Alianza Evangélica de Guatemala (AEG) (Evangelical Alliance of Guatemala).
R = Conferencia Episcopal de Guatemala (CEG) (Episcopal Conference of Guatemala).
OTHER PROTESTANT DENOMINATIONS. These include: Apostolic Ch of Pentecost (Canada, 2 missionaries), Apostolic Lutheran Ch of America (Laestadians), Baptist International Missions (1969), Baptist Missionary Association of America (1964), Children of God International, Christian and Missionary Alliance (1970), Christian Nationals Evangelism Commission (1963), Conservative Mennonite Fellowship (1964), Iglesia Bautista Libre, Pentecostal Ch of God of America, Salvation Army, Union Church (Guatemala City), United Evangelical Churches, World Baptist Fellowship Mission Agency (1967).
OTHER INDIGENOUS CHURCHES. These include: Assembly of Christian Churches (1962) from Puerto Rico, Iglesia Cinco Calles Misionera Primitiva, Iglesia de Dios del Séptimo Día, Iglesia Fuenta de Vida (Fountain of Life Ch), Iglesia La Luz del Mundo (Aaronistas), Iglesias del Aposento Alto (Churches of the Upper Room), and churches among the West Indian Black population. A USA Black mission, National Baptist Convention USA, also began work in 1964.
OTHER MARGINAL PROTESTANT BODIES. Church of Christ, Scientist (Guatemala Society).

PEOPLES (ethnolinguistic). Christians: 55.2% Ladino (Mestizo), 41.8% Amerindian (13.9% Quiché, 8.5% Cakchiquel, 7.2% Mam, 5.9% Kekchí, 1.3% Pocomchí, 1.3% Tojolabali, 1.0% Ixil, 0.6% Tzutuhil, 0.5% Uspantec, Carib), 2.0% Black, 0.9% Guatemalan White, 0.1% Chinese (5,300), Black Carib (1,500), Palestinian Arab.

COUNTRY-WIDE TOTALS
EVANGELIZATION (see Part 5). 1900: 100%. 1970: 100%. 1980: 100%. *Mass evangelism.* Among recent campaigns: 1963, Evangelism-in-Depth (6,036 prayer cells, 50,000 participants for 2-month training course in personal evangelism; 250,000 homes visited distributing 500,000 gospels and a million tracts, 15,000 professions of faith; 30,000 attenders at final rally in Guatemala City); March 1971, Luis Palau 22-day crusade (35 sponsoring churches, 128,800 attenders, 19 one-hour telecasts, 3,148 enquirers); August 1976, Baptist crusade (E. J. Daniels and 85 USA preachers) with 1,500 decisions; 1977, Luis Palau 8-day crusades (over 30,000 attenders and 1,000 decisions); 1978, Here's Life Guatemala City (CCCI). *Radiophonic evangelism.* Annual listeners' letters (1975): 3,600 TGNA, 480 FEBC, 326 HCJB, et alia. Bible correspondence courses: TGNA (6,000), ICI (1,150 enrolments).
FOREIGN MISSIONARIES AND PERSONNEL (nationals serving abroad) (1973). Total 152 in 6 countries: about 140 Roman Catholics, 6 Protestants, 6 Guatemalan indigenous.
FOREIGN MISSIONARIES AND PERSONNEL (aliens from abroad) (1973). Total 2,135. *From Western world.* 1,388: 735 Roman Catholics, 349 Protestants (330 in 36 USA societies, 13 in 2 Canada societies, 4 in 1 New Zealand society, 2 in 1 UK society), about 300 marginal Protestants (275 Mormons) from USA, 4 Anglicans in 1 USA society. *From Communist world.* 3 Roman Catholics from Poland. *From Third World.* 744: 714 Roman Catholics from other Latin American countries, 20 Protestants and 10 indigenous from Mexico and Jamaica.
INSTITUTIONS (church-operated) (1973). Total 215, including 102 higher schools (5 minor seminaries), 43 medical centres (13 hospitals), 13 radio stations, 1 religious community (monastery), 34 seminaries (25 Protestant, 6 RC, 2 Guatemalan indigenous, 1 Anglican), 10 study centres, 2 universities.
PERIODICALS. About 40 titles.
PERSONNEL. About 3,985 (1,850 national, 2,135 foreign).
RELIGIOUS LIBRARIES. About 60.
SCRIPTURE DISTRIBUTION (1975). Annual totals: 81,925 Bibles (39% subsidized, 61% commercial), 59,310 NTs (15% free, 52% subsidized, 33% commercial), 68,835 UBS portions, 1,471,526 UBS selections. *Translations completed.* Portion: 18 languages since 1898. NT: 9 languages since 1931.
SERVICE AGENCIES. About 50, including ACUG, AEG, CCCI, CEF, CEG, CEPA, CNT, CONFREGUA, COSDEGUA, CRS-USCC, CWS, FGER, ICM, IDESAC, LWR, MFC, WBT, WLC(EHC).

ADDITIONAL DATA ON CHURCHES
ASAMBLEAS DE DIOS. By 1975, congregations had increased to 1,248.
IGLESIA CATOLICA EN GUATEMALA. Including 5,300 Chinese Catholics (1975). *Annual baptisms.* (1972) 99.6% infant, 0.4% adult. *National priests.* 93 diocesan, 21 religious. *Expatriate priests.* 71 diocesan, 419 religious. *Religious priests and brothers* (1970). 13% Guatemalans, 6% from other Latin American countries, 81% from other continents (mainly Spanish, Italians and North Americans). *Sisters* (1970). 14% Guatemalans, 66% from other Latin American countries, 19% from other continents. *Main religious orders and congregations.* Priests: OFM, SJ. Brothers: FSC, PFM. Sisters: Hijas de la Caridad, Hijas de María Auxiliadora, Religiosas de la Sagrada Familia, Religiosas de la Asunción.
*Catholic organizations.* The Episcopal Conference of Guatemala (Conferencia Episcopal de Guatemala, CEG) is a member of SEDAC and CELAM. The Confederation of Religious of Guatemala (Confederación de Religiosos de Guatemala, CONFREGUA), serving both men and sisters, is a member of SERCAP and CLAR. Among national lay organizations may be mentioned Acción Católica, Acción Católica Rural Obrera, Movimiento Familiar Cristiano, Cursillos de Cristiandad and Legión de María.
The Holy See has diplomatic relations with Guatemala and is represented to government and the Catholic hierarchy by a nuncio in Guatemala City.
The Confederation of Priests and Laity in Guatemala (Confederación de Sacerdotes y Seglares Diocesanos en Guatemala, COSDEGUA), founded in Guatemala City in 1968, groups together priests of Guatemalan origin dedicated to the vigorous application of Vatican II and the Medellín reforms, to the assumption of control of the church by nationals, and to political and social change aimed at terminating oligarchical rule. This group has entered into conflict with the Spanish cardinal-archbishop who suspended many of its adherents. Of 42 founding members in 1968, only a handful were still active in 1975.
The Institute for Socio-Economic Development in Central America (Instituto para el Desarrollo Económico Social de América Central, IDESAC), founded in Guatemala City in 1964, with a branch in Panama, carries on studies and research concerning the problems of Guatemala and Central America, prepares projects aimed at resolving these problems, trains social service leaders, creates and maintains social work teams and provides technical assistance to co-operative ventures. Another agency engaged in social and socio-religious research is CIAS, run by Jesuits in Guatemala City.
Several diocesan institutes and centres for social and human development are active: Centro San Benito de Promoción Humana (diocese of Vera Paz), Instituto de Capacitación Tecnica del Petén (INCATEP) (jurisdiction of Petén), Centro de Capacitación Emaús (prelature of Escuintla), Centro de Capacitación Campo de Dios (jurisdiction of Izabal), Instituto Católico de Capacitación Social (diocese of Quezaltenango), Centro de Desarrollo Integral (diocese of Huehuetenango), Centro de Formación Social (diocese of Quiché). Moreover, in 1972 there were 11 parish centres for promoting development. In the same category is the network of Catholic radiophonic schools.
The Social Workers' Training Centre (Centro de Adiestramiento para Promotores Sociales) in Guatemala City is associated with Landivar University in training social workers, as well as engaging in philosophical reflection regarding human dignity.
Workers' federations and co-operatives include the following: Confederación Nacional de Trabajadores, Federación Campesina de Guatemala, Movimiento Nacional de Pobladores, Federación de Cooperatives de Consumo, Federación de Cooperativas de Ahorro y Crédito, and Federación de Cooperativas de Productores de Café.
The Missionary Training Institute (Instituto de Capacitación Misionera, ICM), founded in Guatemala City in 1952, is open to all Catholic missionaries in Central America (priests, religious and lay) and offers courses in language, catechesis, economics, anthropology and theology. There are also 5 centres of training for the rural pastorate, with a total of 1,500 students.
The Catholic educational programme consisted in 1970 of 77 mostly primary day schools with 32,000 pupils, 110 religious primary and secondary boarding colleges with 31,000 students, one rural school with 950 pupils and 402 literacy centres with 42,473 students. By 1973 schools numbered 139 primary (59,844 pupils) and 88 secondary (38,849). The Raphael Landivar Catholic University (Universidad Católica Rafael Landivar), founded by Jesuits in Guatemala City, with 2,500 students in 1973, has faculties relating to the political, economic, juridical, human and social sciences, and also industrial engineering. Other affiliated bodies include an institute of political and social sciences and a training centre for social workers. The university offers extension programmes in Antigua, Quezaltenango and San Marcos.
Medical and social services in the archdiocese of Guatemala in 1969 included 12 state or private hospitals maintained by religious personnel, 16 dispensaries, and 9 other institutions (homes for children, handicapped and aged) also run by religious. Caritas de Guatemala was founded in Guatemala City in 1961 but did not become active until 1969. It is involved in the distribution of food and medicines furnished by CRS in the USA, health care, agricultural development and literacy.
IGLESIA CENTROAMERICANA EN GUATEMALA. The statistics in the table refer to the year 1970. By 1976 communicant members had increased to 23,000, and congregations to 535.
IGLESIA DE DIOS DE LA PROFECIA. By 1975, congregations had increased to 82.
IGLESIA DE DIOS DEL EVANGELIO COMPLETO. By 1975, congregations had increased to 769.
IGLESIA DEL EVANGELIO CUADRANGULAR. By 1975, congregations had increased to 52.
IGLESIA EVANGELICA DEL NAZARENO DE GUATEMALA. By 1975, congregations had increased to 117.
MISION EMANUEL (JALAPA). By 1975, congregations had increased to 50.

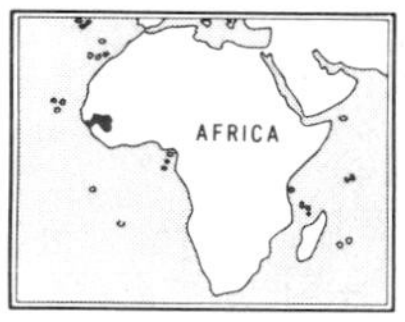


# GUINEA

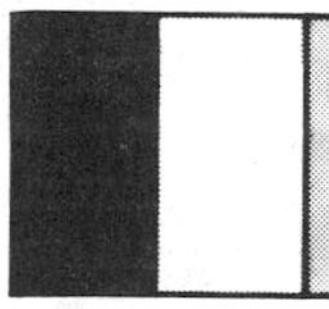

## SECULAR DATA

**STATE. Official name:** The Revolutionary People's Republic of Guinea (La République de Guinée). Adjective of nationality: Guinean (guinéen).
**Flag** (shown above right): Red, yellow, and green bars.
**Area:** 245,857 sq.km. (94,926 sq.miles). Agricultural land: 29.1%.
**Government:** One-party socialist state, since 1958 (12th century in empire of Ghana, 1849 French protectorate, 1958 Independence as republic).
**Legislature:** National Assembly, 75 members.
**Official language:** French (*Français*).
**Capital:** Conakry 197,270 (1967).
**Armed forces** (1976): Total 5,850 regular: army 5,000, navy 350, air force 500 (15 combat aircraft). Paramilitary forces: 8,000.
**Foreign forces** (1973): 100 USSR military advisers.

**DEMOGRAPHY. Population:** 2,570,219 (census of 15.I-31.V. 1955. For 1970–2000 (UN), see last row of Table 1). Population density (1975): 18/sq.km. (47/sq.mile). Under 15 years: 42%. Growth rate (1975–80): 2.54% per year (births 4.61%, deaths −2.07%). Life expectancy (1975–80): 43.5 years. Household size: 4.9 persons.
**Major languages:** Fulani, Mandingo, French, Susu, Kpelle, Loma, Kissi, and about 15 smaller languages.
**Urban dwellers** (1970): 11.2%. Urban growth rate (1950–70): 6.5% per year.
**Labour force:** 48%.
**Refugees** (1977): From abroad, none. Exiles abroad: over a million Guineans in several African countries and France.

**ETHNOLINGUISTIC GROUPS:** 46% Mande [29% Malinke (Mikifore, Toubacaye, 2% Kuranko, Lele, 2% Konianke, Soninke), 13% Susu, 3.2% Dialonke, Bambara], 35% Fulani (Fula Djalon, Fulacunda, Tukulor), 11% Mande-Fu (4.8% Kpelle, 3.2% Loma, 1.1% Vai, 0.5% Mano, Kono), 7% Kissi, 0.4% Tenda (Badyaranke, Bassari, Boeni, Coniagui, Mayo), Temne, Baga, Gbande, Papel, Cuban (500).

**MONEY** (1977). **Monetary unit:** syli (= 100 cauris); US$1 = GS 21.34.
**National income per person:** US$130. Average annual family income: US$637.
**Cost of living in capital** (1976): Daily cost of living: US$44.

**EDUCATION.** Adult literacy: (1965) 9%, (1975) 10%. Education rate: 18%. Schools: 1,984.

**HEALTH.** Hospitals: 83 (6,858 beds). Doctors: 142. Lepers: 161,000 (36.5 per 1,000). Blind: 45,000. Psychotics: 31,000.

**LITERATURE.** Annual new book titles (1966): 8. Newspapers: 1 daily.

**COMMUNICATION** (per 1,000 people). Phones: 3. Radios: 24. Daily newspaper circulation: 1 copy.

TABLE 1. RELIGIOUS ADHERENTS IN GUINEA

| Year | 1900 | | mid-1970 | | Annual change, 1970–1980 | | | | mid-1975 | | mid-1980 | | 2000 | |
|---|---|---|---|---|---|---|---|---|---|---|---|---|---|---|
| *Name* | *Adherents* | *%* | *Adherents* | *%* | *Natural* | *Conversion* | *Total* | *Rate* | *Adherents* | *%* | *Adherents* | *%* | *Adherents* | *%* |
| Muslims | 574,200 | 58.0 | 2,666,280 | 68.0 | 74,871 | 4,501 | 79,372 | 2.62 | 3,025,000 | 68.5 | 3,460,000 | 69.0 | 6,426,000 | 76.0 |
| Ahmadis | 0 | 0.0 | 1,000 | 0.0 | 30 | 10 | 40 | 3.33 | 1,200 | 0.0 | 1,400 | 0.0 | 3,000 | 0.0 |
| Tribal religionists | 414,015 | 41.8 | 1,194,364 | 30.5 | 32,785 | −4,095 | 28,690 | 2.16 | 1,324,580 | 30.0 | 1,481,260 | 29.5 | 1,921,700 | 22.7 |
| **Christians** | **1,785** | **0.2** | **55,256** | **1.4** | **1,485** | **−511** | **974** | **1.62** | **60,000** | **1.4** | **65,000** | **1.3** | **90,000** | **1.1** |
| crypto-Christians | 285 | 0.0 | 5,756 | 0.1 | 124 | −200 | −76 | −1.52 | 5,000 | 0.1 | 5,000 | 0.1 | 6,000 | 0.1 |
| professing | 1,500 | 0.2 | 49,500 | 1.3 | 1,361 | −311 | 1,050 | 1.91 | 55,000 | 1.2 | 60,000 | 1.2 | 84,000 | 1.0 |
| Roman Catholics | 1,500 | 0.2 | 45,500 | 1.2 | 1,252 | −282 | 970 | 1.92 | 50,600 | 1.1 | 55,200 | 1.1 | 78,700 | 0.9 |
| Protestants | 0 | 0.0 | 3,000 | 0.1 | 82 | −22 | 60 | 1.82 | 3,300 | 0.1 | 3,600 | 0.1 | 4,000 | 0.0 |
| Anglicans | 0 | 0.0 | 1,000 | 0.0 | 27 | −7 | 20 | 1.82 | 1,100 | 0.0 | 1,200 | 0.0 | 1,300 | 0.0 |
| affiliated | 1,785 | 0.2 | 55,256 | 1.4 | 1,485 | −511 | 974 | 1.62 | 60,000 | 1.4 | 65,000 | 1.3 | 90,000 | 1.1 |
| total practising | 1,610 | *90* | 38,680 | *70* | 1,040 | −358 | 682 | 1.62 | 42,000 | *70* | 45,500 | *70* | 63,000 | *70* |
| non-practising | 180 | *10* | 16,580 | *30* | 445 | −153 | 292 | 1.62 | 18,000 | *30* | 19,500 | *30* | 27,000 | *30* |
| Roman Catholics | 1,785 | 0.2 | 48,356 | 1.2 | 1,293 | −495 | 798 | 1.53 | 52,220 | 1.2 | 56,340 | 1.1 | 76,500 | 0.9 |
| Protestants | 0 | 0.0 | 4,200 | 0.1 | 118 | −8 | 110 | 2.31 | 4,750 | 0.1 | 5,300 | 0.1 | 8,000 | 0.1 |
| Evangelicals | 0 | 0.0 | 4,100 | 0.1 | 114 | −14 | 100 | 2.17 | 4,600 | 0.1 | 5,100 | 0.1 | 7,600 | 0.1 |
| Anglicans | 0 | 0.0 | 2,000 | 0.1 | 54 | −14 | 40 | 1.82 | 2,200 | 0.0 | 2,400 | 0.0 | 3,000 | 0.0 |
| Marginal Protestants | 0 | 0.0 | 500 | 0.0 | 14 | 2 | 16 | 2.76 | 580 | 0.0 | 660 | 0.0 | 1,500 | 0.0 |
| African indigenous | 0 | 0.0 | 200 | 0.0 | 6 | 4 | 10 | 4.00 | 250 | 0.0 | 300 | 0.0 | 1,000 | 0.0 |
| Non-religious | 0 | 0.0 | 4,000 | 0.1 | 124 | 76 | 200 | 4.00 | 5,000 | 0.1 | 6,000 | 0.1 | 13,000 | 0.2 |
| Atheists | 0 | 0.0 | 1,000 | 0.0 | 32 | 28 | 60 | 4.62 | 1,300 | 0.0 | 1,600 | 0.0 | 4,000 | 0.0 |
| Baha'is | 0 | 0.0 | 100 | 0.0 | 3 | 1 | 4 | 3.33 | 120 | 0.0 | 140 | 0.0 | 300 | 0.0 |
| Country's population | 990,000 | 100.0 | 3,921,000 | 100.0 | 109,300 | 0 | 109,300 | 2.48 | 4,416,000 | 100.0 | 5,014,000 | 100.0 | 8,455,000 | 100.0 |

COLUMNS, ROWS. For meanings and definitions, see Codebook (Part 6). Note that, by definition, total 'Christians' = professing + crypto-Christians, which also = affiliated + nominal Christians. Percentages may not always total exactly, due to rounding.
CENSUSES. **1958** (estimated): 62.0% Muslims, 36.5% tribal religionists, 1.5% Christians.

NOTES ON RELIGIONS
AFRICAN INDIGENOUS. Isolated radio believers (see Table 2).
ATHEISTS. Intellectuals, a few communists; also 100 USSR military advisers (1973).

BAHA'IS. In 1 local spiritual assembly (1973).
COUNTRY'S POPULATION. In the 1970s, several hundred thousand had fled as refugees to neighbouring countries.
CRYPTO-CHRISTIANS. Christians affiliated to churches but unknown as such to state or society; unorganized individuals in the recognized churches, members of clandestine churches, and a few isolated radio believers.
MUSLIMS. Sunnis (of the Malikite rite). Islamized tribes: Dialonke, Sarakole, Susu (85%). Most Muslims belong to the Tijaniya brotherhood; there are also some Ahmadis, Qadianis linked with Pakistani missionaries (enumerated here under Muslims although declared non-Muslim by Pakistan). *Conver-*

*sions to Islam.* These are taking place among tribal religionists, although the forest tribes, Guerze, Loma (Toma) and Kissi form a resistant barrier. The Kissi remain only 8% islamized, the Coniagui-Bassari 3%. A number of Christians also defect to Islam each year, mostly through marriage to Muslims. *Hajj pilgrims to Mecca.* (1970) 2,631; (1974) 988; (1975) 986; (1976) 1,334.
TRIBAL RELIGIONISTS. Tribes over 60% traditionalist (animist) in 1972: Kissi (95%), Loma (91%), Gbande (80%), Koranko (70%, and 30% Muslim), Malinke (60%), Guerze (Kpelle) (60%). The Yalunka and Konyanke are about 60% Muslim and 40% traditionalist.

---

## NON-CHRISTIAN RELIGIONS. **Islam** was introduced into Guinea by the Fulani during the 18th century in a jihad from 1725 on, and is now the majority religion of the country. The Dialonke, Sarakole and Susu peoples are highly islamized. Most Guinean Muslims belong to the Tijaniya brotherhood.

**Traditional religions** are followed by nearly 30% of the population. The Kissi, Loma and Gbande in the forests of the southeast have remained highly resistant to both Islam and Christianity, and the Malinke and Kpelle are each 60% traditionalist. As in other parts of Africa, magical practices, ancestral veneration and a belief in God are characteristic of these religions. The supreme being is called Hala by the Kissi; and Hounounga (Unknown) by the Tenda. The Malinke have 3 names for God: Gala, Guele and Jalang.

## CHRISTIANITY. Guinea was part of the large medieval empires of Ghana (prior to the 13th century) and of Malinke, which began to decline 2 centuries later. During the 15th century, Portuguese ships

**Tribal religionists.** Masked traditional dancers at Nzérékoré among Guerze (Kpelle), who are still 60% pagans.

penetrated further south along the West African coast, passing Guinea by 1462. An attempt was made to introduce Christianity when the Portuguese tried to establish trading posts along the Atlantic coast, but these Christian overtures diminished as Portugal declined in power. A Muslim holy war was proclaimed in 1725 which initiated the process of islamization among the indigenous peoples. French rights to the Guinea coast were affirmed at the Treaty of Paris in 1814, and in 1849 the area was declared a French protectorate. By 1882 France had begun to occupy the interior, and in 1891 Guinea became a colony. Catholic missionaries entered in 1877 and Protestants in 1918, but Christians today still constitute less than 2% of the population.

CATHOLIC CHURCH. Holy Ghost priests opened a mission at Boff in 1877 and a second one near Conakry in 1890, with White Fathers beginning work in the southeast in 1896. In 1897 Guinea became a prefecture. By 1900 there were 1,800 Catholics, rising to 6,000 (including catechumens) in 1920, 20,000 in 1949 and 26,500 in 1965. The first Guinean priest was ordained in 1940, and by 1949 another priest and 13 African sisters had been added. In 1955 an archdiocese was established at Conakry, with the first African appointed archbishop in 1962.

Up to 1967, the archdiocese of Conakry in the west and the apostolic prefecture of Kankan in the centre were entrusted to the Holy Ghost mission and the diocese of N'Zékékoré to White Fathers. In 1967 all foreign missionaries were expelled (including 73 priests, 10 brothers, 55 sisters and 16 women lay missionaries), and only 8 Guinean priests were left to carry the entire work, which created a serious pastoral crisis. However, by 1976 there were 15 African priests, including one from Mali, and 24 sisters, 4 being from Upper Volta. In addition there are 18 major seminarians, and 60 minor seminarians at Kindia in the archdiocese of Conakry.

OTHER CHURCHES. The Christian and Missionary Alliance from the USA began work in 1918 at Baro in the Niger valley, and since then has built a number of other stations throughout the country. Although its weekly radio broadcasts from Radio ELWA in Liberia cover large Muslim areas, its converts have come primarily from traditionalist peoples. The CMA distributes scripture portions in 8 languages, and the New Testament is now available in Fulani. When foreign missionaries were ordered to leave Guinea in 1967, an arrangement was made for 26 CMA missionaries to remain, although their activity was restricted. The church is said to have grown in strength through the increased responsibility assumed by its 80 national workers. Foreign missionaries were also expelled belonging to the Open Bible Standard Mission, which began work among Muslims and traditionalists in both rural and urban areas in 1952; the Paris Evangelical Missionary Society; and the Anglican Church which is still part of the Diocese of Gambia and the Rio Pongas, in the Church of the Province of West Africa. There are no African indigenous churches in Guinea, except for isolated radio believers.

CHURCH AND STATE. According to the constitution of 10 November 1958, Guinea is a secular state (Article 1) which assures to all citizens equal rights without distinction of religion (Article 39). In 1961 all denominational schools (Quranic, Catholic and Protestant) were nationalized, and the Catholic archbishop of Conakry, a Frenchman, was deported. In 1962 a Guinean who had worked for the integration of the Catholic minority into the life of the nation, Msgr R. Tchidimbo, was consecrated as the new archbishop. In 1964 two Christian ministers served in the government for a period. In May 1967, all foreign missionaries were given one month to leave the country, the 2 Swiss Catholic bishops of Kankan and N'Zékékoré having already left. Thirteen African priests and several African sisters from neighbouring countries arrived to take their place; but the national political office of the Democratic Party of Guinea, the country's only political party, declared in June

**Muslims.** Fulah boy reads Quranic tablet at Gaoual, northwest of Fouta Djallon.

that 'no foreign persons, not even priests, will be tolerated in Guinea without the prior consent of the government'. African priests already present were confined to the city of Conakry prior to their subsequent repatriation. Following an attempted invasion with Portuguese backing in 1970, archbishop Tchidimbo was arrested on Christmas Eve, 1970; and although widely known as a militant anti-colonialist, he was sentenced on 24 January 1971 to life imprisonment with hard labour for 'collaboration with the enemy'.

In September 1973 the apostolic delegate met with president Sékou Touré and later concelebrated mass with all the Guinean priests in the cathedral, which provoked considerable discussion over Radio Conakry. Since then other signs have appeared indicating a relaxation of tension between the Catholic Church and the state. In December 1973, 3 priests from Cameroon were authorized to visit Conakry; and at the new year in 1974 Msgr Tchidimbo, in prison, received permission to write a letter to the pope. Moreover, in September 1974 Sékou Touré received a delegation of African priests from Upper Volta, Mali and Benin (Dahomey), who had come for the ordination of a Guinean priest.

Archbishop Tchidimbo was finally released from prison in 1978.

BROADCASTING. There are Protestant recording studios at Kissidougou and Labe, operated by the Mission Protestante (CMA); the Catholic organizer is at Conakry under the archdiocese. Christian programmes from abroad can be easily heard from ELWA (Liberia) in the Fula, Toma, Guerze, Kissi, Susu, Malinke and French languages.

BIBLIOGRAPHY
'Le culte de Zié: éléments de la religion Kono (Haute Guinée Française)', B. Holas, *Mémoires de l'IFAN* (Dakar), 39 (1954), 217–221. (Study of a river cult).
'The Church in Guinea', *International Fides Service* (Rome), No. 2695 (7 January 1976), NE 6–9.

TABLE 2. ORGANIZED CHURCHES AND DENOMINATIONS IN GUINEA

| Official name 1 | Begun 2 | Type 3 | Counc 4 | Congs 5 | Adults 6 | Affiliated 7 | Names, notes, and other statistics (see Codebook) 8 |
|---|---|---|---|---|---|---|---|
| Egl Anglicane (D Gambia & Rio Pongas) | 1935 | A ACa | awaV. | 9 | 740 | 2,000 | *Anglican Ch.* In CPWA. Declining; many reverting to Islam. 2n,1x,W=45%,5Y,25y. |
| **Eglise Catholique au Guinée:** | 1877 | R Lat | P.SFR | 46 | 28,100 | 48,356 | *Catholic Ch in G.* 1968, all foreigners expelled. C=0+0+4. 13n,1m,26w,935Yy. |
| M Conakry | 1897 | R Lat | Ps | 30 | 10,600 | 18,200 | Area 1% Catholic. 1971, archbishop imprisoned for life. 10 0 16 247 |
| D N'Zérékoré | 1937 | R Lat | Ps | 8 | 8,800 | 15,108 | 55% Kpelle, 27% Toma, 13% Kono. 1.1% baptized. 2 0 8 369 |
| PA Kankan | 1949 | R Lat | Ps | 8 | 8,700 | 15,048 | Rapid growth. 1.5% Catholic. Kissi, some Kpelle. P=30%. 1 1 2 319 |
| Eglise de la Bible Ouverte | 1952 | P Pe2 | Z.... | 2 | 50 | 100 | *Open Bible Standard Churches.* Formerly based at Kindia, with M=OBSC(USA). |
| Eglise Evangélique Protestante | 1918 | P Hol | xF... | 203 | 1,473 | 3,000 | *Ev Protestant Ch.* M=CMA(USA). Toma (Loma), Kissi, few Malinke. 80m,17f,1h,1p. |
| Eglise Libre Pentecôtiste | c1960 | P Pe2 | Z.... | 2 | 500 | 1,000 | Formerly M=SFM(Sweden). Begun by mass-movement Liberians (Kissi, Loma, Gbande). |
| Eglise Réformée | | P Ref | ..... | | 50 | 100 | *Reformed Ch.* Former chaplaincy work to Frenchmen by Eglise Réformée de France. |
| Eglise radiophoniques isolées | c1965 | I rad | ..... | | 100 | 200 | Isolated radio believers, mostly youths. R=10(ELWA, Radio Vatican, &c). |
| Témoins de Jéhovah | c1955 | M Jeh | x.... | 5 | 204 | 500 | *Jehovah's Witnesses.* Active witnessing by 1959. 626 at 1973 Memorial. 27Y. |
| **Total affiliated (mid-1970)** | | | | **280** | **31,217** | **55,256** | **Total denominations (1970) . . . 8.** |
| **Total affiliated (mid-1975)** | | | | **290** | **33,900** | **60,000** | **Total denominations (1975) . . . 8.** |
| **Total affiliated (mid-1980)** | | | | **300** | **36,700** | **65,000** | **Total denominations (1980) . . . 8.** |

**NOTES ON TABLE ABOVE**
COLUMNS: for meanings and CODES (cols. 1, 3, 4, 8), see Codebook (Part 6). Column 1: **Boldface type** = church with over 10% of country's affiliated Christians.
NATIONAL COUNCILS (Column 4, 5th letter).
R = Conférence Episcopale Nationale de la République de Guinée (National Episcopal Conference of the Republic of Guinea).

**PEOPLES** (ethnolinguistic). Christians: about 68% Mande-Fu (53% Kpelle (Guerze), 11% Loma (Toma), 4% Kono), 16% Kissi, 10% expatriate African (Senegalese, Ivory Coast, Guinea-Bissau: Wolof, Serer, Kru), 6% Gbande, a few Malinke.

**COUNTRY-WIDE TOTALS**
EVANGELIZATION (see Part 5). 1900: 7%. 1970: 12%. 1980: 16%.
FOREIGN MISSIONARIES AND PERSONNEL (aliens from abroad) (1973). Total 26. *From Western world.* 18 Protestants (17 in 2 USA societies, 1 from France). *From Third World.* 8: 5 Roman Catholics (4 Upper Volta, 1 Mali), 2 Protestants from Liberia, 1 Anglican.
INSTITUTIONS (church-operated) (1973). Total 2, including 1 minor seminary, 1 medical centre.
PERIODICALS. 3 titles.
PERSONNEL. About 201 (175 national, 26 foreign).
SCRIPTURE DISTRIBUTION. *Translations completed.* Portion: 7 languages since 1869. NT: 4 languages since 1884
SERVICE AGENCIES. About 3.

**ADDITIONAL DATA ON CHURCHES**
EGLISE CATHOLIQUE AU GUINEE. *Catechumens.* (1959) 6,492 in whole country; (1961) 9,593; (1963) 10,918; (1969) 8,407 in D N'Zérékoré. *Annual baptisms.* (1972) 64.8% infant, 35.2% adult. *National priests.* The first national was ordained in 1940. *Personnel.* All Africans (1972). *Seminarians* (1969). 7, studying in Senegal, Upper Volta and Rome. *Catechists.* (1970) 170 in D N'Zérékoré. (1975) 15 in Conakry, 20 in Kankan, 50 in N'Zérékoré. *Religious congregations.* Sisters: Soeurs de l'Immaculée-Conception de Ouagadougou, Petites Servantes des Pauvres de Ouidah (Dahomey), N-D de Guinée.
*Catholic organizations.* The National Episcopal Conference of the Republic of Guinea (Conférence Episcopale Nationale de la République de Guinée) is in principle a member of the Inter-territorial Conference of French-speaking West Africa (Conférence Inter-territoriale de l'Afrique de l'Ouest Francophone) and of SECAM. There are no national organizations for religious personnel, priests or laity nor is there a pastoral council.
The Holy See has no diplomatic relations with Guinea; it is represented to the Catholic hierarchy by an apostolic delegate who also serves as pro-nuncio to the Ivory Coast and resides in Abidjan.
EGLISE EVANGELIQUE PROTESTANTE. By 1976 the church had a very large number of adherents and sympathizers. In addition to 2,300 baptized adults, there were about 12,700 others (believers, interested and sympathizers). The statistics in the table above, and of Christians in Table 1, only include committed, affiliated and/or professing Christians, the others being at present (using this survey's definitions) still traditionalists with a few Muslims.

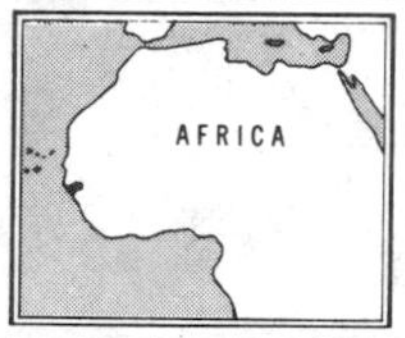


# GUINEA-BISSAU

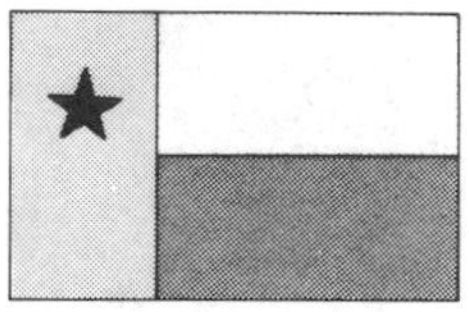

## SECULAR DATA

**STATE. Official name:** The Republic of Guinea-Bissau (A República da Guiné Bissau).
**Flag** (shown above right): Red vertical bar at hoist with black star; 2 horizontal stripes, yellow above green.
**Area:** 36,125 sq.km. (13,948 sq.miles). Agricultural land: 43.3%.
**Government:** Military socialist state, since 1980 (1446 Portuguese possession, 1879 colony, 1952 overseas province, 1973 Independence, 1980 military coup).
**Legislature:** National Assembly, 48 members.
**Official language:** Portuguese (*Português*).
**Capital:** Bissau 60,000.

**DEMOGRAPHY. Population:** 487,448 (census of 15.XII.1970. For 1970–2000 (UN), see last row of Table 1). Population density (1975): 15/sq.km. (38/sq.mile). Under 15 years: 36%. Growth rate (1975–80): 1.76% per year (births 4.08%, deaths −2.32%).
Life expectancy (1975–80): 41.0 years. Household size: 4.9 persons.
**Major languages:** Fulani, Mandingo, Portuguese, Portuguese Creole, Felup, Papel (Pepel), Balante, Manjaco, and 15 other tribal languages.
**Urban dwellers** (1970): 18.1%. Urban growth rate (1950–70): 3.4% per year.
**Labour force:** 37%.
**Refugees** (1977): None. Exiles abroad: 100,000 former refugees in Senegal and Guinea returned to Guinea-Bissau in 1975.

**ETHNOLINGUISTIC GROUPS:** 93.5% African (30.0% Balante, 20.0% Fulani, 13.0% Manjaco, 12.0% Malinke, 6.5% Papel (including Bram, Mancanha), 3.0% Biafada, 3.0% Nalu, 2.6% Diola (Felup, Bayot, et alii), 2.0% Bijogo (Bijago), 0.4% Susu, 0.4% Soninke, Tenda, Bassari), 4.5% White (Portuguese military, with some civilian, declining after 1974 to 0.4%), 2.0% Mestiço (Caboverdian, Guinean), Lebanese Arab.

**MONEY** (1977). **Monetary unit:** peso (= 100 centavos); US$1 = PG 31.00.
**National income per person:** US$300. Average annual family income: US$1,470.
**Cost of living in capital** (1976): Daily cost of living: US$29.

**EDUCATION.** Adult literacy: (1962) 5%. Education rate: 12%. Schools: 346.

**HEALTH.** Hospitals: 34 (889 beds). Doctors: 30. Lepers: 16,800 (32.0 per 1,000). Blind: 5,000. Psychotics: 3,700.

**LITERATURE.** Periodicals: 4. Newspapers: 1 daily, 2 non-daily.

**COMMUNICATION** (per 1,000 people). Phones: 6. Radios: 17. Daily newspaper circulation: 1 copy.

TABLE 1. RELIGIOUS ADHERENTS IN GUINEA-BISSAU

| Year | 1900 | | mid-1970 | | Annual change, 1970–1980 | | | | mid-1975 | | mid-1980 | | 2000 | |
|---|---|---|---|---|---|---|---|---|---|---|---|---|---|---|
| *Name* | *Adherents* | *%* | *Adherents* | *%* | *Natural* | *Conversion* | *Total* | *Rate* | *Adherents* | *%* | *Adherents* | *%* | *Adherents* | *%* |
| Tribal religionists | 97,200 | 81.0 | 264,700 | 52.2 | 4,538 | −1,623 | 2,915 | 1.05 | 277,050 | 52.8 | 293,850 | 51.3 | 382,000 | 45.4 |
| Muslims | 18,000 | 15.0 | 177,450 | 35.0 | 3,214 | 981 | 4,195 | 2.14 | 196,200 | 37.4 | 219,400 | 38.3 | 353,600 | 42.0 |
| **Christians** | **4,800** | **4.0** | **64,300** | **12.7** | **−1,166** | **572** | **−594** | **−1.17** | **50,880** | **9.7** | **58,360** | **10.2** | **99,100** | **11.8** |
| professing | 4,800 | 4.0 | 64,300 | 12.7 | −1,166 | 572 | −594 | −1.17 | 50,880 | 9.7 | 58,360 | 10.2 | 99,100 | 11.8 |
| Roman Catholics | 4,800 | 4.0 | 61,000 | 12.0 | −1,225 | 565 | −660 | −1.40 | 47,250 | 9.0 | 54,400 | 9.5 | 92,600 | 11.0 |
| Protestants | 0 | 0.0 | 3,000 | 0.6 | 54 | 6 | 60 | 1.82 | 3,300 | 0.6 | 3,600 | 0.6 | 6,000 | 0.7 |
| Anglicans | 0 | 0.0 | 300 | 0.1 | 5 | 1 | 6 | 1.82 | 330 | 0.1 | 360 | 0.1 | 500 | 0.1 |
| nominal | 0 | 0.0 | 1,834 | 0.4 | 78 | 301 | 379 | 8.04 | 4,710 | 0.9 | 5,620 | 1.0 | 9,600 | 1.1 |
| affiliated | 4,800 | 4.0 | 62,466 | 12.3 | −1,244 | 271 | −973 | −2.11 | 46,170 | 8.8 | 52,740 | 9.2 | 89,500 | 10.6 |
| total practising | 4,560 | *95* | 49,970 | *80* | −958 | −137 | −1,095 | −3.08 | 35,550 | *77* | 39,030 | *74* | 58,170 | *65* |
| non-practising | 240 | *5* | 12,490 | *20* | −286 | 408 | 122 | 1.15 | 10,620 | *23* | 13,710 | *26* | 31,330 | *35* |
| Roman Catholics | 4,800 | 4.0 | 59,626 | 11.8 | −1,295 | 262 | −1,033 | −2.40 | 43,050 | 8.2 | 49,300 | 8.6 | 84,200 | 10.0 |
| Protestants | 0 | 0.0 | 2,640 | 0.5 | 48 | 8 | 56 | 1.93 | 2,900 | 0.6 | 3,200 | 0.6 | 5,000 | 0.6 |
| Evangelicals | 0 | 0.0 | 2,600 | 0.5 | 47 | 7 | 54 | 1.89 | 2,850 | 0.5 | 3,140 | 0.5 | 4,800 | 0.6 |
| Anglicans | 0 | 0.0 | 200 | 0.0 | 3 | 1 | 4 | 1.82 | 220 | 0.0 | 240 | 0.0 | 300 | 0.0 |
| Non-religious | 0 | 0.0 | 500 | 0.1 | 11 | 29 | 40 | 5.71 | 700 | 0.1 | 900 | 0.2 | 5,000 | 0.6 |
| Baha'is | 0 | 0.0 | 50 | 0.0 | 1 | 3 | 4 | 5.71 | 70 | 0.0 | 90 | 0.0 | 300 | 0.0 |
| Atheists | 0 | 0.0 | 0 | 0.0 | 2 | 38 | 40 | 40.00 | 100 | 0.0 | 400 | 0.1 | 2,000 | 0.2 |
| **Country's population** | **120,000** | **100.0** | **507,000** | **100.0** | **6,600** | **0** | **6,600** | **1.26** | **525,000** | **100.0** | **573,000** | **100.0** | **842,000** | **100.0** |

COLUMNS, ROWS. For meanings and definitions, see Codebook (Part 6). Note that, by definition, total 'Christians' = professing + crypto-Christians, which also = affiliated + nominal Christians. Percentages may not always total exactly, due to rounding.
CENSUSES. **1950:** 62.5% tribal religionists, 35.0% Muslims, 2.4% Roman Catholics (1.5% civilized, 0.9% non-civilized), 0.04% Protestants (185 civilized, 43 non-civilized), 0.02% Druzes (85 persons, Lebanese).

**NOTES ON RELIGIONS**
COUNTRY'S POPULATION. From 1959–74 a large Portuguese military presence was in Portuguese Guinea, averaging 20,000 and as high as 35,000 at one period. After Independence in 1973, the 20,000 troops with some civilians (almost all Roman Catholics), who made up about 4.1% of the 1974 population, departed for Portugal. The table therefore includes them for the year 1970, excludes them for 1975–2000, and under 'Annual change' gives the resulting averages for the decade 1970–80.
MUSLIMS. Predominant in the east and south; Sunnis (of the Malikite rite). Islamized tribes: Soninke, Fula, Susu. Others: Diola (60% Muslim), Biafada (33%), Balante (10%), Manjaco (5%). The total includes Druzes from Lebanon (85 in 1950). *Hajj pilgrims to Mecca.* (1976) 1.
TRIBAL RELIGIONISTS. Strongest in the west. Tribes over 60% traditionalist in 1972: Banyun (92%), Bijago (88%), Manjaco-Papel (84%), Balante (79%), Biafada (60%), Bassari.

**NON-CHRISTIAN RELIGIONS. Traditional religions** are strongest among the western tribes: Banyun who in 1972 were 92% traditionalist, Bijago 88%, Manjaco-Papel 84%, Balante 79%, and Biafada 60%. The proportion of traditionalists is declining rapidly due to conversions to Christianity and Islam. The idea of a supreme being is universal, God being identified as Emit among the Diola and Orrebuco-Ocoto among the Bijago. The ancestral cult, called Choro by the Banyun, is also highly developed. The use of wooden images (*Irus*) to represent the ancestral presence is common among the Papel, Balante and Manjaco.

**Islam,** which has the allegiance of 38% of the population, is predominant among the eastern and southern peoples. The Soninke of the northeast are almost entirely Muslim, and the southeastern Fula and southern Susu are strongly influenced by Islam. Islam has also made inroads in the west, with the Diola about 60% Muslim, the Biafada 33%, the Balante 10%, and the Manjaco 5% Muslim.

## CHRISTIANITY

CATHOLIC CHURCH. The first Catholic

missionaries (OFM) arrived in 1462. When the diocese of St James of Cape Verde (Santiago do Cabo Verde) was erected in 1532, it was given responsibility for the mission on the mainland. Although Jesuits later joined the Franciscans, the work progressed slowly. In 1694 there were only 2,000 Catholics, nor were significant gains achieved later. Indeed in 1929 only one priest remained in the territory. When the concordat was signed between

Portugal and the Holy See in 1940, Guinea became a mission sui juris independent of the diocese of Cape Verde; and in 1955 the mission was raised to the status of prefecture apostolic, and in 1977 to diocese. The diocese is now composed of 3 ecclesiastical districts: Bissau, Bafatá and Cumura. After the outbreak of armed insurrection under the PAICG in 1962, missions retreated from the interior area held by nationalists to regrouped villages and cities along the western coast.

OTHER CHURCHES. Protestantism was not introduced until 1939, when missionaries of the Worldwide Evangelization Crusade arrived in Bissau. The Igreja Evangélica da Guiné is the product of this effort and is the only large Protestant church in the country. Ten mission posts have been erected, 3 on the Arquipelago dos Bijagos. All are concentrated in western Guinea. In 1950 there were 228 Protestants, 43 being indigenous Africans. The Church has no schools but carries on general medical and maternity work among the Papel of Biombo. A clinic is functioning and a small maternity hospital is planned. An extensive leprosy control programme among the Balante at Bissora was abandoned due to guerrilla activity. On the Bijagos Islands, a rural development scheme provides training in improved agricultural methods and better care of livestock. Literacy work is carried on among the Bijago, Papel and Balante. There is also a small Anglican community which is part of the diocese of Gambia and the Rio Pongas.

CHURCH AND STATE. The concordat of 1940 between Portugal and the Holy See provided for the special status of the Catholic Church in all Portuguese territories. Protestants were tolerated but looked upon with suspicion. The civil war which began in the territory in 1962 adversely affected the ability of the churches to carry on evangelistic activity in the interior, and they tended to concentrate their attention in the western part of the country. However, with the proclamation of independence by the African Party for the Independence of Guinea Bissau and Cape Verde (PAIGC) in 1973, a new situation was created. The constitution passed by the PAIGC in 1973 stipulates in Article 13 that all citizens are equal before the law, without regard to their ethnic origin, social class, philosophy or religion. Article 17 guarantees the 'freedom to practise a religion'; the name 'God' however does not appear. Since Independence was recognized by Portugal in September 1974, this has now become the constitution of Guinea-Bissau.

BROADCASTING. The radio network Emissora Provincial permitted religious programmes up to 1975, and Catholic groups transmitted regular religious programmes on secular radio and TV.

**Tribal religionists.** Bassaris (from extreme northeast of country) playing traditional religio-musical instruments.

**Igreja Evangélica da Guiné.** Congregation at Binar outside thatch church, with WEC missionary.

## BIBLIOGRAPHY

*Atlas missionário português.* A Rego & E. dos Santos. Lisboa: Junta de Investigações do Ultramar, 1964. (Maps and data on Catholic missions in Guinea-Bissau).

Several of the country's postage stamps have had Christian themes: here, the 1951 Exposition of Missionary Art.

TABLE 2.  ORGANIZED CHURCHES AND DENOMINATIONS IN GUINEA-BISSAU

| Official name 1 | Begun 2 | Type 3 | Counc 4 | Congs 5 | Adults 6 | Affiliated 7 | Names, notes, and other statistics (see Codebook) 8 |
|---|---|---|---|---|---|---|---|
| Assembleias de Deus | 1974 | P Pe2 | ZP... | 2 | 30 | 100 | *Assemblies of God.* M = Assembleias de Deus (Brazil). Classical Pentecostals. 2f. |
| Igreja Adventista | 1965 | P Adv | x.... | 2 | 20 | 40 | *SDA.* União Portuguesa dos Adventistas do Sétimo Dia. In Portuguese Union Mission. |
| Igr Anglicana (D Gambia & Rio Pongas) | | A ACa | awaV. | | 100 | 200 | *Anglican Ch.* In Ch of the Province of West Africa. HQ Banjul (Gambia.) |
| Igreja Católica: D Bissau | 1462 | R Lat | H,S.. | 13 | 40,000 | 59,626 | Included 20,000 military until 1974 peace. C=2+0+3. 28x,10m,23w,521Y,812y,8144z. |
| Igreja Evangélica da Guiné | 1939 | P int | xP... | 24 | 1,252 | 2,500 | *IEPG.* Evangelical Church of Guinea Bissau. M=MEGP(WEC,UK). 9m,14f,1h,1k,W=90%. |
| Total affiliated (mid-1970) | | | | 43 | 41,402 | 62,466 | Total denominations (1970) . . . 4. |
| Total affiliated (mid-1975) | | | | 46 | 30,600 | 46,170 | Total denominations (1975) . . . 5. |
| Total affiliated (mid-1980) | | | | 49 | 35,000 | 52,740 | Total denominations (1980) . . . 6. |

**NOTES ON TABLE ABOVE**
COLUMNS: for meanings and CODES (cols. 1, 3, 4, 8), see Codebook (Part 6). Column 1: **Boldface type** = church with over 10% of country's affiliated Christians.

PEOPLES (ethnolinguistic). Christians: (1970): 33% Portuguese (including military), 16% Mestiço (Caboverdian, Guinean), 14% Balante, 11% Papel, 9% Manjaco, 7% Mancanha, 5% Bijogo, 2% Banyun, 1.5% Biafada, 1% Diola. (1975): 22% Mestiço (Caboverdian, Guinean), 20% Balante, 16% Papel, 13% Manjaco, 10% Mancanha, 7% Bijogo, 5% Portuguese, 3% Banyun, 2% Biafada, 1% Diola.

COUNTRY-WIDE TOTALS
EVANGELIZATION (see Part 5). 1900: 8%. 1970: 30%. 1980: 36%. The Papel (Pepel) tribe of the Biombo region are virtually 100% evangelized, but only a few hundred have become Protestants; every village has been visited by Protestants (all ex-animistic Papels themselves), and probably every single non-Christian has been spoken to. Well over half of the Balante have also been as thoroughly evangelized.
FOREIGN MISSIONARIES AND PERSONNEL (nationals serving abroad) (1973). Total 2 Roman Catholic sisters in Portugal.
FOREIGN MISSIONARIES AND PERSONNEL (aliens from abroad) (1973). Total 86. *From Western world.* 81: 61 Roman Catholics, 20 Protestants (14 in 1 UK society, 5 in 2 USA societies, 1 in 1 Netherlands society). *From Third World.* 5 (3 Roman

Catholics, 2 Protestants (Assemblies of God)) from Brazil.
INSTITUTIONS (church-operated) (1973). Total 17, including 1 higher school (minor seminary), 12 medical centres, 2 presses, 2 research centres.
PERIODICALS. 3 titles.
PERSONNEL. About 96 (10 national, 86 foreign).
RELIGIOUS LIBRARIES. 4.
SCRIPTURE DISTRIBUTION (1975). Annual totals: 100 Bibles (commercial). *Translations completed.* Portion: 1 language in 1973.
SERVICE AGENCIES. 1.

**ADDITIONAL DATA ON CHURCHES**
IGREJA CATOLICA. The prefecture of Guinea-Bissau was set up in 1955, and was regarded by the Portuguese as part of the ecclesiastical province of Angola. In 1974 it was placed under Propaganda in Rome, and in 1977 was raised to a diocese immediately subject to the Holy See. In 1972, there were 20,000 Portuguese military present, until Independence in 1973. Local Catholics are 25% Cape Verdians (Whites), 18% Papel, 18% Balante, 12% Manjaco, 12% Mancanha, 7% Bijogo. *Priests.* No Guineans, no secular priests; all OFM (Portuguese and Italians), PIME (Italians). *Brothers.* Portuguese and Italians. *Sisters.* All Portuguese except for 2 Africans (in 1972) who by 1975 had left to work in Portugal. *Indigenous religious congregations.* None. *Foreign religious orders and congregations.* Priests: OFM (Portuguese province). PIME. Sisters: Franciscan Hospital

Sisters of Mary Immaculate (Portuguese, Italian), Irmãs do Santo Nome de Deus (Italian).
*Catholic organizations.* Guinea-Bissau has no episcopal conference, association of religious personnel, pastoral or presbyteral councils, nor national lay organizations.
The Holy See had diplomatic relations with Portugal during the colonial regime when it was represented to government and the Catholic hierarchy by a nuncio residing in Lisbon. Subsequent to Independence there have been no diplomatic relations but the Holy See is represented to the Catholic hierarchy by an apostolic delegate who serves also as pro-nuncio to Senegal, with residence in Dakar.
Franciscans run a printing press in Bissau and publish a periodical *A Voz da Guiné* (The Voice of Guinea). They have also directed since 1946 the Museum of Guinea Bissau (Museu da Guiné Bissau) and the Study Centre of Guinea-Bissau (Centro de Estudos da Guiné Bissau). The latter, which aims to study and promote local culture, maintains a library and publishes a cultural journal *Boletin Cultural.*
In 1970 the Catholic Church was responsible for 30 schools with 5,400 pupils, and 11 medical and social service centres (1 leprosarium). By 1973 schools had increased to 78 primary, with 10,457 pupils. By 1976 all schools and hospitals had been nationalized, but religious personnel were asked to continue operating them.

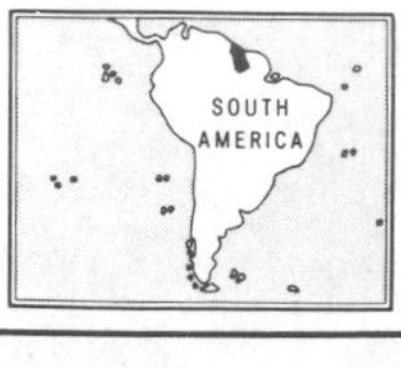


# GUYANA

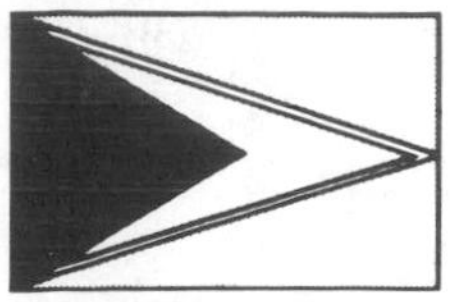

## SECULAR DATA

**STATE. Official name:** The Republic of Guyana. Adjective of nationality: Guyanese. Guyana = Land of Waters.
**Flag** (shown above right): Green field with black-edged red triangle superimposed on white-edged yellow triangle.
**Area:** 214,969 sq.km. (83,000 sq.miles). Agricultural land: 15.0%.
**Government:** Parliamentary republic, since 1970 (1620 Dutch colony, 1831 British Guiana, 1966 Independence).
**Legislature:** National Assembly, 53 members.
**Official language:** English.
**Capital:** Georgetown 99,989 (1970).
**Armed forces** (1976): Total 2,000 regular army. Paramilitary forces: 2,250.

**DEMOGRAPHY. Population:** 699,848 (census of 7.IV.1970. For 1970–2000 (UN), see last row of Table 1). Population density (1975): 4/sq.km. (10/sq.mile). Under 15 years: 47%. Growth rate (1975–80): 2.22% per year (births 3.11%, deaths −0.55%, emigrants −0.34%). Life expectancy (1975–80): 69.1 years. Household size: 5.3 persons.
**Major languages:** English, Guyanese Creole, Hindi, Urdu, Arawak, Portuguese, Chinese, and about 8 other languages.
**Urban dwellers** (1970): 35.0%. Urban growth rate (1950–70): 4.1% per year.
**Labour force:** 32%.

**ETHNOLINGUISTIC GROUPS:** 50.8% East Indian (from North India: Hindi, Urdu), 30.4% Black (African Negro & Bush Negro), 11.4% Mulatto, 4.7% Amerindian (33,000) (2.1% Carib (Arawaio, Galibi, Makushi, Patamona), 0.8% Arawak (Wapishana)), 1.8% White (1.3% Portuguese), 0.6% Chinese (4,680) (Cantonese, Hakka), 0.3% USA Black, Jewish.

**MONEY** (1977). **Monetary unit:** dollar (= 100 cents); US$1 = G$2.55.
**National income per person:** US$410. Average annual family income: US$2,173.

**Inflation:** (1970–75) 7.6% per year (1975: consumer price index 152).
**Cost of living in capital** (1976): index 85 (Washington DC = 100). Daily cost of living: US$40.

**EDUCATION.** Adult literacy: (1946) 76%, (1960) 87%. Education rate: 81%. Schools: 388. Universities: 1.

**HEALTH.** Hospitals: 42 (2,969 beds). Doctors: 191. Lepers: 4,100 (5.2 per 1,000). Blind: 1,300. Psychotics: 6,300. Criminals: 39,866.

**LITERATURE.** Annual new book titles (1972): 24. Periodicals: 20. Newspapers: 4 dailies, 6 non-daily.

**COMMUNICATION** (per 1,000 people). Phones: 23. Radios: 133. TV sets: 4. Daily newspaper circulation: 54 copies.

TABLE 1. RELIGIOUS ADHERENTS IN GUYANA

| Year | 1900 | | mid-1970 | | Annual change, 1970–1980 | | | | mid-1975 | | mid-1980 | | 2000 | |
|---|---|---|---|---|---|---|---|---|---|---|---|---|---|---|
| *Name* | *Adherents* | *%* | *Adherents* | *%* | *Natural* | *Conversion* | *Total* | *Rate* | *Adherents* | *%* | *Adherents* | *%* | *Adherents* | *%* |
| **Christians** | **167,300** | **58.7** | **382,900** | **54.0** | **8,122** | **−462** | **7,660** | **1.83** | **418,800** | **52.9** | **459,500** | **52.0** | **602,900** | **48.0** |
| professing | 167,300 | 58.7 | 382,900 | 54.0 | 8,122 | −462 | 7,660 | 1.83 | 418,800 | 52.9 | 459,500 | 52.0 | 602,900 | 48.0 |
| Protestants | 68,400 | 24.0 | 141,900 | 20.0 | 2,915 | −1,205 | 1,710 | 1.14 | 150,300 | 19.0 | 159,000 | 18.0 | 188,400 | 15.0 |
| Anglicans | 76,100 | 26.7 | 127,600 | 18.0 | 2,599 | −1,219 | 1,380 | 1.03 | 134,000 | 17.0 | 141,400 | 16.0 | 163,300 | 13.0 |
| Roman Catholics | 22,800 | 8.0 | 113,400 | 16.0 | 2,608 | 1,962 | 4,570 | 3.40 | 134,500 | 17.0 | 159,100 | 18.0 | 251,200 | 20.0 |
| nominal | 22,000 | 7.7 | 48,067 | 6.8 | 1,146 | 1,317 | 2,463 | 4.17 | 59,100 | 7.5 | 72,700 | 8.2 | 71,700 | 5.7 |
| affiliated | 145,300 | 51.0 | 334,833 | 47.2 | 6,976 | −1,779 | 5,197 | 1.44 | 359,700 | 45.5 | 386,800 | 43.8 | 531,200 | 42.3 |
| total practising | 116,240 | *80* | 234,380 | *70* | 4,883 | −1,245 | 3,638 | 1.44 | 251,790 | *70* | 270,760 | *70* | 345,300 | *65* |
| non-practising | 29,060 | *20* | 100,450 | *30* | 2,093 | −534 | 1,559 | 1.44 | 107,910 | *30* | 116,040 | *30* | 185,900 | *35* |
| Roman Catholics | 21,700 | 7.6 | 110,000 | 15.5 | 2,424 | 806 | 3,230 | 2.58 | 125,000 | 15.8 | 142,300 | 16.1 | 219,800 | 17.5 |
| Catholic pentecostals | 0 | 0.0 | 0 | 0.0 | 19 | 281 | 300 | 30.00 | 1,000 | 0.1 | 3,000 | 0.3 | 20,000 | 1.6 |
| Anglicans | 62,700 | 22.0 | 100,000 | 14.1 | 1,962 | −1,792 | 170 | 0.17 | 101,200 | 12.8 | 101,700 | 11.5 | 113,000 | 9.0 |
| Protestants | 59,900 | 21.0 | 96,733 | 13.6 | 1,918 | −1,511 | 407 | 0.41 | 98,900 | 12.5 | 100,800 | 11.4 | 119,300 | 9.5 |
| Evangelicals | 42,750 | 15.0 | 41,800 | 5.9 | 1,051 | 159 | 1,210 | 2.55 | 47,500 | 6.0 | 53,900 | 6.1 | 81,600 | 6.5 |
| Guyanan indigenous | 1,000 | 0.3 | 19,500 | 2.8 | 460 | 420 | 880 | 3.71 | 23,700 | 3.0 | 28,300 | 3.2 | 50,200 | 4.0 |
| Orthodox | 0 | 0.0 | 6,000 | 0.8 | 136 | 104 | 240 | 3.43 | 7,000 | 0.9 | 8,400 | 1.0 | 17,600 | 1.4 |
| Marginal Protestants | 0 | 0.0 | 2,600 | 0.4 | 76 | 194 | 270 | 6.92 | 3,900 | 0.5 | 5,300 | 0.6 | 11,300 | 0.9 |
| Hindus | 71,200 | 25.0 | 226,550 | 32.0 | 7,260 | 500 | 7,760 | 2.95 | 262,950 | 33.2 | 304,150 | 34.4 | 474,900 | 37.8 |
| Muslims | 18,000 | 6.3 | 63,800 | 9.0 | 1,381 | 199 | 1,580 | 2.22 | 71,200 | 9.0 | 79,600 | 9.0 | 103,000 | 8.2 |
| Ahmadis | 0 | 0.0 | 1,000 | 0.1 | 25 | 35 | 60 | 4.62 | 1,300 | 0.2 | 1,600 | 0.2 | 3,500 | 0.3 |
| Tribal religionists | 22,800 | 8.0 | 20,000 | 2.8 | 384 | −444 | −60 | −0.30 | 19,800 | 2.5 | 19,400 | 2.2 | 18,800 | 1.5 |
| Afro-American spiritists | 5,700 | 2.0 | 7,000 | 1.0 | 138 | −118 | 20 | 0.28 | 7,100 | 0.9 | 7,200 | 0.8 | 6,300 | 0.5 |
| Non-religious | 0 | 0.0 | 3,000 | 0.4 | 91 | 309 | 400 | 8.51 | 4,700 | 0.6 | 7,000 | 0.8 | 37,700 | 3.0 |
| Buddhists | 0 | 0.0 | 2,000 | 0.3 | 39 | −39 | 0 | 0.00 | 2,000 | 0.3 | 2,000 | 0.2 | 1,000 | 0.1 |
| Baha'is | 0 | 0.0 | 1,700 | 0.2 | 43 | 57 | 100 | 4.55 | 2,200 | 0.3 | 2,700 | 0.3 | 5,000 | 0.4 |
| Atheists | 0 | 0.0 | 1,000 | 0.1 | 27 | 53 | 80 | 5.71 | 1,400 | 0.2 | 1,800 | 0.2 | 6,300 | 0.5 |
| Chinese folk-religionists | 0 | 0.0 | 1,000 | 0.1 | 15 | −55 | −40 | −5.00 | 800 | 0.1 | 600 | 0.1 | 0 | 0.0 |
| Jews | 0 | 0.0 | 50 | 0.0 | 0 | 0 | 0 | 0.00 | 50 | 0.0 | 50 | 0.0 | 100 | 0.0 |
| **Country's population** | **285,000** | **100.0** | **709,000** | **100.0** | **17,500** | **0** | **17,500** | **2.21** | **791,000** | **100.0** | **884,000** | **100.0** | **1,256,000** | **100.0** |

COLUMNS, ROWS. For meanings and definitions, see Codebook (Part 6). Note that, by definition, total 'Christians' = professing + crypto-Christians, which also = affiliated + nominal Christians. Percentages may not always total exactly, due to rounding.
CENSUSES. **9.IV.1946** (adjusted to include 6,023 Amerindians in remote districts): 46.4% Protestants & Anglicans, 31.5% Hindus (0.7% Arya Samajists), 11.6% Roman Catholics, 7.8% Muslims, 2.6% tribal religionists, 0.1% other religionists. **7.IV.1960**: 33.4% Hindus, 22.1% Protestants, 19.6% Anglicans, 14.9% Roman Catholics, 8.8% Muslims, 1.0% tribal religionists, 0.2% marginal Protestants. **7.IV.1970** (incomplete): 37.3% Hindus, 17.4% Anglicans, 13.8% Protestants, 13.5% Roman Catholics, 17.9% all others (Muslims, tribal religionists, other religionists, also other Protestants and Christians, and a large number of unknown religion). The figures in the table above represent the most likely ones for the period 1970–80.

NOTES ON RELIGIONS
AFRO-AMERICAN SPIRITISTS. Vodoun (Voodoo) is widely practised. Bush Negroes have cults derived from Ashanti religion (from Ghana). There are also a few Rastafarians (from Jamaica).
AHMADIS. Most adherents are Qadianis, with missionaries from Pakistan. The rival faction, Lahoris, have in Guyana virtually their only mission outside Pakistan.
ATHEISTS. People's Progressive Party (PPP) (legal; pro-Soviet): membership (1970) 100 communists, 20,000 others; Communist voters (election of 16.XII.1968) 113,027 (37% of all votes).
BAHA'IS. Rapid growth from 1 local spiritual assembly (1964) to 17 (1973).
BUDDHISTS. Chinese.
CATHOLIC PENTECOSTALS (or, Catholic charismatics). Totals (January 1974): 500 involved adults; total charismatic community including children, 1,000. (Mid-1975): 400 involved adults in 8 prayer groups.
GUYANAN INDIGENOUS. In 12 denominations in 1970, among Blacks and Amerindians (see Table 2). The first began around 1870 among Amerindians.
HINDUS. Hindi-speaking; 70% of the Indian population, with a few Blacks. About 2% of all Hindus are Arya Samajists, who gain a number of Black converts each year. The Hindu community has been growing for some years faster than others due to higher fertility.
MUSLIMS. Urdu-speaking; 18% of all Indians, with a few Black converts each year; mostly rural; Sunnis, some adherents of Ahmadiya (enumerated here under Muslims, though declared non-Muslim by Pakistan). There is also a political party, the Guyana United Muslim Party (GUMP).
TRIBAL RELIGIONISTS. Of the over 33,000 pure tribal jungle or lowland Amerindians in the interior, a large proportion are still animists, including among the Taruma and Arawak.

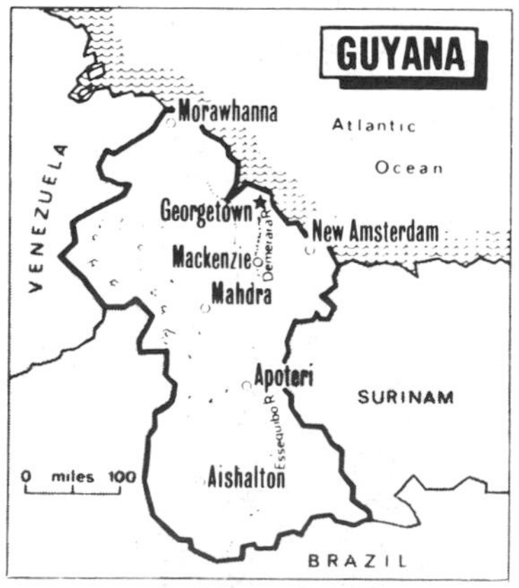


**NON-CHRISTIAN RELIGIONS. Hinduism** is followed by 34% of the population of Guyana and by 70% of the East Indian population. Various organizations are active including the American Aryan League, which represents the reformed wing of Hinduism, and the traditionalist Hindu Orthodox Guyana Sanathan Dharma Maha Sabha whose influence extends beyond the borders of the country.
**Islam,** with 9% of the population and 18% of all East Indians, has its main strength among rural Asians. Organizationally Muslims are divided into orthodox Sunni and heterodox Ahmadiya sects.
**Traditional Amerindian religions** still exist among the Taruma of the extreme south as well as among members of the Arawak family in the southwest.
**Vodoun** (Voodoo) beliefs and practices are observed by non-Christians of African descent (Afro-American spiritists), and also by many nominal Christians. A small number of other Blacks also have been converted to Hinduism and Islam.

**CHRISTIANITY.** Christians make up about 53% of the population. They include a majority of the Black and Mulatto populations and are most frequently found in urban areas. A considerable number of East Indians, around 35,000, have been converted to Christianity. Other ethnic groups are largely Christian.
CATHOLIC CHURCH. Although Guyana was evangelized initially during the 16th century, Catholicism was virtually erased during the long Dutch occupation after 1620. The first Catholic priest of the modern era arrived in 1826, and in 1837 a vicariate was erected. In spite of the fact that Catholicism has been active in Guyana for the past century and a half, only 15 of its 78 priests in 1971 were natives. A Jesuit survey in 1967 reported that approximately 60% of nominal Catholics were of African and mixed descent, 20% were Amerindians and 6% Portuguese. The remaining 14% were East Indians, Chinese and Europeans. The number of nominal Catholics is increasing in relation to population growth, notwithstanding the emigration of a high percentage of the Portuguese, who at one time formed the bulk of the Catholic population. With the exception of the Amerindians, a high proportion of Catholics live in the greater Georgetown area, with relatively few in the rural areas of Berbice and Essequibo.
ANGLICAN CHURCH. The London Missionary Society began work in Guyana in 1807, sponsored by several churches including Anglicans. In 1810 the Anglican Church itself was established in Georgetown, later the archiepiscopal see of the West Indies. The Anglican Church is today the second largest denomination in Guyana. It is strongly Anglo-Catholic in churchmanship and maintains close ties with the Guyana Catholic Church.
PROTESTANT CHURCHES. Guyana has a long

history of missionary endeavour and displays a proliferation of churches and mission agencies, both long-established denominations and more recent arrivals especially in the urban areas. The racially mixed population is reflected in its church membership. Of the 15 churches belonging to the Council of Churches, 5 have a mixed population, 7 are predominantly Black and 2 are mostly East Indian.

Guyana was a colony of the Netherlands until the early 19th century when it passed into British hands. The first Protestant Church was founded in 1743 by Dutch Lutherans to cater for the settler community. From 1766 planters from Scotland began what is now the Presbytery of Guyana, which remained part of the Church of Scotland until its autonomy in 1967. During 1837–1945 it was supported by state subsidies. The first Methodists were freed slaves who emigrated from Nevis in 1802 and were followed later by British Methodists.

The Guyana Presbyterian Church began in 1885 with missionaries from Canada, but its growth remains slow. Seventh-day Adventists on the other hand have established a large community since their arrival in 1887. Of the many new denominations coming after World War II the most significant growth rates have been experienced by Assemblies of God and Southern Baptists. The Unevangelized Fields Mission works with several Indian tribes in the interior near the Brazilian border.

INDIGENOUS CHURCHES. A number of indigenous bodies have arisen, including the Jordanites of the 1920s and the Hallelujah Church. The latter began over a hundred years ago and extends into Venezuela; it remains an Amerindian prophet movement syncretizing traditional religion with Christianity. The recent entrance of missionaries into the area where it originated has resulted in its revival after a period of decline. Several Black denominations from the USA have also been active, including the AME and the AME Zion churches both of which are members of the Guyana Council of Churches.

CHURCH AND STATE. The constitution, promulgated 26 May 1966, begins in its Preamble: 'Whereas the people of Guyana acknowledge that reverence for the Deity (is) the foundation of freedom, justice and peace in society. . .'. It then goes on to guarantee freedom of religion in its Chapter II. The government gives a grant to those churches concerned with social work among Amerindians. Recognized elementary and secondary schools founded by churches receive financial aid from the Ministry of Education, but no further aid is to be offered church schools in the future. Churches are exempt from a number of taxes.

Expatriate ministers of religion need a permit to enter and work in Guyana. Since Independence in 1966, most denominations, especially those dependent on manpower and finance from abroad, have been engaged in a process of reassessing their role in a strongly nationalistic society.

Religious matters are dealt with by the Ministry of Home Affairs. Church buildings must be registered insofar as this is necessary for the calling of marriage banns, and ministers of religion must be appointed as marriage officers in order to officiate at weddings.

In September 1976 the government nationalized all private schools, in the face of vocal Catholic and Anglican opposition.

In November 1978, Peoples Temple, a Protestant cult with 90% USA Black membership, which had had close illegal dealings with the ruling political party, organized a mass suicide-murder at Jonestown in the northwestern jungle, killing 912 persons.

INTERDENOMINATIONAL ORGANIZATIONS. In 1937, through the efforts of an Anglican layman, a Christian Social Council was established, to which both Catholics and Protestants belonged. In 1967 it merged with an Evangelical Council, formed in 1960, to become the present Guyana Council of Churches. The council now numbers 15 churches and includes 4 autonomous regional councils. It sponsors the David Rose Centre, a self-help community project in the poorest sections of Georgetown, providing medical and social services and self-employment training in collaboration with several governmental agencies.

There is also a diocesan Catholic Ecumenical Commission.

BROADCASTING. The government Guyana Broadcasting Service allocates Catholics 15 minutes daily from Monday to Saturday, 15 minutes on

**Anglican Church, Diocese of Guyana.** *Above.* 'And He entered into a boat. . .' Emulating practice of Jesus beside Galilee, a priest of USPG preaches to small crowd from boat.
*Below.* Ecumenical rally of 20,000 people at Bourda Green called by Christian Social Council protesting against government's seizure of 51 denominational schools (Anglican, Catholic and Protestant).

Sundays, and for Protestants 6 hours from Monday to Saturday and one and a half hours on Sundays. The commercial station Radio Demerara, The Voice of Guyana, allows Catholics 15 minutes every day, and Protestants 5.5 hours during the week and 3 hours on Sundays. All broadcasts are in English. Less than half of Protestant programmes are produced locally. There is no television in Guyana. In Georgetown there is a Catholic Communications, Catechetics and Youth (CCY) Training Centre, founded in 1970, with radio and cinema studios. Also in Georgetown

are the Christian Association of Broadcasters, Catholic Broadcast Commission, and Commission on Communications.

BIBLIOGRAPHY

*A history of the Lutheran Church in Guyana.* P. Beatty. South Pasadena, CA(USA): William Carey Library, c1972. 245p.
*Journal of the proceedings of the Annual Synod, Diocese of Guyana, 1969–1970.* Georgetown: Diocesan Office, 1970.
'The birth of a religion: the origins of Hallelujah, the semi-Christian religion of the Carib-speaking people of the borderlands of British Guiana, Venezuela and Brazil', A. J. Butt, *Timehii,* 38 (September, 1959), 37–48.

TABLE 2. ORGANIZED CHURCHES AND DENOMINATIONS IN GUYANA

| Official name 1 | Begun 2 | Type 3 | Counc 4 | Congs 5 | Adults 6 | Affiliated 7 | Names, notes, and other statistics (see Codebook) 8 |
|---|---|---|---|---|---|---|---|
| African Methodist Episcopal Church | | I Met | VwM.K | | 230 | 1,000 | *Guyana-Surinam Annual Conference*. 16th Episcopal District. M=AMEC(USA Blacks). |
| African Methodist Episcopal Zion Ch | 1911 | I Met | Vw..K | 17 | 1,586 | 3,000 | M=AMEZC(USA Blacks). 2 schools. Many emigrants to UK. HQ Lacytown. 13n,1r. |
| **Anglican Church: D Guyana** | 1810 | A ACa | AWMRK | 180 | 25,118 | 100,000 | 1842, Diocese in Ch of Province of West Indies. M=USPG(UK). 33n,18x,68Y,2946y. |
| Assemblies of God in Guyana | 1952 | P Pe2 | ZFH.L | 59 | 2,766 | 6,000 | M=AoG(USA). 53% Black, 42% East Indians. 79n,1x,2f,G=8%pa,1s(125),W=90%,250Y,200z. |
| Baptist Mid-Missions | 1958 | P Bap | x.... | | 100 | 200 | *Regular Baptists*. M=BMM(USA). Fundamentalists from North America. 2f. |
| Bible Missionary Church | 1957 | P Hol | x.H.L | 10 | 120 | 300 | M=Bible Missionary Church)(USA). Holiness denomination. 2n,2x,1p,1s,22Y,10z. |
| Bible Protestant Congregational Chs | | I Con | .TT.T | 2 | 1,000 | 2,000 | Fundamentalist schism ex Congregational Union, with USA support. HQ Georgetown. |
| **Catholic Church: D Georgetown** | 1548 | R Lat | PxNMK | 25 | 58,000 | 110,000 | Under M Port-of-Spain. 60% Black. M=SJ. C=2+0+3. 15n,63x,4m,81w,P=28%,1p,3200Yy. |
| Christadelphian Ecclesias | | P Ade | x.... | 4 | 50 | 100 | *Christadelphian Bible Mission*. 4 ecclesias in New Amsterdam. M=Birmingham(UK). |
| Christian Brethren Assemblies | c1835 | P CBr | x.H.L | 35 | 1,000 | 2,000 | *Plymouth (Open) Brethren*. M=CMML(UK,USA). No HQ, but mainly Georgetown. 4f. |
| Christian Catholic Church | 1948 | P Con | x.H.L | 6 | 100 | 200 | M=CCC(Zion,Illinois,USA). Healing emphases. Small group in Bel Air Park. |
| Church of Christ, Scientist | | M Sci | x.... | 1 | 50 | 100 | *Christian Science*. M=CCS(Boston,USA). First Church, Georgetown. |
| Church of God of Prophecy | 1956 | P Pe3 | Z.... | 2 | 60 | 200 | M=CGP(USA). Holiness Pentecostals. Split in USA ex CoG(Cleveland). HQ Albouystown. |
| Church of God (Anderson) | 1914 | P Hol | x...K | 20 | 1,360 | 2,000 | *General Assembly of CoG(Guyana)*. M=CoG(Anderson)(USA). All races. 6n,2f,1j,28t. |
| Church of the Nazarene | 1945 | P Hol | xF..K | 34 | 971 | 4,000 | M=CoN.Urban Blacks, rural East Indians. 7n,2x,2f,G=6%pa,52t(3233),W=54%,150Y,239z. |
| Elim Pentecostal Churches | | P Pe2 | ZGH.L | 4 | 622 | 1,000 | M=EFGA(UK). Classical Pentecostals (2-stage). HQ Georgetown. 4f. |
| Episcopal Orth Ch (Greek Communion) | c1940 | I Lib | x.... | | 200 | 300 | Black. Ex AOC(USA). Begun 1920 in Trinidad. HQ in Bridgetown (Barbados). |
| Ethiopian Orthodox Church | | O Eth | Nwa.. | 23 | 4,000 | 6,000 | *EOC*. Under P Addis Ababa (Ethiopia). Blacks. M=EOC(Jamaica,Trinidad). 2x. |
| Evangelical Methodist Ch in Guyana | 1960 | P Hol | xTT.T | 2 | 100 | 200 | *Bible Methodists*. M=EMC(USA). Fundamentalists from Holidaysburg, PA(USA). 4f. |
| Guyana Baptist Mission | 1962 | P Bap | T...K | 40 | 1,012 | 3,609 | M=SBC,NBCUSA. Mostly along coast. Rapid growth. 8n,6x,14f,42h,2s(29),W=60%,244Y. |
| Guyana Congregational Union | 1807 | P Con | R.M.K | 37 | 7,000 | 17,000 | M=LMS(UK), now CWM. HQ New Amsterdam. Black. 3n,3x,G=−2.3%pa,W=60%,768Yy,253z. |
| Guyana Presbyterian Church | 1885 | P Ref | R.M.K | 56 | 2,238 | 6,000 | M=PCC(Canada). A=1945. All East Indians till 1945. HQ Queenstown. 15n,1s. |
| Hallelujah Church | c1870 | I mar | ..... | | 5,000 | 10,000 | Begun by prophet Abel. Macushi and tribes for 200 miles near Brazil & Venezuela. |
| Isolated radio churches | c1965 | I rad | ..... | | 100 | 200 | Isolated radio believers, in the southern forests, mostly youths and pupils. |
| Jehovah's Witnesses | 1900 | M Jeh | x.... | 28 | 1,111 | 2,000 | *Watch Tower. IBSA*. Active witnessing under way by 1926. HQ Georgetown. 89Y. |
| Jordanites | c1920 | I pen | ..... | | 500 | 1,000 | *WEMP Church*. Blacks, in Georgetown. Earliest indigenous pentecostal church. |
| Lutheran Church in Guyana | 1683 | P Lut | LvM.K | 50 | 5,000 | 13,058 | Dutch origins. M=LCA(USA). A=1943. East Indians. HQ New Amsterdam. 5f. |
| Methodist Ch in Caribbean & Americas | 1802 | P Met | VwM.K | 51 | 5,428 | 10,000 | *MCCA*(1967 union), *Guyana District*. M=MMS(UK). Black. 7n,5x,G=0.3%pa,5Y,570y. |
| Moravian Church | 1878 | P Mor | xwM.K | 9 | 867 | 2,500 | First attempt 1735–38. *Guyana Province*, *UoB*. M=Moravian Ch(USA). Black. 3x,43y. |
| New Testament Church of God | 1956 | P Pe3 | ZFH.a | 16 | 334 | 600 | M=CoG(Cleveland)(USA). 15 churches, 1 mission. 16n,4f,1p. |
| Presbytery of Guyana | 1766 | P Ref | R.M.K | 25 | 3,250 | 5,600 | Begun by Scots planters. In Ch of Scotland till 1967 autonomy. Black. 9n,1x. |
| Salvation Army | 1895 | P Sal | xwM.K | | 1,000 | 3,000 | *SA, Guyana Division*, Caribbean\|&\CAmerica Territory. All races. HQ Georgetown. |
| Seventh Day Baptist Church | 1920 | P Bap | Tw... | 6 | 146 | 300 | *Guyana Conference*. Sabbatarian Baptists. M=SDBC(USA). HQ Kitty. 2f. |
| Seventh-day Adventist Church | 1887 | P Adv | x.... | 56 | 8,162 | 12,000 | *SDA, Guyana Mission* Caribbean Union Conf. 8nx,142mw,6f,1H,1r,78t(6500),1053Y. |
| Unevangelized Fields Mission | 1949 | P int | xM... | 1 | 500 | 1,000 | M=UFM(UK,USA). In jungle, Brazil border. Indians: Wai–Wai, Wapishana, Macushi. 5f. |
| Wesleyan Church in Guyana | 1909 | P Hol | VFH.L | 53 | 810 | 3,866 | Formerly Pilgrim Holiness Ch until 1968 merger. 10n,1x,3f,G=−1.8%pa,W=22%,482Y. |
| Other Protestant denominations | | P | ..... | | 1,000 | 2,000 | Total about 20 (see list below) |
| Other Black indigenous churches | | I | ..... | | 1,000 | 2,000 | Incl African Apost Ch, FDPMM, Good Shepherd Universal Ch of Christ, House of Israel (USA). |
| Other marginal Protestant bodies | | M | ..... | | 200 | 500 | Total over 5, including: Christian Mystic Faith, New Jerusalem Ch, Unitarian Ch. |
| **Total affiliated (mid-1970)** | | | | **945** | **142,091** | **334,833** | **Total denominations (1970) . . . 67.** |
| **Total affiliated (mid-1975)** | | | | **960** | **152,600** | **359,700** | **Total denominations (1975) . . . 70.** |
| **Total affiliated (mid-1980)** | | | | **980** | **164,100** | **386,800** | **Total denominations (1980) . . . 73.** |

NOTES ON TABLE ABOVE

COLUMNS: for meanings and CODES (cols. 1, 3, 4, 8), see Codebook (Part 6). Column 1: **Boldface type** = church with over 10% of country's affiliated Christians.

NATIONAL COUNCILS (Column 4, 5th letter).
- a = member of both GCC and GEF.
- K = Guyana Council of Churches (GCC) (1967 merger of Christian Social Council, and Council of Evangelical Churches).
- L = Guyana Evangelical Fellowship (GEF).
- T = Guyana Council of the ICCC.

*Local councils*. 4 regional councils, related to GCC.

OTHER PROTESTANT DENOMINATIONS. These include: Association of Baptists for World Evangelism, Christian Mission Chs (member of GEF), Chs of Christ (Instrumental) (1959), Chs of Christ, Exclusive Brethren (Kelly-Continental), Full Gospel Fellowship (member of GEF), Guyana Mennonite Mission (35 adherents), Guyana Missionary Baptist Ch (member of GCC), Independent Assemblies of God, Missionary Aviation Fellowship (1958: a few congregations in areas without other missions), Open Bible Standard Chs, Peoples Temple (1974 exodus from USA to Jonestown in jungle; 1,200 followers, 90% USA Blacks; November 1978, mass suicide-murder of 912), Streams of Power Movement (Stromen van Kracht, Netherlands), Worldwide Evangelization Crusade, World-Wide Missions (1967).

PEOPLES (ethnolinguistic). Christians: 60% Black, 23% Mulatto, 10% Indian (East Indian), 4% White (2.7% Portuguese), 2% Amerindian, 0.6% USA Black, 0.2% Chinese.

COUNTRY-WIDE TOTALS

EVANGELIZATION (see Part 5). 1900: 59%. 1970: 94%. 1980: 95%. *Mass evangelism*. In 1974 and in February 1975 large 7-day crusades were conducted under the auspices of the Evangelistic Association, Pentecostal Assemblies of the West Indies, in the National Park, Georgetown, and in the bauxite centre Lyndon. In Georgetown in the 1975 campaign, there were 2,000 professions of faith in 7 days. *Radiophonic evangelism*. Bible correspondence courses: Presbyterian Ch of Canada, ICI (6,300 enrolments, 180 conversions).

FOREIGN MISSIONARIES AND PERSONNEL (nationals serving abroad) (1973). Total about 2 Guyanan indigenous in UK.

FOREIGN MISSIONARIES AND PERSONNEL (aliens from abroad) (1973). Total 193. *From Western world*. 176: 96 Roman Catholics, 59 Protestants (48 in 23 USA societies, 10 in 4 UK societies, 1 in 1 France society), 20 Anglicans in 2 UK societies, 1 Black indigenous from USA. *From Third World*. 17: 11 Roman Catholics (6 from India, 3 Trinidad & Tobago, 2 Barbados), 4 Protestants and Anglicans from Jamaica, 2 Orthodox from Ethiopia.

INSTITUTIONS (church-operated) (1973). Total 60, including 1 ecumenical centre, 6 higher schools (1 minor seminary), 45 medical centres (2 hospitals), 1 research centre, 5 seminaries (Protestant).

PERIODICALS. About 20 titles.

PERSONNEL. About 880 (687 national, 193 foreign).

RELIGIOUS LIBRARIES. 7.

SCRIPTURE DISTRIBUTION (1975). Annual totals: 2,450 Bibles (8% free, 88% subsidized, 4% commercial), 20,300 NTs (86% free, 14% commercial), 5,100 UBS portions, 36,700 UBS selections. *Translations completed*. Portion: 5 languages since 1850. NT: Patamuna in 1974.

SERVICE AGENCIES. About 19, including CJGS, CLC, GCC, MAF, SPCK, YMCA, YWCA.

ADDITIONAL DATA ON CHURCHES

CATHOLIC CHURCH. *Catholics*. 60% Black (African and mixed descent), 20% Amerindian, 6% Portuguese; remainder East Indian, Chinese (290 in 1975), European. *Annual baptisms*. (1972) 95.1% infant, 4.9% adult. *Priests*. Nationals: 8 Jesuits, 3 secular. The first Guyanan priest was ordained in 1954. Expatriates: 58 Jesuits, 5 secular priests on loan. *Brothers*. All nationals. *Sisters*. 48 nationals, 33 expatriates. *Catholic charismatics* (January 1974). About 500 adults including religious personnel are active in over 5 prayer groups in Georgetown. *Catechists*. Total (1970) 187. Training at Diocesan Catechetical Training Centre, Georgetown. *Indigenous (Caribbean) religious congregations*. Sisters: Ursuline Nuns of the Roman Union of the South Caribbean Province (Barbados), Corpus Christi Carmelites of the West Indies Province (Trinidad & Tobago). *Foreign orders and congregations*. Priests: SJ, SFM (Scarboro Fathers, secular priests but not diocesan). Sisters: Sisters of Mercy. *Catholic organizations*. The diocese of Georgetown belongs to the Antilles Episcopal Conference with headquarters in Kingston, Jamaica. Religious personnel in Guyana are part of the Conference of the Major Superiors of the Antilles, centred in Montego Bay, Jamaica. Both a Pastoral Council and a Senate of Priests have been established, the former consisting mostly of appointed members while the membership of the latter is mainly elected. The most active Catholic lay associations are the St Vincent de Paul Society and the Ladies of Charity.

The Holy See has no diplomatic relations with Guyana. It is represented to the Catholic hierarchy by an apostolic delegate based in Port-au-Prince, Haiti.

The Catholic Church is now trying to become more involved in the fields of economic and social development through the Guyana Institute for Social Research and Action. It sponsors community development projects, co-operatives and credit unions, working in close relation with the Guyana Council of Churches. In addition to schools found elsewhere in the country, a system of schools has recently been built up among the scattered Amerindians in the interior. In 1974 Catholic institutions included 63 schools (60 primary, 3 secondary) with 20,980 pupils, one hospital, one dispensary, 5 homes for the aged and infirm, 3 orphanages, a hostel for boys and one for girls.

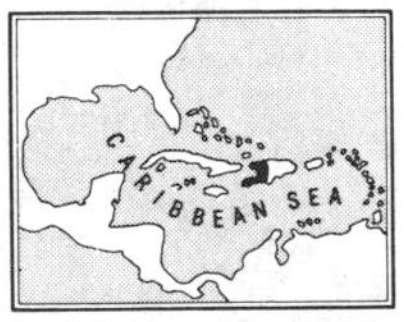


# HAITI

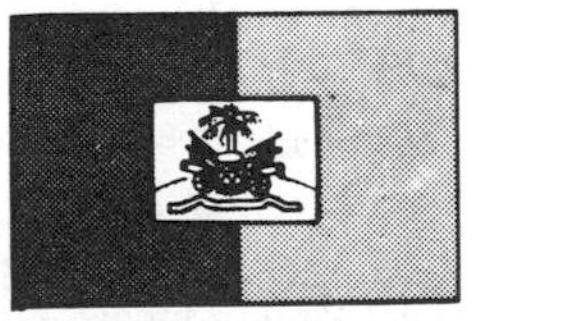

## SECULAR DATA

**STATE. Official name:** The Republic of Haiti (La République d'Haïti). Adjective of nationality: Haitian (haïtien).
**Flag** (shown above right): Black and red bars; centred white rectangle with emblems of war around palm tree.
**Area:** 27,750 sq.km. (10,714 sq.miles). Agricultural land: 52.8%.
**Government:** Republic under authoritarian rule, since 1971 (1492 Spanish possession, 1697 French colony, 1804 Independence as empire, 1915–34 USA rule, 1957 dictatorship).
**Legislature:** National Assembly, 58 members.
**Official language:** French (*Français*).
**Capital:** Port-au-Prince 493,930 (1971).
**Political divisions:** 9 Départements.
**Armed forces** (1976): Total 6,550 regular: army 6,000, navy 300, air force 250. Paramilitary forces: 14,900 National Security Volunteers/Tontons Macoutes).

**DEMOGRAPHY. Population:** 4,329,991 (census of 31.VIII.1971. For 1970–2000 (UN), see last row of Table 1). Population density (1975): 164/sq.km. (425/sq.mile). Under 15 years: 42%. Growth rate (1975–80): 1.70% per year (births 3.62%, deaths −1.46%, emigrants −0.46%). Life expectancy (1975–80): 52.2 years. Household size: 4.4 persons.
**Major languages:** French, French Creole (Haitian Creole),

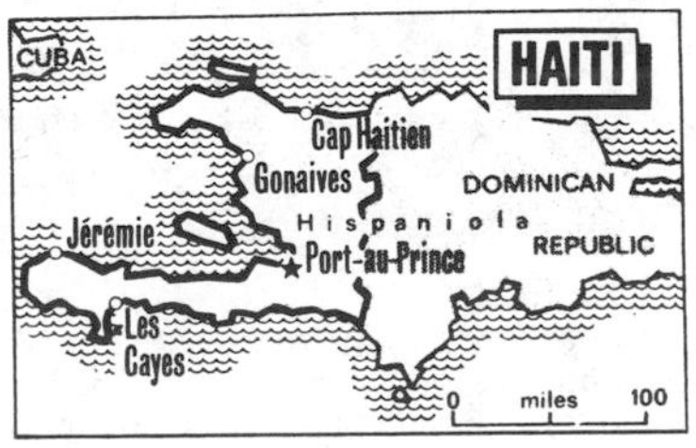


Spanish, Arabic.
**Urban dwellers** (1970): 17.8%. Urban growth rate (1950–70): 4.6% per year.
**Labour force:** 56%.
**Refugees** (1977): From abroad, none. Exiles abroad: 370,000 Haitians (300,000 in Dominican Republic, 50,000 in USA (1,851 since 1972), 15,000 in Bahamas, 5,000 in Puerto Rico).
**Tourists** (1973): 206,000. (1974) 47,600. (1976) 200,000.

**ETHNOLINGUISTIC GROUPS:** 94.5% Black (pure Negro), 5.0% Mulatto (Black/French), 0.4% Dominican Mulatto, Levantine Arab (2,000), European White (500) (USA, UK, French, German, Italian), Chinese (180), Jewish.

**MONEY** (1977). **Monetary unit:** gourde (= 100 centimes); US$1 = Gde 5.00.
**National income per person:** US$140. Average annual family income: US$616.
**Inflation:** (1970–75) 12.6% per year (1975: consumer price index 195).
**Cost of living in capital** (1976): index 109 (Washington DC=100). Daily cost of living: US$39.

**EDUCATION.** Adult literacy: (1950) 11%, (1971) 23%. Education rate: 22%. Schools: 2,083. Universities: 1.

**HEALTH.** Hospitals: 48 (3,494 beds). Doctors: 412. Lepers: 900 (0.2 per 1,000). Blind: 9,000. Psychotics: 32,000.

**LITERATURE.** Annual new book titles (1967): 18. Periodicals: 70. Scientific journals: 10. Newspapers: 7 dailies.

**COMMUNICATION** (per 1,000 people). Phones: 2. Radios: 17. TV sets: 3. Daily newspaper circulation: 16 copies.

TABLE 1. RELIGIOUS ADHERENTS IN HAITI

| Year | 1900 | | mid-1970 | | Annual change, 1970–1980 | | | | mid-1975 | | mid-1980 | | 2000 | |
|---|---|---|---|---|---|---|---|---|---|---|---|---|---|---|
| *Name* | *Adherents* | *%* | *Adherents* | *%* | *Natural* | *Conversion* | *Total* | *Rate* | *Adherents* | *%* | *Adherents* | *%* | *Adherents* | *%* |
| **Christians** | **1,499,100** | **99.9** | **4,179,200** | **98.5** | **71,070** | **–980** | **70,090** | **1.56** | **4,880,000** | **98.6** | **4,880,100** | **98.5** | **6,891,500** | **97.8** |
| professing | 1,499,100 | 99.9 | 4,179,200 | 98.7 | 71,070 | –980 | 70,090 | 1.56 | 4,487,000 | 98.6 | 4,880,100 | 98.5 | 6,891,500 | 97.8 |
| Roman Catholics | 1,428,100 | 95.2 | 3,570,000 | 84.3 | 60,137 | –7,867 | 52,270 | 1.38 | 3,796,700 | 83.4 | 4,092,700 | 82.6 | 5,577,700 | 79.2 |
| Spiritist Catholics | 1,357,000 | 90.5 | 3,214,400 | 75.9 | 54,138 | –7,378 | 46,760 | 1.37 | 3,418,000 | 75.1 | 3,682,000 | 74.3 | 4,741,000 | 67.3 |
| Protestants | 70,000 | 4.7 | 489,200 | 11.6 | 8,796 | 5,724 | 14,520 | 2.61 | 555,300 | 12.2 | 634,400 | 12.8 | 1,056,800 | 15.0 |
| Black indigenous | 0 | 0.0 | 80,000 | 1.9 | 1,457 | 1,143 | 2,600 | 2.83 | 92,000 | 2.0 | 106,000 | 2.1 | 190,000 | 2.7 |
| Anglicans | 1,000 | 0.1 | 40,000 | 0.9 | 680 | 20 | 700 | 1.63 | 43,000 | 0.9 | 47,000 | 0.9 | 67,000 | 1.0 |
| nominal | 218,100 | 14.5 | 161,465 | 3.8 | 2,770 | 1,513 | 4,283 | 2.45 | 174,900 | 3.8 | 204,300 | 4.1 | 321,200 | 4.5 |
| affiliated | 1,281,000 | 85.4 | 4,017,735 | 94.9 | 68,300 | –2,493 | 65,807 | 1.53 | 4,312,100 | 94.7 | 4,675,800 | 94.3 | 6,570,300 | 93.3 |
| doubly-affiliated | –52,000 | –3.5 | –350,000 | –8.3 | –6,130 | –1,970 | –8,100 | 2.09 | –387,000 | –8.5 | –431,000 | –8.7 | –634,000 | –9.0 |
| total practising | 1,216,950 | *95* | 3,415,070 | *85* | 58,055 | –2,119 | 55,936 | 1.53 | 3,665,280 | *85* | 3,974,430 | *85* | 5,256,200 | *80* |
| non-practising | 64,050 | *5* | 602,660 | *15* | 10,245 | –374 | 9,871 | 1.53 | 646,820 | *15* | 701,370 | *15* | 1,314,100 | *20* |
| Roman Catholics | 1,270,000 | 84.7 | 3,797,400 | 89.7 | 64,241 | –6,371 | 57,870 | 1.43 | 4,055,800 | 89.1 | 4,376,100 | 88.3 | 5,988,000 | 85.0 |
| Catholic pentecostals | 0 | 0.0 | 0 | 0.0 | 32 | 568 | 600 | 30.00 | 2,000 | 0.0 | 6,000 | 0.1 | 60,000 | 0.9 |
| Protestants | 60,000 | 4.0 | 447,883 | 10.6 | 8,003 | 4,699 | 12,702 | 2.51 | 505,300 | 11.1 | 574,900 | 11.6 | 958,100 | 13.6 |
| Evangelicals | 30,000 | 2.0 | 402,300 | 9.5 | 7,210 | 4,600 | 11,810 | 2.59 | 455,200 | 10.0 | 520,400 | 10.5 | 915,900 | 13.0 |
| Black indigenous | 2,000 | 0.1 | 79,000 | 1.9 | 1,441 | 1,069 | 2,510 | 2.76 | 91,000 | 2.0 | 104,100 | 2.1 | 183,200 | 2.6 |
| Anglicans | 1,000 | 0.1 | 38,452 | 0.9 | 656 | 49 | 705 | 1.70 | 41,400 | 0.9 | 45,500 | 0.9 | 64,000 | 0.9 |
| Marginal Protestants | 0 | 0.0 | 5,000 | 0.1 | 89 | 31 | 120 | 2.14 | 5,600 | 0.1 | 6,200 | 0.1 | 11,000 | 0.2 |
| Non-religious | 0 | 0.0 | 41,000 | 1.0 | 774 | 916 | 1,690 | 3.46 | 48,800 | 1.1 | 57,900 | 1.2 | 123,800 | 1.8 |
| Baha'is | 0 | 0.0 | 9,700 | 0.2 | 166 | 34 | 200 | 1.90 | 10,500 | 0.2 | 11,700 | 0.2 | 20,000 | 0.3 |
| Afro-American spiritists | 500 | 0.0 | 2,000 | 0.0 | 33 | –13 | 20 | 0.95 | 2,100 | 0.0 | 2,200 | 0.0 | 2,000 | 0.0 |
| Muslims | 400 | 0.0 | 1,500 | 0.0 | 25 | –5 | 20 | 1.25 | 1,600 | 0.0 | 1,700 | 0.0 | 2,500 | 0.0 |
| Atheists | 0 | 0.0 | 500 | 0.0 | 10 | 10 | 20 | 3.33 | 600 | 0.0 | 700 | 0.0 | 2,000 | 0.0 |
| Jews | 0 | 0.0 | 100 | 0.0 | 2 | –2 | 0 | 0.00 | 100 | 0.0 | 100 | 0.0 | 200 | 0.0 |
| Other religionists | 0 | 0.0 | 1,000 | 0.0 | 20 | 40 | 60 | 4.62 | 1,300 | 0.0 | 1,600 | 0.0 | 3,000 | 0.0 |
| **Country's population** | **1,500,000** | **100.0** | **4,235,000** | **100.0** | **72,100** | **0** | **72,100** | **1.58** | **4,552,000** | **100.0** | **4,956,000** | **100.0** | **7,045,000** | **100.0** |

COLUMNS, ROWS. For meanings and definitions, see Codebook (Part 6). Note that, by definition, total 'Christians' = professing + crypto-Christians, which also = affiliated + nominal Christians. Percentages may not always total exactly, due to rounding.
CENSUSES. **31.VIII.1971**: 84.3% Roman Catholics, 14.2% Protestants, 1.0% non-religious, 0.6% other Christians and other religionists.

NOTES ON RELIGIONS
AFRO-AMERICAN SPIRITISTS. Non-Christian (mostly immigrant) adherents of Afro-Caribbean non-Christian spirit-possession cults syncretizing African religion with elements of Christianity. There are also a few Rastafarians (from Jamaica).
ATHEISTS. There are small numbers, of 2 varieties: (1) Unified Party of Haitian Communists (PUCH) (proscribed under penalty of death); membership a few hundred; and (2) de facto atheists among Tontons Macoutes and other secret police thugs.
BAHA'IS. Rapid growth from 12 local spiritual assemblies (1964) to 65 (1973). Missionary pioneers from Haiti have settled in Benin (Dahomey), the Central African Republic and Guadeloupe.
BLACK INDIGENOUS. In about 34 denominations in 1970 (see Table 2).
CATHOLIC PENTECOSTALS (or, Catholic charismatics). Begun 1972 at a Carmelite monastery in Cap-Haïtien. The total persons personally involved grew from 8 (mid-1973) to over 400 adults weekly in Cap-Haïtien alone (January 1975), including 25 priests and the bishop (July 1975); mid-1975 total charismatic community including children, 2,000, growing very rapidly and having spread to surrounding towns, Port-au-Prince and Les Cayes (by January 1976).
DOUBLY-AFFILIATED. The term covers those affiliated to, or claimed by, both the Catholic Church and also an Evangelical church (Protestant, Anglican, marginal Protestant, Black indigenous), i.e. baptized Catholics who have recently become Evangelicals. Because their statistics represent a duplication, they are shown in the table as a negative quantity (with a minus sign).
MUSLIMS. Immigrant Syrian and Lebanese Arab traders since 1880, also East Indians and others.
OTHER RELIGIONISTS. Adherents of smaller religions and cults, including Rosicrucians (5 AMORC centres).
PRACTISING CHRISTIANS. About 20% of Roman Catholics practise regularly (weekly), a majority on festivals, and about 80% at least once a year.
PROTESTANTS. Conversions to Protestantism come primarily from active participants of Vodoun (Voodoo); often whole families are converted at the same time.
ROMAN CATHOLICS (affiliated). 1872: 927,000. 1880: 970,000. 1890: 1,000,000. 1900: 1,270,000. 1937: 2,663,000. 1940: 2,666,300. 1942: 2,688,000.
SPIRITIST CATHOLICS. Some 90% of all Catholics, mainly the rural peasantry but not the upper and middle urban classes, regularly practise a form of spiritist christo-paganism termed Vodoun (Voodooism, or The Gods, of Fon (Dahomean) origin), including Arada (Rada) and many other cults.

**NON-CHRISTIAN RELIGIONS. Vodoun** (Vodun, Voodooism) first appeared in the 17th century, a syncretism of African rites mainly from Dahomey with Catholic practices, resulting in a form of spiritism often termed christo-paganism in other countries. Vodoun priests and priestesses *(hounganor)* have great prestige and power among their followers, their word being taken as law in many regions. Under their leadership Vodoun worship revolves around offerings, bloody and bloodless, to the spirits *(loa)* who control nature and daily human life. It includes ritual dances accompanied by a heady rhythm and heavy drinking and often involves spirit-possession. Black and white magic and divining the future are also important features. While ancient African spirits have often been identified with Christian saints, Vodoun has been subject to attack by the Catholic Church, such as the anti-superstition campaign of 1941–42. It was placed under the penal code, but this was revoked in 1946 by president Estimé. Widely practised by the peasantry and urban proletariat and by a majority of Catholics, its influence has begun to diminish recently, in part due to the growing tourist trade.

**Baha'i** has recently experienced rapid growth, from 12 local spiritual assemblies in 1964 to 65 by 1973, and has sent missionaries to West and Central Africa.

**CHRISTIANITY.** The island of which Haiti forms part was the first land colonized by the Spanish, and within a century the indigenous Indian population had disappeared. Catholic missionaries arrived in 1493, and the first Franciscan college was established in 1503. Dominicans entered in 1511, including the renowned Bartolomeu de las Casas, and St Thomas University was opened in 1538. The west became more heavily occupied after 1630 by buccaneers, with African slaves and indentured Frenchmen working the land. Jesuits came in 1704, and in 1777 the island was divided between Spain and France, the latter receiving Haiti. Plantations were developed at the expense of the Negroes who finally revolted in 1791 and seized their own independence in 1804. Three years later Protestant missionary activity was begun. Political control of the island shifted frequently during the 19th century with different European governments, the Dominican republic, Colombia and Haiti itself alternating in power. During 1915–34 the island was occupied by the military forces of the USA.

CATHOLIC CHURCH. The modern era of the Catholic Church in Haiti dates from the signing of a concordat with the Holy See in 1860. The following year 5 episcopal sees were erected, including the archdiocese of Port-au-Prince. As a result of the concordat, the Catholic Church was organized on a parochial basis instead of a missionary basis. For many years most of its missionaries were French, especially from Brittany, although this began to change in 1942 with the arrival of Canadian missionaries from Quebec. An important effort has also been put into the creation of an indigenous clergy by the opening of the Seminary of Haiti in 1872 and the St James Seminary in 1894, and later through the creation of a major seminary by Jesuits in 1948. At the present time, some 150 Haitian priests remain at work in Haiti. The continued control of the church by the political regime remains one of the major problems of Catholicism in the country and has greatly hampered its pastoral work.

PROTESTANT CHURCHES. Haiti has the largest number of Protestants in the Latin Caribbean. Most denominations are experiencing rapid growth, particularly among the lower classes. The conversion of whole families from Voodooism is common although individual conversions also take place among migrants to the cities. In addition there are large numbers of unbaptized adherents. Pastors are scarce, but most are nationals. While there are Bible institutes in Haiti, there are no Protestant higher-level seminaries, and the level of theological training is low. Because of this, missionaries tend to remain in leadership positions, with missions rather than national church organizations often being recognized by government. Most pastors and churches continue to rely heavily on financial subsidies from North America. Protestant expansion was initially aided by the USA military occupation between 1915 and 1934.

The first 2 Protestant missionaries, sent by British Methodists to Haiti in 1807, went to serve the large number of English-speaking Negroes who had emigrated there to seek their freedom. They were expelled eleven years later when their preaching and teaching attracted increasing crowds and they were considered a threat to the shifting all-Black governments in control. The Methodist Church nevertheless continued, one of its missionaries later devising a system for writing Creole which has enabled thousands to learn to read and write. The church is identified with the elite class of towns and cities, which con-

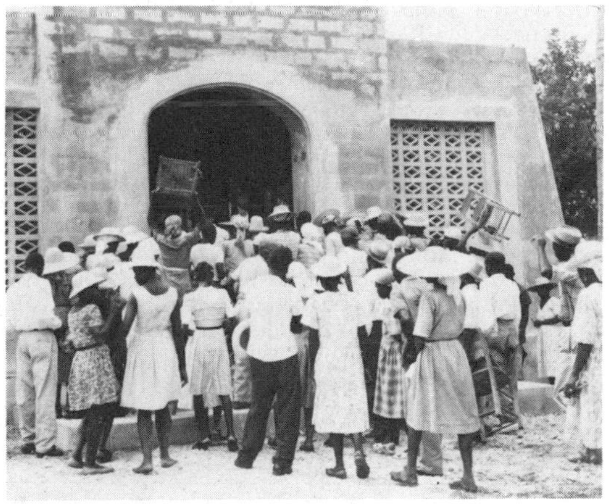

**Eglise Méthodiste d'Haïti.** Crowd enter church at Oliviers, Petit-Goâve.

tributes to its slow growth, due partly to the emigration of many of these elite to Europe and North America for political and other reasons. Since 1823 different British and American Baptist missions have attempted to start churches. Little success was achieved until the entrance of the American Baptists in 1923 while the country was under USA occupancy. Other conservative Baptist societies followed, the rapidity of increase of Baptist churches since then constituting almost a mass conversion. They are today the largest Protestant tradition and are active in all parts of the country. The pastoral training given Haitian Baptist pastors is said to provide the highest educational standards of any Protestant church. Seventh-day Adventists, with heaviest membership in the north, form the second largest Haitian Protestant church, their greatest strength residing in their effective use of lay workers. The Church of God of Prophecy and the Church of God (Cleveland) are next in size, indicating the rapid development of Pentecostal churches in Haiti. Other North American groups, many of which have entered Haiti since World War II, are characterized by a regional orientation.

INDIGENOUS CHURCHES. Over 90,000 persons are found in indigenous Black churches. Some were begun by USA Black churches, the earliest being the AMEC in 1823. But over 25 others have been begun by Haitians independent of any outside aid.

ANGLICAN CHURCH. The Episcopal Church dates back to 1861 when 110 American Blacks settled there and, with proselytes from Roman Catholicism, began the Eglise Orthodoxe Apostolique Haïtienne. In 1911 the Haitian clergy requested that their church become a missionary district of the Protestant Episcopal Church of the USA, due to inadequacies in local leadership, and this took place in 1913. Members today are mostly of the elite class, this church suffering also from the migration of much of its leadership to Europe and the USA.

**CHURCH AND STATE.** Freedom of religion is guaranteed, on paper, by the constitution of 1964 (Article 27). Catholicism enjoys a unique status as a result of the concordat of 1860 when it was considered a priori the religion of the majority of Haitians. According to this concordat, the Catholic Church and its ministers are especially protected (Article 1). The bishops are paid by the state (Article 3), nominated by the president of the republic, subject to the approval of the Holy See (Article 4), and are obliged, as are other members of the clergy and directors of religious institutions, to take an oath the text of which is provided in Article 5. The president must approve the nomination of vicars-general and parish clergy as well as any modifications within the ecclesiastical jurisdictions (Article 11). Homage must be made to him through special prayers at the end of each mass (Article 15). Churches are obliged to register with the Department of Foreign Affairs and Religions.

The regime established by president François Duvalier exercised progressive control over the Catholic Church through intimidation and violence, in particular through: (1) the expulsion of the archbishop of Port-au-Prince in 1960, followed by his Haitian auxiliary, Msgr Rémi Augustin, in 1961, by the bishop of Gonaïves in 1962, and by at least 17 French missionaries and 18 Canadian Jesuits expelled between 1959 and 1964; (2) the arrest or placing under surveillance of several Haitian priests under the apostolic administrator of Port-au-Prince in 1964; (3) the closure of the interdiocesan major seminary in 1964–65; (4) the dissolution of the Christian trade union; and (5) the banning of the Catholic daily *La Phalange* in 1961, the pastoral review *Eglise en marche* and the cultural review *Rond-Point* in 1964. These measures at first caused the Holy See to break off de facto diplomatic relations in October 1962. In face of the institutional vacancies thus created, Rome signed on 15 August 1966 a common protocol, assuring the renewal of the concordat; the filling with Haitian bishops of the 3 vacant episcopal sees, including that of Cayes, whose bishop had died; the nomination of 2 auxiliary Haitian bishops; the reinstallation of Msgr Augustin and the re-establishment of diplomatic relations. This agreement permitted president Duvalier to present himself as the champion of the indigenization of the church. He was assured at the same time of the unconditional fidelity of the newly-nominated hierarchy. Nevertheless, under the pretext of subversive activities, arrests of priests continued. In 1969 the expulsion of 21 priests, including 10 Haitians (most CSSp), resulted in the voluntary withdrawal of all Holy Ghost priests but aroused no reaction on the part of the episcopate. The Episcopalian bishop, a USA citizen, was also expelled in 1964.

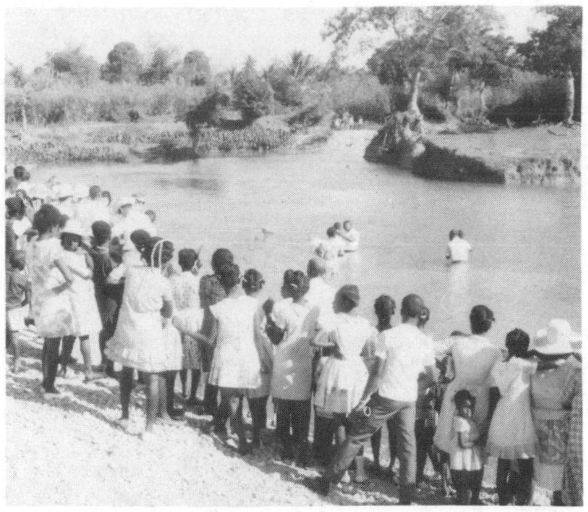

**Mission Evangélique Baptiste du Sud-Haïti.** Adult (believer's) baptism near Les Cayes, 1970.

In August 1974 the journal *World evangelism* published on its cover a photograph of a naked and undernourished child with the caption 'Hunger in Haiti'. In reaction the Ministry of the Interior let it be known that president Jean-Claude Duvalier, who succeeded his father after his death in April 1971, 'could not but criticize the methods used by certain missions to obtain assistance' and that authorization accorded to guilty missions would simply be withdrawn.

**INTERDENOMINATIONAL ORGANIZATIONS.** Although there is no national ecumenical Christian council, 11 of Haiti's conservative denominations have joined together to form the Council of Evangelical Churches of Haiti. The Ecumenical Research Group, founded in January 1968, has representatives from Catholic, Episcopal, Methodist and African Methodist Episcopal churches, as well as the Salvation Army. It includes also some Baptist pastors as individuals. In addition to a library and common religious activities, it sponsors joint social action projects. In 1971 its activities were limited to Port-au-Prince. The Haitian Commission of the Churches for Development (Commission Haïtienne des Eglises pour le Développement, CHED), founded at Port-au-Prince in 1974, brings together delegates from some 30 churches (including the Catholic Church) and interconfessional organizations for the following purposes: to encourage co-operation between churches, co-ordinate their efforts in development and integrate their initiatives into the national plan for the country as a whole.

**BROADCASTING.** The state Radio Haïti accepts Protestant programmes for up to 3 hours from Monday to Saturday. All commercial stations accept Christian programmes. Protestant broadcasting is carried on primarily through 2 missionary radio stations, Radio 4VEH and Radio Lumière. The former was established in 1950 and has been operated by the Oriental Missionary Society since 1958. Located on the northern coast, 4VEH broadcasts some 163 hours of programmes weekly in English, Spanish, French and Creole. Radio Lumière, operated by the West Indies Mission from the southern peninsula and in the south-central areas, began daily operation in January 1959; co-operating missions include the Missionary Church Association and the Unevangelized Fields Mission. Radio Lumière broadcasts some 17 hours a day. Battery-operated transistor radios have been distributed to several hundred churches throughout southern Haiti, particularly to those without regular mail service. Regular Catholic programmes are also transmitted on secular radio and TV stations. International stations from abroad easily received in Haiti include Trans World Radio (Netherlands Antilles), and Radio PJD-2 (Netherlands Antilles). In 1978 a Catholic station, Radio Soleil, began functioning.

**BIBLIOGRAPHY**

*Annuaire de l'Eglise d'Haïti* (Numéro Spécial 1972). Port-au-Prince: Archevêché de Port-au-Prince, 1973. (Catholic).
*Annuaire Protestant 1971–1972*. Port-au-Prince: Centre d'Information et de Statistiques Evangéliques, 1973.
*Haiti, status of Christianity*. Monrovia, California: Missions Advanced Research and Communication Center, 1971.
'Le role du Vaudou dans l'indépendance d'Haïti', A. M. Rigaud, *Présence africaine* (Paris), (February–March, 1958), 43–67.
'Médicine et Vodou en Haïti', A. Metraux, *Acta tropica*, Separatum Vol. 10, 1 (1953), 28–68.
'Réactions psychologiques à la christianisation de la Valée de Marbial (Haïti)', A. Metraux, *Revue de psychologie des peuples*, 8 (1953), 250–267. (Official government attempt to destroy Voodoo in Haiti, and its failure).
*Religion and politics in Haiti*. H.Courlander & R.Bastien. Washington, DC: Institute for Cross-Cultural Research, 1966. 81p.
'Survivance des cultes africains et syncrétisme en Haïti', J. M. Salgado, in *Devant les sectes non-chrétiennes* (Louvain: Desclée de Brouwer, 1961), p. 225–252.
'The belief system of Haitian Vodun', G. E. Simpson, *American anthropologist*, (January, 1945), 35–59.
*The growing church in Haiti*. H. A. Johnson. Coral Gables, Florida: West Indies Mission, 1970. 88p.
'The Vodun service in northern Haiti', G. E. Simpson, *American anthropologist*, (April, 1940), 236–254.

TABLE 2. ORGANIZED CHURCHES AND DENOMINATIONS IN HAITI

| Official name 1 | Begun 2 | Type 3 | Counc 4 | Congs 5 | Adults 6 | Affiliated 7 | Names, notes, and other statistics (see Codebook) 8 |
|---|---|---|---|---|---|---|---|
| Armée du Salut | 1950 | P Sal | xwM.. | | 500 | 1,000 | *Salvation Army, Haiti Division*, Carribbean & CAmerica Territory (HQ Jamaica). 1h. |
| Assemblées de Dieu | 1945 | P Pe2 | ZF... | 99 | 8,713 | 20,000 | M = Assemblies of God(USA). Splits. 5 schools. HQ Port-au-Prince. 89n,6f,1s(14). |
| Convention Baptiste d'Haïti | 1823 | P Bap | T.H.E | 669 | 36,000 | 60,000 | *Baptist Conv.* 1923, M = ABHMS(USA). 65n,2x,11f,G = 2.7%pa,5p,1s,W = 85%,3920Y,10840z. |
| Eglise Adventiste du Septième Jour | 1879 | P Adv | x.... | 79 | 34,657 | 60,000 | *Seventh-day Adventists, N&S Haiti Missions*. 25nx,10f,1h,1j,1r,1s,320t(47707),3330Y. |
| **Eglise Catholique au Haïti:** | 1493 | R Lat | B.L.R | 250 | 2,202,500 | 3,797,400 | *Catholic Ch in Haiti*. C = 8 + 3 + 21. 150n,1p,2s(89),W = 20%. 391nx,194m,799w,103370Yy. |
| M Port-au-Prince | 1861 | R Lat | Bs | 56 | 782,000 | 1,348,000 | Capital, urban. Extreme impoverishment in slums. 1s. 129 110 309 48000 |
| D Cap Haïtien | 1861 | R Lat | Bs | 51 | 431,300 | 743,800 | Northeast. Rural. 27 priests are Haitians. 1p. 109 26 193 17644 |
| D Les Cayes | 1861 | R Lat | Bs | 53 | 539,000 | 930,000 | Extreme southwest peninsula. Rural. Voodoo strong. 87 18 166 26500 |
| D Les Gonaïves | 1861 | R Lat | Bs | 25 | 322,200 | 555,600 | Rural. 7 priests are Haitians. 600 catechumens. 41 24 91 6812 |
| D Port-de-Paix | 1861 | R Lat | Bs | 65 | 128,000 | 220,000 | Extreme northwest. Rural. Voodoo strong. 25 16 40 4415 |
| Eglise de Dieu de Prophétie | 1931 | P Pe3 | Z.H.E | 249 | 16,800 | 34,000 | *Ch of God of Prophecy*. M = CGP(USA), split in USA from Ch of God (Cleveland). |
| Eglise de Dieu en Christ | | I pe3 | Z.... | 96 | 10,697 | 15,000 | *Ch of God in Christ*. M = CoGiC(Black mission from USA). HQ Port-au-Prince. |
| Eglise de Dieu Pentecôtiste | 1952 | P Pe2 | Z.... | 196 | 9,000 | 18,889 | *Pentecostal Ch of God*. M = PCG(Puerto Rico). HQ Port-au-Prince. 153n,2f,1s. |
| Eglise de Dieu (Cleveland) | 1934 | P Pe3 | ZFH.E | 390 | 20,655 | 40,000 | M = Ch of God(Cleveland)(USA). 15 Districts. HQ Port-au-Prince. 173n,5f,1p(30). |
| Eglise du Nazarène | 1946 | P Hol | xFH.E | 390 | 19,826 | 30,000 | M = CoN. 40 schools. 10n,5x,154m,11f,G = 21%pa,1h,1j,1r,1s(33),159t,W = 72%,975Y,13427z. |
| Eglise Episcopale d'Haïti | 1861 | A Hig | aw.R. | 176 | 15,092 | 38,452 | Begun by US Blacks. Since 1913 in PECUSA Province II. 26n,1x,1s,W = 40%,36Y,921y. |
| Eglise Evangélique d'Haïti | 1946 | P Hol | xFH.E | 76 | 688 | 2,915 | *Ev Ch of H*. Begun by M = EWIBM; 1958, M = OMS(USA). Radio station 4VEH. 4n,39f,1h,24Y. |
| Eglise Mennonite | 1966 | P Men | G.... | | 74 | 190 | *Mennonite Ch.* M = Ch of God in Christ(Mennonite)(USA). 2 schools. 13f. |
| Eglise Méthodiste d'Haïti | 1807 | P Met | VwM.. | 123 | 5,440 | 22,500 | *MCCA, Haiti District*. M = MMS(UK). Urban. 30 schools. 4n,5x,11f,1h,3r,341Yy,2182z. |
| Eglise Méthodiste Episcopale Africaine | 1823 | I Met | VwM.. | | 8,000 | 15,000 | In 16th Episcopal District, AMEC (USA). Begun by 500 USA Negroes invited in. |
| Eglise Méthodiste Libre | 1949 | P Hol | VFH.E | 21 | 1,165 | 2,000 | *Free Methodist Ch.* Begun 1949 by Haiti Inland Mission; 1964 joined M = FMC(USA). 5f,1h,1s. |
| Eglise Missionnaire | 1900 | P Hol | xFH.E | 16 | 1,840 | 3,000 | 1951, M = MCA, now MC(USA). Central Plateau. Strong Vodun area. 14 schools, 11f,1h,1p. |
| Eglise Pentecôtiste Unie | 1962 | P Pe1 | x.... | 125 | 4,300 | 10,000 | *United Pentecostal Ch/Jesus Only*. M = UPC(USA). Unitarian Pentecostals. 60n,1p(28). |
| Eglise Réorganisée de J-C des SDJ | | M LdS | x.... | | 400 | 766 | M = Reorganized Ch of Jesus Christ of Latter-day Saints (USA). Schism in USA ex Mormons. |
| Eglise Wesleyenne d'Haïti | 1946 | P Hol | VFH.E | 148 | 6,420 | 8,000 | *Wesleyan Ch. M* = WC(USA). 32 schools. 6n,3x,13f,G = −0.3%pa,2H,3h,W = 62%,344Y,210z. |
| Eglises Baptistes Indépendantes | | I Bap | .T... | 5 | 500 | 1,000 | *Independent Baptist Churches of Cap Haïtien*. HQ Port-au-Prince. Fundamentalists. |
| Eglises Ebenezer | 1960 | I Bap | ..M.. | 50 | 4,000 | 8,000 | *Ebenezer Mission*. Rejected 1960 formation of Baptist Convention. Jacmel area. |
| Mission Baptiste | 1949 | P Bap | x.... | | 530 | 1,000 | *Baptist Mid-Missions*. M = BMM(USA). Fundamentalist Baptists. 6f. |
| Mission Baptiste Conservatrice | 1946 | P Bap | xFH.E | 115 | 5,572 | 24,000 | *Conservative Baptist Haiti Mission*. M = CBFMS(USA). Many splits. 93 schools. 13n,1H. |
| Mission Ev Baptiste du Sud-Haïti | 1936 | P Bap | xMH.E | 609 | 19,910 | 35,000 | *Baptist Mission of South Haiti*. M = WIM(USA). 38 Districts. 117n,40f,1h,1r,1s(57). |
| Mission Evangélique Baptiste d'Haïti | 1928 | P Bap | xMH.E | 217 | 10,113 | 35,389 | *Baptist Mission of Haiti*. 1943, M = UFM(USA). 20n,9x,45f,1H,2h,1p(4),W = 57%,858Y,1238z. |
| Missions Mondiales | 1961 | P ind | x.... | | 15,000 | 30,000 | M = World-Wide Missions(USA). Evangelicals based on Pasadena, CA (USA). |
| Témoins de Jéhovah | 1944 | M Jeh | x.... | 34 | 1,882 | 4,234 | *Jehovah's Witnesses. Watch Tower*. 1944, Brooklyn branch responsible. 197Y. |
| Other Black indigenous churches | | I | ..... | | 20,000 | 40,000 | Total about 30 (see below), mainly splits from Baptist and other denominations. |
| Other Protestant denominations | | P | ..... | | 5,000 | 10,000 | Total over 130 (see list below). |
| Doubly-affiliated (duplication) (1970) | | | | | −203,000 | −350,000 | Evangelicals who also are or were baptized Roman Catholics. |
| **Total affiliated (mid-1970)** | | | | **4,520** | **2,282,274** | **4,017,735** | **Total denominations (1970) . . . 190.** |
| **Total affiliated (mid-1975)** | | | | **4,570** | **2,449,500** | **4,312,100** | **Total denominations (1975) . . . 210.** |
| **Total affiliated (mid-1980)** | | | | **4,630** | **2,656,100** | **4,675,800** | **Total denominations (1980) . . . 230.** |

NOTES ON TABLE ABOVE
COLUMNS: for meanings and CODES (cols. 1, 3, 4, 8), see Codebook (Part 6). Column 1: **Boldface type** = church with over 10% of country's affiliated Christians.
NATIONAL COUNCILS (Column 4, 5th letter).
E = Concile des Eglises Evangéliques d'Haïti (Council of Evangelical Churches of Haiti, CECH).
R = Conférence Episcopale d'Haïti (CEH) (Episcopal Conference of Haiti).
OTHER BLACK INDIGENOUS CHURCHES. These are largely a vast number of independent congregations, either unorganized, or in groupings or organized ephemerally in associations. Among the latter are: African-Negro Mission (under a bishop), Foi Apostolique Nationale, Mission Patriotique Chrétienne. Also there are various USA Black missions at work, including: AME Zion Ch, National Baptist Convention of America, Pentecostal Assemblies of the World, Progressive National Baptist Convention (1965).
OTHER PROTESTANT DENOMINATIONS. These number over 130, mostly smaller bodies from the USA, and include the following: Ch of God Holiness (1966), Ch of the Faith (Faith Holiness Mission/World Gospel Mission, 1965), Chs of God in North America (1967), Elim Missionary Assemblies (1968), Ev Bible Mission (1963), Ev Methodist Ch (1962), Haiti Mountain Mission, Maranatha Baptist Mission (1968), Strict Baptist Mission, Worldwide Evangelization Crusade.

PEOPLES (ethnolinguistic). Christians: 94.5% Black, 5.0% French-speaking Mulatto, 0.4% Dominican Mulatto, European (White), Lebanese Arab.

COUNTRY-WIDE TOTALS
EVANGELIZATION (see Part 5). 1900: 100%. 1970: 100%. 1980: 100%. *Mass evangelism.* Among recent campaigns: 1969, Assemblies of God 2-week campaign (25,000 attenders, 500 enquirers); 1970, 3 denominations initiated major saturation evangelism campaign 'To every Haitian' (also called 'Christ for All' by Ev Baptist Mission of South Haiti, 'Christ in Every Home' by Baptist Convention of Haiti, and 'Every Creature Crusade' by Ev Ch of Haiti). *Radiophonic evangelism.* Many programmes and courses (785 active ICI students).
FOREIGN MISSIONARIES AND PERSONNEL (nationals serving abroad) (1973). Total 26: about 20 Protestants in Bahamas, Canada, Dominican Republic, Guadeloupe, USA, and Gambia and other African countries, about 5 Roman Catholics, 1 Anglican.
FOREIGN MISSIONARIES AND PERSONNEL (aliens from abroad) (1973). Total 1,195. *From Western world.* 1,160: 792 Roman Catholics, 339 Protestants (299 in 44 USA societies, 14 in 2 UK societies, 14 in 3 Canada societies, 8 in 3 New Zealand societies, 3 in 1 Switzerland society, 1 in 1 WGermany society), about 20 Black indigenous from USA, 9 Anglicans in 2 USA societies. *From Third World.* 35 (about 30 Roman Catholics and Protestants, about 5 indigenous) from Puerto Rico, Guadeloupe, Jamaica et alia.
INSTITUTIONS (church-operated) (1973). Total 220, including 87 higher schools (7 minor seminaries), 98 medical centres, 2 radio stations, 1 religious community (monastery), 2 research centres, 13 seminaries (10 Protestant, 2 RC, 1 Anglican), 2 study centres.
PERIODICALS. About 40 titles.
PERSONNEL. About 2,745 (1,550 national, 1,195 foreign).
RELIGIOUS LIBRARIES. About 20.
SCRIPTURE DISTRIBUTION (1975). Annual totals: 40,475 Bibles (88% subsidized, 12% commercial), 69,443 NTs (52% free, 41% subsidized, 7% commercial), 232,469 UBS portions, 1,765,410 UBS selections. *Translations completed.* Haitian Creole: Portion in 1927, NT 1951.
SERVICE AGENCIES. About 35, including ACISJF, ACO, CCCI, CECH, CEH, CHED, CHR, COHORTE, CRH, CWS, FHSC, JEC, JOC, JUC, MAF, SU, URH, WVI.

ADDITIONAL DATA ON CHURCHES
EGLISE CATHOLIQUE AU HAITI. *Annual baptisms.* (1972) 98.0% infant, 2.0% adult. *National priests.* By 1970, a total of 213 Haitians had been ordained priest in the history of the church (70% since 1940), and 193 were still alive, though 12 had been reduced to lay status. Among the 181 priests in 1970, 136 were secular and 45 religious; but since about 30 of the latter were in exile in 1970, the actual number of Haitian priests at work in Haiti was about 150. *Expatriate priests.* 44% secular, 56% religious. *Male religious personnel.* Total including contemplatives (1970): 420 (21% nationals, 0.4% from Latin American countries, 78% from Europe and North America). Foreign priests and brothers in 1970: 50 from Canada, 49 Belgium, 31 USA, 29 France, 13 Netherlands, and 2 from elsewhere. *Brothers.* Of the total of 108 Haitian brothers since the early days, 39 were still at work in 1969. Expatriates are mostly from Canada and France. *Sisters.* Total including contemplatives (1970): 1,000. About 52% Haitians, 30% from Canada, 9% France, 2% USA, 2% Belgium, and 2% Italy. *Indigenous religious congregations.* Petits Frères de Ste-Thérèse de l'Enfant-Jésus (begun 1960), Petites Soeurs de Ste-Thérèse de l'EJ (begun 1946, 154 professed in 1970). *Foreign congregations.* Priests: SMM, CSSR, SDB, OMI, CSC, CICM, CSV, Voluntas Dei. Brothers: FICP, SC. Sisters (congregations with over 100 members): St-Joseph de Cluny, Filles de la Sagesse, Filles de Marie, Immaculée Conception.
*Catholic organizations.* The Episcopal Conference of Haiti (Conférence Episcopale d'Haïti, CEH) is the only French-speaking member of CELAM. The Haitian Conference of Religious Personnel (Conférence Haïtienne des Religieux, CHR) co-ordinates the activities of the Conférence des Religieux d'Haïti (CRH, men) and the Union des Religieuses d'Haïti (URH, women) and is the sole francophone member of CLAR. There are no national presbyteral or pastoral councils. The principal lay movements are Moun Apostola, Légion de Marie, Croisade Eucharistique, Kiro, Rallye, JOC, JEC, Scouts and Guides.
The Holy See has diplomatic relations with Haiti and is represented to government and the Catholic hierarchy by a nuncio in Port-au-Prince. In 1973 he also served as apostolic delegate in the Caribbean territories.
There were 308 parish primary schools in 1962–63 supervised by pastors of rural parishes and 153 public and private schools in 1968–69 operated by religious congregations. By 1973 schools had increased to 742 primary (420,570 pupils) and 68 secondary (9,920). In addition there were, in 1968, 69 hospitals and dispensaries under Catholic supervision as well as workshops in nutrition and rural development. At the end of 1969 each of 7 communities of religious sisters had charge of a literacy centre, with about 1,000 adults and 1,550 children enrolled; and in Cap Haïtien there exists a diocesan institute of adult education. Three other important accomplishments have been: (1) Christian Community Development of Laborde (Développement Communautaire Chrétien de Laborde) in the Cayes Plain, sponsored by the Antilles Fraternal Association, which comprises 12 community groups with about 20 members each, 25 literacy centres for adults, one co-operative, one medical-social centre, one rural development project and one local savings foundation; (2) Community Development of Dondon (Développement Communautaire du Dondon), which was founded by St Viateur priests, St Joseph sisters and numerous lay persons; and (3) Centre for Hospitality and Community Development on the Iles de la Tortue, consisting of the following: a dispensary, a hospital, a school for medical helpers, courses in management, crafts, agriculture and nutrition, 10 literacy centres for adults and 5 primary schools. In 1969, Fr Riou, founder of the latter centre, was expelled by the paramilitary Tontons Macoutes; his work continues although different methods are now used.
EGLISE EPISCOPALE D'HAITI. The church was founded in 1861 by a group of 110 immigrant US Negroes. In 1874, the Episcopal Church USA granted the new church autonomy under the name Apostolic Orthodox Haitian Church. In 1913 it merged again with PECUSA as a missionary district under Province II.

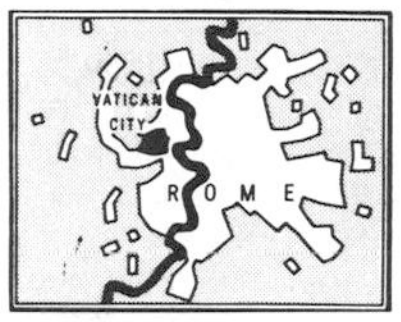


# HOLY SEE

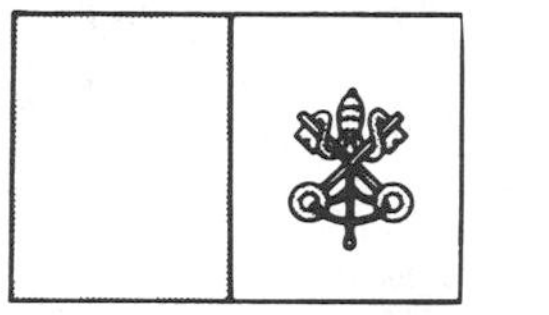

## SECULAR DATA

**STATE. Official name:** The Holy See (Sancta Sede). This title is also United Nations' usage; but for UPU and ITU, official name is: Vatican City State (Stato della Città del Vaticano).
**Flag** (shown above right): Yellow and white bars; crossed keys of St Peter under papal tiara on white bar.
**Area:** 0.44 sq.km. (0.17 sq.miles). Agricultural land: 0.0%.
**Government:** Ecclesiastical sovereign state, since 1929 (in papal lands before 1850, 1870 part of Italian kingdom, 1929 sovereign state).
**Official language:** Latin.
**Capital:** Vatican City.
**Armed forces** (1976): 50 Swiss Guards.
**Dependencies:** 13 buildings have extra-territorial rights.

**DEMOGRAPHY. Population** (de jure): 890 (census of 30.IV.1948. For 1970–2000 (UN), see last row of Table 1). Population density (1975): 12,500/sq.km. (32,375/sq.mile). Under 15 years: 3%. Growth rate (1975–80): 0.0% per year (births 0%, deaths –0%). Household size: 3 persons.
**Major languages:** Latin, Italian, English, French, Spanish, Portuguese, German.
**Urban dwellers** (1970): 100%.

**ETHNOLINGUISTIC GROUPS:** 65% Italian, 35% non-Italian (mainly European, also USA, Latin American, Asian (50 Chinese), African, Oceanian).

**MONEY** (1977). **Monetary unit:** Vatican City lira (= 100 centesimi); US$1 = VL 650.3.
**National income per person:** US$5,000. Average annual family income: US$15,000.

**EDUCATION.** Adult literacy: 100%. Education rate: 100%. Universities: 5.

**LITERATURE.** Annual new book titles (1973): 417. Periodicals: 100. Scientific journals: 20. Newspapers: 1 daily, 6 non-daily.

**COMMUNICATION** (per 1,000 people). Daily newspaper circulation: 250 copies.

TABLE 1. RELIGIOUS ADHERENTS IN THE HOLY SEE

| Year | 1900 | | mid-1970 | | Annual change, 1970–1980 | | | | mid-1975 | | mid-1980 | | 2000 | |
|---|---|---|---|---|---|---|---|---|---|---|---|---|---|---|
| *Name* | *Adherents* | *%* | *Adherents* | *%* | *Natural* | *Conversion* | *Total* | *Rate* | *Adherents* | *%* | *Adherents* | *%* | *Adherents* | *%* |
| **Christians** | **2,000** | **100.0** | **4,950** | **100.0** | **105** | **0** | **105** | **1.91** | **5,500** | **100.0** | **6,000** | **100.0** | **10,000** | **100.0** |
| professing | 2,000 | 100.0 | 4,950 | 100.0 | 105 | 0 | 105 | 1.91 | 5,500 | 100.0 | 6,000 | 100.0 | 10,000 | 100.0 |
| Roman Catholics | 2,000 | 100.0 | 4,950 | 100.0 | 105 | 0 | 105 | 1.91 | 5,500 | 100.0 | 6,000 | 100.0 | 10,000 | 100.0 |
| affiliated | 2,000 | 100.0 | 4,950 | 100.0 | 105 | 0 | 105 | 1.91 | 5,500 | 100.0 | 6,000 | 100.0 | 10,000 | 100.0 |
| total practising | 1,980 | *99* | 4,850 | *98* | 102 | –11 | 91 | 1.71 | 5,330 | *97* | 5,760 | *96* | 9,200 | *92* |
| non-practising | 20 | *1* | 100 | *2* | 3 | 11 | 14 | 8.24 | 170 | *3* | 240 | *4* | 800 | *8* |
| Roman Catholics | 2,000 | 100.0 | 4,950 | 100.0 | 105 | 0 | 105 | 1.91 | 5,500 | 100.0 | 6,000 | 100.0 | 10,000 | 100.0 |
| **Country's population** | **2,000** | **100.0** | **4,950** | **100.0** | **105** | **0** | **105** | **1.91** | **5,500** | **100.0** | **6,000** | **100.0** | **10,000** | **100.0** |

COLUMNS, ROWS. For meanings and definitions, see Codebook (Part 6). Note that, by definition, total 'Christians' = professing + crypto-Christians, which also = affiliated + nominal Christians. Percentages may not always total exactly, due to rounding.
COUNTRY'S POPULATION. In 1853 the Pontifical States in Italy had a population of 3,134,188 (99.7% Roman Catholics, 0.3% Jews); in 1870 they became part of the Italian state. The territory that is now the Vatican state was part of Italy until its creation as a sovereign state in 1929. In 1975 it consisted of Vatican City proper, together with a number of extra-territorial buildings (churches and offices) in Rome. The population figures above refer to the de facto population in these territories and properties.
PRACTISING CHRISTIANS. Vast numbers of Catholics attend services in St Peter's basilica regularly. *Pilgrims.* The first Holy Year in Rome in AD 1300 attracted 200,000 pilgrims. In the 1950 Holy Year the total was 2.5 million; and in the 1975 Holy Year, 8,370,000 pilgrims.

## CHRISTIANITY

CATHOLIC CHURCH. The Holy See is the supreme organ of the Roman Catholic Church and is, at the same time, a widely-international juridical entity. The existence of the City of the Vatican and of the state dates from the signing of the Lateran Agreements with Italy in November 1929, as a result of which the Holy See possesses full ownership of the Vatican territory, with exclusive power and sovereign jurisdiction. The creation of this state had as its purpose the assurance of a territorial base essential to the exercise of international sovereignty. Prior to this, in the intervening period after 1870 when the last papal states were annexed by the kingdom of Italy, the papacy had nevertheless continued to exercise its traditional state prerogatives, particularly those concerned with the sending and receiving of diplomatic personnel and the conclusion of treaties and concordats. These prerogatives were validated through an Italian law according a series of privileges to the Holy See because of its spiritual role but refusing it all territorial sovereignty. The Holy See had never ceased protesting against this dispossession.

In international public law, the state character of the Vatican has not been unanimously accepted. Some authorities hold that since the demographic element essential to statehood is lacking, Vatican citizenship is not a permanent tie between citizen and state but a purely functional qualification in which the individual retains the nationality of his country of origin. Vatican citizenship does in fact have only a provisional character and ceases when the function ceases for which it has been accorded. The question has therefore been raised whether the sovereign pontiff can exercise any real political power in the absence of any real population base.

The terminology of the Lateran Agreements involves certain ambiguities, particularly in relation to the term 'state', which is used sometimes with reference to the Holy See and sometimes with reference to Vatican City. Nevertheless, the latter regards itself as a true sovereign state and is a member of several international organizations including the Universal Postal Union, International Telecommunications Union, International Wheat Council, International Union for the Protection of Literary and Artistic Works and the International Union for the Protection of Industrial Property.

*Vatican City.* With an area of only 44 hectares (0.44 square kilometres), Vatican City (Stato della Città del Vaticano) is the smallest country in the

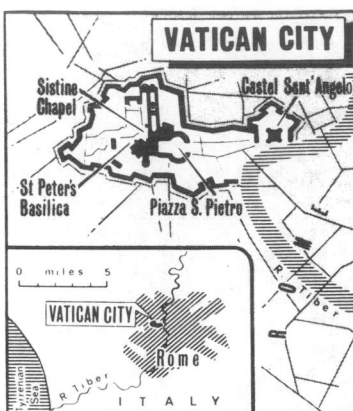

world. It includes St Peter's square and basilica, the apostolic palace and the papal gardens. Twelve other buildings in the vicinity of Rome but outside the City have extra-territorial rights, including exemption from expropriation and taxes: the Lateran basilica and palace, the basilicas of St Mary Major and St Paul Outside-the-Walls, the papal summer residence at Castelgandolfo 25 kms south of Rome, as well as the palaces of the Dataria, Chancellery, Propagation of the Faith, St Calixtus of Trastevere, Congregation for the Eastern Churches, Holy Office, ancient vicariate of Rome at the Villa della Pigna, and College of the Propaganda. Since 1951, the area holding the transmitting antennas of Radio Vatican at Santa Maria di Galeria 20 kms out of Rome has also been extra-territorialized; the recording studios themselves are lodged in an old tower in the centre of the papal gardens. In 1972, Vatican City had as its population, the pope, 358 citizens (33 cardinals, 153 representatives of the Holy See serving abroad, 34 secular and 4 religious priests, 66 members of the Swiss Guard and 68 laymen), and also 325 juridically-defined 'residents', all of whom retain in addition their nationality of origin. Furthermore, 4,268 people in 1972 were residing in buildings belonging to the Holy See but located on Italian territory. The Vatican issues its own currency and postage stamps, and has its own flag, police force, radio station, museums, art galleries, printing press, daily newspaper and its own railway station.

*Secular administration.* According to the founding Law of the Vatican City (7 June 1929), the pope has full legislative, executive and judicial powers. Diplomatic relations with foreign countries and treaty-making are also his prerogatives but are carried out through an intermediary, the cardinal secretary of state. The pope today delegates his legislative and executive powers to the Pontifical Commission for the State of Vatican City (Pontificia Commissione per lo Stato della Città del Vaticano), composed of cardinals named by him for 5-year terms, assisted by a special delegate also appointed by the pope and on whom executive powers are conferred except in those areas where the commission decides otherwise. This commission has been aided since 1968 by a consultative council of 24 laymen residing in Rome (Consultà dello Stato). The pope's judicial powers are exercised by 3 courts: Apostolic Penitentiary, Rota and Apostolic Signature. The judicial system is based on canon law where applicable; in other cases, the laws of the city of Rome are used.

*Religious administration.* Vatican City is an integral part of the Diocese of Rome; nevertheless it has its own religious administration, the Vicariate of Vatican City (Vicariato della Città del Vaticano), under the direction of a vicar-general whose jurisdiction extends over the whole of the Vatican City with the exception of St Peter's Basilica and its sacristy, the Lateran palace and the papal villa of Castelgandolfo. St Anne's Church is the parish church of Vatican City, and the Basilica of St John Lateran, which dates back to AD 324, is the pope's personal patriarchal basilica. The Basilica of St Peter, built between 1506 and 1626, is the largest Catholic church building in the world and is where most papal ceremonies take place.

*The papacy.* At the summit of the ecclesiastical hierarchy of the Catholic Church is the bishop of Rome, also called pope, sovereign pontiff, holy father, and head of the universal church. Catholic dogma considers the papal primacy as being of divine origin, the pope receiving this primacy as the successor to the apostle Peter appointed by Jesus as head of the college of apostles. According to Vatican Council I

(1870), in virtue of his charge as vicar of Christ and pastor of the whole church, the pope has direct authority over the entire body of the faithful and bishops, and over each one in particular, a power greater than the usual authority of a bishop. As patriarch of the West, also, he exercises a special authority over Western Christendom, over Italy and over the ecclesiastical province of Rome. Lastly, he is temporal sovereign of the Vatican state. The sum of his titles, therefore, is as follows: bishop of Rome, vicar of Jesus Christ, successor of the prince of the apostles, supreme pontiff of the universal church, patriarch of the West, primate of Italy, archbishop and metropolitan of the Roman province, and sovereign of Vatican City.

The scope of papal powers has not been the same at all periods of history. In particular, the relation between the authority of the pope and that of bishops has not always followed the pattern of centralization which was at its peak between Vatican Council I (1869–70) and Vatican II (1962–65). In the Dogmatic Constitution on the Church ('Lumen gentium'), of November 1964, Vatican II returned to an honoured position the doctrine of collegiality in which the whole body of bishops, in union with the pope, exercises the supreme teaching and pastoral authority over the entire church, in addition to the authority which they have in their own dioceses. Lumen Gentium affirms that this collegiality of bishops with the pope is exercised in a solemn way through an ecumenical council, and can also be effected in other ways, 'provided that the head of the college calls them to collegiate action, or at least so approves or freely accepts the united action of the dispersed bishops, that it is made a true collegiate act' (paragraph 22). All ecumenical councils must be convoked, presided over and confirmed, or at least accepted, by the pope himself. This doctrine is based on the fact that 'by the institution of the Lord', 'St Peter and the other apostles constituted one apostolic college' (paragraph 22). In this spirit, Paul VI created in 1965 the Synod of Bishops to make permanent the exercise of collegiate authority. In practice, however, the doctrine of collegiality is still nascent and is difficult to reconcile with the prerogatives of papal primacy.

Prior to the visit of John XXIII to Assisi and Loreto in 1963, no official papal visits had been made outside the Vatican since 1857, and until Paul VI no pope had left Italy since Pius VII was forced out by Napoleon between 1809 and 1814. In January 1964, Paul VI began his international journeys with a pilgrimage to the Holy Land where he met Athenagoras of Constantinople, the first meeting of a pope with an ecumenical patriarch in 900 years. Thereafter he visited Bombay, India for a eucharistic congress in November 1964; New York and the UN in October 1965; Fatima, Portugal in May 1967; Constantinople and Ephesus, Turkey in July 1967; Bogotá, Colombia in August 1968; Geneva, Switzerland for visits to the World Council of Churches and the International Labour Organization in June 1969; Kampala, Uganda in July 1969; and the Far East in November-December 1970 for visits to Manila, Pago Pago (American Samoa), Sydney, Jakarta, Hong Kong and Colombo.

In 1978-79 this tradition was taken further by John Paul II's extensive visits abroad, of which the most

notable were to Mexico, Poland, Ireland and the USA.

*College of Cardinals.* Formed by the whole body of cardinals, the Sacred College or Council of the Pope has the crucial role of meeting in conclave to elect a new pope when the seat of Peter falls vacant. Individually, cardinals counsel the pope and many serve in the Curia.

The College of Cardinals received its definitive form in 1150. In 1586, their number was fixed at 70, which is still the norm established by canon law (Canon 231 of 1917). In 1959 John XXIII deviated for the first time from this principle in raising the number to 79, in order to assure greater international representation within the college. After several fluctuations, the number was finally brought to 145 by Paul VI at the time of the consistory or general meeting of cardinals in March 1973. Meanwhile, by motu proprio 'Ingravescentem aetatem' of 21 November 1970, the pope established 80 years as the maximum age for cardinals to continue in office, both within the Roman Curia and as papal electors. Thus only 117 of the 145 cardinals at the 1973 consistory were eligible as electors. By March 1973, the number of cardinals in each continent (with electors in brackets) was: Africa 9 (9), North America (Canada and USA) 15 (13), Latin America 21 (18), Asia 11 (11), Europe 84 (61), and Oceania 5 (5). Countries with the largest number of cardinals were: Italy 40 (30), USA 11 (10), France 11 (8), Spain 7 (5), West Germany 6 (4), and Brazil 6 (5). Altogether, 51 countries were represented in the college, 34 of which had a single cardinal, several of whom in addition were over 80 years of age.

*Synod of Bishops.* Since 1965 the Synod of Bishops (Synodus Episcoporum) has been a permanent, central ecclesiastical institution with the function of counselling and assisting the pope in the government of the universal church. Its constitutive charter (motu proprio 'Apostolica sollicitudo'), promulgated by Paul VI on 15 September 1965 during the last session of Vatican II, presents as the purposes of the Synod of Bishops 'to encourage close union and valued assistance between the Sovereign Pontiff and the bishops of the entire world; to ensure that direct and real information is provided on questions and situations touching upon the internal action of the Church and its necessary activity in the world today; to facilitate agreement on essential points of doctrine and on methods of procedure in the life of the Church'. The Synod is under the direct and immediate authority of the pope, who alone fixes dates of sessions, sets the agenda, confers deliberative power on its members when judged useful, presides over the sessions personally or by delegation and ratifies decisions taken. The Synod has a permanent or general secretary with several assistants, while the assemblies have a special secretary, all secretaries being nominated by the pope. Three types of assembly (general, extraordinary, and special) are provided for. (1) A general assembly is made up of patriarchs, leading archbishops and metropolitans of Eastern-rite churches not under patriarchs, elected bishops from national episcopal conferences (regional conferences such as CELAM not being represented as such), 10 male religious personnel elected by the Union of General Superiors, the cardinals in charge of the dicasteries of the Roman Curia, together with other bishops, priests and religious appointed directly by the pope up to 15% of the total membership. (2) A

St Peter's Basilica, largest church in Christendom, accommodates 100,000 inside at one time. *Above.* Fish-eye view of Vatican from dome, with (left) Apostolic Palace.

special assembly may be convoked at the regional level, and is made up of those members of the general assembly who belong to the region. Lastly (3) an extraordinary assembly has the same membership as the general assembly except that only presidents of episcopal conferences and 3 delegates from the Union of Male General Superiors may be members. The extraordinary assembly of 1969 decided that general assemblies should be convened every 2 years, but this was extended to 3 years in 1971 to permit better preparation. The 1969 assembly also fixed the organization of the permanent secretariat and requested that bishops be consulted before the agenda of any succeeding assembly was determined. The pope ratified this proposition and created in 1970 the Council of the General Secretariat of the Synod of Bishops to assist the secretary-general in maintaining liaison with episcopal conferences and in determining agendas. This council, composed of 15 members (12 elected by the assembly and 3 named by the pope), continues its work between assembly sessions.

By 1980, 6 assemblies had been held: the general assembly of October 1967, which had as its objective 'to preserve and reinforce the Catholic faith, its integrity, its strength, its development, its doctrinal and historical cohesiveness'; the extraordinary assembly of October 1969 which defined the principles of episcopal collegiality; the general assembly of October 1971 on justice in the world and the priestly ministry; the general assembly of October 1974 on evangelization in the modern world; 1977 on 'Catechetics in Our Time', 1980 the Christian family.

*Roman Curia.* The Curia is the church's highest-level centralized administrative and judicial body in Rome whose function is to assist the pope to govern. It consists of the Office of Secretary of State (the private secretariat of the pope), the Council for the Public Affairs of the Church, 10 congregations, 3 tribunals, 3 secretariats, as well as a large number of commissions, councils and offices. The Roman Curia has developed progressively over a lengthy period. It was reorganized in March 1968 by Paul VI who internationalized both its top executive posts, until then held exclusively by Italians, and also its entire personnel; whereas in 1961 its staff including consultants consisted of 749 Italians (57%) and 573 non-Italians (43%), by 1970 Italians were 854 (38%) and non-Italians 1,406 (62%). In 1970, Italians headed 11 of the 28 principal dicasteries of the Curia. However, the Office of Secretary of State, whose staff in 1974 was still almost 80% Italian, is presided over by a Frenchman. The number of laymen has also increased, from 40 in 1961 to 200 in 1970.

In the organization and functioning of the Curia, several procedures are commonly followed. Joint councils are constituted among the various congregations for dealing with common issues and problems. Seven diocesan bishops are appointed as members of each congregation, with full rights in annual plenary assemblies. The heads of dicasteries are now appointed for 5 years only and their posts automatically become vacant on the death of the pope. The new pope has 3 months to reconfirm them in their functions. Each congregation is directed by a cardinal prefect, assisted by a secretary and an under-secretary, all 3 appointed by the pope. Both prefect and secretary are appointed for 5 years and require similar reconfirmation. Laymen may be named as consultants of the Curia's departments, all appointed for 5 years which is renewable. Lastly, each congregation has its own direct liaison with episcopal conferences and communicates to the bishops decisions which concern them before they are promulgated.

*Office of Secretary of State.* Until recently this was simply one of several offices on the Holy See, ranking lower than the Curia's congregations and courts. However, in 1967 Paul VI elevated it to its present position of pre-eminence in the Curia. Its head, the cardinal secretary of state, is the principal adviser to the pope, is received regularly by him and accompanies him on all travels of note. His position corresponds to that of prime minister and minister of foreign affairs for the pontiff. The responsibilities of the secretary of state extend to any matters referred to him by the pope, in addition to his role as co-ordinator of the Curia's activities. He exercises authority over heads of dicasteries and can convene them whenever he requires. He supervises the Council for the Public Affairs of the Church, and serves as president of the Cor Unum Council, commissions for the Vatican State, Administration of Property of the Holy See, and Special Administration of the Holy See. He is also a member of 4 congregations (Doctrine of the Faith,

Bishops, Evangelization of Peoples, Cause of the Saints) and of the commissions for the revision of Canon Law and Eastern Canon Law. He controls the diplomatic service of the Holy See, the Commission for Social Communications, and also General Services which is responsible for 2 important publications: *Annuario Pontificio*, and *Acta Apostolica Sedis*, the official journal of the Holy See (begun 1908) which publishes definitive texts of all official acts. Legal texts have the force of law 3 months

After his 1978 election Pope John Paul I addresses 2 million faithful from balcony of St Peter's Basilica.

after their publication in the *Acta*. Because of the sporadic publication of the *Acta*, *L'Osservatore Romano*, the official daily newspaper of the Holy See, gives temporary authority for such documents. The editing of *AP* is carried on in collaboration with the Central Office of Statistics of the church, now also under the secretary of state.

*Council for the Public Affairs of the Church.* Begun in 1814 under the title Congregation of Extraordinary Ecclesiastical Affairs, in 1967 the council changed its name and assumed its present importance. Directed by the secretary of state, the council is charged with diplomatic and all other relations with foreign governments, and functions through nunciatures, apostolic delegations and other representatives of the Holy See. The Pontifical Commission for Russia also is under this council. It has also been the congregation responsible for ecclesiastical affairs in Portugal and in Portuguese overseas territories; in 1975, however, the latter were in process of being transferred to the jurisdiction of Propaganda.

*Papal representatives.* There are 3 types of pontifical representative: nuncios (for nations with a Catholic majority) and pro-nuncios (for nations with a Catholic minority) are accredited to countries which have diplomatic relations with the Holy See; permanent observers or delegates are appointed to certain international organizations; and apostolic delegates, with no diplomatic status, represent the Holy See to bishops in countries which have no diplomatic relations with the Holy See. A nuncio, according to customary law, is dean of the diplomatic corps in the country to which he is appointed, as stated in the Treaty of Vienna of 1815 and confirmed by the convention on diplomatic relations of Vienna in 1961. The development of diplomatic relations with non-Catholic countries led Paul VI in 1965 to adopt the term pro-nuncio to describe a representative with the powers of a nuncio but not given the honour by a country of being dean of its diplomatic corps.

In June 1974, the Holy See was represented throughout the world by 37 nunciatures with a nuncio (3 in Africa, 19 in America, 3 in Asia, and 12 in Europe including one for the European Community); 42 nunciatures headed by a pro-nuncio (22 in Africa, one in America, 12 in Asia, 5 in Europe including Turkey and 2 in Oceania); and 26 apostolic delegations (15 in Africa (including the Red Sea), 2 in America, 4 in Asia, 2 in Europe and 3 in Oceania).

The Holy See maintains diplomatic relations with

2 Communist countries, Cuba and Yugoslavia, and informal relations with several other Eastern European Communist countries at the level of the Council for the Public Affairs of the Church. Western countries having apostolic delegations and not nunciatures include the USA (although there is a personal representative of the US president at the Vatican), UK, Mexico and the Scandinavian countries with the exception of Finland. There was no representative of the Holy See in Greece until 1977. Recent years

have witnessed a significant increase in the number of nunciatures and apostolic delegations in Third-World countries, especially Africa and the Middle East. Under Paul VI, in fact, diplomatic ties had been established with, in 1975, 5 more Arab countries than in 1963: Algeria, Iraq, Kuwait, Sudan and Tunisia.

Nine permanent representatives of the Holy See to international governmental organizations include: permanent observers at the UN in New York; WHO, ILO and UN in Geneva; FAO in Rome; UNESCO in Paris; one to the Council of Europe in Strasbourg; delegates in Vienna to the International Agency for Atomic Energy and the UN Organization for Industrial Development, one to the Council for Cultural Co-operation of the Council of Europe, International Committee of Military Medicine and Pharmacy, and Union of Official Organizations for Tourism; the Holy See is also represented at the International Geographical Union.

Six permanent representatives of the Holy See are appointed to non-governmental international organizations including permanent observers or delegates to international committees concerned with the historical sciences, paleography, history of art, anthropology, and of medicine, as well as the International Study Centre for the Conservation and Restoration of Culture. Long considered an Italian domain, papal representation has recently been broadened to include a number of high-level representatives of other European countries; and in 1970 the Holy See began the recruitment of priests from the Third World for diplomatic work. By 1974 there were Korean, Japanese, Kenyan and Zairean representatives in the diplomatic service. After having completed their studies of canon law, candidates study diplomacy at the Pontifical Ecclesiastical Academy in Rome, which was founded in 1701 and is now located outside Vatican City.

In mid-1974, diplomats accredited to the Holy See represented 81 countries, including Great Britain which maintains an ambassador at the Vatican in spite of the fact that there is no official Vatican representative in London. Switzerland on the other hand has no ambassador at the Vatican although the Holy See is represented in Bern by a nuncio.

*Sacred Congregations.* The 9 congregations are primarily executive offices, each charged with a specific area in the government of the universal church and placed under the supervision of the cardinal secretary of state.

(1) The Congregation for the Doctrine of the Faith was created in 1542 under the title Congregation of the Universal Inquisition; it became the Congregation of the Holy Office in 1908 and received its present name in 1965. Vatican II called for reorganization and reform in the methods of the Holy Office, and Paul VI undertook this, suppressing inter alia the Index of prohibited books. The congregation is responsible for all questions of faith and morals. It examines new doctrines; promotes study and

if the faith of the believing spouse is considered to be in danger. The congregation is served by 2 commissions, the Theological Commission and the Pontifical Biblical Commission.

(2) The Congregation for Bishops was erected in 1588 under the title Consistorial Congregation and reorganized under its present name in 1967. It is responsible for all matters concerning bishops and dioceses with the exception of the Eastern churches and the church's foreign missions under Propaganda. It includes in its jurisdiction the Pontifical Commission

3rd Synod of Bishops, Rome, 1974: 'The Evangelization of the Modern World', attended by 207 prelates. *Above.* First session, in new synod hall. *Below.* At concelebrated mass, in Sistine Chapel.

general meetings; criticizes doctrines judged contrary to the faith, after consultation with interested bishops; examines and condemns books, after having alerted the ordinary and having given the author a hearing and the right to defend himself and his work; it also administers the 'privilege of faith' (or Pauline privilege), which is the right to dissolve a legitimate marriage between a Catholic and a so-called infidel

for Latin America, and the Pontifical Commission for Migration and Tourism.

(3) The Congregation for the Eastern Churches was created in 1862, united with Propaganda, then finally became autonomous in 1917 under the name Congregation for the Eastern Church. The last word in the title was changed from the singular to the plural in 1967 to show more respect for the distinctive

character of the churches of the Eastern rite. This was also manifest in the appointment by John XXIII of 5 Eastern-rite patriarchs as members of the congregation, as well as Eastern-rite consultants by Paul VI. The responsibility of the congregation extends to all affairs concerning dioceses, personnel (bishops, clergy, religious and laity), and discipline in churches of the Eastern rite. Similar matters are handled for the Church of the Latin rite by the congregations for Bishops, Sacraments and Divine Worship, Clergy, Religious Personnel and Catholic Education. The congregation exercises exclusive authority over all jurisdictions independent of rite in the following countries: Afghanistan, southern Albania, Bulgaria, Cyprus, Egypt, Eritrea and northern Ethiopia, Greece, Iran, Iraq, Jordan, Lebanon, Palestine (Gaza, Israel, West Bank), Syria, and Turkey. It includes the Special Commission for the Liturgy and issues an information service bulletin in Italian, French and English.

(4) The Congregation for the Sacraments and Divine Worship was formed in July 1975 by joining together the former Congregation for the Discipline of the Sacraments (created in 1908) and the Congregation for Divine Worship (created in 1969), the latter having taken over some of the responsibilities of the former Congregation of Rites. The new congregation is responsible for all matters relating to the discipline of the 7 sacraments, with the exception of those which fall under the competence of the Congregation for the Doctrine of the Faith, the courts of the Rota and Apostolic Signature; it is also responsible for the liturgical and extra-liturgical worship and life of the Latin church. Its jurisdiction extends over all territories of the Latin church and includes countries under Propaganda.

(5) The Congregation for the Clergy was established in 1564 under the name Congregation of the Council, its first task being to interpret the decrees of the Council of Trent. Its responsibility was later extended to cover general discipline of clergy and laity, but it was reorganized in 1967 to fulfil a more pastoral function. Its province now includes all that concerns the persons, pastoral work and ministry of clergy exercising their apostolate in dioceses, that is diocesan priests, deacons and religious personnel engaged in normal pastoral work in a diocese. It operates through 3 offices, dealing with the training and spiritual growth of clergy, the preaching of the Word of God and the material needs of clergy and church properties.

(6) The Congregation for Religious Personnel and Secular Institutes was created in 1586. After a variety of changes, it became in 1908 the Congregation for Religious Personnel and was reorganized and renamed in 1967. Being concerned with personnel in a non-territorial manner its jurisdiction extends to all male and female religious personnel, secular institutes and third orders of the Latin church. It consists of 2 sections: one for institutes and societies of male and female religious personnel; and the other for secular institutes, that is institutes of laymen who have professed the evangelical counsels and wish to implement them in the world. It sponsors a council for relations between the congregation and the international unions of general superiors.

(7) The Congregation for the Evangelization of Peoples was formed in 1622 as the Congregation of Propaganda Fide (Spreading the Faith), and received its present name in 1967. It is responsible for all foreign mission territories, with the exception of Portuguese territories and Goa, which came under the Council for the Public Affairs of the Church until 1975. Its territories are independent of those included under the Congregation for the Eastern Churches and include almost all of Africa, Asia and Oceania, several areas in the 2 Americas, and several countries and regions of Europe (Denmark, Norway, Finland, Sweden, Gibraltar, northern Albania and 5 ecclesiastical districts in Yugoslavia). Its authority is final within these territories, except in matters which are in the competence of the congregations for the Doctrine of the Faith, Cause of Saints, and Sacraments and Divine Worship, including such matters as non-consummated marriages. Its authority also extends over the efforts of mission-sending countries in aid of mission-receiving countries. It sponsors a supreme council for administration of papal missionary works (in 51 countries, to promote missionary co-operation), which in turn is responsible for the Missionary Union of Clergy (in 53 countries), Society for the Propagation of the Faith, Society of St Peter the Apostle (for training clergy of mission countries, operating 85 major seminaries) and Society of the Holy Childhood (in 36 countries),

One-month reign of Pope John Paul I. *Above.* After election in conclave of cardinals, 1978. *Below left.* Public audience. *Below right.* At his funeral.

in addition to 4 commissions including those for catechesis and catechists. The congregation also sponsors the Agenzia Internazionale Fides (AIF) which produces bulletins in Italian, French, English, Spanish and German.

(8) The Congregation for the Cause of Saints was erected in 1969 with some of the responsibilities of the former Congregation of Rites, first established in 1588. It is concerned with beatifications, canonizations and the conservation of relics.

(9) The Congregation for Catholic Education was created in 1915 under the title Congregation of Seminaries, Universities and Studies, and was reorganized under its present name in 1967. It supervises the work and institutions of Catholic education, with the exception of those in territories under the congregations for the Eastern Churches and Evangelization of Peoples. It has 3 offices, dealing with seminaries, higher education (church-related universities and faculties) and lower schools of all types. In addition it sponsors the pontifical work for priestly vocations.

*Courts.* The Holy See's courts are colleges of cardinals and prelates handling judicial cases relating to internal questions of conscience and external matters. They consist of 3 distinct entities.

(1) The Apostolic Penitentiary originated in the 13th century, with its most recent reorganization in 1935. As a court, it is concerned with questions of conscience, both of a sacramental and extra-sacramental nature, and rules on the usage and concession of indulgences, absolutions and dispensations.

(2) The Rota, dating back to 1331, is the court of appeal of the Holy See and is particularly well known for its decisions concerning requests for nullifying marriages.

(3) The Apostolic Signature was established in the 13th century and reorganized by Paul VI. It is the supreme court of the church, composed of cardinals chosen by the pope, and is divided into 2 sections: one corresponding to a court of appeals which judges the competence of other courts as well as the observance of laws and rights at the highest level, and the second serving as a council of state which pronounces on controversies concerning acts of ecclesiastical administration, appeals against decisions of the Roman dicasteries and conflicts over areas of competence among the dicasteries. Decisions of the Rota may also be appealed to this body.

*Secretariats.* Three secretariats created after Vatican II are related to new concerns of the conciliar church.

(1) The Secretariat for Christian Unity was established by John XXIII in 1960 in preparation for Vatican II, received the rank of conciliar commission in 1962 and was definitively confirmed by Paul VI in 1966. Its general aim is to promote unity among Christians, to which end it creates relations with other ecclesiastical communities, sends Catholic observers to their meetings and invites them to send representatives to Catholic functions, co-ordinates at both the national and international levels efforts to promote unity, enters into dialogue on ecumenical questions, engages in activities with other churches, interprets and watches over the execution of the principles of ecumenism and conciliar decrees touching ecumenical questions and supports Catholic ecumenical groups. Each staff member is a specialist either concerning a particular Christian denomination or tradition, or concerning the World Council of Churches or theological questions, and there are also regional desks. The Office for Catholic-Jewish Relations was added to its responsibilities in 1967, and in 1974 the Commission for Religious Relations with Judaism was formed. The statutes of the latter define it as a distinct body attached to the secretariat.

(2) The Secretariat for Non-Christians was formed by Paul VI in 1964. It is concerned with promoting dialogue and studies to develop mutual understanding and respect between Catholics and all persons professing religions other than Christianity and to prepare manuals on dialogue with other religions. Its sub-sections include Asia, Hinduism, Buddhism, and Africa; and in October 1974 a new Commission for Religious Relations with Islam was created as a distinct body but attached to the secretariat. In 1970 the Islamic Council of Cairo and the Holy See agreed on a mutual exchange of appointed representatives.

(3) The Secretariat for Non-Believers was created in 1965 by Paul VI. Its purpose is to study the bases of theoretical and situational atheism, the latter being concerned with atheism not supported by philosophical or theoretical conceptualizations. It seeks to open up and pursue dialogue with non-believers, and in particular to develop national

commissions and secretariats, without itself becoming a substitute for them. By August 1973 there were 21 national secretariats (2 in Africa, 2 in North America, 6 in Latin America, 5 in Asia and 6 in Europe) and 2 regional bodies (Middle East and CELAM), as well as a large number of correspondents.

The number of these secretariats is expected to increase rapidly.

*Councils, commissions and committees.*

(1) The Council of the Laity (Consilium de Laicis) was established in 1967 by Paul VI to implement the conciliar decree 'Apostolicam actuositatem' as a service to the whole church, to be a means of communication and dialogue and a sign of the co-responsibility of all the faithful. Its aim is to promote the development of the apostolate of the laity by co-ordinating apostolic work; establish bonds between laity and hierarchy; carry out doctrinal and practical studies, with special emphasis on opening the way for more lay participation in the church's pastoral programme; as well as to serve as a documentation centre. It publishes a journal.

(2) The Pontifical Commission on Justice and Peace (Justitia et Pax) was created by Paul VI to implement Vatican II's pastoral constitution 'Gaudium et Spes'. Its purposes are to promote social justice at the international level, stimulate development in poor countries, and examine means of furthering peace in the world. National commissions for justice and peace had been established in 63 countries by June 1972, but their role and influence varies. Some have been very effective in bringing about a change of mentality and influencing action at the level of the local church. Nevertheless, the statutes of the pontifical commission are ambiguous and tensions have arisen with the office of the secretary of state because of the political nature of the problems with which the commission is confronted.

(3) The Pontifical Commission for the Revision of the Code of Canon Law was instituted by John XXIII in 1963 to prepare, in the light of the conciliar decrees of Vatican II, a revision of the 1917 Code of Canon Law.

(4) The Pontifical Commission for the Reform of the Code of Eastern Canon Law was reconstituted by Paul VI in 1972 to replace an earlier commission dating back to 1935.

(5) The Pontifical Commission for the Interpretation of the Decrees of Vatican Council II was created in 1967 to provide for an exact interpretation of the letter and spirits of the documents of the council according to decisions reached by the Holy See. It is composed of 13 cardinals and bishops.

(6) The Pontifical Commission for Social Communications was established in 1948, acquired a permanent character in 1959 and received its present name in 1964. Its purpose is to put into affect the norms of the 1964 conciliar decree 'Inter mirifica' on social communications. Placed under the supervision of the secretary of state, it controls the press office of the Holy See, which was created in 1966, and administers the Vatican film library formed in 1959 to assemble and preserve films and TV programmes dealing with the life of the church.

(7) The Pontifical Commission for Latin America (CAL) was instituted in 1958 by Pius XII and placed under the supervision of the Congregation for Bishops in 1969. Its principal aim is to follow the activities of the Latin American Episcopal Council (CELAM) and national episcopal organizations in order to provide personnel and funds in aid of the Latin American church. Attached to it is the General Council for Latin America (COGECAL), formed in 1963 by Paul VI to integrate CAL; CELAM; presidents of the national episcopal organizations for Latin America found in Europe, USA and Canada; and presidents of the Union of Male General Superiors, International Union of Female General Superiors and Latin America Confederation of Religious Personnel. Its purpose is to study topics contributing to better co-operation in service to Latin America.

(8) The Pontifical Commission for Migration and Tourism was formed in 1970 by Paul VI to offer pastoral assistance to migrants and travellers. It falls under the supervision of the Congregation for Bishops and includes 5 specialized sectors: Emigrants and Refugees, co-ordinating the work of 26 national directors (1971) without encroaching on the work of the International Catholic Commission on Migration (CICM) located in Geneva; Apostolatus Maris (Apostolate of the Sea), founded in 1922 with 29 national administrations and 2 regional organizations

(Latin America and French West Africa), whose activities cover the maritime world; Apostolatus Aeris (Apostolate of the Air), which in 1971 co-ordinated the work of 19 airport chaplains; Apostolatus Nomadum (Apostolate for Nomads), which included 22 episcopal promoters and national directors in 1971; and the general pastoralia of tourism.

(9) The Cor Unum Pontifical Council, created by Paul VI in 1971 and placed under the direct authority of the cardinal secretary of state, is neither an operational agency nor a regrouping of agencies. Rather it is a body dedicated to furthering the harmonization and co-ordination of aid by various Catholic organizations to the church in developing countries and as such is concerned with the integration of their efforts with the directives of the hierarchy, especially the pope. The particular purpose of the council is to enable those representing the receiving or mission churches to have a stronger voice. It is composed of some 30 members, representing sending agencies, dicasteries of the Roman Curia, national churches and laity.

(10) The Committee for the Family was established by Paul VI in 1973 on a 3-year experimental basis. Its purpose is pastoral study and research, with an emphasis on promoting and safeguarding the spiritual, moral and social realities of the family. It is part of the Council of the Laity, without however being dependent upon it. In addition to a co-ordinating group of 7 persons, it is composed of 18 members and 9 consultants, all appointed by the pope.

(11) The Study Commission on the Role of Woman in Society and Church, composed of 15 women and 10 men (7 priests and 3 laymen), was established by Paul VI in 1973 following the recommendation of the 1971 Synod of Bishops.

(12) The Theological Commission is an international body instituted by Paul VI in 1969 on the recommendation of the first Synod of Bishops in 1967 to assist, on a consultative basis, the Congregation for the Doctrine of the Faith. The commission is under the prefect of this congregation and includes not more than 30 specialists representing different schools of thought. The latter are appointed by the pope after nomination by the prefect.

(13) The International Council for Catechesis was founded in 1975 by Paul VI to respond to the wish expressed by the Second International Catechetical Congress. It serves as a consultative organ to the Congregation for Clergy.

(14) The Pontifical Biblical Commission was created in 1902 and restructured in 1971 by Paul VI who placed it under the Congregation for the Doctrine of the Faith. It is a study commission to prepare instructions and decrees which are then promulgated by the congregation with the approval of the pope. The commission must be consulted on all proposals for new biblical norms.

(15) The Abbey of St Jerome for the Revision and Correction of the Vulgate was instituted by Pius XI in 1933 with the aim of improving the original text of St Jerome's 4th-century Latin translation of the Bible and also to prepare a scholarly edition as well.

(16) The Pontifical Commission for the New Vulgate was established in 1965 in order to amend the Vulgate's text to bring it into conformity with the original Hebrew and Greek texts of the Bible. The first volume appeared in 1969. This is to be the official text for the liturgy and documents of the Latin church.

(17) The Pontifical Commission for Sacred Archeology was created in 1852 for the preservation of the catacombs and other ancient buildings and Christian cemeteries in Rome and vicinity. Its authority has been extended by the Lateran Agreements to all other catacombs in Italy.

(18) The Pontifical Commission for Historical Sciences was formed in 1954 to represent the Holy See before the International Committee of Historical Sciences.

(19) Other commissions of lesser importance include: Pontifical Commission for Ecclesiastical Archives of Italy (founded in 1955); Central Pontifical Commission for Sacred Art in Italy (1924); Cardinal Commission for the Pontifical Sanctuaries of Pompei and Loreto (19th century); Pontifical Commission for Russia (1930; at present placed under the supervision of the Council for the Public Affairs of the Church, treating matters relating to clergy and faithful of the Latin rite in Russia); Commission for the Protection of Historical and Artistic Monuments of the Holy See (1923, reorganized in 1963); Pontifical Work for the Preservation of the Faith and for the

Erection of New Churches in Rome (1930); Cardinal Commission of the Institute for the Work of Religion (1942, which administers funds for religious work); and the Pontifical Commission for the State and City of the Vatican.

*Offices.* Vatican offices of particular significance include: (1) Prefecture of Economic Affairs, created in 1967 to supervise all financial agencies of the Holy See; (2) Apostolic Chamber, formed in 1934 to administer property and temporal rights during a vacancy in the Holy See; (3) Administration of the Patrimony of the Apostolic See, established in 1878 and reorganized in 1967; (4) Prefecture of the Pontifical House, instituted in 1967 under the name Prefecture of the Apostolic Palace and renamed in 1968, which caters for audiences and non-liturgical pontifical ceremonies and, in collaboration with the secretary of state, arranges for papal voyages and the reception of foreign heads of state; (5) Service of the Assistance of St Peter, formed in the 13th century as a charitable agency and reorganized in 1968, which distributes alms and assistance to persons in need and supervises and administers charitable institutions under the auspices of the Holy See; (6) Archives of Vatican Council II; (7) Office for Relations with the Personnel of the Holy See, created in 1971; (8) Central Office of Statistics of the Church, created in 1967, and under the direct supervision of the secretary of state, which analyses data on the state of the church and its pastoral ministry; (9) Palatine Administrations, maintaining the various apostolic palaces; (10) Works of St Peter, to administer the Basilica of St Peter; (11) Vatican Apostolic Library, founded in the 15th century with some 60,000 manuscripts, 7,000 incunabula and 900,000 other volumes, which includes a Christian museum (founded 1745), a secular museum (1767), a Numismatic Cabinet (1738) and a School of Librarianship (1934); (12) Secret Archives of the Vatican, created in 1611, which were open for research until 1878 but are now inaccessible except on the authorization of the secretary of state; (13) Vatican School of Paleography and Diplomacy, founded in 1884, which is annexed to the administration of the secret archives and offers an advanced 2-year course; (14) Vatican Polyglot Printing Press (founded 1587) and Vatican Publishing House (1926), under the supervision of Salesians; and (15) *L'Osservatore Romano*, founded in 1861, the official newspaper of the Holy See published daily in Italian with weekly editions in French, English, Italian, Portuguese, Spanish and German. The latter is also responsible for *L'Osservatore della Domenica*, a less official and more popular illustrated weekly distributed at the parish level throughout Italy.

*Pontifical academies.* The most important of these is the Pontifical Academy of Sciences, founded in 1603, which is a unique scientific body composed of 70 pontifical academicians who are scholars of world repute in the applied sciences. It is the only academy actually located within Vatican City. Others in Rome include the Roman Academy of St Thomas Aquinas and the Catholic Religion (1879), Pontifical Academy of Roman Theology (1718), Pontifical Academy of the Immaculate Conception (1835), International Marian Pontifical Academy (1946), Academy of the Liturgy (1740), Academy of the Virtuous of the Pantheon (1542), Roman Pontifical Academy of Archeology (1740), and College of the Cults of the Martyrs (1879).

## INTERDENOMINATIONAL ORGANIZATIONS.
A number of joint international commissions have been formed between the Roman Catholic Church (through its Secretariat for Christian Unity) and other Christian denominations.

(1) The Joint Working Group of the Roman Catholic Church and the World Council of Churches was created in 1966 and reorganized in 1969, and by May 1973 had held 12 plenary meetings.

(2) The Roman Catholic/Anglican International Commission (ARCIC) was officially established in 1968 but owes its origin to a meeting of the pope and the archbishop of Canterbury in Rome in 1966. A preparatory commission was established and met 3 times in 1967–68. The report of the last of these meetings, the Report of Malta, was accepted by the heads of both churches during the course of the year and led to the creation of the International Commission. Meetings since then were held at Windsor (England, January 1970), Venice (September 1970), Windsor (September 1971), Gazzada (Italy, August–September 1972), Canterbury (August–September 1973), Grottaferrata (Italy, August–September 1974), and Venice (1976); and in April 1977 the pope and

the archbishop of Canterbury met and issued a Common Declaration.

(3) The Joint Roman Catholic/Lutheran International Commission goes back to 1966 when a working group appointed by LWF and the Secretariat for Christian Unity began preparation for its formation. A joint Catholic/Lutheran commission for study of 'The Gospel and the Church' was established in 1967 and held 5 meetings between 1967 and 1971. Its meeting in Geneva during March 1973 had as its theme 'The significance of the world and the self-understanding of the Church', and its meeting in Rome in January 1974 dealt with 'The ministry'.

(4) The Methodist/Roman Catholic Joint Commission was created in 1966 and reorganized in 1972. The first commission considered theological questions and ecclesiastical problems at annual meetings held between 1967 and 1970: Ariccia (Rome, 1967); London (1968); Malta (1969); and Lake Junaluska (USA, 1970).

Pope John Paul II at audience.

(5) The Roman Catholic/Reformed Study Commission on 'The presence of Christ in the Church and in the world' was formed in 1969 on the basis of preparations begun in June 1968 by WARC and the Secretariat for Christian Unity. Meetings have been held at Rome (April 1970); Carigny-Geneva (March 1971); Bievres-Paris (January–February 1972); Zeist (Netherlands, February 1974); and Rome (March 1975).

(6) The Joint Roman Catholic/Lutheran/Reformed Study Commission on 'The theology of marriage and the problems of mixed marriages' was formed in 1970 following a consultation of the 3 churches in 1969 dealing with the same theme. Meetings have taken place in Strasbourg (November 1971), Madrid (December 1972) and Basel (October 1973).

(7) The Joint Catholic/Coptic Orthodox Commission was initiated by the heads of the 2 churches at the time of their meeting in Rome in May 1973. The Catholic group includes, in addition to its chairman, 6 Coptic Catholics and 6 Latins. Its first meeting at Cairo in March 1974 was devoted to a review of theological studies and issues.

(8) Without taking on the formal substance of commissions, non-official conversations have been carried on between representatives of the Roman Catholic Church, through its Secretariat for Christian Unity, and representatives of the Russian Orthodox Church, Pentecostal churches and charismatic movements within various Protestant, Anglican and Orthodox churches. Joint Russian Orthodox/Catholic meetings have been held in Leningrad (December 1967), Bari (Italy, December 1970), and Zagorsk (USSR, June 1973). Joint Catholic/Pentecostal meetings, including representatives of churches and

movements, have been held in Zurich-Horgen (Switzerland, June 1972), and Rome (June 1973) on the role of the Holy Spirit and gifts of the Spirit in mystical tradition, particularly in the mystical tradition of the East.

(9) The International Catholic/Jewish Liaison Committee was formed in 1971 and is composed of 5 Catholic members appointed (with papal approval) by the prefect of the Secretariat for Christian Unity, and 5 Jewish members representing the World Jewish Congress, B'nai B'rith (Anti-Defamation League), Synagogue Council of America, American Jewish Committee and the Jewish Council of Inter-religious Contacts in Israel. Meetings held thus far include Paris (December 1971), Marseilles (December 1972) and Antwerp (December 1973).

**BROADCASTING.** The official voice of the Vatican state is Radio Vaticana, inaugurated in 1931 by Pius XI in the gardens of Vatican City. Subsequently it has become a powerful international station broadcasting to 157 countries of the world in 32 languages for 16 hours a day. It has 2 centres of transmission, one within the Vatican and since 1957 another in Santa Maria di Galeria 20 km outside Rome; it has no other foreign or overseas studio nor transmitters. Of note are the programmes directed to Communist countries in 15 languages of Eastern Europe and the USSR. There are also regular programmes in Spanish for Latin America, in Portuguese for Angola and Mozambique and for Japan and China. Recording studios are in the Vatican, and Vatican Radio also has a regular service of producing programmes in Spanish, French, Portuguese and English for transmission over Western radio chains and stations in Latin America and Africa. The Holy See is a member of UNDA.

## BIBLIOGRAPHY
*Annuario Pontificio per l'anno 1978.* Città del Vaticano: Segreteria di Stato, 1978. 1,960p. (Annual).
*Annuario statistico della Chiesa, 1974.* Annuarium statisticum Ecclesiae, MCMLXXIV. Città del Vaticano: Segreteria di Stato, 1974. (Annual; tables for all countries).
*Annuario 1976.* Roma: SC Propaganda, 1976. 482p. (Annual yearbook, in Italian).
*Breve compendium informationum de Conferentiis Episcoporum, MCMLXXI.* Città del Vaticano: Cura Secretariae Generalis Synodi Episcoporum, 1971. 183p.
*Connaissance du Vatican.* P. Poupard. Paris: Beauchesne. 1st edition 1968, 230p. 2nd edition, 1974, 205p.
*Guida delle missioni cattoliche.* Città del Vaticano: SC Propaganda, 1975. 1,628p. (Earlier editions 1934, 1946, 1950, 1970).
*La Diocesi di Roma, 1972–73.* Roma: Editoriale Italiana, 1972.
*Oriente cattolico.* Cenni storici e statistiche. Città del Vaticano: SC per le Chiese Orientali, 1974. 857p. (Earlier editions 1929, 1932, 1962).
*The Vatican empire.* N. Lo Bello. New York: Trident Press, 1968. 186p. (Unfavourable but well-documented account of Vatican finances).

TABLE 2. ORGANIZED CHURCHES IN THE HOLY SEE

| Official name 1 | Begun 2 | Type 3 | Counc 4 | Congs 5 | Adults 6 | Affiliated 7 | Names, notes, and other statistics (see Codebook) 8 |
|---|---|---|---|---|---|---|---|
| **Chiesa Cattolica: V Città del Vaticano** | c 40 | R LEr | b,B.. | 60 | 4,000 | 4,950 | *Vicariato della Città del Vaticano.* Part of D Rome under pastoral care of pope. |
| **Total affiliated (mid-1970)** | | | | **60** | **4,000** | **4,950** | **Total denominations (1970) . . . 1.** |
| **Total affiliated (mid-1975)** | | | | **60** | **4,400** | **5,500** | **Total denominations (1975) . . . 1.** |
| **Total affiliated (mid-1980)** | | | | **65** | **4,800** | **6,000** | **Total denominations (1980) . . . 1.** |

NOTES ON TABLE ABOVE
COLUMNS: for meanings and CODES (cols. 1, 3, 4, 8), see Codebook (Part 6). Column 1: **Boldface type** = church with over 10% of country's affiliated Christians.

PEOPLES (ethnolinguistic). Christians: 65% Italian, 35% non-Italian (mainly European, also USA, Latin American, Asian, African, Oceanian).

COUNTRY-WIDE TOTALS
EVANGELIZATION (see Part 5). 1900: 100%. 1970: 100%. 1980: 100%.
FOREIGN PERSONNEL (nationals serving abroad) (1973). Total about 500 Roman Catholics, mostly diplomatic representatives in 79 nunciatures and 26 apostolic delegations abroad; also cardinals, et alii.
FOREIGN PERSONNEL (aliens from abroad) (1973). Total about 360 Roman Catholics. *From Western world.* About 300. *From Communist world.* About 20. *From Third World.* About 40.
INSTITUTIONS (church-operated) (1973). Total 50 (in Vatican City, or with privilege of extraterritoriality), including 1 radio station (Vatican Radio), 1 press (Polyglotta Vaticana), 30 research centres, 4 seminaries, 5 universities (with Atenei Romani).
PERIODICALS. About 100 titles.
PERSONNEL. About 1,044 (684 national, 360 foreign).
RELIGIOUS LIBRARIES. About 60.
SCRIPTURE DISTRIBUTION (1975). Annual totals: 1,000 Bibles (50% free, 50% commercial), 1,000 NTs (50% free, 50% commercial), 40,000 UBS portions. From 1964–76 the pope financed the free distribution to visiting bishops, government leaders, pilgrims and schoolchildren in Rome (with a few external causes) of 750,000 portions in various languages, nearly 10,000 Latin New Testaments, and 2.5 million scripture selections through UBS and WCFBA.
SERVICE AGENCIES. About 150.

ADDITIONAL DATA ON CHURCHES
CHIESA CATTOLICA. Also part of the Vicariate, and an extra-territorial part of Vatican City, is the Abbey Nullius of San Paolo fuori le Mura; et alia.

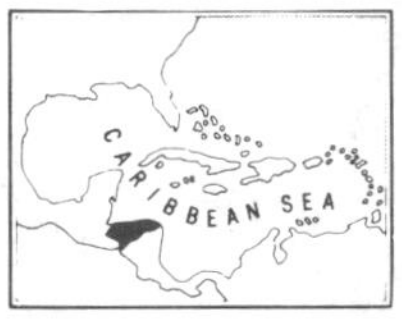


# HONDURAS

## SECULAR DATA

**STATE. Official name:** The Republic of Honduras (La República de Honduras). Adjective of nationality: Honduran (hondureño). **Flag** (shown above right): Stripes of blue, white, and blue, with 5 blue stars in centre.
**Area:** 112,088 sq.km. (43,277 sq.miles). Agricultural land: 25.6%.
**Government:** Republic under military control, since 1972 (1524 Spanish possession, 1838 Independence, several military regimes).
**Legislature:** Unicameral, Congress of Deputies (suspended).
**Official language:** Spanish (*Español/Castellano*).
**Chief cities:** capital Tegucigalpa 302,480 (1973), San Pedro Sula 153,310.
**Political divisions:** 18 Departments.
**Armed forces** (1976): Total 14,200 regular: army 13,000, air force 1,200 (12 combat aircraft). Paramilitary forces: 3,000.

**DEMOGRAPHY. Population:** 2,653,857 (census of 6.III.1974. For 1970–2000 (UN), see last row of Table 1). Population density (1975): 27/sq.km. (70/sq.mile). Under 15 years: 48%. Growth rate (1975–80): 3.37% per year (births 4.63%, deaths −1.27%). Life expectancy (1975–80): 56.2 years. Household size: 5.7 persons.
**Major languages:** Spanish, English, Miskito, Pipil, Lenca, Chinese, Arabic.
**Urban dwellers** (1970): 26.2%. Urban growth rate (1950–70): 5.1% per year.
**Labour force:** 33%.
**Tourists** (1972): 140,000.

**ETHNOLINGUISTIC GROUPS:** 86.1% Honduran Mestizo (predominance of Indian blood), 5.9% Amerindian (150,000) (Miskito, Pipil, Lenca, Paya, Maya, Jicaque, Half-Indian), 2.0% Honduran Black (African Negro), 2.0% Honduran White, 1.1% Salvadorian Mestizo, 0.8% Black Carib (Amerindian/Black), 0.8% Palestinian Arab (20,000), 0.5% Jamaican, 0.5% other West Indian Black, 0.2% White (European, North American), 0.1% Chinese (1,800), Syro-Lebanese Arab, Jewish, Turkish, Armenian.

**MONEY** (1977). **Monetary unit:** lempira (=100 centavos); US$1 = L 2.00.
**National income per person:** US$306. Average annual family income: US$1,744.
**Inflation:** (1970–74) 6.3% per year (1975: consumer price index 139).
**Cost of living in capital** (1976): index 107 (Washington DC=100). Daily cost of living: US$40.

**EDUCATION.** Adult literacy: (1950) 35%, (1974) 57%. Education rate: 53%. Schools: 4,098. Universities: 1.

**HEALTH.** Hospitals: 37 (4,508 beds). Doctors: 780. Lepers: 600 (0.2 per 1,000). Blind: 1,000. Psychotics: 24,000.

**LITERATURE.** Annual new book titles (1973): 173. Periodicals: 175. Scientific journals: 15. Newspapers: 12 dailies, 95 non-daily.

**COMMUNICATION** (per 1,000 people). Phones: 5. Radios: 56. TV sets: 8. Daily newspaper circulation: 42 copies.

TABLE 1. RELIGIOUS ADHERENTS IN HONDURAS

| Year | 1900 | | mid-1970 | | Annual change, 1970–1980 | | | | mid-1975 | | mid-1980 | | 2000 | |
|---|---|---|---|---|---|---|---|---|---|---|---|---|---|---|
| *Name* | *Adherents* | *%* | *Adherents* | *%* | *Natural* | *Conversion* | *Total* | *Rate* | *Adherents* | *%* | *Adherents* | *%* | *Adherents* | *%* |
| **Christians** | **524,000** | **97.0** | **2,520,250** | **98.7** | **102,736** | **−886** | **101,850** | **3.40** | **2,994,320** | **98.6** | **3,538,750** | **98.4** | **6,696,100** | **97.3** |
| professing | 524,000 | 97.0 | 2,520,250 | 98.7 | 102,736 | −886 | 101,850 | 3.40 | 2,994,320 | 98.6 | 3,538,750 | 98.4 | 6,696,100 | 97.3 |
| Roman Catholics | 524,000 | 97.0 | 2,458,950 | 96.3 | 100,128 | −1,548 | 98,580 | 3.38 | 2,918,320 | 96.1 | 3,444,750 | 95.8 | 6,483,100 | 94.2 |
| Christo-pagans | 38,000 | 7.0 | 130,000 | 5.1 | 5,215 | −615 | 4,600 | 3.03 | 152,000 | 5.0 | 176,000 | 4.9 | 275,000 | 4.0 |
| Spiritist Catholics | 5,000 | 1.0 | 51,000 | 2.0 | 2,093 | 7 | 2,100 | 3.44 | 61,000 | 2.0 | 72,000 | 2.0 | 138,000 | 2.0 |
| Evangelical Catholics | 500 | 0.1 | 16,654 | 0.7 | 791 | 614 | 1,405 | 6.09 | 23,050 | 0.8 | 30,700 | 0.9 | 88,600 | 1.3 |
| Protestants | 0 | 0.0 | 61,300 | 2.4 | 2,608 | 662 | 3,270 | 4.30 | 76,000 | 2.5 | 94,000 | 2.6 | 213,000 | 3.1 |
| nominal | 2,700 | 0.5 | 29,495 | 1.1 | 1,249 | 471 | 1,720 | 4.73 | 36,400 | 1.2 | 46,700 | 1.3 | 206,000 | 3.0 |
| affiliated | 521,300 | 96.5 | 2,490,755 | 97.6 | 101,487 | −1,357 | 100,130 | 3.38 | 2,957,920 | 97.4 | 3,492,050 | 97.1 | 6,490,100 | 94.3 |
| total practising | 469,170 | *90* | 1,992,600 | *80* | 81,190 | −1,086 | 80,104 | 3.38 | 2,366,340 | *80* | 2,793,640 | *80* | 4,543,100 | *70* |
| non-practising | 52,130 | *10* | 498,150 | *20* | 20,297 | −271 | 20,026 | 3.38 | 591,580 | *20* | 698,410 | *20* | 1,947,000 | *30* |
| Roman Catholics | 520,800 | 96.4 | 2,412,601 | 94.5 | 98,080 | −2,633 | 95,447 | 3.34 | 2,858,630 | 94.1 | 3,367,070 | 93.6 | 6,188,000 | 89.9 |
| Catholic pentecostals | 0 | 0.0 | 0 | 0.0 | 549 | 3,451 | 4,000 | 25.00 | 16,000 | 0.5 | 40,000 | 1.1 | 200,000 | 2.9 |
| Protestants | 500 | 0.1 | 64,339 | 2.5 | 2,853 | 1,353 | 4,206 | 5.06 | 83,100 | 2.7 | 106,400 | 3.0 | 262,000 | 3.8 |
| Evangelicals | 500 | 0.1 | 48,500 | 1.9 | 2,189 | 1,231 | 3,420 | 5.36 | 63,800 | 2.1 | 82,700 | 2.3 | 241,000 | 3.5 |
| Marginal Protestants | 0 | 0.0 | 6,405 | 0.3 | 281 | 79 | 360 | 4.38 | 8,200 | 0.3 | 10,000 | 0.3 | 25,000 | 0.4 |
| Orthodox | 0 | 0.0 | 5,200 | 0.2 | 178 | −170 | 8 | 0.15 | 5,240 | 0.2 | 5,280 | 0.1 | 6,500 | 0.1 |
| Non-White indigenous | 0 | 0.0 | 2,000 | 0.1 | 86 | 14 | 100 | 4.00 | 2,500 | 0.1 | 3,000 | 0.1 | 8,000 | 0.1 |
| Anglicans | 0 | 0.0 | 210 | 0.0 | 9 | 0 | 9 | 3.60 | 250 | 0.0 | 300 | 0.0 | 600 | 0.0 |
| Baha'is | 0 | 0.0 | 8,000 | 0.3 | 337 | 23 | 360 | 3.67 | 9,800 | 0.3 | 11,600 | 0.3 | 28,000 | 0.4 |
| Spiritists | 0 | 0.0 | 7,000 | 0.3 | 416 | 684 | 1,100 | 9.09 | 12,100 | 0.4 | 18,000 | 0.5 | 55,000 | 0.8 |
| Afro-American spiritists | 1,000 | 0.2 | 5,000 | 0.2 | 189 | −89 | 100 | 1.82 | 5,500 | 0.2 | 6,000 | 0.2 | 12,000 | 0.2 |
| Tribal religionists | 15,000 | 2.8 | 5,000 | 0.2 | 154 | −254 | −100 | −2.22 | 4,500 | 0.1 | 4,000 | 0.1 | 3,000 | 0.0 |
| Non-religious | 0 | 0.0 | 2,500 | 0.1 | 165 | 555 | 720 | 15.32 | 4,700 | 0.2 | 9,700 | 0.3 | 68,000 | 1.0 |
| Muslims | 0 | 0.0 | 1,600 | 0.1 | 54 | −30 | 24 | 1.40 | 1,710 | 0.1 | 1,840 | 0.1 | 2,500 | 0.0 |
| Atheists | 0 | 0.0 | 1,000 | 0.0 | 55 | 65 | 120 | 7.50 | 1,600 | 0.1 | 2,200 | 0.1 | 13,000 | 0.2 |
| Buddhists | 0 | 0.0 | 1,000 | 0.0 | 34 | −34 | 0 | 0.00 | 1,000 | 0.0 | 1,000 | 0.0 | 1,000 | 0.0 |
| Chinese folk-religionists | 0 | 0.0 | 500 | 0.0 | 14 | −34 | −20 | −5.00 | 400 | 0.0 | 300 | 0.0 | 0 | 0.0 |
| Jews | 0 | 0.0 | 150 | 0.0 | 6 | 0 | 6 | 3.53 | 170 | 0.0 | 210 | 0.0 | 400 | 0.0 |
| Other religionists | 0 | 0.0 | 1,000 | 0.0 | 40 | 0 | 40 | 3.33 | 1,200 | 0.0 | 1,400 | 0.0 | 2,000 | 0.0 |
| **Country's population** | **540,000** | **100.0** | **2,553,000** | **100.0** | **104,200** | **0** | **104,200** | **3.43** | **3,037,000** | **100.0** | **3,595,000** | **100.0** | **6,881,000** | **100.0** |

COLUMNS, ROWS. For meanings and definitions, see Codebook (Part 6). Note that, by definition, total 'Christians' = professing + crypto-Christians, which also = affiliated + nominal Christians. Percentages may not always total exactly, due to rounding.
CENSUSES. **24.VI.1945:** 97.8% Roman Catholics, 1.9% Evangelicals, 0.3% other religionists. The religion question has subsequently not been asked.

NOTES ON RELIGIONS
AFRO-AMERICAN SPIRITISTS. Non-Christian adherents of Afro-Caribbean spirit-possession cults (low spiritism) syncretizing Christianity with African religion; mostly Jamaicans and other Blacks.
ATHEISTS. Communist Party of Honduras (PCH) (proscribed since 1957; pro-Soviet) and rival faction: membership (1970) 300.
BAHA'IS. Rapid growth from 15 local spiritual assemblies (1964) to 60 (1973).
BUDDHISTS. Chinese.
CATHOLIC PENTECOSTALS (or, Catholic charismatics). In January 1976, over 10,000 adults were attending charismatic prayer meetings in Honduras, mainly led by laymen (only a few priests being charismatics) and with up to 1,000 people to each assembly. Total charismatic community (mid-1975) including children, 16,000, growing very rapidly. In 1976 the charismatic Catholic bishop of Olancho was relieved of his duties after violent opposition by landowners to his calls for social reform. In February 1978, over 8,000 attended a healing service in San Pedro Sula.
CHRISTO-PAGANS. Maya Amerindians, and 20,000 Black Caribs (Amerindian/Black), syncretizing Catholicism with pre-Columbian Maya religion.
COUNTRY'S POPULATION. In 1974 a major hurricane struck the north coast, leaving 10,000 dead.
EVANGELICAL CATHOLICS. This term is used here to describe persons who are affiliated to churches termed by the state Evangélica (Protestant, marginal Protestant, Anglican or Non-White indigenous churches), but who are regarded by state and society as, or who profess to be, Roman Catholics.
MUSLIMS. Palestinian Arab immigrants from 1910 onwards, with some Syro-Lebanese traders, mainly around San Pedro Sula.
ORTHODOX. Palestinian Arab settlers with some Syrians and Lebanese, immigrating from Jordan from 1910 onwards, most of whom have been and are Christians. Living mainly in San Pedro Sula, they form the backbone of the nation's industrial and commercial classes.
OTHER RELIGIONISTS. Including Rosicrucians (2 AMORC centres).
SPIRITIST CATHOLICS. Roman Catholics actively and regularly involved in the practice of high or low spiritism, mainly Afro-American low spiritism.
SPIRITISTS. Non-Christian adherents of high spiritism. The rapid growth of spiritism comes mostly from the ranks of nominal Catholics. In 1930 a large new spiritist movement began among the Miskito and Suma Indians.
TRIBAL RELIGIONISTS. Of the 150,000 Amerindians in 1969, a small proportion were still animists, including among the Miskito, Suma, Torrupan (Jicaque) and Lenca.

## NON-CHRISTIAN RELIGIONS.

**Traditional religions** are still practised by a small proportion of the Amerindian tribes: Miskito, Suma, Torrupan (Jicaque) and Lenca; many others follow traditional practices but also profess at the same time to be Catholics.

**Spiritism** has grown in recent years, taking its converts from the nominal fringe of Catholicism.

## CHRISTIANITY

**CATHOLIC CHURCH.** Honduras was a major centre of the ancient Mayan culture before the 10th century. It was first sighted by Columbus in 1502. In 1524 Cortes entered from Mexico, attracted by tales of gold. The territory became part of Spanish-controlled Guatemala in 1538, but evangelization did not get under way until the arrival of Spanish Franciscans about 1550. By 1807 there were 145 churches. Honduras became independent in 1838, and church and state were legally separated in 1880.

The great majority of the population has been baptized in the Catholic Church, although the proportion of Catholics relative to the population as a whole is diminishing due to conversions to Protestantism and spiritism. Catholic concern and activity in the realms of society, laity and evangelization are recent phenomena dating only from the 1960s. This has taken such forms as the creation of new movements of the lay apostolate, concern for social and human development, integration of nuns (until recently confined to education) into wider parish structures, and an attempt to achieve a global understanding of the pastoral function. A first national meeting of diocesan pastoral teams took place in August 1970.

Although expatriate priests have continued to increase in number, from 45 in 1955 to 188 in 1970, the number of national priests has not grown in proportion, falling from 55 in 1955 to 48 in 1970.

**PROTESTANT CHURCHES.** Although the origins of Methodism in Honduras go back to 1860, the first major organized Protestant activity in Honduras began in 1896 with the arrival of the Central American Mission. Other early pioneers include Friends in 1902, Adventists in 1891, Evangelical and Reformed Church (ERC) in 1920 and Moravians in 1930. Pentecostalism made its initial appearance in 1937 when the first Assemblies of God missionaries entered from nearby El Salvador; and such other USA-based Pentecostal denominations as the Church of God (Cleveland), International Church of the Foursquare Gospel and Church of God of Prophecy followed after World War II. Many other small missions have also appeared since the war. Although Adventists and Assemblies of God have the largest Protestant constituencies, no single church or tradition stands out as predominant.

Protestants have through the years shown a keen interest in educational and medical work. The Central American Mission built an important hospital at Siguatepegue in 1960 and operates a nursing school there as well. The United Church of Christ, formerly the ERC, is noted for its educational and medical programme, and other Protestant bodies have also devoted considerable resources to social work.

**CHURCH AND STATE.** Since the separation of church and state in 1880, in advocating the freedom of religion and worship the various constitutions of Honduras have borne the stamp of the masonic influence of the age; instruction was lay and clergy had no right of vote. These characteristics are not retained in the new constitution of 1965, which invokes in its Preamble the 'protection of God' and from whose text on educational instruction the term 'lay' has been removed. The state has therefore not renounced its original religious character. On education, the present constitution merely states that 'The organization and technical direction of education is the prerogative of the State. Official instruction shall be free; moreover, primary schooling shall be obligatory and paid for entirely by the State' (Article 150). A supplementary decree of February 1967 allows for the establishment of a course on religion in state schools, if requested by parents and teachers. In addition, the new constitution does not deprive clergy of their right to vote. Article 187 'assures the free exercise of all religions and of worship without any pre-eminence', prohibits ministers of the various religious bodies from holding public office and from carrying on 'in any fashion political propaganda by invoking religious motives or by making use of the religious beliefs of the people for this purpose'. A constitutional decree published in September 1969, 2 months after the short war between Honduras and El Salvador, placed the armed forces of Honduras under the protection of the Virgin of Suyapa and compelled the entire military corps to render her public homage. Although the Catholic Church is not recognized as the state church, it nevertheless still figures prominently in state and government activities.

The hierarchy and clergy of the Catholic Church in general are tending to use more and more the constitutional guarantees of freedom of expression to address themselves to the country's social problems, as evidenced by numerous recent episcopal and clerical declarations. Indeed, the involvement of clergy in social affairs has caused a certain uneasiness on the part of governmental authorities. The Catholic clergy are opposed by the ruling class which, through the mass media, threatens foreign priests with expulsion and accuses the church's centres for social training of being responsible for the occupation of lands by the poor in the southern part of the country. Because of these difficulties, the clergy of Honduras in their June 1971 meeting underlined the necessity of adopting a unified position and passed a resolution calling for solidarity in the face of any attacks which might arise.

There is no ministry nor ministerial department responsible for religious affairs nor registration of churches as such by government. Nevertheless, every secular or religious group desiring to obtain or sell property must, according to the law, first obtain a juridical personality.

**INTERDENOMINATIONAL ORGANIZATIONS.** The Honduras Evangelical Alliance (Alianza Evangélica Hondureña), founded in 1945, has 12 member churches and meets annually. Its activities are limited and its unity threatened by the incipient withdrawal of several members in recent years.

CONCORDE is an agency for the co-ordination of the work of private institutions, both confessional and non-confessional, in social development. A pioneer in central America, CONCORDE is also engaged in applied research and long-range planning.

**BROADCASTING.** Radio and TV networks all accept religious programmes. There are 4 Catholic radio transmitters: La Voz de Suyapa (Tegucigalpa), Radio Paz La Voz del Desarrollo (Choluteca), La Voz de San Isidro (La Ceiba) and Emisora Católica (Yoro). Radio schools are widely used for both education and evangelization; in Honduras there are the Suyapa Radio Schools and also Acción Cultural Popular Hondureña, founded in July 1960, with 1,136 radio schools and 21,630 students in 1971 covering 12 of the 18 provinces of the republic. Radio HRVC is operated by the Conservative Baptist Mission, and has enrolled 10,000 correspondence course students. Foreign Christian programmes can easily be heard on the international stations FEBC (California), TWR (Netherlands Antilles) and HCJB (Ecuador). For Catholics, Honduras is a member of UNDA.

## BIBLIOGRAPHY

*Anuario de la Iglesia en Honduras, 1970.* Tegucigalpa: Arzobispado, 1971.
'Observations on a Lenca ceremony in Honduras', W. W. Plowden, *El Palacio* (Santa Fe), 66 (6 December 1959), 203–5.
'Planting the church in Honduras: the development of a culturally relevant witness'. E. F. Mathews. Thesis, Fuller Theological Seminary, Pasadena (CA), 1970.

Factory worker (left) purchases New Testament from Bible colporteur (right).

TABLE 2. ORGANIZED CHURCHES AND DENOMINATIONS IN HONDURAS

| Official name 1 | Begun 2 | Type 3 | Counc 4 | Congs 5 | Adults 6 | Affiliated 7 | Names, notes, and other statistics (see Codebook) 8 |
|---|---|---|---|---|---|---|---|
| Asambleas de Dios | 1937 | P Pe2 | ZF... | 92 | 3,400 | 8,000 | *Assemblies of God.* M=AoG(USA). 2 fields, begun from El Salvador. 97n,8f,1s(50). |
| Consejo de Igls Luteranas en CA & P | 1964 | P Lut | x.... | 9 | 16 | 200 | *Council of Lutheran Chs in CAmerica & Panama (Misuri).* M=LCMS(USA). 1m,1t(142). |
| Convención Bautista Hondureña | 1954 | P Bap | T...C | 42 | 839 | 2,000 | *Honduras Baptist Convention.* M=SBC(USA). HQ San Pedro Sula. 20n,21f,1h,1s,209Y. |
| Hermanos Libres | 1898 | P CBr | x.... | 70 | 600 | 1,500 | *Christian Brethren.* Plymouth (Open) Brethren. M=CMML(UK,USA). 12f,1j. |
| Iglesia Adventista del Séptimo Día | 1891 | P Adv | x.... | 28 | 4,442 | 8,000 | *Seventh-day Adventists, Honduras Mission,* CAmerican UM. 8nx,8f,1r,48t(4581),355Y. |
| Iglesia Católica en Honduras: | 1550 | R Lat | B.LDR | 110 | 1,254,000 | 2,412,601 | *Catholic Ch in Honduras.* C=11+1+23. 2p,1s(19).   48n,188x,29m,286w,89280Yy. |
| M Tegucigalpa | 1561 | R Lat | B₂ | 36 | 324,000 | 624,013 | Capital.Serious shortage of priests in rural areas.   20   75   15   142   19785 |
| D Comayagua | 1963 | R Lat | B₂ | 11 | 118,000 | 227,000 | In centre. Acute agrarian problem of latifundia.   7   7   0   5   9045 |
| D San Pedro Sula | 1916 | R Lat | P₂ | 17 | 235,000 | 451,620 | North coast. 2 Mission Zones, among Aborigines. M=CM. 2   34   8   57   16594 |
| D Santa Rosa de Copán | 1916 | R Lat | Bₓ | 28 | 351,000 | 675,250 | Extreme west of Honduras. Population 80% rural.   18   32   3   29   25578 |
| PN Choluteca | 1964 | R Lat | B₂ | 11 | 151,000 | 290,000 | 1,000s of impoverished squatters. Bishop a charismatic.   1   33   3   51   13850 |
| PN Inmaculada CBVM en Olancho | 1949 | R Lat | B₂ | | 75,000 | 144,718 | *CBVM=Concepción de la BVM.* Bishop a charismatic.   0   7   0   2   4428 |
| Iglesia Centroamericana | 1896 | P int | xM..C | 100 | 1,417 | 4,868 | *Central American Ch.* M=CAM(USA). 1 school. HQ Choluteca. 38f,1H,2k,1r,1s. |
| Iglesia de Dios de la Profecía | 1952 | P Pe3 | z.... | 15 | 200 | 500 | M=Ch of God of Prophecy(USA). Holiness Pentecostals. Split in USA ex CoG(Cleveland). |
| Iglesia de Dios (Anderson) | | P Hol | x.... | 42 | 2,473 | 3,000 | M=Ch of God (Anderson)(USA). Holiness denomination. 1 primary school. |
| Iglesia de Dios (Cleveland) | 1944 | P Pe3 | ZF... | 111 | 2,838 | 6,675 | M=CoG(Cleveland)(USA). Congs: 17 English-speaking (Blacks), 36 Spanish. 77n,4f. |
| Iglesia de JC de los Santos de los UD | 1952 | N LdS | x.... | | 1,950 | 3,314 | *Latter-day Saints.* Mormons. M=CJCldS(USA). Many USA personnel. 70f,G=12.6%pa. |
| Igl de los Hermanos Unidos en Cristo | 1944 | P Hol | xF..C | 20 | 300 | 1,000 | *United Brethren in Christ Ch.* M=UBC(USA). HQ La Ceiba. 2f. |
| Iglesia del Evangelio Cuadrangular | 1952 | P Pe2 | ZF..C | 27 | 2,258 | 6,000 | *Internat Ch of the Foursquare Gospel.* M=ICFG(USA). 33nn,5f,2p(35),W=45%,141Y. |
| Iglesia del Nazareno | 1971 | P Hol | xF... | 4 | 385 | 2,083 | *Ch of the Nazarene.* M=CoN(USA). Holiness denomination. 2f. |
| Iglesia Episcopal Hondureña | | A ACa | aw₂R₂ | 4 | 132 | 210 | *Episcopal Ch.* 1969, missionary diocese, PECUSA, Province IX. 90% Black. 3x,W=82%. |
| Iglesia Ev Luterana de CR,ES,H,N,P | 1954 | P Lut | 1.... | 3 | 30 | 116 | *ELC of Costa Rica, El Salvador, H, Nic, Panama.* Germans, Scandinavians. 1n,1x,3Yy. |
| Iglesia Evangélica Menonita | 1950 | P Men | G...C | 18 | 376 | 1,000 | *Honduras Mennonite Ch.* M=EMBMC(USA). NCoast, Aguan, Agalta, Central. 36f,1h,1s. |

*Continued overleaf*

*Table 2 – continued*

| Official name 1 | Begun 2 | Type 3 | Counc 4 | Congs 5 | Adults 6 | Affiliated 7 | Names, notes, and other statistics (see Codebook) 8 |
|---|---|---|---|---|---|---|---|
| Iglesia Filadelfia | 1967 | P Pe2 | Z.... | 16 | 283 | 500 | *Philadelphia Ch.* M=SFM(Sweden). Classical Pentecostals (2-stage). 6n,10x,49Y,6z. |
| Iglesia Independiente | | I ind | ..... | | 245 | 300 | *Independent Church.* Small indigenous Honduran body. |
| Iglesia Metodista | 1860 | P Met | VwM.. | 13 | 466 | 1,500 | In Belize District, MCCA. Bay Islands. M=MMS(UK). Blacks. 1n,1x,5f,110Yy. |
| Iglesia Morava: Provincia de Honduras | 1930 | P Mor | xv..C | 26 | 2,020 | 5,000 | *Moravians. Unity of Brethren.* M=MC(USA). Miskito Indians. 3n,2x,7f,1H,3h,44Y,99y. |
| Iglesia Ortodoxa (P Jerusalem) | c1910 | O Ara | Cwo.. | 10 | 1,100 | 4,400 | Under Greek Orthodox Patriarchate of Jerusalem. Palestinian Arabs. HQ San Pedro Sula. |
| Iglesia Reorganizada de JC de los SUD | | M LdS | x.... | | 50 | 91 | M=Reorganized Ch of Jesus Christ of Latter-day Saints (USA). Schism ex Mormons. |
| Iglesia Unida de Cristo | 1920 | P Ref | ....C | | 1,000 | 2,000 | *United Ch of Christ.* Formerly M=ERC, now UCBWM(USA). Northeast. Schools. 3f,1s. |
| Iglesia Wesleyana | 1957 | P Hol | VF..C | 9 | 1,000 | 2,000 | M=WC(USA). English-speaking Blacks on north coast. 1n,1x,2f,1h,1k,W=33%,37Y. |
| Iglesias Ev Amigos de Centroamérica | 1902 | P Qua | QF..C | 43 | 279 | 1,947 | *Junta Anual. YM of Friends.* M=California YM(USA). 10n,5x,G=9%pa,2p,W=29%,48Y. |
| Misión Bautista | 1955 | P Bap | x.... | | 20 | 150 | M=Baptist Mid-Missions(USA). Fundamentalist Baptists. 10f. |
| Misión Bautista Conservador | 1951 | P Bap | xF..C | 53 | 1,235 | 2,000 | *Conservative Baptist Mission.* M=CBHMS(USA). Radio HRVC: T=10000, V=1000. 16f,1s,275Y. |
| Misión Bíblica Pioneira | 1949 | P ind | x.... | 4 | 100 | 300 | M=Pioneer Bible Mission (1967, United Missionary Fellowship, USA). Medical, dental. 4f,2h. |
| Misión Evangelical Mundial | 1943 | P Hol | xF..C | 63 | 800 | 2,000 | *World Gospel Holiness Ch.* M=World Gospel Mission(USA). 2 schools. 27f,1s. |
| Sinodo Evangélico y Reformada | c1970 | I Ref | .v..C | | 200 | 500 | *Evangelical and Reformed Synod.* HQ San Pedro Sula. 1973, membership enquiry made to WCC. |
| Testigos de Jehová | 1930 | M Jeh | x.... | 22 | 1,432 | 3,000 | *Jehovah's Witnesses. Watch Tower.* Missionary visit 1930; work restarted 1945. 194Y. |
| Unión de los Hermanos | | I Mor | ..... | | 70 | 200 | *Unity of the Brethren.* Small indigenous split ex Moravian Church. |
| Other Protestant denominations | | P | ..... | | 1,000 | 2,000 | Total about 20 (see list below). |
| Other Black indigenous churches | | I | ..... | | 500 | 1,000 | Mostly begun by, and spread among, Jamaicans and other West Indian Blacks. |
| Other Orthodox churches | | O | ..... | | 600 | 800 | Syrian Orthodox (Palestinian Arab immigrants), Armenian Apostolics. |
| **Total affiliated (mid-1970)** | | | | **1,020** | **1,288,056** | **2,490,755** | **Total denominations (1970) . . . 55.** |
| **Total affiliated (mid-1975)** | | | | **1,050** | **1,529,600** | **2,957,920** | **Total denominations (1975) . . . 60.** |
| **Total affiliated (mid-1980)** | | | | **1,080** | **1,805,900** | **3,492,050** | **Total denominations (1980) . . . 65.** |

NOTES ON TABLE ABOVE
COLUMNS: for meanings and CODES (cols. 1, 3, 4, 8), see Codebook (Part 6). Column 1: **Boldface type** = church with over 10% of country's affiliated Christians.
NATIONAL COUNCILS (Column 4, 5th letter).
C = Alianza Evangélica Hondureña (AEH) (Honduras Evangelical Alliance).
R = Conferencia Episcopal de Honduras (CEH) (Episcopal Conference of Honduras).
OTHER PROTESTANT DENOMINATIONS. These include: Associated Brotherhood of Christians (Jesus Only Pentecostals), Baptist Faith Missions (1972), Christian Reformed Ch (1971), Ch of Christ (Non-Instrumental), Churches of Christ in Christian Union, Congregational Holiness Ch (1968), Congregational Methodist Ch, Ev Methodist Ch (1964), Evangelistic Faith Missions (1970), World Baptist Fellowship (1967), World-Wide Missions.

PEOPLES (ethnolinguistic). Christians: 86.5% Honduran Mestizo, 5.7% Amerindian (Miskito, Pipil, Lenca, Paya, Maya, Jicaque, Half-Indian), 2.0% Honduran Black, 2.0% Honduran White, 1.1% Salvadorian Mestizo, 0.8% Black Carib, 0.7% Palestinian Arab, 0.5% Jamaican Black, 0.5% other West Indian Black, 0.2% White (European, North American), Syro-Lebanese Arab, Chinese (120), Armenian.

COUNTRY-WIDE TOTALS
EVANGELIZATION (see Part 5). 1900: 99%. 1970: 100%. 1980: 100%. *Mass evangelism.* Among recent campaigns: 1963–64, Evangelism-in-Depth (296 participating churches from 14 denominations, 15,000 Christians in 2,636 prayer groups, 6,000 enrolled in evangelism training courses, 205,520 homes visited, 6,204 professions of faith, 110 new congregations formed doubling of Protestant church membership in San Pedro Sula); April 1971, Luis Palau crusade in Tegucigalpa (25 sponsoring churches, 57,000 attenders, 2,424 enquirers). *Radiophonic evangelism.* HCJB, FEBC, ICI.
FOREIGN MISSIONARIES AND PERSONNEL (nationals serving abroad) (1973). Total about 50 Roman Catholics in Guatemala, Mexico et alia.
FOREIGN MISSIONARIES AND PERSONNEL (aliens from abroad) (1973). Total 699. *From Western world.* 559: 271 Protestants (239 in 34 USA societies, 18 in 4 UK societies, 10 in 1 Sweden society, 4 in 1 Norway society), 215 Roman Catholics, about 70 marginal Protestants (65 Mormons) from USA, 3 Anglicans in 1 USA society. *From Third World.* 140: 130 Roman Catholics from other Latin American countries, about 6 Protestants from Guatemala, Puerto Rico et alia, about 4 Black indigenous from Jamaica et alia.
INSTITUTIONS (church-operated) (1973). Total 90 including 35 higher schools (1 minor seminary), 30 medical centres (8 hospitals), 6 radio stations, 11 seminaries (10 Protestant, 1 RC), 2 study centres.
PERIODICALS. About 20 titles.
PERSONNEL. About 1,674 (975 national, 699 foreign).
RELIGIOUS LIBRARIES. About 19.
SCRIPTURE DISTRIBUTION (1975). Annual totals: 52,807 Bibles (2% free, 41% subsidized, 57% commercial), 76,905 NTs (29% free, 32% subsidized, 39% commercial), 372,560 UBS portions, 50,670 UBS selections.
SERVICE AGENCIES. About 35, including: ACPOH, AEH, CCCI, CEH, CIRH, CNR, JEC, JOC, MAF, MFC, WBT.

ADDITIONAL DATA ON CHURCHES
IGLESIA CATOLICA EN HONDURAS. *Annual baptisms.* (1972) 98.5% infant, 1.5% adult. *Priests.* Nationals: 42 diocesan, 6 religious. Expatriates: 65 Spanish, 51 Canadian, 43 USA, 13 other nationalities including 13 Latin American priests. Growth of number of priests (nationals + expatriates): 1955, 50 + 45; 1960, 39 + 131; 1965, 32 + 111; 1970, 48 + 188. *Male religious.* Total (1970): 116 (5% nationals, 9% from other Latin American nations, 86% from other continents). *Brothers.* All expatriates (16 being Spanish). *Sisters.* Total all sisters (1970): 286 (18% nationals, 42% from other Latin American nations, 40% from other continents). *Catechists.* Total (1970) 485. Training schools: Paul VI interdiocesan school, and Tegucigalpa catechetical centre. *Main religious orders and congregations.* Priests: PME, CM, SJ, OFM, CP, SDB. Brothers: FSC. Sisters: Salesians (Daughters of Marie-Auxiliatrice), Daughters of Charity of St Vincent de Paul, School Sisters of St Francis (Milwaukee, USA), Franciscans de la Purisima (Spain).
*Catholic organizations.* The Episcopal Conference of Honduras (Conferencia Episcopal de Honduras) is a member of SEDAC and CELAM. The Honduras National Conference of Religious Institutes (Conferencia Nacional de Religiosos) for men and women, is a member of CLAR and SERCAP. There are no national presbyteral or pastoral councils. The principal lay movements are Legión de Maria, MFC, Cursillos de Cristiandad, JOC, JEC, and Dinámicos (for children 8–14 years of age).
The Holy See has diplomatic relations with Honduras and is represented to government and the Catholic hierarchy by a pro-nuncio.
The work of the Catholic Church in development is co-ordinated by the Consejo de Coordinación para el Desarrollo, with the following organizations represented on the council. (1) Popular Cultural Action in Honduras (Acción Cultural Popular Hondureña, ACPOH) is a society with juridical personality founded to combat, on the cultural and technical levels, the ignorance and misery of adult peasants. The society supervises an educational system by radio, the first school being founded in 1960. (2) The Association for Human Development (Asociación de Promoción Humana) furnishes technical assistance and credit to co-operatives and pre-cooperatives, as well as a programme of low-cost housing. (3) Development, savings and credit co-operatives (Fomento Cooperativo, Cooperativos de Ahorro y Credito) have the purpose of educating adults in group action. The first co-operative was established in 1963, and by 1971 there were 122 credit union co-operatives. (4) Caritas of Honduras has since 1958 promoted numerous community development projects. Each diocese also has one or more centres for rural development (Centros de Capacitación Campesina). There are in all 9: at San Pedro Sula, Comayagua, Pinalejo, El Progresso, Nueva Ocotepegue, Station Rosa de Copán, Juticalpa and 2 at Choluteca. Working in the various Catholic development centres are about 300 full-time lay persons.
The Catholic Church supervises 29 parochial schools (3,190 pupils), 21 colleges and institutes, 2 technical and professional schools (13,833 students); and priests and religious personnel also teach in the Autonomous National University of Honduras (Universidad Nacional Autónoma de Honduras). Medical and philanthropic action includes popular clinics, 2 nursing schools, 3 homes for the aged and 5 homes for children. In addition religious personnel work in 2 public health centres.

# HONG KONG

## SECULAR DATA

**STATE. Official name:** The Crown Colony of Hong Kong (in Chinese, Kong-O).
**Flag** (shown above right): British Blue Ensign with arms of the Colony on white disc in the fly.
**Area:** 1,034 sq.km. (403.7 sq.miles). Agricultural land: 10.6%.
**Government:** British crown colony, since 1842.
**Legislature:** Legislative Council, up to 30 members.
**Official languages:** Chinese and English.
**Chief cities:** administrative capital, Victoria 520,930; New Kowloon 1,478,580, Kowloon 716,270.
**Foreign forces (1973): 9,000 British (UK), falling to 8,000 by 1976.**

**DEMOGRAPHY. Population:** 3,948,179 (census of 9.III.1971. For 1970–2000 (UN), see last row of Table 1). Population density (1975): 4,086/sq.km. (10,583/sq.mile). Under 15 years: 41%. Growth rate (1975–80): 1.36% per year (births 1.94%, deaths –0.58%). Life expectancy (1975–80): 71.2 years. Household size: 4.5 persons.
**Major languages:** Chinese (Cantonese, Hoklo, Hakka), English, Japanese.
**Urban dwellers** (1970): 92.0%. Urban growth rate (1950–70): 4.5% per year.
**Labour force:** 41%.
**Refugees** (1974): 114,730 from People's Republic of China. After 1974 all refugees were declared illegal and are not counted. About 2 million have entered from China in recent years.
**Tourists** (1974): 1,295,462.

**ETHNOLINGUISTIC GROUPS:** 98.3% Chinese [81.5% Cantonese (including Tanka), 8.1% Hoklo (South Fukienese), 3.3% Hakka, 3.0% Sze Yap, 2.8% Shanghai & Mandarin], 0.7% British (29,000), 0.3% Indo-Pakistani, 0.2% USA White, 0.2% Anglo-Australian, 0.1% Portuguese, 0.1% Malay, 0.1% Filipino, Korean, Japanese, Vietnamese, German, French, Dutch, Sinhalese, Indonesian, Persian, USA Black, Jewish.

**MONEY** (1977). **Monetary unit:** dollar (= 100 cents); US$1 = HK$4.75.
**National income per person:** US$1,500. Average annual family income: US$6,750.
**Inflation:** (1970–74) 10.3% per year.

**Chinese folk-religionists.** Festival of Sea Goddess in Hong Kong, with dragon.

Cost of living in capital (1976): index 116 (Washington DC=100). Daily cost of living: US$52.

EDUCATION. Adult literacy: (1961) 71%, (1971) 77%, (1976) 81%. Schools: 1,339. Universities: 2.

HEALTH. Hospitals: 118 (16,733 beds). Doctors: 2,533. Lepers: 13,000 (3.1 per 1,000). Blind: 6,500. Psychotics: 50,000. Drug addicts: 300,000. Criminals: 30,105, plus 80,000 in underworld gangs.

LITERATURE. Annual new book titles (1973): 806. Periodicals: 203. Scientific journals: 2. Newspapers: 81 dailies, 36 non-daily.

COMMUNICATION (per 1,000 people). Phones: 147. Radios: 182. TV sets: 106. Daily newspaper circulation: 371 copies.

### TABLE 1.    RELIGIOUS ADHERENTS IN HONG KONG

| Year | 1900 | | mid-1970 | | Annual change, 1970–1980 | | | | mid-1975 | | mid-1980 | | 2000 | |
|---|---|---|---|---|---|---|---|---|---|---|---|---|---|---|
| Name | Adherents | % | Adherents | % | Natural | Conversion | Total | Rate | Adherents | % | Adherents | % | Adherents | % |
| Chinese folk-religionists | 339,900 | 89.4 | 2,050,000 | 52.0 | 28,850 | -19,295 | 9,555 | 0.45 | 2,101,620 | 49.7 | 2,145,550 | 47.4 | 2,207,200 | 39.2 |
| Buddhists | 30,400 | 8.0 | 630,000 | 16.0 | 5,152 | 9,628 | 14,780 | 2.11 | 701,350 | 16.6 | 777,800 | 17.2 | 1,091,000 | 19.4 |
| Christians | 8,200 | 2.1 | 620,050 | 15.7 | 9,686 | 8,349 | 18,035 | 2.56 | 705,600 | 16.7 | 800,400 | 17.7 | 1,181,200 | 21.0 |
| professing | 8,200 | 2.1 | 620,050 | 15.7 | 9,686 | 8,349 | 18,035 | 2.56 | 705,600 | 16.7 | 800,400 | 17.7 | 1,181,200 | 21.0 |
| Roman Catholics | 3,700 | 1.0 | 280,000 | 7.1 | 4,350 | 3,370 | 7,720 | 2.44 | 316,900 | 7.5 | 357,200 | 7.9 | 534,400 | 9.5 |
| Protestants | 3,800 | 1.0 | 250,000 | 6.3 | 3,948 | 3,987 | 7,935 | 2.76 | 287,650 | 6.8 | 329,350 | 7.3 | 461,600 | 8.4 |
| Chinese indigenous | 0 | 0.0 | 60,000 | 1.5 | 928 | 762 | 1,690 | 2.50 | 67,600 | 1.6 | 76,900 | 1.7 | 118,100 | 2.1 |
| Anglicans | 700 | 0.2 | 25,000 | 0.6 | 371 | 29 | 400 | 1.48 | 27,000 | 0.6 | 29,000 | 0.6 | 45,000 | 0.8 |
| Marginal Protestants | 0 | 0.0 | 5,000 | 0.1 | 88 | 202 | 290 | 4.53 | 6,400 | 0.2 | 7,900 | 0.2 | 12,000 | 0.2 |
| Orthodox | 0 | 0.0 | 50 | 0.0 | 1 | -1 | 0 | 0.00 | 50 | 0.0 | 50 | 0.0 | 100 | 0.0 |
| nominal | 1,600 | 0.4 | 59,796 | 1.5 | 870 | -70 | 800 | 1.26 | 63,400 | 1.5 | 67,800 | 1.5 | 45,000 | 0.8 |
| affiliated | 6,600 | 1.7 | 560,254 | 14.2 | 8,816 | 8,419 | 17,235 | 2.68 | 642,200 | 15.2 | 732,600 | 16.2 | 1,136,200 | 20.2 |
| total practising | 5,940 | 90 | 392,180 | 70 | 6,171 | 5,893 | 12,064 | 2.68 | 449,540 | 70 | 512,820 | 70 | 681,720 | 60 |
| non-practising | 660 | 10 | 168,070 | 30 | 2,645 | 2,526 | 5,171 | 2.68 | 192,660 | 30 | 219,780 | 30 | 554,480 | 40 |
| Roman Catholics | 3,000 | 0.8 | 256,227 | 6.5 | 3,944 | 2,544 | 6,488 | 2.26 | 287,300 | 6.8 | 321,100 | 7.1 | 460,000 | 8.2 |
| Protestants | 3,000 | 0.8 | 222,609 | 5.6 | 3,580 | 4,644 | 8,224 | 3.15 | 260,750 | 6.2 | 304,850 | 6.7 | 513,300 | 9.1 |
| Evangelicals | 2,700 | 0.7 | 153,700 | 3.9 | 2,610 | 5,080 | 7,690 | 4.05 | 190,100 | 4.5 | 230,600 | 5.1 | 450,000 | 8.0 |
| Chinese indigenous | 0 | 0.0 | 53,800 | 1.4 | 870 | 990 | 1,860 | 2.93 | 63,400 | 1.5 | 72,400 | 1.6 | 112,500 | 2.0 |
| Anglicans | 600 | 0.2 | 23,200 | 0.6 | 343 | 37 | 380 | 1.52 | 25,000 | 0.6 | 27,000 | 0.6 | 39,400 | 0.7 |
| Marginal Protestants | 0 | 0.0 | 4,368 | 0.1 | 78 | 205 | 283 | 4.96 | 5,700 | 0.1 | 7,200 | 0.2 | 11,000 | 0.2 |
| Orthodox | 0 | 0.0 | 50 | 0.0 | 1 | -1 | 0 | 0.00 | 50 | 0.0 | 50 | 0.0 | 100 | 0.0 |
| Non-religious | 0 | 0.0 | 300,000 | 7.6 | 4,525 | 1,655 | 6,180 | 1.88 | 329,600 | 7.8 | 361,800 | 8.0 | 495,000 | 8.8 |
| Atheists | 0 | 0.0 | 200,000 | 5.1 | 3,074 | 1,796 | 4,870 | 2.18 | 223,900 | 5.3 | 248,700 | 5.5 | 337,500 | 6.0 |
| New-Religionists | 0 | 0.0 | 110,000 | 2.8 | 1,741 | 1,729 | 3,470 | 2.74 | 126,800 | 3.0 | 144,700 | 3.2 | 225,000 | 4.0 |
| Muslims | 1,000 | 0.3 | 18,000 | 0.5 | 263 | -13 | 250 | 1.30 | 19,200 | 0.5 | 20,500 | 0.5 | 26,000 | 0.5 |
| Hindus | 300 | 0.1 | 7,500 | 0.2 | 110 | -10 | 100 | 1.25 | 8,000 | 0.2 | 8,500 | 0.2 | 9,500 | 0.2 |
| Sikhs | 100 | 0.0 | 1,000 | 0.0 | 14 | -14 | 0 | 0.00 | 1,000 | 0.0 | 1,000 | 0.0 | 1,000 | 0.0 |
| Baha'is | 0 | 0.0 | 400 | 0.0 | 7 | 13 | 20 | 4.00 | 500 | 0.0 | 600 | 0.0 | 1,200 | 0.0 |
| Jews | 0 | 0.0 | 400 | 0.0 | 6 | -1 | 5 | 1.16 | 430 | 0.0 | 450 | 0.0 | 600 | 0.0 |
| Other religionists | 100 | 0.0 | 4,650 | 0.1 | 96 | 639 | 735 | 10.50 | 7,000 | 0.2 | 12,000 | 0.3 | 50,000 | 1.0 |
| Country's population | 380,000 | 100.0 | 3,942,000 | 100.0 | 58,000 | 0 | 58,000 | 1.37 | 4,225,000 | 100.0 | 4,522,000 | 100.0 | 5,625,000 | 100.0 |

COLUMNS, ROWS. For meanings and definitions, see Codebook (Part 6). Note that, by definition, total 'Christians' = professing + crypto-Christians, which also = affiliated + nominal Christians. Percentages may not always total exactly, due to rounding.

CENSUSES. The religion question has not been asked.

NOTES ON RELIGIONS

ANGLICANS. Including many expatriate British military and civilians.

ATHEISTS. In 1972 there were at least 95,400 workers in Hong Kong who were either communists or affiliated with Communist organizations (Communist Federation of Trade Unions, etc.).

BAHA'IS. Growth from 1 local spiritual assembly (1964) to 3 (1973).

BUDDHISTS. Mahayana, introduced in the 5th century AD In 1968 there were over 500 Buddhist temples in Hong Kong, and 180 monasteries with 250 monks and 1,400 nuns, with a growing emphasis on social commitment. Since 1956, the following institutions have been begun: 30 Buddhist primary schools, 8 middle schools, 1 post-secondary school, one 350-bed hospital, 2 dental clinics, 2 youth associations, 4 youth centres, and 3 homes for the aged. Much of the work of the various Buddhist branches in Hong Kong is performed through the Hong Kong Buddhist Association (6,000 members).

CHINESE FOLK-RELIGIONISTS. Including (1) about 650,000 Taoists in 400 temples with over 500 priests, whose institutions include 4 primary schools, 1 middle school and 3 homes for old people and over 50 smaller retirement homes; (2) 250,000 worshippers of T'ien Hou (Tin Hau, goddess of heaven and protectress of seafarers), mostly fishermen; (3) worshippers of Kwan Yam (Buddhist goddess of mercy), Kwan Tai (god of war), Hung Shing (god of south seas), Pak Tai (lord of the north), Lo Ban Sin (patron of building contractors); (4) Triad Societies (over 200 religio-political secret blood brotherhoods, involving half a million people); and (5) Swatow Ghosts' Festival Association. Of all Chinese folk-religionists in Hong Kong, 55% are ancestor-venerators and 45% are virtually non-religious except in name.

CHINESE INDIGENOUS. In about 110 Chinese indigenous denominations in 1970 (see Table 2).

COUNTRY'S POPULATION. Rapid increase by immigration from 24,774 in 1845 (23,817 Chinese, 595 Europeans, 362 Indians) to 120,000 in 1861, 1.5 million in 1941, a fall to 600,000 in 1945, 1.8 million in 1947, and a rise to 2,360,000 in 1950. In one month in May 1962, 250,000 refugees from mainland China forced their way in.

HINDUS. Indian merchants and businessmen, with 2 large temples (capacity 1,200) and 2 priests. ISKCON (Hare Krishna) operates 1 centre, and Ananda Marga others.

MUSLIMS. Begun in the 1880s with immigrants from Western

China (Sunnis of the Hanafite rite). Races (1970): 13,000 Chinese, 3,500 Pakistanis, the rest from India, Sri Lanka, Malaysia, Indonesia, Iran. In 1970, there were 6 mosques (capacity 2,150) and 4 imams (2 Chinese, 1 Indian, 1 Pakistani).

NEW-RELIGIONISTS. (1) 100,000 followers of Heavenly Virtue Holy Church (T'ien Te Sheng Hui), a syncretistic combination of Confucianism, Taoism, Buddhism, Islam and Christianity, widespread among the Chinese diaspora; (2) followers of Soka Gakkai (Value Creation Society), from Japan, begun in 1964 and rapidly growing by 1970 to 3,000 (500 Japanese and 2,500 Chinese converts) and by 1975 to 25,500; (3) World Red Swastika Society (Hong Kong Branch), a syncretistic religion combining Buddhism, Taoism, Christianity, Islam and Confucianism, which operated 2 clinics; and small branches of other new syncretistic religions.

NON-RELIGIOUS. Including large numbers of alienated Chinese youth.

OTHER RELIGIONISTS. These include: Parsis (or Parsees: Persians, who arrived in the 19th century), Masonic Benevolent Association, and other groups.

PROTESTANTS. Among recent conversions have been numerous former Buddhist monks, 11 of whom were ordained to the Lutheran ministry in 1972.

SIKHS. Immigrants in the 1840s. Indians, with 1 temple and priest. Declining gradually in numbers.

## NON-CHRISTIAN RELIGIONS.
Chinese folk religion is the religion with the largest following in Hong Kong. It is a mixture of Buddhism, Confucianism, Taoism, polytheism and ancient ancestor-veneration. The emphasis given to each of these varies according to the individual and the region in China with which he identifies. Taoism has 650,000 followers with 400 temples and 500 priests, and about 60 social institutions. Educated youth have become increasingly alienated from folk religion and often declare themselves to be without religion.

Buddhism of the Mahayana school retains considerable importance at the cultural level as a time-honoured element of Chinese life. There are over 500 Buddhist temples in Hong Kong, and in 1968 there were 180 monasteries with 250 monks and 1,400 nuns. There are numerous social institutions including 39 schools and a hospital.

Heavenly Virtue Holy Church (T'ien Te Sheng Hui)

is a widespread syncretistic new religious movement, claiming 100,000 Chinese adherents in Hong Kong, which attempts to combine the 5 major religions of Confucianism, Buddhism, Taoism, Islam and Christianity. Founded in 1920 in Yunnan (China) by a Chinese Buddhist, it has only recently spread widely among the Chinese diaspora, especially in Malaysia, and receives support from many wealthy

Chinese. It emphasizes social and ethical conduct, virtue, wisdom, and aims to establish harmony between heaven and earth. It has a cosmological concept of history, a low level of folk religion content, and has developed an emphasis on healing.

Soka Gakkai, the largest of the New Religions in Japan, also has a following of 500 Japanese in Hong Kong, with 2,500 Chinese converts as well by 1970.

Catholic Church, Diocese of Hong Kong. Pope Paul VI (centre) on 1970 visit celebrates open-air mass with bishops and clergy.

# CHRISTIANITY

CATHOLIC CHURCH. The apostolic prefecture of Hong Kong was erected in 1841, being detached at that time from the diocese of Macao. However, the territory was not opened up to Christian evangelization until after it was ceded to Great Britain following the Opium War and the Treaty of Nanking in 1842. The first Catholic missionaries were French MEP priests in 1847, and in 1867 the prefecture was confided to Italian PIME priests. A vicariate was erected in 1874, and following the

**Assemblies of God.** Packed congregation at Sunday morning dedication service, First Assembly of God, Hong Kong.

Japanese occupation during World War II, a diocese was formed in 1946. The vast influx of refugees from China after 1949 and extensive evangelistic activity during the 1950s resulted in an increase of baptized members from 32,000 in 1949 to nearly 175,000 in 1961 and over 250,000 in 1970.

Approximately 90% of all Catholics are Chinese, with the remaining 10% divided between British, Portuguese (2,000), Filipino (800) and other nations. A decrease in refugees from mainland China since 1965 has resulted in a substantial drop in adult baptisms.

The numbers of both expatriate and Chinese priests have increased since the 1950s, the former rising from 204 in 1957 to 217 in 1966, while the latter grew from 84 to 115 during the same period.

PROTESTANT CHURCHES. After Hong Kong was ceded to Great Britain in 1842, James Legge, a talented linguist and scholar of the Chinese classics, became chief representative of the London Missionary

Society and played a major role in the establishment of the British colony's educational system. The American Board (ABCFM) also sent missionaries to Hong Kong at that time, followed by American Lutheran and Baptist missions. A number of German societies began working there during the last quarter of the century.

The greatest influx of missionaries came following the forced exodus of missionaries from the People's Republic of China, with over 30 new American mission groups entering the colony since 1949. As has characterized much Chinese mission activity in the past, most missionary staff have engaged in education and social service to meet the problems of refugees from the mainland.

The Baptist Church and the Church of Christ in China are the largest of the non-Catholic churches in Hong Kong. The rapid church growth which characterized most churches in the 1950s and early 1960s has begun to level off, primarily due to the decrease in new refugees.

INDIGENOUS CHURCHES. Independent Chinese churches have also made their appearance since the 1930s, and are now rapidly growing in numbers and influence. By 1970, more than 100 separate denominations had been formed, the largest being the Spiritual Food Worldwide Evangelistic Mission and the Assembly Hall Churches, the latter having begun on the mainland in 1926.

CHURCH AND STATE. As a British colony, Hong Kong has always been a secular and non-religious dependency with no religion enjoying a privileged status. For a long time, fear of Communist China and aid to refugees absorbed all the energies of both the colonial administration and the churches. Since 1965 the urgency of these problems has lessened, and the churches have become more critical of the social policies of the British administration. As one result, in 1970 several churches assumed a public position opposing limitations placed on the right to strike.

## INTERDENOMINATIONAL ORGANIZATIONS.
The Hong Kong Christian Council was established in 1954 to minister to the social needs of the rapidly increasing population. It conducts surveys on housing, industrial work conditions, problems of youth; publishes descriptive reports; conducts tours, and initiates a wide variety of programmes to enable churches and church members to serve the community more effectively. The Catholic Church co-operates with these programmes and surveys through the Diocesan Ecumenical Commission and the Joint Development Committee, which serves as the Sodepax

Committee in Hong Kong. The Christian Study Centre on Chinese Religion and Culture publishes materials regularly to which Protestants, Anglicans and Catholics contribute.

BROADCASTING. The first Christian Broadcasting Service over the government station began in 1935, run by Anglican, Roman Catholic and Union churches. By 1975, the government station Radio Hong Kong was still broadcasting religious services and brief religious programmes in Cantonese and English, prepared in turn by Anglicans, Baptists,

**Hong Kong Methodist Church.** Choir, Ward Memorial Methodist Church.

Free Church, Lutherans and Catholics. The international station FEBC from Manila (Philippines) broadcasts to Hong Kong in 5 Chinese dialects and English. Several studios prepare Christian programmes, including the Audio-Visual Evangelism Committee of the Christian Council, Assemblies of God, FEBC, Alliance Bible Seminary. LWFBS produced programmes in Mandarin for release over RVOG (Ethiopia) until 1977. A Catholic body, Chinese Provincial Broadcast, founded in July 1967, publishes radio texts in Chinese.

For Catholics, Hong Kong is a member of UNDA.

## BIBLIOGRAPHY
*Hong Kong Catholic directory and yearbook, 1972.* Hong Kong: Catholic Truth Society, 1972.
*Hong Kong church directory, 1976.* Hong Kong: Chinese Christian Literature Council, 1976.
'The diakonia function of the Church in Hong Kong'. M. Berndt. Dissertation, Concordia Seminary, St Louis (MO), 1970.
*Urban church growth in Hong Kong, 1958–1962.* L. E. Noren. Hong Kong: American Baptist Foreign Mission Society, 1962. 60p.

TABLE 2.    ORGANIZED CHURCHES AND DENOMINATIONS IN HONG KONG

| Official name 1 | Begun 2 | Type 3 | Counc 4 | Congs 5 | Adults 6 | Affiliated 7 | Names, notes, and other statistics (see Codebook) 8 |
|---|---|---|---|---|---|---|---|
| Anglican Ch in China: D HK & Macao | 1843 | A Eva | AvEAW | 44 | 16,075 | 23,200 | *Chung Hua Sheng Kung Hui. Holy Cath Ch.* M=CMS. 39n,21x,G=3.4%pa,1s,W=31%,2Y,506y. |
| Assemblies of God | 1907 | P Pe2 | ZF... | 24 | 3,797 | 10,000 | 3 Districts. M=AoG; 1948, PAoC. 4,840 in schools. 25n,11f,1h,1j,1s(17),W=61%,226Y. |
| Assembly Hall Churches | c1950 | I EBr | x..... | 6 | 4,500 | 8,000 | *Chu Hui So. Church Assembly Hall. Little Flock.* Begun on mainland in 1926. |
| Assoc of Baptists for World Evangelism | 1945 | P Bap | x,T,T | 10 | 240 | 850 | M=ABWE. Filipino missionaries. 2 schools. 1n, 7x,22Y,G=3.7%pa,2h,1p,W=32%,20Y,23z. |
| Canadian Holiness Mission | 1954 | P Hol | ..... | 4 | 595 | 1,000 | M=Independent Holiness Ch(Canada). Links with, but not merger with, FMC(USA). |
| Catholic Church: D Hong Kong | 1841 | R Lat | PxF... | 54 | 151,200 | 256,227 | Suffragan of M Canton. C=11+3+22. 128n,231x,125m,804w,P=64%,1s(50),3378Y,2926y,3424z. |
| China Free Methodist Church | 1951 | P Hol | VF... | 9 | 1,194 | 5,300 | *Chung Wah Chun Lei Wui.* M=FMC(USA). 5 schools. 5n,3x,10f,G=5%pa,9t(822),W=43%,74Y. |
| China Peniel Missionary Society | 1909 | P Hol | x..... | 7 | 4,675 | 10,000 | M=Voice of China & Asia Miss Soc (USA). Cantonese. 5 schools, orphanage. W=23%,151Y. |
| Chinese Christian Church of Amoy | 1938 | I ind | ..... | 4 | 500 | 1,100 | Dialect church, part of CCC before 1950 but refused to join it in Hong Kong. W=50%,40Yy. |
| Chinese Ev Lutheran Church, Far East | 1964 | P Lut | ..... | 5 | 500 | 1,450 | *CELC.* Lutheran refugees from China. M=Wisconsin ELS(USA). 5n,6f,1r,1s,156Y. |
| Chinese Evangelistic Zion Church | 1950 | P Con | x..... | 5 | 205 | 950 | *Wang Tau Hom Sion.* M=Swedish Alliance Mission. 2n,1x,5f,G=5%pa,W=16%,31Y,16z. |
| Chinese Evangelistic Crusade | 1951 | I ind | ..... | 7 | 979 | 2,000 | *Chinese Native Evangelistic Crusade.* Churches: HK 1, Kowloon 5, New Territories 1. |
| Chinese Full Gospel Church | 1955 | P Pe2 | Z..... | 5 | 2,560 | 5,000 | *Zion Churches.* M=Swedish Free Mission. HQ Kowloon. 2f,1h,W=27%,60Y. |
| Chinese Methodist Church | 1880 | P Met | VwE,W | 10 | 5,213 | 7,200 | *Hong Kong Meth Ch(UK).* M=MMS. Cantonese. 4n,2x,8f,1h,1r,W=31%,240Yy. |
| Chinese Rhenish Ch, Hong Kong Synod | 1847 | P Lut | L,..,. | 7 | 3,000 | 7,682 | M=RM,VEM(Germany). Other 5 Districts were in mainland China. 5f,1h,W=14%,161Yy. |
| Christian & Missionary Alliance | 1933 | P Hol | xF... | 32 | 3,570 | 8,000 | *HK Church Union, Tong Chs.* M=CMA(USA). 11n,6x,18f,G=9%pa,1j,3k,1s(70),W=80%,246Y. |
| Christian Brethren | | P CBr | x..... | 6 | 200 | 400 | *Plymouth (Open) Brethren.* M=CMML(UK,USA,NZ,Australia). 4 schools. 13f,1h. |
| Chr Nationals Evangelism Commission | 1950 | P int | xF... | 13 | 1,886 | 3,000 | *CNEC.* Begun China 1942. HQ Kowloon. 9 schools. 6f,3h,1j,2s,W=61%,107Y. |
| Church of Christ in China, HK Council | 1863 | P unt | WWE,W | 33 | 22,329 | 30,000 | *CCC.* Cantonese. 72 schools(47000),22n,7x,61m,32f,1H,10r,1s,184t(3527),W=27%,650Yy. |
| Church of Christ, Scientist | 1905 | M Sci | x..... | 1 | 20 | 50 | *Christian Science.* M=CCS(Boston, USA). No licensed practitioners. |
| Church of Hong Kong | c1950 | I pen | ..... | 3 | 100 | 200 | Schism ex CCC led by prophetess, former film star; died 1967. Most back in CCC. |
| Church of Jesus C of Latter-day Saints | 1949 | M LdS | x..... | 11 | 2,000 | 3,598 | *Southern Far East (Hong Kong-Taiwan) Mission.* Mormons. M=CJCLdS(USA). 80f,G=5%pa. |
| Churches of Christ | 1925 | P Dis | x..... | 16 | 500 | 1,000 | M=CC(Non-Instrumental)(USA). Mostly expatriates and USA naval personnel. 10f. |
| Conservative Baptist Association | 1963 | P Bap | xF... | 8 | 261 | 545 | M=CBFMS(USA). Cantonese, English. 7 primary schools. 1n,3m,1w,14f,2h,W=95%,57Y. |
| Cumberland Presbyterian Church | 1949 | P Ref | R..... | 7 | 338 | 780 | *South China Mission.* M=CPC (USA Whites). 10% refugees. 3 schools. 3n,4m,2f,W=70%,5Y,4y. |
| Elim Church | c1963 | P Pe2 | ZG... | 3 | 410 | 800 | M=EMA(USA),EFGA(UK). Classical Pentecostals (2-stage). 1f. |
| Emmanuel Church | 1927 | P Pen | ..... | 4 | 450 | 750 | *Ling Kuang Tong.* Pentecostals. 1 school. 1n,1x,G=4.6%pa,2h,1k,W=44%,40Y,9z. |
| English Methodist Church | 1890 | P Met | Vwc,W | 2 | 500 | 1,000 | *District, Methodist Ch (UK).* English-speaking. Sailors and Soldiers Home. 1x. |
| Evangelical Free Church of China | 1937 | P Con | KF..h | 8 | 1,500 | 2,000 | M=EFCA,China Mission(USA). HQ Kowloon. 4n,2x,20f,1H,1j,1k,1s,W=82%,56Yy. |
| Evangelical Hakka Church | 1846 | R LuR | L...,W | 16 | 4,301 | 7,600 | *Tsung Tsin Hui.* From mainland. M=Basel Mission. Hakka. 13n,2x,12f,1.,1s,W=50%,325Yy. |
| Evangelical Lutheran Ch of Hong Kong | 1890 | P Lut | L...,W | 38 | 5,310 | 9,819 | *Hsiang Kang Hsin Yi Hui.* M=CMA(USA). Mandarin, Cantonese. Hakka. 33n,4x,1j,1s(8),W=45%,298Yy. |
| Evangelize China Fellowship | 1949 | I int | x..... | 5 | 1,650 | 3,000 | *HK-Macau Synod.* Begun in China by Chinese. M=ECF(USA). 2 schools. 1j,2s,W=84%,52Y. |
| German Evangelical Lutheran Church | 1965 | P Lut | ...,W | 2 | 130 | 500 | For German-speaking expatriates. In Hong Kong. 1n,G=4.5%pa,W=10%,12Yy,5z. |
| Grace Evangel Mission | | P ind | ..... | 2 | 384 | 800 | M=Grace Evangel Mission. Small independent mission. 2 schools. 1n,1w,1f,2h. |
| Harbour Mission | 1914 | P ind | ..... | | 1,200 | 2,000 | Early independent mission in Hong Kong. In Aplichau, Aberdeen. 185Y. |
| Heap Gay Churches | 1950 | I ind | ..... | 5 | 699 | 2,000 | *Hip Kei Tong (Conservative Co-operative Christian).* Rooftop school. 1h,1j. |
| Hong Kong Evangelical Churches | 1954 | P Hol | xF... | 9 | 1,103 | 2,000 | *Yan Poon. Grace Rock.* M=OMS Internat(USA). 8n,3x,7f,G=0.7%pa,1h,W=58%,67Y,72z. |
| Hong Kong Methodist Church | 1952 | P Met | VwE,W | 10 | 2,082 | 3,500 | *Wei Li Kung Hui.* M=UMC(USA). A=1972. Mandarin. 16n,4x,18f,1H,1s,9t,106Yy,369z. |
| Hong Kong Union Christian Church | 1900 | P Ref | | 7 | 3,500 | 6,497 | From mainland China. English Presbyterian background. No missionaries. W=35%,291Y. |
| Jehovah's Witnesses | 1933 | M Jeh | x..... | 8 | 251 | 720 | 1933 placed under Australian branch. 1970: 678 at one meeting. 9(Filipinos),22Y. |
| Joyous Word Christian Chs Association | 1947 | I ind | ..... | 5 | 1,188 | 2,000 | *Lock Tao (Joyous Word) Baptist Mission.* Ex CCC. Swatow. 3 schools. 1h,W=56%,65Y. |
| Lutheran Church, Hong Kong Synod | 1950 | P Lut | l..... | 27 | 3,076 | 9,021 | M=LCMS(USA). Refugee Bible camp. 19n,9x,G=−0.8%pa,1s(5),W=49%,348Yy. |
| New Life Temple | 1959 | P Pen | ..... | 1 | 300 | 1,000 | M=Lester Sumrall Evangelistic Association(USA). Church is one floor of skyscraper. |
| Norwegian Lutheran Mission | 1946 | P Lut | ..... | | 500 | 1,375 | Refugees from church begun 1891 in Honan, Hupeh, N Manchuria. M=NLM(Norway). 10f. |
| Oriental Christian Churches Association | 1950 | P Bap | ..... | 8 | 430 | 650 | *Tung Fong Kei Tuk Kaau Wooi.* Formerly M=Oriental Boat M. 1x,G=−4%pa,W=80%,73Y,35z. |

*Continued opposite*

*Table 2–continued*

| Official name 1 | Begun 2 | Type 3 | Counc 4 | Congs 5 | Adults 6 | Affiliated 7 | Names, notes, and other statistics (see Codebook) 8 |
|---|---|---|---|---|---|---|---|
| Pentecostal Church of God | | P Pe2 | Z.... | 6 | 350 | 1,000 | M=PCG in America(USA). Classical 2-stage Pentecostals. World HQ Joplin, MO(USA). |
| Pentecostal Holiness Church | 1907 | P Pe3 | ZF... | 16 | 2,613 | 6,000 | *Hong Kong Conference.* M=PHC(USA). 2 schools. HQ Kowloon. 21nm,11f,1h,W=30%,58Y. |
| Russian Orthodox Church | | O Sla | ..... | 1 | 30 | 50 | Small congregation of Russians and Russian-speaking Chinese. |
| Salvation Army | 1930 | P Sal | xwE.W | 40 | 1,395 | 5,345 | *Kau Shai Kwan/Chiu Shih Chiin*(Cantonese/Mandarin). 35n,18x,G=8%pa,6h,1s,W=65%,143Y. |
| Seventh-day Adv Ch, HK-Macao Mission | 1888 | P Adv | x...W | 13 | 2,801 | 7,000 | *SDA.* South China Island UM. 1 boat. 6nx,105mw,15f,2H,3h,4r,20t(3267),W=64%,155Y. |
| South China Foursquare Gospel Church | 1936 | P Pe2 | ZF... | 4 | 448 | 1,500 | *Internat Ch of Foursquare Gospel.* M=ICFG(USA). 6nm,2x,5f,G=−1.6%pa,W=58%,14Y,90z. |
| Spiritual Food Worldwide Ev Mission | 1950 | I int | x.... | 8 | 4,500 | 9,000 | *Ling Liang WEM.* Chinese missionaries to 10 nations. HQ Kowloon. 1s,W=29%,220Y. |
| True Jesus Church | | I pel | x.... | 5 | 1,000 | 1,500 | *TJC, World Conference* (HQ Taiwan). Chinese indigenous church begun 1917 on mainland. |
| Union Churches | 1923 | P com | ....W | 2 | 1,000 | 2,000 | *Union Ch, Hong Kong; Union Ch, Kowloon.* English-speaking. Expatriates. 2x. |
| United HK Chr Baptist Churches Assoc | 1842 | P Bap | T...d | 60 | 22,391 | 50,000 | 1842, M=ABFMS; 1949 SBC(USA). 40n,21x,80f,G=2.9%pa,1H,1j,1k,4r,1s,W=45%,730Y. |
| West China Evangelistic Band | 1949 | P ind | ..... | 1 | 124 | 300 | *HK Christian Ev Preaching Band.* Begun 1936 in Szechwan. Spiritual Light Centre. 2f,1h. |
| Other indigenous churches | | I | ..... | 100 | 10,000 | 20,000 | Total about 70 non-pentecostal (see below), also scores of single congregations. |
| Other Protestant denominations | | P | ..... | 50 | 3,000 | 7,000 | Total about 25 (see list below). |
| Other indigenous pentecostal churches | | I pen | ..... | 50 | 2,000 | 5,000 | Total about 30 (see list below). |
| **Total affiliated (mid-1970)** | | | | **870** | **307,143** | **560,254** | **Total denominations (1970) . . . 181.** |
| **Total affiliated (mid-1975)** | | | | **910** | **352,100** | **642,200** | **Total denominations (1975) . . . 196.** |
| **Total affiliated (mid-1980)** | | | | **990** | **401,600** | **732,600** | **Total denominations (1980) . . . 211.** |

NOTES ON TABLE ABOVE
COLUMNS: for meanings and CODES (cols. 1, 3, 4, 8), see Codebook (Part 6). Column 1: **Boldface type** = church with over 10% of country's affiliated Christians.
NATIONAL COUNCILS (Column 4, 5th letter).
- d = member of both HKCC and HKCCCU.
- h = Hong Kong Chinese Christian Churches Union (HKCCCU) (observer member of HKCC; members, 125 out of the 400 Chinese congregations in HK).
- T = Hong Kong Consultative Council of the ICCC (begun 1969, 31 member congregations).
- W = Hong Kong Christian Council (HKCC).

*Other national councils.* Chinese Churches Evangelical Fellowship. Hong Kong Evangelical Fellowship. Hong Kong Lutheran Association.
OTHER INDIGENOUS CHURCHES. There are a large number of independent single congregations, with a smaller number of groupings. These latter include: Canaan Ch (1955), Chinese Christian Evangelists Mission (200 adults), Chinese Christians Trinity Ch, Christian Ch of Living Faith (1956), Christian En-Chao Tong, Christian True Gospel Centre, Christian World-Saving Work, HK Japanese Christian Fellowship, Holy Spirit Association for Unification of World Christianity (from Korea), New Life Ch of Christ (350 adults), Tsang Tai Uk Christian Ch (Brethren; 250 adults).
OTHER PROTESTANT DENOMINATIONS. These smaller bodies include: Apostolic Faith (1951), Baptist Bible Fellowship International (1968), Baptist Mid-Missions (1958), Bethel Mission of China (1940), Calvary Baptist Ch (UK), China Missionary and Evangelistic Association (1931), Christadelphian Ecclesia, Christian Ch of Love (200 adults), Ch of God (Anderson) (1969), Ch of God (Cleveland), Ch of the Living Stones (200 adults), Chs of Christ (Christian Chs)(1963), Ev Methodist Ch (1960), Exclusive Brethren (Continuing Tunbridge Wells), Far Eastern Gospel Crusade (1958), Fellowship of Ev Baptist Chs of Canada, Glad Tidings Missionary Society (1959), HK Mennonite Mission (1965), HK Pentecostal Tabernacle Ch (500 adults), International Missions (1950), International Pentecostal Assemblies (1930), Overseas Missionary Fellowship (1949), Pentecostal Apostolic Ch, Reformed Presbyterian Ch, Religious Society of Friends (Quakers), Swedish Free Baptist Mission, United Brethren in Christ (1949), World-Wide Missions (1962).
OTHER INDIGENOUS PENTECOSTAL CHURCHES. These include: Chinese Pentecostal Ch, Ch of Celestial Grace, Fan Hing Christian Association (1,300 adults), New Life Temple (210 adults), Tsuen Wan Truth Centre (117 adults). A Black USA mission is also at work: Pentecostal Assemblies of the World.
UNITING CHURCHES. Negotiations for organic union were under way in 1974 between: (1) Anglican Church in China, Chinese Methodist Church, Church of Christ in China; and (2) in October 1975, the 2 Methodist churches (Chinese Methodist Ch, Hong Kong Methodist Church) agreed to unite and function for 5 years as 2 Districts of a united Methodist Ch of Hong Kong.

**PEOPLES** (ethnolinguistic). Christians: 93.1% Chinese (about 88% Cantonese), 3.5% British, 1.0% USA White, 1.0% Anglo-Australian, 0.5% Portuguese, 0.4% Filipino, 0.2% German, 0.1% French, 0.1% Dutch, 0.1% Korean, Japanese, USA Black, Indian.

**COUNTRY-WIDE TOTALS**
EVANGELIZATION (see Part 5). 1900: 16%. 1970: 98%. 1980: 99%. *Mass evangelism.* Billy Graham rally in 1956, also in November 1975 a 5-day crusade (500 participating churches, 10,000 workers, 500,000 homes visited; 217,000 attenders (85% aged 16–21 years), 20,400 enquirers); August 1976, international conference, Chinese Congress on World Evangelization (CCOWE); 1977–8, Here's Life Hong Kong (CCCI) (15,000 workers, 359 participating churches, 28,174 decisions). *Radiophonic evangelism.* Many programmes and courses, including ICI (5,793 enrolments, 1,502 active, 776 conversions). *Literature evangelism.* By 1976, 17,494 Chinese decision cards had been received out of 10,382,608 leaflets delivered to homes among all Chinese of the diaspora (a rate of 0.17% or 1 in 600).
FOREIGN MISSIONARIES AND PERSONNEL (nationals serving abroad) (1973). Total 190 in 25 countries: 62 Chinese indigenous, 60 Roman Catholics (2 Jesuits in USA), 30 Protestants, 23 Anglicans, 15 marginal Protestants. 17 Protestant sending bodies are co-ordinated through the Hong Kong Association of Christian Missions.
FOREIGN MISSIONARIES AND PERSONNEL (aliens from abroad) (1973). Total 1,405. *From Western world.* 1,279: 632 Roman Catholics, 523 Protestants (351 in 57 USA societies, 47 in 10 UK societies, 30 in 3 Norway societies, 28 in 5 Canada societies, 22 in 3 Sweden societies, 18 in 9 Australia societies, 14 in 4 WGermany societies, 10 in 1 Finland society, 2 in 2 New Zealand societies, 1 in 1 Switzerland society), about 100 marginal Protestants (75 Mormons) from USA, 23 Anglicans (20 in 2 UK societies, 2 in 1 USA society, 1 in 1 Canada society), 1 Black indigenous from USA. *From Communist world.* About 2 Roman Catholics from Yugoslavia. *From Third World.* 124: about 50 indigenous from Japan, Taiwan and Korea, about 40 Roman Catholics from Japan, Taiwan, Korea, Mexico et alia, about 20 Protestants from Philippines, Taiwan, Japan et alia, about 14 marginal Protestants (9 Filipino Jehovah's Witnesses from Philippines, 5 Mormons).
INSTITUTIONS (church-operated) (1973). Total 250, including 140 higher schools, 50 medical centres, 10 presses, 6 religious communities, 2 research centres, 25 seminaries (20 Protestant, 3 Chinese indigenous, 1 RC, 1 Anglican), 6 study centres, 1 university.
PERIODICALS. About 220 titles.
PERSONNEL. About 2,825 (1,420 national, 1,405 foreign).
RELIGIOUS LIBRARIES. About 50.
SCRIPTURE DISTRIBUTION (1975). Annual totals: 96,551 Bibles (1% free, 71% subsidized, 28% commercial), 52,885 NTs (12% free, 69% subsidized, 19% commercial), 624,313 UBS portions, 773,364 UBS selections.
SERVICE AGENCIES. About 110, including APCTE, CCCI, CCF, CEF, CNA, CORE, EMF, FABC, FEBC, HKACM, HKCC, HKCCCU, HKCEC, HKCWC, HKCYC, HKFCS, IFES, IMCS, LWR, MTS, SCM, SGM, SU, WLC(EHC), WVI, YFC, YMCA, YWAM, YWCA.

**ADDITIONAL DATA ON CHURCHES**
ANGLICAN CHURCH IN CHINA. Name in Cantonese: Sheng Kung Hui Kong O Kau Kiu. Membership is 92% Cantonese-speaking, 8% English. The main Anglican missionary society has been the CMS (UK). The diocese is the only remaining part of the former Holy Catholic Church in China, whose 14 dioceses in mainland China had ceased to exist by 1965. Members include many UK military and dependants. *Priests* (1977). Including 4 women. *Lay workers* (1977). 27 men, 25 women. *Lay readers* (1977). 124 men, 30 women.
CATHOLIC CHURCH. In Cantonese, Tin Chue Kau (Heaven Lord Assembly). The diocese is divided into an English-speaking urban pastoral zone (HK island, Kowloon) with 39 parishes, and a Cantonese-speaking mission zone (in the New Territories) with 15 ecclesiastical districts. *Catechumens.* (1959) 12,780; (1961) 17,463; (1963) 15,791. *Annual baptisms.* (1972) 36.3% infant, 63.7% adult. *Priests.* 'Nationals' means Chinese here: 2 bishops, 65 secular (41 from Hong Kong, the rest from the mainland), 65 religious (most from the mainland). Expatriates: 79 Italians, 54 Irish, 41 USA, 13 Belgians, 12 Spanish, 11 French. Of the total 359 priests, 132 are secular and 227 religious. Numbers (Chinese + expatriates): 1957, 84 + 204; 1961, 109 + 212; 1966, 115 + 217. *Brothers.* 55 Chinese, 70 expatriates (22 Irish, 11 Italians). *Sisters.* 447 Chinese, 357 expatriates (96 Italians, 71 USA, 31 Irish, 30 French, 26 Canadians, 26 Filipinos, 21 Belgians, 15 Portuguese, 10 British). *Seminarians.* 50, increasing to 65 (1972), of which 27 were secular, 38 religious. *Catechists.* Total (1971) 120 (47 men, 73 women); (1973) 156 (86 full-time). Two-year training at Diocesan Catechetical Centre. *Chinese religious congregations.* Brothers: 2 in the Congregation of St John the Baptist. Sisters: 109 Sisters of the Precious Blood (begun 1922), 26 Sisters of the Immaculate Heart of Mary, 24 Sisters Announcers of the Lord, 12 Chinese Sisters of the Immaculate Conception. *Main foreign orders and congregations.* Priests (congregations with over 20): 115 SDB, 65 PIME, 58 SJ, 30 MM, 21 OCSO, 20 OFM. Brothers: 36 FSC, 27 PFM. Sisters (congregations with over 40): 166 Canossian Daughters of Charity, 130 Sisters of St Paul of Chartres, 77 Maryknoll Sisters of St Dominic, 47 Missionary Sisters of the Immaculate Conception, 46 Franciscan Missionaries of Mary, 41 Salesian Sisters.
*Catholic organizations.* There is at present no episcopal conference; but until 1968 Hong Kong was part of the Regional Conference of Chinese Bishops based in Taipei, Taiwan. Religious personnel are represented by 2 organizations: the Association of Major Religious Superiors of Men in Hong Kong, and the Association of Major Religious Superiors of Women in Hong Kong. A Senate of Priests and a Pastoral Council were formed in 1967, the latter consisting of 26 lay members, 20 secular and regular priests, 8 sisters and 2 brothers. Elected members predominate in both organizations. The Lay Apostolate Central Council Diocesan Office is divided into 2 specialized branches: the Hong Kong Catholic Women's Council, and the Hong Kong Catholic Youth Council. The 36 organizations and clubs of the lay apostolate include 42,534 members (19,774 men and 22,760 women).
The Holy See has diplomatic relations with Hong Kong and is represented to government and the Catholic hierarchy by the Apostolic Nunciature in China, based in Taiwan.
Hong Kong is the headquarters for the general secretariat of the Federation of Asian Bishops' Conferences (FABC), formed in 1972, which in 1975 included all the episcopal conferences from Pakistan to Indonesia and Japan: Bangladesh, Burma, Cambodia, India, Indonesia, Japan, Malaysia-Singapore, Pakistan, Philippines, Sri Lanka, South Korea, South Vietnam, Taiwan (Regional Conference of Chinese Bishops) and Thailand. The dioceses of Hong Kong and Macao are also associate members. To facilitate its work, sub-regions have been created, and specialized offices have been opened in the Philippines (Office of Human Development; Office of Education and Student Chaplains), Taiwan (Office of Ecumenical and Inter-Religious Affairs) and Sri Lanka (Office of Social Communications).
Two local Catholic institutions are of special note: (1) the Catholic Centre, which is a diocesan organization carrying on press and cultural activities; and (2) China News Analysis, a documentation centre, which publishes materials relating to mainland China.
The Catholic Education Council in 1971 supervised 48 pre-primary schools, 123 primary, 54 secondary, 17 middle, 11 technical and commercial and 37 night schools. The great majority (84%) of their students are non-Catholic in background. The church also maintains a variety of medical and social centres (6 hospitals, 2 hospices, 3 orphanages).
CHURCH OF CHRIST IN CHINA. This is the continuing union church mostly of Presbyterian and Reformed background founded in China in 1925. In Hong Kong, overseas supporting churches and missionary societies are: CWM (UK), formerly CCWM or LMS; Disciples of Christ (USA); New Zealand Presbyterian Mission; Presbyterian Ch of Australia; Reformed Ch in America; United Ch of Canada; UCBWM; UPUSA.
EVANGELICAL LUTHERAN CHURCH OF HONG KONG. Work was begun in mainland China in 1842, and large numbers of members migrated to Hong Kong after 1948. The work of the present 8 missionary bodies (including LCA, ALC, NMS, FMS) is co-ordinated by the HK Lutheran Missions Conference.

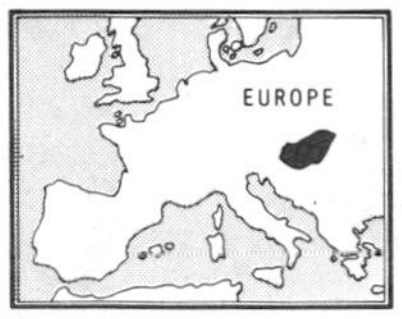


# HUNGARY

## SECULAR DATA

**STATE. Official name:** The Hungarian People's Republic (Magyar Népköztársaság). Adjective of nationality: Hungarian.
**Flag** (shown above right): Red, white, and green tricolour.
**Area:** 93,030 sq.km. (35,929 sq.miles). Agricultural land: 72.9%.
**Government:** One-party Communist state, since 1949 (1001 independent kingdom, 1919 independent republic).
**Legislature:** National Assembly, 349 members.
**Official language:** Hungarian (*Magyar*).
**Chief cities:** capital Budapest 2,043,960 (1973), Miskolc 192,270, Debrecen 175,030, Pécs 158,150.
**Political divisions:** 19 Counties (megyek), 5 County Boroughs, Capital.
**Armed forces** (1976): Total 100,000 regular (60,000 conscripts): army 80,000, air force 20,000 (140 combat aircraft). Reserves: 148,000. Paramilitary forces: 70,000 (50,000 Workers' Militia).
**Foreign forces** (1973): 38,000 USSR troops, rising (1978) to 90,000.

**DEMOGRAPHY. Population:** 10,322,099 (census of 1.1.1970. For 1970–2000 (UN), see last row of Table 1). Population density (1975): 113/sq.km. (293/sq.mile). Under 15 years: 25%. Growth rate (1975–80): 0.35% per year (births 1.54%, deaths −1.19%). Life expectancy (1975–80): 70.3 years. Household size: 3.0 persons.
**Major languages:** Hungarian, Romany, German, Russian, Slovak, Serbo-Croatian, Romanian.
**Urban dwellers** (1970): 46.8%. Urban growth rate (1950–70): 1.7% per year.
**Labour force:** 48%.
**Tourists** (1974): 4,655,200.

**ETHNOLINGUISTIC GROUPS:** 91.1% Magyar (including 2.9% Magyarized (Hungarian-speaking) Ruthenian), 5.6% Gypsy (4.5% Hungarian-speaking), 1.0% Jewish, 0.5% German (51,000), 0.4% other nationality (44,000), 0.4% USSR military (38,000), 0.3% Slovak (31,000), 0.3% Croatian (25,000), 0.2% Serbian (20,000), 0.2% Romanian (16,000), Slovene.

**MONEY** (1977). **Monetary unit:** forint (= 100 filler); US$1 = Ft 20.83.
**National income per person:** US$2,200. Average annual family income: US$6,600.
**Inflation:** (1970–74) 2.5% per year (1975: consumer price index 117).
**Cost of living in capital** (1976): index 107 (Washington DC=100). Daily cost of living: US$39.

**EDUCATION.** Adult literacy: (1949) 95%, (1970) 98%. Education rate: 56%. Schools: 5,197. Universities: 4.

**HEALTH.** Hospitals: 267 (86,517 beds). Doctors: 21,742. Blind: 10,000. Psychotics: 105,000.

**LITERATURE.** Annual new book titles (1973): 7,581. Periodicals: 780. Scientific journals: 250. Newspapers: 27 dailies, 75 non-daily.

**COMMUNICATION** (per 1,000 people). Phones: 93. Radios: 243. TV sets: 211. Daily newspaper circulation: 221 copies.

TABLE 1. RELIGIOUS ADHERENTS IN HUNGARY

| Year | 1900 | | mid-1970 | | Annual change, 1970–1980 | | | | mid-1975 | | mid-1980 | | 2000 | |
|---|---|---|---|---|---|---|---|---|---|---|---|---|---|---|
| *Name* | *Adherents* | *%* | *Adherents* | *%* | *Natural* | *Conversion* | *Total* | *Rate* | *Adherents* | *%* | *Adherents* | *%* | *Adherents* | *%* |
| **Christians** | **6,411,000** | **93.5** | **8,683,928** | **84.0** | **32,019** | **–8,452** | **23,567** | **0.27** | **8,806,600** | **83.6** | **8,919,600** | **83.2** | **9,018,300** | **81.5** |
| crypto-Christians | 0 | 0.0 | 725,928 | 7.0 | 2,728 | 2,109 | 4,837 | 0.64 | 750,300 | 7.1 | 774,300 | 7.2 | 837,600 | 7.6 |
| professing | 6,411,000 | 93.5 | 7,958,000 | 77.0 | 29,291 | –10,561 | 18,730 | 0.23 | 8,056,300 | 76.5 | 8,145,300 | 76.0 | 8,180,700 | 73.9 |
| Roman Catholics | 4,404,000 | 64.2 | 5,634,000 | 54.5 | 20,758 | –6,298 | 14,460 | 0.25 | 5,709,400 | 54.2 | 5,778,600 | 53.9 | 5,833,400 | 52.7 |
| Protestants | 1,933,000 | 28.3 | 2,274,000 | 22.0 | 8,349 | –4,179 | 4,170 | 0.18 | 2,296,400 | 21.8 | 2,315,700 | 21.6 | 2,302,300 | 20.8 |
| Orthodox | 70,000 | 1.0 | 50,000 | 0.5 | 184 | –84 | 100 | 0.20 | 50,500 | 0.5 | 51,000 | 0.5 | 45,000 | 0.4 |
| Marginal Protestants | 4,000 | 0.1 | 0 | 0.0 | 0 | 0 | 0 | 0.00 | 0 | 0.0 | 0 | 0.0 | 0 | 0.0 |
| nominal | 340,000 | 5.0 | 0 | 0.0 | 0 | 0 | 0 | 0.00 | 0 | 0.0 | 0 | 0.0 | 0 | 0.0 |
| affiliated | 6,071,000 | 88.6 | 8,683,928 | 84.0 | 32,019 | –8,452 | 23,567 | 0.27 | 8,806,600 | 83.6 | 8,919,600 | 83.2 | 9,018,300 | 81.5 |
| total practising | 5,463,900 | *90* | 6,078,750 | *70* | 22,414 | –5,917 | 16,497 | 0.27 | 6,164,620 | *70* | 6,243,720 | *70* | 5,861,900 | *65* |
| non-practising | 607,100 | *10* | 2,605,180 | *30* | 9,605 | –2,535 | 7,070 | 0.27 | 2,641,980 | *30* | 2,675,880 | *30* | 3,156,400 | *35* |
| Roman Catholics | 4,153,000 | 60.6 | 6,124,328 | 59.2 | 22,567 | –6,552 | 16,015 | 0.26 | 6,206,970 | 58.9 | 6,284,480 | 58.6 | 6,357,100 | 57.4 |
| Protestants | 1,850,000 | 27.0 | 2,489,500 | 24.1 | 9,192 | –1,912 | 7,280 | 0.29 | 2,528,200 | 24.0 | 2,562,300 | 23.9 | 2,601,200 | 23.5 |
| Evangelicals | 190,000 | 2.8 | 1,033,800 | 10.0 | 3,868 | 2,102 | 5,970 | 0.56 | 1,063,900 | 10.1 | 1,093,500 | 10.2 | 1,162,000 | 10.5 |
| Neo-pentecostals | 0 | 0.0 | 0 | 0.0 | 4 | 196 | 200 | 20.00 | 1,000 | 0.0 | 2,000 | 0.0 | 10,000 | 0.1 |
| Orthodox | 65,000 | 0.9 | 66,500 | 0.6 | 246 | 0 | 246 | 0.36 | 67,700 | 0.6 | 68,960 | 0.6 | 55,300 | 0.5 |
| Marginal Protestants | 3,000 | 0.0 | 2,100 | 0.0 | 8 | 12 | 20 | 0.91 | 2,200 | 0.0 | 2,300 | 0.0 | 3,000 | 0.0 |
| Catholics (non-Roman) | 0 | 0.0 | 1,500 | 0.0 | 6 | 0 | 6 | 0.39 | 1,530 | 0.0 | 1,560 | 0.0 | 1,700 | 0.0 |
| Non-religious | 23,000 | 0.3 | 841,672 | 8.1 | 3,153 | 5,980 | 9,133 | 1.03 | 885,000 | 8.4 | 933,000 | 8.7 | 1,107,000 | 10.0 |
| Atheists | 10,000 | 0.2 | 720,000 | 7.0 | 2,720 | 2,480 | 5,200 | 0.70 | 748,000 | 7.1 | 772,000 | 7.2 | 841,000 | 7.6 |
| Jews | 410,000 | 6.0 | 90,000 | 0.9 | 400 | 0 | 400 | 0.43 | 92,000 | 0.9 | 94,000 | 0.9 | 100,000 | 0.9 |
| Muslims | 0 | 0.0 | 2,000 | 0.0 | 7 | –7 | 0 | 0.00 | 2,000 | 0.0 | 2,000 | 0.0 | 2,000 | 0.0 |
| Buddhists | 0 | 0.0 | 300 | 0.0 | 1 | –1 | 0 | 0.00 | 300 | 0.0 | 300 | 0.0 | 500 | 0.0 |
| Baha'is | 0 | 0.0 | 100 | 0.0 | 0 | 0 | 0 | 0.00 | 100 | 0.0 | 100 | 0.0 | 200 | 0.0 |
| **Country's population** | **6,854,000** | **100.0** | **10,338,000** | **100.0** | **38,300** | **0** | **38,300** | **0.36** | **10,534,000** | **100.0** | **10,721,000** | **100.0** | **11,069,000** | **100.0** |

COLUMNS, ROWS. For meanings and definitions, see Codebook (Part 6). Note that, by definition, total 'Christians' = professing + crypto-Christians, which also = affiliated + nominal Christians. Percentages may not always total exactly, due to rounding.
CENSUSES. Note: before 1920, boundaries referred to Hungary proper, but differed from present ones. **1857:** 57.9% Roman Catholics (10.1% Greek Catholics), 20.8% Protestants, 17.9% Greek Orthodox, 3.0% Jews, 0.4% marginal Protestants (Unitarians). **1870:** 58.9% Roman Catholics (10.2% Greek Catholics), 20.3% Protestants, 16.8% Greek Orthodox, 3.6% Jews, 0.4% Unitarians. **1900** (Hungary proper): 59.6% Roman Catholics (10.9% Greek Catholics), 21.9% Protestants, 13.1% Greek Orthodox, 4.9% Jews, 0.4% Unitarians. **1910** (Hungary proper, old boundaries): 60.3% Roman Catholics (11.0% Greek Catholics), 21.4% Protestants, 12.8% Greek Orthodox, 5.0% Jews, 0.4% Unitarians. **1920** (new boundaries): 66.1% Roman Catholics (2.2% Greek Catholics), 27.2% Protestants (21.0% Reformed, 6.2% Lutherans), 5.9% Jews, 0.6% Greek Orthodox, 0.1% Unitarians. **1930:** 67.1% Roman Catholics (2.3% Greek Catholics), 27.1% Protestants (20.9% Reformed, 6.1% Lutherans), 5.1% Jews, 0.5% Greek Orthodox.

NOTES ON RELIGIONS
ATHEISTS. Hungarian Socialist Workers' Party (in power; pro-Soviet): membership (1970) 724,000; Communist voters (election of 25.IV.1971) 7,334,918 (98.7% of all votes). Of Communist party members, only around 25% are estimated to be committed atheists, the rest being non-religious with a large minority of professing Christians. Unlike the clearcut division between the party and the churches in Bulgaria and the USSR, in Hungary a large number of party members have their children baptized, although for preference at churches where they are not known.
BAHA'IS. In 1 centre.
BUDDHISTS. Centred on a Buddhist mission in Budapest.
CRYPTO-CHRISTIANS. Christians affiliated to churches but not known as such to the state, being (1) unorganized individuals in the legal churches, (2) members of illegal or underground churches, and (3) a few isolated radio believers.
JEWS. Before 1939, they numbered 800,000, but 600,000 perished in the Nazi massacres. Of the present total, 80% live in Budapest with 32 synagogues, a seminary and a library of 60,000 volumes. In 1976, there were in Hungary 130 synagogues and 26 rabbis.
MUSLIMS. A small minority including a community in Budapest.
NEO-PENTECOSTALS. Charismatics within the non-Pentecostal Protestant churches.
NON-RELIGIOUS. Agnostics, indifferent to religion, including most Communist party members. In addition to this total, there are another 7% of the population who are regarded by state and society as non-religious but who are affiliated to the churches and so are classified here as crypto-Christians.
PRACTISING CHRISTIANS. Church attenders 14% of the whole population weekly, rising to 20% at Easter and festivals.

**NON-CHRISTIAN RELIGIONS. Atheism** and **agnosticism** are professed by most members of the Communist party and their circles, amounting to around 15% of the population.

**Judaism** had about 92,000 adherents in 1975, 80% of whom live in Budapest. Before World War II they numbered more than 800,000, but 600,000 died in the Nazi holocaust. Judaism's principal organization is the Central Board of Hungarian Jews in Budapest. Also found in Budapest are 32 synagogues, a Jewish secondary school for boys and girls, and a rabbinic seminary with a Jewish library of 60,000 volumes; this is the only seminary for rabbis in eastern Europe. In those exceptional cases when the USSR government agrees, rabbis from the USSR are trained here.

**Islam** has a small minority of followers including a community in Budapest.

**Buddhism** is represented by a Buddhist mission in the capital.

**CHRISTIANITY.** Christians in Hungary trace their history back to the 3rd century, Christianity having entered the northern Pannonian and Dacian provinces of the Roman empire at that period. Arian, Roman and Orthodox missionaries were also active among the Goths, Huns, Avars, Franks and Slavs, who played significant roles at various periods of Hungarian history. The greatest missionaries were Cyril and Methodius, Catholics who worked in Moravia, introduced the Greek rite and translated the liturgy and Bible into the Slavic language. Moravian converts were later dispersed, spreading the Byzantine rite throughout Bulgaria and Russia, and the Roman rite in Hungary. The Magyars (Hungarians), who invaded from the east, although having had strong ties with the Byzantine church, finally opted for the Latin church under prince Geza and his son, Stephen I. The latter was given by the pope the title apostolic king. Aided by Italian, German and Bohemian missionaries, Stephen established Catholicism in AD 1001; and he and his son were later canonized by the Catholic Church. In the 13th century, Hungarian missionaries set out for the Urals to christianize kinsmen left behind centuries before. There they were met by Mongolians who captured the entire Magyar kingdom in 1241, with great loss of life and property. After their withdrawal, the task of reconstruction was begun. Two centuries later the expanding power of the Ottoman empire reached the country's southern borders. Although the Hungarian army resisted the Turks for 100 years, they were finally defeated in 1526; and for the next 150 years the central part of the country was occupied by Turkey. During the Reformation period, Hungary was divided into 3 regions: the west (the kingdom of Hungary) under the control of the Austrian Hapsburgs, the central plains under the Turks, and the principality of Transylvania in the east, which remained independent.

The Lutheran Reformation entered in 1518 under the influence of the writings of Luther and the return of Hungarian reformers from Wittenberg. The Augsburg Confession was adopted in 1545 and the Lutheran catechism in 1550. During the latter part of the 16th century, the Swiss Reformation gained more ground, and the emerging Reformed church adopted the Second Helvetic Confession at Debrecen in 1567. Later the Heidelberg Catechism was adopted and became influential in the church. In Transylvania, the law of the land granted freedom of worship to the Catholic, Lutheran, Reformed and Unitarian churches in 1568; and by the end of the 16th century the majority of Hungarians were Protestants, mostly of the Reformed faith. A century later the Hapsburgs had expelled the Turks and the country was reunited under Vienna, whereupon Counter-Reformation activities, until then limited to the kingdom in the West, were extended to the whole country and launched with new vigour. The war of liberation of Ferenc Rákoóczi II in 1703–11, attempting to wrest political and religious freedom from Austria, was ultimately lost and was followed by an even more vigorous oppression, as well as the arrival of Catholic settlers in the regions left desolate by Turks and wars. At the close of the 18th century the number of Protestants had been reduced to one-third of the population. Legal guarantees of religious freedom were given by the royal decree of 1780, the Edict of Toleration of Joseph II, and were reaffirmed at the Diet of 1791. In that year Lutheran and Reformed churches were reorganized with the laity assuming greater control. Further steps towards religious equality were taken progressively before the unsuccessful political uprising of 1848–49, and also in 1867 when the Austro-Hungarian dual monarchy came into being. Hungary achieved independence from the Hapsburgs following World War I but suffered a great loss of territory and population. The Lutheran Church, formerly with over a million adherents, lost more than half its membership, a large number being dispersed to areas with no Lutheran churches. In 1881 the Reformed Church adopted its book of church law affirming a synodal-presbyterian form of government, but with bishops. It also faced new difficulties after World War I, not only because of loss of membership through the reduction of Hungarian territory, but also through rationalism and theological liberalism. However, a theological renewal inspired by dialectical theology and a popular revival movement, particularly during the years following World War II, gave the church new strength and identity.

During all these years when Protestantism was repressed, the Catholic Church had grown in influence, and it experienced a new awakening towards the end of the 19th century. Religious vocations increased, parishes were reorganized, lay and missionary movements developed and publications increased. As a result, the Catholic Church remains the dominant spiritual influence in the country up to the present day.

CATHOLIC CHURCH. Catholics live mostly in western Transdanubia, in the area between the Danube and Tisza rivers and in the mountains of the north. They form the majority in 70% of the towns and are especially strong among the ethnic minorities: Croats, Germans, Slovaks and Gypsies. Catholics of the Byzantine rite live in Budapest and in the rural communities of the northern Great Plains.

The Catholic Church has had to face the double problem of secularization accompanied by official atheistic propaganda. Nevertheless, institutional religious life in Hungary remains active and influential, especially in rural areas and among intellectuals. Christmas midnight mass, Easter offices and places of pilgrimage continue to hold a strong attraction. These external manifestations of religiosity are no longer concealed, nor engaged in merely as open opposition to the regime. In part they are an expression of popular folk religion, but in part also of genuine spiritual needs. In both rural and urban communities, the

3 major events of life (birth, marriage, death) are usually accompanied by religious ceremonies. Marriages and burials are carried out as solemn occasions with massive participation, while baptisms are often carried out secretly for fear of reprisals, real or imaginary. The number of clergy has declined drastically, from 5,948 priests in 1950 before the dissolution of religious orders, to 4,014 in 1969. Since 1968, there have been only about 20 ordinations each year in contrast to about 70 deaths of priests annually. In June 1969, 45% of all priests were under 50 years of age (7% under 30) and 55% were over 50, indicating that in 1974 more than half the Hungarian clergy were over 60.

PROTESTANT CHURCHES. Protestant churches consider that discrimination against them in favour of Rome finally ended following World War II, when the new Communist government made individual

Pentecostals each have several thousand members. Other bodies are the Apostolic Church, Church of God, Nazarenes and several groups of Brethren. Sunday church attendance for Protestants averages 14% of the entire population weekly, rising to 20% at Easter and festivals.

ORTHODOX CHURCH. The Orthodox Church in Hungary has 10 parishes consisting mostly of Serbian and Romanian ethnic minorities in Szentendre and Budapest. Hungarian Orthodoxy is under the authority of the Moscow Patriarchate. The Bulgarian, Romanian, Russian and Serbian Orthodox churches also have their own jurisdictions.

CHURCH AND STATE. Hungary, a religious state in the year 1900, became an atheistic state in 1949. Relations of churches with the state are now governed by the constitution of April 1972 and a series of laws

continues to be extended. (5) Agreements were reached between the state and the Lutheran and Reformed churches in 1948, and in 1950 with the Catholic Church. The latter agreement provided for collaboration between the Catholic Church and the regime, particularly in economic affairs. The state guaranteed freedom of worship and undertook to return the 8 schools and to provide subsidies. (6) Partial agreements were reached with the Holy See in 1964, 1969 and 1972. That of 1964, the first of its kind concluded by the Holy See with a Communist country, recognized the right of the Holy See to nominate bishops approved by the government, this being a modification of the agreement of April 1951 when the right of patronage held by the former Austro-Hungarian empire was taken over by the Communist regime. The 1964 agreement also provided for a compromise in the oath of loyalty taken by

**Reformed Church of Hungary.** *Top.* Confirmands at 1973 confirmation service in village near River Tisza. *Right.* Interior, Calvin Square Reformed Church, Budapest (19th century). The major problem facing Christianity in Hungary is that all church activities, including worship, are heavily infiltrated by incognito agents of the state. *Above.* Elders and pillars of the church in Sunday dress of farmers walk to church in small town in Trans-Tibiscan Church District.

agreements with each body and the Roman Catholic Church was no longer given special preference. Moreover, the government subsidized the reconstruction of churches extensively damaged during the war, and continues to finance religious education with teachers provided by the churches. The Reformed Church of Hungary, with about 19% of the population, has 2,000 autonomous parishes in 4 church districts or dioceses. Organized on the synodal-presbyterian principle, it has a dual chairmanship, with ministerial and lay chairmen. There are 2 theological academies. The Church also administers several institutions of higher learning and 20 charitable organizations. It is attempting to move from its earlier status as a folk church with automatic membership based on birth, to a gathered church with membership voluntarily chosen through a decision based on faith. The Evangelical Lutheran Church with 4% of the population, is divided into 2 districts with 500 parishes forming 16 seniorates. It has one theological academy and operates 18 social service institutions. The largest of the smaller denominations is the Baptist Church begun in 1846. It has 500 congregations and maintains a theological seminary and 3 institutions for social service. Methodists entered Hungary in 1900 and now have 55 congregations and one charitable institution. Seventh-day Adventists and Evangelical-Christian

regulating religious life. The constitution guarantees freedom of conscience, the free exercise of worship (paragraph 67, item 1) and proclaims the separation of church and state 'in the interests of freedom of conscience' (paragraph 63, item 2).

The following laws and agreements are of significance. (1) Decree 600 of 1945, passed by the provisional government, concerned the nationalization of eccesiastical estates mostly belonging to the Catholic Church. Half of all ecclesiastical estates, forest and pasture land, passed into the hands of the state, and the other half was distributed among peasants in the interests of agrarian reform. (2) Law 33 of 1948 proclaimed the nationalization of all church schools. Eight Catholic and 2 Protestant schools were eventually returned to the churches in 1950. (3) Law 34 of 1950 ordered the dissolution of 53 religious orders and congregations. All congregations were banned with the exception of Benedictines, Franciscans, Piarists and congregations of sisters involved in public teaching, who are still authorized to operate Catholic schools and to recruit a maximum of 2 novices per year. (4) Decree 170 (1951) of the Presidium Council created a fund for churches. The state deposits a sum of 80 million forints (4 million US dollars) for the churches according to their numerical importance. This decree was originally designed to last only 15 years, but its application

bishops to the People's Republic. Moreover, it made possible the reopening of the Hungarian Institute of Rome under the direction of priests agreed upon by the Budapest government. Five apostolic administrators for Hungary were then nominated in 1964. Four more, and 4 bishops, were nominated in 1969.

The churches may collect voluntary financial contributions amounting in the case of the Catholic Church to 1% of the income of each head of family. The property of the churches, including church buildings, rectories, seminaries and schools, are exempt from taxes. All clergy must take an oath of loyalty to the state, to the effect that they regard the regime as lawful and respect its lawful decisions. Except for the free churches which have never received government aid, the salaries of both Catholic and Protestant clergy are partially subsidized by the state. In the case of Protestant clergy the state contribution amounts to about 25% of the total stipend.

Religious instruction may be offered in state primary schools in the form of optional courses outside regular school hours to reach pupils of up to 14 years of age. All schools do not organize such courses, especially in the cities. In 1973 an official Hungarian source estimated that only 60% of all schools offer such courses and that only 23% of Hungarian youth participate. Priests and lay persons teaching in the programme draw a salary from the state. There is no teaching of religion in state secondary schools, although religious training for older youth prior to confirmation is common. For Catholics this usually consists of a 6-weeks accelerated course, whereas in the Reformed Church there are two 10–12 week courses over a 2-year period. Religion courses are obligatory in church schools and students have the right to the services of chaplains. Teachers

*Above.* Miskolc Reformed Church (16th century), with state television tower.
**Evangelical-Christian Pentecostal Church.** *Below .* New Pentecostal church in Budapest being built by Baptist workers in 1974.

in confessional schools receive their salaries from the state, but other school expenses are the responsibility of the sponsoring organization and also of parents. Students educated in these schools have no difficulty in obtaining access to Hungary's universities.

The State Office for Ecclesiastical Affairs (Allami Egyhazügyi Hitaval) was created in May 1951; and except for 1957 and 1959, when it was temporarily suspended, it has continued to function up to the present time. Its head has the rank of minister. The office exercises strict control over all activities of the churches. It controls the religious press, church organizations and institutions, suggests or opposes appointments, supervises admissions to seminaries,

provides subsidies to schools exempt from nationalization and pays the expenses of religious education in state schools. Its diocesan delegates are present at festivals and religious ceremonies and participate actively in semi-official meetings, such as synods and meetings held by Priests for Peace. It should be noted that the intervention of the state in ecclesiastical appointments and activities did not begin with the Communist regime. Under the former monarchy there was also a State Secretariat for Ecclesiastical Affairs, although its ideological orientation was very different.

The Protestant churches, which are termed national ecclesiastical communities, have succeeded better in accommodating themselves to the People's Republic than the Catholic Church. The latter was bound to the old regime politically, as the official church under the Austro-Hungarian empire and later the Horthy regency, and also economically, as exemplified by the feudal character of its hierarchy. Reformers before 1939 were aware of the dangers facing the church but were unsuccessful in changing existing structures. The struggle of the Catholic Church against the new regime began in 1945 and was characterized by public manifestations of strength, including pilgrimages, public novenas, meetings, the celebration of the Marian year 1948, and open hostility to nationalization. This campaign was conducted personally under the direction of cardinal Mindszenty, who was finally arrested on 25 December 1948, and sentenced the following February to life imprisonment. Between 1950 and 1956, the church engaged in passive resistance, characterized by a will to survive; but already there began to manifest itself a will to collaborate with the regime, as shown by the Movement of Priests for Peace, and other peace campaigns. A more liberal course has been followed since 1956, partly due to the new approach of the Vatican, which has had an effect on the willingness of bishops and clergy to speak out more freely. A definite thaw began in relations between church and state in 1960, when discussions were initiated between governmental and ecclesiastical authorities concerning the development of socialism, freedom of travel outside the country for priests and bishops, and publication of religious books. This has become even more marked since 1971. In that year the Catholic Church in Hungary celebrated its millennium with the government permitting the organization of local pilgrimages, authorizing for the first time the publication of a children's catechism and ignoring its right to review such lower ecclesiastical appointments as vicars and parish priests. After October 1971, priests accused of collaborating with the regime were no longer excommunicated by the hierarchy, and the number of imprisoned priests began to diminish. In 1970 there were 35 imprisonments of priests, most of whom were accused of clandestine work with young people. Four more were arrested at the beginning of 1971 but none subsequently; and at the end of 1972 only 3 priests

remained in prison.

In 1972 the Hungarian government agreed to the appointment of 4 new bishops, and 9 more in January 1975: 5 residential bishops, 3 auxiliary bishops and one apostolic administrator. In the meantime, during 1973 the state accepted the election of the new abbot nullius of Pannonhalma. By 31 May 1975 only 2 dioceses were still lacking residential bishops: Esztergom and Györ. On 15 January 1975, the government signed a decree officially authorizing religious teaching in churches and other worship places.

The evolution of this detente was made possible by the desire of the Hungarian government to normalize its relations with the Catholic Church, at the same time ensuring that the church would not be hostile to the state. A factor contributing to the latter was the growing role of Opus Pacis within Catholicism, the importance of which can be appreciated when one remembers that the general secretary of the Catholic Committee for Peace is a member of the supreme presidium of the republic. Of equal importance has been the new policy of the Vatican towards Eastern Europe began under pope John XXIII and continued under cardinal Casaroli, secretary of the Council for the Public Affairs of the Church, in Rome.

For a long time the major obstacle to the realization of this new policy was the refusal of cardinal Mindszenty to renounce his see at Esztergom and his title as primate of Hungary. The cardinal considered himself not only as Hungary's religious leader but also as the representative of the monarchy, the country's only legitimate government. According to the constitution of the former regime, when the throne became vacant and in the absence of the regent (which was the case after the departure of the regent Horthy following World War II), the primate as the first member of the Council of the Crown was invested with full political powers during the interregnum. For this reason Mindszenty never recognized the Communist state which he considered illegal, although the constitution of the People's Republic had abolished the political role of the archbishop of Esztergom. The Mindszenty affair was resolved when, on 28 September 1971, through papal pressure he agreed to leave the American Embassy in Budapest where he had lived since 1956. In 1974, Paul VI withdrew his titles as archbishop of Esztergom and primate of Hungary, and on 6 May 1975 he died in Vienna at the age of 83. Finally, the pope appointed a new primate who was installed early in 1976; all 11 dioceses now had bishops for the first time under the Communist regime.

In 1978, diplomatic relations with the Holy See were finally established.

**INTERDENOMINATIONAL ORGANIZATIONS.** A Union of Free Churches, which brought together most of the leaders of the smaller churches of Hungary, was formed prior to World War II, becoming in 1948 the Council of Free Churches. Members include Adventists, Apostolic Church, Baptists, Church of God, Free Christians (a Brethren group), Methodists, Open Brethren, and Pentecostals. The Nazarenes are not members.

In 1943 an Ecumenical Committee composed of Reformed and Lutheran representatives was established to prepare the ground for the formation in 1948 of the Ecumenical Council of Churches (Magyarországi Egyházak Ökumenikus Tanásca). Members include the Reformed, Lutheran, Baptist, Methodist and Orthodox churches as well as the Council of Free Churches as a corporate member. The Ecumenical Council has from the beginning been active in the international Faith and Order movement as well as at all World Council of Churches assemblies. It sponsors a theological academy and issues 2 journals, the monthly *Theological review* and the fortnightly *Hungarian Church Press* in both English and German. Faculty and student exchanges take place among the various denominational theological academies.

**BROADCASTING.** The longstanding tradition of Sunday church broadcasting has never been entirely revoked by the Communist regime, Hungary being the only Eastern European country at the present time to permit the use of regular religious radio programmes. Every Sunday morning on Radio Hungary (Petöfi Adó) in Budapest, transmitted nation-wide, Christians are allowed 30 minutes at 7.30 a.m. This is a recorded service, and is prepared in rotation among the different churches. The Catholic Church is allowed

18 half-hour programmes a year produced under Catholic Action. The Orthodox Church prefers a whole hour for its liturgy at less frequent intervals, about twice a year. The churches are not allowed to broadcast on television, and there is a subtle background of anti-religious propaganda every day on both radio and TV. Christian programmes in Hungarian are easily received from foreign international stations over VOA, BBC, Radio Free Europe, Europe I (15 minutes on Fridays), TWR (5 hours weekly), and Radio Vatican (3.5 hours weekly).

## BIBLIOGRAPHY


*Beiträge zur Lage der Katholischen Kirche im Ungarn in Jahre 1961*. Wien: Ungarisches Katholische Institut für Kirchliche Sozialforschung, 1962.

*Bilanz des ungarischen Katholizismus: Kirche and Gesellschaft in Dokumenten, Zahlen und Analysen*. I. Andras & J. Mrel. München: Heimatwerk Verlag, 1969. 255p.

*Der Protestantismus in Ungarn, 1521-1977: Ungarns Reformationskirche in Geschichte und Gegenwart*. M. Bucsay. Leiden: Brill, 1978. 320p.

*Die Lage der Katholischen Kirche in Ungarn im Jahre 1960*. Wien: Ungarisches Katholische Institut für Kirchliche Sozialforschung, 1960.

*Five years of Hungarian Protestantism, 1945-1950*. Ed I. Kadar. Budapest: Hungarian Church Press, 1950. 129p.

*Handbuch des ungarischen Katholizismus*. Wien (Austria): UKI, 1975. 208p.

*Hungarian Protestantism, its past and present*. Budapest: Ecumenical Council of Churches, 1956.

'Hungary', I. Varga, in H. Mol (ed), *Western religion* (The Hague: Mouton, 1972), p. 277–294.

'L'Eglise de Hongrie sous le Régime Communiste', *Informations catholiques internationales*, 36 (1956).

*The Church in the storm of time*. I. Kadar. Budapest: Bibliotheca, 1957. 175p. (History of the Hungarian Reformed Church).


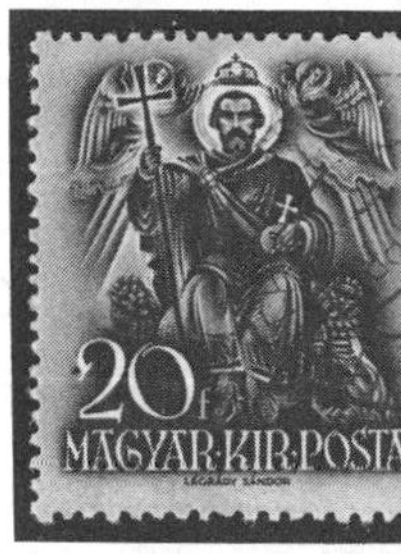

The Church and its beliefs are often featured on state postage stamps.
*Left*. Apostolic King Stephen I establishes Christianity, AD 1001.
*Right*. Summer Drama Festival in front of Szeged Cathedral, 1963.

TABLE 2. ORGANIZED CHURCHES AND DENOMINATIONS IN HUNGARY

| Official name 1 | Begun 2 | Type 3 | Counc 4 | Congs 5 | Adults 6 | Affiliated 7 | Names, notes, and other statistics (see Codebook) 8 |
|---|---|---|---|---|---|---|---|
| Apostolic Christian Church (Nazarean) | | P Hol | x.... | 112 | 3,380 | 4,000 | Holiness Christians of Swiss origin, related to Mennonites. In 17 nations. |
| Apostolic Ch (Primitive Chr Brethren) | 1930 | P PeA | Z...C | 60 | 2,532 | 5,000 | *Öskeresztyén Felekezet*. Centrally organized: 4 apostles, 6 prophets, 14 preachers. |
| Baptist Church in Hungary | 1846 | P Bap | TW..d | 500 | 20,000 | 40,000 | *Magyarországi Baptista Egyház. Hungarian Baptist Union*. 2 homes for aged. 92n,2s(23). |
| Bulgarian Orthodox Church | | O Sla | Mwc.. | 2 | 70 | 100 | *Balgarskata Pravoslavna Crkva*. Under jurisdiction of P Sofia. Bulgarian residents. |
| **Catholic Church in Hungary:** | c 250 | R LEr | B.B.R | 2,295 | 4,593,200 | 6,124,328 | *Római Katolikus Egyház*. C=3+0+1. 71m,57w,6s,62Y. 3678n,90700y. |
| M Eger | c 950 | R Lat | Bs | 302 | 645,900 | 861,257 | *Egri Föegyhàzmegye*. 60% urban. Suffragan Ds in Czechslovakia. 1s. 413 13068 |
| M Esztergom | c 950 | R Lat | Bs | 205 | 570,000 | 760,000 | *Esztergomi Föegyhàzmegye*. Primatial see, in Budapest. 32m,4w,1s. 609 11180 |
| D Györ | c1050 | R Lat | Bs | 211 | 311,000 | 415,000 | *Györi egyhàzmegye*. Rural, very religious. Pilgrimage centres. 1s. 382 6698 |
| D Hajdudorog (*Byzantine*) | 1912 | R Byz | Os | 121 | 184,000 | 245,000 | Hungarian-speaking. Ruthenian and a few Romanian parishes. 1s. 169 3329 |
| D Pécs | 1009 | R Lat | Bs | 205 | 333,000 | 444,000 | 'Five Churches'. Rural and town of Pecs. German minority. 250 7125 |
| D Székesfehérvár | 1777 | R Lat | Bs | 162 | 289,100 | 385,425 | Rural. First royal capital, site of St Stephen's coronation 314 6574 |
| D Szombathely | 1777 | R Lat | Bs | 176 | 239,400 | 319,279 | *Szombathelyi egyhàzmegye*. Rural, well-developed. 243 5242 |
| D Vác | c1050 | R Lat | Bs | 283 | 975,000 | 1,300,000 | *Vàci egyhàazmegye*. Catholics urban, many Protestant minorities. 1s. 453 20000 |
| D Veszprém | 1009 | R Lat | Bs | 351 | 565,100 | 753,538 | *Veszprémi egyhàzmegye*. Tourist region (Lake Balaton). Villages. 402 10014 |
| M Kalocsa | 1000 | R Lat | Bs | 81 | 163,900 | 218,529 | *Kalocsai Föegyhàzmegye*. Rural villages and scattered hamlets, 139 2560 |
| D Csanád | 1035 | R Lat | Bs | 151 | 278,800 | 371,700 | *Csanàdi egyhàzmegye*. Mixed Catholics/Protestants in towns. 55w,1s. 168 4405 |
| AN Pannonhalma | 997 | R Lat | bosb | 19 | 19,900 | 26,500 | Long tradition of Catholic education. 52m,19w. 104 300 |
| EA Miskolc (*Byzantine*) | 1923 | R Byz | Os | 28 | 18,100 | 24,100 | Magyarized Ruthenians living outside D Hajdudorog; same bishop 32 203 |
| Christian Brethren | c1910 | P CBr | x...C | 25 | 2,000 | 3,000 | *Keresztyén Testvérgyülekezetek. Open Brethren*. Many intellectuals are members. |
| Church of God | 1960 | P Pe3 | ZF..C | 20 | 3,700 | 5,000 | *Isten Egyhàza. Church of the Living God*. Link with M=CoG(Cleveland)(USA). 1n. |
| Evangelical Lutheran Ch in Hungary | 1518 | P Lut | LWC.W | 500 | 300,000 | 450,000 | *Magyarországi Evangélikus Egyház*. Diaspora church. Dioceses: North, South. 400n,1s(55). |
| Evangelical-Christian Pentecostal Ch | 1926 | P Pe2 | ZF..C | 190 | 5,000 | 13,000 | *Evangéliumi Keresztyének-Pünkösdiek. Pünkösdi Egyház*. Links M=AoG(USA). 22n,1s(13). |
| Free Christians (Brethren) | | P EBr | ....C | 10 | 500 | 1,000 | *Szabad Keresztyének Gyülekezete*. Many professionals, doctors et alii. |
| Hungarian Methodist Church | 1900 | P Met | VvC.d | 55 | 2,250 | 6,000 | Autonomous, but links with Central & Southern Europe Central Conf, UMC(USA). 13n. |
| Hungarian Orthodox Greek Catholic Ch | 1933 | O Hun | ..... | | 200 | 400 | *Greek Oriental HOC*. Split begun by Serbian P Belgrade. Jacobite succession. Also in USA. |
| Isolated radio churches | c1950 | P rad | ..... | | 200 | 500 | Isolated radio believers, mostly youths aged 12–25. R=1000(TWR,Radio Vatican, &c). |
| Jehovah's Witnesses | c1910 | M Jeh | x.... | 205 | 1,410 | 2,000 | First missionaries arrived c1910. Legally proscribed; underground, very active. |
| New Apostolic Church | | C CAp | x.... | | 500 | 1,000 | In Bezirk Schweiz (Switzerland District). Germans. World HQ Dortmund (Germany). |
| Old Catholic Church of Hungary | 1945 | C CCa | ..... | | 200 | 500 | Schism ex Rome. Close links with, and succession from, Mariavite Ch (Poland). |
| Orthodox Church in Hungary | c1200 | O Hun | Mwc.W | 10 | 5,000 | 40,000 | Autonomous, under P Moscow. Greek/Serbian/Romanian, but no longer Greek churches. 8n. |
| **Reformed Church of Hungary:** | 1530 | P Ref | RWC.W | 2,077 | 1,585,000 | 1,950,000 | *Magyarorzsági Reformàtus Egyház*. 4 Districts & bishops. 85% farmers. 1650n,1j,2s. |
| Cistibiscan Church District | c1600 | P Ref | R | 450 | 370,000 | 450,000 | North Tibiscan District (north of River Tisza). HQ in Miskolc. 4 Seniorates. |
| Danubian Church District | 1560 | P Ref | R | 450 | 365,000 | 450,000 | *Puspoki Hitaval*. HQ Budapest; 53 Reformed churches in capital. 8 Seniorates. |
| Trans-Danubian Church District | 1591 | P Ref | R | 227 | 80,000 | 100,000 | West of river Danube, Veszprém. Strong Counter-Reformation area. 6 Seniorates. |
| Trans-Tibiscan Church District | 1560 | P Ref | R | 950 | 770,000 | 950,000 | East of river Tisza. HQ Debrecen. 9 Seniorates. Heartland of Reformed Church. 2s. |
| Romanian Orthodox Church | c1200 | O Rum | Cwc.. | 10 | 10,000 | 15,000 | *Biserica Ortodoxa Romana*. Parishes under jurisdiction of P Bucharest. |
| Russian Orthodox Church | c1920 | O Sla | Mwc.. | | 700 | 1,000 | *Russkaya Pravoslavnaya Cerkov*. Under jurisdiction of P Moscow. One archpriest. |
| Serbian Orthodox Church: D Budim | 1552 | O Ser | Cwc.. | 400 | 7,000 | 10,000 | Under jurisdiction of P Belgrade. Yugoslav clergy prohibited. 11n,35b,1d,W=90%. |
| Seventh-day Adventist Church | 1912 | P Adv | x...C | 142 | 5,485 | 10,000 | *SDA, Hungarian UC* (*Duna & Tisza Confs*). Declining 6% pa. 32n,1s(20),142t(5585),132Y. |
| Unitarian Church in Hungary | 1568 | M Unt | Iv... | 10 | 50 | 100 | *Unitárius Egyház*. Links with UUA,(USA). Transylvanians. HQ Budapest. 1 bishop. |
| Other Protestant denominations | | P | ....- | | 1,000 | 2,000 | Including Ch of God (Anderson)(6 churches), Ch of the Nazarene, World-Wide Mission. |
| **Total affiliated (mid-1970)** | | | | **6,650** | **6,549,377** | **8,683,928** | **Total denominations (1970) . . . 24.** |
| **Total affiliated (mid-1975)** | | | | **6,660** | **6,641,900** | **8,806,600** | **Total denominations (1975) . . . 25.** |
| **Total affiliated (mid-1980)** | | | | **6,670** | **6,727,100** | **8,919,600** | **Total denominations (1980) . . . 25.** |

### NOTES ON TABLE ABOVE

COLUMNS: for meanings and CODES (cols. 1, 3, 4, 8), see Codebook (Part 6). Column 1: **Boldface type** = church with over 10% of country's affiliated Christians.

NATIONAL COUNCILS (Column 4, 5th letter).

- C = Council of Free Churches in Hungary (CFCH) (Magyarországi Szabadegyházak Tanácsa) (before 1948, Union of Free Churches; since 1965, member of ECHC).
- d = member of both CFCH and ECHC.
- R = Assembly of Catholic Bishops of Hungary, or Hungarian Episcopal Council (HEC)(Magyar Püspöki Kar).
- W = Ecumenical Council of Hungarian Churches (ECHC) (Magyarországi Egyházak Ökumenikus Tanácsa).
- w = observer member of ECHC.

PEOPLES (ethnolinguistic). Christians: 92.8% Magyar (including 2.9% Magyarized (Hungarian-speaking) Ruthenian), 5.6% Gypsy (4.5% Hungarian-speaking), 0.5% German, 0.3% Slovak, 0.2% Croatian, 0.2% Romanian, 0.1% Serbian, Russian, Slovene.

### COUNTRY-WIDE TOTALS

EVANGELIZATION (see Part 5). 1900: 100%. 1970: 94%. 1980: 96%. *Mass evangelism*. In September 1977, Billy Graham (USA) made a one-week preaching visit (27,000 attenders). *Radiophonic evangelism*. TWR (690 listeners' letters a year), HCJB, Radio Vatican, et alia.

FOREIGN MISSIONARIES AND PERSONNEL (nationals serving abroad) (1973). Total 44 in Brazil, Canada, Kenya, Switzerland, UK, USA et alia: about 38 Roman Catholics (6 priests in Switzerland, 8 sisters in the Netherlands; and in 6 other countries), 6 Protestants (Reformed; in Kenya, Brazil). In addition to these personnel serving abroad legally, sent by their churches, there are large numbers of Hungarian priests and others who are refugees or in exile serving abroad, often in process of acquiring other citizenship. In 1975 there were 24 Hungarian Jesuits in the USA and 9 in Canada.

FOREIGN MISSIONARIES AND PERSONNEL (aliens from abroad) (1973). Total 14. *From Western world*. 9 Protestants (6 in 5 USA societies, 3 in 2 UK societies). *From Communist world*. About 5 Orthodox from Romania, USSR et alia.

INSTITUTIONS (church-operated) (1973). Total 25, including 7 higher schools (1 minor seminary), 1 medical centre, 2 religious communities (monasteries), 11 seminaries (6 RC, 5 Protestant).

PERIODICALS. About 27 titles.

PERSONNEL. About 6,214 (6,200 national, 14 foreign).

RELIGIOUS LIBRARIES. About 45.

SCRIPTURE DISTRIBUTION (1975). Annual totals: 19,000 Bibles (subsidized), 5,000 NTs (20% free, 80% subsidized), 11,012 UBS selections. *Translations completed*. Portion: 2 languages since 1533. NT: Hungarian in 1541, Bible in 1590.

SERVICE AGENCIES. About 24, including CFCH(MST), ECHC(MEOT), HEC(MPK).

### ADDITIONAL DATA ON CHURCHES

CATHOLIC CHURCH IN HUNGARY. *Annual baptisms*. (1972) 100% infants, very few adults. *Personnel*. All nationals. *Priests*. 3,510 secular, 168 religious (including SJ). *Brothers*. Only 74 are known of. *Sisters*. Only 57 professed sisters are known of. *Seminaries*. There are 5 Latin-rite seminaries and one Byzantine-rite, with an average of 55 seminarians in each for 5- or 6-year courses. Budapest Central Seminary is also the Theological Academy, the latter with (1971) 50 seminarians, 27 priests and 24 laymen. *Religious congregations* (active in teaching). Benedictines (in Pannonhalma), Franciscans (at Szentendre), Piarists (in Budapest), Sisters of Our Lady (Budapest).p.

*Catholic organizations*. The secretariat of the Hungarian Episcopal Conference (Magyar Püspöki Kar) was organized in Budapest in 1972 at the express demand of the government. There are no associations of religious personnel, nor pastoral or presbyteral councils. The Holy See had no diplomatic relations with Hungary until they were set up in 1978.

Organized Catholic associations, movements and groups are few in number. After the forcible dissolution of such older organizations as Scouts, YCW and Marian congregations, only a few groups remain at the parish level. The main ones are parish choirs, rosary circles and a few informal groups of mass servers. At the national level, there are 5 main associations. (1) Catholic Action (Actio Catholica) is the most important organization of the lay apostolate. It co-ordinates parish and regional activities, and serves a protocol role, including meeting visiting foreign churchmen. It also arranges festivals, jubilees, masses; directs Catholic radio programmes and edits 3 Catholic journals: *Uj Ember* (weekly; 68,000 copies); *Vigilia* (monthly; 13,000); and *Theologia* (tri-monthly; 2,000 copies). (2) Work of Peace (Opus Pacis) is an old movement of priests for peace, which was founded in 1950 and re-established by the episcopate in 1957. The Vatican approved Opus Pacis in order to avoid a schism in the Hungarian church. The movement justifies its political position relating to peace with scriptural and theological arguments, its members working in collaboration with their bishops and with civil authorities. In reality, however, Opus Pacis exercises control over all the major Catholic bodies: Catholic Action, the secretariat of the Hungarian episcopate, the Committee for Foreign Relations of Catholics and the Hungarian Episcopate founded in 1972, and the Secretariat of the Catholic Committee for Peace, founded in 1973, which is responsible for the internal activities of Hungarian Catholics. (3) The Society of St Stephen (Szent István Tarsulat) is dedicated to the preservation and development of Hungarian religious culture through the publication of books and organization of conferences. Its field of action is limited to Budapest. (4) The Hungarian Association of St Cecilia (Orszagos Magyar Cecilia Egyesület) organizes concerts and meetings to promote liturgical music and singing in churches. (5) Two co-operatives have been formed: Ecclesia, founded in 1951, which sells religious articles and publishes ecclesiastical books; and Solidaritas, a craft co-operative, in which several hundred elderly religious personnel are employed producing works of art and articles for practical use.

The church owns 8 schools serving 3,000 primary and secondary students, under the supervision of the 4 religious orders which have received permission to remain in Hungary and which may engage in no other religious activity: OSB at Györ and Pannonhalma; OFM at Esztergom and Szentendre; SP at Budapest and Kecskemét; and Sisters of the Schools at Budapest and Debrecen. They each have a noviciate, averaging 15 novices each, and may accept 2 new vocations a year to assure continuity of teaching staff.

With regard to social-service institutions, the Catholic Church administers one clinic for priests in Budapest and finances 7 of the 14 homes for aged religious personnel built after the suppression of religious orders; the other 7 are financed by the state. In 1969 these homes cared for 710 sisters, 100 brothers, 75 priests and 20 laymen.

REFORMED CHURCH OF HUNGARY. By 1976, totals had fallen to 1,502 churches and chapels, and 1,306 clergy. *Seminarians* (1976) 185.

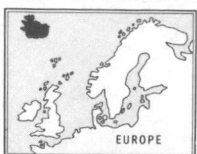

# ICELAND

## SECULAR DATA

**STATE. Official name:** The Republic of Iceland (Lydveldid Island). Adjectives of nationality: Icelandic, an Icelander.
**Flag** (shown above right): White-bordered red cross on blue field.
**Area:** 103,000 sq.km. (39,768 sq.miles). Agricultural land: 22.1%.
**Government:** Parliamentary republic, since 1944 (1262 Norwegian possession, 1874 home rule, 1918 sovereign state under Danish crown, 1944 Independence as republic).
**Legislature:** Parliament (Althing): Upper House, 20 members; Lower House, 40 members.
**Official language:** Icelandic (*islenzka*).
**Capital:** Reykjavik 98,190 (1973).
**Political divisions:** 16 Provinces (syslur); 14 Urban Municipalities, 213 Rural Municipalities.
**Armed forces** (1976): None. The USA is responsible for defence, under NATO.

**Foreign forces** (1973): 3,000 USA troops.

**DEMOGRAPHY. Population:** 204,930 (census of 1.XII.1970. For 1970–2000 (UN), see last row of Table 1). Population density (1975): 2/sq.km. (5/sq.mile). Under 15 years: 35%. Growth rate (1975–80): 1.17% per year (births 1.93%, deaths −0.77%). Life expectancy (1975–80): 74.1 years. Household size: 2.9 persons.
**Major languages:** Icelandic, Danish, Norwegian.
**Urban dwellers** (1970): 71.7%. Urban growth rate (1950–70): 2.7% per year.
**Labour force:** 42%.
**Tourists** (1972): 68,000.

**ETHNOLINGUISTIC GROUPS:** 98.6% Icelander, 1.4% alien (Danish, USA military).

**MONEY** (1977). **Monetary unit:** króna (= 100 aurar); US$1 = IKr 190.00.

**National income per person:** US$5,000. Average annual family income: US$14,500.
**Inflation:** (1970–74) 19.1% per year (1975: consumer price index 339); (1975) 44% per year.
**Cost of living in capital** (1976): index 147 (Washington DC=100). Daily cost of living: US$42.

**EDUCATION.** Adult literacy: 100%. Education rate: 68%. Schools: 184. Universities: 1.

**HEALTH.** Hospitals: 48 (2,923 beds). Doctors: 299. Blind: 434. Psychotics: 2,000. Criminals: 5,000.

**LITERATURE.** Annual new book titles (1972): 617. Periodicals: 176. Scientific journals: 30. Newspapers: 5 dailies, 90 non-daily.

**COMMUNICATION** (per 1,000 people). Phones: 387. Radios: 311. TV sets: 220. Daily newspaper circulation: 449 copies.

TABLE 1.    RELIGIOUS ADHERENTS IN ICELAND

| Year / Name | 1900 Adherents | % | mid-1970 Adherents | % | Annual change, 1970–1980 Natural | Conversion | Total | Rate | mid-1975 Adherents | % | mid-1980 Adherents | % | 2000 Adherents | % |
|---|---|---|---|---|---|---|---|---|---|---|---|---|---|---|
| Christians | 77,900 | 99.9 | 199,940 | 98.0 | 2,441 | −152 | 2,289 | 1.08 | 210,890 | 97.6 | 222,830 | 97.3 | 265,330 | 95.4 |
| professing | 77,900 | 99.9 | 199,940 | 98.0 | 2,441 | −152 | 2,289 | 1.08 | 210,890 | 97.6 | 222,830 | 97.3 | 265,330 | 95.4 |
| Protestants | 77,880 | 99.8 | 198,440 | 97.3 | 2,421 | −185 | 2,236 | 1.07 | 209,130 | 96.8 | 220,800 | 96.4 | 261,930 | 94.2 |
| Roman Catholics | 20 | 0.0 | 1,200 | 0.6 | 16 | 24 | 40 | 2.86 | 1,400 | 0.6 | 1,600 | 0.7 | 2,500 | 0.9 |
| Marginal Protestants | 0 | 0.0 | 300 | 0.1 | 4 | 9 | 13 | 3.61 | 360 | 0.2 | 430 | 0.2 | 900 | 0.3 |
| nominal | 300 | 0.4 | 1,726 | 0.8 | 23 | 57 | 80 | 4.04 | 1,990 | 0.9 | 2,530 | 1.1 | 4,530 | 1.6 |
| affiliated | 77,600 | 99.5 | 198,214 | 97.2 | 2,418 | −209 | 2,209 | 1.06 | 208,900 | 96.7 | 220,300 | 96.2 | 260,800 | 93.8 |
| total practising | 62,080 | 80 | 118,930 | 60 | 1,451 | −126 | 1,325 | 1.06 | 125,340 | 60 | 132,180 | 60 | 130,400 | 50 |
| non-practising | 15,520 | 20 | 79,280 | 40 | 967 | −83 | 884 | 1.06 | 83,560 | 40 | 88,120 | 40 | 130,400 | 50 |
| Protestants | 77,580 | 99.5 | 196,646 | 96.5 | 2,400 | −239 | 2,161 | 1.04 | 207,390 | 96.0 | 218,550 | 95.4 | 257,800 | 92.7 |
| Evangelicals | 23,000 | 29.5 | 16,300 | 8.0 | 200 | 0 | 200 | 1.16 | 17,300 | 8.0 | 18,300 | 8.0 | 23,600 | 8.5 |
| Neo-pentecostals | 0 | 0.0 | 0 | 0.0 | 12 | 388 | 400 | 40.00 | 1,000 | 0.5 | 4,000 | 1.7 | 20,000 | 7.2 |
| Roman Catholics | 20 | 0.0 | 1,018 | 0.5 | 14 | 21 | 35 | 2.93 | 1,200 | 0.6 | 1,370 | 0.6 | 2,200 | 0.8 |
| Marginal Protestants | 0 | 0.0 | 250 | 0.1 | 4 | 9 | 13 | 4.19 | 310 | 0.1 | 380 | 0.2 | 800 | 0.3 |
| Non-religious | 100 | 0.1 | 1,900 | 0.9 | 29 | 91 | 120 | 4.80 | 2,500 | 1.2 | 3,100 | 1.4 | 5,900 | 2.1 |
| Atheists | 0 | 0.0 | 1,000 | 0.5 | 15 | 45 | 60 | 4.62 | 1,300 | 0.6 | 1,600 | 0.7 | 3,000 | 1.1 |
| Spiritists | 0 | 0.0 | 600 | 0.3 | 7 | −3 | 4 | 0.65 | 620 | 0.3 | 640 | 0.3 | 600 | 0.2 |
| Baha'is | 0 | 0.0 | 300 | 0.1 | 4 | 6 | 10 | 2.86 | 350 | 0.2 | 400 | 0.2 | 800 | 0.3 |
| Pagan religionists | 0 | 0.0 | 100 | 0.0 | 2 | 11 | 13 | 8.13 | 160 | 0.1 | 230 | 0.1 | 2,000 | 0.7 |
| Hindus | 0 | 0.0 | 60 | 0.0 | 1 | 3 | 4 | 5.00 | 80 | 0.0 | 100 | 0.0 | 170 | 0.1 |
| Other religionists | 0 | 0.0 | 100 | 0.0 | 1 | −1 | 0 | 0.00 | 100 | 0.0 | 100 | 0.0 | 200 | 0.1 |
| Country's population | 78,000 | 100.0 | 204,000 | 100.0 | 2,500 | 0 | 2,500 | 1.16 | 216,000 | 100.0 | 229,000 | 100.0 | 278,000 | 100.0 |

**COLUMNS, ROWS.** For meanings and definitions, see Codebook (Part 6). Note that, by definition, total 'Christians' = professing + crypto-Christians, which also = affiliated + nominal Christians. Percentages may not always total exactly, due to rounding.
**CENSUSES. 1920:** 99.7% Protestants (91.9% state church, 7.6% other Lutherans, 0.2% SD Adventists), 0.2% non-religious, 0.1% Roman Catholics. **1930:** 99.1% Protestants (90.8% state church, 7.8% other Lutherans, 0.4% SD Adventists), 0.7% non-religious, 0.2% Roman Catholics. **1940:** 98.2% Protestants (90.7% state church, 6.9% other Lutherans, 0.4% SD Adventists, 0.1% Pentecostals), 1.5% non-religious, 0.3% Roman Catholics. **1950:** 98.1% Protestants (90.6% state church, 6.8% other Lutherans, 0.3% SD Adventists, 0.2% Pentecostals), 1.6% non-religious. 0.3% Roman Catholics. **1.XII.1960:** 98.3% Protestants (91.6% state church, 6.1% other Lutherans, 0.3% SD Adventists, 0.3% Pentecostals), 1.1% non-religious and atheists, 0.5% Roman Catholics, 0.1% other Christians.

**NOTES ON RELIGIONS**
**ATHEISTS.** People's Alliance (Altydubandalagid, AB) (legal; pro-Soviet): membership (1970, 1974) 2,500; Communist voters (election of VI.1946) 13,049 (19.5% of all votes), (13.VI.1971) 18,055 (17.1% of all votes), (VI.1974) 20,922 (18.1% of all votes).
**BAHA'IS.** Growth of local spiritual assemblies: 1964, none; 1973, 5. Mostly youths.
**HINDUS.** Adherents of a new Hindu sect, the Bengali Sri Chinmoy Centre (HQ New York, USA). In Iceland the Theosophical Society in 1975 had 13 Lodges and 611 members, many being Hindus.
**NEO-PENTECOSTALS.** The total (1975) includes about 300 lay charismatics and 5 clergy within the national church in 15 organized prayer groups, with about 50 in other non-Pentecostal Protestant denominations; total charismatic community including children, about 1,000.
**NON-RELIGIOUS.** Mainly in the southwest, with a few in the south.
**OTHER RELIGIONISTS.** Including Rosicrucians (1 AMORC centre).
**PAGAN RELIGIONISTS.** Begun about 1962, the Fellowship of Norse-god Believers (Asa, or Asatruarmenn, Believers in the Great Gods) is a heathen revival of pre-Christian Icelandic religion. In 1974 there were 100 adherents, 10 priests and a high priest. The movement aims to dechristianize Iceland by the year 2000.
**SPIRITISTS.** Arising out of liberalism around 1900, interest in Spiritism, occultism and Theosophy has grown considerably. Though supported by numerous state church clergy and exercising considerable influence, the movement has been hostile to the state church and critical of it.

**National Church of Iceland.** *Left.* Hallgrims Memorial Church (Hallgrimskirkju), Reykjavik, consecrated 1974. *Above.* Sermon in Hallgrims Church.

**NON-CHRISTIAN RELIGIONS. Norse pagan religion** has recently been reintroduced in Iceland. The Fellowship of Norse-god Believers or Asatruarmenn, meaning believers in the Aesir or 'greatest gods' and commonly known in Icelandic as Asa, is a heathen revival begun during the early 1960s and officially recognized as a religion and subsidized by the state from 1973 on. Founded by an Icelandic farmer, a former Lutheran, who is the present high priest of the sect, Asa is a revival of traditional Norse pre-Christian religion. The principal deities worshipped include Odin, king of the gods; Erica, Odin's wife; Thor, Odin's son and god of thunder, whose symbol is a hammer; Frey, god of farming and fertility, who is known for his magic sword and is identified with a red plastic graven image with a large phallus; Freyja sister of Frey and goddess of love; Idun, a king of northern Atlanta; Loge, god of fire; Ull, god of archery and skiing; and a large pantheon of lesser deities. Plans to revive ancient animal sacrifices (Iceland's renowned small ponies) and the brewing of mead, the potent Norse drink formerly used in religious ceremonies, have thus far been thwarted by Icelandic law. The Asa community, which at present consists of 100 adherents (many Danish) and 10 priests, hopes to dechristianize Iceland by AD 2000, the one thousandth anniversary of the christianization of the country.

**CHRISTIANITY.** The first missionaries were monks from Ireland around AD 740. Norwegians established themselves in Iceland in 874, and a parliament was formed in 930. Christianity became the state religion shortly afterwards, and by 1005 there were 2 dioceses and many monasteries and abbeys. Iceland was ruled by Norway after 1262, with Danish influence exercised following the creation of the Danish-Norwegian state in 1381. Iceland followed Denmark in becoming Lutheran at the time of the Reformation and Catholicism was proscribed from 1544 to 1874. Free Protestant denominations and Catholics then began work at the end of the 19th century.

**PROTESTANT CHURCHES.** Lutheranism became the state religion of Iceland in 1550, following the Reformation in 1544, and remains so today. The overwhelming majority of the population (91%) belong to the National Church of Iceland, also called the Evangelical Lutheran Church and the People's Church. The church is organized into 21 deaneries, 120 parishes, and 288 congregations, served by 114 national clergy. There is one seminary for the training of Lutheran ministers. Annual baptisms number 3,600 and 12% of the church's membership attend weekly services.

Apart from the state church, the most influential grouping is known as the Lutheran Free Churches of Iceland, organized in 1899. Two denominations which entered Iceland earlier but have been less successful in attracting members are the Salvation Army (1895) and the Seventh-day Adventists (1897). After the turn of the century came Plymouth Brethren (1911) and Swedish Pentecostals (1920), the latter now having the largest constituency outside the Lutheran tradition, and also the largest church building in the country.

**CATHOLIC CHURCH.** In 1896 the Roman Catholic Church opened work again, concentrated in the Reykjavik area. It is small but continues to grow slowly. Reykjavik's 2 parishes are served by secular priests, Dutch SMM priests and 3 congregations of sisters. In 1977 Iceland was transferred from the jurisdiction of Propaganda to that of the Congregation for Bishops.

**CHURCH AND STATE.** The only legal religion was the Lutheran state church until religious liberty, or freedom for all religions to enter, was proclaimed in 1874. The constitution, promulgated in 1917, assures freedom of conscience and worship, as well as freedom to found religious associations (Article 63). The Evangelical Lutheran Church, or National Church of Iceland (Thjódkirkja Islands), or People's Church (Pjookirkan), is still recognized as the official state church (Article 62) and receives complete subsidies which pay the salaries of ministers, as well as the cost of building and maintaining churches and schools; however, other churches and religions are now recognized and receive state subsidies, including the Norse religion Asa. Acts of baptism, marriage and burial, and their corresponding certificates, are also legally valid for other communities, including the Catholic Church since 1896, Christian Brethren (1911), Seventh-day Adventists (1912), the Sjonarhaed Community (1926) and Asatruarmenn (1973). The state imposes a church tax, but citizens who are not members of the National Church may give the corresponding sum instead to the University of Iceland or one of the foundations which support it. In the same way, gifts given to religious associations whose heads are recognized by the Ministry of Finance may be deducted from one's tax. All religious associations are exempt from the land tax on buildings. Religious matters are dealt with by the Ministry of Justice and Ecclesiastical Affairs (Doms-og Kirkjumáláraduneytid).

**INTERDENOMINATIONAL ORGANIZATIONS.** The Ecumenical Centre (Centrum for Kontakt og Ekumenisme) is a Catholic diocesan organization charged with ecumenical relations.

**BROADCASTING.** The Iceland State Broadcast Service allows religious broadcasting, usually Lutheran, for one hour on Sundays and 5 minutes each day.

**BIBLIOGRAPHY**
'Church and religion', in P. Thorsteinsson (ed), *Iceland 1946* (Reykjavík, 1946).
'The Church', in Nordal & Kristinsson (eds), *Iceland 1966* (Reykjavík, 1966).
'The Church in Iceland', S. Einarsson, *Iceland review*, V, 5 (1967).

**National Church of Iceland.** *Above.* Consecration in 1963 of new church at Skalholt by Lutheran bishop (*Inset.* Postage stamp illustrating old Skalholt church, 1056-1956). *Above right.* Congregation in another newly-opened church.

TABLE 2.　　ORGANIZED CHURCHES AND DENOMINATIONS IN ICELAND

| Official name 1 | Begun 2 | Type 3 | Counc 4 | Congs 5 | Adults 6 | Affiliated 7 | Names, notes, and other statistics (see Codebook) 8 |
|---|---|---|---|---|---|---|---|
| Catholic Church: D Reykjavik | 1896 | R Lat | bxBQ. | 5 | 660 | 1,018 | *Rómversk Kathólska Kirkjan, Reykjavík Bispedomme.* C = 1 + 0 + 3. 2n,6x,62w,P = 42%,21y. |
| Christian Brethren | 1911 | P CBr | x.... | 2 | 100 | 200 | *Open Brethren.* Originated from Faeroe Islands. One congregation in Akureyri. 4f. |
| Church of Christ | | P Dis | x.... | 1 | 100 | 200 | M = CC(Non-Instrumental)(USA). Meeting on USA naval base. Largely USA military. |
| Ev Lutheran Free Churches of Iceland | 1899 | P Lut | ..... | 3 | 6,500 | 10,000 | Free local churches. Schism from state church. 2 in Reykjavik, 1 Hafnarfjörour. |
| Independent Lutheran Churches | c1930 | P Lut | ..... | 4 | 1,000 | 1,846 | Secessions from state church stressing complete liberty of thought and action. |
| Jehovah's Witnesses | 1932 | M Jeh | x.... | 3 | 135 | 200 | *Watch Tower.* IBSA. Work began via Scandinavia. Widespread activity. 15Y. |
| National Church of Iceland | 931 | P Lut | LWC.. | 303 | 117,000 | 180,000 | *Thjódkirkja Islands.* State church since 1550. 114n,G = 1.6%pa,1s,W = 12%,3600Yy. |
| Pentecostal Movement in Iceland | 1920 | P Pe2 | z.... | 50 | 600 | 2,000 | *Hvítasunnusofnourinn a Islandi.* Largest building. M = SFM(Sweden). 15n,G = 7%pa,37Y. |
| Salvation Army | 1895 | P Sal | xwc.. | 6 | 100 | 300 | *Hjálpraedisherinn. Iceland & the Faroes Division. Norway & Iceland Territory.* 16n. |
| Seventh-day Adventist Church | 1897 | P Adv | x.... | 7 | 492 | 1,000 | *Sjounda-Dags Adventistar. Iceland Conf.* 4n,G = 1.3%pa,1j,1r,9t(576),W = 75%,20Y. |
| Southern Baptist Mission | 1963 | P Bap | T.... | 1 | 50 | 100 | M = SBC(USA). Missionary 1963 as pastor Keflavik English-language church. 1x,2f. |
| Unitarian Church | | M Unt | I.... | 1 | 30 | 50 | Small, but has 20 congregations in Canada (United Conference of Icelandic Chs in NAmerica). |
| Worldwide European Fellowship | c1960 | P int | .N... | 2 | 100 | 200 | M = WEF(Canada, USA); 1972 merger with Harvesters International Mission. Broadcasting. 7f. |
| Other Protestant denominations | | P | ..... | | 650 | 1,100 | Including: European Missionary Fellowship, and USA military chaplaincies. |
| | | | | | | | |
| **Total affiliated (mid-1970)** | | | | 394 | 127,517 | 198,214 | **Total denominations (1970) . . . 15.** |
| **Total affiliated (mid-1975)** | | | | 405 | 134,400 | 208,900 | **Total denominations (1975) . . . 15.** |
| **Total affiliated (mid-1980)** | | | | 415 | 141,700 | 220,000 | **Total denominations (1980) . . . 16.** |

**NOTES ON TABLE ABOVE**
COLUMNS: for meanings and CODES (cols. 1, 3, 4, 8), see Codebook (Part 6). Column 1: **Boldface type** = church with over 10% of country's affiliated Christians.

PEOPLES (ethnolinguistic). Christians: 98.6% Icelander, 1.4% alien (Danish, USA military).

COUNTRY-WIDE TOTALS
EVANGELIZATION (see Part 5). 1900: 100%. 1970: 100%. 1980: 100%. *Literature evangelism.* Every Home Crusade conducted nationwide coverage campaigns in 1970 and 1976,

FOREIGN MISSIONARIES AND PERSONNEL (nationals serving abroad) (1974). Total 11 Protestants in 2 societies (10 in Ethiopia, 1 Switzerland).
FOREIGN MISSIONARIES AND PERSONNEL (aliens from abroad) (1973). Total 63. *From Western world.* 63: 44 Roman Catholics, 19 Protestants (9 in 2 USA societies, 3 in 2 Finland societies, 2 in 1 Norway society, 2 in 1 Sweden society, 2 in 1 Faeroes society, 1 in 1 UK society).
INSTITUTIONS (church-operated) (1973). Total 7, including 1 higher school, 3 medical centres (hospitals), 1 press, 1 seminary (Protestant).
PERIODICALS. About 20 titles (2 SDA).
PERSONNEL. About 253 (190 national, 63 foreign).
RELIGIOUS LIBRARIES. 2.
SCRIPTURE DISTRIBUTION (1975). Annual totals: 3,860 Bibles (16% free, 84% subsidized), 11,238 NTs (53% free, 47% subsidized), 282 UBS portions, 39 UBS selections. *Translations completed.* Icelandic: NT 1540, Bible 1584.
SERVICE AGENCIES. About 20, including IMS(SIK), KFUK (YWCA), KFUM(YMCA), NEC, SCA, SU, WLC(EHC).

ADDITIONAL DATA ON CHURCHES
CATHOLIC CHURCH. Most Catholics (Rooms-katholieken) live in the 2 parishes in Reykjavík. *Annual baptisms.* 100% infants, no adults. *Priests.* Nationals: secular (first Iceland national since Reformation ordained 1924, bishop 1942). Expatriates: religious (SMM). By 1977 priests had increased to 3 diocesan and 15 religious. *Sisters.* One indigenous, 23 others who have taken citizenship. *Foreign religious congregations* Priests: SMM (Dutch province). Sisters: St-Joseph de Chambéry, Missionary Franciscans of Mary, Carmelites OCD.
*Catholic organizations.* The Nordic or Scandinavian Episcopal Conference (Nordiske Bispekonferense or Conferentia Episcopalis Scandiae) based in Copenhagen, Denmark, is a member of CCEE. A Presbyteral Council and a Pastoral Council have been formed, but no associations of religious personnel exist. Three small groups are engaged in lay activities: Leikmanna-Félag, which is dedicated to deepening religious experience and to assisting priests; Kathólska Kvennafélag, which works with Catholic women; and Félag Kathólska Unglinga, which is a youth organization.
The Holy See had no diplomatic relations with Iceland until 1976, when they were set up with a pro-nuncio in Reykjavík.
The Catholic Church sponsors 2 nursery schools, one primary school, 2 summer camps and 3 hospitals.
NATIONAL CHURCH OF ICELAND. The church is divided into 21 Deaneries. The Icelandic Mission Society works within the church as a home mission, as well as overseas. *Parishes.* Reduced in 1879 from 174 to 142, then in 1907 to 105; now 120, with a total of 288 congregations in 1966 increasing gradually with population increase. *Bishops.* 3 (including 2 suffragans).

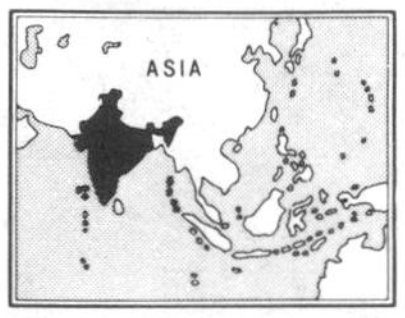


# INDIA

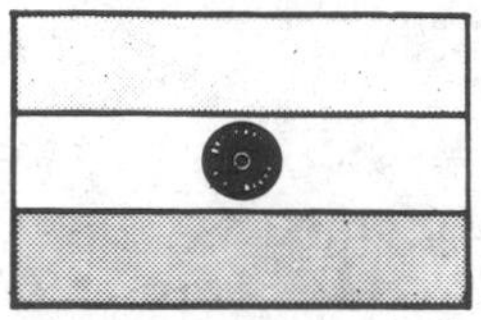

## SECULAR DATA

**STATE. Official name:** The Republic of India (Bharat). Adjective of nationality: Indian.
**Flag** (shown above right): Deep saffron, white, and green stripes, with centred 24-spoke Wheel of Asoka in blue.
**Area:** 3,287,590 sq.km. (1,269,346 sq.miles). Agricultural land: 54.3%.
**Government:** Parliamentary federal republic or union of states, since 1950 (19th century under Britain, 1947 Independence, 1950 republic).
**Legislature:** Parliament: Rajya Sabha (Council of States), 240 members; Lok Sabha (House of the People), 521 members.
**Official languages:** Hindi (Devanagari script) and English. Fourteen others are official in one or more states: Assamese, Bengali, Gujarati, Kannada, Kashmiri, Malayalam, Marathi, Oriya, Punjabi, Sanskrit, Sindhi, Tamil, Telugu, Urdu.
**Chief cities:** capital New Delhi 301,800 (1971), Calcutta 7,031,380, Bombay 5,970,570, Delhi 3,647,020, Madras 3,169,930, Hyderabad 1,796,340.
**Political divisions:** 21 States and 9 Union Territories.
**Armed forces** (1976): Total 1,055,500 regular: army 913,000, navy 42,500, air force 100,000 (950 combat aircraft). Reserves: 240,000. Paramilitary forces: 180,000.
**Foreign forces** (1973): 200 USSR military advisers.
**Dependencies:** Sikkim (claimed as 22nd state of India since 1975).

**DEMOGRAPHY. Population:** 548,159,652 (census of 1.IV.1971. For 1970–2000 (UN), see last row of Table 1). Population density (1975): 187/sq.km. (483/sq.mile). Under 15 years: 41%. Growth rate (1975–80): 2.48% per year (births 3.87%, deaths −1.39%). Life expectancy (1975–80): 52.1 years. Household size: 5.4 persons.
**Major languages:** As listed above under **Official languages.** There are about 1,650 other mother tongues (103 non-Indian).
**Urban dwellers** (1970): 19.7%. Urban growth rate (1950–70): 2.9% per year.
**Labour force:** 33%. Other categories: 10 million nomads, 13 million beggars.
**Refugees** (1977): Over 100,000, including 70,000 Tibetans from China. After Partition in 1947, 18 million fled from Pakistan to India or vice versa. In 1971, 9 million Bengalis fled from East Pakistan.
**Tourists** (1974): 423,161.

**ETHNOLINGUISTIC GROUPS:** 24.0% Hindi (Hindustani), 9.0% Marathi, 8.1% Bengali, 7.9% Telugu, 7.6% Tamil, 5.4% Kanarese, 4.9% Gujarati, 4.7% Rajasthani, 4.5% Urdu, 4.3% Punjabi, 4.0% Oriya, 3.9% Malayali, 3.6% non-tribal Bihari, 2.6% Assamese, 0.8% Santali, 0.8% Kashmiri, 0.6% Gond, 0.5% Bhil, 0.3% Pahari (Kumauni), 0.3% Sindhi, 0.3% Tripuri, 0.2% Oraon, 0.2% Munda, 0.2% Ho, 0.2% Manipuri, 0.2% Goanese (Konkani), 0.1% Mizo (Lushai), 0.1% Gypsy, 0.1% Saora, 0.1% Garo, 0.1% Khasi, 0.1% Naga, European (150,000), Chinese (75,000), Tibetan (120,000), Anglo-Indian, Armenian, Parsi, Jewish, and a large number of smaller peoples.

**MONEY** (1977). **Monetary unit:** rupee (= 100 paisa); US$1 = IRs 8.70.
**National income per person:** US$125. Average annual family income: US$675.
**Inflation:** (1970–74) 13.0% per year (1975: consumer price index 173).
**Cost of living in capital** (1976): index 92 (Washington DC = 100). Daily cost of living: US$32.

**EDUCATION.** Adult literacy: (1951) 19%, (1971) 33%. Education rate: 41%. Schools: (1969) 517,864 (400,210 primary, 117,654 secondary). Universities: 92 (and 101 medical colleges).

**HEALTH.** Hospitals: 15,731 (325,500 beds). Doctors: 112,000. Lepers: 3,200,000 (5.2 per 1,000). Blind (1976): 9,000,000. Psychotics: 3,600,000. Drug addicts: 93,000 (on opium). Criminals: 311,780.

**LITERATURE.** Annual new book titles (1973): 14,064. Periodicals: 7,080. Scientific journals: 670. Newspapers: 793 dailies, 4,053 non-daily.

**COMMUNICATION** (per 1,000 people). Phones: 3. Radios: 23. TV sets: 0.1: Daily newspaper circulation: 16 copies.

TABLE 1. RELIGIOUS ADHERENTS IN INDIA

| Year | 1900 | | mid-1970 | | Annual change, 1970–1980 | | | | mid-1975 | | mid-1980 | | 2000 | |
|---|---|---|---|---|---|---|---|---|---|---|---|---|---|---|
| *Name* | *Adherents* | *%* | *Adherents* | *%* | *Natural* | *Conversion* | *Total* | *Rate* | *Adherents* | *%* | *Adherents* | *%* | *Adherents* | *%* |
| Hindus | 184,022,700 | 80.0 | 433,556,472 | 79.8 | 11,676,965 | −320,262 | 11,356,703 | 2.34 | 486,093,000 | 79.3 | 547,123,500 | 78.8 | 806,366,000 | 76.1 |
| Muslims | 31,552,000 | 13.7 | 60,877,000 | 11.2 | 1,955,800 | 10,500 | 1,966,300 | 2.81 | 69,907,000 | 11.4 | 80,540,000 | 11.6 | 127,131,000 | 12.0 |
| Ahmadis | 40,000 | 0.0 | 90,000 | 0.0 | 2,800 | 1,200 | 4,000 | 3.64 | 110,000 | 0.0 | 130,000 | 0.0 | 300,000 | 0.0 |
| **Christians** | **3,820,200** | **1.7** | **19,231,528** | **3.5** | **610,000** | **174,647** | **784,647** | **3.46** | **22,689,000** | **3.7** | **27,078,000** | **3.9** | **49,793,000** | **4.7** |
| crypto-Christians | 1,150,200 | 0.5 | 5,110,528 | 0.9 | 164,861 | 87,786 | 252,647 | 4.12 | 6,132,000 | 1.0 | 7,637,000 | 1.1 | 15,891,000 | 1.5 |
| professing | 2,670,000 | 1.2 | 14,121,000 | 2.6 | 445,139 | 86,861 | 532,000 | 3.21 | 16,557,000 | 2.7 | 19,441,000 | 2.8 | 33,902,000 | 3.2 |
| Roman Catholics | 1,470,000 | 0.6 | 6,393,000 | 1.2 | 207,017 | 56,283 | 263,300 | 3.42 | 7,700,000 | 1.2 | 9,026,000 | 1.3 | 15,891,000 | 1.5 |
| Protestants | 505,000 | 0.2 | 5,761,000 | 1.1 | 179,243 | 42,457 | 221,700 | 3.33 | 6,667,000 | 1.1 | 7,978,000 | 1.1 | 13,911,000 | 1.3 |
| Orthodox | 220,000 | 0.1 | 1,108,000 | 0.2 | 31,187 | −18,287 | 12,900 | 1.11 | 1,160,000 | 0.2 | 1,237,000 | 0.2 | 1,700,000 | 0.2 |
| Indian indigenous | 60,000 | 0.0 | 859,000 | 0.2 | 27,692 | 6,408 | 34,100 | 3.31 | 1,030,000 | 0.2 | 1,200,000 | 0.2 | 2,400,000 | 0.2 |
| Anglicans | 415,000 | 0.2 | 0 | 0.0 | 0 | 0 | 0 | 0.00 | 0 | 0.0 | 0 | 0.0 | 0 | 0.0 |
| affiliated | 3,820,200 | 1.7 | 19,231,528 | 3.5 | 610,000 | 174,647 | 784,647 | 3.46 | 22,689,000 | 3.7 | 27,078,000 | 3.9 | 49,793,000 | 4.7 |
| total practising | 3,438,180 | *90* | 16,346,800 | *85* | 518,499 | 148,451 | 666,950 | 3.46 | 19,285,600 | *85* | 23,016,200 | *85* | 39,834,000 | *80* |
| non-practising | 382,020 | *10* | 2,884,730 | *15* | 91,501 | 26,196 | 117,697 | 3.46 | 3,403,400 | *15* | 4,061,700 | *15* | 9,959,000 | *20* |
| Roman Catholics | 1,920,000 | 0.8 | 8,469,075 | 1.6 | 271,541 | 61,852 | 333,393 | 3.30 | 10,100,000 | 1.6 | 11,803,000 | 1.7 | 21,100,000 | 2.0 |
| Catholic pentecostals | 0 | 0.0 | 2,000 | 0.0 | 807 | 8,993 | 9,800 | 32.67 | 30,000 | 0.0 | 100,000 | 0.0 | 500,000 | 0.0 |
| Protestants | 650,000 | 0.3 | 7,431,091 | 1.4 | 237,254 | 116,297 | 353,551 | 4.01 | 8,824,700 | 1.4 | 10,966,600 | 1.6 | 20,015,000 | 1.9 |
| Evangelicals | 500,000 | 0.2 | 2,172,000 | 0.4 | 82,433 | 116,957 | 199,390 | 6.50 | 3,066,100 | 0.5 | 4,165,900 | 0.6 | 10,594,000 | 1.0 |
| Neo-pentecostals | 0 | 0.0 | 1,000 | 0.0 | 538 | 5,362 | 5,900 | 29.50 | 20,000 | 0.0 | 60,000 | 0.0 | 300,000 | 0.0 |
| Indian indigenous | 90,000 | 0.0 | 1,857,460 | 0.3 | 59,148 | 20,105 | 79,253 | 3.60 | 2,200,000 | 0.4 | 2,650,000 | 0.4 | 6,357,000 | 0.6 |
| Orthodox | 610,000 | 0.3 | 1,438,100 | 0.3 | 40,866 | −24,076 | 16,790 | 1.10 | 1,520,000 | 0.2 | 1,606,000 | 0.2 | 2,200,000 | 0.2 |
| Catholics (non-Roman) | 0 | 0.0 | 20,000 | 0.0 | 645 | 155 | 800 | 3.33 | 24,000 | 0.0 | 28,000 | 0.0 | 60,000 | 0.0 |
| Marginal Protestants | 200 | 0.0 | 15,552 | 0.0 | 538 | 312 | 850 | 4.25 | 20,000 | 0.0 | 24,050 | 0.0 | 60,000 | 0.0 |
| Anglicans | 550,000 | 0.2 | 250 | 0.0 | 8 | 2 | 10 | 3.33 | 300 | 0.0 | 350 | 0.0 | 1,000 | 0.0 |
| Sikhs | 2,180,000 | 0.9 | 10,287,000 | 1.9 | 330,000 | 29,900 | 359,900 | 3.00 | 12,000,000 | 2.0 | 13,886,000 | 2.0 | 23,307,000 | 2.2 |
| Tribal religionists | 6,670,000 | 2.9 | 9,230,000 | 1.7 | 241,872 | −123,372 | 118,500 | 1.21 | 9,811,000 | 1.6 | 10,415,000 | 1.5 | 11,654,000 | 1.1 |
| Buddhists | 200,000 | 0.1 | 3,779,000 | 0.7 | 113,404 | 64,096 | 177,500 | 3.86 | 4,600,000 | 0.8 | 5,554,000 | 0.8 | 10,594,000 | 1.0 |
| Jains | 1,320,000 | 0.6 | 2,582,000 | 0.5 | 66,000 | −4,200 | 61,800 | 1.99 | 3,100,000 | 0.5 | 3,200,000 | 0.5 | 4,238,000 | 0.4 |
| Non-religious | 10,000 | 0.0 | 2,000,000 | 0.4 | 75,685 | 140,915 | 216,600 | 7.06 | 3,070,000 | 0.5 | 4,166,000 | 0.6 | 21,189,000 | 2.0 |
| Baha'is | 100 | 0.0 | 730,000 | 0.1 | 21,448 | 10,552 | 32,000 | 3.68 | 870,000 | 0.1 | 1,050,000 | 0.2 | 1,900,000 | 0.2 |
| Atheists | 5,000 | 0.0 | 700,000 | 0.1 | 22,188 | 17,812 | 40,000 | 4.44 | 900,000 | 0.1 | 1,100,000 | 0.2 | 3,000,000 | 0.3 |
| Parsis | 93,000 | 0.0 | 90,000 | 0.0 | 2,490 | 10 | 2,500 | 2.45 | 102,000 | 0.0 | 115,000 | 0.0 | 160,000 | 0.0 |
| Chinese folk-religionists | 10,000 | 0.0 | 60,000 | 0.0 | 1,602 | −602 | 1,000 | 1.54 | 65,000 | 0.0 | 70,000 | 0.0 | 80,000 | 0.0 |
| Jews | 17,000 | 0.0 | 9,000 | 0.0 | 246 | 4 | 250 | 2.50 | 10,000 | 0.0 | 11,500 | 0.0 | 17,000 | 0.0 |
| **Country's population** | **229,900,000** | **100.0** | **543,132,000** | **100.0** | **15,117,700** | **0** | **15,117,700** | **2.47** | **613,217,000** | **100.0** | **694,309,000** | **100.0** | **1,059,429,000** | **100.0** |

COLUMNS, ROWS. For meanings and definitions, see Codebook (Part 6). Note that, by definition, total 'Christians' = professing + crypto-Christians, which also = affiliated + nominal Christians. Percentages may not always total exactly, due to rounding.
CENSUSES. The following censuses for 1881, 1891, 1901 and 1911 refer to the area of the present India, Pakistan, Bangladesh and Burma. The figures for 1900 in the table above have therefore been adjusted to cover the 1975 boundaries of India only. **1881:** 74.3% Hindus, 19.7% Muslims, 2.6% tribal religionists, 1.4% Buddhists, 0.7% Christians, 0.7% Sikhs, 0.5% Jains. **1891:** 72.3% Hindus, 20.0% Muslims, 3.2% tribal religionists, 2.5% Buddhists, 0.8% Christians, 0.7% Sikhs, 0.5% Jains. **1.III.1901:** 70.4% Hindus, 21.2% Muslims, 3.2% Buddhists, 2.9% tribal religionists, 1.0% Christians (1,524,755 Roman Catholics, 453,462 Anglicans, 250,450 Orthodox, 221,040 Baptists, 155,455 Lutherans, et alii), 0.7% Sikhs, 0.4% Jains. **1911:** 69.4% Hindus, 21.2% Muslims, 3.4% Buddhists, 3.3% tribal religionists, 1.2% Christians (1,904,005 Roman Catholics, 492,752 Anglicans, 337,226 Baptists, 240,789 Orthodox, 218,500 Lutherans, et alii), 1.0% Sikhs, 0.4% Jains. **1921** (India only): 84.4% Hindus, 9.6% Muslims, 3.3% tribal religionists, 1.8% Christians, 0.5% Jains, 0.4% Sikhs. **26.II.1931** (India excluding Assam, West Bengal and Punjab): 84.3% Hindus, 9.9% Muslims, 2.7% tribal religionists, 2.1% Christians, 0.5% Jains, 0.5% Sikhs. **1941** (with race/caste/tribe definition of religion): 63.3% Hindus (1.4% scheduled castes), 12.6% Muslims, 7.9% tribal religionists, 1.8% Christians, 1.3% Sikhs, 0.5% Jains. **1.III.1951** (de jure; excluding Kashmir-Jammu and Assam tribal areas): 85.0% Hindus, 9.9% Muslims, 2.3% Christians, 1.7% Sikhs, 0.5% Jains, 0.5% tribal religionists, 0.1% Buddhists. **1.III.1961:** 83.5% Hindus, 10.7% Muslims, 2.4% Christians, 1.8% Sikhs, 0.7% Buddhists, 0.5% Jains, 0.3% tribal religionists. **1.IV.1971:** 82.7% Hindus (including Hindu crypto-Christians and many tribal animists), 11.2% Muslims, 2.6% Christians, 1.9% Sikhs, 0.7% Buddhists, 0.5% Jains, 0.4% tribal religionists. *Notes.* (1) The definition of 'tribal religionists' has varied considerably from census to census, often covering only a part of the animistic population. (2) All figures for Hindus in these censuses include the persons this survey is calling crypto-Christians, and also many tribals who are in fact still animists.

NOTES ON RELIGIONS
AHMADIS. A messianic schism from Shia Islam, the movement was founded in 1889 and had its headquarters in Qadian, Punjab, until forced to emigrate to Pakistan in 1947. Ahmadis in India are Qadianis, and are strongest in Kashmir and Bihar.
ANGLICANS. In the year 1900, Anglicans were 67% Indians, 25% Europeans, 8% Eurasians (Anglo-Indians). The Anglican Church (CIPBC) remained a major denomination until its merger in the CSI in South India (1947) and in the CNI in North India (1970), united churches here classified as Protestant. Thereafter there were no specifically Anglican churches in India except for the miniscule Reformed Episcopal Church.
ATHEISTS. Three rival parties since 1964 split: Communist Party of India (CPI) (pro-Soviet, 90,000), Communist Party of India/Marxist (CPM) (pro-Chinese, 75,000), Communist Party of India/Marxist-Leninist (Naxalites): total membership (1970) 175,000; Communist voters (election of 1.III.1971) 14,531,978 (10% of all votes). Most party members are atheists, though anti-religious persons opposed to all religion are not numerous. Communist voters are mainly in Kerala and Bengal, with little or no atheistic connotation. In Kerala, the Communist vote is related to 2 Malayalam-speaking castes, Pulayas and Ezhavas, both regarded as outcaste by Hindus.
BAHA'IS. Origins in India began around 1860. Until 1960 most

Baha'is in India were Persians. In 1961, when there were only 850 Baha'is, mass conversions began; by 1963, there were 65,355 Baha'is with 10,000 adult converts a month. Very rapid growth then took place from 1,064 local spiritual assemblies (1964) to 4,869 (1973), with 17,034 other isolated centres or groups (1973). From 1964–73, 157,000 converts were enrolled. Radio, TV, press and correspondence courses are widely used.

BUDDHISTS. After flourishing in India from the 6th century BC to the 6th century AD, Buddhism declined in India and was eventually finally extinguished by Islam in the 12th century. In 1956, the neo-Buddhist movement began, leading to the conversion to Buddhism of over 3 million Mahars and other Harijans (scheduled-caste Hindus) over 5 years. Subsequently, large numbers have been converted back to Hinduism by the Arya Samaj. The Maha Bodhi Society of Ceylon has developed centres throughout India to spread the Buddhist religion. In the 1970s Harijan leaders have been claiming that Harijan converts are vastly more numerous than those professing to be Buddhists in the census; thus they claim 7 million in 1961 and 20 million by 1973. In 1970 also there were about 100,000 Tibetans and 10,000 Chinese Buddhists (Mahayana), also Burmese.

CATHOLIC PENTECOSTALS (or, Catholic charismatics). Totals (January 1974): 8,000 involved adults (over 15 years old) in over 50 prayer groups; total charismatic community including children, 16,000. In 1974, 4,000 attended a rally led by Catholic charismatic evangelists in Bombay. The renewal has subsequently mushroomed across India, especially in the south. By 1976, prayer groups numbered 200, mostly English-speaking. In October 1976, 3,400 attended the Second All-India Charismatic Convention sponsored by several Catholic bishops.

COUNTRY'S POPULATION. Immediately after Partition in 1947, about 7 million Muslims fled from homes in India to Pakistan, with a further 2 million following over the 2 subsequent decades; and about the same number of non-Muslims fled from Pakistan to India. Some 7% (1.1 million) were massacred or starved to death en route. This was the greatest population transfer in history.

CRYPTO-CHRISTIANS. At every government census since before 1900 the number of Christians enumerated (here termed professing Christians) has been considerably less than the aggregate of Christians reported then by the churches (here termed affiliated Christians). These affiliated Christians unknown to the state (here termed crypto-Christians) are of 3 distinct kinds. (1) The great majority have been, and continue to be, Christians who are scheduled-caste persons (formerly, outcastes) regarded as Hindus by society and state. If such backward-class persons declare themselves to be Christians, they lose their scheduled-caste status and privileges (education, employment quotas in government, university places, etc). (2) A substantial minority however are high-caste Hindus, mostly unorganized individuals belonging to known and recognized Christian churches. Since 1887 and the formation of the Calcutta Christo Samaj, there have also been a number of organized movements of believers in Christ who regard themselves, corporately as well as individually, as still Hindus. Of these Hindu-Christian movements, the largest is the Subba Rao movement which rejects Christian baptism (see Table 2). (3) Since 1952, a completely new type of crypto-Christian has arisen all over India, namely isolated radio believers unrelated to existing denominations (see Table 2, and methodology in Part 3).

HINDUS. (1961) 82.4% high-caste and other caste (totalling over 26,000 castes in the 4 categories of Vedic theory: Brahman (1,886 castes), Ksatriya (warriors), Vaisya (merchants), Sudra (servants)), 17.6% Scheduled Caste (formerly, Outcastes, Untouchables, or (Gandhi's term) Harijans (Children of God); in 1975 totalling 83 million). Scheduled Castes can only be Hindus or Sikhs (clause 3 of constitution (Scheduled Castes) Order, 1950); in 1961 they were 98.6% Hindus, 1.4% Sikhs. There are hundreds of Hindu sects, of 3 main types. (A) 0.5% of all Hindus belong to intellectual reform movements opposed to polytheism and idol-worship: Arya Samaj (92,419 in 1901, 243,445 in 1911), which rejects belief in incarnations of gods, Shankar Acharya (Vedanta Hinduism), and the Ramakrishna Mission, all of whom claim to be converting large numbers of non-Hindus back to Hinduism. The Ramakrishna Mission has 150 centres in over 12 countries (126 in India). (B) 98% of all Hindus, popularly called idol-worshippers or Sanatanists (Sanskrit: Old Ways), believe in incarnations of gods and are either (a) Shaivites (followers of Siva), predominant in south India (AP, Kerala, Tamil Nadu, also West Bengal), or (b) Vaishnavites (followers of Vishnu), predominant in all other states, especially in western, northern, eastern India and Assam, or (c) Saktas, worshippers of the divine mother, Sakti, female aspect of the deity. As well as organized priesthoods with 9 million priests, these 3 groupings have also produced around 15 million sadhus (holy beggars) at the present time. (C) Lastly, there are many newer sects and neo-Hindu movements. Among the largest are (1) the Divine Light Mission, a Vedantist movement first spread in north India in the 1920s, organized and founded in 1960, and now of Europeanized type centred on devotion to the internationally-known Guru Maharaj Ji (born 1958); 5 million followers in India are claimed; (2) Ananda Marga (Path of Bliss), a violent politico-religious Bengali sect with 2.5 million converts in India and a network of branches in 30 countries; (3) 50,000 followers of Sri Aurobindo (died 1950) and the divine mother (died 1973) at the international city-state of Auroville (Pondicherry) with 1,800 devotees in India's largest ashram and hundreds of action centres throughout India, with centres in 23 other countries also; (4) the Theosophical Society, a neo-Hindu movement with marked Hindu influences, begun in 1875 in New York (USA), moved to India, with in 1912 a Hindu youth Krishnamurti proclaimed Supreme World Teacher, in 1975 with 34,357 members in 1,227 Lodges in 63 countries across the world (in India, 9,263 members in 480 Lodges) and headquarters in Adyar, Madras; and (5) the Self-Realization Fellowship (in India known as the Yogoda Satsang) begun in the USA in 1920 and now with 150 centres on 4 continents. *Conversions.* Many Hindu women marry non-Hindus and take their spouses' religion. A number of conversions to Baha'i, Sikhism, Buddhism and Christianity take place every year; the Arya Samaj claims to be winning back to Hinduism large numbers of such converts. *Fertility.* The major reason for the gradual proportionate decline of the Hindu community over the last 100 years is markedly lower fertility due to the prohibition of widow remarriage. *Pilgrims.* Pilgrimages to shrines (in Sanskrit, *tirthayatra*) play a major role in Hindu practice, and increasing millions of pilgrims visit the 7 holy cities of Varanasi (Benares), Ayodhya (UP), Mathura (UP), Dvaraka (Gujarat), Kanchipuram (Tamil Nadu), Hardwar (UP), and Ujjain (MP); the sources or confluences of the 7 sacred rivers; and the 4 great abodes of the gods, Badrinath in the north, Dvaraka in the west, Rameswaram in the south, and Puri in the east. The largest religious mass festival in the world is the 43-day bathing festival Kumbh Mela, held every 12 years at the confluence of the Ganges and the Jumna near Allahabad, with over 10 million pilgrims in January-February 1977.

INDIAN INDIGENOUS. In about 85 denominations in 1970 (see Table 2).

JAINS. In 3 sects: Digambaras, Svetambaras, Sthanakyasis. Largely in Gujarat and Rajasthan. Since 1880 Jains have declined proportionately due to low fertility, itself due to the taboo on widow remarriage.

JEWS. 2,000 Cochin Jews from Kerala: and Bney Israel in Bombay province (5,500 in 1850), who are Marathi-speaking.

MUSLIMS. About 65% Sunnis (of the Hanafite and Shafiite rites), and 35% Shias mostly in Uttar Pardesh (Ithna-Asharis, Ismailis (Bombay), Bohoras); also Ahmadis (enumerated here under Muslims though declared non-Muslim by Pakistan). The disputed territory of Kashmir is 78% Muslim. *Proportional increase.* Since 1881 the Muslim community has increased faster than the total population increase, due to higher Muslim than Hindu fertility, itself due to greater Muslim tolerance of widow remarriage. *Hajj pilgrims to Mecca.* (1968) 15,826; (1969) 16,057; (1970) 16,470; (1971) 16,657; (1972) 18,306; (1973) 19,879; (1974) 21,874; (1975) 18,863; (1976) 17,510.

NEO-PENTECOSTALS. Charismatics in organized groups within the non-Pentecostal Protestant denominations, mainly the CSI (5 dioceses), CNI, Lutherans, Baptists and Christian Brethren, and especially in the Madras area. There are young Jesus Movement adherents in several areas, including a few communes in Goa.

PARSIS. Zoroastrians, Gujarati-speaking; originally refugees from Persia in the 8th century AD; mainly in Bombay. Since 1900 they have been declining proportionately to the total population, due to their very low marital fertility.

PRACTISING CHRISTIANS. *Pilgrims.* Among the large number of Catholic pilgrimage centres is the 16th-century shrine at Velankanni ('The Lourdes of India'), 270 miles south of Madras which attracts pilgrims all the year round and 500,000 (many being non-Christians) during the Feast of the Nativity of Our Lady (28 August–8 September). Another centre is Old Goa, where 600,000 venerated the body of St Francis Xavier from 23 November 1974 for 6 weeks.

PROFESSING CHRISTIANS. In the year 1900, Christians were 91% Indians, 6% Europeans, and 3% Anglo-Indians.

SIKHS. Sects: Akali, Nanapanthi, Udasi, Khalsa, Nirmali, Sewapanthi. The Namdharis and Nirankaris are groups worshipping living Gurus. At Partition in 1947, the 2.5 million Sikhs living in Pakistan were either compelled to flee to India or all massacred. *Conversions.* Although up to the early part of the 20th century converts from Hinduism were still numerous due to the Akali proselytizing movement among depressed classes, by the 1970s the rate of lapsing back to Hinduism had become appreciable. However, numbers of Hindu women in the Punjab (which is 60% Sikh) were still becoming Sikhs through marriage, and in addition a number of full-time Sikh missionaries were active including some posted to international airports at New Delhi and elsewhere. *Fertility.* A major reason for the rapid proportionate growth of the Sikh community since 1880 is that Sikhs, being the most rural of the major religions, and tolerating widow remarriage, have a higher fertility than Hindus and also a lower mortality.

TRIBAL RELIGIONISTS. This term refers to animists among the Aboriginal and tribal peoples including hill tribes. The total tribal population of India was 22,615,708 (6.7%) in 1931, rising in 1941 to 25,441,489 (7.9%), of whom 8,775,000 (2.26% of the total population) were animists, in 1961 to (scheduled tribes) 29,883,470 (6.8%), and by 1970 to about 38 million (7.0%). The proportion of animists (tribal religionists) to total population increased slightly from 2.6% in 1881, to 2.9% in 1901, and to 3.2% in 1911; and has since declined slowly from 3.0% in 1921 to 2.7% (7,630,000) in 1931. Before 1941, government census reports termed these persons animists; in 1941 the category was dropped and all tribals (7.9% of the population) were classed as tribals irrespective of religion. From 1951 large numbers of these animists were henceforth for political reasons enumerated as Hindus. Various analysts from Kingsley Davis (1951) onwards have shown however that tribal religion has persisted remarkably, numerically, over the decades, despite consistent and widespread underenumeration, and hence this category can be estimated to have declined only slightly to 1.7% of the population by 1970. In the 1971 census, the category 'Other religions and persuasions' (2,184,556 persons) covered only a quarter of these animists, namely those who refused to allow themselves to be classified as Hindus. These formed 63.5% of the entire population in Arunachel Pradesh, 31.5% of Meghalaya, 20.9% of Nagaland, 7.8% of Manipur, and 1.8% of Bihar. Among the larger tribes in India either predominantly-animist, or with large numbers of animists, are the Gond (3 million), Santal (20% animist), Bhil, Oraon (20% animist), Kond (900,000), Munda (20% animist), Ho (still 70% animist), Korku (250,000), and Kaipeng-Koloi (200,000). *Conversions.* There is in 1979 a steady number of animists each year who are either hinduized, i.e. assimilated into Hinduism (the more numerous), or converted to Christianity (less numerous). Conversions to Islam are almost non-existent. Several tribes have been completely christianized during the 20th century: thus the Mizo (Lushai), numbering 300,000 now, were all animists when the first missionary arrived in 1891; in the 1901 census, only 45 Mizo were Christians, but by 1975 all were Christians with not a single known Mizo animist remaining.

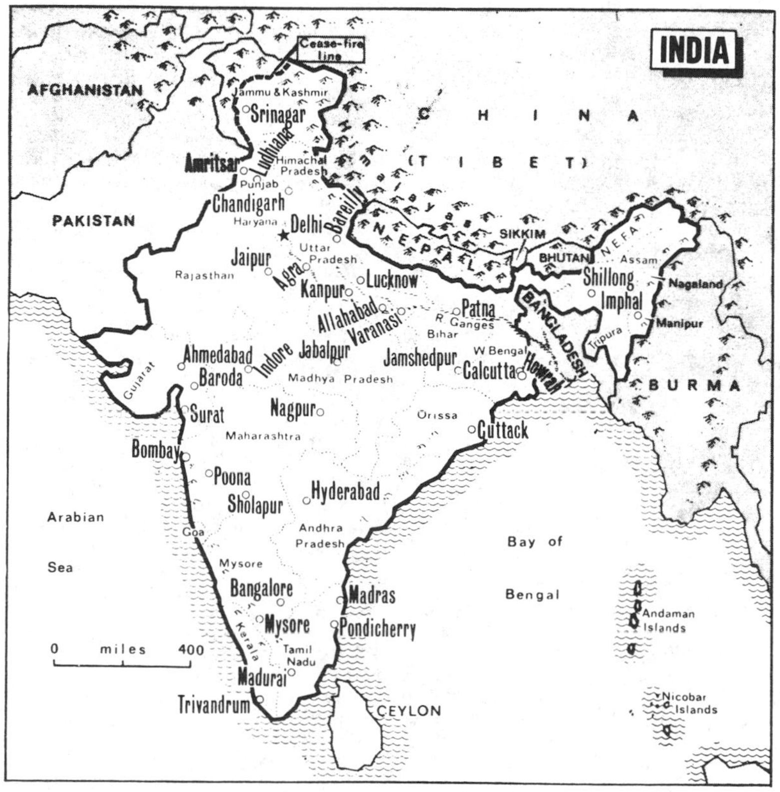


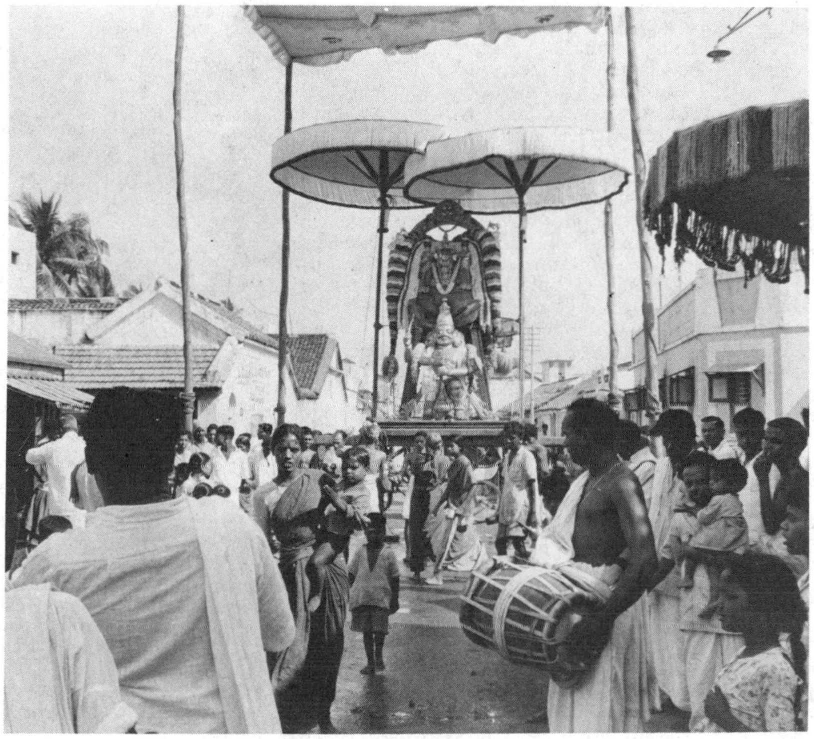

**Hindus.** Festival of god Subrahmanya (with, behind his statue, his 2 wives, Lord Shiva and his sacred bull Nandi) in Saidapet district, Madras.

**NON-CHRISTIAN RELIGIONS. Hinduism** is the principal religion of India, having developed over the past 5 millenia through a series of definite periods each with its own distinctive emphases: Vedic, Brahmanic, Philosophic, Devotional and Reformed Hinduism. Strongly influenced by both Islam and Christianity, the principal reform movements have been the Brahmo Samaj (1828), Arya Samaj (Assembly of Noble Men, 1875), Ramakrishna Mission (1886) and Servants of India. Unifying factors are esteem for the Vedas; the ideas of Karma, reincarnation and

(Kerala). The Arya Samaj also claims many reconversions of Christians in Assam, Orissa and central India, and to have won back a large number of outcaste Hindus who converted to neo-Buddhism in 1956 under their leader Ambedkar. The Divine Light Mission claims 5 million followers in India including many former nominal Indian Christians and also European and American youth; Auroville and other neo-Hindu centres also have many Western converts; and Ananda Marga claims 2.5 million converts in India and a network of branches in 30

(4) Gandhi Smarak Sangrahalaya, in Ahmedabad and New Delhi, which promotes the Gandhi heritage; and (5) Banaras Hindu University, in Varanasi (Banaras), which has a faculty of oriental learning and theology.

**Islam** is the second largest religion and has been active in India since the 8th century AD. Virtually the whole gamut of Muslim sects are found on the sub-continent. The principal Sunni law schools are the Hanafite and Shafiite; and Shias are represented in their Ithna-Ashari, Ismaili Khoja and Bohora branches, the Dawoodi Bohoras having their headquarters in Bombay. The Ahmadiya Movement in Islam, which began in Lahore in 1890 and is considered heretical by other Muslims, is also numerous. India has been noted for its reform movements going back to the Moghul emperor Akbar in the 16th century. Among the early reformers were Shakykh Ahmad Sirhindi Shah Wali Allah of Delhi, Sayyid Ahmad and Hajji Shariat Allah; while more recent influential thinkers have been Jamal al-Din al-Afghani, Muhammed Abduh, Sayyid Ahmad Khan, Sayyid Amir Ali and Muhammad Iqbal.

At Partition in 1947, the proportion of Muslims in India fell drastically due to the violent exchange of population with Pakistan; it has since increased gradually, from 9.9% in 1951 to 10.7% in 1961 and to 11.2% in 1971. After the serious rioting and massacres between Hindus and Muslims at Partition, communal riots against Muslims have erupted periodically especially in northwestern cities. Conversions both to and from Hinduism have taken place; the Arya Samaj claims converts from Islam, and Ahmadiya attempts conversions to Islam.

The principal Muslim organizations in India are: (1) Muslim Community of India (Jamaate Islami Al-Hind), in Delhi, which is the most important co-ordinating body for Indian Islam; (2) Islam and Modern Age Society, in New Delhi, whose aim is to reinterpret Islam in the light of modern needs; (3) Indian Institute of Islamic Studies, in New Delhi, which has a large library and engages in research; (4) Darul-Musannifin, in Azamgarh, UP, which is a research centre dealing mostly with Arabic and Persian sources; (5) Islamic Research Association founded in Bombay in 1933, which publishes research on Islam; and (6) Aligarh Muslim University, which has a faculty of theology and also sponsors the Islamic Research Circle.

**Hindus.** Largest mass gathering in world: 10 million pilgrims at 12-yearly 43-day Kumbh Mela ritual bathing festival seeking salvation at confluence of Ganges and Jumna, Allahabad, in January 1977.

non-violence *(ahimsa)*; respect for the holy man *(sanyasi)*; and the acceptance of caste as the socio-religious framework of society. The Hindu proportion of the population has decreased gradually over the last century by on average 1% every 10 years, due to the influx and growth of immigrant religions and also to Muslim fertility being higher than that of the Hindu population.

Hinduism is divided into hundreds of sects centering on various deities (totalling 3 million in number), which can be classified under 3 heads. (1) About 0.5% of Hindus belong to the more intellectual reform movements opposed to polytheism and idol worship which reject belief in incarnations of gods; these include Arya Samaj, Shankar Acharya (Vedanta Hinduism), and the Ramakrishna Mission (and also Sikhism). (2) The vast majority of 98%, popularly called Sanatanists or idol-worshippers, believe in incarnations of gods and are either Shaivites (followers of Siva, the goddess Kali and other deities), or, by far the larger number, Vaishnavites (followers of Vishnu, Ram, Krishna and other deities). There are also Saktas, worshippers of the divine mother Sakti, female aspect of the deity. Shaivites predominate in South India, whereas Vaishnavites predominate in western and northern India, the east (Bihar, Orissa) and Assam. (3) Lastly, there are many newer sects several of which have spread abroad to the Western world. These include the Divine Light Mission, a Vedantist movement first spread in north India in the 1920s, organized and founded in 1960, and now of Europeanized type centred on devotion to the internationally-known Guru Maharaj Ji (born 1958); Ananda Marga (Path of Bliss), a violent politico-religious Bengali sect; followers of Sri Aurobindo, Sri Chinmoy, et alii.

Although traditionally Hinduism has not been a missionary religion, the reform movements and newer sects have been active in proselytism and conversion. In South India, Shankar Acharya followers have recently converted 4,000 Christians back to Hinduism at Rameshwaram, Madras; and they have other conversion centres at Ujjain (MP), Jaganath Puri, Kedarnadh (UP), Badrinath (Kashmir), and Shringeri

**Sikhs.** Golden Temple (Harimandir, or Darbar Sahib), Amritsar, chief gurdwara (house of worship) of Sikhs and their most important pilgrimage centre. Built in 1604, it stands in amrit-sar ('pool of nectar') tank of water approached on west by marble causeway.

countries abroad.

Among the principal orthodox Hindu organizations in India are: (1) Bharat Sevak Samaj, founded by Pandit Nehru in New Delhi in 1952, which works in the social field (famine relief, housing reconstruction, schools) irrespective of caste and community, acts as liaison between the needs of people and governmental agencies, and fosters interreligious co-operation; (2) Bharatiya Vidya Bhavan, in Bombay, whose aims are cultural and religious; (3) Ramakrishna Institute of Culture, in Calcutta, which works in the field of religion and culture;

**Sikhism** owes its origin to Guru (teacher) Nanak (AD 1469–1538) who was a follower of the poet Kabri. Although a Hindu by birth, Nanak was influenced by the Islam of his native Lahore. He repudiated caste, found little help in the Hindu scriptures, refused to accept the Brahman priesthood, and emphasized the oneness of God. On the other hand he continued the Hindu belief in Karma and reincarnation and taught release through *bhakti*, the way of faith or devotion. Arjun, the fifth Guru, was responsible for the compilation of the Granth, the Sikh scriptures, which consist of the songs of Nanak, Kabri and others; and the tenth Guru declared that thereafter the Granth should be their Guru. Sikhism, which is therefore a reform movement out of Hinduism, has its centre in Amritsar where the Golden Temple has been built. Sikhs grew from 4,335,771 in 1931 to 6,219,134 (1.74%) in 1951, 7,845,915 (1.79%) in 1961, and 10,378,797 (1.90%) in 1971.

**Traditional religions,** collectively described as animism, continue to exist among India's 40 million tribal peoples, and are particularly strong among hill tribesmen especially in Assam. Tribal religionists have been consistently underenumerated in recent government censuses (as described below Table 1), but the fact is that numerically they have persisted remarkably since 1880 despite the inroads of Hindu proselytism and the constant pressure towards detribalization and acculturation with rural and urban Hindu society. From being 2.6% of the total population in 1881, animists increased slightly to 2.7% in 1931; but this proportion then declined gradually to 1.7% by 1970 largely due to mass conversions to Christianity. Their total in absolute numbers has however increased meanwhile, from 6.7 million in 1900 to 9.2 million in 1970.

Tribal religions are particularly widely followed by a number of tribes of Aboriginal peoples: the Naga people of western India, who have an elaborate ancestral cult using megalithic monuments and elaborate ceremonies for their 5 rites of passage; the Kandyans of Bengal, who formerly made human sacrifice to Tari Pennu, old Mother Earth, at the planting season; and the pastoral Toda of Nilgiris

**Buddhists.** The Dalai Lama, exiled god-king of Tibet, officiates at conversion of 2,000 Hindu Untouchables to Buddhism at Ram Lila Maidan, New Delhi, on 11 March 1973.

whose religions are centred in their cattle and sacred milk houses. Among the Birhors of Chota Nagpur, both ancestral spirits (Haprom) and clan divinities (Buru-Bongas or Ora-Bongas) are venerated, and the mother goddesses Devi Mai and Bushi Mai are appealed to in times of severe illness, barrenness or famine. Also recognized is the existence of a supreme being, Singabonga, who is creator but takes little interest in men. Although virtually devoid of witchcraft beliefs, the Birhors place great reliance on the powers of the diviner-medicine man *(mati)* who is adept at offering sacrifices and exorcizing evil spirits. Other traditionalist Indian peoples include the Bhils, Garo, Ho, Kaipeng-Koloi, Khasi, Kolam, Kond, Korku and Santal. Most are rapidly becoming hinduized.

**Buddhism** began in India where its founder, Gautama Buddha (BC 560–480), lived out his life; and it enjoyed great prestige for a thousand years thereafter under outstanding emperors including Asoka, Kanishka, Chandragupta II and Harsha. Between the 3rd and 1st centuries BC, Mahayana Buddhism took form in northwestern India, from which it later spread to China and Japan. By the 7th century AD Indian Buddhism began to decline, sparked by internal rivalries, the resurgence of Hinduism and the later arrival of Islam. The virtual eclipse of Buddhism in India continued until 1956 when the neo-Buddhist movement, led by the untouchables' leader B. R. Ambedkar, swept across the country resulting in the conversion of over 3 million scheduled-caste Hindus to Buddhism in a period of 5 years. This movement began in Maharashtra, and spread from UP to Mysore and Madras states, where it rejuvenated a 1909 Buddhist movement. The major tribes affected were the Mahars, Jatavs or Chamars, and leather workers in UP, Punjab, Jammu and Kashmir. This dramatic growth in the 1950s is evident in the census figures, rising from 180,828 Buddhists (0.05% of the population) in 1951 to 3,250,227 (0.74%) in 1961. However, momentum has not been maintained over the past decade, and in the 1971 census the proportion of Buddhists had dropped slightly to 0.70% (3,812,325 persons). In several areas large numbers have been reconverted back to Hinduism by the Arya Samaj, and in Kolhapur (southeast of Bombay) 12,000 neo-Buddhists asked the Church of North India for Christian baptism in 1971.

**Jainism** is a Hindu reform movement dating back to the 6th century BC. Its founder, Mahavira (BC 599–527), better known as the Great Hero, was the last of the 24 Tirthankaras, those who obtained salvation *(moksha)* through self-abnegation. Jains emphasize asceticism, the Three Jewels (knowledge, faith and right conduct), non-violence *(ahimsa)* and a modified view of transmigration from that prevalent among Hindus. Jains have some of India's most beautiful temples. The Jain community declined numerically from 1,378,596 in 1891 to 1,178,596 in 1921, then increased to 1,252,105 in 1931, 0.45% in 1951, 0.46% in 1961 and 2,604,646 (0.50%) in 1971.

**Baha'i** has had in India its most spectacular successes in any country, numerically. Baha'i was introduced into India from Persia around 1860, and until 1960 most Baha'is in India (850 in 1961) were Persians. In that year, however, mass conversion of Indian Hindus began. By 1963, 10,000 adult converts a month were being claimed. There has subsequently been very rapid expansion from 1,064 local spiritual assemblies in 1964 to 4,869 assemblies with 17,034 other isolated centres and groups by 1973, the largest Baha'i community of any country in the world.

**Other religions** are numerous, including Parsiism (90,000) descended from the ancient Zoroastrianism of Persia and found mainly in Bombay, and a number of smaller new syncretistic religions mostly of Hindu background. There are also 9,000 Jews (Cochin Jews, and Bney Israel in Bombay) and a large growing number of atheists and non-religious persons.

**CHRISTIANITY.** According to Malabar tradition, Christianity was introduced into India by the Apostle Thomas in AD 52. By 200, the Orthodox tradition is considered to have been established in the south. A bishop is known to have been sent from Jerusalem to India in AD 345, and a traveller in 530 reported Christian communities in the southwest and in Ceylon. The Franciscan, John of Monte Corvino, spent a year in Malabar prior to going on to China in 1294, and in 1498 Vasco da Gama claimed India for the Portuguese monarchy.

In 1514 pope Leo X accorded to the kings of Portugal the right of patronage, the development of missions in Asia; and the diocese of Goa was established in 1533. Francis Xavier arrived in India in 1542, and in subsequent years the Jesuits worked for the conversion to Catholicism of both non-Christians and the Orthodox. Although the Thomas Christians at one point affirmed their allegiance to Rome, in 1653 a sizeable number declared their autonomy.

During the first half of the 17th century, the Jesuit Robert de Nobili developed the missionary method of 'adaptation' to Indian life as a way of winning high-caste Brahmins to Catholicism, but the rites controversy which this provoked proved to be a serious blow to Catholic outreach in subsequent years.

From 1612 onwards, Anglican clergy served in India as chaplains under the East India Company. Although occasional converts were made in the early days, the policy of the company was opposed to missionary activities.

Protestant missions began in 1706 with the arrival of the Danish-Halle Lutherans, B. Ziegenbalg and H. Plutschau, at Tranquebar on the coast of Coromandel, which at that time was under Danish control; and by 1800 a Christian community of 20,000 had been formed. In 1793 the BMS missionary William Carey arrived at Serampore and the modern era of Protestant missions began. He was soon followed by other British missionaries, those of the LMS in 1798, CMS in 1813, Methodists in 1819 and Scottish Presbyterians in 1823. American missionaries were also active during this period: Congregationalist (American Board) in 1810, Presbyterians in 1834, Baptists in 1836, Lutherans in the 1840s and Methodists in 1856. The German Gossner Mission sent missionaries to India as early as 1839, and the first Scandinavian Lutherans arrived in 1867.

The numerical growth of professing Christians over the last century has been remarkable: from 1,506,098 in British India in 1881 to 8,392,038 (2.35%) in 1951, 10,728,086 (2.44%) in 1961 and 14,223,382 (2.60%) in 1971.

Christianity is the second largest religious minority, after Islam, but the geographical spread of Christians is very uneven. The faithful are concentrated mostly in the extreme south, where Christianity was first established, and the east, where important minority groups have been converted. The states of Kerala, Tamil Nadu and Andhra Pradesh together account for more than 60% of India's Christians. The following states and territories had in 1971 the highest proportion of Christians in comparison to total population: Nagaland (66.8%); Meghalaya (47.0%); Goa, Daman and Diu (31.8%); Andaman and Nicobar Islands (26.35%); Manipuri (26.03%); and Kerala (21.05%). Kerala has the largest number of denominations in India; but outside Kerala, Christianity is strongest in states and territories with relatively small populations. On the other hand, Christians are extremely scattered in the west (except in the Bombay area) and in the centre and north of the country including the Ganges Valley, areas of high population density. Concerning the nationality of ministers and religious personnel, Indian Christianity is now firmly in the hands of nationals since the government discourages the arrival of new foreign missionaries. According to official statistics published in New Delhi in 1971, the number of professional foreign missionaries known to the government of India diminished by one third between 1968 and 1970 (from 6,420 in 1968 to 4,903 in 1970); in addition, there were in 1973 over a thousand others. All of these, however, amounted to less than 6% of the total of all Indian church workers.

One of the most remarkable examples of the indianization of the church has been in the growth of Christian ashrams. Following the ideal of ancient and modern Hindu ashrams, these aim primarily at being centres for prayer where people may experience union with God in an atmosphere conducive to silence and meditation. Study, research and social work may be carried on but these are subordinate to the main objectives. The role of Christian ashrams in India is to bear witness to the importance of contemplation in the life of the church which is usually associated in the minds of non-Christians with institutions only; to provide a place where all who wish, irrespective of race, caste, religion or nationality, may find a spiritual oasis for meeting God in prayer; to give an example of a wholly Indian life-style, simple and austere, but always welcoming to guests, thus showing non-Christians that Christianity is not necessarily Western; and

**Catholic Church in India.** 'Inasmuch as you did it unto the least of these My brethren, you did it unto Me'. Mother Teresa at her Home for Dying Destitutes, Calcutta.

where possible, to use Indian forms of liturgical worship. In 1973, there were almost 40 Christian ashrams in India, about 30 being Protestant or Anglican, 7 Catholic and 2 ecumenical. These latter 2 are Kirisumala Ashram, founded in 1956 at Vagamon, Kerala, with about 20 monks (mostly Catholics); and Christa Prema Seva Ashram, one of the most noted Christian ashrams in India, in 1973 run by 10 Catholic nuns of the Society of the Sacred Heart and 3 Anglican nuns of the Church of North India, with a programme consisting of common prayer, study of languages, Indian philosophy and culture and dialogue seminars to promote ecumenical and interreligious relations. The most important Catholic ashrams are the Saccidananda Ashram near Tiruchirappally (Tamil Nadu, begun 1950), Shantinavam Ashram near Kulitalai (Tamil Nadu), and the Jyotiniketan Ashram in Kareli, North India.

CATHOLIC CHURCH. The ecclesiastical hierarchy was established in 1558, with the formation of the metropolitan archdiocese of Goa, and was re-established for the whole of India in 1878. The total Catholic population was nearly 8.5 million in 1970 compared to 1.9 million in 1900, 2,606,000 in 1921 and 6,282,000 in 1961. Most Catholics are of the Latin rite, but the Syro-Malabar rite is also strong, and a not insignificant number belong to the Syro-Malankara rite.

Through the impetus given by Vatican II, the Indian Catholic Church has shown a remarkable dynamism in recent years, although the traditional folk-religiosity of the majority of Catholics and the clerical authoritarianism of many priests are still strong realities. A long evolution is still necessary to eradicate the remnants of Western dependence among Catholics of the Latin rite or the ethnic particularity of those of the Syrian rites. Nevertheless, the meeting of the All India Seminar at Bangalore in May 1969, as well as its various extensions, marked a major turning point in Indian Catholic life and its post-conciliar renewal. Created through the initiative of a joint Committee of the Episcopal Conference (CBCI) and the Conference of Religious Personnel (CRI), the All India Seminar was the result of 2 years' preparatory work by a series of regional seminars (diocesan and specialized by subjects), whose results were published in 5 volumes. A seminar of the clergy, with 70% of its delegates elected by their peers, met at Poona in January 1969. The national seminar of 1969 brought together 502 participants, including those invited from foreign churches and observers from other Christian denominations. Six working groups studied the following subjects: spirituality, liturgy and catechesis, evangelization, dialogue with other religions, Indian culture, education, socio-economic activities, civic and political life, means of social communication, leadership, family, work, ecumenism, personnel and resources, medical and social service, and pastoral life. Seen from the standpoint of work accomplished and conclusions adopted, the seminar proved to be a highly important medium for the expression of new ideas concerning the church in India. Among the tendencies which came increasingly to the fore may be mentioned the desire to further the indianization of the liturgy (for the first time, a mass was celebrated officially according to a ritual using certain symbolic gestures with the imprint of Hindu culture), the participation of laity in the organs of the church, a less intransigent attitude concerning birth control, a clearer position regarding social justice, a more open training for clergy and religious personnel, and a greater concern for ecumenism. An important agreement was reached concerning rites guaranteeing unity of jurisdiction and plurality of rites in North India. Moreover, a permanent committee was elected to prepare a constitution for a national pastoral council.

Several important meetings followed the All India Seminar. The first was the All India Christian Consultation on Development, which met in an ecumenical atmosphere in New Delhi in February 1970, with its focus on the idea that integral development necessarily includes institutional and structural changes in society. The idea of distributive justice is central, the church having an essential role in education and an important contribution to make to the urban and rural development of the country. A second meeting was the National Consultation on Evangelization, at Patna in October 1973, which was prepared for by 2 other non-official consultations: the International Theological Conference on Evangelization and Dialogue in Asia, at Nagpur in October 1971, with contemporary mission theology

as its theme; and the Asian Seminar on Religion and Development, at Bangalore in July-August 1973 sponsored by the National Catechetical, Liturgical and Biblical Centre. The Patna consultation included 50 Indians among its 85 participants from 9 Asian countries and centred on methods for analyzing social and religious reality and theological reflection (including liberation theology) concerning these realities. Thus evangelization, liberation and development were closely associated.

The recent development of Indian Catholicism has been accompanied by an important ecumenical rapprochement and new contacts between the religions. In this latter domain, the way had already been prepared by the various Catholic ashrams beginning in 1950.

PROTESTANT CHURCHES. India's principal united churches are the Church of North India and the Church of South India. In 1901, 2 Reformed bodies joined together in the South India United Church, followed by the amalgamation of 2 Congregational groups in the Congregational General Union of South India in 1905. In 1908 these 2 united churches in turn merged to form the United Church of South India, and in 1947 a further union with Anglicans and Methodists created the Church of South India. The church in 1973 consisted of 16 dioceses, with a Christian community exceeding 1.5 million. Merger talks with 5 Lutheran churches are under way towards a united Church of Christ in South India; also with the Methodist Church in Southern Asia, the CNI and the Mar Thoma Syrian Church towards a future Bharath Christian Church.

community of nearly 800,000.

The Salvation Army has made extraordinary progress in India since its arrival from the UK in 1882. Organized into 5 territories, they now have more than 4,000 congregations and a Christian community of half a million.

As with the Baptists, not all Presbyterians entered into the CNI in 1970. The large Presbyterian Church in North East India, with a Christian community of nearly 325,000, continues to maintain its identity as a separate denomination. Consisting of 3 synods, the church maintains its historic links with Welsh Presbyterianism. Negotiations for organic union in a Church of North East India are however under way with the Council of Baptist Churches in North East India and remaining elements of the Church of North India.

Western Pentecostalism has not been as successful in India as in many other parts of the world. The largest group is the United Pentecostal Church, related to the church of the same name in the USA. Two Assemblies of God groups related to the USA and UK denominations are active, as are the Swedish Free Mission, Norwegian Free Mission, Church of God (Full Gospel), and the Church of God of Prophecy.

Other important groups include the Plymouth Brethren, Seventh-day Adventists, Mennonites, Evangelical Congregationalists and Church of God (Anderson). In addition there are nearly 200 smaller Protestant denominations.

Protestants have been heavily involved in education and social service. Protestant churches related to the

**Orthodox Syrian Church of the East, Diocese of Quilon.** Blessing of censer during liturgy by vicar and assistant vicar, in Trivandrum Church.

Church union first came to North Indian in 1924 with the merger of the Presbyterian and Congregational churches. By 1929, 11 different denominations had joined while negotiations continued with other bodies. In 1970 the Anglican, Baptist, Brethren, Disciples, Methodist (British and Australian conferences) and United churches came together to form the Church of North India. Negotiations are still going on regarding merger with the even larger Methodist Church in Southern Asia, related to American Methodism, which if effected would make the CNI comparable in size to the CSI.

Although many Baptists went into the Church of North India in 1970, a larger number remained outside. The Council of Baptist Churches in North East India was (in 1975) the second largest Protestant community in the country; it consists of 4 conventions. Another important Baptist group which refused to enter the CNI in 1970 was the Baptist Church of Mizo District. Baptists in Southern India are found principally in the Convention of Telugu Baptist Churches and the Convention of Baptist Churches in the Northern Circars.

Nine autonomous Lutheran bodies owing their origin to German, Scandinavian and American missionary outreach as early as 1706, came together to form in 1975 the United Evangelical Lutheran Churches in India (UELCI). Spread throughout the country, Lutherans in 1970 had a combined Christian

National Christian Council of India continue to sponsor 316 secondary schools and 53 degree-granting colleges, while Protestant, Orthodox and Mar Thoma Christians are responsible for 279 hospitals and 115 dispensaries, with 23,726 beds. Two renowned Christian medical colleges, Vellore and Ludhiana, have produced thousands of medical graduates. Since the 1920s the churches have also been engaged in rural reconstruction and community development, including road-building, improving agriculture, distributing improved seed and fertilizer, well-drilling, irrigation schemes and education in nutrition. Urban industrial mission is carried on through programmes in Calcutta, Durgapur, Nagpur, Madras, Bangalore, Coimbatore and Alwaye.

Theological colleges of the member churches of the NCCI number over 15, of which the better known are Bishop's College (Calcutta), Leonard Theological College (Jabalpur), Serampore College (Serampore), Tamilnad Theological College (Tirumaraiyur), and the United Theological College at Bangalore. In addition there are 50 other Protestant seminaries.

ORTHODOX CHURCHES. The Orthodox Syrian Church of the East traces its history to the Apostle Thomas and originally maintained spiritual ties with the Nestorians of Mesopotamia. When the Portuguese Catholics arrived in the 16th century, they attempted to convert the Syrians forcibly to Catholicism and actually succeeded in doing so at the Synod of Diamper in 1599. However, in 1653 a group met at Koonen Cross in the Mattancheri churchyard which proclaimed its autonomy and consecrated its own bishop, Mar Thoma I. Although the Church of Rome later recovered nearly two-thirds of these Syriac Malankara-rite Christians, the autonomous Orthodox body succeeded in maintaining its independence. In 1665 Mar Gregorios, an Eastern bishop long sought by the Thomas Christians, arrived in Kerala to take charge of the work. Ironically he was a Monophysite from Diarbekir rather than a Nestorian from Mesopotamia, which accounts for the present christological stance of the church. A major schism from the Syrian Orthodox occurred in the 19th century when the Mar Thoma Syrian Church of Malabar broke off. In spite of the divisions which the church has suffered through the years, largely due to foreign ecclesiastical intervention, the Orthodox Syrian Church of the East has continued to grow numerically though only by natural population increase. Today there are 10 dioceses and a Christian community of nearly 1.5 million.

Other small Orthodox communities include the Chaldean Syrian Church (Nestorian), Armenian Apostolic Church (Gregorian) and Greek Orthodox Church under Constantinople.

INDIGENOUS CHURCHES. A large number of independent indigenous churches begun by Indians have been formed in India, the most important being the Mar Thoma Syrian Church of Malabar. In 1816 the Anglican CMS sent 4 missionaries to assist the Orthodox Syrian Church of the East in the training of its priests. They began a theological school at Kottayam, translated the Bible into Malayalam and became the centre of a reform movements which led to conflict within the church by 1829. At the Mavelikkara Synod in 1836, the missionaries were severed from the church, although they continued to carry on their educational work. The vision of reform affected a significant element within the Orthodox Church, led by a teacher of Syriac at the Kottayam seminary, Abraham Malpan, leading to conflict and ultimately schism. The Mar Thoma Church maintains many Orthodox elements including priestly vestments, ecclesiastical structures and liturgical emphases.

From 1858 began the first of many indigenous attempts to form a Hindu-Christian church affirming faith in Jesus Christ but rejecting Western missionary control and retaining Hindu culture and Indian nationalism. The first bodies to be formed were: 1858, Hindu Church of the Lord Jesus (Tinnevelly); 1868, the proposal for a National Church of Bengal; 1870, Chet Ramis (Punjab); 1880, Church of the New Dispensation (Nava Vidhana, Calcutta); 1886, National Church of Madras; 1887, Calcutta Christo Samaj; and 1893, the proposal for an all-embracing National Church in India. Others followed in 1920, 1921, 1933 (Fellowship of the Followers of Jesus, begun by Kandiswamy Chetti in Madras), and in 1942 the largest still existing in 1975, the Subba Rao movement. Begun among the Telugu in Andhra Pradesh, the latter is strongly opposed to all churches, stresses elements of Hindu culture as well as study of the Bible, is virtually unorganized, and holds massive healing crusades reaching 300,000 people by 1966.

Altogether, from 1858 to 1975 there have been over 150 such indigenous Hindu-Christian movements or churches. Many other modern movements in Hinduism and Neo-Hinduism group together devotees of Jesus who explicitly acknowledge Jesus as their central source of inspiration and message.

Other indigenous movements have been more strictly Christian. The Assemblies (Jehova Shammah) of Brother Bakht Singh, with headquarters in Hyderabad, form one of India's faster-growing denominations. Noted for its large open-air Bible conferences, this completely self-supporting group of churches has spread beyond the borders of India to Africa and the Middle East.

Several splits have occurred within the Church of South India, the first being the London Mission Church composed of LMS Christians who opposed the union scheme in 1947 and kept litigation going for 17 years. In 1966 a schism of Pulaya outcastes from the CSI produced the large CMS Anglican Church of India, and in 1970 dissident Methodists formed the Wesleyan Methodist Church of India.

Among important indigenous pentecostal bodies may be mentioned the Indian Pentecostal Church of God (120,000) begun among the Telugu in 1924, the Pentecostal Church of God of Andhra Pradesh (30,000), the Ceylon Pentecostal Mission (40,000), and the Nagaland Christian Revival Church (40,000).

CHURCH AND STATE. India is a multi-religious state in which 'secularism' means equal protection for all religions and non-interference by the state in purely religious concerns. This philosophy has been expounded in the pronouncements and writings of former chief justice P. B. Gajendragadkar and former attorney-general M. C. Setalvad, and is illustrated in various judgements and legislations as noted below. The following articles of the constitution of 1950 are of note. (1) Article 15: the state may not discriminate against any citizen on the ground of

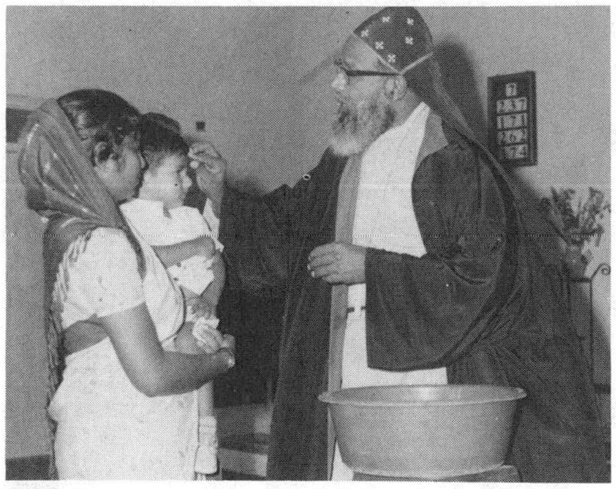

**Mar Thoma Syrian Church of Malabar.** Bishop of Outside Kerala baptizes an infant.

religion only, and no citizen shall be subject to disability in a public context on the ground of religion only. The state may discriminate in favour of socially and educationally backward classes of citizens among whom Christians are found (Article 15, item 4); but in order to extend educational and other preferences to them, the state must not equate 'backwardness' with religion per se nor with caste (documented in the case Harihara vs State, All India Reporter 1968, Kerala 42 Full Bench). (2) Article 25: all persons have 'freedom of conscience and the right freely to profess, practise and propagate religion'. Religion includes practices associated with religion and essential to it (Durgah Committee vs Syed, AIR 1961, Supreme Court 1402, 1415). The right to worship in a particular place and form is a right protected by civil courts (Ujamsingh vs Kesrimal, 1971 1, SCWR9). The freedom thus guaranteed is subject to public order, morality and health, and to other fundamental rights. The state may legislate concerning financial and other secular activities associated with religion and provide for social welfare and reform (Article 25, item 2). (3) Article 26: subject to public order, morality and health, a religious denomination or a section thereof may (a) establish and maintain institutions for religious and charitable purposes, (b) manage its own affairs in matters of religion, (c) own or acquire property, and (d) administer the same in accordance with law. (4) Article 27: no taxes may be levied to assist a particular religion or religious denomination. (5) Article 28: religious instruction is forbidden in schools or colleges wholly maintained out of state funds, unless the state administers a trust originally founded with a requirement of religious instruction. No pupils may be compelled to attend religious instruction in any institutions recognized by the state or receiving funds from it. (6) Article 29: where the state maintains or aids a school or college, no-one may be denied entry on the grounds of religion only. (7) Article 30: minorities (including the churches) may establish and administer educational institutions of their choice. A judicious balance is to be preserved between the state's desire for efficiency within the state's educational framework, and the minorities' desire to manage their institutions on their own principles. On the whole, internal independence is safeguarded (see Bishop Patro vs State, AIR 1970, SC259), but aliens have no right at the present time to set up institutions of their choice. The state aids all recognized educational institutions without discrimination on the ground of religion (Article 30, item 2).

There is no ministry of religious affairs, nor other government department dealing specifically with religion. In the states of Maharashtra and Gujurat all religious and charitable trusts must be registered, in the interests of their own efficiency and security against misappropriation by trustees, with powers of alienation of trust assets controlled significantly by the state (Bombay Public Trusts Act, No 29 of 1950).

Persons promoting feelings of enmity between classes or religious groups are liable to detention (Defence of India Act, No 51 of 1962, Section 3 (5); Defence of India Rules, 1962, R35,6,g). Papers or documents tending to promote feelings of enmity between classes, or to insult religion, may be seized by the state (Criminal Procedure Code, Section 99 A). It is a criminal offence to promote enmity between different groups on the grounds of religion or to prejudice the maintenance of harmony between religious groups (Indian Penal Code, No 45 of 1860, Section 153A as amended by Section 2 of Act 41 of 1961); or to damage or defile a place of worship or any object held sacred (ibid, Section 295); to outrage religious feelings or insult religion (Section 295A, amended in 1961); to disturb religious ceremonies (Section 296); or to wound religious feelings by sounds or gestures (Section 298).

Foreign missionaries who have not previously entered India are not necessarily granted visas, and those already admitted find the reissue of visas facilitated by a 'No objection to return' endorsement made on their passports before leaving India. In fact it is increasingly difficult for foreign missionaries to obtain visas although those involved in medical or educational work obtain them more readily than those engaged in other forms of service or witness.

Many churches serve members of the scheduled castes or the recognized tribes, some of these tribes living in areas under emergency legislation. The status of the church is indirectly affected by the rule that for purposes of serving as representatives in state or union legislatures, no non-Hindu or non-Sikh may be deemed to be a member of a scheduled caste (Scheduled Castes and Scheduled Tribes Orders Amendment Act, No 63 of 1956, Sch. I(1); for the various orders themselves see H. M. Seervai, *Constitutional law of India*, 1967, P.A-96, concerning Article 341). This discrimination has been challenged. The novel concept of dual religious affiliation (a person being both a Christian and a Hindu) is tentatively arising in social terms and also beginning in law. Several forces including the growth of secularism are contributing to the elimination of legal discrimination on the ground of religion.

An attempt by the legislature of Orissa and Madhya Pradesh to make it a punishable offence to attempt to convert any person from one religious faith to another by offering him any 'inducement' has been struck down by the High Court as a violation of the right conferred by the constitution (Article 25, item 1) guaranteeing to Christians the right to propagate their faith (Yulitha Hyde vs State of Orissa, AIR 1973, Or. 116). On the other hand, in the Subansiri District of Arunachel Pradesh in northeast India, Christians have experienced severe harassment at the hands of anti-Christian elements since 1971, including the burning of churches and dwellings. Urgent appeals to the prime minister by the North East India Christian Council (NEICC) have thus far gone unheeded.

**INTERDENOMINATIONAL ORGANIZATIONS.** The National Christian Council of India (NCCI) was founded in 1953, building on the foundations laid by the Missionary Council of 1912, the National Christian Council of India, Burma and Ceylon in 1921, and the National Christian Council of India and Pakistan in 1947. The NCCI is an associate council of the WCC and affiliated to CWME, as well as being a member council of the Christian Conference of Asia. Eighteen of its member churches are also members of CCA. Fourteen regional Christian councils are part of the NCCI, namely those of Andhra Pradesh, Bengal, Bihar, Gujurat, Karnataka, Kerala, Madhya Pradesh, Maharashtra, North East India, North West India, Santal, Tamilnad, Uttar Pradesh and Uktal.

In 1950 the Evangelical Fellowship of India (EFI) came into being; by 1973 it had 94 member denominations and local congregations. The Fellowship sponsors its own Indian missionaries and in 1965 was responsible for the creation of the indigenous Indian Evangelical Mission. The autonomous Union of Evangelical Students of India is also active. A more recent council formed after 20 year's endeavour is the Federation of Evangelical Churches of India (FECI); although it co-operates with the EFI, it limits membership to non-conciliar Evangelical bodies, numbering 30 denominations by 1978.

A Commission for Ecumenism of the Catholic Bishops' Conference of India (CBCI) has been formed,

**Subba Rao Movement.** Prayer meeting: note garlanded crucifix with bloodstained body of Jesus, always present on special table, perpetuating founder's 1942 vision. Movement is anti-churches and anti-baptism, and is a high-caste Hindu revival featuring massive healing crusades.

and ecumenical interest among Catholics has increased significantly since the All India Seminar of 1969.

The first meeting of the All-India Liaison Body was held at Bangalore in July 1973 between the NCCI (4 delegates), the Syrian Orthodox Church (4 delegates) and the CBCI (4 delegates). Its aims were: (1) to diminish obstacles to Christian unity in order to promote understanding and dialogue at the levels both of hierarchy and also of local groups and communities; (2) to foster common witness in a non-Christian country by joint collaboration in common works in the fields of health, education, development and peace. The formal name and other details concerning this organization have yet to be decided upon. It has been tentatively called the Co-ordinating Body of the CBCI, NCCI and the Orthodox Church, with a secretariat in Bangalore.

The most important and active joint working group in India today is the Joint Faith and Order Study Project which was formed in August 1972 at the Nasrapur Consultation near Poona, bringing together for the first time Indian representatives of the Protestant, Syrian Orthodox and Catholic churches. Subjects studied were the structure of visible unity, priesthood, ministry and ordination, scripture, tradition, authority and mariology. The committee asked officials of their respective churches to continue to sponsor, and support with funds and personnel, a continuation committee of the conference at the national level.

At the national level, at least 7 other inter-church bodies are active. (1) The Christian Agency for Social Action, Relief and Development (CASA) is the social service arm of the NCCI. (2) Action for Food Production (AFPRO), founded in New Delhi in 1966, is a non-profit joint service agency co-ordinating food production projects of church-related and voluntary agencies without regard for race, caste, community or creed. This secular agency of Christian inspiration brings together the resources of voluntary agencies in a single programme. Accomplishments up to 1972 include water development, groundwater investigation, small credit schemes, poultry, livestock and technical information services. AFPRO member organizations are Caritas-India, CASA (NCCI), CRS/USCC, Indian Social Institute, Indo-German Social Service Society (IGSSS) representing MISEREOR, OXFAM, Church World Service (CWS), Lutheran World Federation (LWF) and the Society for Developing Gramdans. (3) Skills for Progress (SKIP) is an all-India organization of church-related technical institutions, which co-ordinates technical assistance and information to

**True Jesus Church of India.** Baptism in 1974 of first Indian convert to this large Chinese indigenous church.

institutions offering training in vocational skills for industry. Founder members are CASA, Caritas India, OXFAM and the Presbyterian churches. (4) The Co-ordinating Agency for Health Planning (CAHP), founded in New Delhi in 1970, is a small group endeavouring to develop the ecumenical aspect of Catholic and Protestant medical work in India, working through some 5 national seminars a year. In 1971 the CAHP described a new secular concept, the voluntary health association (VHA), open to all medical institutions in the voluntary non-profit class. By 1972 a VHA had been established in 9 states. (5) The Ecumenical Industrial Service, founded in 1970, is an inter-church service (Catholic, Orthodox, Anglican, and 2 Protestant churches) catering for 40,000 industrial workers. (6) The All India Association for Christian Higher Education provides for ecumenical contacts between the 171 Catholic, Protestant and Orthodox institutions associated with India's official universities. In 1972 a Christian Association of India was being formed, and in 1974 the Catholic, Protestant and Orthodox representatives of seminaries, theological colleges and faculties decided to form a federation of all theological institutes in India. This union is regarded as the first step towards the eventual creation of a theological university in India.

At the regional level, several inter-church bodies have come into existence in Kerala. Two are working at the city-wide level in Trivandrum. The United Christmas Celebration Committee, founded in 1957, is a permanent body consisting of leaders of all the

Christian churches in Trivandrum (Catholic, Jacobite, Mar Thoma and the Church of South India) which organizes in the city every year a joint Christmas celebration and other festivals of common interest, including St Thomas Day. A related body is the United Christian Housing Committee, set up in 1971 to engage in social welfare in the slums of Trivandrum. Importance is given to a housing scheme for the poor and homeless, and by 1972 a number of houses had been built and donated. On the state level in Kerala, several other organizations are active. Home for All is a registered body comprising the leaders of all churches and also of non-Christian communities. It builds low-cost houses and distributes them to homeless people irrespective of religion or caste. Secondly, the Kerala Social Action Council is an ecumenical committee founded in 1972 in Christhavashram (Kottayam) which is involved in conscientization concerning social justice and stimulates social action aimed at improving the living conditions of the poor. Thirdly, the Committee for the Kerala Ecumenical Mental Hospital was formed in 1972 in order to begin a service for mental patients under the auspices of all churches in Kerala. Fourthly, the embryo of a Kerala Christian Bishops' Conference is also in existence. Although not yet formally constituted, it is worthy of note that the bishops of all the Christian churches in Kerala gather together regularly once or twice a year to study and discuss important issues of common interest.

Organizations at the regional level in Bihar include: (1) the Bihar Association of Voluntary Agencies (BAVA), a permanent registered body founded after the Bihar famine; and (2) Vikas Maitri, founded in Ranchi in 1968, which is an ecumenical association for agricultural, socio-economic and health projects in the Chota Nagpur region of Bihar and contiguous districts of neighbouring states. The Catholic, Lutheran, Anglican, Mennonite and Mar Thoma churches participate in this association, whose satellite body, the Development Board of Vikas Maitri (Vikas Maitri Kalyan Sanstha) functions as a guarantor and mediator for farmers and small-scale entrepreneurs in their relations with commercial banks and donor agencies.

Several institutes and research centres carry on their work in an ecumenical context. The Christian Institute for the Study of Religion and Society (CISRS), founded in Bangalore in 1953, is an interdenominational study and research institute with emphasis on dialogue with non-Christian religions. The Ecumenical Christian Centre, founded in Whitefield, Bangalore in 1963, is sponsored by 20 national churches (Catholic, CNI, CSI, Lutheran, Methodist, Mar Thoma, Baptist et alia) and such ecumenical national Christian organizations as the YMCA and YWCA. This is a study, research and inspirational centre open to Christians and non-Christians, which offers schools of politics, economics and other subjects. The Christian Retreat and Study Centre, founded at Dehra Dun (Rajpur, UP) in 1954, is an ecumenical action centre affiliated to and sponsored by all of the major Protestant denominations working in North India. The Ecumenical Centre Sneha Sena Office, founded at Cochin in 1964, is a Catholic-sponsored but interdenominationally-oriented study and conference centre for writers and journalists. The related Shanthinilayan (Place of Peace), founded at Kottayam by Jesuits in 1971, organizes the Ecumenical Christian Writers Fellowship. Lastly, there are various ecumenical groups in the major cities, including the Fellowship of St Thomas and St Paul (Adur, Travancore) and the Lumen Institute (Ernakulam, Cochin).

A number of world interreligious organizations, which include to varying degrees co-operation with Christian churches, have their headquarters in India. (1) The Theosophical Society was founded in New York in 1875 and its world headquarters was transferred to Adyar, Madras in 1882. It considers itself as a religion or school of thought providing a synthesis of all religions. In 1973 it had 32,000 members belonging to 1,223 lodges in 62 countries. (2) The World Fellowship of Religions was founded in New Delhi in 1957, its principal aim being to foster religious tolerance and co-operation. Membership is open to both individuals and organizations, and in 1972 there were 45 regional councils throughout the world. Five world religious conferences have been held, all in India, since 1957. The association also maintains links with the World Alliance of Religions in Paris, France. (3) The World Union, founded in Pondicherry in 1958, is a body dedicated to the search for the unity of mankind and the world built on spiritual values. The union sponsors seminars, conferences (the 4th taking place in Pondicherry in 1973) and a world parliament of youth with affiliated centres found in various countries.

Among India's non-denominational institutes of religious studies, a major one is the Department of Religious Studies (Guru Gobind Singh Bhavan) affiliated to the Faculty of Humanities and Religious Studies of the Punjab University in Patiala. Founded in 1967, the department sponsors studies and research in 5 major religious traditions: Hinduism, Buddhism, Christianity, Islam and Sikhism. At present the department is preparing an *Encyclopedia of Sikhism*. Other centres and institutes for the study of world religions and dialogue are: (1) Henry Martyn Institute of Islamic Studies (HMI), founded in Lahore in 1930 and now located at Hyderabad, AP; (2) Christian Institute of Sikh Studies, founded at Patiala, Punjab in 1966; (3) Aikya Alayam, founded at Madras by Jesuits in 1966, a Tamil culture and inter-faith research and dialogue centre; (4) Centre for the Study of World Religions, founded at Bangalore by the CMI in 1971; (5) Institute of Indian Culture, founded in Bombay by the SVD; and (6) Chavara Library and Cultural Centre, founded in Cochin by the CMI, which maintains a library and sponsors discussions involving Christians, Hindus, Muslims and Marxists. Still other interreligious dialogue centres are Shanti-Bhavan and Santi-Sadan in Calcutta, Signasu Kendra in Allahabad and Masih Vidya Bhavan in Indore. The Kerala Philosophical Congress, founded in Cochin in 1968, also sponsors an annual 3-day symposium on religio-philosophical topics in the Malayalam language.

**BROADCASTING.** In India, broadcasting is the exclusive responsibility of the central government, and All India Radio does not accept religious broadcasting, except for cathedral services at Easter and Christmas and Christmas music (in fact mostly secular) on Christmas Day. The television service does not accept religious material either. Christian programmes for India were carried over Radio Ceylon until 1957, and also over Radio Goa for a time. Increasingly, Indian stations have proved unwilling to take religious material, and so churches have turned to providing programmes instead for the foreign Christian stations which can easily be heard, namely FEBC (Manila) since 1958, and FEBA (Seychelles). In 1973, there were 20 recording studios in India co-operating with FEBC in the production of programmes for 50 hours weekly. RVOG (Ethiopia) also broadcast in Tamil, Telugu and Hindi from 1963–77; it averaged 15 hours a week until its closure in 1977. In addition Christian programmes in Indian languages are again carried over Radio Sri Lanka. These studios, entirely inadequate for such a vast nation, include the Christian Association for Radio and Audio Visual Service (CARAVS, NCCI) in Jabalpur, Christian Arts and Communications Service (CACS, Lutheran Hour) in Madras, and Suvartha Vani (Andhra Christian Council) in Vijayawada.

For Catholics, India is a member of UNDA. Catholics have recently taken great interest in the use of media for general education on a large scale, including the use of television via satellite for mass education in the towns. In 1972 a contract was signed with the USA to put a communications satellite into orbit over the northern part of India. At first some 5,000 towns will receive programmes, with a goal of 100,000 in the future.

**BIBLIOGRAPHY**


*An introduction to Indian church history*. C. B. Firth. Madras: Christian Literature Society, 1961. 263p.
*Catholic directory of India, 1972*. New Delhi: St Paul International Book Centre, 1973. (In 1969 edition, 826p. Biennial or triennial).
*Christian handbook of India, 1970*. Nagpur: National Christian Council of India, 1971. 74p. (Previous edition 1959).
*Christianity in India and a brief history of the Mar Thoma Syrian Church*. J. Mar Thoma. Madras: K. M. Cherian, 1968. 50p.
*Iconographic dictionary of the Indian religions*. G. Liebert. Leiden: Brill, 1976. 377p. (Hindu iconographic terminology).
'Indian church growth dynamics'. K. C. Daniel. Thesis, Fuller Theological Seminary, Pasadena (CA), 1971. 161p.
*Kerala Christian directory, 1969*. Ernakulam: Women Welfare Services, 1969. 747p. (All denominations).
*Living religions of the Indian people*. N. MacNicol. New Delhi: YMCA, 1964.
*Modern religious movements in India*. J. N. Farquar. London: Macmillan, 1929. (66 movements described).
'Nagaland church growth'. N. Y. Sema. Thesis, Bethel Theological Seminary (USA), 1972. 127p. (Baptist expansion).
*Pioneers of indigenous Christianity*. K. Baago. Madras: Christian Literature Society, 1969.
*Rebellious prophets: a study of messianic movements in Indian religions*. S. Fuchs. New York: Asia Publishing House, 1965. (77 movements described).
'Religion: numerical aspects', in *The population of India and Pakistan*, Kingsley Davis (New York: Russel & Russel, 1951), p. 177–194. (Analysis of decennial censuses).
*St Thomas Christian encyclopedia of India*. Ed G. Menachery. Trichur: St Thomas Encyclopedia, 1973–76. 2 vols.
*The Catholic community in India*. K. N. Subramanyam. Madras: Macmillan, 1970. 148p.
'The first independence movement among Indian Christians', K. Baago, *Indian church history review*, I, 1 (June, 1967), 65–78.
'The growth of Pentecostal churches in South India'. T. C. George. Thesis, Fuller Theological Seminary, Pasadena (CA), 1975.
*The Indian church: identity and fulfilment*. M. Zachariah. Madras: CLS, 1971. 220p.
*The movement around Subba Rao: a study of the Hindu-Christian movement around K. Subba Rao in Andhra Pradesh*. K. Baago. Madras: CLS, 1968. 32p.
*The religion of India: the sociology of Hinduism and Buddhism*. Max Weber. New York: Free Press, 1958. 392p.
'The role of Christian education in the evangelization of India'. G. V. Mathai. Thesis, Talbot Theological Seminary (USA), 1970.
'The role of the Christian community in a secular state: India as a case study'. A. V. Thomas. Dissertation, University Microfilms, 1970. 536p.
*The Syrian Christians of Kerala*. S. G. Pothan. Bombay: Asian Publishing House, 1963.


TABLE 2. ORGANIZED CHURCHES AND DENOMINATIONS IN INDIA

| Official name 1 | Begun 2 | Type 3 | Counc 4 | Congs 5 | Adults 6 | Affiliated 7 | Names, notes, and other statistics (see Codebook) 8 |
|---|---|---|---|---|---|---|---|
| Advent Christian Conference | 1882 | P Adv | xF..E | 33 | 1,734 | 5,000 | M=AAM(USA). 89% Tamil, 8% Telugu. 17 schools. 13n,5x,6f,G=5.8%pa,1h,1p,W=75%,175Y. |
| Apostolic Church of Pentecost in India | 1946 | P Pe1 | x.... | 45 | 2,500 | 5,000 | M=ACP(Canada). Malayalam-speaking, in Kerala state. HQ Kottayam. 6f,1. |
| Apostolic Church (GB) | 1929 | P PeA | ZG..E | 2 | 1,500 | 2,000 | M=Apostolic Church Missionary Movement (Great Britain). HQ Bangalore, Madras. 2f. |
| Apostolic Fellowship Tabernacle (Ind) | | I pen | .TT.T | 15 | 1,200 | 3,000 | *Ind=Independent*. Madras area. Workers' training centre, 2 orphanages. 18n,12m. |
| Armenian Apostolic Church: D India | 1704 | O Arm | Ewc.. | 7 | 6,000 | 10,000 | *D India & Far East. Gregorians*. Based on Calcutta. Under C Echmiadzin (USSR). 2r. |
| Assemblies of God | 1933 | P Pe2 | ZG..H | 30 | 3,000 | 5,000 | 1933, M=AoG(Australia), HQ Poona; 1936, AoG(UK), around Madras, Bombay. 4f. |
| Assemblies of God (NI, SI) | 1906 | P Pe2 | ZF..Z | 275 | 17,681 | 40,000 | *AGNI*(NIndia), *SIAG*(SIndia), M=AoG(USA). 70% in south. 290n,41f,6h,6s(214). |
| Assemblies of Jesus Christ | | I ind | .TT.T | | 500 | 1,000 | Local independent congregations, in Kakinada (Andhra Pradesh). Telugu-speaking. |
| Assemblies (Jehova Shammah) | c1950 | I CBr | x.... | 450 | 18,000 | 120,000 | Brother Bakht Singh. Chaubra/Sikh converts. Strong in AP; also abroad. M=WEC. 30f. |
| Association of Oriya Baptist Churches | 1910 | P Bap | ....W | 61 | 2,901 | 8,442 | *Ganjama Mala OB Mandali*. M=CBOMB. 90% Madiga Harijan. 11n,4x,G=2.1%pa,W=50%,205Y. |
| Assoc of Regular Indep Chs of India | 1935 | P Bap | xTT.T | 58 | 1,200 | 4,000 | *Fell of Bapt Chs, NT Bapt Ch Assoc*. M=BMM. Assam. 3n,3x,19f,G=8%pa,2H,W=85%,140Y. |
| Baptist Bible Believers Assembly | 1968 | I Bap | .TT.T | 5 | 250 | 500 | Begun for Koya Aborigines (Hill Tribes) in Hyderabad area, AP. 2n. |
| Baptist Christian Association | 1945 | P Bap | xF..E | 132 | 1,200 | 2,500 | *Ev Baptist Assoc*. M=CIBM(CBFMS). Took over KCIHM(UK). 1n,3x.24f,G=9%pa,2h,1s,120Y. |
| Baptist Church of Mizo District | 1902 | P Bap | ..... | 200 | 27,593 | 50,411 | *Zoram Baptist Kohhran*. 1970 refused to join CNI. M=BMS. 20n,5x,G=5%pa,1p,W=30%,2261Y. |
| Bengal-Orissa-Bihar Baptist Convention | 1836 | P Bap | TuE.W | 112 | 4,837 | 8,000 | M=ABFMS. 37% Santal, 25% Orlya, 12% Bengali, 12% Hindi, 15n,G=2.4%pa,W=75%,183Y. |
| Bethel Pentecostal Church | 1917 | P Pen | ..... | 48 | 1,000 | 2,500 | M=Bethel Pentecostal Temple (Seattle,USA). In Bihar, UP. 55n,2x,W=52%,537Y. |
| Bhartiya General Conf Mennonite Chs | 1900 | P Men | G...x | 133 | 3,220 | 6,394 | M=GCMC(USA). 95% Harijan Gara. Raipur. 13n,7x,29f,G=0.9%pa,3H,1s,W=35%,165Y,100z. |
| Bible Believing Churches in India | | I Bap | .TT.T | 3 | 500 | 1,000 | Baptist schism in Hubli (Mysore) and Salem district, South India. 1n,2m. |
| Bible Crusade Missionary Society | 1934 | P ind | ..... | 19 | 965 | 2,800 | Formerly Victory Prayer Crusade. Madras. Tract work. 10n,G=6%pa,1h,W=45%,36Y,42z. |
| Bible Mission | 1938 | I Lut | ..... | 100 | 10,000 | 15,000 | Guntur district, AP. Telugu-speaking. HQ Railpet. 40n,G=9.3%pa,W=70%,150Y. |
| Bible Pattern Church | | P Pe2 | ..... | 5 | 200 | 1,000 | Mission from UK, split ex Elim Foursquare Gospel Alliance. British-Israelite. |
| Bible Presbyterian Church of India | 1936 | P Ref | .TT.T | 4 | 100 | 200 | *BPCI*. M=IBPFM(USA). HQ Kanpur, UP. Declining in numbers; defections to RPCES. |
| Brethren in Christ Church in India | 1904 | P Men | GF..x | 28 | 900 | 1,800 | In Bihar state. M=BiCC(USA). HQ Barjora. 4n,3x,15f,G=6.4%pa,1H,1p,W=39%,65Y,20z. |
| Bundelkhand Friends Church | 1896 | P Qua | QF..x | 4 | 231 | 500 | *Bundelkhand* (town in MP) *Masihi Mitra Samaj*. M=EFC(USA). 2n,4f,G=−1%pa,1H,1s,W=57%. |
| **Catholic Church in India:** | 1319 | R LEr | PxF.R | 4,315 | 4,996,800 | 8,469,075 | C=35+15+122. 7p,31p,20s(3679). 8060n,1071x,2291m,34059w,P=70%,273406Yy,136884z. |
| P Goa/East Indies (AD Goa, Damao) | 1533 | R Lat | hs | 152 | 146,900 | 249,037 | Goa, DNH. Konkani. 1s. 539 6 44 627 70 85855 0 |
| M Agra | 1886 | R Lat | Pofmc | 5 | 3,200 | 5,458 | UP, Rajasthan. Hindi, Urdu. 21 0 6 112 48 103 852 |
| D Ajmer-Jaipur | 1913 | R Lat | Ps | 14 | 12,000 | 20,390 | Rajasthan, MP. Hindi, Bhil Boli. 63 10 8 471 71 1265 1464 |
| D Allahabad | 1886 | R Lat | Ps | 21 | 5,100 | 8,604 | UP. Hindi, Urdu, Bengali. 1s. 53 3 175 225 50 307 270 |
| D Jhansi | 1940 | R Lat | Ps | 12 | 1,500 | 2,472 | UP. Hindi. 20 1 30 77 94 103 5 |
| D Lucknow | 1940 | R Lat | Ps | 23 | 3,500 | 5,872 | UP. Formerly M=OFMCap. Hindi. 39 12 18 154 79 267 161 |
| D Meerut | 1956 | R Lat | Pofmc | 22 | 8,000 | 13,481 | UP. Hindi, Urdu. 23 11 44 210 48 488 656 |
| D Varanasi (Benares) | 1946 | R Lat | Ps | 20 | 5,300 | 9,034 | UP. Hindi, Bhodjpuri. 40 11 20 236 34 162 112 |
| M Bangalore | 1940 | R Lat | Ps | 58 | 76,600 | 129,758 | Karnataka. Kannada, Tamil. 1s. 216 41 75 942 67 2839 65 |
| D Bellary | 1928 | R Lat | Pofmc | 17 | 6,800 | 11,520 | Karnataka. Kannada, Tamil. 19 7 1 118 58 517 1085 |
| D Chikmagalur | 1963 | R Lat | Ps | 26 | 21,600 | 36,578 | Karnataka. Kannada, Konkani. 38 0 2 180 64 1787 78 |
| D Mangalore | 1886 | R Lat | Ps | 120 | 129,400 | 219,282 | Karnataka. Kannada, Konkani. 1s. 262 3 35 948 71 4842 32 |
| D Mysore | 1886 | R Lat | Ps | 28 | 25,000 | 42,401 | Karnataka. Kannada, Konkani. 46 14 5 284 71 1298 789 |
| M Bhopal | 1963 | R Lat | Pmsfs | 7 | 2,300 | 3,818 | MP. Hindi, some Urdu. 16 6 0 87 95 104 18 |
| D Indore | 1935 | R Lat | Psvd | 28 | 18,400 | 31,232 | MP. Hindi, Bhili, Korku, Malvi. 47 19 29 179 42 3565 907 |
| D Jabalpur | 1932 | R Lat | Ps | 19 | 9,900 | 16,762 | MP. Hindi. 28 expatriates. 40 7 6 99 80 214 1548 |
| D Raigarh-Ambikapur (split 1977) | 1951 | R Lat | Ps | 33 | 106,400 | 180,329 | MP. Hindi. 81 5 20 167 60 6147 3435 |
| D Raipur | 1964 | R Lat | Psac | 27 | 17,400 | 29,500 | MP. Hindi, 7 others. Fast growth. 36 6 8 116 48 720 3600 |
| M Bombay | 1832 | R Lat | Ps | 100 | 257,080 | 435,995 | Maharashtra. Marashi. 1s. 411 93 142 876 74 9303 722 |
| D Ahmedabad | 1934 | R Lat | Psj | 23 | 28,800 | 48,876 | Gujarat. Gujarati, Konkani. 46 38 23 240 63 2114 1070 |
| D Baroda | 1966 | R Lat | Ps | 15 | 6,600 | 11,269 | Gujarat. Gujarati, Adivasi. 17 15 9 77 95 299 503 |
| D Belgaum | 1953 | R Lat | Ps | 42 | 32,900 | 55,759 | Karnataka. Konkani, Kannada. 105 2 12 206 77 1609 171 |
| D Poona (Pune) | 1886 | R Lat | Ps | 41 | 72,500 | 122,950 | Maharashtra. Marathi. 1p,1s. 117 67 48 356 91 5048 3950 |
| M Calcutta | 1886 | R Lat | Ps | 34 | 48,600 | 82,389 | West Bengal. Bengali, Hindi. 1s. 94 83 93 538 50 2906 610 |
| D Bhagalpur | 1956 | R Lat | Ptor | 24 | 14,200 | 24,093 | Bihar. Santali, Hindi, Malto. 41 7 14 68 78 936 1577 |
| D Darjeeling | 1929 | R Lat | Ps | 23 | 15,700 | 26,694 | WB, Sikkim. Nepali, Tibetan. 31 56 36 194 78 1258 393 |
| D Dumka | 1952 | R Lat | Psj | 21 | 27,300 | 46,198 | Bihar. Santali, Hindi, Mundari. 16 34 10 77 50 1851 1810 |
| D Jalpaiguri | 1952 | R Lat | Ps | 9 | 28,100 | 47,571 | WBengal. Oraon, Munda, Sadri. 20 0 0 25 73 522 309 |
| D Krishnagar | 1886 | R Lat | Psdb | 51 | 8,700 | 14,665 | West Bengal. Bengali, Santali. 11 14 13 226 85 746 286 |
| M Changanacherry (*Syro-Malabar*) | 1896 | R SyM | Os | 184 | 228,800 | 387,870 | Kerala. Malayalam, Tamil. 1s. 459 0 0 2065 70 7800 1100 |
| D Kottayam (*Syro-Malabarese*) | 1887 | R SyM | Os | 84 | 49,800 | 84,342 | Malayalam. For Southists. 136 0 8 488 70 2624 200 |
| D Palai (*Syro-Malabarese*) | 1950 | R SyM | Os | 123 | 157,300 | 266,560 | Kerala. Malayalam. 448 0 28 1729 70 6849 500 |
| M Delhi | 1910 | R Lat | Ps | 15 | 14,700 | 24,855 | UTC. Hindi, Punjabi, Urdu. 1s. 52 16 34 139 80 671 222 |
| D Jullundur | 1952 | R Lat | Pofmc | | 13,000 | 21,983 | Punjab, Chandigarh, Hariyana, HP. 17 0 0 145 57 460 4104 |
| D Simla & Chandigarh | 1959 | R Lat | Ps | 18 | 4,100 | 6,866 | In 4 states. Punjabi. M=SDR. 34 1 16 123 68 346 1989 |
| M Ernakulam (*Syro-Malabarese*) | 1896 | R SyM | Os | 221 | 178,200 | 302,000 | Kerala. Malayalam. 364 0 47 2141 70 8685 232 |
| D Kothamangalam (*Syro-Malab*) | 1956 | R SyM | Os | 155 | 121,600 | 206,129 | Kerala. Malayalam, Tamil. 207 0 11 1495 70 5884 100 |
| D Tellicherry (*Syro-Malabarese*) | 1953 | R SyM | Os | 225 | 184,500 | 312,711 | Kerala. Malayalam. 252 0 38 940 70 9741 100 |
| D Trichur (*Syro-Malabarese*) | 1887 | R SyM | Os | 235 | 262,600 | 445,101 | Kerala, Malayalam. 1s. 346 0 79 2936 70 10000 100 |
| M Hyderabad | 1886 | R Lat | Ps | 19 | 21,900 | 37,070 | AP. Telugu, Kannada. 1s. 34 11 30 373 67 1445 150 |
| D Guntur | 1940 | R Lat | Ps | 36 | 44,700 | 75,815 | AP. Telugu. 10 expatriate RCs. 66 4 3 347 41 4940 3015 |
| D Kurnool | 1967 | R Lat | Ps | 26 | 22,700 | 38,523 | AP. Telugu, Urdu, Kannada, Tamil. 29 5 0 61 44 1918 3400 |

*Continued overleaf*

*Table 2 – continued*

| Official name 1 | Begun 2 | Type 3 | Counc 4 | Congs 5 | Adults 6 | Affiliated 7 | Names, notes, and other statistics (see Codebook) 8 |
|---|---|---|---|---|---|---|---|
| D Nellore | 1928 | R Lat | Ps | 24 | 30,000 | 50,000 | AP. Telugu. Formerly M=MHM. 53 3 2 72 65 1798 3758 |
| D Vijayawada | 1933 | R Lat | Ps | 59 | 101,400 | 171,785 | AP. Telugu. Formerly M=PIME. 1p. 76 2 6 406 38 8705 16457 |
| D Visakhapatnam | 1886 | R Lat | Pmsfs | 33 | 52,700 | 89,377 | AP, Orissa. Telugu, Oriya. 69 2 38 193 59 2309 18093 |
| D Warangal | 1953 | R Lat | Ppime | 35 | 42,600 | 72,156 | AP. Telugu, Urdu. 27 15 24 329 60 3961 9016 |
| M Madras & Mylapore | 1606 | R Lat | Ps | 76 | 97,100 | 164,558 | TN. Tamil, Telugu. 1p,1s. 175 20 93 908 84 6912 1761 |
| D Coimbatore | 1886 | R Lat | Ps | 47 | 54,700 | 92,640 | TN. Tamil, Malayalam. 90 0 24 560 69 2511 690 |
| D Ootacamund | 1955 | R Lat | Ps | 34 | 30,900 | 52,450 | TN. Tamil, Kanarese. 1s. 51 5 26 365 56 1731 1450 |
| D Vellore | 1952 | R Lat | Ps | 41 | 48,000 | 81,284 | TN. Tamil, Telugu. M=SDB. 69 15 19 182 79 2539 1256 |
| M Madurai | 1938 | R Lat | Ps | 84 | 151,600 | 256,876 | TN. Tamil, Malayalam. M=SJ. 1s. 174 27 151 1210 57 7134 256 |
| D Kottar | 1930 | R Lat | Ps | 72 | 161,800 | 274,156 | TN. Tamil. No expatriates. 122 0 17 405 57 12560 3324 |
| D Tiruchchirappalli | 1886 | R Lat | Ps | 41 | 102,900 | 174,351 | TN. Tamil. Trichinopoly. 1s. 118 16 92 855 60 6633 103 |
| D Tuticorin | 1923 | R Lat | Ps | 56 | 97,500 | 165,325 | TN. Tamil. No expatriates. 93 0 41 475 73 4900 300 |
| M Nagpur | 1889 | R Lat | Ps | 13 | 6,700 | 11,383 | Maharashtra, MP. Marathi. 1s. 75 15 10 174 86 233 44 |
| D Amravati | 1955 | R Lat | Pmsfs | 22 | 11,800 | 19,951 | M. Marathi, Korku Gondi, Urdu. 29 0 2 120 43 498 386 |
| M Pondicherry & Cuddalore | 1886 | R Lat | Ps | 54 | 98,900 | 167,555 | Pondicherry. Tamil, French. 1p. 95 25 52 698 67 8259 293 |
| D Kumbakonam | 1899 | R Lat | Ps | 57 | 84,700 | 143,627 | Tamil Nadu. Tamil. 17 expatriates. 94 0 4 368 61 4030 265 |
| D Salem | 1930 | R Lat | Ps | 37 | 36,700 | 62,195 | Tamil Nadu. Tamil, Telugu. 56 18 32 352 53 2083 227 |
| D Tanjore (Thanjavur) | 1952 | R Lat | Ps | 44 | 76,800 | 130,045 | Tamil Nadu. Tamil, Telugu. 79 0 2 331 95 4210 245 |
| M Ranchi | 1927 | R Lat | Psj | 59 | 188,000 | 318,665 | Bihar, ANI. Santali. 1p,1s. 173 86 102 735 86 9289 2589 |
| D Cuttack (M Cuttack from 1974) | 1937 | R Lat | Ps | 7 | 27,800 | 47,088 | Orissa. Oriya, Kui, Savara. 46 13 7 102 49 2080 10000 |
| D Daltonganj | 1971 | R Lat | Psj | 11 | 20,700 | 35,000 | Bihar. Santali, Hindi. 26 26 25 85 50 1418 1000 |
| D Jamshedpur | 1962 | R Lat | Psj | 10 | 12,300 | 20,794 | Bihar, WB. Santali, Ho, Mundari. 17 23 0 99 95 1236 1455 |
| D Patna | 1919 | R Lat | Psj | 40 | 27,100 | 45,917 | Bihar. Hindi, Nepali, Tibetan. 58 65 26 368 32 1430 2625 |
| D Sambalpur | 1951 | R Lat | Psvd | 28 | 74,500 | 126,267 | Orissa. Oriya, Kharia, Kisani. 37 23 7 226 87 4537 1000 |
| M Shillong-Gauhati | 1934 | R Lat | Psdb | 22 | 80,400 | 136,352 | Meghalaya. Assamese, tribals. 1s. 37 44 86 191 52 5816 4788 |
| D Dibrugarh | 1951 | R Lat | Psdb | 17 | 45,700 | 77,523 | Nagaland, ARP. Assam, tribals. 40 3 2 155 78 4920 4893 |
| D Silchar (Haflong) | 1952 | R Lat | Ps | 9 | 5,800 | 9,856 | Tripura, Mizoram. Nizo, Khasi. 13 5 0 34 57 416 600 |
| D Tezpur | 1964 | R Lat | Ps | 19 | 42,700 | 72,448 | Assam, ARP. Assamese, tribals. 34 0 7 69 88 4821 494 |
| M Trivandrum (*Syro-Malankarese*) | 1932 | R Mal | Os | 89 | 97,400 | 165,016 | Kerala. Malayalam, Tamil. 1p. 177 0 33 353 80 5242 2200 |
| D Tiruvalla (*Syro-Malankarese*) | 1932 | R Mal | Os | 166 | 21,600 | 36,573 | Kerala, TN, Karnataka. Malayalam. 129 0 25 152 80 850 400 |
| M Verapoly | 1886 | R Lat | Ps | 64 | 132,600 | 224,779 | Kerala. Malayalam. 1s. 175 14 32 506 60 6226 500 |
| D Alleppey | 1952 | R Lat | Ps | 24 | 52,700 | 89,306 | Kerala. Malayalam. No aliens. 55 0 2 150 90 2758 8 |
| D Calicut (Kozikhode) | 1923 | R Lat | Psj | 15 | 18,000 | 30,571 | Kerala. Malayalam. 28 expatriates. 93 8 21 497 92 1051 158 |
| D Cochin | 1558 | R Lat | Ps | 31 | 77,900 | 131,955 | Kerala. Mother Latin diocese. 63 0 2 117 97 3339 12 |
| D Quilon | 1845 | R Lat | Ps | 46 | 96,500 | 163,569 | Kerala. Diocese first in 1349 98 0 13 462 73 4723 927 |
| D Trivandrum of the Latins | 1937 | R Lat | Ps | 309 | 193,400 | 327,748 | Kerala, TN. Malayalam, Tamil. 137 3 30 260 52 10010 548 |
| D Vijayapuram | 1930 | R Lat | Ps | 112 | 40,200 | 68,213 | Kerala. Malayalam, Tamil. M=OCD. 95 2 10 159 76 1945 250 |
| EA Bijnor (*Syro-Malabarese*)(1977,D) | 1972 | R SyM | Ocmi | 2 | 50 | 83 | UP. Hindi. Detached D Meerut. 3 1 0 5 70 5 0 |
| EA Chanda (*Syro-Malab*)(1977,D) | 1962 | R SyM | Ocmi | 11 | 5,400 | 9,235 | Maharashtra, AP. Marathi, Telugu. 41 0 0 73 70 535 2000 |
| EA Jagdalpur (*Syro-Malabarese*) | 1972 | R SyM | Ocmi | 2 | 160 | 278 | Detached from PA Raipur. 5 2 1 11 70 13 0 |
| EA Sagar (*Syro-Malabarese*)(1977,D) | 1968 | R SyM | Ocmi | 26 | 950 | 1,612 | MP. Hindi. Under M Bhopal. 19 1 2 40 70 56 0 |
| EA Satna (*Syro-Malabarese*)(1977,D) | 1968 | R SyM | Ocvm | 3 | 400 | 685 | M. Hindi. Under M Bhopal. 13 0 0 19 70 17 3 |
| EA Ujjain (*Syro-Malabarese*)(1977,D) | 1968 | R SyM | Osmst | 1 | 260 | 440 | MP. Hindi. Under M Bhopal. 9 0 1 4 70 19 0 |
| PA Balasore | 1968 | R Lat | Pcm | 3 | 1,700 | 2,956 | Orissa. Oriya, Santali, Hindi. 6 1 2 23 95 774 127 |
| PA Jammu & Kashmir | 1952 | R Lat | Pmhm | 4 | 2,100 | 3,619 | J & K. Kashmiri, Urdu, Dogri. 1 9 0 63 36 134 693 |
| Ceylon Pentecostal Mission | 1927 | I pe2 | Z.... | 350 | 25,000 | 40,000 | 1927 ex AoG. From Sri Lanka. Strong in Madras, Kerala, Andaman/Nicobar Is, Nagaland. |
| Chaldean Syrian Church: D Trichur | 1814 | O Nes | Yw..W | 4 | 1,000 | 2,000 | *Chaldia Suriyani Sabha. Ancient Ch of the East.* 1874 ex Rome. 13n,W=50%,250y. |
| Chaldean Syrian Church: P (Baghdad) | 1969 | O Nes | y.... | 31 | 9,000 | 13,000 | Schism ex Shimun XXIII (USA) supporting rival patriarch Addai (Iraq). 27n. |
| Christ Church the Full Gospel Church | 1966 | I pen | .v... | 31 | 1,206 | 2,000 | Churches in southern Orissa. 1969 applied to join WCC. 4n,1p(7),W=80%,86Y,50z. |
| Christian & Missionary Alliance of India | 1887 | P Hol | xF..x | 79 | 8,000 | 25,000 | M=CMA(USA). Central eastern India. HQ Bombay. 21n,34f,G=3.2%pa,2s(12),W=90%,285Y. |
| Christian Assemblies in India | 1829 | P CBr | x.... | 800 | 40,000 | 100,000 | *Plymouth Brethren. Open Brethren.* M=CMML(UK,Australia,NZ,USA). E Godavari. 99f,4p. |
| Christian Community Ch, Bhilai Nagar | 1957 | P com | ....C | 8 | 1,000 | 5,000 | Begun for all Protestants in major new steel city Bhilai (MP). Steel, mines. 3n. |
| Christian Mission | 1918 | P Pe3 | x.... | 5 | 200 | 500 | 1923, M=International Pentecostal Assemblies (USA). Hamirpur (UP), Kerala. 2f. |
| Church of Christ, Scientist | | M Sci | x.... | 4 | 110 | 300 | *Christian Science.* M=CCS(Boston,USA). Bombay, Bangalore, Calcutta, Delhi. 5w. |
| Church of God of Prophecy | 1957 | P Pe3 | Z.... | 44 | 5,893 | 10,000 | M=CGP(USA). Holiness Pentecostals (3-stage). 33n,G=13.6%pa,1p,W=58%,280Y,100z. |
| Church of God (Anderson) | 1904 | P Hol | x.... | 774 | 35,992 | 50,000 | M=Ch of God(Anderson) (USA). In Assam, WBengal, Orissa, SIndia. 95n,6f,1s. |
| Church of God (Full Gospel) in India | 1913 | P Pe3 | ZF..Z | 436 | 25,300 | 30,000 | M=Ch of God(Cleveland) (USA). HQ Chengannur, Kerala. 331 churches. 274n,6f,3p. |
| Ch of Jesus C of Latter-day Saints | | M LdS | x.... | | 150 | 252 | *Mormons.* M=CJCLdS(Utah,USA). Mainly expatriate North Americans. |
| Church of North India: | 1612 | P uni | RWE.W | 2,000 | 230,959 | 579,554 | *CNI.* 1970 union. 60% Harijan (Chamar, Sweepers). 4s,1u. 917nx,1118m,290f. |
| D Amritsar with Chandigarh | 1970 | P uni | R | | 17,191 | 72,727 | Former Anglican area; M=CMS,USPG(UK),also UPUSA in Chandigarh. 102 39 43 |
| D Andaman & Nicobar Islands | 1970 | P uni | R | | 5,000 | 14,429 | 30% Christian (Car Nicobar 99%). M=USPG; Anglicans. Bengali. 19 17 0 |
| D Assam | 1970 | P uni | R | | 10,000 | 35,000 | Former Anglican D Assam. Kachari, Mundari, Oraon, Khasi. 31 3 1 |
| D Barrackpore | 1970 | P uni | R | | 8,979 | 19,126 | Rural. Formerly Methodist (M=MMS,CSM,CWM),Anglican(USPG),CBCNI. 37 7 9 |
| D Bhopal | 1970 | P uni | R | | 5,610 | 18,232 | M=UCCan(Canada), CSM, Anglicans. 49 24 12 |
| D Bombay | 1970 | P uni | R | | 6,643 | 12,049 | Begun 1718. Mainly Anglican D Bombay; also CSM, UCBWM, MMS. 1H. 22 10 8 |
| D Calcutta | 1970 | P uni | R | | 5,021 | 11,319 | Churches in city, Hooghly, Howrah. M=USPG,CMS,CCWM,CSM,MMS. 30 10 6 |
| D Chota Nagpur | 1970 | P uni | R | | 26,551 | 55,693 | Formerly Anglican diocese. M=USPG, CSM(among Santals). 68 361 23 |
| D Cuttack with Sambalpur | 1970 | P uni | R | | 24,662 | 53,959 | Formerly CBCNI(Baptists); M=BMS. Some Anglicans. Severe floods. 79 187 45 |
| D Darjeeling | 1970 | P uni | R | | 8,400 | 22,670 | Previously in UCNI. M=CSM, also USPG. Many tribes. 26 38 1 |
| D Delhi & Rajasthan | 1970 | P uni | R | | 9,195 | 21,356 | Formerly Anglican, also CBCNI. M=USPG,UPUSA,MMS,CSM. 4H,1r. 56 16 27 |
| D Durgapur | 1972 | P uni | R | | 3,000 | 10,000 | Heavy industry, dynamic city. Rural tribal Santals. M=MMS. 10 0 0 |
| D Gujarat | 1970 | P uni | R | | 15,899 | 31,948 | M=Ch of Brethren(USA), Irish Presb. Some Anglicans (CMS, USPG). 77 50 6 |
| D Jabalpur | 1970 | P uni | R | | 5,461 | 15,399 | Formerly Disciples of Christ, Anglicans. M=UCMS,CSM. Bhils. 30 0 0 |
| D Kolhapur | 1970 | P uni | R | 55 | 25,572 | 48,338 | 1970, 12,000, neo-Buddhists request baptism. M=UPUSA,CSM,USPG. 80 100 6 |
| D Lucknow | 1970 | P uni | R | 121 | 18,066 | 40,018 | 62% Anglican, 30% UCNI, 7% Methodist. 7H,44r. M=MMS,BCMS. 77 51 74 |
| D Nagpur | 1970 | P uni | R | | 1,534 | 4,486 | Former UCNI area. M=CSM,Episcopal Ch of Scotland,USPG. 22 23 6 |
| D Nandyal (later transferred to CSI) | 1970 | P uni | R | | 14,800 | 41,500 | Former Anglicans. M=SPG(UK); 1947 refused to join CSI. Telugu. 24 15 0 |
| D Nasik | 1970 | P uni | R | | 13,405 | 38,600 | Formerly UCNI, Anglicans. M=UCBWN.CSM,USPG,CMS. 2H. 58 63 8 |
| D Patna | 1970 | P uni | R | | 5,970 | 12,705 | Formerly Anglicans, UCNI, CBCNI. M=USPG,CSM,MMS,CMS. 24 68 11 |
| Church of South India: | 1640 | P uni | .WE.W | 8,435 | 515,700 | 1,555,902 | *CSI.* 70% former Harijans. 56x,1s,3u(142). 1071nx,1609m,577w,81f,11440Y,24311y. |
| D Coimbatore | 1951 | P uni | . | 328 | 15,558 | 43,383 | M=LMS. Tamil. 1H,6r. 51 31 4 7 182 654 |
| D Dornakal | 1947 | P uni | . | 985 | 38,642 | 135,324 | M=CMS,SPG. Telugu. 5H,4r. Mass rural exodus. 68 168 14 8 1323 2197 |
| D Kanniyakumari | 1947 | P uni | . | 334 | 41,176 | 163,280 | M=LMS. Tamil. 1947, 25% seceded. 6H,19r. 69 282 59 0 2653 2289 |
| D Karnataka Central (C Mysore) | 1969 | P uni | . | 75 | 14,430 | 28,560 | M=MMS,Basel Mission. Kanarese. 3H,5h,9r. 54 6 8 8 227 490 |
| D Karnataka Northern | 1969 | P uni | . | 105 | 10,092 | 22,600 | Mysore. M=MMS. Kanarese. 3H,11h,9r. 43 33 11 5 181 577 |
| D Karnataka Southern | 1969 | P uni | . | 113 | 14,728 | 27,023 | Mysore. M=MMS,CMS,LMS. Kanarese. 3H,7h,3r. 41 39 8 0 193 335 |
| D Krishna-Godavari | 1947 | P uni | . | 921 | 43,349 | 135,858 | M=CMS,LMS. Telugu. 2H,1h,8r. 86 147 20 2 1507 2363 |
| D Madhya Kerala (Central Kerala) | 1947 | P uni | . | 342 | 40,342 | 95,140 | 1816, M=CMS. Malayalam. 1966, schism. 6H,1j,26r. 88 170 29 0 600 1647 |
| D Madras | 1947 | P uni | . | 915 | 55,775 | 136,206 | M=CMS,SPG,MMS. Tamil. 6H,3h,28r. 123 43 50 22 827 2837 |
| D Madurai-Ramnad | 1947 | P uni | . | 639 | 29,900 | 68,275 | M=LMS,SPG. Tamil. 3H,4h,17r. 58 82 3 1 263 1097 |
| D Medak | 1947 | P uni | . | 812 | 42,469 | 153,945 | M=MMS. Telugu. 1970, 20% secede. 4H,12r. 67 167 189 11 284 1140 |
| D North Kerala | 1947 | P uni | . | 139 | 16,071 | 33,756 | M=CMS,United Basel Mission Ch. 1H,2h,10r. 57 39 5 3 410 729 |
| D Rayalaseema | 1947 | P uni | . | 582 | 18,911 | 72,534 | M=CMS,LMS. Telugu. Poorest diocese. 3H,7r. 55 21 32 7 382 1007 |
| D South Kerala | 1947 | P uni | . | 229 | 20,162 | 95,580 | M=LMS. Tamil, Malayalam. 6H,5r,1u. 61 85 20 1 737 1084 |
| D Tiruchchirappalli-Thanjavur | 1947 | P uni | . | 770 | 24,235 | 58,920 | Tanjore. M=SPG,MMS.Tamil. 2H,14h,14r. 39 75 38 5 307 694 |
| D Tirunelveli (Tinnevelly) | 1947 | P uni | . | 1,146 | 89,860 | 285,518 | M=CMS,SPG. Tamil. 6H,38r. 111 221 87 1 1364 5171 |
| Church of the Apostolic Faith | 1955 | P Pe3 | ..... | 2 | 300 | 1,000 | M=CAF(USA). Holiness Pentecostals (3-stage). 2n,W=50%,15Y,30z. |
| Church of the Nazarene of Bharat | 1902 | P Hol | xF..x | 40 | 1,195 | 2,260 | M=CoN(USA). HQ Buldana. 17n,55mw,15f,G=2.4%pa,1H,4h,1s(16),63t,W=90%,140Y,266z. |
| Churches of Christ | c1892 | P Dis | x.... | 10 | 519 | 1,129 | *MKPK. Mandivon ki Pratinidhi Kaunsil.* M=CC(GB & Ireland). HQ Bhandaria. 6f. |
| Churches of Christ in Western India | 1905 | P Dis | x...x | 14 | 1,100 | 2,000 | *Conference of CCWI.* M=CC(Australia). Institutions closed, declining. 7n,W=60%. |
| Churches of Christ (Instrumental) | 1928 | P Dis | x.... | 600 | 10,000 | 20,000 | M=CCCC(Instrumental)(USA). Across entire nation, including Assam. 37f. |
| Churches of Christ (Non-Instrumental) | 1963 | P Dis | x.... | 100 | 2,000 | 3,000 | M=CC(Non-Instrumental) (USA). Main cities of North India, also Madras. 31f. |
| Churches of God | 1908 | P Ref | x...E | | 500 | 1,000 | *India Eldership.* M=Chs of God in NA, General Eldership(USA). Howrah, WBengal. 4f. |
| CMS Anglican Church of India | 1966 | I Ang | .TT.T | 300 | 80,000 | 107,000 | *D Travancore & Cochin.* Pulaya outcaste schism ex CSI(M Kerala). 24n,W=83%,7500Yy. |
| Conv of Bapt Chs in Northern Circars | 1874 | P Bap | T...W | 180 | 40,000 | 80,000 | *CBCNC.* M=CBOMB. 90% Madigas(Telugu,Oriya). 160n,G=1.5%pa,5H,1p,W=77%,300Y. |
| Convention of Telugu Baptist Churches | 1836 | P Bap | TWE.a | 1,785 | 228,767 | 500,000 | *Samavesam of TBC.* M=ABFMS.99% Mala,Madiga. 140n,G=4%pa,2s(120),W=40%,4091Y. |
| Council of Baptist Chs in NE India | 1836 | P Bap | T.E.W | 3,075 | 230,200 | 1,064,990 | *CBCNEI.* M=ABFMS(USA). Doubled 1950–70. 97n,1x,5704m,54w,9f,6H,12p,1s(110),16363Y. |
| Dhulia Nandurbar Church | 1900 | P Con | x...W | 10 | 1,062 | 2,000 | Dhule/Nandurbar: NE of Bombay. M=SAM(Sweden).90% Bhil. 6n,3x,16f,W=61%,27Y,45y. |
| Dipti Mission | 1925 | I int | ....E | 1 | 20 | 150 | *Mission of Light.* Begun by Bengali woman. 2 schools in Sahibgunj, Bihar. 2f,1k. |
| Disciples of Christ, India Ch Council | 1882 | P Dis | x...C | 17 | 1,500 | 3,000 | *ICCDC. Continuing Chr Chs in India.* Formerly M=UCMS; 1970 refused to join CNI. 12n,1H. |
| Dohnavur Fellowship | 1901 | P int | ..... | 2 | 400 | 1,000 | Boys and girls nurseries, Tirunelveli. Tamil. Medical and evangelistic work. 11f. |
| Elim Church | | P Pe2 | Z.... | 1 | 30 | 100 | M=NZ Full Gospel Mission (New Zealand). HQ Karmala, Scholapur district, Bombay. |
| Elim Churches of India | 1929 | P Pe2 | ZG... | 5 | 500 | 1,000 | M=Elim Foursquare Gospel Alliance(UK). HQ Mirzapur district, UP. 6f. |
| Evangelical Christian Church of India | 1941 | P Hol | xF..E | 165 | 1,739 | 2,465 | M=OMS (USA). Rapidly growing in Madras area. 60n,9f,G=1.8%pa,3s(38),207Y,274z. |
| Evangelical Congregational Church | 1910 | P ind | ....E | 354 | 18,778 | 49,599 | M=NEIGM(IBPM, now BFTW) (USA). Manipur. Paite, Thado, Hmar. 50n,1r,1s,W=62%,396Y. |
| Evangelical Free Church of India | 1973 | I ind | ....E | 125 | 1,557 | 12,082 | Manipuris. HQ Sielmat, Churachandpur, Manipur. M=BFTW(USA). 35n,180m. |
| Ev Missionary Society in Mayurbhanj | 1895 | P int | ..... | 9 | 52 | 314 | All churches in Orissa state. Oriya. M=EMSM(Australia). 4f,2h,1j,1n,W=74%,1Y. |
| Fell of Ev Churches in North Bihar | 1899 | P int | xM..C | 11 | 355 | 1,000 | M=RBMU(UK). Conservative Evangelical. Located in north Bihar. 10f,W=62%,4Y,3z. |
| Fell of Free Baptist Chs in North India | 1908 | P Pe2 | Z...Z | 40 | 915 | 2,430 | M=Örebro M(Sweden). A=1967. HQ Deoria (UP). 8n,G=3.3%pa,1H,4h,12t(1083),W=70%,59Y. |
| Fellowship of Indigenous Gospel Chs | 1954 | I ind | ..... | 160 | 10,000 | 15,000 | Members mostly Telugu, 20% converts from Hinduism. 50n,G=5.7%pa,W=99%,384Y. |
| Fell of Pentecostal Chs of God, India | 1962 | I pen | Z.... | 250 | 1,000 | 2,000 | HQ Itarsi, MP. Schism ex India Pentecostal CoG. 80n,G=15%pa,1p(25),W=75%,150Y,250z. |
| Free Methodist Church of India | 1881 | P Hol | VF..x | 46 | 1,415 | 2,000 | M=FMC(USA). HQ Yeotmal, also Chikalda (Maharashtra). 13n,10f,G=8%pa,1H,1p,661z. |

*Continued opposite*

*Table 2–continued*

| Official name 1 | Begun 2 | Type 3 | Counc 4 | Congs 5 | Adults 6 | Affiliated 7 | Names, notes, and other statistics (see Codebook) 8 |
|---|---|---|---|---|---|---|---|
| Free Will Baptist Conference of India | 1935 | P Bap | xF••x | 13 | 800 | 2,000 | Members Tamil. M=NAFWB(USA). HQ Nilgiris; also in Bihar. 2n,4x,4f,G=9%pa,42Y,50z. |
| Full Gospel Church Fellowship | 1911 | P Pen | ••••• | 16 | 200 | 2,000 | *FGCF.* M=Bharosa Ghar Mission(USA).HQ Jabalpur. A=1952. 4n,G=1.4%pa,W=80%,25Y,30z. |
| Goalpara Boro Baptist Church Union | 1927 | P Bap | •v••• | 37 | 1,918 | 5,550 | In Assam. M=ABMS(Australia). Migration losses. 1962 applied to WCC. 4n,W=70%,37Y. |
| God's Church of Visible Salvation | 1921 | I mar | ••••• | | 1,000 | 5,000 | Outcastes ex Mar Thoma SCEA. Led by founder's wife. Claims to be Hindu revival. |
| Gospel Association of India | c1945 | I Bap | ••••• | 60 | 5,000 | 10,000 | *GAI.* Schism ex CBOMB. Healing. Telugu, 50% former Kamma (Sudra) high-caste Hindus. |
| Greek Orthodox Ch (D New Zealand) | | O Gre | Cwc•• | 2 | 600 | 1,000 | Part of D New Zealand, under jurisdiction of EP Constantinople. Greeks. |
| Gypsy Evangelical Movement | | P Pe2 | x•••• | | 1,000 | 2,000 | Nomadic caravan communities among 300,000 Gypsies. M=GGMS(Switzerland,France). 8m. |
| Himalayan Free Church | 1892 | P Pen | ••••• | 19 | 220 | 425 | HQ Ghoom, Darjeeling. Work also in Sikkim. Pentecostals. G=9.5%pa,W=31%,36Y,20z. |
| Hindustani Covenant Church | 1940 | P Con | ••••W | 6 | 383 | 760 | M=Swedish Mission Covenant Ch. HQ Bombay. Ministry to Muslims. 5n,W=24%,44Y,12z. |
| Indep Chr Bible Believers Gospel Fell | 1966 | I ind | •TT•T | 427 | 12,185 | 20,000 | Telugu members. In Northern Circars. HQ Ramachandrapuram, AP. 20n,W=75%,823Y. |
| Independent Church of India | 1930 | I ind | ••••E | 132 | 22,000 | 45,000 | Ex IBPM, now aided by them. Manipur. Hmars. 42n,226m,G=10.5%pa,5p,W=39%,520Y. |
| Independent Full Gospel Church | 1953 | I pe3 | •TT•T | 18 | 1,500 | 5,000 | Revival movement in Coimbatore and E Godavari, AP. Telugu. 6n,G=6.3%pa,84Y. |
| Independent Local Churches of Kerala | 1969 | I ind | •TT•T | 7 | 166 | 400 | In Cochin district, Kerala state. Malayalam-speaking. 6n,1s. |
| Independent Syrian Church of Malabar | 1771 | I ReO | ••••• | 16 | 2,280 | 3,780 | *Malabar Swathanthra Suriani Sabha.* D Thozhiyur. Orthodox split. 8n,1s,W=50%,52y. |
| India Bible Church Fellowship | 1952 | I ind | ••••• | 36 | 800 | 1,200 | Agricultural work. Ahmednagar, Maharashtra. 8n,1x,G=9.8%pa,1p,W=40%,75Y,100z. |
| India Bible Mission Church | | I ind | ••••• | 120 | 2,200 | 3,200 | Revival movement in E Godavari, AP; HQ Rajahmundry. Split ex Baptist mission. |
| India Christian Assemblies | 1938 | P Pe2 | Z•••H | 18 | 2,500 | 5,000 | *ICA.* M=Finnish Free Foreign Mission(Finland). Mainly in Krishna district, AP. |
| India Christian Mission | 1897 | I int | ••••E | 65 | 5,329 | 9,593 | Eluru, AP. Formerly USA aid. Healing, revivals among Hindus. 6n,W=71%,534Y,681z. |
| India Gospel Fellowship Mission | | I ind | ••••• | 2 | 100 | 200 | Independent body in Nilgiris: indigenous Indian origin. |
| India Gospel League | 1906 | P Bap | ••••• | 40 | 1,500 | 2,000 | M=IGL(USA). Medical work around Salem (Tamil Nadu). 8n,4f,1H,25h,1p,W=85%,31Y,40z. |
| India Mennonite Brethren Church | 1899 | P Men | GF••x | 766 | 22,000 | 120,000 | M=Menonnite Brethren Ch of NAmerica. 99% Telugu. 126n,14f,G=2.4%pa,3H,3h,9p,100Y. |
| India Mission | 1933 | P int | xM••• | 60 | 5,000 | 7,000 | M=International Mission(USA). Good News Literature Centre, AP. 30n,27f,4h,2s,W=70%,150Y. |
| India United Evangelical Mission | 1924 | P ind | ••••• | 4 | 443 | 1,345 | M=IUEM(USA). Independent mission, now indigenous workers only. HQ Bangalore. 1h. |
| India (Bihar) Mennonite Church | 1940 | P Men | G•••w | 21 | 529 | 1,000 | M=MCNA(Bihar MM). Tribal; 85% Oraon, 15%Munda. 9n,3x,6f,1H,1k,1p,1s,W=60%,19Y. |
| Indian National Church | 1955 | I ARo | ••••• | 20 | 500 | 1,000 | Schism ex D Bombay, CIPBC(Anglican). Bishops in Vilatte succession. HQ Delhi. |
| Indian Orthodox Church: P India | 1956 | I CCa | •v••• | 30 | 1,000 | 2,000 | *Eastern Orthodox Catholic P India.* Ex RCC. 5 Dioceses, no buildings; services in homes. |
| Indian Pentecostal Church of God | 1924 | I pe2 | Z•••• | 1,850 | 51,250 | 120,000 | Ex CPM, AoG. Largest pentecostal church. 80% Malayali. 154n,G=4.6%pa,3p,1s,1500Y. |
| International Christian Fellowship | 1893 | P int | xM••x | 7 | 180 | 500 | M=Ceylon & India General M, Poona & Indian Village M. HQ Poona. 4n,2x,41f,1H,2h. |
| Isolated radio churches | 1952 | I rad | ••••• | 16,300 | 300,000 | 650,000 | Radio believers (youths &c). R=75000(FEBA,RVOG),T=2810000(ICI,TEAM,EHC,&c). |
| Jehovah's Witnesses | 1905 | M Jeh | x•••• | 64 | 3,644 | 10,000 | *Watch Tower.* Active witnessing by 1925. 25% ex RCs. HQ Santa Cruz, Bombay. 328Y. |
| Lakher Independent Evangelical Church | 1907 | P ind | ••••• | 94 | 11,115 | 19,991 | Church is 95% of whole Lakher headhunting tribe (Assam & Burma). M=LPM(UK). 13n,3f. |
| Laymen's Evangelical Union/Fellowship | 1935 | I Bap | ••••• | 100 | 5,000 | 10,000 | Founder Brother Daniels, ex CBOMB. Telugu, now also Tamil. 2 factions. |
| London Mission Church | 1947 | I Con | •TT•T | 100 | 10,000 | 40,000 | Schism ex LMS opposing 1947 CSI union (D Kannyiakumari). Litigation from 1947–64. |
| Madras Pentecostal Assembly Church | 1920 | I pen | ••••• | 24 | 570 | 1,238 | Rapid growth. Healing, exorcism. HQ Royapettah. 4n,G=16.4%pa,1p,W=85%,128Y,40z. |
| Malabar Basel German Mission Church. | c1970 | I LuR | •TT•T | 5 | 1,000 | 2,000 | Fundamentalist split ex CSI, D North Kerala (United Basel Mission Ch). HQ Calicut. |
| Mar Thoma Syrian Church of Malabar: | 1843 | I ReO | xWE•W | 642 | 207,000 | 350,017 | Reform ex Orthodox Syrian Ch. Syrians. 272n,6H,1j,1k,P=95%,30r,2s,575t,W=37%. |
| AD Tiruvalla (Niranam) | 1889 | I ReO | xm | 45 | 17,000 | 29,000 | Original diocese. Four mission centres, several schools. HQ Tiruvalla. 27n,7r. |
| D Bahya Kerala (Outside Kerala) | 1953 | I ReO | xb | 60 | 23,000 | 39,000 | 60 Parishes in India (8 in Andaman Is), others from Arabian Gulf to Singapore. 30n. |
| D Kottarakara (Southern) | 1953 | I ReO | xb | 173 | 68,000 | 113,000 | Kottarakara Convention annually since 1958. HQ Hermon Aramana, Adoor. 60n. |
| D Kottayam | 1953 | I ReO | xb | 136 | 52,000 | 88,000 | Orphanage, rest house, Mar Thoma Centre for evangelization. 55n,2H,6r. |
| D Maramon (Central) | 1937 | I ReO | xb | 110 | 42,000 | 72,000 | Centre of reforms. Annual Maramon Convention since 1896. HQ Maramon. 59n. |
| MTS Christian E Assoc of Malabar | 1888 | I ReO | x | 118 | 5,000 | 9,017 | *E=Evangelistic.* Non-Syrian outcaste converts: Harijan, Cheramar, Sambava. 40n. |
| Mara Independent Evangelical Church | 1907 | P Con | ••••• | 93 | 15,000 | 30,000 | Member of NEIndia Christian Council. Manipuris. 17n,G=5.7%pa,500Y,100z. |
| Mennonite Church in India | 1899 | P Men | G•••z | 16 | 1,830 | 3,000 | M=Mennonite Ch NA(USA). HQ Dhamtari, MP. 11n,2x,13f,G=1.3%pa,2H,2r,1u,W=60%,76Y. |
| Methodist Church in Southern Asia: | 1856 | P Met | VwE•W | 2,508 | 421,109 | 901,306 | *MCSA. SAsia CC, UMC*(USA). 80% Harijan (Madiga). 20H,4s. 612n,118f,11057Yy. |
| Agra Annual Conference | 1893 | P Met | V | 55 | 73,756 | 150,000 | Sweepers, Chamars, Mazhabi Sikhs. Very large, many nominal. 64 5 617 |
| Bengal Annual Conference | 1888 | P Met | V | 35 | 10,927 | 20,000 | Bengalis, Santals, some Oraons and Mundas. 47 3 195 |
| Bombay Annual Conference | 1892 | P Met | V | 75 | 15,840 | 40,000 | 8 languages including Malayalam churches; also Mangs, Mahars. 59 5 755 |
| Delhi Annual Conference | 1893 | P Met | V | 79 | 31,747 | 70,000 | 70% Chuhra, Mazhabi Sikhs, and artisan classes from Rajasthan. 48 25 977 |
| Gujarat Annual Conference | 1922 | P Met | V | 531 | 26,732 | 60,000 | 80% low caste Dherds. Many Sweepers. Outstanding preachers. 75 13 584 |
| Hyderabad Annual Conference | 1926 | P Met | V | 697 | 77,763 | 111,306 | Telugu. 90% Madiga; Sudra. 20,000 at November Dharur Jathra. 55 10 3512 |
| Lucknow Annual Conference | 1921 | P Met | V | 88 | 15,313 | 40,000 | 70% depressed Chamars, Doms. Nur Manzil psychiatric centre. 41 17 410 |
| Madhya Pradesh Annual Conference | 1905 | P Met | V | 102 | 14,738 | 40,000 | 70% Lal Begis, Bhils, tribals. Iron and sulphur mine workers. 38 5 231 |
| Moradabad Annual Conference | 1958 | P Met | V | 113 | 39,452 | 90,000 | 80% Sweepers, Chamars, Doms. Part of mass movement area. 62 2 622 |
| North India Annual Conference | 1864 | P Met | V | 116 | 39,855 | 90,000 | First conference, organized 1864. 80% Sweepers, Chamars, Doms. 48 3 476 |
| South India Annual Conference | 1876 | P Met | V | 617 | 74,986 | 190,000 | Kannada. 80% Sudra, Madiga; farmers. Many women workers. 75 30 2678 |
| Metropolitan Church Association | 1904 | P Hol | x•••E | 20 | 5,000 | 7,000 | Southern India; some camp work in north India. M=MCA(USA). HQ Siwait, UP. 2n,2x. |
| Mid-India Yearly Meeting of Friends | 1866 | P Qua | Q•••• | 6 | 323 | 1,000 | *Quakers.* M=Religious Society of Friends (UK). A=1953. HQ Itarsi, MP. |
| Nagaland Christian Revival Church | 1952 | I pen | ••••• | 84 | 20,000 | 40,000 | *NCRC.* Pentecostal split ex Nagaland Baptists. Nagas. M=DNR(USA). At Kohima, 1p(25). |
| National Missionary Society of India | 1905 | I ind | ••••• | 10 | 500 | 1,000 | *NMS. Bharat Christya Sevak Samaj.* Aids CSI & ELC, but has own churches. 40n,300mw. |
| Native Church (Protestant) | | I ind | ••••• | 70 | 5,000 | 8,000 | Independent separatist body, of indigenous Indian origin. 12n,10m,1p. |
| New Apostolic Church | 1969 | C CAn | x•••• | | 14,325 | 20,000 | Canada Bezirk. HQ Dortmund (Germany). Rapid growth. 1973 mission in Kenya, Africa. |
| North Bank Baptist Association | c1930 | P Bap | •F••E | 253 | 13,500 | 25,500 | *Uttor Par Bapt Christian Sanmilan.* M=BGC. Assam. 3f,G=6.3%pa,2H,3h,2p,W=55%,650Y. |
| North Goalpara Garo Baptist Union | 1908 | P Bap | •H••• | 33 | 1,173 | 2,202 | In Assam. M=ABMS(Australia). HQ Chhaibari. 3n,G=4.8%pa,W=75%(90%in towns),99Y. |
| Norwegian Free Evangelical Church | 1910 | P Pe2 | Z•••Z | 284 | 17,285 | 43,018 | M=NPY(Norway),SFM(Sweden),FFFM(Finland),Elim(Denmark). NIndia. HQ Banda, UP. 1H. |
| Open Bible Church of God | | I pe2 | •TT•T | 10 | 300 | 500 | Independents in Nilgiris & Coimbatore districts. Village evangelism. HQ Tatabad. |
| Orthodox Syrian Church of the East: | c 180 | O SyM | DWE•• | 937 | 833,000 | 1,412,100 | *Malankara OSC, Catholicate of the East.* Syrians. 942n,G=1.1%pa,1s(85),W=55%,7820Yy. |
| D Angamaly (Ankamaly) | 1886 | O SyM | Dm | 96 | 85,400 | 144,700 | HQ Trikkunnathu Seminary. Alwaye. Orthodox Youth League. 50 units. 130n,12r,123t. |
| D Bahya Keralam (Outside Kerala) | 1959 | O SyM | Dm | 41 | 36,500 | 61,800 | Across India. 5 further parishes abroad. HQ Devalokam, Kottayam. |
| D Chingavanom (Knanaya) | 1910 | O SyM | Dm | 43 | 38,200 | 64,800 | Knanaya Syrian Christians date from AD 350 in unbroken line. 35n,1e,1H,4r,1s. |
| D Cochin | 1876 | O SyM | Dm | 80 | 71,100 | 120,600 | HQ Zion Seminary, Kuratty, via Alwaye. Strong Sunday schools, youth work. |
| D Kandanad | 1876 | O SyM | Dm | 73 | 65,000 | 110,000 | HQ Muvattupuzha. Scattered churches to east of Cochin. 5 bishops since 1876. |
| D Kottayam | 1876 | O SyM | Dp | 128 | 113,800 | 192,900 | Diocese of Catholicos of the East, but with own bishop. 1s(Kottayam). |
| D Malabar | 1953 | O SyM | Dm | 84 | 74,700 | 126,600 | 22,000 converts through Servants of the Cross mission. HQ Calicut. 3r. |
| D Niranam | 1876 | O SyM | Dm | 75 | 66,700 | 113,000 | Site of one of St Thomas' 7 churches. HQ Pathanapuram. 2H,6r,1s. |
| D Quilon | 1876 | O SyM | Dm | 185 | 164,200 | 278,800 | HQ Cross Junction, Quilon. Medical missions, many schools. 2d,2e,11r, |
| D Thumpamon (Thumpaman) | 1876 | O SyM | Dm | 132 | 117,400 | 198,900 | HQ Pathanamthitta. Active Orthodox youth movement. 9 bishops since 1876. |
| Pentecostal Ch of God of Andhra Prad | | I pe3 | ••••• | 700 | 20,000 | 30,000 | *Prad=Pradesh.* Large indigenous pentecostal body. M=PCG(Jamaican Blacks from UK). |
| Pentecostal Free Will Baptist Church | c1960 | P Pe3 | ••••• | 10 | 200 | 500 | M=PFWBC(USA), schism in USA ex Free Will Baptists. 80 workers. 1p. |
| Pentecostal Holiness Church | 1920 | P Pe3 | ZF••H | 25 | 1,152 | 3,000 | M=PHC(USA). In Bihar. HQ Jha Jha. Member, All India Pentecostal Fellowship. 62nm,8f. |
| Presbyterian Ch in North East India | 1812 | P Ref | ••••• | 1,836 | 135,135 | 324,091 | 3 Synods, Bangladesh,Burma. M=PCW. 60% Mizo,30% Khasi. 165n,3H,2j,2s,W=70%,13709Yy. |
| Pure Church | 1925 | I Ang | ••••• | 1 | 500 | 1,500 | *Suttangam Sabhi. Alvaneri's Ch.* Split of 7,000 ex CMS (D Tinnevelly). Declining. |
| Rabha Baptist Church Union | 1959 | P Bap | ••••• | 8 | 265 | 500 | In Goalpara district, Assam. HQ Debitala. 1n,G=8.0%pa,4p,1s,W=20%,45Y. |
| Ramabai Mukti Mission | 1905 | I Hol | •M••E | 2 | 400 | 800 | Begun by woman, Pandita Ramabai, at Mukti. 2,000 widows and orphans. 32f,1H,3h. |
| Reformed Episcopal Church | 1890 | A sEv | x•••E | 2 | 100 | 250 | *Calvary Church.* M=REC(USA), Anglican schism. HQ Lalitpur, Jhansi, UP. 2f,1H,1h. |
| Reformed Presbyterian Ch, Ev Synod | 1860 | P Ref | x•••• | 8 | 230 | 337 | M=RPCES(USA),WPM(USA). HQ Roorkee, UP. 6n,4x,10f,G=4.8%pa,1s,W=61%,12Yy. |
| St Thomas Evangelical Church of India | 1961 | I ReO | •TT•C | 192 | 15,000 | 25,000 | *Pathiopadesa Samiti.* Split ex Mar Thoma Syrian Ch. 29n,G=4.6%pa,2p,1r,W=75%,254Yy. |
| Salvation Army | 1882 | P Sal | xwE•W | 4,252 | 300,000 | 500,000 | *Muktifauj.* 5 Territories: Madras & AP, NE, SE, SW, Western. 1952nx,34f,9H,3s. |
| Saora Association of Baptist Churches | c1900 | P Bap | ••••• | 200 | 4,000 | 18,000 | Orissa and AP. M=CBOMB(Canada). 90% Harijan (Madiga, Saora). Rapid growth. |
| Separate Baptists in Christ | 1917 | P Bap | ••••• | 3 | 1,200 | 4,000 | *India Mission.* Covers 70 villages in Ahmednagar district. HQ Vambori. 7n,W=75%. |
| Seventh Day Baptist Church | | P Bap | Tw••• | | 18,500 | 25,000 | M=SDBC(USA). Sabbatarian Baptist with USA and UK links. |
| Seventh-day Adventist Church | 1895 | P Adv | x•••• | 408 | 49,658 | 80,000 | *SDA,C,N,SIndia Unions.* 164n,44x,95f,G=12%pa,6H,1j,2p,11r,1s(60),882t(55721),W=94%,5784Y. |
| Southern Baptist Mission | 1962 | P Bap | T•••• | 8 | 466 | 1,000 | M=SBC(USA). Mainly USA residents. Sunday-school enrolment 264. 1n,14f,1h,60Y. |
| Subba Rao Movement | 1942 | I non | ••••• | 300 | 30,000 | 100,000 | High-caste Hindus. Anti-churches, anti-baptism. Massive healing crusades. Telugu. |
| Swedish Free Mission | | P Pe2 | Z•••H | 155 | 25,275 | 50,000 | M=Svenska Fria Missionen(Sweden). In UP. Member, All India Pentecostal Fellowship. |
| Tamil Baptist Churches | 1861 | P Bap | ••••• | 70 | 1,100 | 3,000 | M=Strict Baptist Mission(UK). Around Tiruchi. Tamils. HQ Kovilpatti. 7n,9f,G=0%pa,30Y. |
| TEAM Christian Churches | 1892 | P int | xM••C | 48 | 3,000 | 7,000 | M=TEAM(USA), Swedish Alliance M. Bhils. 6n,5x,64f,G=3.7%pa,2H,3h,1p,W=80%,193Y. |
| Telugu Baptist Churches | 1968 | I Bap | •TT•T | 20 | 1,000 | 2,000 | Schism ex Convention of Telugu Baptist Chs. Many years' lawsuits against ABFMS. |
| Theistic Church of India | 1795 | M Unt | I•••• | 50 | 2,000 | 5,000 | *Brahmo Samaj. Unitarian Union.* 1795 Madras; Assam(Khasi), Calcutta. M=UUA(Canada). |
| Tripura Baptist Christian Union | 1938 | P Bap | •v••• | 166 | 5,442 | 12,000 | M=NZBMS(New Zealand). 1962, applied to join WCC. 16n,2x,G=6.3%pa,1p,W=67%,262Y. |
| True Jesus Church of India | 1969 | I pe1 | x•••• | 5 | 180 | 300 | *TJC, World Conference* (HQ Taiwan). Chinese. Indian pastors in South India. |
| Undenominational Ch of the Lord in I | 1958 | P Hol | ••••• | 100 | 4,000 | 15,000 | Mission from USA. Members Telugu, tribals. 15n,G=14.9%pa,250Y,500z. |
| United Evangelical Lutheran Chs in India: | 1706 | P Lut | LWE•W | 7,933 | 339,690 | 790,440 | *UELCI.* Formed 1975. Large % Harijan. Missionaries sent to Malaysia, Burma, Tanzania. |
| Andhra Evangelical Lutheran Church | 1842 | P Lut | Lwe•W | 3,000 | 96,060 | 288,461 | 5 synods. First M=LCA(USA). 98% Telugu-speaking outcastes. 225n,4x,1p,10265Yy. |
| Arcot Lutheran Church | 1861 | P Lut | Lwe•W | 109 | 9,792 | 18,267 | Madras. Tamil-speaking. First M=DMS(Denmark). 22n,G=3.4%pa,1p,1u,545Yy. |
| Gossner Evangelical Lutheran Church | 1844 | P Lut | Lwe•W | 2,478 | 122,908 | 256,174 | M=Gossner MS(Germany). A=1919. Tribal Munda, Oraon. 134n,1x,3f,1s,W=90%,677Yy. |
| India Evangelical Lutheran Church | 1895 | P Lut | Lwe•W | 416 | 15,803 | 41,107 | Tamil; 1 Malayalam district. M=LCMS. 87 schools. 112n,14x,23f,G=5%pa,1s(39),2427Yy. |
| Jeypore Evangelical Lutheran Church | 1885 | P Lut | Lwe•• | 819 | 30,245 | 53,324 | M=Breklum M. 1910 outcastes mass movement. A=1928. 61n,3x,9f,2s(30),W=55%,2135Yy. |
| Madhya Pradesh Ev Lutheran Church | 1887 | P Lut | Lwe•W | 34 | 3,612 | 6,275 | *MPEL Kalisiya.* M=SEMS. Episcopal. Hindi-speaking. Oraon, Gond. 19n,G=5%pa,1p,171Y. |
| Northern Evangelical Lutheran Church | 1867 | P Lut | Lwe•W | 327 | 18,435 | 42,069 | *Santal Mission of Northern Chs. Ebenezer ELC.* Santals. 58n,2x,6p,1s,W=60%,1686Yy. |
| South Andhra Lutheran Church | 1865 | P Lut | Lwe•W | 253 | 6,000 | 14,970 | First M=Hermannsburg(Germany),ALC(USA). A=1945. Work among depressed classes. 17n. |
| Tamil Evangelical Lutheran Church | 1706 | P Lut | Lwe•W | 497 | 36,835 | 69,793 | First Lutheran mission in Orient. M=CoS(Sweden). Tamil. 79n,G=3%pa,1u,W=67%,2064Yy. |
| United Missionary Church of India | 1908 | P Hol | xF••E | | 1,000 | 2,000 | Mennonite. West Bengal. M=UMS(USA). 1969 Missionary Church. HQ Calcutta. 1 school. 3f. |
| United Pentecostal Church in India | 1949 | P Pe1 | x•••• | 341 | 38,531 | 100,000 | M=UPC. Fields: NE(Assam)123 congs,S(Kerala)41. 145n,3x,G=6%pa,2p(74),W=80%,1600Y. |
| Wesleyan Church of India | 1910 | P Hol | VF••E | 39 | 491 | 836 | *India Conference.* M=WC(USA). HQ Surat, Bombay. 7n,1x,2f,2H,3h,1p,W=66%,42Yy. |
| Wesleyan Methodist Ch of India | 1970 | I Met | •TT•C | 12 | 25,000 | 30,000 | Schism ex Diocese of Medak, Church of South India, opposing new bishop. Telugu. |
| World Missions | 1965 | P int | x•••• | | 3,125 | 5,000 | M=World Missions (USA). North American Evangelicals based on Long Beach, CA(USA). |
| World-Wide Missions of India | 1960 | P ind | x•••• | | 15,000 | 30,000 | M=World-Wide Missions(USA). Evangelicals linked with Pasadena, CA(USA). |
| Other Protestant denominations | | P | ••••• | | 11,500 | 35,000 | Total about 100 (see list below). |
| Other Indian indigenous churches | | I | ••••• | | 10,000 | 20,000 | Total about 40 (see list below). |
| **Total affiliated (mid-1970)** | | | | **69,500** | **9,734,823** | **19,231,528** | **Total denominations (1970) . . . 286.** |
| **Total affiliated (mid-1975)** | | | | **79,000** | **11,484,900** | **22,689,000** | **Total denominations (1975) . . . 306.** |
| **Total affiliated (mid-1980)** | | | | **91,000** | **13,706,600** | **27,078,000** | **Total denominations (1980) . . . 330.** |

NOTES ON TABLE ABOVE

COLUMNS: for meanings and CODES (cols. 1, 3, 4, 8), see Codebook (Part 6). Column 1: **Boldface type** = church with over 10% of country's affiliated Christians.

NATIONAL COUNCILS (Column 4, 5th letter).

a = member of both NCCI and EFI.
C = Federation of Evangelical Churches of India (FECI) (non-conciliar Evangelicals only).
E = Evangelical Fellowship of India (EFI) (conciliar and non-conciliar Evangelicals).
H = All-India Pentecostal Fellowship (AIPF) (Northern and Southern Regions; formed 1957).
R = Catholic Bishops' Conference of India (CBCI).
T = Council of Christian Churches in India (formerly India Bible Christian Council, IBCC).
W = National Council of Churches of India (NCCI).
x = Member of both EFI and FECI.
Z = member of AIPF, FECI and/or EFI.
z = member of both NCCI, EFI and FECI.

*Other national councils.* (1) All-India Ecumenical Coordinating Body (AECB) (leading eventually to a National Council of Churches of India, including the Catholic Church). (2) Two councils link a number of indigenous churches, and aim to create an independent indigenous national church of India: All India Federation of National Churches, and Fellowship of Christ in India (Bharat Khrist Sangh). (3) Various Western bodies belong to the Christian Holiness Association, Mennonite Christian Fellowship of India, and other bodies. (4) A Joint Council, formed 1978, links the CSI, CNI and Mar Thoma Syrian Church of Malabar.

*Local councils.* Many bodies not in national councils belong to local Christian councils; there are 14 regional councils affiliated to the NCCI.

OTHER PROTESTANT DENOMINATIONS. In addition to those listed, there is a large number of over 90 small Protestant denominations. These include (with year begun and/or total affiliated in parentheses where known): Amazing Grace Missions, American Baptist Association, Apostolic Faith, Assembly of Yahvah, Baptist Bible Fellowship International (1955), Behat Village Mission, Bible Holiness Mission (Canada), Bible Missionary Ch, Brethren Ch (Ashland) (1971), Calvary Pentecostal Ch, Central Asian Mission, Children of God International (many communes; work with hippies and drug addicts), Chowpatta Agricultural & Industrial Mission, Christian Ch of North America, Christian Churches (Direct-support Mission), Christian Nationals Evangelism Commission (1967), Ch of Christ (Bailey Mission), Ch of God (General Conference) (1964), Ch of God (Queen's Village), Ch of God (Seventh-day), Chs of God in the British Isles & Overseas, Exclusive Brethren (Kelly-Continental), Free Ch of Finland Mission (1909, Darjeeling), Free Ch of Scotland Mission (85), Free Gospel Church Mission (begun 1928; 300), Glad Tidings Missionary Society (1965), Grace Mission (1969), International Ch of the Foursquare Gospel, Moravian Ch (Tibetan Unity Undertaking), National Revival Crusade, Nepal Evangelistic Band, New Tribes Mission (1945), Peniel Chs of VOCA (1950), Pilgrims Mission (1908, Pentecostal), South India Ch of Christ Mission, United World Mission (begun 1958; 65), World Gospel Mission (begun 1937; 100), Worldwide Evangelization Crusade (1926).

OTHER INDIAN INDIGENOUS CHURCHES. Since the early movements in 1843, 1858, 1880, 1886, 1887, 1921 and 1925 (see above, and text under Indigenous Churches) there have been numerous Christian and Hindu-Christian indigenous churches formed. In addition to those given in the table above, others still existing in 1970 include: Anglican Episcopal Ch of India (HQ Dehra Dun, UP), Apostolic Christian Assembly (member of ICCC), Apostolic Pentecostal Faith, Baptist Christian Chs (member of ICCC), Bharat Ev Mission, Bible Brethren Assemblies (member of ICCC), Bible Mission, Bible Standard Ch (member of ICCC), Church of the Country (Nattusabai), Delhi Bible Fellowship, Elim Bible Fellowship (member of ICCC), Independent Assembly, Independent Ch of South India (South Kerala Diocese) (member of ICCC), India Independent Ch of God, Indian Orthodox Catholic Apostolic Ch (bishop consecrated 1967 in New York, USA), Madras Bethesda Mission (member of ICCC), Masihi Mandali (Pentecostal Church), Nagaland Suffering Ch, National Ch of India, New Testament Baptist Christian Association (member of ICCC), Revival Centre, South India United Mission, Voice of Full Gospel Assembly, Zion Assembly (Siyon Sangham). In addition, certain USA Black missions are assisting, including: Apostolic Overcoming Holy Ch of God, Lott Carey Baptist Foreign Mission Convention, NBCUSA. There are also indigenous bodies from other races, including the Spiritual Food Worldwide Evangelistic Mission (Chinese from Hong Kong).

OTHER MARGINAL BODIES. The Reorganized Ch of Jesus Christ of Latter-day Saints (USA) maintains a small work based on Madras 24 and Berhampur (Orissa), with 805 members.

UNITING CHURCHES. In 1979, 4 separate sets of negotiations for organic union were under way, as follows: (1) Church of Christ in South India (in 1975, agreement reached to unite in 1979): Andhra Ev Lutheran Ch, Arcot Lutheran Ch, Ch of South India, India Ev Lutheran Ch, South Andhra Lutheran Ch, Tamil Ev Lutheran Ch. (2) North East India Christian Council (to become Church of North East India): Ch of North India, Council of Baptist Churches in NE India, Presbyterian Ch in NE India. (3) Methodist Ch in Southern Asia (withdrew from CNI in 1970 before union) is in preliminary negotiations with CNI, CSI and Mar Thoma Syrian Ch. (4) Bharath Christian Church (to be formed on a certain specific future date): Ch of North India, Ch of South India, Mar Thoma Syrian Ch.

PEOPLES (ethnolinguistic). Christians (1971; ethnolinguistic groups are followed by, in italics, the Indian state or union in which they are concentrated): 31.6% Malayali (21% Syrian) (*Kerala*), 16.9% Tamil (*Tamil Nadu*), 12.8% Telugu (*Andhra Pradesh*), 5.0% Marathi (*Maharashtra*), 4.6% Bihari tribal (2.2% Oraon, 1.1% Munda, 0.5% Kharia, 0.2% Santal and other Aboriginal) (*Bihar*), 4.3% Kannada (Kanarese) (*Mysore*), 3.2% Hindi (*Uttar Pradesh, Madhya Pradesh, Delhi*), 2.7% Oriya (*Orissa*), 2.5% Assamese (*Assam*), 2.4% Naga (*Nagaland*), 2.0% Manipuri (*Manipur*), 1.9% Goanese (Konkani; *Goa*), 1.8% Bengali (*West Bengal*), 1.5% Mizo (Lushai) (*Mizoram*), 1.2% Khasi (*Meghalaya*), 1.2% Punjabi (*Punjab, Haryana*), 1.0% Anglo-Indian, 0.9% Garo (*Meghalaya*), 0.8% Gujarati (*Gujarat*), 0.8% European, 0.5% Bhil, 0.2% Rajasthani (*Rajasthan*), 0.2% Gypsy, 0.1% Tripuri (*Tripura*), 0.1% Saora (Savara), Pawi, Lakher, Armenian (10,000), Chinese (4,000), Gond, Sindhi, Kashmiri, Nicobarese, et alii. Within these ethnolinguistic groups, the majority of all Christians (who are found in South India) come from 6 of the 26,000 castes, almost all being Shudra (Vellala, Kamma, Reddi, Lambadi, Yerakula, Syrian), and from 14 of the scheduled castes (outcastes, Harijans): mainly from the Madiga, Mala, Nadar, and Pariah (Paraya); together with lesser numbers from the Balahi, Bhangi, Chamar, Dherd, Gara, Mahar, Mehra, Mukkuva, Namasudra, Parava, Sambava, et alii. About 50% of all Christians are Harijans. Over the years in the past, strong people movements have developed in some 20 castes.

COUNTRY-WIDE TOTALS

EVANGELIZATION (see Part 5). 1900: 27%. 1970: 58%. 1980: 73%. *Mass evangelism.* Among the large number of recent campaigns: 1956 Billy Graham rallies in Bombay, Delhi, Kottayam, Madras (800,000 attenders, 29,034 enquirers); 1969, All Kerala United Evangelistic Movement formed for city campaigns; Diocese of Dornakal (CSI) holds annual Week of Witness; 1970, first All-India Congress on Evangelism, in Bombay (300 workers); 1972, Billy Graham Nagaland crusade (460,000 attenders); 1972 India Every Home Crusade; 1972, City-wide Gospel Campaign in Bangalore led by India Herald International; campaigns led by Asian Fellowship and Study Centre, also Evangelical Fellowship of India (Poona Penetration Plan, Shillong Penetration Plan, also for Lucknow, Yeotmal, Indore, Nagpur); 1972 Nellore campaigns by Hindustan Bible Institute (100 decisions for Christ); 1974 Operation Mobilization's Reach Up '74 campaign in Uttar Pradesh (over 1,000 decisions for Christ); 1976–77, Here's Life Kerala (run by CCCI), saturating the whole of Kerala state, with 99% of 2,700,000 homes reached with the gospel, 9,900,352 persons evangelized, and 1,850,982 decisions for Christ (1,470,954 through person-to-person presentations, 380,028 at public meetings; of the total, 10% were formerly Hindu or Muslim); December 1977, 4 Billy Graham 'Good News Festival' crusades, including Calcutta (attenders 40% Hindus), Hyderabad, Kottayam, Madras (totals 676,000 attenders, 13,291 decisions); 1978, Here's Life Bangalore, Tirunelveli and others (CCCI). From 1956–76 the Billy Graham/Akbar Haqq ministry alone reached nearly 4 million persons. In January 1977 was held the All-India Congress on Mission and Evangelism (AICOME), in Devlali, Maharashtra. *Radiophonic evangelism.* There are vast numbers of programmes and courses. In 1976, FEBC/FEBA alone was broadcasting for 185 hours per week: FEBC (Manila) for 14 hours 45 minutes per day in English and 45 minutes per day in vernaculars, and FEBA (Seychelles) for 3 hours 15 minutes per day in English and 7 hours 45 minutes per day in vernaculars; with a total audience of over 10 million. Annual listeners' letters (1975): 75,000 (44,000 FEBC/FEBA, 22,884 RVOG, HCJB, TWR, Radio Vatican, et alia). Bible correspondence courses: numerous, with 2,810,000 enrolments (2 million Light of Life/TEAM, 783,846 ICI (with 9,211 conversions reported), 25,000 EHC, et alia). Over a million Hindus are known to be studying the Bible regularly. *Literature evangelism.* In January 1976, Every Home Crusade began its second nation-wide coverage, Project Calvary, aiming to deliver booklets to every home by the end of 1980. By a year later, the city of Calcutta (7,540,000) had been completely reached by EHC, with a continuing 5,000 written decisions each month. By early 1977, 40,000 written decision cards per month were being received from all India, with a goal of 100,000 per month anticipated soon.

FOREIGN MISSIONARIES AND PERSONNEL (nationals serving abroad) (1973). Total 3,931 in over 54 countries: about 3,420 Roman Catholics in 47 countries (including 34 Jesuits in the USA; and also 2,000 Kerala nuns recruited to fill vacancies in monasteries in France, Germany, Italy, Switzerland, UK), about 300 Protestants, 200 Indian indigenous (Jehova Shammah et alia), 9 Orthodox priests, 2 Catholics (non-Roman).

FOREIGN MISSIONARIES AND PERSONNEL (aliens from abroad) (1973). Total 5,979. *From Western world.* 5,673: about 3,400 Roman Catholics, 2,149 Protestants (1,150 in 109 USA societies, 530 in 26 UK societies, 110 in 10 Canada societies, 85 in 17 Australia societies, 80 in 7 Sweden societies, 72 in 15 New Zealand societies, 39 in 7 Norway societies, 34 in 7 WGermany societies, 25 in 4 Denmark societies, 12 in 3 Finland societies, 9 in 1 Switzerland society, 3 in 1 Netherlands society), 115 Anglicans (90 in 6 UK societies, 10 in 1 Australia society, 5 in 1 New Zealand society, 4 in 2 Ireland (Eire) societies, 3 in 2 USA societies 3 in 1 Canada society), about 7 Catholics (non-Roman), about 2 Orthodox. By 1975 North American missionaries had fallen to 783. *From Communist world.* About 39 Roman Catholics (30 from Yugoslavia, 9 Poland). *From Third World.* 267: about 100 Roman Catholics from Burma, Brazil, Philippines, Sri Lanka et alia, about 100 Protestants from Japan, South Africa, Philippines et alia, 53 indigenous from Sri Lanka, Japan, Taiwan, Hong Kong, Jamaica et alia, 12 Anglicans from Japan, Sri Lanka et alia, 2 Orthodox.

INSTITUTIONS (church-operated) (1973). Total 5,300, including 3,100 higher schools (105 minor seminaries), 1,440 medical centres (620 hospitals), 200 religious communities (50 ashrams), 13 research centres, 122 seminaries (65 Protestant, 51 RC, 5 Indian indigenous, 1 Orthodox), 50 study centres, 130 universities (including degree-granting colleges: 78 RC, 45 Protestant, 7 Orthodox, mostly in Madras, AP, Kerala, Mysore; with 117,500 students out of India's 1.1 million).

PERIODICALS. About 650 titles (350 Protestant (44 SDA, 19 Salvation Army), 170 RC, 40 indigenous).

PERSONNEL. About 120,479 (114,500 national, 5,979 foreign).

RELIGIOUS LIBRARIES. About 580.

SCRIPTURE DISTRIBUTION (1975). Annual totals: 122,746 Bibles (8% free, 68% subsidized, 24% commercial), 1,564,952 NTs (57% free, 30% subsidized, 13% commercial), 2,186,420 UBS portions, 16,854,569 UBS selections. *Translations completed.* Portion: 94 languages since 1714. NT: 55 languages since 1715. Bible: 25 languages since 1727.

SERVICE AGENCIES. About 320, including AECB, AFPRO, AICUF, AIFCTG, AIPF, BMMF, CAHP, CARAVS, CASA, CBAI, CBCI, CCCI, CCCS, CCIC, CEF, CHA, CLC, CLS, CLSA, CNI, CRI, CSU, CWM, CWS, EFI, ELFI, ESII, FEBA, FECI, IEM, IMS, LWR, NCCI, NCCWI, NMSI, OM (1964; 50 missionaries), SCM, SCS, SGM, SU, TAFTEE, TAVES, UESI, WBT, WLC(EHC), WVI, YCW, YFC, YMCA, YWAM, YWCA.

ADDITIONAL DATA ON CHURCHES

ANDHRA EVANGELICAL LUTHERAN CHURCH. Name in Telugu: Andhra Suvisesha Lutheran Sanghamu.

ASSEMBLIES (JEHOVA SHAMMAH). From headquarters in Hyderabad, AP, extensive missionary work is undertaken across India, in Nepal, and in several Middle Eastern countries.

CATHOLIC CHURCH IN INDIA. Name in Hindi: Katholic Kaleesia. (Archdiocese = Mahadharm Pradesh. Diocese = Dharm Pradesh. Exarchate Apostolic = Preritik Dharmkshetra). *New dioceses.* In 1974, D Cuttack became M Cuttack-Bhubaneswar with as suffragans D Sambalpur and a new diocese, D Berhampur. Other dioceses created since 1972: Kohima-Imphal, Manantoddy (Syro-Malabarese), Palayamkottai, Palghat (Syro-Malabarese), Tura. In 1977 a large number of new dioceses were erected, including 7 Syro-Malabarese (Bijnor, Chanda, Jagdalpur, Kanjirapally, Rajkot, Sagar, Satna, Ujjain), also Ambikapur, Baruipur, Cuddapah, Eluru, Karwar, Khandwa, Nalgonda, and in 1978 Aurangabad, Raiganj and the Malankara Eparchy of Battery (from D Tiruvalla). By mid-1977 Catholic jurisdictions in India numbered 100 (82 Latin-rite, 16 Syro-Malabarese, 2 Syro-Malankara), 93 headed by Indians and 7 by foreign missionaries. *Catechumens.* Totals: (1959, under SC Propaganda only) 78,693; (1961) 78,609; (1963) 81,685; (1969, under SC Propaganda plus 6,935 under SC Oriental Chs) 136,884. Statistics are given above for each diocese in column 8 in order to highlight the range of response met, from mass movement areas with thousands of catechumens to resistant areas with few or no converts. These figures are also included in column 7. *Column 8.* The first word indicates which state(s) the diocese is in (ANI = Andaman & Nicobar Islands, AP = Andhra Pradesh, ARP = Arunachal Pradesh, DNH = Dadra & Nagar Haveli, HP = Himachal Pradesh, MP = Madhya Pradesh, TN = Tamil Nadu (formerly Madras State), UP = Uttar Pradesh, UTD = Union Territory of Delhi, WB = West Bengal). Then follow the diocese's main languages, in order of importance. The major lingua franca, English, is used in almost all dioceses and hence is not shown in column 8. *National priests.* 70% diocesan (5,682), 30% religious (2,378). *Expatriate priests.* 4% diocesan (43), 96% religious (1,028). *Brothers.* 87% Indians, 13% expatriates. *Sisters.* 94% Indians, 6% expatriates. *Catholic charismatics* (January 1974). 8,000 adults including many religious personnel are active in over 50 prayer groups in the Charismatic Renewal. *Baptisms.* (1970) 83% infant, 17% adult. (1972) 86.0% infant, 14.0% adult. *Seminaries.* In addition to the 20 diocesan ones, there are 31 seminaries for religious priests. *Seminarians.* 2,150 secular, 1,529 religious (1972). *Catechists.* Total about 50,000 (96% part-time, 4% full-time). *Indigenous religious congregations* (1972). Priests: 1,149 Carmelites of Mary Immaculate (CMI, begun 1831 in Kerala), 175 Missionary Society of St Francis Xavier (begun 1887 in Goa), 146 Little Flower Congregation (begun 1947 in Kerala), 103 Order of the Imitation of Christ (begun 1919), Malabar Vincentian Congregation (begun 1927 in Kerala), 69 Missionary Congregation of the Blessed Sacrament (begun 1933 in Kerala), 49 Indian Missionary Society (begun 1945; HQ in UP), 48 Rosarians (begun 1928 in Jaffna, Ceylon), 33 Oblates of the Sacred Heart (begun 1930 in Kerala), 15 Kirisumala Ashram (begun 1957), 5 Oblates of St Joseph (begun 1962 in Kerala), Missionary Society of St Thomas the Apostle (SST, begun 1968). Brothers: 179 Franciscan Missionary Brothers (begun 1901 in Bombay), 138 Brothers of the Sacred Heart (begun 1903 in Kerala), 75 Missionary Brothers of Charity (begun in 1963 by Mother Teresa in Calcutta), 29 Franciscan Brothers of the Blessed Sacrament (begun 1937, in UP), 28 Malabar Missionary Brothers (begun 1948 in Kerala), 16 Brothers of St Michael the Archangel (begun 1916 in Coimbatore), 13 Olivet Brothers (begun 1934 in Mangalore), 12 Snehagiri Society for Brothers (Kerala). Sisters: total over 60 local congregations (20 founded before 1900, the first being the Sisters of St Louis of Gonzague, begun 1750). Main ones: 3,125 Franciscan Clarist Congregation (begun in 1888 in Kerala), 2,907 Congregation of Mother of Carmel (begun 1886 in Kerala), 2,105 Sisters of the Adoration of the Blessed Sacrament (begun 1908 in Kerala), 1,228 Apostolic Carmel (with houses outside India also), 1,157 Franciscan Missionaries of Mary (begun 1877 in Kerala). The best known are the 750 Missionary Sisters of Charity (begun 1950 in Calcutta by Mother Teresa; 41 houses in India, 14 abroad). *Foreign religious orders and congregations.* Priests: 3,090 SJ, 882 SDB, 487 OFMCap, 269 SVD. Brothers: 295 Brothers of St Gabriel, 136 Christian Brothers; and others. Sisters: about 60 foreign congregations.

*Catholic organizations.* The Catholic Bishops' Conference of India (CBCI), founded in 1944, now a member of FABC, was divided in 1973 into 11 regional councils: Kerala, Tamil Nadu, Andhra Pradesh, Karnataka, Western Region, Uttar Pradesh, North, Madhya Pradesh, Eastern, Bengal and North-Eastern. The national conference leaves to the competence of the regional councils all matters concerning the specific needs of their respective regions and the raising of funds to meet those needs (Article 54, Statutes of the CBCI). The Conference of Religious of India (CRI), founded in 1960, has sections for men and women and a sub-section for brothers. There are also regional conferences which follow generally the pattern of the CBCI regional councils. In 1969, a 10-day meeting of bishops, priests, nuns and laity at Bangalore drew up plans for a National Pastoral Council for all India. This meeting had been prepared for by 2 years of intensive work and consultation at the diocesan, regional and national levels, followed by advanced plans approved by the bishops. However, in 1973 Rome vetoed the project, arguing that the time for national pastoral councils was not 'opportune'. Following consultation at various levels (including Rome) during 1973, the CBCI General Meeting in Calcutta in January 1974 decided to go ahead with the establishment of the National Pastoral Council, using the same constitution but changing its name to National Advisory Council. The council met at Pentecost 1974 with 75 members in attendance: 8 bishops; 22 representatives of the clergy, male and female religious personnel; 20 representatives of Catholic organizations; and 25 well-known personalities of the church.

The CBCI Commission for the Family and Laity, and CBCI Commission for Youth, co-ordinate the lay activities of Catholics, the principal movements with their 1972 statistics being as follows. (1) The All India Catholic University Federation (AICUF), founded in the 1930s and commissioned by the hierarchy in 1948 as the 'official organ of Catholic Action for the universities of India', is the most important lay apostolic movement in India with 220 units divided in 12 regions with 20,000 members. The AICUF works through 2 branches: Christian Students Union (students) and Newman Association (for intellectuals); and conducts every year an average of 40 to 50 leadership camps, seminars and study weeks throughout India; it is a member of Pax Romana in Fribourg, Switzerland. (2) The Catholic Union of India, founded in 1945, is recognized as the representative all-India organization of laymen by both Catholic hierarchy and civil authorities. (3) The Christian Workers' Movement (CWM), affiliated to the World Movement of Christian Workers (MMTC) in Brussels, Belgium, collaborates with YCW and Christian Service to Industrial Mission. (4) The National Council of Catholic Women of India (NCCWI) has 50 member units in 50 dioceses representing 100,000 women. (5) The Legion of Mary, founded in 1931, has 3 senatus in Madras, Bombay and Kerala, totalling 178 curiae. (6) The Society of St Vincent de Paul has 681 conferences and 6,230 active members. (7) The Christian Family Movement has 33 groups mainly in the bigger cities. (8) The YCW has units in 31 dioceses and sections for boys and girls. (9) The Sodality of Our Lady has approximately 2,000 sodalities and a membership of about 8,000. Lastly there are (10) the Apostleship of Prayer for Adults, and (11) the Eucharistic Crusade for Children.

The Holy See has diplomatic relations with India and is represented to government and the Catholic hierarchy by a pronuncio based in New Delhi.

The Regional Secretariat for Asia of Teaching Teams (Equipes Enseignantes), which has its international headquarters in Paris, France, is located at Karaikal, Kerala. There were in 1973 approximately 30 teams in Tamil Nadu and Kerala, as well as others in Sri Lanka, Thailand and Singapore.

A militantly traditionalist non-official opinion group is the

Blue Army of Our Lady of Fatima with its international headquarters in Switzerland and its national secretariat in Calcutta, the latter serving also as the regional secretariat for Asia. On the progressivist side, by contrast, there are no organized movements.

A number of organizations are engaged in research and social action. The Indian Social Institute (ISI), founded in New Delhi by Jesuits in 1951, is a centre for research, training and action in the socio-economic field. The Institute for Social Studies and Community Development (Seva Sadan Institute), founded at Bhopal (MP) in 1968, is a socio-pastoral institute set up by the bishops of the state of Madhya Pradesh with the approval of the CBCI for training in community development, social leadership and pastoral responsibility. The Xavier Institute, founded by Jesuits at Jamshedpur, Bihar in 1949, is one of the leading centres for education in management and labour relations in India and is recognized by the government of India. Xavier's Institute of Social Service, founded by Jesuits at Ranchi (Bihar) in 1955, is a postgraduate institute, with 250 students in 1972, which provides for training in social service and in business management, as well as extension courses.

Pastoral and religious training is provided by several institutions. The Pontifical Athenaeum, sponsored by Jesuits at Poona, was first erected in 1893 as the Pontifical College in Kandy, Ceylon. In 1940 it was constituted as the Pontifical Athenaeum and transferred to Poona in 1955. The Pontifical Theological Institute, sponsored by the OCD at Alwaye (Kerala), was erected in 1682 as the Seminary of Verapoly, transferred to Alwaye in 1932, and constituted as a theological institute in 1972. The National Biblical, Catechetical and Liturgical Centre (NBCLC), founded in Bangalore in 1967 under the auspices of the CBCI, promotes and co-ordinates biblical, catechetical and liturgical renewal in the whole of India. The Lumen Institute, founded by Jesuits at Cochin (Kerala) in 1961, its present name being adopted in 1965, promotes the integral doctrinal formation of an educated laity, with special reference to university students, and diffuses the message of Christ among the educated classes outside the church. In addition there is a Common Training Centre for Brothers in Bangalore, founded in 1969, as well as 4 others for sisters in Old Goa, Bangalore (1968), Tindivanam (1968) and Hyderabad (1973).

There is considerable foreign missionary activity. Five Indian Jesuit priests work in Sudan, Africa: and the Congregation of the Missionary Sisters of Charity, founded in Calcutta in 1950 by Mother Teresa Bojaxhiu, is devoted to service of the poor with 13 houses in 11 foreign countries (Australia 2, Great Britain 2, and one each in Sri Lanka, USA, Northern Ireland, Italy, Jordan, Mauritius and Tanzania). In addition, a number of Catholic priests, brothers and sisters work among Indian-born persons in Mauritius, Tanzania, Fiji and Guyana. The largest lay home missionary movement is the Cherupushpa (Little Flower) Mission League, with 1,200 branches and 315,700 members, which aims to foster a missionary spirit, to provide aid for missions and to promote vocations both for India and abroad.

The Catholic educational programme is co-ordinated by the Xavier Board of Higher Education in India, founded at Mangalore in 1952, and the Xavier Association of Catholic Secondary Schools, founded at Poona in 1953. In 1973 there were 5,752 Catholic primary schools (1,456,617 pupils), 2,607 secondary schools (1,261,886 pupils), and 122 institutions of higher education (69,095 students in colleges, of whom 28% are Catholics, and 76,495 in universities). Catholic schools thus enrol about 3% of the total school population in India (2.8 million out of more than 85 million pupils), whereas Catholic education absorbs 29% of all priests, 23% of all brothers and 46% of all sisters in India.

Caritas India was founded in New Delhi in 1962 under the name Catholic Charities of India and received its present name in 1969. Affiliated to Caritas Internationalis in Rome, it is the official national organization established by the hierarchy to co-ordinate the church's involvement in social service and has an all-India network with 85 diocesan directors. Its activities include development aid (credit unions, fisheries, participation in government programmes of well-boring) and emergency relief. Three regional offices at the ports of Bombay, Madras and Calcutta are responsible for clearing relief supplies and controlling their distribution. The Catholic Hospital Association (CHA) in New Delhi co-ordinates 358 Catholic hospitals, maternity homes and health centres. Statistics for the total Catholic medical and social service programme include 328 hospitals, 533 dispensaries, 694 orphanages, 724 hostels and 213 other charitable institutions including homes for the aged. Several agricultural co-operatives have been formed, most notably the Chotanagpur Catholic Mission Co-operative Credit Society at Ranchi, the Maharashtra Prabodan Seva Mandal at Bombay, and the St Joseph's Co-operative Farming Society at Isanagar, Meerut. A Catholic rural organization of a more general type is Catholic Social Action in Cochin, Kerala.

CHALDEAN SYRIAN CHURCH. There are 2 rival factions within the church claiming jurisdiction: the largest is the Metropolitan or anti-patriarchal party (13,000 faithful, 13 priests, 14 deacons), followed by the Patriarchal party (2,000, 7 priests, 6 deacons). The major part of the church in Kerala has thus since 1969 been in schism from the Assyrian catholicos in California (USA) over rival episcopal appointments, with a lawsuit over the possession of the cathedral in Trichur. The church operates a clinic, a press, 2 schools and a seminary.

CHURCH OF NORTH INDIA. 1970 union of: Council of Baptist Churches in Northern India (Baptist Union of NI, Bengal Baptist Union, Uktal Christian Ch); Ch of India, Pakistan, Burma & Ceylon (CIPBC); Ch of the Brethren in India; Disciples of Christ; Methodist Ch (British & Australasian Conferences); United Ch of Northern India (UCNI). *Dioceses.* (1978) 22, after transfer of D Nandyal to the CSI. *New dioceses* (since 1972). D Agra D Chandigarh, D Sambalpur.

CHURCH OF SOUTH INDIA. 1947 union of: Ch of India, Pakistan, Burma & Ceylon (CIPBC) (500,000 in 4 dioceses in 1947); Methodist Ch of South India (British Conference; 220,000 in 1947); South India United Ch (Congregational, Presbyterian, Reformed) (290,000 in 1947). The original or major missionary societies in each diocese were as indicated in the table above, although in most cases they have few or no remaining personnel. *New dioceses* (since 1969). D Nandyal (transferred from Church of North India), D Vellore. *Membership.* Largely former outcastes: Nadar (Shanar, Parayah); and Vellala. 95% of members have a background in only 5 of the hundreds of castes or scheduled castes (outcastes, Harijans). The CSI had in 1970: 1,051 pastorates, 298,128 church families, 464,407 baptized adults who are not communicants, 450,248 baptized children under 16 years, 40,055 catechumens (included in column 7 above) of whom 19,000 were new in 1970, 16,966 newly-confirmed persons a year; of the annual adult baptisms, 13,375 were second-generation (belated baptisms of adult children of Christian parents) and 8,535 were first-generation (converts from other religions); Sunday schools had 175,549 Christian children and 34,810 of other religions; in youth organizations there were 46,732 boys and 27,764 girls; women's organizations numbered 75,135 women; annual emigration of Christians going elsewhere numbered 20,000 and immigration 5,400; and literate Christians numbered 597,535 (40%) in 1968, increasing to 647,174 (41%) in 1970. The total of affiliated Christians increased over 1968–70 by 1.9% per year. *Institutions.* The CSI has developed a vast complex of church-operated technical and vocational institutions, resulting in a heavy burden of plant. *Neo-pentecostals.* By 1975, charismatics were growing rapidly in 5 of the 16 dioceses.

COUNCIL OF BAPTIST CHURCHES IN NORTH EAST INDIA. HQ Gauhati. There are 12 Associations, divided among: Assam Baptist Convention (18,100 adults, Assamese), Garo Baptist Convention (56,300 adults, Garos), Manipur Baptist Convention (52,800 adults, Manipuris), Nagaland Baptist Convention (103,000 adults, 16 Naga tribes). Nagaland province is predominantly Baptist. *Main languages.* Abor, Anal, Assamese, Garo, Hmar, Kom-Rem, Kuki, Manipuri, Mao, Maring, Mikir, Miri. *Growth rate* (1970). 3.6% pa.

INDEPENDENT SYRIAN CHURCH OF MALABAR. In 1977, the archbishop was converted to Roman Catholicism.

MAR THOMA SYRIAN CHURCH OF MALABAR. *Language.* Malayalam. *Institutions.* 5 ashrams (with schools, dispensaries, village preaching, literature distribution): Christumitra (Ankola), Christubandhukulom (Satna), Suvartapremi Samity (Ranthi on Tibetan border), Christa Panthi Sangh (Sihora). Other organizations: Association of Women for Evangelistic Work (Sevika Sangham), Episcopal Jubilee Institute of Evangelism, Mar Thoma Theological Seminary (Kottayam), Medical Missions Board, Sunday School Samajam.

ORTHODOX SYRIAN CHURCH OF THE EAST. Although in communion with the Syrian Orthodox Patriarchate of Antioch (Syria) which follows the Old (Julian) Calendar, this church follows the New (Gregorian) Calendar. Members are ethnic Syrians, speaking Malayalam, and a few Kanarese speaking Kannada. Institutions include 8 monasteries, 7 convents, 3 hospitals, one dispensary, 18 schools of higher education and one engineering college (in D Angamaly). By 1975 there were 6 splits and factions, some attempting to organize work in Britain and elsewhere abroad. *Bishops.* Total 13. *Priests.* 77% married, 23% unmarried.

SALVATION ARMY. Name in Indian languages: (Tamil) Ratchania Senai, (Telugu) Rakshana Sineyamu, (Bengali) Mukthi Sena, (Hindi, Punjabi) Muktifauj, (Malayalam) Raksha Sainyam, (Gujarati, Marathi) Muktifauj.

SOUTH ANDHRA LUTHERAN CHURCH. Name in Telugu: Dakshana Andhra Lutheran Sangham.

TAMIL EVANGELICAL LUTHERAN CHURCH. Name in Tamil: Thamizh Suvisesha Lutharan Thiruchchabai.

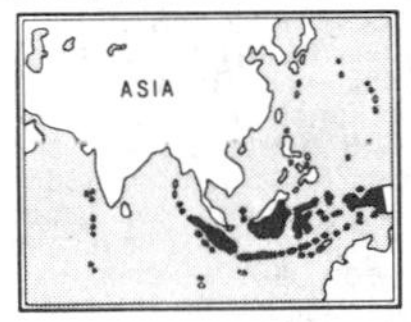


# INDONESIA

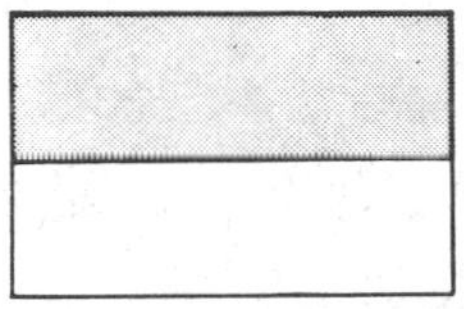

## SECULAR DATA

**STATE. Official name:** The Republic of Indonesia (Republik Indonesia). Adjective of nationality: Indonesian.
Flag (shown above right): Red stripe above white stripe.
**Area:** 1,934,198 sq.km. (746,798 sq.miles). Description: 13,677 islands (992 inhabited). Agricultural land: 14.9%.
**Government:** Republic, since 1971 (1800 Dutch possession (East Indies), 1945 Independence, 1957 dictatorship, 1967 military junta).
**Legislature:** House of Representatives, 460 members. People's Consultative Congress, 920 members.
**Official language:** Indonesian (*Bahasa Indonesia*).
**Chief cities:** capital Jakarta 4,576,000 (1971), Surabaja 1,556,260, Bandung 1,201,730, Semarang 646,590.
**Political divisions:** 26 Provinces.
**Armed forces** (1976): Total 246,000 regular: army 180,000, navy 38,000, air force 28,000 (30 combat aircraft). Paramilitary forces: 112,000.
**Dependencies:** East Timor (1976, claimed as 27th Province).

**DEMOGRAPHY. Population:** 119,391,290 (census of 24.IX.1971. For 1970–2000 (UN), see last row of Table 1). Population density (1975): 70/sq.km. (182/sq.mile). Under 15 years: 44%. Growth rate (1975–80): 2.59% per year (births 4.09%, deaths −1.50%). Life expectancy (1975–80): 50.0 years. Household size: 5.1 persons.
**Major languages:** Indonesian, English, Javanese, Sundanese, Madurese, Chinese, Balinese, Batak, Bugi, and about 840 other local ones. Some 13 are used by over 1 million speakers each.
**Urban dwellers** (1970): 17.2%. Urban growth rate (1950–70): 3.7% per year.
**Labour force:** 34%.
**Refugees** (1976): 40,000 from Portuguese Timor.
**Tourists** (1968): 40,000. (1974) 313,452.

**ETHNOLINGUISTIC GROUPS:** 42.0% Javanese, 13.6% Sundanese, 7.0% Madurese, 3.3% Minangkabau, 2.9% Batak (Toba, Mandailing, Angkola, Simalungan, Karo, Dairi, Pakpak), 2.9% Chinese [2.0% Indonesian-speaking Peranakan (Indonesian-born), 0.9% Totok (China-born, Chinese-speaking); from Fukien, Kwangtung], 2.9% Coast Malay, 2.8% Buginese, 2.1% Balinese, 2.0% Achinese, 1.6% Dayak, 1.6% Jakartan, 1.5% Banjarese, 1.2% Sasak, 1.2% Makassarese, 0.9% Borneo Malay, 0.9% Toraja, 0.7% Irianese (Papuan) (896,000) (Asmat, Bentoeni, Biak-Numfoor, Damal, Dani, Djabi, Jali, Marind-Anim, Moni, Sentani, Waropen, Wondama, & 340 other tribes), 0.6% Minahasan (Menadonese), 0.5% Gorontalese, 0.5% Rejong-Lebonger, 0.5% Ngadju, 0.5% Butung, 0.4% Lamponger, 0.4% Mandarese, 0.4% Ambonese, 0.4% Atoni, 0.4% Niassan, 0.3% Bimi, 0.3% Sangihe-Talaud, 0.3% Sumban, 0.3% Manggaraj, 0.3% Savu, 0.2% Kenyah, 0.2% Sumbawan, 0.2% Lio, 0.2% Sikka, 0.2% North Halmaheran, 0.2% Solor, 0.2% Alor, 0.1% Bolaang-Mogondow, 0.1% Eurasian, 0.1% Arab, 0.1% other Indonesian,

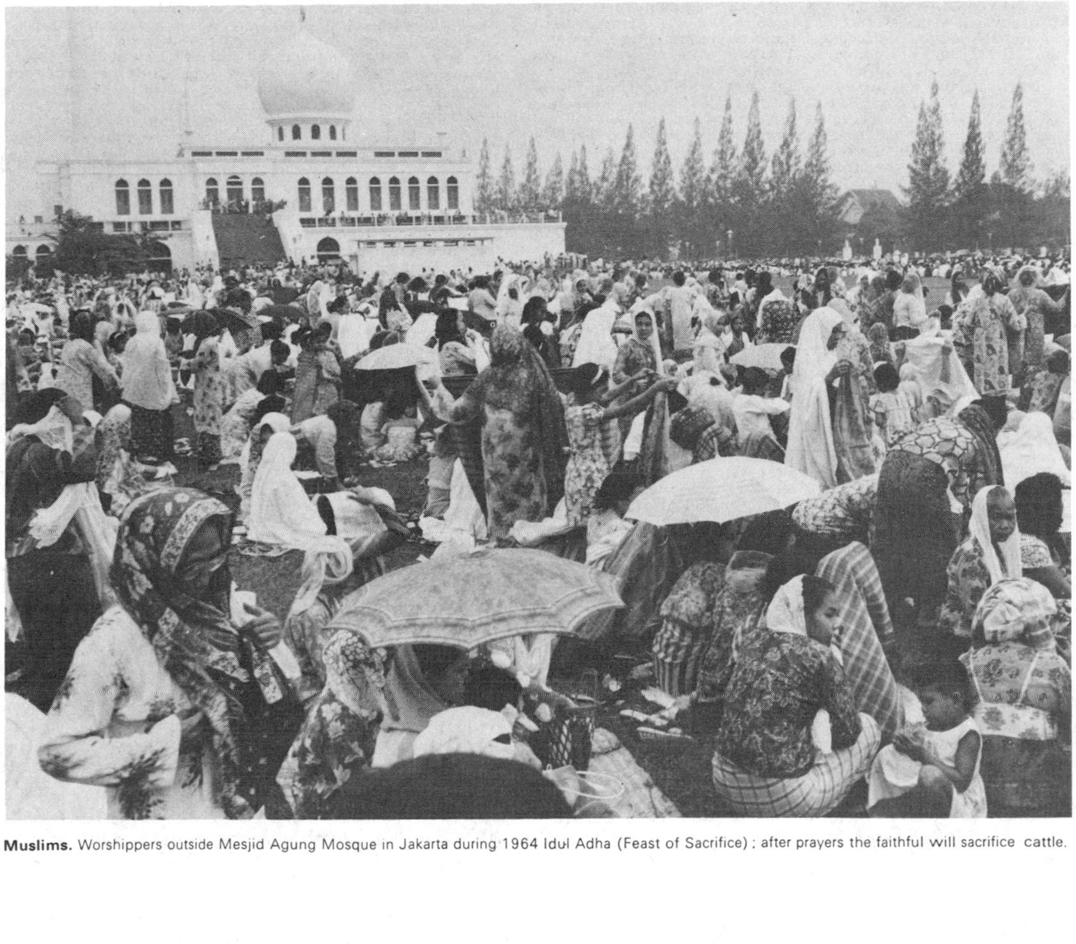

**Muslims.** Worshippers outside Mesjid Agung Mosque in Jakarta during 1964 Idul Adha (Feast of Sacrifice); after prayers the faithful will sacrifice cattle.

Ekari (Kapauku), Indian (40,000), European (20,000), Iban, Mentaweian, Tapiro Pygmy, Jewish, et alii.

**MONEY** (1977). **Monetary unit:** rupiah (= 100 sen); US$1 = Rp 415.00.
**National income per person:** US$200. Average annual family income: US$1,020.
**Inflation:** (1970–74) 19.6% per year (1975: consumer price index 279). In 1967, inflation reached a peak of 600% per year.

**Cost of living in capital** (1976): index 120 (Washington DC=100). Daily cost of living: US$47.

**EDUCATION.** Adult literacy: (1961) 43%, (1971) 57%. Education rate: 44%. Schools: 73,310 (64,250 elementary, 9,060 high). Universities: 59 (29 state, 30 private).

**HEALTH.** Hospitals: 1,199 (86,022 beds). Doctors: 4,561. Lepers: 133,200 (1.0 per 1,000). Blind (1974): 1,000,000. Psychotics: 810,000. Criminals: 74,010.

**LITERATURE.** Annual new book titles (1973): 1,180. Periodicals: 900. Scientific journals: 90. Newspapers: 85 dailies.

**COMMUNICATION** (per 1,000 people). Phones: 2. Radios: 114. TV sets: 2. Daily newspaper circulation: 18 copies.

TABLE 1. RELIGIOUS ADHERENTS IN INDONESIA

| Year | 1900 | | mid-1970 | | Annual change, 1970–1980 | | | | mid-1975 | | mid-1980 | | 2000 | |
|---|---|---|---|---|---|---|---|---|---|---|---|---|---|---|
| *Name* | *Adherents* | % | *Adherents* | % | *Natural* | *Conversion* | *Total* | *Rate* | *Adherents* | % | *Adherents* | % | *Adherents* | % |
| Muslims (Quranic) | 15,520,000 | 40.0 | 51,370,800 | 43.0 | 1,529,367 | 54,853 | 1,584,220 | 2.70 | 58,771,000 | 43.2 | 67,213,000 | 43.4 | 104,503,000 | 44.0 |
| Ahmadis | 0 | 0.0 | 81,000 | 0.1 | 2,602 | 1,298 | 3,900 | 3.90 | 100,000 | 0.1 | 120,000 | 0.1 | 300,000 | 0.1 |
| New-Religionists | 3,880,000 | 10.0 | 44,680,120 | 37.4 | 1,288,428 | −254,040 | 1,034,388 | 2.09 | 49,512,100 | 36.4 | 55,024,000 | 35.5 | 77,005,800 | 32.4 |
| **Christians** | **536,050** | **1.4** | **11,288,280** | **9.4** | **364,283** | **213,879** | **578,162** | **4.13** | **13,998,800** | **10.3** | **17,069,900** | **11.0** | **31,656,000** | **13.3** |
| crypto-Christians | 51,050 | 0.1 | 2,477,280 | 2.1 | 81,107 | 61,755 | 142,862 | 4.58 | 3,116,800 | 2.3 | 3,905,900 | 2.5 | 7,905,000 | 3.3 |
| professing | 485,000 | 1.2 | 8,811,000 | 7.4 | 283,176 | 152,124 | 435,300 | 4.00 | 10,882,000 | 8.0 | 13,164,000 | 8.5 | 23,751,000 | 10.0 |
| Protestants | 434,000 | 1.1 | 5,197,000 | 4.3 | 162,849 | 60,851 | 223,700 | 3.57 | 6,258,000 | 4.6 | 7,434,000 | 4.8 | 13,300,000 | 5.6 |
| Roman Catholics | 50,000 | 0.1 | 2,706,000 | 2.3 | 88,476 | 59,024 | 147,500 | 4.34 | 3,400,000 | 2.5 | 4,181,000 | 2.7 | 7,363,000 | 3.1 |
| Indonesian indigenous | 1,000 | 0.0 | 908,000 | 0.8 | 31,851 | 32,249 | 64,100 | 5.24 | 1,224,000 | 0.9 | 1,549,000 | 1.0 | 3,088,000 | 1.3 |
| affiliated | 536,050 | 1.4 | 11,288,280 | 9.4 | 364,283 | 213,879 | 578,162 | 4.13 | 13,998,800 | 10.3 | 17,069,900 | 11.0 | 31,656,000 | 13.3 |
| total practising | 482,440 | *90* | 9,143,510 | *81* | 295,069 | 173,242 | 468,311 | 4.13 | 11,339,030 | *81* | 13,826,620 | *81* | 22,159,200 | *70* |
| non-practising | 53,610 | *10* | 2,144,770 | *19* | 69,214 | 40,637 | 109,851 | 4.13 | 2,659,770 | *19* | 3,243,280 | *19* | 9,496,800 | *30* |
| Protestants | 473,000 | 1.2 | 6,302,682 | 5.3 | 198,254 | 85,208 | 283,462 | 3.72 | 7,618,500 | 5.6 | 9,137,300 | 5.9 | 16,625,000 | 7.0 |
| Evangelicals | 210,000 | 0.5 | 4,778,700 | 4.0 | 148,689 | 54,861 | 203,550 | 3.56 | 5,713,800 | 4.2 | 6,814,200 | 4.4 | 13,063,000 | 5.5 |
| Neo-pentecostals | 0 | 0.0 | 5,000 | 0.0 | 260 | 4,240 | 4,500 | 45.00 | 10,000 | 0.0 | 50,000 | 0.0 | 300,000 | 0.1 |
| Roman Catholics | 55,650 | 0.1 | 2,620,140 | 2.2 | 88,504 | 83,082 | 171,586 | 5.05 | 3,401,000 | 2.5 | 4,336,000 | 2.8 | 8,075,000 | 3.4 |
| Catholic pentecostals | 0 | 0.0 | 0 | 0.0 | 52 | 948 | 1,000 | 50.00 | 2,000 | 0.0 | 10,000 | 0.0 | 100,000 | 0.0 |
| Indonesian indigenous | 3,000 | 0.0 | 2,341,778 | 2.0 | 76,766 | 45,256 | 122,022 | 4.14 | 2,950,000 | 2.2 | 3,562,000 | 2.3 | 6,888,000 | 2.9 |
| Marginal Protestants | 0 | 0.0 | 11,580 | 0.0 | 390 | 252 | 642 | 4.28 | 15,000 | 0.0 | 18,000 | 0.0 | 40,000 | 0.0 |
| Catholics (non-Roman) | 400 | 0.0 | 10,000 | 0.0 | 312 | 88 | 400 | 3.33 | 12,000 | 0.0 | 14,000 | 0.0 | 25,000 | 0.0 |
| Anglicans | 0 | 0.0 | 2,000 | 0.0 | 57 | −7 | 50 | 2.27 | 2,200 | 0.0 | 2,500 | 0.0 | 3,000 | 0.0 |
| Orthodox | 4,000 | 0.0 | 100 | 0.0 | 0 | 0 | 0 | 0.00 | 100 | 0.0 | 100 | 0.0 | 0 | 0.0 |
| Tribal religionists | 17,692,950 | 45.6 | 6,570,000 | 5.5 | 180,544 | −109,644 | 70,900 | 1.02 | 6,938,000 | 5.1 | 7,279,000 | 4.7 | 7,363,000 | 3.1 |
| Hindus | 776,000 | 2.0 | 2,318,000 | 1.9 | 71,562 | 21,638 | 93,200 | 3.39 | 2,750,000 | 2.0 | 3,250,000 | 2.1 | 5,225,000 | 2.2 |
| Buddhists | 200,000 | 0.5 | 1,099,000 | 0.9 | 33,829 | 6,271 | 40,100 | 3.08 | 1,300,000 | 1.0 | 1,500,000 | 1.0 | 2,613,000 | 1.1 |
| Chinese folk-religionists | 195,000 | 0.5 | 980,000 | 0.8 | 26,413 | −19,413 | 7,000 | 0.69 | 1,015,000 | 0.7 | 1,050,000 | 0.7 | 1,188,000 | 0.5 |
| Non-religious | 0 | 0.0 | 950,000 | 0.8 | 38,930 | 82,870 | 121,800 | 8.14 | 1,496,000 | 1.1 | 2,168,000 | 1.4 | 7,125,000 | 3.0 |
| Atheists | 0 | 0.0 | 200,000 | 0.2 | 6,506 | 3,494 | 10,000 | 4.00 | 250,000 | 0.2 | 300,000 | 0.2 | 800,000 | 0.3 |
| Baha'is | 0 | 0.0 | 10,700 | 0.0 | 338 | 92 | 430 | 3.31 | 13,000 | 0.0 | 15,000 | 0.0 | 28,000 | 0.0 |
| Jews | 0 | 0.0 | 100 | 0.0 | 0 | 0 | 0 | 0.00 | 100 | 0.0 | 100 | 0.0 | 200 | 0.0 |
| **Country's population** | **38,800,000** | **100.0** | **119,467,000** | **100.0** | **3,540,200** | **0** | **3,540,200** | **2.60** | **136,044,000** | **100.0** | **154,869,000** | **100.0** | **237,507,000** | **100.0** |

COLUMNS, ROWS. For meanings and definitions, see Codebook (Part 6). Note that, by definition, total 'Christians' = professing + crypto-Christians, which also = affiliated + nominal Christians. Percentages may not always total exactly, due to rounding.
CENSUSES. In 1930 a partial census produced these figures for the whole country: 48.7% Muslims, 47.2% animists, 1.9% Hindus and Buddhists, 1.6% Protestants, 0.6% Roman Catholics. The *Statistical pocketbook of Indonesia* has for many years published annual religion statistics provided by the government Department of Religion, compiled in each region by local government officials using in the main information direct from the churches. The only census claiming complete enumeration for religion is as follows. **24.IX.1971:** 87.50% Muslims (Quranic and syncretistic), 7.38% Christians (4.35% Protestants, 2.27% Roman Catholics, 0.76% other Christians), 1.94% Hindus, 0.92% Buddhists, 0.82% Confucians (Chinese folk-religionists), 1.42% others.

**NOTES ON RELIGIONS**
AFFILIATED PROTESTANTS. Conversions have been very numerous since 1965. On Kalimantan alone, there were 300,000 persons baptized from 1965–74.
AHMADIS. Ahmadiya has 57 mosques and numerous foreign missionaries (Pakistanis), scattered across the nation. Both Ahmadi factions, Qadianis and Lahoris, are present.
ATHEISTS. The Communist Party of Indonesia (PKI) was suppressed in 1966 after an abortive coup, with over 250,000 massacred, and was driven underground with 90,000 imprisoned, and only a few thousand remained in 1973. However, something over 100,000 members and sympathizers are believed still to exist, making a total atheistic community of around 200,000, with at least a million more non-religious.
BAHA'IS. Local spiritual assemblies: 62 (1964), increasing slightly to 71 (1973).
BUDDHISTS. Prevalent among urban Chinese, and Javanese military and government officials. There are 30 Buddhist monasteries, and (in 1970) 355 temples (*rumah ibadat*). Since 1965 a large movement of nominal Muslims into Buddhism and Hinduism has taken place in East and Central Java. The resurgence of Buddhism has taken a neo-Theravada form.
CATHOLIC PENTECOSTALS (or, Catholic charismatics). The charismatic renewal was first introduced by Protestant groups, hence numerous prayer groups in 1976 were ecumenical with equal Protestant and Catholic membership. In 1975 only one Catholic priest was known to be active, but in 1976 bishops and priests became widely involved, with numerous retreats and conferences.
CHRISTIANS. Over 95% have come into Christianity from an animistic background, particularly the Batak church and those of Nias, Timor and Minahasa; the Java churches have arisen out of a Muslim background; and the Bali church has 11,000 converts from Hinduism. The large numbers of annual converts during 1965–1980 (over 2.5 million Protestant and Catholic converts) are mainly former nominal Muslim, animists, Hindus and Chinese.
COUNTRY'S POPULATION. In 1965 at least 250,000 alleged communists were massacred in the wake of an abortive communist coup.
CRYPTO-CHRISTIANS. Protestants and indigenous Christians affiliated to churches but in areas of strong Muslim hostility, and therefore not known to state or society as professing Christians nor recorded as such in censuses; including organized and unorganized isolated radio believers, and numbers of illegal or underground churches.
HINDUS. Predominant among the Balinese, also in some mountainous areas of Java, and among the Tenggarese (400,000). In addition, though not enumerated here as Hindus, 50% of the national population mostly in Java are strongly hinduized; they are enumerated here as New-Religionists. Since 1965 many hundreds of thousands of nominal Muslims have become Hindus, mostly in East and Central Java. *Temples.* In 1970, there were 411,678 houses of worship (*rumah ibadat*). ISKCON (Hare Krishna) operates 1 centre. In 1975 the Theosophical Society had 21 Lodges with 761 members.
INDONESIAN INDIGENOUS. In over 140 denominations in 1970 (see Table 2).
MUSLIMS. This line in the table enumerates only Quranic Muslims properly so called. Indonesian Islam has been characterized as malleable, tentative, syncretistic and multi-voiced. The government Department of Religion in its annual enumerations and in the 1971 census classifies 87.5% of the population as Muslims (the term *Islam statistik*, i.e. nominal or 'statistical Muslims', is used), by extending the term to include all peoples who are islamized or who are under Muslim influence, covering the 4 distinct groups shown as separate categories in the table above: (1) 43% who are Quranic Muslims, or strict Muslims, or Muslims properly so called; these are Sunnis (of the Shafiite rite), mostly coastal peoples including Sumatra Malays, Achinese, Buginese, Makassarese, with Wahhabi reform movement centres in north Sumatra and southwest Celebes, in 2 groups of similar size: (a) reformist favouring arabization, and (b) traditionalist; and also Ahmadiya (enumerated here under Muslims although declared non-Muslim by Pakistan); Islam is most strictly practised in Atjeh (west Sumatra), west Java, southeast Kalimantan, and some of the Lesser Sunda islands; (2) 29.4% belonging to islamized and hinduized new religions and mystical sects syncretizing Islam, Hinduism, Buddhism and animism (here termed New-Religionists); (3) 12.6% who are animistic tribal religionists either partially islamized or completely non-islamized; and (4) 2% who, while labelled 'statistical Muslims', are in fact (unknown to the state) either atheists, or non-religious, or Chinese folk-religionists, or crypto-Christians. Peoples strongly Muslim include the Achinese, Minangkabau, Sundanese, Madurese, Banjarese, Buginese and Javanese. *Mosques.* The total of mosques (*mesdjid*) was 58,059 in 1958, 62,976 in 1962, rising to 83,914 in 1970, and houses of worship (*langgar, surau*) 198,832 (1958), 219,745 (1962) and 240,520 (1970). *Mosque attendance.* About 3% of the population attend mosques regularly or occasionally. Total capacity of all mosques is about 7% of the population. *Hajj pilgrims to Mecca.* (1963) 8,637; (1968) 17,565; (1969) 10,615; (1970) 14,633; (1971) 22,753; (1972) 22,659; (1973) 40,668; (1974) 68,872; (1975) 55,617; (1976) 25,624. From the early days of Islam in Indonesia (9th century), pilgrims to Mecca have been a main means of communication, especially for Muslim reform movements.
NEO-PENTECOSTALS. Charismatics within the non-Pentecostal Protestant denominations.
NEW-RELIGIONISTS. These fall into 2 categories, the first indigenous to Indonesia and found there only, the second international movements introduced from outside. (1) By far the larger group are followers of new Muslim or islamized and hinduized syncretistic religions (syncretizing Islam, Hinduism, Buddhism and animism). The origins of these religions go back several centuries, when the traditional animistic element was predominant. Since 1800 this element has receded in importance as Muslim, Hindu and Christian elements have come to the fore. In this survey, they are classified among the so-called New Religions of Asia because of this recent syncretistic development, and also because they have become especially widespread since 1950. They include: Javanese religion (Agama Jawa), Java-Sundanese religion (Agama Jawa-Sunda), Javanese and other mystical sects (Golongan-golongan Kebatinan: including Budi Setia, Sumarah, Kawruh Bedja, Ilmu Sejati), and similar syncretistic religions outside Java. A representative movement is Pangestu, a syncretistic religion with 100,000 adherents (mainly intellectuals) on Java, teaching 'one Divine Being' derived from Islam, Christianity, Buddhism and Hinduism. A number of these new religions have been banned for alleged subversion but continue to operate underground. The total of all such sects is probably over 300, less than half of which are registered with government. A handful have followings outside Indonesia, such as the experiential cult Subud begun by Bapak on Java in 1933 and since 1956 spread abroad, with centres in over 70 USA cities alone. (2) There are also a few followers of Japanese and Chinese New Religions, including (1975) 2,600 in Soka Gakkai (Nichiren Shoshu).
NON-RELIGIOUS. Three separate groupings: (1) those related to the underground communist movement, (2) former Chinese folk-religionists who have abandoned religion, and (3) intellectuals and other humanists.
ORTHODOX. Armenians rapidly emigrating since the year 1900.
PRACTISING CHRISTIANS. This Encyclopedia's questionnaire survey of major Protestant churches (1972) showed an average weekly church attendance of 61%, which indicates annual practice of around 80%. Catholic Easter practice was 64% in 1969, and all practising Catholics about 74%; Sunday mass attenders in many areas are as high as 95%. The indigenous churches have even higher attendance, around 90% annually.
ROMAN CATHOLICS. In the year 1900, there were 54,909 baptized (29,009 indigenous, including 1,461 in West Irian, and 25,900 Europeans) and 729 catechumens.
TRIBAL RELIGIONISTS. Two groupings: (a) partially-islamized folk-religionists and animists, and (b) predominantly or completely animistic peoples. Animists are numerically significant among Bataks, Dayaks, Torajas, Halmaherans, Irianese, and in Nias, Mentawei, Aru, Seram, Buru, and Nusatenggara (16% animist; Sumba island was 68.7% animist in 1968). In West Irian, many of the 350 tribes (800,000 population) are still predominantly animist, and for some decades nativistic and messianic or cargo-cult movements have been frequent among them. On Kalimantan, about one million follow the primal religion Kaharingan.

**NON-CHRISTIAN RELIGIONS.** Islam was introduced into northern Sumatra in 1272. In general, western Indonesia is more islamized than the east where Muslims are confined largely to coastal areas. The principal ethnic groups accepting Islam include the following: Achinese, a small part of the Bataks, Sumatra Coastal Malays, Minangkabaus, Palembangese, Jambirese, Rejong-Lebongers and Lampongers of Sumatra; Bantamese, Sundanese, Madurese and a portion of the Javanese in Java and Madura; Banjarese and Kutanese of Kalimantan; Gorontalese, Makassarese, Buginese, Butungese of Sulawesi; Ternatenese, Tidorese of Maluku; Sasaks of Lombok; Bimans, and Sumbawans. The percentage of adherents attributed to Islam varies considerably according to how Muslims are defined. The government Department of Religion uses the figure of 89% of the population in 1965 rising to 91% in 1970, based on the principle that whoever is not Catholic, Protestant, Hindu or Buddhist must be married in a Muslim ceremony and is therefore counted as Muslim (the term 'statistical Muslims' is used). On the other hand, many sociologists and observers estimate that only 43% of the population are Quranic Muslims (Muslims in the strict or correct sense of the term), a figure which is based on the percentage of votes obtained by the 5 Islamic political parties in 1955, since during the electoral campaign this vote was considered a minimal requirement for being called a Muslim, and also on the voting percentage in 1959 on the proposition to transform Indonesia into an Islamic state.

According to a recent investigation, Muslims on

Java are slightly less urbanized than Christians or Buddhists, whereas on the other islands the reverse is true. Most Muslims are peasants, but in coastal areas there are many who are merchants and seafarers. Particularly in Central and East Java, one finds relatively more convinced Muslims in the middle class and among the wealthier portion of the peasant class than among the very poor. Quranic Muslims are Sunnis of the Shafiite rite. They are divided into 2 groups: (1) a reformist branch which favours the arabization of Indonesian Islam, purifying it of pre-Islamic customs, and seeking to prepare Muslims for their encounter with modernity; and (2) a traditionalist branch which does not favour secular education and wishes to maintain the present mixture of Islamic and Indonesian customs. At the first general elections held in 1955, the reformist party obtained 20.9% of the votes and the traditionalist party 18.4%. Since the accession to power of general Suharto as acting president in 1967, the position and influence of Muslims in national affairs has been noticeably reduced.

**New Religions** syncretizing traditional animism with, firstly, Hinduism and Buddhism, and later Islam, have arisen over the centuries mainly on Java. They are of the same generic synthetic kind as the other new Asiatic syncretistic religions of Japan, China, Korea, Viet Nam et alia, except that in Indonesia today the main background religion is Islam. The following 3 distinct religions are in this category; from one point of view they may be described as islamized new religions.

**Javanese religion** (Agama Jawa), composed of animistic, Hindu, Buddhist and Muslim elements, is the religion of a large number of Javanese of the urbanized upper classes among whom Hindu elements predominate, as well as being found among poor peasants of the Central and East Javanese plains, among whom animistic elements are more significant. Originally these were all considered animists, as in the census of 1930 which listed Indonesia as 47.2% animist and 48.7% Muslim. The Department of Religion today classes the adherents of Agama Jawa as Muslims; but many, reacting against the campaign of islamization, are turning towards Hinduism, Buddhism and Christianity.

**Java-Sundanese religion** (Agama Jawa-Sunda) was not widely recognized as a distinct religion until 1964 when Muslims tried forcibly to islamize its adherents. The religious head, followed by some of his faithful, sought refuge in the Catholic Church. The exact number of members is not known, but it appears to be found only among the Sundanese in the interior of West Java. This religion categorically rejects practices permitted by Muslims such as polygamy, divorce and child marriage.

**Mystical sects** (Golongan-golongan Kebatinan) are also important in Indonesia. There has never been any lack of mystical movements in Java and elsewhere, but their number has grown considerably since 1950 mainly as a result of the general social disorder. Mystical movements are most common in Java and are found among members of all social classes. Representing a great diversity of beliefs from pantheism to monotheism, most of them evidence belief in spirits and the use of magical practices. In varying degrees they engage in occultism, theosophy and metapsychical phenomena. A number have been banned by government for alleged subversion but continue to operate underground. Their attraction lies in the emphasis they give to certain indigenous religious values and concerns which are ignored by Indonesia's others religions. In general they manifest uneasiness and even animosity towards the established religions, especially to legalistic Islam. Nevertheless, one occasionally finds Javanese Christians among their members.

**Traditional tribal religion,** commonly called animism, still exists among the Bataks of northern Sumatra; the inhabitants of Nias and Mentawai; the Dayaks of Kalimantan; the Torajas of Sulawesi; the inhabitants of the archipelago of Aru; the peoples of Seram and Buru, and Halmaherans in Maluku; the Irianese of West Irian; as well as on the islands of Nusatenggara. These peoples are for the most part the inhabitants of small islands or isolated regions of the interior. Some, such as several of the Papuan tribes, follow stone age culture. Most tribal religions are complex, with numerous names for God; among the Toba Bataks the supreme being is called Mula

**Tribal religionists.** Head of Batak sorcerer's carved staff, Sumatra.

Dyadi, while Batara Guru (Sanskrit: Bhattara Guru) is the name more commonly used by the Dairi and Karo Bataks. Their adherents can be classified into 2 groups: partially islamized folk-religionists and animists, and predominantly or completely animistic peoples. Islam is making an effort to reach them, but most are more attracted to Christianity. In West Irian by 1973 a total of over 21 distinct cargo cults of animistic origin had arisen, mainly in Geelvink Bay and in the highlands.

**Hinduism** and **Buddhism** are the most ancient of Indonesia's immigrant religions. Both have shown a new flowering since Independence in 1945. Hinduism is the predominant religion among the Balinese who mix with it pre-Hindu and Hindu-Javanese elements. Denpasar, the capital of Bali, has a university for training Hindu teachers. Hinduism also exists in some of the mountainous areas of Java where, lately, the Parisada Hindu Dharma Society has been actively engaged in literature distribution and establishment of Hindu schools. Buddhism is especially prevalent among the Chinese who are largely city-dwellers, and also among Javanese army officers and government officials. In 1970 there were 30 Buddhist monasteries and 355 temples in Indonesia. There are in addition large numbers of 'statistical Muslims' among whom Hindu elements predominate, and who account for much of the estimated half a million conversions from nominal Islam to Hinduism since 1965.

**CHRISTIANITY.** A Catholic community established itself on the island of Sumatra as early as the 7th century, and in 1323 Franciscans had some contacts with Sumatra, Java and Borneo. Portuguese colonial expansion was extended to the Moluccas and the Celebes in 1522 and the evangelization of Timor began in 1530. The first Portuguese missionary to the Moluccas arrived in 1534. Francis Xavier spent nearly a year there in 1546, and was followed by other Jesuits and Dominicans in 1562. By the end of the 16th century, there were 18 Catholic mission posts and 25,000 Christians. With the defeat of Portugal by the Dutch in 1605, Catholic missionaries were expelled and replaced by Dutch Reformed chaplains supported by the Dutch East India Company. The Dutch Reformed Church was virtually the only Christian influence in the islands for the next 300 years. The beginning of the 19th century saw a change in both the political and religious climates. France conquered Holland in 1799 and disbanded the Dutch East India Company, and England began to

**Hindus.** Balinese song-and-dance drama in Hindu village on Bali.

exert its colonial influence in the area in 1811. This was accompanied by the Protestant awakening epitomized by William Carey's missionary journey to India. In 1827 the Netherlands Missionary Society began work in the Celebes and the Rhenish Mission among the Dayaks of Borneo. These beginnings were followed by many others, including the notable work of German Lutherans among the Bataks of Sumatra beginning in 1861. Catholic missionaries also returned to Indonesia during the 19th century. In 1807 the prefecture apostolic of Batavia was erected, which

**Protestants.** North Sumatran choir sing at DGI ecumenical worship service in football stadium at Pematang Siantar, 1971.

was eventually in 1961 renamed as the archdiocese of Jakarta. Dutch Jesuits appeared on the scene in 1859 and Catholic evangelization of all the major islands began. The 20th century has witnessed the influx of many new Protestant missionary groups, as well as the continued growth of Catholicism and of large regional Reformed and Lutheran churches.

Since 1966 Protestants and Catholics have experienced massive growth in membership. During July–August 1966 the East Java Christian Church (then with 63,000 followers) baptized nearly 10,000 persons. The Karo Batak Protestant Church (30,000 in 1965) baptized over 26,000 persons in 1966–67. Prolonged revival movements broke out, notably on Timor where the Evangelical Christian Church in Timor grew by over 100,000 members in 4 years. In the 8 months before March 1967, 250,000 joined member churches of the Christian Council of Indonesia alone. Altogether, Protestants and Catholics received well over 2.5 million converts from nominal Islam (former 'statistical Muslims') since 1965. The largest numbers came from the following areas (in order of magnitude): Central Java, East (but not West) Java, north Sumatra, Alor, Timor (eastern part), Lampung, Sulawesi (among the Torajas), and the interiors of Kalimantan and West Irian.

Part of this whole widespread increase is explained by the violence of anti-communist repression following the abortive coup d'etat of 1965, and also by the requirement, subsequently enforced on all citizens, that everyone belong to one of the 4 recognized religions. In the Catholic Church this phenomenon has manifested itself since 1966 by a sudden rise in the number of catechumens and since 1967 by a marked increase in adult baptisms. Not uncommonly the vigorous campaign aimed at islamizing animists and 'atheists' (communist sympathizers being automatically considered as atheists) has paradoxically resulted in pushing many towards Christianity, Hinduism and Buddhism rather than towards Islam. This sudden growth is more evident in areas with a relatively large proportion of animists, Chinese or 'statistical Muslims', the latter being the animists and Javanese religionists listed as Muslims by the Department of Religion. There has been virtually

no additional growth in strongly Muslim areas or where Christians already form a large part of the population. Irian Barat is an exception in that the events of 1965–66 have had little influence; and Muslims, who in any case are few in number and largely confined to the coast, show little interest in the Irianese peoples.

PROTESTANT CHURCHES. Of the 17.1 million affiliated Christians in Indonesia (1980), 9.1 million (54%) are Protestants. Eight million belong to churches which are members of the Council of Churches in Indonesia (DGI), with a few Western-related Pentecostal and other Protestant groups outside the council. Protestant strength by regions may be listed in order as follows: West Irian 65% (Protestants as % of total population), Moluccas 57%, Sulawesi 18%, northern Sumatra 15%, south-east Indonesia and Bali 10%, Kalimantan 6%, Java 2%. Indonesia has several very large Protestant churches, the largest and most extensive being the Protestant Church in Indonesia; totalling nearly 2 million members in 1970, it serves as the General Synod for 7 component churches. Initials based on the Indonesian names of churches and organizations

are widely used to identify them. The most significant churches in Sumatra are the Batak Christian Protestant Church (HKBP) with more than a million members, the Nias Christian Protestant Church (BNKP) with 220,000 and the Simalungun Protestant Christian Church (GKPS) with 109,500. Sulawesi churches of particular importance include the Christian Evangelical Church in Minahasa (GMIM), Evangelical Christian Church in Sangihe-Talaud (GMIST), the Toraja Christian Church, and the Christian Church in Central Sulawesi (GKST), with (1970) respectively 556,000, 183,000, 175,000, and 125,000 adherents. Among the Java churches may be mentioned the East Java Christian Church (GKJW) and the Christian Churches of Java (GKJ), each with more than 120,000 members. The Moluccan Protestant Church (GPM) then had 505,000 adherents. On Irian Barat, the Evangelical Christian Church in West Irian has some 360,000 adherents, while the Evangelical Church in Kalimantan has over 90,000 followers. In addition to these large churches, most of which represent the fruit of early European missionary work, there are numerous smaller bodies, most representing recent missionary activity by conservative missions from North America. Of these the largest is the Gospel Tabernacle Christian Church (KINGMI), a product of the missionary activity of the Christian and Missionary Alliance. The Pentecostal movement has expanded rapidly both in numbers of denominations and in membership since the arrival of the first Pentecostal missionaries in the late 1920s. Altogether, there were in 1973 over 1,150 Western Protestant missionaries, 750 in 64 societies being from the USA.

The Protestant churches are heavily involved in education, and medical and social services. Of the 49 members of the DGI, 28 reported the following statistics in 1971: 230 kindergartens, 2,158 elementary schools, 75 junior and 62 senior secondary schools, plus 75 junior and 78 senior trade and vocational schools. Also there are 17 Christian universities and institutes of higher education. These include 4 well-established universities whose degrees are fully certified by government (Christian University of Indonesia in Jakarta, Nommensen University in North Sumatra, Satya Wacana Christian University in Central Java, Petra Christian University in East Java), and a school of social work at the under-

**Catholic Church in Indonesia.** Pope Paul VI gives homily at mass in Jakarta during December 1970 visit.

graduate level. Medical facilities operated by 23 churches include: 22 hospitals, 10 clinics, 7 dispensaries, 8 maternity hospitals, 8 maternity clinics, 7 health centres, 41 family planning clinics and 3 leprosaria. At least 9 churches operate technical and agricultural schools at the secondary level, and others are involved in numerous smaller development projects. This effort has been intensified since 1971 with the establishment of one national and 3 regional development centres under the DGI. In various parts of Indonesia churches are engaged in lumbering, irrigation, upgrading cattle, poultry and fisheries, planting and improving rice, maize, vegetables, coconut and coffee groves, and road and bridge building. One of the Christian universities has an agricultural faculty.

CATHOLIC CHURCH. In 1949, 90,000 of the 791,000 Catholics were Europeans, mostly Dutch. Following Independence, and especially the nationalization of foreign-owned installations in 1958, Dutch citizens returned en masse to Europe, the only exception being priests and religious personnel. By 1969 there were only 2,000 Europeans out of a total of 2.2 million Catholics (rising to 2,538,000 baptized Catholics in 1972). In 1969 Chinese, both Indonesian and foreign, made up 7.1% of the total Catholic population. The largest percentages of Chinese by dioceses include the following: Pangkal Pinang 60.6%, Padang 56.3%, Malang 42.9%, Bogor 39.2%, Jakarta 38.2%, Surabaya 38.1%, Palembang 32.6%, Bandung 29.7%. By ecclesiastical provinces, the percentages are as follows: Jakarta 35.7%, Semarang 19.1%, Pontianak 12%, Medan 10.4%, Makassar 6%, Merauke 0.5% and Ende 0.5%. The ecclesiastical province with the greatest number of Catholics (Ende: 1,073,911 out of 2,220,428 in 1969) is also the one which has the smallest percentage of Chinese; and the smallest number of Chinese are in the province of Merauke. On the island of Flores which has 1% of the nation's population, 73% are Catholic, which figure is 36% of all Indonesian Catholics. On Java live 63.8% of the total population, but only 19% of all Catholics. In 8 dioceses (5 of them on Java) less than 0.5% of the population is Catholic, whereas in 5 other dioceses (3 of them on Flores) more than half are Catholics. This inequality in geographical distribution was even more evident 20 years ago, due in part to the Dutch colonial policy of prohibiting certain territories to Catholic work. Java was never closed to Catholics, but Bali was until 1935. The Torajas of Sulawesi and the inhabitants of Nias became accessible only in 1939. Ambon and the northern part of Western Irian were opened after 1925; but the Bataks and the inhabitants of Sumba were closed until 1929. The geographical inequality is now being modified because since Independence many Catholics from outlying islands have joined in the widespread migration to Java and particularly to Jakarta.

INDIGENOUS CHURCHES. Since 1891 there have been numerous secessions led by Indonesians from the major Protestant missions, and numbers of other churches independent of Western missions have been begun by Indonesians and Chinese since 1866. In 1970 there were around 150 such indigenous denominations, of which over 100 were known to, and listed by, the government Department of Religion. With an estimated 2.3 million affiliated adherents in 1970, they represent a powerful factor in the evolution of an indigenous Christianity. At least half of these are adherents of around 50 indigenous pentecostal denominations. Most of these are clearly-defined denominations; but the largest of these, the Pentecostal Church of Indonesia (GPI), is in reality less an organized denomination than a vast unstructured agglomeration of relatively independent congregations.

CHURCH AND STATE. The constitution of 1945 stipulates: 'The State is based on the recognition of one all-powerful God' (Chapter XI, paragraph 29, Article 1), and 'The State guarantees to each citizen the freedom to embrace the religion of his choice and to fulfil the religious obligations which conform to his faith' (Article 2). Liberty to propagate religion is guaranteed 'on condition that it does not disturb religious peace'. The Indonesian state is based on 5 principles, called *pancasila:* faith in one all-powerful God, humanity, national consciousness, sovereignty of the people, and social justice. In reality, since January 1965 freedom of religion has been legally confined to free choice between 4 recognized religions: Islam, Protestantism, Catholicism and 'Hindu-Buddhism', the latter 2 being grouped together as one religion. Every good citizen is expected to adhere formally to one of these. Belief in one God (monotheism) makes formal adherence to any other than the 4 recognized religions practically impossible, and a person who derides any of the monotheistic religions is punishable with 5 years' imprisonment. This situation was modified in 1973 when the New Religions (Kebatinan), of which president Suharto himself was a member, were finally granted official recognition and equal status.

The recognized religions are subject to parliamentary law although the terms 'churches' and 'religious societies' do not appear in legal texts. Statutes and

**Church of Christ.** 1974 Christmas Eve candlelight service held by Gereja Kristus, a Chinese pentecostal church in West Java, one of 140 indigenous denominations in Indonesia.

internal regulations relating to each religion are approved by the Ministry of Justice which confers on them a juridical personality. The government Department of Religion (Departemen Agama Republik Indonesia), created in January 1946, has final jurisdiction over religious questions. This ministry has the responsibility for proposing all religious legislation to parliament, which however can only be adopted by unanimous vote. Religious questions are regulated by various principles. Recognized religions are free to erect places of worship 'wherever there are numerous adherents'. They are free to build and direct schools, hospitals, orphanages and so on, and also to create political and social movements. The state does not concern itself with the internal affairs of the religions, and it confers certain advantages on religious leaders and exempts them from taxes. Religion courses are obligatory in all state schools and universities. In state institutions, students may choose one of the 4 recognized religions, courses on any being provided if 10 or more students request them. Teachers of religion are paid by the state. Religious marriages have legal validity, but a civil marriage ceremony is considered legal for all Christians on Java, Madura, Minahasa, Ambon and Banda, as well as for non-native Indonesians of Asian extraction. Chinese have to contract a civil marriage in addition to any religious ceremony. Finally, under pain of prison or fine, it is prohibited to offend or insult, orally or in written form, any of the recognized religions or religious groups. It is also worthy of note that the Christian New Year, Good Friday, Ascension Day, and Christmas are considered national holidays. Nevertheless, in practice the government Department of Religion, which is in the hands of conservative Muslims, favours Islam over the 3 other recognized religions. The major portion of the budget, reputedly as much as 95%, is given to Muslims who according to the department compose around 90% of the population. Large subsidies are provided for the construction of mosques and Quranic schools, the printing and diffusion of Muslim literature, and the like. The entire nation down to the smallest village is divided into a network of 'offices for religious affairs' whose personnel, paid by the state, are almost exclusively Muslim. Altogether these personnel number 180,000 employees.

The constitutional liberty to propagate religion suffers from the numerous ways such terms can be defined and the many ways of claiming that religious peace has been 'disturbed'. In the same way, the phrase 'wherever there are numerous adherents' is also interpreted differently depending on whether the projected place of worship is Muslim or non-Muslim. Locally, Muslim pressure sometimes turns to violence resulting in the destruction of churches or Christian schools. The treatment received by churches depends on the administrative level concerned, distance from the capital, and personal relations with local officials of the Department of Religion. However, private

schools conforming to established norms receive subsidies, as do orphanages and some Christian hospitals. Churches and ministers are exempted from certain taxes. The churches' proposals for social and economic development projects receive authorization from the central government. In spite of Muslim opposition, visas are accorded to new foreign missionaries and their residence permits are regularly renewed. Muslim religious fanaticism is exercised principally against alleged communists and atheists, of whom hundreds of thousands were massacred in 1965–66 after the abortive coup d'etat. By 1973, most of the 95,000 political prisoners and communist suspects had been released, leaving 15,000 in prisons and detention camps. On the island of Buru in the Maluku chain, there is a farming penal colony for some 7,500 of them. Although labelled atheists, they also are required to choose a religion in conformity with the law.

Christian political parties have had a certain history. The Partai Katolik (Roman Catholic) and PARKINDO (Protestant) had considerable influence; but in 1972 they were fused with 3 other national parties into the secular Democracy Party of Indonesia (Partai Demokrasi-Gereja Indonesia).

In July 1978, the appointment of a new head of the Department of Religion resulted in government edicts banning all proselytism, conversions and house churches, and calling for the expulsion of all foreign missionaries within 2 years (Decrees Nos. 70 and 77). These were however later toned down considerably.

**INTERDENOMINATIONAL ORGANIZATIONS.** The major Protestant body is the Council of Churches in Indonesia, referred to in English as either the CCI or ICC (Dewan Gereja-Gereja di Indonesia, DGI), begun in 1950 with 27 members, and by 1973 greatly enlarged in size and activities with 44 autonomous member churches (49 by 1978). A number of indigenous pentecostal and non-pentecostal churches are members; the first pentecostal body being the Church of Jesus the Messiah which joined in 1960. The DGI has a wide range of activities, and has in addition 14 affiliated regional councils across the nation. There are also 2 smaller Christian councils, Christian Laymen's Evangelical Fellowship (1969), and the Association of Evangelical Churches of Indonesia (Dewan Gereja-Gereja Injil di Indonesia) (1970). Further, some 23 separate pentecostal bodies were at one time members of the United Pentecostal Full Gospel Churches of Indonesia (Alamat Jamaat-Jemaat Dari Gereja-Gereja Injil Penuh) mainly based on Jakarta, but this has for some time ceased to function. Other Protestant co-operating bodies include the Christian Publishing Body (Badan Penerbit Kristen), and organizations serving youth, women, farmers, labourers and intellectuals. Ecumenical relations between Protestants and Catholics have improved considerably since Vatican II, with such activities as joint celebration of Christian feast days in several regions. Sodepaxi Indonesia, founded in 1969, is an organ of the DGI and the Catholic episcopal conference (MAWI) for the promotion of social justice, peace and economic development. Catholic activities are co-ordinated through the Ecumenical Commission of MAWI.

**BROADCASTING.** There are many commercial and private stations in Indonesia in addition to the government Radio Republic Indonesia. Whereas the latter will not accept foreign-made religious programmes, some private stations will. Most material must therefore be locally produced. Very short religious spots are allowed in some cities in rotation among various churches from Monday to Saturday, together with one hour on Sundays for both Catholic and Protestant material. The predominant language used is Indonesian, but some shortwave services are in English, French, Dutch and Chinese. FEBC has a studio and supplies private stations with tapes every week, in addition to sending others from Jakarta to FEBC (Manila) for transmission to Indonesia. The Sanggar Prathivi Radio and TV Production Centre in Jakarta is the principal producer of Catholic radio and TV programmes. It supplies 25 radio programmes weekly to more than 80 government and private radio stations, plus a 25-minute nationwide TV programme and a longer educational drama every 2 months. In Jakarta there is an Educational Radio and TV Centre for development, which produces 18 radio programmes a week and 6 TV programmes a month, all sent to local and national stations. These programmes are aimed at adult education. SEARV, the Protestant Filipino Service from Manila, was for a time the major Christian service in the area and supplemented local broadcasting. For Catholics, Indonesia is a member of UNDA.

In 1976 Indonesia's first domestic satellite was launched, carrying religious programmes free of charge, including 23-minute TV programmes 8 times a year (produced by Southern Baptists in Jakarta).

**BIBLIOGRAPHY**


*Batak blood and Protestant soul: the development of national Batak churches in North Sumatra.* P. B. Pedersen. Grand Rapids: Eerdmans, 1970. 212p.

*Bibliography of Indonesian peoples and cultures.* R. Kennedy. Southeast Asia Studies, Yale University, 1962, 2nd revised edition. 207p. (About 12,000 entries, many on religion).

(Bibliography of the scientific study of religions and Christian theology in the Indonesian language. Vol. 2) *Bibliografi Ilmu Agama dan Theologia Kristen Dalam Bahasa Indonesia,* Jilid II. J. A. B. Jongeneel. Jakarta: Unit Pemasaran BPK, 1976. 477p. (Vol. I, 1975).

*Church growth in the central highlands of West New Guinea.* J. Sunda. Lucknow: Lucknow Publishing House, 1963. 51p.

'Cultural contact and culture change in Western New Guinea', J. M. van der Kroef, *Anthropological quarterly*, 32 (1959), 134–60.

'Das Christentum in Indonesien', T. Müller-Krüger, in H. Kähler (ed), *Indonesien, Malaysia und die Philippinen* (Leiden: Brill, 1975).

*Der Protestantismus in Indonesien.* T. Müller-Krüger. Stuttgart: Evangelisches Verlagswerk, 1968.

(Directory of the Catholic Church in Indonesia) *Buku Petunjuk Gereja Katolik Indonesia, 1974.* Jakarta: Kantor Waligereja Indonesia, 1974.

*Entwicklung im Paradies: Socialer Fortschrift und die Kirchen in Indonesien.* U. Beyer. Frankfurt: Lembeck, 1974.

*God's miracles: Indonesian church growth.* E. C. Smith. South Pasadena: William Carey Library, 1970. 217p.

(History of the Catholic Church in Indonesia) *Sejarah Gereja Katolik Indonesia.* Ed M. P. M. Muskens. Ende (Flores): Arnoldus Press (SVD), 1974. 4 vols; 2,800p. (In Bahasa Indonesia language. English version 1977, Melbourne University Press).

'Indonesia', *Pro Mundi Vita bulletin*, 64 (Jan–Feb, 1977): 1–32.

*Indonesia: church and society.* F. L. Cooley. New York: Friendship Press, 1968. 128p.

*Indonesian revival: why two million came to Christ.* A. T. Willis, Jr. South Pasadena, CA: William Carey Library, 1978. 288p.

'Islam in Indonesia', A. Mukti Ali, in H. Kähler (ed) *op. cit.*

'Messianic movements in the Celebes, Sumatra and Borneo', J. M. van der Kroef, in S. Thrupp (ed), *Millennial dreams in action* (The Hague: Mouton, 1962), p. 80–121.

'Messianic movements in Western New Guinea', F. U. Kamma, *International review of missions*, 41, 162 (1952), 148–60.

'Pentecostalism among the Bandjalang', M. Calley, in M. Reay (ed), *Aborigines now* (Sydney, 1964), p. 44–58.

*Religious texts of the oral tradition from Western New Guinea.* Part A: The origin and sources of life. Part B: The threat to life and its defence against natural and supernatural phenomena. Ed F. C. Kamma. Leiden: Brill, 1975, 1978. 140p, 196p. (Papuan tribal religions).

(Survey of the Christian Evangelical Church of Timor). Ed F. L. Cooley. Jakarta: DGI, 1976. 413p.

*The Catholic Church in Indonesia.* Jakarta: Kantor Waligereja Indonesia, 1975. 95p.

*The growing seed: the Christian Church in Indonesia.* 20 vols. Jakarta: DGI Institute for Research and Study, 1976—. (Comprehensive 7-year project covering whole country. In Indonesian, *Benih Yang Tumbuh*).

*The Kalimantan Kenyah: a study of tribal conversion in terms of dynamic cultural themes.* W. Conley. Nutley, NJ (USA): Presbyterian & Reformed Publishing Co., 1975. 476p.

*The religion of Java.* C. Geertz. Glencoe, IL (USA): Free Press, 1958.

*The struggle of Islam in modern Indonesia.* B. J. Boland. The Hague: H. H. L. Smits, 1970.


TABLE 2. ORGANIZED CHURCHES AND DENOMINATIONS IN INDONESIA

| Official name 1 | Begun 2 | Type 3 | Counc 4 | Congs 5 | Adults 6 | Affiliated 7 | Names, notes, and other statistics (see Codebook) 8 |
|---|---|---|---|---|---|---|---|
| Anglican Ch (D Papua & New Guinea) | | A Hig | awpK. | 5 | 800 | 2,000 | Papuans from PNG working in West Irian; British expatriates in Jakarta, Surabaya, Sumatra. |
| Armenian Apostolic Church | | O Arm | Ev... | 1 | 50 | 100 | *Gereja Armenia.* In 1904, 4,000 Armenians in prelature of Batavia; rapid emigration. |
| Assemblies of God | c1930 | P Pe2 | ZF..I | 248 | 17,975 | 40,000 | *Sidang Jumat Allah.* Java, Sumatra, Ambon, Sulawesi. M=AoG(USA). 267n,32f,4s(91). |
| Association of Christian Foundations | | I pen | ..... | 175 | 30,000 | 70,000 | *Persekutuan Jajasan Kristen.* Unregistered Javanese autonomous congregations. |
| Australian Baptist Missionary Society | 1955 | P Bap | .H... | 79 | 7,174 | 20,000 | In West Irian. 1955 began among Dani tribe. Works with CMA, UFM, RBMU. 15f,1H. |
| Bali Christian Protestant Church | 1932 | P Ref | Ru..W | 36 | 6,000 | 11,000 | *GKPB.* Ex Hindus. HQ Denpasar. 1975: intense persecution. 25n,G=−3.0%pa,40Yy. |
| Baptist Churches in Indonesia | 1951 | P Bap | T...E | 983 | 10,748 | 20,000 | *GGBI. G2 Baptis I.* M=SBC(USA). Urban. 6 schools. 62n,42x,121f,1H,2h,1s,W=70%,1715Y. |
| Baptist Gospel Association of Indonesia | 1961 | P Bap | xF... | 38 | 288 | 5,893 | *Perhimpunan Injil Baptis I.* WKalimantan. M=CBFMS(USA). 3m,2x,25f,1H,W=66%,82Y,35z. |
| Batak Christian Church | 1927 | I Lut | .TT.T | 30 | 3,000 | 7,000 | *Huria Kristen Batak.* Split ex HKBP, rejecting all Western influences. 10n. |
| Batak Christian Community Church | 1927 | I Lut | LuE.W | 35 | 6,250 | 10,000 | *PKB. Punguan Kristen Batak.* HQ Jakarta. Branches in N & S Sumatra. 16n,W=75%. |
| Batak Christian Protestant Church | 1861 | P Lut | LWE.W | 1,676 | 465,457 | 1,044,382 | *HKBP. Huria Kristen Batak Protestan.* Toba Bataks. 298n,25x,1v,W=45%,1657Y,40928y. |
| Batak Ev Lutheran Christian Church | 1965 | I Lut | ..... | 30 | 5,672 | 15,560 | *Huria Kristen Batak Protestan Luther.* Schism ex HKBP. 6n,G=14.1%pa,W=65%,435Yy. |
| Bethel Church in Indonesia | 1946 | P Pe3 | ZF... | 958 | 240,000 | 400,000 | *GBI. G Bethel Indonesia (G=Gereja).* 50% Chinese. M=CoG(Cleveland)(USA). 4f,1p. |
| Bethel Full Gospel Church | 1970 | I pe3 | Z...b | 372 | 7,531 | 51,279 | *GBIS. GB Injil Sepenuh.* 50% Chinese. Ex GBI(GBIS) retaining name. 450n,1p. |
| Bethel Tabernacle Church | 1957 | I pe2 | ....I | 200 | 30,000 | 80,000 | *GBT. G Bethel Tabernakel.* Work throughout nation. HQ Jakarta. 102n. |
| Calvary Pentecostal Mission Church | 1948 | P Pen | ..... | 60 | 4,500 | 5,000 | *G Calvari Pantekosta Missi.* Based on Ternate. 15n,G=10.7%pa,1s,W=60%,1000Y. |
| **Catholic Church in Indonesia:** | c 650 | R Lat | P.F.R | 698 | 1,467,000 | 2,620,140 | *Gereja Katolik I.* C=19+9+70. 5p,10s(651). 373n,1062x,737m,3500w,P=64%,147962Yy. |
| M Ende (Endeh) | 1913 | R Lat | Psvd | 81 | 243,000 | 434,065 | Central Flores. Rural. Florinese. 2s. 41 88 68 205 68 18134 |
| D Atambua | 1936 | R Lat | Psvd | 24 | 134,300 | 239,777 | Timorese on west central Timor. Rural. 10 42 22 70 54 13558 |
| D Denpasar | 1950 | R Lat | Psvd | 2 | 4,600 | 8,281 | Bali, Lombok. Balinese, urban Chinese. 6 10 4 32 55 477 |
| D Kupang | 1967 | R Lat | Psvd | 14 | 18,800 | 33,569 | Timorese, SW Timor. Rural. 4 9 1 6 54 2969 |
| D Larantuka | 1951 | R Lat | Psvd | 32 | 99,600 | 177,809 | Flores, islands. Florinese. 8H,15h. 26 30 9 111 69 8916 |
| D Ruteng | 1951 | R Lat | Psvd | 45 | 152,600 | 272,570 | Flores. Rural Florinese. Many schools. 1p. 18 32 15 22 69 12967 |
| D Weetebula | 1959 | R Lat | Pcssr | 11 | 14,000 | 25,054 | Sumba, Sumbawa. Rural. Sumbans & migrants. 1 19 7 10 44 1061 |
| M Jakarta | 1807 | R Lat | Psj | 24 | 45,700 | 81,702 | *Keuskupan Agung Jakarta.* 38% Chinese. 1s. 31 69 48 306 96 5621 |
| D Bandung | 1932 | R Lat | Posc | 15 | 20,000 | 35,639 | *Keuskupan Bandung.* 30% urban Chinese. 1s. 7 33 8 171 94 2433 |
| D Bogor | 1948 | R Lat | Pofm | 24 | 5,800 | 10,338 | 39% urban Chinese. 6 16 11 75 68 626 |
| M Medan | 1911 | R Lat | Pofmc | 32 | 122,300 | 218,344 | NSumatra. Rural. Bataks. 4% Chinese. 2s. 14 67 34 294 49 15062 |
| D Padang | 1952 | R Lat | Psx | 18 | 11,900 | 21,309 | Sumatra, Mentawei. 56% Chinese; Javanese. 1 36 8 35 69 1462 |
| D Palembang | 1923 | R Lat | Pscj | 20 | 16,000 | 28,585 | SE Sumatra. 33% Chinese, migrant Javanese. 2 30 16 121 40 1957 |
| D Pangkal Pinang | 1923 | R Lat | Psscc | 7 | 7,300 | 13,101 | Bangka, Belitung, Riau. 61% Chinese; Batak. 1 17 16 38 91 642 |
| D Tanjungkarang | 1952 | R Lat | Pscj | 10 | 25,800 | 46,040 | S Sumatra. Mostly rural Javanese migrants. 3 18 1 90 85 3401 |
| PA Sibolga | 1959 | R Lat | Pofmc | 12 | 37,800 | 67,491 | NW Sumatra, Nias, Batu. Rural. Bataks. 5h. 3 16 9 32 77 4749 |
| M Merauke | 1950 | R Lat | Pmsc | 27 | 44,800 | 80,005 | Southern W Irian. Rural. Irianese/Papuans. 3 32 30 48 60 4518 |
| D Agats | 1969 | R Lat | Posc | 10 | 12,500 | 22,354 | Formerly northwest M Merauke. Irianese. 0 12 7 5 60 850 |
| D Jayapura | 1949 | R Lat | Pofm | 34 | 19,600 | 34,960 | Until 1966, Sukarnapura. Irianese. 1s. 3 48 14 27 63 1477 |
| D Manokwari-Sorong | 1959 | R Lat | Posa | 7 | 5,500 | 9,798 | Islands and west of W Irian. Irianese. 2 12 1 28 60 651 |
| M Pontianak | 1905 | R Lat | Pofmc | 18 | 43,400 | 77,540 | W Kalimantan. Dayaks, urban Chinese. 6H,9h. 3 42 37 168 63 6889 |
| D Banjarmasin | 1938 | R Lat | Pmsf | 9 | 6,200 | 11,113 | SE Kalimantan. Dayaks, Javanese, Chinese. 2 11 10 19 58 1012 |
| D Ketapang | 1954 | R Lat | Pcp | 8 | 5,300 | 9,449 | W Kalimantan. Rural. Mostly Dayaks. 1H,2h. 2 17 11 26 68 756 |
| D Samarinda | 1955 | R Lat | Pmsf | 12 | 11,500 | 20,494 | E Kalimantan. Rural. Dayaks. 3 16 2 27 52 728 |
| D Sintang | 1948 | R Lat | Psmm | 7 | 13,500 | 24,177 | W Kalimantan. Rural. Dayaks. 4 21 4 39 59 1097 |
| PA Sekadau | 1968 | R Lat | Pcp | 4 | 12,100 | 21,533 | W Kalimantan. Rural. Dayaks. 0 10 1 0 95 1328 |
| M Semarang | 1940 | R Lat | P | 65 | 136,600 | 243,975 | Central Java. Javanese & urban Chinese. 1s. 99 116 171 541 46 14070 |
| D Malang | 1927 | R Lat | Pocar | 25 | 27,400 | 48,942 | E Java, Madura. Javanese; 43% Chinese. 1s. 24 31 36 290 87 2670 |
| D Purwokerto | 1932 | R Lat | Pmsc | 12 | 14,400 | 25,770 | C Java. Javanese, urban Chinese. 7H,8h. 8 17 34 135 92 1618 |
| D Surabaya | 1928 | R Lat | Pcm | 20 | 42,100 | 75,141 | E Java. Javanese; 38% Chinese. 12H,32h,1s. 22 35 32 201 73 4720 |
| M Ujung Pandang (Makassar) | 1937 | R Lat | Pcicm | 21 | 35,900 | 64,159 | S,SE Sulawesi. Torajas, Chinese. 6H,7h. 3 49 21 101 67 4975 |
| D Amboina | 1902 | R Lat | Pmsc | 22 | 37,800 | 67,541 | Naluku. Rural. Mainly Kayese, Tanimbarese. 9 21 29 126 83 3397 |
| D Manado | 1919 | R Lat | Pmsc | 26 | 38,900 | 69,515 | N,C Sulawesi. Mainly rural Minahasans. 1s. 12 40 20 101 56 3171 |
| Christian Bible Circle | 1946 | I Lut | ..... | 24 | 500 | 1,000 | *KPB. Kristen Panangkosi Bibelkring.* HKBP background. Bataks. No ministers. |
| Christian Ch in Central Sulawesi | 1893 | P Ref | .WE.W | 254 | 50,000 | 125,000 | *GKST. G Kristen Sulawesi Tengh.* M=NZG. 1909 mass influx. Poso Torajas. 68n,1x. |
| Christian Church in Luwuk Banggai | 1966 | P Ref | .v..W | 177 | 20,000 | 52,500 | *GKLB. GK di Luwuk Banggai.* Formerly in GKST. 1972 applied to WCC. Loinangs. 21n,1u. |
| Christian Church in South Sulawesi | 1933 | P Ref | R...W | 25 | 2,000 | 5,500 | *GKSS. GK Sulawesi Selatan.* NZG attempts failed 1851, 1895. Makassarese. 14n. |
| Christian Ch of North Central Java | 1891 | I Ref | ....W | 43 | 3,000 | 7,896 | *GKJTU. GK Jawa Tengh Utara. Salatiga Mission.* HQ Semarang. Javanese. 14n,2x. |
| Christian Church of Sumba | 1870 | P Ref | F...W | 52 | 20,000 | 43,121 | *GKS. G Kristen Sumba.* Begun by Sawu immigrants; 1881 M=NCRMS. A=1947. 50n,117m. |
| Christian Churches & Chs of Christ | 1968 | P Dis | x.... | 10 | 200 | 500 | *SJK. Sidang Jumat Kristus.* M=CCCC(Instrumental)(USA). 13f. |
| Christian Churches of Java | 1858 | P Ref | FWE.W | 916 | 91,205 | 121,500 | *GKJ. G2 Kristen Jawa.* M=NCRMS. 99% Javanese. 1949 merger. 136n,11x,1u,W=70%. |
| Christian Reformed Chs of Indonesia | 1925 | P Ref | ..... | 12 | 2,000 | 5,000 | *G Gereformeerd Indonesia.* A=1969. Javanese living in Sumatra. HQ Medan. 3n,2x. |
| Church of Christ | 1905 | I pe2 | ....W | 13 | 6,000 | 20,000 | *G Kristus.* Chinese pentecostal church in West Java. HQ Jakarta. 12n,W=70%. |
| Church of Christ, Scientist | | M Sci | x.... | 5 | 300 | 1,000 | *G Kesatu Kristus Ahli Ilmu.* M=CCS(Boston,USA). In 5 cities. Many Indonesians. 6w. |
| Ch of Jesus C of Latter-day Saints | | M LdS | x.... | | 400 | 580 | *Mormons.* M=CJCLdS(Utah,USA). Mainly USA personnel, few indigenous. |
| Church of Jesus Christ (the Messiah) | 1945 | I pe2 | Z.E.b | 30 | 13,599 | 20,000 | *G Isa Almasih/Sing Ling Kauw Hui.* Java Chinese. 15n,G=4%pa,1s(35),W=67%,1000Y. |
| Church of the Lord Jesus Christ | 1956 | I Ref | ....W | 15 | 4,000 | 9,834 | *GKT. G Kristus Tuhan.* Chinese. HQ Malang. 8n,W=60%. |
| Churches of Christ | 1967 | P Dis | x.... | 10 | 200 | 500 | M=CC(Non-Instrumental)(USA). Loosely affiliated churches. 10f. |
| East Java Christian Church | 1815 | P Ref | RWE.W | 244 | 50,000 | 126,000 | *GKJW. GK Jawi Waten.* 1848, M=NZG. 99% Javanese. HQ Malang. 74n,1x,5H,16h. |
| Evangelical Alliance Mission | 1952 | P int | xM... | 90 | 3,415 | 11,000 | M=TEAM(USA). Entirely working in West Irian. 1 school. 49f,1H,8h,3x. |
| Ev Christian Ch in Bolaang-Mongondow | 1904 | P Ref | R...W | 100 | 35,000 | 41,250 | *GMIBM. G Masehi Injili Bolaang-Mongondow.* Sulawesi. M=NZG. A=1950. 14n,1x,5r,W=60%. |
| Ev Christian Church in Halmahera | 1866 | P Ref | ....W | 280 | 31,000 | 82,000 | *GMIH.* 1546, first converts. 1866, M=UMS. 30n,G=3.6%pa,4p,1s,W=60%,1045Yy. |
| Ev Christian Church in Java | 1851 | P Men | G...W | 22 | 18,500 | 38,000 | *GITJ. G Injili di Tanah Jawa.* M=European Mennonites (also USA). 32n,2x,1u,W=75%. |
| Ev Christian Ch in Sangihe-Talaud | 1568 | P Ref | RWE.W | 311 | 70,000 | 183,344 | *GMIST. GMI Sangihe-Talaud.* 1856, M=NRMB. A=1947. 90n,189m,1H,8h,4r,1s(50),W=50%. |
| Ev Christian Church in West Irian | 1862 | P Ref | RWE.W | 800 | 150,000 | 360,000 | *GKI Ir-Jay. Irian Java/Barat.* M=UM,RM,VEM. A=1956. 200 tribes. 77n,8x,1p,1s,W=40%. |
| Evangelical Church in Kalimantan | 1836 | P Ref | RWE.W | 301 | 40,000 | 90,000 | *GKE. G Kalimantan Evangelis* (former Dayak Ev Ch). M=RM,BM. 88n,1x,15f,1s(53),W=60%. |
| Evangelical Church of South Sumatra | 1964 | P ind | ..... | 7 | 2,250 | 4,000 | *GEKISUS. GK Sumatera Selatan.* M=IMF. 50% Serawai (Rejang-Lebong) ex Muslims. |
| Fellowship of Preaching Gosp of Christ | 1947 | P int | xM... | 61 | 20,000 | 50,000 | *PPIK* (Borneo), Chinese, Dayaks; *GGIK* (WIrian), Dani. M=RBMU. 23n,57f,1H,3p,W=68%. |
| Free Methodist Church of Indonesia | 1964 | I Met | ..... | 6 | 500 | 1,500 | *GMMI. G Methodis Merdeka Indonesia.* Schism ex GMI by indigenous Indonesians. 4n. |

*Continued opposite*

*Table 2 – continued*

| Official name 1 | Begun 2 | Type 3 | Counc 4 | Congs 5 | Adults 6 | Affiliated 7 | Names, notes, and other statistics (see Codebook) 8 |
|---|---|---|---|---|---|---|---|
| Gospel Tabernacle Christian Ch of I | 1929 | P Hol | xF..E | 650 | 84,320 | 150,000 | *KINGMI. Kemah Injil G Masehi I.* M=CMA (USA). 135n,21x,128f,23h,3p,6s(370),2816Y. |
| Holy Spirit Church of Indonesia | | I pe2 | ..... | | 6,914 | 20,000 | *GSRKI. G Sidang Rohul Kudus Indonesia.* Indigenous pentecostals. HQ Medan. |
| Holy Word Christian Church | 1951 | I int | x.... | 20 | 1,375 | 7,000 | *GKKK. GK Kalam Kudus.* HQ Malang. M=Evangelize China Fellowship. 200m,5f,8r (5000),1s(100). |
| Indigenous cargo cult churches | | I mar | ..... | | 2,000 | 3,000 | Several of the over 21 cargo cults in West Irian have had christianized features. |
| Indonesia Pentecostal Church | | I pe2 | ....I | | 15,475 | 40,000 | *G Pantekosta di Indonesia.* Indigenous Batak and other pentecostals on Sumatra. |
| Indonesia Protestant Christian Church | 1963 | I Lut | LW..W | 417 | 63,378 | 128,424 | *GKPI. GK Protestan I.* N Sumatra. Ex HKBP. Batak. 79n,1x,G=15.3%pa,1s,W=55%,7634Yy. |
| Indonesian Baptist Gospel Fellowship | | P Bap | ..... | | 10,000 | 30,000 | *Persekutuan Injil Baptis I.* Western Kalimantan. Loose connection with USA bodies. |
| Indonesian Christian Ch in Central Java | 1866 | I Ref | FWE.W | 57 | 11,697 | 31,044 | *GKI Ja-Teng. Jawa Tengah.* Chinese. HQ Semarang. 37n,2x,G=8%pa,1p,2s(50),W=70%,837Yy. |
| Indonesian Christian Ch in East Java | 1898 | I Ref | RwE.W | 11 | 7,835 | 10,005 | *GKI Ja-Tim. Jawa Timur.* Chinese, begun by Chinese. HQ Surabaya. 13n,2x. |
| Indonesian Christian Ch of West Java | 1867 | I Ref | RvE.W | 35 | 8,000 | 23,361 | *GKI Ja-Bar. Jawa Barat.* Chinese origin and members. HQ Jakarta. 32n,W=70%. |
| Indonesian Christian Church (HKI) | 1927 | I Lut | LWE.W | 501 | 100,000 | 242,500 | *Huria Kristen Indonesia.* Ex HKBP. Bataks. 71n,1x,560m,G=2.1%pa,4p,W=50%,3923Yy. |
| Indonesian Ev Christian Church | | I ind | ..... | | 1,000 | 2,075 | *GMEI. G Masehi Evangelis Indonesia.* Indigenous grouping based on Makassar, Sulawesi. |
| Isolated radio churches | 1952 | I rad | ..... | 1,700 | 30,000 | 66,300 | Isolated radio believers (youths &c). R=15000(FEBC,&c),T=55000(ICI,FEBC,&c). |
| Jehovah's Witnesses | 1933 | M Jeh | x.... | 80 | 2,731 | 10,000 | *Perkumpulan Siswa Alkitab.* 1933 under Australia branch. 1937 Celebes, Borneo. 452Y. |
| Jesus Christ Church | 1952 | I Lut | ..... | 5 | 500 | 1,000 | *Huria Hatopan ni Kristus Jesus.* N Sumatra. Schism ex HKBP. HQ Hutadipar. 2n,5m. |
| Karo Batak Protestant Church | 1890 | P Ref | RWE.W | 300 | 30,000 | 72,492 | *GBKP. G Batak Karo Protestan.* M=NZG,RM,VEM. 1965, mass conversions. 30n,5x,W=60%. |
| Mentawei Protestant Christian Church | 1901 | P Lut | ..... | 124 | 10,500 | 35,000 | *PKPM. Paamian Kristen Protestan Mentawei.* M=HKBP,RM,VEM on Mentawei Is. 11n,3x,9f. |
| Methodist Church in Indonesia | 1903 | P Met | VvE.W | 209 | 33,221 | 70,000 | *GMI. G Methodis I.* M=UMC(USA),A=1964. Chinese, Batak. 45n,19f,1p,148t,W=93%,1506Yy. |
| Minahasa Protestant Ch Association | | I Ref | ..... | | 10,000 | 25,000 | *KGPM. Kerapatan Gereja Protestan Minahasa.* Schism ex GMIM. HQ Jakarta. |
| Muria Christian Church in Indonesia | 1925 | P Men | G...W | 12 | 3,190 | 7,000 | *GKMI. G Kristen Muria Indonesia* (formerly United Muria Christian Ch of I). Chinese. 11n,1u. |
| New Apostolic Church | 1881 | C CAp | x.... | | 7,000 | 10,000 | Begun on Java. M=NAC(Germany). Chief Apostle and world HQ in Dortmund (Germany). |
| Nias Christian Protestant Church | 1865 | P Lut | .WE.W | 350 | 100,000 | 220,000 | *BNKP. Banua Niha Keriso Protestan.* Since 1865, M=RM,VEM. A=1940. 53n,2x,14f,1s. |
| Nias Christian Protestant Organization | 1952 | I Lut | ..... | 52 | 10,000 | 32,000 | *ONKP. Orahua Niha Keriso Protestan.* Indigenous schism ex BNKP. 15n. |
| Nias Indonesian Christian Association | 1940 | I Lut | ..... | 11 | 20,000 | 60,000 | *AMIN. Angawuloa Masehi Indonesia Nias.* Large indigenous schism ex BNKP. 6n. |
| Pasundan Christian Church | 1861 | P Ref | RWE.W | 38 | 8,000 | 18,890 | *GKP. G Kristen Pasundan.* West Java. 1863, M=NZG. 30% Chinese. Islam strong. 21n. |
| Pentecostal Church in Sorong | 1948 | I pe2 | ..... | 13 | 500 | 13,000 | *GPS. G Pantekosta Sorong.* Salawati and Irianese. 5n,G=25%pa,W=40%,75Y,125z. |
| Pentecostal Church of God | 1950 | P Pe2 | Z.... | 60 | 45,983 | 100,000 | M=PCG(USA). Classical Pentecostals. HQ Calvary Mission, Ternate. 1 school. 4f. |
| Pentecostal Church of Indonesia | 1920 | I pe1 | Z...I | 1,500 | 750,000 | 1,000,000 | *GPI,GPdI. G Pantekosta di Indonesia.* 25% Chinese. Many splits, including GBIS. 1500n,3s. |
| Pentecostal Church (Sihombing) | | I pe2 | ..... | 210 | 38,000 | 100,000 | *G Pantekosta* (*Sihombing*)(=name of present leader). HQ Pematang Siantar, Sumatra. |
| Pentecostal Missionary Church | 1935 | I pe2 | ..... | 41 | 9,034 | 20,000 | *GUP. G Utusan Pantekosta.* Indigenous pentecostals (2-stage). 19n,11m. |
| Pentecostal Movement Church | | I pe2 | ....b | | 10,892 | 30,000 | *G Gerakan Pantekosta.* In several regions; HQ Jakarta. 1975: 12,261 adult members. |
| **Protestant Church in Indonesia:** | 1615 | P Ref | RW..W | 2,680 | 987,000 | 1,958,710 | *GPI. Gereja Protestan Indonesia.* Former state-controlled Church of the Indies. 770n. |
| Christian Ev Church in Minahasa | 1568 | P Ref | RWE.W | 532 | 200,000 | 556,432 | *GMIM. G Masehi Injili Minahasa.* 1822 M=NZG. A=1934. 174n,5x,G=2.1%pa,1s(130),W=60%. |
| Ev Christian Church in Timor | 1612 | P Ref | RWE.W | 1,258 | 200,000 | 517,779 | *GMIT. G Masehi Injili Timor.* First Dutch pastor 1612; 1821 M=NZG. 106n,9x,1s,W=48%. |
| Indonesian Prot Church in Donggala | 1964 | P Ref | ....W | 71 | 6,000 | 15,340 | *GPID. G Protestan Indonesia Donggala.* HQ Maesa-Palu (Central Sulawesi). Palus. 11n,W=65%. |
| Indonesian Prot Church in Gorontalo | 1964 | P Ref | ....W | 5 | 3,000 | 7,000 | *GPIG. G Protestan Indonesia di Gorontalo.* HQ Gorontalo. 5n,W=50%. |
| Moluccan Protestant Church | 1534 | P Ref | RWE.W | 678 | 425,000 | 505,000 | *GPM. GP Maluku.* Oldest Protestant church in Asia. 462n,3x,G=1.0%pa,1s(30),W=60%,2183Yy. |
| Protestant Ch in Western Indonesia | 1620 | P Ref | R.E.W | 126 | 150,000 | 350,000 | *GPIB. GP Indonesia Bagian Barat.* HQ Jakarta. Ambonese, Timorese, Minahasans. 54n,2x. |
| Protestant Ch of I in Buol-Toli-toli | 1964 | P Ref | ..... | | 3,000 | 7,159 | *GPI Buol-Toli 2.* Sulawesi. Gorontalo, Tomini, Buginese, Orang-Laut (Sea Gypsies). |
| Protestant Ch in South East Sulawesi | 1915 | P Ref | ....W | 36 | 4,000 | 9,000 | *GEPSULTRA. G Protestan Sulawesi Tenggara.* M=NZG. First baptism 1929. 14n,1x,W=75%. |
| Ray of the Gospel Christian Church | 1960 | I Lut | ....W | 46 | 15,000 | 30,000 | *GKPI. GK Pemancar Injil.* NE Kalimantan. Very rapid growth. 15n,9x,1s,W=90%. |
| Salvation Army | 1894 | P Sal | xwE.w | 228 | 63,460 | 200,000 | *Bala Keselamatan. Indonesia Territory.* 253n,24x,G=4.5%pa,5H,1p,1s(30),W=79%,627Y. |
| Seventh-day Adventist Church | 1900 | P Adv | x.... | 532 | 44,981 | 70,677 | *GMAHKT.* 137n,9x,29f,G=8%pa,2H,23h,1j,9r,2s(92),662t(58746),W=80%,3220Y. |
| Simalungun Protestant Christian Ch | 1903 | P Lut | LW..W | 275 | 40,000 | 109,500 | *GNPS. GK Protestan Simalungun.* M=RM,VEM. In HKBP till 1962. 33n,1x,3f,1p(27),W=60%. |
| Spiritual Food Church of Indonesia | | I int | xTT.T | | 2,015 | 6,000 | *GSRI. G Santopan Rohani Indonesia.* M=LLWEM(Hong Kong). Linked ICCC. HQ Singkawang. |
| Surabaya Pentecostal Church | 1959 | I pe2 | Z...b | 250 | 40,000 | 100,000 | *GPPS. G Pantekosta Pusat Surabaya.* East Java. Largely Chinese. 250n. |
| Toraja Christian Church | 1913 | P Ref | RWE.W | 432 | 85,000 | 175,000 | *G Toraja/Makale-Rantepao.* Doubled 1947–54. 64n,5x,G=5%pa,1H,1p,1s(110),W=30%,7317Yy. |
| Toraja Church in Mamasa | 1929 | P Ref | JTT.W | 270 | 36,000 | 53,923 | *GTM. G Toraja/Mamasa.* M=NCRMA. HQ Mamasa. 30n,2x,G=6.3%pa,W=60%,1500Yy. |
| True Jesus Church | 1939 | I pe1 | x.... | 9 | 1,400 | 2,000 | *GJJS. G Jesus Jang Sejati.* Chinese indigenous church. 4n,G=12.7%pa,W=70%,140Y. |
| Unevangelized Fields Mission | 1952 | P int | xM... | 40 | 2,500 | 40,000 | M=UFM(USA). West Irian among Dani tribe. 4 schools. 36f,1H,3h,2s. |
| United Pentecostal Church | 1938 | P Pe1 | x.... | 114 | 16,200 | 40,000 | *GPS. G Pantekosta Serikat.* M=UPC(USA). HQ Semarang. 1970, schism. 73n,4f,1p(29). |
| West Kalimantan Christian Church | 1938 | I ind | ..... | 31 | 2,500 | 5,000 | *GKKB. G Kristen Kalimantan Barat.* 60% Chinese. 3n,1x,G=13.6%pa,W=75%,140Y. |
| Worldwide Evangelization Crusade | 1949 | P int | xF... | 100 | 10,000 | 20,000 | *Fellowship of Independent Gospel Assemblies in I.* M=WEC. In West Borneo; 6,000 Dayaks in 2 years. |
| World-Wide Missions of Indonesia | 1963 | P ind | x.... | | 3,500 | 7,000 | M=World-Wide Missions(USA). Links with Evangelicals from Pasadena, CA (USA). |
| Other Indonesian indigenous churches | | I | ..... | | 20,000 | 50,000 | Total over 100 (see list below). |
| Other Protestant denominations | | P | ..... | | 15,000 | 30,000 | Total about 30 (see list below). |
| **Total affiliated (mid-1970)** | | | | **22,410** | **5,756,615** | **11,288,280** | **Total denominations (1970) . . . 220.** |
| **Total affiliated (mid-1975)** | | | | **25,400** | **7,138,900** | **13,998,800** | **Total denominations (1975) . . . 240.** |
| **Total affiliated (mid-1980)** | | | | **28,500** | **8,705,000** | **17,069,900** | **Total denominations (1980) . . . 270.** |

NOTES ON TABLE ABOVE
COLUMNS: for meanings and CODES (cols. 1, 3, 4, 8), see Codebook (Part 6). Column 1: **Boldface type** = church with over 10% of country's affiliated Christians.
ABBREVIATIONS ABOVE (columns 1 & 8). G=Gereja (Church); G2=Gereja-Gereja (Churches). GK=Gereja Kristen (Christian Church). I=Indonesia. Note that English names of many Protestant churches are in use in 2 forms: (1) as shown in column 1, and (2) with the last part of the name first.
NATIONAL COUNCILS (Column 4, 5th letter).
- b = member of both DGI and UPFGCI.
- E = Association of Evangelical Churches of Indonesia (Dewan Gereja-Gereja Injil di Indonesia) (Evangelical Fellowship of Indonesia, Indonesian Evangelical Fellowship) (80 associations and denominations).
- I = United Pentecostal Full Gospel Churches of Indonesia (UPFGCI) (Alamat Jemaat-Jemaat Dari Gereja-Gereja Injil Penuh) (23 members; inoperative by 1974).
- R = Bishops' Conference of Indonesia (Majelis Agung Para Waligereja Indonesia, MAWI).
- T = Indonesian Council of Christian Churches.
- W = Council of Churches in Indonesia (CCI, ICC) (Dewan Gereja-Gereja di Indonesia, DGI).
- w = associate (extraordinary) member of DGI.

*Other national councils.* The Council of Chinese Christian Churches in Indonesia (Dewan Gereja-Gereja Kristen Tionghoa di Indonesia), formed in 1949, has now merged in the DGI. *Local councils.* 14 regional councils are affiliated to the DGI.
OTHER INDONESIAN INDIGENOUS CHURCHES. Most of these 100 are registered with the government's Department of Religion, and were begun for either Indonesians or Chinese. They include: Ch of the New Apostolate, Ev Christian Ch of S Sumatra, Holy Ghost Guided Christian Assembly, Voice of Salvation Ch.
OTHER PROTESTANT DENOMINATIONS. Most are recent missions with only small followings. These include: Apostolic Christian Ch of I, Baptist Mid-Missions, Bethany Fellowship Missions (1971), Bethel Pentecostal Temple (Seattle, USA), Christadelphian Ecclesias, Christian Faith Missionary Union, Christian Nationals' Evangelism Commission (1971), Ch of God of Prophecy (1971), First Baptist Ch, Grace Christian Ch, Oriental Missionary Society (1970), Overseas Missionary Fellowship (1954; 39 missionaries), United Evangelical Chs, West Java United Baptist Chs, West Kalimantan Pioneer Mission (member of ICCC), Wisconsin Evangelical Lutheran Synod (1969), World Baptist Fellowship Mission Agency (1969), World Gospel Mission (1968).
UNITING CHURCHES. In 1974 there were no known negotiations for organic union under way.

PEOPLES (ethnolinguistic). Christians: 24.8% Batak (Toba, also Simalungun, Karo, Angkola, Pakpak), 11.9% Chinese (Peranakan (Indonesian-born and -speaking), of Fukienese or Kwangtung origin), 9.0% Javanese, 7.8% Florinese (Laruntuk, Lio, Manggarai, Nageh, Ngada, Sikka), 7.2% Timorese (Atoni, Kupang, Mare (Bunak), Rotinese, Tetum (Belu)), 6.3% Irianese (Papuan) (Damal, Dani, Djabi, Marind-Anim, Sentani), 5.9% Minahasan (Menadonese), 4.2% Ambonese, 3.7% Toraja (Koro, Palu, Poso, Sadang), 2.8% Niassan, 2.5% Dayak, 1.6% Sangihe-Talaud, 1.0% Sundanese, 1.0% Madurese, 0.9% Eurasian, 0.7% Gorontalese, 0.5% Loinang, 0.5% North Halmaheran (Galelo, Ibu, Lolod, Makian, Ternate, Tidore, Tobelo), 0.5% Sumban, 0.4% Bolaang-Mongondow, 0.4% Minangkabau, 0.3% Mentaweian, 0.3% Maba, 0.3% Seramese, 0.2% European, 0.2% Balinese, 0.1% Sumbawan, 4.0% other Indonesian, Laki (Tolaki), Kayan, Kenyah, Indian, Iban, Filipino, Ekari (Kapauku), Tapiro Pygmy, et alii.

COUNTRY-WIDE TOTALS
EVANGELIZATION (see Part 5). 1900: 24%. 1970: 62%. 1980: 76%. *Mass evangelism.* There has been a long history of evangelism. Up to 1944, the Chinese evangelist John Sung trained 5,000 3-man evangelistic teams who made a major impact across Indonesia. Among the many more recent campaigns have been: 1967, Oral Roberts crusade; 1967–69, Southern Baptists '1 + 1 = 80' Campaign (each of existing 40 churches being expected to plan a further one, ditto each believer; after 2 years, 149 churches, and the 4,000 members growing to 9,700); 1969, Japanese and Pakistani evangelistic teams; 1970, consultation on evangelism; 1975, Asian Evangelists Commission (AEC) crusade in several cities, including Palembang (535 converts of whom 150 were Muslims), and Medan (1,229 decisions for Christ); 1976, LCWE-sponsored 8-day crusade at Kupang, Timor (250,000 attenders, mass burning of fetishes); 1978, Here's Life Jakarta (CCCI). *Radiophonic evangelism.* Annual listeners' letters (1975): 15,000 (12,000 FEBC, et alia). In 1976, FEBC was broadcasting into Indonesia for 3.5 hours per day, plus 15 minutes per week over 60 local stations. Bible correspondence courses: 55,000 enrolments (43,491 ICI (with 6,541 conversions reported), 7,392 FEBC et alia). In 1975, 21,000 (mainly Muslims) enrolled in an AMG Bible correspondence course, of whom 3,500 later professed faith in Christ. In 1976, advertisements placed in Muslim newspapers resulted in 48,000 enquiries, 21,000 enrolled in Bible correspondence courses, and 3,400 known conversions.
FOREIGN MISSIONARIES AND PERSONNEL (nationals serving abroad) (1973). Total 203 in 16 countries: about 155 Roman Catholics, 40 Protestants, 8 Indonesian indigenous.
FOREIGN MISSIONARIES AND PERSONNEL (aliens from abroad) (1973). Total 4,360. *From Western world.* 4,004: 2,850 Roman Catholics, 1,151 Protestants (750 in 64 USA societies, 85 in 7 WGermany societies, 80 in 18 Australia societies, 75 in 11 Netherlands societies, 59 in 6 UK societies, 41 in 15 New Zealand societies, 31 in 8 Canada societies, 22 in 2 Switzerland societies, 8 in 4 Finland societies), 3 Catholics (non-Roman). By 1975, North American missionaries had increased to 858. *From Communist world.* About 50 Roman Catholics (44 from Poland, others from Yugoslavia). *From Third World.* 306: about 200 Roman Catholics, about 60 Protestants from about 15 countries, about 46 indigenous from Taiwan, Hong Kong, Japan, Philippines, et alia.
INSTITUTIONS (church-operated) (1973). Total 2,800, including 1,950 higher schools (650 Protestant schools; 23 minor seminaries), 700 medical centres (190 hospitals), 1 pharmaceutical factory, 10 religious communities, 6 research centres, 95 seminaries (75 Protestant, 10 RC, 10 Indonesian indigenous), 22 universities.
PERIODICALS. About 220 titles (100 RC, 90 Protestant, 20 indigenous).
PERSONNEL. About 32,684 (28,324 national, 4,360 foreign).
RELIGIOUS LIBRARIES. About 150.
SCRIPTURE DISTRIBUTION (1975). Annual totals: 155,703 Bibles (7% free, 67% subsidized, 26% commercial), 86,290 NTs (21% free, 55% subsidized, 23% commercial), 1,746,796 UBS portions, 16,205,686 UBS selections. *Translations completed.* Portion: 42 languages since 1815. NT: 20 languages since 1829. Bible: 8 languages since 1854.
SERVICE AGENCIES. About 105, including CCCI(LIFE), CEF, CLC, CWS, DGI, IBSI, IMKA(YMCA), ISKI, KESPEKRI, LAI, LPPS, LWR, MABRI, MAF (1954; 62 missionaries), MASI, MAWI, NTM, OC, PGK, PPSK, PSKI, PTL, SU, UPFGCI, WBT, WKRI, WLC(EHC), WVI.

ADDITIONAL DATA ON CHURCHES
BALI CHRISTIAN PROTESTANT CHURCH. Also called, Protestant Christian Church in Bali.
BATAK CHRISTIAN PROTESTANT CHURCH. The HKBP has 13 Districts. *Foreign missionary aid.* Work was begun by the Rhenish Mission. In 1973, aiding bodies were: Lutheran Church in America, Lutheran Church of Australia, Vereinigte Evangelische Mission, LWF. *Members.* 89% Toba Bataks, 3.8% Pakpak Bataks, 2.9% Angkola Bataks, 5,000 Simalungun Bataks, 2,500 Javanese, 250 Chinese. *Catechumens* (1973). 22,179. *Lay workers* (1973). 15,266 men (183 expatriates), 95 women (10 expatriates). *Growth.* By 1976, 1,160,000 members.
BETHEL CHURCH IN INDONESIA. This body was formerly called GBIS until 1970 when the government awarded this name to a schismatic body, shown above as Bethel Full Gospel Church.
CATHOLIC CHURCH IN INDONESIA. *Column 5.* In addition to the 698 parishes shown, there are 1,120 missions with a church or chapel, and 2,320 missions without. *Catholics.* Including about 7% Chinese: (1966) 123,147, (1970) 179,000, (1975) 220,000. *Catechumens.* (1959) 75,868, (1961) 79,288, (1963) 88,265; (1970) 165,319, divided among the 33 dioceses as follows, in the order shown: 3121, 9832, 285, 6709, 943, 1554, 2051; 3159, 3505, 607; 16578, 3104, 1298, 422, 4233, 4521; 7015, 7665, 3874, 49; 18663, 924, 1352, 4000, 8032, 520, 24855; 9252, 1391, 5915; 4036, 633, 451. *Annual baptisms.* (1972) 72.7% infant (98,364), 27.3% adult (38,927). *Priests.* The first Indonesian priest was ordained in 1926, followed by 372 others up to 1970. M Semarang has 215 priests and 171 brothers, and also 29 contemplatives (priests and brothers) not listed above. In 1970, there were 121 secular clergy (8.4%) and 1,314 regular clergy (91.6%). Numbers of national and expatriate clergy have grown as follows: (1949) 62 + 586, (1954) 130 + 858, (1959) 151 + 921, (1964) 224 + 1001, (1968) 373 + 1062, (1977) 500 + 1100. *Brothers.* (1970) 387 nationals, 359 expatriates (from 3 countries; almost all Dutch). Nearly half these brothers serve schools in densely-populated Java. *Sisters.* (1970) 2,064 nationals, 1,435 expatriates (from 23 countries; 76% Dutch), half in Java in schools and medical care. Total all sisters, including contemplatives: 4,019 (1968). *Seminaries.* Secular and regular clergy are often trained together, especially in the diocesan seminaries of Manado (MSC and secular), Medan (OFMCap and secular), Semarang, Jakarta, et alia. Ende, however, has a diocesan seminary for SVD clergy, and Medan one for Carmelite priests. Most seminaries date from 1949. One of the 10 seminaries is actually the Philosophical Institute. *Seminarians.* Total 473 (1970); 651 (1972) of which 229 are secular, 422 religious; 784 (1977) in 9 major seminaries, with 2,000 more in 25 minor seminaries. *Catechists.* Total (1974) 9,424 (1,635 in D Ruteng). *Catechist training schools.* Total 5 for ex-secondary school pupils, and at least 14 of lower standard (including one in D Jayapura). *Indigenous religious congregations.* Brothers: Tarekat Frater Hamba Kristus (Institute of the Servants of Christ), begun 1958, 14 professed. Sisters: Maria Pengantara (Maria Mediatrix), begun 1927, 72 professed; Tarekat Suster-

Suster Pengikat Jesus (Congregatio Imitatio Jesu, CIJ), begun 1935, 157 professed; Abdi Dalam Sang Kristus, ADSK (Soeurs Servantes du Christ), begun 1938, 42 professed; Tarekat Putri Reinha Rosari (Sisters of the Rosary), begun 1958, 23 professed; Dina Keluarga Sutji (Servants of the Holy Family), begun 1960, 17 professed. *Main foreign orders and congregations.* Total 78 (1970). Priests (orders with over 50 in 1968): 482 SVD, 290 SJ, 212 MSC, 185 OFMCap, 141 OFM, 107 OCarm, 91 SCJ, 57 CM, 53 CICM, 52 OSC. Brothers (orders with over 50 professed in 1968): 108 FIC, 66 Our Lady of Lourdes (Ghent), 54 Oudenbosch. Sisters (orders with over 100 professed in 1968): 333 Ursulines of the Roman Union, 314 Missionaries of the Holy Spirit of Steyl, 270 Charity of St Charles Borromeo, 267 Franciscans of Heijthuisen, 203 Society of Jesus Mary & Joseph, 104 Our Lady of Amersfoort.
*Catholic organizations.* The national episcopal conference is known as MAWI (Majelis Agung Para Waligereja Indonesia: General Conference of the Ordinaries of Indonesia) and is a member of FABC. Religious personnel are served by MASI (Majelis Serikat Imam: National Association of Clerical Institutes), MABRI (Majelis Bruder Indonesia: National Association of Institutes of Brothers), and IBSI (Ikatan Biarawati Seluruh Indonesia: Association of Sisters of All Indonesia). There is no national pastoral council, nor priests' senate. Youth organizations include: Association of Catholic Secondary Pupils (Ikatan Siswa Katolik Indonesia), Catholic Primary Pupils (Persuatan Pelajar Sekolah Katolik), University Students' Association (Perhimpunan Mahasiswa Katolik Republik Indonesia), Catholic Youth (Pemuda Katolik), and Scouts (Pramuka). Adult lay organizations include: Legion of Mary, Congregation of Mary, Catholic Women (Wanita Katolik Republik Indonesia), Catholic Intellectuals (Ikatan Sarjana Katolik), and Catholic Social Movement (Perkumpulan Sosial Katolik Indonesia). For the armed forces, Indonesia forms a military vicariate.
The Holy See has diplomatic relations with Indonesia, and is represented to government and the Catholic hierarchy by the Apostolic Nunciature of Indonesia, with a pro-nuncio in Jakarta.
Catholic schools represent a wide range of interests and activities: 359 kindergartens, 2,991 primary schools (with 571,370 pupils in 1973), 609 lower secondary, 138 higher secondary, 66 teacher-training, 82 domestic science, 22 commercial, 14 agricultural, 18 nursing, 6 midwifery, 36 technical, 9 social work and 195 other specialized schools. The 3 dioceses on Flores alone have 767 primary schools and 80 secondary schools. Institutions of higher education include 4 universities: Atma Jaya (with campuses in Jakarta, Yogyakarta, Kediri, Ujung Pandang, Malang, Palembang, Surakarta and Semarang), Wydia Mandala (campuses in Surabaya and Madiun), Sanata Dharma (Yogyakarta) and Parahijangan (Bandung). In addition there is a Philosophical Institute (Drijakara in Jakarta), and 8 academies: 5 for catechists, 2 for nurses and one for community development. An Association of Catholic Academic Institutions of Indonesia has also been formed and is a member of the International Federation of Catholic Universities (FIUC) in Paris.
Medical facilities consist of 145 hospitals and maternity centres including 5 leprosaria and one sanatorium, 318 clinics and dispensaries, 70 orphanages (3 for the deaf and dumb, one for the blind, and one for the mentally retarded), one home for the aged, and one centre for training former lepers.
The Lembaga Penelitian Dan Pembangunan Social (LPPS), a member of CIDSE in Belgium, co-ordinates social and community development activities which may be classified as follows: (1) Pancasila (Five-principle) unions, for farmers, workers, fishermen, and the like; (2) Socio-Economic Development Committee of the Bishops' Conference; (3) Institute for Social Research and Development, which advises bodies intending to set up development projects; (4) Institute for the Education and Counselling of Credit Union Leaders; (5) Soegijapranata Social Foundation, which aids slum-dwellers of Central Java to migrate to Kalimantan; (6) Community Organization Committee, dealing with the needs of urban industrial Jakarta; (7) Social Programme of the Cardinal, which seeks to ameliorate the plight of political prisoners, mostly communists; (8) aid programme for the 60,000 Chinese who fled from the Dayaks of interior Kalimantan towards the coast in 1967–68; and (9) participation in Sodepaxi Indonesia.
INDONESIA PROTESTANT CHRISTIAN CHURCH. Also called: Christian Protestant Church in Indonesia, and Protestant Christian Church in Indonesia. By 1976 there were 536 congregations, 150,000 members (mostly Bataks), 87 pastors, 536 preacher-teachers, 17 elementary schools, 3 junior high schools, 1 Bible school, 2 rice-planting estates, and 1 small radio station.
MOLUCCAN PROTESTANT CHURCH. The oldest Protestant church in Asia. Headquarters are on Ambon, and membership is all Moluccan (mainly Ambonese and Menadonese). Of the total population of the Moluccas, about 50% are Christians and 47% Muslims.
SEVENTH-DAY ADVENTIST CHURCH. GMAHKT = Gereja Masehi Adven Hari Ke Tujuh.

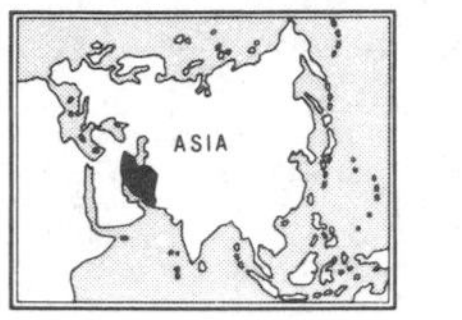


# IRAN

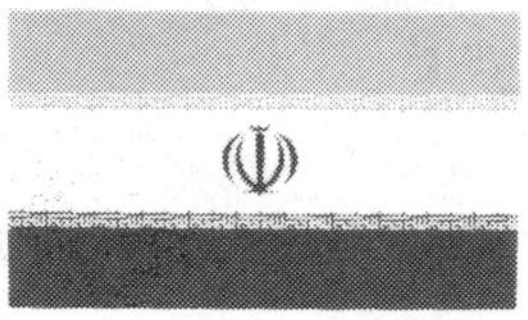

## SECULAR DATA

**STATE. Official name:** The Islamic Republic of Iran, formerly the Empire of Iran (Keshvaré Shahanshahiyé Irân). Adjective of nationality: Iranian; an Irani.
**Flag** (shown above right): Green, white, and red stripes; Monograph of Allah in centre.
**Area:** 1,648,000 sq.km. (636,296 sq.miles). Agricultural land: 16.6%.
**Government:** One-party Islamic revolutionary republic, since 1979 (1921 military dictatorship, 1953 absolute monarchy, 1979 revolution).
**Legislature** (Until revolution of 1979): Parliament: Senate, 60 members; Majlis, 268 members.
**Official language:** Persian (*Faris*).
**Chief cities:** capital Tehran 3,774,050 (1973), Isfahan 575,000, Mashad 562,000, Tabriz 493,000.
**Political divisions:** 14 Provinces (ustán), 6 Governor-generalships, 151 Governorships, 459 Districts.
**Armed forces** (1976): Total 300,000 regular: army 200,000, navy 18,500, air force 81,500 (317 combat aircraft). Reserves: 300,000. Paramilitary forces: 70,000 gendarmerie.
**Foreign forces** (1973): 1,000 USA troops.

**DEMOGRAPHY. Population:** 25,785,210 (census of 1–20.XI. 1966. For 1970–2000 (UN), see last row of Table 1). Population density (1975): 20/sq.km. (52/sq.mile). Under 15 years: 45%. Growth rate (1975–80): 3.13% per year (births 4.48%, deaths −1.37%, immigrants 0.02%). Life expectancy (1975–80): 53.5 years. Household size: 5.0 persons.
**Major languages:** Persian, Azerbaijani, Kurdish, Arabic, Turkish, Armenian, English, French, Baluchi, Brahui, and about 30 other languages.
**Urban dwellers** (1970): 40.8%. Urban growth rate (1950–70): 4.7% per year.
**Labour force:** 27%.
**Refugees** (1977): 35,000 Kurds from Iraq.
**Tourists** (1974): 389,992.

**ETHNOLINGUISTIC GROUPS:** 45.0% Persian, 16.0% Azerbaijanian, 8.2% Kurdish, 5.8% Gilaki, 4.6% Mazanderani, 3.4% Lur, 2.2% Baluchi, 1.9% Bakhtiari, 1.9% Arab Gypsy, 1.6% Turkmen, 1.5% Kashkai, 1.5% Afshar, 1.1% Tat, 1.0% Turkic tribal, 0.7% Armenian, 0.7% Shahseven, 0.5% Hazara-Berberi, 0.3% Teymur, 0.2% Talysh, 0.2% Jewish, 0.2% Afghani, 0.3% Assyrian (Aissor, Chaldean), 0.1% Jamshidi, 0.1% Galesh, 0.1% Tadzhik, 0.1% Kajar, 0.1% Indo-Pakistani, 0.1% Karapapakh, 0.1% USA military & civilian (rising to 41,000 by 1978 before mass exodus), Black African (Bantu) (10,000), British (3,000), Korean (3,000), Russian, Georgian, Brahui, other Arab, other European.

**MONEY** (1977). **Monetary unit:** rial (= 100 dinars); US$1 = Rls 70.35.
**National income per person:** US$960. Average annual family income: US$4,800.
**Inflation:** (1970–74) 8.6% per year (1975: consumer price index 163), (1978) 50% per year.
**Cost of living in capital** (1976): index 117 (Washington DC = 100). Daily cost of living: US$44.

**HEALTH.** Hospitals: 519 (42,000 beds). Doctors: 10,053. Lepers: 12,000 (0.4 per 1,000). Blind: 200,000. Psychotics: 230,000. Drug addicts: 350,000 (on opium).

**EDUCATION.** Adult literacy: (1956) 13%, (1971) 37%. Education rate: 35%. Schools: 28,357. Universities: 7.

**LITERATURE.** Annual new book titles (1973): 3,353. Periodicals: 201. Scientific journals: 10. Newspapers: 39 dailies, 100 non-daily.

**COMMUNICATION** (per 1,000 people). Phones: 18. Radios: 229. TV sets: 33. Daily newspaper circulation: 24 copies.

TABLE 1. RELIGIOUS ADHERENTS IN IRAN

| Year | 1900 | | mid-1970 | | Annual change, 1970–1980 | | | | mid-1975 | | mid-1980 | | 2000 | |
|---|---|---|---|---|---|---|---|---|---|---|---|---|---|---|
| *Name* | *Adherents* | *%* | *Adherents* | *%* | *Natural* | *Conversion* | *Total* | *Rate* | *Adherents* | *%* | *Adherents* | *%* | *Adherents* | *%* |
| Muslims | 9,518,800 | 98.1 | 27,727,072 | 97.8 | 996,600 | 123 | 996,723 | 3.09 | 32,209,000 | 97.8 | 37,694,300 | 97.9 | 65,370,000 | 98.2 |
| **Christians** | **116,200** | **1.2** | **272,528** | **1.0** | **6,246** | **−169** | **6,077** | **2.01** | **302,500** | **0.9** | **333,300** | **0.9** | **460,000** | **0.7** |
| crypto-Christians | 35,200 | 0.4 | 109,128 | 0.4 | 2,426 | −9 | 2,417 | 2.00 | 121,100 | 0.4 | 133,300 | 0.3 | 180,000 | 0.3 |
| professing | 81,000 | 0.8 | 163,400 | 0.6 | 3,820 | −160 | 3,660 | 2.02 | 181,400 | 0.5 | 200,000 | 0.5 | 280,000 | 0.4 |
| Orthodox | 60,000 | 0.6 | 132,600 | 0.5 | 3,120 | −150 | 2,970 | 2.02 | 147,200 | 0.4 | 162,300 | 0.4 | 221,000 | 0.3 |
| Roman Catholics | 20,000 | 0.2 | 21,800 | 0.1 | 500 | −10 | 490 | 2.02 | 24,200 | 0.1 | 26,700 | 0.1 | 37,000 | 0.1 |
| Protestants | 1,000 | 0.0 | 8,000 | 0.0 | 200 | 0 | 200 | 2.22 | 9,000 | 0.0 | 10,000 | 0.0 | 20,000 | 0.0 |
| Anglicans | 0 | 0.0 | 1,000 | 0.0 | 0 | 0 | 0 | 0.00 | 1,000 | 0.0 | 1,000 | 0.0 | 2,000 | 0.0 |
| affiliated | 116,200 | 1.2 | 272,528 | 1.0 | 6,246 | −169 | 6,077 | 2.01 | 302,500 | 0.9 | 333,300 | 0.9 | 460,000 | 0.7 |
| total practising | 110,390 | *95* | 218,020 | *80* | 4,997 | −135 | 4,862 | 2.01 | 242,000 | *80* | 266,640 | *80* | 322,000 | *70* |
| non-practising | 5,810 | *5* | 54,510 | *20* | 1,249 | −34 | 1,215 | 2.01 | 60,500 | *20* | 66,660 | *20* | 138,000 | *30* |
| Orthodox | 90,000 | 0.9 | 223,200 | 0.8 | 4,965 | −200 | 4,765 | 1.93 | 246,600 | 0.7 | 270,850 | 0.7 | 347,000 | 0.5 |
| Roman Catholics | 22,900 | 0.2 | 23,978 | 0.1 | 552 | −20 | 532 | 2.00 | 26,600 | 0.1 | 29,300 | 0.1 | 40,500 | 0.1 |
| Protestants | 3,000 | 0.0 | 14,000 | 0.0 | 310 | −10 | 300 | 1.94 | 15,500 | 0.0 | 17,000 | 0.0 | 30,000 | 0.0 |
| Evangelicals | 2,500 | 0.0 | 8,000 | 0.0 | 206 | 194 | 400 | 4.00 | 10,000 | 0.0 | 12,000 | 0.0 | 25,000 | 0.0 |
| Iranian indigenous | 0 | 0.0 | 8,400 | 0.0 | 320 | 80 | 400 | 3.85 | 10,400 | 0.0 | 12,400 | 0.0 | 35,000 | 0.1 |
| Anglicans | 300 | 0.0 | 2,600 | 0.0 | 92 | −22 | 70 | 2.33 | 3,000 | 0.0 | 3,300 | 0.0 | 6,500 | 0.0 |
| Evangelicals | 300 | 0.0 | 2,000 | 0.0 | 50 | 30 | 80 | 3.33 | 2,400 | 0.0 | 2,800 | 0.0 | 6,000 | 0.0 |
| Marginal Protestants | 0 | 0.0 | 350 | 0.0 | 7 | 3 | 10 | 2.50 | 400 | 0.0 | 450 | 0.0 | 1,000 | 0.0 |
| Baha'is | 5,000 | 0.1 | 250,000 | 0.9 | 9,079 | −79 | 9,000 | 3.05 | 295,000 | 0.9 | 340,000 | 0.9 | 590,000 | 0.9 |
| Jews | 44,000 | 0.5 | 58,900 | 0.2 | −440 | 0 | −440 | −0.78 | 56,700 | 0.2 | 54,500 | 0.1 | 32,000 | 0.0 |
| Parsis | 10,000 | 0.1 | 22,500 | 0.1 | 803 | −3 | 800 | 3.06 | 26,100 | 0.1 | 30,500 | 0.1 | 50,000 | 0.1 |
| Non-religious | 0 | 0.0 | 10,000 | 0.0 | 400 | 200 | 600 | 4.62 | 13,000 | 0.0 | 16,000 | 0.0 | 50,000 | 0.1 |
| Hindus | 1,000 | 0.0 | 8,000 | 0.0 | 283 | −43 | 240 | 2.61 | 9,200 | 0.0 | 10,400 | 0.0 | 16,000 | 0.0 |
| Mandaeans | 5,000 | 0.1 | 5,000 | 0.0 | 172 | −52 | 120 | 2.14 | 5,600 | 0.0 | 6,200 | 0.0 | 9,000 | 0.0 |
| Sikhs | 0 | 0.0 | 3,000 | 0.0 | 80 | 0 | 80 | 2.35 | 3,400 | 0.0 | 3,800 | 0.0 | 6,000 | 0.0 |
| Atheists | 0 | 0.0 | 2,000 | 0.0 | 77 | 23 | 100 | 4.00 | 2,500 | 0.0 | 3,000 | 0.0 | 10,000 | 0.0 |
| **Country's population** | **9,700,000** | **100.0** | **28,359,000** | **100.0** | **1,013,300** | **0** | **1,013,300** | **3.08** | **32,923,000** | **100.0** | **38,492,000** | **100.0** | **66,593,000** | **100.0** |

COLUMNS, ROWS. For meanings and definitions, see Codebook (Part 6). Note that, by definition, total 'Christians' = professing + crypto-Christians, which also = affiliated + nominal Christians. Percentages may not always total exactly, due to rounding.
CENSUSES. **1–15.XI.1956:** 98.7% Muslims (including Baha'is), 0.6% Christians (114,528 persons), 0.3% Jews (65,232 persons), 0.3% other religionists, 0.1% Parsis (15,723 persons). **1–20.XI. 1966:** 98.8% Muslims (including Baha'is), 0.6% Christians (0.5% Orthodox, 0.1% Roman Catholics) (149,427), 0.3% other religionists, 0.2% Jews (60,683 persons), 0.1% Parsis (19,816 persons). In censuses, Baha'is are recorded as Muslims.

NOTES ON RELIGIONS
ATHEISTS. Communist Party of Iran (Tudeh/Masses) (proscribed; pro-Soviet): membership (1970) 500. A growing number of Iranian intellectuals are atheists.
BAHA'IS. Iran has been the original homeland since 1844 of the Baha'i World Faith. There have been sporadic persecutions and confiscations from 1850 up to the present day, especially 1955, at which time there were 200,000 Baha'is in Iran (40,000 in Tehran alone); many then were forced underground. There has since been rapid growth from 530 local spiritual assemblies (1964) to 949 (1973), with 2,037 other isolated centres or groups. In 1970 there were about 20,000 active adult Baha'is in Tehran in 300 groups, and a similar number in the provinces, making a total of about 40,000 active adults, a total adult community of 80,000, and a total Baha'i community including children, infants and adherents of about 250,000. A large number of Persian Baha'is work abroad as missionaries, and many others resident abroad form the nucleus of the Baha'i communities in Pakistan, India, and elsewhere. From 1964–73, 3,500 Persian pioneers and 5,000 travelling teachers were active. Over 184 books and periodicals have been published (mimeographed due to the prohibition on printing). *Schisms.* About 5,000 unorganized and underground Babis (Azalis) still exist, followers of the Bab (Baha'i forerunner) of 1850 and of a schism out of Baha'i since 1868. Statistics of this group, and of other very small schisms, are included in the total for Baha'is given in the table.
COUNTRY'S POPULATION. In 1971, about 55,000 Persians from Iraq were deported to Iran.
CRYPTO-CHRISTIANS. Iranian Christians affiliated to churches (mostly Orthodox) but recorded as Muslims in government censuses.
HINDUS. Indians. ISKCON (Hare Krishna) operates 1 centre.
IRANIAN INDIGENOUS. Isolated radio and Bible correspondence course believers (see Table 2).
MANDAEANS. Descendants of the Jewish-Christian Gnostic religion of the 2nd century AD, the Mandaeans call themselves Gnostics and are also called Christians of St John, Followers of John the Baptist, Dippers, Sabaeans (the name used by Arabs) or (the priestly caste) Nasoreans. They are found in Khuzistan in the southwest. The only other organized Mandaean community abroad is in Iraq. The cult is centred on fertility worship.
MUSLIMS. 90% Shia Imamites (Ithna-Asharis (Twelvers), also Ismailis (Seveners) in the west), 8% Sunnis (mainly Shafiite

Kurds, Hanafite Afghanis, Turkmen); also some Yazidis. The Shias include 500,000 Ahl-i-Haqq (Men of God), Kurds accepting 7 incarnational manifestations of God. *Priests* (mullahs, imams). Total 60,000. *Hajj pilgrims to Mecca.* (1968) 22,903; (1969) 15,132; (1970) 48,367; (1971) 30,299; (1972) 45,298; (1973) 57,230; (1974) 57,314; (1975) 74,095; (1976) 39,296.

NON-RELIGIOUS. Expatriate Europeans, also Iranian intellectuals.
PARSIS. Descendants of Zoroastrians, now concentrated in Yazd in central Iran, Kerman to the south, and Tehran. Also called Guebers.
PRACTISING CHRISTIANS. Weekly attenders: about 30%

of all Christians.
PROTESTANTS. Including a number of expatriate USA military and civilians.
SIKHS. Indians, first arriving in 1920.

**NON-CHRISTIAN RELIGIONS. Islam** is the professed religion of 98% of the population, of which the majority are Shia Imamites, also called Ithna-Asharis or Twelvers. Indeed, Iran is in many ways the major centre of Shiite Islam in the world. There are also over 2.6 million Sunnis, mainly Kurds of the Shafiite rite and Afghanis of the Hanafite rite. During recent years the power of the Shiite religious leadership has been limited by the imperial government, until the 1979 revolution. Virtually all mosques and shrines have endowments which are at present used for educational and charitable purposes under the control of the Ministry of Education. The veneration of Muslim saints is widely practised, and the shrines of popular saints are extensively endowed. Iran's most important pilgrimage centres are the cities of Qum and Meshed. The universities of Tehran and Meshed each have Muslim theological faculties.

**Baha'i** owes its origin to a Persian, Sayyid Ali Muhammed, who in 1844 added his name as Bab al-Din (Gate of the Faith) to the list of the Twelve Imams of Shiite Islam. His followers were called Babis. His successor was Baha'u'llah (Glory of God), from whose name comes the term Baha'i. Accused of complicity in a plot to assassinate the Persian shah in 1852, Baha'is fled from Iran en masse. Baha'i is still legally banned, but the sizeable Baha'i community residing in the country have not been molested since the persecution and confiscations of 1955 which drove them underground for a time. Now they are found in commerce and the professions, and in censuses are regarded by the government as Muslims. As a missionary religion the Baha'i World Faith in Iran doubled the number of its organized centres from 1960–75, has sent abroad large numbers of missions, and has Persian Baha'is forming the nuclei of Baha'i communities in Pakistan, India and elsewhere. A separate group also exists in Iran named Babis, being 5,000 followers of those who accepted the Bab but refused to recognize Baha'u'llah.

**Judaism** is still represented by an influential community, in spite of the large numbers of Jews who have emigrated to Israel. The majority reside in Tehran. They operate one hospital, 3 recreation centres and 2 centres for marriage registration, in addition to several synagogues and schools.

**Parsiism** began in the 6th century BC as Zoroastrianism, with the preaching of Zarathustra who succeeded in eliminating all deities of the Iranian pantheon except Ahura Mazda, the One True God. During the period of Sassanid rule in Persia, from the 7th to 3rd centuries BC, Zoroastrianism became the symbol of national and cultural identity as well as the state religion, although later it was unable to withstand the Muslim onslaught which began in the 7th century AD. In 1966 there were 7,000 Parsis in Tehran, 7,000 in Yazd, 4,000 at Kerman and 3,000 at Isfahan. Altogether there are 20 places of Parsi worship.

**Mandaeanism** is an ancient Jewish-Christian Gnostic syncretistic religion begun in the 2nd century AD, centred on fertility worship, whose followers call themselves Mandaiia (Gnostics) and who are also variously called Mandaeans, Sabaeans (so termed by Arabs), Nasoreans, Followers of John the Baptist, Dippers, or Christians of St John. They are found only in Khuzistan (southwest Iran) and in Iraq.

**Sikhism,** which is a reform movement out of Hinduism with a strong monotheistic emphasis, entered Iran about 1920. Sikhs remain for the most part expatriate Indians.

**CHRISTIANITY.** About 98% of all Christians in Iran belong to non-Persian ethnic minorities. Only a few converts from Islam have become members of the Anglican and Evangelical (Presbyterian) churches.
ORTHODOX CHURCHES. The Armenian Apostolic Church is the largest church in Iran. It terms itself Apostolic because it traces its origin to the work of the 1st-century Apostles Thaddeus and Bartholomew in Armenia and northwest Persia. Until 1946, its 3 dioceses in Iran were under the Catholicate of Echmiadzin in the USSR, and the bishops were Soviet Armenians. In 1959 the communal councils of the dioceses asked to be placed instead under the jurisdiction of the rival Armenian Catholicate of Cilicia (Sis) based on Antelias, Lebanon. The Armenian community in Iran operates numerous schools, publishes books in its own language and maintains good rapport with civil authorities.

The Assyrian or Ancient Church of the East has traditionally been termed Nestorian, a name which is however rejected by the church itself on the grounds that it existed before the Greek patriarch Nestorius and reached its theological position independently of him. Membership in Iran consists largely of refugees from persecution in Turkey and Iraq. Concentrated in the northern part of the country at an earlier period, the Assyrian population has gradually moved to the Tehran area. The church sponsors one school. Since 1976, the new Patriarch of the East, Mar Dinkha IV, has been based in Tehran.

The Russian Orthodox Church was established in Tehran in 1863 and is directly related to the synod of bishops of the Russian Orthodox Church Outside of Russia whose primate lives in New York, USA. Activities in Tehran include a school, a library and a club.

Greeks came to Iran largely by way of Russia between 1917 and 1936, and in the early years they worshipped with the Russian Orthodox. A separate Greek Orthodox Church was established in Tehran in 1943, whose leader, an archimandrite, serves under the Patriarchate of Antioch through the archbishop of Baghdad. A small school is attached to the church in Tehran.
CATHOLIC CHURCH. Roman Catholicism is represented by 3 rites. (1) The Chaldean Catholic Church is the largest with about two-thirds of the total Catholic population (15,000). It has roots identical with the Assyrian Church of the East and consists of converts to Rome from the year 1552 on. (2) The Latin Church has 7,000 members, more than half being expatriates. Latin missionaries came to Iran in the 13th and in the 17th centuries, but each time their work was destroyed. Another mission entered in 1840 and several new ones since World War II. (3) The Armenian Catholic Church, a uniate church created through Dominican activity, dates its founding to 1605, although the establishment of its own patriarchate came later. Armenian Catholics suffered under the Afghan persecutions of the 18th century and now number only 2,000.
PROTESTANT CHURCHES. The pioneer Protestant mission was the American Board (ABCFM) in 1832. Its Presbyterian and Congregationalist missionaries did not intend to organize a separate church but called themselves the Mission to the Nestorians, which was organized in 1834. The Nestorian Church, however, resisted reforms, and instead the mission found itself converting numbers of Assyrians. As a result, the Evangelical Church, which is Presbyterian in polity, came into existence in 1855. It is today the largest Protestant church in the country and has had an influence out of all proportion to its size. Its membership is 55% Assyrian, 21% Armenian and 24% of other ethnic origins. The church maintains 19 schools and is related through its Christian Service Board to the Nurbakhsh School for Practical Nurses.

Persians who became Pentecostals while living in Chicago (USA) brought Pentecostalism to their homeland in 1909; but during World War I many of them were killed or scattered and their work came

to a halt. Missionaries from the Assemblies of God, USA were active during 1924–38 and returned again in 1966. An Armenian group of Pentecostals, Filadelfia, which began in Iran in 1958, has also received support from the Assemblies of God since 1965.

Seventh-day Adventists arrived in 1911 and the first Brethren work began in 1920, but both of these groups have remained small, two-thirds of the Adventist community having emigrated to the USA. There are now numerous small American missions in Iran, the majority having arrived since 1955. Many have only expatriate membership. Protestants have mainly grown at the expense of the Orthodox churches, Armenian and Assyrian, with very few Persian converts.
ANGLICAN CHURCH. The first Anglican to enter Iran (1811) was Henry Martyn, a chaplain of the East India Company, who displayed extraordinary gifts in the translation of the scriptures into the Persian language. In 1844 the London Society for the Propagation of Christianity among the Jews sent missionaries to the Jewish community of Tehran. The Church Missionary Society made its appearance in 1869, and the diocese of Persia was formed in 1912. At the present time an Iranian bishop presides over the church whose membership is 10% expatriate. In contrast to the Protestant churches, however, it has not won converts from Orthodoxy but is, rather, a church of converts from Judaism, Islam and Parsiism. The church operates 2 hospitals, 2 schools and a school for the blind.

**CHURCH AND STATE.** The official religion of the state is the Ithna-Ashariya branch of Shia Islam. Two important laws govern the status of non-Muslim religious minorities. (1) A law of 1928 reserves a certain number of parliamentary seats for representatives of a few religious communities, the representatives being elected solely by the faithful of those communities. In the legislature of 1971, the religious minorities were represented by 6 deputies (2 Gregorian Armenians, 2 Jews, one Zoroastrian, one Chaldean Assyrian) and by one senator, a Gregorian Armenian. (2) A law of 1943, known as the 'Law concerning the observance of the personal statute of Iranian Non-Shiites', guarantees respect for the customs observed by each religious community, provided that they continue to respect public order. Three cases are clearly provided for, where courts must base their judgement on the established customs of the religious community in question, after having consulted the appropriate religious authorities: (a) matters relative to marriage and divorce, which are subject to the established customs of the religion of the husband; (b) matters relative to wills and inheritance, which are subject to the established customs of the religion of the deceased; and (c)

**Episcopal Church of Iran.** Blind evangelist reads Bible in Braille to group at Fawzia hospital.

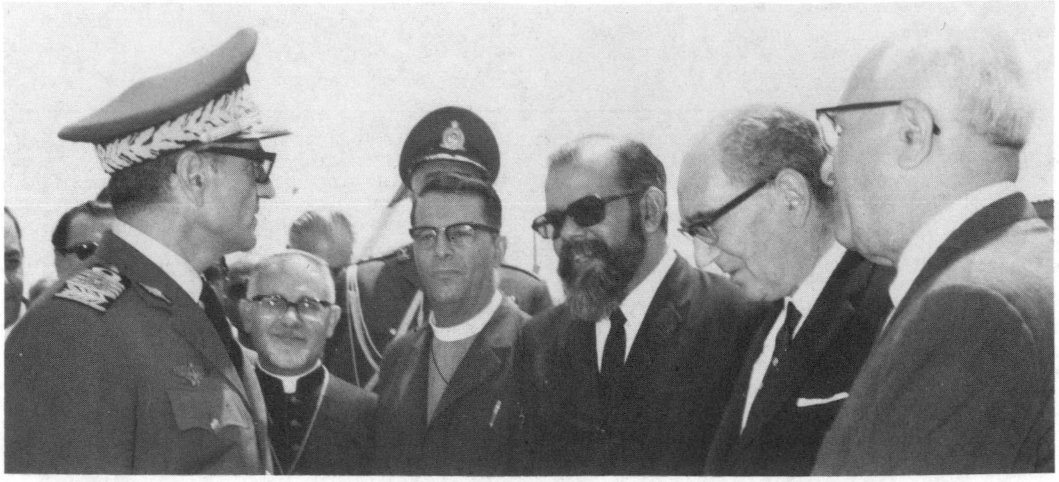

Former Shah of Iran in audience with Anglican, Orthodox, Catholic and Protestant leaders including secretary of Iran Council of Churches.

matters which concern the adoption of children, which follow the established customs of the religion of the adopting parents.

In practice, each religious community, Christian and non-Christian, of all rites, has its own tribunal which handles questions relating to marriage and hereditary succession. The civil tribunal makes legally binding the decisions of the religious courts.

**INTERDENOMINATIONAL ORGANIZATIONS.** The Iran Council of Churches was formed in 1951 to 'strengthen Christian Churches in their internal life; to encourage evangelistic outreach; (and) to work toward a united Church'. There are only 3 members at present (Anglican, Presbyterian and Tehran Community churches), but unofficial co-operation also exists with the Catholic Church. Projects include literature development, youth activity, correspondence courses and preparation of programmes in Farsi for Radio Voice of the Gospel in Addis Ababa (until 1977). There exists also a Youth Committee of the Churches in Iran which is in contact with the Ecumenical Office for Students and Youth in the Middle East (SOJEMO) with its headquarters in Lebanon. The Bible Society also has wide Protestant and Catholic support.

**BROADCASTING.** Since Iran is a Muslim state, it is extremely difficult to get Christian programmes accepted by official stations. In Tehran there is however a station owned by the US Air Force which accepts Christian programmes, but this is conditional on approval from the Armed Forces Chaplaincy Board. All programmes are in English. International stations from abroad easily heard in Iran were RVOG (Ethiopia) until its closure in 1977 and FEBA (Seychelles), both using Farsi (Persian). There are 2 Christian production studios, those of International Missions for release over FEBA, and of the Near East Council of Churches Radio Programme Centre for Iran.

## BIBLIOGRAPHY

'A handbook of the Christian community in Iran, 1970'. N.A. Horner. Tehran: United Presbyterian Commission in Iran, 1970. 19p.

*Christians in Persia*. R. E. Waterfield. London: Allen & Unwin, 1973.

*Design of my world*. H. B. Dehqani-Tafti. London: Lutterworth, 1960. (Autobiography of Anglican bishop).

'Islam et babysme', R. Leniir, *Revue de synthèse*, 78, 8 (Nov–Dec, 1957), 471–7.

*Religion and politics in contemporary Iran: clergy-state relations in the Pahlavi period*. S. Akhavi, Leiden: E.J. Brill, 1980.

*Religion and state in Iran 1785-1906*. H. Algar. Leiden: E.J. Brill, 1970. 304p.

'The Armenian Apostolic Church in Iran', J. Hananian, *Al-Mushir* (Rawalpindi, Pakistan), XII, 7–8 (July–August, 1970), 1–10.

'The Presbyterian Church in Iran'. J. Elder. New York: United Presbyterian Church, n.d.

TABLE 2. ORGANIZED CHURCHES AND DENOMINATIONS IN IRAN

| Official name 1 | Begun 2 | Type 3 | Counc 4 | Congs 5 | Adults 6 | Affiliated 7 | Names, notes, and other statistics (see Codebook) 8 |
|---|---|---|---|---|---|---|---|
| Ancient Church of the East: P Tehran | c 50 | O Nes | Yw... | | 13,500 | 20,000 | *D Urmia/Rezayeh*. Assyrians. 2,700 families. No dissidents as in Iraq. Patriarch,6n,1s. |
| **Armenian Apostolic Church:** | c 64 | O Arm | Sw.N. | 118 | 134,900 | 202,000 | *Gregorians*. Under jurisdiction of C Sis (Lebanon). Armenians. 73,000 in 1908. |
| D Julfa-Isfahan | c1600 | O Arm | Sa | 38 | 26,000 | 40,000 | Armenians in eastern Iran, transferred en masse in c1600 from Julfa. 17n,1H. |
| D Tabriz (Azerbaijan) | c 64 | O Arm | Sa | 45 | 8,900 | 12,000 | Azerbaidzhan province of Iran. Until c1820, named D Artaz. 3n,2d. |
| D Tehran | 1944 | O Arm | Sb | 35 | 100,000 | 150,000 | Irak province. Archbishop, 16n,1h,3r(and 14 primary schools). Many youth clubs. |
| Armenian Closed Brethren | 1945 | P EBr | ..... | 1 | 30 | 100 | Exclusive separation from Armenian Ev Spiritual Brethren in 1945. Armenians. |
| Armenian Ev Spiritual Brethren | c1920 | P CBr | x.... | 1 | 55 | 150 | *Holiness Brethren*. Schism ex various Armenian churches. Tehran. No ministers. |
| Assemblies of God (Assyrian) | 1909 | P Pe2 | ZF... | 9 | 450 | 1,000 | Assyrians, in Azerbaijan Province. M=AoG(USA) since 1924. 55% of members in Tehran. |
| Assemblies of God (Filadelfia) | 1958 | P Pe2 | Z.... | 16 | 1,701 | 3,000 | Armenians. Origin USSR. M=AoG(USA). Correspondence courses (8000). 15n,4f,1s(9). |
| Catholic Church in Iran: | 1552 | R LEr | O...R | 46 | 13,200 | 23,978 | *Kelisa-ye-Katolik*. Mainly proselytes from Nestorians. C=3+1+5. 55nx,5m,75w,296Yy. |
| M Urmya (Rezayeh) (*Chaldean*) | 1890 | R Cha | Os | 7 | 2,200 | 4,000 | Chaldeans (Kaldani), united with Rome 1552. Under P Babylon. 4 0 4 45 |
| D Salmas (Shahpur) (*Chaldean*) | 1847 | R Cha | Os | 2 | 400 | 700 | For some time counted as part of M Urmya. HQ Rezayeh. 1 0 0 0 |
| M Tehran (*Chaldean*) | 1850 | R Cha | Os | 8 | 5,200 | 9,500 | In capital. Until 1971, M Sehna. Many former Nestorians. 2r. 7 0 11 126 |
| AD Ahwaz (*Chaldean*) | 1966 | R Cha | Os | 6 | 400 | 778 | Suffragan diocese of P Babilonia (Iraq). Declining. HQ Ahwaz. 1 0 0 11 |
| AD Ispahan (*Latin*) | 1632 | R Lat | os | 20 | 3,900 | 7,000 | *Kelisa-ye-Latini-e-Katolik*. Latin-rite. 60% expatriates. 40 5 50 97 |
| D Ispahan (*Armenian*) | 1605 | R Arm | Os | 3 | 1,100 | 2,000 | 340 Armenian families, mostly in Tehran. HQ Tehran. 1r. 2 0 10 17 |
| Church of Christ, Scientist | 1960 | M Sci | x.... | 1 | 20 | 50 | *Christian Science*. M=CCS(Boston,USA). In Tehran. |
| Church of Jesus C of Latter-day Saints | 1965 | M LdS | x.... | 3 | 137 | 200 | Under Swiss Mission, LdS. Mainly Americans, Europeans. Tehran, Bandar Abbas, Ahwaz. |
| Episcopal Church of Iran | 1811 | A Eva | Aw.NK | 12 | 700 | 2,600 | *D Iran*, in *ECJME*. M=CMS,CMJ,CB. 10% expatriates. 6n,5x,39f,2k,2H,3r,W=61%,7Y,18y. |
| Evangelical Church of Iran | 1832 | P Ref | RW.NK | 36 | 3,067 | 6,000 | 1835,M=UPUSA. A=1934. North. 55% Assyrian, 21% Armenian. 19 schools. 12n,37f,1r,1s. |
| French Evangelical Church | 1967 | P Ref | ..... | 1 | 20 | 50 | *Eglise Evangélique Française*. French-speaking congregation in Tehran. |
| German Evangelical Church in Iran | c1930 | P Lut | ..... | 1 | 300 | 400 | *Deutsche Evangelische Kirche*. Serving large German community in Tehran. 1x,1k. |
| Greek Orth P Antioch (D Baghdad) | 1917 | O Gre | Cw.N. | 2 | 400 | 600 | Greeks, Arabs, also former Nestorians; in Tehran, Abadan. 1x. |
| International Missions | 1955 | P int | xM... | 3 | 30 | 100 | M=IM(USA). Faraman Church (rural), Good Shepherd Church (Tehran). 25f. |
| Isolated radio churches | c1970 | I rad | ..... | 210 | 4,000 | 8,400 | Isolated radio believers (youths etc). R=900(RVOG,TWR),T=53500(IM,ICI,VOP). |
| Jehovah's Witnesses | 1926 | M Jeh | x.... | 1 | 30 | 100 | *Watch Tower. IBSA*. 1926, missionaries' arrival; 1954, active witnessing under way. |
| Khuzestan Church Council | c1970 | P uni | ..... | 8 | 200 | 300 | Joint project of Episcopal Ch/Evangelical Ch/ICC. Abadan and Ahwaz. 1n,2x. |
| Russian Orthodox Church | 1863 | O Sla | x.... | 3 | 400 | 600 | Related to ROC Outside of Russia (New York, USA). Tehran. 15,000-volume library. |
| Seventh-day Adventist Church | 1911 | P Adv | x.... | 7 | 225 | 300 | *Iran Field*. 60% emigrated to USA. 5n,4x,17mw,14f,G=−1.3%pa,1h,1r,5t(176),W=83%,8Y. |
| Tehran Bible Church | 1964 | P int | .M... | 1 | 50 | 100 | English-speaking. Linked with International Missions. 1x. |
| Tehran Community Church | c1930 | P com | ....K | 2 | 119 | 500 | English-speaking congregation in Tehran. Mostly expatriates. |
| Tehran Lutheran Church | 1970 | P Lut | ..... | 1 | 40 | 100 | English-speaking congregation in Tehran. Mostly expatriates. 1x. |
| Union of Armenian Ev Chs in Near East | | P Con | Rw.N. | 2 | 100 | 300 | Armenian Protestants. HQ Beirut. 2 congregations and 1 school in Tehran. |
| United Pentecostal Church | 1930 | P Pel | x.... | 4 | 35 | 100 | *Jesus Only Church*. M=UPC(USA). Early work not followed up until much later. 2m,2f. |
| Other Protestant denominations | | P | ..... | | 500 | 1,500 | Total about 10 (see list below). |
| **Total affiliated (mid-1970)** | | | | **550** | **174,209** | **272,528** | **Total denominations (1970) . . . 35.** |
| **Total affiliated (mid-1975)** | | | | **560** | **193,400** | **302,500** | **Total denominations (1975) . . . 40.** |
| **Total affiliated (mid-1980)** | | | | **570** | **213,000** | **333,300** | **Total denominations (1980) . . . 45.** |

**NOTES ON TABLE ABOVE**

COLUMNS: for meanings and CODES (cols. 1, 3, 4, 8), see Codebook (Part 6). Column 1: **Boldface type** = church with over 10% of country's affiliated Christians.

NATIONAL COUNCILS (Column 4, 5th letter).
K = Iran Council of Churches (ICC) (Shovraye Kelissye Iran).
R = Iranian Episcopal Conference (formerly Inter-Rite Episcopal Conference), begun 1977.

OTHER PROTESTANT DENOMINATIONS. These include: Baptist Bible Fellowship International (1966), Ch of Christ (Non-Instrumental), International Christian Fellowship (1969), Lutheran Orient Mission Society (1911), Southern Baptist Convention (1968), United Evangelical Chs, Worldwide Evangelization Crusade (1963); also USA military chaplaincies.

UNITING CHURCHES. Negotiations for organic union were under way in 1974 between: Episcopal Ch of Iran, Ev Ch of Iran.

**PEOPLES** (ethnolinguistic). Christians: 77% Armenian, 15% Assyrian (Chaldean), 4% European (2.5% Italian & French, 1.4% British & USA, 0.1% German, Russian), 2% Persian, 1% Arab, Korean.

**COUNTRY-WIDE TOTALS**

EVANGELIZATION (see Part 5). 1900: 13%. 1970: 27%. 1980: 32%. *Mass evangelism*. Autumn 1970, meetings in Tehran led by evangelist from Iowa, USA. *Radiophonic evangelism*. RVOG, TWR, et alia. Bible correspondence courses: 53,500 enrolments (IM, ICI (with 400 conversions reported), VOP, et alia).

FOREIGN MISSIONARIES AND PERSONNEL (nationals serving abroad) (1973). Total about 2 Orthodox and Protestants in USA et alia.

FOREIGN MISSIONARIES AND PERSONNEL (aliens from abroad) (1973). Total 300. *From Western world*. 279: 145 Protestants (113 in 18 USA societies, 13 in 2 UK societies, 9 in 2 WGermany societies, 4 in 4 Australia societies, 2 in 1 Denmark society, 2 in 1 Canada society, 1 in 1 New Zealand society, 1 in 1 Netherlands society), about 95 Roman Catholics, 39 Anglicans (33 in 2 UK societies, 4 in 1 Australia society, 2 in 1 USA society). *From Communist world*. About 2 Roman Catholics from Yugoslavia. *From Third World*. 19: about 10 Roman Catholics, 8 Protestants (1 Presbyterian from Korea), 1 Orthodox.

INSTITUTIONS (church-operated) (1973). Total 32, including 18 higher schools (1 minor seminary), 8 medical centres (3 hospitals), 3 seminaries (2 Protestant, 1 Orthodox), 1 study centre.

PERIODICALS. About 18 titles.

PERSONNEL. About 440 (140 national, 300 foreign).

RELIGIOUS LIBRARIES. 5.

SCRIPTURE DISTRIBUTION (1975). Annual totals: 2,181 Bibles (23% free, 72% subsidized, 5% commercial), 1,928 NTs (21% free, 74% subsidized, 5% commercial), 80,934 UBS portions, 512,325 UBS selections. *Translations completed*. Portion: 4 languages since 1546. NT: Persian in 1815. Bible: Persian in 1838.

SERVICE AGENCIES. About 24, including BMMF, CCCI, CEF, ICC, MECC, OM, WV.

**ADDITIONAL DATA ON CHURCHES**

CATHOLIC CHURCH IN IRAN. *Annual baptisms*. (1972) 96.3% infant, 3.7% adult. *Priests*. Latin priests are expatriates, and in religious orders; for the other rites, almost all priests are nationals and secular (except 2 Chaldean religious). The Latins nowadays work only in schools or in the Latin-rite parishes. *Main religious congregations*. Priests: CM, SDB. Sisters: Daughters of Charity, Armenian Sisters of the Immaculate Conception, Chaldean Sisters of the Immaculate Conception.

*Catholic organizations*. There is no episcopal conference in Iran. However, the ordinaries representing all Catholic rites have constituted an Inter-Rite Episcopal Conference without compromising the autonomy of any rite. There are no national presbyteral or pastoral councils and no associations for religious personnel.

The Holy See has diplomatic relations with Iran and is represented to government and the Catholic hierarchy by a pro-nuncio in Tehran.

Together the 3 Catholic rites operate 15 schools, with the majority of teaching personnel being Iranians; 4 orphanages; 2 homes for the aged; and 2 dispensaries.

EPISCOPAL CHURCH OF IRAN. Diocese of Iran, in the Episcopal Church in Jerusalem and the Middle East (formerly Jerusalem Archbishopric). *Converts*. Whilst all other immigrant churches have won their converts at the expense of the Armenians and Nestorians, the Episcopal Church is a church of converts from Judaism, Islam and Parsiism.

EVANGELICAL CHURCH OF IRAN. In 1975, a Korean congregation, Teheran Korean Christian Church, was formed to work among the 3,000 Koreans in Iran (in construction and transport companies, 65% in Tehran), with (1976) 160 communicants and 215 total community, served by a Korean pastor sent as a missionary by the Presbyterian Church of Korea.

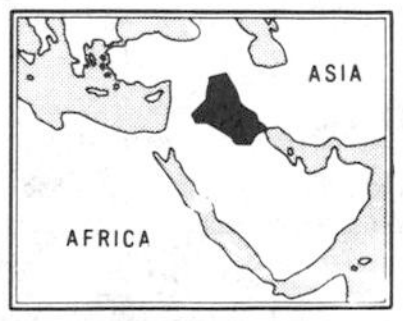


# IRAQ

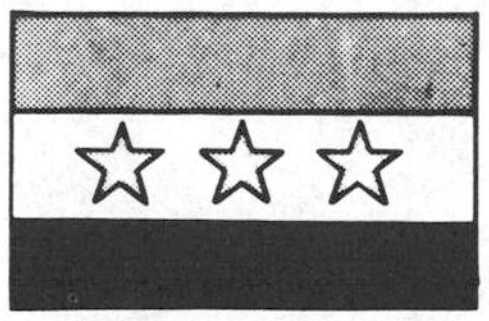

## SECULAR DATA

**STATE. Official name:** The Republic of Iraq (Al Jumhouriyah al Iraqiyah). Adjective of nationality: Iraqi.
**Flag** (shown above right): Red, white, and black stripes, with 3 green stars.
**Area:** 434,924 sq.km. (167,925 sq.miles). Agricultural land: 21.3%.
**Government:** One-party socialist-military state, since 1963 (1920 monarchy, 1958 military junta).
**Legislature:** National Council, 100 members.
**Official language:** Arabic. Kurdish also is official in Kurdish districts.
**Chief cities:** capital Baghdad 1,657,400 (1965), Basra 310,950, Mosul 264,150, Kirkuk 183,900.
**Political divisions:** 10 Governorates.
**Armed forces** (1976): Total 158,000 regular: army 140,000, navy 3,000, air force 15,000 (299 combat aircraft). Reserves: 250,000. Paramilitary forces: 54,800 (50,000 People's Army).
**Foreign forces** (1974): 1,000 USSR military advisers.

**DEMOGRAPHY. Population:** 8,047,415 (census of 14.X.1965. For 1970–2000 (UN), see last row of Table 1). Population density (1975): 25/sq.km. (66/sq.mile). Under 15 years: 46%. Growth rate (1975–80): 3.44% per year (births 4.73%, deaths −1.30%). Life expectancy (1975–80): 55.2 years. Household size: 6.0 persons.
**Major languages:** Arabic, Kurdish, Chaldean (Aramaic-Syriac), Persian, Turkish, Turkoman, Armenian, English, French, Circassian, and several others.
**Urban dwellers** (1970): 47.1%. Urban growth rate (1950–70): 4.4% per year.
**Labour force:** 29%.
**Refugees** (1977): From abroad, about 14,000. Internally displaced: 300,000 Kurds. Exiles abroad: 35,600 Iraqi Kurds (35,000 in Iran, 400 in USA, et alia).
**Tourists** (1974): 544,800.

**ETHNOLINGUISTIC GROUPS.** 75.9% Arab (Iraqi, Syrian, 0.1% Palestinian (14,000), Egyptian), 17.9% Kurdish, 3.3% Assyrian (Chaldean), 1.2% Persian, 1.2% Turkmen, 0.2% Armenian, 0.1% Lur, 0.1% Turkish, 0.1% Circassian, European, USSR military (1,000), Jewish (700), Chinese (600).

**MONEY** (1977). **Monetary unit:** dinar (=5 riyals = 20 dirhams = 1,000 fils); US$1 = ID 0.295.
**National income per person:** US$750. Average annual family income: US$4,500.
**Inflation:** (1970–74) 5.5% per year (1975: consumer price index 149), (1979) 8% per year.
**Cost of living in capital** (1976): index 125 (Washington DC=100). Daily cost of living: US$54.

**HEALTH.** Hospitals: 151 (18,565 beds). Doctors: 4,123. Lepers: 3,500 (0.3 per 1,000). Blind: 75,000. Psychotics: 90,000. Criminals: 14,459.

**EDUCATION.** Adult literacy: (1947) 11%, (1965) 24%, (1975) 40%. Education rate: 49%. Schools: 6,269. Universities: 6.

**LITERATURE.** Annual new book titles (1972): 623. Periodicals: 74. Scientific journals: 10. Newspapers: 5 dailies, 6 non-daily.

**COMMUNICATION** (per 1,000 people). Phones: 12. Radios: 106. TV sets: 52. Daily newspaper circulation: 18 copies.

TABLE 1. RELIGIOUS ADHERENTS IN IRAQ

| Year | 1900 | | mid-1970 | | Annual change, 1970–1980 | | | | mid-1975 | | mid-1980 | | 2000 | |
|---|---|---|---|---|---|---|---|---|---|---|---|---|---|---|
| *Name* | *Adherents* | *%* | *Adherents* | *%* | *Natural* | *Conversion* | *Total* | *Rate* | *Adherents* | *%* | *Adherents* | *%* | *Adherents* | *%* |
| Muslims | 2,012,790 | 89.5 | 8,916,318 | 95.3 | 367,228 | 60 | 367,288 | 3.47 | 10,570,600 | 95.5 | 12,589,200 | 95.8 | 23,444,900 | 95.9 |
| Yazidis | 15,000 | 0.7 | 80,000 | 0.9 | 3,287 | −87 | 3,200 | 3.33 | 96,000 | 0.9 | 112,000 | 0.9 | 210,000 | 0.9 |
| **Christians** | **144,110** | **6.4** | **379,982** | **4.1** | **9,152** | **−800** | **8,352** | **1.99** | **420,500** | **3.8** | **463,500** | **3.5** | **707,900** | **2.9** |
| crypto-Christians | 62,110 | 2.8 | 127,382 | 1.4 | 3,682 | −300 | 3,382 | 2.35 | 143,800 | 1.3 | 161,200 | 1.2 | 243,400 | 1.0 |
| professing | 82,000 | 3.6 | 252,600 | 2.7 | 5,470 | −500 | 4,970 | 1.80 | 276,700 | 2.5 | 302,300 | 2.3 | 464,500 | 1.9 |
| Roman Catholics | 25,000 | 1.1 | 195,100 | 2.1 | 4,130 | −90 | 4,040 | 1.88 | 214,900 | 1.9 | 235,500 | 1.8 | 390,700 | 1.6 |
| Orthodox | 57,000 | 2.5 | 56,000 | 0.6 | 1,370 | −400 | 970 | 1.60 | 60,500 | 0.5 | 65,700 | 0.5 | 73,000 | 0.3 |
| Protestants | 0 | 0.0 | 1,500 | 0.0 | −30 | −10 | −40 | −3.08 | 1,300 | 0.0 | 1,100 | 0.0 | 800 | 0.0 |
| affiliated | 144,110 | 6.4 | 379,982 | 4.1 | 9,152 | −800 | 8,352 | 1.99 | 420,500 | 3.8 | 463,500 | 3.5 | 707,900 | 2.9 |
| total practising | 129,700 | *90* | 303,990 | *80* | 7,322 | −641 | 6,681 | 1.99 | 336,400 | *80* | 370,800 | *80* | 495,530 | *70* |
| non-practising | 14,410 | *10* | 75,990 | *20* | 1,830 | −159 | 1,671 | 1.99 | 84,100 | *20* | 92,700 | *20* | 212,370 | *30* |
| Roman Catholics | 44,000 | 2.0 | 278,953 | 3.0 | 6,435 | −150 | 6,285 | 2.03 | 309,600 | 2.8 | 341,800 | 2.6 | 537,800 | 2.2 |
| Orthodox | 100,000 | 4.4 | 75,450 | 0.8 | 2,003 | −848 | 1,155 | 1.43 | 81,000 | 0.7 | 87,000 | 0.7 | 97,800 | 0.4 |
| Non-White indigenous | 0 | 0.0 | 22,500 | 0.2 | 753 | 197 | 950 | 3.52 | 27,000 | 0.2 | 32,000 | 0.2 | 70,000 | 0.3 |
| Protestants | 60 | 0.0 | 2,579 | 0.0 | −59 | 1 | −58 | −2.52 | 2,300 | 0.0 | 2,000 | 0.0 | 1,500 | 0.0 |
| Evangelicals | 50 | 0.0 | 1,300 | 0.0 | −21 | 1 | −20 | −1.67 | 1,200 | 0.0 | 1,100 | 0.0 | 1,000 | 0.0 |
| Anglicans | 50 | 0.0 | 500 | 0.0 | 20 | 0 | 20 | 3.33 | 600 | 0.0 | 700 | 0.0 | 800 | 0.0 |
| Non-religious | 0 | 0.0 | 30,000 | 0.3 | 1,369 | 631 | 2,000 | 5.00 | 40,000 | 0.4 | 50,000 | 0.4 | 200,000 | 0.8 |
| Mandaeans | 3,000 | 0.1 | 18,000 | 0.2 | 736 | −36 | 700 | 3.25 | 21,500 | 0.2 | 25,000 | 0.2 | 40,000 | 0.2 |
| Atheists | 0 | 0.0 | 10,000 | 0.1 | 445 | 155 | 600 | 4.62 | 13,000 | 0.1 | 16,000 | 0.1 | 50,000 | 0.2 |
| Jews | 90,000 | 4.0 | 700 | 0.0 | −60 | 0 | −60 | −20.00 | 300 | 0.0 | 100 | 0.0 | 200 | 0.0 |
| Buddhists | 0 | 0.0 | 500 | 0.0 | 10 | −10 | 0 | 0.00 | 500 | 0.0 | 500 | 0.0 | 0 | 0.0 |
| Baha'is | 100 | 0.0 | 500 | 0.0 | 20 | 0 | 20 | 3.33 | 600 | 0.0 | 700 | 0.0 | 2,000 | 0.0 |
| **Country's population** | **2,250,000** | **100.0** | **9,356,000** | **100.0** | **378,900** | **0** | **378,900** | **3.42** | **11,067,000** | **100.0** | **13,145,000** | **100.0** | **24,445,000** | **100.0** |

COLUMNS, ROWS. For meanings and definitions, see Codebook (Part 6). Note that, by definition, total 'Christians' = professing + crypto-Christians, which also = affiliated + nominal Christians. Percentages may not always total exactly, due to rounding.
CENSUSES. **19.X.1947:** 93.6% Muslims, 3.1% Christians, 2.4% Jews, 0.7% Yazidis, 0.1% Mandaeans. **12.X.1957** (including 49,984 nationals abroad): 95.6% Muslims, 3.3% Christians (206,206 persons), 0.9% Yazidis, 0.2% Mandaeans (Followers of St John), 0.1% Jews. **14.X.1965:** 96.0% Muslims, 2.9% Christians (232,406 persons), 0.9% Yazidis, 0.2% Mandaeans, 0.0% Jews (3,187 persons).

**NOTES ON RELIGIONS**
ANGLICANS. Expatriates, largely Whites.
ATHEISTS. Communist Party of Iraq (CPI) (proscribed; internal factions): hard-core membership (1970) 2,000. Also 1,000 USSR military advisers (1974).
BAHA'IS. Begun in Iraq from Persia about 1850. In 1964, 6 local spiritual assemblies; 1970, banned by decree and property confiscated; 1973, only 19 isolated centres or groups.
BUDDHISTS. Chinese. Buddhism was first introduced into Iraq around AD 550.
COUNTRY'S POPULATION. In 1971 about 55,000 Persians in Iraq were deported to Iran.
CRYPTO-CHRISTIANS. Iraqi Christians affiliated to churches but recorded in government censuses as Muslims.
JEWS. Rapid decline from 250,000 in 1945 by massive emigration to Israel from 1950 onwards, to 4,906 in 1957 and 3,187 in 1965.
MANDAEANS. Calling themselves Mandaiia (Gnostics), and descendants of the Jewish-Christian Gnostic religion of the 2nd century AD, the Mandaeans are also called Christians of St John, Followers of John the Baptist, Dippers, Sabaeans (the name used by Arabs) or (the priestly caste) Nasoreans. The only other organized Mandaean community abroad is in Iran.
MUSLIMS. 62% Shias (Ithna-Asharis (Twelvers), and Ismailis (Seveners) in the southeast), 38% Sunnis (of the Hanafite rite, and Shafiite rite including the Kurds). Shias are all Arabs; Sunnis are Arabs, Turkmen, Turkish and Kurdish. The figures for Muslims here include Yazidis. *Hajj pilgrims to Mecca.* (1968) 19,475; (1969) 24,902; (1970) 19,482; (1971) 17,628; (1972) 24,681; (1973) 35,567; (1974) 58,983; (1975) 10,368; (1976) 49,703.
NON-WHITE INDIGENOUS. Isolated Arab radio and Bible correspondence course believers, also 2 Nestorian schisms (see Table 2).
PROFESSING CHRISTIANS. In recent years there has been a steady emigration to Kuwait, Australia, the USA and Canada, amounting in the 1970s to 300 known families a year or, allowing for unrecorded and individual emigrants, around 4,000 professing Christians a year, compared with the natural (biological) increase of 9,470 a year, and defections (losses by conversion, mostly to Islam) of about 500 a year. As can be seen from the line above for affiliated Christians, affiliated losses are considerably higher.
YAZIDIS (Yezidis, Devil-Worshippers). A 12th-century Muslim syncretistic religion; enumerated here under Muslims. Yazidis speak a Kurdish dialect and are thought to be descendants of the original Iraqi population.

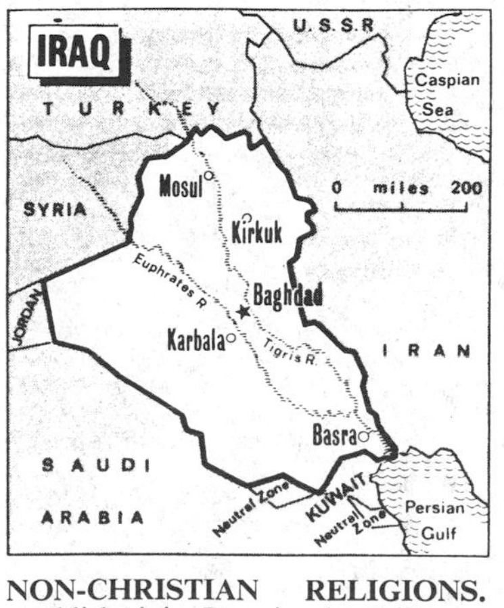


**NON-CHRISTIAN RELIGIONS. Islam** was established in Iraq in the 7th century. Shias form a majority of the population (62% of the 96% who are Muslims), but the influence exercised by Sunnis of both the Hanafite and Shafiite rites is preponderant. Sunnis in fact form the urban middle class and are predominant among government officials. The important Kurdish community follows basically the Shafiite rite, but there are also Kurds who are Christians and also Yazidis. Iraq is noted for its Shia sanctuaries, Karbala and An Najaf west of the Euphrates as well as Samarra and Al Khadimain (a suburb of Baghdad) bordering the Tigris. There is an Institute of Islamic Studies at Baghdad.

**Yazidi religion** is a syncretistic mixture of traditional, Manichaean, Zoroastrian, Jewish, Nestorian and Muslim elements of which the latter are predominant. Yazidis are often called devil-worshippers because of the prominence given to the fallen angel Malak Ta'us who manifested himself in Shaikh Adi, the founder of the religion in the 12th century. They have 2 sacred books, the Black Book and the Book of Revelation. Yazidis live mostly in the Jebel Sinjar west of Mosul; but they are also found in other parts, notably northeast of Mosul where their religious and civil leaders live and where the principal sanctuary dedicated to Shaikh Adi is located.

**Mandaeanism** began in the 2nd century AD as Gnosticism, a syncretistic religion with Mesopotamian, Iranian, Jewish and Christian elements. Its followers today call themselves Mandaiia (Gnostics), and are also variously called Mandaeans, Christians of St John, Followers of John the Baptist, Dippers, Sabaeans (so termed by Arabs) and (the priestly caste) Nasoreans. The religion is centred on fertility worship. The principal sacred books are the Kinza or Treasure, which is a collection of hymns, with cosmological and doctrinal texts; the Book of John, a late popular account of the life of John the Baptist; and the Qolasta, a book of hymns. Mandaeans live in lower Mesopotamia, centred at Basra, Kut and Suq al-Shuyukh; the only other community is in Khuzistan (southwest Iran). They have a hierarchical clergy and rudimentary temples, and worship on Sundays.

**Judaism** is practised by a very small remnant community in Baghdad. Until recent times Jews were relatively numerous; at the end of World War II, Iraqi Jews numbered 250,000. After 1950 they began to emigrate massively to the new state of Israel. Due to the prolonged Israeli-Arab conflict their situation has become increasingly precarious, and in 1972 only 600 remained, decreasing rapidly.

**Baha'i** has a history of over 120 years in Iraq, but due to severe repression and confiscations, and banning by decree in 1970, only a handful of scattered assemblies remain.

**CHRISTIANITY.** In the first century of the Christian era, Jewish colonies were evangelized, an activity

**Muslims.** Interior of Cheik Abd el-Qadir el-Gailani Mosque in Baghdad.

traditionally ascribed to the Apostle Thomas. Church structures developed under the patriarch of Antioch in the 4th century, but a century later the church in Mesopotamia declared its independence from Antioch and subsequently became almost entirely Nestorian. Up until the 10th century the Nestorians exercised an energetic missionary activity towards the east; but Islam, which entered the country in the 7th century, became increasingly more important. From the 13th century onwards, Latin missionaries made strenuous efforts towards obtaining Nestorian reunion with Rome, which resulted in the establishment of the uniate Chaldean Catholics in Baghdad in 1553. A Latin diocese was formed in 1632, but no resident Latin bishop was permitted until 1820. Protestantism also made its appearance during the 19th century.

Christians who today use a Syriac liturgy are divided into Chaldeans, Nestorians (Assyrian Church of the East), Syrian Catholics and Syrian Orthodox, the latter also called Jacobites. These churches are of Mesopotamian origin, and in certain villages Syriac is still the spoken as well as the liturgical language. After the dismemberment of the Ottoman empire in 1917, Armenian Orthodox (Gregorians) and Armenian Catholics fled from Turkish massacres and established themselves in Iraq. Greek Orthodox and Greek Catholics are small communities composed largely of immigrants from Syria, Lebanon and Palestine. Latin Catholics are mostly foreigners and their clergy (OP, OCD, CSSR) are occupied with schools, youth, medical and seminary work, along with parish and inter-rite activities.

Christians live grouped in northern villages, in the large cities and in a few southern villages where they form a minority. In 1970 there were in the north 104 villages which were entirely Christians or with a strong Christian majority. Five of these had each between 2,000 and 7,000 inhabitants. These Christian villagers have emigrated in increasing numbers towards the cities, especially Baghdad. In 1939, 70% of all Christians were found in 192 towns and villages in the northern half of the country, with 30% in 8 localities in the south mostly at Baghdad. By 1968 these proportions had changed to 40% of the Christian population in 165 localities in the north and 60% in 15 centres in the south, with 54% of all Christians living in Baghdad itself. This exodus from northern villages has been due to insecurity created by Kurdish revolts and their repression in mountain villages; the greater opportunity for schooling and employment for youth in urban areas; the attractions of city life; and the anonymity of cities in which Christians can pass unnoticed in a Muslim society. To this internal migration can be added an annual emigration of some 300 families (about 1,800 persons) to Australia, Canada, the USA and Kuwait.

Religious instruction in Christianity is given to all Christian children in state schools having a Christian majority. Christian students in state schools with a Christian minority receive no religious instruction, except that provided irregularly by churches during holiday periods and in preparation for first communion. Of Catholic students of all rites, 44% receive catechetical instruction during primary

schooling, 22% being students in private schools and 22% in state schools. In the latter case, however, the teacher is often a Christian layman with no special qualifications. The remaining 56% receive instruction only sporadically or not at all. At the secondary level, the corresponding proportions are respectively 13.6% and 23.7%, with 62.7% receiving no instruction.

CATHOLIC CHURCH. Catholics are more numerous than all other Iraqi Christians combined. They have in fact a higher percentage of the Christian population (74%) than in any other Middle East country. Most of them belong to the Chaldean Church which was organized in union with Rome under its own patriarchate in 1553 following dissension within the Assyrian (Nestorian) community. Chaldean Catholics now number 242,000 divided into 10 dioceses served by 10 bishops and 102 priests. The patriarch of Babylon lives in Baghdad. Chaldean and Syrian Catholics jointly sponsor the Pontifical Seminary at Mosul, Iraq's main major seminary; and a number of minor seminaries exist in various parts of the country. In 1972 there were 10 married Catholic priests in Iraq, all Chaldeans. They were for the most part aged and some no longer exercise their ministry. There has been no ordination of married priests since 1948. However, in 1970 a group of innovative Chaldean priests founded the Chaldean Sacerdotal Alliance (Al-Rabita al-Kahnutiya al-Kaldaniya) with 31 members in 1971, to renew missionary zeal and to implement the decisions of Vatican II.

Syrian Catholics number 30,000 in 2 dioceses, the first established in 1790, with 2 bishops and 32 priests. Five Syrian and Chaldean priests, 3 of whom are teachers in the Pontifical Seminary, have formed a semi-monastic community in Mosul dedicated to the advancement of lay education and church renewal.

The 3,000 Armenian Catholics belong to the archdiocese of Baghdad created in 1954, with an archbishop and 4 priests. The Greek Catholic community of 350 members is served by a priest residing in Baghdad. Latin Catholics also have a small membership (3,500) composed mostly of expatriates with only a handful of native Iraqis. The apostolic administrator in 1973 was a French Carmelite missionary. There were 14 Dominican, 8 Carmelite and 5 Redemptorist priests engaged in parish and school work, the Christian Student Centre in Baghdad, the Pontifical Seminary in Mosul and also in scholarly research. About 200 Dominican and Presentation sisters, mostly Iraqis, are involved in education and medical work, and a number of other Iraqi sisters serve abroad.

ORTHODOX CHURCHES. The Ancient Church of the East, or the Assyrian Church, is the oldest Christian church in Iraq. It became regarded as Nestorian in tradition because its theology was similar to that of the Orthodox patriarch of Constantinople, Nestorius, and for this reason also can be regarded as a branch of Orthodoxy. The Nestorian centre, Seleucia-Ctesiphon near Baghdad, was at one time the most important patriarchate beyond the borders of the Roman empire, and was

largely responsible for the early extension of the Christian faith to other parts of the Middle East and Asia. Several schisms have rent the church down the ages, and several such bodies have followers in present-day Iraq. The major split is between the faction of Mar Addai, claimed to have been recognized as patriarch by the state since 1972, and the larger grouping under Mar Dinkha IV, who is recognized as Patriarch of the East by the Vatican, WCC, Anglican Communion, et alia. Since 1976 his headquarters has been based in Tehran.

Syrian Orthodox entered Iraq in the 6th century; and although later in time than the Nestorians, they still consider themselves the true Iraqis among the various Orthodox groups in the country. The oldest Christian monastery in Iraq is Mar Matta near Mosul with 6 resident monks. Its historic importance to Syrian Orthodoxy equals that of the monasteries of Tur Abdin in Turkey. Three bishops and 18 priests serve a community of 20,000.

The Armenian Apostolic Church, Diocese of Baghdad, is related to the Catholicate of Echmiadzin (USSR) as contrasted with dioceses in Iran which are attached to the Catholicate of Cilicia (Sis) in Antelias, Lebanon. Primary schools exist in the 5 cities where there are congregations and resident priests, and a large high school is maintained in Baghdad. School enrolment is entirely Armenian, and the Armenian tongue is taught as an auxiliary language.

Greek Orthodox have one congregation in Baghdad under the jurisdiction of the Patriarchate of Antioch. The titular archbishop of Baghdad resides, however, in Kuwait.

OTHER CHURCHES. The first British missionary contact in Iraq was made by the London Jews Society in 1820 followed by the opening of an American Board (ABCFM) station in Mosul shortly after 1850. The Church Missionary Society arrived in Baghdad in 1882 where it was active until World War I. The Arabian Mission of the Reformed Church in America entered Basra in 1889, initiating work which during the 1920s received support from 2 other American denominations, the Evangelical and Reformed Church, and the United Presbyterian Church in the USA. The United Mission, as it was later called, was joined in 1957 by yet a fourth body, the Presbyterian Church in the US. Strongly involved in educational work, the United Mission had little success in the evangelistic sphere. No present-day Iraqi church resulted directly from this activity, but undoubtedly converts were made, mostly from the Nestorian and Orthodox milieux, who now participate in the life of a handful of autonomous Arab, Assyrian and Armenian evangelical churches. Other influences at work on the formation of these churches were Presbyterian and American Board activities in neighbouring Turkey and Iran. The Arab Evangelical churches are composed of 3 congregations in Baghdad, Kirkuk and Basra, all served by Egyptian pastors. There are 2 Assyrian Evangelical churches in Baghdad and Mosul which are independent of each other and in 1973 were without pastoral leadership. The Armenian Eva-

**Ancient Assyrian Church of the East.** World hierarchy in 1979 (from left) : Mar Youkhanan (Iraq), Mar Timotheous (India), Mar Claudio (Sicily), Patriarch-Catholicos Mar Dinkha IV (Iran), Mar Narsay (Lebanon), Mar Aprim (USA), Mar Bascio (Italy).

ngelical Church is related to the international Union of Armenian Evangelical Churches and consists of one small congregation in Baghdad.

The Episcopal Church is part of the diocese of Cyprus & the Gulf in the Episcopal Church in Jerusalem and the Middle East, formerly the Jerusalem Archbishopric. Membership is almost entirely expatriate Arab and British.

The Lutheran Orient Mission entered in 1911, but in spite of many years of work among the Kurds, few converts have been made. Other small Protestant bodies include the Assemblies of God, Basra Assembly, Evangelical Alliance Mission and Seventh-day Adventists. In 1969 all USA missionaries were expelled from the country and their schools nationalized or closed. However, most of their churches continue to function, under national leadership.

**CHURCH AND STATE.** According to the provisional constitution of 16 July 1970, 'Islam is the State religion' (Article 4), but all citizens are equal before the law without distinction of religion (Article 19a). Freedom of religion, belief and worship are equally guaranteed (Article 25).

The cultural rights of Syriac-speaking Iraqi Christians were recognized by Decree 251 promulgated by the Revolutionary Council on 22 April 1972. According to the terms of the decree, which concerns 'Assyrians, Chaldeans and Syrians', the use of Syriac is authorized in primary and secondary schools where this is the mother tongue of a majority of the pupils, although the teaching of Arabic is also obligatory. Moreover, provision is made for the study of Syriac, as an ancient language, in the University of Bagdad. The decree equally makes provision for radio and television broadcasts in Syriac and encourages the publication of books and journals, the formation of theatrical and artistic groups, as well as the participation of Syriac writers in the cultural life of the country. In Decree 110 of October 1972, the Revolutionary Council also recognized the existence of 3 religious holidays for Christians (25 December, and 2 days at Easter) and 5 for Jews.

The General Bureau of Waqf in Baghdad is the official Muslim service agency of the administration responsible for religious trusts and finances. It oversees maintenance and construction of mosques and religious schools, training and payment of religious personnel, and the like. Religious judges *(qadi)* regulate the individual affairs and rights of Muslims. For non-Muslims there is no governmental bureau of religious affairs, and everything pertaining to the administration of church property or individual rights is regulated by civil courts. In each such court, one judge is especially charged with the affairs of non-Muslims. He renders his verdict, taking into consideration the particular customs of each community, after having consulted with its leader. The 2 basic laws governing the organization of courts for Christian and Jewish communities and the personal status of non-Muslims are Law 32 of 1947, which was modified for Catholics by several decrees in 1948, and Law 188 of 1959. Customary law regulates a number of other matters, such as the recognition by the state of leaders of dioceses and religious communities. The appointment of a new diocesan head is not valid until his name appears in the official governmental journal, after an inquiry has been made by the responsible judge concerning his reliability as a candidate and the legal status of the community, and after this has been confirmed by the head of state.

**INTERDENOMINATIONAL ORGANIZATIONS.** There are no formal nation-wide ecumenical councils or bodies. In Mosul, a committee composed of members of the various Christian confessions and rites has recently been formed to decide what measures should be taken when Christians are requested to participate in organizations or programmes of the state. Resulting joint actions include publication of a common catechism for use in schools having a Christian majority in Mosul province, and the preparation of television broadcasts at Christmas.

**BROADCASTING.** No Christian broadcasting is permitted, nor are there studios preparing them. However, Christian programmes in Arabic are easily received over the foreign stations, FEBA (Seychelles), ELWA (Liberia), TWR (Monaco and Cyprus), and Radio Vatican for 3 hours 30 minutes a week. ELWA prepares programmes in its Beirut studio and broadcasts them from Liberia to Iraq 4 nights a week, chanting the Scriptures in a Quranic/Byzantine style. There has been good response, and letters are regularly received at the studios of these stations abroad, although strict mail censorship makes it almost impossible to answer.

## BIBLIOGRAPHY


*A history of Eastern Christianity.* A. S. Atiya. London: Methuen, 1968. 486p.

'Die nestorianische Kirche', B. Spuler, in *Handbuch der Orientalistik*, Abt I, Bd VIII (Leiden-Köln, 1961), p. 120–169.

*The history and doctrine of this most ancient Church of Christ.* Shimun XXIII (Patriarch). Trichur (India): Church of the East, 1961. 27p.


TABLE 2. ORGANIZED CHURCHES AND DENOMINATIONS IN IRAQ

| Official name 1 | Begun 2 | Type 3 | Counc 4 | Congs 5 | Adults 6 | Affiliated 7 | Names, notes, and other statistics (see Codebook) 8 |
|---|---|---|---|---|---|---|---|
| Ancient Church of the East: P Tehran | c 50 | O Nes | YW... | | 16,000 | 30,000 | *Assyrian Ch. Nestorians.* 3 Dioceses. Patriarch Mar Dinkha IV lives in Tehran. 26n. |
| Ancient Church of the East: P Baghdad | 1972 | O Nes | y.... | | 7,000 | 12,000 | 1972 split under rival state-recognized patriarch Mar Addai. Old Calendar. |
| Arab Evangelical Churches | c1855 | P Ref | ..... | 3 | 500 | 1,100 | Formerly M=ABCFM,UPUSA,RCA. Baghdad, Kirkuk, Basra, all with Egyptian pastors. |
| Armenian Apostolic Ch: D Baghdad | c 300 | O Arm | Ewc.. | 9 | 7,000 | 13,000 | *Gregorians.* Under C Echmiadzin (USSR). 1917 Turkish refugees. 6 schools. 7n. |
| Armenian Ev Spiritual Brethren | c1930 | P CBr | x.... | 1 | 50 | 100 | *Holiness Brethren.* Ex Armenian churches. Origins M=ABCFM(USA) in Turkey. Baghdad. |
| Assemblies of God | c1965 | P Pe2 | ZF... | 1 | 30 | 100 | M=AoG(USA). Church built up by 1972 visit by students from Lebanon. |
| Assyrian Evangelical Churches | c1855 | P Ref | ..... | 2 | 100 | 200 | Formerly M=ABCFM,UPUSA,RCA. Baghdad, Mosul, without pastors in 1973. |
| **Catholic Church in Iraq:** | c1250 | R LEr | O...R | 145 | 150,700 | 278,953 | *Al-Kanissa al-Kathoulikiah.* C=4+0+5. 3s. 136n,25x,40m,219w,5387Yy. |
| P Babilonia (Baghdad) (*Chaldean*) | 1553 | R Cha | Os | 27 | 94,600 | 174,800 | Patriarchal diocese. Rapid Catholic influx from north. 30 0 27 95 2272 |
| D Alquoch (Alqos) (*Chaldean*) | 1960 | R Cha | Os | 7 | 6,600 | 12,300 | *Al-Kaldan al-Kathoulik* (*Chaldeans*). Rapid decline. 11 0 12 13 362 |
| D Al-Amadiyah (*Chaldean*) | 1785 | R Cha | Os | 14 | 1,100 | 2,000 | Turkish-Syrian frontier. Rapid Catholic emigration. 6 0 0 18 62 |
| D Aqrah (Akra) (*Chaldean*) | 1850 | R Cha | Os | 2 | 100 | 180 | In north. Arab/Kurdish fighting; Catholic emigration. 1 0 0 0 8 |
| D As-Sulaymaniyah (*Chaldean*) | 1968 | R Cha | Os | 1 | 300 | 565 | Patriarchal vicariate. On Iran border. 1 0 0 0 22 |
| D Zakhu (Zakho) (*Chaldean*) | 1850 | R Cha | Os | 37 | 6,600 | 12,292 | On Turkish frontier. Catholic migration to Baghdad. 13 0 0 0 450 |
| M Kirkuk (Kerkuk) (*Chaldean*) | 1789 | R Cha | Os | 5 | 3,200 | 6,000 | Founded c350 AD. Northeast. Petroleum area. 5 0 0 3 129 |
| AD Al-Basrah (Basra) (*Chaldean*) | 1953 | R Cha | Os | 10 | 4,100 | 7,646 | Founded as M Perat of Maishan around AD 450. 8 0 0 11 159 |
| AD Al-Mawsil (Mosul) (*Chaldean*) | 1789 | R Cha | Os | 8 | 9,700 | 18,000 | Second city. Patriarchal seat until 1947. 21 0 1 1 580 |
| AD Al-Mawsil (Mosul) (*Syrian*) | 1790 | R Syr | Os | 12 | 8,000 | 14,750 | *Al-Sourian al-Kathoulik* (*Syrian Catholics*). 23 0 0 25 518 |
| AD Baghdad (*Latin*) | 1632 | R Lat | Os | 3 | 1,900 | 3,500 | Includes Mission Sui Juris in south (1896). 1s. 2 21 0 50 30 |
| AD Baghdad (*Syrian*) | 1862 | R Syr | Os | 8 | 8,400 | 15,550 | Syrian-rite, dependant on P Antioch (Lebanon). 9 0 0 0 435 |
| AD Baghdad (*Armenian*) | 1954 | R Arm | Os | 4 | 1,600 | 3,000 | Under Armenian Catholic P Cilicia (Lebanon). 0 4 0 0 30 |
| AD Irbil (Arbil) (*Chaldean*) | 1968 | R Cha | Os | 7 | 4,500 | 8,370 | Kurdistan. Catholic emigration from villages in north. 6 0 0 3 330 |
| Christian Brethren | | P CBr | x.... | 1 | 30 | 50 | *Basra Assembly. Open Brethren.* Begun by British; mainly expatriates. |
| Church of the East | c1962 | I Nes | .v... | | 3,000 | 5,000 | Assyrian schism ex Patriarchate (P Baghdad). 3 Dioceses, 3 bishops. 11n. |
| Ch of the Virgin Mary & Mar Gaura | | I Nes | ..... | 2 | 150 | 200 | Assyrian (Nestorian) schism in dispute over ecclesiastical authority. 2 priests. |
| Coptic Orthodox Church(PAlexandria) | c1970 | O Cop | NwaN. | 1 | 100 | 300 | Egyptian doctors, lecturers: 60 families by 1977. Church in Baghdad. 1 priest monk. |
| Episcopal Ch in Jerusalem & the MEast | 1882 | A Cen | aw... | 2 | 300 | 500 | In D Cyprus & the Gulf. Formerly in Jerusalem Archbishopric. 70% Whites, 30% Arabs. |
| Greek Orthodox P Antioch: D Baghdad | | O Ara | Cw.N. | 1 | 250 | 450 | Arabs, Greeks, and former Nestorians. Archbishop of Baghdad lives in Kuwait. 1n. |
| Isolated radio churches | c1950 | I rad | ..... | 430 | 8,000 | 17,300 | Isolated Arab radio believers (students &c). R=1400(TWR,RSB,RVatican),T=16000(ICI). |
| Lutheran Orient Mission | 1911 | P Lut | ..... | 1 | 20 | 29 | Kurdistan. 1958, USA missionaries expelled, now run by nationals. HQ Arbil. |
| Seventh-day Adventist Church | 1923 | P Adv | x.... | 3 | 152 | 300 | *SDA, Iraq Field.* Middle East Union. HQ Baghdad. 2n,26mw,2f,1r,5t(132),5Y. |
| Syrian Orthodox Church (P Antioch) | 550 | O Syr | Dw.N. | | 11,900 | 19,700 | *Jacobites.* 3 Dioceses: Baghdad, Mar Matta (Sheikh-Matti), Mosul. 18n,1d(6) |
| World-Wide Missions | 1967 | P ind | x.... | | 100 | 200 | M=World-Wide Missions(USA). Evangelicals with links in Pasadena, CA(USA). |
| Other Protestant denominations | | P | ..... | | 200 | 500 | Including Ev Alliance Mission, Union of Armenian Ev Chs (1 group in Baghdad). |
| **Total affiliated (mid-1970)** | | | | **690** | **205,582** | **379,982** | **Total denominations (1970) . . . 20.** |
| **Total affiliated (mid-1975)** | | | | **700** | **227,500** | **420,500** | **Total denominations (1975) . . . 21.** |
| **Total affiliated (mid-1980)** | | | | **710** | **250,800** | **463,500** | **Total denominations (1980) . . . 23.** |

NOTES ON TABLE ABOVE
COLUMNS: for meanings and CODES (cols. 1, 3, 4, 8), see Codebook (Part 6). Column 1: **Boldface type** = church with over 10% of country's affiliated Christians.
NATIONAL COUNCILS (Column 4, 5th letter).
R = Inter-Rite Bishops' Meeting of Iraq.

PEOPLES (ethnolinguistic). Christians: 79.4% Assyrian (Chaldean), 14.9% Arab (Syrian, Iraqi, Palestinian, Egyptian), 4.4% Armenian, 1.2% European (French, Italian, Greek, British).

COUNTRY-WIDE TOTALS
EVANGELIZATION (see Part 5). 1900: 22%. 1970: 32%. 1980: 35%. *Radiophonic evangelism.* TWR, RSB, Radio Vatican, ICI (5,000 enrolments).
FOREIGN MISSIONARIES AND PERSONNEL (nationals serving abroad) (1973). Total 29: 20 Roman Catholics in Kuwait and United Arab Emirates, 9 Orthodox priests in Syria and USA.
FOREIGN MISSIONARIES AND PERSONNEL (aliens from abroad) (1973). Total 66. *From Western world.* 59: 51 Roman Catholics, 8 Protestants in 7 USA societies. *From Third World.* 7: about 5 Roman Catholics, 2 Orthodox.
INSTITUTIONS (church-operated) (1973). Total 28, including 16 higher schools (4 minor seminaries), 2 medical centres (1 hospital), 5 religious communities (monasteries), 3 seminaries (RC).
PERIODICALS. About 15 titles.
PERSONNEL. About 556 (490 national, 66 foreign).
RELIGIOUS LIBRARIES. 8.

SCRIPTURE DISTRIBUTION (1975). Annual totals: 287 Bibles (90% subsidized, 10% commercial), 787 NTs (subsidized), 1,197 UBS portions, 6,443 UBS selections. *Translations completed.* Portion: 2 languages since 1840. NT: 2 languages since 1555. Bible: 2 languages since 1645.
SERVICE AGENCIES. About 15, including CCCI, JEC, OM, YWCA.

ADDITIONAL DATA ON CHURCHES
CATHOLIC CHURCH IN IRAQ. *Catholics.* Statistics are taken from *Annuario Pontificio 1973* and represent the situation as at approximately 1970. Other sources give lower figures for Chaldeans but have not taken account of the rapid increase in D Baghdad due to Catholics migrating from the northern dioceses. *Annual baptisms.* (1972) 99.8% infant, 0.2% adult. *Priests.* All Chaldean, Syrian and 2 Latin religious (OP, OCD) are Iraqi nationals; the rest, expatriates. In addition to those listed by diocese, there are about 20 other nationals and 6 expatriates in various occupations. Out of 187 priests, 40 (21%) are religious, including only 12 Eastern-rite (Chaldeans). *Brothers.* All nationals. *Sisters.* In addition, there are about 166 others in contemplative and other duties. Total 385: 365 nationals, 20 expatriates. *Seminaries.* Chaldean Patriarchal Seminary, Baghdad: no seminarians, no ordination since 1968. Syro-Chaldean Seminary, Mosul: 28 seminarians. *Oriental religious congregations.* Priests: Antonians of St Hormisdas (Chaldean monks and priests). Sisters: Daughters of Mary Immaculate (Chaldeans, begun 1920); Daughters of the Sacred Heart (Chaldeans, begun 1922); Dominican Sisters of St Catherine of Siena (Chaldean, Syrian and Armenian, begun 1928); Sisters of the Immaculate Conception (Armenian); Little Sisters of Jesus, who have adopted Chaldean rite in Baghdad and the Syrian in Mosul. At Mosul, there is also a community of secular priests, Priests of Christ the King, begun 1942. *Foreign orders and congregations.* Priests: OP, OCD, CSSR. Sisters: Sisters of the Presentation.
*Catholic organizations.* The Inter-Rite Bishops' Meeting of Iraq has met annually since 1972. Each rite is attached to its own patriarchate, the Latin jurisdiction being part of the Conference of Latin Bishops of the Arab Regions (CELRA) with its headquarters in East Jerusalem. The principal lay movements are: Legion of Mary (49 praesidia, 400 members), JEC (16 groups, 130 members), Friends of Jesus (former university student members of JEC, 2 teams), and 17 study circles serving different social levels in the cities and large villages.

The Holy See has diplomatic relations with Iraq and is represented to government and the Catholic hierarchy by a pronuncio in Baghdad.

Catholic educational institutions in 1970 numbered 31 kindergartens and primary schools (9,748 pupils), and 8 intermediary and secondary schools (1,519 pupils). Of Catholic pupils 20% attended Catholic private schools, 21% state schools with a Christian majority (33 primary schools, 9 intermediary and secondary schools), and 59% state schools with a Muslim majority. Medical and charitable institutions in 1971 included one hospital, one dispensary, 5 orphanages, one day nursery, one home for the aged and 9 welfare committees in the larger cities.

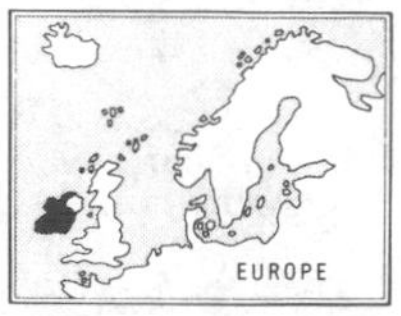


# IRELAND

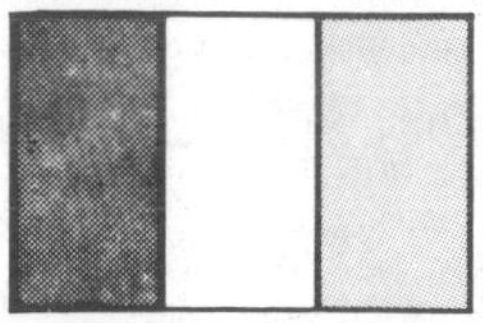

## SECULAR DATA

**STATE. Official name:** Irish Republic (Poblacht Na H'Eireann/ Eire). Adjectives of nationality: Irish, an Irishman, the Irish.
**Flag** (shown above right): Green, white, and orange bars.
**Area:** 70,283 sq.km. (27,136 sq.miles). Agricultural land: 69.0%.
**Government:** Parliamentary republic, since 1949 (1800 part of UK, 1922 Independence as Irish Free State, 1949 republic).
**Legislature:** National Parliament (Oireachtas): Seanad Eireann (Senate), 60 members; Dáil Eireann (House), 144 members.
**Official languages:** Irish (Gaelic) and English.
**Chief cities:** capital Dublin 650,150 (1971), Cork 128,240.
**Political divisions:** 4 Provinces, 32 Counties and County Boroughs.
**Armed forces** (1976): Total 14,000 regular: army 12,800, navy 500, air force 700 (9 combat aircraft). Reserves: 18,100.

**DEMOGRAPHY. Population:** 2,978,248 (census of 18.IV.1971. For 1970–2000 (UN), see last row of Table 1). Population density (1975): 45/sq.km. (115/sq.mile). Under 15 years: 31%. Growth rate (1975–80): 1.04% per year (births 2.19%, deaths −1.00%, emigrants −0.15%). Life expectancy (1975–80): 72.5 years. Household size: 4.0 persons.
**Major languages:** Irish (Gaelic) (spoken by 20%, used by 5%), English.
**Urban dwellers** (1970): 46.9%. Urban growth rate (1950–70): 0.7% per year.
**Labour force:** 36%.
**Tourists** (1970): 1,758,000. (1974) 1,619,000.

**ETHNOLINGUISTIC GROUPS:** 96.3% Irish, 1.4% English, 1.0% Ulster Irish, 0.4% USA, 0.3% Scottish, 0.2% Welsh, 0.2% Irish Traveller (nomad, Gypsy, Shelta), 0.1% Jewish, Greek, Russian., Chinese.

**MONEY** (1977). **Monetary unit:** pound (= 100 new pence); US$1 = I£0.592 (operational rate of exchange).

**National income per person:** US$2,042. Average annual family income: US$8,168.
**Inflation:** (1970–74) 11.4% per year (1975: consumer price index 206); (1977) 16% per year.
**Cost of living in capital** (1976): index 109 (Washington DC = 100). Daily cost of living: US$25.

**HEALTH.** Hospitals: 241 (34,520 beds). Doctors: 3,565. Blind: 7,000. Psychotics: 28,000.

**EDUCATION.** Adult literacy: 99%. Education rate: 28%. Schools: 3,829. Universities: 2.

**LITERATURE.** Annual new book titles (1973): 491. Periodicals: 278. Scientific journals: 50. Newspapers: 7 dailies, 50 non-daily.

**COMMUNICATION** (per 1,000 people). Phones: 121. Radios: 201. TV sets: 176. Daily newspaper circulation: 233 copies.

TABLE 1. RELIGIOUS ADHERENTS IN IRELAND

| Year | 1900 | | mid-1970 | | Annual change, 1970–1980 | | | | mid-1975 | | mid-1980 | | 2000 | |
|---|---|---|---|---|---|---|---|---|---|---|---|---|---|---|
| *Name* | *Adherents* | *%* | *Adherents* | *%* | *Natural* | *Conversion* | *Total* | *Rate* | *Adherents* | *%* | *Adherents* | *%* | *Adherents* | *%* |
| **Christians** | **3,227,000** | **99.9** | **2,942,000** | **99.6** | **34,240** | **−370** | **33,870** | **1.09** | **3,116,450** | **99.5** | **3,280,700** | **99.5** | **3,971,500** | **99.2** |
| professing | 3,227,000 | 99.9 | 2,942,000 | 99.6 | 34,240 | −370 | 33,870 | 1.09 | 3,116,450 | 99.5 | 3,280,700 | 99.5 | 3,971,500 | 99.2 |
| Roman Catholics | 2,894,000 | 89.6 | 2,807,800 | 95.1 | 32,750 | 870 | 33,620 | 1.13 | 2,980,850 | 95.2 | 3,144,000 | 95.3 | 3,832,400 | 95.8 |
| Anglicans | 265,500 | 8.2 | 98,000 | 3.3 | 1,066 | −1,266 | −200 | −0.21 | 97,000 | 3.1 | 96,000 | 2.9 | 96,000 | 2.4 |
| Protestants | 67,000 | 2.1 | 28,200 | 1.0 | 308 | −378 | −70 | −0.25 | 28,000 | 0.9 | 27,500 | 0.8 | 24,000 | 0.6 |
| Marginal Protestants | 500 | 0.0 | 6,500 | 0.2 | 99 | 401 | 500 | 5.56 | 9,000 | 0.3 | 11,500 | 0.3 | 17,000 | 0.4 |
| Orthodox | 0 | 0.0 | 1,500 | 0.1 | 17 | 3 | 20 | 1.25 | 1,600 | 0.1 | 1,700 | 0.1 | 2,100 | 0.1 |
| nominal | 30,000 | 0.9 | 127,388 | 4.3 | 1,595 | 2,076 | 3,671 | 2.53 | 145,150 | 4.6 | 164,100 | 5.0 | 253,700 | 6.3 |
| affiliated | 3,197,000 | 99.0 | 2,814,612 | 95.3 | 32,645 | −2,446 | 30,199 | 1.02 | 2,971,300 | 94.9 | 3,116,600 | 94.5 | 3,717,800 | 92.9 |
| total practising | 3,133,000 | *98* | 2,702,030 | *96* | 31,013 | −8,256 | 22,757 | 0.81 | 2,822,740 | *95* | 2,929,600 | *94* | 2,974,200 | *80* |
| non-practising | 64,000 | *2* | 112,580 | *4* | 1,632 | 5,810 | 7,442 | 5.01 | 148,560 | *5* | 187,000 | *6* | 743,600 | *20* |
| Roman Catholics | 2,866,000 | 88.7 | 2,682,342 | 90.8 | 31,204 | −853 | 30,351 | 1.07 | 2,840,060 | 90.7 | 2,985,850 | 90.5 | 3,589,880 | 89.7 |
| Catholic pentecostals | 0 | 0.0 | 1,000 | 0.0 | 950 | 23,950 | 24,900 | 27.67 | 90,000 | 2.9 | 250,000 | 7.6 | 800,000 | 20.0 |
| Anglicans | 264,000 | 8.2 | 97,520 | 3.3 | 1,060 | −1,282 | −222 | −0.23 | 96,500 | 3.1 | 95,300 | 2.9 | 90,000 | 2.2 |
| Evangelicals | 193,800 | 6.0 | 60,000 | 2.0 | 688 | −88 | 600 | 0.96 | 62,600 | 2.0 | 66,000 | 2.0 | 76,000 | 1.9 |
| Anglican pentecostals | 0 | 0.0 | 100 | 0.0 | 5 | 85 | 90 | 18.00 | 500 | 0.0 | 1,000 | 0.0 | 5,000 | 0.1 |
| Protestants | 66,500 | 2.1 | 27,450 | 0.9 | 275 | −692 | −417 | −1.66 | 25,050 | 0.8 | 23,280 | 0.7 | 20,000 | 0.5 |
| Evangelicals | 60,000 | 1.9 | 20,000 | 0.7 | 209 | −409 | −200 | −1.05 | 19,000 | 0.6 | 18,000 | 0.5 | 17,000 | 0.4 |
| Marginal Protestants | 500 | 0.0 | 5,800 | 0.2 | 89 | 381 | 470 | 5.80 | 8,100 | 0.3 | 10,500 | 0.3 | 16,000 | 0.4 |
| Orthodox | 0 | 0.0 | 1,500 | 0.1 | 17 | 0 | 17 | 1.07 | 1,590 | 0.1 | 1,670 | 0.1 | 2,000 | 0.1 |
| Non-religious | 0 | 0.0 | 6,200 | 0.2 | 88 | 292 | 380 | 4.75 | 8,000 | 0.3 | 10,000 | 0.3 | 20,000 | 0.5 |
| Jews | 3,000 | 0.1 | 4,000 | 0.1 | 46 | −6 | 40 | 0.95 | 4,200 | 0.1 | 4,400 | 0.1 | 4,000 | 0.1 |
| Atheists | 0 | 0.0 | 1,200 | 0.0 | 18 | 62 | 80 | 5.00 | 1,600 | 0.1 | 2,000 | 0.1 | 5,000 | 0.1 |
| Baha'is | 0 | 0.0 | 600 | 0.0 | 8 | 22 | 30 | 4.00 | 750 | 0.0 | 900 | 0.0 | 1,500 | 0.0 |
| **Country's population** | **3,230,000** | **100.0** | **2,954,000** | **100.0** | **34,400** | **0** | **34,400** | **1.10** | **3,131,000** | **100.0** | **3,298,000** | **100.0** | **4,002,000** | **100.0** |

COLUMNS, ROWS. For meanings and definitions, see Codebook (Part 6). Note that, by definition, total 'Christians' = professing + crypto-Christians, which also = affiliated + nominal Christians. Percentages may not always total exactly, due to rounding.
CENSUSES. **1861:** 89.6% Roman Catholics, 8.5% Anglicans, 1.9% Protestants. **1901:** 89.6% Roman Catholics, 8.2% Anglicans, 2.1% Protestants, 0.1% Jews. **1926:** 92.6% Roman Catholics, 5.5% Anglicans, 1.7% Protestants, 0.1% Jews. **1936:** 93.7% Roman Catholics, 4.9% Anglicans, 1.3% Protestants, 0.1% Jews. **12.V.1946:** 94.5% Roman Catholics, 4.2% Anglicans, 1.1% Protestants, 0.1% Jews. **9.IV.1961:** 95.0% Roman Catholics, 3.7% Anglicans, 1.1% Protestants, 0.1% Jews. **18.IV.1971:** 95.1% Roman Catholics, 3.3% Anglicans, 1.0% Protestants, 0.3% non-religious and atheists, 0.2% marginal Protestants, 0.1% Jews.

POLLS. February 1970: 96% Roman Catholics, 4% Anglicans and Protestants. Results for church attendance are given below. *Charismatic renewal.* 1977 poll (*Catholic Standard*): 86% were aware of the renewal, 7% were not; 20% approved, 17% did not, 35% were undecided; 19% had attended a prayer meeting.

**NOTES ON RELIGIONS**
ATHEISTS. Communist Party of Ireland (CPI) (legal; pro-Soviet): membership (1970, 1974) 300; Communist voters (election of II.1973) 466.
BAHA'IS. Growth from 1 local spiritual assembly (1964) to 4 (1973).
CATHOLIC PENTECOSTALS (or, Catholic charismatics). Totals (January 1974): 2,500 involved priests, monks, nuns and lay adults (over 15 years old) in 60 prayer groups; total charismatic community including children, 5,000. The movement began before 1970, because noticeable in Dublin about 1972, and then spread outwards; by 1975 most towns and large villages in the republic had prayer groups. In October 1975, a Dublin charismatic conference drew 3,500 adults from all the churches; a year later, 6,000, of whom over 30% were nuns. During the year 1976 prayer groups throughout Ireland (North and South) more than doubled to 220 by the year's end, with 20,000 people active, mostly Catholics, rising by mid-1978 to 300 groups with 35,000 members. The June 1978 International Conference on the Charismatic Renewal in the Catholic Church was held in Dublin with 15,000 participants. By 1980, active charismatics numbered 250,000, including 21% of all Irish nuns and clergy.
PRACTISING CHRISTIANS. *Weekly mass attendance.* Average 91% of population. University College, Dublin: 83.5%. Rural areas: 95–100% of eligible Catholics. Urban areas: 80% for young men, 95% young women.

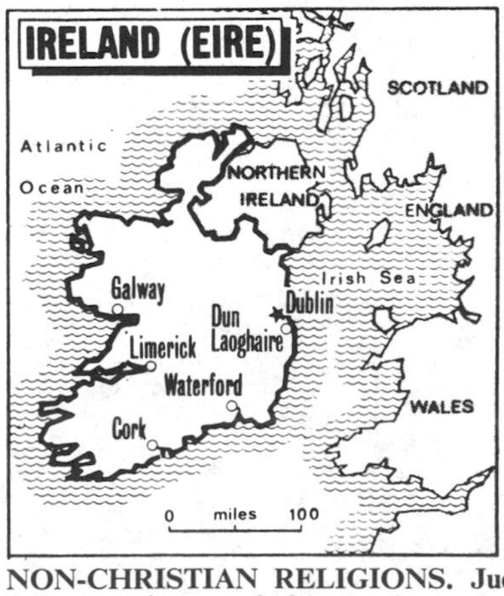


**NON-CHRISTIAN RELIGIONS. Judaism** with its followers increased in numbers, largely through immigration, during the last quarter of the 19th century. Since World War II, however, a moderate exodus has taken place, and Jews who numbered about 4,000 in 1970 are declining again in percentage.

**CHRISTIANITY.** Missionary work in Ireland was begun by Palladius in AD 431 and Patrick in 432, and Ireland soon became a centre for the evangelization of several other countries. A century later, Columba founded a monastery at Iona, off the west coast of Scotland, in 563, whose influence spread south to England and east to continental Europe. Charlemagne also appealed to Ireland for missionaries when he became Roman emperor in 800. Government from England became the rule after 1200. In 1537 the English king was declared head of the church of Ireland and submission to Roman authority was forbidden. Following this establishment of the Church of England as the official church, the Irish suffered persecution in their insistence on identifying Roman Catholicism with patriotism. Baptists and Presbyterians entered Ireland during the Reformation era, followed by Methodists a century later after many notable preaching tours in Ireland by John Wesley.

CATHOLIC CHURCH. The importance of Irish Catholic religious life extends far beyond the borders of Ireland, in part as a result of the large Irish emigration of the 19th century. Ireland has produced several missionary organizations peculiar to the Anglo-Saxon world and today still contributes in large measure to their work. In 1971, there were 61 Catholic ordinations of priests in religious orders and congregations and 24 for the 3 main missionary societies. Since the Middle Ages in fact the country has played a remarkable missionary role. In 1970, 5,954 foreign missionaries were supported by the Irish Catholic Church, although this was a marked decrease from the 7,085 missionaries of 1965. Irish Catholicism has supplied significant numbers of priests to Anglo-Saxon countries. Thus, between 1790 and 1936, of the 260 Catholic bishops then serving in the USA, 103 were from Ireland, with many others being of Irish descent. To this day, ordinations of secular priests each year are still divided into those for home and those for abroad: in 1971, 75 priests were ordained for Irish dioceses, and 63 for foreign dioceses, 37 of which were for the USA, 24 for Great Britain, one for Australia and one for South America.

Whereas Catholics constituted 90% of the population of the Irish nation in 1861, the proportion rose to 95% after 1946. Meanwhile, however, the actual number of Catholics decreased considerably during that period as a result of the constant emigration of Irish to other lands.

Catholic religious practice is extremely high. A survey in 1968 by the national university indicated that Sunday mass attendance in the country was as high as 84% of the population every week. Another study in 1969, limited to an urban zone, concluded that 95% of young women attended Sunday mass and 80% of young men. In rural areas, where social pressure is stronger, from 95–100% of those under obligation to attend Sunday mass do in fact do so.

Irish Catholicism is still profoundly marked by its historic past: the imposition of Anglicanism as the state religion in the 16th century, persecutions, massacres and deportations. It was not until 1829 that Roman Catholics were formally emancipated in Great Britain and Ireland; and in 1867 the Anglican Church ceased to be the state religion in Ireland.

The long period of British occupation, until 1921, has resulted in the firm identification of Catholicism with Irish nationalism. This explains the present notable cohesion of Irish Catholicism, its popularity (with its clergy always drawn from all ranks of the people and remaining close to the people) and its all-pervasive influence in all sectors of social life. Strongly attached to tradition, the church has been and remains little prepared to accept Vatican II with all that is implied therein in questioning Ireland's commonly-held system of values. This is perhaps less conservatism than national independence, for it should be noted that the Irish bishops were also reserved in accepting the full implications of Vatican I in 1870.

ANGLICAN CHURCH. The Church of Ireland, disestablished in 1867, is the largest non-Catholic denomination in the country. It also claims its origin in Patrick in the 5th century, and its dioceses trace their origins to those early centuries. Although 76% of their membership live in Northern Ireland, Anglicans have played a significant role in the south as well. Their numbers however have fallen drastically, largely by emigration, falling continually from 8.5% of the population in 1861 to 3.3% by 1971. By 1975, 5 dioceses had less than 2,000 communicants each. In 1976–7, several smaller dioceses were regrouped with larger ones.

PROTESTANT CHURCHES. Over the same period since 1861, Protestants have likewise fallen from 1.9% of the total population to 1.0% by 1971. They are even fewer today. This decrease again has been largely due to the great emigration from Ireland, which began with the Potato Famine of the last century and continues to the present time. Of the total population decrease of more than one million people between 1881 and 1961, a disproportionate number were Protestants who left during this period. In Northern Ireland 350 years ago, Presbyterians arrived from Scotland, later spreading to the south. Theologically conservative, the church is a founder member of the World Alliance of Reformed Churches and the World Council of Churches. Methodism was brought to Ireland by John Wesley in the mid-18th century. Today 93% of its members live in Northern Ireland, with the remaining 7% located in the south. Methodist membership in the south again fell by 50% from 1861 to 1971. A number of other small Protestant churches are also active.

CHURCH AND STATE. Ireland has always been a specifically Christian state. Article 44 of the 1937 constitution of the republic of Ireland included the following stipulations regarding religion: (i) The State acknowledges that homage of public worship is due to Almighty God. It shall hold His Name in reverence and shall respect and honour religion; (ii) the State recognizes the special position of the Holy Catholic Apostolic and Roman Church as the guardian of the Faith professed by the great majority of the citizens; (iii) the State also recognizes the Church of Ireland, the Presbyterian Church in Ireland, the Methodist Church in Ireland, the Religious Society of Friends in Ireland, as well as the Jewish Congregations and other religious denominations existing in Ireland at the date of the coming into operation of this constitution. Article 41 of the 1937 constitution, which has been challenged but which nevertheless remains valid, states that the institution of marriage is especially protected and that 'No law shall be enacted providing for the grant of a dissolution of marriage'.

Although recognized, the churches have no juridical personality, and parishes and bishoprics are not considered to be persons in civil law. Thus church properties are generally held through trustees.

There is in fact no official legal relationship between any church and the state. The state does not subsidize the churches, nor does it give the churches the right to levy taxes. No assistance or salary is paid by the state to ministers of religion. There is no ministry or government department in charge of religious affairs or responsible for relations with church authorities.

Two legal types of marriage are possible in Ireland, civil and religious. Each is sufficient of itself before the law. For historical reasons, the marriages of Protestants, and only Protestants, come within the field of civil law. In mixed marriages, spouses are bound before the law by pre-nuptial written promises even though they be given before a priest (decision of the Supreme Court, 1951).

The churches on their part do not intervene directly in the functioning of the state. This represents a change in church involvement, since prior to

**Catholic Church in Ireland.** *Above.* Catholics on barefoot pilgrimage (every last Sunday in July) up Cruach Phadraig (Croagh Patrick), a 2,510-foot quartzite peak west of Westport, County Mayo. *Below.* Cardinal L.-J. Suenens celebrates charismatic mass with 190 priests and 5,000 charismatics from all over Ireland, with joyous dancing around altar, use of tambourines, etc (2nd National Conference on the Charismatic Renewal, Dublin, 1975). At Dublin's 1978 international conference, Cardinal Suenens concelebrated on TV with 17 bishops and 1,500 priests in the presence of 20,000.

Independence in 1921 it was not unusual for priests to be actively and openly involved in politics. Unofficially, however, there have been recent cases where church influence has been brought to bear on national and local government decisions. When discovered by the public, this has been resented. State authorities have also given opinions in a private capacity on the election of bishops.

In 1967, a committee was set up by all political parties to reconsider and possibly to repeal Articles 41 and 44 of the constitution, which were considered to be an impediment to the reunification of the republic (with its majority of Catholics) and Northern Ireland (with its majority of Protestants). A national referendum held during 1972 resulted in the abolition of Article 44 with its giving to the Catholic Church a 'special position' within the republic.

In December 1973, the Supreme Court judged unconstitutional a part of the law concerning contraceptives. Because of this the minister of justice submitted to parliament a proposed law making possible the importation and sale of contraceptives to married couples by pharmacists. This proposal was rejected by the House of Representatives by a vote of 75 to 61, with 7 government ministers including the prime minister voting with the majority.

In this largely Catholic state, Anglicans and Protestants play a more important role than their numbers would suggest. In 1973, an Anglican, E. Childers, was elected president of the republic.

INTERDENOMINATIONAL ORGANIZATIONS. The Irish Council of Churches, established in Belfast in 1922, serves both the republic and Northern Ireland. In the republic it includes the Anglican and 6 Protestant churches. It has 10 local councils. However, the British Council of Churches based in London is more active and influential. The Irish School of Ecumenics, founded in 1970, is sponsored by Anglican, Methodist, Presbyterian and Catholic churches. Interdenominational and international in its teaching staff and students, it offers a systematically-organized programme of postgraduate courses relating to movements for Christian unity. Other interdenominational groups in the republic include the Irish Commission on Justice and Peace, in Dublin, a Catholic group with some Anglican and Protestant members, which serves as an official Catholic commission as well as the recognized Sodepax committee in Ireland. Ecumenical groups based in Northern Ireland but with activities in the south include the Corrymeela Ecumenical Community near Belfast, the Industrial Council in Belfast and Londonderry, and Protestant and Catholic Encounter (PACE), founded in Belfast in 1968, which is an ICC/RCC working group dealing with social problems. Established with the aim of providing an alternative to violence through dialogue, PACE functions through some 30 local groups and a central council. In 1970, a Young PACE Association was formed to reach youth 14 to 25 years of age. Lastly, a significant ecumenical impact is being made by the charismatic movement in Ireland, with several thousand Catholics and Protestants involved.

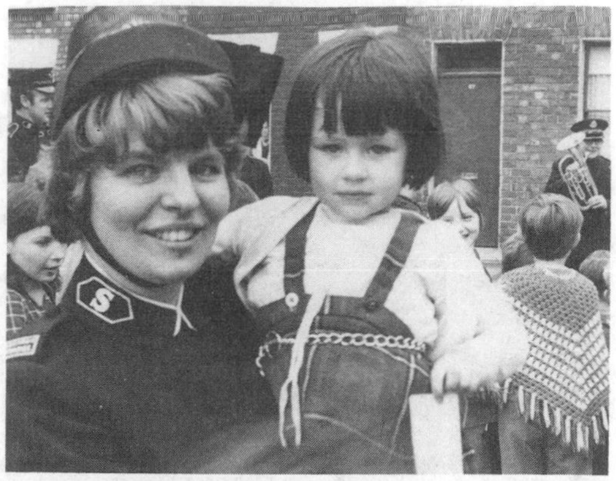

**Salvation Army.** Officers with band in street evangelism.

**BROADCASTING.** Radio Telefis Eireann (RTE), the national network, makes available time to religious programmes. Catholics produce a weekly radio programme on current religious affairs and filmed documentaries on RTE TV. Masses are also broadcast. In Dublin there is a Catholic communication centre founded in 1969 by the Catholic hierarchy, with radio and TV studios. Ireland is a member of UNDA.

## BIBLIOGRAPHY


*Church of Ireland directory, 1971.* Dublin: Irish Church Publications, 1971. 258p.

'Ireland', C. K. Ward, in H. Mol (ed), *Western religion* (The Hague: Mouton, 1972), p. 295–303.

*Irish Anglicanism 1869–1969.* Ed M. Hurley. Dublin: Figgis, 1970. 236p.

*Irish Methodism.* F. Jeffery. London: Epworth House, 1964.

'Religion in Ireland: preliminary analysis', M. N. Ghiolla Phadraig, in *Social studies*, 5, 2 (Summer 1976).

*The changing face of Catholic Ireland.* D. Fennel. Washington, DC: Corpus Instrumentorum, 1968. 223p.

*The Church in contemporary Ireland.* J. Blanchard. Dublin: Clonmore & Reynolds, 1963.

*The Church of Ireland.* K. Milne. Dublin: APCK, 1966. 72p.

*The Church of Ireland, 1869–1969.* R. B. McDowell. London: Routledge, 1975.

*The Irish Catholic directory, 1971.* Dublin: James Duffy, 1971. 878p.

'The Irish conflict and the Christian conscience'. Special note, *Pro Mundi Vita* (Brussels), 30 (1973).


TABLE 2. ORGANIZED CHURCHES AND DENOMINATIONS IN IRELAND

| Official name 1 | Begun 2 | Type 3 | Counc 4 | Congs 5 | Adults 6 | Affiliated 7 | Names, notes, and other statistics (see Codebook) 8 |
|---|---|---|---|---|---|---|---|
| Assemblies of God in GB & Ireland | c1915 | P Pe2 | ZG... | 2 | 100 | 300 | M=AoG(GB). Originally Pentecostal Missionary Union, until 1924. 2f. |
| Baptist Union of Ireland | 1642 | P Bap | ..... | 7 | 300 | 400 | Not in BUGBI. 92% of Union (75 churches) is in Northern Ireland. |
| **Catholic Church in Ireland:** | c 350 | R Lat | B.B.P | 999 | 1,850,800 | 2,682,342 | *Eaglais Chaitliceach Rómhánach.* C=34+11+104. W=96%. 5068n,2958m,12868w,61477Yy. |
| M Cashel & Emly | c 350 | R Lat | Bs | 46 | 55,900 | 81,064 | South. Mainly rural. HQ (residence) Thurles. 1s. 197 58 439 1565 |
| D Cloyne | 580 | R Lat | Bs | 46 | 74,400 | 107,881 | In south, with coastal strip. Mainly rural. HQ Cobh. 166 76 439 2364 |
| D Cork & Ross | 570 | R Lat | Bs | 52 | 134,600 | 195,097 | South. 50% urban. Growing industrialization in Cork. 322 188 950 5242 |
| D Kerry | c 570 | R Lat | Bs | 51 | 86,600 | 125,500 | Southwest. Rural, depopulation. Gaelic survivals. 157 50 590 9120 |
| D Killaloe | c 450 | R Lat | Bs | 58 | 69,600 | 100,872 | In west centre. Rural, depopulation. HQ Ennis. 211 58 489 2134 |
| D Limerick | c 650 | R Lat | Bs | 55 | 80,200 | 116,200 | 50% urban. Growing industries in Limerick. 266 92 610 2733 |
| D Waterford & Lismore | 659 | R Lat | Bs | 39 | 69,800 | 101,165 | 50% urban. Waterford being industrialized. 1s. 200 146 766 2509 |
| M Dublin | 633 | R Lat | Bs | 134 | 598,000 | 867,000 | Capital, east coast. Urban, industrialized. 1s. 1579 1521 3939 22591 |
| D Ferns | 600 | R Lat | Bs | 42 | 55,000 | 80,000 | In southeast. All rural. HQ Wexford. 1s. 153 35 490 1937 |
| D Kildare & Leighlin | 519 | R Lat | Bs | 51 | 90,800 | 131,600 | Southwest of Dublin. All rural. HQ Carlow. 1s. 219 140 586 2928 |
| D Ossory | 459 | R Lat | Bs | 42 | 43,600 | 63,152 | Rural. HQ Kilkenny. 1s. 165 96 430 1423 |
| M Tuam | 550 | R Lat | Bs | 56 | 78,100 | 113,199 | West. Rural, depopulation. Marked Gaelic survivals. 202 118 419 2140 |
| D Achonry | 560 | R Lat | Bs | 22 | 27,600 | 40,000 | All rural. 99% Catholic. HQ Ballaghaderreen. 78 8 192 565 |
| D Clonfert | 550 | R Lat | Bs | 24 | 23,300 | 33,755 | In west centre of country. All rural. HQ Loughrea. 96 21 175 673 |
| D Elphin | 450 | R Lat | Bs | 34 | 53,600 | 77,731 | Almost all rural. HQ Sligo. 142 96 411 1315 |
| D Galway,Kilmacduagh,Kilfenore | c 650 | R Lat | Bs | 38 | 42,400 | 61,379 | 50% urban. Industrializing. Gaelic areas. 151 95 335 1527 |
| D Killala | c 550 | R Lat | Bs | 22 | 26,100 | 37,847 | Northwest extreme. Rural depopulation. HQ Ballina. 59 4 118 674 |
| D Ardagh (HQ in NIreland) | c 450 | R Lat | Bs | 41 | 45,000 | 65,323 | Next 5 Dioceses are under M Armagh (in NI). 114 19 386 1294 |
| D Clogher | 454 | R Lat | Bs | 20 | 28,000 | 40,000 | 50% in Eire, 50% in NI. HQ Monaghan. 70 10 160 800 |
| D Kilmore | c 450 | R Lat | Bs | 33 | 36,000 | 52,000 | Rural, depopulation. HQ Cavan. 10% of diocese in NI. 130 10 210 880 |
| D Meath | 552 | R Lat | Bs | 66 | 89,700 | 130,000 | Southern part of province. Rural. HQ Mullingar. 1s. 301 94 620 2931 |
| D Raphoe | c 450 | R Lat | Bs | 27 | 42,500 | 61,577 | Extreme north. Rural depopulation. Some Gaelic areas. 90 23 114 1332 |
| Christian Brethren | 1827 | P CBr | x...., | 18 | 1,000 | 2,000 | *Open.* 1827, JNDarby left Anglican ministry, began Brethren in Dublin. 21f(UK,USA). |
| Christian Brethren (Exclusive) | 1849 | P EBr | ..... | | 500 | 1,000 | *Darbyites.* Kelly-Continental, Glanton, Raven-Taylor, Continuing Tunbridge Wells. |
| Church of Christ | | P Dis | x.... | 1 | 50 | 100 | M=CC(Non-Instrumental) (USA). Independents from USA. One congregation in Dublin. |
| Church of Christ, Scientist | | M Sci | x.... | 3 | 140 | 300 | *Christian Science.* M=CCS(Boston,USA). Dublin, Cork. 1m,3w. |
| Church of God (Anderson) | | P Hol | x.... | 1 | 50 | 100 | M=CoG(Anderson) (USA). Holiness denomination. 1n,W=50%. |
| Church of Ireland: | c 350 | A Low | AWc.K | 880 | 50,100 | 97,520 | *Eaglais na hEireann.* Declining fast. M=ICM(London). 12f,1s,W=60%. 364n,1406y. |
| Province of Armagh: | | A plu | A | 255 | 13,178 | 21,021 | Major problem rural depopulation. Half of Province is in Ulster. 86 381 |
| D Clogher | 1128 | A Eva | A | 24 | 678 | 2,218 | Other 90% of diocese is in NI(UK). Rural. W=50%. 10 28 |
| UDs Derry & Raphoe | 927 | A Eva | A | 63 | 4,000 | 6,693 | Other 80% of diocese is in NI(UK). Rural. 1s. 21 90 |
| UDs Kilmore & Elphin & Ardagh | 454 | A Eva | A | 129 | 7,000 | 10,000 | Union of 3 Celtic dioceses. 25,000 annual visitors. W=55%. 40 224 |
| UDs Tuam, Killala & Achonry | 500 | A Low | A | 39 | 1,500 | 2,110 | Rural. West coast, widely scattered churches. Small farmers. W=55%. 15 39 |
| Province of Dublin: | 1152 | A plu | A | 625 | 36,922 | 76,499 | Southern half of Ireland (Catholic Provinces of Dublin, Cashel). 278 1025 |
| UDs Dublin & Glendalough | 790 | A Cen | A | 163 | 15,000 | 45,000 | Anglicans 8% of population, rest Roman Catholic. 118 600 |
| UDs Cashel, Waterford & Lismore | 764 | A Cen | A | 45 | 2,000 | 3,000 | 4 dioceses united 1834–1977. Rural, one urban centre. W=55%. 19 45 |
| UDs Cork, Cloyne & Ross | 870 | A Cen | A | 109 | 6,000 | 8,500 | 3 dioceses united 1583. Rural. Decline 1% per year. W=60%. 42 100 |
| UDs Limerick & Killaloe | 1050 | A Cen | A | 106 | 3,149 | 4,452 | Decline 1920–70. Some Irish-speaking. Tourism ministry. G=−3.6%pa. 34 85 |
| UDs Meath & Kildare | 520 | A Cen | A | 64 | 2,773 | 3,547 | Mostly rural. 15 churches closed since 1960. Scattered. W=40%. 20 45 |
| UDs Ossory, Ferns & Leighlin | 598 | A Low | A | 138 | 8,000 | 12,000 | 3 dioceses united 1835. Mainly rural, widely scattered. 1r. 45 150 |
| Church of Jesus C of Latter-day Saints | c1880 | M LdS | x.... | 22 | 2,500 | 3,500 | *Ireland Mission. Mormons.* M=CJCLdS(USA). Growing. 140f,G=6.2%pa,W=16%,365Yy,325z. |
| Church of the Nazarene | | P Hol | xF... | 2 | 50 | 100 | M=CoN(USA). Small Holiness denomination with links in UK and USA. |
| Cooneyites | 1894 | P ind | x.... | | 500 | 1,000 | *Go-Preachers.* Communal itinerants; founder Edward Cooney. Also NI,USA,Canada. |
| Elim Foursquare Gospel Alliance | 1910 | P Pe2 | Z.... | 2 | 40 | 200 | Movement begun in Monaghan by Welsh evangelist George Jeffreys. Few converts. |
| Evangelical Presbyterian Church | 1927 | P Ref | J...h | 10 | 403 | 950 | *Irish Ev Ch.* Split ex PCI over heresy trial. HQ Belfast. 6n,G=0.9%pa,W=49%,4Yy. |
| Greek Orthodox Church (AD Thyateira) | | O Gre | Cwc.. | 1 | 500 | 1,000 | Under EP Constantinople. HQ London (UK). One parish of Greek Cypriots. |
| Jehovah's Witnesses | 1891 | M Jeh | x.... | 21 | 1,076 | 2,000 | Missionary attempt at entry 1926; by 1948, witnessing under way. G=10%pa,79Y. |
| Lutheran Church in Ireland | 1952 | P Lut | L...K | 3 | 300 | 400 | Begun due to influx of refugees after World War II. In Dublin, Cork, Killarney. |
| Methodist Church in Ireland | 1747 | P Met | Vwc.K | 70 | 3,000 | 5,000 | Also 70,000 adherents in NIreland. Linked to British Methodist Conference. W=76%. |
| Non-Subscribing Presbyterian Church | 1649 | P Ref | I...K | 2 | 200 | 300 | Unitarian. Bulk of church in Northern Ireland (UK). Churches: Dublin, Cork. 2n. |
| Presbyterian Church in Ireland | 1642 | P Ref | Rw..K | 108 | 9,000 | 14,000 | 3 Presbyteries: Dublin, Donegal, Monaghan. Decline from 56,498 in 1881. G=0,W=60%. |
| Religious Society of Friends | | P Qua | Qv..K | 8 | 500 | 600 | *Dublin Yearly Meeting. Quakers.* Rapid decline. HQ Dublin. |
| Russian Orthodox Ch Outside of Russia | | O Sla | x.... | 1 | 100 | 200 | M=ROCOR (New York, USA). Church of emigre Russians in exile. |
| Russian Orth Ch (PE Western Europe) | | O Sla | Mwc.. | 1 | 100 | 300 | Under P Moscow. One parish (Russian emigres) under bishop in London (UK). |
| Salvation Army | 1880 | P Sal | xwc.K | 3 | 200 | 500 | *SA, Ireland Division.* 3 Corps (2 in Dublin, and Cork). 4 officers. |
| Other Protestant denominations | | P | ..... | | 200 | 500 | Total about 10 (see list below). |
| **Total affiliated (mid-1970)** | | | | **2,196** | **1,921,719** | **2,814,612** | **Total denominations (1970) . . . 33.** |
| **Total affiliated (mid-1975)** | | | | **2,200** | **2,028,700** | **2,971,300** | **Total denominations (1975) . . . 34.** |
| **Total affiliated (mid-1980)** | | | | **2,205** | **2,127,900** | **3,116,600** | **Total denominations (1980) . . . 36.** |

NOTES ON TABLE ABOVE

COLUMNS: for meanings and CODES (cols. 1, 3, 4, 8), see Codebook (Part 6). Column 1: **Boldface type** = church with over 10% of country's affiliated Christians.

NATIONAL COUNCILS (Column 4, 5th letter).
- h = British Evangelical Council (BEC).
- K = Irish Council of Churches (ICC).
- P = Episcopal Conference of Ireland.

*Other national councils.* Evangelical Fellowship of Ireland (EFI) (members not churches but individuals; not affiliated to WEF or EEA).

*Local councils.* 2 affiliated to BCC and ICC.

OTHER PROTESTANT DENOMINATIONS. There are several other groups with very small memberships, mostly well under 100 adults, including: Apostolic Ch of Pentecost of Canada, Barreiro Bible Ch (European Evangelistic Crusade, 1954; 72 members), Children of God International (Dublin), Congregational Union of Ireland, Gospel Halls (independent congregations), Irish Missionary Fellowship, Moravian Ch, Reformed Presbyterian Ch of Ireland (1811), Seventh-day Adventist Ch (Irish Mission).

UNITING CHURCHES. Negotiations for organic union were under way in 1980 between: Church of Ireland, Methodist Ch in Ireland, Presbyterian Ch in Ireland.

PEOPLES (ethnolinguistic). Christians: 96.4% Irish, 1.4% English, 1.0% Ulster Irish, 0.4% USA, 0.3% Scottish, 0.2% Welsh, 0.2% Irish Traveller (nomad, Gypsy, Shelta), Greek, Russian, German.

COUNTRY-WIDE TOTALS

EVANGELIZATION (see Part 5). 1900: 100%. 1970: 100%. 1980: 100%.

FOREIGN MISSIONARIES AND PERSONNEL (nationals serving abroad) (1973). Total 9,537: 9,524 Roman Catholics (5,954 foreign missionaries (2,318 priests, 487 brothers, 2,831 sisters, 318 lay) (decline from 7,085 in 1965 and 6,517 in 1968) in 55 societies and groups serving in Third-World countries, and 3,570 other personnel serving in Western nations, especially UK and USA), 13 Anglicans in 3 societies in 12 countries.

FOREIGN MISSIONARIES AND PERSONNEL (aliens from abroad) (1973). Total 242. *From Western world.* 232: about 150 marginal Protestants (140 Mormons from USA, UK), 65 Protestants (44 in 6 UK societies, 17 in 8 USA societies, 2 in 1 Denmark society, 2 in 1 Canada society), 12 Anglicans in 1 UK society, 5 Roman Catholics. *From Third World.* About 10 Roman Catholics mostly from Nigeria.

INSTITUTIONS (church-operated) (1973). Total 990, including 820 higher schools (22 minor seminaries), 110 medical centres, 5 religious communities, 2 research centres, 34 seminaries (33 RC, 1 Anglican), 3 study centres, 2 universities.

PERIODICALS. About 160 titles (80% RC).

PERSONNEL. About 21,642 (21,400 national, 242 foreign).

RELIGIOUS LIBRARIES. About 60.

SCRIPTURE DISTRIBUTION (1975). Annual totals: 25,340 Bibles (13% free, 28% subsidized, 59% commercial), 110,360 NTs (56% free, 16% subsidized, 27% commercial), 55,000 UBS portions, 4,000 UBS selections. *Translations completed.* Irish: NT 1602, Bible 1685.

SERVICE AGENCIES. About 105, including ACISJF, CCCI, CCII, CEF, CMCSS, HCMS, IMU, SPS, SSC, SU, YWAM.

ADDITIONAL DATA ON CHURCHES

CATHOLIC CHURCH IN IRELAND. Diocesan boundaries in Ireland do not follow political boundaries or national frontiers. The last 5 dioceses in the table are part of the Province of Armagh

with seat in Northern Ireland. D Clogher is almost equally divided between Eire and Ulster; 90% of D Kilmore is in Eire, and in Eire there are also small parts of the 2 Ulster dioceses of Derry and Dromore. *Annual baptisms.* (1972) 99.7% infant, 0.3% adult. *Personnel.* Virtually all nationals. *Priests.* In addition to those listed above by dioceses, there were in 1970 about 1,000 others in various occupations making a grand total of 6,082 (2,025 regular clergy, and 4,057 secular clergy, the latter total being composed of 3,389 in Irish parishes, chaplaincies and administration, 105 in major seminaries, 23 in university colleges, 339 in secondary schools, 103 in temporary overseas service, 58 retired or sick, and 35 engaged on higher studies). *Catholic charismatics* (January 1974). 2,500 adults including many religious personnel are active in 60 prayer groups in the Charismatic Renewal. *Seminarians.* Total (1971) 1,917, divided as follows: 1,015 diocesan, 240 in missionary institutes, 662 for religious orders and congregations. *Decline of diocesan seminarians.* (1965) 1,545, (1966) 1,465, (1967) 1,433, (1968) 1,297, (1969) 1,226, (1970) 968. *Seminaries.* 8 major seminaries for secular clergy (6 diocesan, and 2 interdiocesan: Kildare & Leighlin, Waterford & Lismore); Pontifical Irish College in Rome; All Hallows College in Dublin for secular clergy for work with overseas Irish, 5 major seminaries for home and foreign missions; 3 missionary seminaries (SMA, SPS, Maynooth); and 16 study houses for religious orders and congregations. *Major religious orders and congregations* (excluding those for overseas missions). Priests: SJ, CSSp, OFMCap, OP, OFM, SDB, OESA, CSSR. Brothers: Christian Brothers, St Patrick Brothers and Presentation Brothers (3 Irish institutes), FSC. Sisters (main Irish congregations): Sisters of Mercy, Loreto Nuns, Presentation Sisters, Irish Dominicans, Sisters of St John of God, Irish Sisters of Charity, St Louis Sisters.
*Catholic organizations.* The Episcopal Conference of Ireland, which includes the bishops of the republic and also of Northern Ireland, is a member of CCEE. It was first organized in 1882, its latest statutes being approved in 1969. The Conference of Major Religious Superiors, for men and women, was formed in 1961. There are no national pastoral nor presbyteral councils. The National Council for the Apostolate of the Laity co-ordinates lay activities, the major organizations in 1970 being: Legion of Mary (27,000 members), Society of St Vincent de Paul (9,500), Knights of St Columbanus (6,400), Catholic Boy Scouts of Ireland (8,000) and Catholic Girl Guides (2,300).

The Holy See has diplomatic relations with Ireland and is represented to government and the Catholic hierarchy by a nuncio based in Dublin.

An international Catholic organization with its headquarters in Ireland is the Legion of Mary. Founded in Dublin in 1921, it undertakes different forms of the apostolate including the sick and aged, caring for the homeless and sponsoring discussion groups concerned with moral and religious questions. The Legion of Mary is a member of the Conference of the OIC and exists in 1,200 dioceses on 5 continents.

There are at present no organized underground or progressivist opinion groups in Ireland. A Catholic leftist movement called Grille has ceased to exist for lack of recruits. However, an Irish branch of the rightist Latin Mass Society, with headquarters in London, was founded in 1970 to work for the full restoration of the liturgy in Latin.

Research and social service training are undertaken by several centres and organizations. (1) The Research and Development Unit, founded in 1970, is dependent on the hierarchy and is part of a larger centre, the Catholic Communications Institute of Ireland (Dublin). (2) The Dublin Institute of Adult Education, founded in 1950 by the archbishop of Dublin, with 1,800 adult students in 1970, offers courses in religion, the humanities and socio-religious subjects. (3) The College of Industrial Relations, founded by Jesuits, with 1,078 students in 1971 offers courses for employers and unionists covering the whole field of industrial relations. (4) The National Farmers' Association in Dublin, which is a member of ICRA in Italy, is a trade-union type of organization. (5) The Irish Creamery Milk Suppliers Association is also a member of ICRA in Italy. (6) Trocaire ('Solidarity', in Gaelic), founded in Dublin in 1973 and at present a member of CIDSE in Belgium, provides financial aid to Third-World development and conscientization of Irish Catholics with respect to the Third World. (7) Concern, founded in Dublin in 1968, recruits voluntary lay personnel for Third-World development. It was earlier involved in Biafra and is now most active in Bangladesh. (8) Muintir na Tire (People of the Country), which is also a member of ICRA in Italy, is an organization founded about 1930 for the improvement of conditions of rural life. Several other community development projects, begun or directed by priests, have produced significant results, the most important being the Glencolumcille Project (County Donegal), Fastnet Co-operative (West Cork), Northern Counties Co-operative and Aherlow Co-operative (County Tipperary).

Pastoral and religious training is provided by 5 main organizations: (1) St Patrick's College, founded in 1795 in Maynooth, County Kildare, under the direction of the Episcopal Conference, which includes, beyond the secular faculties attaching it to the National University, faculties of canon law, theology and philosophy; (2) Milltown Institute of Theology and Philosophy, founded by Jesuits in Dublin in 1889; (3) Dublin Institute of Adult Education; (4) Mater Dei Institute, founded in 1966 by the archbishop of Dublin, which is attached to the St Thomas Aquinas Pontifical University in Rome and offers a diploma in religious education recognized by the state for teaching religion in secondary schools; and (5) the Catechetical and Pastoral Institute in Dundalk, under the bishops of the province of Armagh.

The Irish Missionary Union, founded in 1970, is an association of (in 1973) 58 missionary societies and groups aiding missions, with the aim of co-ordinating the missionary action of the Irish Church. In 1970 there were 2,318 missionary priests serving overseas, 487 brothers, 2,831 sisters and 318 lay missionaries, making a total of 5,954 persons; this represented a decline from the 1965 total of 7,085 (2,797 priests, 486 brothers, 3,547 sisters, 255 lay). Distribution of missionary personnel by continents was 3,686 in Africa (including 1,089 in South Africa); 1,697 in Asia and Oceania and 571 in America (including 102 in Canada, but excluding personnel in the USA). The principal missionary congregations and institutes are: SSC and SSP (clerical congregations founded in Ireland); SMA, SVD, MHM, CSSp and WF; Medical Missionaries of Mary, St Columban Missionary Sisters, Holy Rosary Sisters, Franciscan Missionaries for Africa (all founded in Ireland); and Sisters of St Joseph of Cluny.

The Irish educational system is based for the most part on national primary schools which are Catholic but receive state subsidies through the intermediary role of local authorities. In 1970 there were 5,232 primary schools (595,709 pupils), 746 secondary schools (206,703), 6 normal schools (1,106) and one university (St Patrick's College, Maynooth University Section, with 809 students), a total of 802,327 students. To that must also be added 5,272 students of 'lay schools', which are privately run by lay Catholics and have a Catholic orientation. It is also important to note that state vocational schools have entirely Catholic teaching staff who co-operate in religious education. Higher education is provided at the Catholic University of Ireland founded in 1854.

Medical work in 1969 included 100 health centres and public hospitals (16,802 beds) run by sisters, some of which are owned by them, in addition to a number of private hospitals also run by sisters. Social service work in 1970 was co-ordinated by the Catholic Social Service Conference, a federation of numerous charitable bodies involving the distribution of food and clothing, maternity care and youth work, and the Catholic Social Welfare Bureau. The latter caters for emigration, family care, sports, aid to primary schools, youth work, preparation for marriage and marriage counselling. There has also been a recent development of social centres providing meals for the aged and infirm, 30 homes for the aged (14 of which are in Dublin) and aid programmes for the itinerant population, there being about 20,000 nomads or vagrants in Ireland.
CHURCH OF IRELAND. The total of members in the Republic has declined annually from 317,576 in 1881. *Reorganization.* In a major reorganization in 1976 (shown in column 1), 7 combined dioceses (Aghadoe, Ardfert, Clonfert, Kilfenora, Killaloe, Kilmacduagh, Limerick) were reorganized as UDs Limerick & Killaloe; and Kildare was detached from UDs Dublin and attached to D Meath, which was then transferred from the Province of Armagh to that of Dublin. Later, in 1977, Ossory, Ferns & Leighlin were joined to Cashel, Waterford & Lismore; Emly was detached and added to Limerick & Killaloe. By 1981 it was hoped further to unite Kilmore, Elphin & Ardagh with Tuam, Killala & Achonry. *Bishops.* In the newly-united dioceses, bishops are known by the first place name only. *Type of churchmanship* (column 3). The Church of Ireland has traditionally been Low Church in ritual, although most dioceses now have pluralistic traditions.

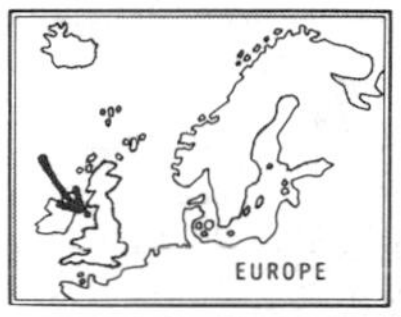


# ISLE OF MAN

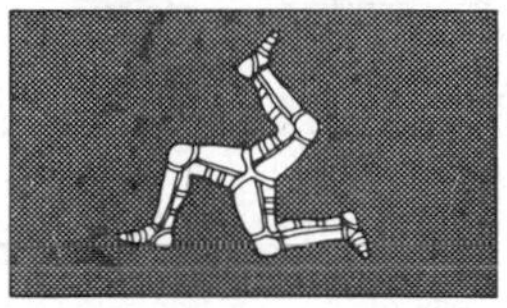

## SECULAR DATA

**STATE. Official name:** The Isle of Man. Alternative name: Mona. **Flag** (shown above right): Red, with 3 steel-coloured legs armoured and spurred (knees and spurs, yellow) in the centre.
**Area:** 588 sq.km. (227 sq.miles). Agricultural land: 50.8%.
**Government:** Self-governing British crown possession, since 1765 and 1828.
**Legislature:** Court of Tynwald, 11 members. House of Keys, 24 members. Executive Council, 7 members.
**Official language:** English.
**Chief cities:** capital Douglas 20,390 (1971), Ramsey 5,048.
**Political divisions:** 6 Sheadings and 4 Municipalities.

**DEMOGRAPHY. Population:** 56,289 (census of 25.IV.1971. For 1970–2000 (UN), see last row of Table 1). Population density (1975): 99/sq.km. (255/sq.mile). Under 15 years: 23%. Growth rate (1975–80): 0.78% per year. Household size: 3.1 persons.
**Major languages:** English, Irish, Manx (Celtic).
**Urban dwellers** (1970): 56.5%. Urban growth rate (1950–70): 0.3% per year.
**Labour force:** 38%.
**Tourists** (1975): 529,913.

**ETHNOLINGUISTIC GROUPS:** 88.8% British, 10% Irish, 1% Manx (Celtic), 0.1% Jewish.

**MONEY** (1977). **Monetary unit:** pound (= 100 new pence); US$1 = IoM£0.585.
**National income per person:** US$2,300. Average annual family income: US$7,130.

**HEALTH.** Hospitals: 3 (717 beds). Doctors: 67. Blind: 60. Psychotics: 400.

**EDUCATION.** Adult literacy: 99%. Schools: 42 (36 primary, 6 secondary).

**LITERATURE.** Periodicals: 30. Newspapers: 4 non-daily.

**COMMUNICATION** (per 1,000 people). Phones: 248. Radios: 365. TV sets: 340.

TABLE 1. RELIGIOUS ADHERENTS IN THE ISLE OF MAN

| Year | 1900 | | mid-1970 | | Annual change, 1970–1980 | | | | mid-1975 | | mid-1980 | | 2000 | |
|---|---|---|---|---|---|---|---|---|---|---|---|---|---|---|
| *Name* | *Adherents* | *%* | *Adherents* | *%* | *Natural* | *Conversion* | *Total* | *Rate* | *Adherents* | *%* | *Adherents* | *%* | *Adherents* | *%* |
| **Christians** | **37,600** | **98.9** | **52,030** | **92.9** | **372** | **0** | **372** | **0.69** | **53,890** | **92.9** | **55,750** | **92.9** | **61,140** | **89.9** |
| professing | 37,600 | 98.9 | 52,030 | 92.9 | 372 | 0 | 372 | 0.69 | 53,890 | 92.9 | 55,750 | 92.9 | 61,140 | 89.9 |
| Anglicans | 25,820 | 67.9 | 34,800 | 62.1 | 249 | –8 | 241 | 0.67 | 36,010 | 62.1 | 37,210 | 62.0 | 40,420 | 59.4 |
| Protestants | 10,070 | 26.5 | 11,200 | 20.0 | 80 | 0 | 80 | 0.69 | 11,600 | 20.0 | 12,000 | 20.0 | 12,240 | 18.0 |
| Roman Catholics | 1,710 | 4.5 | 5,600 | 10.0 | 40 | 0 | 40 | 0.69 | 5,800 | 10.0 | 6,000 | 10.0 | 7,480 | 11.0 |
| Marginal Protestants | 0 | 0.0 | 430 | 0.8 | 3 | 8 | 11 | 2.29 | 480 | 0.8 | 540 | 0.9 | 1,000 | 1.5 |
| nominal | 1,120 | 2.9 | 7,730 | 13.8 | 55 | 1 | 56 | 0.70 | 7,990 | 13.8 | 8,290 | 13.8 | 13,540 | 19.9 |
| affiliated | 36,480 | 96.0 | 44,300 | 79.1 | 317 | –1 | 316 | 0.69 | 45,900 | 79.1 | 47,460 | 79.1 | 47,600 | 70.0 |
| total practising | 32,830 | *90* | 31,010 | *70* | 222 | –1 | 221 | 0.69 | 32,130 | *70* | 33,220 | *70* | 28,560 | *60* |
| non-practising | 3,650 | *10* | 13,290 | *30* | 95 | 0 | 95 | 0.69 | 13,770 | *30* | 14,240 | *30* | 19,040 | *40* |
| Anglicans | 25,080 | 66.0 | 28,000 | 50.0 | 200 | 0 | 200 | 0.69 | 29,020 | 50.0 | 30,000 | 50.0 | 30,400 | 44.7 |
| Evangelicals | 25,080 | 66.0 | 20,000 | 35.7 | 145 | 55 | 200 | 0.95 | 21,000 | 36.2 | 22,000 | 36.7 | 23,000 | 33.8 |
| Protestants | 9,880 | 26.0 | 10,900 | 19.5 | 78 | –9 | 69 | 0.61 | 11,270 | 19.4 | 11,590 | 19.3 | 9,600 | 14.1 |
| Evangelicals | 7,000 | 18.4 | 4,000 | 7.1 | 28 | 2 | 30 | 0.73 | 4,100 | 7.1 | 4,300 | 7.2 | 5,400 | 7.9 |
| Roman Catholics | 1,520 | 4.0 | 5,000 | 8.9 | 36 | 1 | 37 | 0.72 | 5,160 | 8.9 | 5,370 | 8.9 | 6,800 | 10.0 |
| Marginal Protestants | 0 | 0.0 | 400 | 0.7 | 3 | 7 | 10 | 2.22 | 450 | 0.8 | 500 | 0.8 | 800 | 1.2 |
| Non-religious | 380 | 1.0 | 3,920 | 7.0 | 28 | 0 | 28 | 0.69 | 4,060 | 7.0 | 4,200 | 7.0 | 6,800 | 10.0 |
| Jews | 20 | 0.1 | 50 | 0.1 | 0 | 0 | 0 | 0.00 | 50 | 0.1 | 50 | 0.1 | 60 | 0.1 |
| **Country's population** | **38,000** | **100.0** | **56,000** | **100.0** | **400** | **0** | **400** | **0.69** | **58,000** | **100.0** | **60,000** | **100.0** | **68,000** | **100.0** |

COLUMNS, ROWS. For meanings and definitions, see Codebook (Part 6). Note that, by definition, total 'Christians' = professing + crypto-Christians, which also = affiliated + nominal Christians. Percentages may not always total exactly, due to rounding.
CENSUSES. The religion question has not been asked.
JEWS. One congregation of 30 members.

**NON-CHRISTIAN RELIGIONS.** Unlike neighbouring Britain the island has not been subject to massive immigration of adherents of non-Christian religions. There are only a few Jews, with no synagogue. Those claiming to be without religion have grown from 1% of the population in 1900 to 7% in 1970.

**CHRISTIANITY.** The island was converted to Christianity prior to AD 600, probably through the outreach of missionaries from Iona. Vikings first visited the island around AD 800, but it was primarily during the second Scandinavian period (1079–1266) that the church was organized. Prior to 1266 the diocese of Sodor and Man was formed, with a metropolitan in Trondheim, Norway, and its cathedral of St German in Man. It was also during this period that in 1134 Cistercian monks from Furness, Lancashire, built the Rushen abbey which played a significant role in the later religious life of the island. Other early institutions include a convent near Douglas and Kirk Arbory founded by Franciscans in 1373.

At the time of the 16th-century English Reformation, Christianity in Man became a part of the Church of England; and this has continued to the present day, the diocese of Sodor and Man being part of its Province of York. Each year the diocese receives from the Church Commissioners for England (in London) a larger subsidy per Anglican than most

Christian topics proliferate on the Isle's postage stamps: *top*, Bi-Centenary of the Manx Bible (1775); *bottom*, John Wesley preaching outside Braddan Church, 1777.

English dioceses. Nevertheless, there are certain distinctive aspects to the administration of the diocese which give it a national character, including retention of its own canon law, its own convocation and a special relationship with the state. The island's Anglican diocese is Evangelical in churchmanship, and with 43 parishes and one primary school it remains the principal denomination.

The main Protestant community is the Methodist Church which traces its history to successful visits to Man by John Wesley in the 18th century from 1777. The Methodist Isle of Man District is divided into 4 circuits (Douglas, Castletown, Peel and Ramsey), with 30 congregations served by 19 ministers. Other bodies each with a congregation in Douglas include the United Reformed Church, begun as a Congregationalist church in 1808, the Baptist Union begun in 1893, and a more recent independent Pentecostal Revival Church. The Assemblies of God in Great Britain and Ireland have a congregation at Port St Mary.

Catholics in the Isle of Man are part of the diocese of Liverpool in the Catholic Church in England and Wales. There are 7 parishes and one chapel served by 8 priests and 6 Sisters of Mercy, the primary responsibility of the latter being educational work.

**CHURCH AND STATE.** Since the English Reformation, there has been a close relationship between the Anglican diocese and the state. The chief secular administrative officer is the lieutenant governor, appointed as lord by the British monarch, while the island's legislative council consisting of 2 houses is called the Tynwald court. The Anglican bishop and archdeacon are chosen by the lord, while the Tynwald retains control over the church's marriage laws as well as the appointment of its vicar general and churchwardens. The Anglican bishop of Sodor and Man is himself a member of the Tynwald council. The Church of England is the established church, but measures from the Church Assembly (now General Synod) of the Church of England and of Parliament in London have to be approved by the Tynwald before they become law. Measures passed in this way specifically related to the Isle of Man include the Isle of Man Purchase Act, 1765; and others still in force as legislation there including the Ecclesiastical Commissioners (Sodor and Man) Measure, 1930; and Episcopal Pensions (Sodor and Man) Measure, 1931. No moves towards disestablishment are under way.

**INTERDENOMINATIONAL ORGANIZATIONS.** The Isle of Man Council of Churches is an associate member of the British Council of Churches and is in working relationship with the WCC. It has a Douglas Regional Committee in the capital.

TABLE 2.    ORGANIZED CHURCHES AND DENOMINATIONS IN THE ISLE OF MAN

| Official name 1 | Begun 2 | Type 3 | Counc 4 | Congs 5 | Adults 6 | Affiliated 7 | Names, notes, and other statistics (see Codebook) 8 |
|---|---|---|---|---|---|---|---|
| Assemblies of God in GB & Ireland | | P Pe2 | ZG... | 1 | 50 | 100 | HQ Nottingham (UK). One church in Port St Mary. Classical Pentecostals. |
| Baptist Union of GB & Ireland | 1893 | P Bap | Twc,K | 1 | 100 | 200 | *General and Particular Baptists.* One church in Douglas. |
| Catholic Ch in E & W (D Liverpool) | 1814 | R Lat | B,B,s | 8 | 3,800 | 5,000 | *E&W=England & Wales.* Mostly Irish. 3 schools. C=0+0+1. 8nx,6w(Sisters of Mercy). |
| Church of Christ, Scientist | | M Sci | x.... | 1 | 30 | 50 | *Christian Science.* M=CCS(Boston,USA). Small group linked to UK body. |
| Church of England: D Sodor & Man | 447 | A Eva | avc,K | 43 | 18,000 | 28,000 | Includes 400 Manx (Celts). Tourism. HQ Peel. 1 school. 43n,P=23%,W=17%,16Y,392y. |
| Greater World Christian Spiritualist Ch | | M Spi | x.... | 1 | 50 | 150 | *Greater World Sanctuary.* Christian spiritualists. Church in Douglas. |
| Jehovah's Witnesses | | M Jeh | x.... | 3 | 100 | 200 | *Watch Tower. IBSA.* Active branches related to Witnesses in England. |
| Methodist Church of Great Britain | | P Met | Vwc,K | 30 | 2,548 | 8,000 | *Isle of Man District.* 4 Circuits: Douglas, Castletown, Peel, Ramsey. 19nx. |
| Pentecostal Revival Church | | P Pe4 | ..... | 1 | 50 | 100 | Independent congregation in Douglas. Radical Pentecostals. |
| Salvation Army | | P Sal | x...,K | 3 | 100 | 200 | *SA.* Branches in Douglas, Peel, Port Erin. Linked to SA in UK (HQ London). |
| United Reformed Church | 1808 | P Ref | Rwc,K | 2 | 150 | 300 | *URC.* Formerly Presbyterians, till 1970 URC union. One church in Douglas. |
| Other Protestant denominations | | P | ..... | 20 | 1,000 | 2,000 | Total about 10, including Christian Brethren (Open), Religious Society of Friends. |
| **Total affiliated (mid-1970)** | | | | 114 | 25,978 | 44,300 | Total denominations (1970) . . . 21. |
| **Total affiliated (mid-1975)** | | | | 118 | 26,900 | 45,900 | Total denominations (1975) . . . 21. |
| **Total affiliated (mid-1980)** | | | | 122 | 27,800 | 47,460 | Total denominations (1980) . . . 21. |

**NOTES ON TABLE ABOVE**
COLUMNS: for meanings and CODES (cols. 1, 3, 4, 8), see Codebook (Part 6). Column 1: **Boldface type** = church with over 10% of country's affiliated Christians.
NATIONAL COUNCILS (Column 4, 5th letter).
K = Isle of Man Council of Churches (IOMCC) (associated council of the British Council of Churches (BCC); in working relationship with WCC).
s = represented on Catholic Bishops' Conference of England and Wales, also associate member of IOMCC.
*Local councils.* Douglas Regional Committee of IOMCC.

PEOPLES (ethnolinguistic). Christians: 89% British, 10% Irish, 1% Manx (Celtic).

**COUNTRY-WIDE TOTALS**
EVANGELIZATION (see Part 5). 1900: 100%. 1970: 100%. 1980: 100%.
FOREIGN MISSIONARIES AND PERSONNEL (nationals serving abroad) (1973). Total about 4 Anglicans.
FOREIGN MISSIONARIES AND PERSONNEL (aliens from abroad) (1973). Total 3. *From Western world.* About 2 Anglicans, 1 Protestant from UK.
PERIODICALS. About 15 titles.

PERSONNEL. About 93 (90 national, 3 foreign).
SCRIPTURE DISTRIBUTION (1975). Annual totals: 1,650 Bibles (9% subsidized, 91% commercial), 950 NTs (16% subsidized, 84% commercial), 1,000 UBS portions, 2,000 UBS selections. *Translations completed.* Manx: portion in 1748, NT 1767, Bible 1773.
SERVICE AGENCIES. About 8.

**ADDITIONAL DATA ON CHURCHES**
CATHOLIC CHURCH IN ENGLAND AND WALES. *Catholic organizations.* The church sponsors 3 primary schools.

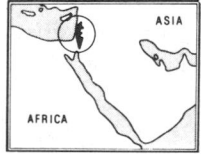

# ISRAEL

## SECULAR DATA

STATE. **Official name:** The State of Israel (Medinat Yisrael).
Adjective of nationality: Israeli.
**Flag** (shown above right): White field bearing blue Star of David between 2 blue stripes.
**Area:** 20,700 sq.km. (7,993 sq.miles). In addition, since 1973 Israel claims the disputed territory of East Jerusalem, and (1977) over 25,000 sq.miles of Arab territory. Agricultural land: 60.3%.
**Government:** Parliamentary republic, since 1948 (1917 British mandated territory, 1948 Independence proclaimed).
**Legislature:** Parliament (Knesset), 120 members.
**Official languages:** Hebrew (*Ivrit*) and Arabic.
**Chief cities:** capital Jerusalem 326,400 (1973), Tel Aviv-Jaffa 367,600, Haifa 225,800.
**Political divisions:** 29 Municipalities (2 Arab), 118 Local Councils (47 Arab and Druze), 48 Regional Councils (1 Arab) comprising 695 villages.
**Armed forces** (1976): Total 158,500 regular (123,000 conscripts): army 135,000, navy 4,500, air force 19,000 (543 combat aircraft). Reserves: 450,000. Paramilitary forces: 9,000.

DEMOGRAPHY. **Population:** 3,147,683 (census of 20.V.1972. For 1970–2000 (UN), see last row of Table 1). Population density (1975): 163/sq.km. (422/sq.mile). Under 15 years: 36%. Growth rate (1975–80): 2.64% per year (births 2.64%, deaths −0.67%, immigrants 0.67%). Life expectancy (1975–80): 72.0 years. Household size: 5.2 persons.
**Major languages:** Hebrew, Yiddish, Ladino, Arabic, English, French, German, Aramaic, Circassian, and numerous others.
**Urban dwellers** (1970): 79.5%. Urban growth rate (1950–70): 4.6% per year.
**Labour force:** 35%.
**Refugees** (1977): From abroad 83,634 (71,634 from USSR during 1973–76, 12,000 from Romania during 1973–76).
**Tourists** (1950): 33,122. (1974): 569,622. (1978) 800,000 (60% Jewish, 30% Christian).

**ETHNOLINGUISTIC GROUPS:** 83.1% Jewish (65.9% Hebrew, 4.8% Yiddish, 1.9% Romanian, 1.3% German, 1.2% Spanish

Jewish President Shazar greets church dignitaries (Coptic, Armenian, Greek, Syrian, Roman Catholic, Protestant) on New Year's Eve, 1968.

(Ladino), 1.2% French), 15.4% Palestinian Arab, 1.3% Bedouin Arab, 0.1% Gazan Arab (5,500), 0.1% Circassian (2,000), Egyptian Arab, Ethiopian, Lebanese Arab, Armenian, Polish (1,000), Hungarian (1,000), Greek, other European (French, Italian, German, British), USA White.

**MONEY** (1977). **Monetary unit:** pound (= 100 agorot); US$1 = Is£9.07 (operational rate of exchange).
**National income per person:** US$3,000. Average annual family income: US$15,600.
**Inflation:** (1970–74) 20.6% per year (1975: consumer price index 333); (1977) 35% per year; (1979) 60% per year.
**Cost of living in capital** (1976): index 103 (Washington DC = 100). Daily cost of living: US$37.

**HEALTH.** Hospitals: 87 (18,221 beds). Doctors: 8,453. Lepers: 250 (0.1 per 1,000). Blind: 5,285. Psychotics: 40,000. Criminals: 72,731.

**EDUCATION.** Adult literacy: (1961) 84%, (1971) 88%. Education rate: 81%. Schools: 1,767 (1,490 primary). Universities: 5.

**LITERATURE.** Annual new book titles (1973): 2,147. Periodicals: 425. Scientific journals: 30. Newspapers: 26 dailies, 107 non-daily.

**COMMUNICATION** (per 1,000 people). Phones: 214. Radios: 221. TV sets: 120. Daily newspaper circulation: 208 copies.

TABLE 1. RELIGIOUS ADHERENTS IN ISRAEL (excluding East Jerusalem)

| Year | 1900 | | mid-1970 | | Annual change, 1970–1980 | | | | mid-1975 | | mid-1980 | | 2000 | |
|---|---|---|---|---|---|---|---|---|---|---|---|---|---|---|
| *Name* | *Adherents* | *%* | *Adherents* | *%* | *Natural* | *Conversion* | *Total* | *Rate* | *Adherents* | *%* | *Adherents* | *%* | *Adherents* | *%* |
| Jews | 32,000 | 8.6 | 2,566,000 | 87.8 | 85,774 | –2,274 | 83,500 | 2.81 | 2,973,900 | 88.2 | 3,401,000 | 88.4 | 4,855,500 | 88.4 |
| Karaites | 500 | 0.1 | 10,000 | 0.3 | 200 | 0 | 200 | 1.82 | 11,000 | 0.3 | 12,000 | 0.3 | 16,000 | 0.3 |
| Samaritans | 30 | 0.0 | 230 | 0.0 | 4 | 0 | 4 | 1.60 | 250 | 0.0 | 270 | 0.0 | 300 | 0.0 |
| Muslims | 308,200 | 83.3 | 260,500 | 8.9 | 4,890 | –200 | 4,690 | 1.65 | 283,900 | 8.4 | 307,400 | 8.0 | 357,000 | 6.5 |
| Druzes | 3,700 | 1.0 | 34,600 | 1.2 | 620 | 0 | 620 | 1.64 | 37,700 | 1.1 | 40,800 | 1.1 | 60,000 | 1.1 |
| Ahmadis | 0 | 0.0 | 1,500 | 0.1 | 26 | 24 | 50 | 2.86 | 1,750 | 0.1 | 2,000 | 0.1 | 4,000 | 0.1 |
| **Christians** | **29,700** | **8.0** | **72,150** | **2.5** | **1,385** | **–90** | **1,295** | **1.65** | **78,600** | **2.3** | **85,100** | **2.2** | **109,000** | **2.0** |
| crypto-Christians | 5,100 | 1.4 | 14,350 | 0.5 | 285 | 640 | 925 | 5.17 | 17,900 | 0.5 | 23,600 | 0.6 | 46,000 | 0.8 |
| professing | 24,600 | 6.6 | 57,800 | 2.0 | 1,100 | –730 | 370 | 0.61 | 60,700 | 1.8 | 61,500 | 1.6 | 63,000 | 1.1 |
| Roman Catholics | 7,000 | 1.9 | 35,000 | 1.2 | 667 | –400 | 267 | 0.71 | 37,400 | 1.1 | 37,670 | 1.0 | 33,000 | 0.6 |
| Orthodox | 17,000 | 4.6 | 15,000 | 0.5 | 285 | –290 | –5 | –0.03 | 14,980 | 0.4 | 14,950 | 0.4 | 18,000 | 0.3 |
| Protestants | 100 | 0.0 | 7,000 | 0.2 | 133 | –20 | 103 | 1.37 | 7,500 | 0.2 | 8,030 | 0.2 | 11,000 | 0.2 |
| Anglicans | 500 | 0.1 | 800 | 0.0 | 15 | –10 | 5 | 0.61 | 820 | 0.0 | 850 | 0.0 | 1,000 | 0.0 |
| affiliated | 29,700 | 8.0 | 72,150 | 2.5 | 1,385 | –90 | 1,295 | 1.65 | 78,600 | 2.3 | 85,100 | 2.2 | 109,000 | 2.0 |
| total practising | 26,730 | *90* | 54,110 | *75* | 1,039 | –68 | 971 | 1.65 | 58,950 | *75* | 63,820 | *75* | 76,300 | *70* |
| non-practising | 2,970 | *10* | 18,040 | *25* | 346 | –22 | 324 | 1.65 | 19,650 | *25* | 21,280 | *25* | 32,700 | *30* |
| Roman Catholics | 9,000 | 2.4 | 41,900 | 1.4 | 799 | –70 | 729 | 1.60 | 45,600 | 1.4 | 49,190 | 1.3 | 60,000 | 1.1 |
| Orthodox | 20,000 | 5.4 | 18,200 | 0.6 | 357 | –50 | 307 | 1.56 | 19,670 | 0.6 | 21,270 | 0.6 | 27,000 | 0.5 |
| Protestants | 200 | 1.0 | 9,550 | 0.3 | 181 | 10 | 191 | 1.82 | 10,500 | 0.3 | 11,460 | 0.3 | 16,000 | 0.3 |
| Evangelicals | 200 | 0.1 | 7,600 | 0.3 | 148 | 52 | 200 | 2.33 | 8,600 | 0.3 | 9,600 | 0.2 | 14,000 | 0.3 |
| Neo-pentecostals | 0 | 0.0 | 0 | 0.0 | 10 | 110 | 120 | 20.00 | 600 | 0.0 | 1,200 | 0.0 | 2,000 | 0.0 |
| Israeli indigenous | 0 | 0.0 | 1,100 | 0.0 | 21 | 20 | 41 | 3.15 | 1,300 | 0.0 | 1,510 | 0.0 | 3,000 | 0.0 |
| Anglicans | 500 | 0.1 | 900 | 0.0 | 17 | –10 | 7 | 0.75 | 930 | 0.0 | 970 | 0.0 | 1,500 | 0.0 |
| Anglican pentecostals | 0 | 0.0 | 100 | 0.0 | 4 | 16 | 20 | 10.00 | 200 | 0.0 | 300 | 0.0 | 400 | 0.0 |
| Marginal Protestants | 0 | 0.0 | 500 | 0.0 | 10 | 10 | 20 | 3.33 | 600 | 0.0 | 700 | 0.0 | 1,500 | 0.0 |
| Non-religious | 0 | 0.0 | 20,000 | 0.7 | 506 | 2,494 | 3,000 | 8.90 | 33,700 | 1.0 | 50,000 | 1.3 | 165,000 | 3.0 |
| Atheists | 0 | 0.0 | 1,000 | 0.0 | 20 | 40 | 60 | 4.62 | 1,300 | 0.0 | 1,600 | 0.0 | 4,000 | 0.1 |
| Baha'is | 100 | 0.0 | 400 | 0.0 | 8 | 12 | 20 | 4.00 | 500 | 0.0 | 600 | 0.0 | 1,500 | 0.0 |
| Other religionists | 0 | 0.0 | 950 | 0.0 | 17 | 18 | 35 | 3.18 | 1,100 | 0.0 | 1,300 | 0.0 | 2,000 | 0.0 |
| **Country's population** | **370,000** | **100.0** | **2,921,000** | **100.0** | **92,600** | **0** | **92,600** | **2.74** | **3,373,000** | **100.0** | **3,847,000** | **100.0** | **5,494,000** | **100.0** |

COLUMNS, ROWS. For meanings and definitions, see Codebook (Part 6). Note that, by definition, total 'Christians' = professing + crypto-Christians, which also = affiliated + nominal Christians. Percentages may not always total exactly, due to rounding.
CENSUSES. **1919** (Holy Land): 81.7% Muslims, 9.4% Jews, 8.9% Christians. **23.X.1922** (Holy Land): 78.0% Muslims, 11.1% Jews, 9.6% Christians (73,024). **18.XI.1931** (Holy Land): 73.3% Muslims, 16.9% Jews, 8.9% Christians (91,938). **1934:** 67.6% Muslims, 23.1% Jews, 8.2% Christians (99,500). **1939:** 59.5% Muslims, 33.1% Jews, 7.4% Christians (100,000). **22.V.1961** (Israel: de jure, excluding aliens): 88.7% Jews, 7.8% Muslims, 2.3% Christians (50,543), 1.1% Druzes, 0.1% non-religious. **19-20.V.1972:** 85.4% Jews, 11.2% Muslims, 2.3% Christians (72,131: 0.8% Orthodox, 0.7% Roman Catholics), 1.2% Druzes. Comparing these censuses is extremely complex because of varying definitions and territories included or excluded; our Tables 1 for Israel, Jordan and Palestine attempt to include and reconcile all the available data.
POLLS. March 1967 (adults nationwide; PORI): 'Do you consider yourself religious (orthodox)?' — 30% Yes, 70% No. About 70% of all Jews are non-observing on any regular basis. 1971 (Harris): 13% defined themselves as religious, 40% non-religious, 47% traditionalists observing at least major holy days.

NOTES ON RELIGIONS
AHMADIS. Qadianis; there is a strong community of over 700 adults in Kababir near Haifa, mainly Palestinian Arabs.
ANGLICAN PENTECOSTALS (or, Anglican charismatics). An ecumenical charismatic renewal began in 1970, initially among English-speaking Anglican expatriates, later among Arab and Hebrew Christians.
ANGLICANS. In the year 1900 there was a strong Anglican Arab community with numerous Anglican schools around Nazareth.
ATHEISTS. 2 parties since 1965: Israel Communist Party (MAKI), 1,000 members (mainly Ashkenazi Jews), and New Communists (RAKAH), 1,000 members (70% Arabs); Communist voters (election of 28.X.1969) 15,712 (1% of all votes) for MAKI, 38,827 (3%) for RAKAH. Many Communist party members are Muslims or Christians, often practising.
BAHA'IS. Reached Palestine before 1892. World headquarters now on Mount Carmel, Haifa.
CHRISTIANS. 80% Arabic-speaking, and mostly urban or in Galilee and the Central Plain (Yafo, Lod, Jerusalem). The total excludes 11,000 Christians in East Jerusalem, a disputed area claimed by Israel since 1967 to be part of the state of Israel, but before 1967 part of Jordan (and hence included in this survey under Palestine).
COUNTRY'S POPULATION. This table refers to the territory of Israel proper, i.e. that before June 1967, excluding the administered territories (West Bank, Northern Sinai, Gaza Strip, Golan Heights) and excluding also East Jerusalem; the latter is excluded because the reunification of Jerusalem by Israel has not been internationally accepted. In 1948 the population was 758,700 Jewish, and 120,300 Arabs. From 1948–70, about 1,300,000 Jewish immigrants entered and 200,000 left. In 1970 Arabs numbered 490,000 including refugees. In the column 'Natural change' above are included both biological increase and also the average 1970–80 immigration rate of around 40,000 Jews a year.
CRYPTO-CHRISTIANS. Secret believers, Israeli Arabs and Israeli Jewish, in all churches and also a number of isolated radio churches amongst Arab and Jewish communities.
DRUZES. An 11th-century Muslim Shia Ismaili schism with Christian and Jewish elements. In 18 Galilean villages and on Mount Carmel. Arabic-speaking.
ISRAELI INDIGENOUS. Isolated radio believers among the Israeli population (see Table 2); mostly Arab, with some Jewish.
JEWS. The Jewish population of Palestine (including present Israel) rose gradually from 10,000 in 1800 to 25,000 in 1880 to 40,000 in 1900, mostly residing in the 4 holy towns (Jerusalem, Hebron, Tiberias, Safad), Jaffa and Haifa. *Immigration.* After 1920 immigration became massive, 35,000 entering in 1925 and 65,000 in 1935. Jewish immigrants from 1919–32: 84,093. 1933–39: 218,099. 1940–47: 92,563. 1948–51: 702,779. 1952–61: 334,000. 1962–69: 299,424. 1970: 36,928. 1971: 42,000. 1972: 55,888. *Origin.* In 1951, Jews were 25% Sabras (born in Israel), 47% born in Europe or USA (Ashkenazis), 28% born in Africa or Asia (Sefardi-Orientals). By 1970, the composition had changed to: 46% Sabras, 28% Ashkenazis, 26% Sefardi-Orientals. In addition to Orthodox and Reformed Jews, there are other parties: Neturei Karta, Agudat Israel, Mizrachis. *Synagogues.* 1970: 6,000 synagogues, 400 rabbis in 175 local communities; the great majority are Orthodox, with a few Reformed and Conservative. *Practice.* 15% observe all commandments, 15% most, 46% some traditions, 24% none.
KARAITES (Readers of the Scriptures). An 8th-century AD Jewish sect similar to the Sadducees, rejecting Jewish Talmudic oral tradition. Now around Ramla, with 9 synagogues, each with its own minister-reader.
MUSLIMS. Mainly Palestinians, with 37,000 Bedouin, and a few Circassians in Galilee; mostly Sunnis (of Shafiite, Hanafite and Hanbalite rites), Shahiliya Sufis (HQ Acre); also Ahmadis and Druzes, both here enumerated under Muslims. 1970: 150 mosques, with 200 imams paid by the state. *Hajj pilgrims to Mecca.* (1970) 838 Palestinians from Israel and Jordan. *Conversions to Islam.* In 1971, 200 Jews converted to Islam (190 in Jaffa), almost all Jewish girls marrying Muslim men.
NON-RELIGIOUS. An increasing number of Jews each year regard themselves as having abandoned religion, as the column 'Conversion' above shows.
ORTHODOX. Tens of thousands of Orthodox were displaced, in the 1947–48 fighting, out of Israel to Lebanon, Jordan, Syria and overseas.
OTHER RELIGIONISTS. Adherents of other non-Christian religions, including Theosophists (in 1975, in 6 Lodges with 102 members) and Rosicrucians (AMORC, 2 centres).
PROTESTANTS. About 200 Jewish by 1970 and 800 by 1973; the rest Arabs, or European or USA expatriates (the latter including in 1973 over 700 young USA Jews converted through the Jews for Jesus movement, and USA non-Jewish persons who convert to Judaism without giving up belief in Christ and then move to Israel as missionaries).
SAMARITANS. A Jewish sect dating from the 8th century BC, accepting only the Pentateuch and Book of Joshua. Now in Holon, near Tel-Aviv (with 250 more in Nablus, West Bank).

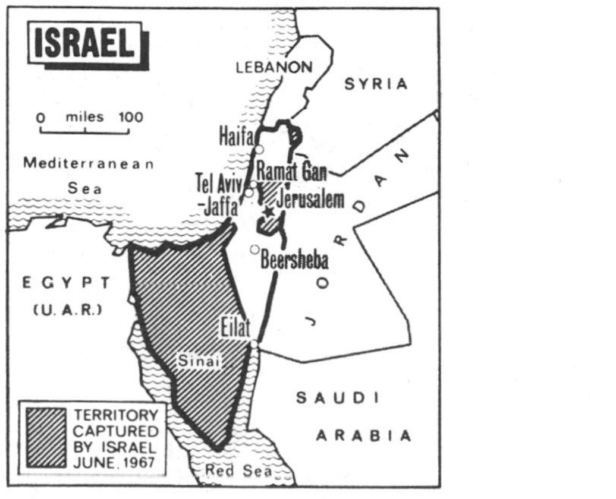


**NON-CHRISTIAN RELIGIONS. Judaism** is the principal religion of Israel, and today Israel is the only nation in the world where Jews are in the majority. At the end of 1970, the composition of the Jewish population in Israel included 46% Sabras (Jews born in Israel); 28% Jews originally from Europe or America, the great majority being Ashkenazis (Jews of the western tradition who speak or whose ancestors spoke Yiddish or Judeo-German); and 26% Jews originally from Africa or Asia, almost all Sefardis (whose traditional language was Latin or Judeo-Spanish) or Orientals (coming from Arab countries). In 1951, these percentages were respectively 25%, 47% and 28%. Immigration and the higher birth rate of the Sefardi-Orientals has resulted in their continued increase. In 1970 the Sefardi-Oriental family size averaged 4.6 persons as against 2.9 for Ashkenazis, although they composed only 20% of the world Jewish population. Tension exists between Ashkenazis and Sefardi-Orientals, due to the former holding leading positions in government and the economy, leaving the latter who were later immigrants in subordinate positions in the social and professional spheres.

Jewish worship is well-organized. In 1970 there were almost 6,000 synagogues, and 400 rabbis paid by the state were officiating in 175 local communities. The synagogues of Sefardi and Ashkenazi rites usually each have a congregation from one particular overseas country and maintain their foreign traditions. Some 178 religious councils and almost 320 religious committees in the villages care for the religious needs of the population. These are under the administrative control of the Ministry of Religion but are also accountable to the Chief Rabbinate of Israel for religious questions. The rabbinate consists of the 2 chief rabbis, one Ashkenazi and the other Sefardi, and the Supreme Rabbinical Council; the latter constitutes the highest religious authority, interpreting the law and supervising the rabbinical courts.

Israeli life is deeply permeated by the Bible and by Jewish traditions and festivals; and also by the Sabbath (Saturday) during which public transport does not operate. Each morning the national radio station Qol Israel begins its day with a religious chant and the reading of a psalm. There are also Biblical and Talmudic commentaries on radio and television. Bible study has an important place in the elementary and secondary schools, and a Bible is solemnly given to soldiers at the end of their period of instruction. Jewish food regulations are observed in the army and in all other official institutions.

According to a survey by the Israeli Institute of Applied Social Research published in 1963, 15% of Israeli Jews observe all the commandments, 15% observe most of them, 46% observe the traditions to some extent, the minimum being synagogue attendance once or twice a year, at Yom Kippur (Day of Atonement) and Rosh Hashana (New Year); and 24% do not observe any of the traditions. The 30% making up the first 2 categories, who practise their religion, corresponds to the attendance at religious elementary schools, governmental for the most part, by a third of the school population. Attendance at the Yeshivoth (secondary and higher studies, principally Talmudic) has witnessed a notable increase, from under 7,000 students in 1960 to 18,795 in 1969–70 (including a large number of non-Israelis, especially Americans). Among the universities is the Religious University of Bar-Ilan at Ramat-Gan near Tel-Aviv, which had 3,641 students in 1968–69 and is being expanded to cater for 6,000.

The Orthodox branch of Judaism plays a far more important role in Israel than the 2 other worldwide Jewish branches, the Reformed (liberal or progressive)

**Baha'is.** Headquarters of Baha'i World Faith on Mount Carmel, Haifa; with (left) Shrine of the Bab; in foreground, Baha'is from many lands on site of new Universal House of Justice building (1973).

and the Conservative which takes an intermediate position. According to law and in actuality, the Orthodox enjoy a complete monopoly over synagogues, marriages, courts, rabbis paid or recognized by the state, military rabbis, religious political parties (14.7% of the votes in the 1969 elections), as well as 3 government ministries which have been in the hands of these parties for many years (Interior, Social Affairs and Religious Affairs). A few non-Orthodox rabbis and institutions are fighting to obtain legal status. In the face of this kind of institutionalized orthodoxy and its theocratic designs, there is often manifest in Israel the irritation of believers towards the rigidity of organizations, compromised as well by political and financial matters. Orthodox Judaism does not seem able to free itself from the defence mentality which has made possible the survival of the Jewish people during the long centuries of their exile. In Israel, the original widespread aspirations for a completely renewed Judaism have not come to fruition in any observable fashion.

International Jewish organizations with their headquarters in Israel include the Agudas Israel World Organization (AJWO), founded in 1912 in Katowice, Upper Silesia, and now located in Jerusalem, which seeks to find a solution for the problems of Jewish people, both in Israel and the diaspora, in the traditional spirit of Judaism.

**Karaism** emerged out of Judaism in Babylon in the 8th century AD. The Karaites (Readers of the Scriptures) only recognize the books of the Bible and reject Jewish oral tradition as found in the Talmud. Spiritual descendants of the Sadducees, they had a flourishing period during the Middle Ages. In Israel

they now number about 10,000, the majority located in the vicinity of Ramla.

**Samaritan religion** is followed by descendants of Jews who intermarried with colonists placed in Samaria by Assyrian kings during the 8th century BC. Samaritans accept only the Pentateuch and the Book of Joshua. They number about 500, of whom 250 are in Palestine (West Bank) at Nablus near Mount Gerizim where the ruins of their ancient temple are located, and 250 in Israel at Holon, a suburb of Tel-Aviv.

**Islam** has decreased radically both in numbers and percentage of the population during the present century, from 83% in 1900 to 8.2% in 1977. Religious councils direct Muslim affairs and administer their religious foundations (waqfs). The highest dignitaries are the kadis of the 4 religious courts (sharia) and the Court of Appeal in Jerusalem. There are about 200 imams paid by the state and 150 mosques of which the most important are those of Omar and al-Aqsa in East Jerusalem, al-Jazzar at Acre and the new Mosque of Peace at Nazareth. According to the Israeli Ministry of Religions, 200 Jewish nationals were converted to Islam in 1971. Of these 190 live at Jaffa where Arabs are most numerous. Most of them are Jewish women whose husbands are Muslims.

**Druze religion** is a sect which emerged from Islam in the 11th century. The Druze's faith today includes Muslim, Jewish and Christian elements. They are found in Galilean villages and at Mount Carmel.

**Baha'i** arose in Persia in the 19th century, claiming to synthesize all religions. Its world centre and Universal House of Justice are in Haifa, Israel, where its founder, Baha'u'llah (Glory of God) is buried. The 400 Baha'is in Israel live in both Haifa and Acre.

**CHRISTIANITY.** The Jewish state in Palestine with its capital Jerusalem was destroyed by the Romans in AD 70 and again in AD 132, resulting in the dispersal of the Jews, and also of Jewish Christians, throughout the Mediterranean world and the Near East. Subsequently Palestine came under the rule of Byzantines (324), Arabs (636), Crusaders (1099), Mamluks (1291), Ottoman Turks (1517), British (1917), finally leading to the founding of the new state of Israel in 1948.

After the conversion of the emperor Constantine in the 4th century, Jerusalem became a place of pilgrimage for Christians. In 451 it was acknowledged as one of the 4 major patriarchates. The Crusades were initially encouraged by pope Hildebrand to heal the growing separation between the Western and

Eastern churches but in fact contributed to the Great Schism of 1054. Rome then established a separate Latin patriarchate in Jerusalem in 1099. This was suppressed in 1291 by the Mamluks and not restored until 1847, when Latin clergy were once more allowed to return to Palestine. In 1333 an exception was made for Franciscans who were permitted to return as caretakers of the Christian holy places. During Turkish rule from the 16th to the 19th centuries, the patriarch of Constantinople was given official jurisdiction over all Christians in areas under Turkish control. Only the Greek Melkites in Palestine were able to maintain any relationship with Rome.

In 1882 Zionist agitation began calling for Palestine to become a Jewish state. Following the increasing Jewish immigration to Israel, Britain in 1917 issued the Balfour Declaration, recognizing Palestine as the national homeland of the Jews. This marked the beginning of Jewish-Arab hostility.

The great majority of all Christians living in Israel are Palestinian Arabs. About 85% of them live in Galilee, 61% being city-dwellers and 39% rural peasants living in some 25 villages. Christians thus tend to be more urbanized than Muslims. However, the emigration of Christians which began in the Turkish period and has been intensified since 1948, and especially since 1967, may eventually result in the complete evacuation of Christian Arabs from the region, for political, social, psychological and religious reasons. Many Palestinian Christians, especially those with better education, live in the diaspora, in Lebanon, Jordan, Kuwait, as well as in Canada, USA, Brazil, Argentina and Australia.

Non-Arab Christians are mostly married to Jews or are the children of mixed marriages. Their exact number is unknown because many baptized immigrants are identified as Jews on their official papers, and they often have no relations with local churches. There is also a small group of persons known as Jewish Christians, coming from mixed marriages where the father or mother is ethnically Jewish. Some Catholic priests and laymen have formed a group called the work of St James the Apostle, consisting of from 200 to 300 members, which attempts to develop a community speaking Hebrew and using it in its liturgy. The presence of a minority of Christians among a Jewish majority constitutes a situation unique in the world and without precedent in history, at least since the first Christian communities of the early church.

A special problem for religions in Israel concerns the holy places. Within a radius of one kilometre in Jerusalem are the sacred sites of 3 great mono-theistic religions: the Wailing Wall from 1st-century Judaism, 2 mosques from the 7th and 8th centuries which make Jerusalem the third holy city of Islam after Mecca and Medina, and the Christian holy places. The most important of the latter are the Holy Sepulchre built by Constantine and often renovated, the Cenacle on the site of the Last Supper, the Tomb of the Virgin and the Chapel of the Ascension in Jerusalem, as well as the basilica and the Grotto of the Nativity at Bethlehem. The status of these holy places, especially the Christian ones, has always been the subject of controversy involving not uncommonly the great political powers, such as Tsarist Russia and France in the 19th century and Italy and Greece in the 20th. As a result of the rights and prerogatives established in 1757 by the Ottoman empire, and which contribute to the lack of Christian unity in the Holy Land, rival and privileged communities share the possession, disposition and exploitation of the holy places, to the exclusion of all other Christian groups. Thus, the Holy Sepulchre is in the possession of Armenian Apostolic, Greek Orthodox and Latin Catholics and the basilica in Bethlehem belongs to Greeks, Armenians, Copts and Syrians. In this way the holy places continue to present and project the spectacle of a divided Christianity.

**CATHOLIC CHURCH.** Catholics form the majority of the Christian population of Israel, and 3 different Catholic rites exist in the country. (1) Melkites are the most important group. The Greek Melkite patriarch of Antioch resides in Damascus, Syria and is represented by a patriarchal vicar in Jerusalem who has responsibility for East Jerusalem and the West Bank as well as a parish at Jaffa. The archdiocese of Acre serves the faithful in Galilee. (2) Latin Catholics are under the jurisdiction of the Latin Patriarchate of Jerusalem, which includes Israel, Jordan and Cyprus as well as the Catholic parish of Gaza. The patriarch lives in East Jerusalem. He is represented by 3 patriarchal vicars: at Nazareth for Israel, at Amman for Jordan and at Nicosia for Cyprus. The entire patriarchate in 1973 included 51,730 Catholics, 62 parishes or quasi-parishes, 77 secular priests, 255 religious priests, 1,192 sisters and 28 major seminarians. Of these parishes 13 were in Israel proper, one in East Jerusalem, one in Gaza, 15 on the West Bank, 22 in Jordan and 4 in Cyprus. (3) Maronites are under the archbishopric of Tyre in Lebanon, represented at Jaffa by a vicar-general who with 4 priests supervises 5 'Palestinian' parishes (Jaffa, Haifa, Nazareth, Jish and Acre). On the other hand, West Bank Catholics in Jerusalem, Bethlehem and Ramallah are dependent on the Maronite patriarch of Lebanon. The patriarch is represented by a patriarchal vicar at Jerusalem whose jurisdiction extends also to Jordan. The total number of Maronites in Israel proper is about 2,800.

ORTHODOX CHURCHES. The Greek Orthodox are the second largest Christian denomination in Israel. Nevertheless, their strength has steadily decreased since the early 19th century when their members made up nearly 80% of the entire Christian population of the Holy Land. Factors which have contributed to their decline are a shortage of priests, inadequate finances, conversions to other denominations, emigration, and a conflict between the hierarchy who are mostly Greeks and the priests and laity who are Palestinian Arabs. The church continues to claim precedence among Christian communities in the Holy Land as the direct successor to the first church in Jerusalem under James the Apostle. The patriarch is assisted by 14 titular archbishops.

Prior to 1917 the Russian Orthodox Church built numerous churches, convents, schools and hostels to cater for pilgrims from Russia to the Holy Land. At the present time there is an ecclesiastical mission under the jurisdiction of the patriarch of Moscow.

Four Oriental Orthodox or Monophysite churches have followings in Israel: Armenian, Coptic, Syrian and Ethiopian Orthodox. The largest is the Armenian Apostolic Church, led by a patriarch; the Copts and Syrians have archbishops and the Ethiopians a bishop.

PROTESTANT CHURCHES. Of active Protestant groups, the one with the oldest history is the Church of Scotland, which dates back to 1839 and continues to sponsor a school and 2 hostels. The Christian and Missionary Alliance opened 3 centres in 1890 and a fourth in 1911. At present it has a bookshop in Beersheba and serves an international congregation in Jerusalem.

The largest Protestant denomination in Israel today is the Baptist Convention which owes its origin to the arrival of Southern Baptist missionaries in 1911 but which undertook its greatest expansion in evangelism, education and social service after 1948. With a staff of 50 missionaries, this is the largest Southern Baptist mission in Europe and the Near East. Although 7 congregations are directly related to the Baptist Convention, 9 other Arab Baptist groups joined together in 1965 to form the Association of Baptist Churches in Israel. There are several other denominations also. Most are recent arrivals with very small followings. Jewish newspapers have as a result recently expressed concern about the proselytizing efforts of these bodies.

ANGLICAN CHURCH. In 1820 the London Church's Ministry among the Jews (CMJ), arrived in Jerusalem, where it continues work today with a few centres for worship, education, social relations and a book store. In 1851 the Church Missionary Society took up work among Arabs and built several hospitals and an orphanage. The Jerusalem and the East Mission began in 1888. The Anglican community developed considerably during the British mandate with the presence of large numbers of British personnel. However, Anglican membership was reduced by three-fourths following the exodus of Christians, mostly Arabs, in 1948. The Jerusalem Archbishopric was enlarged in 1957 to include 8 Near East and North African countries and in 1975 became the Episcopal Church in Jerusalem and the Middle East.

**CHURCH AND STATE.** While a constitution originally expected to be promulgated on 1 October 1948 was being prepared, the Provisional National Council which was acting as Provisional State Assembly declared in its proclamation of independence of 14 May 1948 that the State of Israel 'shall be founded on the principles of liberty, justice and peace as taught by the Prophets of Israel; it shall assure complete equality of social and political rights to all its citizens without distinction of belief, race or sex; it shall guarantee full freedom of conscience, worship, education and culture; it shall assure the protection and inviolability of the holy places and sanctuaries of all religions and respect the principles of the charter of the United Nations'.

The constitution has in fact still not been completed, but several fundamental laws dealing with religion have been adopted by the parliament, the Knesset. Among these is the Law of Return of 1950 which accords to all Jews anywhere the right to establish themselves in Israel and become naturalized Israelis. In May 1971 a new law permitted the granting of Israeli nationality to all Jews in other nations who express a desire to emigrate to Israel. There was also a law in 1952, giving to non-Jews Israeli nationality under conditions similar to immigration policy in other countries. In the 1950 law, the term 'Jew' was not defined, and this remained the case

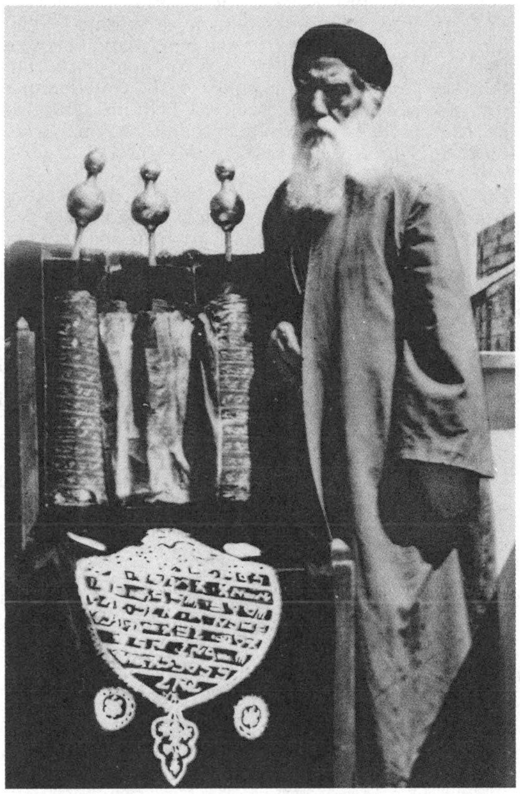

**Samaritans.** A Samaritan (Shamerim) priest based on Holon, near Tel Aviv, with ancient manuscript of Torah. This Jewish sect dates from the 8th century BC.

until in 1970 the Knesset adopted the following definition: 'A Jew is one who was born of a Jewish mother and has not been converted to any other religion, or one who, not being Jewish, is converted to Judaism'. In this way a Jew who becomes a Christian is refused the status of Jew but not the convinced atheist. The Supreme Court has made several pronouncements on the definition of this term, notably in 1962 when it dismissed a suit against the Minister of the Interior by a Catholic priest, Father Daniel (Oswald Ruffeissen), who was originally Jewish, but to whom the minister had refused to grant citizenship. In January 1970, a month before the passage of the law defining the term, the Supreme Court rendered a liberal verdict granting the status of Jews (always in the ethnic sense of the term) to the children of a marine officer who had been originally a Jew by religion, was now married to a Christian, and who both now declared themselves to be atheists. Israel's religious parties desire that conversions to Judaism be refused recognition unless they are conducted by an Orthodox rabbi according to a long and complex procedure, which would have the effect of excluding from the benefit of the Law of Return those who for the most part are of Jewish background but do not have Jewish mothers and who were converted by liberal or 'conservative' (in the sense of American Judaism) rabbis, these latter, (especially American rabbis) being considered too lenient. Nevertheless, neither the Knesset nor the government has shown any interest in following these traditionalist circles.

Before the establishment of the State of Israel the law defined the personal status of citizens primarily in Islamic terms, and this law is still partially in effect. This follows basically the Ottoman millet system, in that each person is regarded as under the authority of his religious community in matters concerning marriage, divorce and funerals. The recognized religious authority reports marriages to the Ministry of the Interior who then registers them. There is thus no civil marriage in Israel, and agnostic or atheist citizens must submit to religious laws. Moreover, mixed marriages exist neither in rabbinical law nor in Muslim law, and conversion of one party is required if a mixed marriage is to take place involving these religions. The millet system also involves the recognition of legal status for religious communities. Those religions which were recognized under the Turks have kept this status in the State of Israel. In addition to Orthodox Judaism and Islam, these include the following Christian communities: Greek Orthodox, Melkite, Latin, Maronite, Armenian and Coptic. Since the proclamation of the State of Israel in 1948, 3 others have been recognized: Druzes (1957), Anglicans (1970) and Baha'i (1971). Protestant churches have no legal status which means, as one example, that church weddings are not recognized by the state. The United Christian Council in Israel is serving as an intermediary in negotiations concerning this. The legal situation as it existed under the Ottoman regime and the British mandate prevails also in the domain of the activities, properties and legal rights of religious communities, and the State of Israel continues to support it.

Within the government, religious questions are the responsibility of the Ministry of Religions (Misrad Hadatoth). One of its tasks is to inform religious communities as to how many of their members are converted to other religions. A law forbids changes of religion for young people under 18 years of age unless both parents consent to it. The ministry has a Department of Muslim Affairs and a Department of Christian Affairs. Within the same ministry is also the Keren Yaldenou, a body whose aim is to prevent Jewish children from being influenced by Christian institutions.

The internal policies of Israel primarily revolve around 3 questions with important religious implications: (1) the relationship between religious leaders and lay persons, which will undoubtedly have a growing importance in the years to come and which will probably result in a formula somewhere between the 2 extremes of a theocracy and complete separation of religion and state; (2) the economic tension between socialism and liberalism, which overlays to a great extent the conflict between Sefardi Orientals and Ashkenazis; and (3) relations between Jews and Arabs, which is affected both by the government's policies and by the external situation. Concerning these last 2 questions, a significant role has been played by the World Conference of Christians for Palestine, with headquarters in Paris. This conference was created to help explain the situation of Palestinian Christians, and it has in fact sensitized Christians across the world to the problem involved.

It is also necessary to stress the importance of the function performed by the Greek Catholic Church in defence of the rights of the Palestininan people, which has manifested itself in 2 different ways. First has been the activity of Msgr Joseph Raya, archbishop of Haifa (Acre) from 1968 to 1974, who is well-known for his public interventions in favour of Palestinians forced out of their villages. In 1974 he felt obliged to withdraw from his position as archbishop due to pressures from the patriarchate and the Vatican because he accepted, in spite of everything, the reality of the Jewish state and especially because of his declaration that Jerusalem should remain under Israeli control. A second important person has been Msgr Capucci, of Syrian origin and patriarchal vicar of Jerusalem, who has supported the Palestinian resistance and who was arrested on 18 August 1974 and sentenced to 15 years in prison. The prelate denied the Israeli accusation that, at the moment of his arrest, he was transporting arms in his vehicle; but he also refused to answer questions at his trial because he rejected the competence of the court, calling it an 'occupation court'.

A certain tension has existed between Christians and Jews since 1972 due to attacks on Christian institutions committed by extremist Jews linked to rabbi Meir Kahane's Jewish Defence League. The Israeli government has vigorously condemned such attacks, but it has also expelled since 1972 about 10 Christian missionaries and put such pressure on others that they have left the country.

**INTERDENOMINATIONAL ORGANIZATIONS.** The United Christian Council in Israel was founded in 1957 and through its 14 sub-committees carries out studies on Christian problems in Israel, has a literature programme with emphasis on the use of Hebrew in Bible studies, works on liturgy and music, maintains an educational programme, updates Christian tourist information, and prepares contingency plans for emergencies in any area affecting the Christian minority. On the Catholic side, the Latin patriarchate of Jerusalem has an ecumenical commission.

There are 3 co-operative ecumenical centres dedicated to contacts between the churches. (1) The Ecumenical Institute for Advanced Theological Studies (EIATS), located at Tantur between Jerusalem and Bethlehem, was begun in 1971 in accordance with a wish expressed by pope Paul VI on his trip to the Holy Land in 1964. The first director is a Catholic but those who follow will be successively Protestant then Orthodox. The institute is devoted especially to a study of the 'mystery of salvation' in all its aspects. (2) The Ecumenical Theological Research Fraternity in Israel was founded in Jerusalem in 1967. It brings together specialists of different Christian confessions to jointly study aspects of Judeo-Christian relations. (3) The Near East Christian Centre, begun by the White Fathers in 1951, is a research centre dedicated to the renewal of the churches of the Near East and the furthering of ecumenical contacts among them. It has a library of 30,000 volumes. Also of importance is the ecumenical role played by the first Catholic university in the Holy Land, Bethlehem Regional University, described in this survey under Palestine.

Five further groups are dedicated to interreligious dialogue. (1) The Israeli Committee for Religious Understanding (or, Interface) (Ha'vad lehavana bein-datith) was begun in Jerusalem in 1960 and provides a meeting ground for representatives of Judaism, Islam and Christianity. (2) The House of Isaiah (Beit Yeshayaou) in Jerusalem is a centre for Jewish studies run by Dominicans, with links at the Hebrew University of Jerusalem. (3) The Rainbow, an English-speaking group with 20 members founded in Jerusalem in 1965, brings together Jews and Christians of diverse tendencies. (4) The Tel-Aviv Inter-religious Group (Ha'houg bein dati) is a Hebrew-speaking body consisting of about 100 members who engage in Jewish-Christian dialogue. (5) The Oasis of Peace (Neveshalom), a community of Jews, Christians and Muslims who engage in dialogue and prayer, was founded in Jerusalem in 1972. In 1973 it was attempting to establish a kibbutz for work in the former no-man's-land between East and West Jerusalem. Also of note is the fact that the 5th annual meeting of the International Catholic-Jewish Committee was held in Jerusalem in March 1976, previous meetings having taken place in Paris, Marseilles, Antwerp and Rome.

**BROADCASTING.** The Israel Broadcasting Authority accepts Jewish religious programmes and to a much smaller extent Christian programmes. Network I has a daily Old Testament reading and a 10-minute commentary, and on Saturday 5 minutes of psalm chanting. Television ends daily with scripture or other sacred literature verse, usually one or 2 minutes in length. IBA radio has church music on Sundays, a programme for the Christian community entitled 'Music for Sunday'. There are a number of foreign international stations easily received in Israel: ELWA (Liberia), FEBA (Seychelles), RVOG (Ethiopia) until 1977, TWR (Monaco), and the Protestant programmes over CBC (Cyprus). All these stations transmit to Israel in Arabic only, except TWR who also transmit in Hebrew and Yiddish for 45 minutes a week. TWR also has its own studio preparing Christian programmes in Hebrew and Yiddish.

## BIBLIOGRAPHY


*Annuaire de l'Eglise Catholique en Terre Sainte, 1972.* Jerusalem: Franciscan Printing Press, 1972.

*Asian and African Jews in the Middle East, 1860–1971: annotated bibliography.* Ed H. J. Cohen & Z. Yehuda. Leiden: Brill, 1976. 453p.

*Christianity in the Holy Land, past and present.* S. P. Colbi. Tel Aviv: Am Hassefer, 1969. 272p.

'Judaism', Part 1 in A. J. Arberry (ed), *Religion in the Middle East: 3 religions concord & conflict*, Vol. 1 (Cambridge: Cambridge University Press, 1969), p.3–235.

'Les forces religieuses d'Israël', A. Chouraqui, *Evidences* (1957), 44–47.

'Panorama religieux d'Israël', S. Z. Klausner, *Revue Nouvelle*, XIX, 1 (1963), 74–83.

*Religious life and communities.* Israel Pocket Library. Jerusalem: Keter Publishing House, 1974. 214p.

*Renaissance des Eglises locales: Israël.* R. Laurentin. Paris: Seuil, 1973. 172p.


TABLE 2. ORGANIZED CHURCHES AND DENOMINATIONS IN ISRAEL (excluding East Jerusalem)

| Official name 1 | Begun 2 | Type 3 | Counc 4 | Congs 5 | Adults 6 | Affiliated 7 | Names, notes, and other statistics (see Codebook) 8 |
|---|---|---|---|---|---|---|---|
| Armenian Apostolic P of Jerusalem | c 500 | O Arm | Ew.N. | 3 | 400 | 600 | *Gregorians.* 2 Vicariates; Haifa, Jaffa. 1950–73: 90% emigrated. |
| Association of Baptist Chs in Israel | 1965 | P Bap | T...K | 9 | 250 | 700 | Scattered Arab congs, loose link with Baptist Conv. 2n,G=4.6%pa,1p,W=40%,16Y,10z. |
| Baptist Convention in Israel | 1911 | P Bap | T...K | 7 | 315 | 1,000 | *BCI.* M=SBC(USA). 5n,50f,1j,2k,1r,1s(Central Training Centre),1 art gallery,23Y. |
| Bible Evangelistic Mission | 1927 | P Pen | ....K | 1 | 30 | 100 | *BEM.* Linked with Pentecostal Jewish Mission (UK). 1k (Bakaa, Jerusalem). |
| Brethren Assemblies | | P CBr | x.... | 5 | 250 | 500 | *Christian Brethren. Plymouth (Open) Brethren.* M=CMML(UK). 4f. |
| **Catholic Church in Israel:** | 1099 | R LEr | O...P | 46 | 26,400 | 41,900 | *Hakenessia Hacatholit.* Includes 2,800 Maronites. C=17+2+32. 35n,39x,461w. |
| P Jerusalem (*Latin*) | 1099 | R Lat | Os | 15 | 6,900 | 11,000 | Patriarchate restored 1847. 75% Arabs, 25% non-Arabs. Nazareth, et alia. 7n,456w. |
| AD Akka (Acre) (*Melkite*) | 1753 | R Mel | Os | 31 | 19,500 | 30,900 | *St John of Acre and Galilee.* Arab laity, alien hierarchy. 28n,3x,2m,5w,1024Yy. |
| Christian & Missionary Alliance of I | 1890 | P Hol | xF..K | 2 | 25 | 100 | M=CMA(USA). Beersheba; also International Evangelical Ch (Jerusalem). 8f,1k,1Y. |
| Church of God of Prophecy | 1965 | P Pe3 | Z.... | 3 | 100 | 300 | M=CGP(USA). Memorial built on Horns of Hittin. |
| Church of Scotland in Israel | 1839 | P Ref | Rwc.K | 3 | 100 | 300 | Educational work, formerly hospital also. 1 school (205), 2 hospices. 11f. |
| Church of the Nazarene | 1921 | P Hol | xF..K | 2 | 30 | 100 | M=CoN(USA). Nazareth, Haifa. Arab congregations. 2m,4f,1t(92),W=70%. |
| Churches of Christ | | P Dis | x.... | 3 | 200 | 500 | M=CC(Non-Instrumental)(USA). West Jerusalem, Nazareth, Bat Yam. 1r(Galilee). |
| Coptic Orthodox Church: D Jerusalem | c 850 | O Cop | NwaN. | 2 | 200 | 300 | Egyptians. Jaffa, Nazareth (church built 1950). Under bishop in Jerusalem. 2n,2d. |
| Episcopal Ch in Jerusalem & the MEast | 1820 | A plu | Aw.NK | 5 | 600 | 900 | *D Jerusalem.* Formerly Jerusalem Archbishopric. 86% Arabs. M=CMS,CMJ,JEM. 8n,5x,27f,1s. |
| Ethiopian Orthodox Ch: D Jerusalem | c1172 | O Eth | Nwa.. | 1 | 40 | 50 | Under P Addis Ababa. Church and monastery in West Jerusalem. 12 monks. |
| **Greek Orth Patriarchate of Jerusalem** | 30 | O Ara | CW.N. | 30 | 10,000 | 17,000 | Decline. 99% Arab (laity and priests); 1% Greek (bishops and monks). P=60%,W=10%. |
| Isolated radio churches | c1950 | I rad | ..... | 50 | 500 | 1,100 | Isolated radio believers (Arabs, Jewish). R=300(TWR, Radio Vatican), T=10000(ICI). |
| Jehovah's Witnesses | c1920 | M Jeh | x.... | 4 | 100 | 500 | Active witnessing under way in Palestine by 1926, and in Israel from 1951. 10Y. |
| Messianic Assembly in Israel | 1948 | P Bap | ..... | 1 | 30 | 100 | M=American Messianic Fellowship (formerly Chicago Hebrew Mission). Jerusalem. 1f. |
| Norwegian Lutheran Mission | 1949 | P Lut | ....K | 5 | 100 | 200 | *Hakuesia Haluteranit.* M=NLM,LWF. Jewish Christians from Romania, Hungary. 2x,9f. |
| Russian Orthodox Church | 1848 | O Sla | Mwc.. | 5 | 100 | 200 | Ecclesiastical mission under P Moscow. Churches in Jaffa, Mt Carmel, Galilee. |
| Scandinavian Seamen's Church | 1949 | P Lut | ..... | 2 | 100 | 500 | For sailors in ports of Haifa, Ashdod. Visited by 6,000 seamen a year. |
| Seventh-day Adventist Church | 1932 | P Adv | x.... | 4 | 59 | 150 | *SDA, Israel Mission*, Southern European Union Mission. 2x,3mw,5t(102),W=93%,1Y. |
| Syrian Orth P of Antioch: D Jerusalem | 30 | O Syr | Dw.N. | 1 | 40 | 50 | *Jacobites.* Small community of Israeli adherents. HQ Damascus (Syria). |
| Other Protestant denominations | | P | ..... | | 2,500 | 5,000 | Total about 40 (see list below), mainly USA and European expatriates. |
| **Total affiliated (mid-1970)** | | | | **280** | **42,469** | **72,150** | **Total denominations (1970) . . . 63.** |
| **Total affiliated (mid-1975)** | | | | **290** | **46,300** | **78,600** | **Total denominations (1975) . . . 65.** |
| **Total affiliated (mid-1980)** | | | | **300** | **50,100** | **85,100** | **Total denominations (1980) . . . 67.** |

NOTES ON TABLE ABOVE

COLUMNS: for meanings and CODES (cols. 1, 3, 4, 8), see Codebook (Part 6). Column 1: **Boldface type** = church with over 10% of country's affiliated Christians.

NATIONAL COUNCILS (Column 4, 5th letter).

K = United Christian Council in Israel (UCCI).

OTHER PROTESTANT DENOMINATIONS. A certain number of USA and European bodies cater mainly for USA and European expatriate civilians. A number of other bodies, especially USA missions and denominations, have small local followings and church services, and so may be considered as denominations or para-denominations: American Association for Jewish Evangelism in Israel, American Baptist Association (1967; 1 Arab church), Assemblies of God, Children of God International, Christian Catholic Ch (USA; 1948), Ch of God (Seventh-day), Ev Missions to the Muslims (1964), Exclusive Brethren (Kelly-Continental), Finnish Missionary Society (1924), Independent Assemblies of God, Jews for Jesus movement (1,500 converts by 1973: 50% Jewish Christians from USA, registered as Jews in rabbinical courts, who work in Israel as evangelists; the other 50% are Israeli Jewish converts baptized in the Dead Sea or Lake Galilee), Mennonite Association in Israel (1953), Norwegian Pentecostal Mission, Slavic Gospel Association (1959), Swedish Free Mission, Swiss Pentecostal Mission, United Evangelical Chs, United Fundamentalist Ch (USA; 1952), World-Wide Missions (1961).

**PEOPLES** (ethnolinguistic). Christians: 81.8% Palestinian Arab, 8.0% Western European (French, Italian, German, British, USA), 3.9% Lebanese Arab, 2.0% Jewish (Hebrew), 1.3% Polish, 1.3% Hungarian, 0.8% Armenian, 0.4% Egyptian Arab, 0.2% Greek, 0.1% Ethiopian, 0.1% Syrian Arab, et alii.

COUNTRY-WIDE TOTALS

EVANGELIZATION (see Part 5). 1900: 24%. 1970: 66%. 1980: 81%. *Mass evangelism.* Among recent campaigns: March 1960, Billy Graham rallies in Haifa, Nazareth, Jaffa, Jerusalem (2,500 attenders, 350 enquirers). Subsequently many conferences held in Jerusalem have either been evangelistic or held evangelistic meetings. *Radiophonic evangelism.* TWR, Radio Vatican, RVOG, ELWA, RSB, ICI (about 10,000 enrolments).

FOREIGN MISSIONARIES AND PERSONNEL (nationals serving abroad) (1973). Total about 8 Roman Catholics in Cyprus, Morocco et alia.

FOREIGN MISSIONARIES AND PERSONNEL (aliens from abroad) (1973). Total 534. *From Western world.* 449: 300 Roman Catholics, 129 Protestants (about 40 in 15 USA societies, 30 in 4 UK societies, 18 in 2 Finland societies, 15 in 1 Sweden society, 12 in 2 Norway societies, 12 in 2 WGermany societies, 1 in 1 Canada society, 1 in 1 Denmark society), 15 Anglicans in 2 UK and 1 USA societies, about 5 Orthodox. *From Communist world.* 30: 20 Roman Catholics from Poland, about 10 Orthodox priests, monks and nuns. *From Third World.* 55: about 30 Roman Catholics, 10 Protestants, about 10 Orthodox priests and monks from Egypt, Ethiopia, Syria, 5 Anglican.

INSTITUTIONS (church-operated) (1973). Total 60, including 3 ecumenical centres, 7 higher schools, 21 medical centres (6 hospitals), 1 press, 4 religious communities, 10 research centres, 6 seminaries (3 Protestant, 2 RC, 1 Anglican).

PERIODICALS. About 80 titles.

PERSONNEL. About 764 (230 national, 534 foreign).

RELIGIOUS LIBRARIES. About 32.

SCRIPTURE DISTRIBUTION (1975). Annual totals: 9,363 Bibles (10% free, 79% subsidized, 10% commercial), 6,359 NTs (16% free, 68% subsidized, 16% commercial), 3,240 UBS portions, 23,470 UBS selections. *Translations completed.* In Hebrew: portion 1477, OT 1487, Bible 1599.

SERVICE AGENCIES. About 60, including AAJE, CEF, CELRA, CRS, EMMS, FOI, IHCA, IJS, MCC, OM, UCCI, URI, YMCA, YWCA.

ADDITIONAL DATA ON CHURCHES

CATHOLIC CHURCH IN ISRAEL. *Catholics.* Latins include 2,000 Polish and Hungarian Catholic refugees. Statistics for AD Akka include the 2,800 Maronites in Israel. *Annual baptisms.* (1972) 97.5% infant, 2.5% adult. *Priests.* Latin-rite: OFM (Custody) has 39 in Israel; also 3 OCD in parish work, and also priests in monastic life. Nationality: OFM (Custody): 50% Italians, 25% Spanish, 25% Canadians, French et alii. Priests of the Patriarchate: mostly Arabs. *Brothers.* OFM (Custody). *Sisters.* Latins: 456 in Israel. *Melkite religious congregations.* Priests: several Basilian Salvatorians in parish work, monks of Laure Netoufa (Lake Tiberias), Paulists. Sisters: Salvatorians, Nuns of the Annunciation (Nazareth), Little Sisters of Jesus, Carmelites. *Chaldean congregations.* Sisters: Dominicans of St Catherine of Siena. *Main Latin orders and congregations.* Priests: OFM, OCD, Sion Fathers, OP, SDB, OSB, Bétharram Fathers, Little Brothers of Jesus, AA, SJ, CP, CM, OCSO. Brothers: OH, FSC. Sisters (with over 50 members): St Joseph of the Apparition, Rosary Sisters (Palestinians), Franciscans of the Immaculate Heart of Mary, Cloistered Carmelites, St Charles Borromeo, N–D de Sion, Daughters of Charity. In addition to these orders and congregations at work, there is a large number of others which maintain a small or nominal presence in Israel. *Catholic organizations.* The Latin patriarchate forms part of the Latin Episcopal Conference of the Arab Regions (CELRA) which has its seat in Jerusalem and since 1967 has held its meetings in Beirut, Lebanon. Melkites are part of the Melkite Patriarchal Synod in Syria. There are no national associations of priests or brothers but one for sisters exists, the Union of Sisters of Israel. Lay movements include the Legion of Mary, Third Order Franciscans, Scouts and JEC.

The Holy See has no diplomatic relations with Israel. It is represented to the Catholic hierarchy by the Apostolic Delegation of Jerusalem and Palestine, with its seat in East Jerusalem. The apostolic delegate in Jerusalem is also pro-nuncio in Cyprus.

Catholic institutions are influential but not numerous. (1) The Bible School and French Archaeological School (Ecole Biblique et Ecole Archéologique Française), founded in Jerusalem by the OP in 1890, engages in teaching, research, biblical and oriental studies and archaeological excavation. With a library of 50,000 volumes, the school produces a quarterly journal and the Jerusalem Bible. (2) The Franciscan Biblical Institute, founded in Jerusalem by the OFM in 1924, is also involved in teaching, archaeological excavation and publication. (3) The Pontifical Biblical Institute, founded in Jerusalem by Jesuits in 1927, is a branch of the same institute in Rome and offers study courses. (4) Caritas Jerusalem, founded after the 1967 war, co-ordinates and distributes relief supplies. Its administrative council is composed of the heads of all West Bank Catholic communities, and supervises agricultural projects, equipment for manual workers, and dispensaries.

In education, in 1971 the Latin patriarchate was responsible for 3,240 students in Israel and Jordan. The Custody had responsibility for 993 students in East Jerusalem, 2,898 in Israel and 1,629 on the West Bank; Latin religious congregations had 10,677 students in Israel, the West Bank and East Jerusalem; Melkites had 564 students at Jerusalem and 1,727 in Galilee and on the West Bank; Maronites were responsible for 160 students in Israel; and Syrian Catholics had 79 students on the West Bank. These schools cover the whole spectrum from pre-primary to secondary and professional.

Medical and social action in 1971 included the following.

In Jerusalem there were 2 hospitals, 6 dispensaries, 6 orphanages, and one home for handicapped children and the aged. In Israel there were 3 hospitals, 9 dispensaries, 2 orphanages and one home for the aged. On the West Bank there were 5 hospitals, 22 dispensaries, 4 orphanages, 2 homes for the aged, one home for handicapped children and the Paul VI Ephphatha Institute for deaf-mute children.

GREEK ORTHODOX PATRIARCHATE OF JERUSALEM. There are 2 dioceses in Israel: Jerusalem, and Nazareth & Ptolemais. Main centres include Lod, Jaffa, Acre, Tiberias. The bishops, monks, several priests and a few laity are Greeks and still largely Greek citizens (as are also those in the Church of Sinai). Greeks total about 1% only, and Arabs 99%.

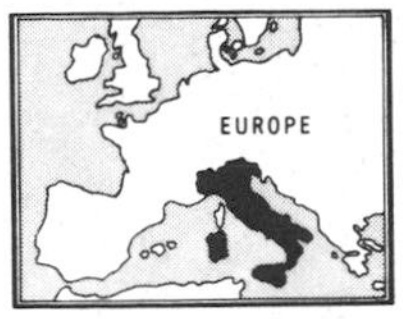


# ITALY

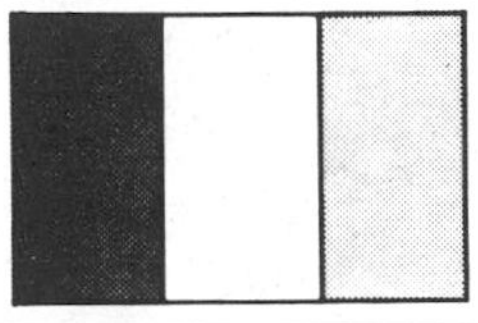

## SECULAR DATA

**STATE. Official name:** The Italian Republic (La Repubblica Italiana). Adjective of nationality: Italian.
**Flag** (shown above right): Green, white, and red bars.
**Area:** 301,225 sq.km. (116,304 sq.miles). Agricultural land: 58.1%.
**Government:** Parliamentary republic, since 1946 (1861 Kingdom of Italy proclaimed, 1923 fascist dictatorship, 1946 republic).
**Legislature:** Parliament: Senate, 232 members; Chamber of Deputies, 630 members.
**Official language:** Italian (*Italiano*).
**Chief cities:** capital Rome 2,799,840 (1971), Milan 1,724,170, Naples 1,232,880, Turin 1,177,940.
**Political divisions:** 20 Autonomous Regions (regioni), divided into Provinces (province) and Municipalities (comuni).
**Armed forces** (1976): Total 352,000 regular (234,100 conscripts): army 240,000, navy 42,000, air force 70,000 (296 combat aircraft). Reserves: 737,800. Paramilitary forces: 80,000 carabinieri.
**Foreign forces** (1973): 10,000 USA troops, falling to 3,000 by 1976.
**Dependencies** (semi-autonomous): Sardinia, Sicily.

**DEMOGRAPHY. Population:** 53,744,737 (census of 24.X.1971. For 1970–2000 (UN), see last row of Table 1). Population density (1975): 183/sq.km. (473/sq.mile). Under 15 years: 25%. Growth rate (1975–80): 0.47% per year (births 1.52%, deaths −1.01%, emigrants −0.04%). Life expectancy (1975–80): 72.7 years. Household size: 3.6 persons.
**Major languages:** Italian, German, French, Slovenian, Romansh, English, Albanian, Sardinian, Latin.
**Urban dwellers** (1970): 53.0%. Urban growth rate (1950–70): 1.9% per year.
**Labour force:** 35%.
**Refugees** (1977): From abroad, about 14,000 (13,000 from Eastern Europe, 700 from Chile).
**Tourists** (1974): 12,441,657. Arrivals at borders, including excursionists (1970): 33 million.

**ETHNOLINGUISTIC GROUPS:** 95.9% Italian (including 8.5% Sicilian), 2.2% Sardinian, 0.7% Romansh, 0.4% Austrian, 0.2% French, 0.2% Slovene, 0.2% Albanian, 0.1% Jewish, British (25,000), Greek (19,700), Gypsy (9,400), Catalonian, German, Croat, USA White, Chinese (1,200), & over 100 other nationalities.

**MONEY** (1977). **Monetary unit:** lira (= 100 centesimi); US$1 = L 875.00 (operational rate of exchange).
**National income per person:** US$2,442. Average annual family income: US$8,791.
**Inflation:** (1970–74) 10.0% per year (1975: consumer price index 185), (1976) 22% per year, (1977) 15% per year.
**Cost of living in capital** (1976): index 123 (Washington DC = 100). Daily cost of living: US$35.

**HEALTH.** Hospitals: 2,318 (568,520 beds). Doctors: 99,341. Lepers: 700. Blind: 110,000. Psychotics: 550,000. Criminals: about 2,000,000.

**EDUCATION.** Adult literacy: (1951) 86%, (1971) 94%. Education rate: 48%. Schools: 35,691. Universities: 73 (26 state).

**LITERATURE.** Annual new book titles (1973): 8,122. Periodicals: 8,153. Scientific journals: 1,530. Newspapers: 78 dailies, 119 non-daily.

**COMMUNICATION** (per 1,000 people). Phones: 230. Radios: 227. TV sets: 208. Daily newspaper circulation: 133 copies.

TABLE 1. RELIGIOUS ADHERENTS IN ITALY

| Year | 1900 | | mid-1970 | | Annual change, 1970–1980 | | | | mid-1975 | | mid-1980 | | 20 | |
|---|---|---|---|---|---|---|---|---|---|---|---|---|---|---|
| *Name* | *Adherents* | *%* | *Adherents* | *%* | *Natural* | *Conversion* | *Total* | *Rate* | *Adherents* | *%* | *Adherents* | *%* | *Adherents* | *%* |
| **Christians** | **32,903,000** | **99.7** | **48,657,800** | **90.8** | **239,426** | **−394,756** | **−155,330** | **−0.32** | **47,835,650** | **86.9** | **47,104,500** | **83.6** | **46,472,000** | **76.3** |
| professing | 32,903,000 | 99.7 | 48,657,800 | 90.8 | 239,426 | −394,756 | −155,330 | −0.32 | 47,835,650 | 86.9 | 47,104,500 | 83.6 | 46,472,000 | 76.3 |
| Roman Catholics | 32,872,700 | 99.6 | 48,476,800 | 90.5 | 238,341 | −401,326 | −162,985 | −0.34 | 47,618,820 | 86.5 | 46,846,950 | 83.2 | 46,132,500 | 75.8 |
| Spiritist Catholics | 1,650,000 | 5.0 | 2,000,000 | 3.7 | 9,910 | −12,910 | −3,000 | −0.15 | 1,980,000 | 3.6 | 1,970,000 | 3.5 | 1,830,000 | 3.0 |
| Evangelical Catholics | 31,300 | 0.1 | 366,073 | 0.7 | 1,857 | −464 | 1,393 | 0.38 | 371,000 | 0.7 | 380,000 | 0.7 | 586,000 | 1.0 |
| Protestants | 30,000 | 0.1 | 150,000 | 0.3 | 926 | 6,574 | 7,500 | 4.05 | 185,000 | 0.3 | 225,000 | 0.4 | 304,000 | 0.5 |
| Orthodox | 200 | 0.0 | 30,000 | 0.1 | 154 | −4 | 150 | 0.49 | 30,800 | 0.1 | 31,500 | 0.1 | 34,000 | 0.1 |
| Anglicans | 100 | 0.0 | 1,000 | 0.0 | 5 | 0 | 5 | 0.49 | 1,030 | 0.0 | 1,050 | 0.0 | 1,500 | 0.0 |
| affiliated | 32,903,000 | 99.7 | 48,657,800 | 90.8 | 239,426 | −394,756 | −155,330 | −0.32 | 47,835,650 | 86.9 | 47,104,500 | 83.6 | 46,472,000 | 76.3 |
| disaffiliated | −50,000 | −0.1 | −4,825,845 | −9.0 | −35,423 | −386,543 | −421,966 | 5.96 | −7,077,350 | −12.9 | −9,045,500 | −16.1 | −8,336,000 | −13.7 |
| doubly-affiliated | −61,600 | −0.2 | −588,973 | −1.1 | −3,064 | −6,113 | −9,177 | 1.46 | −630,430 | −1.1 | −680,750 | −1.2 | −952,500 | −1.6 |
| total practising | 31,257,850 | *95* | 38,926,240 | *80* | 189,147 | −407,620 | −218,473 | −0.58 | 37,790,160 | *79* | 36,741,510 | *78* | 32,530,400 | *70* |
| non-practising | 1,645,150 | *5* | 9,731,560 | *20* | 50,279 | 12,864 | 63,143 | 0.63 | 10,045,490 | *21* | 10,362,990 | *22* | 13,941,600 | *30* |
| Roman Catholics | 32,953,000 | 99.9 | 53,483,645 | 99.8 | 274,849 | −8,213 | 266,636 | 0.48 | 54,913,000 | 99.8 | 56,150,000 | 99.7 | 54,788,000 | 90.0 |
| Catholic pentecostals | 0 | 0.0 | 0 | 0.0 | 30 | 3,970 | 4,000 | 66.67 | 6,000 | 0.0 | 40,000 | 0.1 | 500,000 | 0.8 |
| Protestants | 60,000 | 0.2 | 430,566 | 0.8 | 2,227 | 4,996 | 7,223 | 1.56 | 464,000 | 0.8 | 502,800 | 0.9 | 650,000 | 1.1 |
| Evangelicals | 20,000 | 0.1 | 380,000 | 0.7 | 2,102 | 6,898 | 9,000 | 2.14 | 420,000 | 0.8 | 470,000 | 0.8 | 640,000 | 1.1 |
| Marginal Protestants | 800 | 0.0 | 85,307 | 0.2 | 455 | 814 | 1,269 | 1.39 | 91,000 | 0.2 | 98,000 | 0.2 | 220,000 | 0.4 |
| Orthodox | 200 | 0.0 | 30,000 | 0.1 | 154 | 6 | 160 | 0.52 | 30,800 | 0.1 | 31,600 | 0.1 | 34,000 | 0.1 |
| Catholics (non-Roman) | 500 | 0.0 | 32,900 | 0.1 | 123 | −3 | 120 | 0.36 | 33,600 | 0.1 | 34,100 | 0.1 | 37,000 | 0.1 |
| Anglicans | 100 | 0.0 | 10,000 | 0.0 | 5 | 0 | 5 | 0.05 | 10,030 | 0.0 | 10,050 | 0.0 | 11,500 | 0.0 |
| Third-World indigenous | 0 | 0.0 | 200 | 0.0 | 100 | 300 | 400 | 40.00 | 1,000 | 0.0 | 4,200 | 0.0 | 20,000 | 0.0 |
| Non-religious | 50,000 | 0.2 | 3,740,000 | 7.0 | 29,133 | 361,407 | 390,540 | 6.71 | 5,820,400 | 10.6 | 7,654,400 | 13.6 | 12 150,000 | 20.0 |
| Atheists | 10,000 | 0.0 | 1,071,000 | 2.0 | 6,334 | 32,966 | 39,300 | 3.11 | 1,265,500 | 2.3 | 1,464,000 | 2.6 | 2,130,000 | 3.5 |
| Muslims | 1,000 | 0.0 | 43,000 | 0.1 | 225 | 25 | 250 | 0.56 | 45,000 | 0.1 | 45,500 | 0.1 | 49,000 | 0.1 |
| Jews | 35,000 | 0.1 | 37,000 | 0.1 | 190 | 0 | 190 | 0.50 | 38,000 | 0.1 | 38,900 | 0.1 | 42,000 | 0.1 |
| Baha'is | 0 | 0.0 | 4,200 | 0.0 | 22 | 18 | 40 | 0.91 | 4,400 | 0.0 | 4,600 | 0.0 | 6,000 | 0.0 |
| Buddhists | 0 | 0.0 | 2,000 | 0.0 | 10 | 0 | 10 | 0.49 | 2,050 | 0.0 | 2,100 | 0.0 | 2,000 | 0.0 |
| Other religionists | 1,000 | 0.0 | 10,000 | 0.0 | 60 | 340 | 400 | 3.33 | 12,000 | 0.0 | 14,000 | 0.0 | 25,000 | 0.0 |
| **Country's population** | **33,000,000** | **100.0** | **53,565,000** | **100.0** | **275,400** | **0** | **275,400** | **0.50** | **55,023,000** | **100.0** | **56,319,000** | **100.0** | **60,876,000** | **100.0** |

COLUMNS, ROWS. For meanings and definitions, see Codebook (Part 6). Note that, by definition, total 'Christians' = professing + crypto-Christians, which also = affiliated + nominal Christians; and, total 'affiliated' = affiliated Roman Catholics + affiliated Protestants (+ the other 4 major blocs), *minus* doubly-affiliated persons, *minus* disaffiliated persons. Percentages may not always total exactly, due to rounding.
CENSUSES. **1931:** 99.6% Roman Catholics. The religion question has generally not been asked in government censuses.
POLLS. A number of public-opinion polls and sample surveys since 1940 have included religion. *Religious preference.* February 1970: 90% Roman Catholics, 9% non-religious and atheists, 1% Protestants. Some results for practice are given below.

NOTES ON RELIGIONS
AFFILIATED. By adding up diocesan totals in *Annuario Pontificio* (as is done in Table 2 below), it may been seen that (as is shown in the table above) the Roman Catholic Church in the 1960s and 1970s claimed 99.8% of the total population as affiliated members, on the grounds that that number were, or had once been, baptized Catholics and were still on the church's rolls. However, as elaborated below, in 1975 over 600,000 were also Protestants or other Christians and so were doubly-affiliated, and over 7 million regarded themselves as having disaffiliated completely from Christianity and were now non-religious (agnostics) and atheists. Subtracting these 2 groups from the aggregate totals claimed by the churches produces the figures on the line 'affiliated', i.e. 47.8 million distinct individuals in 1975.
ATHEISTS. Partito Comunista Italiano (PCI) (legal; split on Sino-Soviet issue): membership (1943) 6,000, (1951) 2,300,000 (plus 463,000 in youth federation), (1970) 1,596,000 in PCI (decline of 13,000 per year), 110,785 in FCGI (Federation of Italian Communist Youth); (1974, PCI) 1,622,861; (1976, PCI) 1.7 million; Communist voters (election of 1921) 4.6% of all votes, (VI.1946) 4,356,686 (19% of all votes), (V.1958) 6,704,454 (22.7% of all votes), (7.V.1972) 9,085,927 (27.2% of all votes), (20.VI.1976) 10,631,871 (33.8% of all votes) winning 116 seats in the Senate, and 12,620,509 (34.4% of all votes) winning 227 seats in the Chamber of Deputies. In 1976 the PCI was still the largest non-ruling Communist party in the world. Of Communist party members, 20% are estimated to be professing atheists, 40% non-religious, and 40% professing Catholics (including a number of priests and nuns), this latter despite clear statements in 1975 by the pope and the Italian Episcopal Conference that 'One cannot be simultaneously Marxist and Christian' (CEI, 15 December 1975). Communist militants fell from 8% of the PCI in 1955 to 5% (90,000) by 1966. Of Communist voters, 30% are agnostics, 70% Catholics. The highest % Communist vote is in the former papal states, due to their long anti-clerical history. The south with its depressed rural areas also has a high % Communist vote but this is found together with the highest traditional religious practice (processions, etc). A poll survey in 1974 (Doxa) found 2.2% of the whole country's population to be militant atheists (men 3.4%, women 1.1%), concentrated mainly in the northeast.
BAHA'IS. La Fede Baha'i. Entered before 1921. Local spiritual assemblies: 1964, 16; 1973, 28, including centres in 15 cities.
BUDDHISTS. In 5 centres. As well as the Associazione Buddista Italiana (HQ Florence), there are Tantric centres and a Centro di Illuminazione Lamaista (in Rome).
CATHOLIC PENTECOSTALS (or, Catholic charismatics). The charismatic renewal began in Rome in 1971 among foreigners, and by 1977 had involved numerous Italian bishops, clergy and nuns. Totals (January 1974): 450 involved adults (over 15 years old) in 7 prayer groups; total charismatic community including children, 1,000. On Pentecost Sunday 1975, the pope addressed and celebrated mass with 20,000 persons (50% charismatics from 58 countries) in St Peter's Basilica in Rome. In January 1976 there were numerous groups in Rome, Turin (200 in 1 group), and over 15 other cities. Regional groups and conferences then began to proliferate; in October 1977, over 2,000 gathered for a regional charismatic conference in Salerno cathedral with widespread radio/TV coverage.
DISAFFILIATED. This term is used here to describe dechristianized persons who, although baptized Roman Catholics and therefore regarded by the Catholic Church as still affiliated to it (and hence enumerated in Table 2 as such), have recently withdrawn or disaffiliated themselves completely from Christianity and now profess to be either non-religious (agnostics) or atheists. Because their statistics represent a duplication, they are shown in the table above as a negative quantity (with a minus sign). The vast majority of these 7 million or so persons in 1975 are in and around the so-called 'Red region' in the northeast, the heavily-communist regions of Emilia-Romagna, Lombardia, Veneto, Marche, Umbria and part of Tuscany, where polls show that at least 4% of the population are militant atheists and about 20% profess to be non-religious or have no religion. Despite this, Catholic dioceses claim virtually the whole population; the archdiocese of Bologna, for instance, reports in *AP 1975* a total population of 974,279 within its borders, out of whom 970,375 are baptized Catholics (99.6%). The table above incorporates all of these data and interpretations.
DOUBLY-AFFILIATED. The term covers those affiliated to, or claimed by, both the Catholic Church and also a church termed Evangelica by state or society (Protestant, Anglican, marginal Protestant) or a Catholic (non-Roman) or Orthodox church, i.e. baptized Catholics who have recently become Evangelicals or others. Because their statistics represent a duplication, they are shown in the table as a negative quantity (with a minus sign).
EVANGELICAL CATHOLICS. This term is used here to describe persons who are affiliated to churches termed by the state Evangelica (Protestant, Anglican, or marginal Protestant churches), but who in censuses or polls are regarded by state and society as, or who profess to be, Roman Catholics.
JEWS. In 22 communities, mainly in Rome, Milan, Florence and Trieste. Ashkenazis in the north, Sefardis in central Italy.
MUSLIMS. Including 25,000 refugees after World War II from Albania, Bulgaria, Hungary, Yugoslavia, 15,000 university students of various nationalities, diplomats and technical personnel.
OTHER RELIGIONISTS. Small numbers adhering to a large number of groups, including Japanese New-Religionists (Soka Gakkai in Rome, Florence and Naples since 1960, with 400 adherents by 1975), Theosophy (Theosophical Society, with in 1975 24 Lodges with 639 members), Rosicrucianism (Rosacroce, with 4 AMORC centres), Alaya, Yogasangha and others. Freemasons in Italy are, largely, openly hostile to Christianity and operate as a quasi-religion. ISKCON (Hare Krishna) operates 1 centre and a farm; and Ananda Marga has several centres.
PRACTISING CHRISTIANS. In the years 1744–53, 99.6% of the urban population were regularly practising Catholics, and 99.9% in rural areas. In 1880–82, practice varied from 82.3% to 77.6% in different areas. *Easter practice.* 1952: Mantova region, 60%. 1957: Diocese of Padova, 78.8%. 1966: urban 50%, rural 58%. *Church attendance.* June 1959: 57% of population attend at least weekly, 24% once in a while, 9% only on major festivals, 5% never, 3% non-religious. February 1970: 12% of population attend church several times a week, 44% once a week (only 6% taking communion every week), 30% from time to time, 5% never, 9% non-religious and atheists. 1971: mass attenders in Rome 38% weekly (women 50%, men 33%), 34% more than once a month. 1974: Italian adults over 14 (sample of 2,000 in 150 areas throughout Italy; Instituto Doxa-EP): 54.4% regularly-practising believers, 32.9% non-practising believers, 10.5% non-religious (but not opposed to religion), 2.2% militant atheists (opposed to religion on principle). 1975: mass attenders in Rome 40% weekly. 1977: Sunday mass attenders 28% regularly

(men 18%, women 38%), 19% fairly regularly, 33% rarely, 20% never. Protestants: church attendance weekly is much higher, around 70%. A detailed presentation and analysis of Catholic practice in Italy are given in S. Acquaviva, 'Italy', in H. Mol (ed), *Western religion* (1972), p. 305–324. *Pilgrims*. During the

1975 Holy Year, 8,370,000 pilgrims visited Rome and Vatican City. Other pilgrimage centres in Italy include the cathedral of Turin with its Shroud (3.3 million pilgrims when exposed for 43 days in September–October 1978).
SPIRITIST CATHOLICS. Nominal Catholics in the rural south

who follow spiritism, magical practices and traditional pre-Christian pagan customs and beliefs syncretized with Catholicism. THIRD-WORLD INDIGENOUS. In about 5 denominations by 1976 (see Table 2).

**Chiesa Cattolica in Italia.** Cathedral of Archdiocese of Pisa with (left) baptistery and (right) campanile (the Leaning Tower).

## NON-CHRISTIAN RELIGIONS. Spiritism continues

to exist in Italy, especially among southern peasants. It is a remnant of the old religion (*la vecchia religione*) with its emphasis on magic and spirit communication, as well as a strong belief in fate (*destino*) believed to be controllable by magical practices. The most renowned medium in Italian history was Eusapie Polladino who plied her art in Naples at the turn of the century, but other lesser-known figures exist in many Italian villages. Today the practices of traditional and pagan religion are so intertwined with Catholicism, especially its religious festivals and veneration of saints, that it is impossible to separate the two. Indeed virtually all spiritists claim also to be Catholics.

**Islam** is the professed religion of some 44,000 Muslims (1973), of whom 25,000 came for political reasons from Albania, Yugoslavia, Bulgaria and Hungary after World War II and continue to live in refugee camps near Venice, Trieste, Naples, Capobasso and Latina; some 15,000 are university students of different nationalities; 2,000 are residents, with their families, employed as staff members of FAO, and various airlines, businesses and professions; in addition to 2,000 members of diplomatic and consular offices, also with their families. The construction of a mosque in Rome, long opposed by the Vatican in its concern to maintain the 'special character' of the city as the world centre of Catholicism in accordance with the concordat of 1929, was finally sanctioned by the Holy See in 1974, with the proviso that specific conditions concerning its location and external dimensions be observed. A mosque flanked by a Muslim cultural centre is expected to be built on the edge of the city by 1985. Rome already has 3 Islamic organizations: the Islamic Cultural Centre of Italy (Centro Islamico Culturale d'Italia), the Islamic Union in the West (Unione Islamica in Occidente) and the Centre for Islamic Publications and Studies (Centro Editoriale Studi Islamici, CESI). The first 2 provide social services to Muslims, while the latter is an independent body begun in 1972 with the aim of making Islam better known and providing opportunities for dialogue with Christianity, in order to further understanding, justice and peace. It produces a bulletin entitled *CESI: Agenzia d'Informazione Islamica*.

**Judaism** is represented in 22 communities with a total of 37,000 members in 1973. The number declined during the fascist period from 47,485 Jews in 1931 to 35,146 in 1939. Jews were forced out of public employment and those who had entered the country after 1919 were forced to leave. In 1943 Jews of the

north and centre, where the Germans had gained control, were systematically seized, and more than 1,000 were exterminated at Auschwitz. At the end of the war there were only 29,117 left in the country. Of some 26,300 Jewish refugees from central and eastern Europe who passed through Italy, only a few remained permanently. The civil rights of Jews were restored after the war, and they received support as immigrants from Libya, Egypt and other countries of the Middle East as well as from certain European countries, particularly Hungary.

The principal Jewish communities are located in Rome (with 15,000), Milan (9,500), Florence (1,400) and Trieste (1,200), with very few found in southern Italy. Sefardis predominate in central Italy, Ashkenazis in the north. There is also in Rome a very small community of Jews of the Italian rite dating back to pre-Christian times, whose influence is evident in the liturgy of the Sefardic synagogues of Rome. All Italian synagogues are traditional and the 2 principal rabbinical schools are in Rome and Turin. The Jewish educational system is recognized by the state and follows the official programme in addition to accenting Jewish concerns. The principal co-ordinating organization is the Union of Italian Israelite Communities (Unione delle Comunità Israelitiche Italiane) in Rome which organizes cultural activities and represents Jewish interests before government. Religious matters are under the jurisdiction of the Italian Rabbinical Council. In Milan is located the Centre for Contemporary Hebrew Documentation (Centro di Documentazione Ebraica Contemporanea) which undertakes research concerning anti-Semitic persecutions and Jewish participation in the war-time Resistance.

**Buddhism** is also present. Although still sporadic, the Communità Buddista Italiana is in the process of formation. The following groups and study centres are active: Zendo Rinzai in Rome; Zen Sôto in Milan; Centre for Zen Buddhist Studies on the island of Murano near Venice; Ljanna Tibetan Buddhist Centre in Rome; and Association for Buddhist Studies in Turin.

## CHRISTIANITY. Christianity came to Rome prior

to the first visits of either the apostles Peter or Paul. During the first 2 centuries, periodic persecutions against Christians took place, as internal conflicts and barbarian invasions increased. In 324 the emperor Constantine officially recognized Christianity as the state religion and moved his capital to Constantinople, the division between the eastern and western Roman

empire being completed by 395. As Lombards and Goths continued to push from the north, Rome was sacked and the emperor deposed in 476. Theological disputes, exemplified by Arianism and Manicheism, further weakened the structure of Christianity, while such northern bishops as Ambrose of Milan (374) contributed to the strengthening of the western church and Benedict of Nursia (c500) initiated monasticism in the west. In 752 the Roman pope appealed to Pepin of France for protection, and in 800 Charlemagne was crowned Holy Roman emperor. Sicily and southern Italy fell to the Muslims, while Hungarians began pressing from the northeast. Otto I of Germany re-established the Holy Roman empire in 962, and from then until the Napoleonic invasion of 1796, Italy was the scene of constant power conflicts between the papacy and the growing political powers to the north: Germans and Normans during the 11th and 12th centuries, French during the 13th and 14th centuries, Spanish during the 15th and 16th centuries, followed by the Austrian Hapsburgs. Such city-states as Venice, Bologna and Florence, which became flourishing centres of trade and the arts largely as a result of the Crusades, also entered into the power struggle.

The beginning of the second millenium AD saw the final separation of Greek and Roman Christianity (1054) and the rise of such western pre-Reformation movements as that of Peter Waldo (1173) and his Waldenses in southeastern France and northern Italy. With France's reascendency, the papacy was taken to Avignon in 1309, and this was followed by the schism of rival popes during 1378–1417. The success of Luther and Calvin in the 16th century contributed to the growth of the Waldenses in northern Italy during the 16th century, but this was quickly extinguished by the Counter-Reformation following the Council of Trent (1545–1563) and new reforming bodies, the Capuchins (1525) and Jesuits (1540).

Following the Napoleonic conquest (1796–1814), the Austrian Hapsburgs again attempted to re-establish the power of Italy's former ruling families, but the Risorgimento movement continued to grow throughout the century, resulting in the eventual unification of Italy under Victor Emmanuel I in 1870 and the emergence of the Holy See as a state separate from Italy. The first Protestant missionaries began to enter Italy during the 1860s.

CATHOLIC CHURCH. In Italy, 99% of the population are baptized Roman Catholics, 95% of all children receive first communion, 82% receive confirmation and 99.5% are married in the church, though this latter figure is beginning to decrease. Italy is thus a country with a fundamentally Catholic culture, insofar as this religion historically and psychologically forms the foundation for the life of the people. While these figures demonstrate fidelity to many traditional religious rites, other statistics raise questions regarding the degree of Catholic practice. Only 6% take communion every Sunday, 50% of the children are given no catechetical instruction, and 30% of the population do not receive the sacrament of extreme unction before death. Of those attending Sunday mass, 41% are under 17 years of age and 31% are over 65, with the majority of the 28% in between being women. For the most part, those attending Sunday mass are farmers, artisans, technicians and clerks. The almost total absence of manual workers and the high proportion of middle-income participants suggest a certain identification of Catholicism with the bourgeois classes.

In a survey of the sub-cultures within Italian Catholicism, S. Burgalassi distinguishes 5 strata of society: (1) the indifferent sub-culture, representing a major and growing portion of the population (55–60%), mostly men (77%) and adults (75%) of higher income and education (55%), found primarily in cities (72%) in the centre of the country (64%) and the north (11%), which is more agnostic than opposed to religion and pays virtually no attention to the church or what it says; (2) the magical-sacred sub-culture, representing a minority (20%) of mostly rural people (93%), of advanced years (60% over 50 years of age), with modest cultural attainment (58%) and generally reduced income, who are characterized by high weekly mass attendance (70 to 75%), attachment to private devotions, utilitarian attitudes, fatalism (especially in the south), conservatism, and an absence of social involvement; in addition to a large number of priests (44%) who are extremely traditional and legalistic in attitude; (3) the official sub-culture, including 15% of the population and 46% of all priests, who are realistically oriented to the present, obedient to pope and bishops, who adjust to change in social and religious life and advocate reforms in church life and organization; (4) the atheistic sub-culture, consisting of 5% of all Italians and about 20% of university students (27% of the Catholic University of Milan), who are predominantly male (92%), adult (78%), urban (78%), upper class (64%) with higher income (60%), located in the centre (54%) and north (31%) of Italy, whose individual and social involvement is commendable but whose religious practice, if any, is sporadic; and (5) the prophetic sub-culture, including about 5% of the population and 10% of all clergy, consisting mostly of students and workers who are mainly young idealists (70%), oriented to the future and actively engaged in work for others (86%) against misery and social injustice for the sake of the gospel.

There has also been a breaking up of the monolithic nature of the church in Italy, in part due to Vatican II which permitted existing divergent forces to come to the surface and in part the result of deep socio-political changes which took place in Italian society during the 1960s. Different controversial currents have thus developed during the past decade, including the Italian Catholic University Federation (FUCI) at universities and the Christian Association of Italian Workers (ACLI) among workers. They bear witness to the pressure for greater latitude within the church for such movements and more freedom of choice in temporal matters. The 11th Congress of ACLI, held at Turin in 1969, marked for Italian Catholics an open manifestation of a new concern for social problems. An example of change in political attitudes was the emergence of a block of 'Catholics for No' opposing the repeal of the law permitting divorce, in contrast to other Catholic groups and the official church which urged its repeal. In the past the Italian Catholic Church exercised great political power due to its role in the Christian Democratic party, its function in education and public assistance programmes, its privileged legal position as defined in the concordat, and the presence in Italy of the Holy See with its diplomatic pomp and international prestige. However, the unexpected size of the 'No' vote in the 1974 anti-divorce referendum demonstrated the new limits which Catholic laity intend to exercise in reference to the political influence of the episcopate and the Christian Democratic party. The latter is no longer able to lay claim to being the sole party of Catholics.

It is difficult to define precisely the control exercised by the Holy See over Italian Catholic life, since authority is often used in ways scarcely perceptible outwardly. Nevertheless, it is clear that the Holy See exerts its influence on at least 3 levels: through its geographic proximity, which permits permanent surveillance and immediate interventions; through the concordat, which created several power zones administered more or less directly by the Holy See; and especially through the Italian Episcopal Conference whose president is named by the pope as primate of the Italian Church.

A final characteristic of Italian Catholicism is the exceptionally high number of dioceses (283) as well as the presence in Italy of the most prestigious diocese of them all, that of Rome. In the teeth of local and conservative opposition, efforts have been under way since Vatican II to reduce the number of dioceses by the pope's refusal to nominate new bishops for the smaller ones. By 1974, 22 had already been eliminated and another 20 were about to be removed,

but there still remained 48 dioceses with less than 50,000 residents, found mostly in the centre and in the south, and 69 with from 50,000 to 100,000, all well below the Catholic world average size of 200,000 for a diocese. Of the large dioceses, 88 had from 100,000 to 200,000, and only 25 dioceses had more than 400,000 residents, of which 4 exceeded one million (Milan, Naples, Rome and Turin). In contrast, some parishes in the suburbs of Rome had up to 80,000 residents.

The diocese of Rome itself has a particular status. The pope as bishop of the diocese is responsible for its administration and spiritual direction. In reality, the pope, engrossed as he is in other responsibilities, delegates his powers to a cardinal-vicar who is responsible for the administration of the diocese. The offices of the vicariate are in the city of Rome, not in the Vatican, which is itself an integral part of the diocese. The power and influence of the Catholic Church is at its most visible in the diocese of Rome, with its 17 pontifical universities, institutes and faculties of theology; its 89 ecclesiastical institutes of education and instruction for secular or religious seminarians; and its 10 pontifical academies. According to the directory of the diocese of Rome, 5,127 clergy (cardinals, archbishops, bishops, diocesan and regular priests, approximately one-third being of foreign nationality) lived and worked in Rome in 1972. Of this number, 1,173 priests were destined for the parish ministry, though only 463 were locally incardinated and dependent directly on the vicariate. There were relatively few religious vocations from Rome itself, 241 of the 463 incardinated priests having come from other localities. The number of parishes has now been raised to 249, 53% being under religious priests. Their population varies from 2,000 to 82,000 residents, with 65 suburban parishes having more than 20,000 inhabitants. The reorganization of the diocese of Rome began some time ago and should ultimately resolve many of its pastoral problems, including the reallocation of its clergy. A socio-religious study in 1971 indicated that Rome had one of the highest proportions of Sunday mass attenders in European cities, averaging between 35% and 40% every Sunday. It also revealed, however, that actual participation was weak, with only 10–25% of those attenders receiving communion.

**PROTESTANT CHURCHES.** The Evangelical Waldensian Church is the oldest Protestant denomination in Italy and still the largest of the non-Pentecostal bodies. Originating in southern France during the 12th century through the preaching of Peter Waldo, the so-called Poor Men of Lyons spread across the border and established themselves

**Chiesa Cattolica in Italia.** *Above.* The ancient Sacconi Association of hooded laymen lead annual Via Crucis procession inside Colosseum, Rome. *Below.* **Diocese of Feltre & Belluno.** Bishop of Belluno says mass for the dead on spot where a church stood until washed away in dam disaster at Longarone in October 1963.

as a people's church with local autonomy in the valleys of Turin in northwestern Italy. By the middle of the 16th century, the church had grown to more than 100,000 members, but severe persecution under the Counter-Reformation during the next hundred years reduced the Waldenses to less than 5,000. By 1900 they had built up their community again to over 20,000. A further period of decline during the early part of this century has been reversed.

Lutheranism, which dates back to the Reformation,

over 350 with an adult membership of 30,000, expanding to 600 churches with 100,000 members by 1961. Expansion continued at the same pace through the next decade. The Assemblies of God are by far the most important Protestant church in Italy at the present time. In 1957 another Pentecostal body, the International Evangelical Church, was formed. Becoming a member of the WCC, this denomination has grown rapidly, more by drawing into its membership small unaffiliated Pentecostal groups than by

and independence which culminated in the capture of Rome by Italian troops in 1870 and the royal decree of 1871 making Rome the capital of the kingdom, were seen as placing in jeopardy the Catholic Church which considered its temporal sovereignty indispensable for the exercise of its divine mission. The Roman question was resolved by the formation of a new pontifical state, small but sovereign, Vatican City, while the problem of reparations was covered by a joint financial convention in the same treaty. The first article of the treaty states: 'Italy recognizes and affirms the principle that the Roman, Apostolic and Catholic religion is the only religion of the state'. Annex II of the treaty lists the properties of the Holy See in Italy which have the privilege of extra-territoriality with exemption from expropriation and taxes. Annex III lists other properties such as the Gregorian University and the Biblical Institute which, without benefit of extraterritoriality, are also exempt from expropriation and taxes.

The purpose of the concordat is 'to regulate the conditions of religion and the Church in Italy'. Its principal stipulations are as follows: (1) the state recognizes Catholic jurisdiction over ecclesiastics and grants its protection (difesa) to them when necessary for carrying out their ministerial responsibilities (Article 1, paragraph 1); (2) the state agrees to protect the city of Rome from all that would contradict its sacred character, insofar as it is the seat of the papacy, the centre of the Catholic world and a place of pilgrimage (Article 1, paragraph 2). It was in the application of this second paragraph that the government in 1965 refused to permit the presentation in Rome of the play 'The Vicar' by R. Hochhuth, and that it consulted with the pope in 1973–74 concerning the construction of a mosque in the Eternal City; (3) clergy in charge of souls are excused from military service, even in the case of general mobilization (Article 3); (4) all clergy desiring employment with the state must obtain permission from their diocesan ordinary; if anyone has been suspended, he may not teach nor receive employment which would place him in direct contact with the public (Article 5); (5) clergy accused of common law misdemeanors receive privileged treatment (Article 8); (6) the appointment of military chaplains is subject to the prior consent of the Italian government, which may oppose particular cases and make other appointments (Articles 13 and 15); (7) the state may oppose appointments of particular diocesan bishops and parish priests (Articles 19 and 21); (8) newly-appointed bishops must take the oath of fidelity to the head of state (Article 20); (9) clergy benefit from a wage supplement, paid since 1887, to cover deficiencies in ecclesiastical allowances (Article 30).

In Article 34 of the concordat, the state gives civil recognition to marriages performed under canon law, justifying this on the basis of returning to the institution of marriage its 'dignity in conformity with the Catholic traditions' of the Italian people. It renounces all rights to the judicial nullification of marriages, these rights being reserved to ecclesiastical courts. The Holy See, in turn, agrees that civil courts have jurisdiction in cases of separation. Called into question already because of the introduction of divorce in Italy in the Fortuna-Baslini Law of January 1970, Article 34 was for all practical purposes annulled by the results of the referendum on divorce of May 1974, which went against the expressed wishes of Catholic political and ecclesiastical leaders. Only a few bishops invoked freedom of conscience for the faithful; all others as well as the Episcopal Conference campaigned for a 'Yes' vote. The large resulting 'No' vote averaging 59% in each of the 20 civil regions of the country (being largest in the north and centre and in the major cities and including those regions considered most Catholic, namely Venice and the south), gives strong support to existing divorce laws in Italy. Prior to the passage of the Fortuna-Baslini Law, non-Catholics were unable to secure annulment of marriage, since such authority lay exclusively with ecclesiastical courts. Article 34 of the concordat was also the basis for the law of June 1929 requiring that non-Catholic clergy wishing to secure civil recognition for marriages performed by them should in each and every case request through their church president such authority from the state, the choice of celebrant being left to the discretion of the civil officer. Thus Protestant pastors were deemed not competent to judge the validity of marriages they themselves celebrated. Despite declarations of its unconstitutionality, this law of 1929 has remained in effect. In August 1972, the first united synod of Waldensians and Methodists

**Chiesa Evangelica Valdese.** Open-air Waldensian service. Founded in 1173, Waldensians are Italy's oldest Protestants.

grew among Germans in the north during the 18th century, but only in recent years have efforts been made by Lutherans to evangelize Italians. The Christian Church of the Brethren is an indigenous body which traces its origin back to small groups of converts meeting together in Florence in 1833. Working under the guidance of lay elders without ordained clergy, their strength remains in northwest Piemonte, where they have recently begun tent campaigns to develop new assemblies.

The 1860s saw the arrival of Protestant missionaries from England: Methodists in 1859, Baptists in 1863, the first Adventists in 1864 and later the Salvation Army in 1886. These were followed during the next decade by their counterparts from America. British Baptists turned their churches over to American Southern Baptists in 1920, and in 1956 the Italian Baptist Union was formed. The majority of its pastors are nationals, but few churches are as yet self-supporting. Following an initial evangelistic ministry, Methodists began directing their efforts to developing institutions. The British and American Methodist missions worked in close co-operation prior to their merger in 1946, and the Evangelical Methodist Church of Italy became autonomous in 1962. Social and ecumenical concerns are carried on at present, but with little increase in membership.

Seventh-day Adventist work was begun by a converted Polish Roman Catholic priest, and Adventists established their first organized mission in 1877. By 1909, 44 converts had been made and the church has continued to grow slowly during the present century. Its publishing house quadrupled its output between 1950 and 1968, and its Bible correspondence courses and radio programmes are widely known.

The Assemblies of God were introduced in 1908 with the return of an American immigrant. With the aid of other returned immigrants, membership increased rapidly throughout the south, numbering about 5,000 in 1934, at the time the fascist regime imposed its severest persecutions, prohibiting services and imprisoning pastors. When work was reopened in 1944, there were 120 churches, 129 having been lost. However, by 1955 they had increased again to

making new converts.

Protestant groups entering Italy since World War II include the Churches of Christ (1947), Church of the Nazarene (1948) and Mennonites (1949). The most successful has been the Churches of Christ, which reached a membership of 2,000 in 15 years. In spite of severe persecution in the early years, rapid growth has resulted from its policy of church-planting and its use of Italian evangelists.

OTHER CHURCHES. Anglicans, under the Anglican Church in Europe and in the diocese of Gibraltar of the Church of England, have maintained chaplaincy services in Italy since 1559; and the New Apostolic Church has built up a large German-speaking constituency since its arrival after World War II. Several Orthodox communities are also present: Armenian, Greek, Russian and Serbian. The largest is the Greek Orthodox Church which is part of the Ecumenical Patriarchate of Constantinople, under the archbishop of London. Marginal churches include Christian Scientists, Mormons and Jehovah's Witnesses, the largest being the latter.

CHURCH AND STATE. In church-state relations in Italy, it is well to distinguish between the realm of law and that of practice. As far as the law is concerned, relations between the 2 powers are regulated by the Lateran Agreements (Patti Lateranensi) between pope Pius XI and Mussolini on 2 November 1929 and confirmed by Article 7 of the Republican constitution of 1 January 1948: 'The State and the Catholic Church have each their own independent and sovereign order. Their relations are regulated by the Lateran Agreements. Modifications of the Agreements, when accepted by both parties, do not require a constitutional revision'. Concerning other religions, Article 8 of the constitution stipulates that they 'have the right to organize themselves according to their own statutes, insofar as they are not contrary to Italian law'.

The Lateran Agreements consist of 2 protocols, a treaty and a concordat. The treaty concerns the 'Roman question', the conflict which developed in the 19th century between the new kingdom of Italy and the papacy. At the time, the struggle for unity strongly urged its formal abrogation.

Article 36 of the concordat declares that Italy considers as 'fundamental to public education the teaching of Christian doctrine in the form received through the Catholic tradition'. Accordingly the teaching of the Catholic religion has been made obligatory in the state educational system. The latter pays, in conformity to the law of 5 May 1930, all teachers of religion, to whom are accorded the same rights and duties as other teachers, except that their

**Italian Pentecostals.** *Below right.* Protestant charismatics in Rome. *Above.* Catholic charismatics in Rome, led by a bishop and an archbishop (with crosses).

employment is submitted each year to their bishop for his approval. A law of 28 February 1930 allows for the possibility of other religions offering religious education courses in local schools, provided that parents request them, that there are a sufficient number of pupils, and that 'for well-founded reasons' the school chapel is not used for this purpose.

The pre-eminence of the Catholic religion as the 'religion of the State' affects also the Italian penal code, as reflected in a number of decisions of the Court of Appeals. The court affirmed on 29 December 1949 and again on 16 January 1950 that the first article of the Lateran treaty forms the foundation of the penal code. In the same manner, the Constitutional Court declared on 17 December 1958 that the Catholic religion, professed by 'almost all the citizens', 'merits a particular penal protection'. Thus remaining in effect are Articles 402 and 406 of the Penal Code, which concern the crime of 'offence' (*vilipendio*) against the religion of the state. These articles stipulate that there is an aggravating circumstance if the offence is directed against a Catholic clergyman, and extenuating circumstance if directed against a non-Catholic sect or one of its ministers. There is also Article 724 which punishes blasphemy.

In practice, although the concordat of 1929 functioned during the whole period of the fascist dictatorship (with some conflicts between the 2 parties, notably on the subject of Catholic Action and the suppression of Catholic youth organizations) and is still in effect, serious differences of opinion concerning church-state relations remain. Article 7 of the constitution, earlier described, was adopted by the Constituent Assembly in March 1947 by a majority of the 2 principal parties, the Christian Democrats and Communists, plus liberals and neo-fascists, against the socialists, republicans and a few minor parties. The article itself envisaged the possibility of future modifications to the concordat, and this question was taken up for serious discussion at the end of Vatican II. In the course of the debate which quickly became violently polemical, positions crystallized around 2 poles: (1) those who were partisans of revision (Christian Democrats, Communists and Neo-Fascists) and who invoked the importance of maintaining the 'religious peace' of Italy, not wishing to go beyond the stage of a bilateral modification of a few clauses as envisaged in the concordat itself; and (2) those who, convinced of the inadequacies of the concordat, were in favour of its complete abolition. Following a favourable vote in the chamber on 5 October 1967, the government appointed (in

October 1968) a commission to make a preparatory study. The Holy See gave its approval for the negotiations, and meetings were begun. However, all discussion was interrupted between 1970 and February 1975 because of the introduction of divorce in Italy despite the Holy See's strenuous opposition. In the spring of 1972, several socialist deputies presented to the Chamber of Representatives a proposed law modifying certain articles of the constitution in such a way as to make the concordat unconstitutional.

By 1976, a draft revised concordat had been drawn up and seemed likely to be ratified within a year or two. Although stopping short of full separation of church and state, it removes the original provision recognizing Catholicism as the official state religion, removes the status of Rome as a 'sacred city', and gives parents or students over the age of 16 the option of retaining or eliminating religious education. By thus lessening the chances of conflict between church and state in a secularized Italy, the new

concordat is recognized as an acceptable compromise by the Holy See and the Catholic Church.

Relations between the Catholic world and the political world of the Italian parties are extremely complex, today more so than previously. A complicating factor is the socio-political situation of the country, characterized by class conflicts and regional disequilibrium. The situation is also confused by the contradictions and divergent attitudes held within the Catholic world, both at the top and bottom. The ties between the Catholic Church and the Christian Democrats, strong in the past, are less in evidence today. The ability of the Holy See thus to intervene in Italian life through the party is not nearly so significant as previously. While maintaining its identification as Catholic, the party, in pursuing the interests of the middle classes, has created an infrastructure of power which is to an extent autonomous vis-a-vis the church. The Catholic world remains the major support of the party, but it is not alone in this. Efforts to disassociate themselves from the party continue among Catholics, and the hierarchy intervenes with much greater prudence than in the past. The Italian Communist Party (PCI), the second strongest political force in the country and the foremost Communist party in Western Europe, has always given great attention to the Catholic world, seeking to establish ties with it. If in the past the response of the Catholic hierarchy was for the most part negative, culminating in the celebrated excommunication of 1948, today there are less differences between them. The ideological impasse remains, but its practical importance has decreased. Thus the Episcopal Conference of Emilia has recently sought agreements with leftist civil regional authorities. With the small traditional 'lay' parties, which in the past have been mostly anticlerical, present relations are ambiguous. On the one hand, these parties retain an appearance of anticlericalism, while in practice they support the Catholic Church and the Christian Democrats, which

are considered to be a sure and necessary protection against Communism. On the other hand, the church easily accepts these contacts which enable it to maintain its power. In yet another direction, certain sectors of the hierarchy and the Catholic world have contact with the Italian Social Movement (MSI), which has clearly fascist tendencies.

**INTERDENOMINATIONAL ORGANIZATIONS.**
Protestant interdenominational activities are centred

in the Federation of Evangelical Churches in Italy (Federazione delle Chiese Evangeliche in Italia), while the principal agency for co-ordination within the Catholic Church is the Commission for Ecumenism (Commissione per l'Ecumenismo) of the Italian Episcopal Conference. A number of ecumenical centres and organizations are active, of which 17 may be mentioned. (1) International Documentation on the Contemporary Church (IDOC), founded in Rome in 1962, is an independent centre, which through research, publications and symposia seeks to inform the churches concerning international and interconfessional matters of ecumenical interest. (2) Sezione Ecumenico, Patristica Greco-Bizantina S Nicola, founded in Bari in 1969 as a department of the theological faculty of St Thomas Aquinas Pontifical University in Rome, with Catholic and Orthodox students and faculty, has special interest in stimulating Orthodox and Catholic dialogue in the field of patristics and the recovery of an ecclesiology of communion. (3) Centro Pro Unione, founded in Rome in 1968 by Friars of the Atonement (USA), provides opportunities for ecumenical encounter through conferences, study and information. (4) Associazione Cattolica Italiana per l'Oriente Cristiano, founded in Palermo, promotes unity between Catholic and Orthodox churches. (5) Centro Ecumenico Ut Unum Sint, founded in Rome in 1935 by the Catholic religious congregation Pia Società San Paolo and since 1973 related to the Vatican's Sacred Congregation for the Clergy, is concerned especially for spiritual, doctrinal and pastoral ecumenism and offers biblical and theological correspondence courses for laymen in conjunction with the Lateran Pontifical University. (6) Associazione Internazionale Unitas, founded in Rome in 1945, is a Catholic centre for ecumenical spirituality responsible for the creation of a Eucharistic Prayer Centre for Christian Unity at the basilica of Santa Maria in Via Lata; it is linked to Unidad Cristiana (Madrid) and Unité Chrétienne (Lyons). (7) The Anglican Centre (Centro Anglicano) is the representative in Rome of the faith and practice of the Anglican Communion, working for the reconciliation of the Catholic and Anglican communions. (8) Agape Centro Comunitario, founded in Prali in 1943, is an international ecumenical centre founded by Waldensian youth with support from the WCC. (9) Comunità Ecumenica di Bose, founded in Magnano in 1968, is an interconfessional Catholic/Protestant community of men and women living the gospel together in common and celibate life while remaining in communion with their own churches. A similar group was formed in Switzerland in 1972. (10) Comunità Evangelica Ecumenica di Ispra-Varese unites members of different Protestant denominations and nationalities who remain faithful to their own confessions. (11) Centro Internazionale della Pace (Studi Ecumenici) was founded in Turin in 1967. (12) Segretariato Attività Ecumeniche, founded in Rome in 1963, is an association for ecumenical lay training, especially university students. (13) Centro UNO per l'Unità dei Cristiani, founded in Rome in 1960, is a centre for ecumenical spirituality, especially for Focolarini. (14) Piccoli Operai Missionari Ecumenici, founded at Riano in 1947, is a pious society of religious and lay personnel of both sexes and all ages and social classes dedicated to union of Christians. Affiliated with the dioceses of Porto and Santa Rufino, it has founded ecumenical communities in Italy, Spain, USA, Chile and Malta, as well as other prayer and study centres throughout the world. It publishes periodicals, and organizes pilgrimages and international conferences. (15) Centro di Studi Ecumenici Giovanni XXIII, in Sotto il Monte, Berg, is a Catholic ecumenical study centre. (16) Studi Ecumenici is a Catholic institution involved in ecumenical research in Turin. (17) Other Catholic ecumenical centres mostly of local interest which aid visitors of other denominations are: Foyer & Casa Unitas (Bethany Sisters); Centro Ecumenico Santa Rita (Daughters of the Divine Providence of Don Orioni), founded in 1968 in Rome; Centro Ecumenico Nordico (Nordisk Ekumenisk Centrum), for Scandinavians, founded in 1966; Centro Francescano d'Azione Ecumenica (OFM), founded in 1969; Hospitium Oecumenicum di S Damiano (OFM), founded in 1965, in Assisi; Centro Ecumenico Pastorale, for Catholics of the Italo-Albanian rite, founded in 1967 in Lungro, Consenza; and Centro Ecumenico e Universitario San Martino (for university students) at Perugia.

Italy's first ecumenical sanctuary, the St Gregory the Great chapel, which is open to all member churches of the WCC, was dedicated at Assisi in November 1972.

Several agencies are dedicated to improving relations between the Catholic Church and other religions. (1) The Pontifical Institute of Arab Studies (IPEA) was founded in Tunisia in 1960 and transferred to Rome under its present title in 1964. It is directed by White Fathers and offers linguistic studies and training in Islamics for those wishing to specialize, from a missionary of view, in Muslim-Christian dialogue. Classes are in French and Arabic. (2) The International Information Service for Jewish-Christian Relations, founded in Rome in 1965 by a group of bishops and Vatican II experts and at present supervised by the Congregation of Notre-Dame de Sion, has for its purpose the development of mutual understanding and esteem among Christians and Jews. It has a specialized international library in 5 languages, offers a documentation service, publishes *Sidic*, a review aimed at aiding the development of Judeo-Christian relations throughout the world, sponsors receptions, courses, study sessions and conferences, and conducts visits and trips. (3) The Judeo-Christian Fellowship of Florence (Amicizia Ebraico-Cristiana di Firenze) founded in 1951, has members in other Italian cities, conducts conferences and meetings, produces a liaison bulletin, and is affiliated with the International Council of Christians and Jews in London. (4) The Institute for Religious Science (Istituto per le Scienze Religiose), founded in Bologna, is an independent centre for socio-religious, historical and theological research. The institute is under the direction of the Association for the Development of Religious Science, founded in 1952, and has its international headquarters in Italy.

**BROADCASTING.** The Italian Radio and TV Company (RAI) is government-owned and controlled. It allows numerous Catholic programmes. In addition, the Federation of Protestant Churches is responsible for a 20-minute radio programme each week and since 1973 a 15-minute weekly TV magazine.

In Rome the station La Voce Amica, founded in 1956, gives spiritual aid and comfort 24 hours a day by broadcasting the telephone service Tele-Bibbia, which gives commentaries on biblical passages. Over 35,000 calls were made to La Voce Amica in 1969. For Catholics, Italy is a member of UNDA. From Vatican City, Radio Vatican broadcasts 11 hours a week in Italian. Trans World Radio (Monaco) beams Protestant programmes in Italian for 4 hours 50 minutes a week.

## BIBLIOGRAPHY


*Annuario cattolico d'Italia, 1972–1973.* Roma: CNEC. 1973.

*Annuario evangelico 1972–73: indirizzi e orari di tutte le chiese ed opere evangeliche in Italia.* Torino: Editrice Claudiana, 1972. 346p.

*Church and state in Italy, 1850–1950.* A. C. Jemelo. Oxford: Blackwell, 1960. 340p.

*Cristianesimo Evangelico, 1967–1968.* Torino: Editrice Claudiana, 1968. 219p.

*Dati statistici delle diocesi italiane.* Roma: Conferenza Episcopale Italiana, 1967. 319p.

'Elementi per uno studio della practica religiosa in Italia'. C. D. Michelis. Rome: Gregorian Pontifical University, 1965. (Mimeographed).

*Il comportamento religioso degli Italiani.* S. Burgalassi. Firenze: Vallecchi, 1967.

'Italy', S. Acquaviva, in H. Mol (ed), *Western religion* (The Hague: Mouton, 1972), p. 305–324.

*La Chiesa e la organizzazioni cattoliche in Italia, 1945–1955.* C. Falconi. Torino: Einaudi, 1956.

'La Chiesa italiana: tensioni e problemi', *Humanitas* (Brescia), 31 (1976), 603–754. (28 articles).

'La religiosità in Italia', G. De Rosa, *Civiltà Cattolica*, 2960 (October, 1973), 168–173.

*L'altra Chiesa in Italia: Gli Evangelici.* G. Bouchard & R. Turinetto. Torino: Editrice Claudiana, 1976.

*Minoranze religiose in Italia.* A. Santini et al. Roma: Edizioni Religioni Oggi, 1969. 390p.

'Politics and religion in Italy', *Social compass*, XXIII, 2–3(1976), 97–278. (11 articles and a bibliography).

'Sociologie religieuse et sociologie des religions en Italie', S. Acquaviva, *Archives de sociologie des religions*, 12 (1961).

'The Church in Italy', M. Castelli, *Pro Mundi Vita bulletin*, 66 (May-June, 1977), 1–29.

*The Protestant movement in Italy: its progress, problems and prospects.* E. R. Hedlund. South Pasadena, CA(USA): William Carey Library, 1970. 257p.


TABLE 2. ORGANIZED CHURCHES AND DENOMINATIONS IN ITALY

| Official name 1 | Begun 2 | Type 3 | Counc 4 | Congs 5 | Adults 6 | Affiliated 7 | Names, notes, and other statistics (see Codebook) 8 |
|---|---|---|---|---|---|---|---|
| Assemblea Evangelica Battista | 1947 | P Bap | xF... | 18 | 225 | 593 | M=Associazione Missionaria Battista Italiana (CBFMS,USA). 10x,5m,27f,1k,W=55%,34Y,60z. |
| Assemblee di Dio in Italia | 1908 | P Pe2 | ZF..k | 759 | 166,736 | 300,000 | *CCEP* (see below). *Assemblies of God.* M=AoG(USA). 1934–58 persecution. 363n,15f,1s(17). |
| Associazione Missionaria Ev Italiana | 1866 | P Bap | .G..K | 18 | 520 | 1,500 | *AMEI. Italian Ev Missionary Association.* M=Spezia Mission, also WEC(UK) in Sardinia. 3f. |
| Chiesa Anglicana (D Gibraltar) | 1559 | A plu | awc.. | 18 | 3,000 | 10,000 | *Ch of England*, also M=PECUSA. Chaplaincies: 2 Rome, 2 Sicily, 2 seasonal. 9x. |
| Chiesa Apostolica Armena: V Milano | | O Arm | Ewc.. | 1 | 500 | 1,000 | *Armenian Apostolic Ch, Vicariate of Milan. Gregorians.* Armenian refugees from USSR. |
| Chiesa Apostolica in Italia | 1926 | P PeA | ZG..k | 74 | 2,400 | 5,000 | *Apostolic Ch.* M=ACMM(UK). HQ Grosseto. Large % are students. 18n,2f,G=4.8%pa,1j,90Y. |
| **Chiesa Cattolica in Italia:** | c 30 | R LEr | B.B.R | 28,150 | 40,110,280 | 53,483,645 | 64008n,6840m,153293w,838950Yy. *Holy Catholic Apostolic & Roman Church.* 169q,145s. |
| P Roma (Rome): D Roma | c 40 | R Lat | Bs | 270 | 1,864,500 | 2,486,000 | 5977 1471 15600 47743 D Rome. 90 bishops, 800 schools. In Lazio Conciliar Region. |
| *CR Abruzzi:* | | R Lat | Bs | 827 | 958,200 | 1,278,634 | *Conferenza Episcopale Abruzzeze.* This end column contains notes on the 18 Conciliar |
| M Chieti & Vasto | c 450 | R Lat | Bs | 147 | 222,900 | 297,200 | 292 27 508 3959 Regions (Regioni Conciliari) given in italics |
| M Lanciano & Ortona | c 450 | R Lat | Bs | 39 | 59,400 | 79,200 | 95 19 135 1027 after CR in column 1. *Abruzzi Conciliar Region.* |
| M L'Aquila | 1257 | R Lat | Bs | 149 | 72,700 | 96,959 | 178 19 265 1290 Under Abruzzi Episcopal Conference. Roughly civil |
| D Marsi | c 850 | R Lat | Bs | 94 | 97,400 | 129,800 | 144 8 240 2600 region of Abruzzi. Area 11,000 km2, population 1,298,000; |
| D Valva & Sulmona | c 450 | R Lat | Bs | 64 | 83,000 | 110,725 | 120 5 164 870 since 1961, 25,000 emigrants a year for work |
| D Penne-Pescara | c 450 | R Lat | bs | 104 | 202,000 | 270,000 | 138 10 400 2500 elsewhere. 6 diocesan pastoral councils, 1 regional |
| D Teramo & Atri | c 450 | R Lat | bs | 168 | 158,000 | 211,000 | 243 14 302 3713 and 8 diocesan priests' councils. Suppressed |
| D Trivento | c 950 | R Lat | bs | 62 | 62,800 | 83,750 | 79 2 45 1015 diocese: Trivento (absorbed by D Isernia & Venafro). |
| *CR Beneventano:* | | R Lat | Bs | 627 | 1,105,200 | 1,473,834 | *Conferenza Epis Beneventana.* *Benevento Conciliar Region.* Southern Italy. Parts |
| M Benevento | c 90 | R Lat | Bs | 163 | 230,800 | 307,741 | 298 60 446 4315 of 4 civil regions: Molise, Campania, Basilicata, |
| D Alife | c 450 | R Lat | Bs | 20 | 30,500 | 40,690 | 41 5 81 700 Puglia. Area 13,993 km2, population 1,548,900, |
| D Ariano | c1050 | R Lat | Bs | 35 | 48,900 | 65,200 | 37 0 75 590 mainly in agriculture. 12 diocesan pastoral |
| D Ascoli Satriano & Cerignola | c1050 | R Lat | Bs | 37 | 62,900 | 83,876 | 69 4 141 1853 councils and 15 presbyteral councils (1971). |
| D Avellino | c 150 | R Lat | Bs | 55 | 93,700 | 125,000 | 93 8 59 2200 Molise civil region has the highest emigration |
| D Bovino | c 450 | R Lat | Bs | 14 | 26,400 | 35,200 | 31 0 29 619 rate in Italy, 0.96% of the population per year |
| D Larino | c 450 | R Lat | Bs | 23 | 45,000 | 60,000 | 40 2 106 800 leaving Italy permanently. Suppressed dioceses: |
| D Lucera | c 350 | R Lat | Bs | 25 | 72,800 | 97,000 | 77 9 105 1675 Larino (absorbed by D Termoli), Lucera (absorbed |
| D San Severo | c1050 | R Lat | Bs | 18 | 68,500 | 91,382 | 50 3 81 1967 by D San Severo). In 1974, D Boiano-Campobasos was |
| D Sant'Agata de' Goti | c 950 | R Lat | Bs | 34 | 26,500 | 35,385 | 55 3 86 652 elevated to AD, and in 1976 to M. |
| D Telese (Cerreto Sannita) | c450 | R Lat | Bs | 26 | 36,900 | 49,158 | 56 3 118 665 |
| D Termoli | c 950 | R Lat | Bs | 24 | 42,000 | 56,000 | 44 0 51 985 |
| M Boiano-Campobasso | c1050 | R Lat | Bs | 51 | 72,000 | 96,000 | 98 25 159 1385 **N.B.** Note that the complex listing of P, CR, M, D et alia |
| M Manfredonia & Vieste | c 250 | R Lat | Bs | 44 | 106,600 | 139,505 | 122 32 214 2890 in column 1, with some indented and others not, is an |
| D Foggia | 1855 | R Lat | bs | 87 | 121,600 | 162,000 | 147 31 300 3200 exactly correct picture of the structure of the Church's |
| D Troia | c1050 | R Lat | bs | 11 | 14,700 | 19,712 | 33 0 39 290 jurisdictions (see Parts 3 and 6). |
| AN Monte Vergine | c1150 | R Lat | bs | 10 | 7,500 | 9,985 | 45 12 56 187 |
| *CR Calabrie:* | | R Lat | Bs | 1,042 | 1,538,100 | 2,050,874 | *Conferenza Episcopale Calabrese.* *Calabria Conciliar Region.* Southern Italy; |
| M Reggio Calabria | c 90 | R Lat | Bs | 113 | 173,200 | 231,000 | 206 8 536 5208 co-terminous with Calabria civil region. Poverty, |
| D Bova | c 650 | R Lat | Bs | 19 | 18,700 | 24,950 | 27 0 35 190 exploitation, violence. Area 15,011 km2, |
| D Cariati | c1350 | R Lat | Bs | 31 | 54,200 | 72,230 | 36 0 33 2099 population 2,070,000, mainly agricultural. 9 |

*Continued opposite*

*Table 2–continued*

| Official name 1 | Begun 2 | Type 3 | Counc 4 | Congs 5 | Adults 6 | Affiliated 7 | Names, notes, and other statistics (see Codebook) 8 | | | | |
|---|---|---|---|---|---|---|---|---|---|---|---|
| D Cassano all'Ionio | c 450 | R Lat | Bs | 53 | 98,000 | 130,600 | 76 | 0 | 125 | 1999 | diocesan pastoral councils and 16 presbyteral councils (1971). One diocese for Italians of the Italo-Albanian Eastern Catholic rite. Suppressed dioceses: Bova (absorbed by M Reggio Calabria), Nicotera & Tropea (absorbed by D Mileto), Squillace (absorbed by AD Catanzaro). |
| D Crotone | c 550 | R Lat | Bs | 15 | 45,700 | 61,000 | 38 | 2 | 54 | 1351 | |
| D Gerace-Locri | c 450 | R Lat | Bs | 88 | 97,500 | 130,000 | 88 | 0 | 140 | 3672 | |
| D Nicastro | c 550 | R Lat | Bs | 69 | 102,000 | 136,000 | 92 | 6 | 127 | 2331 | |
| D Nicotera & Tropea | c 550 | R Lat | Bs | 42 | 26,500 | 35,302 | 49 | 4 | 54 | 621 | |
| D Oppido Mamertina | c1250 | R Lat | Bs | 21 | 19,400 | 25,872 | 34 | 0 | 38 | 455 | |
| AD Catanzaro | 1121 | R Lat | bs | 54 | 105,000 | 140,000 | 91 | 18 | 201 | 2000 | |
| AD Cosenza | c 650 | R Lat | bs | 148 | 220,200 | 293,608 | 255 | 39 | 489 | 4585 | |
| AD Rossano | c 650 | R Lat | bs | 51 | 84,300 | 112,400 | 70 | 0 | 129 | 2080 | |
| AD Santa Severina | c 650 | R Lat | bs | 25 | 48,000 | 64,000 | 40 | 7 | 52 | 1721 | |
| D Lungro per gli Italo-Albanesi | 1919 | R IAb | os | 24 | 25,400 | 33,900 | 35 | 2 | 47 | 527 | |
| D Mileto | c1050 | R Lat | bs | 141 | 217,500 | 290,000 | 200 | 6 | 255 | 5167 | |
| D San Marco & Bisignano | c 950 | R Lat | bs | 79 | 105,000 | 140,000 | 103 | 10 | 176 | 1370 | |
| D Squillace | c 350 | R Lat | bs | 69 | 97,500 | 130,012 | 128 | 17 | 157 | 2408 | |
| *CR Campania:* | | R Lat | Bs | 1,105 | 2,760,900 | 3,681,190 | *Conferenza Epis Campana.* | | | | *Campania Conciliar Region*. Southern Italy. Covers part of Campania civil region, and part of Lazio. Area 5,115 km2, population 4,107,500 mainly in agriculture with some in industry in D Caserta, AN Montecassino, D Pozzuoli. High population density (803 persons per square km, compared to national average of 183 km2). Rapid industrial growth, heavy emigration of 0.5% per year leaving Italy permanently. 11 diocesan pastoral councils and 16 presbyteral councils (1971). Suppressed diocese: Castellammare di Stabia (absorbed by M Sorrento). |
| M Capua | c 150 | R Lat | Bs | 72 | 97,300 | 129,800 | 117 | 4 | 405 | 2425 | |
| D Caiazzo | c 850 | R Lat | Bs | 36 | 24,400 | 32,540 | 39 | 0 | 42 | 360 | |
| D Calvi & Teano | c 450 | R Lat | Bs | 106 | 64,500 | 86,000 | 97 | 5 | 50 | 950 | |
| D Caserta | c1150 | R Lat | Bs | 55 | 99,100 | 132,100 | 110 | 10 | 172 | 3300 | |
| D Isernia & Venafro | c 450 | R Lat | Bs | 42 | 36,400 | 48,490 | 68 | 2 | 37 | 560 | |
| D Sessa Aurunca | c 450 | R Lat | Bs | 51 | 63,300 | 84,450 | 69 | 3 | 95 | 1370 | |
| M Napoli (Naples) | c 90 | R Lat | Bs | 283 | 1,200,000 | 1,600,000 | 1112 | 50 | 250 | 30000 | |
| D Acerra | c1050 | R Lat | Bs | 23 | 52,700 | 70,242 | 71 | 16 | 98 | 1387 | |
| D Ischia | c1150 | R Lat | Bs | 24 | 28,800 | 38,348 | 64 | 1 | 50 | 643 | |
| D Nola | c 150 | R Lat | Bs | 125 | 277,500 | 370,000 | 274 | 45 | 980 | 7559 | |
| D Pozzuoli | c 90 | R Lat | Bs | 48 | 315,800 | 421,050 | 123 | 11 | 245 | 6952 | |
| M Sorrento | c 450 | R Lat | Bs | 40 | 60,800 | 81,090 | 152 | 21 | 337 | 2450 | |
| D Castellammare di Stabia | c 350 | R Lat | Bs | 47 | 90,800 | 121,000 | 123 | 62 | 396 | 3745 | |
| D Aversa | c1050 | R Lat | bs | 79 | 254,700 | 339,650 | 247 | 15 | 488 | 5815 | |
| AN Montecassino & Atina | 1323 | R Lat | bs | 71 | 82,500 | 110,000 | 85 | 12 | 190 | 1211 | |
| PN Pompei | 1926 | R Lat | bs | 3 | 12,300 | 16,430 | 53 | 25 | 253 | 390 | |
| *CR Emilia:* | | R Lat | Bs | 1,360 | 1,180,900 | 1,574,480 | *Conferenza Epis Emiliana.* | | | | *Emilia Conciliar Region*. Northern Italy. Western half of Emilia-Romagna (the 'Red region', because of heavy Communist vote). Area 10,430 km2, population 1,591,000. 1964–69, 20% drop in vocations to priesthood. 7 diocesan pastoral councils and 7 presbyteral councils. Suppressed diocese: Guastalla (absorbed by D Reggio-Emilia). |
| M Modena & AN Nanontola | c 250 | R Lat | Bs | 238 | 285,800 | 381,093 | 411 | 33 | 694 | 6707 | |
| D Carpi | 1779 | R Lat | Bs | 40 | 79,200 | 105,600 | 89 | 1 | 150 | 1258 | |
| D Guastalla | 1828 | R Lat | Bs | 30 | 48,400 | 64,487 | 57 | 1 | 155 | 800 | |
| D Reggio-Emilia | c 90 | R Lat | Bs | 280 | 265,000 | 353,300 | 455 | 25 | 713 | 4642 | |
| D Fidenza | 1601 | R Lat | bs | 61 | 47,600 | 63,500 | 96 | 4 | 161 | 650 | |
| D Parma | c 350 | R Lat | bs | 328 | 228,800 | 305,000 | 485 | 143 | 880 | 3709 | |
| D Piacenza | c 350 | R Lat | bs | 383 | 226,100 | 301,500 | 560 | 41 | 829 | 5544 | |
| *CR Etruria:* | | R Lat | Bs | 3,090 | 2,577,000 | 3,436,418 | *Conferenza Episcopale Toscana.* | | | | *Etruria (Tuscany) Conciliar Region*. Central Italy. Roughly same as civil region of Tuscany, also a few islands. Major centre of Italian culture. Heavily dechristianized. Area 23,870 km2, population 3,553, in industry and agriculture; heavily working-class. 14 diocesan pastoral councils and 22 presbyteral councils (1971). |
| M Firenze (Florence) | c 90 | R Lat | Bs | 499 | 592,500 | 790,000 | 859 | 157 | 2710 | 11302 | |
| D Colle di Val d'Elsa | 1592 | R Lat | Bs | 75 | 41,200 | 54,900 | 70 | 3 | 102 | 966 | |
| D Fiesole | c 90 | R Lat | Bs | 261 | 101,400 | 135,193 | 313 | 82 | 620 | 1750 | |
| D Pistoia | c 250 | R Lat | Bs | 172 | 151,000 | 201,919 | 216 | 16 | 549 | 2547 | |
| D Prato | 1653 | R Lat | Bs | 55 | 113,000 | 150,650 | 123 | 7 | 280 | 2108 | |
| D San Miniato | 1622 | R Lat | Bs | 107 | 103,700 | 138,311 | 131 | 4 | 262 | 1742 | |
| D Sansepolcro | 1515 | R Lat | Bs | 136 | 33,800 | 45,000 | 99 | 3 | 135 | 580 | |
| M Pisa | c 350 | R Lat | Bs | 170 | 229,900 | 306,500 | 328 | 23 | 850 | 4130 | |
| D Apuania | 1822 | R Lat | Bs | 218 | 151,700 | 202,300 | 228 | 9 | 351 | 3560 | |
| D Livorno | 1806 | R Lat | Bs | 49 | 153,800 | 205,000 | 154 | 4 | 680 | 3600 | |
| D Pescia | 1726 | R Lat | Bs | 47 | 69,200 | 92,239 | 57 | 4 | 240 | 1080 | |
| D Pontremoli | 1797 | R Lat | Bs | 132 | 30,000 | 39,980 | 132 | 2 | 87 | 309 | |
| D Volterra | c 450 | R Lat | Bs | 107 | 64,600 | 86,158 | 107 | 0 | 245 | 851 | |
| M Siena | c 350 | R Lat | Bs | 121 | 75,000 | 99,950 | 179 | 30 | 560 | 1000 | |
| D Grosseto | 1138 | R Lat | Bs | 59 | 97,200 | 129,576 | 115 | 3 | 189 | 1512 | |
| D Massa Marittima | c 450 | R Lat | Bs | 45 | 99,100 | 132,200 | 71 | 2 | 150 | 1428 | |
| D Sovana-Pitigliano | c 650 | R Lat | Bs | 63 | 51,600 | 68,830 | 65 | 0 | 64 | 610 | |
| AD Lucca | c 90 | R Lat | bs | 260 | 198,300 | 264,359 | 467 | 22 | 807 | 4171 | |
| D Arezzo | c 250 | R Lat | bs | 330 | 145,500 | 194,000 | 381 | 15 | 500 | 3225 | |
| D Chiusi & Pienza | c 250 | R Lat | bs | 60 | 26,300 | 35,089 | 79 | 1 | 101 | 304 | |
| D Cortona | 1325 | R Lat | bs | 61 | 17,500 | 23,340 | 68 | 6 | 83 | 247 | |
| D Montalcino | 1462 | R Lat | bs | 38 | 19,200 | 25,640 | 5 | 0 | 54 | 159 | |
| D Montepulciano | 1561 | R Lat | bs | 18 | 10,900 | 14,597 | 26 | 1 | 43 | 161 | |
| AN Monte Oliveto Maggiore | 1319 | R Lat | bs | 7 | 600 | 687 | 23 | 13 | 13 | 5 | |
| CR *Lazio* (D Roma, & 3 subdivisions): | | R Lat | Bs | 1,454 | 3,429,280 | 4,572,609 | *Conferenza Episcopale Laziale.* | | | | *Lazio Conciliar Region*. The Region covers 4 areas: (a) the *Diocese of Rome* (P Roma), which is listed separately at the head of this list of Italian dioceses, but whose statistics are included in the sub-total for Lazio Conciliar Region; (b) *Traditional Suburban Churches* (*Chiese Suburbicarie*), which are all immediately subject to the Holy See; (c) *Lower Lazio* (*Lazio Inferiore*); (d) *Upper Lazio* (*Lazio Superiore*). Lazio Conciliar Region is in central Italy, and its boundaries are almost the same as those of the civil region. Area 13,955 km2, population 4,600,000 (rural and urban, including Rome). 1964–69, 16% rise in vocations to the priesthood. 15 diocesan pastoral councils and 18 presbyteral councils (1971). Suppressed diocese: Montefiascone (absorbed by D Viterbo-Tuscania). Abbreviation in column 1: in D Terracina-Latina, S=Sezze. D Viterbo: SM=San Martino. |
| (1) Chiese Suburbicarie: | | R Lat | bs | 233 | 491,400 | 655,398 | *Traditional Suburban Churches.* | | | | |
| D Albano | c 350 | R Lat | bs | 48 | 185,400 | 247,170 | 269 | 152 | 1138 | 2955 | |
| D Frascati | c 250 | R Lat | bs | 19 | 56,200 | 74,950 | 255 | 172 | 634 | 988 | |
| D Ostia | c 250 | R Lat | bs | 1 | 2,900 | 3,920 | 4 | 5 | 22 | 60 | |
| D Palestrina | c 350 | R Lat | bs | 30 | 43,300 | 57,800 | 96 | 8 | 174 | 840 | |
| D Porto & Santa Rufina | c 250 | R Lat | bs | 48 | 87,500 | 116,700 | 125 | 40 | 751 | 1312 | |
| D Sabina & Poggio Mirteto | c 450 | R Lat | bs | 78 | 76,600 | 102,158 | 168 | 4 | 350 | 1561 | |
| D Velletri | c 450 | R Lat | bs | 9 | 39,500 | 52,700 | 54 | 22 | 108 | 761 | |
| (2) Lazio Inferiore: | | R Lat | bs | 539 | 706,370 | 941,961 | *Lower Lazio.* | | | | |
| AD Gaeta | c 750 | R Lat | bs | 50 | 94,600 | 126,123 | 122 | 12 | 320 | 2072 | |
| D Alatri | c 550 | R Lat | bs | 22 | 23,400 | 31,260 | 48 | 1 | 119 | 524 | |
| D Anagni | c 450 | R Lat | bs | 33 | 30,500 | 40,683 | 94 | 5 | 208 | 695 | |
| D Aquino, Sora & Pontecorvo | c 250 | R Lat | bs | 105 | 112,700 | 150,251 | 171 | 15 | 256 | 1898 | |
| D Ferentino | c 350 | R Lat | bs | 34 | 40,900 | 54,500 | 60 | 4 | 130 | 690 | |
| D Segni | c 450 | R Lat | bs | 20 | 35,100 | 46,800 | 42 | 4 | 136 | 886 | |
| D Terracina-Latina, Priverno & S | c 90 | R Lat | bs | 99 | 166,800 | 222,459 | 157 | 2 | 270 | 4124 | |
| D Tivoli | c 150 | R Lat | bs | 89 | 98,800 | 131,800 | 131 | 6 | 256 | 1721 | |
| D Veroli-Frosinone | c 750 | R Lat | bs | 57 | 84,000 | 112,038 | 151 | 32 | 341 | 1231 | |
| AN Santa Maria di Grottaferrata | 1937 | R IAb | os | 1 | 80 | 88 | 18 | 12 | 7 | 17 | |
| AN Subiaco | c1050 | R Lat | bs | 29 | 19,500 | 25,959 | 83 | 20 | 47 | 382 | |
| (3) Lazio Superiore: | | R Lat | bs | 412 | 367,000 | 489,250 | *Upper Lazio.* | | | | |
| D Acquapendente | 1649 | R Lat | bs | 12 | 15,700 | 20,999 | 20 | 0 | 97 | 236 | |
| D Bagnoregio | c 550 | R Lat | bs | 29 | 15,900 | 21,155 | 36 | 2 | 135 | 215 | |
| D Civita Castellana, Orte, Gallese | c 650 | R Lat | bs | 42 | 60,060 | 80,825 | 69 | 2 | 98 | 800 | |
| D Montefiascone | c1450 | R Lat | bs | 19 | 26,000 | 34,682 | 53 | 4 | 110 | 432 | |
| D Nepi & Sutri | c 90 | R Lat | bs | 37 | 53,400 | 71,174 | 86 | 25 | 305 | 1049 | |
| D Rieti | c 450 | R Lat | bs | 203 | 83,600 | 111,415 | 143 | 11 | 304 | 965 | |
| D Tarquinia & Civitavecchia | c 350 | R Lat | bs | 24 | 55,500 | 74,000 | 70 | 0 | 246 | 930 | |
| D Viterbo-Tuscania & AN SM | c 250 | R Lat | bs | 46 | 56,300 | 75,000 | 106 | 108 | 358 | 1025 | |
| *CR Liguria:* | | R Lat | Bs | 1,362 | 1,611,400 | 2,148,490 | *Conferenza Episcopale Ligure.* | | | | *Liguria Conciliar Region*. Northern Italy. Civil region of Liguria, and part of Lombardy (D Tortona), and Genoa the largest Italian port. Area 7,404 km2, population 2,200,000, in industry and agriculture. 8 diocesan pastoral councils and 8 presbyteral councils (1971). D Luni (La Spezia), Sarzana & B: B=Brugnato. |
| M Genova (Genoa) | c 250 | R Lat | Bs | 270 | 700,500 | 934,000 | 1161 | 282 | 3321 | 10331 | |
| D Albenga-Imperia | c 450 | R Lat | Bs | 203 | 115,800 | 154,450 | 264 | 25 | 913 | 1853 | |
| D Bobbio | c1050 | R Lat | Bs | 71 | 14,900 | 19,916 | 80 | 0 | 28 | 143 | |
| D Chiavari | 1892 | R Lat | Bs | 136 | 106,500 | 142,000 | 208 | 51 | 600 | 1300 | |
| D Luni (La Spezia), Sarzana & B | c 450 | R Lat | Bs | 190 | 183,800 | 245,009 | 295 | 21 | 390 | 3083 | |
| D Savona & Noli | c 950 | R Lat | Bs | 77 | 126,800 | 169,000 | 214 | 8 | 842 | 1921 | |
| D Tortona | c 150 | R Lat | Bs | 315 | 230,000 | 306,615 | 413 | 11 | 670 | 3200 | |
| D Ventimiglia-San Remo | c 650 | R Lat | Bs | 100 | 133,100 | 177,500 | 185 | 12 | 755 | 1169 | |
| *CR Lombardia:* | | R Lat | Bs | 3,171 | 5,484,700 | 7,313,572 | *Conferenza Epis Lombarda.* | | | | *Lombardy Conciliar Region*. Northern Italy. Area 20,081 km2, nearly co-terminous with civil region of Lombardy. Population 7,400,000. Milan is the economic capital of the country, and Lombardy the centre for internal immigration. 1964–69, 10% rise in vocations. Milan has Italy's only Catholic (non-pontifical) university, 8 diocesan pastoral councils; 1 regional and 9 diocesan presbyteral councils. |
| M Milano (Milan) | c 90 | R Lat | Bs | 1,081 | 3,007,000 | 4,010,000 | 3637 | 0 | 12300 | 81000 | |
| D Bergamo | c 350 | R Lat | Bs | 427 | 521,400 | 695,200 | 1148 | 98 | 4231 | 12651 | |
| D Brescia | c 90 | R Lat | Bs | 489 | 637,500 | 850,000 | 1276 | 217 | 3953 | 16288 | |
| D Como | c 350 | R Lat | Bs | 382 | 343,500 | 458,000 | 722 | 178 | 2100 | 8171 | |
| D Crema | 1579 | R Lat | Bs | 60 | 56,200 | 74,967 | 150 | 43 | 370 | 1733 | |
| D Cremona | c 350 | R Lat | Bs | 236 | 270,100 | 360,178 | 447 | 67 | 1460 | 5000 | |
| D Lodi | c 350 | R Lat | Bs | 124 | 153,900 | 205,212 | 308 | 17 | 700 | 2795 | |
| D Mantova | 804 | R Lat | Bs | 168 | 240,900 | 321,180 | 335 | 13 | 780 | 4588 | |
| D Pavia | c 90 | R Lat | Bs | 111 | 116,000 | 154,735 | 212 | 19 | 516 | 1402 | |
| D Vigevano | 1529 | R Lat | Bs | 93 | 138,100 | 184,100 | 192 | 5 | 343 | 2251 | |
| *CR Lucania & Salernitano:* | | R Lat | Bs | 863 | 1,355,900 | 1,807,663 | *Conf Epis Salernitano-Lucana.* | | | | *Salerno-Lucania Conciliar Region*. Southern Italy. Covers parts of 2 civil regions (Basilicata, Campania). Area 16,748 km2, population 1,864,200, in agriculture. 1964–69, 30% rise in vocations. 14 diocesan pastoral councils and 18 presbyteral councils (1971). Suppressed dioceses: Campagna |
| M Acerenza | c 350 | R Lat | Bs | 22 | 45,100 | 60,100 | 38 | 0 | 75 | 807 | |
| D Muro Lucano | c1050 | R Lat | Bs | 19 | 27,000 | 36,000 | 30 | 0 | 34 | 364 | |
| D Venosa | c 450 | R Lat | Bs | 13 | 28,400 | 37,877 | 33 | 1 | 72 | 667 | |
| M Conza, S'Angelo dei Lombardi | c 750 | R Lat | Bs | 24 | 60,000 | 80,000 | 55 | 7 | 78 | 860 | |
| D Lacedonia | c1050 | R Lat | Bs | 13 | 21,000 | 28,050 | 19 | 0 | 24 | 372 | |

*Continued overleaf*

*Table 2–continued*

| Official name 1 | Begun 2 | Type 3 | Counc 4 | Congs 5 | Adults 6 | Affiliated 7 | Names, notes, and other statistics (see Codebook) 8 | | | | |
|---|---|---|---|---|---|---|---|---|---|---|---|
| M Matera | c 850 | R Lat | Bs | 41 | 101,200 | 135,000 | 93 | 10 | 135 | 1828 | (absorbed by M Salerno & Acerno), Cava & Sarno (absorbed by AD Amalfi and D Nocera dei Pagani), M Conza (absorbed by D Nusco). In 1973, D Potenza was elevated to AD and to M in 1976; in 1976, D Anglona-Tursi became D Tursi-Lagonegro. |
| D Anglona-Tursi (Lagonegro) | 968 | R Lat | Bs | 62 | 86,500 | 115,300 | 59 | 0 | 104 | 2029 | |
| D Tricarico | c1050 | R Lat | Bs | 31 | 49,900 | 66,506 | 39 | 1 | 93 | 828 | |
| M Salerno & Acerno | c 550 | R Lat | Bs | 176 | 285,000 | 380,051 | 372 | 50 | 635 | 8825 | |
| D Diano-Teggiano | 1850 | R Lat | Bs | 54 | 68,200 | 90,904 | 75 | 2 | 131 | 1100 | |
| D Nocera dei Pagani | c 650 | R Lat | Bs | 29 | 105,800 | 141,053 | 98 | 22 | 326 | 3235 | |
| D Nusco | c1050 | R Lat | Bs | 21 | 27,200 | 36,224 | 26 | 2 | 44 | 405 | |
| D Policastro | c1050 | R Lat | Bs | 44 | 60,700 | 80,883 | 71 | 2 | 140 | 1401 | |
| D Vallo di Lucania | c1150 | R Lat | Bs | 118 | 120,700 | 160,950 | 125 | 3 | 140 | 1900 | |
| M Potenza & Marsico Nuovo | c 350 | R Lat | Bs | 35 | 82,500 | 110,000 | 97 | 6 | 240 | 2015 | |
| AD Amalfi | c 550 | R Lat | bs | 49 | 32,900 | 43,850 | 80 | 5 | 135 | 812 | |
| D Campagna | 1525 | R Lat | bs | 34 | 48,000 | 64,000 | 36 | 2 | 52 | 1020 | |
| D Cava & Sarno | c1050 | R Lat | bs | 34 | 42,700 | 56,915 | 64 | 5 | 118 | 1172 | |
| D Melfi & Rapolla | c1050 | R Lat | bs | 19 | 36,800 | 49,000 | 35 | 3 | 62 | 860 | |
| AN S Trinità di Cava dei Tirreni | 1394 | R Lat | bs | 25 | 26,300 | 35,000 | 60 | 10 | 90 | 405 | |
| *CR Marche:* | | R Lat | Bs | 1,402 | 1,036,000 | 1,381,585 | *Conferenza Epis Marchigiana.* | | | | *Marche Conciliar Region.* Central Italy. Area roughly same as civil region, also part of Republic of San Marino (in D Montefeltro). Area 9,141 km2, population 1,390,000, mainly in agriculture with some industry. 14 diocesan pastoral councils and 17 presbyteral councils (one interdiocesan: Treia, Macerata, Tolentino) (1971). Celebrated Marian pilgrimage centre in PN Loreto. Suppressed dioceses: Fano (absorbed by D Fossombrone), Osimo & Cingoli (absorbed by M Ancona & Numana), Ripatransone (absorbed by D Montalto). In 1977, D Montefeltro was renamed D San Marino-Montefeltro. |
| M Ancona & Numana | c 250 | R Lat | Bs | 56 | 115,500 | 154,000 | 203 | 24 | 281 | 2291 | |
| D Iesi | c 550 | R Lat | Bs | 38 | 56,200 | 75,000 | 88 | 12 | 202 | 994 | |
| D Osimo & Cingoli | c 450 | R Lat | Bs | 40 | 40,100 | 53,464 | 100 | 22 | 150 | 796 | |
| M Fermo | c 250 | R Lat | Bs | 165 | 165,000 | 220,000 | 422 | 88 | 550 | 3329 | |
| D Macerata & Tolentino | c 450 | R Lat | Bs | 37 | 51,500 | 68,697 | 159 | 28 | 206 | 926 | |
| D Montalto | 1586 | R Lat | Bs | 38 | 21,200 | 28,250 | 47 | 1 | 56 | 218 | |
| D Ripatransone | 1571 | R Lat | Bs | 31 | 64,300 | 85,800 | 102 | 37 | 176 | 1510 | |
| D San Severino & Treia | 1586 | R Lat | Bs | 39 | 17,400 | 23,234 | 85 | 9 | 143 | 214 | |
| M Urbino | c 550 | R Lat | Bs | 111 | 28,900 | 38,500 | 89 | 0 | 96 | 402 | |
| D Cagli & Pergola | c 350 | R Lat | Bs | 57 | 18,800 | 25,098 | 54 | 8 | 61 | 315 | |
| D Fossombrone | c 450 | R Lat | Bs | 42 | 14,300 | 19,105 | 59 | 0 | 23 | 240 | |
| D Montefeltro (1977, San M) | c 850 | R Lat | Bs | 124 | 30,000 | 40,000 | 110 | 2 | 104 | 700 | |
| D Pesaro | c 250 | R Lat | Bs | 59 | 76,100 | 101,500 | 122 | 4 | 178 | 1808 | |
| D Senigallia | c 550 | R Lat | Bs | 57 | 85,800 | 114,378 | 148 | 5 | 272 | 1466 | |
| D Urbania & S'Angelo in Vado | 1635 | R Lat | Bs | 63 | 9,800 | 13,000 | 114 | 19 | 148 | 2838 | |
| AD Camerino | c 250 | R Lat | bs | 173 | 38,600 | 51,471 | 154 | 4 | 192 | 500 | |
| D Ascoli Piceno | c 350 | R Lat | bs | 146 | 76,500 | 102,000 | 186 | 4 | 241 | 1155 | |
| D Fabriano & Matelica | c 450 | R Lat | bs | 47 | 27,900 | 37,261 | 96 | 30 | 141 | 453 | |
| D Fano | c 90 | R Lat | bs | 52 | 56,200 | 75,000 | 124 | 12 | 230 | 1500 | |
| D Recanati | 1239 | R Lat | bs | 23 | 33,700 | 44,932 | 76 | 5 | 82 | 658 | |
| PN Loreto | 1965 | R Lat | bs | 4 | 8,200 | 10,895 | 58 | 32 | 172 | 139 | |
| *CR Piemonte:* | | R Lat | Bs | 2,585 | 3,203,700 | 4,271,177 | *Conferenza Epis Piemontese.* | | | | *Piedmont Conciliar Region.* Northern Italy. Civil regions of Piemonte and Valle d'Aosta (the latter bilingual, Italian/French). Area 29,404 km2, population 4,501,000, mostly industrial. 15 diocesan pastoral councils and 18 presbyteral councils (1971). End of 1971: the 2 councils of Turin produced a notable pastoral letter setting out a plan for joint pastoral action and centring on the themes of poverty, liberty and brotherhood. D Pinerolo in the extreme west on the French frontier contains the major Waldensian strongholds. |
| M Torino (Turin) | c 450 | R Lat | Bs | 405 | 1,365,000 | 1,820,000 | 1850 | 776 | 7475 | 31720 | |
| D Acqui | c 350 | R Lat | Bs | 151 | 122,200 | 163,000 | 235 | 9 | 465 | 2011 | |
| D Alba | c 350 | R Lat | Bs | 140 | 90,200 | 120,236 | 261 | 117 | 562 | 1581 | |
| D Aosta | c 350 | R Lat | Bs | 94 | 81,200 | 108,300 | 175 | 16 | 244 | 1484 | |
| D Asti | c 250 | R Lat | Bs | 139 | 112,500 | 150,000 | 238 | 9 | 480 | 840 | |
| D Cuneo | 1817 | R Lat | Bs | 89 | 78,000 | 104,000 | 204 | 12 | 699 | 1575 | |
| D Fossano | 1592 | R Lat | Bs | 35 | 26,600 | 35,420 | 85 | 4 | 105 | 535 | |
| D Ivrea | c 450 | R Lat | Bs | 196 | 148,050 | 198,040 | 270 | 58 | 929 | 2815 | |
| D Mondovi | 1388 | R Lat | Bs | 190 | 99,500 | 132,660 | 335 | 30 | 320 | 1200 | |
| D Pinerolo | 1748 | R Lat | Bs | 66 | 57,200 | 76,250 | 144 | 22 | 565 | 1342 | |
| D Saluzzo | 1511 | R Lat | Bs | 109 | 75,000 | 99,950 | 233 | 7 | 248 | 1370 | |
| D Susa | 1772 | R Lat | Bs | 64 | 43,500 | 58,000 | 97 | 2 | 395 | 350 | |
| M Vercelli | c 250 | R Lat | Bs | 144 | 147,200 | 196,251 | 261 | 44 | 865 | 2015 | |
| D Alessandria | 1175 | R Lat | Bs | 73 | 114,800 | 153,000 | 175 | 9 | 450 | 1737 | |
| D Biella | 1772 | R Lat | Bs | 128 | 151,000 | 201,327 | 219 | 18 | 421 | 2410 | |
| D Casale Monferrato | 1474 | R Lat | Bs | 147 | 94,300 | 125,743 | 246 | 20 | 396 | 1208 | |
| D Novara | c 350 | R Lat | Bs | 415 | 397,000 | 529,000 | 799 | 106 | 2015 | 9000 | |
| *CR Puglie:* | | R Lat | Bs | 679 | 2,261,600 | 3,015,538 | *Conferenza Epis Pugliese.* | | | | *Puglia Conciliar Region.* Southern Italy. Area almost identical with civil region. Area 12,237 km2, population 3,028,000, in agriculture. 1964–69, rise of 20% in vocations. 14 diocesan pastoral councils and 17 presbyteral councils. Suppressed dioceses: Conversano (absorbed by D Monopoli, and M Otranto. PN Altamura: the abbreviation F= Fonti. D Molfetta: T = Terlizzi. |
| M Bari | c 350 | R Lat | Bs | 83 | 469,100 | 625,500 | 411 | 94 | 1325 | 11630 | |
| D Conversano | c 450 | R Lat | Bs | 28 | 79,100 | 105,500 | 120 | 13 | 230 | 2200 | |
| D Ruvo & Bitonto | c 550 | R Lat | Bs | 25 | 52,900 | 70,563 | 61 | 1 | 145 | 1583 | |
| M Brindisi & Ostuni | c 350 | R Lat | Bs | 48 | 186,500 | 248,615 | 153 | 6 | 390 | 4466 | |
| M Otranto | c 650 | R Lat | Bs | 66 | 142,100 | 189,450 | 145 | 12 | 283 | 3122 | |
| D Gallipoli | c 550 | R Lat | Bs | 14 | 21,000 | 28,000 | 29 | 0 | 82 | 571 | |
| D Ugento-SMaria di Leuca | c1250 | R Lat | Bs | 35 | 82,500 | 110,000 | 79 | 0 | 140 | 1745 | |
| M Taranto | c 550 | R Lat | Bs | 69 | 269,200 | 358,900 | 215 | 19 | 522 | 7358 | |
| D Castellaneta | c1050 | R Lat | Bs | 25 | 51,700 | 68,972 | 38 | 3 | 90 | 1388 | |
| D Oria | 1591 | R Lat | Bs | 31 | 115,100 | 153,440 | 151 | 24 | 375 | 2896 | |
| M Trani, Barletta & Bisceglie | c 550 | R Lat | Bs | 49 | 182,100 | 242,840 | 179 | 15 | 440 | 5500 | |
| D Andria | c1050 | R Lat | Bs | 29 | 92,300 | 123,018 | 105 | 2 | 157 | 2680 | |
| D Gravina & Irsina | c 850 | R Lat | bs | 14 | 33,200 | 44,267 | 33 | 4 | 139 | 889 | |
| D Lecce | 1057 | R Lat | bs | 56 | 170,100 | 226,780 | 224 | 30 | 558 | 4111 | |
| D Molfetta, Giovinazzo & T | c1050 | R Lat | bs | 24 | 77,400 | 103,261 | 98 | 22 | 203 | 2053 | |
| D Monopoli | c1050 | R Lat | bs | 24 | 72,900 | 97,200 | 82 | 5 | 75 | 1815 | |
| D Nardo | 1413 | R Lat | bs | 40 | 118,200 | 157,630 | 133 | 7 | 160 | 2406 | |
| PN Altamura & Acquaviva delle F | 1248 | R Lat | bs | 19 | 46,200 | 61,602 | 57 | 5 | 141 | 1403 | |
| *CR Romagna:* | | R Lat | Bs | 1,506 | 1,716,500 | 2,288,791 | *Conferenza Epis Flaminia.* | | | | *Romagna Conciliar Region.* Northern Italy. Eastern half of civil region of Emilia-Romagna, also part of Republic of San Marino (in D Rimini). Area 10,519 km2, population 2,296,800, mainly agriculture with some industry. 1964–69, 32% drop in vocations. 9 diocesan pastoral councils and 11 presbyteral councils (1971). |
| M Bologna | c 250 | R Lat | Bs | 469 | 684,800 | 913,127 | 923 | 177 | 2331 | 10804 | |
| D Faenza | c 250 | R Lat | Bs | 123 | 97,500 | 130,000 | 221 | 8 | 368 | 1704 | |
| D Imola | c 350 | R Lat | Bs | 135 | 108,900 | 145,200 | 200 | 7 | 524 | 1408 | |
| D Modigliana | 1850 | R Lat | Bs | 83 | 17,100 | 22,845 | 61 | 0 | 93 | 148 | |
| M Ravenna & Cervia | c 90 | R Lat | Bs | 84 | 145,500 | 194,000 | 173 | 8 | 490 | 3414 | |
| D Bertinoro | 1360 | R Lat | Bs | 65 | 28,800 | 38,444 | 74 | 3 | 99 | 535 | |
| D Cesena | c 90 | R Lat | Bs | 87 | 96,100 | 128,136 | 191 | 27 | 207 | 2392 | |
| D Comacchio | c 550 | R Lat | Bs | 43 | 49,200 | 65,600 | 61 | 1 | 125 | 880 | |
| D Forli | c 150 | R Lat | Bs | 69 | 96,900 | 129,150 | 125 | 8 | 298 | 1750 | |
| D Rimini | c 250 | R Lat | Bs | 171 | 180,000 | 240,000 | 276 | 12 | 685 | 2000 | |
| D Sarsina | c 350 | R Lat | Bs | 52 | 9,700 | 13,000 | 47 | 0 | 15 | 266 | |
| AD Ferrara | c 350 | R Lat | bs | 125 | 202,000 | 269,289 | 224 | 25 | 500 | 3272 | |
| *CR Sardegna:* | | R Lat | Bs | 564 | 1,078,300 | 1,437,985 | *Conferenza Episcopale Sarda.* | | | | *Sardinia Conciliar Region.* Central Italy. Covers whole island. Area 24,091 km2, population 1,447,900; population density at 60 per km2 only one-third of national average; mainly agriculture and breeding, with some industrial centres. Steady emigration to northern Italy and abroad. 1964–69, 35% drop in vocations. 6 diocesan pastoral councils; one regional and 7 diocesan presbyteral councils (1971). Suppressed diocese: Alghero (absorbed by D Bosa). |
| M Cagliari | c 350 | R Lat | Bs | 118 | 300,000 | 400,000 | 368 | 45 | 1065 | 9859 | |
| D Iglesias | 1763 | R Lat | Bs | 59 | 106,700 | 142,300 | 105 | 7 | 183 | 1980 | |
| D Nuoro | c1150 | R Lat | Bs | 40 | 91,600 | 122,162 | 102 | 8 | 268 | 2342 | |
| D Ogliastra | 1824 | R Lat | Bs | 30 | 54,700 | 72,962 | 56 | 6 | 61 | 1219 | |
| M Oristano | c1050 | R Lat | Bs | 85 | 105,000 | 140,000 | 165 | 11 | 404 | 2338 | |
| D Ales & Terralba | c 650 | R Lat | Bs | 49 | 78,200 | 104,310 | 93 | 7 | 132 | 2729 | |
| M Sassari | c 450 | R Lat | Bs | 54 | 135,000 | 180,000 | 216 | 24 | 502 | 3917 | |
| D Alghero | c1150 | R Lat | Bs | 34 | 60,500 | 80,720 | 82 | 4 | 129 | 1296 | |
| D Ampurias & Tempio | c 350 | R Lat | Bs | 44 | 77,000 | 102,712 | 88 | 1 | 168 | 1847 | |
| D Bosa | c 450 | R Lat | Bs | 22 | 26,200 | 35,000 | 48 | 1 | 64 | 389 | |
| D Ozieri | c1250 | R Lat | Bs | 29 | 43,400 | 57,819 | 75 | 0 | 75 | 876 | |
| *CR Sicilia:* | | R Lat | Bs | 1,672 | 3,643,900 | 4,858,694 | *Conferenza Episcopale Sicula.* | | | | *Sicily Conciliar Region.* Southern Italy. Area covers islands of Sicily, Lipari (a separate diocese), Pelagian isles (in D Agrigento), Pantellaria in the extreme south of Italy (in D Mazara del Vallo), and others. Sicily is relatively poor, industrialization being obstructed by the criminal activities of the Mafia. In consequence, there is heavy emigration, to Lombardy and Piemonte and also abroad, giving a very high rate of 0.6% per year leaving Italy permanently. Area 25,710 km2, population 4,948,800, mainly in agriculture except industrial areas of Catania, Messina, Palermo, Syracuse. Diocesan councils: 14 pastoral, 17 presbyteral; and 1 regional presbyteral council (1971). |
| M Messina & Ssmo Salvatore | c 450 | R Lat | Bs | 261 | 365,200 | 487,000 | 545 | 215 | 1030 | 6634 | |
| D Lipari | c 450 | R Lat | Bs | 26 | 9,900 | 13,200 | 31 | 0 | 22 | 150 | |
| D Nicosia | 1816 | R Lat | Bs | 40 | 82,700 | 110,200 | 88 | 2 | 119 | 1630 | |
| D Patti | c1150 | R Lat | Bs | 82 | 150,000 | 200,000 | 185 | 7 | 188 | 3476 | |
| M Monreale | 1176 | R Lat | Bs | 80 | 148,500 | 198,000 | 180 | 18 | 340 | 3120 | |
| D Agrigento | c 90 | R Lat | Bs | 197 | 352,500 | 470,000 | 371 | 29 | 990 | 8448 | |
| D Caltanissetta | 1844 | R Lat | Bs | 65 | 119,200 | 159,000 | 177 | 11 | 492 | 4001 | |
| M Palermo | c 90 | R Lat | Bs | 148 | 610,500 | 814,000 | 645 | 160 | 1971 | 16979 | |
| D Cefalù | 1131 | R Lat | Bs | 44 | 83,800 | 111,703 | 149 | 17 | 286 | 1547 | |
| D Mazara del Vallo | 1093 | R Lat | Bs | 57 | 169,600 | 226,183 | 140 | 9 | 226 | 3735 | |
| D Trapani | 1844 | R Lat | Bs | 81 | 154,900 | 206,533 | 166 | 16 | 368 | 3494 | |
| M Siracusa | c 150 | R Lat | Bs | 65 | 201,000 | 268,000 | 188 | 14 | 420 | 5062 | |
| D Caltagirone | 1818 | R Lat | Bs | 58 | 120,400 | 160,500 | 135 | 9 | 237 | 2415 | |
| D Noto | 1844 | R Lat | Bs | 80 | 141,700 | 188,950 | 143 | 18 | 338 | 3328 | |
| D Piazza Armerina | 1817 | R Lat | Bs | 69 | 180,000 | 240,000 | 169 | 6 | 316 | 5274 | |
| D Ragusa | 1950 | R Lat | Bs | 47 | 122,300 | 163,115 | 144 | 7 | 362 | 2779 | |
| AD Catania | c 90 | R Lat | bs | 136 | 460,900 | 614,547 | 555 | 152 | 1314 | 12207 | |
| D Acireale | 1844 | R Lat | bs | 110 | 132,400 | 176,550 | 279 | 66 | 458 | 3159 | |
| D Pinna degli Albanesi | 1937 | R IAb | os | 15 | 25,200 | 33,600 | 34 | 2 | 71 | 336 | |
| PN Santa Lucia del Mela | 1206 | R Lat | bs | 11 | 13,200 | 17,613 | 21 | 0 | 21 | 249 | |

*Continued opposite*

*Table 2–continued*

| Official name 1 | Begun 2 | Type 3 | Counc 4 | Congs 5 | Adults 6 | Affiliated 7 | Names, notes, and other statistics (see Codebook) 8 | |
|---|---|---|---|---|---|---|---|---|
| *CR Umbria:* | | R Lat | Bs | 1,186 | 624,200 | 832,456 | *Conferenza Episcopale Umbra.* | *Umbria Conciliar Region.* Central Italy. Area |
| M Perugia | c 150 | R Lat | Bs | 205 | 139,700 | 186,280 | 328 10 589 2926 | covers the civil region of Umbria and also part of |
| D Assisi | c 250 | R Lat | Bs | 37 | 33,700 | 45,000 | 176 89 533 539 | Abruzzi. Area 11,254 km2, population 942,900, in |
| D Città della Pieve | 1600 | R Lat | Bs | 34 | 21,800 | 29,112 | 39 0 95 295 | agriculture and manual work. 1964–69, drop of 31% |
| D Città di Castello | c 650 | R Lat | Bs | 156 | 43,500 | 58,013 | 110 0 245 775 | in vocations. 8 diocesan pastoral councils (one |
| D Foligno | c 90 | R Lat | Bs | 67 | 44,300 | 59,020 | 106 40 210 870 | interdiocesan: Terni-Narni) and 12 presbyteral |
| D Gubbio | c 450 | R Lat | Bs | 67 | 32,200 | 43,000 | 74 1 116 506 | councils (one interdiocesan: Amelia-Terni-Narni) |
| D Nocera Umbra & Gualdo T | c 450 | R Lat | Bs | 85 | 30,000 | 40,000 | 118 8 182 361 | (1971). Celebrated St Francis of Assisi pilgrimage |
| AD Spoleto | c 90 | R Lat | bs | 189 | 64,800 | 86,350 | 183 5 389 975 | centre (in D Assisi). Suppressed dioceses: Gubbio |
| D Amelia | c 450 | R Lat | bs | 21 | 14,600 | 19,500 | 32 2 86 233 | (absorbed by D Città di Castello), Norcia |
| D Norcia | c 450 | R Lat | bs | 101 | 16,100 | 21,480 | 79 7 151 165 | (absorbed by AD Spoleto), Todi (absorbed by D |
| D Orvieto | c 550 | R Lat | bs | 57 | 39,800 | 53,000 | 65 10 200 527 | Orvieto). D Nocera: T=Tadino. |
| D Terni & Narni | c 150 | R Lat | bs | 66 | 104,200 | 139,000 | 98 10 196 1450 | |
| D Todi | c 150 | R Lat | bs | 101 | 39,500 | 52,701 | 115 7 172 664 | |
| *CR Veneto (Triveneta):* | | R Lat | Bs | 3,655 | 4,544,600 | 6,059,655 | *Conferenza Epis Triveneta.* | *Venetian Conciliar Region.* Northern Italy. Area |
| P Venezia (Venice) | 1170 | R Lat | Bs | 121 | 300,000 | 400,000 | 602 95 1670 5790 | covers Triveneta, the 3 northeastern civil regions |
| D Adria | c 650 | R Lat | Bs | 111 | 151,900 | 202,568 | 266 4 619 2819 | of Trentino-Alto Adige (bilingual, Italian, |
| D Chioggia | c 650 | R Lat | Bs | 71 | 92,800 | 123,750 | 138 8 320 1915 | German), Friuli-Venezia-Giulia (both these latter |
| D Concordia-Pordenone | c 350 | R Lat | Bs | 194 | 222,200 | 296,246 | 405 38 665 4706 | 2 being intensely Catholic areas), and Veneto, |
| D Feltre & Belluno | c 150 | R Lat | Bs | 168 | 153,500 | 204,630 | 348 28 591 2761 | Area 40,256 km2, population 6,119,400, mainly |
| D Padova | c 90 | R Lat | Bs | 442 | 645,000 | 860,000 | 1340 368 4300 12000 | agricultural, some industry. Considerable |
| D Treviso | c 350 | R Lat | Bs | 251 | 431,200 | 575,000 | 807 201 1911 10306 | emigration: 1961–71, 0.13% of population per year. |
| D Verona | c 250 | R Lat | Bs | 372 | 525,000 | 700,000 | 1196 434 4255 12350 | Diocesan councils: 14 pastoral and 14 presbyteral |
| D Vicenza | c 150 | R Lat | Bs | 347 | 465,600 | 620,879 | 941 214 2717 10899 | (1971). |
| D Vittorio Veneto | c 550 | R Lat | Bs | 175 | 208,400 | 277,896 | 434 35 970 3575 | |
| M Gorizia & Gradisca | 1751 | R Lat | Bs | 105 | 133,500 | 178,000 | 233 31 620 2295 | |
| D Trieste & Capo d'Istria | c 550 | R Lat | Bs | 54 | 217,500 | 290,000 | 261 22 488 3067 | |
| M Trento | c 150 | R Lat | Bs | 450 | 319,500 | 426,000 | 1149 176 1897 7300 | |
| D Bolzano-Bressanone | c 550 | R Lat | Bs | 341 | 310,300 | 413,637 | 905 126 1415 8510 | |
| M Udine | 1751 | R Lat | bs | 453 | 368,300 | 491,049 | 820 63 1270 6635 | |
| Chiesa Cattolica Riformata d'Italia | 1881 | C ReC | ••••• | 6 | 200 | 500 | Schism ex RCC by 12 priests, 6 churches. Support from Swiss Old Catholics. Milan. | |
| Ch Cristiana Avventista del 7 Giorno | 1864 | P Adv | x•••k | 62 | 3,523 | 7,000 | *SDAs. Seventh-day Adventists. Italian Mission.* 30nx,76mw,1j,1p(30),1s,62t,201Y. | |
| Chiesa Cristiana Cattolica | | C OCa | U•••• | 1 | 50 | 100 | *Old Catholic Ch.* In Scandiano (Reggio Emilia). Links with Union of Utrecht. 1n. | |
| Chiesa Cristiana Ev dei Fratelli in I | 1833 | P CBr | x•••k | 174 | 11,500 | 20,000 | *Christian Ch of the Brethren. Plymouth (Open) Brethren.* Piedmont, Puglie. 25f. | |
| Chiesa di Dio | 1966 | P Pe3 | ZF••• | 10 | 350 | 1,000 | *Ch of God.* M=CoG(Cleveland)(USA). Calabria and southern Italy. 8n,2f,W=50%,5Y,20z. | |
| Chiesa di Gesú Cristo dei Santi dUG | 1850 | M LdS | x•••• | 20 | 1,000 | 2,307 | *dUG=degli Ultimi Giorni, Ch of JC of Latter-day Saints. Mormons.* HQ USA, 50f. | |
| Chiesa Evangelica del Nazareno | 1948 | P Hol | xF••• | 19 | 1,107 | 2,000 | *Ch of the Nazarene.* M=CoN(USA). 7n,1x,6m,2f,G=9.8%pa,1p,10t (287),W=43%,37Y. | |
| Chiesa Evangelica Internazionale | 1957 | P Pe2 | ZW••• | 200 | 3,000 | 15,000 | *International Ev Ch.* Ex AoG. Rapidly-growing merger of independents. 70n,1p. | |
| Chiesa Evangelica Luterana in Italia | 1648 | P Lut | L•C•K | 59 | 5,000 | 7,000 | Germans. Member of VELKD. 1948 union of 9 congregations (Venice, 1648). 2n,8x,400z. | |
| Chiesa Evangelica Mennonita | 1949 | P Men | G•••• | 3 | 60 | 200 | *Ev Mennonite Ch.* M=Mennonite Ch of N America. HQ Florence. 7f. | |
| Chiesa Evangelica Metodista d'Italia | 1859 | P Met | VWC•K | 75 | 3,423 | 6,000 | *Ev Methodist Ch of Italy* (since 1946). A=1962. 32n,48m,G=−1.3%pa,W=63%,47Yy,228z. | |
| Chiesa Evangelica Riformata Svizzera | | P Ref | Rwc•• | 4 | 300 | 500 | *Swiss Evangelical Reformed Ch.* Swiss immigrants. Florence, Genoa, Milan, Naples. | |
| Chiesa Evangelica Valdese | 1173 | P Wal | RWC•K | 121 | 20,753 | 29,413 | *Waldensians.* Decreasing (emigration). 75n,8x,G=−0.9%pa,1p,1s(6),W=40%,320Yy,4135z. | |
| Chiesa Neo-Apostolica | c1950 | C CAp | x•••• | | 10,000 | 20,000 | *New Apostolic Ch.* In Bezirk Schweiz. Germans. World HQ Dortmund (Germany). | |
| Chiesa Ortodossa Greca (D Austria) | | O Gre | Cwc•• | 8 | 15,000 | 25,000 | *Greek Orthodox Ch.* Under Ecumenical Patriarchate of Constantinople. Greeks. 5x. | |
| Chiesa Ortodossa Russa | 1823 | O Sla | Mwc•• | 6 | 1,500 | 2,000 | *Russian Orthodox Ch.* 1929, state recognition. Rome, Florence, Bari, Merano. 4x. | |
| Chiesa Ortodossa Russa (ROCOR) | | O Sla | x•••• | 2 | 500 | 1,000 | *Russian Orthodox Ch Outside of Russia.* M=ROCOR(USA). HQ New York. Conservative. | |
| Chiesa Pentecostal Unite | 1972 | P Pel | x•••• | 9 | 125 | 300 | *United Pentecostal Ch. Jesus Only Church.* M=UPC(USA). Palermo area. 2n,2f. | |
| Chiesa Presbiteriana Scozzese | 1862 | P Ref | Rwc•• | 3 | 50 | 160 | M=Ch of Scotland(UK). English-speaking congregations: Rome, Genoa, Milan. 2f. | |
| Chiesa Universale Giuris-Davidica | 1878 | C mar | ••••• | 6 | 1,000 | 1,800 | *Universal Ch of Law revealed to David* (=Catholic heretic, shot 1878). 20n,24Yy. | |
| Chiese di Cristo in Italia | 1947 | P Dis | x•••• | 49 | 3,000 | 6,000 | *Churches of Christ.* M=CCCC(Instrumental)(USA). Rapid growth. 42n,15f,1j,1p,230Y. | |
| Comunità Catt dei SS Andrea Ap e di C | | C ReC | •V••• | 1 | 300 | 500 | *C=Caffa. Comunità Ecclesiale Ecumenica*, Roma. 1972 applied to join WCC. | |
| Comunità Religiosa Serbo-Ortodossa | 1782 | O Ser | Cwc•• | 1 | 700 | 1,000 | *Serbian Orthodox Ch.* In Trieste. 1944, rejected P Belgrade; under USA bishop. | |
| Esercito della Salvezza | 1886 | P Sal | xwc•k | 36 | 1,715 | 4,000 | *Salvation Army, Italy Territory.* 8 institutions. 43n,6x,G=2.2%pa,W=80%,15Y,30z. | |
| Società della Scienza Cristiana | | M Sci | x•••• | 9 | 300 | 1,000 | *Ch of Christ, Scientist. Christian Science.* M=CCS(Boston,USA). 2m,7w. | |
| Testimoni di Geova | 1891 | M Jeh | x•••• | 433 | 22,196 | 80,000 | *Jehovah's Witnesses.* 1903 first magazines printed. G=15.1%pa,W=95%,2873Y,2187z. | |
| Unione Cristiana Ev Battista d'Italia | 1863 | P Bap | TuC•K | 130 | 5,014 | 10,100 | *UCEBI. 1956 Baptist Union of I.* M=SBC(USA). 55n,3x,25f,G=2.3%pa,1s,W=75%,174Y,80z. | |
| Other Protestant denominations | | P | ••••• | | 7,900 | 14,800 | Total over 120 smaller groups (see list below). | |
| Other Catholic (non-Roman) churches | | C | ••••• | | 5,000 | 10,000 | Total over 30 small bodies (see list below), 15 being under bishops-at-large. | |
| Other marginal Protestant bodies | | M | ••••• | | 1,000 | 2,000 | Total over 30 (see list below). | |
| Other Third World indigenous churches | | T | ••••• | | 100 | 200 | Rapidly-growing immigrant bodies, totalling 5 by 1976 (see below). | |
| Doubly-affiliated (duplication) (1970) | | | | | −427,500 | −588,973 | Evangelicals and other minorities who also are or were baptized Roman Catholics. | |
| Disaffiliated (duplication) (1970) | | | | | −3,619,400 | −4,825,845 | Baptized Catholics who are now completely disaffiliated agnostics or atheists. | |
| **Total affiliated (mid-1970)** | | | | **30,800** | **36,362,427** | **48,657,800** | **Total denominations (1970) . . . 220.** | |
| **Total affiliated (mid-1975)** | | | | **30,600** | **35,748,000** | **47,835,650** | **Total denominations (1975) . . . 225.** | |
| **Total affiliated (mid-1980)** | | | | **30,400** | **35,201,600** | **47,104,500** | **Total denominations (1980) . . . 230.** | |

NOTES ON TABLE ABOVE

COLUMNS: for meanings and CODES (cols. 1, 3, 4, 8): see Codebook (Part 6). Column 1: **Boldface type** = church with over 10% of country's affiliated Christians.

NATIONAL COUNCILS (Column 4, 5th letter).

K = Federazione delle Chiese Evangeliche in Italia (FCEI) (Federation of Evangelical Churches in Italy) (up to 1967, Consiglio Federale).

k = affiliated member of FCEI (Salvation Army), or member of Legal Advisory Board (all other churches).

R = Conferenza Episcopale Italiana (CEI) (Italian Episcopal Conference).

*Other national councils.* Alleanza Evangelica Italiana (AEI) (Italian Evangelical Alliance, IEA) (affiliated to EEA and also to WEF; members individuals only, not denominations). *Local councils.* 5 regional councils affiliated to FCEI.

OTHER PROTESTANT DENOMINATIONS. There are a large number of smaller denominations. Names are given here in Italian unless more commonly known by English or French names. They include: Action Biblique, Avventisti del 7 Giorno Movimenti di Reforma, Baptist Mid-Missions (1951: 8 missionaries), Baptist Missionary Association of America, Chiesa Battista Autonoma, Chiesa Cristiana Biblica (Bible Christian Union) (1950; 15 missionaries), Chiesa Cristiana Evangelica, Chiesa Cristiana Ev dei Fratelli Stretti (Darbisti) (Strict Brethren, Darbyites; Raven-Taylor group), Chiesa Cristiana Protestante, Chiesa di Cristo, Chiesa Presbiteriana Autonoma di Milano, Children of God International (Rome), Christian Ch of North America, Ch of God (Anderson), Communion of Free Churches, Comunità Cristiana Evangelica, Comunità Evangelica Ecumenica di Ispra-Varese, Congregazione Olandese-Alemanna, Crusaders for Christ, Gospel Missionary Union (1950), Greater Europe Mission (1954), Gypsy Ev Movement (France, Switzerland), Independent Faith Mission, International Pentecostal Assemblies, L'Abri Fellowship, Missionary & Soul-Winning Fellowship, Missione Cristiana Europea (European Christian Mission), Missione di Beatenberg, Missione Norvegese per Marittimi (10,000 visitors a year to Seamen's Mission, Genoa), SDA Movement of Reform, Slavic Gospel Association, Società Religiosa degli Amici (Quaccheri), Unione delle Chiese Libere, US Armed Forces chaplaincies (for 10,000 Protestants), West Indies Mission (1972), World Baptist Fellowship Mission Agency (1970), Worldwide European Fellowship, World-Wide Missions (1963).

OTHER CATHOLIC (NON-ROMAN) CHURCHES. These bodies, mostly schisms from the Roman Catholic Church, are very small, and include: Antoinists (Belgium), Chiesa Cattolica Apostolica Ortodossa, Chiesa Cattolica Liberale, Chiesa Vetero-Cattolica, and about 15 miniscule bodies with few lay followers under episcopi vagantes (bishops-at-large). One larger dissident body follows the papal claimant Clement XV (Michel Collin, died 1974) and his Renewed Church of Christ the King (HQ Dijon, France).

OTHER THIRD-WORLD INDIGENOUS CHURCHES. A large Korean movement has opened centres in Rome and Milan: Associazione dello Spirito Santo per l'Unificazione del Cristianesimo nel Mondo (Holy Spirit Association for the Unification of World Christianity). In 1976, Nigerian students in Rome had formed a small congregation of the Christ Apostolic Church from Ibadan (Nigeria). There is also a church of the Father Divine Peace Mission Movement (USA Blacks).

OTHER MARGINAL PROTESTANT BODIES. These include: Amis de l'Homme, Associazione Universale Alaya (1953), Chiesa del Regno di Dio (Amis de l'Homme/Freytag; begun in Italy 1946; HQ Turin), Ch of Our Lord Jesus Christ (Bickertonites), Missione degli Apostoli della Fede (begun 1936), Missione di Fede (begun 1944), New Ch, Reorganized Ch of Jesus Christ of Latter-day Saints (USA).

UNITING CHURCHES. Negotiations for organic union were under way in 1974 between: Ev Waldensian Ch, and Ev Methodist Ch of Italy. Federation (not merger) took place in 1979.

**PEOPLES** (ethnolinguistic). Christians: 95.9% Italian (including 8.5% Sicilian), 2.2% Sardinian, 0.7% Romansh, 0.4% Austrian, 0.2% French, 0.2% Slovene, 0.2% Albanian, British, Greek, Catalonian, German, Croat, Gypsy, USA White, Chinese (350), & over 100 other nationalities.

**COUNTRY-WIDE TOTALS**

EVANGELIZATION (see Part 5). 1900: 100%. 1970: 100%. 1980: 100%. *Mass evangelism.* Among the many recent campaigns: 1967, Billy Graham for 2 days in Turin (3,000 attenders, 100 enquirers); 1967, Brethren Assemblies summer tent crusade in Naples; 1968, 6-week Conservative Baptist campaign in Naples area, also Assemblies of God tent meetings in Sicily after local earthquake, also country-wide Southern Baptist crusade; 1969, Brethren Assemblies tent ministry in Terni; 1969, formation of Operation Mobilization in Naples; 1970, crusade in Messina (Sicily) led by American evangelist di Giongi. *Radiophonic evangelism.* Annual listeners' letters (1975): 14,000 Radio Vatican, 1,900 TWR, 154 HCJB, RVOG, RSB, et alia. Bible correspondence courses: numerous, including ICI (1,835 enrolments). *Literature evangelism.* By the end of 1976, Every Home Crusade had distributed 44 million gospel booklets to homes across Italy.

FOREIGN MISSIONARIES AND PERSONNEL (nationals serving abroad) (1973). Total 25,321: 25,269 Roman Catholics (15,769 foreign missionaries (70 bishops and prelates, 8,299 priests and brothers in over 54 institutes, 6,800 sisters, 600 lay), serving in Third-World countries (rising to 16,950 in 1977), and about 9,500 personnel serving in Western nations including 440 in Switzerland), about 30 marginal Protestants (mainly Jehovah's Witnesses), about 20 Protestants (Pentecostals, and Waldensians in FR Germany, Switzerland, USA), about 2 Catholics (non-Roman).

FOREIGN MISSIONARIES AND PERSONNEL (aliens from abroad) (1973). Total 9,388. *From Western world.* 8,284: about 8,000 Roman Catholics, 266 Protestants (180 in 39 USA societies, 63 in 13 UK societies, 9 in 3 Australia societies, 7 in 3 New Zealand societies, 1 in 1 Netherlands society), 9 Anglicans, about 5 Orthodox, about 4 Catholics (non-Roman). *From Communist world.* 104: about 100 Roman Catholics, about 4 Orthodox from USSR and Yugoslavia. *From Third World.* About 1,000, mostly Roman Catholics from over 150 countries. In the diocese of Rome, about 1,700 priests of foreign nationality are listed in its directory.

INSTITUTIONS (church-operated) (1973). Total 13,500, including 30 ecumenical centres, 2,200 higher schools (536 minor seminaries), around 10,000 social service/welfare/medical institutions, 30 study centres, 30 presses, 300 monasteries, 80 research centres, 330 seminaries (314 RC, 11 Protestant), 5 universities.

PERIODICALS. About 1,400 titles (1,100 RC, including many periodicals of religious orders and congregations, and 117 diocesan bulletins in 1976; 100 Protestant, others non-denominational).

PERSONNEL. About 225,888 (216,500 national, 9,388 foreign).

RELIGIOUS LIBRARIES. About 850.

SCRIPTURE DISTRIBUTION (1975). Annual totals: 1,431,519 Bibles (2% subsidized, 98% commercial), 851,347 NTs (4% free, 2% subsidized, 94% commercial), 500,949 UBS portions, 2,043,513 UBS selections. *Translations completed.* Portion: 21 languages or dialects since 1830. NT: 3 languages since 1835. Bible: Latin in 1456, Italian in 1471.

SERVICE AGENCIES. About 850, including ACI, ACIOC, ACLI, ADI, AFI, AFMM, AIMC, ALAM, ASCA, ASCI, CCCI, CCMM, CDUCE, CEF, CEI, CIMS, CISL, CISM, CLC, CMM, COSEI, CUAMM, CUMIF, ECM, EISS, EMI, FCEI, FICIR, FIDAE, FIRAS, FUCI, GLAM, ICRA, IEA, IMC, IPAS, MHM, MIIC, MIR, MMAC, OFM, OM, OMI, OP, PIME, SICO, SIRC, SJ, SMA, STAM, SU, TVC, UCASI, UCEI, UCP, UCSEI, UCSI, UCSS, UISG, UISPER, UMMI, USG, USMI, WLC(EHC), WUCT, WVI, YMCA, YWCA.

**ADDITIONAL DATA ON CHURCHES**

ASSEMBLEA DI DIO IN ITALIA (ADI). Also known as CCEP, Chiesa Cristiana Evangelica Pentecostale (Evangelical Pentecostal Christian Church), a name derived from the Christian Church of North America which the Italian Pentecostal movement followed closely for many years. *Regions.* Pentecostals are particularly strong in the central regions (Abruzzi, Lazio) and southern regions (Campania, Basilicata, Calabria, and in Sicily where they work in every provincial capital). *Growth.* Expansion has been rapid, from 173 congregations in 1940, to 447 in 1960, and to 782 in 1976.

CHIESA ANGLICANA. Church of England chaplaincy work was begun in Messina in 1559, in Venice in 1624, and in Leghorn in 1706.

CHIESA CATTOLICA IN ITALIA. *Dioceses.* The list of dioceses in column 1 includes the 21 dioceses which (end of 1973) had been gradually suppressed de facto (but not de jure) by the Holy See (by leaving them vacant without bishops) in the attempt to reduce the excessive number of Italian dioceses (283); the list also includes the 52 others under threat of suppression. *Regions*. The table shows the division of all dioceses into 18 Conciliar Regions introduced in 1889, 1919 and 1933. Since 1967 each region has had its own regional episcopal conference with elected officers. Each region is described in the right-hand part of column 8. *Structure*. The table above gives the structure of regions, archdioceses, dioceses, etc, as in 1973. Note that the situation changes slightly from year to year, as reported in successive issues of *AP*. *Councils*. By 1977 almost all Italian dioceses had priests' councils, and 80% had also established pastoral councils. *Annual baptisms*. (1972) 99.9% infant, 0.1% adult. *Personnel*. About 96% nationals, 4% expatriates. *Priests*. In 1971, the 64,008 in diocesan service consisted of 42,698 secular and 21,310 regular. Secular priests declined from 44,031 (1967) to 41,818 (1973). *Sisters*. In 1971, 153,293 in diocesan service. *Catholic charismatics*. In January 1974, 450 adults including priests, brothers and sisters were active in 7 organized prayer groups in the Charismatic Renewal (one in the Gregorian University in Rome). During the following months, however, the movement grew rapidly, and at Pentecost 1975 an international charismatic conference of 10,000 pilgrims met in Rome, addressed by the pope and cardinals. *Seminaries*. The total of 314 is made up of 169 major religious seminaries (for religious clergy); and 145 secular major seminaries, these being made up as follows: (1) 33 Roman ecclesiastical institutes of education and instruction in Rome for secular seminarians (not including 24 colleges for priests-students, nor the 56 for male religious personnel); among these are Pontificia Accademia Ecclesiastica, and seminaries and colleges of various nationalities and rites for candidates to the priesthood; (2) 14 regional pontifical seminaries (one for each Conciliar Region except Emilia, Liguria, Lombardy, Sicily and Venice); (3) 94 diocesan seminaries; (4) 2 interdiocesan seminaries; and (5) Seminaria America Latina (Verona). *Seminarians*. (1972) 22,220 secondary schools students, 8,131 theological students (philosophy and theology). *Catechetical training institutes*. At the primary level, Magistero Maria Assunta (for sisters; Rome), Pontificio Istituto Jesus Magister (male religious and lay), and many other local courses. *Religious congregations and orders*. Total C = 100 (male clerical) + 13 (brothers) + 356 (sisters). These numbers are of religious institutes with Italian members, and also international institutes with headquarters in Rome (44 for sisters). Male institutes: 3 canons regular, 11 monks, 15 frati, 8 regular clergy, 51 clerical congregations, 8 societies of common life without vows, 11 lay congregations, 6 diocesan institutes. Female institutes: 102 with generalate in Rome, 151 in northern Italy and 103 in central or southern Italy. The addition of foreign institutes makes a grand total of 516 different congregations and orders, occupying 15,000 convents. *Main orders and congregations* (1973). The first number is of members in Italy, the second (in parentheses) is of Italian members serving abroad. Priests: 4,660 (1,571) SDB, 4,210 (576) OFM, 3,061 (782) OFMCap, 1,448 (186) SJ, 1,307 (147) OFM-Conv. Brothers: 660 (13) FSC, 178 (14) Fatebenefratelli, 140 (4) PFM, 135 (14) FIC. Sisters: Figlie di Maria SS Ausiliatrice, Figlie della Carità di S Vincenzo, Suore di Maria SS Bambina, Figlie di S Paolo, Suore della Carità Canossiane, Suore di S Giovanna Antida, Figlie di S Anna, Suore dell'Immacolata Concezione di Ivrea, Suore della Consolata, Suore Francescane Missionarie di Maria.

*Catholic organizations*. The Italian Episcopal Conference (Conferenza Episcopale Italiana, CEI) was founded in 1952 and since 1967 has been divided into regional conferences corresponding to the 18 conciliar regions set up for the church in 1889, 1919 and 1933. In 1973 there were 18 conferences which were only approximately similar to the 19 civil regions. Unlike other countries, the president of the Episcopal Conference is appointed by the pope, and a representative of the Holy See has the right to intervene in meetings and add items to the agenda. For the armed forces, Italy forms a military vicariate.

Two organizations of religious personnel are the Conferenza Italiana dei Superiori Maggiori (CISM) for men and Unione Superiore Maggiori d'Italia (USMI) for sisters. There are no national pastoral or presbyteral councils; but in 1972, 4 conciliar regions (Abruzzi, Lombardy, Sardinia and Sicily) held regional presbyteral councils.

The Consulta Generale dell'Apostolato dei Laici is the principal agency for co-ordinating studies and activities relating to lay organizations in Italy. In 1971, 59 bodies were full members and 24 others associate members. The most important groups by categories are: Associazione Scouts Cattolici Italiani (ASCI), Centro Sportivo Italiano (CSI) and Associazione Guide Cattolici Italiani (AGI) among youth; Azione Cattolica Italiana (ACI) for youth and adults; Associazione Cristiane Lavoratori Italiani (ACLI), Centro Italiano Femminile (CIF), Federazione Nazionale delle Congregazioni Marianae (CCMM), Federazione Universitaria Cattolica Italiana (FUCI), Legio Mariae, Società di S Vincenzo de Paoli, Unione Cattolica della Stampa Italiana (UCSI) and Unione Cristiana Imprenditori Dirigenti (UCID), all for adults. Of groups outside the Consulta, the most important is the Movimento dei Focolari which is widespread, especially in urban parishes throughout Italy.

The Holy See has diplomatic relations with Italy and is represented by a nuncio in Rome.

Catholic international organizations with their headquarters in Italy are numerous. Major ones include the following 24 bodies: (1) Aid to the Church in Distress (Aiuto alla Chiesa che soffre) founded in 1948 in Belgium to aid German refugees and now centred in Rome, which at present gives major attention to pastoral aid for the church in Communist countries; (2) Apostolate of Prayer (Apostolato della Preghiera), founded in Rome in 1849 with 20,000 members throughout the world in 1972, which emphasizes prayer and personal sacrifice (especially through performance of the mass, daily offerings, Sacred Heart worship and Marian devotion) as the bases of the Christian life; (3) International Catholic Rural Association (ICRA), founded in Rome in 1962 under the name International Catholic Liaison Body for Agricultural and Rural Organizations, its new name being adopted in 1966, which brings together 2 international agricultural organizations (MIJARC and FIMARC, both with headquarters in Belgium) and 37 national organizations in 22 countries of Asia, America, Europe and Oceania; (4) Associationes Juventutis Salesianae, founded in Rome in 1847, which coordinates the activities of youth groups in 50 countries (1970) undergoing training according to the spirit of St John Bosco; (5) Caritas Internationalis, founded in Rome in 1955 under the name Caritas Catholica, which, through its 90 affiliated agencies in 86 countries (Africa 28, America 21, Asia 14, Europe 20 and Oceania 3) and its Latin American secretariat in Rio de Janeiro, Brazil, is engaged in charitable and development activities throughout the world, including studies of the problems of need, promotion of co-operation between bodies dedicated to aiding those in need and co-ordination of activities of its members, especially in times of national disaster; (6) Consociatio Internationalis Musicae Sacrae (CIMS), founded in Rome in 1963 with member bodies in 12 countries in 1971, whose purpose is to stimulate the training of qualified persons in sacred music, promote its use for divine worship, conserve the traditional treasure of church music and search out new expressions; (7) Consociatio Internationalis Studio Iuris Canonici Promovendo, founded in Rome in 1970 with 129 regular members from 10 European and 3 extra-European countries, which is dedicated to the study of canon law through research, seminars and international meetings; (8) Cooperatori Salesiani, founded in Rome in 1876, which provides Christian training for youth in the spirit of St John Bosco, for service to the church; (9) International Federation of Catholic Men/Fédération Internationale des Hommes Catholiques (FIHC), also known as Unum Omnes, founded in Rome in 1948 with a regional office in Mexico, which co-ordinates the activities of Catholic men in 32 countries (1972) in the areas of civic life, social and family questions, religious training, promotion of vocations and Third-World development; (10) International Federation of Pueri Cantores, with statutes approved by the Holy See in 1965 and national federations in 29 countries, which seeks to promote the use of liturgical chant among youth as an aid to spiritual and cultural development; (11) World Federation of Christian Life Communities/Fédération Mondiale des Communautés de Vie Chrétienne (FMCVC), founded in Rome in 1953 under the name World Federation of Marian Congregations, its new name being adopted in 1967, which attempts to inspire the development of the Christian life among its members in 45 countries through the use of the spiritual exercises of the Jesuit founder St Ignatius Loyola; (12) Movimento dei Focolari, founded at Trent in 1943 by a young woman, Chiara Lubich, with more than a million members now in 25 countries, which through its international lay training centre at Loppiano (near Florence), its publishing house Città Nuova and its annual world conventions (Mariapoli), spreads abroad its concern for charity, unity and spirituality; (13) International Catholic Independent Youth/Jeunesse Indépendante Catholique Internationale (JICI), founded in 1946 at Brussels with headquarters now in Rome and members in 12 countries, which promotes contacts between member youth groups, helps to create new movements and facilitates cooperation between existing bodies; (14) Mouvement International d'Apostolat des Milieux Sociaux Indépendants (MIAMSI), founded in Rome in 1963 with 21 movements throughout the world in 1972, which is dedicated to the evangelization of the middle and upper classes; (15) Movimento per un Mondo Migliore, founded in Rome in 1952 with representation in 30 countries in 1972, which is a loose organization (without formal membership) dedicated to the improvement of Christian community primarily through retreats; (16) Carmelite Third Order, with its headquarters in Rome; (17) Dominican Third Order, founded in 1285 by St Dominic; (18) Franciscan Third Order, founded by St Francis of Assisi, with its first rule approved in 1221; (19) Union of Worshippers of the Most Holy Sacrament, founded in Rome in 1937 with member associations in 15 countries in 1972, for lay women; (20) General Union of Pastoral Works for Youth/Union Générale des Oeuvres Pastorales pour la Jeunesse (UGOPJ), founded in Rome in 1966, which co-ordinates Catholic educational and recreational activities among youth; (21) International Union of Female General Superiors/Union Internationale des Supérieures Générales (UISG), founded in Rome in 1965; (22) World Union of Catholic Teachers/Union Mondiale des Enseignants Catholiques (UMEC), founded in Rome in 1951 with 53 national associations and correspondents in 50 countries in the world in 1972, which caters for the spiritual, pedagogical and cultural training of Catholic teachers as well as their economic and social conditions of work; (23) Union of Male General Superiors/Union des Supérieurs Généraux (USG), founded in Rome in 1957, which co-ordinates all national unions of male major superiors; and (24) Sovereign Military Hospitalier Order of St John of Jerusalem, commonly called the Order of Malta or Order of Rhodes, whose headquarters has been established in Rome since 1834. This latter order was founded in Jerusalem in the 11th century to aid and protect pilgrims to the Holy Land, then withdrew successively to Cyprus (1291), Rhodes (1309), and Malta (1530), where it remained until the island was captured by Napoleon in 1798. The Order of Malta has played an important military role in the past, especially in the struggle against the Turks; but at present it is devoted only to charitable activities. It is extensively involved in medical service in 75 countries, including: organized emergency teams in 10 countries, assistance to hospitals some of which it owns, shipment of medicines, and participation in programmes to combat leprosy and cancer. The order has national branches in many countries of Europe, America, Africa and Oceania and in unique in maintaining diplomatic relations with 40 states including the Holy See. The maintenance of these privileged relations is today due more to courtesy and ancient tradition than international juridical rights. The Order of Malta is represented in the Cor Unum council of the Holy See, and the grand master of the Order is appointed by the pope. Italy is also the home of the Filmis department of OCIC in Belgium, which provides information on films serving Christian missions in the Third World, and the International Secretariat of Catholic Jurists, which is the professional secretariat of MIIC in Switzerland.

Opinion groups representing both progressivist and traditionalist tendencies are active. The birth and development of groups expressing Catholic dissent (*dissenso cattolico*) date from the 1960s, caused both by structural changes in the country and by the new dynamism arising from Vatican II. Even before the council several journals had begun to examine critically the Catholic Church and its role in society: *Il Regno* (The Kingdom) of Bologna, *Adesso* (Now) of Milan, *Il Gallo* (The Cock) of Genoa, *Questitalia* (This Italy) of Venice and *Testimonianze* (Testimonies) of Florence. After the council, other movements appeared, even within organizations dependent on the hierarchy, of which the prototypes were the communities of Isolotto (Florence), Pratorotondo (Rome), Oregina (Genoa) and Vandalino (Turin). These were more radical in their criticism of Catholic political involvement and existing ecclesiastical structures. More than 1,000 such groups were in existence by 1967–69, and were especially strong in the centre and north of Italy. More organized structures were formed from these early initiatives and began to express themselves at the level of social action. At the same time traditionalist groups were formed, few in number but of considerable significance, with emphasis on spirituality and an attempt at resurrecting the old Catholic blending of faith and politics. The principal point of contention has not been over inter-ecclesiastical questions or individual problems but on the relations of faith and politics, church and society, because of the involvement of the Catholic Church in the structure of Italian political power, both in the past and in the present.

Progressivist groups include: (1) Secretariat for Basic Communities (Segreteria delle Comunità di Base), founded in Rome in 1969, which seeks to unite basic communities and stimulate joint action by them, especially through its weekly journal *Com*; (2) National Secretariat of Christians for Socialism (Segreteria Nazionale Cristiani per il Socialismo), founded in Bologna in 1973 following a congress of more than 2,000 persons, whose secretariat is now located at Florence and includes representatives from Protestantism and other left-wing Catholic organizations; (3) 7th of November National Movement (Movimento Nazionale 7 Novembre), founded in Rome in April 1972 with 1,000 members (mostly priests) in 1974, which was inspired by its French counterpart Echanges et Dialogue and owes its name to the closing date of the Third Synod of Bishops (7 November 1971), proving, according to the group, the impossibility of resolving at the summit the grave crisis facing the church, and advocating a bypassing of the bureaucratic, sacral and authoritarian church and the liberation of priests from the cultural, political and economic conditioning to which they are subject; (4) Secretariat for Counter-Information Journals (Segreteria delle Riviste di Controinformazione), founded in Rome in 1971, which co-ordinates the activities of the following journals: *Com-Nuovi Tempi*, *IDOC-Internazionale*, *Testimonianze*, *Il Tetto*, *La Rocca* and *Ricerca*.

Traditionalist movements are: (1) Communione e Liberazione, consisting for the most part of youth groups following the spirit of the conservative GS (student youth) movement founded by Giussani prior to the council and structured similarly to the student movement in Milan and other northern cities, whose national congress attracted 5,000 students in 1973; (2) National Civics Committee (Comitato Civico Nazionale), founded in Rome in 1948 and officially recognized by some bishops, which co-ordinates the activities of 300 zonal civics committees (one per diocese) and 20,000 local committees (one per parish), charged with publicizing the Christian Democrats; (3) M Fani Circles (Circoli M Fani); (4) Youth Groups of the Year 2000 (Gruppi GIAD/Gioventù Anno Duemila), which are dedicated to propagandizing the right-wing personalities of Christian Democrats and organizing initiatives to make Italy 'Catholic'; (5) Comitato Internationale per la Difesa della Civiltà Cristiana, Sezione Italiana, established in Rome in 1956, which is the Italian Section (the only section still active) of the International Committee for the Defence of Christian Civilization, orginally founded in Germany under the inspiration of Konrad Adenauer; (6) Una Voce Italia, the Italian subsidiary of Una Voce International Federation with headquarters in Switzerland. Other groups are dedicated to fighting communist materialism among clergy and intellectuals, using as their channel of expression such publications as *L'Ordine*, *Lo Specchio*, *Il Borghese* and *Renovatio*.

Organizations for research and social action include: (1) International Centre for Social Research (Centro Internazionale di Ricerche Sociali, CIRIS), founded in Rome in 1964 and affiliated to the Gregorian University and FERES (Belgium), which trains students in social research and carries on studies at the request of various Catholic institutions; (2) Institute of Applied Research, Documentation and Study (Istituto di Ricerche Applicata Documentazione e Studi, IRADES), founded in Rome in 1967, affiliated to FERES, which is an independent institute working in collaboration with diocesan research centres; (3) Servizio di Documentazione e Studi (SEDOS), founded in Rome in 1964 and affiliated to FERES, which co-ordinates the activities of 24 male and 15 female international missionary religious institutes (1973) to serve the church in its missionary task; (4) Associazione Internazionale Pro Deo, founded in 1965, at whose central headquarters in Rome function: The Free International University of Pro Deo Social Studies, Higher Institute of Public Opinion Sciences and Techniques, Institute of Latin American Studies, Higher Institute of Social Training, and courses for secretarial candidates, and at whose subsidiary headquarters in Milan and Turin are offered technical and business courses, marketing, organization of production and economics; (5) Christian Association of Italian Workers (Associazione Cristiane Lavoratori Italiani, ACLI), founded in Rome in 1944 to aid workers and counter-balance Italy's only existing trade union, which began by working closely with Christian Democrats, became socialistic in orientation by 1969, numbered 700,000, was renounced by the Episcopal Conference and the pope in 1971, suffered 2 schisms of 200,000 members in 1971 (MOCLI and FEDERACLI which later united to form MCL), and is now seeking reform and reintegration under episcopal guidance; (6) Associazione Nazionale della Comunità di Lavoro (ANCOL) formerly known as ONARMO, founded in Rome in 1943, which is an organization of working communities dedicated to the creation of new forms of association and participation in Italian life in order to aid social development and, through its Institute of Patronage for Social Assistance, to serve the needs of workers and other citizens; (7) Confederazione Nazionale Coltivatori Diretti, founded in Rome in 1944, with 14,385 local groups including female and youth sections, which is aimed at improving the socio-economic conditions of life of small rural farmers through the improvement of production, formation of co-operatives and instruction concerning legal rights, and which is a member of ICRA; (8) Comunità dei Braccianti, founded in Rome in 1966, which provides assistance for rural workers and small farmers through training and co-operative projects; (9) Central Office for Italian Emigration (Ufficio Centrale per l'Emigrazione Italiana, UCEI), founded in Rome in 1965, the executive organ of the Episcopal Conference for providing spiritual and social assistance to Italian emigrants, carrying on at the present time the former activities of the Italian Catholic Board for Emigration; (10) Centro Studi Emigrazione Roma (CSER), founded in 1963 by Scalabrinians, which engages in statistical research relating to migration patterns and sponsors several publications; (11) Hands Extended (Mani Tese), an independent organization in Milan, working in collaboration with FAO, Misereor and Oxfam, which attempts to stimulate public opinion and raise funds in aid of Third-World development projects; (12) Federation of Christian Organizations for International Voluntary Service (Federazione Organismi Cristiani di Servizio Internazionale Volontario, FOCSIV), with headquarters in Milan, which co-ordinates the activities of its 18 federated bodies (1973), including Feminine Medical Missionary Association, Association of Lay Volunteers, and Laymen for Latin America (CEIAL), in sending technical personnel to developing countries; and (13) Council of Agencies for Foreign Students in Italy (Consiglio degli Organismi per Student Esteri in Italia, COSEI), co-ordinating 13 agencies (1973) aiding foreign students, most of whom are from the Third World.

Institutions for pastoral and religious training include the following. (1) There are 17 pontifical universities and higher institutes in Rome (Atenei Romani): Pontificia Università Gregoriana (Gregorian; founded in 1552 by Jesuits); Pontificio Istituto Biblico (1909; SJ); Pontificio Istituto di Studi Orientali (1917; SJ); Pontificia Università Lateranense (Lateran; 1824); Pontificia Università Urbaniana (founded 1627 by pope Urban VIII); Pontificia Università S Tommaso d'Aquino (St Thomas Aquinas or Angelicum; 1580; OP); Pontificio Ateneo S Anselmo (1687; OSB); Pontificio Ateneo Antonianum (1933; OFM); Pontificia Università Salesiana (1933; SDB); Pontificio Istituto Superiore di Latinita (dependent on the Salesian Atheneum; 1971); Pontificio Istituto di Musica Sacra; Pontificio Istituto di Archeologia Cristiana (1925); Pontificia Facoltà Teologica S Bonaventura (Seraphicum; 1905; OFMConv); Pontificia Facoltà Teologica dei SS Teresa di Gesú e Giovanni della Croce (Teresianum; 1935; OCD); Facoltà Teologica Marianum (1955; OSM); Pontificio Istituto di Studi Arabi; and Pontificio Istituto Regina Mundi (1954). (2) There are 3 faculties of theology and canon law outside Rome: Facoltà Teologica Interregionale, in Milan; Pontificia Facoltà Teologica del SS Cuore di Gesù, in Nuoro, Sardinia; and Facoltà Teologica Napoletana, in Naples. (3) There are 2 liturgical institutes: Istituto Liturgico di S Anselmo, founded in Rome in 1961; and Istituto di Liturgia Pastorale per le Tre Venezie, in Padua; in addition to the Centro di Azione Liturgica (CAL), in Rome, which co-ordinates all Italian liturgical action. (4) Six university-related pastoral and catechetical institutes exist: Istituto di Catechetica (Faculty of Educational Sciences of Salesian University); Pontificio Istituto Pastorale (Lateran University); Pontificia Facoltà di Scienze dell'Educazione (supervised by the Daughters of Mary Helper in Turin and associated with Salesian University); Istituto di Scienze Religiose (Gregorian University); Istituto Superiore di Scienze Religiose Ecclesia Mater (for laymen, dependent on Lateran University); Scuola di Vallombrosa (with courses organized by CENAC). (5) There are 10 catechetical centres: Centro Nazionale di Attività Catechistiche (CENAC) (Rome); Centro Catechistico Salesiano (Turin; SDB); Centro Catechistico Dehoniano (Bologna; SCJ); Centro Catechistico Paolino (Rome; Sisters of St Paul); Centro Ut Unum Sint; Ufficio Catechistico Nazionale (Rome), which provides national co-ordination for catechesis; Centro Salesiano di Pastorale Giovanile (CPG) (Rome and Turin), specializing in youth pastoralia; Centro Cattolico di Preparazione al Matrimonio (Rome; begun 1966) and Centro di Preparazione alla Famiglia (Turin), specializing in family problems; and Centro Italiano di Sessuologia (Rome), specializing in conjugal and sexual problems in the light of Christian ethics. (6) Two pontifical institutes exist for sacred music: Pontificio Istituto di Musica Sacra (Rome; 1911); and Pontificio Istituto Ambrosiano di Musica Sacra (Milan; 1940). (7) There are 3 research centres for pastoral study: Centro di Orientamento Pastorale (COP) (Rome; 1953), associated with IRADES; Centro Internazionale Pio XII per un Mondo Migliore (Rocca di Papa, Rome), which studies pastoralia and spirituality according to recent Jesuit orientation; and Pro Civitate Cristiana (Assisi; 1939), which studies spirituality in its relation to culture and art and runs a publishing house, Cittadella.

Organizations for missionary action include the following 5 groupings: (1) four co-ordinating agencies: Commissione Episcopale per la Cooperazione tra le Chiese, in Rome, which is part of the Episcopal Conference and is divided into 2 subcommissions, one for missions in general and the other for Latin America, the latter being responsible for Centro Ecclesiale Italiano per l'America Latina (CEIAL) and Seminario ND de Guadelupe per l'America Latina in Verona; Consiglio Missionario Nazionale, in Rome, an agency for the Episcopal Conference promoting missionary interest and activity in the Italian church; Conference of Major Superiors of Missionary Institutes of Italian Origin, in Rome; and Joint Secretariat of Missionary Institutes, also in Rome; (2) three specialized agencies for missionary co-operation: Agrimissio (Rome; founded 1970), concerned with rural development and working closely with FAO; Centro Internazionale Aviazione Motorizzazione Missionaria (CIAMM) (Turin; 1959), which promotes the use of aviation and other mechanized transport to aid missionary activity; and Lay Association Pro-Missions (Venice), providing aid and scholarships to Third-World countries; (3) six centres for study, training and information: Scientific Missionary Institute (Urbaniana University); Facoltà di Missionologia (Gregorian University); Centro Studi Asiatici (Milan; PIME); Collegio Universitario Aspiranti Medici Missionari (CUAMM) (Padova), for medical students intending to work in Third-World countries; Servizio Missionario per l'Africa e l'Asia (Rome), offering orientation for diocesan priests going overseas; International Centre for Missionary Promotion (CIAM) in Rome (1974), organizing conferences and retreats on missionary themes; and Editrice Missionaria Italiana (EMI) (Bologna, Milan, Parma, Turin), publishing house of Italy's 4 male missionary institutes; (4) four Italian male missionary institutes: Pontificio Istituto Missioni Estere (PIME) (Rome, 1850), a secular institute with 451 members in Asia, Africa and America; Missioni Africane di Verona (Combonians, FSCJ) (Rome; begun 1867), with 730 members in Africa, North and South America; Pia Società di S Francesco Saverio per le Missioni (SX) (Rome; 1895), with about 800 members in Africa, Asia and South America; Istituto Missioni Consolata (IMC) (Rome; begun 1900 at Turin), with 781 members in Africa, North and South America; and (5) six Italian female missionary institutes: Pie Madri della Nigrizia (Combonian Sisters) (Rome; 1872), with about 1,200 members in Africa, the Near East and Latin America; Suore Missionarie della Consolata (Grugliasco/Turin; 1910), with several hundred members in Africa and Latin America; Missionarie dell'Immacolata (Milan; 1936), with about 170 members in Asia, Africa and Latin America; Missionarie di Maria (Xaverian Sisters) (San Lazzaro/Parma; 1945), with about 170 members in Africa, Asia and Latin America; Ancelle Missionarie del SS Sacramento (Venice; 1933); and Francescane Ausiliarie Laiche Missionarie Immacolata (FALMI) (Rome; 1945), a lay society living in common, whose members work in West Africa. The total number of Italian personnel in overseas mission countries in 1973 was 70 bishops and other prelates, 7,700 religious priests and brothers (belonging to more than 54 institutes), 6,800 sisters (in more than 36 congregations) 599 Fidei Donum priests (484 in Latin America, 115 in Africa) and 600 lay missionaries.

The Catholic educational programme is co-ordinated by: Ufficio per la Pastorale Scolastica in Italia in Rome. Statistics for 1970 listed more than a million infants in Catholic pre-primary schools (65% of the total at this level); 140,000 primary pupils (8%); 120,000 lower secondary students (4.5%); 25,000 classic lyceum students (12%); 15,000 scientific lyceum students (6%); 500,000 language lyceum students (50%); 40,000 normal school students at the primary level (19.5%); 22,500 technical institute students (3.4%); 3,200 professional institute students (1.4%); artistic institute students (3.5%); and 17,000 Froebelian normal school students (61%). Beyond the pontifical universities, higher institutes and faculties already mentioned, there is also the non-pontifical Università Cattolica del Sacro-Cuore, founded in 1920 in Milan, with faculties also at Rome, Brescia, Piacenza and Castelnuovo Fogliani, which had a total of 22,207 students in 1968.

Social service and medical work is co-ordinated through Caritas-Italiana, in Rome, founded in 1971 to replace Pontificia Opera di Assistenza, formed during World War II, which is affiliated to Caritas Internationalis. There are thousands of welfare institutions in Italy, most maintained by religious congregations. Italian Catholicism's principal social service agencies are: (1) Consulta Generale dei Laici, Apostolatus Maris, founded in 1932 and existing in 65 dioceses to aid sailors through its clubs in the principal ports and 50 other centres; (2) Associazione Cattolica Nazionale delle Opere per la Protezione della Giovane, founded in 1902, dedicated to the protection of youth; (3) Patronato ACLI, which provides social assistance to travellers; (4) Centro Italiano Femminile (CIF), providing social and cultural services for individuals and communities; (5) Compagnia della Carità di S Vicenzo de Paoli, for aid to the poor; (6) Ente Italiano di Servizio Sociale (EISS), founded in 1964, for study, research and social services; (7) Società di S Vicenzo de Paoli, also for aid to the poor; (8) Catholic Relief Service, in Rome, the regional office of CRS/USCC in the USA for Europe, North Africa, the Middle East, India and Pakistan; (9) Associazione Nazionale Famiglie degli Emigrati, for aid to emigrants; (10) Associazione Volontari Italiani del Sangue, a blood donor agency; (11) Ente Nazionale per la Protezione e l'Assistenza ai Sordomuti, with 22 institutions for deaf-mutes; (12) Federazione Italiana Centri e Istituti per la Riabilitazione (FICIR), founded in 1964 for mental health; (13) Istituto di Patronato per l'Assistenza Sociale (IPAS) for social assistance for travellers; (14) Movimento FAC, for assistance at the parish level; (15) Opera Assistenza Spirituale Nomadi in Italia, for aid to nomads; (16) Opera Divino Redentore per la Redenzione Sociale dei Libertati del Carcere Casa dell'Amore Fraterno, which aids ex-prisoners; (17) Unione Nazionale fra gli Enti di Beneficenza e di Assistenza (UNEBA), for technical, fiscal legal, and other services to more than 11,000 social service institutions, the great majority of which are Catholic.

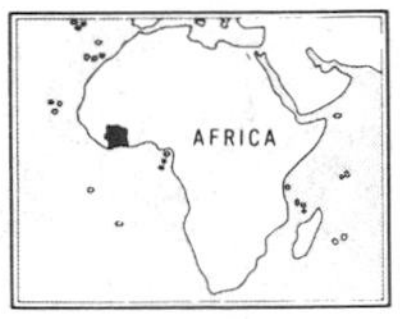


# IVORY COAST

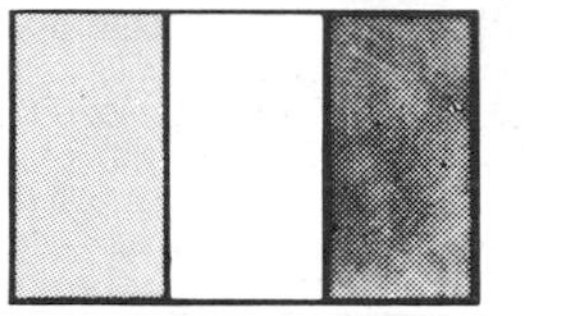

## SECULAR DATA

**STATE. Official name:** The Republic of the Ivory Coast (La République de Côte d'Ivoire). Adjective of nationality: ivoirien.
**Flag** (shown above right): Tricolour of orange, white, and green bars.
**Area:** 322,463 sq.km. (124,504 sq.miles). Agricultural land: 53.0%.
**Government:** One-party republic (1842 French protectorate, 1893 colony, 1958 autonomous state, 1960 Independence).
**Legislature:** National Assembly, 100 members.
**Official language:** French (*Français*).
**Capital:** Abidjan 500,000 (1970).
**Political divisions:** 4 Departments: North, West, Central, South-East.
**Armed forces** (1976): Total 4,100 regular: army 3,500, navy 200, air force 400 (7 combat aircraft). Paramilitary forces: 2,800.
**Foreign forces** (1978): 500 French troops.

**DEMOGRAPHY. Population:** 6,673,013 (census of 14.IV–15.V.1975. For 1970–2000 (UN), see last row of Table 1). Population density (1975): 15/sq.km. (39/sq.mile). Under 15 years: 42%. Growth rate (1975–80): 2.66% per year (births 4.53%, deaths −1.87%). Life expectancy (1975–80): 46.0 years. Household size: 4.9 persons.
**Major languages:** Mandingo, French, Baule, Kru, Dioula, Mande, Senufo, Lagoon, and about 60 other languages.
**Urban dwellers** (1970): 21.3%. Urban growth rate (1950–70): 7.7% per year.
**Labour force:** 53%.
**Tourists** (1974): 86,392.

**ETHNOLINGUSTIC GROUPS:** 20% Baule, 17% Kru (9.3% Bete, Dida, Guere, Wobe, Godie), 14% Mande (Malinke, Bambara, Diula, Mahon), 12% Senufo (Minianka), 9% Lagoon (Abidji, Ajukru, Ebrie, Abe, Alladian, Avikam), 7% Dan (with Yakuba), 6% Lobi (with Kulango), 6% Agni (Nzima, Abure, Abron), 4.0% Mossi, 3.0% Guro, 0.9% French (40,000), 0.6% Gagu, Attie, Yoruba, et alii. Total aliens: 17% (7.8% from Upper Volta, 5.6% from Mali, 0.9% French).

**MONEY** (1977). **Monetary unit:** CFA franc (= 100 centimes); US$1 = CFAF 250.00.
**National income per person:** US$600. Average annual family income: US$2,940.
**Inflation:** (1970–74) 6.5% per year (1975: consumer price index 149).
**Cost of living in capital** (1976): index 163 (Washington DC = 100). Daily cost of living. US$50.

**HEALTH.** Hospitals: 207 (8,682 beds). Doctors: 324. Lepers: 183,000 (37.5 per 1,000). Blind: 50,000. Psychotics: 39,000. Criminals: 10,934.

**EDUCATION.** Adult literacy: (1962) 5%, (1975) 30%. Education rate: 52%. Schools: 2,390. Universities: 1.

**LITERATURE.** Annual new book titles (1973): 260. Periodicals: 37. Scientific journals: 5. Newspapers: 3 dailies, 8 non-daily.

**COMMUNICATION** (per 1,000 people). Phones: 6. Radios: 17. TV sets: 9. Daily newspaper circulation: 10 copies.

TABLE 1. RELIGIOUS ADHERENTS IN THE IVORY COAST

| Year | 1900 | | mid-1970 | | Annual change, 1970–1980 | | | | mid-1975 | | mid-1980 | | 2000 | |
|---|---|---|---|---|---|---|---|---|---|---|---|---|---|---|
| *Name* | *Adherents* | *%* | *Adherents* | *%* | *Natural* | *Conversion* | *Total* | *Rate* | *Adherents* | *%* | *Adherents* | *%* | *Adherents* | *%* |
| Tribal religionists | 949,300 | 94.9 | 2,113,000 | 49.0 | 58,760 | −25,800 | 32,960 | 1.46 | 2,261,700 | 46.3 | 2,442,600 | 43.8 | 3,224,500 | 33.5 |
| **Christians** | **700** | **0.1** | **1,206,800** | **28.0** | **38,070** | **19,780** | **57,850** | **3.95** | **1,465,500** | **30.0** | **1,785,300** | **32.0** | **3,654,500** | **38.0** |
| professing | 700 | 0.1 | 1,206,800 | 28.0 | 38,070 | 19,780 | 57,850 | 3.95 | 1,465,500 | 30.0 | 1,785,300 | 32.0 | 3,654,500 | 38.0 |
| Roman Catholics | 700 | 0.1 | 709,800 | 16.5 | 22,208 | 10,022 | 32,230 | 3.77 | 854,900 | 17.5 | 1,032,100 | 18.5 | 2,067,600 | 21.5 |
| African indigenous | 0 | 0.0 | 323,000 | 7.5 | 10,287 | 5,953 | 16,240 | 4.10 | 396,000 | 8.1 | 485,400 | 8.7 | 1,057,900 | 11.0 |
| Protestants | 0 | 0.0 | 172,000 | 4.0 | 5,510 | 3,770 | 9,280 | 4.38 | 212,100 | 4.3 | 264,800 | 4.7 | 521,600 | 5.4 |
| Catholics (non-Roman) | 0 | 0.0 | 1,000 | 0.0 | 31 | 9 | 40 | 3.33 | 1,200 | 0.0 | 1,400 | 0.0 | 2,400 | 0.0 |
| Marginal Protestants | 0 | 0.0 | 1,400 | 0.0 | 34 | 26 | 60 | 4.62 | 1,300 | 0.0 | 1,600 | 0.0 | 5,000 | 0.1 |
| nominal | 150 | 0.0 | 124,022 | 2.9 | 3,936 | 2,072 | 6,008 | 3.97 | 151,500 | 3.1 | 184,100 | 3.3 | 384,500 | 4.0 |
| affiliated | 550 | 0.1 | 1,082,778 | 25.1 | 34,134 | 17,708 | 51,842 | 3.95 | 1,314,000 | 26.9 | 1,601,200 | 28.7 | 3,270,000 | 34.0 |
| total practising | 520 | *95* | 757,940 | *70* | 23,894 | 12,396 | 36,290 | 3.95 | 919,800 | *70* | 1,120,840 | *70* | 2,125,500 | *65* |
| non-practising | 30 | *5* | 324,830 | *30* | 10,240 | 5,312 | 15,552 | 3.95 | 394,200 | *30* | 480,360 | *30* | 1,144,500 | *35* |
| Roman Catholics | 550 | 0.1 | 626,855 | 14.5 | 19,475 | 8,479 | 27,954 | 3.73 | 749,700 | 15.3 | 906,400 | 16.2 | 1,762,300 | 18.3 |
| African indigenous | 0 | 0.0 | 300,000 | 7.0 | 9,645 | 6,105 | 15,750 | 4.24 | 371,300 | 7.6 | 457,500 | 8.2 | 1,019,400 | 10.6 |
| Protestants | 0 | 0.0 | 153,923 | 3.6 | 4,949 | 3,089 | 8,038 | 4.22 | 190,500 | 3.9 | 234,300 | 4.2 | 480,900 | 5.0 |
| Evangelicals | 0 | 0.0 | 120,700 | 2.8 | 3,933 | 2,967 | 6,900 | 4.56 | 151,400 | 3.1 | 189,700 | 3.4 | 423,000 | 4.4 |
| Catholics (non-Roman) | 0 | 0.0 | 1,000 | 0.0 | 31 | 9 | 40 | 3.33 | 1,200 | 0.0 | 1,400 | 0.0 | 2,400 | 0.0 |
| Marginal Protestants | 0 | 0.0 | 1,000 | 0.0 | 34 | 26 | 60 | 4.62 | 1,300 | 0.0 | 1,600 | 0.0 | 5,000 | 0.1 |
| Muslims | 50,000 | 5.0 | 982,700 | 22.8 | 29,822 | 5,808 | 35,630 | 3.10 | 1,148,000 | 23.5 | 1,339,000 | 24.0 | 2,693,000 | 28.0 |
| Ahmadis | 0 | 0.0 | 1,000 | 0.0 | 34 | 26 | 60 | 4.62 | 1,300 | 0.0 | 1,600 | 0.0 | 4,000 | 0.0 |
| Baha'is | 0 | 0.0 | 4,000 | 0.1 | 130 | 70 | 200 | 4.00 | 5,000 | 0.1 | 6,000 | 0.1 | 20,000 | 0.2 |
| Non-religious | 0 | 0.0 | 2,000 | 0.0 | 78 | 122 | 200 | 6.67 | 3,000 | 0.1 | 4,000 | 0.1 | 20,000 | 0.2 |
| Other religionists | 0 | 0.0 | 1,500 | 0.0 | 40 | 20 | 60 | 3.33 | 1,800 | 0.0 | 2,100 | 0.0 | 5,000 | 0.1 |
| **Country's population** | **1,000,000** | **100.0** | **4,310,000** | **100.0** | **126,900** | **0** | **126,900** | **2.60** | **4,885,000** | **100.0** | **5,579,000** | **100.0** | **9,617,000** | **100.0** |

COLUMNS, ROWS. For meanings and definitions, see Codebook (Part 6). Note that, by definition, total 'Christians' = professing + crypto-Christians, which also = affiliated + nominal Christians. Percentages may not always total exactly, due to rounding.
CENSUSES. **1957–58** (sample survey, CHEAM): 64.3% tribal religionists, 22.4% Muslims, 9.4% Roman Catholics, 1.7% Protestants, 1.4% Harrists.

NOTES ON RELIGIONS
AFRICAN INDIGENOUS. In about 34 denominations in 1970 (see Table 2). Strongly Harrist tribes include: Ajukru, Assini, Attie, Dida, Ebrie.
AHMADIS. Begun 1961; Qadianis in Abidjan (Yorubas from Nigeria), also in northeast from around Wa in Ghana.
BAHA'IS. Growth from 1 local spiritual assembly (1964) to 27 (1973).
MUSLIMS. Sunnis (of the Malikite rite): strongest among the Malinke (70%), Bambara (70%), Senufo (30%), Minianka (30%). Islam is growing numerically in 4 different ways, in addition to natural increase: (1) conversions to Islam among tribal religionists,

especially among the Bete and Dida; (2) conversions to Islam in the cities among foreign migrant labourers (especially from Upper Volta; a 1963 survey in Abidjan found that out of 17,260 Mossi, pagans on arrival, over 12,000 had been converted to Islam and 4,300 to Christianity); (3) conversions of Christians to Islam, especially among the Baule; and (4) the growing influx of foreign Muslims from Mali, Niger and Upper Volta, mostly itinerant businessmen. There is also an Ahmadiya Mission (enumerated here under Muslims although declared non-Muslim by Pakistan). Muslims in Abidjan: (1955) 37%, (1963) 38.4%, (1965) 40%, (1970) 45%. *Hajj pilgrims to Mecca*. (1970) 567; (1974) 1,165; (1976) 916.

NON-RELIGIOUS. French and, after 1970, African intellectuals and others.

OTHER RELIGIONISTS. Adherents of smaller religions and cults, including Rosicrucians (21 AMORC centres).
TRIBAL RELIGIONISTS. Tribes over 60% traditionalist (animist) in 1972: Gagu Pygmies (99%), Lobi (99%), Kulango (92%), Negre (90%), Wobe (79%), Baule (75%), Guro (75%), Anyi (70%), Dan (Yakuba) (70%), Senufo (65%), Bete (60%), Brong (60%). Many peoples remain resistant to Islam.

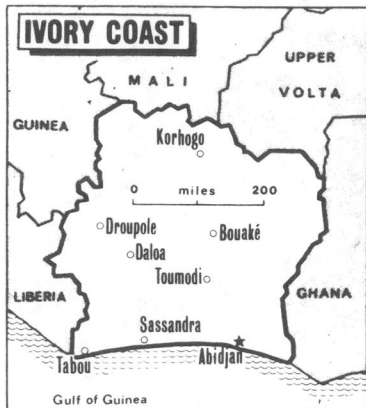

## NON-CHRISTIAN RELIGIONS. African traditional
**religions** remain very influential. The Kulango, Lobi, Ngere and Gagu are still more than 90% traditionalist; the Anyi, Dan, Baule, Guro and Wobe more than 70%; the Bete, Brong and Senufo more than 60%; and the population as a whole 46% in 1975. Names for God include Nyam (among the Ajukru), Nyangka (Ebrie) and Zra (Dan): Zra is the creator and all other spirits owe their origin to him. All these spirits are good except Kogbin-dy who incites men to practise witchcraft, which is considered to be man's greatest crime and the only one judged by Zra after death. God is the witchcraft eradicator par excellence, but the good spirit Zole-dy is also active in enlisting living men in the service of witchcraft eradication. The rites of several secret societies of eradicators, of which the most important is Yuomi, have as their aim the transformation of their initiates into animals to better observe the activities of witches.

**Islam** is growing in numbers largely because of the influx of foreign ethnic groups from Mali, Niger and the Upper Volta. The principal agents of its propagation are itinerant traders and small businessmen. Its strength is in the northwest, the Malinke and Bambara being 70% Muslim and the Senufo and Minianka 30%. The capital Abidjan is around 47% Muslim.

## CHRISTIANITY.
CATHOLIC CHURCH. French missionaries worked briefly in the Ivory Coast in 1637, but the difficult coastline discouraged the opening of European ports. France established a protectorate over the area in 1842 which stimulated a renewal of Catholic interest. A prefecture was created in 1895 with responsibility for evangelization given to the African Missions of Lyons (SMA), and missionaries of the Sisters of Our Lady of the Apostles arrived in 1898. The prefecture of Korhogo was erected to serve the north in 1911.

The first indigenous priests were ordained in 1934

**Eglise Catholique en Côte d'Ivoire.** Monk in Benedictine monastery, Bouaké (a strongly animist Baule area), where OSB/AIM organized its 1964 international monastic conference.

**Eglise Harriste.** Temple Biblique Harriste in Abidjan, showing highly original architecture characteristic of this largest of over 34 Ivorian indigenous churches.

and the first local archbishop was consecrated in 1960. The hierarchy was established with its metropolitan see at Abidjan in 1955. A diocesan synod was organized in Abidjan between March 1969 and November 1971, one session being held each year during the 3-year period. These assemblies brought together all active priests, lay persons chosen by their parishes, and movements and delegates elected by sisters, novices and seminarians. After the second session, lay delegates became more numerous than priests.

Catholicism is localized largely in the south where evangelization was begun in 1895. The church is especially strong in the cities. Surveys undertaken by the Ministry of Planning indicate that more than 50% of the population of Abidjan is Catholic. A desire to rise socially is undoubtedly one of the reasons for becoming Christians; but one notes also among the baptized elite, especially in the capital, a certain dechristianization which is linked to the process of urbanization.

INDIGENOUS CHURCHES. The Harris Church arose through the preaching of the Liberian Grebo prophet William Wadé Harris during 1913–15, through whose ministry 120,000 adults were converted and baptized. About 20,000 later became Catholics and 35,000 Methodists, but the majority organized themselves as an independent church. Though they have a central committee, Harrists are divided into various branches, the principal one being that among the Ebrie at Petit Bassam, near Abidjan. Others are located at Toukouzou and Grand Lahou on the Atlantic coast. Harrism is still strong in rural areas, especially among the Ebrie and Attie of the southeast; but adherents are decreasing in the cities. Other indigenous churches include a large schism in 1922 from Catholicism, the Eglise Déimatiste, and 2 schisms from Methodism, the Eglise Adaïste (1932) mainly among the Dida and the Eglise Protestante Libre in 1968. Approximately 30 other small independent churches are also active, some of which have entered the Ivory Coast from Ghana and Nigeria. Schisms from Harrism have been especially numerous.

PROTESTANT CHURCHES. Protestantism did not enter the Ivory Coast until after World War I, the first British Methodist missionary arriving in 1924. Other missions followed soon afterwards, the Mission Biblique (France) in 1927, CMA (USA) in 1930 and WEC in 1934. Protestant work is characterized by comity agreements which tend to give to the principal churches a regional orientation. Methodists, active among the Alagya, Attie, Ari, Avikam and Dida in the southeastern part of the country, are the strongest Protestant denomination. Other groups include the Evangelical Protestant Church (related to CMA) and the Protestant Church (WEC) among the Baule, Guro and Gagu of central Ivory Coast; the Union of Evangelical Churches (Mission Biblique, UFM) among the Dan, Bete, Wobe and Ngere of the southwest; Freewill Baptists (1957) among the Lobi, Kulango and Diula of the northeast; and Conservative Baptists (1947) among the Senufo of the northwest. Seventh-day Adventists are also at work on the southwest coast and Assemblies of God in Abidjan, and there has been a Yoruba community of the Nigerian Baptist Convention in the Ivory Coast since 1930.

**CHURCH AND STATE.** According to the constitution of November 1960, which was further modified in January 1963, the Ivory Coast is a secular republic (Article 2), and 'The Republic . . . shall respect all religious beliefs' (Article 6).

Religious education in public schools is conducted outside class hours, and chaplains are supplied for Catholic and Protestant instruction when at least 10 students make the request. Private confessional education must obey laws common to all private schools.

The president of the republic participates personally in important religious ceremonies. In 1966, without prior consultation with the religious authorities, the government established a special and progressive tax intended to finance the construction of Catholic, Protestant, Harrist and Muslim cathedrals 'worthy of the urbanism' of Abidjan. At the same time president Houphouet-Boigny has repeatedly urged

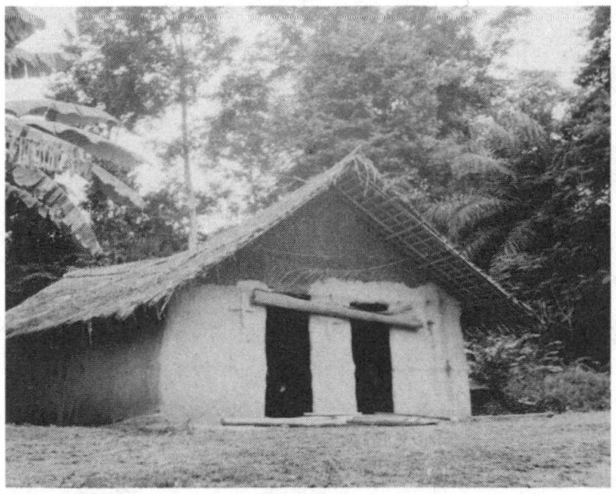

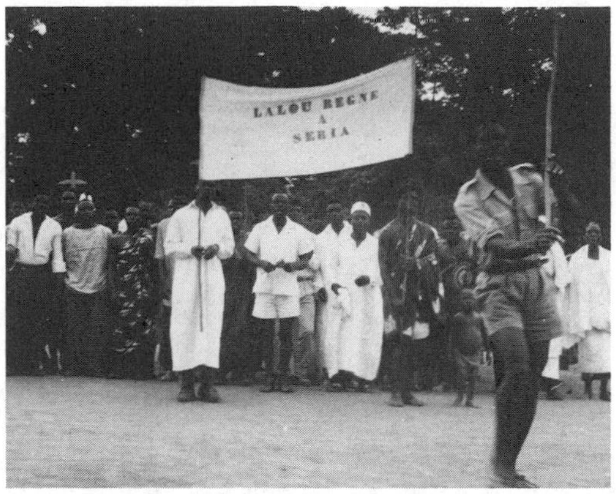


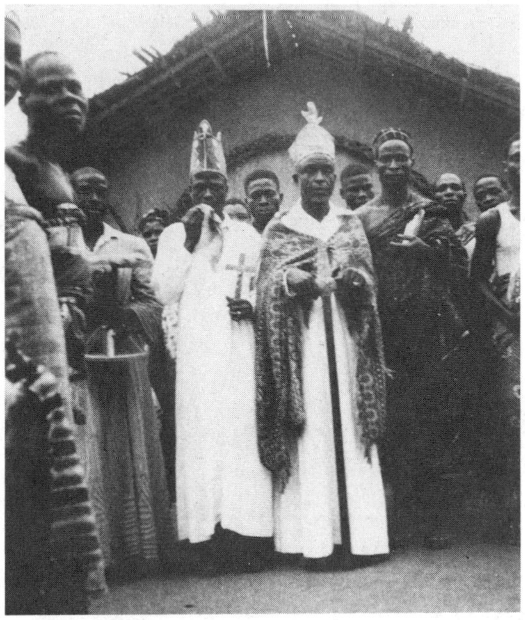

**Eglise Déimatiste.** *Left.* Church in Seria among Bete tribe. Note crosses in relief, also 2 entrance doors (men's on right, women's on left). *Centre.* Procession before church service. The banner reads: 'Pope Lalou rules in Seria'. *Right.* Officiants vested for the liturgy, with chief prophet (centre).

the population to cease being animists or traditionalists and to be converted to one of the 3 major religions.

Although at present authorizations for the opening of new classes are suspended, the development of Catholic schools during the colonial period resulted in the presence of a high percentage of Catholics in the upper classes and in the new national bourgeousie. Because of this fact, the influence of the Catholic Church in the country, and above all in Abidjan, is greater than its numerical size would indicate.

In 1974 a convention was concluded between the state and Catholic education authorities, guaranteeing a financial contribution towards the salaries of personnel teaching in Catholic schools, at the rate of 66% to 80% of equivalent salaries in the public educational sector. The convention also renewed the guarantee of freedom regarding the exercise of Catholic instruction and allocated to the state the duties of inspection, control of programmes and financial oversight of Catholic schools.

**INTERDENOMINATIONAL ORGANIZATIONS.** There is no national ecumenical Christian council, but most Protestant bodies belong to the Evangelical Federation of the Ivory Coast, composed of churches and missions related to the CMA, WEC, UFM, Conservative and Freewill Baptists, and the Mission Biblique. The Taizé Community from France attempts to promote dialogue between Protestants and Catholics.

**BROADCASTING.** The government Radiodiffusion Télévision Ivoirienne accepts Christian programmes. Both Protestants and Catholics are allowed 20 minutes radio time each on Sundays and 30 minutes each on TV every second Sunday. The Commission de la Communication (Catholic) and the Commission des Mass Media (Methodist) are responsible for production. Protestant programmes from abroad, especially in French, can be heard over ELWA (Liberia), with a recording studio in the Ivory Coast. For Catholics, UNDA is represented by a national association.

## BIBLIOGRAPHY

*Annuaire du clergé, des religieux et religieuses de Côte d'Ivoire, 1971.* Abidjan: Secrétariat de l'Episcopat, 1971.
'Avec Christ à l'oeuvre en Côte d'Ivoire aujourd'hui'. S. A. Nandjui et al. Abidjan: Eglise Méthodiste, 1969.
'Carte des religions de l'Afrique de l'Ouest: République de la Côte d'Ivoire' (maps). Paris: Université de Paris, n.d. (c1960).
*Le séparatisme religieux en Afrique noire: l'exemple de la Côte d'Ivoire.* B. Holas. Paris: Presses Universitaires de France, 1965. 410p.
'L'Eglise Harriste'. R. Bureau. Bregbo, Côte d'Ivoire, 1968. 79p. (Manuscript).
*Sorciers, féticheurs et guérisseurs de la Côte d'Ivoire.* J. Kerharo & A. Bouquet. Paris: Vigot, 1950.
*The prophet Harris: a study of an African prophet and his mass-movement in the Ivory Coast and the Gold Coast, 1913–1915.* G. M. Haliburton. London: Longmans, 1971. 250p.
'Une guérisseur de la Basse Côte d'Ivoire: Josué Edjro', H. Memel-Foté, *Cahiers d'études africaines*, VII (1967), 547–605. (On the founder of the Eglise Protestante Libre).
'Une religion syncrétique en Côte d'Ivoire' D. Paulme, *Cahiers d'études africaines*, III, 1 (1963), 5–90. (Déima among the Dida).

TABLE 2. ORGANIZED CHURCHES AND DENOMINATIONS IN THE IVORY COAST

| Official name 1 | Begun 2 | Type 3 | Counc 4 | Congs 5 | Adults 6 | Affiliated 7 | Names, notes, and other statistics (see Codebook) 8 |
|---|---|---|---|---|---|---|---|
| Assemblées de Dieu | 1927 | P Pe2 | ZF... | 41 | 3,500 | 5,000 | *Assemblies of God.* M=AdD(France),AoG(USA). Abidjan area. 2 schools. 24n,16f,2s. |
| Assoc des Eglises Baptistes du Nord | 1947 | P Bap | xFG.G | 52 | 607 | 2,300 | *ABN. Northern Baptist Chs.* M=CBFMS. Senufo, Diula. 4n,83m,90f,G=19%pa,1H,2h,2s,84Y. |
| Convention Baptiste Nigérienne | 1930 | P Bap | T.... | 22 | 1,400 | 2,000 | M=NBC(Nigeria), 1966 SBC(USA). Begun by traders. 95% Yoruba. 2x,8f,W=80%,8Y,20z. |
| Eglise Adaïste | 1932 | I mar | ..... | 50 | 2,000 | 5,000 | Schism ex MMS under prophet Boto Adaï (died 1963). Dida. Major womens' roles. |
| Eglise Adventiste du Septième Jour | 1946 | P Adv | x.... | 24 | 654 | 3,672 | *Seventh-day Adventists, IC Mission,* WAfrica UM. 38% Dida, 35% Bete. 5nx,16f,1s,W=80%,66Y. |
| Eglise Baptiste Libre | 1957 | P Bap | xFG.G | 24 | 525 | 1,000 | *Free Will Baptist Ch.* M=NAFWB(USA). Northeast. Lobi ,Kulango, Diula. 2n,24f,1H,1h. |
| **Eglise Catholique en Côte d'Ivoire:** | 1637 | R Lat | P.SFR | 122 | 363,600 | 626,855 | *Catholic Ch in IC.* C=15+2+17. 4p,1s(40). 60n,320x,98m,419w,P=33%,19821Yy. |
| M Abidjan | 1895 | R Lat | Ps | 34 | 190,800 | 329,000 | 20% urban. Catholic HQ of West Africa. 1p,1s. 38 107 33 150 28 8873 |
| D Abengourou | 1963 | R Lat | Ps | 16 | 53,800 | 92,708 | 90% Agni, Brong, Attie. Only South evangelized. 2 32 3 34 30 2086 |
| D Bouaké | 1951 | R Lat | Psma | 16 | 42,900 | 73,943 | Strongly animist. 70% Baule, 15% Agni. 4 53 25 81 39 2601 |
| D Daloa | 1940 | R Lat | Psma | 11 | 6,200 | 10,685 | 18% Yakuba, 16% Wobe, 14% Bete, 14% Guro. 0 24 7 40 40 753 |
| D Gagnoa | 1956 | R Lat | Psma | 22 | 43,200 | 74,543 | 27% Bete, 21% Avikam, 20% Dida, 8% Bakwe. 1p. 6 42 17 45 38 3108 |
| D Katiola | 1911 | R Lat | Psma | 6 | 11,600 | 20,000 | 51% Tagwana, 15% Niarafolo, 15% Tiembara. 4 25 5 30 40 800 |
| D Korhogo | 1971 | R Lat | Ps | 4 | 5,800 | 10,000 | Peoples highly islamized Senufo, Malinke. 2 13 3 14 40 400 |
| D Man | 1968 | R Lat | Ps | 13 | 9,300 | 15,976 | High % animist, but open to evangelism. 1p. 4 24 5 25 68 1200 |
| Eglise Déimatiste | 1922 | I mar | ..... | 500 | 50,000 | 90,000 | *Ch of Ashes of Purification.* Schism ex Catholics led by female pope Lalou. Bete. |
| Egl Episcopale Prot Libre (D WAfrica) | 1972 | C ARo | x.... | 1 | 650 | 1,000 | *Free Protestant Episcopal Ch.* HQ Monrovia (Liberia). M=FPEC(UK,USA). Abidjan. |
| Eglise Harriste | 1913 | I ind | .vI.. | | 50,000 | 150,000 | *Temples Bibliques Harristes.* Ebrie, Attie, Ajukru, Dida. 1968 applied to join WCC. |
| Eglise Protestante du Centre | 1934 | P int | xFG.G | 51 | 685 | 5,000 | M=MEAO(WEC,WEK). 57% Guro, 29% Baule. Animistic area. 8n,10f,G=28%pa,W=75%,40Y. |
| Eglise Protestante Ev du Centre | 1930 | P Hol | xFG.G | 392 | 9,326 | 20,583 | *EPEC. Prot Ch of Central IC.* M=CMA(USA). 90% Baule, 4% Agni. 65n,25f,G=5.4%pa,1h,1s. |
| Eglise Protestante Libre | 1968 | I Met | ..... | | 3,000 | 5,000 | *Free Protestant Ch.* 1965 mass movement under Ajukru Methodist healer Edjro; 1968 schism. |
| Eglise Protestante Méthodiste en CI | 1924 | P Met | VwA.f | 684 | 41,495 | 99,068 | *Prot Methodist Ch.* M=MMS(UK). 25n,8x,73m,27f,1H,1h,2r,237t(12581),692Y,4054y,3189z. |
| Témoins de Jéhovah | c1945 | M Jeh | x.... | 11 | 502 | 1,000 | *Jehovah's Witnesses. Watch Tower. IBSA.* Active witnessing under way by 1950. 92Y. |
| Union des Egls Ev du Sud Ouest de CI | 1927 | P Bap | .MG.G | 192 | 2,772 | 15,000 | *Chs of SW.* M=MB,UFM. 56% Yakuba, 35% Wobe. 48n,8x,G=10.6%pa,1p,1s(5),W=60%,200Y. |
| Other African indigenous churches | | I | ..... | | 20,000 | 50,000 | Total about 30 (see list below). |
| Other Protestant denominations | | P | ..... | | 100 | 300 | Total about 8 (see list below). |
| **Total affiliated (mid-1970)** | | | | **3,070** | **550,816** | **1,082,778** | **Total denominations (1970) . . . 53.** |
| **Total affiliated (mid-1975)** | | | | **3,400** | **668,400** | **1,314,000** | **Total denominations (1975) . . . 60.** |
| **Total affiliated (mid-1980)** | | | | **3,750** | **814,500** | **1,601,200** | **Total denominations (1980) . . . 67.** |

NOTES ON TABLE ABOVE
COLUMNS: for meanings and CODES (cols. 1, 3, 4, 8), see Codebook (Part 6). Column 1: **Boldface type** = church with over 10% of country's affiliated Christians.
NATIONAL COUNCILS (Column 4, 5th letter).
f = formerly in FECI, from 1960–63.
G = Fédération Evangélique de la Côte d'Ivoire (FECI) (Evangelical Federation of the Ivory Coast).
R = Conférence Episcopale de la Côte d'Ivoire (CECI) (Episcopal Conference of the Ivory Coast).
OTHER AFRICAN INDIGENOUS CHURCHES. There are numerous Ghanaian spiritual churches in the southeast of the country, especially around Port Bouet, also Nigerian bodies, as well as about 20 others indigenous to the Ivory Coast including a large number of unorganized Harrist schisms and groupings. Among the total are: African Faith Tabernacle Ch, Chérubin et Séraphin (Nigeria), Christ Apostolic Ch (1968; from Nigeria), Eglise Akéiste (Harrisme Libéral) (1926), Eglise Aladura (Ch of the Lord (Aladura) from Nigeria), Eglise de Papa Nouveau (1954, Bete), Eglise du Christ (Krastchotche) (c1935, Dida), Eglise du Christ (Mission Harris), Eglise du Christianisme Céleste de Dahomey (Abidjan; HQ Porto Novo), Eglise Protestante de Jésus-Christ, Episcopal Foursquare Gospel Ch. Indigenous bodies from outside Africa include the Unification Church, from Korea.
OTHER PROTESTANT DENOMINATIONS. These smaller missions include: Christian Ch of North America, Churches of Christ (USA), Eglise Ev Chrétienne de l'Ouest Africa (EECOA) (Sudan Interior Mission, ECWA; 1968), United Pentecostal Ch (1975), World-Wide Missions (1967).

PEOPLES (ethnolinguistic). Christians: 32.0% Lagoon (Abidji, Ajukru, Ebrie, Abe, Alladian, Avikam), 28.0% Kru (Dida, Bete, Guere, Wobe), 17.6% Baule, 9.3% Agni, 4.3% Dan, 3.4% French, 2.5% Guro, 2.2% Senufo, 0.2% Lobi (Kulango), 0.2% Yoruba, 0.1% Diula, Attie, Mossi, et alii.

COUNTRY-WIDE TOTALS
EVANGELIZATION (see Part 5). 1900: 5%. 1970: 79%. 1980: 84%. *Radiophonic evangelism.* Annual listeners' letters: about 2,200 (ELWA, RVOG, et alia). Bible correspondence courses: Roman Catholic courses with 6,000 active students, VOP (SDA), ICI (4,700 active students, 110 conversions reported).
FOREIGN MISSIONARIES AND PERSONNEL (nationals serving abroad) (1973). Total 153 in 6 countries: about 135 Roman Catholics, 10 Protestants, 8 African indigenous.
FOREIGN MISSIONARIES AND PERSONNEL (aliens from abroad) (1973). Total 1,087. *From Western World.* 1;014: 740 Roman Catholics, 274 Protestants (176 in 12 USA societies, 49 in 5 UK societies, 27 in 2 France societies, 5 in 3 Australia societies, 5 in 2 WGermany societies, 4 in 1 Switzerland society, 4 in 1 Canada society, 2 in 1 Netherlands society, 2 in 1 New Zealand society). *From Communist world.* 3 Roman Catholics from Poland. *From Third World.* 70: about 50 Roman Catholics, 15 African indigenous from Ghana, Nigeria and Liberia, about 5 Protestants.
INSTITUTIONS (church-operated) (1973). Total 98, including 40 higher schools (7 minor seminaries), 35 medical centres, 5 religious communities, 2 research centres, 8 seminaries (7 Protestant, 1 RC).
PERIODICALS. About 18 titles.
PERSONNEL. About 4,307 (3,220 national, 1,087 foreign).
RELIGIOUS LIBRARIES. About 13.
SCRIPTURE DISTRIBUTION (1975). Annual totals: 9,000 Bibles (22% free, 67% subsidized, 11% commercial), 34,000 NTs (44% free, 53% subsidized, 3% commercial), 20,000 UBS portions, 93,000 UBS selections. *Translations completed.* Portion: 15 languages since 1927. NT: 2 languages. Bible: Gouro, 1980.
SERVICE AGENCIES. About 56, including ACF, ACISJF, CECI, CLC, CV/AV, FECI, GBUAF, IFES, INADES, ISCR, JAC/F, JEC/F, JECI, JOC/F, SPCA, SU, WBT.

ADDITIONAL DATA ON CHURCHES
EGLISE CATHOLIQUE EN COTE D'IVOIRE. *Catechumens.* Totals: (1959) 62,898; (1961) 75,512; (1963) 92,796; and (1970) 113,000, divided approximately as follows among the 8 dioceses in order (and included in column 7): 50000, 25000, 10000, 2000,

10000, 7000, 5000, 6000. *Annual baptisms.* (1972) 41.7% infant, 58.3% adult. *Sisters.* Including 49 nationals. *Catechists.* Total (1974) 2,500. *Indigenous religious congregations.* Sisters: 42 N-D de la Paix (begun 1965). *Main foreign congregations.* Priests: SMA. Sisters: N-D des Apôtres.

*Catholic organizations.* The Episcopal Conference of the Ivory Coast is a member of SECAM and also of the International Episcopal Conference of French-speaking West Africa. Religious personnel are represented in the Union of Major Superiors of Native Congregations of French-speaking West Africa (called 'Anima Una') in Bamako, Mali. There are no national pastoral or presbyteral councils. The National Council of the Lay Apostolate, founded in 1968, forms a liaison between lay organizations and the hierarchy, while the National Office of Works co-ordinates the activities of all movements of the lay apostolate, including: CV/AV (12,000 members); JAC/F (5,000); JEC/F (2,600); Legion of Mary (2,000); Scouts (1,800); JOC/F, ACF and Teaching Teams (1,000 each).

The Holy See has diplomatic relations with the Ivory Coast and is represented to government and the Catholic hierarchy by a pro-nuncio in Abidjan, who serves also as pro-nuncio to Benin and apostolic delegate to Togo and Guinea.

The Ivory Coast serves as headquarters for 4 supra-national organizations serving francophone Africa (especially West Africa): (1) Conférence Episcopale Interterritoriale de l'Ouest Africain; (2) Institut Africain pour le Développement Economique et Social (INADES), founded in Abidjan by Jesuits in 1962, which maintains a training centre (CAF) and an extensive library and provides correspondence courses and lectures concerning the rural world, with special emphasis on training for women; (3) Institut Supérieur de Culture Religieuse (ISCR), whose functions were expanded in 1973 by the creation of a Catholic faculty of theology, a normal school for catechists and a centre for pastoralia where all African priests in francophone West Africa are expected to spend a period of time in study and reflection; (4) Sécretariat Permanent du Clergé Africain (SPCA), in Yopoungen near Abidjan. The secretariat for francophone Africa of Dialogue et Coopération/Equipes Enseignantes, founded in Paris in 1963, which organizes exchanges between Catholic teachers of the world, is also located in Abidjan.

National organizations serving the social sector include: (1) Centre for Studies and Social Action, which has as its goal the education of the middle and upper classes in their social responsibilities; (2) Church and Development Commission of the Synod of Abidjan, which was established to study and promote national development; and (3) Caritas de Côte d'Ivoire, affiliated to Caritas Internationalis in Rome, which administers emergency aid and stimulates small development projects.

The Catholic school system is co-ordinated by the National Office for Catholic Education. In 1970 the church was responsible for 404 pre-primary and primary schools with 99,281 pupils (22.9% of the total) and 24 secondary and technical schools with 5,968 students (12.1% of the total). In 1970 Catholic sisters were at work in 53 Catholic and state medical institutions.

EGLISE PROTESTANTE METHODISTE EN COTE D'IVOIRE. *Membership.* 75% Lagoon (Abidji, Ajukru, Ebrie, Attie, Abe, Alladian, Avikam), 20% Dida, 4% Agni, some French.

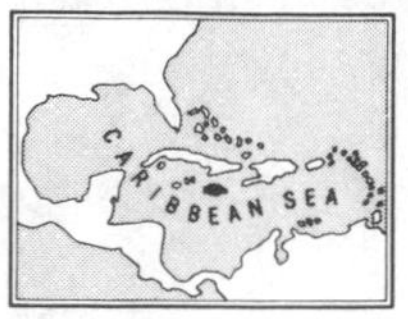


# JAMAICA

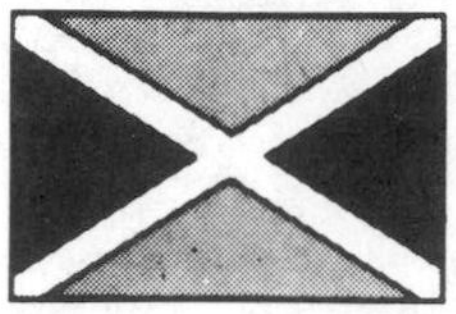

## SECULAR DATA

**STATE. Official name**: The Dominion of Jamaica. Adjective of nationality: Jamaican.
**Flag** (shown above right): Gold cross with green field in top and bottom quarters, black to left and right.
**Area**: 10,962 sq.km. (4,232 sq.miles). Agricultural land: 43.8%.
**Government**: Parliamentary state (constitutional monarchy), since 1962 (1509 Spanish possession, 1866 British crown colony, 1953 internal autonomy, 1958 in Federation of the West Indies, 1962 Independence).
**Legislature**: Parliament: Senate, 21 members; House of Representatives, 53 members.
**Official language**: English.
**Capital**: Kingston 475,550 (1970).
**Political divisions**: 14 Parishes.
**Armed forces** (1976): Jamaica Defence Force, with Air Wing.

**DEMOGRAPHY. Population**: 1,865,400 (census of 7.IV.1970. For 1970–2000 (UN), see last row of Table 1). Population density (1975): 185/sq.km. (479/sq.mile). Under 15 years: 42%. Growth rate (1975–80): 1.37% per year (births 3.06%, deaths −0.66%, emigrants −1.03%). Life expectancy (1975–80): 70.6 years. Household size: 4.3 persons.
**Major languages**: English, Jamaican Creole (Bongo Talk, Quashie Talk), Hindi, Chinese, Spanish.
**Urban dwellers** (1970): 37.6%. Urban growth rate (1950–70): 4.4% per year.
**Labour force**: 35%.
**Tourists** (1974): 432,987.

**ETHNOLINGUISTIC GROUPS**: 79.0% Black (African Negro), 14.6% Mulatto (Black/White), 1.7% Indo-Pakistani (East Indian), 1.6% Afro-East-Indian, 1.2% Chinese (Hakka) (23,000), 0.8% White (European) (British, North American, Portuguese, German), 0.6% Afro-Chinese (9,670), 0.3% Cuban, 0.1% Jewish, 0.1% Arab (1,350) (Syrian, Lebanese, Palestinian).

**MONEY** (1977). **Monetary unit**: dollar (= 100 cents); US$1 = J$0.91.

**National income per person**: US$1,065. Average annual family income: US$4,580.
**Inflation**: (1970–74) 14.4% per year (1975: consumer price index 210).
**Cost of living in capital** (1976): index 116 (Washington DC=100). Daily cost of living: US$43.

**HEALTH.** Hospitals: 28 (7,100 beds). Doctors: 490. Lepers: 2,100 (1.0 per 1,000). Blind: 3,100. Psychotics: 16,000. Criminals: about 50,000.

**EDUCATION.** Adult literacy: (1953) 77%, (1960) 82%. Education rate: 66%.Schools: 713. Universities: 1.

**LITERATURE.** Annual new book titles (1972): 120. Periodicals: 70. Scientific journals: 2. Newspapers: 3 dailies, 13 non-daily.

**COMMUNICATION** (per 1,000 people). Phones: 43. Radios: 376. TV sets: 55. Daily newspaper circulation: 100 copies.

TABLE 1. RELIGIOUS ADHERENTS IN JAMAICA

| Year | 1900 | | mid-1970 | | Annual change, 1970–1980 | | | | mid-1975 | | mid-1980 | | 2000 | |
|---|---|---|---|---|---|---|---|---|---|---|---|---|---|---|
| *Name* | *Adherents* | % | *Adherents* | % | *Natural* | *Conversion* | *Total* | *Rate* | *Adherents* | % | *Adherents* | % | *Adherents* | % |
| **Christians** | **679,700** | **94.4** | **1,718,400** | **91.3** | **26,302** | **−2,484** | **23,818** | **1.29** | **1,840,240** | **90.7** | **1,956,580** | **90.1** | **2,389,300** | **87.6** |
| professing | 679,700 | 94.4 | 1,718,400 | 91.3 | 26,302 | −2,484 | 23,818 | 1.29 | 1,840,240 | 90.7 | 1,956,580 | 90.1 | 2,389,300 | 87.6 |
| Protestants | 301,500 | 41.9 | 1,053,900 | 56.0 | 16,054 | −2,666 | 13,388 | 1.19 | 1,123,190 | 55.4 | 1,187,780 | 54.7 | 1,374,400 | 50.4 |
| Anglicans | 353,000 | 49.0 | 338,800 | 18.0 | 4,930 | −4,060 | 870 | 0.25 | 344,900 | 17.0 | 347,500 | 16.0 | 381,600 | 14.0 |
| Roman Catholics | 14,400 | 2.0 | 161,900 | 8.6 | 2,638 | 2,022 | 4,660 | 2.52 | 184,600 | 9.1 | 208,500 | 9.6 | 308,000 | 11.3 |
| Black indigenous | 10,800 | 1.5 | 143,300 | 7.6 | 2,348 | 2,002 | 4,350 | 2.65 | 164,300 | 8.1 | 186,800 | 8.6 | 289,000 | 10.6 |
| Marginal Protestants | 0 | 0.0 | 13,000 | 0.7 | 214 | 186 | 400 | 2.67 | 15,000 | 0.7 | 17,000 | 0.8 | 24,500 | 0.9 |
| Orthodox | 0 | 0.0 | 5,600 | 0.3 | 89 | 31 | 120 | 1.94 | 6,200 | 0.3 | 6,800 | 0.3 | 9,000 | 0.3 |
| Catholics (non-Roman) | 0 | 0.0 | 1,900 | 0.1 | 29 | 1 | 30 | 1.46 | 2,050 | 0.1 | 2,200 | 0.1 | 2,800 | 0.1 |
| nominal | 115,000 | 16.0 | 769,129 | 40.9 | 11,976 | 1,649 | 13,625 | 1.63 | 837,940 | 41.3 | 905,380 | 41.7 | 1,108,300 | 40.7 |
| affiliated | 564,700 | 78.4 | 949,271 | 50.4 | 14,326 | −4,133 | 10,193 | 1.02 | 1,002,300 | 49.4 | 1,051,200 | 48.4 | 1,281,000 | 47.0 |
| total practising | 536,460 | *95* | 854,340 | *90* | 12,893 | −3,719 | 9,174 | 1.02 | 902,070 | *90* | 946,080 | *90* | 1,024,800 | *80* |
| non-practising | 28,240 | *5* | 94,930 | *10* | 1,433 | −414 | 1,019 | 1.02 | 100,230 | *10* | 105,120 | *10* | 256,200 | *20* |
| Protestants | 250,700 | 34.8 | 533,498 | 28.3 | 7,730 | −7,016 | 714 | 0.13 | 540,820 | 26.6 | 540,640 | 24.9 | 554,400 | 20.3 |
| Evangelicals | 230,000 | 31.9 | 395,200 | 21.0 | 5,800 | −4,050 | 1,750 | 0.43 | 405,800 | 20.0 | 412,700 | 19.0 | 490,700 | 18.0 |
| Roman Catholics | 13,000 | 1.8 | 160,873 | 8.5 | 2,610 | 1,933 | 4,543 | 2.49 | 182,600 | 9.0 | 206,300 | 9.5 | 300,000 | 11.0 |
| Catholic pentecostals | 0 | 0.0 | 0 | 0.0 | 14 | 186 | 200 | 20.00 | 1,000 | 0.0 | 2,000 | 0.1 | 10,000 | 0.4 |
| Black indigenous | 20,000 | 2.8 | 138,300 | 7.3 | 2,263 | 1,937 | 4,200 | 2.65 | 158,300 | 7.8 | 180,300 | 8.3 | 278,100 | 10.2 |
| Anglicans | 281,000 | 39.0 | 100,000 | 5.3 | 1,449 | −1,239 | 210 | 0.21 | 101,400 | 5.0 | 102,100 | 4.7 | 117,200 | 4.3 |
| Marginal Protestants | 0 | 0.0 | 10,600 | 0.6 | 179 | 211 | 390 | 3.12 | 12,500 | 0.6 | 14,500 | 0.7 | 21,800 | 0.8 |
| Orthodox | 0 | 0.0 | 5,000 | 0.3 | 80 | 40 | 120 | 2.14 | 5,600 | 0.3 | 6,200 | 0.3 | 8,000 | 0.3 |
| Catholics (non-Roman) | 0 | 0.0 | 1,000 | 0.1 | 15 | 1 | 16 | 1.48 | 1,080 | 0.1 | 1,160 | 0.1 | 1,500 | 0.1 |
| Afro-American spiritists | 36,000 | 5.0 | 130,000 | 6.9 | 2,029 | 371 | 2,400 | 1.69 | 142,000 | 7.0 | 154,000 | 7.1 | 204,000 | 7.5 |
| Non-religious | 0 | 0.0 | 17,800 | 0.9 | 414 | 1,986 | 2,400 | 8.25 | 29,100 | 1.4 | 41,800 | 1.9 | 106,000 | 3.9 |
| Hindus | 1,900 | 0.3 | 5,600 | 0.3 | 86 | −6 | 80 | 1.33 | 6,000 | 0.3 | 6,400 | 0.3 | 8,000 | 0.3 |
| Baha'is | 0 | 0.0 | 3,100 | 0.2 | 57 | 133 | 190 | 4.75 | 4,000 | 0.2 | 5,000 | 0.2 | 8,000 | 0.3 |
| Muslims | 2,000 | 0.3 | 3,000 | 0.2 | 46 | −6 | 40 | 1.25 | 3,200 | 0.2 | 3,400 | 0.2 | 4,200 | 0.2 |
| Jews | 300 | 0.1 | 1,800 | 0.1 | 28 | 0 | 28 | 1.44 | 1,940 | 0.1 | 2,080 | 0.1 | 2,600 | 0.1 |
| Chinese folk-religionists | 100 | 0.0 | 1,000 | 0.1 | 13 | −33 | −20 | −2.22 | 900 | 0.0 | 800 | 0.0 | 600 | 0.0 |
| Buddhists | 0 | 0.0 | 300 | 0.0 | 5 | −1 | 4 | 1.25 | 320 | 0.0 | 340 | 0.0 | 300 | 0.0 |
| Other religionists | 0 | 0.0 | 1,000 | 0.1 | 20 | 40 | 60 | 4.62 | 1,300 | 0.1 | 1,600 | 0.1 | 3,000 | 0.1 |
| **Country's population** | **720,000** | **100.0** | **1,882,000** | **100.0** | **29,000** | **0** | **29,000** | **1.43** | **2,029,000** | **100.0** | **2,172,000** | **100.0** | **2,726,000** | **100.0** |

COLUMNS, ROWS. For meanings and definitions, see Codebook (Part 6). Note that, by definition, total 'Christians' = professing + crypto-Christians, which also = affiliated + nominal Christians. Percentages may not always total exactly, due to rounding.

CENSUSES. **1943**: 61.0% Protestants (25.8% Baptists, 8.9% Methodists, 7.5% Presbyterians, 4.1% Moravians, 3.5% Ch of God, 2.2% SD Adventists, 1.7% Congregationalists, 1.1% Salvation Army), 28.4% Anglicans, 5.7% Roman Catholics, 4.0% Afro-American spiritists (Pocomania, etc) and Black indigenous Christians and non-religious, 0.3% Hindus, 0.1% Jews. **1953**: 61.7% Protestants (22.7% Baptists, 7.7% Methodists, 6.2% Ch of God, 5.6% Presbyterians, 4.0% SD Adventists, 3.6% Moravians, 1.3% Congregationalists, 1.3% Salvation Army), 23.5% Anglicans, 7.9% Afro-American spiritists (Pocomania, etc), Black indigenous Christians and non-religious, 6.9% Roman Catholics. **7.IV.1960** (de jure): 59.2% Protestants (20.1% Baptists, 12.6% Ch of God, 7.1% Methodists), 21.0% Anglicans, 12.1% Afro-American spiritists (Pocomania, etc), and Black indigenous Christians and non-religious, 7.6% Roman Catholics, 0.1% Hindus. **7.IV.1970**: 64.3% Protestants (including Black indigenous), 18.0% Anglicans, 8.6% Roman Catholics, 8.0% other religionists,

NOTES ON RELIGIONS

AFRO-AMERICAN SPIRITISTS. There are 2 distinct types of movement in this category. (1) There are numerous Afro-Caribbean spirit-possession cults syncretizing Christianity with African religion, which are usually referred to as the Revival Zion-Pocomania-Obeah complex, or Afro-Christian cults. In this survey we classify Revival Zion as more Christian than non-Christian and so include it under Black indigenous churches; we classify Pocomania, however, as more non-Christian than Christian, hence include it under our category of non-Christian Afro-American spiritism. Other, related, non-Christian cults include the Black Israelites, a cult band invoking Satan and fallen angels, begun in 1900 and with 811 adherents in 1960; Convince and Cumina cults, Obeah, and Myalismo (now almost extinct). Members of these cults wear turbans, use the colours black, white, red and blue, sing Sankey hymns, take the sacrament of communion (bread and wine) frequently, and perform counter-clockwise dancing-trumping to induce possession; Pocomania in addition uses strong liquor and marijuana. Numerically, censuses have not clearly enumerated these cults, because the name Pocomania is regarded unfavourably and most adherents call themselves Baptists or Revivalists, though usually recorded in the censuses under 'No religion'. But a 1953 survey estimated participants in the Revival Zion-Pocomania-Obeah complex to be 8,000 (10.0% of the population) in West Kingston alone. (2) A different type of cult is the Ras Tafari movement begun in 1930, with 50,000 followers and over 30,000 sympathizers. Some of its offshoots and branches (e.g. in UK) are specifically Christian. Of all Rastafarians 80% are aged 17–35 years, predominantly male, and most were formerly members of Christian churches.

BAHA'IS. Rapid growth from 6 local spiritual assemblies (1964) to 21 (1973). Mainly East Indians. In 1971 a mass teaching project enrolled 1,000 new believers.

BLACK INDIGENOUS. In over 60 denominations in 1970 (see Table 2). Three groups: (1) Black pentecostals from the USA, Methodists (AMEC) and others founded with aid from USA Black churches; (2) indigenous Jamaican bodies (e.g. New Testament Church of Christ the Redeemer); and (3) Revival Zionists, Shouters, Shakers, Spiritual Baptists and other indigenous Jamaican Afro-Christian cults syncretizing Christianity, spiritism and African religions.

CATHOLIC PENTECOSTALS (or, Catholic charismatics). Totals (mid-1975): 500 involved adults (over 15 years) in 10 prayer groups; total charismatic community including children, 1,000.

COUNTRY'S POPULATION. Annual emigration has averaged 30,000 a year since 1960, mainly to the UK at first, then to the USA and Canada.

HINDUS. East Indians. Among Hindu sects, Ananda Marga has a following.

JEWS. United Congregation of Israelites, with synagogues in Kingston; Sefardic.

MUSLIMS. East Indians, Syrians; with one mosque.

NOMINAL CHRISTIANS. There are vast numbers of nominal Methodists, Anglicans and Presbyterians, many of whom participate in Afro-American spiritist cults whilst continuing to regard themselves as Protestants or Anglicans.

NON-RELIGIOUS. Chinese and Europeans; with Blacks who either have abandoned religion or have no interest in it.

OTHER RELIGIONISTS. Adherents of smaller religions and cults, including Rosicrucians (1 AMORC centre).

PRACTISING CHRISTIANS. 1953 census (a sample survey for population of 10 years and over): 31.2% attended church frequently, 43.7% infrequently, and 25.1% did not attend church. Since then, attenders have declined in numbers appreciably.

## NON-CHRISTIAN RELIGIONS. Afro-Caribbean

**syncretistic religions,** a mixture of spiritism, Christianity and traditional African rites, abound in Jamaica. The first Afro-Christian movement was the Native Baptist cult begun by an ex-slave in 1783 and which played a significant role in the political disturbances at Port Morant in 1865. During 1861 the Great Awakening came to prominence featuring wild dancing, trances, sexual orgies and public confession. Another marginal Christian group was Bedwardism began in 1920 by Alexander Bedward, who considered himself to be Christ and who predicted his own ascension into heaven and second coming. One of the largest of contemporary sects is the Ras Tafari movement, which built on the back-to-Africa ideas of Marcus Garvey, became a significant politico-religious force in the 1930s, attracted masses of poverty-stricken slum-dwellers, attempted to prepare for repatriation to Ethiopia in the 1960s and numbered in 1975 some 50,000 members with tens of thousands more supporters and sympathizers. More recent nativistic cults are the Black Israelites, Pocomania, Convince and Cumina cults, and other revivalist groups.

**Other religions** include Baha'i (0.2% of the population), Hinduism (0.3%), Chinese folk religion, and a small Sefardic Jewish community

## CHRISTIANITY.

PROTESTANT CHURCHES. Protestant work in Jamaica was pioneered by the Friends (Quakers) in 1671, followed by Moravians and Methodists during the 18th century and many other groups since then. The first Baptist missionary to the West Indies was George Lisle, a freed slave from Virginia who arrived in Kingston in 1783. His first Baptist congregation later evolved into both the Native Baptist cult and also the Jamaica Baptist Union. British Baptists were invited in after 1813, but the local church has been entirely independent since 1842. Indeed, the indigenous Jamaica Baptist Missionary Society sent its own missionaries to Fernando Poo off the coast of equatorial Africa as early as 1884. The total community of the Jamaica Baptist Union, numbering 100,000, is now equal in size to the Anglican and Seventh-day Adventist churches, the latter having been at work in Jamaica since 1893. In the present century, a number of Baptist missionary societies from the USA have begun work in the country: Baptist International Missions, Baptist Mid-Missions, General Baptists, National Baptists, Seventh-day Baptists and Southern Baptists.

The Methodist Church, related to British

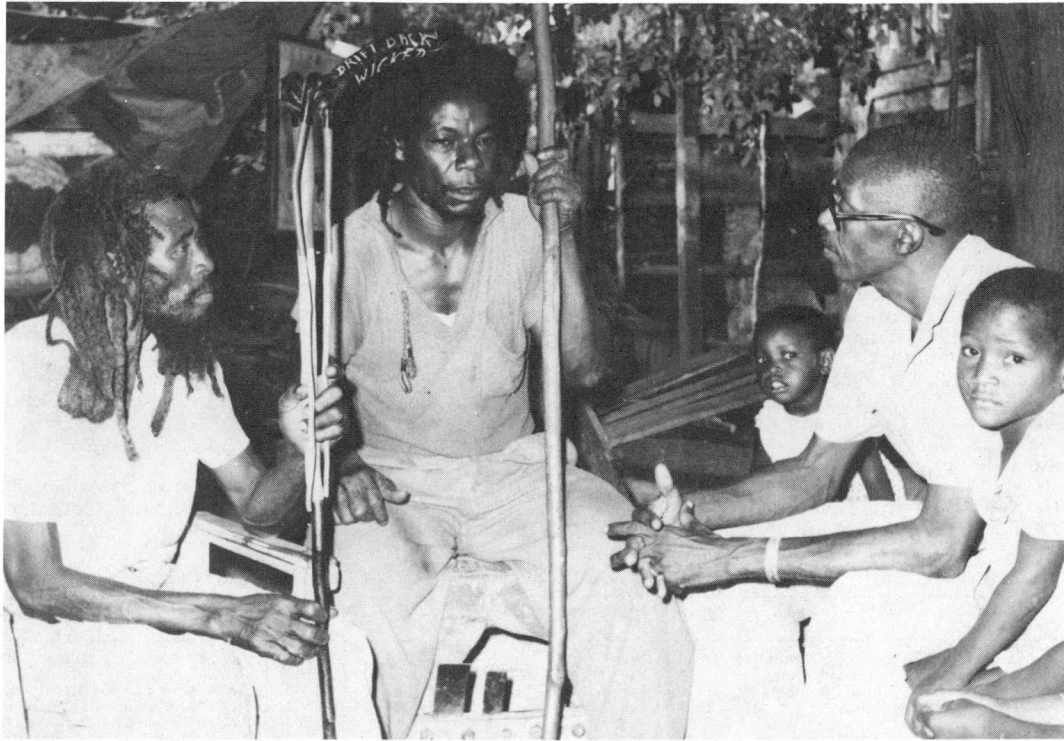

**Afro-American spiritists.** Two of the 50,000 Rastafarians (left) talk with a Methodist minister (right).

**Revival Zion.** A charismatic Black church begun in 1783. *Left.* Leader with staff. *Above.* 'Table' (combined religious service and feast) at new church's dedication.

Methodism, has built up a Christian community of 50,000 since its inception in 1789; and the United Church of Jamaica and Grand Cayman, a merger of Presbyterians and Congregationalists in 1965, has a similar constituency. Another early arrival, the Moravian Church (1754), is half as large.

The predominant Protestant tradition in terms of total membership is now Pentecostalism. The first Pentecostal mission was the Church of God (Cleveland) from the USA in 1917; and its affiliated daughter church, the New Testament Church of God, remains Jamaica's largest Pentecostal denomination. Of some 12 other Pentecostal groups, the next largest is the Church of God of Prophecy (1923).

The Brethren, Church of God (Anderson), Disciples, Friends, Salvation Army and a host of small independent missions from the USA are also at work.

CATHOLIC CHURCH. Jamaica was discovered by Columbus in 1494, and within 14 years the first sugar cane plantations had been established.

Early Catholic missionary efforts produced limited results due to lack of clergy, but by 1655 when England attacked Spanish possessions in the Caribbean and took over Jamaica, most of the population was Catholic. Catholicism was prohibited thereafter and was not begun again until the arrival of Jesuits in 1837. However, its growth has been rapid since then, and at the present time the Catholic Church has more members than any other denomination in Jamaica.

A significant proportion of Catholics is found among the poorer classes of the population. Of all

Jamaica's ethnic groups, the Chinese have the highest proportion of Catholics.

INDIGENOUS CHURCHES. The earliest specifically-Christian indigenous movement was Revival Zion, which began in 1783 as the Native Baptist Church and which spread rapidly during the Great Christian Revival of 1861–62 and subsequently. Despite numerous syncretistic features, it remains today as basically a charismatic Christian movement.

Black denominations from the USA including the AME Church (1912) have been at work in Jamaica since before World War I, but the majority of Jamaica's many indigenous churches were formed after World War II. Most are small, some consisting of only a single congregation, although the New Testament Church of Christ the Redeemer has 40,000 adherents. Jamaica's 60 or so independent churches generally display pentecostal-type features in their mode of worship. As a result of mass emigration to Britain since 1960, many of them now have extensive missionary work in that country.

ANGLICAN CHURCH. The Anglican Church is one of Jamaica's oldest and largest denominations, dating back to chaplaincy work in the 17th century. The first Anglican bishoprics in the Caribbean were established in Jamaica and Barbados in 1824, and the diocese of Jamaica has since 1883 been part of the automous Church of the Province of the West Indies.

CHURCH AND STATE. There is freedom of conscience and worship in Jamaica. The state neither favours nor supports any church or religion, but

**Anglican Church, Diocese of Jamaica.** Choir in St Stephen's Church, Majesty Pen.

financial aid is provided for private schools, and the churches are exempt from taxation. Provision is made for religious instruction in the lower grades of the public school system (junior secondary, primary, infant schools), by means of an ecumenical syllabus prepared through the co-operation of the Protestant and Catholic churches. A similar syllabus is also being prepared for secondary schools. Churches and their properties are registered with government, but there is no ministry or government office dealing specifically with religious affairs.

**INTERDENOMINATIONAL ORGANIZATIONS.** The Jamaica Council of Churches was established in 1939 as a Protestant organization, but since November 1971 it has included in its membership the Anglican and Catholic churches as well. The council is affiliated to the World Council of Churches and the CWME. The Catholic archdiocese of Kingston has a Commission on Ecumenism. There is also a fundamentalist council, the Jamaica Association of Evangelical Churches.

**BROADCASTING.** Television studios and a closed-circuit TV system are in use at St John's University.

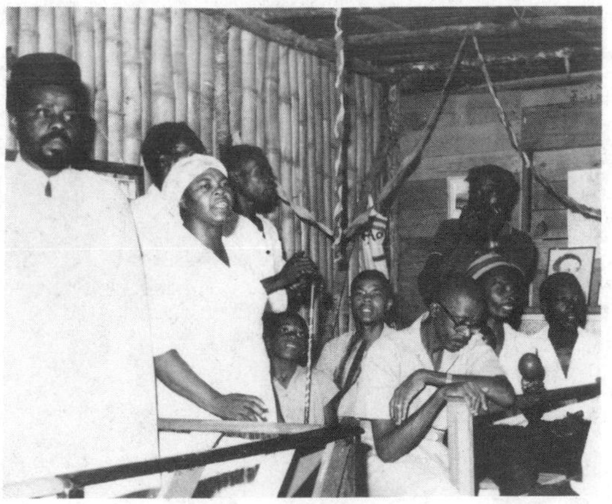

**Ethiopian Orthodox Church.** Priest and faithful in Kingston church, 1964.

Its School of General Studies has over one hundred students, including many active churchmen, learning all aspects of social communication.

## BIBLIOGRAPHY


'A comparative study of acculturation in Morant Bay and West Kingston, Jamaica', J. G. Moore & G. E. Simpson, *Zaire*, XI (Nov–Dec, 1957), 979–1020, and XII (January, 1958), 65–88.

*Black religions in the New World.* G. E. Simpson. New York: Columbia University Press, 1978. 415p.

*Caribbean Catholic directory, 1971.* Kingston: Antilles Episcopal Conference Executive Secretariat, 1971.

*Church growth in Jamaica.* D. A. McGavran. Lucknow (India): Lucknow Publishing House, 1962.

*History of Bedwardism: or the Jamaica Native Baptist Free Church.* A. A. Brooks. Kingston, 1917.

'Jamaican revivalist cults', G. E. Simpson, *Social and economic studies* (Jamaica), V, 4 (1956), 231–442.

*Obeah, Christ and Rastaman: Jamaica and its religion.* I. Morrish. London: Brill, 1978. 224p.

'Protest and mysticism: the Ras Tafari cult of Jamaica', S. Kitzinger, *Journal for the scientific study of religion*, VIII, 2 (1969), 240–262.

'Religion of Jamaican Negroes: a study of Afro-Jamaican acculturation'. J. G. Moore. Dissertation, Northwestern University, Evanston (Illinois), 1954.

'Religious syncretism in Jamaica', J. G. Moore, *Practical anthropology*, XII, 2 (1965), 63–70.

*The Church in the new Jamaica.* J. M. Davis. New York: International Missionary Council, 1942.

'The Convince Cult in Jamaica', D. Hogg, in S. Mintz (ed), *Papers in Caribbean anthropology* (New Haven: Yale University, 1960), p. 21–28.

'The Ras Tafari movement in Jamaica: a study of race and class conflict', G. E. Simpson, *Social forces*, XXXIV (December, 1955), 167–171.

'The Rastafarian brethren of Jamaica', S. Kitzinger, *Comparative studies in society and history*, IX, 1 (1966), 33–39.


TABLE 2. ORGANIZED CHURCHES AND DENOMINATIONS IN JAMAICA

| Official name 1 | Begun 2 | Type 3 | Counc 4 | Congs 5 | Adults 6 | Affiliated 7 | Names, notes, and other statistics (see Codebook) 8 |
|---|---|---|---|---|---|---|---|
| African Methodist Episcopal Church | 1912 | I Met | VwM.N | | 520 | 1,500 | *Jamaica Annual Conference*, 16th Episcopal District. M=AMEC(USA Blacks). |
| African Methodist Episcopal Zion Ch | 1965 | I Met | Vw... | 241 | 10,000 | 24,500 | Revival movement, later invited in M=AMEZC(USA Blacks). Very rapid growth. 65n. |
| African Reformed Coptic Church of God | 1959 | I mar | ..... | | 1,000 | 4,000 | *God's Army Camp*, *Back to Africa*. 1960–70 jailings; 1970 New Creation Peacemakers. |
| **Anglican Church: D Jamaica** | 1655 | A Cen | AwMRN | 280 | 52,584 | 100,000 | In *CPWI*. Declining 3% pa. 3 episcopal regions. 90% Black. 71n,22x,1u,4851Yy. |
| Apostolic Church | | P PeA | Z.... | 3 | 3,000 | 5,000 | M=Apostolic Church Missionary Movement(UK). Based in Walderston. |
| Apostolic Church of Pentecost | | P Pe1 | x.... | | 200 | 500 | M=Apostolic Ch of Pentecost(Canada). HQ Cambridge. Unitarian Pentecostals. 1f. |
| Assemblies of God | 1937 | P Pe2 | ZF... | 69 | 3,414 | 11,000 | M=AoG(USA). Classical Pentecostals. HQ Kingston. 71n,3f,1p,1s(118). |
| Assemblies of the First-Born | c1950 | I pen | ..... | 20 | 2,000 | 3,000 | Related to Church of the First-Born, but now pentecostal. HQ Kingston. |
| Associated Gospel Assemblies | 1925 | P CBr | x.Y.1 | 72 | 3,500 | 7,000 | *Association of Ev Chs. Open Brethren.* M=CMML(UK,USA). 6n,1x,8f,G=3.7%pa,2H,200Y. |
| Baptist Mid-Missions | 1939 | P Bap | xTY.1 | | 1,000 | 3,000 | M=BMM(USA). Regular Baptists; fundamentalists. 19f,1s. |
| **Catholic Church in Jamaica:** | 1509 | R Lat | P.NMN | 42 | 93,300 | 160,873 | 12% Chinese. C=5+0+9. 2H,37r(10582),1s. 22n,98x,12m,247w,P=22%,7641Yy. |
| M Kingston in Jamaica | 1837 | R Lat | Ps | 25 | 81,100 | 139,870 | Eastern Jamaica. M=SJ. D=pc,PC. 11r,1s. 20 75 11 204 20 6516 |
| D Montego Bay | 1967 | R Lat | Ps | 17 | 12,200 | 21,003 | Western part of Jamaica. M=CP. 4r. 2 23 1 43 33 1125 |
| Christadelphian Ecclesias | | P Ade | x.... | 7 | 150 | 300 | *Christadelphian Bible Mission* (*CBM*). 7 ecclesias (churches). Pacifist, adventist. |
| Christian Churches & Chs of Christ | c1935 | P Dis | x.... | | 2,000 | 4,000 | M=CCCC(Instrumental)(USA). Independent congregations, mainly split ex UCMS. 21f. |
| Church of Christ, Scientist | | M Sci | x.... | 1 | 200 | 400 | *Christian Science.* First Church, Kingston. M=CCS(Boston, USA). 3w. |
| Church of God Holiness | 1933 | P Hol | x.... | 35 | 300 | 1,000 | M=CoG Holiness(Overland Park,Kansas,USA). 1 school. Emigration to UK. 2f,1s. |
| Church of God in Christ | | I pe3 | Z.... | 20 | 400 | 800 | M=CoGiC(Black pentecostals from USA). Emigration to UK. HQ Kingston. |
| Church of God in Jamaica | 1907 | P Hol | x...N | 92 | 3,400 | 11,000 | *General Assembly of CoG* (*Jamaica*). M=CoG(Anderson)(USA). SS=6,000. 24n,6f,1k,1r,1s. |
| Church of God of Prophecy | 1923 | P Pe3 | Z.... | 171 | 15,480 | 25,000 | M=CGP(USA). Theocratic government. Many emigrants to UK to form church there. |
| Church of the First-Born | c1950 | I ind | x.... | 20 | 1,000 | 2,000 | Strict ethics. Branches by emigration in UK, Canada, USA, Barbados. HQ Kingston. |
| Church of the Nazarene | 1966 | P Hol | xF... | 7 | 65 | 1,000 | M=CoN(USA). Small holiness denomination. 3m,7f,6t(715). |
| Churches of Christ (Non-Instrumental) | 1965 | P Dis | x.... | 16 | 1,000 | 2,000 | M=CC(Non-Instrumental)(USA). Many split ex UCMS. In Kingston. 20f. |
| Disciples of Christ in Jamaica | 1858 | P Dis | x.M.N | 60 | 5,500 | 12,000 | Rejected 1968 United Ch merger. M=UCMS(USA). 16n,2x,3f,G=1.9%pa,1p,1u,W=66%,510Y. |
| Ethiopian Orthodox Ch (D Trinidad) | 1959 | O Eth | Nwa.N | 6 | 2,800 | 5,000 | *EOC*. Under P Addis Ababa, Ethiopia. Blacks, formerly in Ras Tafari cult. W=10%,1000z. |
| Evangelical Church of the West Indies | 1945 | P int | xM... | | 1,000 | 2,000 | M=West Indies Mission(USA). Interdenominational mission. 15f,1s. |
| General Baptist Mission | 1966 | P Bap | TF... | 12 | 440 | 1,000 | *General Association of General Baptists.* M=GBFMS(USA). 2f. |
| Independent Jamaica Baptist Mission | c1947 | P Bap | .TY.1 | 2 | 200 | 400 | Fundamentalist Baptists with USA connections. HQ Glenrock, Ramble. |
| Internat Ch of the Foursquare Gospel | 1947 | P Pe2 | ZF... | 35 | 591 | 3,000 | M=ICFG(USA). Classical Pentecostals. HQ Hagley Park. 23nm,2f,1p(35),W=49%,26Y. |
| International City Mission | c1950 | I pen | ..... | 20 | 1,000 | 2,000 | Healing, schools, orphanages. HQ Kingston. Work in UK, USA, Belize. Women bishops. |
| **Jamaica Baptist Union** | 1814 | P Bap | T.M.N | 430 | 33,120 | 100,000 | 1814, M=BMS(UK); 1963, SBC. 92% Black, 3% Indian. 71n,4f,G=0.9%pa,1u,W=50%,1794Y. |
| Jehovah's Witnesses | 1898 | M Jeh | x.... | 149 | 5,053 | 9,000 | *Watch Tower. IBSA.* Active witnessing under way by 1926. HQ Kingston. 296Y. |
| Mennonite Church | 1955 | P Men | G.... | | 314 | 785 | *Jamaica Mennonite Mission.* M=MCC,Virginia Mennonite Conference(USA). 40f. |
| Methodist Church in Jamaica | 1789 | P Met | VwM.N | 198 | 20,106 | 50,000 | *MCCA, Jamaica District.* M=MMS(UK). 42n,16x,27f,G=−1.3%pa,6r,1u,21Y,1608y,1272z. |
| Missionary Church | 1949 | P Hol | xF... | 39 | 2,538 | 5,000 | Before 1969 merger, M=Missionary Church Association(USA); now MC(USA). 6f,1s. |
| Moravian Church in Jamaica | 1754 | P Mor | xWM.N | 51 | 8,500 | 23,298 | *Jamaica Province, UoB.* A=1966. Rural. 50 schools. 13n,6x,1r,1u,W=40%,739Yy,260z. |
| New Apostolic Church | | C CAp | x.... | | 500 | 1,000 | *NAC*. In Canada Bezirk (District). Ex Irvingites. World HQ Dortmund (Germany). |
| New Testament Ch of Christ the R | | I ind | ..... | 86 | 18,000 | 40,000 | *R=Redeemer.* Founded in Kingston, churches across island. 14,000 in Sunday schools. |
| New Testament Church of God | 1917 | P Pe3 | ZF... | 255 | 32,218 | 50,000 | M=CoG(Cleveland)(USA). Members 70% women; large emigration to UK. 232n,4f,4r,1s. |
| Open Bible Standard Churches of J | 1948 | P Pe2 | ZFY.1 | 23 | 1,000 | 3,000 | M=OBSC(USA). Black. Classical Pentecostals. HQ Kingston. 12n,2x,3f,4H,1s,12Y. |
| Pentecostal Assemblies of the World | | I pe1 | x.... | | 200 | 500 | M=PAoW(Blacks from USA). Also in Barbados. Branches in UK through emigration. |
| Pentecostal Church of God | 1954 | P Pe2 | Z.... | 46 | 701 | 2,000 | *PCG of America Branch.* M=PCG. 1 school. 18n,3x,4f,1p,1s(10),W=99%,213Y. |
| Pentecostal Holiness Church | | P Pe3 | ZF... | 44 | 1,528 | 2,000 | M=PHC(USA). Holiness Pentecostals (3-stage). 2f. |
| Religious Society of Friends | 1671 | P Qua | Q...N | 15 | 750 | 1,300 | *Jamaica Yearly Meeting.* M=FUM(USA). 10 schools. 2n,2x,5f,G=−3.6%pa,1r,W=50%,50z. |
| Revival Zion | 1783 | I pen | ..... | 300 | 17,000 | 35,000 | 1861–62, Great Christian Revival. Charismatics similar to Shouters, Shakers. |
| Salvation Army | 1887 | P Sal | xwM.N | 70 | 8,000 | 11,000 | *SA*, Caribbean & CAmerica Territory (HQ for 12 nations is in Kingston). 1s. |
| Seventh Day Baptist Church | 1927 | P Bap | Tw... | 28 | 965 | 2,000 | *SDB, Jamaica Conference.* M=SDBC(USA). 1 school. 1966, Black mission to UK begun. 2f. |
| **Seventh-day Adventist Church** | 1893 | P Adv | x.... | 363 | 59,834 | 100,000 | *SDA, Central, E, W Jamaica Conferences.* 55nx,323mw,1H,1h,6r,1s,397t,(73750),5423Y. |
| Unitarian Universalist Church | | M Unt | I.... | | 100 | 200 | M=Unitarian Universalist Service Committee. HQ Mandeville. |
| United Brethren in Christ | 1945 | P Hol | xF... | | 200 | 300 | M=UBC(USA). Small holiness denomination. |
| United Ch of Jamaica & Grand Cayman | 1800 | P uni | RWM.N | 160 | 18,000 | 47,000 | 1965 union: Congr Union of J, Presb Ch of J; 1968 Disciples of Christ. 50n,6r,1u. |
| United Pentecostal Church | 1933 | P Pe1 | x.... | 61 | 5,452 | 10,000 | *Jesus Only Church.* M=UPC(USA). Mission to UK through emigration. 35n,4f,1p(12). |
| Wesleyan Church | 1911 | P Hol | VF... | 82 | 1,549 | 4,015 | M=WMM(USA), Pilgrim Holiness, Missionary Bands. 26n,3x,5f,G=−7%pa,1p,W=46%,411Y. |
| World Missions | 1966 | P int | x.... | | 300 | 600 | M=World Missions(USA). North American Evangelicals based on Long Beach, CA. 1f. |
| World-Wide Missions of Jamaica | 1961 | P ind | x.... | | 10,000 | 20,000 | M=World-Wide Missions(USA). Evangelicals with links in Pasadena, CA (USA). |
| Other Black indigenous churches | | I | ..... | | 15,000 | 25,000 | Total over 50 bodies, with many single congregations (see list below). |
| Other Protestant denominations | | P | ..... | | 6,000 | 12,000 | Total about 20 (see list below). |
| Other marginal Protestant bodies | | M | ..... | | 400 | 1,000 | Including: Divine Science Fed International (1 church), Unity School of Christianity (2 churches). |
| **Total affiliated (mid-1970)** | | | | **4,080** | **473,372** | **949,271** | **Total denominations (1970) . . . 125.** |
| **Total affiliated (mid-1975)** | | | | **4,200** | **499,800** | **1,002,300** | **Total denominations (1975) . . . 135.** |
| **Total affiliated (mid-1980)** | | | | **4,350** | **524,200** | **1,051,200** | **Total denominations (1980) . . . 145.** |

NOTES ON TABLE ABOVE

COLUMNS: for meanings and CODES (cols. 1, 3, 4, 8), see Codebook (Part 6). Column 1: **Boldface type** = church with over 10% of country's affiliated Christians.

NATIONAL COUNCILS (Column 4, 5th letter).

1 = Jamaica Association of Evangelical Churches (or National Council of Fundamentalist Churches in Jamaica) (affiliated to both Evangelical Association of the Caribbean (EAC) and ICCC).

N = Jamaica Council of Churches (JCC).

OTHER BLACK INDIGENOUS CHURCHES. These, mostly pentecostal, include: Apostolic Churches (several Jesus-Only independent pentecostal congregations; including Apostolic Ch of God in Christ), Assembly of Yahweh, Bethel Apostolic (Shilo) Ch, Blood-Bought Ch of God, Ch of God Fellowship (split ex NTCoG), Ch of God Pentecostal, Ch of Jesus (Watt Town, St Ann), Ch of the Lord (Aladura) from Nigeria, Emanuel Apostolic United Ch of Christ, First Glorious Temple Ch of God Apostolic, Jamaica Native Baptist Free Ch (Bedwardites; 1891–1921 enormous following throughout Jamaica), Model Ch of God, Ras Tafari Melchizedek Orthodox Ch, Remnant Chs of God, Sanctified Ch of God, Shakers, Shouters, Spiritual Baptists, Universal Ch of the Master. There are also several other USA Black missions at work including: Bible Way Chs of Our Lord Jesus Christ World Wide (1958).

OTHER PROTESTANT DENOMINATIONS. Other smaller denominations total about 20, including: Baptist Bible Fellowship International (1972), Baptist International Missions (1971), Children of God International (Mona, Kingston), Christian Catholic Ch, Ch of God Seventh-day, Elim Fellowship (1966), Evangelical Methodist Ch (1960), Exclusive Brethren (groups: Raven-Taylor and Kelly-Continental), Independent Assemblies of God, Lutheran Ch in America, Methodist Protestant Ch, United Ev Chs, United World Mission.

UNITING CHURCHES. In 1974, 2 separate sets of negotiations for organic union were under way, as follows: (1) Disciples of Christ in Jamaica (partly in United Ch of Jamaica & GC), Moravian Ch in Jamaica, United Ch of Jamaica & Grand Cayman. (2) Ch of the Province of the West Indies (Anglican), Methodist Ch in the Caribbean & the Americas.

**PEOPLES** (ethnolinguistic). Christians: 79.5% Black, 14.6% Mulatto, 2.1% Chinese, 1.6% Afro-East Indian, 0.8% White (European), 0.6% Afro-Chinese, 0.5% East Indian, 0.3% Cuban.

COUNTRY-WIDE TOTALS

EVANGELIZATION (see Part 5). 1900: 100%. 1970: 100%. 1980: 100%. *Mass evangelism.* Among recent campaigns: 1968. Crusade for World Revival (from UK) 8-day campaign (8,000 attenders a night). *Radiophonic evangelism.* Annual listeners' letters (1975): 1,050 TWR, 255 HCJB, et alia.

FOREIGN MISSIONARIES AND PERSONNEL (nationals serving abroad) (1973). Total 376 in 33 countries: 187 Black indigenous in 22 countries including UK, USA, India, 105 Protestants in 16 countries including UK, 44 Anglicans in 6 countries including Zambia, 40 Roman Catholics in 3 countries.

FOREIGN MISSIONARIES AND PERSONNEL (aliens from abroad) (1973). Total 597. *From Western world.* 558: 264 Protestants (198 in 49 USA societies, 53 in 7 UK societies, 11 in 4 Canada societies, 1 in 1 Finland society, 1 in 1 Norway society), about 250 Roman Catholics, 24 Anglicans (22 in 2 UK societies, 1 in 1 USA society, 1 in 1 Canada society), about 20 Black indigenous from USA. *From Third World.* 39: about 20 Roman Catholics, 10 Protestants and Anglicans from 5 countries including Japan, 5 Orthodox from Ethiopia, 4 Black indigenous.

INSTITUTIONS (church-operated) (1973). Total 85, including 50 higher schools, 11 medical centres, 14 seminaries (13 Protestant,

1 RC).
PERIODICALS. About 40 titles.
PERSONNEL. About 2,097 (1,500 national, 597 foreign).
RELIGIOUS LIBRARIES. About 15.
SCRIPTURE DISTRIBUTION (1975). Annual totals: 75,100 Bibles (1% free, 98% subsidized), 76,600 NTs (85% free, 14% subsidized), 46,000 UBS portions, 159,000 UBS selections.
SERVICE AGENCIES. About 29, including AEC, JBMU, JCC, JCCEA, SCM, SPCK, SU, WVI, YMCA, YWCA.

ADDITIONAL DATA ON CHURCHES
CATHOLIC CHURCH IN JAMAICA. M Kingston includes the Cayman Islands, and it has 3 other suffragan dioceses outside Jamaica: Belize, Hamilton (Bermuda), and Nassau (Bahamas). *Annual baptisms.* (1972) 79.3% infant, 20.7% adult. *Priests.* 22 Jamaicans, 98 expatriates mostly from USA. From 1959–70, 12 Jamaican priests were ordained. *Catechists.* 3. *Main religious orders and congregations.* Priests: SJ (New England province, USA), CP (St Paul of the Cross province, USA), OFM (Holy Name province, USA). Sisters (1970): 75 Franciscan Missionary Sisters of Our Lady of Perpetual Help of Jamaica, 60 Sisters of Mercy, 60 Sisters of St Francis of Alleghany.
*Catholic organizations.* The Catholic Church is a member of the Antilles Episcopal Conference (AEC), itself a member of CELAM, and also belongs to the Conference of Major Superiors of the Antilles (HQ Kingston), a member of CLAR. The archdiocese of Kingston has a Senate of Priests and a Pastoral Council. Major national lay organizations are: Catholic Women's League, Catholic Youth Organization, Chinese Catholic Action Organization, Apostleship of Prayer, Catholic Boy Scouts and Girl Guides, Legion of Mary, and St Vincent de Paul Society.
The Holy See has no diplomatic relations with Jamaica. It is represented to the Catholic hierarchy by the Apostolic Delegation for the Antilles, based on Port-au-Prince, Haiti.
The Social Action Centre of the Extension Department, St George's College, Kingston, offers training courses as well as assistance in developing programmes in the fields of credit unions, and construction and industrial co-operatives. Statistics for 1974 include the following Catholic institutions: 2 nursery schools (117 infants), 88 primary schools (28,959 pupils), 13 secondary schools (8,156 pupils), 9 commercial and other schools (3,483 pupils), one college for primary school teachers (245 students), 2 hospitals or clinics (8,850 patients), one leprosarium (115 in-patients), 2 orphanages (375 boarders) and 2 homes for the aged (66 residents). In addition, Catholic Relief Services is involved in relief and development projects.

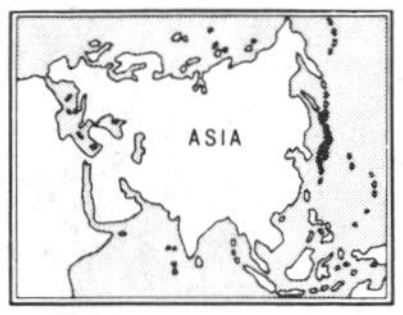


# JAPAN

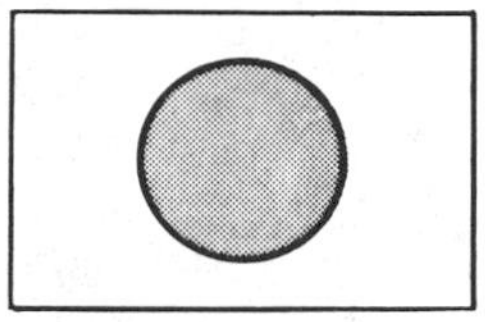

## SECULAR DATA

**STATE. Official name:** Japan (Nippon/Nihon). Adjective of nationality: Japanese.
**Flag** (shown above right): Red sun on white field.
**Area:** 372,269 sq.km. (143,751 sq.miles). Agricultural land: 15.7%.
**Government:** Constitutional monarchy, since 1946 (1601 unified empire, 1889 constitutional monarchy with bicameral parliament, 1932 military-ruled empire).
**Legislature:** Diet: House of Councillors, 252 members; House of Representatives, 491 members.
**Official language:** Japanese (*Nihongo*).
**Chief cities:** capital Tokyo 11,612,310 (1973), Osaka 2,841,940, Yokohama 2,494,980, Nagoya 2,075,250, Kyoto 1,435,250, Kobe 1,338,700.
**Political divisions:** 46 Prefectures (Todofuken).
**Armed forces** (1976): Total 235,000 regular: army 153,000, navy 39,000, air force 43,000 (448 combat aircraft). Reserves: 39,600.
**Foreign forces** (1973): 18,000 USA troops in Japan, 40,000 on Ryukyu Islands.

**DEMOGRAPHY. Population:** 111,933,818 (census of 1.X.1975. For 1970–2000 (UN), see last row of Table 1). Population density (1975): 298/sq.km. (773/sq.mile). Under 15 years: 30%. Growth rate (1975–80): 1.12% per year (births 1.80%, deaths –0.68%). Life expectancy (1975–80): 74.3 years. Household size: 3.6 persons.
**Major languages:** Japanese, Ryukyuan (Amami), English, Korean, Chinese, Okinawan (Luchu), Sakishima, and others.
**Urban dwellers** (1970): 53.2%. Urban growth rate (1950–70): 3.1% per year.
**Labour force:** 48%.
**Tourists** (1970): 850,000. (1974) 764,246.

**ETHNOLINGUISTIC GROUPS:** 98.3% Japanese, 0.9% Ryukyuan (Okinawan), 0.7% alien [0.6% Korean (607,300), Chinese (50,800) (Mandarin, Fukienese, Cantonese), USA (25,000), 21,200 European, Jewish, & others], 0.02% Ainu (20,000).

**MONEY** (1977). **Monetary unit:** yen (= 100 sen); US$1 = Y 295.00.
**National income per person:** US$3,330. Average annual family income: US$11,988.
**Inflation:** (1970–74) 11.2% per year (1975: consumer price index 187).
**Cost of living in capital** (1976): index 154 (Washington DC = 100). Daily cost of living: US$59.

**HEALTH.** Hospitals: 38,175 (1,364,327 beds). Doctors: 123,382. Lepers: 16,500 (0.1 per 1,000), 2,000 being on Ryukyu Islands. Blind (1976): 256,455. Psychotics: 1,300,000. Criminals: 519,985.

**EDUCATION.** Adult literacy: (1960) 98%, (1975) 100%. Education rate: 66%. Schools: 24,325. Universities: 75 national.

**LITERATURE.** Annual new book titles (1973): 35,857. Periodicals: 6,027. Scientific journals: 2,820. Newspapers: 172 dailies.

**COMMUNICATION** (per 1,000 people). Phones: 357. Radios: 658. TV sets: 229. Daily newspaper circulation: 519 copies.

TABLE 1. RELIGIOUS ADHERENTS IN JAPAN

| Year | 1900 | | mid-1970 | | Annual change, 1970–1980 | | | | mid-1975 | | mid-1980 | | 2000 | |
|---|---|---|---|---|---|---|---|---|---|---|---|---|---|---|
| *Name* | *Adherents* | *%* | *Adherents* | *%* | *Natural* | *Conversion* | *Total* | *Rate* | *Adherents* | *%* | *Adherents* | *%* | *Adherents* | *%* |
| Buddhists | 35,666,000 | 79.6 | 64,685,000 | 62.0 | 802,576 | –269,952 | 532,624 | 0.79 | 67,485,640 | 60.7 | 70,011,240 | 59.6 | 67,701,000 | 50.9 |
| non-religious Buddhists | 10,000 | 0.0 | 47,992,000 | 46.0 | 604,351 | –48,067 | 556,284 | 1.09 | 50,817,640 | 45.7 | 53,554,840 | 45.6 | 54,408,000 | 40.9 |
| religious Buddhists | 35,656,000 | 79.5 | 16,693,000 | 16.0 | 198,225 | –221,885 | –23,660 | –0.14 | 16,668,000 | 15.0 | 16,456,400 | 14.0 | 13,293,000 | 10.0 |
| New-Religionists | 2,000,000 | 4.5 | 21,300,000 | 20.4 | 282,805 | 220,195 | 503,000 | 2.12 | 23,780,000 | 21.4 | 26,330,000 | 22.4 | 37,220,000 | 28.0 |
| Non-religious | 0 | 0.0 | 9,737,200 | 9.3 | 128,361 | 71,554 | 199,915 | 1.85 | 10,793,400 | 9.7 | 11,736,350 | 10.0 | 15,303,500 | 11.5 |
| Shintoists | 6,720,000 | 15.0 | 4,173,000 | 4.0 | 46,252 | –110,914 | –64,662 | –1.66 | 3,889,200 | 3.5 | 3,526,380 | 3.0 | 2,658,000 | 2.0 |
| **Christians** | **430,000** | **1.0** | **3,100,000** | **3.0** | **39,645** | **2,995** | **42,640** | **1.28** | **3,333,600** | **3.0** | **3,526,400** | **3.0** | **5,317,000** | **4.0** |
| crypto-Christians | 30,000 | 0.1 | 520,000 | 0.5 | 6,759 | –1,119 | 5,640 | 0.99 | 568,300 | 0.5 | 576,400 | 0.5 | 605,000 | 0.5 |
| professing | 400,000 | 0.9 | 2,580,000 | 2.5 | 32,886 | 4,114 | 37,000 | 1.34 | 2,765,300 | 2.5 | 2,950,000 | 2.5 | 4,712,000 | 3.5 |
| Protestants | 169,000 | 0.4 | 866,000 | 0.8 | 10,882 | –1,082 | 9,800 | 1.07 | 915,000 | 0.8 | 964,000 | 0.8 | 1,446,000 | 1.1 |
| Japanese indigenous | 23,000 | 0.1 | 755,000 | 0.7 | 9,715 | 2,585 | 12,300 | 1.51 | 817,000 | 0.7 | 878,000 | 0.7 | 1,470,000 | 1.1 |
| Roman Catholics | 124,000 | 0.3 | 643,000 | 0.6 | 8,265 | 2,235 | 10,500 | 1.51 | 695,000 | 0.6 | 748,000 | 0.6 | 1,236,000 | 0.9 |
| Anglicans | 25,000 | 0.1 | 174,000 | 0.2 | 2,204 | –4 | 2,200 | 1.19 | 185,300 | 0.2 | 196,000 | 0.2 | 294,000 | 0.2 |
| Marginal Protestants | 0 | 0.0 | 95,000 | 0.1 | 1,225 | 375 | 1,600 | 1.55 | 103,000 | 0.1 | 111,000 | 0.1 | 187,000 | 0.1 |
| Orthodox | 59,000 | 0.1 | 47,000 | 0.0 | 595 | 5 | 600 | 1.20 | 50,000 | 0.0 | 53,000 | 0.0 | 79,000 | 0.1 |
| nominal | 252,919 | 0.6 | 1,492,339 | 1.4 | 17,214 | –27,928 | –10,714 | –0.74 | 1,447,400 | 1.3 | 1,385,200 | 1.2 | 2,182,000 | 1.6 |
| affiliated | 177,081 | 0.4 | 1,607,661 | 1.5 | 22,431 | 30,923 | 53,354 | 2.83 | 1,886,200 | 1.7 | 2,141,200 | 1.8 | 3,135,000 | 2.4 |
| total practising | 159,370 | *90* | 1,286,130 | *80* | 17,945 | 24,738 | 42,683 | 2.83 | 1,508,960 | *80* | 1,712,960 | *80* | 2,194,500 | *70* |
| non-practising | 17,710 | *10* | 321,530 | *20* | 4,486 | 6,185 | 10,671 | 2.83 | 377,240 | *20* | 428,240 | *20* | 940,500 | *30* |
| Japanese indigenous | 10,000 | 0.0 | 595,847 | 0.6 | 9,250 | 25,165 | 34,415 | 4.42 | 777,800 | 0.7 | 940,000 | 0.8 | 1,595,000 | 1.2 |
| Protestants | 75,000 | 0.2 | 516,848 | 0.5 | 6,565 | 150 | 6,715 | 1.22 | 552,000 | 0.5 | 584,000 | 0.5 | 670,000 | 0.5 |
| Evangelicals | 73,000 | 0.2 | 313,000 | 0.3 | 4,222 | 4,978 | 9,200 | 2.59 | 355,000 | 0.3 | 405,000 | 0.3 | 502,000 | 0.4 |
| Neo-pentecostals | 0 | 0.0 | 0 | 0.0 | 12 | 488 | 500 | 50.00 | 1,000 | 0.0 | 5,000 | 0.0 | 20,000 | 0.0 |
| Roman Catholics | 55,090 | 0.1 | 365,662 | 0.4 | 4,698 | 1,236 | 5,934 | 1.50 | 395,000 | 0.4 | 425,000 | 0.4 | 530,000 | 0.4 |
| Catholic pentecostals | 0 | 0.0 | 0 | 0.0 | 12 | 488 | 500 | 50.00 | 1,000 | 0.0 | 5,000 | 0.0 | 50,000 | 0.0 |
| Marginal Protestants | 0 | 0.0 | 53,702 | 0.1 | 951 | 4,179 | 5,130 | 6.41 | 80,000 | 0.1 | 105,000 | 0.1 | 230,000 | 0.2 |
| Anglicans | 10,997 | 0.0 | 49,100 | 0.0 | 632 | 188 | 820 | 1.54 | 53,200 | 0.0 | 57,300 | 0.0 | 76,000 | 0.1 |
| Orthodox | 25,994 | 0.1 | 26,502 | 0.0 | 335 | 5 | 340 | 1.20 | 28,200 | 0.0 | 29,900 | 0.0 | 34,000 | 0.0 |
| Atheists | 0 | 0.0 | 1,280,000 | 1.2 | 21,145 | 85,955 | 107,100 | 6.02 | 1,778,000 | 1.6 | 2,351,000 | 2.0 | 4,652,000 | 3.5 |
| Chinese folk-religionists | 5,000 | 0.0 | 40,000 | 0.0 | 507 | –7 | 500 | 1.17 | 42,600 | 0.0 | 45,000 | 0.0 | 50,000 | 0.0 |
| Baha'is | 0 | 0.0 | 9,800 | 0.0 | 131 | 139 | 270 | 2.45 | 11,000 | 0.0 | 12,500 | 0.0 | 16,000 | 0.0 |
| Jews | 0 | 0.0 | 1,000 | 0.0 | 13 | 0 | 13 | 1.23 | 1,060 | 0.0 | 1,130 | 0.0 | 1,500 | 0.0 |
| Other religionists | 4,000 | 0.0 | 5,000 | 0.0 | 65 | 35 | 100 | 1.82 | 5,500 | 0.0 | 6,000 | 0.0 | 10,000 | 0.0 |
| **Country's population** | **44,825,000** | **100.0** | **104,331,000** | **100.0** | **1,321,500** | **0** | **1,321,500** | **1.19** | **111,120,000** | **100.0** | **117,546,000** | **100.0** | **132,929,000** | **100.0** |

COLUMNS, ROWS. For meanings and definitions, see Codebook (Part 6). Note that, by definition, total 'Christians' = professing + crypto-Christians, which also = affiliated + nominal Christians. Percentages may not always total exactly, due to rounding.
RELIGIOSITY IN JAPAN. It is important to note that contemporary Japanese usually interpret the word 'religion' (and the question 'What is your religion?') to mean 'personal religion' as opposed to 'family religion'. This leads to 2 apparently contradictory sets of statistics. (a) In nation-wide polls and surveys, only 33–35% profess to have a personal religion, and 65–70% (mostly young people who have abandoned the traditional religions) profess no religion. (b) Government statistics of religion, however, are based on family religion, and show that around 85% have a family religion. In our table above both sets of data are combined and reconciled.
CENSUSES. The religion question is not asked in national population censuses, but the Ministry of Education (and earlier, the Ministry of Home Affairs) has for many years published annual statistics of affiliated members returned by headquarters of the various religions (*Religion year book*). Although methods of counting have varied, and sects not recognized by the state are usually ignored, the series does provide an idea of chronological progression, as follows. **1919**: 81.3% Buddhists (in 56 sects), 15% Sect Shintoists (including 5.0% in Shinto New Religions), 0.42% Christians. **1943** (sects recognized by state only): 62.0% Buddhists (in 28 sects), 14.3% Sect Shintoists, 0.45% Christians. **1959** (sects recognized by state only): 64.8% Buddhists (in 167 sects), 10.9% Sect Shintoists (in 129 sects), 0.75% Christians. **1966** (all sects, including those not recognized by state, and with Shrine Shinto claiming most Buddhists also): 80.8% Buddhists (in 165 sects; about 27% in Buddhist New Religions), 80.2% Shintoists (in 143 sects; including about 12.5% Sect Shintoists in 127 sects), 0.75% Christians. Total of all sects known to the state: 376. **1970**: 81.2% Buddhists (including in New Religions), 79.6% Shintoists (including in New Religions), 0.77% Christians, 9.4% other religionists (including non-Buddhist non-Shintoist New Religions).
POLLS. A large number on religion have been taken, especially every 5 years since 1953 through the Research Committee, Japanese National Character (JNC), National Institute of Statistical Mathematics, Tokyo, and by the Oriens Institute. 1952–53 (Odaka and Nishira, in the 6 major cities): Buddhism is the family religion for 90.8%, a personal religion for 32.0%; Shinto (same 2 categories) 3.4% and 2.4%; Protestantism 0.6% and 1.7%; Catholicism 0.3% and 0.3%; no religion 3.9% and 61.3%. JNC, OR answers to the question 'Have you a personal faith?': 1958: 35% Yes, 65% No. 1963: 31% Yes, 69% No. 1968: 30% Yes, 70% No. 1968: 34% Yes, 66% No. *Christianity.* 1955: 0.35% stated that Christianity was their family religion, and 2.15% their personal religion. A detailed presentation of all these polls is given in Spae, *Japanese religiosity*.

NOTES ON RELIGIONS
AFFILIATED CHRISTIANS. The totals are over twice as large as government statistics in the *Religion year book* because the latter omits or does not know of many indigenous and Protestant bodies.
ATHEISTS. Japan Communist Party (JCP) (legal; independent of USSR and China): membership (1970) 320,000; Communist voters (election of 10.XII.1972, House of Representatives) 5,496,477 (10% of all votes). Among youths aged 18–24 in 1974, 6% professed to be atheists and 74% to have no religious affiliation or interest (Gallup). Persons who openly and outspokenly oppose religion and religious structures are well under 5% of the population.
BAHA'IS. Entered in 1914. Recent rapid growth from 13 local spiritual assemblies (1964) to 64 (1973). Converts include a number of Ainus.
BUDDHISTS. This category here excludes those New Religions which are radical sects of or schisms from Buddhism. Buddhists are of the Mahayana school, including Zen, Amida (Pure Land), and hundreds of other sects. There are 70,000 temples. In the first 3 days of the 1976 New Year, a record 64.8 million people visited Buddhist temples and shrines throughout Japan to pray to Buddhist and Shintoist deities.
CATHOLIC PENTECOSTALS (or, Catholic charismatics). Totals (January 1974): 200 involved adults (over 15 years old) in 12 prayer groups: total charismatic community including children, 400. By 1975 there were bishops as well as priests involved. In December 1975 the first National Catholic Charismatic Leadership Conference was held in Ohatano, Tokyo.
CHRISTIANS. Since the Meiji period (1868–1912), the number of those who call themselves Christians but are not baptized nor enrolled in any Christian church has been consistently higher than those known to churches. In addition to affiliated Christians, there has long been a large number of unaffiliated persons who, influenced particularly by the Christian scriptures (found in 50% of all Japanese homes), regard themselves as Christians, sometimes as anonymous or latent Christians. An example is a Buddhist leader at a Catholic conference who said: 'Whether I shall ever be baptized is not for me to say, but one thing is certain: in my own mind I am already an anonymous

Christian' (quoted in Spae 1968: 23). Another example is the high degree of interest evident from polls: one survey found that of all Japanese university students, 53.5% of the men and 73.1% of the women professed interest in Christianity. Often there is personal belief in Christ accompanied by disinterest in or rejection of organized Christianity on the grounds that the churches have adulterated the Christian faith by institutionalizing it. Estimates in 1959, 1965 and 1971 have all put the total of all persons regarding themselves as Christians at 3.0% of the population (Spae, et alia). From the public's point of view, this 3% consists of around 2.5% who openly profess in polls (as indicated above in the footnote POLLS), leaving 0.5% as crypto-Christians. From the churches' point of view, this 3% consists of 1.6% affiliated to churches (as shown in Table 2), which leaves 1.4% non-affiliated or nominal Christians; this is the very large number of unchurched persons, youths in particular, who either have had contact with Christianity through its educational institutions, or who grew up in Christian families or environments and know no other religious background, and who answer the question 'What is the religion of your home or family?' with the reply 'Christian'.

CRYPTO-CHRISTIANS. The oldest community is that of the 30,000 Kakure Kirishitan (Hidden Christians, former Catholics) who existed underground (at the same time acting externally as Buddhists) from 1638–1859, after which because of their refusal to return to the Church of Rome they were termed Hanare Kirishitan (Separated Christians). To this day they do not appear in the government's annual census of known religious bodies. The wider term Sempuku Kirishitan (Hidden Christians) is also used, to denote all Christians who maintained their faith throughout the 2 centuries of isolation. In addition, there are a large number of unorganized individuals who are committed Christians affiliated or known to churches but who either do not publicly profess their faith or do not attend church; together with a large number of isolated radio believers.

JAPANESE INDIGENOUS. In about 44 denominations in 1970 (see Table 2), in 3 groupings: (1) most are in Japanese indigenous churches, the oldest being the Hidden Christians of the South Japan islands; (2) there are also some Chinese indigenous and Korean indigenous Christians, and chaplaincy work among USA armed forces on Okinawa by USA Black churches including the Church of God in Christ; and (3) there are large numbers of isolated radio believers who listen regularly to Christian broadcasts but are not, or not yet, in touch with organized denominations.

MARGINAL PROTESTANTS. Totals were growing rapidly in the 1970s; Mormons (Latter-day Saints) in 1970 were claiming 1,500 Japanese converts a year, and Jehovah's Witnesses 2,160 adult baptisms in 1970.

NEO-PENTECOSTALS. Charismatics spread throughout the non-Pentecostal Protestant denominations, including many USA foreign missionaries.

NEW-RELIGIONISTS. This term describes adherents of the so-called New Religions (Shinko Shukyo), more correctly termed New Religious Movements, or crisis religions, which are mostly post-1945 sects of, or schisms from, Buddhism and Shinto, but which also include new religions syncretizing the major world religions. In 1962, the Union of New Religious Organizations in Japan (Nihon Shin Shukyo Dantai Rengo Kai) had 86 member denominations with 5,442,240 adherents. In 1966, the government's *Religion year book* listed over 150 New Religions, 8 of which had over 500,000 adherents each and totalled 26,691,259. It is widely held by analysts that the actual total of active adult adherents is less than half of this figure (especially Soka Gakkai, which then claimed 15,234,136 adherents although observers estimated it at 6,500,000 adults, and at 8 million by 1972). By 1970, all adherents including children and fringe members totalled around 21 million, with the 7 largest bodies as follows: (1) Nichiren Shoshu, or Soka Gakkai (Value Creation Society; in 1969, it claimed 6,876,000 families as members), (2) Reiyukai-kyodan (Association of Friends of the Spirit; Buddhist, 4,079,000 in 1962, 4,719,988 in 1970), (3) Tenrikyo (Religion of Divine Wisdom; a Shinto sect, founded in 1838; 2,459,000 in 1962, 2,342,131 in 1970), (4) Izumo-taishakyo (begun 1873; 2,261,382), (5) Rissho-koseikai (Society for the Establishment of Righteousness and Friendly Intercourse; 2,205,728 in 1970, rising by (1978 to 4,600,000), (6) Seicho no Ie (House of Growth; neither Buddhist nor Shintoist; founded 1929; 1,457,778 rising to 3 million worldwide by 1974), and (7) PL Kyodan (Perfect Liberty Church, begun 1946; 1,265,422, growing to 2.5 million worldwide by 1975). Growth, backed by detailed statistics, has been most spectacular for Soka Gakkai, as follows: (1937) 60 members, (1940) 350, (1941) 3,000, (1953) 20,000 (families; also all following figures), (1956) 194,000, (1959) 1,050,000, (1964) 3,950,000, (1966) 5,000,000, (1968) 6,720,000, (1969) 6,876,000. Along with other New Religions it has large followings abroad among the Japanese diaspora in Asia and the Americas, and has mission work in (1975) 88 countries.

NOMINAL CHRISTIANS. As described in the note above on CHRISTIANS, nominal Christians consist of a very large number of unchurched or unaffiliated persons, youths in particular, who either have had contact with Christianity through its schools and colleges, or who grew up in Christian circles and know no other religious background, and who answer the question 'What is the religion of your home or family?' with the reply 'Christian'.

NON-RELIGIOUS. The term covers those having neither family religion nor personal religion, i.e. agnostics, freethinkers and (the vast majority) those indifferent to religion. Among young men aged 20–40 years, one survey found that 82% have no religious beliefs at all. The rapid growth of this category in the 20th century is due to abandonment of religion by Japanese youth who are highly critical of the major traditional religions. Converts to Christianity come mainly from this group.

NON-RELIGIOUS BUDDHISTS. This term covers persons, mostly young people, whose family religion is Buddhism and who may visit the shrines annually, but who regard themselves as having no personal religion nor personal commitment to Buddhism. In polls, they are usually around 46% of the population.

ORTHODOX. In the year 1900, there were about 20,000 Russians who were Orthodox.

OTHER RELIGIONISTS. There are traditional tribal religionists among the aboriginal Ainus of Hokkaido (20,000). The few Hindus and Muslims are mostly foreign residents (expatriates). There were 100 Japanese Muslims in 1967, formerly Central Asian Turks now settled in Japan, with 2 mosques (Tokyo, Kobe) and a Turkish school in Tokyo. The Quran in Japanese has been printed, with 100,000 copies. In 1970, 404 Muslims from Japan performed the Hajj pilgrimage to Mecca. Muslims are assisted by the Japan Muslim Association, in Tokyo. Among Hindus there is 1 ISKCON (Hare Krishna) centre, also Ananda Marga centres.

PRACTISING CHRISTIANS. *Protestants.* Weekly attendance: UCCJ 38%, all Protestants about 60%. Annual practice about 85%. *Roman Catholics.* Sunday mass attendance 40% weekly, Easter practice 64%, annual practice about 74%. *Pilgrims* (1978). There are many Christians among the 500,000 Japanese who visit Rome (Italy) every year.

RELIGIOUS BUDDHISTS. This term covers those who profess Buddhism as both a family religion and also a personal religion. In polls, this category is usually around 16% of the population (excluding New-Religionists).

SHINTOISTS. There are 2 categories of Shintoists: Shrine Shintoists (before 1945 a state politico-religious organization, disestablished 1945) who form the majority of Shintoists, and Sect Shintoists (whose numbers have declined slightly from 15.0% in 1919 to 12.5% in 1966). Shrine Shintoists are usually Buddhists simultaneously, and so are termed Buddhists in this table; Sect Shinto (Kyoha Shinto) with its 13 sects is usually considered as a part of the New Religions, and is treated as such in our table. Shrine Shintoists were never enumerated before 1945, and government statistics since have claimed around 65% for them. However, a private study in 1952–53 by Odaka and Nishira, with residents of the 6 most important cities, showed that Shinto was a family religion for only 3.4% and a personal religion for 2.4%. In polls in the 1960s, around 4% claimed to be Shintoists and only 1.5% professed active Shinto affiliation. Our definition of the category Shintoist in the table also follows this usage, namely persons who profess, or still profess, Shinto as their first or major religion.

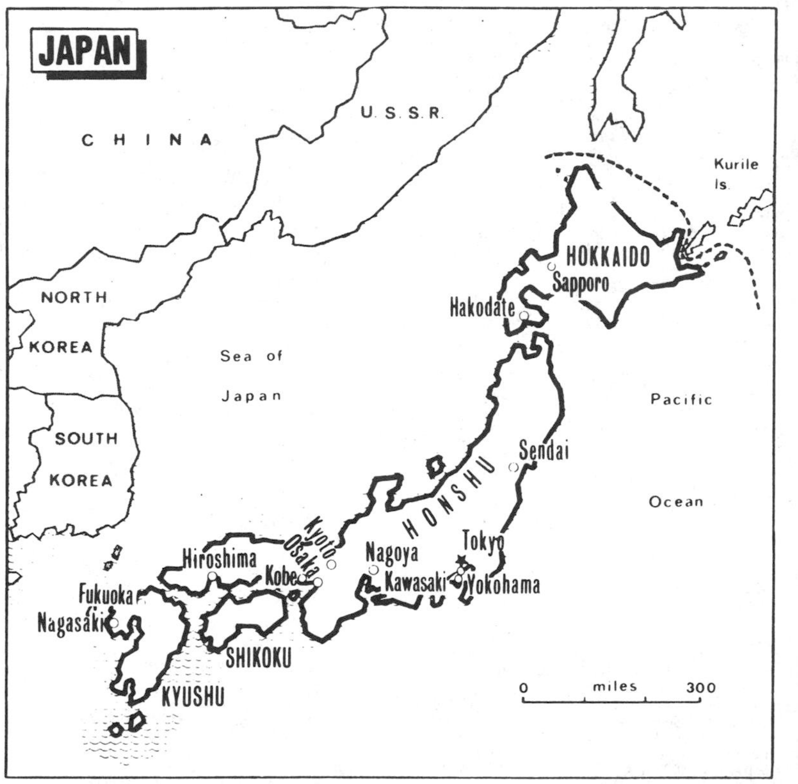


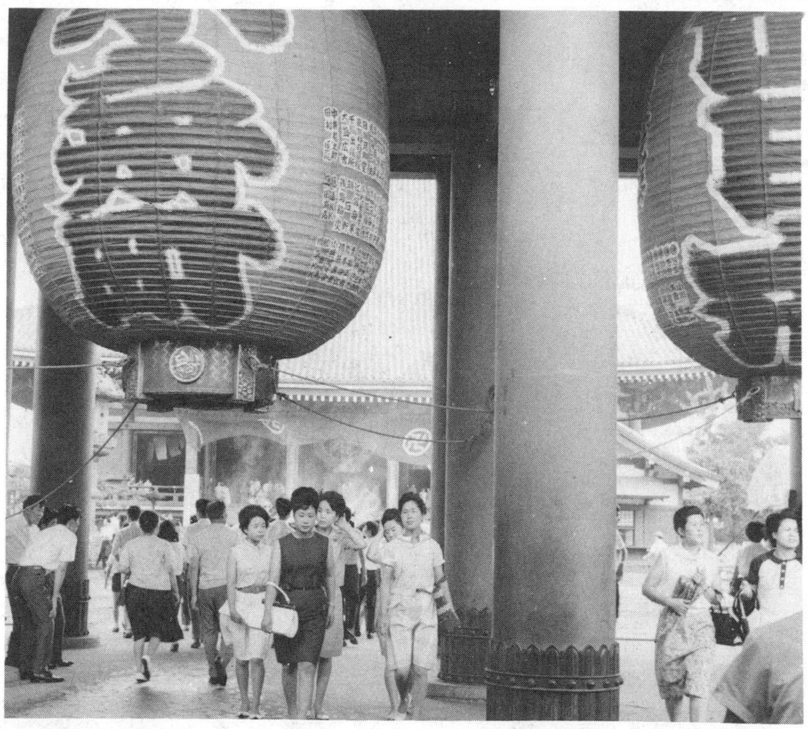

**Buddhists.** In the first 3 days of the 1976 New Year, a record 64.8 million Japanese visited and prayed in Buddhist temples and shrines across Japan. *Above.* Worshippers at Tokyo temple of Asakusa Kannon (Bodhisattva or 'Buddha-to-be', also regarded as female goddess of mercy).

**NON-CHRISTIAN RELIGIONS.** In 1961, 40% of all Japanese claimed to follow both Buddhism and Shinto as their family religion. The role played by religion in individual behaviour is much less than at the familial, cultural and national levels; in polls, only one third answer the question 'Have you a personal faith?' in the affirmative. In the 6 most important cities, Buddhism is a family religion for 91% of residents but a personal religion for only 32%.

**Buddhism** was introduced into Japan during the 6th century and since the 7th century has been Japan's principal religion. Its spread among the lower classes began in the 9th century, after having settled on the Mahayana school accompanied by the rapid development of 2 esoteric schools based on severe asceticism: Tendaï-shû and Shingon-shû. Although at one point Tendaï-shû completely dominated Japanese Buddhism, it was later reduced to a secondary although still important position. In 1975 it had 2.9 million faithful and 4,383 temples, with its mother temple and pilgrimage centre at Mount Hiei near Kyoto. Tendaï-shû has recently again become very demanding in its training of monks. As for Shingon-shû, it has now taken the lead in the study and application of Tantric Mahayanist doctrine and numbers 11.9 million faithful and 12,328 temples. Its centre at Koya-San consists of a small city with a university of Buddhism (Koya-San Daigaku), which possesses one of the finest specialized libraries in the world. The Rinzaï, Sôtô and Obaku sects of Zen Buddhism arrived from China in respectively the 12th, 13th and 17th centuries and represent a further development of the Ch'an school of meditation. All have had a profound effect on Japanese culture (arts, flowers, gardens, tea, et alia). The popularity of Zen today, with 13 million followers and 20,494 temples, is due primarily to its techniques of meditation: Zazen and Sanzen of Rinzaï and Zazen of Sôtô. Its expansion in the Western world is well-known, and of note is the Zen temple of the Jesuit father Lassalle which uses the techniques of Zen meditation while removing it from Buddhist doctrine.

Nevertheless, the Japanese masses have been most attracted to the 2 pietist schools Amita Jodo (Pure Land School) and Nichiren-shû. Jodo-shû and its reformed wing, Jôdoshin-shû, have the largest number of followers, about 17.7 million with 29,876 temples. An important Jôdoshin-shû university, Bukkyô Daigaku, is found at Kyoto; and from its major temple, Nishi-Honganji, Jôdoshin-shû is making an effort to expand its influence among non-Japanese in Europe and America.

Founded in the 13th century by the monk Nichiren, whose principal concerns were religious austerity and social justice, Nichiren-shû has gained a popular following among the lower classes and at present has 13 million members with 5,782 temples.

A number of organizations have emerged in recent years to help Buddhism deal with the problems and challenges of the modern era. One of the largest is the Japan Buddhist Federation (Zen-Nihon Buddyo-kai), which includes in its membership 60 Buddhist sects, 37 regional associations and 19 other groups.

**Shinto** is the ancestral religion of Japan. It came under the influence of Confucianism towards the end of the 5th century, then was eclipsed by Buddhism from the 7th to the 9th centuries before its revival during the Meiji era. This religion, after having lost its dogmatic hold little by little, ended by being a national cult to which all citizens had to submit. The suppression of state Shinto in 1945 on the one hand swept away the institution of shrine Shinto (Jinja Shinto) whose basic unity was a territorial community grouped about a shrine, and on the other hand gave rise to a large number of new heterogeneous sects of Shinto inspiration. Most Shinto shrines are now legally incorporated within the Association of Shinto Shrines (Jinja-honcho) and are concerned more with administrative than doctrinal questions.

As a whole, Shinto includes all groups which revere the Japanese gods, the Kami. A collective religion more than an individual one, the influence of Shinto is especially marked at the family level. Recent sociological studies, however, show a certain evolution towards the formation of bonds with the shrines, bonds that are more spiritual than familial or geographical, and which result thus in a process of delocalization. In addition to Jinja-honcho, which includes 90% of all Shinto shrines, there exist other Shinto organizations including the Federation of Sectarian Shinto (Kyoha Shinto Rengokai). The latter includes the 11 traditional sects although the

**Buddhists.** *Left.* The 49-ft-high bronze Great Buddha (Daibutsu) of Kamakura, formerly housed in a temple, now a popular pilgrimage centre (with a stairway inside). *Right.* Massive 170-foot colossus of Kwannon

(Kannon), Goddess of Mercy, garlanded with streamers, on Otsubo-yama Hill overlooking Tokyo Bay, completed 1961.

total number of Shinto sects is much higher. There are 2 Shinto universities, Kokugakuin Daigaku in Tokyo and Kogakukan at Ise, the latter having been reopened in 1962.

**New Religions** or, more correctly, New Religious Movements (Shinko Shukyo), a term in use since 1930, are recently-begun religions or sects as contrasted with the older-established ones of orthodox Shinto, Buddhism and Christianity. Many of them are not, strictly speaking, distinct new religions but are only renewals or new religious movements or sects within either Shinto or Buddhism, although at the same time being radical breaks, with new and distinct religious systems and other innovations. However, a number are quite new in the sense that they syncretize in a new form elements of Shinto, Buddhism and Christianity; and because they almost all attempt to adapt religion to the modern age, it is best to follow the popular usage of regarding them together forming a new grouping, termed for convenience Shinko Shukyo.

The first of these New Religions were formed in the 19th century at the close of the feudal era and the beginning of the Meiji restoration; Tenrikyo was begun about 1838 and Konkokyo in 1859. The New Religions have had 3 periods of marked development: the first around 1920, the second about 1935, and the third during the decade 1945–55, corresponding respectively to the 3 periods of most rapid social change in Japan: World War I, the rise of fascism and the Sino-Japanese war, and the defeat of 1945. The religious characteristics of these religions can be summarized as follows: the promise of salvation, miracles and the practice of magic, belief in the existence of a divine spirit, shamanism and authoritarianism, syncretism in doctrinal sources, and community morale. More than 10 New Religions have branches in North and South America, as well as in Southeast Asia. Although several New Religions are very large, many others are small local groups with barely a few hundred members. Eighty-six of the religions belong to the Union of New Religious Organizations in Japan, which includes many of the major religions with the exception of Soka Gakkai, Reiyukai, Seicho no Ie (House of Growth) and Sekai Kyusei-kyo (Church of World Messianity).

Five of the so-called New Religions each have over 2 million adherents in 1970. In order of size, these are as follows. (1) Soka Gakkai (Value Creation Society) or Nichiren Shoshu, which stems from Nichiren Buddhism, has an active adult membership of around 8 million, though 15,234,136 faithful were officially claimed in 1966. With its central organization in Tokyo, it was founded in 1930 but has developed extensively only since 1951. It has its strength among persons excluded from the evident economic prosperity of Japan, including small businessmen, the independently employed, and poorly-paid workers in the large cities. Soka Gakkai is based on the fundamental unity of religion and politics, conducts intensive propaganda, and has created a political party Komei-to which has fascist tendencies and which gives political expression to the middle classes. Soka Gakkai did not develop until after most of the other New Religions and is distinguished from them by its political ambitions and its religious intolerance. However, its practice

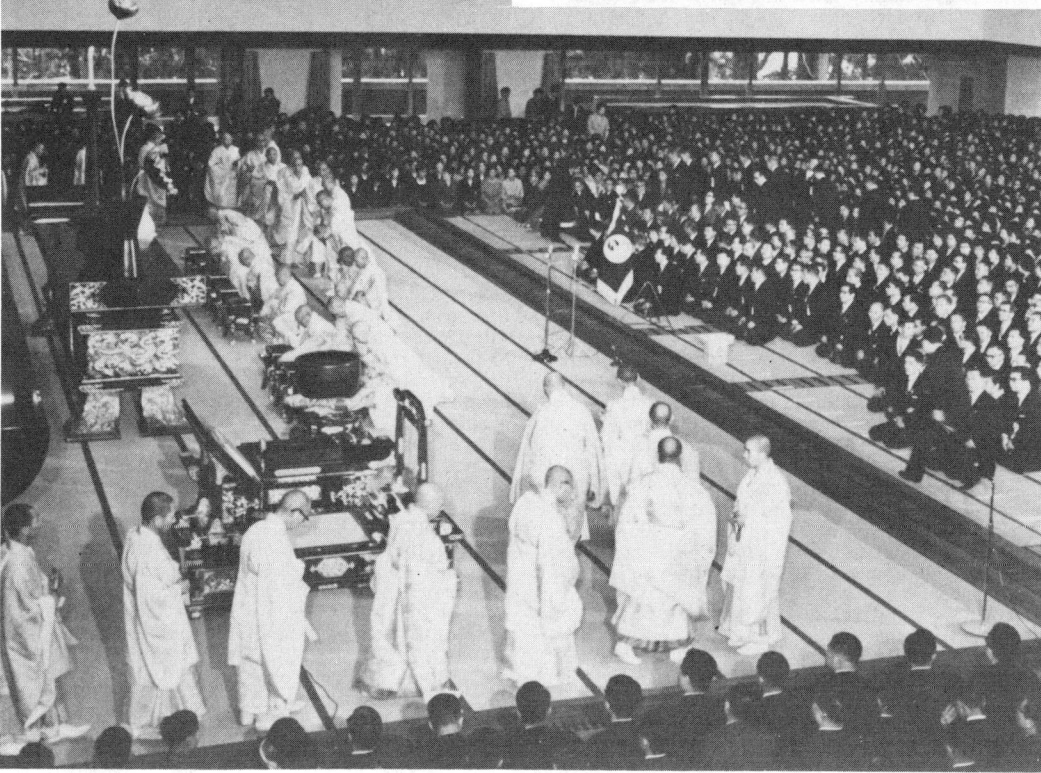

**New-Religionists (1).** Soka Gakkai (Value Creation Society), largest of Japan's 150 New Religions. *Above.* Opening service in new temple by Mount Fuji, 1964. *Inset.* New earthquake-proof Sho-Hondo/Grand Main

Temple/High Sanctuary ('largest temple on earth', opened 1972) for 60,000 worshippers at headquarters on lower slopes of Mount Fuji, with shrine for Nichiren's sacred tablet Dai-Gohonson.

**New-Religionists (2)**. Rissho-koseikai (Society for Establishment of Righteousness). *Left*. Its Great Sacred Hall, Tokyo. *Right*. Great Sacred Hall's radio/TV studio, with 100 closed-circuit TV sets for internal viewing.

of forced conversion (*shakubuku*) and the more virulent of its anti-Christian aspects have become less prominent since 1970. (2) Reiyukai (Association of Friends of the Spirit) was founded in Tokyo in 1923 and in 1970 had a following of 4,719,988. It follows the lay Buddhist tradition, with a doctrine combining emphasis on temporal concerns with the ancestral cult and patriarchal morals. (3) Tenrikyo (Religion of Divine Wisdom) founded in 1838 with its central organization at Tenri, Nara, had 2,342,131 adherents in 1970. It is a popular religion characteristic of the Meiji period which expanded on a national scale during the 1880s. Originally it developed as a subversive religious movement within the feudal order preceding the Meiji regime, but it then placed itself at the service of the imperial government and became, under government pressure, a sect of National Shinto (Kokka-shinto) in 1890. (4) Izumo-taishakyo began in 1873 and is based on Shinto. The headquarters for its 2,261,382 adherents is in Taisha, Shimane prefecture. (5) Rissho-koseikai (Society for the Establishment of Righteousness), with 2,042,590 adherents, is based on Buddhism and has its central organization in Tokyo. It separated from Reiyukai in 1938, but its doctrine is still centred in the Reiyukai emphasis on personal perfection of the individual realized through faith in Hokke Buddhism. Around 1948 its influence spread rapidly in Tokyo and in the eastern part of the country.

Two other religions had under 2 million adherents in 1970 but by 1975 had grown to over 2.5 million each worldwide: Seicho no Ie, and PL Kyodan (Perfect Liberty Church).

*Interreligious organizations.* A number of bodies are at present active in promoting interreligious understanding and dialogue between all religions. (1) The Japan Religions League (Nihon Shukyo Remmei) is a nation-wide interreligious organization established in 1945 to promote religious co-operation and to ensure religious liberty. Each prefecture in the country has its own related religions league. Official members are: the Japan Buddhist Federation (Zen-Nihon Bukkyo-kai), the Association of Shinto Shrines (Jinja-honcho), the Federation of Sectarian Shinto (Kyoha Shinto Rengokai), the Japan Christian Federation (Nihon Kirisutokyo Rengokai), and the Union of New Religious Organizations in Japan (Shinshu-remmei). (2) The NCC Centre for the Study of Japanese Religions was founded in Kyoto in 1962 and is affiliated to the National Christian Council of Japan. This study centre provides both national clergy and others interested in Japanese religions with detailed information about the thought and activities of contemporary religions in Japan. It collaborates with the Oriens Institute, maintains liaison with Buddhists and Shintoists, and publishes an English quarterly *Japanese religions* and a Japanese quarterly *Deai*. (3) The Oriens Institute for Religious Research, established in Tokyo in 1961, is a Catholic research centre sponsored by the Scheut Fathers and engaged in the study of present-day religious trends in Japan. There are numerous publications and emphasis is placed on social questions and subsequent action on an ecumenical basis. (4) The International Institute

for the Study of Religions (Kokusai Shukyo Kenkyu Sho) is an interreligious organization with headquarters in Sophia University (Catholic) in Tokyo. The institute studies present-day Japanese religions and publishes a journal, *Contemporary religions in Japan*.

A World Conference on Religion and Peace was held in Kyoto in October 1970 bringing together 1,600 delegates and observers from 22 world religions. This conference was the culmination of several smaller interreligious conferences and consultations held in New York in 1965, Washington in 1966, New Delhi in 1968 and Kyoto in 1968. The conference established a permanent interreligious body called the World Conference of Religion for Peace, with headquarters in New York.

**Traditional tribal religion** is practised by the hunting and fishing Ainus who inhabit Sakhalin, Hokkaido and the southern part of the Kurile Islands. An unusual feature of their cult is the ceremonial sacrifice of a bear each year in October. While the bear is eaten by the community, its spirit serves as intermediary taking messages from the living to their first ancestor, the Mountain Spirit. Demons, nature divinities and family ancestral spirits have a place in their belief system as well as the idea of a supreme being and a conception of an after-life with rewards and punishments.

## CHRISTIANITY.

PROTESTANT CHURCHES. Several unsuccessful attempts were made by Protestants to reach Japan in the first half of the 19th century, and it was not until the Townsend Harris treaty of 1858, 4 years after the appearance of admiral Mathew Perry, that they were permitted entry. The first to arrive in 1859 were USA missionaries of the Protestant Episcopal Church, the Presbyterian Board and the Dutch Reformed Church, a number of whom had formerly served in China. Faced with Japanese hostility towards all things Western as the result of the period of exclusion from 1606–1854, they were initially confined to Yokohama and Nagasaki. The first Protestant baptism did not take place until 1864. During these early difficult years, they prepared dictionaries and grammars, translated the Bible and assisted government in building a new system of education. They also developed hospitals and private schools and educated some of the most influential men in Japan's later political development.

American Baptists began their first permanent mission in Yokohama in 1872, the same year a revival took place as a result of work by Reformed missionaries, and converts established the first Japanese Protestant church in Yokohama. The first missionary conference was also held in Yokohama in 1872 with representatives from the Presbyterian, Reformed and Congregational missions. As a result of their concern for non-denominational emphases, the first converts called their group the Church of Christ. They also joined forces in establishing the Union Theological Seminary in Tokyo in 1877, and in the same year 5 Presbyterian and 4 Church of Christ denominations united to form the United

Church of Christ in Japan.

In 1878 all anti-Christian restrictions were removed, and the number of foreign missionaries doubled from 29 to 58, including newly-arrived Methodists and Anglicans. Work spread to Osaka, Kobe, Kyoto and the northern island of Hokkaido. Revivals again broke out in 1883 in Yokohama and spread throughout central Japan in the next few years largely due to the zeal of converts in bringing others to Christ. Foreign missionaries increased from 145 to 383 and congregations grew from 83 to 448. In a 7-year period the number of ordained pastors tripled and the number of evangelists quadrupled. The century closed with missionaries from several newly-organized interdenominational faith missions beginning to arrive, including the Evangelical Alliance Mission and Christian and Missionary Alliance in 1891 and the Oriental Missionary Society in 1901.

Nationalism increased in fervour under the Meiji regime, and a reaction against Western Christianity set in once again. Although the government in 1884 declared Buddhism and Shinto no longer state religions, in 1890 the Imperial Rescript on Education rejected Christian theology and morality and ordered all Japanese to publicly revere the ancestral gods of Shinto. Missionaries and Japanese Christians at first refused to comply but later made an effort to demonstrate their loyalty during the Chinese and Russian wars.

During the 15-year period following the overthrow of the Meiji regime in 1912, Christianity again gained ground through evangelistic campaigns and literature distribution. Church membership increased from 79,000 to 110,000, with numerous high officials becoming Christians. At the same time there was also a revival of Buddhism, which adopted such traditionally Christian activities as the establishment of schools and hospitals. Militarism also grew as Japan gained territory in Manchuria during the 1930s. Moreover, the government increasingly relied on subservience to Shinto to unite all Japanese in order to further imperialist expansion. Christianity in turn was severely restricted and Japanese Christians were divided as to where to place their loyalty. A special problem was to what extent Christians might acquiesce in the Shinto requirements which the government defined as political rather than religious, although they involved public acknowledgement of the divine ancestry of the emperor.

In 1940 to gain further control, the government ordered the formation of the Kyodan, which was intended to include all Protestant churches in a single United Church of Christ. Denominations which refused to join, including the Salvation Army, Anglican, Adventist and Holiness churches, all ceased to exist officially. The Kyodan survived the war and in 1948 included a majority of all Protestant churches and members.

Following the war, the American general MacArthur called for '1,000 missionaries' from the USA to Japan. Foreign missionaries poured in, totalling over 2,500 Protestants by 1973. Many of these were new to the Orient, the majority being from conservative groups in the USA. The result has been a vast proliferation of almost 200 different churches and missions working in the country. In 1963, 2 Lutheran churches and 6 missions joined to form the Japan Evangelical Lutheran Church, but 7 other Lutheran missions remain independent. More than 20 Baptist denominations work in Japan, and 7 Presbyterian groups remain outside the Kyodan.

The largest Protestant church continues to be the United Church of Christ in Japan, consisting of those churches which remained part of the Kyodan. It has 1,610 ordained pastors assisted by 305 foreign missionaries and in 1975 sponsored 47 of its own Japanese missionaries serving in 12 overseas countries.

INDIGENOUS CHURCHES. The oldest indigenous group of Christians are 33,000 former Roman Catholics who survived the persecutions of 1606–1859, but who have since 1865 consistently refused to rejoin the Catholic Church. Known as Hidden Christians (Kakure Kirishitan), or Separated Christians (Hanare) by the Catholics, they inhabit islands in southern Japan and have their own ceremonies and rites embodying Buddhist and Shinto elements.

An early reaction to the proliferation of Protestant foreign missions after the 1860s was the forming by Japanese nationals of anti-missionary indigenous movements. One of the earliest was Mukyokai or the No-Church Movement began by a former Methodist, Kanzo Uchimura, based on small Bible study groups. Later a large number of independent churches were begun by Japanese, often as schisms from Western denominations. By 1972 there were about 50 Japanese indigenous denominations and groups in Japan. The largest is the Spirit of Jesus Church which split from the Assemblies of God in 1937 and now has its own Japanese missionaries in the USA and Brazil. Another important denomination is the Original Gospel (Tabernacle) Movement, a pentecostal schism from the No-Church Movement. Another body is the Unification Church, from Korea (Holy Spirit Association for the Unification of World Christianity), which has a large student following.

CATHOLIC CHURCH. The first Christian mission to Japan began with the visit of Francis Xavier to Kagoshima in 1549. Catholics expanded rapidly, and there were 300,000 baptized by 1593, many in the Nagasaki region. In 1613 Christianity was prohibited and severe persecution followed. Foreign missionaries were not able to return until 1859, when the present era of missions began.

By 1971 there was a total of 360,000 baptized, or 0.4% of the total population. The archdiocese of Nagasaki has the greatest number and concentration of Catholics in the country; its 69,190 baptized are 4.5% of the local population, and 19% of all Catholics in Japan. None of the other 15 dioceses has a local proportion of Catholics above 0.5%, and the Tokyo archdiocese has 0.4%. The only exceptions are a few small islands off south Kyushu, populated by fishermen and farmers; Catholics number 16% on the island of Goto in the archdiocese of Nagasaki, and 5% on the island of Amami-Oshima in the diocese of Kagoshima.

So far as social distribution is concerned, in the archdiocese of Nagasaki Catholics constitute sociologically a closed milieu, with hardly any adult conversions taking place but with numerous infant baptisms and marriages among Catholics, especially in the countryside. A large proportion of the Catholics in this region are descendants of the Old Christians (Kirishitan) who survived the persecutions of the 16th and 17th centuries and who were rediscovered by missionaries in 1865; all but 33,000 of these have now rejoined the Catholic Church. On the islands of Honshu, Hokkaido and Shikoku, most Catholics are young adult converts with the same social characteristics as Protestants. The vast majority of Catholics live in urban areas. On Honshu, 45% of Catholics are high school graduates, 60% are women, 50% are unmarried, over 75% are adult converts, and over 80% belong to the middle class. The importance of women among Japanese Catholics is the result, in large part, of the disproportionately large number of girls educated in Catholic schools. Equally to be noted is the large number of Japanese sisters, who numbered 5,348 in 1971 in contrast to 950 foreign sisters. This is a remarkably high number in comparison with the total Catholic population, being one sister for every 57 Catholics.

One important Catholic immigrant group are the Koreans, and pastoral work for them is well organized, with centres in Tokyo, Osaka and Kyoto where a priest and Korean sister are assigned to this task.

Catholics also form a large minority among Japanese emigrants, especially those who have moved to Brazil and other parts of Latin America; and special efforts have been made to minister to them. In 1971 there were 68 priests, 53 sisters and 24 catechists working with these emigrants in overseas countries. The total number of emigrant Catholics is in fact higher than the number residing in Japan.

There are 2 major characteristics of recent Catholic demography in Japan. In the first place, there has been a marked decrease in the annual rate of Catholic population growth, in contrast to the rapid increases that took place after World War II. From a total of 108,324 baptized Catholics in 1946, the number increased to 357,478 in 1971, an average annual increase of 5%. The decline in growth is illustrated by the following annual growth rates: 10.4% in 1951, 7.9% in 1953, 0.85% in 1970, and 0.34% in 1971. The number of annual adult baptisms in Japan, including the Ryukyu Islands, reached a peak of 10,669 in 1953, but since then has decreased annually to 5,269 in 1971, almost back to the level of the 1946 figure of 4,242. The number of infant baptisms reached a peak of 7,521 in 1964, and then began to decrease, to 6,413 in 1971. Most of the converts during the post-war years were young adults; therefore there should have been a substantial increase in the number of baptized infants, but this has not been the case. One explanation of this is that many Catholics

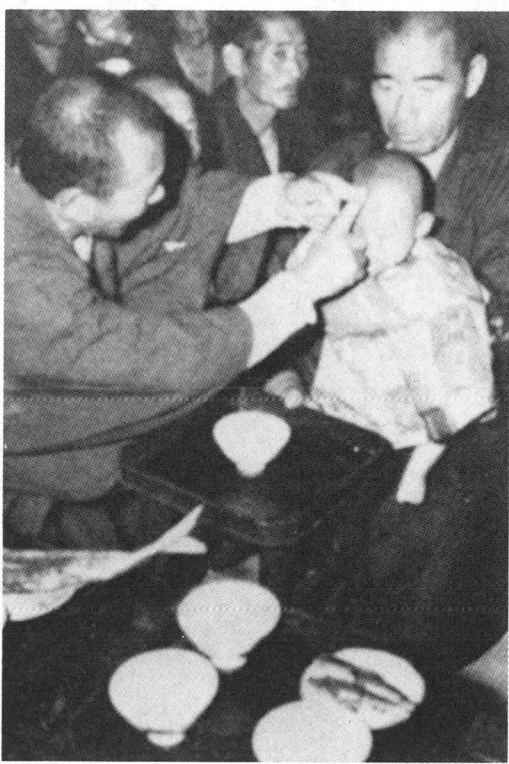

**Japanese indigenous churches.** Dating from year 1549, the Hidden Christians (Kakure Kirishitan) are earliest of Japan's 44 indigenous churches. Here, a child is baptized in ceremony with Christian, Buddhist and Shinto elements.

lose touch with the church as a result of widespread internal migration; another is that the Catholic annual birth rate fell from 4.4% per year in 1946 to 1.9% in 1968, though it continues to remain slightly higher than the national birth rate, which fell from 3.3% per year in 1946 to 1.85% in 1968.

A second factor in recent Catholic demography is the increasing Catholic migration from rural dioceses in the south to dioceses in the highly urbanized and industrialized centre of the country: Tokyo, Nagoya, Yokohama and Osaka. Thus 4 of the 5 dioceses on Kyushu and Shikoku (Takamatsu, Fukuoka, Nagasaki and Kagoshima) experienced a decline in membership from 108,839 baptized in 1970 to 107,586 in 1971. The diocese most affected by this exodus is that of Nagasaki: between June 1970 and June 1971, 255 Catholics took up residence in the archdiocese but 2,999 others departed. In 1903 Nagasaki had 77% of all Catholics in Japan; this proportion declined to 45% in 1951, and to 19% by 1971. The exodus is due to population mobility caused by urbanization, but also to the frequent shifting of public officials and employees of private businesses, social categories in which many Catholics are to be found. From 1970–71, 13,201 Catholics

took up residence elsewhere outside their dioceses. Of these, 10,061 registered their arrival in other dioceses but 3,140 failed to register in their new parishes and so were lost from Catholic records. In 1971, the 3 major urban dioceses (Tokyo, Yokohama and Osaka) had 140,248 Catholics, almost 40% of the total in Japan. Nevertheless in 1971 for the first time the archdiocese of Tokyo registered an annual decrease of 842 Catholics, from 57,931 in 1970 to 57,089 in 1971, despite the fact that Catholic migrants from the countryside were continuing to pour in.

ANGLICAN CHURCH. Two USA Episcopal missionaries from China were the first to arrive in Japan following the 1858 treaty. The CMS from Britain sent missionaries in 1869 and the Woman's Union Missionary Society opened a girls' school in Yokohama in 1871. In 1887 the CMS, SPG and the Protestant Episcopal Church of the USA organized the Japan Holy Catholic Church (NSKK). Its first Japanese bishops were consecrated in 1923. During World War II the church remained underground rather than comply with government decrees. It is the sixth largest church in Japan after the Catholic Church, Kyodan, Unification Church, Spirit of Jesus Church, and the No-Church Movement.

ORTHODOX CHURCH. The Holy Orthodox Church of Japan was begun in 1861 and now consists of 108 congregations with a total Christian community of nearly 25,000, in 3 dioceses. It has ties with the Russian Orthodox Church, Patriarchate of Moscow.

**CHURCH AND STATE.** The constitution of 1946 states in Article 20: 'Freedom of religion is guaranteed to all. No religious organization may receive any privileges whatsoever from the State, nor may it exercise any political authority. No one may be forced to take part in a religious act, service, rite, or ceremony. The State and its agencies shall refrain from religious education and all other religious activities.' Article 89 states: 'No public funds or property of the State may be used for the profit or maintenance of a religious institution or association, of whatever kind, nor for any charitable, educational or benevolent enterprise not under the control of public authorities.'

The Meiji constitution of 1889 had made Shinto the state religion, a state of affairs not ended until the separation of Shinto from the state became effective in December 1945 by order of the supreme commander for the Allied Powers. An imperial rescript of 1 January 1946 clearly repudiates the divine character of the emperor, and Imperial Ordinance 719 of 1945, revised in 1946 as Imperial Ordinance 70, suppressed all ancient laws, ordinances and regulations protecting Shinto or limiting the liberty of other religions. This legislation permits all religious corporations, including the Great Shinto Shrine of Ise, to possess a 'religious juridical personality' (Shukyo-hojin). Today religious corporations wishing to benefit from this statute must register with an ad hoc department (Shukyo-hojin Bunga-cho) within the Ministry of Public Instruction (Mombusho). Registered groups, churches, dioceses, parishes and religious communities, enjoy certain privileges, notably exemption from taxes on purchase of land and construction of buildings for church use. In return, they must comply with other legal requirements: submission of annual reports, inspection of their worship buildings, and the like.

Christian schools have the same rights and obligations as other private schools. In addition to the secular syllabus applied in all schools by the Ministry of Public Instruction, religious education courses are authorized both within and outside the schools.

In 1979 for the first time a professing Christian, M. Ohira, became premier.

**INTERDENOMINATIONAL ORGANIZATIONS.** The National Christian Council of Japan (NCCJ) was founded in 1923, building on earlier ecumenical efforts which began with the first National Christian Conference in Tokyo in 1878. The Conference was part of the World Evangelical Alliance between 1884 and 1906 after which it went out of existence. The Christian Church Federation was formed in 1911, taking the name NCCJ in 1923. The Federation of Christian Missions turned over its work to the Council in 1936 and became simply a Fellowship of Christian Missionaries which continues to exist.

The Japan Evangelical Association was formed in 1968, merging the Japan Evangelical Fellowship, Japan Evangelical Missionary Association, and Japan Protestant Council. There is also a Japan

Church Growth Research Association, formed in 1968, which co-ordinates research into the factors which foster or inhibit church growth.

Relations between Protestants and Catholics have improved considerably since Vatican II. The Catholic Episcopal Commission for Ecumenism is active as are such other groups as the Sodepax Committee, which was set up in Tokyo in 1970.

The Japan Ecumenical Association (JEA) is an interdenominational organization, founded in 1969, with the following aims: to promote contact, dialogue, study and mutual help between its members, who are the major Protestant churches and the Catholic Church; to study from the ecumenical point of view all problems which the churches face in their proclamation of the gospel to Japan and to promote contact, dialogue and co-operation with the other religions of Japan and with the leaders of Japanese society. In particular, the JEA promotes ecumenism at the grass-roots level through joint social action. One such instance is the Friendship Volunteers, inaugurated in 1970 by the Oriens Institute and which brings together Protestants and Catholics in helping poor people in Tokyo.

Another ecumenical project is the telephone counselling services in Japanese and English. The former of these is Inochi no Denwa (Live-saving Telephone) begun in 1971. This Christian service was the first of its kind in Japan and has had great success. More than 30,000 calls from persons lonely or in distress were received during its first 5 months of operation. A volunteer staff of 185 counsellors and 26 supervisors from the principal churches, Protestant and Catholic, operate this service from headquarters located in the Lutheran Centre in Tokyo. A similar service in the English language was inaugurated in 1973, known as the Tokyo English Life Line (TELL).

Other joint activities have included the Christian Pavilion at the 1970 World Exposition in Osaka, and during the same year a mass distribution of ecumenical posters inviting non-Christians to participate in Christmas midnight services in any denomination.

**BROADCASTING.** There are many radio and TV networks in Japan, and although in principle all accept Christian programmes, very little time is in fact allocated. The only Christian radio stations have been the 3 operated by the Far East Broadcasting Company in the Ryukyu Islands (phased out in 1977), and in Tokyo a private Catholic station Saint Paul Radio Centre which is in partnership with a commercial company and produces its own programmes. Foreign international stations transmitting Christian programmes in Japanese include HCJB (Ecuador), FEBC (5 hours a day), Radio Veritas (Manila), HLKX (Korea), and Radio Vatican (45 minutes a week). There are many studios preparing Christian programmes, all in Japanese. AVACO (National Christian Council of Japan) supplies tapes from its 3 Tokyo studios. A total of 40 Christian bodies in 1973 were offering 70 radio broadcasts a week over 157 stations. The Catholic Good Shepherd Movement produces two 5-minute daily radio programmes for 115 radio stations and two 15-minute weekly TV programmes for networks, reaching about 10 million people. Several Catholic dioceses and prefectures are also involved in preparing programmes for local stations. In Tokyo there are several information centres and schools including the Department of Communications of Sophia University which gives courses in journalism and television, and summer seminars are held on the educational aspects of television. For Catholics, Japan is a member of UNDA. Two missions, the Far Eastern Gospel Crusade, and the Evangelical Alliance Mission, have formed an autonomous radio recording ministry to serve the Protestant churches in Japan. Twenty-one radio programmes are produced for 25 mission boards, and time is purchased over about 80% of the commerical stations. Since 1961 several series of telecasts have been aired, a ministry undertaken by the Pacific Broadcasting Association. The LWFBS has a regional office in Tokyo.

## BIBLIOGRAPHY


*A history of Christianity in Japan.* R. H. Drummond. Grand Rapids (MI): Eerdmans, 1971. 398p.

*Catholicism in Japan.* J. J. Spae. Tokyo: ISR Press, 1963. 85p.

*Christianity encounters Japan.* J. J. Spae. Tokyo: Oriens Institute for Religious Research, 1968. 285p.

*Church growth in Japan.* T. Yamamori. South Pasadena: William Carey Library, 1974. 196p. (Dissertation, Duke University (USA), 1970. 262p. 8 denominations, 1859–1939).

*Folk religion in Japan: continuity and change.* I. Hori. Chicago: University of Chicago, 1968. 278p.

*Japan Catholic directory, 1972.* Tokyo: National Catholic Committee of Japan, 1972.

*Japan's new Buddhism: an objective account of Soka Gakkai.* K. Murata. Tokyo: Walker/Weatherhill, 1969. 194p.

*Japanese religion: unity and diversity.* H. B. Earhart. Belmont (CA): Dickenson, 1969.

*Japanese religiosity.* J. J. Spae. Tokyo: Oriens Institute for Religious Research, 1971. 313p.

*Japanese religious attitudes.* F. M. Basabe. New York: Orbis, 1972.

'Planting house churches in Japan through household evangelism and household conversion'. K. Takagi. Thesis, Dallas Theological Seminary (USA), 1970. 104p.

*Protestant theologies in modern Japan.* C. Germany. New York: Friendship Press, 1967.

*Religion and society in modern Japan: continuity and change.* E. Norbeck. Houston: Tourmaline Press, 1970.

*Religion in changing Japanese society.* K. Morioka. Tokyo: University of Tokyo Press, 1975.

*Religions in Japan.* Ed W. K. Bunce. Rutland, Vermont: Tuttle, 1967. 194p.

'Sociology of religion in Japan', *Social compass*, XVII, 1 (1970), 1–208. (9 articles, bibliography of 420 items).

*The Catholic Church in Japan since 1859.* J. L. Van Hecken. Tokyo: Herder, 1963.

*The Japan Christian yearbook 1969–1970.* Tokyo: Christian Literature Society of Japan, 1969. 429p. (Early editions mainly annual).

*The New Religions of Japan: a bibliography of Western language materials.* H. B. Earhart. Monumenta Nipponica Monograph. Tokyo: Sophia University, 1970. (810 items on 50 New Religions).

*The religions of Japan.* H. Thomsen. Rutland, Vermont: Tuttle, 1963.

*The rush hour of the Gods: a study of new religious movements in Japan.* H. N. McFarland. New York: Macmillan, 1967. 267p.


TABLE 2. ORGANIZED CHURCHES AND DENOMINATIONS IN JAPAN

| Official name 1 | Begun 2 | Type 3 | Counc 4 | Congs 5 | Adults 6 | Affiliated 7 | Names, notes, and other statistics (see Codebook) 8 |
|---|---|---|---|---|---|---|---|
| Apostolic Christian Church of Japan | 1952 | P Hol | ••••• | 3 | 30 | 100 | *Nippon Shito Kirisuto Kyokai.* M=ACC of America(USA). 1 school. 3n,5f,W=92%,3Y. |
| Assoc of Baptists for World Evangelism | 1953 | P Bap | x•••• | 9 | 240 | 500 | *Bankoku Baputesuto Fukuin Dendo Kyokai.* M=ABWE(USA). HQ Kobe. 16f,W=73%. |
| Association of Evangelical Churches | 1952 | P int | •M••• | 25 | 340 | 1,000 | *Fukuin Kirisutokyokai Kyogikai.*M=OMF(CIM). Hokkaido, Aomori. 5n,33f,1s,W=99%,10Y. |
| Baptist Bible Fellowship of Japan | 1949 | P Bap | x•••• | 31 | 930 | 3,000 | *Nippon Baputesuto Baiburi Ferouship.* M=BBFI(USA). 17n,26f,1s,150Y. |
| Baptist Mid-Missions in Japan | 1949 | P Bap | x•T•T | 7 | 100 | 300 | *Zen Nippon Baputesuto Mid-Mission Senkyodan.* M=BMM(USA). HQ Fukushima. 1n,19f. |
| Bible Study Circle | | I ind | ••••• | 23 | 262 | 331 | *Seisho Kenkyu Kai.* Japanese founder. HQ Ukyo (Kyoto). 2n,W=99%,35Y. |
| Brethren in Christ Church | 1953 | P Men | GF••• | 16 | 141 | 250 | *Nippon Kirisutokyo Keiteinda.* M=BiCC(USA). HQ Koganei, Tokyo. 3x,8f,1p,W=58%,12Y. |
| **Catholic Church in Japan:** | 1549 | R Lat | P•F•R | 730 | 256,000 | 365,662 | *Nippon Katorikku Kyokai.* C=37+4+86. 3s(352). 791n,1167x,420m,6298w,P=64%,11585Yy. |
| M Nagasaki | 1891 | R Lat | Ps | 63 | 48,600 | 69,379 | SW Kyushu. Many RCs in 16th century. 100 15 23 323 81 1780 |
| D Fukuoka | 1927 | R Lat | Ps | 68 | 17,400 | 24,918 | W Kyushu. D=pc(priests' council) begun 1970. 48 59 7 433 66 807 |
| D Kagoshima | 1927 | R Lat | Ps | 24 | 6,300 | 8,993 | SW Kyushu. D=PC(1968),pc(1971). 25 26 12 174 59 339 |
| D Naha | 1972 | R Lat | Ps | 10 | 3,500 | 4,983 | Ryukyu Isles. D=pc. Chinese exodus to Guam. 5 17 1 44 60 216 |
| D Oita | 1928 | R Lat | Ps | 23 | 4,300 | 6,211 | N Kyushu. D=pc(1970). 18 32 9 180 60 231 |
| M Osaka | 1891 | R Lat | Ps | 90 | 37,300 | 53,355 | S Honshu. D=pc(1967),PC(1967). 88 146 36 915 50 1656 |
| D Hiroshima | 1923 | R Lat | Ps | 45 | 12,700 | 18,151 | SW Honshu. D=PC(1970),pc(1971) 41 64 8 286 56 600 |
| D Kyoto | 1937 | R Lat | Ps | 63 | 13,200 | 18,797 | C Honshu. D=pc(1966),PC(1972). 30 82 20 311 61 686 |
| D Nagoya | 1922 | R Lat | Ps | 39 | 11,500 | 16,421 | C Honshu. 44 80 8 247 66 531 |
| D Takamatsu | 1904 | R Lat | Ps | 24 | 3,800 | 5,381 | On Shikoku. D=pc(1968),PC(1970). 10 38 1 90 52 178 |
| M Tokyo | 1891 | R Lat | Ps | 64 | 40,900 | 58,272 | D=pc(1966),PC(1968),Synod. 194 290 174 1589 60 1953 |
| D Niigata | 1912 | R Lat | Ps | 24 | 4,900 | 7,013 | NW Honshu. D=pc(1967),PC(1967). 19 31 1 115 52 209 |
| D Sapporo | 1915 | R Lat | Ps | 60 | 12,500 | 17,830 | Hokkaido. D=pc(1970). 70 61 61 412 71 601 |
| D Sendai | 1891 | R Lat | Ps | 64 | 8,600 | 12,297 | NE Honshu. D=pc(1969). Bishop a charismatic. 29 56 5 382 65 349 |
| D Urawa | 1939 | R Lat | Ps | 45 | 7,900 | 11,341 | C Honshu. D=pc(1971). 25 56 8 148 68 342 |
| D Yokohama | 1937 | R Lat | Ps | 24 | 22,600 | 32,320 | EC Honshu. D=pc(1966),PC(1968). 45 114 46 649 64 1107 |
| Central Japan Pioneer Mission | 1925 | P int | ••••• | | 500 | 1,000 | *Chuo Nippon Fukuin Senkyodan.* M=CJPM(UK). A=1962. HQ Fukushima. 1p. |
| Christian Brethren | c1925 | P CBr | x•••• | 60 | 3,000 | 5,000 | *Kirisuto Shinto no Shukai. Open Brethren.* M=CMML(USA,UK,NZ,Germany). 64f,W=99%. |
| Christian Brotherhood Church | 1946 | I Hol | ••••• | 200 | 2,586 | 7,000 | *Kirisuto Kyodai Dan.* Throughout Japan. HQ Tokyo. 39n,G=2.6%pa,1s(15),W=90%,140Y. |
| Christian Canaan Church | 1948 | I pen | ••••• | 14 | 2,797 | 5,000 | *Kirisutokyo Kanan Kyodan.* Indigenous pentecostals. HQ Sakai(Osaka). 9n,W=22%. |
| Christian Catholic Church | 1950 | P Con | x•••W | 2 | 500 | 1,000 | *Kirisuto Kodo Kyokai.* M=CCC(Zion,Illinois,USA). Holiness emphasis. HQ Osaka. 5f. |
| Christian Ch of the Glorious Gospel | 1936 | I Hol | ••••• | 21 | 3,680 | 6,000 | *Eiko no Fukuin Kirisuto Kyokai.* Ex Holiness missions. 12n(5 women). HQ Kumamoto. |
| Christian Churches & Chs of Christ | 1883 | P Dis | x•••• | 100 | 6,100 | 15,000 | *Kirisuto no Kyokai.* M=CCCC(Instrumental)(USA). USA military bases. 30n,55f,W=33%. |
| Christian Evangelistic Church | 1951 | I pen | ••••• | 9 | 101 | 165 | *Kirisuto Dendo-dan.* Founded on Early Church lines (tongues, &c). 3n,W=77%,6Y. |
| Christian Holy Convention | | I Hol | ••••• | 53 | 1,651 | 3,000 | *Kirisuto Seikyodan.* Merger with Japan Holiness Church (Arahara-ha). 10n,1p,59Y. |
| Christian Oriental Salvation Church | | I ind | ••••• | 3 | 25 | 100 | *Kirisutokyo Toyo Kyureidan.* Small independent group. HQ Nada (Kobe). 1n,W=99%. |
| Christian Spiritual Church | 1927 | I ind | ••••• | 26 | 858 | 1,193 | *Kirisuto Shinsu Kyodan. Christ Heart Church.* Completely indigenous life. 4n,G=2.1%pa. |
| Ch of Christ in Japan (Presb & Ref) | 1951 | I Ref | R•••• | 125 | 5,402 | 15,772 | *Nippon Kirisuto Kyokai.* 1945 schism ex Kyodan (UCCJ). HQ Tokyo. 110n,W=28%,328Yy. |
| Church of Christ, Scientist | | M Sci | x•••• | 3 | 90 | 200 | *Kirisutokyo Kagaku Daiichi Kyokai.* M=CCS(Boston,USA). Tokyo, Kyoto, Okinawa. 4w. |
| Ch of God in Christ in Japan: D Japan | 1969 | I pe3 | Z•••• | 3 | 600 | 1,500 | M=CoGiC(USA Blacks). HQ Urasoe City, Okinawa; also Tokyo. USA military. |
| Church of God (Cleveland) | 1952 | P Pe3 | ZF••• | 11 | 113 | 438 | *Kami no Kyokai.* M=CoG(Cleveland)(USA). 5 churches, 6 missions. 5n,2x,2f,1p,37Y. |
| Church of God (Independent Holiness) | 1953 | P Hol | ••••• | 10 | 200 | 500 | *Independent Holiness People* (USA). HQ Kanagawa. 5n,G=8.1%pa,W=73%,17Y. |
| Ch of Jesus Christ of Latter-day Saints | 1901 | M LdS | x•••• | 106 | 10,537 | 19,902 | *Matsujitsu Seito Iesu Kirisuto Kyokai.* M=CJCLdS(USA). 620nx,940f,G=5.6%pa,1500Y. |
| Church of Jesus the Victor | 1949 | P int | ••••• | 5 | 150 | 300 | *Shorisha Iesu Kyodan. Bible Institute Mission.* M=Life M(USA). 6f,1j,1k,1p,W=33%. |
| Church of the Resurrected Christ | | I ind | ••••• | 12 | 585 | 1,000 | *Fukkatsu no Kirisuto Kyodan.* Indigenous body. HQ Nagano. 13n,W=56%,6Y. |
| Church of the Way | | I ind | ••••• | 26 | 2,172 | 4,000 | *Do Kai.* Indigenous Japanese grouping of congregations. 34n. |
| Churches of Christ (Non-Instrumental) | 1890 | P Dis | x•••• | 40 | 2,000 | 5,000 | M=CC(Non-Instrumental)(USA). Ex Disciples of Christ (UCMS). 2 schools. 20f,2s. |
| Conservative Baptist Assoc of Churches | 1947 | P Bap | xF••• | 28 | 692 | 2,000 | *Hoshu Baputesuto Domei.* M=CBFMS(USA). HQ Yamagata. 1n,16m,7w,47f,1s,W=82%,101Y. |
| Cumberland Presbyterian Church | 1950 | P Ref | ••••W | 6 | 466 | 500 | *Kanbarando Choro Kyokai.* M=CPC(USA). HQ Kanagawa. 3 schools. 6nx,2f,W=51%,41Yy. |
| Evangelical Alliance Mission | 1891 | P int | xM••C | 108 | 4,238 | 6,000 | *NDKK. Nippon Domei Kirisuto Kyodan.* M=TEAM,SAM. Tokyo. 74n,50x,142f,G=4.8%,1s,267Y. |
| Evangelical Covenant Church of Japan | 1949 | P Con | K•••• | 15 | 320 | 1,000 | *Nippon Seikei Kirisuto Kyodan.* M=ECCA(USA). HQ Meguro. 4n,3x,12f,1s(5),W=64%,38Y. |
| Evangelical Free Church in Japan | 1949 | P Con | KF••C | 18 | 617 | 1,622 | *Nippon Fukuin Jiyu Kyokai.* M=EFCA(USA). HQ Urawa. 16n,19f,G=7.3%pa,W=90%,105Y. |
| Evangelical Missionary Church | | I ind | ••••• | 44 | 692 | 1,000 | *Fukuin Dendo Kyodan. Gospel Evangelistic Ch.* HQ Maebashi (Gumma). 20n,W=95%,67Y. |
| Evangelical Orient Mission | 1951 | P int | ••••• | 19 | 160 | 220 | *Toyo Fukuin Senkyokai.* M=NEOM(Norway). HQ Fukushima. 6n,W=91%,15Y. |
| Fellowship of Ev Baptist Churches | 1964 | P Bap | ••••• | 8 | 200 | 500 | *Nippon Fukuin Baputesuto Senkyo Dan.* M=FEBC(Canada). HQ Takaoka. 9f. |
| Free Methodist Church of Japan | 1895 | P Hol | VF••C | 33 | 4,246 | 5,800 | *Nippon Jiyu Mesojisuto Kyodan.* M=FMC(USA). HQ Osaka. 1 school. 20n,8f,1s,W=68%. |
| German Alliance Mission | 1955 | P int | ••••• | 16 | 200 | 430 | *Domei Fukuin Kirisuto Kyokai.* M=AMB. Nagoya-Gifu area. 6n,5x,9f,G=11%pa,W=99%,30Y. |
| Gospel of Jesus Church | 1947 | I ind | ••••• | 13 | 875 | 1,018 | *Iesu Fukuin Kyodan.* Tokyo, Honshu. Work in Brazil. 11n,G=–0.4%pa,W=70%,23Y,200z. |
| Hidden Christians | 1549 | I CCa | ••••• | 4 | 15,000 | 33,000 | *Kakure I Kirishitan.* Catholic survivors of persecution 1606–1859. South (Hanare) Japan islands. |
| Holy Jesus Society | | I pen | ••••• | 78 | 3,767 | 4,633 | *Sei Iesu Kai.* HQ Shinjuju Ku, Tokyo. No foreign mission. 27n,W=84%,224Y. |
| Holy Orthodox Church of Japan | 1861 | O Sla | MW••• | 108 | 15,000 | 24,502 | *Nippon Harisutosu Seikyo Kei.* Dioceses: Tokyo, Kyoto, Sendai. 70n,1x,19m,1s. |
| Holy Spirit Association for U of WC | c1956 | I mar | x•••• | 121 | 85,035 | 117,020 | *Sekai Kirisutokyo Toitsu Shinrei Kyokai. Unification Ch.* Korean; many Japanese students. 1023n. |
| Immanuel General Mission of Japan | 1919 | I Hol | •F••C | 123 | 8,129 | 10,775 | *Imanuero Sogo Dendo Dan.* M=WC(USA). HQ Chiyoda. 19n,2f,G=4%pa,1H,1j,1s,W=40%,339Y. |
| International Christian University Ch | 1949 | P int | ••••W | | 200 | 500 | *Kokusai Kirisuto Daigaku Kyokai* (*ICU Kyokai*). M=Japan ICU Foundation. 27f. |

*Continued opposite*

*Table 2 – continued*

| Official name 1 | Begun 2 | Type 3 | Counc 4 | Congs 5 | Adults 6 | Affiliated 7 | Names, notes, and other statistics (see Codebook) 8 |
|---|---|---|---|---|---|---|---|
| Internat Ch of the Foursquare Gospel | 1951 | P Pe2 | ZF... | 12 | 437 | 1,300 | *Kokusai Foosukuea Fukuin Kyodan.* M=ICFG(USA). HQ Saitama. 12nm,2f,1p(2),W=50%,48Y. |
| Isolated radio churches | 1952 | I rad | ..... | 4,100 | 80,000 | 165,000 | Isolated radio believers; mostly students and youths. R=164400,T=850000. |
| Japan Advent Christian Association | 1898 | P Adv | xF... | 13 | 415 | 1,000 | *Nippon Adobento Kirisuto Kyodan.* 1948, M=American Advent MS. 4n,10f,1p,W=78%,25Y. |
| Japan Alliance Church | 1891 | P Hol | xF... | 40 | 4,086 | 5,000 | *Nippon Araiansu Kyodan.* M=CMA(USA). A=1935. 26n,11f,G=3.3%pa,1s,W=50%,88Y. |
| Japan Apostolic Mission | 1917 | P Pe2 | ..... | 13 | 1,404 | 3,000 | *Nippon Shilo Kyodan.* M=Far East Apostolic Mission(USA). HQ Ikoma (Nara). |
| Japan Assemblies of God | 1913 | P Pe2 | ZF..C | 166 | 11,562 | 25,000 | *Nippon Assenburi Kyodan.* M=AoG(USA,UK). 9 schools. 211n,27f,1s(39),W=70%,311Y. |
| Japan Baptist Association | 1952 | P Bap | x.... | 9 | 180 | 500 | *Nippon Baputesuto Rengo.* M=American Baptist Assoc(USA). HQ Kashiwa. 6n,3f,18Y. |
| Japan Baptist Conference | 1951 | P Bap | TF... | 7 | 159 | 400 | *Nippon Baputesuto Senkyodan.* M=NABGMS(USA). Linked with USA German Baptists. 4n,18f. |
| Japan Baptist Convention | 1889 | P Bap | T...W | 258 | 22,924 | 30,000 | *Nippon Baputesuto Renmei.* M=SBC(USA). 142n,53x,142f,G=3.3%pa,1H,2s(21),W=46%,906Y. |
| Japan Baptist Union | 1872 | P Bap | T...W | 84 | 4,478 | 8,000 | *Nippon Baputesuto Domei.* M=ABFMS(USA),SBM(Sweden). 3 schools. 84n,26f,60Y. |
| Japan Christ Society | c1937 | I Ref | ..... | 8 | 212 | 300 | *Nippon Kirisuto Kai.* Presbyterian schism. Uses Buddhist, Shinto terms. 9n,24Yy. |
| Japan Church of God | 1908 | P Hol | x.... | 18 | 850 | 2,000 | *Nippon Kami no Kyokai Renmei.* M=CoG(Anderson)(USA). S Japan. 13n,4x,7f,W=72%,15Y. |
| Japan Church of Jesus Christ | 1903 | P int | .G... | 75 | 8,181 | 15,000 | *Nippon Iesu Kirisuto Kyodan.* M=JEB(UK). HQ Kobe. 186n,135m,21f,1s(60),W=40%,237Y. |
| Japan Church of the Nazarene | 1905 | P Hol | xF..C | 168 | 5,431 | 10,000 | *Nippon Nazaren Kyodan.* M=CoN(USA). 50n,216m,18f,G=0.7%pa,1s(5),73t(4561),W=61%,208Y. |
| Japan Evangelical Christian Church | 1918 | I ind | ..... | 2 | 224 | 500 | *Nippon Fukuin Kirisuto Kyodan.* Indigenous group. HQ Chofu (Tokyo). 5n,W=34%,5Y. |
| Japan Evangelical Church | 1951 | P Hol | .TT.T | 61 | 1,210 | 2,000 | *Nippon Fukuin Kirisuto Kyodan.* Links with USA fundamentalist bodies. 87n. |
| Japan Evangelical Church of Christ | 1948 | P Bap | TF... | 27 | 474 | 1,326 | *Nippon Kirisuto Baputesuto Rengo Senkyodan.* M=BGC(USA). 3n,2x,17f,1u,W=38%,91Y. |
| Japan Evangelical Lutheran Church | 1892 | P Lut | LvE.W | 145 | 6,719 | 17,225 | *Nippon Fukuin Ruteru Kyokai. JELC.* M=LCA(USA),ALC,et alia. 126nx,105f,W=61%,515Yy. |
| Japan Evangelical Mission | 1949 | P Bap | .M... | 12 | 1,115 | 2,177 | *Nippon Dendo Fukuin Kyodan.* M=JEM(Canada). HQ Niigata. 4n,54f,1s(18),W=99%. |
| Japan Free Religious Association | | M Unt | I.... | 4 | 1,365 | 3,000 | *Nippon Jiyu Shukyo Renmei.* Unitarians. HQ Minato (Tokyo). 3n. |
| Japan Free Will Baptist Mission | 1954 | P Bap | xF... | 14 | 145 | 300 | *Fukuin Baputesuto Kyodan.* M=NAFWB(USA). HQ Tsukisappu (Sapporo). 4n,10f,W=95%. |
| Japan Gospel Church | 1930 | I Hol | .T..C | 50 | 1,143 | 3,000 | *Nippon Fukuin Kyodan.* Japan Bible Seminary. 34n,G=2.9%pa,W=50%,68Y. |
| Japan Gospel Fellowship Association | | P int | ..... | 5 | 166 | 300 | *Nippon Fukuin Koyukai.* M=Gospel Fellowship Missions(USA). HQ Sakai, Osaka. 8n,6f. |
| Japan Gospel League Church of Christ | 1945 | P int | ..... | 5 | 177 | 500 | *Japan Gosuperu Rigu Kirisuto Kyokai.* M=International Gospel League(USA). 4n,2f. |
| Japan Gospel Pentecostal Church | 1951 | P Pel | x.... | 9 | 230 | 380 | *Nippon Pentekosute Kyodan.* M=ACP(Canada). Unitarian. HQ Nagoya. 7n,4f,W=22%. |
| Japan Holiness Church | 1901 | P Hol | xF... | 127 | 5,435 | 10,000 | *Toyo Senkyokai.* M=OMS(USA). Severe persecution 1939–45. 60n,20f,1s,W=89%,351Y. |
| Japan Holy Catholic Church: | 1859 | A plu | AWE.W | 311 | 25,860 | 49,100 | *NSKK. Nippon Sei Ko Kai.* M=CMS,USPG,PECUSA. 27f,4s. 318n,22x,W=26%,744Y,504y. |
| D Hokkaido | 1896 | A Eva | A | 25 | 1,112 | 2,680 | Churches: 17 urban, 6 rural. 30 Ainu members. 21 2 26 42 11 |
| D Kobe | 1923 | A plu | A | 28 | 2,705 | 4,433 | *Kobe Kyoku.* Southwestern mainland from Kobe to Ube. 43 6 25 91 51 |
| D Kyoto | 1898 | A plu | A | 45 | 1,700 | 5,507 | Industrial apartment mission. M=USPG,PECUSA. 2r,1s. 33 2 18 74 48 |
| D Kyushu | 1896 | A Low | A | 23 | 1,329 | 2,348 | Southermost islands of Japan (Kushu). HQ Fukuoka. 18 0 29 17 16 |
| D Mid-Japan (Chubu) | 1912 | A Cen | A | 24 | 1,463 | 3,500 | *Chubu Kyoku.* Rural. M=Anglican Ch of Canada. HQ Nagoya. 27 1 23 46 33 |
| D North Kanto (Kitakanto) | 1893 | A plu | A | 24 | 1,768 | 3,692 | Area north of Tokyo. HQ Omiya (north Tokyo suburb). 27 2 36 46 21 |
| D Okinawa | 1967 | A Cen | A | 14 | 902 | 1,700 | In PECUSA Province VIII till 1972. 400 members are lepers. 13 0 50 46 53 |
| D Osaka | 1896 | A Eva | A | 23 | 3,896 | 5,289 | *Osaka Kyoku.* M=CMS(UK). 80% urban. 3 orphanages, 2H,6r. 30 0 20 80 53 |
| D Tohoku | 1920 | A plu | A | 29 | 1,034 | 3,068 | Parishes: 27 urban, 2 rural. Very conservative culture. 17 1 53 47 25 |
| D Tokyo | 1923 | A plu | A | 42 | 6,910 | 12,833 | Secularized city. M=CMS,SSJE,USPG,PECUSA. 1H,4r,1s(5). 62 7 25 155 115 |
| D Yokohama | 1941 | A plu | A | 34 | 3,041 | 4,050 | Largest industrial complex in Japan. 8 rural churches. 27 1 24 100 78 |
| Japan Inland Mission | 1949 | P Pe2 | ..... | 10 | 200 | 500 | *Nippon Kaitaku Dendo Kyokai.* Mission from UK. Kyoto, Hyogo, Shiga. 3f,5m. |
| Japan Jesus Christ Church | | I pen | ..... | 33 | 4,000 | 10,000 | *Nippon Iesu Kirisuto Kyokai.* HQ Akashi Shi. Indigenous Japanese pentecostals. |
| Japan Jesus Christ Society | | I ind | ..... | | 500 | 1,000 | *Nippon Iesu Kirisuto Kai.* Indigenous grouping of congregations. |
| Japan Lutheran Church (Missouri Synod) | 1948 | P Lut | l.... | 70 | 2,308 | 2,987 | *Nippon Ruteru Kyodan.* M=LCMS. Kanto,Hokkaido,Okinawa. 23n,27x,28f,G=4.1%pa,117Yy. |
| Japan Mennonite Brethren Conference | 1950 | P Men | GF... | 14 | 613 | 2,000 | *Nippon Menonaito Burezaren Kyodan.* M=Mennonite Brethren Ch of NA. 14n,13f,1s. |
| Japan Mennonite Church Conference | 1949 | P Men | G.... | 19 | 352 | 1,000 | *Nippon Menonaito Kyokai Kyogikai.* M=Mennonite CNA. 6n,3x,24f,G=3.2%pa,1p,W=63%,4Y. |
| Japan New Testament Church | 1947 | P Bap | xM... | 23 | 390 | 1,500 | *Nippon Shinyaku Kyodan.* M=Far Eastern GC(USA). 13n,16x,78f,G=12.1%pa,W=90%,31Y. |
| Japan Open Bible Church | 1950 | P Pe2 | ZF... | 10 | 200 | 450 | *Nippon Opun Baiburu Kyodan.* M=OBSC(USA). HQ Nishinomiya (Hyogo). 3n,7f, W=50%. |
| Japan Orthodox Church | 1967 | O Sla | M.... | 3 | 825 | 2,000 | *Nippon Christos Sei Kyo Kai.* Schism aided by Orthodox P Moscow. 10n. |
| Japan Regular Baptist Church | | P Bap | ..... | | 200 | 500 | *Japan Regyura Baputesuto Mission.* M=Regular Baptist Churches (USA). |
| Japan Union Mission of SD Adventists | 1896 | P Adv | x.... | 131 | 7,695 | 20,000 | *Nippon Rengo Dendo Bukai.* 72n,40f,G=3.6%pa,3H,2h,1j,1r,1s(100),111t,W=95%,287Y. |
| Japan United Pentecostal Church | 1947 | P Pel | x.... | 43 | 1,000 | 2,000 | *Nippon Unaito Pentekosute Kyodan.* M=UPC(USA). HQ Kita (Kyoto). 26n,1f,1p(25),75Y. |
| Jehovah's Witnesses | 1911 | M Jeh | x.... | 284 | 12,133 | 30,000 | *Monomi no Toh Seisho Sasshi Kyokai.* Colporteurs 1913, Branch 1926. 74f,1j,2160Y. |
| Kinki Evangelical Lutheran Church | 1950 | P Lut | lv... | 25 | 1,164 | 1,315 | *Kinki Fukuin Ruteru Kyokai.* M=NMS,Free Ch of Norway. 15nx,15f,G=4.6%pa,W=50%,71Yy. |
| Korean Christian Church in Japan | 1907 | P Ref | RuE.W | 53 | 2,761 | 3,000 | *Zainichi Daikan Kirisuto Kyokai.* M=PCC(Canada). Korean residents in Japan. 30n,8f. |
| Kyushu Mennonite Christian Church | | P Men | G.... | 15 | 192 | 421 | *Kyushu Menonaito Kirisuto Kyokai Kaigi.* HQ Miyazaki. 1n,6f,W=79%. |
| Liebenzell Mission, Japan | 1927 | P int | xM... | 26 | 455 | 1,000 | *Riibenzera Nippon Dendokai.* M=LM(Bad Liebenzell, Germany). 18n,32f,W=99%,50Y. |
| Living Water Christian Church | | I pen | ..... | 23 | 805 | 2,044 | *Kassui Kirisuto Kyodan.* Ex Japan Evangelistic Band. HQ Odawara. 7n,W=36%,32Y. |
| Lutheran Brethren Mission of Japan | 1949 | P Lut | x.... | 11 | 241 | 346 | *Nippon Ruteru Doho Senkyodan.* M=CLB(USA) begun from China. HQ Akita. 7n,6f,W=90%. |
| Lutheran Mission of J, Wisconsin Synod | 1952 | P Lut | x.... | | 200 | 500 | M=Wisconsin EL Synod(USA). Radio ministries. HQ Mito (Ibaraki). 3n,4x. |
| Mino Mission | 1918 | P int | ..... | 23 | 366 | 1,000 | Work in Mino district (Gifu) also Mie & Aichi Prefectures. HQ Yokkaichi. 5n,2f. |
| Mission Covenant Church of Japan | | P Con | ..... | 9 | 575 | 1,500 | *Nippon Seikei Kirisuto Kyodan.* Links with Swedish mission SMF. 4n,6f,36Y. |
| New Christ Union Church | | I ind | ..... | 127 | 5,000 | 11,370 | *Union Kirisuto Kyokai.* Independent Japanese grouping of congregations. 50n. |
| Next Towns Crusade in Japan | 1957 | P Pe4 | ..... | 17 | 330 | 1,000 | *Nippon NTC.* M=Revival Temple, San Antonio,TX(USA). HQ Higashi (Osaka). 10n,8f. |
| No-Church Movement | 1900 | I non | ..... | 600 | 20,000 | 50,000 | *Mukyokai.* Small Bible study groups. No buildings, no clergy, unorganized. |
| Okinawa Baptist Convention | | P Bap | T...W | 31 | 2,673 | 5,000 | *Okinawa Baptist Renmei.* M=SBC(USA). After 1972, in Japan Baptist Conv. 17n,4f,248z. |
| Okinawa Christian Association | | I ind | .v... | | 200 | 500 | Small independent group on Okinawa island. 1948, applied to join WCC. |
| Orebro Mission | 1949 | P Pe2 | Z.... | 15 | 650 | 1,000 | *Sueden Oreburo Senkyokai.* M=Örebro M(Sweden). 12n,13x,1s(7),SS=1413,W=85%,47Y. |
| Oriental Boat Mission | 1966 | P int | xM... | | 200 | 500 | *Toyo Boat Mission.* M=International Missions (USA). |
| Oriental Chr Ch for Ev of the Deaf | | P ind | ..... | 56 | 500 | 1,000 | *Ev=Evangelization. Toyo Rowa Kirisuto Dendo Kyokai.* HQ Iruma (Saitama). 7n. |
| Original Gospel (Tabernacle) Movement | | I pe2 | ..... | 746 | 20,000 | 46,000 | *Genshi Fukuin. Primitive Gospel Ch. Makuya.* Split ex Mukyokai. 160n,W=34%, 1000Y. |
| Pentecostal Church of God in Japan | 1953 | P Pe2 | Z.... | 9 | 600 | 1,200 | *Nippon Pentekosute Kami no Kyokai Kyodan.* M=PCG(USA). HQ Kita. 3n,4f,W=45%. |
| Praising Church | | I ind | ..... | 7 | 122 | 200 | *Sanbi Kyodan.* Small Japanese indigenous grouping. HQ Hiroshima. 2n,W=57%. |
| Presbyterian Church in Japan | | P Ref | R.... | 12 | 452 | 541 | *Nippon Kirisuto Choro Kyokai.* HQ Suginami (Tokyo). 10nx,W=99%,33Yy. |
| Reformed Church in Japan | 1946 | P Ref | JF... | 86 | 5,317 | 6,000 | *Nippon Kirisuto Kaikakuha Kyokai.* M=CRC,OPC. 1 school. 81nx,32f,G=6%pa,W=66%,199Yy. |
| Reformed Presbyterian Christian Church | 1950 | P Ref | ..... | 3 | 70 | 80 | *Nippon Kirisuto Kaikaku Choro Kyokai.* Missionary split. No hymns. 1n,5f,W=94%. |
| Religious Society of Friends | 1884 | P Qua | Q...w | 9 | 275 | 500 | *Kirisuto Tomo no Kai Nenkai. Japan Yearly Meeting* (1917). *Quakers.* HQ Tokyo. W=19%. |
| Reorganized Ch of JC of Latter-day S | | M LdS | x.... | 2 | 38 | 100 | *Fukugen Iesu Kirisuto Kyokai.* Schism ex Mormons (USA). On Okinawa. 4n,1f,W=69%,2Y. |
| Salvation Army in Japan | 1895 | P Sal | xwE.. | 104 | 14,198 | 20,000 | *Kyusei Gun Nippon Honei. Japan Territory.* 178n,12f,G=0.2%pa,2H,1s(10),W=24%,1203z. |
| Spirit of Jesus Church | 1937 | I pel | x.... | 453 | 37,000 | 62,726 | *Iesu no Mitama Kyokai Kyodan.* Ex AoG. Missions to USA, Brazil. 185n(94 women). |
| Swedish Alliance Mission in Japan | 1950 | P ind | x.... | 13 | 366 | 600 | *Nippon Domei Kirisuto Kyodan.* M=SAM(Sweden). Zainichi Sweden Kirisutokyo DSD. 14f. |
| Swedish Evangelical Mission in Japan | 1951 | P int | ..... | 20 | 173 | 300 | *Zainichi Sweden FS.* M=Svenska Mongol- och Japanmissionen. 1n,7x,W=80%,7Y,12z. |
| Swedish Evangelical Orient Mission | 1950 | P Lut | ..... | 4 | 106 | 200 | *Sweden Toyo Fukuin Dendodan.* HQ Numazu (Shizuoka). 2n,6f,G=11.7%pa,W=40%,4Y,10z. |
| Swedish Free Mission | 1950 | P Pe2 | Z.... | 20 | 2,000 | 5.000 | *Sweden Jiyu Dendodan.* M=SFM(Sweden),NPY(Norway), Elim(Denmark),FFFM(Finland). |
| True Jesus Church in Japan | 1941 | I pel | x.... | 7 | 360 | 700 | *Shin Iesu Kyokai Nippon Sokai.* Chinese begun mainland 1917. HQ Osaka. 6n,W=28%. |
| United Baptist Church | | P Bap | ..... | 29 | 497 | 737 | *Nippon Baputesuto Kyokai Rengo.* Japan Baptist Church Assoc. 14n,9f,W=81%,64Y. |
| **United Church of Christ in Japan:** | 1859 | P uni | RWE.W | 1,654 | 144,269 | 205,051 | *Nippon Kirisuto Kyodan.* 59x,282f,G=0.4%pa,8s,1434t. 1610n,305f,W=38%,2738Y,353y. |
| CD Chubu (Chubu Church District) | 1941 | P uni | R | 113 | 8,301 | 12,105 | *Chubu Kyoku.* Rural, high-rise apartments, commerce. 79 8 39 140 31 |
| CD Higashi Chugoku/East Chugoku | 1941 | P uni | R | 59 | 4,534 | 5,664 | Rural, agriculture, commerce. No cities over 300,000. 41 6 35 105 5 |
| CD Hokkaido | 1941 | P uni | R | 62 | 4,721 | 5,722 | Least populated island. Fishing. Formerly UPUSA. 54 20 40 80 6 |
| CD Hyogo | 1941 | P uni | R | 101 | 11,033 | 14,317 | Hyogo prefecture. Rural. Kobe city industrial. 111 41 39 192 13 |
| CD Kanagawa | 1941 | P uni | R | 85 | 8,226 | 10,835 | Yokohama. Suburban high-rise, commerce, manufacture. 94 9 40 150 22 |
| CD Kanto | 1941 | P uni | R | 132 | 7,004 | 9,170 | Near Tokyo. Rural, high-rise. 110 7 42 150 23 |
| CD Kyoto | 1941 | P uni | R | 79 | 6,893 | 13,052 | Cultural centre, old capital of traditional Japan. 92 19 39 136 20 |
| CD Kyushu | 1941 | P uni | R | 134 | 10,486 | 15,131 | West. Rural/agriculture/manufacture. Methodist area. 114 21 38 201 37 |
| CD Nishi Chugoku/West Chugoku | 1941 | P uni | R | 81 | 5,460 | 7,697 | Commerce, high-rise. Formerly Southern Methodist. 60 9 34 49 9 |
| CD Okinawa | 1969 | P uni | R | 24 | 1,652 | 2,286 | *United Ch of Christ in Okinawa.* Tourism. US bases. 20 9 56 39 0 |
| CD Osaka | 1941 | P uni | R | 126 | 14,365 | 18,820 | Mainly urban high-rise, shipping, commercial. 122 18 38 237 33 |
| CD Ou | 1941 | P uni | R | 54 | 3,189 | 6,582 | North central Honshu. Rural; rich farming. 47 6 39 54 6 |
| CD Shikoku | 1941 | P uni | R | 90 | 6,043 | 9,875 | Shikoku prefecture (island). Mainly rural. 71 8 42 155 12 |
| CD Tohoku | 1941 | P uni | R | 90 | 5,245 | 7,957 | North Honshu. Mainly rural, poorest farmers. 79 18 37 119 6 |
| CD Tokai | 1941 | P uni | R | 96 | 6,614 | 8,697 | Rural, some high-rise apartments, commerce. 97 6 43 156 23 |
| CD Tokyo | 1946 | P uni | R | 328 | 40,503 | 57,141 | Capital. Mainly urban, high-rise, commercial. 405 95 37 775 107 |
| United Universalist Church | c1912 | M Unt | I.... | 5 | 200 | 500 | *Kirisutokyo Dojin Shadan.* M=Unitarian Univ Assoc(USA). HQ Bunkyo (Tokyo). 2n. |
| Universal Evangelical Church | | I ind | ..... | 31 | 1,000 | 2,000 | *Bankoku Fukuin Kyodan.* Ex Japan Evangelistic Band. HQ Matsumoto (Nagano). 20n. |
| West Japan Evangelical Lutheran Church | 1949 | P Lut | l.... | 18 | 1,004 | 1,500 | *Nishi Nippon Fukuin Ruteru Kyokai.* N=NLM(Norway). 8nx,12f,G=5.3%pa,1s,W=48%,65Yy. |
| Worldwide Evangelization Crusade | 1950 | P int | xF... | 12 | 93 | 552 | *Sekai Fukuin Dendodan.* M=WEK(Germany). HQ Kanzaki. 10n,20x,3f,G=11%pa,W=80%,9Y. |
| Zion Christian Church | | I ind | ..... | 9 | 500 | 1,000 | *Shion Kirisuto Kyokai.* Independent Japanese grouping of congregations. 9n,W–60%. |
| Other Protestant denominations | | P | ..... | | 19,390 | 38,700 | Total about 40 (see list below). |
| Other Japanese indigenous churches | | I | ..... | | 10,000 | 27,000 | Total about 20 (see list below). |
| **Total affiliated (mid-1970)** | | | | **13,800** | **951,087** | **1,607,661** | **Total denominations (1970) . . . 185.** |
| **Total affiliated (mid-1975)** | | | | **15,300** | **1,115,900** | **1,886,200** | **Total denominations (1975) . . . 192.** |
| **Total affiliated (mid-1980)** | | | | **17,000** | **1,266,700** | **2,141,200** | **Total denominations (1980) . . . 200.** |

NOTES ON TABLE ABOVE

COLUMNS: for meanings and CODES (cols. 1, 3, 4, 8), see Codebook (Part 6). Column 1: **Boldface type** = church with over 10% of country's affiliated Christians.

NATIONAL COUNCILS (Column 4, 5th letter).

C = Japan Evangelical Association (JEA), composed of Japan Evangelical Fellowship (JEF) (Nippon Fukuin Renmei), Japan Protestant Council (JPC), Japan Evangelical Missionary Association (JEMA).

R = Catholic Bishops' Conference of Japan (CBCJ).

T = Japan Bible Christian Council (Nippon Seisho Kirisutokyo Kyogikai), or Japan Evangelical Council, or Bible Council of Japan.

W = National Christian Council of Japan (NCCJ) (Nippon Kirisutokyo Kyogikai).

w = associate member of NCCJ.

*Other national councils.* Okinawa Christian Council (separate from Japan until 1972).

*Local councils.* About 40, loosely affiliated to NCCJ.

OTHER PROTESTANT DENOMINATIONS. These smaller groups include: Apostolic Faith Mission, Baptist International Missions (1966; 23 missionaries), Baptist Missionary Association of America, Bethel Pentecostal Temple (Seattle, USA), Bible Protestant Ch (1953), Children of God International (Tokyo), Ch of the Lutheran Confession (USA) (1 church in Tokyo), Community Baptist Ch Mission, Ev Congregational Ch (1963), Ev Methodist Ch (1968), Exclusive Brethren (Continuing

Tunbridge Wells), Free Christian Mission, Grace Mission (1969), International Missions (1950), International Pentecostal Assemblies, Japan Rural Mission, Kobe Union Ch, Maranatha Baptist Mission, Missionary Ch, North American Baptist General Conference (1951), Orthodox Presbyterian Ch, Philadelphia Ch Mission, Reformed Presbyterian Ch of NAmerica (1950), Swedish Holiness Mission (1950), Tokyo Union Ch, World Baptist Fellowship Mission Agency (1966), World Gospel Mission (1952), World-Wide Missions (1964). In addition to these bodies with Japanese membership, there were in 1970 about 20,000 Protestants in USA military chaplaincies (65% in the Ryukyu Islands).
OTHER JAPANESE INDIGENOUS CHURCHES. These smaller groups include: Amen Church, International Evangelical Convention; and a number of marginal bodies including: Japan Free Religious Association (Unitarian). The few bodies from abroad include the Spiritual Food Worldwide Evangelistic Mission (from Hong Kong).
OTHER CATHOLIC (NON-ROMAN) CHURCHES. The New Apostolic Ch (Germany) has a small work.

PEOPLES (ethnolinguistic). Christians: 86.8% Japanese, 8.9% Korean, 1.6% USA, 1.4% Ryukyuan (Okinawan), 1.0% European, 0.3% Chinese.

COUNTRY-WIDE TOTALS
EVANGELIZATION (see Part 5). 1900: 20%. 1970: 65%. 1980: 76%. *Mass evangelism*. Japan has had a long history of co-operative evangelism, notably the Kingdom of God Movement (Dr T. Kagawa) which lasted from 1930–34 and which drew over 1 million attenders (75% non-Christian), producing 35,000 enquirers; it was succeeded by the Nation-Wide United Evangelistic Movement. Among the many recent campaigns: 1956, Billy Graham rally; 1960, Oral Roberts in Tokyo; 1961, World Vision crusade; 1967, Billy Graham 10-day visit to Tokyo (191,750 attenders, 15,854 enquirers); 1969, 9 visits by E. Stanley Jones sponsored by NCCJ; Honda Crusades (Japanese evangelist Koji Honda; 1960–71, 158 crusades, with 377,951 attenders, 49,934 decisions); 1969, 'Total Mobilization Evangelism' (Sodoin Dendo) for saturation evangelism of Shikoku (1970), Kobe (1971), Okinawa (1972), Western Japan (1972–74), Kyushu (1974–76), Tohoku (1974–76), and whole of Japan by 1980; 1974, first nation-wide Japan Congress on Evangelism (Kyoto); 1976, Japan Multimedia Evangelism Project (JMEP), in Hokkaido; 1978, Here's Life Nagoya, Here's Life Okinawa (CCCI). *Radiophonic evangelism*. Annual listeners' letters: 140,000 FEBC (in 1976, 5 broadcast hours per day), 17,488 HCJB, 5,000 Radio Vatican, 1,360 TWR, 527 RVOG, et alia. Bible correspondence courses: numerous, with 800,000 enrolments (200,000 EHC, FEBC, Roman Catholic, ICI, et alia). TV evangelism: 1974–78 Rex Humbard (Cathedral of Tomorrow, Akron, USA) weekly TV programmes and campaigns on Channel 12, Tokyo (weekly audience 4 million; 1,500 letters a week in Tokyo). *Literature evangelism*. The first Every Home Crusade (WLC) took 13 years to complete; by 1976 EHC work had increased greatly in rapidity.
FOREIGN MISSIONARIES AND PERSONNEL (nationals serving abroad) (1973). Total 518 in 35 countries; about 230 Protestants in 27 countries, 170 Roman Catholics in 9 countries (including 68 priests, 53 sisters, 24 catechists serving the Japanese diaspora in the Americas), 65 Japanese indigenous in 8 countries, 41 marginal Protestants in 5 countries, 12 Anglicans in 5 countries.
FOREIGN MISSIONARIES AND PERSONNEL (aliens from abroad) (1973). Total 6,116. *From Western world*. 5,765: 2,486 Protestants (1,854 in 112 USA societies (including 135 on Okinawa, Ryukyu Islands), 139 in9 Norway societies, 113 in 6 Canada societies, 84 in 8 WGermany societies, 78 in 9 UK societies, 66 in 7 Sweden societies, 49 in 3 Finland societies, 34 in 10 Australia societies, 21 in 9 New Zealand societies, 6 in 2 Denmark societies, 6 in 1 Switzerland society, 3 in 2 Netherlands societies), about 2,250 Roman Catholics, about 1,000 marginal Protestants (900 Mormons from USA, 54 Jehovah's Witnesses), 27 Anglicans (12 in 2 USA societies, 12 in 3 UK societies, 3 in 1 Canada society), 2 Orthodox. By 1975, North American missionaries had declined to 1,545. *From Communist world*. 41: about 38 Roman Catholics (28 from Poland, 10 Yugoslavia), 3 Orthodox from USSR. *From Third World*. 310: about 130 Roman Catholics from 20 countries, 88 Protestants (about 80 from Korea, Singapore, Philippines, Taiwan et alia, 8 in 2 South Africa societies), about 60 marginal Protestants (40 Mormons, 20 Jehovah's Witnesses), 32 indigenous from Korea, Hong Kong and Taiwan.
INSTITUTIONS (church-operated) (1973). Total 670, including 390 higher schools (282 RC, 92 Protestant), 118 medical centres (72 Protestant, 44 RC), 25 presses, 3 radio stations, 30 religious communities, 14 research centres, 50 seminaries (36 Protestant, 7 RC, 4 Anglican, 2 Japanese indigenous, 1 Orthodox), 21 universities (12 RC, 9 Protestant).
PERIODICALS. About 280 titles (150 Protestant (8 SDA), 80 RC, 20 indigenous, 12 Anglican).
PERSONNEL. About 19,251 (13,135 national, 6,116 foreign).
RELIGIOUS LIBRARIES. About 120.
SCRIPTURE DISTRIBUTION (1975). Annual totals: 255,158 Bibles (88% subsidized, 12% commercial), 2,156,903 NTs (47% free, 49% subsidized, 4% commercial), 170,123 UBS portions, 5,807,808 UBS selections. *Translations completed*. Portion: 3 languages since 1837. NT: 2 languages since 1879. Bible: Japanese in 1883. About 1,800 bookshops sell the Bible.
SERVICE AGENCIES. About 250, including AMF, AVACO, BAVACO, CBCJ, CCCI, CEF, CLC, FABC, FEBC, HOREMCO, JBS(NSK), JCMC, JEA, JEF, JEMA, JEMS, JEOM, MTS, NCCJ, NTM, PTL, RVOG, TEAM-AVED, WLC(EHC), WSCF, WVI, YCW, YLC, YMCA, YWAM, YWCA.

ADDITIONAL DATA ON CHURCHES
The names of churches in Japanese can use either the spelling 'Nippon' or 'Nihon' for 'Japan'; the former is government usage and has nationalistic connotations, the latter has more liberal overtones.
CATHOLIC CHURCH IN JAPAN. In addition to the jurisdictions listed, there is a disputed area in the South Kuriles (Sakhalin), PA Karafuto, founded 1932 but since 1945 occupied by Soviets and so in the USSR. *Catholics*. About 33% are descendants of the Nagasaki or Kirishitan (Hidden Christian) communities rediscovered in 1865. *Catechumens*. (1959) 19,700; (1961) 19,197; (1963) 18,436. In column 7, figures include catechumens, which in Japan means not only candidates for baptism but also 'persons who are at present studying religion and have begun to live a Christian life, and who can be presumed to eventually receive baptism'. Total (1971) 7,184, divided among the 16 jurisdictions as follows, in the order shown: 189, 524, 224, 132, 219; 1658, 642, 664, 353, 148; 1183, 243, 482, 297, 368,858. *Annual baptisms*. (1972) 57.2% infant, 42.8% adult. *Column 8. Diocesan councils*. The code D shows progress in internal diocesan conciliarism to December 1971, indicating which dioceses had: pc = priests' or presbyteral council or senate, lc = council of laity, PC = pastoral council (laity, priests and religious), and the dates when begun. M Tokyo prepared a unique synod, 1968–72. *Priests*. Of the Japanese priests (1971), 447 were secular, 322 religious. *Bishops*. The 22 bishops were all Japanese (first Japanese bishop, 1927). Numbers of Japanese and expatriate clergy have grown as follows: (1911) 31 + 60, (1920) 37 + 71, (1930) 61 + 227, (1940) 159 + 308, (1950) 187 + 556, (1960) 426 + 1246, (1970) 738 + 1188. In 1971 there were 2 Japanese worker-priests in a restaurant chain. *Brothers*. 241 Japanese, 179 expatriates. *Sisters*. 5,348 Japanese, 950 expatriates. *Catholic charismatics* (January 1974). 200 adults including a number of religious personnel in 12 organized prayer groups are active in the Charismatic Renewal in M Osaka, and there are others elsewhere. *Seminaries*. There are 4 for religious clergy; and 3 for secular clergy, being Tokyo Catholic Seminary, St Sulpice Interdiocesan Seminary (Fukuoka), Seminary for Late Vocations (Osaka). *Seminarians*. 30% secular, 70% religious. *Catechist training school*. St Mary's (Nagoya) trains most catechists. *Catechists*. Total (1971) 535, of whom 275 work in one diocese, Nagasaki. *Indigenous religious congregations*. Sisters (1974): Sisters of the Holy Maid (begun 1959, 332); Daughters of the Sacred Heart of Jesus (begun 1920, 333); Sisters of Miyazaki Caritas (begun 1937, 263); Sisters of the Immaculate Heart of Mary (begun 1934, 282); Secular Institute of the Catechists of MaryVirgin and Mother (begun 1954, 212); Sisters of the Visitation (begun 1925, 185); Congregation of the Japanese Sisters of Bethany (begun 1937, 137); Missionary Sisters of St Joseph of Osaka (begun 1948, 112); Franciscan Sisters of Militia Immaculatae (begun 1949, 105); Franciscan Sisters of the Annunciation (begun 1938, 51); Missionary Sisters of St John the Evangelist (begun 1944, 41); Franciscan Sisters of the Immaculate Heart of Mary (begun 1954, 35); Sisters of the Light of the Gospel (begun 1949, 31); Society of Seminary Auxiliaries (begun 1941, 7); Aikukai Community in Japan (begun 1884; 10 members in 1973); Religious of the Most Holy Cross and Passion of Our Lord (begun 1957; 16 members). *Main foreign orders and congregations*. Priests (with over 50 in 1974): 385 SJ, 247 OFM, 139 SDB, 112 SVD, 95 SMI, 94 OFMConv, 90 MEP, 86 SSC, 82 CICM, 67 OP, 61 MM, 61 CSSR. Sisters (with over 150): 423 Franciscan Missionaries of Mary, 325 Congregation of the Infant Jesus of Chauffailles, 273 Daughters of Mary Help of Christians, 230 Franciscan Sisters of St George, 227 Order of Cistercians of Strict Observance, 200 Sisters of St Paul of Chartres, 174 Society of the Sacred Heart of Jesus, 169 Sisters of the Holy Infant Jesus, 155 Missionary Sisters Servants of the Holy Spirit.
*Catholic organizations*. The Catholic Bishops' Conference of Japan is a member of FABC in Hong Kong. According to Japanese legislation, the Catholic Church is officially registered under the title of 'The National Catholic Committee of Japan' (Katorikku Chuo Kyogikai), which acts as a general secretariat for the Catholic Bishops' Conference of Japan. Two national organizations cater for religious personnel: Superiors Conference of Japan, for men, and National Conference of Major Superiors of Women Religious.
Japan has no national pastoral or presbyteral councils, and Tokyo is the only diocese to have the uniquely progressive programme known as a pastoral synod. Established in 1968 by cardinal Doi at the request of the diocesan pastoral council, the Pastoral Synod of Tokyo was begun in order to 'form a truly Christian community in the archdiocese'. A preparatory commission of elected priests, religious and lay personnel worked on it from the beginning of 1969. The first general assembly consisting of 335 members for the most part elected by their peers met in January 1972 and adopted several concrete measures aimed at integrating the entire Christian community into the material and pastoral organization of the archdiocese.
Active membership in the main lay movements in 1971 was as follows: Catholic Boy Scouts 3,156; Girl Scouts 1,038; Legion of Mary 3,097; Catholic High School Students Association 2,949; St Vincent de Paul 306; and YCW 250.
The Holy See has diplomatic relations with Japan, and is represented to government and the Catholic hierarchy by an Apostolic Nunciature, with a pro-nuncio in Tokyo.
Two major Catholic research centres have been established, the Catholic Social Research Institute in Tokyo run by MEP personnel, and the St Thomas Aquinas Institute in Kyoto run by OP personnel, the latter specializing in the study of Christian philosophy. Several others are also at work.
The involvement of the Catholic Church in education is extensive, and in 1976 included 593 kindergartens (118,580 children), 54 primary schools (22,589 pupils), 94 middle schools (27,155), 114 high schools (71,370), 32 junior colleges (12,445), 12 universities (21,887), 35 special schools (8,338) and 492 Sunday schools (30,050). All these schools include a higher proportion of girls than of boys, especially from the primary to the junior college levels; junior colleges have 7,610 girls and 1,288 boys. There are 3 principal Catholic universities. Sophia University (Jochi Daigaku) in Tokyo has 7,940 students and is run by SJ personnel. Attached to this university is a Faculty of Theology, a Theology Course for Laymen, and an Institute of Christian Culture. Nanzan University (Nanzan Daigaku) in Nagoya has 4,047 students and is run by SVD personnel. The International University of the Sacred Heart in Tokyo has 1,482 women students and is run by the Society of the Sacred Heart. The average proportion of Catholic pupils and students to total enrolment is 41% in kindergartens, 8.3% at university level and 6.2% for Catholic schools in general.
Medical activity and welfare are also extensive, and include 31 hospitals (4,961 beds), 15 dispensaries (117,089 consultations a year), 55 orphanages (3,818 orphans), 146 day nurseries (13,535 children), 42 homes for aged (2,721 inmates), 11 institutions for the handicapped (1,254), 19 institutions for the mentally retarded (1,175), 21 infant homes (1,067), and 83 student residences (5,466 men and women students). By way of comparison, public and private institutions for the whole of Japan in 1970 numbered 1,014 homes for the aged (75,397 inmates), 522 orphanages (34,241), 196 institutions for the handicapped (14,606), and 235 institutions for the retarded (37,161). Other important programmes include the Stella Maris Centre for seamen in Kobe, Japan Catholic Migration Council (JCMC) and Caritas Japan. Caritas was established after World War II and reorganized in 1967, and comprises 6 autonomous organizations including the Japan Catholic Nurses' Association and the Association for Social Welfare.
JAPAN HOLY CATHOLIC CHURCH. *Lay workers* (1977). Nationals: 3 men, 15 women. Expatriates: 4 men, 6 women. *Lay readers* (1977). 42 men. *Seminarians* (1977). 10.
UNITED CHURCH OF CHRIST IN JAPAN. Several long-standing USA missionary societies, which until 1973 worked through the Interboard Committee for Christian Work in Japan, have now joined other USA societies to work through the Japan North America Commission on Co-operative Mission (JNAC). *Statistics*. Although membership and the number of congregations increases very slightly from year to year, the number of adult baptisms is declining; but exact comparison is difficult because congregations that do not submit statistics for 3 years are dropped from the tabulations and totals. In 1972, 154 congregations did not report in this way. *Membership*. In 1973, 23% of the active adult membership (15 years and over) were non-resident, 77% resident.

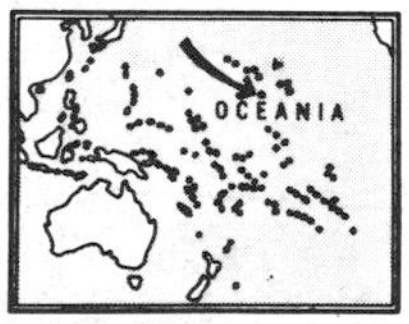


# JOHNSTON ISLAND

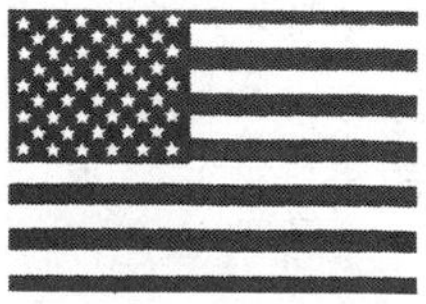

## SECULAR DATA

**STATE. Official name:** Johnston and Sand Islands.
**Flag** (shown above right): That of the USA.
**Area:** 1 sq.km. (0.4 sq.miles). Description: Atoll with a reef 12 miles round, and 2 islets. Agricultural land: 0.0%.
**Government:** Island dependency of the USA, since 1934.
**Official language:** English.
**Armed forces** (1973): Total 1,000 USA troops.

**DEMOGRAPHY. Population:** 1,007 (census of 1.IV.1970. For 1970–2000 (UN), see last row of Table 1). Population density (1975): 1,000/sq.km. (2,500/sq.mile). Under 15 years: 44%. Growth rate (1975–80): 0% per year (births 3.49%, deaths −0.79%, emigrants −2.70%). Life expectancy (1975–80): 63.8 years. Household size: 5.7 persons.
**Major language:** English.

**ETHNOLINGUISTIC GROUPS:** 99% USA military (79% White, 20% Black).

**MONEY** (1977). **Monetary unit:** US dollar (= 100 cents).

TABLE 1. RELIGIOUS ADHERENTS IN JOHNSTON ISLAND

| Year | 1900 | | mid-1970 | | Annual change, 1970–1980 | | | | mid-1975 | | mid-1980 | | 2000 | |
|---|---|---|---|---|---|---|---|---|---|---|---|---|---|---|
| *Name* | *Adherents* | *%* | *Adherents* | *%* | *Natural* | *Conversion* | *Total* | *Rate* | *Adherents* | *%* | *Adherents* | *%* | *Adherents* | *%* |
| **Christians** | **0** | **0.0** | **900** | **90.0** | **0** | **−10** | **−10** | **−1.18** | **850** | **85.0** | **800** | **80.0** | **1,050** | **70.0** |
| professing | 0 | 0.0 | 900 | 90.0 | 0 | −10 | −10 | −1.18 | 850 | 85.0 | 800 | 80.0 | 1,050 | 70.0 |
| Protestants | 0 | 0.0 | 800 | 80.0 | 0 | −8 | −8 | −1.05 | 760 | 76.0 | 720 | 72.0 | 960 | 64.0 |
| Roman Catholics | 0 | 0.0 | 100 | 10.0 | 0 | −2 | −2 | −2.22 | 90 | 9.0 | 80 | 8.0 | 90 | 6.0 |
| nominal | 0 | 0.0 | 560 | 56.0 | 0 | 4 | 4 | 0.69 | 580 | 58.0 | 600 | 60.0 | 900 | 60.0 |
| affiliated | 0 | 0.0 | 340 | 34.0 | 0 | −14 | −14 | −5.19 | 270 | 27.0 | 200 | 20.0 | 150 | 10.0 |
| total practising | 0 | 0.0 | 240 | *70* | 0 | −10 | −10 | −5.26 | 190 | *70* | 140 | *70* | 90 | *60* |
| non-practising | 0 | 0.0 | 100 | *30* | 0 | −4 | −4 | −5.00 | 80 | *30* | 60 | *30* | 60 | *40* |
| Protestants | 0 | 0.0 | 300 | 30.0 | 0 | −12 | −12 | −5.00 | 240 | 24.0 | 180 | 18.0 | 130 | 9.0 |
| Roman Catholics | 0 | 0.0 | 40 | 4.0 | 0 | −2 | −2 | −6.67 | 30 | 3.0 | 20 | 2.0 | 20 | 1.4 |
| Non-religious | 0 | 0.0 | 100 | 10.0 | 0 | 10 | 10 | 6.67 | 150 | 15.0 | 200 | 20.0 | 450 | 30.0 |
| **Country's population** | **0** | **100.0** | **1,000** | **100.0** | **0** | **0** | **0** | **0.00** | **1,000** | **100.0** | **1,000** | **100.0** | **1,500** | **100.0** |

COLUMNS, ROWS. For meanings and definitions, see Codebook (Part 6). Note that, by definition, total 'Christians' = professing + crypto-Christians, which also = affiliated + nominal Christians. Percentages may not always total exactly, due to rounding.

**CHRISTIANITY.** There are no organized denominations or parishes on the island although Protestant and Catholic worship services and activities are organized by USA military chaplains. Johnston Island is part of the Catholic diocese of Honolulu, itself part of the Province of San Francisco, USA.

**CHURCH AND STATE.** The island was uninhabited when first discovered in 1807. Annexed by the USA in 1858, jurisdiction was transferred to the USA Navy in 1934 and to the US Air Force in 1948. The religious life of Johnston Island is entirely dependent upon the activity of US military chaplains who are recruited and paid by the government.

TABLE 2. ORGANIZED CHURCHES AND DENOMINATIONS IN JOHNSTON ISLAND

| Official name 1 | Begun 2 | Type 3 | Counc 4 | Congs 5 | Adults 6 | Affiliated 7 | Names, notes, and other statistics (see Codebook) 8 |
|---|---|---|---|---|---|---|---|
| Catholic Church (D Honolulu) | | R Lat | B.... | 1 | 20 | 40 | Under D Honolulu, province of San Francisco (USA). No parish. USA expatriates. |
| USA military chaplaincy | | P int | ..... | 1 | 200 | 300 | Protestant chaplaincy to USA armed services; interdenominational. |
| Total affiliated (mid-1970) | | | | 2 | 220 | 340 | Total denominations (1970) . . . 2. |
| Total affiliated (mid-1975) | | | | 2 | 170 | 270 | Total denominations (1975) . . . 2. |
| Total affiliated (mid-1980) | | | | 2 | 130 | 200 | Total denominations (1980) . . . 2. |

**NOTES ON TABLE ABOVE**
COLUMNS: for meanings and CODES (cols. 1, 3, 4, 8), see Codebook (Part 6). Column 1: Boldface type = church with over 10% of country's affiliated Christians.

**PEOPLES** (ethnolinguistic). Christians: 99% USA military (79% White, 20% Black).

**COUNTRY-WIDE TOTALS**
EVANGELIZATION (see Part 5). 1900: 0%. 1970: 100%. 1980: 100%.

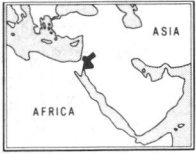

# JORDAN

## SECULAR DATA

**STATE. Official name:** The Hashemite Kingdom of Jordan (Al Mamlakah al Urduniyah al Hashemiyah). Adjective of nationality: Jordanian.
**Flag** (shown above right): Black, white, and green stripes, with 7-pointed white star in red triangle on left.
**Area:** 89,715 sq.km. (34,639 sq.miles), excluding West Bank and East Jerusalem (occupied by Israel; 5,879 sq.km.). Agricultural land: 14.9%.
**Government:** Absolute monarchy, since 1946 (in Ottoman empire, 1920 British mandated territory of Transjordan, 1946 Independence).
**Legislature:** Parliament: Senate, 30 members; House of Representatives, 60 members.
**Official language:** Arabic.
**Chief cities:** capital Amman 580,000 (1973), Zarka 220,000, Irbid 116,000.
**Political divisions:** (1977): Transjordan: 5 Districts (muhafaza) of Amman, Irbid, Balqa, Karak, Ma'an. West Bank (under Israeli occupation since 1967). 3 Districts of Jerusalem, Hebron, Nablus.

**Armed forces** (1976): Total 67,900 regular: army 61,000, navy 250, air force 6,650 (66 combat aircraft). Reserves: 30,000. Paramilitary forces: 10,000.

**DEMOGRAPHY. Population:** 1,706,226 (census of 18.XI.1961. For 1970–2000 (UN), see last row of Table 1). Population density (1975): 22/sq.km. (56/sq.mile). Under 15 years: 44%. Growth rate (1975–80): 3.34% per year (births 4.62%, deaths −1.28%). Life expectancy (1975–80): 55.7 years. Household size: 5.2 persons.
**Major languages:** Arabic, Circassian, Armenian, Kurdish, English.
**Urban dwellers** (1970): 46.6%. Urban growth rate (1950–70): 4.3% per year.
**Labour force:** 25%.
**Refugees** (1977): 645,857 (625,857 Palestinians under UNRWA, 20,000 from Lebanon).
**Tourists** (1974): 554,913.

**ETHNOLINGUISTIC GROUPS:** 51.9% Palestinian Arab (850,000), 46.4% Jordanian & Syrian Arab (6% Bedouin), 1.2% Circassian, 0.1% Armenian, 0.1% Kurdish, 0.1% Turkmen, Chechen.

**MONEY** (1977). **Monetary unit:** dinar (= 100 fils); US$1 = JD 0.333.
**National income per person:** US$370. Average annual family income: US$1,924.
**Inflation:** (1970–74) 10.6% per year (1975: consumer price index 206).
**Cost of living in capital** (1976): index 114 (Washington DC=100). Daily cost of living: US$41.

**HEALTH.** Hospitals: 35 (3,160 beds). Doctors: 1,043. Lepers: 270 (0.1 per 1,000). Blind: 9,000. Psychotics: 18,000. Criminals: 10,000.

**EDUCATION.** Adult literacy: (1961) 32%, (1975) 45%. Education rate: 70%. Schools: 1,866 (1,482 government, 213 private, 171 UNRWA). Universities: 1.

**LITERATURE.** Annual new book titles (1973): 89. Periodicals: 23. Newspapers: 4 dailies, 7 non-daily.

**COMMUNICATION** (per 1,000 people). Phones: 16. Radios: 203. TV sets: 31. Daily newspaper circulation: 24 copies.

TABLE 1. RELIGIOUS ADHERENTS IN JORDAN (Transjordan only)

| Name | 1900 Adherents | % | mid-1970 Adherents | % | Natural | Conversion | Total | Rate | mid-1975 Adherents | % | mid-1980 Adherents | % | 2000 Adherents | % |
|---|---|---|---|---|---|---|---|---|---|---|---|---|---|---|
| Muslims | 235,400 | 94.2 | 1,533,290 | 93.7 | 60,454 | −1,519 | 58,935 | 3.28 | 1,799,120 | 93.3 | 2,122,640 | 93.0 | 3,861,500 | 91.4 |
| Druzes | 100 | 0.0 | 200 | 0.0 | 8 | −2 | 6 | 2.61 | 230 | 0.0 | 260 | 0.0 | 500 | 0.0 |
| Christians | 14,600 | 5.8 | 84,010 | 5.1 | 2,985 | −110 | 2,875 | 2.93 | 98,130 | 5.1 | 112,760 | 4.9 | 194,400 | 4.6 |
| crypto-Christians | 4,600 | 1.8 | 14,010 | 0.8 | 512 | 103 | 615 | 3.65 | 16,830 | 0.9 | 20,160 | 0.9 | 40,300 | 1.0 |
| professing | 10,000 | 4.0 | 70,000 | 4.3 | 2,473 | −213 | 2,260 | 2.78 | 81,300 | 4.2 | 92,600 | 4.1 | 154,100 | 3.6 |
| Orthodox | 6,000 | 2.4 | 33,000 | 2.0 | 1,156 | −156 | 1,000 | 2.63 | 38,000 | 2.0 | 43,000 | 1.9 | 68,000 | 1.6 |
| Roman Catholics | 3,600 | 1.4 | 29,000 | 1.8 | 1,034 | −34 | 1,000 | 2.94 | 34,000 | 1.8 | 39,000 | 1.7 | 67,600 | 1.6 |
| Protestants | 100 | 0.0 | 5,000 | 0.3 | 177 | −17 | 160 | 2.76 | 5,800 | 0.3 | 6,600 | 0.3 | 12,000 | 0.3 |
| Anglicans | 300 | 0.1 | 3,000 | 0.2 | 106 | −6 | 100 | 2.86 | 3,500 | 0.2 | 4,000 | 0.2 | 6,500 | 0.2 |
| affiliated | 14,600 | 5.8 | 84,010 | 5.1 | 2,985 | −110 | 2,875 | 2.93 | 98,130 | 5.1 | 112,760 | 4.9 | 194,400 | 4.6 |
| total practising | 13,140 | 90 | 67,210 | 80 | 2,388 | −88 | 2,300 | 2.93 | 78,500 | 80 | 90,210 | 80 | 136,100 | 70 |
| non-practising | 1,460 | 10 | 16,800 | 20 | 597 | −22 | 575 | 2.93 | 19,630 | 20 | 22,550 | 20 | 58,300 | 30 |
| Orthodox | 10,000 | 4.0 | 38,500 | 2.4 | 1,374 | −24 | 1,350 | 2.99 | 45,200 | 2.3 | 52,000 | 2.3 | 84,100 | 2.0 |
| Roman Catholics | 4,000 | 1.6 | 30,400 | 1.9 | 1,065 | −105 | 960 | 2.74 | 35,000 | 1.8 | 40,000 | 1.8 | 71,900 | 1.7 |
| Protestants | 200 | 0.1 | 7,210 | 0.4 | 259 | 0 | 259 | 3.05 | 8,500 | 0.4 | 9,800 | 0.4 | 17,000 | 0.4 |
| Evangelicals | 200 | 0.1 | 6,500 | 0.4 | 235 | −5 | 230 | 2.99 | 7,700 | 0.4 | 8,800 | 0.4 | 16,000 | 0.4 |
| Arab indigenous | 0 | 0.0 | 4,300 | 0.3 | 158 | 22 | 180 | 3.46 | 5,200 | 0.3 | 6,100 | 0.3 | 13,000 | 0.3 |
| Anglicans | 400 | 0.2 | 3,500 | 0.2 | 125 | −5 | 120 | 2.93 | 4,100 | 0.2 | 4,700 | 0.2 | 8,000 | 0.2 |
| Evangelicals | 200 | 0.1 | 2,000 | 0.1 | 73 | 7 | 80 | 3.33 | 2,400 | 0.1 | 2,800 | 0.1 | 6,000 | 0.1 |
| Marginal Protestants | 0 | 0.0 | 100 | 0.0 | 4 | 2 | 6 | 4.62 | 130 | 0.0 | 160 | 0.0 | 400 | 0.0 |
| Non-religious | 0 | 0.0 | 16,000 | 1.0 | 839 | 1,211 | 2,050 | 8.17 | 25,100 | 1.3 | 36,500 | 1.6 | 126,800 | 3.0 |
| Atheists | 0 | .0 | 3,000 | 0.2 | 194 | 416 | 610 | 10.51 | 5,800 | 0.3 | 9,100 | 0.4 | 42,300 | 1.0 |
| Baha'is | 0 | 0.0 | 700 | 0.0 | 28 | 2 | 30 | 3.53 | 850 | 0.0 | 1,000 | 0.0 | 2,000 | 0.0 |
| Country's population | 250,000 | 100.0 | 1,637,000 | 100.0 | 64,500 | 0 | 64,500 | 33.4 | 1,929,000 | 100.0 | 2,282,000 | 100.0 | 4,227,000 | 10.0 |

COLUMNS, ROWS. For meanings and definitions, see Codebook (Part 6). Note that, by definition, total 'Christians' = professing + crypto-Christians, which also = affiliated + nominal Christians. Percentages may not always total exactly, due to rounding.
CENSUSES. 18.XI.1961 (including West Bank and Jerusalem, and including 933 nationals abroad): 93.6% Muslims, 6.4% Christians (109,000). 18.XI.1961 (Transjordan only): 6.9% Christians (63,000). 18.XI.1961 (West Bank and East Jerusalem, termed in this survey Palestine): 5.7% Christians (46,000).

**NOTES ON RELIGIONS**
AFFILIATED CHRISTIANS. In 1970–71 the Greek Catholic archbishop and his staff conducted an exceptionally detailed and careful head count, by name and family, of all Roman Catholics in Transjordan, taking great care to avoid mobile individuals being counted twice in more than one parish. Other similar enquiries have led to the totals above for affiliated Orthodox, Anglicans and Protestants, whose accuracy is therefore much higher than similar totals in most other countries.
ARAB INDIGENOUS. Isolated radio believers in scattered areas, and a couple of small denominations (see Table 2).
ATHEISTS. Communist Party of Jordan (CPJ) (illegal; split over Sino-Soviet dispute): membership (1970) 500.
BAHA'IS. Growth from 2 local spiritual assemblies (1964) to 7 (1973). Strong around Al-Adasiyah, in Jordan valley.
COUNTRY'S POPULATION. The table refers to Jordan's de facto territory and population in 1970–79, i.e. to Transjordan only, excluding West Bank and East Jerusalem (shown in this survey under Palestine) which have been occupied by Israel since 1967, but including the 305,000 Palestinian refugees who entered between 1947 and 5 June 1967 and also the 433,866 refugees who entered after the 1967 war. In 1970, Jordan had a population of 2,317,000 (including West Bank, East Jerusalem, and 818,000 Palestinian refugees) and 2,739,000 in 1975 (UN estimate and projection). West Bank and East Jerusalem in 1970 had a population of 680,000, almost all Palestinian Arabs.
CRYPTO-CHRISTIANS. Secret believers, i.e. Christians affiliated to churches but not known as such to the state nor recorded in censuses as Christians.
DRUZES. An 11th-century Muslim Shia Ismaili schism with Christian and Jewish elements. On border with Syria, and in and around Amman.
MUSLIMS. Mostly Sunnis (of the Shafiite rite), including Circassians (Cherkess), Kurds and Turkmen, also about 1,000 Chechen (Shishan) Shias; also Druzes, here enumerated under Muslims; and 3,000 Alawites. *Hajj pilgrims to Mecca.* (1969) 6,376; (1970) 10,909; (1971) 15,933; (1972) 25,819; (1973) 12,851; (1974) 19,391; (1975) 17,331; (1976) 23,427.

**NON-CHRISTIAN RELIGIONS. Islam** is the religion of 93% of the population. Most Muslims are Sunnis of the Shafiite rite. The Chechens, a small group of Caucasian extraction, are Shias. Most well-established families living in urban and village areas observe orthodox Muslim customs and practices, but the nomadic Bedouin give first place to the *urf,* their pre-Islamic tribal law.
**Baha'i** is practised by a small community at Adasiya in the northern part of the Jordan valley.

**Druze religion** is a schism from the Muslim Ismaili sect, whose principal belief is that Hakim (the divine sixth Fatimid caliph) is alive and in hiding. Druzes are found mostly on the Jordanian border with Syria.

An Arab Muslim by ruins of old Nabatean city of Petra (biblical Sela), dug into rose sandstone cliffs, which became part of Roman province of Arabia in AD 106 when Christians lived there.

**CHRISTIANITY.** Christians are descended from the ancient Palestinian and Transjordanian inhabitants of the Apostolic era, who have become progressively more arabized in the course of time. They are nevertheless proud of their origin and deeply attached to their ethnic and religious traditions. The survival of Christianity in a world which has become Muslim is explained religiously by the extraordinary zeal of the Orthodox clergy and sociologically by existing tribal structures which have conditioned and stabilized the various religious allegiances. It is in fact in the villages among the farmers (*fellahin*) that Christianity is best preserved. Because of their historic antecedents, one finds Christians today in all strata and classes of society, except among the nomads who make up 6% of the population and, with rare exceptions, among those residing in Palestinian refugee camps. The absence of Christians in these strata is due to their social success. Christians tend to be involved increasingly in rapid urbanization and are now found principally in the merchant and office-worker middle classes and the professions. The inauspicious conditions of life in Jordan, especially due to the economic crises created by 3 Palestinian wars, cause Christians to emigrate in large numbers which is thus the principal problem facing the churches.

ORTHODOX CHURCHES. The largest Christian denomination in Jordan is the Greek Orthodox Church, with 36,000 members on the East Bank. The Orthodox theological seminary in Jerusalem has a smaller student body than formerly from Transjordan due to the difficulties of travel between the 2 areas. Parish priests and laity are for the most part Palestinian Arabs; whereas the patriarch, bishops and monks are Greeks. The patriarchate sponsors 34 schools of which 2 offer full secondary training for 4,700 students, one orphanage, and one home for the aged.

The Armenian Apostolic Church has 1,500 members on the East Bank in Amman. Until recently they were much more numerous, but Armenians have suffered more from emigration than any other church. The church operates one parish school and a programme of charitable relief service. The Syrian Orthodox Church is composed of 1,000 East Bank adherents grouped in one parish served by an Arab priest. The church is also responsible for one school. Russian, Coptic and Ethiopian Orthodox, which all have

small congregations on the West Bank in Jerusalem, have no presence east of the Jordan.

CATHOLIC CHURCH. Catholicism is divided into several communities, the 2 largest groups being Latin-rite and Greek (Melkite) Catholics. The reason for the success of Latin-rite Catholicism in Jordan, as contrasted with other countries of the Middle East, is the extraordinary missionary effort of the Franciscans after the medieval Crusades and the restoration of Jerusalem's Latin patriarchate in 1847. Parish clergy are 90% Palestinian Arabs.

Greek Catholics number 15,000 on the East Bank, which is the archbishopric of Petra and Filadelfia. The Catholic Melkite hierarchy is more indigenous and progressive than its Greek Orthodox counterpart.

Armenian Catholics are found on both sides of the Jordan, about 400 living on the East Bank; whereas Maronites and Syrian Catholics are confined to the West Bank. The Armenian patriarch resides in Jerusalem.

OTHER CHURCHES. Anglicans, who entered Jordan in 1860, have a strong work with 3,500 adherents on the East Bank. Arab congregations are found in the northern part of Transjordan as well as in Amman and Zerqa. The Episcopal Church has 3 schools, of which 2 provide a complete secondary programme (1,100 students), one school for the deaf, dumb and blind, and one home for the aged.

The Evangelical Church of the CMA is an autonomous body resulting from the missionary activity of the Christian and Missionary Alliance following World War I. Another denomination which established itself in Jordan during the 1920s was the Assemblies of God, followed by the Church of the Nazarene in 1948. The latter group is found mostly in Salt and Amman where a secondary school has been built. The Assemblies of God have a clinic in Amman. Lutherans are strongest on the West Bank, with only one small congregation of 100 in Amman. East Bank activities, mostly of a welfare and development nature supported by the Lutheran World Federation, include the Schneller School of Agricultural and Manual Training in addition to a secondary school and an orphanage. Two American Baptist denominations exist, one related to the Southern Baptist Convention and the other to Conservative Baptists. The former group has its centre at Er Rumman north of Amman and at Ajlun where a hospital and nursing school have been built. They also have a secondary school. The Seventh-day Adventists have 6 congregations east of the Jordan, 2 being in Amman, and a secondary school. The Free Evangelical Church and German Alliance Mission are also present on the East Bank.

**CHURCH AND STATE.** The constitution of 1952, subsequently amended several times, establishes Islam as the state religion (Article 2), prohibits all religious discrimination (Article 6) and guarantees the free exercise of religion and belief (Article 14).

There is no government ministry or department dealing with religious affairs. To be recognized and to receive state protection, minority religious groups must be registered with the Ministry of the Interior. Official recognition may be of 2 types: either basic recognition, including the right to conduct worship services, teach, open churches and schools (which has been granted to the Armenian Orthodox,

Armenian Catholic, Syrian Orthodox, Anglican and a few other communities); or a more complex recognition granting the right to have communal ecclesiastical courts and to pass sentences for the civil authorities (which has been granted only to the Greek Orthodox and the Greek and Latin Catholic churches). The state sometimes refuses to recognize a community, as it did when Jehovah's Witnesses were declared a prohibited society because of alleged subversive activities.

The state does not provide financial aid to churches except for such minor assistance as occasional gifts to Christian work of national significance, gratuitous offers by municipalities of water and electricity to churches and schools at two-thirds the normal cost, or a minimal charge for the upkeep of cemeteries. Nevertheless, churches and private schools are exempt from land taxes. Christian communities possess real autonomy, and their leaders have authority over their members in the personal domain, including questions of marriage, separation, divorce, inheritance, the training of youth, and the like.

The status of private schools, both Christian and Muslim, was established by Rule 16 of the Ministry of Education (26 May 1964) and additional ministerial instructions issued since then. No school can be opened without the Ministry's permission; this may then have permanent validity, although this is difficult to obtain, or it may be renewable on an annual basis. From a practical standpoint, the Ministry of Education, which is somewhat under the influence of the Muslim Brotherhood, tends more to frustrate than to facilitate the functioning of Christian schools.

In official schools, Muslim religious instruction is obligatory for Muslim students and constitutes a subject for examination. Christian students are exempt, but many frequent the courses in order to improve their knowledge of literary Arabic, of which the Quran is the classic example. The absence of a course in the Christian religion in public schools, such as that used in Syria and which the Jordanian Ministry of Education would like to initiate, may be traced to the small number of Christian students, their division into many churches and the inability of the churches to agree on a common basic syllabus.

With some reservations in view of the power of social pressure, one can say that Christians enjoy a considerable number of advantages in Jordan. They are well represented in government ministries and administrative circles, and in cases of conflict between Christians and Muslims, the Hashemite monarchy has often played a conciliatory role. Paradoxically the Muslim state has occasionally served as arbiter

A fair number of Jordan's postage stamps have carried Christian themes. *Above.* Christ's Passion: Stations of the Cross (1966).

between rival Christian groups. In the conflict over Palestine, the 3 Christian bishops of Transjordan (Greek Orthodox and Greek Catholic archbishops, and the Latin patriarchal vicar) have several times taken clear positions against the policies of Israel. In so doing, they have also on each occasion been careful not to say or do anything to offend the Hashemite monarchy, a policy which is also followed in internal social and political questions. After 1969 the continued support of some Orthodox and Catholic priests for Palestinian resistance organizations placed them in opposition to the government. In 1970, 2 Catholic priests and 2 nuns, who had created workers' wards in the Arab sector of Nazareth in Israel, at Bethlehem and at Brit-Saheur in Jordan, were expelled from the country by the Jordanian authorities for their association with a group of fedayeen Marxists (FDPLP). They had created in the same year, at Hosn, near Irbid, a farm and workshops in aid of refugees. Among the mass of Christian laymen, all political positions are found, from monarchists to revolutionaries. One notes also the presence of many Christians among militant communists, in the Baathist party and in all Palestinian resistance organizations. Many are in fact initiators and leaders of these movements.

**INTERDENOMINATIONAL ORGANIZATIONS.** Although the Ecumenical Youth Committee in Amman, created by SOJEMO in Lebanon, is the only formal interdenominational organization in Jordan, since 1971 informal but regular meetings of leaders of the different Christian communities, in addition to the 3 Catholic and Orthodox bishops, have been held in Amman. The Greek Orthodox, Episcopal, Armenian Apostolic, Syrian Orthodox and Lutheran churches are all members of the Middle East Council of Churches with its seat in Beirut, Lebanon.

**BROADCASTING.** No regular Christian broadcasting is permitted on government radio or TV. However, Christian broadcasts are allowed from time to time, especially during Christian holidays. Also a few Christian programmes have been allowed on TV, but these are very rare. From abroad, Christian programmes in Arabic can be easily heard on the international stations FEBA (Seychelles), RVOG (Ethiopia) until 1977, TWR (Monaco) for 4 hours a week over CBC (Cyprus), and Radio Vatican for 3 hours 30 minutes a week.

**BIBLIOGRAPHY**

'Religion', in *Area handbook for the Hashemite Kingdom of Jordan* (Washington, DC: US Government Printing Office, 1969), p. 131–139.

TABLE 2. ORGANIZED CHURCHES AND DENOMINATIONS IN JORDAN (Transjordan only)

| Official name 1 | Begun 2 | Type 3 | Counc 4 | Congs 5 | Adults 6 | Affiliated 7 | Names, notes, and other statistics (see Codebook) 8 |
|---|---|---|---|---|---|---|---|
| Armenian Apostolic Church: V Amman | | O Arm | Ew.N. | 1 | 800 | 1,500 | *Gregorians*. Under Armenian Patriarchate of Jerusalem. Massive emigration. 1n. |
| Assemblies of God | 1929 | P Pe2 | ZF... | 15 | 280 | 600 | M=AoG(USA). In Amman area. 1972, revival. Classical Pentecostals. 5n,2f,1h. |
| Bible Preaching Church | 1963 | P ind | x.... | | 150 | 300 | M=World-Wide Missions(USA). Evangelicals based on Pasadena, CA (USA). |
| **Catholic Church in Jordan:** | 1099 | R LEr | O.... | 58 | 17,000 | 30,400 | *Al-Kanissa al-Kathoulikiah.* Latins, Melkites, Armenians. 54n,5x,8m,204w,637Yy. |
| P Jerusalem (V Amman)(*Latin*) | 1869 | R Lat | Os | 30 | 8,400 | 15,000 | *Al-Latinn.* Member of CELRA. Priests 90% Palestinian Arabs. 30 4 8 171 400 |
| AD Petra & Filadelfia (Amman) | 1932 | R Mel | Os | 28 | 8,600 | 15,400 | In Melkite Patriarchal Synod. Including 400 Armenians (1n). 24 1 0 33 237 |
| Christian Brethren | | P CBr | x.... | 8 | 400 | 1,000 | Plymouth (Open) Brethren/Baptist type. All indigenous Arab congregations. |
| Church of God (Cleveland) | | P Pe3 | ZF... | | 50 | 100 | M=CoG(Cleveland) (USA). Holiness Pentecostals (3-stage). |
| Church of the Nazarene | 1948 | P Hol | xF... | 14 | 222 | 1,000 | M=CoN(USA). Arabs and some Armenians. 4n,1x,28m,2f,G=5.7%pa,1r,11t(825),W=68%,4Y. |
| Conservative Baptist Mission | 1956 | P Bap | xF... | 4 | 50 | 530 | M=CBFMS(USA). Autonomous Baptist congregations. 1n,4f,4t(330),W=99%,7Y. |
| Epis Ch in Jerus & ME: D Jerusalem | 1860 | A Low | Aw.N. | 17 | 2,300 | 3,500 | HQ Jerusalem. M=CMS. 30% rural. 87% Arab, 13% White. 9n,1x,4f,3r,W=40%,84y. |
| Evangelical Church of the CMA | 1921 | P Hol | xF... | 6 | 300 | 1,000 | M=CMA(USA). Autonomous church, related to similar body in Lebanon et alia. |
| Evangelical Lutheran Church in Jordan | | P Lut | 1..N. | 1 | 50 | 100 | 1,254 members on West Bank, in Israel since 1967 war. Amman only. Arabs. 1r. |
| Free Evangelical Church | | P ind | ..... | 1 | 200 | 500 | In Amman. Small independent mission. 1x. |
| German Alliance Mission | | P int | ..... | 16 | 200 | 430 | Small independent evangelical mission. 6n,5x,W=81%,30Y,25z. |
| **Greek Orth Patr of Jerusalem: D Amman** | 30 | O Ara | Cw.N. | 31 | 20,000 | 36,000 | 99% Palestinian Arabs (laity, priests); bishops, monks are Greeks. 35n,1x,2r. |
| Isolated radio churches | c1950 | I rad | ..... | 100 | 2,000 | 4,100 | Isolated radio believers (students, pupils). R=510(TWR,&c),T=11000(ICI,GMU). |
| Jehovah's Witnesses | 1918 | M Jeh | x.... | 1 | 32 | 100 | *Watch Tower. IBSA.* Active witnessing under way by 1945. No recent baptisms. Banned. |
| Jordan Baptist Convention | c1943 | P Bap | T.... | 5 | 310 | 750 | 1952, M=SBC(USA). Strongest north of Amman. 5 schools. 8n,14f,1H(Ajlun),2h,1r,13Y. |
| Religious Society of Friends | 1869 | P Qua | Q.... | 1 | 40 | 100 | In Near East Yearly Meeting. Quakers. M=FUM(USA). 2 schools. 2f. |
| Seventh-day Adventist Church | | P Adv | x.... | 6 | 200 | 500 | *SDA, Jordan Station.* East Mediterranean Field, Middle East Union. In Amman. 2f,1r. |
| Syrian Orth P Antioch (D Jerusalem) | 30 | O Syr | Dw.N. | 1 | 500 | 1,000 | *Jacobites.* 2,500 West Bank members now in Israel since 1967. 1 school. 1n. |
| Other Protestant denominations | | P | ..... | | 100 | 300 | Total about 3, including: BMM (1970), RPCES. |
| Other Arab indigenous churches | | I | ..... | | 100 | 200 | Including: Essene Church in the Hashemite Kingdom of Jordan (Gnostic). |
| **Total affiliated (mid-1970)** | | | | **301** | **45,284** | **84,010** | **Total denominations (1970) . . . 25.** |
| **Total affiliated (mid-1975)** | | | | **316** | **52,100** | **98,130** | **Total denominations (1975) . . . 26.** |
| **Total affiliated (mid-1980)** | | | | **335** | **59,800** | **112,760** | **Total denominations (1980) . . . 27.** |

NOTES ON TABLE ABOVE
COLUMNS: for meanings and CODES (cols. 1, 3, 4, 8), see Codebook (Part 6). Column 1: **Boldface type** = church with over 10% of country's affiliated Christians.
SOURCES AND DATES OF STATISTICS. The table refers to the de facto 1973 situation in Jordan, with 5 East Bank provinces (Amman, Balqa, Irbid, Kerak, Ma'an) but excluding the 3 West Bank provinces (Jerusalem, Nablus, Hebron) under Israeli occupation since 1967.
UNITING CHURCHES. Negotiations for organic union were under way in 1974 between: Episcopal Ch, Ev Lutheran Ch in Jordan.

PEOPLES (ethnolinguistic). Christians: 97.1% Arab (50.7% Palestinian, 45.2% Jordanian, 1.2% Syrian), 2.4% Armenian, 0.4% Greek, European.

COUNTRY-WIDE TOTALS
EVANGELIZATION (see Part 5). 1900: 16%. 1970: 53%. 1980: 61%. *Mass evangelism.* 1969, Youth for Christ Teen Team in Amman. *Radiophonic evangelism.* TWR, RSB, et alia. Bible correspondence courses: about 11,000 enrolments (ICI, GMU, RSB, et alia).
FOREIGN MISSIONARIES AND PERSONNEL (nationals serving abroad) (1973). Total 20 in Egypt, Kuwait, Lebanon, Palestine and Syria: about 15 Roman Catholics, 2 Anglicans, 2 Protestants, 1 Orthodox.
FOREIGN MISSIONARIES AND PERSONNEL (aliens from abroad) (1973). Total 129. *From Western world.* 109: 54 Protestants (40 in 14 USA societies, 14 in 2 WGermany societies), about 50 Roman Catholics, 4 Anglicans in 1 UK society, about 1 Orthodox. *From Third World.* About 20 Roman Catholics from India, Palestine et alia.
INSTITUTIONS (church-operated) (1973). Total 27, including 12 higher schools, 12 medical centres (4 hospitals).
PERIODICALS. About 8 titles.
PERSONNEL. About 449 (320 national, 129 foreign).
SCRIPTURE DISTRIBUTION (1975). Annual totals: 2,064 Bibles (48% free, 52% subsidized), 2,014 NTs (95% subsidized, 5% commercial), 10,893 UBS portions, 29,820 UBS selections. *Translations completed.* Portion: 2 languages since 1645.
SERVICE AGENCIES. About 8, including LWR, OM, YWCA.

ADDITIONAL DATA ON CHURCHES
CATHOLIC CHURCH IN JORDAN. *Annual baptisms.* (1972) 97.4% infant, 2.6% adult. *Priests.* Melkite: 21 secular (15 married, 6 unmarried), 3 religious. Latin: 32 secular, 2 OFM(Custody). *Brothers.* Latin are FSC. *Sisters.* 126 Rosary Sisters under patriarchate, 30 Sisters of Nigrizia (in 2 hospitals), 3 Irish, 7 Missionaries of Charity (Calcutta), 5 Missionary Franciscans of Mary (refugee work). *Melkite religious congregations.* Priests: Basilian Salvatorians. Sisters: Ladies of Nazareth, 26 Basilian Salvatorians of Our Lady of the Annunciation, Little Sisters of Jesus. Also 6 ordained Melkite lay women (Auxiliaires Féminines Internationales, AFI). *Latin religious orders and congregations.* Priests: OFM. Brothers: FSC. Sisters: 126 Rosary Sisters (Palestinians), 30 Pie Madri della Nigrizia (Italians).
*Catholic organizations.* The Latin patriarchate is part of the Latin Episcopal Conference of the Arab Regions (CELRA) with its seat in Jerusalem. The Greek patriarchate is attached to the Greek Melkite Catholic patriarchal synod in Syria.
The Holy See has no diplomatic relations with Jordan. It is represented to the Catholic hierarchy by the Apostolic Delegation of Jerusalem and Palestine, with its headquarters in East Jerusalem.
In 1971 Latin Catholics had 40 schools, of which 5 provided secondary education for 10,070 students; 2 specialized secondary schools not dependent on the patriarchate, one of 850 students run by OFM and the other 1,150 students under FSC; and 2 hospitals. Likewise, Greek Catholics sponsored 19 schools, 3 with a complete secondary programme (4,600 students), hospital and 3 dispensaries. Armenian Catholics had one parish school.
Jordan Caritas, which has been historically linked to the Latin church, has now become independent and attempts to serve the whole country in co-operation with all confessions. Its activities include 3 nutritional centres for children (20,000 meals each month) and support for 10 other centres not under Caritas' own supervision; 2 Mother and Infant centres providing food and clothing for 5,000 infants; summer camps for girls and boys; 30 relief centres attached to private schools; 2 dispensaries and 2 clinics at Amman treating 3,000 patients each month; 11 sewing centres; a scholarship programme; and agricultural and development projects at Kerak in the south.

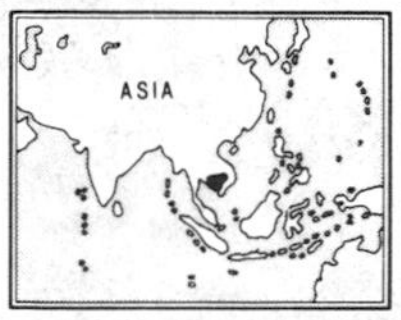


# KAMPUCHEA

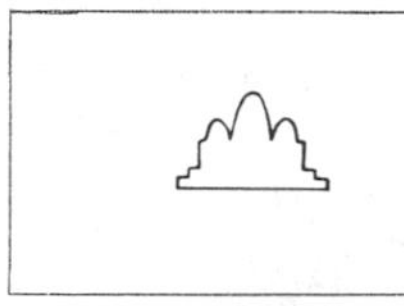

## SECULAR DATA

**STATE. Official name:** Democratic Kampuchea. Earlier names: Khmer Republic (Sathearnak Roath Khmer); Cambodia.
**Flag** (shown above right): Red field with Angkor Wat pagoda in yellow.
**Area:** 181,035 sq.km. (69,898 sq.miles). Agricultural land: 20.0%.
**Government:** One-party Communist state, since 1975 (1863 French protectorate, 1947 constitutional monarchy, 1953 Independence, 1970 Khmer Republic).
**Legislature:** People's Representative Assembly, 250 members.
**Official language:** Khmer.
**Capital:** Phnom Penh 20,000 (1976); decline from 600,000 in 1968 and 2.5 million in 1974).
**Armed forces** (1976): Total 80,000 regular army (45 combat aircraft). (1980) 200,000 Viet Nam troops.

**DEMOGRAPHY. Population:** 5,728,771 (census of 17.IV.1962. For 1970–2000 (UN), see last row of Table 1). Population density (1975): 45/sq.km. (116/sq.mile). Under 15 years: 46%. Growth rate (1975–80): 2.97% per year (births 4.65%, deaths −1.68%). Life expectancy (1975–80): 48.4 years. Household size: 5.1 persons.
**Major languages:** Khmer, French, Chinese, Vietnamese, Cham, Malay, Brao, Kui, Mnong, Pear, and numerous others.
**Urban dwellers** (1970): 12.2%. Urban growth rate (1950–70): 4.4% per year. From 1975 urbanization has been forcibly reversed and even nullified.
**Labour force:** 42%.
**Refugees** (1977): From abroad, none. Internally displaced: 2,500,000 forcibly moved from urban to rural areas. Exiles abroad: 24,926 Cambodians (18,600 in Thailand, 6,326 in USA).
**Tourists** (1973): 16,505.

**ETHNOLINGUISTIC GROUPS:** 82.1% Khmer, 7.5% Chinese (450,000) (5.5% Teochew, 2.0% Cantonese, Hokkien, Hakka), 6.2% Vietnamese, 2.4% Cham & Cham-Malay, 0.7% Kui, 0.6% Lao, 0.4% Mnong & Brao, 0.1% French (5,000), Stieng, Jarai, Tai, Malay, South Indian, USA, British, Eurasian.

**MONEY** (1977). **Monetary unit:** riel (= 100 sen); US$1 = CRls 970.
**National income per person:** US$100. Average annual family income: US$510.
**Inflation:** (1970–74) 73.7% per year, (1975) 158% per year (consumer price index 3,233).
**Cost of living in capital** (1976): Daily cost of living: US$25.

**HEALTH.** Hospitals: 94 (7,500 beds). Doctors: 438. Lepers: 34,400 (4.2 per 1,000). Blind: 40,000. Psychotics: 110,000. Criminals (1972): 4,000.

**EDUCATION.** Adult literacy: (1958) 31%, (1962) 36%, (1975) 41%. Education rate: 48%. Schools: 1,534 (closed 1976; decline from 5,699 primary and 95 secondary in 1970). Universities: 1.

**LITERATURE.** Annual new book titles (1972): 29. Newspapers: 16 dailies, 15 non-daily.

**COMMUNICATION** (per 1,000 people). Phones: 1. Radios: 154. TV sets: 7. Daily newspaper circulation: 10 copies.

TABLE 1. RELIGIOUS ADHERENTS IN KAMPUCHEA (Cambodia)

| Year | 1900 | | mid-1970 | | Annual change, 1970–1980 | | | | mid-1975 | | mid-1980 | | 2000 | |
|---|---|---|---|---|---|---|---|---|---|---|---|---|---|---|
| Name | Adherents | % | Adherents | % | Natural | Conversion | Total | Rate | Adherents | % | Adherents | % | Adherents | % |
| Buddhists | 2,137,590 | 85.5 | 6,161,131 | 87.3 | 217,516 | −1,939 | 215,577 | 3.00 | 7,187,200 | 88.6 | 8,316,900 | 88.4 | 13,763,000 | 87.0 |
| Tribal religionists | 175,000 | 7.0 | 250,000 | 3.5 | 7,751 | −4,521 | 3,230 | 1.21 | 267,600 | 3.3 | 282,300 | 3.0 | 158,000 | 1.0 |
| Muslims | 50,000 | 2.0 | 170,000 | 2.4 | 5,636 | −56 | 5,580 | 2.87 | 194,600 | 2.4 | 225,800 | 2.4 | 364,000 | 2.3 |
| Non-religious | 100 | 0.0 | 150,000 | 2.1 | 5,793 | 9,207 | 15,000 | 7.50 | 200,000 | 2.5 | 300,000 | 3.2 | 949,000 | 6.0 |
| Chinese folk-religionists | 100,000 | 4.0 | 141,000 | 2.0 | 3,760 | −6,560 | −2,800 | −2.16 | 129,800 | 1.6 | 113,000 | 1.2 | 79,000 | 0.5 |
| New-Religionists | 0 | 0.0 | 100,000 | 1.4 | −7,500 | −500 | −8,000 | −40.00 | 20,000 | 0.2 | 20,000 | 0.2 | 30,000 | 0.2 |
| Christians | 37,310 | 1.5 | 35,269 | 0.5 | 105 | 1,968 | 2,073 | 4.38 | 47,300 | 0.6 | 56,000 | 0.6 | 100,000 | 0.6 |
| crypto-Christians | 7,310 | 0.3 | 12,269 | 0.2 | 315 | 1,958 | 2,273 | 13.14 | 17,300 | 0.2 | 35,000 | 0.4 | 67,000 | 0.4 |
| professing | 30,000 | 1.2 | 23,000 | 0.3 | −210 | 10 | −200 | −0.67 | 30,000 | 0.4 | 21,000 | 0.2 | 33,000 | 0.2 |
| Roman Catholics | 30,000 | 1.2 | 16,000 | 0.2 | −460 | −40 | −500 | −5.00 | 10,000 | 0.1 | 11,000 | 0.1 | 13,000 | 0.1 |
| Protestants | 0 | 0.0 | 7,000 | 0.1 | 250 | 50 | 300 | 1.50 | 20,000 | 0.2 | 10,000 | 0.1 | 20,000 | 0.1 |
| affiliated | 37,310 | 1.5 | 35,269 | 0.5 | 105 | 1,968 | 2,073 | 4.38 | 47,300 | 0.6 | 56,000 | 0.6 | 100,000 | 0.6 |
| total practising | 33,580 | 90 | 24,690 | 70 | 74 | 1,377 | 1,451 | 4.38 | 33,110 | 70 | 39,200 | 70 | 80,000 | 80 |
| non-practising | 3,730 | 10 | 10,580 | 30 | 31 | 591 | 622 | 4.38 | 14,190 | 30 | 16,800 | 30 | 20,000 | 20 |
| Roman Catholics | 37,310 | 1.5 | 20,069 | 0.3 | −357 | −50 | −407 | −2.91 | 14,000 | 0.2 | 16,000 | 0.2 | 20,000 | 0.1 |
| Protestants | 0 | 0.0 | 12,800 | 0.2 | 400 | 1,820 | 2,220 | 7.40 | 30,000 | 0.4 | 35,000 | 0.4 | 65,000 | 0.4 |
| Evangelicals | 0 | 0.0 | 12,000 | 0.2 | 387 | 1,813 | 2,200 | 7.59 | 29,000 | 0.3 | 34,000 | 0.4 | 63,000 | 0.4 |
| Asian indigenous | 0 | 0.0 | 2,200 | 0.0 | 87 | 193 | 280 | 9.33 | 3,000 | 0.0 | 5,000 | 0.1 | 15,000 | 0.1 |
| Anglicans | 0 | 0.0 | 200 | 0.0 | −25 | 5 | −20 | −6.67 | 300 | 0.0 | 0 | 0.0 | 0 | 0.0 |
| Atheists | 0 | 0.0 | 30,000 | 0.4 | 1,014 | 1,986 | 3,000 | 8.57 | 35,000 | 0.4 | 60,000 | 0.6 | 316,000 | 2.0 |
| Baha'is | 0 | 0.0 | 22,600 | 0.3 | 825 | 415 | 1,240 | 4.35 | 28,500 | 0.4 | 35,000 | 0.4 | 60,000 | 0.4 |
| Country's population | 2,500,000 | 100.0 | 7,060,000 | 100.0 | 234,900 | 0 | 234,900 | 2.90 | 8,110,000 | 100.0 | 9,409,000 | 100.0 | 15,819,000 | 100.0 |

COLUMNS, ROWS. For meanings and definitions, see Codebook (Part 6). Note that, by definition, total 'Christians' = professing + crypto-Christians, which also = affiliated + nominal Christians. Percentages may not always total exactly, due to rounding.

### NOTES ON RELIGIONS

AFFILIATED PROTESTANTS. During 1970–74 there were on average 100 professions of faith each week (5,000 a year) due to a series of mass evangelistic campaigns and house meetings. As a result, there was a mass influx into the churches during 1970–75, including large numbers of young people, although after the Communist takeover large numbers were killed, imprisoned or forced underground. The figures 'Annual change' above incorporate emigration in the column 'Natural', and are averaged over the decade 1970–80.
ASIAN INDIGENOUS. Chinese and Cambodian indigenous congregations and groups, mostly isolated radio believers (see Table 2).
ATHEISTS. People's Party (Pracheachon) (forced underground in 1962): membership about 1,000; also Cambodian People's Revolutionary Party (PRP) and Khmer Rouge, membership (1973) 30,000 insurgents (1975: 50,000); in power after mid-1975 victory.
BAHA'IS. Very rapid growth from 1 local spiritual assembly (1964) to 151 (1973), with 425 other isolated centres or groups. Many Vietnamese before 1974.
BUDDHISTS. Theravada (Hinayana, Little Vehicle), with 2 main religious orders (1970): the aristocratic Thommayutt (Order of the Law) with 104 monasteries and 2,053 monks, and Mohanikay (Great Order) with 2,722 monasteries and 66,092 monks. Mainly Khmers with over 200,000 Chinese, also Vietnamese, Lao and others. From 1970–71, communists destroyed 208 Buddhist temples and killed 40 monks; losses up to 1979 are far higher.
CHRISTIANS. The column 'Natural' includes mass emigration and deportations, especially of Catholics, averaged over the decade 1970–80.
COUNTRY'S POPULATION. In the year after mid-1975, 800,000 people are estimated to have been killed by the new regime, many in the forced reduction of the population of Phnom Penh from 2.5 million to 20,000. In 1977, there were 10,000 Cambodian refugees in Thailand. By 1978, 2.5 million deaths had taken place through starvation, disease and execution.
CRYPTO-CHRISTIANS. Christians affiliated to churches but unknown as such to state or society.
MUSLIMS. Sunnis (of the Shafiite rite); mainly among the Cham-Malays (known as Khmer Islam) along the Mekong river.
NEW-RELIGIONISTS. Vietnamese followers of the Cao Daist syncretistic religion, mainly in Phnom Penh, Siem Reap and on the shores of the Tonlé Sap lake.
NON-RELIGIOUS. In the year 1900, French and other expatriates; by 1970, mostly Chinese.
ROMAN CATHOLICS. In the year 1900, 36,107 baptized Catholics and 1,200 catechumens. During the year 1970, Catholics fell from 60,000 to 20,000 by the expulsion or deaths in war of 40,000 Vietnamese Catholics, and continued to decline by 1,200 a year over the following 3 or 4 years.
TRIBAL RELIGIONISTS. Animists among the Montagnard tribes (Khmer-Loeu, i.e. Upland Khmer) of the northeast adjoining the Laos border, including the Mnong, Brao, Stieng and Kui.

### NON-CHRISTIAN RELIGIONS.

Theravada Buddhism (or Hinayana) has been the predominant religion of Cambodia since the 14th century. There are 2 main religious orders whose doctrine and rules are similar: the Thommayutt (Order of the Law) which is by nature aristocratic, with 104 monasteries and 2,053 monks; and the Mohanikay (Great Order), having wider support, with 2,722 monasteries and 66,092 monks. Buddhism has always played an important social role, with the clergy exercising an intermediary function between government and people. The majority of Cambodian boys at age 12 serve a period of several weeks in a monastery in order to learn Buddhism's main precepts, and when adult often return for retreats. Annexed to the monasteries is a vast primary school network, in addition to the Buddhist lyceum and university in Phnom Penh. A hereditary caste of Brahmans, called Bakou, a witness to the survival of Brahmanic influence in Buddhism, exercised an important function among officials at the royal palace of former regimes.

**Traditional tribal religion** continues to exist among the Montagnard tribes (Khmer-Loeu) of the northeast near the border with Laos, including the Mnong, Brao, Stieng and Kui.

**Islam** was first introduced by Malays in 1550. Cambodian Muslims are Sunnis of the Shafiite rite. Although strongest among the Cham-Malays who are descended from the people of the ancient kingdom of Champa and who continue to perform its rites in Malay, Islam is fully integrated in Khmer society. It is strongest along the banks of the Mekong river and its affluents, in the province of Kompong-Cham and the region of Phnom Penh, as well as at Battambang and Kampot. In addition to an active Muslim religious life, there are numerous Quranic schools.

**Cao Dai,** a syncretistic new religion composed of Buddhist, Christian and animistic elements, existed among the Vietnamese, especially at Phnom Penh, Siem Reap and along the banks of Lake Tonlé Sap, until April 1970 when most were deported.

### CHRISTIANITY.

Evangelization began with the arrival of Jesuits and Dominicans in 1555, but permanent stations were not opened until the 17th century. By 1842 there were only 4 churches and 222 Catholics. The apostolic prefecture of Cambodia (Phnom Penh) was erected in 1850, and the territory was elevated to the rank of vicariate in 1924. Protestants began work in the country only after World War I.

CATHOLIC CHURCH. The events of 1970 and 1975 profoundly changed the situation of the Catholic Church in Cambodia. In 1969 the church reported 62,000 baptized members, of which 55,000 (88%) were Vietnamese, 3,000 Khmers, 2,000 Chinese and 2,000 Europeans. The clergy were predominantly

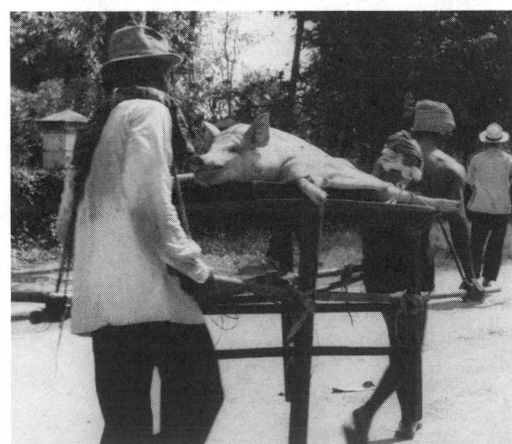

**Buddhists.** (*Left*). Pilgrims visit ruins of Angkor Wat temple complex ('City of Water', dating from AD 1100) symbolizing universe as understood in Hindu cosmology. By 1431, Shiva and Vishnu cults had been replaced by Mahayana Buddhism.
**Chinese folk-religionists.** (*Above*). Chinese funeral in Cambodia. The cortege includes varieties of food (here, a pig) to sustain the departed on his voyage into eternity.

French (58) and Vietnamese (16), with only 5 Khmer priests out of 80, one of whom was resident in Paris. There was also one Chinese priest. The 4 Khmer priests resident in the country included a bishop (the Franco-Khmer apostolic prefect of Battambang), an OSB and 2 secular priests. Although the first ordination of a Vietnamese priest in Cambodia took place in 1888, the first Khmer was not ordained until 1957. Between 1888 and 1970, 163 local priests were ordained, 156 being Vietnamese, 5 Khmers and 2 Chinese. Of those enrolled in the major seminary of Phnom Penh in 1970, 6 were Vietnamese, 2 Laotians and one Khmer. There were also 2 training centres for catechists, one for Khmers and the other for Vietnamese. Other religious personnel included 27 Vietnamese and 2 Khmer brothers and 266 sisters (183 Europeans, 75 Vietnamese and 8 Khmers). In addition the church maintained 50 primary and 4 secondary schools, 2 hospitals, a dispensary, 2 day nurseries, an orphanage, a home for the destitute, a training centre for girls, a hostel for students, a co-operative and a community centre.

The Catholic Church was primarily the church of the Vietnamese and Europeans and was little integrated into Khmer society. The languages commonly in use in the church were French and Vietnamese, only 14 priests being capable of preaching in Khmer. Catholic Vietnamese with Khmer citizenship were little integrated into Cambodian society and tended to form so-called Catholic villages along the Mekong river and its tributaries. In addition the majority of Khmer Catholics were descendants of mixed Khmer-Portuguese and Khmer-Spanish people whose origins go back to the 17th century. Only a few Catholics were Khmers in the full sense of the term. The episcopate was slow in expressing concern about the situation, its joint pastoral letter of 3 September 1969 being the first serious attempt to call for the integration of the church into Khmer society. This letter was followed by a conference on missionary pastoralia conducted by the French sociologist canon Boulard, which proved to be the most important event in the life of the Cambodian Catholic church during this period.

Given Catholicism's particularly vulnerable situation in Cambodia, the anti-Vietnamese campaign which followed the coup d'etat of March 1970 by the Lon Nol faction proved to be a disaster for the church. In April 1970 thousands of resident Vietnamese were massacred and Catholic villages were among the first attacked. About 40,000 Catholics were killed while others escaped to Viet Nam. Missionaries were also involved; 5 were killed and a sixth disappeared in the area held by the Communist revolutionaries. Several churches in Phnom Penh were set on fire, and the new regime closed all private schools, which were for the most part Catholic and frequented by Vietnamese. Many MEP missionaries followed their members into South Viet Nam, to which also local Vietnamese feminine congregations fled en masse. Social and medical institutions and programmes were severely restricted or completely abandoned although some were begun again later. Only the infirmary of the Chruy Changvar community centre continued to function normally. The major seminary of Phnom Penh was also closed, due to a lack of Khmer students, and was turned into a transit centre for Vietnamese refugees. At the end of 1970 there remained in Cambodia only about 20,000 Catholics, 29 priests (12 Vietnamese and 4 Khmers, the rest being missionaries), 3 brothers and 54 sisters. Three years later official statistics showed a decline to 16,835 Catholics, with 29 priests, 3 brothers and 68 sisters. The only priests left in the prefecture of Kompong Cham was the apostolic vicar, a Frenchman, while 2 (a Khmer, the apostolic vicar; and a French missionary) remained in the prefecture of Battambang. The figure of 16,835 also included Catholics living in liberated zones who had no contact with the rest of the church, as well as Khmers in the republican zone who chose after 1970 to keep their distance from a religion which they considered too Vietnamese. In 1974 another Khmer was ordained priest; and on 15 April 1975 (2 days before the fall of the capital), a Khmer priest was consecrated bishop of the vicariate of Phnom Penh.

On 17 April 1975, when Phnom Penh fell, the situation of the Catholic Church was as follows: (1) the prefecture of Kompong Cham had no religious personnel, although a few hundred Catholics remained; (2) the prefecture of Battambang had a Khmer bishop, a French OSB priest, a Khmer and 4 Vietnamese sisters and about 2,000 Vietnamese and Khmer Catholics; and (3) the vicariate of Phnom Penh had one Khmer and 2 French bishops, 3 Khmer and 10 French priests, 2 Khmer OSB brothers and 5 Khmer and 4 French sisters. Shortly after taking the city, the revolutionaries expelled all Europeans including religious personnel, while Khmer and Vietnamese were forced out of the cities into the countryside. Khmer bishops and priests were generally involved in leading Catholic groups during the exodus. In the whole of Cambodia, including zones held for a long time by the Communists, the Catholic

**Eglise Evangélique Khmère.** Some of 4,681 professions of faith at April and November 1972 mass evangelistic rallies in Phnom Penh. Many were subsequently murdered.

population at the end of May 1975 was estimated to be not more than 15,000, widely-dispersed.

PROTESTANT CHURCHES. Protestant work in Cambodia has also suffered from the political events of the last decade. The major Protestant denomination in the country is the Eglise Evangélique Khmère which was created through the work of the Christian and Missionary Alliance. Since its origins in 1922, the CMA has been strongest in the Phnom Penh area, while also gradually spreading its influence to other parts of the country. In addition to its work among Cambodians, Chinese and Vietnamese, the church has opened work among the Mnong Biet and Kuoy (Kui) tribes of northeastern Cambodia. By 1964 it had established 13 churches in 9 of the 17 provinces. In 1961 it invited the Far Eastern Gospel Crusade to pioneer work in eastern Cambodia; but due to anti-American feeling all missionaries except for one French couple were withdrawn in 1965. Because of a broader base among Cambodians, rather than Vietnamese, Protestants were not adversely affected by the events of 1970 and registered phenomenal membership growth during the early part of the decade. Indeed, American CMA missionaries were allowed to return in 1970 and during 1970–75 they were extensively involved in relief work as well as evangelistic activities. As with the Catholics, all foreign Protestant religious personnel were evacuated again in 1975. Prior to 1975, Cambodia's small Seventh-day Adventist Church was served by an Indonesian missionary.

**CHURCH AND STATE.** The royal constitution of May 1947, which was further modified in January 1956, remained in effect until the coup d'etat of 18 March 1970. It proclaimed Buddhism the state religion and assured freedom of religion for all (Article 8). The Ministry of Religion (Krasuong Thommaka) dealt with all matters relating to religious observance, and leaders of the 2 Buddhist orders were nominated by the king. Higher clergy also participated in certain government activities. Buddhist monks were exempt from fiscal responsibilities and enjoyed other juridical privileges. The Ministry of Religion, working in close co-operation with the heads of the Buddhist orders, prepared legislation to cover religious matters and saw to its implementation. It organized and controlled Buddhist schools

and provided lay diplomas for them. The king also nominated the supreme head of the Islamic community, and the Ministry of Religion controlled the appointment of mosque leaders (Hakem). Other religions were considered to be private affairs. The opening of new worship centres required the authorization (Prakas) of the Ministry of Religion, and any other acts of worship, beyond those of Catholics and Protestants, required the sanction of the king.

The republican government of Lon Nol came to power in March 1970 and in its constitution of 30 April 1972 proclaimed Buddhism as the state religion. The government attempted to gain the support of Buddhist leaders and clergy through the Khmer Buddhist Congress, but most monks remained faithful to prince Sihanouk. During this period, Sihanouk's revolutionary government-in-exile maintained a Ministry of Religion and continued to affirm its recognition of Buddhism as the state religion.

After the victory of the Communist forces on 17 April 1975, an important meeting was held in Phnom Penh (April 25–27) to define the major political policies of the new government. Among the 311 delegates were Buddhist monks representing the Buddhist clergy. The revolutionary government maintains a Ministry of Religious and Social Affairs, and the new authorities affirmed their desire to respect freedom of conscience and religion while insisting on the social role that the religions should play in the development of the country. This was also emphasized in the zones held by revolutionaries before the fall of Phnom Penh, where monks were forbidden to beg and instead were required to work. However, in practice, churches and religions have all suffered together in the reign of terror that followed in the next year, when 800,000 persons were killed across the country.

**BROADCASTING.** Christian programmes can only be heard over foreign international stations. FEBC (Manila), which beams programmes in English, French, Vietnamese, Cambodian, Thai, Lao, Burmese, Chinese and tribal languages, also runs correspondence courses. Until 1975 it had a studio at Phnom Penh operated by the Christian and Missionary Alliance, preparing programmes in Cambodian. Radio Veritas, in Manila, is a Catholic station broadcasting in Thai. For Catholics, prior to 1975 the Khmer Republic was a member of UNDA.

**BIBLIOGRAPHY**
'Cambodia: Buddha's burden', R. Norton, *Far Eastern economic review* (Hong Kong), May 1971.
'Church and State in Cambodia', J. C. Haughley, *America* (New York), October 1971.
*1972 Mission directory of Thailand, Cambodia and Laos.* Ed B. Bray. Bangkok: Newsasia, 1972.

TABLE 2. ORGANIZED CHURCHES AND DENOMINATIONS IN KAMPUCHEA (Cambodia)

| Official name 1 | Begun 2 | Type 3 | Counc 4 | Congs 5 | Adults 6 | Affiliated 7 | Names, notes, and other statistics (see Codebook) 8 |
|---|---|---|---|---|---|---|---|
| Congrégations Chinoises indépendantes | | I Hol | ••••• | 2 | 100 | 200 | Independent congregations of Chinese, of CMA origin. Holiness doctrines. |
| Eglise Adventiste du Septième Jour | c1937 | P Adv | x•••• | 1 | 100 | 200 | *SDA. Seventh-day Adventists*, in Vietnam Mission, Southeast Asia Union Mission. 8f. |
| Eglise Anglicane (D Singapore) | | A Cen | aweA. | 2 | 150 | 200 | *Anglican Church. Trinity Congregation*, Phnom Penh. 60% USA, 40% British. W=27%. |
| **Eglise Catholique au Cambodge:** | 1555 | R Lat | P.F.P | 36 | 10,800 | 20,069 | *Catholic Ch.* Decline from 62,000 in 1969. C=2+0+1. 4n,24x,3m,60w,P=42%,653Yy. |
| VA Phnum-Pénh (Phnom Penh) | 1850 | R Lat | Pmep | 8 | 3,500 | 6,569 | Capital. 50% Vietnamese, 30% Europeans, 15% Chinese. 2 19 3 40 25 121 |
| PA Batdambang (Battambang) | 1968 | R Lat | Ps | 8 | 2,400 | 4,500 | Thailand border; forest. 70% Vietnamese, 20% Khmer. 1 2 0 13 51 332 |
| PA Kampóng Cham (Kompong C) | 1968 | R Lat | Pmep | 20 | 4,900 | 9,000 | Viet-Nam border; forest. 90% Vietnamese. 1 3 0 7 50 200 |
| **Eglise Evangélique Khmere** | 1922 | P Hol | xF... | 50 | 3,000 | 10,000 | *Khmer Ev Ch.* M=ACM(France),CMA(USA). Tenfold expansion, 1971–73. 13n,9f,1p,1s. |
| Eglises Evangéliques | 1961 | P int | xM... | 25 | 1,000 | 2,000 | Begun by M=Far Eastern Gospel Crusade; left 1965. 1971, M=OMF, rapid growth. |
| Eglises radiophoniques isolées | 1952 | I rad | ••••• | 500 | 1,000 | 2,000 | Isolated radio believers, mostly youths, across nation. R=50(FEBC),S=2000(CMA). |
| Other Protestant denominations | | P | ••••• | | 300 | 600 | Small French and USA Pentecostal missions. |
| **Total affiliated (mid-1970)** | | | | **176** | **16,450** | **35,269** | **Total denominations (1970) . . . 9.** |
| **Total affiliated (mid-1975)** | | | | **250** | **22,100** | **47,300** | **Total denominations (1975) . . . 9.** |
| **Total affiliated (mid-1980)** | | | | **150** | **26,100** | **56,000** | **Total denominations (1980) . . . 8.** |

NOTES ON TABLE ABOVE
COLUMNS: for meanings and CODES (cols. 1, 3, 4, 8), see Codebook (Part 6). Column 1: **Boldface type** = church with over 10% of country's affiliated Christians.
NATIONAL COUNCILS (Column 4, 5th letter).
P = Conférence Episcopale du Laos et Cambodge (CELAC)/ Sapha (Sangharat) Lao-Kmen (Episcopal Conference of Laos & Cambodia).

PEOPLES (ethnolinguistic). Christians (end of 1970): about 52% Vietnamese, 22% Chinese, 18% Khmer, 6% European (French), 0.6% South Indian, 0.5% USA, 0.3% British, Mnong, Kui, Eurasian.

COUNTRY-WIDE TOTALS
EVANGELIZATION (see Part 5). 1900: 7%. 1970: 30%. 1980: 32%. *Mass evangelism.* April and November 1972, Khmer Ev Ch/CMA/World Vision campaigns in Phnom Penh (4,681 professions of faith). *Radiophonic evangelism.* FEBC (in 1976, 3 broadcast hours per day), CMA/BCC (2,000 enrolled in 1973).
FOREIGN MISSIONARIES AND PERSONNEL (aliens from abroad) (1973). Total 77. *From Western world.* 55: 40 Roman Catholics, 15 Protestants (9 in 3 USA societies, 6 others). *From Third World.* 22: about 15 Roman Catholics from South Viet Nam (decline from 37 Vietnamese in 1970), about 4 Protestants, 3 indigenous from Hong Kong.
INSTITUTIONS (church-operated) (1973). Total 7, including 5 medical centres.
PERIODICALS. 3 titles.
PERSONNEL. About 218 (141 national, 77 foreign) in 1973.
SCRIPTURE DISTRIBUTION (1975). Annual totals: 5,464 Bibles (subsidized), 14,920 NTs (subsidized), 216,797 UBS portions, 180,302 UBS selections. *Translations completed.* In Khmer: portion 1899, NT 1929, Bible 1954.
SERVICE AGENCIES. About 4, including CELAC, WVI.

ADDITIONAL DATA ON CHURCHES
EGLISE CATHOLIQUE AU CAMBODGE. The statistics describe the situation at shortly after mid-1970 and towards the close of the year. During this year, the number of Catholics fell from 62,000 (55,000 Vietnamese (88%), 3,000 Khmer (5%), 2,000 Chinese (3.5%), 2,000 Europeans (3.5%)) to 20,000 due to the expulsion from the country or deaths in war of 40,000 Vietnamese Catholics, and the defection of many Khmer Catholics who abandoned Catholicism as being a purely Vietnamese religion. *Catholics* (close of 1970). 15,000 Vietnamese, 2,000 Chinese, 2,000 Europeans, South Indians, and about 1,000 Khmer. *Catechumens.* (1959) 314, (1961) 442, (1963) 259. *Annual baptisms.* (1972) 92.0% infant, 8.0% adult. *Priests.* The first Khmer was ordained priest in 1957. In 1970 there were 4 ordained nationals (Khmer) including one OSB, 2 secular, one bishop (Battambang); with a fifth serving in Paris, France. Expatriate priests: 3 Vietnamese, 21 French. The first ordination of a Vietnamese priest in Cambodia was in 1888. From 1888 to 1970, 163 local priests were ordained: 156 Vietnamese, 5 Khmer, 2 Chinese. *Brothers.* 2 Khmer OSB brothers. *Sisters.* Including 9 Khmer, 30 Vietnamese, 4 Chinese, 11 French. All belong to Province de Portieux except 7 Vietnamese of Filles de Marie de Russey Kéo. *Seminarians.* There being none in 1970, the major seminary at Phnom Penh was closed. *Catechists.* Total (1969) 82, with one Khmer training school; the school for Vietnamese was closed in 1970. *Foreign religious orders and congregations.* **Priests: MEP, OSB. Sisters: Providence de Portieux.**
*Catholic organizations.* The Episcopal Conference of Laos-Cambodia (Conférence Episcopale du Laos-Cambodge, CELAC) has its headquarters in Vientiane, Laos and is a member of FABC in Hong Kong. There are no national presbyteral or pastoral councils, no associations of religous personnel and no Catholic lay organizations.
The Holy See has had no diplomatic relations with Cambodia either before or after 1975. It is represented to the Catholic hierarchy by an apostolic delegate based in Saigon, Viet Nam.

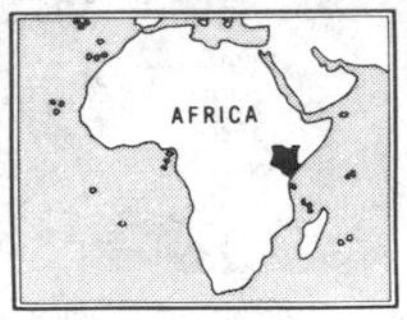


# KENYA

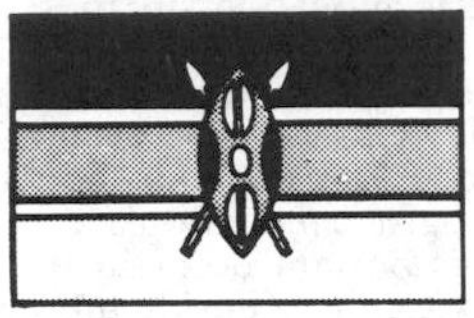

## SECULAR DATA

**STATE. Official name:** The Republic of Kenya (Jamhuri ya Kenya). Adjective of nationality: Kenyan.
**Flag** (shown above right): Black, red, and green bands separated by white stripes; red, black, and white shield over crossed white spears in centre.
**Area:** 582,645 sq.km. (224,961 sq.miles). Agricultural land: 9.5%.
**Government:** One-party republic, since 1969 (1887 British possession, 1920 British crown colony with coastal protectorate, 1963 Independence (Uhuru) as parliamentary republic).
**Legislature:** National Assembly, 170 members.
**Official language:** English. National language: Swahili.
**Chief cities:** capital Nairobi 630,000 (1973), Mombasa 301,000.
**Political divisions:** 7 Provinces, and Nairobi Area.
**Armed forces** (1976): Total 7,600 regular: army 6,500, navy 340, air force 760 (15 combat aircraft). Paramilitary forces: 1,800.

**DEMOGRAPHY. Population:** 10,942,705 (census of 24–25. VIII.1969. For 1970–2000 (UN), see last row of Table 1). Population density (1975): 23/sq.km. (59/sq.mile). Under 15 years: 47%. Growth rate (1975–80): 3.38% per year (births 4.80%, deaths −1.43%). Life expectancy (1975–80): 52.5 years. Household size: 5.6 persons.
**Major languages:** Swahili, English, Kikuyu, Luo, Luhya, Kamba, Kalenjin, Gusii, Somali, Turkana, Maasai, Hindi, Gujarati, Punjabi, Taita, and about 50 smaller languages.
**Urban dwellers** (1970): 10.2%. Urban growth rate (1950–70): 6.2% per year.
**Labour force:** 39%.
**Refugees** (1977): From abroad, about 100,000 (mainly from Uganda; also 10,000 from Ethiopia; and others from Tanzania, Sudan, Somalia). In early 1977, another 10,000 fled from Uganda to Kenya.
**Tourists** (1970): 276,000. (1974) 377,510.

**ETHNOLINGUISTIC GROUPS:** 20.1% Kikuyu, 13.9% Luo, 13.3% Luhya, 11.0% Kamba, 9.7% Kalenjin (4.3% Kipsigis, 2.4% Nandi, 1.2% Tugen, 1.0% Elgeyo, 0.7% Marakwet), 6.4% Gusii, 5.1% Meru, 4.8% Mijikenda (2.8% Giriama, 1.1% Digo, 0.9% Duruma), 2.3% Somali, 1.9% Turkana, 1.4% Maasai, 1.3% Indo-Pakistani (150,000) (Gujarati, Hindi, Bengali, Punjabi, Goanese, Malayali), 1.1% Embu, 1.1% Taita, 0.9% Suk (Pokot), 0.8% Teso, 0.6% Kuria, 0.5% Tharaka, 0.5% Mbere, 0.5% Samburu, 0.5% alien African, 0.4% European (44,900), 0.4% Sabaot, 0.3% Arab (33,800), 0.3% Boran, 0.3% Pokomo, Baluchi, Jewish, & a large number of smaller peoples. British Asians declined from 180,000 in 1968 to 15,000 by 1977 through emigration.

**MONEY** (1979). **Monetary unit:** shilling (= 100 cents); US$1 = KShs 7.5.
**National income per person:** US$197. Average annual family income: US$1,103.
**Inflation:** (1970–74) 9.0% per year, (1975) 25% per year (consumer price index (1976) 178).
**Cost of living in capital** (1976): index 97 (Washington DC=100). Daily cost of living: US$35.

**HEALTH.** Hospitals: 194 (15,904 beds). Doctors: 766. Lepers: 67,000 (5.1 per 1,000). Blind: 65,000. Psychotics: 110,000. Criminals: 19,530 (excluding 389,682 petty offenders).

**EDUCATION.** Adult literacy: (1962) 19%, (1975) 60%. Education rate: 39%. Schools: 10,516 (8,893 primary, 1,623 secondary). Universities: 2.

**LITERATURE.** Annual new book titles (1973): 224. Periodicals: 160. Scientific journals: 10. Newspapers: 4 dailies.

**COMMUNICATION** (per 1,000 people). Phones: 8. Radios: 41. TV sets: 3. Daily newspaper circulation: 14 copies.

TABLE 1. RELIGIOUS ADHERENTS IN KENYA

| Year | 1900 | | mid-1970 | | Annual change, 1970–1980 | | | | mid-1975 | | mid-1980 | | 2000 | |
|---|---|---|---|---|---|---|---|---|---|---|---|---|---|---|
| *Name* | *Adherents* | *%* | *Adherents* | *%* | *Natural* | *Conversion* | *Total* | *Rate* | *Adherents* | *%* | *Adherents* | *%* | *Adherents* | *%* |
| **Christians** | **5,000** | **0.2** | **7,141,800** | **63.5** | **306,429** | **124,611** | **431,040** | **4.71** | **9,143,200** | **69.0** | **11,452,200** | **73.0** | **25,399,000** | **81.9** |
| professing | 5,000 | 0.2 | 7,141,800 | 63.5 | 306,429 | 124,611 | 431,040 | 4.71 | 9,143,200 | 69.0 | 11,452,200 | 73.0 | 25,399,000 | 81.9 |
| Roman Catholics | 2,700 | 0.1 | 2,700,000 | 24.0 | 114,133 | 30,027 | 144,160 | 4.23 | 3,405,500 | 25.7 | 4,141,600 | 26.4 | 9,032,000 | 29.1 |
| Protestants | 300 | 0.0 | 1,829,500 | 16.3 | 79,945 | 39,885 | 119,830 | 5.02 | 2,385,400 | 18.0 | 3,027,800 | 19.3 | 6,197,000 | 20.0 |
| African indigenous | 0 | 0.0 | 1,610,000 | 14.3 | 71,051 | 44,059 | 115,110 | 5.43 | 2,120,000 | 16.0 | 2,761,100 | 17.6 | 7,030,000 | 22.7 |
| Anglicans | 2,000 | 0.1 | 742,300 | 6.6 | 30,642 | 8,078 | 38,720 | 4.23 | 914,300 | 6.9 | 1,129,500 | 7.2 | 2,290,000 | 7.4 |
| Orthodox | 0 | 0.0 | 260,000 | 2.3 | 10,658 | 2,562 | 13,220 | 4.16 | 318,000 | 2.4 | 392,200 | 2.5 | 850,000 | 2.7 |
| nominal | 0 | 0.0 | 1,056,265 | 9.4 | 48,408 | 18,525 | 66,933 | 4.63 | 1,444,400 | 10.9 | 1,725,500 | 11.0 | 2,475,000 | 8.0 |
| affiliated | 5,000 | 0.2 | 6,085,535 | 54.1 | 258,021 | 106,086 | 364,107 | 4.73 | 7,698,800 | 58.1 | 9,726,600 | 62.0 | 22,924,000 | 73.9 |
| total practising | 4,750 | *95* | 4,868,430 | *80* | 206,417 | 84,869 | 291,286 | 4.73 | 6,159,040 | *80* | 7,781,280 | *80* | 17,193,000 | *75* |
| non-practising | 250 | *5* | 1,217,110 | *20* | 51,604 | 21,217 | 72,821 | 4.73 | 1,539,760 | *20* | 1,945,320 | *20* | 5,731,000 | *25* |
| Roman Catholics | 2,700 | 0.1 | 1,934,811 | 17.2 | 81,715 | 32,284 | 113,999 | 4.67 | 2,438,200 | 18.4 | 3,074,800 | 19.6 | 6,824,000 | 22.0 |
| Catholic pentecostals | 0 | 0.0 | 0 | 0.0 | 67 | 933 | 1,000 | 50.00 | 2,000 | 0.0 | 10,000 | 0.1 | 300,000 | 1.0 |
| Protestants | 300 | 0.0 | 1,687,760 | 15.0 | 71,058 | 26,866 | 97,924 | 4.62 | 2,120,200 | 16.0 | 2,667,000 | 17.0 | 6,212,000 | 20.0 |
| Evangelicals | 300 | 0.0 | 1,552,000 | 13.8 | 65,726 | 26,944 | 92,670 | 4.73 | 1,961,100 | 14.8 | 2,478,700 | 15.8 | 5,738,700 | 18.5 |
| Neo-pentecostals | 0 | 0.0 | 500 | 0.0 | 67 | 483 | 550 | 27.50 | 2,000 | 0.0 | 6,000 | 0.0 | 70,000 | 0.2 |
| African indigenous | 0 | 0.0 | 1,625,264 | 14.5 | 70,377 | 36,097 | 106,474 | 5.07 | 2,099,900 | 15.8 | 2,690,000 | 17.1 | 7,010,000 | 22.6 |
| Anglicans | 2,000 | 0.1 | 582,600 | 5.2 | 24,425 | 8,305 | 32,730 | 4.49 | 728,800 | 5.5 | 909,900 | 5.8 | 2,016,000 | 6.5 |
| Evangelicals | 2,000 | 0.1 | 570,000 | 5.1 | 23,795 | 7,905 | 31,700 | 4.46 | 710,000 | 5.4 | 887,000 | 5.7 | 1,985,000 | 6.4 |
| Anglican pentecostals | 0 | 0.0 | 1,000 | 0.0 | 335 | 2,565 | 2,900 | 29.00 | 10,000 | 0.1 | 30,000 | 0.2 | 200,000 | 0.6 |
| Orthodox | 0 | 0.0 | 250,000 | 2.2 | 10,222 | 2,428 | 12,650 | 4.15 | 305,000 | 2.3 | 376,500 | 2.4 | 838,000 | 2.7 |
| Marginal Protestants | 0 | 0.0 | 4,100 | 0.0 | 184 | 106 | 290 | 5.27 | 5,500 | 0.0 | 7,000 | 0.0 | 20,000 | 0.1 |
| Catholics (non-Roman) | 0 | 0.0 | 1,000 | 0.0 | 40 | 0 | 40 | 3.33 | 1,200 | 0.0 | 1,400 | 0.0 | 4,000 | 0.0 |
| Tribal religionists | 2,779,700 | 95.8 | 3,158,430 | 28.1 | 100,948 | −119,576 | −18,628 | −0.62 | 3,012,060 | 22.7 | 2,972,150 | 18.9 | 3,257,000 | 10.5 |
| Muslims | 100,000 | 3.4 | 719,800 | 6.4 | 27,638 | −5,488 | 22,150 | 2.70 | 821,600 | 6.2 | 941,300 | 6.0 | 1,706,000 | 5.5 |
| Ahmadis | 0 | 0.0 | 2,000 | 0.0 | 84 | 16 | 100 | 4.00 | 2,500 | 0.0 | 3,000 | 0.0 | 7,000 | 0.0 |
| Baha'is | 0 | 0.0 | 121,000 | 1.1 | 5,027 | 873 | 5,900 | 3.93 | 150,000 | 1.1 | 180,000 | 1.1 | 450,000 | 1.4 |
| Hindus | 10,000 | 0.3 | 60,000 | 0.5 | 2,346 | −346 | 2,000 | 2.86 | 70,000 | 0.5 | 80,000 | 0.5 | 100,000 | 0.3 |
| Jains | 3,000 | 0.1 | 30,000 | 0.3 | 1,173 | −173 | 1,000 | 2.86 | 35,000 | 0.3 | 40,000 | 0.3 | 60,000 | 0.2 |
| Sikhs | 2,000 | 0.1 | 13,000 | 0.1 | 400 | 0 | 400 | 2.67 | 15,000 | 0.1 | 17,000 | 0.1 | 25,000 | 0.1 |
| Non-religious | 0 | 0.0 | 2,000 | 0.0 | 101 | 99 | 200 | 6.67 | 3,000 | 0.0 | 4,000 | 0.0 | 20,000 | 0.1 |
| Jews | 100 | 0.0 | 700 | 0.0 | 27 | 1 | 28 | 3.41 | 820 | 0.0 | 980 | 0.0 | 2,300 | 0.0 |
| Parsis | 200 | 0.0 | 270 | 0.0 | 11 | −1 | 10 | 3.12 | 320 | 0.0 | 370 | 0.0 | 700 | 0.0 |
| **Country's population** | **2,900,000** | **100.0** | **11,247,000** | **100.0** | **444,100** | **0** | **444,100** | **3.35** | **13,251,000** | **100.0** | **15,688,000** | **100.0** | **31,020,000** | **100.0** |

COLUMNS, ROWS. For meanings and definitions, see Codebook (Part 6). Note that, by definition, total 'Christians' = professing + crypto-Christians, which also = affiliated + nominal Christians. Percentages may not always total exactly, due to rounding.
CENSUSES. Before 1948, censuses enumerated non-Africans only. 1921 (non-Africans): 20,986 Muslims, 12,284 Christians (5,701 Anglicans, 3,609 Roman Catholics, 1,037 Dutch Reformed Ch), 9,308 Hindus, 1,619 Sikhs, 688 Jains, 215 Jews, 155 Parsis, 153 non-religious or atheists. 1926 (non-Africans): 22,615 Muslims, 15,418 Christians, 10,859 Hindus, 2,089 Sikhs, 1,405 Jains, 256 Jews, 179 Parsis. 1931 (non-Africans only; total 73,947): 36.8% Muslims, 28.9% Christians (13.2% Anglicans, 8.5% Roman Catholics, 2.8% Presbyterians), 24.9% Hindus, 6.0% Sikhs, 1.8% Jains, 0.3% Parsis. II-VIII.1948 (including Northern Frontier District): 59.9% tribal religionists, 11.2% Protestants, 10.4% Anglicans, 8.6% Muslims, 8.1% Roman Catholics, 0.8% Hindus, 0.7% African indigenous, 0.2% Sikhs, 0.1% Jains. 15.VIII.1962: 36.8% tribal religionists, 33.6% Protestants, Anglicans and African indigenous, 20.3% Roman Catholics, 7.9% Muslims, 1.1% Hindus and Jains, 0.3% Sikhs. The religion question was not asked after 1962.

### NOTES ON RELIGIONS

AFRICAN INDIGENOUS. In about 154 denominations in 1970 (see Table 2), growing rapidly in number.
AHMADIS. Begun 1934: Qadiani Ahmadiya from Pakistan; since 1963 most Asian followers have emigrated or been expelled, leaving mainly African followers.
ANGLICAN PENTECOSTALS. The charismatic renewal in the Anglican Church since 1970 has been largely amongst secondary school and other students.
BAHA'IS. Rapid growth from 166 local spiritual assemblies (1964) to 805 (1973). Most new converts are Bantu (especially

Luhya), including many former Muslims and Christians, but there are also a number of Asians, previously Hindus.
CATHOLIC PENTECOSTALS (or, Catholic charismatics). In Kenya the movement began in 1975.
COUNTRY'S POPULATION. In 1900, 32,000 coolies imported from India were at work building the Uganda railway. After its completion in 1901, only 6,700 stayed on permanently in Kenya. In the 1911 census there were 11,886 Asians (of whom 5,939 were Muslims, 3,205 Hindus, and 97 Parsis). The table above shows the 1900 situation.
HINDUS. Asians (Indians), with about 2,500 Black African converts. There are over 50 different Hindu organizations in Kenya (speaking Gujarati, Hindi, Bengali, Punjabi), most co-operating in the Hindu Council of Kenya. The Arya Samaj reform movement has (1975) around 9,000 members (1,000 being Africans). ISKCON (Hare Krishna movement) began in 1971 and has about 500 African converts. These gains are offset by considerable emigration and also losses by conversion to Baha'i. In 1975 the Theosophical Society had 17 Lodges with 280 members.
JAINS. First immigrants from India were in 1886. In 1970, 80% Svetambara sect, 20% Digambara; 50 centres in Kenya. Recently there have been numerical losses due to emigration, with some conversions to Baha'i.
MUSLIMS. In 1970, all were Africans who were Shafiite Sunnis, except for 30,800 Arabs (Shafiites), 32,000 Asian Sunnis (22,000 Shafiites, 10,000 Hanafites), and 18,000 Asian Shias (13,000 Ismailis, 3,000 Ithna-Asharis, 2,000 Bohoras). There were also 2,000 Ahmadis (enumerated here under Muslims although declared non-Muslims by Pakistan). Conversions. Although small numbers of pagans are being converted to Islam in the north, the proportion of Muslims in Kenya has declined markedly since 1948 due to (1) emigration of Somalis and other non-Kenyan Muslims; and (2) several coastal peoples formerly

labelled nominal Muslims when subject to the Mombasa sultanate are now reclassifying themselves as traditional religionists (animists). In Nyanza, 200 Luhyas were recently converted by an Arab. A few hundred Muslims a year also are becoming Christians, almost all through church-related evangelism, and about half that number of Christians become Muslims (usually when marrying Muslim husbands). Organized missions. Active proselytism is under way through the Ahmadiya Muslim Mission, and also through the Bilal Muslim Mission operated by the Shia Ithna-Asharis based in Mombasa who by 1976 were claiming 5,000 Kikuyu converts from an African indigenous church, the Christian Theocratic Holy Church of God. In 1976, 2 Egyptian sheikhs from Al-Azhar University (Cairo) were also at work; and 2 Pakistani Sunni missionaries were working among the Luhya. Hajj pilgrims to Mecca. (1970) under 30; (1974) 531; (1975) 598; (1976) 791.
NON-RELIGIOUS. Europeans and a small but growing number of African intellectuals.
PROFESSING CHRISTIANS. Persons publicly professing to be Christians. Amongst other Christian and quasi-Christian groupings, this category includes 3,400 Freemasons, a quasi-religious male secret brotherhood begun in Nairobi in 1905 and now with 36 lodges; mostly British members, but with some Hindu, Ismaili, non-religious and other non-Christian members.
SIKHS. From 21,169 in 1962, there was a decline by emigration to 13,000 in 1970, continuing into the 1970s. In 1973 there was a large temple in Nairobi and 21 gurdwaras (centres) throughout Kenya. There are several hundred Africans interested in Sikhism, but full acceptance into the Khalsa is not encouraged.
TRIBAL RELIGIONISTS. Animists. Tribes over 60% traditionalist in 1972: Dorobo (99% animist), El Molo (97%), Samburu (97%), Turkana (96%), Pokot (Suk) (90%), Giriama (82%), Maasai (78%), Mbere (66%), Tharaka (61%), Sagala (60%).

---

NON-CHRISTIAN RELIGIONS. Traditional religions, adhered to by over 95% of the population in the year 1900, had declined to 60% in 1948, to 37% in 1962, and to about 27% in 1972. The peoples most resistant to conversion are the Samburu (still 97% traditionalists), Turkana (96%), Pokot or Suk (90%), Giriama (82%), and Maasai (78%). Other peoples with traditionalists over 50% include the Mbere, Tugen, Elgeyo and Meru. As in other

parts of Africa, beliefs relating to mystical power (uganga in Kiswahili), medicine men (ombila in Luhya), diviners (chebsageyot among the Kipsigis), taboo (kwer in Luo) and witchcraft (murogi in Kikuyu) continue to exert their influence. The ancestral cult is less prevalent than formerly, whereas God receives more emphasis. All of Kenya's peoples have a traditional belief in a supreme being who is known by different names: Akuj (Turkana), Asis (Dorobo, Elgeyo, Kipsigis, Marakwet, Nandi), Engai (Maasai), Erioba (Gusii), Mlungu (Taita), Mulungu (Digo, Kamba, Rabai), Mungu (Swahili), Murungu (Meru), Muungu (Pokomo), Ngai (Embu, Kikuyu, Mbere), Nyasaye (Luhya, Luo), Tororut (Pokot), Wah (Rendille), Waqa (Boran, Galla) and Wele (Luhya). Some Kenyan peoples associate God with the phenomena of nature. The Suk speak of the moon as God's firstborn son. Engai in Maasai means sky and rain as well as God, while Asis (Nandi) and Erioba (Kuria) refer to both God and the sun. Several attempts have been made to renew traditional religions over the last 3 decades. In 1944 the Religion of the Ancestral Spirits (Dini ya Msambwa) arose in western Kenya, followed by witchcraft eradication movements from the coast led by Kabwere and Kajiwe in the mid-1960s. In 1971 the Medicine Men's Society (Waganga wa Miti Shamba) was organized and registered with govern-

**Hindus.** Three Africans, who have become Hindus, in Arya Samaj temple, Nairobi. About 2,500 Black Kenyans have become converts to Arya Samaj or Hare Krishna.

ment, with 110 medicine men as members, mostly Kamba.

**Islam** is strongest at the coast and in northeast Kenya, with its main strength among the Somalis (100% Muslim), Digo (91%), Boran (90%), Pokomo (85%), and Duruma (25%). Islam has had little or no success among the large and rapidly-growing peoples of the interior, resulting in its declining in percentage relative to the population since 1945. Since Independence in 1963, large numbers of Coastal peoples formerly classified as Muslims when subject to the Mombasa sultanate have reclassified themselves as traditional religionists, and numbers of Muslim Somalis have returned to Somalia. In 1970 Muslims were estimated to make up 6.4% of the total population. Muslims of Arab (30,800) and African (637,000) origin are mostly Sunnis and Shafiites, while Asian Muslims (50,000) are divided into Shafiite (22,000), Hanafite (10,000) and Shia (18,000) communities. Shias are further sub-divided as Ismaili Khojas (13,000), Ithna-Asharis (3,000) and Dawoodi Bohoras (2,000). In addition there are 2,000 Africans who have become Ahmadis.

**Hinduism, Jainism** and **Sikhism** are confined almost entirely to the Asian population. There are no African Jains or Sikhs and not more than 2,500 African Hindus, most of whom are converts to the Arya Samaj plus a few to the Hare Krishna movement. In 1970 Kenya had 60,000 Hindus, 30,000 Jains and 13,000 Sikhs.

**Other religions** are Baha'i (121,000), Judaism (700) and Parsiism (270); only Baha'i has an African constituency, most of its members being Luhya Bantu.

**CHRISTIANITY.** The Christian faith first came to Kenya in 1498, when Vasco da Gama set anchor off Malindi bay. Contacts were made with the local population, followed later by evangelistic work at various points along the coast. By the end of the

(Tsume Washe), a traditional religious practitioner of witchcraft eradication, in action as a witchfinder at the Kenya coast.

**Tribal religionists.** Left. The cattle of a deceased Luhya elder are driven over his grave in the last rite of respect due to his spirit. Right. Kajiwe

16th century there were missionary priests at Lamu and Augustinian friars in Mombasa with 600 African converts. This mission later collapsed and Catholic work lapsed until started again by Holy Ghost Fathers in 1889. Anglican activity began in Mombasa with the arrival of CMS missionary J: L. Krapf in 1844, and in 1862 British Methodists appeared on the scene. Scottish Presbyterians entered in 1891, followed by the Africa Inland Mission in 1895; and the opening of the railway to Kisumu in 1902 resulted in a Protestant influx into western Kenya. The first of Kenya's many independent indigenous churches, the Nomiya Luo Mission, was begun in Nyanza in 1914.

African response to Christianity was instantaneous and immense from the earliest days of this mass influx of missions, the number of converts doubling or even trebling every year for the first 10 years after 1900. By 1916 a mass movement into all the churches, Protestant, Anglican and Catholic, had begun, and by 1948, 30% of the population professed to be Christians, this figure rising to 54% in 1962 and to over 63% in 1970. By 1970, 206 distinct denominations had been begun, of which 154 were independent indigenous churches. In mid-1970 about 6,085,000 persons (54.1% of the total population) were affiliated to churches of which 1,935,000 were Roman Catholics, 1,688,000 Protestants, 1,625,000 African independents, 583,000 Anglicans and 250,000 Orthodox.

As to ethnic composition, Christianity has now become the majority religion of Kenya's largest peoples, each with over one million in population: the Bantu-speaking Luhya (94% Christian in 1972), Gusii (82%), Kikuyu (77%) and Kamba (61%); as well as the Nilotic Luo (89%).

CATHOLIC CHURCH. Following the recommencement of its mission in 1889, Catholicism grew rapidly under the Holy Ghost priests at the coast and among the Kamba; Consolata priests in Kikuyu country; and Mill Hill priests in western Kenya, in addition to many institutes of brothers and sisters. Growth became even more rapid after World War II. In 1948, 8.1% of the populations professed to be Catholics, rising to 20.3% in 1962, and to about 24% in 1970. However, a major problem for the Catholic church has been its slow progress in the development of indigenous vocations. Although the first African priests were ordained in 1927, in 1974 less than 100 of the country's 700 priests were Africans, keeping the Catholic Church still heavily dependent on foreign missionaries and village catechists. On the other hand, the church has been much more successful in challenging Kenyan women and girls to enter the sisterhood. African priests have no indigenous religious congregations of their own and, except for 5 in monasteries, all Kenyan priests are secular. In contrast, 5 indigenous congregations of brothers and 11 of sisters have been founded in Kenya. Sisters led the way founding a sodality in 1918 called the Immaculate Heart of Mary Sisters, which became a religious congregation in 1927. The first African mother superior was elected in 1946.

In 1953, the Catholic ecclesiastical province of Kenya was created, with one archdiocese (Nairobi) and 3 dioceses: Kisumu, Meru and Nyeri. By 1979 the work had expanded to 14 dioceses and a prefecture. The first Kenyan bishop was consecrated in 1957, and in 1974 there were 7 African bishops, including the cardinal archbishop of Nairobi.

PROTESTANT CHURCHES. The largest Protestant body is the Africa Inland Church (AIC) which owes its origin to the activity of the interdenominational Africa Inland Mission from 1895 and which became autonomous in 1971. The AIC consists of 2,500 congregations divided into 10 regions and 67 districts. Theological education is provided at Scott Theological College in Machakos, in addition to 7 Bible schools, functioning in various parts of the country. The church also sponsors 667 primary schools and is responsible for 30 harambee (self-help) schools. Other activities include Kenya's largest religious broadcasting studio, a press and a number of medical institutions.

The most important Protestant churches of Central Province are the Presbyterian Church of East Africa (PCEA) among the Kikuyu, and the Methodist Church in Kenya (MCK) among the Meru; the latter also maintains work at the coast and in the lower Tana river area. The PCEA was established as an independent body in 1943, while the MCK became an autonomous Methodist conference in 1967. Both churches are heavily involved in education and social service. The PCEA sponsors 275 primary schools (1973), a number of harambee secondary schools and 3 hospitals, the Methodists in turn having 166 primary schools, 10 harambee secondary schools and 2 hospitals.

Western Kenya also has been the scene of extensive Christian activity, the principal denominations being the Friends (FAM, later EAYM) in 1902, Church of God in 1905 and Seventh-day Adventists (SDA) in 1906. The first two have established large Christian communities and extensive educational and medical institutions among the Luhya, while SDAs have been active among the Luo of Nyanza. Primary schools founded by the 3 churches number 400 for the SDA, 254 for EAYM and 96 by the CoG. Theological education is provided by Kima Theological School (CoG) and several Bible schools belonging to the various denominations.

Pentecostalism also is strong in western Kenya as well as in other parts of the country. The 2 most important communities are the Pentecostal Assemblies of God (PAG) and the Pentecostal Evangelistic Fellowship of Africa (PEFA). The former, begun among the Luhya in 1910 but now widely spread throughout Kenya, is related to the Pentecostal Assemblies of Canada and has as many members in Kenya as in Canada. PEFA on the other hand was formed in 1962 by bringing together 2 societies, the International Pentecostal Assemblies (1938) and the Elim Missionary Assemblies (1942). Other Pentecostal bodies are the Full Gospel Churches of Kenya, founded by Finnish missionaries in 1949, and the small Norwegian Pentecostal Mission since 1955.

Another large church with extensive evangelistic, educational, medical and social service interests is the Salvation Army which entered Kenya in 1921. It has its main strength among the Kamba and Luhya, but it also maintains work in Elgon, Eldoret, Embu, Kisumu, Mombasa and Thika.

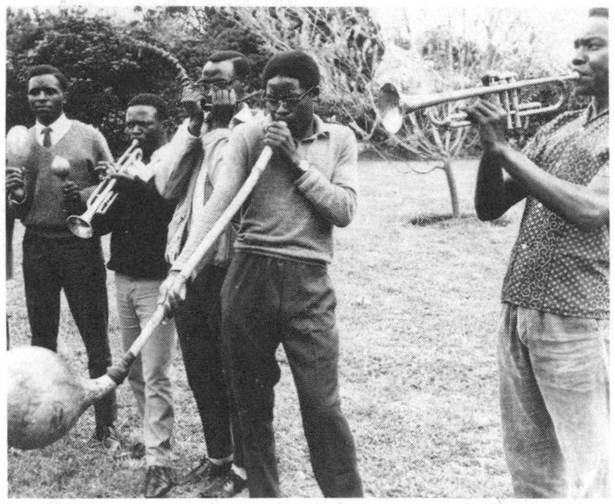

**Protestants.** 'Let everything that hath breath praise the Lord!'. Theological students of Africa Inland Church combine traditional musical instruments (drums, rattles, horns) and Western musical instruments in their choirs. In centre, *abu* (bugle) of the Luo.

Among Kenya's smaller Protestant denominations may be mentioned the Africa Gospel Church, Baptist Churches of Kenya, Gospel Furthering Bible Church, Lutheran Church in Kenya and the Reformed Church of East Africa.

INDIGENOUS CHURCHES. In 1979 there were over 220 distinct independent African indigenous denominations in Kenya, with a combined Christian community of 2,600,000. The first to be begun was the Nomiya Luo Mission, a schism in Nyanza from the Anglican Church in 1914. Other important Luo schisms have been the Church of Christ in Africa, which began as an Anglican revival movement (called Johera or People of Love) in 1952 and separated in 1957; and Maria Legio of Africa, the largest split from Roman Catholicism anywhere in Africa. The most important of the many Luhya indigenous denominations is the African Israel Church Nineveh (AICN), which is noted for its lengthy charismatic worship services and its custom of running through the streets in formation in white robes; while the African Brotherhood Church (ABC) is the largest such body among the Kamba. Both the AICN and the ABC are members of the National Christian Council of Kenya, and the AICN joined the World Council of Churches in 1975.

During the late 1920s and early 1930s, Kikuyu country was the scene of serious conflicts over land, schools and female circumcision, which resulted in the formation of some of Kenya's most important independent churches: the African Independent Pentecostal Church (AIPC) and the African Orthodox Church (AOC). The former is today Kenya's largest indigenous Christian community, while in 1946 the AOC was accepted into Greek Orthodoxy and is now in the diocese of Eirenopolis under the patriarchate of Alexandria. Other Kikuyu pentecostal independents tracing their origin to the same period are known collectively as Wakorino, although they are divided into many separate denominations: African Mission of Holy Ghost Church, Chosen Church of the Holy Spirit, Christian Holy Ghost Church of East Africa, Holy Ghost Church of East Africa, Holy Spirit Church of Zayun, and Kenya Foundation of the Prophets Church. The Wakorino are noted for the white turbans worn by their members.

ANGLICAN CHURCH. Anglicanism is second only to Catholicism both in date of arrival and size of its present Christian community. Two missions playing an important role in evangelism and the early formation of the church have been the Church Missionary Society, beginning in 1844, and the Bible Churchmen's Missionary Society from 1931.

The first African ordinations to the Anglican ministry took place in 1885, and the first 2 African bishops were appointed in 1955. In 1960 the church obtained its autonomy from Canterbury as the Church of the Province of East Africa, which included the Anglican churches of Kenya, Tanganyika and Zanzibar. The 2 latter were separated off in 1970 and the Church of the Province of Kenya (CPK) was formed. As with Catholicism, the CPK is found in all parts of the country although it is strongest among the Kikuyu, Luo and Luhya. The church is organized with a metropolitan diocese in Nairobi and 5 other dioceses (with a sixth added in 1975) with responsiblitity for property and finance handled by the Church Commissioners for Kenya. Ministerial training is provided at St Paul's United Theological College and at several diocesan Bible schools. Interest in education is maintained through its continued sponsorship of 775 primary schools and 60 harambee secondary schools, and the CPK is still indirectly responsible for 2 hospitals.

**CHURCH AND STATE.** In affirming freedom of religion, the 1969 constitution of Kenya follows the United Nations' 1948 *Universal Declaration of Human Rights*. Chapter V, paragraph 78 states: 'No person shall be hindered in the enjoyment of his freedom of conscience... freedom of thought and of religion, freedom to change his religion or belief, and freedom to manifest and propagate his religion or belief in worship, teaching, practice and observance'; 'Every religious community shall be entitled, at its own expense, to establish and maintain places of education...; and no such community shall be prevented from providing religious instruction for persons of that community'; 'No person attending any place of education shall be required to receive religious instruction or to take part in or attend any religious ceremony or observance'; and 'No person shall be compelled to take any oath which is contrary to his religion or belief'.

The churches continue to participate in education, although in 1968 the government took over the management of all mission-founded primary schools, nearly 5,000 in all. The policy of 'participation' as defined in the Education Act of 1968 seeks to avoid the extremes of a secular school system on the one hand and the use of schools to further religious objectives on the other. It allows for religious sponsorship of primary schools and grants representation to the churches on the governing boards of their former secondary schools and teacher-training colleges. The Education Act also makes provision for religious education in government-maintained schools while stipulating that such courses are purely voluntary. The Kenya government and the churches (Protestant, Anglican and Catholic) co-operate through the Joint East African Religious Education Committee in the development of syllabuses and text books, and the government assumes responsibility for training religious education teachers at the University of Nairobi and Kenyatta University College.

Government co-operation and aid is also provided to other church-sponsored projects including hospitals, dispensaries, village polytechnic schools and socio-economic development programmes.

Leaders representing all religious traditions are given prominent roles at major government functions, such as the opening of parliament; and the churches are permitted chaplaincy services in the prisons and

**African indigenous churches.** In Kenya, there are over 220 indigenous denominations, with 2.7 million adherents. As elsewhere in Africa, these churches can be described by one or more of 3 adjectives illustrated here: (1) (*left*) *African* (dress, drums, and other traditional African features; shown here in African Israel Church Nineveh); (2) (*centre*) *Charismatic* (glossolalic, prophetic, Spirit-possessed; shown here, Local Churches of Kenya); (3) (*right*) *Liturgical* (rich robes, written liturgies, crosses, beads and other symbols; shown here, Maria Legio of Africa).

armed forces. Major Muslim and Christian holidays are also respected.

Officially a secular state, Kenya makes no attempt to regulate religious observance unless such practices are deemed subversive. The only cases of recent government intervention in religion have been the proscribing in 1968 of the Religion of the Ancestral Spirits, and the banning of Jehovah's Witnesses with the deportation of its 34 European missionaries for 7 months in 1973 before the ban was lifted.

**INTERDENOMINATIONAL ORGANIZATIONS.**
Two Africa-wide interdenominational councils of churches have their headquarters in Kenya. The All Africa Conference of Churches (AACC), formed in 1963 and based in Nairobi, has 100 member churches and councils throughout the continent and represents the conciliar wing of Protestant, Anglican and Orthodox ecumenism in Africa. Secondly, the Association of Evangelicals of Africa and Madagascar (AEAM), founded in Nairobi in 1966 and united with the Africa Evangelical Office in 1971, has member national associations in 10 countries and provides for co-operation and fellowship among Conservative Evangelical Christians.

Nairobi is also the centre for 2 international organizations: the United Bible Societies (UBS) (Africa Regional Centre), which serves as a consultative and co-ordinating body for Africa's 24 national Bible societies; and the World Students Christian Federation (WSCF) (Africa Region). Several national bodies of an interdenominational nature are active. The National Christian Council of Kenya (NCCK) was founded in 1943 as the Christian Council of Kenya, building on the Alliance of Protestant Missions of 1918 and the Kenya Missionary Council of 1924, and received its present name in 1966. The council has 25 member denominations and carries on its work through 8 regional branches and 6 departments: Biblical Study and Research; Christian Communication; Christian Education and Training; Christian Service, Home and Family Life; Relief, Rehabilitation and Rural Development; and Youth. With 120 full-time employees it is one of the largest such national councils in the world. Over 100 social service projects (including rural training centres and village polytechnics) are directly under NCCK sponsorship,

with assistance provided for 50 others belonging to its member churches.

The Christian Churches Educational Association (CCEA) was founded in 1957 to co-ordinate the work of Protestant and Anglican churches in education. Membership consists of 15 churches, 6 teacher-training colleges and 59 secondary schools. In 1971 the CCEA sponsored 2,613 primary schools and 149 secondary schools. The Protestant Churches Medical Association (PCMA) was established in 1962 to promote Protestant medical services and in 1970 co-ordinated the work of 15 hospitals and 19 dispensaries. Training for the ministry is provided at St Paul's United Theological College, Limuru, which came into existence in 1955 as a joint venture of the Anglican, Presbyterian and Methodist churches, with the Reformed Church joining later. In addition to these, there were in 1973 about 300 other Christian organizations of significance at the national level.

Indigenous churches in Kenya have over the years made 14 different attempts to form national councils of independent churches. Most have foundered due to lack of funds and personnel, and several have been refused registration by government. A pioneer was the Kenya Independent Churches Fellowship formed in 1960, and in 1973 the most important were the East African Christian Alliance begun in 1965 and affiliated to the International Council of Christian Churches, and the United Orthodox Independent Churches of East Africa begun in 1971.

**BROADCASTING.** Since its inception the government Voice of Kenya (VOK) has welcomed religious broadcasting; in 1971, 13.5 hours a week were given free to religious programmes, plus TV epilogues and religious music programmes, rising to 22 hours by 1977 and to 30 hours by 1979, the most generous of any government radio facility in the world. The Voice of Kenya has a National Service in Swahili, a General Service in English, and also services in Kenya's vernacular languages. In a rotation system among the major churches, the VOK Religious Department produces programmes on radio and television: morning 'Lift up Your Hearts', 4-minute epilogues every night, Sunday church services with discussions, church news and music, and special programmes for Christmas and Easter. Most of the recording is done in VOK studios in Nairobi, Kisumu and Mombasa.

In this way the Communications Department of the Kenya Catholic Secretariat produces over 31 Catholic programmes each month in Swahili, Meru, Kikuyu and English. In 1972 there were 4 Protestant production centres in Kenya, operated by the WGM (Kericho), AIM (Kijabe) which produces 100 programmes a month, AACC (Nairobi) which trains churchmen from across Africa in radio-TV, and SBC (Nairobi). Afromedia (Nairobi) is a Protestant television production centre, to serve other African countries as well. From abroad RVOG (Ethiopia) was easily received, in Swahili and English, until its closure in 1977. For Catholics, UNDA is represented in Kenya by a national association.

**BIBLIOGRAPHY**
'Bibliography of Christianity and religion in Kenya', in *Kenya churches handbook* (Kisumu: Evangel Press, 1973), p. 315–332. (600 titles, annotated).
*Catholic directory of Eastern Africa 1977–1979*. Tabora (Tanzania): TMP Book Department, 1977. 258p.
*Kenya churches handbook: the development of Kenyan Christianity, 1498–1973*. Eds D. B. Barrett, G. K. Mambo, J. MacLaughlin, M. J. McVeigh. Kisumu: Evangel Press, 1973. 349p.
*Luo religion and folklore*. H. E. Hauge. London: Brill, 1976. 154p.
*New Testament eschatology in an African background; a study of the encounter between New Testament theology and African traditional concepts*. J. S. Mbiti. London: Oxford University Press, 1971. (A study of the Kamba people).
'The Maria Legio: the dynamics of a breakaway church among the Luo of East Africa'. P. J. Dirven. Dissertation, Pontificia Universitas Gregoriana, Rome, 1970. 343p.
*The Presbyterian Church in Kenya: an account of the origin and growth of the PCEA*. R. Macpherson. Nairobi: PCEA, 1970. 151p.

TABLE 2.    ORGANIZED CHURCHES AND DENOMINATIONS IN KENYA

| Official name 1 | Begun 2 | Type 3 | Counc 4 | Congs 5 | Adults 6 | Affiliated 7 | Names, notes, and other statistics (see Codebook) 8 |
|---|---|---|---|---|---|---|---|
| Africa Gospel Church | 1935 | P Hol | xPG.a | 250 | 6,500 | 15,000 | *AGC.* 5 Dioceses. M=WGM(USA). A=1961. 95% Kipsigis. 20n,33f,1H,2h,1s,W=84%,266Y. |
| Africa Gospel Unity Church | 1964 | I Hol | .T.,T | 19 | 1,000 | 1,500 | *AGUC.* Split ex AGC when moderator deposed. Kipsigis. HQ Silibwet. 10n,W=85%,250Y. |
| Africa Inland Church | 1895 | P int | xMG.a | 1,700 | 150,000 | 300,000 | M=AIM. 33% Kamba, 27% Kalenjin, 20% Kikuyu. 80n,50x,226f,4H,30h,5p,1s,W=65%,2000Y. |
| African Brotherhood Church | 1945 | I ind | xvA.K | 342 | 30,869 | 64,030 | *ABC.* Schism ex AIM, Salvation Army. Kamba. HQ Mitaboni, Machakos. 100n,1s,W=68%,1010Y. |
| African Christian Church & Schools | 1947 | I Bap | .WA,K | 33 | 8,000 | 30,500 | *ACC&S.* Split ex AIM. 1967, invited in M=CBOMB(Canada). 99% Kikuyu. 7n,2x,8f,1500Y. |
| African Church | 1961 | I Bap | .T.,T | 19 | 15,000 | 30,000 | *AC.* Kamba split ex AIM, first known as Kenya African Ch. HQ Machakos. 6n,W=19%. |
| African Church Mission | 1941 | I Ang | ..... | 12 | 2,000 | 3,000 | *ACM.* Ex Nomiya Luo Mission, permitting post-baptismal polygamy. 3n,W=35%, 90Y,80y. |
| African Ch of Jesus Christ in Kenya | 1970 | I Ang | ..... | 4 | 300 | 1,000 | *ACJC.* Kikuyu split ex Anglican D Mount Kenya, linked with CCA. 1n,W=50%,15Y,6y. |
| African Church of the Holy Spirit | 1927 | I pen | .U.,K | 54 | 3,352 | 5,455 | *ACHS. Dini ya Msalaba (Religion of the Cross)*, ex Quakers. 29n,W=75%,460Y,271y. |
| African Divine Church | 1949 | I pen | ....I | 82 | 2,000 | 3,850 | *ADC.* Maragoli schism ex PAoC over desire to wear uniforms. 21n,W=95%,186Y,106y. |
| African Evangelical Presbyterian Ch | 1962 | P Ref | .T..T | 30 | 338 | 800 | *AEPC.* M=WPM(USA). 88% Kamba, rest Mbere and Embu. HQ Mwingi. 8n,5f,W=67%,30Y,20y. |
| African Holy Zionist Church | 1959 | I Sal | ....I | 3 | 1,200 | 3,000 | Luhya schism formerly called Africa Zion Church. HQ Kegomori, Maragoli. 20n,W=90%. |

*Continued overleaf*

*Table 2–continued*

| Official name 1 | Begun 2 | Type 3 | Counc 4 | Congs 5 | Adults 6 | Affiliated 7 | Names, notes, and other statistics (see Codebook) 8 |
|---|---|---|---|---|---|---|---|
| African Independent Church of Kenya | 1943 | I Ang | ..... | | 500 | 1,000 | Kamba schism ex Anglican Church, declining since 1960. HQ Machakos. |
| African Indep Pentecostal Ch of Africa | 1925 | I ind | .vA.K | 454 | 200,000 | 496,000 | *AIPC*. 4 Dioceses. Persecution 1930–57; 1964, massive rural growth. 136n,1p,6000Y. |
| African Interior Church | 1943 | I Hol | ....K | 29 | 10,650 | 30,000 | *AIC*. Luhya split ex Church of God (Anderson) mission. 5n,W=68%,160Y,200y. |
| African Israel Church Nineveh | 1942 | I pen | .W..K | 274 | 36,904 | 76,200 | *AICN*. HQ holy city Nineveh. Ex PAoC. 51% Luhya, 49% Luo. 91n,W=80%,160Y,83y. |
| African Mission of Holy Ghost Church | 1930 | I pen | ..... | 14 | 2,500 | 7,000 | *AMHGC*. Early Kikuyu Spirit church, formed from Watu wa Mungu. 14n,W=99%,120Y,50y. |
| African Orthodox Church of Kenya | 1928 | O Gre | CwA.k | 230 | 99,000 | 248,000 | *D Eirenopolis*, in P Alexandria. 80% Kikuyu, 15% Luhya. 33n,3x,1s,10000Y,15000y. |
| Apostolic Faith of Africa | 1959 | I pen | ..... | 50 | 4,000 | 7,000 | Kikuyu split ex PCEA; spread west through Pokot into Uganda. HQ Thogoto. 5n,W=98%. |
| Apostolic Hierarchy Church | 1940 | I CCa | ..... | | 580 | 1,500 | Kikuyu. Ex RCC, formerly African God Worshippers Fellowship Church Society. |
| Assemblies of God, Kenya District | 1968 | P Pe2 | ..... | 212 | 3,000 | 12,000 | Split ex IPA by 2 missionaries as Kenya Pentecostal Fellowship. 4n,4x,W=50%,876Y. |
| Baptist Convention of Kenya | 1956 | P Bap | T...K | 205 | 5,985 | 25,000 | *BCK*. M=BMEA(SBC,USA). 25% Kikuyu, rest Coast, Nyanza. 35n,18x,89f,11h,W=50%,1200Y. |
| Bible Fellowship Church | c1940 | P Bap | ....K | 1 | 210 | 500 | Independent group in Thika begun by former GMS woman missionary, ex GMS. |
| **Catholic Church in Kenya:** | 1498 | R Lat | PzSER | 578 | 1,025,200 | 1,934,811 | *Kanisa Katoliki*. C=9+11+40. 1s(194). 86n,580x,205m,1299w,P=41%,45618Y,54078y. |
| M Nairobi | 1860 | R Lat | Ps | 62 | 121,000 | 228,274 | 60% Kikuyu, 14% Luhya, 6% Whites. 1s. 8 86 35 291 54 6161 9338 |
| D Eldoret | 1959 | R Lat | Ps | 20 | 31,800 | 60,050 | 30% Bukusu, 20% Kikuyu, 18% Elgeyo. 1 24 11 48 40 2086 2522 |
| D Kisii | 1960 | R Lat | Ps | 21 | 148,400 | 279,950 | 52% Luo, 47% Kisii. 3,000 Muslims. 12 33 29 93 34 4408 6386 |
| D Kisumu | 1925 | R Lat | Pmhm | 43 | 266,200 | 502,374 | 47% Luhya, 34% Luo, 7% Nandi, 6% Teso. 13 91 30 245 32 5264 11602 |
| D Kitui | 1956 | R Lat | Psps | 13 | 11,200 | 21,205 | 99% Kamba. 3,000 Muslims, 200 Hindus. 1 37 0 28 51 2226 623 |
| D Machakos | 1969 | R Lat | Pcssp | 66 | 54,400 | 102,596 | 99% Kamba. Very rapid growth. 6 35 10 6 50 4060 2204 |
| D Marsabit | 1964 | R Lat | Pimc | 12 | 2,300 | 4,347 | 94% animist, 3% Muslim, 2% Catholic. 0 26 3 54 59 708 213 |
| D Meru | 1926 | R Lat | Pimc | 26 | 98,600 | 186,043 | 45% Meru, 45% Embu, 4% Turkana. 14 49 15 96 46 5000 5000 |
| D Mombasa | 1955 | R Lat | Pcssp | 24 | 37,700 | 71,206 | 40% Taita, 20% Giriama, 10% Duruma. 5 46 0 93 46 1700 2089 |
| D Nakuru | 1968 | R Lat | Ps | 238 | 58,100 | 109,726 | Mostly Kikuyu; 1% expatriate. 1 52 20 39 47 2818 4173 |
| D Nyeri | 1905 | R Lat | Ps | 37 | 188,100 | 355,000 | 99% Kikuyu. M=IMC. 23 73 49 266 42 10400 8800 |
| PA Lodwar (1978, D Lodwar) | 1968 | R Lat | Psps | 7 | 800 | 1,550 | In extreme northwest desert. 0 13 0 7 60 87 28 |
| PA Ngong (1976, D Ngong) | 1959 | R Lat | Pmhm | 9 | 6,600 | 12,490 | 40% Kikuyu, 14% Maasai, 12% Kipsigis. 2 15 3 33 45 700 1100 |
| Children of God Regeneration Church | 1947 | I ind | ..... | 90 | 1,000 | 3,542 | *Ayie Remb Yesu* (*I accept the Blood of Jesus*). 95% Luo, 5% Bantu. 42n,124Y,52y. |
| Chosen Ch of the Holy Spirit in Kenya | 1930 | I pen | ..... | 33 | 1,500 | 2,500 | Early Kikuyu movement out of Watu wa Mungu (People of God). 3n,W=95%,78Y,64y. |
| Christadelphian Bible Mission (Kenya) | c1970 | P Ade | x.... | 5 | 50 | 150 | *CBMK*. M=CBM(UK). Small ecclesias (churches) across Kenya. Pacifist, adventist. |
| Christian Brotherhood Church | 1952 | I Ang | ..... | 144 | 3,000 | 9,000 | *CBC*. Schism ex Anglicans. 45% Luhya, 30% Luo, 18% Gusii, 6% Ganda. 8n,30Y,36y. |
| Christian Evangelical Church | 1948 | I Ang | ..... | 45 | 1,920 | 4,000 | *CEC*. First Balokole (Revival) schism ex Anglicans among Luo. 11n,W=94%,65Y. |
| Christian Holy Ghost Ch of EAfrica | 1934 | I pen | ..... | 18 | 660 | 1,500 | *CHGC*. Conservative wing of the Aroti (Dreamers, Seers). All Kikuyu. 9n,W=95%,60Y. |
| Christian Science Ch of East Africa | 1925 | M Sci | x.... | 1 | 30 | 100 | *Church of Christ, Scientist*. M=CCS(Boston,USA). 70% Africans. 1w,W=90%. |
| Christian Theocratic Holy Ch of God | 1958 | I ind | ..... | 77 | 3,000 | 3,870 | Kikuyu movement. Finally registered 1971. HQ Kawangware Village. 70n,W=75%. |
| Church of Christ in Africa | 1957 | I Ang | xT.TT | 545 | 75,000 | 120,000 | *CCA*. Schism of 40% D Maseno. 8 Dioceses. 81% Luo, 10% Luhya. 81n,1p,W=60%,2400Y,8640y. |
| Church of God in East Africa | 1905 | P Hol | x.G.a | 385 | 40,000 | 260,000 | *CGEA*. M=CoG(Anderson) (USA). 78% Luhya, 20% Gusii. 375n,26f,2H,4h,1s,W=75%.1800Y. |
| Church of Saviour, Diocese of Nyakoko | 1968 | I Ang | ..... | 33 | 2,000 | 3,293 | Schism of clergy ex HTCA (itself a schism ex CCA). All Luo. 7n,W=50%,39Y,65y. |
| Church of the Kenya Family | 1948 | I ind | ..... | 13 | 1,049 | 4,000 | Embu movement; healing, rejection of word 'Amen' after prayers. W=75%,54Y,96y. |
| Church of the Province of Kenya: | 1844 | A Eva | AWAVK | 1,629 | 239,383 | 582,600 | *CPK. Kanisa la Jimbo la Kenya*. M=CMS,BCMS. 176f. 224n,51x,W=41%,26853Y,20132y. |
| D Nairobi | 1964 | A Eva | A | 105 | 15,000 | 50,000 | City, with Maasai and Kamba areas. 1p. 23 22 20 700 1700 |
| D Maseno North | 1970 | A Eva | A | 400 | 20,000 | 100,000 | Rural. 90% Luhya, 10% Teso. Revival splits. 1H,2r. 37 3 40 1000 1000 |
| D Maseno South | 1970 | A Eva | A | 402 | 20,400 | 150,000 | Rural. 94% Luo, 500 Kipsigis, 250 Gusii, 100 White. 31 3 30 1891 1043 |
| D Mombasa | 1898 | A Eva | A | 75 | 15,000 | 40,000 | Coastal. 80% Taita, 20% Giriama, Luo labourers. 1H. 33 4 35 800 1000 |
| D Mount Kenya East | 1975 | A Eva | A | 140 | 50,000 | 70,000 | Kikuyu, Embu. Very rapid growth,G=10%pa. 20 2 70 3000 2000 |
| D Mount Kenya South | 1975 | A Eva | A | 210 | 109,925 | 129,900 | 99% Kikuyu. Formed 1961, divided 1975. 1u. 40 6 60 17910 11940 |
| D Nakuru | 1961 | A Eva | A | 297 | 9,058 | 42,700 | 55% Kikuyu, 20% Nandi, 10% White. G=10%pa. 40 11 25 1552 1449 |
| Cross Church of East Africa | c1940 | I Ang | ..... | 70 | 5,000 | 15,000 | *Roho Musalaba* (*Spirit Cross Church*). Luo schism ex MHGC. HQ Kabondo. 10n. |
| Deliverance Church | 1969 | I pe4 | x.... | 3 | 1,000 | 3,000 | *YCAF. Young Christian Ambassadors Fellowship*. Youths; healing, shouting for victory. 2n. |
| East Africa Pentecostal Churches | 1953 | P Pe4 | ..... | 74 | 10,000 | 20,000 | *EAPC*. M=Kenya Faith Mission(Norway), ex SFM. 80% Meru. 117n,2x,2p,W=80%,7000Y. |
| East Africa Yearly Meeting of Friends | 1902 | P Qua | Q.A.K | 1,200 | 33,860 | 100,000 | *EAYM*. M=FUM. Largest Quaker church after USA. 99% Luhya. 130n,2x,16f,3H,1s,W=50%. |
| Episcopal Church of Africa | 1968 | I Ang | ....K | 39 | 2,000 | 5,000 | *ECA. Diocese of Kenya*. 3 Parishes. Schism ex CCA. 99% Luo. Also in Tanzania. 4n. |
| Evangelical Free Mission in Kenya | 1960 | P Pe2 | Z.... | 35 | 4,000 | 8,000 | M=SFM(Sweden). 57% Kikuyu, 34% Luhya, 5% Turkana, 4% Maasai. 60n,8x,W=75%,850Y. |
| Evangelical Lutheran Ch in Tanzania | 1967 | P Lut | Lwa.K | 17 | 1,500 | 3,284 | *Kenya Synod*. M=ELCT(Tanzania). Tanzanians. Merger talks with LCK. 73Y,322y. |
| Friends of the Holy Spirit | 1946 | I pen | ..... | 10 | 1,000 | 2,000 | *Arata a Roho Mutheru* (=*FHS*). Unorganized Kikuyu, Kamba Anglican revivalists. 10n. |
| Full Gospel Churches of Kenya | 1949 | P Pe2 | Z...K | 353 | 22,000 | 60,000 | *FGCK*. M=FFFM(Finland). 39% Luo, 33% Kikuyu, 14% Kalenjin. 182n,6x,W=95%,1604Y. |
| God of the Universe Church | 1962 | I pen | ..... | 18 | 500 | 1,274 | *GUC*. Luo schism ex PAG. Successful evangelism directed by prophecy. 7n,W=75%,80Y. |
| Good News Church of Africa | 1958 | I Bap | .T..T | 120 | 11,050 | 30,000 | *GNCA*. Schism of 70% ex GFF over polygamy. 50% Kamba, 25% Kikuyu, Coastal. 60n. |
| Gospel Assemblies of Kenya | 1960 | I pen | ..... | 102 | 2,000 | 6,000 | *Local Chs of Kenya*. 35% Luo, 25% Luhya, 25% Kikuyu, 15% Teso. 52n,1x,500Y,50y. |
| Gospel Furthering Bible Church | 1936 | P Bap | .M... | | 3,000 | 10,000 | *GFBC*. M=GFF(USA), 1936 schism ex AIM. Kamba. 1958 massive schism, GNCA. 18f,1s. |
| Gospel of God Church | 1967 | I peA | x.... | 30 | 800 | 1,800 | *Vapostori* (*Apostles*) of Johane Masowe. M=ACJM(Shona from Rhodesia). 20n,W=95%. |
| Gospel Tabernacle Church | c1943 | I Bap | ..... | 15 | 2,650 | 8,000 | Kamba schism ex GFF led by missionary; now autonomous, with M=GFF(USA). 15n,1x. |
| Holy Ch of Evangelistic Apostles Faith | 1958 | I pen | ..I.. | 30 | 2,000 | 11,000 | Ex AFM(SAfrica) over polygamy. 80% Kikuyu, 7% Luo, 5% Maasai. 19n,W=85%,200Y. |
| Holy Ghost Church of East Africa | 1934 | I pen | ..... | 30 | 6,000 | 10,000 | *HGCEA*. Liberal wing of Aroti, modern views. Kikuyu. 31n,W=90%,100Y,100y. |
| Holy Ghost Coptic Church of Africa | 1964 | I CCa | ..... | 7 | 1,700 | 5,000 | Ex RCC, with Catholic terminology, Holy Father, basilica, mass. Luo. 8n,W=55%. |
| Holy Spirit Church of East Africa | 1927 | I pen | ..... | 25 | 660 | 3,000 | *Dini ya Roho*. Luhya revival ex Quakers. White robes, turbans. 8n,W=65%,52Y,187y. |
| Holy Spirit Church of Zayun | c1962 | I pen | ..... | | 470 | 1,500 | Known as '*M*' *Aroti* (red M on robes, red or blue turbans, green forbidden). Kikuyu. |
| Holy Trinity Church in Africa | 1960 | I Ang | ..... | 174 | 20,000 | 50,000 | *HTCA*. Ex CCA over leadership. 75% Luo, 10% Luhya, 5% Kikuyu. 15n,W=55%,600Y,1000y. |
| Independent Baptist Churches of EA | 1964 | P Bap | .T..T | 28 | 400 | 2,400 | *IBCEA*. Kamba churches aided by M=Grace Independent Baptist Mission(USA). 7n,2x. |
| Independent Lutheran Church of Africa | 1961 | I Lut | .T..T | 20 | 500 | 1,000 | *ILC. Loyalist Religion*. No Lutheran connections. Luhya. 1n,W=80%,31Y,25y. |
| Independent Presbyterian Church of EA | 1946 | P Ref | .T..T | 9 | 1,000 | 3,000 | *IPCEA*. Kamba, north of Kitui. M=IBPFM(USA). 1957 split by WPM(now AEPC). 3x. |
| International Fellowship for Christ | 1969 | I pen | ..... | 120 | 1,000 | 3,000 | *IFFC*. Indigenous pentecostals, with links with USA and Canada bodies. 8n. |
| Jehovah's Witnesses | 1931 | M Jeh | x.... | 25 | 1,082 | 3,000 | *IBSA*. Missionaries 1956 (1973, 34f expelled). Whites; first Africans 1962. 164Y. |
| Jerusalem Seventh-day Church of God | 1959 | I pen | ..... | 20 | 1,020 | 3,000 | Kikuyu. 17 Kenyans ordained in 1970 by M=Ch of God Seventh-day(USA).15n,30Y. |
| Judah Israel Mission | 1961 | I Ang | ..... | 3 | 900 | 3,009 | Bukusu split ex DYM. Temple in Kimilili, sacrifices. 10n,W=95%,70Y,80y. |
| Kenya Church of Christ | 1965 | P Dis | x.... | 26 | 600 | 2,000 | M=CC(Non-Instrumental) (USA). Nairobi, Kakamega. 50% Kikuyu. 12x,340Y. |
| Kenya Foundation of the Prophets Ch | 1927 | I pen | ..... | 17 | 15,000 | 41,325 | *KFPC*. Kikuyu. Led by 92-year-old founder. Prayer facing Mt. Kenya. W=20%,220Y,405y. |
| Last Ministry Church | c1965 | I pen | ..... | | 1,485 | 4,000 | Coast. Taita body stressing ministry in last days before Second Coming of Christ. |
| Lavington Church, Nairobi | 1960 | P uni | .aw.k | 2 | 500 | 1,500 | First united parish (Angl,Meth,Presb); no other subsequently. 1x,W=50%,20Y,30y. |
| Lost Israelites of Kenya | 1960 | I ind | ..... | | 10,000 | 20,000 | *Israel with 10 Commandments*. Flags, uniforms, marching. HQ Kitale. 12n,W=95%,1000Y. |
| Luo Spirit Church | 1968 | I Ang | ..... | 21 | 1,669 | 3,744 | *Luo Roho Church*. Split ex NLC to assert glossolalia, exorcism. 36n,W=95%,41Y,82y. |
| Lutheran Church in Kenya | 1948 | P Lut | L...K | 69 | 4,204 | 8,694 | *LCK. Kanisa la Kilutheri*. M=SLM(Sweden). 85% Gusii, 15% Luo. 8n,2x,W=50%,250Y. |
| Maranatha Church | 1967 | P Pe4 | x.... | 45 | 1,169 | 1,922 | M=Swedish Maranatha (Aramaic for 'Our Lord, come') Mission. Luo. 42n,1x,7Y. |
| Maria Legio of Africa | 1962 | I CCa | x.... | 600 | 48,264 | 150,000 | *MLA*. Largest RCC schism in Africa. 90% Luo. 9 Dioceses, 7 cardinals, pope. 500n. |
| Mennonite Church of Kenya | 1965 | P Men | G...K | 15 | 550 | 2,000 | M=EMBMC(MCNA,USA). Luo immigrants from Tanzania in SNyanza. 2n,22f,1h,W=20%,50Y. |
| Methodist Church in Kenya | 1862 | P Met | VWA.K | 624 | 18,729 | 100,000 | *MCK*. M=MMS(UK). A=1967. 3 Districts. 30n,10x,40f,2H,1u,W=75%,2258Y,1989y. |
| Miracle Revival Fellowship Pente Ch | c1948 | I pen | ..... | | 600 | 2,000 | *Weni Mwanguvu/People of Power*. Taita split ex Anglicans after TLOsborn crusades. |
| Musanda Holy Ghost Church of EA | 1934 | I pen | ..... | 65 | 1,673 | 5,073 | *MHGC*. First Luo Roho (Spirit) movement. Ex CMS. HQ Musanda. 13n,W=64%,80Y,111y. |
| National Independent Church of Africa | 1929 | I Ang | ..... | 53 | 5,691 | 6,928 | *NICA*. Embu and Meru ex-Anglicans formerly in AIPC. 41n,W=75%,80Y,165y. |
| New Apostolic Church | 1973 | C CAp | x.... | | 500 | 1,000 | M=NAC(World HQ Dortmund,Germany). Catholic Apostolic. Begun from Bombay, India. |
| New East African Church | c1970 | I ind | ..... | | 3,500 | 10,000 | *NEAC*. Kamba schism at Mitaboni. HQ Kwakivanyu, Mitaboni, Machakos. |
| Nomiya Luo Church | 1914 | I Ang | ..... | 420 | 65,000 | 120,000 | *NLC*. Nomiya=The Word of God was given to me. Ex CMS. 3 Dioceses. 31n,2076Y,3504y. |
| Nomiya Luo Sabbath | c1957 | I Ang | ..... | 184 | 6,800 | 10,680 | *NLS*. Schism ex NLC. Muslim features stressed. HQ Nairobi. 23n,W=68%,340Y,860y. |
| Norwegian Pentecostal Mission in Kenya | 1955 | P Pe2 | Z...K | 74 | 5,200 | 15,000 | *NPMK*. M=NPY(Norway). 48% Luo, 38% Kipsigis, 10% Gusii. HQ Ukwala. 60n,W=65%,924Y. |
| Pentecostal Assemblies of God | 1910 | P Pe2 | ZPG.a | 710 | 90,000 | 192,000 | *PAG*. M=PAoC. 73% Luhya, 10% Luo, 10% Gusii. 314n,11x,53f,1j,1s(71),W=65%,15000Y. |
| Pentecostal Evangelistic Fell of Africa | 1938 | P Pe2 | ZG..K | 791 | 48,200 | 150,000 | *PEFA*. 1962 union of IPA(USA) & Elim(USA). 526n,9x,40f,G=15%pa,5000Y. |
| Power of Jesus Around the World Ch | 1955 | I pen | ..... | 200 | 10,000 | 20,000 | Luo schism ex Voice of Salvation & Healing Ch after TLOsborn crusade in Uganda. |
| Presbyterian Church of East Africa | 1891 | P Ref | RWA.K | 350 | 62,000 | 100,000 | *PCEA*. M=CSM(UK). 60% Kikuyu, 30% Meru. 71n,6x,14f,3H,9h,1p,18r,1u,W=80%,2450Y,5000y. |
| Reformed Church of East Africa | 1909 | P Ref | Rv..K | 62 | 3,031 | 6,487 | *RCEA*. M=DRC(SA),now NHK(Holland). A=1963. 50% Nandi.4n, 3x,9f,1u,W=45%,508Y,478y. |
| Religion of the Ancestral Spirits | 1944 | I mar | ..... | | 10,000 | 50,000 | *Dini ya Msambwa* (*DYM*).*Israel Anglican Ch*.Schism ex Quakers.Banned 1948,again in 1968.Mt Elgon. |
| Ruwe Holy Ghost Ch of East Africa | 1939 | I pen | ..... | 114 | 2,615 | 5,000 | Schism ex MHGC over uniforms, setting up rival HQ at Ruwe. Luo. 5n,W=95%,16Y,86y. |
| Salvation Army | 1921 | P Sal | xwa.K | 1,150 | 34,929 | 110,000 | *Jeshi la Wokovu*. 8 Divisions, East Africa Territory. 70% Luhya. 447n,23x,1s,W=75%. |
| Seventh-day Adventist Church | 1906 | P Adv | x...k | 861 | 73,116 | 171,023 | *East African Union*. 45% Luo, 45% Gusii. 105n,16x,37f,1H,11h,1j,1r,906t(159570),W=64%,8601Y. |
| Sinai Church of East Africa | 1965 | I pen | .T..T | 6 | 350 | 1,200 | *SCEA*. Luhya schism ex AICN, growing very slowly. HQ North Maragoli. 3n,W=50%. |
| Spirit Church of God of Israel | 1960 | I pen | .v... | 25 | 12,300 | 40,000 | *Roho CGI*. Schism ex AICN as World Spiritual Israel Ch. 60% Luo, 30% Luhya. 36n. |
| United Pentecostal Church | 1971 | P Pel | x.... | 20 | 1,000 | 2,000 | *Jesus Only Church*. M=UPC(USA). Unitarian Pentecostals. HQ Nairobi. 30n,2f,1p. |
| Voice of Prophecy Church | c1960 | I Adv | ..... | | 700 | 2,000 | Luo sabbatarian church led by blind charismatic prophetess Susanna Nyabulwa. |
| Voice of Salvation & Healing Church | 1954 | I pen | ..... | 50 | 6,000 | 12,000 | Early Luo schism ex AIM over faith-healing and charismata. 50n,W=70%. |
| Wokofu (Salvation) African Church | 1966 | I Sal | .T.TT | 120 | 3,900 | 15,000 | *WAC*. Ex Salvation Army; yellow uniforms, symbol 'W'. 60% Luhya, 30% Kamba. 35n,160Y. |
| World Christian Soldiers Church | c1966 | I ind | ..... | | 300 | 1,000 | Luo movement requiring all members to use musical instruments in worship. |
| Other African indigenous churches | | I | ..... | | 15,000 | 30,000 | Total about 90 (see list below). |
| Other Protestant denominations | | P | ..... | | 2,000 | 5,000 | Total about 20 (see list below). |
| Other Orthodox churches | 1973 | O | ..... | 2 | 1,000 | 2,000 | Ethiopian Orthodox Ch, and Apostolic Ch of St Mark (see below). |
| Other marginal Protestant bodies | | M | ..... | | 700 | 1,000 | Bodies mainly from USA (see below), including Branhamites, Worldwide Ch of God. |
| **Total affiliated (mid-1970)** | | | | **18,200** | **2,683,047** | **6,085,535** | **Total denominations (1970) . . . 206.** |
| **Total affiliated (mid-1975)** | | | | **21,000** | **3,394,300** | **7,698,800** | **Total denominations (1975) . . . 246.** |
| **Total affiliated (mid-1980)** | | | | **24,000** | **4,288,300** | **9,726,600** | **Total denominations (1980) . . . 296.** |

NOTES ON TABLE ABOVE

COLUMNS: for meanings and CODES (cols. 1, 3, 4, 8), see Codebook (Part 6). Column 1: **Boldface type** = church with over 10% of country's affiliated Christians.

NATIONAL COUNCILS (Column 4, 5th letter).

a = member of both NCCK and EFK.
b = member of both OAICK and NCCK.
G = Evangelical Fellowship of Kenya (EFK).
I = Organization of African Independent Churches of Kenya (OAICK).
K = National Christian Council of Kenya (NCCK) (Jumuiya ya Wakristo wa Kenya).

k = consultative associate member of NCCK.
R = Kenya Episcopal Conference (KEC).
T = East Africa Christian Alliance (EACA) (all members are Kenyan churches).

*Other national councils.* These number at least 11, all being attempts to unite African indigenous churches: African Independent Communion Churches, Council of East African Evangelist Societies of God (1970), East African United Churches and Orthodox Coptic Communion (1962), Ethiopian Orthodox Holy Spirit & United Churches of East Africa (1970), Indigenous African Christian Churches (IACC) (1974), Kenya African United Christian Churches (1961), Kenya Independent Churches Fellowship (1960), National United Churches Association of East Africa (1969), United Churches of Africa (1969), United Churches of East Africa (1969), United Independent Churches of East Africa (1969), United Orthodox Independent Churches of East Africa (1971), United Orthodox Independent Zion Churches of Kenya (1971).

*Local councils.* 6 local branches of the NCCK.

OTHER AFRICAN INDIGENOUS CHURCHES. In 1973 there were about 90 other smaller bodies, mostly pentecostal, and mostly with well under 1,000 adult members each; about 80 of these were registered with government as lawful societies. The larger of these bodies include the following (with, in brackets, year of founding, and present total of adult members): African Holy Ghost Christian Ch (1968; 600), African Sinai Ch (1965; 350), Apostles Christian Ch of Africa (1968; 542), Christ Evangelistic Association (c1959; 10,000 claimed), Christian Association (1,100), Christian Chs (Chs of Christ) (1968), Ch of Holy Communion of God (1969; 550), Ch of Messiah (1948; 5,000), Ch of Spirit in Grace and Truth in Africa (c1967; 600), Ch of the Living God (c1964; 429), Communion Ch of Africa (c1970; 400), Disciples of Christ in Africa (1970; 700), Divine Christian Ch of East Africa (1962; 3,500), Full Gospel Fellowship Mission of Africa (c1964; 829), Independent African Orthodox Ch (c1965; 968), Israel Holy Ghost Ch of Kenya (1971; 936), Kimbanguist Ch (EJCSK, from Zaire), Miracles and Wonders Ch (1975 application WCC), Muolo Roho Israel Ch (1950; 600), Pentecostal Christian Universal Ch (1968; 970), Sabina Church of the Ark (700), Seventh-day Missionary Ch (1936; 500), Truth of the Apostles (c1966; 300). By 1975 indigenous bodies from other continents were beginning to enter, including the Unification Ch (Moon Ch) from Korea (HSAUWC).

OTHER PROTESTANT DENOMINATIONS. These smaller bodies include: Children of God International (from USA, UK), Christian Faith Mission of Kenya (85), Dutch Reformed Ch (20), East African Mission (1970; 231), Kenya Revival Centre (c1960; 400), Nairobi Baptist Ch (1958; 140), Nairobi Undenominational Ch (Open Brethren) (c1930; 45), Restoration (House-Church Movement/Pyramid Ch/Ch of the Great Shepherd; neo-charismatic split ex mainline Charismatic Renewal), Scriptural Holiness Mission (1948; 150 members; member of NCCK), Seventh-day Adventist Reform Movement (c1968; 400), World-Wide Missions (1961).

OTHER ORTHODOX CHURCHES. After several years of contact with indigenous federations of churches in Kenya, 2 churches have opened teaching missions and churches in Nairobi: in 1973, the Ethiopian Orthodox Church (HQ Addis Ababa); and in 1976, the Coptic Orthodox Church (HQ Cairo), registered in Kenya as the Apostolic Church of St Mark, with an Egyptian bishop set aside solely for ministry with African indigenous churches.

OTHER MARGINAL PROTESTANT BODIES. These include Branhamites (Kenya Local Believers, End Time Believers; begun 1970 from HQ Jeffersonville, IN, USA; Jesus-Only Unitarians), Worldwide Ch of God (Radio Ch of God, USA; begun 1975; visiting teams from Japan et al), et alia.

UNITING CHURCHES. In 1974, 2 separate sets of negotiations for organic union were under way, as follows: (1) Ch of the Province of Kenya, Methodist Ch in Kenya, Presbyterian Ch of East Africa. (2) Lutheran Ch of Kenya, Ev Lutheran Ch in Tanzania (Kenya Synod).

**PEOPLES** (ethnolinguistic). Christians: 22.3% Kikuyu, 18.9% Luhya, 18.9% Luo, 10.1% Kamba, 8.4% Kalenjin (4.4% Kipsigis, 2.1% Nandi, 0.7% Tugen, 0.7% Elgeyo, 0.5% Marakwet), 8.0% Gusii, 3.5% Meru, 1.6% Mijikenda (0.6% Giriama, 0.5% Duruma), 1.2% Embu, 1.1% Taita, 1.0% Teso, 0.5% European (White), 0.5% Maasai, 0.5% Kuria, 0.5% Sabaot, 0.3% Tharaka, 0.2% Mbere, 0.2% Indian (Goanese, Malayali), 0.1% Pokot, 0.1% Pokomo, 0.1% Turkana, Samburu, Boran, et alii.

**COUNTRY-WIDE TOTALS**

EVANGELIZATION (see Part 5). 1900: 7%. 1970: 96%. 1980: 98%. *Mass evangelism.* Among the many recent campaigns: 1960, Billy Graham crusades in Kisumu and Nairobi (16,600 attenders, 4,755 enquirers); several campaigns by T. L. Osborn, Oral Roberts, E. J. Daniels; East African Revival (Balokole) conventions in Butere 1961 (7,000 attenders), Mombasa 1964 (20,000), Kitui 1965 (5,000), Meru 1966 (10,000), Kabare 1967 (5,000), Wundanyi 1969 (10,000), Kikuyu 1970 (30,000), Mumias 1971 (6,000); 1969 United Christian Mission to Nairobi (Crossroads Mission) sponsored by Africa Enterprise; 1970–75, numerous campaigns; December 1976, Pan-African Christian Leadership Assembly (PACLA) with 800 participants, including Billy Graham rally in Nairobi with 55,000 attenders and 985 enquirers; 1978, Here's Life Africa (CCCI) in Nairobi (18,300 enquirers). *Radiophonic evangelism.* TWR, RVOG, FEBA, et alia. Bible correspondence courses: ICI Emmaus Bible School, Word of Life BCC (24,660 enrolments, 10,300 active), Every Home Crusade (184,000 enrolled), VOP, et alia. *Literature evangelism.* By June 1976, Every Home Crusade had distributed 4,840,995 tracts or booklets (198,000 per month) resulting in 256,026 decision cards being received (13,848 per month), a rate of 5–7%. In February 1977, 26,990 decision cards were received.

FOREIGN MISSIONARIES AND PERSONNEL (nationals serving abroad) (1973). Total 112 in Tanzania, Uganda et alia: 52 Roman Catholics, 46 African indigenous, 10 Protestants, 4 Anglicans.

FOREIGN MISSIONARIES AND PERSONNEL (aliens from abroad) (1973). Total 2,969. *From Western world.* 2,788: about 1,500 Roman Catholics, 1,062 Protestants (580 in 44 USA societies, 153 in 11 UK societies, 136 in 6 Canada societies, 52 in 3 Sweden societies, 44 in 4 Finland societies, 40 in 2 Norway societies, 30 in 2 Australia societies, 12 in 5 WGermany societies, 9 in 1 Netherlands society, 3 in 2 Denmark societies, 3 in 1 Switzerland society), 188 Anglicans (143 in 6 UK societies, 30 in 1 Australia society, 9 in 1 New Zealand society, 3 in 2 Ireland (Eire) societies, 3 in 2 USA societies), 34 marginal Protestants (Jehovah's Witnesses), 4 Orthodox from Greece. By 1975, North American missionaries had risen to 929. *From Communist world.* 6: 4 Protestants from Hungary, 2 Roman Catholics from Poland. *From Third World.* 175: 138 Roman Catholics from 14 countries (50 from Tanzania, 38 Uganda, 28 Mexico, 10 India, 3 Philippines, 3 Colombia), 20 Protestants from Egypt, India, Sri Lanka, Japan et alia, 15 indigenous from Rhodesia, Uganda et alia, about 2 Catholics (non-Roman) from India.

INSTITUTIONS (church-operated) (1973). Total 970, including 660 higher schools (9 minor seminaries), 250 medical centres (80 hospitals), 5 presses, 5 religious communities, 7 research centres, 11 seminaries (9 Protestants, 1 RC, 1 Orthodox).

PERIODICALS. About 120 titles (70 Protestant (15 SDA), 28 RC, 10 indigenous). For details, see *Kenya Churches handbook.*

PERSONNEL. About 11,813 (8,844 national, 2,969 foreign).

RELIGIOUS LIBRARIES. About 28.

SCRIPTURE DISTRIBUTION (1975). Annual totals: 96,018 Bibles (7% free, 82% subsidized, 10% commercial), 218,380 NTs (14% free, 81% subsidized, 5% commercial), 611,818 UBS portions, 1,333,998 UBS selections. *Translations completed.* Portion: 22 languages since 1848. NT: 15 languages since 1902. Bible: 8 languages since 1908.

SERVICE AGENCIES. About 180, including AACC, AEAM, AEATC, AICMB, AMECEA, AOSK, BB, CA, CACC, CCCI, CCEA, CCUC, CHF, CITC, CORAT, CRS, CSC, CSLC, DMA, EACA, EFK, FOCUS, JRSK, KALM, KCGF, KCMS, KCS, KCTPF, KEC, KHCF, KSCF, LCWE, LIFE, MAF, MTS, NCCK, NCCW, OCU, OCYAK, PCMA, RSAK, SAFE, SU, TF, UBS, WLC(EHC), WSCF, WVI, YCS, YMCA, YWCA.

**ADDITIONAL DATA ON CHURCHES**

AFRICA INLAND CHURCH. *Membership.* 33% Kamba, 27% Kalenjin, 20% Kikuyu, 12% Coastal, 5% Maasai, 2% Luo. *Growth.* The figures in the table above represent the situation in 1970. An official survey in 1978, based on 30% replies from all churches, produced the following 1978 estimates: total congregations 2,500, divided among 10 Regions and 67 Districts (DCCs); adult membership (on rolls) 197,400; total Christian community 440,000; total professing any relation to AIC, 630,800. *Growth rate.* Over 1970–78, this represents growth at 5.0% per year.

AFRICAN BROTHERHOOD CHURCH. By 1977 the total community had increased to 78,622 in 14 Pastorates (13 in Kenya, 1 in Uganda, with 4 churches also in Tanzania).

BAPTIST CONVENTION OF KENYA. In 1977 among the coastal Giriama tribe, 2,177 persons were baptized and 145 new congregations begun during a 24-week period.

CATHOLIC CHURCH IN KENYA. In Kenya Swahili, Kanisa Katoliki ya Kenya. *New dioceses.* In 1976, PA Ngong was raised to diocese, and PA Garissa was erected out of D Meru and D Mombasa. In 1978, PA Lodwar was raised to diocese, and D Kakamega was erected out of D Kisumu. *Churches.* The 578 parishes and quasi-parishes had 1,868 churches or mass centres in 1972. *Catechumens.* Total: (1959) 168,023; (1961) 184,018; (1963) 173,324; and (1970) 166,137, divided as follows among the 13 dioceses in order (and included in column 7): 25967, 10550, 6218, 8260, 3467, 23094, 2500, 15220, 7420, 22401, 40000, 550, 490. *Annual baptisms.* (1972) 56.0% infant, 44.0% adult. *Priests.* The first 2 Africans were ordained in 1927. Almost all African priests are secular except 5 religious in monasteries. Expatriates: almost all religious, except for a few in secular institutes. *Brothers.* (1967) 17% African, 83% expatriate. *Sisters.* (1967) 41% African, 59% expatriate. *Seminarians* (1972). 166 secular, 28 religious. *Growth.* By 1977, these totals had risen to 837 priests (142 being Africans), 207 brothers (67 Africans), 1,711 sisters (738 Africans), and 239 seminarians. *Catechists.* Total (1967) 2,344, (1978) 2,338. *Indigenous religious congregations.* Brothers: Bannakaroli (Brothers of St Charles Lwanga), Brothers of St Joseph (Nyeri), St Joseph of Kisumu, Brothers of St Joseph Mukaza (Meru), St Peter Claver Brothers (Machakos). Sisters: Sisters of the Assumption of the BVM of Eldoret, Our Lady of Kilimanjaro, Nazareth Sisters of the Annunciation, Sisters of St Joseph, St Joseph of Mombasa, St Joseph of Patricroft, Assumption of the BVM of Nairobi, Sisters of the BVM (Kisumu), Franciscan Sisters of St Joseph, Sisters of St Mary, Sisters of Mary Immaculate. *Main foreign orders and congregations.* Priests: OCSO, IMC, SPS, SM, MM, MHM, Missionaries of Our Lady of Guadalupe (Mexico), CP, CSSp. Brothers: Christian Instruction, Christian Schools, Fraters of Tilburg, Fraters of Utrecht, Sacred Heart, St Francis Xavier, St Patrick. Sisters (main congregations): Assumption, BVM of Loreto, Carmel, Our Lady of Charity, Consolata, Dominicans, Franciscan Sisters of Oudenbosch, Immaculate Heart, Little Sisters of Jesus, Little Sisters of the Child Jesus, Medical Missionaries of Mary, Mercy Sisters, N-D de Namur, Sisters of Our Lady of Africa, Our Lady of the Holy Rosary, Our Lady of Mercy (Sligo; and Dublin), Our Lady of the Missions, Precious Blood, Third Order of St Francis, Ursulines, Franciscan Missionary Sisters for Africa.

*Catholic organizations.* The Kenya Episcopal Conference (KEC) is a member of the regional conference AMECEA and the all-Africa conference SECAM. There are 2 organizations of religious personnel: the Religious Superiors' Association of Kenya, for men, and the Association of Sisterhoods of Kenya (AOSK); and a Priests' Association of Kenya was formed in 1972. The Catholic Lay Council of Kenya, begun in 1968 as the National Lay Council, co-ordinates the work of such organizations as Catholic Action, Catholic Forum, Legion of Mary, National Council of Catholic Women, St Vincent de Paul Society and Young Christian Students. For the armed forces, Kenya forms a military vicariate.

The Holy See has diplomatic relations with Kenya and is represented to government and the Catholic hierarchy by a pro-nuncio resident in Nairobi.

Nairobi is the headquarters for the Association of the Episcopal Conferences of Eastern Africa (AMECEA), which acts as a regional co-ordinating body for the 5 episcopal conferences of Kenya, Uganda, Tanzania, Malawi and Zambia, including also the Seychelles. In February 1977, the Conference of the Catholic Bishops of Ethiopia also joined; also the Sudan Episcopal Conference.

On the national level, the Kenya Catholic Secretariat serves the episcopal conference and the dioceses through its education, medical and social, catechetical, communication and lay apostolate, and youth departments.

Pastoral and theological training is provided by one major seminary (St Thomas Aquinas National Seminary outside Nairobi) and 9 minor seminaries at Eldoret, Kakamega, Kaimosi, Kisii, Kitui, Nkubu, Kwale, Nairobi and Nyeri. Catechist training centres have also been established at Kisumu, Mombasa and Nyeri.

The Education Department of the Kenya Catholic Secretariat co-ordinates the activities of schools sponsored by the Catholic Church. In 1970 there were 1,876 Catholic-sponsored primary schools (maintained by government), 73 maintained secondary schools and 98 unaided harambee (self-help) secondary schools.

Medical and social service work is also supervised by the Secretariat. In 1970 the church sponsored 63 general and maternity hospitals and 120 dispensaries. Catholic Relief Services caters for relief and development projects.

CHURCH OF THE PROVINCE OF KENYA. *New dioceses.* In 1975, D Mount Kenya was divided, the northern and north-eastern parts being formed into the new D Mount Kenya East, the remainder being renamed D Mount Kenya South. By 1977 D Mount Kenya East had opened 30 new churches and there were 100,000 regular Sunday worshippers in the diocese. In 1979 a new Northern Diocese was being formed. *East African Revival.* Members of the Revival, which reached Kenya from Rwanda in 1937, numbered in 1975 about 150,000 committed adults, or a total community of around 300,000, divided among 3 factions. Members are about 70% Anglicans, 20% Presbyterians, 10% Methodists; main ethnic groups are Kikuyu, Luo, Luhya, Kamba, Kalenjin. *Personnel.* (1977) 365 priests, 25 deacons, 2 deaconesses, 1,000 lay workers (evangelists), 510 lay readers (10 women).

LUTHERAN CHURCH IN KENYA. *Growth.* Increasing to 15,000 members by 1977, in 95 congregations.

NORWEGIAN PENTECOSTAL MISSION IN KENYA. Alternative name (1979), Free Pentecostal Fellowship in Kenya. *Congregations* (1979). 183. *Personnel* (1979). 110 pastors, 24 missionaries. *Baptized members* (1979). 7,500. *Institutions.* 1 Bible school, 1 maternity clinic, 2 dispensaries.

PENTECOSTAL ASSEMBLIES OF GOD. *Growth.* In 1975, 315 new congregations were formed, making a total of 1,600.

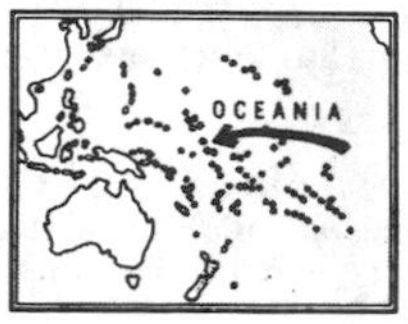


# KIRIBATI

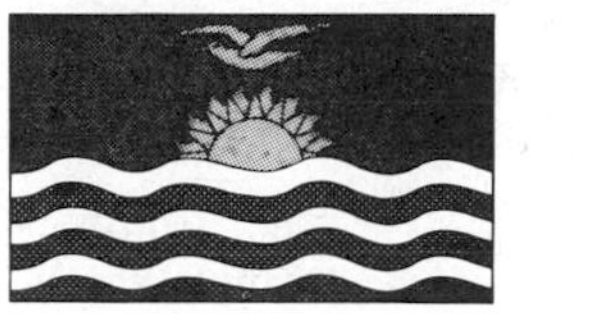

## SECULAR DATA

**STATE. Official name:** The Republic of Kiribati. Former name: The Gilbert Islands. Alternative name: Kingsmill Islands.
**Flag** (shown above right): (of the colony) British Blue Ensign with shield of the Colony in the fly. (1979) Sun, waves, bird.
**Area:** 860 sq.km. (332 sq.miles). Description: 33 main islands across a million square miles of ocean. Agricultural land: 50.7%.
**Government:** Parliamentary state, since 1979 (1892 British protectorate, 1916 British crown colony of the Gilbert and Ellice Islands; 1976 self-governing British crown colony, 1979 Independence).
**Official language:** English.
**Capital:** Bairiki 10,616 (1968).

**DEMOGRAPHY. Population:** 57,819 (census of 8.XII.1973. For 1970–2000 (UN), see last row of Table 1). Population density (1975): 68/sq.km. (177/sq.mile). Under 15 years: 44%. Growth rate (1975–80): 2.94% per year (births 3.49%, deaths −0.79%, immigrants 0.24%). Life expectancy (1975–80): 63.8 years. Household size: 6.0 persons.
**Major languages:** English, Gilbertese, Chinese.

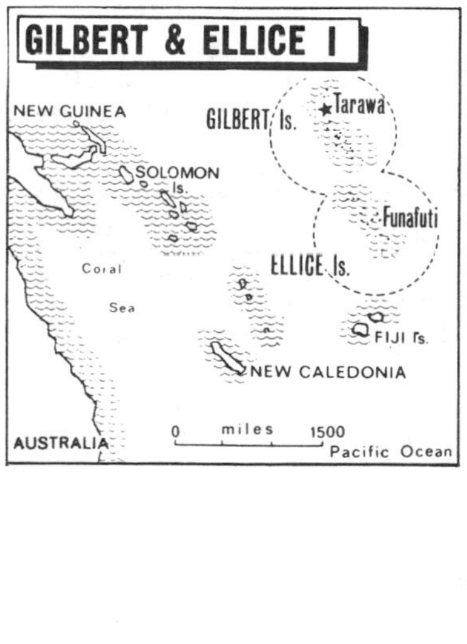


**Urban dwellers** (1970): 18.3%. Urban growth rate (1950–70): 12.4% per year.
**Labour force:** 25%.

**ETHNOLINGUISTIC GROUPS:** 97.2% Gilbertese (Micronesian), 1.3% Euronesian (part-European) (700), 0.9% European (400), 0.5% Ellice Islander (Polynesian), 0.1% Chinese.

**MONEY** (1977). **Monetary unit:** Australian dollar (= 100 cents); US$1 = A$0.94.
**National income per person:** US$700. Average annual family income: US$4,200.
**Cost of living in capital** (1976): Daily cost of living: US$32.

**EDUCATION.** Adult literacy: 95%. Schools: 118.

**HEALTH.** Hospitals: 28 (778 beds). Doctors: 25. Lepers: 700 (11.9 per 1,000). Blind: 100.

**LITERATURE.** Periodicals: 14. Newspapers: 3 non-daily.

**COMMUNICATION** (per 1,000 people). Phones: 8. Radios: 214.

TABLE 1.    RELIGIOUS ADHERENTS IN KIRIBATI (GILBERT ISLANDS)

| Year / Name | 1900 Adherents | % | mid-1970 Adherents | % | Natural | Conversion | Total | Rate | mid-1975 Adherents | % | mid-1980 Adherents | % | 2000 Adherents | % |
|---|---|---|---|---|---|---|---|---|---|---|---|---|---|---|
| Christians | 20,500 | 100.0 | 48,740 | 97.5 | 1,777 | −146 | 1,631 | 2.91 | 55,980 | 9.50 | 65,050 | 95.7 | 102,800 | 493.4 |
| professing | 20,500 | 100.0 | 48,740 | 97.5 | 1,777 | −146 | 1,631 | 2.91 | 55,980 | 95.0 | 65,050 | 94.7 | 102,800 | 93.4 |
| Protestants | 11,300 | 55.1 | 24,520 | 49.0 | 862 | −205 | 657 | 2.42 | 27,150 | 46.1 | 31,090 | 45.3 | 46,880 | 42.6 |
| Roman Catholics | 9,200 | 44.9 | 24,000 | 48.0 | 907 | 59 | 966 | 3.38 | 28,570 | 48.5 | 33,660 | 49.0 | 55,440 | 50.4 |
| Anglicans | 0 | 0.0 | 220 | 0.4 | 8 | 0 | 8 | 3.08 | 260 | 0.4 | 300 | 0.4 | 480 | 0.4 |
| nominal | 100 | 0.5 | 260 | 0.5 | 35 | 116 | 151 | 13.85 | 1,090 | 1.9 | 1,770 | 2.6 | 3,690 | 3.3 |
| affiliated | 20,400 | 99.5 | 48,480 | 97.0 | 1,742 | −262 | 1,480 | 2.70 | 54,890 | 93.2 | 63,280 | 92.1 | 99,110 | 90.1 |
| total practising | 18,360 | 90 | 38,780 | 80 | 1,394 | −210 | 1,184 | 2.70 | 43,910 | 80 | 50,620 | 80 | 69,380 | 70 |
| non-practising | 2,040 | 10 | 9,700 | 20 | 348 | −52 | 296 | 2.70 | 10,980 | 20 | 12,660 | 20 | 29,730 | 30 |
| Protestants | 11,200 | 54.6 | 24,380 | 48.8 | 832 | −323 | 509 | 1.94 | 26,200 | 44.5 | 29,470 | 42.9 | 43,580 | 39.6 |
| Evangelicals | 5,100 | 24.9 | 5,000 | 10.0 | 181 | −31 | 150 | 2.63 | 5,700 | 9.7 | 6,500 | 9.5 | 9,900 | 9.0 |
| Roman Catholics | 9,200 | 44.9 | 23,900 | 47.8 | 903 | 59 | 962 | 3.38 | 28,450 | 48.3 | 33,520 | 48.8 | 55,000 | 50.0 |
| Anglicans | 0 | 0.0 | 150 | 0.3 | 5 | 0 | 5 | 2.94 | 170 | 0.3 | 200 | 0.3 | 330 | 0.3 |
| Marginal Protestants | 0 | 0.0 | 50 | 0.1 | 2 | 2 | 4 | 5.71 | 70 | 0.1 | 90 | 0.1 | 200 | 0.2 |
| Baha'is | 0 | 0.0 | 1,160 | 2.3 | 89 | 145 | 234 | 8.36 | 2,800 | 4.7 | 3,500 | 5.1 | 6,800 | 6.2 |
| Non-religious | 0 | 0.0 | 100 | 0.2 | 4 | 1 | 5 | 4.17 | 120 | 0.2 | 150 | 0.2 | 400 | 0.4 |
| Country's population | 20,500 | 100.0 | 50,000 | 100.0 | 1,870 | 0 | 1,870 | 3.17 | 58,900 | 100.0 | 68,700 | 100.0 | 110,000 | 100.0 |

**COLUMNS, ROWS.** For meanings and definitions, see Codebook (Part 6). Note that, by definition, total 'Christians' = professing + crypto-Christians, which also = affiliated + nominal Christians. Percentages may not always total exactly, due to rounding.
**CENSUSES.** Figures for the Gilbert and Ellice Islands combined: **30.IV.1963:** 56.4% Protestants (54.9% LMS), 42.1% Roman Catholics, 1.0% non-religious, 0.3% Anglicans, 0.2% non-religious. **6.XII.1968:** 55.6% Protestants (53.5% Congregationalists, 1.5% SD Adventists), 42.9% Roman Catholics, 0.8% Baha'is (440 persons), 0.4% Anglicans, 0.2% non-religious.

**NOTES ON RELIGIONS**
**BAHA'IS.** Begun 1955. Rapid growth in the Gilbert and Ellice Islands from 16 local spiritual assemblies (1964) to 54 (1973) with 72 other isolated centres or groups (total localities in 1973, 126); with a total of 151 Baha'i centres by the end of 1973, including a Baha'i Temple site on Tarawa. In 1973 at the end of the worldwide Baha'i Nine Year Plan, Baha'i claimed 2,460 followers in the Gilbert and Ellice Islands, and asserted that the name of Baha'ullah was already universally known there. Converts are mostly former Congregationalists. Government figures do not yet document this adequately. In the 1963 census, 508 Baha'is

were recorded. In the 1968 census only 440 Baha'is were recorded, but since the number of assemblies has grown extremely rapidly, it is likely that a number of new Baha'is were recorded then under their previous Christian denomination (mostly Congregationalist), which points to the analysis as shown in the table above for 1970–80. Only a small proportion of all Baha'is are on Tuvalu (Ellice Islands), as shown under that country.
**NON-RELIGIOUS.** Europeans and Chinese.
**PROTESTANTS.** Since 1900, Congregationalists have suffered losses to Catholicism, newer Protestant bodies, and since 1955 to Baha'i.

**Gilbert Islands Protestant Church.** The GIPC, autonomous since 1968, is Congregationalist in polity. *Left.* GIPC Chapel, Tarawa on postage stamp (1975). *Right.* A Sunday congregation. *Below.* Sunday-school pupils on parade.

**Catholic Church, Diocese of Tarawa, Nauru & Funafuti.** (*Right*). Church on Ocean Island, on postage stamp (1975).

**NON-CHRISTIAN RELIGIONS. Baha'i** has grown rapidly in numbers since its introduction into the Gilbert and Ellice Islands in 1955, though with a decline from 1963–68; in 1973 there were 54 local spiritual assemblies and 72 other isolated centres and groups.

**Traditional Micronesian and Polynesian religions** have ceased to exist as separate entities although local beliefs and customs continue to persist among Christians.

## CHRISTIANITY
PROTESTANT CHURCHES. The pioneer missionary Hiram Bingham opened the first American Board station at Abaiang in 1856, thus beginning the evangelization of the northern Gilbert Islands. Before long Samoan pastors had been placed on Arorae, Tamana, Onotoa and Beru in the southern Gilberts. In 1917 the American Board agreed to hand over all its work to the LMS, thereby providing for a single witness. Because of ethnic tensions, Congregationalists in the formerly united church of the Gilbert and Ellice Islands have since 1968 divided themselves into 2 separate autonomous churches, one serving the Gilbert Islands (now Kiribati) and the other the Ellice Islands (now Tuvalu). They form the largest single church tradition, with 47% of the population in the Gilberts in 1968.

Following World War II, Seventh-day Adventists built their first church at Abemama in the Gilbert Islands. By 1963, 497 persons claimed to be Adventists increasing to 813 by 1968. Two Church of God groups have been active since the mid-1950s, but growth has been slower.

Most LMS schools and medical institutions have now been taken over by government, there being only one primary school and one teacher-training college still under church sponsorship. However, Adventists continue to operate 8 primary schools and there is one Church of God school.

CATHOLIC CHURCH. Catholicism was introduced into the islands by 2 native Gilbertese, Petero and Tiroi, who were converted while working in Tahiti and who then brought their new faith back to Nonouti with them. When the first priests appeared in 1888, they found that there was already a Catholic community of 500 believers.

Catholics in the Gilbert Islands constitute 48% of the population. In the Gilbert archipelago, the vast distances make pastoral visits difficult and links between parishes tenuous.

The diocese of Tarawa, Nauru and Funafuti encompasses all the Gilbert Islands (except for the Line Islands which belong to the diocese of Honolulu in the USA) as well as Tuvalu, Nauru, and Canton and Enderbury. Nevertheless, because the Line Islands are peopled by the same ethnic group, pastoral care in the form of Gilbertese catechists is provided by the bishop of Tarawa.

INDIGENOUS CHURCHES. Although nothing survives today, there was an indigenous religious movement in 1929 called Religion of Barane, or

Swords of Gabriel. It was begun on Onotoa Island in the Congregational Church (now the GIPC) by Barane who was identified as the prophet of God, with a female prophetess Nei Kamaitia and Nei Baate. The movement lasted only a year or two before disappearing.

**CHURCH AND STATE.** Theoretically all denominations enjoy equal freedom before the law, but local anti-Catholic sentiment prevents the building of Catholic churches on the islands of Tamana and Arorae in the Gilberts.

Although many LMS schools were placed under government supervision after World War II, the churches continue to play an important role in education. Government subsidies are provided for their operation as well as for teachers' salaries.

The churches exert an important influence on the life of the islands and the surrounding area. In December 1970, the Catholic bishop of Tarawa placed before the pope and the bishops of the Pacific and Australia his concern at the over-population and lack of resources of the territory, in the hope that Australia might be requested to open its doors to Gilbertese immigration.

**INTERDENOMINATIONAL ORGANIZATIONS.** No organizations exist at the national level. In 1969, the Catholic Church announced that intercommunion with Anglicans was permitted.

**BROADCASTING.** Religious programmes are broadcast over the government radio on Sundays for 20 minutes, in addition to a 5-minute devotional weekday mornings and one-hour programmes at Christmas and Easter. Of these, Catholics are responsible for one Sunday and 7 weeks per month. All programmes are in Gilbertese. For Catholics, an association grouping Kiribati with Tuvalu and Fiji is a member of UNDA.

**BIBLIOGRAPHY**
'The Swords of Gabriel', H. E. Maude, *Journal of Pacific history*, 2 (1967), 113–136.

TABLE 2. ORGANIZED CHURCHES AND DENOMINATIONS IN KIRIBATI (GILBERT ISLANDS)

| Official name 1 | Begun 2 | Type 3 | Counc 4 | Congs 5 | Adults 6 | Affiliated 7 | Names, notes, and other statistics (see Codebook) 8 |
|---|---|---|---|---|---|---|---|
| Anglican Church (D Polynesia) | | A Hig | awPK. | | 100 | 150 | In Diocese of Polynesia, Ch of the Province of New Zealand. Indians. |
| **Catholic Ch: D Tarawa, Nauru, Funafuti** | 1850 | R Lat | P.PY. | 18 | 13,000 | 23,900 | Begun by 2 locals. 1888, M=MSC. 62 aliens. C=1+0+2. 6n,14x,5m,42w,P=46%,2p,1385Yy. |
| Church of God | 1954 | P Pen | ..... | | 50 | 100 | M=South Carolina Memorial Church of God (USA). On Tarawa only. 1 school. 1f. |
| Church of God (Cleveland) | 1955 | P Pe3 | ZF... | 19 | 306 | 500 | M=CoG(Cleveland)(USA), based on Tarawa. 13 churches, 6 missions. 15n,2f,1p. |
| **Gilbert Islands Protestant Church** | 1856 | P Con | .vP.. | | 10,000 | 23,000 | *GIPC.* 1857,M=ABCFM(USA);1917,LMS(UK),CCWM. A=1968. 1972 applied to WCC. 1f,1j,1s. |
| Jehovah's Witnesses | c1960 | M Jeh | x.... | 1 | 14 | 50 | *Watch Tower. IBSA.* Active witnessing under way by 1962. 2Y. |
| Presbyterian Church | | P Ref | ..... | 1 | 30 | 50 | Small church of Presbyterian immigrants from other Pacific areas. |
| Seventh-day Adventist Church | 1947 | P Adv | x.... | 5 | 572 | 730 | *SDA, G & EI Mission,* Central Pacific Union Mission. 2nx,25mw,1r,5t(510),52Y. |
| **Total affiliated (mid-1970)** | | | | **174** | **24,072** | **48,480** | **Total denominations (1970) . . . 8.** |
| **Total affiliated (mid-1975)** | | | | **179** | **27,250** | **54,890** | **Total denominations (1975) . . . 8.** |
| **Total affiliated (mid-1980)** | | | | **185** | **31,420** | **63,280** | **Total denominations (1980) . . . 9.** |

NOTES ON TABLE ABOVE
COLUMNS: for meanings and CODES (cols. 1, 3, 4, 8), see Codebook (Part 6). Column 1: **Boldface type** = church with over 10% of country's affiliated Christians.

**PEOPLES** (ethnolinguistic). Christians: 97.3% Gilbertese (Micronesian), 1.3% Euronesian, 0.9% European (White), 0.5% Ellice Islander (Polynesian), Chinese.

COUNTRY-WIDE TOTALS
EVANGELIZATION (see Part 5). 1900: 100%. 1970: 100%. 1980: 100%.
FOREIGN MISSIONARIES AND PERSONNEL (nationals serving abroad) (1973). Total 3 Protestants in Nauru.
FOREIGN MISSIONARIES AND PERSONNEL (aliens from abroad) (1973). Total 51. *From Western world.* 49: 46 Roman Catholics, 3 Protestants in 2 USA societies. *From Third World.* About 2 Protestants.
INSTITUTIONS (church-operated) (1973). Total 13, including 7 higher schools, 1 hospital, 1 press, 1 religious community, 1 seminary (Protestant).
PERIODICALS. About 10 titles (4 SDA).
PERSONNEL. About 392 (341 national, 51 foreign).
RELIGIOUS LIBRARIES. 3.
SCRIPTURE DISTRIBUTION (1975). Annual totals: 1,000 Bibles (subsidized), 1,200 NTs (subsidized), 1,500 UBS portions, 21,700 UBS selections. *Translations completed.* Gilbertese: portion in 1864, NT in 1873, Bible in 1893.
SERVICE AGENCIES. About 4.

ADDITIONAL DATA ON CHURCHES
CATHOLIC CHURCH. The diocese, which is a suffragan of the archdiocese of Suva (Fiji), also covers Tuvalu (the Ellice Islands), Nauru (1,200 Catholics) and the Canton and Enderbury Islands (30). *Annual baptisms.* (1972) 93.9% infant, 6.1% adult. *Priests.* The first Gilbertese priest was ordained in 1964. 17 priests out of 20 are MSC. *Brothers.* Including 3 indigenous (nationals). *Sisters.* About a quarter are nationals, the rest Australians. *Catechists.* Total (1974) 221. *Catechist training schools.* Manoku, Abaiang. *Indigenous religious congregations.* Sisters of St Teresa. *Foreign religious congregations.* Priests: MSC. Sisters: Daughters of Our Lady of the Sacred Heart.
*Catholic organizations.* The diocese is represented on the Pacific Episcopal Conference (CEPAC). There are no associations of religious personnel, nor pastoral or presbyteral councils; and only one lay organization is active, the Legion of Mary, which had 1,245 active members and 433 helpers in 1971.
The Holy See has no diplomatic relations with the Islands but is represented to the Catholic hierarchy by the Apostolic Delegation of New Zealand and the Pacific Islands based on Wellington, New Zealand.
The Catholic Church has developed an important school programme which is well integrated into the government's educational system. Gilbertese youth receive instruction in the school nearest their home, irrespective of their religion or the type of school. The state pays 50% of the expenses of recognized mission schools. It also trains church teachers in its teacher-training college and pays the salaries of qualified instructors. In 1969 there were 14 Catholic primary schools and 5 other schools, catering for 1,449 Catholic and 2,232 non-Catholic pupils. In the same year the mission operated one maternity hospital and 4 orphanages with 331 children. By 1973 schools had increased to 45 primary (5,893 pupils) and 3 secondary (234 pupils).

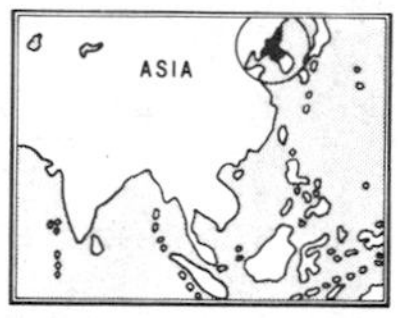


# KOREA, North

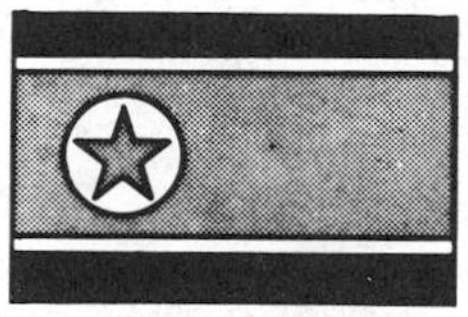

## SECULAR DATA

**STATE. Official name:** The Democratic Peoples' Republic of Korea (Chosun Minchu-chui Inmin Konghwa-guk). Unofficial name: North Korea.
**Flag** (shown above right): Large red centre stripe bordered by thin white stripes and wider blue stripes; white circle near hoist enclosing red 5-pointed star.
**Area:** 120,538 sq.km. (46,540 sq.miles). Agricultural land: 17.8%.
**Government:** One-party Communist state, formed 1948 (1910 Japanese possession).
**Legislature:** Supreme People's Assembly, 541 members.
**Official language:** Korean (*Chosenmal*).
**Chief cities:** capital Pyongyang 1,500,000, Chongjin 184,300, Hungnam 143,600, Kaesong 139,900.
**Political divisions:** 11 administrative units: 2 Cities (Pyongyang, Kaesong), 9 Provinces.
**Armed forces** (1976): Total 495,000 regular: army 430,000, navy 20,000, air force 45,000 (655 combat aircraft). Paramilitary forces: 1,840,000.

**DEMOGRAPHY. Population:** 11,568,000 (official estimate of 1.X.1963. For 1970–2000 (UN), see last row of Table 1). Population density (1975): 132/sq.km. (341/sq.mile). Under 15 years: 44%. Growth rate (1975–80): 2.46% per year (births 3.27%, deaths –0.82%). Life expectancy (1975–80): 62.8 years. Household size: 5.0 persons.
**Major languages:** Korean, Chinese (Mandarin), Russian.
**Urban dwellers** (1970): 38.1%. Urban growth rate (1950–70): 4.9% per year.
**Labour force:** 43%.

**ETHNOLINGUISTIC GROUPS:** 99.3% Korean, 0.7% Chinese, Russian, Mongolian.

**MONEY** (1977). **Monetary unit:** won (= 100 chon); US$1 = NKW 2.06 (operational rate of exchange).
**National income per person:** US$380. Average annual family income: US$1,900.
**Inflation:** (1970–74) nil.
**Cost of living in capital** (1976): Daily cost of living: US$40.

**HEALTH.** Hospitals: about 100 (55,000 beds). Doctors: 11,919. Lepers: 27,300 (1.7 per 1,000). Blind: 48,000. Psychotics: 140,000.

**EDUCATION.** Adult literacy: 90%. Education rate: 53%. Schools: 9,260. Universities: 3.

**LITERATURE.** Periodicals: 200. Scientific journals: 60.

**COMMUNICATION** (per 1,000 people). Radios: 70. TV sets: 0.2. Daily newspaper circulation: 20 copies.

TABLE 1. RELIGIOUS ADHERENTS IN NORTH KOREA

| Year / Name | 1900 Adherents | % | mid-1970 Adherents | % | Annual change, 1970–1980 Natural | Conversion | Total | Rate | mid-1975 Adherents | % | mid-1980 Adherents | % | 2000 Adherents | % |
|---|---|---|---|---|---|---|---|---|---|---|---|---|---|---|
| Non-religious | 0 | 0.0 | 6,337,000 | 45.6 | 196,945 | 102,935 | 299,880 | 3.87 | 7,739,150 | 48.8 | 9,335,800 | 52.1 | 16,738,000 | 61.0 |
| Shamanists | 3,766,100 | 94.2 | 3,000,000 | 21.6 | 75,020 | –95,420 | –20,400 | –0.69 | 2,948,000 | 18.6 | 2,796,000 | 15.6 | 2,200,000 | 8.0 |
| Atheists | 0 | 0.0 | 2,133,000 | 15.4 | 62,930 | 7,000 | 69,930 | 2.83 | 2,472,900 | 15.6 | 2,832,300 | 15.8 | 4,558,000 | 16.6 |
| New-Religionists | 20,000 | 0.5 | 2,000,000 | 14.4 | 57,258 | –7,258 | 50,000 | 2.22 | 2,250,000 | 14.2 | 2,500,000 | 13.9 | 3,570,000 | 13.0 |
| Buddhists | 200,000 | 5.0 | 280,000 | 2.0 | 7,380 | –5,380 | 2,000 | 0.69 | 290,000 | 1.8 | 300,000 | 1.7 | 200,000 | 0.7 |
| **Christians** | **13,900** | **0.3** | **142,000** | **1.0** | **3,867** | **–1,877** | **1,990** | **1.31** | **151,950** | **1.0** | **161,900** | **0.9** | **191,000** | **0.7** |
| crypto-Christians | 0 | 0.0 | 142,000 | 1.0 | 3,867 | –1,877 | 1,990 | 1.31 | 151,950 | 1.0 | 161,900 | 0.9 | 191,000 | 0.7 |
| professing | 13,900 | 0.3 | 0 | 0.0 | 0 | 0 | 0 | 0.00 | 0 | 0.0 | 0 | 0.0 | 0 | 0.0 |
| Protestants | 12,900 | 0.3 | 0 | 0.0 | 0 | 0 | 0 | 0.00 | 0 | 0.0 | 0 | 0.0 | 0 | 0.0 |
| Roman Catholics | 1,000 | 0.0 | 0 | 0.0 | 0 | 0 | 0 | 0.00 | 0 | 0.0 | 0 | 0.0 | | 0.0 |
| affiliated | 13,900 | 0.3 | 142,000 | 0.1 | 3,867 | –1,877 | 1,990 | 1.31 | 151,950 | 1.0 | 161,900 | 0.9 | 191,000 | 0.7 |
| total practising | 12,510 | *90* | 99,400 | *70* | 2,707 | –1,314 | 1,393 | 1.31 | 106,360 | *70* | 113,330 | *70* | 133,700 | *70* |
| non-practising | 1,390 | *10* | 42,600 | *30* | 1,160 | –563 | 597 | 1.31 | 45,590 | *30* | 48,570 | *30* | 57,300 | *30* |
| Protestants | 12,900 | 0.3 | 118,000 | 0.8 | 3,156 | –1,956 | 1,200 | 0.97 | 124,000 | 0.8 | 130,000 | 0.7 | 140,000 | 0.5 |
| Evangelicals | 11,000 | 0.3 | 60,000 | 0.4 | 1,600 | –1 000 | 600 | 0.95 | 63,000 | 0.4 | 66,000 | 0.4 | 80,000 | 0.3 |
| Roman Catholics | 1,000 | 0.0 | 15,000 | 0.1 | 433 | –33 | 400 | 2.35 | 17,000 | 0.1 | 19,000 | 0.1 | 25,000 | 0.1 |
| Korean indigenous | 0 | 0.0 | 8,000 | 0.1 | 254 | 146 | 400 | 4.00 | 10,000 | 0.1 | 12,000 | 0.1 | 25,000 | 0.1 |
| Marginal Protestants | 0 | 0.0 | 1,000 | 0.0 | 24 | –34 | –10 | –1.05 | 950 | 0.0 | 900 | 0.0 | 1,000 | 0.0 |
| **Country's population** | **4,000,000** | **100.0** | **13,892,000** | **100.0** | **403,400** | **0** | **403,400** | **2.54** | **15,852,000** | **100.0** | **17,926,000** | **100.0** | **27,457,000** | **100.0** |

COLUMNS, ROWS. For meanings and definitions, see Codebook (Part 6). Note that, by definition, total 'Christians' = professing + crypto-Christians, which also = affiliated + nominal Christians. Percentages may not always total exactly, due to rounding.
CENSUSES. No religion question has ever been asked in population censuses.

NOTES ON RELIGIONS
ATHEISTS. Korean Workers' Party (KWP) (in power; neither pro-Soviet nor pro-China): Communist membership (1970) 1,600,000. Of party members about a third are atheists and the rest non-religious.
BUDDHISTS. Mahayana.
COUNTRY'S POPULATION. After the Korean war (1950–53) in which about 5 million persons were killed, a further 2 million fled from North to South Korea, including vast numbers of Protestants.
CRYPTO-CHRISTIANS. Since 1950 all Christians have been forced underground. Although there is now no organized religion, there is much private activity including radio listening. In 1957, 2,000 active Christians in 500 small units were discovered by the regime and 10 leaders were executed.
KOREAN INDIGENOUS. Organized and unorganized isolated radio believers (see Table 2) exist across the nation even though radio sets are relatively few in number.
NEW-RELIGIONISTS. Chondogyo (Religion of the Heavenly Way), begun in 1860, had 2 million followers in North Korea in 1945. In 1948, 10,000 of its leaders and members were arrested. In 1970 its members were believed to be still as numerous and active as in 1945, though the leadership is underground.
NON-RELIGIOUS. Agnostics, secularists, indifferent to religion, including most communists.
PROFESSING CHRISTIANS. Since 1950, there have been no professing Christians, because so far as the state is concerned Christianity has been eradicated and completely destroyed.
SHAMANISTS. Unorganized remnants of earlier folk religion blending animism, spirit-worship and folk-healing.

**NON-CHRISTIAN RELIGIONS. Shamanism,** belief in the existence of good and evil spirits residing in material objects such as rocks and trees, which may be controlled by priests *(mudang)*, combined with Confucianist concepts, is still widespread in the rural north. Propitiatory rites are centred in the exorcism of evil spirits in times of illness and misfortune. Shamanism's individualistic mixture of ancestor veneration and magical practices and its lack of central organization are assets for survival in an anti-religious state.

**Chondogyo,** the Religion of the Heavenly Way, began in 1860 and had 2 million followers in North Korea in 1945. Despite the arrest of 10,000 of its members in 1948, it continues underground with somewhat the same numerical strength in 1975 as 30 years previously.

**Buddhism** continues to exist among a small minority of the population in spite of the suppression of Buddhist temples and monasteries.

## CHRISTIANITY.

The earliest Catholic contacts with North Korea were through China at the end of the 18th century. In 1831 a vicariate was erected, and the following year the first Protestant missionary made a short visit to Korea. Religious freedom became a reality after the signing of the Korean treaty with the USA in 1882, and within 3 years Presbyterian and Methodist missionaries were at work. Catholics also took up their duties with renewed vigour, having suffered severely from persecution and martyrdom for most of a century.

PROTESTANT CHURCHES. Prior to 1945, the Christian population of Korea was second in size in Asia only to that of the Philippines. The Presbyterian Church was the largest denomination, followed by the Methodists, with smaller numbers of adherents belonging to the Salvation Army, Holiness Church and Seventh-day Adventists. The strongest sections of the Presbyterian Church were found in North and South Pyongan provinces, an area which forms part of present-day North Korea. Reports during the 1930s listed entire rural villages as having become Christian, with 50% of the whole population of Sonchon and 10% of Pyongyang cities worshipping in Presbyterian churches on Sundays.

After the coming of the Communist regime to power following World War II, many Christians fled south; those who remained suffered severe persecution in the government's anti-religion campaign. Towards the end of the Korean war in 1953, migrations southwards increased again and rose to massive proportions. In 1972, Seventh-day Adventists estimated that there were 26 SDA congregations and churches in North Korea. Although no other organized churches can be identified today, many crypto-Christians are known to exist.

CATHOLIC CHURCH. In 1945, North Korea had 2 dioceses, suffragans of Seoul: Ham Heung and Pyongyang, founded respectively in 1920 and 1927. In addition Korean Catholics in southeastern Manchuria (China) were served by the Chinese diocese of Yenki (founded 1937) and the abbey nullius of Deok Weon established at Tokwon, North Korea, in 1940. All of these have been suppressed, and their administrators and priests now reside in South Korea or abroad. Half the Catholic population fled south after World War II, leaving only 25,000 adherents in 1950; and of these a large proportion subsequently fled as well.

Tracts and literature are sent by balloon across skies of North Korea and China by Christian Mission to the Communist World (Christ to Far East's Millions), based in Seoul. Each balloon scatters 250,000 small paper tracts. In return, the regime sends Communist propaganda material to the South in covers disguised as gospels.

CHURCH AND STATE. Less is known about Christianity in North Korea than in other Communist countries except Mongolia and Albania. Christianity was subject to considererable persecution during the Japanese occupation (1910–45), especially so during the 1930s with the increase of Japanese pressure to adopt Shinto as the national religion. During the short period between the fall of Japan and the introduction of the Communist regime, Presbyterians formed a temporary northern General Assembly. They also launched a country-wide Freedom Memorial Evangelistic Campaign and reopened the Presbyterian theological seminary in Pyongyang which in 1947 had 164 students. Communist suppression of religion took place in several stages. In 1946 Christian organizations seeking political freedom were suppressed, and their leaders were imprisoned or disappeared. A Christian League was organized by the government to foster church support for the new regime, and in 1950 the Methodist and Presbyterian seminaries were combined into one 'Christian seminary'. When the League was consistently boycotted by the Christian population, a systematic attempt to exterminate Christianity was initiated. Church buildings were confiscated and leaders imprisoned. As the Korean war progressed, retreating Communist soldiers massacred many Christians to prevent their liberation. When United Nations forces temporarily gained control of North Korea and the Communist capital fell, many Christians were observed attending church. However, when these forces later withdrew and over 2 million fled south, a virtually-complete blackout on the fate of remaining Christians descended which has continued to the present day.

BROADCASTING. No religious broadcasting of any kind is permitted within the country. Over radio station HLKX from South Korea, passages of scripture are read at dictation speed for 10 minutes daily.

BIBLIOGRAPHY
*A history of the church in Korea.* A. D. Clark. Seoul: Christian Literature Society of Korea, 1971.
*Catholic Korea, yesterday and now.* J. C. Kim and J. J. Chung. Seoul: Catholic Korean Publishing Co, 1964.
*The history of Protestant missions in Korea, 1832–1910.* I. G. Park. Seoul: Yonsei University Press, 1970.

TABLE 2.     ORGANIZED CHURCHES AND DENOMINATIONS IN NORTH KOREA

| Official name 1 | Begun 2 | Type 3 | Counc 4 | Congs 5 | Adults 6 | Affiliated 7 | Names, notes, and other statistics (see Codebook) 8 |
|---|---|---|---|---|---|---|---|
| **Catholic Church in Korea** | 1777 | R Lat | P.... | | 10,000 | 15,000 | Formerly M=MM(USA). 1950, 25,000 Catholics remain in 3 jurisdictions; suppressed. |
| Church of the New Jerusalem | 1933 | M Swe | x.... | 40 | 500 | 1,000 | Before 1950, 40 congregations in the North. Suppressed, underground. |
| Isolated radio churches | | I rad | ..... | 200 | 4,000 | 8,000 | Isolated radio believers (students, youths). FEBC is heard 2.5 hours per day. |
| Methodist Church | 1888 | P Met | ..... | | 2,000 | 5,000 | Slow growth in 1930s. Suppressed from 1945 onwards, but underground activity. |
| **Presbyterian Church of Korea** | 1887 | P Ref | ..... | | 40,000 | 108,000 | Mass influx 1907–10. In 1940, 85,115 communicants in North. Suppressed after 1945. |
| Seventh-day Adventist Church | 1934 | P Adv | x.... | 26 | 866 | 3,000 | *North Korean Mission*, Korean Union Mission. 2,265 enrolled in sabbath schools. |
| Other Protestant denominations | | P | ..... | | 1,000 | 2,000 | Remnants of other bodies strong before 1945: Holiness Ch (OMS), et alia. |
| Total affiliated (mid-1970) | | | | 2,100 | 58,366 | 142,000 | Total denominations (1970) . . . 8. |
| Total affiliated (mid-1975) | | | | 2,000 | 62,400 | 151,950 | Total denominations (1975) . . . 7. |
| Total affiliated (mid-1980) | | | | 1,900 | 66,500 | 161,900 | Total denominations (1980) . . . 6. |

NOTES ON TABLE ABOVE
COLUMNS: for meanings and CODES (cols. 1, 3, 4, 8), see Codebook (Part 6). Column 1: **Boldface type** = church with over 10% of country's affiliated Christians.

PEOPLES (ethnolinguistic). Christians: 99.9% Korean.

COUNTRY-WIDE TOTALS
EVANGELIZATION (see Part 5). 1900: 19%. 1970: 23%. 1980: 25%. *Radiophonic evangelism.* Many programmes from South Korea are heard. International stations include FEBC (2.5 hours per day in Korean).
PERSONNEL. About 20 national (clandestine).

ADDITIONAL DATA ON CHURCHES
CATHOLIC CHURCH IN KOREA. Before 1945, the church had 3 jurisdictions: D Ham Heung and D Pyongyang (both suffragans of M Seoul); also AN Tokwon. All were suppressed from 1945 onwards. In 1950, there were 25,000 Catholics remaining, 25,000 others having fled to South Korea. *Personnel.* In 1963, there were about 47 national priests and about 75 sisters.

---

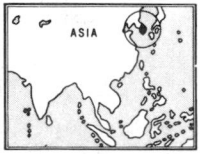

# KOREA, South

## SECULAR DATA

STATE. Official name: The Republic of Korea (Taehan Min'guk/ Han Kook). Unofficial name: South Korea. Adjective of nationality: Korean.
Flag (shown above right): White field with circular emblem (red top and blue bottom); black bar design in each corner.
Area: 98,477 sq.km. (38,025 sq.miles). Agricultural land: 24.8%.
Government: Republic under dictatorship, since 1972 (1910 Japan possession, 1948 republic, 1961 military junta).
Legislature: National assembly, 219 members.
Official language: Korean (*Chosenmal*).
Chief cities: capital Seoul 5,433,200 (1970), Pusan 1,842,260, Taegu 1,063,550, Inchon 634,050.
Political divisions: 9 Provinces, 2 Cities with provincial status (Seoul, Pusan).
Armed forces (1976): Total 595,000 regular: army 520,000, navy 25,000, marines 20,000, air force 30,000 (204 combat aircraft). Reserves: 1,148,000. Paramilitary forces: 750,000 Homeland Defence Reserve Force.

Foreign forces (1973): 42,000 USA troops. (1977) 41,300 USA troops (65 combat aircraft, 50 ships of Seventh Fleet).

DEMOGRAPHY. Population: 34,688,000 (census of 1.X.1975. For 1970–2000 (UN), see last row of Table 1). Population density (1975): 345/sq.km. (893/sq.mile). Under 15 years: 44%. Growth rate (1975–80): 1.96% per year (births 2.76%, deaths −0.80%). Life expectancy (1975–80): 62.8 years. Household size: 5.2 persons.
Major languages: Korean, English, Chinese.
Urban dwellers (1970): 37.9%. Urban growth rate (1950–70): 5.9% per year.
Labour force: 36%.
Tourists (1974): 517,590.

ETHNOLINGUISTIC GROUPS: 99.8% Korean, 0.1% USA military (42,000), 0.1% Chinese (33,000) (Shantung), Eurasian (8,000) (Korean/USA).

MONEY (1977). Monetary unit: won (= 100 chon); US$1 = SKw 480.00.

National income per person: US$455. Average annual family income: US$2,366.
Inflation: (1970–74) 12.5% per year (1975: consumer price index 223), (1976) 12% per year.
Cost of living in capital (1976): index 105 (Washington DC=100). Daily cost of living: US$41.

HEALTH. Hospitals: 170 (16,373 beds). Doctors: 16,363. Lepers: 72,700 (2.1 per 1,000). Blind: 110,000. Psychotics: 300,000. Criminals: 430,802.

EDUCATION. Adult literacy: (1955) 77%, (1970) 88%, (1975) 91%. Education rate: 67%. Schools: 8,957 (6,085 elementary, 1,974 middle, 898 high). Universities: 80.

LITERATURE. Annual new book titles (1973): 7,396. Periodicals: 882. Scientific journals: 100. Newspapers: 33 dailies, 111 non-daily.

COMMUNICATION (per 1,000 people). Phones: 31. Radios: 127. TV sets: 30. Daily newspaper circulation: 136 copies.

TABLE 1. RELIGIOUS ADHERENTS IN SOUTH KOREA

| Year: | 1900 Adherents | % | mid-1970 Adherents | % | Annual change, 1970–1980 Natural | Conversion | Total | Rate | mid-1975 Adherents | % | mid-1980 Adherents | % | 2000 Adherents | % |
|---|---|---|---|---|---|---|---|---|---|---|---|---|---|---|
| Shamanists | 6,507,300 | 81.3 | 11,806,000 | 38.4 | 214,580 | −423,640 | −209,060 | −1.93 | 10,835,400 | 31.9 | 9,715,400 | 25.9 | 6,768,700 | 13.0 |
| Christians | 42,700 | 0.5 | 5,828,000 | 19.0 | 168,120 | 390,060 | 558,180 | 6.57 | 8,489,700 | 25.0 | 11,409,800 | 30.5 | 21,607,300 | 41.6 |
| professing | 42,700 | 0.5 | 5,828,000 | 19.0 | 168,120 | 390,060 | 558,180 | 6.57 | 8,489,700 | 25.0 | 11,409,800 | 30.5 | 21,607,300 | 41.6 |
| Korean indigenous | 50 | 0.0 | 2,575,000 | 8.4 | 77,980 | 196,220 | 274,200 | 6.96 | 3,938,000 | 11.6 | 5,317,000 | 14.2 | 10,399,600 | 20.0 |
| Protestants | 6,500 | 0.1 | 2,150,000 | 7.0 | 63,200 | 167,380 | 230,580 | 7.23 | 3,191,200 | 9.4 | 4,455,800 | 11.9 | 8,319,700 | 16.0 |
| Roman Catholics | 36,000 | 0.4 | 1,002,000 | 3.3 | 24,202 | 21,628 | 45,830 | 3.75 | 1,222,200 | 3.6 | 1,460,300 | 3.9 | 2,547,900 | 4.9 |
| Marginal Protestants | 0 | 0.0 | 58,000 | 0.2 | 1,762 | 4,438 | 6,200 | 6.97 | 89,000 | 0.3 | 120,000 | 0.3 | 260,000 | 0.5 |
| Anglicans | 100 | 0.0 | 40,000 | 0.1 | 911 | 389 | 1,300 | 2.83 | 46,000 | 0.1 | 53,000 | 0.1 | 75,000 | 0.1 |
| Orthodox | 50 | 0.0 | 3,000 | 0.0 | 65 | 5 | 70 | 2.12 | 3,300 | 0.0 | 3,700 | 0.0 | 5,100 | 0.0 |
| nominal | 0 | 0.0 | 943,116 | 3.1 | 21,940 | 10,148 | 32,088 | 2.90 | 1,107,800 | 3.3 | 1,264,000 | 3.4 | 2,377,300 | 4.6 |
| affiliated | 42,700 | 0.5 | 4,884,884 | 15.9 | 146,180 | 379,912 | 526,092 | 7.13 | 7,381,900 | 21.7 | 10,145,800 | 27.1 | 19,230,000 | 38.5 |
| total practising | 38,430 | *90* | 4,054,450 | *83* | 121,330 | 315,326 | 436,656 | 7.13 | 6,126,980 | *83* | 8,421,010 | *83* | 15,384,000 | *80* |
| non-practising | 4,270 | *10* | 830,430 | *17* | 24,850 | 64,586 | 89,436 | 7.13 | 1,254,920 | *17* | 1,724,790 | *17* | 3,846,000 | *20* |
| Korean indigenous | 50 | 0.0 | 2,151,558 | 7.0 | 68,320 | 196,684 | 265,004 | 7.68 | 3,450,000 | 10.2 | 4,801,600 | 12.8 | 9,360,000 | 18.0 |
| Protestants | 6,500 | 0.1 | 1,820,428 | 5.9 | 55,940 | 164,567 | 220,507 | 7.81 | 2,825,000 | 8.3 | 4,025,500 | 10.8 | 7,510,000 | 14.4 |
| Evangelicals | 6,400 | 0.1 | 1,751,000 | 5.7 | 40,339 | 24,161 | 64,500 | 3.17 | 2,037,000 | 6.0 | 2,396,000 | 6.4 | 4,056,000 | 7.8 |
| Neo-pentecostals | 0 | 0.0 | 100,000 | 0.3 | 9,902 | 130,098 | 140,000 | 28.00 | 500,000 | 1.5 | 1,500,000 | 4.0 | 3,000,000 | 5.8 |
| Roman Catholics | 36,000 | 0.4 | 828,133 | 2.7 | 19,496 | 13,771 | 33,267 | 3.38 | 984,500 | 2.9 | 1,160,800 | 3.1 | 2,027,900 | 3.9 |
| Catholic pentecostals | 0 | 0.0 | 0 | 0.0 | 500 | 10,500 | 11,000 | 55.00 | 20,000 | 0.1 | 110,000 | 0.3 | 700,000 | 1.3 |
| Marginal Protestants | 0 | 0.0 | 48,329 | 0.2 | 1,584 | 4,583 | 6,167 | 7.71 | 80,000 | 0.2 | 110,000 | 0.3 | 260,000 | 0.5 |
| Anglicans | 100 | 0.0 | 32,436 | 0.1 | 753 | 304 | 1,057 | 2.78 | 38,000 | 0.1 | 43,000 | 0.1 | 65,000 | 0.1 |
| Orthodox | 50 | 0.0 | 3,000 | 0.0 | 65 | 5 | 70 | 2.12 | 3,300 | 0.0 | 3,700 | 0.0 | 5,100 | 0.0 |
| Catholics (non-Roman) | 0 | 0.0 | 1,000 | 0.0 | 22 | −2 | 20 | 1.82 | 1,100 | 0.0 | 1,200 | 0.0 | 2,000 | 0.0 |
| Buddhists | 800,000 | 10.0 | 5,069,000 | 16.5 | 107,571 | −34,071 | 73,500 | 1.35 | 5,432,000 | 16.0 | 5,804,000 | 15.5 | 6,760,000 | 13.0 |
| Confucians | 640,000 | 8.0 | 4,516,000 | 14.7 | 94,125 | −47,725 | 46,400 | 0.98 | 4,753,000 | 14.0 | 4,980,000 | 13.3 | 5,356,000 | 10.3 |
| New-Religionists | 10,000 | 0.1 | 3,380,000 | 11.0 | 84,710 | 109,000 | 193,710 | 4.53 | 4,277,600 | 12.6 | 5,317,100 | 14.2 | 10,400,000 | 20.0 |
| Non-religious | 0 | 0.0 | 100,000 | 0.3 | 2,673 | 6,027 | 8,700 | 6.44 | 135,000 | 0.4 | 187,000 | 0.5 | 1,040,000 | 2.0 |
| Baha'is | 0 | 0.0 | 14,000 | 0.0 | 317 | 83 | 400 | 2.50 | 16,000 | 0.0 | 18,000 | 0.0 | 30,000 | 0.1 |
| Atheists | 0 | 0.0 | 5,000 | 0.0 | 139 | 261 | 400 | 5.71 | 7,000 | 0.0 | 9,000 | 0.0 | 30,000 | 0.1 |
| Muslims | 0 | 0.0 | 3,000 | 0.0 | 65 | 5 | 70 | 2.12 | 3,300 | 0.0 | 3,700 | 0.0 | 6,000 | 0.0 |
| **Country's population** | **8,000,000** | **100.0** | **30,721,000** | **100.0** | **672,300** | **0** | **672,300** | **1.98** | **33,949,000** | **100.0** | **37,444,000** | **100.0** | **51,998,000** | **100.0** |

COLUMNS, ROWS. For meanings and definitions, see Codebook (Part 6). Note that, by definition, total 'Christians' = professing + crypto-Christians, which also = affiliated + nominal Christians. Percentages may not always total exactly, due to rounding.
CENSUSES. The religion question has never been asked in government censuses. The Ministry of Culture and Information does however collect statistics of affiliation returned by the major religious bodies, and publishes them in *Chongkyo Pyonlam* (Handbook of Religions). The 1969 edition reported as follows for 1967: 16.5% Buddhists, 13.1% Christians (10.6% Protestant including Korean indigenous, 2.5% Roman Catholics), 14.7% Confucians, 8.0% New-Religionists (2.1% Chondogyo, 2.1% Won), the remaining 47.7% being regarded as having no religion.
POLLS. 1971 (sample of 3,321 intellectuals): 'Is there a Being which transcends human beings?' — 38% Yes, 18% No, 44% Don't know.

NOTES ON RELIGIONS
AFFILIATED CHRISTIANS. The number of annual conversions has risen markedly since 1960. From 1971–73, 150,000 soldiers in the Korean army professed conversion (75,000 a year), followed by mass baptism services, raising the proportion of Christians in the army from 12% in 1970 to 35% in 2 years. By 1977, 47% of the army were church members. In the table above, the column 'Conversion change' gives the averages for the decade 1970–80.
ATHEISTS. No communist party is tolerated. Atheism is however prevalent in intellectual circles.
BAHA'IS. Entered first in 1921; new surge in 1950 through USA military personnel. Rapid growth from 12 local spiritual assemblies (1964) to 99 (1973); 120,000 booklets distributed.
BUDDHISTS. Mahayana. Adherents were served by 2,135 temples with 14,361 monks, priests and nuns in 1967 (in 1972, 1,912 sanctuaries and 18,629 clergy). Sects: 78% Chogye sect, 10% Pop-hwa sect, 5% Chingak sect; Miruk (Maitreya Buddha), Yongwhagyo and other sects.
CATHOLIC PENTECOSTALS (or Catholic charismatics). Total involved adults (1974) about 300; total charismatic community including children, 1,000, increasing rapidly.
CONFUCIANS. Adherents are 70% men, 30% women, in 231 centres with 11,831 teachers in 1967. Confucianism was introduced from China in AD 885, and remained the state religion until 1910. Although its Korean adherents are also usually involved both in Buddhism and in shamanism, the separation of the 3 into separate statistical categories by the Ministry of Culture and Information indicates that in Korea they are distinct religious systems, unlike the situation in China and among the Chinese diaspora.
COUNTRY'S POPULATION. After the Korean war (1950–53) in which about 5 million persons were killed, a further 2 million arrived after fleeing from North Korea, including several hundred thousand Protestants.
KOREA INDIGENOUS. In about 96 denominations in 1970 (see Table 2).
MUSLIMS. First introduced in 1953 by Turkish battalion among United Nations' troops; Hanafite Sunnis.
NEO-PENTECOSTALS. Charismatics in the non-Pentecostal Protestant denominations, especially Presbyterians.
NEW-RELIGIONISTS. Of the over 250 new non-Christian syncretistic religions (Sin Jonggyo, or Shinhung (Newly-risen) Jonggyo) in Korea, most sprang up after religious freedom was promulgated in 1945. The oldest, however, is Chondogyo (Religion of the Heavenly Way), begun in 1860 as Tonghak (Eastern Learning), syncretizing Confucianism, Buddhism, Taoism, Roman Catholicism and Korean shamanism, with (in 1969) 636,067 members in 119 churches with 977 clergy, in South Korea (rising in 1972 to 718,000 members in 141 churches with 1,526 clergy), and 2 million members underground in North Korea. Other leading New Religions are Jingsan-gyo (a system of traditionalist revitalization sects, begun 1901); Wonri (with syncretistic christology), Tangun, Ilbu, Bongnam, Kwansonggyo (with a shrine centre in Kyeryongsan representing all known gods including Jesus and Buddha), Sangjegyo (a sect of Jingsan-gyo, incorporating ideas of Christian Sunday worship), Ilsimgyo (now called Yudo; HQ Namwon; with a claimed reincarnation of Jesus); the Zen (Son, in Korean) sects Bochongyo, Bohwagyo and Samdoggyo; Ilkwando, Musul; and also Soka Gakkai from Japan since 1963 with around 10,000 followers (in Korea called Ch'angga Hakhoe, Value Creation Learning Society). The Won Buddhism sect, making Buddhism more relevant to secular life, began in 1924 and claimed 619,219 members in 1969, and 682,000 members in 1972 with 348 sanctuaries and 805 clergy. Other sects (1972): Daechongkyo (145,000 members), Chunrikyo (368,000), Taegukdo (152,000), Chungilhae (307,000), and International Moral Association (429,000 in 95 sanctuaries with 309 clergy).
NON-RELIGIOUS. Mainly young Koreans and Chinese who have abandoned family religion.
PRACTISING CHRISTIANS. *Roman Catholics*. Easter communicants, 66%; annual attenders of all kinds, 76%. *Protestants*. Weekly attendance, 70%; annual 85%.
SHAMANISTS. Shamanism in Korea is a folk religion, a blend of animism, spirit-worship, geomancy, folk-healing and fortune-telling. In 1968, 7,074 shamans (*mudang*, *paksu*, exorcisers) were reported, 995 working in Seoul (*Korean statistical yearbook 1969*). Rural shamans remain unorganized, but in the cities associations of shamans exist.

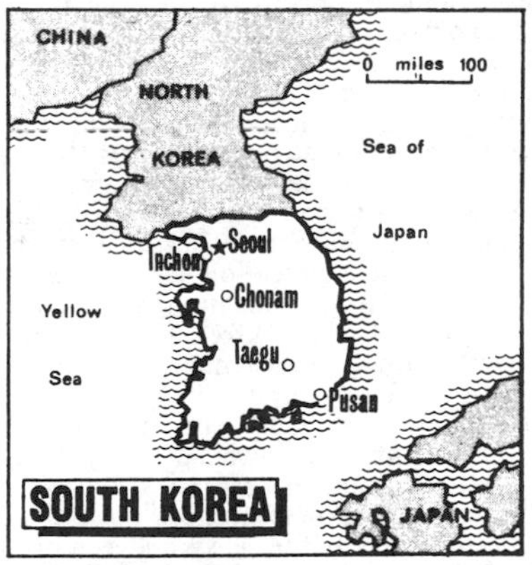


**NON-CHRISTIAN RELIGIONS. Shamanism** is the traditional religion, and still the most widely practised one, in Korea. It involves a strong belief in the influence of departed ancestral spirits as well as nature spirits who inhabit trees, rocks and other natural phenomena. These in turn must be propitiated or otherwise controlled either by individuals or by priests (shamans, *mudang*) to ensure health, fertility and success in life's ventures. There is a strong emphasis on exorcism and healing, with extensive use of chanting and drums. Belief in a supreme being also appears to be ancient; and this idea has been strenthened by contact with Christianity. A census by the Ministry of Education in June 1964 reported 87% of the population as 'non-religious'. However, this category undoubtedly includes many, perhaps a majority, who practise these unorganized nature religions. In 1968 there were 7,074 shaman medicine men, of whom 995 operated in Seoul. When in addition one realises that Korean nature religion is carried on for the most part by private individuals, without recourse to the intermediary function of shamans, the significance of this religion becomes apparent.

**Mahayana Buddhism** continues to be active. Suppressed and eclipsed during the Yi dynasty (1392–1910) under which Confucianism was the official religion, Buddhism took on a new life at the time of the Japanese occupation. Nevertheless it was only at the end of the Korean war in 1954 that it assumed a position of importance in Korean religious and social life. The marriage of monks, imposed by the Japanese, was forbidden from 1954, although celibacy has not yet been widely introduced except among the younger generation. The Chogye sect, which represents 78% of Buddhists in South Korea, has at its head a primate and has about 4,000 monks and 6,000 nuns. Its practices include Zen meditation and Amita pietism, both Mahayana schools, and it works vigorously for the renewal and modernization of Buddhism in close co-operation with organizations of Buddhist youth (7,000 adherents), the very active Union of Korean Students, the General Union of Buddhist Believers (3.85 million adherents) and the daily newspaper *Korean Buddhism*. It is engaged in social and charitable work as well as the renewal and spread of Buddhist doctrine. A Buddhist university, Dongguk, exists in Seoul.

**Confucianism,** which is a system of social ethics rather than a religion, was introduced into Korea from China in AD 885, and remained the state religion from 1392 until 1910. It still encourages the practice of ancestor veneration.

**New Religions,** a loose term for syncretistic religions begun in Asia over the last hundred years, are numerous, over 250 distinct non-Christian sects being known in present-day Korea. The largest is

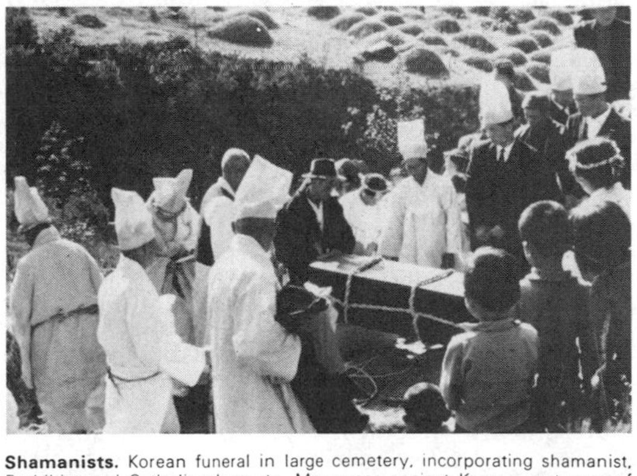

**Shamanists.** Korean funeral in large cemetery, incorporating shamanist, Buddhist and Catholic elements. Men wear ancient Korean costumes of white (colour of mourning). Burial of an ancestor must take place, traditionally, on a sun-warmed site.

Chondogyo (Religion of the Heavenly Way), an eclectic blend of shamanistic, Buddhist, Confucian and Christian elements which arose in the 19th century as a reaction against Western, especially Catholic, influence. The Tonghak Revolt of 1894 had its roots in Chondogyo, and it has maintained its political orientation.

Another large movement, arising out of Buddhism but completely separate from it, is popular Won Buddhism, which in 1972 claimed 682,000 faithful, 348 sanctuaries and 805 clergy. Begun in 1924 in an attempt to purify Buddhist doctrine, it permits the marriage of monks, authorizes the religious service of women, imitates Christianity in its worship service and stresses the importance of social work.

**Atheism** and **agnosticism** are prevalent in intellectual circles, a mood originally encouraged by the neo-

Confucianist state ideology of the Yi Dynasty (1392–1910).

**Islam** was introduced in 1953 by Turkish troops among the United Nations occupying forces. There are at present about 3,000 believers served by one imam, and one mosque has been built. The Korea Muslim Federation in Seoul co-ordinates all Muslim work.

**CHRISTIANITY.** The first contacts between Christians and Korea were in 1592 when Hideyoshi, accompanied by a Catholic general and a Jesuit priest, invaded Korea from Japan. Catholic books were brought from Peking to Seoul in 1777; and a Korean baptized in China returned home in 1784 to begin the church. The first of many Catholic martyrs was recorded in 1791; 3 years later in 1794, 4,000 Christians greeted the first Chinese missionary on his arrival in Korea. A vicariate was created in 1831, but martyrdom was the principal characteristic of the church until freedom of religion was declared in the early 1880s. A Protestant missionary touched Korea briefly in 1832 and another was martyred in 1865. By 1876, Korean Protestants were being baptized in Manchuria. The doors to Christian evangelization in Korea itself were opened by the 1882 Korean treaty with the USA. The first Presbyterian missionary entered in 1884 and a Methodist soon after. Extensive missionary itineration was begun in 1887.

PROTESTANT CHURCHES. Korea remained true to its name the Hermit Kingdom until forced to capitulate to Japanese forces in 1876. When missionaries arrived in Korea during the next decade communities of professing Christians were found waiting for further teaching, the combined result of decades of indigenous evangelization and the

resulted in the formation of the Korea Holiness Church which has been self-governing since the 1940s. These, with more recent Pentecostal and Baptist groups, have also grown rapidly in recent years. Many Korean churches experienced internal divisions after World War II for a wide variety of reasons. Since 1945 many new missionary societies from the USA have also entered the country.

Protestantism had entered Korea in the first rush of Western technological advance and had created Korea's first modern schools both at lower and university levels. During the Japanese occupation, Protestant laymen and socialist politicians shared leadership in resistance movements against Japan, as well as in the new liberation government after World War II. In spite of Japanese Shinto persecutions during the 1930s and 1940s, followed by the

**Pentecostals.** *Below.* 10th Pentecostal World Conference with 3,000 delegates in session at 10,000-seat 21,000-member Full Gospel Central Church, Seoul, 1973. *Above right.* A choir item in Hyo Chang stadium during Conference's final rally.

distribution of scriptures in China which gradually made their way into Korea as early as 1830. Korea has been the most fruitful field in Asia for Protestant missions. By 1890 Koreans were openly asking for instruction en masse. In the year 1900 alone, church membership increased by over 30%. Bible classes and the earnest simple witness of Korean Christians were primarily responsible. A third factor was the revival of 1907 which spread from Korea into Manchuria and China. The memory of this early spirit of prayer and piety has remained with Koreans over many years.

Four Presbyterian groups from northern and southern USA, Canada and Australia, began work between 1884 and 1898. A central committee was set up, and in 1907 the 4 missions united to form the Presbyterian Church of Korea. Presbyterianism remains the principal church tradition of Korea up to the present time. However, many serious schisms have occurred in recent years, particularly since World War II, resulting in the division of 4 major bodies and a host of smaller groups. Two American Methodist societies from northern (1884) and southern (1896) USA, worked together closely and in 1930 established the autonomous Korean Methodist Church, the largest single Protestant denomination in Korea. Seventh-day Adventists pioneered in 1903, followed by the Oriental Missionary Society in 1907. The latter's activity

Communist invasion from the north in 1950 and schisms from within during the 1950s, the Protestant community has continued to double in size every 10 years since 1940.

Protestant education in Korea pioneered an intellectual revolution. The first school was opened in 1886 by Methodists, and Protestants also pioneered in education for women. Today there are 11 Protestant colleges and universities, 85 high schools, 79 middle schools and innumerable primary schools, all legally recognized as private schools but subject to the Ministry of Education's curriculum requirements.

The first recognized Protestant medical institution in Korea was a hospital built in 1885. There are now 21 Protestant hospitals in operation and a great many smaller clinics, all having legal status under the Ministry of Health and Public Welfare. Protestants have also been involved in medical education. Severance Medical College of Yosei University has over the years produced a large proportion of Korea's trained doctors. Recent emphases in Christian medicine are rural medical service and family planning.

The Protestant churches have been active in land reclamation projects, slum resettlement and development, rural agricultural projects and city planning. Protestants pioneered in literacy; but with the country now over 90% literate, this work is no longer emphasized.

CATHOLIC CHURCH. The minor role played by the Catholic Church in the independence movement, as well as its failure to become involved earlier in education, considerably reduced its influence which had already been shaken by the 19th-century persecutions. However, this state of affairs has been largely reversed since World War II. Owing mostly to adult conversions, a huge increase occurred in the Catholic population between 1950 and 1968: the number of baptized Catholics rose from 163,471 in 1953 to 731,628 in 1967. Adult baptisms totalled 574,636 during the period 1959–70. This numerical growth was maintained throughout the Korean war of 1950–53 and the following period of national reconstruction. One of the factors contributing to this increase was the important and varied aid received by or through the Catholic Church during this period. There has also been mass immigration; between 1946 and 1951, a total of 25,000, more than half the Catholic population of North Korea, joined with other Christians in the huge wave of refugees to the south; and after 1952, a further 2 million refugees including another 10,000 or so Catholics fled from North to South Korea.

A serious problem facing the church has been the migration of Catholics from the countryside to the large cities, especially Seoul, which results in the loss of a large number of church members each year. In an attempt to remedy the situation, the episcopal conference established in 1973 an Office of the Apostolate to Migrants whose role is to trace migrant Christians and to help re-establish them in urban parishes. Six rural dioceses are especially affected by internal migration. Today Catholics tend to be more urbanized than the average population.

INDIGENOUS CHURCHES. Over 100 distinct indigenous denominations existed in the 1970s. The first of many schisms from the Presbyterian Church of Korea took place in 1938, although the situation became much more serious after World War II. A conservative split appeared in 1946 which resulted in the establishment of the Koryo Presbyterian Church, followed by a much larger conservative split in 1951 which formed the Presbyterian Church in Korea (Reunited Anti-Ecumenical), and later in 1954 by a liberal split to organize the Presbyterian Church in the ROK. Methodists have also had their problems with schisms; but except for a few small groups, they were reunited by 1959.

Many Korean indigenous churches blend mysticism with reverence for the forces of nature, this being reflected in a variety of incantations, charms, omens and a preoccupation with exorcism and healing. They profess stern moral codes, which are vestiges of Confucianism, and a concern for cleansing and ritual purity, drawn from Taoist, Shinto and Buddhist practices. Resting primarily on shamanistic traditions, the most rapidly-expanding of these new denominations are conspicuously influenced by Christian ideas, but the presence of strong syncretistic and non-Christian elements has led some observers to classify them as syncretistic new religions rather than (as here) as indigenous churches. The 2 largest of these movements are the Unification Church (Holy Spirit Association for the Unification of World Christianity, 1954) and the Olive Tree Church (1955). Both are strongly messianic. Sun Myung Moon, founder of the Unification Church, is widely regarded by his followers as the final messiah and the mediator between man and the powers of the spiritual world. Pak T'ae-son, founder of the Olive Tree Church, is able to cure sickness because he is filled with magical power and holy fire. He is the immortal Olive Tree (Revelation 11.4) and oracle of God. Both movements have developed widespread urban-industrial complexes and vast property holdings. At least 10 other self-proclaimed or acclaimed messiahs have appeared since the end of the Korean war in 1953.

CHURCH AND STATE. Religious liberty, guaranteed by Article 16 of the Yushin constitution of 27 December 1972, prohibits the government from establishing any state church and also proclaims that religion and politics shall be separated. Article 17 guarantees freedom of conscience; and Article 9, which is concerned with the equality of all citizens before the law, stipulates that no religion may practise any kind of discrimination. These articles represent no change over the constitution of 1962. However, the present constitution also states that these rights may be withdrawn by the president of the republic who has full powers, especially 'in case the national security or the public order is seriously

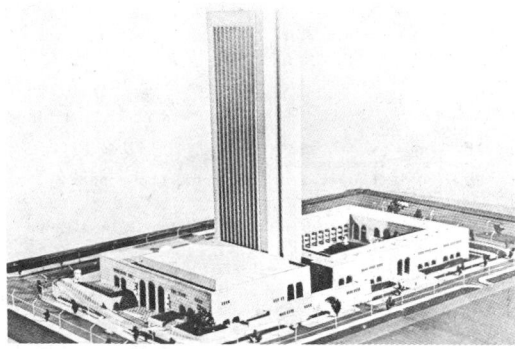

**Unification Church International.** *Above.* Projected world headquarters of Tong-il (Holy Spirit Association for the Unification of World Christianity), Seoul. *Right.* In golden robes and crown, founder Sun Myung Moon (centre front) and wife perform their 7th mass-wedding ceremony since 1960, this one for 1,800 couples from 20 countries (half Japanese) in Changchung Gymnasium, Seoul, on 8 February 1975.

threatened or anticipated to be threatened' (Article 53, paragraph 1 and 2).

The Religious Bodies Registration Law, included in the general registration law of December 1968 and amended in December 1969, requires religions and churches to register with the Ministry of Culture (Munhwa Kongbo-bu) before being authorized to hold public meetings or services. The Ministry of Education (Munkyo-bu) supervises the lands, buildings and finances of religious bodies. This supervision most directly concerns the considerable properties (including many designated as national treasures) of Buddhist temples and Confucian shrines.

Religions which offend patriotism are banned until they remove their offensive features. Thus Japanese Shinto is effectively banned because it implies loyalty to a foreign government; and Soka Gakkai from Japan was forced to omit bows towards Japan from its ritual before being allowed to register.

The government has had the power to tax religions since 1965, but it has chosen not to exercise this power and taxes neither property belonging to religions nor the incomes of their clergy.

Religions receive no direct support from government. By regulation of the Ministry of Education, religious instruction is forbidden during normal class hours, in both public and private primary and secondary schools, although schools often circumvent these rules. In May 1973, the minister of Education ordered that the law be enforced in Christian secondary schools, recommending also that teaching clergy be replaced by lay persons.

The Christians of Korea have behind them a long tradition of active resistance to the former Japanese colonial regime. Hence after World War II, although

Christians were still a small minority, many government ministers and officials were chosen from among the Christian community, mostly Protestants, including president Syngman Rhee. This explains the close collaboration between the churches and the regime and why they registered practically no reaction when Park Chong Hi became president in a military coup d'etat in 1961. The churches maintain the right to have military chaplains, and the government took the initiative in creating a corps of evangelists attached to the police who were authorized to preach to prisoners and policemen. The party in power in 1976 (DRP) clearly has the ear of the churches.

The first indication of Christian dissent appeared among a small group of Protestant pastors and lay persons who had been involved in an industrial mission since 1961 (extended into a wider urban mission in 1965) and who later received support from Catholic members of JOC. Opposition was first centred on the conditions faced by migrants and the misery of the masses. At the end of the 1960s, unrest grew due to new dictatorial tendencies evidenced by the regime: changes in the constitution in 1969, the state of emergency decreed in October 1971, proclamation of martial law in February 1972 and promulgation of the new Yushin

('Restoration') constitution giving to the president virtually unlimited powers. Centred in the Student Christian Movement, the opposition became increasingly public and active with as spokesmen a number of well-known Catholic and Protestant personalities including the Catholic cardinal arch-bishop of Seoul, Kim Soo Hwan; Catholic bishop of Wonju, Chi Hak Soon; Protestant leaders Kim Chae Hoon and Kang Won Young; the president of Ewha Protestant University for Women; Catholic poet Kim Chi Ha; and others. The first collective letter of the Catholic episcopate relating to these questions, dated 18 February 1968, provided support for militant members of JOC and their chaplain, while the second letter, 'Let's defeat today's injustice' (14 November 1971), criticized more directly the endemic corruption and unjust practices of the government. Numerous Korean militants, pastors and priests were arrested and a number of foreign missionaries were expelled. Msgr Chi Hak Soon was arrested in July 1974 and sentenced to 15 years in prison, but on 17 February 1975 he was freed along with others as a peace gesture by government.

**INTERDENOMINATIONAL ORGANIZATIONS.** The Federal Council of Churches and Missions was organized in 1919, with the name changed to National Christian Council in 1924. It became the National Council of Churches in 1946. Although only 7 churches are members, the NCC represents about one-third of Korean Christians. Thirteen other churches form the National Association of Evangelicals, a fundamentalist body. Church members work together in many interdenominational groups with specialized functions, including the Christian School Association, Korean Student Movement, and Christian Broadcasting System, under the overall supervision of the NCC. Through its Justice and Peace Committee, Catholics collaborate with their Protestant counterparts in socio-economic development; and Protestant-Catholic co-operation is also maintained through the Sodepax Korea Committee and Association of Christian Hospitals, the latter founded in Seoul in 1972. Anglican and Catholic priests conduct an Institute for Ecumenical Inter-Religious Studies.

Working in close co-operation with the government, the Korean Association of Voluntary Agencies, with 36 of its 74 members church-related Protestant and Catholic groups, co-ordinates the distribution of relief and development aid.

**BROADCASTING.** The government Korean Broadcasting System allows religious broadcasting, but only a very small amount takes place; most is done by the 9 Protestant and Catholic radio stations. The Evangelical Alliance Mission operates TEAM Radio in Seoul (HLKX), with 100 hours of Protestant programming from Monday to Saturday and 20 hours on Sunday; and the Korean Christian Association has Protestant programming for 10.5 hours from Monday to Saturday and 4.5 hours on

**True Jesus Church, Korea Assembly.** Members, mainly Chinese, in front of their church building.

Sundays. FEBC transmits from the Cheju Islands in Korean, Chinese and Russian. The Lutheran Church—Missouri Synod produces radio and TV programmes. The US Army station AFRTS broadcasts a small amount of religious material. The Christian Broadcasting System has a 5-station network, most of the programmes being prepared in their studios in Seoul (HLKX). In Sogang College (Seoul), the Department of Communications produces radio and TV programmes. For Catholics, Korea is a member of UNDA.

## BIBLIOGRAPHY


*A history of the church in Korea*. A. D. Clark. Seoul: Christian Literature Society of Korea, 1971. (First edition 278p).

*Catholic Korea, yesterday and now*. J. C. Kim & J. J. Chung. Seoul: Catholic Korean Publishing Co, 1964.

*Chongkyo P'yonlam* (Handbook of religions). Seoul: Ministry of Culture and Information, 1969.

(*Christian yearbook 1970*). Seoul: National Council of Churches in Korea, 1970. 688p. (Korean-language only. First edition, 1957).

*Korea and Christianity*. S. J. Palmer. Seoul: Hollym Corporation, 1967.

*Korea struggles for Christ*. Eds H. S. Hong et al. Seoul: Christian Literature Society of Korea, 1966. 254p.

*Korean Catholicism in the 70s*. W. E. Biernotzai et al. New York: Orbis, 1975.

'Receptivity of Korea and Taiwan mountain people'. E. S. Chae. Thesis, Fuller Theological Seminary, Pasadena (CA), 1973. 133p.

'Revival and church growth in Korea, 1884–1910'. H. T. Watson. Thesis, Fuller Theological Seminary, Pasadena (CA).

*The Christians of Korea*. S. H. Moffett. New York: Friendship Press, 1962. 174p.

*The history of Protestant missions in Korea, 1832–1910*. I. G. Park. Seoul: Yonsei University Press, 1970.

*The new religions of Korea*. Ed S. J. Palmer. Transactions of the Korea Branch, Royal Asiatic Society, Seoul, vol XLIII (1967). 180p.

*Wildfire: church growth in Korea*. R. E. Shearer. Grand Rapids (MI): Eerdmans, 1962. 242p.


TABLE 2. ORGANIZED CHURCHES AND DENOMINATIONS IN SOUTH KOREA

| Official name 1 | Begun 2 | Type 3 | Counc 4 | Congs 5 | Adults 6 | Affiliated 7 | Names, notes, and other statistics (see Codebook) 8 |
|---|---|---|---|---|---|---|---|
| Bible Presbyterian Church of Korea | 1955 | I Ref | .TT.T | 89 | 2,834 | 13,951 | Schism ex Koryo Presbyterian Ch. M=IBPFM(USA). Fundamentalists. HQ Seoul. 91n. |
| **Catholic Church in Korea:** | 1592 | R Lat | P.F.R | 472 | 463,800 | 828,133 | *Ch'onju Kyohwe*. C=14+2+32. 2p,2s(709),W=63%. 533n,369x,113m,2150w,P=66%,53917Yy. |
| M Kwangju (Kwang Ju) | 1937 | R Lat | Ps | 36 | 37,700 | 67,393 | *Kwangju Tae Kyogu*. Rural. Heavy emigration. 20 70 13 126 59 3728 |
| D Chonju (Jeon Ju) | 1937 | R Lat | Ps | 31 | 30,400 | 54,207 | *Chonju Kyogu*. Mountainous. Heavy emigration. 45 4 1 78 54 3214 |
| M Soul (Seoul) | 1831 | R Lat | Ps | 119 | 104,000 | 185,769 | *Seoul Tae Kyogu*. Rapid urban growth. 145 96 37 664 87 14160 |
| D Ch'unch'on (Chun Cheon) | 1939 | R Lat | Pssc | 25 | 18,500 | 33,005 | Mountainous, mining. Many military bases. 12 33 0 44 45 2063 |
| D Inch'on | 1961 | R Lat | Pmm | 20 | 32,100 | 57,293 | Second largest port city, many islands. 11 22 17 130 53 2971 |
| D Suwon (Su Won) | 1963 | R Lat | Ps | 30 | 31,200 | 55,722 | Rural, recent industry. Military bases. 53 3 1 58 56 3689 |
| D Taejon (Tae Jon) | 1948 | R Lat | Ps | 34 | 36,900 | 65,900 | Rural, and a major transportation centre. 43 13 4 120 77 4335 |
| D Wonju (Won Ju) | 1965 | R Lat | Ps | 21 | 17,600 | 31,420 | Mountainous, rural, mining. 15 23 0 37 93 1924 |
| M Taegu (Tae Gu) | 1911 | R Lat | Ps | 46 | 47,800 | 85,309 | Rural, 3 developing industrial centres. 92 29 37 438 57 5359 |
| D Andong | 1969 | R Lat | Pmep | 18 | 15,800 | 28,149 | Mountainous, rural, mining. 7 19 0 34 65 1086 |
| D Ch'ongju (Cheong Ju) | 1958 | R Lat | Pmm | 23 | 25,600 | 45,664 | Rural, agricultural industrialization. 10 20 2 61 60 2002 |
| D Masan | 1966 | R Lat | Ps | 25 | 17,100 | 30,554 | Mountains, port. Least Catholic area (1.4%). 25 6 0 49 50 2060 |
| D Pusan | 1957 | R Lat | Pmep | 36 | 42,900 | 76,586 | Urban, largest port (population 1.9 million). 51 17 0 299 55 6676 |
| PA Cheju-do (1977, D Cheju) | 1971 | R Lat | Pssc | 8 | 6,200 | 11,162 | Created out of M Kwangju. 4 14 1 12 65 650 |
| Central Jerusalem Church in Korea | 1957 | I ind | ..... | 5 | 320 | 1,470 | Indigenous group. 420 Sunday-school children. 40 deacons,5n,3m. |
| Chinese Christian Church | 1912 | I ind | ..... | 9 | 300 | 582 | *Chung-hwa Kidokyohwei*. Chinese. Declining rapidly in numbers. HQ Seoul. 10n. |
| Choson Christian Church | 1918 | I ind | ..... | 13 | 1,000 | 3,030 | *Choson Kidokyo Whei* (Choson=old name for Korea). Korean Christianity. 20n. |
| Christian Brethren | c1895 | P CBr | x.... | 20 | 1,000 | 2,000 | *Gospel Halls. Plymouth* (*Open*) *Brethren*. M=CMML(USA,UK). Work re-begun c1955. 20f. |
| Christian Church of Emmanuel | 1950 | I ind | ..... | 29 | 896 | 3,441 | Grouping of indigenous Korean congregations. 20n. |
| Christian Independent Church | | I ind | ..... | 13 | 1,000 | 2,300 | Small group of indigenous independent congregations. 18n. |
| Christian Korean Pentecostal Ch of God | 1964 | I pen | ..... | 2 | 355 | 1,000 | *Kidokyo Hankuk Osungol Hananim-e Kyowhei*. Korean indigenous. HQ Seoul. 3nx. |
| Christian Reformed Church in Korea | 1967 | P Ref | .F... | 136 | 3,000 | 19,015 | Recent North American work. M=CRC(USA). 52n,2f. |
| Christian Rehabilitated Ch in Korea | 1945 | I ind | ..... | 48 | 2,773 | 4,329 | One of many splinter renewal movements. Large indigenous grouping. 12n. |
| Christ's Assembly | 1947 | I Adv | ..... | 5 | 200 | 550 | *Kurisudo Sohoe*. Small sabbatarian group. HQ Seoul. 4 evangelists, 1 minister. |
| Church of Christ, Scientist | 1963 | M Sci | x.... | 1 | 50 | 200 | *Christian Science*. M=CCS(Boston,USA). Seoul Society. Expatriate Americans. |
| Church of God (Cleveland) | 1966 | P Pe3 | ZF... | 38 | 5,109 | 10,000 | M=GoC(Cleveland) (USA). Holiness Pentecostals. 30 churches, 8 missions. 40n,1p. |
| Church of God (Seventh-day) | 1962 | P Adv | x.... | 3 | 32 | 154 | Related to Ch of God (Seventh-day), Adventist group in USA. |
| Church of Jesus C of Latter-day Saints | 1950 | M LdS | x.... | 16 | 4,000 | 6,329 | *Malil Songdo Yesu Kristo Kyowhei. Mormons*. M=CJCLdS(USA). 116n,300f,G=14.6%pa. |
| Constitutional Korean Presbyterian Ch | 1962 | I Ref | ..T.T | 75 | 1,500 | 4,000 | *Tae-Han Yesukyo Changno Whei* (*Ho-hon*) (*Legal*). 47n,1p,1s(23),W=75%,40Yy,300z. |
| Episcopal Church in Korea: | 1889 | A ACa | AwEAN | 70 | 4,321 | 32,436 | *Tae-Han Song-Kong-hwei* (*Korea Holy Catholic Ch*). G=6.1%pa,1s(11). 44n,6x,650Yy. |
| D Soul (Seoul) | 1965 | A ACa | a | 31 | 2,540 | 12,436 | *Seoul Kyogu*. 70% urban. 2m,5w,1p,W=72%,182Y,250z. 16 1 260 |
| D Taejon | 1965 | A ACa | a | 39 | 1,781 | 20,000 | *Taejon Kyogu*. M=USPG,MU,KM(UK). 45% rural. Growing. W=60%, 150z. 28 5 390 |
| Evangelical Alliance Mission in Korea | 1953 | P int | xM... | 15 | 582 | 2,000 | *Hankuk Pokumjui Tongmaeng Sonkyo Whei*. M=TEAM(USA). HQ Seoul. 1 school. 14n,30f. |
| Far East Apostolic Mission | 1958 | P Pe2 | ..... | 19 | 1,420 | 3,000 | M=FEAM(Texas,USA), in Korea and Japan only. 19n,4x,G=15.4%pa,1p(Seoul),W=70%,80Y. |
| Full Gospel Central Church | 1958 | I pe3 | Z.... | 1 | 12,500 | 23,000 | FGCC. Rapid grouth in adult members: (1961) 800, (1969) 8,000, (1978) 75, 361. 100 staff, 5,000 cells. |
| Greek Orthodox Ch (D New Zealand) | 1896 | O Gre | Cw..N | 2 | 1,000 | 3,000 | Under EP Constantinople; until 1970 in AD N& S America. 2n,1x,G=0,1p(3),W=25%,61Yy. |
| Heavenly Gospel Tabernacle Church | | I mar | ..... | 30 | 2,000 | 5,000 | 1976, leader arrested for selling absolution tickets; died in police custody. |
| Holy Spirit Association for U of WC | 1954 | I mar | xv... | 936 | 100,000 | 304,750 | *T'ongil Kyohoe*. Unification Ch. Missions to USA, Japan, 120 nations. HQ Seoul. 1013n. |
| Independent Korean Presbyterian Church | 1949 | I Ref | ..T.T | 9 | 600 | 1,380 | Split with USA fundamentalist support. Rapid growth. 11n,W=95%, 158Yy,212z. |
| Internat Ch of the Foursquare Gospel | 1970 | P Pe2 | ZF... | 6 | 958 | 3,000 | M=ICFG(USA). Classical Pentecostals. High proportion of youths. 4nm,4f,29Y. |
| Jehovah's Witnesses | 1912 | M Jeh | x.... | 300 | 13,668 | 40,000 | *Wach'ui Ta-wo Songso Ch'aekja Hyop-hwei/Watchtower*. G=17.3%pa,W=53%,3290Y,16251z. |
| Jesus End of the World Gospel Mis Soc | 1963 | I ind | ..... | 42 | 1,926 | 9,802 | Revivalist, evangelistic. Large grouping of indigenous congregations. 5n. |
| Jesus Korean Holiness Church | 1961 | I Hol | .TT.T | 133 | 6,388 | 44,525 | *Yesukyo Tae-Han Songkyol-kyohwei*. HQ Seoul. 185n,1p(140),W=95%,617Y. |
| Jesus Korean Methodist Church | 1962 | I Met | .TT.T | 45 | 6,788 | 19,960 | *Yesukyo Tae-Han Kamni-Whei*. No foreign mission connections. HQ Seoul. 48n. |
| Jesus Presbyterian Ch, Head Presbytery | 1949 | I Ref | ..... | 14 | 2,000 | 5,016 | *Tae-Han Yesukyo Changno Whei Tok-nowhei*. HQ Seoul. 17n. |
| Korea Baptist Bible Fellowship | 1950 | P Bap | x.... | 49 | 6,000 | 12,108 | *Hankuk Songso Chimnekyo Whei*. M=BBFI(USA). Fundamentalists. HQ Seoul. 61n,20f,1s. |
| Korea Baptist Convention | 1890 | P Bap | TTT.T | 463 | 13,678 | 51,613 | *Hankuk Chimnehwei Yonmaeng*. East Asia Ch. 1950, M=SBC(USA). 365n,72f,1H,1s,3122Y. |
| Korea Church of Christ (Instrumental) | 1936 | P Dis | x.... | 123 | 10,120 | 20,000 | *Hankuk Kristo-e Kyohwei* (*ak-ki*). M=KCM(CCCC,USA). 89n,25f,G=9.1%pa,2p(202),1080Y. |
| Korea Ch of Christ (Non-Instrumental) | 1927 | P Dis | x.... | 41 | 1,000 | 2,550 | *Hankuk Kristo-e Kyohwei* (*mu-ak-ki*). M=CC(USA). USA servicemen on bases. 41nx. |
| Korea Church of God | c1932 | P Hol | x.... | 17 | 3,637 | 5,000 | Linked since 1961 with M=CoG(Anderson) (USA). No missionaries now. 24n,1p,W=43%. |
| Korea Holiness/Evangelical Church | 1907 | P Hol | xF... | 617 | 28,856 | 177,305 | *Kidokyo Tae-Han Songkyol Kyohwei*. M=OMS. 354n,14f,G=–10.5%pa,3s(500),W=65%,1567Y. |
| Korea Jesus Bible Presbyterian Church | 1961 | I Ref | .TT.T | | 1,000 | 2,000 | *Tae-Han Yesukyo Songkyong Changno-Whei*. Presbyterian schism over doctrine. Seoul. |
| Korea Lutheran Church | 1958 | P Lut | L.... | 6 | 700 | 1,100 | *Hankuk Lutokyo Sonkyobu*. M=LC Missouri Synod(USA). 6n,6x,G=16.8%pa,1s,W=75%,220Yy. |
| Korea Peniel Church | 1958 | I Hol | ..... | 5 | 277 | 1,651 | Small indigenous group of churches in holiness tradition. 4n. |
| Korea Presbyterian Ch (Conservative) | 1965 | I Ref | ..... | 3 | 250 | 851 | One of Presbyterian schisms over doctrine. Expanding. HQ Seoul. 3n. |
| Korea Reformed Presbyterian Church | 1955 | I Ref | ..... | 139 | 3,000 | 7,260 | *Tae-Han Yesukyo Kaehyok Changno-Whei*. One of many fundamentalist schisms. 187n. |
| Korea Tabernacle Temple | 1965 | I ind | ..... | 3 | 1,000 | 1,350 | Small indigenous grouping of independent congregations. |
| Korean Bethel Presbyterian Church | | I Ref | ..... | 9 | 500 | 1,005 | Small fundamentalist indigenous group of Presbyterian background. 14n. |
| Korean Bible Presbyterian Church | | I Ref | ..T.T | 58 | 7,000 | 21,190 | One of larger Presbyterian schisms over fundamentalism. Now anti-ICCC. 62n. |
| Korean Christian Assemblies of God | 1952 | P Pe2 | ZF... | 160 | 55,353 | 100,000 | *Tae-Han Kidokyo Hananim-e Song-Hwei*. M=AoG. 205n,19f,G=24%pa,1s(300),W=77%,700Y. |
| Korean Christian Pentecostal Church | | I pen | ..... | 6 | 590 | 1,000 | Small grouping of indigenous Korean pentecostals. 6n. |
| Korean Christian Reformed Presb Ch | | I Ref | ..... | 51 | 3,000 | 8,225 | Presbyterian schism over doctrine and fundamentalism, with USA support. 58n. |
| Korean Conservative Baptist Church | | P Bap | x.... | 2 | 350 | 1,000 | M=CBFMS(USA). Independent Baptist churches aided by North American mission. 4nx. |
| Korean Evangelical Church of Christ | 1925 | I ind | ....N | 15 | 6,000 | 12,000 | *Kidokyo Tae-Han Pokum Kyohwei*. Founder a Korean. 20n,G=3.7%pa,W=83%,400Y,4000z. |
| Korean Evangelical Movement | 1951 | I ind | .TT.T | | 295 | 1,105 | Small indigenous grouping of Korean fundamentalist congregations. 1 minister. |
| Korean Jesus Free Methodist Church | 1961 | I Hol | .TT.T | 20 | 5,000 | 8,000 | *Hankuk Yesukyo Chayu Kamni-hwei*. No foreign mission. 15n,G=9.3%pa,1p(25),950Y,4000z. |
| **Korean Methodist Church** | 1884 | P Met | VWE.N | 1,679 | 301,810 | 600,000 | *Kidokyo Tae-Han Kamni-hwei*. M=UMC. 914n,51f,G=4.3%pa,2s(375),W=89%,1850Yy,85000z. |
| Korean Nazarene Church | 1948 | P Hol | xF... | 73 | 6,242 | 20,000 | *Tae-Han Kidokyo Nazaret-kyowhei*. M=CoN. 64n,3x,10f,G=13%pa,1s,71t(9657),W=69%,320Y. |
| Korean United Pentecostal Church | 1965 | P Pel | x.... | 20 | 2,658 | 6,000 | *Hankuk Yunhang Osoonch Kyohwei. Jesus Only*. M=UPC. 20n,9x,12f,4p(173),W=21%,170Y. |
| Koryo Presbyterian Church | 1946 | I Ref | JTT.T | 513 | 40,000 | 102,125 | *Tae-Han Yesukyo Changno-Hwei* (*Ko-Sin*). Koryo=Korea. M=IPM,OPM,WPM(USA). 702n. |
| Meeting of Christians | 1896 | I ind | ..... | 23 | 550 | 1,110 | *Kristo-in-a Chip Whei-so*. Small indigenous independent groups. HQ Seoul. |
| New Apostolic Church | | C CAp | x.... | | 500 | 1,000 | *NAC*. In Canada Bezirk, NAK. Catholic Apostolic. World HQ Dortmund (FR Germany). |
| New Jerusalem Church of Korea | 1933 | M Swe | x.... | 7 | 316 | 800 | *Swedenborgians*. Had 40 congs in NKorea. Declining. 2n,G=5.5%pa,2p(5),W=85%,24Y. |
| No-Church Movement Association of BS | 1924 | I non | ..... | 3 | 100 | 300 | BS=Bible Students. Influenced by Japanese Mukyokai (Non-Church). No buildings. |
| **Olive Tree Church (Evangelical Church)** | 1955 | I mar | ..... | 1,768 | 200,000 | 700,520 | *Chondokwon. Preaching Tabernacle. Korean Christian Revival Society*. Vast towns. |
| Peniel Churches of VOCA | 1946 | P Hol | x.... | 10 | 1,215 | 5,115 | M=Voice of China AMS(USA). 50% students. 3 schools. 15n,G=9%pa,1s(23),W=36%,562Y. |
| **Presb Ch in K(Reunited Anti-Ecumenical)** | 1951 | I Ref | J.T.T | 1,991 | 200,000 | 550,790 | *Tae-Han Yesukyo Changno-hwei* (*Hap-Dong*). *NAE*. Anti-ecumenical schism. 2096n,1s(850). |
| Presbyterian Church in the RoK | 1954 | I Ref | RWE.N | 688 | 129,931 | 218,287 | *Hankuk Kidokyo Changno-hwei*. Liberal schism. 459n,5x,23f,2s(150),W=70%,5720Yy. |
| **Presbyterian Church of Korea** | 1884 | P Ref | RWE.N | 2,348 | 253,616 | 534,368 | *Tae-Han Yesukyo Changno-hwei* (*T'ong-hap*). 1303n, 109f,G=0.9%pa,6H,15p,3s,16240Yy. |
| Presbyterian Ch of K (Non-Assembled) | 1960 | I Ref | ..... | 18 | 2,500 | 7,500 | Ex Koryo Presbyterian Church in long-standing fundamentalist controversy. 14n. |
| Presbyterian Ch of K (Reformed Faith) | 1954 | I Ref | ..... | 7 | 315 | 1,465 | Small Presbyterian schism over fundamentalism. 5n. |
| Presbyterian Ch of K (Restored) | 1966 | I Ref | .TT.T | 5 | 200 | 960 | Small Presbyterian schism over controversy on fundamentalism. 5n. |
| Presbyterian Church (Neutral) | 1950 | I Ref | ..... | 51 | 2,550 | 7,743 | One of numerous splits over fundamentalism ex Presbyterian Church of Korea. 30n. |
| Presbyterian Ch (Revolutionary Rehab) | 1949 | I Ref | ..... | 3 | 300 | 967 | *Revolutionary Rehabilitated*. Schism claiming return to Reformed origins. |
| Pure Presbyterian Church of Korea | 1939 | I Ref | ..... | 14 | 545 | 4,299 | Presbyterian fundamentalist schism. Rapid decline: G=–9.8%pa. 6n,1p,W=80%,50Yy. |
| Reconstruction Presbyterian Church | 1945 | I Ref | ..... | 53 | 1,000 | 3,449 | *Tae-Han Yesukyo Changno Whei* (*Chae-Kon*). HQ Seoul. 35n,1s(in Dong-ku, Pusan). |
| Religious Society of Friends | 1955 | P Qua | Q.... | 1 | 26 | 100 | *Chongkyo Ch'in-u-whei* (*Kwei-ko*). *Quakers*. Small group meeting in Seoul. |
| Reorganized Ch of JC of Latter-day S | 1960 | M LdS | x.... | 5 | 200 | 1,000 | *RLDS Church*. Schism ex Mormons. HQ Seoul. World HQ Independence, MO (USA). 7nx. |
| Salvation Army, Korea Territory | 1908 | P Sal | xwE.N | 94 | 71,161 | 150,000 | *Ku-se-kun Tae-Han Pon-Yong*. 5 Divisions. 213 Officers, 16 institutions. 1s. |
| Seventh-day Adventist Church | 1903 | P Adv | x.... | 554 | 25,637 | 50,000 | *SDA, Korea Council*. 91n,26f,2H,1h,1j,7r,1s,W=85%,1532Y. |
| True Jesus Church, Korea Assembly | 1944 | I pel | x.... | 27 | 1,348 | 3,000 | *Ch'am Yesukyo Whei Han-kuk Chongwhei*. Chinese. 21n,G=–1.5%pa,1s,W=43%,74Y. |
| World Evangelical Mission of Korea | | I pen | ..... | 121 | 1,900 | 5,000 | Indigenous body with seminary in Seoul. 64 priests, 72 missionaries. |
| Worldwide Evangelization Crusade | 1956 | P int | xF... | 11 | 1,900 | 4,000 | Small interdenominational evangelical body. M=WEC(UK). 16n,1f. |
| World-Wide Missions of Korea | 1961 | P ind | x.... | | 500 | 1,000 | M=World-Wide Missions(USA). Evangelicals with links in Pasadena, CA(USA). |
| Zion Presbyterian Church of Christ | 1938 | I Ref | ..... | 5 | 200 | 320 | *Sionan Yesukyo Changrohoe*. Presbyterian schism, near Kyongju. G=4.9%pa,W=63%,15Yy. |
| Other Korean indigenous churches | | I | ..... | 1,000 | 10,000 | 30,000 | Total about 50 (see list below). |
| Other Protestant denominations | | P | ..... | 800 | 25,000 | 40,000 | Total about 30 (see list below), including USA military chaplaincies. |
| **Total affiliated (mid-1970)** | | | | 16,400 | 2,072,146 | 4,884,884 | **Total denominations (1970) . . . 158.** |
| **Total affiliated (mid-1975)** | | | | 20,500 | 3,131,400 | 7,381,900 | **Total denominations (1975) . . . 173.** |
| **Total affiliated (mid-1980)** | | | | 29,600 | 4,303,800 | 10,145,800 | **Total denominations (1980) . . . 188.** |

NOTES ON TABLE ABOVE
COLUMNS: for meanings and CODES (cols. 1, 3, 4, 8), see Codebook (Part 6). Column 1: **Boldface type** = church with over 10% of country's affiliated Christians.
NATIONAL COUNCILS (Column 4, 5th letter).
N = National Council of Churches in Korea (NCCK) (Hankuk Kidokyo Yonhap-hui).
R = Bishops' Conference of Korea (Hanguk Jukyo Hweoi).
T = Korean Evangelical Council of Christian Churches (formerly Korea Fundamentalist Association of Churches, sometimes called National Association or Assembly of Evangelicals, NAE).
OTHER KOREAN INDIGENOUS CHURCHES. These include: Assembly of God's House, Christian Revolutionary Ch, Ch of God of Korea (member of ICCC), Jehovah's Saeil (New Work) Church, Korea Christian Ch of God, Korea Independent Lutheran Ch, Korean Christian Chs (member of ICCC), Mount Yongmun Prayer Centre, Original Jesus Christ Ch, True Gospel Ch (pentecostal).
OTHER PROTESTANT DENOMINATIONS. These smaller bodies include: American Baptist Association, Apostolic Faith Mission (1967), Baptist Mid-Missions (1966), Ch of God of Prophecy (1969), Ev Methodist Ch (1964), Evangelistic Faith Missions (1971), Far East Missionary Society (1968), International Gospel League (1954), Japanese Christian Ch in Korea (Seoul), Korea Christian Ch, Maranatha Baptist Mission, Mennonite Mission, Methodist Protestant Ch, Overseas Missionary Fellowship (1968), Pentecostal Holiness Ch (1979, merger with 30,000 Korean members, 142 pastors), Slavic Gospel Association, Swedish Free Mission, United World Mission (1955). There are also USA military chaplaincies among the 42,000 USA troops (1970–79).

PEOPLES (ethnolinguistic). Christians: 99.3% Korean, 0.7% USA military, Chinese, Eurasian.

COUNTRY-WIDE TOTALS
EVANGELIZATION (see Part 5). 1900: 16%. 1970: 90%. 1980: 94%. *Mass evangelism.* Among the many recent campaigns: 1956, Billy Graham rally; 1965, nation-wide 17-denomination campaign (80th anniversary of Protestantism in Korea; 20,000 professions of faith); 1966, launching of Operation Lighthouse by Jesus Presbyterian Ch in Soonchun (emphasis on local evangelism), extended in 1970 to Chinju and Mokpo presbyteries; 1967, Crusade for World Revival (from UK) (30,000 attenders a night); 1973, 5-day crusade in Seoul (3,210,000 attenders, 75,000 registered enquirers and 200,000 unregistered), when Billy Graham preached to largest single evangelistic gathering in history (1,100,000 attenders), with associate evangelists in 6 provincial cities (1,312,300 attenders); August 1974, EXPLO 74 training conference on evangelism and discipleship (323,419 workers from 78 countries in residence, Seoul, invited by Campus Crusade for Christ; largest attendance at a single rally 1.5 million; 6.5 million persons involved in one week (1,250,000 salvation decisions recorded), resulting a year later in 33% increase of membership in a sample of 1,000 churches); 1977, National Evangelization Crusade 1977 on Yoido Island; 1978, Here's Life Korea (CCCI). *Radiophonic evangelism.* Annual listeners' letters (1975): 39,768 FEBC. Bible correspondence courses: LCMS (250,000 enrolled in 10 years), ICI, et alia. *Literature evangelism.* Widespread campaigns; one in 1975 reached 640,000 homes with evangelistic leaflets. During the initial Every Home Crusade saturation crusade, 6 years of work resulted in 19,757 decisions for Christ; the second took 5 years with over 70,482 decisions.
FOREIGN MISSIONARIES AND PERSONNEL (nationals serving abroad) (1973). Total 620 in 30 countries: about 270 Protestants (Presbyterians, Methodists, et alii, 80% serving Korean communities abroad), 250 Korean indigenous (mainly HSAUWC), about 90 Roman Catholics, about 10 marginal Protestants. There has been a long tradition since 1913 of Koreans serving abroad as foreign missionaries, but in the 1970s the numbers involved have increased rapidly.
FOREIGN MISSIONARIES AND PERSONNEL (aliens from abroad) (1973). Total 1,537. *From Western world.* 1,423: 590 Roman Catholics, 524 Protestants (467 in 57 USA societies, 25 in 2 Canada societies, 17 in 4 UK societies, 13 in 7 Australia societies, 2 in 1 Denmark society), about 300 marginal Protestants (260 Mormons, 30 Jehovah's Witnesses) from USA, 8 Anglicans (7 in 3 UK societies, 1 in 1 USA society), 1 Orthodox from Greece. *From Communist world.* About 2 Roman Catholics from Yugoslavia. *From Third World.* 112: about 50 Roman Catholics (22 from Mexico), 22 indigenous from Japan, Taiwan and Hong Kong, 20 Protestants from Japan and Taiwan, about 20 marginal Protestants (Mormons) from Japan, Philippines, et alia.
INSTITUTIONS (church-operated) (1973). Total 580, including 190 higher schools (2 minor seminaries), about 200 medical centres (80 hospitals), 9 radio/TV stations, 12 religious communities, 6 research centres, 108 seminaries (90 Protestant, 15 Korean indigenous, 2 RC, 1 Anglican), 21 universities. By 1977, Protestant seminaries were increasing rapidly in numbers, with the 23 major ones producing over 500 graduates annually.
PERIODICALS. About 90 titles, including 6 well-known weekly newspapers.
PERSONNEL. About 17,025 (15,488 national, 1,537 foreign).
RELIGIOUS LIBRARIES. About 160.
SCRIPTURE DISTRIBUTION (1975). Annual totals: 373,897 Bibles (1% free, 96% subsidized, 3% commercial), 2,132,975 NTs (42% free, 55% subsidized, 2% commercial), 985,67. UBS portions, 17,918,885 UBS selections. *Translations completed.* In Korean: portion 1882, NT 1887, Bible 1911.
SERVICE AGENCIES. About 120, including CBS, CCCI, CEF, CEI, CRS-USCC, ILM, KAATS, KAVA, KAVACO, KCCE, KCHI, KCMC, KCSA, KCWM, NAE, NCCK, NCCW, NCLA, SU, WLC(EHC), WMMC, WVI, YCW, YMCA, YWAM, YWCA.

ADDITIONAL DATA ON CHURCHES
CATHOLIC CHURCH IN KOREA. The statistics in the table refer to the situation in 1970. *Catechumens.* (1959) 86,144; (1961) 82,948; (1963) 59,746. In column 7, figures include (1970) 40,053 catechumens, divided among the 14 jurisdictions as follows, in the order shown: 3000, 590; 19847, 1137, 2045, 2012, 2719, 740; 2968, 922, 1518, 946, 1109, 500. *Baptisms.* Adult baptisms remain at over 60% of the total (e.g. 1973: 33,505 adult, 18,962 infant). *Priests.* The first Korean priest was ordained in China in 1845 and martyred in Korea in 1846. 1976 figures: 700 Koreans, 983 total. *Brothers.* Of the 112, 84 were Koreans (1969); by 1974 there were 143 Koreans out of 176. *Sisters.* Of the 2,150, 1,958 were Koreans in 1969; by 1974, 2,645 Koreans and 186 expatriates. *Catholic charismatics* (January 1974). 120 adults including a number of religious personnel are active in 4 organized prayer groups in the Charismatic Renewal; (January 1975) 200 in 5 groups. *Seminarians.* At the 2 regional seminaries of Seoul and Kwangju; major seminarians (secular) 609 (1970), 570 (1974); (religious) 121 (1972). *Catechist schools.* University level, non-accredited, 2-year; at Seoul, National Catholic Catechetical Institute, for lay catechists; and at Taegu, mainly for sisters. Total catechists (1970): 1,707 men, 581 women. *Indigenous religious congregations.* Priests: Order of the Blessed Korean Martyrs (4 priests and 19 professed Korean Martyr Brothers in 1972). Sisters: Handmaids of the Sacred Heart (begun 1935, 353 members); Sisters of the Blessed Korean Martyrs (begun 1946, 164 members); Caritas (Congregation of the Blessed Sacrament) (157 members); Holy Family Sisters (begun 1943, 112 members); Sisters of Our Lady of Perpetual Help (begun 1932, 98 members). *Main foreign orders and congregations.* Priests: WM, MEP, SSC, SJ, SDB, MSC, OSB, OFM. Sisters: St Paul de Chartres, Benedictines, Missionary Benedictines.
*Catholic organizations.* The Bishops' Conference of Korea (Hanguk Jukyo Hweoi) is a member of FABC in Hong Kong. There are no national presbyteral or pastoral councils, but religious personnel are represented in the Conference of Major Superiors of Men in Korea, and the Association of Majaor Superiors of Religious Women in Korea. The National Council for the Lay Apostolate co-ordinates lay activities, the most active organizations being YCW (3,000 members), Cursillos de Cristiandad (2,350 members), National Council of Catholic Women, Korean Catholic Students' Association (3,000 members) and Pax Romana.
The Holy See has diplomatic relations with Korea and is represented to government and the Catholic hierarchy by a pro-nuncio in Seoul.
After a slow start the Catholic Church has increasingly become involved in education and social service. Their various activities, in 1970 included the following: 126 kindergartens; 14 primary, 42 middle, 33 high and 10 professional schools; 3 post-secondary colleges; Sogang University; 46 hospitals; 15 dispensaries; 22 leper colonies; 12 homes for the aged; and 18 orphanages. Organizations include Caritas Coreana, Catholic Leprosy Service, National Catholic Hospital Association and Catholic Relief Services (USCC Korean Division).
In addition the Maryknoll Sisters have pioneered in credit unions. The Co-operative Education Institute (CEI) has since 1962 trained 7,300 leaders for the country's 400 voluntary credit unions, with 80,000 members, as well as for co-operatives. A large number of co-operatives have also been organized by the Columban Fathers on Cheju Island, under the name Isidore Development Association which is a member of ICRA in Italy. The YCW has concentrated on improving conditions for girls working in textile mills, and since 1966 the Institute for Labour and Management (ILM) of Sogang University has trained more than 560 labour leaders and management representatives.
Major Catholic centres include the National Pastoral Institute, National Catholic Catechetical Institute, Social Research Institute, and Korean Church History Institute.
EPISCOPAL CHURCH IN KOREA. *New diocese* (1974). D Pusan, formed out of D Taejon. *Lay personnel* (1977). 20 lay workers (13 women), 16 lay readers (men). *Seminarians* (1977). 4.
FULL GOSPEL CENTRAL CHURCH. The FGCC is an indigenous pentecostal body, claimed by 1979 to be the largest single congregation in Asia. Begun in 1958 as the Full Gospel Revival Centre, renamed FGCC in 1962, full members have increased phenomenally, as follows: (1961) 800 advent baptized members, (1969) 8,000, (1974) 19,500, (1976) 35,794, (1978) 75,361 members, with over 5,000 cells, 100 fulltime pastoral staff, 3,750 deacons and deaconesses. *Facilities* (1978). 10,000-seat main auditorium, 2,000 more via closed-circuit TV; publishing company; TV studio; 10-storey World Mission Centre.
HOLY SPIRIT ASSOCIATION FOR UNIFICATION OF WORLD CHRISTIANITY. Full name, Segye Kidokyo T'ongil Sillyong Hyophwei. Known also as the Unification Church International, it has branches or members in 122 countries and controls a network of industries in Korea and vast properties abroad, especially in the USA. *Theology.* Originally a Christian movement, by 1976 its theology had become clearly marginal: 'Judaism was God's first central religion, and Christianity was the second. The Unification Church is the third, coming with the new revelation that will fulfil the final chapter of God's Providence' (Sun Myung Moon, Washington, DC (USA), September 1976).
KOREAN METHODIST CHURCH. 119 institutions, 1,479 Sunday schools.
OLIVE TREE CHURCH. Founder Elder Pak T'ae-son claims to be olive tree of Revelation 11.4. Some estimates put professing adherents at 2 million by 1964, expanding very rapidly. *Ministers.* 1,515 (1970). *Industries.* The church operates vast urban-industrial complexes manufacturing Zion brand products: Christian Towns I and II in the Seoul area, and a third industrial Christian town in Pusan; including what is claimed as the world's largest temple seating 50,000. Headquarters is in the Castle of the Millennium 6 miles outside Seoul.
PRESBYTERIAN CHURCH IN KOREA. Known as Haptong, the church has the largest seminary in Asia, with (1977) over 800 students. By 1977, the church had grown very rapidly from the 1970 statistics given in the table above to: 2,896 churches, 722,682 members and 4,300 ministers. Its expansion programme has a goal of 10,000 churches. In 1975, 351 new churches were planted; in 1977, the goal was 600 a year. *Membership growth.* (1970) 550,790, (1975) 680,000, (1977) 722,682, (1979) 1,100,000.
PRESBYTERIAN CHURCH IN THE ROK. ROK = Republic of Korea. Foreign mission: United Ch of Canada.
PRESBYTERIAN CHURCH OF KOREA. *Missions.* Foreign missions assisting this church are: UPUSA, PCUS, PCA. (Australia). *Growth.* Statistics in the table above refer to the year 1970. By 1976, total constituent membership had grown to 700,000 (36% being baptized members), with 3,000 churches. During 1976, 200 new churches were established, and 60,000 new members added.
SEVENTH-DAY ADVENTIST CHURCH. Full name in Korean: Jechilil Ansikil Yesoo Jaerimkyo Hankookyunhaphoe.

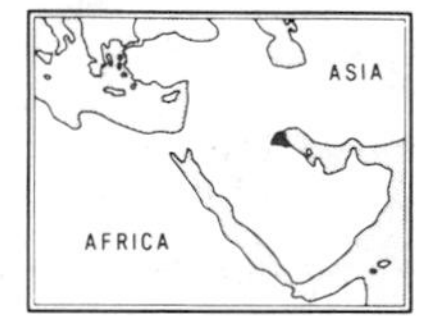


# KUWAIT

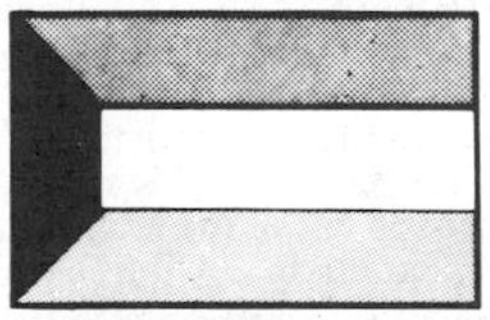

## SECULAR DATA

**STATE. Official name:** The State of Kuwait (Dowlat al Kuwait) Adjective of nationality: Kuwaiti.
**Flag** (shown above right): Green, white, and red stripes, with black trapezoid at flagstaff.
**Area:** 24,280 sq.km. (9,375 sq.miles). Agricultural land: 7.6%.
**Government:** (Absolute monarchy (emirate), since 1976 (1756 emirate, 1899 British quasi-protectorate, 1961 independence as monarchy).
**Legislature:** National Assembly, 50 members (dissolved 1976).
**Official language:** Arabic.
**Chief cities:** capital Kuwait City 295,270 (1970), Hawalli 106,540.
**Political divisions:** 3 Governorates.
**Armed forces** (1976): Total 9,700 regular: army 8,500, navy 200, air force 1,000 (33 combat aircraft).

**DEMOGRAPHY. Population:** 994,837 (census of 21.IV.1975). For 1970–2000 (UN), see last row of Table 1). Population density (1975): 45/sq.km. (116/sq.mile). Under 15 years: 35%. Growth rate (1975–80): 5.63% per year (births 4.54%, deaths −0.45%, immigrants 1.54%). Life expectancy (1975–80): 68.8 years. Household size: 6.2 persons.
**Major languages:** Arabic, Persian (Farsi), English, Kurdish.
**Urban dwellers** (1970): 56.3%. Urban growth rate (1950–70): 7.2% per year.
**Labour force:** 32% (92% non-Kuwaiti).
**Refugees** (1977): 150,000 Palestinians.
**Tourists** (1970): 617,900.

**ETHNOLINGUISTIC GROUPS:** 52.8% non-Kuwaiti [19.3% Palestinian (147,000) & 10.6% Jordanian Arab, 10.0% Kurd (rising to 150,000 by 1980), 4.2% Iranian (30,800), 3.5% Iraqi (26,000) 2.8% Lebanese (20,900), 0.8% Armenian, also Omani, Syrian, Pakistani, South Indian, Egyptian, Saudi Arabian, South Arabian, Sudanese, 0.3% British (2,000), 0.2% Assyrian, 0.2% USA White, European], 45.6% Kuwaiti Arab, 1.6% Black African (Bantu).

**MONEY** (1977). **Monetary unit:** dinar (= 10 dirhams = 1,000 fils); US$1 = KD 0.288.
**National income per person:** US$9,900. Average annual family income: US$61,380.
**Inflation:** (1970–74) 11.0% per year (1975: consumer price index 139).
**Cost of living in capital** (1976): index 138 (Washington DC=100). Daily cost of living: US$90.

**HEALTH.** Hospitals: 26 (4,009 beds). Doctors: 1,050. Lepers: 140 (0.1 per 1,000). Blind: 1,000. Psychotics: 8,000. Criminals: 18,039.

**EDUCATION.** Adult literacy: (1957) 34%, (1975) 60%. Education rate: 79%. Schools: 161. Universities: 1.

**LITERATURE.** Annual new book titles (1973): 138. Periodicals: 21. Newspapers: 6 dailies, 11 non-daily.

**COMMUNICATION** (per 1,000 people). Phones: 108. Radios: 13. TV sets: 137. Daily newspaper circulation: 66 copies.

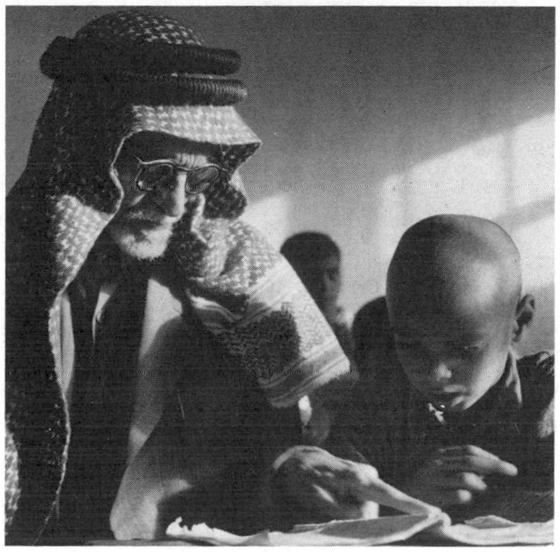

**Muslims.** (*Right*). Kuwaiti headmaster of village school at Fahaheel, with 120 pupils.

TABLE 1.   RELIGIOUS ADHERENTS IN KUWAIT

| Year / Name | 1900 Adherents | % | mid-1970 Adherents | % | Natural | Conversion | Total | Rate | mid-1975 Adherents | % | mid-1980 Adherents | % | 2000 Adherents | % |
|---|---|---|---|---|---|---|---|---|---|---|---|---|---|---|
| Muslims | 66,800 | 99.7 | 719,300 | 94.6 | 65,015 | −85 | 64,930 | 6.31 | 1,029,200 | 94.9 | 1,368,600 | 95.1 | 3,040,500 | 95.5 |
| Christians | 200 | 0.3 | 35,850 | 4.7 | 2,485 | 90 | 2,575 | 5.25 | 49,000 | 4.5 | 61,600 | 4.3 | 122,000 | 3.8 |
| crypto-Christians | 100 | 0.1 | 2,350 | 0.3 | 215 | 80 | 295 | 7.76 | 3,800 | 0.3 | 5,300 | 0.4 | 21,000 | 0.6 |
| professing | 100 | 0.1 | 33,500 | 4.4 | 2,270 | 10 | 2,280 | 5.04 | 45,200 | 4.2 | 56,300 | 3.9 | 101,000 | 3.2 |
| Roman Catholics | 50 | 0.1 | 17,500 | 2.3 | 1,260 | 10 | 1,270 | 5.31 | 23,900 | 2.2 | 30,200 | 2.1 | 57,000 | 1.8 |
| Orthodox | 50 | 0.1 | 12,000 | 1.6 | 810 | 0 | 810 | 4.97 | 16,300 | 1.5 | 20,100 | 1.4 | 35,000 | 1.1 |
| Anglicans | 0 | 0.0 | 1,500 | 0.2 | 60 | 0 | 60 | 3.33 | 1,800 | 0.2 | 2,100 | 0.1 | 3,000 | 0.1 |
| Protestants | 0 | 0.0 | 1,300 | 0.2 | 60 | 0 | 60 | 3.75 | 1,600 | 0.1 | 1,900 | 0.1 | 3,000 | 0.1 |
| Asian indigenous | 0 | 0.0 | 1,200 | 0.2 | 80 | 0 | 80 | 5.00 | 1,600 | 0.1 | 2,000 | 0.1 | 3,000 | 0.1 |
| affiliated | 200 | 0.3 | 35,850 | 4.7 | 2,485 | 90 | 2,575 | 5.25 | 49,000 | 4.6 | 61,600 | 4.3 | 122,000 | 3.8 |
| total practising | 190 | 95 | 32,260 | 90 | 2,236 | 82 | 2,318 | 5.26 | 44,100 | 90 | 55,440 | 90 | 97,600 | 80 |
| non-practising | 10 | 5 | 3,590 | 10 | 249 | 8 | 257 | 5.24 | 4,900 | 10 | 6,160 | 10 | 24,400 | 20 |
| Roman Catholics | 100 | 0.1 | 17,700 | 2.3 | 1,250 | 10 | 1,260 | 5.25 | 24,000 | 2.2 | 30,300 | 2.1 | 58,000 | 1.8 |
| Orthodox | 100 | 0.1 | 12,150 | 1.6 | 805 | 0 | 805 | 4.88 | 16,500 | 1.5 | 20,200 | 1.4 | 36,000 | 1.1 |
| Asian indigenous | 0 | 0.0 | 3,100 | 0.4 | 315 | 75 | 390 | 7.80 | 5,000 | 0.5 | 7,000 | 0.5 | 22,000 | 0.7 |
| Anglicans | 0 | 0.0 | 1,500 | 0.2 | 60 | 0 | 60 | 3.33 | 1,800 | 0.2 | 2,100 | 0.1 | 3,000 | 0.1 |
| Protestants | 0 | 0.0 | 1,400 | 0.2 | 55 | 5 | 60 | 3.53 | 1,700 | 0.2 | 2,000 | 0.1 | 3,000 | 0.1 |
| Evangelicals | 0 | 0.0 | 1,000 | 0.1 | 42 | 18 | 60 | 4.62 | 1,300 | 0.1 | 1,600 | 0.1 | 1,500 | 0.1 |
| Hindus | 0 | 0.0 | 3,800 | 0.5 | 310 | −10 | 300 | 5.66 | 5,300 | 0.5 | 6,800 | 0.5 | 14,500 | 0.5 |
| Baha'is | 0 | 0.0 | 1,050 | 0.1 | 90 | 5 | 95 | 6.33 | 1,500 | 0.1 | 2,000 | 0.1 | 6,000 | 0.2 |
| Country's population | 67,000 | 100.0 | 760,000 | 100.0 | 67,900 | 0 | 67,900 | 6.26 | 1,085,000 | 100.0 | 1,439,000 | 100.0 | 3,183,000 | 100.0 |

COLUMNS, ROWS. For meanings and definitions, see Codebook (Part 6). Note that, by definition, total 'Christians' = professing + crypto-Christians, which also = affiliated + nominal Christians. Percentages may not always total exactly, due to rounding.

CENSUSES. 28.II.1957: 94.4% Muslims, 4.7% Christians, 0.9% other religionists. 25.IV.1965: 94.1% Muslims, 5.3% Christians (24,506 non-Kuwaitis, 134 Kuwaitis), 0.6% other religionists (all non-Kuwaitis). 19.IV.1970 (including 754 nationals abroad): 94.7% Muslims, 4.6% Christians (34,179 persons), 0.6% other religionists.

NOTES ON RELIGIONS

ASIAN INDIGENOUS. South Indian and Arab indigenous congregations, in 3 denominations or groupings in 1970 (see Table 2).

BAHA'IS. Growth from 3 local spiritual assemblies (1964) to 7 (1973). Including several Indians, former Hindus and Muslims.

CHRISTIANS. Since 1965, the proportion of Christians has declined gradually as a percentage of total population (as shown under CENSUSES above and also as a percentage of the non-Kuwaiti population (from 11.6% in 1957, to 9.9% in 1965, to 8.7% in 1970, to about 8.3% in 1980, and to around an estimated 6.0% in the year 2000, due to the much greater influx of Muslim immigrants.

COUNTRY'S POPULATION. The non-Kuwaiti population, mostly immigrant workers (37.6% Palestinian and Jordanian Arabs, 12.5% Iranians (Persians, 10.5% Iraqis, 8.4% Lebanese, 7.9% Omanis, 6.8% Syrians) has risen from 92,800 in 1957 (40% of the population) to 247,000 in 1965 (52.9%), to 400,000 in 1970 (52.8%), to 593,000 in 1975 (54.7%), and is expected to reach 1.7 million by the year 2000 (53%). During 1970–80, annual nett immigration averaged 17,000.

HINDUS. South Indians.

MUSLIMS. Kuwaitis are Sunnis of various rites including Malikite, at one time strongly influenced by the Wahhabi movement; foreign Muslims mostly Shias. There are over 300 mosques. *Hajj pilgrims to Mecca.* (1968) 8,783; (1970) 8,072; (1975) 8,808; (1976) 4,908.

NON-CHRISTIAN RELIGIONS. **Islam** is the religion of virtually all Kuwaitis, who are Muslim Sunnis of the Malikite rite and are strongly influenced by the Wahhabi movement. Foreign Muslims are mainly Shias. There is a total of over 300 mosques.

CHRISTIANITY. The massive influx of workers into the oilfields from both western and eastern countries has included a wide variety of Christians of different denominations and rites. However, the foreign community is now decreasing due to gradual improvement in the technical skills of native Kuwaitis, and Christianity's influence has begun to diminish. Seven of Kuwait's 42 private schools are under Christian management (4 Catholic, plus one each serving the Greek, Armenian, and Protestant communities), and there is also a Catholic hospital.

CATHOLIC CHURCH. Although an American Catholic priest entered Kuwait as early as 1795, the first resident cleric did not arrive until 1948. Individual Catholics represent many Eastern-rite traditions (Melkites, Maronites, Chaldeans and others), but all are part of the Latin-rite vicariate of Kuwait. Aided by OCD priests and 3 congregations of sisters, Catholicism is the principal Christian denomination in Kuwait.

ORTHODOX CHURCHES. Five different Orthodox groups are present, 3 belonging to the Oriental Orthodox (Non-Chalcedonean) tradition: Armenian, Coptic and Syrian churches. The Armenian Apostolic Church, Kuwait's largest Orthodox community, built its own church in 1958 and has had a resident priest since that time. In addition the church operates a school with 600 pupils. Copts and Syrians also have resident priests.

The Greek Orthodox are Kuwait's second largest Orthodox body and only representative of Eastern Orthodoxy. Although having had resident priests since 1962, they continue to hold services in the Protestant churches of Kuwait and Ahmadi. The church also sponsors Al Salam School, which was begun in 1968 and has 700 pupils.

The Ancient Church of the East (Assyrians or Nestorians), forms a small community led by a resident deacon.

OTHER CHURCHES. The Protestant pioneer was Samuel Zwemer of the Reformed Church in America who entered Kuwait in 1903. The first Arabic church service of the National Evangelical Church was held in 1926, and the first building constructed in 1931. The church consists of Arabic, English and Indian congregations, each with their own resident ministers.

The first Anglican services were held in Ahmadi in 1947, and a permanent building, St Paul's church, was completed there in 1956.

A large Mar Thoma congregation serving South Indian Christians and a small Brethren group are also active.

CHURCH AND STATE. According to the 1962 constitution, Islam is the religion of the state and the Islamic Sharia constitutes one of the principal sources of legislation (Article 2). Religious liberty is guaranteed, and the state protects the free practice of religion in conformity with established customs (Article 35). Relations between Christian churches and the government are amicable, but by implicit agreement with the Kuwaiti authorities, no overt attempt is made to convert Muslims.

The government agency responsible for religion is the Ministry of Awqaf and Religious Affairs. It has a large staff numbering over 2,500.

INTERDENOMINATIONAL ORGANIZATIONS. The Anglican, Catholic and Evangelical churches work closely together through the Council of Churches in Kuwait, which was founded in 1960. Co-operation is also maintained with the Orthodox in the joint use of church buildings in Kuwait and Ahmadi.

BROADCASTING. As Kuwait is a Muslim state, no Christian broadcasting is allowed on government radio or TV. However, foreign Christian programes in Arabic can easily be heard from FEBA (Seychelles), TWR (Monaco) for 4 hours a week, Radio Vatican for 3 hours 30 minutes a week, and also over CBC (Cyprus).

BIBLIOGRAPHY
*Christians in Kuwait.* V. Sanmiguel. Beirut: Beirut Printing Press, 1970. 107p. (By the Catholic bishop).

TABLE 2.   ORGANIZED CHURCHES AND DENOMINATIONS IN KUWAIT

| Official name (1) | Begun (2) | Type (3) | Counc (4) | Congs (5) | Adults (6) | Affiliated (7) | Names, notes, and other statistics (see Codebook) (8) |
|---|---|---|---|---|---|---|---|
| Ancient Church of the East | | O Nes | Yv... | 1 | 290 | 450 | *Assyrians (Nestorians).* Patriarch in USA. 1 congregation, with resident deacon. |
| Anglican Church (D Cyprus & the Gulf) | 1947 | A plu | av..C | 2 | 500 | 1,500 | In Episcopal Ch in Jerusalem & the Middle East. 77% British, 23% Arabs. W=10%. |
| Armenian Apostolic Church: V Kuwait | | O Arm | Sv.N. | 2 | 3,600 | 5,600 | Under P Cilicia (Lebanon). Since 1958, own church and priest. 1 school (600). |
| Assemblies (Jehova Shammah) | | I CBr | x.... | 1 | 30 | 50 | Indian missionaries (Brother Bakht Singh), HQ Hyderabad, AP (India). |
| Catholic Church: VA Kuwait | 1795 | R Lat | P..LC | 4 | 11,000 | 17,700 | 58% Latins (31% Indian,21% Arab),42%Eastern. M=OCD. C=1+0+3. 5x,31w,1H,10Y,293y. |
| Christian Brethren | | P CBr | x.... | 2 | 70 | 200 | *Plymouth Brethren. Open Brethren.* 50% Arabs, 50% Indians. |
| Coptic Orthodox Church (P Alexandria) | 1960 | O Cop | Nva.. | 1 | 600 | 950 | By 1977, 600 families. Resident priest, with Coptic papal representative. |
| Greek Orthodox Church (P Antioch) | | O Ara | Cv... | 2 | 2,700 | 4,200 | Resident priest since 1962, using Protestant buildings. 1 school (700), 1 bishop. |
| Isolated radio churches | c1950 | I rad | .... | 50 | 900 | 1,900 | Isolated radio believers (students). R=500(FEBA,TWR,&c),T=4000(RSB,ICI). |
| Mar Thoma Syrian Ch (D Bahya Kerala) | | I ReO | .... | 1 | 700 | 1,150 | In Diocese of Outside Kerala. Largest Mar Thoma congregation outside India. 1x. |
| National Evangelical Church in Kuwait | 1903 | P Ref | ...NC | 3 | 500 | 1,200 | Arab, Indian, USA congregations. M=RCA(USA). 3x,4f,1H(until 1968),1k,1t(50). |
| Orthodox Syrian Church of India | | O Syr | Dwe.. | 1 | 600 | 950 | Malayalis. Resident priest since 1959, using National Ev Ch building. |
| Total affiliated (mid-1970) | | | | 70 | 21,490 | 35,850 | Total denominations (1970) . . . 12. |
| Total affiliated (mid-1975) | | | | 75 | 29,400 | 49,000 | Total denominations (1975) . . . 15. |
| Total affiliated (mid-1980) | | | | 80 | 36,900 | 61,600 | Total denominations (1980) . . . 20. |

NOTES ON TABLE ABOVE

COLUMNS: for meanings and CODES (cols. 1, 3, 4, 8), see Codebook (Part 6). Column 1: **Boldface type** = church with over 10% of country's affiliated Christians.

NATIONAL COUNCILS (Column 4, 5th letter).
C = Council of Churches in Kuwait.

PEOPLES (ethnolinguistic). Christians: 48.8% Arab (Jordanian, Palestinian, Lebanese, Syrian, Egyptian), 23.3% South Indian (23.0% Malayali, 0.3% Telugu, Tamil), 16.6% Armenian, 4.6% Assyrian (Chaldean), 4.0% British, 2.0% USA White, 0.6% Greek, Pakistani.

COUNTRY-WIDE TOTALS
EVANGELIZATION (see Part 5). 1900: 7%. 1970: 35%. 1980: 41%. *Radiophonic evangelism.* Annual listeners' letters (1975): 380 FEBA, 120 TWR. Bible correspondence courses: about 4,000 enrolled (RSB, ICI).
FOREIGN MISSIONARIES AND PERSONNEL (aliens from abroad) (1973). Total 48. *From Western world.* 8: 6 Protestants (4 in 1 USA society, 2 in 1 Denmark society), about 2 Roman Catholics. *From Third World.* 40: about 34 Roman Catholics from India, Palestine, Jordan and Iraq, 5 Orthodox from Egypt, Lebanon, Syria and India, 1 indigenous from India.
INSTITUTIONS (church-operated) (1973). Total 5, including 3 higher schools.

PERIODICALS. About 5 titles.
PERSONNEL. About 52 (4 national, 48 foreign).
SCRIPTURE DISTRIBUTION (1975). Annual totals: 100 NTs (subsidized).
SERVICE AGENCIES. 2.

ADDITIONAL DATA ON CHURCHES
CATHOLIC CHURCH. Catholics: 9,400 Latins (5,000 Indians, 3,500 Palestinian and Jordanian Arabs, 900 Europeans and Americans); 6,900 Eastern-rite (2,900 Melkites, 2,000 Maronites, 1,200 Chaldeans, 350 Armenians, 200 Syrians, 200 Syro-Malankar & Malabar, 50 Copts). *Foreign religious orders and congregations.* Priests: OCD (India, Italy, Malta, Spain). Sisters: Rosary Sisters

(Jordan), Immaculate Conception (Chaldean Iraqi), Carmelites (India).
*Catholic organizations.* The vicariate is part of the Conference of Latin Bishops of the Arab Regions (CELRA) with headquarters in East Jerusalem. There are no presbyteral or pastoral councils, associations of religious personnel or lay organizations.
  The Holy See maintains diplomatic relations with Kuwait and is represented to government and the Catholic hierarchy by a pro-nuncio resident in Lebanon.
  The Catholic Church is responsible for 4 schools (4,025 primary and 1,663 secondary pupils in 1973) and one hospital.

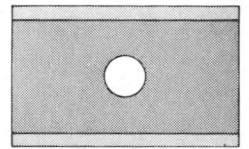

# LAOS

## SECULAR DATA

STATE. Official name: The Lao Peoples' Democratic Republic (Pathet Sathalanalath Pasathipathay Pasason Lao). Earlier name: The Kingdom of Laos (Phrarasa-Anachak Lao). Adjective of nationality: Lao, a Lao, the Lao.
Flag (shown above right): Narrow red stripes top and bottom; wide blue stripe in middle with large white circle.
Area: 236,800 sq.km. (91,429 sq.miles). Agricultural land: 7.4%.
Government: One-party Communist state, since 1975 (14th century kingdom of Laos, 1893 French protectorate, 1947 constitutional monarchy, 1949 Independence).
Official language: Lao.
Chief cities: capital Vientiane 132,250 (1966), Luang Prabang 42,000.
Political divisions: 16 Provinces.
Armed forces (1976): Total 42,500 regular: army 40,000, navy 500, air force 2,000 (73 combat aircraft).
Foreign forces (1973): 30,000 China troops; 17,000 USA troops.

DEMOGRAPHY. Population: 3,257,000 (estimate of 1.VII.1974).

For 1970–2000 (UN), see last row of Table 1). Population density (1975): 14/sq.km. (36/sq.mile). Under 15 years: 42%. Growth rate (1975–80): 2.38% per year (births 4.41%, deaths −2.03%). Life expectancy (1975–80): 43.5 years. Household size: 5.1 persons.
Major languages: Lao, French, Thai, Chinese, Vietnamese, English, and 70 other languages.
Urban dwellers (1970): 15.0%. Urban growth rate (1950–70): 6.7% per year.
Refugees (1977): From abroad, none. Internally displaced: 700,000. Exiles abroad: 63,466 Laotians (52,900 in Thailand, 10,566 in USA).
Tourists (1973). 23,102.

ETHNOLINGUISTIC GROUPS: 61.2% Thai Lao (including Lao-Lum/Valley Lao), 5.4% Tai (tribal) (Lao-Tai: Black Tai, Red Tai, Phon Tai, Tai Neua, Tai Phuan), 5.4% Khmu, 5.4% Phuteng, 3.2% Miao (Lao-Soung), 3.2% Sui & Alak, 3.2% Boloven (Loven), 3.0% Chinese (Mandarin, Cantonese), 2.2% Bo & So, 2.2% Lu, 1.6% Yuang, 1.6% Lamet, 1.1% Yao, 0.8% Vietnamese, 0.3% Khmer, French, British, USA, Filipino,

Cham, & 60 others.

MONEY (1977). Monetary unit: kip (= 100 at); US$1 = Kp 200.
National income per person: US$150. Average annual family income: US$765.
Inflation: (1970–74) 25.5% per year (1975: consumer price index 432).
Cost of living in capital (1976): index 108 (Washington DC=100). Daily cost of living: US$40.

HEALTH. Hospitals: 15 (2,411 beds). Doctors: 234. Lepers: 11,300 (3.4 per 1,000). Blind: 10,000. Psychotics: 25,000.

EDUCATION. Adult literacy: (1962) 28%. Education rate: 25%. Schools: 3,413.

LITERATURE. Annual new book titles (1972): 179. Periodicals: 15. Newspapers: 2 dailies, 26 non-daily.

COMMUNICATION (per 1,000 people). Phones: 2. Radios: 47. Daily newspaper circulation: 3 copies.

TABLE 1.  RELIGIOUS ADHERENTS IN LAOS

| Year | 1900 | | mid-1970 | | Annual change, 1970–1980 | | | | mid-1975 | | mid-1980 | | 2000 | |
|---|---|---|---|---|---|---|---|---|---|---|---|---|---|---|
| Name | Adherents | % | Adherents | % | Natural | Conversion | Total | Rate | Adherents | % | Adherents | % | Adherents | % |
| Buddhists | 905,000 | 60.3 | 1,715,490 | 57.9 | 43,904 | −418 | 43,486 | 2.28 | 1,910,580 | 57.8 | 2,150,350 | 57.8 | 3,268,700 | 57.1 |
| Tribal religionists | 581,000 | 38.7 | 1,007,080 | 34.0 | 25,654 | −1,342 | 24,312 | 2.18 | 1,116,400 | 33.8 | 1,250,200 | 33.6 | 1,878,000 | 32.9 |
| Non-religious | 0 | 0.0 | 100,000 | 3.4 | 2,732 | 1,408 | 4,140 | 3.48 | 118,900 | 3.6 | 141,400 | 3.8 | 286,000 | 5.0 |
| Christians | 8,000 | 0.5 | 51,330 | 1.7 | 1,356 | 211 | 1,567 | 2.65 | 59,000 | 1.8 | 67,000 | 1.8 | 109,000 | 1.9 |
| crypto-Christians | 3,000 | 0.2 | 21,330 | 0.7 | 598 | 369 | 967 | 3.72 | 26,000 | 0.8 | 31,000 | 0.8 | 52,000 | 0.9 |
| professing | 5,000 | 0.3 | 30,000 | 1.0 | 758 | −158 | 600 | 1.82 | 33,000 | 1.0 | 36,000 | 0.1 | 57,000 | 1.0 |
| Roman Catholics | 5,000 | 0.3 | 25,000 | 0.8 | 632 | −132 | 500 | 1.82 | 27,500 | 0.8 | 30,000 | 0.8 | 46,000 | 0.8 |
| Protestants | 0 | 0.0 | 5,000 | 0.2 | 126 | −26 | 100 | 1.82 | 5,500 | 0.2 | 6,000 | 0.2 | 11,000 | 0.2 |
| affiliated | 8,000 | 0.5 | 51,330 | 1.7 | 1,356 | 211 | 1,567 | 2.65 | 59,000 | 1.8 | 67,000 | 1.8 | 109,000 | 1.9 |
| total practising | 7,200 | 90 | 33,360 | 65 | 881 | 138 | 1,019 | 2.66 | 38,350 | 65 | 43,550 | 65 | 65,400 | 60 |
| non-practising | 800 | 10 | 17,970 | 35 | 475 | 73 | 548 | 2.65 | 20,650 | 35 | 23,450 | 35 | 43,600 | 40 |
| Roman Catholics | 8,000 | 0.5 | 41,480 | 1.4 | 1,092 | 60 | 1,152 | 2.43 | 47,500 | 1.4 | 53,000 | 1.4 | 83,200 | 1.5 |
| Protestants | 0 | 0.0 | 9,150 | 0.3 | 245 | 145 | 390 | 3.65 | 10,680 | 0.3 | 13,050 | 0.4 | 24,000 | 0.4 |
| Evangelicals | 0 | 0.0 | 9,000 | 0.3 | 241 | 139 | 380 | 3.62 | 10,500 | 0.3 | 12,800 | 0.3 | 23,600 | 0.4 |
| Anglicans | 0 | 0.0 | 300 | 0.0 | 7 | −7 | 0 | 0.00 | 300 | 0.0 | 300 | 0.0 | 500 | 0.0 |
| Asian indigenous | 0 | 0.0 | 300 | 0.0 | 9 | 11 | 20 | 5.00 | 400 | 0.0 | 500 | 0.0 | 1,000 | 0.0 |
| Marginal Protestants | 0 | 0.0 | 100 | 0.0 | 3 | 2 | 5 | 4.17 | 120 | 0.0 | 150 | 0.0 | 300 | 0.0 |
| Chinese folk-religionists | 3,000 | 0.2 | 30,000 | 1.0 | 735 | −335 | 400 | 1.25 | 32,000 | 1.0 | 34,000 | 0.9 | 40,000 | 0.7 |
| Muslims | 3,000 | 0.2 | 30,000 | 1.0 | 758 | −58 | 700 | 2.12 | 33,000 | 1.0 | 37,000 | 1.0 | 57,000 | 1.0 |
| Atheists | 0 | 0.0 | 28,000 | 0.9 | 758 | 532 | 1,290 | 3.91 | 33,000 | 1.0 | 40,900 | 1. | 86,000 | 1.5 |
| Baha'is | 0 | 0.0 | 100 | 0.0 | 3 | 2 | 5 | 4.17 | 120 | 0.0 | 150 | 0.0 | 300 | 0.0 |
| Country's population | 1,500,000 | 100.0 | 2,962,000 | 100.0 | 75,900 | 0 | 75,900 | 2.30 | 3,303,000 | 100.0 | 3,721,000 | 100.0 | 5,725,000 | 100.0 |

COLUMNS, ROWS. For meanings and definitions, see Codebook (Part 6). Note that, by definition, total 'Christians' = professing + crypto-Christians, which also = affiliated + nominal Christians. Percentages may not always total exactly, due to rounding.
CENSUSES. The religion question has not been asked.

NOTES ON RELIGIONS
AFFILIATED PROTESTANTS. In 1975–76, 450 Protestant families with 17 pastors (about 2,500 persons) fled from Laos and settled as a community in central Thailand.

ASIAN INDIGENOUS. Isolated radio believers scattered across the nation (see Table 2).
ATHEISTS. Lao People's Party (Phak Passaon Lao, LPP) (Communist; neutral in Sino-Soviet dispute): membership (1970) 14,000, with 43,000 troops.
BUDDHISTS. Theravada (or Hinayana, Little Vehicle); predominantly Lao, with 20,000 Vietnamese and about 10,000 Chinese (Mandarin-speaking).
MUSLIMS. Mainly Sunnis of the Shafiite rite among the Cham and other peoples from Cambodia, Viet Nam and surrounding countries.

NON-RELIGIOUS. Communist forces and sympathizers, also Chinese (Mandarin-speaking), including 30,000 Chinese engaged on road-building, and (in 1976) 30,000 North Vietnamese troops.
TRIBAL RELIGIONISTS. Animists among non-Lao ethnic minorities and Montagnard tribes. Tribes over 95% animist: Alak (population 80,000), Brao (80,000), Galler (50,000), Jeng (500), Kasseng (800), Loven (50,000), Makong (50,000), Ngeq (50,000), Nyaheun (15,000), Oi (10,000), Phu Thai (100,000), So (15,000), and Ta-Oi (100,000).

**NON-CHRISTIAN RELIGIONS. Theravada** or **Hinayana Buddhism** is the principal and official

religion and that professed by about 58% of the Laotian population. The head of the Buddhist community is the Phra Sangharaja, who is advised by the Religious Council consisting of 5 members known as Chao Rajakhana. Two Buddhist monastic orders are active, the Thammayut and the Mahanakay, the latter being the more important. Village life is generally centred around a pagoda. In 1966 the number of pagodas in Laos was estimated to be about 1,900. The principal national institution is the Buddhist Institute in Vientiane, founded in 1947, which makes available religious information and supervises Pali schools for training future monks. In 1958 some 100 Pali schools were functioning, with a total enrolment of 5,000 students.
  **Traditional tribal religion** remains important among the non-Lao ethnic minorities: Alak, Brao, Galler, Jeng, Kasseng, Loven, Makong, Ngeq, Nyaheun, Oi, Phu Thai, So and Ta-oi. Buddhist

**Buddhists.** *(Right).* That Luang, biggest national shrine in Laos, a Buddhist stupa in Vientiane built in 1566, where the Buddha's chest-bone is believed to be deposited.

**Tribal religionists.** Keeping funeral vigil after death of village schoolteacher in Laos.

missionary attempts among them have met with a mixed reaction, some tribes being more resistant than others. Traditionalists numbered over 30% of the population in 1970. The belief in spirits, Phi, is fundamental to tribal religion, and ancestor veneration forms an essential part of the cult of such groups as the Black Tai. The Black Tai affirm that each person has 32 souls, some of which go 'beyond the sky' at death while others remain on the ancestral altar. Of special concern are spirits of the soil (called *ten*), which exist at the district (*pi muong*) and village (*pi ban*) levels, in addition to the chief of soil spirit (*ten luong*). The priests of the soil cult are known as Mo.

## CHRISTIANITY

CATHOLIC CHURCH. The first efforts by the Catholic Church to evangelize the country were begun in 1630 and were concentrated among the Thai Lao of the plains, the major ethnic group of Laos. All the mission centres are located along the border with Thailand, and the Thai Lao faithful are dominant (59%) in the 3 vicariates of Vientiane, Savannakhet and Paksé. Beginning in 1950, due to the increase in missionaries and insufficient evangelistic results among the Lao, the attention of the church has been turned increasingly to the tribal mountain peoples. In 1970 they were 21% of all Catholics but their catechumens made up 80% of the total catechumens in the country. Foreigners have also traditionally constituted a significant part of the Catholic community: French (1%), Americans, Filipinos (0.2%), Chinese (1.2%), and Vietnamese

(15%). Since 1974 the foreign community has decreased. The first Lao priest was ordained in 1963 and the first Lao bishop consecrated in 1974, the latter as auxiliary bishop of Vientiane.

PROTESTANT CHURCHES. The Protestant pioneers in Laos were Swiss Brethren. They began work in 1902 and translated the entire Bible into Lao, their work being strengthened by the arrival of Overseas Missionary Fellowship workers after 1957. However, the Gospel Church of Laos, affiliated with the CMA, which entered in 1929, has had the greatest numerical success. After World War II missionary effort was intensified. Although the Lao have been resistant to Christian evangelization, there has been considerable penetration among the Montagnard tribal groups, largely due to the increase in numbers of native catechists. Chrisian work is also carried on among the thousands of refugees created by the prolonged fighting.

CHURCH AND STATE. The constitution, promulgated in May 1947 and amended in 1956 and 1961, 'recognizes as fundamental principles the rights of the Lao, notably equality before the law, legal protection of the means of existence, freedom of conscience. . .' (Preamble). 'Buddhism is the State religion. The King is its official protector' (Article 7), and he 'should be a fervent Buddhist' (Article 8). There is a certain imprecision in the constitution, lacking as it does any declaration regarding freedom of religion or worship. Successive amendments have tended to be more restrictive than the initial text adopted in 1947 which declared: 'Laos recognizes as

the fundamental rights of Laotians individual freedom, freedom of conscience. . . and freedom of meeting and association. . .'. However, although the Christian churches have enjoyed considerable freedom, the slogan 'A good patriot follows the religion of his King' is still heard.

The statute relating to church property depends on a law passed by the Ministry of Colonies of the French Republic in January 1939, which was incorporated into Laotian legislation. Congregations and associations, having as their purpose the exercise of public worship, are directed by administrative councils and endowed with a religious and moral personality. Since 1970, the government has refused to recognize the ecclesiastical ownership of Catholic and Protestant schools but rather considers them private schools under the names of individual priests and pastors. Property used for worship, education, medical and social service is not subject to fiscal legislation; and in practise priests and nuns, as with Buddhist bonzes, are exempt from personal taxes.

Until its reorganization in 1967, the Ministry of Religion only concerned itself with Buddhist questions. In 1967 the Department of Religious Administration (Kom Pokkhong Satsana) was established to cater for other religions, although no director was appointed until 1971. Church registration is not required. Administrative councils are free to be registered or not at will.

In the government of national union which came to power on 5 April 1974, following the agreement of 22 February 1973 providing for the reconciliation of rightist and leftist elements in Laos, the Ministry of Religion was given to a representative of the Pathet Lao. A Buddhist monk, the minister was at first flanked, as with all the ministers of the left and right (with the exception of the 2 neutralist ministries), by a secretary of state representing the opposite political tendency. This pattern subsequently became less significant as the Pathet Lao has increasingly assumed control of the government.

By 1976, the Communist regime had taken over all Catholic schools, orphanages, residences and churches, and religious education had been eliminated. Only 2 of Vientiane's 87 Buddhist pagodas remained open also.

## INTERDENOMINATIONAL ORGANIZATIONS.
No council of churches exists. In 1971 the Catholic Church established an Office of Buddhism with the purpose of stimulating Buddhist-Christian dialogue.

BROADCASTING. Only in the early 1970s was religious broadcasting permitted over the military station Lao Armed Forces in Savannakhet, heard all over the country. Due to lack of trained national personnel, production of Lao material has been quite inadequate. However, foreign Christian programmes can be easily heard from the international stations: FEBC (Manila), in many languages; and Radio Veritas (Manila, Catholic) mainly in Thai. There have been 2 studios preparing Christian programmes, at Vientiane operated by the CMA for release over FEBC (Manila), and at Savannakhet.

## BIBLIOGRAPHY
'Religion', in *Area handbook for Laos*. D. P. Whitaker et al. Washington, DC: US Government Printing Office, 1972.
*1972 Mission directory of Thailand, Cambodia, Laos*. Ed B. Bray. Bangkok: Newsasia, 1972.

TABLE 2.    ORGANIZED CHURCHES AND DENOMINATIONS IN LAOS

| Official name 1 | Begun 2 | Type 3 | Counc 4 | Congs 5 | Adults 6 | Affiliated 7 | Names, notes, and other statistics (see Codebook) 8 |
|---|---|---|---|---|---|---|---|
| Eglise Adventiste du Septième Jour | 1957 | P Adv | x.... | 2 | 62 | 100 | *SDA. Seventh-day Adventists.* In Thailand Mission. Meo, some Chinese. 1x,W=99%,10Y. |
| Eglise Anglicane (D Singapore) | | A Cen | aweA. | 2 | 100 | 300 | *Church of the Holy Spirit*, Vientiane; in D Singapore. 99% expatriates (UK,USA). |
| Eglise Catholique au Laos: | 1630 | R Lat | P,F,P | 90 | 24,000 | 41,480 | *Catholic Ch. Phrakristachak Katolik.* C=2+0+6.    16n,95x,8m,152w,P=49%,1818Yy,6896z. |
| VA   Luang Prabang | 1963 | R Lat | Pomi | 10 | 1,800 | 3,134 | Royal/Buddhist centre. Montagnards; 26 dialects.    1    25    3    5    87    143    1800 |
| VA   Paksé | 1967 | R Lat | Pmep | 48 | 4,500 | 7,700 | South. Rural. 50% from ethnic minorities.    3    14    0    52    56    479    1920 |
| VA   Savannakhet | 1950 | R Lat | Pmep | 15 | 4,300 | 7,494 | Centre of country. Rural, one mining centre.    7    9    0    58    55    424    124 |
| VA   Vientiane | 1938 | R Lat | Pomi | 17 | 13,400 | 23,152 | Capital; vast influx of refugees. Many tribes.    5    47    5    37    40    772    3052 |
| Eglise Evangélique du Laos | 1929 | P Hol | xFE.. | 93 | 3,086 | 6,000 | *Gospel Ch of Laos.* M=CMA(USA). 90% tribal (Meo, Khmu) in north. 39n,27f,2h,1s. |
| Eglise radiophoniques isolées | 1952 | I rad | ..... | 10 | 100 | 300 | Isolated radio believers (FEBC), mostly students and youths, across nation. |
| Mission Evangélique au Laos | 1902 | P CBr | xM... | 30 | 1,500 | 3,000 | *Ev Mission.* M=Swiss Brethren(Open); and 1957, OMF. Hill tribes in south. 20f,1H. |
| Témoins de Jéhovah | c1955 | M Jeh | x.... | 1 | 28 | 100 | *Jehovah's Witnesses. Watch Tower. IBSA.* Active witnessing from 1959. 6Y. |
| Other Protestant denominations | | P | ..... | | 20 | 50 | Including: Eglise Réformée de France, Southern Baptist Convention (1971). |
| Total affiliated (mid-1970) | | | | 321 | 28,896 | 51,330 | Total denominations (1970) . . .    9. |
| Total affiliated (mid-1975) | | | | 250 | 33,200 | 59,000 | Total denominations (1975) . . .    10. |
| Total affiliated (mid-1980) | | | | 200 | 37,700 | 67,000 | Total denominations (1980) . . .    9. |

NOTES ON TABLE ABOVE
COLUMNS: for meanings and CODES (cols. 1, 3, 4, 8), see Codebook (Part 6). Column 1: Boldface type = church with over 10% of country's affiliated Christians.
NATIONAL COUNCILS (Column 4, 5th letter).
P = Conférence Episcopale du Laos et Cambodge (CELAC)

(Episcopal Conference of Laos & Cambodge) (Sapha (Sangharat) Lao-Kmen).

PEOPLES (ethnolinguistic). Christians: 47.8% Thai Lao, 33.6% Montagnard (Miao (Meo), Khmu, et alia), 15.0% Vietnamese, 1.2% Chinese, 1.0% French, 0.8% British and USA, 0.2%

Filipino.

COUNTRY-WIDE TOTALS
EVANGELIZATION (see Part 5). 1900: 4%. 1970: 38%. 1980: 42%. *Mass evangelism.* 1968, Tamil evangelist G. D. James (Malaysia Evangelistic Fellowship) campaign (average attenders

800); a number of Japanese evangelists have also been active in Laos. *Radiophonic evangelism.* In 1976, FEBC was broadcasting into Laos for 2 hours per day.
FOREIGN MISSIONARIES AND PERSONNEL (aliens from abroad) (1973). Total 223. *From Western world.* 178: about 100 Roman Catholics, 78 Protestants (52 in 7 USA societies, 12 in 1 Switzerland society, 8 in 1 UK society, 2 in 1 Canada society, 1 in 1 WGermany society, 1 in 1 New Zealand society, 1 in 1 Netherlands society, 1 in 1 Australia society). *From Third World.* 45: about 30 Roman Catholics from Viet Nam, Philippines and Taiwan, 15 Protestants from Viet Nam, Hong Kong, Philippines and Thailand.
INSTITUTIONS (church-operated) (1973). Total 80, including 10 higher schools, 60 medical centres, 1 research centre, 1 seminary (Protestant).
PERIODICALS. 3 titles.
PERSONNEL. About 493 in 1973 (270 national, 223 foreign).
RELIGIOUS LIBRARIES. 2.
SCRIPTURE DISTRIBUTION (1975). Annual totals: 1,800 Bibles (22% free, 78% subsidized), 20,000 NTs (free), 700 UBS portions, 25,000 UBS selections. *Translations completed.* Portion: 4 languages since 1918. NT: Tai Lu in 1933.
SERVICE AGENCIES. About 15, including ABS, CELAC, CV/AV, JEC/F, JOC/F, MAF, SEC, WVI.

ADDITIONAL DATA ON CHURCHES
EGLISE CATHOLIQUE AU LAOS. VA Luang Prabang = (in Laotian) Sangkha Monton Luang Prabang. The government discourages use of the word Sangkha because it wishes to reserve it for Buddhist religious groupings. *Catholics.* Members (1970) were 59% Thai Lao (half in VA Vientiane, quarter each in VA Paksé and Savannakhet), 21% ethnic minorities and hill tribes, and 20% expatriates (mainly Vietnamese, French, Americans, Filipinos, and some 600 Chinese). *Catechumens.* (1959) 2,565; (1961) 4,089; (1963) 4,366; (1969) 6,896, as shown above in column 8, and included in column 7. In 1970, 80% of catechumens were mountain tribes. *Annual baptisms.* (1972) 78.6% infant, 21.4% adult. *Priests.* The first Lao priest was ordained in 1963. *Brothers.* 2 nationals, 6 expatriates. *Sisters.* 125 nationals, 27 expatriates. *Foreign missionaries.* Expelled at Easter 1976. *Seminarians.* 5 secular, 2 religious; no seminary in Laos. *Catechists.* Total (1970) 50 full-time, 30 part-time. 4 catechist training schools, with 133 students. *Indigenous religious congregations* (Vietnamese or Lao-Vietnamese). Sisters: Amantes de la Croix, Paksong (6 members); Amantes de la Croix, Hué (4). *Main foreign congregations.* Priests: MEP, OMI (French and Italian provinces). Sisters: Charité de St-Vincent de Paul, Oblats Missionnaires de Marie Immaculée, Filles de Marie de la Croix.
*Catholic organizations.* The Episcopal Conference of Laos-Cambodia (Sapha (Sangharat) Lao-Kmen) has its headquarters in Vientiane and is a member of FABC in Hong Kong. There are no national presbyteral or pastoral councils, nor associations of religious personnel. The principal lay movements are CV/AV (100 members) and Légion de Marie (8 groups). JOC/F (40 members) and JEC/F (20 members) have also been started in Vientiane.
The Holy See has no diplomatic relations with Laos. It is represented to the Catholic hierarchy by the apostolic delegate to Laos, Malaysia and Singapore based in Bangkok, Thailand.
In 1970 Catholic schools accounted for about 5% of the total student population of Laos, including 233 primary classes (11,030 pupils) and 20 secondary classes (663), in addition to work with 257 students in domestic science classes. Medical work consists of 50 dispensaries and 3 leprosaria. Between 1968 and 1971 Caritas-Laos sponsored 79 rural development projects, in addition to its involvement in refugee resettlement. In 1971 Caritas formed a committee for socio-economic development, with the aim of providing co-ordination for all Catholic development projects.

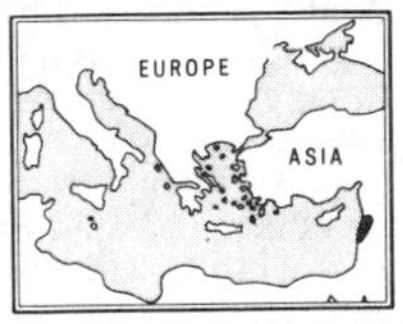


# LEBANON

## SECULAR DATA

**STATE. Official name:** The Lebanese Republic (Al-Jumhouriya al-Lubnaniya/La République Libanaise). Adjective of nationality: Lebanese (libanais).
**Flag** (shown above right); Red, white, and red stripes, with green cedar tree in centre.
**Area:** 10,400 sq.km. (4,015 sq.miles). Agricultural land: 34.4%.
**Government:** Parliamentary republic, since 1941 (1919 French mandate, 1926 republic, 1941 Independence proclaimed).
**Legislature:** Chamber of Deputies, 99 members.
**Official language:** Arabic.
**Chief cities:** capital Beirut 938,940 (1970), Tripoli 127,610.
**Armed forces** (1976): Total 18,250 regular: army 17,000, navy 250, air force 1,000 (27 combat aircraft). Paramilitary forces: 5,000 gendarmerie.
**Foreign forces** (1976): 13,000 Syrian troops, increasing; others from Saudi Arabia, Libya, et alia.

**DEMOGRAPHY. Population:** 2,126,325 (census of 15.XI.1970. For 1970–2000 (UN), see last row of Table 1). Population density (1975): 276/sq.km. (714/sq.mile). Under 15 years: 44%. Growth rate (1975–80): 3.16% per year (births 4.04%, deaths −0.88%). Life expectancy (1975–80): 65.2 years. Household size: 5.2 persons.
**Major languages:** Arabic, French, English, Armenian, Kurdish, Greek, Turkish, Italian, Chaldean (Aramaic), and numerous others.
**Urban dwellers** (1970): 40.6%. Urban growth rate (1950–70): 5.8% per year.
**Labour force:** 23%.
**Refugees** (1977): 196,855 Palestinians under UNRWA (and others totalling 300,000). Internally displaced: 450,000. Exiles abroad: 374,700 Lebanese (250,000 in Syria, 50,000 in UAE, 20,000 in Jordan, 15,000 in France, 12,000 in Egypt, 10,000 in UK, 7,000 in Greece, 5,000 in Sierra Leone, 3,000 in Cyprus; and in numerous other countries).
**Tourists** (1974): 2,261,767.

**ETHNOLINGUISTIC GROUPS:** 91.0% Arab (12.1% Palestinian (300,000), 6.8% Armenian, 0.7% Kurdish, 0.5% Assyrian (Chaldean), 0.5% French, 0.1% Jewish, 0.1% Greek, 0.1% Turkish, 0.1% Italian, 0.1% USA White, British.

**MONEY** (1977). **Monetary unit:** pound (= 100 piastres); US$1 = L£2.85.
**National income per person:** US$1,200. Average annual family income: US$6,240.
**Inflation:** (1970–74) 5.9% per year (1975: consumer price index 129).
**Cost of living in capital** (1976): index 135 (Washington DC = 100). Daily cost of living: US$36.

**HEALTH.** Hospitals: 143 (10,727 beds). Doctors: 2,300. Lepers: 910 (0.3 per 1,000). Blind: 5 000. Psychotics: 25,000. Criminals (1972): 1,100,000.

**EDUCATION.** Adult literacy: (1970) 69%, (1975) 86%. Education rate: 71%. Schools: 735. Universities: 5.

**LITERATURE.** Annual new book titles (1967): 427. Periodicals: 323. Scientific journals: 20. Newspapers: 52 dailies, 46 non-daily.

**COMMUNICATION** (per 1,000 people). Phones: 87. Radios: 215. TV sets: 108. Daily newspaper circulation: 88 copies.

TABLE 1. RELIGIOUS ADHERENTS IN LEBANON

| Year | 1900 | | mid-1970 | | Annual change, 1970–1980 | | | | mid-1975 | | mid-1980 | | 2000 | |
|---|---|---|---|---|---|---|---|---|---|---|---|---|---|---|
| *Name* | *Adherents* | *%* | *Adherents* | *%* | *Natural* | *Conversion* | *Total* | *Rate* | *Adherents* | *%* | *Adherents* | *%* | *Adherents* | *%* |
| **Christians** | **317,400** | **77.4** | **1,541,743** | **62.4** | **47,451** | **−935** | **46,516** | **2.65** | **1,752,700** | **61.1** | **2,006,900** | **59.7** | **3,214,000** | **52.5** |
| crypto-Christians | 0 | 0.0 | 215,943 | 8.7 | 7,827 | 149 | 7,976 | 3.19 | 249,700 | 8.7 | 295,700 | 8.8 | 441,000 | 7.2 |
| professing | 317,400 | 77.4 | 1,325,800 | 53.7 | 39,624 | −1,084 | 38,540 | 2.56 | 1,503,000 | 52.4 | 1,711,200 | 50.9 | 2,773,000 | 45.3 |
| Roman Catholics | 303,300 | 74.0 | 949,600 | 38.5 | 27,270 | −600 | 26,670 | 2.50 | 1,067,300 | 37.2 | 1,216,300 | 36.2 | 1,927,000 | 31.5 |
| Orthodox | 12,000 | 2.9 | 350,000 | 14.2 | 11,400 | −400 | 11,000 | 2.72 | 405,000 | 14.1 | 460,000 | 13.7 | 777,000 | 12.7 |
| Protestants | 2,000 | 0.5 | 24,700 | 1.0 | 901 | −71 | 830 | 2.86 | 29,000 | 1.0 | 33,000 | 1.0 | 67,000 | 1.1 |
| Anglicans | 100 | 0.0 | 1,500 | 0.1 | 53 | −13 | 40 | 2.35 | 1,700 | 0.1 | 1,900 | 0.1 | 2,000 | 0.0 |
| affiliated | 317,400 | 77.4 | 1,541,743 | 62,3 | 47,451 | −935 | 46,516 | 2.65 | 1,752,700 | 61.1 | 2,006,900 | 59.7 | 3,214,000 | 52.5 |
| total practising | 285,660 | *90* | 1,156,310 | *75* | 35,590 | −704 | 34,886 | 2.65 | 1,314,520 | *75* | 1,505,170 | *75* | 2,250,000 | *70* |
| non-practising | 31,740 | *10* | 385,430 | *25* | 11,861 | −231 | 11,630 | 2.65 | 438,180 | *25* | 501,730 | *25* | 964,000 | *30* |
| Roman Catholics | 300,000 | 73.2 | 1,141,622 | 46.2 | 33,958 | −700 | 33,258 | 2.58 | 1,289,450 | 44.9 | 1,474,200 | 43.9 | 2,291,000 | 37.4 |
| Catholic pentecostals | 0 | 0.0 | 0 | 0.0 | 12 | −188 | 200 | 50.00 | 400 | 0.0 | 2,000 | 0.1 | 30,000 | 0.5 |
| Orthodox | 12,300 | 3.0 | 356,600 | 14.4 | 11,840 | −500 | 11,340 | 2.76 | 410,000 | 14.3 | 470,000 | 14.0 | 795,000 | 13.0 |
| Protestants | 5,000 | 1.2 | 32,495 | 1.3 | 1,211 | 40 | 1,251 | 3.21 | 39,000 | 1.3 | 45,000 | 1.3 | 92,000 | 1.5 |
| Evangelicals | 4,000 | 1.0 | 12,300 | 0.5 | 447 | 3 | 450 | 3.13 | 14,400 | 0.5 | 16,800 | 0.5 | 37,000 | 0.6 |
| Arab indigenous | 0 | 0.0 | 5,100 | 0.2 | 217 | 173 | 390 | 5.57 | 7,000 | 0.2 | 9,000 | 0.3 | 20,000 | 0.3 |
| Marginal Protestants | 0 | 0.0 | 3,126 | 0.1 | 124 | 63 | 187 | 4.69 | 4,000 | 0.1 | 5,000 | 0.1 | 10,000 | 0.2 |
| Anglicans | 100 | 0.0 | 1,800 | 0.1 | 64 | −14 | 50 | 2.44 | 2,050 | 0.1 | 2,300 | 0.1 | 3,000 | 0.0 |
| Catholics (non-Roman) | 0 | 0.0 | 1,000 | 0.0 | 37 | 3 | 40 | 3.33 | 1,200 | 0.0 | 1,400 | 0.0 | 3,000 | 0.0 |
| Muslims | 84,300 | 20.6 | 874,257 | 35.4 | 39,676 | −1,442 | 38,234 | 3.66 | 1,044,300 | 36.4 | 1,256,600 | 37.4 | 2,533,000 | 41.4 |
| Druzes | 24,600 | 6.0 | 155,000 | 6.3 | 5,590 | 10 | 5,600 | 3.11 | 180,000 | 6.3 | 211,000 | 6.3 | 385,000 | 6.0 |
| Ahmadis | 0 | 0.0 | 1,000 | 0.0 | 37 | 3 | 40 | 3.33 | 1,200 | 0.0 | 1,400 | 0.0 | 3,000 | 0.0 |
| Non-religious | 0 | 0.0 | 37,000 | 1.5 | 1,602 | 1,758 | 3,360 | 6.51 | 51,600 | 1.8 | 70,600 | 2.1 | 245,000 | 4.0 |
| Atheists | 0 | 0.0 | 12,000 | 0.5 | 534 | 616 | 1,150 | 6.69 | 17,200 | 0.6 | 23,500 | 0.7 | 122,000 | 2.0 |
| Jews | 8,200 | 2.0 | 3,000 | 0.1 | −200 | 0 | −200 | −10.00 | 2,000 | 0.1 | 1,000 | 0.0 | 1,000 | 0.0 |
| Baha'is | 100 | 0.0 | 1,000 | 0.0 | 37 | 3 | 40 | 3.33 | 1,200 | 0.0 | 1,400 | 0.0 | 3,000 | 0.0 |
| **Country's population** | **410,000** | **100.0** | **2,469,000** | **100.0** | **89,100** | **0** | **89,100** | **3.11** | **2,869,000** | **100.0** | **3,360,000** | **100.0** | **6,118,000** | **100.0** |

COLUMNS, ROWS. For meanings and definitions, see Codebook (Part 6). Note that, by definition, total 'Christians' = professing + crypto-Christians, which also = affiliated + nominal Christians. Percentages may not always total exactly, due to rounding.
CENSUSES. The last government census of religion was held in **1932**, as follows: 53.7% Christians (29.0% Maronites, 10% Greek Orthodox, 6.3% Greek Catholics, 6.2% Armenians, 2.2% other Christians), 39.0% Muslims (excluding Druzes: 20.8% Sunnis, 18.2% Shias), 6.3% Druzes, 1% other religionists including Jews. **1958** (semi-official estimate): 55.0% Christians (29.9% Maronites, 10.6% Greek Orthodox, 7.5% other Catholics, 4.9% Armenian Orthodox, 1.0% Protestants), 37.9% Muslims (20.2% Sunnis, 17.7% Shias) 6.2% Druzes, 0.5% Jews (6,600 persons).

NOTES ON RELIGIONS
AHMADIS. Begun about 1930; Qadianis (world HQ Rabwah, Pakistan); 10 branches in Lebanon. HQ Beirut.
ATHEISTS. Lebanese Communist Party (LCP) (only legal party in Arab world (since 1970); split on Sino-Soviet dispute): membership (1970) 3,000. There is also an illegal Armenian Communist Party.
BAHA'IS. Reached Lebanon before 1892. Growth of local spiritual assemblies: 1964, none: 1973, 8.
CHRISTIANS. The column 'Natural change' includes considerable annual emigration by Maronites and others. The column 'Conversion change' indicates that many young persons abandon Christianity each year to become agnostics or atheists.
COUNTRY'S POPULATION. (a) There has long been large-scale emigration of Lebanese. In 1963 Lebanese emigrants living abroad (in North and South America, Africa, Australia) numbered 1,214,000. (b) During the civil war between Muslims and Christians from 1975 onwards, hundreds of thousands fled the country temporarily, and many thousands of others were killed (60,000 in the 24 months from April 1975). The column 'Annual change' above gives averages for the whole decade 1970–80; the column 'Natural' includes considerable annual emigration by Christians (mainly Maronites) and annual immigration by Muslims (Palestinians, refugees, guerrillas and others); it also includes higher Muslim than Christian fertility (birth-rate).
CRYPTO-CHRISTIANS. Christians unknown to and unrecognized by the state, which in 1975 still held to the official figure of 53.7% for all Christians. They are mainly Roman Catholics, who have increased their proportion considerably since the 1932 census, although their proportion of the total population has decreased.
DRUZES. Followers of Hakimiya, an 11th-century Muslim Shia Ismaili schism with Christian and Jewish elements. Druzes are Arabic-speaking and regard themselves as the pure Monotheists. They are treated here as a sect within the wider Muslim community, and in Lebanon they form 14% of all Muslims (6.3% of total population).
JEWS. Decline from 10,000 in 1956, by emigration to Israel.
MUSLIMS. There has been large-scale immigration of Muslims in the 20th century (especially by 300,000 Palestinian Arabs). In 1975, 46% of all Muslims were Sunnis (along the coast and in Beirut, Tripoli, Sidon), 40% of all Muslims were Shias (mountainous east (Bekaa) and south; mostly Twelvers or Ithna-Asharis); and 14% of all Muslims were Druzes (included here under Muslims though not usually counted as Muslims in Lebanon). There is also a small Ahmadiya Mission (enumerated here under Muslims although declared non-Muslim by Pakistan). Muslims are mainly Arabs with some Kurds, Turks and others. In addition to Muslims as enumerated here (35.4% in 1970), there are a further 3% or 4% of the population in Muslim areas who profess publicly to be Muslims but who are affiliated to churches and so are classified here as crypto-Christians. As the column 'Conversion change' shows, many Muslim youths abandon Islam each year to become agnostics, atheists, or (a growing number) crypto-Christians. *Hajj pilgrims to Mecca.* (1970) 6,712; (1974) 9,528; (1975) 1,208; (1976) 1,069.
ORTHODOX. In the 20th century, there has been massive immigration into Lebanon of Orthodox from Syria, Israel, Egypt, Jordan and Turkey. In 1905, there were only 1,000 Armenian Apostolics in the diocese of Beirut, but after 1915 vast numbers of refugees arrived from Turkey.
PROFESSING CHRISTIANS. Since this category refers to Christians as known to the state, the 1970–75 figures are those of the 1932 census which were still officially adhered to in 1975 as the state's estimate of size.

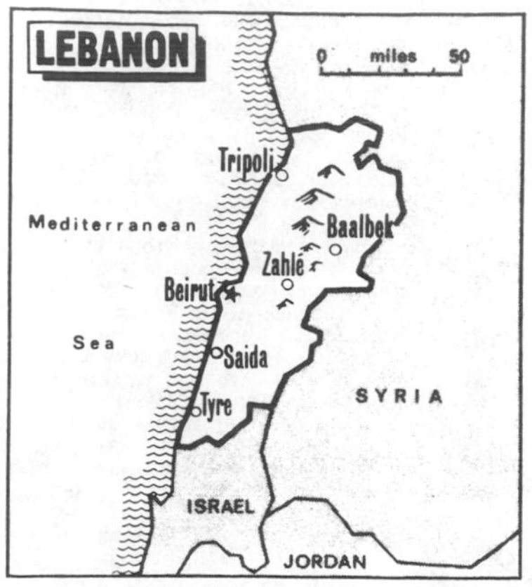


**NON-CHRISTIAN RELIGIONS.** The principal religions of Lebanon are divided internally into communities which although not always coinciding with Lebanon's different ethnic groups nevertheless form coherent social groups each with their own property, hierarchy, courts and representatives in parliament. The state recognizes 15 of these communities.

**Islam** is represented by both Sunnis and Shias. Sunnis are found along the coast, with very important groups also in Beirut, Tripoli and Sidon. Shias occupy for the most part the mountainous area in the east (Bekaa) and the south. Community councils and diverse associations for schools, hospitals, dispensaries and clubs all contribute to the vitality and unity of the Muslim community. Religious leaders are known as muftis among the Sunnis and imams among the Shias. The Near East regional bureau of the World Muslim Congress, with its international headquarters in Pakistan, is located in Beirut. For the first time in Lebanon's history a national Islamic Congress met from 3–10 June 1974. This congress was mainly concerned with analysing Lebanese Islamic institutions and with setting out possible reforms to deal with the impact of the Western world in the social and pastoral fields. Sunnis, Shias and Druzes were all represented at the congress.

**Druze religion** is an off-shoot from Islam, and is a Muslim sect which originated in the 11th century through the preaching of Darasi, who identified the Egyptian Fatimid caliph al-Hakim as the incarnation of Allah. Druzes are governed by a council of judges whose supreme head is known as the Cheikh-al-Aql. As well as being numerous in Lebanon, Druzes are also found in Syria, Jordan and Israel.

**Judaism** is known as the Community of Moses, the name adopted by the Jewish community of 1973. Numbering now about 2,000, Jews have lived in peace in Lebanon for centuries.

**CHRISTIANITY.** Christianity came to Lebanon in the 1st century AD and over the centuries has continued to play an important role in the country in spite of the numerical encroachment of Islam. Lebanon has the highest proportion of Christians of any country in the Middle East, and their influence in government and commercial life is even greater than their size would indicate. Christianity in Lebanon displays great variety. Catholics, the predominant Christian body, are represented by 6 different rites: Maronite, Melkite, Armenian, Syrian, Chaldean and Latin. The Orthodox include both Chalcedonians (Greek and Russian) and non-Chalcedonians (Armenian, Syrian and Coptic), as well as Nestorians in the Ancient Church of the East. There are also significant Anglican and Protestant communities, in addition to marginal Protestant groups including Jehovah's Witnesses and Mormons.

In the past 50 years Lebanon has passed from a feudal to a commercial capitalistic economy which is increasingly secular in outlook. This in turn offers new challenges to ancient church structures which are no longer adequate in the new situation. A significant element is the role assumed by youth, especially Catholic Action and the Orthodox Youth Movement, in the renewal of the churches.

CATHOLIC CHURCH. The largest community is that of the Maronites, who formed their own hierarchy in the 7th century. At that time Greek Orthodox, centred on the 5th-century monastery of Mar Maroun (St Maron) in the Apamée region in northern Syria, detached themselves from the Orthodox patriarch of Antioch in order to elect their own patriarch and form a church embodying the Syriac culture. Fleeing from harassment by various Orthodox and Muslim groups, they took refuge in the deep valleys of northern Lebanon where they mixed with the indigenous population, Qadisha (Holy Valley) being their principal location. Moving gradually to the south they formed with the Druzes the nucleus of Mt Lebanon's resistance to the Ottoman occupation. This was the historic role of the Maronite patriarchate in the rise of the Lebanese nation during the 19th century, until the creation of Great Lebanon in 1920. Lebanon was under French mandate until 1943 when full independence was granted. By that time the Maronite community, which had united with Rome in 1357, had become the major part of the Roman Catholic community.

Maronites are mostly land-owners and small farmers in the mountains, merchants at the coast, civil servants or members of the professions. Although deeply rooted in Lebanon, they are also found in neighbouring Arab countries as well as in other parts of the world. The Maronite community enjoys certain privileges in national life. By common agreement a Maronite is always president of the republic and commander-in-chief of the army; and other key posts in several ministries are reserved for Maronites. Maronite bishops form the majority in the commissions of the Assembly of Catholic Patriarchs and Bishops of Lebanon, the principal inter-rite episcopal organization in the country.

The Greek Catholics or Melkites form that part of the Orthodox patriarchate of Antioch which united with Rome in the 18th century. It includes faithful in Lebanon, Syria, Jordan, Palestine, Egypt, the Americas, Australia, Europe and Africa. Its head has the title of patriarch of Antioch, Alexandria and Jerusalem, with residences at Damascus and

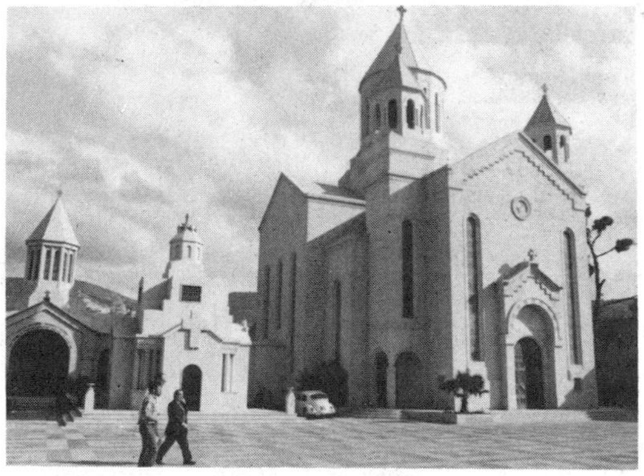

**Armenian Apostolic Church, Catholicate of Cilicia.** Cathedral in Antélias (right), with (centre) martyrion, and (left) burial chapel of former patriarchs.

Beirut. Melkites are found equally in the towns of the coast and in the mountains, and form the third largest Christian community in Lebanon (after the Catholic Maronites and the Greek Orthodox). They play a dynamic part in both inter-Catholic and inter-denominational relations. The Congress of Melkite Catholic Clergy, which was founded in 1969 and holds an annual general assembly, is an organ of dialogue between elected representatives of secular and religious clergy and the episcopate for all questions concerning the priestly ministry. A Synodal Commission for Renewal, created in August 1974, is the principal force for renewal in the Melkite Catholic Church.

Other Catholic rites participating in the Assembly of Catholic Patriarchs and Bishops of Lebanon include Armenians and Syrians, for the most part refugees since World War I who have their patriarchs in Lebanon (Charfeh and Mount Lebanon); Chaldeans, a branch originating from the Assyrian (Nestorian) Church, who have one diocese for the whole of Lebanon, with their patriarchal see at Baghdad; and Latins, who first became fully organized in Lebanon in 1953 and have been represented by a Lebanese vicar apostolic since 1973. The Latin bishop of Beirut is a member of the Conference of Latin Bishops of the Arab Regions (CELRA), with its headquarters in East Jerusalem.

ORTHODOX CHURCHES. The Greek Orthodox Patriarchate of Antioch consists almost entirely of Arabs and uses Arabic in its liturgy. Beginning with the loss of the Maronites in the 7th century, and the Melkites in the 18th century, it has continued to lose members both to Latin-rite Catholicism and to Protestantism. Nevertheless, the patriarchate as a whole, with its see in Damascus, numbers more than 500,000 faithful, not counting its dioceses which serve immigrants to North and South America and Australia. The church in Lebanon has a total community of 200,000. With members consisting of rural agricultural communities in the north and south of Lebanon, as well as urban merchants, officials and members of the liberal professions, the church has experienced a significant renewal since World War II. This has been manifested in several ways: creation of the Orthodox Youth Movement (OYM) in 1942; re-organization of the basic statutes of the patriarchate, the Holy Synod and diocesan councils; appointment of a new generation of bishops; re-establishment of monastic life through the new convent of Mar Yacoub-Deddé in north Lebanon and the monastery at Deir al-Harf, Mt Lebanon; a new emphasis on catechesis in liaison with Syndesmos, the World Fellowship of Orthodox Youth Organizations; promotion of the ecumenical movement regionally, nationally and world-wide; establishment of a theological seminary at Balamand near Tripoli in 1970; and the participation of Orthodox in Arab nationalist, progressive socialist and Palestinian movements. The Antioch patriarchate maintains 25 elementary schools, 12 secondary schools, a hospital in Beirut, together with clinics, homes for the aged and orphanages.

The non-Chalcedonian Armenian Apostolic Church, officially termed the Catholicate (or Catholicossate) of Cilicia (Sis), has its see at Antelias, a suburb of Beirut. Originating from Armenia and established in Cilicia, southern Asia Minor, in AD 1441, Armenian Orthodox flooded into northern Syria and Lebanon as refugees from the Turkish massacres of 1915–1920. They are now fully integrated into Lebanese society, with 4 deputies in parliament in addition to one for the Armenian Catholic community, and are well represented in skilled industry, commerce and the liberal professions. They have also been involved in the creation of secondary schools, cultural associations, hospitals and housing projects. Their School of Theology at Antelias, founded in 1930, provides for renewal of the clergy and also furnishes priests to serve the diaspora communities of Cyprus, Syria, Iraq, Iran, USA, Canada and Australia. The Catholicate of Cilicia, which has long recognized the spiritual primacy of the Catholicate of Echmiadzin in the USSR severed relations with Echmiadzin in 1956 in a dispute over Cilicia's right to appoint its own catholicos. In Lebanon, Cilicia has also played an important role in helping to develop relations between Chalcedonian and non-Chalcedonian churches, as well as between Orthodox and Catholics. Its vitality as a church was not seriously weakened by the separation of the Uniate Armenian Catholics who submitted to Rome in the 16th century, nor by the creation of the Armenian Evangelical Union in the 19th century.

Other smaller Orthodox churches represented in Lebanon include the Russian Orthodox Church, and its rival the Russian Orthodox Church Outside of Russia; 2 Oriental bodies, the Coptic and Syrian Orthodox Churches; and the Ancient Church of the East (Nestorians).

PROTESTANT CHURCHES. The National Evangelical Synod of Syria and Lebanon, which owes its origin to the missionary outreach of the American Board (ABCFM) as early as 1823 and later American United Presbyterians, has the largest Protestant constituency in both countries, with a Christian community of 10,000 in Syria and the same in Lebanon. The church became autonomous in 1920 and has its headquarters in Beirut. It sponsors 2 hospitals, 12 primary schools, 11 secondary schools, Beirut University College for Women, in addition to being the original sponsor in 1866 of the American University of Beirut. Church union discussions with the third largest Protestant body, the National Evangelical Church of Beirut, failed in 1958 but were begun again and broadened to include Anglicans in 1973. The National Evangelical Church has the most important Protestant parish in Beirut, plus 2 small village congregations.

There are 2 Armenian Protestant churches, the Union of Armenian Evangelical Churches and the Armenian Evangelical Spiritual Brethren. American Board work among the Armenian Orthodox in Istanbul resulted in the formation of the first Armenian Evangelical congregation in 1846. Taking refuge in Lebanon in 1918 during the Turkish massacres, the Union of Armenian Evangelical Churches is the second strongest Protestant community in the country with an extensive primary and secondary school programme serving 20% of the entire Armenian school population. The Armenian Evangelical Spiritual Brethren, formed in 1920 in Aleppo, consists of a small community of Plymouth Brethren type which separated from the various Evangelical, Catholic and Orthodox Armenian communities.

Although a small community, the Lebanese Baptist Convention (related to USA Southern Baptists) has established an important theological school, Arab Baptist Seminary, in Mansourieh.

Other groups include those formed through the missionary activity of Seventh-day Adventists, Church of God (Anderson), Pentecostal Church of God, Assemblies of God, Christian and Missionary Alliance and several smaller bodies.

**CHURCH AND STATE.** The Lebanese political regime rests on an original system called 'confessionalism' which guarantees each religious community participation in the government proportional to its numerical importance. In Article 9 of the constitution, amended several times since its promulgation on 23 May 1926, the state guarantees freedom of conscience and respect for all faiths in these words: 'The state in rendering homage to the Most High shall respect all religions and creeds'. Article 95 stipulates that 'Provisionally in order to further justice and concord, the communities shall be equally represented in public employment and in the composition of ministries'. The basic agreement, constantly enforced and invoked, was enshrined in an unwritten National Pact (Al Mithak al-Watani) concluded in 1943 at the beginning of independence.

As a result, confessional representation is continuously maintained at all levels of public service up to the highest positions of state. Thus the president of the republic must be a Maronite, the president of the legislative assembly a Shia, the premier a Sunni, and vice-presidents of both the assembly and government must be Greek Orthodox. The distribution of parliamentary seats is governed by the same system, with the electoral re-organization of 1960 maintaining the previously existing proportion of 6 Christian deputies to 5 Muslims. Distribution of ministerial portfolios is also made on the basis of religious affiliation, somewhat differently from that of parliament because of the small number of posts. There is no government ministry of religions, but each ministry has an ad hoc section charged with the application within itself of proportional community representation.

No new government census of population has been taken since 1932. The system of proportional community representation remains therefore based on an official numerical estimate published by the Ministry of the Interior and expressed (in the 1932 percentages) as follows: Christians 53.7% (Maronites 29%, Greek Orthodox 10%, Greek Catholics 6.3%, Armenians 6.2%, other Christians 2.2%), Muslims 39.0% (Sunnis 20.8%, Shias 18.2%), Druzes 6.3%, and 1% for others including Jews.

In virtue of Article 9 of the constitution, religious communities are recognized by the state as juridical personalities with specific prerogatives, notably in the field of law. Thus religious courts enact laws concerning marriage, separation, divorce, and inheritance. Each head of a community is assisted by a community council. The religion of each citizen is registered with the state as well as on his identity card. As yet there is no civil marriage although campaigns have been conducted for it. Religious chanceries issue certificates of baptism and death, which have official validity; and in the Muslim community judicial officers are civil servants of the state. All communities receive subsidies for their social work, courts and schools. Article 10 of the constitution, which concerns educational freedom, provides for the involvement of the various religious communities in education. At the present time there are in Lebanon approximately 1,500 confessional or private schools as contrasted with 1,300 government schools.

In addition to demands for 'participation' by those communities which feel left out, as well as for 'deconfessionalization' of the state by recent political parties, especially the younger generation, other problems include government bureaucracy, financial distribution, economic development, social justice, cultural unity and plurality, integration with the Arab world, unemployment, emigration and relations with immigrant groups including Syrian workers, stateless Kurds and expelled Palestinians.

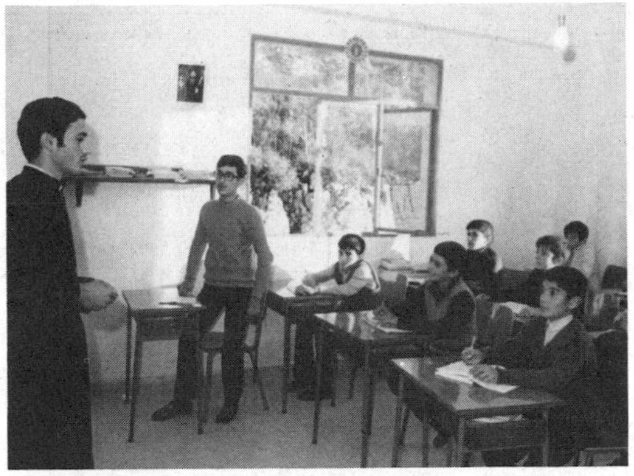

**Syrian Orthodox Patriarchate of Antioch, Diocese of Beirut.** Class at Mar Ephrem seminary, Atshana.

The fact that the Christian population, though only slightly the majority block in the country, has continued over the years to dominate Lebanon's political and economic scene has led to increasing unrest on the part of the Muslim minority and was the principal cause of the outbreak of civil war between Christian and Muslim factions during 1975.

**INTERDENOMINATIONAL ORGANIZATIONS.** Ecumenical agencies are numerous in Lebanon, considering the small size of the country. Several are mainly national with extensions to the Middle East region; others are for the most part regional with national branches.

At the national level there are 4 official commissions for ecumenical relations. The first emanates from the Armenian Catholicate of Cilicia; the second from the Assembly of Catholic Patriarchs and Bishops of Lebanon; the third from the Greek Orthodox patriarchate; and the fourth from the Supreme Council of Evangelical Churches in Lebanon and Syria. Their joint executive secretariat is the Ecumenical Pastoral Group (Groupe Oecuménique de Pastorale, GOP), founded in 1968, which co-ordinates the activities of the following 8 mixed working groups some of which were operating prior to the creation of the official commissions. (1) The Centre for Religious Sociology conducts studies on specific problems of the country and its institutions, in collaboration with the WCC. (2) Common Prayer (Prière Commune) is a service which publishes and distributes each year material used for the Week of Prayer for Unity, in conjunction with the ad hoc commissions in Rome and Geneva. (3) Joint Catechesis (Catéchèse Harmonisée) is a group which develops catechetical programmes for Christian students in government schools and prepares curricula and lessons for catechists. (4) Evangelization Teams for different age groups and milieux handle the problem of the re-evangelization of modern Lebanese society, in collaboration with the Catholic Centre for Catechesis and Pastoralia (Centre de Catéchèse et de Pastorale Notre Dame des Dons). (5) Parables and Symbols for Today (Paraboles et Symboles pour Aujourd'hui, PSA) is an ecumenical service for audio-visual catechesis, in collaboration with the Catholic Centre for Catechesis and Pastoralia, which produces notable material on liturgical renewal especially for Maronites and Orthodox. (6) The Lebanese Ecumenical Committee for Development, Justice and Peace, founded in 1972, serves as the executive office of the Ecumenical Secretariat for Youth and Students of the Middle East in conjunction with Sodepax and ad hoc international Catholic organizations. (7) The Co-ordination Committee for Christian Movements promotes the training of lay leaders. Lastly, there is (8) the Assembly of Involved Christians (Rassemblement des Chrétiens Engagés), founded in 1974, which joins together Christians with a social and political orientation who seek to discover a new Christian identity through their solidarity in the liberation struggle of the Arab world.

Several monasteries and convents have become ecumenical prayer centres, notably the Orthodox monastery of St Georges at Deir el-Harf, created through the efforts of the Orthodox Youth Movement; the Orthodox Convent of St James the Persian at Deddé near Tripoli; the Catholic monastery of Our Lady of Unity at Yarzé; and the Carmelites of Harissa Catholic convent near Jounieh.

At the regional level, with headquarters in Beirut, an organization which has played an especially important role is the Middle East Council of Churches (MECC), an organization founded in Nicosia in May 1974, replacing the Near East Council of Churches (NECC) which was formed in 1927 as the Council of Western Asia and Northern Africa, later called the Near East Christian Council and finally in 1944 the Near East Council of Churches with a new constitution in 1967. The MECC represents the interests of 3 church families: the Chalcedonian (Eastern Orthodox), Non-Chalcedonian (Oriental Orthodox) and Anglican/Protestant churches; and each of these 3 groups is accorded an equal number of delegates in the general assembly. The council carries on its work through 4 divisions: (1) Radio Broadcasting, which includes programme production in the main studio in Beirut and in 2 associated studios in Egypt and the Sudan and until 1977 broadcast over Radio Voice of the Gospel in Ethiopia; (2) Literature, which co-ordinates the publishing and distribution policy of member churches through their publishing houses and bookshops throughout the Middle East; (3) Christian Education, which seeks to train leaders and teachers and produces the Faith and Work curriculum; and (4) Outreach and Witness, which is involved in training Christians for dialogue with non-Christians and undertakes research and studies in Christian-Muslim relations.

Other specialized organizations and institutions include the following: (1) the Ecumenical Secretariat for Youth and Students of the Middle East (ESYSME), founded in 1962, with a sub-regional secretariat in Cairo, which is involved in research, leadership training, development programmes (conscientization and literacy) and consultations concerning the role of Christianity in the Middle East; (2) Association for Theological Education in the Near East (ATENE), with headquarters in Cairo and a sub-secretariat in Beirut; (3) Near East School of Theology (NEST), founded in Beirut in 1931 to serve the Protestant churches; (4) World Conference of Christians for Palestine, with headquarters in Paris and a Secretariat for Arab countries in Beirut; (5) Near East Ecumenical Information and Interpretation Bureau (NEEBII), founded in 1971, which provides information and theological insight for the Christian world concerning the region, especially Palestine; (6) Common Translation Service for the Bible in Arabic, initiated by the regional secretariat of the United Bible Societies; (7) Near East Ecumenical Committee for Palestinian Refugees (NEECPR), with headquarters in Nicosia and a sub-secretariat in Beirut; and (8) the Middle East secretariat of the World Student Christian Federation (WSCF or FUACE).

**BROADCASTING.** All radio stations in Lebanon are government-owned, and fixed percentages of weekly broadcasting are allowed to the various religious groups, Maronites, Orthodox, Armenians, Lutherans and other Protestants. Protestant programmes are usually Sunday morning services broadcast live. Recently, the Middle East Communication Fellowship has started a 15-minute daily religious broadcast in Arabic beamed into Lebanon and other Middle East countries from the transmitters of Radio Cyprus. Foreign Christian programmes in Arabic can also easily be heard on the international stations RVOG (Ethiopia) (until 1977), ELWA (Liberia), FEBA (Seychelles), TWR (Monaco and Cyprus), and Radio Vatican for 3 hours 30 minutes a week. In Beirut there are 5 studios preparing Christian programmes for these stations. The ELWA studio has developed a new approach, different from the usual preaching, in order to reach Muslims: Scriptures are chanted in a mixed Quranic/Byzantine style for 4 nights a week; response has been good. The 90-minute daily programmes in Arabic broadcast by RVOG were also produced in Beirut.

## BIBLIOGRAPHY

*Histoire de l'Eglise Maronite*. P. Dib. Beirut, 1962.

*Rediscovering Christianity where it began: a survey of contemporary churches in the Middle East and Ethiopia*. N. A. Horner. Beirut: Near East Council of Churches, 1974. 110p.

'Religion', chapter 11 in *Area handbook for Lebanon*. Washington, DC: US Government Printing Office, 1969, p. 123–133.

*The Catholic Church in the Middle East*. B. Etteldorf. New York: Macmillan. 1958.

The effect of Twentieth-century Arab nationalism on the Christian witness in the Near East'. C. Smith. Thesis, Wheaton College (Illinois), 1970.

TABLE 2. ORGANIZED CHURCHES AND DENOMINATIONS IN LEBANON

| Official name 1 | Begun 2 | Type 3 | Counc 4 | Congs 5 | Adults 6 | Affiliated 7 | Names, notes, and other statistics (see Codebook) 8 |
|---|---|---|---|---|---|---|---|
| Ancient Church of the East: D Beirut | | O Nes | Yw... | | 3,400 | 6,000 | *Assyrian Church. Nestorians.* Under Tehran Patriarchate. No dissidents as in Iraq. 3n. |
| Armenian Apostolic Ch, C Cilicia (Sis) | 1440 | O Arm | SW.N. | 250 | 75,600 | 135,000 | *AD Beirut, Catholicate of Sis.* Broke with C Echmiadzin in 1956. 180n,6r,1s(50). |
| Armenian Ev Spiritual Brethren | 1920 | P CBr | x.... | 3 | 100 | 250 | Beirut. Split ex Armenian Evangelicals. Holiness Brethren. 1r. |
| Assemblies of God | c1920 | P Pe2 | ZF... | 3 | 150 | 400 | M=AoG(USA). 1972, university campaign; 9,000 student attenders. 3n,10f,1s(13). |
| Baptist Bible Church | 1956 | P Bap | ..... | 1 | 50 | 150 | Arabic and English services; 1 Lebanese pastor. Formerly M=BBFI(USA). |
| Beirut Community Church | | P com | ..... | 1 | 300 | 400 | English-speaking community church. 1 North American pastor. W=75%. |
| **Catholic Church in Lebanon:** | c 300 | R LEr | O...R | 1,075 | 639,300 | 1,141,622 | *Al-Kanissa al-Kathoulikiah.* C=21+2+53. 2p,2q,5s(328). 1400nx,541m,3402w,19486Yy. |
| P Antiochia (VP Lebanon) (*Syrian*) | c1650 | R Syr | Os | 8 | 10,100 | 18,000 | *Patriarchal Vicariate.* Growing numerically. 6 schools. 13 0 9 221 |
| M Beirut & Gibail (*Melkite*) | 1881 | R Mel | Os | 104 | 44,800 | 80,000 | First founded c350. Rapid expansion. 26 schools. 4h. 83 0 31 1300 |
| M Tyre (*Melkite*) | 1683 | R Mel | Os | 12 | 3,400 | 6,000 | Sour. *Al-Rounn al-Malakioun al-Kathoulik.* 9 schools. 9 0 5 170 |
| AD Baniyas (*Melkite*) | 1886 | R Mel | Os | 16 | 2,300 | 4,162 | Paneas. Caesarea Philippi. Golan area. 5 schools. 4 0 12 52 |
| AD Saida (*Melkite*) | 1683 | R Mel | Os | 56 | 14,600 | 26,000 | Sidon & Deir el Qamar. Expanding. 10 schools. 23 0 12 463 |
| AD Tripoli (*Melkite*) | 1879 | R Mel | Os | 16 | 3,600 | 6,500 | Tarabulus (4th century). HQ Tripoli. 11 schools. 7 0 23 142 |
| AD Baalbek (*Melkite*) | 1701 | R Mel | Os | 10 | 8,400 | 15,000 | Heliopolis, dating from c350. 27 schools. 20 0 100 321 |
| AD Beirut (*Maronite*) | 1577 | R Mar | Os | 115 | 106,300 | 190,000 | *Al-Mawarinah* (Maronites). 101 schools. 3H. 178 25 183 3128 |
| AD Cyprus (Antelias) (*Maronite*) | 1357 | R Mar | Os | 100 | 42,000 | 75,000 | 5% of AD is in Cyprus, 95% in Lebanon. 12 schools. 100 40 260 1973 |
| AD Tripoli (*Maronite*) | c1650 | R Mar | Os | 121 | 98,600 | 176,000 | Extremely rapid numerical growth. 208 schools. 169 18 114 1926 |
| AD Tyre (*Maronite*) | 1838 | R Mar | Os | 33 | 12,300 | 22,000 | Sour. Rapid expansion. HQ Tyr. 12 schools. 19 3 30 500 |
| AD Zahleh & Furzul (*Melkite*) | 1724 | R Mel | Os | 44 | 22,400 | 40,000 | Formerly suffragan of AD Damascus. 21 schools. 1H. 27 0 70 660 |
| D Baalbek (*Maronite*) | c1650 | R Mar | Os | 78 | 51,100 | 91,200 | Heliopolis. Rapid growth. 80 schools. 1H. 68 2 170 1920 |
| D Beirut (*Armenian*) | 1742 | R Arm | Os | 10 | 13,600 | 24,300 | *Patriarchal Diocese* (1928) of P Cilicia. 12 schools. 28 0 60 245 |
| D Beirut (*Chaldean*) | 1957 | R Cha | Os | 3 | 3,200 | 5,800 | *Al-Kaldan al-Kathoulik.* Under P Babylon. 1 school. 8 0 0 47 |
| D Gibail & Batrun (*Maronite*) | 1848 | R Mar | Os | 188 | 103,500 | 184,763 | *Patriarchal Diocese* (P Antiochia). 69 schools. 1H. 206 35 131 2145 |
| D Saida (*Maronite*) | 1900 | R Mar | Os | 107 | 58,200 | 103,970 | Sidon. Rapid growth. 40 schools. Covers Israel also. 86 10 127 3140 |
| D Sarba (*Maronite*) | 1959 | R Mar | Os | 43 | 29,700 | 52,927 | HQ Sarba, Achkut. Rapid growth. 33 schools. 1H. 108 172 260 893 |
| VA Beirut (*Latin*) | 1953 | R Lat | Oofm | 11 | 11,200 | 20,000 | *Al-Latinn* (*Latins*). Rapid growth. 189 schools. 244 236 1805 240 |
| Christian Brethren (Exclusive) | | P EBr | x.... | 2 | 60 | 200 | *Plymouth* (*Closed*) *Brethren* (*Kelly-Continental*), in 2 meetings. |
| Christian Brethren (Open) | | P CBr | x.... | 4 | 200 | 400 | *Plymouth* (*Open*) *Brethren. Gospel Halls.* M=CMML(USA,UK). 6f. |
| Church of Christ | | P Dis | x.... | 3 | 80 | 200 | M=CC(Non-Instrumental) (USA). Independents. Mainly USA expatriates. 1p. |
| Church of God (Anderson) | 1910 | P Hol | x...C | 3 | 200 | 500 | M=CoG(Anderson) (USA). No missionaries now except visitors from Egypt. 4n,W=55%. |
| Church of Jesus C of Latter-day Saints | | M LdS | x.... | | 250 | 426 | *Mormons.* M=CJCLdS(Utah,USA). Mostly USA expatriates. |
| Coptic Orthodox Church | | O Cop | NwaN. | 1 | 200 | 300 | Under P Cairo. Egyptians. Congregation in Beirut, new building. 1 deacon, 1x. |
| Epis Ch in Jerusalem & ME (D Jerusalem) | | A Low | aw.NC | 3 | 1,000 | 1,800 | Formerly Jerusalem Archbishopric. 67% Arab, 33% British. M=JEM. 1n,2x,W=50%,13y. |
| Evangelical Baptist Church | | P Bap | ..... | 1 | 50 | 100 | Independent Lebanese congregation in Beirut. No foreign missionaries. |
| Evangelical Church of the Nazarene | 1952 | P Hol | xF..C | 6 | 108 | 400 | *Kniset Innasari Il Injiliyeh.* M=CoN(USA). 1n,1x,39m,6f,1p(4),6t(268),W=39%. |
| French Evangelical Church | | P Ref | ..... | 1 | 20 | 30 | French-speaking. In Beirut, for francophone expatriates. 1 Armenian pastor. 1r. |
| German Evangelical Church in Beirut | | P Lut | ..... | 1 | 50 | 150 | *Deutschsprachige Evangelische Kirche.* German-speaking congregation. 1x(German). |
| Gospel Preaching Church | | P ind | ..... | 1 | 50 | 100 | Arabic and English. Small independent congregation. 1 Lebanese pastor. |
| **Greek Orth Patriarchate of Antioch:** | 30 | O Ara | Cw.N. | 295 | 112,000 | 200,000 | Arabic-speaking. Patriarch in Damascus. 210n,15d,1H,P=60%,12r,1s(Tripoli),W=10%. |
| D Akkar (Arkadia) | | O Ara | Cm | 45 | 17,000 | 30,000 | HQ Archevêché Grec-Orthodoxe, Halba. 2 monasteries (6 monks). 40n. |
| D al-Hadath (Byblos & Botrus) | | O Ara | Cm | 110 | 42,000 | 75,000 | *Diocese of Mount Lebanon.* HQ Hadeth. 5 monasteries (12 monks). 65n. |
| D Beirut (Berytos) | | O Ara | Cm | 13 | 6,000 | 10,000 | Seat of archbishop in Beirut. Summer residence Souk El-Gharb. 15n,3d(30). |
| D Marj Uyun (Tyre & Sidon) | | O Ara | Cm | 32 | 11,000 | 20,000 | HQ Archevêché Grec-Orthodoxe, Marj Uyun (in southeast near Israel border). 28n. |
| D Tripoli | | O Ara | Cm | 70 | 28,000 | 50,000 | HQ Archevêché Grec-Orthodoxe, Tripoli. 40n,5d,1s(in monastery). |
| D Zahla (Heliopolis & Seleucia) | | O Ara | Cm | 25 | 8,000 | 15,000 | HQ Zahlah, in Lebanon Mountains east of Beirut. 22 parish priests. |
| Independent Evangelical Church | | P int | .T.T. | 1 | 50 | 100 | One congregation in Beirut. Fundamentalist. 1 American pastor. |
| Internat Ch of the Foursquare Gospel | 1962 | P Pe2 | ZF... | 2 | 49 | 200 | M=ICFG(USA). Classical Pentecostals (2-stage). 2nm,2f,1p(8),W=41%,12Y. |
| Isolated radio churches | c1950 | I rad | ..... | 130 | ·2,500 | 5,100 | Isolated radio believers in Muslim areas. R=1200,T=180000(ICI & 17 others). |
| Jehovah's Witnesses | c1930 | M Jeh | x.... | 29 | 1,356 | 2,700 | *Watch Tower. IBSA.* Active witnessing under way by 1940. HQ Beirut. 74Y. |
| Lebanese Baptist Convention | 1895 | P Bap | T...C | 15 | 517 | 1,540 | 1948, M=SBC. 13 Arabic-speaking congs. 10n,4x,30f,G=10.1%pa,1r,1s,W=95%,50Y,50z. |
| Lebanon Evangelical Mission | 1860 | P int | .G... | | 1,000 | 2,000 | M=LEM(UK)/MECO, formerly British Syrian Mission; 1963, expelled. 104n,32f,1p,1s,2r. |
| National Ev Christian Alliance Church | 1921 | P Hol | xF..C | 5 | 175 | 275 | M=CMA. 50% Arabic-speaking, 50% English-speaking. 1n,9f,G=38%pa,1p,W=45%,5Y,3z. |
| National Evangelical Church of Beirut | c1950 | P Ref | ...NC | 3 | 2,000 | 3,500 | Arabs. Beirut, and 2 mountain village churches. 1958, refused to join NESynod. 3r. |
| National Ev Synod of Syria & Lebanon | 1823 | P Ref | RW.NC | 35 | 1,500 | 10,000 | M=UPUSA,UCBWM. A=1920. Emigration 4%pa. 9n,2x,25f,G=–4.1%pa,2H,8r,1u,W=70%,39Yy. |
| New Apostolic Church | | C CAp | x.... | | 500 | 1,000 | *NAC.* In Wiesbaden Bezirk (District); world HQ Dortmund (Germany). Germans. |
| Pentecostal Church of God of America | 1950 | P Pe2 | Z.... | 5 | 210 | 500 | M=PCG(USA). Classical Pentecostals. Work with Jews in Beirut. 1 school. 3f,1p. |
| Religious Society of Friends | 1869 | P Qua | Q...C | 2 | 50 | 100 | In Near East Yearly Meeting. Quakers. 1 high school by HQ in Broumana. |
| Russian Orthodox Church | | O Sla | Mwc.. | 1 | 100 | 200 | Under P Moscow. Uses Greek Orthodox building in Beirut. 1x(sent from Russia). |
| Russian Orthodox Ch Outside of Russia | | O Sla | x.... | 1 | 50 | 100 | Related to ROCOR(New York). 1 Russian priest. In Ain Mraissé, Beirut. |
| Seventh-day Adventist Church | 1908 | P Adv | x...C | 13 | 1,000 | 3,000 | *SDA*, East Mediterranean Field, Middle East Union. 8nx,51f,1j,6r,14t(1000),40Y. |
| Syrian Orth Patr of Antioch: D Beirut | 30 | O Syr | Dw.N. | | 8,400 | 15,000 | *Jacobites.* Patriarch in Damascus. Summer residence, Zahle. 1r,1s(Atshana),W=10%. |
| Union of Armenian Ev Chs in Near East | 1918 | P Con | RW.NC | 9 | 4,000 | 7,000 | Refugees from 1914–18 massacres. 1918,M=AMAA(USA). HQ Beirut. 28n,1H,1j,5r,1u,1v. |
| Other Protestant denominations | | P | ..... | | 500 | 1,000 | Total about 10 (see list below). |
| **Total affiliated (mid-1970)** | | | | **1,990** | **857,125** | **1,541,743** | **Total denominations (1970) . . . 46.** |
| **Total affiliated (mid-1975)** | | | | **2,270** | **974,400** | **1,752,700** | **Total denominations (1975) . . . 48.** |
| **Total affiliated (mid-1980)** | | | | **2,570** | **1,115,700** | **2,006,900** | **Total denominations (1980) . . . 50.** |

**NOTES ON TABLE ABOVE**

COLUMNS: for meanings and CODES (cols. 1, 3, 4, 8), see Codebook (Part 6). Column 1: **Boldface type** = church with over 10% of country's affiliated Christians.

NATIONAL COUNCILS (Column 4, 5th letter).

C = Supreme Council of Evangelical Churches in Lebanon and Syria (Conseil Suprème des Eglises Evangélique au Liban et en Syrie).

R = Assembly of Catholic Patriarchs and Bishops of Lebanon Assemblée des Patriarches et Evêques Catholiques du (Liban).

OTHER PROTESTANT DENOMINATIONS. These smaller bodies include: Bible Preaching Ch (World-Wide Missions, 1961), Ch of God (Abrahamic Faith) (1967), Ch of the Brethren, Elim Missionary Assemblies, Fellowship of Independent Missions, World Gospel Mission, Worldwide Evangelization Crusade (1970).

UNITING CHURCHES. Negotiations for organic union were under way in 1974 between: Episcopal Ch, Ev Synod of Syria & Lebanon, National Ev Ch of Beirut.

**PEOPLES** (ethnolinguistic). Christians: 87.0% Arab (10% Palestinian, 1% Syrian, 0.2% Egyptian), 10.8% Armenian, 1.0% Latin (French, Italian, et alii), 0.8% Assyrian, 0.1% Greek, 0.1% USA White, British.

**COUNTRY-WIDE TOTALS**

EVANGELIZATION (see Part 5). 1900: 80%. 1970: 99%. 1980: 100%. *Radiophonic evangelism.* Annual listeners' letters (1975): 620 TWR, 500 ELWA, Radio Vatican et alia. Bible correspondence courses: 180,000 enrolled, by 18 organizations (LCMS 23,000 active students in 1968).

FOREIGN MISSIONARIES AND PERSONNEL (nationals serving abroad) (1973). Total 173 in 15 countries: about 150 Roman Catholics, 19 Orthodox priests in 6 countries, 4 Protestants.

FOREIGN MISSIONARIES AND PERSONNEL (aliens from abroad) (1973). Total 1,080. *From Western world.* 966: about 700 Roman Catholics, 262 Protestants (194 in 27 USA societies, 24 in 4 UK societies, 19 in 4 WGermany societies, 9 in 4 Australia societies, 6 in 5 New Zealand societies, 5 in 1 Canada society, 3 in 1 Netherlands society, 2 in 1 Switzerland society), 3 Orthodox, 1 Anglican in 1 UK society. *From Communist world.* 10: 9 Roman Catholics from Poland, 1 Orthodox. *From Third World.* 104: about 70 Roman Catholics from Palestine et alia, 22 Orthodox from Syrian and Egypt, 10 Protestants, 2 Anglicans.

INSTITUTIONS (church-operated) (1973). Total 290, including 170 higher schools, 45 medical centres, 1 press, 30 religious communities, 5 research centres, 15 seminaries (7 RC, 5 Protestant, 3 Orthodox), 3 universities.

PERIODICALS. About 60 titles (9 SDA).

PERSONNEL. About 6,680 (5,600 national, 1,080 foreign).

RELIGIOUS LIBRARIES. About 55.

SCRIPTURE DISTRIBUTION (1975). Annual totals: 11,000 Bibles (54% subsidized, 46% commercial), 45,880 NTs (13% free, 65% subsidized, 22% commercial), 25,000 UBS portions, 255,000 UBS selections.

SERVICE AGENCIES. About 140, including ACI, ATENE, BMMF, CALL, CCCI, CCMC, CEC, CEEC, CMCP, CV/AV, DORB-MECC, ELWA, ESYSME(SOJEMO), EYSS, FEBA, GOP, ICYE, IYCS, JEC, JOC/F, LES, MECC (NECC/CEPO), MELM, MJO, NEEBII, NEECPR, OIEC, OM, PSA, RVOG, SIRLAS, SYNDESMOS, TEE, TWR, UCIL, WSCF, YFC, YMCA, YWCA.

**ADDITIONAL DATA ON CHURCHES**

CATHOLIC CHURCH IN LEBANON. Several jurisdictions extend over Cyprus, Israel and Syria. In addition to the Syrian Patriarchate shown above, there is also a Maronite Patriarchate (HQ Dimane, in D Gibail & Batrun). *New diocese.* (1977) D Baalbek & Zahté (Maronite), with the former D Baalbek changing its name to D Jounieh of the Maronites. *Annual baptisms.* (1972) 99.8% infant, 0.2% adult. *Sisters.* (1970) 66% Lebanese, 13% Europeans, 11% Arabs from neighbouring countries. *Catholic charismatics* (January 1974). 100 adults including some religious personnel are active in 2 organized prayer groups in the Charismatic Renewal. *Seminaries.* In 1973, 5 for secular clergy and 2 for religious clergy. From 1974, Université Saint-Esprit, Kaslik, with training schools at Raboua, Charfé. *Seminarians* (1972). 120 secular, 208 religious. *Oriental religious congregations.* Priests (1972): (Maronites) 500 Ordre Libanais Maronite, 100 Ordre Mariamite (formerly Alépin), 100 Ordre Antonin Maronite, 100 Congrégation des Missionnaires Libanais (Krémistes); (Melkites) 100 Ordre Basilien Salvatorien, 75 Ordre Basilien Chouérite, 50 Ordre Basilien Alépin, 50 Congrégation des Missionnaires de St-Paul; (Armenians) Méchitaristes de Venise (Bifkaya), Méchitaristes de Vienne (Hazmieh); Petits Frères de Jésus (now with Maronite rite). Sisters: (Maronites) Baladites, Antonines, Mariamites, Sainte-Famille Maronite (Abrine), Ste-Thérèse; (Melkites) 170 Basiliennes Chouérites, 100 Missionnaires de N-D du Perpétuel Secours, 90 Basiliennes Salvatoriennes, 40 Basiliennes Alépines: (Syrians) Ephrémites (Charfeh), Dominicaines de Ste-Catherine (Iraqis of Chaldean rite, under Latin jurisdiction); (Armenians) Immaculée-Conception (Jounieh); also Petites Soeurs de Jésus and Clarisses du Monastère de l'Unité (Yarzé) (adopting Maronite rite), and Carmélites Déchaussées du Monastère de Harissa (Greek Catholic rite). *Latin religious orders and congregations.* Numerous; either Latin or inter-rite under Latin jurisdiction; majority of members mainly of Middle East origin. Priests: OFMCap, OCD, OP, OFM, SJ, CM, SDB, PB, CSSR, Bénédictins Olivétains. Brothers: FSC, PFM. Sisters: nearly 40 congregations (3 exclusively oriental: Soeurs des Saints-Coeurs de Jésus et Marie (538 professed in 1974, including 82 serving abroad: 60 in Syria, 9 in Morocco, 7 in Chad, 6 in Algeria), Franciscaines de la Croix du Liban, Soeurs du Rosaire (Palestinians)).

*Catholic organizations.* Inter-rite organizations include: (1) Assembly of Catholic Patriarchs and Bishops of Lebanon founded in 1967 with a permanent secretariat since 1973; (2) Assembly of (Male) Major Superiors, and Assembly of (Female) Religious Superiors; and (3) Co-ordinating Committee for Movements of the Lay Apostolate, founded in 1966 with responsibility for 16 movements including the Legion of Mary; Scouts and Guides; Society of St Vincent de Paul; JEC; JOC/F; La Flamme (an association aiding clergy and maintaining parishes without priests); a movement known popularly as the 'Congregations' (450 congregations with 35,000 members in 14 geographical regions in 1972 including 95% of the Maronite parishes and many Greek Catholic parishes as well); Knights of the Virgin (Fursan El Adra), youth group founded in 1958 with 7,000 members (10 to 16 years of age) in 1972; and the Pioneers, a group catering for youth of 15 to 18 years of age. There are no national pastoral or presbyteral councils.

The Holy See has diplomatic relations with Lebanon and is represented to government and the Catholic hierarchy by a nuncio in Beirut.

Movements for renewal since Vatican II have been stimulated, slowly but profoundly, by a group called Priests of Christ the King (Prêtres du Christ-Roi), with about 100 members, and the Church for Our Times (Eglise pour Notre Temps) movement, an activist and study group consisting of laity, priests and religious personnel.

Inter-rite institutions for pastoral and religious training include: (1) Institut Supérieur de Formation Religieuse (ISFR), founded in 1963 at St Joseph University in Beirut, which offers courses given in French; (2) Faculté des Sciences Philosophiques et Religieuses founded in 1974 also at St Joseph University, which serves both lay persons and clerics; (3) Institut Supérieur de Formation Théologique, founded in 1969 at the St Anthony Convent in Beirut, which offers courses given in Arabic; (4) Centre de Catéchèse et de Pastorale Notre Dame des Dons, founded in Beirut in 1963, which provides catechetical instruction and pastoral training in both Arabic and French, and in an ecumenical atmosphere; (5) Institut Supérieur de Liturgie, at the Holy Spirit University in Kaslik; and (6) Centre Religieux d'Etudes Arabes (CREA), at St Joseph University in Beirut. The Holy Spirit and St Joseph universities each have a faculty of theology which were united at Kaslik in 1974 for a trial period of 2 years.

In 1970 brothers were responsible for 38 schools and sisters for 282 schools in addition to collaboration in 106 other schools. Sisters were also responsible for 13 hospitals and clinics, 25 dispensaries, 23 orphanages, 16 centres offering sewing courses, 3 homes for the aged and 57 other projects, in addition to their collaboration in 93 medical and charitable works. The Pontifical

Mission for Palestine, founded in Beirut in 1949 to aid Palestinian refugees and with local centres also in Jerusalem and Amman, is supported by USA Catholics and presided over by an American prelate. Also active in relief and development work is Caritas-Liban-Sud, founded in 1972, which is a member of Caritas Internationalis in Rome. The Regional Secretariat for the Near and Middle East of OIEC (International Office of Catholic Education, in Belgium) is located in Beirut.

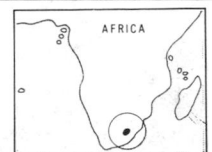

# LESOTHO

## SECULAR DATA

**STATE. Official name:** The Kingdom of Lesotho.
**Flag** (shown above right): Parallel bars of green, and red at hoist, with white conical Basuto hat on blue field. **Agricultural land:** 93.9%.
**Area:** 30,355 sq.km. (11,720 sq.miles).
**Government:** Parliamentary constitutional monarchy, since 1966 (1818 Basotho nation, 1868 under British protection as Basutoland, 1959 self-government, 1966 Independence).
**Legislature:** Parliament: National Assembly, 60 members; Senate, 33 members.
**Official languages:** English and Sesotho.
**Capital:** Maseru 29,050 (1972).
**Political divisions:** 9 Districts.
**Armed forces** (1976): Paramilitary police force, 1,295.

**DEMOGRAPHY. Population:** 852,361 (census of 14-24.IV.1966).

For 1970–2000 (UN), see last row of Table 1). Population density (1975): 38/sq.km. (98/sq.mile). Under 15 years: 38%. Growth rate (1975–80): 2.23% per year (births 4.01%, deaths −1.79%). Life expectancy (1975–80): 48.5 years. Household size: 5.1 persons.
**Major languages:** Sotho (Sesotho), English, Afrikaans, Zulu, Xhosa, French.
**Urban dwellers** (1970): 4.0%. Urban growth rate (1950–70): 3.2% per year.
**Labour force:** 54%.
**Refugees** (1977): About 1,000 from South Africa.

**ETHNOLINGUISTIC GROUPS:** 99.7% Bantu (90% Sotho, 6% Zulu, Xhosa), 0.2% White (1,600) (Afrikaner, British), 0.1% Asian (800), Mulatto (Coloured).

**MONEY** (1977). **Monetary unit:** South African rand (= 100 cents); US$1 = R 0.867.
**National income per person:** US$140. Average annual family income: US$714.
**Cost of living in capital** (1976): Daily cost of living: US$27.

**HEALTH.** Hospitals: 89 (1,919 beds). Doctors: 46. Lepers: 24,000 (20.9 per 1,000). Blind: 3,000. Psychotics: 7,000. Criminals: 20,000.

**EDUCATION.** Adult literacy: (1946) 35%, (1966) 59%. Education rate: 42%. Schools: 1,085. Universities: 1.

**LITERATURE.** Annual new book titles (1972): 33. Periodicals: 40.

**COMMUNICATION** (per 1,000 people). Phones: 3. Radios: 10.

### TABLE 1. RELIGIOUS ADHERENTS IN LESOTHO

| Year Name | 1900 Adherents | % | mid-1970 Adherents | % | Annual change, 1970–1980 Natural | Conversion | Total | Rate | mid-1975 Adherents | % | mid-1980 Adherents | % | 2000 Adherents | % |
|---|---|---|---|---|---|---|---|---|---|---|---|---|---|---|
| Christians | 33,800 | 11.1 | 895,900 | 85.9 | 21,761 | 7,799 | 29,560 | 2.85 | 1,036,600 | 90.3 | 1,191,500 | 92.8 | 1,942,400 | 95.8 |
| professing | 33,800 | 11.1 | 895,900 | 85.9 | 21,761 | 7,799 | 29,560 | 2.85 | 1,036,600 | 90.3 | 1,191,500 | 92.8 | 1,942,400 | 95.8 |
| Roman Catholics | 4,600 | 1.5 | 421,300 | 40.4 | 10,217 | 3,503 | 13,720 | 2.82 | 486,700 | 42.4 | 558,500 | 43.5 | 910,100 | 44.9 |
| Protestants | 25,900 | 8.5 | 292,100 | 28.0 | 7,037 | 2,013 | 9,050 | 2.70 | 335,200 | 29.2 | 382,600 | 29.8 | 610,700 | 30.1 |
| Anglicans | 2,700 | 0.9 | 109,500 | 10.5 | 2,700 | 1,120 | 3,820 | 2.97 | 128,600 | 11.2 | 147,700 | 11.5 | 239,200 | 11.8 |
| African indigenous | 600 | 0.2 | 73,000 | 7.0 | 1,807 | 1,163 | 2,970 | 3.45 | 86,100 | 7.5 | 102,700 | 8.0 | 182,400 | 9.0 |
| nominal | 6,100 | 2.0 | 119,600 | 11.5 | 2,844 | 736 | 3,580 | 2.64 | 135,500 | 11.8 | 155,400 | 12.1 | 202,700 | 10.0 |
| affiliated | 27,700 | 9.1 | 776,300 | 74.4 | 18,917 | 7,063 | 25,980 | 2.88 | 901,100 | 78.5 | 1,036,100 | 80.7 | 1,739,700 | 85.8 |
| total practising | 26,310 | 95 | 698,670 | 90 | 17,025 | 6,357 | 23,382 | 2.88 | 810,990 | 90 | 932,490 | 90 | 1,391,800 | 80 |
| non-practising | 1,390 | 5 | 77,630 | 10 | 1,892 | 706 | 2,598 | 2.88 | 90,110 | 10 | 103,610 | 10 | 347,900 | 20 |
| Roman Catholics | 4,000 | 1.3 | 410,600 | 39.4 | 9,979 | 3,531 | 13,510 | 2.84 | 475,300 | 41.4 | 545,700 | 42.5 | 889,800 | 43.9 |
| Protestants | 20,200 | 6.6 | 222,600 | 21.3 | 5,393 | 1,597 | 6,990 | 2.72 | 256,900 | 22.4 | 292,500 | 22.8 | 501,300 | 24.7 |
| Evangelicals | 18,000 | 5.9 | 62,600 | 6.0 | 1,543 | 927 | 2,470 | 3.36 | 73,500 | 6.4 | 87,300 | 6.8 | 170,000 | 8.4 |
| Anglicans | 2,500 | 0.8 | 80,000 | 7.7 | 1,975 | 805 | 2,780 | 2.95 | 94,100 | 8.2 | 107,800 | 8.4 | 182,400 | 9.0 |
| African indigenous | 1,000 | 0.3 | 62,000 | 5.9 | 1,543 | 1,117 | 2,660 | 3.62 | 73,500 | 6.4 | 88,600 | 6.9 | 162,200 | 8.0 |
| Marginal Protestants | 0 | 0.0 | 1,100 | 0.1 | 27 | 13 | 40 | 3.08 | 1,300 | 0.1 | 1,500 | 0.1 | 4,000 | 0.2 |
| Tribal religionists | 271,200 | 88.9 | 137,210 | 13.2 | 2,106 | −7,807 | −5,701 | −5.68 | 100,310 | 8.7 | 80,200 | 6.2 | 61,000 | 3.0 |
| Baha'is | 0 | 0.0 | 8,700 | 0.8 | 204 | −4 | 200 | 2.06 | 9,700 | 0.8 | 10,700 | 0.8 | 20,000 | 1.0 |
| Muslims | 0 | 0.0 | 530 | 0.1 | 12 | −1 | 11 | 1.90 | 580 | 0.1 | 640 | 0.0 | 1,000 | 0.0 |
| Non-religious | 0 | 0.0 | 500 | 0.0 | 13 | 7 | 20 | 3.33 | 600 | 0.1 | 700 | 0.1 | 2,000 | 0.1 |
| Atheists | 0 | 0.0 | 100 | 0.0 | 3 | 7 | 10 | 6.67 | 150 | 0.0 | 200 | 0.0 | 500 | 0.0 |
| Hindus | 0 | 0.0 | 60 | 0.0 | 1 | −1 | 0 | 0.00 | 60 | 0.0 | 60 | 0.0 | 100 | 0.0 |
| **Country's population** | **305,000** | **100.0** | **1,043,000** | **100.0** | **24,100** | **0** | **24,100** | **2.10** | **1,148,000** | **100.0** | **1,284,000** | **100.0** | **2,027,000** | **100.0** |

**COLUMNS, ROWS.** For meanings and definitions, see Codebook (Part 6). Note that, by definition, total 'Christians' = professing + crypto-Christians, which also = affiliated + nominal Christians. Percentages may not always total exactly, due to rounding.
**CENSUSES. 1904** (Census of the British Empire) Basutoland: 85.5% tribal religionists, 11.7% Protestants, 1.6% Roman Catholics, 1.0% Anglicans, 0.2% African indigenous (AMEC). **23.IV.1911:** 82.4% tribal religionists, 17.6% Christians (11.5% Protestants, 3.3% Roman Catholics, 2.1% Anglicans, 0.7% African indigenous). **1921:** 72.2% tribal religionists, 14.7% Protestants (13.5% French Reformed, 0.3% Methodists, 0.1% Dutch Reformed), 7.9% Roman Catholics, 4.0% Anglicans, 1.2% African indigenous. **1936:** 54.2% tribal religionists, 20.1% Roman Catholics, 17.5% Protestants (14.8% French Reformed, 0.7% Methodists), 6.7% Anglicans, 1.5% African indigenous.

**7.V.1946** (Basutoland): 38.2% tribal religionists, 26.9% Roman Catholics, 23.4% Protestants, 8.9% Anglicans, 2.2% African indigenous, 0.4% non-Christians. **8.IV.1956:** 33.7% Roman Catholics, 28.8% tribal religionists, 23.0% Protestants (21.9% PEMS), 9.5% Anglicans, 5.0% African indigenous. **14-24.IV.1966** (Africans only): 38.7% Roman Catholics, 26.7% Protestants, 18.2% tribal religionists, 10.4% Anglicans, 6.0% African indigenous.

### NOTES ON RELIGIONS
**AFRICAN INDIGENOUS.** There were 798 members of the AME Church in the 1904 census, 6,181 in the 1921 census, and 8,642 in the 1936 census. In 1970, there were about 210 indigenous denominations (see Table 2).
**ATHEISTS.** Lesotho Communist Party (proscribed 1970); membership very small.

**BAHA'IS.** Rapid growth from 1 local spiritual assembly (1964) to 37 (1973).
**COUNTRY'S POPULATION.** The figures, as with official censuses in Lesotho since 1966, do not include temporarily absentee workers. The massive labour migration of men to the Rand and OFS in South Africa amounts to 12% of the entire population; as a result there are far more women than men in the churches throughout Lesotho.
**MUSLIMS.** About 100 Asian traders with their families, with a mosque at Butha-Buthe since 1972.
**PRACTISING CHRISTIANS.** 80% of Roman Catholics are regular churchgoers, and 90% practise annually; however, due to difficulties of terrain and travel, only 50% attend mass every Sunday and 50% are Easter communicants.

**NON-CHRISTIAN RELIGIONS. African traditional religions** are practised by a minority of under 10% of the population. The Sotho name for God is Molimo, and the Balimo are ancestral spirits. Another term, Medimo, is used to refer to such divinities as Cosa who is responsible for fixing man's destiny, and Nape to whom appeal is made during divination. A diviner is called *moitse-a-Nape*, one who knows Nape. Other Medimo associated with the initiation ceremonies are Tintibane, Thobege-a-phachwa and Thanakana. Mathuela, a spirit-possession cult among women, utilizes dancing, drumming, songs and medicines and places emphasis on divination.
**Islam** has made no gains among the indigenous peoples, but a small group of about 100 Asian traders built a mosque at Butha-Buthe in 1972.

## CHRISTIANITY
**CATHOLIC CHURCH.** French OMI priests arrived in 1862 and in 1930 turned over their work to Canadian OMI missionaries. The Catholic population grew from 60,000 in 1930, when the first Mosotho priest was ordained, to 205,000 in 1953, the latter year being notable for the consecration of Lesotho's first indigenous bishop.

Catholics are spread very evenly over all areas, and over all types and groups of people. According to a recent official parish survey, 80% of all Catholics are regular churchgoers, although many are unable to attend mass every Sunday because of distance and hazards of travel. A 1970 analysis (Lesotho Oblate Questionnaire) showed that the church is placing greater overall emphasis on building new institutions, such as schools, churches, roads, convents and rectories, rather than on deepening personal faith, a finding which disturbed many Catholics. For the coming years, one of the primary needs of the church is to hand over to lay leadership institutions which are now largely managed, directed and administered by clergy.

**PROTESTANT CHURCHES.** The Lesotho Evangelical Church is the oldest Christian denomination in the country, tracing its history to the arrival of the Paris Mission in 1833. The church became autonomous in 1964 and is strongly ecumenical in outlook, with membership in the Christian Council of Lesotho, All Africa Conference of Churches, World Council of Churches and World Alliance of Reformed Churches. In the population census of 1966, 24.2% of the population professed to belong to this body, making it second only to the Catholic church in size; and as with the latter its 6 presbyteries cover the entire country. The church's commitment to education is large: 541 primary, 3 secondary and 3 junior-secondary schools, 2 teacher-training colleges, a trades school, and training colleges for boys and girls. Other activities include 2 hospitals, one dispensary, the Mophato oa Morija youth centre, a church newspaper called *Leselinyana*, and several development projects conducted along ecumenical lines through Sodepax.

The Methodist and Dutch Reformed churches of South Africa have initiated work in Lesotho, as have several North American Pentecostal groups: Assemblies of God, Church of God (Cleveland) and Pentecostal Holiness Church. Seventh-day Adventists are also active.

**ANGLICAN CHURCH.** The third largest church in Lesotho, dating from 1875, is the Anglican Church, which is of Anglo-Catholic tradition and is a diocese

**Anglican Church in Lesotho.** *Left.* Bishop arrives on horseback at Lereko's. *Above.* After robing, he administers confirmation.

in the Church of the Province of Southern Africa. Among social service activities may be mentioned a number of primary and 2 secondary schools, one teacher-training college, one hospital and a clinic.

INDIGENOUS CHURCHES. Lesotho was the scene of the first independent church in southern Africa, a secession in 1872 from the Herman congregation of the Paris Mission. Although this group later went out of existence, many more have been formed since then; and there are now estimated to be about 210 such bodies spread throughout the country. The largest Lesotho-originated indigenous church continues to be the Moshoeshoe Berean Bible Readers' Church, a schism from the Paris Mission in 1909, in spite of the fact that it has of late lost many of its supporters. Some indigenous churches have entered Lesotho from South Africa, including Zion Christian Church; whereas others owe their origin to the outreach of such USA-based Black denominations as the African Methodist Episcopal Church and the National Baptist Convention.

**CHURCH AND STATE.** During the political crisis of 1970, the 1965 constitution was suspended, and a state of emergency was declared. The first step in the crisis was the imprisonment by the ruling prime minister (a Roman Catholic, as was his Nationalist Party) of the leftist opposition which appeared about to win the national elections. The Catholic Church is still identified with this party; the other Christian denominations have no such affiliations. In 1970 when riots spread throughout the country, the Christian Council's call for reconciliation achieved little due to lack of Catholic support. However, the Catholic Church itself joined the council in 1972, and this has had its effect on the church-state situation. In April 1973 the Lesotho Ecumenical

Association (with Catholic, Protestant and Anglican membership) launched an appeal for reconciliation between government and the opposition party. Following the riots of 1974, 32 members of the opposition Basotho Congress Party were imprisoned without trial; and the Christian Council hired a lawyer to defend them. Although 17 were convicted, the sentences meted out were lighter than expected, a fact which Christian leaders hope will open the door to dialogue.

There is no official government ministry or department dealing with religion, but 2 cabinet members have had special responsibility for church affairs. The 1965 constitution guaranteed freedom of religion, which has remained unaltered by events since 1970.

**INTERDENOMINATIONAL ORGANIZATIONS.** The Christian Council of Lesotho was founded in 1964 as a successor to the General Missionary Conference. It is a member of the AACC and an associate council of the South African Council of Churches. Member churches subscribe to the doctrinal basis of the World Council of Churches, and other Christian bodies prepared to co-operate are associate members. The Catholic Church also had associate status for many years prior to becoming a full member in November 1972. The council carries on its work through 3 commissions: (1) Lesotho Sodepax Commission, which is related to Sodepax in Switzerland and is a member of the Movement for Ecumenical Action in National Development (MEND) in Malawi, and whose projects include the establishment of an ecumenical agricultural school at Thaba Khupa in 1972; (2) Social Services Commission, which is especially concerned for the integration of political refugees from South Africa; and (3) Lesotho Ecumenical Association, which studies such topics

as peace and justice and attempts to influence the government to take a Christian position.

Other signs of ecumenical progress in Lesotho are: joint study by Anglican and Catholic seminarians at the Catholic major seminary in Roma since 1971; the establishment of a nursing school to train Catholic Protestant and Anglican nurses; and the opening of the first ecumenical primary school at Ntsane in 1971.

**BROADCASTING.** The state Radio Lesotho accepts Protestant programmes in Sesotho and English. The Catholic Church has 2 stations, one a predominantly educational station in Maseru, Radio ZNF 4V (Lesotho Communication Centre), founded in 1959 and with its own studio. Programmes are produced also for Radio Lesotho. For Catholics, Lesotho is registered as a member of UNDA.

**BIBLIOGRAPHY**
*A century of mission work in Basutoland, 1833–1933.* V. F. Ellenberger. Morija: Paris Mission, 1938. 382p.
*L'expérience de la conversion chez les Basotho.* J. L. Richard. Documata Missionalia 12. Rome: Università Gregoriana Editrice, 1977.
*The biblical concept of messianism and messianism in Southern Africa.* M. L. Martin. Morija: Sesuto Book Depot, 1964.
*The Catholic Church of Lesotho at the hour of Independence.* Maseru: Catholic Information Bureau, 1966.
*The Mabilles of Basutoland.* E. W. Smith. London: Hodder & Stoughton, 1939.
'The Sotho notion of the Supreme Being and the impact of the Christian proclamation', K. Nürnberger, *Journal of religion in Africa*, VII (1975).
'Walter Matitta and Josiel Lefela: a prophet and a politician in Lesotho', G. M. Haliburton, *Journal of religion in Africa*, VII (1975).

**Moshoeshoe Berean Bible Readers' Church.** Annual Easter Conference at Peka, 1972, of Nazarite Association (Mokhatlo oa Banazari). *Above.* Male leaders in Nazarite uniform arriving; (right) Nazarite leader Rev. Albert Maloi. White robe is given to those elected to lay hands on the sick. *Right.* White-robed Nazarite women leaders in procession in silence except for Bible quoting or singing. At death, leaders are buried in these robes.

TABLE 2. ORGANIZED CHURCHES AND DENOMINATIONS IN LESOTHO

| Official name 1 | Begun 2 | Type 3 | Counc 4 | Congs 5 | Adults 6 | Affiliated 7 | Names, notes, and other statistics (see Codebook) 8 |
|---|---|---|---|---|---|---|---|
| African Methodist Episcopal Church | c1892 | I Met | Vw..K | | 9,000 | 16,000 | *AMEC.* USA Black mission. In 18th Episcopal District, AMEC. 1 USA bishop. HQ Maseru. |
| **Anglican Church in Lesotho** | 1875 | A ACa | AwaVK | 247 | 39,600 | 80,000 | *Kereke ea Chache.* In CPSA (diocese 1950). M=SSM,USPG. 25n,14x,1H,W=40%,692Y,2531y. |
| Apostolic Faith Mission of SAfrica | 1904 | P Pe3 | Z.... | 12 | 600 | 1,500 | M=AFM(SA). Mission of large South African body. Classical Pentecostals (2-stage). 2f. |
| Assemblies of God in Lesotho | 1916 | P Pe2 | ZF..K | 45 | 830 | 2,000 | M=AoG(USA,SA),PAoC,NPY,SPM. Classical Pentecostals. HQ Maseru. 17n,2f,1s(14). |
| Bantu Baptist Church | | I Bap | ..... | 10 | 300 | 1,000 | Links with African United National Baptist Ch(SA), & NBCUSA. HQ Maseru. 4n,1r,1s. |
| **Catholic Church in Lesotho:** | 1862 | R Lat | P.SSS | 69 | 254,600 | 410,600 | *Kereke ea Roma.* C=1+1+7. 2p,1q,1s(32). 37n,109x,97m,733w,P=50%,17780Yy. |
| M Maseru (divided 1977) | 1894 | R Lat | Pomi | 42 | 150,900 | 243,292 | Densely-populated lowlands. 1p,1s. 19 81 82 420 57 11768 |
| D Leribe | 1952 | R Lat | Ps | 16 | 55,500 | 89,563 | Agricultural, most fertile part of country. 15 9 7 191 24 3042 |
| D Qacha's Nek | 1961 | R Lat | Pomi | 11 | 48,200 | 77,745 | Mountainous, arid. Large % pagan. 1p. 3 19 8 122 57 2970 |
| Church of God | 1951 | P Pe3 | ZF... | 28 | 2,589 | 5,000 | Branch from South Africa. M=CoG(Cleveland) (USA),FGCoG(SA). 32n. |
| Dutch Reformed Church | 1957 | P Ref | F.... | 3 | 100 | 200 | *NGK. Nederduitse Gereformeerde Kerk*, from Orange Free State, SA. White Afrikaners. |
| Dutch Reformed Church in Africa | 1957 | P Ref | F.... | | 500 | 1,000 | *NGK in Afrika* (mission body from South Africa); Bantu work. 1r. |
| Ethiopian Catholic Ch of South Africa | c1920 | I pen | ....I | | 500 | 1,000 | Branch of indigenous body in South Africa. Sotho, Xhosa members. |
| Galilean Mission Church | | I pen | ....I | | 500 | 1,000 | Basotho United Church. Small body in FCAC. Local Sotho members. |
| Jehovah's Witnesses | c1945 | M Jeh | x.... | 9 | 472 | 1,000 | *Watch Tower. IBSA.* Active witnessing under way by 1949. 25Y. |
| **Lesotho Evangelical Church** | 1833 | P Ref | RWA.K | 526 | 64,500 | 200,000 | M=PEMS,SM,UCCan. A=1964. 541 schools (83,000). 36n,8x,38f,2H,1h,1j,1p,17r,1s. |
| Methodist Church of Sou'h Africa | c1900 | P Met | Vwa.K | | 3,327 | 5,000 | Part of Northern Free State & Lesotho District. All Sotho. Numerical decline. |
| Moshoeshoe Berean Bible Readers' Ch | 1909 | I pen | ..I.I | 15 | 2,200 | 5,500 | *MBBRC. Kereke ea Moshoeshoe.* Founder prophet Mattita, ex PEMS. 5 schisms. 3n,3m. |
| New Chûrch of South Africa | | M Swe | x.... | | 50 | 100 | *Swedenborgians.* From mother church in South Africa. |
| Pentecostal Holiness Church | | P Pe3 | ZF... | | 200 | 400 | M=PHC(USA), from South Africa. Holiness Pentecostals (3-stage). |
| St Paul's Church of Africa | c1960 | I ind | .v..I | | 200 | 500 | Indigenous group based on Lefihlile Mission, Maseru. Leader termed cardinal. |
| Seventh-day Adventist Church | 1899 | P Adv | x.... | 14 | 1,200 | 2,000 | *Lesotho Field*, Southern Union(Black), SAfrican UC(White). 7nx,2f,1H,23t(1700),130Y. |
| Union Apostolic Church | | I pen | ....I | | 500 | 1,000 | *Union Apostole Mission.* In FCAC. Birettas, stoles. Local Sotho members. |
| United Church, Maseru | | P com | ..... | 1 | 300 | 500 | Union church in capital. Expatriate Whites, mainly. |
| Zion Christian Church | c1920 | I pen | x.... | | 500 | 1,000 | *ZCC.* Lekganyane's church, from South Africa. Strong in Teyateeaneng. |
| Zion Foundation Church of Lesotho | c1965 | I pen | ....I | | 4,000 | 7,000 | A merger/union of 45 small Zionist bodies. Member of FCAC. |
| Other African indigenous churches | | I | ..... | | 18,000 | 28,000 | Total about 200 (see list below), including many Zulu bodies from South Africa. |
| Other Protestant denominations | | P | ..... | | 2,000 | 5,000 | Total about 40 (see list below), many based in South Africa. |
| **Total affiliated (mid-1970)** | | | | **1,750** | **406,568** | **776,300** | **Total denominations (1970) . . . 263.** |
| **Total affiliated (mid-1975)** | | | | **2,100** | **471,900** | **901,100** | **Total denominations (1975) . . . 293.** |
| **Total affiliated (mid-1980)** | | | | **2,450** | **542,600** | **1,036,100** | **Total denominations (1980) . . . 330.** |

NOTES ON TABLE ABOVE
COLUMNS: for meanings and CODES (cols, 1, 3, 4, 8), see Codebook (Part 6). Column 1: **Boldface type** = church with over 10% of country's affiliated Christians.
NATIONAL COUNCILS (Column 4, 5th letter).
I = Federal Council of African Churces (FCAC) (Federation of African Independent Churches; links with AICA of South Africa); begun 1925–27; 23 members (1980).
K = Christian Council of Lesotho (CCL) (Lekhotla la Likereke la Lesotho).
S = Episcopal Conference of Lesotho (ECL), and also full member of CCL.
OTHER AFRICAN INDIGENOUS CHURCHES. There are many immigrant groups from the republic of South Africa, especially Zulu bodies, in addition to many scores of short-lived Zionist groupings indigenous to Lesotho in remote areas. The total includes: Apostolic Ch in Zion of the New Jerusalem (1919, ex AFM of South Africa), Basuto Redemption Episcopal Ch, Christian Apostolic Catholic Church in Zion (member of FCAC), Ethiopian Ch of Lesotho, Melchizedek Ch of Salem (member of FCAC), St Joseph's Apostolic Ch, The Lord's New Church.
OTHER PROTESTANT DENOMINATIONS. These smaller bodies, many related to denominations in South Africa, include: Metropolitan Church Association, United Missionary Ch of South Africa.

PEOPLES (ethnolinguistic). Christians: 93.8% Sotho, 6% Nguni (5% Zulu, Xhosa), 0.2% White (Afrikaner, British), Mulatto.

COUNTRY-WIDE TOTALS
EVANGELIZATION (see Part 5). 1900: 31%. 1970: 100%. 1980: 100%. *Mass evangelism.* 1966, 'Lesotho Christian Mission' held in Maseru stadium by Africa Enterprise (South Africa) at invitation of Protestant churches. *Radiophonic evangelism.* FEBA, TWR, ICI (660 enrolments), et alia.
FOREIGN MISSIONARIES AND PERSONNEL (nationals serving abroad) (1973). Total 18 mainly in South Africa: about 10 Roman Catholics, 4 African indigenous, 4 Protestants.
FOREIGN MISSIONARIES AND PERSONNEL (aliens from abroad) (1973). Total 655. *From Western world.* 482: about 400 Roman Catholics, 49 Protestants (21 in 1 Switzerland society, 6 in 1 France society, 6 in 1 WGermany society, 6 in 6 USA societies, 4 in 1 Netherlands society, 4 in 2 Canada societies, 2 in 1 Denmark society), 33 Anglicans in 5 UK societies. *From Communist world.* 2 Roman Catholics from Poland. *From Third World.* 171: 86 Protestants in 7 South African societies, about 40 Roman Catholics (15 from South Africa), about 40 African indigenous and 8 Anglicans from South Africa.
INSTITUTIONS (church-operated) (1973). Total 140, including 42 higher schools (3 minor seminaries), 2 lay training centres, 75 medical centres (9 hospitals), 1 press, 2 radio stations, 3 religious communities, 5 seminaries (2 RC, 2 Protestant, 1 African indigenous).
PERIODICALS. About 20 titles.
PERSONNEL. About 2,302 (1,647 national, 655 foreign).
RELIGIOUS LIBRARIES. About 14.
SCRIPTURE DISTRIBUTION (1975). Annual totals: 6,000 Bibles (83% subsidized, 17% commercial), 2,400 NTs (17% subsidized, 83% commercial), 1,000 UBS portions, 2,000 UBS selections. *Translations completed.* In 1 language, Sesotho: portion 1839, NT 1855, Bible 1878.
SERVICE AGENCIES. About 55, including AICA, CCL, ECL, LCRS, LCTF, LCUL, LOF, LPC, SCM.

ADDITIONAL DATA ON CHURCHES
CATHOLIC CHURCH IN LESOTHO. *Catechumens.* Total (1959) 16,964; (1961) 15,104; (1963) 15,903; and (1970) 13,827, divided as follows among the 3 dioceses in the order shown (and included in column 7): 7367, 2473, 3987. *Annual baptisms.* (1972) 82.7% infant, 17.3% adult. *Priests.* 17% secular, 83% regular (all OMI). *National priests.* The first Mosotho priest was ordained in 1931. A number now belong to OMI. *Expatriate priests.* Whites born outside Southern Africa (there are also many Whites born in the republic of South Africa). *Brothers.* 37 Africans (18 OMI, 19 Teaching Brothers of the Sacred Heart), 41 expatriates (26 OMI, 15 Sacred Heart). There are also contemplatives. *Sisters.* 423 Africans, 59 expatriates. There are also contemplatives. *Catholic charismatics* (January 1974). 100 adults including religious personnel are active in 2 organized prayer groups in the Charismatic Renewal. *Seminarians.* All religious. *Catechists.* Total (1971) 797, mostly part-time. (1976) 67 full-time, 1,010 part-time. *Indigenous religious congregations.* None; however, there is a recently-founded secular institute for priests called Christ the Priest. *Main foreign congregations.* Priests: OMI. Brothers: Brothers of the Sacred Heart.
*Catholic organizations.* The Episcopal Conference of Lesotho, founded in 1972, is a member of SECAM. Until the beginning of 1972, the dioceses of Lesotho belonged to the Southern Africa Catholic Bishops' Conference. There is no national pastoral council, but in 1972 the Lesotho Priests Council was formed. Religious personnel have representation in the Conference of Clerical Religious Superiors in Southern Africa and the Association of Women Religious, both with headquarters in South Africa. The strongest and most active Catholic lay association is the Legion of Mary with 156 praesidia and 1,560 members in 1970. A significant youth association is the Cadets (2,000 youth aged 10–18 years), in addition to Boy Scouts and Girl Guides. Other lay groups are mostly pious associations including Sodalities.

The Holy See has diplomatic relations with Lesotho and is represented to government and the Catholic hierarchy by pronuncio based in Pretoria, South Africa.

Church-sponsored institutions include: Mazenod Institute, a printing and publishing house which disseminates, among others the weekly *Moeletsi oa Basotho;* and Lesotho Observatory Foundation (LOF), or Institute of Natural Revelation, founded in 1967 to develop a modern synthesis between science and religion and to delineate a world-view based on both science and the Christian faith.

An extensive educational programme is in evidence, with, in 1973, 476 primary and 27 secondary schools (with respectively 92,120 and 4,521 pupils) as well as 42 teacher-training colleges. The total enrolment in Catholic schools at 96,641 pupils is about 20,000 less than those in Protestant and government schools. There are also 2 homecraft and 8 sewing schools. The former Pius XII University College, founded at Roma in 1945, became in 1964 the University of Botswana, Lesotho and Swaziland (UBLS), under government management.

Medical aid is provided through 4 well-equipped hospitals, 44 dispensaries, 13 maternity hospitals, 41 pre-school clinics and the only leprosarium in the country. Outstanding achievements in social developments are: Rome Valley Agricultural Project, a large 9-year pilot project (1968–77), which is the result of a contract between the Maseru archdiocese and the government; Lesotho Credit Union League, which during 1961 to 1968 was responsible for the formation of 38 credit unions with 10,000 members; and self-help projects founded and backed by Lesotho Catholic Relief Services since 1966 and by Caritas-Lesotho since 1970.
LESOTHO EVANGELICAL CHURCH. Kereke ea Evangeli Lesotho. Also known popularly as Fora (French), after PEMS.
MOSHOESHOE BEREAN BIBLE READERS' CHURCH. In Sesotho, Kereke ea Moshoeshoe Berea ea Babali Ba Bibele. *Membership.* Mostly Sotho, with a few Zulu, and 2 Pedi congregations. Membership has declined since the schisms beginning after Mattita's death in 1935. *Missions abroad.* In the republic of South Africa, the church uses the same name and has 10 congregations with 8 pastors in the Orange Free State. In Botswana and Namibia, the Spiritual Healing Church originated in a disciple of Mattita's in OFS who later migrated to Bechuanaland; it uses the same hymns and liturgy as the MBBRC. The link between them has only been rediscovered by them, since 1974, and subsequently there has been considerable fellowship and interrelations. *Nazarites Association.* Since 1935, the Mokhatlo oa Banazari has operated as an interdenominational body, though mainly within the Moshoeshoe Church, working across Lesotho, OFS and Transvaal, and emphasizing Bible study, Bible memorizing, prayer, and prayer for the sick. It holds an annual Easter conference at Peka.

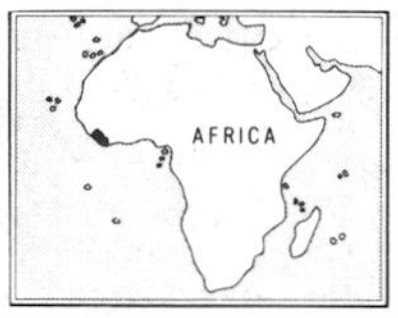


# LIBERIA

## SECULAR DATA

STATE. **Official name:** The Republic of Liberia. Adjective of nationality: Liberian.
**Flag** (shown above right): Alternative stripes of red and white, with blue square containing white star in upper hoist corner.
**Area:** 111,369 sq.km. (43,000 sq.miles). Agricultural land: 6.5%.
**Government:** Republic under military junta (1822 colony founded by ex-slaves, 1847 Independence as republic, 1980 military coup).
**Legislature:** Congress: Senate, 18 members; House of Representatives, 52 members.
**Official language:** English.
**Capital:** Monrovia 96,230 (1970).
**Political divisions:** 9 Counties and 5 Territories.
**Armed forces** (1976): Total 5,520 regular: army 5,020, navy (coastguard) 200. Paramilitary forces: 21,300.

DEMOGRAPHY. **Population:** 1,016,443 (census of 2.IV.1962. For 1970–2000 (UN), see last row of Table 1). Population density (1975): 18/sq.km. (40/sq.mile). Under 15 years: 38%. Growth rate (1975–80): 2.52% per year (births 4.42%, deaths −1.90%). Life expectancy (1975–80): 46.0 years. Household size: 4.2 persons.

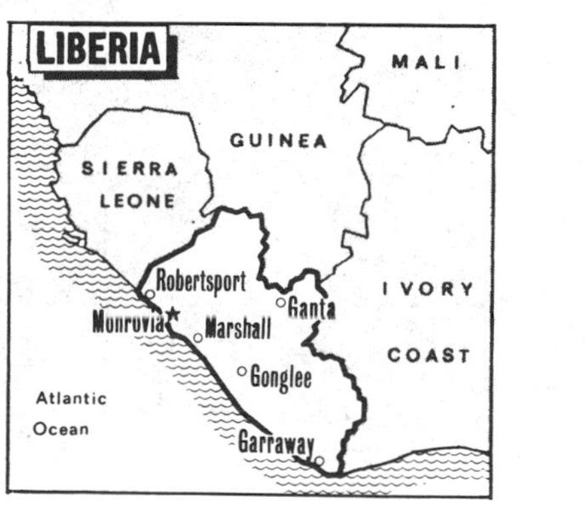


**Major languages:** English, Kpelle, Bassa, Kru, Grebo, Kissi, Mandingo, Arabic, Yoruba, and over 25 other tribal languages.
**Urban dwellers** (1970): 10.1%. Urban growth rate (1950–70): 4.4.% per year.
**Labour force:** 31%.

ETHNOLINGUISTIC GROUPS: 21% Kpelle, 16% Bassa, 8% Gio (Dan), 8% Kru, 8% Grebo, 8% Gola-Kissi, 7% Mano, 6% Loma (Toma), 5% Krahn, 3% Vai, 3% Gbande (with Belle), 3% Mandingo, 2.3% alien (1.4% Ghanaian (22,000), 0.7% Lebanese Arab (10,000), 1% Americo-Liberian (Kwi), USA, Nigerian (Yoruba), British, Congolese, Guinean, Sierra Leonian, Ivorian), Fanti, Sapo, Mende, Kono, et alii.

MONEY (1977). **Monetary unit:** dollar (= 100 cents); US$1 = L$1.00.
**National income per person:** US$260. Average annual family income: US$1,092.
**Inflation:** (1970–74) 10.5% per year (1975: consumer price index 172).
**Cost of living in capital** (1976): index 137 (Washington DC=100). Daily cost of living: US$47.

HEALTH. Hospitals: 32 (2,181 beds). Doctors: 132. Lepers: 21,500 (12.6 per 1,000). Blind: 15,000. Psychotics: 12,000.

EDUCATION. Adult literacy: (1962) 9%, (1975) 10%.

Education rate: 10%. Schools: 1,155. Universities: 3.

LITERATURE. Annual new book titles (1966): 11. Periodicals: 60. Newspapers: 1 daily, 4 non-daily.

COMMUNICATION (per 1,000 people). Phones: 2. Radios: 132. TV sets: 5. Daily newspaper circulation: 4 copies

### TABLE 1.    RELIGIOUS ADHERENTS IN LIBERIA

| Year | 1900 | | mid-1970 | | Annual change, 1970–1980 | | | | mid-1975 | | mid-1980 | | 2000 | |
| Name | Adherents | % | Adherents | % | Natural | Conversion | Total | Rate | Adherents | % | Adherents | % | Adherents | % |
|---|---|---|---|---|---|---|---|---|---|---|---|---|---|---|
| Tribal religionists | 271,000 | 87.4 | 759,000 | 49.8 | 19,319 | −10,879 | 8,440 | 1.06 | 797,100 | 46.7 | 843,400 | 43.5 | 1,097,000 | 34.1 |
| Christians | 32,800 | 10.6 | 472,000 | 31.0 | 13,662 | 6,938 | 20,600 | 3.66 | 563,600 | 33.0 | 678,000 | 35.0 | 1,288,000 | 40.0 |
| professing | 32,800 | 10.6 | 472,000 | 31.0 | 13,662 | 6,938 | 20,600 | 3.66 | 563,600 | 33.0 | 678,000 | 35.0 | 1,288,000 | 40.0 |
| Protestants | 17,000 | 5.5 | 246,600 | 16.2 | 7,206 | 4,164 | 11,370 | 3.83 | 297,200 | 17.4 | 360,300 | 18.6 | 740,400 | 23.0 |
| Black indigenous | 13,000 | 4.2 | 132,800 | 12.0 | 5,240 | 2,250 | 7,490 | 3.46 | 216,200 | 12.7 | 257,700 | 13.3 | 423,700 | 13.2 |
| Roman Catholics | 0 | 0.0 | 25,900 | 1.7 | 744 | 346 | 1,090 | 3.55 | 30,700 | 1.8 | 36,800 | 1.9 | 74,000 | 2.3 |
| Anglicans | 2,800 | 0.9 | 13,700 | 0.9 | 390 | 170 | 560 | 3.48 | 16,100 | 0.9 | 19,300 | 1.0 | 41,800 | 1.3 |
| Catholics (non-Roman) | 0 | 0.0 | 3,000 | 0.2 | 82 | 8 | 90 | 2.65 | 3,400 | 0.2 | 3,900 | 0.2 | 8,100 | 0.3 |
| nominal | 4,500 | 1.5 | 182,700 | 12.0 | 5,382 | 3,468 | 8,850 | 3.99 | 222,000 | 13.0 | 271,200 | 14.0 | 483,200 | 15.0 |
| affiliated | 28,300 | 9.1 | 289,300 | 19.0 | 8,280 | 3,470 | 11,750 | 3.44 | 341,600 | 20.0 | 406,800 | 21.0 | 804,800 | 25.0 |
| total practising | 25,470 | 90 | 202,510 | 70 | 5,796 | 2,429 | 8,225 | 3.44 | 239,120 | 70 | 284,760 | 70 | 563,360 | 70 |
| non-practising | 2,830 | 10 | 86,790 | 30 | 2,484 | 1,041 | 3,525 | 3.44 | 102,480 | 30 | 122,040 | 30 | 241,440 | 30 |
| Protestants | 15,000 | 4.8 | 126,997 | 8.3 | 3,588 | 1,202 | 4,790 | 3.24 | 148,000 | 8.7 | 174,900 | 9.0 | 334,800 | 10.4 |
| Evangelicals | 3,000 | 1.0 | 76,100 | 5.0 | 2,235 | 1,385 | 3,620 | 3.93 | 92,200 | 5.4 | 112,300 | 5.8 | 225,300 | 7.0 |
| Black indigenous | 11,000 | 3.5 | 122,306 | 8.0 | 3,519 | 1,681 | 5,200 | 3.58 | 145,200 | 8.5 | 174,300 | 9.0 | 355,500 | 11.0 |
| Roman Catholics | 0 | 0.0 | 23,697 | 1.6 | 703 | 417 | 1,120 | 3.86 | 29,000 | 1.7 | 34,900 | 1.8 | 70,800 | 2.2 |
| Catholic pentecostals | 0 | 0.0 | 0 | 0.0 | 10 | 90 | 100 | 25.00 | 400 | 0.0 | 1,000 | 0.1 | 5,000 | 0.2 |
| Anglicans | 2,200 | 0.7 | 11,000 | 0.7 | 320 | 130 | 450 | 3.41 | 13,200 | 0.8 | 15,500 | 0.8 | 29,000 | 0.9 |
| Catholics (non-Roman) | 0 | 0.0 | 3,800 | 0.2 | 104 | 6 | 110 | 2.56 | 4,300 | 0.2 | 4,900 | 0.2 | 8,500 | 0.3 |
| Marginal Protestants | 100 | 0.0 | 1,500 | 0.1 | 46 | 34 | 80 | 4.21 | 1,900 | 0.1 | 2,300 | 0.1 | 6,500 | 0.2 |
| Muslims | 6,200 | 2.0 | 289,000 | 19.0 | 8,322 | 3,838 | 12,160 | 3.54 | 343,300 | 20.1 | 410,600 | 21.2 | 824,000 | 25.6 |
| Ahmadis | 0 | 0.0 | 500 | 0.0 | 14 | 6 | 20 | 3.33 | 600 | 0.0 | 700 | 0.0 | 1,500 | 0.0 |
| Baha'is | 0 | 0.0 | 3,000 | 0.2 | 97 | 103 | 200 | 5.00 | 4,000 | 0.2 | 5,000 | 0.3 | 10,000 | 0.3 |
| Country's population | 310,000 | 100.0 | 1,523,000 | 100.0 | 41,400 | 0 | 41,400 | 2.42 | 1,708,000 | 100.0 | 1,937,000 | 100.0 | 3,219,000 | 100.0 |

COLUMNS, ROWS. For meanings and definitions, see Codebook (Part 6). Note that, by definition, total 'Christians' = professing + crypto-Christians, which also = affiliated + nominal Christians. Percentages may not always total exactly, due to rounding.
CENSUSES. The religion question has not been asked in any census or sample survey.

NOTES ON RELIGIONS
AHMADIS. Mission begun in 1956; little response. There are 6 branches.
ANGLICANS. In 1885 there were 419 communicants and 30 preaching places; in 1895, 1,237 communicants and 63 preaching places; in 1900, 1,507 communicants; in 1930, 6,152 communicants and a total baptized community of 8,190. These data indicate that from 1900–1970 this church remained exactly the same size, numerically, relative to the total population of the country. In 1970, of the 11,000 members, over 1,200 baptized members (with 700 day-school students and over 400 in Sunday school) belonged to one congregation, Trinity Cathedral in Monrovia. After the election in 1970 of the first Liberian bishop, a gradual increase in membership began.
BAHA'IS. Growth from 3 local spiritual assemblies (1964)

to 20 (1973). Expansion is particularly rapid among youth.
BLACK INDIGENOUS. Originally begun by Black denominations from the USA, by 1970 there were 81 denominations of which the great majority were African indigenous bodies unrelated to USA Black missions (see Table 2).
CATHOLIC PENTECOSTALS (or, Catholic charismatics). The renewal has only grown slowly since 1970, with 200 or so involved adults (many being religious personnel) scattered across the country.
MUSLIMS. Africans, mostly Sunnis (of the Malikite rite), with some Ahmadis (Qadianis; enumerated here under Muslims, though declared non-Muslim by Pakistan) with missionaries from Pakistan; Qadiriya and Tijaniya orders; and numerous Mandingo (Wangara) traders. Muslims in tribes: Gola and Vai (75%), both recently islamized; Kissi, Gbande (10%), and Mande and other Guinean, Sierra Leonian and Ivorian tribesmen. Since 1955 numbers of whole Gbande villages have become Muslim; and conversions to Islam have been numerous among the Gio (Dan, Yakuba). In addition, Mandingo small traders from Guinea, all Muslims, have been infiltrating from the north (3% of the population); and there are Lebanese Arabs (0.7%) and alien migrant workers from Muslim areas in Ghana and Nigeria. Hajj pilgrims to Mecca. (1970) 85; (1975) 61; (1976) 98.

NOMINAL CHRISTIANS. As in Nigeria and Ghana, this category is very numerous due to widespread Christian schools and complete freedom of religion, and consists of persons professing to be Christians but not affiliated to or known by the churches.
PRACTISING CHRISTIANS. Weekly church attendance (1970): 25% of Methodists, 20% Lutherans, less for Catholics and Episcopalians, more for Pentecostals; average for country, 25% of all Christians. Annual attenders: about 70%.
PROFESSING CHRISTIANS. Persons publicly professing to be Christians. Amongst other Christian and quasi-Christian groups, this category includes the quasi-religious movement Freemasonry, a worldwide male secret brotherhood. Most of its members in Liberia are Protestants, and its influence on Liberia is very strong.
TRIBAL RELIGIONISTS. The Loma and Kpelle (in which the Poro and Sande secret societies have been especially powerful) have resisted Islam. Tribes over 75% traditionalist (animist) in 1972: Gio (95%), Mano (95%), Kpelle (90%), Gbande (80%), Kran (Tchien) (80%), Loma (Toma) (80%), Sapo (80%). Pagan areas unreached by Christians mission include a Loma clan, Gola, several clans of Bush Grebo, 2 clans of Belle, et alia.

---

## NON-CHRISTIAN RELIGIONS.    Traditional religions are the living faith of well over half the population and are strongest among the inland peoples. Tribes over three-quarters traditionalist are: Gbande 80%, Gio 95%, Kpelle 90%, Loma 80%, Mano 95%, Sapo 80% and Tchien 80%. Names for God include Zra (among the Dan), Kamba

(Vai), Hala (Kissi), Yala (Kpelle) and Gala (Loma). Nevertheless, veneration of ancestors forms the core of Liberian traditional religious experience. The Mandingo are especially noted as diviners, their principal method being the observation of the pattern formed by bones thrown in the sand. Medicine men (zo in Loma) are active, and belief in witchcraft

is strong. Secret societies (Poro for men, Sande for women among the Loma) also play a dominant role and are characterized by elaborate initiation ceremonies.

Islam is strongest among the Vai who are more than 75% islamized. Muslim minorities are also found among the northwestern peoples, especially the Kissi and Gbande, largely due to the influence of Mandingo traders. Muslims make up 8% of the population, and Ahmadiya missionaries from Egypt and Pakistan have been active since 1956.

### CHRISTIANITY
PROTESTANT CHURCHES. The United Methodist Church is the largest denomination in Liberia. Some Methodists were among the pioneer settlers from America in 1822, but the church generally dates its origin to the arrival of the first missionary in 1833. For many years during this century the church was served by Black bishops from the USA, the first Liberian bishop being elected in 1965. In Monrovia, Methodists have active Americo-Liberian communities, but attention has also been given to the peoples of the interior. Ganta mission station was opened on the northern border in 1925, followed by Gbarnga in 1948; and important evangelistic initiatives have also been taken on the Kru coast. Methodists maintain 13 primary and 4 secondary schools, including the College of West Africa which was established in Monrovia in 1939. They also sponsor a hospital, a nursing school and an extensive leprosy programme.

The Lutheran Church had its beginnings in a mission to the interior tribes in 1860 undertaken by the United Lutheran Church in America. The work produced few conversions although a school system was developed. In 1908 a new expansion into the interior began with the opening of a mission at Kpoloelle, and during the next 50 years, 6 more stations were begun. In 1947 the Evangelical Lutheran Church in Liberia was organized. By 1965 the Lutheran mission ceased to exist as a separate entity, and the church changed its name to the Lutheran Church in Liberia. The church is still basically rural although new work has been started in urban areas where educated tribal peoples have

**United Methodist Church of Liberia.** Choir in Ganta church.

Modern communications: *left*, light aircraft used by Evangelical missionary societies; *above*, prisoners in South Beach jail listening to Christian program over Radio ELWA.

gone to find employment. The Lutheran Church is responsible for 9 primary schools, 4 secondary schools, 2 hospitals, 8 dispensaries, a nursing school, 3 literacy centres, 3 community centres and an agricultural extension programme.

Pentecostal missionaries from the USA opened the first of their mission stations at Newaka in 1908. Since then more than a dozen stations have been established in the eastern part of the country. Churches are completely indigenous and response to the gospel from tribal peoples has been marked, with entire villages burning their traditional charms. There are 3 Bible schools, and a co-educational school in Monrovia, a girls' school at Newaka, a leper colony in New Hope Town and a new work begun on a Firestone rubber plantation. Several other Pentecostal groups are also working in Liberia including the United Pentecostal Church and Free Pentecostal Church.

Seventh-day Adventists entered Liberia in 1927, and the United Liberia Inland Church was started by the Worldwide Evangelization Crusade in 1938. In addition to medical, educational, literacy and evangelistic work in the interior, the latter has a ministry at one of the large Firestone plantations, and operates a bookstore in Monrovia and an aircraft service.

In 1954 the Sudan Interior Mission built the first mission radio station in Africa, ELWA (Eternal Love Winning Africa). It broadcasts in 40 languages covering Africa and the Middle East, and in addition runs a hospital.

A number of other small Protestant societies and churches are also at work in Liberia.

INDIGENOUS CHURCHES. The first church built in Liberia, and the oldest Baptist congregation in Africa, was the Providence Baptist Church in Monrovia, begun by 2 USA Black Baptist missionaries, Lott Carey and Colin Teague, who took part in the expedition of American Negro settlers to Liberia in 1822. The church later received support from the Lott Carey Baptist Foreign Mission Convention, a Negro society formed in 1897. A second Black society was the National Baptist Convention USA which established missions in 1897 at Brewerville and Monrovia and later took over the work of the independent Klay Mission. Today these various initiatives are combined in the Liberian Baptist Convention. Aid is also received from Southern Baptists who entered Liberia in 1960. The Convention sponsors 14 primary schools, 3 secondary schools, a hospital and industrial academy in Monrovia and a rubber farm at Bamboota. In addition to their work with the Convention, Southern Baptists also provide support for the churches begun by independent Baptist missionaries including Mother George, who founded 13 congregations in the area of Greenville in Simoe Country prior to 1961, and Daniel Horton who was originally a missionary of the National Baptist Convention. Horton organized a separate conference among Bassa tribesmen in 1938 which included 36 congregations by 1968.

The influence of Blacks from the USA has also been felt in the creation of the African Methodist Episcopal Church (1873), AME Zion Church (1876), Pentecostal Assemblies of the World (1919) and other smaller groups. Independent churches from other parts of West Africa have also spread to Liberia. The Church of the Lord (Aladura) is a Nigerian body which entered Liberia in 1947 at the request of a Liberian judge who had visited Nigeria for healing the previous year. Healing has in fact been a major emphasis in the witness of many independent churches. Contrary to the situation in other parts of West Africa, no large or powerful indigenous churches have arisen within Liberia itself. Prophet Harris was himself a native Grebo but his ministry in 1914–15 was carried on almost entirely in neighbouring Ivory Coast. Nevertheless, many small denominations exist.

CATHOLIC CHURCH. Although the coast of Liberia was first touched by Portuguese mariners as early as 1462 and was included in the diocese of Cape Verde in 1533, no permanent Catholic work was established until the present century. When the first Negroes emigrated to Liberia in 1822, Catholic bishops in the USA attempted to begin a mission. Edward Barron and 2 others went to Monrovia in 1841 but were unsuccessful in gaining a foothold. In 1848 Holy Ghost priests opened a church and school in Monrovia, but the project was abandoned in 1887 due to opposition. The church today is the outgrowth of work established in 1906 by a different body, the Society of African Missions. Attention was at first given to Monrovia and Kakata. However, when the Kru coast appeared to be more receptive, other missions were closed and efforts were concentrated on the Kru. Catholics have also had some success with the Grebo in the southeastern part of the country, the Bassa, and the Mano to the north. At present there are 2 vicariates. There have not been great numbers of converts, and greater success has attended Catholic educational work in schools.

ANGLICAN CHURCH. The Protestant Episcopal Church of the USA opened a station among the Grebo at Cape Palmas in 1836. The first Black bishop was appointed in 1885 and was largely responsible for developing the extensive educational programme which today includes 41 primary schools, 10 secondary schools and a university, Cuttington College and Divinity School. Since the 1920s the church has given more attention to evangelistic work at Cape Mount in western Liberia and at Bolahun among the Gbande and other northwestern peoples. The church is an extra-provincial missionary diocese of the Episcopal Church in the USA, and has resisted joining in the Anglican Province of West Africa until in 1975 it agreed on a trial membership period.

CHURCH AND STATE. Founded and organized by the American Colonization Society in the early part of the 19th century in order to resolve the problem of Blacks in the USA, Liberia was first led by Protestant ministers. In the beginning the laws and regulations were based on Christian principles and often legislative, executive and judicial powers were exercised by churchmen. In the history of the country, 4 of the presidents of the republic have been pastors, including president Tolbert who was an ordained Baptist minister. The latter announced in 1971 that the teaching of religion would henceforth form part of the programme of all schools.

The constitution of 1847 which is still in force provides for liberty of conscience and worship. It specifies that 'No sect of Christians shall have exclusive privileges or preference over any other sect; but all shall be alike tolerated' (Article 1, section 3). The civil authorities stress that Liberia terms itself a Christian country but that all religions are protected. The churches receive financial help of various kinds from the government. There is no ministry charged with religious affairs, and churches are not required to register with government.

INTERDENOMINATIONAL ORGANIZATIONS. Liberia has had no national Christian council nor other ecumenical body fostering co-operation among the churches. The United Ecumenical Organization (UEO), founded in 1970, is a lay group composed mostly of Methodists and Episcopalians, with some Catholic participation, whose major interest is social work. There is also an ad hoc National Interdenominational Conference of Bishops which provides an opportunity for Catholics, Episcopalians, Methodists and Lutherans to discuss together the special problems of Christian presence in slum areas. The Christian Rural Fellowship was begun in 1967. In 1968 a conservative grouping, the Liberian Evangelical Fundamental Fellowship was formed, which 6 years later joined the AEAM as the Liberian Evangelical Fellowship.

BROADCASTING. Radio ELWA, operated by the Sudan Interior Mission and located on the coast southeast of Monrovia, is a major Protestant international radio station, beaming programmes to Liberia, West Africa, Central Africa, North Africa, the Far East and also to South America. It produces its own programmes in French, English, Arabic and some 30 vernacular languages and has enrolled over 10,000 students in Bible correspondence courses. Plans include the installation of a bigger long-wave transmitter for better coverage of Liberia. SIM-produced programmes are also broadcast over national television by the Liberia Broadcasting Corporation. For Catholics, UNDA is represented by an national association.

BIBLIOGRAPHY
'Change strategies initiated in the Protestant Episcopal Church in Liberia from 1836 to 1950 and their effects'. D. A. Holt. Dissertation, Boston University School of Education (USA), 1970.
God's impatience in Liberia. J. C. Wold. Grand Rapids, Michigan: Eerdmans. 1968. 227p.
'History of the Methodist Church mission in Liberia'. W. J. King. Monrovia: Methodist Church, n.d. (c1950). 77p. (Mimeographed. By the Methodist bishop).
The Catholic story of Liberia. M. J. Bane. New York: Declan MacMullen. 1950.
'The growth of Christianity in the Liberian environment'. J. W. Cason. Dissertation, Columbia University, New York, 1962. 484p.

TABLE 2. ORGANIZED CHURCHES AND DENOMINATIONS IN LIBERIA

| Official name 1 | Begun 2 | Type 3 | Counc 4 | Congs 5 | Adults 6 | Affiliated 7 | Names, notes, and other statistics (see Codebook) 8 |
|---|---|---|---|---|---|---|---|
| African Disciples of Christ | 1968 | I ind | ..... | 11 | 992 | 2,000 | *Soul-Winning Mission Ch of L.* 74% Bassa, 16% Kru, 10% Kpelle. 9n,4m,72Y,60y. |
| African Methodist Episcopal Church | 1873 | I Met | VwA.. | 83 | 6,222 | 8,576 | M=AMEC(USA). Part of 14th Episcopal District. 16 schools. 71n,3w,1h,3r. |
| African Methodist Episcopal Zion Ch | 1876 | I Met | Vw... | 21 | 2,586 | 7,500 | In 9th Episcopal District. M=AMEZC(USA). 20 schools. HQ Monrovia. 20n. |
| African Salvation Army Church | 1964 | I ind | ..... | 8 | 342 | 1,000 | A Bassa church on Firestone plantation. HQ Buchanan. Declining. 5n,4m,54Y,34y. |
| Apostolic God of Mercy Church | 1957 | I pen | ..... | 12 | 500 | 1,569 | On Firestone Plantation. Bassa. Buchanan area. HQ Owensgrove. 25n,15w,160Y. |
| Army of the Cross of Christ Church | c1950 | I pen | ..... | | 400 | 585 | *MDCC. Musama Disco Christo Ch.* Immigrant church from Ghana (Fante). |
| Bafu Bay Church | 1952 | I Bap | ..... | 37 | 1,804 | 4,000 | Begun by USA roadbuilder, continued by Sapo tribesmen. HQ Juarzon. 5n,5m,288Y. |
| Believe in God Healing Church | 1960 | I pen | ..... | 4 | 45 | 200 | *Poe Yonswah-tah un jae por* (Sapo). Woman bishop. 60% Sapo. 75% lost in splits. |
| Catholic Church in Liberia: | 1906 | R Lat | P.SGP | 35 | 14,700 | 23,697 | 3 failed starts; finally 1906 M=SMA. C=2+2+7. 1s. 5n,45x,20m,80w,P=27%,1277Yy. |
| VA Cape Palmas | 1950 | R Lat | Psma | 22 | 6,400 | 10,380 | 80% Kru, 15% Grebo, 5% Kran, Lebanese. Emigration. 2 20 0 29 24 560 |
| VA Monrovia | 1903 | R Lat | Psma | 13 | 8,300 | 13,317 | Heavy Catholic immigration from VA Cape Palmas. 3 25 20 51 30 717 |
| Church of God by Faith | 1959 | I pen | ..... | 5 | 438 | 1,000 | 25% Bassa,23% Kpelle,23% Mano,18% Dei,11% Gio. HQ Barnardsville. 1n,5m,1s(6),23Y. |
| Church of God in Christ | c1945 | I pe3 | Z...I | 3 | 200 | 500 | M=CoGiC(Black mission from USA). Main work among Grebo, Bassa. HQ Monrovia. |
| Ch of the Lord JC of Apostolic Faith | 1963 | I pe1 | x...I | 9 | 385 | 1,000 | Linked with M=COLJCAF(USA) Black pentecostals. 90% Bassa. HQ Fortsville. 2n,135Y. |
| Church of the Lord (Aladura) | 1947 | I pen | xwi.. | 45 | 7,000 | 10,000 | M=CLA(Nigeria). 9 Districts. Widespread Bassa, Kru, Kpelle. 60n,70m,20w,5h,3r. |
| Churches of Christ | 1966 | P Dis | x.... | 17 | 700 | 1,500 | M=CCCC(Instrumental)(USA). 5 churches in Monrovia. School, mobile clinic. 4f,1p. |
| ELWA Chapels | 1951 | P int | xMG.G | 9 | 120 | 590 | M=SIM. 1954 radio station ELWA, 43 languages. 29% White. 1n,4x,80f,1H, W=78%,Y5. |
| Episcopal Church of Liberia | 1836 | A Cen | awAV. | 66 | 8,000 | 11,000 | D in PECUSA Prov II. M=OHC. Grebo, Kru, Kissi. 22n,4x,3h,1p,10r,1s,1v,202Y,356y. |
| Evangelical Church of Christ | c1968 | I ind | .T... | 20 | 400 | 800 | Begun by former ELWA radio programmer. 7 churches in Muslim areas. Most Bassa. |
| Ev Congregational Ch of Liberia | 1971 | P Hol | xFG.G | | 300 | 500 | M=Ev Congregational Ch(USA), formerly East Pennsylvania Conference. 2f. |
| Fire-Baptized Holiness CoG of Africa | | I pen | x...I | 100 | 3,000 | 6,000 | M=FBHC(USA). 4 Districts across nation. Mainly Kru, Bassa, Gola, Kran. 60nm,75Y. |
| Free Pentecostal Church | 1920 | P Pe2 | Z...I | 5 | 2,250 | 5,000 | M=SFM(Sweden). Mass movement. 40% Kissi, 40% Loma, 20% Gbande. 3 schools. |
| Free Protestant Episcopal Church | 1957 | C ARo | xv... | 40 | 1,025 | 3,800 | *D WAfrica. ECF.* M=FPEC(UK,USA). 50% Nigerians. 3n,6x,8r,1s(10),W=39%,615Y,200y. |
| General Assoc of Regular Baptist Chs | 1938 | P Bap | xT... | | 300 | 600 | M=BMM,GARB(Canada,USA). HQ Monrovia. Gio, Mano, Bassa, Kran, Kpelle. 44f,1H,2h,2s. |
| Gethsemane Church of Liberia | 1959 | I pen | ..... | 19 | 740 | 1,500 | 54% Bassa, 27% Kpelle, 14% Mano, 5% Gio. 2 schools. 19n,10m,9w,W=75%. |
| Jehovah's Witnesses | 1887 | M Jeh | x.... | 15 | 774 | 1,500 | 1887, Grebo secession Russelite Ch, ex PECUSA. HQ Monrovia. Baptisms in 1970: 101Y. |
| Liberia Assemblies of God | 1908 | P Pe2 | ZFG.G | 196 | 7,103 | 20,000 | M=AoG(USA),PAoC(Canada). A=1967. 95% Kru. 4 schools. 242n,21f,1H,3p,1s(63). |
| **Liberian Baptist Convention** | 1822 | I Bap | T.A.. | 201 | 22,500 | 50,000 | *LBMEC.* M=NBCUSA,LCBFMC; 1960,SBC(USA). Grebo. 140n,39f,1H,7h,4r,2s,1318Y. |
| Liberian Christian Assemblies of God | 1920 | P Pe4 | ....I | 10 | 200 | 500 | *Sinoe Bible Institute.* M=IAoG(Scandinavians from USA). 5 schools. 33f,2h,1p. |
| Liberian Gospel Crusade Church | 1952 | I pen | ..... | 13 | 600 | 2,000 | *LGCC.* Director in Liberian senate. Mainly Bassa; Kpelle. 23n,30m,10w,W=75%,46Y. |
| Lighthouse Fellowship of Churches | 1936 | I pen | .T... | 20 | 1,000 | 2,000 | *Mother Blatch's Chs.* M=Lighthouse Full Gospel Ch(USA). Americo-Liberians. Monrovia. |
| Lutheran Church in Liberia | 1860 | P Lut | LWA.. | 350 | 9,000 | 20,507 | *LCL.* First M=Muhlenberg M, LCA(USA). A=1947. Kpelle, Loma. 39f,2H,8h,4r,1s,W=20%. |
| Mary Sharp Memorial Church | 1876 | I Met | ..... | 1 | 100 | 300 | Kru. Begun by USA missionary MSharp. Aid from M=Defenders of the Faith(USA). |
| Open Bible Standard Churches | 1935 | P Pe2 | ZFG.G | 20 | 300 | 800 | Schism ex AoG by a USA woman missionary. HQ River Cess. 2 schools. 11f,1h,1p. |
| Pentecostal Assemblies of the World | 1919 | I pe1 | xv..I | 36 | 5,280 | 10,000 | M=PAW(USA Blacks). 90% Kru, 3% Dey, 2% Bassa. 43n,2x,24m,17w,3f,1H,1h,W=87%,153Y. |
| Pillar of Fire | 1961 | P Hol | x.... | 20 | 300 | 500 | M=Pillar of Fire West African Missions(USA). At River Cess. 2 schools. 45n,5f,1h,1s. |
| Presbytery of Liberia in West Africa | 1831 | P Ref | RuA.. | 11 | 1,136 | 2,000 | *Presbyterian Ch in Liberia.* M=UPUSA. A=1890. Many women evangelists. 16n(5 women). |
| Seventh-day Adventist Church | 1927 | P Adv | x.... | 30 | 3,494 | 7,000 | *Liberian Mission.* 67% Bassa, 29% Kpelle, 4% Gio. 7n,13f,1s(7),1v,W=60%,529Y. |
| Star of Bethlehem Church | 1960 | I Ang | ..... | 11 | 792 | 1,776 | Sinoe, Gedeh countries. 84% Sapo, 11% Kran, 4% Kru. 18n,26m,10w,1p,W=75%,32Y,17y. |
| United Liberia Inland Church | 1938 | P int | xFG.G | 35 | 3,000 | 5,000 | *LIM. Liberia Inland Mission.* M=WEC. Bassa, Mano, Gio, Kpelle. 9m,9w,40f,6h,1p,1r. |
| **United Methodist Church of Liberia** | 1823 | P Met | VwA.. | 274 | 22,968 | 50,000 | *Liberia CC,* UMC(USA). 33% Bassa, 19% Kru. 75n,5x,34f,1H,10h,4r,W=25%,931Y,1205y. |
| United Pentecostal Church of Liberia | 1936 | P Pe1 | x...I | 32 | 2,000 | 5,000 | *Jesus Only Ch.* Unitarians. M=UPC(USA). Belle. 1 school. 29n,4f,1h,1p(30),1r. |
| World-Wide Missions of Liberia | 1961 | P ind | x.G.G | | 2,000 | 4,000 | M=World-Wide Missions(USA). Evangelicals with base in Pasadena, CA(USA). |
| Other African indigenous churches | | I | ..... | | 5,000 | 10,000 | Total about 60 (see list below). |
| Other Protestant denominations | | P | ..... | | 1,500 | 3,500 | Total about 15 (see list below). |
| **Total affiliated (mid-1970)** | | | | **2,100** | **141,496** | **289,300** | **Total denominations (1970) . . . 114.** |
| **Total affiliated (mid-1975)** | | | | **2,400** | **167,000** | **341,600** | **Total denominations (1975) . . . 130.** |
| **Total affiliated (mid-1980)** | | | | **2,900** | **198,900** | **406,800** | **Total denominations (1980) . . . 146.** |

**NOTES ON TABLE ABOVE**
COLUMNS: for meanings and CODES (cols. 1, 3, 4, 8), see Codebook (Part 6). Column 1: **Boldface type** = church with over 10% of country's affiliated Christians.

NATIONAL COUNCILS (Column 4, 5th letter).
- G = Liberia Evangelical Fellowship (LEF) (formerly Liberian Ev Fundamental Fellowship, LEFF).
- I = Pentecostal Fellowship Union of Liberia.
- P = Inter-Territorial Episcopal Conference of the Gambia, Liberia & Sierra Leone.

*Other national or plurinational councils.* National Interdenominational Conference of Bishops. Association of Independent Churches of African (supported by Peoples Church, Toronto, Canada). United Pentecostal Assemblies of the World in Liberia & Sierra Leone (HQ Monrovia).

OTHER AFRICAN INDIGENOUS CHURCHES. In addition to immigrant groups from Ghana and Nigeria, there are at least 50 more Liberian-founded churches. The dominant tribe of each, together with date of founding, are given in parentheses below where known. The total includes: Abosso Apostolic Faith Ch of Jesus Christ (Kru, 1938), African Faith Tabernacle Ch, African Glory Prophet Ch Number One (Bassa, 1955), African National Pentecostal Ch (Kru, 1945), Assemblies of God Kissi Ch (Kissi, 1963), Cavalla River Ch (Krahn, 1966), Cherubim & Seraphim (Nigeria), Christ Apostolic Ch (Nigeria), Ch of Heaven (Kru, 1955), Emissaries of Divine Light (Ghana), First United Ch of Jesus Christ (Apostolic) (Jamaica pentecostals), Grace Pentecostal Ch (Kru, 1949), Healing Ch of Christ (Bassa, 1969), House of Prayer (Grebo, 1953), Morning Star Ch of God in Christ (Bassa, 1945), Mount Hermon Holy Ch (Kru, 1969), Mount Sinai Ch (Bassa, 1968), Shepherd looking for Lost Sheep Ch (Bassa, 1966), Twelve Apostles Ch (Bassa, 1956), Universal House of Prayer (Gbande, 1955), Zion Christian Ch (Bassa, 1948). There are in addition a number of other USA Black pentecostal missions, including: Bible Way Chs of Our Lord Jesus Christ World Wide (1958), Ch of the Living God (1947), Kodesh Ch of Immanuel (1956), United Holy Ch of America; there is also the National Baptist Convention of America.

OTHER PROTESTANT DENOMINATIONS. The many smaller bodies are mostly missions from the USA. Among these and other foreign bodies are: American Soul Clinic (1959), Baptist International Missions (1972), Baptist Mid-Missions (Mid-Liberian Mission), Christian Nationals' Evangelism Commission (1965), Christian Reformed Ch, Christian Union General Mission Board (1969), International Gospel League (1947), Voice of Africa Mission (1966), West African Gospel Mission (1954).

UNITING CHURCHES. Negotiations for organic union were under way in 1975 between: United Methodist Ch of Liberia, and Lutheran Ch in Liberia.

**PEOPLES** (ethnolinguistic). Christians: 31.0% Kru, 22.8% Grebo, 18.0% Bassa, 7.5% Kpelle, 5.0% Americo-Liberian (Kwi), 3.5% Ghanaian (Akan) (10,000), 3.5% Loma (Toma), 2.0% Sapo, 1.8% Kissi, 1.0% White (European, USA, British), 0.7% Nigerian (Yoruba), 0.6% Krahn, 0.5% Mano, 0.5% Gio, 0.5% Lebanese Arab, 0.4% Gbande, 0.4% Gola.

**COUNTRY-WIDE TOTALS**
EVANGELIZATION (see Part 5). 1900: 27%. 1970: 91%. 1980: 95%. *Mass evangelism.* Among recent major campaigns: January 1960, Billy Graham 5-day Monrovia crusade (12,800 attenders, 1,297 enquirers); 1978, major United Methodist Church campaign in every city and county. *Radiophonic evangelism.* Annual listeners' letters (1974): 65,821 ELWA. Bible correspondence courses: ELWA (7,089 active students in English courses), ICI (1,312 enrolments).
FOREIGN MISSIONARIES AND PERSONNEL (nationals serving abroad) (1973). Total 14 (8 African indigenous, 4 Catholics (non-Roman), 2 Protestants) in Equatorial Guinea, Guinea, Ivory Coast, Nigeria, Sierra Leone et alia.
FOREIGN MISSIONARIES AND PERSONNEL (aliens from abroad) (1973). Total 753. *From Western world.* 676: 487 Protestants 388 in 39 USA societies, 42 in 2 Sweden societies, 22 in 3 UK societies, 19 in 3 Canada societies, 12 in 1 Norway society, 2 in 2 Australia societies, 1 in 1 Netherlands society, 1 in 1 WGermany society), 139 Roman Catholics, about 40 Black indigenous from USA, 10 Anglicans in 2 USA societies. *From Third World.* 77: 40 African indigenous from Ghana and Nigeria, about 20 Protestants, 10 Roman Catholics, 6 Catholics (non-Roman) from Nigeria, 1 Anglican.
INSTITUTIONS (church-operated) (1973). Total 125, including 50 higher schools (1 minor seminary), 50 medical centres (9 hospitals), 1 radio station, 14 seminaries (10 Protestant, 2 African indigenous, 1 Anglican, 1 RC).
PERIODICALS. About 30 titles (many indigenous).
PERSONNEL. About 2,057 (1,304 national, 753 foreign).
RELIGIOUS LIBRARIES. About 16.
SCRIPTURE DISTRIBUTION (1975). Annual totals: 7,366 Bibles (27% free, 73% subsidized), 15,189 NTs (39% free, 47% subsidized, 13% commercial), 20,400 UBS portions, 19,887 UBS selections. *Translations completed.* Portion: 11 languages since 1838. NT: 3 languages since 1967.
SERVICE AGENCIES. About 35, including CCCI, CEF, CLC, ELWA, LEF(LEFF), LWR, NSCC, SU, UEU, YMCA, YWCA.

**ADDITIONAL DATA ON CHURCHES**
CATHOLIC CHURCH IN LIBERIA. *Catechumens.* The total was 1,034 in 1959; 1,010 in 1961; 912 in 1963; and 846 in 1970. *Annual baptisms* (1972). 78.3% infant, 21.7% adult. *Priests.* The first Liberian was ordained in 1946, others from 1961 onwards. *Brothers.* All expatriates. *Sisters.* Of whom 6 are Liberians. *Seminarians.* Total 4 (1971), studying in Nigeria and Ghana till local seminary opened at Gbarnga in 1974. *Catechists.* Total (1971) 12, mostly part-time and voluntary; (1973) 57 (55 full-time). *Indigenous religious congreg ations.* Nil. *Foreign congregations.* Priests: SMA (Irish and USA provinces), WF. Brothers: Holy Cross, FSC. Sisters: Franciscan Missionaries of Mary, Bernardines, Consolata, Holy Child, et alia.
*Catholic organizations.* The Inter-Territorial Episcopal Conference of Liberia, Sierra Leone and Gambia is a member of SECAM and of the Regional Episcopal Conference of Ghana, Liberia, Sierra Leone and Gambia, the latter having its secretariat in Sierra Leone. There are no national pastoral or presbyteral councils, nor associations of religious personnel. Several lay groups are active: Legion of Mary, Knights of St John, Ladies Auxiliaries, and Catholic Boy Scouts.
The Holy See has diplomatic relations with Liberia and is represented to government and the Catholic hierarchy by a pro-nuncio, who serves also as apostolic delegate to Sierra Leone and the Gambia.
The National Secretariat of Catholic Education is responsible for 30 elementary and junior high schools (12,000 pupils), 5 senior high schools (1,000 pupils) and a teacher training college (50 students). The church sponsors one 100-bed hospital in Monrovia which caters for about 350 out-patients daily, and 5 clinics spread throughout the country. The Torino College of Medicine, founded originally by the Catholic Church, was integrated into the University of Monrovia in 1971. The church's social welfare programme also includes credit unions and co-operatives, orphanages, and rehabilitation of the handicapped.
CHURCH OF THE LORD (ALADURA). By 1976, the Liberia church had become known as the Liberia Province.
EPISCOPAL CHURCH OF LIBERIA. The table above gives statistics for 1970. By 1977, these had increased to: 105 preaching stations, 10,000 communicants, 13,000 baptized, with 32 priests.
LIBERIAN BAPTIST CONVENTION. Full name: Liberia Baptist Missionary and Educational Convention (LBMEC).
LUTHERAN CHURCH IN LIBERIA. *Growth.* 30,000 members by 1977, in 150 congregations.

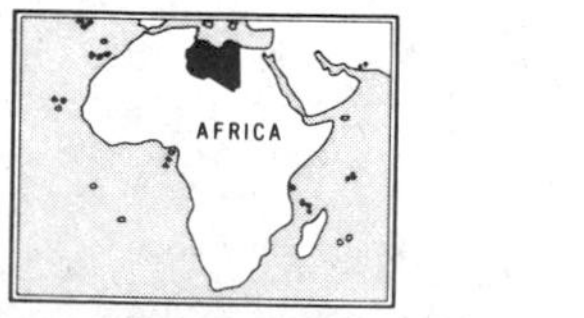


# LIBYA

## SECULAR DATA

**STATE. Official name:** The Socialist People's Libyan Arab Jamahiriya, before 1977, the Libyan Arab Republic (Al-Jumhuriyah al-Arabiya al-Libiyah). Adjective of nationality: Libyan.
**Flag** (shown above right): Green.
**Area:** 1,759,540 sq.km. (679,358 sq.miles). Agricultural land: 5.3%.
**Government:** Socialist military junta, since 1969 (1911 Italian colony, 1943 under British military rule, 1951 Independence as United Kingdom of Libya).
**Official language:** Arabic.
**Chief cities:** capital, Tripoli 213,510 (1964), Bengazi 137,300.
**Political divisions:** 10 Divisions.
**Armed forces** (1976): Total 29,700 regular: army 22,000, navy 2,700, air force 5,000 (129 combat aircraft).

**DEMOGRAPHY. Population:** 2,257,037 (census of 31.VII.1973. For 1970–2000 (UN), see last row of Table 1). Population density (1975): 1/sq.km. (3/sq.mile). Under 15 years: 43%. Growth rate (1975–80): 3.14%per year (births 4.43%, deaths –1.30%). Life expectancy (1975–80): 55.4 years. Household size: 4.7 persons.
**Major languages:** Arabic, English, Italian, Tuareg, Maltese, French, Berber, and 5 others.
**Urban dwellers** (1970): 26.6%. Urban growth rate (1950–70): 4.6% per year.
**Labour force:** 26%.
**Refugees** (1977): About 5,000 Palestinians and others.

Tourists (1974): 295,984.

**ETHNOLINGUISTIC GROUPS:** 79.7% Libyan Arab (with strong Negro element), 7.7% Egyptian Arab (till 1972, then declining by expulsion), 5.8% Oasis & Arabized Berber (Cyrenaican), 2.9% Tunisian Arab, 1.0% Pakistani, 1.0% Palestinian & other Arab, 0.5% Yugoslav, 0.4% Tuareg, 0.3% Italian, 0.2% Tubu, 0.2% USA & British, 0.1% Maltese, 0.1% French, 0.1% Greek, Teda, Zagawa, Arab/Negro (Fezzan), Chinese (600), Jewish, Sudanese, Bulgarian. By 1978, foreign workers had risen to include 160,000 Egyptians, 70,000 Tunisians, 24,000 Pakistanis, 15,000 Yugoslavs, 10,000 Italians and 5,000 British.

**MONEY** (1977). Monetary unit: dinar (= 100 dirhams); US$1 = LD 0.296.
**National income per person:** (1975): US$4,000. (1978): US$6,000.
Average annual family income: US$28,200.
**Inflation:** (1970–74) 4.3% per year (1975: consumer price index 135.
**Cost of living in capital** (1976): index 134 (Washington DC=100). Daily cost of living: US$37.

**HEALTH.** Hospitals: 86 (9,079 beds). Doctors: 1,655. Lepers: 2,800 (1.2 per 1,000). Blind: 10,000. Pyschotics: 16,000. Criminals: 5,222.

**EDUCATION.** Adult literacy: (1954) 13%, (1964) 22%, (1975) 35%. Education rate: 32%. Schools: 1,707. Universities: 1.

**LITERATURE.** Annual new book titles (1972): 218. Newspapers: 6 dailies, 10 non-daily.

**COMMUNICATION** (per 1,000 people). Phones: 18. Radios: 46. TV sets: 2. Daily newspaper circulation: 20 copies.

### TABLE 1.  RELIGIOUS ADHERENTS IN LIBYA

| Year | 1900 | | mid-1970 | | Annual change, 1970–1980 | | | | mid-1975 | | mid-1980 | | 2000 | |
| --- | --- | --- | --- | --- | --- | --- | --- | --- | --- | --- | --- | --- | --- | --- |
| *Name* | Adherents | % | Adherents | % | Natural | Conversion | Total | Rate | Adherents | % | Adherents | % | Adherents | % |
| Muslims | 749,980 | 93.7 | 1,877,610 | 96.9 | 71,185 | −30 | 71,155 | 3.23 | 2,200,470 | 97.6 | 2,589,160 | 98.1 | 4,608,800 | 97.3 |
| **Christians** | **10,020** | **1.2** | **57,750** | **3.0** | **−1,268** | **13** | **−1,255** | **−2.44** | **51,440** | **2.3** | **45,200** | **1.7** | **118,500** | **2.5** |
| crypto-Christians | 5,020 | 0.6 | 50,150 | 2.6 | −1,328 | 13 | −1,315 | −3.02 | 43,540 | 1.9 | 37,000 | 1.4 | 105,500 | 2.2 |
| professing | 5,000 | 0.6 | 7,600 | 0.4 | 60 | 0 | 60 | 0.76 | 7,900 | 0.4 | 8,200 | 0.3 | 13,000 | 0.3 |
| Roman Catholics | 5,000 | 0.6 | 4,000 | 0.2 | 20 | 0 | 20 | 0.49 | 4,100 | 0.2 | 4,200 | 0.2 | 6,000 | 0.1 |
| Orthodox | 0 | 0.0 | 2,000 | 0.1 | 60 | 0 | 60 | 2.61 | 2,300 | 0.1 | 2,600 | 0.1 | 5,000 | 0.1 |
| Protestants | 0 | 0.0 | 1,400 | 0.1 | 0 | 0 | 0 | 0.00 | 1,400 | 0.1 | 1,400 | 0.1 | 2,000 | 0.0 |
| Anglicans | 0 | 0.0 | 200 | 0.0 | −20 | 0 | −20 | −20.00 | 100 | 0.1 | 0 | 0.0 | 0 | 0.0 |
| affiliated | 10,020 | 1.2 | 57,750 | 3.0 | −1,268 | 13 | −1,255 | −2.44 | 51,440 | 2.3 | 45,200 | 1.7 | 118,500 | 2.5 |
| total practising | 8,020 | *80* | 40,420 | *70* | −888 | 10 | −878 | −2.44 | 36,010 | *70* | 31,640 | *70* | 71,100 | *60* |
| non-practising | 2,000 | *20* | 17,330 | *30* | −380 | 3 | −377 | −2.44 | 15,430 | *30* | 13,560 | *30* | 47,400 | *40* |
| Orthodox | 0 | 0.0 | 47,000 | 2.4 | −1,400 | 0 | −1,400 | −3.50 | 40,000 | 1.8 | 33,000 | 1.3 | 100,000 | 2.1 |
| Roman Catholics | 10,000 | 1.2 | 5,850 | 0.3 | 115 | 0 | 115 | 1.80 | 6,400 | 0.3 | 7,000 | 0.3 | 10,000 | 0.2 |
| Protestants | 20 | 0.0 | 3,900 | 0.2 | 0 | 0 | 0 | 0.00 | 3,900 | 0.2 | 3,900 | 0.1 | 5,000 | 0.1 |
| Evangelicals | 10 | 0.0 | 1,600 | 0.1 | 10 | 0 | 10 | 0.61 | 1,650 | 0.1 | 1,700 | 0.1 | 2,100 | 0.0 |
| Arab indigenous | 0 | 0.0 | 620 | 0.0 | 25 | 13 | 38 | 4.75 | 800 | 0.0 | 1,000 | 0.0 | 3,000 | 0.1 |
| Anglicans | 0 | 0.0 | 380 | 0.0 | −8 | 0 | −8 | −2.35 | 340 | 0.0 | 300 | 0.0 | 500 | 0.0 |
| Non-religious | 0 | 0.0 | 2,000 | 0.1 | 75 | 15 | 90 | 3.75 | 2,400 | 0.1 | 2,900 | 0.1 | 9,000 | 0.2 |
| Buddhists | 0 | 0.0 | 400 | 0.0 | 0 | 0 | 0 | 0.00 | 400 | 0.0 | 400 | 0.0 | 700 | 0.0 |
| Baha'is | 0 | 0.0 | 200 | 0.0 | 8 | 2 | 10 | 4.00 | 250 | 0.0 | 300 | 0.0 | 700 | 0.0 |
| Jews | 40,000 | 5.0 | 40 | 0.0 | 0 | 0 | 0 | 0.00 | 40 | 0.0 | 40 | 0.0 | 0 | 0.0 |
| Country's population | 800,000 | 100.0 | 1,938,000 | 100.0 | 70,000 | 0 | 70,000 | 3.10 | 2,255,000 | 100.0 | 2,638,000 | 100.0 | 4,737,000 | 100.0 |

**COLUMNS, ROWS.** For meanings and definitions, see Codebook (Part 6). Note that, by definition, total 'Christians' = professing + crypto-Christians, which also = affiliated + nominal Christians. Percentages may not always total exactly, due to rounding.
**CENSUSES. 30.VII.1954:** 95.5% Muslims, 4.0% Christians (43,888 persons: 37,954 Italians, 1,849 British, 688 Greeks, 590 USA), 0.4% Jews (4,743 persons). **31.VII.1964** (de jure): 97.2% Muslims, 2.4% Christians (38,274 persons: 21,167 Italians, 6,737 USA, 6,672 British, 1,554 Greeks), 0.2% Jews (3,866 persons), 0.1% other religionists.

### NOTES ON RELIGIONS
**ARAB INDIGENOUS.** Isolated radio believers (see Table 2).
**BAHA'IS.** 1973, 1 local spiritual assembly.
**BUDDHISTS.** Chinese.
**COUNTRY'S POPULATION.** At the beginning of 1970 the bulk of the Italian population, and other expatriates, finally left or were expelled. By 1978, large numbers of expatriates had returned as technical advisers and other foreign workers.
**CRYPTO-CHRISTIANS.** Arab Christians. In general the state has tended either to ignore or not to recognize the existence of Arab Christians (mostly from Egypt).
**JEWS.** Decline from 30,000 in 1931 and 35,000 in 1948, to 6,300 in 1964 (all in Tripolitania), due to mass emigration to Israel. Languages used: Hebrew, also Arabic and Italian.
**MUSLIMS.** Almost all Sunnis of the Hanafite and Shafiite rites, with Sanusis (a militant reform order inaugurated in Cyrenaica in 1843; Sunnis of the Malikite rite) still predominant in Cyrenaica. Libyan Berbers, few in number, belong to a rival Ibadi (Kharijite) sect, in Zuwara (12,000) and Jabal Nafusa (30,000) in Tripolitania. *Missionaries.* There is a fluctuating number of Egyptians sent by Al-Azhar University (Cairo). *Haji pilgrims to Mecca.* (1964) 6,000; (1968) 10,444; (1969)

13,547; (1970) 11,835; (1971) 16,861; (1972) 23,774; (1973) 30,705; (1974) 30,715; (1975) 52,718; (1976) 18,057.
**NON-RELIGIOUS.** Expatriate Europeans and some Chinese.
**ORTHODOX.** In the 1964 census, only 8,521 alien Arabs were enumerated. By 1972 the number of immigrant Arabs from Egypt was estimated to be over 150,000, of whom 50,000 were Christians (45,000 Coptic Orthodox). The latter however remained largely unorganized and the Coptic Orthodox Church in Egypt was able to open for them only a handful of parishes with priests before expulsions of Egyptians began in 1974.
**ROMAN CATHOLICS.** Italian settlers since their beginnings in 1912 reached a peak of 110,000 in 1941. After 1945 most were expelled, and in 1963 there were only 22,840 Catholics left in Tripoli, 2,000 in Bengazi and 300 in Derna. By mid-1970 this had dropped further to 5,850.

### NON-CHRISTIAN RELIGIONS. Islam spread to
Libya from Arabia and Egypt in the second half of the 7th century. Almost the entire Libyan population are Sunnis of the Hanafite and Shafiite rites, with Sanusis (Malikite rite) predominant in Cyrenaica. Sanusiya, a militant reform order founded in 1843, plays a significant role in Libyan life. Important Islamic institutions and organizations in Libya are the Faculty of Arabic Language and Islamic Studies of the University of Libya in Bengazi created in 1970 to replace the Ali Sanusi Islamic University; and the Islamic Vocation Association (Jamiat al-Dawah al-Islamiah), founded by the government in Tripoli in 1973, which fosters Islam's international missonary role.

### CHRISTIANITY. In North Africa, Christianity
has had an ancient history, being the scene of the church's early expansion and the home of some of its most distinguished theologians. However, the combination of a failure to convert the Berbers and internal divisions due in part to Donatism weakened the church and made it impotent in the face of Muslim expansion in the 7th century. There are today almost no indigenous professing Christian believers, and Christianity is made up of Catholics and Orthodox

from Greece and the Near East, in addition to a decreasing number of Protestants and Anglicans from Europe and North America. The expulsion of Italian colonists and American and British military personnel, together with Egyptians since 1974, has radically reduced Catholic, Orthodox and Protestant communities.

**CATHOLIC CHURCH.** Before the departure of Italians at the beginning of 1970, the Catholic Church was divided into 4 ecclesiastical jurisdictions: the vicariates of Bengazi, Derna, and Tripoli, and the prefecture of Misurata. In 1969 there were 39,300 faithful of the Latin rite in 23 parishes, served by 30 Franciscan priests, 20 brothers, and 200 sisters of different congregations. By 1972, 3 of the 4 jurisdictions had been closed, leaving the vicariate of Tripoli, and only 2 churches remained open for worship: St Francis in Tripoli and another in the Berka quarter of Bengazi. Between 1970 and 1976, when Egyptians were expelled from Libya en masse,

**Muslims.** Sunni Muslims meet on market day in coastal village of Garabulli 25 miles east of Tripoli.

Coptic Catholics made up a substantial proportion of the Catholic community.

ORTHODOX CHURCHES. During 1970–76 the principal Christian tradition present in Libya was that of the Coptic Orthodox Church. For many years Coptic Orthodox, estimated to number in 1972 up to 45,000 in Libya, had no formal church structures or worship centres. However, following the visit of patriarch Shenouda in 1971, authorization was granted by the government to form 2 Coptic congregations, one in Bengazi using a Greek Orthodox church and another in Tripoli using a former Catholic church. Greek Orthodox, mostly expatriate residents, have organized churches in both Tripoli and Bengazi.

OTHER CHURCHES. The North Africa Mission entered Tripoli in 1889; and for many years an Anglican body, Church Missions to Jews (now the Church's Ministry among the Jews) carried on work in the country. All non-Catholic missionaries were expelled by the Italians in 1936 but were allowed re-entry in 1946 after Libya was placed under United Nations' trusteeship. Seventh-day Adventists followed, and between 1960 and 1970, 10 Protestant churches existed serving the expatriate community, the largest being the Union Church in Tripoli with 1,500 members. Since the 1969 revolution which resulted in the evacuation of British and American military bases, missionaries are no longer permitted, and expatriate Protestants and Anglicans have been greatly reduced in numbers.

In Tripoli 4 congregations continue active: the Union Church which has its own building, Anglicans who use the Union Church building, Southern Baptists who have a rented hall, and the Church of Christ which uses the Baptist hall. In Bengazi, the Anglican community worships in a Catholic church building. All these congregations in both Tripoli and Bengazi are composed of expatriates. The Union Church has been substantially weakened by the exodus of military personnel and oil company employees and the more recent expulsion of Egyptians (including Coptic Evangelicals) in 1976.

Beginning in 1972, the Children of God International, an outgrowth of the Jesus Movement in the USA, have visited Libya on over 12 missions and been received several times by the Muslim president Gaddaffi, whom the group regards as a latter-day prophet, and who has given them permission to stage musical tours, has supported them financially and has even composed a religious song they perform.

**CHURCH AND STATE.** The provisional constitution of 1970 stipulates that 'Islam is the religion of the State' and that 'The State protects freedom of worship according to observed traditions' (Article 2). There are also a number of articles referring explicitly to Islamic tradition, Article 3 dealing with the foundations of the family and Article 8 with inheritance.

The Libyan revolution which came to power on 1 September 1969 has adopted as its national anthem *Allah Akbar* (Allah is Great) and confers upon Islam an ideological role, considering it as a radically different alternative to both capitalism and communism. It insists on total respect for all Islamic religious regulations and traditions. By a 1971 law, the Libyan government called for the submission of all existing laws to the Muslim Sharia (Holy Law), even if this required their abolition. Another 1971 law institutionalized zakat (giving of alms), one of the 5 ritual obligations of the Muslim believer, under the form of an additional tax of 2.5% on land, flocks, money deposits and other possessions. In a speech delivered at Zware on 15 April 1973 to mark the birthday of the Prophet Mohammed, president Gaddaffi, a Muslim fundamentalist, called for the suspension of all existing laws and the implementation of the thoughts of the Prophet. The austerity of life of the chief of state and members of government, as well as that imposed on the entire population (such as the prohibition of alcohol), are due directly to the influence of the Sanusiya.

An agreement between the Holy See and the Libyan government was signed in Tripoli on 10 October 1970 whereby the Catholic Church renounced all its property, including churches, convents, schools, and welfare projects. In return the Libyan government conceded use of 2 churches for worship, and also permission for 10 priests to reside in Libya (6 at Tripoli and 4 at Bengazi) to serve the spiritual needs of Catholics. These church buildings are used by other Christian communities as well. The Ministry of Unity and Foreign Affairs (Wizarat al-Wihda wa al-Kharijia) is the branch of government responsible for all matters relating to Christian churches.

By 1975 the government was once more recognizing the value of foreign missionaries: in 1975, 12 Catholic nurse sisters were invited in by government; and in 1976, 23 sisters and 2 priests arrived from Poland.

**BROADCASTING.** Christian programmes in Arabic can only be heard over foreign international stations, in particular ELWA (Liberia), TWR (Monaco and Cyprus) for 4 hours a week, and Radio Vatican for 3 hours 30 minutes a week.

**BIBLIOGRAPHY**

*Baal, Christ and Mohammed: religion and revolution in North Africa.* J. K. Cooley. New York: Holt, Rinehart & Winston, 1965. 369p.

TABLE 2. ORGANIZED CHURCHES AND DENOMINATIONS IN LIBYA

| Official name 1 | Begun 2 | Type 3 | Counc 4 | Congs 5 | Adults 6 | Affiliated 7 | Names, notes, and other statistics (see Codebook) 8 |
|---|---|---|---|---|---|---|---|
| Anglican Church (D Egypt) | c1900 | A Cen | aw.U. | 2 | 200 | 380 | In Episcopal Ch in Jerusalem & M East. M=ICS(UK). Use of Union building. Expatriates. 2x. |
| Baptist Church in Tripoli | 1965 | P Bap | T.... | 1 | 378 | 500 | M=SBC(USA). Expatriate Americans with oil companies. 2f,17Y. |
| **Catholic Church in Libya:** | 1642 | R Lat | P.SH. | 32 | 3,900 | 5,850 | Italians, French, Egyptians, Maltese. 1969 exodus. C=1+0+1. 15x,110w,4Y,39y. |
| VA Bengasi (Bengazi) | 1927 | R Lat | Pofmc | 1 | 200 | 350 | 1969: 9,971 expatriate Catholics, 11 nationals. One congregation left. Closed. 3x. |
| VA Derna | 1939 | R Lat | Pofmc | 1 | 0 | 0 | 1969: 2,500 expatriate Italian and French Catholics. Closed since 1972. |
| VA Tripoli | 1913 | R Lat | Pofmc | 29 | 1,700 | 3,000 | Decline from 39,300 Catholics (expatriates) in 1969. 10x,100w,38y. |
| PA Misurata | 1939 | R Lat | Pofmc | 1 | 0 | 0 | 1969: 1,146 expatriate Italian and French Catholics. Closed since 1972. |
| Coptic Catholics | c1970 | R Cop | Os | | 2,000 | 2,500 | Egyptian workers resident in Libya. No separate jurisdiction by 1976. |
| Church of Christ in Tripoli | | P Dis | x.... | 1 | 20 | 50 | Among USA military, strong until US Wheelus air base closed. |
| Coptic Evangelical Church | c1968 | P Ref | RwaN. | | 1,000 | 2,500 | Part of the growing Egyptian immigrant worker community. |
| **Coptic Orthodox Ch: D North Africa** | c1968 | O Cop | NwaN. | 10 | 18,000 | 42,000 | Under P Cairo. Egyptian workers. Requisitioned churches, 2 resident priests. |
| Greek Orth P Alexandria: D Carthage | | O Ara | Cw.N. | 16 | 600 | 2,000 | 16 parishes (8 Russian Orthodox chapels). Greeks, Arabs. Archbishop, 6 priests. |
| Isolated radio churches | c1950 | I rad | ..... | 15 | 300 | 620 | Isolated radio believers, mostly students and youths. R=50,T=2200(GMU,ICI,RSB). |
| Seventh-day Adventist Church | c1950 | P Adv | x.... | 1 | 20 | 50 | Formerly in SDA, North African Union. Hospital in Benghazi now commandeered. 37f. |
| Union Church of Tripoli | | P com | ..... | 1 | 400 | 700 | Expatriate Americans, declining rapidly in membership. 1x. |
| Other Orthodox churches | | O | ..... | | 2,000 | 3,000 | Yugoslav and other migrant workers from Serbian Orthodox Church et alia. |
| Other Protestant denominations | | P | ..... | 4 | 50 | 100 | Children of God (1972), NAM (1889; a few believers left), Tripoli Bible Ch, WEC. |
| **Total affiliated (mid-1970)** | | | | **89** | **26,868** | **57,750** | **Total denominations (1970) . . . 12.** |
| **Total affiliated (mid-1975)** | | | | **60** | **23,900** | **51,440** | **Total denominations (1975) . . . 9.** |
| **Total affiliated (mid-1980)** | | | | **50** | **21,000** | **45,200** | **Total denominations (1980) . . . 8.** |

NOTES ON TABLE ABOVE

COLUMNS: for meanings and CODES (cols. 1, 3, 4, 8), see Codebook (Part 6). Column 1: **Boldface type** = churches with over 10% of country's affiliated Christians.

CLOSED CHURCHES. In 1972, 3 Catholic jurisdictions were closed (VA Bengasi, VA Derna, and PA Misurata; with 13,617 expatriate Catholics in 1969); also several independent English-language congregations in Tripoli (Church of Christ, Tripoli Bible Church, Worldwide Evangelization Crusade).

PEOPLES (ethnolinguistic). Christians: 79.0% Egyptian Arab, 5.0% Italian, 3.5% Serbian, 2.4% Maltese, 2.4% USA & British, 2.0% Greek, 2.0% Palestinian Arab, 1.7% French, 1.1% Libyan Arab, Sudanese Arab, Croatian, Bulgarian, Armenian.

COUNTRY-WIDE TOTALS

EVANGELIZATION (see Part 5). 1900: 8%. 1970: 14%. 1980: 18%. *Radiophonic evangelism.* TWR, ELWA, RVOG, Radio Vatican, et alia. Bible correspondence courses: 2,200 enrolled (GMU, ICI, RSB, et alia).

FOREIGN MISSIONARIES AND PERSONNEL (aliens from abroad) (1973). Total 179. *From Western world.* 116: about 75 Roman Catholics, 39 Protestants in 3 USA societies, 2 Anglicans. *From Communist world.* About 3 Roman Catholics (2 from Yugoslavia, 1 Poland). In 1976, a further 25 (23 sisters, 2 priests) arrived from Poland. *From Third World.* 60: about 50 Roman Catholics from Egypt, Palestine, Syria, Lebanon, India et alia, 9 Orthodox from Egypt, 1 Protestant.

PERIODICALS. 2 titles.

PERSONNEL. About 179 (all foreign) in 1973.

SCRIPTURE DISTRIBUTION (1975). Annual totals: 30 Bibles (subsidized).

ADDITIONAL DATA ON CHURCHES

CATHOLIC CHURCH IN LIBYA. In Arabic, al-Kanissa al-Katholikia. *Catholics.* The decline from 39,300 in 1969 is due to expulsion or repatriation of Italians and other Europeans, with the expropriation by government of 35 church buildings. In 1969 there were also about 3,000 Maltese. The only growing community is of Coptic Catholics from Egypt. *Parishes.* Only 2 parishes remained open by 1973. *Mission.* Priests: OFMCap. *Sisters.* In 3 congregations, working in government schools and hospitals: Sisters of Mercy (Maltese), Franciscan Sisters, Franciscan Sisters of Mercy (Italians). In 1975, 12 more nurse sisters (4 Consolata) were invited in by the government, and in 1976, 23 sisters and 2 priests from Poland for work in the hospitals of El-Beida and Bengazi.

*Catholic organizations.* Libya is part of the Episcopal Conference of North Africa, with headquarters in Algiers, which is a member of SECAM. There are no national presbyteral or pastoral councils, no associations of religious personnel and no lay organizations.

The Holy See has no diplomatic relations with Libya. It is represented to the Catholic hierarchy by an apostolic delegate based in Algiers.

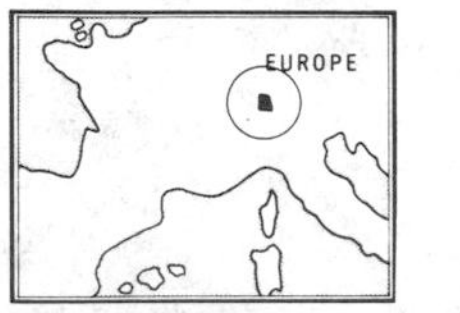


# LIECHTENSTEIN

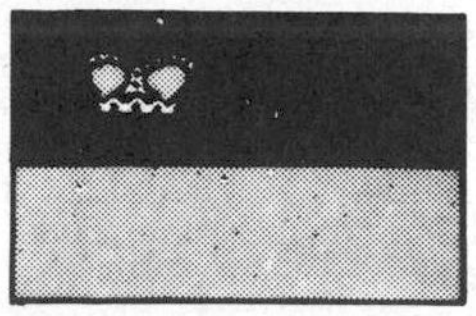

## SECULAR DATA

**STATE. Official name:** The Principality of Liechtenstein (Fürstentum Liechtenstein).
**Flag** (shown above right): Blue and red: gold crown in blue stripe.
**Area:** 157 sq.km. (61 sq.miles) Agricultural land: 56.3%.
**Government:** Constitutional principality, created 1719 (1342 country of Vaduz).
**Legislature:** Diet, 15 members.
**Official language:** German (*Deutsch*).
**Capital:** Vaduz 4,020.
**Armed forces:** Switzerland is responsible for defence; police force, 33.

**DEMOGRAPHY. Population:** 21,350 (census of 1.XII.1970. For 1970–2000 (UN), see last row of Table 1). Population density (1975): 141/sq.km. (366/sq.mile). Under 15 years: 23%. Growth rate (1975–80): 0.88% per year. Household size: 3.8 persons.
**Major languages:** German (Alemannish).
**Urban dwellers** (1970): 28.6%.
**Labour force:** 44%.
**Tourists** (1972): 86,456. (1974) 73,615.

**ETHNOLINGUISTIC GROUPS:** 87% Austrian, 12% Swiss, 0.1% Jewish.

**MONEY** (1977). **Monetary unit:** Swiss franc (= 100 centimes); US$1 = SwFr 2.44.
**National income per person:** US$8,000. Average annual family income: US$30,400.
**Inflation:** (1975) consumer price index 147.

**EDUCATION.** Adult literacy: 98%. Education rate: 45%. Schools: 16.

**LITERATURE.** Periodicals: 9. Newspapers: 1 daily, 2 non-daily.

**COMMUNICATION** (per 1,000 people). Phones: 667. Radios: 225. TV sets: 190. Daily newspaper circulation: 286 copies.

TABLE 1.    RELIGIOUS ADHERENTS IN LIECHTENSTEIN

| Year | 1900 | | mid-1970 | | Annual change, 1970–1980 | | | | mid-1975 | | mid-1980 | | 2000 | |
|---|---|---|---|---|---|---|---|---|---|---|---|---|---|---|
| *Name* | *Adherents* | *%* | *Adherents* | *%* | *Natural* | *Conversion* | *Total* | *Rate* | *Adherents* | *%* | *Adherents* | *%* | *Adherents* | *%* |
| Christians | 9,380 | 99.8 | 20,960 | 98.9 | 197 | −6 | 191 | 0.87 | 21,920 | 98.7 | 22,870 | 98.6 | 27,260 | 97.4 |
| professing | 9,380 | 99.8 | 20,960 | 98.9 | 197 | −6 | 191 | 0.87 | 21,920 | 98.7 | 22,870 | 98.6 | 27,260 | 97.4 |
| Roman Catholics | 9,180 | 97.7 | 19,100 | 90.1 | 178 | −49 | 129 | 0.65 | 19,760 | 89.0 | 20,390 | 87.9 | 23,340 | 83.4 |
| Protestants | 200 | 2.1 | 1,860 | 8.8 | 19 | 43 | 62 | 2.87 | 2,160 | 9.7 | 2,480 | 10.7 | 3,920 | 14.0 |
| nominal | 50 | 0.5 | 575 | 2.7 | 5 | 10 | 15 | 2.27 | 640 | 2.9 | 720 | 3.1 | 1,120 | 4.0 |
| affiliated | 9,330 | 99.2 | 20,385 | 96.1 | 192 | −16 | 176 | 0.83 | 21,280 | 95.8 | 22,150 | 95.5 | 26,140 | 93.4 |
| total practising | 8,860 | *95* | 17,330 | *85* | 163 | −13 | 150 | 0.83 | 18,090 | *85* | 18,830 | *85* | 18,300 | *70* |
| non-practising | 470 | *5* | 3,060 | *15* | 29 | −3 | 26 | 0.82 | 3,190 | *15* | 3,320 | *15* | 7,840 | *30* |
| Roman Catholics | 9,150 | 97.3 | 19,000 | 89.6 | 177 | −52 | 125 | 0.63 | 19,660 | 88.5 | 20,250 | 87.3 | 23,060 | 82.4 |
| Protestants | 180 | 1.9 | 1,385 | 6.5 | 15 | 36 | 51 | 3.18 | 1,620 | 7.3 | 1,900 | 8.2 | 3,080 | 11.0 |
| Evangelicals | 50 | 0.5 | 210 | 1.0 | 2 | 9 | 11 | 4.07 | 270 | 1.2 | 320 | 1.4 | 560 | 2.0 |
| Non-religious | 0 | 0.0 | 170 | 0.8 | 2 | 5 | 7 | 3.50 | 200 | 0.9 | 240 | 1.0 | 560 | 2.0 |
| Baha'is | 0 | 0.0 | 40 | 0.2 | 1 | 1 | 2 | 4.00 | 50 | 0.2 | 60 | 0.3 | 150 | 0.5 |
| Jews | 20 | 0.2 | 30 | 0.1 | 0 | 0 | 0 | 0.00 | 30 | 0.1 | 30 | 0.1 | 30 | 0.1 |
| Country's population | 9,400 | 100.0 | 21,200 | 100.0 | 200 | 0 | 200 | 0.90 | 22,200 | 100.0 | 23,200 | 100.0 | 28,000 | 100.0 |

COLUMNS, ROWS. For meanings and definitions, see Codebook (Part 6). Note that, by definition, total 'Christians' = professing + crypto-Christians, which also = affiliated + nominal Christians. Percentages may not always total exactly, due to rounding. CENSUSES. 1.XII.1960: 92.3% Roman Catholics, 6.8% Protestants, 0.7% non-religious, 0.2% Jews. 1.XII.1970: 90.1% Roman Catholics, 8.8% Protestants, 0.9% others (non-religious, Baha'is), 0.1% Jews (also 4 Old Catholics).

# CHRISTIANITY

**CATHOLIC CHURCH.** As Liechtenstein is surrounded on 3 sides by Switzerland, the development of the Catholic Church in the principality corresponds to that in Switzerland, the earliest Christian contacts taking place during the Roman occupation in the first centuries of the Christian era. At the present time the principality forms a single deanery within the diocese of Chur in Switzerland. In 1972 it consisted of 12 parishes, with 31 priests (10 religious), one Italian mission and several sisters.

**PROTESTANT CHURCHES.** The major Protestant body is the united or interdenominational Evangelical Church in the Principality of Liechtenstein, which consists of one parish with about 1,000 active members. It was originally formed in 1881 by skilled textile workers immigrating from neighbouring countries, most of whom were members of Lutheran or Reformed churches. Following World War II, there was an influx of trained artisans and university graduates to meet the needs of industrial expansion, and the parish now consists of young families occupying relatively high positions in the country. Continuing the tradition of avoiding denominational limitations, they observe a variety of worship services each month. In 1954 the Evangelical Church entered into a patronage agreement (Patronatsvertrag) with the Protestant Church of the Canton of St Gallen in Switzerland. This agreement assures support and help, especially in pastoral appointments, but leaves the church free to arrange its own affairs in conformity with its interdenominational character. A separate Lutheran congregation was formed in 1954 and belongs to the Association of Evangelical Lutheran Churches in Switzerland and the Principality of Liechtenstein, a body of 12,000 Lutherans based in Zurich. There also is a small Seventh-day Adventist community.

**CHURCH AND STATE.** According to the constitution of 1921, 'The Roman Catholic Church is the State church (Landeskirche) and as such enjoys the full protection of the State'; nevertheless, freedom of religion and of conscience is guaranteed to all (Article 37). Article 39 states: 'The exercise of national and political rights is independent of one's religious confession; national duties shall not be prejudiced on account of an individual's religious profession'. Also safeguarded are the rights to ownership and utilization of property by religious communities and groups, for worship, education or charitable activity (Article 38). The state guarantees to protect the 'religious and moral interests' of the populace (Article 14); and in collaboration with family, school, and church, it assumes responsibility for insuring to the younger generation a moral and religious education (Article 15). Religious education is therefore placed under state supervision (Article 16).

In conformity with the law of 1 August 1870 concerning the administration of church property in parishes, such property is administered by a church council composed of the parish priest, members designated by the community council and one member elected by the local citizens.

**Katholische Kirche.** *Left.* Parish church (centre), under Vaduz Castle (left). *Above.* Catholic nun works the fields with 2 peasant women.

TABLE 2.    ORGANIZED CHURCHES AND DENOMINATIONS IN LIECHTENSTEIN

| Official name 1 | Begun 2 | Type 3 | Counc 4 | Congs 5 | Adults 6 | Affiliated 7 | Names, notes, and other statistics (see Codebook) 8 |
|---|---|---|---|---|---|---|---|
| Evangelische Kirche im Fürstentum L | 1881 | P uni | Rwc.. | 1 | 700 | 1,100 | *Ev Ch in L.* Migrant skilled professionals. Linked to Prot Ch of St Gallen. 1x. |
| Evangelisch-Lutherische Kirche | 1954 | P Lut | 1.... | 1 | 150 | 185 | *Assoc of Ev Lutheran Chs in Switzerland & L.* HQ Zurich. 1x,G=6.4%pa,W=20%,3Yy. |
| Katholische Kirche (D Chur) | c 450 | R Lat | b.B.. | 12 | 14,600 | 19,000 | *Catholic Ch in L.* One deanery in D Chur (Switz). One Italian mission. 31nx. |
| Siebenten-Tags-Adventisten | | P Adv | x.... | 1 | 30 | 100 | *SDA. Seventh-day Adventists*, part of German Swiss Conference, Swiss Union Conf. |
| Total affiliated (mid-1970) | | | | 15 | 15,480 | 20,385 | Total denominations (1970) . . . 4. |
| Total affiliated (mid-1975) | | | | 15 | 16,200 | 21,280 | Total denominations (1975) . . . 4. |
| Total affiliated (mid-1980) | | | | 16 | 16,800 | 22,150 | Total denominations (1980) . . . 5. |

**NOTES ON TABLE ABOVE**
COLUMNS: for meanings and CODES (cols. 1, 3, 4, 8), see Codebook (Part 6). Column 1: **Boldface type** = church with over 10% of country's affiliated Christians.

PEOPLES (ethnolinguistic). Christians: 87% Austrian, 12% German-Swiss, Italian, German.

**COUNTRY-WIDE TOTALS**
EVANGELIZATION (see Part 5). 1900: 100%. 1970: 100%. 1980: 100%.
FOREIGN MISSIONARIES AND PERSONNEL (nationals serving abroad) (1973). Total about 10 Roman Catholics (2 in Angola, several in European countries).
FOREIGN MISSIONARIES AND PERSONNEL (aliens from abroad) (1973). Total 23. *From Western world.* 23: about 20

Roman Catholics, 3 Protestants.
PERIODICALS. 3 titles.
PERSONNEL. About 37 (14 national, 23 foreign).
SCRIPTURE DISTRIBUTION (1975). Annual totals: 120 Bibles (17% subsidized, 83% commercial), 90 NTs (67% subsidized, 33% commercial), 100 UBS portions.
SERVICE AGENCIES. About 3.

# LUXEMBOURG

## SECULAR DATA

**STATE. Official name:** The Grand Duchy of Luxembourg (Le Grand-Duché de Luxembourg/Grossherzogtum Luxemburg). Adjective of nationality: Luxembourgeois.
**Flag** (shown above right): Red, white, and light blue stripes.
**Area:** 2,586 sq.km. (998 sq.miles). Agricultural land: 51.0%.
**Government:** Parliamentary constitutional grand duchy, since 1839 (1354 duchy, 1839 autonomy).
**Legislature:** Council of Ministers, 7 members. Chamber of Deputies, 56 members.
**Official languages:** Luxemburgish (*Lezebuurjesh*) and French (*Français*).
**Capital:** Luxembourg-ville 78,270 (1973).
**Political divisions:** 4 Electoral Districts.
**Armed forces** (1976): Total 625 (regular army). Paramilitary forces: 420 gendarmerie.

**DEMOGRAPHY. Population:** 332,434 (census of 31.XII.1970).

For 1970–2000 (UN), see last row of Table 1). Population density (1975): 132/sq.km. (342/sq.mile). Under 15 years: 21%. Growth rate (1975–80): 0.15% per year (births 1.36%, deaths – 1.21%). Life expectancy (1975–80): 71.6 years. Household size: 3.2 persons.
**Major languages:** Luxemburgish, French, Italian, German, English.
**Urban dwellers** (1970): 64.4%. Urban growth rate (1950–70): 1.3% per year.
**Labour force:** 42%.

**ETHNOLINGUISTIC GROUPS:** 81.8% Luxemburger, 18.2% alien (7.3% Italian, 2.4% West German, 2.1% French, 1.8% Belgian, 0.2% Jewish, Dutch, UK, USA, Greek, Russian, Danish).

**MONEY** (1977). **Monetary unit:** franc (= 100 centimes); US$1 = LFr 36.50.
**National income per person:** US$5,050. Average annual family

income: US$16,160.
**Inflation:** (1970–74) 6.3% per year (1975: consumer price index 152).
**Cost of living in capital** (1976): index 134 (Washington DC=100). Daily cost of living: US$45.

**HEALTH.** Hospitals: 30 (3,948 beds). Doctors: 375. Blind: 204. Psychotics: 3,000. Criminals: 6,406.

**EDUCATION.** Adult literacy: 98%. Education rate: 48%. Schools: 1,667. Universities: 1.

**LITERATURE.** Annual new book titles (1971): 180. Periodicals: 224. Scientific journals: 30. Newspapers: 7 dailies, 1 non-daily.

**COMMUNICATION** (per 1,000 people). Phones: 384. Radios: 263. TV sets: 208. Daily newspaper circulation: 463 copies.

TABLE 1.    RELIGIOUS ADHERENTS IN LUXEMBOURG

| Year | 1900 | | mid-1970 | | Annual change, 1970–1980 | | | | mid-1975 | | mid-1980 | | 2000 | |
|---|---|---|---|---|---|---|---|---|---|---|---|---|---|---|
| *Name* | *Adherents* | *%* | *Adherents* | *%* | *Natural* | *Conversion* | *Total* | *Rate* | *Adherents* | *%* | *Adherents* | *%* | *Adherents* | *%* |
| **Christians** | **234,560** | **99.4** | **323,000** | **95.3** | **569** | **−302** | **267** | **0.08** | **324,290** | **94.8** | **325,670** | **94.4** | **325,170** | **92.1** |
| professing | 234,560 | 99.4 | 323,000 | 95.3 | 569 | −302 | 267 | 0.08 | 324,290 | 94.8 | 325,670 | 94.4 | 325,170 | 92.1 |
| Roman Catholics | 232,390 | 98.5 | 318,300 | 93.9 | 560 | −300 | 260 | 0.08 | 319,560 | 93.4 | 320,900 | 93.0 | 319,790 | 90.6 |
| Evangelical Catholics | 1,130 | 0.5 | 3,773 | 1.1 | 6 | 79 | 85 | 2.02 | 4,200 | 1.2 | 4,620 | 1.3 | 6,100 | 1.7 |
| Protestants | 2,170 | 0.9 | 3,950 | 1.2 | 7 | 0 | 7 | 0.18 | 3,980 | 1.2 | 4,020 | 1.2 | 4,600 | 1.3 |
| Anglicans | 0 | 0.0 | 400 | 0.1 | 1 | −1 | 0 | 0.00 | 400 | 0.1 | 400 | 0.1 | 420 | 0.1 |
| Orthodox | 0 | 0.0 | 350 | 0.1 | 1 | −1 | 0 | 0.00 | 350 | 0.1 | 350 | 0.1 | 360 | 0.1 |
| nominal | 3,300 | 1.4 | 17,527 | 5.2 | 36 | 551 | 587 | 2.86 | 20,500 | 6.0 | 23,400 | 6.8 | 35,300 | 10.0 |
| affiliated | 231,260 | 98.0 | 305,473 | 90.1 | 533 | −853 | −320 | −0.11 | 303,790 | 88.8 | 302,270 | 87.6 | 289,870 | 82.1 |
| total practising | 219,700 | *95* | 277,980 | *91* | 480 | −1,376 | −896 | −0.33 | 273,410 | *90* | 269,020 | *89* | 217,400 | *75* |
| non-practising | 11,560 | *5* | 27,490 | *9* | 53 | 523 | 576 | 1.90 | 30,380 | *10* | 33,250 | *11* | 72,470 | *25* |
| Roman Catholics | 227,960 | 96.6 | 296,500 | 87.5 | 517 | −929 | −412 | −0.14 | 294,360 | 86.1 | 292,380 | 84.7 | 277,850 | 78.7 |
| Protestants | 3,300 | 1.4 | 6,923 | 2.0 | 12 | 20 | 32 | 0.45 | 7,080 | 2.1 | 7,240 | 2.1 | 8,100 | 2.3 |
| Evangelicals | 1,900 | 0.8 | 1,400 | 0.4 | 2 | 8 | 10 | 0.69 | 1,450 | 0.4 | 1,500 | 0.4 | 1,700 | 0.5 |
| Marginal Protestants | 0 | 0.0 | 1,000 | 0.3 | 2 | 58 | 60 | 4.62 | 1,300 | 0.4 | 1,600 | 0.5 | 2,800 | 0.8 |
| Catholics (non-Roman) | 0 | 0.0 | 500 | 0.1 | 1 | −1 | 0 | 0.00 | 500 | 0.1 | 500 | 0.1 | 540 | 0.2 |
| Orthodox | 0 | 0.0 | 350 | 0.1 | 1 | −1 | 0 | 0.00 | 350 | 0.1 | 350 | 0.1 | 360 | 0.1 |
| Anglicans | 0 | 0.0 | 200 | 0.1 | 0 | 0 | 0 | 0.00 | 200 | 0.1 | 200 | 0.1 | 220 | 0.1 |
| **Non-religious** | **100** | **0.0** | **10,800** | **3.2** | **21** | **209** | **230** | **1.92** | **12,000** | **3.5** | **13,100** | **3.8** | **17,700** | **5.0** |
| Atheists | 0 | 0.0 | 3,000 | 0.9 | 6 | 74 | 80 | 2.35 | 3,400 | 1.0 | 3,800 | 1.1 | 7,000 | 2.0 |
| Baha'is | 0 | 0.0 | 1,000 | 0.3 | 2 | 10 | 12 | 1.13 | 1,060 | 0.3 | 1,120 | 0.3 | 1,400 | 0.4 |
| Jews | 1,210 | 0.5 | 700 | 0.2 | 1 | 0 | 1 | 0.14 | 700 | 0.2 | 710 | 0.2 | 730 | 0.2 |
| Other religionists | 80 | 0.0 | 500 | 0.1 | 1 | 9 | 10 | 1.82 | 550 | 0.2 | 600 | 0.2 | 1,000 | 0.3 |
| **Country's population** | **235,950** | **100.0** | **339,000** | **100.0** | **600** | **0** | **600** | **0.18** | **342,000** | **100.0** | **345,000** | **100.0** | **353,000** | **100.0** |

COLUMNS, ROWS. For meanings and definitions, see Codebook (Part 6). Note that, by definition, total 'Christians' = professing + crypto-Christians, which also = affiliated + nominal Christians. Percentages may not always total exactly, due to rounding.
CENSUSES. **1871:** 99.5% Roman Catholics, 0.3% Jews, 0.2% Protestants. **1.XII.1900:** 98.5% Roman Catholics, 0.9% Protestants, 0.5% Jews. **1922:** 97.4% Roman Catholics, 1.1% Protestants, 0.5% Jews. **1935:** 97.0% Roman Catholics, 1.1% Protestants, 1.1% Jews. **31.XII.1947** (de jure): 98.3% Roman Catholics, 0.9% Protestants, 0.3% Jews, 0.2% non-religious, 0.2% other religionists. **31.XII.1960** (de jure): 98.2% Roman Catholics, 1.0% Protestants, 0.2% Catholics (non-Roman), 0.2% Jews, 0.2% non-religious, 0.1% marginal Protestants,

0.1% Orthodox. **31.XII.1970:** 93.9% Roman Catholics, 4.1% non-religious and atheists, 1.2% Protestants, 0.2% Jews, 0.6% other Christians and non-Christian religionists.

NOTES ON RELIGIONS
ATHEISTS. Parti Communiste de Luxembourg (PCL) (legal; pro-Soviet): membership (1970) 500, (1974) 1,000; Communist voters (election of I.1959)220,425 (9.1% of all votes), (15.XII.1968) 402,610 (15.5% of all votes). Communists are mostly urban, and are found in the heavily industrialized south near the French border. Many consider themselves still Roman Catholics.
BAHA'IS. Growth from 4 local spiritual assemblies (1964) to 7 (1973).
EVANGELICAL CATHOLICS. This term (the term Protestant

might also be used) is used here to describe persons who are affiliated to churches termed Evangélique by state or society (Protestant, marginal Protestant, Anglican), but who in government censuses or polls are regarded as, or profess to be, Roman Catholics.
OTHER RELIGIONISTS. Recent immigrants from a variety of non-Christian bodies.
PRACTISING CHRISTIANS. February 1970: 9% of population attend church several times a week, 43% once a week, 30% from time to time, 17% never, 1% non-religious.
PROTESTANTS. In the 20th century there has been a gradual increase in the number of Protestants (and other non-Catholics) largely due to immigration. Many however remain nominal only and are unaffiliated to churches.

**NON-CHRISTIAN RELIGIONS. Baha'i** has a small following in 7 local spiritual assemblies.
**Judaism,** with a population of 2,000 in 1940, was decimated by the Nazi occupation in World War II. The Jewish community numbered 700 in 1970 of whom 30% were non-citizens.

## CHRISTIANITY
CATHOLIC CHURCH. Catholicism, organized in Luxembourg by the French missionary Willibrord who built the monastery of Echternach in 698, is the traditional religion of Luxembourg, although the proportion of professing Catholics has decreased slightly since World War II. Catholics represented 93.9% of the total population in the census of 1970 as contrasted with 98.3% in 1947. The role played by Christian labour unions, the Christian Socialist Party (which has been in power for more than 50 years and claims to represent the 'social doctrine of the church') and the newspaper *Luxemburger Wort* (the largest daily in the country whose 70,000 copies are said to reach 80% of all Luxembourg readers), all witness to the institutional force of Catholicism in the Grand Duchy. The diocese of Luxembourg is administratively directly under the Holy See.
OTHER CHURCHES. The Protestant community is a small minority, composed mostly of non-citizens or those of foreign extraction whose numbers have grown slightly with the founding of the European Economic Community. There are English, Dutch, French and German-speaking congregations in the country. Protestants are found mostly in the urban

**Eglise Catholique, Diocèse de Luxembourg.** Postage stamp commemorating 1870 founding of Diocese.

areas of Luxembourg city and in the mining basin. The largest denomination is the Protestant Church of the Grand Duchy, which is Lutheran and Reformed in tradition and owes its origin to Prussian soldiers who occupied Luxembourg after 1813. German Mennonites built farms near Echternach in eastern

Luxembourg in 1844 and since 1951 American Mennonite missionaries have carried on urban industrial work in Esch-sur-Alzette and Dudelange. Of the denominations established more recently, most success has been recorded by Jehovah's Witnesses and the New Apostolic Church.

Small Russian and Greek Orthodox groups also exist.

**CHURCH AND STATE.** The Napoleon concordat of 1801, concluded well before the independence of the country in 1839, has never been expressly abolished, with the exception of a few articles which have been superseded by subsequent laws. Nevertheless, because the context of the document has little utility today, one may conclude that for all practical purposes the concordat no longer exists.

The legal status of the churches, as found in the constitution of 1868 (Articles 19, 20, 21, 26) and other legislative texts, follows essentially the provisions of the constitution of Belgium: reciprocal independence of state and church and protection of the freedom of the latter, payment of clergy by the state, and the like. The only difference is the law of 30 April 1873 concerning the nomination of the Catholic bishop, who must pledge his oath to the crown, and the recognition of the Bishopric of Luxembourg created in 1870. Article 26 of the constitution, which provides that 'the establishment of all religious corporations must be authorized by law', has given rise to divergent interpretations. However, ancient practice dictates that legal authorization is only required for obtaining juridical personality. In such cases, where the buying and selling of property is involved, the state treats religious congregations in the same way as public benevolent organizations.

In state primary education, a course in the Catholic religion is obligatory, except where parents specifically request that their children be excused. In secondary schools, since 1968 parents have been able to choose between a course in the Catholic religion (85% so choose), non-confessional ethics (12.5%) or no course at all (2.5%). Beyond its role in the secondary education of girls, the Catholic Church has not generally established schools. However, one of the five persons termed curators exercising supervision over state schools represents the Catholic Church. Moreover, 5 'episcopal dormitories' are attached to the country's main secondary schools and many

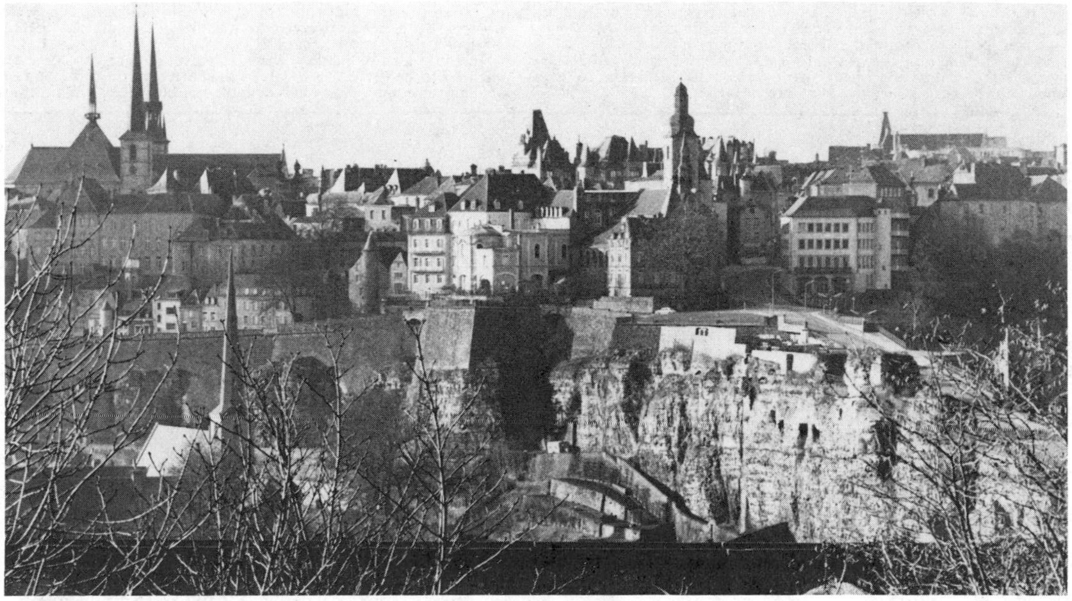

**Eglise Catholique.** Capital city with (left) late-Gothic Catholic Cathedral of Notre-Dame, built 1613-21, and other churches. During the Octave (national pilgrimage) for 2 weeks after 3rd Sunday after Easter, tens of thousands flock to its miraculous shrine.

such schools have priests teaching both secular and religious courses.

Ecclesiastical affairs are handled by the Ministry of Religions (Ministère des Cultes).

**INTERDENOMINATIONAL ORGANIZATIONS.** The Luxembourg Interconfessional Association, founded in 1965 as the Interconfessional Luxembourg Committee and reorganized in 1970, brings together Catholics, Protestants and Jews for the study of common problems and to promote mutual understanding. The association, which is a member of the International Council of Christians and Jews in London, enjoys the moral and financial support of the 3 communities, each of which appoints to the association a theological counsellor. There is also an Ecumenical Homestead (Oekumenische Heimstätte) run by Protestants, and the Benedictine abbey of Cleraux serves as a centre for study and reflection oriented towards the Scandinavian countries.

**BROADCASTING.** Radio Luxembourg, the world's most powerful commercial radio station, has long been known for its international religious broadcasting, with programmes on Tuesdays, Wednesdays, Thursdays and Saturdays in English, German, Slovak and other languages. Global Gospel Broadcasts (USA) have had religious programmes in French since beginning in 1946. For Catholics, Luxembourg is a member of UNDA.

**BIBLIOGRAPHY**

*Annuaire diocésain de Luxembourg, 1971.* Luxembourg-Ville: Evêché, 1971.

TABLE 2. ORGANIZED CHURCHES AND DENOMINATIONS IN LUXEMBOURG

| Official name 1 | Begun 2 | Type 3 | Counc 4 | Congs 5 | Adults 6 | Affiliated 7 | Names, notes, and other statistics (see Codebook) 8 |
|---|---|---|---|---|---|---|---|
| Communauté des Protestants CECA | c1960 | P LuR | ..... | 3 | 150 | 250 | *Protestant Community for CECA*. In capital. Mostly Germans. 1n,W=20%,10Yy,31z. |
| Communauté Protestante Anglaise | | P com | ..... | 1 | 100 | 200 | English-speaking Protestant Community. Expatriates, mostly temporary residents. |
| Eglise Adventiste du Septième Jour | c1900 | P Adv | x.... | 1 | 19 | 50 | *SDA. Seventh-day Adventists, Belgium-Luxembourg Conference*. 1x,W=99%,3Y. |
| Eglise Anglicane (J Fulham) | c1910 | A plu | awc.. | 1 | 100 | 200 | *Anglican Ch.* English-speaking chaplaincy, for 900 UK citizens. 1 chapel. |
| **Eglise Catholique: D Luxembourg** | c 250 | R Lat | bzB.h | 274 | 234,200 | 296,500 | *Cath Ch. Katoulesch Kiirch*. C=8+2+17. 535nx,149m,1597w,1p,1q,1s(20),W=46%,4318Yy. |
| Eglise Mennonite | c1830 | P Men | G.... | 4 | 65 | 200 | *Mennonite Ch.* M=EMBMC(USA). Agricultural, German-speaking. 2x,2f,1k,W=67%,5Y,4z. |
| Eglise Néo-Apostolique | | C CAp | x.... | | 350 | 400 | *New Apostolic Ch.* Schism ex Catholic Apostolic Ch. World HQ Dortmund (Germany). |
| Eglise Orthodoxe Grecque (D Belgique) | | O Gre | Cwc.. | 1 | 150 | 200 | *D Belgique, Hollande et Luxembourg. Greek Orthodox Ch.* Under EP Constantinople. |
| Eglise Orthodoxe Russe Hors-Frontières | | O Sla | x.... | 1 | 100 | 150 | *Russian Orthodox Ch Outside of Russia*. M=ROCOR(NewYork,USA). Russian exiles. |
| Eglise Protestante du Canton d'Esch | | P ind | ..... | 3 | 200 | 400 | *Consistory of the Protestant Ch of Esch Canton*. HQ Esch-sur-Alzette. Independent. |
| Eglise Protestante du Grand-Duché de L | 1813 | P LuR | .v..h | 8 | 3,000 | 4,843 | *Protestant Ch.* 1918 influx from Netherlands. A state church. 85% Reformed. 4n. |
| Eglise Protestante Européenne | | P com | ..... | 1 | 100 | 200 | *European Protestant Ch* (French-speaking). Expatriates, mostly temporary residents. |
| Eglise Protestante Néerlandaise | 1958 | P Ref | ..... | 1 | 42 | 80 | *Nederlandse Protestantse Gemeenschap*. Dutch. HQ Muhlenbach. 1x,W=56%,8Yy,2z. |
| Mission Intérieure au Luxembourg | | P ind | ..... | 1 | 100 | 200 | *Inner Luxembourg Mission*. Independent body with congregation in Luxembourg city. |
| Témoins de Jéhovah | 1929 | M Jeh | x.... | 13 | 591 | 1,000 | *Jehovah's Witnesses. Watch Tower*. First activity 1929, subsequent expansion. 37Y. |
| Other Protestant denominations | | P | ..... | | 200 | 500 | Total about 10 (see list below). |
| Other Catholic (non-Roman) churches | | C | ..... | | 50 | 100 | Including: Reformiert-Apostolischen Gemeindebund (schism ex New Apostolic Ch). |
| **Total affiliated (mid-1970)** | | | | **330** | **239,517** | **305,473** | **Total denominations (1970) . . . 25.** |
| **Total affiliated (mid-1975)** | | | | **333** | **238,300** | **303,790** | **Total denominations (1975) . . . 27.** |
| **Total affiliated (mid-1980)** | | | | **336** | **237,100** | **302,270** | **Total denominations (1980) . . . 29.** |

NOTES ON TABLE ABOVE

COLUMNS: for meanings and CODES (cols. 1, 3, 4, 8), see Codebook (Part 6). Column 1: **Boldface type** = church with over 10% of country's affiliated Christians.

NATIONAL COUNCILS (Column 4, 5th letter).

h = Association Interconfessionnelle du Luxembourg (formerly Comité Interconfessionnelle Luxembourgeois) (Luxembourg Interconfessional Association); includes also Jews.

OTHER PROTESTANT DENOMINATIONS. These small groups include: Assemblies of God, Christian Ch of North America (Pentecostal), Eglise Libre du Grand-Duché, Free Ev Ch, Worldwide European Fellowship, and a few chaplaincies and union congregations for other language groups.

PEOPLES (ethnolinguistic). Christians: 82% Luxemburger, 18% alien (7.3% Italian, 2.4% West German, 2.1% French, 1.8% Belgian, 1.8% British and USA White, 0.9% Dutch, 0.1% Greek, Russian, Danish).

COUNTRY-WIDE TOTALS

EVANGELIZATION (see Part 5). 1900: 100%. 1970: 100%. 1980: 100%.

FOREIGN MISSIONARIES AND PERSONNEL (nationals serving abroad) (1973). Total about 90 Roman Catholics serving in Europe, Africa et alia.

FOREIGN MISSIONARIES AND PERSONNEL (aliens from abroad) (1973). Total 32. *From Western world.* 32: about 20 Roman Catholics, 11 Protestants (6 in 3 USA societies, 2 in 1 UK society), 1 Anglican.

INSTITUTIONS (church-operated) (1973). Total 25, including 8 higher schools, 12 medical centres (hospitals), 2 religious communities, 1 seminary (RC).

PERIODICALS. About 25 titles.

PERSONNEL. About 2,312 (2,280 national, 32 foreign).

RELIGIOUS LIBRARIES. About 10.

SCRIPTURE DISTRIBUTION. (1975) Annual totals; 2,000 Bibles (8% subsidized, 92% commercial), 1,500 NTs (67% subsidized, 33% commercial), 1,000 UBS portions.

SERVICE AGENCIES. About 45, including ACE, ACHPF, ACIEMP, ACISJF, ALUC, CNAL, CNM, JAC/F, JBJW, JEC/F, JOC/F, LCGV, UIRF.

ADDITIONAL DATA ON CHURCHES

EGLISE CATHOLIQUE. In German: Katholische Kirche, Bistum Luxemburg. In Luxembourger language: Katoulesch Kiirch, Letzebuurger Diözes. The diocese was founded in 1870. The south of this missionary diocese is heavily industrialized. In 1955 a European Parish was founded for CECA officials. *Catholics.* About 10% expatriate. *Annual baptisms.* (1972) 100% infants, no adults. *Personnel.* About 99% nationals, 1% expatriates. *Priests.* 436 secular, 99 religious. There are many chaplains to immigrant workers. *Seminaries.* One secular, one for religious clergy. *Religious orders and congregations.* Priests: 33 OSB, 28 SCJ, 11 CSSR, 9 SJ, 7 PB(WF), 5 CS, 3 OMI, 3 SDB. Brothers: 12 FSC, 10 Frères de la Miséricorde. Sisters (with over 100 professed): 501 Soeurs de Ste-Elisabeth, 384 Soeurs de la Doctrine Chrétienne, 338 Franciscaines de la Miséricorde, 176 Tiers-Ordre de Notre-Dame du Mont-Carmel.

*Catholic organizations.* There is no episcopal conference, but the diocese is part of the CCEE. A diocesan synod, which in Luxembourg corresponds to a national pastoral council, was opened in 1972. At its first session there were 191 members, of whom 88 were diocesan clergy and 8 religious personnel. The synod was preceded by extensive consultations involving the whole population (Catholic and non-Catholic) of over 16 years of age, with remarkably high participation through questionnaire replies (45%). A Presbyteral Council has also been formed consisting of 18 elected, 6 appointed and 2 ex-officio members. One association for religious personnel has been formed: the Union of Feminine Institutes (Union des Instituts Féminins). The National Council for the Lay Apostolate (Conseil National pour l'Apostolat des Laïcs) co-ordinates the activities of male and female Catholic Action with their specialized movements, those for youth (JAC/F, JEC/F, JOC/F, Scouts and Guides), Catholic Action of Children (Action Catholique de l'Enfance) and Luxembourg Action of Catholic University Students (Action Luxembourgeoise des Universitaires Catholiques, ALUC).

The Holy See has diplomatic relations with Luxembourg and is represented to government and the Catholic hierarchy by a nuncio based in Brussels, Belgium.

An international organization having its headquarters in the Grand Duchy is the International Catholic Association for the Study of Medical Psychology (Association Catholique Internationale d'Etudes Médico-Psychologiques, ACIEMP), founded in 1949 as the International Catholic Congress of Psychiatry and Clinical Psychology, with its present name and statutes adopted in 1957. The association has individual members in 22 countries.

An important organization for social action is the Luxembourg Christian Trade Union (Letzeburger Chreschtleche Gewerkschaftsbond). Concern for foreign missionary work is promoted and co-ordinated through the National Council for Missions (Conseil National pour les Missions).

Although it has the right to establish whatever schools it wishes, the Catholic Church has confined its attention to the education of girls. Catholic nuns are in fact responsible for 50%

of all secondary education of girls in Luxembourg, for which no state subsidies are received. In addition the church has built a small girls' primary school.

In the realm of medical care, 12 hospitals are run by sisters with 1,215 beds (28.2% of all in the nation); and Catholic nuns also provide major services in most public medical institutions.

Relief and charity work is co-ordinated by the Office of Charity (Office de Charité); while the principal Catholic organization for development assistance is Bridderlech Delen, which is a member of CIDSE in Belgium.

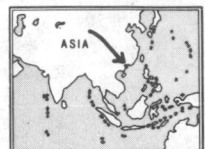

# MACAO

## SECULAR DATA

**STATE. Official name:** The Province of Macao (A Província de Macau).
**Flag** (shown above right): That of Portugal.
**Area:** 16 sq.km. (6 sq.miles). Agricultural land: 10.0%.
**Government:** Overseas province of Portugal, since 1952 (1557 Portuguese colony).
**Official language:** Portuguese (*Português*).
**Capital:** Macao City 241,410 (1970).
**Political divisions:** 2 Wards.
**Armed forces** (1976): Portuguese.

**DEMOGRAPHY. Population:** 248,636 (census of 15.XII.1970. For 1970–2000 (UN), see last row of Table 1). Population density (1975): 16,938/sq.km. (43,868/sq.mile). Under 15 years: 41%. Growth rate (1975–80): 1.54% per year. Household size: 5.0 persons.
**Major languages:** Chinese (Cantonese), Portuguese, Burmese, English.
**Urban dwellers** (1970): 100.0%. Urban growth rate (1950–70): 2.6% per year.
**Labour force:** 27%.
**Refugees** (1977): 25,000 from People's Republic of China, 10,000 from Burma.
**Tourists** (1973): 2,500,000, especially Chinese and Japanese (to gambling casinos).

**ETHNOLINGUISTIC GROUPS:** 96.6% Chinese (including 4% Burmese-speaking, & many other refugees), 2.7% Macanese (Eurasian, Portuguese-Chinese), 0.4% Portuguese, 0.3% British, Indonesian, USA White.

**MONEY** (1977). **Monetary unit:** pataca (= 100 avos); US$1 =

Pat 6.15.
**National income per person:** US$200. Average annual family income: US$1,000.
**Cost of living in capital** (1976): Daily cost of living: US$20.

**HEALTH.** Hospitals: 6 (1,275 beds). Doctors: 104. Lepers: 610 (2.3 per 1,000). Blind: 800. Psychotics: 2,400. Drug addicts: over 1,000 (800 morphine addicts).

**EDUCATION.** Adult literacy: (1950) 53%, (1970) 79%. Schools: 117 (84 elementary, 33 secondary).

**LITERATURE.** Newspapers: 7 dailies, 1 non-daily.

**COMMUNICATION** (per 1,000 people). Phones: 36. Radios: 47. Daily newspaper circulation: 114 copies.

### TABLE 1. RELIGIOUS ADHERENTS IN MACAO

| Year | 1900 | | mid-1970 | | Annual change, 1970–1980 | | | | mid-1975 | | mid-1980 | | 2000 | |
| --- | --- | --- | --- | --- | --- | --- | --- | --- | --- | --- | --- | --- | --- | --- |
| Name | Adherents | % | Adherents | % | Natural | Conversion | Total | Rate | Adherents | % | Adherents | % | Adherents | % |
| Chinese folk-religionists | 52,600 | 82.2 | 145,830 | 58.8 | 2,737 | −1,429 | 1,308 | 0.85 | 153,520 | 56.6 | 158,910 | 54.4 | 167,800 | 45.1 |
| Buddhists | 6,400 | 10.0 | 37,900 | 15.3 | 677 | 63 | 740 | 1.77 | 41,700 | 15.4 | 45,300 | 15.5 | 59,100 | 15.9 |
| **Christians** | **5,000** | **7.8** | **31,993** | **12.9** | **312** | **122** | **434** | **1.26** | **34,290** | **12.7** | **36,330** | **12.4** | **44,100** | **11.8** |
| crypto-Christians | 1,000 | 1.6 | 6,733 | 2.7 | 176 | 44 | 220 | 2.82 | 7,790 | 2.9 | 8,930 | 3.0 | 12,800 | 3.4 |
| professing | 4,000 | 6.2 | 25,260 | 10.2 | 136 | 78 | 214 | 0.81 | 26,500 | 9.8 | 27,400 | 9.4 | 31,300 | 8.4 |
| Roman Catholics | 4,000 | 6.2 | 23,360 | 9.4 | 134 | 100 | 234 | 0.95 | 24,700 | 9.1 | 25,700 | 8.8 | 29,800 | 8.0 |
| Protestants | 0 | 0.0 | 1,800 | 0.7 | 0 | −20 | −20 | −1.18 | 1,700 | 0.6 | 1,600 | 0.5 | 1,300 | 0.3 |
| Anglicans | 0 | 0.0 | 100 | 0.0 | 2 | −2 | 0 | 0.00 | 100 | 0.0 | 100 | 0.0 | 200 | 0.1 |
| affiliated | 5,000 | 7.8 | 31,993 | 12.9 | 312 | 122 | 434 | 1.26 | 34,290 | 12.7 | 36,330 | 12.4 | 44,100 | 11.8 |
| total practising | 4,500 | 90 | 25,590 | 80 | 250 | 97 | 347 | 1.26 | 27,430 | 80 | 29,060 | 80 | 30,870 | 70 |
| non-practising | 500 | 10 | 6,400 | 20 | 62 | 25 | 87 | 1.26 | 6,860 | 20 | 7,270 | 20 | 13,230 | 30 |
| Roman Catholics | 5,000 | 7.8 | 27,000 | 10.9 | 270 | 100 | 370 | 1.27 | 29,000 | 10.7 | 30,700 | 10.5 | 37,200 | 10.0 |
| Protestants | 0 | 0.0 | 4,543 | 1.8 | 36 | 20 | 56 | 1.17 | 4,800 | 1.8 | 5,100 | 1.7 | 6,000 | 1.6 |
| Evangelicals | 0 | 0.0 | 4,200 | 1.7 | 33 | 17 | 50 | 1.14 | 4,400 | 1.6 | 4,700 | 1.6 | 5,500 | 1.5 |
| Chinese indigenous | 0 | 0.0 | 200 | 0.1 | 4 | 2 | 6 | 2.61 | 230 | 0.1 | 260 | 0.1 | 500 | 0.1 |
| Anglicans | 0 | 0.0 | 200 | 0.1 | 2 | −2 | 0 | 0.00 | 200 | 0.1 | 200 | 0.1 | 300 | 0.1 |
| Marginal Protestants | 0 | 0.0 | 50 | 0.0 | 0 | 2 | 2 | 3.33 | 60 | 0.0 | 70 | 0.0 | 100 | 0.0 |
| Non-religious | 0 | 0.0 | 24,560 | 9.9 | 528 | 1,136 | 1,664 | 5.12 | 32,500 | 12.0 | 41,200 | 14.1 | 83,700 | 22.5 |
| Atheists | 0 | 0.0 | 5,000 | 2.0 | 97 | 103 | 200 | 3.33 | 6,000 | 2.2 | 7,000 | 2.4 | 13,000 | 3.5 |
| Muslims | 0 | 0.0 | 110 | 0.0 | 2 | 0 | 2 | 1.62 | 120 | 0.0 | 130 | 0.0 | 100 | 0.0 |
| Baha'is | 0 | 0.0 | 107 | 0.0 | 2 | 0 | 2 | 1.92 | 120 | 0.0 | 130 | 0.0 | 200 | 0.1 |
| Other religionists | 0 | 0.0 | 2,500 | 1.0 | 45 | 5 | 50 | 1.82 | 2,750 | 1.0 | 3,000 | 1.0 | 4,000 | 1.1 |
| Country's population | 64,000 | 100.0 | 248,000 | 100.0 | 4,400 | 0 | 4,400 | 1.62 | 271,000 | 100.0 | 292,000 | 100.0 | 372,000 | 100.0 |

**COLUMNS, ROWS.** For meanings and definitions, see Codebook (Part 6). Note that, by definition, total 'Christians' = professing + crypto-Christians, which also = affiliated + nominal Christians. Percentages may not always total exactly, due to rounding.
**CENSUSES. 15.XII.1960:** 71.0% Chinese folk-religionists and Buddhists, 17.0% non-religious and atheists (and some Chinese folk-religionists), 10.0% Roman Catholics, 2.0% Protestants and Anglicans (3,360 persons). **15.XII.1970:** 76.7% Chinese folk-religionists and Buddhists, 11.9% non-religious and atheists, 9.4% Roman Catholics, 0.8% Protestants and Anglicans (1,899

persons), 1.1% other religionists (including 117 Muslims and 13 Jews).

### NOTES ON RELIGIONS
**ATHEISTS.** Although there is (in 1975) no communist party, there are many Maoist sympathizers.
**BAHA'IS.** Begun about 1958. In 1 local spiritual assembly (1973).
**BUDDHISTS.** Increasing due to the influx of numerous refugee Chinese groups (10,000 Burmese-speaking from Burma, et alia). There are several Buddhist temples.
**CHINESE INDIGENOUS.** Isolated radio believers (see Table 2).

**CHRISTIANS.** Declining gradually as a percentage of the population due to continual emigration of Chinese to Hong Kong and beyond, also of Portuguese.
**CRYPTO-CHRISTIANS.** Christians affiliated to churches but not known to the state or society as such, nor recorded as Christians in censuses.
**NON-RELIGIOUS.** Many Chinese have abandoned all religion and favour instead mainland China's Marxist philosophy.
**OTHER RELIGIONISTS.** Adherents of other non-Christian religions, including New-Religionists and 13 Jews in 1970.

**Igreja Católica, Diocese de Macau.** (*Left*). During procession of Our Lord of Passos (in 1968, Sunday 3 March), statue of Christ carrying the Cross passes by Communist slogan reading 'Cheering the glorious formation of the Revolutionary Committee'. Many Portuguese from Hong Kong return for this annual occasion.

**NON-CHRISTIAN RELIGIONS.** The population is over 96% Chinese. A majority are said to be sympathetic to mainland Communism, and the teachings of Mao Tse-tung are the main focus of many of Macao's residents. There is also a substratum of traditional popular religion (Chinese folk religion) which is an amorphous mixture of animism, Taoism, Buddhism and Confucianism. Several Buddhist temples exist in the territory.

## CHRISTIANITY
CATHOLIC CHURCH. Catholicism came to Macao in 1557 when the Portuguese installed themselves as a tiny settlement at the mouth of the Canton river, and Macao was made a Catholic diocese in 1576. The pioneer missionary Matteo Ricci studied the Chinese language here in the 16th century, prior to receiving permission in 1583 to settle in Chaoch'ing. In 1964 Macao had a population of 170,000 of whom 24,000 (14%) were Catholics, the majority being Macanese (native Portuguese-Chinese Eurasians). Over the past decade, the total population has grown substantially, but Catholic membership has not increased proportionally. The relatively high number of 80 priests and 28 religious personnel is mainly the result of the forced exodus of missionaries from China after 1949.

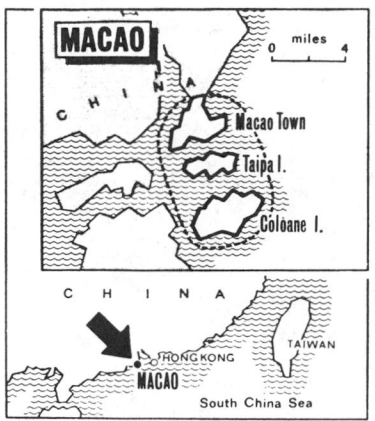

missionary to China (1807), lived periodically in Macao while continuing his translation of the Bible; and he is buried there today. Baptists affiliated with the Southern Baptist Convention USA entered Macao in 1910, and today form the largest of the non-Catholic churches, although a number of other North American missions have entered since World War II. Anglicanism is also represented by a small community.

**CHURCH AND STATE.** Since Macao in 1978 was still a Portuguese territory, its religio-political situation continues to be governed by 3 special agreements between Portugal and the Holy See; the Concordat (1940), Missionary Agreement (1940) and Missionary Statute (1941).

**BROADCASTING.**
Christian radio programmes totalling nearly 8 hours a week are broadcast over Macao stations, including daily Catholic programmes in Portuguese and Cantonese, and Protestant programmes produced in Hong Kong.

Official charity tax postage stamp (proceeds going to public charities) of 1945, showing bishop and monks in acts of mercy.

OTHER CHURCHES. Robert Morrison of the London Missionary Society, the first Protestant

TABLE 2.    ORGANIZED CHURCHES AND DENOMINATIONS IN MACAO

| Official name 1 | Begun 2 | Type 3 | Counc 4 | Congs 5 | Adults 6 | Affiliated 7 | Names, notes, and other statistics (see Codebook) 8 |
|---|---|---|---|---|---|---|---|
| Assembleias de Deus | 1954 | P Pe2 | ZF... | 1 | 300 | 600 | *Assemblies of God.* M=PAoC(Canada). Radio broadcast to China, aided by FEBC. 1n. |
| Igreja Adventista do Sétimo Dia | 1949 | P Adv | x.... | 1 | 200 | 500 | *SDA. Seventh-day Adventists,* in Hong Kong-Macao Mission, South China Island UM. |
| Igreja Anglicana: D Hong Kong & Macao | c1940 | A Cen | AwoA. | 2 | 75 | 200 | *Sheng Kung Hui Kong O Kau Kiu.* Anglican Ch. Cantonese. 4 schools. 1n,W=80%,2Y,6y. |
| Igreja Baptista | 1910 | P Bap | T.... | 4 | 532 | 2,000 | *Baptist Ch.* M=SBC(USA). 7 schools. Sunday-school enrolment 414. 4n,25Y. |
| Igreja Católica: D Macau | 1557 | R Lat | HzF.. | 9 | 16,000 | 27,000 | *Catholic Ch in Macao.* Suffragan of P Goa (India). C=3+0+13. 80nx,14m,224w,831Yy. |
| Igreja Luterana (Missouri) | 1952 | P Lut | x.... | 2 | 84 | 513 | In Hong Kong Mission. M=LCMS(USA). 1 primary school. 13m,2t(222),5Yy. |
| Igreja Metodista Livre | | P Hol | VF... | 1 | 50 | 200 | *Free Methodist Ch.* M=FMC(USA). Small holiness congregation. |
| Igreja Sion (Zion) | 1954 | P Con | x.... | 3 | 60 | 230 | *Chinese Ev Zion Ch.* M=SAM(Sweden). 1 orphanage, 50 orphans. 4f,G=0,W=26%,12z. |
| Igrejas radiofónicas isoladas | 1950 | I rad | ..... | 5 | 100 | 200 | Isolated Chinese radio believers, mostly youths, pupils and students aged 12–25. |
| Testemunhas de Jeová | c1960 | M Jeh | x.... | 1 | 30 | 50 | *Jehovah's Witnesses. Watch Tower. IBSA.* First activity reported 1961. |
| Other Protestant denominations | | P | ..... | | 200 | 500 | About 8, incl Ch of Christ in China, CMA, CNEC (1962), ECF, ICFG, PCG, WWM (1965). |
| Total affiliated (mid-1970) | | | | 32 | 17,631 | 31,993 | Total denominations (1970) . . . 18. |
| Total affiliated (mid-1975) | | | | 34 | 18,900 | 34,290 | Total denominations (1975) . . . 19. |
| Total affiliated (mid-1980) | | | | 36 | 20,020 | 36,330 | Total denominations (1980) . . . 20. |

**NOTES ON TABLE ABOVE**
COLUMNS: for meanings and CODES (cols. 1, 3, 4, 8): see Codebook (Part 6). Column 1: **Bold face type** = church with over 10% of country's affiliated Christians.

PEOPLES (ethnolinguistic). Christians: 75.1% Chinese (about 70% Cantonese), 20.6% Macanese (Eurasian), 2.6% Portuguese, 1.6% British, USA White.

**COUNTRY-WIDE TOTALS**
EVANGELIZATION (see Part 5). 1900: 30%. 1970: 83%. 1980: 86%. *Mass evangelism.* 1978, Here's Life Macao (CCCI). *Literature evangelism.* In 1975, Operation Mobilization with teams of local youths distributed 80,000 tracts and gospels.
FOREIGN MISSIONARIES AND PERSONNEL (nationals serving abroad) (1973). Total about 2 Roman Catholics.
FOREIGN MISSIONARIES AND PERSONNEL (aliens from abroad) (1973). Total 324. *From Western world.* 292: about 280 Roman Catholics, 12 Protestants (8 in 7 USA societies, 4 in 1 Sweden society). *From Third World.* 32: about 30 Roman Catho-

lics, 2 indigenous.
INSTITUTIONS (church-operated) (1973). Total 40, including 23 higher schools (1 minor seminary), 12 medical centres, 1 seminary.
PERIODICALS. 2 titles.
PERSONNEL. About 356 (32 national, 324 foreign).
RELIGIOUS LIBRARIES. 1.
SCRIPTURE DISTRIBUTION (1975). Annual totals: 100 Bibles (commercial, 100 NTs (subsidized).
SERVICE AGENCIES. About 12, including CCCI, CRS/USCC, OM, WLC(EHC), WVI.

**ADDITIONAL DATA ON CHURCHES**
IGREJA CATOLICA. The diocese includes a Portuguese parish in Singapore and one in Malacca, Malaysia (7 priests, 2 churches, 3 chapels, 3 schools). *Catholics.* 72.4% Chinese, 24.5% Macanese (Eurasian), 3.1% Portuguese. *Annual baptisms.* (1972) 42.5% infant, 57.5% adult. *Priests.* 45 secular, 35 religious. Many are Chinese. *Seminarians.* (1971) 17. *Indigenous religious congregations.* None. *Foreign orders and congregations.* Priests: SJ, SDB, OFM.

Sisters: Canossians (houses in Macao, Malacca, Singapore), Missionary Franciscans of Mary; and others.
*Catholic organizations.* Macao as a diocese forms part of the Federation of Asian Bishops' Conferences (FABC), with its seat in Hong Kong. There are no organizations for religious personnel, although a Presbyteral Council has been formed. Two lay organizations are the Legião de Maria and the Conferencias de São Vicente de Paulo.
The Holy See has diplomatic relations with Portugal and is therefore represented to government and the Catholic hierarchy in Macao by a nuncio residing in Lisbon.
The Secretariat for Diocesan Social Assistance Services (Secretariado dos Servicos Diocesanos de Assistência Social) sponsors an extensive relief and aid programme in co-operation with Catholic Relief Services in the USA. Another important institution is the Pius X Academy of Music (Academia de Musica São Pio X). In 1970 the church operated 73 schools and 12 medical and social service centres, changing by 1978 to 51 schools (20,000 pupils) and 24 health and social welfare centres.

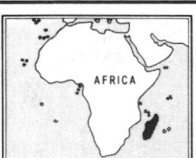

# MADAGASCAR

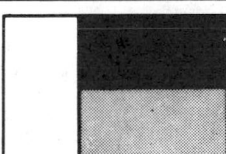

**SECULAR DATA**

STATE. Official name: The Democratic Republic of Madagascar (Repoblika Demokratika Malagasy/La République Démocratique de Madagascar). Adjective of nationality: Malagasy (malgache).
Flag (shown above right): White bar; stripes of red over green.
Area: 587,041 sq.km. (226,657 sq.miles). Agricultural land: 62.9%.
Government: One-party socialist state, since 1975 (16th century monarchy, 1896 French colony, 1958 self-government, 1960 Independence, 1972 military junta).
Legislature: Parliament (in formation).
Official languages: Malagasy and French (*Français*).
Capital: Tananarive 377,600 (1971).
Political divisions: 6 Provinces.
Armed forces (1976): Total 4,760 regular: army 4,000, navy 600, air force 160. Paramilitary forces: 6,600.
Foreign forces (1973): 6,500 French. (1980): 4,000 North Korean.

DEMOGRAPHY. Population: 6,200,000 (census of 9.V–11.XI.1966. For 1970–2000 (UN), see last row of Table 1). Population density (1975): 14/sq.km. (35/sq.mile). Under 15 years: 45%. Growth rate (1975–80): 3.02% per year (births 4.93%, deaths −1.91%). Life expectancy (1975–80): 46.0 years. Household size: 4.9 persons.
Major languages: Malagasy, French, English, Swahili, Hindi, Arabic, Chinese.
Urban dwellers (1970): 13.7%. Urban growth rate (1950–70): 4.6% per year.
Labour force: 48%.
Refugees: Aliens: in 1975, 90,000 of the 140,000 French settlers fled.

ETHNOLINGUISTIC GROUPS: 97.3% Malagasy (26.1% Merina (Hova), 14.9% Betsimisaraka, 12.0% Betsileo, 7.2% Tsimihety, 5.9% Sakalava, 5.7% Antaisaka, 5.3% Antandroy, 4.0% Bara, 4.0% Tanala, 3.3% Antaimoro, 2.8% Antanosy, 2.0% Sihanaka), 2.7% alien (0.8% French (39,800), 0.6% Comorian (36,500), 0.4% Reunionese, 0.3% Indo-Pakistani (14,000), 0.3% Arab (Yemeni, et alii), 0.2% Swahili, 0.1% Chinese (9,500), Korean, Jewish; some in these groups have become citizens).

MONEY (1977). Monetary unit: franc (= 100 centimes); US$1 = FMG 250.00.
National income per person: US$190. Average annual family income: US$931.
Inflation: (1975) consumer price index 161.
Cost of living in capital (1976): index 145 (Washington DC=100). Daily cost of living: US$30.

HEALTH. Hospitals: 846 (18,787 beds). Doctors: 667. Lepers: 72,000 (9.0 per 1,000). Blind: 40,000. Psychotics: 100,000. Criminals: 10,000.

EDUCATION. Adult literacy: (1953) 34%, (1970) 40%. Education rate: 44%. Schools: 6,054. Universities: 1.

LITERATURE. Annual new book titles (1973): 154. Periodicals: 60. Scientific journals: 2. Newspapers: 13 dailies, 19 non-daily.

COMMUNICATION (per 1,000 people). Phones: 4. Radios: 104. TV sets: 2. Daily newspaper circulation: 15 copies.

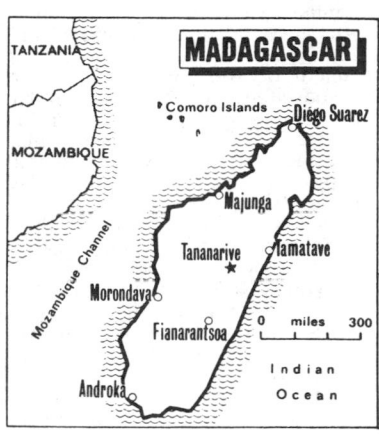

TABLE 1. RELIGIOUS ADHERENTS IN MADAGASCAR

| Year | 1900 | | mid-1970 | | Annual change, 1970–1980 | | | | mid-1975 | | mid-1980 | | 2000 | |
|---|---|---|---|---|---|---|---|---|---|---|---|---|---|---|
| *Name* | *Adherents* | *%* | *Adherents* | *%* | *Natural* | *Conversion* | *Total* | *Rate* | *Adherents* | *%* | *Adherents* | *%* | *Adherents* | *%* |
| Tribal religionists | 1,556,000 | 60.3 | 3,408,050 | 49.2 | 115,360 | −17,147 | 98,213 | 2.54 | 3,859,780 | 48.1 | 4,390,180 | 47.0 | 7,591,000 | 42.7 |
| **Christians** | **1,010,200** | **39.2** | **3,396,700** | **49.0** | **119,841** | **16,279** | **136,120** | **3.39** | **4,009,700** | **50.0** | **4,757,900** | **51.0** | **9,781,600** | **55.0** |
| professing | 1,010,200 | 39.2 | 3,396,700 | 49.0 | 119,841 | 16,279 | 136,120 | 3.39 | 4,009,700 | 50.0 | 4,757,900 | 51.0 | 9,781,600 | 55.0 |
| Roman Catholics | 464,400 | 18.0 | 1,739,800 | 25.1 | 61,362 | 7,208 | 68,570 | 3.34 | 2,053,100 | 25.6 | 2,425,500 | 26.0 | 4,801,100 | 27.0 |
| Protestants | 541,800 | 21.0 | 1,476,500 | 21.3 | 51,775 | 5,815 | 57,590 | 3.32 | 1,732,300 | 21.6 | 2,052,400 | 22.0 | 4,214,300 | 23.7 |
| Malagasy indigenous | 0 | 0.0 | 124,800 | 1.8 | 4,782 | 3,258 | 8,040 | 5.03 | 160,000 | 2.0 | 205,200 | 2.2 | 569,000 | 3.2 |
| Anglicans | 4,000 | 0.2 | 55,000 | 0.8 | 1,901 | −1 | 1,900 | 2.99 | 63,600 | 0.8 | 74,000 | 0.8 | 195,600 | 1.1 |
| Orthodox | 0 | 0.0 | 600 | 0.0 | 21 | −1 | 20 | 2.86 | 700 | 0.0 | 800 | 0.0 | 1,600 | 0.0 |
| nominal | 140,000 | 5.4 | 289,133 | 4.2 | 9,943 | −126 | 9,817 | 2.95 | 332,680 | 4.1 | 387,300 | 4.2 | 885,200 | 5.0 |
| affiliated | 870,200 | 33.7 | 3,107,567 | 44.8 | 109,898 | 16,405 | 126,303 | 3.43 | 3,677,020 | 45.8 | 4,370,600 | 46.8 | 8,896,400 | 50.0 |
| total practising | 783,180 | *90* | 2,175,300 | *70* | 76,928 | 11,484 | 88,412 | 3.43 | 2,573,910 | *70* | 3,059,420 | *70* | 5,337,800 | *60* |
| non-practising | 87,020 | *10* | 932,270 | *30* | 32,970 | 4,921 | 37,891 | 3.43 | 1,103,110 | *30* | 1,311,180 | *30* | 3,558,600 | *40* |
| Roman Catholics | 387,000 | 15.0 | 1,595,241 | 23.0 | 56,329 | 8,047 | 64,376 | 3.42 | 1,884,700 | 23.5 | 2,239,000 | 24.0 | 4,445,500 | 25.0 |
| Protestants | 480,000 | 18.6 | 1,351,040 | 19.5 | 47,462 | 4,943 | 52,405 | 3.30 | 1,588,000 | 19.8 | 1,875,100 | 20.1 | 3,734,200 | 21.0 |
| Evangelicals | 310,000 | 12.0 | 346,600 | 5.0 | 12,224 | 1,626 | 13,850 | 3.39 | 409,000 | 5.1 | 485,100 | 5.2 | 978,000 | 5.5 |
| Malagasy indigenous | 200 | 0.0 | 109,532 | 1.6 | 4,316 | 3,391 | 7,707 | 5.34 | 144,400 | 1.8 | 186,600 | 2.0 | 533,500 | 3.0 |
| Anglicans | 3,000 | 0.1 | 50,414 | 0.7 | 1,742 | 17 | 1,759 | 3.02 | 58,300 | 0.7 | 68,000 | 0.7 | 177,800 | 1.0 |
| Marginal Protestants | 0 | 0.0 | 800 | 0.0 | 30 | 10 | 40 | 4.00 | 1,000 | 0.0 | 1,200 | 0.0 | 4,000 | 0.0 |
| Orthodox | 0 | 0.0 | 540 | 0.0 | 19 | −3 | 16 | 2.58 | 620 | 0.0 | 700 | 0.0 | 1,400 | 0.0 |
| Muslims | 13,000 | 0.5 | 111,900 | 1.6 | 3,946 | 764 | 4,710 | 3.57 | 132,000 | 1.6 | 159,000 | 1.7 | 356,000 | 2.0 |
| Chinese folk-religionists | 400 | 0.0 | 4,000 | 0.1 | 137 | −17 | 120 | 2.61 | 4,600 | 0.1 | 5,200 | 0.1 | 10,000 | 0.1 |
| Baha'is | 0 | 0.0 | 4,000 | 0.1 | 143 | 17 | 160 | 3.33 | 4,800 | 0.1 | 5,600 | 0.1 | 12,000 | 0.1 |
| Non-religious | 100 | 0.0 | 4,000 | 0.1 | 149 | 51 | 200 | 4.00 | 5,000 | 0.1 | 6,000 | 0.1 | 20,000 | 0.1 |
| Buddhists | 200 | 0.0 | 2,000 | 0.0 | 69 | −1 | 68 | 2.96 | 2,300 | 0.0 | 2,680 | 0.0 | 5,100 | 0.0 |
| Hindus | 100 | 0.0 | 1,250 | 0.0 | 51 | 54 | 105 | 6.18 | 1,700 | 0.0 | 2,300 | 0.0 | 6,000 | 0.0 |
| Jews | 0 | 0.0 | 100 | 0.0 | 4 | 0 | 4 | 2.99 | 120 | 0.0 | 140 | 0.0 | 300 | 0.0 |
| **Country's population** | **2,580,000** | **100.0** | **6,932,000** | **100.0** | **239,700** | **0** | **239,700** | **2.99** | **8,020,000** | **100.0** | **9,329,000** | **100.0** | **17,782,000** | **100.0** |

COLUMNS, ROWS. For meanings and definitions, see Codebook (Part 6). Note that, by definition, total 'Christians' = professing + crypto-Christians, which also = affiliated + nominal Christians. Percentages may not always total exactly, due to rounding.
CENSUSES. The religion question has not been asked.

NOTES ON RELIGIONS
ATHEISTS. Malagasy Communist Party (MCP) (pro-Soviet): membership negligible.
BAHA'IS. Founded 1955; growth from 3 local spiritual assemblies (1964) to 27 (1973). Peoples: Hova, Betsileo, Comorians, Antaimoro, Antaifasy, Antambahoaka and Antaisaka.
CHRISTIANS. After the mass conversion of the Merina from 1869–1900, growth by conversions has been very small during the 20th century.
HINDUS. Originally immigrants from India. In 1975 a new Hindu sect, the Divine Light Mission led by Guru Maharaj Ji, began to spread and obtained 500 young converts before being banned by the military government in August 1975.
MALAGASY INDIGENOUS. In 21 denominations in 1970 (see Table 2).
MUSLIMS. Strongest on northwest coast among the Sakalava. In 1971, 100,000 Sunnis (58% Malagasy, 40% Comorians, 1,700 Indian Karanas, 200 Somalis), 5,000 Bohoras, 2,600 Ismaili Khojas, 2,500 Ithna-Asharis, 1,800 Yemeni Zaydis. About 10,000 are Asians (Indo-Pakistanis and others). There are at least 75 mosques. Among Malagasy peoples, the Antanosy, Antaimoro, Antambahoaka and Sakalava have been superficially islamized to some extent; the Antankarana (40,000; mixture of Sakalava, Betsimisaraka and Arabs) have been strongly islamized. By 1976 there were 60,000 Comorian citizens, all Muslims; in riots in Majunga, 1,400 were massacred, and the Comorian government agreed to repatriate all the rest. *Hajj pilgrims to Mecca*. (1970) 31; (1976) 13.
NON-RELIGIOUS. Mainly French.
PROTESTANTS. As a result of the mass movement among the Merina, LMS adherents grew from 5,000 in 1861 (the end of Ranavalona I's persecution) to 13,000 with 100 congregations in 1867, 37,112 in 1868 (7,066 being communicants), 230,000 with 600 congregations by 1870, and 455,000 by 1895. After 1900, the mass conversions ceased, and the proportion of affiliated Protestants (known to the churches) in the total population increased only slightly from 18.6% in 1900 to 19.5% in 1970.
ROMAN CATHOLICS. The 19th-century mass movement produced growth from 1,150 Catholics in 1870 to 387,000 (112,000 baptized including 3,000 French, 3,500 Reunionese, and 1,000 Mauritians; and 275,000 catechumens) by 1900. Thereafter, annual conversions rapidly slowed down.
TRIBAL RELIGIONISTS. Animists, especially among the Sihanaka (60% animist in 1972) and Antanosy (50%). Among the southern Betsimisaraka, cult leaders known as Tangalamena officiate at the cult of the ancestors.

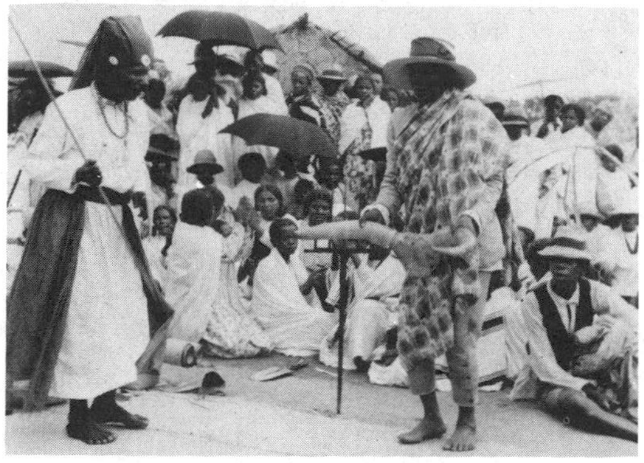

**Tribal religionists.** Witchdoctor and accomplice practising divination and traditional medicine. Traditional Malagasy religion is still followed by 47% of the population.

**NON-CHRISTIAN RELIGIONS. Traditional religions** retain the allegiance of a substantial proportion of the population in 1975 and are especially strong among the Sihanaka and Antanosy. In spite of tribal differences, a certain unity of belief and religious practice exists among the various tribal religions. The central element is a belief in the spiritual survival of the personality after death and the continuation of relations between the living and the dead. God the creator (Zahahary) exists, but the most important rituals are those concerned with maintaining the proper relationship of the living to their ancestral spirits (Razana). The ceremony of turning the corpses of the dead *(famadihana)* is a major occasion, when corpses wrapped in cloths are moved around, fed, and even danced with. Belief in the negative effects of witchcraft *(mpamosavy)* and the beneficial function of amulets *(ody)* is less strong today than previously, but the ancestral cult has been little affected by modern developments in the country.

**Islam** is strongest on the northwest coast among the Sakalava of the Majunga region. In addition to the indigenous peoples, there are also Muslim immigrants from the Comoro Islands, forced to emigrate because of the overpopulation of their homeland, and Indo-Pakistani Muslims scattered throughout the country. In 1971 there were approximately 100,000 Sunnis, including 1,700 Indian Karanas, 200 Somalis and 40,000 Comorians, the rest being natives of Madagascar. Among other smaller Muslim groups are 2,500 Ithna-Asharis, 2,600 Khojas (Ismailis), 5,000 Bohoras and 1,800 Yemeni Zaydis.

**Other religions** include 1,250 Hindus, 100 Jews, a number of followers of Chinese folk religion, some Chinese Buddhists, and a rapidly-growing number of Baha'is.

**CHRISTIANITY.** The dominant people, the Merina, immigrated to the islands from the south Pacific, beginning before the Christian era and continuing up to the 15th century. While they were settling in the central highlands, newcomers from Africa and Arabia were occupying the coastal areas. Europeans first sighted the island in 1500. During the 17th century, sporadic efforts were made to establish Catholic missions, and a number of missionaries died or were killed, but little was accomplished. King Radama (1810–28) introduced European culture and welcomed missionaries who opened schools and churches and developed a written form of the Malagasy language. The translation of the Bible completed in 1836 is still used. Queen Ranavalona I (1828–61) turned against Christianity in 1836, expelling all Europeans and ordering the death of hundreds of Christians. However, the Christian community continued to grow, and their numbers actually increased by the time the missionaries returned in 1861. Queen Ranavalona II became a Christian at her coronation in 1869 and welcomed new missionary activity. Indeed Christianity was then recognized as the faith of the island. For the next 30 years a phenomenal mass movement into the churches began, and professing Christians increased from 5,000 in 1861 to over a million by 1900 (39% of the total population). After 1900, however, mass conversions ceased, and 70 years later the proportion of Christians had only increased slightly to 49%.

Meanwhile, dissension between Merina rulers and the French caused the wars of 1883–85 and 1895–96 and resulted in the French taking possession of the island and making it a French colony in 1896. A new wave of terror followed with more Christians killed and many churches destroyed. Moreover, French anti-clericalism resulted in severe restrictions being placed on church work. This was alleviated to some degree by the entrance of the Paris Mission in 1897, whose strong protests to the French government helped to bring about a more stable situation.

Approximately 50% of the population now consider themselves Christians, with varying degrees of commitment, some being third-generation Christians, some being recent converts from traditional religion. Most are found in the highlands, among the progressive Merina and Betsileo, with Catholics slightly more numerous than Protestants Most Protestant clergy are Malagasy, whereas only a quarter of the Catholic clergy are nationals, celibacy being a major stumbling block. Politically, Protestants have been more nationalistic, particularly in the north, and the leader of the main opposition party during the 1960s was a Protestant pastor. However, one of the earliest church statements in favour of political independence was issued by the Catholic episcopate in 1953.

CATHOLIC CHURCH. Following the failure of the Catholic efforts to establish missions in Madagascar during the 17th century, work was quietly resumed in the southern part of the island during the 19th century persecution, although the later arrival of more Jesuits in 1861 is generally given as the official date for the beginning of the present Malagasy Catholic Church. By 1875 there were 15,000 Catholics. Catholic missions benefitted for a time after Madagascar became a French colony but later suffered from the anti-religious bias of the French government. A vicariate was established in the south in 1896, and 2 others were formed in 1900. At the turn of the century 78 priests and 100 religious were serving 112,000 baptized Catholics and 275,000 catechumens. In 1925, 9 Malagasy priests were ordained, and in 1939 the first Malagasy bishop was consecrated. The Malagasy hierarchy was established in 1955 and divided into 3 provinces, and a Malagasy became archbishop in 1960. An attempt to involve the wider Catholic communities in the affairs of the church has also been evident in recent years, and in 1972 the bishops decided to call a National Synod to be prepared by diocesan synods; this Synod was in fact begun in 1975.

With Protestantism firmly rooted in the high plateaux and among the upper classes of Merina society, the Catholic Church has orientated its work towards the peasant masses and the coastal regions. This continues to characterize Catholicism, although it has also penetrated the intellectual and social elites through its schools.

PROTESTANT CHURCHES. The London Missionary Society was the first mission to arrive, in 1818. Through its efforts, by 1836 30,000 had learned to read, 2,000 had become Christians and the

**Eglise Luthérienne Malgache.** *Left.* Antaimoro revivalist prophetess Nenilava ('My tall Mother'). Mrs Volahavana Germaine, catechist's widow who leads 40-year-old Lutheran revival at Ankaramalaza. *Right.* Nenilava conducts healings in Ankaramalaza Lutheran Church, assisted by 2 Lutheran foreign missionaries. On the wall are the words of Jesus concerning John the Baptist: 'What did you go out to see? Someone dressed in fine clothes? A prophet? Yes, I tell you, and far more than a prophet!'.

translation of the Bible had been completed. All missionaries were expelled in 1836 and none was permitted to return until the death of the anti-Christian queen in 1861. At that time the LMS found 5,000 disciples who had retained their faith throughout the persecution. The baptism of the new queen and her husband in 1869 resulted in a mass movement into the church, membership rising from 13,000 in 1867 to 230,000 in 600 congregations by 1870. By 1895 there were 455,000 Merina Protestants, 74 missionary pastors and 1,313 catechists. The entrance of French Catholics and other missions in the 1860s resulted in growing tension between Christians associated with English missions and those of French missions. French Jesuits actually took over most of the schools for a time, after Madagascar became a French colony. British Friends arrived in 1869 and the Paris Mission in 1897; and when comity agreements were reached among Protestant missions in 1913, the LMS released 1,290 schools and 500 of its 700 churches to these other societies. All of these groups have been concentrated in the northern half of the island, and in 1968 they united to form the Church of Jesus Christ in Madagascar, which now includes nearly two-thirds of all Malagasy Protestants.

In 1866 the Norwegian Missionary Society sent workers to the southern part of the island, and 2 American Lutheran bodies entered in 1892 and 1895. In 1950 these 3 Lutheran groups united to form the Malagasy Lutheran Church with 6 independent synods. In 1967, at their centenary, there were 344 ordained national pastors and 1,440 trained evangelists. It is now Madagascar's second largest Protestant church.

Seventh-day Adventists entered in the 1920s, and 2 small Pentecostal groups are also at work: Swedish Free Missions, and the United Pentecostal Church.

Protestants have always placed great emphasis on the development of schools and now operate more than 800 primary schools and nearly 300 secondary schools.

INDIGENOUS CHURCHES. A total of about 21 independent churches have been founded by Malagasy leaders, both as a result of schisms from parent mission-related bodies and also from the numerous revival movements since the Soatanana revival in 1895. The first to emerge was the Malagasy Protestant Church Tranozozoro Antranobiriky, a schism from the LMS in 1894. Many others have subsequently broken from the LMS and Lutheran missions. Of the Revivalists (Fifohazana), the best known are the Disciples of the Lord who, after remaining for 60 years inside the Lutheran Church, finally seceded in 1955. Another important schism in 1955, but from the LMS, was that of the Evangelical Reformed Church. In 1966, the Bible Baptist Church, which split from the LMS in 1930, invited Conservative Baptists from the USA to send missionaries to aid them in their work.

ANGLICAN CHURCH. Both the SPG and CMS arrived in 1864, but the latter withdrew after 10 years. The SPG began along the east coast and later expanded its work to the far north and the general area of the capital. The Anglican Church is found throughout the country and has shown remarkable growth since 1965. The 3 Madagascar dioceses are part of the Church of the Province of the Indian Ocean since the latter's formation in 1973.

ORTHODOX CHURCH. The Greek Orthodox Church was established in Madagascar in 1927 and is under the Patriarchate of Alexandria. There are 3 churches, but no priest has been resident for several years.

CHURCH AND STATE. Since the end of the persecutions in 1861, freedom of religion and worship has been consistently recognized. The constitution of 1959 was suspended by the new military regime in 1972 and replaced for 5 years by a 'Referendary Law', but no radical changes in the government's attitude towards religion have appeared. The constitution of 1959 made reference to God, guaranteed freedom of worship in the preamble and affirmed the 'neutrality' of the state with regard to the various religions (Article 2). After Madagascar achieved independence, the Malagasy government passed legislation on specifically Malagasy religions, taking into account local factors, which differs slightly from the old French legislation. According to Ordinance 62–117 of October 1962, followed by the present regime: (1) the state provides no salaries or subsidies to any religion; (2) it is not necessary to secure authorization for holding religious meetings, whether public or private; (3) when the number of faithful who regularly attend private religious meetings reaches one hundred, a religious association may be formed and can obtain legal recognition; (4) a religious association can always integrate itself with a recognized church if the majority of the members so desire; (5) several religious associations may group themselves together to form a church to whose juridical existence and moral personality the government, through the Ministry of the Interior, may give recognition. An amendment to Ordinance 62–117 recognized at the outset the juridical existence and moral personality of 6 churches each of which had a long history in Madagascar and had proved its vitality and carried out activities judged profitable to the country in the cultural and social domains. These included the Catholic Church (Eglizy Katolika Apostolika Romana), Anglicans (Fiangonana Episkopal Malagasy), LMS (Fianfonan'i Kristy eto Madagasikara), Lutherans (Fiangonana Loterana Malagasy), PEMS (Fiangonana Ara-Pilazantsara eto Madagasikara), and the Friends (Fiangonana Frenjy Malagasy). In addition, Decrees 63–586 (15 October 1963) and 73–6127 (18 May 1973) recognize 3 other churches: the Church of the Revival (Fifohazan' ny Mpianatry ny Tompo), the FMTA (Fiangonana Protestanta Malagasy Tranozozoro Antranobiriky), and the Seventh-day Adventist Church.

Each year there is held a census of worship places, which are exempt from taxation, and their personnel. Each denomination may provide religious instruction within the primary or secondary school system; and the provincial budgets subsidize Christian schools according to the number of teachers employed and their level of eduation. In 1974 following the publication of an open letter from the president of the Episcopal Commission for Catholic Education, the Malagasy government decided to subsidize private schools, both confessional and non-confessional, of which many were in serious financial difficulties.

Until May 1972 when riots put an end to the concentration of power in the hands of president Tsiranana, the Protestant churches were considered more autonomous and less tied to the state than the Catholic Church. Protestants seemed less concerned than Catholics about state subsidies for private schools. They also followed a teaching programme more closely in touch with the realities of the situation. The Catholic Church followed the official programme but saw its own influence over educational policy decrease after independence. In the face of the

**Eglise Réformée Evangélique de Madagascar.** Evangelistic revival service at main Tananarive church of one of the 21 Malagasy indigenous denominations.

arbitrary regime of Tsiranana, the Catholic hierarchy adopted a policy of not involving itself in politics, explicable in part by the slow rate of malgachisation (indigenization of leadership). At the end of 1971, 10 of the 16 bishops were Europeans and only one of the 4 bishops consecrated between 1967 and 1971 was Malagasy; and by 1973, 9 out of 19 were expatriates. Nevertheless, 2 Catholic journals, *Lumière* and *Lakroan'i Madagasikara*, are noted for their freedom of expression. Several Catholics and Protestants, including priests, were arrested in 1971; and the leaders of the Hery Malagasy Association (HEMA), a programme for the social and political training of young Catholic adults modelled after the New Life Movement in France, were thrown into prison for alleged 'Maoist subversion'. Because of the political troubles which shook the country in 1972, and also due to the influence of Vatican II, the Catholic bishops have called for wide-ranging reforms in the area of development (pastoral letter of 26 March 1972 on 'The Church and development in Madagascar') and the involvement of Christians in politics (Christmas pastoral letter of 1973 on 'The Church and politics'). In a joint pastoral letter published at the end of 1972, the Catholic episcopate broke all ties with the old order; and in 1975 in a decision unique among Catholic hierarchies, the bishops refused to organize a national pilgrimage to Rome to celebrate the Holy Year, arguing that because of the poverty of Madagascar such would be a negative witness. From the ranks of the military regime of May 1972 has appeared a new generation of young technicians, many of whom are Catholics and who appear to be more socially aware than their predecessors.

## INTERDENOMINATIONAL ORGANIZATIONS

The Christian Council of Madagascar (Fiomban' ny Fiangonana Protestanta eto Madagasikara ,FFPM) was created in 1958, replacing the Missionary Conference formed in 1913 by the LMS and 2 Lutheran missions. It consists of the 2 major churches, the Church of Jesus Christ in Madagascar in the north and the Malagasy Lutheran Church in the south. Anglicans were members of the former missionary conference until 1927 when comity conflicts caused their withdrawal. However, relations between the FFPM and both the Anglican and Catholic churches are good, and the council sponsors a Commission for the Study of Church Unity. In addition to denominational seminaries a united theological college has been established. There is also a Mixed Commission of Theologians which includes Catholics. The Catholic Episcopal Conference has attached to it a Commission for Ecumenism.

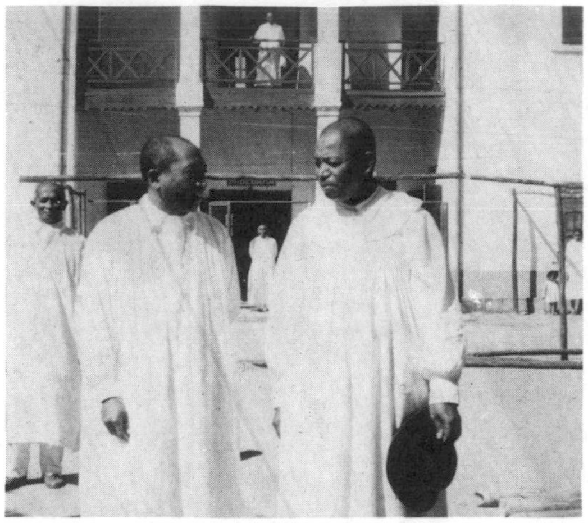

**Eglise du Réveil Spirituelle Malgache.** White-robed priests and faithful meet after Sunday liturgy in their headquarters church, a converted mansion, in Tananarive. The Spiritual Head of the church stands in background under a Malagasy text which reads simply: *Mibebaha* ('Repent').

**BROADCASTING.** The state Radiodiffusion Nationale Malagache has a large number of Christian programmes. The Catholic Church and the Protestant Federation each have 5 programmes per week (4 in Malagasy, one in French) comprising a total of 2 hours 30 minutes. Smaller Christian groups also have some short programmes. To date, the state Télévision Malagache has no regular Christian output. At Antsirabé is located a Lutheran studio which prepares 2 daily programmes in Malagasy for release over RVOG (Ethiopia), until the station's closure in 1977. RVOG also broadcast to Madagascar in French. In Tananarive the Bureau de Liaison de l'Information Religieuse dans l'Océan Indien (BLIROI), founded in 1970, handles ecumenical broadcasting. For Catholics, Madagascar is registered as a member of UNDA.

## BIBLIOGRAPHY


'A study in the self-propagating church: Madagascar', C. W. Forman, in W. C. Harr (ed), *Frontiers of the Christian world mission since 1938* (New York: Harper, 1962), p. 115–170. (The Soatanana Revival, p. 150–165).

*Agenda 1973: annuaire de l'Eglise Catholique à Madagascar.* Tananarive, 1973.

*Diary Malagasy 1966.* Antsahamanitra, Tananarive: Imprimerie Luthérienne, 1965.

'John Ratsizehena: a self-ordained Malagasy bishop', B. A. Gow, *Journal of religious history* (North Ryde, NSW, Australia), December 1976, 158–172.

*La Mission Luthérienne à Madagascar.* P. Buchsenschutz. Tananarive: Imprimerie de la Mission Norvégienne, 1938. 34p.

*La mort et les coutumes funéraires à Madagascar.* R. Decary. Paris: G.-P. Maisonneuve et Larose, 1962. 305p. (Excellent illustrations of ancestral cult).

*Les esprits de la vie à Madagascar.* J. Faublée. Paris: Presses Universitaires, 1954. 139p.

*Madagascar and the Protestant impact.* B. A. Gow. London: Longmans, 1978.

*Madagascar on the move.* J. T. Hardyman. London: Livingstone Press, 1950.

'Madagascar', in *Annuaire des missions catholiques, 1968–1969: Afrique francophone et al* (Paris: ONPC, 1969), p. 1070–1156.

*Taboo: a study of Malagasy customs and beliefs.* J. Ruud. London: George Allen & Unwin, 1960.

'The Church and Christians in Madagascar today', P. Gérard, *Pro Mundi Vita*, Africa Dossier 6 (July–August, 1978), 1–39.

*The waiting isle: Madagascar and its church.* G. F. Burton. London: Livingstone Press, 1953.


TABLE 2. ORGANIZED CHURCHES AND DENOMINATIONS IN MADAGASCAR

| Official name 1 | Begun 2 | Type 3 | Counc 4 | Congs 5 | Adults 6 | Affiliated 7 | Names, notes, and other statistics (see Codebook) 8 |
|---|---|---|---|---|---|---|---|
| Assemblées de Dieu | c1968 | I pen | ••••• | 4 | 400 | 1,000 | *Assemblies of God.* Schism of 50% ex FPM after founder deported. M=SFM(Sweden). |
| Eglise Adventiste du Septième Jour | 1926 | P Adv | x•••• | 160 | 7,200 | 20,700 | *Seventh-day Adventists*, Indian Ocean Union Mission. 31nx,1h,1j,5r,164t(10504),520Y. |
| Eglise Apostolique de Madagascar | 1968 | I Ang | xT••• | 52 | 2,600 | 15,000 | *Apostolic Ch.* Schism ex Episcopal Ch. M=AOC(USA). 5n,25m,1p,1s(5),W=50%,22Y,90y. |
| Eglise Baptiste Biblique à Madagascar | 1930 | I Bap | •F••• | | 2,065 | 5,000 | *FBMB. Bible Baptist Ch in M.* Schism ex LMS. 1966, M=CBFMS(USA). Mail courses. 10f. |
| **Eglise Catholique au Madagascar:** | 1540 | R Lat | P•S•S | 2,480 | 877,400 | 1,595,241 | *Eglizy Katolika. Cath Ch.* C=14+5+55. 8p,2s. 168n,569x,437m,1583w,P=44%,61345Yy. |
| M Diégo-Suarez | 1896 | R Lat | Ps | 22 | 45,800 | 83,257 | 55% Betsimisaraka, 25% Tsimihety. M=CSSp. 13 42 25 43 39 3304 |
| D Ambanja | 1848 | R Lat | Pofmc | 14 | 14,800 | 26,822 | 50% Tsimihety, 35% Sakalava, 10% Makoa. 1p. 4 35 17 69 45 1058 |
| D Majunga | 1923 | R Lat | Ps | 373 | 25,300 | 46,003 | Sakalava, Betsileo, Tsimihety. M=CSSp. 1p. 7 46 21 96 34 1637 |
| M Fianarantsoa | 1913 | R Lat | Psj | 8 | 201,100 | 365,740 | 82% Betsileo, 8% Merina, 7% Tanala. 1p. 24 98 87 246 37 14639 |
| D Farafangana | 1957 | R Lat | Pcm | 18 | 38,200 | 69,500 | 38% Antaimoro, 32% Antaisaka, 9% Antaifasy. 4 22 8 62 21 1823 |
| D Fort-Dauphin | 1896 | R Lat | Pcm | 13 | 11,600 | 21,000 | Very poor. Antandroy, Antanosy. 1971 riots. 2 22 10 65 ·19 1025 |
| D Ihosy | 1967 | R Lat | Pcm | 117 | 8,600 | 15,697 | Bara tribe, 36 Whites. M=CM (Italy). 1 16 1 33 36 925 |
| D Mananjary | 1968 | R Lat | Pmep | 208 | 18,000 | 32,732 | Antaimoro tribe, 500 Whites. 2 17 7 24 37 725 |
| D Morombe | 1960 | R Lat | Pmsf | 148 | 7,100 | 12,917 | 44% Betsileo, 31% Sakalava, 14% Bara. 0 20 3 20 28 633 |
| D Morondava | 1938 | R Lat | Pms | 8 | 12,600 | 22,871 | Sakalava, Bara, 210 Whites. M=MS (USA). 2 19 7 30 25 502 |
| D Tuléar | 1957 | R Lat | Paa | 113 | 19,900 | 36,150 | 50% Sakalava, 17% Mahafaly, 4% Betsileo. 2 21 25 71 69 1502 |
| M Tananarive (Antananarivo) | 1643 | R Lat | Ps | 565 | 170,100 | 309,201 | Catholics 90% Merina. M=SJ,OSB,OCar. 1p,1s. 58 83 114 453 59 12414 |
| D Ambatondrazaka | 1959 | R Lat | Posst | 10 | 32,400 | 58,909 | 34% Merina, 32% Sihanaka, 20% Bezanozano. 1p. 0 20 13 84 31 1175 |
| D Antsirabé | 1913 | R Lat | Pms | 590 | 160,500 | 291,833 | 95% Merina, 5% Betsileo, 678 Whites. 27 29 53 152 51 13329 |
| D Miarinarivo | 1933 | R Lat | Ps | 256 | 40,700 | 73,989 | 95% Merina, 5% Betsileo, 34 Whites. 18 2 4 35 42 3008 |
| D Tamatave | 1935 | R Lat | Psmm | 6 | 42,700 | 77,714 | Betsimisaraka, 2,854 Whites. 1p. 3 51 33 64 37 1918 |
| D Tsiroanomandidy | 1949 | R Lat | Posst | 11 | 28,000 | 50,906 | Sakalava, 1,095 Whites. M=OSST(Spain). 1p. 1 26 9 36 37 1728 |
| **Eglise de Jesus-Christ a Madagascar** | 1818 | P uni | RWA•N | 3,500 | 250,000 | 881,487 | *FJKM.* 1968 union of FKM, FPM. M=CCWM,PEMS,FSC. 830n,75r(61000),4s,1u,W=34%. |
| E du Réveil des Disciples du Seigneur | 1955 | I pen | ••••• | 322 | 4,247 | 11,534 | *Fihohanaza.* 1895, Soatanana Revival; 1955, schism ex FIM. Betsileo. 104n. |
| Eglise du Réveil Spirituelle Malgache | 1958 | I pen | ••••• | 50 | 5,000 | 10,000 | *FPPM. Malagasy Spiritual Ch of Revival. Vomiters.* Schism ex Mandoa Revival in FIM. |
| Eglise Episcopale de Madagascar: | 1864 | A Hig | AW•V• | 353 | 18,302 | 50,414 | *Eklesia Episkopaly Malagasy.* 1973, in CPIO. M=USPG(UK). 7f. 57n,4x,163Y,1959y. |
| D Tananarive (Antananarivo) | 1872 | A Hig | A | 100 | 10,000 | 30,694 | Mostly Merina, Betsimisaraka. 1s. P=80%,W=40%. 25 1 60 750 |
| D Diégo Suarez | 1969 | A Hig | A | 84 | 2,471 | 4,353 | *Diosesin'i Diego-Suarez.* Extreme north. Rural. 1p,W=75%. 10 1 8 259 |
| D Tamatave | 1969 | A ACa | A | 169 | 5,831 | 15,367 | Rural. 35% Betsimisaraka, 35% Antaimoro, 15% Antambahoaka. 22 2 95 950 |
| Eglise Grecque Orthodoxe | 1927 | O Gre | Cw••• | 3 | 300 | 540 | *Greek Orth Ch*, AD Rhodesia (P Alexandria). In Majunga, Italy, Greeks. No priest. |
| **Eglise Lutherienne Malgache** | 1866 | P Lut | LWA•N | 2,034 | 105,585 | 448,253 | *FLM. Malagasy Lutheran Ch.* M=NMS,ALC(USA). 444nx,128f,6p,1s(52),1943Y,14290y. |
| Eglise Malgache du Réveil | 1962 | I pen | ••••• | 2 | 500 | 1,000 | *Malagasy Revivalist Ch, Jesus Saves. Jesosy Mamonjy.* Pentecostals. Banned 1970. |
| Eglise Malgache Luthérienne Evangile | c1960 | I Lut | ••••• | 4 | 500 | 1,000 | *FALM. Lutheran Gospel Ch. Fiangonana Ara-pilazantsara Loterana Malagasy.* Ex FLM. |
| Eglise Pentecostale Unie | 1969 | P Pel | x•••• | 3 | 275 | 600 | *United Pentecostal Ch. Jesus Only Church.* Unitarians. M=UPC(USA). 2n,4f,1p(58). |
| Eglise Pentecôtiste en Madagascar | 1961 | I pen | ••••• | 1 | 100 | 200 | *FPM. Pentecostal Full Gospel Ch.* Lebanese founder MADaoud; healings, deported. |
| Eglise Protestante Malgache TA | 1894 | I Con | •vI•• | 111 | 10,000 | 23,401 | *FMTA.* Ex LMS. 1967, applied to join WCC. 36n,10m,5w,1s(5),W=25%,5000Yy. |
| Eglise Protestante Témoin à Jésus | 1967 | I Ref | ••••• | 1 | 50 | 100 | *FPVJ. Vavolombelon'i Jesosy. Protestant Witness to Jesus Church.* Schism ex FJKM. |
| Eglise Réformée Evangélique de M | 1955 | I Con | •T••• | 246 | 5,134 | 36,297 | *Mission Ev de Tananarive. MET.* Ex LMS Museum. 33n,124m,1p,1s(8),60Y,126y. |
| Témoins de Jéhovah | 1933 | M Jeh | x•••• | 11 | 398 | 800 | *Jehovah's Witnesses. Vavolombelon'i Jehovah.* Banned 1970, but underground. 41Y. |
| Other Malagasy indigenous churches | | I | ••••• | | 2,000 | 5,000 | Total about 10 (see list below). |
| **Total affiliated (mid-1970)** | | | | **9,490** | **1,292,056** | **3,107,567** | **Total denominations (1970) . . . 29.** |
| **Total affiliated (mid-1975)** | | | | **11,100** | **1,528,800** | **3,677,020** | **Total denominations (1975) . . . 34.** |
| **Total affiliated (mid-1980)** | | | | **12,700** | **1,817,200** | **4,370,600** | **Total denominations (1980) . . . 39.** |

**NOTES ON TABLE ABOVE**

COLUMNS: for meanings and CODES (cols. 1, 3, 4, 8): see Codebook (Part 6). Column 1: **Boldface type** = church with over 10% of country's affiliated Christians.

NATIONAL COUNCILS (Column 4, 5th letter).

N = Fédération Chrétien de Madagascar (Fiombonan' ny Fiongonana Kristiana eto Madagasikara, FFKM) (Christian Council of Madagascar).

S = Conférence Episcopal de Madagascar (CEM) (Episcopal Conference of Madagascar), also member of FFKM.

OTHER MALAGASY INDIGENOUS CHURCHES. In addition to those listed in the table, there are about 10 others, including those following. Schisms ex LMS: Malagasy Christian Ch, Ankazomasina, Malagasy Christian Protestant Ch Ankadilalana, Malagasy Protestant Church Antanimena (1916). Schism ex FMTA: Malagasy Protestant Tranozozoro Antanifotsy Ch. Schisms ex Lutheran Church: Malagasy Christian Protestant Church Antanetikely (c1960), Malagasy Christian Protestant Church Morarano II (c1960). Many of the 50,000 adults in the Soatanana revival (Disciples of the Lord) are still members of Protestant churches (FJKM, FLM). Other Third-World indigenous bodies: in 1975 the Korean movement, Holy Spirit Association for the Unification of World Christianity, began work; but, soon after, was suppressed by the state and its workers expelled.

PEOPLES (ethnolinguistic). Christians: 98.0% Malagasy (43.0% Merina (Hova), 23.0% Betsileo, 5.6% Betsimisaraka, 4.2% Sakalava, 3.3% Antaimoro, 3.3% Antaisaka, 3.1% Bara, 2.6% Antanosy, 2.3% Antandroy, 1.7% Tanala, 1.6% Tsimihety, 1.3% Sihanaka, 0.8% Mahafaly, 0.4% Bezanozano, 0.2% Antaifasy, 0.2% Antankarana, 0.1% Makoa), 1.3% French, 0.6% Reunionese, 0.1% Chinese (4,000).

**COUNTRY-WIDE TOTALS**

EVANGELIZATION (see Part 5). 1900: 55%. 1970: 96%. 1980: 97%. *Mass evangelism.* Among recent campaigns: in early 1960s, evangelist M.A. Daoud held healing crusades in several cities. *Radiophonic evangelism.* RVOG (2,984 listeners' letters a year), ICI.

FOREIGN MISSIONARIES AND PERSONNEL (nationals serving abroad) (1973). Total 104: about 100 Roman Catholics in Reunion and France, 3 Anglicans, 1 Protestant (FJKM pastor) in Senegal.

FOREIGN MISSIONARIES AND PERSONNEL (aliens from abroad) (1973). Total 1,872. *From Western world.* 1,828: 1,534 Roman Catholics, 287 Protestants (151 in 1 Norway society, 83 in 5 USA societies, 30 in 3 France societies, 10 in 2 UK societies,

9 in 1 Switzerland society, 4 in 1 Sweden society), 7 Anglicans in 1 UK society. *From Communist world.* About 29 Roman Catholics (15 from Yugoslavia, 14 Poland). *From Third World.* About 15 Roman Catholics (5 from Mauritius, 3 Brazil, 2 Reunion).
INSTITUTIONS (church-operated) (1973). Total 380, including 270 higher schools (7 minor seminaries), 80 medical centres (12 hospitals), 11 religious communities, 11 seminaries (7 Protestant, 2 RC, 1 Anglican, 1 Malagasy indigenous).
PERIODICALS. About 35 titles (4 SDA).
PERSONNEL. About 14,773 (12,900 national, 1,872 foreign).
RELIGIOUS LIBRARIES. About 23.
SCRIPTURE DISTRIBUTION (1975). Annual totals: 16,554 Bibles (94% subsidized, 6% commercial), 20,704 NTs (90% subsidized, 10% commercial), 38,002 UBS portions, 252,960 UBS selections. *Translations completed.* Portion: 2 languages since 1828. NT: in Malagasy in 1830. Bible: in Malagasy in 1835.
SERVICE AGENCIES. About 58, including AIM, ATTM, BLASC, BLIROI, CCSM, CEM, CWS, FFPM, FIM, FMB, FTMTK(MIJARC), GBUAF, JAC/F, JEC/F, LWR, MKM, SU, URM, USMM, YMCA, YWCA.

ADDITIONAL DATA ON CHURCHES
EGLISE APOSTOLIQUE DE MADAGASCAR. Diocèse de Madagascar. Fiangonana Apostolika eto Madagasikara.
EGLISE CATHOLIQUE AU MADAGASCAR. *Catholics.* Including (1966) 3,820 Chinese, rising to 6,700 by 1975. *Catechumens.* (1959) 83,211; (1961) 95,778; (1963) 103,494. The total in 1971 was 45,887, divided as follows among the 17 dioceses in the order shown (and included in column 7): 4043, 5117, 510, 1000, 1500, 2000, 1500, 432, 774, 1039, 1150, 1687, 450, 14327, 2070, 2700, 5588. *Annual baptisms.* (1972) 89.2% infant, 10.8% adult. *National priests.* The first 9 Malagasy were ordained in 1925. In 1973, 10 bishops (including 2 auxiliaries) out of 19 were Malagasy. *Brothers.* 295 Malagasy, 142 expatriate. *Sisters.* 48% Malagasy, 52% expatriate. In addition there are a number of contemplatives. *Missionaries.* Almost all foreign missionaries in 1970 were French, except in the dioceses of Ihosy (from Italy), Morombe (Switzerland), Morondava (USA), Ambatondrazaka (Italy), Tsiroanomandidy (Spain). *Seminarians* (1972). 94, all secular. *Catechists.* Total (1970) about 10,000, mostly heads of rural communities with a few hundred part-time, guided by 581 catechist-inspectors working under the clergy. *Indigenous religious congregations.* Sisters: 27 Soeurs du Coeur Immaculé de Marie de Diégo-Suarez (begun 1955). *Foreign orders and congregations.* Priests: AA, CM, CSSp, MEP, MS, MSF, OC, OFM, OFMCap, OSB, OSST, SJ, SMM, SOC. Brothers: FSC, PFM, St-Gabriel, Sacré-Coeur, Doctrine Chrétienne de Matzenheim. Sisters: 181 Filles de la Charité, 158 St-Joseph de Cluny, 129 Franciscaines Missionnaires de Marie, 122 La Providence de Corenc, 85 Salésiennes Missionnaires de Marie Immaculée. *Catholic organizations.* The Episcopal Conference of Madagascar is a member of SECAM. There are no national pastoral or priests' councils, but 2 associations for religious personnel exist: the Union of Major Superiors of Madagascar (Union des Supérieurs Majeurs de Madagascar) for men, and the Union of Religious Sisters of Madagascar (Union des Religieuses de Madagascar). The following lay organizations are active (using the Malagasy names): Vovonam-Pirenena ny Tanora Katolika (National Catholic Youth Council), Tanora Mpiasa Kristianina (TAK, JAC/F), Tanora Mpianatra Kristianina Tampikri (JEC/F), Fivondronan' ny Tanora Malagasy Tantsaha Katolika (FTMTK, MIJARC), Antilin'i Madagasikara (AIM, Scouts), Fanilon'i Madagasikara (FIM, Guides), Aintsika ny Fivavahana (Prayer and Life).
The Holy See has diplomatic relations with Madagascar and is represented to government and the Catholic hierarchy by a pro-nuncio in Tananarive, who also serves as pro-nuncio for Mauritius and apostolic delegate for Reunion and the Comoro Islands.
An international organization has been formed to serve the region, the Liaison Bureau for Religious Information in the Indian Ocean (Bureau de Liaison d'Information Religieuse dans l'Océan Indien, BLIROI), with its headquarters in Tananarive.
The Catholic Church has been heavily involved in education. In 1972, there were 856 pre-primary schools (37,764 pupils), 702 primary schools (155,736), 103 short-cycle secondary schools (17,083), 18 long-cycle secondary schools (10,125), 3 industrial technical schools (232), 27 domestic science technical schools (1,134), 2 teacher training schools (76), and 8 centres for rural training providing short courses for a variable number of trainees. At the beginning of 1973, public primary schools accounted for 74% of all pupils and the private sector 26%, the latter consisting of 1,577 institutions catering for 260,726 pupils. At the general secondary level, however, public education accounted for only 33% of the students with private education responsible for the remaining 67%, that is 70,318 students in 420 institutions.
Medical work and social service in 1973 included the following: 4 hospitals, one clinic, 6 leprosaria, one maternity centre, 55 dispensaries, one centre for the physically and mentally handicapped, 4 orphanages and one home for the aged. In addition Catholic sisters work in 12 public hospitals, 5 public leprosaria and one public home. Caritas Madagascar was founded in 1947.
EGLISE DE JESUS-CHRIST A MADAGASCAR. FJKM = Fiangonan'i Jesosy Kristy eto Madagasikara (Church of Jesus Christ in Madagascar). Formed in 1968 as a union of 3 churches: (1) FKM (Eglise du Christ à Madagascar; Fiangonana i Kristy eto Madagasikara), with a membership 73% Merina, 13% Betsileo, 6% Sihanaka, supported since 1818 by LMS (UK), now by CCWM (UK); (2) FPM (Eglise Evangélique de Madagascar; Fiangonana Protestanta Malagasy), with a membership 50% Merina, 32% Betsileo, 10% Betsimisaraka, supported since 1896 by PEMS (Paris Mission); and (3) FFM (Eglise des Amis en Madagascar; Fiangonana Frenjy Malagasy), with a membership 92% Merina, 8% Sakalava, supported since 1864 by British Friends, now FSC (UK). *Combined membership.* 61.5% Merina, 22.6% Betsileo, 5.2% Betsimisaraka, 2.7% Sihanaka, 0.2% Sakalava.
EGLISE EPISCOPALE DE MADAGASCAR. The first Anglican mission was the CMS (UK), around 1860, replaced shortly after by SPG (now USPG). A diocese was formed in 1872, which with its subsequent divisions remained extra-provincial under the archbishop of Canterbury (Church of England) until 1973 when the Church of the Province of the Indian Ocean (CPIO) was formed. *Membership.* 41% Merina, 27% Betsimisaraka, 11% Antankarana.
EGLISE LUTHERIENNE MALGACHE. FLM = Fiangonana Loterana Malagasy. The church has 6 Synods (4 Norwegian, 2 USA) and works in the southern half of the island. *Revival movements.* Many widely-separated revivals have broken out since that at Soatanana in 1895, but all except those of Soatanana and Mandoa (begun 1955) have remained inside the church without schism. Those within the FLM are (named after their respective centres): Farihimena (begun 1947), Manakara, Vohipeno or Ankaramalaza (1939; in 1970 still under the prophetess Nenilava), Farafangana, Vangaindrano (1938), Antsirabe (1928). Huge multitudes flock to these villages; Farihimena had one million pilgrims visiting it during the 4 years 1947–51.
EGLISE PROTESTANTE MALGACHE TA. FMTA = Fiangonana Protestanta Malagasy Tranozozoro Antranobiriky (Malagasy Protestant Church, formerly made of *zozoro* (jonc) reeds but now built with bricks). This was the first indigenous Malagasy church to be founded in opposition to foreign missions. *Membership.* 73% Merina, 10% Betsileo, 5% Betsimisaraka, 5% Antaimoro and Antanosy, 4% Tsimihety, 3% Sakalava.

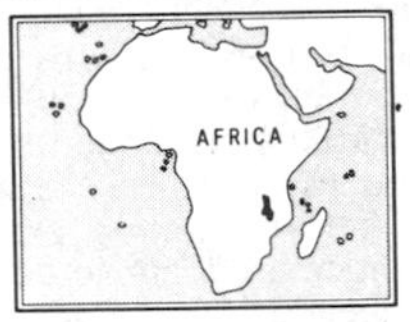


# MALAWI

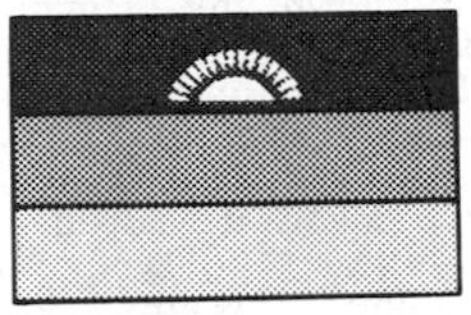

## SECULAR DATA

SECULAR DATA
**STATE. Official name:** The Republic of Malawi. Adjective of nationality: Malawian.
**Flag** (shown above right): Black, red, and green stripes, with red rising sun on black stripe.
**Area:** 118,484 sq.km. (45,747 sq.miles). Agricultural land: 40.0%.
**Government:** One-party republic, since 1970 (1891 British protectorate of British Central Africa later Nyasaland, 1953 in Central African Federation, 1963 self-government, 1964 Independence, 1966 republic).
**Legislature:** National Assembly, 75 members.
**Official languages:** Chichewa and English.
**Chief cities:** capital Lilongwe 19,176 (1966), Blantyre-Limbe 160,060.
**Political divisions:** 3 Regions and 24 Districts.
**Armed forces** (1976): Total 2,300 regular army.

**DEMOGRAPHY. Population:** 4,039,583 (census of 9.VIII.1966. For 1970–2000 (UN), see last row of Table 1). Population density (1975): 41/sq.km. (107/sq.mile). Under 15 years: 45%. Growth rate (1975–80): 2.52% per year (births 4.63%, deaths −2.11%). Life expectancy (1975–80): 43.5 years. Household size: 4.9 persons.
**Major languages:** Chewa (Chichewa, similar to Chinyanja), English Tumbuka (Chitumbuka), Yao, Ngoni (Zulu), Hindi, Portuguese and 10 smaller languages.
**Urban dwellers** (1970): 5.9%. Urban growth rate (1950–70): 6.5% per year.
**Labour force:** 46%. 250,000 adult Malawian males are working in the mines of Zambia and South Africa.
**Refugees** (1976): 32,000 from Mozambique. Exiles abroad: 34,000 Malawians in Mozambique, others in neighbouring countries.
**Tourists** (1972): 34,000. (1974) 28,400.

**ETHNOLINGUISTIC GROUPS:** 50% Maravi cluster (26% Chewa, 13% Nyanja, 6% Tumbuka, 5% Sena, Zimba), 19% Lomwe, 14% Yao, 9% Ngoni, 3% Fipa, 3% Nyakyusa, 0.3% Indo-Pakistani (11,300, including Goanese), 0.2% British (7,400), Wandya, Lambya, Shona, Greek, Swahili, Portuguese. British Asians declined from 10,000 in 1968 to 3,000 in 1977.

**MONEY** (1977). **Monetary unit:** kwacha (= 100 tambala); US$1 = MK 0.91.
**National income per person:** US$130. Average annual family income: US$637.
**Inflation:** (1970–74) 8.0% per year (1975: consumer price index 170).
**Cost of living in capital** (1976): index 92 (Washington DC = 100). Daily cost of living: US$25.

**HEALTH.** Hospitals: 147 (6,951 beds, Doctors: 114. Lepers: 43,000 (8.7 per 1,000). Blind: 18,400. Psychotics: 48,000. Criminals: 18,967.
**EDUCATION.** Adult literacy: (1945) 6%, (1966) 22%. Education rate: 18% Schools: 1,994. Universities: 1.

**LITERATURE.** Annual new book titles (1973): 32. Periodicals: 45. Newspapers: 3 non-daily.

**COMMUNICATION** (per 1,000 people). Phones: 4. Radios: 23. Daily newspaper circulation: 6 copies.

TABLE 1. RELIGIOUS ADHERENTS IN MALAWI

| Year | 1900 | | mid-1970 | | Annual change, 1970–1980 | | | | mid-1975 | | mid-1980 | | 2000 | |
|---|---|---|---|---|---|---|---|---|---|---|---|---|---|---|
| *Name* | *Adherents* | % | *Adherents* | % | *Natural* | *Conversion* | *Total* | *Rate* | *Adherents* | % | *Adherents* | % | *Adherents* | % |
| **Christians** | **13,500** | **1.8** | **2,572,400** | **59.0** | **75,456** | **27,004** | **102,460** | **3.36** | **3,048,000** | **62.0** | **3,597,000** | **64.5** | **6,829,000** | **71.6** |
| professing | 13,500 | 1.8 | 2,572,400 | 59.0 | 75,456 | 27,004 | 102,460 | 3.36 | 3,048,000 | 62.0 | 3,597,000 | 64.5 | 6,829,000 | 71.6 |
| Protestants | 8,300 | 1.1 | 1,273,200 | 29.2 | 37,239 | 11,093 | 48,332 | 3.21 | 1,504,250 | 30.6 | 1,756,520 | 31.5 | 3,320,000 | 34.8 |
| Roman Catholics | 800 | 0.1 | 1,090,000 | 25.0 | 32,007 | 12,913 | 44,920 | 3.47 | 1,292,900 | 26.3 | 1,539,200 | 27.6 | 2,890,000 | 30.3 |
| African indigenous | 0 | 0.0 | 109,000 | 2.5 | 3,285 | 1,985 | 5,270 | 3.97 | 132,700 | 2.7 | 161,700 | 2.9 | 353,000 | 3.7 |
| Anglicans | 4,400 | 0.6 | 87,200 | 2.0 | 2,555 | 995 | 3,550 | 3.44 | 103,200 | 2.1 | 122,700 | 2.2 | 238,000 | 2.5 |
| Catholics (non-Roman) | 0 | 0.0 | 12,000 | 0.3 | 342 | 18 | 360 | 2.61 | 13,800 | 0.3 | 15,600 | 0.3 | 26,000 | 0.3 |
| Orthodox | 0 | 0.0 | 1,000 | 0.0 | 28 | 0 | 28 | 2.43 | 1,150 | 0.0 | 1,280 | 0.0 | 2,000 | 0.0 |
| nominal | 3,000 | 0.4 | 300,598 | 6.9 | 8,521 | 2,119 | 10,640 | 3.09 | 344,200 | 7.0 | 407,000 | 7.3 | 723,400 | 7.6 |
| affiliated | 10,500 | 1.4 | 2,271,802 | 52.1 | 66,935 | 24,885 | 91,820 | 3.40 | 2,703,800 | 55.0 | 3,190,000 | 57.2 | 6,105,600 | 64.0 |
| total practising | 9,980 | *95* | 1,908,310 | *84* | 56,225 | 20,904 | 77,129 | 3.40 | 2,271,190 | *84* | 2,679,600 | *84* | 4,884,500 | *80* |
| non-practising | 520 | *5* | 363,490 | *16* | 10,710 | 3,981 | 14,691 | 3.40 | 432,610 | *16* | 510,400 | *16* | 1,221,100 | *20* |
| Protestants | 6,800 | 0.9 | 1,036,096 | 23.8 | 30,479 | 9,494 | 39,973 | 3.25 | 1,231,150 | 25.0 | 1,435,820 | 25.7 | 2,666,600 | 28.0 |
| Evangelicals | 6,400 | 0.9 | 523,200 | 12.0 | 15,822 | 9,938 | 25,760 | 4.03 | 639,100 | 13.0 | 780,800 | 14.0 | 1,717,000 | 18.0 |
| Roman Catholics | 500 | 0.1 | 993,448 | 22.8 | 29,086 | 10,989 | 40,075 | 3.41 | 1,174,900 | 23.9 | 1,394,200 | 25.0 | 2,671,000 | 28.0 |
| African indigenous | 100 | 0.0 | 99,758 | 2.3 | 3,042 | 2,042 | 5,084 | 4.14 | 122,900 | 2.5 | 150,600 | 2.7 | 334,000 | 3.5 |
| Anglicans | 3,100 | 0.4 | 76,500 | 1.8 | 2,312 | 1,188 | 3,500 | 3.75 | 93,400 | 1.9 | 111,500 | 2.0 | 229,000 | 2.4 |
| Anglican pentecostals | 0 | 0.0 | 0 | 0.0 | 12 | 88 | 100 | 20.00 | 500 | 0.0 | 1,000 | 0.0 | 10,000 | 0.1 |
| Marginal Protestants | 0 | 0.0 | 55,000 | 1.3 | 1,703 | 1,157 | 2,860 | 4.16 | 68,800 | 1.4 | 83,600 | 1.5 | 181,000 | 1.9 |
| Catholics (non-Roman) | 0 | 0.0 | 10,000 | 0.2 | 285 | 15 | 300 | 2.61 | 11,500 | 0.2 | 13,000 | 0.2 | 22,000 | 0.2 |
| Orthodox | 0 | 0.0 | 1,000 | 0.0 | 28 | 0 | 28 | 2.43 | 1,150 | 0.0 | 1,280 | 0.0 | 2,000 | 0.0 |
| Tribal religionists | 714,000 | 95.2 | 1,075,200 | 24.7 | 26,236 | −28,016 | −1,780 | −0.17 | 1,059,800 | 21.6 | 1,057,400 | 19.0 | 1,049,000 | 11.0 |
| Muslims | 22,500 | 3.0 | 698,000 | 16.0 | 19,594 | 956 | 20,550 | 2.60 | 791,500 | 16.1 | 903,500 | 16.2 | 1,622,000 | 17.0 |
| Baha'is | 0 | 0.0 | 8,400 | 0.2 | 260 | 60 | 320 | 3.20 | 10,000 | 0.2 | 11,600 | 0.2 | 28,300 | 0.3 |
| Hindus | 0 | 0.0 | 5,000 | 0.1 | 139 | −9 | 130 | 2.32 | 5,600 | 0.1 | 6,300 | 0.1 | 9,000 | 0.1 |
| Non-religious | 0 | 0.0 | 500 | 0.0 | 15 | 5 | 20 | 3.33 | 600 | 0.0 | 700 | 0.0 | 2,000 | 0.0 |
| Other religionists | 0 | 0.0 | 500 | 0.0 | 0 | 0 | 0 | 0.00 | 500 | 0.0 | 500 | 0.0 | 1,700 | 0.0 |
| **Country's population** | **750,000** | **100.0** | **4,360,000** | **100.0** | **121,700** | **0** | **121,700** | **2.48** | **4,916,000** | **100.0** | **5,577,000** | **100.0** | **9,540,000** | **100.0** |

COLUMNS, ROWS. For meanings and definitions, see Codebook (see Part 6). Note that, by definition, total 'Christians' = professing + crypto-Christians, which also = affiliated + nominal Christians. Percentages may not always total exactly, due to rounding.
CENSUSES. None have included the religion question for the whole population. **8.V.1956** (non-Africans): 7,523 Christians, 5,748 Muslims, 2,506 Hindus, 378 non-religious, 134 Sikhs, 37 Jews, 109 other religionists. **26.IX.1861** (non-Africans): 7,730 Christians, 7,570 Muslims, 3,010 Hindus, 720 non-religious, 1,850 other religionists.

**NOTES ON RELIGIONS**
AFRICAN INDIGENOUS. In about 82 denominations in 1970 (see Table 2), this number increasing annually.
ANGLICAN PENTECOSTALS (or, Anglican charismatics). The charismatic renewal began in 1973 and by 1977 involved several Anglican parishes, and was beginning to involve Roman Catholics also.
BAHA'IS. Growth from 1 local spiritual assembly (1964) to 27 (1973); including numerous Indians formerly Muslim or Hindus.

CHRISTIANS. In 1921, some 103,001 Africans claimed to be Christians (8.6% of the known population then).

COUNTRY'S POPULATION. From 1965–75, around 500,000 Mozambican refugees, mostly Catholics and traditional religionists, with some Anglicans, Protestants and Muslims, fled from Mozambique, settled in Malawi and have become absorbed into Malawian life. From 1969–76, over 10,000 Jehovah's Witnesses fled the country to Mozambique, then were deported back to Malawi.

HINDUS. Indians, mostly traders.

MUSLIMS. The first effective Muslim proselytism did not begin till 1890 after the defeat of the slave traders; by 1921, 73,015 (6%) of the population, mostly Yao and Lakeside Chewa) claimed to be Muslims. Africans are Sunnis (of the Shafiite rite), including 90% of the Yao who still form the majority of Muslims. There has been no spread of Islam for a long time, no Muslim militancy, and there is among the Yao considerable interconversion between both Islam and Christianity. There are also several thousand Indo-Pakistani Muslims, as well as some Arabs and Swahili. *Hajj pilgrims to Mecca* (figures for all Central Africa). (1970) 121; (1974) 232.

NON-RELIGIOUS. Europeans.

OTHER RELIGIONISTS. Including (1956) 134 Sikhs and 37 Jews; emigrating during the 1970s. Rosicrucians (AMORC) are also present.

PRACTISING CHRISTIANS. Protestants: weekly attenders 60% of affiliated members in towns, 50% in rural areas. Affiliated members tend to be those who attend communion at least once a year, so annual practice (as defined here) is about 95%. Catholics: Easter communicants 45%, total all annual attenders about 70%.

TRIBAL RELIGIONISTS. Animistic remnants among various tribes, including Tumbuka and Tonga (both about 50% pagan with no Muslims).

## NON-CHRISTIAN RELIGIONS. Traditional

**religions** continue to exist among all tribes, but among none are they the dominant influence. The total population remains about 25% traditionalist. God is known among many peoples as Mulungu, but other names are also prevalent: Ciuta (among the Tumbuka and Matengo), Kyala (Ngonde), Unkurukuru (Ngoni), Tilo (Tonga) and Chisumphi (northern Chewa). In an earlier day the Chisumphi cult was highly developed, with its main centre at Kaphirintiwa. The symbol of God was a sacred drum, and Chisumphi regularly possessed the Makewana, cultic spirit wives who served as mediums at the shrine. The shrine was also cared for by a priesthood whose chief was called Mfumu ya Chisumphi. During the slave-raiding days of the middle of the 19th century, the sacred drum was removed to Msekere in Mozambique and was later returned to a new shrine at Tsang'oma in Nyasaland. The cult still exists but in attenuated form. A more durable movement is the M'Bona cult of the southern Chewa which is centred in the divinity M'Bona who was once human. Since the arrival of Christianity, the cult has taken on syncretistic elements including the identification of M'Bona as a Black Jesus. There is also a strong emphasis among the Chewa on secret societies (Nyau), with a cultic use of masks representing ancestral spirits and elaborate ceremonies *(pembero lalikulu)* performed at burials and tribal initiations. In 1930 a highly important witchcraft eradication movement, Mchape (Medicine), arose in Nyasaland and ultimately spread through Northern and Southern Rhodesia, Tanganyika and Mozambique.

**Islam** is strongest among the Yao tribesmen of eastern Malawi, 90% of the 380,000 Yao claiming to be Muslims. Malawi Muslims, who are Sunnis and almost all Africans, number about 15% of the population. Because of their numerical strength and vitality, they form the southern frontier of Islam in Africa.

**Baha'i** has spread considerably in the last 15 years and 1973 had 27 local spiritual assemblies.

## CHRISTIANITY

PROTESTANT CHURCHES. David Livingstone explored the Zambesi and Shire rivers during 1858–64 and attracted others to begin missionary work in Malawi. Protestant pioneers were Presbyterians from the Free Church of Scotland in 1875 and the Church of Scotland the following year, the former concentrating its work at the renowned Livingstonia station in the north, with the latter active in the southern region of Blantyre. The next to arrive (1888) were Dutch Reformed missionaries from South Africa at Nkhoma. These 3 groups joined together in 1926 to create the large Church of Central Africa Presbyterian (CCAP), now with 2,172 churches in 3 synods. The church as a whole has continued to grow at a rapid rate, and this is especially true of the Blantyre Synod.

Seventh-day Adventists opened their first mission in 1891 and have shown significant gains since then. Malawi Adventists form the South-East Africa Union of the SDA Church, which was organized in 1925. At present the church has 3 fields covering the northern, central and southern regions of the country.

Two groups of Disciples entered Malawi in the early part of the century, the Church of Christ (Non-Instrumental) from the USA in 1907, the Churches of Christ from the UK in 1909. The former is larger although both have succeeded in establishing sizeable communities in Malawi.

Notable by their relative absence are Pentecostals, there being only 7 relatively small Pentecostal denominations. In 1978, the Pentecostal Fellowship of Malawi was formed to co-ordinate them.

Other Protestant denominations include the Zambesi Evangelical Church, Evangelical Church of Malawi, Seventh-day Baptist Church and several smaller bodies.

Protestants on the churches' rolls make up about 24% of the population and have been heavily involved in education, medical and social service. Churches belonging to the Christian Council of Malawi, which is mostly Protestant, operate 22 hospitals, 36 clinics, one school for the blind, 5 teacher-training colleges, one technical school, one village co-operative, 3 lay training centres, 4 printing presses, and 24 bookshops, in addition to 8 Bible schools and 2 theological colleges.

CATHOLIC CHURCH. Catholic missionaries entered what is now Malawi from Mozambique during the 16th century but established no permanent stations until the arrival of the White Fathers in 1889. The first indigenous priest was ordained in 1937 and the church now has over 70 national priests in addition to 288 Malawian sisters and 1,580 catechists. An African bishop was consecrated in 1956 and the hierarchy established in 1959. Three indigenous religious congregations have been formed for sisters and in 1929 one for brothers, although the latter had only 2 members remaining by 1972. The Catholic Church has increased enormously in size since 1950 and its members are now 23% of the total population of the country. The church is heavily involved in education and social service.

OTHER CHURCHES. The Anglican UMCA, heeding the call of David Livingstone, appeared briefly in Malawi during 1861 and definitively after 1879. The work is now organized into 2 dioceses which are part of the Church of the Province of Central Africa.

Jehovah's Witnesses have built up an important community since their arrival from South Africa in 1907. Following a government ban on their activities in 1969, many fled to Mozambique but have attempted to return since Mozambique obtained its independence in 1975. Witnesses continue to

**Catholic Church in Malawi.** Overflow Sunday congregation in a small bush church/school building. Note children of all ages including infants.

**Church of Central Africa Presbyterian.** Main CCAP church in Blantyre.

suffer from virulent state persecution both in Mozambique and Malawi.

Some 90 African indigenous churches are active in Malawi. The first and still the most important is the Providence Industrial Mission, begun in 1898. Other early groups include the Achewa Church (1920), African Covenant Church (1923) and the Last Church of God and His Christ (1924). The influence of Black churches from the USA has been felt through the African Methodist Episcopal Church. Another foreign church is the African Apostolic Church of Johane Maranke, which entered Malawi from Rhodesia in 1958.

**CHURCH AND STATE.** The constitution of 1963 adheres to the United Nation's Declaration of Human Rights and so affirms freedom of conscience for all. There is no established church and Malawi leans towards the principle of separation of church and state. Because of its extreme poverty, the state accepts the churches as partners in development. Hospitals and clinics in operation when the Federation of Rhodesia and Nyasaland was disbanded in 1963 still receive a small grant-in-aid, but new medical institutions since that date receive no subsidies. Teachers' salaries are paid by government and church institutions are not taxed. Religious instruction is a compulsory subject in primary schools; in post-primary institutions, provision is made for the religious instruction of teachers of religion. Churches are not required to register, and no government body is specifically charged with responsibility for religious affairs.

In June 1969 the government banned the Jehovah's Witnesses as 'dangerous to the good government of the state'. In 1976 some 5,000 were estimated to be held in prison or prison camps, often subjected to torture, others having suffered the loss of their jobs or similar privations. The Youth League of the ruling Malawi Congress Party has been involved in deliberate harassment of the Witnesses, which has caused many to flee to Mozambique. Others attempting to return to Malawi from the increasingly hostile situation in Mozambique have experienced even more serious persecution. By 1976 their plight had aroused widespread international protest.

**INTERDENOMINATIONAL ORGANIZATIONS.** The Christian Council of Malawi was founded in 1939, building on foundations laid earlier by the Consultative Board of Federative Missions of Nyasaland. At present 13 churches and several other bodies are members, including a wide spectrum of church traditions from high-church Anglicans to African indigenous churches. The council is affiliated to CWME of the World Council of Churches and 5 of its Protestant members also belong to the Evangelical Association of Malawi, a constituent member body of the Association of Evangelicals of Africa and Madagascar. The principal Catholic body responsible for interdenominational relations is the National Catholic Commission for Ecumenism.

Two national committees co-ordinating the work of CCM churches and the Catholic Church are: (1) the Private Hospital Association of Malawi (PHAM), established in 1965 with the support of the WCC, which provides for co-operation in Christian medical work with the Ministry of Health; and (2) the Christian Service Committee of the Churches of Malawi (CSC), founded in Blantyre in 1968, which sponsors social service and development projects in liaison with government and Sodepax in Switzerland. The CSC is a member of CIDSE in Belgium. An important institution fostering a spirit of ecumenism is the Chilema Training Centre, sponsored by the Anglican and Presbyterian churches, with a Catholic member on its board of government. A regional Sodepax-type group based in Blantyre (but serving also Botswana, Lesotho, Kenya, Tanzania, Uganda and Zambia) is the Movement for Ecumenical Action in National Development (MEND).

**BROADCASTING.** The national network Radio Malawi gives 3.5 hours a week for religious programmes, which are divided among the various churches. These include vernacular and English church services on Sundays and epilogues during the week. There are also special programmes at Easter and Christmas. A Religious Advisory Board composed of representatives from the churches, meets periodically to plan and co-ordinate these programmes. There is no television in the country. For Catholics, UNDA is represented by a national association.

## BIBLIOGRAPHY


'A general survey of the history of Independent Churches in Malawi, 1900–1976'. H. J. Sindima. Nairobi: AACC, 1977. 10p.

*Catholic directory of Malawi, 1970.* Limbe, Malawi: Catholic Secretariat in Malawi, 1970.

*Five years in the life of the Christian Service Committee of the churches in Malawi, 1968 to 1972.* J. D. Mein. Blantyre: Christian Council of Malawi, 1972.

*Independent African: John Chilembwe and the origins, setting and significance of the Nyasaland native rising of 1915.* G. Shepperson & T. Price. Edinburgh: Edinburgh University Press, 1958. 564p.

'Missions to Malawi'. F. Alexander. Thesis, Fuller Theological Seminary, Pasadena (USA), 1969.

'Political removal and deportation of African separatist church leaders in Nyasaland, 1909–1925'. K. Lohrentz. Seminar paper, Syracuse University (NY), 1970.

*Politics and Christianity in Malawi, 1875–1940: the impact of the Livingstonia Mission in the northern province.* J. McCracken. London: Brill, 1977. 324p.

*Sectarianism in Sothern Nyasaland.* R. L. Wishlade. London: Oxford University Press, 1964. 162p.

*The beginnings of Nyasaland and North-Eastern Rhodesia, 1859–95.* A. J. Hanna. Oxford: Clarendon Press, 1956.

'The Nyasaland Government's policy toward African Muslims, 1900–1925'. R. Greenstein. N.d. 27p. (Duplicated).


TABLE 2. ORGANIZED CHURCHES AND DENOMINATIONS IN MALAWI

| Official name 1 | Begun 2 | Type 3 | Counc 4 | Congs 5 | Adults 6 | Affiliated 7 | Names, notes, and other statistics (see Codebook) 8 |
|---|---|---|---|---|---|---|---|
| Achewa Church | 1920 | I ind | ••••• | | 1,000 | 2,500 | Schism ex PIM, Dedza district; Chewa (Achewa) tribe. 9 ministers (unsalaried). |
| Africa Evangelical Church of Malawi | 1900 | P int | xMG•a | 63 | 2,000 | 5,000 | M=AEF(SAGM). 55% Mang'anja, 30% Sena, 9% Zimba. 5n,3x,10f,2h,2k,2p,W=80%,60Y. |
| African Apostolic Ch of Johane Maranke | 1934 | I peA | x•••• | 14 | 1,000 | 2,000 | *AACJM. Mpingo wa Apositoli.* Shonas from Umtali (Rhodesia). 14 pasakas held. |
| African Covenant Church | 1923 | I Ref | ••••• | 100 | 2,000 | 10,000 | *Chipangano (Covenant), or Ch of Abraham.* Ex CCAP(CSM). All over north. Tumbuka. |
| African Methodist Episcopal Church | 1924 | I Met | Vw••N | 71 | 2,000 | 4,000 | M=AMEC(Black mission from USA). Chewa-speaking. HQ Kasungu. |
| African National/International Church | 1928 | I Ref | ••••• | 28 | 2,000 | 4,000 | *ANC.* Schism ex CCAP(Free Ch of Scotland). In north. OT theology, polygamous. |
| Anglican Church in Malawi: | 1861 | A ACa | AWAVN | 260 | 25,149 | 76,500 | In Anglican CPCA. M=USPG. Rural. 60 schools. 26f,10H,P=60%. 61n,7x,1936Y,3269y. |
| D Lake Malawi | 1971 | A ACa | A | 172 | 15,104 | 46,500 | West of lake. 80% Chewa, 15% Tonga, 5% Tumbuka. 1p,W=59%. 40 1 1121 1839 |
| D Southern Malawi | 1971 | A ACa | A | 88 | 10,045 | 30,000 | 1 Archdeaconries. 65% Chewa, 30% Yao, 5% Ngoni. 5H,W=62%. 21 6 815 1430 |
| Apostolic Ch of Pentecost of Malawi | 1947 | P Pe1 | x•••• | 157 | 2,000 | 4,000 | M=ACP(Canada). North of Lilongwe. HQ Mponela. 5n,3x,56m,4w,4f,105Y. |
| Apostolic Faith Mission of Malawi | 1933 | P Pe2 | Z•••• | 8 | 700 | 1,500 | M=AFM(South Africa). 8 Bantu congregations, one White missionary pastor. |
| Assemblies of God in Malawi | 1930 | P Pe2 | ZFG•a | 77 | 3,621 | 10,000 | M=AoG(USA). HQ Limbe. 80% Chewa, 10% Tumbuka. 10n,5x,50m,16f,1j,4k,1s(115),200Y. |
| Baptist Mission of Central Africa | 1926 | P Bap | ••G•a | 99 | 5,584 | 10,000 | 1959, M=SBC(USA). 67% Lomwe, 13% Chewa, 13% Nyanja. 1 school. 61n,28f,6h,1s,1609Y. |
| Blackman's Presbyterian Ch of Africa | 1933 | I Ref | ••••• | 3 | 300 | 500 | *Mpingo wa Afipa wanu Africa. African Ch.* Ex FCSM. Also Zambia, Tanzania.Tonga,Tumbuka. |
| **Catholic Church in Malawi:** | 1561 | R Lat | PzSER | 711 | 546,400 | 993,448 | C=4+3+10. 109,900 catechumens. 3p,1s(53). 70n,235x,106m,529w,P=45%,37143Yy. |
| M Blantyre | 1903 | R Lat | Ps | 39 | 181,600 | 330,078 | 60% Lomwe, 25% Ngoni, 15% Yao. 1p. 25 49 35 157 39 8023 |
| D Chikwawa | 1965 | R Lat | Psmm | 12 | 35,200 | 64,043 | 40% Sena, 30% Lomwe, 30% Nyanja. 4 20 0 34 40 2162 |
| D Dedza | 1956 | R Lat | Ps | 24 | 71,600 | 130,164 | 65% Ngoni, 35% Nyanja. 1p. 21 25 16 36 60 6723 |
| D Lilongwe | 1889 | R Lat | Pwf | 317 | 134,400 | 244,305 | New capital. 90% Chewa, 10% Ngoni. 1s. 9 55 20 145 40 10990 |
| D Nzuzu | 1947 | R Lat | Pwf | 121 | 37,100 | 67,469 | 80% Tumbuka, 20% Tonga. 1p. 5 40 25 93 66 1704 |
| D Zomba | 1952 | R Lat | Ps | 62 | 55,300 | 100,595 | 30% Muslims. 50% Lomwe, 20% Ngoni, 10% Yao. 4 28 10 42 45 4754 |
| PA Fort Johnston (Mangochi) | 1969 | R Lat | Psmm | 136 | 31,200 | 56,794 | In extreme south. 1973, elevated as D Mangochi. 2 18 3 35 50 2787 |
| Christadelphian Ecclesias | 1960 | P Ade | x•••• | 8 | 150 | 300 | *Abale a Yesu.* M=Christadelphian Bible Mission(USA). Work in Zomba. Pacifist. |
| **Church of Central Africa Presbyterian:** | 1875 | P Ref | RvA•N | 2,172 | 282,171 | 766,000 | *CCAP*, formed 1926. 6H,1j,P=90%,1s(34),W=55%. 151nx,15148Y,14291y,51670z. |
| S Blantyre (Synod of Blantyre) | 1876 | P Ref | • | 570 | 129,329 | 344,000 | M=CSM(UK). Nyanja, some Yao, 28f,G=7%pa,1H,5h,3k,1p. 45 6632 8199 14289 |
| S Livingstonia | 1875 | P Ref | • | 476 | 47,056 | 172,000 | M=FCSM. 69% Tumbuka, 18%Tonga, 13% Konde. 4H,10h,5k,1p. 42 1500 2267 6090 |
| S Nkhoma (Mkhoma) | 1888 | P Ref | F | 1,126 | 105,786 | 250,000 | M=DRC(SA). 99% Chewa. In EAM. 11x,G=4.4%pa,4H,6h,1s. 64 7016 3825 31291 |
| Church of Christ (Non-Instrumental) | 1907 | P Dis | x•••• | 1,000 | 20,000 | 50,000 | 1957, M=CC(Non-Instrumental)(USA). 80% Chewa, 20% Tumbuka. 10f,1H,2p. |
| Church of God/Full Gospel Ch of God | 1970 | P Pe3 | ZF••• | 8 | 1,267 | 2,000 | M=CoG(Cleveland)(USA), Full Gospel Ch of God(South Africa). 6n. |
| Church of the Ancestors | 1942 | I Adv | ••••• | | 500 | 1,000 | *Calici ca Makolo. Ethiopian Ch.* Nyanja-speaking schism ex Seventh-day Adventists. |
| Church of the Nazarene in Malawi | 1957 | P Hol | xFG•G | 42 | 494 | 3,000 | M=CoN(USA). 99% Nyanja, 1% Yao. HQ Limbe. 2n,4x,10f,G=12.0%pa, 1s,W=76%,567z. |
| Church of the Watch Tower/Mikael Ch | 1908 | I Jeh | ••••• | | 2,500 | 4,000 | Tonga mass revival; collapsed. 1937, restarted as Mikael Church. Banned 1969. |
| Churches of Christ | 1909 | P Dis | x•••N | 62 | 10,000 | 20,000 | M=CC(UK). 2 Synods. 20% Lomwe, 20% Tumbuka,20% Nyanja,16n,4f,1H,1h,2i,1p,W=50%,227Y. |
| Congregation of the Lamb | 1932 | I ind | ••••• | 3 | 300 | 500 | *Kagulu ka Nkhosa.* Indigenous body ex Zambesi Industrial Mission. Nyanja. Mlanje. |
| Evangelical Church of Malawi | 1893 | P int | xMG•a | 126 | 5,000 | 15,000 | Formerly Nyasa Industrial M, Nyasa Ev Ch. M=TEAM(USA,SA). Cholo. Nyonja. 1h,1k,1p. |
| Faithful Church of Christ | 1949 | I ind | ••••• | 30 | 500 | 1,000 | *Wendewende Mission.* Schism ex African Chs of Christ. Nyanja. Many splits. |
| Greek Orth Archbishopric of Rhodesia | c1920 | O Gre | Cw••• | 1 | 500 | 1,000 | In AD Rhodesia, under Greek P Alexandria. No resident priest. Greek settlers. |
| Independent Assemblies of God | 1958 | P Pe2 | ••••N | 25 | 1,000 | 3,000 | Formerly African Gospel Ch, AoG in S&C Africa. Ex AoG, led by White missionary. |
| Jehovah's Witnesses | 1906 | M Jeh | x•••• | 432 | 23,398 | 55,000 | 1972, 1975 vicious persecutions of 36,000 to Mozambique. 1973: G=10%pa,1577Y. |
| Last Church of God & His Christ | 1924 | I Ref | ••••• | | 2,000 | 5,000 | Schism ex Chipangano; many ex CCAP. Growing very rapidly north of Mzimba. Tumbuka. |
| Lutheran Church of Central Africa | 1962 | P Lut | x•••• | 14 | 264 | 796 | *African Lutheran Ch.* M=Wisconsin ELSynod(USA). Chewa. 3x,2m,5f,3p,W=69%,46Y,68y. |
| New Apostolic Church | 1923 | C CAp | x•••• | | 5,000 | 10,000 | *Zambia-Malawi Church District.* M=NAC(Chief Apostle in Dortmund,Germany). |
| Pentecostal Holiness Association | 1932 | P Pe3 | ZFG•G | 14 | 769 | 2,000 | Lambya, Winamwanga from PHA in Zambia; extreme north. M=PHC(USA). 4n,2f,1p,19Y. |
| Providence Industrial Mission | 1898 | I Bap | ••••N | 419 | 10,000 | 25,258 | *African Baptist Assembly Malawi.* M=NBCUSA(Black). 70% Lomwe, 10% Yao, 2f,2H,2h. |
| Seventh Day Baptist Church | 1899 | P Bap | Tw••N | 50 | 3,949 | 8,000 | Central Africa Conf. Ex FCSM.1947, M=SDB(USA). 50% Lomwe, 20% Ngoni. 4f,1H,2h,1k. |
| Seventh-day Adventist Church | 1891 | P Adv | x•••N | 823 | 30,748 | 100,000 | South-East Africa U. 86% Chewa. 63n,9x,40f,2H,12h,1j,3k,3r,454t(47831),W=72%,3513Y. |
| United Apostolic Faith Church | | P Pe2 | x•••• | | 2,000 | 5,000 | M=UAFC(UK). HQ Pretroia(SA). British-Israelite Pentecostals. All Africans. |
| Zambesi Evangelical Church | 1892 | P ind | ••G•a | 258 | 10,000 | 30,000 | M=ZM(UK), formerly Zambesi Industrial Mission. HQ Blantyre. 9f,1H,2h,1j,2k,1p. |
| Other African indigenous churches | | I | ••••• | | 20,000 | 40,000 | Total about 70 (see list below), including numerous very small bodies. |
| Other Protestant denominations | | P | ••••• | | 200 | 500 | Total about 5 (see list below). |
| **Total affiliated (mid-1970)** | | | | **8,160** | **1,026,464** | **2,271,802** | **Total denominations (1970) . . . 110.** |
| **Total affiliated (mid-1975)** | | | | **9,200** | **1,221,600** | **2,703,800** | **Total denominations (1975) . . . 120.** |
| **Total affiliated (mid-1980)** | | | | **10,300** | **1,441,300** | **3,190,000** | **Total denominations (1980) . . . 130.** |

**NOTES ON TABLE ABOVE**

COLUMNS: for meanings and CODES (cols. 1, 3, 4, 8): see Codebook (Part 6). Column 1: **Boldface type** = church with over 10% of country's affiliated Christians.

NATIONAL COUNCILS (Column 4, 5th letter),
- a = member of both CCM and EAM.
- G = Evangelical Association of Malawi (EAM).
- N = Christian Council of Malawi (CCM).
- R = Episcopal Conference of Malawi (ECM).

OTHER AFRICAN INDIGENOUS CHURCHES. These, some of which are branches of Zambian or Rhodesian or South African bodies, include: African Abraham Ch (1929; Tonga), African Assemblies of God (1969; ex IAoG), African Ch (c1953, ex Zambesi Industrial Mission), African Ch Crucified Mission (1960), African Chs of Christ (1933; ex Ch of Christ; several small factions), African Emmanuel Ch (1927; 10 congregations in north), African Nyasa Mission (1946, in south, ex Nyasa Industrial Mission), African Pentecostal Ch (in north), African United Baptist Ch (1946, in south, ex PIM), Apostolic Zion Ch (1928), Bantu Ch (Tonga), Chitemwano cha Chiuta Ch, Christian Catholic Apostolic Ch in Zion (1923), Ch of God in Africa (1931; ex Ch of Christ), Emmanuel Chs of Christ, Episcopal Holiness Ch, Full Gospel Ch (Zionist, pentecostal; ex CCAP), Galilea Ch (ex RCC), Gospel of God Ch (Apostolic Ch of Johane Masowe; 1946; 4 congregations, 2,000 followers), Independent Baptist Convention (1971; split ex PIM; 10 churches, 20 ministers), Jordan Ch (1961, ex CCAP Blantyre Synod), Last Reformed Ch, Light African Ch (1970, ex CCAP), New Jerusalem of God Ch, Presbyterian Ch of Africa (from South Africa), Sent of the Holy Ghost Ch/Holy Ghost Evangelical Ch in Africa (1927, ex ZIM), Sons of God (1929; ex Ch of Christ), Sons of God/Ana a Mulungu (1935; ex SDA), Watchman Healings Mission/Ine wa Jehova ndi Mikaeli (1937), Yesu Ch, Zion Christian Ch, Zion Ch (ex SDA

Ch), Zion Prophet Ch (1978), Zion Restoration Ch. Many others are small schisms from ZEC, CCAP, Ch of Christ, Baptists. In 1975 a Korean movement began work, with 2 Japanese missionaries: Holy Spirit Association for the Unification of World Christianity.
OTHER PROTESTANT DENOMINATIONS. These smaller bodies include: Religious Society of Friends, Salvation Army (1967).
UNITING CHURCHES. In 1974, separate sets of negotiations for organic union were under way, as follows: (1) Ch of Central Africa Presbyterian, Churches of Christ, Ch of the Province of Central Africa; and (2) 3 Evangelical Protestant churches. In 1977, the Evangelical Ch of Malawi united with the Zambesi Evangelical Ch to form the United Evangelical Ch.

**PEOPLES** (ethnolinguistic). Christians: 31.0% Chewa, 20.0% Nyanja, 14.0% Lomwe, 12.0% Tumbuka (2.4% Tonga), 9.8% Ngoni, 3.4% Yao, 3.0% Sena, 2.5% Fipa, 2.0% Nyakyusa (1.0% Konde), 0.3% British, 0.1% Shona, 0.1% Lambya, Greek, Zimba.

**COUNTRY-WIDE TOTALS**
EVANGELIZATION (see Part 5). 1900: 17%. 1970: 93%. 1980: 96%. *Mass evangelism.* 1970, New Life for All campaign. *Radiophonic evangelism.* TWR, RVOG, ICI (11,626 enrolments, 650 conversions reported). *Literature evangelism.* Every Home Crusade in 1976 completed its first nationwide coverage (visitation of every home with literature).
FOREIGN MISSIONARIES AND PERSONNEL (nationals serving abroad) (1973). Total 92 in Mozambique, Rhodesia, South Africa, Tanzania and Zambia: about 35 Protestants, 30 Roman Catholics, 10 African indigenous, 10 marginal Protestants (Jehovah's Witnesses), 7 Anglicans.
FOREIGN MISSIONARIES AND PERSONNEL (aliens from abroad) (1973). Total 994. *From Western world.* 847: 576 Roman Catholics, 238 Protestants (135 in 15 USA societies, 91 in 7 UK societies, 8 in 3 Canada societies, 2 in 1 WGermany society, 2 in 1 Australia society), 26 Anglicans (24 in 3 UK societies, 1 in 1 USA society, 1 in 1 Canada society), about 4 Black indigenous from USA, about 3 Catholics (non-Roman). *From Third World.* 147: 90 Protestants (78 in 6 South Africa societies, 5 Swaziland), 40 African indigenous from South Africa, Rhodesia and Zambia, about 15 Roman Catholics (4 from South Africa, 3 Philippines, Mexico et alia), 2 Anglicans.
INSTITUTIONS (church-operated). Total 170, including 40 higher schools (4 minors eminaries), about 90 medical centres, 4presses, 4 religious communities, 1 research centre, 5 study centres, 7 seminaries (6 Protestant, 1 RC).
PERIODICALS. About 30 titles.
PERSONNEL. About 3,514 (2,520 national, 994 foreign).
RELIGIOUS LIBRARIES. About 22.
SCRIPTURE DISTRIBUTION (1975). Annual totals: 31,657 Bibles (6% free, 90% subsidized, 3% commercial) 18,265 NTs (5% free, 40% subsidized, 55% commercial), 43,075 UBS portions, 213,756 UBS selections. *Translations completed.* Portion: 6 languages since 1880. NT: 6 languages since 1886. Bible: 3 languages since 1905.
SERVICE AGENCIES. About 50, including AMRIM, ARIMA, CCM, CLAIM, CSC, CSM, CWS, EAM, ECM, MEND, NCL, NCLA, NLFA, PHAM, SCO, SU, TEEM, WLC(EHC), YCS, YCW.

**ADDITIONAL DATA ON CHURCHES.**
AFRICAN NATIONAL/INTERNATIONAL CHURCH. Before 1970 known as the African National Church, since 1970 also as the African International Church. *Branches abroad.* The ANC is also found in Zambia (especially Kitwe) and Tanzania.
CATHOLIC CHURCH IN MALAWI. *Catechumens.* Totals: (1959) 66,592; (1961) 99,100; (1963) 86,225; (1970) 109,911, divided as follows among the 7 dioceses in the order shown (and included in column 7 above): 11649, 2838, 10300, 58559, 20565, 4000, 2000. *Annual baptisms.* (1972) 73.0% infant, 27.0% adult. *Priests.* The first Malawian was ordained in 1937. *Brothers.* Including 6 nationals. *Sisters.* Including 288 nationals. *Catechists.* Total (1969) 1,580 (472 being full-time). *Indigenous religious congregations.* Brothers: Oblates of the Holy Family (begun 1929; only 2 members remaining). Sisters: 140 Servants of the BVM (begun 1928), 76 Theresian Sisters (begun 1932), 44 Rosarian Sisters (begun 1951). *Main foreign congregations.* Priests: SMM, WF. Brothers: Marists, Immaculate Conception. Sisters: Montfort Sisters, Daughters of Wisdom, Medical Mission Sisters. *Catholic organizations.* The Episcopal Conference of Malawi (ECM) is a member of AMECEA and SECAM. Two organizations of religious personnel are the Association of Men's Religious Institutes in Malawi (AMRIM), and the Association of Religious Institutes in Malawi (ARIMA) for sisters. A National Council of Priests has been formed, consisting of 2 priests representing each diocesan council of priests, and plays a role in unifying pastoral planning in Malawi. Lay organizations include the National Council of the Laity, and the National Chaplain Lay Apostolate. The latter co-ordinates the activities of the Legion of Mary (700 praesidia, 12,000 members), Young Christian Students (YCS) with 430 members and Young Christian Workers (YCW) with 60 members in 15 groups.
The Holy See has diplomatic relations with Malawi and is represented to government and the Catholic hierarchy by a pro-nuncio who resides in Lusaka, Zambia.
The Catholic Church has a strong educational programme, including 619 primary schools (70,559 boys; 40,269 girls); 11 secondary schools (1,440 boys; 812 girls); 2 technical schools (214 boys); several homecraft schools (213 girls); 6 teacher-training colleges (282 boys; 335 girls); 3 minor seminaries; and one junior seminary.
Regarding social action and welfare work, most of the 103 parishes are engaged in agricultural and water schemes, through local farmers' clubs, illiteracy campaigns, credit-unions, and rural preventive and curative health work. Recently, each diocese appointed a development animator to co-ordinate overall planning and to assist in the implementation of development plans. The Catholic Church also administers homes for the aged and children in need at Limbe. Since the problem of migration is one of the major pastoral concerns of the church, a permanent chaplaincy for Malawi workers in Rhodesia was established in November 1971, and a survey of the pastoral needs of immigrants in South Africa is being made.
CHURCH OF CENTRAL AFRICA PRESBYTERIAN. In Chewa, Eklesia wa Pakati pa Afrika Chipresbiterio, Sinodi wa Blantyre/Livingstonia/Nkhoma.
CHURCH OF THE WATCH TOWER/MIKAEL CHURCH. This body has been the major separatist church in Central Africa. At its beginnings in 1908, 10,000 Tonga were baptized by Elliott Kamwana before his deportation. Returning in 1937, he restarted the movement as the Mikael Church, still mainly among the Tonga of Nkhata Bay.
PROVIDENCE INDUSTRIAL MISSION. Mainly in the south. By 1978, many members were defecting. *Name.* After 1945, the alternative name African Baptist Assembly Malawi Inc. was used.

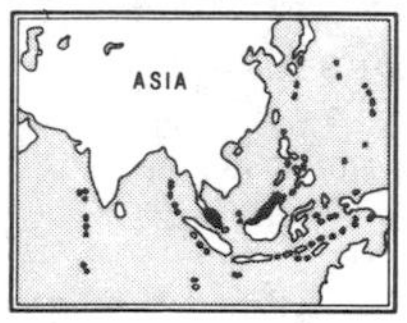


# MALAYSIA

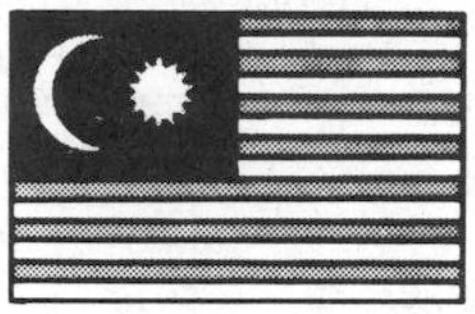

## SECULAR DATA

**STATE. Official name:** The State of Malaysia. Adjective of nationality: Malaysian.
**Flag** (shown above right): Red and white stripes with blue field containing gold crescent and 14-pointed gold star.
**Area:** 329,749 sq.km. (127,317 sq.miles). Agricultural land: 18.3%.
**Government:** Federal constitutional monarchy, since 1963 (by 1900 British-protected, 1946 Union of Malaya, 1948 Federation of Malaya, 1957 Independence).
**Legislature:** Parliament: Senate (Dewan Negara), 58 members; House of Representatives (Dewan Ra'ayat), 154 members.
**Official languages:** Malay and English.
**Chief cities:** capital Kuala Lumpur 451,980 (1970), George Town 269,600, Ipoh 247,950.
**Political divisions:** Peninsular Malaysia (former West Malaysia, or Malaya), Sarawak and Sabah (the latter 2 formerly called East Malaysia); divided into 9 States.
**Armed forces** (1976): Total 62,300 regular: army 52,500, navy 4,800, air force 5,000 (50 combat aircraft). Reserves: 26,500. Paramilitary forces: 82,000.
**Foreign forces** (1973): 1,400 Australian troops.

**DEMOGRAPHY. Population:** 10,319,324 (census of 24–25.VIII.-1970. For 1970–2000 (UN), see last row of Table 1). Population density (1975): 37/sq.km. (95/sq,mile). Under 15 years: 47%. Growth rate (1975–80): 2.93% per year (births 3.78%, deaths −0.86%). Life expectancy (1975–80): 61.8 years. Household size: 5.1 persons.
**Major languages:** Malay, English, Chinese (Fukienese), Tamil, Javanese, Iban, Dusun, Banjarese, Telugu, Punjabi, Arabic, Dayak, and about 170 smaller languages.
**Urban dwellers** (1970): 41.1%. Urban growth rate (1950–70): 5.8% per year.
**Labour force:** 33%.
**Refugees** (1977): 90,000, in Sabah, from the Philippines; 1,440 from Viet Nam.
**Tourists** (1974): 1,080,720.

**ETHNOLINGUISTIC GROUPS:** 40.6% Malay, 36.4% Chinese (Hokkien Fukienese, Cantonese, Hakka, Teochew, Hainanese, Kwangsi, Hokchiu Fukienese), 7.2% Tamil, 3.1% Javanese, 2.6% Iban (Sea Dayak), 2.0% Dusun (Kadazan), 1.1% Banjarese, 0.8% Bajau (Sea Nomad, Sea Gypsy, Orang-Laut), 0.8% Dayak, 0.6% Malayali, 0.6% Melanau, 0.4% Kedayan, 0.4% Telugu, 0.4% Riau, 0.4% Punjabi, 0.3% Senoi, 0.3% Kayan, 0.3% Murut, 0.2% Kanarese, 0.2% Hindi, 0.2% Buginese, 0.2% Minangkabau, 0.2% Euronesian (Eurasian), 0.1% Sulu-Samal, 0.1% Kenyah, 0.1% British, Afghani, Arab, Bengali, Sinhalese, Thai, Semang, Filipino, Kelabit, Bisaya, Punan, Tidong, et alii.

**MONEY** (1977). **Monetary unit:** ringgit (dollar) (= 100 cents); US$1 = m$2.52.
**National income per person:** US$570. Average annual family Income: US$2,907.
**Inflation:** (1970–74) 8.0% per year (1975: consumer price index 145).
**Cost of living in capital** (1976): index 119 (Washington DC=100). Daily cost of living: US$39.

**HEALTH.** Hospitals: 244 (37,311 beds). Doctors: 2,054. Lepers: 17,600 (1.5 per 1,000). Blind: 50,000. Psychotics: 85,000. Criminals: 10,000.

**EDUCATION.** Adult literacy: (1947) 38%, (1970) 56%. Education rate: 60%. Schools: 6,357. Universities: 3.

**LITERATURE.** Annual new book titles (1973): 1,082. Periodicals: 747. Newspapers: 39 dailies, 14 non-daily.

**COMMUNICATION** (per 1,000 people). Phones: 21. Radios: 40. TV sets: 31. Daily newspaper circulation: 85 copies.

TABLE 1. RELIGIOUS ADHERENTS IN MALAYSIA

| Year | 1900 | | mid-1970 | | Annual change, 1970–1980 | | | | mid-1975 | | mid-1980 | | 2000 | |
|---|---|---|---|---|---|---|---|---|---|---|---|---|---|---|
| *Name* | *Adherents* | *%* | *Adherents* | *%* | *Natural* | *Conversion* | *Total* | *Rate* | *Adherents* | *%* | *Adherents* | *%* | *Adherents* | *%* |
| Muslims | 1,024,000 | 48.8 | 5,181,000 | 49.5 | 174,658 | −458 | 174,200 | 2.91 | 5,980,000 | 49.4 | 6,923,000 | 49.4 | 10,806,000 | 49.0 |
| Ahmadis | 0 | 0.0 | 1,000 | 0.0 | 38 | 22 | 60 | 4.62 | 1,300 | 0.0 | 1,600 | 0.0 | 4,000 | 0.0 |
| Chinese folk-religionists | 525,000 | 25.0 | 2,608,373 | 24.9 | 87,476 | −2,863 | 84,613 | 2.83 | 2,995,000 | 24.8 | 3,454,500 | 24.7 | 5,570,000 | 25.2 |
| Hindus | 210,000 | 10.0 | 774,500 | 7.4 | 26,137 | −7 | 26,130 | 2.92 | 894,900 | 7.4 | 1,035,800 | 7.4 | 1,544,000 | 7.0 |
| Buddhists | 105,000 | 5.0 | 669,800 | 6.4 | 22,606 | −586 | 22,020 | 2.84 | 774,000 | 6.4 | 890,000 | 6.4 | 1,323,000 | 6.0 |
| **Christians** | **32,000** | **1.5** | **561,827** | **5.4** | **20,418** | **9,579** | **29,997** | **4.29** | **699,100** | **5.8** | **861,800** | **6.2** | **1,649,000** | **7.5** |
| crypto-Christians | 7,000 | 0.3 | 101,327 | 1.0 | 3,887 | 4,960 | 8,847 | 6.65 | 133,100 | 1.1 | 189,800 | 1.4 | 392,000 | 1.8 |
| professing | 25,000 | 1.2 | 460,500 | 4.4 | 16,531 | 4,619 | 21,150 | 3.74 | 566,000 | 4.7 | 672,000 | 4.8 | 1,257,000 | 5.7 |
| Roman Catholics | 16,000 | 0.8 | 262,500 | 2.5 | 9,551 | 3,399 | 12,950 | 3.96 | 327,000 | 2.7 | 392,000 | 2.8 | 750,000 | 3.4 |
| Protestants | 1,000 | 0.0 | 136,000 | 1.3 | 4,848 | 1,152 | 6,000 | 3.61 | 166,000 | 1.4 | 196,000 | 1.4 | 353,000 | 1.6 |
| Anglicans | 8,000 | 0.4 | 62,000 | 0.6 | 2,132 | 68 | 2,200 | 3.01 | 73,000 | 0.6 | 84,000 | 0.6 | 154,000 | 0.7 |
| affiliated | 32,000 | 1.5 | 561,827 | 5.4 | 20,418 | 9,579 | 29,997 | 4.29 | 699,100 | 5.8 | 861,800 | 6.2 | 1,649,000 | 7.5 |
| total practising | 28,800 | *90* | 421,370 | *75* | 15,314 | 7,184 | 22,498 | 4.29 | 524,320 | *75* | 646,350 | *75* | 1,154,300 | *70* |
| non-practising | 3,200 | *10* | 140,460 | *25* | 5,104 | 2,395 | 7,499 | 4.29 | 174,780 | *25* | 215,450 | *25* | 494,700 | *30* |
| Roman Catholics | 20,000 | 0.9 | 301,449 | 2.9 | 10,950 | 5,105 | 16,055 | 4.28 | 374,900 | 3.1 | 462,000 | 3.3 | 882,000 | 4.0 |
| Catholic pentecostals | 0 | 0.0 | 0 | 0.0 | 29 | 371 | 400 | 40.00 | 1,000 | 0.0 | 4,000 | 0.0 | 20,000 | 0.1 |
| Protestants | 2,000 | 0.1 | 160,478 | 1.5 | 5,651 | 2,101 | 7,752 | 4.01 | 193,500 | 1.6 | 23[illegible],000 | 1.7 | 463,000 | 2.1 |
| Evangelicals | 2,000 | 0.1 | 105,000 | 1.0 | 3,884 | 2,416 | 6,300 | 4.74 | 133,000 | 1.1 | 168,000 | 1.2 | 352,900 | 1.6 |
| Neo-pentecostals | 0 | 0.0 | 0 | 0.0 | 29 | 271 | 300 | 30.00 | 3,000 | 0.0 | 3,000 | 0.0 | 10,000 | 0.0 |
| Anglicans | 10,000 | 0.5 | 69,600 | 0.7 | 2,687 | 1,753 | 4,440 | 4.83 | 92,000 | 0.8 | 114,000 | 0.8 | 190,000 | 0.9 |
| Asian indigenous | 0 | 0.0 | 27,700 | 0.3 | 1,051 | 679 | 1,730 | 4.81 | 36,000 | 0.3 | 45,000 | 0.3 | 110,000 | 0.5 |
| Orthodox | 0 | 0.0 | 1,500 | 0.0 | 44 | −44 | 0 | 0.00 | 1,500 | 0.0 | 1,500 | 0.0 | 2,000 | 0.0 |
| Marginal Protestants | 0 | 0.0 | 900 | 0.0 | 28 | −18 | 10 | 1.05 | 950 | 0.0 | 1,000 | 0.0 | 2,000 | 0.0 |
| Catholics (non-Roman) | 0 | 0.0 | 200 | 0.0 | 7 | 3 | 10 | 4.00 | 250 | 0.0 | 300 | 0.0 | 500 | 0.0 |
| Tribal religionists | 200,000 | 9.5 | 533,000 | 5.1 | 16,925 | −7,375 | 9,550 | 1.65 | 579,400 | 4.8 | 628,500 | 4.5 | 657,000 | 3.0 |
| New-Religionists | 0 | 0.0 | 50,000 | 0.5 | 1,752 | 248 | 2,000 | 3.33 | 60,000 | 0.5 | 70,000 | 0.5 | 220,000 | 1.0 |
| Baha'is | 0 | 0.0 | 42,700 | 0.4 | 1,519 | 411 | 1,930 | 3.71 | 52,000 | 0.4 | 62,000 | 0.4 | 125,000 | 0.6 |
| Sikhs | 4,000 | 0.2 | 20,000 | 0.2 | 686 | 14 | 700 | 2.98 | 23,500 | 0.2 | 27,000 | 0.2 | 45,000 | 0.2 |
| Non-religious | 0 | 0.0 | 16,000 | 0.2 | 672 | 728 | 1,400 | 6.09 | 23,000 | 0.2 | 30,000 | 0.2 | 80,000 | 0.4 |
| Atheists | 0 | 0.0 | 8,000 | 0.1 | 321 | 279 | 600 | 5.45 | 11,000 | 0.1 | 14,000 | 0.1 | 30,000 | 0.1 |
| Other religionists | 0 | 0.0 | 800 | 0.0 | 30 | 30 | 60 | 5.45 | 1,100 | 0.0 | 1,400 | 0.0 | 5,000 | 0.0 |
| **Country's population** | **2,100,000** | **100.0** | **10,466,000** | **100.0** | **353,200** | **0** | **353,200** | **2.92** | **12,093,000** | **100.0** | **13,998,000** | **100.0** | **22,054,000** | **100.0** |

COLUMNS, ROWS. For meanings and definitions, see Codebook (Part 6). Note that, by definition, total 'Christians' = professing + crypto-Christians, which also = affiliated + nominal Christians. Percentages may not always total exactly, due to rounding.
CENSUSES. (a) *Malaya* (West Malaysia). **1931**; 45.1% Muslims, 38.4% Chinese folk-religionists and Buddhists, 12.0% Hindus, 2.3% Christians, 0.7% tribal religionists, 0.4% Sikhs. **23.IX.1947:** 44.0% Muslims, 43.8% Chinese folk-religionists and Buddhists,

8.7% Hindus, 2.1% Christians, 0.6% tribal religionists, 0.3% Sikhs. **24.VIII.1970**: 53.2% Muslims, 34.9% Chinese folk-religionists and Buddhists, 8.7% Hindus, 2.5% Christians, 0.4% tribal religionists, 0.2% Sikhs. (b) *Sabah* (formerly North Borneo), **1921**: 52.5% tribal religionists, 31.8% Muslims, 13.0% Chinese folk-religionists and Buddhists, 2.7% Christians. **1931**: 48.7% tribal religionists, 32.1% Muslims, 15.3% Chinese folk-religionists and Buddhists, 3.9% Christians. **3.IV.1951**: 40.3% tribal religionists, 34.5% Muslims, 16.5% Chinese folk-religionists and Buddhists, 8.7% Christians. **9. VIII. 1960**: 37.9% Muslims, 29.0% tribal religionists, 16.5% Chinese folk-religionists and Buddhists, 16.6% Christians. **24.VIII.1970**: 40.1% Muslims, 9.7% Christians (rest incorrectly recorded: probably 33.7% tribal religionists, 16.5% Chinese folk-religionists and Buddhists). (c) *Sarawak*. **23.IX.1947**: 45.7% tribal religionists, 24.6% Muslims, 21.8% Chinese folk-religionists and Buddhists, 7.9% Christians (3.7% Protestants, 2.4% Roman Catholics, 1.8% Anglicans). **14.VI.1960**: 37.3% tribal religionists, 23.5% Chinese folk-religionists and Buddhists, 23.4% Muslims, 15.8% Christians. **23.VIII.1970**: 30.9% tribal religionists, 25.8% Muslims, 24.0% Chinese folk-religionists and Buddhists, 19.3% Christians. (d) *Malaysia* (all parts). **24.VIII.1970**: 50.0% Muslims, 32.8% Buddhists and Chinese folk-religionists, 7.4% Hindus, 5.1% tribal religionists, 4.4% Christians, 0.2% Sikhs, 0.2% non-religious.

## NOTES ON RELIGIONS

**AHMADIS.** Qadianis from Pakistan. There are now 5 mosques in Sabah among the Dusun.

**ASIAN INDIGENOUS.** In 12 denominations or groupings in 1970 (see Table 2); Chinese, Indian and Malay indigenous Christians.

**ATHEISTS.** Communist Party of Malaya (proscribed; pro-Chinese): membership (1970) 2,000, all underground.

**BAHA'IS.** 1962, mass conversions in Sarawak of 6,000 in 4 months to Baha'i, then rapid growth from 97 local spiritual assemblies (1964; 70 in Sarawak) to 287 (1973; 165 in Sarawak). There are many Iban teachers.

**BUDDHISTS.** Chinese adherents of Mahayana and Tantric Buddhism, with small areas of Theravada (Sinhalese et alii).

**CATHOLIC PENTECOSTALS** (or, Catholic charismatics). The renewal is largely ecumenical. Total Catholics involved (1976), over 500 adults, with their children.

**CRYPTO-CHRISTIANS.** Mostly unorganized individuals in legal or recognized churches in Sabah; in the 1960 census there, 16.6% Christians were recorded, but in 1970 (under strong state-aided Muslim pressure) only 9.7% publicly professed to be Christians. There are also numerous organized and unorganized isolated radio believers.

**HINDUS.** Mostly Tamils from South India. Every year 200,000 Hindus make the pilgrimage to the Batu Caves for the Thaipusam festival, doing penance by carrying spiked cages (*Kavadis*) whilst in a trance. Sects include the Ramakrishna Mission.

**MUSLIMS.** Sunnis (with Shia and Sufi elements), consisting of: all Malays (all Shafiite), all Pakistanis, most Javanese, 50,000

Indians in West Malaysia, 10,200 Indonesians in Sabah, and 33% of the Aboriginal population of East Malaysia. There are also a few Ahmadis (enumerated here although declared non-Muslim by Pakistan). *Hajj pilgrims to Mecca.* (1968) 6,236; (1969) 8,353; (1970) 10,361; (1971) 10,650; (1972) 10,395; (1973) 12,983; (1974) 15,366; (1975) 15,835; (1976) 3,373. *Conversions.* With state support many Aboriginals and others in Sabah are being converted to Islam, and state pressure on the Iban to become Muslim is particularly strong. A Chinese Muslim trained at Al-Azhar University (Cairo, Egypt) is training Chinese Muslim missionaries in Kuala Lumpur. At the same time, many Muslims in West Malaysia are being converted to Baha'i, atheism and non-religion (with a few to Christianity), so that the nett balance is a small annual numerical loss to Islam in Malaysia.

**NEO-PENTECOSTALS.** A charismatic renewal began around 1972 involving a number of senior Protestant church leaders.

**NEW-RELIGIONISTS.** Adherents of (1) Heavenly Virtue Holy Church (T'ien Te Sheng Hui), a syncretistic combination of Confucianism, Taoism, Buddhism, Islam and Christianity, begun in 1920 in China and widespread among the Chinese diaspora; and (2) Soka Gakkai (Nichiren Shoshu) from Japan, numbering 6,500 by 1975.

**NON-RELIGIOUS.** Mainly Chinese.

**OTHER RELIGIONISTS.** Including Rosicrucians (1 AMORC centre).

**TRIBAL RELIGIONISTS.** Animists in East Malaysia among the Dusun, Iban (Sea Dayak), Land Dayak and other tribes.

---

**NON-CHRISTIAN RELIGIONS. Islam** is the state religion and is adhered to by virtually all Malays, who constitute 50% of the population of West Malaysia, by all Pakistanis and by about 50,000 Indians in West Malaysia; the latter being low-caste farmer immigrants from southern India; approximately one-third of the aboriginal population of East Malaysia also are Muslims. In 1970 Malaya was 53% Muslim, Sabah 40% and Sarawak 26%.

Islam was brought to Malaya by Arab traders in the 13th century, and within the next 200 years became the predominant religion of the region. By the end of the 16th century Malayan Islam tended to be Sunni in form, although today Shia elements and a Sufi spirit are also evident. Malays are attracted to the more mystical aspect of Islam but freely retain and adapt them to early Hindu and animistic traditions. Ancestor veneration, belief in the omnipresence of spirits, sacrifices, astrology, amulets, magicians and shamans all have a place in popular devotion. As elsewhere, Muslim religious education tends to concentrate on memorizing passages from the Quran; but in recent years educated Malay Muslims, influenced by British secular education, have turned to various modern Islamic movements such as those expounded at the University of Al-Azhar in Cairo or the Muhammadiyah party of Indonesia. The Southeast Asia regional bureau of the World Muslim Congress, with headquarters in Pakistan, is located in Kuala Lumpur.

**Chinese folk religion** and **Buddhism** are the predominant religions among the Chinese, who make up 40% of the population of West Malaysia and 25% in Sarawak. Buddhism arrived in Malaya in the 3rd century, the original Hinayana form being displaced in the 12th century by Mahayana. A still later manifestation is Tantric Buddhism, a result of the influence of early Malayan Hinduism. Most Chinese immigrants, however, have come from the lower classes of south and central China and observe a popular folk religion centred in ancestral veneration rituals and magical practices together with elements taken from Buddhism, Confucianism and Taoism.

**Hinduism** was introduced during the first century AD. Immigrants from the Indian sub-continent, most of whom have come since the end of the 19th century, make up 11% of the population of West Malaysia and are predominantly Hindus. There is also a small community of Sikhs originating in the Punjab of northwest India.

**Tribal religions** are still strong among the indigenous peoples of Sarawak and Sabah. Although there are variations between the different tribes (Dusan, Iban or Sea Dayak, Land Dayak), they share many beliefs and rituals in common. All believe in the existence

**Muslims.** One of the most modern mosques in Asia, the National Mosque (Masjid Negara) in Kuala Lumpur, opened in 1965, accommodates 15,000 worshippers. Its spire and roof depict, respectively, a folded umbrella and unfurled parasol, both symbolic of Malaysian royalty.

**Chinese folk-religionists.** In Confucian temple near Kuala Lumpur.

of good and evil spirits whose favour is sought or whose anger must be placated. Omens, tabus, divination and magical practices are also important, and elaborate rites are performed at burials as well as at rice-planting and harvesting seasons. Traditional tribal religions, including head-hunting customs, continue to exist among the Dayaks in Sarawak. Possession of a skull is believed to ensure fertility of the soil, safe arrival of the deceased to the land of the dead and enlistment of the spirit of the dead enemy in the service (after death) of the one possessing his skull. Among some Dayaks, marriage arrangements cannot be formalized until a skull has been captured.

**Heavenly Virtue Holy Church** (T'ien Te Sheng Hui) is a syncretistic new religion widespread among the Chinese diaspora, especially in Hong Kong (100,000 adherents) and in Malaysia where it is supported by wealthy Chinese and has a following among medical doctors because of its emphasis on healing. It was founded in Yunnan (China) in 1920 by a Chinese Buddhist, and it attempts to combine the 5 major religions of Confucianism, Taoism, Buddhism, Islam and Christianity. It stresses ethical conduct, virtue and wisdom, and aims to establish harmony between heaven and earth. It has a cosmological concept of history and a low level of folk-religion content.

**Baha'i** has grown rapidly since its mass conversion of 6,000 in Sarawak in 4 months in 1962. By 1973 there were 287 local spiritual assemblies.

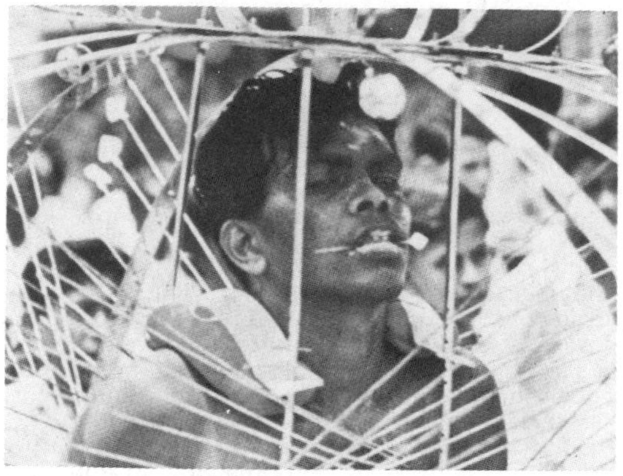

**Hindus.** Thaipusam festival in Batu Caves (14 miles from Kuala Lumpur): devotee in trance carries a *kavadi* (cage of metal spikes) to shrine of Hindu deity Lord Subramaniam, the Spotless One. Every year 200,000 Hindus make this pilgrimage.

**CHRISTIANITY.** The first Christians were Catholics who arrived in the 16th century after the conquest of Malacca by the Portuguese. Protestantism appeared in the 17th century with the Dutch occupation, but Protestant missions made little advance until the arrival of the British in the early part of the 19th century. Christianity is most highly developed among the Chinese, somewhat less so among the Indians and Aboriginals, and has made no inroads at all among the Malays who remain almost entirely Muslim. By 1975 Christians made up 5.4% of the total population of Malaysia, with Catholics 3% and Protestants 1.5%. In 1970 Christians formed 10% of the population of Sabah and 19% in Sarawak. Several denominations consist of jurisdictions covering both Malaysia and Singapore, a state of affairs which remained unaltered even after Singapore's withdrawal from the Federation in 1965. A few have since redrawn their ecclesiastical boundaries to accord with the new political situation. However, the Council of Churches of Malaysia and Singapore remained undivided and based in Singapore, as one of the major centres of Christian activity in southeast Asia, until 1975 when it split up into 2 separate national councils, one for each nation.

CATHOLIC CHURCH. The first Catholic priest arrived in Malacca with the Portuguese in 1511, and Francis Xavier spent 3 years there in the 1540s. Malacca became a diocese in 1557, but the bishop was forced to leave in 1641 when the Dutch took over Malaysia. In 1841 the area was formed into the vicariate of West Siam. The diocese of Malacca was reconstituted in 1888 with Singapore as its seat, and in 1953 an archdiocese was established. Singapore became a separate archdiocese in 1972.

In West Malaysia the majority of Catholics are Indians with a substantial number of Chinese and Eurasians; in fact, almost all Eurasians are Catholics. The present diocese of Malacca-Johore has a Catholic population of 18,000 Chinese, 5,000 Indians and 3,000 Eurasians. Of its 21 priests, 12 are Chinese, 3 Indians, 2 Eurasians and 4 Europeans (MEP). In East Malaysia most Catholics are either Aboriginal or Chinese. In the state of Sabah, whose Catholic population consists of 50,000 Aboriginals and 40,000 Chinese, plus a few in other ethnic groups, the Catholic Church has been under attack by provincial authorities which has not been the case in the adjoining state of Sarawak with its larger Chinese constituency. The vicar apostolic of Kota Kinabalu, although a naturalized Malaysian citizen, has in fact never been granted permission to reside permanently in Sabah. While living in the neighbouring vicariate of Miri (Sarawak), he is authorized to make only one pastoral visit to Sabah every 2 weeks. A general problem for the church has been its failure to develop local clergy to replace foreign missionaries, in contrast to Protestant churches which are well provided with local leaders.

According to the Office of the Apostolic Visitor for the Chinese of the Diaspora in Singapore, in 1969 there were in Malaysia, Brunei and Singapore an estimated 166,900 Chinese Catholics among a total Chinese population of 5,802,000, with 183 Chinese priests working among them in 85 churches.

An anachronistic vestige of the old Portuguese patronage system is the presence of a Portuguese parish within the diocese of Malacca-Johore but under the jurisdiction of the diocese of Macao.

PROTESTANT CHURCHES. Protestant missions and churches have been characterized by great diversity since the arrival of numerous new missionaries after World War II, including many forced out of mainland China and others sent by autonomous national churches in Japan, Korea and the Philippines. Many congregations are composed of immigrants from China and India, which has militated against unity within denominations as well as between them. The various conservative ethnic churches, particularly among the large Chinese population, generally give more attention to their national traditions and the social needs of their members than to broader Christian concerns. This pattern of ethnic isolation has been further aggravated by certain government policies. Out of fear of infiltration by Chinese communists in the early 1950s, new inland villages were created in West Malaysia composed of Chinese who had formerly been living in slum settlements along the Thailand border. In East Malaysia, rapid conversion to Christianity is taking place among Aboriginals, which however does not preclude the continuation of many traditional beliefs. This is also true of conversions to Islam. In both East and West Malaysia, the influence of Christian mission schools and hospitals far outweighs their numerical significance.

Protestantism first entered Malaya with the conquest of Malacca by the Dutch in 1641 but was confined to the European population. When Malacca passed into the hands of the British at the beginning of the 19th century, a first Protestant missionary was sent by the London Missionary Society in 1814. Soon after, the Anglo-Chinese College was established in Malacca to train Chinese missionaries for work in China, which was then closed to Europeans. The LMS left Malaya for China when the door opened for missionary work there in 1843.

Another early LMS missionary, a Presbyterian, worked among Malays but with little success. Presbyterian growth has been slow due to the restriction of its sphere of activity to the east coast of the Malay peninsula, and also due to Presbyterian Chinese immigrants importing their own structures. Nevertheless, the Presbyterian Church in Singapore and Malaysia, also called the Chinese Christian Church began to register important gains during the 1960s and in fact doubled in size.

Methodists have the largest Protestant church in Malaysia. The first American Methodist missionaries arrived in Singapore in 1885, followed later by others from Australia and Britain. Chinese and Tamil pastors came from China, India and Ceylon; and the first annual conference was held in 1902. The Sarawak Annual Conference was formed in 1956 and the Sarawak Iban Provisional Annual Conference in 1962. The church has 35 primary and 43 secondary schools, but these are now coming increasingly under government control. There are also 5 medical institutions (one hospital and 4 clinics), an agricultural extension service and a rural community development programme for Ibans in Sarawak and a community centre in Kuala Lumpur. The Methodist Church of Malaysia and Singapore became autonomous in 1968, with its first local bishop elected at that time.

The second largest Protestant denomination is the Evangelical Church of Borneo, which was founded in 1963 and has 278 local congregations in more than 10 tribes. This church owes its beginnings to the outreach of the Borneo Evangelical Mission from Australia among East Malaysian tribesmen, particularly the Dusuns, in 1928. From the beginning emphasis was placed on indigenous principles of evangelization, and its Central Bible School now has a largely local staff and 150 students.

Seventh-day Adventists are growing rapidly in East Malaysia, particularly in Sabah; church membership tripled in size during the early 1960s. The Basel Mission opened work among Chinese Christian Hakka families in Northern Borneo in 1882. There congregations have grown through continual Chinese immigration, as well as by conversion and natural increase; and the Basel Christian Church was formally established in 1926.

Pentecostal bodies include the Assemblies of God and the Finnish Free Foreign Mission. Also present are Baptists, Brethren, Lutherans, Salvation Army and several smaller denominations.

OTHER CHURCHES. The first Anglican touched Malaysia in 1809. An Anglican opened the first English-speaking school in 1816, but systematic work did not begin for another 30 years. In 1841 Sarawak was ceded to the British settler James Brook, who arranged for the arrival of the first

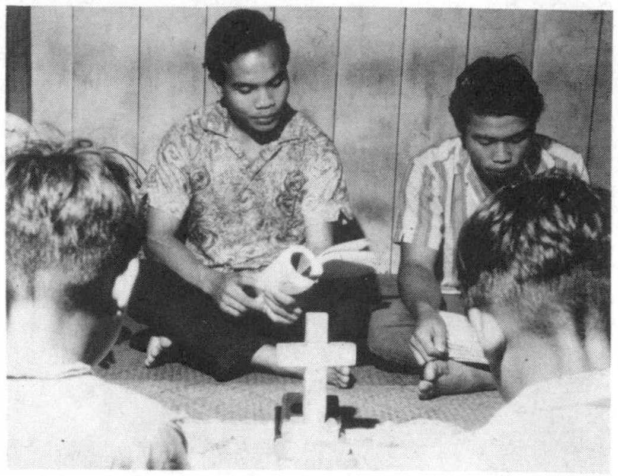

**Methodist Church in Malaysia.** Iban pastor conducts service on long-house verandah in Sarawak.

SPG missionaries in 1848. The missionary staff was later enlarged by the addition of CMS members from the UK and Australia. Evangelistic, educational and medical work was undertaken among Chinese residents, Tamil immigrants from India, and the Sea Dayaks whose language was then reduced to writing. The church is now responsible for 59 primary schools, 6 secondary schools, 3 clinics and an agricultural programme in Kuching. The 3 Anglican dioceses in Malaysia are missionary dioceses under the archbishop of Canterbury, England, and in 1974 they formed part of the Council of the Church of South East Asia (from 1975 renamed East Asia).

Several independent churches have been formed in Malaysia, especially among the Chinese. The major group is the True Jesus Church which was brought to Malaysia by immigrants from mainland China. Other immigrant bodies are the Tamil-speaking Ceylon Pentecostal Church of Malaya, which was established in 1936, and the Mar Thoma Syrian Church which serves Indians from Kerala. Of groups entirely indigenous to Malaysia, the largest is the Bible Presbyterian Church which was created through a schism in the Chinese Christian Church.

There is also a small community of the Orthodox Syrian Church composed of immigrants from Kerala, South India.

**CHURCH AND STATE.** According to the constitution of 1957 (Article 3, item 1), 'Islam is the religion of the Federation'; but when Sabah and Sarawak joined the federation in 1963, safeguards covering their special interests were included. The head of state or king is the recognized head of Islam (the Muslim community) in his home state and also in 2 other states, Malacca and Penang. These latter states have no Muslim sultans but governors are appointed by the king, and their provincial constitutions provide that the king will also serve as the head of Islam in their areas. In Sabah and Sarawak there is no head of Islam, but Article 3 is also applicable there. Although the constitution does not specifically enjoin that the head of state should be a Muslim, as a matter of fact only a Muslim can be elected because he is always chosen from the Muslim sultans of the 9 states of West Malaysia. Furthermore, while it is not stated in the constitution that the king is officially the defender of the faith or head of Islam throughout the federation, nevertheless when taking the oath of office the king declares that he will 'at all times protect the Muslim religion', and he is constitutionally empowered to undertake action in minor matters such as fixing uniform dates for religious functions and festivals.

Article 11, item 1, stipulates: 'Every person has the right to profess and practise his religion and, subject to clause 4, to propagate it'. Clause 4 provides that any state law may control and restrict the propagation of any religious doctrine or belief among persons professing the Muslim religion. Nevertheless, Article 161D affirms that in the 2 Borneo states no law controlling or restricting the propagation of any religious doctrine or belief among Muslims may be passed, except with the consent of a two-thirds majority in the state legislature.

In each state there is a council of religion, called by various names, to advise the sultan in the exercise of his functions as head of Islam. In Malacca and Penang, the council advises the king and in Sabah and Sarawak the state governments. To provide for a more efficient co-ordination of religious affairs, on 17 October 1968 the National Council for Islamic Affairs of West Malaysia was established. Usually the prime minister is appointed chairman of this council, and the secretariat with a small staff works at the prime minister's office in Kuala Lumpur. Its functions are, firstly, to advise and make recommendations concerning any religious matters referred to it by any state government or state religious council; and secondly, to advise the Conference of Rulers, state governments and state religious councils on matters concerning islamic law, the administration of Islam, and islamic education. Nevertheless, the National Council has no jurisdiction over the position, privileges, rights, sovereignty or other powers of any ruler as head of Islam in his state.

Although Islam is the official religion of the whole federation, the power to legislate on matters of Islamic law is vested solely in the state legislatures. Today Islamic law in Malaysia is restricted entirely to religious matters and the personal status and rights of Malays.

Recently the Catholic Church has had a prolonged dispute with the state government of Sabah. Between March 1970 and December 1974, 37 Mill Hill priests and all expatriate sisters were deported and others were refused permits to enter Sabah. At the same time there has been since 1969 an upsurge in Muslim missionary activities with the formation of the United Sabah Islamic Association (USIA). The secretary-general of the USIA, a prominent lawyer, recently claimed that 'leaders of the USIA have made tremendous progress in winning converts all over Sabah, particularly in the interior'. There have been allegations that some conversions to Islam from among the Aboriginal and Christian populations have been based on coercion or bribery. The Sabah chief minister in 1972 held that Islam alone could bring national unity to Malaysia and did not hide his antipathy towards Christian conversions in his state. These anti-Catholic developments do not have the approval of Kuala Lumpur, but the federal government is unwilling to involve itself in Sabah's internal religious affairs. By 1977 all Protestant missionaries also had been deported or withdrawn from Sabah.

## INTERDENOMINATIONAL ORGANIZATIONS.

The Council of Churches of Malaysia and Singapore, begun in 1948, had its headquarters in Singapore until 1975. It operated through 11 regional councils, 10 in Malaysia and one in Singapore. The council continued to have difficulty in breaking through denominational self-sufficiency due to the large number of national and tribal churches and the multiplicity of languages and dialects, both foreign and local. Other problems included divisions created by pro- and anti-ecumenical factions, the conservative attitude of the large Chinese Christian population, and the government's uncompromising opposition to mission work among Malays. The latter policy also restricted co-operative efforts in radio broadcasting. Finally in 1975 the Council split into 2 separate national councils, one for Malaysia and one for Singapore.

Church union discussions among several members of the Council have been in progress for a number of years. In both Malaysia and Singapore, discussions have begun concerning the creation of a Sodepax committee.

**BROADCASTING.** Neither radio nor TV stations in Malaysia accept regular Christian programmes, which can only be heard over the foreign stations FEBC (Manila) and Radio Vatican (20 minutes a week in Malay). However, radio programmes prepared in Chinese and Tamil are broadcast at Christmas. Catholics have recently opened a small recording and training studio for radio and educational TV in Kuala Lumpur, and a Protestant studio is located in Lawas, Sarawak, sponsored by the Evangelical Church of Borneo, which prepares programmes for release over FEBC. For Catholics, Malaysia/Singapore is a member of UNDA.

## BIBLIOGRAPHY


*Buddhism in Malaya*. C. McDougall. Singapore: Donald Moore, 1956.

*Catholic directory and diary 1973*. Kuala Lumpur: Bishop's House, 1973.

*Christ and crisis in southeast Asia*. G. H. Anderson. New York: Friendship Press, 1968. 176p. (On Malaysia and other countries).

'Church structure issues in Asian ecumenical thought with particular reference to Malaysia and Singapore'. K. H. Yap. Dissertation, University Microfilms (USA), 1970. 260p.

'Into a new age'. R. Nyce. Kuala Lumpur: Area Research Report, 1972. (Mimeographed).

*The Catholic Church in Malaya*. F. G. Lee. Singapore: Donald Moore, 1963.

*The Centenary of the Methodist Church in southeast Asia*. J. N. Hollister. Lucknow: Lucknow Publishing House, 1956.

'The form of a North Borneo nativistic behavior', T. R. Williams, *American antropologist*, 65, 3 (1963), Part I, 543–551. (During Japanese contact in 1941).


TABLE 2. ORGANIZED CHURCHES AND DENOMINATIONS IN MALAYSIA

| Official name 1 | Begun 2 | Type 3 | Counc 4 | Congs 5 | Adults 6 | Affiliated 7 | Names, notes, and other statistics (see Codebook) 8 |
|---|---|---|---|---|---|---|---|
| Advent Christian Church | 1959 | P Adv | xF••• | 2 | 50 | 200 | M=American Advent Mission Society(USA). Begun from India. Tamils. |
| **Anglican Church of Malaysia:** | 1809 | A Cen | AwEAW | 139 | 47,365 | 69,600 | In CCEA. 3 missionary dioceses under D Canterbury. 3h,6r. 35n,34x,1643Y,2200y. |
| D Sabah (Jesselton) | 1962 | A Cen | a | 32 | 16,000 | 30,000 | M=CMS(Australia),USPG. Chinese, Kadazan, Murut, Indians. 4 3 700 900 |
| D Kuching (Sarawak) | 1855 | A Hig | a | 47 | 25,635 | 29,600 | 53% Iban, 35% Chinese, 12% other Dayak. P=46%,1s(10),W=18%. 16 16 783 996 |
| D West Malaysia | 1970 | A Cen | a | 60 | 5,730 | 10,000 | Language: 53% English, 24% Tamil, 23% Chinese. P=60%,W=35%. 15 15 160 300 |
| Apostolic Bible Christian Church | 1960 | I pen | ••••• | 3 | 43 | 100 | Small group of indigenous pentecostals. Members all South Indians. 1n,W=80%,10Y. |
| Assemblies of God | 1928 | P Pe2 | ZF••• | 28 | 2,755 | 6,000 | *Sidang Jumat Allah*. M=AoG(USA,UK). Classical Pentecostal. 1 school. 61n,12f,1s(39). |
| Bible Presbyterian Church | | I Ref | •TT•T | | 500 | 1,500 | Schism ex Chinese Christian Ch. Sponsors Malaysia Christian Pioneer Mission. |
| **Catholic Church in Malaysia:** | 1511 | R Lat | P•F•P | 154 | 159,800 | 301,449 | 53% West Malaysia, 47% East. C=7+4+12. 3p,1s(35). 251nx,175m,597w,P=61%,13606Yy. |
| M Kuala Lumpur | 1955 | R Lat | Ps | 32 | 28,600 | 53,885 | *Diocesi Agong Kuala L.* Indian, Chinese, Eurasian. 52 55 238 74 1744 |
| D Malacca-Johore | 1972 | R Lat | Pmep | 13 | 13,800 | 25,975 | 69% Chinese, 19% Indian, 12% Eurasian. 1p. 21 29 60 48 700 |
| D Penang | 1955 | R Lat | Ps | 56 | 32,500 | 61,237 | *Diocesi Penang*. Major centre of Buddhism. 1p,1s. 72 74 129 75 1771 |
| VA Kota Kinabalu (1976, D) | 1927 | R Lat | Pmhm | 28 | 42,700 | 80,837 | Sabah.55% Aborigines,45% Chinese. Underground. 12n. 38 0 60 49 4483 |
| VA Kuching (from 1976, M Kuching) | 1927 | R Lat | Pmhm | 16 | 34,700 | 65,380 | Sarawak. 1976, archdiocese. Majority Chinese. 9n. 41 14 98 58 4008 |
| VA Miri (1976, D) | 1959 | R Lat | Pmhm | 9 | 7,500 | 14,135 | Chinese, Indian, European. Includes Brunei. 2n,1p. 27 3 12 64 900 |
| Christian Brethren | c1865 | P CBr | x•••• | 55 | 2,500 | 5,000 | *Open Brethren*. M=CMML(UK,NZ,Australia). Chinese in West Malaysia. 11f. |
| Chr Nationals Evangelism Commission | 1951 | P int | xF••• | 8 | 80 | 265 | *CNEC. Keristen Nasionals Pengar Injil*. 5 schools. Fast growth. 1n,1p,W=62%. |
| Church of Jesus C of Latter-day Saints | | M LdS | x•••• | | 200 | 500 | *Mormons*. M=CJCLdS(Utah,USA). Mainly expatriates (Asians, USA, Oceanians). |
| Churches of Christ | | P Dis | x•••• | 10 | 400 | 1,000 | M=CC(Non-Instrumental)(USA). In Ipoh, Penang, Seremban, Kuala Lumpur, et alia. |
| Evangelical Church of Borneo | 1928 | P int | •H••• | 278 | 6,700 | 40,000 | *Sidang Injil Borneo*. M=BEM. 60% in Sabah. All ex-animists. 150n,46f,G=9.8%pa,6p,2s. |
| Evangelical Free Ch of M & Singapore | 1957 | P Con | KF••• | 5 | 100 | 200 | M=EFCA(USA). Several preaching points, related to 2 churches in Singapore. 10f. |
| Ev Lutheran Church in M & Singapore | 1907 | P Lut | L•••W | 31 | 873 | 1,831 | M=Tamil ELC(India). 1961, M=SKM(Sweden). A=1962. Tamils. 9n,G=3.2%pa,1p(2),57Yy. |
| Evangelize China Fellowship | 1951 | I int | x•••• | 3 | 50 | 100 | Begun in China by a Chinese, 1947. M=ECF(HQ,USA). Chinese members. HQ Singapore. |
| Isolated radio churches | 1952 | I rad | ••••• | 350 | 7,000 | 13,800 | Isolated believers, R=2400(FEBC,&c),T=31000(ICI,FEBC). ICI: S=5000,V=1500. |
| Jehovah's Witnesses | 1932 | M Jeh | x•••• | 7 | 207 | 400 | Placed under Australian branch 1932. Activity by 1957 in Sarawak. 32Y. |
| Jemaluang Community Church Mission | | P ind | ••T•T | 1 | 50 | 100 | Mission from Kaimuki Community Church, Hawaii(USA), in Johore (West Malaysia). |
| Lutheran Ch in Malaysia & Singapore | 1949 | P Lut | L•••W | 48 | 598 | 1,476 | *Ma Sin Tsue Dtuk Tsau Sin Yi Whei*. M=ULCA(now LCA)(USA). Some Aborigines. 16f,1s. |
| Malaysia-Singapore Baptist Convention | 1951 | P Bap | T•••• | 41 | 2,325 | 4,000 | Begun from China. M=SBC(USA). In west. 8 schools. SS=2,076. 16n,40f,1s,269Y. |
| Mar Thoma Syrian Church in Malaysia | | I ReO | xwe•W | 26 | 1,300 | 2,200 | In Diocese of Bahya Kerala (Outside Kerala). Syrians from South India. 2 priests. |
| **Methodist Church in Malaysia** | 1885 | P Met | VWE•W | 240 | 30,000 | 65,000 | M=UMC(USA),45f; MMS(UK),9f. 50% West, 50% Sarawak (Chinese, Iban). 50n,1H,43r,1s. |
| New Apostolic Church | | C CAp | x•••• | | 100 | 200 | In Canada Bezirk, Neuapostolische Kirche. M=NAK(world HQ Dortmund, Germany). |
| Orthodox Syrian Church in Malaya | | O SyM | Dwe•W | 3 | 500 | 1,500 | In Diocese of Bahya Keralam (Outside Kerala). Syrians from South India. 3x. |
| Overseas Missionary Fellowship | 1952 | P int | xM••• | 10 | 500 | 1,000 | OMF has a few congregations but mostly works with BEM and other denominations. 66f. |
| Pentecostal Church of Malaya | 1936 | I pe2 | Z•••• | 7 | 500 | 1,000 | *CPM*. M=Ceylon Pentecostal Mission(Sri Lanka). Tamil-speaking. HQ Singapore. |
| Pentecostal Evangelical Churches | | P Pe2 | Z•••• | 5 | 380 | 1,000 | *Free Ev Pentecostal Ch. Glad Tidings Ch.* M=FFFM(Finland). Classical Pentecostals. |
| Presbyterian Church in Malaysia | 1851 | P Ref | Rw••W | 4 | 500 | 1,000 | *Malaysia Presbytery, Presbyterian Ch of England*. British expatriate chaplaincy. |
| Presbyterian Church in Singapore & M | 1881 | P Ref | R•••W | 42 | 2,720 | 4,106 | *Chinese Christian Ch.* M=LMS,PCE(UK). Doubled 1960–70. 10n,6x,G=5.7%pa,W=43%,136Yy. |
| Protestant Church in Sabah | 1882 | P LuR | lu••W | 150 | 8,800 | 13,000 | *Basel Chr Ch.* Hakka Chinese, Rungus. M=BM. 64n,2x,200m,7f,G=5.9%pa,W=56%,155Yy. |
| Salvation Army in Malaya | 1935 | P Sal | xwe•W | 6 | 1,000 | 2,000 | *Bala Keselamatan* (Malay). *Chiu Shi Chen* (Mandarin). Singapore/M Command. 20n,5f. |
| Seventh-day Adventist Church | 1911 | P Adv | x•••• | 150 | 7,000 | 10,000 | *Masehi Advent Hari Ketujah. SDA Chs.* Kadazans. 3n,3x,10f,G=8%pa,1H,3r,W=85%,400Y. |
| True Jesus Church | 1927 | I pel | x•••• | 44 | 5,000 | 8,000 | *Gereja Jesus Jang Sejati*. Chinese. Begun China 1917. 33 churches in Sabah. |
| World-Wide Missions of Malaysia | 1961 | P ind | x•••• | | 150 | 300 | M=World-Wide Missions(USA). Evangelicals with base in Pasadena, CA(USA). |
| Other Protestant denominations | | P | ••••• | | 1,500 | 3,000 | Total about 10 (see list below). |
| Other indigenous churches | | I | ••••• | | 500 | 1,000 | Total about 5 (see list below). |
| **Total affiliated (mid-1970)** | | | | **1,930** | **292,048** | **561,827** | **Total denominations (1970) . . . 48.** |
| **Total affiliated (mid-1975)** | | | | **2,200** | **363,400** | **699,100** | **Total denominations (1975) . . . 50.** |
| **Total affiliated (mid-1980)** | | | | **2,500** | **448,000** | **861,800** | **Total denominations (1980) . . . 52.** |

NOTES ON TABLE ABOVE

COLUMNS: for meanings and CODES (cols. 1, 3, 4, 8): see Codebook (Part 6). Column 1: **Boldface type** = church with over 10% of country's affiliated Christians.

NATIONAL COUNCILS (Column 4, 5th letter).
- P = Catholic Bishops' Conference of Malaysia-Singapore.
- T = Malaysia Council of Christian Churches.
- W = Council of Churches of Malaysia (CCM) (until 1975 '& Singapore').

*Other national councils*. National Evangelical Fellowship of Malaysia (NEFM) (begun 1975; member of WEF; members individuals, not denominations). *Local councils*. 10 regional councils.

OTHER PROTESTANT DENOMINATIONS. These include: American Baptist Convention FMS (1967), Baptist Churches, Christian & Missionary Alliance (31 missionaries), Malaysia Evangelistic Fellowship, Malaysia Faith Mission, New Tribes Mission, Peniel Chs of VOCA (Voice of China & Asia Missionary Society) (1963), Worldwide Evangelization Crusade.

OTHER INDIGENOUS CHURCHES. These include: Ch of Christ of Malaya, Fishermen of Christ Fellowship, Jesus Saves Mission.

UNITING CHURCHES. Negotiations for organic union were under way in 1974 between: (1) Anglican Ch in M & S, Ev Lutheran Ch in M & S, Mar Thoma Syrian Ch in M, Presbyterian Ch in S & M; and (2) Evangelical Ch of Borneo (BEM) and Overseas Missionary Fellowship (integrated in 1975).

**PEOPLES** (ethnolinguistic). Christians: 50% Chinese (Mandarin, Hakka), 35% tribal indigenous (Dayak, Iban (Sea Dayak), Murut, Dusun (Kadazan), Sea Nomad, Kayan, Kenyah, Kelabit), 9% South Indian (Tamil, Malayali, Telugu, Kanarese), 3% Euronesian (Eurasian), 2% British and other European, Javanese, Banjarese, Malay, Filipino.

COUNTRY-WIDE TOTALS

EVANGELIZATION (see Part 5). 1900: 12%. 1970: 58%. 1980: 69%. *Mass evangelism*. Among recent campaigns: 1968, Asian Evangelistic Crusade; 1969, Grady Wilson Crusade in Kuala Lumpur (36,700 attenders, 1,461 enquirers); also Malacca and Ipoh; 1969, Methodist renewal team visited many centres helping pastors develop district evangelism programmes; 1977, Here's Life Kuala Lumpur (CCCI); April 1978, Congress on Evangelism for Malaysia and Singapore (COEMAS). *Radiophonic evangelism*. Annual listeners' letters (1975): 2,400 (2,027 FEBC). Bible correspondence courses: 31,000 enrolments (ICI 30,000, with 5,000 active students, 1,500 conversions reported).

FOREIGN MISSIONARIES AND PERSONNEL (nationals

serving abroad) (1973). Total about 5 Protestants in Thailand et alia.
FOREIGN MISSIONARIES AND PERSONNEL (aliens from abroad) (1973). Total 928. *From Western world.* 792: 413 Protestants (188 in 20 USA societies, 107 in 9 UK societies, 79 in 5 Australia societies, 15 in 5 New Zealand societies, 7 in 1 Canada society, 7 in 1 WGermany society, 4 in 2 Finland societies, 2 in 1 Sweden society, 2 in 1 Norway society, 2 in 1 Switzerland society), about 340 Roman Catholics, 39 Anglicans (24 in 2 UK societies, 15 in 2 Australia societies). *From Third World.* 136: about 60 Protestants from 14 countries including India, Korea, Philippines, Singapore and Taiwan, about 40 indigenous (19 from Taiwan, 6 India, 4 Philippines, 4 Sri Lanka, 3 Hong Kong), about 30 Roman Catholics, 3 Anglicans, 3 Orthodox from India.
INSTITUTIONS (church-operated) (1973). Total 185, including 150 higher schools (2 minor seminaries), about 20 medical centres, 1 religious community, 8 seminaries (7 Protestant, 1 RC).
PERIODICALS. About 30 titles.
PERSONNEL. About 2,798 (1,870 national, 928 foreign).
RELIGIOUS LIBRARIES. About 10.
SCRIPTURE DISTRIBUTION (1975). Annual totals: 12,000 Bibles (8% free, 92% subsidized), 184,242 NTs (91% free, 9% subsidized), 92,000 UBS portions, 140,000 UBS selections. *Translations completed.* Portion: 12 languages since 1629. NT: 6 languages since 1668. Bible: High Malay in 1733.
SERVICE AGENCIES. About 41, including AMSW, CCCI, CCM, CSS, CWL, MEF, MRF, NEFM, SCM, SCMS, SCW, SU, YCS, YCW, YMCA, YWCA.

### ADDITIONAL DATA ON CHURCHES
CATHOLIC CHURCH IN MALAYSIA. In Malay, Gereja Katolik. In D Malacca-Johore there is also a small Portuguese parish dependent on D Macau. *New dioceses.* The hierarchy in East Malaysia was set up in 1976 as M Kuching, D Miri and D Kota Kinabalu. *Catholics.* Including about 90,000 Chinese, and virtually all the Eurasians in Malaysia. *Catechumens.* (1963) 8,000. *Annual baptisms.* (1972) 66.4% infant, 33.6% adult. *National priests.* This includes Chinese who came from China after 1949. The 3 bishops in West Malaysia, and of Kota Kinabalu,

are nationals (1973). In East Malaysia almost all the national priests are Chinese. *Expatriate priests.* In West Malaysia, 64 priests are Australians and 9 are missionaries from Asia (2 OFMCap Indians, 4 CDD Chinese from Taiwan, 3 OMI from Sri Lanka). In East Malaysia, all expatriates are MHM Europeans. *Seminary.* The major seminary (College General, in Penang) was founded in 1665 and moved to Penang in 1807, and has served many Far Eastern countries. Seminarians now are from Malaysia and Singapore. *Catechists.* Total (1974) about 550. *Chinese religious congregations.* Priests: CDD. Sisters: Sisters of St Francis (Sarawak). *Foreign orders and congregations.* Priests: MEP, CSSR, SJ, OFMCap, OMI (West Malaysia), MHM (East Malaysia). Brothers: FSC, PFM, Brothers of Mercy, Brothers of St Gabriel. Sisters: Sisters of the Holy Infant Jesus, Canossian Daughters of Charity, Little Sisters of the Poor, Good Shepherd Sisters, Franciscan Missionaries of the Divine Motherhood, Franciscan Missionaries of Mary, Sisters of the Foreign Mission, Daughters of St Paul, Carmelites, Franciscan Sisters of the Immaculate Conception, Franciscan Sisters of St Joseph.
*Catholic organizations.* The close relations existing between the church in Malaysia and that in Singapore are reflected in the fact that most Catholic organizations have been structured to cover both nations. The Catholic Bishops' Conference of Malaysia–Singapore, which is a member of FABC and to which belong all the bishops of the area including the Apostolic Visitor for the Chinese of the Diaspora, has its seat in Miri, East Malaysia. Also in Malaysia are the headquarters of the Superiors' Conference of Malaysia and Singapore, serving men, as well as the Association of Major Superiors of Women of Malaysia and Singapore. A senate of priests exists in Singapore, but there is nothing comparable for Malaysia. Lay organizations serving both countries are the Joyful Vanguard (children), YCW, YCS, Catholic Students' Society (university students), Catholic Women's League, Christian Family and Social Movement, Legion of Mary and Society of St Vincent de Paul.
The Holy See has no diplomatic relations with either Singapore or Malaysia. It is represented to the Catholic hierarchy by the Apostolic Delegation to Laos, Malaysia and Singapore, with headquarters in Bangkok. The apostolic delegate also serves as

pro-nuncio in Thailand.
The Catholic Church sponsors 183 schools in Malaysia (117,630 students, 14,219 of whom are Catholics), including the following: 25 kindergartens (2,244 children, 246 being Catholics), 90 primary schools (61,896 pupils, 8,501 being Catholics), 59 lower secondary schools (49,623 pupils 12–16 years of age, 5,264 being Catholics), 9 upper secondary schools (3,967 pupils above 15 years of age, 208 being Catholics) and one residential technical training college. The medium of instruction has traditionally been English, but for the past 10 years Catholic schools have been increasingly using the Malay language in line with national policy. Kindergarten, upper secondary and the training college are private schools, while primary and lower secondary are government schools run by Catholics, with school fees paid to government.
Concerning social service projects, Sabah Catholic Welfare was founded in 1961 to serve Jesselton and Sabah and is affiliated to Caritas International. It is involved in the distribution of USA food from the CRS/USCC programme and development projects at Bunda Tuhan opposite Mount Kinabalu. In addition, government boys' towns are run by St Gabriel Brothers. The medical programme includes a general hospital in Petaling Jaya (Kuala Lumpur) and 2 smaller hospitals in Ipoh (Penang). There are also several dispensaries, orphanages and homes for the aged.
EVANGELICAL CHURCH OF BORNEO. Predominantly Muruts, with some Kelabits, Kayans and Kenyahs, also some Sea Dayaks and Chinese.
PRESBYTERIAN CHURCH IN SINGAPORE AND MALAYSIA. In 1975 the church divided into separate, autonomous synods for the 2 countries.
PROTESTANT CHURCH IN SABAH. Formerly 2 distinct churches, both associated with the Basel Mission (Switzerland): (1) Basel Christian Church of Malaysia (Gereja Basel Malaysia, or Borneo-Basel Self-Established Church), which began with a migration of Chinese Hakkas around 1882 from China; and (2) from 1952 work has taken place among the Rungus and Dusun tribes in north Sabah; this church became autonomous in 1967, and has 7 Districts.

---

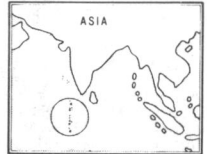

# MALDIVES

## SECULAR DATA

STATE. **Official name:** The Republic of Maldives (Divehi Raajje). Alternative names: Maldives, The Maldives. Adjective of nationality: Maldivian.
**Flag** (shown above right): Red field with green panel containing white crescent.
**Area:** 298 sq.km. (115 sq.miles). Description: over 2,000 small coral islands (220 inhabited) extending over 550 miles. Agricultural land: 13.3%.
**Government:** Republic with no political parties, since 1975 ruled by decree (1887 British protectorate, 1965 Independence as constitutional monarchy, 1968 republic, 1975 rule by decree).
**Legislature:** Majlis, 54 members.
**Official language:** Divehi (Maldivian Sinhalese).
**Capital:** Malé 16,000 (1972).

**Political divisions:** 19 administrative groups of islands.

**DEMOGRAPHY. Population:** 128,697 (census of 1974. For 1970–2000 (UN), see last row of Table 1). Population density (1975): 399/sq.km. (1,034/sq.mile). Under 15 years: 44%. Growth rate (1975–80): 2.10%. Household size: 5.4 persons.
**Major languages:** Divehi, Arabic, Sinhalese, Tamil.
**Urban dwellers** (1970): 11.8%. Urban growth rate (1950–70): 2.0% per year.
**Tourists** (1975): 7,000.

**ETHNOLINGUISTIC GROUPS:** 99% Maldivian (Sinhalese), Sinhalese (Sri Lanka), Arab, Dravidian (Tamil, Malayali), Malay.

**MONEY** (1977). **Monetary unit:** rupee (= 100 lareas); US$1 =

MvRs 3.93.
**National income per person:** US$100. Average annual family income: US$540.
**Cost of living in capital** (1976): Daily cost of living: US$34.

**HEALTH.** Hospitals: 1 (20 beds). Doctors: 2. Lepers: 90 (0.8 per 1,000). Blind: 128. Psychotics: 700.

**EDUCATION.** Adult literacy: 40%. Education rate: 10%. Schools: 2.

**LITERATURE.** Annual new book titles (1965): 24. Periodicals: 4. Newspapers: 4 non-daily.

**COMMUNICATION** (per 1,000 people). Phones: 3. Radios: 20.

### TABLE 1.    RELIGIOUS ADHERENTS IN THE MALDIVES

| Year | 1900 | | mid-1970 | | Annual change, 1970–1980 | | | | mid-1975 | | mid-1980 | | 2000 | |
|---|---|---|---|---|---|---|---|---|---|---|---|---|---|---|
| *Name* | Adherents | % | Adherents | % | Natural | Conversion | Total | Rate | Adherents | % | Adherents | % | Adherents | % |
| Muslims | 72,000 | 100.0 | 107,840 | 99.9 | 2,397 | 0 | 2,397 | 2.02 | 118,825 | 99.9 | 131,805 | 99.9 | 204,660 | 99.9 |
| Christians | 0 | 0.0 | 140 | 0.1 | 3 | 0 | 3 | 2.02 | 155 | 1.0 | 170 | 0.1 | 300 | 0.1 |
| professing | 0 | 0.0 | 140 | 0.1 | 3 | 0 | 3 | 2.02 | 155 | 0.1 | 170 | 0.1 | 300 | 0.1 |
| Roman Catholics | 0 | 0.0 | 120 | 0.1 | 3 | 0 | 3 | 2.02 | 135 | 0.1 | 145 | 0.1 | 260 | 0.1 |
| Protestants | 0 | 0.0 | 20 | 0.0 | 0 | 0 | 0 | 2.02 | 20 | 0.0 | 25 | 0.0 | 40 | 0.0 |
| affiliated | 0 | 0.0 | 140 | 0.1 | 3 | 0 | 3 | 2.02 | 155 | 0.1 | 170 | 0.1 | 300 | 0.1 |
| total practising | 0 | 0 | 85 | 60 | 2 | 0 | 2 | 2.02 | 95 | 60 | 105 | 60 | 150 | 50 |
| non-practising | 0 | 0 | 55 | 40 | 1 | 0 | 1 | 2.02 | 60 | 40 | 65 | 40 | 150 | 50 |
| Roman Catholics | 0 | 0.0 | 120 | 0.1 | 3 | 0 | 3 | 2.02 | 135 | 0.1 | 145 | 0.1 | 260 | 0.1 |
| Protestants | 0 | 0.0 | 20 | 0.0 | 0 | 0 | 0 | 2.02 | 20 | 0.0 | 25 | 0.0 | 40 | 0.0 |
| Baha'is | 0 | 0.0 | 20 | 0.0 | 0 | 0 | 0 | 2.02 | 20 | 0.0 | 25 | 0.0 | 40 | 0.0 |
| Country's population | 72,000 | 100.0 | 108,000 | 100.0 | 2,400 | 0 | 2,400 | 2.02 | 119,000 | 100.0 | 132,000 | 100.0 | 205,000 | 100.0 |

COLUMNS, ROWS. For meanings and definitions, see Codebook (Part 6). Note that, by definition, total 'Christians' = professing + crypto-Christians, which also = affiliated + nominal Christians. Percentages may not always total exactly, due to rounding.

CENSUSES. 18.VI.1965: 100% Muslims.

NOTES ON RELIGIONS.
BAHA'IS. In 1 isolated group.
CHRISTIANS. All expatriate Sinhalese from Sri Lanka.

MUSLIMS. Sunnis (of the Shafiite rite), since the conversion of the Maldives to Islam in 1153.

---

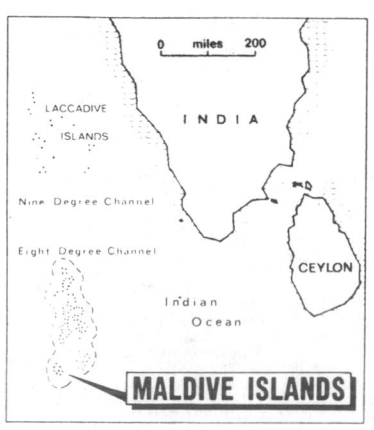

Several postage stamps have carried religious themes: (*left*) the Maldives embrace Islam in AD 1153; also the Apostles Peter *(centre)* and Paul *(right)*, both by Michelangelo.

**NON-CHRISTIAN RELIGIONS. Islam** is the religion of virtually the entire indigenous population. Originally Buddhists, the Maldivian people were converted to Sunni Islam in 1153.

**CHRISTIANITY.** The Maldive Islands have historical links with the Catholic Church in Sri Lanka. In 1972 there were 120 Catholics, mostly Ceylonese teachers, working in the islands. There are no priests resident or assigned there, and no parish structures. Catholic religious services consist largely of informal Bible readings. Small groups of expatriate Protestants, mostly Adventists, also meet together for worship.

**CHURCH AND STATE.** Following the conversion to Islam in 1314 of the Buddhist ruler of the Maldives, Dharumasantha Rasgefanu, he took the name Sultan Muhammed bin Abdullah, and the islands were ruled as a Muslim sultanate until the 20th century. In 1953 the sultanate was abolished and attempts were made to initiate progressive social legislation. However, Muslim traditionalists strongly opposed the changes, and the sultanate was restored. On 11 November 1968 the sultan was deposed once more and a republic proclaimed. According to the constitution of 1964, revised in 1968, Islam is the official religion of the Maldives; and the fundamental rights of individuals are recognized, provided that they do not contradict the stipulations of Islam. The nation's legal system has its basis in Islamic law, the Sharia.

TABLE 2. ORGANIZED CHURCHES AND DENOMINATIONS IN THE MALDIVES

| Official name 1 | Begun 2 | Type 3 | Counc 4 | Congs 5 | Adults 6 | Affiliated 7 | Names, notes, and other statistics (see Codebook) 8 |
|---|---|---|---|---|---|---|---|
| Catholic Church (M Colombo) | | R Lat | P.P.. | 1 | 70 | 120 | 95% Ceylonese (mostly teachers). No parish or priest. Lay-led Bible studies. |
| Seventh-day Adventist Church | | P Adv | X.... | 1 | 10 | 20 | Under SDA, Ceylon Union, Southern Asia Division. Expatriates, occasional meetings. |
| Total affiliated (mid-1970) | | | | 2 | 80 | 140 | Total denominations (1970) ... 2. |
| Total affiliated (mid-1975) | | | | 2 | 90 | 155 | Total denominations (1975) ... 2. |
| Total affiliated (mid-1980) | | | | 2 | 100 | 170 | Total denominations (1980) ... 2. |

**NOTES ON TABLE ABOVE.**
COLUMNS: for meanings and CODES (cols. 1, 3, 4, 8): see Codebook (Part 6). Column 1: **Boldface type** = church with over 10% of country's affiliated Christians.

PEOPLES (ethnolinguistic). Christians: 95% Sinhalese, 4% South Indian (Tamil, Malayali).

**COUNTRY-WIDE TOTALS**
EVANGELIZATION (see Part 5). 1900: 0%. 1970: 11%. 1980: 12%.

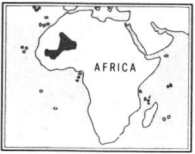

# MALI

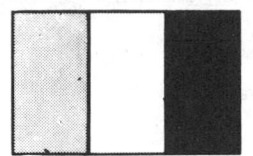

## SECULAR DATA

**STATE. Official name:** The Republic of Mali (La République du Mali). Adjective of nationality: Malian (malien).
**Flag** (shown above right): Bars of green, yellow, and red.
**Area:** 1,240,000 sq.km. (478,767 sq.miles). Agricultural land: 33.6%.
**Government:** Military dictatorship, since 1974 (1904 French Soudan, 1958 self-government, 1960 Independence, 1968 military junta).
**Official language:** French (*Français*).
**Capital:** Bamako 196,800 (1972).
**Political divisions:** 19 Districts.
**Armed forces** (1976): Total 4,200 regular army (7 combat aricraft). Paramilitary forces: 5,700.

**DEMOGRAPHY. Population:** 3,484,500 (census of 15.VI.1960–V.1961. For 1970–2000 (UN), see last row of Table 1). Population density (1975): 5/sq.km. (12/sq.mile). Under 15 years: 44%. Growth rate (1975–80): 2.54% per year (births 4.94%, deaths

–2.40%). Life expectancy (1975–80): 40.0 years. Household size: 4.9 persons.
**Major languages:** French, Bambara, Fulani, Senufo, Soninke, Dioula, Dogon, Tuareg, Mandingo, Arabic, Mossi, and 15 smaller languages.
**Urban dwellers** (1970): 12.0%. Urban growth rate (1950–70): 4.0% per year.
**Labour force:** 56%.
**Refugees** (1977): None. Exiles abroad: due to the drought of 1969–74, 700,000 Tuareg nomads migrated to Niger, Algeria and Nigeria, who later refused to repatriate them.

**ETHNOLINGUISTIC GROUPS:** 31% Bambara, 13% Fulani (Macina, Kita), 7% Soninke (Sarakole), 6% Serufo, 6% Dogon, 5% Songhai, 5% Tuareg, 5% Malinke, 4% Minianka (Suppire), 3% Diula, 3% Moorish (Mauri), 2.4% Samo (Samogo), 2.0% Bobo (Bwa), 2% Kasonke, 1.7% Bozo (Sorogo), 1.4% Saharan Arab, 0.8% Kagoro, 0.6% Nono, 0.5% Tukulor, 0.5% Mossi, French, Ivorian, Sanu, Wolof, Moroccan, Libyan, Syrian, Karaboro, et alii.

**MONEY** (1977). **Monetary unit:** franc (= 100 centimes); US$1 = FM 500.00.
**National income per person:** US$73. Average annual family income: US$358.
**Cost of living in capital** (1976): index 153 (Washington DC=100). Daily cost of living: US$35.

**HEALTH.** Hospitals: 54 (3,718 beds). Doctors: 135. Lepers: 153,000 (26.9 per 1,000). Blind: 110,000. Psychotics: 35,000. Criminals: 4,000.

**EDUCATION.** Adult literacy: (1962) 3%, (1975) 10%. Education rate: 15%. Schools: 1,018.

**LITERATURE.** Periodicals: 10. Newspapers: 3 dailies, 10 non-daily.

**COMMUNICATION** (per 1,000 people). Phones: 2. Radios: 14. Daily newspaper circulation: 0.6 copies.

TABLE 1. RELIGIOUS ADHERENTS IN MALI

| Year | 1900 | | mid-1970 | | Annual change, 1970–1980 | | | | mid-1975 | | mid-1980 | | 2000 | |
|---|---|---|---|---|---|---|---|---|---|---|---|---|---|---|
| Name | Adherents | % | Adherents | % | Natural | Conversion | Total | Rate | Adherents | % | Adherents | % | Adherents | % |
| Muslims | 390,312 | 30.0 | 3,935,300 | 78.0 | 112,309 | 12,078 | 124,387 | 2.77 | 4,496,320 | 78.9 | 5,179,170 | 80.0 | 9,451,600 | 84.0 |
| Tribal religionists | 909,000 | 69.9 | 1,030,000 | 20.4 | 27,476 | –13,476 | 14,000 | 1.27 | 1,100,000 | 19.3 | 1,170,000 | 18.1 | 1,520,000 | 13.5 |
| Christians | 688 | 0.1 | 81,164 | 1.6 | 2,498 | 1,386 | 3,884 | 3.88 | 100,000 | 1.8 | 120,000 | 1.9 | 281,400 | 2.5 |
| crypto-Christians | 388 | 0.0 | 40,764 | 0.8 | 1,360 | 744 | 2,104 | 3.87 | 54,420 | 1.0 | 61,800 | 1.0 | 146,300 | 1.3 |
| professing | 300 | 0.0 | 40,400 | 0.8 | 1,138 | 642 | 1,780 | 3.91 | 45,580 | 0.8 | 58,200 | 0.9 | 135,100 | 1.2 |
| Roman Catholics | 300 | 0.0 | 30,300 | 0.6 | 854 | 646 | 1,500 | 4.39 | 34,180 | 0.6 | 45,300 | 0.7 | 101,300 | 0.9 |
| Protestants | 0 | 0.0 | 10,100 | 0.2 | 284 | –4 | 280 | 2.46 | 11,400 | 0.2 | 12,900 | 0.2 | 33,800 | 0.3 |
| affiliated | 688 | 0.1 | 81,164 | 1.6 | 2,498 | 1,386 | 3,884 | 3.88 | 100,000 | 1.8 | 120,000 | 1.9 | 281,400 | 2.5 |
| total practising | 654 | 95 | 60,873 | 75 | 1,874 | 1,039 | 2,913 | 3.88 | 75,000 | 75 | 90,000 | 75 | 196,980 | 70 |
| non-practising | 34 | 5 | 20,291 | 25 | 624 | 347 | 971 | 3.88 | 25,000 | 25 | 30,000 | 25 | 84,420 | 30 |
| Roman Catholics | 688 | 0.1 | 60,740 | 1.2 | 1,874 | 1,052 | 2,926 | 3.90 | 75,000 | 1.3 | 90,000 | 1.4 | 202,600 | 1.8 |
| Protestants | 0 | 0.0 | 20,424 | 0.4 | 624 | 334 | 958 | 3.83 | 25,000 | 0.4 | 30,000 | 0.5 | 78,800 | 0.7 |
| Evangelicals | 0 | 0.0 | 20,424 | 0.4 | 624 | 334 | 958 | 3.83 | 25,000 | 0.4 | 30,000 | 0.5 | 78,800 | 0.7 |
| Baha'is | 0 | 0.0 | 20,436 | 0.0 | 13 | 7 | 20 | 3.78 | 540 | 0.0 | 640 | 0.0 | 3,000 | 0.0 |
| Other religionists | 0 | 0.0 | 100 | 0.0 | 4 | 5 | 9 | 6.43 | 140 | 0.0 | 190 | 0.0 | 1,000 | 0.0 |
| Country's population | 1,300,000 | 100.0 | 5,047,000 | 100.0 | 142,300 | 0 | 142,300 | 2.50 | 5,697,000 | 100.0 | 6,470,000 | 100.0 | 11,257,000 | 100.0 |

**COLUMNS, ROWS.** For meanings and definitions, see Codebook (Part 6). Note that, by definition, total 'Christians' = professing + crypto-Christians, which also = affiliated + nominal Christians. Percentages may not always total exactly, due to rounding.
CENSUSES. **1960–61:** 76.4% Muslims, 22.8% tribal religionists, 0.5% Roman Catholics, 0.2% Protestants.

**NOTES ON RELIGIONS**
BAHA'IS. In 3 local spiritual assemblies (1973).
CRYPTO-CHRISTIANS. In 1961, the government census

reported 20,100 Roman Catholics and 7,300 Protestants, whereas soon after (1963) the Catholic Church reported 28,653 baptized Catholics and 18,247 catechumens, which total 46,900; and Protestants reported about 12,000. Crypto-Christians (Christians unknown to the state) therefore amount to half the total Christian community.
MUSLIMS. Almost all Sunnis (of the Malikite rite). Hamaliya (using an 11-bead rosary) is still especially strong in Mali. Conversions to Islam are taking place among tribal religionists, through family conversion in areas remote from Western influence, and by individual conversion in urban areas. *Hajj pilgrims to Mecca.*

(1970) 113; (1974) 2,628; (1975) 2,719; (1976) 2,072.
OTHER RELIGIONISTS. Including Rosicrucians (1 AMORC centre).
ROMAN CATHOLICS. In the year 1900, there were 101 baptized Catholics and 587 catechumens.
TRIBAL RELIGIONISTS. Animists. Tribes over 30% traditionalist in 1972: Kagoro (95% animist), Bobo (70%), Minianka (65%), Dogon (60%), Kita (43%), Bambara (30%), Malinke (30%). Fetish altars are still prominent in many villages.

**NON-CHRISTIAN RELIGIONS. Islam** was first propagated in the 11th century and is now the principal religion of Mali claiming the allegiance of 78% of the population. Important cities include Timbuktu, one of the most famous holy places of African Islam, Djenne, a law school centre, Oualata and Nioro, the cradle of Hamaliya, a 20th-century sect which split from Tijaniya. In 1976 a large new mosque in Bamako was completed, paid for by Saudi Arabia.

**Traditional African religions** retain the allegiance of about 19% of the population and are especially strong among the Dogon, Bobo, Kagoro and Minianka, all of whom are more than 60% traditionalist. The Bambara name for God is Jalang while the Dogon term is Amma, Creator. Dogon myths of creation are extremely complex and essential for understanding traditional conceptions of the individual, family and society. Key elements are the creation of the primordial egg (*aduno tal*) with twin placenta, each with twin male and female Nommo, recognized as children of God and ideal models of man. The key event revolves around the premature emergence of the first man (Yurugu) from the male principle of one of the egg's placentas, resulting in imperfection and impurity, with a fragment of Yurugu's placenta forming earth. Secret societies, with extensive rituals and rich mask symbolism, play an important role in the life of the Dogon.

## CHRISTIANITY
CATHOLIC CHURCH. Bamako was reached in 1895 by White Fathers coming from Senegal, and White Sisters followed soon afterwards. The vicariate

**Muslims.** Village mosque with mud walls in Sikasso region (Minianka tribe, 10% Muslims).

of cult in the Republic of Mali', specifies that the creation of religious establishments, missions, and congregations must be submitted for authorization beforehand to the Ministry of the Interior (Article 4). Duly-recognized councils of administration represent such religious bodies in all the affairs of civil life (Article 8), and religious education may be given to children frequenting the public schools outside the time scheduled for classes (Article 25).

A convention dealing with Catholic education in Mali called 'Catholic private education' ('Enseigne-ment privé catholique', EPC), was concluded on 8 August 1973 between the minister of National Education and the archbishop of Bamako in the name of the Episcopal Conference of Mali. Renewable every 3 years, the convention deals with all Catholic educational institutions except kindergartens, catechetical schools and training centres for religious personnel. EPC is defined as being 'of private service in the general interest'; and while retaining its specific organization and its relationship to the Episcopal Conference (Article 8), it remains part of the national school system (Article 3). EPC accepts control by the state (Article 13) and pledges fidelity to official programmes and recognizes that Mali is a secular state (Article 5). It cannot give diplomas, since all its students are required to take official examinations (Article 16). EPC is entitled to regular financial subsidies for teachers' salaries, at least

**Tribal religionists.** *Left.* Animistic Minianka with their fetish house (a form of pagan temple) in Koutiala region. *Above.* A massive fetish in Koutiala, covered with libations.

of Bamako was erected in 1921 and the first African priest ordained in 1936. New vicariates were formed at Gao in 1942 and at Kayes and Sikasso in 1947; and the archdiocese of Bamako was established in 1955. The first Malian bishop was consecrated in 1962. Numerically, the progress of the Catholic Church is slow, only just over 1% of the population being affiliated Catholics. The most christianized ethnic groups are the Bobo and Wala in the diocese of San and the Dogon in the diocese of Mopti.

PROTESTANT CHURCHES. Of the 7 Protestant groups at work in Mali, the first to arrive was the Gospel Missionary Union in 1919. The most significant success has been recorded by the Evangelical Christian Church of Mali in its work among the Dogon people. Aided by the CMA, which began work in southeastern Mali in 1923, this church is now active throughout the country and maintains Bible schools for training church leaders. Several other missions have entered since World War II, but Protestants still form less than 0.5% of the population. No indigenous church movements have yet appeared in Mali, though there have been a few unsuccessful attempts.

**CHURCH AND STATE.** According to the con-stitution of September 1960, modified in January 1961, the republic is secular, and equality before the law without distinction of religion is assured for all (Article 1). Law 86 AN-RM of 21 July 1961, 'On the organization of religious liberty and the exercise

**Eglise Catholique au Mali.** Small rural church in Mandiakui.

70% of the amount available for those in state schools, and occasionally receives personnel and supplementary financial grants for equipment and the administrative costs of lycées and second-cycle schools (Articles 21 and 29).

## INTERDENOMINATIONAL ORGANIZATIONS.
The Association of Evangelical Protestant Churches and Missions in Mali, with 4 member churches, is a member of the Association of Evangelicals of Africa and Madagascar (AEAM) based in Nairobi, Kenya.

**BROADCASTING.** The government Radio Mali accepts a weekly 30-minute Catholic programme and others touching on the subject of man and society, and other social problems. Missionaries of the Gospel Missionary Union produce a daily broadcast in the Bambara language which is transmitted from Radio ELWA (Liberia), the only international station easily received, although the Radio Vatican French programmes for West Africa can also be heard (15 minutes daily, 1 hour 20 minutes weekly). The government has offered Malian Christians time on a new radio station in Bamako as soon as it begins operation. For Catholics, UNDA in Mali is represented by a national association.

## BIBLIOGRAPHY
*Conversations with Ogotemmeli: an introduction to Dogon religious ideas.* M. Griaule. London: Oxford University Press, 1965. (1948, in French).
*Essai sur la religion bambara.* G. Dieterlen. Paris: Presses Universitaires de France, 1950.
*La rencontre de Jésus-Christ en milieu Bambara.* S.P.M. Sidibe. Leiden: Brill, 1978. 318p.
'Le Nya: changements spirituels modernes d'une société ouest-africaine', B. Holas, *Acta tropica* (Basel), 12, 2 (1955), 97–122. (Nya and Massa cults among the Minianka).
*L'Islam et le terroir africain.* M. Cardaire. Bamako-Koulouba: IFAN, 1954.
'Mali: prestige du passé, destin nouveau', *Vivant univers* (Namur), 267 (1970), 1–47.
'The Dogon', M. Griaule & G. Dieterlen, in D. Forde (ed), *African worlds* (London: Oxford University Press, 1954), p.83–110.

### TABLE 2. ORGANIZED CHURCHES AND DENOMINATIONS IN MALI

| Official name 1 | Begun 2 | Type 3 | Counc 4 | Congs 5 | Adults 6 | Affiliated 7 | Names, notes, and other statistics (see Codebook) 8 | | | | | | |
|---|---|---|---|---|---|---|---|---|---|---|---|---|---|
| Eglise Catholique au Mali: | 1895 | R Lat | P,SFR | 39 | 34,000 | 60,740 | *Catholic Ch.* Minority church. C=1+1+16. 4p. | 14n,146x,29m,141w,P=65%,2231Yy. | | | | | |
| M Bamako | 1921 | R Lat | Ps | 8 | 7,500 | 13,374 | 65% Muslim, 34% animist. Catholics 70% Bambara. | 6 | 38 | 7 | 54 | 50 | 552 |
| D Kayes | 1947 | R Lat | Pwf | 7 | 3,200 | 5,649 | 60% Muslim, 40% animist. 50% Bambara, 25% Kasonke. | 3 | 25 | 1 | 19 | 77 | 150 |
| D Mopti | 1942 | R Lat | Pwf | 7 | 8,200 | 14,739 | 81% Muslim, 19% animist. Catholics 80% Dogon. | 0 | 24 | 1 | 13 | 72 | 304 |
| D San | 1962 | R Lat | Pwf | 5 | 9,800 | 17,548 | 76% animist, 18% Muslim. 90% Bobo Oulé. | 3 | 19 | 6 | 15 | 73 | 725 |
| D Ségou | 1962 | R Lat | Pwf | 6 | 3,300 | 5,853 | 79% Muslim, 20% animist. Mostly Bambara. | 2 | 18 | 3 | 22 | 63 | 267 |
| D Sikasso | 1947 | R Lat | Pwf | 6 | 2,000 | 3,557 | 50% Muslim, 49% animist. Catholics Minianka. | 0 | 22 | 11 | 18 | 57 | 233 |
| Eglise Chrétienne Evangélique du Mali | 1923 | P Hol | xPG,G | 277 | 7,477 | 14,074 | *ECEM. Ev Christian Ch.* M=CMA. 80% Dogon (Kado). 65n,6x,27f,6h,2s(3),W=68%,1384Y. | | | | | | |
| Eglise Ev Protestante au Mali | 1919 | P Hol | xMG,G | 70 | 3,000 | 5,000 | *EEPM. Ev Protestant Ch.* M=GMU(USA). Bambara. 2 schools. 5n,12x,16m,45f,4h,1s,23Y. | | | | | | |
| Eglise Protestante de Kayes | 1953 | P int | xPG,G | 8 | 350 | 1,000 | *United World Mission.* M=UWM(USA). 86% Malinke, 15% Kasonke. 16f,1H,2h,1s,45Y. | | | | | | |
| Mission Evangélique Baptiste | 1950 | P Bap | xTG,G | 4 | 20 | 50 | *Ev Baptist Missions.* M=EBM(USA). Gao area (99% Muslim). Songhais, Tuaregs. 14f. | | | | | | |
| Other Protestant denominations | | P | ....G | | 100 | 300 | CBFMS(Ivory Coast migrants), Coopération Ev Mondiale, World-Wide Missions(1964). | | | | | | |
| Total affiliated (mid-1970) | | | | 415 | 44,947 | 81,164 | Total denominations (1970) ... 9. | | | | | | |
| Total affiliated (mid-1975) | | | | 455 | 55,400 | 100,000 | Total denominations (1975) ... 9. | | | | | | |
| Total affiliated (mid-1980) | | | | 500 | 66,400 | 120,000 | Total denominations (1980) ... 10. | | | | | | |

**NOTES ON TABLE ABOVE**
**COLUMNS:** for meanings and CODES (cols. 1, 3, 4, 8): see Codebook (Part 6). Column 1: **Boldface type** = church with over 10% of country's affiliated Christians.
**NATIONAL COUNCILS** (Column 4, 5th letter).
　G = Association des Groupements d'Eglises et Missions Protestantes Evangéliques au Mali (Association of Evangelical Protestant Churches & Missions in Mali).
　R = Conférence Episcopale du Mali (CEM) (Episcopal Conference of Mali).

**PEOPLES** (ethnolinguistic). Christians: 33% Dogon, 31% Bambara, 22% Bobo, 5% Minianka, 4% Kita (Fulani, Fuladugu), 2% Kasonke, 2% Mossi, 1% Malinke, Ivorian, French.

**COUNTRY-WIDE TOTALS**
**EVANGELIZATION** (see Part 5). 1900: 4%. 1970: 26%. 1980: 28%. *Mass evangelism.* 1970, New Life for All campaign, supported by all Protestant churches.
**FOREIGN MISSIONARIES AND PERSONNEL** (nationals serving abroad) (1973). Total 1 Roman Catholic priest in Guinea.
**FOREIGN MISSIONARIES AND PERSONNEL** (aliens from abroad) (1973). Total 396. *From Western world.* 374: 280 Roman Catholics, 94 Protestants in 5 USA societies. *From Third World.* 22: about 20 Roman Catholics, 2 Protestants.
**INSTITUTIONS** (church-operated) (1973). Total 70, including 22 higher schools (2 minor seminaries), 35 medical centres (7 hospitals), 1 religious community, 1 study centre, 4 seminaries (Protestant).
**PERIODICALS.** About 7 titles.
**PERSONNEL.** About 1,026 (630 national, 396 foreign).
**RELIGIOUS LIBRARIES.** 6.
**SCRIPTURE DISTRIBUTION** (1975). Annual totals: 1,200 Bibles (92% subsidized, 8% commercial), 1,600 NTs (94% subsidized, 6% commercial), 1,500 UBS portions, 5,000 UBS selections. *Translations completed.* Portion: 6 languages since 1923. NT: 4 languages since 1933. Bibles: 1 language in 1961.
**SERVICE AGENCIES.** About 17, including ACF, BGEA, CCCI, CEC, CEM, GBUAF, JOC, NLFA, SU, WRC, WVI.

**ADDITIONAL DATA ON CHURCHES**
**EGLISE CATHOLIQUE AU MALI.** *Catechumens.* (1963) 18,247, divided among the 6 dioceses in the order shown above, as follows (and included in column 7): 1374, 1203, 10708, 2448, 1293, 1221; (1971) 18,094. *Annual baptisms.* (1972) 72.7% infant, 27.3% adult. *Priests.* The first African was ordained in 1936. *Brothers.* All expatriates. *Sisters.* 29 African, 112 expatriate. *Seminarians.* Total 7, at Koumi seminary, Upper Volta. *Catechists.* Total (1974) about 500. *Catechist training schools.* The 4 each handle one language: Bambara (Bamako), Malinke (Kayes), Dogon (Mopti), Bobo (San). D Sikasso has closed its former school and chooses catechists from rural literacy classes. *Indigenous religious congregations.* Sisters: Daughters of the Immaculate Heart of Mary (formerly Sudanese Daughters of Mary, begun 1934; 29 professed in 1970). *Foreign congregations.* Priests: WF. Brothers: FSC. Sisters: White Sisters.
*Catholic organizations.* The Episcopal Conference of Mali (Conférence Episcopale du Mali) is a member of the Conférence Plénière des Ordinaires de l'Afrique Occidentale, and also of SECAM. There are no national presbyteral or pastoral councils, but religious personnel are represented on the Union des Supérieures des Congrégations Autochtones d'Afrique de l'Ouest Francophone, commonly known as Anima Una. The secretariat is in Bamako, and the following countries are represented in the union: Benin, Ivory Coast, Mali, Senegal, Togo and Upper Volta. The principal lay movements are Jeunes Travailleurs Chrétiens (similar to JOC), Communauté Etudiante Catholique, Equipes Enseignantes and ACF.
The Holy See has no diplomatic relations with Mali. It is represented to the Catholic hierarchy by an apostolic delegate based in Dakar, Senegal.
The Catholic Church supervises 16% of the total enrolment of Mali schools; 21 dispensaries; 5 maternity hospitals; a leprosy institute; 5 rural community development centres; 2 trades schools; numerous literacy centres; and the important cultural centre of Diulila, at Bamako, with 7 subsidiaries and 18 dependent libraries throughout the country.
**EGLISE CHRETIENNE EVANGELIQUE DU MALI.** Work is among the Dogon, Bambara, Bobo, Senoufo and Mianka. By 1976, response to the gospel was greatest among the Dogon, Bobo and Mianka.

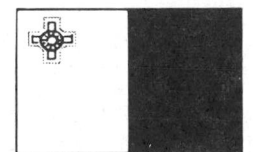

# MALTA

## SECULAR DATA

**STATE.** Official name: The Republic of Malta (Ir-Republika ta' Malta). Adjective of nationality: Maltese.
**Flag** (shown above right): White and red bars, with George Cross in silver on white bar.
**Area:** 316 sq.km. (122 sq.miles). Agricultural land: 43.8%.
**Government:** Parliamentary republic, since 1974 (1814 British crown colony, 1962 self-government, 1964 Independence, 1974 republic).
**Legislature:** House of Representatives, 65 members.
**Official languages:** Maltese and English.
**Chief cities:** capital Valletta 14,152 (1973), Sliema 22,000.
**Foreign forces** (1973): 3,500 British (UK) marines and Royal Air Force; almost all left by 1978.

**DEMOGRAPHY. Population:** 315,765 (census of 26.XI.1967. For 1970-2000 (UN), see last row of Table 1). Population density (1975): 1,041/sq.km (2,697/sq.mile). Under 15 years: 37%. Growth rate (1975-80): 0.34% per year (births 1.87%, deaths -0.93%, emigrants -0.60%). Life expectancy (1975-80): 71.6 years. Household size: 4.0 persons.
**Major languages:** Maltese, English, Italian, Arabic, Greek.
**Urban dwellers** (1970): 87.4%. Urban growth rate (1950-70): 1.9% per year.
**Labour force:** 33%.
**Tourists** (1974): 273,516.

**ETHNOLINGUISTIC GROUPS:** 95.7% Maltese, 2.1% British, 1.5% Italian, Greek, Jewish, Arab.

**MONEY** (1977). Monetary unit: pound (= 100 cents = 1,000 mils); US$1 = M£0.433.
**National income per person:** US$1,119. Average annual family income: US$4,476.
**Inflation:** (1970-74) 5.1% per year (1975: consumer price index 129).
**Cost of living in capital** (1976): index 99 (Washington DC=100). Daily cost of living: US$28.

**HEALTH. Hospitals:** 9 (3,431 beds). Doctors: 334. Lepers: 440 (1.3 per 1,000). Blind: 570. Psychotics: 2,600. Criminals: 1,000.

**Catholic Church in Malta, Archdiocese of Malta.** St Publius Church, Floriana, Valetta. The numerous silos are granaries in use during the Knights' occupation (1530-1802).

EDUCATION Adult literacy: (1948) 60%, (1963) 66%, (1973) 88%. Education rate: 55%. Schools: 154. Universities: 1.

LITERATURE. Annual new book titles (1973): 123. Periodicals: 160. Scientific journals: 2. Newspapers: 6 dailies, 4 non-daily.

COMMUNICATION (per 1,000 people). Phones: 145. Radios: 401. TV sets: 189. Daily newspaper circulation: 195 copies.

## TABLE 1.    RELIGIOUS ADHERENTS IN MALTA

| Year | 1900 | | mid-1970 | | Annual change, 1970–1980 | | | | mid-1975 | | mid-1980 | | 2000 | |
|---|---|---|---|---|---|---|---|---|---|---|---|---|---|---|
| Name | Adherents | % | Adherents | % | Natural | Conversion | Total | Rate | Adherents | % | Adherents | % | Adherents | % |
| Christians | 207,800 | 100.0 | 324,300 | 99.5 | 893 | −172 | 721 | 0.22 | 326,440 | 99.2 | 331,510 | 99.0 | 328,270 | 97.7 |
| professing | 207,800 | 100.0 | 324,300 | 99.5 | 893 | −172 | 721 | 0.22 | 326,440 | 99.2 | 331,510 | 99.0 | 328,270 | 97.7 |
|   Roman Catholics | 185,000 | 89.0 | 318,770 | 97.8 | 878 | −159 | 719 | 0.22 | 320,900 | 97.5 | 325,960 | 97.3 | 323,870 | 96.4 |
|   Anglicans | 14,600 | 7.0 | 3,900 | 1.2 | 11 | −11 | 0 | 0.00 | 3,900 | 1.2 | 3,900 | 1.2 | 3,000 | 0.9 |
|   Protestants | 8,000 | 3.8 | 1,300 | 0.4 | 3 | −3 | 0 | 0.00 | 1,300 | 0.4 | 1,300 | 0.4 | 1,000 | 0.3 |
|   Marginal Protestants | 0 | 0.0 | 230 | 0.1 | 1 | 1 | 2 | 0.83 | 240 | 0.1 | 250 | 0.1 | 300 | 0.1 |
|   Orthodox | 200 | 0.1 | 100 | 0.0 | 0 | 0 | 0 | 0.00 | 100 | 0.0 | 100 | 0.0 | 100 | 0.0 |
| nominal | 12,800 | 6.2 | 6,499 | 2.0 | 20 | 134 | 154 | 2.13 | 7,240 | 2.2 | 8,040 | 2.4 | 13,400 | 4.0 |
| affiliated | 195,000 | 93.8 | 317,801 | 97.5 | 873 | −306 | 567 | 0.18 | 319,200 | 97.0 | 323,470 | 96.6 | 314,870 | 93.7 |
|   total practising | 189,000 | 97 | 311,440 | 98 | 856 | −300 | 556 | 0.18 | 312,820 | 98 | 317,000 | 98 | 283,400 | 90 |
|   non-practising | 6,000 | 3 | 6,360 | 2 | 17 | −6 | 11 | 0.17 | 6,380 | 2 | 6,470 | 2 | 31,500 | 10 |
|   Roman Catholics | 184,000 | 88.5 | 314,261 | 96.4 | 863 | −298 | 565 | 0.18 | 315,650 | 95.9 | 319,910 | 95.5 | 312,270 | 92.9 |
|     Catholic pentecostals | 0 | 0.0 | 0 | 0.0 | 1 | 199 | 200 | 50.00 | 400 | 0.1 | 2,000 | 0.6 | 6,000 | 1.8 |
|   Anglicans | 10,000 | 4.8 | 3,000 | 0.9 | 8 | −8 | 0 | 0.00 | 3,000 | 0.9 | 3,000 | 0.9 | 2,000 | 0.6 |
|   Marginal Protestants | 0 | 0.0 | 230 | 0.1 | 1 | 1 | 2 | 0.83 | 240 | 0.1 | 250 | 0.1 | 300 | 0.1 |
|   Protestants | 800 | 0.4 | 210 | 0.1 | 1 | −1 | 0 | 0.00 | 210 | 0.1 | 210 | 0.1 | 200 | 0.1 |
|     Evangelicals | 600 | 0.3 | 100 | 0.0 | 0 | 0 | 0 | 0.00 | 100 | 0.0 | 100 | 0.0 | 200 | 0.1 |
|   Orthodox | 200 | 0.1 | 100 | 0.0 | 0 | 0 | 0 | 0.00 | 100 | 0.0 | 100 | 0.0 | 100 | 0.0 |
| Non-religious | 0 | 0.0 | 1,000 | 0.3 | 5 | 130 | 135 | 8.23 | 1,640 | 0.5 | 2,350 | 0.7 | 5,000 | 1.5 |
| Atheists | 0 | 0.0 | 500 | 0.2 | 2 | 38 | 40 | 5.71 | 700 | 0.2 | 900 | 0.3 | 2,300 | 0.7 |
| Baha'is | 0 | 0.0 | 100 | 0.0 | 0 | 4 | 4 | 3.33 | 120 | 0.0 | 140 | 0.0 | 300 | 0.1 |
| Hindus | 30 | 0.0 | 50 | 0.0 | 0 | 0 | 0 | 0.00 | 50 | 0.0 | 50 | 0.0 | 60 | 0.0 |
| Jews | 60 | 0.0 | 50 | 0.0 | 0 | 0 | 0 | 0.00 | 50 | 0.0 | 50 | 0.0 | 70 | 0.0 |
| Country's population | 207,890 | 100.0 | 326,000 | 100.0 | 900 | 0 | 900 | 0.27 | 329,000 | 100.0 | 335,000 | 100.0 | 336,000 | 100.0 |

COLUMNS, ROWS. For meanings and definitions, see Codebook (Part 6). Note that, by definition, total 'Christians' = professing + crypto-Christians, which also = affiliated + nominal Christians. Percentages may not always total exactly, due to rounding.
CENSUSES. 1901 Census of the British Empire: as in 1900 column above, adjusted to include the 23,000 resident British military personnel. No question on religion has been asked recently.

NOTES ON RELIGIONS
ANGLICANS. Mostly expatriate British military and civilians.
ATHEISTS. Communist Party of Malta (CPM) (founded 1970, legal; pro-Soviet): membership (1970, 1974) 100. It is assumed in Malta that good Christians cannot be communists, and vice versa.
CATHOLIC PENTECOSTALS (or, Catholic charismatics). The first meetings were held in mid-1975. 1980: 35 prayer groups.
COUNTRY'S POPULATION. In 1968 there were 1,608 foreign residents; of these 480 were Italians, almost all Roman Catholics.

Many more Maltese citizens are of Italian origin.
HINDUS. Indian traders.
JEWS. With a synagogue in Valletta.
NOMINAL CHRISTIANS. Largely British military.
NON-RELIGIOUS. Mainly British military.
PRACTISING CHRISTIANS. 1967: weekly mass attendance 82% of the population. 1980: mass attendance 87% every Sunday, 20% daily.
ROMAN CATHOLICS. About 3,000 emigrate annually, mostly to Australia.

---

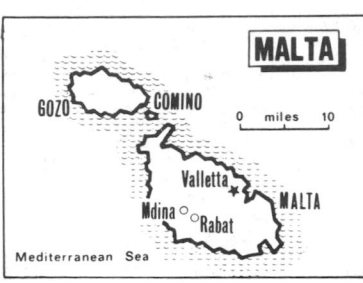

NON-CHRISTIAN RELIGIONS. Small Jewish and Hindu groups are found among the expatriate community, and there is a Jewish synagogue in Valletta.

## CHRISTIANITY

CATHOLIC CHURCH. According to the Acts of the Apostles, the apostle Paul was shipwrecked on Malta and remained there for 3 months on his way to Rome. A bishop from Malta was later in attendance at the Council of Chalcedon in 451. The island fell to the Arabs in 870 but was recaptured by Normans in 1090 and given to the Knights of St John of Jerusalem in 1530. Virtually all native Maltese are baptized Roman Catholics. In a survey taken on 17 December 1967, those attending Sunday mass numbered 82% of the population, 77% of all men and 86% of women. A total of 198,150 persons participated in one or other of the 803 masses celebrated that day.

Catholicism is practised in Malta in the Italian manner, with its religious ceremonies such as the celebration of the apostle Paul's shipwreck on 10 February being transformed into popular feasts with decorated and lighted streets. Catholicism is an institutional power of exceptional significance in Malta. In addition to publishing the influential daily newspaper, *Il-Hajj*, the church organizes social and cultural movements, credit unions and emigration services. Annual emigration figures are about 3,000, mostly to Australia.

In 1970, 351 Maltese priests were working outside the islands in foreign lands: 138 as foreign missionaries, 61 as chaplains for Maltese communities abroad, and 152 in other work including service as priests in Europe or the USA. In 1966, there were also 395 nuns serving abroad. The church has its own institute for foreign missions, the Missionary Society of St Paul, which had 45 priests in 1969 and received pontifical recognition in 1973.

The church in Malta owns large properties, a fact which has become increasingly controversial in recent years. In 1973 the pope approved the proposals of a commission set up in 1971 under the chairmanship of a Vatican diplomat to carry out reforms in Maltese church administration. The commission reached its conclusions on the basis of recommendations made by a USA management consultant firm which had been called in to establish the relevant facts. The annual income of the Catholic Church in Malta was revealed to be approximately US dollars 840,000. It owns 17% of the island's urban and 18% of its rural property. A major problem noted in the report is that 'financial administration is the uncontrolled and undirected responsibility of about 1,500 administrations that are in turn the responsibility of 280 separate administrators'. Recent financial scandals in Malta involving church funds have highlighted the need for reform.

OTHER CHURCHES. Several denominations serve the expatriate community: Greek Orthodox, Anglicans and Church of Scotland in Valletta; Methodists, Gospel Hall and Salvation Army in Floriana; Anglicans in Sliema; and Christian Scientists in Marsa. Jehovah's Witnesses are also active.

CHURCH AND STATE. The constitution which became effective at Independence on 21 September 1964 affirms that 'The religion of Malta is the Roman Catholic and Apostolic Religion' (Article 2, item 1), but guarantees full freedom to all other religions (Article 41). It stipulates that the Catholic Church is entitled to run its own affairs (Article 2, item 2) and that the Catholic religion is to be taught in state schools (Article 10). State legislation on marriage runs parallel with canon law, since there is no provision for civil marriage nor for divorce.

There is no concordat between church and state, which remain in practice quite separate. Catholic and other religious bodies, as well as their clergy and personnel, receive neither remuneration nor subsidies from the state, although they are usually exempt from tax. The only exceptions to this are secular clergy who have to pay taxes and private Catholic schools which receive small subsidies which totalled £36,720 in 1965–66.

The Catholic Church largely controls social and cultural life in Malta. Before Independence the church was the natural representative of the people vis-a-vis both the French imperial and British colonial governments. At the local level, parish priests are still community leaders in the absence of non-religious local authorities. During the early years of the movement seeking national independence, Catholic clergy led political movements and were elected to parliament. This is now no longer the case; and the most important episcopal statement in recent years, that of Easter 1969, both announced the settlement of the dispute between the church and the Labour Party, and at the same time affirmed the separation of ecclesiastical and political affairs. During 1974–75 contacts were made between the

Since 1899, Malta's stamps have commemorated St Paul's shipwreck: here in 1960, its 19th centenary and that of episcopal consecration of Publius.

Maltese government and the Vatican to discuss the possibility of constitutional change effecting the Church in Malta.

There is no ministry or government department in charge of religious matters, and churches are not obliged to register with any state office.

INTERDENOMINATIONAL ORGANIZATIONS. The Catholic episcopal conference has an Ecumenical Commission, and there is also a wider Ecumenical Group including other bodies which meets periodically in Valletta.

BROADCASTING. There are 3 governing bodies for radio and TV: the Broadcasting Authority, Malta Rediffusion and Malta Television Service. Religious programmes were first properly organized and co-ordinated in 1961 when the Broadcasting Authority came into being. A religious broadcasting adviser is attached to the Authority to supervise all religious programmes, assisted by panels of priests and laymen. About 7 hours a week of religious programmes are broadcast on Rediffusion, and 3.5 hours monthly are presented on Malta Television. For Catholics, Malta is a member of UNDA. The international Pentecostal association IBRA has recently begun regular broadcasts from Malta (Radio Mediterranean) in 7 languages including Greek, Turkish, Hungarian and Bulgarian.

## BIBLIOGRAPHY
*Catholic directory of Malta and Gozo, 1963.* Floriana, Malta: Empire Press, 1963.
*Report on the Sunday mass census of 17 December 1967.* B. Tonna & A. Depasquale. Valletta: Pastoral Research Services, 1969. 156p.
*Saints and fireworks: religion and politics in rural Malta.* J.F. Boissevain. London: Athlone Press, 1965.
*The Maltese church amid social and political upheaval.* London: Herder Correspondence, 1966.
*What is happening to religion in Malta?* M. Gonzi. Valletta: Pastoral Research Services, 1969. 38p. (By the Catholic archbishop).

TABLE 2. ORGANIZED CHURCHES AND DENOMINATIONS IN MALTA

| Official name 1 | Begun 2 | Type 3 | Counc 4 | Congs 5 | Adults 6 | Affiliated 7 | Names, notes, and other statistics (see Codebook) 8 |
|---|---|---|---|---|---|---|---|
| **Catholic Church in Malta:** | 60 | R Lat | BxB.R | 73 | 198,000 | 314,261 | Il-Knisja Kattolika. C=10+1+23,1p,4q,2s(233),W=82%. 1038n,3x,143m,1641w,5265y. |
| M Malta | 1831 | R Lat | Bs | 58 | 181,400 | 288,000 | Arcidjocesi ta' Malta. Industries, tourism. 1s. 878 3 121 1420 4921 |
| D Gozo | 1863 | R Lat | Bs | 15 | 16,600 | 26,261 | Djocesi ta' Ghaiodex. Rural island, 99.8% RC. 1s. 160 0 22 221 344 |
| Church of Christ, Scientist | | M Sci | x.... | 1 | 20 | 30 | Christian Science. One informal group in Marsa. M=CCS(Boston,USA). |
| Church of England (D Gibraltar) | 1798 | A plu | awc.. | 9 | 1,000 | 3,000 | British residents and military. Has co-cathedral of diocese. 6x,W=50%,29Yy. |
| Church of Scotland | | P Ref | Rwc.. | 1 | 30 | 50 | St Andrew's Church, Valletta. Expatriate Scots, mostly temporary. 1f. |
| Gospel Hall | c1926 | P CBr | x.... | 1 | 15 | 30 | Plymouth Brethren. One group (Open) in Floriana. Expatriate British. W=99%,20Y. |
| Greek Orthodox Church (AD Thyateira) | | O Gre | Cwc.. | 1 | 50 | 100 | St George's Church, Valletta. Under jurisdiction of EP Constantinople. 1 bishop. |
| Jehovah's Witnesses | c1939 | M Jeh | x.... | 1 | 48 | 200 | Watch Tower. 1939, placed under Syrian branch; active witnessing since 1952. 3Y. |
| Methodist Church | | P Met | Vwc.. | 1 | 20 | 30 | Under Methodist Church of GB. Church in Floriana. Mostly expatriate British. |
| Salvation Army | 1896 | P Sal | xwc.. | 2 | 50 | 100 | Under British Territory. Red Shield work, Floriana (British armed forces). |
| **Total affiliated (mid-1970)** | | | | **90** | **199,233** | **317,801** | **Total denominations (1970) . . . 9.** |
| **Total affiliated (mid-1975)** | | | | **92** | **200,100** | **319,200** | **Total denominations (1975) . . . 9.** |
| **Total affiliated (mid-1980)** | | | | **94** | **202,800** | **323,470** | **Total denominations (1980) . . . 9.** |

NOTES ON TABLE ABOVE
COLUMNS: for meanings and CODES (cols. 1, 3, 4, 8): see Codebook (Part 6). Column 1: **Boldface type** = church with over 10% of country's affiliated Christians.
NATIONAL COUNCILS (Column 4, 5th letter).
R = Malta Episcopal Conference (MEC).

PEOPLES (ethnolinguistic). Christians: 96.5% Maltese, 1.5% Italian, 1.3% British (English, Scottish), Greek, other European.

COUNTRY-WIDE TOTALS
EVANGELIZATION (see Part 5). 1900: 100%. 1970: 100%. 1980: 100%. *Mass evangelism.* 1976, Operation Mobilization campaign following visit by ship MV Logos.
FOREIGN MISSIONARIES AND PERSONNEL (nationals serving abroad) (1970). Total 746 Roman Catholics (351 priests, 395 sisters; 90 in the Missionary Society of St Paul) serving in Europe and USA, or as foreign missionaries (including 138 priests) in Third-World countries.
FOREIGN MISSIONARIES AND PERSONNEL (aliens from abroad) (1973). Total 18. *From Western world.* 18: 10 Roman Catholics, 6 Anglicans, 1 Protestant in 1 UK society, 1 Orthodox.
INSTITUTIONS (church-operated) (1973). Total 20, including 2 higher schools (1 minor seminary), 3 medical centres (hospitals), 2 research centres, 1 study centre, 5 seminaries (RC).
PERIODICALS. About 56 titles.
PERSONNEL. About 3,593 (3,575 national, 18 foreign).
RELIGIOUS LIBRARIES. 8.
SCRIPTURE DISTRIBUTION (1975). Annual totals: 5,220 Bibles (77% free, 23% commercial), 8,400 NTs (83% free, 5% subsidized, 12% commercial), 60 UBS portions, 6,000 UBS selections. *Translations completed.* Maltese: portion in 1822, NT 1847, Bible 1952.
SERVICE AGENCIES. About 48, including CNRM, CRS, GCR, IBRA, KDAL, KNC, MAS, MBS, MCATM, MEC, MSC, MUT, PRS, SCD, ZHN(YCW).

ADDITIONAL DATA ON CHURCHES
CATHOLIC CHURCH IN MALTA. *Annual baptisms.* (1972) 99.9% infant, 0.1% adult. *Priests.* Of the 1,038 priests, 554 are secular (Malta 405, Gozo 149), and 487 religious. All are Maltese except 3 SDB Italians. *Brothers.* 136 nationals, 7 expatriates. *Sisters.* Figure includes novices; and 157 contemplatives (Malta). All are Maltese. *Seminaries.* One diocesan, 4 religious. Seminarju ta' l-Arcisqof (M Malta), Seminarju ta' l-Isqof (D Gozo). *Seminarians.* 101 for secular clergy, 132 religious. *Catechists.* Total 750 (1964). Each year Kummissjoni Kateketika Nazzjonali (KKN) runs a course for catechists to work in public or private schools. *Religious orders and congregations.* Priests (congregations with 50 or more): 94 OFMCap, 90 OP, 87 SJ, 78 OC, 67 OFM, 66 OSA. Brothers: 38 FSC. Sisters (congregations with 100 or more, including novices): 385 Franciscan Sisters of the Heart of Jesus, 222 Sisters of Charity, 156 Dominican Sisters, 137 Augustinian Sisters, 136 Daughters of the Sacred Heart, 100 Sisters of St Joseph.
*Catholic organizations.* The Malta Episcopal Conference is a member of CCEE. Organizations for religious personnel are the National Council of Religious Men of Malta (Consilium Nationale Religiosorum Melitensium) and the Malta Sisters Conference. A Pastoral Council (Kunsill Pastorali) has been formed in each diocese composed of priests, religious personnel and lay members, the latter being in the majority except in Gozo. A Presbyteral Council (Kunsill Presbiterali) also exists with the majority of its members elected by the clergy. Each diocese has its own organization for the co-ordination of the lay apostolate, called in Malta the Kunsill Djocezan ta' l'Apostolat tal Lajci (KDAL) and in Gozo the Kommissjoni Djocezana ghall-Apostolat tal-Lajci. The principal movements of the 2 dioceses are Maltese Catholic Action (Azzjoni Kattolika Maltija) (4,340 members in 1969); Society of Christian Doctrine (also called Museum, 1,750 members in 1969); Legion of Mary (2,603 members in 1969); Sodality of Our Lady (Kongregazzjoni Marjana) (3,140 members in 1967); YCW (Zghazagh Haddiema Nsara) (1,750 members in 1967); and Cana Movement (Moviment ta' Kana) (8,000 members in 1967).
The Holy See has diplomatic relations with Malta and is represented to government and the Catholic hierarchy by a nuncio based in Valletta.
The Ghaqda Christus Rex, founded in 1971, is a non-official association of priests advocating radical reform in the administration of the church's wealth and property, which it considers to be an obstacle to the church's credibility and pastoral work. The association has not assumed a radical position in regard to doctrinal matters. Other agencies include Pastoral Research Services in Valletta, and, for religious training, the Catholic Institute (Institut Kattoliku) and the Faculty of Theology of Royal University of Malta.
In 1968 the Catholic Church was responsible for 69 nursery schools (3,170 children), 22 primary schools (9,369 pupils), 27 secondary schools (3,752), and 2 post-secondary schools (391), making a total of 120 schools and 16,682 pupils as contrasted with 156 government schools with 58,844 pupils.
Medical work in 1970 included 3 Catholic hospitals (154 beds), 16 children's homes (450 residents) and 8 homes for the aged (305 residents). Malta is served by Catholic Relief Services, and Caritas (Kunsill Nazzjonali Caritas).

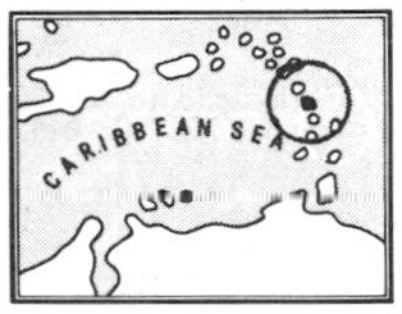


# MARTINIQUE

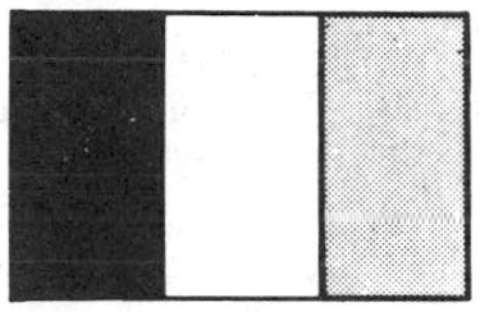

## SECULAR DATA

**STATE. Official name:** The Department of Martinique (Le Département de la Martinique).
**Flag** (shown above right): That of France.
**Area:** 1,102 sq.km. (425 sq.miles). Agricultural land: 44.5%.
**Government:** Overseas department of France, since 1946 (1635 French possession).
**Legislature:** General Council, 36 members.
**Official language:** French (*Français*).
**Capital:** Fort-de-France 104,420 (1967).
**Political divisions:** 34 Communes.

**DEMOGRAPHY. Population:** 320,030 (census of 16.X.1967. For 1970–2000 (UN), see last row of Table 1). Population density (1975): 329/sq.km. (853/sq.mile). Under 15 years: 43%. Growth rate (1975–80): 1.44% per year (births 2.72%, deaths −0.62%, emigrants −0.66%). Life expectancy (1975–80): 71.0 years. Household size: 4.4 persons.
**Major languages:** French, French Creole, Tamil, English, Chinese, Arabic, Vietnamese.
**Urban dwellers** (1970): 50.1%. Urban growth rate (1950–70): 5.1% per year.
**Labour force:** 33%.
**Tourists** (1973): 64,600. (1976) over 150,000 annually.

**ETHNOLINGUISTIC GROUPS:** 94.7% Mulatto (Black/French/Chinese/Indian/Vietnamese), 2.3% metropolitan French (7,440), 1.9% East Indian (Tamil) (6,100), 0.7% Creole (Martinique White) (French) (1,760), 0.3% other West Indian Black (1,000), Chinese, Vietnamese, Syrian.

**MONEY** (1977). **Monetary unit:** French franc (= 100 centimes); US$1 = Fr 5.00.

**National income per person:** US$1,500. Average annual family income: US$6,600.
**Inflation:** (1970–74) 9.6% per year.
**Cost of living in capital** (1976): index 153 (Washington DC = 100). Daily cost of living: US$39.

**HEALTH.** Hospitals: 15 (3,281 beds). Doctors: 214. Lepers: 3,600 (9.9 per 1,000). Blind: 100. Psychotics: 2,500.

**EDUCATION.** Adult literacy: (1954) 74%, (1967) 88%. Schools: 227.

**LITERATURE.** Periodicals: 8. Newspapers: 2 dailies, 13 non-daily.

**COMMUNICATION** (per 1,000 people). Phones: 70. Radios: 103. TV sets: 41. Daily newspaper circulation: 137 copies.

TABLE 1. RELIGIOUS ADHERENTS IN MARTINIQUE

| Year | 1900 | | mid-1970 | | Annual change, 1970–1980 | | | | mid-1975 | | mid-1980 | | 2000 | |
|---|---|---|---|---|---|---|---|---|---|---|---|---|---|---|
| *Name* | *Adherents* | *%* | *Adherents* | *%* | *Natural* | *Conversion* | *Total* | *Rate* | *Adherents* | *%* | *Adherents* | *%* | *Adherents* | *%* |
| **Christians** | **207,500** | **99.8** | **332,800** | **98.5** | **5,199** | **−259** | **4,940** | **1.39** | **356,090** | **98.1** | **382,200** | **97.7** | **462,200** | **95.3** |
| professing | 207,500 | 99.8 | 332,800 | 98.5 | 5,199 | −259 | 4,940 | 1.39 | 356,090 | 98.1 | 382,200 | 97.7 | 462,200 | 95.3 |
| Roman Catholics | 207,500 | 99.8 | 325,700 | 96.4 | 5,085 | −295 | 4,790 | 1.37 | 348,290 | 95.9 | 373,600 | 95.5 | 450,600 | 92.9 |
| Evangelical Catholics | 0 | 0.0 | 6,700 | 2.0 | 118 | 192 | 310 | 3.83 | 8,100 | 2.2 | 9,800 | 2.5 | 17,100 | 3.5 |
| Spiritist Catholics | 10,000 | 4.8 | 6,000 | 1.8 | 90 | −64 | 26 | 0.42 | 6,170 | 1.7 | 6,260 | 1.6 | 6,300 | 1.3 |
| Protestants | 0 | 0.0 | 7,100 | 2.1 | 114 | 36 | 150 | 1.92 | 7,800 | 2.2 | 8,600 | 2.2 | 11,600 | 2.4 |
| nominal | 4,200 | 2.0 | 19,000 | 5.6 | 318 | 302 | 620 | 2.84 | 21,800 | 6.0 | 25,200 | 6.4 | 38,800 | 8.0 |
| affiliated | 203,300 | 97.7 | 313,800 | 92.8 | 4,881 | −561 | 4,320 | 1.29 | 334,300 | 92.1 | 357,000 | 91.3 | 423,400 | 87.3 |
| total practising | 182,970 | *90* | 238,490 | *76* | 3,612 | −1,757 | 1,855 | 0.75 | 247,380 | *74* | 257,040 | *72* | 254,040 | *60* |
| non-practising | 20,330 | *10* | 75,310 | *24* | 1,269 | 1,196 | 2,465 | 2.84 | 86,920 | *26* | 99,960 | *28* | 169,360 | *40* |
| Roman Catholics | 203,300 | 97.7 | 300,000 | 88.7 | 4,649 | −789 | 3,860 | 1.21 | 318,400 | 87.7 | 338,600 | 86.6 | 394,700 | 81.4 |
| Protestants | 0 | 0.0 | 10,800 | 3.2 | 180 | 150 | 330 | 2.68 | 12,300 | 3.4 | 14,100 | 3.6 | 21,300 | 4.4 |
| Evangelicals | 0 | 0.0 | 7,000 | 2.1 | 117 | 93 | .210 | 2.63 | 8,000 | 2.2 | 9,100 | 2.3 | 14,000 | 2.9 |
| Marginal Protestants | 0 | 0.0 | 2,000 | 0.6 | 36 | 74 | 110 | 4.40 | 2,500 | 0.7 | 3,100 | 0.8 | 5,800 | 1.2 |
| Black indigenous | 0 | 0.0 | 1,000 | 0.3 | 16 | 4 | 20 | 1.82 | 1,100 | 0.3 | 1,200 | 0.3 | 1,600 | 0.3 |
| Non-religious | 0 | 0.0 | 2,800 | 0.8 | 56 | 147 | 203 | 5.37 | 3,780 | 1.0 | 4,830 | 1.2 | 13,600 | 2.8 |
| Atheists | 0 | 0.0 | 1,000 | 0.3 | 20 | 70 | 90 | 6.43 | 1,400 | 0.4 | 1,900 | 0.5 | 4,900 | 1.0 |
| Baha'is | 0 | 0.0 | 1,000 | 0.3 | 19 | 41 | 60 | 4.62 | 1,300 | 0.4 | 1,600 | 0.4 | 3,000 | 0.6 |
| Muslims | 500 | 0.2 | 200 | 0.1 | 3 | −1 | 2 | 0.95 | 210 | 0.1 | 220 | 0.1 | 300 | 0.1 |
| Other religionists | 0 | 0.0 | 200 | 0.1 | 3 | 2 | 5 | 2.27 | 220 | 0.1 | 250 | 0.1 | 1,000 | 0.2 |
| **Country's population** | **208,000** | **100.0** | **338,000** | **100.0** | **5,300** | **0** | **5,300** | **1.46** | **363,000** | **100.0** | **391,000** | **100.0** | **485,000** | **100.0** |

COLUMNS, ROWS. For meanings and definitions, see Codebook (Part 6). Note that, by definition, total 'Christians = professing + crypto-Christians, which also = affiliated + nominal Christians. Percentages may not always total exactly, due to rounding.
CENSUSES. The religion question has not been asked.

NOTES ON RELIGIONS
ATHEISTS. Communist Party of Martinique (legal; pro-Soviet): membership (1970) 1,000; Communist voters (election of 23.VI. 1968) 13,342 (17% of all votes).
BAHA'IS. Rapid growth in local spiritual assemblies: 1964, none; 1973, 10.
EVANGELICAL CATHOLICS. This term is used here to describe persons who are affiliated to churches termed by the state Evangélique (Protestant, marginal Protestant, or Black indigenous churches), but who are regarded by state and society as, or who profess to be, Roman Catholics.
MUSLIMS. Syrian Arabs.
NON-RELIGIOUS. Mostly metropolitan French, French Creoles, a few Chinese, with Martiniquan communists and sympathizers.
OTHER RELIGIONISTS. Including Rosicrucians (3 AMORC centres).
SPIRITIST CATHOLICS. Martinique East Indians (originally 25,000 Tamils from South India, declining through repatriation by 1900 to 10,000) are now all Roman Catholics, speaking Creole,

but they follow the cult of Maldevidan, a hybrid Hindu-Catholic spirit-possession religion based on the worship of a pantheon of Tamil Hindu village gods, centred on Maldevidan as chief deity (identified as Vishnu Christ or St Michael), and Mari-eman

(the Virgin Mary, also Mari the South Indian goddess of disease). There are many temples, and the northern half of the island is dotted with small masonry structures (*chapelles*) and statues, to which on Sundays during the cane harvest several hundred

East Indians come to participate in rites devoted to *les bons dieux coolies*. The rites include drumming, animal sacrifice (sheep, goats, cocks), ecstatic possession, and dancing on sharpened machettes.

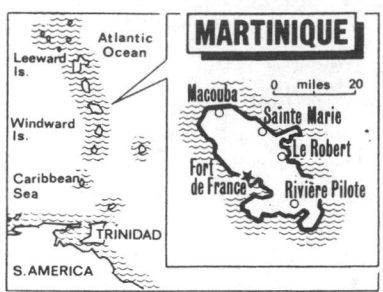

## NON-CHRISTIAN RELIGIONS. The **cult of Maldevidan** is a syncretistic mixture of Hinduism and Catholicism found among East Indians, commonly referred to at an earlier period of history as 'coolies'. Virtually all are now Roman Catholics, but claim to be Hindus as well. Scores of temples are found in the northern part of the island, where Sunday ceremonies are led by a ritual leader known as l'abbé coolie, the rites performed being devoted to 'the good coolie gods' (les bons dieux coolies). The principal deity of the pantheon is Maldevidan who is represented as riding on a horse and is commonly identified with Jesus Christ. The second most important is Mari-eman, a female divinity corresponding to the Virgin Mary except that she is not the mother of Maldevidan. The extensive pantheon also includes Katarai, identified as St Michael, and Buminaman, who is said to be an evil saint. Ritual ceremonies, which are most common during the harvest season (January to June), involve drumming, dancing, spirit possession, the sacrifice of a sheep and cock and an elaborate community feast.

**Islam** exists among a small community of Syrian Muslims.

## CHRISTIANITY

CATHOLIC CHURCH. There was missionary activity by Dominicans, Jesuits and Capuchins during the 16th century, but the first apostolic

prefect was not appointed until 1816. The island was made a diocese in 1850. Because of the difficulty of obtaining clergy, Martinique was placed under the jurisdiction of Propaganda Fide in Rome at the beginning of the present century and confided to the Holy Ghost Fathers in 1909. Although often at a superficial level, the majority of the people are Catholics. According to a Boulard study in 1957, Sunday practice varies, according to parishes, from 9% to 21% for men and 15% to 60% for women, with very little participation between the ages of 14 and 25. Since this study, in spite of some increase among youth, general Sunday church attendance has decreased even more.

PROTESTANT CHURCHES. Protestant activity is recent and not extensive. Independent Baptists have developed a limited work in 4 areas since their arrival in 1945, and the Reformed Church caters almost entirely for metropolitan Frenchmen. The greatest advance is being made by Seventh-day Adventists who entered in 1924 and have both an urban and a rural following among the lower classes.

CHURCH AND STATE. Legal statutes regarding religious liberty are the same as in metropolitan France. In practice, the hierarchy has more influence than in France since the civil authorities tend to seek their support. It appears to public opinion that the interventions of the hierarchy in burning social and political questions (immigration, political status of the island, unemployment) remain rather cautious by contrast with the initiatives of individual priests and laymen. However, this has tended to change since 1973, when for the first time a Martinique national became archbishop.

INTERDENOMINATIONAL ORGANIZATIONS. A group made up of Catholics and French Reformed was constituted in November 1970 and meets regularly for dialogue and Bible study.

BROADCASTING. The state-operated Radiodiffusion Télévision Française allows Catholic

**Eglise Catholique, Archdiocèse de Fort-de-France.** Cathedral in Fort-de-France.

programming for quarter of an hour daily from Monday to Saturday, and half an hour on Sundays. Protestants are given 15 minutes on Sundays only.

## BIBLIOGRAPHY

*Annuaire ecclésiastique 1971*. Fort-de-France, Martinique: Imprimerie Antillaise Saint-Paul, 1971.
'The Martiniquan East Indian cult of Maldevidan', M. Horowitz & M. Klass, *Social and economic studies*, X, 1 (March, 1961), 93–100.

TABLE 2.    ORGANIZED CHURCHES AND DENOMINATIONS IN MARTINIQUE

| Official name 1 | Begun 2 | Type 3 | Counc 4 | Congs 5 | Adults 6 | Affiliated 7 | Names, notes, and other statistics (see Codebook) 8 |
|---|---|---|---|---|---|---|---|
| Communautés Evangéliques Libres | | I CBr | x•••• | 12 | 600 | 1,000 | Indigenous congregations, Plymouth (Open) Brethren influence. Fort-de-France. |
| Eglise Adventiste du Septième Jour | 1924 | P Adv | x•••• | 38 | 4,446 | 10,000 | *Seventh-day Adventists, Martinique Mission.* Working-class. 8nx,1r,63t(5819),279Y. |
| Eglise Baptiste Indépendante | 1945 | P Bap | ••••• | 4 | 200 | 400 | *Independent Baptist Ch.* M=Ev Baptist Missions(USA). Bible shops, radio work. 10f. |
| **Eglise Catholique: M Fort-de-France** | 1635 | R Lat | PzNMr | 48 | 171,000 | 300,000 | *Catholic Ch in M.* 2.0% East Indian. C=2+0+6. 85n,89x,24m,274w,W=40%,8150Yy. |
| Eglise Réformée de France | | P Ref | Rwc•• | 1 | 100 | 200 | Serving almost entirely short-term metropolitan French, military and civilian. |
| Témoins de Jéhovah | c1945 | M Jeh | x•••• | 7 | 724 | 2,000 | *Jehovah's Witnesses. Watch Tower. IBSA.* Activity first reported 1950. 97Y. |
| Other Protestant denominations | | P | ••••• | | 100 | 200 | Assemblées de Dieu, Ch of the Nazarene, Streams of Power, World-Wide Missions. |
| **Total affiliated (mid-1970)** | | | | **116** | **177,170** | **313,800** | **Total denominations (1970) ... 8.** |
| **Total affiliated (mid-1975)** | | | | **118** | **188,700** | **334,300** | **Total denominations (1975) ... 9.** |
| **Total affiliated (mid-1980)** | | | | **120** | **201,600** | **357,000** | **Total denominations (1980) ... 10.** |

### NOTES ON TABLE ABOVE

COLUMNS: for meanings and CODES (cols. 1, 3, 4, 8): see Codebook, (Part 6). Column 1: **Boldface type** = church with over 10% of country's affiliated Christians.
NATIONAL COUNCILS (Column 4, 5th letter).
r = member of Conférence Episcopale de France (CEF) (Episcopal Conference of France).

PEOPLES (ethnolinguistic). Christians: 94.7% Mulatto, 2.3% French, 1.9% East Indian, 0.7% Creole (Martinique White, French), 0.3% alien West Indian Black, Chinese, Vietnamese.

COUNTRY-WIDE TOTALS
EVANGELIZATION (see Part 5). 1900: 100%. 1970: 100%. 1980: 100%. *Radiophonic evangelism.* Christ Vous Appelle (Assemblées de Dieu, France).
FOREIGN MISSIONARIES AND PERSONNEL (nationals serving abroad) (1973). Total about 50 Roman Catholics in French Guiana, Guadeloupe, France et alia.
FOREIGN MISSIONARIES AND PERSONNEL (aliens from abroad) (1973). Total 177. *From Western world.* 119: 110 Roman

Catholics, 9 Protestants (8 in 2 USA societies, 1 in 1 France society). *From Third World.* About 58, mostly Roman Catholics from Guadeloupe.
INSTITUTIONS (church-operated) (1973). Total 10, including 6 higher schools (1 minor seminary), 1 religious community, 1 study centre.
PERIODICALS. 4 titles.
PERSONNEL. About 2,087 (1,910 national, 177 foreign).
RELIGIOUS LIBRARIES. 2.
SCRIPTURE DISTRIBUTION (1975). Annual totals: 6,000 Bibles (17% free, 67% subsidized, 16% commercial), 7,464 NTs (85% free, 13% subsidized, 1% commercial), 2,800 UBS portions, 16,000 UBS selections.
SERVICE AGENCIES. About 25, including AFC, CEF, CMR, CV/AV, DAL, JAC, JEC, UCF, UCH.

ADDITIONAL DATA ON CHURCHES
EGLISE CATHOLIQUE. *Catholics.* Including all 6,100 East Indians in Martinique, with some Chinese and Vietnamese. *Jurisdiction.* Fort-de-France was erected as a diocese in 1850, and a metropolitan see in 1967. *Annual baptisms.* (1972) 100% infants, no adults. *Brothers.* 10 from Martinique and Guadeloupe. *Sisters.* 202 from Martinique and Guadeloupe. *Catechists.* Total

(1968) 1,635. *Indigenous religious congregations.* None. *Foreign orders and congregations.* Priests: CSSp, OSB. Sisters: St Paul de Chartres, Dominicaines de la Délivrance, St-Joseph de Cluny. *Catholic organizations.* The diocese is a member of the Episcopal Conference of France (Conférence Episcopale de France), and the ecclesiastical province of Martinique-Guadeloupe-French Guiana has been a member with consultative voice of the Antilles Episcopal Conference since February 1971. There is a Council of Sisters and also a Presbyteral Council, a majority of the latter's members being elected. The Bureau of the Lay Apostolate (Direction de l'Apostolat des Laïcs) co-ordinates the youth work of CV/AV, Scouts and Guides, Chrétiens dans le Monde Rural, JEC and Jeunesse Mariale; and the adult work of Union Catholique des Hommes, Union Catholique des Femmes, Equipes Enseignantes, Association Familiale Catholique, Légion de Marie and Equipes Ouvrières.
The Holy See has no diplomatic relations with Martinique. It is represented to the Catholic hierarchy by an apostolic delegate based in Port-au-Prince, Haiti.
The Catholic Church operates 7 primary and 4 secondary schools, 2 orphanages, a centre for educational extension (COPES), JAC action in agrarian reform, domestic science schools, a union for fishermen, and Catholic Aid.

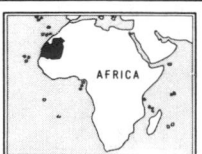

# MAURITANIA

## SECULAR DATA

STATE. **Official name:** The Islamic Republic of Mauritania (Al-Jumhuriyah al-Islamiyah al-Muritaniyah/La République Islamique de Mauritanie). Adjective of nationality: Mauritanian (mauritanien).
**Flag** (shown above right): Gold star and crescent on green field.

**Area:** 1,030,700 sq.km. (397,950 sq.miles). Agricultural land: 39.1%.
**Government:** One-party republic, since 1964 (1903 French protectorate, 1920 colony in French West Africa, 1958 self-government, 1960 Independence).
**Legislature:** National Assembly, 50 members.
**Official language:** French (*Français*).
**Capital:** Nouakchott 100,000 (1973).

**Political divisions:** 8 Administrative Areas divided into 12 Districts.
**Armed forces** (1976): Total 4,750 regular: army 4,500, navy 100, air force 150. Paramilitary forces: 1,300.

**DEMOGRAPHY. Population:** 1,030,000 (census of XII.1964-XII.1965. For 1970–2000 (UN), see last row of Table 1). Population density (1975): 1/sq.km. (3/sq.mile). Under 15 years: 42%.

Growth rate (1975–80): 2.13% per year (births 4.47%, deaths −2.35%). Life expectancy (1975–80): ˙40.0 years. Household size: 4.9 persons.
**Major languages:** French, Hassaniyah (Arabic), Fulani (Poulah), Berber, Spanish, Soninke, Zenaga, and about 5 others.
**Urban dwellers** (1970): 7.4%. Urban growth rate (1950–70): 5.1% per year.
**Labour force:** 32%.
**Tourists** (1972): 10,300.

**ETHNOLINGUISTIC GROUPS:** 81% Moor (Mauri) (53%

White Moor (Bidan), 28% Black Moor) speaking Hassaniyah, 8% Tukulor, 5% Fulani, 3% Soninke, 1.3% Zenaga, 0.5% French, 0.5% Bambara, 0.4% Wolof, 0.3% Malinke, Senegalese, Dahomean, Togolese, Ivorian, Spaniard.

**MONEY** (1977). **Monetary unit:** ouguiya (= 5 khoums); US$1 = U 50.00.
**National income per person:** US$200. Average annual family income: US$980.
**Cost of living in capital** (1976): index 177 (Washington DC=100).

**Daily cost of living:** US$44.

**HEALTH.** Hospitals: 6 (440 beds). Doctors: 71. Lepers: 4,600 (3.6 per 1,000). Blind: 15,000. Psychotics: 8,000

**EDUCATION.** Adult literacy: 1977 17%. Education rate: 4%. Schools: 50.

**LITERATURE.** Periodicals: 2. Newspapers: 3 non-daily.

**COMMUNICATION** (per 1,000 people). Phones: 1. Radios: 64.

### TABLE 1.   RELIGIOUS ADHERENTS IN MAURITANIA

| Year | 1900 | | mid-1970 | | Annual change, 1970–1980 | | | | mid-1975 | | mid-1980 | | 2000 | |
|---|---|---|---|---|---|---|---|---|---|---|---|---|---|---|
| *Name* | Adherents | % | Adherents | % | Natural | Conversion | Total | Rate | Adherents | % | Adherents | % | Adherents | % |
| Muslims | 214,950 | 97.7 | 1,154,100 | 99.3 | 26,476 | 34 | 26,510 | 2.08 | 1,275,220 | 99.4 | 1,419,200 | 99.4 | 2,262,200 | 99.2 |
| **Christians** | 50 | 0.0 | 6,200 | 0.5 | −11 | −3 | −14 | −0.23 | 6,050 | 0.5 | 6,060 | 0.4 | 16,000 | 0.7 |
| crypto-Christians | 0 | 0.0 | 1,200 | 0.1 | 29 | 1 | 30 | 2.14 | 1,400 | 0.1 | 1,500 | 0.1 | 2,000 | 0.1 |
| professing | 50 | 0.0 | 5,000 | 0.4 | −40 | −4 | −44 | −0.95 | 4,650 | 0.4 | 4,560 | 0.3 | 14,000 | 0.6 |
| Roman Catholics | 50 | 0.0 | 5,000 | 0.4 | −40 | −4 | −44 | −0.95 | 4,650 | 0.4 | 4,560 | 0.3 | 14,000 | 0.6 |
| affiliated | 50 | 0.0 | 6,200 | 0.5 | −11 | −3 | −14 | −0.23 | 6,050 | 0.5 | 6,060 | 0.4 | 16,000 | 0.7 |
| total practising | 45 | *90* | 4,340 | *70* | −8 | −2 | −10 | −0.24 | 4,230 | *70* | 4,240 | *70* | 9,600 | *60* |
| non-practising | 5 | *10* | 1,860 | *30* | −3 | −1 | −4 | −0.22 | 1,820 | *30* | 1,820 | *30* | 6,400 | *40* |
| Roman Catholics | 50 | 0.0 | 6,160 | 0.5 | −12 | −4 | −16 | −0.27 | 6,000 | 0.5 | 6,000 | 0.4 | 15,500 | 0.7 |
| Protestants | 0 | 0.0 | 40 | 0.0 | 1 | 1 | 2 | 4.00 | 50 | 0.0 | 60 | 0.0 | 500 | 0.0 |
| Tribal religionists | 5,000 | 2.3 | 1,000 | 0.1 | 18 | −38 | −20 | −2.22 | 900 | 0.1 | 800 | 0.1 | 500 | 0.0 |
| Non-religious | 0 | 0.0 | 600 | 0.1 | 14 | 6 | 20 | 2.86 | 700 | 0.1 | 800 | 0.1 | 2,000 | 0.1 |
| Baha'is | 0 | 0.0 | 100 | 0.0 | 3 | 1 | 4 | 3.08 | 130 | 0.0 | 140 | 0.0 | 300 | 0.0 |
| **Country's population** | **220,000** | **100.0** | **1,162,000** | **100.0** | **26,500** | **0** | **26,500** | **2.07** | **1,283,000** | **100.0** | **1,427,000** | **100.0** | **2,281,000** | **100.0** |

**COLUMNS, ROWS.** For meanings and definitions, see Codebook (Part 6). Note that, by definition, total 'Christians' = professing + crypto-Christians, which also = affiliated + nominal Christians. Percentages may not always total exactly, due to rounding.

**NOTES ON RELIGIONS**
BAHA'IS. In 2 local spiritual assemblies (1973).

**CHRISTIANS.** The total has fluctuated considerably during the 1970s due to arrivals and departures of expatriates, French and Africans (nett immigration is included in the column 'Natural change'). The projection to AD 2000 envisages a rapid increase in the number of African expatriates from francophone Africa, mainly Catholics.
**CRYPTO-CHRISTIANS.** African expatriates and a few nationals who attend church services.

**MUSLIMS.** Sunnis (of the Malikite rite). The majority follow Qadiriya (Sufi) maraboutism, which is widespread; others follow Tijaniya, and a few Shadhiliya. The Black minorities are all Muslims but are opposed to arabization. *Hajj pilgrims to Mecca.* (1970) 724; (1975) 914; (1976) 1,654.
NON-RELIGIOUS. Mainly French.
TRIBAL RELIGIONISTS. A few pockets of animists among Blacks (Negroes), following pre-Islamic customs.

**MAURITANIA**

**NON-CHRISTIAN RELIGIONS. Islam** reached the nomadic Berbers of this region in the 10th century and a century afterwards produced the warrior-like Almoravides who later took control of Morocco and Spain for a period. Arabs appeared in the 15th century and the present population is a mixture of Berbers and Arabs who speak a dialect of Arabic similar to the language used in the Quran. The southern region is inhabited by Blacks, but all are united by Islam which is the official religion of the country. All Mauritanians, Moors and Blacks are Sunnis of the Malikite rite, although Mauritanians also continue to follow some pre-Muslim customs. An institute of higher Islamic studies has been established at Boutilimit.

## CHRISTIANITY

**CATHOLIC CHURCH.** The Catholic Church dating from the beginning of the present century is the only organized Christian body existing in Mauritania at the present time. All Catholics are foreigners. Most are French, a transitory group generally spending terms of 3 years' service in government institutions. Other Christians include some Senegalese, Togolese, Dahomeans and Spanish from the Canary Islands, who form a sub-proletariat at the port of Nouadhibou. Ten Holy Ghost Fathers are divided between Nouakchott, Nouadhibou, Atar, Zouerate, Russo and Kaedi. Living in a country whose citizens are virtually 100% Muslims, their pastoral efforts are directed largely towards immigrant workers from Black Africa. This involves literacy work and, for a small number of adults, catechetical study leading to baptism.

**PROTESTANT CHURCHES.** Protestants have on several occasions attempted to begin activity in Mauritania, but without success. The last Protestant group to work in the country, the Worldwide Evangelization Crusade, withdrew its missionaries in 1965. A small expatriate congregation exists in the capital.

## CHURCH AND STATE.
The preamble to the constitution of May 1961 invokes the All-Powerful God. Article 2 stipulates that Islam is the religion of the Mauritanian people and guarantees to each person liberty of conscience and the right to practise his religion. In practice, conversion from Islam is prohibited and virtually non-existent.

Postage stamps with religious themes: (*top*) Nouakchott Mosque, (*bottom*) 90th anniversary of birth of Protestant missionary Albert Schweitzer.

**BROADCASTING.** No Christian broadcasting is permitted. However, programmes from Radio ELWA (Liberia) can easily be heard.

## BIBLIOGRAPHY
*Islam and social order in Mauritania.* C.C. Stewart. London: Oxford University Press, 1973. 224p.

### TABLE 2.   ORGANIZED CHURCHES AND DENOMINATIONS IN MAURITANIA

| Official name 1 | Begun 2 | Type 3 | Counc 4 | Congs 5 | Adults 6 | Affiliated 7 | Names, notes, and other statistics (see Codebook) 8 |
|---|---|---|---|---|---|---|---|
| Eglise Catholique: D Nouakchott | c1900 | R Lat | p.SFP | 7 | 3,600 | 6,160 | *Catholic Ch.* 90% French. C=1+0+1. 10x(CSSp),12w(St Joseph Apparition),P=19%,85Yy. |
| Eglise Evangélique | c1964 | P ind | ••••• | 1 | 20 | 40 | Expatriate Protestant believers in Nouakchott. Links with M=WEC(UK). |
| **Total affiliated (mid-1970)** | | | | 8 | 3,620 | 6,200 | Total denominations (1970) . . . 2. |
| **Total affiliated (mid-1975)** | | | | 6 | 3,530 | 6,050 | Total denominations (1975) . . . 2. |
| **Total affiliated (mid-1980)** | | | | 7 | 3,540 | 6,060 | Total denominations (1980) . . . 2. |

**NOTES ON TABLE ABOVE**
COLUMNS: for meanings and CODES (cols. 1, 3, 4, 8): see Codebook (Part 6). Column 1: **Boldface type** = church with over 10% of country's affiliated Christians.
NATIONAL COUNCILS (Column 4, 5th letter).
P = Conférence Episcopale de Sénégal-Mauritanie (CESM) (Episcopal Conference of Senegal & Mauritania).

PEOPLES (ethnolinguistic). Christians: 90% French, 10% Senegalese (Serer, Diola, Wolof), Dahomean, Togolese, Ivorian, Spaniard, Bambara.

**COUNTRY-WIDE TOTALS**
EVANGELIZATION (see Part 5). 1900: 3%. 1970: 10%. 1980: 12%. *Radiophonic evangelism.* RSB, ELWA, ICI (100 enrolments).
FOREIGN MISSIONARIES AND PERSONNEL (aliens from abroad) (1973). Total 22. *From Western world.* 22 Roman Catholics.
PERIODICALS. 1 title.
PERSONNEL. 22 (all foreign).
SERVICE AGENCIES. 1.

**ADDITIONAL DATA ON CHURCHES**
CATHOLIC CHURCH IN MAURITANIA. *Catholic organiz-*

*ations.* The diocese is attached to the Episcopal Conference of Senegal-Mauritania (Conférence Episcopale de Sénégal-Mauritanie) with headquarters in Dakar, Senegal. It is also a member of the Conférence Plénière des Ordinaires de l'Afrique Occidentale, and of SECAM. There are no presbyteral or pastoral councils, nor associations of religious personnel.
The Holy See has no diplomatic relations with Mauritania. It is represented to the Catholic hierarchy by an apostolic delegate based in Dakar.
The Catholic Church operates no service institutions except 2 kindergartens. However, Catholic nuns work in hospitals and centres for maternal and infant care belonging to the government.

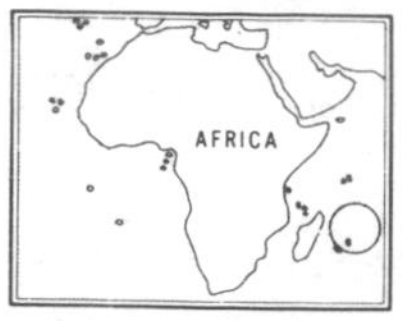


# MAURITIUS

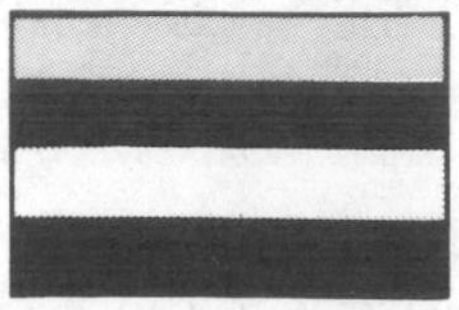

## SECULAR DATA

**STATE. Official name:** The Dominion of Mauritius (Maurice). Adjective of nationality: Mauritian (mauricien).
**Flag** (shown above right): Red, blue, yellow, and green stripes.
**Area:** 2,045 sq.km. (790 sq.miles). Agricultural land: 60.8%.
**Government:** Parliamentary state (constitutional monarchy), since 1968 (1589 Dutch settlement, 1810 British protectorate, 1903 British colony, 1968 Independence).
**Legislature:** Legislative Assembly, 70 members.
**Official language:** English.
**Capital:** Port-Louis 141,100 (1971).
**Political divisions:** 22 Constituencies.
**Armed forces** (1976): Special Mobile Force, 341. Paramilitary forces Mauritius Police, 2,373.

**DEMOGRAPHY. Population:** 851,335 (census of 30.VI.1972. For 1970–2000 (UN), see last row of Table 1). Population density (1975): 440/sq.km. (1,139/sq.mile). Under 15 years: 44%. Growth rate (1975–80): 1.49% per year (births 2.14%, deaths −0.65%). Life expectancy (1975–80): 67.1 years. Household size: 5.0 persons.
**Major languages:** English, Creole, Hindi, Urdu, French, Tamil, Punjabi, Bihari, Telugu, Chinese (Cantonese), Malagasy.
**Urban dwellers** (1970): 41.7%. Urban growth rate (1950–70): 2.7% per year.
**Labour force:** 30%.
**Refugees:** In 1976, 1,400 persons from Diego Garcia, BIOT, were resettled on Agalega Islands.
**Tourists** (1973): 60,000. (1974) 34,884.
**ETHNOLINGUISTIC GROUPS:** 67.2% Indo-Pakistani (pure and mixed or Indo-Mauritian) (59.1% Hindustani, 2.2% Tamil, 2.2% Punjabi, 2.2% Bihari & other North Indian, 0.7% Telugu), 25.8% French/Franco-Mauritian (Creole, Mulatto), 3.7% English, 3.1% Chinese (Cantonese) (25,000), Bantu, Malagasy.

**MONEY** (1977). **Monetary unit:** rupee (= 100 cents); US$1 = MRs 6.60.

**National income per person:** US$600. Average annual family income: US$3,000.
**Inflation:** (1970–74) 11.5% per year (1975: consumer price index 189).
**Cost of living in capital** (1976): index 97 (Washington DC = 100). Daily cost of living: US$30.

**HEALTH.** Hospitals: 39 (3,121 beds). Doctors: 155. Lepers: 400 (0.4 per 1,000). Blind: 250. Psychotics: 7,000. Criminals: 28,144.

**EDUCATION.** Adult literacy: (1952) 52%, (1962) 61%, (1975) 80%. Education rate: 49%. Schools: 360. Universities: 1.

**LITERATURE.** Annual new book titles (1973): 86. Periodicals: 12. Newspapers: 12 dailies, 14 non-daily.

**COMMUNICATION** (per 1,000 people). Phones: 27. Radios: 128. TV sets: 32. Daily newspaper circulation: 78 copies.

TABLE 1. RELIGIOUS ADHERENTS IN MAURITIUS

| Year | 1900 | | mid-1970 | | Annual change, 1970–1980 | | | | mid-1975 | | mid-1980 | | 2000 | |
|---|---|---|---|---|---|---|---|---|---|---|---|---|---|---|
| *Name* | *Adherents* | *%* | *Adherents* | *%* | *Natural* | *Conversion* | *Total* | *Rate* | *Adherents* | *%* | *Adherents* | *%* | *Adherents* | *%* |
| Hindus | 206,200 | 54.5 | 379,560 | 46.1 | 7,146 | –432 | 6,714 | 1.62 | 414,400 | 46.1 | 446,700 | 46.1 | 578,100 | 46.0 |
| **Christians** | **126,600** | **33.5** | **296,640** | **36.0** | **4,531** | **45** | **4,576** | **1.43** | **320,600** | **35.7** | **342,400** | **35.3** | **428,000** | **34.0** |
| crypto-Christians | 600 | 0.2 | 19,840 | 2.4 | 314 | 152 | 466 | 2.10 | 22,200 | 2.5 | 24,500 | 2.5 | 29,000 | 2.3 |
| professing | 126,000 | 33.3 | 276,800 | 33.6 | 4,217 | –107 | 4,110 | 1.38 | 298,400 | 33.2 | 317,900 | 32.8 | 399,000 | 31.7 |
| Roman Catholics | 118,000 | 31.2 | 263,700 | 32.0 | 4,015 | –155 | 3,860 | 1.36 | 284,100 | 31.6 | 302,300 | 31.2 | 377,000 | 30.0 |
| Anglicans | 4,000 | 1.1 | 6,600 | 0.8 | 94 | –74 | 20 | 0.30 | 6,700 | 0.7 | 6,800 | 0.7 | 7,000 | 0.6 |
| Protestants | 4,000 | 1.1 | 5,800 | 0.7 | 95 | 95 | 190 | 2.84 | 6,700 | 0.7 | 7,700 | 0.8 | 13,000 | 1.0 |
| Marginal Protestants | 150 | 0.0 | 700 | 0.1 | 13 | 27 | 40 | 4.44 | 900 | 0.1 | 1,100 | 0.1 | 2,000 | 0.2 |
| affiliated | 126,600 | 33.5 | 296,640 | 36.0 | 4,531 | 45 | 4,576 | 1.43 | 320,600 | 35.7 | 342,400 | 35.3 | 428,000 | 34.0 |
| total practising | 113,940 | *90* | 237,310 | *80* | 3,625 | 36 | 3,661 | 1.43 | 256,480 | *80* | 273,920 | *80* | 321,000 | *75* |
| non-practising | 12,660 | *10* | 59,330 | *20* | 906 | 9 | 915 | 1.43 | 64,120 | *20* | 68,480 | *20* | 107,000 | *25* |
| Roman Catholics | 118,300 | 31.3 | 280,000 | 34.0 | 4,221 | –51 | 4,170 | 1.38 | 302,000 | 33.6 | 321,700 | 33.2 | 400,000 | 31.8 |
| Anglicans | 4,100 | 1.1 | 8,000 | 1.0 | 150 | –10 | 140 | 1.61 | 8,700 | 1.0 | 9,400 | 1.0 | 10,000 | 0.8 |
| Protestants | 4,200 | 1.1 | 7,000 | 0.8 | 126 | 44 | 170 | 2.18 | 7,800 | 0.9 | 8,700 | 0.9 | 14,000 | 1.1 |
| Evangelicals | 3,000 | 0.8 | 3,000 | 0.4 | 55 | 25 | 80 | 2.35 | 3,400 | 0.4 | 3,800 | 0.4 | 6,000 | 0.5 |
| Marginal Protestants | 0 | 0.0 | 1,640 | 0.2 | 34 | 62 | 96 | 4.57 | 2,100 | 0.2 | 2,600 | 0.3 | 4,000 | 0.3 |
| Muslims | 41,200 | 10.9 | 131,800 | 16.0 | 2,507 | 203 | 2,710 | 1.86 | 145,600 | 16.2 | 158,900 | 16.4 | 213,700 | 17.0 |
| Ahmadis | 0 | 0.0 | 13,000 | 1.6 | 263 | 177 | 440 | 2.88 | 15,300 | 1.7 | 17,400 | 1.8 | 32,700 | 2.6 |
| Baha'is | 0 | 0.0 | 6,500 | 0.8 | 137 | 163 | 300 | 3.77 | 7,950 | 0.9 | 9,500 | 1.0 | 16,600 | 1.3 |
| Buddhists | 3,100 | 0.8 | 5,800 | 0.7 | 96 | –136 | –40 | –0.71 | 5,600 | 0.6 | 5,400 | 0.6 | 4,000 | 0.3 |
| Chinese folk-religionists | 1,000 | 0.3 | 1,600 | 0.2 | 26 | –46 | –20 | –1.33 | 1,500 | 0.2 | 1,400 | 0.1 | 1,000 | 0.1 |
| Non-religious | 80 | 0.0 | 1,600 | 0.2 | 46 | 184 | 230 | 8.52 | 2,700 | 0.3 | 3,900 | 0.4 | 12,600 | 1.0 |
| Atheists | 20 | 0.0 | 400 | 0.0 | 9 | 11 | 20 | 4.00 | 500 | 0.1 | 600 | 0.1 | 2,000 | 0.2 |
| Other religionists | 0 | 0.0 | 100 | 0.0 | 2 | 8 | 10 | 6.67 | 150 | 0.0 | 200 | 0.0 | 1,000 | 0.1 |
| **Country's population** | **378,200** | **100.0** | **824,000** | **100.0** | **14,500** | **0** | **14,500** | **1.61** | **899,000** | **100.0** | **969,000** | **100.0** | **1,257,000** | **100.0** |

COLUMNS, ROWS. For meanings and definitions, see Codebook (Part 6). Note that, by definition, total 'Christians' = professing + crypto-Christians, which also = affiliated + nominal Christians. Percentages may not always total exactly, due to rounding.
CENSUSES. **1881.** 56.6% Hindus, 30.0% Roman Catholics, 9.9% Muslims, 1.5% Protestants, 1.0% Anglicans, 0.9% Buddhists, 0.1% Parsis. **1891:** 56.5% Hindus, 31.2% Roman Catholics, 9.4% Muslims, 1.0% Protestants, 1.0% Anglicans, 0.9% Buddhists. **1901** (excluding foreign military personnel): 55.0% Hindus, 31.2% Roman Catholics, 11.0% Muslims, 0.9% Protestants, 0.9% Anglicans, 0.9% Buddhists. (The figures for 1900 in the above table are adjusted to 1900 and to include 2,313 foreign military personnel). **19.VI.1952:** 47.0% Hindus (41.1% self-termed Sanatanists, 5.6% Arya Samajists), 34.6% Roman Catholics, 15.0% Muslims (1.3% Ahmadis), 1.5% Buddhists, 1.0% Anglicans, 0.5% Protestants, 0.2% non-religious, 0.2% Chinese folk-religionists, 0.1% marginal Protestants. **30.VI.1962** (including European military): 47.6% Hindus (23.0% self-termed Sanatanists, 13.7% Arya Samajists), 33.8% Roman Catholics, 15.8% Muslims, 1.0% Anglicans, 0.9% Buddhists, 0.5% Protestants, 0.2% Chinese folk-religionists, 0.1% Baha'is, 0.1% non-religious. **30.VI.1972:** 49.7% Hindus (30.4% self-termed Sanatanists, 11.8% Arya Samajists), 33.3% Christians (31.8% Roman Catholics, 0.8% Anglicans, 0.7% Protestants, 0.1% marginal Protestants), 16.1% Muslims, 0.6% Buddhists, 0.1% Baha'is, 0.1% non-religious.

NOTES ON RELIGIONS
AHMADIS. Begun in 1915; Qadianis (the main body in Pakistan), with a small Lahori faction. There are 6 mosques, and considerable proselytizing activity with many converts claimed.
ATHEISTS. Mauritian Communist Party (MCP) (legal): membership very small.
BAHA'IS. Growth from 18 local spiritual assemblies (1964) to 57 (1973). Many are Indians converted from Hinduism.
BUDDHISTS. Chinese.
COUNTRY'S POPULATION. There has been heavy emigration since 1966, mainly of Catholics leaving for Australia.
CRYPTO-CHRISTIANS. As always in a majority non-Christian society, a small number of Christians affiliated to churches are recorded in government censuses as, or are regarded as, or profess in those censuses to be (for family or employment reasons), non-Christians (in this case Hindus).
HINDUS. 75% Sanatanists (Orthodox, or idol-worshippers, of whom in 1972 61% were identified as Sanatanists in the census), with (in 1956) 178 temples (48 Northern Hindu, 2 Marathi, 25 Telugu, 103 Tamil), and 25% Arya Samaj (Reform) (of whom over 90% are Northern Hindu). Hare Krishna (ISKCON) has 1 centre, the Ramakrishna Mission others. In the table above, the total of Hindus is less than the 1972 census indicates because many Hindus are classified here as crypto-Christians.
MARGINAL PROTESTANTS. In the 1901 census, 138 adherents of the New Jerusalem Church were recorded; in the 1972 census, 849 Jehovah's Witnesses.
MUSLIMS. Mainly Indians; 88.9% Urdu-speaking Sunnis (82% Hanafite, 6.9% Shafiite), 0.8% Shias, 0.3% Bohras, 10.0% adherents of Ahmadiya (the latter enumerated here under Muslims, though declared non-Muslim by Pakistan). *Hajj pilgrims to Mecca.* (1975) 214; (1976) 315.
NON-RELIGIOUS. Largely Chinese abandoning traditional folk religion.
OTHER RELIGIONISTS. Including Rosicrucians (1 AMORC centre).
ROMAN CATHOLICS. Declining since 1960 by emigration, largely to Australia. The column 'Natural change' includes about 650 Catholic emigrants a year.

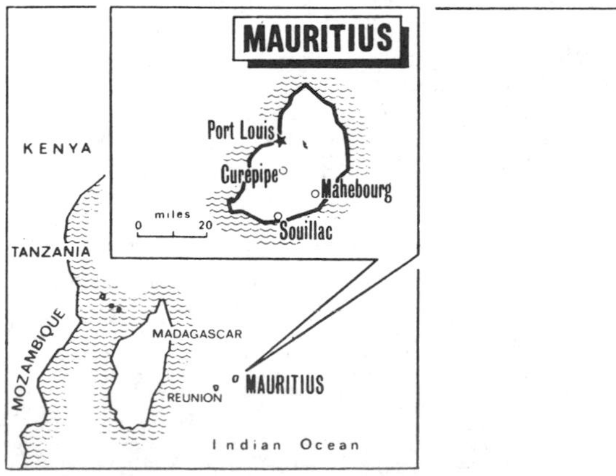


**NON-CHRISTIAN RELIGIONS. Hinduism** is the principal religion of Mauritius, the professed faith of nearly half the population. Hindus can be divided into 2 groups: Sanatanists (Orthodox, or idol-worshipper) and Arya Samaj (Reform). The latter, present in Mauritius since 1913, number over 100,000. They do not frequent temples and they use simplified rites. Many Hindus however participate in the ceremonies and activities of both groups. In 1956, there were 48 temples for northern Indians, 25 for Telugus and 103 for Tamils, although northern Indians are more numerous. By 1954 the rural Hindus had established 416 *baitkas* (sitting-places) which are religious and mutual aid societies, used for religious conferences and teaching courses in Indian languages. In cities, the baitkas are generally replaced by clubs. The caste system is less complex than in India and can be reduced to 2 principal classes: the 'great nations', including the priestly caste of the Marazes and the old warrior caste of the Baboojee; and the 'little nations' where are gathered the old servile castes. In between one finds a middle class or bourgeoisie composed of those who have acquired property or high governmental positions. There are no pariahs (untouchables).

**Islam** is primarily of Indian origin, about 16% of the population considering itself Muslim. Although Muslims come from different parts of India, 90% are Sunnis whose common language is Urdu. The remaining 10% belong to the Ahmadiya Muslim Mission, considered heretical by Sunnis, plus some descendants of merchants of Surat and Gujarat on the northwestern coast of India. Speaking Gujarati, they belong to 2 different sects: Dutchi Maiman and Sunni Surti. Their imams are trained at the Jummah mosque in Port-Louis, but some continue to come from abroad in which case they often do not know English.

**Buddhism** and **Confucianism** are still practised by a few aged Chinese but are tending to disappear.

## CHRISTIANITY

CATHOLIC CHURCH. Lazarist Fathers began the evangelization of Mauritius in 1722, which they then carried on for nearly a century. In 1819 the work was given to the Benedictines and Port-Louis was made the centre of a vicariate which included Madagascar, South Africa and Australia until 1837 and the Seychelles and St Helena until 1852. In 1847 Port-Louis was made a diocese, and the first Holy Ghost (CSSp) and Jesuit priests appeared after the middle of the century. The Catholic Church counts in its membership about 34% of the total population of the territory, including 98% of Rodriguez Island. Catholics are 60% urban, and there are a disproportionate number of Catholic emigrants, mostly to

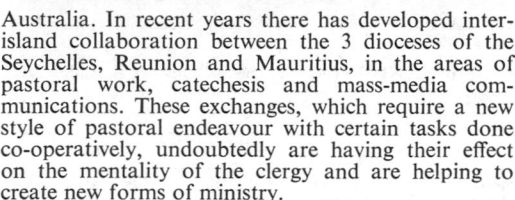

*Left.* Catholic, Anglican and other cathedrals and churches are visible here in Port-Louis.
**Protestants.** (*Above*). Prime Minister, Sir Seewoosagur Ramgoolam, opens book exhibition on evangelistic ship MV Logos during July 1977 visit to Mauritius.
**Catholic Church, Diocese of Port-Louis.** (*Right*) Catholic parish at Curepipe.

Australia. In recent years there has developed inter-island collaboration between the 3 dioceses of the Seychelles, Reunion and Mauritius, in the areas of pastoral work, catechesis and mass-media communications. These exchanges, which require a new style of pastoral endeavour with certain tasks done co-operatively, undoubtedly are having their effect on the mentality of the clergy and are helping to create new forms of ministry.

OTHER CHURCHES. Anglicans first entered in 1810 and continue to be the largest portion of the non-Catholic Christian community. The Anglican diocese of Mauritius is part of the Church of the Province of the Indian Ocean. The first Protestant missionaries to Mauritius were LMS in 1814, a work which is now incorporated into the Church of Scotland. Seventh-day Adventists, who belong to the Indian Ocean Union Mission, have built up 15 congregations and a substantive community since their arrival in 1914. Several small marginal Protestant groups are also active.

CHURCH AND STATE. The constitution of Mauritius of March 1968, incorporated in the Mauritius Independence Order 1968, presents in detail in 5 paragraphs of Article 11 the multiple aspects of liberty of conscience recognized in the country, especially liberty of thought and of religion and the right to manifest and propagate one's belief and religion. Article 14 gives to any body or grouping, religious or not, the right to found and maintain schools at its own expense. In 1810, when Mauritius passed from French to British control, the Napoleonic concordat of 1801 was implicitly maintained by the English governor. Article 8 of the act of capitulation stipulated that all 'the religious establishments in the colony will be maintained with their privileges and revenues, without any change'; and the validity of this agreement was never contested by the colonial authorities. The independent state of Mauritius does not recognize explicitly the existence of a state religion in its constitution of 1968, and no other document recognizes any differences between the Catholic Church and other churches or religions. Nevertheless, the budget includes each year an allocation to the Catholic and Anglican churches under the headings 'personal emoluments' and 'other recurrent charges'. The Church of Scotland gets only the second of these. Under the title 'subsidization of religions', other registered religious associations also receive government funds. In 1971–72, the total of these different allocations added up to Rs 842,630 (US$151,550), of which Rs 275,640 were for the Catholic Church, Rs 98,470 for the Church of England, Rs 18,120 for the Church of Scotland, and Rs 450,400 for other religions. Religious matters are dealt with by the office of the prime minister.

INTERDENOMINATIONAL ORGANIZATIONS. A Mixed Committee, composed of ecclesiastical and lay representatives of the Ecumenical Commission of the Catholic Church, the Church of England and the Church of Scotland, meets 4 times yearly for discussion and prayer. A conference and spiritual retreat centre in the south of the island, called Centre Unita, is directed by a Catholic priest but serves all religions and churches. In 1974 on the island of Rodrigues, the Catholic and Anglican colleges joined to form one ecumenical institution, Rodrigues College, with 400 students.

Mauritius is unusual in having a multi-religious council, the Mauritius Interreligious Committee (Comité Interreligieux Mauricien), also known as World Fraternal Solidarity (Solidarité Fraternelle Mondiale). It is composed of representatives of 17 churches and religious groups, including the Catholic, Anglican, Presbyterian, Adventist and Christian Science churches, and the principal Hindu and Muslim associations. Its aim is the promotion of contacts, understanding and peace among Mauritians.

BROADCASTING. The government Mauritius Broadcasting Corporation only accepts Christian programmes on special occasions. The Bureau de Liaison de l'Information Religieuse dans l'Océan Indien (BLIROI) in Madagascar supplies information for radio and TV programmes in this area of the world. From abroad, French programmes from RVOG (Ethiopia) were easily heard until its closure in 1977. For Catholics, UNDA is represented by a national association.

BIBLIOGRAPHY
*A short history of Mauritius.* P. J. Barnwell & A. Toussaint. London, 1949.
*Annuaire du Diocèse de Port-Louis, 1971.* Port-Louis, Ile Maurice: Evêché, 1971.

TABLE 2.    ORGANIZED CHURCHES AND DENOMINATIONS IN MAURITIUS

| Official name 1 | Begun 2 | Type 3 | Counc 4 | Congs 5 | Adults 6 | Affiliated 7 | Names, notes, and other statistics (see Codebook) 8 |
|---|---|---|---|---|---|---|---|
| Anglican Church: D Mauritius | 1810 | A Rig | AW,Vh | 30 | 4,000 | 8,000 | 1973, in Ch of the Province of the Indian Ocean. Poverty, cyclones. 10n,10x,2r,1s. |
| Assemblies of God | | P Pe2 | z.... | | 400 | 800 | Assemblées de Dieu. M=AdD(France). On Mauritius and Rodriguez. |
| Catholic Church: D Port-Louis | 1722 | R Lat | pxS,r | 58 | 157,000 | 280,000 | Catholic Ch. Includes Rodriguez Is, 98% RC. C=3+2+7. 54n,39x,32m,318w,1p,5733Yy. |
| Church of Christ | | P Dis | x.... | 6 | 155 | 500 | Eglise du Christ. M=CC(Non-Instrumental)(USA). Rose Hill. 1p(12)(Indian Ocean BS). |
| Church of Christ, Scientist | | M Sci | x...h | 1 | 20 | 40 | Christian Science. M=CCS(Boston,USA). Rose Hill Society. |
| Church of Scotland | 1814 | P Ref | Rwc,h | 1 | 500 | 1,000 | Eglise Réformée Indépendante de l'Ile Maurice. 1814, M=LMS(UK); now M=CSM(UK). 1f. |
| Church of the New Jerusalem | c1850 | M Swe | x.... | 2 | 50 | 100 | Swedenborgian Ch. M=GCNJ(South Africa,USA). Decline from 140 adherents in 1900. |
| Jehovah's Witnesses | 1933 | M Jeh | x.... | 7 | 297 | 1,500 | Association Les Témoins de Jéhovah. IBSA. Rose Hill. Hindi, Telugu, Tamil. 49Y. |
| Pentecostal Church | | P Pe2 | ..... | | 300 | 700 | English-speaking Pentecostals on both Mauritius and Rodriguez. |
| Seventh-day Adventist Church | 1914 | P Adv | x...h | 15 | 1,460 | 3,000 | SDA, Mauritius Mission, Indian Ocean Union Mission. 4nx,34mw,1r,13t(1141),109Y. |
| Other Protestant denominations | | P | ..... | | 500 | 1,000 | Total about 5 (see list below). |
| **Total affiliated (mid-1970)** | | | | 126 | 164,682 | 296,640 | Total denominations (1970) ...  15. |
| **Total affiliated (mid-1975)** | | | | 130 | 178,000 | 320,600 | Total denominations (1975) ...  16. |
| **Total affiliated (mid-1980)** | | | | 135 | 190,100 | 342,400 | Total denominations (1980) ...  17. |

NOTES ON TABLE ABOVE
COLUMNS: for meanings and CODES (cols. 1, 3, 4, 8): see Codebook (Part 6). Column 1: **Boldface type** = church with over 10% of country's affiliated Christians.
NATIONAL COUNCILS (Column 4, 5th letter).
h = Mauritius Inter-Religious Committee/Comité Interreligieux Mauricien (World Fraternal Solidarity); its 17 members also include the Catholic Church, and Hindu and Muslim associations.
r = attached to Conférence Episcopale de Madagascar (Episcopal Conference of Madagascar).

OTHER PROTESTANT DENOMINATIONS. Including: Africa Evangelical Fellowship (1969), Christadelphian Ecclesias, Methodist Ch, Mission Salut et Guérison (on Rodriguez).

PEOPLES (ethnolinguistic). Christians: 71% French/Franco-Mauritian (Creole), 16% Indo-Mauritian, 6% Chinese, 4% British (English, Scottish), 0.4% pure Indian (Hindi, Tamil, Telugu).

COUNTRY-WIDE TOTALS
EVANGELIZATION (see Part 5). 1900: 46%. 1970: 90%. 1980: 92%.
FOREIGN MISSIONARIES AND PERSONNEL (nationals serving abroad) (1973). Total about 31 Roman Catholics in Madagascar, Reunion, Seychelles and South Africa.
FOREIGN MISSIONARIES AND PERSONNEL (aliens from abroad) (1973). Total 151. *From Western world.* 126: 110 Roman Catholics, 9 Protestants (4 in 2 UK societies, 2 in 1 France society, 2 in 1 Australia society, 1 in 1 USA society), 7 Anglicans in 2 UK societies. *From Third World.* 25: about 20 Roman Catholics from India, 3 Anglicans, 2 Protestants from Taiwan.
INSTITUTIONS (church-operated) (1973). Total 20, including

16 higher schools, 1 medical centre, 1 religious community, 1 seminary (Anglican).
PERIODICALS. 4 titles.
PERSONNEL. About 678 (527 national, 151 foreign).
RELIGIOUS LIBRARIES. 2.
SCRIPTURE DISTRIBUTION (1975). Annual totals: 4,334 Bibles (77% subsidized, 23% commercial), 7,429 NTs (99% subsidized, 1% commercial), 39,469 UBS portions, 69,801 UBS selections. *Translations completed.* Portion: Mauritius Creole in 1885.
SERVICE AGENCIES. About 41, including AOC, BCE, CEM, CV/AV, CWS, FEC, IMCA, JEC/F, JOC/F, LAOC, USM, YMCA.

**ADDITIONAL DATA ON CHURCHES**
CATHOLIC CHURCH. The first mission (Lazarists) arrived in 1722. In 1847, the diocese was erected. *Catholics.* Including 6% Chinese. *Catechumens.* (1959) 367; (1961) 440; (1963) 500. *Annual baptisms.* (1972) 95.9% infant, 4.1% adult. *Priests.* The first Mauritian priest was ordained in 1821. National priests: 49 secular, 5 religious. Expatriates: 9 nationalities, including 1 Chinese, 2 Indians, 2 from Reunion. *Brothers.* 6 nationals. *Sisters.* 230 nationals. *Catechists.* Total (1970) 162. One training

school and 7 up-dating centres. *Indigenous religious organizations.* Sisters of the Charity of Our Lady of Good and Perpetual Help (begun 1850, 70 professed including 5 expatriates). *Foreign religious congregations.* Brothers: Christian Doctrine, St Gabriel. Sisters: Daughters of Mary (Reunion), Franciscan Missionaries of Mary, Institute of Loreto, Marie Réparatrice, Notre-Dame du Perpétuel Secours, Missionnaires de la Charité (Mother Theresa sisters from Calcutta), Carmélites.
*Catholic organizations.* The diocese is attached to the Episcopal Conference of Madagascar. Mauritius has a Union of Major Superiors (Union des Supérieures Majeures) for sisters, a Pastoral Council and a Presbyteral Council, the majority of whose members are elected. The Centrale des Oeuvres co-ordinates lay activities, the principal movements being JOC/F, JEC/F, Scouts and Guides, CV/AV, Union Catholique de l'Ile Maurice, Indo-Maurician Catholic Association, Action Familiale, Action Ouvrière Catholique and Légion de Marie (with 220 praesidia).
The Holy See has diplomatic relations with Mauritius and is represented to government and the Catholic hierarchy by a pro-nuncio based in Tananarive, Madagascar.
The Catholic Church sponsors 53 primary schools, with 37,970 pupils (in contrast to the public sector with 108,000 pupils); 14

secondary schools, 11,075 pupils (public sector: 28,000 pupils). Other institutions include 3 clinics (59 beds), 2 dispensaries, 6 homes for the aged (450 boarders), one nursery, 3 homes for orphans and one home for unmarried mothers. A government leprosarium has also been placed in the care of a religious congregation, and in 1973 the Brothers of St John of God (OH) took charge of the preventive medical programme and an itinerant dispensary on the island of Rodriguez.
Social service and development projects are promoted by Caritas of Mauritius and the Institute for Development and Progress, founded respectively in 1963 and 1970. The latter works on the level of information; research and leadership, development, and maintains 57 domestic science training schools.
Other institutions and programmes include the Emigration Bureau, founded in 1965, which aids and provides loans to emigrants; and Family Action, founded in 1963 by Catholics although the organization is non-confessional, which educates families in responsible parenthood and the natural methods of birth control in the spirit of the papal encyclical 'Humanae Vitae'.
CHURCH OF SCOTLAND. In Phoenix. Members: British, Creoles.

---

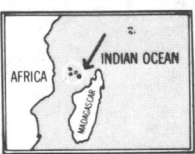

# MAYOTTE

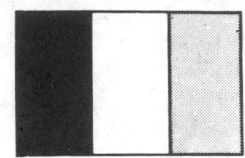

## SECULAR DATA

STATE. Official name: The Department of Mayotte (Le Département de Mayotte).
Flag (shown above right): That of France.
Area: 373 sq.km. (144 sq.miles). Agricultural land: 50.0%.
Government: Overseas department of France, since 1976 (1843 annexed by France, 1886 part of Comoros, 1975 secession).
Official language: French (*Français*).
Capital: Dzaoudzi.
Foreign forces (1976): About 300 French troops, increasing to 2,000 by 1978.

DEMOGRAPHY. Population: 43,000 (estimate of mid-1975. For 1970–2000 (UN), see last row of Table 1). Population density (1975): 115/sq.km. (299/sq.mile). Under 15 years: 45%. Growth rate (1975–80): 2.51% per year (births 4.45%, deaths −1.95%). Life expectancy (1975–80): 45.0 years. Household size: 4.9 persons.
Major languages: French, Swahili, Arabic, French Creole, Malagasy.
Urban dwellers (1970): 3.0%.

ETHNOLINGUISTIC GROUPS: 97.3% Comorian (Swahili), 1.6% Makua, 0.7% European (French), 0.2% Malagasy (Sakalava), 0.2% Reunionese Creole, Arab, Malay.

MONEY (1977). Monetary unit: CFA franc (= 100 centimes); US$1 = CFAF 250.00.
National income per person: US$103. Average annual family income: US$505.
Cost of living in capital (1976): Daily cost of living: US$46.

HEALTH. Hospitals: 2 (150 beds). Doctors: 7.

EDUCATION. Adult literacy: 60%. Education rate: 70%. Schools: 30.

COMMUNICATION (per 1,000 people). Phones: 4. Radios: 120.

### TABLE 1. RELIGIOUS ADHERENTS IN MAYOTTE

| Year | 1900 | | mid-1970 | | Annual change, 1970–1980 | | | | mid-1975 | | mid-1980 | | 2000 | |
|---|---|---|---|---|---|---|---|---|---|---|---|---|---|---|
| Name | Adherents | % | Adherents | % | Natural | Conversion | Total | Rate | Adherents | % | Adherents | % | Adherents | % |
| Muslims | 9,970 | 99.7 | 37,140 | 99.0 | 1,079 | −3 | 1,076 | 2.53 | 42,500 | 98.8 | 47,900 | 98.8 | 76,000 | 98.7 |
| Christians | 30 | 0.3 | 360 | 1.0 | 21 | 3 | 24 | 4.80 | 500 | 1.2 | 600 | 1.2 | 1,000 | 1.3 |
| professing | 30 | 0.3 | 360 | 1.0 | 21 | 3 | 24 | 4.80 | 500 | 1.2 | 600 | 1.2 | 1,000 | 1.3 |
| Roman Catholics | 30 | 0.3 | 260 | 0.7 | 17 | 2 | 19 | 5.43 | 350 | 0.8 | 450 | 0.9 | 700 | 0.9 |
| Protestants | 0 | 0.0 | 100 | 0.3 | 4 | 1 | 5 | 3.33 | 150 | 0.3 | 150 | 0.3 | 300 | 0.4 |
| affiliated | 30 | 0.3 | 360 | 1.0 | 21 | 3 | 24 | 4.80 | 500 | 1.2 | 600 | 1.2 | 1,000 | 1.3 |
| total practising | 25 | 80 | 250 | 70 | 15 | 2 | 17 | 4.86 | 350 | 70 | 420 | 70 | 600 | 60 |
| non-practising | 5 | 20 | 110 | 30 | 6 | 1 | 7 | 4.67 | 150 | 30 | 180 | 30 | 400 | 40 |
| Roman Catholics | 30 | 0.3 | 260 | 0.7 | 17 | 2 | 19 | 5.43 | 350 | 0.8 | 450 | 0.9 | 700 | 0.9 |
| Protestants | 0 | 0.0 | 100 | 0.3 | 4 | 1 | 5 | 3.33 | 150 | 0.3 | 150 | 0.3 | 300 | 0.4 |
| Country's population | 10,000 | 100.0 | 37,500 | 100.0 | 1,100 | 0 | 1,100 | 2.56 | 43,000 | 100.0 | 48,500 | 100.0 | 77,000 | 100.0 |

COLUMNS, ROWS. For meanings and definitions, see Codebook (Part 6). Note that, by definition, total 'Christians' = professing + crypto-Christians, which also = affiliated + nominal Christians. Percentages may not always total exactly, due to rounding.

NON-CHRISTIAN RELIGIONS. Islam, the predominant religion, dates back to Arab settlement 6 centuries ago. Muslims are Sunnis of the Shafiite rite.

CHRISTIANITY. Catholics are metropolitan French and Reunionese with some Malagasy. Mayotte is part of the apostolic administration of the Comoro Islands. Protestants are mostly Malagasy with a few French.

CHURCH AND STATE. Since the secession of Mayotte in 1975, the island has, as a French territory, come under French law with its separation of church state.

### TABLE 2. ORGANIZED CHURCHES AND DENOMINATIONS IN MAYOTTE

| Official name 1 | Begun 2 | Type 3 | Counc 4 | Congs 5 | Adults 6 | Affiliated 7 | Names, notes, and other statistics (see Codebook) 8 |
|---|---|---|---|---|---|---|---|
| Eglise Catholique (AA Comoro Islands) | 1517 | R Lat | P,S,r | 3 | 140 | 260 | *Parish of Dzaoudzi* (begun 1845), AA Comoro Islands (HQ Moroni). French, Reunionese. |
| Eglise de Jésus-Christ aux Comores | | P Ref | ••••• | 1 | 50 | 100 | *EJCC.* Malagasy Protestants (seasonal workers, officials), French military. M=AIM. |
| Total affiliated (mid-1970) | | | | 4 | 190 | 360 | Total denominations (1970) ... 2. |
| Total affiliated (mid-1975) | | | | 4 | 260 | 500 | Total denominations (1975) ... 2. |
| Total affiliated (mid-1980) | | | | 5 | 320 | 600 | Total denominations (1980) ... 2. |

NOTES ON TABLE ABOVE
COLUMNS: for meanings and CODES (cols. 1, 3, 4, 8): see Codebook (Part 6). Column 1: **Boldface type** = church with over 10% of country's affiliated Christians.
NATIONAL COUNCILS (Column 4, 5th letter).

r = Conférence Episcopale de Madagascar (Episcopal Conference of Madagascar).

PEOPLES (ethnolinguistic). Christians: (mid-1975) 60% French (metropolitan), 20% Reunionese Creole, 20% Malagasy.

COUNTRY-WIDE TOTALS
EVANGELIZATION (see Part 5). 1900: 1%. 1970: 35%. 1980: 45%.

---

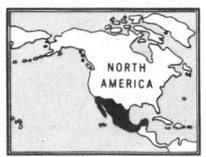

# MEXICO

## SECULAR DATA

STATE. Official name: The United Mexican States (Los Estados Unidos Mexicanos). Adjective of nationality: Mexican (mexicano).
Flag (shown above right): Green, white, and red bars; coat of arms in centre (eagle devouring serpent, and Aztec legend).
Area: 1,972,547 sq.km. (761,605 sq.miles). Agricultural land: 47.3%.
Government: Federal republic, since 1823 (1519 Spanish possession (New Spain), 1821 Independence as empire, 1823 republic).
Legislature: Congress: Senate, 60 members; Chamber of Deputies, 210 members.
Official language: Spanish (*Español/Castellano*).

Chief cities: capital Mexico City 10,766,790 (1974), Guadalajara 1,856,880, Monterrey 1,543,400, Juárez 497,270.
Political divisions: 29 States, 1 Federal District, 2 Territories.
Armed forces (1976): Total 89,500 regular (and 250,00 part-time conscripts): army 69,000, navy 14,500, air force 6,000 (42 combat aircraft).

DEMOGRAPHY. Population: 48,225,238 (census of 28.I.1970. For 1970-2000 (UN), see last row of Table 1). Population density (1975): 30/sq.km. (78/sq.mile). Under 15 years: 46%. Growth rate (1975–80): 3.34% per year (births 4.17%, deaths −0.76%, emigrants −0.07%). Life expectancy (1975–80): 65.5 years. Household size: 4.9 persons.
Major languages: Spanish, English, Nahuatl, Maya, Otomí, Zapotec, Mixtec, Arabic, Chinese, Yiddish. There are in addition

over 200 other Indian languages. Usage: 92.2% Spanish-speaking only, 5.6% bilingual Indian, 2.1% monolingual Indian (no Spanish).
Urban dwellers (1970): 56.5%. Urban growth rate (1950–70): 4.8% per year.
Labour force: 26%.
Refugees (1977): About 2,000 from Chile.
Tourists (1971): 2,769,987. (1974) 3,360,900.

ETHNOLINGUISTIC GROUPS: 55.0% Mestizo (Spanish/ Amerindian), 29.0% Amerindian (pure-blooded) [21.3% speaking Spanish only, 5.6% bilingual, 2.1% monolingual (Indian only)] [9.0% Half-Indian (non-tribal, detribalized), 6.0% Aztec (Nahuatl), 3.3% Maya (1.4% Tzeltal, Yucatec, Huastec, Tzotzil, Chol, chontal, &c), 2.6% Otomí, 2.3% Zapotec, 2.0% Mixtec,

0.3% Totonac, 0.2% Mazahua, 0.2% Mazatec, 0.1% Mixé, Tarahumara, &c], 15.0% Mexican White, 0.5% Black (Negro), 0.3% Spaniard (160,000), 0.1% Arab (Lebanese, Palestinian, Syrian), 0.1% Jewish, Chinese (14,200), USA, Greek, Russian, French, Italian, Galician, Catalonian, German, British, Basque, Japanese, Gypsy, et alii.

**MONEY** (1977). **Monetary unit:** peso (= 100 centavos); US$1 = mn$20.00 (operational rate of exchange).

**National income per person:** US$1,070. Average annual family income: US$5,243.
**Inflation:** (1970–74) 10.9% per year (1975: consumer price index 197).
**Cost of living in capital** (1976): index 98 (Washington DC = 100). Daily cost of living: US$39.

**HEALTH.** Hospitals: 1,521 (62,566 beds). Doctors: 38,000. Lepers: 26,000 (0.4 per 1,000). Blind: 60,000. Psychotics: 480,000.

**EDUCATION.** Adult literacy: (1950), 57%, (1970) 74%. Education rate: 51%. Schools: 47,234. Universities: 39.

**LITERATURE.** Annual new book titles (1973): 5,455. Periodicals: 1,642. Scientific journals: 225. Newspapers: 216 dailies, 347 non-daily.

**COMMUNICATION** (per 1,000 people). Phones: 40. Radios: 311. TV sets: 80. Daily newspaper circulation: 85 copies.

TABLE 1. RELIGIOUS ADHERENTS IN MEXICO

| Year | 1900 | | mid-1970 | | Annual change, 1970–1980 | | | | mid-1975 | | mid-1980 | | 2000 | |
|---|---|---|---|---|---|---|---|---|---|---|---|---|---|---|
| *Name* | *Adherents* | *%* | *Adherents* | *%* | *Natural* | *Conversion* | *Total* | *Rate* | *Adherents* | *%* | *Adherents* | *%* | *Adherents* | *%* |
| **Christians** | **13,493,900** | **99.2** | **49,319,000** | **98.0** | **1,917,972** | **–63,182** | **1,854,790** | **3.21** | **57,781,200** | **97.6** | **67,866,900** | **97.0** | **125,588,000** | **95.0** |
| professing | 13,493,900 | 99.2 | 49,319,000 | 98.0 | 1,917,972 | –63,182 | 1,854,790 | 3.21 | 57,781,200 | 97.6 | 67,866,900 | 97.0 | 125,588,000 | 95.0 |
| Roman Catholics | 13,442,100 | 98.8 | 48,366,000 | 96.1 | 1,877,376 | –86,226 | 1,791,150 | 3.17 | 56,558,200 | 95.5 | 66,277,500 | 94.7 | 121,112,300 | 91.6 |
| Christo-pagans | 2,721,000 | 20.0 | 1,861,000 | 3.7 | 70,736 | –11,936 | 58,800 | 2.76 | 2,131,000 | 3.6 | 2,449,000 | 3.5 | 2,645,000 | 2.0 |
| Evangelical Catholics | 11,800 | 0.1 | 969,780 | 1.9 | 41,807 | 23,655 | 65,462 | 5.20 | 1,259,500 | 2.1 | 1,624,400 | 2.3 | 3,716,100 | 2.8 |
| Mexican indigenous | 0 | 0.0 | 410,000 | 0.8 | 17,686 | 11,284 | 28,970 | 5.44 | 532,800 | 0.9 | 699,700 | 1.0 | 1,983,700 | 1.5 |
| Protestants | 45,380 | 0.4 | 400,000 | 0.8 | 15,335 | –335 | 15,000 | 3.25 | 462,000 | 0.8 | 550,000 | 0.8 | 1,320,000 | 1.8 |
| Marginal Protestants | 1,420 | 0.0 | 100,000 | 0.2 | 5,895 | 12,095 | 17,990 | 10.13 | 177,600 | 0.3 | 279,900 | 0.4 | 1,058,000 | 0.0 |
| Orthodox | 1,000 | 0.0 | 37,000 | 0.1 | 1,444 | –4 | 1,440 | 3.31 | 43,500 | 0.1 | 51,400 | 0.1 | 97,000 | 0.1 |
| Anglicans | 4,000 | 0.0 | 5,000 | 0.0 | 196 | 4 | 200 | 3.39 | 5,900 | 0.0 | 7,000 | 0.0 | 14,000 | 0.0 |
| Catholics (non-Roman) | 0 | 0.0 | 1,000 | 0.0 | 40 | 0 | 40 | 3.32 | 1,200 | 0.0 | 1,400 | 0.0 | 3,000 | 0.0 |
| nominal | 1,090,100 | 8.0 | 1,700,696 | 3.4 | 70,683 | 25,197 | 95,880 | 4.50 | 2,129,400 | 3.6 | 2,659,500 | 3.8 | 6,612,000 | 5.0 |
| affiliated | 12,403,800 | 91.1 | 47,618,304 | 94.6 | 1,847,289 | –88,379 | 1,758,910 | 3.16 | 55,651,800 | 94.0 | 65,207,400 | 93.2 | 118,976,000 | 90.0 |
| doubly-affiliated | –40,000 | –0.3 | –1,350,000 | –2.7 | –56,993 | –24,897 | –81,890 | 4.77 | –1,717,000 | –2.9 | –2,168,900 | –3.1 | –5,290,000 | –4.0 |
| total practising | 9,923,040 | *80* | 30,951,900 | *65* | 1,200,738 | –57,447 | 1,143,291 | 3.16 | 36,173,670 | *65* | 42,384,810 | *65* | 71,385,600 | *60* |
| non-practising | 2,480,760 | *20* | 16,666,400 | *35* | 646,551 | –30,932 | 615,619 | 3.16 | 19,478,130 | *35* | 22,822,590 | *35* | 47,590,400 | *40* |
| Roman Catholics | 12,380,200 | 91.0 | 47,028,524 | 93.5 | 1,821,215 | –110,187 | 1,711,028 | 3.12 | 54,866,300 | 92.7 | 64,138,800 | 91.7 | 116,028,200 | 87.7 |
| Catholic pentecostals | 0 | 0.0 | 0 | 0.0 | 664 | 6,336 | 7,000 | 35.00 | 20,000 | 0.0 | 70,000 | 0.1 | 700,000 | 0.5 |
| Mexican indigenous | 0 | 0.0 | 929,792 | 1.8 | 39,305 | 21,636 | 60,941 | 5.15 | 1,184,100 | 2.0 | 1,539,200 | 2.2 | 3,967,300 | 3.0 |
| Protestants | 55,800 | 0.4 | 733,675 | 1.5 | 31,444 | 14,128 | 45,572 | 4.81 | 947,300 | 1.6 | 1,189,400 | 1.7 | 2,777,100 | 2.1 |
| Evangelicals | 50,000 | 0.4 | 603,700 | 1.2 | 25,549 | 12,031 | 37,580 | 4.88 | 769,700 | 1.3 | 979,500 | 1.4 | 2,513,000 | 1.9 |
| Marginal Protestants | 1,800 | 0.0 | 212,432 | 0.4 | 9,825 | 10,932 | 20,757 | 7.01 | 296,000 | 0.5 | 420,000 | 0.6 | 1,322,400 | 1.0 |
| Orthodox | 1,000 | 0.0 | 54,000 | 0.1 | 2,108 | 2 | 2,110 | 3.32 | 63,500 | 0.1 | 75,100 | 0.1 | 143,000 | 0.1 |
| Anglicans | 5,000 | 0.0 | 8,881 | 0.0 | 345 | 7 | 352 | 3.38 | 10,400 | 0.0 | 12,400 | 0.0 | 25,000 | 0.0 |
| Evangelicals | 5,000 | 0.0 | 8,000 | 0.0 | 315 | 35 | 350 | 3.68 | 9,500 | 0.0 | 11,500 | 0.0 | 23,000 | 0.0 |
| Catholics (non-Roman) | 0 | 0.0 | 1,000 | 0.0 | 40 | 0 | 40 | 3.32 | 1,200 | 0.0 | 1,400 | 0.0 | 3,000 | 0.0 |
| Non-religious | 10,160 | 0.1 | 838,900 | 1.7 | 41,104 | 63,106 | 104,210 | 8.41 | 1,238,300 | 2.1 | 1,881,000 | 2.7 | 6,053,000 | 4.6 |
| Tribal religionists | 100,000 | 0.7 | 50,000 | 0.1 | 1,692 | –1,492 | 200 | 0.39 | 51,000 | 0.1 | 52,000 | 0.1 | 50,000 | 0.0 |
| Jews | 150 | 0.0 | 35,000 | 0.1 | 1,361 | –1 | 1,360 | 3.32 | 41,000 | 0.1 | 48,600 | 0.1 | 91,000 | 0.1 |
| Atheists | 0 | 0.0 | 20,000 | 0.0 | 996 | 1,004 | 2,000 | 6.67 | 30,000 | 0.1 | 40,000 | 0.1 | 300,000 | 0.2 |
| Baha'is | 0 | 0.0 | 15,100 | 0.0 | 631 | 159 | 790 | 4.16 | 19,000 | 0.0 | 23,000 | 0.0 | 50,000 | 0.0 |
| Buddhists | 2,090 | 0.0 | 15,000 | 0.0 | 581 | –1 | 580 | 3.31 | 17,500 | 0.0 | 20,800 | 0.0 | 37,000 | 0.0 |
| Muslims | 1,000 | 0.0 | 15,000 | 0.0 | 584 | 6 | 590 | 3.35 | 17,600 | 0.0 | 20,900 | 0.0 | 39,000 | 0.0 |
| Chinese folk-religionists | 0 | 0.0 | 3,000 | 0.0 | 113 | –33 | 80 | 2.35 | 3,400 | 0.0 | 3,800 | 0.0 | 6,000 | 0.0 |
| New-Religionists | 0 | 0.0 | 1,000 | 0.0 | 116 | 384 | 500 | 14.29 | 3,500 | 0.0 | 6,000 | 0.0 | 20,000 | 0.0 |
| Other religionists | 0 | 0.0 | 1,000 | 0.0 | 50 | 50 | 100 | 6.67 | 1,500 | 0.0 | 2,000 | 0.0 | 10,000 | 0.0 |
| **Country's population** | **13,607,300** | **100.0** | **50,313,000** | **100.0** | **1,965,200** | **0** | **1,965,200** | **3.32** | **59,204,000** | **100.0** | **69,965,000** | **100.0** | **132,244,000** | **100.0** |

COLUMNS, ROWS. For meanings and definitions, see Codebook (Part 6). Note that, by definition, total 'Christians' = professing + crypto-Christians, which also = affiliated + nominal Christians. Percentages may not always total exactly, due to rounding.
CENSUSES. **1900:** 99.4% Roman Catholics, 0.4% Evangelicals, 0.2% non-religious and pagans. **1910:** 99.2% Roman Catholics, 0.5% Evangelicals, 0.3% non-religious, pagans and others. **1921:** 97.1% Roman Catholics, 0.5% Evangelicals, 0.8% non-religious. **1930:** 97.7% Roman Catholics, 1.0% non-religious and pagans, 0.8% Evangelicals, 0.3% other religionists. **1940:** 96.6% Roman Catholics, 2.3% non-religious and pagans, 0.9% Evangelicals, 0.1% Jews, 0.2% other religionists. **6.VI.1950** (de jure): 98.2% Roman Catholics, 1.3% Evangelicals, 0.4% others religionists, 0.1% Jews. **8.VI.1960:** 97.1% Roman Catholics, 1.8% Evangelicals, 0.6% non-religious, 0.3% Jews, 0.3% marginal Protestants. **28.I.1970** (de jure): 96.2% Roman Catholics, 1.8% Evangelicals (Protestants, Mexican indigenous, marginal Protestants, Anglicans), 1.6% non-religious, 0.3% other religionists, 0.1% Jews. Exact interpretation and comparison of these censuses is difficult because the census term 'Evangélicos' includes Protestants, Anglicans, marginal Protestants and some Mexican indigenous, but some of the latter appear under other categories also ('Católicos', 'Otros', 'Ninguna'). 'Otra' is defined in the census as 'Islam, Buddhism, Taoism, Shinto, Confucianism, Brahmanism, Orthodoxy, etc'.

NOTES ON RELIGIONS
ATHEISTS. Partido Comunista de México (PCM) (legal; no longer pro-Soviet): membership (1970) 5,000; pro-Communist voters (election of 5.VII.1970) 188,000.
BAHA'IS. Rapid growth from 10 local spiritual assemblies (1964) to 96 (1973). Converts include Seri and Tarahumara Indians.
BUDDHISTS. Chinese and Japanese; mainly in Lower California and Sonorá.
CATHOLIC PENTECOSTALS (or, Catholic charismatics). Begun in 1971 with (in June) one prayer group of 40 people in Mexico City. Totals (January 1974): 3,000 involved adults (over 15 years old) in 100 prayer groups; total charismatic community including children, 6,000. By mid-1975 there were 10,000 adults involved (20,000 total community). In January 1976, over 5,000 attended a National Day of Renewal in Mexico City; in 1978, 7,000 attended the national renewal conference in San Luis.
CHRISTO-PAGANS. Over 95% of Mexico's 2.1% monolingual Amerindians, and around 30% of the 5.6% bilingual Amerindians, still practise strong christo-paganism, which is the term usually given to their syncretistic folk-Catholicism as a religion combining 17th-century Spanish Catholicism with traditional Amerindian religion (in particular, Aztec and Mayan religious concepts and world-views). At the same time, however, they remain baptized Roman Catholics and are enumerated as such by the Catholic Church and also by the state and its census enumerators.
COUNTRY'S POPULATION. The UN estimate for mid-1970 population used in this table is 2.1 million higher than the 28.I.1970 census figure to compensate for known underenumeration.
DOUBLY-AFFILIATED. The term covers those affiliated to, or claimed by, both the Catholic Church and also a church termed by the state Evangélica (Protestant, Mexican indigenous, Anglican or marginal Protestant) or other church, i.e. baptized Catholics who have recently become Evangelicals or others. Because their statistics represent a duplication, they are shown in the table as a negative quantity (with a minus sign).
EVANGELICAL CATHOLICS. This term is used to describe persons who are affiliated to churches termed by the state Evangélica (Protestant, Anglican, Mexican indigenous, marginal Protestant), but who in government censuses are regarded as, or profess to be, Roman Catholics.
EVANGELICALS. The English term is used here in the sense understood within the churches (not as understood by the state), and embraces the following 4 groupings: (1) Conservative Evangelicals, namely all persons affiliated to Protestant denominations which are Conservative Evangelical in theology and emphasis, (2) Conciliar Evangelicals, within the non-Evangelical or conciliar Protestant denominations usually affiliated to the Ecumenical Movement, (3) Fundamentalists, namely all persons affiliated to Protestant denominations linked with the ICCC or other fundamentalist councils, and (4) Anglican (Episcopalian) Evangelicals. This definition excludes non-Protestant groupings such as the Mexican indigenous pentecostal churches.
JEWS. Mostly in Mexico City. Ashkenazi and Sefardi synagogues, and one congregation of Indian Jews; 55% Yiddish-speaking Ashkenazi, 15% Spanish-speaking Sefardi, 10% Arabic-speaking.
MEXICAN INDIGENOUS. In about 120 denominations in 1970 (see Table 2). The 1970 total above was obtained by totalling column 7 in Table 2 for the indigenous churches listed there (coded 'I' in column 3).
MUSLIMS. Lebanese, Palestinian and Syrian Arab immigrants.
NEW-RELIGIONISTS. By 1975, 3,500 converts to the Japanese movement Nichiren Shoshu (Soka Gakkai).
OTHER RELIGIONISTS. Adherents of other non-Christian religions and syncretistic cults, including Hindus, Rosicrucians (AMORC, 22 Lodges and centres), and Theosophists (27 Lodges with 272 members in 1974).
PRACTISING CHRISTIANS. Attendance has declined drastically since 1959. *Roman Catholics.* June 1959: 70% attend at least weekly, 22% once in a while, 1% only on major festivals, under 1% never. 1970: weekly mass attendance 10% urban, 25% rural; annual communicants 55% urban, 73% rural, averaging 60%, or 65% of affiliated Christians including irregular annual attenders. *Pilgrims.* Up to 1970, around 500,000 pilgrims a year visited the shrine of the Virgin at Guadalupe, north of Mexico City. In 1976 the total was 2 million, increasing in 1977 with the growing popularity of the new basilica.
TRIBAL RELIGIONISTS. A small proportion of monolingual Amerindians in 100 tribes have resisted and still resist both Catholicism, christo-paganism and also Protestant missions; among them are 10,000 Huichols in western Mexico who eventually forced missions to give up and now live with their own culture and religion, and the Tepehuans of northern Mexico who in 1956 began a traditionalist fertility cult movement of reaction away from both christo-paganism and Mexican culture.

**NON-CHRISTIAN RELIGIONS. Traditional Indian religions** retain a strong attraction for the more than 100 tribes in Mexico, each of which has its own distinctive language (Aztec, Ch'ol Sabanilla, Chamula, Huave, Mixteco, Otomí, Yaqui, Zinacanteco, et alia). The vast majority of all monolingual Indians still practise strong christo-paganism, namely a syncretistic folk-Catholicism combining 17th-century Spanish Catholicism with traditional Amerindian religion, and in particular with Aztec and Mayan religious concepts and world-views. A further small proportion of monolingual Indians including the Huichols and Tepehuans have resisted and still resist both Catholicism, christo-paganism and Protestant missions and retain their traditional religions.

**Judaism** is represented in Mexico by about 35,000 Jews who reside mostly in Mexico City. There are both Ashkenazi and Sefardi synagogues and also one congregation of Indian Jews. The principal Jewish co-ordinating organization is the Israelite Central Committee of Mexico (Comité Central Israélita de México).

**Baha'i** has recently had rapid growth, from 10 local spiritual assemblies in 1964 to 96 by 1973.

**Islam** also has followers, mostly immigrant Lebanese, Palestinian and Syrian Arabs.

**Buddhism** and other Asiatic religions are found among small groups of immigrant Asians in the northwestern part of the country in Lower California and Sonorá.

## CHRISTIANITY

CATHOLIC CHURCH. Amerigo Vespucci landed near Tampico in 1497, and the first Spanish settlers arrived in 1518. Franciscan missionaries came in 1522, soon followed by other religious orders. The first bishop was appointed in 1528, and by 1551 the University of Mexico had been founded. The Catholic Church had been the principal organized influence in Mexico for nearly 5 centuries. Today it is the major example of self-support and self-

**Iglesia Católica en México.** *Above.* At right, old Basilica of Our Lady of Guadalupe (dedicated 1709; accommodating 2,000 worshippers), north of Mexico City, which is rapidly tilting and subsiding into ground, to which came 500,000 pilgrims a year up to 1970; and (*left*) ultramodern new Basilica inaugurated 12 October 1976 in presence of half a million pilgrims from around the world, to which greatly increased crowds have since come (in 1976, 2 million). *Below.* Interior of new basilica during inaugural mass with 100 Mexican and other bishops present; it accommodates 20,000 people with visibility unobstructed by a single pillar.

propagation of all the Catholic communities in Latin America, with the highest proportion of citizen personnel in the continent. The majority of the church's clergy are nationals, and in 1972 all the bishops except one prelate nullius were Mexicans. By 1974 there were 11 archdioceses, 48 dioceses and 7 other jurisdictions.

In 1971, 87% of members of male religious orders and congregations were Mexicans, of whom 1% were from other Latin American countries and 12% from other continents, principally from the USA, Spain and Italy. Of sisters, 93% were from Mexico, 3% from other Latin American countries and 4% from the USA and Spain. There are 26 diocesan or interdiocesan major seminaries in addition to a Mexican major seminary in New Mexico (USA),

and a seminary for missionaries in Mexico. The work of catechists is being taken over increasingly by sisters, aided by young girls.

The religious attitudes and customs of Mexican Catholics are extremely varied, differing from region to region. Over 90% of the population are baptized Catholics; more than 80% have been confirmed and 77% married in the church.

Apart from christo-paganism among Amerindians, Mexican Catholicism among Mestizos also has syncretistic elements in it, of which one of the best-known is the cult of the Virgin of Guadalupe. From 9–12 December 1531, an Indian, Juan Diego, claimed visions of the Virgin Mary. Today this has grown into an intense and impassioned cult, a uniquely Mexican creation with a vast iconography, in which

the Aztec worship of the earth goddess Cuauhtli (Coatlicue, or Tonantzin, Madre Antigua) has become fused with veneration of Virgin Mary (Madre Nueva, Madre Nuestra). Each year hundreds of thousands of pilgrims from across the world visit the shrine and basilica.

PROTESTANT CHURCHES. Protestant efforts began with the distribution of scriptures by the American Bible Society in 1824; but until the revolution of 1857 Mexico was virtually closed to Protestant missions. Juarez, the new president at that time, encouraged Protestant activities and several independent missionaries entered Monterrey during the late 1850s. Lutheran immigrants formed a German-speaking congregation in 1861, and the following year the first Baptist church was begun. Encouraged by their success, the American Baptist Home Mission Society established a station in 1870; and 2 years later American Board missionaries were also found in Monterrey and Guadalajara. American Presbyterians entered Mexico City in 1872 and the Methodists a year later. In 1901 the Presbyterian Synod of Mexico was formed and the autonomous Methodist Church of Mexico in 1930. The Southern Baptist Convention came to Mexico in 1880, its first Latin American field; and another important early arrival was the Seventh-day Adventist church in 1893.

The number of Protestant churches continued to grow until 1910 when anti-church laws, created to continue the government's attack on the Catholic Church, limited equally the activities of all the other churches. Many missions left. Membership in established Protestant churches fell noticeably during the next 25 years. In contrast, however, church groups originating during this period grew in membership.

A comity arrangement, agreed upon by 9 of the earliest missions in 1917 to prevent overlapping of effort, created bitterness as congregations were separated from their original sponsoring bodies and several missions refused to observe the new lines of demarcation.

Since the mid-1930s, with greater social stability in Mexico and a shift in attitude of government and the Catholic Church towards Protestants, the number of Evangelicals (Evangélicos) or Protestants has increased. In one instance, the government attempted to eradicate them completely in the state of Tabasco in 1930; but 5 years later when the persecution ceased, there were twice as many Presbyterians as before.

The National Presbyterian Church increased eightfold between 1935 and 1960 making this the largest Protestant denomination in Mexico today. Presbyterianism is especially strong in the states of Chiapas and Tabasco. Of the many USA-based groups which have entered Mexico since World War II, some of the most significant gains have been registered by the Church of God (Anderson).

Pentecostalism was brought by Mexicans returning from the USA as early as 1915 and has grown very rapidly during the present century. Much of the growth of such Pentecostal groups as the Assemblies of God is due to strong leadership-training programmes carried on in numerous Bible schools and to the fact that churches have been completely autonomous since their origin.

Work among the large Indian population of Mexico has been slow because of the over 100 different languages spoken by them. Wycliffe Bible Translators, with their main training centre for Latin America in Mexico, had by 1971 published portions of the Bible in 79 of these languages. The Mexican Indian Mission has trained 30 national evangelists in its Bible school. An aid in this work has been the Mission Aviation Fellowship which opened its first field in Mexico in 1946.

INDIGENOUS CHURCHES. Numerous independent churches, large and small, have developed in Mexico, particularly during the government persecution in the first third of this century. Some were started by migrant Mexican workers returning from the USA, while others are the result of local schisms. Most are pentecostal and are characterized by an apostolic and biblical faith built on the Catholic culture they inherited. The earliest, the Apostolic Church of the Faith in Jesus Christ, begun in 1914, has churches in all but one of Mexico's 29 states. In 1967 it had 425 organized churches, 13 bishops and over 1,000 preachers.

The largest of these churches is the Union of Evangelical Independent Churches, which began in 1923 and has its strength among the Otomí Indians.

The largest schism from Catholicism took place in 1926, leading to the formation of the Orthodox Catholic Apostolic Mexican Church, also known as the National Church.

OTHER CHURCHES. Two marginal Protestant bodies from the USA have built up large constituencies in Mexico during the present century, namely the Mormons and Jehovah's Witnesses who arrived respectively in 1879 and 1893. Mormons have had spectacular successes among Indians, with 40,000 baptisms reported in 1976 alone.

Three Eastern Orthodox groups are active, representing the Russian, Greek and Antiochene traditions. The Russian Orthodox community is the largest and is an exarchate of the Orthodox Church in America (OCA).

The Episcopal Church traces its origins to 1857 as a mass secession from the Roman Catholic Church demanding ecclesiastical reforms, named Iglesia de Jesus and supported by several leading government officials. By 1865 there were 72 congregations, with over 7,000 members in Mexico City alone. Their appeal for bishops to the Episcopal Church in the USA met with interminable delays during which time the movement declined catastrophically before an Englishman was consecrated as the first bishop in 1879. Finally in 1904 the church became a missionary district of the Episcopal Church in the USA, with 34 Mexican and 27 English-speaking congregations, with 16 Mexican and 12 USA clergy. Since then the church has continued to decline in comparison with the demographic increase in the country.

CHURCH AND STATE. The federal constitution of the United States of Mexico, ratified in 1917, recognizes in Article 24 freedom of conscience and freedom of the practice of religion, both public and private. Nevertheless, the law recognizes no juridical personality for either the Catholic Church or other churches (Article 130). Building on this basic principle, a series of precise constitutional dispositions has been developed, tending to regulate the internal structure of the churches especially the Catholic Church, and to limit their function as social entities. (1) The religious ministry is considered as a profession, subject to regulation by the state. The government has the power to determine the maximum number of clergy and to authorize the opening of any place of worship. Clergy do not have the right to vote nor to participate in politics; they may not criticize in public or at religious meetings either the laws of the country or public authorities. Their right to inheritance is limited (Article 130). (2) The nation is assured complete control of all landed property that churches may hold in their own right or that of an intermediary. Churches thus do not have any property rights (Article 27). (3) All activities in education are forbidden to clergy and religious associations (Article 3). The establishment of monastic orders by any denomination for any purpose is also forbidden (Article 5).

These constitutional dispositions put into a general framework all the anti-clerical laws developed in Mexico after Independence in 1821. They testify to the violence and past scars of the struggle between the Catholic Church, which was the state religion until 1857, and the revolutionary forces which became victorious in 1910. Today the majority of these anti-clerical laws are rarely applied, but the legislation continue to exist. Relations between the state and the Catholic Church may therefore be interpreted as a kind of modus vivendi, translated in practice into peaceful-existence without reconciliation.

Since 1971 several bishops have publicly denounced institutionalized oppression and violence, and the modus vivendi has been placed in jeopardy by the move towards the right by government and towards the left by a section of the Catholic Church which includes several bishops as well as progressivist priests and laymen. Bishop Mendes Arceo of Cuernavaca has been considered the leader of this Latin American emphasis which has become known as Christians for Socialism.

In 1974 the Mexican parliament over Catholic objections adopted an education law which establishes state control over private schools and prohibits religious authorities from intervening in any way in any type of degree of education. The same law warns that the state may withdraw the licences of private schools if they contravene Article 3 of the constitution prohibiting clergy and religious associations from involvement in educational activities.

INTERDENOMINATIONAL ORGANIZATIONS. The Evangelical Federation of Mexico (Federación Evangélica de México), begun in 1927, includes 13 churches, of which the largest is the Methodist Church. Also members of the federation are a number of interdenominational bodies including the National Anti-Alcoholic Association (Asociación Nacional Antialcoholica), Audio-Visual Education Centre (Centro Audiovisual Educativo, CAVE), Christian Student Movement (Movimiento Estudiantil Cristiano), Evangelical Literature Committee (Comité de Literatura Evangélica) and National Union of Christian Women's Societies (Unión Nacional de Sociedades Femeniles Cristianas).

A significant number of indigenous pentecostal churches are grouped in the Pentecostal Fraternal Association (Asociación Fraternal de Iglesias Pentecostales, also known as the Asociación Fraternal Pentecostés).

Catholic involvement in the ecumenical movement is maintained through the National Secretariat for Ecumenism (Secretariado Nacional de Ecumenismo), founded in 1963 under the name Centre for Christian Unity, which is dependent on the Episcopal Commission for the Doctrine of the Faith (Comisión Episcopal para la Doctrina de la Fe).

The Centre for Ecumenical Studies (Centro de Estudios Ecuménicos), founded in 1969, provides for dialogue and co-operation between Catholics and Protestants, as well as sponsoring research and programmes of social action.

BROADCASTING. Until recently, religious broadcasts were forbidden in Mexico; but today there are hundreds of such broadcasts every week in all parts of the country. All commercial radio and television networks accept religious material although most are reluctant to accept programmes because they are often poorly prepared. They usually have no objections to short evangelistic spots. Unlike the USA and other Latin American states, there are no Catholic or Protestant radio stations or TV channels. Catholics have however developed radiophonic schools. In Huayacocotla region there is the Sistema Educativo Radiofónico de México (SER). In 1970 there were 60 radio schools in Sisoguichi (Escuelas Radiofónicas de la Tarahumara), founded in 1955 and now with over 1,500 students. For Catholics, Mexico is a member of UNDA

There are numerous regular Protestant programmes and studios. The Evangelical Latin League (TELL) has a radio broadcast in Spanish, the Radio Bible Institute, which reaches most of Mexico. Southern Baptists and CAVE (Centro Audio Visual Educativo), amongst others, have recording studios in Mexico City. In 1968, Seventh-day Adventists were broadcasting over 44 stations. From abroad, international stations easily received are FEBC (California), TWR (Bonaire, Netherlands Antilles) and HCJB (Ecuador), also Radio Vatican.

Since 1977, official hostility towards proliferating Protestant broadcasts has become marked. In July 1978, religious radio programmes on 50 stations were suspended by government order.

## BIBLIOGRAPHY

'A study of the number, distribution and growth of the Protestant population in Mexico'. J.C. Bridges. Thesis, University of Florida (USA), 1969. 108p.
*Anuario de la Iglesia en México, 1970.* México: Secretariado General del Episcopado, 1970.
*Christo-paganism: a study of Mexican religious syncretism.* W. Madsen. New Orleans: Middle American Research Institute, Tulane University, 1957. Publication 19: 105–180.
*Church growth in Mexico.* D.A. McGavran, J. Huegel & J. Taylor. Grand Rapids, Michigan: Eerdmans, 1963. 136p. (Protestantism).
*Directorio evangélico de la Ciudad de México, 1969–70.* México: CINCOMEX, 1970. 72p.
*Directorio evangélico de México, 1970.* Mexico City: Mexico Missionary Services, 1970.
*El guadalupanismo mexicano.* F. de la Maza. México: Porrúa y Obregón, 1953. 130p. (Aztec/Catholic syncretism in the Guadalupe cult).
*La Iglesia en Méjico: estructuras eclesiásticas.* R. Rama, I. Alonso & D. Garre. Fribourg: Feres, 1963. 119p. (Roman Catholic).
*La serpiente y la paloma.* M. Gaxiola. South Pasadena, CA: William Carey Library, 1970. 177p. (On IAFCJ indigenous church).
'Mexico', *Pro Mundi Vita* (Brussels), 7 (1965).
*Mito y magia del mexicano.* J. Carrión. México: Porrúa y Obregón, 1952. 104p.
'Pagan and Christian concepts in a Mexican Indian culture', W.L. Wonderly, *Practial anthropology,* 5, 5–6 (1958), 197–202. (Review of W. Madsen, *op. cit.*).
'Peyote: giver of visions', R. Shonle, *American anthropologist,* XXVII (1925), 53–75. (Peyote cult in Mexico and Oklahoma; bibliography).
'Seventh-day Adventism in a Mexican village: a study in motivation and culture change', O. Lewis, in *Process and pattern* (Chicago, 1960), p.63–83.
'The cult of the Holy Cross: an analysis of cosmology and Catholicism in Quintana Roo', C. Zimmerman, *History of religions,* III, 1 (1963), 50–71.
'The "Luz del Mundo" movement in Mexico', R.S. Greenway, *Missiology,* I, 2 (1973), 113–124.
*Tinder in Tabasco: a study of church growth in tropical Mexico.* C. Bennett. Grand Rapids, Michigan: Eerdmans, 1968. 213p.

**Union de Iglesias Evangélicas Independientes.** Otomí Indians (theological students under Rev. Ramundo Ramirez, centre) redecorate rural Bible institute near pentecostal stronghold of Pachuca. This indigenous pentecostal church is the second largest denomination in Mexico.

**Protestants.** Chol Indians at dedication service in Tumbala, in mountains in northern Chiapas state, for New Testament in their Mayan language (completed 1960).

Family Festival in Acapulco, a 5-day evangelistic crusade with Argentinian evangelist Luis Palau: some of the 2,266 public decisions for Christ (December 1978).

TABLE 2. ORGANIZED CHURCHES AND DENOMINATIONS IN MEXICO

| Official name 1 | Begun 2 | Type 3 | Counc 4 | Congs 5 | Adults 6 | Affiliated 7 | Names, notes, and other statistics (see Codebook) 8 | | | | |
|---|---|---|---|---|---|---|---|---|---|---|---|
| Asambleas de Dios de México | 1915 | P Pe2 | ZF..I | 835 | 45,177 | 100,000 | Begun by Mexicans. M=AoG. Aids Igl Cri Nacional. Rapid growth. 950n,23f,14s(450). | | | | |
| Asociación de Igls Cristianas Ev en M | 1895 | P Dis | x.u.N | 45 | 2,000 | 3,000 | *Igl Cristiana Discípulos. Disciples of Christ.* M=UCMS. 1960 expansion. 6f,1s,1u. | | | | |
| Bando Evangelistico Gedeón | 1938 | I pen | ..... | | 1,000 | 3,000 | *Gideon's Ev Band.* White suits, ties, dresses. Mass Bible distribtors. HQ Jalapa. | | | | |
| Concilio Latino-Americano de Igls Cris | c1925 | I pen | ....I | 55 | 2,200 | 5,000 | *Latin American Council of Christian Chs.* Begun in USA (Los Angeles) by Mexicans. | | | | |
| Congregación Escandinava en México | 1953 | P Lut | 1...N | 1 | 700 | 1,100 | *Scandinavian Congregation in Mexico.* Set up with support from LWF. 2n,W=15%,10Yy. | | | | |
| Congregaciónes Ev Lut de habla Alemana | 1861 | P Lut | L.u.N | 24 | 2,640 | 4,613 | *German Ev Congs in Mexico.* German immigrants. 3 parish districts. 4x,58Yy,324z. | | | | |
| Convención National Bautista de México | 1862 | P Bap | T.... | 668 | 15,386 | 35,000 | *National Baptists* (1902). 1880, M=SBC(USA); 1971, CBHMS. 172n,73f,1H,1s,1276Y. | | | | |
| Cruzada Evangelistica Mundial | 1950 | P Hol | xF... | 9 | 66 | 200 | *World Gospel Crusade. World Gospel Church.* M=WGM(USA). HQ Tijuana. 7m,5f,1p. | | | | |
| Ejército de Salvación | 1937 | P Sal | xwu.N | 100 | 2,000 | 5,000 | *Salvation Army, Mexico Division,* USA Southern Territory. In 25 cities. 1s. | | | | |
| Hermanos Menonitas | 1950 | P Men | GF... | 3 | 200 | 300 | M=Mennonite Brethren Ch of NAmerica(USA). HQ Durango. 5f,1H,1h. | | | | |
| Iglesia Adventista del Séptimo Día | 1893 | P Adv | x.... | 269 | 51,160 | 100,000 | *Seventh-day Adv, Mexico Union Mission.* 88nx,651m,26f,1H,6h,5r,1376t(76491),5415Y. | | | | |
| Iglesia Alianza Cristiana y Misionera | 1954 | P Hol | xF... | 11 | 108 | 200 | *Christian & Missionary Alliance Ch.* M=CMA(USA). HQ Mexico City 15. 14m, 2f. | | | | |
| Iglesia Apostólica de la Fe en CJ | 1914 | I pel | x.... | 954 | 16,064 | 48,192 | *IAFCJ, Apost Ch of Faith in CJ.* Mestizos. 441n,776m,G=4.2%pa,14s(100),W=50%,1115Y. | | | | |
| Iglesia Bautista del Séptimo Día | | P Bap | Tw... | 20 | 478 | 1,000 | *Seventh Day Baptist Ch.* Ch of Christ of the 7th Day. Under Gen Conf, SDBC(USA). | | | | |
| Igl Católica Apostólica Ortodoxa en M | 1957 | I CCa | ..... | 7 | 9,333 | 18,000 | *Catholic Apostolic Orth Ch.* Ex RCC. Lebanese Arabs. 12n,G=6.9%pa,1s(5),W=68%,208Yy. | | | | |
| **Iglesia Católica en México:** | 1518 | R Lat | B.L.R | 3,529 | 25,395,400 | 47,028,524 | *Catholic Ch.* C=37+3+146. 10p,22q,32s,W=25%. 9369nx,1976m,23063w,1804400Yy. | | | | |
| M Antequera (Oaxaca) | 1535 | R Lat | Bs | 129 | 755,800 | 1,399,618 | 50% urban. Indians: many monolingual. W=5%. | 622 | 3 | 208 | 58989 |
| D San Cristóbal de las Casas | 1539 | R Lat | Bs | 31 | 391,800 | 725,632 | 90% rural. 80% Indian. Strong christo-paganism. | 58 | 8 | 92 | 20132 |
| D Tapachula | 1957 | R Lat | Bs | 13 | 244,800 | 453,318 | 80% rural. 70% Indian. 80% RC. New farming areas. | 35 | 0 | 69 | 16436 |
| D Tehuantepec | 1891 | R Lat | Bs | 26 | 155,400 | 287,850 | 90% rural. 30% monolingual Indians. | 31 | 3 | 78 | 11373 |
| D Tuxtla Gutiérrez | 1964 | R Lat | Bs | 16 | 217,000 | 402,000 | 80% rural. 70% Indian. New farming areas. | 32 | 6 | 96 | 18150 |
| PN Mixe (Mixes) | 1964 | R Lat | Bs | 8 | 48,800 | 90,360 | Entirely rural, all Indian (monolingual). M=SDB. | 15 | 1 | 19 | 1231 |
| M Chihuahua | 1891 | R Lat | Bs | 50 | 446,000 | 825,843 | Rapid urban growth, rich agricultural areas. 1s. | 107 | 5 | 310 | 28800 |
| D Ciudad Juárez | 1957 | R Lat | Bs | 24 | 298,600 | 552,908 | 80% urban. Industrial expansion very recent. | 60 | 7 | 213 | 17463 |
| PN Madera (Ciudad Madera) | 1966 | R Lat | Bs | 14 | 88,000 | 163,000 | In northwest. 90% rural. M=OAR. | 21 | 3 | 18 | 6110 |
| M Durango | 1623 | R Lat | Bs | 56 | 351,700 | 651,371 | 50% urban, mass city immigration. Tepehuanas. 1s. | 148 | 17 | 397 | 18115 |
| D Culiacán | 1884 | R Lat | Bs | 35 | 393,600 | 728,935 | Prosperous rural areas, intensively farmed. 1s. | 95 | 6 | 316 | 38128 |
| D Mazatlán | 1958 | R Lat | Bs | 19 | 181,000 | 336,000 | Recent tourist industry. Insufficient clergy. 1s. | 52 | 1 | 92 | 10517 |
| D Torreón | 1957 | R Lat | Bs | 195 | 246,300 | 456,142 | Rural, farming, industries. Clergy inadequate. | 62 | 5 | 12 | 17664 |
| PN El Salto | 1966 | R Lat | Bs | 10 | 50,800 | 94,090 | 100% rural. 90% Indian. Underdeveloped. M=OCD. | 8 | 0 | 23 | 4329 |
| M Guadalajara | 1548 | R Lat | Bs | 191 | 1,336,100 | 2,474,168 | 90% urban. Traditional catholicism. 1p,2s. | 1008 | 608 | 3080 | 120415 |
| D Aguascalientes | 1899 | R Lat | Bs | 42 | 237,000 | 438,936 | Little development, mass emigration elsewhere. 1s. | 156 | 15 | 569 | 24709 |
| D Autlán | 1961 | R Lat | Bs | 22 | 122,900 | 227,581 | Intensively farmed. Very high practice: W=75%. | 60 | 0 | 169 | 10117 |
| D Colima | 1881 | R Lat | Bs | 37 | 205,000 | 379,570 | Tourism. Rural. High religious practice. 1s. | 140 | 0 | 152 | 12285 |
| D Tepic | 1891 | R Lat | Bs | 20 | 319,000 | 591,000 | 60% urban. Rich new farming. Few Indians. 1s. | 142 | 6 | 138 | 25798 |
| D Zacatecas | 1863 | R Lat | Bs | 93 | 545,000 | 1,010,000 | 50% urban. Much emigration. Some Indians. W=50%. | 208 | 1 | 418 | 21207 |
| PN Jesús María (Nayar) | 1962 | R Lat | Bs | 10 | 29,000 | 53,000 | 100% rural. 95% monolingual Indians. M=OFM. | 14 | 11 | 20 | 2210 |
| M Hermosillo | 1779 | R Lat | Bs | 37 | 296,500 | 549,119 | Mass immigration from other parts of Mexico. 1s. | 64 | 10 | 112 | 16839 |
| D Ciudad Obregón | 1959 | R Lat | Bs | 23 | 268,400 | 497,125 | Very rapid urban expansion and immigration. | 50 | 11 | 166 | 17150 |
| D Mexicali | 1966 | R Lat | Bs | 101 | 357,900 | 662,707 | 80% urban. Immigration, rapid industrialization. | 46 | 8 | 169 | 17882 |
| D Tijuana | 1874 | R Lat | Bs | 27 | 309,000 | 572,000 | 90% urban. Intensive industrialization, 1s. | 81 | 9 | 342 | 17075 |
| M Jalapa | 1863 | R Lat | Bs | 89 | 585,400 | 1,084,140 | Rich farming areas, expanding urban areas. 1s. | 181 | 15 | 442 | 56175 |
| D Papantla | 1922 | R Lat | Bs | 22 | 297,000 | 550,000 | 70% rural. Bilingual (Indian/Spanish) Indians. | 57 | 3 | 186 | 20075 |
| D San Andrés Tuxtla | 1959 | R Lat | Bs | 26 | 381,000 | 705,000 | 60% urban. Rich farm land, petroleum, Few Indians. | 40 | 1 | 110 | 28592 |
| D Tuxpan | 1962 | R Lat | Bs | 28 | 375,700 | 695,812 | 50% urban. Area in farm land, petroleum. | 43 | 0 | 45 | 22439 |
| D Veracruz | 1962 | R Lat | Bs | 24 | 326,000 | 604,000 | 70% urban. Port, tourism. 20% Pesquera Indians. | 50 | 0 | 246 | 24452 |
| M México | 1530 | R Lat | Bs | 251 | 3,916,400 | 7,250,000 | Capital. 100% urban. 93% RC. 5p,1s. | 1568 | 475 | 5800 | 258340 |
| D Acapulco | 1958 | R Lat | Bs | 40 | 248,800 | 460,800 | Towns, ports, tourism and seasonal influx. 1s. | 53 | 7 | 149 | 17000 |
| D Chilapa | 1863 | R Lat | Bs | 73 | 431,400 | 798,825 | 50% urban. Subsistence level rural Indians. 1s. | 111 | 0 | 158 | 28051 |
| D Cuernavaca | 1891 | R Lat | Bs | 56 | 335,000 | 620,000 | Tourism. Diocesan experiments. HQ of CIDOC. | 119 | 12 | 281 | 15056 |
| D Texcoco | 1960 | R Lat | Bs | 62 | 457,600 | 847,411 | 80% urban, imigration, industry. Rural Indians. | 110 | 3 | 213 | 38637 |
| D Tlalnepantla | 1964 | R Lat | Bs | 160 | 796,000 | 1,475,000 | 90% urban, rapid industrialization. 1s. | 272 | 60 | 45 | 40826 |
| D Toluca | 1950 | R Lat | Bs | 112 | 481,200 | 891,112 | 60% urban, immigrants. Monolingual Indians. 1s. | 203 | 53 | 110 | 60161 |
| D Tula | 1961 | R Lat | Bs | 24 | 214,000 | 397,000 | 80% rural. 30% monolingual Indians. Subsistence. | 35 | 4 | 88 | 15555 |
| D Tulancingo | 1862 | R Lat | Bs | 55 | 366,900 | 679,384 | 60% rural. Metals, mining. Indians monolingual. | 91 | 6 | 231 | 30458 |
| M Monterrey | 1777 | R Lat | Bs | 55 | 730,800 | 1,353,251 | 70% urban. Rich farming areas. 1s,W=70%. | 184 | 119 | 689 | 57924 |
| D Ciudad Valles | 1960 | R Lat | Bs | 31 | 238,000 | 440,000 | 80% rural. Recent petroleum industry. Huastecos. | 47 | 3 | 64 | 18270 |
| D Ciudad Victoria | 1964 | R Lat | Bs | 25 | 151,200 | 279,994 | 50% urban. Rural areas subsistence level. | 34 | 5 | 40 | 9697 |
| D Linares | 1962 | R Lat | Bs | 11 | 134,000 | 248,200 | 80% rural. Subsistence farming. Indian groups. | 24 | 0 | 54 | 8598 |
| D Matamoros | 1958 | R Lat | Bs | 38 | 319,000 | 590,000 | Rich farming and petroleum areas. Rapid growth. | 64 | 15 | 93 | 20473 |
| D Saltillo | 1891 | R Lat | Bs | 38 | 389,000 | 720,000 | 80% urban, rapid industrialization; coal mining. | 95 | 17 | 336 | 30300 |
| D San Luis Potosí | 1854 | R Lat | Bs | 59 | 422,300 | 782,106 | 50% urban. Traditional Indian catholicism. 1s. | 178 | 68 | 631 | 38306 |
| D Tampico | 1870 | R Lat | Bs | 27 | 251,200 | 465,120 | 60% urban. Rich petroleum area. Few Indians. | 62 | 2 | 150 | 17408 |
| M Morelia | 1536 | R Lat | Bs | 155 | 1,026,000 | 1,900,000 | Formerly M Michoacán. 2p,1s. | 533 | 50 | 1275 | 95100 |
| D Apatzingán | 1962 | R Lat | Bs | 20 | 155,600 | 288,145 | 80% rural. Recently-opened farming areas. | 46 | 11 | 47 | 14016 |
| D Ciudad Altamirano | 1964 | R Lat | Bs | 30 | 188,000 | 349,000 | 80% rural. Traditional Indian catholicism. | 41 | 0 | 28 | 16842 |
| D León | 1862 | R Lat | Bs | 53 | 644,700 | 1,193,819 | 80% urban. Moderate urbanization. 1p,1s,W=60%. | 354 | 69 | 1098 | 53874 |
| D Querétaro | 1862 | R Lat | Bs | 66 | 294,200 | 544,800 | 60% urban. Impoverished Indians. 1s. | 180 | 67 | 447 | 22838 |
| D Tacámbaro | 1913 | R Lat | Bs | 30 | 116,600 | 215,903 | 70% rural. Traditional Indian catholicsm. 1s. | 60 | 0 | 95 | 11169 |
| D Zamora | 1862 | R Lat | Bs | 75 | 419,500 | 776,774 | 50% urban. Rich farms. Monolingual Indians. W=60%. | 241 | 40 | 840 | 34348 |
| M Puebla de los Angeles | 1525 | R Lat | Bs | 155 | 989,400 | 1,832,141 | 60% urban. Traditional catholicism. 1s,W=60%. | 394 | 53 | 750 | 35924 |
| D Huajuápan de León | 1902 | R Lat | Bs | 40 | 181,000 | 336,000 | Rural; Indian groups. Unevangelized areas. 1s. | 88 | 0 | 16 | 7995 |
| D Huejutla | 1922 | R Lat | Bs | 28 | 151,000 | 280,000 | Rural. Indian groups. Insufficient clergy. | 54 | 0 | 53 | 8803 |
| D Tehuacán. | 1962 | R Lat | Bs | 29 | 143,000 | 265,000 | 60% rural. Intensive colonization. Some Indians. | 63 | 5 | 90 | 10000 |
| D Tlaxcala | 1959 | R Lat | Bs | 46 | 221,000 | 409,340 | 50% urban. Traditional Indian catholicism. 1s. | 87 | 5 | 136 | 18608 |
| M Yucatán | 1561 | R Lat | Bs | 69 | 386,700 | 716,182 | Mérida. 60% urban, Major tourist centre of future. | 146 | 21 | 268 | 13582 |
| D Campeche | 1895 | R Lat | Bs | 25 | 137,000 | 254,000 | Towns, ports, tourism. Rich farming. W=60%. | 34 | 14 | 41 | 9560 |
| D Tabasco | 1880 | R Lat | Bs | 35 | 393,500 | 728,792 | 50% urban. Immigration: farms, petroleum. W=10%. | 55 | 0 | 94 | 26600 |
| PN Chetumal | 1970 | R Lat | Bs | 11 | 49,000 | 90,000 | Prelature formed out of M Yucatán. M=LC. | 12 | 2 | 21 | 3144 |
| VA La Paz en la Baja California | 1957 | R Lat | Pfscj | 19 | 77,900 | 144,200 | Area recently opened to colonization. P=29%. | 26 | 5 | 115 | 5898 |
| VA Tarahumara | 1950 | R Lat | Psj | 108 | 78,000 | 145,000 | Rural. 40% monolingual Indians. Poor economy. P=10%. | 19 | 22 | 110 | 6178 |

*Continued opposite*

*Table 2 – continued*

| Official name<br>1 | Begun<br>2 | Type<br>3 | Counc<br>4 | Congs<br>5 | Adults<br>6 | Affiliated<br>7 | Names, notes, and other statistics (see Codebook)<br>8 |
|---|---|---|---|---|---|---|---|
| Iglesia Católica Romana Antigua | 1935 | I CCa | .v... | 2 | 100 | 200 | *Ecclesia Veteris Romanae Catholicae. Old Roman CC.* 1965 applied to WCC, rejected. |
| Iglesia Cristiana Bethel | 1953 | I pe2 | ....I | | 1,200 | 2,000 | *Bethel Assemblies of Latin America.* Ex CoG in RM. 1956, M=BFMF(USA). 20f. |
| Iglesia Cristiana Interdenominacional | | I pe2 | ....I | 500 | 20,000 | 50,000 | *Interdenominational Christian Ch.* Rapidly expanding. 10 churches in Mexico City. |
| Igl Cristiana Nacional de las AdD | 1934 | I pe2 | Z.... | 329 | 14,954 | 30,000 | *National Christian Ch of the Assemblies of God.* Indigenous, working with M=AoG. |
| Iglesia Cristiana Unida | c1938 | P ind | ..u.N | | 2,900 | 4,000 | *United Christian Ch.* Spanish refugees from 1936 Spanish civil war. HQ Mexico 12. |
| Iglesia de Dios de la Profecía | 1944 | P Pe3 | Z...I | 50 | 2,200 | 4,000 | *Ch of God of Prophecy.* M=CGP(USA). Holiness Pentecostals. HQ Mexico City 8. |
| Iglesia de Dios del Séptimo Día | 1920 | I Adv | ..... | 185 | 8,000 | 15,000 | *Ch of God (Seventh-day).* Ex SDAs. Link with M=CGSD(USA). Rapidly growing. 185n. |
| Iglesia de Dios en Cristo | 1933 | P Men | G.... | | 1,000 | 2,000 | *Ch of God in Christ.* M=Ch of God in Christ, Mennonite(USA). 48f. |
| Iglesia de Dios en Cristo por El ES | 1969 | I pen | ..... | 8 | 250 | 400 | ES=Espiritu Santo. *Ch of God in Christ through the Holy Spirit.* 8n,W=90%,86Y,18z. |
| Igl de Dios en la República Mexicana | 1920 | I pen | ....I | | 40,000 | 80,000 | *Ch of God in Republic of M.* Schism ex AoG and 1946 CoG(Cleveland). 9 Districts. |
| Iglesia de Dios en México | 1893 | P Hol | x.u.N | 629 | 33,542 | 50,000 | *Ch of God in Mexico.* M=CoG(Anderson)(USA). In 5 states. HQ Mexico 14. 7f,2h,2s. |
| Iglesia de Dios Pentecostal | 1942 | P Pe2 | Z...I | 45 | 750 | 2,000 | *Igl de Dios Pentecostés.* M=Pentecostal Ch of God of America(USA). HQ Veracruz. 4f. |
| Iglesia de Dios (Evangelio Completo) | 1932 | P Pe3 | ZF..I | 827 | 28,129 | 50,000 | *Ch of God (Full Gospel).* Begun by Mexicans. M=CoG(Cleveland). Schisms. 568n,7f,5s. |
| Iglesia de JC de los Santos de los UD | 1879 | M LdS | x.... | | 60,000 | 112,232 | *Latter-day Saints. Mormons.* M=CJCLdS(USA). Indians. 900f,G=8%pa, 40000Yy(in 1976). |
| Iglesia de los Amigos | 1871 | P Qua | QF... | 2 | 200 | 300 | *Ch of the Friends. Quakers.* M=California YMF,FUM(USA). HQ Mexico City 1. 2f. |
| Iglesia del Evangelio Cuadrangular | 1943 | P Pe2 | ZF..I | 59 | 3,205 | 10,000 | *Int Ch of Foursquare Gospel.* M=ICFG(USA). HQ Monterrey. 57nm,8f,3p(32),W=40%,170Y. |
| Iglesia del Nazareno en México | 1903 | P Hol | xFu.N | 250 | 24,420 | 30,000 | *Ch of the Nazarene.* M=CoN(USA). 4 Districts. Very rapid growth. HQ Guadalajara. 74n. |
| Iglesia El Buen Pastor | 1942 | I pel | ..... | 65 | 2,000 | 5,000 | *Church of the Good Shepherd.* Schism ex Iglesia La Luz del Mundo (Aaronistas). 75n. |
| Iglesia Episcopal Mexicana | 1857 | A Low | awuRN | 100 | 4,508 | 8,881 | Ex Ch of Rome. 3 Dioceses, in PECUSA IX. 31n,11x,G=1.7%pa,2s(14),W=75%,213Yy. |
| Igl Evangélica de los Hermanos Libres | c1895 | P CBr | x.... | 60 | 3,000 | 5,000 | *Ev Ch of Open Brethren.* Plymouth Brethren. M=CMML(USA,UK). HQ Mexico 3. 19f,1p. |
| Iglesia Ev de los Peregrinos | 1920 | P Hol | VF... | 128 | 16,476 | 30,000 | M=Pilgrim Holiness (Wesleyan) Ch. HQ San Luis Potosí. 28n,1f,G=0,1s(24),W=44%,742Y. |
| Igl Ev del Consejo Espiritual Mexicano | 1928 | I pel | ..... | 175 | 6,000 | 18,000 | *Mexican Ch of Spiritual Council.* Schism ex IAFCJ. Many splits. Declining. Rural. |
| Iglesia Evangélica Menonita | 1954 | P Men | GF... | 7 | 100 | 300 | M=Ev Mennonite Ch(USA). South central Mexico. Rapid growth. 1n,5x,12f,W=50%,8Y,5z. |
| Iglesia Evangélica Misionera | 1954 | P int | ..... | | 200 | 500 | *Ev Missionary Ch.* M=Mexican Militant Mission (Texas,USA). Mestizos only. 1p. |
| Iglesia La Luz del Mundo (Aaronistas) | 1940 | I pel | x.... | 20 | 15,000 | 30,000 | *Light of the World Ch.* Messiah Aaron, died 1964. Vast tabernacle Guadalajara. 1h. |
| Iglesia Luterana Mexicana | 1947 | P Lut | L.u.N | 12 | 500 | 1,000 | *Mexican Lutheran Ch.* Begun by 2 Nazarene pastors with M=ALC(USA). A=1957. 1s. |
| Iglesia Menonita | 1922 | P Men | G.... | | 18,250 | 32,000 | 11,750 Old Colony Mennonites (first settlers in Latin America) from Canada. Germans. |
| Iglesia Metodista de México | 1873 | P Met | VWu.N | 350 | 32,935 | 70,000 | *Methodist Ch* (A=1930), affiliated UMC(USA). 2 Confs. 79n,37f,1H,13r,1s,178t,1u. |
| Iglesia Metodista Libre Mexicana | 1912 | P Hol | VF..N | 37 | 879 | 2 000 | *Mexican Free Meth Ch.* M=FMC(USA). HQ Nogales. 11n,6f,G=6.3%pa,1h,1p,1s(18),206z. |
| Iglesia Misionera Mexicana | 1951 | I pen | ..... | 5 | 500 | 1,000 | *Mexican Missionary Ch.* Founded by Methodist woman. Charismatic, enthusiastic. |
| Igl Nacional Presbiteriana de México | 1872 | P Ref | R.... | 1,010 | 35,994 | 120,000 | *National Presb Ch.* M=PCUS,UPUSA,RCA. Many Indians. 180n,85f,3H,4h,14p,1s(33). |
| Iglesia Nueva Apostólica | | C CAp | x.... | | 500 | 1,000 | *New Apostolic Ch*, USA Bezirk (District). Germans. World HQ Dortmund (Germany). |
| Igl Ortodoxa Cat Apostólica Mexicana | 1926 | I CCa | ..... | 752 | 40,000 | 60,000 | National Ch. State-aided schism ex RCC. Decline since 1940. 10 bishops. 200n. |
| Iglesia Ortodoxa Católica de México | c1890 | O Sla | Mwo.. | 22 | 20,000 | 30,000 | *Orth Cath Ch.* Exarchate of OCA(USA), 1972. Russians. Veracruz. Bishop, 7n,11f,15i, |
| Iglesia Ortodoxa Griega | c1970 | O Gre | Cwo.. | 2 | 2,000 | 4,000 | In 12th Archdiocesan District, Greek Orthodox AD of N&SAmerica. Greeks, Arabs. |
| Iglesia Ortodoxa: D México & CAmerica | c1890 | O Ara | Cwo.. | | 12,000 | 20,000 | Under Antiochian Orth Ch (USA), & Greek P Antioch. Lebanese Arab émigrés. |
| Igl Presbiteriana Asociada Reformada | 1878 | P Ref | R.u.N | 82 | 2,500 | 5,000 | M=ARPC(USA). A=1964. 1975, left WARC. 14n,3x,6f,G=2.7%pa,1H,1s(3),W=25%,340Yy. |
| Igl Presbiteriana Independiente de M | 1962 | P Ref | JF... | 100 | 1,000 | 2,000 | Indep Presb Ch of Mexico. M=Iglesia Cristiana Reformada(CRC)(USA). 40f,1p,3s. |
| Iglesia Santa Pentecostés Mexicana | 1931 | P Pe3 | ZF..I | 55 | 3,505 | 5,000 | *Pentecostal Holiness Ch.* M=PHC(USA). Holiness Pentecostals (3-stage). 95nm,12f,2s. |
| Iglesias Congregationales de México | 1872 | P Con | ..u.N | 13 | 750 | 1,110 | *Junta General de IC. Congregational Ch in M.* M=UCBWM(USA). 5n,2f,1u,W=93%,47Y. |
| Iglesias de Cristo | 1933 | P Dis | x.... | 170 | 3,000 | 5,000 | M=Churches of Christ(Non-Instrumental)(USA). HQ Mexico City 7. 12f,2s,W=88%. |
| Iglesias de Cristo (Instrumental) | 1902 | P Dis | x.... | 200 | 5,000 | 10,000 | M=CCCC(Instrumental)(USA). Splits ex UCMS. Independents. 89f. |
| Iglesias Evangélicas Independientes | c1930 | I pe2 | ....I | 400 | 30,000 | 70,000 | *Independent Chs.* Vast grouping of separate bodies under SFM (Sweden) influence. |
| Iglesias Evangélicas Independientes | 1961 | P ind | ..... | 11 | 15,000 | 20,000 | *Independent Evangelical Chuches.* M=Mexican Border Missions (USA). 8m,4f. |
| Misión Centroamericana | 1955 | P int | xM... | 6 | 56 | 250 | M=Central American Mission(USA). Interdenominational. 1 school. 54f,1s. |
| Misión Cristiana, México Poniente | 1950 | P ind | ..... | 15 | 525 | 1,000 | *Western Mexico Christian M.* HQ Hermosillo, Sonora. 6n,2x,G=5.6%pa,1p(9),50Y,25z. |
| Misión Evangelistica Mexicana | 1926 | I Hol | ..... | 180 | 1,960 | 4,000 | *MEM. Mexican Ev M.* 1946, M=EMC(USA). Tarahumaras. 23n,10x,1j,1s(6),W=82%,45Y. |
| Misión Menonita Mexicana | 1958 | P Men | G.... | 7 | 104 | 300 | *Mennonite Mexican Mission.* M=Mennonite Ch of NAmerica. 3 schools. 14f,1H,1h. |
| Misiones Mundiales de México | 1960 | P ind | x.... | | 1,500 | 3,000 | M=World-Wide Missions(USA). Evangelicals based in Pasadena, CA (USA). |
| Movimiento Igls Ev Pentecostales Indep | 1930 | I pe2 | ..... | 600 | 15,000 | 40,000 | *MIEPI. Movement of Ev Indep Pentecostal Chs.* In 12 states. Rapid growth. 115n. |
| Sínodo Luterano de México | 1940 | P Lut | x.... | 21 | 705 | 1,502 | Formerly Conferencia Concordia de México. M=LCMS(USA). 17m,2f,16t(581),42Yy. |
| Sociedad de la Ciencia Cristiana | | M Sci | x.... | 2 | 100 | 200 | *Ch of Christ, Scientist. Christian Science.* M=CCS(Boston,USA). 1w. |
| Testigos de Jehová | 1893 | M Jeh | x.... | 1,439 | 54,384 | 100,000 | *Jehovah's Witnesses.* Witnessing under way by 1925, literature from 1929. 5683Y. |
| Unión de Iglesias Ev Independientes | 1923 | I pe2 | Z...I | 489 | 150,000 | 350,000 | *Union of Ev Independent Chs. Igl Cristiana Indep Pentecostés.* Otomí Indians. |
| Unión de Iglesias Ev Mexicanas | 1930 | P int | .M... | 250 | 3,000 | 6,000 | *Union of Ev Mexican Chs.* M=Mexican Indian M(USA). Aztecs, others. 45mn,18f,1p. |
| Other indigenous pentecostal churches | | I pen | ..... | | 50,000 | 100,000 | Total about 100 (see list below). |
| Other Protestant denominations | | P | ..... | | 5,000 | 10,000 | Total about 70 (see list below). |
| Doubly-affiliated (duplication)(1970) | | | | | –729,000 | –1,350,000 | Evangelicals who also are or were baptized Roman Catholics. |
| **Total affiliated (mid-1970)** | | | | **18,400** | **25,609,693** | **47,618,304** | **Total denominations (1970) . . . 238.** |
| **Total affiliated (mid-1975)** | | | | **21,000** | **29,930,100** | **55,651,800** | **Total denominations (1975) . . . 260.** |
| **Total affiliated (mid-1980)** | | | | **25,700** | **35,069,300** | **65,207,400** | **Total denominations (1980) . . . 285.** |

NOTES ON TABLE ABOVE
COLUMNS: for meanings and CODES (cols. 1, 3, 4, 8): see Codebook (Part 6). Column 1: **Boldface type** = church with over 10% of country's affiliated Christians.
NATIONAL COUNCILS (Column 4, 5th letter).

- I = Asociación Fraternal de Iglesias Pentecostales en la República de México (Asociación Fraternal Pentecostés) (Pentecostal Fraternal Association), representing over 200,000 adult pentecostals, including a number of bodies listed below under 'Other indigenous pentecostal churches'.
- N = Federación Evangélica de México (FEM) (Evangelical Federation of Mexico).
- R = Conferencia del Episcopado Mexicano (CEM) (Conference of the Mexican Episcopate).

OTHER INDIGENOUS PENTECOSTAL CHURCHES. There are at least 100 other distinct Mexican denominations and para-denominations, in addition to a large number of independent single congregations. A number belong to the Asociación Fraternal Pentecostés. Among this total of 100 are the following: Acción Cristiana Independiente de Nuevos Pentecostés, Pente- Asambleas Pentecostés Beteles de México, Comunión de Iglesias costales Libres, Comunión de los Creyentes, Iglesia Apostólica de Dios, Iglesia Berea de Pentecostales, Iglesia de Dios Separado, Iglesia de la Fe en Jesucristo Dios (Mexicana), Iglesia Defensores de la Fe, Iglesia Ev Independiente, Iglesia Gideon Cristiana, Iglesia Libre Pentecostés, Iglesia Presbiteriana Nacional Independiente (member of ICCC), Iglesia Pentecostés La Hermosa, Iglesia Universal de Jesucristo, Iglesias del Aposento Alto (Chs of the Upper Room), Movimiento Cristiano Independiente Pentecostés, Movimiento Ev Independiente Pentecostés Debora, Movimiento Libre Pentecostés.
OTHER PROTESTANT DENOMINATIONS. About 70 other smaller Protestant denominations are at work, most being missions from denominations in the USA retaining their identity as separate bodies. They include the following: American Advent Mission Society (1956), American Baptist Association (1955; 10 churches), Apostolic Ch of Pentecost of Canada (1963), Apostolic Faith Mission (Oregon) (1966), Associated Brotherhood of Christians, Baptist Bible Fellowship International (1950), Baptist International Missions (1968), Baptist Mid-Missions (1960), Baptist Missionary Association of America (1950), Baptist World Mission (1965), Bethany Fellowship Missions (1971), Bible Missionary Ch, Children of God International (from USA), Christian Nationals Evangelism Commission (1968), Ch of Christ (Holiness), Ch of God Holiness (1967), Chs of Christ in Christian Union (1944; 6 churches), Congregational Holiness Ch (1963), Congregational Methodist Ch, Conservative Baptist Home Mission Society (1951), Elim Missionary Assemblies (1960), Ev Congregational Ch (1965), Exclusive Brethren (Continuing Tunbridge Wells), Free Will Baptist Mission, Gospel Missionary Union (1956), Independent Bible Baptist Missions (1960), International Pentecostal Assemblies (1952), Maranatha Baptist Mission (1966), Metropolitan Ch Association, Mexican Mission of the Churches of Christ (1917), Mexican Missions (Pentecostal) (1960), National Fellowship of Brethren Chs (1951), New Testament Missionary Union, Open Bible Standard Chs (1965), Pentecostal Free Will Baptist Ch (1963), Reformed Baptists (USA), Southern Methodist Ch, Spanish America Inland Mission (1955), Unevangelized Fields Mission (1971), Union Ev Ch (English-speaking), United Ev Chs (16 missionaries), United Pentecostal Ch (1974), Wisconsin Ev Lutheran Synod (1968), World Baptist Fellowship Mission Agency (1956), World Missions (1959).
OTHER MARGINAL BODIES. The Reorganized Ch of Jesus Christ of Latter-day Saints (USA) has a small work based in Mexico City 10 (358 members); also Friends of Man (Switzerland), Ch of Our Lord Jesus Christ (Bickertonites), Ch of Christ (Temple Lot) (200 members among Indians).

**PEOPLES** (ethnolinguistic). Christians: 55.1% Mestizo, 29.0% Amerindian (pure-blooded) [21.3% speaking Spanish only, 5.6% bilingual, 2.1% monolingual (Indian only)] [9.0% Half-Indian) 6.0% Aztec, 3.3% Maya, 2.6% Otomí, 2.3% Zapotec, 2.0% Mixtec, &c], 15.0% Mexican White, 0.5% Black, 0.3% Spaniard, 0.1% Arab (Lebanese, Palestinian, Syrian), Russian, USA, Greek, French, Italian, Galician, Catalonian, German, British, Basque, Chinese, Gypsy.

**COUNTRY-WIDE TOTALS**
EVANGELIZATION (see Part 5). 1900: 100%. 1970: 100%. 1980: 100%. *Mass evangelism.* Among the many recent campaigns: 1969, Luis Palau campagin in Monterrey (25 supporting churches; 30,000 attenders, 2,340 enquirers), Tampico (15 supporting churches; 9,000 attenders, 827 enquirers) and Mexico City (20 supporting churches; 32,600 attenders, 2,203 enquirers), also in 1970 Mexico City again (110 supporting churches; 106,000 attenders, 6,640 enquirers); 1969, Hermano Pablo Cruzada Unida in Guaymas, Sonora (10,400 attenders, 5,171 enquirers), also 1970 in Ciudad Obregón (5,500 attenders, 276 enquirers); 1970, month-long 'Operation Amigo' by Assemblies of God; 1971, Evangelism-in-Depth nation-wide campaign (over half of the 10,000 Evangelical congregations in Mexico involved, over 13,000 prayer cells formed, one million scriptures distributed); 1976, Luis Palau campaigns in 8 cities in Yucatán peninsula (5,350 decisions in 3 weeks); 1977, Here's Life Tijuana and Pachuca (CCCI; 930,000 exposed, 10,767 decisions), 1978 Mexico City Billy Graham crusade. *Radiophonic evangelism.* Annual listeners' letters (1975): 2,445 FEBC, 541 HCJB, Radio Vatican, and many smaller stations. Bible correspondence courses: very numerous, over 200,000 enrolments (ICI 25,000). Radiophonic Schools (Catholics): about 500,000 enrolled. *Literature evangelism.* 1976, Every Home Crusade distributed one million booklets each month; in March 1977, 1,230,000 booklets, producing 1,000 decision cards a month.
FOREIGN MISSIONARIES AND PERSONNEL (nationals serving abroad) (1973). Total 2,086 in 24 countries: about 1,990 Roman Catholics in 22 countries (most in Latin America; also 28 in Kenya, 22 in Korea, 14 in Japan), 66 Mexican indigenous, about 30 Protestants.
FOREIGN MISSIONARIES AND PERSONNEL (aliens from abroad) (1973). Total 5,648. *From Western world.* 4,642: about 2,200 Roman Catholics, 1,401 Protestants (1,295 in 122 USA societies, 50 in 1 Sweden society, 35 in 3 Canada societies, 16 in 2 UK societies, 3 in 3 New Zealand societies, 2 in 1 Finland society), about 1,000 marginal Protestants (900 Mormons, 100 Jehovah's Witnesses) from USA, about 30 Orthodox mostly from USA, 11 Anglicans in 1 USA society. *From Communist world.* 1 Roman Catholic from Poland. *From Third World.* 1,005: about 970 Roman Catholics from other Latin American countries, about 30 Protestants from Costa Rica, Korea, Puerto Rico et alia, about 5 Orthodox.
INSTITUTIONS (church-operated) (1973). Total 1,260, including 980 higher schools (95 minor seminaries), about 60 medical centres, 2 radio stations, 5 religious communities, 9 research centres, 10 study centres, 151 seminaries (70 Protestant, 54 RC, 25 Mexican indigenous, 2 Anglican).
PERIODICALS. About 500 titles (130 Protestant, many indigenous).
PERSONNEL. About 43,148 (37,500 national, 5,648 foreign).
RELIGIOUS LIBRARIES. About 180.
SCRIPTURE DISTRIBUTION (1975). Annual totals: 259,164 Bibles (4% free, 58% subsidized, 38% commercial), 286,120 NTs (38% free, 27% subsidized, 35% commercial), 332,606 UBS portions, 5,484,581 UBS selections. *Translations completed.* Portion: 91 languages since 1833. NT: 28 languages since 1951.
SERVICE AGENCIES. About 205, including AC, ACF(YWCA), ACISJF, ACJM, ACM, ACO, CAVE, CCCI, CEF, CEM, CIDOC, CIRM, CNEP, CNM, CRS-USCC, FEM, FMJFC, IMES, JCFM, MAF, MEC, MEP, MFC, MJ, MMM, MSC, MSpS, NTM, OM, OSLAM, PTL, SER, SESOMEX, SU, UCM, UFCM, UFEC, UMTS, WBT (1935; 306 missionaries), WLC(EHC), WVI.

**ADDITIONAL DATA ON CHURCHES**
ASAMBLEAS DE DIOS DE MEXICO. *Congregations.* Rapid growth from 835 (1970) to 1,070 (November 1974), the latter being 584 organized churches and 486 missions and outstations.
IGLESIA CATOLICA EN MEXICO. *New dioceses.* Created 1974: Celaya; created 1977, PN Nuevo Casas Grandes. *Catholics.* 55% Mestizos, 29% Amerindians (2.1% monolingual), and 15% Mexican White (of European origin); there were also 5,650 Chinese (in 1966), rising to 12,800 by 1975. As shown for certain dioceses in the table, 2% of all Indians are monolingual, i.e. speaking only their mother tongue but not Spanish; and 6% are bilingual, speaking Spanish as well. *Joint Pastoral Regions.* The episcopate has created 13 regions (Regiones Pastoral de Conjunto) as follows: Noroeste (Ecclesiastical Province (EPr) of Hermosillo, PA La Paz, D Culiacán, D Mazatlán); Norte (EPr Chihuahua, EPr Durango except D Culiacán and D Mazatlán, PA Tarahumara); Noreste (EPr Monterrey except D Ciudad Valles and D San Luis Potosí); Occidente (M Guadalajara, D Tepic, D Aguascalientes, PN Jesús Maria); Bajio (M Morelia, D Ciudad Valles, D Zacatecas, D San Luis Potosí, D León, D Querétaro); Golfo (EPr Jalapa); Pacifico Medio (D Autlán Colima, D Zamora, D Apatzingán, D Tacámbaro); Metropolitana (M México, D Cuernavaca, D Toluca, D Texcoco, D Tlalnepantla); Centro (D Huejutla, D Tula, D Tulancingo); Sur (D Acapulco, D

Chilapa, D Ciudad Altamirano); Oriente (EPr Puebla except D Huejutla); Peninsula Yucatán (EPr Yucatán); and Pacifico Sur (EPr Oaxaca/Antequera). *Rites.* In addition to Latin-rite Catholics, there are 11,000 Melkite Greek Catholics. *Annual baptisms.* (1972) 99.3% infant, 0.7% adult. *Priests.* 6,292 secular, 3,077 religious. *Religious priests and brothers.* Mexico has the highest proportion of religious nationals in all Latin America; in 1971, 87% of all religious priests and brothers were Mexicans, 1% were other Latin Americans, and 12% were from other continents (mainly from USA, Spain and Italy). *Sisters.* Total all sisters including contemplatives, non-diocesan and others (1970): 30,000, with the highest proportion of nationals in Latin America; 93% of all sisters were Mexicans, 3% were other Latin Americans, and 4% were from other countries (USA 140, Spain 70). *Catholic charismatics* (January, 1974). 3,000 adults including many religious personnel are active in 100 prayer groups in the Charismatic Renewal. The renewal is spearheaded by most of the 319 priests of the Mexican congregation Misioneros del Espíritu Santo (MSpS), which also has work in Bolivia, Guatemala and Peru. *Seminaries.* In 1973, 32 major seminaries for secular clergy, and 22 for religious clergy. The Mexican church also operates the interdiocesan Montezuma Seminary in New Mexico, USA and a seminary for foreign missions in Mexico. *Catechists.* There are now very few qualified lay catechists in Mexico, and only a few male catechists among Indian groups. In towns and villages, catechesis is the work of sisters assisted by young girls. *Religious orders and congregations* (1972). Several are of indigenous Mexican origin, several foreign or international. Priests (with over 100 members): 662 SJ, 567 OFM, 358 SDB, 319 MSpS (Mexican), 303 OSA, 165 MJ (Mexican), 138 OP, 130 OdeM, 117 CMF, 113 Legionnaires of Christ (a diocesan congregation), 103 OCD. Brothers (with over 100 members): 499 PFM, 287 FSC. Sisters (with over 500 members): 923 Franciscans of the Immaculate Conception of Mexico, 830 Poor Servants of the Sacred Heart, 761 Missionary Franciscans of Guadalupe, 755 Daughters of Mary Immaculate of Guadalupe, 726 Servants of the Sacred Heart of Jesus and the Poor, 717 Servants of Jesus Present in the Blessed Sacrament, 682 Josephite Sisters of Mexico, 566 Carmelites of the Sacred Heart, 531 Sisters of the Incarnate Word.
*Catholic organizations.* The Conference of the Mexican Episcopate (Conferencia del Episcopado Mexicano, CEM) is a member of CELAM. The Conference of the Religious Institutes of Mexico (Conferencia de Institutos Religiosos de México, CIRM) is a member of CLAR. There are no pastoral or presbyteral councils. The principal movements attached to the Episcopal Commission of the Lay Apostolate (Comisión Episcopal de Apostolado de los Laicos) are: Mexican Catholic Action (Acción Católica Mexicana, ACM), Catholic Association of Mexican Youth (Asociación Católica de la Juventud Mexicana, ACJM), Guadalupe National Association of Mexican Workers (Asociación Nacional Guadalupana de Trabajadores Mexicanos), Knights of Columbus (Caballeros de Colon), Corporation of Mexican Students (Corporación de Estudiantes Mexicanos, CEM), Christian Study Courses (Cursillos de Cristiandad), Catholic Young Women of Mexico (Juventud Católica Femenina Mexicana, JCFM), Legion of Mary (Legión de Maria), Children's Movement (Movimiento de Infancia), Christian Family Movement (Movimiento Familiar Cristiano), Movement for a Better World (Movimiento por un Mundo Mejor), Union of Mexican Catholics (Unión de Católicos Mexicanos, UCM), Union of Mexican Catholic Women (Unión Feminina Católica Mexicana, UFCM), Union of Catholic Women Students (Unión Feminina de Estudiantes Católicas, UFEC), and Stages of the Christian Life (Jornadas de Vida Cristiana).

The Holy See has no diplomatic relations with Mexico. It is represented to the Catholic hierarchy by an apostolic delegate based in Mexico City.

Latin American agencies based in Mexico include: (1) Departamento de Ministerios, Secretaria de Seminarios, which is part of CELAM; (2) Organización de Seminarios Latinoamericanos (OSLAM), founded in 1958 and composed of national federations of associations of diocesan seminaries, which furnishes technical assistance to the secretariat for seminaries of CELAM, provides for exchange of experiences and joint study of common problems of Latin American seminaries and seeks to improve training for the priesthood; and (3) Centro Intercultural de Documentación (CIDOC) and Centro de Formación Intercultural (CIF), the latter being the financial and juridical arm of the former, founded in 1961 by Ivan Illich and legally registered in 1963, which is an independent, non-confessional, Catholic-inspired intercultural centre financed by membership fees and sales of publications and microfilms. CIDOC has 5 distinct sections: an ultra-modern language school, a programme of conferences given by specialists, a fine Latin American library, a publications service and working seminars (15% of its students being priests and religious personnel).

Two Latin American secretariats of international organizations are based in Mexico: Secretariado para Latinoamérica del Movimiento Familiar Cristiano (MFC); and Secretariado Regional para América Latina de la Federación Mundial de la Juventud Femenina Católica (FMJFC), the latter with its headquarters in Brussels, Belgium.

No militantly traditionalist opinion groups have been formed in Mexico, but 2 progressivist groups are active: Sacerdotes para el Pueblo, founded in 1972, which unites bishops, secular and regular priests with several well-known Catholic personalities; and Cristianos para el Socialismo, founded after the continental meeting of progressives in Santiago in 1971, which is an ecumenical but predominantly Catholic movement of laymen, priests and pastors who accept 'Marxism as a scientific method of analysing society' (but not atheism, nor Marxist philosophy) and are willing to criticize certain attitudes of the hierarchy and other Christian groups as contrary to the interests of people fighting for their liberation.

Organizations for research and social action include: (1) Secretariado Social Mexicano (SESOMEX), founded in 1945 and serving now as the executive organ of the Episcopal Commission for Social Action in co-ordinating the work of 58 diocesan social secretariats, whose lay and priestly members are involved in doctrinal and sociological studies, provide courses in sociological training and promote the formation of credit unions (Cajas Populares de Ahorro); (2) Centro de Investigación y Acción Social (CIAS), founded by Jesuits; (3) Instituto Mexicano de Estudios Sociales (IMES), a non-confessional association of Catholic inspiration dedicated to social research related to development, which is divided into 3 departments: family and population, socio-economic, and socio-cultural; (4) Sociedad Teológica Mexicana, which is especially interested in the creation of a theology of development and organized a national congress in 1969 on the theme 'Theology and integral development' (Congreso Nacional de Teologia); (5) Centro Nacional de Comunicación Social (CENCOS, AC), an independent institution of Catholic inspiration, whose aim is to promote the liberation and dignity of man by means of social communication and publishes the weekly *Comunicación CENCOS*; and (6) Centro Nacional de Ayuda a las Misiones Indigenas (CENAMI) and Centro Nacional de Pastoral Indigena (CENAPI), the 2 executive bodies of the Episcopal Commission for Indigenous Peoples, CENAMI being dedicated to awakening the country to the problems of indigenous peoples (Amerindians) and acting as a channel for those desiring to work among them, with CENAPI studying living conditions and the apostolate in each Indian region. CENAPI has also undertaken pastoral work, including the organization of the first national encounter for indigenous pastoralia (Primer Encuentro Nacional de Pastoral Indigenista) at Xicotepec in January 1970. The diocese of Chiapas maintains an Institute of Anthropological Educative and Economic Research and Application (INAREMAC) at San Cristobal de las Casas. This institute organized at the end of 1974 an Indian Congress, with the participation among others of 1,500 Indian delegates from various Indian tribes.

Institutions for pastoral and religious training include: (1) Instituto Superior de Estudios Eclesiásticos, which offers complete courses and special programmes of advanced religious studies for diocesan major seminarians, priests, religious personnel and laity; (2) Instituto de Pastoral Catequístico 'Sedes Sapientiae', mostly for priests and religious personnel which is the only higher school for catechesis in Mexico; and (3) Centro Informaciones Pastorales (CIP) which provides pastoralia courses for priests and religious personnel. In 1972 the bishops decided to establish a theological faculty.

Missionary action is co-ordinated by the Consejo Nacional Misiones which is the executive organ of the Episcopal Commission for Missions. The Seminario Nacional de Misiones was founded in 1948 and the following Mexican missionary congregations are active: Misioneros del Espirito Santo (MSpS) for men; Misioneros Josefinos de México (MJ) for men (with work in Peru); Misioneros del Sagrado Corazón y Sta Maria de Guadalupe (MSC) for men, founded in 1949 with 40 priests working in foreign countries in 1974 (Japan, Korea, Hong Kong and Kenya); Misioneras Clarisas del Santissimo Sacramento for women (Japan, Costa Rica, Mexico and the USA); Misioneras del Sagrado Corazón y Sta Maria de Guadalupe for women.

In spite of a constitutional prohibition, there exists in fact a system of Catholic schools which are part of the National Confederation of Private Schools (Confederación Nacional de Escuelas Particulares), which includes institutions from the kindergarten level to the Ibero-American University. In 1973 there were 1,470 Catholic primary schools with 514,547 pupils, and 832 secondary schools with 149,369 pupils.

Catholic Social Aid in Mexico (Ayuda Social Católica de México, AC), founded in 1961, is a member of Caritas Internationalis, and co-operates with Catholic Relief Services/USCC (USA).

UNION DE IGLESIAS EVANGELICAS INDEPENDIENTES. This indigenous pentecostal movement is also known as the Iglesia Cristiana Independiente Pentecostés (Independent Pentecostal Christian Church: HQ Pachuca, Hidalgo), and as Iglesias Evangélicas Independientes. It was founded by Andrés Ornelas Martinez, a miner, in Pachuca in 1923. By amalgamation with other independent pentecostal groups including ones begun by missionaries of the Swedish Free Mission (e.g. Filadelfia Church in Mexico City, now Saron), and many others under the influence of SFM teaching and concepts, the church became a large union of congregations known as Iglesia Evangélica Independiente. In 1941 Ornelas dissociated himself from the SFM missionaries. In 1955 the church merged with the Iglesia Cristiana Independiente, and after further amalgamations became known by the 2 names shown in the table. Many members are from the Otomí and other tribes, and there is a strong Otomí cultural background in the churches. Half of all Otomí are monolingual, speaking Otomí but no Spanish; and a third are illiterate. The churches have suffered a long history of Catholic persecution. All are self-supporting, and there are pentecostal co-operatives, large collective farms and textile factories, and in consequence members experience phenomenal upward social mobility.

# MIDWAY ISLANDS

## SECULAR DATA

**STATE. Official name:** The Midway Islands.
**Flag** (shown above right): That of the USA.
**Area:** 5 sq.km. (1.9 sq.miles). Description: Sand Island, Eastern Island. Agricultural land: 0.0%.
**Government:** Island dependency of the USA (1867 annexed by USA; under US Navy).
**Official language:** English.

**Foreign forces** (1973): About 1,000 USA troops.

**DEMOGRAPHY. Population:** 2,220 (census of 1.IV.1970. For 1970–2000 (UN), see last row of Table 1). Population density (1975): 444/sq.km. (1,150/sq.mile). Under 15 years: 44%. Growth rate (1975–80): 1.31% per year (births 3.49%, deaths −0.79%, emigrants −1.39%). Life expectancy (1975–80): 63.8 years. Household size: 5.0 persons.
**Major languages:** English.

**ETHNOLINGUSTIC GROUPS:** 99% USA military (90% White, 9% Black).

**MONEY** (1977). **Monetary unit:** US dollar (= 100 cents). **National income per person:** US$4,000. Average annual family income: US$20,000.

**COMMUNICATION** (per 1,000 people). Phones: 600.

TABLE 1. RELIGIOUS ADHERENTS IN THE MIDWAY ISLANDS

| Year | 1900 | | mid-1970 | | Annual change, 1970–1980 | | | | mid-1975 | | mid-1980 | | 2000 | |
|---|---|---|---|---|---|---|---|---|---|---|---|---|---|---|
| *Name* | *Adherents* | *%* | *Adherents* | *%* | *Natural* | *Conversion* | *Total* | *Rate* | *Adherents* | *%* | *Adherents* | *%* | *Adherents* | *%* |
| **Christians** | **20** | **100.0** | **1,920** | **86.5** | **0** | **0** | **0** | **0.00** | **1,920** | **86.5** | **1,920** | **86.5** | **2,000** | **80.0** |
| professing | 20 | 100.0 | 1,920 | 86.5 | 0 | 0 | 0 | 0.00 | 1,920 | 86.5 | 1,920 | 86.5 | 2,000 | 80.0 |
| Protestants | 20 | 100.0 | 1,320 | 59.5 | 0 | 0 | 0 | 0.00 | 1,320 | 59.5 | 1,320 | 59.5 | 1,380 | 55.0 |
| Roman Catholics | 0 | 0.0 | 600 | 27.0 | 0 | 0 | 0 | 0.00 | 600 | 27.0 | 600 | 27.0 | 620 | 25.0 |
| nominal | 20 | 100.0 | 620 | 27.9 | 0 | 0 | 0 | 0.00 | 620 | 27.9 | 620 | 27.9 | 750 | 30.0 |
| affiliated | 0 | 0.0 | 1,300 | 58.6 | 0 | 0 | 0 | 0.00 | 1,300 | 58.6 | 1,300 | 58.6 | 1,250 | 50.0 |
| total practising | 0 | *0* | 650 | *50* | 0 | 0 | 0 | 0.00 | 650 | *50* | 650 | *50* | 620 | *50* |
| non-practising | 0 | *0* | 650 | *50* | 0 | 0 | 0 | 0.00 | 650 | *50* | 650 | *50* | 630 | *50* |
| Protestants | 0 | 0.0 | 800 | 36.0 | 0 | 0 | 0 | 0.00 | 800 | 36.0 | 800 | 36.0 | 750 | 30.0 |
| Roman Catholics | 0 | 0.0 | 500 | 22.5 | 0 | 0 | 0 | 0.00 | 500 | 22.5 | 500 | 22.5 | 500 | 20.0 |
| Non-religious | 0 | 0.0 | 300 | 13.5 | 0 | 0 | 0 | 0.00 | 300 | 13.5 | 300 | 13.5 | 500 | 20.0 |
| **Country's population** | **20** | **100.0** | **2,220** | **100.0** | **0** | **0** | **0** | **0.00** | **2,220** | **100.0** | **2,220** | **100.0** | **2,500** | **100.0** |

COLUMNS, ROWS. For meanings and definitions, see Codebook (Part 6). Note that, by definition, total 'Christians' = professing + crypto-Christians, which also = affiliated + nominal Christians. Percentages may not always total exactly, due to rounding.
CENSUSES. The religion question has not been asked.

**NOTES ON RELIGIONS**
CHRISTIANS. USA military personnel.

**CHRISTIANITY.** There are no organized parishes, but the island is served by Catholic and Protestant chaplains of the US armed forces. Midway Island is under the Catholic diocese of Honolulu, itself part of the province of San Francisco in the USA.

**CHURCH AND STATE.** Midway was uninhabited when it was first discovered in 1859. The USA took possession of it in 1867 and placed it under the jurisdiction of the US Navy in 1903. Since the only religious activity at Midway is that organized by armed forces chaplains, who are recruited and paid by the USA government, church and state are closely identified.

**TABLE 2. ORGANIZED CHURCHES AND DENOMINATIONS IN THE MIDWAY ISLANDS**

| Official name 1 | Begun 2 | Type 3 | Counc 4 | Congs 5 | Adults 6 | Affiliated 7 | Names, notes, and other statistics (see Codebook) 8 |
|---|---|---|---|---|---|---|---|
| Catholic Church (D Honolulu) | | R Lat | B.... | 1 | 200 | 500 | Under D Honolulu, province of San Francisco (USA). No parish. USA expatriates. |
| USA military chaplaincies | 1903 | P unt | ..... | 2 | 300 | 800 | USA armed forces personnel on naval and air bases, with military chaplaincies. |
| Total affiliated (mid-1970) | | | | 3 | 500 | 1,300 | Total denominations (1970) ... 2. |
| Total affiliated (mid-1975) | | | | 4 | 500 | 1,300 | Total denominations (1975) ... 2. |
| Total affiliated (mid-1980) | | | | 5 | 500 | 1,300 | Total denominations (1980) ... 2. |

**NOTES ON TABLE ABOVE**
COLUMNS: for meanings and CODES (cols. 1, 3, 4, 8): see Codebook (Part 6). Column 1: **Boldface type** = church with over 10% of country's affiliated Christians.

PEOPLES (ethnolinguistic). Christians: 99% USA military (90% White, 9% Black).

**COUNTRY-WIDE TOTALS**
EVANGELIZATION (see Part 5). 1900: 100%. 1970: 100%.

1980: 100%.
FOREIGN MISSIONARIES AND PERSONNEL (aliens from abroad) (1973). Total 3. *From Western world.* About 3. PERSONNEL. 3 (foreign).

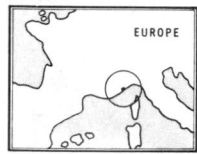

# MONACO

## SECULAR DATA

STATE. Official name: The Principality of Monaco (La Principauté de Monaco). Adjective of nationality: Monegasque (monégasque).
Flag (shown above right): Red stripe over white stripe.
Area: 1.49 sq.km. (0.58 sq.miles). Agricultural land: 0.0%.
Government: Constitutional principality, since 1911 (1524 Spanish protectorate, 1641 French protectorate).
Legislature: National Council, 18 members.
Official language: French (*Français*).
Capital: Monaco-Ville 3,000.
Political divisions: 3 Sections.

DEMOGRAPHY. Population: 23,035 (census of 1.III.1968. For 1970–2000 (UN), see last row of Table 1). Population density (1975): 16,779/sq.km. (43,456/sq.mile). Under 15 years: 26%. Growth rate (1975–80): 0.81% per year. Household size: 3.6 persons.
Major languages: French, English, Italian, Monegasque.
Urban dwellers (1970): 100.0%.
Labour force: 45%.
Tourists (1973): 137,094.

ETHNOLINGUISTIC GROUPS: 84.9% expatriate (57.8% French, 16.6% Italian, 3.0% USA, 2.0% British, 1.7% Jewish, 1.4% Belgian, 1.0% Spaniard, 1.0% Slav (Russian, et alii), 0.4% Greek), 15.1% citizen (Monégasque) (3,000).

MONEY (1977). Monetary unit: French franc (= 100 centimes); US$1 = FF 5.00.
National income per person: US$6,000. Average annual family income: US$21,600.
Cost of living in capital (1976): Daily cost of living: US$40.

HEALTH. Hospitals: 1 (282 beds). Doctors: 53. Blind: 15. Criminals: 496.

EDUCATION. Adult literacy: 99%. Education rate: 72%. Schools: 8.

LITERATURE. Annual new book titles (1967): 114. Periodicals: 8.

COMMUNICATION (per 1,000 people). Phones: 965. Radios: 660. TV sets: 262.

**TABLE 1. RELIGIOUS ADHERENTS IN MONACO**

| Year Name | 1900 Adherents | % | mid-1970 Adherents | % | Annual change, 1970–1980 Natural | Conversion | Total | Rate | mid-1975 Adherents | % | mid-1980 Adherents | % | 2000 Adherents | % |
|---|---|---|---|---|---|---|---|---|---|---|---|---|---|---|
| **Christians** | **15,300** | **98.7** | **23,570** | **98.2** | **196** | **1** | **197** | **0.80** | **24,555** | **98.2** | **25,540** | **98.2** | **28,460** | **98.1** |
| professing | 15,300 | 98.7 | 23,570 | 98.2 | 196 | 1 | 197 | 0.80 | 24,555 | 98.2 | 25,540 | 98.2 | 28,460 | 98.1 |
| Roman Catholics | 15,690 | 94.8 | 21,770 | 90.7 | 181 | 1 | 182 | 0.80 | 22,675 | 90.7 | 23,590 | 90.7 | 25,850 | 89.1 |
| Protestants | 460 | 3.0 | 1,100 | 4.6 | 9 | 1 | 10 | 0.87 | 1,150 | 4.6 | 1,200 | 4.6 | 1,740 | 6.0 |
| Anglicans | 150 | 1.0 | 550 | 2.3 | 5 | 0 | 5 | 0.86 | 580 | 2.3 | 600 | 2.3 | 580 | 2.0 |
| Orthodox | 0 | 0.0 | 150 | 0.6 | 1 | −1 | 0 | 0.00 | 150 | 0.6 | 150 | 0.6 | 290 | 1.0 |
| nominal | 110 | 0.7 | 345 | 1.4 | 3 | 1 | 4 | 1.10 | 365 | 1.5 | 380 | 1.5 | 880 | 3.0 |
| affiliated | 15,190 | 98.0 | 23,225 | 96.8 | 193 | 0 | 193 | 0.80 | 24,190 | 96.8 | 25,160 | 96.8 | 27,580 | 95.1 |
| total practising | 12,150 | 80 | 13,930 | 60 | 116 | 0 | 116 | 0.80 | 14,510 | 60 | 15,100 | 60 | 13,790 | 50 |
| non-practising | 3,040 | 20 | 9,290 | 40 | 77 | 0 | 77 | 0.80 | 9,680 | 40 | 10,060 | 40 | 13,790 | 50 |
| Roman Catholics | 14,640 | 94.5 | 21,675 | 90.3 | 180 | 0 | 180 | 0.80 | 22,570 | 90.3 | 23,480 | 90.3 | 25,230 | 87.0 |
| Protestants | 450 | 2.9 | 1,000 | 4.2 | 8 | 1 | 9 | 0.86 | 1,050 | 4.2 | 1,090 | 4.2 | 1,630 | 5.6 |
| Anglicans | 100 | 0.6 | 450 | 1.9 | 4 | 0 | 4 | 0.85 | 470 | 1.9 | 490 | 1.9 | 490 | 1.7 |
| Orthodox | 0 | 0.0 | 100 | 0.4 | 1 | −1 | 0 | 0.00 | 100 | 0.4 | 100 | 0.4 | 230 | 0.8 |
| **Jews** | 200 | 1.3 | 400 | 1.7 | 4 | −1 | 3 | 0.72 | 415 | 1.7 | 430 | 1.7 | 490 | 1.7 |
| **Baha'is** | 0 | 0.0 | 30 | 0.1 | 0 | 0 | 0 | 0.00 | 30 | 0.1 | 30 | 0.1 | 50 | 0.2 |
| **Country's population** | **15,500** | **100.0** | **24,000** | **100.0** | **200** | **0** | **200** | **0.80** | **25,000** | **100.0** | **26,000** | **100.0** | **29,000** | **100.0** |

COLUMNS, ROWS. For meanings and definitions, see Codebook (Part 6). Note that, by definition, total 'Christians' = professing + crypto-Christians, which also = affiliated + nominal Christians. Percentages may not always total exactly, due to rounding.

CENSUSES. 10.III.1946: 94.6% Roman Catholics, 3.2% Protestants, 1.0% Orthodox, 0.9% Jews, 0.2% Muslims, 0.1% non-religious. The religion question was not asked in subsequent censuses.

**NOTES ON RELIGIONS**
BAHA'IS. Begun 1955. In 1 local spiritual assembly (1964, 1973). JEWS. In over 150 families, using an equipped oratory but with no synagogue.

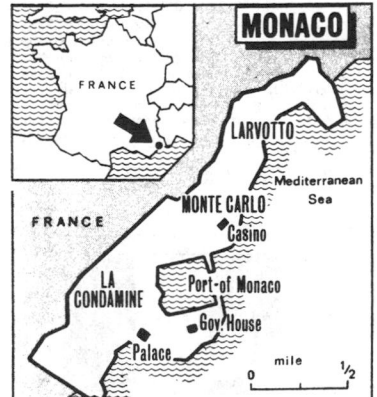

NON-CHRISTIAN RELIGIONS. **Judaism** has been represented by a cultural association since 1947. A resident rabbi serves the Jewish community, with Sabbath and feast days celebrated in a chapel built in 1960. The construction of a synagogue is anticipated.
**Baha'i** also has a small community.

## CHRISTIANITY
CATHOLIC CHURCH. Catholicism is the majority religion of Monaco. A parish was formed in 1247 as part of the diocese of Nice. It became a diocese in its own right in 1887 and is, ecclesiastically, immediately subject to the Holy See. Diocesan clergy and several religious congregations are active

**Eglise Catholique, Diocèse de Monaco.** Cathedral in Monaco.

in 5 Catholic parishes, as well as in the official schools and social service institutions of the principality.

OTHER CHURCHES. Monaco's large English-speaking community is served by St Paul's Church, which was built in 1925 and is attached to the Anglican diocese of Gibraltar. The building is also used by Greek Orthodox who are part of the Parish of the Riviera and the Principality, and under the ecumenical patriarch of Constantinople, services being conducted by an archimandrite from Nice. The Reformed Church of Monaco also made use of the Anglican building until 1959 when their own was opened.

CHURCH AND STATE. The constitution of 17 December 1962 stipulates that 'The Catholic Apostolic and Roman religion is the religion of the State' (Article 9). Since the preceding constitution lacked such a declaration, the Department of the Interior of the Ministry of State justified this inclusion by reference to the following: (1) the papal bull 'Quemadmodum sollicitus pastor' of 15 March 1887, which listed the guarantees, endowments and juridical status accepted by the state prior to the creation of the diocese; and (2) the 'organic law' of 28 September 1887, which gave legal sanction to this bull. The government considers that these texts bear the significance of a concordat, in contrast to the ecclesiastical authorities for whom, according to canon law, a concordat is a solemn bilateral treaty, and who do not speak of Catholicism as the state religion. Nevertheless, the prince plays the role of patron; and when there is a vacancy in the episcopal see, he presents a list of 3 candidates for papal selection. In return the Catholic Church receives financial compensation including salaries of many clergy, upkeep of buildings, and the covering of parish deficits by the state. Article 23 of the constitution guarantees freedom of religion and expression of opinion. For the construction or opening of a building destined for worship, authorization from the Department of the Interior is required. All official community schools, the hospital as well as 2 hostels and 3 orphanages, are run by Catholic religious personnel.

Headquarters of Trans World Radio on Mount Agel, Monaco.

INTERDENOMINATIONAL ORGANIZATIONS. Although no formal organization exists, there are good relations between Monaco's religious confessions. The Anglican building is available to other denominations, and the Catholic bishop has on numerous occasions participated in ecumenical services at the Anglican and Reformed churches.

BROADCASTING. Monaco is the centre of operations for Trans World Radio, which operates through the commercial station Radio Monte Carlo and broadcasts over 800 programmes a month in 25 languages to 100 nations in Europe, Africa, Asia and the USSR. To supplement its station on Mount Agel, Monaco, TWR has established a major radio station on the island of Bonaire in the Netherlands Antilles, and maintains full-time production studios in a number of countries. There are also transmitting facilities on Cyprus. For Catholics, Monaco is a member of UNDA.

TABLE 2.    ORGANIZED CHURCHES AND DENOMINATIONS IN MONACO

| Official name 1 | Begun 2 | Type 3 | Counc 4 | Congs 5 | Adults 6 | Affiliated 7 | Names, notes, and other statistics (see Codebook) 8 |
|---|---|---|---|---|---|---|---|
| Eglise Anglicane (D Gibraltar) | 1925 | A plu | awc.. | 1 | 300 | 450 | *St Paul's Anglican Ch.* Chaplaincy in D Gibraltar. English residents, tourists. 1x. |
| Eglise Catholique: D Monaco | 1247 | R Lat | bxB.. | 5 | 16,000 | 21,675 | *Catholic Ch in Monaco.* Diocese under Holy See. C=5+1+7. 32nx,17m,104w,274Yy. |
| Eglise Orthodoxe Grecque | 1957 | O Gre | Cwc.. | 1 | 50 | 100 | *Parish of Monte Carlo, Greek Orthodox Ch.* Greek residents. Use Anglican building. |
| Eglise Réformée de Monaco | 1959 | P Ref | Rwc.. | 1 | 500 | 1,000 | *Reformed Ch of M.* Chapel of Eglise Réformée de France (Menton). |
| Total affiliated (mid-1970) | | | | 8 | 16,850 | 23,225 | Total denominations (1970) ... 4. |
| Total affiliated (mid-1975) | | | | 9 | 17,550 | 24,190 | Total denominations (1975) ... 4. |
| Total affiliated (mid-1980) | | | | 10 | 18,250 | 25,160 | Total denominations (1980) ... 5. |

NOTES ON TABLE ABOVE
COLUMNS: for meanings and CODES (cols. 1, 3, 4, 8): see Codebook (Part 6). Column 1: **Boldface type** = church with over 10% of country's affiliated Christians.
OTHER MARGINAL BODIES. Société des Antonistes (12 adherents in 1946).

PEOPLES (ethnolinguistic). Christians: 84.9% expatriate (58.8% French, 16.9% Italian, 3.0% USA, 2.0% British, 1.4% Belgian, 1.0% Spaniard, 1.0% Slav, 0.4% Greek, Russian), 15.1% citizen (Monégasque).

COUNTRY-WIDE TOTALS
EVANGELIZATION (see Part 5). 1900: 100%. 1970: 100%. 1980: 100%.
FOREIGN MISSIONARIES AND PERSONNEL (aliens from abroad) (1973). Total 147. *From Western world.* 147: about 100 Roman Catholics, 46 Protestants in 2 USA societies, 1 Anglican.

INSTITUTIONS (church-operated) (1973). Total 7, including 4 higher schools, 1 radio station.
PERIODICALS. 6 titles.
PERSONNEL. About 202 (55 national, 147 foreign).
RELIGIOUS LIBRARIES. 1.
SCRIPTURE DISTRIBUTION (1975). Annual totals: 150 Bibles (33% subsidized, 67% commercial), 100 NTs (70% subsidized, 30% commercial), 100 UBS portions.
SERVICE AGENCIES. About 20, including ACI, ACO, CV/AV, JEC/F, JOC/F, TWR.

ADDITIONAL DATA ON CHURCHES
EGLISE CATHOLIQUE. The area became a parish of the diocese of Nice in 1247, and a diocese in 1887. *Annual baptisms.* 100% infants, no adults. *Priests.* 15 diocesan, 17 religious. *Religious orders and congregations.* Priests: OFM, OCD, SJ, OSFS, Clercs de la Mère de Dieu. Brothers: FSC. Sisters: Dames de St-Maur, Filles de la Charité de St-Vincent de Paul, Bon Secours de Troyes,

Ste-Enfance de Digne, St-Rosaire de Grenoble, Dominicaines de la Ste-Famille de Vence, Pieuse Union Ste-Croix de Jérusalem. *Catholic organizations.* The diocese is not a member of a national episcopal conference but it is attached to the CCEE. A Presbyteral Council consisting of elected members, and a Pastoral Council composed of priests, religious personnel and lay members, have been formed. There are no organizations of religious personnel. The Bureau of Diocesan Works (Direction des Oeuvres Diocésaines) co-ordinates the activities of CV/AV, Scouts, Guides, JEC/F and JOC/F with youth; and Action Catholique Ouvrière, Action Catholique des Indépendants, Légion de Marie and Conférence de St-Vincent de Paul with adults.
The Holy See does not maintain diplomatic relations with Monaco.
In 1973 there were 4 Catholic primary schools with 1,648 pupils and 4 secondary with 1,769.

# MONGOLIA

## SECULAR DATA

STATE. Official name: The Mongolian People's Republic, MPR (Büged Nayramdakh Mongol Arad Ulas). Adjective of nationality: Mongolian.
Flag (shown above right): Red, blue, and red bars, with national emblem (soyombo symbol) in gold below 5-pointed gold star.
Area: 1,565,000 sq.km. (604,250 sq.miles). Agricultural land: 89.9%.
Government: One-party Communist state, since 1924 (1200 Mongolian empire, 1691 Chinese province, 1911 autonomy, 1921 republic).
Legislature: Great People's Hural, 287 members.
Official language: Mongolian (Khalka Mongol).
Capital: Ulan Bator 287,000 (1970).
Political divisions: 2 Cities, 18 Provinces (aimag) divided into Districts (somon).
Armed forces (1976): Total 30,000 regular: army 28,000, air force 2,000 (10 combat aircraft). Reserves: 30,000. Paramilitary forces: 18,000.

Foreign forces: (1973) 200,000 USSR troops; (1977) 180,000 plus 20,000 USSR civilian work force.

DEMOGRAPHY. Population: 1,197,600 (census of 10.I.1969. For 1970–2000 (UN), see last row of Table 1). Population density (1975): 1/sq.km. (3/sq.mile). Under 15 years: 44%. Growth rate (1975–80): 2.87% per year (births 3.67%, deaths −0.81%). Life expectancy (1975–80): 62.8 years. Household size: 4.4 persons. Major languages: Mongolian (Khalka), Russian, Kazakh, Buryat, Chinese.
Urban dwellers (1970): 36.9%. Urban growth rate (1950–70): 4.9% per year.
Labour force: 38%.
Tourists (1976): 4,000.

ETHNOLINGUISTIC GROUPS: 67.0% Khalkha, 13.8% USSR military (200,000), 4.0% Kazakh, 2.7% Durbet (Oyrat), 2.4% Buryat, 2.0% Tuvinian, 1.7% Bayat, 1.6% Chinese, 1.5% Dariganga, 1.1% Uryankhai (Darkhat), 1.1% Dzakhchin, Evenki, Khoton, Uriankhai-Monchak.

MONEY (1977). Monetary unit: tughrik (= 100 möngö); US$1 = T 3.33.
National income per person: US$500. Average annual family income: US$2,200.
Cost of living in capital: (1976): Daily cost of living: US$51.

HEALTH. Hospitals: 351 (11,926 beds). Doctors: 2,578. Lepers: 100 (0.1 per 1,000). Blind: 4,000. Psychotics: 13,000.

EDUCATION. Adult literacy: (1956) 95%, (1975) 100%. Education rate: 50%. Schools: 504. Universities: 1.

LITERATURE. Annual new book titles (1973): 587. Periodicals: 28. Newspapers: 2 dailies, 8 non-daily.

COMMUNICATION (per 1,000 people). Phones: 20. Radios: 129. TV sets: 25. Daily newspaper circulation: 103 copies.

TABLE 1.    RELIGIOUS ADHERENTS IN MONGOLIA

| Year | 1900 | | mid-1970 | | Annual change, 1970–1980 | | | | mid-1975 | | mid-1980 | | 2000 | |
|---|---|---|---|---|---|---|---|---|---|---|---|---|---|---|
| Name | Adherents | % | Adherents | % | Natural | Conversion | Total | Rate | Adherents | % | Adherents | % | Adherents | % |
| Non-religious | 0 | 0.0 | 575,000 | 39.7 | 17,639 | 7,331 | 24,970 | 3.62 | 689,650 | 41.9 | 824,700 | 44.1 | 1,517,600 | 52.3 |
| Shamanists | 316,450 | 60.6 | 504,800 | 34.9 | 13,930 | −6,660 | 7,270 | 1.34 | 541,500 | 32.9 | 577,500 | 30.9 | 667,200 | 23.3 |
| Atheists | 0 | 0.0 | 312,000 | 21.5 | 9,054 | −74 | 8,980 | 2.54 | 354,000 | 21.5 | 401,800 | 21.5 | 638,200 | 22.0 |
| Buddhists | 200,000 | 38.3 | 30,000 | 2.1 | 841 | −291 | 550 | 1.67 | 32,900 | 2.0 | 35,500 | 1.9 | 43,500 | 1.5 |
| Muslims | 5,000 | 1.0 | 23,000 | 1.6 | 632 | −312 | 320 | 1.30 | 24,700 | 1.5 | 26,200 | 1.4 | 29,000 | 1.0 |
| **Christians** | **550** | **0.1** | **3,200** | **0.2** | **4** | **6** | **10** | **0.31** | **3,250** | **0.2** | **3,300** | **0.2** | **5,500** | **0.2** |
| crypto-Christians | 550 | 0.1 | 3,200 | 0.2 | 4 | 6 | 10 | 0.31 | 3,250 | 0.2 | 3,300 | 0.2 | 5,500 | 0.2 |
| affiliated | 550 | 0.1 | 3,200 | 0.2 | 4 | 6 | 10 | 0.31 | 3,250 | 0.2 | 3,300 | 0.2 | 5,500 | 0.2 |
| total practising | 500 | 90 | 2,560 | 80 | 3 | 5 | 8 | 0.31 | 2,600 | 80 | 2,640 | 80 | 3,850 | 70 |
| non-practising | 50 | 10 | 640 | 20 | 1 | 1 | 2 | 0.31 | 650 | 20 | 660 | 20 | 1,650 | 30 |
| Orthodox | 500 | 0.1 | 3,050 | 0.2 | 0 | 0 | 0 | 0.00 | 3,050 | 0.2 | 3,050 | 0.2 | 5,000 | 0.2 |
| Mongolian indigenous | 0 | 0.0 | 100 | 0.0 | 4 | 6 | 10 | 6.67 | 150 | 0.0 | 200 | 0.0 | 400 | 0.0 |
| Roman Catholics | 50 | 0.0 | 50 | 0.0 | 0 | 0 | 0 | 0.00 | 50 | 0.0 | 50 | 0.0 | 100 | 0.0 |
| Country's population | 522,000 | 100.0 | 1,448,000 | 100.0 | 42,100 | 0 | 42,100 | 2.56 | 1,646,000 | 100.0 | 1,869,000 | 100.0 | 2,901,000 | 100.0 |

COLUMNS, ROWS. For meanings and definitions, see Code-book (Part 6). Note that, by definition, total 'Christians' = professing + crypto-Christians, which also = affiliated + nominal Christians. Percentages may not always total exactly, due to rounding.
CENSUSES. No census has ever included religion.

NOTES ON RELIGIONS
ATHEISTS. Mongolian People's Revolutionary Party (MPRP) (Communist; in power; pro-Soviet): membership (1970) 58,048 (30% workers, 20% agriculturalists, 50% white-collar); Communist voters (election of 18.VI.1972) 607,000 (99.9% of all voters).

BUDDHISTS. 1900: 200,000 Lamaists (followers of Tibetan Tantrism). 1920: 120,000 lamas in 2,648 temples, and 85,000 followers of the Living Buddha (Bogdo-Guegen) of Urga. 1929: all lamaseries suppressed or destroyed, then nationalized and secularized. 1960: new lamasery permitted at Gandan Djoo, with 40 young monks by 1977.
COUNTRY'S POPULATION. The totals shown above for 1970–2000 include the 200,000 USSR military and dependants permanently stationed in Mongolia, of whom approximately 55% are non-religious, 40% atheists, 2% Muslims, at least 1.5% Christians, also Buddhists and others.
CRYPTO-CHRISTIANS. The existence of Christians has never

been recognized by the state, so all Christians are properly termed crypto-Christians. There are 4 groupings (see Table 2).
MUSLIMS. Mostly Sunnis (of the Hanafite rite), in the west, together with around 4,000 expatriates in the USSR armed forces.
NON-RELIGIOUS. Mongolians, Chinese and USSR military personnel.
MONGOLIAN INDIGENOUS. This term is used here to describe the very small number of scattered and completely isolated indigenous radio believers (see Table 2).
SHAMANISTS. Unorganized traditional religionists, functioning at the family level without public temples or centres; declining since 1930, but increasing again in influence by 1977.

## NON-CHRISTIAN RELIGIONS. Shamanism is
Mongolia's traditional religion. Devoid of public temples, it has its centre in family worship. Although strongly challenged at one time by Tibetan Tantrism, and ruthlessly suppressed by the Communist regime since 1921, it has by no means disappeared; in 1977 it was reported to be again increasing its influence.

**Tibetan Tantrism**, or **Lamaism**, is a form of Buddhism which was introduced in 1575. Encouraged by the Manchu emperors, it exercised great economic, social, political and cultural influence. In 1920 there were 2,648 temples and monasteries with 120,000 lamas, in addition to 85,000 disciples of the Living Buddha, Bogdo-Guegen of Urga (now Ulan Bator), who was monarch and head of the Buddhist clergy. In 1929 the Communist government suppressed or destroyed all lamaseries, nationalized temple properties and integrated the lamas forcibly into civic life; but by 1960 the situation had improved sufficiently to permit the construction of a new temple at Ulan Bator, the lamasery of Gandan Djoo, with (in 1977) 40 young monks and a growing attendance of young people at the temple. Tantrism exerts little influence in Mongolia today.

**Islam** is represented by 20,000 Muslims in the western part of the country, mostly Sunnis of the Hanafite rite.

## CHRISTIANITY. Nestorian missionaries from China
touched Mongolia as early as the 7th century, but Christianity had disappeared there by the 10th century. Franciscans and Dominicans entered in the 13th century, and Lazarists in the 1830s. From 1817–41 the London Missionary Society had 2 missionaries working among the Buryats; they translated the Bible into literary Mongolian. In 1870 the LMS missionary James Gilmour began a ministry which ended 21 years later without having seen a single baptism.

**Buddhists.** *Above right* and *right.* Bogdo-Guegen (Living Buddha) Temple, on outskirts of Ulan Bator. In 1920 there were 120,000 lamas in 2,648 temples; in 1929, all were suppressed; in 1977, 40 young monks and increasing temple attendance by young people.

A Russian Orthodox congregation existed at Mai-mai-ch'eng until the mid-1930s. The government of China, which controlled the country until 1921, and since 1924 the Communist government of Mongolia have made overt Christian evangelization impossible. In 1922 the Holy See established the mission sui juris of Urga and placed it under the theoretical authority of the Scheut Fathers (CICM). Since the jurisdiction has no active work, it has never been officially suppressed. There are no legal organized public churches in Mongolia at present, although Christians of 3 kinds exist: among the expatriate diplomatic community, among European expatriate technical personnel, and thirdly among Orthodox and Evangelical believers among the 200,000 USSR troops stationed permanently in Mongolia.

**CHURCH AND STATE.** The constitution of September 1960 proclaims the separation of religion from state and school, and Article 86 guarantees freedom of religion as well as the right to disseminate anti-religious propaganda. However, these guarantees mean little or nothing. Government pressure is in fact exerted against all religious profession except among old people. The only religious centre recognized is the new lamasery, Gandan Djoo, at Ulan Bator. Its 130 monks live at the expense of the state, serving as propaganda for friendly Buddhist countries.

**BROADCASTING.** No religious broadcasting of any kind is permitted within the country. However, programmes in Mongolian and Russian from FEBC and other foreign Christian stations are regularly heard.

Christian themes on a 1972 series of postage stamps: (*above*) The Presentation in the Temple (Bellini). (*left*) The Transfiguration of Christ (Bellini). (*right*) St John on Patmos.

**BIBLIOGRAPHY**
*James Gilmour of Mongolia.* R. Lovett. London: Religious Tract Society, 1895.
*The Challenge of Central Asia: A brief survey of Tibet and its borderlands, Mongolia, NW Kansu, Chinese Turkestan and Russian Central Asia.* London: World Dominion Press, c1932.
*The Mongol mission: narratives and letters of the Franciscan missionaries in Mongolia in the 13th century.* C.H. Dawson. New York, 1955.

TABLE 2.  ORGANIZED CHURCHES AND DENOMINATIONS IN MONGOLIA

| Official name 1 | Begun 2 | Type 3 | Counc 4 | Congs 5 | Adults 6 | Affiliated 7 | Names, notes, and other statistics (see Codebook) 8 |
|---|---|---|---|---|---|---|---|
| Catholic Church: m Urga (Ulan Bator) | 1798 | R Lat | P.... | 0 | 30 | 50 | Jurisdiction erected in 1922, confided to M=CICM. Scattered secret believers. |
| Isolated radio churches | 1969 | I rad | ..... | 10 | 50 | 100 | Isolated radio believers (through FEBC), mostly youths and students. |
| Orthodox Church | | O Sla | M.... | | 20 | 50 | Remnants of numbers of Russian settlers; last church building suppressed 1937. |
| USSR military groups | 1921 | O Sla | ..... | 100 | 2,000 | 3,000 | Small private prayer groups among mainly Orthodox believers in USSR armed forces. |
| **Total affiliated (mid-1970)** | | | | 112 | 2,100 | 3,200 | Total denominations (1970) ... 4. |
| **Total affiliated (mid-1975)** | | | | 110 | 2,130 | 3,250 | Total denominations (1975) ... 4. |
| **Total affiliated (mid-1980)** | | | | 100 | 2,160 | 3,300 | Total denominations (1980) ... 4. |

**NOTES ON TABLE ABOVE**

COLUMNS: for meanings and CODES (cols. 1, 3, 4, 8), see Codebook (Part 6). Column 1: **Boldface type** = church with over 10% of country's affiliated Christians.

PEOPLES (ethnolinguistic). Christians: 90% Russian, 10% Mongolian.

**COUNTRY-WIDE TOTALS**
EVANGELIZATION (see Part 5). 1900: 10%. 1970: 19%.

1980: 23%. *Radiophonic evangelism.* Broadcasts in Mongolian over FEBC.
SCRIPTURE DISTRIBUTION (1975). Annual totals: Nil. *Translations completed.* Portion: 2 languages since 1819. NT: Literary Mongolian in 1827, and Bible in 1840.

---

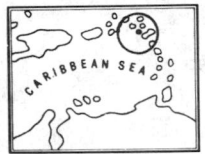

# MONTSERRAT

**SECULAR DATA**

**STATE. Official name:** The Crown Colony of Montserrat.
**Flag** (shown above right): British Blue Ensign with shield of the Colony in the fly.
**Area:** 98 sq.km. (39.5 sq.miles). Agricultural land: 30.0%.
**Government:** Self-governing crown colony of United Kingdom (Britain), since 1960 (1493 Spanish influence, 1782 French rule).
**Legislature:** Executive Council, 6 members. Legislative Council, 10 members.
**Official language:** English.
**Capital:** Plymouth 1,267 (1970).
**Armed forces** (1976): British.

**DEMOGRAPHY. Population:** 11,458 (census of 7.IV.1970. For 1970–2000 (UN), see last row of Table 1). Population density (1975): 125/sq.km. (324/sq.mile). Under 15 years: 43%. Growth rate (1975–80): 0.63% per year (births 2.87%, deaths −0.68%, emigrants −1.56%). Life expectancy (1975–80): 69.1 years. Household size: 3.5 persons.
**Major languages:** English.
**Labour force:** 39%.
**Tourists** (1971): 9,073. (1973) 12,600.

**ETHNOLINGUISTIC GROUPS:** 96.3% Black (African Negro), 2.7% White (European), 0.7% Mulatto, 0.1% Indo-Pakistani.

**MONEY** (1977). **Monetary unit:** East Caribbean dollar (= 100 cents); US$1 = EC$2.70.
**National income per person:** US$1,100. Average annual family income: US$3,850.
**Cost of living in capital** (1976): Daily cost of living: US$31.

**HEALTH.** Hospitals: 2 (86 beds). Doctors: 6.

**EDUCATION.** Adult literacy: (1946) 77%, (1960) 80%. Schools: 15.

**COMMUNICATION** (per 1,000 people). Phones: 127.

TABLE 1.  RELIGIOUS ADHERENTS IN MONTSERRAT

| Year / Name | 1900 Adherents | % | mid-1970 Adherents | % | Annual change, 1970–1980 Natural | Conversion | Total | Rate | mid-1975 Adherents | % | mid-1980 Adherents | % | 2000 Adherents | % |
|---|---|---|---|---|---|---|---|---|---|---|---|---|---|---|
| **Christians** | **12,200** | **100.0** | **11,220** | **97.6** | **146** | **−7** | **139** | **1.17** | **11,920** | **97.3** | **12,610** | **97.0** | **13,440** | **96.0** |
| professing | 12,200 | 100.0 | 11,220 | 97.6 | 146 | −7 | 139 | 1.17 | 11,920 | 97.3 | 12,610 | 97.0 | 13,440 | 96.0 |
| Protestants | 4,270 | 35.0 | 5,500 | 47.8 | 71 | −13 | 58 | 1.00 | 5,800 | 47.3 | 6,080 | 46.8 | 6,270 | 44.8 |
| Anglicans | 6,710 | 55.0 | 4,340 | 37.8 | 56 | −12 | 44 | 0.96 | 4,570 | 37.3 | 4,780 | 36.8 | 4,960 | 35.4 |
| Roman Catholics | 1,220 | 10.0 | 1,330 | 11.6 | 18 | 16 | 34 | 2.28 | 1,490 | 12.2 | 1,670 | 12.8 | 2,100 | 15.0 |
| Marginal Protestants | 0 | 0.0 | 50 | 0.4 | 1 | 2 | 3 | 5.00 | 60 | 0.5 | 80 | 0.6 | 110 | 0.8 |
| nominal | 1,340 | 11.0 | 1,520 | 13.2 | 20 | 3 | 23 | 1.40 | 1,640 | 13.4 | 1,750 | 13.5 | 2,280 | 16.3 |
| affiliated | 10,860 | 89.0 | 9,700 | 84.3 | 126 | −10 | 116 | 1.13 | 10,280 | 83.9 | 10,860 | 83.5 | 11,160 | 79.7 |
| total practising | 8,690 | 80 | 6,790 | 70 | 82 | −109 | −27 | −0.40 | 6,680 | 65 | 6,520 | 60 | 6,140 | 55 |
| non-practising | 2,170 | 20 | 2,910 | 30 | 44 | 99 | 143 | 3.97 | 3,600 | 35 | 4,340 | 40 | 5,020 | 45 |
| Protestants | 3,660 | 30.0 | 4,350 | 37.8 | 56 | −15 | 41 | 0.90 | 4,560 | 37.2 | 4,760 | 36.6 | 4,690 | 33.5 |
| Evangelicals | 3,000 | 24.6 | 2,500 | 21.7 | 32 | −5 | 27 | 1.02 | 2,640 | 21.5 | 2,770 | 21.3 | 2,940 | 21.0 |
| Anglicans | 6,100 | 50.0 | 4,000 | 34.8 | 51 | −12 | 39 | 0.93 | 4,200 | 34.3 | 4,390 | 33.8 | 4,400 | 31.4 |
| Roman Catholics | 1,100 | 9.0 | 1,300 | 11.3 | 18 | 15 | 33 | 2.26 | 1,460 | 11.9 | 1,630 | 12.5 | 1,960 | 14.0 |
| Marginal Protestants | 0 | 0.0 | 50 | 0.4 | 1 | 2 | 3 | 5.00 | 60 | 0.5 | 80 | 0.6 | 110 | 0.8 |
| **Baha'is** | 0 | 0.0 | 150 | 1.3 | 2 | 3 | 5 | 2.94 | 170 | 1.4 | 200 | 1.5 | 280 | 2.0 |
| **Non-religious** | 0 | 0.0 | 130 | 1.1 | 2 | 4 | 6 | 3.75 | 160 | 1.3 | 190 | 1.5 | 280 | 2.0 |
| **Country's population** | **12,200** | **100.0** | **11,500** | **100.0** | **150** | **0** | **150** | **1.22** | **12,500** | **100.0** | **13,000** | **100.0** | **14,000** | **100.0** |

**COLUMNS, ROWS.** For meanings and definitions, see Codebook (Part 6). Note that, by definition, total 'Christians' = professing + crypto-Christians, which also = affiliated + nominal Christians. Percentages may not always total exactly, due to rounding.

CENSUSES. 7.IV.1960: 48.8% Protestants (28.2% Methodists 10.% Pentecostals, 6.5% SDAs), 38.8% Anglicans, 10.4% Roman Catholics, 1.2% non-Christian religionists, 0.7% non-religious, 0.1% marginal Protestants. 7.IV.1970: 47.8% Protestants (28.3% Methodists, 9.5% Pentecostals, 7.0% SDAs), 37.8%

Anglicans, 11.6% Roman Catholics, 1.3% non-Christian religionists, 1.1% non-religious, 0.4% marginal Protestants.

**NOTES ON RELIGIONS**
BAHA'IS. In 2 local spiritual assemblies (1973).

**NON-CHRISTIAN RELIGIONS. Baha'i** has a small following. In addition, a few claim allegiance to other religions or no religion.

**CHRISTIANITY**
ANGLICAN CHURCH. As is true of all the Leeward Islands, the Anglican Church is the principal denomination. Its strength is about the same as the Church of England on Antigua and greater than that of St Kitts-Nevis and Anguilla. All of these

Several postage stamps carry Christian themes: here, at Easter 1971, 'Noli Me tangere (Do not touch Me)', by Orcagna.

islands form the diocese of Antigua, which was founded in 1842 and is part of the Church of the Province of the West Indies.

PROTESTANT CHURCHES. In spite of declining membership in recent years, Methodism remains the largest Protestant body in Montserrat, having had its West Indies beginnings in nearby Antigua as early as 1760. The Methodist Church is now more influential in Montserrat than in Antigua although not quite as much so as in St Kitts-Nevis or Anguilla, the other members of the Leeward chain.

Canadian Pentecostals and American Adventists have been active respectively since 1910 and 1926. Adventists, who lost members during the 1960s, belong to the SDA East Caribbean Conference. The Church of God of Prophecy is also at work, as is the Wesleyan Church, formerly known as the Pilgrim Holiness Church; the latter body has not been as successful here as in St Kitts-Nevis.

CATHOLIC CHURCH. Montserrat belongs to the diocese of Saint John's with its seat in Antigua.

In 1970 Montserrat had one parish, 2 stations, 2 priests, and several Missionary Sisters of the Immaculate Heart of Mary engaged in teaching commercial courses, in addition to school and social work.

CHURCH AND STATE. Unlike Antigua, St Kitts-Nevis and Anguilla, Montserrat has so far not sought either full or partial independence from Great Britain. However, such political differences have little effect on church-state relations, and all the Leeward Islands have similar policies regarding religion: there are no established churches and there is equal status for all religious bodies before the law.

INTERDENOMINATIONAL ORGANIZATIONS. The Anglican, Methodist and Catholic churches belong to the Montserrat Council for Social Action.

BROADCASTING. Both the government Radio Montserrat and Radio Antilles (private, commercial) accept religious programmes.

TABLE 2.    ORGANIZED CHURCHES AND DENOMINATIONS IN MONTSERRAT

| Official name 1 | Begun 2 | Type 3 | Counc 4 | Congs 5 | Adults 6 | Affiliated 7 | Names, notes, and other statistics (see Codebook) 8 |
|---|---|---|---|---|---|---|---|
| Anglican Church (D Antigua) | | A ACa | awMRC | | 2,000 | 4,000 | In Ch of Province of WIndies. M=USPG(UK). 95% WIndian Blacks. Declining. W=58%. |
| Catholic Church (D Saint John's) | | R Lat | P.NMC | 3 | 800 | 1,300 | In D Saint John's (Antigua). 1 parish, 1 school (120). 2nx,4w,P=47%. |
| Church of God of Prophecy | | P Pe3 | Z.... | 6 | 150 | 250 | M=CGP(USA). Schism in USA ex Ch of God (Cleveland). Holiness Pentecostals. |
| Jehovah's Witnesses | | M Jeh | x.... | 1 | 25 | 50 | Watch Tower. IBSA. Small congregation with in 1972 one baptism only. |
| Methodist Ch in Caribbean & Americas | 1820 | P Met | VwM,C | | 1,000 | 2,000 | In MCCA (1967) union, Leeward Islands District. M=MMS(UK). Declining rapidly. 2n. |
| Pentecostal Assemblies of the WIndies | 1910 | P Pe2 | ZP... | | 500 | 1,000 | M=PAoC(Canada). Expanding. Many emigrants to UK (Anglo-West-Indian Assembly). |
| Seventh-day Adventist Church | 1926 | P Adv | x.... | | 650 | 800 | SDA, East Caribbean Conference, Caribbean Union Conference. Decline since 1960. |
| Wesleyan Church | | P Hol | VF... | 2 | 150 | 300 | Before 1968 merger, M=Pilgrim Holiness Church(USA). Holiness denomination. |
| Total affiliated (mid-1970) | | | | 87 | 5,275 | 9,700 | Total denominations (1970) . . . 8. |
| Total affiliated (mid-1975) | | | | 89 | 5,590 | 10,280 | Total denominations (1975) . . . 8. |
| Total affiliated (mid-1980) | | | | 91 | 5,900 | 10,860 | Total denominations (1980) . . . 8. |

NOTES ON TABLE ABOVE
COLUMNS: for meanings and CODES (cols. 1, 3, 4, 8): see Codebook (Part 6). Column 1: **Boldface type** = church with over 10% of country's affiliated Christians.
NATIONAL COUNCILS (Column 4, 5th letter).
C = Montserrat Council for Social Action.

PEOPLES (ethnolinguistic). Christians: 96.3% Black, 2.7% White (European, British), 0.7% Mulatto.

COUNTRY-WIDE TOTALS
EVANGELIZATION (see Part 5). 1900: 100%. 1970: 100%. 1980: 100%. Mass evangelism. In 1975 the Evangelistic Association, Pentecostal Assemblies of the West Indies, held a crusade in Harris, also a deeper life crusade in Dyers.
FOREIGN MISSIONARIES AND PERSONNEL (aliens from abroad) (1973). Total 4. From Western world. About 2. From Third World. About 2 Anglicans.
PERIODICALS. 3 titles.
PERSONNEL. About 9 (5 national, 4 foreign).

SCRIPTURE DISTRIBUTION (1975). Annual totals: 200 Bibles (subsidized), 600 NTs (subsidized), 2,600 UBS selections.
SERVICE AGENCIES. About 4, including YWCA.

ADDITIONAL DATA ON CHURCHES
CATHOLIC CHURCH. Catholic organizations. The diocese is a member of the Antilles Episcopal Conference (AEC) with its headquarters in Kingston, Jamaica, and through it is a member of CELAM. The church sponsors one primary school with 123 pupils and one kindergarten with 112 pupils.

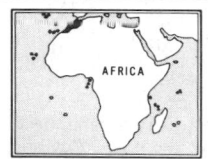

# MOROCCO

## SECULAR DATA

STATE. Official name: The Kingdom of Morocco (Al-Mamlakah al-Maghrebiyah/Le Royaume du Maroc). Adjective of nationality: Moroccan (marocain).
Flag (shown above right): Red field with green 5-pointed star.
Area: 458,730 sq.km. (171,834 sq.miles). Agricultural land: 45.1%.
Government: Absolute (de facto) or constitutional (de jure) monarchy, since 1956 (1912 French and Spanish protectorates, 1956 Independence).
Legislature: Parliament, 240 deputies (in abeyance since 1972).
Official language: Arabic.
Chief cities: capital Rabat-Salé 534,270 (1971), Casablanca 1,561,280, Marrakech 390,480, Fez 379,790, Meknès 362,840, Tangiers 185,850.
Political divisions: 19 Provinces and 2 Urban Prefectures (Casablanca, Rabat-Salé).
Armed forces (1976): Total 73,000 regular: army 65,000, navy 3,000, air force 5,000 (59 combat aircraft). Paramilitary forces: 30,000.
Foreign forces (1973): 1,000 USA troops.
Dependencies: In 1976 Morocco and Mauritania claimed ex-

Spanish Sahara, Morocco taking the northern two-thirds.

DEMOGRAPHY. Population: 15,379,259 (census of 20.VII.1971. For 1970–2000 (UN), see last row of Table 1). Population density (1975): 38/sq.km. (99/sq.mile). Under 15 years: 45%. Growth rate (1975–80): 3.05% per year (births 4.45%, deaths −1.34%, emigrants −0.06%). Life expectancy (1975–80): 55.4 years. Household size: 5.4 persons.
Major languages: Arabic, Berber (Ghomara, Rif, Shilha, Tamazigt), French, Spanish, English, and a few others.
Urban dwellers (1970): 32.5%. Urban growth rate (1950–70): 4.4% per year.
Labour force: 28%.
Refugees (1977): 3,000.
Tourists (1971): 914,292. (1974). 1,204,664.

ETHNOLINGUISTIC GROUPS: 64% Moroccan Arab, 34% Berber (11.1% Shluh, 10.3% Beraber (Tamazigt), 5.9% Rif, 1.3% Oasis Berber; monolingual Berber, 25%), 0.7% Algerian Arab, 0.6% French, 0.3% Maghreb Jewish, 0.2% Spaniard, Sudanese Black, Haratine (Black/Berber), Bedouin, Russian, Byelorussian, USA White, British.

MONEY (1977). Monetary unit: dirham (= 100 centimes); US$1 = DH 4.50.
National income per person: US$360. Average annual family income: US$1,944.
Inflation: (1970–74) 7.3% per year (1975: consumer price index 146).
Cost of living in capital (1976): index 115 (Washington DC=100). Daily cost of living: US$34.

HEALTH. Hospitals: 141 (22,927 beds). Doctors: 1,173. Lepers: 25,000 (1.4 per 1,000). Blind: 35,000. Psychotics: 140,000. Criminals: 52,750.

EDUCATION. Adult literacy: (1960) 14%, (1971) 21%. Education rate: 32%. Schools: 5,248. Universities: 4.

LITERATURE. Annual new book titles (1971): 122. Periodicals: 23. Newspapers: 11 dailies.

COMMUNICATION (per 1,000 people). Phones: 11. Radios: 74. TV sets: 20. Daily newspaper circulation: 15 copies.

TABLE 1.    RELIGIOUS ADHERENTS IN MOROCCO

| Year | 1900 | | mid-1970 | | Annual change, 1970–1980 | | | | mid-1975 | | mid-1980 | | 2000 | |
| Name | Adherents | % | Adherents | % | Natural | Conversion | Total | Rate | Adherents | % | Adherents | % | Adherents | % |
|---|---|---|---|---|---|---|---|---|---|---|---|---|---|---|
| Muslims | 5,012,920 | 96.4 | 14,958,920 | 98.9 | 530,186 | −408 | 529,778 | 3.05 | 17,360,100 | 99.2 | 20,256,700 | 99.4 | 35,748,000 | 99.6 |
| **Christians** | **30,080** | **0.6** | **129,580** | **0.9** | **−3,022** | **294** | **−2,728** | **−2,36** | **115,700** | **0.7** | **102,300** | **0.5** | **132,000** | **0.4** |
| crypto-Christians | 5,080 | 0.1 | 36,580 | 0.2 | 938 | 294 | 1,232 | 2.90 | 42,500 | 0.2 | 48,900 | 0.2 | 88,000 | 0.2 |
| professing | 25,000 | 0.5 | 93,000 | 0.6 | −3,960 | 0 | −3,960 | −5.41 | 73,200 | 0.4 | 53,400 | 0.3 | 44,000 | 0.1 |
| Roman Catholics | 25,000 | 0.5 | 90,000 | 0.6 | −4,000 | 0 | −4,000 | −5.71 | 70,000 | 0.4 | 50,000 | 0.2 | 40,000 | 0.1 |
| Protestants | 0 | 0.0 | 3,000 | 0.0 | 40 | 0 | 40 | 1.25 | 3,200 | 0.0 | 3,400 | 0.0 | 4,000 | 0.0 |
| affiliated | 30,080 | 0.6 | 129,580 | 0.9 | −3,022 | 294 | −2,728 | −2.36 | 115,700 | 0.7 | 102,300 | 0.5 | 132,000 | 0.4 |
| total practising | 24,060 | 80 | 80,340 | 62 | −1,874 | 183 | −1,691 | −2.36 | 71,730 | 62 | 63,430 | 62 | 92,400 | 70 |
| non-practising | 6,020 | 20 | 49,240 | 38 | −1,148 | 111 | −1,037 | −2.36 | 43,970 | 38 | 38,870 | 38 | 39,600 | 30 |
| Roman Catholics | 30,000 | 0.6 | 100,000 | 0.6 | −4,030 | 30 | −4,000 | −5.00 | 80,000 | 0.5 | 60,000 | 0.3 | 50,000 | 0.1 |
| Arab indigenous | 0 | 0.0 | 22,400 | 0.1 | 826 | 234 | 1,060 | 3.85 | 27,500 | 0.2 | 33,000 | 0.2 | 70,000 | 0.2 |
| Protestants | 30 | 0.0 | 5,180 | 0.0 | 112 | 20 | 132 | 2.28 | 5,800 | 0.0 | 6,500 | 0.0 | 8,000 | 0.0 |
| Evangelicals | 20 | 0.0 | 2,500 | 0.0 | 54 | 6 | 60 | 2.14 | 2,800 | 0.0 | 3,100 | 0.0 | 4,000 | 0.0 |
| Orthodox | 0 | 0.0 | 900 | 0.0 | 30 | 0 | 30 | 2.86 | 1,050 | 0.0 | 1,200 | 0.0 | 1,000 | 0.0 |
| Anglicans | 50 | 0.0 | 600 | 0.0 | 20 | 0 | 20 | 2.86 | 700 | 0.0 | 800 | 0.0 | 1,000 | 0.0 |
| Marginal Protestants | 0 | 0.0 | 500 | 0.0 | 20 | 10 | 30 | 4.62 | 650 | 0.0 | 800 | 0.0 | 2,000 | 0.0 |
| Jews | 156,000 | 3.0 | 31,100 | 0.2 | −1,610 | 0 | −1,610 | −8.05 | 20,000 | 0.1 | 15,000 | 0.1 | 5,000 | 0.0 |
| Non-religious | 1,000 | 0.0 | 3,000 | 0.0 | 120 | 80 | 200 | 5.00 | 4,000 | 0.0 | 5,000 | 0.0 | 10,000 | 0.0 |
| Baha'is | 0 | 0.0 | 2,200 | 0.0 | 81 | 19 | 100 | 3.70 | 2,700 | 0.0 | 3,200 | 0.0 | 6,000 | 0.0 |
| Atheists | 0 | 0.0 | 1,200 | 0.0 | 45 | 15 | 60 | 4.00 | 1,500 | 0.0 | 1,800 | 0.0 | 3,000 | 0.0 |
| Country's population | 5,200,000 | 100.0 | 15,126,000 | 100.0 | 525,800 | 0 | 525,800 | 3.00 | 17,504,000 | 100.0 | 20,384,000 | 100.0 | 35,904,000 | 100.0 |

COLUMNS, ROWS. For meanings and definitions, see Code-book (Part 6). Note that, by definition, total 'Christians' = professing + crypto-Christians, which also = affiliated + nominal Christians. Percentages may not always total exactly, due to rounding.
CENSUSES. 31.XII.1950–15.IV.–1951.IV.1952 (excluding military personnel): 92.8% Muslims, 4.9% Christians, 2.3% Jews. 18.VI.1960: 95.2% Moroccan Muslims, 1.4% Moroccan Jews (160,000 persons), 3.4% 'others' (Christians, alien Jews and alien Muslims). 20.VII.1971 (de jure): 99.1% Muslims, 0.7% 'unknown' (111,909 persons, mainly Christians), 0.2% Jews (31,119 persons).

NOTES ON RELIGIONS
ARAB INDIGENOUS. Isolated Moroccan radio and correspon-dence course believers (see Table 2).
ATHEISTS. Moroccan Communist Party (MCP) (outlawed 1959), now Party of Liberation and Socialism (PLS) (banned 1969): membership 500 (1968) declining to 300 (1971). A number of intellectuals however are atheists, as well as many French expatriates.
BAHA'IS. Severe persecution since 1962. Local spiritual assemb-lies: 10 (1964), 13 (1973). Many Baha'is are Berbers.
COUNTRY'S POPULATION. After France declared Morocco a protectorate in 1912, French and Spanish settlers arrived in growing numbers. At Independence in 1956 they numbered 500,000, mostly Roman Catholics; most then left for Europe or (Jews) for Israel. In the 1970s, some 240,000 Moroccans lived in Europe (France, Belgium, Germany, Netherlands) as migrant workers, mostly from the Atlas, Rif and Tafilalt regions.
CRYPTO-CHRISTIANS. Christians affiliated to churches but not known to the state or recorded in censuses, of 3 kinds: (a) a few hundred Moroccan nationals in the recognized churches (in 1973, 500 Catholics and 200 Protestants) who have been baptized but are not allowed to practise their faith openly, (b) expatriates in the churches who prefer not to be publicly known as Christians, and (c) isolated radio and correspondence course believers.
JEWS. Maghreb Jews. Decline from 250,000 in 1952 (2.7% of the population), and 160,000 in 1960 (1.4%), due to emigration to Israel. Most are urban, descendants of Sefardic Jews from Spain and Portugal. There are several ancient Berber-speaking groups, and Arabic-speaking communities.
MUSLIMS. Sunnis (of the Malikite rite). Sufi brotherhoods remain strong, including Qadiriya and Kattaniya. *Hajj pilgrims to Mecca.* (1968) 8,208; (1969) 10,943, (1970) 10,640; (1971) 15,463; (1972) 22,425; (1973) 14,923; (1974) 26,632; (1975) 16,176; (1976) 15,044.
*Attitude polls.* University students self-description (1966): 5% very religious, 53% rather religious, 23% slightly religious, 18% not religious; 67% practise fast of Ramadan strictly, 9% most of time, 9% when required to, 5% rarely, 10% never; 10% pray every day, 8% at least once a week, 42% rarely, 40% never. *Missionaries.* There are a number of Egyptians sent by Al-Azhar University (Cairo).
NON-RELIGIOUS. French, also some Arab intellectuals.
PRACTISING CHRISTIANS. Weekly attenders, 15% of all Christians; annual attenders about 62%.
ROMAN CATHOLICS. In the year 1900, all French and Spanish except 6,260 indigenous Catholics.

## NON-CHRISTIAN RELIGIONS.

**Islam** is the state religion and, with a few exceptions, Moroccans are Sunnis almost all of the Malikite rite. The islamization of the country has been profound, including the Berbers, although in the exercise of religion Berbers often depart from Muslim orthodoxy. There are only a few small dissident sects; but the Sufi brotherhoods and religious congregations remain strong, as was evident during the nationalist revival which led to Independence in 1956. The most important national leader at that time was Allal El-Fassi, the Moroccan representative of the Maghribian Salafiya, a reformist movement advocating a return to Islamic sources, the purification of maraboutistic distortions and the integration of Islamic religion with the forces of modern progress. As a whole, however, Islam has made little accommodation to the secular forces which are increasingly evident in Moroccan life. If the majority of youth still submit to collective religious obligations, a minority, especially among intellectuals and in the cities, call in question the very foundations of Islam.

Two universities are dedicated exclusively to Arabic and Islamic studies: the Université Ben Youssef at Marrakech with more than 1,000 students; and the Université al-Qarawiyin at Rabat, Fez and Marrakech with 400 students. The latter institution was founded in AD 859 and has faculties of Quranic law, theology, Arabic language and literature; an Institute of Islamic Studies; and offers a master's degree in the study of the Quran.

**Judaism** was represented in 1971 by about 30,000 persons as contrasted with 250,000 in 1952, most of whom subsequently emigrated to Israel. Jews have virtually disappeared from the rural areas, and in the cities they are progressively losing their identity as organized groups.

**Baha'i** has a small number of followers but they have been severely persecuted and imprisoned since 1962.

## CHRISTIANITY

CATHOLIC CHURCH. By the end of the 2nd century AD, 4 bishoprics had been established in the Tangier-Rabat-Fez triangle, but in the centuries which followed the church suffered successively from the Diocletian persecution, the Donatist schism, the Arian vandal invasion and finally the triumph of Islam throughout North Africa. A new missionary effort was begun by Franciscans in 1220, and in 1234 the diocese of Marrakech was formed. The diocese was suppressed in 1566; and in spite of attempts by Capuchins in 1624 and Andalusian Franciscans in 1639, the church remained weak. In 1822 there was only one Catholic priest resident in the country, at Tangiers. Nevertheless, a new start was made in 1859 with the creation of the prefecture of Morocco, which was made a vicariate in 1908. In 1923 the vicariate of Rabat was established, becoming an archdiocese in 1955.

The Catholic population, mostly French and Spanish at the time of the protectorate, has tended since Independence to become more diversified as other nations have developed co-operative relations with Morocco. Numbering 420,000 in 1955, Catholics declined to 100,000 in 1970, of whom some 40,000 were adults over 15 years. According to a survey made in Rabat in 1970, between 12% and 15% of adult Catholics participate regularly in Sunday mass.

The positive attitude of Christian leaders, notably Catholics, towards the movement which led to national independence in 1956 has undoubtedly helped the churches. Nevertheless, one cannot speak of any significant influence exercised by them in the country, either as institutions or by means of their doctrine and teaching. The churches, and especially the Catholic Church, tend to reduce to a minimum only outward manifestations which call attention to their presence. Moreover, during the past 6 years, numerous Catholic places of worship have been secularized or closed as expatriate Catholics have left the country.

OTHER CHURCHES. The Bible Churchmen's Missionary Society has had the largest church work in Morocco, beginning in the central area in 1929 as part of the Anglican diocese of Sierra Leone. In 1968 the government closed down 3 stations, but 5 others remain open. Anglicans in Morocco are virtually all expatriates, their first chaplaincy work dating from the British occupation of Tangiers in 1662.

Eastern Orthodox are also expatriates and are divided into a Russian Orthodox congregation in Rabat under the Moscow Patriarchate, a White Russian congregation in Casablanca opposed to the Moscow Patriarchate and 4 Greek Orthodox communities under the Patriarchate of Alexandria.

The first Protestants were from the North Africa Mission which entered Morocco in 1884, establishing the widely-known Tullock Memorial Hospital and Nurses Training School in Tangiers. In 1959 the NAM merged with the Southern Morocco Mission, a Scottish society. These missions have always given special emphasis to health care, 7 of their 9 centres being devoted to medical work. Attention has recently been given to Bible correspondence courses and radio broadcasts from Marseilles, France. Missionaries of 2 Protestant groups were expelled in the late 1960s, those of the Gospel Missionary Union and the Emmanuel Mission Sahara, which had been in the country respectively since 1894 and 1926. The GMU was at the time engaged in a successful Bible correspondence course programme which it then continued to operate from Malaga, Spain, in addition to radio broadcasts from Monaco. Nevertheless, Moroccans originally associated with these missions continue to remain Christians.

The largest Protestant denomination at the present time is the Evangelical Church of Morocco (Eglise Evangélique au Maroc) related to the Reformed Church of France, although this consists almost entirely of French citizens involved in technical assistance in the country. A few expatriate American congregations form the Church of Christ composed of USA military personnel.

A large number of other mission bodies and individual missionaries have entered to work in social service or development projects and have gathered small groups of expatriates and Moroccans into loosely-organized Christian communities. In spite of legal prohibitions against Moroccans becoming Christians, it is estimated that there are now approxi-mately 500 indigenous Protestant Christians of all denominations, some 200 of whom have openly manifested their religious allegiance through public baptism.

**Muslims.** Muslim holy city of Chauen, at foot of Mount Kala y el Magot.

*Above.* Rif women, Berbers from Targuist, singing song of the Rif. *Below.* Shluh men of Tamawar dancing the Haha.

**Isolated radio believers.** A radio convert through ELWA broadcasts in Arabic from Liberia, Efa (above) began a radio church in his home. Over 110,000 such persons in Morocco have enrolled in radio or mail correspondence courses.

long as their activities are confined to serving strictly the religious needs of their essentially expatriate members. Authority granted to the churches to administer their various properties is part of the common right of every group or association, each in its capacity as a moral person. However, proselytism is outlawed, and conversion from Islam to Christianity is prohibited by law. In September 1974, a missionary couple of the North Africa Mission received a 6-month prison sentence for allegedly 'bribing' 2 Moroccan youth to convert to Christianity. While pending appeal in June 1975 they were suddenly expelled from the country. Later during 1975 a baptized Moroccan Christian, Mustapha Jabiri, was given a 6-month prison term for breaking the Muslim fast of Ramadan, an action which discouraged other Moroccan believers from openly acknowledging their faith.

**INTERDENOMINATIONAL ORGANIZATIONS.** Catholics, Protestants, Orthodox and Anglicans have been members of an informal ecumenical council in Casablanca and have engaged in co-operative relief and development projects through the Ecumenical Interchurch-Aid Committee of Morocco (Comité Oecuménique d'Entr'aide au Maroc, COEM). In 1977 this relationship was formalized with the formation of the Morocco Council of Christian Churches, with 5 members. There is also an ecumenical group called the College Oecuménique au Maroc which provides for dialogue between the Christian, Muslim and Jewish communities.

**BROADCASTING.** No religious broadcasting is allowed except for Muslim material, and all stations are government-owned except for Voice of America transmitters. The foreign international station ELWA (Liberia) has a substantial audience in Morocco for their 2 hours of Arabic programmes a week. Trans World Radio (Monaco) has 4 hours weekly in Arabic and a 15-minute programme in Berber every Friday evening for the 7 million Berber-speaking peoples of Morocco. Radio Vatican transmits 3.5 hours of programmes each week in Arabic.

**CHURCH AND STATE.** The Alawite dynasty has ruled Morocco since the 17th century, its rulers having combined the role of political monarch with that of supreme chief in the religious domain. At the present time the Moroccan state is founded on the following 3 attributes of its head of state: (1) sharif, which confers on him a special legitimacy because of his being a descendant of the prophet Mohammed's family; (2) king, a title used since 1956 in place of the traditional appellation, sultan; (3) commander of the faithful (Amir al-Muminin), or caliph, because he is the heir of the prestigious historical caliphates of Cordoba, an Arab dynasty, and Marrakech, a Berber dynasty. The king's authority derives from the holy character of his person, which is described in the constitution of 1972 (Article 23) as 'inviolable and sacred'. Article 19 reads: 'The King, Commander of the Faithful, supreme representative of the nation, symbol of its

unity, guarantor of the perpetuation and continuity of the state, insures that Islam and the constitution are properly respected'. Finally, Article 6 of the constitutional text of 1972 establishes, in a manner similar to the earlier constitutions of 1962 and 1970, that 'Islam is the religion of the state which guarantees to all the free exercise of religion'.

The government is moreover dedicated to the preservation of Islam. As one instance, the practice of Ramadan enters into the Penal Code (Article 222); as another, Muslim prayers in primary and secondary schools have been obligatory since 1966. In October 1968, king Hassan II inaugurated a campaign in favour of Quranic schools. A few months later, he invited Moroccan women to create a National Union, one of whose objects would be 'the advancement of women within the limits of Quranic tradition'. Apart from Islam, other confessions receive no legal recognition but are in fact tolerated by the state so

**BIBLIOGRAPHY**
*Baal, Christ and Mohammed: religion and revolution in North Africa.* J.K. Cooley. New York: Holt, Rinehart & Winston, 1965. 369p.
'Chrétienté et Islam au Maroc (du XVIe à XXe siècle)', G. Matringe, *Revue historique de droit français et étranger,* IV (43), 588–643.
'Eglises chrétiennes en terre d'Islam: essai sur la liberté de culte et la pratique religieuse au Maroc depuis le XIIe siècle', G. Matringe, in *Etudes d'histoire de droit canonique dédiées à Gabriel le Bras* (Paris, 1965), p. 341–349.
*Extinction of the Christian Churches in North Africa.* L.R. Holme. New York: Burt Franklin, 1969.
*La Archdiocesis de Tanger: Anuario 1970.* Tanger: Curia Pastoral, 1970.
'Maghribi brotherhoods'. K.L. Brown. Paper presented at the annual meeting of the American Historical Association, New York, 1968. (Mimeographed).
*Saints of the Atlas.* E. Gellner. London: Weidenfeld & Nicolson, 1969. 317p. (Charismatic Muslim leaders in holy villages among the contemporary Berbers (Rif, Tamazigt, Tashlehait) of the High Atlas).

TABLE 2.    ORGANIZED CHURCHES AND DENOMINATIONS IN MOROCCO

| Official name<br>1 | Begun<br>2 | Type<br>3 | Counc<br>4 | Congs<br>5 | Adults<br>6 | Affiliated<br>7 | Names, notes, and other statistics (see Codebook)<br>8 |
|---|---|---|---|---|---|---|---|
| Assemblées de Dieu | 1945 | P Pe2 | z.... | 1 | 30 | 50 | M=Swedish Free Mission (Sweden),NPM(Norway). Based on Tangiers, radio work. |
| Eglise Adventiste du Septième Jour | 1928 | P Adv | x.... | 2 | 20 | 50 | *Seventh-day Adventists,* in NAfrican M, Euro-Africa Division. Some work in south. |
| Eglise Anglicane (J NCentral Europe) | 1662 | A Cen | av.UK | 5 | 100 | 600 | Till 1974 in D Egypt. English chaplaincies; M=CMJ(1832), BCMS(1929). 9f. |
| Eglise Catholique au Maroc: | 1220 | R Lat | pzSHK | 86 | 56,000 | 100,000 | *Catholic Ch.* French and Spanish. C=11+3+28. W=15%.  167x,59m,690w,P=52%,1916Yy. |
| AD  Rabat | 1923 | R Lat | pofm | 67 | 45,000 | 80,000 | Emigration. French-speaking. C=8+2+21. 1s(closed).  120 27 500  54  1724 |
| AD  Tanger (Tangiers) | 1630 | R Lat | pofm | 19 | 11,000 | 20,000 | *Arquidiocesis (Iglesia Católica).* Spanish. C=3+1+7.  47 32 190  45  192 |
| Eglise Chrétienne de Réveil | | P Pen | ..... | 2 | 20 | 50 | *Christian Revival Ch.* In Casablanca and Rabat. Foreigners, 4 Moroccans. 1x. |
| Eglise du Christ | | P Dis | x.... | 2 | 50 | 100 | *Ch of Christ.* M=CC(Non-Instrumental)(USA). Tangiers, Kenitra. USA naval personnel. |
| Eglise Emmanuel | 1926 | P Hol | x.... | 6 | 200 | 300 | *Emmanuel Holiness Ch. Sahara Mission.* M=EHC(UK) until banned 1968. Meknes. 8f. |
| Eglise Evangélique au Maroc | 1910 | P Ref | R,A,K | 11 | 2,000 | 3,000 | *EEAM. Ev Ch.* In Reformed Ch of France until 1958. All French. 3x,W=20%,5Y,20y. |
| Eglise Orthodox Belorusse | | O Sla | ..... | 1 | 80 | 150 | *Russian Orthodox Ch.* White Russian refugee congregation in Casablanca. |
| Eglise Orthodox Grecque | | O Ara | Cv.NK | 4 | 400 | 600 | *Greek Orthodox Ch.* Under P Alexandria. Half in Casablanca. Arab immigrants. 1x. |
| Eglise Orthodox Russe | | O Sla | Mvc.K | 1 | 80 | 150 | *Russian Orthodox Ch.* Under P Moscow. 1 congregation in Rabat. Russian emigres. |
| Eglise radiophoniques isolées | 1958 | I rad | ..... | 560 | 11,000 | 22,400 | Isolated radio believers, most under 25. R=2300,S=4400,T=110000(RSB,GMU,ICl). |
| Frères Larges | | P CBr | x.... | 3 | 100 | 200 | *Christian Brethren (Open).* M=CMML(UK,USA). Tangiers, Marrakesh. 3f. |
| Mission d'Afrique du Nord | 1884 | P int | xMg.. | 6 | 70 | 150 | M=North Africa M(UK). 70% Moroccans, in legal building. 28f(in secular jobs),1H. |
| Mission Israel | 1950 | P Lut | 1.... | 1 | 20 | 30 | M=Swedish Israel Mission. Small group in Casablanca for Hebrew Christians. |
| Témoins de Jéhovah | c1950 | M Jeh | x.... | 5 | 213 | 500 | *Jehovah's Witnesses.* Active witnessing under way by 1952. All foreigners. 37Y. |
| Union Evangélique Missionnaire | 1894 | P Hol | xM... | 5 | 30 | 50 | M=Gospel Missionary Union(USA). 50 Moroccans. Radio courses. Banned 1969. 4f. |
| Other Protestant denominations | | P | ..... | | 700 | 1,200 | Total about 10 (seee list below). |
| **Total affiliated (mid-1970)** | | | | 725 | 71,113 | 129,580 | Total denominations (1970) ...  27. |
| **Total affiliated (mid-1975)** | | | | 735 | 63,500 | 115,700 | Total denominations (1975) ...  29. |
| **Total affiliated (mid-1980)** | | | | 750 | 56,100 | 102,300 | Total denominations (1980) ...  31. |

**NOTES ON TABLE ABOVE**
COLUMNS: for meanings and CODES (cols. 1, 3, 4, 8): see Codebook (Part 6). Column 1: **Boldface** type = church with over 10% of country's affiliated Christians.
NATIONAL COUNCILS (Column 4, 5th letter).
  K = Conseil des Eglises Chrétiennes au Maroc (Morocco Council of Christian Churches), formed 1977, formerly

Comité Oecuménique d'Entr'aide au Maroc (COEM) (Ecumenical Interchurch-Aid Committee of Morocco).
OTHER PROTESTANT DENOMINATIONS. These consist of (1) small para-denominations begun by foreign mission bodies but now with few or no followers, including: Action Biblique de Genève, Berean Mission (1966, among Berbers), Ch of the Brethren (1959), Fellowship of Independent Missions (1950;

formerly Morocco Evangelistic Fellowship), Light of Africa Mission, Mennonite Central Committee (1958), Southern Baptist Convention (1966, Rabat), Swedish Church Seamen's Mission; and (2) USA military chaplaincies among 1,000 USA servicemen and dependants.

**PEOPLES** (ethnolinguistic). Christians: 76.6% French, 18.0% Spaniard, 5.4% Moroccan Arab, other Arab, Russian, Byelorussian, USA White, British.

COUNTRY-WIDE TOTALS
EVANGELIZATION (see Part 5). 1900: 9%. 1970: 28%. 1980: 35%. *Radiophonic evangelism*. Annual listeners' letters (1975): 2,300 (TWR, RSB, et alia). Bible correspondence courses: 110,000 enrolments (70,000 GMU, 2,518 RSB, 2,000 ICI, et alia).
FOREIGN MISSIONARIES AND PERSONNEL (aliens from abroad) (1973). Total 928. *From Western world*. 891: about 800 Roman Catholics, 82 Protestants (46 in 8 USA societies, 25 in 2 UK societies, 6 in 1 Switzerland society, 3 in 1 France society, 2 in 1 Canada society), 9 Anglicans in 1 UK society. *From Communist world*. 4 Roman Catholics from Poland. *From Third World*. 33: about 30 Roman Catholic Arabs (including 9 sisters from Lebanon), 2 Protestants (Baptists), 1 Orthodox.
INSTITUTIONS (church-operated) (1973). Total 50, including 32 higher schools, about 10 medical centres, 3 religious communities.
PERIODICALS. About 15 titles.
PERSONNEL. About 1,031 (103 national, 928 foreign).
RELIGIOUS LIBRARIES. 4.
SCRIPTURE DISTRIBUTION (1975). Annual totals: 850 Bibles (88% subsidized, 12% commercial), 800 NTs (94% subsidized, 6% commercial), 2,900 UBS portions, 1,200 UBS selections. *Translations completed*. Portion: 4 languages since 1887. NT: Arabic in 1932. Bible: Arabic in 1963.
SERVICE AGENCIES. About 31, including ACISJF, ACE, ACO, COEM, ECAM, IBRA, JEC, TWR, YMCA, YWAM.

ADDITIONAL DATA ON CHURCHES
EGLISE CATHOLIQUE AU MAROC. In Arabic, al-Kanissa al-Katholikia. *Catholics*. All expatriates except for 500 nationals (in 1969, AD Tanger listed 173). *Annual baptisms*. (1972) 97.2% infant, 2.8% adult. *Priests*. In 1955 there were 337 priests (93% religious, 60% in parish ministry). *Sisters*. In 1955 there were 850 sisters (55% in medical care). *Catechists*. Total (1963) 2,332, falling by 1975 to under 20. *Main religious orders and congregations* (1970). Priests: OFM. Brothers: (Rabat) 15 FSC, (Tanger) PFM. Sisters: (Rabat) 270 Missionary Franciscans of Mary, 38 Missionaries of Our Lady of the Apostles, 30 Little Sisters of Jesus; (Tanger) 76 Mijas de la Caridad de SVincente de Paul, 47 Franciscanas Misioneras de la Immaculada Concepción. In the city of Rabat also there is a Melkite convent (Nuns of the Annunciation) with liturgy in Arabic.
*Catholic organizations*. Morocco belongs to the Episcopal Conference of North Africa (Conférence Episcopale d'Afrique du Nord) based in Algiers. A Council of Sisters (Conseil des Religieuses) was formed in 1968 for the archdiocese of Rabat, consisting of elected members. The archdiocese of Rabat also possesses a presbyteral council of elected members, founded in 1967, and a pastoral council, founded in 1968, composed of elected and co-opted members of parishes, movements and sectors, who participate actively in planning pastoral work in the diocese. The archdiocese of Tangiers also has presbyteral and pastoral councils. The most active lay movements in the archdiocese of Rabat in 1972 were Communauté et Vie Fraternelle (formerly General Catholic Action of Women), ACI, ACO, ACE, JEC, Vie Nouvelle, Enseignants et Coopérants Chrétiens, Fraternités de Foucauld, Fraternités Franciscaines and Conférences de St-Vincent de Paul. In the archdiocese of Tangier, in 1971 3 groups were predominant: Cursillos de Cristiandad, Fe Católica, and Conferencia de San Vicente de Paul.
The Holy See has no diplomatic relations with Morocco. It is represented to the Catholic hierachy by an apostolic delegate based in Algiers.
Catholic schools total about 15,000 students in 44 establishments, out of a total school population of 2 million. Except at the pre-primary level, where Catholics cater for more than half the total, and to a lesser extent in professional instruction which is designed to prepare students for entrance into such government courses as nursing, home economics and art for girls, carpentry and agriculture for boys, Catholic education does not reach beyond 1% of Morocco's student body. Catholic instruction is officially recognized. About 90% of its students and 30% of its teachers are Moroccans. One-third of its schools still follow the French system closely, although there is now a rapid evolution towards the adoption of programmes which are more typically Moroccan. Nuns engaging in medical work, 55% of the total, are mostly integrated into the public sector, there being only a few Catholic hostels and dispensaries.
MISSION D'AFRIQUE DU NORD (North Africa Mission). The church in Casablanca was in 1973 the only one in Morocco where Moroccan converts could legally meet. NAM missionaries all work in secular developmental jobs; occasionally (as in 1975) one or 2 missionary families are identified and deported.

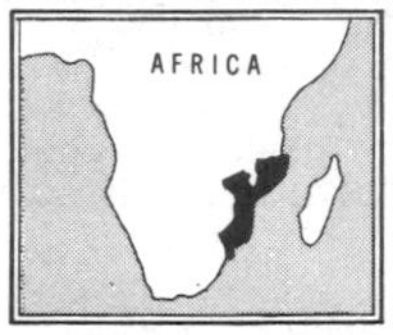


# MOZAMBIQUE

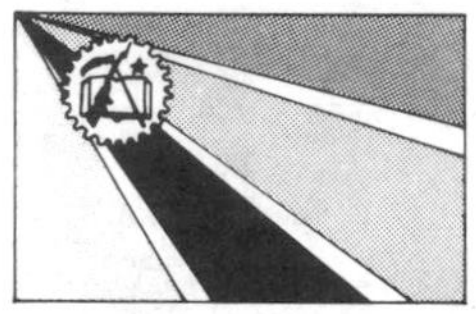

## SECULAR DATA

**STATE. Official name:** The People's Republic of Mozambique (A República de Moçambique). Adjective of nationality: Mozambican.
**Flag** (shown above right): Four triangles separated by white wedges (from hoist upwards: yellow, black, red, green); emblem representing motto 'Study, Produce, Struggle'.
**Area:** 783,030 sq.km. (302,330 sq.miles). Agricultural land: 60.1%.
**Government:** One-party Marxist state, since 1975 (1505 Portuguese possession, 1952 overseas province of Portugal, 1975 Independence).
**Legislature:** Legislative Assembly, 50 members.
**Official language:** Portuguese (*Português*).
**Chief cities:** capital Maputo 383,770 (1970), Beira 115,000.
**Political divisions** (1975): 9 Districts.
**Armed forces** (1976): Total 10,000.
**Foreign forces:** From 1964–74, 70,000 Portuguese troops fought FRELIMO forces. From 1977, Cuban and Russian military personnel.

**DEMOGRAPHY. Population:** 8,233,978 (census of 15.XII.1970. For 1970–2000 (UN), see last row of Table 1). Population density (1975): 12/sq.km. (31/sq.mile). Under 15 years: 39%. Growth rate (1975–80): 2.32% per year (births 4.13%, deaths −1.82%). Life expectancy (1975–80): 46.0 years. Household size: 4.9 persons.
**Major languages:** Portuguese, Makua, Tsonga, Lomwe, Karanga, Chopi, Ronga, Sena, Shona, Ndau (Chishanga), Chewa (Nyanja), Makonde, Yao, and about 20 smaller languages.
**Urban dwellers** (1970): 5.7%. Urban growth rate (1950–70): 5.9% per year.
**Labour force:** 35%.
**Refugees** (1977): From abroad 69,000 (34,000 from Malawi, 35,000 from Zimbabwe). Exiles abroad: 150,000 in Portugal.

**ETHNOLINGUISTIC GROUPS:** 31.6% Makua, 14.7% Ronga, 11.9% Sena, 9.6% Tsonga, 8.6% Lomwe, 7.4% Shona (Ndau, Manyika, Karanga), 4.0% Chopi, 3.3% Portuguese (1970, declining to 30,000 by mid-1976), 2.7% Nyanja, 2.3% Makonde, 2.0% Yao, 0.7% Borore, 0.4% Mestiço (30,000), 0.2% Angoni, 0.2% Indian (15,000), Chinese (3,000), Chuabo, Swahili, Swazi, Zulu, Pakistani, Goanese, Jewish, and numerous smaller tribes; also (1977) Cuban (600 military, 150 civilian), Russian. In 1977 the regime expelled tens of thousands of Indians and Mestiços and most of the remaining Chinese.

**MONEY** (1977). **Monetary unit:** escudo (= 100 centavos); US$1 = MEsc 31.00.
**National income per person:** US$300. Average annual family income: US$1,470.
**Inflation:** (1970–74) 12.3% per year (1975: consumer price index 166).
**Cost of living in capital** (1976): index 124 (Washington DC=100). Daily cost of living: US$32.

**HEALTH.** Hospitals: 989 (13,102 beds). Doctors: 510. Lepers: 11,000 (12.0 per 1,000). Blind: 28,000. Psychotics: 70,000.

**EDUCATION.** Adult literacy: (1950) 2%, (1962) 11%, (1975) 21%. Education rate: 12%. Schools: 4,274.

**LITERATURE.** Periodicals: 40. Newspapers: 4 dailies, 7 non-daily.

**COMMUNICATION** (per 1,000 people). Phones: 6. Radios: 13 TV sets: 1. Daily newspaper circulation: 5 copies.

TABLE 1. RELIGIOUS ADHERENTS IN MOZAMBIQUE

| Year | 1900 | | mid-1970 | | Annual change, 1970–1980 | | | | mid-1975 | | mid-1980 | | 2000 | |
|---|---|---|---|---|---|---|---|---|---|---|---|---|---|---|
| *Name* | *Adherents* | *%* | *Adherents* | *%* | *Natural* | *Conversion* | *Total* | *Rate* | *Adherents* | *%* | *Adherents* | *%* | *Adherents* | *%* |
| Tribal religionists | 2,504,900 | 96.4 | 4,757,300 | 57.8 | 112,292 | −91,652 | 20,640 | 0.43 | 4,832,300 | 52.3 | 4,963,700 | 47.8 | **6,197,000** | **35.1** |
| **Christians** | **16,700** | **0.6** | **2,459,000** | **29.9** | **74,721** | **82,969** | **157,690** | **4.89** | **3,224,400** | **34.9** | **4,035,900** | **38.9** | **8,825,000** | **50.0** |
| professing | 16,700 | 0.6 | 2,459,000 | 29.9 | 74,721 | 82,969 | 157,690 | 4.89 | 3,224,400 | 34.9 | 4,035,900 | 38.9 | 8,825,000 | 50.0 |
| Roman Catholics | 15,000 | 0.6 | 1,979,000 | 24.0 | 60,462 | 67,218 | 127,680 | 4.90 | 2,607,100 | 28.2 | 3,255,800 | 31.4 | 7,075,000 | 40.1 |
| Protestants | 1,500 | 0.0 | 428,000 | 5.2 | 12,845 | 14,905 | 27,750 | 5.01 | 554,300 | 6.0 | 705,500 | 6.8 | 1,588,000 | 9.1 |
| Anglicans | 200 | 0.0 | 50,000 | 0.6 | 1,414 | 846 | 2,260 | 3.70 | 61,000 | 0.7 | 72,600 | 0.7 | 159,000 | 0.9 |
| Orthodox | 0 | 0.0 | 2,000 | 0.0 | 0 | 0 | 0 | 0.00 | 2,000 | 0.0 | 2,000 | 0.0 | 3,000 | 0.0 |
| nominal | 3,400 | 0.1 | 428,844 | 5.2 | 11,562 | −3,607 | 7,955 | 1.59 | 498,900 | 5.4 | 508,400 | 4.9 | 353,000 | 2.0 |
| affiliated | 13,300 | 0.5 | 2,030,156 | 24.6 | 63,159 | 86,576 | 149,735 | 5.49 | 2,725,500 | 29.5 | 3,527,500 | 34.0 | 8,472,000 | 48.0 |
| total practising | 12,630 | *95* | 1,624,120 | *80* | 49,264 | 56,414 | 105,678 | 4.97 | 2,125,890 | *78* | 2,680,900 | *76* | 5,506,800 | *65* |
| non-practising | 670 | *5* | 406,030 | *20* | 13,895 | 30,162 | 44,057 | 7.35 | 599,610 | *22* | 846,600 | *24* | 2,965,200 | *35* |
| Roman Catholics | 12,000 | 0.5 | 1,552,723 | 18.9 | 49,940 | 77,858 | 127,798 | 5.94 | 2,153,100 | 23.3 | 2,830,700 | 27.3 | 6,723,000 | 38.1 |
| Protestants | 1,000 | 0.0 | 349,133 | 4.2 | 9,636 | 5,251 | 14,887 | 3.58 | 415,800 | 4.5 | 498,000 | 4.8 | 1,235,000 | 7.0 |
| Evangelicals | 800 | 0.0 | 329,000 | 4.0 | 9,077 | 4,943 | 14,020 | 3.58 | 391,700 | 4.2 | 469,200 | 4.5 | 1,163,500 | 6.6 |
| Anglicans | 200 | 0.0 | 45,000 | 0.5 | 1,228 | 492 | 1,720 | 3.25 | 53,000 | 0.6 | 62,200 | 0.6 | 141,000 | 0.8 |
| Marginal Protestants | 0 | 0.0 | 45,000 | 0.5 | 1,284 | 1,476 | 2,760 | 4.98 | 55,400 | 0.6 | 72,600 | 0.7 | 194,000 | 1.1 |
| African indigenous | 100 | 0.0 | 36,300 | 0.4 | 1,071 | 1,499 | 2,570 | 5.56 | 46,200 | 0.5 | 62,000 | 0.6 | 176,000 | 1.0 |
| Orthodox | 0 | 0.0 | 2,000 | 0.0 | 0 | 0 | 0 | 0.00 | 2,000 | 0.0 | 2,000 | 0.0 | 3,000 | 0.0 |
| Muslims | 78,300 | 3.0 | 1,005,000 | 12.2 | 26,974 | 7,426 | 34,400 | 2.96 | 1,164,000 | 12.6 | 1,349,000 | 13.0 | 2,471,000 | 14.0 |
| Hindus | 0 | 0.0 | 6,500 | 0.1 | −150 | 0 | −150 | −2 50 | 6,000 | 0.1 | 5,000 | 0.0 | 3,000 | 0.0 |
| Non-religious | 0 | 0.0 | 5,000 | 0.1 | 162 | 538 | 700 | 10.00 | 7,000 | 0.1 | 12,000 | 0.1 | 100,000 | 0.6 |
| Baha'is | 0 | 0.0 | 1,000 | 0.0 | 28 | 12 | 40 | 3.33 | 1,200 | 0.0 | 1,400 | 0.0 | 3,000 | 0.0 |
| Jews | 100 | 0.0 | 200 | 0.0 | −20 | 0 | −20 | −20.00 | 100 | 0.0 | 0 | 0.0 | 0 | 0.0 |
| Atheists | 0 | 0.0 | 0 | 0.0 | 93 | 707 | 800 | 20.00 | 4,000 | 0.0 | 8,000 | 0.1 | 50,000 | 0.3 |
| **Country's population** | **2,600,000** | **100.0** | **8,234,000** | **100.0** | **214,100** | **0** | **214,100** | **2.32** | **9,239,000** | **100.0** | **10,375,000** | **100.0** | **17,649,000** | **100.0** |

COLUMNS, ROWS. For meanings and definitions, see Codebook (Part 6). Note that, by definition, total 'Christians' = professing + crypto-Christians, which also = affiliated + nominal Christians. Percentages may not always total exactly, due to rounding.
CENSUSES. **21.X.1950** (de jure): 81.3% tribal religionists, 10.7% Muslims, 6.2% Roman Catholics, 1.7% Protestants & Anglicans, 0.1% Hindus, 0.1% non-religious. **21.IX.1950** (civilized population only, 91,954 total): 71.8% Roman Catholics, 24.9% non-Christians (Muslims, Hindus, also non-religious), 3.3% Protestants. **1955** (non-Africans only, 117,405 total): 73.0% Roman Catholics, 13.9% Muslims, 4.0% Hindus, 3.3% Protestants, 5.6% non-religious and other religionists.

NOTES ON RELIGIONS
AFRICAN INDIGENOUS. In around 100 denominations in 1970 (see Table 2).
ATHEISTS. In February 1977, the broad Liberation movement FRELIMO (Frente de Libertação de Moçambique) was changed to become a Marxist-Leninist party, cancelling existing membership lists and reducing membership to a revolutionary core of about 5,000.
BAHA'IS. In 1973, in 7 local spiritual assemblies.
COUNTRY'S POPULATION. Portuguese settlers and their families, who numbered 250,000 at the time of the April 1974 coup in Portugal, then rapidly decreased by emigration, as also did Asian traders. By April 1976, only 50,000 remained; by mid-1976, only 30,000. The column 'Natural change' above includes this emigration which was spread in varying degrees over the whole range of churches and religions.
HINDUS. Indians, numbering 4,731 at the 1955 census. After 1965, a number were emigrating; these are incorporated in the column 'Natural change' above.
MUSLIMS. Sunnis (of the Shafiite rite). Mainly among the Yao (80%), Makonde (43%), Makua (18%), in the northern districts of Delgado, Moçambique, Niassa and Zambezia. In 1955, there were also 16,348 Muslim Indo-Pakistanis and others from the Comoro Islands and Mauritius. *Hajj pilgrims to Mecca*. (1976) 47.
NOMINAL CHRISTIANS. Under Portuguese rule until 1975, many Africans professed to be Christians in censuses, although not yet affiliated to churches, thus forming part of a sizeable nominal fringe. After 1975 this fringe rapidly decreased in size.
NON-RELIGIOUS. As in Portugal itself, in 1970 about 2% of the 250,000 Portuguese settlers were non-religious; so were numbers of the Chinese from Macau. As the Portuguese emigrated, workers from the People's Republic of China arrived, most being non-religious.
ROMAN CATHOLICS. After experiencing phenomenal numerical growth from 6.2% of the population in 1950 to about 30% in 1970 and 35% in 1975, professing Catholics ceased to grow so rapidly due to the 1974–76 emigration of 250,000 Portuguese, the state's nationalization of all Catholic schools, and the subsequently-increasing government restrictions placed on Catholic missions.
TRIBAL RELIGIONISTS. All tribes north of the Save river were over 70% traditionalist in 1972, except the Yao, Makonde (36%) and Makua (66%). These included: Chuabo (79% animist), Lomwe (79%), Manyika (75%), Ndau (75%), Sena (75%), Chewa (73%), Gomani (73%), Kunda (73%), Majanga (73%), Nsenga (73%), Tawara (73%), and Zimba (73%).

MOZAMBIQUE

## NON-CHRISTIAN RELIGIONS.

**Traditional religions** are followed by more than half the African population. With the exception of 3 tribes (Yao, Makonde and Makua) where Islam is a significant feature, all peoples north of the Save river are at least 70% traditionalist. The most common names for God are Mulungu north of the Zambezi (among the Yao, Nyanja, Chewa) and Tilo (Sky) among the Chopi and Tsonga of southern Mozambique. The Tsonga do not attribute creation to Tilo, but they insist that he is responsible for such celestial phenomena as thunder and lightning, as well as death. Rain on the other hand is given or withheld by the Psikwembu, the ancestral spirits, who must be placated in time of drought. Part of the rain-making rite is a purification ceremony, *mbelele*, administered by women. Revitalization movements playing an important role during the 20th century include the Murimi of 1915 and Mchape of 1934. The former was a cult of the supreme being Mwirimi (in Hlengwe) who was believed to possess the movement's prophets. Beginning among the Hlengwe, it spread south, the immediate cause being a severe famine in the area between 1913 and 1915. It ultimately took on the characteristics of a witchcraft eradication campaign, the active cleansing agent being the snuffing of tobacco. Mchape (Medicine), another witchcraft eradication movement, began in Nyasaland and spread quickly to Tanganyika, Northern and Southern Rhodesia and among the Ndau of Mozambique, although it never became as important in Mozambique as in the other areas. Mchape took the form of water or maize meal doctored with blood, hair and fingernail clippings. Both movements were suppressed by the Portuguese authorities.

**Islam** has a long history in Mozambique. Arab and Persian traders reached the northern coast about AD 1000; and until the arrival of the Portuguese, the coastal area was controlled by Muslim sultans centred on Zanzibar. The Yao, who inhabit the region east of Lake Malawi, are 80% islamized, the only interior tribe below the equator to experience such a mass conversion to Islam. This is explained by their role as traders between the lake and Kilwa since the 19th century. The northern Makonde are 43% Muslim and the Makua 18% with greatest concentration of Muslims in the coastal area. Islamic influence is also evident along the Zambezi river.

## CHRISTIANITY

CATHOLIC CHURCH. Dominican missionaries arrived in Mozambique as early as 1506 accompanying the advance of Portuguese maritime discoveries. In 1560 came the Jesuits, and during the next century and a half Dominicans, Jesuits and Augustinians were active on the southern coast and in the region of the Zambezi river. This early activity was followed by a period of decline. Sustained work among most of the tribes north of the Save river was not begun until the end of the 19th and early 20th centuries. The northwestern Yao were not reached until 1930.

From a liturgical and catechetical point of view, little effort was made, prior to Independence in 1975, to integrate specifically African religious values into Catholicism. In general the Mozambican Catholic Church still appears as a faithful copy of religion as it is lived and organized in Portugal. The same has been true of the church's leadership, although all this is now changing. In spite of centuries of Portuguese Catholic presence in southern Mozambique, the clergy has been little africanized. Indeed until the coup d'etat of April 1974 in Portugal and the promise of independence for Portugal's colonies which followed, there were no African bishops in

Mozambique. However, since then has come the resignation of the Portuguese archbishop of Maputo (then called Lourenço Marques), who was closely allied with the previous regime; and in December 1974 an African archbishop was appointed. Another indigenous bishop was named to the diocese of Porto Amélia in January 1975. These 2 bishops were consecrated together on 9 March 1975 by the cardinal-prefect of the Congregation for the Evangelization of Peoples who came especially to Maputo for the ceremony. Everything indicates that the africanization of the hierarchy is being rapidly accelerated at the present time.

The war of liberation which began in 1964 took its toll, a number of missions having been abandoned in the northern area of hostilities. Many were established in villages later destroyed by the Portuguese army.

PROTESTANT CHURCHES. Protestant efforts began in 1879 with the arrival of the first American Board missionaries; and although this work was turned over to American Methodists in 1888, there still exists a Congregationalist church dating its origin to 1879. Today United Methodists have a large following in the Inhambane area. Other early Methodist groups include Free Methodists from the USA and Wesleyan Methodists from South Africa. Swiss Presbyterians arrived in 1881 and directed their attention to the Tsonga and Shangaan people northwest of Lourenço Marques.

Following World War I, there was a new missionary upsurge with the entry of Scandinavian Baptists in 1918, International Holiness Mission in 1921, SAGM and Nazarenes in 1922, Seventh-day Adventists in 1933 and 2 Pentecostal bodies from the USA and Canada during the 1930s. The latter group, the Pentecostal Assemblies of God, has now built up the largest Protestant community in Mozambique. The International Holiness work north of Tete has been taken over by Nazarenes who have added this field to the work northeast of Maputo. Baptists are located north of Maputo and Inhambane and Adventists north of the Zambezi among the Lomwe and Chuabo peoples.

In 1962 the Africa Evangelical Fellowship (formerly SAGM) was expelled from Mozambique, but its work among the Lomwe west of Nampula was carried on by its daughter church, the Evangelical Church of Mozambique, with support from the Christian Council of Mozambique. The latter is also responsible for founding the Church of Christ in Manica & Sofala in 1965.

ANGLICAN CHURCH. Although Anglicans exist in the districts of Maputo and Gaza, they exert their greatest influence among the Yao of northwestern Mozambique, the only predominantly Muslim tribe in the country. High Church Anglican missionaries of the UMCA were in fact the Christian pioneers in Yao country. Bishop Steere visited them

in 1875, but it was not until 1893 that a permanent mission station was established at Unango. At the present time there are about twice as many Yao Anglicans as Catholics.

INDIGENOUS CHURCHES. Because of strong government opposition, African indigenous churches have had difficulty in establishing themselves in Mozambique. There exist today over 100 small semi-clandestine bodies, most owing their origin to outside influences. Many have been brought home by Mozambican miners working in South Africa. Several, including the African Apostolic Church of Johane Maranke, have been imported from neighbouring Rhodesia; and the African Methodist Episcopal Church was begun by Blacks from the USA as early as 1883. Several have a purely Mozambican origin, beginning with the Igreja Luso-Africana which split from the Swiss Mission in 1921.

CHURCH AND STATE. Prior to Independence in June 1975, the juridical bases of the relationship of the Catholic Church to the Portuguese government were contained in the Missionary Concordat of 1940 and the Missionary Statute of 1941. By their declarations and acts, the local Catholic hierarchy closely identified the interests of the church with those of the Portuguese state, thereby sanctioning the colonial status quo and remaining silent in the face of injustices perpetrated in the name of 'defence of Christian civilization'. In their pastoral letter of 1970 entitled 'Christian message for ordering right relations in Mozambique' (Mensagem Cristã nas Coordenadas de Moçambique), the bishops noted 'the total absence of racial discrimination in Portuguese laws', condemned 'every kind of guerrilla action *(terrorismo)*' and expressed the wish that social injustices be resolved in a progressive mutual assumption of social, economic and political responsibility.

After 1971, this attitude of the hierarchy was increasingly rejected by European clergy. In May of that year, the 48 White Fathers (natives of 9 Western countries but with none from Portugal) who worked in the dioceses of Beira and Tete withdrew en masse in protest against the identification of the hierarchy with the politics of colonialism. This decision, taken by the general council of the missionary congregation after consultation with the missionaries, was strongly criticized by the Portuguese government and the Episcopal Conference of Mozambique who 'did not believe it to be dictated by an authentic evangelical spirit' and who, on the same occasion, re-emphasized their support of government policy. The exodus of White Fathers had repercussions on other congregations serving in Mozambique, especially those of the Burgos, Consolata and Combonian Fathers, of whom some (including Portuguese) felt constrained to leave the country. Moreover, 4 priests (2 diocesan Portuguese and 2 Spanish IEME), accused of being in contact with Frelimo, were arrested and sentenced to prison in 1972. Only 2 bishops were known for this non-conformist attitude towards Portuguese colonialism; Sebastião Soares Rezenda, former bishop of Beira (died 1967) who courageously defended the rights of Africans (although within the context of integration rather than political independence) and Manuel

**Igreja Anglicana, Diocese de Lebombo.** *Left.* Anglican priest gives Bible teaching at end of sewing class at Mhamauila, Maciene.
**Igreja Católica em Moçambique, Arquidiocese de Maputo.** *Above.* Urban parish church in Maputo.

Vieira Pinto, bishop of Nampula, who was ultimately exiled on 14 April 1974 because of his criticism of the colonial war. About 100 other Catholic missionaries were expelled from Mozambique prior to the coup d'etat in Portugal on 25 April 1974. In addition, many catechists were killed during the hostilities generated by the colonial war.

The Protestant churches had been much more independent than the Catholic Church with respect to the colonial administration, without however serving as any real or effective opposition. This independence, made possible by the absence of privileges, and the educational role of Protestant missions in training an African elite, served indirectly to promote the idea of national emancipation, which explains the attachment of large numbers of Protestants to the liberation movement and the Portuguese police repression of which these churches were often the object, a repression which amounted to religious persecution. Significant elements within Frelimo were of Protestant origin. In 1972 during a police raid that produced several hundred arrests, 31 African Presbyterian leaders were imprisoned, including Zedequias Manganhela and José Sidumo who later died in Machava prison.

Since the coup d'etat of April 1974 in Portugal and especially following Mozambique's Independence on 25 June 1975, a radical change has taken place in church-state relations. On its part, the Catholic Church has made an effort to adjust to the new situation. The episcopal conference, in a pastoral letter of 30 August 1974 entitled 'The Church in an independent Mozambique', expressed its 'profound joy' at the proclamation of the right to independence. Later the Portuguese archbishop of Maputo was replaced by an African in December 1974. In a statement of support for the Mozambique Revolution issued in mid-1975, the Burgos Fathers affirmed: 'We dissociate ourselves from any reactionary and reformist attitude or activity of the Church. In the life of the Church, also, there exists class struggle, often hidden behind a facade of unity. By participating in the revolutionary struggle, we are working for the true unity of the Church, since that unity can only be achieved through the unity of Mankind.' An editorial in the July issue of the Catholic magazine *Nova vida* acknowledged the past errors of the Catholic Church and promised support for the cause of liberation.

For its part the transitional government extended an invitation to return to bishop Manuel Vieira Pinto and other Catholic missionaries who had left in protest against Portuguese policy or been expelled.

Article 19 of the new constitution affirms: 'The People's Republic of Mozambique is a secular State, in which there is an absolute separation between the State and religious organizations. In the People's Republic of Mozambique all activities of religious bodies must conform to the laws of the State.' Article 26 assures to all citizens the same rights and duties 'independent of their colour, race, sex, ethnic origin, place of birth, religion, rank of instruction, social position and profession', with the further proviso that 'all acts with the goal of prejudice, creating divisions or situations of privilege' because of these things 'will be punished by the law'. Article 33 affirms that 'the State guarantees citizens the freedom to practise or not to practise a religion'.

The president of Mozambique, Samora Machel, although from a Free Methodist background, is known for his Marxist sentiments and his attempt to equate religion with superstition, exploitation and divisiveness. Before Independence, in a speech on 4 June 1975, he stated: 'Another factor which divides our people is religion... Therefore, there will be no privileges for any church here in Mozambique. The privileged will be the Mozambican people, and only Frelimo will organize the peoples of Mozambique, no-one else'. Elsewhere, Machel held that 'Religion, and especially Roman Catholicism, contributed enormously towards the cultural and human alienation of the Mozambican, in order to make him into a submissive instrument and the object of exploitation, to smother any manifestation of resistance by appealing to the Christian doctrine of abnegation'. On yet another occasion, before 100,000 people in Maputo's Machava stadium, Machel castigated the Churches for allowing themselves to be ruled from outside Mozambique: Catholics from Rome, Presbyterians from Swizerland and Methodists from America.

Muslims likewise have also been strongly criticized for allegedly allowing themselves to be used by the Portuguese in order to gain material benefits and official recognition.

A major move to reduce the influence of the churches was the nationalization of all educational and social service institutions of the churches, including schools and hospitals. Missionary doctors and teachers wishing to stay were required to sign contracts with government and were in most cases relocated to different areas.

Many missionaries in fact left the country and others were expelled. Three, including 2 Nazarenes and one WEC, were imprisoned and held for trial, though later released. New missionaries are not being sought by churches.

The last of Machel's attacks on the churches was made in a speech on 11 November 1975, Angola's day of independence. Subsequently he has shown a more conciliatory attitude, and on 31 January 1976 received a delegation representing from the Catholic and Protestant churches, and the Christian Council of Mozambique, who sought clarification of the role of the churches in newly-independent Mozambique.

**INTERDENOMINATIONAL ORGANIZATIONS.** The Christian Council of Mozambique (Conselho Cristão de Moçambique), with 8 member churches, was organized in 1944 to implement with church as well as mission representation the work begun by the Evangelical Missionary Association of Mozambique in 1923. In addition to sponsorship of an evangelical newspaper, a youth hostel in Maputo, literature and audio-visual programmes, the CCM has been engaged in evangelistic work in the districts of Manica e Sofala and Zambézia. A direct product of this activity is the Church of Christ in Manica & Sofala. The CCM was also instrumental in the establishment of a united seminary at Ricatla in 1958. Ecumenical affairs for the Catholic episcopal conference are handled by the Episcopal Commission on Ecumenism (Comissão Episcopal do Ecumenismo). Thus far contacts between Anglicans and Catholics have been more cordial than the relations of either of these churches with Protestants.

**BROADCASTING.** Until 1974, as a Portuguese overseas province, Mozambique permitted Catholic broadcasts as in Portugal itself. There has also been a Catholic station Radio Pax in Beira. The South African Broadcasting Corporation controlled the Lourenço Marques Radio and restricted religious broadcasting to 15 minutes a week. After Independence the situation changed radically and no religious broadcasting is permitted now. Programmes can easily be heard, however, over Trans World Radio's station in Swaziland.

## BIBLIOGRAPHY


*Anuário católico de Moçambique, 1971.* R. Dias. Lourenço Marques: Conferência Episcopal de Moçambique, 1971. (1966 edition, 465p.).

'A presença protestante em Moçambique', in J.J. Gonçalves, *Protestantismo em Africa: contribuição para o estudo do protestantismo na Africa Portuguesa* (Lisboa: Junta de Investigações do Ultramar, 1960), p.109–136.

*Historia de Moçambique cristão.* A. Garcia. Lourenço Marques: Diario Grafica, 1969. 208p.

'Le mouvement de mourimi: un réveil au sein de l'animisme thonga', H.A. Junod, *Journal de psychologie normale et pathologique* (Paris), 21, 10 (15 Dec, 1924), 55–69. (Murimi witchfinding movement).

*Missão em Moçambique.* D.E. Nogueira. Vila Gabral, 1970. 480p.

'Mozambique: a church in a socialist state in a time of radical change', *Pro Mundi Vita* (Brussels), Africa Dossier 3 (Jan–Feb, 1977), 1–42.

*Portuguese East Africa: a study of its religious needs.* E. Moreira. London: World Dominion Press, 1936. 104p.

'Seitas religiosas gentilicas de Moçambique', A.I.F. De Freitas. *Estudos ultramarinos* (Lisboa), 1 (1961), 91–122. (Pagan sects).

'The challenge of Mozambique: the unreached five million'. P. Johnstone. Pretoria: Dorothea Mission, 1965. 26p.


TABLE 2. ORGANIZED CHURCHES AND DENOMINATIONS IN MOZAMBIQUE

| Official name 1 | Begun 2 | Type 3 | Counc 4 | Congs 5 | Adults 6 | Affiliated 7 | Names, notes, and other statistics (see Codebook) 8 |
|---|---|---|---|---|---|---|---|
| Assembleias de Deus Pentecostales | 1938 | P Pe2 | ZF... | 400 | 31,000 | 70,000 | *Pentecostal Assemblies of God.* M=PAoC(Canada). HQ Maputo. 385n,4x. |
| Convenção Baptista de Moçambique | 1957 | P Bap | ..... | 12 | 230 | 1,000 | M=CBP,CBB(Brazil). 50% Shangaan, 50% Portuguese. 4n,1f,1p(6),W=65%,26Y. |
| Exército de Salvação | 1916 | P Sal | xwa.. | 5 | 1,000 | 2,000 | *Salvation Army.* Pioneers Bantu miners converts from SAfrica. Organized 1923. Banned. |
| Igreja Adventista do Séptimo Dia | 1933 | P Adv | x.... | 99 | 12,279 | 20,733 | *Seventh-day Adventists, Mozambique UM.* 57% Chuabo. 10n,G=20%pa,1h,1j,1s,W=69%,1270Y. |
| Igreja Africana Metodista Episcopal | 1883 | I Met | Vw... | | 500 | 1,000 | *African Methodist Episcopal Church*, 18th Episcopal District. M=AMEC(USA Blacks). |
| Igreja Anglicana: D Lebombo | 1893 | A ACa | AwaV. | 26 | 5,210 | 45,000 | In CPSA. M=USPG. 30% Nyanja, 20% Shangaan. 30n,3x(2 Brazilian),2H,P=57%,544Y,799y. |
| Igreja Apostólica de Johane Maranke | c1950 | I peA | x.... | | 3,000 | 5,000 | *AACJM.* M=African Apostolic Ch of Johane Maranke(Rhodesia). Shonas. 5 pasakas held. |
| **Igreja Católica em Moçambique:** | 1506 | R Lat | H.SSR | 329 | 947,700 | 1,552,723 | *Catholic Church.* C=15+2+32. 3p,3s(167). 27n,548x,204m,1224w,44591Yy. |
| M Maputo (Lourenço Marques) | 1940 | R Lat | Hs | 77 | 155,200 | 253,519 | Urban. Tsonga majority, 50,000 Europeans in 1974. 6 87 36 404 4311 |
| D Beira | 1940 | R Lat | Hs | 33 | 131,300 | 215,207 | Rural. Commercial, new industries. Shona, Sena. 1p. 3 60 25 197 4170 |
| D Inhambane | 1962 | R Lat | Hs | 25 | 113,700 | 186,381 | Southern coast. Rural. Tsonga, Chopi. 1p. 1 43 14 65 3551 |
| D Lichinga (Vila Cabral) | 1963 | R Lat | Hs | 30 | 43,000 | 70,435 | 80% Makua, 12% Yao, 8% Nyanja. War area until 1975. 3 40 9 74 2093 |
| D Nampula | 1940 | R Lat | Hs | 45 | 151,100 | 247,811 | 95% Makua. Army HQ. Only diocese with D=PC. 1p. 2 92 35 135 8276 |
| D Pemba (Porto Amélia) | 1957 | R Lat | Hs | 23 | 65,100 | 106,754 | 50% Makua, 50% Makonde. 1970s, main guerilla area. 4 44 12 62 2997 |
| D Quelimane | 1954 | R Lat | Hs | 40 | 99,000 | 162,322 | North of Beira. Makua, Sena, Nyanja. 2 94 33 159 10744 |
| D Tete | 1962 | R Lat | Hs | 22 | 59,600 | 97,681 | Maravi, Angoni. Cobara Bassa dam. War area to 1975. 2 50 28 72 4675 |
| D Xai-Xai (João Belo) | 1970 | R Lat | Hs | 34 | 129,700 | 212,613 | Formed from M Maputo. Rural. Predominantly Tsonga. 4 38 12 56 3774 |
| Igreja CCAP | 1913 | P Ref | R.... | | 1,500 | 3,000 | Malawians from CCAP, and their Mozambique missions (formerly Lomweland Mission). |
| Igreja Congregacional Unida de M | 1879 | P Con | Rwa.C | 24 | 3,111 | 7,000 | *Mozambique Region, UCCSA.* M=ABCFM(UCBWM). Tswa, Tsonga, Chopi. 4n,W=98%,40Y,80y. |
| Igreja da Nova Aliança | c1970 | I pe2 | ..... | 46 | 6,000 | 12,000 | *Ch of the New Covenant. Ch of Christ in Zambezi.* Ex AFMSA. 70% Sena, 10% Manyika. |
| Igreja de Cristo em Manica e Sofala | c1965 | P uni | ....C | 25 | 3,000 | 5,000 | *Ch of Christ in M&S.* Joint CCM project, M=UMC,Swiss Mission. HQ Beira. |
| Igreja do Evangelho Completo de Deus | c1931 | P Pe3 | ZF... | 607 | 7,052 | 20,000 | *Assembleias de Deus.* M=FGCoG(SA),AoG(Portugal),CoG(Cleveland)(USA). 724n. |
| Igreja do Nazareno | 1922 | P Hol | xF..C | 291 | 9,219 | 20,000 | M=CoN. 80% Shangaan, 20% Tsonga. 27n,9x,23f,1H,1h,1s(115),245t(8986),W=81%,65Y. |
| Igreja Evangélica Baptista de Moçambique | 1921 | P int | ....C | 60 | 30,000 | 50,000 | First M=CSM; Nyasa M, Zambezi M; then SAGM(AEF), expelled 1962. 60% Lomwe, Makua. |
| Igreja Evangélica dos Irmãos | | P CBr | x.... | 2 | 100 | 200 | *Christian Brethren.* Plymouth (Open) Brethren. Small independent congregations. |
| Igreja Evangélica Portuguesa | 1933 | P int | ....f | | 50 | 200 | *Portuguese Ev Ch.* Protestants from Portugal. 30 families before 1976 evacuation. |
| Igreja Luso-Africana | 1921 | I Ref | ..... | | 100 | 300 | *African Portuguese Ch.* First separatist movement; ex Swiss Mission. Tsonga. |
| Igreja Metodista Livre | 1885 | P Hol | VF..C | 462 | 6,762 | 10,000 | M=Free Meth(USA),ABCFM. Tswa,Chopi,Shangaan. 62n,16f,G=6.8%pa,1H,1h,2s(44),1153z. |
| Igreja Metodista Unida | 1879 | P Met | VwA.C | 900 | 24,000 | 60,000 | *United Meth Ch*, Africa Central Conference. M=UMC(USA). Tswa. 60n,20f,1H,1r,1s. |
| Igreja Ortodoxa | | O Gre | Cw... | 2 | 600 | 2,000 | Part of Greek AD Rhodesia, under P Alexandria. Beira, Maputo. 2x. |
| Igreja Presbiteriana de Moçambique | 1881 | P Ref | R.A.C | 204 | 10,125 | 50,000 | M=Swiss M/Tsonga PC(SA). A=1948. 62% Tsonga, 35% Ronga,3% Chopi. 20n,2H,1u,671Yy. |
| Igreja Reformada em Moçambique | 1908 | P Ref | x.... | 20 | 2,306 | 5,000 | *Reformed Ch.* Formerly M=DRC(Transvaal Synod) until 1922, then CCAP(Nkhoma). |
| Missão Baptista Escandinava | 1918 | P Bap | x...f | | 5,000 | 15,000 | M=SIBU(Free Baptist Union,Sweden). Begun by returning Rand miners. HQ Maputo. 4nm. |
| Missão da Fé Apostólica | | P Pe2 | Z.... | | 1,500 | 3,000 | M=Apostolic Faith Mission of South Africa,AFMSA African Ch(Rhodesia), Umtali. |
| Missão Metodista Wesleyana | 1880 | P Met | ....C | | 2,500 | 6,000 | M=Meth Ch of South Africa. Returning miners from Rand. 65% Ronga, 35% Tsonga. |
| Testemunhas de Jeová | 1933 | M Jeh | x.... | 200 | 10,000 | 45,000 | *Jehovah's Witnesses.* 1973, 36,000 persecuted Malawians; 1975, expelled. 438Y. |
| Other African indigenous churches | | I | ..... | | 9,000 | 18,000 | Total about 100 (see list below). |
| Other Protestant denominations | | P | ..... | | 500 | 1,000 | Total about 5 (see list below). |
| **Total affiliated (mid-1970)** | | | | **4,260** | **1,133,344** | **2,030,156** | **Total denominations (1970) . . .** 131. |
| **Total affiliated (mid-1975)** | | | | **6,200** | **1,521,500** | **2,725,500** | **Total denominations (1975) . . .** 138. |
| **Total affiliated (mid-1980)** | | | | **7,100** | **1,969,200** | **3,527,500** | **Total denominations (1980) . . .** 145. |

**NOTES ON TABLE ABOVE**
COLUMNS: for meanings and CODES (cols. 1, 3, 4, 8): see Codebook (Part 6). Column 1: **Boldface type** = church with over 10% of country's affiliated Christians.
NATIONAL COUNCILS (Column 4, 5th letter).
C = Conselho Cristão de Moçambique (CCM) (Christian Council of Mozambique) (unrelated to WCC and AACC until 1976).
f = formerly member of CCM.
R = Conferência Episcopal de Moçambique (CEM) (Episcopal Conference of Mozambique).
OTHER AFRICAN INDIGENOUS CHURCHES. There are a number of branches of churches from the republic of South Africa, Malawi, Zimbabwe and Swaziland which have not been permitted to become organized or centralized in Mozambique. These include: African Abraham Ch, African Assemblies of God (Malawi), African Catholic Ch of Gaza, African United Gaza Ch, Apostolic Ch of Johane Masowe (1969), Ch of the Holy Ghost, Ch of the Lost Christians (from Rhodesia), Emmanuel Chs of Christ (Malawi), Gazaland Zimbabwe Ethiopian Ch, Igreja Luso-Africana Etiópica, Igreja Luz Episcopal, Luso African Congregational Ch, United Ch of Ethiopian South Africa, VaZioni (Zionists), & 80 unorganized groups.
OTHER PROTESTANT DENOMINATIONS. These include: Pentecostal Holiness Ch (from SA), Southern Baptist Convention (1970), Worldwide Evangelization Crusade (1966).

**PEOPLES** (ethnolinguistic). Christians (1970): 38% Shangaan (29% Ronga-Tsonga, 5% Chopi, 3% Tswa), 17% Makua, 13% Portuguese, 7% Lomwe, 6% Ndau, 5% Sena, 3% Nyanja (Maravi), 3% Makonde, 2% Chuabo, 1.5% Mestiço, 1% Manyika, 1% Tawara, 0.6% Zimba, 0.5% Yao, 0.1% Greek, Nsenga, Angoni, Boroe, Goanese, Macao Chinese (500).

**COUNTRY-WIDE TOTALS**
EVANGELIZATION (see Part 5). 1900: 11%. 1970: 73%. 1980: 77%. *Radiophonic evangelism.* TWR, ICI, Radio Vatican.
FOREIGN MISSIONARIES AND PERSONNEL (nationals serving abroad) (1973). Total about 60 Roman Catholics in neighbouring countries (5 in Angola).
FOREIGN MISSIONARIES AND PERSONNEL (aliens from abroad) (1973). Total 2,048. *From Western world.* 1,907: 1,788 Roman Catholics, 107 Protestants (58 in 9 USA societies, 36 in 1 Switzerland society, 7 in 1 Sweden society, 4 in 1 Canada society, 2 in 1 UK society), 10 Anglicans in 3 UK societies, 2 Orthodox from Greece. *From Communist world.* About 2 Roman Catholics from Yugoslavia. *From Third World.* 139: about 60 Roman Catholics (30 from Brazil), 55 Protestants (47 in 5 South Africa societies, about 8 from Brazil), about 20 African indigenous from Rhodesia and South Africa, 4 Anglicans from Brazil and South Africa. During 1975–76, 611 Roman Catholic foreign missionaries left the country.
INSTITUTIONS (church-operated) (1973). Total 280, including 90 higher schools (12 minor seminaries), 160 medical centres (32 hospitals), 1 radio station, 2 religious communities, 9 seminaries (6 Protestant, 3 RC). In 1976 the state nationalized all schools, hospitals, social works and much other property.
PERIODICALS. About 30 titles.
PERSONNEL. About 6,078 in 1973 (4,030 national, 2,048 foreign).
RELIGIOUS LIBRARIES. About 13.
SCRIPTURE DISTRIBUTION (1975). Annual totals: 9,925 Bibles (95% subsidized, 5% commercial), 92,583 NTs (42% free, 58% subsidized), 22,445 UBS portions, 53,855 UBS selections. *Translations completed.* Portion: 13 languages since 1880. NT: 7 languages since 1890. Bible: 4 languages since 1907.
SERVICE AGENCIES. About 20, including CCM, CEM, CLC, JOC/F, MTS, USAREMO.

**ADDITIONAL DATA ON CHURCHES**
IGREJA ANGLICANA. *Membership.* 30% Nyanja, 20%, Shangaan, 13% Atonga, 12% Chopi, 10% Ronga, 5% Yao, 5% Tswa, 5% Zulu. *New diocese.* In 1978 a new Diocese of Niassa covering the north was inaugurated. Both dioceses have been, and remain, within the Church of the Province of Southern Africa (CPSA).
IGREJA CATOLICA EM MOCAMBIQUE. The name of the capital, and of the archdiocese, has been changed several times after the end of Portuguese rule (1975–76): from Lourenço Marques to Msumbiji, then to Can Phumo, then to Maputo. *Catholics.* Including 500 Macao Chinese (1975). *Catechumens.* Total (1971) 162,315, divided as follows among the 9 dioceses in the order shown (and included in column 7): 21327, 26233, 16708, 6920, 17705, 4402, 34964, 8776, 25280. *Annual baptisms.* (1972) 56.3% infant, 43.7% adult. *National priests.* The first African priest was ordained in 1953. The figures refer to Africans, until 1975 officially called 'autochthonous Portuguese'. *Expatriate priests.* The figures refer to 1971 just before the exodus of 48 WF priests. Total: 328 Portuguese ('non-autochthonous Portuguese') + 220 other Europeans, divided into these same 2 categories among the 9 dioceses in order as follows: 75+12, 38 + 22, 30 + 13, 11 + 29, 63 + 29, 27 + 17, 23 + 71, 29 + 21, 32 + 6. *Situation in 1976.* During 1975–76, 146 priests, 55 brothers and 450 sisters (all but 5, 8 and 27 being foreign missionaries) left the country. *Total priests.* (1960) 54 secular, 289 religious; (1971) 90 secular,
485 religious; (April 1976) 38 local, 336 foreign. *Brothers.* 23 Africans, 181 Whites (103 Portuguese, 78 other Europeans). *Sisters.* 165 Africans, 1,059 Whites (789 Portuguese, 270 other Europeans). *Seminarians* (1972). 102 secular, 65 religious. *Catechists.* Full-time: Beira 13, Tete 5, Quelimane 22. Part-time (same 3 dioceses only): 910. *Indigenous religious congregations.* Sisters: 27 Irmãs de Nossa Senhora da Conceição (begun 1951; D Villa Cabral), 17 Instituto Diocesano das Filhas do Imaculado Coração de Maria (begun 1959: D Porto Amélia). *Foreign orders and congregations.* Priests (with over 25 members): 97 OFM, 82 Portuguese Missionary Society of Cucujães (SMP), 75 FSCJ, 67 IMC, 55 OFMCap, 52 SJ, 47 SCJ, 47 CM, 29 IEME. Sisters (with over 75 members): 172 Franciscans Missionaries of Our Lady of Victories, 171 Franciscans Missionaries of Mary, 92 Sisters of the Presentation, 88 Franciscan Nurses of the Immaculate Conception, 82 Consolata, 81 Sacred Heart of Mary, 76 Franciscans Missionaries of Our Saviour.
*Catholic organizations.* The Episcopal Conference of Mozambique (Conferência Episcopal de Moçambique, CEM) is a member of SECAM. There are no national presbyteral or pastoral councils, but religious personnel are represented in the Federation of Male Religious Institutes of Mozambique (Federação dos Institutos Religiosos Masculinos de Moçambique) founded in 1965, and (until 1975) the Mozambique Section of the National Federation of Feminine Religious Institutes of Portugal (Federação Nacional dos Institutos Religiosos Femininos (Portugal)—Secção para Moçambique) founded in 1968. By 1976 these had been subsumed in the Union of Mozambican Priests and Religious (USAREMO). Catholic Action exists only in the diocese of Nampula, although a small team of JOC/F is also active in the diocese of Porto Amélia. Catholic pious associations are active throughout the country, the most important groups being the Legion of Mary (Legião de Maria) for Africans and Christian Study Courses (Cursos de Cristandade) for Europeans, although the latter has been severely hit by the 1975–76 exodus of Portuguese.
The Holy See has no diplomatic relations with Mozambique and is represented to the Catholic hierarchy by an apostolic delegate based in Maputo since December 1974.
In 1974 there were 3,346 pre-primary schools, 182 primary schools, 20 secondary schools, 58 trade schools, 19 homes for the needy, 4 universities, 120 dispensaries and 25 maternity centres.

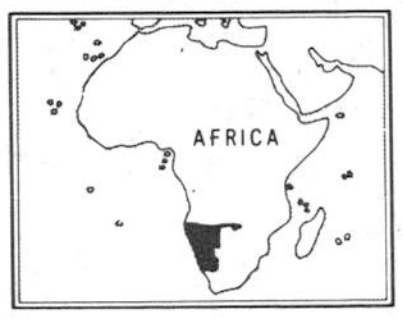


# NAMIBIA

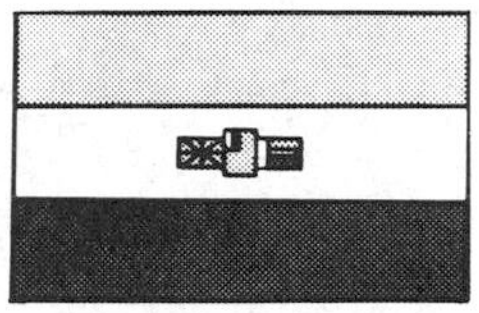

## SECULAR DATA

**STATE. Official name:** (1) (United Nations) Namibia; (2) (Republic of South Africa) The Territory of South West Africa (Suidwes-Afrika).
**Flag** (shown above right): That of the Republic of South Africa.
**Area:** 824,292 sq.km. (318,261 sq.miles). Agricultural land: 65.0%.
**Government:** Self-governing dependency of the Republic of South Africa, since 1949 (1884 German colony, 1920 South African mandated territory, 1949 annexed by South Africa, 1966 named Namibia by UN).
**Legislature:** Legislative Assembly, 18 members; Legislative Council for Ovamboland, 42 members.
**Official languages:** English and Afrikaans.
**Capital:** Windhoek 61,370.
**Political divisions:** 22 Districts.
**Armed forces** (1977): People's Liberation Army of Namibia (military wing of SWAPO).
**Foreign forces** (1977): 50,000 South African troops centred on Grootfontein base (army, air force, paramilitary police).

**DEMOGRAPHY. Population:** 762,184 (census of 6.V.1970. For 1970–2000 (UN), see last row of Table 1). Population density (1975): 1/sq.km. (2/sq.mile). Under 15 years: 39%. Growth rate (1975–80): 2.34% per year (births 4.45%, deaths −2.11%). Life expectancy (1975–80): 43.5 years. Household size: 5.1 persons.
**Major languages:** English, Afrikaans, Ovambo, Nama, Herero, German, Bushman, Tswana (Setswana), and 10 smaller languages.
**Urban dwellers** (1970): 31.8%. Urban growth rate (1950–70): 5.8% per year.
**Labour force:** 31%.
**Refugees** (1977): 22,000 from Angola.

**ETHNOLINGUISTIC GROUPS:** 43.3% Ovambo (Ndonga, Kwangali, Kwanyama), 8.7% Damara (Bergdama), 8.1% Afrikaner, 6.7% Okavango, 6.6% Herero, 5.9% Coloured (& Baster), 4.4% Nama Hottentot, 3.3% East Caprivian, 2.9% Bushman, 2.8% German, 2.5% Tswana, 1.5% Yeye, 1.2% English, 1.1% Subia, 0.9% Kaokovelder Herero, 0.1% Jewish.

**MONEY** (1977). **Monetary unit:** South African rand (= 100 cents); US$1 = R 0.87.
**National income per person:** US$800. Average annual family income: US$4,080.
**Cost of living in capital** (1976): Daily cost of living: US$18.

**HEALTH.** Hospitals: 156 (6,900 beds). Doctors: 170. Lepers: 650 (0.9 per 1,000). Blind: 1,400. Psychotics: 6,000.

**EDUCATION.** (1960) 38%, Schools: 694.

**LITERATURE.** Newspapers: 3 dailies.

**COMMUNICATION** (per 1,000 people). Phones: 58. Radios: 62.

TABLE 1. RELIGIOUS ADHERENTS IN NAMIBIA

| Year | 1900 | | mid-1970 | | Annual change, 1970–1980 | | | | mid-1975 | | mid-1980 | | 2000 | |
|---|---|---|---|---|---|---|---|---|---|---|---|---|---|---|
| *Name* | *Adherents* | *%* | *Adherents* | *%* | *Natural* | *Conversion* | *Total* | *Rate* | *Adherents* | *%* | *Adherents* | *%* | *Adherents* | *%* |
| **Christians** | **12,400** | **8.7** | **599,000** | **94.6** | **15,528** | **1,167** | **16,695** | **2.46** | **678,630** | **95.9** | **765,950** | **96.3** | **1,291,400** | **97.7** |
| professing | 12,400 | 8.7 | 599,000 | 94.6 | 15,528 | 1,167 | 16,695 | 2.46 | 678,630 | 95.9 | 765,950 | 96.3 | 1,291,400 | 97.7 |
| Protestants | 12,000 | 8.4 | 403,000 | 63.7 | 10,357 | 228 | 10,585 | 2.34 | 452,630 | 63.9 | 508,850 | 64.0 | 823,200 | 62.3 |
| Roman Catholics | 400 | 0.3 | 117,000 | 18.5 | 3,078 | 422 | 3,500 | 2.60 | 134,500 | 19.0 | 152,000 | 19.1 | 264,200 | 20.0 |
| Non-White indigenous | 0 | 0.0 | 53,000 | 8.4 | 1,393 | 307 | 1,700 | 2.79 | 60,900 | 8.6 | 70,000 | 8.8 | 132,100 | 10.0 |
| Anglicans | 0 | 0.0 | 21,000 | 3.3 | 567 | 173 | 740 | 2.98 | 24,800 | 3.5 | 28,400 | 3.6 | 59,400 | 4.5 |
| Catholics (non-Roman) | 0 | 0.0 | 4,200 | 0.7 | 110 | 20 | 130 | 2.71 | 4,800 | 0.7 | 5,500 | 0.7 | 10,000 | 0.8 |
| Marginal Protestants | 0 | 0.0 | 800 | 0.1 | 23 | 17 | 40 | 4.00 | 1,000 | 0.1 | 1,200 | 0.2 | 2,500 | 0.2 |
| nominal | 4,200 | 3.0 | 2,466 | 0.4 | 74 | 194 | 268 | 8.31 | 3,230 | 0.5 | 5,150 | 0.6 | 27,200 | 2.0 |
| affiliated | 8,200 | 5.8 | 596,534 | 94.2 | 15,454 | 973 | 16,427 | 2.43 | 675,400 | 95.4 | 760,800 | 95.7 | 1,264,200 | 95.7 |
| total practising | 7,380 | *90* | 447,400 | *75* | 11,591 | 729 | 12,320 | 2.43 | 506,550 | *75* | 570,600 | *75* | 884,900 | *70* |
| non-practising | 820 | *10* | 149,130 | *25* | 3,863 | 244 | 4,107 | 2.43 | 168,850 | *25* | 190,200 | *25* | 379,300 | *30* |
| Protestants | 8,000 | 5.6 | 400,181 | 63.2 | 10,267 | 95 | 10,362 | 2.31 | 448,700 | 63.4 | 503,800 | 63.4 | 802,600 | 60.7 |
| Evangelicals | 7,000 | 4.9 | 180,000 | 28.4 | 4,805 | 1,195 | 6,000 | 2.86 | 210,000 | 29.7 | 240,000 | 30.2 | 422,700 | 32.0 |
| Roman Catholics | 200 | 0.1 | 116,353 | 18.4 | 3,062 | 443 | 3,505 | 2.62 | 133,800 | 18.9 | 151,400 | 19.0 | 258,900 | 19.6 |
| Non-White indigenous | 0 | 0.0 | 55,000 | 8.7 | 1,441 | 189 | 1,630 | 2.59 | 63,000 | 8.9 | 71,300 | 9.0 | 132,100 | 10.0 |
| Anglicans | 0 | 0.0 | 20,000 | 3.2 | 551 | 209 | 760 | 3.15 | 24,100 | 3.4 | 27,600 | 3.5 | 58,100 | 4.4 |
| Catholics (non-Roman) | 0 | 0.0 | 4,200 | 0.7 | 110 | 20 | 130 | 2.71 | 4,800 | 0.6 | 5,500 | 0.7 | 10,000 | 0.8 |
| Marginal Protestants | 0 | 0.0 | 800 | 0.1 | 23 | 17 | 40 | 4.00 | 1,000 | 0.1 | 1,200 | 0.2 | 2,500 | 0.2 |
| Tribal religionists | 129,600 | 91.3 | 33,100 | 5.2 | 648 | −1,178 | −530 | −1.87 | 28,300 | 4.0 | 27,800 | 3.5 | 26,400 | 2.0 |
| Jews | 0 | 0.0 | 600 | 0.1 | 15 | 0 | 15 | 2.24 | 670 | 0.1 | 750 | 0.1 | 1,200 | 0.1 |
| Baha'is | 0 | 0.0 | 300 | 0.0 | 9 | 11 | 20 | 5.00 | 400 | 0.0 | 500 | 0.0 | 2,000 | 0.2 |
| **Country's population** | **142,000** | **100.0** | **633,000** | **100.0** | **16,200** | **0** | **16,200** | **2.29** | **708,000** | **100.0** | **795,000** | **100.0** | **1,321,000** | **100.0** |

COLUMNS, ROWS. For meanings and definitions, see Codebook (Part 6). Note that, by definition, total 'Christians' = professing + crypto-Christians, which also = affiliated + nominal Christians, Percentages may not always total exactly. due to rounding.
CENSUSES. (South West Africa) **9.IV.1960** 60.9% Protestants (40.0% Lutherans, 8.4% NGK), 15.1% tribal religionists, 13.6% Roman Catholics, 7.4% Non-White indigenous (Bantu, Coloured), 2.8% Anglicans, 0.1% Jews. In 1980, estimated population was given as 1,024,000 in some quarters.

**NOTES ON RELIGIONS**
BAHA'IS. In 3 local spiritual assemblies (1973). Members include Ovambo, Herero and some Bushmen.
NON-WHITE INDIGENOUS. In about 40 denominations in 1970, among both Bantu and Coloured races (see Table 2 below).
PROTESTANTS. The Rhenish Mission, begun in 1842, had 2,200 converts by 1874 and 3,600 by 1888; in 1908 alone there were 1,700 baptisms. The Finnish Mission grew from its origin in 1870 to 21 native Christians and 5 missionaries in 1890, to 2,000 baptized Christians and 24 missionaries by 1910.
ROMAN CATHOLICS. By 1907 there were 970 Catholics (800 Europeans, 170 natives).
TRIBAL RELIGIONISTS. Animists among the Heikum and Kung Bushmen (over 90%), and a minority of the Ambo and Herero (Ovahimba, 60% animist).

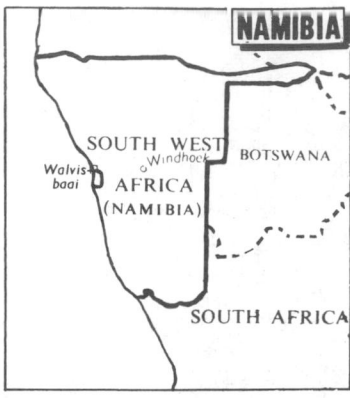

## NON-CHRISTIAN RELIGIONS. Traditional
religions are still followed by a small minority of Ambo and Herero, most of whom have become Christian, as well as by over 90% of the Heikum and Kung bushmen. The traditional name for God among the Ambo is Kalunga, and Nijambi Kalunga among the Herero. In both cases God is conceived as distant and so men's attention is centred on the ancestral spirits called Ovakuamungu by the Ambo and Ovakuru by the Herero. Belief in the efficacy of charms and the reality of witchcraft is also prevalent. Among the Ambo, the medicine man is called *ondudu* and the sorcerer *omulodi*. The Heikum and Kung appellation for God is Xu. Prayers are offered to him on the occasions of drought, illness, hunting and before travel, and offerings are sometimes given following the hunt. The principal minister of Xu is Nawa who is the head of the spirits (Gouab) and executes God's will on earth.

## CHRISTIANITY

PROTESTANT CHURCHES. The Hottentots in southwest Africa were first reached by the London Missionary Society in 1805. At the request of LMS, the Rhenish Missionary Society (German Lutheran) arrived in 1842, followed by Finnish Lutherans in 1870. The largest church today, now under African leadership, is the direct result of this early activity. In 1971 the Evangelical Lutheran Church in South West Africa (outgrowth of the Rhenish Society) and the Evangelical Lutheran Ovambokavango Church (related to the Finnish Lutheran Mission) came together to form the United Evangelical Church of South West Africa. The Christian community of this federated church (over 300,000) formed 50% of the total population of Namibia in 1970. A separate body, the German Evangelical Lutheran Church,

serves the German-speaking White community; in 1975 they reluctantly agreed to join the United Church but the latter had by then itself become reluctant to accept them.

The Reformed tradition is represented by 6 denominations all owing their origin to South Africa and reflecting the racial separation existing within their mother churches. Their impact on South West Africa has been much less than within the republic to the south. The largest of these is the Dutch Reformed Church in South West Africa which is composed entirely of White Afrikaners.

Other groups affiliated to South African denominations are the Methodist and Congregationalist churches and a Pentecostal body with strength among the Afrikaner population, the Apostolic Faith Mission. Seventh-day Adventists have been in Namibia since 1954 and 2 small Baptist communities have also been formed, one originating from South Africa and the other begun by Southern Baptists from the USA. Several other small missions are also at work.

CATHOLIC CHURCH. The Portuguese touched the coast of southwest Africa as early as 1485, but no sustained Catholic influence was felt until the end of the 19th century. Originally part of the prefecture of Cimbebasia in Portuguese Angola, the area south of the Angola border was designated a prefecture in its own right in 1892 and received its first Oblates of Mary Immaculate missionaries after 1896. The vicariate of Windhoek was erected in 1926. The growth of Catholics in the vicariate can be seen from the following statistics: 3,402 in 1921, 15,607 in 1946, 62,000 in 1965, 82,800 in 1946 and 96,000 in 1970. Catholic membership is largely Ovambo with a minority of 3,500 Whites. The Keetmanshoop mission, entrusted to Oblates of St Francis de Sales, became a prefecture in 1909 and was elevated to a vicariate in 1949. Although the Catholic Church in Namibia is 98% African or Coloured in membership, the clergy remains predominantly White; in 1971 there were only 4 African priests.

ANGLICAN CHURCH. The Anglican diocese of Damaraland is part of the Church of the Province of Southern Africa and is 77% Ambo in membership. Anglicans are the fourth largest Christian community in Namibia after the Lutheran, Catholic and Dutch Reformed churches.

INDIGENOUS CHURCHES. Three important schisms from the Rhenish Mission have occurred since World War II. The first, among the Nama Hottentots in 1946 who were dissatisfied with the progress of Lutheran pastoral training, became a branch of the AME Church, a Black denomination from the USA which had been at work in South Africa since 1892. In 1955, unrest in the Herero community erupted, resulting in the establishment

of the Herero Church, commonly called Oruuano (Community), which subsequently produced 2 further schisms, the Church of Africa and the Protestant Unity Church. Then in 1959, a majority of the Baster Coloureds at Rehoboth broke off to form the Independent Rhenish Mission of South Africa, protesting Bantu domination of the Evangelical Lutheran Church after 1957. Numerous independent churches from South Africa have also migrated to Namibia since World War I, but none has a large following.

CHURCH AND STATE. The territory was a German colony until World War I, after which it was transferred as a trust territory to South Africa by the League of Nations in 1919, a mandate later disputed by the United Nations. Unrest under South African rule has manifested itself within the country and in the churches. In 1971, African leaders of the principal church of Namibia, the United Evangelical Church of South West Africa, published a pastoral letter, condemning the politics of apartheid, which received the support of Anglican and Catholic leaders as well. Moreover, in another 'Open Letter' in 1971 the Lutheran bishop called for the granting of independence to Namibia. These attitudes and actions caused SWAPO (South West African People's Organization, a national liberation movement) to write in its bulletin *Namibia today*, in November 1971, that clergy and other persons with religious responsibilities should be considered, along with guerrillas of the bush and workers in the towns, as one of the 3 elements of the Namibian revolution. On 4 March 1972 the Anglican bishop of Damaraland and 2 of his co-workers, all Whites, were expelled from the country. The bishop later declared that during the 3 years of his episcopal ministry, the South African authorities had refused 17 residence permits for Anglican missionaries. Some time later, his successor as bishop (another Englishman) was also deported. The churches today find themselves the sole institutions able to form a bridge between the African masses and their White rulers. Nevertheless, ecclesiastical leaders in Namibia have not yet adopted a precise political position regarding the situation nor have they openly opposed the economic exploitation of the country which is the principal reason for its occupation by South Africa.

INTERDENOMINATIONAL ORGANIZATIONS. Five of Namibia's churches are represented as members and 5 others as observers on the South African Council of Churches founded in 1936. In August 1978 the Namibian Council of Churches was inaugurated.

**Tribal religionists.** Ovambo local headman at Osandi, dressed up for traditional religious cattle festivities. Less than 6% of the Ovambo still adhere to tribal religion.

**Evangelical Lutheran Church.** Contemporary Herero women, who still wear traditional Christian dress dating from a century ago, outside Okahandja mission church.

**BROADCASTING.** The situation is the same as in the republic of South Africa. Programmes in English, Afrikaans and several African languages can be received in most areas.


## BIBLIOGRAPHY

'Die Gemeinschaft der Ahnen and die Gemeinde Jesu Christi bei den Herero'. W.A. Wienecke. Dissertation, University of Hamburg (Germany), 1962.

*Eingeborenenkirchen in Sud-und Sudwestafrika: ihre Geschichte und Sozialstruktur*. K. Schlosser. Kiel: W.G. Mühlau, 1958. 355p.

*Namibia*. C.O. Winter. London: Lutterworth, 1977. (By exiled Anglican bishop).

'The half-opened door', G. Reeh, *International review of missions*, 50, 199 (July, 1961), 293–6. (The Herero Church).


TABLE 2. ORGANIZED CHURCHES AND DENOMINATIONS IN NAMIBIA

| Official name 1 | Begun 2 | Type 3 | Counc 4 | Congs 5 | Adults 6 | Affiliated 7 | Names, notes, and other statistics (see Codebook) 8 |
|---|---|---|---|---|---|---|---|
| African Church | c1965 | I Lut | ••••• | | 500 | 1,000 | One of 3 factions split ex Herero Church. Some Lutheran polity retained. |
| African Methodist Episcopal Church | 1946 | I Met | Vw••K | | 5,000 | 15,000 | Nama Hottentot secession ex Rhenish Mission (RM). Later, affiliated to AMEC. |
| Anglican Ch: D Damaraland/Namibia | 1924 | A Hig | AwaVK | 147 | 4,883 | 20,000 | In CPSA. 77% Ovambo,18% White,5% Colouerd. 17n,3x,15f,1h,P=32%,3r,1s,1382Y,2379y. |
| Apostolic Faith Mission of S Africa | | P Pe2 | Z•••• | 14 | 1,000 | 1,400 | M=AFM(SA). 83% White (Afrikaners), 13% Bantu, 4% Coloured. HQ Lyndhurst, SA. 2f. |
| Baptist Union of South Africa | | P Bap | T•••w | 2 | 100 | 200 | *BUSA*. In Walvis Bay and Windhoek. All Whites. HQ Johannesburg, South Africa. |
| **Catholic Church in Namibia:** | 1880 | R Lat | P•SSK | 62 | 71,000 | 116,353 | 87% African, 10% Coloured. C=2+1+6. 17H,1p. 4n,76x,55m,351w,P=39%,6096Yy,1629z. |
| VA Keetmanshoop | 1909 | R Lat | Posfs | 22 | 11,500 | 18,777 | South. Catholics mostly Basters; 5% Whites. 0 25 9 84 40 991 67 |
| VA Windhoek | 1892 | R Lat | Pomi | 40 | 59,500 | 97,576 | 37% Ambo,34% Kwangare,15% Damara,3% White. 4 51 46 267 39 5105 1562 |
| Christian Assemblies | c1950 | I pen | ••••• | 11 | 2,000 | 5,000 | *Christen Gemeente* (South Africa). 80% Coloured. Strong in N & W Cape, Natal (SA). |
| Christian Reformed Church | | P Ref | x•••• | | 2,000 | 2,500 | *NHK. Nederduitsch Hervormde Kerk van Afrika*. 99% White Afrikaners, in NHK(SA). |
| Church of Africa | c1965 | I Lut | ••••• | | 1,000 | 2,000 | West Hereros. Schism ex Herero Church by members of Mbanderu sub-tribe. |
| Church of Jesus C of Latter-day Saints | | M LdS | x•••• | | 50 | 100 | *Mormons*. M=CJCLdS(Utah,USA). Mainly USA expatriates. HQ Johannesburg, SA. |
| Dutch Reformed Church in SWA | | P Ref | F•••• | | 24,000 | 40,000 | *NGK. Nederduitse Gereformeerde Kerk in SWA. Mother Ch.* White Afrikaners only. |
| Dutch Ref Ch in SWA (Coloured Ch) | | P Ref | F•••• | | 2,000 | 3,000 | *NGK vir SWA*. Coloured section of NGK, based in Kakamas, CP, South Africa. |
| Dutch Reformed Ch Mission in Namibia | 1955 | P Ref | F•••w | 15 | 1,000 | 3,000 | *NGK Sendingkerk*. M=NGK(SA). 3 areas: Herero, Kwangali, Bushmen. 2n,5x. |
| Full Gospel Ch of God in Southern A | | P Pe3 | ZF••• | 12 | 1,148 | 2,000 | M=FGCoG(South Africa),CoG(Cleveland)(USA). HQ Irene (Transvaal, SA). 1p. |
| German Ev Lutheran Church in Namibia | 1896 | P Lut | L••JK | 33 | 8,000 | 14,000 | One of 4 synods of UELCSA. German-speaking Whites only. HQ Oranjezicht, CP. 11nx. |
| Herero Church | 1955 | I Lut | ••••• | | 3,000 | 5,000 | *Oruuano* (Community). Schism of Herero tribe ex Rhenish Mission; now splintered. |
| Independent Rhenish Mission of SA | 1959 | I Lut | ••••• | | 2,000 | 4,000 | Anti-Bantu schism ex Rhenish Mission by 80% all Basters (Coloureds) at Rehoboth. |
| Jehovah's Witnesses | c1945 | M Jeh | x•••• | 5 | 206 | 600 | Active witnessing under way by 1949. Literature in Kwanyama (Ambo). 14Y. |
| Methodist Church of South Africa | | P Met | Vwa•K | | 1,589 | 5,000 | Part of MCSA. HQ Cape Town. 45% White, 37% Coloured, 18% Bantu. |
| New Apostolic Church | c1910 | C CAp | x•••• | | 2,000 | 4,000 | M=NAC(World HQ Dortmund,Germany). Ex Catholic Apostolic Ch. German immigrants. |
| Presbyterian Church of Southern Africa | | P Ref | Rwa•W | | 200 | 500 | *PCSA*. Attached to PCSA in South Africa. HQ Johannesburg. 90% White. |
| Protestant Unity Church | c1965 | I Lut | ••••• | | 10,000 | 18,000 | Hereros. Largest faction to split ex Herero Church. |
| Reformed Church | 1937 | P Ref | J•••• | 15 | 2,200 | 5,000 | *Gereofrmeerde* (*Dopper*) *Kerk*. 2 Classic: Nossob, Etosha. 97% Afrikaners. W=50%. |
| Seventh-day Adventist Church | 1954 | P Adv | x•••• | 3 | 255 | 600 | *SDA*, *SWAfrica Field*, South African UC (White, Coloured). 3nx,5mw,5t(211),34Y. |
| Southern Baptist Mission | 1968 | P Bap | T•••• | 1 | 70 | 200 | M=SBC(USA). Recent independent Baptist work. 4f,7Y. |
| United Congr Ch in Southern Africa | 1805 | P Con | Rwa•K | 12 | 773 | 1,500 | Part of Western Cape Region, UCCSA. 73% Coloured, 22% Bantu, 5% White. 1n. |
| **United Evangelical Church of Namibia:** | 1791 | P Lut | L•••K | 379 | 194,000 | 319,281 | 1971 federation of 2 of the 3 Lutheran churches in SWA; both retain autonomy. 1s. |
| Evangelical Lutheran Ch in Namibia | 1842 | P Lut | L••JK | 150 | 70,000 | 115,391 | M=RM,VEM(Germany). 39% Bergdama,20% Nama,17% Herero,12% Coloured. 54f,150Y,3300y. |
| Ev Lutheran Ovambokavango Church | 1870 | P Lut | L••JK | 229 | 124,000 | 203,890 | ELOC. M=Finnish Missionary Society. A=1954. 90% Ovambo. 90n,10x,200m,81f,13H,24h. |
| Other Non-White indigenous churches | | I | ••••• | | 3,000 | 5,000 | Total over 30, mainly migrant groups from South African bodies (see list below). |
| Other Protestant denominations | | P | ••••• | | 1,000 | 2,000 | Total about 10 (see list below). |
| Other Catholic (non-Roman) churches | | C | ••••• | | 100 | 200 | Including Old Apostolic Church (from Europe). |
| Other marginal Protestant bodies | | M | ••••• | | 20 | 100 | Small groups of German and other bodies, including Horpenites (from Saxony). |
| **Total affiliated (mid-1970)** | | | | **1,510** | **344,094** | **596,534** | **Total denominations (1970) . . . 73.** |
| **Total affiliated (mid-1975)** | | | | **1,650** | **389,600** | **675,400** | **Total denominations (1975) . . . 77.** |
| **Total affiliated (mid-1980)** | | | | **1,790** | **438,800** | **760,800** | **Total denominations (1980) . . . 83.** |

NOTES ON TABLE ABOVE
COLUMNS: for meanings and CODES (cols. 1, 3, 4, 8): see codebook (Part 6). Column 1: **Boldface type** = church with over 10% of country's affiliated Christians.
NATIONAL COUNCILS (Column 4, 5th letter).
- K = Namibian Council of Churches (formed 1978), also member of SACC.
- W = member of South African Council of Churches (SACC).
- w = observer member of SACC.

OTHER NON-WHITE INDIGENOUS CHURCHES. Including: Apostolic Spiritual Healing Ch (Tswana leaders from Botswana), Orujano Ch (schism ex Herero Ch), St John's Apostolic Faith Ch, St Philip Apostolic Ch, Spiritual Healing Ch (Branch of Botswana church, with bishop for Namibia; Herero members; linked with Lesotho body, Moshoeshoe Berean Bible Readers' Ch).
OTHER PROTESTANT DENOMINATIONS. These include: Christian Brethren, Ch of the Latter Rain (Afrikaner Pentecostals, called Blourokkies because of women's blue dresses), Free Gospel Ch, Salvation Army (began 1932).

PEOPLES (ethnolinguistic). Christians: 45.0% Ovambo, 9.2% Damara (Bergdama), 8.5% Afrikaner, 6.6% Okavango, 6.3% Herero, 6.2% Coloured (& Baster), 4.5% Nama Hottentot, 3.0% East Caprivian, 2.9% German, 2.5% Tswana, 1.2% English, 1.0% Yeye, 1.0% Subia, 0.8% Kaokovelder Herero, 0.4% Bushman, other Southwestern Bantu.

COUNTRY-WIDE TOTALS
EVANGELIZATION (see Part 5). 1900: 14%. 1970: 97%. 1980: 100%.
FOREIGN MISSIONARIES AND PERSONNEL (nationals serving abroad) (1973). Total about 10 (Protestants and Non-White indigenous) in South Africa.
FOREIGN MISSIONARIES AND PERSONNEL (aliens from abroad)(1973). Total 711. *From Western world*. 544: about 390 Roman Catholics, 139 Protestants (81 in Finland society, 54 in 2 WGermany societies, 4 in 2 USA societies), 15 Anglicans (13 in 2 UK societies, 2 in 1 USA society). *From Third World*. 167: 65 Protestants (59 in 10 South Africa societies), about 50 Bantu and Coloured indigenous from South Africa and Botswana about 30 Roman Catholics from South Africa, about 20 Anglicans from South Africa, about 2 Catholics (non-Roman) from South Africa.
INSTITUTIONS (church-operated)(1973). Total 140, including 40 higher schools (2 minor seminaries), 80 medical centres (30 hospitals), 1 religious community, 2 seminaries (1 Protestant, 1 Anglican).
PERIODICALS. About 25 titles.
PERSONNEL. About 1,421 (710 national, 711 foreign).
RELIGIOUS LIBRARIES. About 5.
SCRIPTURE DISTRIBUTION (1975). Annual totals: 16,000 Bibles (94% subsidized, 6% commercial), 14,000 NTs (7% free, 57% subsidized, 36% commercial), 10,000 UBS portions, 20,000 UBS selections. *Translations completed*. Portion: 7 languages since 1831. NT: 6 languages since 1866. Bible: 3 languages since 1954.
SERVICE AGENCIES. About 12, including AWR, CRSSA, DM, SACBC, SACC.

ADDITIONAL DATA ON CHURCHES
CATHOLIC CHURCH IN NAMIBIA. Catholics are 87% African (mostly Bantu), 10% Coloured, and 3% White. *Catechumens*. (1959) 2,917; (1961) 3,892; (1963) 2,193; (1969) 1,629. *Annual baptisms*. (1972) 84.1% infant, 15.9% adult. *Priests*. Nationals here refers to Africans, expatriates to Whites. All Whites except one originated outside South Africa. VA Windhoek also has a Spanish-speaking chaplain at Walvis Bay to serve the 45,000 seamen each year who pass through this fishing port. *Brothers*. VA Keetmanshoop: 8 Whites, 1 Coloured. *Sisters*. VA Keetmanshoop: 4 Africans, 12 Coloured, 68 Whites from outside South Africa (8 now naturalized). *Seminarians*. Total (1970) 6. *Catechists*. Total (1971) 116 part-time (Windhoek 100, Keetmanshoop 16). Windhoek has a large training programme. *Indigenous religious congregations*. African Sisters of St Benedict (SSB), in VA Windhoek. *Foreign congregations*. Priests: OSFS (Austrian province), OMI (German province). Brothers: Brothers of Tilburg. Sisters: OSFS Sisters, Sacred Heart Sisters (Hiltrup), OSD, Sisters of the Immaculate Conception, Holy Cross Sisters. *Catholic organizations*. Namibia forms part of the Southern Africa Catholic Bishops' Conference, which is a member of SECAM. Two associations serving religious personnel are the Conference of Clerical Religious Superiors in Southern Africa and the Association of Women Religious, both based in the republic of South Africa. The only active lay organization is the Legion of Mary.

The Holy See has no diplomatic relations with South Africa or Namibia. It is represented to the Catholic hierarchy by an apostolic delegate with residence in Pretoria.

Educational and medical institutions in 1970 included 15 schools for mixed-race pupils, 149 schools for Africans; 17 hospitals; 21 dispensaries; and 59 hostels of which 41 were for Africans, 3 for Whites and 15 for those of mixed race.
EVANGELICAL LUTHERAN CHURCH IN SWA. Afrikaans, = Evangeliese Lutherse Kerk in SWA (Rynse Sendingkerk). By 1975 this church and its partner in federation numbered 340,000 adherents.
EVANGELICAL LUTHERAN OVAMBOKAVANGO CHURCH. Initials ELOC or ELOK. In Kwanyama (Ambo), = Ongarki onkwaEvangeli paLuther yomOvambokavango. The church has experienced very rapid growth of 5% per year since 1960.

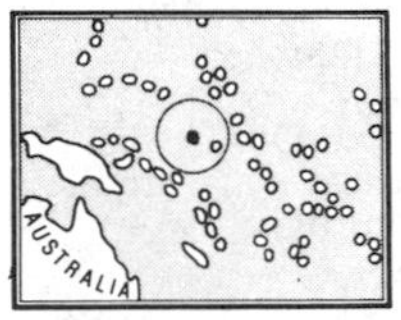


# NAURU

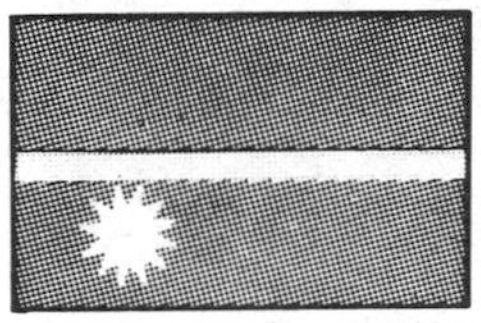

## SECULAR DATA

**STATE. Official name:** The Republic of Nauru (Naoero). Adjective of nationality: Nauruan.
**Flag** (shown above right): Blue field halved by horizontal gold stripe, 12-pointed white star at lower hoist corner (representing the 12 tribes from which Nauruans are descended).
**Area:** 21 sq.km. (8 sq.miles). Agricultural land: 0.0%.
**Government:** Republic, since 1968 (1888 German colony, 1914 Australian occupation, then mandated territory, 1947 trust territory of the UN, 1968 Independence).
**Legislature:** Legislative Assembly, 18 members.
**Official language:** English.
**Capital:** Yaren.

**DEMOGRAPHY. Population:** 6,057 (census of 30.IV.1966. For 1970–2000 (UN), see last row of Table 1). Population density (1975): 357/sq.km. (925/wq.mile). Under 15 years: 44%. Growth rate (1975-80): 1.29% per year. Household size: 6.6 persons.
**Major languages:** English, Nauruan, Gilbertese, Chinese (Cantonese).
**Labour force:** 41%.

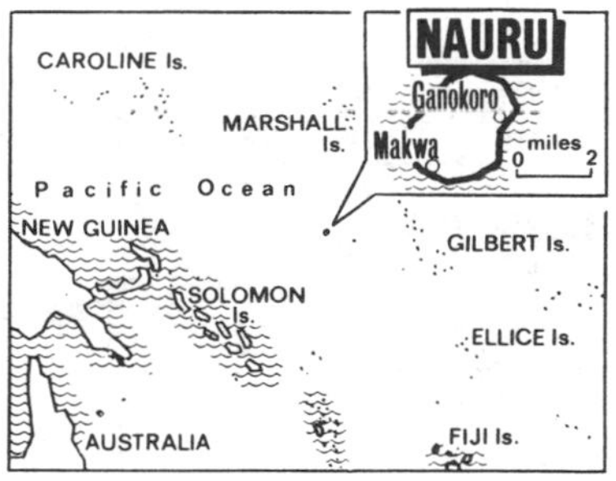


**ETHNOLINGUISTIC GROUPS:** 50.0% Nauruan, 28.2% other Pacific islander (20% Gilbertese), 1.36% Chinese (Cantonese (940), 8.2% European (Anglo-Australian)(570), Filipino.

**MONEY** (1977). **Monetary unit:** Australian dollar (= 100 cents); US$1 = A$0.94.
**National income per person:** US$7,000. Average annual family income: US$46,200.
**Cost of living in capital** (1976): Daily cost of living: US$41.

**HEALTH.** Hospitals: 2 (207 beds). Doctors: 10. Lepers: 90 (12.0 per 1,000).

**EDUCATION.** Adult literacy: 100%. Education rate: 66%. Schools: 11.

**LITERATURE.** Newspapers: 1 non-daily.

**COMMUNICATION** (per 1,000 people). Phones: 88, Radios: 600.

## TABLE 1.    RELIGIOUS ADHERENTS IN NAURU

| Year / Name | 1900 Adherents | % | mid-1970 Adherents | % | Natural | Conversion | Total | Rate | mid-1975 Adherents | % | mid-1980 Adherents | % | 2000 Adherents | % |
|---|---|---|---|---|---|---|---|---|---|---|---|---|---|---|
| | | | | | Annual change, 1970–1980 | | | | | | | | | |
| Christians | 300 | 20.0 | 5,350 | 82.3 | 123 | −5 | 118 | 1.91 | 6,160 | 82.1 | 6,530 | 81.6 | 7,760 | 77.6 |
| professing | 300 | 20.0 | 5,350 | 82.3 | 123 | −5 | 118 | 1.91 | 6,160 | 82.1 | 6,530 | 81.6 | 7,760 | 77.6 |
| Protestants | 300 | 20.0 | 3,590 | 55.2 | 82 | −5 | 77 | 1.86 | 4,130 | 55.1 | 4,360 | 54.5 | 5,160 | 51.6 |
| Roman Catholics | 0 | 0.0 | 1,560 | 24.0 | 0 | 36 | 36 | 2.00 | 1,800 | 24.0 | 1,920 | 24.0 | 2,300 | 23.0 |
| Anglicans | 0 | 0.0 | 200 | 3.1 | 5 | 0 | 5 | 2.17 | 230 | 3.1 | 250 | 3.1 | 300 | 3.0 |
| nominal | 0 | 0.0 | 2,500 | 38.5 | 60 | 20 | 80 | 2.67 | 3,000 | 40.0 | 3,300 | 41.3 | 4,500 | 45.0 |
| affiliated | 300 | 20.0 | 2,850 | 43.8 | 63 | −25 | 38 | 1.20 | 3,160 | 42.1 | 3,230 | 40.4 | 3,260 | 32.6 |
| total practising | 290 | *97* | 2,420 | *85* | 45 | −22 | 32 | 1.19 | 2,690 | *85* | 2,740 | *85* | 2,280 | *70* |
| non-practising | 10 | *3* | 430 | *15* | 9 | −3 | 6 | 1.28 | 470 | *15* | 490 | *15* | 980 | *30* |
| Protestants | 300 | 20.0 | 1,500 | 23.1 | 33 | −21 | 12 | 0.74 | 1,620 | 21.6 | 1,620 | 20.3 | 1,500 | 15.0 |
| Evangelicals | 250 | 16.7 | 350 | 5.4 | 8 | −1 | 7 | 1.75 | 400 | 5.3 | 420 | 5.2 | 500 | 5.0 |
| Roman Catholics | 0 | 0.0 | 1,200 | 18.5 | 27 | −4 | 23 | 1.68 | 1,370 | 18.2 | 1,430 | 17.9 | 1,560 | 15.6 |
| Anglicans | 0 | 0.0 | 150 | 2.3 | 3 | 0 | 3 | 1.76 | 170 | 2.3 | 180 | 2.2 | 200 | 2.0 |
| Chinese folk-religionists | 0 | 0.0 | 600 | 9.2 | 13 | −6 | 7 | 1.06 | 660 | 8.0 | 670 | 8.4 | 800 | 8.0 |
| Non-religious | 0 | 0.0 | 300 | 4.6 | 9 | 14 | 23 | 5.48 | 420 | 5.6 | 530 | 6.6 | 1,000 | 10.0 |
| Buddhists | 0 | 0.0 | 150 | 2.3 | 3 | −4 | −1 | −0.67 | 150 | 2.0 | 140 | 1.7 | 140 | 1.4 |
| Baha'is | 0 | 0.0 | 100 | 1.5 | 2 | 1 | 3 | 2.73 | 110 | 1.5 | 130 | 1.6 | 300 | 3.0 |
| Tribal religionists | 1,200 | 80.0 | 0 | 0.0 | 0 | 0 | 0 | 0.00 | 0 | 0.0 | 0 | 0.0 | 0 | 0.0 |
| **Country's population** | **1,500** | **100.0** | **6,500** | **100.0** | **150** | **0** | **150** | **2.00** | **7,500** | **100.0** | **8,000** | **100.0** | **10.000** | **100.0** |

**COLUMNS, ROWS.** For meanings and definitions, see Codebook (Part 6). Note that, by definition, total 'Christians' = professing + crypto-Christians, which also = affiliated + nominal Christians. Percentages may not always total exactly, due to rounding.
**CENSUSES. 30.IV.1961:** 54.2% Protestants (44.1% Congregationalists), 26.0% Roman Catholics, 16.5% Chinese folk-religionists and Buddhists, 3.0% non-religious, 0.5% non-religious. **30.VI.1966:** 51.6% Protestants (31.1% Congregationalists), 21.8% Roman Catholics, 19.1% Chinese folk-religionists and Buddhists, 4.0% non-religious, 3.0% Anglicans, 0.4% other religionists.

**NOTES ON RELIGIONS**
**BAHA'IS.** In 3 isolated groups.
**BUDDHISTS.** Chinese (from Hong Kong).
**CHINESE FOLK-RELIGIONISTS.** From Hong Kong; mostly labourers without their families.
**COUNTRY'S POPULATION.** The proportion of Nauruans has remained constant at around 50% since 1930; however, Chinese have decreased from 41% in 1930 (43% in 1950) to 16% in 1961, 19% in 1966, 15% in 1968 and 13% in 1971; and other Pacific islanders have increased in numbers from 2.4% in 1950 to 24% in 1961 and 28.2% in 1971.

**NON-RELIGIOUS.** Mainly Chinese from Hong Kong who have abandoned their family religion.
**PROTESTANTS.** Although there is only one organized Protestant church, the NPC with 1,752 Congregationalist adherents in the 1966 census, that census showed professing adherents of at least 6 other traditions; 51 Presbyterian, 30 Methodist, 7 Church of Christ, 5 Lutheran, 5 Baptist, 1 Orthodox, as well as 940 unspecified Protestants and 123 unspecified other Christians.
**TRIBAL RELIGIONISTS.** Pre-Christian traditional Micronesian religion, embracing polytheism and the ancestor cult, did not finally disappear until well into the 20th century.

**Nauru Congregational Church.** *Above.* Two young Christians celebrate Nauru's Independence in 1968. *Right.* Congregational Church, Orro.

Christmas 1977

Catholic Church 1902

Christmas 1977

**Catholic Church, Diocese of Tarawa, Nauru & Funafuti.** *Left.* Fr Kayser and Nauru's first Catholic Church (1902). *Right.* Catholic Church, Arubo.

## NON-CHRISTIAN RELIGIONS.
**Chinese folk religion** is adhered to by most of the Chinese, who are imported labourers from Hong Kong.

**Buddhism** also has followers among the Chinese.

**Baha'i** has begun recently and in 1973 had 3 centres.

## CHRISTIANITY

**PROTESTANT CHURCHES.** The main denomination is the Nauruan Protestant Church (NPC), which was begun by Congregationalist missionaries of the London Missionary Society after Germany assumed control of the island in 1888. By 1902 scripture portions had been translated into the Nauru language, by 1907 the New Testament, and by 1918 the whole Bible. Although the church is basically congregational in polity, the membership includes also those of Presbyterian, Lutheran, Methodist and Baptist background. About 31% of the population professed to be Congregationalists in 1966 although only 23% are actually recognized members. An additional 32% call themselves Protestants but are not affiliated to any church.

**CATHOLIC CHURCH.** Nauru forms part of the diocese of Tarawa, Nauru and Funafuti, with its seat in the Gilbert Islands. In 1972 there were one resident priest and 4 sisters, one of whom was Chinese. The population identifies itself as about 18% Catholic.

**ANGLICAN CHURCH.** Anglicans make up Nauru's smallest church. They belong to the diocese of Polynesia, formed in 1908, which is part of the Church of the Province of New Zealand and the South Pacific Anglican Council (SPAC).

**CHURCH AND STATE.** Nauru was discovered by the British whaling captain, John Fearn, in 1798. Germany annexed the island in 1888 after which European settlement began. Between World War I and independence in 1968, Australia administered the territory. Religion has never been an issue vis-a-vis government. Prior to 1923 all education was in the hands of mission schools which were subsidized by government; and to this day Catholic schools continue to receive state aid. The independent state of Nauru, however, specifically recognizes God in its constitution: 'We the people of Nauru acknowledge God as the almighty and everlasting Lord and the giver of all good things...'

**INTERDENOMINATIONAL ORGANIZATIONS.** Relations between Protestants, Catholics and Anglicans are informal but cordial.

## TABLE 2.    ORGANIZED CHURCHES AND DENOMINATIONS IN NAURU

| Official name 1 | Begun 2 | Type 3 | Counc 4 | Congs 5 | Adults 6 | Affiliated 7 | Names, notes, and other statistics (see Codebook) 8 |
|---|---|---|---|---|---|---|---|
| Anglican Church (D Polynesia) | | A Hig | awpK. | 1 | 50 | 150 | In Ch of the Province of New Zealand. Small chaplaincy work. |
| Catholic Ch: D Tarawa, Nauru, Funafuti | 1902 | R Lat | P.PY. | 1 | 700 | 1,200 | Under Diocese of Tarawa (Gilbert & Ellice Is). M=MSC. 1x,4w(one Chinese),1r. |
| Nauru Congregational Church | 1888 | P Con | ..P.. | 8 | 700 | 1,500 | *NPC. Nauruan Protestant Ch.* M=LMS(UK). 66% Nauruans, 30% other Pacific islanders. |
| **Total affiliated (mid-1970)** | | | | 10 | 1,450 | 2,850 | Total denominations (1970) ... 3. |
| **Total affiliated (mid-1975)** | | | | 10 | 1,610 | 3,160 | Total denominations (1975) ... 3. |
| **Total affiliated (mid-1980)** | | | | 11 | 1,640 | 3,230 | Total denominations (1980) ... 3. |

**NOTES ON TABLE ABOVE**

**COLUMNS:** for meanings and CODES (cols. 1, 3, 4, 8): see Codebook (Part 6). Column 1: **Boldface type** = church with over 10% of country's affiliated Christians.

**PEOPLES** (ethnolinguistic). Christians: about 55% Nauruan, 27% Gilbertese, 8% other Pacific islander, 6% European (Anglo-Australian), 2% Chinese, Filipino.

**COUNTRY-WIDE TOTALS**
**EVANGELIZATION** (see Part 5). 1900: 52%. 1970: 100%. 1980: 100%.
**FOREIGN MISSIONARIES AND PERSONNEL** (aliens from abroad)(1973). Total 8. *From Western world.* About 4 Roman Catholics. *From Third World.* 4: 3 Protestants, 1 Roman Catholic.
**INSTITUTIONS** (church-operated)(1973). Total 2 (1 higher school).
**PERIODICALS.** 2 titles.
**PERSONNEL.** About 12 (4 national, 8 foreign).

**SCRIPTURE DISTRIBUTION** (1975). Annual totals: 200 Bibles (subsidized), 100 NTs (subsidized). *Translations completed.* Nauru: portion in 1902, NT 1907, Bible 1918.

**ADDITIONAL DATA ON CHURCHES**
**CATHOLIC CHURCH.** *Catholic organizations.* In 1971 the church sponsored a primary school (208 pupils) which catered for 27% of all Nauruan primary pupils and also a secondary school with 114 pupils.

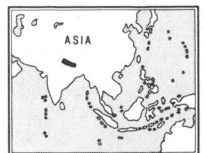

# NEPAL

## SECULAR DATA

**STATE. Official name:** The Kingdom of Nepal (Nepal Adhirajya).
Adjective of nationality: Nepalese.
**Flag** (shown above right): Red bordered in blue with white moon in upper triangle and white sun below.
**Area:** 140,797 sq.km. (54,362 sq.miles). Agricultural land: 28.4%.
**Government:** Absolute (de facto) or constitutional (de jure) monarchical Hindu state, since 1700s.
**Legislature:** National Panchayat, 125 members.
**Official language:** Nepali.
**Capital:** Kathmandu 150,400 (1971).
**Political divisions:** 14 Zones and 75 Development Districts.
**Armed forces** (1976): Total 20,000 regular army.

**DEMOGRAPHY. Population:** 11,555,983 (census of 22.VI.1971. For 1970–2000 (UN), see last row of Table 1). Population density (1975): 89/sq.km. (231/sq.mile). Under 15 years: 42%. Growth rate (1975–80): 2.48% per year(births 4.33%, deaths –1.85%).

**Life expectancy** (1975–80): 46.1 years. Household size: 5.5 persons.
**Major languages:** Nepali (Pahari), Tibetan, Hindi, English, Newari, Tharuhati, and 70 other minor languages.
**Urban dwellers** (1970): 4.6%. Urban growth rate (1950–70): 4.5% per year.
**Labour force:** 42%.
**Refugees** (1977): 10,000 Tibetans from China.
**Tourists** (1974): 89,838.

**ETHNOLINGUSTIC GROUPS:** 54.0% Nepali (Gurkha et alii), 11.5% Maithili, 7.0% Bhojpuri, 4.8% Tamang, 4.3% Tharu, 3.9% Newari, 2.7% Abadhi, 2.5% Magar, 2.0% Rai Kirati, 1.5% Gurung, 1.5% Limbu, 1.2% alien Indian (1.1% Hindustani). 0.7% Bhote Sherpa, 0.5% Rajbansi, Satar, Sunwar, Danuwar, Santali, European, USA, Pakistani.

**MONEY** (1977). **Monetary unit:** rupee (= 100 pice); US$1 = NRs 12.45.

**National income per person:** US$100. Average annual family income: US$550.
**Inflation:** (1970–75) 9.3% per year (1975: consumer price index 188).
**Cost of living in capital** (1976): index 98 (Washington DC=100). Daily cost of living: US$31.

**HEALTH.** Hospitals: 55 (2,006 beds). Doctors: 122. Lepers: 74,490 (5.9 per 1,000). Blind: 60,000. Psychotics: 90,000. Criminals 4,000.

**EDUCATION** Adult literacy: (1953) 5%, (1975) 19%. Education rate: 19%. Schools: (1969) 7,256. Universities: 1.

**LITERATURE.** Periodicals: 168. Newspapers: 26 dailies, 41 non-daily.

**COMMUNICATION** (per 1,000 people). Phones: 1. Radios: 9. Daily newspaper circulation: 3 copies.

### TABLE 1. RELIGIOUS ADHERENTS IN NEPAL

| Year | 1900 | | mid-1970 | | Annual change, 1970–1980 | | | | mid-1975 | | mid-1980 | | 2000 | |
|---|---|---|---|---|---|---|---|---|---|---|---|---|---|---|
| Name | Adherents | % | Adherents | % | Natural | Conversion | Total | Rate | Adherents | % | Adherents | % | Adherents | % |
| Hindus | 3,410,000 | 77.0 | 9,898,590 | 88.1 | 266,380 | 19,504 | 285,884 | 2.56 | 11,166,940 | 88.8 | 12,757,430 | 89.6 | 21,115,600 | 91.0 |
| Buddhists | 886,000 | 20.0 | 842,400 | 7.5 | 20,393 | –17,933 | 2,460 | 0.29 | 854,900 | 6.8 | 867,000 | 6.1 | 1,160,000 | 5.0 |
| Muslims | 44,000 | 1.0 | 331,500 | 3.0 | 9,017 | 233 | 9,250 | 2.45 | 378,000 | 3.0 | 424,000 | 3.0 | 652,000 | 2.8 |
| Tribal religionists | 90,000 | 2.0 | 110,000 | 1.0 | 2,699 | –2,319 | 380 | 0.34 | 113,100 | 0.9 | 113,800 | 0.8 | 116,000 | 0.5 |
| Non-religious | 0 | 0.0 | 30,000 | 0.3 | 883 | 517 | 1,400 | 3.78 | 37,000 | 0.3 | 44,000 | 0.3 | 100,000 | 0.4 |
| Atheists | 0 | 0.0 | 10,000 | 0.1 | 262 | –62 | 200 | 1.82 | 11,000 | 0.1 | 12,000 | 0.1 | 30,000 | 0.1 |
| **Christians** | **0** | **0.0** | **4,010** | **0.0** | **113** | **43** | **156** | **3.28** | **4,760** | **0.0** | **5,570** | **0.0** | **10,600** | **0.0** |
| crypto-Christians | 0 | 0.0 | 3,410 | 0.0 | 95 | 31 | 126 | 3.14 | 4,010 | 0.0 | 4,670 | 0.0 | 9,000 | 0.0 |
| professing | 0 | 0.0 | 600 | 0.0 | 18 | 12 | 30 | 4.00 | 750 | 0.0 | 900 | 0.0 | 1,600 | 0.0 |
| Protestants | 0 | 0.0 | 400 | 0.0 | 12 | 8 | 20 | 4.00 | 500 | 0.0 | 600 | 0.0 | 1,000 | 0.0 |
| Roman Catholics | 0 | 0.0 | 200 | 0.0 | 6 | 4 | 10 | 4.00 | 250 | 0.0 | 300 | 0.0 | 600 | 0.0 |
| affiliated | 0 | 0.0 | 4,010 | 0.0 | 113 | 43 | 156 | 3.28 | 4,760 | 0.0 | 5,570 | 0.0 | 10,600 | 0.0 |
| total practising | 0 | 0 | 3,810 | 95 | 107 | 41 | 148 | 3.27 | 4,520 | 95 | 5,290 | 95 | 9,540 | 90 |
| non-practising | 0 | 0.0 | 200 | 5 | 6 | 2 | 8 | 3.33 | 240 | 5 | 280 | 5 | 1,060 | 10 |
| Asian indigenous | 0 | 0.0 | 3,060 | 0.0 | 86 | 28 | 114 | 3.17 | 3,600 | 0.0 | 4,200 | 0.0 | 8,000 | 0.0 |
| Protestants | 0 | 0.0 | 600 | 0.0 | 18 | 12 | 30 | 4.00 | 750 | 0.0 | 900 | 0.0 | 1,600 | 0.0 |
| Evangelicals | 0 | 0.0 | 400 | 0.0 | 13 | 17 | 30 | 5.45 | 550 | 0.0 | 700 | 0.0 | 1,400 | 0.0 |
| Roman Catholics | 0 | 0.0 | 300 | 0.0 | 8 | 2 | 10 | 2.86 | 350 | 0.0 | 400 | 0.0 | 800 | 0.0 |
| Catholic pentecostals | 0 | 0.0 | 0 | 0.0 | 0 | 3 | 3 | 30.00 | 10 | 0.0 | 30 | 0.0 | 300 | 0.0 |
| Marginal Protestants | 0 | 0.0 | 50 | 0.0 | 1 | 1 | 2 | 3.33 | 60 | 0.0 | 70 | 0.0 | 200 | 0.0 |
| Baha'is | 0 | 0.0 | 3,000 | 0.0 | 83 | 17 | 100 | 2.86 | 3,500 | 0.0 | 4,000 | 0.0 | 7,000 | 0.0 |
| Jains | 0 | 0.0 | 2,500 | 0.0 | 70 | 0 | 70 | 2.50 | 2,800 | 0.0 | 3,200 | 0.0 | 4,800 | 0.0 |
| **Country's population** | **4,430,000** | **100.0** | **11,232,000** | **100.0** | **299,900** | **0** | **299,900** | **2.39** | **12,572,000** | **100.0** | **14,231,000** | **100.0** | **23,196,000** | **100.0** |

**COLUMNS, ROWS.** For meanings and definitions, see Codebook (Part 6). Note that, by definition, total 'Christians' = professing + crypto-Christians, which also = affiliated + nominal Christians. Percentages may not always total exactly, due to rounding.
**CENSUSES. 22.VI.1961:** 87.7% Hindus, 9.3% Buddhists, 3.0% Muslims (also 831 Jains, 458 Christians, 5,716 other religionists). **22.VI.1971:** 89.4% Hindus, 7.5% Buddhsts, 3.0% Muslims, 0.1% other religionists (2,541 Jains, 5,836 others including Christians).

### NOTES ON RELIGIONS
ASIAN INDIGENOUS. In 5 groupings in 1970 (see Table 2); mostly Nepali indigenous Christians and isolated radio believers, with 2 denominations from India.
ATHEISTS. 2 parties: Communist Party of Nepal/Right, Communist Party of Nepal/Left (both proscribed 1960; internal factions; pro-Chinese): membership (1970) 5,000, declining somewhat.
BAHA'IS. Rapid growth from 2 local spiritual assemblies (1964) to 21 (1973); mainly Indians, formerly Hindus and a few ex-Christians.
BUDDHISTS. Both Mahayana and Tentrayana (Tantrism, Lamaism) have large followings, mostly in the north.
CATHOLIC PENTECOSTALS (or, Catholic charismatics). The renewal began in 1975 with one small prayer group (1977, in St Xavier's School).
CHRISTIANS. Nearly half Nepali, with one third expatriate

Indians (out of Indian population of 128,830 in 1971).
CRYPTO-CHRISTIANS. Nepali believers in the legal or recognized (expatriate) churches, and also in organized Nepali churches; together with organized and unorganized isolated radio and correspondence course believers.
MUSLIMS. Sunnis, mainly expatriate traders, also settlers, from India.
NON-RELIGIOUS. Mainly Nepali and Indian intellectuals also Europeans, also Nepali communist sympathizers.
PROFESSING CHRISTIANS. Europeans and some of the Indian Christians only; Nepali believers are not recognized by the state and so exist as crypto-Christians.
TRIBAL RELIGIONISTS. Animists among the hill tribes.

## NON-CHRISTIAN RELIGIONS.
**Hinduism** is the state religion and the religion of the great majority of the population. The king of Nepal is considered by the Hindu faithful to be a reincarnation of Vishnu. An unusual feature is the fertility cult revolving around the worship of the mother goddess Kumari in the form of a human child. This is in fact a cult of female energy as the source of the universe, and the king of Nepal is Kumari's trustee. The human goddess is possessed by Kumari only until her first menstruation when she becomes an ordinary human being, and a successor is then chosen.

**Mahayana Buddhism** and **Tantrism** (Lamaism) have large followings in Nepal, mostly in the northern regions bordering Tibet. The founder of Buddhism, Gautama Buddha, was born about 567 BC in Lumbini near Padaria village in Nepal's Tarai district.

**Islam** is professed by a minority of Indian settlers and foreign traders.

**Traditional tribal religions** are still found among the hill peoples.

## CHRISTIANITY
INDIGENOUS CHURCHES. Churches indigenous to India have been working in Nepal for many years. The first of all missionary societies to arrive was the Peace of Christ Brotherhood of the Mar Thoma Syrian Church, in 1952. The Assemblies (Jehova Shamma) also have work. Both have been expected to confine their ministries to Indians. Since foreign missions are not permitted to open churches among Nepalis, Nepali Christians organized in 1966 their own indigenous body, the Church of Christ in Nepal, which they keep separate from the missions and unrelated to them. This church is a loosely-knit organization consisting in 1970 of approximately 750 baptized members in 30 small congregations with a number of house churches scattered across the land. The Christian community is divided into 3 parts: about 300 baptized Nepali Christians, 150 Indian Christians engaged in secular activities, and 300 missionaries and other foreign Christians involved in educational and medical work. In addition to baptized Nepalis, there are many

**Buddhists.** *Right.* Bodhnath Stupa, pilgrimage centre 5 miles east of Kathmandu; a colossal solid hemisphere, one of biggest stupas in world, built on octagonal base inset with prayer wheels, ringed by houses of lamas. Note all-seeing eyes of Lord Buddha 'keeping eternal watch on human behaviour', repeated on all 4 sides of tower in the 4 cardinal directions.

unbaptized believers, more fringe members who would call themselves Christians, and a sizeable number of secret believers. When Gurkhas served in the British Army in Malaysia, Singapore and elsewhere, many became Christians and on their return to Nepal moved back to remote areas. The church owes its origin to a Nepalese army officer, Prem Pradhan, who was converted to Christianity in India and returned to Nepal in 1959. His evangelistic activity led to conversions and 8 baptisms in Tansen in 1960, which being illegal resulted in the 9 of them being imprisoned for nearly 5 years. More conversions were recorded while he was in prison, and since his release he has continued to preach and baptize. In 1970 there were 9 ordained Nepali pastors.

Another independent group is the Nepali Christian Congregation, a well-attended church in Kathmandu whose pastor Robert Karthak in 1970 was a Lepcha from Sikkim, now a Nepali citizen.

PROTESTANT CHURCHES. Over 50 Protestant foreign missionary societies have been involved in education, medical and community development work since the early 1950s. In 1954 the United Mission to Nepal opened its first medical centre in Kathmandu. Beginning as a co-operative venture of 10 boards, the mission in 1973 had 190 missionaries, with over 700 national staff in its institutions, and was supported in work grants, capital grants and personnel by 30 societies from 15 different countries. The mission operates 7 primary schools, one middle and 3 high schools (a girls' high school in Kathmandu with 630 students, a boys' boarding school in Pokhara and a third high school in Gorkha district), 5 hospitals, a leprosarium, an extensive public health programme, a nurses' training school, a training school for auxiliary nurses and midwives, an industrial training centre and hydroelectric scheme (Butwal Technical Institute), and Nepal's first plywood factory. The Gorkha Community Service project, with heavy emphasis on agriculture, was taken over by the government in 1971.

Other foreign missions, engaging mostly in medical work, include the following: Seventh-day Adventists, with a hospital at Bhanipa 15 miles from the capital; International Nepal Fellowship (which combines the work of the Nepal Evangelistic Band, International Christian Fellowship, and Worldwide Evangelization Crusade) with a hospital, a leprosarium (Green Pastures) and several dispensaries in the Pokhara area; TEAM (Evangelical Alliance Mission) with a hospital in the extreme west at Dandeldhura; Operation Mobilization with 12 missionaries engaged in literature work; Summer Institute of Linguistics (Wycliffe Bible Translators); and a children's mission from over the border in India, Gorakhpur Nurseries, with a clinic, and dispensaries at Semri and Pyersingh run by independent missionaries.

Small Protestant congregations, consisting mostly of expatriates, are sponsored by several of these missions, in addition to Unitarian and Assemblies of God groups and the united English-speaking Protestant Church in Kathmandu.

CATHOLIC CHURCH. Nepal is part of the Catholic diocese of Patna in India. In Nepal in 1973 there were about 300 Catholics, mostly among foreign personnel with embassies and aid groups, and some from India, Pakistan and Bangladesh. Among those from India are about 30 Nepali-speaking families from the Darjeeling area of West Bengal. There are no Catholic parish priests, sisters, brothers, catechists or catechumens; but 15 American-born Jesuit priests, of whom 5 are now Nepali citizens, came in 1951 at the government's invitation to open a school. There are also 14 sisters from the Institute of the Blessed Virgin Mary (Mary Ward, German branch), 10 of whom are Indians, who came to Nepal in 1954 and are involved in education. Two Jesuits, one with a doctorate in Nepali history, live and teach at the University Research Centre, doing research in Himalayan religions, particularly Buddhism and Tantrism. All activities of Catholic priests and sisters are restricted to Kathmandu Valley, although they are allowed to minister to foreign Catholics in other parts of Nepal.

**Protestants.** BMMF missionaries in Nepal in 1978 were testing River Rover hovercraft (shown above), developed by Missionary Aviation Fellowship of Britain.

**CHURCH AND STATE.** The 1967 constitution, Article 3, states that Nepal is 'a monarchical Hindu State', and in fact it is the world's only Hindu kingdom. According to Article 14, 'Every person may profess and practise his own religion as handed down from ancient times, provided that no person shall be entitled to convert another person from one religion to another'. The baptism of Hindu converts is thus illegal, and the United Mission to Nepal has strictly adhered to observance of the law since their arrival. However, Nepali Christians themselves have baptized converts, resulting in imprisonments. In 1973, 7 Christians in Pokhara were given 3-month prison sentences for changing their ancestral faith to Christianity, but the government generally overlooks the law. In fact, prosecution takes place only if a citizen makes a definite charge against a newly-baptized Christian. Foreign residents of Nepal are free to practise their own religions but not to engage in proselytism. The Christian witness of missionaries is restricted to educational and medical work and to pastoral activities among these foreign Christians.

There is no separate government ministry in charge of religious affairs, although the government-supported Guthi Corporation (Guthi Sansthan) looks after the maintenance of Hindu temples, religious buildings and their landed property.

In 1972, a proposition to liberalize the constitution with respect to religion was discussed in parliament but finally rejected. The prohibition against converting Nepalese is directed not only at Christianity but also at Islam.

In August 1973 the government nationalized the administration of 15 hospitals (2 being leprosaria) maintained by Christian missionaries, but their foreign personnel continue to work under the control of the state. In 1976, the government moved against the Wycliffe Bible Translators, ordering its Summer Institute of Linguistics to withdraw its 90 overseas workers.

In 1978, the government requested missionary societies to move into areas previously closed to them.

**INTERDENOMINATIONAL ORGANIZATIONS.** Nepali and foreign Christians, and almost all missionaries, participate in the Nepali-run Nepal Christian Fellowship, which operates an annual Bible school and evangelistic trips. Among missions, the United Mission to Nepal is supported by more foreign societies than any other co-operative missionary venture in the world. Difficulties confronting missionary and evangelistic work have caused these missions to adopt a united front, but there are still other missions not actively co-operating.

**BROADCASTING.** The government Department of Broadcasting does not transmit Christian programmes. From abroad, programmes beamed to India and China by international stations can be heard. FEBA (Seychelles) broadcasts in Nepali; in 1976 there were 3 programmes a week of 15 minutes' duration each.

## BIBLIOGRAPHY

*Nepal: on the potter's wheel.* Kathmandu: United Mission to Nepal, 1970. 50p.
*Nepal and the Gospel of God.* J. Lindell. Kathmandu: United Mission to Nepal, 1979.
*Religion in Nepal.* K.R. van Kooij. Iconography of Religion, *XIII.* Leiden: Brill, 1978. 33p.
*Still in Nepal.* E.W. Oliver. London: RBMU, 1961.

TABLE 2. ORGANIZED CHURCHES AND DENOMINATIONS IN NEPAL

| Official name 1 | Begun 2 | Type 3 | Counc 4 | Congs 5 | Adults 6 | Affiliated 7 | Names, notes, and other statistics (see Codebook) 8 |
|---|---|---|---|---|---|---|---|
| Assemblies of God | c1955 | P Pe2 | ZF... | 2 | 30 | 100 | c1960, M=AoG(USA) had a station for a time. 1971, re-opened; 2 missionaries. |
| Assemblies (Jehova Shammah) | | I CBr | x...C | 2 | 40 | 60 | Missionaries from India (Brother Bakht Singh); HQ Hyderabad, AP. |
| Catholic Church (D Patna) | 1951 | R Lat | P.F.. | 5 | 200 | 300 | 70% expatriates, 30% Nepali-speaking. M=SJ. 5n,10x,14w. 4 schools. |
| **Church of Christ in Nepal** | 1966 | I ind | ....C | 30 | 750 | 2,000 | *Mashi Mandali.* Entirely Nepali-run. 50% Nepali, 30% Indian. Many missionaries. 9n. |
| International Nepal Fellowship | 1951 | P int | .G... | 3 | 70 | 150 | Formerly M=Nepal Evangelistic Band(UK); WEC. In west. Hospitals, boarding school. 50f. |
| **Isolated radio churches** | c1965 | I rad | ..... | 30 | 300 | 600 | Isolated radio believers. T=6000(Bible Correspondence Institute, India; FEBA,ICI,&c). |
| Mar Thoma Syrian Ch (D Bahya Kerala) | 1952 | I ReO | xwe.C | 1 | 50 | 100 | M=MTS Evangelistic Association(HQ Tiruvalla,India). South Indians, some Nepalis. |
| Nepali Christian Congregation | c1968 | I ind | ....C | 1 | 100 | 300 | Begun by a Nepali Lepcha. Packed services; 50% Nepali, 50% expatriates. |
| Protestant Church in Kathmandu | | P com | ....C | 1 | 150 | 300 | English-speaking union church, for expatriates; Indians, British, USA. |
| Seventh-day Adventist Church | 1960 | P Adv | x.... | 1 | 20 | 50 | *SDA.* Under Northern Union (India), Southern Asia Division. Hospital, Bhanipa. 6f. |
| Unitarian Universalist Assoc of K | | M Unt | I.... | 1 | 20 | 50 | K=Kathmandu. Links with Unitarian Universalist Association(USA). |
| **Total affiliated (mid-1970)** | | | | **77** | **1,730** | **4,010** | **Total denominations (1970) . . . 11.** |
| **Total affiliated (mid-1975)** | | | | **90** | **2,050** | **4,760** | **Total denominations (1975) . . . 12.** |
| **Total affiliated (mid-1980)** | | | | **105** | **2,400** | **5,570** | **Total denominations (1980) . . . 13.** |

### NOTES ON TABLE ABOVE

COLUMNS: for meanings and CODES (cols. 1, 3, 4, 8): see Codebook (Part 6) Column 1: **Boldface type** = church with over 10% of country's affiliated Christians.
NATIONAL COUNCILS (Column 4, 5th letter).
C = Nepal Christian Fellowship (NCF).

PEOPLES (ethnolinguistic). Christians: 43% Nepali, 33% Indian (Hindi, Bihari, Malayali, et alii), 20% European, 3.7% Santali, Lepcha, other tribal.

### COUNTRY-WIDE TOTALS

EVANGELIZATION (see Part 5). 1900: 0%. 1970: 26%. 1980: 33%. *Mass evangelism.* About 1968, visit by Indian evangelist Jordan Khan (60 decisions in Kathmandu, 40 in Pokhara). *Radiophonic evangelism.* FEBA (in Nepali), Bible Correspondence Institute (India; 6,000 enrolments), et alia.
FOREIGN MISSIONARIES AND PERSONNEL (aliens from abroad) (1973). Total 307. *From Western world.* 271: 257 Protestants (99 in 7 UK societies, 61 in 18 USA societies, 24 in 3 Norway societies, 19 in 8 Australia societies, 17 in 3 Canada societies, 12 in 2 Finland societies, 11 in 7 New Zealand societies, 10 in 3 WGermany societies, 4 in 1 Sweden society), about 10 Roman Catholics, 4 Anglicans (3 in 1 UK society, 1 in 1 Canada society). *From Third World.* 36: about 20 Protestants (12 from India, 8 Japan). 15 Roman Catholics from India, 1 Indian indigenous.
INSTITUTIONS (church-operated)(1973). Total 25, including 4 higher schools, 20 medical centres (10 hospitals), 1 religious community.
PERIODICALS. 3 titles.
PERSONNEL. About 325 (18 national, 307 foreign).
RELIGIOUS LIBRARIES. 2.
SCRIPTURE DISTRIBUTION (1975). Annual totals: 5,800 NTs (free). *Translations completed.* Portion: Newari in 1964. NT: 2 languages since 1821. Bible: Nepali (Pahari) in 1914.
SERVICE AGENCIES. About 50, including (1) United Mission to Nepal, since 1954, with the following members: American Friends Mission, BMMF, BMS(UK), Central Asian Mission, CMS (UK & Australia), Church of North India, Council of Baptist Churches of Northern India, Disciples of Christ (UCMS), Eastern Himalayan Church Council (CNI), Free Church of Finland, Gorakhpur Nurseries, Gossner Mission, International Christian University Church (Japan), Japan Overseas Co-operative Service, Leprosy Mission, Mennonite Board, Mennonite Central Committee, Methodist Church of Southern Asia, Norwegian Free Evangelical Mission, Orebro (Swedish Baptist) Mission, PECUSA, Protestant Churches in Germany, Swiss Friends for Missions, United Church of Canada, United Methodist Church (USA), UPUSA, Wesleyan Ch of America, Women's Union Missionary Society, World Gospel Mission, World Mission Prayer League (USA, Norway); and (2) other independent agencies: CCCI, ICF, JARS, NCF, OM, RBMU (13 missionaries), SIL, SU, TEAM, WBT, WEC, World-Wide Missions (1964), WVI.

### ADDITIONAL DATA ON CHURCHES

CATHOLIC CHURCH. *Catholic organizations.* In 1972 Catholic sisters from Germany operated Cambridge school with an enrolment of 1,000 girls. The Jesuits conducted 3 schools: a primary boarding school at Godavari with 300 boys, and at Jawalakhel a primary school with 230 boys and a high school with 240 students, including a hostel for 110 boys. The Society of Jesus also operates Alumni Centre, a youth centre in Kathmandu for former pupils; and there is a home for housing and, feeding abandoned boys giving them formal education or vocational training.

# NETHERLANDS

## SECULAR DATA

**STATE. Official name:** The Kingdom of the Netherlands (Koninkrijk der Nederlanden). Unofficial name: Holland. Adjectives of nationality: Netherlands, a Netherlander; (unofficial) Dutch, Dutchman.
**Flag** (shown above right): Red, white, and blue stripes.
**Area:** 40,844 sq.km. (15,770 sq.miles). Agricultural land: 56.6%
**Government:** Constitutional monarchy, since 1815 (1581 republic 1806 Napoleonic kingdom, 1815 independent monarchy).
**Legislature:** First Chamber, 75 members. Second Chamber, 150 members.
**Official language:** Dutch (*Nederlands-Vlaams*).
**Chief cities:** capital Amsterdam 1,023,700 (1972), The Hague (seat of government) 697,870, Rotterdam 1,059,630, Utrecht 463,470.
**Political divisions:** 11 Provinces, and 843 Municipalities.
**Armed forces** (1976): Total 112,200 regular (59,400 conscripts): army 75,000, navy 18,200, air force 19,000 (160 combat aircraft). Reserves: 183,300. Paramilitary forces: 7,700.
**Foreign forces** (1973): 2,000 USA troops.
**Dependencies** (1977): Netherlands Antilles.

**DEMOGRAPHY Population:** 13,045,785 (census of 28.II.1971. For 1970–2000 (UN), see last row of Table 1). Population density (1975): 333/sq. km. (862/sq.mile). Under 15 years: 30%. Growth rate (1975–80): 0.73% per year (births 1.61%, deaths −0.89%, immigrants 0.01%). Life expectancy (1975–80): 73.9 years. Household size: 2.9 persons.
**Major languages:** Dutch, Frisian, Turkish, Creole, Indonesian, Arabic, German, French, English, Chinese (Cantonese), Hindustani, Sranang Tongo (Surinamese).
**Urban dwellers** (1970): 81.0%. Urban growth rate (1950–70): 1.8% per year.
**Labour force:** 34%.
**Refugees** (1977): About 9,000 from Eastern Europe.
**Tourists** (1974): 2,683,442.

**ETHNOLINGUISTIC GROUPS:** 94.1% Dutch, 3.4% Frisian 0.4% Turkish, 0.3% Surinam Creole (45,000), 0.3% Ambonese (South Moluccan) (35,000), 0.2% Moroccan Arab, 0.2% German, 0.2% Belgian, 0.2% Jewish, 0.2% Chinese (30,000) (Cantonese et alii), 0.2% Gypsy (20,000), 0.1% British (16,000), 0.1% Antillean (8,000), 0.1% French, Tunisian, Javanese, other Indonesian, Greek, Italian, Spaniard, Hindi.

**MONEY** (1977). **Monetary unit:** guilder or florin (= 100 cents), US$1 = Fls 2.48.
**National income per person:** US$4,693. Average annual family income: US$13,610.
**Inflation:** (1970–74) 8.2% per year (1975: consumer price index 160), (1977) 5.4% per year.
**Cost of living in capital** (1976): index 137 (Washington DC=100). Daily cost of living: US$51.

**HEALTH.** Hospitals: 330 (156,555 beds). Doctors: 18,142 Lepers: 480. Blind: 8,000. Psychotics: 130,000. Criminals: 126,414.

**EDUCATION.** Adult literacy: 100%. Education rate: 69%. Schools: 9,816 (8,288 primary, 1,528 secondary). Universities: 13.

**LITERATURE.** Annual new book titles (1973): 11,640. Periodicals: 1,800. Scientific journals: 660. Newspapers: 93 dailies, 167 non-daily.

**COMMUNICATION** (per 1,000 people). Phones: 321. Radios: 284. TV sets: 258. Daily newspaper circulation: 311 copies.

TABLE 1. RELIGIOUS ADHERENTS IN THE NETHERLANDS

| Year / Name | 1900 Adherents | % | mid-1970 Adherents | % | Natural | Conversion | Total | Rate | mid-1975 Adherents | % | mid-1980 Adherents | % | 2000 Adherents | % |
|---|---|---|---|---|---|---|---|---|---|---|---|---|---|---|
| **Christians** | **4,998,700** | **96.5** | **11,650,600** | **89.4** | 78,734 | −34,424 | 44,310 | 0.37 | 11,854,500 | 87.2 | 12,093,700 | 85.7 | 12,880,000 | 80.4 |
| professing | 4,998,700 | 96.5 | 11,650,600 | 89.4 | 78,734 | −35,424 | 44,310 | 0.37 | 11,854,500 | 87.2 | 12,093,700 | 85.7 | 12,880,000 | 80.4 |
| Protestants | 3,153,000 | 60.9 | 5,884,800 | 45.2 | 38,857 | −37,027 | 1,830 | 0.03 | 5,862,900 | 43.1 | 5,903,100 | 41.8 | 5,967,000 | 37.3 |
| Roman Catholics | 1,833,700 | 35.4 | 5,603,800 | 43.0 | 38,657 | 1,923 | 40,580 | 0.70 | 5,820,400 | 42.8 | 6,009,600 | 42.6 | 6,660,000 | 41.6 |
| Marginal Protestants | 3,000 | 0.1 | 70,000 | 0.5 | 498 | 502 | 1,000 | 1.33 | 75,000 | 0.5 | 80,000 | 0.6 | 120,000 | 0.7 |
| Catholics (non-Roman) | 9,000 | 0.2 | 69,600 | 0.5 | 482 | 168 | 650 | 0.90 | 72,500 | 0.5 | 76,000 | 0.5 | 100,000 | 0.6 |
| Anglicans | 0 | 0.0 | 10,000 | 0.1 | 80 | 0 | 80 | 0.77 | 10,400 | 0.1 | 10,800 | 0.1 | 13,000 | 0.1 |
| Orthodox | 0 | 0.0 | 7,500 | 0.1 | 70 | 0 | 70 | 0.90 | 7,800 | 0.1 | 8,200 | 0.1 | 10,000 | 0.1 |
| Third-World indigenous | 0 | 0.0 | 5,000 | 0.0 | 90 | 10 | 100 | 1.82 | 5,500 | 0.0 | 6,000 | 0.0 | 10,000 | 0.1 |
| nominal | 56,320 | 1.1 | 1,576,900 | 12.1 | 11,829 | 29,381 | 41,210 | 2.31 | 1,781,000 | 13.1 | 1,989,000 | 14.1 | 2,882,000 | 18.0 |
| affiliated | 4,942,380 | 95.4 | 10,073,700 | 77.3 | 66,905 | −63,805 | 3,100 | 0.03 | 10,073,500 | 74.1 | 10,104,700 | 71.6 | 9,998,000 | 62.4 |
| doubly-affiliated | 0 | 0.0 | −122,819 | −0.9 | −844 | −74 | −918 | 0.72 | −127,000 | −0.9 | −132,000 | −0.9 | −160,000 | −1.0 |
| total practising | 4,448,140 | 90 | 7,857,490 | 78 | 51,517 | −69,309 | −17,792 | −0.23 | 7,756,590 | 77 | 7,679,570 | 76 | 6,998,600 | 70 |
| non-practising | 494,240 | 10 | 2,216,210 | 22 | 15,388 | 5,504 | 20,892 | 0.90 | 2,316,910 | 23 | 2,425,130 | 24 | 2,999,400 | 30 |
| Roman Catholics | 1,816,770 | 35.1 | 5,336,919 | 41.0 | 36,669 | −3,261 | 33,408 | 0.60 | 5,521,000 | 40.7 | 5,671,000 | 40.2 | 6,180,000 | 38.6 |
| Catholic pentecostals | 0 | 0.0 | 500 | 0.0 | 33 | 1,917 | 1,950 | 39.00 | 5,000 | 0.0 | 20,000 | 0.1 | 200,000 | 1.2 |
| Protestants | 3,113,730 | 60.1 | 4,710,335 | 36.1 | 29,964 | −61,188 | −31,224 | −0.69 | 4,552,000 | 33.3 | 4,398,100 | 31.2 | 3,743,000 | 23.4 |
| Evangelicals | 1,554,000 | 30.0 | 1,750,000 | 13.4 | 11,895 | −3,505 | 8,390 | 0.47 | 1,795,100 | 13.2 | 1,833,900 | 13.0 | 1,921,000 | 12.0 |
| Neo-pentecostals | 0 | 0.0 | 2,000 | 0.0 | 332 | 9,468 | 9,800 | 19.60 | 50,000 | 0.4 | 100,000 | 0.7 | 300,000 | 1.9 |
| Marginal Protestants | 3,000 | 0.1 | 67,145 | 0.5 | 478 | 508 | 986 | 1.37 | 72,000 | 0.5 | 77,000 | 0.5 | 120,000 | 0.7 |
| Catholics (non-Roman) | 8,880 | 0.2 | 63,620 | 0.5 | 438 | 200 | 638 | 0.97 | 66,000 | 0.5 | 70,000 | 0.5 | 90,000 | 0.6 |
| Anglicans | 0 | 0.0 | 8,000 | 0.1 | 40 | 0 | 40 | 0.49 | 8,200 | 0.1 | 8,400 | 0.1 | 9,000 | 0.1 |
| Orthodox | 0 | 0.0 | 6,500 | 0.0 | 70 | 0 | 70 | 1.03 | 6,800 | 0.1 | 7,200 | 0.1 | 9,000 | 0.1 |
| Third-World indigenous | 0 | 0.0 | 4,000 | 0.0 | 90 | 10 | 100 | 2.22 | 4,500 | 0.0 | 5,000 | 0.0 | 7,000 | 0.0 |
| **Non-religious** | 65,000 | 1.3 | 1,158,700 | 8.9 | 8,900 | 29,030 | 37,930 | 2.82 | 1,346,000 | 9.9 | 1,538,000 | 10.9 | 2,402,000 | 15.0 |
| Atheists | 10,000 | 0.2 | 100,000 | 0.8 | 900 | 6,100 | 7,000 | 5.15 | 136,000 | 1.0 | 170,000 | 1.2 | 120,000 | 2.0 |
| **Muslims** | 200 | 0.0 | 60,000 | 0.5 | 8,150 | 50 | 8,200 | 6.31 | 130,000 | 0.9 | 142,000 | 1.0 | 192,000 | 1.2 |
| Ahmadis | 0 | 0.0 | 200 | 0.0 | 10 | 10 | 20 | 6.67 | 300 | 0.0 | 400 | 0.0 | 1,000 | 0.0 |
| **Jews** | 105,530 | 2.0 | 30,000 | 0.2 | 200 | 0 | 200 | 0.64 | 31,000 | 0.2 | 32,000 | 0.2 | 35,000 | 0.2 |
| **Chinese folk-religionists** | 0 | 0.0 | 15,000 | 0.1 | 93 | −293 | −200 | −1.43 | 14,000 | 0.1 | 13,000 | 0.1 | 10,000 | 0.1 |
| **Buddhists** | 0 | 0.0 | 4,000 | 0.0 | 27 | −7 | 20 | 0.49 | 4,100 | 0.0 | 4,200 | 0.0 | 5,000 | 0.0 |
| **Baha'is** | 0 | 0.0 | 2,700 | 0.0 | 19 | 21 | 40 | 1.38 | 2,900 | 0.0 | 3,100 | 0.0 | 6,000 | 0.0 |
| **Hindus** | 0 | 0.0 | 1,000 | 0.0 | 10,400 | −500 | 9,900 | 14.14 | 70,000 | 0.5 | 100,000 | 0.7 | 130,000 | 0.8 |
| **Other religionists** | 570 | 0.0 | 10,000 | 0.1 | 77 | 23 | 100 | 0.95 | 10,500 | 0.1 | 11,000 | 0.1 | 30,000 | 0.2 |
| **Country's population** | **5,180,000** | **100.0** | **13,032,000** | **100.0** | 107,500 | 0 | 107,500 | 0.79 | 13,599,000 | 100.0 | 14,107,000 | 100.0 | 16,100,000 | 100.0 |

**COLUMNS, ROWS.** For meanings and definitions, see Codebook (Part 6). Note that, by definition, total 'Christians' = professing + crypto-Christians, which also = affiliated + nominal Christians. Percentages may not always total exactly, due to rounding.

**CENSUSES.** In contrast to most other countries, the Netherlands in its official censuses of religion since 1830, and in its public-opinion polls, has not asked about religious preference ('What is your religion?') but has phrased it to cover only *kerkelijke gezindte*, church denominational affiliation ('With which church are you affiliated?' (census), or 'What is your religious affiliation?' (NIPO)). Consequently, the census categories 'Roman Catholics', 'Protestants', etc imply formal church affiliation or membership; and the category of non-affiliated (*geen kerkelijke gezindte*) does not mean atheists and agnostics alone, but includes both (1) nominal Christians who lack formal membership requirements (baptism, confirmation, etc) or formal affiliation to churches; (2) non-religious and atheists, and those who have withdrawn from Christian profession; and (3) adherents of non-Christian religions. In Table 1 above, nominal Christians are estimated to form half of this category of non-affiliated. Official censuses of religion have been held every 10 years since 1830. **1830:** 59.1% Protestants, 39.0% Roman Catholics, 1.8% Jews, 0.1% other religionists. **1840:** 59.6% Protestants, 38.5% Roman Catholics, 1.8% Jews, 0.1% other religionists. **1869:** 62.5% Protestants (54.7% NHK), 36.5% Roman Catholics, 1.9% Jews, 0.1% other religionists. **1889:** 60.7% Protestants (48.7% NHK), 35.4% Roman Catholics, 2.1% Jews, 1.5% non-affiliated. 0.3% other religionists. **1899:** 60.1% Protestants (48.4% NHK), 35.1% Roman Catholics, 2.3% non-affiliated, 2.0% Jews, 0.2% Old Catholics (Jansenists). **1909:** 56.9% Protestants (44.2% NHK), 35.0% Roman Catholics, 5.0% non-affiliated, 1.8% Jews, 1.1% other religionists, 0.2% Old Catholics. **1920:** 53.3% Protestants (41.2% NHK), 35.6% Roman Catholics, 7.8% non-affiliated, 1.7% Jews, 0.2% Old Catholics. **1930:** 45.5% Protestants (34.4% NHK), 36.4% Roman Catholics, 14.4% non-affiliated, 1.4% Jews, 0.1% Old Catholics. **31.V.1947** (de jure): 42.3% Protestants (31.0% NHK, 7.0% GK), 38.5% Roman Catholics, 17.1% non-affiliated, 1.9% other religionists, 0.1% Jews, 0.1% Old Catholics. **31.V.1960** (de jure): 41.0% Protestants (28.3% NHK, 6.9% GK), 40.4% Roman Catholics, 18.3% non-affiliated, 0.1% Jews, 0.1% Old Catholics, 0.1% marginal Protestants. **28.II.1971** 39.4% Roman Catholics, 37.9% Protestants (22.9% NHK, 7.0% GK), 22.7% non-affiliated. As explained above, the latter figure for Christians (77.3%)

appears in the table above for 1970 under 'affiliated', and the figure for non-affiliated (22.7%) is broken down in the table in 1970 into 12.1% nominal Christians, 8.9% non-religious, 0.8% atheists and 0.9% other religionists.
**POLLS.** Numerous public-opinion polls of religion have been taken by NIPO et alia since 1940; results are given below for practising Christians.

### NOTES ON RELIGIONS
**AHMADIS.** The Ahmadiya Muslim Mission (Qadianis, from Pakistan) was begun in 1949 and now has a mosque in the Hague, with some Dutch converts.
**ATHEISTS.** Communist Party of the Netherlands (Communistische Partij van Nederland, CPN) (large; independent on Sino-Soviet dispute) and miniscule Maoist splinter groups: membership (1970) 10,000, (1974) 12,000; Communist voters (election of III.1959) 144,542 (2.4% of all votes), (29.XI.1972) 329,973 (4.5% of all votes).
**BAHA'IS.** Entered before 1921. Growth from 9 local spiritual assemblies (1964) to 18 (1973).
**BUDDHISTS.** Among the 30,000 Chinese with some Dutch converts.
**DOUBLY-AFFILIATED.** Members of newer Protestant denominations who are still enumerated by the NHK also.
**EVANGELICALS.** As documented for each province in Table 2 below, the NHK classifies 16% of all its churches as Conservative (i.e. Evangelical) in theology, as opposed to Liberal or Central. In addition, Evangelicals are found in over 130 other Protestant denominations of Conservative Evangelical theology.
**HINDUS.** Hindustani-speaking East Indians from Surinam, mostly immigrants (up to 12,000 a month) during 1975 immediately before Surinam's Independence. The column 'Natural change' includes this immigration, averaged over the decade 1970–80. Among Hindu sects, ISKCON (Hare Krishna) operates 1 centre, and Ananda Marga (Path of Bliss) operates others. A neo-Hindu movement, the Theosophical Society in 1975 had 28 Lodges with 1,017 members.
**JEWS.** In 46 communities; Portuguese as well as Dutch Jews.
**MUSLIMS.** Mainly migrant workers, rapidly rising after 1960 to 25,083 registered workers in 1968, to 30,000 in 1970, to 74,651 in 1973, and to 84,275 in 1974. Largest groups in 1974: 53,529 Turks, 29,637 Moroccans, 3,000 Indonesians, 2,600 from Surinam and the Netherlands Antilles, and 1,109 Tunisians. Almost all are Sunnis. There is also an Ahmadiya community (enumerated here under Muslims although declared non-Muslim by Pakistan).

The totals in the table include these adult workers together with their dependants including children, and also other non-worker groups of Muslims. Hajj pilgrims to Mecca. (1976) 29.
**NEO-PENTECOSTALS.** Charismatics within the non-Pentecostal Protestant denominations numbered in 1974 around 25,000 adults, mostly in the NHK, and also 10,000 young Jesus People (1973). Until 1974 the neo-pentecostal movement emphasized demon-possession and exorcism, and experienced little growth. From 1973 the charismatic movement also began to spread within the Old Catholic Church. By 1977 the agency Charismatische Werkgemeenschap Nederland was serving all charismatics including Classical Pentecostals and Roman Catholics.
**NOMINAL CHRISTIANS.** Mainly Protestants who regard themselves as such but who are non-affiliated (unaffiliated to any church).
**NON-RELIGIOUS.** In addition to post-Christian Europeans, this includes a large number of Ambonese (Indonesians) formerly animists but now with no religion; also 15,000 organized humanists. A poll in November 1964 gave these results: 'Do you consider yourself a humanist, or not?': 18% Yes, 75% No, 7% no opinion.
**OTHER RELIGIONISTS.** Adherents of other non-Christian religions and cults, including Rosicrucians (Rozekruisers Genootschap/Lectorium Rosicrucianum, world HQ in Haarlem, with 10 centres; also AMORC with 12 centres; in 1960 census, 1,498 Rosicrucians.
**PRACTISING CHRISTIANS.** Midwinter of 1948: weekly church attenders 60% of whole population (Roman Catholics 77%, Reformed Churches 70%, NHK 29%). June 1964: 'When did you last go to church?': 45% last Sunday, 5% Sunday before last, 3% Sunday 2 weeks ago, 11% over 2 weeks ago, 36% seldom or never. May-June 1968: 42% once weekly, 13% once monthly, 10% once every 2 months, 35% less than annually, or never. February 1970: 5% of population attend several times a week, 37% once a week, 18% from time to time, 8% never, 32% non-affiliated or non-religious. 19 November 1970: 36% of population attended last Sunday (Roman Catholics 46%, NHK 23%, Reformed Churches 69%, other Christians 35%; men 34%, women 36%). This weekly attendance of 36% on Sundays in winter dropped, as elsewhere in Europe, in summer to 26% on cloudy Sundays and 21% on sunny Sundays. *Catholic attendance.* Sunday mass attendance, for all baptized Roman Catholics over 7 years of age, has declined as follows: 1948, 77%; 1966, 64%; 1968, 56%; 1970, 46%; 1972, 41%; 1974, 36%; 1976, 31%. *Total practising.* These data show that, in 1970, annually-practising Christians numbered 60% of the total population,

which was then 78% of all affiliated Christians.
ROMAN CATHOLICS. The percentage of Roman Catholics in the country has risen gradually since 1909 due to a higher illiterate than average and to an increase in mixed Catholic/Protestant marriages.

THIRD WORLD INDIGENOUS. In about 5 denominations in 1970 (see Table 2).

**NON-CHRISTIAN RELIGIONS. Islam** has a growing following; in January 1974, the Muslim population was estimated to be approximately 102,000, according to official information supplied by interested ministries (Justice and Culture, Recreation). Of this total 84,275 were registered officially, having come from 3 countries furnishing the Netherlands with manual labour: Turkey (53,529), Morocco (29,637) and Tunisia (1,109). To this number should be added about 5,000 non-registered Muslim workers. The rest consist of some 10,500 nationals from other Arab, Asian and African countries (including nearly 3,000 Muslim Indonesians), 2,600 nationals from Surinam and the Netherlands Antilles (who constitutionally are of Dutch nationality) and 100 other Dutch, who although born in Holland have converted to Islam. Today's massive Muslim presence is therefore due primarily to the recruitment of manual labour, beginning with Turks in 1960, followed later by Moroccans and most recently Tunisians. Their numbers have continued to increase from 25,083 registered workers and their families in 1968 to 74,651 in 1973 and to over 84,000 in 1974.

Muslims are concentrated in the urbanized and industrialized west, in the provinces of Noord Holland and Zuid Holland. By the end of 1974, worship places consisted of only a few prayer halls and 2 mosques: one in The Hague (built by Ahmadiya in 1950) and the other at Almelo in the eastern part of the country. Several other mosques are being planned for the west. Quranic teaching is given privately and one Turkish Islamic school has been opened in Amsterdam. A federation of the different Muslim organizations active in the Netherlands was also being formed at the end of 1974, of which the following may be mentioned: (1) Islamic Society (Islamitisch Genootschap), of Ahmadiya inspiration, founded in The Hague in 1950; (2) Netherlands Islamic Society, in Vinkeveen, consisting mostly of members from Surinam; (3) Holland Islam Foundation, founded in Amsterdam in 1970, with a branch in The Hague, composed mostly of Ahmadis from Surinam; (4) Netherlands Muslim Association (Ahle Soenat wa Djamaat), founded in Utrecht in 1973, members being mostly Sunnis from Surinam; (5) Islamic Foundation Centre (Islam Merkezi Vakfi), founded in Utrecht in 1972, consisting of Turks; (6) The Mosque Foundation (Stichting 'De Moskee'), founded in Utrecht in 1973 to serve Moroccans; (7) Association for the Promotion of the Interests of Muslims in the Netherlands (Vereniging tot Bevordering van de Belangen van de Islam in Nederland), in Amsterdam and Rotterdam, sponsored by Sunnis and consisting mostly of Turks.

**Judaism** was severely decimated during the Nazi occupation, decreasing from 140,000 members before World War II to about 30,000 by 1974. Half of Holland's Jews live in Amsterdam where Anne Frank House and the Jewish Historical Museum are widely visited. Other cities with Jewish communities include Eindhoven, Groningen, Haarlem, The Hague, 's-Hertogenbosch, Hilversum, Leeuwarden, Middelburg, Nijmegen, Rotterdam, Scheveningen and Utrecht.

**Buddhism** has about 4,000 adherents, mostly Chinese. Holland's principal Buddhist centre is a Theravada shrine, Dhammasucharitanucharee Temple administered by Thai monks at Waalwijk in North Brabant. Other small groups are located in Amsterdam (an Indonesian Theravada group), Utrecht (Tibetan Lamaism) and Amersfoort (Zen). An unusual feature of Dutch Buddhism is its sponsorship of Kosmos in Amsterdam, a meditation centre serving all non-Christian religions. A movement to unify all Buddhists is in progress under the influence of the Stichting Nederlands Buddhistisen Centrum at Hengelo.

**CHRISTIANITY.** Evangelization began in the 7th century, with the Franks establishing a church at Utrecht; but little progress was made before the arrival of the English missionaries Willibrord and Boniface, during the first half of the 8th century. The Netherlands remained under the Holy Roman Empire until its disintegration when such local principalities as Utrecht became dominant; and the cities of Amsterdam and Haarlem rose to prominence following the Crusades. German mysticism became dominant in the 14th century through the influence of John of Ruysbroeck, Gerhard Groot and Thomas à Kempis, with emphasis on union with God as constrasted with churchly observance or good works. Many banded themselves together as Brethren of the Common Life, living essentially a monastic life with common rules but without permanent vows. The Netherlands came under the control of the dukes of Burgundy in the 15th century, followed by the Hapsburgs and then by Spain in 1555. At the same time, Holland became a place of refuge for the followers of Luther, Zwingli and Calvin, the latter ultimately taking precedence. With the attempt by Philip II of Spain to force Catholicism on Europe, the Dutch reformation became closely associated with its struggle for freedom, which lasted from 1568 to 1648. In 1581, 7 Protestant northern provinces began fighting under William of Orange, in turn persecuting Catholics of the southern provinces once Spanish rule had ended at the conclusion of the Thirty Years War.

The Golden Era of the 17th century saw Holland emerge as a great sea and commercial power, with colonies in the East Indies and North and South America. Dutch Reformed missions were established in the East Indies (1598), Formosa (1624), New York (1626), India (1633), Brazil (1640) and South Africa (1652); and the Dutch Reformed Church became Holland's official religion in 1651.

During the 18th century domestic quarrels and competitive wars with France, Britain and Spain brought about a decline, the Netherlands becoming a French dependency from 1795 to 1815. During this period the Catholic Church began once again to gain recognition. The constitution of 1848 affirmed religious liberty for all, and the Catholic hierarchy was re-established in 1853.

CATHOLIC CHURCH. The Dutch Roman Catholic population has remained relatively stable since the middle of the last century. At that time Catholics numbered 38% of the total, which increased slightly to 38.5% in 1947 and 40.4% in 1960, decreasing to 39.3% in 1971. In the years 1955–1964, the Catholic birth rate was still 2.7% above that of the population taken as a whole; but by 1970 the difference had been reduced to 0.7%, indicating that Catholics have by and large adopted family planning as have the rest of the population. The tendency towards non-attachment to a church, long apparent among the Reformed community, is also becoming more prevalent among Catholics. Some 300,000 Catholics in 1960 had been lost to the church by 1971.

The geographic spread of the Catholic population is uneven. The 3 northern provinces (Groningen, Drente and Friesland), which make up the diocese of Groningen, are 8% Catholic and form only 2% of the Catholic population of the country. The centre (dioceses of Utrecht, Haarlem and Rotterdam) are 25 to 30% Catholic, but the percentage is weaker in the strongly urbanized west centre (including Amsterdam and Rotterdam) than in the east. The south (dioceses of 's-Hertogenbosch, Breda and Roermond) is mostly Catholic between 85% and 90%.

Catholic religious practice is still high if one compares it with the situation in other countries or that of the Dutch Reformed Church. Nevertheless, the tendency is towards a weakening of practice, even if it appears to be stabilized in the large cities. Some 6.5% of children born to Catholic parents are no longer baptized. A 1968 survey showed that, of

Catholic Church in the Netherlands, Diocese of Haarlem. Parish church of St Vitus, Hilversum.

1,039,780 couples with both partners Catholic, all but 2.6% had been married in church. The number of mixed marriages in church increased from 6% to 12% between 1955 and 1969. Sunday mass attendance (for all Catholics over 7 years of age) on 2 normal weekends in January 1972 stood at a national average of 41.1%. The largest percentage for a diocese was 50% in Groningen (the so-called Catholic diaspora), and the smallest 32.3% in Rotterdam (the most urbanized area). Although mass attendance has decreased continuously for a number of years (from 64% in January 1966, to 56% in October 1968, 46% in October 1970, and 41% in 1972) it remains higher than in neighbouring countries. This is due principally to the fact that more than in other countries, one is not considered a member of the Netherlands Catholic Church if he ceases to practise his faith. Nevertheless, the tendency towards decreasing practise continues, and by January 1974 the national average of mass attenders had fallen to 36%.

At the beginning of 1971 the Catholic Church in the Netherlands had a total strength of 3,728 secular and 8,583 regular priests. Not counting those retired or sick, about one-third were in the active parish ministry, one-third working overseas (mostly in missions) and one-third involved in administrative or teaching posts. More than a third of the parish priests were over 55 years of age.

Dutch Catholicism has experienced recent changes which have radically altered its character and spirit. After the re-establishment of the Catholic hierarchy in 1853, the Catholic Church tended to emphasize spirituality and was characterized by a defensive attitude towards Protestants, Socialists and liberal Humanists. The effort to reintegrate the Catholic community into the main stream of the country's life, through the achievements of political and cultural equality, resulted in the formation of a system of organizations whose presence continues to be felt: press and media services (Catholic newspapers, radio and TV station), a political party (Katholieke Volkspartij), a trade union and numerous social and professional unions of various types. A similar compartmentalization (known as *verzuiling*) existed also among Protestants and Socialists, a vertical pluralism assuring social equilibrium and reciprocal tolerance. In the Catholic Church, this compartmentalization contributed to a tendency towards introversion, inherent in the theology of the Counter-Reformation, and a deep fidelity to the Roman pontiff whose anti-liberal and anti-Socialist position served to reinforce the existing system.

This traditional situation has changed radically since World War II through the development of urbanization and improvements in the standard of living. The questioning of authority in all sectors of society (family, factory, school, administration of justice) and the growth in desire for co-responsibility helped to prepare the way in 1954 for the first public criticism of the church by a group of Catholic Socialist laymen who refuse to obey the episcopate's demand forbidding the faithful from leaving their political and trade union organizations. This was followed by the evolution of intellectuals pleading for an 'open' Catholicism and a new spirit evident in priests returning from studies in foreign universities, especially Louvain (Belgium). At the same time the ideas of theologians, sociologists and psychologists came increasingly to convergence. Thus, under the guidance of the episcopate aided by a special office of scientific counsellors, began the development of a new image of the church, strongly reinforced by Vatican II. Other events of importance were the creation of the international theological journal *Concilium* in 1965, the first European episcopal conference in 1967, and the publication of the *New Catechism* for adults which attempted to bridge the gap between theology and exegesis on the one side and popular catechesis on the other. This work has enjoyed a wide success and by 1970 had been translated into 10 languages. However, 3 small groups of conservative Dutch Catholics (Confrontation, Legion of St Michael, and Truth and Life) with the aid of a part of the Roman Curia, attacked the catechism and received support from Vatican appointments in 1970 of conservative bishops to the dioceses of Rotterdam and Roermond. Tensions remain although the archbishop of Utrecht has worked strenuously to calm the explosive situation.

Perhaps the most important event of the past decade contributing to Catholic renewal in the Netherlands was the pastoral council held between 1966 and 1970. Creating it largely under the inspiration of the conciliar decree 'Cristus Dominus' of Vatican II, the Dutch bishops invited the faithful to assume a new form of co-responsibility for the church. The pastoral council, which became a deliberative assembly, set for itself 3 objectives: (1) the continuation of work begun at Vatican II, (2) an open study of the situation of the Catholic Church in the Netherlands; and (3) the elaboration of new options for the future. Such a meeting was made possible by the readiness of the Dutch bishops for open dialogue. Six plenary sessions, each of 3 days' duration, were held at Noordwijkerhout between 1968 and 1970. In addition to the bishops, there were 70 members elected by the 7 diocesan pastoral councils, 10 religious personnel, 15 members appointed by the bishops and 5 members of the Catholic secretariat,

in addition to Catholic experts and delegates from other churches, religious communities and the Humanist Union. Among its more startling declarations were the affirmation that the papal encyclical 'Humanae Vitae' was not convincing in its refusal to sanction contraceptives, and its recommendation that the requirement of celibacy for the priesthood be abolished. The council also requested a greater latitude for experiments in intercommunion with other Christian denominations and asked that a permanent body be set up to continue its work. In 1971 the bishops created a National Pastoral Council, with wide deliberative powers (although they retained the right of final decision), an action that was vetoed by Rome. In its place was established in 1972 a National Pastoral Committee (Landelijk Pastoraal Overleg), which would be informal and purely consultative.

The Dutch Catholic Church thus has attempted to transpose to the level of a national church the model of the universal church created at Vatican II. In addressing itself to the pastoral situation, it has not been able to avoid conflicts with Rome. Indeed, 2 different ecclesiologies are opposed: one in which Rome is united vertically with each national church, and the other in which the accent is placed on the horizontal communion of national churches forming together the universal church whose centre of unity is the church in Rome and its bishop the pope. Many Dutch Catholics consider this a test case for other national churches which have not yet gone as far as they have, although the National Pastoral Council model has been followed in the Federal Republic of Germany, Austria and Switzerland.

PROTESTANT CHURCHES. The principal Protestant tradition in the Netherlands is the Dutch Reformed community which is at present divided into 6 different major denominations, together with the Moluccan Protestant Church formed in 1950 by Indonesians resident in Holland. The total affiliated Reformed community is 4.3 million. The mother church is the Netherlands Reformed Church (Nederlandse Hervormde Kerk, NHK) which traces its tradition to the Reformation in 1568 and retains a balance between orthodox and liberal Calvinists. The NHK is divided into 11 church provinces with 2,275 congregations, in addition to 16 Walloon (French-speaking) parishes. Its central legislative body is the general synod, with administrative functions carried on by its general secretariat. Numerous boards and commissions have been established to handle the church's finances, publicity, personnel, missions, youth work, church schools, theological education, catechesis, social service and ecumenical relations. Most NHK ministers are trained in the non-denominational theological faculties (Faculteiten der Godgeleerdheid) in the state universities (Rijksuniversiteiten) of Leiden (founded

in 1575), Groningen (1614) and Utrecht (1636), with the NHK Theological Seminary (Theologisch Seminarium vamwege de NHK) in Driebergen.

Reaction against liberalism and state influence in the mother church have produced a number of neo-Calvinist schisms from the NHK beginning in the early part of the 19th century. The first of these movements (called the Afscheiding or Secession) took place in the village of Ulrum in Groningen in 1834, and within 2 years 100 other so-called free churches had been formed throughout the country. More schisms followed during the 1840s, and in 1886 another large exodus (called the Doleantie or Dissension) took place, with its centre in Amsterdam. The most recent schism in the Reformed community was in 1944, resulting in the formation of the Liberated Reformed Churches. Several groups established during the 19th century have retained their identity as separate denominations, notably the Christian Reformed Churches who date their founding to 1834 and the Old Reformed Churches begun in 1841. However, there have also been unifying forces at work among the neo-Calvinists, and these came together in the creation of the Reformed Churches in the Netherlands (Gereformeerde Kerken in Nederland) in 1892 and the Reformed Communities in the Netherlands (Gereformeerde Gemeenten) in 1907. The Gereformeerde Kerken is now the second largest Protestant denomination after the NHK, with nearly 1,200 parishes in 14 synods in Holland, and an affiliated body (Altreformierte Kirchen in Niedersachsen) in Germany. The church's general synod meets every 2 years with sessions lasting up to 8 weeks in duration. One of the church's most impressive institutions is the Free Reformed University of Amsterdam with 10,000 students.

Calvinism was made the state religion in 1651 but lost its special status in 1795 under French occupation. Nevertheless, the NHK continues to regard itself as the Dutch folk church. Although there was a basis for the claim prior to the 19th century when nearly 60% of the population professed allegiance to the NHK, since that time this percentage has declined continuously from 48.4% (1899), to 44.2% (1909), 41.2% (1920), 34.4% (1930), 31.0% (1947), 28.3% (1960), and 22.9% (1971). During the same period the neo-Calvinist churches have tended to retain a more stable membership of 8% to 9% of the population; the Gereformeerde Kerken, for instance, formed 7.0% of the total population in 1947, 6.9% in 1960 and 7.0% in 1971. The decrease in adherents to the NHK has been accompanied by a continuous increase in those claiming to be without any church allegiance. These trends are due to the declining appeal of the NHK, and the much smaller birth rate (until recently at least) of its members as contrasted with Catholics. The degree of non-allegiance varies considerably from region to region, it being most significant in the industrial area west of Amsterdam.

Of Holland's other Protestant communities, the most important are the Congregationalists, who are divided into 2 groups, the Remonstrant Brotherhood dating from 1618 and the Association of Free Evangelical Congregations from 1834; Mennonites, who entered Holland from West Germany in 1811; Salvation Army, who arrived from England in 1887; and Lutherans, who owe their origin to the early Reformation period. At least 12 distinct Pentecostal bodies are present, the largest being the Apostolic Church in the Netherlands.

OTHER CHURCHES. The Old Catholic Church in the Netherlands traces its history to the 18th century Jansenist controversy which resulted in schism from Rome and its creation in 1724 as an independent Catholic church, with an archbishop in Utrecht. This church has also provided episcopal succession for other European Old Catholic churches established after 1870 by German and Swiss Catholics who rejected papal infallibility and other decisions of Vatican Council I. All these churches are related through acceptance of the common doctrinal basis contained in the 1889 Declaration of Utrecht. A more recent split from Catholicism is the Old Roman Catholic Church, formed in 1970.

The Catholic Apostolic (Irvingite) Church spread from England to Holland in 1867 and has given rise to numerous schisms: the New Apostolic Church and 2 of its splinter groups, the Restored Apostolic Church and the Restored Apostolic Missionary Church, and the Liberal Catholic Church.

Three Orthodox traditions are represented in Holland (Greek, Syrian and Russian), and there are also Anglican chaplaincy services for the British

**Neo-pentecostals.** Members of Jesus People (total 10,000), Protestant charismatics in NHK (50,000) and other committed Christian youths at open-air rally.

expatriate community.

**CHURCH AND STATE.** According to the constitution of 1814 (amended on numerous occasions), each person is free to teach his religious opinions (Article 181) and 'All religious communities enjoy equal protection' (Article 182). No discrimination is tolerated between citizens for religious reasons (Article 183). Religious services of all types are permitted inside buildings and private houses, and the same is true outside 'to the extent that they are authorized by laws and regulations' (Article 184). This last article was introduced in 1848, and Catholic processions are at present allowed only in places where permission was granted prior to that date, although this is not considered an important issue today. Correspondence with superiors of religious communities is free of postal charge, as is the issuing of ecclesiastical instructions (Article 187). In general, religious freedom is not restricted beyond the limitations established in the penal code (Article 181), or in common laws promulgated by the sovereign (Article 186), or in measures necessary to maintain peace and public order (Article 184).

The Netherlands has no concordat with the Holy See nor privileged religion or 'religious community' (Kerkgenootschap in official terminology). In this sense church and state are separate, and there has been no specific government ministry for religious affairs since 1871. An 1853 law, promulgated shortly after the restoration of the Catholic hierarchy, gives to a department of the Ministry of Justice responsibility for verifying that the organization and administration of the various religious communities are in conformity with the law. Thus state approval is required when a church confers an ecclesiastical office on an expatriate (Article 12). Following the Napoleonic Code of France, it has been prohibited since the beginning of the 19th century for clergy to celebrate a religious marriage prior to the civil ceremony, the officiating minister being liable for punishment in case of infraction.

Protection is accorded to religious communities through sanctions related to Sunday observance, prosecution of those who offend religious scruples, and state payment of the salaries of military and prison chaplains. The state provides for legal recognition of the juridical personality of religious communities and their autonomous associations, which are not subject to the laws of 22 May 1855 (concerning the regulation and limitation of the right of association and meeting) and 31 May 1956 (dealing with foundations). In virtue of a law relating to broadcasting, many religious communities are accorded radio and TV time, which may be used by them or be transferred to others. A law of 1962 concerning the construction of churches created temporarily the possibility of state subsidies of up to 30% of the value for such construction. The law was extended until 1 March 1975.

The Netherlands has 14 political parties represented in parliament, of which 2 are Roman Catholic and 4 Protestant. On 17 April 1962, parliament, acting on the preliminary proposal of an ad hoc commission formed in 1946 whose final report was submitted in 1967, repealed Article 185 of the constitution. This article was introduced in 1815 and provided certain religious communities with subsidies in the form of salaries and pensions of ministers and other financial benefits. In reality, since the amounts had remained unchanged for a century and a half, such aid had become negligible in value. The commission's proposal that future financial relations between the state and the churches be regulated by law has been accepted by the government and by parliament, but no concrete decisions have yet been taken. Several denominations, particularly the Netherlands Reformed and Catholic churches, have maintained that a modest annual contribution by the state would not compromise the freedom of the churches.

Since 1876, 3 theological faculties have been attached to the state universities of Groningen, Leiden and Utrecht, serving primarily the NHK, and the state also meets supplementary costs relating to professional posts for training ministers of other religious communities. Since 1963, the theological faculties of the Free Reformed University of Amsterdam and the Catholic University of Nijmegen have been subsidized by the state. In 1970 these subsidies were extended to other higher theological institutions, notably the higher school of Reformed theology of Kampen and the Catholic theological training centres of Amsterdam, Heerlen, Tilburg and Utrecht.

Broadcasting studios in Hilversum near Raadhuis, including NCRV (Netherlands Christian Broadcasting Corporation) and KRO (Catholic Broadcasting Corporation).

Public education is regulated by law, with due respect for the religious principles of each person. Private primary schooling is subsidized on an equal basis with that of the public sector. Private secondary education receives partial state subsidies in accordance with prevailing legal dispositions. Thus, in the domain of education as in the realm of social organizations in general, there exists a triple system of parallel institutions: public, Protestant and Catholic. Nevertheless, these social and cultural organizations are now in the process of deconfessionalization, a slow but seemingly irreversible movement. This is evident in the increasing separation of these organizations from the ecclesiastical hierarchy and their integration into comparable organizations outside the churches. This form of deconfessionalization goes back to the first decade following World War II when the reconstruction of social life required the co-operation of every element in society. The emancipation of the laity in the Catholic Church has also contributed to this evolution. At the same time, Christian organizations are attempting to conserve and deepen the Christian and evangelical foundations for their activities.

**INTERDENOMINATIONAL ORGANIZATIONS.** The Council of Churches in the Netherlands (Raad van Kerken in Nederland) was founded in 1946 as the Ecumenical Council of Churches and received its new name in 1968 when the Catholic Church became a full member. Since then the council has become the principal co-ordinating body of the Dutch churches and has absorbed all the bilateral consultative commissions between the churches, except one (the Rome-Utrecht Commission between the Roman Catholic and Old Catholic churches), transforming them into multilateral organs of the council. In 1973 member churches numbered 11 including associates. The Council carries on its work through 8 sections, working groups and commissions, dealing with social affairs, ecumenical action, theological questions, international affairs (with a Sodepax-type structure), worship, intercommunion and ministry, ecumenical evangelization, and press and publicity.

Seven provincial councils have been formed for Drente, Friesland, Groningen, Limburg, Noord-Holland, Zeeland and Zuid-Holland, together with 2 inter-provincial councils: Noord-Brabant, Zeeland en Limburg; and Overijssel, Gelderland en Utrecht. There are also about 200 local Christian councils.

The Netherlands Missionary Council (Nederlandse Zendingsraad), founded in 1929 and re-organized in 1947, is dedicated to promoting fellowship and co-operation between the mission boards of its member churches (NHK, Gereformeerde, Moravian, Lutheran, Free Evangelical, Baptist, Remonstrant) and other missionary bodies (Reformed Missions League, Netherlands Bible Society, Egypt Mission, Near East Mission). The council is affiliated to the CWME/WCC.

Another body, Inter-ecclesial Advent Action for Latin America (Interkerkelijke Adventsactie voor Latijns Amerika), formed in The Hague by the Catholic episcopate in 1966, with its membership broadened to include Protestants (NHK, Mennonites, Moravians, Remonstrants, Baptists, Netherlands Protestant League) in 1969, provides financial aid for social work to churches and Christian organizations in Latin America.

Regular consultation and joint activities are also carried on between the Catholic and Protestant missionary councils; Catholic and Protestant Bible societies; Catholic Foundation for the Business Apostolate and the Reformed 'Gospel and Industry' Foundation; theological faculties of the state and free universities and the Catholic theological schools of Amsterdam and Utrecht.

Numerous ecumenical institutes and centres have been established; 6 may be mentioned here. (1) The Interuniversitair Instituut voor Missiologie en Oecumenica (IIMO), founded in 1969, has departments for ecumenism (Afdeling Oecumenica) at Utrecht and missiology at Leiden. (2) The Instituut voor Byzantijnse en Oecumenische Studies, founded in Nijmegen in 1948 by Catholic Assumptionist priests, organizes conferences and . encounters on ecumenism with special emphasis on Eastern Orthodoxy. (3) The Ecumenical Research Exchange (ERE), founded in Rotterdam in 1971, is an independent institute related to the Inter-university Institute on Value Research in Rotterdam and the Forschungstätte der Evangelischen Studiengemeinschaft in Heidelberg, West Germany. Its special interest is work for peace. (4) The Liturgisch Oecumenisch Centrum, founded in Rotterdam in 1969, promotes ecumenical dialogue on the liturgy. (5) The Oekumenische Pastorie Oudezijds 100 (OZ 100), founded in Amsterdam in 1955, is an ecumenical pastoral centre serving all churches in Amsterdam. (6) The Hospitium Oecumenicum San Luchesio, founded in Amsterdam in 1967, is a hostel for Catholic and Protestant clergy in Amsterdam, which also organizes pilgrimages to Rome, Taizé, Assisi, Geneva and Moscow.

Other ecumenical organizations include: (1) St Willibrord Vereniging, in 's-Hertogenbosch, which is the official Catholic agency for contacts with Protestants, Jews and non-believers; (2) the Apostolate of Reconciliation (Apostolaat den Hereniging), founded in 1927 in Boxtel, which is the official Catholic agency for contacts with the Eastern churches; (3) the Interecclesiastical Council for Peace (Inter Kerkelijk Vredesberaad, IKV), founded in The Hague in 1966, which organizes annually a Week for Peace (Vredes Week) and includes in its membership 9 churches: Catholic, NHK, Gereformeerde, Baptist, Lutheran, Old Catholic, Quaker, Moravian and Remonstrant; (4) the International League of Religious Socialists, founded in Switzerland in 1922, which has 600 members in Holland and associations in 7 other

European countries; (5) the International Fellowship of Reconciliation (IFOR), established in the Netherlands in 1919, a pacifist organization dedicated to influencing the churches concerning their attitude to peace, war and social justice; and (6) the Ecumenical Co-operative Society for Development, a World Council of Churches organization which was approved in August 1974 and established in Holland in 1976.

Dutch organizations dedicated to the advancement of dialogue between the world religions are numerous, of which 13 may be mentioned: (1) Wereldgesprek der Godsdiensten (WGG), founded in Driebergen in 1948, a branch of the World Congress of Faiths with headquarters in London, which was responsible for establishing in Rotterdam in 1972 the Instituut voor Godsdienstcommunicatie 'Interreligio'; (2) Permanent Comité van Joden, Christenen en Moslims in Europa in Amsterdam, which is a branch of the Standing Conference of Jews, Christians and Muslims in Europe (JCM) in England; (3) Interkerkelijk Contact Israël (ICI) in Utrecht, which promotes Protestant and Catholic dialogue with Jews; (4) Raad voor de Verhouding van Kerk en Israël, in Utrecht, which sponsors Dutch Reformed dialogue with Jews; (5) Katholieke Raad voor Israël (KRI) in 's-Hertogenbosch, which promotes Catholic dialogue with Jews; (6) Nederlandse Vereniging van Jesjoea Hammasjiach-belijdende Joden 'Hadderech', in The Hague, which is a Jewish organization related to the Christian Alliance; (7) Stichting 'Het Leerhuis', in Hilversum, which serves as a Beth NaMidzash for Jews, Christians and others and is a member of the International Council of Christians and Jews in London; (8) Anne Frank Stichting, in Amsterdam; (9) Contactorgaan van Levensovertuigingen, which promotes contacts between the churches and the Humanist Union; (10) Landelijk Werkgroep 'Samenleven Buitenlandse Werknemers', which is responsible for contacts between the churches and foreign workers (especially Muslims); (11) Begrip-Christentom/Islam, founded by White Fathers in Santpoort, which provides for relations between Christians and Muslims; (12) Muslim Foreign Workers section of the Catholic National Pastoral Committee; and (13) numerous local action groups (Rotterdam, Utrecht, Leiderdorp) seeking to aid foreign workers.

**BROADCASTING.** All radio and TV broadcasting is government-sponsored, except Radio Bloemendaal which is owned by the Reformed Church (with Christian services on Sundays and Christian holidays only), and in Hilversum, the Catholic Broadcasting Corporation (Stichting Katholieke Radio en Televisie Omroep, KRO) begun 1925, and operated by Catholics though independent of the hierarchy (60 hours a week radio, 8 hours a week TV). Evangelische Omroep has 2.5 hours per week of prime-time TV and 11 hours of radio. For Catholics, the Netherlands is a member in UNDA.

From abroad, Protestant programmes in Dutch are broadcast by Radio Luxembourg for 30 minutes on Sunday mornings; and Trans World Radio has 22 programmes a week produced in Holland.

## BIBLIOGRAPHY


'Acts and reports of the Reformed Ecumenical Synod'. Amsterdam, 1968.

*Catholica: informatiebron voor het Katholieke leven.* Tomes I, II. Hilversum: Stichting Catholica, 1968.

'La minorité catholique aux Pays-Bas', W. Goddijn, in CISR, Lille (1973).

'Netherlands', L. Layendecker, in H. Mol (ed), *Western religion* (The Hague: Mouton, 1972), p.325–363.

*Nieuw Kerkelijk Handboek 1972-1973* (Van Alphens). Gouda: N.V. Drukkerij Koch & Knuttel, 1972. 613p.

*Pius Almanak: Jaarboek van Katholiek Nederland, 1971.* Amsterdam: N.V. Drukkerij De Tijd, 1971.

'Pluralisme religieux et chrétienté,' W. Goddijn, *Social compass,* X,1(1963), 53–74.

'The case of Dutch Catholicism: a contribution to the theory of the pluralistic society', J.M.G. Thurlings, *Sociologia Neerlandica,* VII,2(1971), 118–136.

*The deferred revolution: a social experiment in church innovation in Holland, 1960–1970.* W. Goddijn. New York: Elsevier Scientific Publishing Co, 1975. (Dutch origin 1973).

'The development of sociology of religion in the Netherlands since 1960', L. Layendecker, *Social compass,* XIV(1967).

'The revolt of the Netherlands: the part played by religion in the process of nation building', J.E. Ellemers, *Social compass,* XIV(1967).

*Vijf jaar Kerkontwikkeling in Nederland, 1967–1971* (Five years in the life of the Duch Church, 1967–71). Amersfoort, The Hague: KASKI/De Horstink, 1973. 152p.


TABLE 2. ORGANIZED CHURCHES AND DENOMINATIONS IN THE NETHERLANDS

| Official name 1 | Begun 2 | Type 3 | Counc 4 | Congs 5 | Adults 6 | Affiliated 7 | Names, notes, and other statistics (see Codebook) 8 |
|---|---|---|---|---|---|---|---|
| Apostolic Church in the Netherlands | 1905 | P PeA | Z.... | | 10,000 | 32,600 | *Apostolische Kerk in Nederland.* Centralized hierarchy. Linked to Apostolic Ch (GB). |
| Apostolic Society | 1940 | C CAp | x.... | | 10,000 | 25,000 | *Apostolisch Genootschap.* Schism of 80% ex New Apostolic Ch. In VAC (Switzerland). |
| Assemblies of God | 1905 | P Pe2 | ZF... | 45 | 4,200 | 10,000 | *Broederschap van Pinkstergemeenten.* M=AoG(USA,UK),SFM. 70n,4f,1j,1s(85),W=75%. |
| Association of Free Ev Congregations | 1834 | P Con | KTT.f | 54 | 8,739 | 30,000 | *Bond van Vrije Evangelische Gemeenten.* In WCC 1947–49. 35n,G=1.3%pa,1s,W=65%,160Y. |
| Baptist Churches | | P Bap | ..... | 4 | 400 | 1,000 | *Baptisten Gemeenten.* Independent congregations of Baptist polity. |
| Baptist Mid-Missions | 1954 | P Bap | x.... | 7 | 55 | 100 | M=BMM(USA). Fundamentalist Baptists. Small autonomous congregations. 4f. |
| Catholic Apostolic Church | 1867 | C CAp | x.... | 18 | 300 | 500 | *Katholiek-Apostolische Gemeenten. Irvingites.* Rapidly declining. HQ The Hague. |
| **Catholic Church in the Netherlands:** | c 650 | R Lat | B.B.S | 1,845 | 3,735,800 | 5,336,919 | *Rooms-Katholieke Kerk.* C=36+16+128. 7q,5s. 7447n,950m,25757w,95735Yy. |
| M Utrecht | c 650 | R Lat | Bs | 375 | 634,200 | 906,000 | Overijssel, Utrecht, part Gelderland. D=PC(22). 1329 450 3500 18345 |
| D Breda | 1803 | R Lat | Bs | 169 | 356,400 | 509,073 | Zeeland, part Noord-Brabant. D=PC(76). 741 480 3091 9009 |
| D Groningen | 1559 | R Lat | Bs | 101 | 87,900 | 125,600 | Groningen, Friesland, Drente. D=PC(19),pc(17). 195 40 558 2200 |
| D Haarlem | 1559 | R Lat | Bs | 204 | 523,600 | 747,972 | Noord-Holland, Amsterdam. D=PC(80),pc(20). 1021 417 2884 11170 |
| D Roermond | 1559 | R Lat | Bs | 350 | 640,200 | 914,625 | Suppressed 1801–53. Limburg province. D=PC(100). 1191 842 5823 15812 |
| D Rotterdam | 1955 | R Lat | Bs | 222 | 564,100 | 805,927 | *Bisdom Rotterdam.* Zuid-Holland province. D=PC(33). 858 190 2301 15474 |
| D 's-Hertogenbosch | 1559 | R Lat | Bs | 424 | 929,400 | 1,327,722 | Part N-Brabant, Gelderland. D=PC(75),pc(28). 2112 1531 7600 23725 |
| Christadelphian Ecclesia | 1960 | P Ade | x.... | 1 | 30 | 100 | *Broeders in Christus. Christadelphian Bible Mission.* Ecclesia (church), The Hague. |
| Christian Brethren | | P CBr | x.... | 40 | 3,000 | 7,500 | *Vergadering van Gelovigen (Assembly of Believers).* Plymouth (Open) Brethren. 2f. |
| Christian Reformed Churches in the N | 1834 | P Ref | Jt... | 184 | 36,157 | 70,051 | *Christelijke Geref Kerken.* 1834, secession ex NHK. 121n,G=1.4%pa,1s,W=65%,1508Yy. |
| Church of Christ, Scientist | | M Sci | n.... | 16 | 1,200 | 1,900 | *Vereniging der Christelijke Wetenschap. Christian Science.* M=CCS(USA). 3m,17w. |
| Church of England (J Fulham) | 1586 | A plu | awc.. | 20 | 3,500 | 8,000 | *Anglikaans Kerkgenootschap.* CCCS chaplaincies (some seasonal), MTS in ports. 8x. |
| Ch of Jesus C of Latter-day Saints | 1864 | M LdS | x.... | | 5,000 | 7,245 | *Kerk van Jezus Christus van de Heiligen der Laatste Dagen.* M=CJCLdS. 80f,G=2.2%pa. |
| Churches of Christ | | P Dis | x.... | 4 | 200 | 500 | *Gemeente van Christus.* M=CC(Non-Instrumental)(USA). In Amsterdam, Haarlem, Hague. |
| Dutch Evangelical Churches | | P Ref | .v... | 10 | 400 | 1,000 | *Evangelische Gemeenten.* HQ Haarlem, Amsterdam. 1972 applied to join WCC. |
| Evangelical Church in Germany | 1857 | P LuR | lwc.. | 3 | 500 | 1,200 | *Duitse Evangelische Gemeenten.* Germans, from EKD. The Hague. 4n,G=0,W=16%,16Yy,8z. |
| Evangelical Lutheran Church in the N | c1520 | P Lut | LWC.W | 137 | 25,195 | 50,355 | *ELK. Evangelisch-Lutherse Kerk.* HQ Arnhem. 74n,1s(University of Amsterdam). Declining. |
| Free Evangelical Churches | | P ind | ..... | | 15,000 | 20,000 | *Vrije Evangelische Gemeenten.* Independent groupings of congregations. |
| Greek Orth Ch (D Belgium,N,Luxemb | | O Gre | Cwc.. | 1 | 2,000 | 3,000 | *Grieks-Orthodoxe Kerk.* Under EP Constantinople. 1 church in Rotterdam. 1x. |
| Jehovah's Witnesses | 1908 | M Jeh | x.... | 238 | 20,285 | 30,000 | *Getuigen van Jehovah. Watch Tower.* Active witnessing under way by 1925. 1647Y. |
| Johan Maasbach World Mission | 1952 | P Pe4 | ..... | 10 | 20,000 | 30,000 | *Stichting Johan Maasbach Wereldzending.* The Hague. Radio. 12n,G=17%pa,W=50%,275Y. |
| Liberal Catholic Church | 1916 | C Lib | xv... | 15 | 800 | 1,120 | *Vrije-Katholieke Kerk* (Centrum London). Decline: G=–2.3%pa. 40n,W=50%,20Yy. |
| Mennonite Brotherhood | 1811 | P Men | GWC.W | 254 | 34,700 | 62,000 | *Algemene Doopsgezinde Broederschap.* Rural. Also in NWGermany. Pacifist. 114n,1s. |
| Moluccan Protestant Church in the N | c1950 | P Ref | Rwn.. | | 10,000 | 20,000 | *Molukse Evangelische Kerk in Nederland* (GPM, from Indonesia). Ambonese separatists. |
| Moravian Church in the Netherlands | 1746 | P Mor | xwc.W | 5 | 1,525 | 2,000 | *Evangelische Broedergemeente. Hernhutters.* UB, European Continental Province. 5n. |
| Netherlands Orthodox Church | | O Gre | Cwc.. | 1 | 300 | 500 | *Nederlandse Orthodoxe Kerk.* Under EP Constantinople. Bishop in The Hague. |
| **Netherlands Reformed Church:** | c 690 | P Ref | RWC.W | 2,275 | 2,203,000 | 3,147,000 | *NHK. Nederlandse Hervormde Kerk.* 2000n,1s. Parishes: 1241. Theology: 13%,71%,16%. |
| CP Drenthe (Kerk Province Drenthe) | | P Ref | R | 87 | 119,000 | 170,000 | Pop: 56% NHK, 9% RC, 16% Geref,16% unaffiliated. 61 37 60 3 |
| CP Friesland | | P Ref | R | 224 | 119,000 | 170,000 | 38 8 24 24 188 31 68 1 |
| CP Gelderland | | P Ref | R | 314 | 350,000 | 500,000 | 40 39 8 9 185 10 65 25 |
| CP Groningen | | P Ref | R | 138 | 126,000 | 180,000 | 39 7 20 29 109 20 77 3 |
| CP Limburg | | P Ref | R | 20 | 17,000 | 24,000 | 3 94 1 1 17 0 99 0 |
| CP Noord-Brabant on Limburg | | P Ref | R | 101 | 63,000 | 90,000 | 3 89 2 2 77 5 73 22 |
| CP Noord-Holland | | P Ref | R | 244 | 287,000 | 410,000 | 20 31 7 37 110 16 79 5 |
| CP Overijssel | | P Ref | R | 164 | 196,000 | 280,000 | 37 32 12 15 82 11 73 16 |
| CP Utrecht | | P Ref | R | 151 | 161,000 | 230,000 | 36 32 11 17 71 3 61 36 |
| CP Zeeland | | P Ref | R | 108 | 84,000 | 120,000 | 43 27 20 8 88 6 86 8 |
| CP Zuid-Holland | | P Ref | R | 452 | 679,000 | 970,000 | 36 25 11 23 183 7 66 27 |
| Waalse Gemeenten | | P Ref | R | 16 | 2,000 | 3,000 | Walloon/French congs. Decline from 10,258 in 1869. 13 parishes. 50 50 0 |
| New Apostolic Ch in the Netherlands | c1900 | C CAp | x.... | 100 | 10,000 | 12,000 | *Nieuw-Apostolische Kerk in Nederland.* Chief Apostle in Germany. HQ Amsterdam. |
| Old Catholic Church in the Netherlands | 1724 | C OCa | UWC.W | 34 | 8,000 | 11,000 | *Oud-Katholieke Kerk. Ch of Utrecht.* Schism ex Ch of Rome. 2 Dioceses. 35n,1s. |
| Old Reformed Churches | 1841 | P Ref | ..... | 66 | 6,500 | 19,000 | *Oud-Gereformeerde Gemeenten.* Ledeboer schism 1841 ex NHK. 57 churches vacant. 9n. |
| Old Roman Catholic Church | 1970 | C CCa | ..... | 3 | 500 | 1,000 | *Oud-Roomsch Katholieke Kerk.* Recent schism ex Ch of Rome opposing centralization. |
| Protestant Union of the Netherlands | 1870 | M Unt | I...w | 115 | 16,400 | 23,000 | *Vereniging Nederlandse Protestantenbond.* Unitarians. Radio VPRO. 40n,G=–1.6%pa. |
| Reformed Churches in the Netherlands | 1892 | P Ref | FWC.W | 1,189 | 472,085 | 881,283 | *Geref Kerken in N.* 1886, the Dissension ex NHK. 1100n,G=1.0%pa,1s,1v,10997Yy. |
| Reformed Churches (Liberated) | 1944 | P Ref | ..... | 274 | 45,735 | 86,451 | *Gereformeerde Kerken (Vrijgemaakt).* Schism over baptismal regeneration. 159n,1s. |
| Reformed Communities in the N | 1907 | P Ref | ..... | 151 | 36,855 | 73,049 | *Gereformeerde Gemeenten in Nederland.* Merger of 1840 NHK schisms. HQ Gouda. 43n,1s. |
| Reformed Congregations in the N | | P Ref | ..... | 51 | 8,000 | 15,946 | Split ex Christian Reformed Ch. Conservative, 18th-century sermons. 3n,G=3%pa. |
| Religious Society of Friends | 1677 | P Qua | Q...W | 10 | 120 | 200 | *Genootschap der Vrienden.* Quaker-centrum, Amsterdam. Quakers. G=4.6%pa,W=50%. |
| Remonstrant Brotherhood | 1618 | P Con | RWC.W | 112 | 19,039 | 40,000 | *Remonstrantse Broederschap.* 1618, NHK expelled 200 clergy. 60n,G=–1.6%pa,1s,330Yy. |
| Restored Apostolic Church | 1897 | C CAp | ..... | | 3,000 | 9,000 | *Hersteld Apostolische Gemeenten in de Eenheid der Apostolen.* Ex New Apostolic Ch. |
| Restored Apostolic Missionary Church | 1897 | C CAp | ..... | 12 | 2,000 | 3,000 | *Hersteld Apostolische Zendingskerk. Stam Juda.* Ex New Apostolic Ch. HQ Amsterdam. |
| Russian Orthodox Church in the N | | O Sla | Mwc.. | 5 | 500 | 1,000 | *Russisch-Orthodoxe Kerk,* AD België & Nederland. Patriarchal Exarchate, Moscow. |
| Russian Orthodox Ch Outside of Russia | | O Sla | x.... | 3 | 800 | 1,500 | In D Western Europe & Austria, ROCOR (HQ New York). 1972, bishop defects. |
| Salvation Army | 1887 | P Sal | xwc.w | 218 | 39,835 | 60,000 | *Leger des Heils. Netherl Territory.* 39 institutions. 428n,G=–1.3%pa,1s,W=33%,618Y. |
| Scandinavian Seamen's Churches | | P Lut | ..... | 4 | 400 | 600 | *Scandinaafse Gemeenten.* Rotterdam: Danish, Finnish, Norwegian, Swedish churches. |
| Seventh Day Baptist Church | | P Bap | Tv... | 5 | 74 | 200 | *Zevendedags Baptisten. Netherlands Conference.* M=SDBC(USA). HQ Rotterdam. |
| Seventh-day Adventist Church | 1898 | P Adv | x.... | 55 | 3,372 | 5,000 | *Zevende Dags Adventisten. Netherlands UC(N,S Confs).* 31nx,G=1.2%pa,1j,1s,W=80%,175Y. |
| Streams of Power Movement | 1948 | P Pe4 | x.... | 13 | 2,000 | 5,000 | *Stromen van Kracht.* Dutch Pentecostalism. Also in West Indies. 8n,G=7.5%pa,350Y. |
| Syrian Orthodox Church: M Nederland | | O Syr | Dw.N. | 3 | 300 | 500 | *Oosters-Orthodoxe Kerk, Syro-Chaldeeuwse Successie.* In P Antioch. Arabs. 1 bishop. |
| Union of Baptist Churches in the N | 1845 | P Bap | T...f | 94 | 9,664 | 18,000 | *Unie van Baptisten Gemeenten in Nederland.* In northeast. 54n,1s(10),W=45%,264Y. |
| United Pentecostal Church | | P Pel | x.... | 1 | 50 | 200 | *Tolle Evangelie Gemeenschappen Filadelfia. Jesus Only Ch.* M=UPC(USA). 2f. |
| Other Protestant denominations | | P | ..... | | 10,000 | 20,000 | Total over 130 (see list below). |
| Other marginal Protestant bodies | | M | ..... | | 2,500 | 5,000 | Total over 30 (see list below). |
| Other Third-World indigenous churches | | I | ..... | | 2,000 | 4,000 | Several Indonesian, Korean and other bodies (see below); mainly pentecostal. |
| Other Catholic (non-Roman) churches | | C | ..... | | 500 | 1,000 | Total about 7 bodies (see below), mostly under episcopi vagantes. |
| Doubly-affiliated (duplication)(1970) | | | | | –86,000 | –122,819 | Members of minority churches still enumerated as members of NHK. |
| **Total affiliated (mid-1970)** | | | | **8,660** | **6,766,515** | **10,073,700** | **Total denominations (1970) . . . 230.** |
| **Total affiliated (mid-1975)** | | | | **8,760** | **6,766,400** | **10,073,500** | **Total denominations (1975) . . . 235.** |
| **Total affiliated (mid-1980)** | | | | **8,890** | **6,787,300** | **10,104,700** | **Total denominations (1980) . . . 240.** |

**NOTES ON TABLE ABOVE**

COLUMNS: for meanings and CODES (cols. 1, 3, 4, 8): see Codebook (Part 6). Column 1: **Boldface type** = church with over 10% of country's affiliated Christians.

CONFESSIONAL COUNCILS. The Remonstrant Brotherhood is a member of WARC and also of IARF.

NATIONAL COUNCILS (Column 4, 5th letter).

f = formerly in Ecumenical Council of Churches.

S = Netherlands Bishops' Conference (Nederlandse Bisschoppen Konferentie), also member of CCN.

W = Council of Churches in the Netherlands (CCN) (Raad van Kerken in Nederland, Conseil des Eglises aux Pays-Bas), replacing 1946–68 Ecumenical Council of Churches.

w = associate (guest) member of CCN.

*Local councils.* 200 local councils and 7 provincial councils are affiliated to CCN.

OTHER PROTESTANT DENOMINATIONS. A large number of these smaller bodies are Reformed schisms which seceded for theological reasons; many others are Pentecostal bodies. Names are given here in Dutch or English depending on which is better known. They include: Bethel Pentecostal Temple, Bible Christian Union (1946), Children of God International (from USA), Christian & Missionary Alliance (1952), Christelijk Afgescheiden Gemeenten, Ch of God of Prophecy, Ch of God (Anderson) (3 isolated congregations), Ch of God (Cleveland), Ch of Norway, Ch of Sweden, Ch of the Nazarene, Communidad Evangélica Española, Estonian Ev Lutheran Ch in Exile, Exclusive Brethren (Continuing Tunbridge Wells, and Kelly-Continental), Full Gospel Churches (Pentecostal; 15 churches in 1978), Gereformeerde Gemeenten onder het Kruis (under the Cross), Gospel Missionary Union (1966), Hervormde Gereformeerde Gemeente, Independent Assemblies of God, Latter Rain Assemblies (from South Africa), Oud-Lutherse Gemeente (Amsterdam), Oud-Baptisten Gemeenten, Portugese Kerk, Presbyteriaanse Gemeente (Rotterdam), Reformiert-Apostolischer Gemeindebund, Seventh-day Adventist Reform Movement, South-East Moluccan Protestant Ch, Vereniging van Uitgetredenen der NHK (Union of Separatists from NHK), Volle-Evangelie Gemeenten, Vrije Baptisten Gemeenten, Vrije Ev Broedergemeente, Vrije Gereformeerde Gemeenten, Vrije Hervormde Gemeenten, World Baptist Fellowship Mission Agency (1969), World Gospel Crusades (1968), World-Wide Missions (1969). There are also USA military chaplaincies among the 2,000 USA troops (1970).

OTHER MARGINAL PROTESTANT BODIES. These include: Amis de l'Homme (Groupe Sayerce), Anthroposophical Society (Christian Community Ch), Centrale Commissie voor het Vrijzinning Protestantisme in Nederland, Ch of the New Jerusalem (1 church), Gralsbewegung, Lord's New Ch, Lou-Gruppe or Lou-mensen (1950 movement begun by Louwrens van Voorthuizen, fisherman prophet claiming to be divine, with 12 wives, died 1968), Reorganized Ch of Jesus Christ of Latter-day Saints (USA; 470 members), Universal Life Church in the Netherlands (HQ Modesto, USA; 1971 applied to join WCC); and other Unitarian bodies.

OTHER THIRD-WORLD INDIGENOUS CHURCHES. Several Indonesian indigenous movements have followers among the Moluccans and others in the Netherlands. There are also: Holy Spirit Association for the Unification of World Christianity in the Netherlands (from Korea; 2,000 adherents by 1976), Moluccan Evangelical Ch (member of ICCC).

OTHER CATHOLIC (NON-ROMAN) CHURCHES. Including Antoinists (from Belgium), Broederschap van het Heilig Sacrament (ex Liberal Catholic Ch), Free Apostolic Ch, and 6 bodies operated by bishops-at-large.

UNITING CHURCHES. Negotiations for organic union were under way in 1974 between: Remonstrant Brotherhood, General Mennonite Society. There are also several smaller Reformed schisms which are in process of re-integration into the NHK.

**PEOPLES** (ethnolinguistic). Christians: 95.5% Dutch, 3.4% Frisian, 0.2% German, 0.2% Belgium, 0.2% Ambonese (Indonesian), 0.1% Antillean, 0.1% British, 0.1% Gypsy, 0.1% French, Chinese (1,000), Greek, Italian, Spaniard.

**COUNTRY-WIDE TOTALS**

EVANGELIZATION (see Part 5). 1900: 100%. 1970: 100%. 1980: 100%. *Mass evangelism.* Among the numerous recent campaigns: Billy Graham campaigns, a 1955 rally in Rotterdam (65,000 attenders, 2,000 enquirers), and in 1970 the Euro '70 TV Crusade in Hilversum televised from Dortmund, Germany; 1958, T.L. Osborn (100,000 in a park at The Hague), followed by his interpreter J. Maasbach; 1979, Here's Life Aalsmeer (CCCI). *Radiophonic evangelism.* Very numerous programmes and courses, including ICI (893 enrolments).

FOREIGN MISSIONARIES AND PERSONNEL (nationals serving abroad) (1973). Total 10,381: 10,008 Roman Catholics (7,608 foreign missionaries (3,720 priests, 1,166 brothers, 2,510 sisters, 212 lay, in over 38 institutes) (decline from 1963 total of 8,866) serving in mission or Third-World countries including 250 in Scandinavia, also 2,400 personnel serving in other Western nations especially Germany, Belgium, Canada, USA et alia), 349 Protestants (178 through 40 Dutch faith missions in Evangelische Zendings Alliantie (Evangelical Missionary Alliance) in 41 countries, 136 (decline from 350 in 1963) through Nederlands Zendingsraad in 16 countries, other independent Pentecostals et alia), about 20 marginal Protestants (Jehovah's Witnesses), about 4 Catholics (non-Roman).

FOREIGN MISSIONARIES AND PERSONNEL (aliens from abroad) (1973). Total 1,771. *From Western world.* 1,697: 1,500 Roman Catholics (1,293 from FR Germany, 118 Belgium, 31 France, 27 Austria, 11 UK, 7 USA), about 100 marginal Protestants (75 Mormons from USA), 85 Protestants (47 in 22 USA societies, 29 in 5 UK societies, 7 in 2 New Zealand societies, 2 in 1 Canada society), 8 Anglicans in 2 UK societies, about 2 Orthodox, about 2 Catholics (non-Roman). *From Communist world.* 30: 29 Roman Catholics (19 from Poland, 8 Hungary, 2 Czechoslovakia), 1 Orthodox from USSR. *From Third World.* 44: about 30 Roman Catholics (18 from Indonesia), 8 Protestants, 5 Asian indigenous from Indonesia and Korea, 1 Orthodox.

INSTITUTIONS (church-operated) (1973). Total 1,800, including 1,400 higher schools (3 minor seminaries), 200 medical centres, 5 radio/TV stations, 20 religious communities, 20 research centres, 27 seminaries (14 Protestant, 12 RC, 1 Catholic/non-Roman), 3 universities.

PERIODICALS. About 500 titles (7 SDA, 6 Pentecostal, 6 Salvation Army).

PERSONNEL. About 43,771 (42,000 national, 1,771 foreign).

RELIGIOUS LIBRARIES. About 300.

SCRIPTURE DISTRIBUTION (1975). Annual totals: 217,431 Bibles (1% free, 53% subsidized, 46% commercial), 369,018 NTs (11% free, 40% subsidized, 49% commercial), 93,052 UBS portions, 352,415 UBS selections. *Translations completed.* Portion: 3 languages since 1477. NT: Frisian in 1933. Bible: Dutch in 1522, Frisian in 1943.

SERVICE AGENCIES. About 340, including AMVJ, BVN, CCCI, CCN, CEBEMO, CEF, CJVF(YWCA), CLC, CMBR, CMC, CNI-N(IVF), ECM, EZA, FIOM, IARF, ICCC, ICI, IFOR, IKV, IRAM, IULCW, KCES, KJN, KLCMD, KNBTB, KOV, KRO, KWJ, MEMISA, MIIC, MIVA, NCRV, NCW, NKOV, NKV, NMR, OM, PMW, RKPN, SALCO, SBCN, SIAC, SIAMA, SIESC, SMB, SNPR, SNVR, TWR, YFC, YWAM.

**ADDITIONAL DATA ON CHURCHES**

CATHOLIC CHURCH IN THE NETHERLANDS. The Archdiocese of Utrecht = (in Dutch) Aartsbisdom Utrecht. *Column 8.* For each diocese, the names given are the civil provinces covered by the diocese. Diocesan boundaries do not follow civil boundaries exactly. *Annual baptisms.* (1972) 99.1% infant, 0.9% adult. *Personnel.* About 96% nationals, 4% expatriates (sisters 6.1% expatriate). *Diocesan councils.* The code D shows progress in internal diocesan conciliarism, indicating which dioceses in 1974 had: PC = pastoral council of laity, priests and religious (with total members in brackets), and pc = priests/presbyteral council or senate (with total members in brackets). In the Netherlands, members of these councils are all elected. Pastoral councils meet each year 10 times (Utrecht, Groningen, Rotterdam), 4 times (The Hague, Roermond), or twice (Haarlem, Breda). Priests' councils meet 5 or 10 times a year. *Catholic charismatics* (January 1974). 64 adults were active in 9 organized prayer groups in the Charismatic Renewal. *Seminaries.* In 1966–67 the bishops closed all major seminaries in favour of 5 institutes or faculties of theology. Of their 1,100 students in 1974, only a few were expecting ordination (there being only 47 ordinations to the priesthood in 1971, and 26 in 1972); most were preparing to be 'pastoral assistants' or laymen. Training for the priesthood is far looser than elsewhere in the Catholic Church and has provoked a continuing controversy with the Holy See. In 1973, there were 7 major seminaries for religious priests. *Main religious orders and congregations* (5 largest in each category only). Priests (1974): 668 OFM, 508 MHM, 473 SJ, 398 CSSp, 367 MSCI. Each of these has also 100–200 brothers. Brothers (1972): 732 Fraters van OLV Moeder van Barmhartigheid (Tilburg), 701 Broeders van de Onbevlekte Ontvangenis der H Maagd Maria (Maastricht), 367 Broeders van OLV van Lourdes (Dongen), 266 Fraters van OLV van het H Hart (Utrecht), 254 Broeders van St Louis (Oudenbosch). Sisters (1972): 2,540 Zusters van Liefde, 1,487 Kleine Zusters van de H Jozef, 1,445 Zusters van de Societeit van Jezus, Maria, Jozef ('s-Hertogenbosch), 1,354 Liefdezusters van de H Carolus Borromeus, 918 Zusters van Liefde van Jezus en Maria.

*Catholic organizations.* The Netherlands Bishops' Conference (Nederlandse Bisschoppen Konferentie) works through a secretariat known as the Sekretariaat van de Rooms-Katholieke Kerkprovincie in Nederland. Organizations of religious personnel include the Association of Dutch Religious Priests (Stichting Nederlandse Priester-Religieuzen, SNPR); Association of the Congregations of Brothers in the Netherlands (Stichting Broeder Congregaties Nederland, SBCN); Association of Dutch Religious Sisters (Stichting Nederlandse Vrouwelijke Religieuzen, SNVR); and Association of Monastic Councils (Stichting Monialen Beraad, SMB). For the armed forces, the Netherlands forms a military vicariate.

Since 1965, when Catholic Action ceased to exist, there have been practically no movements of the lay apostolate in the strict sense, beyond a few pious groups without much impact on Catholic life. On the other hand, specialized pastoralia is considerably developed including the Apostolate of Businesses (Bedrijfsapostolaat); National Catholic Council for the Apostolate of Marriage and the Family (Landelijke Katholieke Raad voor Huwelijks- en Gezinsapostolaat); and Council of Catholic Youth in the Netherlands (Katholieke Jeugdraad voor Nederland). There are also apostolates for itinerants, nomads, sailors, ferrymen, and the sick as well as for prisons, military posts and leisure. There is no co-ordinating agency for these different types of apostolate. Other autonomous lay movements are the Katholieke Werkende Jongeren (young travellers) plus 4 feminine movements, of which the most important is the Unie Nederlandse Katholieke Vrouwenbeweging.

The Holy See has diplomatic relations with the Netherlands and is represented to government and the Catholic hierarchy by a pro-nuncio in Amsterdam.

Catholic international organizations with their headquarters in the Netherlands include: (1) Pax Christi, founded in The Hague in 1944 to further Franco-German reconciliation, which is now a world peace movement; (2) International Secretariat for Catholic Secondary School Teachers (SIESC), in Nijmegen; and (3) International Secretariat of Catholic Artists (SIAC), in Amsterdam.

Opinion groups have been formed representing both progressivist and traditionalist tendencies. In 1973 the episcopate created a Commission of Pluriformity (Commisie Pluriformiteit), composed of 2 working groups (one each for progressivist and conservative movements) to analyse the forces at work behind the creation of informal groups in order to preserve them within the ecclesiastical province and from mutual alienation. Through this commission, the bishops have been able to maintain good relations with both sides.

Progressivist groups may be divided into 3 categories. (1) Critical communities, as they are called, in 1975 included: Amsterdamse Studentenekklesia (at Amsterdam with 384 members, 156 being Catholics), Kritische Gemeente Ijmond (at Beverwijk with 1,000 active members, some being members of the 2 principal Reformed churches), Jongerenkerk Venlo (at Venlo with 125 active members and 750 sympathizers), Leidse Studentenekklesia (at Leiden with 7 full-time Catholic and Reformed pastors), Werkplaats Kritische Gemeente Gooi (at Bussum with 120 members from the Catholic and Reformed churches), Dominicuskerk (at Amsterdam with 1,000 members in one Catholic parish), and Ekklesia Den Haag (in The Hague with 600 members, plus 3 Catholic priests and 2 Reformed pastors). (2) Action groups include Septuagint, founded in Driebergen in 1968, consisting of 70 priests advocating a married priesthood, which was joined by a group of 'critical preachers' of the Netherlands Reformed Church in 1970, and Open Kerk, founded in Heemstede in 1972 as a reaction against the appointment of the new bishop of Roermond. (3) Basic communities include some 50 groups spread throughout the country who held a national meeting at Driebergen in 1972. In addition there are more than 250 religious communes in the Netherlands.

Traditionalist groups include the following 13 bodies: (1) Confrontation (Confrontatie), founded in 1964 in Heerlen, which produces a strongly polemical journal of the same name; (2) For Pope and Church (Voor Paus en Kerk), in Venlo, which is a member of the Union International Pro Fide et Ecclesia in France and publishes the monthly *De Rots;* (3) St Willibrord Association (Sint Willibrord Stichting), founded in Utrecht in 1970, which organizes liturgical services, gives courses, publishes periodicals and has its own broadcasting association (Stichting Sint Willibrord Omroep); (4) Catholic Life Association (Stichting Katholiek Leven), in Heerlen, which produces the monthly *Waarheid en Leven;* (5) St Michael Legion (Michaël Legioen), founded in Amsterdam in 1964, which recognizes Vatican II but minimizes its impact and considers the present changes in the church as sources for the 'dictatorship of modernism'; (6) Rooms Katholiek Nederlands Centrum Pro Fide et Ecclesia, founded in Helmond in 1973, which seeks to co-ordinate the various traditionalist groups in the Netherlands; (7) Rooms Katholieke Partij Nederland (RKPN), founded in Voorburg in 1972, as a political party of traditionalist Catholics (4,000 members, with 70,000 votes in the 1972 elections), which criticizes the Catholic Social Party (Katholieke Volkspartij) for not sufficiently defending the principles of Catholic morals; (8) Vereniging voor Latijnse Liturgie, founded in Amstelveen in 1968, which is not a pressure group but seeks to find places where the liturgy can be celebrated in Latin; (9) Actie Comité voor Paus en Kerk, founded in 1970, which is not related to (2) above; (10) Priestergroep Limburg, founded in 1968, which includes 10% of the priests of the diocese of Roermond; (11) Priestergroep Haarlem, which unites traditionalist priests in the diocese of Haarlem; (12) Rooms Katholiek Jongeren Contact, founded in Stadskanaal in 1972, which caters for youth; and (13) Stichting tot Behoud van het Rooms-Katholieke Leven in Nederland, in Tilburg, which is dedicated to the preservation of Catholic life in Holland and produces the journal *Katholieke Stammen.*

Organizations for research and documentation include 7 centres: (1) Katholiek Sociaal Kerkelijk Instituut (KASKI), founded in The Hague in 1946 and related to FERES (Belgium); (2) Instituut voor Arbeidsvraagstukken (IVA), in Tilburg; (3) Katholiek Studiecentrum voor Geestelijke Volksgezondheid, founded in Utrecht in 1974, which studies the relationship between the Catholic faith and mental health; (4) De Horstink in Amersfoort; (5) Katholiek Documentatie Centrum (KDC) in Nijmegen; (6) Titus Brandsma Instituut in Nijmegen; and (7) Katholiek Nederlands Persbureau (KNP) in The Hague.

The work of Catholic social organizations is co-ordinated by the Raad van Overleg and the Stichting Katholiek Maatschappelijk Beraad, both in The Hague. The principal agencies are: (1) Nederlands Katholiek Vakverbond (NKV), in Utrecht, which unites the various Catholic trade union movements; (2) Katholieke Nederlandse Boeren en Tuindersbond (KNBTB), in The Hague, which is a confederation of farmers and market gardeners; (3) Nederlands Katholiek Ondernemersverbond (NKOV), in Rijswijk, which brings together some 40 professional organizations; and (4) Nederlands Christelijk Werkgeversverbond (NCW), founded in 1970 in The Hague, which unites Catholic and Protestant employers.

Popular education is co-ordinated by the Federatie van Vormingscentra, founded in Driebergen in 1970. Organizations concerned with emigration and immigration are the Bisschoppelijk Gedelegeerde voor Emigratie en Immigratie (Haarlem), Katholieke Centrale Emigratie Stichting (The Hague), and Katholieke Stichting voor Vluchtelingen en Ontheemden ('s-Hertogenbosch). Other bodies concerned with development aid are Bisschoppelijke Vastenactie Nederland (Zeist), which is a member of CIDSE in Belgium; Bisschoppelijk Adventsactie, which serves Latin America; Stichting Landen in Ontwikkeling, founded in The Hague in 1963 and which co-ordinates the work of 26 organizations; and CEBEMO, founded in The Hague in 1969, which serves as an intermediary (especially for obtaining funds) between Third-World Catholic development projects and the co-operative development programme of the Dutch government.

Institutions concerned with pastoral and religious training include: for theology, Theologische Faculteit van de Katholieke Universiteit te Nijmegen, Theologische Faculteit te Tilburg, Katholieke Theologische Hogeschool te Amsterdam, Hogeschool voor Theologie en Pastoraat te Heerlen and Katholieke Theologische Hogeschool Utrecht; for Dutch pastoralia, Mgr Bekkersinstituut in Nijmegen; for European pastoralia, Instituut voor Europese Priesterhulp in Maastricht and Europa-Seminarie in Rothem-Meerssen; for catechesis, Hoger Katechetisch Instituut (HKI), founded in Nijmegen in 1954; and for liturgy, Genootschap voor Liturgiestudie, Nederlandse St-Gregorius-vereniging and Nationale Raad voor Liturgie, all 3 in Utrecht.

Missionary action is co-ordinated by Nederlandse Missieraad (NMR), founded in 's-Hertogenbosch in 1967; Centraal Missionaire Beraad Religieuzen (CMBR); Centraal Missie Commissariat (CMC) in The Hague; and Werkgroep Missieprocuratoren, in Soesterberg. The principal agencies working in aid of missions are the Pauselijke Missiewerken (PMW) in The Hague; Curatorium Week voor de Nederlandse Missionaris in The Hague; Stichting Missie Verkeersmiddelen Actie (MIVA), in Amsterdam; Stichting Medische Missie Actie (MEMISA), in Rotterdam; Carosi, in Wassenaar; Missiehulpkorps; Agromisa, in Wageningen; and Medicus Mundi, in Nijmegen. Missiological study institutes include the missiological department at Leiden of Interuniversitair Instituut voor Missiologie en Oecumenica, and Sektie Missiologie van de Theologische Fakulteit van de RK Universiteit te Nijmegen; while the Centrum Kontakt der Kontinenten, in Soesterberg, is dedicated to the popularization of missions in the Dutch churches. In 1972, there were 7,608 Dutch Catholic foreign missionaries (3,720 priests, 1,166 brothers, 2,510 sisters and 212 lay persons), of which 2,498 serve in Africa (455 in Zaire), 2,133 in North and South America (Surinam 255, Netherlands Antilles 376, Brazil 1,059, plus 2 in Canada), 2,482 in Asia (Indonesia 1,981), 250 in Europe (mostly Scandinavia) and 245 in Oceania. The total of Catholic missionaries has thus declined slightly from the 1963 total of 8,866. Although there are no indigenous Dutch missionary communities, 38 different groups are active. The principal ones are: 436 MHM, 352 WF, 349 CSSp, 319 OFM, 296 Missionaries of the Sacred Heart of Jesus, 148 White Sisters, 146 Ursulines of the Roman Union, 137 Franciscans of Rosendaal, 113 Medical Missionary Sisters and 108 Sisters of Love.

The Catholic educational programme is co-ordinated by Nederlandse Katholieke Schoolraad. The Centraal Bureau voor het Katholiek Onderwijs, serves as a general secretariat for the Schoolraad and provides technical services for all Catholic schools. Both are located in The Hague. In 1971 there were 2,354 pre-primary schools (20,350 infants), 2,881 primary schools (622,319 pupils), 342 special schools for handicapped children (31,650 pupils), 532 secondary schools (253,843 students), 507 technical and lower professional schools (126,167 students), 198 technical and middle professional schools (31,560 students), 89 higher professional schools, one university and one higher school (15,007 students). The total was 6,905 Catholic schools (as contrasted with 12,562 non-Catholic schools), with 1,303,411 students (1,947,070 students in non-Catholic schools). The Katholieke Universiteit te Nijmegen was founded in 1923.

Catholic social service is co-ordinated by 2 organizations. (1) Men in Distress/Netherlands Caritas (Mensen in Nood-Caritas Neerlandica), founded in 's-Hertogenbosch in 1914. Affiliated to Caritas Internationalis in Italy, Netherlands Caritas, is only responsible for a part of the tasks normally fulfilled by Caritas in other countries. Its field of action is restricted to aiding foreigners, refugees and children. (2) The National Catholic Centre for Social Service (Katholiek Landelijk Centrum voor Maatschappelijke Dienstverlening, KLCMD), founded in 's-Hertogenbosch in 1949, is independent of the episcopate but is also affiliated to Caritas Internationalis; it is now in the process of joining with non-Catholic groups to form a non-confessional national body for co-ordinating all social work in the Netherlands. Netherlands social service organizations include: Conference of St Vincent de Paul (St Vincentius Vereniging); Catholic Association of Homes for the Aged (Katholieke Vereniging van Bejaardentehuizen) in The Hague; Netherlands Federation of Institutions for Unwed Mothers and their Children (Nederlandse Federatie van Instellingen voor Ongehuwde Moeder en haar Kind, FIOM) in The Hague; National Catholic Association for Family Social Service (Stichting Nationale Katholieke Gezinszorg) in Utrecht; Catholic Association of Parents for the Care of Children (Katholieke Oudervereniging, Voor het Zorgenkind) in Den Hommel; Catholic Association for the Rehabilitation of Criminals (Katholieke Reclasseringvereniging) in 's-Hertogenbosch); Catholic Alliance for the Protection of Children (Katholiek Verbond voor Kinderbescherming) in 's-Hertogenbosch; National Catholic Foundation for Family and Youth (Katholieke Nationale Stichting voor Bijzonder Gezins- en Jeugdwerk) in Utrecht; National Association of Clubs etc (Stichting Samenwerkende Landelijk Centrale Organen voor Wijk-, buurt- en clubhuiswerk, SALCO); and the Central Bureau for Catholic Hospitals and Clinics (Centraal Bureau voor het Katholieke Ziekenhuiswezen), founded in The Hague in 1933, which in 1971 had 108 medical institutions (2 being in Surinam and the Netherlands Antilles), with 31,909 beds. Other medical organizations are the Yellow and White Cross National Federation (Nationale Federatie Het Wit-Gele Kruis) in Utrecht, which is an association of polyclinics and dispensaries, and the Catholic Union of the Sick and Hospitalized (Katholieke Unie van Verplegenden en Verzorgenden).

MORAVIAN CHURCH IN THE NETHERLANDS. The church grew rapidly to 7,500 in 1975 through immigration of Creoles, Moravians from Surinam.

CHRISTIAN REFORMED CHURCHES IN THE NETHERLANDS. Largest church in the global International Council of Christian Churches until its withdrawal in 1977.

NETHERLANDS REFORMED CHURCH. The church was reformed during the Protestant Reformation in 1568. *Structure.* The church is divided into 11 Church Provinces and 54 Districts. *Column 8.* The first 4 sub-columns refer to the religious profession of the population in each province; the 5th sub-column gives the number of parishes; and the last 3 sub-columns describe the theology of each church province (see below). *Parishes.* In 1970 there were 1,241 village congregations (parishes) (including 30 missions and 27 specialized ministries not included in the Province statistics above) with 2,275 churches and preaching places (including 40 missions and 216 specialized ministries). In 1970, 380 churches were temporarily vacant, and 121 were permanently vacant because of the absence of people, clergy and money. *Theology of Provinces.* The last 3 sub-columns in column 8 in the table give the percentage of churches which are respectively classified by the NHK as Liberal, Central or Conservative in theology. For the whole NHK, of the 2,275 churches and preaching points 286 (13%) were classified in 1970 as Liberal, 1,633 (71%) as Central or orthodox, and 356 (16%) as Conservative. Thus the 224 churches in CP Friesland are classified as 31% Liberal, 68% Central, and 1% Conservative.

# NETHERLANDS ANTILLES

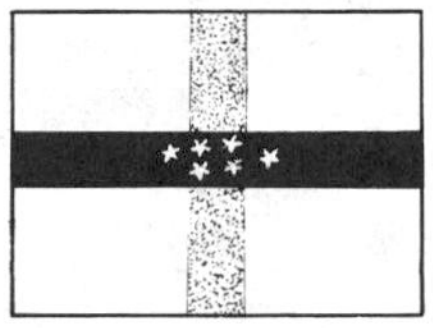

## SECULAR DATA

**STATE. Official name:** The Netherlands Antilles (De Nederlandse Antillen).
**Flag** (shown above right): White background, vertical red stripe, horizontal blue stripe with 6 white stars.
**Area:** 961 sq.km. (371 sq.miles). Description: 6 Antillian islands. Agricultural land: 8.3%.
**Government:** Self-governing integral part of the Kingdom of the Netherlands, since 1954 (1634 Dutch possession, 1954 co-equal part of kingdom).
**Legislature:** Staten, 22 members.
**Official language:** Dutch (*Nederlands-Vlaams*).
**Capital:** Willemstad 149,100.
**Political divisions:** 4 Insular Communities (Aruba, Bonaire, Curaçao, Windward Islands), all self-governing.
**Armed forces** (1976): Dutch.

**DEMOGRAPHY. Population:** 218,390 (census of 31.XII.1971. For 1970–2000 (UN), see last row of Table 1). Population density (1975): 252/sq.km. (652/sq.mile). Under 15 years: 43%. Growth rate (1975–80): 1.96% per year (births 2.87%, deaths −0.68%, emigrants −0.23%). Life expectancy (1975–80): 69.1 years. Household size: 4.4 persons.
**Major languages:** Dutch, Papiamento, English, French, Spanish, Chinese, Hindustani, Sranang Tongo (Surinamese).
**Urban dwellers** (1970): 47.9%. Urban growth rate (1950–70): 2.0% per year.
**Labour force:** 34%.
**Tourists** (1972): 552,776.

**ETHNOLINGUISTIC GROUPS:** 84.0% Antillean Creole (Dutch/Black), 6.1% White (5.3% Dutch, 0.8% USA), 4.9% Black (British & French West Indian), 2.9% Surinam Creole, 1.0% Venezuelan Mestizo, 0.7% Chinese (1,500), 0.4% Jewish, Syrian Arab, Lebanese Arab.

**MONEY** (1977). **Monetary unit:** NA guilder or florin (= 100 cents); US$1 = NAGld 1.77.
**National income per person:** US$1,900. Average annual family income: US$8,360.
**Inflation:** (1970–74) 10.4% per year.
**Cost of living in capital** (1976): index 124 (Washington DC = 100). Daily cost of living: US$46.

**HEALTH.** Hospitals: 11 (2,037 beds). Doctors: 210. Lepers: 30. Blind: 500. Psychotics: 1,900. Criminals: 5,530.

**EDUCATION.** Adult literacy: (1971) 92%. Schools: 280.

**LITERATURE.** Newspapers: 5 dailies.

**COMMUNICATION** (per 1,000 people). Phones: 137. Radios: 556. TV sets: 144. Daily newspaper circulation: 187 copies.

TABLE 1. RELIGIOUS ADHERENTS IN THE NETHERLANDS ANTILLES

| Year | 1900 | | mid-1970 | | Annual change, 1970–1980 | | | | mid-1975 | | mid-1980 | | 2000 | |
|---|---|---|---|---|---|---|---|---|---|---|---|---|---|---|
| *Name* | *Adherents* | *%* | *Adherents* | *%* | *Natural* | *Conversion* | *Total* | *Rate* | *Adherents* | *%* | *Adherents* | *%* | *Adherents* | *%* |
| **Christians** | **32,000** | **100.0** | **215,100** | **96.9** | **4,360** | **2** | **4,362** | **1.86** | **234,490** | **96.9** | **258,720** | **96.9** | **375,600** | **96.6** |
| professing | 32,000 | 100.0 | 215,100 | 96.9 | 4,360 | 2 | 4,362 | 1.86 | 234,490 | 96.9 | 258,720 | 96.9 | 375,600 | 96.6 |
| Roman Catholics | 25,600 | 80.0 | 193,000 | 86.9 | 3,918 | 64 | 3,982 | 1.89 | 210,690 | 87.1 | 232,820 | 87.2 | 339,500 | 87.3 |
| Protestants | 6,400 | 20.0 | 20,000 | 9.0 | 396 | −96 | 300 | 1.41 | 21,300 | 8.8 | 23,000 | 8.6 | 31,100 | 8.0 |
| Anglicans | 0 | 0.0 | 1,100 | 0.5 | 22 | −2 | 20 | 1.67 | 1,200 | 0.5 | 1,300 | 0.5 | 1,900 | 0.5 |
| Marginal Protestants | 0 | 0.0 | 1,000 | 0.5 | 24 | 36 | 60 | 4.62 | 1,300 | 0.5 | 1,600 | 0.6 | 3,100 | 0.8 |
| nominal | 1,600 | 5.0 | 20,670 | 9.3 | 431 | 142 | 573 | 2.47 | 23,200 | 9.6 | 26,400 | 9.9 | 43,600 | 11.2 |
| affiliated | 30,400 | 95.0 | 194,430 | 87.6 | 3,929 | −140 | 3,789 | 1.79 | 211,290 | 87.3 | 232,320 | 87.0 | 332,000 | 85.3 |
| total practising | 25,840 | *85* | 136,100 | *70* | 2,750 | −98 | 2,652 | 1.79 | 147,900 | *70* | 162,620 | *70* | 215,800 | *65* |
| non-practising | 4,560 | *15* | 58,330 | *30* | 1,179 | −42 | 1,137 | 1.79 | 63,390 | *30* | 69,700 | *30* | 116,200 | *35* |
| Roman Catholics | 24,960 | 78.0 | 175,000 | 78.8 | 3,543 | −31 | 3,512 | 1.84 | 190,540 | 78.7 | 210,120 | 78.7 | 303,700 | 78.1 |
| Catholic pentecostals | 0 | 0.0 | 0 | 0.0 | 19 | 181 | 200 | 20.00 | 1,000 | 0.4 | 2,000 | 0.7 | 10,000 | 2.6 |
| Protestants | 5,440 | 17.0 | 17,230 | 7.8 | 338 | −141 | 197 | 1.08 | 18,150 | 7.5 | 19,200 | 7.2 | 23,300 | 6.0 |
| Evangelicals | 5,000 | 15.6 | 9,000 | 4.1 | 181 | −41 | 140 | 1.44 | 9,700 | 4.0 | 10,400 | 3.9 | 14,400 | 3.7 |
| Anglicans | 0 | 0.0 | 1,000 | 0.5 | 20 | 0 | 20 | 1.82 | 1,100 | 0.5 | 1,200 | 0.4 | 1,700 | 0.4 |
| Marginal Protestants | 0 | 0.0 | 1,000 | 0.5 | 24 | 36 | 60 | 4.62 | 1,300 | 0.5 | 1,600 | 0.6 | 3,100 | 0.8 |
| Catholics (non-Roman) | 0 | 0.0 | 200 | 0.1 | 4 | −4 | 0 | 0.00 | 200 | 0.1 | 200 | 0.1 | 200 | 0.1 |
| Non-religious | 0 | 0.0 | 4,000 | 1.8 | 85 | 35 | 120 | 2.65 | 4,530 | 1.9 | 5,200 | 1.9 | 9,500 | 2.4 |
| Jews | 0 | 0.0 | 850 | 0.4 | 17 | 0 | 17 | 1.83 | 930 | 0.4 | 1,020 | 0.4 | 1,600 | 0.4 |
| Chinese folk-religionists | 0 | 0.0 | 700 | 0.3 | 11 | −31 | −20 | −3.33 | 600 | 0.2 | 500 | 0.2 | 300 | 0.1 |
| Buddhists | 0 | 0.0 | 600 | 0.3 | 11 | −11 | 0 | 0.00 | 600 | 0.2 | 600 | 0.2 | 500 | 0.1 |
| Muslims | 0 | 0.0 | 300 | 0.1 | 6 | 0 | 6 | 1.82 | 330 | 0.1 | 360 | 0.1 | 400 | 0.1 |
| Baha'is | 0 | 0.0 | 300 | 0.1 | 7 | 3 | 10 | 2.86 | 350 | 0.1 | 400 | 0.1 | 800 | 0.2 |
| Hindus | 0 | 0.0 | 100 | 0.0 | 2 | −2 | 0 | 0.00 | 100 | 0.0 | 100 | 0.0 | 100 | 0.0 |
| Other religionists | 0 | 0.0 | 50 | 0.0 | 1 | 4 | 5 | 7.14 | 70 | 0.0 | 100 | 0.0 | 200 | 0.1 |
| **Country's population** | **32,000** | **100.0** | **222,000** | **100.0** | **4,500** | **0** | **4,500** | **1.86** | **242,000** | **100.0** | **267,000** | **100.0** | **389,000** | **100.0** |

COLUMNS, ROWS. For meanings and definitions, see Codebook (Part 6). Note that, by definition, total 'Christians' = professing + crypto-Christians, which also = affiliated + nominal Christians. Percentages may not always total exactly, due to rounding.

CENSUSES. **27.VI.1960, 31.XII.1960** (de jure): 82.7% Roman Catholics, 10.5% Protestants, 4.9% other religionists, 1.8% non-religious. (Aruba 81.1% Roman Catholics; Curaçao 83.3% Roman Catholics; Bonaire 94.0% Roman Catholics). **31.XII.1971.** 86.9% Roman Catholics, 10.0% Protestants (including Anglicans and marginal Protestants), 1.5% non-religious, 0.3% Jews, 0.1% Muslims, 0.1% Buddhists.

**NOTES ON RELIGIONS**
BUDDHISTS. Chinese.
CATHOLIC PENTECOSTALS (or, Catholic charismatics). Several prayer groups on Curaçao and elsewhere.
JEWS. The synagogue on Curaçao is a striking edifice.
MUSLIMS. Immigrants from Syria, Lebanon and Surinam, grouped in the Association of the Muslim Community of Curaçao, have a mosque on Curaçao.
OTHER RELIGIONISTS. Including Rosicrucians (2 AMORC centres).

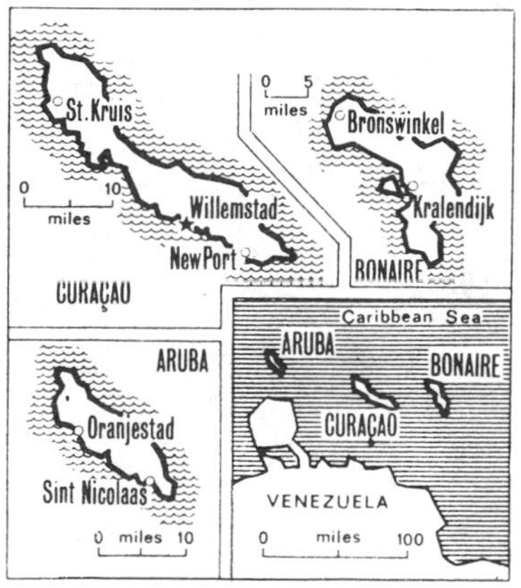
St.Kruis
0 10
miles
Willemstad
NewPort
CURAÇAO
0 5
miles
Bronswinkel
Kralendijk
BONAIRE
ARUBA
Oranjestad
Sint Nicolaas
0 miles 10
Caribbean Sea
ARUBA
BONAIRE
CURAÇAO
VENEZUELA
0 miles 100

**NON-CHRISTIAN RELIGIONS. Judaism** has a number of followers, with a notable synagogue on Curaçao.

**Islam** is followed by a small Muslim minority composed mostly of immigrants from Syria, Lebanon and Surinam. They are organized into the Association of the Muslim Community of Curaçao (Vereniging van der Moslem Gemeente op Curaçao).

**Baha'i** also has a few adherents.

## CHRISTIANITY

CATHOLIC CHURCH. Catholic clergy from the island of Santo Domingo began work during the 16th century, but in 1634 they were expelled and Catholicism prohibited by the Dutch. A few Jesuits were allowed to return in 1705, followed by Augustinians, Flemish secular priests and Franciscans. The vicariate of Curaçao was erected in 1842 and became the diocese of Willemstad in 1958. Catholics, being preponderant in the Windward Islands, have 85% of the population of Curaçao, 80% of Aruba and 94% of Bonaire. Their influence in the Leeward Islands is less, only 37% of the population. The Catholic Church has 20 parishes on Curaçao, 8 on Aruba, 3 on Bonaire, and one each on St Maarten (Dutch part), Saba and St Eustatius.

OTHER CHURCHES. The principal Protestant denomination of the islands is the United Protestant Church of Curaçao which is united Lutheran and Reformed in tradition and traces its origin to early Dutch settlement in 1650. Other churches of the Reformed tradition include the Protestant Church of the Netherlands Antilles in Aruba and Bonaire and 2 smaller Reformed churches on Curaçao. Methodism had its beginnings on St Eustatius which was evangelized by an African slave, Black Henry, and visited by Thomas Coke in 1787. The first missionary was sent to St Maarten in 1819, but it was not until 1929 and 1930 that Methodist work was begun on Aruba and Curaçao. Other active denom-

**Catholic Church, Diocese of Willemstad.** 'Goed Nieuws!' (Good News). Bible bookstall in Catholic church on Curaçao.

Entrance to transmitter and antenna site of most powerful radio facility in Western Hemisphere, TWR's Bonaire station, which beams to Americas, Europe, Africa and Asia.

inations include Seventh-day Adventists, Salvation Army, Anglicans, Moravians and several smaller smaller groups.

**CHURCH AND STATE.** As in Surinam, there is no law regarding religious societies, nor any government ministry specifically charged with religious affairs. However, all denominations receiving government subsidies must be officially registered. The state provides subsidies for the salaries of Catholic bishops and some priests, as well as ordained Protestant ministers, and aids in the administration of private church-sponsored schools but not their construction. Schools may offer courses in religious education if there is a request for such instruction.

**INTERDENOMINATIONAL ORGANIZATIONS.** Four separate church councils serve the Netherlands Antilles: Aruba Council of Churches, Curaçao Ecumenical Council of Churches, St Eustatius Council of Christian Churches and St Maarten Inter-Church Council. Altogether 9 churches are involved, although membership varies from one council to another. Thus Catholics are not members in Curaçao, whereas the chairman of the St Eustatius council in 1975 was a Catholic priest.

**BROADCASTING.** Government stations allow religious broadcasting, and on Netherlands Antilles Television, Catholics have 30 minutes during the week. There are 3 Protestant stations. Radio Victoria, owned by the Evangelical Alliance Mission, transmits Protestant programmes for 6 hours from Mondays to Saturdays and 12 hours on Sundays. A fifth of all programmes are produced locally. The Gospel Voice of the Eastern Carribbean operates from St Maarten. Thirdly, on the island of Bonaire, Trans World Radio has established a major international radio station broadcasting to the Caribbean and South America, Europe, the Middle East, Communist countries and Africa.

**BIBLIOGRAPHY**
*Morgen de eilanden zich verheugen.* J. Hartog. Curaçao: Fortkerk, 1969. 268p. (History of 200 years of Protestantism in the Netherlands Antilles).

TABLE 2.   ORGANIZED CHURCHES AND DENOMINATIONS IN THE NETHERLANDS ANTILLES

| Official name<br>1 | Begun<br>2 | Type<br>3 | Counc<br>4 | Congs<br>5 | Adults<br>6 | Affiliated<br>7 | Names, notes, and other statistics (see Codebook)<br>8 |
|---|---|---|---|---|---|---|---|
| Anglican Church (D Antigua) | | A ACa | awMRK | | 500 | 1,000 | In Ch of the Province of the West Indies. 95% West Indians (90% Black). W=58%. |
| Catholic Church: D Willemstad | c1580 | R Lat | P,NMK | 34 | 100,000 | 175,000 | *Rooms-Katholieke Kerk, Bisdom Willemstad.* C=4+3+7. 6n,57x,115m,309w,P=57%,4298Yy. |
| Christian Brethren | | P CBr | x.... | 1 | 50 | 100 | Plymouth (Open) Brethren. M=CMML. Small group influenced from Britain. |
| Church of God of Prophecy | 1959 | P Pe3 | z.... | 1 | 25 | 100 | M=CGP(USA). Holiness Pentecostals, split ex CoG(Cleveland). On Aruba. 2f. |
| Church of God (Anderson) | | P Hol | x.... | 5 | 200 | 400 | *General Assembly of the Church of God (Curaçao).* M=CoG(Anderson) (USA). 3n,W=50%. |
| Church of God (Cleveland) | | P Pe3 | ZF... | 2 | 50 | 100 | M=CoG(Cleveland) (USA). Holiness Pentecostals. |
| Evangelical Alliance Mission | 1931 | P int | xM... | 10 | 200 | 500 | M=TEAM. Papiamento work on Curaçao, Aruba, Bonaire. Radio Victoria (Aruba). 33f. |
| Jehovah's Witnesses | c1940 | H Jeh | x.... | 10 | 562 | 1,000 | *Getuigen van Jehovah.* 5 congregations on Curaçao, 4 Aruba, 1 Bonaire. 90Y. |
| Largo Community Church | | P com | ....K | 1 | 50 | 100 | Small independent congregation on Aruba, mainly European and other expatriates. |
| Liberal Catholic Church | | C Lib | x.... | 2 | 150 | 200 | *Vrije-Katholieke Kerk.* In Netherlands, UK, USA, Australia, New Zealand, et alia. |
| Methodist Church in Curaçao | 1787 | P Met | VuM,K | | 1,338 | 3,000 | In MCCA, Leeward Islands District. M=MMS(UK). First work St Eustatius. 5n,1x,1f. |
| Moravian Church in Curaçao | | P Mor | xuM,K | | 500 | 700 | In Surinam Province, Unity of Brethren. Work spread from Moravians in Surinam. |
| Reformed Church | | P Ref | ....K | | 100 | 500 | *Gereformeerde Kerk.* On Curaçao. Dutch Calvinist origin. |
| Reformed Church (Liberated) | c1950 | P Ref | ..... | 1 | 60 | 90 | *Gereformeerde Kerk (Vrijgemaakt).* 1944 schism in Holland over baptism. On Curaçao. |
| Salvation Army in Curaçao | 1927 | P Sal | xuM,K | | 1,000 | 2,000 | *Leger des Heils.* Curaçao Region, Caribbean & CAmerica Territory (HQ Jamaica). |
| Seventh-day Adventist Church | 1925 | P Adv | x.... | 14 | 1,254 | 3,000 | *Advent-Zendings Genootschap.* NA Mission. 4n,13mw,G=7%pa,1H,1p,14t(1498),W=83%,125Y. |
| United Protestant Church of Curaçao | 1650 | P LuR | .uM,K | 3 | 500 | 5,500 | *Verenigde Protestantse Gemeente van Curaçao.* M=NHK(Netherlands). 4x,2r. |
| Wesleyan Holiness Church | 1902 | P Hol | VF... | 2 | 67 | 140 | Originally M=Pilgrim Holiness Mission(USA); now Wesleyan Ch(USA). 1n,W=93%,7Y,4z. |
| Other Protestant denominations | | P | ..... | | 500 | 1,000 | Total about 10 (see list below). |
| **Total affiliated (mid-1970)** | | | | 165 | 107,106 | 194,430 | Total denominations (1970) . . . 28. |
| **Total affiliated (mid-1975)** | | | | 175 | 116,400 | 211,290 | Total denominations (1975) . . . 29. |
| **Total affiliated (mid-1980)** | | | | 185 | 128,000 | 232,320 | Total denominations (1980) . . . 30. |

**NOTES ON TABLE ABOVE**
COLUMNS: for meanings and CODES (cols. 1, 3, 4, 8): see Codebook (Part 6). Column 1: **Boldface type** = church with over 10% of country's affiliated Christians.
NATIONAL COUNCILS (Column 4, 5th letter).
  K = Curaçao Ecumenical Council of Churches (Oecumen-ische Raad van Kerken op Curaçao), also Aruba Council of Churches, St Eustatius Council of Christian Churches, St Maarten Inter-Church Council.
OTHER PROTESTANT DENOMINATIONS. These include: Bible Ch (Bethesda Mission), Ch of Christ (Non-Instrumental), Norwegian Seamen's Ch, PEMS (St Martin), Streams of Power.
UNITING CHURCHES. Negotiations for organic union were under way in 1974 between: Methodist Ch, United Protestant Ch of Curaçao; and also between the United Protestant Ch and the Reformed Ch.

PEOPLES (ethnolinguistic). Christians: 86.3% Antillean Creole, 6.1% White (5.3% Dutch, 0.8% USA), 4.9% Black, 1.5% Surinam Creole, 1.0% Venezuelan Mestizo, Chinese (60).

**COUNTRY-WIDE TOTALS**
EVANGELIZATION (see Part 5). 1900: 100%. 1970: 100%. 1980: 100%.
FOREIGN MISSIONARIES AND PERSONNEL (nationals serving abroad) (1973). Total about 10 Roman Catholics in Netherlands et alia.
FOREIGN MISSIONARIES AND PERSONNEL (aliens from abroad) (1973). Total 445. *From Western world.* 433: about 300 Roman Catholics, 133 Protestants (119 in 6 USA societies, 4 in 2 UK societies, 3 in 1 Canada society, 2 in 1 WGermany society, some from Netherlands). *From Third World.* 12: about 10 Roman Catholics, 2 Protestants.
INSTITUTIONS (church-operated) (1973). Total 65, including 43 higher schools, 15 medical centres, 3 radio stations.
PERIODICALS. About 12 titles.
PERSONNEL. About 671 (226 national, 445 foreign).
RELIGIOUS LIBRARIES. About 4.
SCRIPTURE DISTRIBUTION (1975). Annual totals: 3,173 Bibles (54% free, 39% subsidized, 6% commercial), 27,720 NTs (47% free, 53% subsidized), 740 UBS portions, 24,355 UBS selections. *Translations completed.* Papiamentu: portion in 1844, NT 1916.
SERVICE AGENCIES. About 20, including ABS, CCV, JCC, RKO, TWR (1965; Bonaire; 80 missionaries), YMCA.

**ADDITIONAL DATA ON CHURCHES**
CATHOLIC CHURCH. The diocese (erected 1958) is a suffragan of M Port-of-Spain (Trinidad). It operates 4 hospitals. *Annual baptisms.* (1972) 99.5% infant, 0.5% adult. *Seminarians.* 3.

Catechists. 3 full-time. One training school. *Indigenous religious congregations.* Nil. *Main foreign orders and congregations.* Priests: OP. Brothers: Our Lady of Mercy, Our Lady of Lourdes, FSC. Sisters: Dominican Tertiaries, Franciscan Tertiaries (3 different orders).
*Catholic organizations.* The diocese is a member of the Antilles Episcopal Conference, with headquarters in Kingston, Jamaica, itself a member of CELAM. There is no national presbyteral or pastoral council. Religious personnel are represented on the Conference of Major Superiors of the Antilles, with headquarters in Jamaica, which is a member of CLAR. The principal lay movements are Cursillos de Cristianidad; Legion of Mary; Scouts, Antilliaanse Meisjesgilde (for girls), Jonge Wacht (for boys) and Jeugd Centrale Curaçao, the latter serving as the co-ordinating committee for all youth organizations.
The Holy See has no diplomatic relations with the Netherlands Antilles. It is represented to the Catholic hierarchy by an apostolic delegate based in Port-au-Prince, Haiti.
In 1974 the Catholic Church was responsible for 143 schools (45,285 students), 4 hospitals (1,270 beds), 4 homes for the aged (300 residents), numerous medico-social institutions, 57 credit unions (12,000 members), several low-cost housing societies and a Christian labour union serving dock workers and hotel and office personnel.

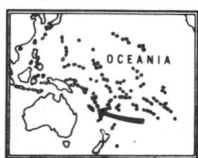

# NEW CALEDONIA

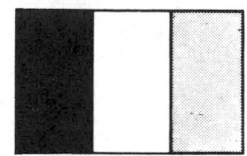

## SECULAR DATA

**STATE. Official name:** The Territory of New Caledonia and Dependencies (Le Territoire de la Nouvelle-Calédonie et Dépendances).
**Flag** (shown above right): That of France.
**Area:** 19,058 sq.km. (7,358 sq.miles). Agricultural land: 21.7%.
**Government:** Overseas territory of France, since 1946 (1853 annexed by France, 1864–94 used as penal colony).
**Legislature:** Territorial Assembly, 35 members.
**Official language:** French (*Français*).
**Capital:** Nouméa 47,966 (1969).
**Armed forces** (1976): French.
**Dependencies:** Bélep Archipelago, Chesterfield Islands, Huon Islands, Isle of Pines, Loyalty Islands, Walpole.

**DEMOGRAPHY. Population:** 100,579 (census of 11.III.1969).

For 1970–2000 (UN), see last row of Table 1). Population density (1975): 7/sq.km. (17/sq.mile). Under 15 years: 42%. Growth rate (1975–80): 2.89% per year (births 4.02%, deaths −1.17%, immigrants 0.04%). Life expectancy (1975–80): 55.9 years. Household size: 4.2 persons.
**Major languages:** French, Melanesian (Houailou, Iai, Lifu, Maré, Ponérihouen), Uvean, Javanese, Tahitian, Vietnamese, and about 20 other local languages.
**Urban dwellers** (1970): 40.9%. Urban growth rate (1950–70): 5.6% per year.
**Labour force:** 45%.
**Tourists** (1966): 7,068. (1968) 17,199. (1972) 10,000.

**ETHNOLINGUISTIC GROUPS:** 48.1% Melanesian, 35.6% French & European & part-European (Euronesian), 6.0% Wallisian (Uvean), 4.5% other Polynesian (1.3% Outlier, 1.3% Tahitian), 1.5% Vietnamese (1,490), some Arab.

**MONEY** (1977). **Monetary unit:** CFP franc (= 100 centimes); US$1 = CFPF 91.00.
**National income per person:** US$5,400. Average annual family income: US$22,680.
**Inflation:** (1970–74) 8.8% per year.
**Cost of living in capital** (1976): Daily cost of living: US$40.

**HEALTH. Hospitals:** 32 (1,296 beds). Doctors: 83. Lepers: 2,540 (20.3 per 1,000). Blind: 30. Psychotics: 900.

**EDUCATION. Adult literacy:** (1976) 91%. Schools: 245.

**LITERATURE. Periodicals:** 15. Newspapers: 3 dailies, 20 non-daily.

**COMMUNICATION** (per 1,000 people). Phones: 127. Radios: 280. TV sets: 101. Daily newspaper circulation: 91 copies.

### TABLE 1. RELIGIOUS ADHERENTS IN NEW CALEDONIA

| Year | 1900 | | mid-1970 | | Annual change, 1970–1980 | | | | mid-1975 | | mid-1980 | | 2000 | |
| Name | Adherents | % | Adherents | % | Natural | Conversion | Total | Rate | Adherents | % | Adherents | % | Adherents | % |
|---|---|---|---|---|---|---|---|---|---|---|---|---|---|---|
| **Christians** | 38,900 | 71.1 | 99,600 | 91.4 | 3,186 | −103 | 3,083 | 2.71 | 113,770 | 91.0 | 130,430 | 90.6 | 219,500 | 88.9 |
| professing | 38,900 | 71.1 | 99,600 | 91.4 | 3,186 | −103 | 3,083 | 2.71 | 113,770 | 91.0 | 130,430 | 90.6 | 219,500 | 88.9 |
| Roman Catholics | 35,100 | 64.2 | 79,500 | 72.9 | 2,545 | −55 | 2,490 | 2.74 | 90,900 | 72.7 | 104,400 | 72.5 | 177,600 | 71.9 |
| Evangelical Catholics | 300 | 0.5 | 1,650 | 1.5 | 39 | −80 | −41 | −2.89 | 1,420 | 1.1 | 1,240 | 0.9 | 1,520 | 0.6 |
| Protestants | 3,800 | 6.9 | 20,100 | 18.4 | 641 | −48 | 593 | 2.59 | 22,870 | 18.3 | 26,030 | 18.1 | 41,900 | 17.0 |
| nominal | 800 | 1.5 | 1,350 | 1.2 | 63 | 128 | 191 | 8.56 | 2,230 | 1.8 | 3,260 | 2.3 | 8,580 | 3.5 |
| affiliated | 38,100 | 69.7 | 98,250 | 90.1 | 3,123 | −231 | 2,892 | 2.59 | 111,540 | 89.2 | 127,170 | 88.3 | 210,920 | 85.0 |
| total practising | 32,380 | 85 | 63,860 | 65 | 2,030 | −150 | 1,880 | 2.59 | 72,500 | 65 | 82,660 | 65 | 126,550 | 60 |
| non-practising | 5,720 | 15 | 34,390 | 35 | 1,093 | −81 | 1,012 | 2.59 | 39,040 | 35 | 44,510 | 35 | 84,370 | 40 |
| Roman Catholics | 34,000 | 62.2 | 76,500 | 70.2 | 2,443 | −103 | 2,340 | 2.68 | 87,250 | 69.8 | 99,900 | 69.4 | 167,500 | 67.8 |
| Protestants | 4,000 | 7.3 | 17,900 | 16.4 | 560 | −100 | 460 | 2.30 | 20,000 | 16.0 | 22,500 | 15.6 | 34,600 | 14.0 |
| Evangelicals | 3,000 | 5.5 | 3,300 | 3.0 | 104 | −14 | 90 | 2.43 | 3,700 | 3.0 | 4,200 | 2.9 | 6,500 | 2.6 |
| Melanesian indigenous | 0 | 0.0 | 3,000 | 2.8 | 92 | −32 | 60 | 1.82 | 3,300 | 2.6 | 3,600 | 2.5 | 6,200 | 2.5 |
| Marginal Protestants | 100 | 0.2 | 800 | 0.7 | 26 | 4 | 30 | 3.23 | 930 | 0.7 | 1,100 | 0.8 | 2,500 | 1.0 |
| Anglicans | 0 | 0.0 | 50 | 0.0 | 2 | 0 | 2 | 2.80 | 60 | 0.0 | 70 | 0.0 | 120 | 0.0 |
| **Muslims** | 0 | 0.0 | 4,400 | 4.0 | 140 | −6 | 134 | 2.70 | 4,970 | 4.0 | 5,740 | 4.0 | 9,400 | 3.8 |
| **Non-religious** | 1,000 | 1.8 | 3,800 | 3.5 | 140 | 130 | 270 | 5.40 | 5,000 | 4.0 | 6,500 | 4.5 | 16,000 | 6.5 |
| **Baha'is** | 0 | 0.0 | 400 | 0.4 | 13 | 4 | 17 | 3.54 | 480 | 0.4 | 570 | 0.4 | 1,200 | 0.5 |
| **Buddhists** | 0 | 0.0 | 400 | 0.4 | 10 | −20 | −10 | −2.86 | 350 | 0.3 | 300 | 0.2 | 200 | 0.1 |
| **Tribal religionists** | 14,800 | 27.1 | 300 | 0.3 | 8 | −8 | 0 | 0.00 | 300 | 0.2 | 300 | 0.2 | 200 | 0.1 |
| **Other religionists** | 0 | 0.0 | 100 | 0.1 | 3 | 3 | 6 | 4.62 | 130 | 0.1 | 160 | 0.1 | 500 | 0.2 |
| **Country's population** | 54,700 | 100.0 | 109,000 | 100.0 | 3,500 | 0 | 3,500 | 2.80 | 125,000 | 100.0 | 144,000 | 100.0 | 247,000 | 100.0 |

**COLUMNS, ROWS.** For meanings and definitions, see Codebook (Part 6). Note that, by definition, total 'Christians' = professing + crypto-Christians, which also = affiliated + nominal Christians. Percentages may not always total exactly, due to rounding.
**CENSUSES. 1961:** 73.1% Roman Catholics, 20.1% Protestants, 5.4% other religionists.

## NOTES ON RELIGIONS

**BAHA'IS.** Begun 1952. Growth from 1 local spiritual assembly (1964) to 3 (1973).

**BUDDHISTS.** Vietnamese, declining since the 1963–69 repatriation of most to North Vietnam for political reasons.
**EVANGELICAL CATHOLICS.** This term is used to describe persons who are affiliated to churches termed by the state Evangélique (Protestant, Anglican, marginal Protestant, indigenous), but who in government censuses are regarded as or profess to be, Roman Catholics.
**MELANESIAN INDIGENOUS.** In one denomination in 1970 (see Table 2).
**MUSLIMS.** Mostly Javanese immigrants from Indonesia, who are Sunnis (of the Shafiite rite), with some Arabs.
**NON-RELIGIOUS.** In 1900, mainly French long-term political prisoners and other Europeans. In 1970, mainly French settlers.
**OTHER RELIGIONISTS.** Including Rosicrucians (1 AMORC centre).
**ROMAN CATHOLICS.** In 1900, Catholics consisted of almost all the 23,000 French (including a majority of the total of 40,000 French political prisoners taken to Ile Nou penal settlement from 1864–1897), many of the 27,700 Melanesians, and some of the 3,280 Chinese and other Asiatics.
**TRIBAL RELIGIONISTS.** In 1970, animists in remote mountain areas, and adherents of occasional traditionalist Melanesian cargo cults, usually introduced from New Hebrides.

## NON-CHRISTIAN RELIGIONS.
**Islam** has over 5,000 adherents, mostly Javanese immigrants from Indonesia, who are Sunnis of the Shafiite rite, with some Arabs.

**Traditional religions** exist only among a few tribes in remote mountain areas. Social rites, during which celebrations give way to orgiastic dancing called Pilou-pilou, are gradually disappearing. Melanesian cargo cults have touched New Caledonia at times, usually from New Hebrides.

## CHRISTIANITY.

**CATHOLIC CHURCH.** Catholic missionaries entered New Caledonia in 1843, and by 1884 the first 4 native priests had been ordained. The majority of the population is now Catholic and includes a large number of Europeans. Parishes with resident priests are found on New Caledonia itself, the islands of Bélep and Pines and the Loyalty Islands of Ouvea, Lifou and Maré. A Vietnamese priest is in charge of a Vietnamese parish in Nouméa, the capital. The majority of the Wallis Islanders (5,980 in 1969) are Catholics. Coming to work in the nickel mines,

they are poorly integrated into the local population and remain particularly dependent on the church. A remarkable programme of pastoral renewal has recently been inaugurated in the territory, characterized by: (1) the preparation (since the beginning of 1973) of a diocesan synod, the first assembly (with 600 participants, mostly Melanesian, 25% representing youth) taking place in May 1974; and (2) the creation of 'apostolic units' involving the regrouping of parishes (5 or 6 per unit) and the formation of sacerdotal teams (3 or 4 priests per team) whose members no longer reside in the parishes but live together, each one being responsible for a functional specialization such as catechesis or school work. This programme began in 1972 and by 1974, 4 apostolic units had been formed. Its purpose is to provide a solution to the isolation of priests and to make lay persons more aware of their responsibility for the church.

**OTHER CHURCHES.** Christianity was first brought to New Caledonia by a native Tongan in 1834. In 1841 the London Missionary Society sent 2 Samoans as teachers and the first White LMS missionaries arrived during the 1850s. The LMS turned over its work to the Paris Mission in 1922. The Evangelical Church, the result of this early effort, is the largest of the non-Catholic churches. A schism by 3 pastors in 1960 produced the country's first indigenous denomination, called the Free Church. Seventh-day Adventists have been active since 1925, with the Assemblies of God entering the field later. There are also Jehovah's Witnesses, and a Mormon schism. The small Anglican community, mostly British nationals, is part of the diocese of New Hebrides in the Church of the Province of Melanesia. In 1971 there were 44 Protestant schools.

**Eglise Evangélique en Nouvelle-Calédonie et Iles Loyauté.** Administration of communion.

**CHURCH AND STATE.** The island was named by Captain James Cook in 1774 and annexed by France in 1853. It served as a penal colony from 1864 to 1894. As a French overseas territory, church-state relations are the same as those in metropolitan France. The large Catholic and Protestant school programmes receive government subsidies.

**BROADCASTING.** The metropolitan France organization ORTF offers on Sundays one hour of broadcast time in the morning for church services and 15 minutes on Thursday evenings for news, discussions and music. These are alternated between the Catholic Church and the Evangelical Church. Broadcasts are in French with excerpts in Lifu and Tahitian. TV time also is offered for showing short films and locally-televised short talks. For Catholics, an associ-ation grouping New Caledonia with New Hebrides is a member of UNDA.

**BIBLIOGRAPHY**
'Forerunners of Melanesian nationalism', J. Guiart, *Oceania*, 22, 2 (December 1951), 81–90. (Cargo cults in New Hebrides and New Caledonia).
'Naissance et avortement d'un messianisme: colonisation et décolonisation en Nouvelle Calédonie', J. Guiart, *Archives de sociologie des religions*, 7 (Jan–June, 1959), 3–44.

TABLE 2. ORGANIZED CHURCHES AND DENOMINATIONS IN NEW CALEDONIA

| Official name 1 | Begun 2 | Type 3 | Counc 4 | Congs 5 | Adults 6 | Affiliated 7 | Names, notes, and other statistics (see Codebook) 8 |
|---|---|---|---|---|---|---|---|
| Assemblées de Dieu de Nouméa | | P Pe2 | ZF... | 5 | 232 | 400 | *Assemblies of God.* M=AdD(France),AoG(USA). 2n,2f,G=39% pa,1s(10),W=50%,18Y,35z. |
| Eglise Adventiste du Septième Jour | 1925 | P Adv | x.... | 5 | 440 | 800 | *Seventh-day Adventists, NC Mission.* Declining 7% pa. 1n,2x,4t(549),W=85%.47Y. |
| Eglise Anglicane (D New Hebrides) | | A ACa | avpK. | 1 | 30 | 50 | *Anglican Ch.* Under D New Hebrides, Ch of the Province of Melanesia. British. |
| **Eglise Catholique: M Nouméa** | 1843 | R Lat | P.,PY. | 33 | 44,400 | 76,500 | *Catholic Ch in NC.* M=SM2. C=2+2+5. 8n,51x,73m,244w,1H,7h,P=42%,1p,1s,2220Yy. |
| Eglise Evangélique en NC & IL | 1841 | P Ref | .WP.. | 95 | 4,000 | 16,700 | *Ev Ch in NC & Loyalty Is.* M=LMS,PEMS. Several schisms. 6n,1s(6),195Yy,135z. |
| Eglise Libre | 1960 | I Ref | ..... | 2 | 1,500 | 3,000 | *Free Ch. French Protestant Ch.* Split ex EENC by 3 pastors. Mission in New Hebrides. |
| Eglise Sanito (Saints) | c1885 | M LdS | x.... | | 200 | 500 | *Sanitos, Kanitos (Saints).* M=Reorganized Ch of JC of LdS(ex CJClLdS,USA). Nouméa. |
| Témoins de Jéhovah | c1950 | M Jeh | x.... | 1 | 189 | 300 | *Jehovah's Witnesses. Watch Tower. IBSA.* Active witnessing under way by 1954. 37Y. |
| **Total affiliated (mid-1970)** | | | | 147 | 50,991 | 98,250 | Total denominations (1970) . . . 8. |
| **Total affiliated (mid-1975)** | | | | 150 | 57,900 | 111,540 | Total denominations (1975) . . . 8. |
| **Total affiliated (mid-1980)** | | | | 153 | 66,000 | 127,170 | Total denominations (1980) . . . 9. |

**NOTES ON TABLE ABOVE**
COLUMNS: for meanings and CODES (cols. 1, 3, 4, 8): see Codebook (Part 6). Column 1: Boldface type = church with over 10% of country's affiliated Christians.

**PEOPLES** (ethnolinguistic). Christians: 51.5% Melanesian, 37.7% French (White) & Euronesian (part-French), 6.6% Wallisian (Uvean), 1.5% other Polynesian, 1.0% New Hebridean Melanesian, 0.7% Vietnamese, 0.6% British, 0.4% Javanese.

**COUNTRY-WIDE TOTALS**
EVANGELIZATION (see Part 5). 1900: 75%. 1970: 99%. 1980: 100%. *Radiophonic evangelism.* ICI (1,897 enrolments, 500 active students).
FOREIGN MISSIONARIES AND PERSONNEL (nationals serving abroad) (1973). Total 13 in Fiji, France and New Hebrides: 6 Roman Catholics, 4 Melanesian indigenous, 3 Protestants.
FOREIGN MISSIONARIES AND PERSONNEL (aliens from abroad) (1973). Total 247. *From Western world.* 226: 210 Roman Catholics, 16 Protestants (9 in 2 France societies, 5 in 1 UK society, 2 in 1 USA society). *From Third World.* 21: about 20 Roman Catholics from Indonesia, Vietnam, Wallis & Futuna et alia, 1 Protestant from New Hebrides.
INSTITUTIONS (church-operated) (1973). Total 38, including 20 higher schools, 10 medical centres, 1 religious community, 1 study centre, 2 seminaries (1 RC, 1 Protestant).
PERIODICALS. 7 titles.
PERSONNEL. About 522 (275 national, 247 foreign).
RELIGIOUS LIBRARIES. 4.
SCRIPTURE DISTRIBUTION (1975). Annual totals: 1,000 Bibles (70% subsidized, 30% commercial), 1,700 NTs (70% subsidized, 30% commercial), 10,200 UBS portions, 27,500 UBS selections. *Translations completed.* Portion: 5 languages since 1855. NT: 4 languages since 1864. Bible: 3 languages since 1890.
SERVICE AGENCIES. About 12, including ACO, CV/AV, JAC/F, JIC/F, JOC/F.

**ADDITIONAL DATA ON CHURCHES**
EGLISE CATHOLIQUE. The archdiocese has 2 suffragans: Port Villa (New Hebrides), and Wallis & Futuna. *Catholics.* 51% White (French), 37% Melanesians, 8% Wallisians, 700 Vietnamese, 420 Indonesians. *Annual baptisms.* (1972) 99.0% infant, 1.0% adult. *Brothers.* Including 33 nationals. *Sisters.* Including 124 nationals. *Seminary.* The major seminary of Nouméa was closed in 1973 through lack of students. *Catechists.* Total (1969) 110. One training school at Ponerihouen. *Indigenous religious congregations.* Sisters: Petites Filles de Marie (begun 1911; in New Hebrides also). *Foreign orders and congregations.* Priests: SM2, OCSO. Brothers: PFM, Frères du Sacré-Coeur. Sisters: Missionnaires de la Société de Marie, St-Joseph de Cluny, Petites Soeurs des Pauvres, Soeurs de la Société de Marie. *Catholic organizations.* New Caledonia is a member of the Bishop's Conference of the Pacific (Conférence des Evêques du Pacifique, CEPAC) with its headquarters in Fiji. Lay organizations include Scouts and Guides, CV/AV, JOC/F, JAC/F, JIC/F, ACO, and the Legion of Mary.
The Holy See is represented to the hierarchy by the Apostolic Delegation for New Zealand and the Pacific Islands, based in Wellington, New Zealand.
In 1970 there were 70 Catholic schools, mostly at the primary level. The number of pupils frequenting 66 of these schools was 9,535 as contrasted with a total school population of 27,644 pupils in 1968. In the same year, the church sponsored one clinic with 60 beds, 6 dispensaries, one leprosarium, one home for the aged and one hostel for girls.

# NEW ZEALAND

## SECULAR DATA

**STATE. Official name:** The Dominion of New Zealand. Adjective of nationality: a New Zealander.
**Flag** (shown above right): Blue field with British Union Jack at upper hoist corner; 4 red stars outlined in white.
**Area:** 268,676 sq.km. (103,747 sq.miles). Agricultural land: 51.8%.
**Government:** Parliamentary state (constitutional monarchy), since 1947 (1840 British possession, 1907 self-governing dominion, 1947 Independence).
**Legislature:** House of Representatives, 87 members (4 being Maoris).
**Official language:** English.
**Chief cities:** capital Wellington 141,800 (1974), Christchurch 292,520, Auckland 291,050.
**Political divisions:** 9 Provincial Districts, divided into Counties, Boroughs and Town Districts.
**Armed forces** (1976): Total 12,575 regular: army 5,432, navy 2,843, air force 4,300 (36 combat aircraft). Reserves: 12,635.
**Foreign forces** (1973): 250 USA troops.
**Dependencies:** Cook Islands, Niue, Ross Dependency, Tokelau Islands. (1971 census: 7 Statistical Divisions and 10 Urban Areas).

**DEMOGRAPHY. Population:** 2,862,631 (census of 23.III.1971. For 1970–2000 (UN), see last row of Table 1). Population density (1975): 11/sq.km. (29/sq.mile). Under 15 years: 33%. Growth rate (1975–80): 1.47% per year (births 2.25%, deaths −0.82%, immigrants 0.04%). Life expectancy (1975–80): 72.4 years. Household size: 3.4 persons. By 1978, 26,000 Whites a year were emigrating to Australia.
**Major languages:** English, Maori, Dutch, Irish, Samoan, Tongan, Chinese (Cantonese), and other languages.
**Urban dwellers** (1970): 79.0%. Urban growth rate (1950–70): 2.7% per year.
**Labour force:** 39%.
**Refugees** (1977): About 3,000 from Eastern Europe.
**Tourists** (1972): 199,695. (1974) 259,336.

**ETHNOLINGUISTIC GROUPS:** 89.3% White (Pakeha) (76.9% Anglo-New Zealander, 7.0% English, 2.1% Scottish, 1.7% Anglo-Australian, 0.8% Dutch, 0.6% Irish, 0.2% Welsh, 0.1% Greek, Polish, Croat, Slovene, Russian, Serbian, Ukrainian, Romanian), 7.9% Maori, 1.9% other Polynesian (0.8% Samoan (22,200), 0.5% Cook Island Maori (13,800), 0.3% Tongan (8,000), 0.2% Niuean (5,460), 0.4% Chinese (12,800) (Cantonese), 0.3% Indo-Pakistani (7,800), 0.1% Jewish, 0.1% Fijian (2,000), Hungarian, Gypsy, Pitcairner, Arab.

**MONEY** (1977). Monetary unit: dollar (= 100 cents); US$1 = NZ$1.07 (operational rate of exchange).
**National income per person:** US$4,100. Average annual family income: US$13,940.

**Church of Jesus Christ of Latter-day Saints.** One of the fastest-growing churches in New Zealand, expanding at 5% per year. Mormon Maori girls from New Zealand perform dance at Polynesian Cultural Centre, Hawaii.

**Inflation:** (1970–74) 9.1% per year, (1975) 15% per year (consumer price index 161).
**Cost of living in capital** (1976): index 108 (Washington DC = 100). Daily cost of living: US$33.

**HEALTH.** Hospitals: 337 (28,723 beds). Doctors: 3,426. Lepers: 31. Blind: 3,687. Psychotics: 27,000. Drug addicts: over 500.

**EDUCATION.** Adult literacy: 98%. Education rate: 78%. Schools: 2,584. Universities: 6.

**LITERATURE.** Annual new book titles (1973): 1,339. Periodicals: 1,455. Scientific journals: 160. Newspapers: 40 dailies, 103 non-daily.

**COMMUNICATION.** (per 1,000 people). Phones: 488. Radios: 911. TV sets: 304. Daily newspaper circulation: 376 copies.

TABLE 1. RELIGIOUS ADHERENTS IN NEW ZEALAND

| Year | 1900 | | mid-1970 | | Annual change, 1970–1980 | | | | mid-1975 | | mid-1980 | | 2000 | |
|---|---|---|---|---|---|---|---|---|---|---|---|---|---|---|
| *Name* | *Adherents* | *%* | *Adherents* | *%* | *Natural* | *Conversion* | *Total* | *Rate* | *Adherents* | *%* | *Adherents* | *%* | *Adherents* | *%* |
| **Christians** | **802,130** | **98.3** | **2,690,080** | **95.4** | **41,288** | **–13,363** | **27,925** | **0.99** | **2,824,890** | **93.2** | **2,969,330** | **91.0** | **3,661,090** | **85.8** |
| professing | 802,130 | 98.3 | 2,690,080 | 95.4 | 41,288 | –13,363 | 27,925 | 0.99 | 2,824,890 | 93.2 | 2,969,330 | 91.0 | 3,661,090 | 85.8 |
| Protestants | 342,700 | 42.0 | 1,085,700 | 38.5 | 16,358 | –9,153 | 7,205 | 0.64 | 1,119,200 | 37.0 | 1,157,750 | 35.5 | 1,321,880 | 31.0 |
| Anglicans | 341,000 | 41.8 | 1,006,740 | 35.7 | 15,151 | –9,125 | 6,026 | 0.58 | 1,036,600 | 34.2 | 1,067,000 | 32.7 | 1,237,430 | 29.0 |
| Roman Catholics | 115,900 | 14.2 | 499,140 | 17.7 | 8,063 | 3,041 | 11,104 | 2.01 | 551,640 | 18.2 | 610,180 | 18.7 | 853,400 | 20.0 |
| Marginal Protestants | 1,000 | 0.1 | 50,000 | 1.8 | 935 | 1,865 | 2,800 | 4.38 | 64,000 | 2.1 | 78,000 | 2.4 | 170,680 | 4.0 |
| Polynesian indigenous | 1,000 | 0.1 | 42,000 | 1.5 | 679 | 11 | 690 | 1.49 | 46,450 | 1.5 | 48,900 | 1.5 | 64,000 | 1.5 |
| Orthodox | 190 | 0.0 | 6,000 | 0.2 | 94 | –4 | 90 | 1.40 | 6,450 | 0.2 | 6,900 | 0.2 | 12,800 | 0.3 |
| Catholics (non-Roman) | 340 | 0.0 | 500 | 0.0 | 8 | 2 | 10 | 1.82 | 550 | 0.0 | 600 | 0.0 | 900 | 0.0 |
| nominal | 59,840 | 7.3 | 457,451 | 16.2 | 7,200 | 34 | 7,234 | 1.47 | 492,600 | 16.3 | 529,790 | 16.2 | 644,320 | 15.1 |
| affiliated | 742,290 | 90.9 | 2,232,629 | 79.2 | 34,088 | –13,397 | 20,691 | 0.89 | 2,332,290 | 76.9 | 2,439,540 | 74.8 | 3,016,770 | 70.7 |
| total practising | 668,060 | *90* | 1,786,100 | *80* | 27,270 | –10,717 | 16,553 | 0.89 | 1,865,830 | *80* | 1,951,630 | *80* | 2,111,740 | *70* |
| non-practising | 74,230 | *10* | 446,530 | *20* | 6,818 | –2,680 | 4,138 | 0.89 | 466,460 | *20* | 487,910 | *20* | 905,030 | *30* |
| Anglicans | 320,000 | 39.2 | 876,570 | 31.1 | 13,113 | –9,080 | 4,033 | 0.45 | 897,180 | 29.6 | 916,900 | 28.1 | 1,066,750 | 25.0 |
| Evangelicals | 220,400 | 27.0 | 397,600 | 14.1 | 6,201 | –601 | 5,600 | 1.32 | 424,300 | 14.0 | 453,600 | 13.9 | 554,700 | 13.0 |
| Anglican pentecostals | 0 | 0.0 | 2,000 | 0.1 | 438 | 7,362 | 7,800 | 26.00 | 30,000 | 1.0 | 80,000 | 2.5 | 200,000 | 4.7 |
| Protestants | 309,600 | 37.9 | 841,383 | 29.8 | 12,537 | –9,225 | 3,312 | 0.39 | 857,800 | 28.3 | 874,500 | 26.8 | 942,110 | 22.1 |
| Evangelicals | 204,000 | 25.0 | 259,400 | 9.2 | 3,987 | –1,217 | 2,770 | 1.02 | 272,800 | 9.0 | 287,100 | 8.8 | 341,400 | 8.0 |
| Neo-pentecostals | 0 | 0.0 | 0 | 0.0 | 44 | 556 | 600 | 20.00 | 3,000 | 0.1 | 6,000 | 0.2 | 25,000 | 0.6 |
| Roman Catholics | 110,100 | 13.5 | 426,128 | 15.1 | 6,911 | 3,010 | 9,921 | 2.10 | 472,840 | 15.6 | 525,340 | 16.1 | 768,060 | 18.0 |
| Catholic pentecostals | 0 | 0.0 | 1,000 | 0.0 | 88 | 812 | 900 | 15.00 | 6,000 | 0.2 | 10,000 | 0.3 | 50,000 | 1.2 |
| Marginal Protestants | 1,000 | 0.1 | 47,156 | 1.7 | 877 | 1,912 | 2,789 | 4.65 | 60,000 | 2.0 | 75,050 | 2.3 | 166,410 | 3.9 |
| Polynesian indigenous | 1,000 | 0.1 | 34,930 | 1.2 | 548 | –14 | 534 | 1.42 | 37,500 | 1.2 | 40,270 | 1.2 | 59,740 | 1.4 |
| Orthodox | 190 | 0.0 | 5,700 | 0.2 | 90 | 0 | 90 | 1.46 | 6,150 | 0.2 | 6,600 | 0.2 | 12,700 | 0.3 |
| Catholics (non-Roman) | 400 | 0.0 | 762 | 0.0 | 12 | 0 | 12 | 1.44 | 820 | 0.0 | 880 | 0.0 | 1,000 | 0.0 |
| Non-religious | 4,800 | 0.6 | 84,360 | 3.0 | 2,285 | 13,120 | 15,405 | 9.85 | 156,390 | 5.2 | 238,410 | 7.3 | 508,010 | 11.9 |
| Atheists | 400 | 0.0 | 15,000 | 0.5 | 266 | 514 | 780 | 4.29 | 18,200 | 0.6 | 22,800 | 0.7 | 64,000 | 1.5 |
| Tribal religionists | 4,000 | 0.5 | 9,000 | 0.3 | 117 | –317 | –200 | –2.50 | 8,000 | 0.3 | 7,000 | 0.2 | 5,000 | 0.1 |
| Chinese folk-religionists | 2,000 | 0.2 | 7,000 | 0.3 | 111 | –1 | 110 | 1.45 | 7,600 | 0.3 | 8,100 | 0.3 | 5,000 | 0.1 |
| Hindus | 0 | 0.0 | 3,800 | 0.1 | 60 | 2 | 62 | 1.52 | 4,090 | 0.1 | 4,420 | 0.1 | 5,800 | 0.1 |
| Jews | 1,600 | 0.2 | 3,800 | 0.1 | 60 | 0 | 60 | 1.47 | 4,080 | 0.1 | 4,400 | 0.1 | 5,700 | 0.1 |
| Baha'is | 0 | 0.0 | 2,600 | 0.1 | 42 | 18 | 60 | 2.07 | 2,900 | 0.1 | 3,200 | 0.1 | 4,500 | 0.1 |
| Buddhists | 430 | 0.0 | 1,360 | 0.0 | 21 | –3 | 18 | 1.24 | 1,450 | 0.0 | 1,540 | 0.0 | 1,900 | 0.0 |
| Spiritists | 500 | 0.1 | 1,000 | 0.0 | 16 | 4 | 20 | 1.82 | 1,100 | 0.0 | 1,200 | 0.0 | 1,500 | 0.0 |
| Muslims | 40 | 0.0 | 1,000 | 0.0 | 16 | 4 | 20 | 1.82 | 1,100 | 0.0 | 1,200 | 0.0 | 2,000 | 0.0 |
| Other religionists | 300 | 0.0 | 1,000 | 0.0 | 18 | 22 | 40 | 3.33 | 1,200 | 0.0 | 1,400 | 0.0 | 2,500 | 0.1 |
| **Country's population** | **816,200** | **100.0** | **2,820,000** | **100.0** | **44,300** | **0** | **44,300** | **1.46** | **3,031,000** | **100.0** | **3,263,000** | **100.0** | **4,267,000** | **100.0** |

COLUMNS, ROWS. For meanings and definitions, see Codebook (Part 6). Note that, by definition, total 'Christians' = professing + crypto-Christians, which also = affiliated + nominal Christians. Percentages may not always total exactly, due to rounding.
CENSUSES. **1901** (adjusted to include 43,143 Maoris): 42.0% Protestants (21.6% Presbyterians, 10.3% Methodists, 2.0% Baptists), 41.8% Anglicans, 14.2% Roman Catholics, 0.6% non-religious, 0.3% Chinese folk-religionists and Buddhists, 0.2% Jews. **25.IX.1945** (excluding foreign military personnel): 80.7% Anglicans & Protestants, 14.8% Roman Catholics, 1.5% Polynesian indigenous (1.2% Ratana, 0.3% Ringatu), 1.3% non-religious, 1.0% marginal Protestants, 0.2% Jews, 0.2% other religionists. **17.IV.1951:** 80.8% Anglicans & Protestants, 14.8% Roman Catholics, 1.3% Polynesian indigenous (1.0% Ratana, 0.3% Ringatu), 1.2% non-religious, 1.0% marginal Protestants, 0.8% other religionists, 0.2% Jews. **17.IV.1956:** 96.8% Christians (including 1.3% Polynesian indigenous (1.0% Ratana, 0.3% Ringatu)), 1.0% non-religious, 0.8% other religionists, 0.2% Jews, 0.1% Hindus. **18.IV.1961** (excluding foreign military): 41.4% Protestants (24.6% Presbyterians), 38.0% Anglicans, 16.6% Roman Catholics, 1.3% marginal Protestants, 1.3% Polynesian indigenous (1.0 Ratana, 0.2% Ringatu), 1.0% non-religious, 0.2% Jews, 0.2% Orthodox, 0.1% Hindus. **22.III.1966** (excluding foreign military): 39.8% Protestants (23.8% Presbyterians, 7.6% Methodists), 36.9% Anglicans, 17.4% Roman Catholics, 1.5% non-religious, 1.4% marginal Protestants, 1.4% Polynesian indigenous (1.1% Ratana, 0.2% Ringatu), 0.3% atheists, 0.2% Jews, 0.1% Orthodox, 0.1% Hindus. **23.III.1971:** 38.2% Protestants (23.1% Presbyterians, 7.2% Methodists, 1.9% Baptists), 35.4% Anglicans, 17.8% Roman Catholics, 3.0% non-religious, 1.7% marginal Protestants, 1.5% Polynesian indigenous (1.2% Ratana, 0.2% Ringatu).

**NOTES ON RELIGIONS**
ANGLICAN PENTECOSTALS (or, Anglican charismatics). Although late-starting by comparison with Anglican churches elsewhere, the charismatic movement has rapidly spread since 1972. It also includes many Anglican youth in the Jesus movement. By 1977 the Charismatic Renewal claimed to involve over 40% of all active Anglicans in New Zealand.
ATHEISTS. In 1970, New Zealand Communist Party (NZCP) (legal; pro-Chinese) and Socialist Unity Party (SUP) (pro-Soviet): communist membership (1970) 300, party sympathizers 3,000.
BAHA'IS. Rapid growth from 3 local spiritual assemblies (1964) to 17 (1973).
BUDDHISTS. Chinese.
CATHOLIC PENTECOSTALS (or, Catholic charismatics). Totals (January 1974): 2,500 involved adults (over 15 years old) in 31 prayer groups; total charismatic community including children, 5,000.
HINDUS. Indians, with a handful of White converts to Hindu sects. ISKCON (Hare Krishna) operates 1 centre, and Ananda Marga (Path of Bliss) operates 6 centres. The Theosophical Society, a neo-Hindu movement, in 1975 had 18 Lodges with 1,360 members.
NEO-PENTECOSTALS. Charismatics in organized groups within the Methodist, Presbyterian and other non-Pentecostal Protestant denominations; also young people in the Jesus Movement.
NON-RELIGIOUS. In the 1901 census, 2,856 freethinkers were recorded, 910 of no religion, 552 agnostics, et alia. In 1970, non-religious were mostly Whites but with small numbers of Chinese.
OTHER RELIGIONISTS. Adherents of a number of small groups, including 380 Sikhs in 1970, Rosicrucians (AMORC) with 7 Lodges, and (1975) 20 converts to Nichiren Shoshu (Soka Gakkai).
POLYNESIAN INDIGENOUS. In about 10 denominations in 1970 (see Table 2).
PRACTISING CHRISTIANS. A survey in 1973 estimated that 482,700 adults (about 45% of all adult Christians) were active (regularly-attending once a month or more) church members. On our definition, therefore, practising Christians (at least once a year) were about 80% of all affiliated Christians.
ROMAN CATHOLICS. In 1900, including 3,600 Maoris.
SPIRITISTS. Adherents of non-Christian Spiritism or Spiritualism.
TRIBAL RELIGIONISTS. A small minority of the Maoris do not identify themselves as Christians but follow traditional Maori religion.

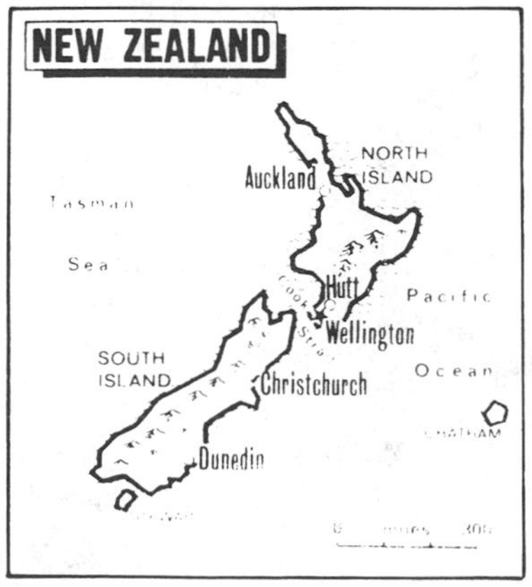


**NON-CHRISTIAN RELIGIONS. Traditional religion** continues to exist among the Maoris, who make up 8% of the population, although a majority today call themselves Christians. In Maori mythology, Rangi, the supreme sky deity, emerged from an initial chaos and, together with Papa (old Mother Earth), was responsible for the propagation of men and other divinities.

**Other religions** include small numbers of Chinese folk-religionists, Hindus, Jews, Baha'is, Buddhists and others.

**CHRISTIANITY.** The history of Christianity in New Zealand includes missions to the oldest of the present inhabitants, the Maoris, and also churches working among White settler immigrants. Maoris are a Malayan-Polynesian people who came to the islands before 1350 and who later were more militantly opposed to European settlers than the Aborigines of Australia. Dutch explorers visited the islands in 1642 and the British in 1769. In the 1790s several English whaling establishments were begun.

ANGLICAN CHURCH. An Anglican chaplain in New South Wales named Samuel Marsden opened the first permanent Anglican mission in 1814. Marsden persuaded the CMS to send missionaries to the Maoris, and by 1838 there was a staff of 35, 21 schools, 178 communicants and 2,176 attending services. A written language was also developed and portions of the Bible and other Christian literature translated. Missionaries had already been working among the Maoris for 25 years before the colonial problem became acute. The CMS attempted to protect the Maoris from British colonization, and when this failed they assisted in the Treaty of Waitangi of 1840, in which the Maoris acknowledged British sovereignty in return for the promise of continued possession of their land. The promise was not kept, and Maori uprisings took place during 1845-48 and 1860-70, to the dismay and demoralization of the missions. Discovery of gold in 1861 and rapidly-expanding commerce in meat and wool soon attracted large numbers of White settlers.

Among the Maoris who remained in the Anglican mission, 23 had been ordained by 1872, and 69 by 1900. In 1883 CMS withdrew and left its responsibilities to the Church of New Zealand which had been developed within the White community. Some time after 1914, Maoris requested and were granted an Anglican organization of their own, with a Maori clergyman consecrated as suffragan bishop. In 1926 a third of all Maoris were Anglicans. Many of the settlers who came to New Zealand following the 1840 treaty were Anglicans. The first bishop was appointed in 1841 with headquarters at Auckland on North Island, originally the most heavily populated. In 1851 a large body of colonists, almost all Anglicans, arrived to establish what is now Christchurch in South Island, which continues to maintain the atmosphere of an English cathedral and university town. Originally the church was part of the diocese of Calcutta, but in 1844 a synod was convened and another in 1847; and finally an ecclesiastical province was created in 1858. A proposal in 1844 that the colonial government should pay part of the bishop's salary was defeated by Presbyterians and Catholics, and the Anglican church was at no time established by law. It remains the largest church in New Zealand, though the number of professing Anglicans has declined from 42% of the population in 1901 to 35% in 1971. Maori Anglicans have also declined, from 34% in 1926 to 26% in 1961. The Church of the Province of New Zealand has 8 dioceses including the missionary diocese of Polynesia with its seat in Fiji. The church administers 25 primary schools, 18 secondary schools and one hospital in New Zealand.

PROTESTANT CHURCHES. Wesleyan Methodists opened a mission on the northern coast of North Island in 1822. The violence of Maori reaction caused them to leave a few years later, but they returned within a year and the first baptism took place in 1830. Missions expanded along the western coast. In 1872 there were 3 districts, 29 circuits, 119 churches, 45 ministers, 181 local preachers and 2,658 members, including Methodists who had arrived as new settlers. In 1874 the first Methodist conference was held in Christchurch, and in 1913 a union took place of several Methodist bodies which had entered New Zealand during the 19th century. Methodists identified themselves as 8.9% of the population in 1926 and 7.2% in 1971; 6.3% of Maoris were Methodists in 1926 and 7.5% in 1961, falling to 7.1% by 1971. Methodists operate one primary and one secondary school.

The first Presbyterian minister came to New Zealand in 1839 among a shipload of colonists to North Island. In 1843 a minister of the Church of Scotland arrived, and in 1850 one from the Free Church of Scotland. The rapid growth of the Presbyterian Church in New Zealand is attributable in part to church disruptions in Scotland in the middle of the 19th century, with New Zealand providing an outlet for the Free Church's outburst of energy. Presbyterians settled in 1844 at what is now Dunedin, in the southern part of South Island, desiring to establish a model Christian community similar to that of the Anglicans at Christchurch. In 1861 gold was discovered in the vicinity and a mixed population grew rapidly. Although most Presbyterians continued to be found in this area, Presbyterian ministers from Scotland, Ireland and Canada spread throughout New Zealand; 17 arrived in 1871-72 from the Free Church alone. Two Presbyterian churches arose, one in the north and the other in the south, which were finally united in 1901. New Zealand Presbyterians began to send out foreign missionaries in 1867, first to the New Hebrides, later to South China and to the Punjab in India. Presbyterians form the second largest church in New Zealand with 23.5% of the population in 1926, declining to 23.1% in 1971. The Presbyterian Church sponsors 9 primary and 12 secondary schools.

Baptist colonists received their first pastor in 1851, and the Baptist Union of New Zealand was formed in 1882 and then undertook both home and foreign missions. Most Baptists are found in the north in the vicinity of Auckland. The Baptist proportion of the population has remained about the same during this century, being 1.6% in 1926 and 1.9% in 1971.

Other smaller denominations include the Christian Brethren, Salvation Army, Disciples, Seventh-day Adventists, Lutherans and Assemblies of God. Adventists have 13 primary and 2 secondary schools.

CATHOLIC CHURCH. An Irish priest entered New Zealand in 1828, although little progress was made until the arrival of French Marists in 1838. A vicariate was established in 1842 and a mission begun also among the Maoris with 1,000 conversions taking place by 1853. Friction developed between Catholics and Protestants, but more serious problems arose with the arrival of European settlers, the Maori revolt and the eventual closing to all Europeans of the area in which Catholics worked. White Catholics were predominantly Irish, and numerous religious orders were sent to serve them. In 1848 Wellington was made a diocese and in 1887 an archdiocese. By 1892 there were 90,000 Catholics of whom more than 3,000 were Maoris, growing to 115,900 by the turn of the century. The Catholic Church, third in size among the churches, continues to expand. Catholics numbered 12.9% of the population in 1926, 17.4% in 1966, and 17.8% in 1971. In 1926, 13.1% of the Maoris were Catholics, rising by 1961 to 17.1%, and by 1971 to 17.3%.

The Catholic population is very evenly distributed both geographically and throughout the income range of the population. The ethnic background of most Catholics is European, predominantly British, with a higher proportion of Irish than in the general population. But there are also substantial racial minorities, the largest being Maori. In recent years Maoris have shown a strong tendency to move from rural to urban areas, with resultant destruction of their traditional style of life and values. About half the Maoris live in Auckland diocese, which also has substantial Samoan and Cook Islands minorities as well. Maoris are served by a separately organized Maori Mission, staffed in Auckland by Mill Hill priests, whereas the rest of New Zealand is served by Marist priests. By 1972 only 5 Maoris had become

priests in New Zealand's 134 years of Catholic history. The first was ordained in 1944 and all 5 were still living at the end of 1972.

MARGINAL CHURCHES. Marginal Protestant bodies from the Western world have a wide following. Mormons grew in numbers from 4,060 (0.3% of the population) in 1926 to 25,564 (1.0%) in 1966 and 1.2% in 1971. Their work is found mostly among Maoris, who increased from 5.4% Mormon in 1926 to 7.2% Mormon in 1961, and to 7.6% by 1971. They also have a secondary school. Jehovah's Witnesses began in New Zealand in 1904. By 1951 they numbered 1,756 (0.1%) and by 1966 had increased to 7,455 (0.3%). Christian Scientists on the other hand have decreased both in numbers and percentage over the period since 1951.

INDIGENOUS CHURCHES. Several churches not begun by Whites are found among the Maoris. During the last half of the 19th century when the Maoris were dying out through inter-tribal warfare

**Church of Jesus Christ of Latter-day Saints.** *Above.* The Mormon Temple, Hamilton.

and continued encroachment by White settlers, one reaction was the development of indigenous cults including the King movement of the 1850s and 1860s, which using biblical ideas, attempted to unite all Maoris under one king. The result however was a colonial war which further weakened them. Later, Hau Hau or Pai Marire, which included indigenous, Protestant, Catholic and Old Testament elements, was started by a Maori who claimed to receive guidance from the archangel Gabriel. Magic associated with the movement was believed to render its members safe from bullets. Two other movements still survive today as organized bodies. The Ratana Church is the third largest denomination among Maoris and was begun in 1918 by a Maori named Takapotiki Ratana. After a vision, Ratana urged his fellow tribesmen to leave their superstitions, with the assurance that God would send angels to help them. Ratana's followers developed their own socio-economic structures and in 1925 became a separate church. Since 1943 they have frequently held all 4 Maori seats in the New Zealand national legislature. Its membership, however, has declined from 18.1% of the Maoris in 1926 to 13.1% in 1961, and to 12.1% in 1971. The second body is Ringatu, which was founded in the 1860s by Te Kooti; Rikirangi, a member of the Rongowhakaota tribe of Poverty Bay, and has a specialized liturgy which all members memorize and are permitted to conduct. It also has declined recently, from 6.0% of the Maoris in 1926 to 3.1% in 1961, and to 2.4% in 1971. During this same period the established churches, with the exception of Anglicans, have all shown a slight increase in proportional membership. The number of Maoris who decline to state their religion in government censuses increased from 5.0% in 1926 to 13.0% in 1961 (and 11.4% in 1971).

ORTHODOX CHURCHES. The Greek and Russian Orthodox churches have followings in New Zealand, mostly of immigrants from Europe since World War II. There is also a community of Old Believers,

CHURCH AND STATE. New Zealand law has 3 sources: the common law of England as it existed in 14 January 1840 when New Zealand became a British colony; certain statutes of the United Kingdom parliament enacted prior to 1947; and statutes of the New Zealand parliament. However, there has been from the beginning one significant difference from English law: there is and has been no established church in New Zealand. Although the Anglican Church has the largest membership, it has no special rights before the law, nor has any special legislation been passed regulating relations between church and

**Ratana Church.** Large central temple in Maori holy city Ratanapa, with archway commemorating Maori founder-healer T.W. Ratana and his 3 sons. Other Ratana churches elsewhere are replicas.

state. No church receives direct financial aid from the state, although charitable institutions are exempt from some forms of taxation and ministers of religion are exempt from military service. Church schools receive financial aid from the state; and church charitable institutions including homes for the aged and hospitals are given state subsidies. In all cases of state assistance, however, aid is given on an equal basis to all institutions, whether denominational, interdenominational or secular; there is no religious basis for the granting or withholding of state aid.

Ministers of religion are gazetted as officiating ministers for the purpose of acting on behalf of the registrar of marriages. There is no ministry or government department in charge of religious or ecclesiastical affairs, nor do the churches have to register themselves with any government body.

There has been very little church-state conflict in New Zealand, except during the period when the Catholic and other churches were trying to obtain state aid for their schools.

**INTERDENOMINATIONAL ORGANIZATIONS.** The National Council of Churches in New Zealand was established in 1941 and now has 10 member denominations, including the Greek Orthodox Church and the Cook Islands Christian Church. An earlier body, the National Missionary Council of New Zealand, was formed in 1926 and became part of the NCC in 1957 as its Commission on Overseas Missions and Inter-Church Aid. There is a joint working group between the National Council and the Catholic Episcopal Conference.

In 1970 an interdenominational parish council was set up in the district of Dunedin. Its 6 member denominations (Anglican, Catholic, Baptist, Presbyterian, Church of Christ and Salvation Army) undertake joint action in youth activities, social problems, relief services and Bible study groups. There is also the Evangelical Alliance of New Zealand, and the Associated Pentecostal Churches of New Zealand formed in 1975.

The Catholic Episcopal Conference created a National Commission on Ecumenism in 1967.

**BROADCASTING.** Until 1970, all radio and TV stations were controlled by the New Zealand Broadcasting Corporation (NZBC), but 3 commercial stations were then granted licences. The national network carries religious programmes co-ordinated by the Central Religious Advisory Committee (CRAC) with members from the major denominations. These consist of 15 minutes each weekday for Bible readings, and a 12-minute programme 'Faith for Today'. On Sundays, there are 2 hours 40 minutes for early morning hymns, morning and evening church services, and an epilogue. The commercial stations also have morning and evening religious slots. On the one NZBC TV channel, 15 minutes each week are given to religious programmes arranged by the Churches Television Commission under CRAC. There are a number of Christian production organizations including Christian Broadcasting Associates, International Radio Crusades, Kiwi Gospel Hour, Wellington Missionary Radio Fellowship and Gospel Radio Fellowship. In Wellington there is a National Catholic Broadcasting Committee, and the secretariat for UNDA/Oceania is established in Christchurch.

## BIBLIOGRAPHY

'New Zealand', H. Mol, in *Western religion* (The Hague: Mouton, 1972), p.365–379.

*Official year book of the Catholic Church of Australia, Papua New Guinea, New Zealand & the Pacific Islands.* Sydney: E.J. Dwyer, n.d. 544p.

'Ratana: the origins and the story of the movement', J.Henderson, Polynesian Society memorandum 36, Wellington, 1963.

*Religion and race in New Zealand.* H. Mol. Christchurch: National Council of Churches, 1966. 80p.

*Survey: a survey of religious opinions and attitudes.* Christchurch: National Council of Churches, 1969. 77p.

'The Maori web', chapter 2 in A.R. Tippett, *People movements in Southern Polynesia* (Chicago: Moody Press, 1971), p.40–75.

'The upraised hand or the spiritual significance of the rise of the Ringatu faith', *Journal of the Polynesian Society*, 51, 1 (1942), 1–80.

TABLE 2. ORGANIZED CHURCHES AND DENOMINATIONS IN NEW ZEALAND

| Official name 1 | Begun 2 | Type 3 | Counc 4 | Congs 5 | Adults 6 | Affiliated 7 | Names, notes, and other statistics (see Codebook) 8 |
|---|---|---|---|---|---|---|---|
| Absolute Maori Established Church | 1941 | I ind | ..... | 2 | 70 | 130 | Maori indigenous church. Decline from 149 adherents (1966 census) to 128 (1971). |
| Apostolic Church of Australia & NZ | 1933 | P PeA | Z...H | 37 | 2,058 | 3,000 | Begun by Apostolic Ch(Australia). Has Maori mission. 31n,G=4.6%pa,1s,W=44%,62Y. |
| Assemblies of God in New Zealand | 1922 | P Pe2 | Z...H | 45 | 3,000 | 6,000 | M=AoG(UK,Austr). HQ Lower Hutt. 10% Samoan. 42n,4x(Samoan),1p,1s(70),W=95%,300Y. |
| Associated Churches of Christ in NZ | 1844 | P Dis | xWE.W | 56 | 4,354 | 10,000 | *Disciples.* Decline since 1951. HQ Lower Hutt. 39n,3x,G=–1.0%pa,1s(7),W=38%,107Y. |
| Baptist Union of New Zealand | 1851 | P Bap | TWE.W | 167 | 17,237 | 45,000 | Pakeha (Whites). Strongest at Auckland. 198n,G=0.1%pa,1s(22),W=76%,589Y,17177z. |
| Bible Presbyterian Ch of New Zealand | | P Ref | .TT.T | 1 | 42 | 100 | Schism ex Presbyterian Church of New Zealand. Fundamentalists. 1n. |
| **Catholic Church in New Zealand:** | 1828 | R Lat | P...R | 285 | 285,500 | 426,128 | 92% White, 8% Maori. C=12+4+22. 1q,3s(145),W=79%. 854nx,438m,2459w,P=82%,11178Yy. |
| M Wellington | 1848 | R Lat | Ps | 92 | 98,500 | 147,000 | Capital. South of North Island. 7 Maori missions. 363 170 866 90 4204 |
| D Auckland | 1848 | R Lat | Ps | 103 | 118,000 | 176,197 | North of North Island. Home of half of all Maoris. 252 147 753 85 4365 |
| D Christchurch | 1887 | R Lat | Ps | 52 | 41,000 | 61,162 | Centre of South Island. Urban, rural. 144 74 470 61 1587 |
| D Dunedin | 1869 | R Lat | Ps | 38 | 28,000 | 41,769 | Southern third of South Island. Urban, rural. 95 47 370 74 1022 |
| Christadelphian Ecclesias | | P Ade | x.... | 16 | 1,000 | 1,700 | *Christadelphian Bible Mission.* 16 ecclesias. Pacifist, adventist. 8n,1s. |
| Christian Brethren | 1853 | P CBr | x.... | 250 | 10,000 | 23,000 | *Brethren Assemblies*(Open). Sends out 210 foreign missionaries. 118m,W=99%. |
| Christian Revival Crusade | 1944 | P Pe2 | x...H | 8 | 253 | 450 | *CRC.* Related to CRC (Australia). On North Island. 11n,1s,W=72%,18Y,9z. |
| Church of Christ, Scientist | | M Sci | x.... | 22 | 500 | 1,100 | *Christian Science.* M=CCS(Boston,USA). Declining (1951: 4,586 adherents). 3m,18w. |
| Church of God of Prophecy | | P Pe3 | Z.... | 1 | 10 | 50 | M=CGP(USA). White Pentecostals, split in USA ex CoG(Cleveland). In Christchurch. |
| Ch of Jesus C of Latter-day Saints | 1851 | M LdS | x.... | | 22,300 | 33,256 | *Mormons*(USA). 70% Maori,30% White. Temple: Hamilton. 141n,500f,G=5%pa,1r,W=50%. |
| Church of the Nazarene | 1952 | P Hol | xF... | 10 | 148 | 1,100 | Home mission area of M=CoN(USA). HQ Auckland. 9n,SS=907,W=75%. |
| **Ch of the Province of New Zealand:** | 1814 | A plu | AWE.W | 1,557 | 122,520 | 876,570 | 94% White, 6% Maori. 37x,1H,18r,790t(48791),300Y. 680n,P=70%,W=33%,15010Yy. |
| D Auckland | 1841 | A Low | A | 340 | 28,432 | 260,000 | M=SSF. 3% expatriates. 10 Maori priests. 1s. 178 74 31 3721 |
| D Christchurch | 1856 | A plu | A | 218 | 29,800 | 140,000 | 50% urban. Some Maoris and Pacific islanders. 1s. 138 53 30 2467 |
| D Dunedin | 1869 | A Hig | A | 110 | 7,300 | 48,600 | Rural. 97% British origin, 3% Maori. 49Y. 44 78 41 692 |
| D Nelson | 1858 | A Low | A | 129 | 5,747 | 44,970 | Mainly rural, population decline. 300 Maoris. 66Y. 47 77 30 804 |
| D Waiapu | 1858 | A Cen | A | 255 | 15,000 | 103,000 | Rural. Maori homeland. 26% Maori (1 bishop, 12 clergy). 65 75 44 2427 |
| D Waikato | 1926 | A Cen | A | 215 | 12,128 | 100,000 | Rural. 93% British, 7% Maori (urban migration). 5r. 60 73 31 1930 |
| D Wellington | 1858 | A Cen | A | 290 | 24,113 | 180,000 | Area 34% Anglican. 5% Maori (5 clergy). 3r,141Y. 148 78 30 2969 |
| Churches of Christ (Non-Instrumental) | 1956 | P Dis | x.... | 14 | 1,000 | 2,000 | M=CC(Non-Instrumental)(USA). In largest cities. 1 school. 18f. |
| Churches of Christ, New Zealand | | P Pen | ..... | 10 | 300 | 700 | Pentecostals, based on HQ in Christchurch. Independent congregations. |
| Commonwealth Covenant Church | | P Pen | ..... | | 300 | 506 | Includes Maori mission with 123 members. Pentecostals, based on HQ Lower Hutt. |
| Congregational Chr Ch of Samoa in NZ | | P Con | Rwp.. | 18 | 1,500 | 3,000 | Samoan immigrants from CCCS. HQ Otara. Mainly Auckland, Wellington. 15x. |
| Congregational Union of New Zealand | 1840 | P Con | RWE.W | 13 | 539 | 1,050 | Union 1884. 1969, 67% of churches join Presbyterian Ch. 67% Pacific islanders. 8n. |
| Cook Islands Christian Church | | P Con | .wp.W | | 5,000 | 12,000 | *CICC.* Cook Islanders working in New Zealand. 3 pastors. Linked Presb Ch of NZ. |
| Elim Church of New Zealand | 1952 | P Pe2 | Z...H | 5 | 170 | 220 | Pentecostals. Based on Wellington. 2 missionaries in Japan. 7n,G=2.5%pa,W=50%,7Y. |
| Evangelistic Church of Christ | | P Pen | ..... | | 100 | 152 | Small independent Pentecostal group based on Christchurch. |
| Greater World Chr Spiritualist League | | M Spi | x.... | 2 | 100 | 200 | *Greater World Sanctuary.* Specifically Christian spiritists. Auckland, Christchurch. |
| Greek Orthodox Ch: D New Zealand | 1924 | O Gre | Cw..W | 5 | 2,000 | 3,000 | Under EP Constantinople. Created Diocese in 1970, includes E India, Japan, Korea. |
| Jehovah's Witnesses | 1904 | M Jeh | x.... | 101 | 5,876 | 10,000 | Witnessing strong by 1926. 1973 International Assembly in Christchurch. 40m,555Y. |
| Liberal Catholic Church | 1916 | C Lib | x.... | 2 | 300 | 462 | Theosophist. Linked to churches and bishops in Australia, UK, USA. HQ Auckland. |
| Lutheran Church of New Zealand | 1843 | P Lut | ..... | 42 | 1,655 | 6,255 | In Luth Ch of Australia. Germans in 1843, now Maoris. 1n,12x,G=2.4%pa,W=35%,102Yy. |
| Methodist Church of New Zealand | 1822 | P Met | VWE.W | 645 | 60,000 | 160,000 | A=1913 (from Australia). 92% White, 8% Maori. 351n,669m,G=–2.2%pa,1r,W=36%. |
| National Revival Church in NZ | | P Pe2 | Z.... | 1 | 50 | 100 | *NRC.* HQ Lower Hutt. Revivalist Pentecostals begun in Australia; split ex CRC. |
| Old Believers Russian Orthodox Church | | O OBe | x.... | | 100 | 200 | *Old Ritualists.* Immigrants from USSR church begun in 1667. HQ Christchurch. |
| **Presbyterian Church of New Zealand** | 1839 | P Ref | RWE.W | 1,637 | 88,566 | 500,000 | A=1901. 23 White Presbyteries (99%), Maori Synod (1%). South. 635n,12r,1s,W=38%. |
| Ratana Church | 1918 | I Met | ..... | | 19,000 | 28,000 | Maori. Begun by Ratana, ex-Methodist. 95% Maori. Declining. 141 apostles. W=20%. |
| Reformed Churches of New Zealand | 1953 | P Ref | JtT.T | 29 | 1,000 | 2,000 | Conservative schism ex Presbyterian Ch of New Zealand. Dutch origin. HQ Auckland. |
| Religious Society of Friends | 1909 | P Qua | Q...W | | 649 | 900 | *New Zealand Yearly Meeting.* Established 1964. Quakers. HQ Christchurch. 1 school. |
| Reorganized Ch of JC of Latter-day S | | M LdS | x.... | | 100 | 152 | S=Saints (Sanitos, Kanitos). Schism in USA ex CJCLdS(Utah), Mormons. |
| Ringatu Church | 1867 | I ind | ..... | | 3,900 | 5,800 | *Ch of the Upraised Hand.* Christian version of Hau Hau. Maori Bible ritual. 73n. |
| Russian Orthodox Ch Outside of Russia | c1950 | O Sla | x.... | 4 | 1,000 | 1,500 | AD Australia & NZ, ROCOR(USA). Auckland, Christchurch. Dunedin, Wellington. 1n. |
| Salvation Army | 1883 | P Sal | xwE.W | 167 | 10,000 | 18,000 | *SA, New Zealand Territory.* 5 Divisions. Officers 356, institutions 47. 6H,1s. |
| Seventh Day Baptist Church of NZ | | P Bap | Tw... | 2 | 58 | 100 | Related to M=SDBC(USA). Sabbatarian. Baptists under General Conference (USA). |
| Seventh-day Adventist Church | 1887 | P Adv | x.... | 170 | 7,486 | 10,000 | *N & South NZ Confs*, Trans-Tasman UC. 60n,G=1.4%pa,1H,3r,1s,70t(7401),W=90%,1000Y. |
| Unitarian Free Churches | 1898 | M Unt | I.... | 2 | 200 | 448 | In General Assembly, UFCC(UK). Churches: Auckland, Wellington. Declining. 1n. |
| United Pentecostal Church | 1969 | P Pe1 | x.... | 40 | 2,000 | 4,000 | *Jesus Only Church.* M=UPC(USA). Unitarian Pentecostals. 40n,2f,1p(25). |
| Other Protestant denominations | | P | ..... | | 20,000 | 30,000 | Total over 30 (see list below). |
| Other marginal Protestant bodies | | M | ..... | | 1,000 | 2,000 | Total 7 (see below), including Ch of Scientology, New Ch, Worldwide Ch of God. |
| Other Orthodox churches | | O | ..... | 6 | 500 | 1,000 | Parishes: Antiochian, Romanian, Serbian, Free Serbian, Ukrainian AOC(2). |
| Other Polynesian indigenous churches | | I | ..... | | 500 | 1,000 | Total about 7 (see list below), mostly Maori in membership. |
| Other Catholic (non-Roman) churches | | C | ..... | | 100 | 300 | About 5, incl Antoinists, Catholic Tridentine Ch, New Apostolic Ch, episcopi vagantes bodies. |
| **Total affiliated (mid-1970)** | | | | **6,150** | **704,041** | **2,232,629** | **Total denominations (1970) . . . 84.** |
| **Total affiliated (mid-1975)** | | | | **6,200** | **735,500** | **2,332,290** | **Total denominations (1975) . . . 90.** |
| **Total affiliated (mid-1980)** | | | | **6,250** | **769,300** | **2,439,540** | **Total denominations (1980) . . . 96.** |

**NOTES ON TABLE ABOVE**

COLUMNS: for meanings and CODES (cols. 1, 3, 4, 8): see Codebook (Part 6). Column 1: **Boldface type** = church with over 10% of country's affiliated Christians.

NATIONAL COUNCILS (Column 4, 5th letter).

H = Associated Pentecostal Churches of New Zealand (formed 1975).
R = New Zealand Episcopal Conference (NZEC).
T = New Zealand Consultative Council of the ICCC (with 8 local committees).
W = National Council of Churches in New Zealand (NCCNZ).

*Other national councils.* Evangelical Alliance of New Zealand (member of WEF; 9 branches; no churches as members). Maori Evangelical Alliance.

*Local councils.* 28 councils linked with NCCNZ.

OTHER PROTESTANT DENOMINATIONS. There are at least 30 other smaller organized denominations. These include: Baptist Bible Fellowship International (1971), Chinese Ch, Christian & Missionary Alliance (1972), Ch of Christ (Life & Advent), Ch of NZ, Churches of God in the British Isles & Overseas (1 church), Exclusive Brethren (groups: Raven-Taylor, Kelly-Continental, Stuarts), Full Gospel Ch, Independent Assemblies of God, United Ch, United Ev Chs, Worldwide Evangelization Crusade.

OTHER MARGINAL PROTESTANT BODIES. These include: Branhamites (HQ Singapore; Jesus-Only Unitarians), Ch of Scientology (1973 licensed for weddings), Ch of the Mystic Christ, New Ch, Order of the Cross (2 centres), Spiritualists, Unity School of Christianity (1 church), Worldwide Ch of God.

OTHER POLYNESIAN INDIGENOUS CHURCHES. There are a small number of other Maori bodies, also a few followers of other Pacific indigenous groups. The former include: Ch of Te Kooti Rikirangi (47 members in 1966), Maori Evangelical Fellowship (1959; 154 members in 1966), United Maori Mission. There are also a few adherents of other Non-White indigenous churches including the Father Divine Peace Mission Movement (USA Blacks).

UNITING CHURCHES. Negotiations for organic union were under way in 1980 between: Associated Churches of Christ in NZ, Ch of the Province of NZ, Congregational Union of NZ, Methodist Ch of NZ, Presbyterian Ch of NZ.

**PEOPLES** (ethnolinguistic). Christians: 90.9% White (Pakeha) (78.3% Anglo-New Zealander, 7.0% English, 2.1% Scottish, 1.7% Anglo-Australian, 0.8% Dutch, 0.6% Irish, 0.2% Welsh, 0.1% Greek, Russian, Serbian, Ukrainian, Romanian), 7.1% Maori, 1.8% Polynesian (0.8% Samoan, 0.5% Cook Island

Maori, 0.3% Tongan, 0.2% Niuean), 0.1% Chinese, 0.1% Fijian, Gypsy, Arab.

**COUNTRY-WIDE TOTALS**

EVANGELIZATION (see Part 5). 1900: 100%. 1970: 100%. 1980: 100%. *Mass evangelism.* Among the many recent campaigns: Billy Graham crusades in 1959 in Auckland, Wellington and Christchurch (355,000 attenders, 16,323 enquirers), also 1969 crusades in Auckland, Christchurch and Dunedin (181,000 attenders, 8,110 enquirers); 1970, Australian evangelist Allan Walker led 'Mission In: the Southland Affair' sponsored by NCCNZ with Roman Catholic parishes and the Apostolic Church (180 professions of faith). *Radiophonic evangelism.* Annual listeners' letters (1975): 611 HCJB, 150 TWR, 106 FEBC, 34 RVOG, Radio Vatican, et alia.

FOREIGN MISSIONARIES AND PERSONNEL (nationals serving abroad) (1973). Total 1,188: 883 Protestants (increase from 350 in 1963) in 48 societies in 121 countries, about 200 Roman Catholics, 75 Anglicans in 2 societies in 8 countries, about 30 marginal Protestants (Mormons, Jehovah's Witnesses).

FOREIGN MISSIONARIES AND PERSONNEL (aliens from abroad) (1973). Total 2,059. *From Western world.* 1,904: about 1,300 Roman Catholics, about 500 marginal Protestants (440 Mormons from USA), 65 Protestants (42 in 13 USA societies, 23 in 5 UK societies), 38 Anglicans (clergy from UK and Australia; also 8 in 4 UK societies), 1 Orthodox. *From Communist world.* 3: about 2 Roman Catholics (Poland, Yugoslavia), and 1 Orthodox from Yugoslavia. *From Third World.* 152: about 60 Roman Catholics from Philippines, India, et alia, about 50 marginal Protestants (Mormons) from Western Samoa, Philippines et alia, about 30 Protestants (25 from Western Samoa, also Cook Islands and Japan), 12 Anglicans from South Africa et alia.

INSTITUTIONS (church-operated) (1973). Total 190, including 120 higher schools, 20 medical centres (hospitals), 5 religious communities, 16 seminaries (10 Protestant, 4 RC, 2 Anglican).

PERIODICALS. About 155 titles (8 LdS, 6 Pentecostals).

PERSONNEL. About 8,859 (6,800 national, 2,059 foreign).

RELIGIOUS LIBRARIES. About 30.

SCRIPTURE DISTRIBUTION (1975). Annual totals: 36,818 Bibles (11% free, 72% subsidized, 16% commercial), 124,649 NTs (60% free, 32% subsidized, 8% commercial), 50,625 UBS portions, 1,295,930 UBS selections. *Translations completed.* Maori: portion in 1833, NT 1837, Bible 1858.

SERVICE AGENCIES. About 150, including BB, BMMF, CARE, CCCI, CEF, CLC, CORSO, CWL EANZ, LAPF, MAF, MTS, NAP, NCCNZ, NTM, NZCMS, NZEC, SCM, SGM, SU, UCS, WBT, WRMF, WV, YCS, YCW, YFC, YMCA, YWAM, YWCA.

**ADDITIONAL DATA ON CHURCHES**

CATHOLIC CHURCH IN NEW ZEALAND. White Catholics are largely of Irish origin. *Annual baptisms.* (1972) 94.8% infant, 5.2% adult. *Priests.* About 60% are New Zealanders. Only 5 Maoris have been ordained, the first in 1944 and all still at work in 1972. Secular priests numbered 520 in 1972, the rest being religious. *Catholic charismatics* (January 1974). 2,500 adults including many religious personnel are active in 31 prayer groups in the Charismatic Renewal. The movement is considered to be more widespread among Catholics in NZ than among any other nation after the USA. *Seminarians* (1972). 74 secular, 71 religious. *Main religious congregations* (1972). Priests: 260 SM2, 35 CSSR, 21 IC, 9 AA. Brothers: 285 PFM, 32 CFC, 25 FSC, 6 OH. Sisters: about 450 Sisters of Mercy, 360 Sisters of Our Lady of the Mission, 233 Sisters of St Joseph of the Sacred Heart, 180 New Zealand Dominican Sisters.

*Catholic organizations.* Major bodies are the New Zealand Episcopal Conference, New Zealand Conference of Major Superiors of Men, Conference of Major Superiors of Women Religious, and the National Association of Priests. The latter was founded in 1969 at Nelson; and although an unofficial organization, it is approved by 2 bishops and had 150 members in 1973. Catholic lay organizations include the Legion of Mary, St Vincent de Paul Society, Catholic Women's League, University Catholic Society, YCW, YCS, Scouts and Guides. For the armed forces, New Zealand forms a military vicariate.

The Holy See has had diplomatic relations with New Zealand since 1973 and is represented to the Catholic hierarchy by a pro-nuncio in Wellington, who serves also as the apostolic delegate to the Pacific Ocean.

Institutions include the Pastoral Centre with headquarters in Palmerston North, specializing in the continuing theological education of the clergy; National Missions Office located in Auckland, for co-ordinating foreign missionary work; New Zealand Catholic Overseas Aid Committee also centred in Auckland, responsible for socio-economic aid to the Third World; Catholic Social Services (a part of each diocese, with New Zealand statistics for 1974 including 11 hospitals, 8 children's homes and 28 other charitable institutions); and the Catholic Education Council with headquarters in Wellington. Educational statistics in 1974 were 259 Catholic primary and 46 secondary schools with respectively 43,467 and 20,647 pupils.

CHURCH OF THE PROVINCE OF NEW ZEALAND. The diocese of Polynesia (HQ Suva, Fiji) is also a member diocese of the CPNZ. *Bishopric of Aotearea.* In 1978 the suffragan bishop of Aotearea (always a Maori) was appointed to head the all-Maori Bishopric coterminous with New Zealand. *Priests.* In 1977, there were 12 women priests.

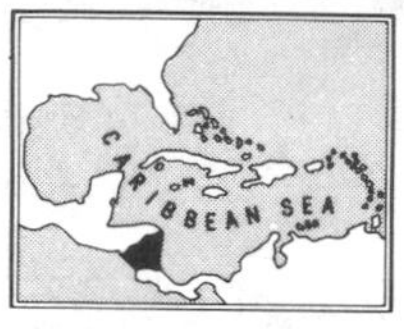


# NICARAGUA

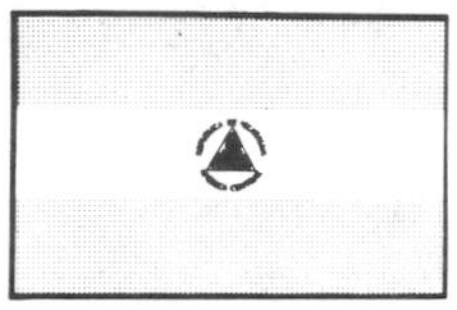

## SECULAR DATA

**STATE. Official name:** The Republic of Nicaragua (La República de Nicaragua). Adjective of nationality: Nicaraguan (nicaragüense).
**Flag** (shown above right): Blue, white, and blue stripes, with coat of arms in centre.
**Area:** 130,000 sq.km. (50,193 sq.miles). Agricultural land: 21.2%.
**Government:** Republic under military rule, since 1936 (1523 Spanish possession, 1821 Independence, 1838 republic, several dictatorships).
**Legislature:** Constituent Assembly, 100 members.
**Official language:** Spanish (*Español/Castellano*).
**Capital:** Managua 398,510 (1971).
**Political divisions:** 16 Departments and 1 Comarca (District); with 123 Municipios.
**Armed forces** (1976): Total 7,100 regular: army 5,400, navy 200, air force 1,500 (16 combat aircraft). Paramilitary forces: 4,000.

**DEMOGRAPHY. Population:** 1,877,952 (census of 20.IV.1971. For 1970–2000 (UN), see last row of Table 1). Population density (1975): 18/sq.km. (46/sq.mile). Under 15 years: 47%. Growth rate (1975–80): 3.29% per year (births 4.66%, deaths −1.22%, emigrants −0.15%). Life expectancy (1975–80): 55.2 years. Household size: 6.1 persons.
**Major languages:** Spanish, English, Miskito, Chinese, and over 12 others.
**Urban dwellers** (1970): 42.1%. Urban growth rate (1950–70): 4.2% per year.
**Labour force:** 27%.
**Tourists** (1972): 148,300.

**ETHNOLINGUISTIC GROUPS:** 68.8% Mestizo (Spanish/Indian), 14% Nicaraguan White, 8% Black (4% Jamaican (70,000), 4% other West Indian), 5% Zambo (Black/Indian), 4% Amerindian (79,000) (1.6% Miskito, Sumu, Rama (Ramaquie), Matagalpa, Monimbo, Subtiaba, Ulva), 0.2% Chinese (3,500), Spaniard, USA White, Jewish, Syro-Lebanese & Palestinian Arab.

**MONEY** (1977). **Monetary unit:** córdoba (= 100 centavos); US$1 = C$7.00.
**National income per person:** US$500. Average annual family income: US$3,050.
**Cost of living in capital** (1976): index 107 (Washington DC = 100). Daily cost of living: US$40.

**HEALTH.** Hospitals: 55 (5,017 beds). Doctors: 1,357. Lepers: 560 (0.2 per 1,000). Blind: 1,800. Psychotics: 18,000.

**EDUCATION.** Adult literacy: (1950) 38%, (1971) 57%. Education rate: 32%. Schools: 2,125. Universities: 2.

**LITERATURE.** Periodicals: 60. Scientific journals: 10. Newspapers: 6 dailies.

**COMMUNICATION** (per 1,000 people). Phones: 8. Radios: 58. TV sets: 30. Daily newspaper circulation: 27 copies.

TABLE 1. RELIGIOUS ADHERENTS IN NICARAGUA

| Year | 1900 | | mid-1970 | | Annual change, 1970–1980 | | | | mid-1975 | | mid-1980 | | 2000 | |
|---|---|---|---|---|---|---|---|---|---|---|---|---|---|---|
| *Name* | *Adherents* | *%* | *Adherents* | *%* | *Natural* | *Conversion* | *Total* | *Rate* | *Adherents* | *%* | *Adherents* | *%* | *Adherents* | *%* |
| **Christians** | **489,000** | **97.8** | **1,954,500** | **99.2** | **75,737** | **243** | **75,980** | **3.30** | **2,300,900** | **99.3** | **2,714,300** | **99.3** | **5,119,700** | **99.3** |
| professing | 489,000 | 97.8 | 1,954,500 | 99.2 | 75,737 | 243 | 75,980 | 3.30 | 2,300,900 | 99.3 | 2,714,300 | 99.3 | 5,119,700 | 99.3 |
| Roman Catholics | 486,000 | 97.2 | 1,881,500 | 95.5 | 72,554 | −1,794 | 70,760 | 3.21 | 2,204,200 | 95.1 | 2,589,100 | 94.7 | 4,844,700 | 94.0 |
| Spiritist Catholics | 5,000 | 1.0 | 99,000 | 5.0 | 3,739 | −519 | 3,220 | 2.83 | 113,600 | 4.9 | 131,200 | 4.8 | 206,200 | 4.0 |
| Evangelical Catholics | 3,000 | 0.6 | 65,489 | 3.3 | 3,644 | 4,007 | 7,651 | 6.91 | 110,700 | 4.8 | 142,000 | 5.2 | 351,700 | 6.8 |
| Christo-pagans | 15,000 | 3.0 | 50,000 | 2.5 | 1,830 | −540 | 1,290 | 2.32 | 55,600 | 2.4 | 62,900 | 2.3 | 103,100 | 2.0 |
| Protestants | 3,000 | 0.6 | 70,000 | 3.6 | 3,051 | 1,969 | 5,020 | 5.42 | 92,700 | 4.0 | 120,200 | 4.4 | 268,000 | 5.2 |
| Anglicans | 0 | 0.0 | 3,000 | 0.2 | 132 | 68 | 200 | 5.00 | 4,000 | 0.2 | 5,000 | 0.2 | 7,000 | 0.1 |
| nominal | 15,000 | 3.0 | 95,016 | 4.8 | 4,012 | 2,116 | 6,128 | 5.03 | 121,900 | 5.3 | 156,300 | 5.7 | 377,700 | 7.3 |
| affiliated | 474,000 | 94.8 | 1,859,484 | 94.4 | 71,725 | −1,873 | 69,852 | 3.20 | 2,179,000 | 94.0 | 2,558,000 | 93.6 | 4,742,000 | 92.0 |
| doubly-affiliated | −5,000 | −1.0 | −60,000 | −3.0 | −2,669 | −2,261 | −4,930 | 6.08 | −81,100 | −3.5 | −109,300 | −4.0 | −258,000 | −5.0 |
| total practising | 450,300 | *95* | 1,580,560 | *85* | 60,966 | −1,592 | 59,374 | 3,20 | 1,852,150 | *85* | 2,174,300 | *85* | 3,556,500 | *75* |
| non-practising | 23,700 | *5* | 278,920 | *15* | 10,759 | −281 | 10,478 | 3.20 | 326,850 | *15* | 383,700 | *15* | 1,185,500 | *25* |
| Roman Catholics | 473,000 | 94.6 | 1,780,995 | 90.4 | 67,567 | −5,656 | 61,911 | 3.02 | 2,052,700 | 88.6 | 2,400,100 | 87.8 | 4,373,300 | 84.9 |
| Catholic pentecostals | 0 | 0.0 | 0 | 0.0 | 494 | 3,506 | 4,000 | 26.67 | 15,000 | 0.6 | 40,000 | 1.5 | 200,000 | 3.9 |
| Protestants | 6,000 | 1.2 | 120,490 | 6.1 | 5,925 | 5,026 | 10,951 | 6.08 | 180,000 | 7.8 | 230,000 | 8.4 | 525,700 | 10.2 |
| Evangelicals | 1,000 | 0.2 | 72,900 | 3.7 | 3,815 | 5,835 | 9,650 | 8.33 | 115,900 | 5.0 | 169,400 | 6.2 | 412,300 | 8.0 |
| Non-White indigenous | 0 | 0.0 | 10,300 | 0.5 | 560 | 810 | 1,370 | 8.06 | 17,000 | 0.7 | 24,000 | 0.9 | 67,000 | 1.3 |
| Marginal Protestants | 0 | 0.0 | 4,499 | 0.2 | 204 | 146 | 350 | 5.65 | 6,200 | 0.3 | 8,000 | 0.3 | 26,000 | 0.5 |
| Anglicans | 0 | 0.0 | 3,200 | 0.2 | 138 | 62 | 200 | 4.76 | 4,200 | 0.2 | 5,200 | 0.2 | 8,000 | 0.2 |
| Non-religious | 0 | 0.0 | 3,800 | 0.2 | 157 | 33 | 190 | 4.00 | 4,750 | 0.2 | 5,700 | 0.2 | 13,000 | 0.3 |
| Baha'is | 0 | 0.0 | 2,800 | 0.1 | 112 | 8 | 120 | 3.53 | 3,400 | 0.1 | 4,000 | 0.1 | 9,000 | 0.2 |
| Tribal religionists | 10,000 | 2.0 | 2,000 | 0.1 | 56 | −116 | −60 | −3.53 | 1,700 | 0.1 | 1,400 | 0.1 | 1,000 | 0.0 |
| Spiritists | 0 | 0.0 | 2,000 | 0.1 | 69 | −49 | 20 | 0.95 | 2,100 | 0.1 | 2,200 | 0.1 | 2,000 | 0.0 |
| Afro-American spiritists | 1,000 | 0.2 | 2,000 | 0.1 | 72 | −32 | 40 | 1.82 | 2,200 | 0.1 | 2,400 | 0.1 | 4,000 | 0.1 |
| Buddhists | 0 | 0.0 | 1,000 | 0.1 | 33 | −33 | 0 | 0.00 | 1,000 | 0.0 | 1,000 | 0.0 | 1,000 | 0.0 |
| Chinese folk-religionists | 0 | 0.0 | 1,000 | 0.1 | 30 | −50 | −20 | −2.22 | 900 | 0.0 | 800 | 0.0 | 500 | 0.0 |
| Atheists | 0 | 0.0 | 500 | 0.0 | 20 | 0 | 20 | 3.33 | 600 | 0.0 | 700 | 0.0 | 1,500 | 0.0 |
| Jews | 0 | 0.0 | 200 | 0.0 | 7 | −7 | 0 | 0.00 | 200 | 0.0 | 200 | 0.0 | 200 | 0.0 |
| Other religionists | 0 | 0.0 | 200 | 0.0 | 7 | 3 | 10 | 4.00 | 250 | 0.0 | 300 | 0.0 | 2,000 | 0.0 |
| **Country's population** | **500,000** | **100.0** | **1,970,000** | **100.0** | **76,300** | **0** | **76,300** | **3.29** | **2,318,000** | **100.0** | **2,733,000** | **100.0** | **5,154,000** | **100.0** |

COLUMNS, ROWS. For meanings and definitions, see Codebook (Part 6). Note that, by definition, total 'Christians' = professing + crypto-Christians, which also = affiliated + nominal Christians. Percentages may not always total exactly, due to rounding.

CENSUSES. **31.V.1950**: 95.9% Roman Catholics, 4.0% Evangelicals (Protestants and Anglicans), 0.1% other religionists. **1963** (partial census): 96.0% Roman Catholics, 3.6% Protestants (1.8% Moravians, 0.2% Baptists), 0.2% Anglicans, 0.1% tribal religionists and others.

**NOTES ON RELIGIONS**

AFRO-AMERICAN SPIRITISTS. Non-Christian adherents of Afro-Caribbean spirit-possession cults (low spiritism) syncretizing Christianity with African religion; mostly Jamaicans and other Blacks.

ATHEISTS. 2 parties: Communist Party of Nicaragua, Socialist Party of Nicaragua (PSN) (banned since 1945): membership (1970) 100.

BAHA'IS. Growth from 11 local spiritual assemblies (1964) to 19 (1973).

BUDDHISTS. Chinese.

CATHOLIC PENTECOSTALS (or, Catholic charismatics). After the 1972 earthquake, cursillo members visited Catholic charismatics in Honduras, then began the charismatic renewal in Nicaragua. In 1975 they numbered 7,000 adults (4,000 in Managua, increasing in June 1974 by 500 new Catholics baptized in the Spirit); total charismatic community, including children, 15,000. By 1977 there were 150 prayer groups in Managua alone. In April 1977 was held in Managua the First Central American Charismatic Conference, with 4,000 attenders. At each evening service, 2 rows were reserved for 30 lepers.

CHRISTO-PAGANS. Amerindians whose syncretistic folk-Catholicism combines a 17th-century Spanish Catholicism with their own traditional pre-Columbian animism, concepts and world-views.

DOUBLY-AFFILIATED. The term covers those affiliated to, or claimed by, both the Catholic Church and also a church termed Evangélica by the state (Protestant, marginal Protestant, Anglican, or Non-White indigenous), i.e. baptized Catholics who have recently become Evangelicals or others. Because their statistics represent a duplication, they are shown in the table as a negative quantity (with a minus sign).

EVANGELICAL CATHOLICS. This term is used here to describe persons who are affiliated to churches termed by the state Evangélica (Protestant, marginal Protestant, Anglican or Non-White indigenous churches), but who in government censuses or polls are regarded as, or who profess publicly to be, Roman Catholics.

NON-WHITE INDIGENOUS. In over 26 denominations in 1970 (see Table 2).

OTHER RELIGIONISTS. Including Rosicrucians (2 AMORC centres), and a few Muslims (Palestinian Arabs).

PROTESTANTS. In 1950, professing Protestants were strongest

(36.8% of inhabitants) in Zelaya department, and in Comarca del Cabo Gracias a Dios (63.8%). Table 2 below represents the 1970 situation; the 1975 figures above come from a CEPAD survey, which shows 550 churches with a total constituency of 180,000 (including 40,000 Moravians). Many Protestant bodies doubled in size in the 3 years after the 1972 earthquake.

SPIRITIST CATHOLICS. Roman Catholics actively and regularly involved in the practice of high or low spiritism, mainly Afro-American low spiritism.
SPIRITISTS. Non-Christian adherents of high spiritism. In 1930 a large new spiritist movement began among the Miskito and Sumu Indians.

TRIBAL RELIGIONISTS. In 1900, many of the 40,000 Amerindians were pagans. Of the 79,000 Amerindians in 1970, small clusters still adhered to their traditional animistic religion, including among the Miskito, Sumu, Ulva and Matagalpa.

Iglesia Católica en Nicaragua, Diocesis de León, State postage stamps of Stations of the Cross in Leon Cathedral, in Holy Week 1975.

**NON-CHRISTIAN RELIGIONS.** Less than 1% of the population are non-Christians, mainly small clusters of Miskito, Sumu, Ulva and Matagalpa Indians adhering to traditional religion, and a slowly-growing community of Baha'is.

## CHRISTIANITY
CATHOLIC CHURCH. The population of Nicaragua is 95% Catholic. Evangelization began on the Atlantic coast in 1522, with missionaries from 4 religious orders arriving in 1526. The following year the diocese of Nicaragua was established by the king of Spain. Christianity did not reach the Pacific coast until 1689, leading to a 'golden age' of the church prior to expulsion of the Jesuits a hundred years later. Under Spanish rule, Nicaragua was part of Guatemala. Nicaragua's first independent constitution in 1826, following its separation from Spain, proclaimed Catholicism as the state religion. During the remainder of the century foreign efforts to gain control of Nicaraguan territory for a proposed canal connecting Atlantic and Pacific oceans, together with internal unrest and civil strife, resulted in periodic shifts in the status of the church. At times the church was placed under the protection of the state: at other times its property was confiscated, religious orders suppressed, and clergy exiled. Nicaragua became an ecclesiastical province in 1912.

By 1970 the church was suffering from a shortage of clergy. In the country as a whole, there was one priest for every 8,300 persons, varying from one priest for 3,313 in the diocese of Bluefields to one for 16,531 in the diocese of Matagalpa.

PROTESTANT CHURCHES. Protestants affiliated to churches numbered 6.1% of the population in 1970, with a higher percentage in the states along the east coast which were at one time

under British control. These states have a large number of Indians and Negroes from Jamaica and include Zelaya (with 36.8% professing Protestants in 1950) and Comarca del Cabo Gracias a Dios (with 63.3% then). The other states averaged less than 2% in 1950, with the exception of Managua (2.5%) and Rio San Juan (2.2%), which continue to show a Protestant increase in growing urban areas. Subsequently Protestant statistics have risen dramatically, and after the 1972 earthquake several denominations doubled in size in 3 years.

Nicaragua was first entered in 1849 by German Moravians, who formed one of the earliest Protestant missions in Central America. Moravians are the largest Protestant denominations in the country and are concentrated along the east coast among the Miskito Indians and the English-speaking Black population. Twelve Miskito Indians are now ordained ministers. Moravians direct a Bible institute and schools for 2,400 students. The Central American Mission came in 1900, but its growth has been slow, reduced in recent years through schisms, which produced the indigenous Central American Convention in 1955 and the National Evangelical Missionary Association in 1965.

Assemblies of God missionaries arrived in 1936, building on the efforts of independent pentecostal missionaries as early as 1912. With 230 congregations and its strength in eastern Nicaragua, this is now the second in size of Nicaragua's Protestant churches. Other important Pentecostal bodies are the International Church of the Foursquare Gospel and the Church of God (Cleveland). The latter doubled in membership between 1962 and 1967.

In 1923 American Baptists took up work begun earlier by an independent Baptist missionary. Heavily involved in education and medical work, including a nurses training programme, the National Baptist Convention also have a large and growing membership. Three other Baptist societies from the USA are also active.

Seventh-day Adventists, who entered in 1904, more than doubled their membership between 1957 and 1967; and the Nazarenes have built up an important community since their arrival in 1943.

INDIGENOUS CHURCHES. As in most Latin American countries, there are a number of Non-White indigenous churches begun on Nicaraguan initiative. In 1970 these numbered 26 denominations with over 10,000 adherents; and 15 of these bodies had by 1976 joined the national relief council CEPAD.

**CHURCH AND STATE.** The state invokes the name of God in the Preamble to its constitution in these words: 'Under the protection of God, we, the representatives of the people of Nicaragua...', although Article 8 affirms that 'The state has no

official religion'.

The institutional separation of the Catholic Church from the state took place in 1893 with the liberal revolution of general Zelaya. The constitution of 1894 elaborated on the meaning of this separation for education, marriage, the financial involvement of the state, and the like, and subsequent constitutions have reflected the same attitude. The constitutions of 1911, 1939 and 1948 contained provisions guaranteeing religious freedom for all.

From 1934 when the Somoza family came to power in Nicaragua, the Catholic Church played an important role in supporting the regime. In 1936 the archbishop of Managua obtained financial concessions from the government including salaries for priests and bishops and a number of other privileges. Twenty years later the church was granted the right to teach catechism in public schools, at its own expense, as an optional subject when requested by parents, and this right was confirmed by the constitutional revision of 1965 (Article 100). It was not until 1969 that the church for the first time withdrew its support from the Somoza regime, with a declaration from the first National Pastoral Meeting supported by CELAM and the apostolic administrator of the archdiocese of Managua. In June 1972, the archbishop of Managua convened a meeting of the Episcopal Conference to take a position concerning the intention expressed by general Somoza to maintain himself in power until 1980 through an illegal amendment to the constitution. A pastoral letter followed, signed by all but one of the bishops, asking for a total change in the political, economic and social structures of the country. Since then, the Catholic Church has been anxious to affirm and consolidate its independence and to avoid any compromise with the Somoza government. Thus, the absence of episcopal representatives at the ceremonies marking the beginning of the second presidential mandate of

Right. Continente '75 3-week mass-communication crusade, involving 56 radio and 100 TV stations in 23 countries, with, above, Argentinian evangelist Luis Palau, then 41 years old. In earthquake-shattered Managua, there were 200,000 attenders and 6,000 decisions for Christ.

general Anastasio Somoza Debayle was widely noted as well as the reduced influence of those priests well-known for their unconditional support of the regime. Such an attitude has caused the state to withdraw Catholic political and financial privilege and to oppose its pastoral programme which is increasingly oriented to the liberation of man.

Churches are expected to register with government, and orders gazetting their date of registration published regularly. From 1948–69, over 62 such decretos for denominations, religious orders or organizations were gazetted.

**INTERDENOMINATIONAL ORGANIZATIONS.** A national evangelical council of churches was formed in 1966 by 9 denominations. In 1972, 5 days after the devastating earthquake of 27 December which levelled the capital and killed nearly 10,000 people, a much larger Evangelical body was formed, the Evangelical Committee for Development Aid (Comité Evangélico Pro-Ayuda al Desarrollo, CEPAD), which after 2 months had as members 30 Evangelical denominations, and after 3 years 35 members of which 15 were Nicaraguan Non-White indigenous denominations. It has mainly supplied relief aid, medicines, food and clothing.

**BROADCASTING.** Stations accept both Catholic and Protestant programmes. The Catholic Church maintains 2 radio stations. Ondas de Luz, owned by the Nicaraguan Cultural Association, transmits Protestant programmes for 7 hours 30 minutes daily. In Puerto Cabezas, Radio Mar transmits Protestant programmes for one hour 30 minutes on Sundays. All these programmes are produced locally. Televisión de Nicaragua also accepts religious programmes. Radio Schools of Nicaragua (Escuelas Radiofónicas de Nicaragua), founded by Catholics in 1965, on the model of Radio Sutatenza in Colombia, provide an integrated education in literacy, mathematics, agriculture, religion, ethics, civics and community development. In 1970 there were 264 radio schools with 6,037 students. From abroad, Protestant programmes can be easily heard on the international stations FEBC (California), TWR (Netherlands Antilles) and HCJB (Ecuador). For Catholics Nicaragua is a member of UNDA.

## BIBLIOGRAPHY


*Anuario eclesiástico de Nicaragua, 1967.* Managua: Conferencia Episcopal de Nicaragua, 1967.

*Evangelizadores laicos para América Latina.* G. Smutko. Quito: Don Bosco, 1970.

*The Evangelism in Depth of the Latin American Mission: a description and evaluation.* R.S. Rosales. Sondeos No. 21. Cuernavaca (Mexico): CIDOC, 1968. 204p.

*Veinticinco años de labor Bautista en Nicaragua, 1917–1942.* A. Parajon. Managua, 1942.


TABLE 2. ORGANIZED CHURCHES AND DENOMINATIONS IN NICARAGUA

| Official name 1 | Begun 2 | Type 3 | Counc 4 | Congs 5 | Adults 6 | Affiliated 7 | Names, notes, and other statistics (see Codebook) 8 |
|---|---|---|---|---|---|---|---|
| Asambleas de Dios | 1912 | P Pe2 | ZF..C | 230 | 10,480 | 20,000 | *Assemblies of God.* M=AoG(USA). In east. Very rapid growth. 115n,11f,1s(57). |
| Associación Misionera Ev Nacional | 1965 | I ind | ....C | 5 | 500 | 1,000 | *National Ev Missionary Association.* Schism ex CAM over delay in self-government. |
| Convención Evangélica Centroamericana | 1955 | I ind | ....C | 12 | 1,000 | 2,000 | *Central American Convention.* 1955 schism of half all CAM's 22 churches. HQ Managua. |
| Convención Nacional Bautista de N | 1917 | P Bap | T...C | 122 | 4,182 | 10,350 | *National Baptist Convention of N.* M=ABHMS(USA). 11f,G=1.9%pa,1s,178Y,195z. |
| Iglesia Adventista del Séptimo Día | 1904 | P Adv | x.... | 14 | 2,605 | 5,000 | *Seventh-day Adventists, Nicaragua Mission,* CAmerican UM. 4nx,10f,1H,1r,30t,357Y. |
| Iglesia Apostólica de la Fe en CJ | 1949 | I pe1 | x...C | 36 | 520 | 2,000 | *IAFCJ. Apostolic Ch of the Faith in Christ Jesus.* Mexican Mestizos. 18n,110z. |
| Iglesia Bando Evangelistico Gedeon | c1960 | I pen | ..... | 1 | 30 | 50 | *Gideon's Evangelistic Band.* Indigenous; HQ Mexico. White suits, dresses. |
| Iglesia Bautista Internacional | 1959 | P Bap | x...C | 18 | 900 | 1,400 | M=Bapt Int Missions(USA). 1 school. 4n,2x,14f,G=14.9%pa,1p,1s(8),W=43%,165Y,50z. |
| **Iglesia Católica en Nicaragua:** | 1522 | R Lat | B.LDR | 176 | 944,000 | 1,780,995 | *Catholic Ch in N.* Shortage of vocations. C=5+1+9. 1p. 312nx,40m,509w,60873Yy. |
| M Managua | 1913 | R Lat | Bs | 49 | 303,000 | 572,000 | Capital. 70% urban. 1972 major earthquake disaster. 152 7 257 3951 |
| D Estelí | 1962 | R Lat | Bs | 15 | 103,600 | 195,939 | 75% rural. Majority of priests nationals (and secular). 21 4 53 5934 |
| D Granada | 1913 | R Lat | Bs | 41 | 94,300 | 177,971 | Southwest coast adjoining Costa Rica. 62% rural. 31 0 36 8595 |
| D León en Nicaragua | 1534 | R Lat | Bs | 32 | 168,100 | 317,085 | Extreme west of country. 48% urban. 52 7 65 15270 |
| D Matagalpa | 1924 | R Lat | Bs | 15 | 153,000 | 288,000 | Central part of country. 83% rural. 19 4 51 14512 |
| PN Juigalpa | 1962 | R Lat | Bs | 10 | 58,000 | 110,000 | Area north of Lake Nicaragua. Rural. 10 0 4 4653 |
| VA Bluefields | 1913 | R Lat | Pofmc | 14 | 64,000 | 120,000 | Rural. Very undeveloped communications, transport.P=30%. 27 18 43 7958 |
| Iglesia de Cristo | | P Dis | x...C | 5 | 600 | 1,200 | *Ch of Christ.* M=CC(Non-Instrumental)(USA). Congs in Mangua, Masatepe. 8m,2f. |
| Iglesia de Dios (Cleveland) | 1950 | P Pe3 | ZF..C | 66 | 2,235 | 5,000 | M=Ch of God(Cleveland)(USA). 42 churches, 24 missions. HQ Managua. 49n,2f,1p. |
| Iglesia de JC de los Santos de los UD | | M LdS | x.... | | 800 | 1,499 | *Ch of JC of Latter-day Saints. Mormons.* M=CJCLdS(USA). 20f. |
| Iglesia de los Hermanos en Cristo | 1965 | P Men | GF..C | 5 | 45 | 400 | *Brethren in Christ Ch.* M=BiCC(USA). HQ Managua. Expanding. 1x,6f,1H,W=80%,5Y,7z. |
| Iglesia del Evangelio Cuadrangular | 1954 | P Pe2 | ZF..C | 31 | 1,428 | 4,000 | *Internat Ch of the Foursquare Gospel.* M=ICFG(USA). 22nm,3f,1k,1p(5),W67%,61Y. |
| Iglesia del Nazareno | 1943 | P Hol | xF..C | 66 | 1,499 | 5,000 | M=CoNazarene(USA). In west. 33n,5x,18f,G=9.3%pa,2h,1s(32),51t(4089),W=67%,208Y. |
| Iglesia del Príncipe de Paz | | I pe2 | x.... | 1 | 100 | 200 | *Ch of the Prnice of Peace.* Pentecostals from Guatemala. Exorcism. In Mangua. |
| Iglesia Episcopal: D Nicaragua | | A ACa | aw.RC | 23 | 1,233 | 3,200 | *Episcopal Ch.* PECUSA, Prov IX. 70% Black, 20% Miskito, 5% Carib. 4n,4x,P=70%,156y. |
| Iglesia Ev Luterana de CR,ES,H,N,P | 1955 | P Lut | l...C | 1 | 200 | 300 | *ELC of Costa Rica,El Sal,Hond,Nic,Pan.* German, Scandinavian diaspora. 1x,W=12%. |
| Iglesia Evangélica Menonita de N | 1968 | P Men | G...C | 3 | 30 | 140 | M=Conservative Mennonite BMC(USA). HQ Managua. 2x,19f,1p,8Y,12z. |
| Iglesia Evangélica Nacional | | I ind | ....C | 1 | 30 | 50 | *National Ev Ch.* Small indigenous congregation in Managua. |
| Iglesia Morava de Nicaragua | 1849 | P Mor | xw..C | 109 | 10,494 | 32,000 | *Moravian Ch, Nicaragua Prov,* UoB. 95% Black. 20n,7x,211m,14f,2H,19i,1s,19Y,1308y. |
| Iglesia Pentecostal Unida | 1970 | P Pe1 | x...C | 5 | 80 | 200 | *United Pentecostal Ch. Jesus Only Church* M=UPC(USA). Unitarians. 2m,2f,1p(10). |
| Iglesias Ev Misión Centroamericana | 1900 | P int | xM..f | 30 | 1,000 | 2,000 | M=Central American Mission. Mainly Indians. Major schisms 1955, 1965. 9f,1s. |
| Testigos de Jehová | 1934 | M Jeh | x.... | 31 | 1,654 | 3,000 | *Jehovah's Witnesses.* 1934, visits; 1943, literature; 1945, missionaries. 204Y. |
| Other Protestant denominations | | P | ..... | | 10,000 | 33,500 | Total about 30 (see list below). |
| Other Non-White indigenous churches | | I | ..... | | 2,500 | 5,000 | Total over 20 (see list below), including several Jamaican bodies. |
| Doubly-affiliated (duplication)(1970) | | | | | –32,000 | –60,000 | Evangelicals who also are or were baptized Roman Catholics. |
| **Total affiliated (mid-1970)** | | | | **1,390** | **966,145** | **1,859,484** | **Total denominations (1970) . . . 74.** |
| **Total affiliated (mid-1975)** | | | | **1,470** | **1,132,200** | **2,179,000** | **Total denominations (1975) . . . 81.** |
| **Total affiliated (mid-1980)** | | | | **1,750** | **1,329,100** | **2,558,000** | **Total denominations (1980) . . . 88.** |

NOTES ON TABLE ABOVE

COLUMNS: for meanings and CODES (cols. 1, 3, 4, 8): see Codebook (Part 6). Column 1: **Boldface type** = church with over 10% of country's affiliated Christians.

The data in the table above refer primarily to the situation in 1970. For 1975–80, see Table 1.

NATIONAL COUNCILS (Column 4, 5th letter).

C = Comité Evangélico Pro-Ayuda al Desarrollo (CEPAD) (Evangelical Committee for Development Aid), with 35 Evangelical denominations as members by 1976.

f = formerly a member of CEPAD.

R = Conferencia Episcopal de Nicaragua (CEN) (Episcopal Conference of Nicaragua).

*Other national councils.* Although there is no nation-wide council of churches, there are 2 local ones: Asociación de Iglesias Cristianas (ADIC), in Puerto Cabezas (members: Baptist, Episcopalian, Pentecostal, Roman Catholic); and Asociación de Cleros, in Bluefields.

OTHER PROTESTANT DENOMINATIONS. These include: American Baptist Association (2 churches), Baptist Bible Fellowship International (1969), Baptist Missionary Association of America (1964), Ch of God of Prophecy (1962), Ev Mennonite Ch (1966), Iglesias Berea (Asociación Cristiana Nicaragüense), Iglesia Cristiana Reformada, Salvation Army (1928), Union Ch (Managua), United Brethren in Christ (1966), United World Mission (1969); and a number of West Indian denominations. Of these, in 1976 over 7 belonged to CEPAD.

OTHER NON-WHITE INDIGENOUS CHURCHES. These include: Apostólica Libre, Asamblea Apostólica, Asambleas de Iglesias Cristianas (Assemblies of Christian Churches) (Puerto Rican pentecostals; 1964), Cristiana Misionera, Embajadora de Cristo, Iglesia Apostólica Libre, Iglesia Bautista Pentecostal, Iglesia Bíblica Nacional, Iglesia Ev Primitiva, Iglesia Fuente de Jacob, Iglesia Pentecostal Libre, Iglesia Poder Pentecostal, Iglesia Sinaí, Misión Cristiana, Misión Obreros de Cristo, Templo Bíblico. Of these, in 1976 about 11 belonged to CEPAD. Several Jamaican bodies have members among the 70,000 Jamaicans resident. A USA Black mission is also at work: National Baptist Convention USA (1964).

**PEOPLES** (ethnolinguistic). Christians: 69.1% Mestizo, 14.0% Nicaraguan White, 8.0% Black (4.0% Jamaican), 5.0% Zambo, 3.9% Amerindian (1.6% Miskito), Chinese (300), Spaniard, USA White, Palestinian & Syro-Lebanese Arab.

COUNTRY-WIDE TOTALS

EVANGELIZATION (see Part 5). 1900: 99%. 1970: 100%. 1980: 100%. *Mass evangelism.* Among recent campaigns: 1959–60, first country to hold an Evangelism-in-Depth campaign (successful, hence LAM sponsored similar campaigns in 10 other Latin American countries by 1971); in 1960, 125 local churches (12 denominations), 65,000 homes visited; 126,000 attenders in 14 local crusades, 2,604 professions of faith, 500 prayer cells formed; 1969, Hermano Pablo 7-day crusades in Managua (52,500 attenders, 1,085 enquirers) and Leon (22,000/567); 1975, Nicaragua '75 3-week crusade (part of Continente '75) in earthquake-shattered Managua, sponsored by most Protestant churches, broadcast by Radio HCJB (Ecuador) to 56 other stations in 20 countries, with tapes over 100 TV stations in 23 countries (Managua: 200,000 attenders, 6,000 decisions for Christ (75% under age 25)). *Radiophonic evangelism.* HCJB,FEBC, ICI (3,500 enrolments, 1,600 active, 25 conversions reported).

FOREIGN MISSIONARIES AND PERSONNEL (nationals serving abroad) (1973). Total about 70 Roman Catholics in Mexico and other Latin American countries.

FOREIGN MISSIONARIES AND PERSONNEL (aliens from abroad) (1973). Total 965. *From Western world.* 545: about 380 Roman Catholics, 141 Protestants (132 in 30 USA societies, 9 in 2 Canada societies), about 20 marginal Protestants (Mormons from USA), 4 Anglicans in 1 USA society. *From Third World.* 420: about 400 Roman Catholics from other Latin American countries, 10 Protestants, about 10 Non-White indigenous from Mexico, Jamaica et alia.

INSTITUTIONS (church-operated) (1973). Total 160, including 105 higher schools (2 minor seminaries), 25 medical centres (7 hospitals), 2 radio stations, 1 research centre, 11 seminaries (10 Protestant, 1 RC), 1 university.

PERIODICALS. About 25 titles.

PERSONNEL. About 1,910 (945 national, 965 foreign).

RELIGIOUS LIBRARIES. About 16.

SCRIPTURE DISTRIBUTION (1975). Annual totals: 15,709 Bibles (87% subsidized, 13% commercial), 33,349 NTs (46% free, 51% subsidized, 3% commercial), 115,059 UBS portions, 832,572 UBS selections. *Translations completed.* Miskito: portion in 1889, NT 1905.

SERVICE AGENCIES. About 40, including CCCI, CEF, CEN, CEPAD, CONFER, CPJ, CRS-USCC, CTN, FENEC, JUC, MAF, MEC, MFC, WVI.

ADDITIONAL DATA ON CHURCHES

IGLESIA CATOLICA EN NICARAGUA. *Annual baptisms.* (1972) 99.7% infant, 0.3% adult. *Priests.* 41% secular, 59% religious. *Male religious.* 265 (1970). *Sisters.* Total including contemplatives (1970): 687. *Seminarians.* There is an acute shortage of vocations; from 1960 to 1969 only 25 Nicaraguans were ordained priests. *Catechists.* Total (1974) 325, in VA Bluefields. *Catechist training school.* The Instituto Catequético Pío XII (OFMCap, Waspam, Rio Coco) trains catechists in the Miskito language. *Main religious orders and congregations.* Priests: OFMCap, SJ, SP, SDB, OFM. Brothers: FSC. Sisters: Josephite Sisters, Salesians, Missionaries of Christ the King, Sisters of the Assumption, Good Shepherd Sisters, Theresians, Sisters of Bethlehem, Missionaries of the Heart of Jesus, Sisters of Charity of St Vincent de Paul. *Catholic organizations.* The Episcopal Conference of Nicaragua (Conferencia Episcopal de Nicaragua) is a member of CELAM and SEDAC. The Nicaraguan National Conference of Religious Institutes (Conferencia Nacional Nicaragüense de Institutos Religiosos, CONFER), which serves both male and female religious personnel, is a member of CLAR and SERCAP. There are no pastoral nor presbyteral councils. Catholic lay organizations include the Juvenile Pastoral Council (Consejo de la Pastoral Juvenil) which co-ordinates all Catholic youth movements, Christian Family Movement (Movimiento Familiar Cristiana), National Federation of Marian Congregations (Federación Nacional de Congregaciónes Marianas), St Vincent de Paul Society (Conferencia de St Vincent de Paul) and Christian Study Courses (Cursillos de Cristiandad). The Central American Conference of Marian Congregations also has its headquarters in Nicaragua.

The Holy See has diplomatic relations with Nicaragua, and is represented to government and the Catholic hierarchy by the apostolic nunciature of Nicaragua, with a nuncio in Managua.

Nicaraguan organizations involved in social and socio-religious action include the following: Nicaraguan Social Institute (Instituto Social Nicaragüense); Nicaraguan Federation of Workers (Central de Trabajadores Nicaragüenses), affiliated with the Latin American Federation of Workers (CLAT) in Venezuela and the World Federation of Workers (CMT) in Brussels, Belgium; and Catholic University Youth (Juventud Universitaria Católica, JUC). Working in the realm of pastoral and religious training is the Mater Ecclesiae Institute of Religious Culture.

There exist 2 rural development centres, one at Rama in the department of Zelaya (Centro de Adiestramiento de Celebradores de la Palabra), and the other at Somoto in the department of Madriz.

In 1969 Catholic schools accounted for 10% of all pupils at primary level (32,884 pupils out of 332,744) and 21.4% at secondary level (9,457 out of 44,155). The Nicaraguan section of the Central American Catholic University was opened in Managua in 1960 and had 2,572 students in 1969–70. In 1973 there were 166 Catholic elementary schools (47,041 pupils) and 98 secondary (24,383).

The archdiocese of Managua operates 3 hospitals, 15 dispensaries, 3 hostels and 2 other social service institutions. Sisters of Charity sponsor several hospitals and dispensaries in various parts of the country. Caritas Nicaragua has since 1959 been involved in the distribution of food, clothing and medicines, most of which comes from Catholic Relief Services in the USA. It co-ordinates the work of 32 Catholic dispensaries, provides aid to tuberculosis patients and sponsors a housing programme called The House of My Brother. Caritas also played an important role in relief and reconstruction following the earthquake of 1972.

IGLESIAS EVANGELICAS MISION CENTROAMERICANA. Also called Fraternidad de Iglesias Centroamericanas. At one time it was a member of CEPAD.

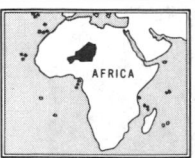

# NIGER

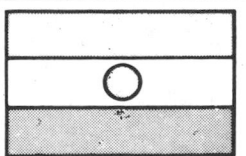

## SECULAR DATA

**STATE. Official name:** The Republic of the Niger (La République du Niger). Adjective of nationality: nigérien.
**Flag** (shown above right): Orange, white, and green stripes with centred orange disc, the sun.
**Area:** 1,267,000 sq.km. (489,191 sq.miles). Agricultural land: 14.2%.
**Government:** Military junta, since 1974 (1890 French penetration, 1922 French colony in French West Africa, 1958 autonomous, 1960 Independence as republic).
**Legislature:** Supreme Military Council, 12 members.
**Official language:** French (*Français*).
**Capital:** Niamey 102,000 (1972).
**Political divisions:** 7 Départements with 33 Arrondissements.
**Armed forces** (1976): Total 2,100 regular: army 2,000, air force 100. Paramilitary forces: 1,800.

**DEMOGRAPHY. Population:** 2,501,800 (census of X.1959–III.1960. For 1970–2000 (UN), see last row of Table 1). Population density (1975): 4/sq.km. (9/sq.mile). Under 15 years: 46%. Growth rate (1975–80): 2.76% per year (births 5.17%, deaths −2.41%). Life expectancy (1975–80): 40.0 years. Household size: 4.9 persons.
**Major languages:** Hausa, Djemar, Fulani, Tuareg, French, Kanuri, Arabic, and about 10 smaller languages.
**Urban dwellers** (1970): 8.2%. Urban growth rate (1950–70): 6.2% per year.
**Labour force:** 30%.
**Refugees** (1977): Large numbers of Tuareg nomads fled Mali during the 1969–74 drought.

**ETHNOLINGUISTIC GROUPS:** 46% Hausa (including Kurfei, Mauri), 19% Zerma-Songhai, 13% Fulani, 10% Tuareg, 7.5% Kanuri (Teda, Tubu), 3.6% Saharan Arab (Shoa), 0.4% alien African (18,000), 0.2% French (6,500), Buduma, Sokoro, Daza, Kanembu, Mober, USA White, Canadian, Lebanese Arab.

**MONEY** (1977). **Monetary unit:** CFA franc (= 100 centimes); US$1 = CFAF 250.00.
**National income per person:** US$100. Average annual family income: US$490.
**Inflation:** (1970–74) 7.2% per year (1975: consumer price index 156).
**Cost of living in capital** (1976): index 149 (Washington DC=100). Daily cost of living: US$34.

**HEALTH.** Hospitals: 57 (2,299 beds). Doctors: 100. Lepers: 41,000 (8.9 per 1,000). Blind: 50,000. Psychotics: 32,000 Criminals: 6,000.

**EDUCATION.** Adult literacy: (1960) 1%, (1975) 6%. Education rate: 8%. Schools: 779.

**LITERATURE.** Periodicals: 5. Newspapers: 1 daily, 1 non-daily.

**COMMUNICATION** (per 1,000 people). Phones: 1. Radios: 36. Daily newspaper circulation: 0.5 copies.

### TABLE 1.   RELIGIOUS ADHERENTS IN THE NIGER

| Year | 1900 | | mid-1970 | | Annual change, 1970–1980 | | | | mid-1975 | | mid-1980 | | 2000 | |
| --- | --- | --- | --- | --- | --- | --- | --- | --- | --- | --- | --- | --- | --- | --- |
| *Name* | *Adherents* | *%* | *Adherents* | *%* | *Natural* | *Conversion* | *Total* | *Rate* | *Adherents* | *%* | *Adherents* | *%* | *Adherents* | *%* |
| Muslims | 410,000 | 45.1 | 3,453,090 | 86.0 | 109,272 | 9,009 | 118,281 | 2.96 | 3,995,050 | 87.0 | 4,635,900 | 87.9 | 8,799,000 | 92.0 |
| Tribal religionists | 500,000 | 54.9 | 545,300 | 13.6 | 15,813 | −8,755 | 7,058 | 1.22 | 578,110 | 12.6 | 615,880 | 11.7 | 742,500 | 7.8 |
| **Christians** | 0 | 0.0 | 16,810 | 0.4 | 489 | −258 | 231 | 1.29 | 17,890 | 0.4 | 19,120 | 0.4 | 23,500 | 0.2 |
| crypto-Christians | 0 | 0.0 | 4,600 | 0.1 | 136 | −44 | 92 | 1.84 | 4,990 | 0.1 | 5,520 | 0.1 | 8,500 | 0.1 |
| professing | 0 | 0.0 | 12,210 | 0.3 | 353 | −214 | 139 | 1.08 | 12,900 | 0.3 | 13,600 | 0.2 | 15,000 | 0.2 |
| Roman Catholics | 0 | 0.0 | 10,110 | 0.3 | 293 | −174 | 119 | 1.11 | 10,700 | 0.2 | 11,300 | 0.2 | 12,300 | 0.1 |
| Protestants | 0 | 0.0 | 2,000 | 0.0 | 57 | −38 | 19 | 0.90 | 2,100 | 0.0 | 2,190 | 0.0 | 2,500 | 0.0 |
| African indigenous | 0 | 0.0 | 100 | 0.0 | 3 | −2 | 1 | 1.00 | 100 | 0.0 | 110 | 0.0 | 200 | 0.0 |
| affiliated | 0 | 0.0 | 16,810 | 0.4 | 489 | −258 | 231 | 1.29 | 17,890 | 0.4 | 19,120 | 0.4 | 23,500 | 0.2 |
| total practising | 0 | *0* | 13,450 | *80* | 391 | −206 | 185 | 1.29 | 14,310 | *80* | 15,300 | *80* | 16,450 | *70* |
| non-practising | 0 | *0* | 3,360 | *20* | 98 | −52 | 46 | 1.28 | 3,580 | *20* | 3,820 | *20* | 7,050 | *30* |
| Roman Catholics | 0 | 0.0 | 13,360 | 0.3 | 386 | −230 | 156 | 1.11 | 14,090 | 0.3 | 14,920 | 0.3 | 16,400 | 0.2 |
| Protestants | 0 | 0.0 | 2,450 | 0.1 | 71 | −42 | 29 | 1.12 | 2,600 | 0.1 | 2,740 | 0.1 | 3,000 | 0.0 |
| Evangelicals | 0 | 0.0 | 2,400 | 0.1 | 70 | −40 | 30 | 1.18 | 2,550 | 0.1 | 2,700 | 0.1 | 2,950 | 0.0 |
| African indigenous | 0 | 0.0 | 950 | 0.0 | 31 | 14 | 45 | 3.91 | 1,150 | 0.0 | 1,400 | 0.0 | 4,000 | 0.0 |
| Marginal Protestants | 0 | 0.0 | 50 | 0.0 | 1 | 0 | 1 | 2.00 | 50 | 0.0 | 60 | 0.0 | 100 | 0.0 |
| Baha'is | 0 | 0.0 | 800 | 0.0 | 26 | 4 | 30 | 3.16 | 950 | 0.0 | 1,100 | 0.0 | 3,000 | 0.0 |
| Country's population | 910,000 | 100.0 | 4,016,000 | 100.0 | 125,600 | 0 | 125,600 | 2.74 | 4,592,000 | 100.0 | 5,272,000 | 100.0 | 9,568,000 | 100.0 |

**COLUMNS, ROWS.** For meanings and definitions, see Codebook (Part 6). Note that, by definition, total 'Christians' = professing + crypto-Christians, which also = affiliated + nominal Christians. Percentages may not always total exactly, due to rounding.
**CENSUSES.** X.1959–III.1960 (Niger Africans only, de jure): 98.5% Muslims, 1.4% tribal religionists, 0.04% Christians. (This survey covered only half the population).

**NOTES ON RELIGIONS**
**AFRICAN INDIGENOUS.** In 3 denominations in 1970 (see Table 2).
**BAHA'IS.** By 1973, 5 local spiritual assemblies established.
**CHRISTIANS.** About 5% citizens (Africans), 95% expatriates (in 1965, 6,000 French, and 8,000 Nigerians and other African expatriates).
**CRYPTO-CHRISTIANS.** Unorganized individuals in the recognized churches, including many citizens and some African expatriates.
**MUSLIMS.** Sunnis (of the Malikite rite), mostly linked to the Tijaniya brotherhood. *Hajj pilgrims to Mecca.* (1970) 1,827; (1974) 7,030; (1975) 685; (1976) 139.
**TRIBAL RELIGIONISTS.** Animists in the south, especially among the Kurfei (90% traditionalist in 1972) and Mauri (95%).

**NON-CHRISTIAN RELIGIONS. Islam** was first propagated in Niger in the 11th century and is the predominant religion in the country. Today most Muslims are linked through their clerics to the Tijaniya brotherhood, which is strong among the Tuareg, Kanuri, Fulani and Hausa city-dwellers, whilst a mixture of Islamic and traditional beliefs is found among the Zerma-Songhai, Beriberi, and rural Hausa. A training school for marabouts exists at Say, the principal Muslim holy city in Niger. A recent development is a powerful Muslim radio station, funded by Arab governments.

**African traditional religions** retain the allegiance of about 13% of the people, most of whom are located in the southern part of the country. The Kurfei and Mauri peoples are almost totally resistant to the claims of both Christianity and Islam.

**CHRISTIANITY.** In the 7th century Berber Christians who had been driven out of North Africa by nascent Islam migrated into the Aïr region and reached as

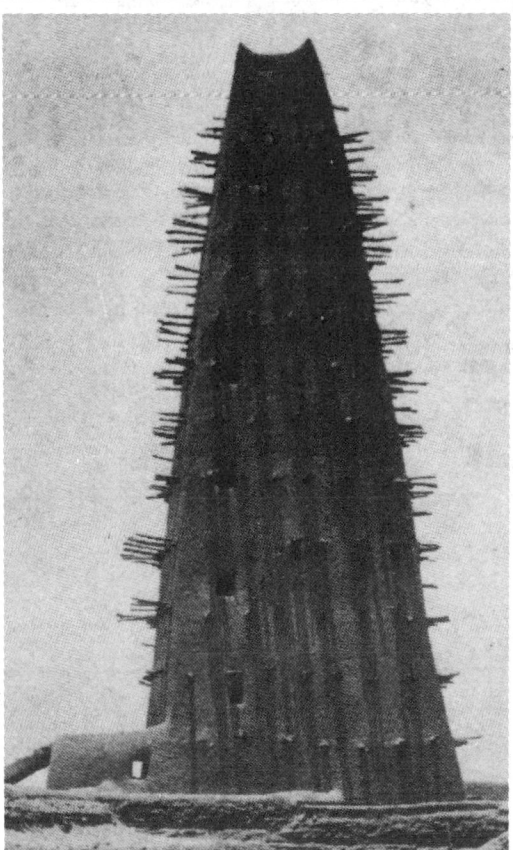

**Muslims.** *Left.* Thousand-year-old mosque. *Right.* Tuareg dance.

**Muslims.** Horseman at edge of Sahara desert near Zinder.

North America, Lebanon and West Africans from Togo, Benin and Upper Volta. Local African Catholics include Hausas from the region of Dogondoutchi, Zerma-Songhai from Dolbel, mixed-race persons and naturalized citizens from Togo and Benin (Dahomey). The number today is considerably smaller than in 1963 when the government deported all Dahomeans, although some subsequently returned clandestinely.

PROTESTANT CHURCHES. The main Protestant work is being carried on by the Evangelical Churches of Niger, supported by the Sudan Interior Mission since its arrival in 1923. Active in the Maradi and Dogondoutchi areas, the church is involved in an extensive school and social service programme including a large hospital at Galmi, a leprosarium at Maradi and numerous dispensaries. The Evangelical Baptist Church is located in southwest Niger at Niamey and along the Niger river. The small Methodist Church confines its activities largely to expatriates from Togo and Dahomey.

INDIGENOUS CHURCHES. There have been no indigenous schismatic churches in Niger, but immigrant Nigerians and Dahomeans have introduced 2 bodies: the Cherubim and Seraphim from the Nigerian coast have made some progress west of Niamey, and the Heavenly Christian Church from Benin works in Niamey.

CHURCH AND STATE. According to the constitution of November 1960, modified in July 1961, Niger is a secular republic (Article 2) which respects all beliefs (Article 6). The churches are neither subsidized nor taxed, except for a small basic tax for occupation of land. The state contributes, nonetheless towards the expenses involved in the functioning of private schools. Courses of religious instruction are given outside school hours and premises. There is no government ministry charged with religious affairs

A number of Niger's postage stamps carry Christian themes: here, Crucifixion (Hugo van der Goes).

nor any obligation for the churches to register with government. Relations between churches on the one hand and the state and Islam on the other are good.

BROADCASTING. The government Radio Niger broadcasts Catholic programmes. For Catholics, Niger is registered as a member of UNDA. Radio Vatican's French programmes are beamed across Niger for one hour 20 minutes weekly; ELWA (Liberia) can also be heard.

BIBLIOGRAPHY

'Un aspect historique des rapports de l'animisme et de l'Islam au Niger', H. Raulin, *Journal de la Société des Africanistes*, XXXII, 2 (1962–3), 249–274. (Syncretism between animism and Islam, hidden by apparent conversions to Islam).

far southwest as the Niger river. They were however isolated from any other Christian support, and eventually disappeared without trace. Christianity did not return again to Niger until the 20th century.

CATHOLIC CHURCH. Catholicism spread from Dahomey to Niger in 1931. The prefecture of Niamey was erected in 1942 and was raised to a diocese in 1961. The first and thusfar only indigenous priest was ordained in 1972 in the presence of senior government officials and the Muslim great imam of Niamey. Of all Catholics 95% are expatriates from Europe,

TABLE 2. ORGANIZED CHURCHES AND DENOMINATIONS IN THE NIGER

| Official name 1 | Begun 2 | Type 3 | Counc 4 | Congs 5 | Adults 6 | Affiliated 7 | Names, notes, and other statistics (see Codebook) 8 |
|---|---|---|---|---|---|---|---|
| Chérubin et Séraphin | c1960 | I peA | x.I.. | 1 | 30 | 50 | *Cherubim & Seraphim* (Nigeria). Schism at Tera of EBM converts among Songhai. |
| Eglise Catholique: D Niamey | 1931 | R Lat | p.SFP | 12 | 7,200 | 13,360 | *Cath Ch.* C=1+1+7. 95% expatriate, 380 Songhai,Hausa. 26x,16m,75w,P=30%,177Yy,860z. |
| Eglise du Christianisme Céleste | | I peA | x.I.. | 2 | 100 | 200 | *Heavenly Christianity* Ch. Ex C & S. Niamey. HQ Porto Novo (Benin). Yoruba et al. |
| Eglise Méthodiste | | P Met | Vva.. | 1 | 30 | 50 | *Methodist Ch.* Migrants from church in Togo and Benin (HQ Contonou, Benin). |
| Eglises Evangéliques du Niger | 1923 | P int | xM.. | 90 | 1,000 | 2,000 | M=ECWA(Nigeria),SIM(USA). 98% Hausa; Tuareg, Beriberi. 4n,16m,30f,2H,5h,1p(14). |
| Eglises radiophoniques isolées | c1960 | I rad | ..... | 20 | 300 | 700 | Isolated radio believers, mostly youths aged 12–25. T=50(ELWA,SIM,ICI). |
| Témoins de Jéhovah | c1960 | M Jeh | x.... | 1 | 24 | 50 | *Jehovah's Witnesses.* Watch Tower. IBSA. Active witnessing under way by 1965. 1Y. |
| Union des Egls Evangéliques Baptistes | 1927 | P Bap | xT... | 5 | 100 | 200 | *Ev Baptist Missions.* M=EBM(USA). 90% Yoruba immigrants, 10% Zerma. 26f,2h,1p. |
| Other Protestant denominations | | P | ..... | | 100 | 200 | Total about 8 (see list below). |
| Total affiliated (mid-1970) | | | | 144 | 8,884 | 16,810 | Total denominations (1970) . . . 16. |
| Total affiliated (mid-1975) | | | | 160 | 9,450 | 17,890 | Total denominations (1975) . . . 16. |
| Total affiliated (mid-1980) | | | | 180 | 10,100 | 19,120 | Total denominations (1980) . . . 17. |

NOTES ON TABLE ABOVE

COLUMNS: for meanings and CODES (cols. 1, 3, 4, 8): see Codebook (Part 6). Column 1: **Boldface type** = church with over 10% of country's affiliated Christians.
NATIONAL COUNCILS (Column 4, 5th letter).
   P = Conférence Episcopale de Haute-Volta et Niger (CEHVN) (Episcopal Conference of Upper Volta & Niger).
OTHER PROTESTANT DENOMINATIONS. These smaller bodies include: Baptist International Missions (1970), Coopération Evangélique Mondiale, Sahara Desert Mission (work among Tuaregs), Southern Methodist Ch, World-Wide Missions.

PEOPLES (ethnolinguistic). Christians: about 39% Nigerian (alien Yoruba, Hausa, et alii, from Nigeria), 37% French, 12% other alien African (Togo, Benin, Upper Volta), 6% other White (European, USA, Canada), 5% Niger citizen (2.8% Songhai, 1.5% Hausa, 0.3% Zerma, 0.1% Tuareg), Lebanese Arab.

COUNTRY-WIDE TOTALS
EVANGELIZATION (see Part 5). 1900: 0%. 1970: 16%. 1980: 20%.
FOREIGN MISSIONARIES AND PERSONNEL (aliens from abroad) (1973). Total 217. *From Western world.* 202: 112 Roman Catholics, 90 Protestants (50 in 7 USA societies, 24 in 1 Canada

society, 9 in 2 UK societies, 2 in 1 WGermany society, 2 in 1 France society, 2 in 2 Australia societies, 1 in 1 New Zealand society). By 1976 USA Protestant missionaries numbered 136. *From Communist world.* 1 Roman Catholic from Poland. *From Third World.* 14: about 7 Roman Catholics from Rwanda, Togo, Nigeria and Upper Volta, 5 Protestants from Nigeria, 2 African indigenous from Nigeria.
INSTITUTIONS (church-operated) (1973). Total 20, including 3 higher schools, 16 medical centres (3 hospitals).
PERIODICALS. 2 titles.
PERSONNEL. About 249 (32 national, 217 foreign).
SCRIPTURE DISTRIBUTION (1975). Annual totals: 300 Bibles (subsidized), 1,200 NTs (subsidized), 1,000 UBS portions, 2,500 UBS selections. *Translations completed.* Portion: 2 languages since 1934. NT: Zerma in 1954.
SERVICE AGENCIES. About 12, including ACF, AMS, CEHVN, GBUAF, JEC, JOC, NLFA.

ADDITIONAL DATA ON CHURCHES
EGLISE CATHOLIQUE. Begun in 1931, the mission became a prefecture in 1942 and a diocese in 1961. *Catholics.* The 12,100 expatriate Catholics are from France, Canada, USA, Upper Volta, Togo, Benin, with some Lebanese and others. *Catechumens.* (1959) 475; (1961) 440; (1963) 630; (1969) 860; (1971) 350. *Annual baptisms.* (1972) 82.8% infant, 17.2% adult. *Priests.* No Africans until first Niger priest was ordained in 1972. *Brothers.* All ex-

patriates. The total includes 4 Protestant brothers of the Taizé Community (France) working in the Catholic missions at Tchirozérine and Makalondi. *Sisters.* Including 5 African sisters from Rwanda, Togo, Upper Volta. *Catechists.* Total (1970) 7 nationals, 4 expatriates. *Indigenous religious congregations.* None. *Foreign religious congregations.* Priests: CSSR. Brothers: FSC. Sisters: Notre-Dame du Perpétuel Secours, Notre-Dame des Apôtres, Petites Soeurs de Jésus du Père de Foucauld, and 4 others. *Catholic organizations.* The Episcopal Conference of Upper Volta-Niger (Conférence Episcopale de Haute-Volta-Niger), with headquarters in Ouagadougou, Upper Volta, is a member of the Inter-Territorial Episcopal Conference of Francophone West Africa and SECAM. There are no presbyteral or pastoral councils, but a Committee of Sisters (Comité de Religieuses) has been formed. Lay groups include ACF (50 members), Scouts and Guides of Niger (200 members), Jeunesse Etudiante Croyante (100 members) and Jeunesse Ouvrière Croyante (30 members).

The Holy See has diplomatic relations with Niger and is represented to government and the Catholic hierarcy by a pronuncio based in Dakar, Senegal.

The Catholic Church supervises 15 primary and 3 secondary schools, all of which permit Muslim students to receive Islamic religious instruction; a co-operative at Tchirozérine; 8 mission posts for work among women and 5 for rural development; 9 dispensaries; and one leprosarium offering mainly outpatient service. Sisters are also at work in 2 government hospitals.

---

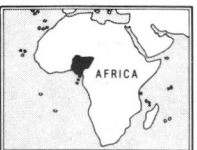

# NIGERIA

## SECULAR DATA

STATE. **Official name:** The Federal Republic of Nigeria. Adjective of nationality: Nigerian (nigérian, in French).
**Flag** (shown above right): Bars of green, white, and green.
**Area:** 923,768 sq.km. (356,669 sq.miles). Agricultural land: 49.8%.
**Government:** Federal parliamentary republic, since 1979 (1861 British colony of Lagos, 1883 Niger Coast protectorate, 1914 unified British colony and protectorate, 1954 federation, 1960 Independence, 1963 republic, 1966 military rule).
**Official language:** English.
**Chief cities:** capital Lagos 1,476,840 (1971), Ibadan 758,330

(metropolitan area 1,496,120 in 1970), Ogbomosho 386,650, Kano 357,100.
**Political divisions:** 12 States: Benue-Plateau, Central-Eastern, Kano, Kwara, Lagos, Mid-Western, North-Central, North-Eastern, North-Western, Rivers, South-Eastern, Western.
**Armed forces** (1976): Total 230,000 regular: army 221,000, navy 3,500, air force 5,500 (24 combat aircraft). Reserves: 12,000.

DEMOGRAPHY. **Population:** 62,925,000 (estimate for mid-1975. For 1970–2000 (UN), see last row of Table 1). Population density (1975): 68/sq.km. (176/sq.mile). Under 15 years: 45%. Growth rate (1975–80): 2.86% per year (births 4.92%, deaths −2.07%). Life expectancy (1975–80): 43.5 years. Household size: 4.9

persons.
**Major languages:** English, Hausa, Yoruba, Ibo, Fulani, Tiv, Kanuri, Efik, Bini, Nupe, Pidgin English, and over 510 other tribal languages.
**Urban dwellers** (1970): 22.8%. Urban growth rate (1950–70): 4.9% per year.
**Labour force:** 41%.
**Refugees:** From 1969–74, large numbers of Tuareg nomads fled from the drought in Mali.

ETHNOLINGUISTIC GROUPS: 17.8% Yoruba (Egba, Ekiti, Ife, Ijebu, Ondo, Oyo, also Igala, Idoma), 17.5% Ibo, 16.8% Hausa (excluding Hausa-speaking Chadic tribal peoples),

10.3% Fulani (1.5% Bororo (pastoral Fulani)), 5.6% Tiv (including Boki, Jarawa and related peoples), 5.5% Plateau Chadic (1.7% Bura, 0.6% Angas, &c), 4.9% Kanuri, 4.7% Ibibio, 3.6% Edo (Bini), 2.1% other Eastern Bantoid (Ekoi, Jukun, Zumper, et alii), 2.0% Ijaw, 2.0% Nupe (with Gbari, Igbira), 1.1% Birom, 1.0% Isoko (with Urhobo), 0.9% Kambari, 0.8% Chamba, 0.3% Mandara, 0.3% Ewe, 0.3% Shoa Arab, 0.3% Katab, 0.3% Mumuye, 0.2% Songhai, 0.2% European, 0.1% Busa, Chinese (5,000), Lebanese & Syrian Arab, & a large number of smaller tribes with around 500 languages.

**MONEY** (1977). **Monetary unit:** naira (= 100 kobo); US$1 = N 0.62.
**National income per person:** US$350. Average annual family income: US$1,715.
**Inflation:** (1970–74) 9.2% per year (1975: consumer price index 213).
**Cost of living in capital** (1976): index 153 (Washington DC=100). Daily cost of living: US$52.

**HEALTH.** Hospitals: 500 (42,101 beds). Doctors: 2,271. Lepers: 675,000 (10.7 per 1,000). Blind: 420,000. Psychotics: 450,000.

Criminals: 120,000.

**EDUCATION.** Adult literacy: (1952) 12%, (1962) 15%, (1975) 25%. Education rate: 19%. Schools: 13,722. Universities: 5.

**LITERATURE.** Annual new book titles (1973): 1,316. Periodicals: 300. Scientific journals: 15. Newspapers: 17 dailies, 23 non-daily.

**COMMUNICATION** (per 1,000 people). Phones: 2. Radios: 73. TV sets: 2. Daily newspaper circulation: 3 copies.

### TABLE 1.    RELIGIOUS ADHERENTS IN NIGERIA

| Year | 1900 | | mid-1970 | | Annual change, 1970–1980 | | | | mid-1975 | | mid-1980 | | 2000 | |
|---|---|---|---|---|---|---|---|---|---|---|---|---|---|---|
| Name | Adherents | % | Adherents | % | Natural | Conversion | Total | Rate | Adherents | % | Adherents | % | Adherents | % |
| Christians | 176,000 | 1.1 | 24,728,000 | 44.9 | 827,069 | 257,331 | 1,084,400 | 3.65 | 12,700,000 | 47.2 | 35,572,000 | 49.0 | 69,081,100 | 51.2 |
| professing | 176,000 | 1.1 | 24,728,000 | 44.9 | 827,069 | 257,331 | 1,084,400 | 3.65 | 29,700,000 | 47.2 | 35,572,000 | 49.0 | 69,081,100 | 51.2 |
| Protestants | 70,000 | 0.4 | 7,710,000 | 14.0 | 256,921 | 75,529 | 332,450 | 3.60 | 9,226,000 | 14.7 | 11,034,50 | 15.2 | 21,129,400 | 15.7 |
| Roman Catholics | 35,000 | 0.2 | 6,060,000 | 11.0 | 204,253 | 69,917 | 274,170 | 3.74 | 7,334,700 | 11.7 | 8,801,700 | 12.1 | 17,135,300 | 12.7 |
| Anglicans | 64,000 | 0.4 | 5,695,000 | 10.3 | 182,239 | 10,521 | 192,760 | 2.95 | 6,544,200 | 10.4 | 7,622,600 | 10.5 | 14,167,000 | 10.5 |
| African indigenous | 7,000 | 0.0 | 4,950,000 | 9.0 | 173,478 | 101,042 | 274,520 | 4.41 | 6,229,600 | 9.9 | 7,695,200 | 10.6 | 15,246,400 | 11.3 |
| Marginal Protestants | 0 | 0.0 | 300,000 | 0.5 | 9,747 | 253 | 10,000 | 2.86 | 350,000 | 0.5 | 400,000 | 0.6 | 1,350,000 | 1.0 |
| Catholics (non-Roman) | 0 | 0.0 | 10,000 | 0.0 | 334 | 66 | 400 | 3.33 | 12,000 | 0.0 | 14,000 | 0.0 | 40,000 | 0.0 |
| Orthodox | 0 | 0.0 | 3,000 | 0.0 | 97 | 3 | 100 | 2.86 | 3,500 | 0.0 | 4,000 | 0.0 | 13,000 | 0.0 |
| nominal | 77,100 | 0.5 | 10,838,915 | 19.7 | 361,953 | 90,125 | 452,078 | 3.48 | 12,997,700 | 20.7 | 15,359,700 | 21.2 | 26,268,100 | 19.5 |
| affiliated | 98,900 | 0.6 | 13,889,085 | 25.2 | 465,116 | 167,206 | 632,322 | 3.79 | 16,702,300 | 26.5 | 20,212,300 | 27.8 | 42,813,000 | 31.7 |
| total practising | 89,010 | 90 | 11,111,270 | 80 | 372,093 | 133,764 | 505,857 | 3.79 | 13,361,840 | 80 | 16,169,840 | 80 | 29,969,100 | 70 |
| non-practising | 9,890 | 10 | 2,777,820 | 20 | 93,023 | 33,442 | 126,465 | 3.79 | 3,340,460 | 20 | 4,042,460 | 20 | 12,843,900 | 30 |
| Protestants | 40,000 | 0.2 | 4,124,001 | 7.5 | 138,433 | 51,717 | 190,150 | 3.83 | 4,971,100 | 7.9 | 6,025,500 | 8.3 | 13,357,500 | 9.9 |
| Evangelicals | 39,000 | 0.2 | 3,822,000 | 6.9 | 127,918 | 48,872 | 176,790 | 3.85 | 4,593,500 | 7.3 | 5,589,900 | 7.7 | 12,413,000 | 9.2 |
| Neo-pentecostals | 0 | 0.0 | 10,000 | 0.0 | 1,392 | 17,608 | 19,000 | 38.00 | 50,000 | 0.1 | 200,000 | 0.3 | 700,000 | 0.5 |
| Roman Catholics | 18,900 | 0.1 | 3,889,688 | 7.1 | 130,950 | 51,991 | 182,941 | 3.89 | 4,702,400 | 7.5 | 5,719,100 | 7.9 | 11,873,300 | 8.8 |
| Catholic pentecostals | 0 | 0.0 | 0 | 0.0 | 278 | 4,772 | 5,000 | 50.00 | 10,000 | 0.0 | 50,000 | 0.1 | 200,000 | 0.1 |
| Anglicans | 35,000 | 0.2 | 2,941,000 | 5.3 | 92,871 | –2,211 | 90,660 | 2.72 | 3,335,000 | 5.3 | 3,847,600 | 5.3 | 7,151,000 | 5.3 |
| Evangelicals | 34,000 | 0.2 | 2,100,000 | 3.8 | 68,340 | 12,040 | 80,380 | 3.28 | 2,454,100 | 3.9 | 2,903,800 | 4.0 | 5,666,800 | 4.2 |
| Anglican pentecostals | 0 | 0.0 | 2,000 | 0.0 | 557 | 6,243 | 6,800 | 34.00 | 20,000 | 0.0 | 70,000 | 0.1 | 300,000 | 0.2 |
| African indigenous | 5,000 | 0.0 | 2,743,371 | 5.0 | 96,377 | 64,866 | 161,243 | 4.66 | 3,460,900 | 5.5 | 4,355,800 | 6.0 | 9,444,700 | 7.0 |
| Marginal Protestants | 0 | 0.0 | 180,300 | 0.3 | 6,126 | 844 | 6,970 | 3.17 | 220,000 | 0.3 | 250,000 | 0.3 | 944,500 | 0.7 |
| Catholics (non-Roman) | 0 | 0.0 | 8,225 | 0.0 | 278 | 0 | 278 | 2.78 | 10,000 | 0.0 | 11,000 | 0.0 | 30,000 | 0.0 |
| Orthodox | 0 | 0.0 | 2,500 | 0.0 | 81 | –1 | 80 | 2.76 | 2,900 | 0.0 | 3,300 | 0.0 | 12,000 | 0.0 |
| Muslims | 4,200,000 | 25.9 | 24,232,000 | 44.0 | 779,784 | 63,816 | 843,600 | 3.01 | 28,002,000 | 44.5 | 32,668,000 | 45.0 | 61,195,200 | 45.4 |
| Ahmadis | 0 | 0.0 | 300,000 | 0.5 | 10,582 | 5,418 | 16,000 | 4.21 | 380,000 | 0.6 | 460,000 | 0.6 | 1,350,000 | 1.0 |
| Tribal religionists | 11,824,000 | 73.0 | 5,970,000 | 10.8 | 139,905 | –326,905 | –187,000 | –3.72 | 5,024,000 | 8.0 | 4,100,000 | 5.6 | 4,047,700 | 3.0 |
| Non-religious | 0 | 0.0 | 100,000 | 0.2 | 3,898 | 4,102 | 8,000 | 5.71 | 140,000 | 0.2 | 180,000 | 0.2 | 400,000 | 0.3 |
| Atheists | 0 | 0.0 | 20,000 | 0.0 | 752 | 748 | 1,500 | 5.56 | 27,000 | 0.0 | 35,000 | 0.0 | 100,000 | 0.1 |
| Baha'is | 0 | 0.0 | 11,400 | 0.0 | 446 | 514 | 960 | 6.00 | 16,000 | 0.0 | 21,000 | 0.0 | 50,000 | 0.0 |
| Buddhists | 0 | 0.0 | 500 | 0.0 | 16 | 0 | 16 | 2.81 | 570 | 0.0 | 660 | 0.0 | 1,000 | 0.0 |
| Other religionists | 0 | 0.0 | 11,100 | 0.0 | 430 | 394 | 824 | 5.34 | 15,430 | 0.0 | 19,340 | 0.0 | 49,000 | 0.0 |
| Country's population | 16,200,000 | 100.0 | 55,073,000 | 100.0 | 1,752,300 | 0 | 1,752,300 | 2.78 | 62,925,000 | 100.0 | 72,596,000 | 100.0 | 134,924,000 | 100.0 |

COLUMNS, ROWS. For meanings and definitions, see Codebook (Part 6). Note that, by definition, total 'Christians' = professing + crypto-Christians, which also = affiliated + nominal Christians. Percentages may not always total exactly, due to rounding.
CENSUSES. 1921: 56.8% tribal religionists, 39.0% Muslims, 1.6% Protestants, 1.0 Anglicans, 0.9% Roman Catholics, 0.8% African indigenous. 1921 (Northern Nigeria): 65.0% Muslims, 34.8% tribal religionists, 0.2% Christians. 1931: 50.0% tribal religionists, 43.6% Muslims, 2.4% Protestants, 1.4% Anglicans, 1.3% Roman Catholics, 1.2% African indigenous. 1931 (Northern Nigeria): 66.0% Muslims, 33.2% tribal religionists, 0.6% Christians (0.5% Protestants). VII.1952–VI.1953 (Africans only): 45.3% Muslims, 32.8% tribal religionists, 21.9% Christians. 1952 (by regions): Western: 36.9% Christians, 32.8% Muslims, 30.3% tribal religionists; Eastern: 49.2% Christians, 50.2% tribal religionists, 0.6% Muslims; Northern: 73.0% Muslims, 24.3% tribal religionists, 2.7% Christians. 5–8.XI.1963 (modified by UN to correct overenumeration): 43.4% Muslims, 37.9% Christians, 18.7% tribal religionists. By plotting the latter census' figure for Christians on a graph together with figures from all previous censuses, and by comparing the result with parallel graphs from other tropical African countries, it may be seen that Christianity is expanding in Nigeria in the 20th century in the manner shown in the table above with its future projections.
POLLS. Public-opinion polls of religious preference have been conducted only in cities and urban areas (Lagos, Enugu, et alia).

NOTES ON RELIGIONS
AFRICAN INDIGENOUS. In about 760 denominations in 1970 (see Table 2).
AHMADIS. The Ahmadiya Mission, begun in 1916, has its adherents mainly in the south among the Yoruba, with some of the 40 mosques also in eastern Nigeria. There are 10 schools. Many of the large number of adherents claimed are children and others influenced by the mission's institutions.
ANGLICAN PENTECOSTALS (or, Anglican charismatics). The movement has been especially strong among young people; in one diocese (Benin), such youth groups have been excommunicated, and in others have become separatist bodies. The strongest areas are: Mid-West, Eastern (strong among Ibo since 1971), Western (new para-denominations among the Yoruba, especially around Oyo).
ATHEISTS. Socialist Workers and Farmers Party (SWAFP) (banned since 1966): membership (1970) around 5,000. Many intellectuals also are atheists.
BAHA'IS. Growth from 15 local spiritual assemblies (1964) to 76 (1973).
BUDDHISTS. Chinese.
CATHOLIC PENTECOSTALS (or, Catholic charismatics). By 1975, the Catholic charismatic renewal was under way on a large scale, with Jos as a major centre.
MUSLIMS. Mainly Sunnis (of the Malikite rite), and mainly in the north among the Hausa, Fulani, Kanuri and Nupe; strongest brotherhoods are Qadiriya, Tijaniya and Ahmadiya (the latter enumerated here under Muslims though declared non-Muslim by Pakistan). There are also Lebanese and Syrian Arabs who are mainly Shias. Conversions to Islam. These have been continuing since 1880 among tribal religionists particularly in Northern Nigeria, and among the Yoruba and a few other southern peoples. The major period for conversions was 1890–1920, whole tribes becoming islamized. In 1964 the Sardauna of Sokoto conducted massive campaigns in Zaria and Niger provinces which converted over 100,000 pagan Maguzawa and other peoples to Islam

(187,216 from December 1963 to June 1965), the largest single-day figure being 7,400 on 8 May 1965. Missionaries. There are a large number of Egyptian missionaries sent by Al-Azhar University (Cairo). Hajj pilgrims to Mecca. (1968) 10,790; (1969) 24,185; (1970) 35,187; (1971) 44,061; (1972) 48,981; (1973) 38,869; (1974) 51,764; (1975) 92,593; (1976) 66,873; (1977) 140,000.
NEO-PENTECOSTALS. Charismatics in the non-Pentecostal Protestant denominations, notably the Tiv Church (NKST), and among university and student groups (SU, NIFES).
NOMINAL CHRISTIANS. These are persons professing in censuses to be Christians, but not affiliated to or known by the churches. In Nigeria they are of 2 kinds: (1) past and present pupils in the vast network of Protestant, Anglican and Roman Catholic schools who have nevertheless not joined those churches, and (2) tribal religionists who have made a clear break with pagan society and regard themselves as Christians but who have not as yet been contacted or initiated by the churches. After 1980 the percentage size of this large nominal fringe around the churches can be seen to decrease as the churches catch up with the vast influx.
OTHER RELIGIONISTS. Including religions of expatriates. Occultist and similar non-Christian religions from Europe and Asia have growing followings. Rosicrucians (AMORC) have 29 Lodges and centres.
TRIBAL RELIGIONISTS. Strongest in the central plateau. Peoples over 90% traditionalist (animist) in 1972: Afo (99%), Ankwe (99%), Bunu (90%), Chawai (90%), Daka (90%), Dibo (90%), Gade (90%), Ibaji (90%), Jaba (90%), Jerawa (90%), Jukun (90%), Kadara (90%), Kamantan (90%), Kamuku (90%), Lungu (90%), Maguzawa (Hausa) (90%), Mumuye (99%), Ngamo (95%), Shanga (90%), Vere (93%), Warjawa (90%).

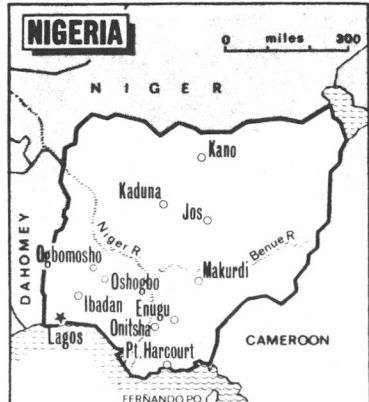

NON-CHRISTIAN RELIGIONS. Islam is numerically parallel to Christianity in Nigeria. Muslims are dominant in the northern states, and they are also important in Western Nigeria. The Hausa, Fulani, Kanuri, Nupe and a significant number of Yoruba provide most of the country's Muslim strength.

Islamic influence was first felt in the 11th and 12th centuries, and by the 15th century Kano had become a flourishing centre for Muslim culture and commerce. A new thrust came in the 19th century when a Fulani crusade swept over the Hausa area leaving permanent marks on the culture and social system. Following a period of disintegration, the British policy of indirect rule through existing Muslim chiefs succeeded in strengthening Islam as well as hindering the entrance of Christian missions. The Qadiriya, Tijaniya and Ahmadiya are the strongest brotherhoods today. The spiritual head of Islam in Nigeria is the Sardauna of Sokoto. In 1962 a faculty of arts and Islamic studies was established at the Amadu Bello University in Zaria and in the same year the Abdullahi Bayero College, founded in Kano in 1960, was attached to the Amadu Bello University as its Kano-based Faculty of Arts and Islamic Studies.

Traditional religions have their main strength in the central plateau. The following peoples are estimated to be more than 90% traditionalist: Afo, Ankwe, Bunu, Chawai, Daka, Dibo, Gade, Ibaji, Jaba, Jerawa, Jukun, Kadara, Kamantan, Kamuku, Lungu, Maguzawa, Mumuye, Ngamo, Shanga, Vere, and Warjawa. As in other parts of Africa, Nigerian traditional religions place considerable emphasis on the importance of ancestral spirits and magical practices, while retaining the idea of a supreme being. God is called Olodumare (among the Yoruba), Chuku (Ibo), Soko (Nupe, Gbari), Abassi (Ibibio), Kashiri (Binawa, Butawa, Dungi, Kaibi, Kitimi, Rishuwa, Rumaiya, Srubu), Gwaza (Kagoro, Katab), Owo (Idoma, Iyala), with other names common among Nigeria's many smaller tribes. A distinctive element is the emphasis placed on divinities, who serve as God's ministers in the theocratic rule of the world. Among the Yoruba there are more than a thousand such divinities each with his own name and function and collectively called orisa.

### CHRISTIANITY
PROTESTANT CHURCHES. British Wesleyan Methodists first came to Yoruba country in 1842, beginning work at Badagry and Abeokuta; and towards the end of the century (1893) Primitive Methodists entered Calabar from Fernando Poo. Today the membership of the autonomous Methodist Church is about equally divided among the Yoruba, Ibibio, Ijebu and Ibo. In 1970 there were 522 Methodist primary schools, 18 secondary schools, 18 teacher training colleges and 13 medical institutions. In January 1976 Methodists completely reorganized

their church in an effort to make it more indigenous. The denomination's leadership now includes 6 bishops and 4 archbishops, with a patriarch as overall head of the church.

The first Presbyterian missionaries were Jamaicans who settled in Calabar, eastern Nigeria, in 1846. They were soon followed by Scottish members of the CSM and more recently (1954) Canadian Presbyterians. The Presbyterian Church of Nigeria has been autonomous since 1954.

Southern Baptists came to Western Nigeria in 1850, and this remains their oldest field anywhere in the world. Although progress was slow in the early years, this has now become one of the most important of Nigeria's churches. The Yoruba Baptist Association was formed in 1914 which later changed its name to the Nigerian Baptist Convention.

In 1887 the interdenominational Qua Iboe Mission of Belfast opened a station at Ibuno on the Qua Iboe river; and in spite of later evangelistic thrusts among the Igala in 1931 and the Bassa in 1936, the strength of the church is still found among the Ibibio. In 1964 the church was responsible for 175 primary schools, 4 secondary schools, 4 teacher training colleges, 2 general hospitals, one maternity hospital, 2 leprosaria and a nurses' training programme.

The Evangelical Churches of West Africa (ECWA),

autonomous since 1956, stem from the outreach of the Sudan Interior Mission as early as 1893. One of the largest denominations in Nigeria, this church both receives and sends missionaries. SIM maintains nearly 400 workers in Nigeria, while ECWA has sent more than 100 Africans to other parts of Africa. The church has had considerable success in northern Nigeria.

Another even larger body is the Fellowship of Churches of Christ in Nigeria (TEKAN) which was formed in 1955 as TEKAS, a loose federation of 8 separate groups, 4 of which were begun by the Sudan United Mission beginning in 1904. Others owe their origin to the missionary activity of the Church of the Brethren, Dutch Reformed Church of South Africa, EUB (now United Methodists) in the USA, and independent Nigerians. Although formal church membership remains relatively low because of high requirements, church attendance is extremely high, exceeding one million each Sunday in 1972.

Two important Pentecostal churches entered Nigeria during the 1930s, the Apostolic Church from UK in 1931 and Assemblies of God from the USA in 1939. Of groups coming after World War II, the greatest progress has been made by the Churches of Christ. A number of smaller but still significant churches include Seventh-day Adventists, Lutherans

**African indigenous Christians.** Totalling 7.7 million by 1980, with 4.4 million church members in about 840 denominations, these largely charismatic believers may be seen everywhere. *Above.* Group of 40 persons pray on Lagos beach (with bottles of holy water to right). At Easter, the beach is packed with such groups. *Below.* A large charismatic church engages in simultaneous audible prayer: The Blood of Jesus Christ Apostolic Church International, Oke-Anu, Ibadan. *Right.* Christ Apostolic Church's Cathedral in Ibadan. This vast indigenous denomination has over 400,000 members.

and the Salvation Army.

CATHOLIC CHURCH. Catholicism first came to Nigeria with the Portuguese in the 15th century, but it had virtually disappeared by the end of the 17th century. The modern era of Catholic missions began in 1865 with the arrival in Lagos of priests belonging to the Society of African Missions of Lyons. Other important groups have been Holy Ghost priests in eastern Nigeria and St Patrick's Society after 1932. A vicariate was erected for Benin in 1870, and in 1950 the archdioceses of Kaduna, Lagos and Onitsha were established. The Catholic Church in Nigeria consisted in 1973 of 25 ecclesiastical divisions.

Intertribal rivalries and the resulting 1967-70 civil war had a serious effect on Catholicism. The mass killings of southerners (mostly Christian Ibos) in the North where they had settled sparked a mass migration homeward which left many northern areas with no Christian community; while in other areas non-Ibo Christians also disappeared. Estimates of the total massacred range from 10,000 to 30,000 and the migration affected around one million people. The diocese of Sokoto in northwestern Nigeria, which had 15,000 Ibo Catholics in 1965, had only 1,650 left in 1970. Nearly two-thirds of the country's Catholics in 1967 were found in 8 dioceses located in eastern Nigeria, which caused a widespread impression that the war was a religious one of Muslims versus Christians. However, the religious aspect of Nigerian inter-cultural rivalries was in fact not important. The subsequent defeat and collapse of the east resulted in a serious interruption in the social and economic development of what was formerly the most dynamic and most Christian part of the country.

At the end of the civil war in January 1970, the church in eastern Nigeria experienced important changes including the expulsion of most foreign missionaries (about 300 priests and 200 sisters) and the nationalization of all primary and secondary schools which had previously played a significant role in evangelization. Nigerian church personnel were relatively numerous, with some 760 priests, brothers and sisters in 1970. Nevertheless, they were inadequate for the task since many priests were responsible for a pastoral charge of more than 5,000 faithful. Nevertheless, vocations continue to be very promising, there being 546 secular major seminarians and 350 novices and postulants in local congregations of sisters in 1973; and among the faithful, especially youth, has emerged the spontaneous Black Rosary Movement which has expanded with great rapidity. This movement gathers people together by house blocks for prayer, singing, Bible study and religious instruction. The movement has been officially recognized by the hierarchy and integrated into parish and diocesan structures.

From 1967 to 1973 the number of Nigerian bishops grew from 8 to 17 and local priests from 108 to 306 which represent one of the most rapid increases of any country in Africa or Asia. Nevertheless, the lack of religious personnel is evident due both to the expulsion of missionaries from eastern Nigeria and the government policy of restricting the entry of foreign priests as much as possible. In March 1974, the Catholic Episcopal Conference meeting in full assembly affirmed that no foreign priest had received authorization to enter Nigeria (not only ex-Biafra) since the civil war. On the same occasion the bishops requested the government to assume a more sympathetic attitude.

In 1972, 3 Nigerian sisters left for Sierra Leone to serve as missionaries with the local church, and in 1975 2 priests were also sent to Sierra Leone.

ANGLICAN CHURCH. The first Anglicans in Nigeria were freed slaves from Sierra Leone, and in 1842 the CMS followed. By 1853 work had begun at Abeokuta, Lagos and Ibadan. In 1864 the first African bishop was consecrated, although he was replaced by a European in 1891. The Church of the Province of West Africa, formed in 1952, now consists of dioceses in Ghana, Gambia and Sierra Leone, as well as 11 dioceses within Nigeria itself. Anglican communicant membership exceeds that of every Nigerian denomination except the Catholic Church. The exceptionally large numbers of adult and infant baptisms are proof of the continued vitality and growth of the Anglican Church in Nigeria.

INDIGENOUS CHURCHES. The first in a long line of independent groups in Nigeria was the Native Baptist Church, splitting from Southern Baptist work among the Yoruba in 1888; however, by 1914 almost the entire body of seceders had been reintegrated into the Nigerian Baptist Convention.

**Church of Nigeria, Diocese of Northern Nigeria.** *Above.* Anglican workers conduct evangelism among Nupe and other pagans around Bida. **Methodist Church, Nigeria.** *Right.* In a 1976 major reorganization to make their church more indigenous, Methodists appointed 6 bishops (5 shown standing here), 4 archbishops (seated), and a patriarch, His Pre-Eminence Bolaji Idowu (centre), complete with vestments.

The first permanent schism was the United Native African Church, a break precipitated by the consecration of a European to replace the first African Anglican bishop in 1891. Other important Anglican schisms include the African Church and Christ Army Church, begun respectively in 1901 and 1915. A conflict among Yoruba Methodists in 1917 resulted in the creation of the United African Methodist Church, commonly called Eledja (Fishmongers). A number of important independent churches owe their origin indirectly to a virulent influenza epidemic which ravaged West Africa in 1918. Believing the mission churches to be impotent in the face of this disaster, Yoruba Christians formed prayer and healing groups which ultimately resulted in the formation of the Cherubim and Seraphim, Church of the Lord (Aladura, or Praying) and Christ Apostolic Church, in addition to a series of other bodies which subsequently split from them. The Cherubim and Seraphim movement itself has spawned some 200 distinct denominations including several of Nigeria's largest churches: the Eternal Sacred Order of Cherubim and Seraphim, Cherubim and Seraphim Church of Zion of Nigeria, and the Holy Order of Cherubim and Seraphim. A large pentecostal prayer-healing church in the eastern sector is the Nigerian Christian Fellowship. Several Black denominations from the USA have also been influential, including the AME and AME Zion Churches.

Nigeria has been fertile soil for the growth of independency. The number of distinct denominations or bodies, in most cases registered with government, was around 760 in 1970, and has increased steadily each year.

**CHURCH AND STATE.** The federal constitution of 1 October 1963 (chapter III, 'Fundamental Rights', Section 24) provides for freedom of religious belief and practice, including the freedom to observe, teach and propagate one's beliefs and also to change one's religion. Religious communities are free to provide religious instruction in educational institutions which they maintain, but no pupil may be required to attend religious ceremonies or receive religious instruction contrary to his wishes. Historically, Christian bodies have provided a major part of Nigeria's basic educational and medical facilities, and the federal, regional and state governments have assumed financial responsibility for a great deal of maintenance and assistance to church-sponsored schools and hospitals. However, this has now been changing as the government has increasingly assumed control over Christian schools.

The government attitude towards church schools varies from state to state. The first to take over all schools was the East Central State (formerly Biafra) on 26 May 1970. By May 1975 all private schools in the following states were in government hands: Mid-Western State, South Eastern State, Rivers State, North Western State and North Central State. In Lagos and in Western and Kwara States, the governments have not in principle taken over schools, but in practice the state school boards appoint

teachers and transfer them indiscriminately. In Kano State and Benue Plateau State, private schools had not yet been nationalized by 1976. However the Federal Government planned to introduce universal free primary education in September 1976, and it was expected that by that date all schools would have passed under government control. Religion is taught in all schools, but the content and time allowed for it vary. Thus in East Central State, one free period a week is made available during which teachers may give religious instruction to willing pupils of their own denomination; in Mid-Western State, 5 periods of religious instruction per week are available also on a denominational basis; and in South Eastern State the Joint Agreed Christian Syllabus of Religious Education is taught for 2 periods a week.

In the largely theocratic northern area where the powers of Muslim emirs remain as strong as under former British colonial policy, non-Islamic religious movements have been limited. Nevertheless, Muslim Nigeria represents a wide spectrum, and numerous Muslim leaders co-operate in the matter of Christian religious education and even over the evangelization of peoples still largely tradtionalist.

Religious bodies must be officially recognized by government in order to acquire property and clergy must be authorized to officiate at legally-registered marriages. Religious groups are exempt from some taxes and a number of other regulations. Until recently the policy of permitting the entrance of foreign missionaries was quite liberal. However, during and following the Biafra war, with its emotional overtones and the search for culprits, the government frequently expressed strong criticism of the churches, notably the Catholic Church. Church relief work on behalf of the Biafran people and the involvement of many locally-based missionaries in propaganda work for them, was especially resented; and one result has been the restriction of visas for further missionaries. Many Catholic expatriate priests in Ibo country indeed were deported after the conflict. Nevertheless, even with the indignation of federal authorities, church-state tensions have been far less serious than might have been expected.

In 1977, with wide support from the churches, the regime introduced a federal government ban on membership in secret societies including Freemasonry for all publicly-employed persons.

**INTERDENOMINATIONAL ORGANIZATIONS.** The Christian Council of Nigeria (CCN), founded in 1930, has 9 member bodies, including the large Anglican, Methodist, Baptist, Presbyterian and Qua Iboe churches. Methodists, Anglicans and Presbyterians are also members of the WCC, and several of Nigeria's churches belong to the AACC. The Nigerian Evangelical Fellowship has 10 member churches and belongs to AEAM, the Association of Evangelicals of Africa and Madagascar. The Catholic Episcopal Conference has no ecumenical commission. Responsibility for ecumenical relations is lodged with the Pastoral Commission, which handles also the lay apostolate, religious education and liturgy.

In 1976 a new ecumenical body was formed, the Christian Association of Nigeria (CAN), with a secretary general the secretary of the CCN, and as members Roman Catholic, Protestant, Anglican and indigenous churches.

Another powerful council of churches is the Nigeria Association of Aladura Churches, founded in 1960, with as members over 95 indigenous denominations and a total constituency of 1.2 million Christians. There are over 10 other similar councils linking indigenous churches.

Three ecumenical institutes have been established: (1) the Institute of Church and Society, founded in 1964 by the Christian Council of Nigeria, which engages in study and dialogue on the church and the world; (2) the Pastoral Institute in Bodija, which is basically Catholic but works in close relationship with the Institute for Church and Society; and (3) the National Institute for Religious Sciences founded in Lagos in 1971, which is involved in the training of secondary school teachers of religion. The latter institution is sponsored and maintained jointly by the Catholic Episcopal Conference and the Christian Council of Nigeria, with help from the WCC.

Four interdenominational associations have been formed to promote medical work and Christian education: (1) Christian Health Association of Nigeria, to review the Christian commitment in health services; (2) Christian Education Review Council (CERC), to discuss with government whenever necessary the church's involvement in education; (3) Association for Christian Higher Education (ACHEN), to influence policy and promote standards of religious education in post-secondary educational institutions; and (4) National Institute of Moral and Religious education, founded in 1971 in the vicinity of the University of Lagos. The latter institution is sponsored and supported jointly by the Catholic Episcopal Conference and the Christian Council of Nigeria and is formally affiliated to the Institute of Education of the University of Ibadan. It promotes a programme called Project TIME (Teachers in Moral Education) held each year, in addition to a research and experimentation centre, a specialist library and a model audio-visual centre. In December 1974 leaders of both the Catholic and Protestant churches held a Retreat of National Concern centred on the moral decadence of Nigeria, at which time they agreed to set up a Moral Leadership Foundation to inspire Christian and moral ideals among the nation's leaders.

Several organizations are dedicated to the promotion of inter-religious contacts and dialogue. The Islam in Africa Project Council began in 1959 and is a joint undertaking of several church groups to prepare Christians for their encounter with and responsibility towards Muslims in Africa south of the Sahara. It has personnel working in Sierra Leone, Liberia, Ghana, Nigeria, Cameroon, Ethiopia and Kenya and is active in other territories including Upper Volta and Malawi. Part of the project is the Study Centre for Islam and Christianity (formerly the Pierre Benignus Study Centre) founded in 1965

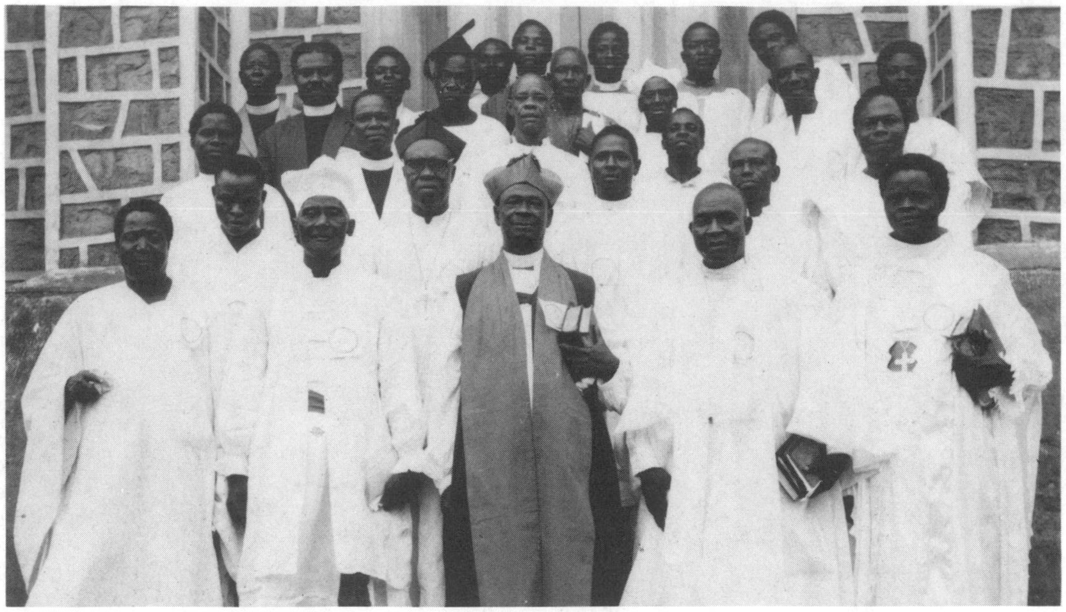

**National Association of Aladura Churches.** Heads of association of 95 Aladura churches, with membership of 2 million, at St Michael's Pro-Cathedral Church of the Cherubim & Seraphim, at Oke Seni headquarters, Ibadan.

in Ibadan. Here Christian students from many parts of Africa study the Quran, Islam and the Christian approach to Muslims. Another body, the Community Development Group (CDG), formerly the Christian Community Development Group, is a private interdenominational body which includes Catholic participation. Open to people of all religions, it functions as a mutual-help society for those involved in community development and social work.

**BROADCASTING.** The Nigerian Broadcasting Corporation has a religious broadcasting department, with 5 hours produced each week by the major churches. Little televising is done. There is more religious broadcasting in local languages in the states than in English, but most of the programmes on the National Network are in English. Extra time for religious broadcasts is provided during lent, at Easter and Christmas, and on Nigeria's National Day. Protestant programmes from abroad can be heard over ELWA (Liberia) which has recording studios at Jos and Igbaja. In addition until 1977, RVOG broadcast to Nigeria in Fulani as well as English. Catholic centres in Kaduna and Lagos produce radio programmes. The Catholic Secretariat in Lagos has a section for radio and TV. For Catholics, UNDA is represented by a national association.

## BIBLIOGRAPHY


*African independent church.* H.W. Turner. 2 vols. I: The Church of the Lord (Aladura), 217p. II: The life and faith of the Church of the Lord (Aladura), 391p. Oxford: Clarendon, 1967.

'African traditional religion in transition'. D.S. Gilliland. Dissertation, Hartford Seminary Foundation (USA), 1971. (On Northern Nigeria).

*Aladura: a religious movement among the Yoruba.* J.D.Y. Peel. London: Oxford University Press, 1968.

*Christianity in Northern Nigeria.* E.P.T. Crampton. c1975. 212p.

*Church growth in central and southern Nigeria.* J.B. Grimley & G.E. Robinson. Grand Rapids, (MI): Eerdmans, 1966. 386p.

*Frontier peoples of central Nigeria and a strategy for outreach.* G.O. Swank. South Pasadena (CA): William Carey Library, 1977. 192p.

'Growth of Churches of Christ among Ibibios of Nigeria'. W.W. Broom. Thesis, Fuller Theological Seminary, Pasadena (CA), 1970. 268p.

*Nupe religion.* S.F. Nadel. Glencoe, IL: Free Press, 1954. 288p.

*Official Nigeria Catholic directory, 1973.* Lagos: Catholic Secretariat of Nigeria, 1973. 163p.

*Sons of Tiv: a study of the rise of the church among the Tiv of central Nigeria.* E. Rubingh. Grand Rapids (MI): Baker, 1969. 263p.

*Tekas Fellowship of Churches: its origin and growth.* E.H. Smith. Jos: Tekas Literature Committee, 1969. 68p. (Now renamed TEKAN).

*The African churches among the Yoruba, 1888–1922.* J.B. Webster. Oxford: Clarendon, 1964. 217p.

'The Celestial Church of Christ: an African independent church'. R. Duckworth. Thesis, London School of Economics, 1978.

'The Christ Apostolic Church: its history, beliefs and organization', *Ecumenical review*, XXVIII, 4 (October, 1976), 418–428.

*The missionary impact on modern Nigeria, 1842–1914: a political and social analysis.* E.A. Ayandele. London: Longmans, Green, 1966. 393p.

*The proposed constitutions and standing orders: Methodist Church, Nigeria.* Lagos: Methodist Church, 1974. 115p. (Introducing patriarchal and archiepiscopal hierarchies).

*Year book of Nigerian churches.* Ed A.A. Akinkusote. Ibadan: Akinniola Associates, 1969. 169p.


TABLE 2. ORGANIZED CHURCHES AND DENOMINATIONS IN NIGERIA

| Official name 1 | Begun 2 | Type 3 | Counc 4 | Congs 5 | Adults 6 | Affiliated 7 | Names, notes, and other statistics (see Codebook) 8 |
|---|---|---|---|---|---|---|---|
| Acts of Apostles Christ Ch, Nigeria | 1961 | I pen | ••••• | 4 | 450 | 1,000 | Indigenous pentecostals. Vision 1957 by founder, ex RCC. HQ Mushin, Lagos. 1p. |
| African Apostolic Ch of Nigeria & Benin | 1942 | I peA | •v••I | 219 | 5,000 | 10,000 | *AAC*. Schism ex CAC by illiterate protesting discrimination. 55% Yoruba, 40% Ibo. |
| African Church, The | 1901 | I Ang | •vA•K | 841 | 25,000 | 48,709 | Schism ex CMS Lagos. 7 Dioceses (4 Yoruba). Applied to join WCC. 91n,1215m,37r,1s. |
| African Methodist Episcopal Church | c1920 | I Met | Vw••• | | 3,000 | 5,000 | M=AMEC(Black mission from USA). Attached to small local indigenous churches. |
| African Methodist Episcopal Zion Ch | 1930 | I Met | Vw••• | 120 | 6,177 | 15,000 | M=AMEZC, 12th Episcopal District. 100 Ibo churches in east 2 in Lagos. 2 schools. |
| American Orthodox Cath Ch in Nigeria | c1970 | O ReO | x•••• | 10 | 200 | 500 | M=AOCC(AD N&SAmerica), Egl Vielle-Cath (Branche Française). Ukrainian origin. |
| **Anglican Church in Nigeria:** | 1842 | A Low | AWAVK | 3,677 | 355,969 | 2,941,000 | In CPWA until Province formed. M=CMS(UK). 68f,1p,1s,1u. 631n,25x,30531Y,76531y. |
| D Aba | 1972 | A Low | A | 217 | 65,000 | 300,000 | 95% Ibo. 1972, widespread charismatic youth movement. 1u. 21 0 2000 8000 |
| D Benin (1977 3 dioceses) | 1961 | A Low | A | 537 | 17,927 | 450,000 | Mid-West. 25% Isoko, 20% Urhobo, 15% Ibo, 13% Bini. 8976z. 50 1 16151 14458 |
| D Ekiti | 1966 | A Low | A | 250 | 15,000 | 100,000 | Cocoa. 1974, potential splits by charismatic youths. 42 0 1000 3000 |
| D Enugu | 1970 | A Eva | A | 101 | 10,659 | 132,000 | Rural, coal, cement. 99% Ibo. W=67%,1295z. Charismatics. 16 0 720 4556 |
| D Ibadan (1974 3 dioceses) | 1952 | A Low | A | 435 | 20,000 | 300,000 | 99% Yoruba. Increasing use of African music. 1s,2446z. 140 10 1629 9484 |
| D Lagos (1976 3 dioceses) | 1919 | A Eva | A | 596 | 63,684 | 600,000 | Capital city. M=CMS. 96% Yoruba, 4% Ibo. W=59%,2333z. 101 3 1130 5085 |
| D Niger Delta | 1952 | A Low | A | 354 | 35,000 | 200,000 | HQ Bonny. Mangrove swamps. Ijaw, Ogoni, Ikwerre. 19 1 1000 7000 |
| D Northern Nigeria | 1953 | A Low | A | 70 | 20,000 | 100,000 | Vast area, 264 000 sq mi, 73% Muslim. 1H,4r. 23 7 1000 3000 |
| D Ondo | 1952 | A Low | A | 526 | 13,944 | 260,000 | 94% Yoruba, 3% Igbira. 250 schools. 16r,W=63%,4554z. 80 2 2329 5559 |
| D Owerri | 1959 | A Eva | A | 373 | 59,838 | 228,000 | 99% Ibo. 8% all Nigeria Anglicans. G=10%,W=55%,3103z. 66 1 1059 8061 |
| D The Niger (Diocese on the Niger) | 1864 | A Eva | A | 218 | 34,917 | 271,000 | 99% Ibo. 1967–70, 35% losses in civil war. 2H,27r,W=80%. 73 0 2513 8328 |
| Apostolic Church of Light | 1957 | I peA | ••••• | 6 | 850 | 1,500 | Schism ex African Apostolic Church by superintendent bishop Aboge. HQ Mushin. |
| Apostolic Church of Nigeria | 1931 | P PeA | ZG••• | 2,048 | 151,706 | 400,000 | M=ACMM(UK). 1931, invited to assist Aladura churches. Southeast. 6 Areas. 5f,3s. |
| Apostolic Life Mission Church | 1942 | I pen | ••••I | 10 | 5,000 | 10,000 | Founded by group of government officials who became evangelists. Yoruba. Ibadan. |
| Assemblies of God | 1939 | P Pe2 | ZFG•G | 867 | 61,234 | 150,000 | M=AoG(USA). A=1960. 48% Ibo, 8% Ishan. 667n,31x,3h,1j,5s(296),W=50%,2593Y. |
| Benin United Baptist Mission of N | 1942 | I Bap | ••••• | 2 | 1,000 | 2,000 | Schism ex Nigerian Baptist Convention opposing missionary decisions. Declining. |
| Bible Holiness Movement | 1952 | P Hol | x•••• | 37 | 5,000 | 10,000 | M=BHM(Canada). 1972 after civil war, merger. HQ Ikot. Ibo, Yoruba. 12n,W=95%. |
| Calvary Church of God in Christ | c1965 | I pe3 | Z•••• | 10 | 800 | 1,500 | M=CCoGiC(Jamaicans HQ London UK). Jamaican and CoGiC (USA Blacks) support. |
| Cameroon Baptist Convention | 1961 | P Bap | TF••• | 105 | 4,000 | 8,000 | *Mambila Baptist Conv.* M=CBC(Cameroon),NABGMS(USA). Station at Wuwar. 12f,1H,1h,1s. |
| **Catholic Church in Nigeria:** | 1487 | R Lat | PzSGV | 577 | 2,139,300 | 3,889,688 | C=11+4+23. 5p,4s(546). 313n,546x,147m,616w,P=40%,245884Yy. |
| M Kaduna | 1911 | R Lat | Psma | 22 | 52,200 | 95,000 | 55% Katab, 10% Koro, 5% Kadara, 5% Gbari. 3 35 2 41 73 6000 |
| D Ilorin | 1960 | R Lat | Psma | 10 | 8,800 | 16,000 | Predominantly Muslim, as throughout north. 0 18 1 6 38 1211 |
| D Jos | 1934 | R Lat | Psma | 18 | 66,000 | 120,000 | 20% Birom, 13% Angas, 13% Ankwe, 10% Kagoro. 11 50 0 26 32 8031 |
| D Lokoja | 1955 | R Lat | Pcssp | 9 | 12,200 | 22,147 | 87% pagan. 40% Igala, 30% Yoruba, 29% Igbira. 6 13 1 7 70 1093 |
| D Maiduguri | 1953 | R Lat | Posa | 18 | 15,200 | 27,696 | 70% Muslim, 22% pagan. 65% Margi, 15% Higi. 0 22 5 4 48 1695 |
| D Makurdi | 1934 | R Lat | Pcssp | 25 | 61,200 | 111,273 | Tiv centre. RCs all Tiv; many animists. 8 53 5 23 51 10714 |
| D Sokoto | 1953 | R Lat | Pop | 6 | 3,000 | 5,400 | 15,000 Ibo Catholics before 1966 massacres. 0 10 3 9 43 280 |
| D Yola | 1950 | R Lat | Posa | 24 | 20,700 | 37,733 | 30% Chamba, 20% Higi, 20% Mumuye, Bachama. 0 21 1 12 48 3024 |
| M Lagos | 1860 | R Lat | Ps | 24 | 77,600 | 141,000 | Mainly urban. 87% Yoruba, 6% Ibo. 1p. 11 39 6 51 35 6194 |
| D Benin City | 1884 | R Lat | Psma | 23 | 98,500 | 179,000 | 34% Ibo, 25% Ishan, 25% Afemai, 15% Bini. 28 38 3 39 55 11811 |
| D Ibadan | 1952 | R Lat | Psma | 15 | 31,200 | 56,700 | Vast ancient Black city. 80% Yoruba. 1p,1s. 3 40 3 34 42 2010 |
| D Ijebu-Ode | 1969 | R Lat | Ps | 7 | 6,300 | 11,450 | Yoruba, Ijebu, Strongly Muslim area. 2 10 0 9 35 564 |
| D Ondo | 1943 | R Lat | Psma | 19 | 48,400 | 88,000 | 99% Yoruba, 1% Urhobo, Ijaw. Many AICs. 10 32 11 36 39 8161 |
| D Oyo | 1949 | R Lat | Pwf | 13 | 27,700 | 50,424 | 88% Yoruba, 7% Ishan, 5% Ibo. 11 21 5 25 30 1657 |
| D Warri | 1964 | R Lat | Ps | 20 | 63,800 | 116,000 | HQ new oil production industry. Ijaw, Urhobo. 15 13 0 11 34 2500 |
| M Onitsha | 1889 | R Lat | Ps | 66 | 283,700 | 515,783 | On Niger. 90% Ibo, 10% Ijaw. 59 0 12 50 42 33147 |
| D Calabar | 1934 | R Lat | Ps | 28 | 131,700 | 239,480 | Port. 50% Ibibio, 40% Efik, 10% Ibo. 11 22 0 30 48 14700 |
| D Enugu | 1962 | R Lat | Pcssp | 34 | 251,900 | 458,000 | Former civil HQ; dying coal industry. 1s. 30 4 23 25 30 28899 |
| D Ikot Ekpene | 1963 | R Lat | Ps | 24 | 34,500 | 62,780 | Devastated in civil war. 95% Annang Ibibio.1s. 10 9 0 12 59 6319 |
| D Ogoja | 1938 | R Lat | Psps | 48 | 50,300 | 91,510 | 85% animist. 48% Ibo, 17% Boki, 7% Iyala. 1p. 6 44 0 57 43 17680 |
| D Owerri | 1934 | R Lat | Ps | 50 | 474,000 | 861,798 | Dense Ibo heartland. 22% of all Nigerian RCs. 51 0 28 40 30 55589 |
| D Port Harcourt | 1961 | R Lat | Ps | 16 | 33,800 | 61,497 | Major sea/river port. Former Ibo dominance. 1 5 0 1 47 2050 |
| D Umuahia | 1958 | R Lat | Pcssp | 30 | 263,000 | 478,201 | 99% Ibo. No foreign priests in former Biafra. 35 0 29 45 44 21138 |
| PA Idah (D from 1978) | 1968 | R Lat | Pcssp | 19 | 20,100 | 36,466 | Mostly Igala; area still 87% pagan.1H,1p,4r. 2 20 5 14 67 1078 |
| PA Minna (D Minna from 1973) | 1964 | R Lat | Psps | 9 | 3,500 | 6,350 | Sparsely settled. 75% animist, 20% Muslim. 0 27 4 9 47 339 |
| Celestial Church of Christ | 1952 | I peA | x•I•F | 150 | 20,000 | 35,000 | Begun Dahomey 1947. Yoruba elites. Healings, incense. Very rapid growth from 1973. |
| Chad Brothers | c1900 | I CBr | ••••• | 10 | 200 | 1,000 | *Gidan Bishara* (*House of the Gospel*). Hausa Chad group antedating White missions. |
| Charismatic youth movements | 1975 | I pen | ••••• | | 5,000 | 10,000 | Begun 1971 among Isoko, Ibo. M=SU(UK). 1974, excommunications ex Anglican Church. |
| Cherubim & Seraphim Ch of Zion of N | 1948 | I peA | x•I•I | 240 | 55,214 | 100,000 | Begun by colleague of Orimolade. 62% West, 23% Mid-West, 13% Lagos, 2% East. 1s. |
| Christ Apostolic Church | 1917 | I peA | x•I•Z | 1,575 | 179,029 | 400,000 | *CAC*(1942). 1920 Faith Tabernacle. 39 Districts. 74% Yoruba. 281n,1224m,28r,2s,12630Y. |
| Christ Apostolic Mission Church | 1952 | I peA | ••••• | 11 | 4,830 | 8,000 | Indigenous pentecostal apostolics. Schism ex CAC and AAC. Yoruba. HQ Mushin. 1s. |
| Christ Apostolic Universal Church | 1962 | I peA | ••••• | 8 | 5,000 | 10,000 | Indigenous pentecostal apostolics. Schism ex CAC by pastor. Yoruba. HQ Mushin. 1s. |
| Christ Army Church | 1915 | I Ang | •T•T• | 40 | 9,800 | 45,760 | Ex CMS founded by Garrick Braide. Annang Ibibio. Many schisms. 12n,6m,W=85%,620Y. |
| Christ Church of the Lord | 1941 | I pen | ••••I | 12 | 1,000 | 2,000 | Schism in Ilesha ex Anglican Ch and CL (Aladura). Yoruba. HQ Yaba. |
| Christ Gospel Apostolic Ch of Nigeria | 1947 | I peA | ••••I | 47 | 10,400 | 20,000 | *CGAC*. Schism ex Christ Apostolic Ch. Yoruba. HQ Ibadan. Work across Nigeria. |
| Christian Brethren | c1925 | P CBr | x•••• | 200 | 10,000 | 20,000 | Plymouth (Open) Brethren. Gospel Halls. M=CMML(USA,UK). 30f. |

*Continued opposite*

*Table 2 – continued*

| Official name 1 | Begun 2 | Type 3 | Counc 4 | Congs 5 | Adults 6 | Affiliated 7 | Names, notes, and other statistics (see Codebook) 8 |
|---|---|---|---|---|---|---|---|
| Christian Churches & Chs of Christ | 1955 | P Dis | x.... | 100 | 3,000 | 5,000 | M=CCCC(Instrumental)(USA). Independent congregations. 4f. |
| Christian Methodist Episcopal Church | | I Met | Vw... | 5 | 200 | 500 | M=CMEC(Black mission from USA); until 1956, Colored ME Ch. 4 churches in Abak. |
| Church of Christ, Scientist | | M Sci | x.... | 2 | 100 | 200 | *Christian Science*. M=CCS(Boston,USA). 2 Societies. |
| Church of God in Christ (Mennonite) | 1963 | P Men | G.... | 16 | 4,850 | 8,000 | M=Ch of God in Christ, Mennonite(USA). HQ Ile Ife. 6f. |
| Church of God in Nigeria | 1949 | P Pe3 | ZFG.G | 62 | 3,500 | 7,000 | M=CoG(Cleveland)(USA). SEastern Nigerian. 93% Efik, 7% Ibo. 28n,1s,100Y. |
| Church of Jesus C of Latter-day Saints | 1953 | I mar | ..... | | 4,000 | 8,000 | Begun by Ibos and Efiks using Mormon literature. M=CJCLdS(USA) but not allowed in. |
| Church of the Lord (Aladura) | 1930 | I pen | xWI.b | 200 | 10,000 | 30,000 | Aladura=Praying (Yoruba). Revival ex CMS. In 7 nations (UK,USA,&c). 1j,1k,1s. |
| Churches of Christ | 1947 | P Dis | x.... | 850 | 52,000 | 100,000 | Begun by Africans. 1950, M=CC(Non-Instrumental)(USA). In SE. 80% Efik,Ibo. 10x,2H,3s. |
| Congregational Holiness Church | | P Pe3 | x.... | 40 | 6,000 | 10,000 | M=CHC(USA). Holiness Pentecostals (3-stage). Work in South Eastern State. |
| Coptic Orthodox Church (P Alexandria) | c1970 | O Cop | NwaN. | | 200 | 500 | Under P Alexandria (Egypt). 200 Egyptian families. 1 priest for short period. |
| Divine Healing Church of Israel | c1960 | I pen | .V... | | 1,000 | 2,000 | Supreme Headquarters, Ibadan. Yoruba pentecostals. 1968, applied to join WCC. |
| Edo National Church of God | 1945 | I mar | ..... | | 5,000 | 10,000 | *Aruosa* (*Holy Place*). Begun by Oba of Benin Akenzua II (ex CMS). Bini syncretism. |
| El-Bethel Church (Mt Silloh) | 1926 | I peA | ..... | 20 | 950 | 2,000 | Pentecostals. Founded by colleague of Moses Orimolade (C&S). HQ Agege. |
| Eternal Sacred Order of Cherubim & S | 1925 | I peA | x.I.b | 1,000 | 100,000 | 300,000 | Original main body of Cherubim & Seraphim. Many schisms, lawsuits. HQ Ebute-Meta. |
| Eternal Sacred Order of C&S, Mt Zion | 1929 | I peA | x...I | 357 | 10,000 | 20,000 | Cherubim & Seraphim. One of many factions claiming first founder. Many schisms. |
| Ethiopian National Church, Nigeria | 1919 | I pen | ....I | 13 | 5,000 | 10,000 | Founded by prophet Adeniran Oke; attempt to introduce Ifa Oracle. 1r,1s. |
| Evangelical Churches of West Africa | 1893 | P int | xMG.G | 1,330 | 60,000 | 500,000 | *ECWA*. M=SIM. A=1956. 800n,500m,50w,672f,3H,88h,31k,22p(692),1s,W=80%,2000Y,3000z. |
| Evangelical Lutheran Church of Nigeria | 1936 | P Lut | L.... | 220 | 20,000 | 46,501 | Begun by M=Ev Luth Synodical Conf,(USA); 1964 LC Missouri S. Ibibio. 26f,2p,1r,1s. |
| **Fell of Chs of Christ in Nigeria:** | 1955 | P uni | ..... | 4,324 | 100,553 | 1,746,000 | *TEKAN*. Federation, in north. 140f,6H177h,1s(80). 262n,37x,3226m,191906Y,7409y. |
| Church of Christ among the Tiv | 1911 | P Ref | JF... | 1,368 | 17,436 | 500,000 | *NKST*. 1911, M=NGK(SAfrica);1940,CRC(USA). 120f,1H. 45 5 243 5344 1617 |
| Ch of Christ in Nigeria: Benue | 1906 | P Ref | JFA.K | 232 | 9,259 | 150,000 | *EKAN Benue*. In BP State. M=SUM(CRC) (USA). 1H. 27 4 113 918 610 |
| Ch of Christ in Nigeria: Gabas | 1923 | P Dun | x...K | 302 | 18,955 | 70,000 | *EKAN Lardin Gabas*(Eastern).M=CBM(USA). 48f,2H,1p,2r. 60 11 317 1677 384 |
| Ch of Christ in N: Mada Hills | 1911 | P int | .GG.G | 310 | 6,135 | 40,000 | *EKAN Dutsen Mada*. M=SUM(SAfrica). 14 1 288 673 271 |
| Ch of Christ in Nigeria: Muri | 1923 | P Met | ..... | 220 | 7,839 | 60,000 | *EKAN Muri*. NE State. M=EUB,now UMC. 18f,1H,1p 24 6 216 1300 490 |
| Ch of Christ in N: Plateau & Bauchi | 1904 | P int | .GG.z | 1,003 | 22,104 | 220,000 | *EKAN Plateau*. M=SUM(UK) 2H,25h,3r. 45 3 1034 4374 2470 |
| Lutheran Ch of Christ in Nigeria | 1913 | P Lut | IG..K | 879 | 18,484 | 700,000 | *EKAN Lutheran*. M=SUM(Danish),ALC. 1H,1k,3p. 45 7 1010 594 1470 |
| United Church of Christ in Nigeria | 1940 | P int | ..... | 10 | 341 | 6,000 | *HEKAN*. Kaduna, Zaria. Begun by soldiers in Kaduna. 3 0 5 226 97 |
| Free Protestant Episcopal Church | 1946 | C ARo | xv... | 17 | 4,000 | 6,225 | *Ecumenical Ch Foundation*, D WAfrica. M=FPEC(UK,USA). Ibibio. 3n,8m,1s(5),520Y,189y. |
| Gospel Faith Mission | 1959 | I peA | ..G.G | 7 | 1,000 | 2,000 | Schism ex CAC on doctrinal grounds. HQ Ibadan. 3-year ministers' training course. |
| Greater World Chr Spiritualist League | | M Spi | x.... | 1 | 200 | 300 | *Redemptive Church Mission*, Enugu. Specifically Christian spiritists. M=GWCSL(UK). |
| Greek Orthodox P Alexandria (D Accra) | | O Gre | Cw... | | 1,000 | 1,500 | HQ Yaoundé(Cameroon). In P Alexandria. Lebanese, Greek traders. 720 in Kaduna. 1x. |
| Holy Apostles Community (Aiyetoro) | 1947 | I ind | ..... | 6 | 3,000 | 5,000 | *Happy City*. 6 self-contained Yoruba fishing communities built over sea. Declining. 1h,1r. |
| Holy Assembly of Christ Church | 1951 | I peA | ....I | 15 | 1,200 | 2,000 | Schism in Lagos ex Holy Flock of Christ Ch. 2s(Lagos, Ibadan). |
| Holy Flock of Christ | 1932 | I peA | ....I | 31 | 10,000 | 20,000 | Indigenous pentecostal apostolics. Split ex Cherubim & Seraphim. HQ Lagos. |
| Holy Order of Cherubim & Seraphim | 1927 | I peA | ..I.I | 200 | 50,000 | 80,000 | One of several Cherubim & Seraphim groupings of pentecostals. HQ Kaduna. 1p. |
| Holy Saviour's Church | 1948 | I pen | ..... | 10 | 2,330 | 4,000 | Schism ex Church of the Lord (Aladura). 1945, praying band. HQ Ile Ife. 15n. |
| Internat Ch of the Foursquare Gospel | 1954 | P Pe2 | ZFG.a | 32 | 1,285 | 3,000 | M=ICFG(USA). 2 Divisions. HQ Yaba, Lagos. 25n,3x,6m,2p(42),W=59%,84Y. |
| Jehovah Jireh Christ Church | 1958 | I peA | ....I | 3 | 2,050 | 4,000 | '*The Lord will provide*'. Schism ex Saviour's Apostolic Ch. Anti-medicine. 1s. |
| Jehovah's Witnesses | 1921 | M Jeh | x.... | 1,281 | 86,843 | 170,000 | Active witnessing under way by 1925. 1972: 200,193 at annual Memorial. 10492Y. |
| Light of Christ Church | 1963 | I pen | ..... | 2 | 400 | 1,000 | Begun in 1963 revival in Ibadan by young woman, ex Christ Apostolic Ch. |
| Methodist Church, Nigeria | 1842 | P Met | VWA.K | 1,540 | 92,762 | 160,000 | M=MMS(UK). 25% Yoruba, 23% Ibibio, 20% Ijebu, 20% Ibo. 40f,15H,33r,1u,4435Y,6401y. |
| National Church of Christ (Aladura) | 1965 | I peA | ..... | | 2,000 | 5,000 | *Mount Pisgah*. Ex Cherubim. Name revealed to founder in vision. HQ Lagos. |
| New Assembly Christian Church | c1950 | I pen | .T.T. | 20 | 2,050 | 4,000 | Linked with Apostolic Faith (Portland,Oregon,USA). HQ Uyo, South East state. 5n. |
| New Church in West Africa | | M Swe | x.... | | 2,000 | 4,000 | M=GCNC(UK). 38% Efik, 30% Yoruba, 18% Ibo. Decline due to secessions. |
| New Eden Light of Jesus Christ | 1958 | I peA | ....I | 8 | 2,000 | 4,000 | Ex Cherubim & Seraphim. HQ Ibadan. Witchcraft eradication. 1s. |
| New Life Church of Christ in Nigeria | | I ind | .T.T. | 7 | 355 | 1,000 | In Vom, Northern Nigeria. Fundamentalists, supported by USA bodies. |
| New Salem Church (Aladura) | 1956 | I pen | ..... | 18 | 1,657 | 4,227 | Schism ex Holy Saviour's Ch led by founder's wife Lucy Adeoti. HQ Ile Ife. |
| New Testament Gospel Church | 1952 | I ind | .v... | 32 | 5,000 | 8,175 | Indigenous independents. Ibibio, in Ikot Ekpene area. 1962 applied to join WCC. |
| Nigeria Mennonite Church | 1957 | P Men | G.... | 49 | 4,518 | 15,000 | M=Mennonite Ch of NAmerica. Churches in SE state (Abak,Ibiono,Itam,Ubium). 2f,1s. |
| Nigerian Baptist Convention | 1850 | P Bap | TWA.K | 1,604 | 89,120 | 300,000 | *NBC*(1914). M=SBC(USA). Yoruba, Gude, Fali, Kamberi. 780n,187f,5H,3s,7852Y. |
| Nigerian Christian Fellowship | | I pen | ..... | 2,122 | 170,352 | 400,000 | A loosely-organized grouping of pentecostal bodies in eastern Nigeria. HQ Uyo. |
| Pentecostal Holiness Church | 1955 | P Pe3 | ZFG.G | 25 | 2,000 | 5,000 | M=PHC(USA). South Eastern state. National HQ Mushin, Lagos. 11n. |
| Pilgrim Baptist Mission | | I Bap | T...K | | 12,000 | 30,000 | M=Lott Carey BFMC,NBCUSA(USA Blacks). West of Niger among Ibo. 11f,1h. |
| Presbyterian Church in West Cameroon | 1959 | P Ref | Rwa.. | 1 | 200 | 500 | Extension of PCWC(Basel Mission) work from Cameroon. Station at Gavva. |
| Presbyterian Church of Nigeria | 1846 | P Ref | RWA.K | 416 | 17,142 | 100,000 | M=CSM(UK),PCC(Canada). 45% Ibo,26% Ibibio,22% Efik. 46n,11f,2p,W=85%,2325Y,1953y. |
| Qua Iboe Church | 1887 | P int | .G..K | 800 | 45,000 | 90,000 | 80% Ibibio, Efik, on Qua Iboe river; Igala, Bassa. M=QIM(NIreland). 25f,5H,8r,2s. |
| Redeemed Christian Church of God | 1952 | I pe2 | ....I | 10 | 1,200 | 2,000 | Ex C&S. Abortive aid: 1957, M=AFM(SAfrica), 1963 Velberter M(Germany). 1p. |
| Reorganized Ch of Jesus Christ of LdS | | M LdS | x.... | | 800 | 1,500 | Ex Mormons/CJLdS(Utah), aiding Nigerians in Abak. World HQ Independence, MO/USA. |
| Salvation Army | 1920 | P Sal | xwA.z | 236 | 14,800 | 35,000 | In Efik, Nka Erinyana. SA, Nigeria Territory. 70% Ibibio. 154n,7x,2r,1s,W=80%. |
| Saviour's Apostolic Ch of Nigeria | 1941 | I peA | ....I | 133 | 12,496 | 20,000 | Indigenous pentecostal apostolics. Schsm ex Christ Apostolic Ch. HQ Ibadan. 1s. |
| Seventh-day Adventist Church | 1914 | P Adv | n.... | 200 | 27,371 | 50,000 | *WAfr UM*(*ECentral*, *NNig*, *Rivers-SE*, *WNig Missions*). 64nx,43f,2H,2h,4r,W=80%,3569Y. |
| Undenominational Ch of the Lord in N | 1958 | I Hol | ..... | 16 | 1,010 | 2,000 | In southeast Nigeria. USA missionaries. 4n,G=2.3%pa,1p,W=85%,82Y,70z. |
| Unitarian Brotherhood Church | 1919 | M Unt | I.... | 1 | 100 | 300 | In General Assembly, Unitarian & Free Christian Chs (UK). One church in Lagos. |
| United African Methodist Church | 1917 | I Met | x.I.F | 300 | 5,000 | 10,000 | *Eledja* (*Fishmongers*, because near Lagos fish market). Schism ex MMS. Yoruba. |
| United Ch of the Cherubim & Seraphim | 1948 | I peA | ....I | 107 | 10,700 | 30,000 | Split ex C&S. 5 Dioceses: Oyo, Ondo, Mid-West, Lagos, Kwara. 8 schools. 1s. |
| United Gospel Apostolic Church | 1943 | I peA | ..... | 7 | 3,100 | 5,000 | 1,000 adults in HQ congregation, Ebute-Meta, Lagos. Revival crusades. Yoruba. 8n. |
| United Missionary Church of Africa | 1901 | P Hol | xFG.G | 191 | 7,000 | 15,000 | M=UMS,MC(USA). 60% Yoruba,30% Nupe,10% Hausa-speaking. 20n,7x,49f,1H,16h,4s,W=40%. |
| United Native African Church | 1891 | I Ang | x.I.F | 276 | 12,000 | 31,000 | *UNAC*. Ex CMS. 36% Ibo, 18% Ijaw, 15% Yoruba. Also in Dahomey. 36n,W=50%,2000Yy. |
| United Pentecostal Church | 1972 | P Pe1 | x.... | 38 | 4,547 | 10,000 | *Jesus Only Church*. M=UPC(USA). Unitarian Pentecostals. 30n,2f,1p(32). |
| World-Wide Missions of Nigeria | 1957 | P ind | x.... | | 20,000 | 30,000 | M=World-Wide Missions(USA). Evangelicals linked to HQ in Pasadena, CA (USA). |
| Zion Methodist Church in Nigeria | 1942 | I Met | .T.T. | 28 | 12,000 | 20,000 | Methodist schism based on Owerri. 99% Ibo. 6n,35m,28w,4p,1r,W=87%,158Y,450z. |
| Other African indigenous churches | | I | ..... | | 380,000 | 940,000 | Total at least 700 (see list below). |
| Other Protestant denominations | | P | ..... | | 100,000 | 300,000 | Total over 60 (see list below). |
| Other marginal Protestant bodies | | M | ..... | | 1,400 | 4,000 | Incl Branhamites (Nigeria Local Believers), COLJCB, Unity School of Christianity. |
| Other Catholic (non-Roman) churches | | C | ..... | | 1,000 | 2,000 | Total about 5, including New Apostolic Ch (Germany). |
| **Total affiliated (mid-1970)** | | | | **41,000** | **4,677,503** | **13,889,085** | **Total denominations (1970) . . . 860.** |
| **Total affiliated (mid-1975)** | | | | **47,000** | **5,624,900** | **16,702,300** | **Total denominations (1975) . . . 910.** |
| **Total affiliated (mid-1980)** | | | | **53,000** | **6,807,000** | **20,212,300** | **Total denominations (1980) . . . 960.** |

NOTES ON TABLE ABOVE

COLUMNS: for meanings and CODES (cols. 1, 3, 4, 8): see Codebook (Part 6). Column 1: **Boldface type** = church with over 10% of country's affiliated Christians.

NATIONAL COUNCILS (Column 4, 5th letter).

- a = member of NEF and CAN.
- b = member of NAAC and CAN.
- F = Christian Association of Nigeria (CAN), only.
- G = Nigeria Evangelical Fellowship (NEF).
- I = Nigeria Association of Aladura Churches (NAAC) (Isokan Ijo Aladura Nigeria (IIAN)/Communion of Aladura Churches, formerly National Council of Aladura Churches (NCAC), founded in 1960, with over 70 denominations as members by 1976 and 95 by late 1977).
- K = Christian Council of Nigeria (CCN), and through it, member of CAN.
- V = National Episcopal Conference of Nigeria (NECN), also full member of CAN.
- Z = member of NAAC, CAN and associate member of CCN.
- z = member of NEF, CCN and CAN.

*Other national councils* (all African indigenous). Christian Council of Praying Bands. Confederation of Nigerian Churches. Federation of Aladura. Inter-denominational Church Council of Nigeria (1962). Prophets' Union of Nigeria (Non-denominational). Spiritual Union of Aladura Churches (1961). Union of Christian Praying Bands. United Independent Churches Fellowship (1959).

OTHER AFFICAN INDIGENOUS CHURCHES. There are a vast number of other churches, mostly each with under 1,000 adult followers in 1970, including an estimated 200 offshoots of the Cherubim and Seraphim. Among the total are the following (with in parenthesis year of origin, and 1970 membership statistics): Abosso Apostolic Faith Ch of Christ, African Ch of the Lord (1959; 72 adults), Agbala Imole Mission Ch Aladura (1964; 500 adults), Apostolic Ch of God (1964; 150 adults), Apostolic Gospel Ch (1964), Army of the Cross of Christ Ch (MDCC from Ghana, begun when leader deported), Associated Gospel Tabernacle Mission Chs (member of ICCC), Bible Methodist Ch (member of ICCC), Bible Presbyterian Ch (member of ICCC), Bible Reformed Ev Ch, Bible Way Baptist Ch (member of ICCC), Blood of Jesus Christ Apostolic Ch International, Brotherhood of the Cross and Star (in Calabar; Efik, Ibibio), Calvary Association of Baptist Chs (member of ICCC), Christ Ch of Jerusalem (1967; 150 adults), Christ Devotional Independent African Ch (120 adults), Christ Ecumenical Ch, Christ Flock of Light, Christ Gospel Apostolic Ch (1956), Christ Healing Ch (1960; 400 adults), Christ Living Ch (member of ICCC), Christ Spiritual Ch (Imisi Jesu) (1964; 250 adults), Christ Temple Baptist Ch (member of ICCC), Church Army of Africa, Ch of Christ (Ijo Enia Krist) (1931; 800 adults), Ch of Philadelphia (member of ICCC), Ebenezer Apostolic Ch (1940), Emissaries of Divine Light Ch (Ilesha, 400 members, 8 groups, bishop, USA missionaries), Evangelical Ch of Apostles Nigeria (1964; 500 adults), First United Ch of Jesus Christ (Apostlic) (Jamaican pentecostals), Free Christian Ch (member of ICCC), God's The Hosts Tabernacle, Gospel Ch or Light (1964; 350 adults), Gospel Pentecostal Assembly (Voice of Deliverance) (1960) (member of NEF), Gospel Team Ch of Nigeria (1950; 400 adults), Holy Assembly Ch (1960; 500 adults), Idapo Mimo Cherubim & Seraphim (1954; 750 adults), Ijo Irapada Kristi (1967; 250 adults), Ijo Ore Ofe Olorun (1965; 100 pentecostals), Latter Rain Assemblies Mission (member of ICCC), Light of the World Ch (1955; 500 adults), Lutheran Bible Reformed Ch (member of ICCC), New Heaven Bible Ch (member of ICCC), Open Door Ch (member of ICCC), Pentecostal Ch of Christ (1954; 580 adults), St Johns' United African Christian Ch (1946; 500 members), St Joseph Gospel Ch of Christ (1968; 200 adults), St Joseph's Chosen Ch of God (1975, applied to join WCC), Saint Moses Ch (1964; 600 adults), Spiritual Ch of Christ (1955), Temple Ch (member of ICCC), Unity Ch of Truth of Nigeria, Universal Christian Ch (member of ICCC), Universal Ch of the Holy Spirit in Nigeria (in southeast), West African Episcopal Ch (1903). Since 1970, 6 of these have applied to join the WCC. In 1976, at least 55 more bodies, in addition to those shown in the table itself, belonged to the Nigeria Association of Aladura Churches. In addition, there is a small number of other UK and USA Black missions, including: Father Divine Peace Mission Movement (USA), Pentecostal Assemblies of the World, Progressive National Baptist Convention USA (1963).

OTHER PROTESTANT DENOMINATIONS. The vast proliferation of smaller Protestant bodies includes: American Advent Mission Society (1966), Brethren Ch (Ashland, USA; 1948), Children of God International (USA; ministry to drug addicts), Christian Nationals Evangelism Commission (1961), Christian Union (USA; 1943), Ch of God General Conference (Abrahamic Faith) (USA; 1967), Ch of God (Queen's Village, USA; 1969, 483 adults), Ch of God (Seventh-day), Ch of the Lutheran Confession (USA) (35 churches), Chs of God in the British Isles & Overseas (7 churches), International Pentecostal Assemblies, Mennonite Brethren Ch of North America (1944), Seventh-day Adventist Reform Movement, Seventh-day Baptist Ch, Southern Methodist Ch (USA), World Missions (1972). There are also a large number of independent single congregations.

UNITING CHURCHES. Negotiations for organic union were under way in 1974 between: Ch of the Province of West Africa (11 dioceses), Methodist Ch Nigeria, Presbyterian Ch of Nigeria (negotiations began 1933, broke down 1966, resumed 1973).

**PEOPLES** (ethnolinguistic). Christians: 36.0% Ibo, 18.8% Yoruba (Egba, Ekiti, Ife, Ijebu, Ondo, Oyo, also Igala, Idoma), 14.0% Hausa-speaking Plateau tribal (Angas, Bachama, Bura, Chamba, Eggon, Fyam, Ganawuri, Higi, Jen, Koro, Kulere, Longuda, Mada, Mambila, Margi, Matakam, Sura, Tigum, Wurkum, et alii), 10.2% Ibibio (Efik), 10.0% Tiv, 4.3% Ijaw, 3.5% Edo (Bini, 0.4% Ishan), 0.9% Isoko, 0.8% Urhobo, 0.6% European (White), 0.4% Ewe, 0.1% Nupe, 0.1% Basakomo, 0.1% Igbira, Hausa, Maguzawa, Jukun, & numerous smaller tribes.

**COUNTRY-WIDE TOTALS**

EVANGELIZATION (see Part 5). 1900: 30%. 1970: 77%. 1980: 86%. *Mass evangelism*. Among the many recent campaigns: 1960, Billy Graham crusades in Lagos, Ibadan, Kaduna, Enugu and Jos (251,125 attenders, 11,405 enquirers); 1963–73, New Life for All campaign throughout nation; 1974, Nigerian Baptist crusades in Ogbomosho (7 days, 75,000 attenders, 1,800 decisions for Christ), Ilorin (4,000 attenders, 500 professions of faith), Ibadan (3,000 professions of faith); 1975, Nigerian National Congress on Evangelization; 1978, Here's Life Africa (CCCI) in Jos; 1978–80, Operation Good News, launched after 1978 2nd National Congress on Evangelization. *Radiophonic evangelism*.

Annual listeners' letters (1975): 24,943 ELWA, 1,024 RVOG, HCJB, Radio Vatican, et alia. Bible correspondence courses (1975): ICI (302,351 enrolments, 58,577 active, 3,745 conversions reported), et alia. *Literature evangelism.* Every Home Crusade: mid-1977, 500,000 leaflets distributed monthly, 5,000 written decisions a month, rising to 10,000.
FOREIGN MISSIONARIES AND PERSONNEL (nationals serving abroad) (1973). Total 344 in 16 countries: about 150 Nigerian indigenous, about 95 Protestants, about 80 Roman Catholics, 12 Catholics (non-Roman), 7 Anglicans.
FOREIGN MISSIONARIES AND PERSONNEL (aliens from abroad) (1973). Total 2,674. *From Western world.* 2,472: 1,543 Protestants (945 in 51 USA societies, 370 in 14 UK societies, 101 in 5 Canada societies, 50 in 1 Denmark society, 26 in 4 WGermany societies, 19 in 4 Australia societies, 19 in 4 New Zealand societies, 8 in 1 Switzerland society, 4 in 2 Netherlands societies, 1 in 1 Finland society), 850 Roman Catholics, 68 Anglicans in 4 UK societies, about 10 Black indigenous from USA, 1 Orthodox from Greece. *From Communist world.* 1 Roman Catholic from Poland. *From Third World.* 201: about 100 Roman Catholics, about 60 African indigenous from Ghana, Benin and Liberia, 35 Protestants from 10 countries (4 in 1 South Africa society), 4 Anglicans, 2 Orthodox.
INSTITUTIONS (church-operated) (1973). Total 730, including 320 higher schools (23 minor seminaries), 280 medical centres (105 hospitals), 8 religious communities, 4 research centres, 50 seminaries (30 Protestant, 14 Nigerian indigenous, 4 RC, 2 Anglicans), 6 study centres.
PERIODICALS. About 150 titles (40 Nigerian indigenous).
PERSONNEL. About 21,274 (18,600 national, 2,674 foreign).
RELIGIOUS LIBRARIES. About 80.
SCRIPTURE DISTRIBUTION (1975). Annual totals: 412,581 Bibles (1% free, 90% subsidized, 9% commercial), 140,718 NTs (16% free, 49% subsidized, 35% commercial), 117,633 UBS portions, 476,348 UBS selections. *Translations completed.* Portion: 66 languages since 1850. NT: 20 languages since 1862. Bible: 10 languages since 1868.
SERVICE AGENCIES. About 105, including AMS, BB, BRAVS, CCCI, CCD, CCN, CDG, CFM, CTEN, ELFON, ELWA, EMS, GB, ICCN, IRETI, LWR, MAF, NAAC(IIAN), NCCWS, NECN, NEF, NFCS, NIFES, NLCN, NLFA, NMCW, RUCOM, SCM, SU, SUAC, UICF, WBT, WLC(EHC), WSCF, WV, YCS, YCW, YMCA, YWCA.

ADDITIONAL DATA ON CHURCHES
ANGLICAN CHURCH IN NIGERIA. Served by the Association of Anglican Dioceses in Nigeria. *New dioceses.* Created 1974: D Ilesha (formerly in D Ibadan), D Kwara (from D Ibadan and D Ondo). Created 1976 out of D Lagos: D Egba-Egbado, D Ijebu, with D Lagos continuing. Created 1977 out of D Benin: D Asaba, D Warri, with D Benin continuing. Nigeria formed part of the Church of the Province of West Africa until 1978 when the Province of Nigeria was being set up. *Membership.* 50% Ibo, 34% Yoruba. *Communicants* (column 6). Rolls of members, names are very inadequately kept, and it is clear from the large numbers of annual baptisms that the figures in column 6 refer to regular communicants only, and that those in column 7 are only general estimates of all such baptized persons.
CATHOLIC CHURCH IN NIGERIA. *New dioceses.* Created 1973: Abakaliki, Issele-Uku; created 1977, Awka. *Catechumens.* (1959) 555,954; (1961) 596,021; (1963) 759,478. In 1971 there were about 454,545 catechumens, divided as follows among the 25 dioceses in the order shown (and included in column 7): 20000, 1000, 20000, 5517, 3647, 43821, 800, 10000; 6000, 17000, 1700, 450, 18000, 934, 22000; 15783, 48500, 50000, 2780, 16510, 64680, 11497, 55702; 17924, 300. *Annual baptisms.* (1972) 62.1% infant, 37.9% adult. *Priests.* The first Nigerian was ordained in 1929. In 1972, all priests in the former secessionist Biafra were nationals (Ibos). *Brothers.* 103 national, 44 expatriate (1970). *Sisters.* 350 national, 266 expatriate (1970); there were also a few contemplatives not included in these totals. *Seminarians* (1972). 546 secular. *Catechists.* Total (1974) 4,400 (966 in D Makurdi). The small number of training schools (5 in 1972) has meant that Catholic teachers have for long had to serve as inadequately-trained catechists. As a result, in 1973 numerous new schools and centres were being planned and opened. *Indigenous religious congregations.* Sisters: 188 Sisters of the Most Pure Heart of Mary (begun 1937) (in 1972, 3 were sent as missionaries to Sierra Leone), 163 Handmaids of the Holy Child Jesus (begun 1931), 17 Sisters of the Eucharistic Heart of Jesus (Lagos, begun 1943), Sisters of the Eucharistic Heart (Ughalli), Daughters of Mary Mother of Mercy (Umuahia). *Main foreign congregations.* Priests: CSSp, SMA, SPS. Sisters: Our Lady of the Apostles, St-Louis, Holy Rosary, Holy Child.
*Catholic organizations.* The National Episcopal Conference of Nigeria is a member of SECAM. Two associations of religious personnel are active: the Nigerian National Conference of Major Superiors, and the Conference of Major Women Religious Superiors; but there is no national pastoral council. The principal lay movements, co-ordinated by the National Laity Council of Nigeria (NLCN), founded in 1973, are the YCS, YCW, Nigeria Federation of Catholic Students, Knights of St Columba, Legion of Mary, Christian Family Movement, Confraternity of Christian Doctrine, National Council of Catholic Women's Societies and St Vincent de Paul Society.

The Holy See has since 1976 had diplomatic relations with Nigeria, and is represented to government and the Catholic hierarchy by a pro-nuncio in Lagos.

There is a Pastoral Institute in Bodija, Ibadan, and the first West African institute for the training of permanent deacons is located at Kabba in the diocese of Lokoja. Other institutions include: (1) the Interdiocesan Religious Education Training Institute (IRETI), in Iperu-Remo (ecclesiastical province of Lagos), which maintains a research centre and trains teachers of religion in the primary schools; and (2) Irawo University Centre, on the campus of the University of Ibadan, which offers theological courses for students.

In 1970 the Catholic Church operated nearly 30% of all primary schools in Nigeria, almost 40% of secondary schools and over 25% of all teacher training colleges, with a total of nearly 900,000 pupils and students. The other Christian bodies together had a comparable number, being somewhat more numerous in the West and the North and less numerous in the East. Subsequently, many Nigerian states have taken over control of church schools since 1970 and all were expected to be nationalized by 1976. By 1975 Catholic primary schools had fallen to 1,028 with 308,200 pupils and secondary schools to 135 with 24,816 pupils. Both Catholics and other Christians have also had major involvement in medical and social service work; in 1967 they ran 76 general hospitals, 19 maternity hospitals, 23 leprosaria, one ophthalmic hospital (belonging to the SIM in Kano) and numerous dispensaries run by Nigeria's various Christian bodies. The Catholic social service programme was co-ordinated by its Social Welfare Department.
CELESTIAL CHURCH OF CHRIST. Name in French: Eglise du Christianisme Céleste. Name in Yoruba: Ijo Mimo Kristi lati Oke wa (Holy Church of Christ from Above). The church was began in Dahomey (now the Republic of Benin) in 1947 as a schism from the Cherubim and Seraphim. The founder was deported to Nigeria in 1952 and founded the church there, but there was little growth until its sudden expansion from 1973 onwards. By 1978 there were churches also in France, Germany, UK and USA. It appeals especially to Yoruba and Egba elites, professionals and businessmen. Members wear white uniforms. By 1977 the headquarters church in Lagos was having 1,800 attenders every Sunday, and there were 48 more branches in Lagos state with others in Ogun, Oyo and Ondo states, and 2 branches in the UK (Britain). The church produces its own musical recordings and other materials. *Leadership.* The Supreme Evangelist in 1977 had 16 wives. Other leaders included Prophets, Apostles and Evangelists.
CHERUBIM AND SERAPHIM (all bodies). Abbreviated in English to C&S, and in Yoruba to K&S (Kerubu ati Serafu).
CHRIST APOSTOLIC CHURCH. Begun in 1917 as a renewal movement within the Anglican Church, by 1920 it had become separate as Precious Stone praying band, or Faith Tabernacle. In 1930 a great revival began originating with a steamroller-driver Babalola. From 1932–39 the church requested and obtained the assistance of the Apostolic Church of Great Britain until the latter was dismissed after disagreements over charismata. Present work extends throughout Nigeria, including a large work among Muslim tribes in the north, and there are foreign missions in Ghana, Ivory Coast, Liberia, Sierra Leone, Italy (Rome) and UK. *Membership.* 74% Yoruba (Western, Lagos, Kwara States), 15% Ibo/Ijaw (eastern states), 5% Edo/Urhobo/Itsekiri (Mid-Western State), 3% Bachama (in northern states), 3% Efik/Ibibio (South-Eastern State), also Cameroonians and Ghanaians. In 1975 there were 400 congregations in Ibadan city alone.
EVANGELICAL CHURCHES OF WEST AFRICA. Work was begun by the Sudan Interior Mission in 1893; and ECWA became autonomous in 1956. There are 13 Districts. *Membership.* Members come from scores of different tribes across the Middle Belt, mainly Hausa-speaking tribes, Afusare, Bariba, Basa, Birom, Gurma, Gwandara, Gwari, Igbira, Jarawa, Karekare, Katab, Koro, Nupe, Saya, Tangale, Tera, Yoruba; also Ibo, Idoma, Igala, Tiv and numerous others. *Mission body.* ECWA's missionary arm, the Evangelical Missionary Society (EMS), in 1978 had 260 African missionaries serving cross-culturally in Nigeria, Niger, Benin, et alia.
FELLOWSHIP OF THE CHURCHES OF CHRIST IN NIGERIA. Also known as the Church of Christ in Nigeria, TEKAN is a federation formed in 1957 by 6 autonomous churches, joined later by 2 others, and known initially as TEKAS after its Hausa name: Tarayyar Ekklesiyoyyin Kristi a Sudan. Of the 8 Churches, 5 each had the initials EKAS (Ekklesiyar Kristi a Sudan, church of Christ in the Sudan); EKAS Lutheran = Ekklesiya Kristi a Cikin Sudan; and the 2 others were: HEKAN (United Church of Christ in Nigeria) and EKAS hen Tiv, which in the Tiv language became NKST (Nongo u Kristu ken Sudan hen Tiv, Church of Christ among the Tiv). After 1975 the ambiguous name Sudan was changed to Nigeria, and TEKAS to TEKAN. *Adult members.* Column 6 gives baptized and enrolled communicant members. These numbers are far smaller than TEKAN attenders or affiliated because of strict membership requirements By 1976 there were 250,000 members of various kinds. *Sunday attenders.* The only statistics for total Christian community which TEKAN churches assemble each year are those attending church on a single specified Sunday during the year; this includes children of 7 years and over but excludes infants. In 1971 the total reported was 1,133,379 (divided among the 8 churches in order thus: 343619, 17975, 30919, 22378, 25040, 111538, 577933, 2980), and in 1972 the total was 1,100,238 (333191, 94104, 30919, 10924, 25700, 110653, 491535, 3212). These attendances have fluctuated a very great deal since 1969 in the civil war disturbances and their aftermath. *Affiliated.* Column 7 above therefore gives conservative estimated totals for all those connected with these churches, including attenders, children and infants, for the year 1970. *Lay leaders.* By 1976, 1,000 were enrolled in TEE courses in 86 centres. *Medical work* (1970). 6 hospitals, 79 dispensaries, 18 maternity centres, 80 leprosy centres and clinics.
GREEK ORTHODOX PATRIARCHATE OF ALEXANDRIA (D ACCRA). The Greek bishop, a Greek citizen, lives in Athens (Greece) and visits West Africa only for Christmas and Easter ceremonies.
METHODIST CHURCH, NIGERIA. In January 1976 the church adopted a new constitution and enthroned its president with the title of patriarch; with 5 archbishops and bishops, these are the only such titles in the world of Methodism.
SALVATION ARMY. Name = (Ibo) Igwe Agha Nzoputa, (Yoruba) Ogun Igbala Na, (Edo) Iyo Kuo Imienfan, (Urhobo) Ofovwi re Arho Na.

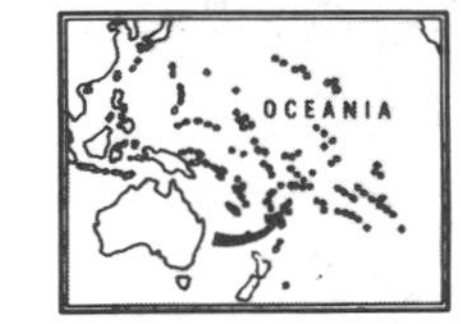


# NIUE ISLAND

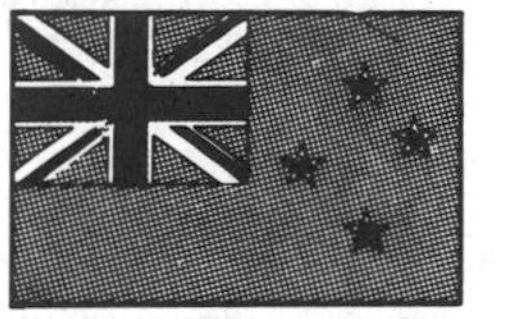

## SECULAR DATA

**STATE. Official name:** The Territory Overseas of Niue Island.
**Flag** (shown above right): That of New Zealand.
**Area:** 259 sq.km. (100 sq.miles). Agricultural land: 77.0%.
**Government:** Territory overseas of New Zealand, since 1903.
**Legislature:** Island Assembly.
**Official language:** English.
**Capital:** Alofi 3,000.

**DEMOGRAPHY. Population:** 4,990 (census of 28.IX.1971. For 1970–2000 (UN), see last row of Table 1). Population density (1975): 21/sq.km. (55/sq.mile). Under 15 years: 44%. Growth rate (1975–80): 1.43% per year. Household size: 6.2 persons.
**Major languages:** English, Niuean, Chinese.
**Labour force:** 28%.

**ETHNOLINGUISTIC GROUPS:** 97.4% Niuean, 2.6% European (130), Chinese.

**MONEY** (1977). **Monetary unit:** New Zealand dollar (=100 cents); US$1=NZ$1.07.
**National income per person:** US$550. Average annual family income: US$3,410.

**Cost of living in capital** (1976): Daily cost of living: US$25.

**HEALTH.** Hospitals: 1 (30 beds). Doctors: 5. Lepers: 120 (21.8 per 1,000).

**EDUCATION.** Adult literacy: (1945) 87%, (1951) 94%. Schools: 10.

**LITERATURE.** Periodicals: 2. Newspapers: 1 non-daily.

**COMMUNICATION** (per 1,000 people). Phones: 53. Radios: 170.

TABLE 1. RELIGIOUS ADHERENTS IN NIUE ISLAND

| Year | 1900 | | mid-1970 | | Annual change, 1970–1980 | | | | mid-1975 | | mid-1980 | | 2000 | |
|---|---|---|---|---|---|---|---|---|---|---|---|---|---|---|
| *Name* | *Adherents* | *%* | *Adherents* | *%* | *Natural* | *Conversion* | *Total* | *Rate* | *Adherents* | *%* | *Adherents* | *%* | *Adherents* | *%* |
| **Christians** | **4,200** | **100.0** | **4,995** | **99.9** | **100** | **–1** | **99** | **1.80** | **5,490** | **99.8** | **5,985** | **99.8** | **6,970** | **99.6** |
| professing | 4,200 | 100.0 | 4,995 | 99.9 | 100 | –1 | 99 | 1.80 | 5,490 | 99.8 | 5,985 | 99.8 | 6,970 | 99.6 |
| Protestants | 4,200 | 100.0 | 4,055 | 81.1 | 78 | –35 | 43 | 1.00 | 4,285 | 77.9 | 4,485 | 74.8 | 4,730 | 67.6 |
| Marginal Protestants | 0 | 0.0 | 605 | 12.1 | 14 | 22 | 36 | 4.65 | 775 | 14.1 | 965 | 16.1 | 1,400 | 20.0 |
| Roman Catholics | 0 | 0.0 | 285 | 5.7 | 7 | 9 | 16 | 4.31 | 360 | 6.5 | 440 | 7.3 | 700 | 10.0 |
| Anglicans | 0 | 0.0 | 50 | 1.0 | 1 | 3 | 4 | 5.71 | 70 | 1.3 | 95 | 1.6 | 140 | 2.0 |
| nominal | 0 | 0.0 | 150 | 10.2 | 11 | 2 | 13 | 2.26 | 575 | 10.4 | 640 | 10.7 | 840 | 12.0 |
| affiliated | 4,200 | 100.0 | 4,485 | 89.7 | 89 | –3 | 86 | 1.75 | 4,915 | 89.4 | 5,345 | 89.1 | 6,130 | 87.6 |
| total practising | 3,990 | *95* | 4,035 | *90* | 80 | –3 | 77 | 1.75 | 4,425 | *90* | 4,810 | *90* | 4,900 | *80* |
| non-practising | 210 | *5* | 450 | *10* | 9 | 0 | 9 | 1.75 | 490 | *10* | 535 | *10* | 1,230 | *20* |
| Protestants | 4,200 | 100.0 | 3,730 | 74.6 | 71 | –32 | 39 | 0.98 | 3,940 | 71.6 | 4,115 | 68.6 | 4,220 | 60.3 |
| Marginal Protestants | 0 | 0.0 | 505 | 10.1 | 12 | 21 | 33 | 5.00 | 660 | 12.0 | 835 | 13.9 | 1,260 | 18.0 |
| Roman Catholics | 0 | 0.0 | 220 | 4.4 | 5 | 6 | 11 | 4.26 | 270 | 5.0 | 335 | 5.6 | 560 | 8.0 |
| Anglicans | 0 | 0.0 | 30 | 0.6 | 1 | 2 | 3 | 6.67 | 45 | 0.8 | 60 | 1.0 | 90 | 1.3 |
| Baha'is | 0 | 0.0 | 5 | 0.1 | 0 | 1 | 1 | 10.00 | 10 | 0.2 | 15 | 0.2 | 30 | 0.4 |
| **Country's population** | **4,200** | **100.0** | **5,000** | **100.0** | **100** | **0** | **100** | **1.82** | **5,500** | **100.0** | **6,000** | **100.0** | **7,000** | **100.0** |

COLUMNS, ROWS. For meanings and definitions, see Codebook (Part 6.) Note that, by definition, total 'Christians, = professing + crypto-Christians, which also = affiliated + nominal Christians. Percentages may not always total exactly, due to rounding.
CENSUSES. **25.IX.1945:** 99.5% Protestants, 0.5% other religionists. **25.IX.1956:** 99.9% Christians. **25.IX.1961:** 84.9% Protestants (84.1% LMS), 9.5% marginal Protestants (8.8% Mormons, 0.7% Jehovah's Witnesses), 4.3% Roman Catholics, 1.2% Anglicans, 0.1% non-religious. **28.IX.1966** 84.7% Protestants (83.4% LMS), 9.8% marginal Protestants (8.2% Mormons, 1.6% Jehovah's Witnesses), 4.7% Roman Catholics,

0.7% Anglicans, 0.1% Baha'is. **28.IX.1971**: 81.1% Protestants (77.8% LMS), 12.1% marginal Protestants (10.4% Mormons, 1.7% Jehovah's Witnesses), 5.7% Roman Catholics, 1.0% Anglicans, 0.1% Baha'is.

**NON-CHRISTIAN RELIGIONS.** Niue is almost entirely Christian, except for a few individuals. In the 1966 census, 5 persons claimed to belong to the Baha'i World Faith.

### CHRISTIANITY
PROTESTANT CHURCHES. The first attempt to evangelize Niue was made in 1830 by the pioneer John Williams of the London Missionary Society. Unsuccessful at the time, the LMS continued to make periodic visits to the island. In 1846 a Niuean, trained as a teacher in an LMS school in Samoa, returned home and was followed 3 years later by a Samoan named Paulo who was instrumental in establishing the church in Niue. There was no resident European missionary until 1861. The early LMS influence was decisive, and Niueans still consider themselves predominantly Congregationalists. There is also a small Seventh-day Adventist church.

MARGINAL CHURCHES. As in other parts of Oceania, Mormons have met with marked success, and the Church of Jesus Christ of Latter-day Saints

**NOTES ON RELIGIONS.**
BAHA'IS. A selection of Baha'i prayers was published in the Niuean language soon after 1970.
COUNTRY'S POPULATION. There is a large Niuean com-

A number of Niue's postage stamps have Christian motifs; here in Easter 1978. (*left*) The Descent from the Cross (Caravaggio), and (*right*) The Burial of Christ (Bellini).

is now the second largest church on the island. Jehovah's Witnesses are also present.

CATHOLIC CHURCH. The small Catholic community is served by a Marist priest at Alofi. In

munity living in New Zealand, and each year about 250 more emigrate there from Niue.

May 1972 Niue was separated from the diocese of Tonga and attached instead to the diocese of Rarotonga with its seat in the Cook Islands.

**CHURCH AND STATE.** Niue was reached by Captain James Cook in 1774 but did not come under British protection until 1889. In 1901 the island was annexed to New Zealand. Religion has not been an issue between church and state and the latter is effectively secular. A resident commissioner and the Niue Island Assembly, with 14 elected members, handle administrative and legislative affairs. Freedom of religion is guaranteed by the constitution of New Zealand.

**BROADCASTING.** The government Niue Broadcasting Service accepts religious programmes from all the churches, Congregationalists and Catholics being allocated more time than Adventists and Mormons.

TABLE 2. ORGANIZED CHURCHES AND DENOMINATIONS IN NIUE ISLAND

| Official name 1 | Begun 2 | Type 3 | Counc 4 | Congs 5 | Adults 6 | Affiliated 7 | Names, notes, and other statistics (see Codebook) 8 |
|---|---|---|---|---|---|---|---|
| Anglican Church (D Polynesia) | | A Hig | awpK. | 1 | 10 | 30 | Under Diocese of Polynesia, Ch of the Province of New Zealand. Expatriates. |
| Catholic Church (D Rarotonga) | | R Lat | P.PY. | 1 | 100 | 220 | Part of D Rarotonga (Cook Is) since 1972; previously under D Tonga. M=SM2. 1x. |
| Church of Jesus C of Latter-day Saints | c1960 | M LdS | x.... | 6 | 200 | 425 | Mormons. M=CJCLdS(Utah,USA). Many expatriates. 2f. |
| Jehovah's Witnesses | | M Jeh | x.... | 1 | 15 | 80 | Watch Tower. IBSA. First activity reported 1961 (36 adherents). 1Y. |
| **Niue Christian Church** | 1846 | P Con | ..P.. | 14 | 1,073 | 3,700 | Ekalesia Niue. 1861, M=LMS(UK). A=1970. 12n,1x,G=−3.9%pa,W=52%,150Yy,55z. |
| Seventh-day Adventist Church | | P Adv | x.... | 1 | 10 | 30 | SDA. Part of Tonga Mission, Central Pacific Union Mission. |
| Total affiliated (mid-1970) | | | | 24 | 1,408 | 4,485 | Total denominations (1970) . . . 6. |
| Total affiliated (mid-1975) | | | | 25 | 1,540 | 4,915 | Total denominations (1975) . . . 6. |
| Total affiliated (mid-1980) | | | | 26 | 1,680 | 5,345 | Total denominations (1980) . . . 6. |

**NOTES ON TABLE ABOVE**
COLUMNS: for meanings and CODES (cols. 1, 3, 4, 8): see Codebook (Part 6). Column 1: **Boldface type** = church with over 10% of country's affiliated Christians.

PEOPLES (ethinolinguistic). Christians: 97.4% Niuean, 2.6% European, Chinese.

**COUNTRY-WIDE TOTALS**
EVANGELIZATION (see Part 5). 1900: 100%. 1970: 100%. 1980: 100%.
FOREIGN MISSIONARIES AND PERSONNEL (aliens from abroad) (1973). Total 7. *From Western world*. 4: 2 marginal Protestants (Mormons), 1 Roman Catholic, 1 Protestant. *From Third World*. About 3 Protestants from Fiji, Tonga and Samoa.

PERIODICALS. 2 titles.
PERSONNEL. About 21 (14 national, 7 foreign).
SCRIPTURE DISTRIBUTION (1975). Annual totals: 100 Bibles (subsidizèd), 20 NTs (subsidized), 80 UBS portions, 270 UBS selections. *Translations completed*. Niuean: portion in 1861, NT 1866, Bible 1904.

# NORFOLK ISLAND

## SECULAR DATA

**STATE. Official name:** The Territory of Norfolk Island.
**Flag** (shown above right): That of Australia.
**Area:** 36 sq.km. (14 sq.miles).
**Government:** Territory of Australia, since 1913 (1856 settlement).
**Legislature:** Norfolk Island Council, 9 members.
**Official language:** English.
**Capital:** Kingston.

**DEMOGRAPHY. Population:** 1,683 (census of 30.IV.1971).

For 1970–2000 (UN), see last row of Table 1). Population density (1975): 47/sq.km. (122/sq.mile). Under 15 years: 42%. Growth rate (1975–80): 0.0% per year (births 4.02%, deaths −1.17%, emigrants −2.85%). Life expectancy (1975–80): 55.9 years. Household size: 3.3 persons.
**Major languages:** English.
**Labour force:** 51%.
**Tourists** (1961): 970. (1970) 9,600. (1974) 10,000.

**ETHNOLINGUISTIC GROUPS:** 63.2% White (35% Anglo-Australian, 16% Anglo-New Zealander, 12% British), 33.8% Pitcairner (Euronesian), 3% other Euronesian.

**MONEY** (1977). **Monetary unit:** Australian dollar (= 100 cents); US$1=A$0.94.
**National income per person:** US$4,300. Average annual family income: US$14,190.

**EDUCATION.** Adult literacy: 95%.

**LITERATURE.** Newspapers: 1 non-daily.

**COMMUNICATION** (per 1,000 people). Phones: 211. Radios: 620.

TABLE 1. RELIGIOUS ADHERENTS IN NORFOLK ISLAND

| Year | 1900 | | mid-1970 | | Annual change, 1970–1980 | | | | mid-1975 | | mid-1980 | | 2000 | |
|---|---|---|---|---|---|---|---|---|---|---|---|---|---|---|
| Name | Adherents | % | Adherents | % | Natural | Conversion | Total | Rate | Adherents | % | Adherents | % | Adherents | % |
| **Christians** | 1,000 | 100.0 | 1,581 | 93.0 | 0 | −10 | −10 | −0.66 | 1,530 | 90.0 | 1,480 | 87.1 | 1,500 | 75.0 |
| professing | 1,000 | 100.0 | 1,581 | 93.0 | 0 | −10 | −10 | −0.66 | 1,530 | 90.0 | 1,480 | 90.0 | 1,500 | 75.0 |
| Anglicans | 770 | 77.0 | 799 | 47.0 | 0 | −20 | −20 | −2.98 | 685 | 40.3 | 595 | 35.0 | 580 | 29.0 |
| Protestants | 200 | 20.0 | 576 | 33.9 | 0 | 5 | 5 | 0.89 | 605 | 35.6 | 630 | 37.1 | 620 | 31.0 |
| Roman Catholics | 30 | 3.0 | 206 | 12.1 | 0 | 5 | 5 | 2.04 | 240 | 14.1 | 255 | 15.0 | 300 | 15.0 |
| nominal | 100 | 10.0 | 411 | 24.2 | 0 | 4 | 4 | 0.91 | 430 | 25.3 | 450 | 26.5 | 600 | 30.0 |
| affiliated | 900 | 90.0 | 1,170 | 68.8 | 0 | −14 | −14 | −1.27 | 1,100 | 64.7 | 1,030 | 60.6 | 900 | 45.0 |
| total practising | 630 | 70 | 585 | 50 | 0 | −7 | −7 | −1.27 | 550 | 50 | 515 | 50 | 450 | 50 |
| non-practising | 270 | 30 | 585 | 50 | 0 | −7 | −7 | −1.27 | 550 | 50 | 515 | 50 | 450 | 50 |
| Anglicans | 720 | 72.0 | 700 | 41.2 | 0 | −20 | −20 | −3.28 | 595 | 35.0 | 505 | 29.7 | 360 | 18.0 |
| Protestants | 160 | 16.0 | 290 | 17.1 | 0 | 2 | 2 | 0.50 | 300 | 17.6 | 305 | 17.9 | 280 | 14.0 |
| Roman Catholics | 20 | 2.0 | 180 | 10.6 | 0 | 4 | 4 | 1.95 | 205 | 12.1 | 220 | 12.9 | 260 | 13.0 |
| Non-religious | 0 | 0.0 | 119 | 7.0 | 0 | 10 | 10 | 5.94 | 170 | 10.0 | 220 | 12.9 | 500 | 25.0 |
| **Country's population** | 1,000 | 100.0 | 1,700 | 100.0 | 0 | 0 | 0 | 0.00 | 1,700 | 100.0 | 1,700 | 100.0 | 2,000 | 100.0 |

COLUMNS, ROWS. For meanings and definitions, see Codebook (Part 6). Note that, by definition, total 'Christians, = professing + crypto-Christians, which also = affiliated + nominal Christians. Percentages may not always total exactly, due to rounding.
CENSUSES. **30.VI.1947**: 92.8% Anglicans & Protestants, 6.9% Roman Catholics, 0.3% non-religious. **30.VI.1954**: 92.8% Anglicans & Protestants, 6.9% Roman Catholics, 0.4% non-religious. **30.VI.1961**: 59.6% Anglicans, 32.8% Protestants

(17.2% Methodists, 9.1% SD Adventists, 4.5% Presbyterians), 7.1% Roman Catholics, 0.5% non-religious. **30.VI.1966**: 55.7% Anglicans, 31.8% Protestants (15.8% Methodists, 7.7% SD Adventists, 5.9% Presbyterians), 9.8% Roman Catholics, 2.6% non-religious. **30.VI.1971**: 47.0% Anglicans, 33.9% Protestants (15.8% Methodists, 7.9% Presbyterians, 5.6% SD Adventists, and followers of about 10 other denominations), 12.1% Roman Catholics, 7.0% non-religious. This census enumerates the population by 20 different categories of religion.

**NOTES ON RELIGIONS**
ANGLICANS. These have decreased rapidly since 1960, whilst Roman Catholics and non-religious have increased markedly.
NON-RELIGIOUS. Europeans of British origin.
PROTESTANTS. Although only 2 denominations have organized congregations, the 1971 census lists the following additional denominational traditions to which persons professed to belong: Baptist, Brethren, Churches of Christ, Congregational, Lutheran, and Salvation Army.

**NON-CHRISTIAN RELIGIONS.** As the inhabitants of the island are either of British stock or Euronesian, non-Christian religions have gained no foothold. Persons without religion however have increased rapidly from one census to the next since 1947 and now number over 10%.

## CHRISTIANITY

**ANGLICAN CHURCH.** The first Christmas service was held in 1788. The Melanesian Mission established its main headquarters on the island in 1867, and St Barnabas chapel there was consecrated as a church in 1880. By 1896 the church claimed 230 members. In 1919 the headquarters were moved to Siota in the British Solomon Islands, but the territory has remained mainly Anglican in denomination, though Anglicans have recently declined in numbers. They form part of the diocese of Sydney in the Church of England in Australia.

**PROTESTANT CHURCHES.** Methodists and Adventists have organized congregations on the island. Both are related to their churches in Australia.

**CATHOLIC CHURCH.** A Marist priest serves one parish, which is attached to the archdiocese of Sydney (Australia). Catholics are growing in numbers, chiefly at the expense of Anglicans.

**CHURCH AND STATE.** In 1774 Captain James Cook discovered an uninhabited island which he

**Church of England in Australia.** St Barnabas Chapel, dedicated in 1880 as memorial to J.C. Patteson, martyred first bishop of Melanesia.

The Island's postage stamps often illustrate Christian themes: (left) the first Christmas service, 1788; (right) St Barnabas Chapel, exterior and interior.

named after the English duke of Norfolk. The island was annexed by Great Britain in 1788, the second of Britain's possessions in the Pacific. Settlement began in 1856 from Pitcairn Island, and in 1914 it became a territory of the Australian Commonwealth. Religion has never been an issue between church and state.

Norfolk Island is today governed by an administrator named by the governor-general of Australia. There is also a Norfolk Island Council, elected every 2 years from the resident community, which acts in an advisory capacity to the administrator. The Australian constitution guarantees freedom of religion.

TABLE 2.   ORGANIZED CHURCHES AND DENOMINATIONS IN NORFOLK ISLAND

| Official name 1 | Begun 2 | Type 3 | Counc 4 | Congs 5 | Adults 6 | Affiliated 7 | Names, notes, and other statistics (see Codebook) 8 |
|---|---|---|---|---|---|---|---|
| Catholic Church (M Sydney) | | R Lat | P.... | 1 | 100 | 180 | Attached to M Sydney (Australia). M=SM2. One parish. 1x. |
| Ch of England in Australia (D Sydney) | 1788 | A plu | awe.. | 1 | 400 | 700 | *Parish of All Saints,* in Diocese of Sydney (Australia). M=Melanesian Mission (UK). |
| Methodist Church | | P Met | Vwe.. | 1 | 100 | 200 | Related to Methodist Church of Australasia. Migrant workers and transients. |
| Seventh-day Adventist Church | c1900 | P Adv | x.... | 1 | 50 | 90 | In Greater Sydney Conference, Trans-Tasman UC. Pitcairn Islanders. |
| Total affiliated (mid-1970) | | | | 4 | 650 | 1,170 | Total denominations (1970) . . . 4. |
| Total affiliated (mid-1975) | | | | 4 | 620 | 1,100 | Total denominations (1975) . . . 4. |
| Total affiliated (mid-1980) | | | | 4 | 590 | 1,030 | Total denominations (1980) . . . 4. |

**NOTES ON TABLE ABOVE**
COLUMNS: for meanings and CODES (cols. 1, 3, 4, 8): see Codebook (Part 6). Column 1: Boldface type = church with over 10% of country's affiliated Christians.

**PEOPLES** (ethnolinguistic). Christians: 63.2% White (European, Anglo-Australian), 33.8% Pitcairner (Euronesian, Eurasian), 3% other Euronesian.

**COUNTRY-WIDE TOTALS**
EVANGELIZATION (see Part 5). 1900: 100%. 1970: 100%. 1980: 100%.
FOREIGN MISSIONARIES AND PERSONNEL (aliens from abroad) (1973). Total 1. *From Western world.* 1 Roman Catholic. PERSONNEL. 1 (foreign).

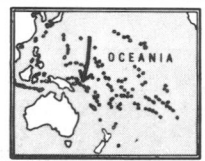

# NORTHERN SOLOMONS

## SECULAR DATA

**STATE. Official name:** The Republic of the Northern Solomons. **Alternative name:** The Province of the North Solomons. **Flag** (shown above right): As of Papua New Guinea **Area:** 11,189 sq.km. (4,320 sq.miles). **Government:** Secessionist party, proclaiming independence 1 September 1975 until 1976; by 1977 a semi-autonomous province loosely in Papua New Guinea. **Official language:** English. **Capital:** Kieta.

**DEMOGRAPHY. Population:** 77,880 (census of 1970. For 1970–2000 (UN), see last row of Table 1). Population density (1975): 8/sq.km. (21/sq.mile). Under 15 years: 41%. Life expectancy (1975–80): 50.2 years. Household size: 5.8 persons. **Major languages:** English, Melanesian (Petats, Teop), Papuan (Koromira, Nasioi, Siwai (Motuna), Telei), Buin, Halia, and about 15 others.

**ETHNOLINGUISTIC GROUPS:** 70.0% Solomoni Papuan, 29.0% Solomoni Melanesian, 1% White (Anglo-Australian, European) (730), Chinese, Banoni.

**MONEY** (1977). **Monetary unit:** kina (= 100 toea); US$1=Ka 0.81. **National income per person:** US$800. Average annual family income: US$4,640.

**EDUCATION. Adult literacy:** 50%.

**COMMUNICATION** (per 1,000 people). Phones: 12.

TABLE 1.   RELIGIOUS ADHERENTS IN THE NORTHERN SOLOMONS

| Year | 1900 | | mid-1970 | | Annual change, 1970–1980 | | | | mid-1975 | | mid-1980 | | 2000 | |
|---|---|---|---|---|---|---|---|---|---|---|---|---|---|---|
| Name | Adherents | % | Adherents | % | Natural | Conversion | Total | Rate | Adherents | % | Adherents | % | Adherents | % |
| **Christians** | 0 | 0.0 | 78,200 | 98.4 | 2,170 | 39 | 2,209 | 2.50 | 88,260 | 98.6 | 100,290 | 98.8 | 163,900 | 98.7 |
| professing | 0 | 0.0 | 78,200 | 98.4 | 2,170 | 39 | 2,209 | 2.50 | 88,260 | 98.6 | 100,290 | 98.8 | 163,900 | 98.7 |
| Roman Catholics | 0 | 0.0 | 66,500 | 83.6 | 1,846 | 23 | 1,869 | 2.49 | 75,060 | 83.9 | 85,190 | 83.9 | 138,700 | 83.5 |
| Evangelical Catholics | 0 | 0.0 | 4,626 | 5.8 | 124 | −29 | 95 | 1.89 | 5,040 | 5.6 | 5,580 | 5.5 | 6,100 | 3.7 |
| Protestants | 0 | 0.0 | 11,700 | 14.7 | 324 | 16 | 340 | 2.58 | 13,200 | 14.8 | 15,100 | 14.9 | 25,200 | 15.2 |
| nominal | 0 | 0.0 | 2,274 | 2.9 | 68 | 44 | 112 | 4.04 | 2,760 | 3.1 | 3,390 | 3.3 | 8,400 | 5.1 |
| affiliated | 0 | 0.0 | 75,926 | 95.5 | 2,102 | −5 | 2,097 | 2.45 | 85,500 | 95.5 | 96,900 | 95.5 | 155,500 | 93.7 |
| doubly-affiliated | 0 | 0.0 | −6,630 | −8.3 | −176 | 39 | −137 | 1.90 | −7,200 | −8.1 | −8,000 | −7.9 | −8,300 | −5.0 |
| total practising | 0 | *0* | 64,540 | *85* | 1,786 | −4 | 1,782 | 2.45 | 72,670 | *85* | 82,360 | *85* | 124,400 | *80* |
| non-practising | 0 | *0* | 11,390 | *15* | 316 | −1 | 315 | 2.45 | 12,830 | *15* | 14,540 | *15* | 31,100 | *20* |
| Roman Catholics | 0 | 0.0 | 66,230 | 83.3 | 1,830 | −31 | 1,799 | 2.42 | 74,460 | 83.2 | 84,220 | 83.0 | 132,500 | 79.8 |
| Protestants | 0 | 0.0 | 11,226 | 14.1 | 312 | 15 | 327 | 2.58 | 12,700 | 14.2 | 14,500 | 14.3 | 24,200 | 14.6 |
| Evangelicals | 0 | 0.0 | 6,000 | 7.5 | 167 | 3 | 170 | 2.50 | 6,800 | 7.6 | 7,700 | 7.6 | 12,900 | 7.8 |
| Melanesian indigenous | 0 | 0.0 | 5,000 | 6.3 | 133 | −33 | 100 | 1.85 | 5,400 | 6.1 | 6,000 | 5.9 | 6,600 | 4.0 |
| Marginal Protestants | 0 | 0.0 | 100 | 0.1 | 3 | 5 | 8 | 5.71 | 140 | 0.2 | 180 | 0.2 | 500 | 0.3 |
| Tribal religionists | 39,600 | 100.0 | 800 | 1.0 | 17 | −37 | −20 | −2.86 | 700 | 0.8 | 600 | 0.6 | 400 | 0.2 |
| Non-religious | 0 | 0.0 | 500 | 0.6 | 13 | −2 | 11 | 2.04 | 540 | 0.6 | 610 | 0.6 | 1,700 | 1.0 |
| **Country's population** | 39,600 | 100.0 | 79,500 | 100.0 | 2,200 | 0 | 2,200 | 2.46 | 89,500 | 100.0 | 101,500 | 100.0 | 166,000 | 100.0 |

**COLUMNS, ROWS.** For meanings and definitions, see Codebook (Part 6). Note that, by definition, total 'Christians' = professing + crypto-Christians, which also = affiliated + nominal Christians. Percentages may not always total exactly, due to rounding.

**NOTES ON RELIGIONS**
DOUBLY-AFFILIATED. This term covers those affiliated to, or claimed by, both the Catholic Church and also either the United Church or the Hahalis Welfare Society. Because their

statistics represent a duplication, they are shown in the table as a negative quantity (with a minus sign).
EVANGELICAL CATHOLICS. This term is used here to describe persons who are affiliated to either the United Church or the Hahalis Welfare Society, but who in government censuses are regarded as, or profess to be, Roman Catholics.
MELANESIAN INDIGENOUS. Among the over 9 cargo cults in this area, some have been direct secessions from Western mission-related churches and have had enough quasi- or semi-Christian elements to be enumerated as Christian movements

(in this case, the Hahalis Welfare Society, and Friday Religion).
NON-RELIGIOUS. Europeans, and a few Chinese.
TRIBAL RELIGIONISTS. Animists following traditional tribal religion, combined with modern non-Christian nativistic or syncretistic revitalization movements termed cargo cults. O these at least 4 have arisen on Bougainville and 5 on Buka, since the first around 1910 on Buka. Other well-known ones have included in 1931 prophet Pako with 5,000 followers, and in 1934 prophet Sanop (on Buka).

**NON-CHRISTIAN RELIGIONS. Traditional religions** continue to exert an influence in the Northern Solomons as in the Solomon Islands and Papua New Guinea. As with the other areas, non-Christian cargo cults have also developed and played an important role in the islands; there have been 4 on Bougainville and 5 on Buka.

## CHRISTIANITY

CATHOLIC CHURCH. Catholicism has been represented in the Northern Solomons since the year 1900 and is now by far the principal religion of the territory. The diocese of Bougainville which continues to form part of the archdiocese of Rabaul in Papua New Guinea is at present served by 5 national and 34 expatriate priests, as well as brothers and sisters who are also predominantly expatriate.

PROTESTANT CHURCHES. Two Protestant churches are active. The United Church has its centre in Papua New Guinea and traces its origin to both New Zealand Methodists and native Christians from other Pacific islands. Tongan and Fijian missionaries are still at work there, although the church is controlled by local personnel. The other Protestants are Seventh-day Adventists, a more recent arrival (1929) but still with substantial membership.

OTHER CHURCHES. The Hahalis Welfare Society is a syncretistic sect formed among Catholic and Methodist Buka villagers in 1957, with a mixture of Christian elements combined with traditional and cargo cult emphases. Friday Religion is an ex-Catholic movement. There is also a small community of Jehovah's Witnesses.

**CHURCH AND STATE.** The Northern Solomons is a secular territory strongly influenced by Christianity, especially Catholicism. The Catholic Church and its bishops are known to have played a significant role in the move towards secession and the declaration in 1975 of independence for the Northern Solomons from Papua New Guinea.

**INTERDENOMINATIONAL ORGANIZATIONS.** The Bougainville Inter-Church Council (BICC), which had formerly been the Kieta Inter-Church Council, has 2 members, the Catholic and United Churches. The BICC is affiliated with the Melanesian Council of Churches with its headquarters in Port Moresby, Papua New Guinea.

## BIBLIOGRAPHY

'Comparative analysis of nativistic movements', chapter 14 in A.R. Tippett, *Solomon Islands Christianity: a study in growth and obstruction* (New York: Friendship Press, 1967), p. 201–216.
'Friday Religion', Brother H. Sipari. Kieta, Catholic Education Office, 1976.
'Le "cargo cult" à Bougainville', M. Lenormand, *Etudes mélanésiennes*, NS No 4 (juillet 1949), 82–83.
'Sorcellerie et civilisation européenne aux Iles Salomon', P. O'Reilly, in *La sorcellerie dans les pays de mission*, Compte rendu de la XIVe Semaine de Missiologie de Louvain 1936 (Brussels: Desclee de Brouwer, 1937), p. 142–156. (Account of an unsuccessful revolution in Buka).
'The continuity of the cults: Buka', in P. Worsley, *The trumpet shall sound: a study of cargo cults in Melanesia* (New York: Schocken, 1968), p. 114–122.
'The Hahalis Welfare Society', H. Griffin, in G.W. Trompf, ed, *Melanesian and Judaeo-Christian traditions* (Port Moresby: University of PNG, 1976), p. 38f.
'The Hahalis Welfare Society of Buka'. M.R. Rimoldi. Dissertation, Australian National University, 1971.
*The United Church in Papua, New Guinea and the Solomon Islands: The development of an indigenous church.* R.G. Williams. Rabaul: Trinity Press, 1972. 320 p.

### TABLE 2. ORGANIZED CHURCHES AND DENOMINATIONS IN THE NORTHERN SOLOMONS

| Official name 1 | Begun 2 | Type 3 | Counc 4 | Congs 5 | Adults 6 | Affiliated 7 | Names, notes, and other statistics (see Codebook) 8 |
|---|---|---|---|---|---|---|---|
| **Catholic Church: D Bougainville** | 1900 | R Lat | P...Q | 34 | 39,100 | 66,230 | Under M Rabaul. M=SM. Copper mines. C=1+3+3. 5n,34x,42m,87w,1p,P=54%,2601Yy,286z. |
| Friday Religion | 1958 | I pen | ..... | | 300 | 500 | Split ex RCC. HQ Pontana, in mountains. 6 Laws. Catholic liturgy. |
| Hahalis Welfare Society | 1957 | I mar | ..... | | 2,700 | 4,500 | Syncretistic cargo cult ex RCC, Methodists. Began at Hahalis (Buka). Baby gardens. |
| Jehovah's Witnesses | 1969 | M Jeh | x,.... | 1 | 20 | 100 | *Watch Tower. IBSA.* Rapid expansion after first arrival in 1969. |
| Seventh-day Adventist Church | 1929 | P Adv | x,.... | 23 | 2,018 | 3,226 | *Bougainville Mission.* HQ Kastiorita, Inus. Highly organized. 3n,1x,4m,6w,4f. |
| United Ch in PNG & the Solomon Is | 1922 | P uni | VWP,K | 60 | 3,026 | 7,500 | *Bougainville Region.* Bishop a Tongan. M=MMB(NZ). 6 Circuits. 10n,5x,41m,3w,4f. |
| Other Protestant denominations | | P | ..... | | 200 | 500 | Including Baptists in Kieta, and Campaigners for Christ (Everyman's Hut). |
| Doubly-affiliated (duplication)(1970) | | | | | −3,900 | −6,630 | Persons claimed as affiliated by both United Church, Catholic Church, and Hahalis. |
| **Total affiliated (mid-1970)** | | | | 170 | 43,464 | 75,926 | Total denominations (1970) . . . 8. |
| **Total affiliated (mid-1975)** | | | | 175 | 48,900 | 85,500 | Total denominations (1975) . . . 8. |
| **Total affiliated (mid-1980)** | | | | 180 | 55,500 | 96,900 | Total denominations (1980) . . . 9. |

NOTES ON TABLE ABOVE
COLUMNS: for meanings and CODES (cols. 1, 3, 4, 8): see Codebook (Part 6). Column 1: Boldface type = church with over 10% of country's affiliated Christians.
NATIONAL COUNCILS (Column 4, 5th letter).
 K = Bougainville Inter-Church Council (BICC) (formerly Kieta Inter-Church Council, in relation with Melanesian Council of Churches).
 Q = Bishops' Conference of Papua New Guinea & the Solomon Islands, also member of BICC.

PEOPLES (ethnolinguistic). Christians: 70.0% Solomoni Papuan, 29.0% Solomoni Melanesian, 1.0% White (Anglo-Australian, European).

COUNTRY-WIDE TOTALS
EVANGELIZATION (see Part 5). 1900: 0%. 1970: 100%. 1980: 100%. *Mass evangelism.* 1972, Ralph Bell Evangelistic Crusade, in Kieta, supported by all churches.
FOREIGN MISSIONARIES AND PERSONNEL (aliens from abroad) (1973). Total 180. *From Western world.* 160: 150 Roman Catholics, 10 Protestants. *From Third World.* 20: about 10 Roman Catholics, 10 Protestants from Tonga, Fiji, Solomon Islands.
INSTITUTIONS (church-operated) (1973). Total about 20, including 13 medical centres (12 hospitals).
PERIODICALS. 3 titles.
PERSONNEL. About 624 (444 national (including 363 RC catechists), 180 foreign).

SCRIPTURE DISTRIBUTION (1975). Annual totals: 300 Bibles (subsidized), 400 NTs (subsidized), 2,000 UBS portions, 2,000 UBS selections.
SERVICE AGENCIES. About 4, including MAF.

ADDITIONAL DATA ON CHURCHES
CATHOLIC CHURCH. *Lay missionaries.* (1975) 13. *Catechists.* (1975) 363. *Seminarians.* (1975) 15.
 *Catholic organizations.* The diocese is part of the Bishops' Conference of Papua New Guinea & the Solomon Islands. The Catholic Church sponsors 91 schools (10,101 pupils), 12 hospitals (521 beds) and one leprosarium (31 patients).

# NORWAY

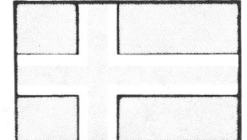

## SECULAR DATA

STATE. Official name: The Kingdom of Norway (Kongeriket Norge). Adjective of nationality: Norwegian.
Flag (shown above right): Blue Latin cross bordered in white on red field.
Area: 324,219 sq.km. (125,182 sq.miles). Agricultural land: 2.8%.
Government: Constitutional monarchy, since AD 900 (1319 united with Sweden, 1905 Independence from Sweden).
Legislature: Storting, 155 members.
Official language: Norwegian (*Norsk*).
Chief cities: capital Oslo 645,410 (1970), Bergen 182,270, Trondheim 112,100.
Political divisions: 19 Counties (fylker), and 47 Urban Districts (by-kommuner) and 396 Rural Districts (herredskommuner).
Armed forces (1976): Total 39,000 regular (25,000 conscripts): army 20,000, navy 9,000, air force 10,000 (131 combat aircraft). Reserves: 170,000.
Foreign forces (1973): 250 USA troops.
Dependencies (Norwegian Overseas Areas): Bouvet Island, Peter I Island, Queen Maud Land, Svalbard and Jan Mayen Islands.

DEMOGRAPHY. Population: 3,874,133 (census of 1.IX.1970. For 1970–2000 (UN), see last row of Table I). Population density (1975): 12/sq.km. (32/sq.mile). Under 15 years: 26%. Growth rate (1975–80): 0.56% per year (births 1.62%, deaths −1.06%). Life expectancy (1975–80): 74.6 years. Household size: 2.9 persons.
Major languages: Norwegian (Bokmal (urban) and Nynorsk (rural) dialects), Lapp, Swedish, Finnish, Danish, English, German.
Urban dwellers (1970): 42.5%. Urban growth rate (1950–70): 2.3% per year.
Labour force: 42%.
Refugees (1977): About 3,000 from Eastern Europe.
Tourists (1972): 4,345,500.

ETHNOLINGUISTIC GROUPS: 97.7% Norwegian, 0.6% Lapp (22,000), 0.5% Swedish, 0.3% Finnish, 0.3% Danish, 0.2% USA White, 0.1% British, 0.1% German, Gypsy, Jewish.

MONEY (1977). Monetary unit: krone (= 100 ore); US$1 = NKr 5.23.
National income per person: US$4,912. Average annual family income: US$14,245.

Inflation: (1970–74) 7.6% per year (1975: consumer price index 161), (1978) 8.3% per year.
Cost of living in capital (1976): index 164 (Washington DC=100). Daily cost of living: US$51.

HEALTH. Hospitals: 835 (52,763 beds). Doctors: 5,995. Blind: 4,000. Psychotics: 40,000. Criminals: 13,384.

EDUCATION. Adult literacy: 100%. Education rate: 57%. Schools: 2,996. Universities: 4.

LITERATURE. Annual new book titles (1973): 5,694. Periodicals: 3,573. Scientific journals: 240. Newspapers: 79 dailies, 80 non-daily.

COMMUNICATION (per 1,000 people). Phones: 330. Radios: 317. TV sets: 249. Daily newspaper circulation: 390 copies.

**Church of Norway.** One of 30 remaining 11th-12th-century stave churches (made of timber with intricate carving), at Borgund, Sognefjord area, western Norway.

## TABLE 1. RELIGIOUS ADHERENTS IN NORWAY

| Year | 1900 | | mid-1970 | | Annual change, 1970–1980 | | | | mid-1975 | | mid-1980 | | 2000 | |
|---|---|---|---|---|---|---|---|---|---|---|---|---|---|---|
| Name | Adherents | % | Adherents | % | Natural | Conversion | Total | Rate | Adherents | % | Adherents | % | Adherents | % |
| Christians | 2,207,060 | 99.4 | 3,830,900 | 98.8 | 24,020 | −2,675 | 21,345 | 0.54 | 3,944,670 | 98.4 | 4,044,350 | 98.1 | 4,349,600 | 97.0 |
| professing | 2,207,060 | 99.4 | 3,830,900 | 98.8 | 24,020 | −2,675 | 21,345 | 0.54 | 3,944,670 | 98.4 | 4,044,350 | 98.1 | 4,349,600 | 97.0 |
| Protestants | 2,204,160 | 99.2 | 3,808,900 | 98.2 | 23,880 | −2,727 | 21.153 | 0.54 | 3,921,710 | 97.9 | 4,020,430 | 97.6 | 4,321,300 | 96.4 |
| Roman Catholics | 2,070 | 0.1 | 11,000 | 0.3 | 70 | 30 | 100 | 0.87 | 11,500 | 0.3 | 12,000 | 0.3 | 14,000 | 0.3 |
| Marginal Protestants | 500 | 0.0 | 8,000 | 0.2 | 52 | 48 | 100 | 1.18 | 8,500 | 0.2 | 9,000 | 0.2 | 11,000 | 0.2 |
| Anglicans | 230 | 0.0 | 2,000 | 0.1 | 12 | −2 | 10 | 0.49 | 2,050 | 0.1 | 2,100 | 0.1 | 2,500 | 0.1 |
| Orthodox | 0 | 0.0 | 600 | 0.0 | 4 | −2 | 2 | 0.33 | 610 | 0.0 | 620 | 0.0 | 700 | 0.0 |
| Catholics (non-Roman) | 100 | 0.0 | 400 | 0.0 | 2 | −22 | −20 | −6.67 | 300 | 0.0 | 200 | 0.0 | 100 | 0.0 |
| nominal | 6,700 | 0.3 | 15,500 | 0.4 | 97 | 3 | 100 | 0.63 | 16,000 | 0.4 | 16,500 | 0.4 | 31,000 | 0.7 |
| affiliated | 2,200,360 | 99.1 | 3,815,400 | 98.4 | 23,923 | −2,678 | 21,245 | 0.54 | 3,928,670 | 98.0 | 4,027,850 | 97.7 | 4,318,600 | 96.3 |
| doubly-affiliated | −9,310 | −0.4 | −222,044 | −5.7 | −1,413 | −683 | −2,096 | 0.90 | −232,000 | −5.8 | −243,000 | −5.9 | −273,000 | −6.1 |
| total practising | 2,090,340 | 95 | 3,052,320 | 80 | 19,138 | −2,142 | 16,996 | 0.54 | 3,142,940 | 80 | 3,222,280 | 80 | 3,239,000 | 75 |
| non-practising | 110,020 | 5 | 763,080 | 20 | 4,785 | −536 | 4,249 | 0.54 | 785,730 | 20 | 805,570 | 20 | 1,079,600 | 25 |
| Protestants | 2,207,000 | 99.4 | 4,010,827 | 103.5 | 25,168 | −2,110 | 23,058 | 0.56 | 4,132,810 | 103.1 | 4,241,400 | 102.9 | 4,555,500 | 101.6 |
| Evangelicals | 1,340,000 | 60.3 | 949,900 | 24.5 | 6,101 | 3,999 | 10,100 | 1.01 | 1,001,800 | 25.0 | 1,050,900 | 25.5 | 1,210,000 | 27.0 |
| Neo-pentecostals | 0 | 0.0 | 1,000 | 0.0 | 61 | 1,839 | 1,900 | 19.00 | 10,000 | 0.2 | 20,000 | 0.5 | 100,000 | 2.2 |
| Marginal Protestants | 500 | 0.0 | 13,283 | 0.3 | 85 | 87 | 172 | 1.23 | 14,000 | 0.3 | 15,000 | 0.4 | 19,000 | 0.4 |
| Roman Catholics | 2,070 | 0.1 | 10,059 | 0.3 | 64 | 30 | 94 | 0.90 | 10,500 | 0.3 | 11,000 | 0.3 | 13,000 | 0.3 |
| Anglicans | 0 | 0.0 | 2,000 | 0.1 | 12 | −2 | 10 | 0.49 | 2,050 | 0.1 | 2,100 | 0.1 | 2,500 | 0.1 |
| Catholics (non-Roman) | 100 | 0.0 | 875 | 0.0 | 5 | 0 | 5 | 0.61 | 900 | 0.0 | 930 | 0.0 | 1,100 | 0.0 |
| Orthodox | 0 | 0.0 | 400 | 0.0 | 2 | 0 | 2 | 0.49 | 410 | 0.0 | 420 | 0.0 | 500 | 0.0 |
| Non-religious | 12,300 | 0.6 | 29,400 | 0.8 | 240 | 1,670 | 1,910 | 4.87 | 39,200 | 1.0 | 48,500 | 1.2 | 86,000 | 1.9 |
| Atheists | 1,000 | 0.0 | 10,000 | 0.3 | 97 | 963 | 1,060 | 6.63 | 16,000 | 0.4 | 20,600 | 0.5 | 36,000 | 0.8 |
| Muslims | 0 | 0.0 | 4,000 | 0.1 | 25 | −5 | 20 | 0.49 | 4,100 | 0.1 | 4,200 | 0.1 | 4,400 | 0.1 |
| Ahmadis | 0 | 0.0 | 200 | 0.0 | 1 | 3 | 4 | 1.82 | 220 | 0.0 | 240 | 0.0 | 300 | 0.0 |
| Baha'is | 0 | 0.0 | 1,200 | 0.0 | 8 | 12 | 20 | 1.54 | 1,300 | 0.0 | 1,400 | 0.0 | 2,000 | 0.0 |
| Jews | 640 | 0.0 | 900 | 0.0 | 6 | −1 | 5 | 0.54 | 930 | 0.0 | 950 | 0.0 | 1,000 | 0.0 |
| Buddhists | 0 | 0.0 | 100 | 0.0 | 0 | 0 | 0 | 0.00 | 100 | 0.0 | 100 | 0.0 | 1,000 | 0.0 |
| Other religionists | 0 | 0.0 | 500 | 0.0 | 4 | 36 | 40 | 5.71 | 700 | 0.0 | 900 | 0.0 | 3,000 | 0.1 |
| Country's population | 2,221,000 | 100.0 | 3,877,000 | 100.0 | 24,400 | 0 | 24,400 | 0.61 | 4,007,000 | 100.0 | 4,121,000 | 100.0 | 4,483,000 | 100.0 |

COLUMNS, ROWS. For meanings and definitions, see Codebook (Part 6). Note that, by definition, total 'Christians' = professing + crypto-Christians, which also = affiliated + nominal Christians. Percentages may not always total exactly, due to rounding.
CENSUSES. 3.XII.1900 (not strictly a census, but a government-sponsored survey of dissenters): 99.3% Protestants (97.6% state church, 1.6% others), 0.6% non-religious, 0.1% Roman Catholics. 3.XII.1946 (de jure): 99.0% Protestants, 0.7% non-religious, 0.2% Roman Catholics. 1.XII.1950 (de jure): 99.1% Protestants, 0.7% non-religious, 0.1% Roman Catholics, 0.1% other religionists. 1.XI.1960 (de jure): 98.8% Protestants (96.3% state church), 0.8% non-religious, 0.2% Roman Catholics, 0.2% marginal Protestants. There was no similar religion question asked in the 1970 census, but church bodies were asked to submit figures of membership. Government estimates are therefore based on church returns and consist of statistics of both professing and affiliated, and also of adults only mixed with adults and children.
POLLS. Many public-opinion polls of religion have been taken since 1940 (Norsk Gallup, VC). Religious preference, February 1970: 99% Protestants, 1% non-religious. Results for practice are given below.

## NOTES ON RELIGIONS

AFFILIATED PROTESTANTS. The totals for 1970–2000 are each over 100% because large numbers of free church members are counted twice (i.e. also by the state church).
AHMADIS. Begun about 1960. Qadianis from Pakistan (Ahmadiya Muslim Mission), with a handful of Norwegian converts.
ATHEISTS. Norwegian Communist Party (Norges Kommunistiske Parti, NKP) (legal; independent in Sino-Soviet dispute):

membership (1970) 2,500, (1974) 5,000; Communist voters (election of X.1945) 176,535 (11.8% of all votes), (7.IX.1969) 22,520 (1% of all votes); declining. Among other atheistic organizations, the Human-Etisk Forbund (founded 1956; 800 members, 200 youth members) specifically aims to promote unbelief and since 1951 has provided an annual civic non-religious confirmation ceremony (200 youths each year).
BAHA'IS. Growth from 4 local spiritual assemblies (1964) to 7 (1973).
BUDDHISTS. With a Tibetan centre in Oslo, based on headquarters in Copenhagen.
DOUBLY-AFFILIATED. A large majority of members of Protestant free churches (especially the Salvation Army) are also regarded as members of the state church which therefore enumerates them all as such.
EVANGELICALS (see p. 71). Although there are many Evangelical free churches, the bulk of all Evangelicals remain within the state church. Experience of new birth. In a 1976 poll, 18% of all Norwegians (or 27% for all young people) considered themselves 'born-again Christians', which is usually regarded as one of the hallmarks of Evangelicalism. Conservative or anti-ecumenical attitudes are stronger in Norway than elsewhere in Scandinavia.
JEWS. Recognized since 1851. Most live in Oslo.
MUSLIMS. Mostly migrant labourers from the Balkans, Turkey and Pakistan, with a small Ahmadiya Mission (enumerated here under Muslims though declared non-Muslim by Pakistan). Muslims are found mostly in Oslo, aided by the Muslim Union of Oslo which has asked both for legal recognition and also for land for a mosque.
NEO-PENTECOSTALS. The total (1975) includes 1,000 lay charismatics and 15 clergy within the state church in 50 organized prayer groups, in a renewal which gathered momentum in 1971

and is now served by the Agape Society; and also about 4,000 in other non-Pentecostal Protestant churches. Total charismatic community including children, 10,000. The Inner Missions in the state church have tended to be anti-charismatic.
OTHER RELIGIONISTS. Including Rosicrucians (2 AMORC centres) and a growing number of cultists and followers of immigrant religions.
PRACTISING CHRISTIANS. In Norway there has never been a widespread tradition of weekly church attendance, mainly due to large distances of homes from churches in snowbound rural areas. However, home religion and radio/TV participation in services (over 50%) are still widespread. 96% of all children are baptized and 80% confirmed in the state church, and 85% of marriages and 95% of funerals are church services. Church attendance. (1948) 17% of population attended weekly. (1957) 0.5% several times a week, 2.2% every Sunday (attending Lutheran high mass), 16% several times a month, 2.0% occasionally, 76.0% never. 1964: 'Are you a practising religious believer?': 11% believe and practise, 29% believe but do not practise, 47% do not believe but some private practice (weddings), 12% neither believe nor practise, 1% opposed to all religions. May-June 1968: church attenders 14% of the population weekly, 8% fortnightly, 5% once every 3 weeks, 10% monthly, 38% once every 2 months, 25% less than annually or never. (1972) 63% attend once a year or more (8% every Sunday, 12% once every 2 weeks), 37% less than once a year or never. Roman Catholics. Weekly mass attenders 15% (low due to distance from a church building); total practising, 75%. Radio service listeners. (1953) 38% every Sunday, 14% every 2 weeks, 30% occasionally, 18% never. (1957) 42.0% every Sunday, 20.0% several times a month, 14.0% occasionally, 17.0% never. (1967) 32% of the population listen daily to either the 8.15 a.m. devotional or a later one.

## NON-CHRISTIAN RELIGIONS.

Islam was represented in Norway by about 4,000 Muslims in 1973, most of them in the capital city. In 1973 the Muslim Union of Oslo asked the city authorities for a plot of land on which to build a mosque, and they have also applied for recognition as a religious congregation.

**Judaism,** which has been accepted since 1851, had some 1,900 adherents in 1973, the majority of whom live in Oslo.

## CHRISTIANITY

PROTESTANT CHURCHES. Christianity was introduced about AD 900 in the region of the Oslofjord through the missionary activity of the Bremen-Hambourg archbishopric, but the greatest influence came from Norwegian kings of the 10th and 11th centuries (the first being Hakon the Good who reigned during 945–960) whose early Christian education took place in England. Resistance to Christianity gradually gave way both in Norway and among those who had established themselves on the islands of the North Atlantic, including Iceland and Greenland. This secular establishment of Christianity led to repeated conflicts between the Norwegian kings and the ecclesiastical authorities in Denmark, who were appointed by Rome to administer the whole of Scandinavia, conflicts which were heightened by the Danish and Swedish political domination of Norway. There was little hesitancy on the part of royalty, therefore, at the time of the Protestant Reformation, in establishing a state church system based on the Lutheran Confession. The evangelical fervour that characterized other European countries during this period did not appear in Norway until the middle of the 19th century. Leaders advocating church reform tended more to emigrate with their followers to America, contributing to the proliferation of Scandinavian Lutheran synods and missionary

societies in the USA.
Lay movements within the state church, leading ultimately to the establishment of free churches as well as a renewal of the Church of Norway, began with a layman and farmer, Hans Nielsen Hauge, at the beginning of the 19th century. After a personal experience of Christ, he began to preach and encouraged the formation of societies of believers, bound together by the Holy Spirit and practising their own fervent devotions while remaining loyal members of the Lutheran Church. In the middle of the century a second awakening took place reaching all social classes through the preaching of Giles Johnson, who also made use of lay evangelists. Small groups were organized throughout the country, frequently calling upon state church ministers to be their leaders. Out of this movement grew the Luther Foundation in 1868, with a strong mission emphasis, which in 1891 became the Lutheran Inner Mission Society (Indremisjon). A similar society developed in western Norway as a result of emigrants returning from America and Britain. In 1891 also the Norwegian Lutheran Mission Society was created, after a revival in 1880–90, to train young people for foreign service. The 20th century has not witnessed renewal movements of comparable intensity to those which characterized the earlier period. Nevertheless, the Church of Norway continues to be a dominant force in Norwegian life.
As compared with other Western nations, membership (96% of the total population) and orthodox religious belief remain high in the Church of Norway, while attendance at weekly worship services is low (about 3%). The origin of this paradox can be traced to patterns established early in Norwegian history, when the population was more scattered and communications difficult or almost non-existent, in which situation habitual churchgoing never developed on a wide scale. Popular religious feeling and practice

is therefore evidenced today in the high level of listener attendance to religious radio broadcasts. Recent polls show that 50% of the population are regular listeners to broadcasts of Sunday High Mass from the state church, with only 18% stating that they 'never listen'. In addition, one-third of the nation's population tunes in to the daily morning radio devotional programmes. Other indications of religious interest are the fact that 96% of all members bring their children to the state church for baptism, 80% of the children are later confirmed, 85% are married in church and 95% are buried with church rites. Moreover, 84% of state church parents claim to teach their children evening prayers, and 50% themselves pray daily. One-third affirm that they have read the Bible recently (the Bible still remains a best-seller) and 95% support programmes of religious education in schools.
When the church became Lutheran in 1537, it retained a diocesan and parish structure basically identical with the pre-reformation Catholic organization, which explains its present high church tradition evidenced in use of vestments and the like. Nevertheless, the Church of Norway defines itself in accordance with the constitution of 1814 as Evangelical Lutheran based on the Apostles' Creed, the Augustana Confession and Luther's Little Catechism. During the German occupation of Norway in World War II, the church was made independent of the state. When its previous relationship with the state was restored after the war, a number of democratic policies were introduced in church administration. At present there are 10 bishoprics subdivided into 91 deaneries, 594 parishes and 1,078 congregational districts. There are about 1,300 churches and chapels served by 1,000 clergy, with since 1961 a small number of women priests. From the 1950s onward, Norway has experienced the richest period of church building in the

country's history, due to large-scale population movements related to new industries. From 1945–65 alone, 150 new churches were built, including several ultra-modern cathedrals.

The first free churches established in Norway owed their origin to foreign, though Scandinavian, influences. A Danish missionary founded a Norwegian Baptist church in 1850, and by 1879 some 18 separate congregations had joined together to form the Baptist Union. Methodism came to Norway in 1853 through the instrumentality among others of a returned Norwegian seaman who was converted and ordained in the USA. With 45 congregations in

abating, and the number of active Norwegian-born priests (16, in 1973) is high in relation to the number of Catholics.

Compared with Denmark and Sweden, there are few migrant workers in Norway. In 1971, they numbered 19,472, 8,000 being from other Scandinavian countries, and only 2,000 from Catholic nations in Europe. In addition, there are some 5,000 seamen from Spain and Portugal serving on Norwegian ships which occasionally visit Norway, and who are not registered in Norwegian Catholic parishes.

About 15% of Catholics participate in Sunday

ably satisfactory arrangement under the circumstances, but many think that these circumstances are changing and that formal church autonomy should be introduced within the next 20 years. In accordance with this view a Royal Commission was appointed in 1970 to evaluate the present system. Meanwhile a number of national church service agencies have been established on a voluntary basis, including the Norwegian Parish Institute (Norsk Menighetinstitutt) to serve pastoral interests at the parish level, the Diaconal Service Council (Diakonirad for den Norske Kirke) to co-ordinate welfare work, and the Christian Institute for Project Aid (Kristen

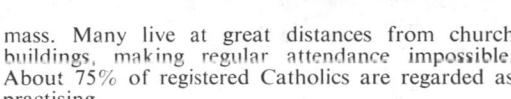

**Church of Norway.** *Left.* Lomskyrkja, old stave church at Lom, dating from 1270, with (*Centre*) interior. *Right.* Cathedral of Diocese of Nidaros, in Trondheim; outstanding example of Gothic style in full flowering.

1905, Norway's Methodism has grown to be the largest Methodist body in Scandinavia.

Other free churches of Lutheran tradition grew out of the renewal within the state church at the end of the 19th century; these included the Evangelical Lutheran Free Church and the Mission Convenant Church. The latter emerged in 1884, though its roots went back to 1856, following the example of the Swedish Bible Readers' movement which had broken ties with the Swedish state church in 1878. These churches wanted all people to be loyal Lutherans but free-thinking in 'non-essential' doctrines. In the beginning, emphasis was placed on Christ as personal Saviour and membership in the state church was retained, but gradually they emerged as separate and exclusive denominations.

Scandinavian Pentecostalism began in Norway when a former Methodist pastor, on a money-raising trip to the USA, came under Pentecostal influence. His meetings in Oslo in 1906 drew large crowds, which disturbed the Methodist Conference and forced his resignation from it. Norwegian Pentecostalism has subsequently grown steadily, from 8,000 adult members in 1930, to 30,000 in 1950, 34,100 in 1960, and 37,500 in 1971. For many years now, Pentecostals, with the Salvation Army, still ranked highest in membership among non-established religious bodies.

Over the last decade, the main free churches have shown considerable growth, except for the Mission Convenant Church, which has declined by 600 members.

CATHOLIC CHURCH. The first Roman Catholic parish was organized in 1842, after the liberalization of the state church system had begun. By 1890 the number of Catholics had reached a thousand, and by 1972 they still represent only 0.3% of the population. The Catholic community consists of 15% converts from other churches, 20% foreign-born immigrants, and 65% native-born Catholics, most of the latter being still minors and children of mixed marriages. Because of its small numbers, its high immigrant membership and its foreign-born clergy (75% of the total) and expatriate personnel (90% of the total), the Catholic Church in Norway has not played an important role in national life. Nevertheless there are signs of change. The widespread prejudice which for so long tended to isolate Catholics is

mass. Many live at great distances from church buildings, making regular attendance impossible. About 75% of registered Catholics are regarded as practising.

In 1977 Norway was transferred from the jurisdiction of Propaganda to that of the Congregation for Bishops.

**CHURCH AND STATE.** A state church system was introduced in 1537 with a royal decree that made the king of Denmark and Norway the head of the church on the basis of the Lutheran Confession. When Norway declared its independence from Denmark in 1814, its constitution specified 'the Evangelical-Lutheran Religion' as the 'official Religion of the State' (Article 2). This provision is still preserved, while various other constitutional terms have been eliminated, including the ban against 'monkish Priests, Jesuits and Jews'. Article 4 states that the king must profess and uphold the state religion, and article 12 rules that at least half the king's cabinet must do the same.

The principal law governing church structure (Norske Kirkes Ordning) dates from 29 April 1953, and prescribes the elements of a self-governing structure: pastors (*sogneprest*), elected parish councils responsible for administration, bishops and diocesan councils. On the national level, the law recognizes the existence of a regular bishops' meeting and a meeting every 4 years of all diocesan councils. A Central Council of Diocesan Councils (Bispedömmeradenes Fellesrad) was established by law in 1969. The real power in church affairs, including the appointment of ministers and bishops and control over finance, is still vested in the government through the Ministry of Church Affairs and Education (Kongelige Kirke- og Undervisningsdepartement) which occupies itself mainly with the state church and public education.

Following the elections of 1973, parliament had for the first time 2 Catholic deputies, one of whom was elected president of the parliamentary Commission for Church Affairs and Education. This election provoked unrest, given the fact that the commission is responsible for preparing a new canon law for the Lutheran state church.

The state church system is at present widely debated. Most people view it as in practice a reason-

Innsats for Ulöste Oppgaver) to finance new church projects.

The financial needs of the state church are provided for partly by the state, with the salaries of state-appointed clergy as its main item; partly by the 440 municipalities which build churches, appoint and pay minor church officials, and provide clergy housing; and also partly by voluntary collections among church members.

The principle that denominations outside the state church system should receive a proportional amount of public money was not recognized until the promulgation of the law of 13 June 1969 (Trudomssamfunn og Ymist Anna, Article 19) which regulates relations between the state and non-established denominations, especially in that which concerns the state budget. In 1970 denominations were subsidized by a small sum per capita, although no system has yet been introduced for sharing out the larger sums involved in municipal church budgets.

Other salient points of the 1969 law are: (1) complete freedom of religion is assured for all religions, Christian and non-Christian; (2) religious bodies must register with the county where their central authority or administration is situated; (3) anyone of 15 years or over may freely join or leave any religious body; (4) it is forbidden for persons under 20 to take perpetually-binding religious vows; (5) children born in wedlock belong to the religion of their parents, but if the parents belong to different bodies, they must choose after birth to which group the child shall belong; (6) children born out of wedlock follow the religion of the mother; and (7) none is permitted to belong to more than one religious body at the same time.

**INTERDENOMINATIONAL ORGANIZATIONS.** Conservative and anti-ecumenical forces are stronger in Norway than in most other Scandinavian countries, which accounts for the fact that there is no national ecumenical council of churches in the country. Pentecostal opposition to a recent proposal to establish such a council proved decisive. Of note also was the refusal of the Norwegian Missionary Council (Norsk Misjonsrad), founded in 1921, to join the CWME at the time of merger in 1961 of the International Missionary Council with the World Council of Churches. Nevertheless, the Church of

Norway is a member of both the Lutheran World Federation and the WCC, and Methodists are also members of the WCC through their association with American Methodism. The Free Church Council (Norsk Frikirkerad) groups non-established Protestant denominations and the Norwegian Evangelical Alliance is also active. A more inclusive ecumenical collaboration exists at the parish level in conjunction with the Week of Prayer for Christian Unity.

The Centre for Ecumenical Theology (Centrum for Okumenisk Teologi) is an interdenominational research institute, founded in 1967, where theologians of different denominations including Catholics work together to promote spiritual and social ecumenism. Emphasis is given to 'church in the world' dialogue and youth training. There is an Ecumenical Institute attached to the University of Oslo; and the Egede Institute (Egede Instituttet), which is affiliated to the International Association for Mission Studies, is also found in Oslo.

**BROADCASTING.** The state Norwegian Broadcasting Company (NRK) has a monopoly on all radio and TV transmission in the country, including an extensive and popular religious broadcasting schedule. A daily early morning devotional programme is heard by 10% of Norway's 3 million adults, while a later daily devotional has an audience of 15–25% of the adult population. Other programmes include a Sunday morning church service (15–20%), religious music on Wednesday afternoon (20%) and a religious news magazine on Thursday (5%). In 1973 there were 250 hours of religious programming on radio, or 4.2% of the total output. The TV schedule includes one religious programme on Sunday afternoon (documentary, interviews, etc), with an audience of 15–25% of the adult population, and a monthly Sunday morning church service (10–15%). In 1973 religious programmes accounted for 42 hours of TV time, or 1.7% of the total output. All broadcasts are prepared by the NRK which maintains good relations with the churches, while the Norwegian Christian Radio and Television Association acts as a watch-dog over the NRK.

From abroad Trans World Radio (Monaco) beams a 30-minute daily programme in Norwegian for a major Protestant service known as Radio Norea, whose production studios and headquarters are in Oslo. Considerable audience research has been done, and the programmes have a widespread appeal in Norway. A Catholic programme in Norwegian is broadcast from Radio Vatican for 15 minutes weekly.

## BIBLIOGRAPHY


*Arbok for den Norske Kirke, 1970*. Oslo: Forlaget Land og Kirke, 1970.

*Den Norske Kirke*. I. Lonning et al. Oslo: Studier i Norge, 1966. 64p.

'Norway', E.D. Vogt, in H. Mol (ed), *Western religion* (The Hague: Mouton, 1972), p.381–401.

*Oversikt over den Katolske Kirke i Norden, 1971*. Oslo: Nordiske Bispekonferanse, 1971.

'Religious change in eleventh-century Norway', P. Hassing, *Missiology*, III, 4 (October, 1975), 17p.

*The Catholic Church in the North*. E.D. Vogt. Bergen, 1962.

'The Church in Norway', O. Lang, in *Norway year book 1967* (Oslo, 1967), 4p.

'The witness of the church of Norway', G. Ostenstad, *International review of mission*, LXII, 245 (January, 1973), 43–50.


TABLE 2. ORGANIZED CHURCHES AND DENOMINATIONS IN NORWAY

| Official name 1 | Begun 2 | Type 3 | Counc 4 | Congs 5 | Adults 6 | Affiliated 7 | Names, notes, and other statistics (see Codebook) 8 |
|---|---|---|---|---|---|---|---|
| Apostolic Church | | P PeA | Z.... | 2 | 50 | 100 | *Apostolske Kirke*. M=Apostolic Ch of Great Britain(UK). Pentecostals. |
| Apostolic Faith | | P Pe3 | x.... | 7 | 200 | 500 | *Apostoliske Tro*. M=AFM(Portland,Oregon,USA). Holiness Pentecostals. HQ Stavanger. |
| Catholic Apostolic Church | c1880 | C CAp | x.... | | 200 | 375 | *Katolsk Apostolisk Menighet*. Remnant of Irvingite church from Britain. Dying out. |
| Catholic Church in Norway: | 1842 | R Lat | B.BQ. | 28 | 7,400 | 10,059 | *Romersk Katolske Kirke*. 20% immigrants. C=8+0+9. 50z. 16n,51x,2m,458w,224Yy. |
| D Oslo | 1868 | R Lat | Bs | 19 | 6,700 | 9,127 | *Oslo Katolske Bispedömme*. 500 aliens (Italians). P=43%. 15 37 0 390 200 |
| VA Central Norway | 1931 | R Lat | Bsscc | 5 | 400 | 579 | *Apostoliske Vikariat Mellom-Norge*. HQ Trondheim. P=65%. 1 7 0 40 14 |
| VA Northern Norway | 1931 | R Lat | Bmaf | 4 | 300 | 353 | Nord-Norge. Includes Svalbard & Jan Mayen Is. HQ Tromso. 0 7 2 28 10 |
| Christadelphian Ecclesias | 1955 | P Ade | x.... | 2 | 50 | 100 | *Christadelphian Bible Mission*. 2 ecclesias (churches) in Bergen. |
| Christian Brethren | c1880 | P CBr | x.... | 3 | 150 | 300 | *Plymouth Brethren. Open Brethren. Gospel Halls*. Links with UK Brethren. |
| Church of Christ, Scientist | | M Sci | x.... | 1 | 134 | 200 | *Christian Science*. M=CCS(Boston,USA). First Church, Oslo. Many expatriates. 2w. |
| Church of England (J Fulham) | c1850 | A plu | awc.. | 14 | 1,000 | 2,000 | English-speaking Anglican chaplaincies, including 4 seasonal and 7 occasional. 1x. |
| Ch of Jesus C of Latter-day Saints | 1850 | M LdS | x.... | | 2,000 | 3,083 | *Jesu Kristi Kirke av Siste Dagers Hellige. Mormoner*. M=CJCLdS(USA). 60f,G=3.2%pa. |
| **Church of Norway:** | c 900 | P Lut | LWX.e | 1,300 | 2,768,000 | 3,740,000 | *Norske Kirke*. 1536, reformed & established. 4p,3s(650). 1044n,586b,W=10%,65012Yy. |
| D Oslo | c1075 | P Lut | L | 130 | 370,000 | 500,000 | *Oslo Bispedömme*. Primatial see. Very small area. 120 47 9 7275 |
| D Agder | 1682 | P Lut | L | 143 | 255,000 | 345,000 | HQ Kristiansand. Southern part of Norway. 108 141 16 5699 |
| D Bjorgvin (Bergen) | c1100 | P Lut | L | 212 | 442,000 | 597,000 | HQ Bergen. Most westerly diocese. 162 207 14 10638 |
| D Borg | 1968 | P Lut | L | 124 | 318,000 | 430,000 | HQ Fredrikstad. Formerly in D Oslo. Extreme southeast. 95 62 10 6993 |
| D Hamar | 1864 | P Lut | L | 135 | 229,000 | 309,000 | HQ Hamar. Separatist charismatic youth movement. 100 115 8 5922 |
| D Nidaros | 1152 | P Lut | L | 170 | 317,000 | 428,000 | AD 1152, Nidaros-Trondheim created out of AD Lund. 132 180 10 8523 |
| D Nord-Halogaland | 1803 | P Lut | L | 79 | 165,000 | 223,000 | HQ Tromasö. Extreme north of country, & Arctic Circle. 62 140 10 4495 |
| D Sör-Halogaland | 1952 | P Lut | L | 93 | 193,000 | 261,000 | HQ Bodö. 1946, D Halogaland divided (N, S). 63 62 10 4525 |
| D Stavanger | 1925 | P Lut | L | 90 | 236,000 | 319,000 | HQ Stavanger. Extreme southwest. 72 47 11 5299 |
| D Tunsberg | 1948 | P Lut | L | 124 | 243,000 | 328,000 | HQ Tönsberg. Between Oslo and Agder dioceses. 90 56 11 5643 |
| Churches of Christ | | P Dis | x.... | 2 | 50 | 100 | *Kristi Kirke*. M=CC(Non-Instrumental) (USA). In Oslo, Bergen. Mainly Americans. |
| Congregation of God at Vegardshei | | P Lut | ..... | | 1,519 | 2,000 | *Guds Menighet pa Vegardshei*. Ex Ch of Norway; Old Lutheran, old Bible versions. |
| Congregation of Jesus Christ | 1880 | P Dis | ..... | | 598 | 1,000 | *Kristi Menighet. Disciples of Christ*. Conservative. From USA via Denmark. |
| Evangelical Lutheran Church Community | 1871 | P Lut | ..... | | 2,700 | 3,618 | *Evangelisk-Lutherske Kirkesamfunn*. Conservative schism ex Church of Norway. |
| Evangelical Lutheran Free Church of N | 1877 | P Lut | ..D.e | 64 | 6,753 | 19,109 | *Evangelisk Lutherske Frikirke i Norge*. Ex Ch of Norway. 69n,G=–0.3%pa,1s(6),151Yy. |
| Free Evangelical Society | c1895 | P Con | ..D.e | | 4,000 | 6,000 | Schism ex Mission Covenant Ch of Norway. 1967, pentecostal trends emerge. |
| Free Pentecostal Friends | 1959 | P Pe4 | ..... | | 1,000 | 2,000 | *Frie Pinsevenner*. Schism ex Maranatha Revival Ch & Pentecostal Revival of Norway. |
| Greek Orthodox Church (D Swedia) | | O Gre | Cwc.. | 1 | 60 | 400 | *Gresk-Ortodokse Kirke*. Under jurisdiction of EP Constantinople. Growing. |
| Jehovah's Witnesses | 1891 | M Jeh | x.... | 158 | 5,857 | 10,000 | *Jehovas Vitner. Watch Tower*. Active witnessing under way by 1926. HQ Oslo 2. 546Y. |
| Maranatha Revival Church | c1955 | P Pe4 | x.... | | 200 | 500 | Schism from Pentecostal Revival of Norway, similar to that in Sweden. |
| Methodist Church of Norway | 1853 | P Met | Vwx.x | 98 | 17,702 | 30,000 | *Norway Annual Conf*, NEurope CC, UMC(USA). 75n,1x,21f,G=–0.1%pa,3H,1j,1s,139Yy. |
| Mission Covenant Church of Norway | 1856 | P Con | K...C | 120 | 7,453 | 11,000 | *Norske Misjonsforbund*. Declining slowly. HQ Oslo 1. 83n,1p,1s(43),W=70%. |
| New Apostolic Church | | C CAp | x.... | | 300 | 500 | *NAC*. Schism ex Catholic Apostolic Ch. World HQ Dortmund (Germany). Germans. |
| Norwegian Baptist Union | 1850 | P Bap | T.D.x | 200 | 6,551 | 12,300 | *Norske Baptistsamfunn*. Africa missions. Declining. 61n,24x,G=–0.4%pa,1s,W=50%,127Y. |
| Norwegian Pentecostal Assemblies | 1906 | P Pe2 | Z.D.x | 770 | 36,105 | 70,000 | *Pinsebevegelsen/Pente Revival of N. Filadelfia*. NPY. 250n,G=2.0%pa,1j,3p,2s,3000Y. |
| Religious Society of Friends | 1818 | P Qua | Q...C | 4 | 119 | 200 | *Vennenes Samfunn* (*Kvekerne*). *Quakers*. In 1900, 175 adherents. G=2.9%pa,W=34%. |
| Salvation Army | 1888 | P Sal | xwx.x | 1,200 | 44,836 | 100,000 | *Frelsesarméen. Norway & Iceland Terr*. 6 Divs. 70 institutions. 518n,G=–2.0%pa,1s. |
| Seventh-day Adventist Church | 1887 | P Adv | x.... | 68 | 5,413 | 10,000 | *Adventistsamfunnet*. East & North & West Norway Confs. 24nx,75mw,4H,1j,1r,187Y. |
| Other Protestant denominations | | P | ..... | | 1,000 | 2,000 | Total about 15 (see list below). |
| Doubly-affiliated (duplication) (1970) | | | | | –164,300 | –222,044 | Salvation Army and other Free church members who retain state church membership. |
| **Total affiliated (mid-1970)** | | | | **4,260** | **2,757,100** | **3,815,400** | **Total denominations (1970) . . . 41.** |
| **Total affiliated (mid-1975)** | | | | **4,300** | **2,839,000** | **3,928,670** | **Total denominations (1975) . . . 43.** |
| **Total affiliated (mid-1980)** | | | | **4,340** | **2,910,600** | **4,027,850** | **Total denominations (1980) . . . 45.** |

NOTES ON TABLE ABOVE

COLUMNS: for meanings and CODES (cols. 1, 3, 4, 8) see Codebook (Part 6). Column 1: **Boldface type** = church with over 10% of country's affiliated Christians.

NATIONAL COUNCILS (Column 4, 5th letter).

C = Norwegian Free Church Council (NFCC) (Norske Frikirkerad).

e = Norwegian Evangelical Alliance (NEA) (Evangeliske Allianse i Norge) (founded about 1850; affiliated to EAA but not to WEF).

x = member of both NFCC and NEA.

OTHER PROTESTANT DENOMINATIONS. These smaller bodies include: Baptist Bible Fellowship International (1971), Baptist Missionary Association of America, Christian Society (Kristensamfunnet), Ch of the Brethren (1972), Evangelical Assembly (Evangeliske Forsamling), Exclusive Brethren (Raven-Taylor), Gypsy Ev Movement (France, Switzerland), World-Wide Missions.

OTHER MARGINAL BODIES. The General Ch of the New Jerusalem has a Circle in Oslo.

**PEOPLES** (ethnolinguistic). Christians: 97.7% Norwegian, 0.6% Lapp, 0.5% Swedish, 0.3% Finnish, 0.3% Danish, 0.2% USA White, 0.1% British, 0.1% German, Gypsy.

COUNTRY-WIDE TOTALS

EVANGELIZATION (see Part 5). 1900: 100%. 1970: 100%. 1980: 100%. *Mass evangelism*. Among recent campaigns: frequent tent campaigns sponsored by Conservative Evangelical groups within the Church of Norway; Billy Graham campaigns in 1955 in Oslo (77,000 attenders, 1,000 enquirers), and the Euro '70 TV Crusade in 1970 televised from Dortmund (Germany) to 10 Norwegian cities; and in 1978, Skandia '78 on radio/TV. *Radiophonic evangelism*. Annual listeners' letters (1975): 2,050 TWR, 358 HCJB, RVOG, et alia. *Literature evangelism*. 90% of all Lapp homes in Finmark in the north have been reached by Every Home Crusade distribution in 1975.

FOREIGN MISSIONARIES AND PERSONNEL (nationals serving abroad) (1974). Total 1,458: 1,428 Protestants (increase from 284 in 1920, to 385 (1933), 658 (1938), 746 (1948), 672 (1951), 849 (1960), 1,014 (1965), and 1,227 in 1971) in about 40 societies in 38 countries, about 20 Roman Catholics (5 in Sweden), about 10 marginal Protestants (Jehovah's Witnesses).

FOREIGN MISSIONARIES AND PERSONNEL (aliens from abroad) (1973). Total 599. *From Western world*. 597: 476 Roman Catholics, 60 Protestants (about 40 from Scandinavian countries, 14 in 8 USA societies, 6 in 3 UK societies), about 60 marginal Protestants (Mormons from USA), 1 Anglican. *From Third World*. About 2 Protestants.

INSTITUTIONS (church-operated) (1973). Total 70, including about 10 higher schools, 20 medical centres (hospitals), 5 presses, 1 religious community, 5 research centres, 10 seminaries (Protestant).

PERIODICALS. About 90 (9 Pentecostal, 5 Salvation Army, 4 SDA; many missionary periodicals).

PERSONNEL. About 3,059 (2,460 national, 599 foreign).

RELIGIOUS LIBRARIES. About 30.

SCRIPTURE DISTRIBUTION (1975). Annual totals: 47,995 Bibles (6% free, 84% subsidized, 10% commercial), 200,580 NTs (2% free, 93% subsidized, 5% commercial), 19,051 UBS portions. *Translations completed*. Portion: 2 languages since 1838. NT: 3 languages since 1819. Bible: 3 languages since 1834.

SERVICE AGENCIES. About 110, including CEF, IAMS, KFUK(YWCA), KFUM(YMCA), NBC, NEA, NFCC, NLM, NMS, NPY, SCM, SU, WLC(EHC), WSCF, WTMA, YFC.

ADDITIONAL DATA ON CHURCHES

CATHOLIC CHURCH IN NORWAY. *Annual baptisms*. (1972) 100% infants, no adults. *Priests*. 20 secular, 37 religious. *Brothers*. All expatriates. *Sisters*. 35 nationals (all in Oslo diocese), 423 expatriates (Dutch, German). *Catechists*. None; work is done by sisters. *Seminarians*. 3 (trained abroad). *Religious orders and congregations*. Priests: OSB, OCSO, OP, OFM, SJ, SM, SSCC, MSF. Sisters: St Joseph of Chambéry, St Francis Xavier, St Elizabeth, Dominican Sisters, St Charles Borromeo Sisters, and others. Most sisters are German or Dutch, running 21 hospitals and several schools.

*Catholic organizations*. The Catholic Church in Norway is represented on the Nordic (or Scandinavian) Bishops' Conference (Nordiske Bispekonferanse). There are no national or priests' councils, nor national organizations of religious personnel. There is however a Lay Council (Legmannsradet) for the diocese of Oslo, as well as rudimentary national Catholic associations for youth, students and women.

The Holy See has no diplomatic relations with Norway but is represented to the Catholic hierarchy by the Apostolic Delegation in Scandinavia based in Copenhagen, Denmark.

The most notable contribution of Catholics to national life is in the field of health. Numerous hospitals have been founded and developed since the middle of the 19th century by different orders of sisters, in particular those from Germany and Holland. Many of these were the first hospitals in their areas. With the present decline in the number of sisters, they are now gradually being taken over by the state hospital system. In 1972, Catholic institutions in Norway were: 17 hospitals and nursing homes, one orphanage, 2 hostels for girl students, 9 kindergartens, 3 grammar schools and one secondary school.

St Francis Aid, founded by Franciscans in Oslo, is a Catholic centre providing relief assistance to those in distress. Caritas-Norge cares for refugees and foreign workers in Norway and gives financial support to development projects in Third-World countries. The Centre for Development Research (Sentrum for Utvikingsforskning) is a socio-religious institution affiliated to a non-profit scientific organization, the Seletun Foundation.

CHURCH OF NORWAY. The 1796 Haugean Awakening, and later ones, have resulted today in the Norwegian Lutheran Inner Mission Society (Indremisjon). There are also Laestadian revivalists (from Finland), and other movements within the state church. About 22% of all members are regularly involved in lay associations.

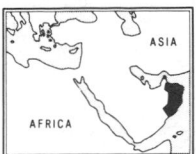

# OMAN

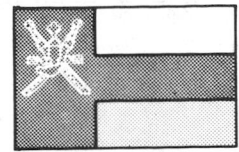

## SECULAR DATA

**STATE. Official name:** The Sultanate of Oman (Saltanat Uman). Adjective of nationality: Omani.
**Flag** (shown above right): Red bar with crossed white swords next to staff; white, red, and green stripes.
**Area:** 212,457 sq.km. (82,030 sq.miles). Agricultural land: 4.9%.
**Government:** Absolute monarchy, since 1741 (Muscat and Oman before 1970; de facto British protectorate).
**Official language:** Arabic.
**Chief cities:** capital Muscat 10,000, Matrah 70,000.
**Armed forces** (1976): Total 14,150 regular: army 13,200, navy 400, air force 550 (44 combat aircraft). Paramilitary forces: 2,000.
**Foreign forces** (1973): 5,000 Iran troops, 200 UK (British) advisers. (1976) 3,000 Iran troops; UK advisers, Jordan engineers.

**DEMOGRAPHY. Population** 600,000 (estimate of 1.VII.1972.

For 1970–2000 (UN), see last row of Table 1). Population density (1975): 4/sq.km. (9/sq.mile). Under 15 years: 44%. Growth rate (1975–80): 3.17% per year (births 4.85%, deaths −1.69%, immigrants 0.01%). Life expectancy (1975–80): 49.5 years. Household size: 5.2 persons.
**Major languages:** Arabic, Persian, Baluchi, Hindi, Tamil, English, Mahri, and a number of minor languages.
**Urban dwellers** (1970): 5.0%. Urban growth rate (1950–70): 4.5% per year.
**Labour force:** 21%.

**ETHNOLINGUISTIC GROUPS:** 87.0% Arab (Hinawi, Ghafiri, &c), 4.0% Baluchi, 3.4% Persian, 2.3% Black African (Bantu, Zanzibari) (along coast), 1.5% Indo-Pakistani (Hindi, Tamil, Malayali), 1.2% Pakistan, 0.3% USA White, 0.3% British (2,000), non-Arab indigenous Omani (Afar, Baharah, Dhaaf, Harasi, Janabah, Mahri (Biljaf, Mahra; non-Mediterranean Australoid Veddoid speaking Semitic languages), Manhil, Qarah, Shahara, Shihuh, et alii).

**MONEY** (1977). **Monetary unit:** Omani rial (= 1,000 baizas); US$1 = OR 0.345.
**National income per person:** US$1,600. Average annual family income: US$8,320.
**Cost of living in capital** (1976): index 126 (Washington DC=100). Daily cost of living: US$88.

**HEALTH.** Hospitals: 10 (825 beds). Doctors: 62. Lepers: 100 (0.1 per 1,000). Blind: 23,000. Psychotics: 5,000.

**EDUCATION.** Adult literacy: 20%. Schools: 65.

**COMMUNICATION** (per 1,000 people). Phones: 6. Radios: 2.

### TABLE 1    RELIGIOUS ADHERENTS IN OMAN

| Year / Name | 1900 Adherents | % | mid-1970 Adherents | % | Natural | Conversion | Total | Rate | mid-1975 Adherents | % | mid-1980 Adherents | % | 2000 Adherents | % |
|---|---|---|---|---|---|---|---|---|---|---|---|---|---|---|
| Muslims | 279,980 | 100.0 | 650,250 | 99.0 | 23,847 | −5 | 23,842 | 3.15 | 757,960 | 98.9 | 888,670 | 98.9 | 1,620,200 | 98.8 |
| Christians | 20 | 0.0 | 2,850 | 0.4 | 106 | 0 | 106 | 3.14 | 3,380 | 0.4 | 3,910 | 0.4 | 7,300 | 0.4 |
| crypto-Christians | 20 | 0.0 | 900 | 0.1 | 38 | 22 | 60 | 5.00 | 1,200 | 0.2 | 1,500 | 0.2 | 3,800 | 0.2 |
| professing | 0 | 0.0 | 1,950 | 0.3 | 68 | −22 | 46 | 2.11 | 2,180 | 0.3 | 2,410 | 0.3 | 3,500 | 0.2 |
| Anglicans | 0 | 0.0 | 1,000 | 0.2 | 35 | −15 | 20 | 1.82 | 1,100 | 0.1 | 1,200 | 0.1 | 1,400 | 0.1 |
| Roman Catholics | 0 | 0.0 | 450 | 0.1 | 16 | −4 | 12 | 2.35 | 510 | 0.1 | 570 | 0.1 | 1,000 | 0.1 |
| Protestants | 0 | 0.0 | 400 | 0.1 | 14 | −2 | 12 | 2.61 | 460 | 0.1 | 520 | 0.1 | 900 | 0.1 |
| Asian indigenous | 0 | 0.0 | 100 | 0.0 | 3 | −1 | 2 | 1.82 | 110 | 0.0 | 120 | 0.0 | 200 | 0.0 |
| affiliated | 20 | 0.0 | 2,850 | 0.4 | 106 | 0 | 106 | 3.14 | 3,380 | 0.4 | 3,910 | 0.4 | 7,300 | 0.4 |
| total practising | 18 | 90 | 2,570 | 90 | 96 | −1 | 95 | 3.13 | 3,040 | 90 | 3,520 | 90 | 5,800 | 80 |
| non-practising | 2 | 10 | 280 | 10 | 10 | 1 | 11 | 3.23 | 340 | 10 | 390 | 10 | 1,500 | 20 |
| Anglicans | 0 | 0.0 | 1,100 | 0.2 | 38 | −18 | 20 | 1.67 | 1,200 | 0.2 | 1,300 | 0.1 | 1,500 | 0.1 |
| Protestants | 20 | 0.0 | 500 | 0.1 | 18 | −6 | 12 | 2.14 | 560 | 0.1 | 620 | 0.1 | 1,000 | 0.1 |
| Evangelicals | 20 | 0.0 | 400 | 0.1 | 15 | 1 | 16 | 3.33 | 480 | 0.1 | 560 | 0.1 | 900 | 0.1 |
| Asian indigenous | 0 | 0.0 | 650 | 0.1 | 27 | 13 | 40 | 4.71 | 850 | 0.1 | 1,050 | 0.1 | 2,500 | 0.2 |
| Roman Catholics | 0 | 0.0 | 470 | 0.1 | 20 | 12 | 32 | 5.08 | 630 | 0.1 | 790 | 0.1 | 2,000 | 0.1 |
| Orthodox | 0 | 0.0 | 130 | 0.0 | 3 | −1 | 2 | 1.43 | 140 | 0.0 | 150 | 0.0 | 300 | 0.0 |
| Hindus | 0 | 0.0 | 2,000 | 0.3 | 73 | −13 | 60 | 2.61 | 2,300 | 0.3 | 2,600 | 0.3 | 5,000 | 0.3 |
| Non-religious | 0 | 0.0 | 1,600 | 0.2 | 63 | 17 | 80 | 4.00 | 2,000 | 0.3 | 2,400 | 0.3 | 5,000 | 0.3 |
| Baha'is | 0 | 0.0 | 300 | 0.0 | 11 | 1 | 12 | 3.33 | 360 | 0.0 | 420 | 0.0 | 1,500 | 0.1 |
| Country's population | 280,000 | 100.0 | 657,000 | 100.0 | 24,100 | 0 | 24,100 | 3.15 | 766,000 | 100.0 | 898,000 | 100.0 | 1,639,000 | 100.0 |

**COLUMNS, ROWS.** For meanings and definitions, see Codebook (Part 6). Note that, by definition, total 'Christians' = professing + crypto-Christians, which also = affiliated + nominal Christians. Percentages may not always total exactly, due to rounding.

**NOTES ON RELIGIONS**
ASIAN INDIGENOUS. South Indian and Arab indigenous congregations, in 5 groupings in 1970 (see Table 2).

BAHA'IS. In 3 local spiritual assemblies (1973).
CRYPTO-CHRISTIANS. Unorganized individual nationals either in the recognized churches, in unrecognized churches, or in isolated radio churches.
HINDUS. Indian merchants, from Gujarat and Bombay.
MUSLIMS. Mostly Hinawis who are Ibadi Kharijites (fundamentalist seceders from both Sunnis and Shias), with Ghafiris in Sunni minorities (Shafiite, Hanbalite and Wahhabi), and 7% Shias (Persians, Arabs, who are Ithna-Asharis or Ismailis) near

Muscat. Most Muslims are Arabs (Omani and expatriate), with some Iranians, Baluchis, Indo-Pakistanis and Zanzibari Blacks. There is also, since 1950, a small Ahmadiya Mission (enumerated here under Muslims although declared non-Muslim by Pakistan). *Hajj pilgrims to Mecca.* (1970) 1,569; (1975) 3,377; (1976) 2,251.
NON-RELIGIOUS. British.
PROFESSING CHRISTIANS. Mainly Europeans and USA personnel; fluctuating in the 1970s due to replacement of expatriate technicians by Omanis.

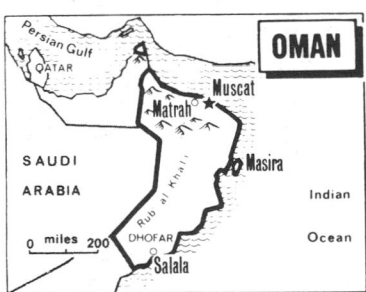

**NON-CHRISTIAN RELIGIONS. Islam** is the official religion, the majority being Ibadi Kharijites. Shafiite, Hanbalite and Wahhabi Sunnis make up important minorities.

### CHRISTIANITY
CATHOLIC CHURCH. Although tradition holds that the Apostle Bartholomew brought Christianity to Arabia, and unquestionably Christian communities were active there in the first centuries of the Christian era, this almost certainly did not include Oman. With the triumph of Islam in the 7th century, Christianity was completely eclipsed in Arabia proper until the 19th century. Meanwhile, Portuguese lived in Muscat from 1508. The first Catholic missionary of the modern era returned to Aden in 1841. Aden became a prefecture in 1854 and a vicariate in 1888, and the following year the vicariate of Arabia was formed. The vicariate which has been administered from Abu Dhabi since 1973, exercises ecclesiastical supervision over the Catholic community of Oman, which in 1972 consisted of 470 Catholics, all foreigners. There are no Catholic institutions, but an American Capuchin has been resident in the capital, Muscat. In November 1977, the first Catholic church building in the Sultanate of Oman was consecrated in Muscat, on land donated by the sultan of Oman himself.

OTHER CHURCHES. The pioneer Protestant missionaries to Oman were James Cantine and

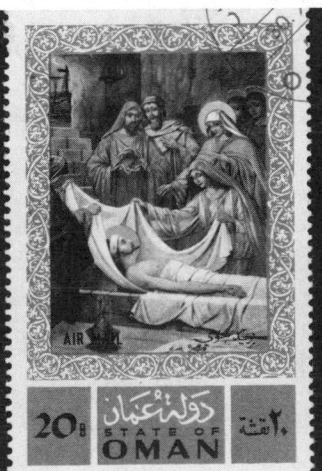

The Passion of Christ, on official postage stamps: from left, Gethsemane, Before Pilate, Carrying the Cross, Behold your Son, Entombment.

Samuel Zwemer who set out respectively in 1889 and 1890 under the American Arabian Mission. In 1894 their work was taken over by the Reformed Church in America which continues to support 16 missionaries and 2 clinics in the country. The Reformed Church also operates a school at Muscat. Anglican chaplaincy work is organized as part of the Episcopal Church in Jerusalem and the Middle East.

**CHURCH AND STATE.** With one of the largest proportions of nomadic populations in the world and few oil resources, Oman remains the least-developed state in the Persian gulf. Although the country is still ruled directly without benefit of a constutition, the new sultan has promised to establish a modern government. Islam is the state religion and the country's judicial system conforms to Islamic law. Nevertheless, Oman places fewer restrictions on

Christian activity than most of its neighbours. In 1973 sultan Qabous officially accorded to the Catholic and Protestant churches the right to found Christian communities in the sultanate.

**BROADCASTING.** No Christian broadcasting is permitted. From overseas, Protestant programmes in Arabic can be easily heard over FEBA (Seychelles).

TABLE 2.    ORGANIZED CHURCHES AND DENOMINATIONS IN OMAN

| Official name 1 | Begun 2 | Type 3 | Counc 4 | Congs 5 | Adults 6 | Affiliated 7 | Names, notes, and other statistics (see Codebook) 8 |
|---|---|---|---|---|---|---|---|
| **Anglican Church** (D Cyprus & the Gulf) | | A plu | av... | 1 | 450 | 1,100 | Chaplaincy, in Episcopal Ch in Jerusalem & ME. For 2,000 UK citizens. |
| **Catholic Church** (VA Arabia) | 1508 | R Lat | P..L. | 1 | 300 | 470 | All expatriates (including Arab Catholics). One USA Capuchin in Muscat (1975). |
| **Isolated radio churches** | c1950 | I rad | ..... | 15 | 100 | 300 | Isolated radio believers, mostly aged 12–25 (ICI, WEC, FEBA, RVOG, RVatican). |
| Mar Thoma Syrian Ch (D Bahya Kerala) | | I ReO | xwe.. | 1 | 50 | 150 | In Diocese of Outside Kerala. South Indians (Malayalis) in Muscat. 1x. |
| Orthodox Syrian Church of the East | 1976 | O Syr | Du... | 1 | 60 | 130 | In D Bahya Kerala (Outside Kerala). South Indians. Meet in RCA church, Muscat. |
| **Protestant Church in Oman** | 1889 | P Ref | Rv... | 5 | 200 | 500 | M=RCA(USA). Ref Ch Synod (Denmark). School in Muscat. 16f(1 Dutch),2h. |
| Other Third-World indigenous churches | | I | ..... | | 100 | 200 | Indian Pentecostals, Christian Brethren (Indians), and others. |
| **Total affiliated (mid-1970)** | | | | 28 | 1,260 | 2,850 | Total denominations (1970) . . .  10. |
| **Total affiliated (mid-1975)** | | | | 31 | 1,490 | 3,380 | Total denominations (1975) . . .  11. |
| **Total affiliated (mid-1980)** | | | | 35 | 1,730 | 3,910 | Total denominations (1980) . . .  12. |

NOTES ON TABLE ABOVE
COLUMNS: for meanings and CODES (cols.1, 3, 4, 8): see Codebook (Part 6). Column 1: **Boldface type** = church with over 10% of country's affiliated Christians.

PEOPLES (ethnolinguistic). Christians: about 32% British, 25% USA White, 22% Arab (11% Omani), 18% South Indian

(Tamil, Malayali), 3% Pakistani.

COUNTRY-WIDE TOTALS
EVANGELIZATION (see Part 5). 1900: 0%. 1970: 13%. 1980: 16%. *Radiophonic evangelism.* WEC, ICI, et alia.
FOREIGN MISSIONARIES AND PERSONNEL (aliens from abroad) (1973). Total 25. *From Western world.* 24: 23 Protestants

(16 in 1 USA society, 7 in 1 Denmark society), 1 Roman Catholic from USA. *From Third World.* 1 Indian indigenous.
INSTITUTIONS (church-operated) (1973). Total 2 (clinics).
PERIODICALS. 2 titles.
PERSONNEL. 25 (all foreign).
SERVICE AGENCIES. 2, including MMG.

---

# PACIFIC ISLANDS

## SECULAR DATA

**STATE.** Official name: United States Trust Territory of the Pacific Islands. Alternative name: Micronesia (= Land of the Small Islands).
**Flag** (shown above right): Blue, with six white stars.
**Area:** 1,857 sq.km. (717 sq.miles). Description: 2,141 atolls and islands (96 inhabited). Agricultural to 43.8%.
**Government:** Self-governing trust territory of the USA, since 1947 (1668 Spanish colony in Marianas, 1885–99 annexed by Germany, 1914 Japanese possession).
**Legislature:** Congress of Micronesia: Senate, 12 members; House of Representatives, 21 members.
**Official language:** English.
**Capital:** Saipan 10,034.
**Political divisions:** 6 Administrative Districts.

**Armed forces** (1976): US troops. Paramilitary Micronesia Police, 222.

**DEMOGRAPHY. Population:** 114,782 (census of 18.IX.1973. For 1970–2000 (UN), see last row of Table 1). Population density (1975): 63/sq.km. (163/sq.mile). Under 15 years: 44%. Growth rate (1975–80): 2.86% per year. Household size: 5.8 persons.
**Major languages:** English, Ponapese, Yapese, Chamorro, Ebon, Kusaie, Mortlock, and several other Micronesian languages.
**Labour force:** 16%.
**Tourists** (1965): 4,100. (1969) 20,600. (1970) 33,000. (1973) 120,000.

**ETHNOLINGUISTIC GROUPS:** 28% Trukese & Nomoian, 19% Marshallese, 15% Ponapean, 13% Palauan, 11% Chamorro, 5% Yapese, 4% Kusaian, 3% Ulithian, 1% Polynesian, 1% USA

White (1,000), Chinese, other Micronesian.

**MONEY** (1977). Monetary unit: USA dollar (= 100 cents).
**National income per person:** US$500. Average annual family income: US$2,900.
**Cost of living in capital** (1976): Daily cost of living: US$39.

**HEALTH.** Hospitals: 9 (539 beds) Doctors: 51. Lepers: 500 (4.3 per 1,000). Blind: 100. Psychotics: 1,000.

**EDUCATION.** Adult literacy: 90%. Schools: 272.

**LITERATURE.** Periodicals: 12. Newspapers: 4 non-daily.

**COMMUNICATION** (per 1,000 people). Phones: 60. Radios: 650. TV sets: 16.

TABLE 1.    RELIGIOUS ADHERENTS IN THE PACIFIC ISLANDS TRUST TERRITORY (Micronesia)

| Year | 1900 | | mid-1970 | | Annual change, 1970–1980 | | | | mid-1975 | | mid-1980 | | 2000 | |
|---|---|---|---|---|---|---|---|---|---|---|---|---|---|---|
| Name | Adherents | % | Adherents | % | Natural | Conversion | Total | Rate | Adherents | % | Adherents | % | Adherents | % |
| **Christians** | 22,700 | 63.1 | 98,470 | 97.5 | 3,315 | 0 | 3,315 | 2.91 | 114,070 | 97.5 | 131,620 | 97.5 | 212,550 | 97.5 |
| professing | 22,700 | 63.1 | 98,470 | 97.5 | 3,315 | 0 | 3,315 | 2.91 | 114,070 | 97.5 | 131,620 | 97.5 | 212,550 | 97.5 |
| Protestants | 18,200 | 50.6 | 49,690 | 49.2 | 1,673 | 0 | 1,673 | 2.91 | 57,560 | 49.2 | 66,420 | 49.2 | 106,820 | 49.0 |
| Roman Catholics | 4,500 | 12.5 | 45,850 | 45.4 | 1,547 | 24 | 1,571 | 2.95 | 53,230 | 45.5 | 61,560 | 45.6 | 101,370 | 46.5 |
| Micronesian indigenous | 0 | 0.0 | 2,930 | 2.9 | 95 | −24 | 71 | 2.16 | 3,280 | 2.8 | 3,640 | 2.7 | 4,360 | 2.0 |
| nominal | 185 | 0.5 | 3,710 | 3.7 | 135 | 45 | 179 | 3.90 | 4,590 | 3.9 | 5,500 | 4.1 | 12,130 | 5.6 |
| affiliated | 22,515 | 62.5 | 94,760 | 93.8 | 3,181 | −45 | 3,136 | 2.86 | 109,480 | 93.6 | 126,120 | 93.4 | 200,420 | 91.0 |
| total practising | 21,390 | 95 | 79,600 | 84 | 2,672 | −38 | 2,634 | 2.86 | 91,960 | 84 | 105,940 | 84 | 160,340 | 80 |
| non-practising | 1,125 | 5 | 15,160 | 16 | 509 | −7 | 502 | 2.86 | 17,520 | 16 | 20,180 | 16 | 40,080 | 20 |
| Roman Catholics | 4,400 | 12.2 | 45,660 | 45.2 | 1,537 | −1 | 1,536 | 2.90 | 52,880 | 45.2 | 61,020 | 45.2 | 98,100 | 45.0 |
| Protestants | 18,115 | 50.3 | 44,700 | 44.2 | 1,505 | 15 | 1,520 | 2.93 | 51,800 | 44.3 | 59,900 | 44.4 | 95,920 | 44.0 |
| Evangelicals | 12,000 | 33.3 | 14,100 | 14.0 | 476 | 4 | 480 | 2.93 | 16,400 | 14.0 | 18,900 | 14.0 | 31,000 | 14.2 |
| Micronesian indigenous | 0 | 0.0 | 4,000 | 4.0 | 124 | −64 | 60 | 1.40 | 4,300 | 3.7 | 4,600 | 3.4 | 4,400 | 2.0 |
| Marginal Protestants | 0 | 0.0 | 400 | 0.4 | 15 | 5 | 20 | 4.00 | 500 | 0.4 | 600 | 0.4 | 2,000 | 0.9 |
| **Tribal religionists** | 13,300 | 36.9 | 1,210 | 1.2 | 38 | −16 | 22 | 1.68 | 1,300 | 1.1 | 1,430 | 1.1 | 1,700 | 0.8 |
| **Baha'is** | 0 | 0.0 | 1,020 | 1.0 | 38 | 25 | 63 | 4.77 | 1,320 | 1.1 | 1,650 | 1.2 | 3,550 | 1.6 |
| **Chinese folk-religionists** | 0 | 0.0 | 300 | 0.3 | 9 | −9 | 0 | 0.00 | 300 | 0.3 | 300 | 0.2 | 200 | 0.1 |
| **Country's population** | 36,000 | 100.0 | 101,000 | 100.0 | 3,400 | 0 | 3,400 | 2.91 | 171,000 | 100.0 | 135,000 | 100.0 | 218,000 | 100.0 |

COLUMNS, ROWS. For meanings and definitions, see Codebook (Part 6). Note that, by definition total 'Christians' = professing + crypto-Christians, which also = affiliated + nominal Christians. Percentages may not always total exactly, due to rounding.
CENSUSES. 18.IX.1973: 49.2% Protestants, 45.4% Roman Catholics, 2.9% traditionalists (termed here Micronesian indigenous Christians), 1.2% non-religious (tribal or traditional religionists), 1.3% other religionists.

NOTES ON RELIGIONS
BAHA'IS. Rapid growth from 1 local spiritual assembly (1964)

to 20 (1973; 17 on Carolines, 2 on Marshalls, 1 on Marianas); and 114 other isolated centres or groups.
COUNTRY'S POPULATION. Japanese permanent settlers arrived in 1914 and by 1920 numbered 3,500; 70,000 in 1940, including 45,000 on Saipan, Tinian and Rota on the sugar plantations; but from 1945–47, USA authorities repatriated all the 70,000 Japanese to Japan, and none remain. In 1945, there were 200,000 USA troops on Saipan alone.
MICRONESIAN INDIGENOUS. In one marginal body in 1970 (see Table 2), regarded as traditional religionists in the government census.
ROMAN CATHOLICS. In 1900, 11,000 on Mariana Islands

with Guam (2,000 on Marianas), 1,700 on Caroline Islands, 703 on Marshall Islands.
TRIBAL RELIGIONISTS. Polytheists, animists and ancestor-venerators among the indigenous Micronesian population. In Yap and some atolls of the central Carolines, traditional Micronesian religions continued to be practised until around 1950, and are still regarded as major alternatives to Christianity in the western and central Carolines. Elements of traditional local religions survive widely in traditional medical practices.

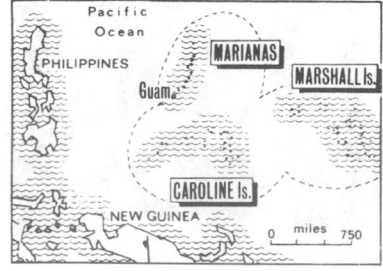

**NON-CHRISTIAN RELIGIONS. Traditional religion** continues to exist as a sub-stratum, although most of the indigenous residents of the islands have accepted Christianity. On Ulithi atoll in the Caroline Islands magic is still important, there being typhoon magicians and navigation, community, fish, house and grave magicians, as well as diviners. A form of ancestor veneration is also practised, with special attention to 2 great community divinities: Iongolap and Marespa. The Great Spirit, Ialulep, is known across the Carolines, as is Solal, lord of the nether regions.

**CHRISTIANITY**
CATHOLIC CHURCH. Catholicism began in the islands in 1668 and the population is now about 45% Catholic. The Chamorros of the Mariana Islands are almost all Catholics and exhibit a way of life similar to other peoples colonized by Spain, such as those of the Philippines or Mexico. In 1971 there were 12 missions, 66 stations, and 61 chapels, of which only one had a resident chaplain. There are no mission hospitals, Catholic or Protestant in the territory, but church schools are common. The

**Protestant Church of East Truk.** Villagers with their simple church in Penia village, Moen Island, Truk District.

**United Church of Christ in Ponape.** Congregationalist women's association meets outside church at Kolonia, Ponape District.

Mariana Islands are part of the diocese of Agaña with its seat in Guam; the Caroline and Marshall Islands form a separate vicariate.

PROTESTANT CHURCHES. American Board missionaries first began work in the Caroline Islands in 1852 and later spread to other parts of Micronesia. From this early activity have grown autonomous Congregationalist churches on Ponape, Truk and the Marshall Islands, which continue to receive support from the United Church of Christ in the USA.

The Liebenzell Mission entered Truk in the eastern Carolines in 1906, meeting the request of the American Board for German missionaries after Germany had claimed sovereignty over the islands in 1885. By 1914, 7 stations had been opened manned by 11 missionaries and 50 nationals. Although all Germany missionaries were evacuated during World War I, they returned again in 1925 and opened new stations on Ponape and Palau by 1928. Following World War II, the work was further extended to Yap.

More recent arrivals have been Seventh-day Adventists and Assemblies of God, the latter with headquarters at Majuro in the Marshall Islands.

Protestant churches supervise 20 elementary and 4 high schools, catering for a total of 3,517 pupils.

INDIGENOUS CHURCHES. Indigenous religious movements have existed in the islands since the early part of the 20th century. One of the most influential has been Modekne, begun on Palau in 1912. Although banned by government in 1945, it continues to function underground as a syncretistic revival of traditional Palauan religion with Christian elements. Modekne's emphasis on healing has had great appeal among the indigenous population.

CHURCH AND STATE. From the 16th to the 19th centuries the islands were Spanish possessions. Germany was sovereign between 1885 and World War I, after which Micronesia became a Japanese territory. Since World War II, the islands have been governed as a trust territory by the USA. The early Spanish period was favourable to the growth of Catholicism; the Liebenzell Mission owes its origin

in the Carolines to the political conditions created by German colonial expansion in 1885; but the present policy of the USA is to maintain complete separation of church and state.

BROADCASTING. The government stations of the 5 districts of Palau, Yap, Truk, Ponape and the Marshalls all make available free time for religious and educational broadcasts in local languages. Catholics began the preparation of programmes on Truk in 1965, and since 1969 each of the 5 districts has had its own small production studio. For Catholics, an association grouping the Caroline and Marshall Islands is a member of UNDA.

In July 1977, the Protestant FEBC (Far East Broadcasting Company) began transmitting on its powerful new medium-wave station KUFE on Saipan, Mariana Islands, to be followed later by short-wave broadcasts to the Soviet Union, China and Japan.

TABLE 2. ORGANIZED CHURCHES AND DENOMINATIONS IN THE PACIFIC ISLANDS TRUST TERRITORY (Micronesia)

| Official name 1 | Begun 2 | Type 3 | Counc 4 | Congs 5 | Adults 6 | Affiliated 7 | Names, notes, and other statistics (see Codebook) 8 |
|---|---|---|---|---|---|---|---|
| Assemblies of God | 1960 | P Pe2 | ZF... | 20 | 1,648 | 4,000 | M=AoG(USA). Classical Pentecostals. Marshall Islands (HQ Majuro). 31n,8f,1s(223). |
| Catholic Church: | 1668 | R Lat | P.... | 28 | 25,600 | 45,660 | 1668, Marianas forcibly converted by Spanish Jesuits. Not in CEPAC. C=1+0+2. |
| D Agaña | 1907 | R Lat | Pofmc | 10 | 5,600 | 10,000 | Mariana Is are part of D Agaña (Guam). Chamorros, 99% practising Catholics. P=68%. |
| VA Caroline & Marshall Islands | 1905 | R Lat | Psj | 18 | 20,000 | 35,660 | Since 1946, excludes Mariana Is. 1n,46x,13m,42w,P=60%,1783Yy. |
| General Baptist Mission | 1947 | P Bap | TF... | | 100 | 200 | *General Association of General Baptists.* M=GBFMS(USA). Autonomous churches. 2f. |
| Jehovah's Witnesses | c1960 | M Jeh | x.... | 2 | 202 | 400 | Congregation on Ponape, also Marshall Is; Witnesses also on Saipan, Truk. 26f,33Y. |
| Modekne (Modekngei) | 1912 | I mar | ..... | | 2,000 | 4,000 | Nativistic healing movement on Palau, 30% population. Banned 1945, underground. |
| Protestant Ch in the Caroline Islands | 1906 | P int | xM... | 60 | 1,000 | 2,000 | M=Liebenzell M(Germany,USA). Yapese, Palauans, Ponapeans. 59m,31f,1s,W=79%,100Y. |
| **Protestant Church of East Truk** | 1885 | P uni | ..... | 24 | 7,500 | 15,000 | *Nomoneas (East) Association.* M=ABCFM,now UCBWM(USA). Trukese. 21n,13m,8f,200Y,100q. |
| Saipan Community Church | | P com | ..... | 1 | 500 | 1,000 | Interdenominational church in capital of PITT. Mainly USA expatriates. 2f. |
| Seventh-day Adventist Church | 1930 | P Adv | x.... | | 200 | 500 | *SDA,* part of Far Eastern Island Mission, Far Eastern Division (HQ Agaña, Guam). 1s. |
| United Ch of Christ in Ponape | 1852 | P uni | ..P.. | | 5,000 | 10,000 | *Pwinen Apwapwali Mwomwodisoen Ponpei.* Caroline Is. M=ABCFM, UCBWM(USA). 2f,G=0. |
| **United Ch of Christ in the Marshall Is** | 1857 | P uni | .vP.. | 88 | 5,000 | 10,000 | *Jarin Rarik Dron.* 1857, M=ABCFM, now UCBWM. 32n,G=0,1p,1r,W=90%,1232Yy. |
| United Pentecostal Church | 1965 | P Pe1 | x.... | 18 | 400 | 1,000 | *Jesus Only Church.* M=UPC(USA). Unitarian Pentecostals. 26m, 2f,3p. |
| Other Protestant denominations | | P | ..... | | 600 | 1,000 | Assoc of Marshall Is Chs, BBFI, Chs of Christ, OMF, Prot Ch of West Truk. |
| **Total affiliated (mid-1970)** | | | | 340 | 49,750 | 94,760 | Total denominations (1970) . . . 17. |
| **Total affiliated (mid-1975)** | | | | 350 | 57,500 | 109,480 | Total denominations (1975) . . . 19. |
| **Total affiliated (mid-1980)** | | | | 360 | 66,200 | 126,120 | Total denominations (1980) . . . 21. |

NOTES ON TABLE ABOVE
COLUMNS: for meanings and CODES (cols,1,3,4,8): see Codebook (Part 6). Column 1: **Boldface type** = church with over 10% of country's affiliated Christians.

PEOPLES (ethnolinguistic). Christians: 28% Trukese & Nomoian, 19% Marshallese, 15% Ponapean, 13% Palauan, 11% Chamorro, 5% Yapese, 4% Kusaiean, 3% Ulithian, 1% Polynesian, 1% USA White, Chinese, other Micronesian.

COUNTRY-WIDE TOTALS
EVANGELIZATION (see Part 5). 1900: 95%. 1970: 100%. 1980: 100%. *Radiophonic evangelism.* FEBC, HCJB, TWR, ICI (655 enrolments, 260 active, 175 conversions reported).
FOREIGN MISSIONARIES AND PERSONNEL (aliens from

abroad) (1973). Total 222. *From Western world.* 190: about 120 Roman Catholics, 62 Protestants (31 in 1 WGermany society, 31 in 7 USA societies), 8 marginal Protestants (Jehovah's Witnesses). *From Third World.* 32: 18 marginal Protestants (Jehovah's Witnesses mostly from Japan), 10 Roman Catholics from Philippines et alia, 4 Protestants from Samoa and Taiwan.
INSTITUTIONS (church-operated) (1973). Total 13, including 8 higher schools (1 minor seminary), 3 seminaries (Protestant).
PERIODICALS. About 8 titles.
PERSONNEL. About 632 (410 national, 222 foreign).
RELIGIOUS LIBRARIES. 3.
SCRIPTURE DISTRIBUTION (1975). Annual totals: 3,029 Bibles (83% subsidized, 17% commercial), 7,945 NTs (87% subsidized, 13% commercial), 29,600 UBS portions, 110,000 UBS selections. *Translations completed.* Portion: 8 languages

since 1862. NT: 6 languages since 1883. Bible: Kusaien in 1928. SERVICE AGENCIES. 3.

ADDITIONAL DATA ON CHURCHES
CATHOLIC CHURCH. *Annual baptisms.* (1972) D Agaña, 98.9% infant, 1.1% adult; VA Carolines, 92.4% infant, 7.6% adult. *Priests.* The one national was ordained (SJ) in 1967. Expatriates are 44 SJ, one secular (USA), one secular (Luxembourg). *Brothers.* SJ (including 2 Micronesians and 2 Spanish). *Catechists.* Total (1974) 200. *Religious orders and congregations.* Priests: SJ (New York province). Sisters: Sisters of Mercy, Maryknoll Sisters.
*Catholic organizations.* In 1971 the Catholic Church was responsible for 13 elementary schools (2,790 pupils) and 3 high schools (365 students). There are no mission hospitals, Catholic or Protestant.

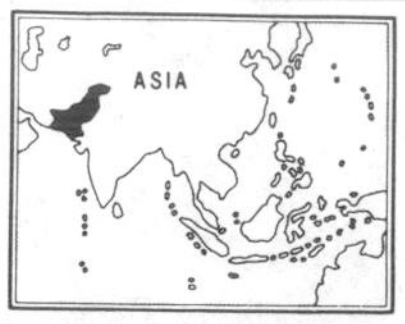


# PAKISTAN

## SECULAR DATA

**STATE. Official name:** The Islamic Republic of Pakistan (Islami Jamhuriya-e-Pakistan). Earlier name: West Pakistan. (Pakistan = Land of the Pure). Adjective of nationality: Pakistani.
**Flag** (shown above right): Green field with white crescent and star; white bar along hoist.
**Area:** 946,719 sq.km. (365,529 sq.miles). Agricultural land: 30.4%.
**Government:** Socialist Islamic republic, since 1971 (1859 British supremacy, 1947 Partition and Independence as dominion, 1956 republic, 1958 military rule).
**Legislature:** Parliament: Senate, 63 members; National Assembly, 210 members.
**Official languages:** Urdu and English.
**Chief cities:** capital Islamabad 77,000 (1972), Karachi 3,469,000, Lahore 2,148,000, Lyallpur 820,000, Hyderabad 624,000, Rawalpindi 615,000.
**Political divisions:** 4 Provinces, 1 Centrally Administered Area (Islamabad), and Azad (Free) Kashmir.
**Armed forces** (1976): Total 428,000 regular: army 400,000, navy 11,000, air force 17,000 (217 combat aircraft). Reserves: 513,000. Paramilitary forces: 75,000.

**DEMOGRAPHY. Population:** 64,979,732 (census of 16.IX.1972. For 1970–2000 (UN), see last row of Table 1). Population density (1975): 75/sq.km. (193/sq.mile). Under 15 years: 46%. Growth rate (1975–80): 3.24% per year (births 4.68%, deaths −1.45%). Life expectancy (1975–80): 52.3 years. Household size: 5.7 persons.
**Major languages:** Urdu, English, Punjabi, Sindhi, Pushtu, Baluchi, Kashmiri, Brahui, Gujarati, Hindi, and 40 smaller languages.
**Urban dwellers** (1970): 22.5%. Urban growth rate (1950–70): 4.6% per year.
**Labour force:** 29%.
**Tourists** (1974): 154,503.

**ETHNOLINGUISTIC GROUPS:** 59.8% Punjabi, 12.6% Sindhi, 8.5% Pathan (Pushtun), 7.6% Urdu, 6.6% Jat, 2.5% Baluchi, 0.9% Brahui, 0.6% Gujarati, 0.3% Kho, 0.2% Hindi, 0.2% Rajasthani, 0.2% Kohistani, Burusho (30,000), Goanese (20,000), Chinese (3,000), Kohli, Thori, British, Anglo-Indian, Jewish, Gypsy, and numerous smaller peoples.

**MONEY** (1977). **Monetary unit:** rupee (= 100 paisa); US$1 = PRs 9.90.
**National income per person:** US$130. Average annual family income: US$741.
**Inflation:** (1970–74) 16.4% per year (1975: consumer price index 222).
**Cost of living in capital** (1976): index 99 (Washington DC = 100). Daily cost of living: US$38.

**HEALTH.** Hospitals: 2,548 (31,565 beds). Doctors: 14,061. Lepers: 70,000 (1.0 per 1,000). Blind: 900,000. Psychotics: 490,000. Drug addicts: 100,000 (on opium).

**EDUCATION.** Adult literacy: (1951) 19%, (1975) 17%. Education rate: 32%. 17%. Schools: 46,660 (41,000 primary, 5,660 secondary). Universities: 4.

**LITERATURE.** Annual new book titles (1972): 1,744. Periodicals: 500. Scientific journals: 90. Newspapers: 71 dailies, 121 non-daily.

**COMMUNICATION** (per 1,000 people). Phones: 3. Radios: 14. TV sets: 2. Daily newspaper circulation: 6 copies.

TABLE 1. RELIGIOUS ADHERENTS IN PAKISTAN

| Year | 1900 | | mid-1970 | | Annual change, 1970–1980 | | | | mid-1975 | | mid-1980 | | 2000 | |
|---|---|---|---|---|---|---|---|---|---|---|---|---|---|---|
| *Name* | *Adherents* | *%* | *Adherents* | *%* | *Natural* | *Conversion* | *Total* | *Rate* | *Adherents* | *%* | *Adherents* | *%* | *Adherents* | *%* |
| Muslims | 20,910,900 | 82.1 | 58,493,968 | 96.8 | 2,181,002 | 1,636 | 2,182,638 | 3.20 | 68,273,500 | 96.8 | 80,320,350 | 96.8 | 142,272,000 | 96.8 |
| Ahmadis | 30,000 | 0.1 | 1,500,000 | 2.5 | 58,043 | 12,957 | 71,000 | 3.90 | 1,820,000 | 2.6 | 2,210,000 | 2.7 | 4,550,000 | 3.1 |
| **Christians** | **90,000** | **0.4** | **1,054,482** | **1.7** | **40,260** | **1,842** | **42,102** | **3.34** | **1,262,400** | **1.8** | **1,475,500** | **1.8** | **2,909,000** | **2.0** |
| crypto-Christians | 25,000 | 0.1 | 208,482 | 0.3 | 8,272 | 1,930 | 10,202 | 3.93 | 259,400 | 0.4 | 310,500 | 0.4 | 679,000 | 0.5 |
| professing | 65,000 | 0.3 | 846,000 | 1.4 | 31,988 | −88 | 31,900 | 3.18 | 1,003,000 | 1.4 | 1,165,000 | 1.4 | 2,230,000 | 1.5 |
| Protestants | 40,000 | 0.2 | 506,000 | 0.8 | 19,167 | −167 | 19,000 | 3.16 | 601,000 | 0.8 | 696,000 | 0.8 | 1,330,000 | 0.9 |
| Roman Catholics | 15,000 | 0.1 | 280,000 | 0.5 | 10,556 | 44 | 10,600 | 3.20 | 331,000 | 0.5 | 386,000 | 0.5 | 750,000 | 0.5 |
| Pakistani indigenous | 0 | 0.0 | 60,000 | 0.1 | 2,265 | 35 | 2,300 | 3.24 | 71,000 | 0.1 | 83,000 | 0.1 | 150,000 | 0.1 |
| Anglicans | 10,000 | 0.0 | 0 | 0.0 | 0 | 0 | 0 | 0.00 | 0 | 0.0 | 0 | 0.0 | 0 | 0.0 |
| affiliated | 90,000 | 0.4 | 1,054,482 | 1.7 | 40,260 | 1,842 | 42,102 | 3.34 | 1,262,400 | 1.8 | 1,475,500 | 1.8 | 2,909,000 | 2.0 |
| total practising | 81,000 | *90* | 738,140 | *70* | 28,182 | 1,289 | 29,471 | 3.34 | 883,680 | *70* | 1,032,850 | *70* | 1,890,900 | *65* |
| non-practising | 9,000 | *10* | 316,340 | *30* | 12,078 | 553 | 12,631 | 3.34 | 378,720 | *30* | 442,650 | *30* | 1,018,100 | *35* |
| Protestants | 50,000 | 0.2 | 581,099 | 1.0 | 22,068 | 322 | 22,390 | 3.24 | 692,000 | 1.0 | 805,000 | 1.0 | 1,470,000 | 1.0 |
| Evangelicals | 25,000 | 0.1 | 285,000 | 0.5 | 10,811 | 289 | 11,100 | 3.27 | 339,000 | 0.5 | 396,000 | 0.5 | 725,000 | 0.5 |
| Neo-pentecostals | 0 | 0.0 | 200 | 0.0 | 64 | 416 | 480 | 24.00 | 2,000 | 0.0 | 5,000 | 0.0 | 20,000 | 0.0 |
| Roman Catholics | 20,000 | 0.1 | 341,231 | 0.6 | 13,076 | 801 | 13,877 | 3.38 | 410,000 | 0.6 | 480,000 | 0.6 | 1,028,000 | 0.7 |
| Catholic pentecostals | 0 | 0.0 | 0 | 0.0 | 32 | 568 | 600 | 60.00 | 1,000 | 0.0 | 6,000 | 0.0 | 30,000 | 0.0 |
| Pakistani indigenous | 0 | 0.0 | 131,852 | 0.2 | 5,102 | 713 | 5,815 | 3.63 | 160,000 | 0.2 | 190,000 | 0.2 | 410,000 | 0.3 |
| Marginal Protestants | 0 | 0.0 | 300 | 0.0 | 13 | 7 | 20 | 5.00 | 400 | 0.0 | 500 | 0.0 | 1,000 | 0.0 |
| Anglicans | 20,000 | 0.1 | 0 | 0.0 | 0 | 0 | 0 | 0.00 | 0 | 0.0 | 0 | 0.0 | 0 | 0.0 |
| Hindus | 3,560,000 | 14.0 | 830,000 | 1.4 | 26,840 | −2,000 | 24,840 | 2.61 | 950,000 | 1.3 | 1,078,400 | 1.3 | 1,616,000 | 1.1 |
| Tribal religionists | 130,000 | 0.5 | 35,000 | 0.1 | 957 | −1,957 | −1,000 | −3.33 | 30,000 | 0.0 | 25,000 | 0.0 | 15,000 | 0.0 |
| Baha'is | 100 | 0.0 | 15,100 | 0.0 | 637 | 353 | 990 | 4.95 | 20,000 | 0.0 | 25,000 | 0.0 | 60,000 | 0.0 |
| Non-religious | 0 | 0.0 | 10,000 | 0.0 | 415 | 185 | 600 | 4.62 | 13,000 | 0.0 | 16,000 | 0.0 | 35,000 | 0.0 |
| Parsis | 4,000 | 0.0 | 5,200 | 0.0 | 0 | 0 | 0 | 0.00 | 5,200 | 0.0 | 5,200 | 0.0 | 5,000 | 0.0 |
| Atheists | 0 | 0.0 | 2,000 | 0.0 | 80 | 20 | 100 | 4.00 | 2,500 | 0.0 | 3,000 | 0.0 | 7,000 | 0.0 |
| Buddhists | 0 | 0.0 | 2,000 | 0.0 | 70 | −30 | 40 | 1.82 | 2,200 | 0.0 | 2,400 | 0.0 | 4,000 | 0.0 |
| Chinese folk-religionists | 0 | 0.0 | 1,000 | 0.0 | 29 | −49 | −20 | −2.22 | 900 | 0.0 | 800 | 0.0 | 500 | 0.0 |
| Jews | 0 | 0.0 | 250 | 0.0 | 10 | 0 | 10 | 3.33 | 300 | 0.0 | 350 | 0.0 | 500 | 0.0 |
| Sikhs | 760,000 | 3.0 | 0 | 0.0 | 0 | 0 | 0 | 0.00 | 0 | 0.0 | 0 | 0.0 | 0 | 0.0 |
| **Country's population** | **25,455,000** | **100.0** | **60,449,000** | **100.0** | **2,250,300** | **0** | **2,250,300** | **3.19** | **70,560,000** | **100.0** | **82,952,000** | **100.0** | **146,924,000** | **100.0** |

COLUMNS, ROWS. For meanings and definitions, see Codebook (Part 6). Note that, by definition, total 'Christians' = professing + crypto-Christians, which also = affiliated + nominal Christians. Percentages may not always total exactly, due to rounding.
CENSUSES. **28.II.1951** (West Pakistan; excluding foreigners): 96.9% Muslims, 1.7% Hindus (1.2% scheduled castes), 1.4% Christians (432,706 persons), 5,320 Parsis, 680 Buddhists. **1.II.1961** (West Pakistan; excluding foreigners and nomads): 97.2% Muslims, 1.5% Hindus (1.0% scheduled castes), 1.4% Christians (583,884 persons), 5,219 Parsis, 2,445 Buddhists.

### NOTES ON RELIGIONS

AHMADIS. A messianic movement out of Shia Islam, the Ahmadiya Movement was founded in 1889 and was based in Qadian (present Punjab in India) until forced to emigrate en masse from India to Pakistan in 1947, to its present headquarters in Rabwah. In 1900 there were about 40,000 adult Ahmadis from Afghanistan right across India, the majority from Orissa, Mysore, Kashmir, the Punjab and Hyderabad (Deccan). Although declared non-Muslim by the state, Ahmadis (who are in majority called Qadianis, with a small faction of 10,000 called Lahoris) regard themselves as devout Muslims and are engaged in Muslim proselytism in 100 countries of the world. Since 1973, social and political discrimination against Ahmadis has increased markedly in Pakistan. An annual convention at Rabwah has attracted 100,000 regularly; and at the 1974 gathering 15,000 converts were made.
ANGLICANS. Formerly one of the larger denominations, the Anglican church disappeared as a separate entity in 1970 when it joined the Protestant union, the Church of Pakistan.
ATHEISTS. Pakistan Communist Party: membership negligible. There are a few intellectuals and humanists.
BAHA'IS. Reached Pakistan area before 1892. Rapid growth from 19 local spiritual assemblies (1964) to 97 (1973). Baha'is are mostly Persian residents.
BUDDHISTS. Chinese and some low-caste Hindu converts.
CATHOLIC PENTECOSTALS (or, Catholic charismatics). The renewal began in mid-1974. The first National Charismatic Renewal Conference (using English) took place in Murree in July 1975 with 150 Catholics and Protestants (particularly from the Church of Pakistan) present; the first using Urdu, with 150 participants, was held in Lahore in January 1977.
CHRISTIANS. Recent conversions have been from among 30 Hindu scheduled castes in Sindh and southern Punjab (8,000 Catholic baptisms and 5,000 Protestant baptisms since 1940).
COUNTRY'S POPULATION. At Partition in 1947, about 5.5 million Hindus and 2.5 million Sikhs fled to India, and about 8 million Muslims fled from India to Pakistan. A total of at least 200,000 were killed en route.
CRYPTO-CHRISTIANS. Christians affiliated to churches but not known as such to state or society, mainly unorganized individual nationals in the recognized churches, or members of Pakistani indigenous churches, or isolated radio believers. There are a lot of secret believers because of family pressure on converts.
HINDUS. Still strong in rural areas of Sindh (500,000) despite continuing emigration to India; strong also in Lahore, Rawalpindi, Peshawar and Karachi. Hindu peoples include: Bagri (20,000), Bajania (20,000), Balmiki (20,000), Bhil (200,000), Kutchi Kohli (50,000), Lohar, Meghwar (100,000), Od (40,000), Parkari Kohli (100,000), Sochi, Tharadari Kohli (40,000), Vagari (30,000), and Wadiara Kohli (40,000). Since 1900 the Hindu community has decreased in size continuously relative to the Muslim community due to (1) lower Hindu fertility resulting from the prohibition of widow remarriage, (2) the mass emigration of 5.5 million at Partition in 1947, and (3) a steady trickle of emigration to India subsequently.
JEWS. With a synagogue in Karachi.
MUSLIMS. Mostly Sunnis (of the Hanafite rite, 67% being under Sufi influence via the 2 major orders Qadiriya and Naqshabandiya) except for 18% Shias mainly in business and banking (Ismailis and Ithna-Asharis), and a few Wahhabi reform movement centres in the northwest. The totals here also include adherents of the 2 Ahmadiya factions (Qadianis and Lahoris) who in 1974 were formally declared by the state to be heretical and so non-Muslim. *Muslim practice.* About 30% of all Muslims are estimated to actually practise all required Muslim duties. *Conversions to Islam.* Since 1965, several low-caste Hindu tribes have become Muslim, including the Batwal (in Sialkot area), Bazigar (in Sindh) and Gagare. *Hajj pilgrims to Mecca.* Pakistan (East and West): (1968) 25,052; (1969) 28,535; (1970) 38,256; (1971) 23,344. West Pakistan only: (1972) 89,373; (1973) 60,688; (1974) 66,534; (1975) 45,017; (1976) 48,327.
NEO-PENTECOSTALS. Mainly in the Church of Pakistan; begun about 1966 among Anglicans.
PAKISTANI INDIGENOUS. In about 11 denominations in 1970 (see Table 2).
PARSIS. Mainly in Karachi.
SIKHS. At Partition in 1947, every one of the 2.5 million Sikhs either left the newly-formed Pakistan or remained and was killed.
TRIBAL RELIGIONISTS. Animists among the tribal peoples including the Gagre (40,000), Kohlis, several thousand Kafir animists in Chitral, Bhils, et alii. The 3,000 Black Kafirs in Chitral are animists with priest-shamans, worshipping Imra as supreme creator.

**NON-CHRISTIAN RELIGIONS. Islam** was proclaimed in 1956 to be the state religion of Pakistan; and in fact the nation had been created in 1947 on the basis of the common Muslim religious identity shared by the peoples inhabiting the eastern and western parts of the Indian sub-continent. Until the outbreak of civil war between East and West Pakistan in 1971, strenuous efforts had been made to remind the population of the earlier struggle for independence and to stress that Pakistan was the most populous Muslim country in the world. Since the secession of the East as Bangladesh, the Islamic character of Pakistan has been even more accentuated, although there are also serious tensions between the rival claims of traditionalism and modernism in providing solutions for present-day problems. Both in mosques and in religious schools, *maulvi* (religious leaders) warn of the dangers of modernism and call for the preservation of traditional religious values. On the other hand, secularizing tendencies are clearly evident and can be seen in the growing influence of socialists, especially in the political parties. The Central Institute of Islamic Research established by the government contributes to this modernizing tendency, particularly through its training programmes for teachers of Islam in government schools. Two Muslim international organizations are based in Pakistan: (1) the World Federation of Islamic Missions, including also the Ahimia Institute of Islamic Studies, the function of which is to prepare Muslim missionaries; and (2) the World Muslim Congress (Motamar al-Alam al-Islami), in Karachi, whose origin goes back to 1926 but which did not become a permanent organization until 1951. The latter is one of the most important of Islam's international organizations, along with the Muslim World

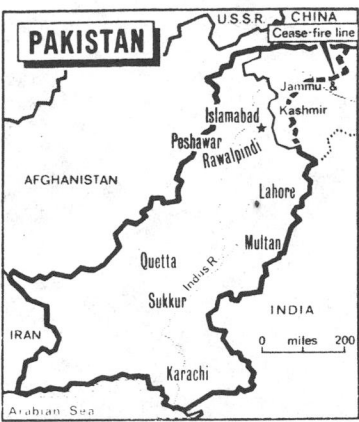

League (from the religious point of view) and the Islamic Conference (from the political point of view), both with headquarters in Saudi. The World Muslim Congress is principally a cultural organization although also religious, whose purpose is to promote unity and co-operation among Muslims. It is a member of the Muslim World League and tends to confine its attention principally to matters internal to the Muslim world. It has affiliated organizations in some 50 countries, with 5 regional offices in Senegal, Somalia, Lebanon, Malaysia and the Philippines.

**Ahmadiya,** begun as a Shia Muslim sect near Lahore in 1889, has grown dramatically in Pakistan and has sent missionaries to spread its doctrines throughout the world. Long considered heretical by other Muslims, it was formally and officially excluded from Islam in 1974 by the Muslim World League in Saudi Arabia and also declared non-Muslim by the Pakistan parliament. Known also as Qadianis, Ahmadis have their strength in the region of Lahore, on the northeast frontier with India and Indian Kashmir. At present there are over 2 million Ahmadis in Pakistan.

**Hinduism** is still strong in Sindh in spite of the continuing tendency, evident since 1947, of Hindus to emigrate to India.

**Traditional religions** are practised by several tribal peoples, including the Gagre, Kohli, Bhil and others.

## CHRISTIANITY.
The first missionaries and Christians were Nestorians who came to the Punjab during the 8th century, although no permanent work resulted. In 1594 Jesuit missionaries arrived at the court of Akbar in Lahore, but no lasting Roman Catholic work was begun until much later.

In the 20th century, the churches are mainly working among Punjabis, and 83% of all Christians in Pakistan are from this ethnic group. This is a result of a mass movement of illiterate low-caste Hindus into Christianity which began after the turn of the century. As Christians form no more than a small minority in a dominant Muslim society, they usually identify themselves first as a community in the religio-caste sense of the term. Their primary loyalties are to families and relatives, and to their caste and

ethnic co-religionists who speak the same language. Participation in national life and civil activities has little attraction for them. In general, Protestants have developed deeper roots than Catholics among rural illiterate communities; and their democratically-oriented ecclesiastical policy has contributed to a more rapid pakistanization of church leadership. Catholicism, on the other hand, is strongest in the cities, especially among the Goan merchant class. There is today a small but rapidly-growing number of well-educated indigenous clergy calling for more dynamic policies to help the churches face the challenge of the modern world.

PROTESTANT CHURCHES. The Church of Pakistan was inaugurated in 1970 through a union of Anglicans, Methodists, Lutherans and Sialkot Presbyterians. The largest of these was the Anglican Church. The Church Missionary Society entered Karachi in 1850, and the Anglican diocese of Lahore was organized in 1877. In 1960 the diocese of Karachi was formed, under the first Pakistani Anglican bishop. American Methodists established themselves in Karachi in 1873 and after 1900 were involved in a mass movement among Hindu outcastes in central Punjab. Between 1902 and 1915 Methodists increased from 1,200 to 15,000, and numbered 60,000 at the time of union. Meanwhile Lutheran work had been begun in the northwest in 1903 by the Danish Pathan Mission, with additional workers from the Finnish Missionary Society lending support in 1959 and the World Mission Prayer League from the USA. Although all 3 were involved in the Pakistan Lutheran Church, the Danish Pathan Mission group refused to go into union in 1970. The Sialkot Church Council was formed through the missionary activity of Scottish Presbyterians and was formerly a member of the United Church of North India and Pakistan.

American Presbyterian missionaries opened their first station at Lahore in 1849 and moved westward outside the Lahore area in 1855. Since this early period the work has been organized separately, and ultimately 2 churches were formed known as the Lahore Church Council and the United Presbyterian Church of Pakistan. The latter church subsequently grew to be the largest Protestant denomination in Pakistan. Widely involved in education, United Presbyterians founded 5 institutions of higher learning, 3 of which are more than 100 years old. The church suffered from a schism in 1968 which carried a portion of the church into the fold of the International Council of Christian Churches (ICCC). It was hoped that the United Presbyterian Church of Pakistan would join the union scheme which produced the Church of Pakistan, but the schisms the church had suffered earlier militated against this. The Lahore Church Council also suffered a schism related to the ICCC in 1968 which played a role in its withdrawal from church union in 1970. Another smaller Presbyterian group is the Associate Reformed Presbyterian Church.

A number of Adventist, Baptist, Pentecostal and other bodies have also begun work in the country, the most important being the Salvation Army. A Pentecostal body, the Full Gospel Assemblies of Pakistan, was of indigenous origin in 1943 but has

for long now been part of Swedish and North American mission work.

CATHOLIC CHURCH. In 1594 Jesuits reached the court of the Mongol emperor Akbar, through whom subsidies were received for the construction of the first Christian church in Lahore. However, few conversions took place. Augustinians and Carmelites were involved in evangelistic activity in Sindh in the 17th century, but their work was interrupted by the persecution of 1672. Work was not begun again until after the conquest of Sindh by the British in 1842. In 1880 the vicariate of the Punjab was erected, being detached from the vicariate of Hindustan; and it became the vicariate of Lahore in 1886. The diocese of Karachi was made an archdiocese in 1950. The Catholic Church is served by 3 indigenous congregations of sisters in addition to 10 foreign orders and congregations of priests, brothers and sisters. Of its 233 clergy in 1972, 74 were nationals. Vocations are still increasing.

INDIGENOUS CHURCHES. During 1968 major Pakistani-led schisms occurred among the Lahore Presbyterians, United Presbyterians, Methodists and Anglicans, influenced by the International Council of Christian Churches. The following year an even larger split appeared among the United Presbyterians, resulting in the formation of the National Virgin Church of Pakistan. Several other small groups have also come into existence.

CHURCH AND STATE. On 23 March 1956 Pakistan was proclaimed an Islamic republic, and this has been re-emphasized in the constitutions of 1962 and 1973. Article 2 of the latter affirms: 'Islam shall be the State religion of Pakistan'. Article 20 guarantees that 'Every citizen shall have the right to profess, practise and propagate his religion; and every religious denomination and every sect thereof shall have the right to establish, maintain and manage its religious institutions'. The constitution outlaws any levy of special taxes for 'the propagation or maintenance of any religion' other than one's own (Article 20), and guarantees that no student will be required to receive religious instruction or attend worship ceremonies against his will (Article 21). Article 31 calls upon the state to take steps to enable Muslims to live in accordance with the fundamental principles of Islam, including the compulsory 'teaching of the Holy Quran and Islamiat'. Article 36 affirms: 'The State shall safeguard the legitimate rights and interests of minorities, including their due representation in the Federal and Provincial services'. In Article 40 mention is made of the need 'to preserve and strengthen fraternal relations among Muslim countries based on Islamic unity', while Article 41 requires that the president of the republic be a Muslim. According to Article 106, a few seats are reserved for members of the minority religions in the provincial assemblies of Baluchistan (1 seat), Punjab (3), North-West Frontier (1) and Sindh (2). Articles 227-231 in part IX of the constitution deal with 'Islamic Provisions', matters relating to the Holy Quran and Sunnah, and the Islamic Council.

In order to demonstrate that its laws are in line with the Quran and with tradition, the government

**Ahmadis.** Annual convention at Rabwah, with in attendance 100,000 devout Ahmadis (who regard themselves as Muslims, though declared non-Muslims by the state), listening to speech by present leader Hazrat Hafiz Mirza Nasir Ahmad, Khalifat-ul-Massih III. At 1974 convention, 15,000 converts were made.

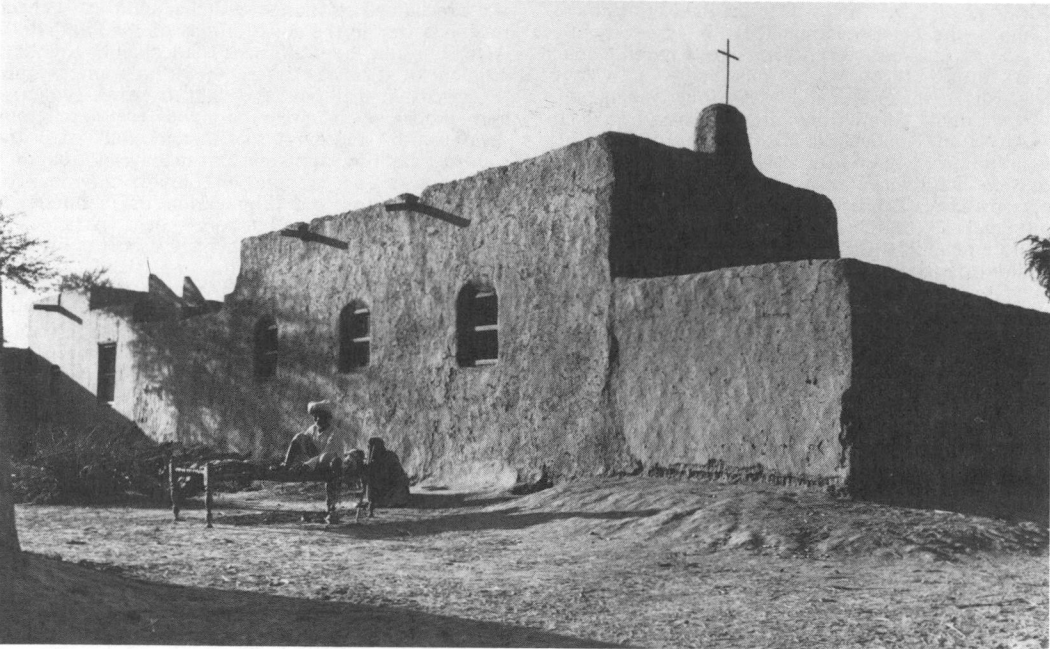

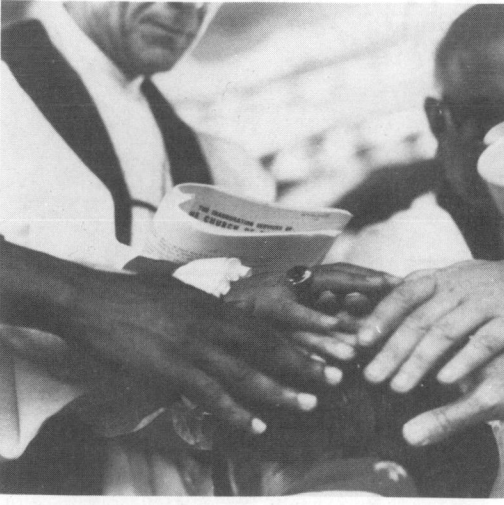

**Church of Pakistan.** *Top left.* Inauguration service in 1970, with clergy at left. *Above.* Laying-on of hands to unify the ministry. *Bottom left.* Khudian Village church (Diocese of Lahore) whose members have more than doubled since church was built.

has established the Central Institute of Islamic Research, with the aim of promoting Islamic studies.

All matters concerning minorities, including religious questions, come under the Ministry of Minority Affairs, a ministry created after 1970. Christians, Hindus, scheduled castes, Sikhs, Parsis, Buddhists, Ahmadis and tribal groups are all defined as minorities. Ahmadis or Qadianis were included in the list of non-Muslim minorities by an amendment to Article 106 of the constitution on 7 September 1974. At the same time the following new clause was added as an amendment to Article 260: 'A person who does not believe in the absolute and unqualified finality of the prophethood of Mohammad (Peace Be Upon Him), the last of the prophets, or claims to be a prophet in any sense of the word or of any description whatsoever, after Mohammad (Peace Be Upon Him) or recognises such a claimant as a prophet or a religious reformer, is not a Muslim for the purposes of the Constitution or Law'.

Churches are not obliged to register officially with government, but as a matter of policy most dioceses and denominations have been registered in the names of individuals, some of whom are foreigners.

Since 1969 the government has exercised increasing control over Christian institutions and the activities of foreign missionaries, it being feared that they are evangelizing and converting people. All private schools and colleges were nationalized between September 1972 and September 1974 in virtue of a government decision taken in 1972. Although this law affects Muslims as well as Christian schools,

Christians believe that its main purpose is to weaken Christian influence in Pakistan in contradiction to Article 20 of the constitution. It is necessary to emphasize that the government has not taken over the ownership of nationalized Christian institutions. They continue to belong to the churches and are rented by the government. Moreover, as of May 1975 no changes had been made in the administration of such schools, their heads and teachers being confirmed in their posts for a period of 2 years. Nevertheless, the situation of Christians in Pakistan is becoming increasingly precarious, due to both a generalized anti-Christian agitation and a growing feeling among numerous members of the federal government that Christianity should be suppressed.

## INTERDENOMINATIONAL ORGANIZATIONS.
Co-operation between Protestant and Anglican missions crystallized in 1913 with the formation of the Punjab Representative Council of Missions. After a visit by John R. Mott it became known in 1923 as the Punjab Christian Council, and was associated with other Christian councils in India. Following national independence in 1947, the name was changed in 1949 to the West Pakistan Christian Council, which in 1971 had as members 6 churches, 6 missions and 9 other Christian organizations. After Bangladesh gained its independence, the name was changed to the Pakistan Christian Council, then again to the National Council of Churches in Pakistan. Another more conservative council is the Evangelical Fellowship of Pakistan, organized in 1956 and

composed of 4 missions and churches. The International Council of Christian Churches (ICCC) has 5 member churches. The Catholic Bishop's Conference sponsors a Commission for Ecumenism.

Co-operative ecumenical institutions and organizations include: (1) Institute for Religious and Social Studies/Ecumenical Section, founded by Franciscans in 1962, which aims at fostering an ecumenical attitude among Catholics, better relations between Catholics and Protestants, and common projects and studies, including the compilation of a joint Dictionary of Christian Terminology, in Urdu; (2) Pakistan Christian Industrial Service, founded in 1969 as an autonomous body by the Catholic, Anglican and Methodist churches of Karachi, which seeks to promote Christian concern for the social, economic and spiritual dimensions of urbanization and industrialization in Pakistan; (3) Adult Basic Education Office, an autonomous group organized by Protestant churches with the help of Catholics and Muslims for the purposes of planning, organizing and promoting adult education programmes for illiterate and newly-literate adults; and (4) Christian Medical Association, which helps to co-ordinate the medical programmes of the various churches.

Three Christian institutes or centres have been established to promote a better understanding of Islam: (1) Christian Study Centre, founded in 1967 by the West Pakistan Christian Council with 2 Catholic members on its board of managers, which aims at creating among the churches an appreciation for Islam and seeks to build up contacts with Muslim schools; (2) Loyola Hall, founded by Jesuits, which is largely academic in nature; and (3) Institute for Religions and Social Studies Islamic Section, founded by Franciscans in 1962, which seeks to encourage dialogue between Christians and Muslims but whose success in this endeavour has thus far been limited.

**BROADCASTING.** As Pakistan is an Islamic state, no regular Christian broadcasting is permitted, but Christmas and Easter programmes in Urdu are allowed and transmitted over government radio for both Protestants and Catholics. From abroad, Protestant programmes in Urdu can be easily heard over the international station FEBA (Seychelles).

**BIBLIOGRAPHY**
*A century for Christ in India and Pakistan, 1855–1955.* Lahore: United Presbyterian Church, c1958.
'Church growth in West Pakistan with special emphasis upon the United Presbyterian Church'. F.E. Stock. Thesis, Fuller Theological Seminary, Pasadena (CA), 1968.
*Focus on Pakistan.* V. Stacey. London: Bible and Medical Missionary Fellowship, 1969. 124p.
*Pakistan Catholic directory, 1966.* Karachi: Archbishop's House, 1966.
'People movements in the Punjab with special reference to the United Presbyterian Church'. F.E. Stock. Thesis, Fuller Theological Seminary, Pasadena (CA), 1974. (Also in published form, 1975: William Carey Library, USA).
*Religion and society in Pakistan.* Ed A. Ahmad. Leiden: Brill, 1971. 105p.
'Secularizing trends in West Pakistan', R.A. Butler, *Al-Mushir* (Rawalpindi), XIII, 1–2 (January-February, 1971), 1–31. (Bibliography of 143 items).
*Survey report of the Church in West Pakistan: a study of the economic, educational and religious condition of the Church, 1955–59.* Lahore: West Pakistan Christian Council, 1960. 55p.
*The Christian minority in the North West Frontier Province of Pakistan.* L. Vemmelund. CSC Series No. 6. Rawalpindi: Christian Study Centre, 1973. 110p.

TABLE 2. ORGANIZED CHURCHES AND DENOMINATIONS IN PAKISTAN

| Official name 1 | Begun 2 | Type 3 | Counc 4 | Congs 5 | Adults 6 | Affiliated 7 | Names, notes, and other statistics (see Codebook) 8 |
|---|---|---|---|---|---|---|---|
| Anglican Orthodox Church: D Pakistan | 1968 | I Ang | xT..T | 196 | 4,393 | 18,057 | *Episcopal Ch of Pakistan.* Schism ex Anglican Ch, Sialkot. M=AOC(USA). 19n,1p(3). |
| Assemblies (Jehova Shammah) | | I CBr | x.... | 90 | 2,000 | 6,000 | Associated with evangelist Brother Bakht Singh (HQ Hyderabad, India). |
| Associate Reformed Presbyterian Church | 1906 | P Ref | FT..a | 29 | 4,300 | 18,000 | M=ARPC(USA),GKN. 3 Presbyteries; Montgomery, Multan. 17 schools. 26f,G=1%pa,1H. |
| Bhai Mission | 1892 | P CBr | x...E | 50 | 2,000 | 5,000 | *Brethren Mission.* M=Brethren Missionary Fellowship(Germany,UK). Multan area. 20f. |
| **Catholic Church in Pakistan:** | 1594 | R Lat | P.F.s | 88 | 184,200 | 341,231 | *Romai Katholik Kalisia.* C=9+6+18. 800f,1p,1q,1s. 74n,159x,71m,585w,P=37%,20311Yy. |
| M Karachi | 1948 | R Lat | Pofm | 17 | 22,700 | 42,000 | *Usqufia-e-Uzma Karachi.* Goans, Punjabis. 1s. 49 20 15 149 45 1615 |
| D Hyderabad in Pakistan | 1958 | R Lat | Pofm | 14 | 12,600 | 23,421 | *Usqufia Hyderabad.* Very poor. Sindhi, Urdu. 6 24 5 56 38 964 |
| D Lahore | 1886 | R Lat | Pofmc | 19 | 80,100 | 148,382 | Most Catholics live in 2,506 scattered villages. 6 43 16 152 30 10772 |
| D Lyallpur (1977, D Faisalabad) | 1960 | R Lat | Pop | 11 | 35,000 | 64,875 | Mainly rural. Urdu and Punjabi. 1p. 9 13 16 79 40 3703 |
| D Multan | 1936 | R Lat | Pop | 8 | 12,600 | 23,304 | Centre. Rural. Mostly Punjabi. M=OCar. 3 18 11 32 63 1260 |
| D Rawalpindi | 1887 | R Lat | Pmhm | 19 | 21,200 | 39,249 | Catholics mostly in villages; many in Islamabad. 1 41 8 117 30 1997 |
| Church of God (Anderson) | 1918 | P Hol | x.... | | 200 | 500 | M=CoG(Anderson) (USA). Holiness denomination aiming to unite all churches. |
| **Church of Pakistan:** | 1850 | P uni | VWE.N | 300 | 150,000 | 250,000 | 1970 union of CIPBC, UCNIP(part), MCSA(UMC), Pakistan Lutheran Ch. 128f. |
| D Karachi | 1970 | P uni | V | | 25,000 | 40,000 | Formerly Anglican D Karachi (CMS), and UMC area. Begun 1850 by M=CMS(UK). |
| D Lahore | 1970 | P uni | V | | 80,000 | 130,000 | Former Anglican D Lahore, UMC, Lutheran. M=FMS(Finland),WMPL(USA). 1s. |
| D Multan | 1970 | P uni | V | | 25,000 | 40,000 | Formerly area of United Methodist Church (UMC). |
| D Sialkot | 1970 | P uni | V | | 20,000 | 40,000 | Formerly Sialkot Ch Council, UCNIP (M=Ch of Scotland); also Lutheran area. |
| Churches of Christ | c1960 | P Dis | x.... | 2 | 50 | 100 | M=CC(Non-Instrumental) (USA). In Karachi, Lahore. Expatriate Americans. 3f. |
| Churches of God | 1911 | P Ref | x.... | 15 | 500 | 1,000 | M=Churches of God in North America, General Eldership (USA). |
| Cooneyites | | P ind | x.... | | 100 | 300 | *Christian Undenominational Church. Go-Preachers.* Irish itinerants from USA, UK. |
| Danish Pathan Mission | 1903 | P Lut | ....N | 5 | 200 | 1,000 | *Tent Mission.* In Pakistan Lutheran Ch until policy split. M=DPM,FMS,WMPL. 3f. |
| Evangelical Alliance Mission | 1946 | P int | xM..E | 10 | 200 | 700 | M=TEAM(USA). In north, adjoining Kashmir. 3 schools. HQ Rawalpindi. 52f,1H,5h. |
| Full Gospel Assemblies of Pakistan | 1943 | P Pe2 | ..... | 34 | 2,400 | 8,000 | *Scandinavian Free Ch.* M=SFM(Sweden),AoG(UK,USA). 16n,20f,G=24%pa,W=83%. |
| Indus Christian Fellowship | 1954 | P Bap | xF..E | 6 | 328 | 799 | M=Conservative Baptist FMS(USA). Work in Sind. HQ Jacobabad. 2n,1m,1w,25f,1H,62Y. |
| International Missions | 1954 | P int | xM... | 5 | 250 | 2,000 | *Pakistan Mission of IM.* M=IM(USA). In Muzaffargah, Dera Ghazi Khan. 12f. |
| Isolated radio churches | c1960 | I rad | ..... | 440 | 8,000 | 17,500 | Isolated radio believers. R=213(FEBA,IBRA),T=120000(90002 PBCS,SFM,VOP,CBFMS,ICI). |
| Jehovah's Witnesses | c1924 | M Jeh | x.... | 4 | 150 | 250 | *Watch Tower Bible & Tract Society.* First missionaries 1926. Little impact. 6Y. |
| Lahore Church Council (ICCC) | 1968 | I Ref | .T..T | 17 | 2,000 | 5,000 | *LCC Sharakpur.* Schism ex LCC. 1968, M=IBPFM(USA). 10n,1p,W=60%,300Yy,500z. |
| National Church of Pakistan | | I pen | ..... | | 500 | 1,000 | Pakistani pentecostals. Headquarters Clarkabad, District Lahore. 1f. |
| National Methodist Church of Pakistan | 1968 | I Met | .T..T | 66 | 5,976 | 22,294 | Schism ex UMC(USA) in Lahore. M=independents(USA). 11n,7f,G=16.6%pa,220Yy. |
| National Virgin Church of Pakistan | 1969 | I Ref | .v... | 50 | 12,452 | 44,701 | *Saint Council.* Ex UPCP. HQ Pasrur, Sialkot. 1969, applied to WCC. 52n,168Yy,230z. |
| Pakistan Christian Fellowship | 1954 | P int | xM... | 7 | 220 | 2,000 | M=International Christian Fellowship (Ceylon & India General Mission). 19f,1p. |
| Philadelphia Pentecostal Church | | P Pe2 | Z.... | 5 | 526 | 1,000 | M=Swedish Baptist(Örebro) Mission (Sweden). HQ Murree. 4n,7t(290),26Y. |
| Salvation Army | 1883 | P Sal | xwE.N | 674 | 40,422 | 60,000 | *Muktifauj. Pakistan Territory.* 7 Divisions. 2 hostels. 192n,21f,G=2%pa,5h,4r,1s. |
| Seventh-day Adventist Church | 1913 | P Adv | x.... | 29 | 2,939 | 8,000 | *Pak Union (& Punjab Section)*, SAsia Div. 17nx,307m,58f,G=7%pa,1H,1h,1j,1r,87Y. |
| Southern Baptist Mission | 1957 | P Bap | T.... | 10 | 291 | 500 | M=Southern Baptist Convention(USA). Sunday-school enrolment 235. 5n,22Y. |
| Unitarian Universalist Fellowship | | M Unt | I.... | 1 | 23 | 50 | *UUF of Lahore.* Small fellowship of expatriates. Links with M=UUA(USA). |
| United Ch in Pakistan: Lahore Ch C | 1849 | P Ref | ....N | 70 | 12,000 | 35,000 | C=Council. In former UCNIP. M=UPUSA. 1968, major schism, property lost. 30n,G=0. |
| United Pentecostal Church | c1960 | P Pe1 | x.... | 140 | 4,200 | 10,000 | *Jesus Only Church.* M=UPC(USA). Unitarian Pentecostals. 29n,4f,2p(33). |
| United Presbyterian Church in Pakistan | 1968 | I Ref | .T..T | | 10,000 | 15,000 | *Synod of UP Ch.* Ex UPCP, opposing WCC, claiming name, property. M=IBPFM(USA). 1s. |
| **United Presbyterian Church of Pakistan** | 1849 | P Ref | RWE.N | 190 | 53,240 | 175,000 | *UPCP.* M=UPUSA. A=1961. 1968, schisms. 1970, union scheme rejected. 158n,48f. |
| World-Wide Missions | 1962 | P ind | x.... | | 60 | 200 | M=World-Wide Missions(USA). Evangelicals with links in Pasadena, CA(USA) |
| Other Pakistani indigenous churches | | I | ..... | | 1,100 | 2,300 | Total about 3 small groupings begun by Pakistanis. |
| Other Protestant denominations | | P | ..... | | 1,000 | 2,000 | Total about 15 (see list below). |
| **Total affiliated (mid-1970)** | | | | **3,590** | **506,220** | **1,054,482** | **Total denominations (1970) . . . 49.** |
| **Total affiliated (mid-1975)** | | | | **3,780** | **606,000** | **1,262,400** | **Total denominations (1975) . . . 53.** |
| **Total affiliated (mid-1980)** | | | | **3,950** | **708,300** | **1,475,500** | **Total denominations (1980) . . . 57.** |

NOTES ON TABLE ABOVE
COLUMNS: for meanings and CODES (cols. 1, 3, 4, 8): see Codebook (Part 6). Column 1: **Boldface type** = church with over 10% of country's affiliated Christians.
NATIONAL COUNCILS (Column 4, 5th letter).
a = member of both NCCP and EFP.
E = Evangelical Fellowship of Pakistan (EFP).
N = National Council of Churches in Pakistan (NCCP) (formerly West Pakistan Christian Council).
s = Catholic Bishops' Conference of Pakistan (CBCP), and also official observer member of NCCP.
T = Pakistan Council of Christian Churches.
*Local councils.* Frontier Regional Conference, Peshawar; Southern Regional Conference, Karachi.
OTHER PROTESTANT DENOMINATIONS. These include: Afghan Border Crusade (1940), Baptist Bible Fellowship International (1954), Central Asian Mission, Christ-Bearers (Christusträger, from West Germany, 1961; 9 missionaries), Evangelical Methodist Ch, Fellowship of Ev Baptist Chs in Canada, Religious Society of Friends (Quakers), Worldwide Evangelization Crusade (1935).

**PEOPLES** (ethnolinguistic). Christians: 82.8% Punjabi (mainly Chuhra caste, formerly Hindu), 7.0% Sindhi, 5.0% Jat, 1.9% Goanese (20,000), 1.0% British, 1.0% Pathan (Afghani, Pushtu), 0.7% Kohli, 0.2% Gujarati, 0.2% Baluchi, 0.1% Brahui, 0.1% Kashmiri (Kho, Kohistani), Thori (Marwari Bhil), Anglo-Indian, Chinese (500).

**COUNTRY-WIDE TOTALS**
EVANGELIZATION (see Part 5). 1900: 17%. 1970: 39%. 1980: 54%. *Mass evangelism.* Recent campaigns: 1960, A.A. Haqq meetings in Lyallpur and Lahore (many enquirers); 1968, 1969, teams of Indonesian evangelists and laymen visited Pakistan's largest cities and towns, and many villages. By 1975 there were an estimated one million enquirers (interested, seekers) in the south, with significant movements among the Bhils and Kohlis (Gujarati- and Sindhi-speaking). Advertisements in Muslim newspapers recently produced 4,500 enquiries. 1978, Here's Life Karachi and Lahore (CCCI). *Radiophonic evangelism.* FEBA, HCJB. Bible correspondence courses: SFM, VOP, CBFMS, ICI, Pakistan Bible Correspondence School (10,000 enrolled before 1964; 1964-76, 90,002 enrolled), et alia.
FOREIGN MISSIONARIES AND PERSONNEL (nationals serving abroad) (1973). Total about 2 Protestants in Afghanistan.
FOREIGN MISSIONARIES AND PERSONNEL (aliens from abroad) (1973). Total 1,160. *From Western world.* 1,120: about 600 Roman Catholics, 495 Protestants (295 in 22 USA societies, 72 in 8 UK societies, 29 in 3 WGermany societies, 22 in 3 Finland societies, 20 in 3 Sweden societies, 15 in 3 Canada societies, 13 in 5 New Zealand societies, 10 in 3 Norway societies, 9 in 7 Australia societies, 6 in 3 Denmark societies, 4 in 1 Netherlands society), 25 Anglicans (19 in 2 UK societies, 6 in 1 New Zealand society). By 1975, North American missionaries had fallen to 208. *From Third World.* 40: about 30 Roman Catholics, about 7 Protestants from Korea, Philippines, Singapore and Sri Lanka, 3 Anglicans.
INSTITUTIONS (church-operated) (1973). Total 210, including 95 higher schools (5 minor seminaries), 75 medical centres (29 hospitals), 3 religious communities, 3 research centres, 7 seminaries (4 Protestant, 2 RC, 1 Pakistani indigenous).
PERIODICALS. About 35 titles.
PERSONNEL. About 2,936 (1,776 national, 1,160 foreign).
RELIGIOUS LIBRARIES. About 15.
SCRIPTURE DISTRIBUTION (1975). Annual totals: 108,657 Bibles (92% free, 7% subsidized, 1% commercial), 37,311 NTs (8% free, 87% subsidized, 5% commercial), 228,384 UBS portions, 789,073 UBS selections. *Translations completed.* Portion: 6 languages since 1805. NT: 5 languages since 1812. Bible: 3 languages since 1843.
SERVICE AGENCIES. About 45, including AMSMP, AMSW, BMMF, CBCP, CCCI, CEF, CLC, CNSP, DU, EFP, NCCP, PACTEE, PBCS, PFES, SCM, WUMS(UFCS), YCW, YMCA, YWCA.

ADDITIONAL DATA ON CHURCHES
CATHOLIC CHURCH IN PAKISTAN. *Members.* Including 20,000 Goanese in Karachi. *Catechumens.* (1963) 64,730. *Annual baptisms.* (1972) 78.8% infant, 21.2% adult. *Brothers.* Including 4 Pakistanis. *Sisters.* Including about 330 Pakistanis. *Seminarians.* 43 secular, 7 regular (1970). Vocations are on the increase, mostly from the Punjab. *Catechists.* Total (1974) 356. *Indigenous religious congregations.* Sisters: 87 Franciscan Missionaries of Christ the King (begun 1930), Orders of the Presentation of the BVM (begun 1775, 18 houses), Franciscan Tertiary Sisters of Lahore. *Main foreign orders and congregations.* Priests: OFM, OFMCap, OP, OCarm, SJ, MHM. Brothers: FSC, FIC, PFM, Brothers of St Patrick. Sisters (major congregations only): Medical Mission Sisters, Franciscan Missionaries of Mary.
*Catholic organizations.* There is a Catholic Bishops' Conference of Pakistan (a member of FABC) and 2 organizations for religious personnel: Association of Major Superiors of Men in Pakistan and Association of Major Superiors of Women. No national presbyteral or pastoral councils have been formed. There is no co-ordinating body for the lay apostolate, although some pious and political movements exist. The YCW has a small membership.
The Holy See has diplomatic relations with Pakistan and is represented to government and the Catholic hierarchy by a pro-nuncio in Islamabad.
The Catholic Church has been heavily involved in literacy, home industries, agriculture and industrial services. The numbers of Catholic institutions in 1970 were: 97 primary schools, 39 middle and 70 high schools, 4 colleges, 25 hospitals, 1 leprosarium with 10 outstations, 32 dispensaries, 3 homes for the aged, and 2 homes for the handicapped. By 1974 schools had been reduced slightly to 87 primary, 22 middle and 74 high.
UNITED PRESBYTERIAN CHURCH OF PAKISTAN. Membership: over 95% Chuhra caste (low-caste, outcaste) since 1880 mass movement of Chuhras began.

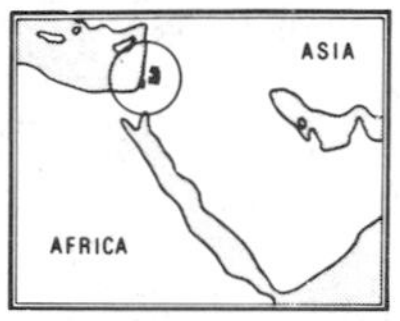


# PALESTINE

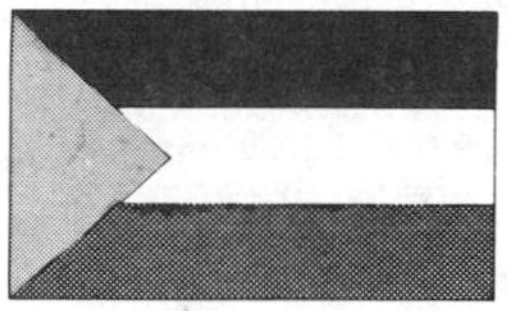

## SECULAR DATA

**STATE. Official name:** Palestine. Adjective of nationality: Palestinian.
**Flag** (shown above right): Stripes of black (top), white, and green, with red triangle in the hoist.
**Area:** 6,257 sq.km. (2,416 sq.miles). Regions: Gaza Strip 378 sq.km., West Bank and East Jerusalem, 5,879 sq.km. (West Bank 5,650 sq.km.).
**Government:** Provisional republic in exile. Status in 1978: Israeli-occupied territory, since 1967. Possible future: non-sovereign independence under UN auspices.
**Official language:** Arabic.
**Capital:** East Jerusalem.
**Armed forces** (1978): Palestine Liberation Organization (PLO) militia, 50,000 men.

**DEMOGRAPHY. Population:** 1,397,000 (estimate for mid-1975. For 1970–2000 (UN), see last row of Table 1). Total Palestinians abroad (in diaspora): 2.3 million (1977). Population density (1975): 223/sq.km. (578/sq.mile). Under 15 years: 40%. Growth rate (1975–80): 3.50% per year (births 4.5%, deaths –1.00%). Life expectancy (1975–80): 60.0 years. Household size: 5.2 persons.
**Major languages:** Arabic, English, Hebrew, French, German, Armenian, Aramaic.
**Refugees** (1977): 625,953 Palestinians under UNRWA mandate (333,031 in Gaza, 292,922 in West Bank). Exiles abroad: 1,006,754 Palestinians under UNRWA (625,857 in Jordan, 196,855 in Lebanon, 184,042 in Syria).

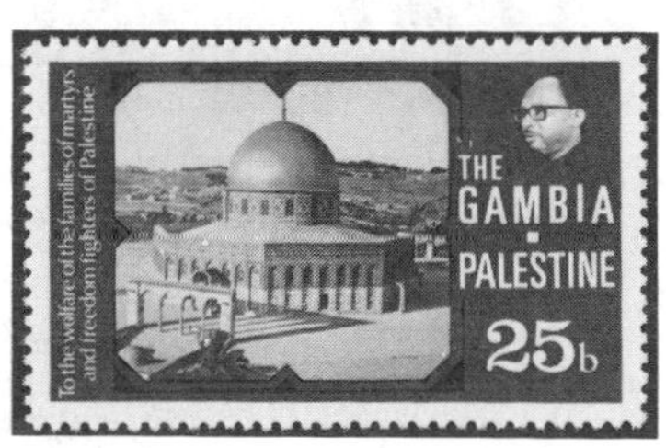

Many countries now recognize Palestine as a state. Here, a Gambia stamp showing the Dome of the Rock (Jerusalem).

**ETHNOLINGUISTIC GROUPS:** 97.2% Palestinian Arab (including Gazan), 2% other Arab, 0.4% European (French, German, Italian, UK, USA), 0.2% Armenian, 0.1% Assyrian (Aramaic), 0.1% Jewish, Greek, Russian, Romanian, Bedouin, Circassian.

TABLE 1. RELIGIOUS ADHERENTS IN PALESTINE (West Bank, Gaza Strip, East Jerusalem)

| Year | 1900 | | mid-1970 | | Annual change, 1970–1980 | | | | mid-1975 | | mid-1980 | | 2000 | |
|---|---|---|---|---|---|---|---|---|---|---|---|---|---|---|
| *Name* | *Adherents* | *%* | *Adherents* | *%* | *Natural* | *Conversion* | *Total* | *Rate* | *Adherents* | *%* | *Adherents* | *%* | *Adherents* | *%* |
| Muslims | 206,700 | 79.5 | 1,120,400 | 94.9 | 44,759 | –54 | 44,705 | 3.38 | 1,323,750 | 94.8 | 1,567,450 | 94.8 | 2,921,500 | 94.8 |
| Ahmadis | 0 | 0.0 | 1,000 | 0.1 | 41 | 9 | 50 | 4.17 | 1,200 | 0.1 | 1,500 | 0.1 | 3,000 | 0.1 |
| **Christians** | **30,300** | **11.7** | **54,930** | **4.7** | **2,225** | –73 | **2,152** | **3.27** | **65,850** | **4.7** | **76,450** | **4.6** | **136,500** | 4.4 |
| crypto-Christians | 4,300 | 1.7 | 11,630 | 1.0 | 539 | 293 | 832 | 5.22 | 15,950 | 1.1 | 19,950 | 1.2 | 39,100 | 1.3 |
| professing | 26,000 | 10.0 | 43,300 | 3.7 | 1,686 | –366 | 1,320 | 2.64 | 49,900 | 3.6 | 56,500 | 3.4 | 97,400 | 3.2 |
| Orthodox | 20,000 | 7.7 | 25,000 | 2.1 | 980 | –180 | 800 | 2.75 | 29,000 | 2.1 | 33,000 | 2.0 | 55,000 | 1.8 |
| Roman Catholics | 5,000 | 1.9 | 15,000 | 1.3 | 574 | –174 | 400 | 2.35 | 17,000 | 1.2 | 19,000 | 1.1 | 34,000 | 1.1 |
| Protestants | 200 | 0.1 | 2,000 | 0.2 | 81 | –1 | 80 | 3.33 | 2,400 | 0.2 | 2,800 | 0.2 | 5,400 | 0.2 |
| Anglicans | 800 | 0.3 | 1,300 | 0.1 | 51 | –11 | 40 | 2.67 | 1,500 | 0.1 | 1,700 | 0.1 | 3,000 | 0.1 |
| affiliated | 30,300 | 11.7 | 54,930 | 4.7 | 2,225 | –73 | 2,152 | 3.27 | 65,850 | 4.7 | 76,450 | 4.6 | 136,500 | 4.4 |
| total practising | 27,270 | *90* | 43,940 | *80* | 1,780 | –58 | 1,722 | 3.27 | 52,680 | *80* | 61,160 | *80* | 95,550 | *70* |
| non-practising | 3,030 | *10* | 10,990 | *20* | 445 | –15 | 430 | 3.26 | 13,170 | *20* | 15,290 | *20* | 40,950 | *30* |
| Orthodox | 23,000 | 8.8 | 27,700 | 2.3 | 1,115 | –85 | 1,030 | 3.12 | 33,000 | 2.4 | 38,000 | 2.3 | 67,000 | 2.2 |
| Roman Catholics | 6,000 | 2.3 | 16,950 | 1.4 | 676 | –71 | 605 | 3.02 | 20,000 | 1.4 | 23,000 | 1.4 | 37,000 | 1.2 |
| Arab indigenous | 0 | 0.0 | 4,500 | 0.4 | 193 | 57 | 250 | 4.39 | 5,700 | 0.4 | 7,000 | 0.4 | 16,000 | 0.5 |
| Protestants | 300 | 0.1 | 3,980 | 0.3 | 166 | 16 | 182 | 3.71 | 4,900 | 0.4 | 5,800 | 0.4 | 11,000 | 0.4 |
| Evangelicals | 200 | 0.1 | 2,700 | 0.2 | 112 | 8 | 120 | 3.64 | 3,300 | 0.2 | 3,900 | 0.2 | 8,000 | 0.3 |
| Neo-pentecostals | 0 | 0.0 | 0 | 0.0 | 5 | 55 | 60 | 20.00 | 300 | 0.0 | 600 | 0.0 | 1,000 | 0.0 |
| Anglicans | 1,000 | 0.4 | 1,400 | 0.1 | 57 | –2 | 55 | 3.23 | 1,700 | 0.1 | 1,950 | 0.1 | 3,500 | 0.1 |
| Evangelicals | 500 | 0.2 | 800 | 0.1 | 33 | 7 | 40 | 4.00 | 1,000 | 0.1 | 1,200 | 0.1 | 2,000 | 0.1 |
| Anglican pentecostals | 0 | 0.0 | 100 | 0.0 | 4 | 16 | 20 | 10.00 | 200 | 0.0 | 300 | 0.0 | 400 | 0.0 |
| Marginal Protestants | 0 | 0.0 | 400 | 0.0 | 18 | 12 | 30 | 5.45 | 550 | 0.0 | 700 | 0.0 | 2,000 | 0.1 |
| Non-religious | 0 | 0.0 | 2,000 | 0.2 | 101 | 99 | 200 | 6.67 | 3,000 | 0.2 | 4,000 | 0.2 | 12,000 | 0.4 |
| Atheists | 0 | 0.0 | 1,000 | 0.1 | 47 | 33 | 80 | 5.71 | 1,400 | 0.1 | 1,800 | 0.1 | 5,000 | 0.2 |
| Jews | 23,000 | 8.8 | 1,000 | 0.1 | 0 | 0 | 0 | 0.00 | 1,000 | 0.1 | 1,000 | 0.1 | 2,000 | 0.1 |
| Samaritans | 70 | 0.0 | 250 | 0.0 | 9 | –7 | 2 | 0.77 | 260 | 0.0 | 270 | 0.0 | 500 | 0.0 |
| Other religionists | 0 | 0.0 | 1,670 | 0.1 | 68 | –5 | 63 | 3.15 | 2,000 | 0.1 | 2,300 | 0.1 | 5,000 | 0.2 |
| **Country's population** | **260,000** | **100.0** | **1,181,000** | **100.0** | **47,200** | **0** | **47,200** | **3.38** | **1,397,000** | **100.0** | **1,653,000** | **100.0** | **3,082,000** | **100.0** |

COLUMNS, ROWS. For meanings and definitions, see Codebook (Part 6). Note that, by definition, total 'Christians' = professing + crypto-Christians, which also = affiliated + nominal Christians. Percentages may not always total exactly, due to rounding.
CENSUSES (Holy Land). **1800** (estimate): 14,000 Christians (about 11,800 being Greek Orthodox). **1919**: 81.7% Muslims, 9.4% Jews (65,000), 8.9% Christians (62,000). **23.X.1922**: 78.0% Muslims, 11.1% Jews, 9.6% Christians (73,024). **1926**: 73% Muslims, 17% Jews, 9.7% Christians (80,000). **18.XII.1931**: 73.3% Muslims, 16.9% Jews, 8.9% Christians (91,938). **1939**: 61.5% Muslims, 30.8% Jews, 7.7% Christians (100,000). **18.XI.1961** (West Bank and Jerusalem): 5.7% Christians (46,000). Gaza Strip, **14.IX.1967**: 99.0% Muslims, 0.6% Christians (2,480), 0.4% others. East Jerusalem, **27.IX.1967**: 10,795 Christians. West Bank (Judea and Samaria), **1967**: 29,434 Christians.

NOTES ON RELIGIONS
AHMADIS. Arab Qadianis. There is also a large Palestinian Arab community of Ahmadis in Haifa, Israel.
ANGLICAN PENTECOSTALS. An ecumenical charismatic renewal began in 1970, initially among English-speaking Anglican expatriates, later among Arab Christians.
ANGLICANS. In the year 1900, there were 1,000 faithful (Arab converts from Greek Orthodoxy and Catholicism); there were also 1,762 pupils in 31 Anglican schools.
ARAB INDIGENOUS. Isolated radio and correspondence course believers scattered across the country (see Table 2).
ATHEISTS. Many Arabs belong to the New Communists (RAKAH), most of whom remain practising Muslims or Christians. In the 28.X.1969 election organized by the state of Israel, 38,827 voted for RAKAH.
CHRISTIANS. The total includes 11,000 Christians in East Jerusalem, a disputed area claimed by Israel since 1967 as part of the state of Israel. Other concentrations of Christians (1969): Ramallah and Bira 7,300, Bethlehem 6,400, Beit Sahour 3,730, Beit Jala 2,270, Gaza 1,650, Bir Zeit 1,350. Over the years since 1948, large numbers of Palestinian Arabs have emigrated, including a high proportion of Christians. Altogether, among all Palestinians in Palestine or abroad, Christians number about 12% (a total of over 300,000) compared with only 4.7% in Palestine itself. The total of all Palestinian Arab Christians in 1975 is made up of 49,000 in Palestine, 50,000 in Jordan, 64,000 in Israel, over 80,000 in Arab countries outside Palestine and Jordan, and over 50,000 outside the Arab world (in the USA, Europe, Latin America, et alia).
COUNTRY'S POPULATION. The statistics in the table refer to the de facto territory and population of West Bank, East Jerusalem and the Gaza Strip. Large numbers of Palestinians fled the territory between 1948 and 5 June 1967, including refugees to Jordan who by 1970 numbered 305,000 (a fair number of whom were Christians) and had become permanent residents in Jordan; but also after the 1967 war a further 433,866 fled to Jordan, almost all Muslims with only a very few Christians. In addition there has been steady emigration of Palestinians to the USA, Canada, Australia, Saudi Arabia, Kuwait, Libya, Lebanon, Syria, et alia. Hence the population of West Bank fell from over 830,000 in 1960 to 680,000 in 1970. In 1970, the population consisted of 680,000 (58% of Palestine as here defined) in West Bank and East Jerusalem, and 501,000 (42%) in Gaza Strip (UN estimates published in 1975).
CRYPTO-CHRISTIANS. Secret believers, i.e. Christians affiliated to churches but not known as such to staate or sociey nor recorded in censuses.
JEWS. In the year 1900, residents from throughout Ottoman rule, mainly in Jerusalem, Hebron and Gaza. In 1970, there remained only Israeli military, administrative and some civilian personnel.
MUSLIMS. Palestinian Arabs with a few Bedouin, all Sunnis (mainly of Shafiite rite, also some of Hanafite and Hanbalite rites); also an Ahmadiya Mission (enumerated here under Muslims, though declared non-Muslim by Pakistan). *Hajj pilgrims to Mecca.* (1970) 838; (1975) 1,445; (1976) 656.
ORTHODOX. The Greek Orthodox Church has since 1850 lost many members as converts to Catholicism, Protestantism and Anglicanism, also by emigration, also by conversion to Islam or non-religion.
OTHER RELIGIONISTS. Including a few Baha'is, and scattered adherents of several other non-Christian religions.
SAMARITANS, or As-Samarah. Around Nablus, West Bank, where their high priest lives.

**NON-CHRISTIAN RELIGIONS. Islam** makes up 95% of the population of the West Bank, Gaza Strip and East Jerusalem, an increase of 15% during the present century due primarily to the emigration of Christians and Jews. Muslims are mostly Shafiites, but there are also some Hanafites and Hanbalites and a small community of Ahmadis.

**Judaism** remains only in the form of security and administrative personnel, who have entered since the 1967 war to supervise Israel's occupation of the territory.

**Samaritan religion** has existed as a sect separate from Judaism since 432 BC. Samaritans number 260 on the West Bank and worship on Mount Gerizim.

**CHRISTIANITY.** As the scene of the birth, death and resurrection of Jesus and the birth and expansion of the early church, Palestine has a long and complex history. Colonized and occupied by Romans, Arabs and Turks for centuries, followed by the British mandate (1917-48), Palestine was the scene of Arab-Jewish hostilities in 1948 as a result of which over 600,000 Palestinians fled the country. In 1949 it was divided between the newly-formed state of Israel and Jordan, the latter annexing Jerusalem and the West Bank, while the Gaza coastal strip was placed under Egyptian administration. In the 1967 war, Israel occupied the latter 3 territories, which provoked a further exodus of Palestinians. By 1970, the total number of Palestinians had reached 3,250,000, divided as follows: Jordan (Transjordan) 850,000; Palestine (West Bank and Gaza) 1,181,000; Israel 450,000; Lebanon 300,000; Syria 180,000; Kuwait 140,000; Egypt 33,000; Gulf countries 30,000; Saudi Arabia 20,000; West Germany 15,000; Iraq 14,000; Libya 10,000; USA 7,000; UK 7,000; and Latin America 5,000.

About 88% of Palestinians are Sunni Muslims, and 12% of the entire Palestinian people are Christians of different denominations. Benefitting from a higher level of education than Muslims, Christian Palestinians have moved quickly into the urban middle

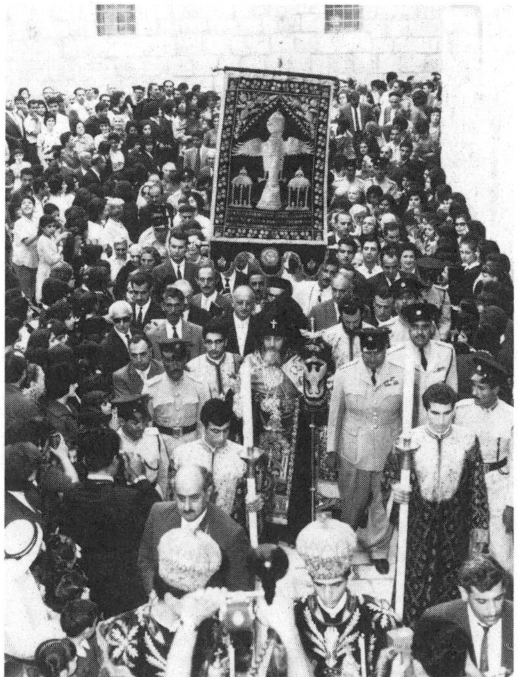

**Armenian Apostolic Patriarchate of Jerusalem.** A huge throng of 4,000 Armenians follows Catholicos of Echmiadzin (USSR), His Holiness Vasken I, Supreme Catholicos of All Armenians (followed by Patriarch of Jerusalem), to Church of the Holy Sepulchre in Jerusalem in 1963. Over quarter of a million Christians visit Jerusalem each year.

class and the professions. Few are in refugee camps, because as doctors, engineers and other professionals they quickly become candidates for emigration. It is estimated that Christians compose almost half of those actively engaged in the Palestinian resistance. In 1974 a Protestant pastor, Elie Khoury, was a member of the executive committee of the Palestine Liberation Organization (PLO), which served to represent all Palestinian resistance organizations as well as leaders of mass movements. Other members and leaders in the PLO are also Christians. At the international and interdenominational level, there is a World Conference of Christians for Palestine, with its principal centre in Paris and an office in Beirut.

The vast Palestinian Christian diaspora is a recent phenomenon of very great importance to the Christian presence in the Muslim world. A majority of Palestinians abroad are Christians. Among them in 1973 were at least 152 full-time Christian workers. About 40% of all Palestinian Roman Catholic religious personnel now live and work outside Palestine, especially in Jordan, Lebanon, Kuwait, United Arab Emirates and Syria. Some 15% have Jordanian citizenship. Among the most notable congregations are the Holy Rosary Sisters with widespread work in the diaspora.

ORTHODOX CHURCHES. The Greek Orthodox Church is the largest Christian denomination, although its community is decreasing rapidly due to the emigration of Orthodox Christians to other parts of the world. A source of tension exists between priests and laity, who are mostly Palestinian Arabs, and the patriarch and bishops, who are Greeks.

Three other Eastern Orthodox communities are the Romanians, who come under the Patriarchate of Bucharest, and 2 Russian groups, one of which is under the Patriarchate of Moscow, the other representing the Russian Orthodox Church Outside of Russia which is opposed to the Moscow Patriarchate.

Five Oriental Orthodox or Monophysite bodies are active: Syrian, Coptic and Ethiopian Orthodox, and the 2 rival Armenian bodies. One of the latter is part of the Catholicate of Cilicia in Lebanon, while the other is related to the Catholicate of Echmiadzin in the Soviet Union through the Armenian Patriarchate of Jerusalem.

The Ancient Church of the East (Nestorians) are

also present in the West Bank.

CATHOLIC CHURCH. Seven different Catholic rites are present in Palestine. (1) Latin Catholics predominate, there being 3,800 in East Jerusalem, 8,800 in the West Bank and 300 in Gaza, making a total of 12,900. All are under the jurisdiction of the Latin Patriarchate of Jerusalem whose patriarch resides in East Jerusalem. Twelve groups of Latin-rite priests are at work, the most important of whom are the OFM who have been granted the Custody of the Holy Places. They number 64 in East Jerusalem and 20 in the West Bank and are 50% Italians, 25% Spanish and 25% other nationalities. A host of other orders and congregations of brothers and sisters are also active. (2) Melkite Catholics number 3,200, 1,200 of which are in East Jerusalem, with 1,700 in West Bank and 300 in Gaza. The Greek Melkite patriarch of Antioch, who lives in Damascus, has a patriarchal vicar in Jerusalem. (3) Maronite Catholics form a small community of 250, with 100 each in Jerusalem and the West Bank and 50 in Gaza. Maronites belong to the archbishopric of Tyre in Lebanon. (4) Syrian Catholics come under the patriarchal vicar of Jerusalem, who is dependent on the Syrian Catholic patriarch of Antioch and the East in Beirut, Lebanon. There are 2 parishes, Jerusalem and Bethlehem, and one other priest. (5) Armenian Catholics, consisting in 1973 of 61 families, are found at Jerusalem, Ramleh, Beirut Jamal and Haifa (in Israel). They are served by 2 priests, including a patriarchal vicar. (6) Chaldean Catholics are dependent on the Chaldean vicariate of Jerusalem under the Chaldean patriarch in Iraq. (7) Coptic Catholics consisted in 1973 of 6 families ministered to by a Franciscan priest attached to the Custody of the Holy Places.

OTHER CHURCHES. Anglicans arrived in 1820 to work with the Jews and were followed in 1860 by Lutherans. The latter are related to German Lutheranism and are confined to the West Bank; while the former, previously in the Jerusalem Archbishopric, now belong to the diocese of Jerusalem of the Episcopal Church in Jerusalem and the Middle East.

Southern Baptists have been at work since 1911 and cater for an extensive programme, with a staff of 18 missionaries in Gaza. The Church of the Nazarene entered in 1921 and has Arab and Armenian congregations in East Jerusalem.

Pentecostalism is widely represented through the presence of 12 denominations, though none has a large membership. The same is true of 30 other small missions mostly from the USA who have appeared on the scene since World War II.

**CHURCH AND STATE.** The PLO has as its objective the establishment of a Palestinian secular state assuring equal rights for Jews, Christian and Muslims. Parallel political organizations also exist in Israel and neighbouring Arab countries. A large number of Arab Christians, both those living in cities (such as the Arab town of Nazareth in Israel proper, which is half Christian and half Muslim) and rural areas, vote for the Arab Communist party RAKAH, because they believe it to be the only officially tolerated party which is concerned about

Church of the Nativity, Bethlehem. Traditional cave birthplace of Jesus, with first church building dating from AD 290; long a source of conflict between Christian traditions, and now divided among Greek Orthodox, Roman Catholic and Armenian Apostolic jurisdictions.

the Palestinian cause. Arab communists are generally religious believers at the same time and insist that their party defends more effectively than others the rights of the disinherited. It is not unusual for militant lay Christians to exercise responsibility within the body of the party.

Because Gaza, the West Bank and East Jerusalem have been under Israeli control since the 1967 Middle East war, church-state relations follow a pattern similar to that of Israel itself.

According to Israeli law, persons are considered to be under specific religious communities much as in the old Turkish millet system, their religious communities in turn being responsible for decisions relating to marriage, divorce and other matters of a personal nature. Recognized community religious authorities report to Israel's Ministry of the Interior which keeps a record of all decisions made.

The occupying Israeli regime also maintains a Ministry of Religions (Misrad Hadatoth), within which are located departments of Muslim affairs and Christian affairs.

**INTERDENOMINATIONAL ORGANIZATIONS.** Anglicans, Baptists, Lutherans and Nazarenes are members of the United Christian Council in Israel (UCCI).

Considerable influence is wielded by the various ecumenical centres and organizations in Israel. In West Bank itself, a significant ecumenical role is

played by the first Catholic university in the Holy Land, Bethlehem Regional University, which was established in 1974. With faculties of arts and sciences, pedagogy and commerce, and schools of nursing and hotel administration, it provides the possibility for young Palestinians to pursue higher studies without leaving Palestine or Israel. It is not a Catholic University in the usual sense of the term, for although the funds and decision to build have come principally from Catholics, local committees composed of Christians of all confessions and Muslims have been formed to assure its development. Courses are given in Arabic. In 1974-75 there were 9 Christian and 6 Muslim teaching staff; 60% of the students were Christians and 40% Muslims.

**BROADCASTING.** Under Israeli occupation, some Christian programmes are heard over the Israel Broadcasting Authority each week. From abroad programmes in Arabic are heard over ELWA, FEBA, RVOG (until 1977), TWR, CBC (Cyprus), and Radio Vatican.

**BIBLIOGRAPHY**
*Annuaire de l'Eglise Catholique en Terre Sainte, 1972.* Jerusalem: Franciscan Printing Press, 1972.
*Christianity in the Holy Land, past and present.* S.P. Colbi. Tel Aviv: Am Hassefer, 1969. 272p.

TABLE 2.    ORGANIZED CHURCHES AND DENOMINATIONS IN PALESTINE (West Bank, East Jerusalem, Gaza)

| Official name 1 | Begun 2 | Type 3 | Counc 4 | Congs 5 | Adults 6 | Affiliated 7 | Names, notes, and other statistics (see Codebook) 8 |
|---|---|---|---|---|---|---|---|
| Ancient Church of the East (P Tehran) | | O Nes | Yw... | | 700 | 1,000 | *Nestorians*, Assyrians, East Syrians. Mostly in Jerusalem, Bethlehem and area. |
| Apostolic Church of Pentecost | | P Pe1 | x.... | 2 | 50 | 100 | M=ACP(Canada). Unitarian Pentecostals (Jesus Only). In Bethlehem, Ramallah. 1f. |
| Armenian Apostolic Ch (C Cilicia) | c1500 | O Arm | Sw.N. | | 40 | 50 | *Gregorians*, related to C Cilicia (Sis) in Lebanon. In Gaza Strip. Armenians. |
| Armenian Apostolic P of Jerusalem | c 500 | O Arm | Ew.N. | 5 | 950 | 1,500 | *Gregorians*. Since 1950, 90% of faithful have emigrated. Armenians. 1d,1j,1s(40). |
| Assemblies of God | | P Pe2 | ZF... | 9 | 80 | 200 | M=AoG(USA). Classical Pentecostals (2-stage). Correspondence courses. 5n. |
| Bible Presbyterian Church | 1946 | P Ref | .T.T. | 1 | 20 | 50 | *Baraka BPC.* M=IBPFM(USA). Educational centre and hospital in Bethlehem. |
| Catholic Church: | 1099 | R LEr | O..P. | 25 | 10,700 | 16,950 | *Al-Kanisa al-Kathoulikiah.* 2 Patriarchates (Latin, Melkite). C=17+2+32. 3q,2s,1v. |
| P  Jerusalem (*Latin*) | 1099 | R Lat | Os | 16 | 8,700 | 13,750 | Patriarchate restored 1847. M=OFM Custody. 65 families in Gaza. 70n,200x,481w,1s. |
| P  Jerusalem (Antiochia) (*Melkite*) | 1932 | R Mel | Os | 9 | 2,000 | 3,200 | *Patriarchal Vicariate.* HQ Damascus (Syria). Includes 300 in Gaza. 7n,11x,65w,190Yy. |
| Church of God of Prophecy | | P Pe3 | Z.... | 3 | 100 | 300 | M=CGP(USA). Holiness Pentecostals. In East Jerusalem, Beit Jala, Ramallah. |
| Church of God (Cleveland) | 1946 | P Pe3 | ZF... | 3 | 20 | 80 | M=CoG(Cleveland) (USA). Holiness Pente. In East Jerusalem. 2n,3f,1p,W=69%,5Y,6z. |
| Church of the Nazarene | 1921 | P Hol | xF..K | 2 | 30 | 100 | M=CoN(USA). Jerusalem: Armenian and Arab congregations. 2m,4f,1t(92),W=70%. |
| Coptic Orthodox Church: D Jerusalem | c 850 | O Cop | NwaN. | 6 | 800 | 1,200 | Egyptians. In Bethlehem, Jericho; 500 in Gaza Strip. 2 schools. 1d(15 monks). |
| Episcopal Ch in Jeru & ME: D Jerusalem | 1820 | A plu | AW.NK | 8 | 1,000 | 1,400 | Formerly Jerusalem Archbishopric. M=CMS,JEM. Arabs (Evangelical Episcopalians). |
| Ethiopian Orthodox Ch: D Jerusalem | 1172 | O Eth | Nva.. | 4 | 40 | 50 | Under P Addis Ababa. In Jerusalem. Mostly priests and monks. 25x,1d(12),4y. |
| Evangelical Lutheran Ch in Jordan | 1860 | P Lut | 1..NK | 4 | 500 | 1,300 | First M=BJ(Germany). West Bank. Arabs, some Germans. 4n,1x,G=−4.0%pa,W=18%,21Yy. |
| Free Pentecostal Church | 1966 | P Pe2 | ..... | 4 | 15 | 400 | *Free Grace Pentecostal Church.* In Beit Jala, Beit Sahour. W=33%. |
| Greek Orth P Jerusalem: D Jerusalem | 30 | O Ara | CW.N. | 60 | 14,000 | 21,950 | 99% Arab (laity, priests); Greek bishops, monks. 19d(18),4e(20),P=60%,1s,W=10%. |
| Isolated radio churches | c1950 | I rad | ..... | 130 | 2,000 | 4,500 | Isolated Arab radio believers, mostly aged 12–25. S=10000,T=33000(ICI,GMU,&c). |
| Jehovah's Witnesses | c1920 | M Jeh | x.... | 2 | 100 | 400 | *Watch Tower. IBSA.* Active witnessing under way in Palestine by 1926. 10Y. |
| Native Church of God | 1959 | P Pen | ..... | 2 | 50 | 150 | *Native Ch (Holy Land) Crusade.* M=Voice of Healing(Christ for the Nations) (USA). |
| Romanian Orthodox Church | 1935 | O Rum | Cvc.. | 2 | 250 | 350 | *Biserica Ortodoxa Romana.* Under jurisdiction of P Bucharest. 3nx,2d,W=70%. |
| Russian Orthodox Church | 1848 | O Sla | Nwc.. | 5 | 200 | 300 | Under P Moscow. In 1918, 100 schools, 12,000 pupils. Now token clergy. 1e(50 nuns). |
| Russian Orthodox Ch Outside of Russia | 1920 | O Sla | x..... | 5 | 100 | 200 | M=ROCOR(USA). Many pre-1917 institutions; some property still. 3e(40 nuns). |
| Southern Baptist Mission | 1911 | P Bap | T...K | 3 | 100 | 300 | M=SBC(USA). Ramallah, Jerusalem. In Gaza: 1x,18f,1H. In Jerusalem: 1k. |
| Syrian Orth P of Antioch: D Jerusalem | 30 | O Syr | Dw.N. | 4 | 700 | 1,100 | *Jacobites.* Largest congregation in Bethlehem, also Jerusalem. 5x,2d. |
| Other Protestant denominations | | P | ..... | | | 500 | 1,000 |  Total about 35 (see list below). |
| | | | | | | | |
| **Total affiliated (mid-1970)** | | | | 350 | 33,045 | 54,930 | Total denominations (1970) . . . 59. |
| **Total affiliated (mid-1975)** | | | | 390 | 39,600 | 65,850 | Total denominations (1975) . . . 64. |
| **Total affiliated (mid-1980)** | | | | 430 | 46,000 | 76,450 | Total denominations (1980) . . . 69. |

NOTES ON TABLE ABOVE
COLUMNS: for meanings and CODES (cols. 1, 3, 4, 8): see Codebook (Part 6). Column 1: **Boldface type** = church with over 10% of country's affiliated Christians.
NATIONAL COUNCILS (Column 4, 5th letter).
K = United Christian Council in Israel (UCCI).
OTHER PROTESTANT DENOMINATIONS. A number of other bodies, especially USA missions, have small followings and church services, and so may be considered as denominations or para-denominations: American Baptist Association (1967), Apostolic Faith Ch of Canada (Bethlehem), Christian Catholic Ch (USA; 1948; 2 groups in Bethlehem area), Ch of Faith (Ramallah), Ch of God (Seventh-day), Churches of Christ (East Jerusalem), Ev Missions to the Muslims (1964), Exclusive Brethren (Kelly-Continental), First Baptist Bible Ch (chapels in East Jerusalem and Ramallah), Independent Assemblies of God, Norwegian Pentecostal Mission, Religious Society of Friends (USA) (1869; in Ramallah), Seventh-day Adventist Ch (East Jerusalem), Slavic Gospel Association (1959), Swedish Free Mission, Swiss Pentecostal Mission, United Evangelical Chs, United Fundamentalist Ch (USA; 1952), World-Wide Missions (1961).

PEOPLES (ethnolinguistic). Christians: about 82% Arab (75% Palestinian, 3% Egyptian, 2% Syrian, Lebanese, Jordanian), 10% European (German, Italian, UK, USA, et alii), 3.3% Armenian, 1.9% Assyrian (Aramaic), 1.0% Greek, 1.0% Russian, 0.7% Romanian.

COUNTRY-WIDE TOTALS
EVANGELIZATION (see Part 5). 1900: 32%. 1970: 95%. 1980: 96%. *Mass evangelism.* Among recent campaigns: 1960 Billy Graham rally in Jerusalem (2,000 attenders, 137 enquirers). *Radiophonic evangelism.* TWR, ELWA, RVOG, FEBA, Radio Vatican, et alia. Bible correspondence courses: ICI (30,000 enrolled, 10,000 active), GMU (1,000).
FOREIGN MISSIONARIES AND PERSONNEL (nationals serving abroad) (1973). Total 152 in 16 countries: 149 Roman Catholics, 3 Protestants.
FOREIGN MISSIONARIES AND PERSONNEL (aliens from abroad) (1973). Total 806. *From Western world.* 595: about 400 Roman Catholics, 160 Protestants (about 80 in 15 USA societies, about 40 in 4 UK societies, about 40 others), about 20 Orthodox from Greece et alia, about 15 Anglicans from UK. *From Communist world.* About 60 Orthodox priests, monks and nuns, from USSR et alia. *From Third World.* 151: about 111 Orthodox priests and monks from Egypt, Ethiopia, Lebanon, Syria et alia, about 40 Roman Catholics.
INSTITUTIONS (church-operated) (1973). Total 160, including about 90 higher schools (2 minor seminaries), 30 medical centres (6 hospitals), 11 religious communities, 10 seminaries (5 RC, 2 Orthodox, 2 Protestants, 1 Anglican), 1 university (RC).
PERIODICALS. About 30 titles.
PERSONNEL. About 1,366 (560 national, 806 foreign).
RELIGIOUS LIBRARIES. About 30.
SCRIPTURE DISTRIBUTION (1975). Annual totals: 19,284 Bibles (5% free, 79% subsidized, 16% commercial), 20,001 NTs (95% subsidized, 5% commercial), 16,097 UBS portions, 25,664 UBS selections.
SERVICE AGENCIES. About 40, including CELRA, CRS, MCC, YMCA, YWCA.

ADDITIONAL DATA ON CHURCHES
CATHOLIC CHURCH. *Catholics.* Including 650 in Gaza Strip (65 families, half Latins, half Melkites (Arabs); and 50 Maronite Catholics). 70 other Catholic families from Gaza now live abroad. *Bishops.* In 1974 the Melkite archbishop Capucci was imprisoned by the Israeli authorities on a charge of gun-running from Jordan and Lebanon. *Priests.* Latin-rite: OFM (Custody) has 64 in East Jerusalem, and 20 in West Bank. Nationality: OFM (Custody): 50% Italians, 25% Spanish, 25% Canadians, French, et alii (only 2 Arabs). Priests directly under the Patriarchates are mostly Arabs. *Brothers.* OFM (Custody). *Sisters.* Latins: 196 in East Jerusalem, 285 in West Bank. *Seminaries.* Latin-rite at Beit Jala; the Melkite seminary moved from East Jerusalem to Lebanon after the 1967 war. *Melkite religious congregations.* Priests: Basilian Salvatorians, Paulists. Sisters: Salvatorians, Benedictines of Emmanuel Convent (Bethlehem), Little Sisters of Jesus, Carmelites. *Chaldean congregations.* Sisters: Dominicans of St Catherine of Siena. *Main Latin orders and congregations.* Priests: OFM, OCD, Sion Fathers, OP, SDB, OSB, Little Brothers of Jesus, AA, SJ, CP, CM, OCSO. Brothers: OH, FSC. Sisters: St Joseph of the Apparition, 96 Rosary Sisters (Palestinians), Franciscans of the Immaculate Heart of Mary, Cloistered Carmelites, St Charles Borromeo, N-D de Sion, Daughters of Charity. In addition to these orders and congregations at work, there is a large number of others which maintain a small or nominal presence in Jerusalem. *Catholic organizations.* The Latin Patriarchate forms part of the Latin Episcopal Conference of the Arab Regions (CELRA), which has its seat in Jerusalem and since 1967 has held its meetings in Beirut, Lebanon. Melkites are part of the Melkite Patriarcha Synod in Syria.
The Holy See is represented to the Catholic hierarchy by the Apostolic Delegation of Jerusalem and Palestine with its seat in East Jerusalem. The apostolic delegate is also pro-nuncio in Cyprus.
In 1971 the Custody of the Holy Land had responsibility for 993 school pupils in East Jerusalem and 1,629 on the West Bank. Syrian Catholics had 79 students on the West Bank. In 1974 the first Catholic university in the Holy Land was established, Bethlehem Regional University.
In 1971, there were in East Jerusalem 2 Catholic hospitals, 6 dispensaries, 6 orphanages and one home serving aged persons and handicapped children. In West Bank there were 5 hospitals, 22 dispensaries, 4 orphanages, 2 homes for the aged, one home for handicapped children and the Paul VI Ephphatha Institute for deaf-mute children.
COPTIC ORTHODOX CHURCH. The diocese of Jerusalem was founded in AD 1237, and later embraced Palestine, Lebanon, Jordan, Iraq, Kuwait, Abu Dhabi, Sinai and the Suez Canal area.
GREEK ORTHODOX PATRIARCHATE OF JERUSALEM. The total includes 2,700 Orthodox (300 Arab families) in Gaza Strip. A similar number from Gaza now live abroad.

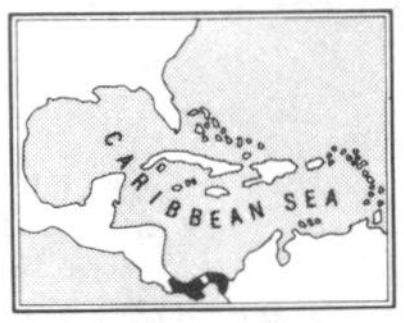


# PANAMA

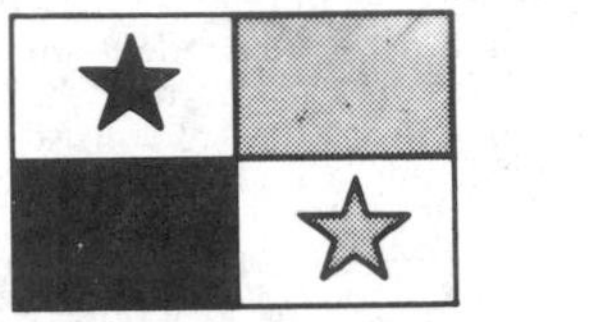

## SECULAR DATA

**STATE. Official name:** The Republic of Panama (La República de Panamá). Adjective of nationality: Panamanian (panameño).
**Flag** (shown above right): Quarters of blue, red, and white, with blue and red stars on the 2 white portions.
**Area:** 75,650 sq.km. (29,209 sq. miles). Agricultural land: 22.3%.
**Government:** Republic under military rule, since 1968 (1502 Spanish possession, 1821 province of Colombia, 1903 Independence from Colombia).
**Legislature:** People's Assembly, 505 members.
**Official language:** Spanish (*Español/Castellano*).
**Capital:** Panama City 392,880 (1974).
**Political division:** 9 Provinces.
**Armed forces** (1976): No regular army. Paramilitary forces: 11,000.

**DEMOGRAPHY. Population:** 1,428,082 (census of 10.V.1970. For 1970–2000 (UN), see last row of Table 1). Population density (1975): 22/sq.km. (57/sq.mile). Under 15 years: 44%. Growth rate (1975–80): 2.80% per year (births 3.55%, deaths –0.66%, emigrants –0.09%). Life expectancy (1975–80): 67.9 years. Household size: 4.9 persons.
**Major languages:** Spanish, English, Guaymí, Cuna, Choco, Hindi, Chinese, Arabic.
**Urban dwellers** (1970): 47.0%. Urban growth rate (1950–70): 4.4% per year.
**Labour force:** 34%.
**Tourists** (1973): 243,667. (1974) 614,100.

**ETHNOLINGUISTIC GROUPS:** 59.5% Mulatto/Mestizo (Spanish/Indian/Black), 14.0% Black (4.6% Jamaican), 12.0% White (USA, European), 7.5% Amerindian (4.6% Guaymí, 2.5% Cuna, Choco, Terraba, Bribri, Half-Indian), 4.0% East Indian (Indo-Pakistani), 1.0% Chinese (14,000), 0.9% Colombian, 0.5% Costarican, 0.5% Nicaraguan, 0.1% Jewish, Palestinian Arab, Spaniard, Italian, Greek, Lebanese, Japanese, Syrian Arab.

**MONEY** (1977). **Monetary unit:** balboa (= 100 centésimos); US$1 = B$1.00.
**National income per person:** US$935. Average annual family income: US$4,582.
**Inflation:** (1970–74) 7.6% per year (1975: consumer price index 142).
**Cost of living in capital** (1976): index 108 (Washington DC = 100). Daily cost of living: US$37.

**HEALTH.** Hospitals: 50 (4,844 beds). Doctors: 1,070. Lepers: 460 (0.3 per 1,000). Blind: 2,000. Psychotics: 13,000.

**EDUCATION.** Adult literacy: (1950) 70%, (1970) 78%. Education rate: 74%. Schools: 2,127, Universities: 2.

**LITERATURE.** Annual new book titles (1971): 97. Periodicals: 156. Scientific journals: 10. Newspapers: 7 dailies.

**COMMUNICATION** (per 1,000 people). Phones: 80. Radios: 162. TV sets: 131. Daily newspaper circulation: 78 copies.

TABLE 1. RELIGIOUS ADHERENTS IN PANAMA

| Year / *Name* | 1900 *Adherents* | *%* | mid-1970 *Adherents* | *%* | Annual change, 1970–1980 *Natural* | *Conversion* | *Total* | *Rate* | mid-1975 *Adherents* | *%* | mid-1980 *Adherents* | *%* | 2000 *Adherents* | *%* |
|---|---|---|---|---|---|---|---|---|---|---|---|---|---|---|
| **Christians** | **193,000** | **96.5** | **1,346,600** | **92.4** | **43,464** | **–884** | **42,580** | **2.75** | **1,545,200** | **92.1** | **1,772,400** | **91.8** | **2,902,600** | **89.9** |
| professing | 193,000 | 96.5 | 1,346,600 | 92.4 | 43,464 | –884 | 42,580 | 2.75 | 1,545,200 | 92.1 | 1,772,400 | 91.8 | 2,902,600 | 89.9 |
| Roman Catholics | 174,000 | 87.0 | 1,252,600 | 85.9 | 40,352 | –1,464 | 38,888 | 2.71 | 1,434,550 | 85.5 | 1,641,480 | 85.0 | 2,657,300 | 82.3 |
| Christo-pagans | 14,000 | 7.0 | 150,000 | 10.3 | 4,816 | –326 | 4,490 | 2.62 | 171,200 | 10.2 | 194,900 | 10.1 | 290,700 | 9.0 |
| Evangelical Catholics | 6,000 | 3.0 | 7,756 | 0.5 | 250 | –106 | 144 | 1.62 | 8,900 | 0.5 | 9,200 | 0.5 | 28,500 | 0.9 |
| Protestants | 14,000 | 7.0 | 65,000 | 4.5 | 2,171 | 399 | 2,570 | 3.33 | 77,200 | 4.6 | 90,700 | 4.7 | 161,500 | 5.0 |
| Anglicans | 5,000 | 2.5 | 15,000 | 1.0 | 484 | 6 | 490 | 2.85 | 17,200 | 1.0 | 19,900 | 1.0 | 36,000 | 1.1 |
| Non-White indigenous | 0 | 0.0 | 7,000 | 0.5 | 228 | 2 | 230 | 2.84 | 8,100 | 0.5 | 9,300 | 0.5 | 23,000 | 0.7 |
| Marginal Protestants | 0 | 0.0 | 6,000 | 0.4 | 197 | 173 | 370 | 5.29 | 7,000 | 0.4 | 9,700 | 0.5 | 22,600 | 0.7 |
| Orthodox | 0 | 0.0 | 1,000 | 0.1 | 32 | 0 | 32 | 2.81 | 1,150 | 0.1 | 1,320 | 0.1 | 2,200 | 0.1 |
| nominal | 4,000 | 2.0 | 6,600 | 0.5 | 371 | 1,159 | 1,530 | 11.59 | 13,200 | 0.8 | 21,900 | 1.1 | 124,800 | 3.9 |
| affiliated | 189,000 | 94.5 | 1,340,000 | 91.9 | 43,093 | –2,043 | 41,050 | 2.68 | 1,532,000 | 91.3 | 1,750,500 | 90.7 | 2,777,800 | 86.0 |
| doubly-affiliated | –10,000 | –5.0 | –78,177 | –5.4 | –2,596 | –396 | –2,992 | 3.24 | –92,300 | –5.5 | –108,100 | –5.6 | –194,000 | –6.0 |
| total practising | 170,100 | *90* | 1,072,000 | *80* | 34,474 | –1,634 | 32,840 | 2.68 | 1,225,600 | *80* | 1,400,400 | *80* | 1,944,500 | *70* |
| non-practising | 18,900 | *10* | 268,000 | *20* | 8,619 | –409 | 8,210 | 2.68 | 306,400 | *20* | 350,100 | *20* | 833,300 | *30* |
| Roman Catholics | 164,000 | 82.0 | 1,316,421 | 90.3 | 42,326 | –2,120 | 40,206 | 2.67 | 1,504,750 | 89.7 | 1,718,480 | 89.0 | 2,698,000 | 83.5 |
| Catholic pentecostals | 0 | 0.0 | 0 | 0.0 | 36 | 264 | 300 | 23.08 | 1,300 | 0.1 | 3,000 | 0.2 | 40,000 | 1.2 |
| Protestants | 18,000 | 9.0 | 72,610 | 5.0 | 2,408 | 331 | 2,739 | 3.20 | 85,600 | 5.1 | 100,000 | 5.2 | 181,000 | 5.6 |
| Evangelicals | 17,000 | 8.5 | 58,900 | 4.0 | 1,952 | 268 | 2,220 | 3.20 | 69,400 | 4.1 | 81,100 | 4.2 | 150,000 | 4.6 |
| Anglicans | 6,000 | 3.0 | 15,000 | 1.0 | 487 | –7 | 480 | 2.77 | 17,300 | 1.0 | 19,800 | 1.0 | 36,000 | 1.1 |
| Non-White indigenous | 1,000 | 0.5 | 7,000 | 0.5 | 225 | 15 | 240 | 3.00 | 8,000 | 0.5 | 9,400 | 0.6 | 32,000 | 1.0 |
| Marginal Protestants | 0 | 0.0 | 6,146 | 0.4 | 211 | 134 | 345 | 4.61 | 7,500 | 0.4 | 9,600 | 5.0 | 22,600 | 0.7 |
| Orthodox | 0 | 0.0 | 1,000 | 0.1 | 32 | 0 | 32 | 2.81 | 1,150 | 0.1 | 1,320 | 0.1 | 2,200 | 0.1 |
| Muslims | 1,000 | 0.5 | 65,000 | 4.5 | 2,110 | –10 | 2,100 | 2.80 | 75,000 | 4.5 | 86,000 | 4.5 | 144,000 | 4.5 |
| Baha'is | 0 | 0.0 | 14,400 | 1.0 | 478 | 82 | 560 | 3.29 | 17,000 | 1.0 | 20,000 | 1.0 | 42,000 | 1.3 |
| Non-religious | 0 | 0.0 | 8,500 | 0.6 | 331 | 529 | 860 | 7.29 | 11,800 | 0.7 | 17,100 | 0.9 | 74,000 | 2.3 |
| Tribal religionists | 6,000 | 3.0 | 8,000 | 0.5 | 197 | –397 | –200 | –2.86 | 7,000 | 0.4 | 6,000 | 0.3 | 3,000 | 0.1 |
| Hindus | 0 | 0.0 | 5,000 | 0.3 | 160 | –10 | 150 | 2.63 | 5,700 | 0.3 | 6,500 | 0.3 | 10,000 | 0.3 |
| Chinese folk-religionists | 0 | 0.0 | 3,000 | 0.2 | 90 | –40 | 50 | 1.56 | 3,200 | 0.2 | 3,500 | 0.2 | 4,500 | 0.1 |
| Buddhists | 0 | 0.0 | 2,000 | 0.1 | 65 | –15 | 50 | 2.17 | 2,300 | 0.1 | 2,500 | 0.1 | 3,500 | 0.1 |
| Jews | 0 | 0.0 | 2,000 | 0.1 | 65 | –5 | 60 | 2.61 | 2,300 | 0.1 | 2,600 | 0.1 | 4,400 | 0.1 |
| Atheists | 0 | 0.0 | 2,000 | 0.1 | 93 | 257 | 350 | 10.61 | 3,300 | 0.2 | 5,500 | 0.3 | 19,000 | 0.6 |
| New-Religionists | 0 | 0.0 | 1,000 | 0.1 | 127 | 473 | 600 | 13.33 | 4,500 | 0.3 | 7,000 | 0.4 | 20,000 | 0.6 |
| Other religionists | 0 | 0.0 | 500 | 0.0 | 20 | 20 | 40 | 5.71 | 700 | 0.0 | 900 | 0.0 | 3,000 | 0.1 |
| **Country's population** | **200,000** | **100.0** | **1,458,000** | **100.0** | **47,200** | **0** | **47,200** | **2.81** | **1,678,000** | **100.0** | **1,930,000** | **100.0** | **3,230,000** | **100.0** |

COLUMNS, ROWS. For meanings and definitions, see Codebook (Part 6). Note that, by definition, total 'Christians' = professing + crypto-Christians, which also = affiliated + nominal Christians. Percentages may not always total exactly, due to rounding.
CENSUSES. 1930: 86.8% Roman Catholics, 7.7% Evangelicals, 3.6% Muslims (with some Hindus), 1.7% non-religious and tribal religionists, 0.2% Jews. Subsequent censuses have not asked the religion question.

NOTES ON RELIGIONS
ATHEISTS. Partido del Pueblo (PDP) (Communist; banned 1968, suppressed; pro-Soviet) and small factions: membership (1970) 500.
BAHA'IS. Rapid growth from 27 local spiritual assemblies (1964) to 96 (1973). Many Indians (Guaymí, Cuna, et alii). Panama City has the first and so far the only Baha'i House of Worship (temple) in Latin America.
BUDDHISTS. Chinese, Japanese.
CATHOLIC PENTECOSTALS. By 1976 one bishop was involved in the Catholic Charismatic Renewal, and numerous clergy and laymen.
CHRISTO-PAGANS. Amerindians whose syncretistic folk-Catholicism combines 17th-century Spanish Catholicism with their own traditional animism, concepts and world-views.
COUNTRY'S POPULATION. From 1855-1900, 30,000 Black immigrants from the Antilles arrived as labourers; but in the 1880s during the French attempts to build a canal some 20,000

workers died of yellow fever.

DOUBLY-AFFILIATED. The term covers those affiliated to, or claimed by, both the Catholic Church and also a church termed Evangélica by the state (Protestant, marginal Protestant, Anglican, or Non-White indigenous), i.e. baptized Catholics Church who have recently become Evangelicals or others. Because their statistics represent a duplication, they are shown in the table as a negative quantity (with a minus sign).

EVANGELICAL CATHOLICS. This term is used here to describe persons who are affiliated to churches termed by the state Evangélica (Protestant, marginal Protestant, Anglican or Non-White indigenous churches), but who in government censuses

or polls are regarded as, or profess publicly to be, Roman Catholics.

HINDUS. East Indians.

MUSLIMS. There is a very heavy population of merchants from the Indian sub-continent, many of whom have contracted mixed marriages. There are also many Palestinian, Syrian, Lebanese and other Arabs from the Middle East. From 1975 Muslim missionaries from Egypt (Sunnis) have been sent by agreement between the governments of Panama and Egypt.

NEW-RELIGIONISTS. By 1975, there were 4,500 converts to the Japanese movement Nichiren Shoshu (Soka Gakkai).

NON-WHITE INDIGENOUS. In about 7 denominations in

1970 (see Table 2). There have been a number of other marginal Christian movements, including from 1962–65 the Mama Chi (Little Mother) movement among the Ngawbe or western Guaymí begun by Delia Atencio and now in decline.

OTHER RELIGIONISTS. Including Rosicrucians (5 AMORC centres).

TRIBAL RELIGIONISTS. Of the 110,000 Amerindians, a proportion still retain traditional animism, including among the Cuna (northeastern coast) and the Guaymí and Terraba (in the west).

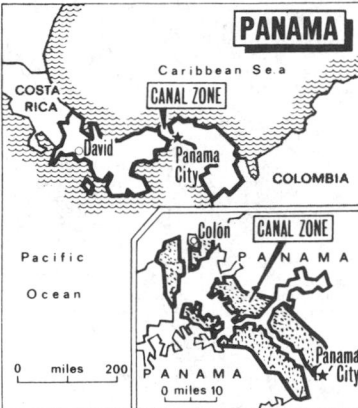

**NON-CHRISTIAN RELIGIONS. Islam** is represented by merchants from the Indian sub-continent and Arabs from the Middle East, who make up about 5% of the population.

**Baha'i** has 96 local spiritual assemblies, and the first Baha'i temple in Latin America has been built outside Panama City.

**Traditional religions** from pre-Hispanic times still exist, in the form of rites and beliefs, among the Cuna Indians of the northeastern coast and the Guaymí and Terraba Indians of western Panama.

## CHRISTIANITY

CATHOLIC CHURCH. Panama formed a part of the first Latin American Catholic diocese, that of Antigua in 1513. Franciscans began the task of evangelization and were followed later by Dominicans, Jesuits (1582), Capuchins and Augustinians in 1648. St Francis Xavier University was founded in 1674 but closed again in 1763 when the Jesuits were expelled from Panama. The ecclesiastical province of Panama was erected in 1925, and in the same year the vicariate of Darien was formed. The diocese of David was created in 1955.

Nearly 65% of Panama's priests, 65% of its brothers and 55% of its sisters are concentrated in the archdiocese of Panama. This pastoral imbalance is further accentuated by the extensive involvement of clergy and religious personnel in education, amounting to 45% of all priests, 90% of brothers and 72% of sisters, and by the small number of students whom they teach (13,885 in 29 schools, amounting to 7.7% of the total student population). The development of indigenous vocations has been slow in Panama. In 1973, Panamanian priests and sisters numbered respectively 44 and 46 as contrasted with 221 expatriate priests and 424 expatriate sisters.

OTHER CHURCHES. The first Protestants in Panama were immigrant Methodists from the Caribbean as early as 1815, and Protestantism was

strengthened through the arrival of 30,000 Black immigrants from the Antilles as rural and contract workers between 1855 and 1900. In 1882 the Methodist Synod in Jamaica sent missionaries to care for its members, and these were followed later by others from the SPG (UK) and the Jamaica Baptist Missionary Society (JBMS). After Panama's declaration of independence from Colombia in 1903, with strong support from the USA, a number of new and mostly North American denominations made their appearance: the Salvation Army in 1904; Church of God (Anderson), American Methodists and Seventh-day Adventists in 1905; and American Episcopalians in 1906, the latter taking over the work of the SPG. Two Pentecostal groups entered after World War I: the International Church of the Foursquare Gospel in 1927 and the Church of God (Cleveland) in 1935. The former has continued to grow rapidly during the 1960s and is now the largest Protestant denomination in the country. Southern Baptists arrived in 1943 to work with the Panama Baptist Convention, formed earlier through the activity of the JBMS. A large number of smaller missionary societies have taken up work in Panama since World War II.

CHURCH AND STATE. Church and state are partially separate in Panama. The constitution of 11 October 1972 stipulates: 'Freedom of religion and worship for all faiths exists with no other limitation than respect for Christian morality and public order. It is recognized that the Catholic religion is that of the majority of Panamanians' (Article 34); and 'Religious associations have authority to direct and administer their property as do other organizations holding juridical personality' (Article 35). Clergy and members of religious orders may not hold public office with the exception of those engaged in social service, public education or scientific research (Article 41). The same article also affirms that 'Leaders of the Catholic Church in Panama, including bishops, vicars-general, episcopal vicars, apostolic administrators and prelates nullius, must be Panamanian citizens by birth. This holds true also for clergymen of other faiths having similar reponsibilities and equivalent jurisdictions'. Since this latter disposition was not made retroactive, it did not alter the status of bishops in office at the time the constitution went into effect. At the end of 1972, in fact, 3 of the bishops in Panama were of Spanish origin and 2 episcopal vicars were American. Article 101 states that 'The Catholic religion shall be taught in public schools, but attendance at classes or religious worship shall not be obligatory for students whose parents or guardians request exemption'.

Relations between the state and the Catholic Church have been strained since the military coup d'etat of 1968. Although the bishops have publicly supported the claims of the new government concerning Panama's sovereignty over the Canal Zone,

at the same time they have criticized (as for example in their joint declaration of 2 August 1973) the general lack of freedom in the country and the marginal economic life of the masses living in poverty. The episcopate has also protested against the obstacles placed by government in the way of efforts by the church to promote social justice, as in its 1973 Lenten Letter. One incident evocative of this tension took place on 9 June 1971 when the police seized Hector Gallego, a Colombian priest actively engaged in programmes of conscientization and development in the diocese of Veraguas which had been begun by bishop MacGrath prior to becoming archbishop of Panama. Gallego disappeared without trace, and several priests who persisted in demanding information about him were expelled from the country. The episcopate was unanimous in expressing its concern about the affair.

INTERDENOMINATIONAL ORGANIZATIONS. The Panama Evangelical Alliance (Alianza Evangélica de Panamá), building on the work of the earlier Isthmian Religious Workers Federation begun in 1941, has 5 members: Assemblies of God, Missouri Lutherans, United Methodists, Conservative Baptists and the Evangelical Mission. For Catholics, the Archdiocesan Department of Ecumenism (Departmento Arquidiocesano de Ecumenismo) co-ordinates interest and activities relating to ecumenism. On the interdenominational level, there is the Pacific Religious Workers' League which engages in co-operative projects.

BROADCASTING. All stations accept religious programmes. In Panama City, La Voz del Istmo (HOXO) owned by the Associación Tropical de Radiodifusión (WRMF, USA) transmits Protestant programmes for half an hour daily from Mondays to Saturdays and for several hours on Sundays. Televisora Nacional transmits Catholic programmes for 3 hours from Mondays to Saturdays and for half

Baha'is. Worshippers in front of one of 9 doors of Baha'i House of Worship (Temple) on Cerro Sonsonate, just outside Panama City, first and so far only temple in Latin America.

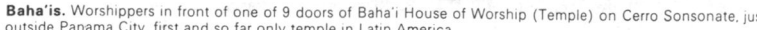

Iglesia Católica en Panamá. *Top.* Modern mass with 3-man combo in foreground, in Church of Christ the Redeemer, San Miguelito. *Bottom.* Priest whose circular church has become a hub of community activity.

an hour on Sundays. There is a Catholic station Radio Hogar in Panama City, and negotiations are going on for another relay station in Colon. In Santiago de Veraguas, a further Catholic station has started operation. From abroad, Protestant programmes can be easily heard on the international stations FEBC (California), TWR (Netherlands Antilles) and HCJB (Ecuador).

## BIBLIOGRAPHY

*Anuario Eclesiástico de Panamá, 1965.* Ciudad de Panamá: Curia Arzobispal. 1965.
'Leadership in the Choco church', J.A. Loewen, *Missiology*, 1 (January, 1973), 73–90.
'Protestant growth and a changing Panama: a study of Foursquare Gospel and Methodist patterns'. C.O. Butler. Thesis, Fuller Theological Seminary, Pasadena, CA (USA), 1964.
'The Church in Central America and Panama', *Pro Mundi Vita* (Brussels), 46 (1973).

TABLE 2. ORGANIZED CHURCHES AND DENOMINATIONS IN PANAMA

| Official name 1 | Begun 2 | Type 3 | Counc 4 | Congs 5 | Adults 6 | Affiliated 7 | Names, notes, and other statistics (see Codebook) 8 |
|---|---|---|---|---|---|---|---|
| Asambleas de Dios | 1967 | P Pe2 | ZF..C | 80 | 1,000 | 2,000 | M=Assemblies of God (USA). Classical Pentecostals. 29n,12f,2s(63),W=75%,150Y,250z. |
| Consejo de Igls Luteranas en CA & P | 1942 | P Lut | x...C | 4 | 40 | 200 | *Council of Lutheran Chs in CAmerica & Panama.* M=LCMS(USA). 2x,2t(100),5Yy,10z. |
| Convención Bautista de Panamá | c1855 | P Bap | T.... | 114 | 6,000 | 8,000 | 1943, M=SBC. 39% Black, 31% Indian, 30% USA. 23n,15x,G=3.7%pa,1h,1s(15),W=33%,374Y. |
| Ecclesias Cristadelfianas | | P Ade | x.... | 2 | 50 | 100 | M=Pacific Coast of America Bible Mission(USA). 2 ecclesias (churches) in Colon. |
| Ejército de Salvación | 1904 | P Sal | xwM.. | | 1,000 | 2,000 | *Salvation Army, Panama Division.* Caribbean & CAmerica Territory (HQ Jamaica). |
| Hermanos Libres | | P CBr | x.... | 1 | 50 | 100 | *Christian Brethren. Plymouth Brethren (Open). Gospel Halls.* |
| Hermanos Menonitas (Iglesia Ev Unida) | 1958 | P Men | GF... | 8 | 345 | 730 | M=Mennonite Brethren(USA). Indians: Choco (Waunana, Empera) in southeast. 2f. |
| Iglesia Adventista del Séptimo Día | 1905 | P Adv | x.... | 60 | 4,000 | 13,000 | *Seventh-day Adventists, Panama Conf*, CAmerican UM. 41% Black,20% Indian. 4f,1r,350Y. |
| Igl Apostólica Pentecostal Nacional | | I pen | ..... | | 1,000 | 2,000 | *National Apostolic Pentecostal Ch.* Indigenous grouping of Mestizos and WI Blacks. |
| Iglesia Bautista Libre | 1962 | P Bap | xF... | 7 | 240 | 500 | *Free Will Baptist Ch.* M=NAFWB(USA). Darien Indians. 2x,6f,G=19%pa,W=81%,30Y,12z. |
| **Iglesia Católica en Panamá:** | 1513 | R Lat | B.LDR | 114 | 737,100 | 1,316,421 | *Catholic Ch in Panama.* C=13+3+22. 1p,1s(17) 44n,221x,62m,470w,32231Yy. |
| M Panamá | 1513 | R Lat | Bs | 49 | 378,000 | 675,000 | Includes southern Canal Zone. 1,236 Cuna Indians. 32 124 39 300 14383 |
| D Chitré | 1962 | R Lat | Bs | 12 | 80,600 | 144,000 | Semi-urban and rural. No Amerindian population. 4 13 0 4 3662 |
| D David | 1955 | R Lat | Bs | 25 | 119,300 | 213,000 | Semi-urban, rural. 11% Indian (25,190 Guaymis). 4 33 7 60 4428 |
| D Santiago de Veraguas | 1963 | R Lat | Bs | 12 | 83,900 | 149,874 | Semi-urban, rural. 2.5% Indian (3,380 Guaymis). 2 13 5 23 3884 |
| PN Bocas del Toro | 1962 | R Lat | Bs | 4 | 12,100 | 21,600 | Rural. 32% Indian (29,700 Guaymis, Bogotas). M=OAR. 0 11 0 18 870 |
| VA Darién | 1925 | R Lat | Pcmf | 12 | 63,200 | 112,947 | Also Canal Zone. 18% Indian(28,930 Cunas). P=4%,2295z. 2 27 11 65 5004 |
| Iglesia Centroamericana | 1944 | P int | xM... | 20 | 500 | 1,000 | M=Central American Mission(USA). Interdenominational mission with HQ Panama 5. 8f. |
| Iglesia de Dios (Anderson) | 1905 | P Hol | x.... | 58 | 1,350 | 4,500 | *Ch of God.* M=CoG(Anderson) (USA). 3n,2f,G=22%pa,1h(medical boat),W=73%,255Y,500z. |
| Iglesia de Dios (Cleveland) | 1935 | P Pe3 | ZF... | 52 | 1,072 | 3,500 | M=CoG(USA). 47% Mestizos, 35% Indians. 57n,4x,4f,G=5.4%pa,1p(15),W=43%,260Y. |
| Iglesia de JC de los Santos de los UD | | M LdS | x.... | | 600 | 1,146 | *Ch of JC of Latter-day Saints. Mormons.* Many Indians. M=CJCLdS(USA). 20f. |
| Iglesia del Evangelio Cuadrangular | 1927 | P Pe2 | ZF... | 268 | 8,152 | 25,000 | *Foursquare.* M=ICFG(USA). 95% Mestizos, 3% Indians. 202nm,7f,2p(28),W=58%,180Y. |
| Iglesia del Nazareno | 1953 | P Hol | xF... | 16 | 350 | 2,000 | *Nazarenes.* M=CoN(USA). 1n,11mw,12f,G=9.7%pa,1s(36),16t(1670),W=67%,75Y,60z. |
| Iglesia Episcopal: D Panamá & Canal Z | c1855 | A Cen | aw.R. | 20 | 4,000 | 15,000 | c1870,M=SPG(UK). 1919, Missionary District, Province IX, PECUSA. 77% Black. 10x,1H. |
| Iglesia Ev Luterana de CR,ES,H,N,P | c1950 | P Lut | 1.... | 1 | 86 | 130 | *Ev Luth Ch in Costa Rica, El Sal,Hond,Nic,Pan.* German-speaking. 1x,G=1.4%pa,W=17%. |
| Iglesia Metodista | 1815 | P Met | VwV.. | 18 | 1,760 | 3,500 | *MCCA, Pan/Costa R Dist.* M=MMS. 90% Blacks; Valiente Indian Circuit. 3n,3x,G=–1.0%. |
| Iglesia Metodista Unida | 1905 | P Met | Vw..C | 30 | 897 | 2,000 | *Panama Provisional Annual Conference*, UMC(USA). 6n,2x,10f,1r,1s(2),17t,W=35%,20Yy. |
| Iglesia Ortodoxa Griega | | O Gre | Cwo.. | 2 | 500 | 1,000 | In 12th Archidiocesan District, Greek Orth AD N&S America. Panama City, Colon. |
| Iglesias de Cristo | | P Dis | x.... | 12 | 500 | 1,000 | *Churches of Christ.* M=CC(Non-Instrumental) (USA). Panama City. USA personnel. |
| Misión Bautista Conservadora | 1962 | P Bap | xF..C | 4 | 35 | 50 | *Conservative Baptist Mission.* M=CBFMS(USA). In Panama City. 2x,6Y,20z. |
| Misión Evangélica de Panamá | 1958 | P ind | ....C | 25 | 500 | 1,000 | M=Pan-American MS(USA). 150 San Blas Indians. 6n,1x,7f,G=15%pa,3p(30),W=90%,120Y. |
| Testigos de Jehová | 1929 | M Jeh | x.... | 45 | 2,013 | 5,000 | *Jehovah's Witnesses. Watch Tower. International Bible Students Association.* 164Y. |
| Unión Misionera Evangélica de Panamá | 1953 | P Hol | xM... | 15 | 152 | 300 | M=Gospel Missionary Union(USA). 1 school. 2x,18f,G=20%pa,1h,1p,1s,W=36%,6Y. |
| Other Non-White indigenous churches | | I | ..... | | 2,000 | 5,000 | Jamaicans, FDPMM(USA),ICAB(Brazil) with bishop, NBCA(USA), USA Black pentecostals. |
| Other Protestant denominations | | P | ..... | | 1,000 | 2,000 | Total about 15 (see list below). |
| Doubly-affiliated (duplication) (1970) | | | | | –43,800 | –78,177 | Evangelicals who also are or were baptized Roman Catholics. |
| **Total affiliated (mid-1970)** | | | | **1,030** | **732,492** | **1,340,000** | **Total denominations (1970) . . . 48.** |
| **Total affiliated (mid-1975)** | | | | **1,100** | **837,400** | **1,532,000** | **Total denominations (1975) . . . 52.** |
| **Total affiliated (mid-1980)** | | | | **1,200** | **956,900** | **1,750,500** | **Total denominations (1980) . . . 56.** |

NOTES ON TABLE ABOVE
COLUMNS: for meanings and CODES (cols. 1, 3, 4, 8): see Codebook (Part 6). Column 1: **Boldface type** = church with over 10% of country's affiliated Christians.
NATIONAL COUNCILS (Column 4, 5th letter).
C = Alianza Evangélica de Panamá (AEP) (Panama Evangelical Alliance).
R = Conferencia Episcopal de Panamá (CEP) (Episcopal Conference of Panama).
OTHER PROTESTANT DENOMINATIONS. These smaller bodies include: Ch of God of Prophecy (1946), Exclusive Brethren (Kelly-Continental), Free Methodist Ch, Iglesia de Dios Pentecostal (1946; from Puerto Rico), New Tribes Mission (1953; 32 missionaries).
UNITING CHURCHES. The Iglesia Metodista Unida was expected to join the Methodist Church in the Caribbean & the Americas after 1974.

**PEOPLES** (ethnolinguistic). Christians: 64.6% Mulatto/Mestizo, 14.0% Black (4.6% Jamaican), 12.0% White (USA, European), 6.8% Amerindian (4.1% Guaymí, 2.1% Cuna, Half-Indian), 0.9% Colombian, 0.5% Costa Rican, 0.5% Nicaraguan, 0.5% Chinese, Spaniard, Italian, Greek, East Indian (Indo-Pakistani), Arab (Palestinian, Lebanese, Syrian).

**COUNTRY-WIDE TOTALS**
EVANGELIZATION (see Part 5). 1900: 99%. 1970: 100%. 1980: 100%. *Mass evangelism.* 1958, Billy Graham campaign (18,000 attenders); subsequently, many campaigns led by evangelist Bolivar De Souza of the Church of God (Cleveland); 1978, Africa-Panama Crusade (Mission '78) (15,000 attenders, 700 decisions; 90 supporting churches). *Radiophonic evangelism.* HCJB, FEBC, ICI (970 enrolments, 515 active), et alia. Radio HOXO is active also.
FOREIGN MISSIONARIES AND PERSONNEL (nationals serving abroad) (1973). Total 354: about 350 Roman Catholics and 4 Protestants in 7 countries.
FOREIGN MISSIONARIES AND PERSONNEL (aliens from abroad) (1973). Total 909: *From Western world.* 566: 360 Roman Catholics, 171 Protestants (147 in 23 USA societies, 8 in 3 Australia societies, 7 in 3 UK societies, 4 in 1 Canada society, 3 in 1 WGermany society, 2 in 2 New Zealand societies), 20 marginal Protestants (Mormons from USA), 10 Anglicans in 1 USA society, about 5 Black indigenous from USA. *From Third World.* 343: about 330 Roman Catholics from other Latin American countries (164 from Colombia, 52 Costa Rica, 28 El Salvador, Mexico et alia), 10 Protestants from Argentina, Costa Rica, Jamaica and Puerto Rico, 3 indigenous from Jamaica and Brazil.
INSTITUTIONS (church-operated) (1973). Total 65, including 28 higher schools (1 minor seminary), 10 medical centres, 3 radio stations, 2 research centres, 7 seminaries (6 Protestant, 1 RC), 5 study centres, 1 university.
PERIODICALS. About 20 titles.
PERSONNEL. About 1,445 (536 national, 909 foreign).
RELIGIOUS LIBRARIES. About 20.
SCRIPTURE DISTRIBUTION (1975). Annual totals: 16,439 Bibles (69% subsidized, 30% commercial), 38,999 NTs (49% free, 38% subsidized, 13% commercial), 35,092 UBS portions, 1,063,532 UBS selections. *Translations completed.* Portion: 4 languages since 1924. NT: Cuna in 1970.
SERVICE AGENCIES. About 47, including ACISJE, AEP, CCCI, CDC, CENCOS, CEP, CRS-USCC, FEPAR(FEDEPAR), FNMC, IDERA, JARS, LAM, MFC, WBT, WRMF.

**ADDITIONAL DATA ON CHURCHES**
IGLESIA CATOLICA EN PANAMA. *Catholics.* Including 7,000 Chinese (1966), and 7,600 in 1975. The totals for M Panamá and VA Darién exclude 12,752 Catholics in these jurisdictions who are enumerated here under Panama Canal Zone. *Annual baptisms.* (1972) 98.2% infant, 1.8% adult. *Priests.* 80 secular, 185 religious. *Male religious* (priests and brothers). 15 Panamanians (including 4 Spanish now naturalized, 22 other Latin Americans, 227 from other continents (175 Spanish, 23 North Americans, 16 Italians). *Sisters.* 46 Panamanians, 300 other Latin Americans (164 Colombians, 52 Costa Ricans, 28 from El Salvador), 124 from other continents (48 Spanish). *Catechists.* Total (1969) 26, in VA Darién. *Main religious congregations* (1972). Priests (with over 25 professed): 48 CMF, 40 OAR, 34 Paulinos, 29 SJ. Brothers (with over 20 professed): FSC. Sisters (with over 30 professed): 84 Franciscanas de Maria Inmaculada, 49 Hijas de la Caridad de SV Paul, 33 Visitandinas. *Catholic organizations.* The Episcopal Conference of Panama (Conferencia Episcopal de Panamá) is a member of CELAM and SEDAC. The Federation of Male and Female Religious of Panama (Federación de Religiosos y Religiosas de Panamá, FEPAR) is a member of CLAR and SERCAP. Lay movements include the Federación Nacional de Mujeres Católicas, Confraternidad de la Doctrina Cristiana, Legión de Maria, Club Serra, Cursillos de Cristiandad, Movimiento Familiar Cristiano, Knights of Colombus, Knights of St John, Damas de la Caridad de St Vincent de Paul.
The Holy See has diplomatic relations with Panama and is represented to government and the Catholic hierarchy by a nuncio in Panama City.
Research and social action bodies include the Centro de Investigaciones Socio-Religiosas de la Arquidiócesis de Panamá (CISRAP), in Panama City, which carries on social science studies with special emphasis on their significance for pastoral work; Instituto Justo Arozamena, in Paitilla, which is related to IDESAC in Guatemala; Centro de Capacitación Social (CCS) in Panama City; and Centro de Estudios, Promoción y Asistencia Social (CEPAS) which is the social agency for the diocese of Veraguas. There exist 2 centres for the training of peasants, one at Chiriquí and the other at Penonomé.
Theological training is provided at the Instituto Teologico Pastoral, in Panama City, which is part of the Universidad Santa María La Antigua; and the Instituto de Estudios Religiosos Avanzados (IDERA), in Panama City, which is dependent on the Department of Pastoralia (Catechesis) of the Episcopal Conference of Panama and which trains lay and religious catechists as well as teachers of religion.
Missionary action is directed towards the interior of the country, national co-ordination being carried on through the Departmento de Misiones, with personnel and evangelistic work sponsored by the Fondo de Apostolado Arquidioceseno.
In 1973 there were about 100 Catholic schools of which 29 were located in the archdiocese of Panama. The Catholic Church is also responsible for the Universidad Santa Maria La Antigua, founded in Panama City in 1965, with 607 students in 1971. Social service is co-ordinated by Caritas Panamá, founded in 1961, which has been responsible for the creation of 140 nutritional centres throughout the country, each dependent on a local committee. Other agencies are Catholic Relief Services (CRS-USCC), with headquarters in the USA, and Fe y Alegria, with its central offices in Venezuela.
IGLESIA DEL EVANGELIO CUADRANGULAR. The church has grown, and is still growing, very rapidly.

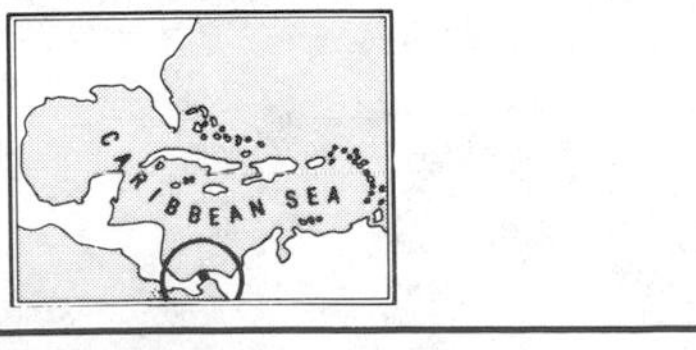

# PANAMA CANAL ZONE

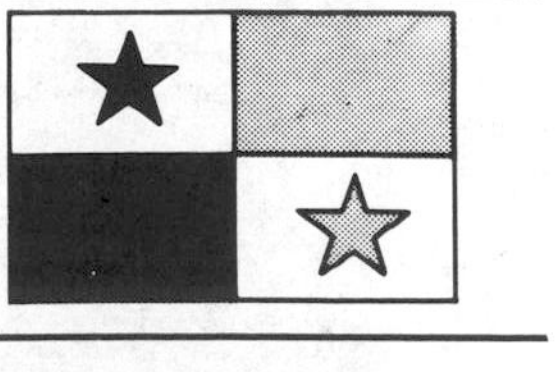

## SECULAR DATA

**STATE. Official name:** The Panama Canal Zone.
**Flag** (shown above right): That of Panama.
**Area:** 1,676 sq.km. (647 sq.miles). Agricultural land: 8.4%.
**Government:** Territory of the USA (opened 1914).
**Official language:** English.
**Chief cities:** administrative centre, Balboa Heights, 232.
**Foreign forces** (1973): 10,000 USA troops.

**DEMOGRAPHY. Population:** 44,198 (census of 1.IV.1970. For 1970–2000 (UN), see last row of Table 1). Population density (1975): 29/sq.km. (74/sq.mile). Under 15 years: 44%. Growth rate (1975–80): 1.81% per year (births 3.55%, deaths –0.66% emigrants –1.08%). Life expectancy (1975–80): 67.9 years. Household size: 4.0 persons.
**Major languages:** English, Spanish, French, Dutch, Hindi, Arabic.
**Labour force:** 34%.

**ETHNOLINGUISTIC GROUPS:** 48% Panamanian (39% Mulatto, 9% black), 36% USA (29% White, 7% Black), 7% Jamaican, 5% other West Indian Black (Negro), 1% Latin American White, 1% Latin American Mestizo, 1% European, 0.5% Jewish, East Indian (Indo-Pakistani), Arab (Palestinian, Lebanese, Syrian), et alii.

**MONEY** (1977). **Monetary unit:** US dollar (= 100 cents).
**National income per person:** US$3,800. Average annual family income: US$15,200.
**Cost of living in capital** (1976): Daily cost of living: US$37.

**HEALTH.** Hospitals: 4 (684 beds). Doctors: 145.

**EDUCATION.** Schools: 22.

**LITERATURE.** Newspapers: 1 non-daily.

**COMMUNICATION** (per 1,000 people). Phones: 330.

TABLE 1. RELIGIOUS ADHERENTS IN THE PANAMA CANAL ZONE

| Year | 1900 | | mid-1970 | | Annual change, 1970–1980 | | | | mid-1975 | | mid-1980 | | 2000 | |
|---|---|---|---|---|---|---|---|---|---|---|---|---|---|---|
| Name | Adherents | % | Adherents | % | Natural | Conversion | Total | Rate | Adherents | % | Adherents | % | Adherents | % |
| Christians | 12,900 | 99.2 | 42,800 | 96.8 | 750 | −53 | 697 | 1.51 | 46,180 | 96.2 | 49,180 | 95.7 | 54,240 | 90.4 |
| professing | 12,900 | 92.9 | 42,800 | 96.8 | 750 | −53 | 697 | 1.51 | 46,180 | 96.2 | 49,770 | 95.7 | 54,240 | 90.4 |
| Protestants | 4,000 | 30.8 | 17,240 | 39.0 | 302 | −19 | 283 | 1.52 | 18,600 | 38.8 | 20,070 | 38.6 | 21,900 | 36.5 |
| Roman Catholics | 6,900 | 53.1 | 15,040 | 34.0 | 264 | −25 | 239 | 1.47 | 16,210 | 33.8 | 17,430 | 33.5 | 18,840 | 31.4 |
| Anglicans | 2,000 | 15.4 | 8,840 | 02.0 | 154 | −19 | 135 | 1.42 | 9,500 | 19.8 | 10,190 | 19.6 | 10,500 | 17.5 |
| Marginal Protestants | 0 | 0.0 | 1,330 | 3.0 | 24 | 9 | 33 | 2.21 | 1,490 | 3.1 | 1,660 | 3.2 | 2,400 | 4.0 |
| Black indigenous | 0 | 0.0 | 350 | 0.8 | 6 | 1 | 7 | 1.84 | 380 | 0.8 | 420 | 0.8 | 600 | 1.0 |
| nominal | 1,300 | 10.0 | 7,440 | 16.8 | 134 | 43 | 177 | 2.14 | 8,260 | 17.2 | 9,210 | 17.7 | 12,000 | 20.0 |
| affiliated | 11,600 | 89.2 | 35,360 | 80.0 | 616 | −96 | 520 | 1.37 | 37,920 | 79.0 | 40,560 | 78.0 | 42,240 | 70.4 |
| total practising | 9,280 | 80 | 21,220 | 60 | 370 | −58 | 312 | 1.37 | 22,750 | 60 | 24,340 | 60 | 21,120 | 50 |
| non-practising | 2,320 | 20 | 14,140 | 40 | 246 | −38 | 208 | 1.37 | 15,170 | 40 | 16,220 | 40 | 21,120 | 50 |
| Protestants | 3,500 | 26.9 | 14,108 | 31.9 | 246 | −29 | 217 | 1.43 | 15,170 | 31.6 | 16,280 | 31.3 | 16,380 | 27.3 |
| Evangelicals | 3,000 | 23.1 | 8,000 | 18.1 | 139 | −9 | 130 | 1.51 | 8,600 | 17.9 | 9,300 | 17.9 | 10,000 | 16.7 |
| Roman Catholics | 6,300 | 48.5 | 12,752 | 28.9 | 221 | −57 | 164 | 1.21 | 13,590 | 28.3 | 14,390 | 27.7 | 15,720 | 26.2 |
| Anglicans | 1,800 | 13.8 | 7,000 | 15.8 | 122 | −21 | 101 | 1.35 | 7,490 | 15.6 | 8,010 | 15.4 | 7,440 | 12.4 |
| Marginal Protestants | 0 | 0.0 | 1,200 | 2.7 | 22 | 9 | 31 | 2.31 | 1,340 | 2.8 | 1,510 | 2.9 | 2,160 | 3.6 |
| Black indigenous | 0 | 0.0 | 300 | 0.7 | 5 | 2 | 7 | 2.12 | 330 | 0.7 | 370 | 0.7 | 540 | 0.9 |
| Muslims | 0 | 0.0 | 700 | 1.6 | 13 | 0 | 13 | 1.69 | 770 | 1.6 | 830 | 1.6 | 1,200 | 2.0 |
| Jews | 0 | 0.0 | 200 | 0.5 | 4 | 2 | 6 | 2.50 | 240 | 0.5 | 260 | 0.5 | 360 | 0.6 |
| Non-religious | 0 | 0.0 | 200 | 0.5 | 6 | 31 | 37 | 9.74 | 380 | 0.8 | 570 | 1.1 | 2,400 | 4.0 |
| Other religionists | 100 | 0.8 | 300 | 0.7 | 7 | 20 | 27 | 6.28 | 430 | 0.9 | 570 | 1.1 | 1,800 | 3.0 |
| Country's population | 13,000 | 100.0 | 44,200 | 100.0 | 780 | 0 | 780 | 1,63 | 48,000 | 100.0 | 52,000 | 100.0 | 60,000 | 100 0 |

**COLUMNS, ROWS.** For meanings and definitions, see Codebook (Part 6). Note that, by definition, total 'Christians' = professing + 'crypto-Christians, which also = affiliated + nominal Christians. Percentages may not always total exactly, due to rounding.

**NOTES ON RELIGIONS**
BLACK INDIGENOUS. Small spirit-possession churches (see Table 2).
MUSLIMS. East Indians, with some Arab immigrants from the Middle East.

OTHER RELIGIONISTS. Unorganized individual adherents of several other non-Christian religions, including Baha'i, Hinduism Chinese folk religion, Buddhism et alia.
PROTESTANTS. Including a large number of USA military and civilians.

## NON-CHRISTIAN RELIGIONS.
Islam and Judaism are represented by small communities.

## CHRISTIANITY
CATHOLIC CHURCH. The Pacific coastal area of the Canal Zone belongs to the archdiocese of Panama, while the Atlantic coastal area is part of the vicariate of Darién, with its seat also in Panama. In 1975 Catholics in the Canal Zone numbered 15% of the 39,000 North Americans and most of the 9,000 Panamanians and expatriates (from the Antilles and Caribbean). The territory is served by Lazarist priests (Vincentins; CM) from the USA.

OTHER CHURCHES. Black Anglican, Baptist and Methodist immigrants from the Caribbean arrived in Panama and the area of the Canal Zone during the 19th century, groups that were later served by missionaries of the SPG (UK), Jamaica Baptist Missionary Society and British Methodism. American Methodists opened work in 1905 but later withdrew as a separate group when the Union Churches of the Canal Zone came into being under the National Council of Churches in the USA. The largest non-Catholic denomination today, with 8 congregations, is the Panama and Canal Zone diocese of Province IX, Episcopal Church in the USA, which in 1906 took over British work begun by the SPG. Seventh-day Adventists arrived shortly after World War I, and Southern Baptists came in 1943. During World War II, Missouri Synod Lutherans built Redeemer Church, Balboa, with a largely expatriate constituency of USA military personnel, and the Assemblies of God opened the first Pentecostal church in the Canal

Cristobal piers at northwestern end of Canal, with several churches visible in distance.

Zone in the latter part of the 1960s.

CHURCH AND STATE. The situation is similar to that in the USA. Freedom of religion is guaranteed, and church and state are separate.

INTERDENOMINATIONAL ORGANIZATIONS. The Union Churches of the Canal Zone are inter-denominational, having been formed through the auspices of the National Council of the Churches of Christ in the USA.

BROADCASTING. The situation is the same as in the republic of Panama; there is an abundance of Christian programmes in Spanish and English.

TABLE 2. ORGANIZED CHURCHES AND DENOMINATIONS IN THE PANAMA CANAL ZONE

| Official name 1 | Begun 2 | Type 3 | Counc 4 | Congs 5 | Adults 6 | Affiliated 7 | Names, notes, and other statistics (see Codebook) 8 |
|---|---|---|---|---|---|---|---|
| Asambleas de Dios | c1967 | P Pe2 | ZP... | 3 | 200 | 500 | *Assemblies of God.* M=AoG(USA). Classical Pentecostals (2-stage). |
| Consejo de Igls Luteranas en CA & P | 1942 | P Lut | x.... | 2 | 260 | 505 | *Lutheran Chs in CA & Panama.* Redeemer Ch, Balboa. M=LCMS(USA). 1x,W=47%,18Yy,40z. |
| Convención Bautista de Panamá | c1870 | P Bap | T.... | | 1,000 | 2,000 | *Panama Baptist Convention.* 1943, M=SBC(USA). Begun by Panamanians. |
| Iglesia Adventista del Séptimo Día | c1920 | P Adv | x.... | 5 | 1,000 | 2,000 | *SDA. Seventh-day Adventists, Panama Conference, Central American UM.* 2f. |
| **Iglesia Católica** | 1513 | R Lat | B,LDR | | 7,100 | 12,752 | *Catholic Ch.* Parts of M Panamá, VA Darién. 55% Panamanians, 45% USA. M=CM. P=10%. |
| Iglesia de Dios (Anderson) | 1905 | P Hol | x.... | 2 | 200 | 500 | *Ch of God.* M=CoG(Anderson) (USA). Holiness denomination. HQ Cristobal, Balboa. 2f. |
| **Iglesia Episcopal: D Panama & Canal Z** | c1870 | A Cen | av,R. | 8 | 2,000 | 7,000 | *Episcopal Ch in P.* 1919, Missionary District, Province IX, PECUSA. 3n,3f,SS=796. |
| Iglesia Metodista | 1815 | P Met | VvV.. | 2 | 1,000 | 2,000 | *Colón Circuit, Panama Costa Rica District, MCCA.* M=MMS(UK). Blacks. 1 school. 3x. |
| Iglesias Benjinitas | | I pen | | | 100 | 300 | *Bedwardites (Jamaica). Jump-Up Churches.* Black. Small spirit-possession churches. |
| Iglesias de Cristo | c1958 | P Dis | x.... | 21 | 1,000 | 2,000 | M=CC(Non-Instrumental) (USA). In Balboa, Cristobal, Margarita. Many USA personnel. |
| Iglesias Unión | | P com | x.... | 4 | 960 | 1,603 | *Union Churches of the Canal Zone.* Interdenominational, English-speaking. |
| Sociedad de la Ciencia Cristiana | | M Sci | x.... | 2 | 70 | 200 | *Ch of Christ, Scientist. Christian Science.* M=CCS. In Balboa and Margarita. |
| Testigos de Jehová | 1929 | M Jeh | x.... | 10 | 450 | 900 | *Jehovah's Witnesses. Watch Tower. International Bible Students Association.* |
| Other Protestant denominations | | P | ..... | | 1,500 | 3,000 | Total about 15, mainly USA bodies serving USA personnel (see list below). |
| Other marginal Protestant bodies | | M | ..... | | 50 | 100 | Including Unitarian Christian Fellowship (24 members in 1964). |
| **Total affiliated (mid-1970)** | | | | 115 | 16,890 | 35,360 | Total denominations (1970) . . . 28. |
| **Total affiliated (mid-1975)** | | | | 125 | 18,100 | 37,920 | Total denominations (1972) . . . 29. |
| **Total affiliated (mid-1980)** | | | | 135 | 19,400 | 40,560 | Total denominations (1980) . . . 30. |

**NOTES ON THE TABLE ABOVE**
COLUMNS: for meanings and CODES (cols.1,3,4,8): see Codebook (Part 6). Column 1: Boldface type = church with over 10% of country's affiliated Christians.
NATIONAL COUNCILS (Column 4, 5th letter).
R = Conferencia Episcopal de Panamá (CEP) (Episcopal Conference of Panama).
OTHER PROTESTANT DENOMINATIONS. Christian Brethren, Ch of God (Cleveland), Ch of the Nazarene, Gospel Missionary Union, International Ch of the Foursquare Gospel, Pan-American Missionary Society (1958), Salvation Army. In addition, most North American Protestants belonging to the major USA ecumenical denominations (Methodist, Presbyterian) belong to additional union congregations in the Canal Zone and the Republic of Panama.

PEOPLES (ethnolinguistic). Christians: 48% Panamanian (39% Mulatto, 9% Black), 36% USA (29% White, 7% Black), 7% Jamaican, 5% other·Black (West Indian), 1% Latin American White, 1% Latin American Mestizo, 1% European, Arab, et alii.

COUNTRY-WIDE TOTALS
EVANGELIZATION (see Part 5). 1900: 100%. 1970: 100%. 1980: 100%. *Mass evangelism.* 1978, Africa-Panama Crusade (Mission '78), based in Panama.
FOREIGN MISSIONARIES AND PERSONNEL (aliens from abroad) (1973). Total 37. *From Western world.* 27: 14 Protestants from USA, about 10 Roman Catholics, 3 Anglicans in 1 USA society. *From Third World.* 10: 6 Roman Catholics, 2 Protestants, 2 Black indigenous.
INSTITUTIONS (church-operated) (1973). Total 3.

PERIODICALS. About 10 titles.
PERSONNEL. About 52 (15 national, 37 foreign).

SCRIPTURE DISTRIBUTION (1975). Annual totals: 3,500 Bibles (86% subsidized, 14% commercial), 1,200 NTs (83% subsidized, 17% commercial), 500 UBS portions, 1,000 UBS selections.
SERVICE AGENCIES. About 10, including ACJ(YMCA), LAM, SU.

ADDITIONAL DATA ON CHURCHES
IGLESIA CATOLICA. *Catholic organizations.* The church sponsors 3 schools maintained by Sisters of Mercy of Brooklyn and Sisters of St Francis.

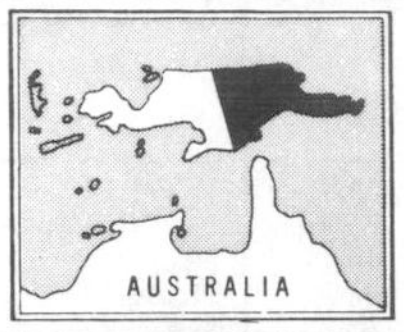


# PAPUA NEW GUINEA

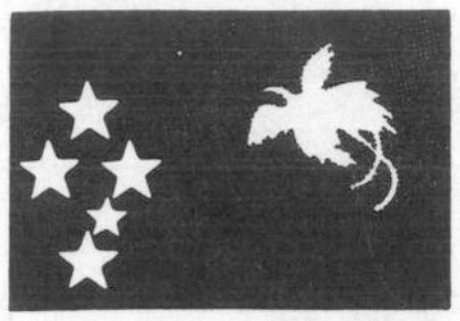

## SECULAR DATA

**STATE. Official name:** The Dominion of Papua New Guinea (Papua-Niugini). Adjective of nationality: a Papua New Guinean. **Flag** (shown above right): Five-star constellation on black triangle on lower left; gold bird of paradise on red triangle on upper right.
**Area:** 461,691 sq.km. (178,260 sq.miles). Agricultural land: 1.0%.
**Government:** Parliamentary state (constitutional monarchy), since 1975 (1884 British protectorate, 1906 Australian territory of Papua, 1920 Australian territory of New Guinea, 1973 self-government, 1975 Independence).
**Legislature:** House of Assembly, 100 members.
**Official language:** English. National language: Pidgin (spoken by 24%).
**Capital:** Port Moresby 76,510 (1971).
**Political divisions:** 19 Districts.

**DEMOGRAPHY. Population:** 2,489,935 (census of 7.VII.1971. For 1970–2000 (UN), see last row of Table 1). Population density (1975): 6/sq.km. (15/sq.mile). Under 15 years: 41%. Growth rate (1975–80): 2.53% per year (births 4.08%, deaths −1.55%). Life expectancy (1975–80): 50.2 years. Household size: 5.8 persons.
**Major languages:** English, Pidgin English (Neo-Melanesian), Motu, Chinese. In addition there are over 950 tribal and other languages.
**Urban dwellers** (1970): 5.9%. Urban growth rate (1950–70): 2.9% per year.
**Labour force:** 51%.

**ETHNOLINGUISTIC GROUPS:** 77.8% New Guinea Papuan, 20.2% New Guinea Melanesian, 1.5% Anglo-Australian, 0.3% Chinese, 0.1% British, 0.1% Euronesian (Australian/Melanesian), Jewish, et alii.

**MONEY** (1977). **Monetary unit:** kina (= 100 toea); US$1 = Ka 0.81.
**National income per person:** US$500. Average annual family income: US$2,900.
**Inflation:** (1975) consumer price index 154.
**Cost of living in capital** (1976): index 130 (Washington DC=100). Daily cost of living: US$48.

**HEALTH.** Hospitals: 456 (16,664 beds). Doctors: 233. Lepers: 10,000 (38 per 1,000). Blind: 9,000. Psychotics: 16,000.

**EDUCATION.** Adult literacy: (1971) 32%. Schools: 1,613 Universities: 1.

**LITERATURE.** Periodicals: 40. Newspapers: 2 non-daily.

**COMMUNICATION** (per 1,000 people). Phones: 13.

TABLE 1. RELIGIOUS ADHERENTS IN PAPUA NEW GUINEA

| Year | 1900 | | mid-1970 | | Annual change, 1970–1980 | | | | mid-1975 | | mid-1980 | | 2000 | |
|---|---|---|---|---|---|---|---|---|---|---|---|---|---|---|
| *Name* | *Adherents* | *%* | *Adherents* | *%* | *Natural* | *Conversion* | *Total* | *Rate* | *Adherents* | *%* | *Adherents* | *%* | *Adherents* | *%* |
| Christians | **45,400** | **4.0** | **2,189,400** | **93.8** | **61,991** | **7,011** | **69,002** | **2.74** | **2,516,510** | **95.8** | **2,879,420** | **96.6** | **4,767,400** | **97.8** |
| professing | 45,400 | 4.0 | 2,128,400 | 93.8 | 61,991 | 7,011 | 69,002 | 2.74 | 2,516,510 | 95.8 | 2,879,420 | 96.6 | 4,767,400 | 97.8 |
| Protestants | 20,000 | 1.8 | 1,325,900 | 56.8 | 37,658 | 3,819 | 41,477 | 2.71 | 1,528,690 | 58.2 | 1,740,670 | 58.4 | 2,895,000 | 59.4 |
| Roman Catholics | 25,000 | 2.2 | 742,000 | 31.8 | 20,899 | 2,661 | 23,560 | 2.78 | 848,400 | 32.3 | 977,600 | 32.8 | 1,608,000 | 33.0 |
| Anglicans | 400 | 0.0 | 121,300 | 5.2 | 3,429 | 531 | 3,960 | 2.84 | 139,200 | 5.3 | 160,900 | 5.4 | 264,000 | 5.4 |
| Orthodox | 0 | 0.0 | 200 | 0.0 | 5 | 0 | 5 | 2.27 | 220 | 0.0 | 250 | 0.0 | 400 | 0.0 |
| nominal | 15,800 | 1.4 | 576,728 | 24.7 | 15,990 | −3,591 | 12,399 | 1.91 | 649,110 | 24.7 | 700,720 | 23.5 | 869,400 | 17.8 |
| affiliated | 29,600 | 2.6 | 1,612,672 | 69.1 | 46,001 | 10,602 | 56,603 | 3.03 | 1,867,400 | 71.1 | 2,178,700 | 73.1 | 3,898,000 | 80.0 |
| total practising | 28,120 | *95* | 1,370,770 | *85* | 39,101 | 9,012 | 48,113 | 3.03 | 1,587,290 | *85* | 1,851,900 | *85* | 3,118,400 | *80* |
| non-practising | 1,480 | *5* | 241,900 | *15* | 6,900 | 1,590 | 8,490 | 3.03 | 280,110 | *15* | 326,800 | *15* | 779,600 | *20* |
| Protestants | 10,000 | 0.9 | 932,928 | 40.0 | 26,646 | 6,596 | 33,242 | 3.07 | 1,081,680 | 41.2 | 1,265,350 | 42.5 | 2,319,900 | 47.6 |
| Evangelicals | 8,500 | 0.8 | 840,000 | 36.0 | 23,981 | 5,899 | 29,880 | 3.07 | 973,500 | 37.1 | 1,138,800 | 38.2 | 2,100,000 | 43.1 |
| Roman Catholics | 19,300 | 1.7 | 606,544 | 26.0 | 17,145 | 2,671 | 19,816 | 2.85 | 696,000 | 26.5 | 804,700 | 27.0 | 1,364,000 | 28.0 |
| Catholic pentecostals | 0 | 0.0 | 100 | 0.0 | 49 | 641 | 690 | 34.50 | 2,000 | 0.1 | 7,000 | 0.2 | 50,000 | 1.0 |
| Anglicans | 200 | 0.0 | 60,000 | 2.6 | 1,811 | 1,129 | 2,940 | 4.00 | 73,500 | 2.8 | 89,400 | 3.0 | 165,700 | 3.4 |
| Melanesian indigenous | 100 | 0.0 | 8,000 | 0.3 | 222 | −22 | 200 | 2.22 | 9,000 | 0.3 | 10,000 | 0.3 | 30,000 | 0.6 |
| Marginal Protestants | 0 | 0.0 | 5,000 | 0.2 | 172 | 228 | 400 | 5.71 | 7,000 | 0.3 | 9,000 | 0.3 | 18,000 | 0.4 |
| Orthodox | 0 | 0.0 | 200 | 0.0 | 5 | 0 | 5 | 2.27 | 220 | 0.0 | 250 | 0.0 | 400 | 0.0 |
| Tribal religionists | 1,074,000 | 95.9 | 128,300 | 5.5 | 2,200 | −7,580 | −5,380 | −6.02 | 89,300 | 3.4 | 74,500 | 2.5 | 29,000 | 0.6 |
| Baha'is | 0 | 0.0 | 9,300 | 0.4 | 323 | 537 | 860 | 6.56 | 13,100 | 0.5 | 17,900 | 0.6 | 49,000 | 1.0 |
| Chinese folk-religionists | 0 | 0.0 | 2,200 | 0.1 | 59 | −19 | 40 | 1.67 | 2,400 | 0.1 | 2,600 | 0.1 | 3,000 | 0.1 |
| Buddhists | 0 | 0.0 | 2,000 | 0.1 | 55 | −5 | 50 | 2.22 | 2,250 | 0.1 | 2,500 | 0.1 | 4,000 | 0.1 |
| Non-religious | 0 | 0.0 | 2,000 | 0.1 | 64 | 56 | 120 | 4.62 | 2,600 | 0.1 | 3,200 | 0.1 | 20,000 | 0.4 |
| Jews | 0 | 0.0 | 300 | 0.0 | 8 | 0 | 8 | 2.35 | 340 | 0.0 | 380 | 0.0 | 600 | 0.0 |
| **Country's population** | **1,119,400** | **100.0** | **2,333,500** | **100.0** | **64,700** | **0** | **64,700** | **2.46** | **2,626,500** | **100.0** | **2,980,500** | **100.0** | **4,873,000** | **100.0** |

COLUMNS. ROWS. For meanings and definitions, see Codebook (Part 6) Note that, by definition, total 'Christians' = professing + crypto-Christians, which also = affiliated + nominal Christians. Percentages may not always total exactly, due to rounding.
CENSUSES. **20.VI–9.VII.1966** (Papua New Guinea, including North Solomons i.e. Bougainville and Buka): 55.5% Protestants (27.4% Lutherans, 14.7% United Church of PNGSI, 3.3% SDA), 31.3% Roman Catholics, 7.5% tribal religionists, 5.2% Anglicans, 0.1% non-religious. No subsequent census has included religion.

NOTES ON RELIGIONS
BAHA'IS. Very rapid growth from 2 local spiritual assemblies (1964) to 67 (1973). Strongest in Gulf district of Papua, Eastern Highlands of New Guinea, and among the Talasea of New Britain.
BUDDHISTS. Chinese.
CATHOLIC PENTECOSTALS (or, Catholic charismatics). By 1975 the movement was rapidly growing, with numerous priests and sisters involved; the archbishop of Madang also is a charismatic leader.
COUNTRY'S POPULATION. All statistics above (all lines) refer to the de facto territory as it was at Independence in 1975, excluding the secessionist islands of Bougainville and Buka (described in this survey under their 1975 self-appellation Northern Solomons) whose population was 39,600 in 1900, 72,393 in mid-1968 (3.09% of total population), 79,500 in 1970 and 89,500 in 1975.
MELANESIAN INDIGENOUS. In about 38 christianized Melanesian (including Papuan) cargo-cult type movements in 1970 (see Table 2).
NOMINAL CHRISTIANS. During the 20th century, the enormous influx into the churches found them unable to provide adequate instruction in Christian initiation, and as a result a huge nominal fringe grew up of professing Christians unaffiliated to churches. By 1970 when remaining tribal religionists numbered under 6%, the nominal fringe stopped expanding, and by 1975 it began to decrease in size as the churches caught up with the expansion of professing Christians.
NON-RELIGIOUS. Europeans and Chinese.
TRIBAL RELIGIONISTS. Animists in several hundred New Guinea mainland tribes following traditional religions including the ancestral cult, together with modern nativistic or sycretistic revitalization movements termed cargo cults. Beginning in 1893, there have been (by 1973) over 115 distinct non-Christian cargo cults (see description in article below).

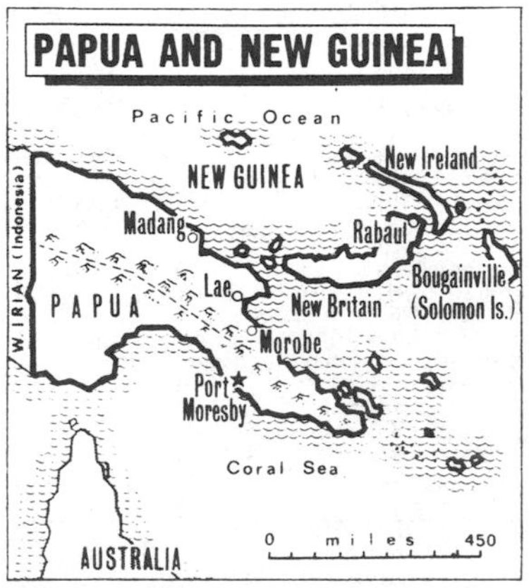


**NON-CHRISTIAN RELIGIONS. Traditional religions** are followed by only about 3% of the population, decreasing rapidly each year, although their influence continues to be felt also among professing Christians. These tribal religions are centred primarily on ancestor veneration coupled with a strong belief in good and evil spirits and the efficacy of magical charms.

**Cargo cults,** the term describing a long series of messianic and syncretistic movements combining traditional elements with Christian and Western secular elements, have arisen under the impact of Western culture since around 1890 and especially since the military campaigns of World War II. Among the earliest of these sects were the Cult of the Prophet Tokerau at Milne Bay in 1893, the Cult of the Three Prophets of Saibai of Torres Strait in 1914, the 'Vailala Madness' among the Orokolo peoples of the Gulf of Papua at the time of World War I, and the Cult of Baigona the Snake among the Orokaivas of New Guinea. Most of these have now been superseded by the rapid spread of the Taro cult initiated in 1914 by Buninia, a Bunadele prophet. After receiving a vision of his slain father's spirit, Buninia developed rites for improving the production of taro crops. Beginning among the Orokaiva, the cult has now spread north and south among neighbouring peoples. Great emphasis is placed on ecstatic singing, dancing, communal meals and spirit possession. Taro spirits substituted for the traditional spirits of the dead are expected to bring prosperity in the form of native-grown produce or European goods. By 1973, a total of over 115 distinct cargo cults had arisen in different areas of the territory, about 30 in Papua, 70 in New Guinea (mostly in the east), and the rest on New Britain, New Ireland and the Admiralty islands.

**Baha'i** has a large following, growing rapidly since 1964 and now strongest in the Gulf district of Papua and in the Eastern Highlands of New Guinea.

**CHRISTIANITY.** By 1966, 92% of the total population had become Christians, 31% being Catholics and 61% in other denominations. Catholicism was strongest in New Guinea with 36% as against only 20% in Papua. Lutherans formed the largest Protestant group with 34% of New Guinea and 27% of the whole population.

PROTESTANT CHURCHES. A pioneer of the London Missionary Society entered southern Papua in 1871 with several Lifu Christians from the Loyalty Islands. During the next few years they were joined by LMS missionaries and Christians from other Pacific islands to the east, including the Cook Islands, and a training school was established at the mouth of the Fly River. A large Christian community resulted. In 1962, the LMS, Presbyterian Church of New Zealand and Kwato Mission joined to form the Papua Ekalesia, at the time the largest single church in Papua. In 1966, 20% of Papua's population were adherents of the Ekalesia. A further union took place in 1968 involving the Papua Ekalesia, the Methodist Church and the Union Church in Port Moresby, producing the United Church of Papua New Guinea and the Solomon Islands. Australian Methodists entered into an early comity arrangement with the LMS and Anglicans, whereby the Methodists were allocated islands to the southeast of Papua. A team including Christians from Fiji and Samoa arrived at the Duke of York Islands in 1875, later moving on to New Britain and New Ireland and finally to Papua itself in 1890. Missionary losses due to cannibalism were not uncommon in the early days; and during World War II other missionaries together with their Christian followers were killed and their buildings destroyed. The stone-age peoples of the Highlands were not reached until 1950 and little progress was made for another decade; by 1961 there were only 200 Methodist members, but by 1967

**Tribal religionists.** Mudmen from Asaro river dance to scare off evil spirits.

the figure had risen to 3,000. Of the local men who serve as pastors and evangelists in this area, 90% are pre-literate. At the time of the merger creating the United Church in 1968, 8.5% of the population professed to be Methodists, 16% in Papua and 5% in New Guinea.

Lutheran pioneers to New Guinea were German missionaries of the Neuendettelsau and Rhenish missions. Beginning in 1886 the work saw little advance in the early years, but since the turn of the century the church has grown rapidly until now

Lutherans form the largest sector of the non-Catholic population. Assistance has also been received from Lutheran churches in Australia and the USA, and since 1951 from the Leipzig Mission. The Evangelical Lutheran Church of New Guinea (ELCONG) became autonomous in 1956. Another Lutheran body is the Wabag Lutheran Church, organized in 1961 as the result of the work of Missouri Synod Lutherans (USA) among the Enga people of the Central Highlands.

Other denominations include the Australian Assemblies of God, Australian Baptists, Plymouth Brethren, Apostlic Church Mission and Seventh-day Adventists. The first interdenominational or faith missions were also from Australia: the Unevangelized Fields Missions among the Gongodala people of the south coast of Papua in 1931 and the South Sea Evangelical Mission at the Sepik River of New Guinea in 1948. These were followed by the New Tribes Mission in 1949, Nazarenes in 1955 and numerous other missions after 1960.

Protestant and Anglican institutions in 1972 included 1,340 primary schools, 10 secondary schools, 4 teacher training colleges, 20 hospitals and 167 clinics.

CATHOLIC CHURCH. Although Catholic missionaries first came to the Bismark archipelago in 1847, little success was recorded prior to the arrival of Sacred Heart missionaries in 1881. In 1885 the first service was held on Papua itself, and the vicariate of British New Guinea was established in 1889. There are now 3 archdioceses and 11 dioceses (excluding Bougainville), the largest in terms of membership being those on mainland New Guinea. The Catholic Church grew enormously during the 1960s, from 423,481 in 1963 to 606,000 in 1970, an average increase of more than 5% per year. However, indigenous vocations are still weak. The first Papuan priest was not ordained until 1937 and became also the first Papuan bishop in 1970. The first ordinations of indigenous priests in New Guinea were in 1953. In 1970 there were in the whole of Papua New Guinea only 15 indigenous priests as contrasted with 475 expatriates. Local brothers and sisters are more numerous.

ANGLICAN CHURCH. Anglican missions began in 1891 at Dogura in eastern Papua. The diocese of Papua New Guinea was erected in 1898 and was a missionary diocese of the Church of England in Australia until the formation in 1977 of an autonomous Anglican province, the Church of the Province of Papua New Guinea, with 5 dioceses.

INDIGENOUS CHURCHES. A number of cargo cults, 35 or so, have incorporated sufficiently strong Christian elements for them properly to be classified as Christian movements, though mostly of a marginal kind. Most also have been short-lived. Among several which began as revivals within mission churches was Eemasang (Cleanup movement) among Kate-speaking tribes in 1927, which lasted as a renewal movement within the Lutheran church until by 1936 it had become a cargo cult which later collapsed. New cults by 1970 included: among Lutherans, a prophet among the Atzera tribe up the Markham river who reintroduced the ancestral cult and promised cargo; and among Baining-speaking United Church adherents near Rabaul, *kivung* (meetings) featuring military drilling, testimonies and simultaneous audible prayer. The only cult to survive for any length of time as an organized church so far is the Paliau Church on Manus Island, a schism from the Catholic Church which has now established co-operative links with the Manus Evangelical Church and other Protestant missions. There are also a number of former cargo-cult groups that have become independent pentecostal congregations.

CHURCH AND STATE. According to the Papua and New Guinea Act 1949-66, Article 8, the Australian administrative authority guaranteed to the inhabitants of the territory 'freedom of conscience and worship and freedom of religious teaching'. There was and is no state church or religion. Neither the administration nor the new state assist the churches or pay clergy engaged in religious work, except army and police chaplains; but churches are exempt from taxation. There is no ministry or government department responsible for religious affairs. Churches must register as corporate bodies in order to obtain titles of property, but they do not have to register as religious organizations.

In accordance with the Education (Papua and New Guinea) Ordinance of 1970, the Australian administration paid the salaries of all qualified teachers in the territory's education system. The Weeden Report which brought about this Ordinance expressed appreciation for the efforts of churches and missions in the field of education. Religious instruction then and subsequently has been provided by church teachers in state schools as well as in church schools.

After their annual conferences of 1969 and 1970, the Catholic bishops issued documents calling for the acceleration of the process leading to independence, and opposing labour conditions which kept indigenous workers away from their families for lengthy periods of time.

**Catholic Church in Papua New Guinea.** *Above.* Seminarians at Regional Seminary of the Holy Spirit, Bomana. Mural at top is an indigenous portrayal of the Holy Spirit. *Right.* Catholic pentecostals in 1972 procession led by (in mitre) Archbishop A.A. Noser of Madang.

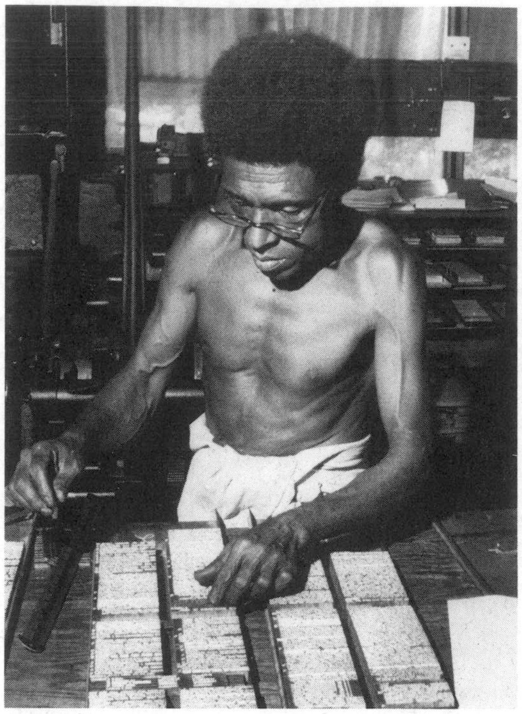

**Evangelical Lutheran Church of Papua New Guinea** (formerly ELCONG). Printer at work in ELCONG press.

The president of the drafting committee for the new constitution was an indigenous Catholic priest who was also an elected deputy in parliament. In 1977, of the 100 members of parliament, 55 were Protestants or Anglicans, 38 Catholics, and 7 non-Christians, with the prime minister a Catholic.

**INTERDENOMINATIONAL ORGANIZATIONS.** The Melanesian Council of Churches (MCC), which covers also the Solomon Islands, was founded at Port Moresby in 1965, and included the Anglican Church, Australian Baptist mission, Evangelical Lutheran Church, Salvation Army and the bodies which in 1968 merged into the United Church. The Catholic Church joined in 1971, and plans are now being made to establish local ecumenical councils in the main towns of Papua New Guinea one of which is the Lae Kristen Kaunsil. The MCC is not affiliated with the WCC (though in working relationship with it), but has strong fraternal ties with the Evangelical Alliance of the South Pacific Islands, Australian Council of Churches, Pacific Conference of Churches, and the Solomon Islands Christian Association. Of the churches working in Papua New Guinea, 20 are members of the Evangelical Alliance of the South Pacific. In 1969 the Melanesian Association of Theological Schools was formed by the theological colleges of the Anglican, Catholic, Lutheran and United churches. Other ecumenical initiatives are the Churches Education Council, which consists of the various denominational education officers responsible for church interests in the newly-formed Education System, and Sodepang (Sodepax Papua New Guinea) which works in collaboration with Sodepax, New Guinea in the field of human development.

**BROADCASTING.** Radio plays a vital role in Christian activities because of the impassable terrain and undeveloped transport and communications; however, no commercial or private missionary stations are permitted. There is a government Department of Information and Extension Services, and 8 regional government stations which broadcast at the village level in Pidgin and vernacular languages. Moreover, services of the Australian Broadcasting Commission (Port Moresby) transmit religious broadcasts, with daily morning Bible readings, evening meditations, and Sunday worship, hymn-singing and Christian discussions. A Churches' Council for Media Coordination, which includes the Catholics, the main Protestant churches and the Evangelical Alliance, was constituted in 1974.

The Christian Radio Missionary Fellowship based on Banz operates an extensive telecommunications network throughout New Guinea linking missionaries on over 40 stations belonging to 20 missionary societies. A radio school of the Air is conducted for 2 hours daily for children of missionaries. Licences for international frequencies have been refused in accordance with government policy. However, the CRMF backed by its 20 societies has received government approval to erect many local stations throughout New Guinea. Programmes are prepared in the CRMF studio at Banz. Since 1966 over 8,000 programmes have been broadcast, including daily Bible readings, Bible studies, devotionals and Bible dramas. Catholics produce a 5-minute devotional 3 mornings and 3 evenings per week and a monthly 15-minute Sunday programme. For Catholics, Papua New Guinea is a member of UNDA.

**BIBLIOGRAPHY**


'A cargo movement in the East Central Highlands of New Guinea', R.M. Berndt, *Oceania*, XXIII, 1 (1952–53), 40–63, and 3, 137–158.

*A Church self-study in Papua New Guinea, 1972–75*. PMV dossier. Brussels: Pro Mundi Vita, 1976.

'A comparison between the Begesin Rebellion and the present Christian Revival movement in the Kein area of the Begesin region'. A. Yagas. Typescript, University of PNG, 1976.

'A history of cargoism in Sio, Northeast New Guinea', T.G. Harding, *Oceania*, XXXVIII, 1 (1967), 1–23.

'Cargo cults and religious beliefs among the Garia', P. Lawrence, *Internationalis Archiv für Ethnographie*, 47 (1955), 1–20.

*Charles W. Abel: Papuan Pioneer*. M.K. Abel. London, 1957. (On the 1891 founder of the Kwato Church).

'Christianity, cargo cults and politics among the Toaripi of Papua', D. Ryan, *Oceania*, XL, 2 (December, 1969), 99–118.

*Church and people in New Guinea*. G.F. Vicedom. London: Lutterworth, 1961. 79p.

'Church growth and urbanization in New Guinea'. G. Fugmann. Thesis, Fuller Theological Seminary, Pasadena (CA), 1969. 244p.

*God, ghosts and men in Melanesia: some religions of Australian New Guinea and the New Hebrides*. Eds P. Lawrence & M.J. Meggitt. London: Oxford, 1965.

*Mambu: a Melanesian millenium*. K. Burridge. London: Methuen, 1961. 296p.

*Manus religion: an ethnological study of the Manus natives of the Admiralty Islands*. R.F. Fortune. Philadelphia: American Philosophical Society, 1935. 391p.

'Native Christianity in a New Guinea village', H.I. Hogbin, *Oceania*, XVIII (1947), 1–35.

*Official year book of the Catholic Church of Australia, Papua New Guinea, New Zealand & the Pacific Islands, 1969–70*. Sydney: E.J. Dwyer, n.d. 544p.

*One hundred years in the islands (1875–1975)*. N. Threlfall. Rabaul: United Church, 1975.

*Orokaiva magic*. F.E. Williams. London: Oxford, 1928.

*Pigs for the ancestors: ritual in the ecology of a New Guinea people*. R.A. Rappaport. New Haven: Yale University Press, 1967.

*Reluctant mission: the Anglican Church in Papua New Guinea, 1891–1942*. D. Wetherell. University of Queensland Press Prentice Hall International, 1977.

'The mission of God in the Wabag area of New Guinea'. E.L. Spruth. Thesis, Fuller Theological Seminary, Pasadena (CA), 1970. 471p.

'The Paliau movement in the Admiralty Islands, 1946–1954', T. Schwartz, *Anthropological papers of the American Museum of Natural History*, XL, Part 2 (1962), 211–413. (Many photographs).

*The trumpet shall sound: a study of 'cargo' cults in Melanesia*. P. Worsley. London: MacGibbon & Kee, 1957. 290 p.

*The United Church in Papua, New Guinea and the Solomon Islands: the development of an indigenous church*. R.G. Williams. Rabaul: Trinity Press, 1972. 320p.

'The view from Hurun: the Peli Association of the East Sepik District'. R.J. May. New Guinea Research Unit, Port Moresby, 1975.

*Towards a Melanesian theology*. Port Moresby: Melanesian Institute, forthcoming.

*United Church directory*. Port Moresby: UCPNGSI, 1975. (Annual).


TABLE 2. ORGANIZED CHURCHES AND DENOMINATIONS IN PAPUA NEW GUINEA

| Official name 1 | Begun 2 | Type 3 | Counc 4 | Congs 5 | Adults 6 | Affiliated 7 | Names, notes, and other statistics (see Codebook) 8 |
|---|---|---|---|---|---|---|---|
| Anglican Church of Papua New Guinea | 1891 | A Hig | AWPKK | 276 | 25,000 | 60,000 | 1977, 5 Dioceses. 92% Papuan. 55n,47x,166f,G=4%pa,3H,27h,2p,3r,1s(20),=W70%,2000Yy. |
| Apostolic Christian Church | 1960 | P Hol | x.... | 25 | 1,250 | 5,000 | M=ACC(USA). Members Wala tribe. Very rapid growth 20% pa. 2x,6f,9p,W=80%,500Y. |
| Apostolic Church Mission | 1954 | P PeA | Z...E | 194 | 10,000 | 17,000 | M=Apostolic Church of Australia & New Zealand. Western Highlands. HQ Kandep. |
| Assemblies of God in Australia | 1948 | P Pe2 | ZH..E | 270 | 1,250 | 20,000 | *New Guinea Miss.* M=AoG(Australia,UK). Wewak. 14n,15x,100f,G=9.5%pa,3p,W=28%,200Y. |
| Assoc of Baptists for World Evangelism | 1967 | P Bap | x.... | | 500 | 1,000 | M=ABWE(USA). Regular Baptists. Fundamentalists. 2f. |
| Bamu River Mission | 1936 | P int | .H..E | 14 | 92 | 2,000 | M=BRM(Aust). Members: Kuvai, Bamu, Duvani tribes. 1 launch. 1n,1x,3f,1H,1p,W=75%,3Y. |
| Baptist Bible Fellowship International | 1961 | P Bap | x.... | | 100 | 150 | M=BBFI(USA). Fundamentalist Baptists. 6f. |
| Baptist Union Western Highlands | 1949 | P Bap | .H..a | 116 | 10,700 | 17,000 | M=ABMS(Australia). Sepik. Engas. 96n,10x,49f,G=5.9%pa,1H,1s(15),W=79%,250Y,300z. |
| Bible Missionary Church | | P ind | x.... | 21 | 500 | 3,000 | M=BMC(USA). Southern Highlands. HQ Kagua, via Mt Hagen. 3f. |
| Bethel Pentecostal Temple | 1948 | P Pe2 | ..... | 120 | 20,000 | 40,000 | M=BPC(Seattle,USA). Classical Pentecostals (2-stage). Growth 7.5%pa,1p,2300Y. |
| **Catholic Church in Papua New Guinea:** | 1847 | R Lat | P...Q | 938 | 357,800 | 606,544 | Many institutions. C=12+8+31. 97H,3q,3s. 15n,475x,308m,745w,P=57%,24337Yy. |
| M Madang | 1896 | R Lat | Psvd | 25 | 32,700 | 55,475 | NG, between Catholic and Lutheran spheres. 9H. 0 61 26 75 49 2195 |
| D Aitape | 1952 | R Lat | Pofm | 26 | 22,000 | 37,337 | NG mainland, extreme north. Underdeveloped. 4 22 16 49 30 1424 |
| D Goroka | 1959 | R Lat | Psvd | 25 | 49,200 | 83,341 | NG rural highlands. Catholics very strong. 1 34 15 30 66 2036 |
| D Lae | 1959 | R Lat | Pcmm | 10 | 6,800 | 11,450 | NG mainland. Lutheran sphere, few Catholics. 0 9 6 5 51 282 |
| D Mount Hagen | 1959 | R Lat | Psvd | 344 | 53,300 | 90,255 | NG mainland, rural highlands. Catholics strong. 0 44 18 36 57 3874 |
| D Vanimo | 1963 | R Lat | Pcp | 7 | 3,400 | 5,700 | NG mainland. Remote, rugged, primitive. 0 9 3 5 63 203 |
| D Wewak | 1913 | R Lat | Psvd | 44 | 44,800 | 75,871 | NG mainland. 43% RC, widespread schools. 0 62 41 50 39 1673 |
| M Port Moresby | 1946 | R Lat | Pmscl | 21 | 13,600 | 23,112 | Papua. Catholics most from other areas. 1s(66). 0 43 24 77 86 917 |
| D Bereina | 1959 | R Lat | Pmscl | 21 | 23,500 | 39,862 | Papua mainland. 199 expatriate Catholics. 3 45 27 86 48 2262 |
| D Daru | 1959 | R Lat | Psmm | 8 | 1,700 | 2,805 | P mainland. Vast wasteland; large mining works. 0 16 13 32 80 126 |
| D Mendi | 1958 | R Lat | Pofmc | 9 | 15,700 | 26,636 | P rural highlands. White influence very recent. 0 33 6 33 84 2492 |
| D Sideia (1975, Alotau-Sideia) | 1946 | R Lat | Pmscl | 11 | 6,800 | 11,500 | Papua: many widely scattered islands. 1 17 15 18 70 450 |
| M Rabaul | 1889 | R Lat | Pmscl | 370 | 64,100 | 109,000 | New Britain. Rich. First RC mission in PNG. 1p. 4 59 83 223 63 5238 |
| D Kevieng | 1957 | R Lat | Pmscl | 17 | 20,200 | 34,200 | NG: New Ireland etc. Fishing, agriculture. 2 21 15 26 63 1165 |
| Christian Brethren | c1955 | P CBr | x...E | 40 | 7,000 | 15,220 | *Plymouth (Open) Brethren*. M=CMML(NZ,Australia,USA). Southern Highlands. 69f. |
| Christian Revival Crusade | 1963 | P Pe2 | x.... | 10 | 500 | 1,000 | M=CRC(Australia). Works also with International Ch of the Foursquare Gospel. 2n,1s. |
| Church of the Nazarene | 1955 | P Hol | xF..E | 34 | 1,026 | 3,000 | M=CoN(USA). HQ Banz. 7x,109m,33f,G=17%pa,1H,1h,1s(23),16t(1945),W=67%,30Y. |
| Churches of Christ in Christian Union | 1963 | P Hol | xF..E | 86 | 5,000 | 9,200 | M=CCCU(USA). Wesleyan doctrine. Southern Highlands. 1 school. 15f,3h. |
| Churches of Christ Mission | 1958 | P Dis | x...E | | 3,000 | 7,000 | M=Australian Churches of Christ Mission. HQ Tung, Wewak. New Guinea. 10f. |
| Evangelical Bible Mission | 1948 | P Hol | ....E | 85 | 1,000 | 2,000 | M=EBM(USA),East & West Indies Bible Mission,Gopel Tidings Mission. 24f,5h,1s. |
| Evangelical Church of Papua | 1931 | P int | xM..E | 154 | 5,246 | 12,601 | M=Asia Pacific Christian Mission,UFM(USA,UK). 160n,139f,G=9.2%pa,7p(80),W=98%,349Y. |
| **Ev Lutheran Ch of Papua New Guinea** | 1886 | P Lut | L.p.K | 2,023 | 230,001 | 365,137 | *ELCONG*. 200 tribes. 275n,98x,2255m,130f,G=3.9%pa,34h,8p,3s(150),W=62%,5161Y,10710y. |
| Faith Mission | | P int | ..... | | 4,000 | 8,730 | Interdenominational mission. In Gono, Goroka, Eastern Highlands. 13f,G=3.8%pa. |
| Greek Orthodox Church: AD Australia | | O Gre | Cw... | 1 | 100 | 200 | Greeks. Under jurisdiction of EP Constaninople, in AD Australia & E All Oceania. |
| Independent Christian Missionary Soc | 1965 | P Pen | ....E | 7 | 1,000 | 3,000 | Port Moresby. Pentecostal. Very rapid growth: 35% pa. 10n,4x,W=99%,21Y. |
| Indigenous cargo-cult churches | 1893 | I mar | ..... | | 600 | 1,000 | Long series of over 30 christianized movements, 1893–1980 (e.g. Wok belong Yali). |
| Indigenous pentecostal congregations | | I pen | ..... | | 500 | 1,000 | Christian pentecostal groups arising from cargo-cult manifestations. |
| Internat Ch of the Foursquare Gospel | 1955 | P Pe2 | ZF..E | 179 | 12,394 | 20,000 | M=ICFG(USA), CRC(Australia). Rapid growth in 5 tribes. 64n,21x,2p,(55),W=76%,359Y. |
| Jehovah's Witnesses | 1938 | M Jeh | x.... | 30 | 1,146 | 5,000 | Congregations: Papua 16; NG 11; Manus 1; New Britain 1; New Ireland 1. 100Y. |
| Kein Independence Group | 1969 | I Lut | ..... | 3 | 200 | 500 | Ex ELCONG. HQ Kein, Begesin District, Madang. '7 Steps and 7 Keys'. |
| Kwato Church | 1917 | I pen | ..... | | 2,400 | 4,000 | Ex LMS; 1977, ex UCPNG. Strong MRA influence. Milne Bay Province. |
| Manus Evangelical Church | 1914 | P int | xM..E | 34 | 2,500 | 4,000 | M=MEM(Liebenzell) (USA). Manus Island, 31 languages. 5n,2x,9f,G=3.2%pa,W=42%,122Y. |
| National Revival Church Mission | | P Pe2 | Z.... | | 200 | 500 | M=National Revival Crusade(Australia). Clasical Pentecostals (2-stage). |
| New Guinea Gospel Mission | 1960 | P int | .H..E | | 500 | 1,000 | M=NGGM(Australia). Interdenominational. HQ Wewak. Schools, medical work. 9f. |
| New Tribes Mission | 1949 | P int | x.... | 100 | 7,000 | 10,000 | M=NTM(USA). HQ Goroka, EHD. 1 school. 21n,37x,88f,G=3.9%pa,1h,2p,W=43%,100Y. |
| Paliau Church | 1946 | I ReC | ..... | | 500 | 1,000 | Schism 25% of RCC on Manus, begun by policeman, Paliau; now links with Manus Ev Ch. |

*Continued opposite*

*Table 2–continued*

| Official name 1 | Begun 2 | Type 3 | Counc 4 | Congs 5 | Adults 6 | Affiliated 7 | Names, notes, and other statistics (see Codebook) 8 |
|---|---|---|---|---|---|---|---|
| Peli (Hawk) Association | 1971 | I mar | ..... | 1 | 300 | 500 | HQ Yangoru, East Sepik. 1972: 200,000 members 1978: M=New Apostolic Ch (Canada). |
| Pentecostal Church | 1968 | P Pe2 | Z.... | 11 | 70 | 850 | M=SFM(Sweden),FFFM(Finland). Classical Pentecostals. 2n,3x,1p,W=47%,10Y,20z. |
| Salvation Army | 1956 | P Sal | xwe.K | 49 | 512 | 2,000 | *PNG Region*, in Eastern Territory, Australia. 24n,22x,G=6%pa,1p,1s(11),W=60%,82Y. |
| Seventh-day Adventist Church | 1908 | P Adv | x.... | 267 | 32,081 | 72,000 | *Coral Sea & Bismarck-Solomons UMs*. 100nx,1127mw,21f,3H,41h,2r,2s,839t(52570),2666Y. |
| South Sea Evangelical Church | 1948 | P int | xH..E | 195 | 2,000 | 5,000 | *SSEC*. M=SSEM(Australia). G=−6.5%pa losses to cargo cult. 10x,2p,W=80%,250Y,120z. |
| Sovereign Grace Baptist Mission | | P Bap | ..... | | 1,500 | 3,000 | Southern Highlands. HQ Tanggi, Koroba, via Mt Hagen; and Goroka EHD. 1f. |
| Swiss Evangelical Brotherhood Mission | | P ind | ..... | | 3,000 | 7,000 | HQ Lae. Districts: Chimbu, Eastern & Western Highlands, New Guinea. 45f. |
| **United Ch in PNG & the Solomon Islands** | 1871 | P uni | VWP.K | 2,082 | 64,278 | 210,540 | 1968 union: Papua Ekalesia (M=LMS), 4 Methodist areas. 276n,58x,5p,2s(80),19138z. |
| Wabag (Gudnius/Good News) Luth Ch | 1948 | P Lut | L...K | 365 | 19,456 | 48,000 | M=NGLM(LCMS,USA). Enga tribe. 23 schools. 80n,17x,58f,G=3.8%pa,1p,2s(35),1696Yy. |
| Wesleyan Church | 1961 | P Hol | VF..E | 37 | 802 | 5,000 | M=WC(USA). HQ Pangia. 2 schools. Rapid growth. 4x,6f,2p,W=87%,17Y,25z. |
| World-Wide Missions | 1971 | P ind | x.... | | 3,000 | 7,000 | M=WWM(USA). Evangelicals based on Pasadena,CA(USA). In Goroka territory, NG. 1f. |
| Other Protestant denominations | | P | ..... | | 2,000 | 5,000 | Total over 20 (see list below). |
| **Total affiliated (mid-1970)** | | | | **8,250** | **842,004** | **1,612,672** | **Total denominations (1970) . . . 97.** |
| **Total affiliated (mid-1975)** | | | | **9,300** | **975,000** | **1,867,400** | **Total denominations (1975) . . . 105.** |
| **Total affiliated (mid-1980)** | | | | **10,400** | **1,137,500** | **2,178,700** | **Total denominations (1980) . . . 115.** |

NOTES ON TABLE ABOVE
COLUMNS: for meanings and CODES (cols. 1, 3, 4, 8): see Codebook (Part 6). Column 1: **Boldface type** = church with over 10% of country's affiliated Christians.
NATIONAL COUNCILS (Column 4, 5th letter).
- a = member of both MCC and EASPI. In addition, the Highland Synod, United Church in PNG & SI, is a member of both.
- E = Evangelical Alliance of the South Pacific Islands (EASPI) (member churches and missions are all in Papua New Guinea, except South Sea Ev Ch in Solomon Is).
- K = Melanesian Council of Churches (MCC) (member churches are all in Papua New Guinea).
- Q = Bishops' Conference of Papua New Guinea & the Solomon Islands, also member of MCC.

*Local councils*. Lae Kristen Kaunsil, and others (related to MCC).
OTHER PROTESTANT DENOMINATIONS. Among the over 20 smaller denominations are the following: Baptist Ch (Boroko), Baptist International Missions (1967), Christadelphians (1 ecclesia), Churches of Christ (USA), Ev Wesleyan Ch, Highlands Christian Mission, Hohola Gospel Mission, Independent Assemblies of God, Independent Baptist Mission, Independent Nazarene Ch, New Guinea Christian Mission, Sola Fide Mission, United Ev Chs, Village Church Mission, Wewak Christian Fellowship.

PEOPLES (ethnolinguistic). Christians: 80.0% New Guinea Papuan, 18.2% New Guinea Melanesian, 1.5% Anglo-Australian, 0.1% British, 0.1% Chinese, 0.1% Euronesian.

COUNTRY-WIDE TOTALS
EVANGELIZATION (see Part 5). 1900: 17%. 1970: 100%. 1980: 100%. *Mass evangelism*. 1976, National Seminar on Evangelism (MCC, EASPI, RCC). *Radiophonic evangelism*. HCJB, FEBC, ICI (1,174 enrolments, 477 active), et alia.
FOREIGN MISSIONARIES AND PERSONNEL (nationals serving abroad) (1973). Total 15 in 4 countries: about 10 Protestants (UCPNGSI) in Australia (4 among Aborigines), Northern Solomons and Solomon Islands, 5 Roman Catholics.
FOREIGN MISSIONARIES AND PERSONNEL (aliens from abroad) (1973). Total 3,328. *From Western world*. 3,177: 1,815 Protestants (785 in 19 Australia societies, 528 in 23 USA societies, 214 in 15 New Zealand societies, 144 in 4 WGermany societies, 76 in 7 UK societies, 49 in 2 Canada societies, 8 in 1 Sweden society, 7 in 2 Finnish societies, 4 in 1 Netherlands society), 1,196 Roman Catholics, 166 Anglicans (91 in 3 Australia societies, 72 in 6 UK societies, 3 in 1 USA society). *From Communist world*. 36 Roman Catholics from Poland. *From Third World*. 115: 55 Protestants (28 from Solomon Islands, 15 from Fiji, Tonga, Samoa, Cook Islands, India), about 50 Roman Catholics from India, Brazil et alia, 10 Anglicans from Solomon Islands.
INSTITUTIONS (church-operated) (1973). Total 570, including 70 higher schools (3 minor seminaries), about 450 medical centres (117 hospitals), 1 religious community, 23 seminaries (16 Protestant, 6 RC, 1 Anglican), 8 study centres.
PERIODICALS. About 30 titles.
PERSONNEL. About 11,712 (8,384 national, 3,328 foreign).
RELIGIOUS LIBRARIES. About 34.
SCRIPTURE DISTRIBUTION (1975). Annual totals: 9,011 Bibles (89% subsidized, 11% commercial), 52,595 NTs (2% free, 94% subsidized, 4% commercial), 43,025 UBS portions, 192,334 UBS selections. *Translations completed*. Portion: 109 languages since 1882. NT: 22 languages since 1891. Bible: 3 languages since 1975.
SERVICE AGENCIES. About 130, including BB, CIP, CLC, CRMF, EASPI, ISO, JARS, LWR, MAF (13 aircraft), MAPNG, MATS, MCC, NCMWS, SIL, SU, WBT (318 missionaries), YMCA, YWCA. There is a total of over 80 Protestant foreign missionary societies at work.

ADDITIONAL DATA ON CHURCHES
ANGLICAN CHURCH OF PAPUA NEW GUINEA. The diocese was a missionary diocese (D Papua New Guinea) in the Province of Queensland, Church of England in Australia, until 1977 when it became an independent Anglican province with 5 dioceses: Aipo Rongo, Dogura, New Guinea Islands, Popondota, Southern Papua. *Members*. 92% Papuans, 8% Whites. *Personnel* (1977). 102 priests (20 expatriate), 12 deacons, 156 lay workers (53 women), 150 lay readers (men), 18 seminarians.
CATHOLIC CHURCH IN PAPUA NEW GUINEA. *Dioceses*. The diocese of Bougainville is excluded here and shown under the secessionist territory of Northern Solomons. *New diocese*. In 1976, D Kerema was created. *Catholics*. Column 7 gives totals of baptized Catholics only, excluding a small number of catechumens. *Catechumens* have decreased rapidly since the nation exceeded 90% Christian in the year 1960. Baptized Catholics have grown rapidly in numbers from 423,481 in 1963 to 672,774 in 1970; in the diocese of Mendi, Catholics grew from 1,412 in 1963 to 26,636 in 1970. Correspondingly, catechumens have decreased from 50,032 (12% of the total baptized) in 1963 to less than 2% by 1973. *Annual baptisms*. (1972) 78.9% infant, 21.1% adult. *Priests*. Nationals: 16 from New Guinea (all diocesan except 3 MSC), 4 from Papua (all MSC except 1 diocesan). The first indigenous priest in Papua was ordained (MSC) in 1937 and appointed the first Papuan bishop in 1970. In New Guinea, the first 4 indigenous priests were ordained (diocesan) in 1953. *Brothers*. Including 92 indigenous. *Sisters*. Including 403 indigenous. *Catholic charismatics*. Growing in M Madang especially. *Seminarians*. (1972) 87 at Port Moresby regional major seminary; half secular, half religious. (1977) 126. *Catechists*. Total (1971) 3,194, of whom 400 graduated from catechetical training schools. (1973) 2,161 (1,527 full-time), plus volunteers. *Indigenous religious congregations* (1973). These include: (brothers) Oblates, St Pius Sarto (Papuans), and (sisters) Daughters of Mary Immaculate (Rabaul; 124 professed), Handmaids of Our Lord (Port Moresby; 80 professed), Sisters of Ste Thérèse of the Child Jesus of Alexishafen (Madang; 32 members), Handmaids of Our Lady. *Major foreign congregations*. Sisters (professed, 1973): 200 Daughtersof Our Lady of the Sacred Heart (Issoudun), 88 Marists. *Catholic organizations*. The Conference of the Bishops of Papua New Guinea and the Solomon Islands has its headquarters in Port Moresby, Papua. Organizations of religious personnel are the Conference of Religious Brothers, and the National Conference of Major Women Superiors. There is no official council of priests; but an unofficial group, the Conference of Indigenous Priests, has shown interest in adapting the local church to Melanesian traditions and seeks consultation with the hierarchy in religious decisions. Lay organizations include a strong and active Legion of Mary, St Vincent de Paul Society in cities and towns, and Catholic Youth which is just beginning.

The Holy See has had no diplomatic relations with Papua New Guinea nor with the former colonial power, Australia. In 1977, however, the Holy See set up relations with the new state.

Organizations involved in research and socio-religious action are the Melanesian Institute for Pastoral and Socio-Economic Service and the Institute of Social Order (ISO).

In 1970 there were 569 Catholic schools with 81,812 students, as follows: 531 primary schools (75,937 pupils), 115 in Papua (14,262) and 416 in New Guinea (61,675); 21 high schools (4,886), 5 in Papua (1,122), 16 in New Guinea (3,764); 6 teacher training colleges (552 students), 1 in Papua (78) and 5 in New Guinea (474); 1 technical school with 35 students in New Guinea; 10 junior technical and vocational schools (402 students), 2 in Papua (57) and 8 in New Guinea (345), and 1 Boys' Town in the diocese of Wewak. By 1973, these had increased to 905 schools with 96,663 pupils. In addition there were, in 1970, 95 hospitals (4,290 beds), 2 leprosy hospitals in New Guinea, 1 Cheshire Home for 12 handicapped children in Port Moresby and numerous dispensaries.
EVANGELICAL LUTHERAN CHURCH OF PAPUA NEW GUINEA. The first missionary society was the Neuendettelsauer Mission, then the Rhenish Mission; supported now by the American Lutheran Church (USA), Leipzig Mission (Germany), and the Lutheran Church in Australia. *Home missionaries*. Large numbers of indigenous evangelists have pioneered inland in the highlands: in 1935, there were 800, in 1961 1,200, and by 1972 there were 3,000. ELCONG (in 1975 renamed ELC/PNG) works among 200 tribes (out of 700 languages in New Guinea). The biggest ELCONG area is in Morobe district among the Kate and Lae, the latter (population 12,000) being 90% Lutheran with 25% as weekly church attenders. The 29 major tribes in ELCONG are: Agarepe, Amari, Amere, Aseki, Atzera, Benabena, Buana, Enga, Fore, Graged, Jabim, Jazub, Jopna, Kafe, Kahuku, Kate, Kaudel, Komano, Komba, Kukakuka, Kuman, Laewomba, Medlpa, Mumeng, Ono, Tairora, Timbe, Waing, Wantoat. *Growth*. By 1977 numbers had grown to 400,000 members, 400 ordained national pastors, 7 Districts (including from 1976 the Siassi Lutheran Church with 7,000 members), 640 primary schools (35,000 pupils), 9 secondary schools (2,200 pupils).
UNITED CHURCH IN PNG AND THE SOLOMON ISLANDS. 6 Regions, each with 5–20 Circuits: Highlands; New Guinea Islands; Papuan Islands; Papua Mainland; Urban Regions (Port Moresby, Lae); Solomon Islands. Languages respectively of these Regions: Mendi & Huli (Tari); Pidgin & Kuanua (biggest tribe in the UC); Dobu; Motu & Police Motu; Pidgin & English; Pidgin & Roviana. *Membership*. Confirmed members increased from 67,504 in 1970 to 85,318 in 1975. *Indigenous pastors*. In 1975, 85% of the church's pastors were indigenous; of its 7 bishops, all were from PNG except 1 Tongan, 1 Fijian and 1 Solomoni. The moderator, in 1976 a Solomoni, resides in Port Moresby. *Expatriate pastors*. The total in 1975 was 41: 20 Australian, 8 British, 7 Fijian, 3 Tongan and 3 Samoan.
WABAG LUTHERAN CHURCH. *Growth*. Rising by 1975 to 53,500 members and in 1977 to 55,000.

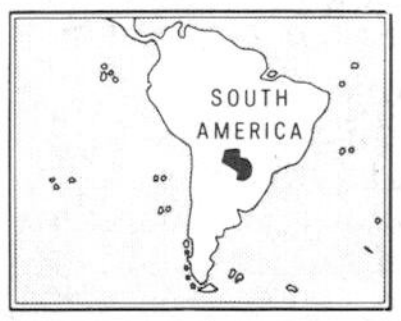


# PARAGUAY

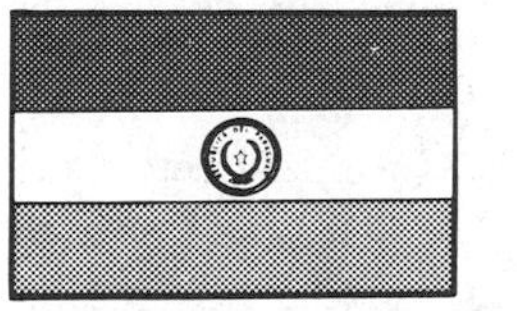

## SECULAR DATA

**STATE. Official name:** The Republic of Paraguay (La República del Paraguay). Adjective of nationality: Paraguayan (paraguayo).
**Flag** (shown above right): Red, white, and blue stripes; national coat of arms in centre.
**Area:** 406,752 sq.km. (157,048 sq.miles). Agricultural land: 39.3%.
**Government:** Republic under dictatorship, since 1954 (1524 Spanish possession, 1811 Independence, several dictatorships and republics).
**Legislature:** Senate, 30 members. Chamber of Deputies, 60 members.
**Official languages:** Spanish (*Español/Castellano*), Guaraní (national).
**Capital:** Asunción 411,500 (1968).
**Political divisions:** (1) Oriental (east of Paraguay river): 13 Departments, divided into 133 partidos. (2) Occidental (west), or Chaco (under military control): 3 Departments with 4 partidos.
**Armed forces** (1976): Total 16,600 regular: army 12,300, navy 1,800, air force 2,500 (12 combat aircraft). Paramilitary forces: 5,000.

**DEMOGRAPHY. Population:** 2,357,955 (census of 9.VII.1972. For 1970–2000 (UN), see last row of Table 1). Population density (1975): 7/sq.km. (17/sq.mile). Under 15 years: 47%. Growth rate (1975–80): 2.91% per year (births 3.91%, deaths −0.81%, emigrants −0.19%). Life expectancy (1975–80): 63.6 years. Household size: 5.5 persons.
**Major languages:** Guaraní, Spanish, Lengua, German, Portuguese, Italian, Ukrainian, and 20 other languages. Usage: 90% speak Guaraní, 75% speak Spanish.
**Urban dwellers** (1970): 38.7%. Urban growth rate (1950–70): 3.6% per year.
**Labour force:** 33%.
**Tourists** (1971): 123,676. (1972) 93,023. (1973) 95,100.

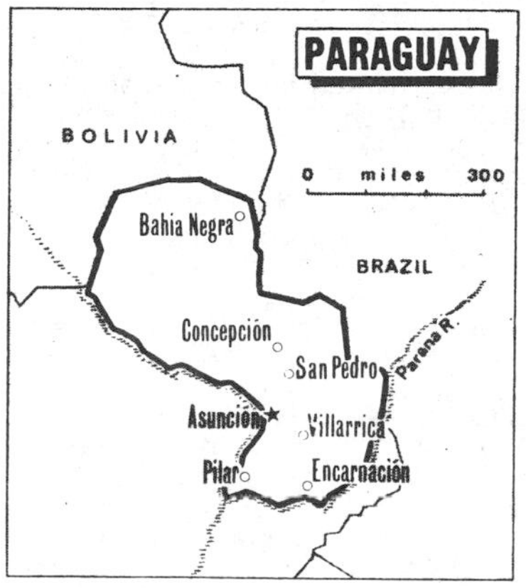


**ETHNOLINGUISTIC GROUPS:** 90.8% Mestizo (Spanish/Guaraní), 3.0% Amerindian (17 tribes, 198 sub-tribes; 70,000; Lengua, Chulupi, Guaraní, Ayoreo, Guana, Sanapana, Tapiete), 1.7% German, 1.4% Argentinian White, 1.0% Black (Negro), 0.6% Brazilian, 0.6% Italian, 0.6% Ukrainian, 0.2% Japanese (5,300), 0.1% Jewish, Greek, Russian, Polish, Chilean, Korean, Australian.

**MONEY** (1977). **Monetary unit:** guaraní (= 100 céntimos); US$1 = G 126.00.
**National income per person:** US$489. Average annual family income: US$2,690.
**Inflation:** (1970–74) 12.8% per year, (1975) 30% per year (consumer price index 183).
**Cost of living in capital** (1976): index 100 (Washington DC=100). Daily cost of living: US$30.

**HEALTH.** Hospitals: 134 (3,875 beds). Doctors: 1,071. Lepers: 7,000 (2.6 per 1,000). Blind: 4,000. Psychotics: 22,000.

**EDUCATION.** Adult literacy: (1950) 66%, (1972) 80%. Education rate: 49%. Schools: 3,200. Universities: 2.

**LITERATURE.** Periodicals: 60. Scientific journals: 15. Newspapers: 11 dailies.

**COMMUNICATION** (per 1,000 people). Phones: 11. Radios: 68. TV sets: 8. Daily newspaper circulation: 38 copies.

TABLE 1. RELIGIOUS ADHERENTS IN PARAGUAY

| Year | 1900 | | mid-1970 | | Annual change, 1970–1980 | | | | mid-1975 | | mid-1980 | | 2000 | |
|---|---|---|---|---|---|---|---|---|---|---|---|---|---|---|
| *Name* | *Adherents* | *%* | *Adherents* | *%* | *Natural* | *Conversion* | *Total* | *Rate* | *Adherents* | *%* | *Adherents* | *%* | *Adherents* | *%* |
| **Christians** | **580,000** | **96.7** | **2,252,700** | **97.9** | **74,677** | **1,183** | **75,860** | **2.92** | **2,597,520** | **98.1** | **3,011,300** | **98.3** | **5,216,000** | **98.9** |
| professing | 580,000 | 96.7 | 2,252,700 | 97.9 | 74,677 | 1,183 | 75,860 | 2.92 | 2,597,520 | 98.1 | 3,011,300 | 98.3 | 5,216,000 | 98.9 |
| Roman Catholics | 579,600 | 96.6 | 2,198,800 | 95.6 | 72,869 | 1,171 | 74,040 | 2.92 | 2,534,620 | 95.8 | 2,939,200 | 96.0 | 5,084,000 | 96.4 |
| Christo-pagans | 24,000 | 4.0 | 50,000 | 2.2 | 1,598 | –478 | 1,120 | 2.01 | 55,600 | 2.1 | 61,200 | 2.0 | 79,100 | 1.5 |
| Protestants | 200 | 0.0 | 42,000 | 1.8 | 1,409 | –9 | 1,400 | 2.86 | 49,000 | 1.9 | 56,000 | 1.8 | 100,000 | 1.9 |
| Orthodox | 0 | 0.0 | 4,200 | 0.2 | 139 | 1 | 140 | 2.89 | 4,850 | 0.2 | 5,600 | 0.2 | 10,000 | 0.2 |
| Marginal Protestants | 0 | 0.0 | 3,100 | 0.1 | 106 | 4 | 110 | 2.97 | 3,700 | 0.1 | 4,200 | 0.1 | 9,000 | 0.2 |
| Anglicans | 200 | 0.0 | 3,000 | 0.1 | 101 | 9 | 110 | 3.14 | 3,500 | 0.1 | 4,100 | 0.1 | 8,000 | 0.2 |
| Latin American indigenous | 0 | 0.0 | 1,600 | 0.1 | 53 | 7 | 60 | 3.24 | 1,850 | 0.1 | 2,200 | 0.1 | 5,000 | 0.1 |
| affiliated | 580,000 | 96.7 | 2,252,700 | 97.9 | 74,677 | 1,183 | 75,860 | 2.92 | 2,597,520 | 98.1 | 3,011,300 | 98.3 | 5,216,000 | 98.9 |
| disaffiliated | 0 | 0.0 | –42,300 | –1.8 | –1,114 | 1,744 | 630 | –1.63 | –38,730 | –1.5 | –36,000 | –1.2 | –32,000 | –0.6 |
| doubly-affiliated | –200 | –0.0 | –54,747 | –2.4 | –1,826 | –49 | –1,875 | 2.95 | –63,500 | –2.4 | –73,500 | –2.4 | –105,000 | –2.0 |
| total practising | 406,000 | *70* | 1,013,710 | *45* | 33,605 | 532 | 34,137 | 2.92 | 1,168,000 | *45* | 1,355,080 | *45* | 2,086,000 | *40* |
| non-practising | 174,000 | *30* | 1,238,990 | *55* | 41,072 | 651 | 41,723 | 2.92 | 1,428,640 | *55* | 1,656,220 | *55* | 3,130,000 | *60* |
| Roman Catholics | 580,000 | 96.7 | 2,294,591 | 99.7 | 75,784 | –643 | 75,141 | 2.85 | 2,636,000 | 99.6 | 3,046,000 | 99.5 | 5,222,000 | 99.0 |
| Protestants | 100 | 0.0 | 43,436 | 1.9 | 1,437 | 119 | 1,556 | 3.11 | 50,000 | 1.9 | 59,000 | 1.9 | 100,000 | 1.9 |
| Evangelicals | 100 | 0.0 | 38,900 | 1.7 | 1,293 | 317 | 1,610 | 3.58 | 45,000 | 1.7 | 55,000 | 1.8 | 94,000 | 1.8 |
| Neo-pentecostals | 0 | 0.0 | 0 | 0.0 | 57 | 443 | 500 | 25.00 | 2,000 | 0.1 | 5,000 | 0.2 | 20,000 | 0.4 |
| Orthodox | 0 | 0.0 | 4,100 | 0.2 | 137 | 3 | 140 | 2.95 | 4,750 | 0.2 | 5,500 | 0.2 | 9,000 | 0.2 |
| Marginal Protestants | 0 | 0.0 | 3,070 | 0.1 | 106 | –3 | 103 | 2.78 | 3,700 | 0.1 | 4,100 | 0.1 | 9,000 | 0.2 |
| Anglicans | 100 | 0.0 | 3,000 | 0.1 | 101 | 9 | 110 | 3.14 | 3,500 | 0.1 | 4,100 | 0.1 | 8,000 | 0.2 |
| Evangelicals | 100 | 0.0 | 2,500 | 0.1 | 86 | 64 | 150 | 5.00 | 3,000 | 0.1 | 4,000 | 0.1 | 7,800 | 0.1 |
| Latin American indigenous | 0 | 0.0 | 1,550 | 0.1 | 52 | 3 | 55 | 3.06 | 1,800 | 0.1 | 2,100 | 0.1 | 5,000 | 0.1 |
| Tribal religionists | 20,000 | 3.3 | 30,000 | 1.3 | 805 | –1,205 | –400 | –1.43 | 28,000 | 1.1 | 26,000 | 0.8 | 10,000 | 0.2 |
| Non-religious | 0 | 0.0 | 9,800 | 0.4 | 322 | –72 | 250 | 2.23 | 11,200 | 0.4 | 12,300 | 0.4 | 26,000 | 0.5 |
| Atheists | 0 | 0.0 | 3,000 | 0.1 | 104 | 16 | 120 | 3.33 | 3,600 | 0.1 | 4,200 | 0.1 | 8,000 | 0.2 |
| Baha'is | 0 | 0.0 | 2,100 | 0.1 | 72 | 8 | 80 | 3.20 | 2,500 | 0.1 | 2,900 | 0.1 | 6,000 | 0.1 |
| Buddhists | 0 | 0.0 | 2,000 | 0.1 | 57 | –57 | 0 | 0.00 | 2,000 | 0.1 | 2,000 | 0.1 | 1,000 | 0.0 |
| Jews | 0 | 0.0 | 1,200 | 0.1 | 40 | 0 | 40 | 2.90 | 1,380 | 0.1 | 1,600 | 0.1 | 3,000 | 0.1 |
| New-Religionists | 0 | 0.0 | 200 | 0.0 | 23 | 127 | 150 | 18.75 | 800 | 0.0 | 1,700 | 0.1 | 4,000 | 0.1 |
| **Country's population** | **600,000** | **100.0** | **2,301,000** | **100.0** | **76,100** | **0** | **76,100** | **2.87** | **2,647,000** | **100.0** | **3,062,000** | **100.0** | **5,274,000** | **100.0** |

COLUMNS, ROWS. For meanings and definitions, see Codebook (Part 6). Note that, by definition, total 'Christians' = professing + crypto-Christians, which also = affiliated + nominal Christians. Percentages may not always total exactly, due to rounding.

CENSUSES. **14.X.1962** (excluding 35,000 jungle Indians): 96.7% Roman Catholics, 2.3% other Christians, 0.6% other religionists, 0.4% non-religious.

NOTES ON RELIGIONS

ATHEISTS. Communist Party of Paraguay (PCP) (proscribed, suppressed) and factions: membership (1970) 4,000 including sympathizers. Many remain Roman Catholics, a number practising.

BAHA'IS. Growth from 3 local spiritual assemblies (1964) to 14 (1973). Many converts are Indians (Yanaigua, Chulupi, Maka).

BUDDHISTS. Among Japanese (since 1956; in Itapua and Alto Paraná) and Korean immigrants.

CHRISTO-PAGANS. Amerindians whose syncretistic folk-Catholicism combines 17th-century Spanish Catholicism with their own traditional pre-Christian animism, concepts and world-views.

COUNTRY'S POPULATION. From 1955–70, about 650,000 Paraguayans (450,000 being men) emigrated principally to Argentina, including large numbers of Catholics and some Protestants.

DISAFFILIATED. This term is used here to describe persons who, although baptized Roman Catholics and therefore regarded by the Catholic Church as still affiliated to it (and hence enumerated as such), have recently disaffiliated themselves from Christianity and now regard themselves as non-Christians. In the 1970s the Catholic Church claimed over 99.5% of the whole population, although 2.1% regarded themselves as non-Christians. Because their statistics represent a duplication, they are shown in the table above as a negative quantity (with a minus sign).

DOUBLY-AFFILIATED. The term covers those affiliated to, or claimed by, both the Catholic Church and also an Evangelical or other non-Catholic church, i.e. baptized Catholics who have recently become Evangelicals or others. Because their statistics represent a duplication, they are shown in the table as a negative quantity (with a minus sign).

LATIN AMERICAN INDIGENOUS. In Paraguayan, Chilean and Brazilian indigenous churches; about 8 denominations in 1970 (see Table 2).

NEO-PENTECOSTALS. A charismatic renewal began in 1972 among the Disciples of Christ and other Protestants, and also within the Anglican Church.

NEW-RELIGIONISTS. By 1975, converts to the Japanese movement Nichiren Shoshu (Soka Gakkai) numbered 800.

PRACTISING CHRISTIANS. *Roman Catholics.* Weekly mass attendance 7% (urban), 25% (rural). Annual practice about 40%. *Protestants.* Weekly attendance about 60%. Annual practice about 80%.

TRIBAL RELIGIONISTS. Of the 70,000 tribal lowland Amerindians in 6 linguistic families and 198 tribes, a large proportion remain animists.

**NON-CHRISTIAN RELIGIONS. Traditional Indian religions** still exist among the tribal lowland Amerindians, over a third of whom remain animists.

There are also a few Baha'is, Buddhists and Jews.

## CHRISTIANITY

CATHOLIC CHURCH. The Spanish arrived in Paraguay in 1524 and founded Asunción in 1537. The diocese of Asunción was erected in 1547, received a bishop in 1556 and 2 years later Jesuits arrived to evangelize the Indian population. In the western Chaco plains of Paraquay, the Jesuits established settlements known as reductions among the Guaraní Indians similar to those at that period in Brazil, Argentina and Bolivia. Each consisted of a small town centred on a large church, with the population engaged in cultivation of crops and cattle-raising. About 100 such reductions were created and a million Indians baptized before the Jesuits were expelled in 1767. A written form of the Guaraní language was also developed, and this is still widely used. In fact more people understand this language than Spanish (90% for Guaraní as contrasted with 75% for Spanish). The paternalistic system enshrined in the reductions left Indians poorly prepared to continue the communities after the Jesuit expulsion, and they therefore disintegrated. Paraguay achieved independence from Spain in 1811 without upheaval, but during the 19th century the country was involved in several disastrous wars. More than half of the population died in the war of 1865-70. The Catholic Church remained subservient to the state, with the government appointing bishops, and the clergy were inadequate to meet the needs of the people. Between 1881 and 1911 only 60 priests were ordained, and only one third of the population was registered on parish rolls.

Today the great majority of Paraguayans have been baptized as Catholics, but sacramental life continues to be impeded by the situation in which many find themselves. The disproportionate number of men to women (at least one man for every 2 women of child-bearing age) is the result both of very high mortality among men during the wars of the Triple Alliance (1865-70) and Chaco (1932-35) and also of the emigration of men to neighbouring countries because of unemployment. This disproportion has caused serious marital instability and in fact a kind of de facto polygamy. Half of all couples are unmarried, and 50% of all infants are born out of wedlock.

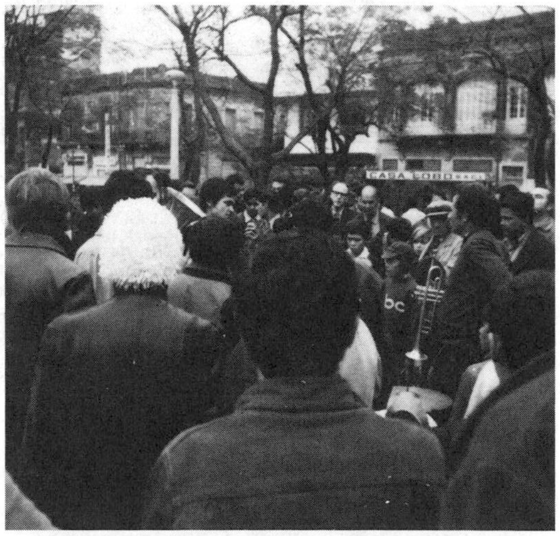

**Protestants.** Preaching at open-air street service in centre of Asunción.

In contrast to the position of the Catholic Church in most Latin American countries, the church in Paraguay owns very little property. Its relative poverty explains in part its present sensitivity to social problems. In 1972, 46% of all priests were nationals, and an even higher proportion (71%) of sisters.

PROTESTANT CHURCHES. The American Bible Society was the first Protestant body to make contact with Paraguay, in 1856, and in 1886 an American Methodist missionary began work there. German Lutheran immigrants organized their first congregations as early as 1893, which came together to form a Lutheran union in 1899. Seventh-day Adventists arrived in 1900, followed by the New Testament Missionary Union 2 years later, the latter directing its attention to the planting of self-supporting churches rather than institutional work. In 1916 the Disciples of Christ (USA) initiated a few small service institutions and later took over Methodist work. The first Mennonites were refugees from Russia following the 1917 Bolshevik revolution. Seeing the needs of local Chaco Indians, they opened work among them and appealed to North American Mennonite groups for assistance. Mennonites at present have the largest Christian community outside the Catholic Church, including over a thousand Indian converts. Another group of German Mennonites from the USSR, Mennonite Brethren, was formed in 1930. The first Baptists (1920) were missionaries of the Baptist Convention of Argentina, and since 1945 the Evangelical Baptist Convention of Paraguay has been aided by Southern Baptist missionaries from the USA. In 1953 they opened the first Baptist hospital in South America.

Assemblies of God missionaries came to Paraguay in 1945 to assist Pentecostal Christians who had left Slavic countries in eastern Europe. Literature, Bible correspondence courses and radio programmes have helped develop a small national church, established in 1958. The Church of God (Cleveland) began in 1954 and has also experienced steady growth. Working in close co-operation with the government's Indian Affairs Department, the New Tribes Mission has since 1946 been active among 6 tribes and in 1973 had 68 missionaries.

ANGLICAN CHURCH. Following the death of its founder Allen Gardiner among Patagonia Indians in southern Argentina, the South American Missionary Society in 1888 moved its work to the Chaco region of Paraguay. Anglican missionaries were the first to live among the Lengua Indians where the language was reduced to writing, scriptures translated and grammars prepared, in addition to evangelistic and social service activity. Fifteen national and 4 missionary clergy continue this work.

**CHURCH AND STATE.** The legal relations between church and state rest on Law 863 of 1963 and on the constitution of 25 August 1967. Law 863 brings together various scattered dispositions made over the years concerning the Catholic Church. The state recognizes the 'perfect character' of the church, confers on it a juridical personality, confirms certain important privileges including exemption from tax on donations and properties, and makes provision for financial contributions to it from the national budget. The constitution of 1967 guarantees respect for religious freedom, but in Article 6 recognizes Roman Catholicism as the official religion of the country, requires that the president be a Roman Catholic, and envisages also that concordats or bilateral treaties should regulate relations between Paraguay and the Holy See. However, no such agreement has as yet been negotiated. Article 189, item 2, makes the archbishop of Asunción a legal member of the Council of State, as the representative of the Catholic Church. In 1971 the archbishop took the oath of office but then publicly renounced his post citing existing institutional injustice throughout the country. Since 1940, and in particular since the rise to power of general Stroessner in 1954, the country has been under a dictatorial regime which has been reconfirmed in office every 3 months.

For several hundred years the Catholic Church in Paraguay has existed in a state of subjection to the political power. The patronage system, which was not abolished until 1967, not only conferred on the government the right of nominating bishops but also the right to censor edicts of the hierarchy with which it did not agree. For many years even the rank and file of priests had been considered officially as chaplains, i.e. religious functionaries of a nominally Catholic government. When general Stroessner disbanded political parties, trade unions and student activities in 1954, only Catholic Action managed to escape suppression, due to its markedly decentralized structure. At the time, Law 863 and its acceptance by the hierarchy were judged anachronistic by Catholic Action militants and lay apostolate activists who saw this as a manoeuvre on the part of government to secure the silence and support of the church at a time when it was preparing for the unconstitutional renewal of Stroessner's presidential mandate. Nevertheless at this period in 1963 the Catholic bishops published several documents criticizing the new constitution: 'Doctrinal orientations concerning constitutional reform' of 25 December 1966, and 'Letter to members of the National Convention' in 1967. The first incidents calling into question existing church-state relations took place in 1969, when there were 3 attempts by the government to intimidate the church: on the occasion of the inauguration of the Paraguayan major seminary, after a sermon given at the cathedral concerning political prisoners, and during a national pilgrimage to Caacupé. These

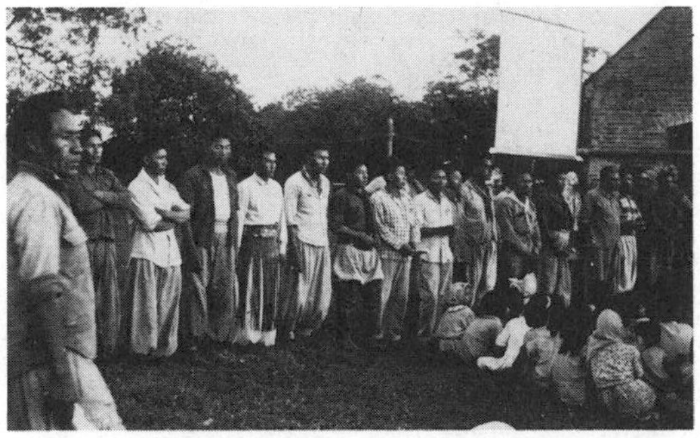

**Iglesia Anglicana Paraguaya.** Amerindian Christians from ranches many miles distant gather for instruction outside their church at Makthlawaiya.

incidents, together with the previous acts of repression against Agrarian Leagues and the Christian Federation of Workers (CCT), made the church decide to take a firm attitude against the abuse of power, not only concerning Christians but also all classes of citizens. Use was therefore made of the refusal to offer Te Deum prayers at government functions, protests against violation of the rights of political prisoners and the excommunication of government officials. The latter, in 1971, involved principally the minister of the Interior and the chief of police. The excommunication was not lifted until the end of 1974 and had a profound effect upon the populace who are unusually religious. This same attitude has also led the church to oppose international Catholic collaboration with the Stroessner regime and to the suspension in 1972 of food distribution by Catholic Relief Services. On its side, the government has attacked foreign clergy. In October 1969, the editor of *Comunidad* was deported although he was a naturalized citizen, and other priests and laymen attached to the Department of the Laity of CELAM, Agrarian Leagues and CCT have also suffered imprisonment, torture and deportation.

Several particularly brutal events became widely known because foreigners were witnesses and victims. On 8 February 1975 the army attacked the village of San Isidro de Jejui, headquarters of the Agrarian League, burning the houses of peasants and sacking the co-operative Experiencia de Fraternidad Campesina. Eight peasants were killed, numerous others wounded and about 50 were arrested. Two American directors of Catholic Relief Services visiting the co-operative at the time and 2 French priests were also arrested although later released. The Episcopal Conference, which is responsible for the co-operative, was not officially informed until several days later and then published a declaration accusing the army's anti-subversion brigade of murder and the theft of more than a million guaranis that had been in the co-operative treasury. Shortly after this attack, several other villages were also victims of similar excesses by the army.

The change in attitude of the hierarchy and clergy since 1954 is due largely to the profound impact on Paraguay of Vatican II, and the Medellín conference in 1968. Four of the 10 Paraguayan bishops participated actively in the latter. The unanimity of the bishops in the face of state power constitutes an important factor within the context of present church-state conflicts in Latin America and reinforces the image of the church as the only structured force opposing the Stroessner regime. In 1973 the episcopate created a consultative organism for relations between church and state.

**INTERDENOMINATIONAL ORGANIZATIONS.** The Paraguayan Episcopal Conference of the Catholic Church maintains a Department of Ecumenism. There is no ecumenical council of churches, but an Evangelical Co-ordinating Commission of Paraguay (Comisión Coordinadora Evangélica de Paraguay), with 5 member churches, has been formed.

**BROADCASTING.** All stations accept Catholic and Protestant programmes. In Asunción there is a Catholic station Radio Charitas and the Centro Experimental de TV Educativa in the Department of Sciences of Communication in the Catholic University prepares courses for educational TV. Paraguay is one of the main target areas of the Protestant Radio La Cruz del Sur in Bolivia.

## BIBLIOGRAPHY


*Anuario Eclesiástico del Paraguay, 1972.* Asunción: Centro de Estudios Socio-Religiosos, 1972.

'Church growth in Paraguay'. J.T. Shumaker. Thesis, Fuller Theological Seminary, Pasadena (CA), 1972. 158p.

*Guia de las iglesias evangélicas en el Paraguay.* 3rd edition. Asunción: Asociación de Obreros, Pastores y Misioneros del Paraguay, 1964. 20p.

'Paraguay: the church confronted by a country in evolution', *Pro Mundi Vita* (Brussels), 38 (1971), 1–32.

*Pilgrims in Paraguay: the story of Mennonite civilization in South America.* J.W. Fretz. Scottdale, PA: Herald Press, 1953. 247p.


TABLE 2. ORGANIZED CHURCHES AND DENOMINATIONS IN PARAGUAY

| Official name 1 | Begun 2 | Type 3 | Counc 4 | Congs 5 | Adults 6 | Affiliated 7 | Names, notes, and other statistics (see Codebook) 8 |
|---|---|---|---|---|---|---|---|
| Asambleas de Dios en el Paraguay | 1945 | P Pe2 | ZF..C | 23 | 545 | 2,000 | *Assemblies of God in P.* M=AoG(USA). Russians, Poles, Germans. 23n,7f,1s(12). |
| Convención Evangélica Bautista del P | 1920 | P Bap | T.... | 40 | 2,000 | 4,000 | *Baptist Conv of P.* 1945, M=SBC(USA). 18n,12x,27f,G=10.8%pa,1H,3h,1s(8),W=40%,225Y. |
| Ejército de Salvación en el Paraguay | 1910 | P Sal | xw... | 10 | 1,000 | 2,000 | *Salvation Army, Paraguay District*, South America East Territory. HQ Asunción. 2f. |
| Hermanos Menonitas | 1930 | P Men | GF... | 7 | 1,458 | 5,000 | 1935 M=MBCNA(USA). Begun USSR Germans; now 87% Lengua, Chulupi, Guaraní. 1H,1h,1s. |
| Iglesia Adventista del Séptimo Día | 1900 | P Adv | x.... | 12 | 781 | 2,000 | *Seventh-day Adventists, Parag M*, Austral UC. 6% Japanese. 2n,15m,6f,G=6%pa,2H,79Y. |
| Iglesia Alianza Cristiana y Misionera | 1966 | P Hol | xF... | 1 | 30 | 50 | *Christian & Missionary Alliance.* M=CMA(USA). Small holiness body. In Asunción. |
| Iglesia Anglicana Paraguaya | 1889 | A Eva | Aw.CC | 74 | 2,000 | 3,000 | *D Paraguay* (begun 1964). Member of CASA. M=SAMS(UK). Indians. 15n,4x,25f,W=58%. |
| **Iglesia Católica en el Paraguay:** | 1524 | R Lat | B.L.R | 250 | 1,216,100 | 2,294,591 | *Catholic Ch in Paraguay.* C=17+1+29. 1p,2q,1s(218). 223n,262x,153m,749w,56995Yy. |
| M Asunción | 1547 | R Lat | Bs | 56 | 365,700 | 690,020 | Capital, and rural Central department. 1s,W=20%. 101 106 92 474 11020 |
| D Caacupé | 1960 | R Lat | Bs | 17 | 101,000 | 190,000 | Mountains. National shrine Virgen de los Milagros. 23 4 0 25 7280 |
| D Concepción | 1929 | R Lat | Bs | 34 | 150,900 | 284,727 | Breeding, forestry, tea, coffee plantations. W=20%. 22 17 10 49 7374 |
| D San Juan Bautista de las M | 1957 | R Lat | Bs | 27 | 75,900 | 143,241 | M=Misiones. Area of 18th-century Jesuit reductions. 16 14 6 14 2478 |
| D Villarrica | 1929 | R Lat | Bs | 39 | 221,700 | 418,500 | Breeding, forestry, sugar cane. 1p,W=25%. 48 22 5 78 7240 |
| PN Alto Paraná | 1968 | R Lat | Bs | 9 | 42,000 | 80,000 | Recent rapid colonization (30%pa); Japanese. M=SVD. 2 11 2 21 3274 |
| PN Coronel Oviedo (1976, D) | 1961 | R Lat | Bs | 13 | 106,000 | 200,000 | East of capital. Forests and mountains. M=TOR. 7 18 8 16 8378 |
| PN Encarnación | 1957 | R Lat | Bs | 38 | 104,900 | 197,953 | Population concentrated around Itapuá. M=SVD. W=15%. 1 42 15 45 8483 |
| VA Chaco Paraguayo | 1948 | R Lat | Psdb | 7 | 17,000 | 32,150 | Forest. Breeding. In western depopulated area. P=14%. 3 8 1 7 482 |
| VA Pilcomayo | 1925 | R Lat | Pomi | 10 | 31,000 | 58,000 | In western depopulated region of country. 10% pagans. 0 20 14 20 986 |
| Iglesia de Dios en el Paraguay | 1954 | P Pe3 | ZF..C | 65 | 1,161 | 2,000 | *Ch of God.* M=CoG(Cleveland)(Chile,USA). German, Spanish, Guaraní. 38n,1s. |
| Iglesia de JC de los Santos de los UD | c1946 | M LdS | x.... | | 600 | 1,070 | *Latter-day Saints. Mormons.* M=CJCLdS(USA). Indians. Rapid growth, 7.5%pa. 10f. |
| Iglesia de los Hermanos Libres | 1919 | P CBr | x.... | 20 | 348 | 870 | *Free (Open) Brethren.* M=CMML(NZ,USA,UK). Strong in south. HQ Asunción. 13f. |
| Iglesia Discípulos de Cristo del P | 1886 | P Dis | x.U.. | 9 | 528 | 1,000 | *Disciples of Christ.* 1886 Methodists(USA); 1916 takeover by M=UCMS(USA). 3n,8f,1r. |
| Iglesia Evangélica del Nuevo Pacto | c1950 | I ind | ..... | 1 | 50 | 100 | *Ev Ch of the New Covenant.* Schism ex NTMU, in Asunción. Small indigenous body. |
| Iglesia Evangélica del Río de la Plata | 1893 | P LuR | L.... | 25 | 1,950 | 3,900 | 1899 union of German diaspora congs (10% Reformed). 2n,3x,G=3.5%pa,1s,W=30%,83Yy. |
| Iglesia Evangélica Filadelfia | 1938 | P Pe2 | Z...C | 28 | 159 | 645 | *Philadelphia Ev Ch.* M=NPY(Norway),SFM(Sweden). Guaraní. 3n,1x,1H,1s,W=62%,46Y,45z. |
| Iglesia Evangélica Gracia y Gloria | c1950 | P Pen | ..... | 6 | 100 | 600 | *Ev Ch of Grace and Glory.* From USA, UK. In Asunción, also among Guaranís. 2n,8m,5x. |
| Iglesia Evangélica Menonita en el P | 1921 | P Men | GF... | | 6,989 | 12,000 | M=GCMC,MCNA. 7 colonies, Germans from USSR, also Lenguas. 35n,1f,5H,2h,1p. |
| Iglesia Evangélica Paraguaya | | I ind | ..... | 1 | 30 | 50 | *Ev Ch of Paraguay.* Schism ex NTMU, in Villa Aurelia. Small indigenous group. 1n. |
| Iglesia Evangélica Plenitud | | I pen | ..... | 1 | 246 | 400 | *Fullness Ev Church.* Small group of indigenous pentecostals. In Asunción. 1n. |
| Iglesia Evangélica Unida de Corea | | P ind | ..... | 1 | 50 | 100 | *Korean United Ev Ch.* Community of immigrants from Korea, with a Korean pastor. |
| Iglesia Luterana (Misuri) | 1936 | P Lut | x.... | 7 | 301 | 600 | *Ev Luth Congr of Holy Cross.* M=LC Missouri Synod(USA). 1x,G=5%pa,W=80%,12Yy,14z. |
| Iglesia Metodista Libre en el Paraguay | 1946 | P Hol | VF..C | 16 | 225 | 301 | M=Free Methodist Ch(USA). Some Japanese. HQ Asunción. 2n,3f,G=4%pa,1h,1p,1r,65z. |
| Iglesia Ortodoxa Griega | c1970 | O Gre | Cwo.. | 1 | 500 | 1,000 | Part of 11th Archidiocesan District, Greek Orthodcx AD of N&S America. Greeks. |
| Iglesia Ortodoxa Russa (D Argentina) | | O Sla | x.... | 2 | 50 | 100 | *Russian Orthodox Ch Outside of Russia.* M=ROCOR (New York, USA). Russian exiles. |
| Iglesia Ortodoxa Ucrania | | O Sla | X.... | | 1,500 | 3,000 | Branch of Ukrainian Orthodox Ch in the USA. Refugee Ukrainians after 1945. 1n. |
| Iglesia Pentecostal de Chile | | I pen | xw... | | 200 | 500 | *Pentecostal Ch of Chile.* Chileans, from large indigenous body in Chile. |
| Iglesia Pentecostal Unida | 1973 | P Pe1 | x.... | 5 | 78 | 200 | *United Pentecostal Ch. Jesus Only Church.* M=UPC(USA). Unitarian Pentecostals. 2f. |
| Misión a las Tribus Nuevas | 1946 | P int | x.... | | 50 | 170 | M=New Tribes Mission(USA). Work among Indians of the north. HQ Asunción. 68f,1h. |
| Sociedad Fraternal Hutterianá | 1941 | P Men | x.... | 3 | 400 | 700 | *Sociedad de Hermanos. Hutterian Brethren, Hutterites.* Primavera Bruderhof. |
| Testigos de Jehová | 1924 | M Jeh | x.... | 21 | 901 | 2,000 | *Jehovah's Witnesses. Watch Tower. IBSA.* Begun by Argentinian in 1925. 121Y. |
| Unión Misionera Neotestamentaria | 1902 | P int | x.... | 20 | 1,640 | 3,000 | M=New Testament Miss Union (UK). In 5 departments: Central, Guiara, et al. 12n,4f. |
| Other Protestant denominations | | P | ..... | | 1,500 | 2,300 | Total about 12 (see list below). |
| Other Non-White indigenous churches | | I | ..... | | 200 | 500 | Including ICAB (with missionary bishop) from Brazil, and similar bodies. |
| Doubly-affiliated (duplication) (1970) | | | | | –29,000 | –54,747 | Evangelicals who also are or were baptized Roman Catholics. |
| Disaffiliated (duplication) (1970) | | | | | –22,400 | –42,300 | Baptized Catholics now disaffiliated agnostics, atheists or traditionalists. |
| **Total affiliated (mid-1970)** | | | | **810** | **1,192,270** | **2,252,700** | **Total denominations (1970) . . . 45.** |
| **Total affiliated (mid-1975)** | | | | **830** | **1,375,900** | **2,597,520** | **Total denominations (1975) . . . 47.** |
| **Total affiliated (mid-1980)** | | | | **880** | **1,595,100** | **3,011,300** | **Total denominations (1980) . . . 49.** |

NOTES ON TABLE ABOVE
COLUMNS: for meanings and CODES (cols.1,3,4,8): see Codebook (Part 6) Column 1: **Boldface type** = church with over 10% of country's affiliated Christians.
NATIONAL COUNCILS (Column 4, 5th letter).
C = Comisión Coordinadora Evangélica de Paraguay (CCEP) (Evangelical Co-ordinating Commission of Paraguay).
R = Conferencia Episcopal Paraguaya (CEP) (Paraguay Episcopal Conference).
OTHER PROTESTANT DENOMINATIONS. These smaller bodies include: Christ-Bearers (Christusträger, W Germany), Chs of Christ, Ev Mennonite Conference (1962), Ev Methodist Ch (1960), Iglesia Cristiana de la Fe, Iglesia Ev Bautista Independiente, Slavic Baptist Chs (Russian), World-Wide Missions (1971).
UNITING CHURCHES. Negotiations for organic union were under way in 1974 between: Iglesia Discípulos de Cristo del Paraguay, with 2 Argentina bodies (Iglesia Ev Metodista Argentina, Iglesia Ev Valdense), and 2 Uruguay bodies (Iglesia Ev Metodista en el Uruguay, Iglesia Ev Valdense del Río de la Plata).

**PEOPLES** (ethnolinguistic). Christians: 92.3% Mestizo, 1.7% Amerindian (Lengua, Chulupi, Guarani), 1.7% German, 1.4% Argentinian White, 1.0% Black, 0.6% Brazilian, 0.6% Italian, 0.6% Ukrainian, Greek, Russian, Polish, Chilean, Korean.

COUNTRY-WIDE TOTALS
EVANGELIZATION (see Part 5). 1900: 98%. 1970: 100%. 1980: 100%. *Mass evangelism.* 1962, Billy Graham 8-day crusade in Asunción: 1968–71, Evangelism-in-Depth (17 denominations, 25,000 active participants); September 1976, Luis Palau 12-day crusade in Asunción (10,000 attenders nightly, total enquirers 5,000, doubling the Evangelical population of the capital). *Radiophonic evangelism.* HCJB (1,263 listeners' letters a year), FEBC, PTL, et alia.
FOREIGN MISSIONARIES AND PERSONNEL (nationals serving abroad) (1973). Total about 180 Roman Catholics in Argentina, Brazil, Chile, Uruguay et alia.
FOREIGN MISSIONARIES AND PERSONNEL (aliens from abroad) (1973). Total 787. *From Western world.* 624: 373 Roman Catholics, 214 Protestants (146 in 18 USA societies, 23 in 1 Norway society, 12 in 3 WGermany societies, 12 in 1 Canada society, 8 in 3 UK societies, 6 in 1 New Zealand society, 4 in 1 Sweden society, 2 in 2 Australia societies, 1 in 1 Finland society), 25 Anglicans in 2 UK societies, about 10 marginal Protestants (Mormons from USA), about 2 Orthodox. By 1975 North American missionaries had increased to 322. *From Communist world.* About 17 Roman Catholics (15 from Poland, others from Yugoslavia). *From Third World.* 146: about 110 Roman Catholics from Argentina, Brazil, Chile, India, Trinidad & Tobago et alia, about 30 Protestants from Argentina, Brazil, Chile at alia, 6 indigenous from Chile, Brazil and Korea.
INSTITUTIONS (church-operated) (1973). Total 220, including 100 higher schools (10 minor seminaries), 98 medical centres (11 hospitals), 1 radio station, 1 religious community, 3 research centres, 10 seminaries (6 Protestant, 3 RC), 1 university.
PERIODICALS. About 20 titles (4 Salvation Army, 2 Mennonite).
PERSONNEL. About 1,949 (1,162 national, 787 foreign).
RELIGIOUS LIBRARIES. About 16.
SCRIPTURE DISTRIBUTION (1975). Annual totals: 12,027 Bibles (58% subsidized, 42% commercial), 38,381 NTs (31% free, 43% subsidized, 26% commercial), 34,190 UBS portions, 486,846 UBS selections. *Translations completed.* Portion: 3 languages since 1900. NT: 3 languages since 1913.
SERVICE AGENCIES. About 54, including CCCI, CCEP, CCT, CELAM, CEP, CFM, CNCML, CRS, Fe-CLAF, FERELPAR, IDER, JAC, JEC, JOC, LAC, MIIC, WLC(EHC).

ADDITIONAL DATA ON CHURCHES
IGLESIA CATOLICA EN EL PARAGUAY. *Annual baptisms.* (1972) 99.8% infant, 0.2% adults. *Priests* (1972). 46% nationals, 54% expatriates (excluding 19 military chaplains of the vicariate castrensis). Nationals: 158 secular, 65 religious. Expatriates: 39 secular, 223 religious; of 19 different nationalities, from (in order of size) Germany, Spain, Italy, USA. The whole clergy are thus 41% secular (197), 59% religious (288). Growth (nationals + expatriates): 1966, 240 + 199; 1969, 267 + 242; 1972, 223 + 262. *Male religious.* 429 (1970). *Sisters.* In 1970, 71% were Paraguayans, 10% were from other Latin American countries, and 19% were from other continents. Total all Paraguayan sisters including contemplatives, non-diocesan and others (1970): 669. *Seminaries.* In addition to the Major Seminary of Paraguay, there are 2 for religious congregations (SDB, SVD). *Catechists.* Total (1969) 32 in jurisdictions under Propaganda. *Main religious orders and congregations.* Priests (1972): SDB, SJ, SVD, OMI, OFM. Sisters (1972): Hermanas Dominicanas del Santisimo Sacramento, Hijas de Maria Auxiliadora, Hermanas de NS de la Inmaculada Concepción, Hijas de la Caridad de San Vincente de Paul, Educacionistas de la Tercera Orden de San Francisco. *Catholic organizations.* The Paraguayan Episcopal Conference (Conferencia Episcopal Paraguaya, CEP) is a member of CELAM. The Federation of Religious Personnel of Paraguay (Federación de Religiosos del Paraguay, FERELPAR), which represents both men and women, belongs to CLAR. For the armed forces, Paraguay forms a military vicariate. There are no pastoral or priests' councils. Attached to the Department of the Laity of the CEP is the National Council for the Co-ordination of Lay Movements (Consejo Nacional de Coordinación de los Movimientos Laicos) which forms a liaison between the episcopate and the following groups: Catholic Action of Paraguay and its specialized branches JOC, JEC, JAC; Focolares; Legion of Mary; Christian Family Movement; Cursillos de Cristiandad; Co-operatores Salesianos; Serra Club; and Tercera Orden, Franciscana.
The Holy See maintains diplomatic relations with Paraguay and is represented to government and to the Catholic hierarchy by a nuncio.
Among Latin American organizations established in Paraguay are several agencies of CELAM: the Department of the Laity which co-ordinates the activities of the Lay Apostolate and ad hoc national commissions and helps to train ecclesiastical counsellors and lay leaders; and the Latin American Committee of Fe-CLAF which provides for theological and technical study of catechesis and biblical pastoralia.
The only continent-wide secretariat of an international organization in Paraguay is the Latin American Secretariat of the International Movement of Catholic Intellectuals (Secretariado Latinoamericano del Movimiento Internacional de Intelectuales Católicos, MIIC) with its international headquarters in Fribourg, Switzerland.
There are several Paraguayan organizations for research and social action. Firstly, the Christian Agrarian Leagues (Ligas Agrarias Cristianas) were founded about 1960 by a group of peasant-priests. Dedicated to conscientization and training of the rural masses, these constitute an important factor in political and social life. Because of their decentralized organization, they have not suffered greatly from government repression. In them one finds the spirit and often the methodology of Paulo Freire. Secondly, the Christian Confederation of Workers (Confederación Cristiana de los Trabajadores, CCT) was founded in 1962 and had 3,000 members in 1971. CCT, the only non-official trade union, is affiliated to the World Confederation of Workers (CMT) and forms a liaison between agrarian leagues and urban unions. The government does not recognize its legal existence and keeps careful watch over its public activities. Its secretary-general was imprisoned for much of 1972 in the regime's political prisons, and other directors and members have suffered systematic intimidation and imprisonment. Thirdly, the Institute of Rural Education (Instituto de Educación Rural, IDER) has since 1966 provided a 9-month training programme of rural leadership for the entire country.
Theological education is catered for at the Superior Institute of Theology and Religious Sciences (Instituto Superior de Teología y Ciencias Religiosas) of Our Lady of Asunción Catholic University (Universidad Católica Nuestra Señora de la Asunción) which was established in 1971. There is also a Centre for Socio-Religious Studies (Centro de Estudios Socio-Religiosos, CESR), founded in 1962, which carries on various studies and gathers statistics for the national episcopal conference.
The Centre for Anthropological Studies of the Catholic University (Centro de Estudios Antropológicos de la Universidad Católica, CEADUC) was formed in 1970 and is engaged in missiological, ethnographic and linguistic investigations, in addition to counselling missionaries working among Indian peoples. The results of its work are published periodically.
Catholic schools in 1973 numbered 174 primary (58,315 pupils) and 86 secondary (15,422). There is a Catholic university with faculties established in Asunción, Villarica, Concepción and Encarnación.
In 1971 the church was responsible for 3 hospitals, 3 clinics or polyclinics, at least 71 dispensaries, 3 sanatoria, one maternity centre, 3 mother-infant centres, 6 homes for infants or the aged, and 10 other institutions. Caritas Paraguaya was founded in 1955 and is involved in social action financed by Caritas Internationalis, including 2 important programmes of agricultural development (Edelira, and Epopeye Nacional). The distribution of food and clothing from CRS in the USA was stopped by the Episcopal Conference because of government interference.

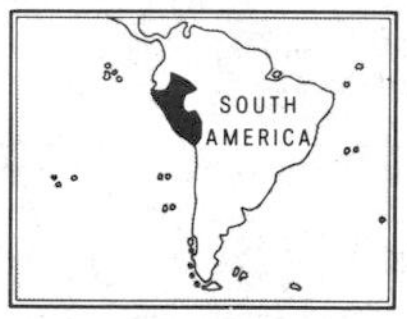


# PERU

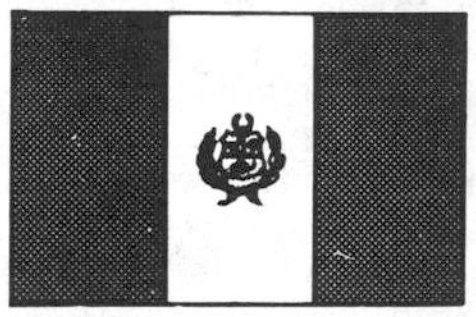

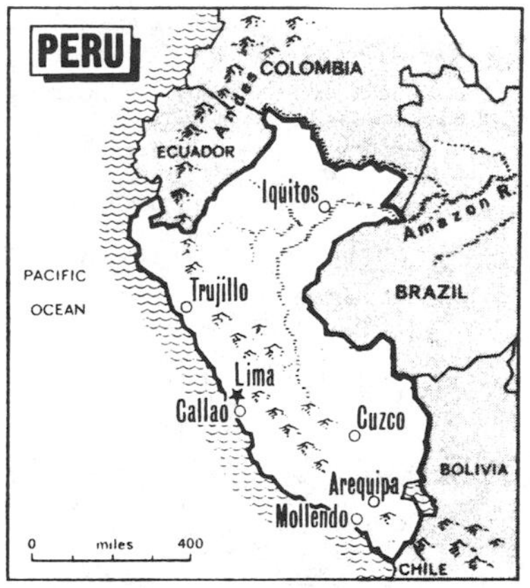


## SECULAR DATA

**STATE. Official name:** The Republic of Peru (La República del Perú). Adjective of nationality: Peruvian (peruano).
**Flag** (shown above right): Red, white, and red bars, with centred coat of arms.
**Area:** 1,285,216 sq.km. (496,225 sq.miles). Agricultural land: 23.3%.
**Government:** Socialist military rule, since 1968 (1533 Spanish conquest, 1821 Independence as republic, several dictatorships).
**Official languages:** Spanish (*Español/Castellano*) and Quechua.
**Chief cities:** capital Lima 3,158,420 (1972), Arequipa 304,650, Callao 296,220, Trujillo 241,880.
**Political divisions:** 23 Departments, divided into 148 Provinces (plus constitutional Province of Callao) and 1,662 Districts.
**Armed forces** (1976): Total 63,000 regular (40,000 conscripts): army 46,000, navy 8,000, air force 9,000 (92 combat aircraft). Paramilitary forces: 20,000 Guardia Civil.

**DEMOGRAPHY. Population:** 13,538,208 (census of 4.VI.1972. For 1970–2000 (UN), see last row of Table 1). Population density (1975): 12/sq.km. (31/sq.mile). Under 15 years: 45%. Growth rate (1975–80): 2.89% per year (births 3.92%, deaths −1.03%). Life expectancy (1975–80): 58.1 years. Household size: 5.3 persons.
**Major languages:** Spanish, Quechua, Aymara, Jivaro, Japanese, Chinese, English, and around 100 minor languages.
**Urban dwellers** (1970): 50.9%. Urban growth rate (1950–70): 3.9% per year.
**Labour force:** 30%.
**Refugees** (1977): 230 from Chile.
**Tourists** (1974): 262,303.
**ETHNOLINGUISTIC GROUPS:** 47.1% Quechua, 32.0% Mestizo (Spanish/Indian), 12.0% Peruvian White, 5.4% Aymara, 1.7% jungle Amerindian (37 tribes, 226,400; Pano, Arawak, Murato, Jivaro, Arabela, Cocama, Campa), 0.5% Black (Negro), 0.5% Japanese (63,000), 0.2% Chinese (25,000), British (3,000), Zambo (Black/Indian), Mulatto, Injerto (White/Chinese or Japanese), Chinocholo (Black/Chinese or Japanese), Chilean, German, Greek, Norwegian, Jewish, Gypsy, et alii.

**MONEY** (1977). **Monetary unit:** sol (= 100 centavos); US$1 = S 69.50.
**National income per person:** US$650. Average annual family income: US$3,445.
**Inflation:** (1970–74) 10.0% per year, (1975) 15% per year (consumer price index 216).
**Cost of living in capital** (1976): index 114 (Washington DC = 100). Daily cost of living: US$43.

**HEALTH.** Hospitals: 435 (29,086 beds). Doctors: 8,023. Lepers: 7,000 (0.5 per 1,000). Blind: 23,000. Psychotics: 130,000. Drug addicts: 270,000 (habitual coca-chewers). Criminals: 60,000.

**EDUCATION.** Adult literacy: (1961) 61%, (1972) 73%. Education rate: 80%. Schools: 19,346. Universities: 22.

**LITERATURE.** Annual new book titles (1973): 943. Periodicals: 827. Scientific journals: 125. Newspapers: 56 dailies, 320 non-daily.

**COMMUNICATION** (per 1,000 people). Phones: 20. Radios: 138. TV sets: 28. Daily newspaper circulation: 122 copies.

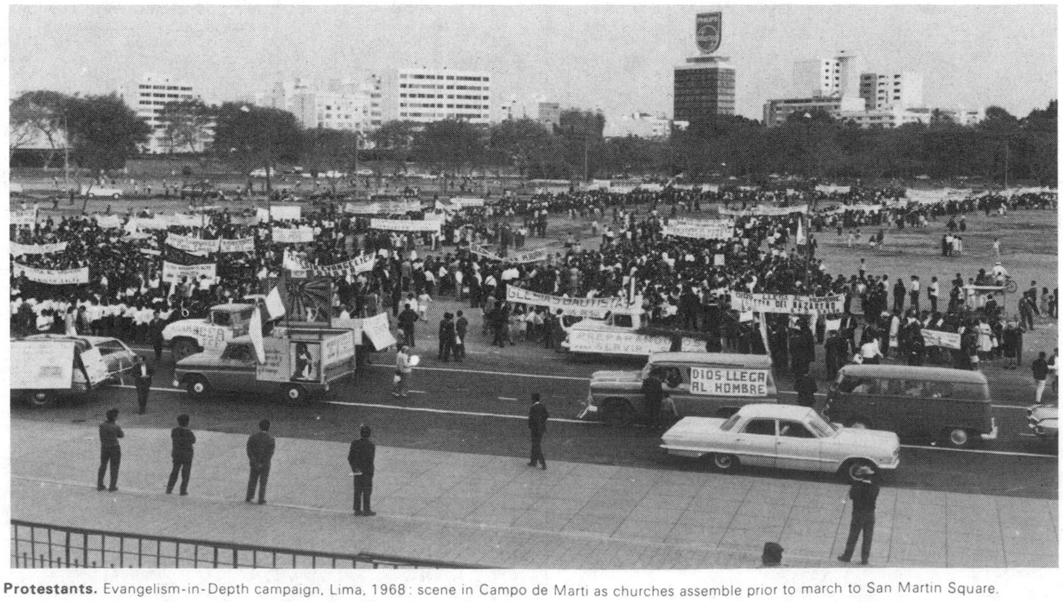


**Protestants.** Evangelism-in-Depth campaign, Lima, 1968: scene in Campo de Marti as churches assemble prior to march to San Martin Square.

TABLE 1. RELIGIOUS ADHERENTS IN PERU

| *Year* | 1900 | | mid-1970 | | Annual change, 1970–1980 | | | | mid-1975 | | mid-1980 | | 2000 | |
|---|---|---|---|---|---|---|---|---|---|---|---|---|---|---|
| *Name* | *Adherents* | *%* | *Adherents* | *%* | *Natural* | *Conversion* | *Total* | *Rate* | *Adherents* | *%* | *Adherents* | *%* | *Adherents* | *%* |
| **Christians** | **3,589,200** | **94.7** | **12,983,400** | **98.0** | **437,574** | **486** | **438,060** | **2.92** | **15,026,350** | **98.0** | **17,364,000** | **98.0** | **29,725,300** | **97.3** |
| professing | 3,589,200 | 94.7 | 12,983,400 | 98.0 | 437,574 | 486 | 438,060 | 2.92 | 15,026,350 | 98.0 | 17,364,000 | 98.0 | 29,725,300 | 97.3 |
| Roman Catholics | 3,586,200 | 94.6 | 12,658,400 | 95.5 | 425,547 | −6,587 | 418,960 | 2.87 | 14,613,350 | 95.3 | 16,848,000 | 95.1 | 28,545,300 | 93·4 |
| Christo-pagans | 2,464,000 | 65.0 | 4,900,000 | 37.0 | 156,202 | −61,702 | 94,500 | 1.76 | 5,364,000 | 35.0 | 5,845,000 | 33.0 | 7,640,000 | 25.0 |
| Evangelical Catholics | 2,000 | 0.1 | 39,593 | 0.3 | 1,425 | 466 | 1,891 | 3.86 | 48,950 | 0.3 | 58,500 | 0.3 | 146,500 | 0.5 |
| Protestants | 3,000 | 0.1 | 300,000 | 2.3 | 11,008 | 6,092 | 17,100 | 4.52 | 378,000 | 2.5 | 471,000 | 2.7 | 1,060,000 | 3.5 |
| Peruvian indigenous | 0 | 0.0 | 25,000 | 0.2 | 1,019 | 981 | 2,000 | 5.71 | 35,000 | 0.2 | 45,000 | 0.3 | 120,000 | 0.4 |
| affiliated | 3,589,200 | 94.7 | 12,983,400 | 98.0 | 437,574 | 486 | 438,060 | 2.92 | 15,026,350 | 98.0 | 17,364,000 | 98.0 | 29,725,300 | 97.3 |
| disaffiliated | 0 | 0.0 | −243,395 | −1.8 | −7,134 | 6,673 | −461 | 0.19 | −245,000 | −1.6 | −248,000 | −1.4 | −244,000 | −0.8 |
| doubly-affiliated | −5,100 | −0.1 | −350,000 | −2.6 | −12,493 | −5,607 | −18,100 | 4.22 | −429,000 | −2.8 | −531,000 | −3.0 | −1,222,000 | −4.0 |
| total practising | 3,409,740 | *95* | 10,386,720 | *80* | 350,059 | 389 | 350,448 | 2.92 | 12,021,080 | *80* | 13,891,200 | *80* | 22,294,000 | *75* |
| non-practising | 179,460 | *5* | 2,596,680 | *20* | 87,515 | 97 | 87,612 | 2.92 | 3,005,270 | *20* | 3,472,800 | *20* | 7,431,300 | *25* |
| Roman Catholics | 3,589,200 | 94.7 | 13,208,702 | 99.7 | 443,631 | −8,120 | 435,511 | 2.86 | 15,234,330 | 99.4 | 17,563,810 | 99.2 | 29,856,800 | 97.7 |
| Catholic pentecostals | 0 | 0.0 | 1,000 | 0.0 | 582 | 3,318 | 3,900 | 19.50 | 20,000 | 0.1 | 40,000 | 0.2 | 200,000 | 0.7 |
| Protestants | 5,000 | 0.1 | 305,012 | 2.3 | 11,153 | 6,146 | 17,299 | 4.52 | 383,000 | 2.5 | 478,000 | 2.7 | 1,070,000 | 3.5 |
| Evangelicals | 4,500 | 0.1 | 248,000 | 1.9 | 9,074 | 5,326 | 14,400 | 4.62 | 311,600 | 2.0 | 392,000 | 2.2 | 880,000 | 2.9 |
| Peruvian indigenous | 0 | 0.0 | 33,150 | 0.3 | 1,369 | 1,316 | 2,685 | 5.71 | 47,000 | 0.3 | 60,000 | 0.4 | 180,000 | 0.6 |
| Marginal Protestants | 0 | 0.0 | 23,931 | 0.2 | 844 | 63 | 907 | 3.13 | 29,000 | 0.2 | 33,000 | 0.2 | 70,000 | 0.2 |
| Anglicans | 100 | 0.0 | 2,500 | 0.0 | 86 | 14 | 100 | 3.39 | 2,950 | 0.0 | 3,500 | 0.0 | 6,500 | 0.0 |
| Evangelicals | 0 | 0.0 | 2,000 | 0.0 | 73 | 37 | 110 | 4.40 | 2,500 | 0.0 | 3,100 | 0.0 | 6,000 | 0.0 |
| Orthodox | 0 | 0.0 | 2,500 | 0.0 | 84 | 1 | 85 | 2.93 | 2,900 | 0.0 | 3,350 | 0.0 | 6,000 | 0.0 |
| Catholics (non-Roman) | 0 | 0.0 | 1,000 | 0.0 | 34 | 0 | 34 | 2.91 | 1,170 | 0.0 | 1,340 | 0.0 | 2,000 | 0.0 |
| Tribal religionists | 200,000 | 5.3 | 160,000 | 1.2 | 4,893 | −3,193 | 1,700 | 1.01 | 168,000 | 1.1 | 177,000 | 1.0 | 214,000 | 0.7 |
| Non-religious | 0 | 0.0 | 44,000 | 0.3 | 1,455 | 1,505 | 2,960 | 5.94 | 49,800 | 0.3 | 73,600 | 0.4 | 405,000 | 1.3 |
| Buddhists | 1,000 | 0.0 | 20,000 | 0.2 | 320 | −1,720 | −1,400 | −12.73 | 11,000 | 0.1 | 6,000 | 0.0 | 10,000 | 0.0 |
| Baha'is | 0 | 0.0 | 13,500 | 0.1 | 495 | 155 | 560 | 3.82 | 17,000 | 0.1 | 20,000 | 0.1 | 38,000 | 0.1 |
| Atheists | 0 | 0.0 | 12,800 | 0.1 | 495 | 325 | 820 | 4.82 | 17,000 | 0.1 | 21,000 | 0.1 | 60,000 | 0.2 |
| New-Religionists | 0 | 0.0 | 5,000 | 0.0 | 772 | 2,528 | 3,300 | 12.45 | 26,500 | 0.2 | 38,000 | 0.2 | 90,000 | 0.3 |
| Jews | 0 | 0.0 | 5,000 | 0.0 | 169 | −9 | 160 | 2.76 | 5,800 | 0.0 | 6,600 | 0.0 | 12,000 | 0.0 |
| Chinese folk-religionists | 500 | 0.0 | 3,000 | 0.0 | 87 | −87 | 0 | 0.00 | 3,000 | 0.0 | 3,000 | 0.0 | 1,000 | 0.0 |
| Muslims | 300 | 0.0 | 300 | 0.0 | 10 | 0 | 10 | 2.86 | 350 | 0.0 | 400 | 0.0 | 700 | 0.0 |
| Other religionists | 0 | 0.0 | 1,000 | 0.0 | 30 | 10 | 40 | 3.33 | 1,200 | 0.0 | 1,400 | 0.0 | 5,000 | 0.0 |
| **Country's population** | **3,791,000** | **100.0** | **13,248,000** | **100.0** | **446,300** | **0** | **446,300** | **2.91** | **15,326,000** | **100.0** | **17,711,000** | **100.0** | **30,561,000** | **100.0** |

COLUMNS, ROWS. For meanings and definitions, see Codebook (Part 6). Note that, by definition, total 'Christians' = professing + crypto-Christians, which also = affiliated + nominal Christians. Percentages may not always total exactly, due to rounding.
CENSUSES. **1940**: 98.6% Roman Catholics, 0.9% Evangelicals, 0.2% Buddhists, 0.1% Chinese folk-religionists, 0.1% non-religious. **2.VII.1961**: 98.1% Roman Catholics, 1.6% Evangelicals, 0.2% non-religious and tribal religionists. **4.VI.1972** (excluding jungle Amerindians): 96.4% Roman Catholics, 2.5% Evangelicals, 0.7% other religionists, 0.4% non-religious and atheists.

NOTES ON RELIGIONS
ATHEISTS. 2 parties: Communist Party of Peru (pro-Soviet) 2,000 members, Communist Party of Peru (pro-Chinese) 1,200 members.
BAHA'IS. Very rapid growth from 13 local spiritual assemblies (1964) to 82 (1973), particularly among the Quechua Indians in the Cuzco area.
BUDDHISTS. Mostly Japanese immigrants, with a few Chinese. Mass conversions to Soka Gakkai have been taking place.
CATHOLIC PENTECOSTALS (or, Catholic charismatics). Totals (January 1974): around 7,000 involved adults, including many priests and sisters, in over 400 prayer groups; total charismatic community including children, 15,000.
CHRISTO-PAGANS. Amerindians syncretizing folk-Catholicism with traditional pre-Columbian animism.
DISAFFILIATED. This term is used here to describe persons who, although either baptized Roman Catholics or claimed and enumerated as affiliated by the Catholic Church in its totals, have recently withdrawn or disaffiliated themselves completely from Christianity and now profess to be or regard themselves as either non-religious (agnostics), atheists, or adherents of non-Christian religions. In particular, it may be noted that in jungle areas Catholic jurisdictions still claim almost the entire population, although a majority of jungle Amerindians there regard themselves as followers of their own tribal religions.
DOUBLY-AFFILIATED. The term covers those affiliated to, or claimed by, both the Catholic Church and also a church termed Evangélica by the state (Protestant, Anglican, Peruvian indigenous, marginal Protestant), i.e. baptized Catholics who have recently become Evangelicals or others. Because their statistics represent a duplication, they are shown in the table as a negative quantity (with a minus sign).
EVANGELICAL CATHOLICS. This term is used here to describe persons who are affiliated to churches termed by the state Evangélica (Protestant, Anglican, Peruvian indigenous or marginal Protestant churches), but who are regarded by state and society as, or profess publicly in censuses to be, Roman Catholics.
NEW-RELIGIONISTS. Japanese adherents of Soka Gakkai (one hall in Lima in 1969) and other New Religions. By 1975, converts to Soka Gakkai, mainly from orthodox Buddhism, numbered 26,000.
OTHER RELIGIONISTS. Adherents of other non-Christian religions and syncretistic cults, including Rosicrucians (AMORC, 4 Lodges).
PERUVIAN INDIGENOUS. In about 22 denominations or groupings in 1970 (see Table 2).
PRACTISING CHRISTIANS. Weekly mass attenders: (1967) in Lima, 20.4% of Catholics. Protestant weekly practice is over 70%.
TRIBAL RELIGIONISTS. A large proportion of the 350,000 lowland or jungle Amerindians in the interior in 1900, and the 226,400 in 1970, were still animists, including among the Aymara and Chayahuita.

NON-CHRISTIAN RELIGIONS. **Traditional religions** are still practised by some Indian peoples including the Chayahuita, usually in combination with Roman Catholic practices. **Aymara religion** is centred in beliefs concerning guardian, nature and evil spirits and the means of controlling them. The divinity of good luck (Ekeko) and old Mother Earth (Pachamama) are also widely venerated. Traditional beliefs once recognized the existence of a supreme being, known as Viracocha, who was creator of all things. However, this name is no longer used, traditional concepts having been supplanted by Catholic ideas of God. Jungle Amerindians also remain largely animist.

## CHRISTIANITY

CATHOLIC CHURCH. Pizarro reached Peru in 1533. At the request of Spain, the diocese of Cuzco was erected in 1536 followed by the diocese of Lima in 1541; and by 1546 Lima had become the metropolitan see for the Pacific coast from Nicaragua to Chile. The 17th century, called 'the religious century' of Peru with 2 canonized saints, was followed by a general decline in monastic and religious life.

In 1845 Catholicism was made the official state religion. Foreigners were given permission to conduct Protestant services, provided that no Peruvians attended. A notable shift in social attitudes away from positions of extreme conservatism has characterized the Catholic clergy in recent years. This is clearly reflected in a document issued by the Peruvian episcopate in 1971, entitled 'Justice in the world'. Some consider this to be the most audacious document on the subject yet to have been issued by any episcopal body. It asserts that evangelization cannot exist 'without engaging in the fight against domination'. It asked the second Synod of Bishops in Rome to condemn the repressive methods of those who employ violence in the name of Christian civilization and to denounce 'the withdrawal of capital by developed nations as well as the pseudo-neutrality of those countries which, by their banking systems, favour the flight of wealth and its accumulation' by a few. A further shift in the practice

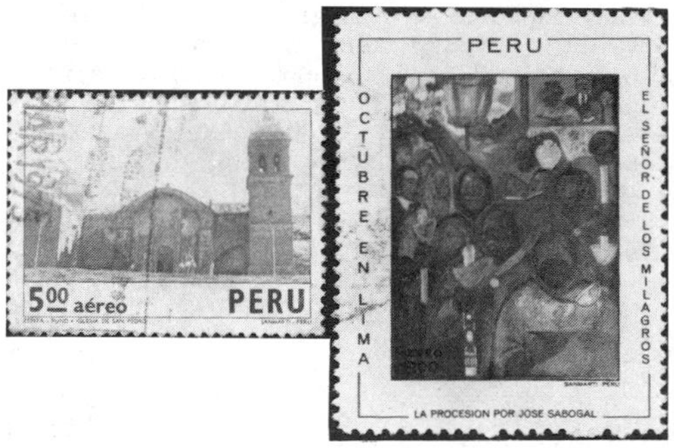


**Iglesia Católica en el Perú.** State postage stamps illustrating: *left,* a parish church; *right,* Lord of the Miracles procession.

and attitudes of Catholics is reflected in the results of a census taken in Lima in May 1967, which revealed that only 20% of the Catholic population attended Sunday mass weekly. Among these 18% were boys, 16% girls, 22% men and 44% women.

Pastoral work has been severely hampered by the lack of priests, there being only one priest for every 6,000 inhabitants. The proportion of Peruvian to expatriate priests has decreased steadily from 1901, when 82% of all priests were nationals, to 39% in 1970. Expatriate brothers are more numerous than Peruvians, whereas there are slightly more Peruvian sisters than expatriates.

PROTESTANT CHURCHES. The earliest Protestant mission workers in Peru, as in surrounding countries, were agents of the Bible societies. These initial efforts dating from 1822 were carried out in collaboration with sympathetic Catholic clergy, whose purpose was to promote a 'spontaneous reformation' from within the church. The first Methodists from the USA arrived in 1877, but little penetration among the Peruvian people was made until the arrival in 1888 of Francisco Penzotti, another Bible society agent. Jailed several times with his Peruvian assistants, he ultimately succeeded in bringing many to a commitment to Christ. In 1891 his work was followed up by the Methodists, whose contribution included the development of an extensive school programme. In spite of its strong start, however, the Methodist Church has been unable to maintain rapid growth in recent years. Independent Brethren missionaries began services in Lima in 1896, a work which was later associated with the Regions Beyond Missionary Union (1897), Evangelical Union of South America (1911) and the Christian and Missionary Alliance (1933) and resulted in the establishment of the Peruvian Evangelical Church, the fourth largest church in Peru at the present time. John Ritchie, perhaps the strongest force in the development of the church, was sent by the RBMU in 1907 and remained influential until his death in 1952. This work included the establishment of a press to address the nation at large, as well as a large farm project where Indians could receive training in agriculture. However, as a result of different mission theories and conflicting personalities, the history of the church has been marked by disagreement and schism. Several foreign missions eventually found it expedient to withdraw from direct and indirect assistance, continuing their efforts with congregations which chose to remain with them.

Seventh-day Adventists, beginning in 1898, have found their greatest response among the Aymara Indians, their schools having a special appeal. While subject to schism, it remains one of the 2 largest Protestant churches. The rapidly growing Pentecostal movement is divided into a number of separate denominations, the Assemblies of God having the largest membership, and indeed, along with the Adventists, the largest Protestant constituency in Peru. Two holiness churches, Wesleyans and Nazarenes, began work in 1903 and 1914 respectively, and the first of several small Baptist missions entered Peru in 1927. Since 1921 the South American Indian Mission has centred most of its work in the jungle lowlands of the east, while the Wycliffe Bible Translators, with a team of 236 in Peru, one of their larger fields, are active in approximately 40 tribes. Small groups from Europe work in Peru, usually in co-operation with other Evangelical bodies; but the

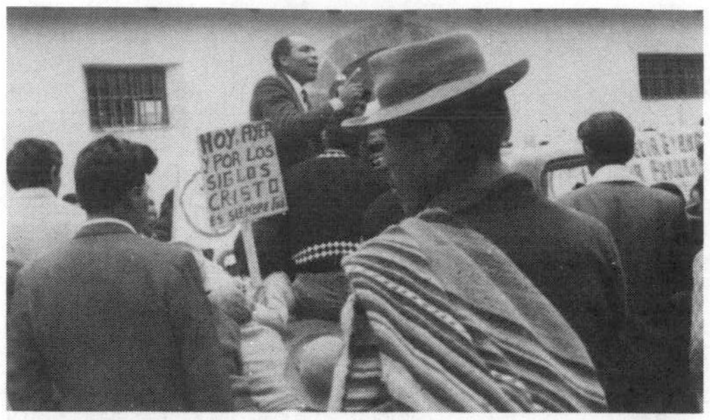


**Protestants.** Open-air preaching to Quechua Indians in Ayaviri, South Peru (12,800 feet above sea level).

major missionary thrust has been from North America.

INDIGENOUS CHURCHES. Many indigenous bodies have been formed during the present century. Most are pentecostal in emphasis, and several have come into existence as schisms from the Assemblies of God. The largest of these independent pentecostal bodies is the Autonomous Pentecostal Churches which receives assistance from Swedish Pentecostals. Another important independent group, resulting from a schism within the Seventh-day Adventist community, is the Evangelical Israelite Church of the New Covenant, whose members are popularly known as Cabañistas or Tabernaclers.

OTHER CHURCHES. The first of Peru's non-Catholic denominations was the Anglican Church which entered the country in 1849. The church's small constituency forms part of the diocese of Chile, Bolivia and Peru under the Anglican Council for South America, CASA.

Two marginal bodies which have had some success during the present century are Jehovah's Witness and the Mormons.

**CHURCH AND STATE.** The constitution of 1933, with several amendments added in 1940 and 1961, was the first in Peruvian history to declare that the state is no longer officially and formally Catholic. It continues, nevertheless, to accord a special status to the Catholic Church, which is placed juridically in the domain of public law. Article 32 states: 'Respecting the feelings of the majority of the nation, the state protects the Roman and Apostolic Catholic religion. The other religions enjoy the freedom of exercising their respective worship'. Article 234 says: 'The rapport between the State and the Catholic Church is governed by the concordats concluded by the executive power and approved by Congress' (Law 9166 of 5 September 1940). Article 235 states that 'To exercise the responsibilities of an archbishop or bishop, it is necessary to be Peruvian by birth or to have had Peruvian national citizenship for at least 3 years before the appointment, with continuous residence in the country during that time' (Law 13739 of 29 November 1961). Article 154 defines the duties of the president as including the power (a) to nominate archbishops and bishops for presentation to the Holy See, and to ensure observance of papal bulls (Law 13739); and (b) to nominate candidates for priestly and other ecclesiastical posts. Finally, Article 123 gives to Congress the authority for 'creating new dioceses and archdioceses, or of suppressing those in existence on the order of the executive power' (Law 9166).

With regard to the constitution and its application, it should be noted that freedom of religion is proclaimed only as the right of individuals; in virtue of Article 232 (by decree since 1945) all meetings and acts of worship or propaganda in public areas are strictly forbidden to non-Catholics. Vatican II caused a definite relaxation in this area, and the decree, of 1945 is rarely observed today. Furthermore, Article 233 confirms the national patronage (Patronato Nacional) conceded to the Peruvian government by the 1874 papal bull 'Preclarainter beneficia', which takes the place of a concordat. The text of Articles 123 and 154 also confirms the right of patronage. To evade the problems posed by the intervention of the state in the nomination of priests, the bishops have substituted for the latter the category of 'steward curates', but this subterfuge caused the withholding of salaries to parish clergy. Nevertheless the state continues to pay the salaries of bishops in office and canons as well as subsidizing seminaries, schools and Catholic hospitals.

Since the 1941 law on public education, Catholic religious instruction is obligatory in all educational institutions in the country, public or private, including penal institutions. Students wishing a dispensation from this must make an explicit request. The National Bureau of Catholic Education (Oficina Nacional de Educación Católica, ONEC), which is recognized and subsidized by the state, supervises religious education at the national level, controls its programmes and licenses teachers. An under-secretariat for religion is in charge of all religious and church affairs, but there is no obligatory registration of churches.

In general, the Catholic Church, urged on by its progressivist members, supports reforms promulgated by the military government resulting from the coup d'etat of 3 October 1968. Thus the episcopate has publicly supported the agrarian reform law of June 1969, the most important act in the area of land reform in Latin America since that in Cuba. It has also given support to the law concerning 'industrial communities' which limits the control of industry by expatriates and requires owners to distribute 10% of all profits to the workers. At the same time, the Catholic Church is now less reticent to speak out concerning authoritarianism or paternalism on the part of government and is working for greater participation by the people. An incident characteristic of this spirit was the arrest of the auxiliary bishop of Lima for supporting a group of squatters in May 1971. He was freed after the intervention of his archbishop, and the minister responsible was removed from his post. The nationalization of foreign property has also been applauded by the episcopate.

**INTERDENOMINATIONAL ORGANIZATIONS.** The National Evangelical Council of Peru (Concilio Nacional Evangélico del Perú) was formed in 1940 by Protestant missions and their national churches. The Methodists withdrew in 1966, asserting it to be a mission-dominated organization. The council in turn remains apprehensive of ecumenical organizations in which Methodists among others participate. An association for theological education was initiated in 1965 with 10 theological colleges in its membership. The Catholic Episcopal Conference maintains a Secretariat for the Union of Christians (Secretariado para la Unión de los Cristianos).

**BROADCASTING.** Commercial networks accept weekly religious programmes. There are 14 Catholic radio stations and one TV station and 3 radio stations belonging to Protestants. Catholics have 2 national associations for radio schools; TEPA (Tele-Escuela Popular Americana) in Arequipa (1,345 students in 1970), which uses television for development programmes, and ERPA (Escuelas Radiofónicas Populares Americanas) with its central radio station in Cañete which covers the regions of Yauyos, Huaochiri and Cañete. Important experiments in radio education are being carried out in the areas of Puno (Escuelas Radiofónicas Onda Azul) and Cuzco, which started in 1967. There are also radio schools in Huallagua (Radio 800) and Yacna (Escuelas Radiofónicas Juan XXIII). Radio San José in Indiana had a system of 72 radio schools with 1,023 students in 1970, the only one in eastern Peru. For Catholics, Peru is a member of UNDA.

For Protestants, the Evangelical Alliance Mission (TEAM) operates a major broadcasting project, Radio del Pacifico (Asociación Cultural Ondas del Perú), which is a commercial station with music, news and Protestant programmes for 17 hours daily. Southern Baptists have a recording studio in Lima.

## BIBLIOGRAPHY


'A Quechua messiah in eastern Peru', A. Metraux, *American Anthropologist*, XLIV, 4 (1942), 721–5.

*A study of the older Protestant missions and churches in Peru and Chile.* J.B.A. Kessler, Jr. Goes (Netherlands): Oosterbaan le Cointre, 1967. 369p.

*Anuario Eclesiástico del Perú,* **1969**. Lima: Secretariado del Episcopado Nacional, 1969.

*Church growth in the high Andes.* K.E. Hamilton. Lucknow (India): Lucknow Publishing House, 1962. 146p.

*La Iglesia en Perú y Bolivia.* I. Alonso et al. Fribourg: FERES, 1962.

*Religion and revolution in Peru,* **1824–1976**. J.L. Klaiber. Leiden: E.J. Brill, 1979. 272p.


TABLE 2. ORGANIZED CHURCHES AND DENOMINATIONS IN PERU

| Official name 1 | Begun 2 | Type 3 | Counc 4 | Congs 5 | Adults 6 | Affiliated 7 | Names, notes, and other statistics (see Codebook) 8 |
|---|---|---|---|---|---|---|---|
| Aaronistas | 1940 | I pen | ••••• | | 1,000 | 3,000 | Revivalists in La Convención jungles. Beards, brown or white robes. 50% Quechuas. |
| Asambleas de Dios del Perú | 1911 | P Pe2 | ZF••E | 368 | 50,750 | 100,000 | *Assemblies of God of Peru.* 1919, M=AoG(USA). HQ Lima. 807n,16f,1j,3s(154). |
| Asociación Bautista Maranatha | 1964 | P Bap | x•••E | | 100 | 300 | M=Maranatha Baptist Mission(USA). Radical Baptists. HQ Ica. 4f. |
| Asoc Bautistas para Ev Mundial | 1931 | P Bap | xT••E | 93 | 550 | 1,000 | Ev=Evangelismo. M=Assoc of Baptists for World Evangelism(USA). 6n,18x,33f,1s(29). |
| Asoc de Igs Ev del Nor-Oriente Peruano | 1897 | P int | xM••E | 54 | 900 | 1,800 | Northeast. M=RBMU(UK,USA) (Misión del Perú Interior). 26f,G=5%pa,1p,1s(16),128Y. |
| Asociación Misionera Ev Nacional | 1946 | I int | ••••• | 5 | 70 | 150 | *AMEN. Nat Ev Missionary Assoc.* Ex IEP, but new churches join IEP. 9n,W=60%,9Y,10z. |
| Convención Evangélica Bautista del P | 1950 | P Bap | T•••E | 49 | 1,006 | 3,000 | *Ev Baptist Convention of Peru.* M=SBC(USA). 16n,34f,1s,162Y. |
| Ejército de Salvación | 1910 | P Sal | xw••E | 12 | 1,500 | 2,000 | *Ejercituman Salvacionman* (Quechua). *Peru District.* 5n,4x,G=6.5%pa,1s,W=78%. |
| Hermanos Libres | c1925 | P CBr | x•••E | 45 | 450 | 1,000 | *Open Brethren. Free Brethren. Brethren Assemblies.* M=CMML(USA,UK). HQ Lima. 33f. |
| Hermanos Menonitas | 1946 | P Men | GF••• | | 311 | 777 | M=Mennonite Brethren Ch of NAmerica. HQ Atalaya, via Pucallpa. 4f. |
| Iglesia Adventista del Séptimo Día | 1898 | P Adv | x•••• | 930 | 48,624 | 100,000 | *7th-day Adv. Inca UM.* 50% Aymara. 60n,20x,38f,G=29%pa,3H,4p,1s,1143t(65270),9159Y. |
| Iglesia Alianza Cristiana y Misionera | 1923 | P Hol | xF••E | 130 | 4,350 | 6,000 | M=CMA(USA). 1954, major split from IEP. HQ Lima. 4n,25x,G=6%pa,1k,1s(20),250Y. |
| Iglesia Anglicana: D Peru | 1849 | A Low | Aw•CE | 4 | 1,300 | 2,500 | *Anglican Ch*, in CASA. 70% English. M=CMS(Austr),SAMS,BCMS. 2x,8f,W=50%,1Y,12y. |
| Iglesia Autónoma Pentecostal del Perú | c1952 | P Pe2 | ••••• | 46 | 1,000 | 2,000 | *Autonomous Pentecostal Ch of Peru.* Schism ex AoG by American missionary. |
| **Iglesia Católica en el Perú:** | 1536 | R Lat | BzL•R | 1,143 | 7,262,300 | 13,208,702 | *Catholic Ch.* 9 Zones. C=40+6+110. 10p,4q,9s(115). 990n,1682x,397m,5064w,344378Yy. |
| M Arequipa | 1577 | R Lat | Bs | 49 | 208,000 | 378,000 | Z:7. Industry, farming. Strong religious. 1p,1s. 92 97 48 454 8429 |
| D Puno | 1861 | R Lat | Bs | 28 | 192,000 | 350,000 | 8 Rural. Quechua, Aymara. Popular religiosity. 49 34 17 76 3200 |
| D Tacna | 1944 | R Lat | Bs | 38 | 104,000 | 190,000 | 7 Urban. Important copper-mining area. 32 18 5 52 4554 |
| PN Ayaviri | 1958 | R Lat | Bs | 41 | 104,000 | 190,000 | 8 Rural, poor; Quechua, Aymara. Very religious. 8 14 0 11 3852 |
| PN Chuquibamba | 1962 | R Lat | Bs | 22 | 54,000 | 98,000 | 7 Rural, farming. West of Arequipa. 13 5 0 23 3126 |
| PN Juli | 1957 | R Lat | Bs | 27 | 220,000 | 400,000 | 8 Rural poverty; Aymara. Religious. M=MM. 4 22 2 23 4160 |
| M Ayacucho | 1609 | R Lat | Bs | 43 | 165,000 | 300,000 | 4 80% rural Quechua. Superficial catholicism. 65 16 4 46 4550 |
| D Huancavelica | 1944 | R Lat | Bs | 26 | 166,800 | 303,263 | 4 Rural Quechua, very poor. Religious. 31 0 0 13 15811 |
| PN Caravelí | 1957 | R Lat | Bs | 23 | 67,000 | 122,000 | 7 Coast, in south. Rural. Partly Quechua. 6 17 1 49 3464 |
| M Cuzco | 1536 | R Lat | Bs | 53 | 245,600 | 446,559 | 8 Ancient Inca capital. Quechua. 1p,1s. 83 22 26 173 5000 |
| D Abancay | 1958 | R Lat | Bs | 15 | 141,000 | 256,000 | 8 Impoverished Quechua. Traditional religion. 11 24 1 52 6950 |
| PN Chuquibambilla | 1968 | R Lat | Bs | 19 | 96,000 | 175,000 | 8 Rural Quechua, very poor; christo-paganism. 3 8 1 15 1654 |
| PN Sicuani | 1959 | R Lat | Bs | 21 | 126,000 | 230,000 | 8 Very poor rural Quechua; christo-paganism. 11 8 0 11 6984 |
| M Huancayo | 1944 | R Lat | Bs | 34 | 330,000 | 600,000 | 4 90% rural Quechua. Transport, mining. 1s. 59 26 12 93 12250 |
| D Huánuco | 1865 | R Lat | Bs | 20 | 223,000 | 405,000 | 4 Rural, mountains, forest. 21 17 12 51 3740 |
| PN Tarma | 1958 | R Lat | Bs | 18 | 143,000 | 260,000 | 4 Rural. Cultivation, produce. 7 30 1 24 7650 |
| M Lima | 1541 | R Lat | Bs | 126 | 1,502,300 | 2,731,488 | 5 39% live in barriadas (slums). 1p,1s,W=20%. 191 628 154 2427 79910 |
| D Callao | 1967 | R Lat | Bs | 14 | 160,000 | 290,000 | 5 Port, industry, commerce. Recent immigrants. 16 43 13 132 6081 |
| D Huacho | 1958 | R Lat | Bs | 35 | 177,000 | 322,000 | 6 Urban, rural with agriculture, fisheries. 22 24 3 48 7365 |
| D Ica | 1946 | R Lat | Bs | 26 | 171,400 | 311,648 | 6 55% urban, with large farming region. 18 47 3 78 8474 |
| PN Yauyos | 1957 | R Lat | Bs | 23 | 88,600 | 161,083 | 6 Rural, agriculture, impoverished. 1p,2s. 1 51 4 7 4500 |
| M Piura | 1940 | R Lat | Bs | 38 | 292,500 | 531,891 | 2 Urban; major petroleum area of Peru. 44 69 9 157 5000 |
| D Chachapoyas | 1805 | R Lat | Bs | 21 | 77,600 | 141,120 | 1 Poor peasantry, living by agriculture. 21 0 1 29 4502 |
| D Chiclayo | 1956 | R Lat | Bs | 37 | 203,800 | 370,500 | 2 80% urban. Commercial, sugar, rice. 1p. 36 50 9 118 15243 |

*Continued opposite*

| Official name 1 | Begun 2 | Type 3 | Counc 4 | Congs 5 | Adults 6 | Affiliated 7 | Names, notes, and other statistics (see Codebook) 8 |
|---|---|---|---|---|---|---|---|
| PN Chota | 1963 | R Lat | Bs | 13 | 143,000 | 260,000 | 1 Rural, agricultural, poor. 2 21 0 20 8991 |
| PN Chulucanas | 1964 | R Lat | Bs | 18 | 203,000 | 370,000 | 1 Rural, agricultural, poor. 6 31 7 37 9185 |
| M Trujillo | 1577 | R Lat | Bs | 42 | 346,500 | 630,000 | 2 Major commercial city, old colonial; sugar. 51 58 5 203 16400 |
| D Cajamarca | 1908 | R Lat | Bs | 24 | 209,000 | 380,000 | 1 Rural. Agriculture. Poor area. 26 28 3 62 15434 |
| D Huáras (Huaraz) | 1899 | R Lat | Bs | 30 | 153,000 | 278,150 | 3 Quechuas. Major earthquake disaster 1970. 36 19 7 41 5844 |
| PN Chimbote | 1962 | R Lat | Bs | 23 | 97,000 | 177,000 | 2 Mass urban immigration; fishing port. 1p. 6 33 7 61 6003 |
| PN Huamachuco | 1961 | R Lat | Bs | 12 | 91,000 | 165,000 | 1 Rural, agricultural, poor. 1 13 1 8 4503 |
| PN Huari | 1958 | R Lat | Bs | 16 | 152,000 | 277,000 | 3 Rural; very impoverished Quechuas. 3p. 9 13 0 7 6250 |
| PN Moyobamba | 1948 | R Lat | Bs | 63 | 121,800 | 221,500 | 1 Mountainous, rural. Quechuas. M=CP. 1 18 2 34 6171 |
| VA Iquitos | 1900 | R Lat | Posa | 12 | 88,000 | 160,000 | 9 27% Amazon tribes: Jivaro, Arabela. P=54%. 1 35 7 45 4690 |
| VA Pucallpa | 1956 | R Lat | Ppme | 10 | 62,400 | 113,500 | 9 Urban, rural. Groups of Cashibo and Shipibo. 0 21 0 52 2554 |
| VA Puerto Maldonado | 1900 | R Lat | Pop | 14 | 50,000 | 90,000 | 9 Poverty. Huarayo, Mashco, Huachipairi. P=75%. 0 32 9 65 3496 |
| VA Requena | 1956 | R Lat | Pofm | 10 | 48,000 | 88,000 | 9 Rural, urban. Dispersed tribes: Cocama. P=2%. 0 12 1 27 5300 |
| VA San Francisco Javier (Jaén) | 1946 | R Lat | Psj | 2 | 59,000 | 108,000 | 1 Aguaruna, Hambisa; genocide tried 1971. 1p. 0 27 9 67 7774 |
| VA San José de Amazonas | 1945 | R Lat | Pofm | 12 | 55,000 | 100,000 | 9 Urban, forest. Huitoto, Bora, Ocaina, Orejon. 0 21 7 56 2725 |
| VA San Ramón | 1900 | R Lat | Pofm | 17 | 96,000 | 175,000 | 9 Urban, forest. Campa, Amuesha tribes. P=61%. 7 16 3 71 10254 |
| VA Yurimaguas | 1921 | R Lat | Pcp | 28 | 29,000 | 52,000 | 9 Forest. Scattered small Indian tribes. P=10%. 0 14 3 46 2355 |
| Iglesia de Cristo | 1935 | I pe2 | ••••• | 9 | 200 | 500 | *Ch of Christ.* Schism ex Assemblies of God. In Lima, Callao, Chimbote. |
| Iglesia de Dios de la Profecía | 1955 | P Pe3 | Z•••• | 14 | 550 | 1,000 | M=Ch of God of Prophecy(USA). Holiness Pentecostals (3-stage). HQ Chimbote. 2f. |
| Iglesia de Dios del Perú | 1947 | P Pe3 | ZF••E | 98 | 1,240 | 5,000 | *Ch of God of P.* M=CoG(Cleveland) (USA). Begun by Chilean missionaries. 25n,4f,1k,1p. |
| Iglesia de Dios en el Perú | 1968 | P Hol | x•••• | 20 | 50 | 500 | *Ch of God in Peru.* M=CoG(Anderson) (USA). Growing. 1n,1x,4f,1s,W=99%,10Y,5z. |
| Iglesia de JC de los Santos de los UD | c1956 | M LdS | x•••• | | 8,000 | 13,831 | *Latter-day Saints. Mormons.* M=CJCLdS(USA). Indians. Rapid growth, 7.9%pa. 250f. |
| Iglesia de los Marineros Escandinavos | | P Lut | l•••• | 1 | 200 | 300 | *Scandinavian Seamens Ch.* Ministry to Norwegian, Swedish &c visiting ships' crews. |
| Iglesia de los Peregrinos del Perú | 1903 | P Hol | VF••E | 212 | 3,508 | 5,492 | *Ch of Pilgrims.* M=Wesleyan Ch(USA). HQ Chiclayo. 17n,2x,7f,G=–1.4%pa,1p,W=79%,778Y. |
| Iglesia del Nazareno | 1914 | P Hol | xF••E | 186 | 4,310 | 15,000 | *Nazarenes.* M=CoN(USA). 2 schools. 15n,8x,80m,21f,G=8.3%pa,1h,1s,166t(12040),W=70%. |
| Iglesia Evangélica de Cristo | | I pen | ••••• | | 100 | 200 | *Ev Ch of Christ.* Indigenous pentecostal split ex Southern Baptists. HQ Chimbote. |
| Iglesia Ev Israelita del Nuevo Pacto | | I Adv | ••••• | | 5,000 | 10,000 | *Ev Israelite Ch of the New Covenant. Cabañistas (Tabernaclers).* Schism ex SDAs. |
| Iglesia Evangélica Luterana en el Perú | 1897 | P Lut | Lv••• | 10 | 1,200 | 2,500 | 1966, M=LCA(USA). Germans, Norwegians, Mestizos. 1n,4x,6f,G=3.7%pa,1h,W=17%,69Yy. |
| Iglesia Ev Pentecostal de Chile | | I pe2 | x•••• | 3 | 500 | 1,000 | *Ev Pentecostal Ch of Chile.* Mission of Chilean indigenous body. Chileans. Curicó. |
| Iglesia Ev Pentecostal del Perú | 1950 | I pe2 | ••••• | 26 | 500 | 1,000 | *Ev Pentecostal Ch of Peru.* Schism ex AoG. Lima area, Ica, Ayacusho. |
| Iglesia Ev Pentecostal Misionera | 1945 | I pe2 | ••••• | 52 | 1,000 | 2,000 | *Missionary Pentecostal Ev Ch. Iglesia Pentecostal Avanzada.* Schism ex AoG. |
| Iglesia Evangélica Peruana | 1896 | P Ref | •G••E | 650 | 10,000 | 25,000 | *IEP.* M=EUSA. 60% Quechua. 8 schisms. 30n,10x,100w,34f,G=7.5%pa,1s(54),W=70%,1000Y. |
| Iglesia Evangélica Presbiteriana del P | | P Ref | •G••E | | 400 | 1,863 | *Ev Presbyterian Ch of Peru.* M=Iglesia Libre de Escocia (Free Ch of Scotland)(UK). |
| Iglesia Metodista Peruana | 1877 | P Met | VuU•f | 52 | 2,753 | 7,000 | *Methodist Ch of Peru.* 1887,M=UMC(USA). HQ Breña. A=1970. 28n,15f,6r(4000),52t,1u. |
| Iglesia Nacional Ev Los Amigos | 1961 | P Qua | QF••E | 24 | 250 | 700 | *National Ev Friends Ch.* M=Oregon YM of Friends(USA). Lake Titicaca. 3x,8f. |
| Iglesia Nueva Apostólica | | C CAp | x•••• | | 500 | 1,000 | In Canada Bezirk, *New Apostolic Ch.* M=NAC(Germany)..World HQ Dortmund. |
| Iglesia Ortodoxa Griega | c1970 | O Gre | Cwo•• | 1 | 1,000 | 2,000 | In 11th Archidiocesan District, Greek Orthodox AD of N&S America. Greeks. Lima. |
| Iglesia Ortodoxa Russa | | O Sla | Mwo•• | 1 | 300 | 500 | *Russian Orthodox Ch.* In D SAmerica, Orthodox Ch in America(USA). Russians. 1x. |
| Iglesia Pentecostal Autónoma del Centro | 1961 | I pen | ••••• | 12 | 167 | 700 | *Autonomous Pentecostal Ch of the Centre.* HQ Huancayo. 4n,13x,1p,W=90%,19Y,45z. |
| Iglesia Pentecostal Unida | 1962 | P Pe1 | x•••• | 42 | 1,069 | 3,000 | *United Pentecostal Ch. Jesus Only.* Unitarians. M=UPC(USA). 23n,6f,1p(75). |
| Iglesia Presbiteriana Nacional del P | 1937 | P Ref | •T••E | 64 | 800 | 2,000 | *Misión Presb Peruana.* M=WPM(RPCES). Quechuas. 4n,6x,17f,G=7.5%pa,1p,W=50%,40Yy. |
| Iglesia Unión de Lima | 1924 | P com | ••••• | 1 | 100 | 300 | *Union Church of Lima.* English-speaking expatriates. 1n,W=50%,6Yy. |
| Iglesias de Cristo | 1965 | P Dis | x•••• | 40 | 500 | 2,000 | *Chs of Christ.* M=CCCC(Instrumental) (USA). Independent congregations. 3x,90Y. |
| Iglesias Pentecostales Autónomas | | I pe2 | ••••• | 76 | 5,000 | 10,000 | *Autonomous Pentecostal Churches.* Some aid from M=SFM(Sweden), and USA. |
| Iglesias radiofónicas solitarias | c1950 | I rad | ••••• | | 300 | 600 | Isolated radio believers (HCJB, FEBC) across Amazon jungles. T=3000(ICI). |
| Misión a los Indios de Sud-América | 1921 | P int | xN••E | | 600 | 2,000 | *South America Indian Mission.* M=SAIM(USA). HQ Pucallpa. 4 schools. 50f,3h,2s. |
| Misión Alianza Evangélica | 1962 | P int | xM••E | 1 | 200 | 500 | M=TEAM(Ev Alliance Mission) (USA). HQ Lima. 13f,1p. |
| Misión Evangélica Bautista Irlandesa | 1927 | P Bap | ••••E | 78 | 1,122 | 2,000 | M=IBFM(Baptist Union of Ireland) (UK). South. Indians. 6x,13f,G=8.8%pa,W=75%,200Y. |
| Misión Suiza de Cooperación Evangélica | 1963 | P Pe2 | Z•••• | 15 | 265 | 780 | *Swiss Mission for Ev Cooperation.* M=SPM(Switz). 4n,3x,1p,1s(5),W=65%,100Y,150z. |
| Sociedad de la Ciencia Cristiana | | M Sci | x•••• | 1 | 50 | 100 | *Christian Science. Ch of Christ, Scientist.* M=CCS(Boston,USA). First Church, Lima. |
| Sinodo Evangélico Luterano | 1968 | P Lut | ••••• | 1 | 100 | 200 | M=Ev Lutheran Synod(USA). Small mission in Trinidad (Lima). 5f. |
| Templos de Avivamiento | 1965 | I pen | ••••• | 114 | 1,353 | 2,000 | *Revival Temples. MEM.* Mestizo,Aymara,Quechua. 28n,5x,G=25.9%pa,1s(10),W=90%,221Y. |
| Testigos de Jehová | c1930 | M Jeh | x•••• | 90 | 5,384 | 10,000 | *Jehovah's Witnesses. Watch Tower. IBSA.* Active witnessing under way by 1932. 974Y. |
| Other Protestant denominations | | P | ••••• | | 5,000 | 10,000 | Total about 30 (see list below). |
| Other indigenous pentecostal churches | | I pen | ••••• | | 1,000 | 2,000 | Total about 10 (see list below). |
| Doubly-affiliated (duplication) (1970) | | | | | –192,500 | –350,000 | Evangelicals who also are or were baptized Roman Catholics. |
| Disaffiliated (duplication) (1970) | | | | | –133,900 | –243,395 | Baptized Catholics now disaffiliated agnostics, atheists, or traditionalists. |
| **Total affiliated (mid-1970)** | | | | **5,230** | **7,112,382** | **12,983,400** | **Total denominations (1970) . . . 91.** |
| **Total affiliated (mid-1975)** | | | | **5,700** | **8,231,500** | **15,026,350** | **Total denominations (1975) . . . 100.** |
| **Total affiliated (mid-1980)** | | | | **6,500** | **9,512,100** | **17,364,000** | **Total denominations (1980) . . . 109.** |

NOTES ON TABLE ABOVE
COLUMNS: for meanings and CODES (cols, 1, 3, 4, 8): see Codebook (Part 6). Column 1: **Boldface type** = church with over 10% of country's affiliated Christians.
NATIONAL COUNCILS (Column 4, 5th letter).
E = Concilio Nacional Evangélico del Perú (CNEP) (National Evangelical Council of Peru).
f = member of CNEP until withdrawal in 1966.
R = Conferencia Episcopal Peruana (CEP) (Peru Episcopal Conference).
OTHER PROTESTANT DENOMINATIONS. These smaller bodies include: American Baptist Association (1960; 5 churches), Andes Ev Mission (1969; 8 missionaries), Asociación de Iglesias Bautistas de la Selva (member of ICCC), Asociación Misionera de Iglesias Ev de la Selva (member of ICCC), Baptist Bible Fellowship International (1959), Baptist Faith Missions (1935), Baptist Gospel Fellowship, Baptist International Missions (1967), Baptist Mid-Missions (1937), Bethany Missionary Association, Children of God International (over 1 million letters distributed), Chinese Christian (Gospel) Fellowship, Elim Missionary Assemblies (1964), Exclusive Brethren (Continuing Tunbridge Wells, Kelly-Continental), German Ev Ch, Iglesia Adventista Reformada, Iglesia de Dios Pentecostal, International Ch of the Foursquare Gospel, Mid-Peruvian Mission, Misión a los Andes, Peruvian Fellowship (1933), United Ev Chs, United World Mission (1955), World Baptist Fellowship Mission Agency (1961), World Missions (1963).
OTHER INDIGENOUS PENTECOSTAL CHURCHES. These include: Iglesia Pentecostal Independiente, and other immigrant bodies from Chile. In addition, there is a USA Black pentecostal mission, Ch of God (Holiness).
OTHER MARGINAL BODIES. The Reorganized Ch of Jesus Christ of Latter-day Saints (USA) maintains a small work based on Miraflores, Lima (65 members).

**PEOPLES** (ethnolinguistic). Christians: 47.9% Quechua, 32.6% Mestizo, 12.0% Peruvian White, 5.4% Aymara, 0.5% jungle Amerindian, 0.5% Black, 0.2% Chinese, Japanese, Zambo, Mulatto, Injerto, Chinocholo, British, Chilean, German, Greek, Norwegian, Gypsy.

**COUNTRY-WIDE TOTALS**
EVANGELIZATION (see Part 5). 1900: 97%. 1970: 99%. 1980: 100%. *Mass evangelism.* Among recent campaigns: 1962, Billy Graham 8-day crusade in Lima; 1967, Evangelism-in-Depth (EAF) (over 800 participating churches from 26 denominations, 24,220 trained lay Christians, 27,842 houses visited the first day, 4,725 prayer cells formed, over 3,000 professions of faith); 1967, Luis Palau EAF crusades in Huancayo (10 supporting churches, 18,400 attenders, 346 professions), in Arcquipa (6 sponsoring churches, 12,000 attenders, 658 professions), and in 1971 in Lima (50 supporting churches, 103,000 attenders, 4,585 professions); 1970, Hermano Pablo 2-week campaign in Lima (113,500 attenders, 5,572 enquirers). *Radiophonic evangelism.* Annual listeners' letters (1974): 3,337 HCJB, 437 FEBC, Radio Vatican, et alia. Bible correspondence courses: ICI (3,000 enrolments, 150 conversions reported), et alia.
FOREIGN MISSIONARIES AND PERSONNEL (nationals serving abroad) (1973). Total 270 in 6 countries: about 250 Roman Catholics, 20 Protestants.
FOREIGN MISSIONARIES AND PERSONNEL (aliens from abroad) (1973). Total 5,458. *From Western world.* 5,145: about 4,100 Roman Catholics, 765 Protestants (640 in 46 USA societies, 74 in 7 UK societies, 18 in 3 Canada societies, 9 in 2 Norway societies, 6 in 2 WGermany societies, 6 in 6 Australia societies, 4 in 1 Sweden society, 4 in 2 New Zealand societies, 3 in 1 Switzerland society, 1 in 1 Netherlands society), about 270 marginal Protestants (240 Mormons from USA), 8 Anglicans in 2 UK and 1 Australia societies, 2 Orthodox. *From Communist world.* About 23 Roman Catholics (13 from Poland, 10 from Yugoslavia). *From Third World.* 290: 240 Roman Catholics from other Latin American countries and Japan, about 30 Protestants from Argentina, Brazil, Chile, Hong Kong, Japan, Korea, Puerto Rico et alia, about 20 Latin American indigenous from Chile and Ecuador.
INSTITUTIONS (church-operated) (1973). Total 450, including 310 higher schools (21 minor seminaries), about 60 medical centres, 20 radio stations, 4 religious communities, 3 research centres, 32 seminaries (18 Protestant, 13 RC, 1 Peruvian indigenous), 4 universities.
PERIODICALS. About 50 titles.
PERSONNEL. About 10,996 (5,538 national, 5,458 foreign).
RELIGIOUS LIBRARIES. About 65.
SCRIPTURE DISTRIBUTION (1975). Annual totals: 139,390 Bibles (57% subsidized, 43% commercial), 392,161 NTs (52% free, 28% subsidized, 20% commercial), 249,114 UBS portions, 3,984,743 UBS selections. *Translations completed.* Portion: 34 languages since 1880. NT: 4 languages since 1947.
SERVICE AGENCIES. About 130, including ACF, ACJ, ACP, AEDET, CASA, CCCI, CCPM, CEC, CEOC, CEP, CIDE-COC, CNEP, CONAMCOS, CPR(CRP), CWS, DECOS, EAF, IFES, ILV(SIL), IPA, JAC, JARS, JEC, JECI, JOC, JUDCA, MEC(SCM), MFC, MIEC, MOSICP, MSCP, MSsA, NA, ONEC, ONIS, SAL-OCIC, SEC, SU, TEPA, UNEC, WBT (218 missionarics), WLC(EHC), YFCI, YLC.

**ADDITIONAL DATA ON CHURCHES**
IGLESIA CATOLICA EN EL PERU. *Catholics.* Including (1966) 21,000 Chinese, and some Japanese in Lima. In January 1972 the first stage in an overall pastoral reorganization took place with the division of Peru into 9 Zones, with in each a zonal assembly bringing together bishops, diocesan directors, bishops' appointees and 'pastoral agents' (priests, religious and laity). The names of the zones are as follows; the zone in which each diocese is may be seen from the first sub-column in column 8 of the table above. Zone 1: Sierra Notre (HQ in Cajamarca). 2: Costa Norte (HQ in Trujillo). 3: Huaraz (HQ in Huaraz). 4: Sierra Centro (HQ in Huancayo). 5: Lima (HQ in Lima). 6: Costa Centro (HQ in Ica). 7: Sur Peruano (HQ in Arequipa). 8: Sur Andino (HQ in Cuzco). 9: Selva (HQ in Pucallpa), *Annual baptisms.* (1972) 95.6% infant, 4.4% adult. *Priests.* In 1970, 65% were religious priests in 65 distinct religious families. Growth of numbers of priests (Peruvians + expatriates): 1901: 897 (82%) + 192 (18%). 1949: 763 (57%) + 565 (43%). 1953: 845 (56%) + 663 (44%). 1963: 1,005 (47%) + 1,153 (53%). 1970: 991 (39%) + 1,577 (61%). *Bishops.* In 1971, numbers (included under priests in the table) were as follows: 51 bishops and auxiliaries, 24 of whom were born in Peru and 27 naturalized. In addition there were 5 retired bishops (all Peruvians), and an Italian bishop expelled from Chile and serving as episcopal vicar for the Chinese colony in Peru. *Expatriate priests.* In 1970, these came from 35 different countries, in this order: from Spain 785 (691 religious + 94 secular), USA 227 (204 + 23), Canada 118 (92 + 26), Italy 117 (103 + 14), France 64 (49 + 15), Ireland 57 (48 + 9), FR Germany 51 (44 + 7), UK 27 (25 + 2), Mexico 23 (21 + 2). The remaining 108 priests (22 being Latin Americans) were from 26 other nations. *Male religious personnel.* Total: 2,514 (1970). In 1969, 32% of all religious priests and brothers had been born in Peru, and 68% had come from outside of whom 1% were from other Latin American countries. *Brothers.* Including 160 Peruvians and 237 expatriates (1971). *Sisters.* Including 2,629 Peruvians and 2,435 expatriates (1971). Of the latter, about 195 were from other Latin American countries. *Catholic charismatics* (January 1974). Around 7,000 adults are active in over 400 prayer groups in the Catholic Charismatic Renewal. *Catechists.* Total (1974) about 200, in jurisdictions under Propaganda. *Religious orders and congregations.* Priests (with over 50 members): 403 SDB, 397 OFM, 156 SJ, 124 OP, 89 OSA, 87 CM, 81 MM, 72 CP, 67 OdeM, 60 SM1, 58 Missionary Society of St James the Apostle (Boston, USA), 56 CSSR, 51 CMF. Brothers (with over 50 members): 158 PFM, 71 FSC. Sisters (with over 100 members): 277 Dominicans Missionaries of the Sacred Rosary (Madrid, Spain), 239 Franciscans of the Immaculate Conception (Lima, Peru), 219 Franciscans Missionaries of Mary (Rome, Italy), 208 Daughters of Charity of St Vincent de Paul, 190 Daughters Helpers of Mary or Salesians (Rome), 184 Sisters of the Sacred Heart of Jesus (Rome), 151 Mercedarians Missionaries of St Gervais (Barcelona, Spain), 150 Clarissians (Rome), 129 Dominicans (Second Order), 125 Discalced Carmelites, 125 Good Shepherd of Angers, 114 Missionaries of the Sacred Heart (Hiltrup, Germany).
*Catholic organizations.* The Peruvian Episcopal Conference (Conferencia Episcopal Peruana) is a member of CELAM. In January 1972, zonal assemblies (Asembleas Zonales) were instituted, the first step towards a national pastoral plan. These consist of bsihops, diocesan directors, episcopal delegates and pastoral agents (priests, religious personnel and lay members). Peru is now divided into 9 zones numbered as follows: (1) Sierra Notre (with headquarters in D Cajamarca), (2) Costa Notre (Trujillo), (3) Huaraz, (4) Sierra Centro (Huancayo), (5) Lima y Callao (Lima), (6) Costa Centro (Ica), (7) Sur Peruano (Arequipa), (8) Sur Andino (Cuzco), and (9) Selva (Pucallpa). The Peruvian Conference of Religious Personnel (Conferencia Peruana de Religiosos) which serves both male and female religious, is a member of CLAR. There is no national patsoral council nor national presbyteral council. However, an Episcopal Commission of the Clergy (Comisión Episcopal del Clero, CEC) was formed in 1970, composed of delegates elected by secular and regular priests from each jurisdiction (7 delegates for Lima and one for each prelature). For the armed forces, Peru forms a military vicariate.

Peruvian Catholic Action (Acción Católica Peruana) coordinates the activities of the following specialized movements: Union Nacional de Estudiantes Católicos (UNEC) for university students; Juventud Obrera Católica (JOC) with its strength in Lima, Pucallpa, Arequipa and Cuzco; Juventud Agraria Católica (JAC), for rural youth; Juventud Estudiantil Católica (JEC) for secondary students; and Movimiento Familiar Cristiano (MFC), found among the middle class in all dioceses. Other important lay movements are Consorcio Nacional de Educadores Católicos, for directors of Catholic colleges; Legión de Maria, Federación Nacional de Asociación de Padres de Familia de Colegios Católicos, for family fathers of Catholic colleges; Movimiento Obrero Sindical Cristiano (MOSIC), the Christian Workers union; Secretariado Nacional de Trabajadores (CNT), and Hermandades del Trabajo, both for workers.

The Holy See has diplomatic relations with Peru and is represented to government and the Catholic hierarchy by a nuncio in Lima.

Several organizations serving Latin America are based in Peru. (1) Noticias Aliadas (NA), is an independent Catholic press agency which keeps up regular contact with the hierarchy; with 740 correspondents throughout the continent, it gathers and disseminates news concerning the Latin American church (2) Misioneros de los Santos Apóstolos (MSsA) is a Latin American priestly society founded in Peru by a Canadian missionary in 1950 and receiving pontifical recognition in November 1971, which works for priestly vocations among youth and adults. Training centres are found in Connecticut (USA), at Chosica (in the diocese of Yauyos, Peru), and at Porto Alegre and Campinas (Brazil). Since 1971 it has furnished 80 priests and trained 205 major seminarians. (3) The Centro Latinoamericano de Lenguaje Total, which is at the service of SAL-OCIC, is engaged in research, publication and training courses concerning methods of social communication and their pedagogical implications in the social context of Latin America. Another similar centre is found at Saith-Etienne, France.

Latin American secretariats in Peru for international organizations include: Oficina Católica International del Cine, Secretariado para América Latina (SAL-OCIC) with its international headquarters at Brussels; Juventud Obrera Católica, Secretariado Latinoamericano (JOC), international HQ Brussels; Movimiento Internacional de Estudiantes Católicos (MIEC), international HQ Fribourg, Switzerland; and Juventud Estudiantil Católica Internacional (JECI), international HQ Paris.

The Oficina Nacional de Información Social (ONIS), also known as Movimiento ONIS Sacerdotal, is a non-official movement of progressivist priests, independent of the hierarchy but in dialogue with it. Founded in 1968, it is dedicated to renewal of the church by confronting theology with the realities of Peruvian social and church life. Politically revolutionary and economically anti-capitalist, its ideology is to the left of the nationalist junta which assumed political power in 1968. In 1971 it numbered 200 member priests with its strength in the dioceses of Lima, Arequipa and Trujillo. ONIS has also dedicated itself to teaching Christian people the social dimensions of the faith. Another association of lay persons with objectives similar to ONIS is 'For Action in Solidarity'.

Three research and social action centres are at work. (1) Oficina Arquidocesana de Investigación y Planeamiento, in Lima, engages in socio-religious studies, statistical analyses and pastoral planning for the whole of Peru. (2) The Centro de Investigaciones Sociales, Economicas, Politicas y Antropologicas is dependent on the Catholic University of Peru in Lima. One of its sections is responsible for socio-religious research. (3) The Instituto de Pastoral Andina (IPA) founded in Cuzco in 1968, engages in research concerning popular religiosity, mentality, traditions and myths of the Altiplano Indians, with the aim of furthering pastoral adaptation. This important institute also organizes training courses for priests, religious personnel and laity in applied anthropology, ethnology, folklore, catechesis, applied liturgics, research methods and religious sociology. (4) The Centro de Investigación y Acción Social (CIAS) is maintained by Jesuits in Lima. CIAS has also been established in Argentina, Chile, Colombia and Mexico.

Theological training is provided by the Facultad de Teologia de Lima Pontificia y Civil, founded in 1551 and recognized by government as the Official Institute of Higher Ecclesiastical Studies of Peru. Its seat is at the Major Seminary of Lima and it is associated with the Pontificia Universidad Católica del Perú, although it retains its own administration. In 1972 it numbered 213 students (44 being enrolled in the Major Seminary of Lima), including secular priests, religious personnel (male and female) and laity.

The Oficina Nacional de Educación Católica (ONEC), coordinates Catholic education. In 1970 there were 469 pre-primary and primary schools (204,569 pupils); 214 secondary schools (55,123) and 4 universities; the Pontificia Universidad Católica del Perú founded in Lima in 1917 (the most important); Universidad Particular San Martin de Porres, founded in Lima in 1952; Universidad Feminina Sagrado Corazón, in Lima, legally approved in 1962; and Universidad Católica Santa Maria, founded in Arequipa in 1962. By 1973 these numbered 507 primary schools (156,793 pupils) and 278 secondary school (85,166).

In 1970 Caritas Peruana was responsible for 4 hospitals, 5 clinics, 44 dispensaries, 13 homes for the aged and 7 nurseries. In addition aid was provided to 33 government hospitals, 4 clinics, 10 dispensaries and one home for the aged. Since 1955 453 credit co-operatives (90 being parish-based) have been formed throughout the country, with more than 260,000 members. Other projects in the Amazon region of the northeast include 255 schools (20,000 pupils), 45 medical centres, 20 workshops for women, 21 nurseries, 16 social service officers, 15 nutrition centres for infants, 2 art schools, 2 experimental farms, 5 agricultural schools and one normal school.

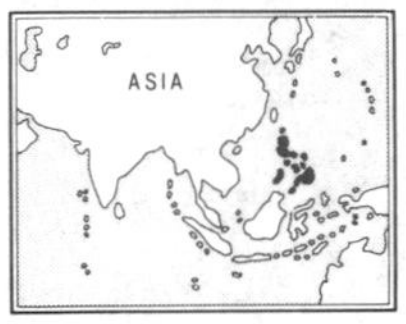


# PHILIPPINES

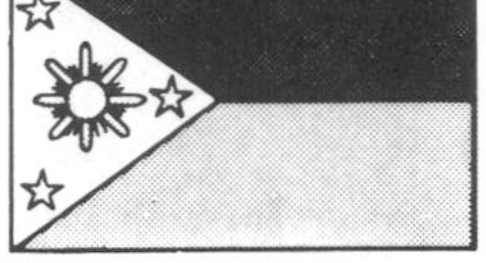

## SECULAR DATA

**STATE. Official name:** The Republic of the Philippines (Republika ñg Pilipinas/República de Filipinas). Adjectives of nationality: Philippine, a Filipino.
**Flag** (shown above right): Blue and red stripes bordered by white triangle containing yellow stars and sun.
**Area:** 300,000 sq.km. (115,830 sq.miles). Description: 7,107 islands. Agricultural land: 36.5%.
**Government:** One-party republic under martial law, since 1972 (1564 Spanish colony, 1898 independence declared but USA rule established, 1946 Independence as republic).
**Legislature:** Congress: Senate, 24 members; House of Representatives, 120 members.
**Official languages:** Filipino and English; according to 1973 constitution, English and Pilipino (Tagalog); also Spanish.
**Chief cities:** capital Manila-Quezon City 7,800,000 (1973), Davao 591,500, Cebu 384,800, Iloilo 232,800.
**Political divisions:** 68 Provinces; 61 Chartered Cities, 1,433 Municipalities, 21 Municipal Districts.
**Armed forces** (1976): Total 78,000 regular: army 45,000, navy 17,000, air force 16,000 (56 combat aircraft). Reserves: 45,000. Paramilitary forces: 60,000.
**Foreign forces** (1973): 15,000 USA troops.

**DEMOGRAPHY. Population:** 41,831,045 (census of 1.V.1975. For 1970–2000 (UN), see last row of Table 1). Population density (1975): 148/sq.km. (384/sq.mile). Under 15 years: 46%. Growth rate (1975–80): 3.22% per year (births 4.12%, deaths −0.91%). Life expectancy (1975–80): 60.7 years. Household size: 5.1 persons.
**Major languages:** Filipino, English, Spanish, Cebuano, Tagalog, Ilocan, Ilongo, Bicol, Pampango, Chinese. In addition, there are about 150 local languages. Usage: Tagalog 44%, English 39%, Spanish 2%, Chinese 0.5%.
**Urban dwellers** (1970): 34.1%. Urban growth rate (1950–70): 4.2% per year.
**Labour force:** 38%.
**Refugees** (1977): 1,405 from Viet Nam.
**Tourists** (1974): 400,238.

**ETHNOLINGUISTIC GROUPS:** 28.0% Visayan (Cebuano), 21.0% Tagalog, 11.7% Ilocan, 10.4% Hiligaynon (Ilongo), 7.8% Bicol, 3.2% Pampango, 3.0% Euronesian (Eurasian, Mestizo: Spanish/Filipino, Filipino/USA), 2.8% Pangasinan, 2.0% Montagnard, 1.7% Sulu-Samal (Tau Sug), 1.4% Ibanag, 1.2% Magindanao, 1.1% Chinese-Filipino (400,000), 0.8% Maranao, 0.6% Ifugao, 0.5% Sambal, 0.5% Bukidnon, 0.3% Kankanai, 0.3% Nabaloi, 0.3% Chinese national (120,000) (Amoy, Cantonese), 0.3% Palawan, 0.2% Bontoc, 0.2% Manobo, 0.1% Negrito (30,000) (Pygmy, Aeta, Baluga), USA White (10,000), Indian (1,500), Spaniard (1,000), Indonesian, Aklan, Subanon, Bilaan, Yakan, Jewish, & around 140 smaller peoples.

**MONEY** (1977). **Monetary unit:** Philippine peso (= 100 centavos); US$1 = PP 7.40.
**National income per person:** US$314. Average annual family income: US$1,601.
**Inflation:** (1970–74) 17.2% per year (1975: consumer price index 211).
**Cost of living in capital** (1976): index 83 (Washington DC = 100). Daily cost of living: US$34.

**HEALTH.** Hospitals: 764 (43,492 beds). Doctors: 14,000. Lepers: 40,000 (0.9 per 1,000). Blind: 80,000. Psychotics: 350,000. Criminals: 33,417.

**EDUCATION.** Adult literacy: (1948) 60%, (1970) 83%. Education rate: 87%. Schools (1965): 35,067. Universities: 34.

**LITERATURE.** Annual new book titles (1971): 706. Periodicals: 400. Scientific journals: 110. Newspapers: 18 dailies.

**COMMUNICATION** (per 1,000 people). Phones: 10. Radios: 46. TV sets: 10. Daily newspaper circulation: 21 copies.

TABLE 1. RELIGIOUS ADHERENTS IN THE PHILIPPINES

| Year | 1900 | | mid-1970 | | Annual change, 1970–1980 | | | | mid-1975 | | mid-1980 | | 2000 | |
|---|---|---|---|---|---|---|---|---|---|---|---|---|---|---|
| *Name* | *Adherents* | *%* | *Adherents* | *%* | *Natural* | *Conversion* | *Total* | *Rate* | *Adherents* | *%* | *Adherents* | *%* | *Adherents* | *%* |
| **Christians** | **6,550,000** | **86.2** | **35,359,600** | **94.0** | **1,373,818** | **10,392** | **1,384,210** | **3.31** | **41,816,800** | **94.1** | **49,201,700** | **94.3** | **84,218,500** | **93.9** |
| professing | 6,550,000 | 86.2 | 35,359,600 | 94.0 | 1,373,818 | 10,392 | 1,384,210 | 3.31 | 41,816,800 | 94.1 | 49,201,700 | 94.3 | 84,218,500 | 93.9 |
| Roman Catholics | 5,550,000 | 73.0 | 31,963,000 | 85.0 | 1,235,144 | −39,174 | 1,195,970 | 3.18 | 37,595,800 | 84.6 | 43,922,700 | 84.1 | 70,082,500 | 78.1 |
| Evangelical Catholics | 800,100 | 10.5 | 5,209,895 | 13.8 | 216,533 | 65,777 | 282,310 | 4.28 | 6,591,000 | 14.8 | 8,033,000 | 15.4 | 12,065,000 | 13.4 |
| Filipino indigenous | 1,000,000 | 13.2 | 2,090,900 | 5.6 | 84,663 | 29,847 | 114,510 | 4.44 | 2,577,000 | 5.8 | 3,236,000 | 6.2 | 9,868,000 | 11.0 |
| Protestants | 0 | 0.0 | 1,165,700 | 3.1 | 48,163 | 17,967 | 66,130 | 4.51 | 1,466,000 | 3.3 | 1,827,000 | 3.5 | 3,768,000 | 4.2 |
| Marginal Protestants | 0 | 0.0 | 100,000 | 0.3 | 4,271 | 1,729 | 6,000 | 4.62 | 130,000 | 0.3 | 160,000 | 0.3 | 400,000 | 0.4 |
| Anglicans | 0 | 0.0 | 40,000 | 0.1 | 1,577 | 23 | 1,600 | 3.33 | 48,000 | 0.1 | 56,000 | 0.1 | 100,000 | 0.1 |
| nominal | 570,000 | 7.5 | 1,317,600 | 3.5 | 58,440 | 36,970 | 95,410 | 5.36 | 1,778,800 | 4.0 | 2,271,700 | 4.4 | 6,711,500 | 7.5 |
| affiliated | 5,980,000 | 78.7 | 34,042,000 | 90.5 | 1,315,378 | −26,578 | 1,288,800 | 3.22 | 40,038,000 | 90.1 | 46,930,000 | 89.9 | 77,507,000 | 86.4 |
| doubly-affiliated | −1,800,100 | −23.7 | −5,375,088 | −14.3 | −217,190 | −44,601 | −261,791 | 3.96 | −6,611,000 | −14.9 | −7,993,000 | −15.3 | −14,318,000 | −16.0 |
| total practising | 5,382,000 | *90* | 27,233,600 | *80* | 1,052,303 | −21,263 | 1,031,040 | 3.22 | 32,030,400 | *80* | 37,544,000 | *80* | 54,254,900 | *70* |
| non-practising | 598,000 | *10* | 6,808,400 | *20* | 263,075 | −5,315 | 257,760 | 3.22 | 8,007,600 | *20* | 9,386,000 | *20* | 23,252,100 | *30* |
| Roman Catholics | 5,980,000 | 78.7 | 30,810,093 | 81.9 | 1,177,340 | −97,329 | 1,080,011 | 3.01 | 35,836,350 | 80.6 | 41,610,200 | 79.7 | 65,622,000 | 73.1 |
| Catholic pentecostals | 0 | 0.0 | 3,000 | 0.0 | 1,314 | 8,386 | 9,700 | 24.25 | 40,000 | 0.1 | 100,000 | 0.2 | 600,000 | 0.7 |
| Filipino indigenous | 1,800,000 | 23.7 | 6,661,038 | 17.7 | 274,125 | 83,571 | 357,696 | 4.29 | 8,344,000 | 18.8 | 10,238,000 | 19.6 | 19,700,000 | 22.0 |
| Protestants | 100 | 0.0 | 1,716,256 | 4.6 | 71,522 | 28,352 | 99,874 | 4.59 | 2,177,000 | 4.9 | 2,715,000 | 5.2 | 5,741,000 | 6.4 |
| Evangelicals | 100 | 0.0 | 1,360,000 | 3.6 | 56,836 | 27,164 | 84,000 | 4.86 | 1,730,000 | 3.9 | 2,200,000 | 4.2 | 4,620,000 | 5.2 |
| Marginal Protestants | 0 | 0.0 | 165,925 | 0.4 | 7,063 | 3,345 | 10,408 | 4.84 | 215,000 | 0.5 | 270,000 | 0.5 | 600,000 | 0.7 |
| Anglicans | 0 | 0.0 | 63,276 | 0.2 | 2,497 | 75 | 2,572 | 3.38 | 76,000 | 0.2 | 89,000 | 0.2 | 160,000 | 0.2 |
| Catholics (non-Roman) | 0 | 0.0 | 500 | 0.0 | 21 | 9 | 30 | 4.62 | 650 | 0.0 | 800 | 0.0 | 2,000 | 0.0 |
| Muslims | 266,000 | 3.5 | 1,617,000 | 4.3 | 62,750 | −3,450 | 59,300 | 3.10 | 1,910,000 | 4.3 | 2,210,000 | 4.3 | 3,857,000 | 4.3 |
| Ahmadis | 0 | 0.0 | 3,000 | 0.0 | 131 | 69 | 200 | 5.00 | 4,000 | 0.0 | 5,000 | 0.0 | 10,000 | 0.0 |
| Tribal religionists | 760,000 | 10.0 | 338,400 | 0.9 | 11,680 | −8,980 | 2,700 | 0.76 | 355,500 | 0.8 | 365,400 | 0.7 | 448,500 | 0.5 |
| Non-religious | 2,000 | 0.0 | 78,000 | 0.2 | 3,812 | 3,688 | 7,500 | 6.49 | 115,500 | 0.3 | 153,000 | 0.3 | 585,000 | 0.7 |
| Chinese folk-religionists | 15,000 | 0.2 | 70,000 | 0.2 | 2,135 | −3,135 | −1,000 | −1.54 | 65,000 | 0.1 | 60,000 | 0.1 | 30,000 | 0.0 |
| Baha'is | 0 | 0.0 | 67,500 | 0.2 | 2,957 | 1,793 | 4,750 | 5.28 | 90,000 | 0.2 | 115,000 | 0.2 | 250,000 | 0.3 |
| Buddhists | 7,000 | 0.1 | 50,000 | 0.1 | 1,708 | −1,308 | 400 | 0.77 | 52,000 | 0.1 | 54,000 | 0.1 | 60,000 | 0.1 |
| Atheists | 0 | 0.0 | 20,000 | 0.1 | 854 | 646 | 1,500 | 5.77 | 26,000 | 0.1 | 35,000 | 0.1 | 240,000 | 0.3 |
| Hindus | 0 | 0.0 | 1,000 | 0.0 | 36 | −16 | 20 | 1.82 | 1,100 | 0.0 | 1,200 | 0.0 | 2,000 | 0.0 |
| New-Religionists | 0 | 0.0 | 1,000 | 0.0 | 100 | 300 | 400 | 13.33 | 3,000 | 0.0 | 5,000 | 0.0 | 10,000 | 0.0 |
| Jews | 0 | 0.0 | 500 | 0.0 | 20 | 0 | 20 | 3.33 | 600 | 0.0 | 700 | 0.0 | 1,000 | 0.0 |
| Other religionists | 0 | 0.0 | 1,000 | 0.0 | 30 | 70 | 100 | 6.67 | 1,500 | 0.0 | 2,000 | 0.0 | 5,000 | 0.0 |
| **Country's population** | **7,600,000** | **100.0** | **37,604,000** | **100.0** | **1,459,900** | **0** | **1,459,900** | **3.29** | **44,437,000** | **100.0** | **52,203,000** | **100.0** | **80,707,000** | **100.0** |

COLUMNS, ROWS. For meanings and definitions, see Codebook (Part 6). Note that, by definition, total 'Christians' = professing + crypto-Christians, which also = affiliated + nominal Christians. Percentages may not always total exactly, due to rounding.
CENSUSES. **1939:** 78.8% Roman Catholics, 10.0% Filipino indigenous (9.8% Aglipayans), 4.2% Muslims, 4.0% tribal religionists, 2.4% Protestants and Anglicans, 0.3% Buddhists, 0.1% Shintoists, 0.1% non-religious, 0.1% Chinese folk-religionists. **1.X.1948:** 83.0% Roman Catholics, 8.0% Filipino indigenous (7.6% Aglipayans, 0.3% Iglesia ni Cristo), 4.1% Muslims, 2.2% Protestants, 1.8% tribal religionists, 0.5% other religionists, 0.2% Buddhists, 0.1% Anglicans. **15.II.1960:** 83.8% Roman Catholics, 6.7% Filipino indigenous (5.2% Aglipayans, 1.0% Iglesia ni Cristo), 4.9% Muslims, 2.7% Protestants, 1.3% tribal religionists, 0.2% Anglicans, 0.2% Chinese folk-religionists, 0.1% Buddhists, 0.1% non-religious. **6.V.1970:** 85.0% Roman Catholics, 5.6% Filipino indigenous (3.9% Aglipayans, 1.3% Iglesia ni Cristo, 0.4% others), 4.3% Muslims, 3.1% Protestants, 0.1% Episcopalians, 0.1% Buddhists, 1.8% other religionists or non-religious (0.9% tribal religionists).

NOTES ON RELIGIONS
AHMADIS. Begun about 1950; Qadianis from Pakistan, mainly on Sulu and Mindanao (HQ Bongao, Sulu).
ATHEISTS. Communist Party of the Philippines (PKP) (illegal 1932, outlawed 1957) and several factions: membership (1970) 8,000 in PKP, 1,000 Maoist dissidents, 100,000 sympathizers (many in the New People's Army, People's Liberation Army (Huks), and Maoist New People's Army).
BAHA'IS. 1961, only 200 Baha'is in 40 centres, then rapid growth to 1,600 Baha'is in 182 centres within year, then from 150 local spiritual assemblies (1964) to 268 (1973), with 3,110 other isolated

centres or groups. From 1967–72, 64 young Persian pioneers from Iran entered as students; by 1971, 3,100 students in 5 universities had become Baha'is. Over 4,000 were enrolled in 1973 in Baha'i correspondence courses. Many Baha'is are former Hindus.

BUDDHISTS. About 10% of all Chinese are Buddhists.

CATHOLIC PENTECOSTALS (or, Catholic charismatics). Totals (January 1974): 15,000 involved adults (over 15 years old), including 100 priests and 500 nuns, in over 200 prayer groups; total charismatic community including children, 30,000. In March 1978, 380 leaders attended a National Leaders Conference in Manila.

DOUBLY-AFFILIATED. The term covers those affiliated to, or claimed by, both the Roman Catholic Church and also a church termed or regarded as Evangelical by the state (Protestant, Aglipayan or other Filipino indigenous, Anglican, or marginal Protestant), i.e. baptized Catholics who have recently become Evangelicals or others. Because their statistics represent a duplication, they are shown in the table as a negative quantity (with a minus sign).

EVANGELICAL CATHOLICS. This term is used here to describe persons who are affiliated to churches termed or regarded by the state as Evangélica or Evangelical (Protestant, Aglipayan or other Filipino indigenous, Anglican, or marginal Protestant

churches), but who in government censuses are regarded as, or who profess publicly to be, Roman Catholics. Many Aglipayans regard themselves as Católicos and report themselves as such in censuses.

FILIPINO INDIGENOUS. After its founding in 1890, the Philippine Independent Church (PIC) numbered at its peak nearly half of all Roman Catholics in the Philippines. Since 1906, however, this Aglipayan segment with its splinter groups has declined rapidly with each successive decade. After 1960, other types of Filipino indigenous churches began to increase markedly, especially the Iglesia ni Cristo (INC). By 1970 there were over 330 such indigenous denominations (see Table 2), and the PIC itself was again increasing.

HINDUS. Including adherents of the Ananda Marga sect; and a neo-Hindu movement, the Theosophical Society with (1975) 19 Lodges and 291 members. Many Hindus have become Baha'is.

JEWS. With a synagogue in Manila.

MUSLIMS. All Sunnis (of the Shafiite rite); commonly termed Moros (Moors). Mainly in the south on Mindanao, Sulu archipelago and Palawan. Of all Muslims, 96.0% belong to these predominantly-Muslim peoples: Sulu-Samal (640,000, including 200,000 Tau Sug), Magindanao (450,000), Maranao (300,000), Yakan (50,000), Sangir (7,500), Melebuganon, Bajau (Sea-

Gypsies). There is also an Ahmadiya Mission (Qadianis; enumerated here under Muslims though declared non-Muslim by Pakistan). *Hajj pilgrims to Mecca.* (1970) 150; (1974) 1,564; (1975) 1,154; (1976) 357.

NEW-RELIGIONISTS. Adherents of Asian syncretistic New Religions from China, Japan, Korea and Indonesia, including by 1975, 1,700 converts to the Japanese movement Nichiren Shoshu (Soka Gakkai).

OTHER RELIGIONISTS. Followers of numerous other smaller Western cults including Rosicrucians (1 AMORC centre).

PRACTISING CHRISTIANS. Roman Catholics (1969): 26.4% weekly attendance in barrios (urban slums), 33% in non-urban lowland areas. Among youths aged 18–24, 65% claimed to attend church every weekend in 1974 (Gallup).

TRIBAL RELIGIONISTS. Animists or shamanists among mountain tribes, especially the Ifugao (95,000), Igorot and Bontoc (20,000) of Luzon. Other pagan tribes and peoples: Apayao, Atta (10,000), Bagobo, Bukidnon, Dumagat (1,000), Gadang (5,500), Kalagan (19,000), Kalinga, Mandaya, Mangyan (60,000), Manobo (35,000), Negritos, Subanon (20,000), Tagbanua (Palawan), Tboli (67,500), Tinggian, and Tiruray.

## NON-CHRISTIAN RELIGIONS. Islam was

introduced in 1380 by Malay immigrants. Filipino Muslims are Sunnis of the Shafiite rite. They are commonly referred to as Moros (the Spanish word for Moor), but this term is not acceptable to most because of its negative connotations dating from the Spanish occupation of the islands. Filipino Muslims are concentrated in the relatively undeveloped islands of Mindanao, the Sulu archipelago and Palawan in the south of the nation. The Muslim population in 1977 was around 2 million. There are 9 different Filipino linguistic groups professing Islam, all belonging to the Central Philippine sub-group and closely related to the major languages spoken by Filipinos, namely Tagalog and Cebuano. The following groups account for 92% of all Muslims: Magindanao, the largest group of Muslims in the country, living along the banks of Rio Grande de Cotabato, Mindanao; Maranao, of whom 90%

live in the province of Lanao del Sur and 10% in Lanao del Norte, Mindanao; and Tau Sug, who occupy the archipelago and province of Sulu where Muslims constitute 95% of the total population. Other Muslim groups are the Samals, Bajaus and Yakan. The Bajaus, often called Sea Gypsies, are of Arab and Malay ancestry and live in southern Sulu; the Yakan of Basilan island are part Polynesian in origin. Other provinces with a Muslim minority are Zamboanga del Sur, Davao del Norte, Davao del Sur and Davao Oriente. Ethnically, Filipino Muslims along with most other Filipinos are of Malayan and Indonesian stock.

Muslims showed unyielding resistance to Spanish military domination and attempts at christianization and were not completely conquered by Spanish forces until 1876, nor were they ever integrated into Philippine political life. In 1938, the head of state, president Quezon, coined the mottos 'Land for the landless' and 'Go south, young man' and offered farms in the Muslim south to Christian Filipinos from the nation's more congested areas. Cotabato was first chosen for this settlement, and other areas in the south were opened to the influx of settlers beginning in 1939. With a pause during World War II, this influx has continued up to the present time. Although they had occupied the land for centuries, most Muslims lacked written titles for their property; consequently, many lost their land to thousands of new Christian settlers.

In 1970 the bitterness of Muslims on Mindanao broke out in armed revolt directed against both government and Christian colonists. The resulting civil war has spread to other predominantly Muslim regions, and, aggravated by massive and indiscriminate military repression, has threatened to cause the secession of all Muslims from the Filipino state. The conflict has continued now since 1945

and has taken on new vitality recently as a result of the cultural awakening of the elite, more thorough training for Muslim religious leaders (imams) some of whom have studied abroad in Egypt and other countries, interference by president Gaddaffi of Libya, and recent increases in the numbers of Quranic schools and Muslim religious associations.

In certain regions, such as Sulu and Cotabato, the Muslim insurrection has lost its character as a religious conflict, either because it has the support of the Catholic clergy or because it is directed equally against the ruling Muslim class (the Datus) who hold vast properties and enjoy government support. In other areas, however, where the Ilagas (Catholic terrorists dedicated to hunting Muslims) carry on their savage activities, many bishops fear that Muslims will hold the Catholic Church responsible for atrocities committed against them. In 1974 attempts at conciliation took place between the government and Muslim insurgents, without however achieving an end to hostilities. The government created a loan bank without interest and accepted the installation of a permanent delegation for the South from the Islamic Conference, the major Muslim political body with headquarters in Saudi Arabia, which would divide the aid and prepare plans for the development of those regions inhabited by Muslims.

The Far east regional office of the World Muslim Congress, with its headquarters in Pakistan, is located in Manila.

**Traditional religions** are still prevalent among the mountain-dwellers dispersed throughout the nation, including the Bontoc, Gadang, Ifugao and Igorot of Luzon, Mangyan of Mindoro, Tagbanua of Palawan, and Atta, Manobo and Subanon of Mindanao. Tribal religion, with emphasis on magic, spirits and an originator supreme being, is followed by the nomadic Negritos who inhabit the wooded mountains

**Catholic Church in the Philippines.** *Left.* Pope Paul VI greets crowd of 1.5 million Catholics in Quezon Park before mass on November 1970 visit. *Above.* Radio Veritas, in Archdiocese of Manila.

of the smaller islands. The Kalinga of Northern Luzon, with a population of 100,000, are still head-hunters, although a few have now become Christians. Their religion consists of 3 principal elements: (1) the work of the medium or shaman *(Mangalisig)* who is usually a woman and wears a turban; (2) belief in spirits (Anitos); and (3) a creator God (Kaboniyan). Traditionalists fell from 4% of the population in 1939 to 1.3% in 1960, and to 0.8% by 1975. The influence of these religions persists however in popular Christianity.

**Baha'i** is rapidly growing, from 40 centres in 1961 to 3,378 centres by 1973. Agents in producing many conversions are Persian missionaries from Iran, and extensive correspondence courses.

**Other religions** include Buddhism, Taoism and Confucianism, often mixed. There are also some Hindus and Jews.

## CHRISTIANITY

CATHOLIC CHURCH. The explorer Magellan's world expedition brought the first priest to the Philippines in 1521, and the first Augustinian missionary arrived in 1565. Dominicans established the University of St Thomas in 1611 and Jesuits their first college in 1695. During the 17th and 18th centuries, the Philippines served as a base for missions to Japan, China and Cambodia. For much of the 19th century the church retained its Spanish character and discriminated against the few national priests. The latter participated in various revolutionary efforts, and 3 priests were shot in 1872. Following the war of 1898, 500 missionary priests were expelled and the church lost its favoured position. From 1890 onwards, a leading Filipino priest Gregorio Aglipay with others rebelled against the continued failure to indigenize the Catholic Church and founded the Philippine Independent Church. The Catholic hierarchy was reorganized in 1907 and several new missionary congregations arrived for new work in mountainous regions. In 1905 the first Filipino bishop was consecrated, followed in 1934 by the first archbishop and in 1960 by the first cardinal.

The republic of the Philippines has the highest percentage of Catholics of all countries of Asia (84%). Nevertheless, traditional beliefs retain much of their vigour and give to the practice of Christianity the quality of a folk religion. In 1960 there was on average one priest to every 8,363 inhabitants, one priest for every 7,004 Catholics and one priest in the parish ministry for every 10,950 Catholics. These averages conceal a wide range of divergence. At St Teresita, Quezon City, the ratio was one priest to 4,170 persons and one for every 3,150 Catholics, while in Tondo, the slums of Manila, there was one priest to every 55,400 and one for every 52,000 Catholics. In the countryside there is frequently only one priest for rural communities *(barrios)*. Only 13% of barrios have a resident priest, minister or imam; 67% are visited only once a year by a minister of religion, and the remaining 20% are left unvisited. In 1968, 65% of all Catholic jurisdictions were under Filipino bishops. Chinese Catholics are numerous, numbering 104,000 in 1975, and since 1955 have been grouped under a National Office for Chinese Missions in the Philippines. In 1970 Chinese work included 13 parishes, 13 missions, one bishop, 68 priests, 22 sisters, 45 schools with 16,511 students, and in the year there were 2,328 infant baptisms and 514 adult baptisms.

Several characteristics of the Catholic Church in the Philippines are similar to those found in Latin American countries. Its triumphalism, long autocratic tradition, and social and theological conservatism, have created for it an image which was widely criticized by the press and the student world prior to the promulgation of martial law in September 1972. The former cardinal-archbishop, Rufino J. Santos, who died in September 1973, became the principal focus of criticism and indeed the object of public demonstrations in the streets of the capital during 1969 and 1970. Under martial law, these manifestations have been no longer permitted, but the position of the institutional church continues to provoke tension in many dioceses.

The forces of change are however also at work, especially since 1965 when priests and lay persons began to become involved in social action. This movement consists essentially of groups not recognized by the majority of bishops and often in conflict with them. A number of Jesuits figure among the principal progressivist leaders of the church, which has led president Marcos to state that the Society of Jesus 'foments violent revolution' in the country. A new factor is the active involvement of several younger bishops in the committees of the Federation of Asian Bishops' Conferences (FABC), formed in Hong Kong in 1972, which may in the long run aid the Catholic Church in the Philippines to discover its Asian identity and to depart from the model of Western Christianity which has characterized it to date. It was with this in view that the Office for Human Development of the FABC was located in Manila.

By 1973 some 60 activist sisters of various congregations had formed a group to live and work together in full-time rural social action in collaboration with the radical Free Farmers' Federation (FFF) the Trade Union of Sugar Industry Workers. On the conservative side, one notes also the expansion of the Cursillos de Cristiandad, with about 100,000 members in 1970. Though criticized for their anti-conciliar theological approach and outmoded methods of indoctrination nevertheless from their ranks have come many noted parish leaders.

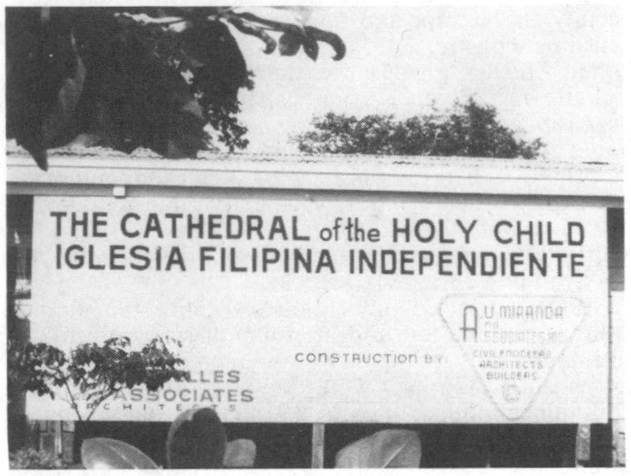


**Philippine Independent Church.** *Above.* Noticeboard of Manila cathedral of the PIC, largest (with 3.5 million members including President Ferdinand Marcos) of the over 330 Filipino indigenous churches.
**Banner of the Race Church.** *Below.* Catholic-type hierarchy of Iglesia Watawat ng Lahi (a Rizalist spiritist body with 50,000 members) in front of their church in Calamba, Laguna.

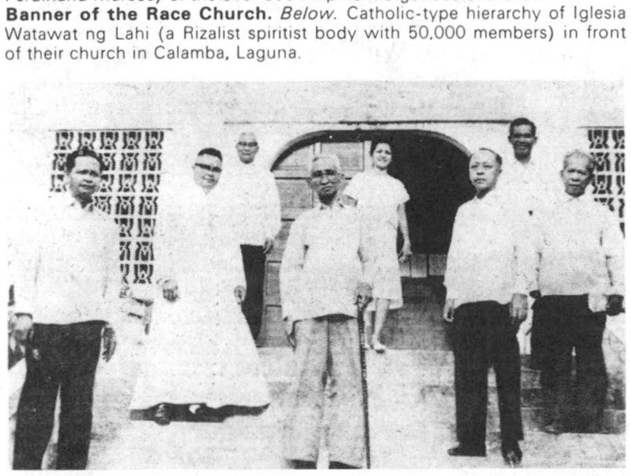

INDIGENOUS CHURCHES. In 1840 the first peasant protest movement against Spanish Catholicism took place, with the formation of an independent brotherhood, the Confraternity of St Joseph. It won thousands of followers in Tayabas, Laguna and Batangas before the leader, known as king of the Tagalogs, was captured and executed in 1841. Subsequently, many similar movements of religious protest and independence have arisen, most becoming institutionalized as independent churches. By 1970 there were over 330 such denominations begun by Filipinos in the Philippines, as well as some pseudo-Christian groups which mix Christian, tribal and nationalistic traditions, including cults deifying the nationalist leader José Rizal, who was executed in 1896.

The largest of these churches is the Philippine Independent Church which was founded in 1890 and organized in 1902 by a Catholic priest Gregorio Aglipay and a nationalist leader Isabelo de Los Reyes. The PIC attracted a vast following in its early years, including many priests and nearly 50% of the entire Catholic community. However, when the Supreme Court in 1906 ordered the return of all Catholic properties appropriated by the PIC, peoples' attachment to their parish churches resulted in large numers returning to Catholicism. The PIC went into decline with only a few poorly-trained clergy, no funds, inadequate buildings, and a liturgy and dogma which became increasingly unitarian and rationalist. Following the death of its 2 founders in the late 1930s, a new Declaration of Faith and Articles of Religion were prepared and arrangements made for the consecration of bishops by the Philippine Episcopal Church (Anglican) in 1948. Priests are now trained in the Episcopalian seminary, and in 1961 the 2 churches entered into full communion with each other. As with other churches, the PIC has experienced a series of schisms, several of which arose from its new direction in 1948. While over the years it declined in influence from 14% of the population in 1918 to 7% in 1948, and to 6% in 1960, it is now experiencing rapid growth and today accounts for 77% of the numerical strength of the National Council of Churches (NCCP). Of the 330 Filipino indigenous churches today at least 120 may be classed as Catholic-type groups similar to the PIC.

The Church of Christ (Iglesia ni Cristo), which also has a larger membership than any mission-founded Protestant church, was begun by Felix Manalo, a Catholic who entered and left several other churches before declaring that he had been divinely appointed to revive the original Christian church, outside of which there is no salvation. Its aggressive nationalistic emphasis, authoritarian organization and all-Filipino leadership have attracted many followers, who form a major force in politics by practising block voting in government elections. The church now has 3,000 congregations and 35 large and lavishly-appointed cathedrals, and tripled its membership between 1948 and 1960. Other important indigenous churches include Crusaders of the Divine Church of Christ.

PROTESTANT CHURCHES. American Protestant missionaries entered the Philippines following its annexation by the USA in 1898. The first Presbyterian began in 1899, founding the well-known Silliman University in 1901. Presbyterians early involved themselves in ecumenical dialogue with other churches and jointly formed, with Congregationalists, the United Evangelical Church in 1929. This church in turn became part of the United Church of Christ in the Philippines in 1948.

American Methodists arrived in 1899, and the first annual conference was held in 1908. Schisms took place in the Methodist Church in 1905, 1909 and 1933, the result in part of the Filipino desire for independence which was frustrated by American rule. The first Filipino Methodist bishop was elected in 1944, and all key administrative positions are now held by nationals. Methodists continue their heavy involvement in education, medicine, social service and agricultural development. Among their many institutions are a large hospital in Manila and a school of nursing. The Methodist Church in 1973 was supporting 8 missionaries in Okinawa and Sarawak.

American Baptists entered in 1900 for work on the islands of Panay and Negros. They opened several hospitals, completed translation of the Bible in Panayan Visayan, and began an industrial centre which later became the Central Philippine University. The Convention of Philippine Baptist Churches was organized in 1935 and now has over 700 full-time workers.

Disciples of Christ sent missionaries in 1901 to work in northern Luzon. In 1943 their church joined with the United Brethren to form the Evangelical Church which in 1948 joined the United Church of Christ. Churches established by missionaries of the American Board also became part of the United Church in 1948.

Entering in 1902, the Christian and Missionary Alliance grew into an autonomous church in 1947 and in 1970 had over 600 congregations, 4 Bible schools and 200 self-supporting laymen in charge of small parishes, preaching in 30 dialects. It has a publishing centre and is also involved in radio.

Seventh-day Adventists have since 1906 built up the third largest Protestant church membership. They continue to sponsor a large number of secondary schools and hospitals, in addition to having more than 1,000 churches. During the past 20 years the church has sent 175 missionaries overseas.

Pentecostals are also active, the largest group at present being the Assemblies of God, which began with the return of Filipino converts from the USA in the 1920s; there are now over 700 national workers.

The United Church of Christ came into being in 1948 as a re-organization of a union of evangelical churches created during the Japanese occupation. Participating churches included the United Evangelical Church, the independent Philippine Methodist Church and the Evangelical Church. It has sent more than 35 missionaries overseas since 1953.

A large number of other small mostly American missions work in the Philippines, the majority of which have made their appearance since World War II. There are now several times as many foreign missionaries serving non-ecumenical churches in the Philippines as those serving ecumenical churches. This represents a clear reversal of the distribution prior to World War II. Comity lines have broken down with the influx of new missions and shifting populations, and no common strategy for the location of new work has been developed among Evangelicals. On the other hand these new bodies have contributed to Protestant growth which has been extremely rapid since 1948.

ANGLICAN CHURCH. The Episcopal Church in the USA sent its first missionaries to the Philippines in 1902, directing their attention to unchurched and minority groups such as Chinese in greater Manila, tribal groups in northern Luzon, and tribal people and Muslims in western Mindanao and Sulu. The Philippine Episcopal Church continues to maintain elementary and secondary schools, hospitals and St Andrew's Seminary. The first Filipino bishop was consecrated in 1967, and 80% of his clergy are nationals. From 1945–61 the number of Filipino clergy increased from 3 to 48 and the number of baptized members more than doubled. In 1961 the church entered into full communion with the Philippine Independent Church.

**CHURCH AND STATE.** Separation of church and state in the Philippines coincides with the beginning of American rule, as delineated in the Treaty of Paris of December 1898. It is stated as follows in the new constitution of January 1973: 'The separation of Church and State shall be inviolable' (Article XV, section 15). According to the new constitution, the state guarantees freedom of religion and worship 'without discrimination or preference' (Article IV, section 8) and it also affords protection in employment and ensures equal work opportunities for all regardless of sex, race or creed (Article II, section 9). No public money or property may be paid to or used by any religious institution or any priest, minister or other religious teacher, except clergy assigned to armed forces, penal institutions, government orphanages or leprosaria (Article VIII, section 18, 2). The property of churches, mosques, non-profit cemeteries and other charitable institutions is exempt from taxation (Article VIII, section 17, 3), and this includes denominationally-owned institutions such as radio and TV stations. An exception to this is the recent requirement that private and confessional schools must now pay taxes. Finally, the constitution stipulates that 'At the option expressed in writing by the parents or guardians, and without cost to them and the government, religion shall be taught to their children or wards in public elementary and high schools as may be provided by law' (Article XV, section 8, 8). This religious education, the sanction for which came from the former constitution of 1935, was approved by vote of parliament in 1965.

Being the only predominantly Christian country in Asia, the Philippines has always tended towards a loose interpretation of the separation of church and state. Consequently, the preamble of the new constitution begins with this invocation: 'We, the sovereign Filipino people, imploring the aid of the Divine Providence. . .'. One result of this religious milieu is that seminarians in San Jose Major Seminary, who are enrolled in 4-year courses at Ateneo University, are exempt from military training, although all able-bodied male citizens are required by law to follow a 2-year basic course in the Reserve Officers' Training Corps.

The influence of the Catholic Church remains preponderant. On the one hand, the government hesitates to oppose the hierarchy openly in such fields as divorce and birth control; on the other hand, the Catholic Church has successfully expressed opposition to several proposed laws of a nationalistic character, including the proposal in 1956 to make compulsory in schools the study of the 2 principal literary works of José Rizal, 'The Father of the Nation' who was executed in 1896. Catholics opposed this because Rizal had often attacked the church. They also opposed the proposal of a Catholic senator who in 1958 wished to place Filipinos as heads of all Catholic schools run by foreign missionaries. On this subject the constitution of 1973 states that 'Educational institutions other than those established by religious orders and mission boards shall be owned solely by citizens of the Philippines' (Article XV, section 8, 8).

By virtue of the separation of church and state, there is no governmental department in charge of religious or ecclesiastical affairs. According to Section 154 of the Corporation Law, Act 1459, as amended on 1 April 1906, for the administration of the temporal affairs of any religious denomination

**Church of Christ** (Iglesia ni Cristo). Second largest Filipino indigenous church (1.5 million members), organized like an army, with some ministers carrying revolvers. *Above* One of its 35 cathedrals, in Manila. *Below.* Executive Minister (and son of 1913 Founder), Brother Eraño G. Manalo (centre), greets and blesses followers after packed church service in House of Worship, Moriones (Tondo, Manila), before he drives off.

or church and the management of the estates and properties thereof, it is lawful for the bishop, chief priest or other leader to become a corporation in himself. According to Section 155, for purposes of affording public notice of the existence of such a corporation, the head of the religious body must file with the government's Securities and Exchange Commission articles of incorporation setting forth the facts required by law. Further, in order to be legally permitted to solemnize marriages, priests, ministers and rabbis must register their names with the National Library.

On 21 September 1972, president Marcos declared martial law throughout the country. Since then, only the president has power to decide when the constitution is to be implemented, and when not. Faced with this situation, the Catholic Church has been very much divided. Most bishops and a segment of the clergy approve this at least implicitly and have shown no opposition to it. Some bishops have gone as far as forbidding their priests and religious personnel from engaging in social action, thus adding support to the position of the army which considers social action to be subversive. Only a minority of 17 bishops and 18 religious superiors have protested

against the regime of martial law through a joint declaration in November 1973 in addition to a few individual statements. Other episcopal declarations, when there have been any, have been content to protest against certain abuses such as police searches of convents. On the other hand, some 20 priests and many militant lay persons have been arrested since the proclamation of martial law, in some cases for things done (such as involvement in social action) prior to its promulgation. Others have been arrested since. In most cases the period of detention for priests has been relatively short. Several foreign missionaries also have been expelled from the country.

**INTERDENOMINATIONAL ORGANIZATIONS.** The National Council of Churches in the Philippines (NCCP), founded in 1963, evolved out of 4 previous changes in the original Evangelical Union of 1901, Filipino leaders assuming greater control with each change in name and structure. The NCCP now has as members 9 churches and 4 associate organizations, and includes 52% of all Protestants in 1970. There is also an Inter-Church Commission on Medical Care, and an Association of Christian Schools and Colleges, the latter being affiliated with the NCCP.

Two other more conservative councils are the Philippine Council of Evangelical Churches (PCEC) and the Philippine Council of Fundamental Evangelical Churches.

The John XXIII Ecumenical Center (JEC) was founded in 1968 and functions as the permanent secretariat of the Roman Catholic Bishops' Commission for Promoting Christian Unity (BCPCU) and deals directly with the NCCP in all joint ecumenical endeavours. This service centre also promotes ecumenical study and research, through the training of personnel who teach ecumenical subjects and are involved in ecumenical activities, and also by theological and pastoral reflection on those problems which are of interest to the ecumenical movement in general and to the Philippine situation in particular.

The Cardinal Bea Institute for Ecumenical Studies (CBI), founded by Jesuits in 1968, is involved in research, dialogue and ecumenical training in connection with the Ateneo de Manila University. The CBI shares the same offices and personnel as the JEC. As a research centre it provides materials and personnel for both the Philippines and also southeast Asia. Special emphasis is given to doctrinal and theological questions.

The Interchurch Committee on Urban Squatter Resettlement (ICUSR) was founded in 1969 by Catholic, Independent and Protestant leaders. The ICUSR is a co-operative agency which complements and strengthens the government programme to resettle squatters and ameliorate the living conditions of slum-dwellers in greater Manila.

**BROADCASTING.** The vast network of radio and TV stations all accept both Protestant and Catholic programmes. A total of 21 Catholic radio stations are associated in the Philippine Federation of Catholic Broadcasters working with Radio Veritas in Manila, which has an Overseas Department and a Home Service and is owned and operated by the Philippine Radio Educational and Information Centre, a non-profit organization with 7 Filipino bishops as board members. Radio Veritas reaches throughout East Asia and beyond with musical, religious and educational programmes. In emission power across Asia, it is second only to Radio Peking and the Voice of America in the middle- and short-wave bands. Most Catholic programmes are produced by Mountain Province Broadcasting Corporation in Baguio City, but there are at least 4 other production centres in Manila. A radio school in Cotabato City is mainly intended for educating the indigenous Tyrurags. Catholics are also heavily involved in the preparation of regular and educational TV programmes. The Visayan Educational Radio and Television Association (VERTA) has its headquarters at Bacolod City. This is a radio and TV station owned and run by a group of laymen. The chairman of their board is the bishop of the diocese, a prominent progressivist. It sponsors an adult literacy programme in the language of the area, Hiligayen; local, national and international information; health and sanitary suggestions; and a programme for women. VERTA is a member of the National Federation of Christian Broadcasters, as are Station DZJU in the province of Quezon and Station DXCD (Tagum Community Development Radio Corporation in Davao del Norte) which also broadcasts development programmes. The Philippines is a member of UNDA.

For Protestants, the Far East Broadcasting Company (FEBC) has a very large station in Manila which beams to over 50% of the entire world's population for 19 hours each day. Programmes include correspondence courses. Around 100 Protestant churches and missions co-operate with FEBC in preparing material for Asia and Latin America. Another service has been the ecumenical SEARV (South East Asia Radio Voice), located 20 miles north of Manila, which has served Christian councils in many nations around.

## BIBLIOGRAPHY


'A study of the Iglesia Ni Cristo: a political-religious sect in the Philippines', H. Ando, *Pacific affairs*, XLII, 3 (Fall 1969), 334–345.

*Catholic directory of the Philippines, 1971*. Manila: Catholic Trade School, 1971.

*Churches and sects in the Philippines: a descriptive study of contemporary religious group movements*. D.J. Elwood. Dumaguete City: Silliman University, 1968. 213p.

'Iglesia ni Cristo: an angel and his church', A.L. Tuggy, in D.J. Hesselgrave (ed), *Dynamic religious movements* (Grand Rapids: Baker, 1978), p. 85-101.

*Islands under the Cross: the story of the church in the Philippines*. P.G. Gowing. Manila: NCCP, 1967. 286p.

*Nationalism and Christianity in the Philippines*. R.L. Deats. Dallas, TX: Southern Methodist University Press, 1967.

*New Testament fire in the Philippines*. J. Montgomery. C-GRIP, c1975. 210p. (On Pentecostal growth).

*Revolt in Mindanao: the rise of Islam in Philippine politics*. T.J.S. George. Leiden: E.J. Brill, 1980. 290p.

'Some theological aspects of Roman Catholic responses to lowland Filipino spirit-world beliefs'. D.J. Schneider. Thesis, Concordia Lutheran Seminary, St Louis (MO), 1971.

*Studies in Philippines church history*. Ed G.H. Anderson. Ithaca (NY): Cornell University Press, 1969.

*The Catholic Church in the Philippines today*. Manila: Bookmark (Historical Conservation Society), 1968. 131p.

*The discipling of a nation*. J.H. Montgomery & D.A. McGavran. Global Church Growth Bulletin, 1980. 175p.

*The Philippine church: growth in a changing society*. A.L. Tuggy. Grand Rapids: Eerdmans, 1971. 191p.

'The Philippine Iglesia ni Cristo: a study in independent church dynamics'. A.L. Tuggy. Dissertation, Fuller Theological Seminary, Pasadena (CA), 1974.

'The Sapilada religion: reformation and accommodation among the Igorots of Northern Luzon', F. Eggan & A. Pacyaya, *Southwestern journal of anthropology*, XVIII, 2 (1962).


TABLE 2. —ORGANIZED CHURCHES AND DENOMINATIONS IN THE PHILIPPINES

| Official name 1 | Begun 2 | Type 3 | Counc 4 | Congs 5 | Adults 6 | Affiliated 7 | Names, notes, and other statistics (see Codebook) 8 | | | | |
|---|---|---|---|---|---|---|---|---|---|---|---|
| Advent Christian Church | 1953 | P Adv | xF... | | 800 | 2,000 | M=AAM(ACC)(USA). HQ Lagonglong, Misamis Oriental. 11f,1s. | | | | |
| Alaph Divine Temple | | I mar | ..... | | 50,000 | 90,000 | *Alaph Catolico Filipino*. Split ex RCC. HQ Sagay, Negros Occidental. 1p. | | | | |
| Alpha & Omega Christian Church | 1966 | I pen | ..... | 48 | 280 | 1,000 | M=AOCC(Honolulu,USA). Churches in Ilocos Norte (Luzon). 6n,1s(40),W=75%,180Y. | | | | |
| Anchor Bay Evangelistic Assoc of the P | 1955 | P Pe2 | ..... | | 1,400 | 3,000 | M=ABEA(USA). Fundamentalists. HQ Kabacan, Cotabato. 2p,2s. | | | | |
| Apostolic Church of God Christians | 1964 | I pen | ..... | 16 | 521 | 1,421 | HQ Initao, Misamis Oriental. Indigenous. 20n,G=21.1%pa,W=80%,1010Y,200z. | | | | |
| Apostolic Door of Faith | 1965 | I pen | ..... | 10 | 200 | 500 | Indigenous pentecostals. All members Ilocanos. 6n,G=12.2%pa,1p,W=25%,80Y. | | | | |
| Apostolic Faith Mission | 1962 | P Pe3 | x.... | 24 | 250 | 1,000 | M=AFM(Portland,Oregon,USA). HQ Cabanatuan City. 4n,G=5.7%pa,W=60%,64Y,40z. | | | | |
| Assemblies of Christians | 1956 | I ind | ..... | | 800 | 2,000 | Independent groups with no central organization. HQ Rosales, Pangasinan. | | | | |
| Assemblies of God | 1926 | P Pe2 | ZF... | 1,228 | 71,000 | 150,000 | *Philippine General Council*. M=AoG(USA). Rapid growth. 621n,47f,G=15.6%pa,6s(255). | | | | |
| Assemblies of the Lord Jesus Christ | 1949 | I pel | x.... | 6 | 50 | 800 | M=COLJCAF(USA) Black pentecostals. In central Luzon. 17n,1p,W=80%,506Y,100z. | | | | |
| A of BC in Luzon, Visayas, Mindanao | 1965 | P Bap | .TT.T | 88 | 10,000 | 30,000 | AofBC=Association of Baptist Chs. ABCLVM. Rapidly-growing church-planting body. | | | | |
| Assoc of Bible Chs of the Philippines | 1951 | P int | xM..E | 80 | 900 | 2,000 | *ABCOP*. M=OMF(formerly CIM). HQ Calapan, Oriental Mindoro; also Manila. 51f,1s. | | | | |
| Assoc of Fundamental Baptist Chs in P | 1927 | P Bap | xTT.T | | 16,000 | 40,000 | *Doane Baptists*. M=ABWE(Regular Baptists) (USA). Growing very rapidly. 76f,3h,2s. | | | | |
| Banner of the Race Church | 1936 | I Lib | ..... | | 30,000 | 50,000 | *Iglesia Watawat ng Lahi*. Ex RCC. Catholic-type hierarchy. Rizalist, spiritist. | | | | |
| Baptist Bible Fellowship of the P | 1950 | P Bap | x.T.T | | 4,000 | 10,000 | Fundamentalist Baptists. M=BBFI(USA). HQ Manila. 38f,6s. | | | | |
| Baptist General Conference of the P | 1949 | P Bap | xF..E | 37 | 1,114 | 2,250 | M=BGCA(USA). HQ Cebu. Cebuano. 10n,13x,26f,G=19.3%pa,1s(30),W=65%,210Y,150z. | | | | |
| Believers in Christ | 1957 | I ind | ..... | | 1,010 | 2,000 | HQ Tondo, Manila. Small local grouping of independents. | | | | |
| Bethel Temples | 1952 | P Pen | ..... | 10 | 3,000 | 7,000 | M=Lester Sumrall Evangelistic Association(USA), formerly World Temples. Manila. | | | | |
| Bible Holiness Movement | 1960 | P Hol | x.... | 8 | 237 | 800 | M=Bible Holiness Movement(Canada). Body with holiness doctrines. 6n,W=99%. | | | | |
| Bumila Fellowship of Baptist Churches | 1951 | P Bap | ..... | 32 | 350 | 800 | M=International Missions(USA). On Mindanao. 4n,G=8.0%pa,W=75%,32Y,30z. | | | | |
| **Catholic Church in the Philippines:** | 1521 | R Lat | B.F.R | 1,836 | 16,637,000 | 30,810,093 | *Iglesia Catolica*. C=34+3+66. 6p,16q,21s(1841). 4388nx,1307m,6791w,1143472Yy. | | | | |
| M Gáceres | 1595 | R Lat | Bs | 64 | 586,800 | 1,086,739 | SLuzon. Rural, poor. Strongly Catholic. 1s. | 130 | 1 | 89 | 41338 |
| D Legazpi | 1951 | R Lat | Bs | 55 | 426,400 | 789,610 | SLuzon. Densely populated. Many priests vocations. | 96 | 11 | 55 | 37891 |
| D Masbate | 1968 | R Lat | Bs | 21 | 234,700 | 434,652 | An island. Poor (including priests) exploited. | 25 | 0 | 8 | 17313 |
| D Sorsogón | 1951 | R Lat | Bs | 22 | 211,400 | 391,560 | Southern end of Luzon. Poor, especially priests. | 47 | 0 | 47 | 16439 |
| M Cagayán de Oro | 1933 | R Lat | Bs | 36 | 261,400 | 484,038 | NMindanao. Catholics from Visayan islands. 1s. | 64 | 4 | 94 | 17088 |
| D Butuan | 1967 | R Lat | Bs | 14 | 227,700 | 421,705 | Mindanao. Recent Visayan Christian immigrants. | 30 | 0 | 14 | 14841 |
| D Surigao | 1939 | R Lat | Bs | 30 | 229,000 | 425,000 | Mindanao, northeast coast. Visayan immigrants. | 36 | 7 | 32 | 14834 |
| PN Iligan | 1971 | R Lat | Bs | 18 | 128,300 | 237,577 | Mindanao Moroland. Politico-religious disturbances. | 36 | 4 | 32 | 8794 |
| PN Malaybalay | 1969 | R Lat | Bs | 23 | 193,100 | 357,659 | Primitive pagans in interior of Bukidnon. | 29 | 8 | 23 | 16284 |
| M Cebú | 1595 | R Lat | Bs | 92 | 987,500 | 1,828,759 | M Cebú (Nominis Iesu) Cradle of Christianity. 1s. | 269 | 21 | 201 | 45947 |
| D Borongan | 1960 | R Lat | Bs | 34 | 193,400 | 358,203 | SSamar. Poorest province, isolated. | 44 | 0 | 27 | 13510 |
| D Calbayog | 1910 | R Lat | Bs | 36 | 313,600 | 580,802 | NSamar. Populace very poor but strongly Catholic. | 61 | 8 | 32 | 20997 |
| D Dumaguete | 1955 | R Lat | Bs | 42 | 450,100 | 833,581 | Eastern Negros Is. Developed; rich-poor cleavage. | 79 | 8 | 90 | 29833 |
| D Naasin | 1968 | R Lat | Bs | 26 | 205,000 | 379,000 | SLeyte. Poor, very religious (site of first mass). | 45 | 1 | 42 | 9000 |
| D Palo | 1937 | R Lat | Bs | 54 | 474,000 | 877,865 | NLeyte. Developed. First island christianized. 1s. | 106 | 9 | 66 | 30310 |
| D Tagbilaran | 1941 | R Lat | Bs | 54 | 335,200 | 620,718 | Bohol Island. Strongly religious. | 99 | 1 | 28 | 25897 |
| VA Palawan | 1910 | R Lat | Porsa | 23 | 106,200 | 196,761 | West of Visayas. Many mines. 57 aliens. P=28%. | 36 | 0 | 47 | 8440 |
| M Davao | 1949 | R Lat | Bs | 29 | 446,700 | 827,249 | SMindanao. Catholic immigrants from Luzon. 1s. | 117 | 14 | 209 | 33125 |
| PN Cotabato (1976, D Cotabato) | 1950 | R Lat | Bs | 26 | 350,300 | 648,714 | Southwest Mindanao. Strong Muslim population. 1p. | 59 | 36 | 109 | 20239 |
| PN Marbel | 1960 | R Lat | Bs | 15 | 210,500 | 389,790 | Catholic immigrants from Luzon, Visayas. | 33 | 46 | 85 | 18124 |
| PN Tagum | 1962 | R Lat | Bs | 22 | 305,000 | 565,000 | East Mindanao. Muslims, Catholic immigrants. | 45 | 2 | 56 | 24300 |
| M Jaro | 1865 | R Lat | Bs | 72 | 558,300 | 1,033,934 | SPanay. Mostly very poor. Original RC centre. 1s. | 161 | 5 | 263 | 37179 |
| D Bacolod | 1932 | R Lat | Bs | 47 | 612,700 | 1,134,637 | NNegros. Social unrest due to sugar magnates. 1s. | 183 | 23 | 207 | 29970 |
| D Capiz (M from 1976) | 1951 | R Lat | Bs | 52 | 410,200 | 759,644 | MPanay. Developed farms. Many priest vocations. | 96 | 0 | 32 | 27931 |
| PN San José de Antique | 1962 | R Lat | Bs | 24 | 114,400 | 211,820 | Many sects due to lengthy shortage of priests. | 42 | 16 | 50 | 6851 |
| M Lingayen-Dagupan | 1928 | R Lat | Bs | 57 | 599,500 | 1,110,244 | CLuzon. Rural prosperity. Many Protestant bodies. | 102 | 0 | 68 | 33421 |
| D Cabanatuan | 1963 | R Lat | Bs | 36 | 366,700 | 679,120 | CLuzon. Prosperity and poverty. Little religiosity. | 52 | 0 | 41 | 22827 |
| D San Fernando de la Unión | 1970 | R Lat | Bs | 26 | 177,000 | 328,000 | NWCLuzon. Hocos region, Hocan-speaking. Emigration. | 40 | 4 | 2 | 11407 |
| D Tarlac | 1963 | R Lat | Bs | 27 | 226,700 | 419,831 | Land owned by 2% populace; Huku communist hotbed. | 32 | 3 | 33 | 14970 |
| M Lipa | 1910 | R Lat | Bs | 47 | 479,700 | 888,247 | Near Manila. Very progressive farmers. | 88 | 11 | 168 | 25288 |
| D Lucena | 1950 | R Lat | Bs | 58 | 486,600 | 901,121 | SLuzon. Mountainous, self-supporting. Religious. | 91 | 0 | 120 | 27462 |
| PN Infanta | 1950 | R Lat | Bs | 9 | 59,500 | 110,142 | Eastern coast of Luzon. Poor roads and economy. | 15 | 0 | 22 | 2753 |
| VA Calapan | 1936 | R Lat | Psvd | 28 | 213,900 | 396,090 | Vast Mindoro island, stone-age Mangyans. 1s. P=28%. | 60 | 6 | 38 | 15466 |
| M Manila | 1579 | R Lat | Bs | 150 | 1,988,500 | 3,682,435 | SLuzon. Vast slums, little church action. 2p.2s. | 1069 | 498 | 3062 | 164688 |
| D Imus | 1961 | R Lat | Bs | 27 | 196,600 | 364,057 | Very backward province near Manila. No industry. | 38 | 150 | 79 | 14686 |
| D Malolos | 1961 | R Lat | Bs | 46 | 449,900 | 833,220 | Near Manila. Very developed, industry. | 75 | 9 | 115 | 28750 |
| D San Fernando (M from 1975) | 1948 | R Lat | Bs | 62 | 354,900 | 657,289 | CLuzon. Very developed. Communism began here. | 111 | 3 | 18 | 39976 |
| D San Pablo | 1966 | R Lat | Bs | 45 | 343,300 | 635,723 | SLuzon. Big landowners. Farming. Religious area. | 72 | 80 | 72 | 23111 |
| PN Iba | 1955 | R Lat | Bs | 20 | 117,600 | 217,814 | Coast of western Luzon. No industry, poor farmland. | 38 | 0 | 67 | 14622 |
| VA Mountain Province | 1932 | R Lat | Pcicm | | 175,200 | 324,480 | Montañosa. Mines. 30% pagan. Headhunters. P=36%. | 108 | 293 | 315 | 11815 |
| M Nueva Segovia | 1595 | R Lat | Bs | 34 | 177,300 | 328,307 | Early Catholic area. Farming, backward. 1p,1s. | 72 | 0 | 183 | 6031 |
| D Ilagan | 1970 | R Lat | Bs | 34 | 281,000 | 520,000 | NELuzon. Many immigrants. PIC, Protestants strong. | 40 | 4 | 41 | 13311 |
| D Laoag | 1961 | R Lat | Bs | 24 | 95,800 | 177,337 | NLuzon. Emigration due to poverty. PIC stronghold. | 30 | 0 | 42 | 5200 |
| D Tuguegarao (M from 1974) | 1910 | R Lat | Bs | 34 | 254,700 | 471,740 | Northern end of Luzon. Still mostly uncultivated. | 51 | 2 | 45 | 16000 |
| PN Bangued | 1955 | R Lat | Bs | 19 | 62,300 | 115,327 | NLuzon. Very poor. Hocos; Fingians in mountains. | 38 | 4 | 29 | 3738 |
| PN Batanes & Babuyán Islands | 1950 | R Lat | Bs | 7 | 9,700 | 17,922 | Islands north of Luzon. Marginal subsistence. | 8 | 0 | 10 | 517 |
| PN Bayombong | 1966 | R Lat | Bs | 16 | 78,000 | 145,000 | CLuzon. Undeveloped, moutainous. Immigrant Hocanos. | 16 | 0 | 30 | 4719 |

*Continued opposite*

Table 2 – continued

PHILIPPINES 567

| Official name 1 | Begun 2 | Type 3 | Counc 4 | Congs 5 | Adults 6 | Affiliated 7 | Names, notes, and other statistics (see Codebook) 8 |
|---|---|---|---|---|---|---|---|
| M Zamboanga | 1910 | R Lat | Bs | 41 | 377,100 | 698,376 | WMindanao. Poor. Visayan Catholics, rest Muslims. 76 4 73 35843 |
| D Dipolog | 1967 | R Lat | Bs | 15 | 189,100 | 350,112 | North of Zamboanga. Poor, mountainous, bad roads. 23 1 14 14668 |
| D Ozamis | 1951 | R Lat | Bs | 16 | 120,800 | 223,758 | NMindanao. Catholics Visayan immigrants. 1p. 29 0 65 9409 |
| D Pagadían | 1971 | R Lat | Bs | 13 | 156,000 | 288,884 | New diocese covering east of Zamboanga del Sur. 23 3 13 12362 |
| PN Isabela | 1963 | R Lat | Bs | 6 | 22,000 | 40,000 | Basilian City, island. Badly neglected area. 9 3 4 2555 |
| VA Jolo | 1953 | R Lat | Pomi | 8 | 5,700 | 10,500 | Southwest. Mostly Muslims, with Catholics 2%. P=72%. 14 4 22 402 |
| Children of God | 1965 | I ind | ••••• | 8 | 60 | 300 | Filipinos unrelated to USA body. HQ San Juan, Rizal. 8n,G=35%pa,1p,W=25%,25Y. |
| Chinese Christian Gospel Centre | 1931 | I EBr | x•••• | | 1,000 | 3,000 | *Chu Hui So. Little Flock*. Chinese indigenous body. HQ Santa Cruz, Manila. |
| Christ Jesus' Holy Church | 1958 | I CCa | ••••• | | 3,000 | 7,000 | Indigenous Catholic-type body, split ex Church of Rome. HQ Sta Maria, Pangasinan. |
| Christian & Missionary Alliance Chs | 1902 | P Hol | xF••E | 611 | 16,724 | 56,354 | M=CMA(USA). 1,000 Indonesians. 101n,45f,G=4.9%pa,1h,3p,1s(12),W=73%,500Y,5142z. |
| Christian Catholic Ch (Evangelical) | 1947 | P Con | x•••• | 25 | 2,000 | 3,500 | M=CCC(Zion City,Illinois,USA). Congregationalist polity. HQ Ormoc City. 1p. |
| Christian Ecumenical Faith of the P | 1966 | I ReC | ••••• | | 3,000 | 10,000 | Filipino attempt to unite all Catholic and Protestant churches in world. 55nm. |
| Christian Evangelical Mission | 1950 | P int | ••••• | 129 | 12,000 | 20,000 | HQ Davao City. M=Midwest Evangelistic Assoc(USA). 94n,G=8.0%pa,1p,W=99%,104Y,60z. |
| Christian Mission in the Far East | 1946 | I ind | ••••E | | 9,500 | 20,000 | An indigenous Filipino pioneer mission organization. HQ Singalong, Manila. 1p. |
| Christian Missions in the Philippines | 1922 | P CBr | x•••• | 20 | 1,600 | 3,000 | *Christian Brethren. Plymouth (Open) Brethren*. M=CMML(USA,NZ,UK). HQ Rizal. 26f. |
| Christian Reformed Church of the P | 1962 | P Ref | xF••• | 8 | 150 | 225 | M=CRC(USA). HQ Bacolod City. 3x,12f,G=32%pa,1s(7),W=98%,40Y,25z. |
| Christian Settlement Association | 1945 | I EBr | ••••• | | 3,000 | 7,000 | *Christohanon*. A Filipino version of the Chinese Little Flock. Rapid growth. |
| Christian Spiritist Union of the P | 1920 | I Spi | ••••• | | 50,000 | 100,000 | *Union Espiritista Cristiana de Filipinas*. Spiritualist body. HQ Malabon, Rizal. |
| Christian Union for True Knowledge | 1950 | I mar | ••••• | | 675 | 2,000 | *CUTK and Spiritual Living*. Indigenous body, marginal doctrines. HQ Dagupan City. |
| Church Founded by JC in the Far East | 1923 | I ind | ••••• | | 500 | 1,000 | *Iglesia ng Itinayo ni Jesucristo sa Malayong Silangan*. HQ Cabanatuan City. |
| Church of Christ | 1913 | I ind | x•••• | 3,000 | 400,000 | 1,500,000 | *INC. Iglesia ni Cristo* (*Manalista*). 35 cathedrals, 2 radio stations. 1902n. |
| Church of Christ upon the Rock | 1932 | I Adv | ••••• | 7 | 200 | 300 | *Iglesia ni Cristo sa Ibabaw ng Bato*. Declining: G=–5.4%pa. 7n,1p,1s(2),W=60%,23Y. |
| Church of Christ (Matt 16.18) in the P | 1949 | I ind | ••••• | | 800 | 2,000 | Indigenous body based on Tondo, Manila; independents. 1p. |
| Church of Christ, Scientist | | M Sci | x•••• | 3 | 100 | 300 | *Christian Science*. M=CCS(Boston,USA). In Manila and Baguio. |
| Ch of Father of Fathers & Mother of Ms | 1951 | I mar | ••••• | | 10 000 | 15,457 | Ms=Mothers. *Samahan ng Amang Ka-Amahan at Inang Ka-Inainahan*. Rizalist. Bongabon. |
| Church of God | 1956 | I ind | ••••• | | 1,000 | 2,000 | *Iglesia ng Dios*. Indigenous group in Manila. |
| Church of God in Christ Jesus | 1922 | I ind | ••••• | | 15,000 | 30,000 | *Iglesia ng Dios kay Kristo Jesus*. Indigenous group based on Tondo, Manila. |
| Church of God of Prophecy | 1952 | P Pe3 | Z•••• | 10 | 3,200 | 7,000 | M=CGP(USA). Mission split in USA from CoG (Cleveland)(USA). HQ Ilocos Sur. 2f. |
| Church of God (Anderson) | 1963 | P Hol | x•••• | 10 | 300 | 1,000 | M=CoG(Anderson)(USA). HQ Valenzuela, Bulacan. No missionaries remain. 3n,W=17%. |
| Church of God (Ecclesiae Dei) | 1957 | I pen | ••••E | 132 | 60,000 | 83,000 | Indigenous pentecostals. 300n,10x,G=8.4%pa,1s(300),W=70%,5000Y,5000z. |
| Church of God (Seventh-day) | | P Adv | x•••• | | 1,000 | 2,000 | M=CGSD(USA). Mission from one of several small USA bodies using same name. |
| Church of Jesus Christ New Jerusalem | 1918 | I ind | ••••• | | 30,000 | 50,000 | *Iglesia ni Jesucristo Bagong Jerusalem*. Indigenous body based on Tondo, Manila. |
| Ch of Jesus C of Latter-day Saints | 1955 | M LdS | x•••• | | 6,500 | 11,625 | *Mormons*. M=CJCLdS. HQ Pasay City. Many Filipino missionaries abroad. 240f,G=12%pa. |
| Church of the Holy Trinity | 1952 | I pen | ••••• | | 1,000 | 2,000 | Indigenous pentecostal group based on Cebu City. |
| Church of the Living God | 1962 | I pen | ••••• | 265 | 60,000 | 100,000 | *Iglesia ti Dios a Sibibiag. Revival Fellowship*. Daily radio ministry. 126n,2p. |
| Church of the Nazarene | 1942 | P Hol | xF••• | 93 | 1,076 | 6,000 | M=CoN(USA). Across nation. 21n,8x,28mw,13f,G=19.7%pa,2s(60),93t(4948),W=37%,350z. |
| Churches of Christ | 1901 | P Dis | x•••• | 51 | 1,200 | 2,500 | M=CCCC(USA). Rejected 1948 UCCP merger. Luzon, Mindanao. 24n,22f,1s(19),W=90%,151Y. |
| Churches of Christ (New Testament) | 1966 | I ind | ••••• | | 5,600 | 10,000 | One of many indigenous Churches of Christ groupings. HQ Caloocan City. |
| Churches of Christ, Philippine Mission | 1924 | P Dis | x•••• | 150 | 54,000 | 100,000 | *Wolfe Group* (split ex Disciples). M=CC(USA). Growing very rapidly. 21f,2p. |
| Conservative Baptist Assoc of the P | 1952 | P Bap | xF••E | 45 | 1,903 | 5,713 | *CBAP*. M=CBFMS(USA). Tagalog-speaking. 19n,9x,35f,G=19.3%pa,1p,1s(25),W=46%,189Y. |
| Convention of Philippine Baptist Chs | 1900 | P Bap | T•••W | 359 | 33,331 | 60,000 | M=ABFMS(USA). Organized 1935. 2 schools. 66n,5x,16f,2H,1h,1p,1s(19),1v,1499Y. |
| Crusaders of the Divine Ch of Christ | 1955 | I ind | ••••• | 750 | 100,000 | 300,000 | Very rapid expansion. HQ Pangasinan. 60% Ilocano. 200n,G=25%pa, 1p(3),W=66%,3000Y. |
| Davao Fell of Fundamental Baptist Chs | 1952 | P Bap | •TT•T | 20 | 1,000 | 2,000 | Regular Baptists. Fundamentalists. HQ Davao City. 11n,G=10.8%pa,W=85%,50Y. |
| Divine Filipino Catholic Church | 1954 | I CCa | ••••• | 15 | 5,000 | 10,000 | Aglipayan. Widespread. HQ Valenzuela, Bulacan. 15n,G=18%pa,5s(20),W=80%,800Y,1000z. |
| Divine Trinity of Jesus (Catholic Ch) | 1962 | I CCa | ••••• | | 7,000 | 15,000 | Indigenous Catholic-type body, Catholic elements. HQ San Francisco, Agusan. |
| Edified Church of Jesus Christ | 1956 | I ind | ••••• | | 12,000 | 20,000 | *Iglesia Edificada de Jesucristo*. Independents. HQ Malabon, Rizal. |
| Equifrilibricum World Religion | 1925 | I mar | ••••• | | 8,000 | 16,000 | *Equality-Fraternity-Liberty Church. Moncadistas*. Begun 1925 by Filipinos in USA. |
| Ev Christian Catholic Apostolic Ch | 1957 | I CCa | ••••• | | 500 | 1,000 | Indigenous group in Davao City. Catholic features, beliefs and rituals. |
| Evangelical Church of Christ | 1956 | I ind | ••••• | 8 | 400 | 600 | Small Filipino indigenous group. On Mindanao, Cebu. 11n,1x,G=8.1%pa,W=75%,20Y. |
| Evangelical Church of God | 1955 | P ind | ••••• | | 2,140 | 4,000 | *Philippine District Council*. M=Ev Bible Ch(Maryland,USA). 1p. |
| Evangelical Church of God | 1928 | I pen | ••••• | 175 | 10,000 | 20,000 | One of many pentecosal bodies. Declining. HQ Cotabato. 50n,1p,1s,W=85%,95Y,1000z. |
| Evangelical Free Philippine Church | 1951 | P Con | KF••E | 12 | 181 | 750 | *EFPC*. M=EFCA(USA). First pastors 1969. 2n,4x,14f,G=38%pa,1p(5),W=53%,46Yy,30z. |
| Evangelical Full Gospel Revival Center | 1965 | I pen | ••••• | 80 | 5,000 | 7,000 | Indigenous pentecostal group based on Davao City. 10n,G=22.2%pa,1s(57),600Y,5000z. |
| Evangelical Methodist Church in the P | 1909 | I Met | VWE•W | 68 | 25,000 | 70,000 | *IEMELIF. Iglesia Ev Metodista en las Islas F*. First Filipino schism. HQ Tondo. 1p. |
| Evangelical Spiritist Church | 1946 | I Spi | ••••• | | 500 | 1,000 | *Iglesia Evangelica Espiritista*. Spiritualist group in Caloocan City. |
| Far Eastern Gospel Crusade | 1947 | P ind | xM••E | 39 | 1,300 | 2,500 | M=FEGC(USA). Members Tagalog-speaking. 25n,84f,G=8.4%pa,1H,2s(40),W=76%,163Y,200z. |
| Filipino Christian Church | 1928 | I ReC | ••••• | | 500 | 1,500 | Indigenous group based on Quezon City. Catholic beliefs and practices. |
| Free Methodist Ch in the Philippines | 1949 | P Hol | VF••E | 25 | 927 | 3,000 | M=FMC(USA). Members Cebuano, Samareno, Manobo. 20n,10f,1s(25),W=83%,222Y,250z. |
| General Baptist Ch of the Philippines | 1957 | P Bap | TF••E | 21 | 921 | 1,147 | M=GBFMS(USA). HQ Davao City. 19n,9x,G=12.1%pa,3s(48),W=70%,37Y,142z. |
| Glorious Seventh-day Adventist Mission | 1921 | I Adv | ••••• | | 800 | 2,000 | *Iglesia Adventista del Septimo Dia Glorioso*. Schism ex SDAs. HQ Manila. |
| God of the World Association | 1952 | I mar | ••••• | | 4,000 | 8,000 | *Ang Bathala ng Daigdig Asosasyon*. Based on Tondo, Manila. Marginal in doctrine. |
| God, Mysterious Mother | 1948 | I mar | ••••• | | 100,000 | 200,000 | *Bathalismo* (*Inang Mahiwaga*). Large Rizalist movement. HQ Nueva Ecija. |
| Good Shepherd's Fold | 1946 | I Bap | ••••• | 20 | 200 | 1,200 | Radio station, M=FEBC(USA). HQ Buenavista, Iloilo. 2n,G=5.9%pa, 2p,W=99%,26Y,180z. |
| Gospel Mission | 1960 | I ind | ••••• | 10 | 1,000 | 2,000 | Indigenous grouping. HQ Valenzuela, Bulacan. 4n,G=20.1%pa,W=25%,25Y,100z. |
| Grace & Truth Tabernacle | 1936 | I pen | ••••• | 32 | 2,000 | 5,000 | Open-air crusades begun 1969. HQ Mlang, Cotabato. 10n,G=5.9%pa,1p,W=50%,450Y,200z. |
| Grace Gospel Church of Christ | 1958 | P Adv | ••••• | 112 | 2,000 | 5,000 | M=Things to Come Mission(USA). HQ Ozamis City. 8f,2p. |
| Grace Gospel Church of Manila | 1952 | I Bap | ••••E | 1 | 250 | 760 | Chinese body. Sends out Grace Mission, 33 missionaries. 1n,G=4.6%pa,W=66%,74Y,10z. |
| Holy Stone of Cath Apost Ch of Spirit | 1938 | I Lib | ••••• | | 878 | 2,000 | Began among migrant settlers from the Visayas to Davao province. HQ Mati, Davao. |
| Independent Ch of Filipino Christians | 1946 | I Lib | ••••• | | 1,000 | 1,700 | *Fonacier Group*. Schism ex Philippine Independent Ch by deposed primate Fonacier. |
| Independent Republican Christian Ch | c1960 | I ind | ••••• | 50 | 10,000 | 50,000 | Rapidly-growing indigenous group. 20n,G=38.0%pa,2p,1s(20),1000Y,2000z. |
| Internat Ch of the Foursquare Gospel | 1927 | P Pe2 | ZF••E | 450 | 15,661 | 25,000 | M=ICFG(USA). Rapid growth. 213n,5x,13f,G=6.6%pa,11p,3s(117),W=74%,3197Y,7716z. |
| Jehovah's Witnesses | 1912 | M Jeh | x•••• | 1,380 | 56,078 | 150,000 | *Watch Tower*. Active witnessing by 1929. Rapid growth. G=9.7%pa,1j,6224Y. |
| Kingdom of God through Jesus Christ | 1958 | I ind | ••••• | | 200 | 1,000 | Indigenous body. HQ Butuan City. Baptism not until 30 years of age. 3n,3p,W=50%. |
| Light & Spirit of Truth | 1907 | I mar | ••••• | | 10,000 | 20,000 | *Tipan ng Panginoon*. Marginal group based on Caloocan City. |
| Lutheran Church in the Philippines | 1946 | P Lut | L•••W | 114 | 3,059 | 10,200 | *LCP*. M=LCMS(USA). A=1963. Radio, TV. 17n,20x,30f,G=5.3%pa,1s(11),612Yy,624z. |
| National Catholic Apostolic Church | 1930 | I CCa | ••••• | 102 | 800 | 35,000 | *Iglesia Catolica Apostolica Nacional*. Ex RCC. HQ Cabanatuan City. 85n,1s(7),250Yy. |
| National Catholic Church | 1930 | I CCa | ••••• | | 5,400 | 10,000 | *Iglesia Catolica Nacional*. Catholic-type body based on Ormoc City, Leyte. |
| National Schismatic Church of the P | 1938 | I CCa | ••••• | | 5,400 | 10,000 | *Iglesia Cismatica Filipina Nacional*. Schism ex Ch of Rome, Misamis Occidental. |
| New Testament Church of God | 1947 | P Pe3 | ZF••• | 192 | 8,192 | 17,000 | M=Ch of God(Cleveland)(USA). 140 churches, 52 missions. 250n,6f,3s. |
| New Tribes Mission of the Philippines | 1951 | P int | x•••E | 89 | 872 | 2,967 | M=NTM(USA). Work among jungle tribes. 10n,20x,62f,G=13.8%pa,1h,1p,W=95%,66Y,348z. |
| Oriental Missionary Crusade | 1958 | P Pen | ••••• | | 5,000 | 10,000 | Pentecostals with USA links. M=OMC(USA). HQ Sampaloc, Manila. 40m,3f. |
| Patriotic Ch of Our Lord Jesus Christ | 1938 | I pen | ••••• | 83 | 30,000 | 40,000 | *Iglesia Patriota de Nuestro Senor JC*. Rizalist. 45n,G=3.7%pa,1s(20),W=27%,500Y. |
| Pentecostal Bible Way Church | 1948 | I pel | ••••• | 16 | 300 | 1,000 | M=BWCOLJCWW(USA Black pentecostals). 5n,G=31.6%pa,1p,W=50%,50Y. |
| Pentecostal Church of God of the P | 1950 | P Pe2 | Z•••• | 160 | 1,000 | 3,000 | M=PCG(USA). Classical Pentecostals. HQ Caudon, Ilocos Sur. 2 schools. 4f. |
| Pente Ev Assembly of Christ Elect | 1962 | I pen | ••••• | | 2,000 | 4,000 | Pente=Pentecostal. Indigenous Filipino pentecostal group based on Quezon City. |
| People's Missionary Church | 1964 | I pen | ••••• | 15 | 570 | 1,500 | Indigenous churches around HQ Sampaloc, Manila. 8n,G=17.0%pa,1p,W=90%,65Y,18z. |
| Philippine Baptist Mission | 1948 | P Bap | T•••E | 300 | 14,492 | 30,000 | M=SBC(USA). Rapid growth. 6 schools. 152n,98f,G=9.5%pa,1H,1h,1p,1s(67),2138Y. |
| Philippine Church (Adarnista) | 1901 | I mar | ••••• | | 8,000 | 15,000 | *Iglesia Filipina* (*Adarnistas*). Followers of bishop Adarna. Rizalist. HQ La Union. |
| Philippine Episcopal Church | 1901 | A ACa | awEAW | 268 | 24,283 | 63,276 | *PEC. Igl Epis*. M=PECUSA. 3 Dioceses. 83n,9x,15f,G=0.9%pa,3H,12r,1u(135),147Y,1875y. |
| **Philippine Independent Church** | 1890 | I ReC | UWEAW | 3,400 | 1,860,000 | 3,500,000 | *PIC. Iglesia Filipina Independiente*. Ex RCC. Many breakoffs. 470n,1u(with PEC). |
| Philippine Missionary Fellowship | 1956 | I ind | ••••E | | 2,000 | 4,000 | An indigenous Filipino pioneer mission organization. HQ Silang, Cavite. 1p. |
| Philippine Unitarian Church | 1955 | I Lib | ••••• | | 500 | 1,000 | Catholic-type independent church; unitarian doctrines. HQ Urdaneta, Pangasinan. |
| Sacred Church of the Race | 1949 | I mar | ••••• | 40 | 18,000 | 35,000 | *Iglesia Sagrada ng Lahi*. Christian rites, traditional beliefs, Rizalist. HQ Tondo. |
| Sacred Philippine Ch of the 5 Vowels | 1926 | I mar | ••••• | | 550 | 1,000 | *SPC5V and Virtues. Iglesia Sagrada Filipina*. Rizalist. HQ Candelaria, Quezon. |
| Salvation Army | 1937 | P Sal | xwE•W | 79 | 6,526 | 20,000 | *Hukbo ng Kaligtasan. SA, Philippines Command*. Officers 64, 1 girls' home, 1s. |
| Seventh-day Adventist Church | 1906 | P Adv | x•••• | 1,194 | 139,138 | 200,000 | *C,N&S Philip Unions*. 4 launches. 190n,30f,G=9.9%pa,6H,3h,1j,18r,2s,2027t,10211Y. |
| Seventh-day Adventist Reform Movement | 1957 | P Adv | x•••• | | 515 | 1,000 | M=SDARM(USA). Schism ex SDAs. HQ Manila. World HQ Charlottenlund, Denmark. |
| Teachings of God the Father | 1953 | I mar | ••••• | | 5,000 | 10,000 | *Pagtulun-an sa Dios nga Amahan* (*Iglesia ni Tinago*). San Carlos, Negros Occidental. |
| Temple of God, Jehovah's Witnesses JC | 1960 | I Jeh | ••••• | | 500 | 1,000 | JC=for Jesus Christ. *Templo ng Dios* (*Mga Saksi ni Jehovah kay Kristo Jesus*). Rizal. |
| The Church, the Body of Christ | 1966 | I ind | ••••• | | 869 | 2,000 | Indigenous group in Pagadian, Zamboanga del Sur. |
| The Rock, Christ Jesus | 1957 | I mar | ••••• | | 2,000 | 4,000 | *White Rock*. Rizalist tendencies. HQ Rizal, Zamboanga del Norte. |
| True Spiritual Ch of the Holy Spirit | 1904 | I Spi | ••••• | | 3,000 | 6,000 | *Iglesia Espirita Veridica del Espiritu Santo*. HQ Caloocan City. Spiritists. |
| United Church of Christ in the P | 1899 | P uni | WWE•W | 1,600 | 211,053 | 500,000 | 1948 union 4 bodies. M=PInterboard Comm(USA). 342n,47f,G=1.6%pa,10H,16r,2s,1u,1v. |
| United Evangelical Church of Christ | 1931 | I ind | •v••W | | 7,000 | 15,000 | *Iglesia Ev Unida de Cristo*. Filipino attempt at united church. 1973 applied to WCC. |
| United Evangelical Church (Reformed) | 1929 | I ind | ••••• | | 15,000 | 30,000 | Chinese independent indigenous church. HQ Manila. 1p. |
| United Filipino Church | 1962 | I CCa | ••••• | 14 | 8,000 | 25,000 | *Iglesia Filipinista*. Expanding. HQ Labazon. 4n,G=14.9%pa,1s(7),W=63%,1800Yy,5000z. |
| United Methodist Church in the P | 1899 | P Met | VwE•W | 1,500 | 130,000 | 300,000 | *Philippines Central Conf*, *UMC*(USA). 6 Annual Confs. 750n,33f,5H,1j,2p,14r,1u. |
| United Pentecostal Church | 1957 | P Pel | x•••• | 520 | 15,000 | 40,000 | *Jesus Only Ch*. M=UPC(USA). Unitarians. HQ Pampanga. 1 school. 220n,52m,8f,4p(98). |
| Universal Church of Christ | 1924 | P ind | ••••• | | 500 | 1,000 | *Iglesia Universal de Cristo* (*Carlson Group*). Mission from USA. HQ Cebu City. |
| Universal Family of Yahweh of the FB | 1956 | I pen | ••••• | 25 | 1,000 | 2,000 | FB=Firstborn. Pentecostal, holiness. HQ Manila. 25n,W=60%,70Yy. |
| Universalist Church of the Philippines | 1955 | M Unt | I•••• | | 2,000 | 4,000 | M=Unitarian Universalist Association (USA). HQ San Carlos, Negros Occidental. |
| Visayan Associated Gospel Chs of the P | 1948 | P Bap | ••••• | 23 | 1,000 | 2,000 | M=Associated Gospel M(USA). HQ Cauayan. 2n,G=7.4%pa,1p,2r,W=80%,270Y,250z. |
| Way of Salvation Church of the P | 1948 | I pen | ••••• | 27 | 5,000 | 10,000 | M=WSC(founded Honolulu,Hawaii). HQ Narvacan, Ilocos Sur. 4n,G=10.8%pa,1p,W=85%. |
| Wesleyan Church of the Philippines | 1932 | P Hol | VF••E | 100 | 2,612 | 6,550 | 1936 Pilgrim Holiness(USA), 1950 WMC; 1968 union. 42n,5x,11f,G=12.4%pa,3p,W=46%,222Y. |
| Other Filipino indigenous churches | | I | ••••• | | 20,000 | 50,000 | Total about 250 (see list below). |
| Other Protestant denominations | | P | ••••• | | 7,000 | 13,000 | Total about 50 (see list below), including USA military chaplaincies. |
| Other marginal Protestant bodies | | M | ••••• | | 500 | 1,000 | Incl: New Ch, Reorganized Ch of Jesus Christ of Latter-day Saints (on Pangasinan). |
| Other Catholic (non-Roman) churches | | C | ••••• | | 300 | 500 | Including: New Apost Ch (Germany), and a few related to European episcopi vagantes. |
| Doubly-affiliated (duplication)(1970) | | | | | –2,876,500 | –5,375,088 | Evangelicals, Aglipayans and others who also are or were baptized Roman Catholics. |
| **Total affiliated (mid-1970)** | | | | 26,300 | 17,700,198 | 34,042,000 | **Total denominations (1970) . . . 430.** |
| **Total affiliated (mid-1975)** | | | | 30,100 | 20,817,800 | 40,038,000 | **Total denominations (1975) . . . 460.** |
| **Total affiliated (mid-1980)** | | | | 36,200 | 24,401,300 | 46,930,000 | **Total denominations (1980) . . . 490.** |

**NOTES ON TABLE ABOVE**
COLUMNS: for meanings and CODES (cols. 1, 3, 4, 8): see Codebook (Part 6). Column 1: **Boldface type** = church with over 10% of country's affiliated Christians.
**NATIONAL COUNCILS (Column 4, 5th letter).**
E = Philippines Council of Evangelical Churches (PCEC).
R = Catholic Bishops' Conference of the Philippines (CBCP).
T = Philippine Council of Fundamental Evangelical Churches.
W = National Council of Churches in the Philippines (NCCP) (Sangguniang Pambansa ng mga Simbahan sa Pilipinas).
*Other national councils.* Joint Council of the Philippine Episcopal Church & the Philippine Independent Church.
OTHER FILIPINO INDIGENOUS CHURCHES. The table lists 69 bodies with 1,000 or more adherents, and 6 with under 1,000. In addition, there are over 250 other Filipino indigenous churches, about 180 being small bodies with under 1,000 but over 100 adherents. These latter include: Apostolic Philippine Pentecostal Mission, Association of the Holy Family, Association of Three Persons One God, Brotherhood of Faith, Christian Brethren of the Gospel of St John, Ch in the Community, Ch of Christ (Pilipino Movement), Ch of God Christ Buildeth, Ch of God (Acts 20.28), Ch of Liberty, Ch of Philadelphia, Ch of the Holy Family, Ch of the Mystic City of God, Churches of the Saints, Ev Catholic Ch of the Philippines, Free Faith Organisation, God of Truth Ch, Holy Catholic Apostolic Christian Ch, Independent Ch of Free Independent Christians (Unitarian), Independent Filipino Ch of the Most Holy Trinity (c1935 schism ex Philippine Independent Ch), Kingdom of God, March of Faith (begun 1970 ex AoG), Moncadian Ch of God, Mystic Ch of the Philippines, New Testament Ch, Philippine Liberal Ch, Sacred Family of God, Spirit and Life, Spiritual Filipino Catholic Ch, Temple of the Holy Spirit, True Ch, Universal Christian Ch, Universal Dei Ecclesia, World Christian Movement.
OTHER PROTESTANT DENOMINATIONS. The table gives bodies with 200 or more adherents (total 48). In addition, there are over 40 others including: American Baptist Association (1961), Assembly of Yahvah, Berean Mission (1952), Bethany Fellowship Missions (1971), Bethany Home, Bible Protestant Ch of the Philippines, Christadelphian Ecclesias, Christian Ch of North America, Christian Nationals Evangelism Commission (1968), Church of God (Abrahamic Faith), Free Gospel Ch, International Missions (1951), Liebenzell Mission (1970), Missionary Ch, Peniel Chs of VOCA (Voice of China & Asia MS, 1948), Philippine Miracle Missions, Slavic Gospel Association, Union Ch of Manila, United Followers of Christ Ch, United World Mission (1946), World Baptist Fellowship Mission Agency (1972), World-Wide Missions (1962). In addition to these bodies with Filipino membership, there were in 1970 about 10,000 Protestants in USA military chaplaincies.
OTHER MARGINAL PROTESTANT BODIES. The Reorganized Ch of Jesus Christ of Latter-day Saints (USA) maintains a small work based on Pangasinan (283 members); and the New Ch (Swedenborgian) has a society in Malabon, Rizal.

**PEOPLES** (ethnolinguistic). Christians: 30.8% Visayan (Cebuano), 23.0% Tagalog, 11.7% Ilocan, 10.4% Hiligaynon (Ilongo), 7.8% Bicol, 3.2% Pampango (Pampangan), 3.0% Euronesian (Eurasian, Mestizo), 2.8% Pangasinan, 1.4% Ibanag, 1.0% Chinese-Filipino, 0.5% Bukidnon, 0.4% Chinese, 0.2% Bontoc, 0.1% Palawan, USA White, Spaniard, Indonesian, Sulu-Samal, et alii.

**COUNTRY-WIDE TOTALS**
EVANGELIZATION (see Part 5). 1900: 93%. 1970: 98%. 1980: 99%. *Mass evangelism.* Among the many recent campaigns and events: Billy Graham 1956 rally, and in 1963 a 3-week crusade in Davao, Iloilo City, Manila and Cebu (175,000 attenders, 4,641 enquirers); 1970, Philippines Congress on Evangelism; 1973, 'Christ the Only Way' 3-day total mobilization event (Overseas Crusades; 2,000 CORE groups meeting weekly for fellowship, each CORE member in turn leading one Lay Evangelistic Group Study (LEGS), these numbering 3,000; 55 supporting denominations; aim, to establish 1,000 new churches); 1973, launching of Operation 200, to form 200 new churches by 1981, February-August 1974, One Way '74 mass campaign in 20 key cities, with results followed by up 5,000 CORE groups and 10,000 LEGS; 1976–77, Here's Life Manila (and other cities; run by CCCI; 209,830 responses and 9,242 decisions); 1976, Christ for Greater Manila showed films to over 112,000 persons, with 5,000 enquirers; November 1977, Billy Graham 5-day crusade in Manila (412,000 attenders, 22,512 enquirers). *Radiophonic evangelism.* Annual listeners' letters (1975): 12,000 FEBC, Radio Vatican, et alia. Bible correspondence courses: there are many agencies, the largest being FEBC (1.5 million enrolments) and ICI (50,230 enrolments, 38,375 active, 17,420 conversions reported). *Film evangelism.* Philippines Action International Ministries: (1977) 143,797 attenders, 8,262 decisions.
FOREIGN MISSIONARIES AND PERSONNEL (nationals serving abroad) (1973). Total 1,159 in 38 countries including USA: about 850 Roman Catholics, 135 Protestants, 94 marginal Protestants (Mormons, Jehovah's Witnesses) in Hong Kong, Japan, Korea, New Zealand, Samoa et alia, about 80 Filipino indigenous in Guam, Indonesia, Malaysia, USA, Viet Nam et alia. By 1977 Protestant and indigenous sending agencies were rapidly increasing their totals of personnel sent abroad.
FOREIGN MISSIONARIES AND PERSONNEL (aliens from abroad) (1973). Total 5,990. *From Western world.* 5,732: about 4,180 Roman Catholics, 1,287 Protestants (1,140 in 87 USA societies, 55 in 5 Canada societies, 32 in 4 UK societies, 24 in 7 Australia societies, 21 in 10 New Zealand societies, 9 in 2 WGermany societies, 4 in 3 Netherlands societies, 2 in 1 Finland society), about 250 marginal Protestants (210 Mormons from USA), 15 Anglicans in 1 USA society. *From Communist world.* About 6 Roman Catholics (4 from Yugoslavia, 2 Poland). *From Third World.* 252: about 200 Roman Catholics from 12 countries, 20 Protestants (3 in 1 South Africa society, 2 from Japan, Singapore), about 20 marginal Protestants (Mormons), 10 indigenous from Hong Kong and Taiwan, 2 Anglicans.
INSTITUTIONS (church-operated) (1973). Total 1,490, including 1,100 higher schools (47 minor seminaries), about 180 medical centres, 30 radio stations, 33 religious communities, 7 research centres, 107 seminaries (49 Protestant, 37 RC, 20 Filipino indigenous, 1 Anglican), 11 universities.
PERIODICALS. About 170 titles (70 Protestant (16 SDA), 50 RC, many Filipinos indigenous).
PERSONNEL. About 33,090 (27,100 national, 5,990 foreign).
RELIGIOUS LIBRARIES. About 195.
SCRIPTURE DISTRIBUTION (1975). Annual totals: 177,138 Bibles (15% free, 28% subsidized, 57% commercial), 1,306,303 NTs (53% free, 16% subsidized, 31% commercial), 524,418 UBS portions, 11,492,392 UBS selections. *Translations completed.* Portion: 66 languages since 1887. NT: 10 languages since 1902. Bible: 8 languages since 1905.
SERVICE AGENCIES. About 190, including ACMI, AMRSMP, AMRSWP, CBCP, CCCI, CEAP, CEF, CFM, CLC, CWLP, CWS, FABC, FEBC, FFF, FFW, ISO, IVCF, JARS, LIT-LIT, LWR, MAF, NAFE, NASSA, NCCP, NCPF, NFCB, NFSW, OC, OCSC, OIEC, PABATS, PAFTEE, PATS, PCEC, PISA, PPI, PTL, SATC, SCA, SCM, SEARSOLIN, SIL, SU, UNDA, VERTA, WBT, WLC(EHC), WVI, YCS, YCW, YLAC, YLC, YMCA, YWAM, YWCA.

**ADDITIONAL DATA ON CHURCHES**
CATHOLIC CHURCH IN THE PHILIPPINES. *New jurisdictions.* In 1974, D Tuguegarao became M Tuguegarao with as suffragans D Ilagan, PN Batanes and PN Bayombong. In 1975, D San Fernando became M San Fernando. New dioceses: created in 1974, Daet, Virac; in 1975, Balanga, Catarman, Romblon; in 1976, Kalibo. In 1976, D Capiz became M Capiz; PN Cotabato became D Cotabato; and PN Kidapawan was created. In 1977, D Boac was erected, and PN Marawi was created. *Catholics.* Including 80,838 Chinese (1966), rising to 104,000 in 1975, and to 121,581 by 1977. *Catechumens* (jurisdictions under Propaganda only). (1959) 3,535; (1961) 2,066; (1963) 3,594. *Annual baptisms.* (1972) 97.6% infant, 2.4% adult. *Priests.* Total includes 2,264 religious priests (482 Filipino, 1,782 expatriate). *Brothers.* Including 216 Filipinos. *Sisters.* Including 5,325 Filipino sisters. *Catholic charismatics* (January 1974). 15,000 adults including many religious personnel (100 priests, 500 nuns) are active in over 200 prayer groups in the Charismatic Renewal. *Seminarians* (1972). 1,841 secular, 728 religious. *Catechists.* Total (1974) about 12,000, with 1,220 in the 4 jurisdictions under Propaganda. *Indigenous religious congregations.* Sisters: Religious of the Virgin Mary (begun 1684, now with 559 professed), Augustinian Sisters of the Philippines (begun 1883; 278), Religiosas Dominicas de Sta Catalina de Sena (begun 1706; 249), Augustinian Recollect Sisters (begun 1719; 240), Oblates of Notre Dame (begun 1956; 101), Missionary Catechists of St Theresa (begun 1963; 74), Order of St Clare (begun 1621; 63), Missionary Daughters of St Theresa (begun 1960; 52), Sisters of the Immaculate Heart of Mary (begun 1952; 38), Franciscan Apostolic Sisters (begun 1953; 33), Order of the Most Blessed Virgin of Mt Carmel (Ancient Observance; begun 1958; 22), Missionary Sisters of Mary (begun 1958; 21), Poor Sisters of St Francis of Perpetual Adoration (begun 1962; 20), Dominican Sisters of the Most Holy Rosary of the Philippines (begun 1925; 18), Congregation of Our Lady of the Retreat in the Cenacle (begun 1967; 15), Sisters of Our Lady of La Salette (begun 1968; 6), Missionary Catechists of the Holy Infant Jesus. *Main foreign orders and congregations.* Priests (with over 160 professed in 1970): 430 SVD, 373 SJ, 259 SSC, 254 CICM, 234 OMI, 175 OP, 147 OFM, 140 SDB, 138 ORSA, 120 MSC, 114 CM. Brothers (with over 100 professed in 1970): 112 FSC. Sisters (with over 200 professed in 1970): 676 Sisters of St Vincent de Paul, 409 Daughters of Charity of St Vincent de Paul, 328 Missionary Sisters Servants of the Holy Spirit, 315 Missionary Sisters of the Immaculate Heart of Mary, 259 Order of the Most Blessed Virgin of Mt Carmel, 247 Missionary Benedictine Sisters, 206 Franciscan Missionaries of Mary, 206 Franciscan Sisters of the Immaculate Conception, 202 Religiosas Misioneras de Sto Domingo.
*Catholic organizations.* There is a Catholic Bishops' Conference of the Philippines (CBCP), which is a member of FABC, and 2 organizations of religious personnel: Association of Major Religious Superiors of Men in the Philippines (AMRSMP) and Association of Major Religious Superiors of Women in the Philippines (AMRSWP). For the armed forces, the Philippines forms a military vicariate. There is no official council of priests. The main national mandated lay organizations, co-ordinated by the National Secretariat of Catholic Action, include the following: Association of the Children of Mary Immaculate, Barangay San Virgen (an organization of voluntary catechists), Catholic Women's League of the Philippines, Christian Family Movement, Daughters of Isabela, Knights of Columbus, Legion of Mary, Society of St Vincent de Paul, Sodality of Our Lady, Student Catholic Action, YCW (boys), YCW (girls), and Young Ladies Association of Charity.
The Holy See has diplomatic relations with the Philippines, and is represented to government and the Catholic hierarchy by a nuncio in Manila.
International organizations based in Manila are: (1) Asian Working Groups for Cursillos de Cristiandad (an international movement begun in Spain) covering the Philippines, Korea, Japan, Australia, Taiwan, Thailand, Sri Lanka, Hong Kong, Macao and Viet Nam; (2) Working Committee of UNDA in East Asia, with its headquarters in Switzerland; and (3) Catholic International Education Office, Regional Secretariat for Asia, with its headquarters in Belgium. Two of the offices of the FABC are also located in the Philippines, the Office of Human Development and the Office of Education and Student Chaplaincies.
There are a number of Philippine organizations and associations. The Philippine Priests Incorporated (PPI) is the only national organization of priests and is duly registered with the government Securities and Exchange Commission, although it is not officially recognized by the church's hierarchy. The PPI was organized in November 1968, beginning with 11 priests representing different parts of the country. Membership increased rapidly and rose to 1,164 by October 1972, despite the fact that some bishops explicitly warned their priests against joining. The PPI became nationally accepted as spokesman for progressive issues within the church and a moral force on social and political questions. Three national conventions were held by the end of 1972, and the resolutions of the last convention called for a protracted struggle for liberation from all forms of oppression: church structural oppression (to awaken bishops to the need to be 'more just and brotherly' with their priests), feudalism (landlord tenant system), imperialism (American capitalist exploitation) and corrupt bureaucracy (politicians). This clearly put the PPI on the left, both in the eyes of the bishops and also before the military. The PPI was responsible for a high-quality intellectual and spiritual publication *The Philippine Priests' Forum*, and also concerned itself with the economic security of priests by means of health and sickness insurance, group accident insurances, and its plans for developing retirement pensions for priests. Some PPI leaders were detained shortly after martial law was declared in 1972. Since then the organization has changed its political orientation, lending its support to the side of president Marcos. However, there has been internal dissension. Another body is Christians for National Liberation (CNL), a clandestine association formed in September 1972 which groups together Christians favourable to the position of the Communist Party (PKP).
The following organizations are involved in research and socio-religious action. (1) The Priests' Institute for Social Action (PISA) is an independent organization which owes its origin to a month-long Priests' Institute for Social Action, a meeting of priests from all over East Asia with the exception of India, which was held in Hong Kong in August 1965. The Philippine institute is almost the only group still in existence. It produces a major monthly magazine, *Impact*, which has considerable influence in the Far East. PISA provided the initial impetus to church involvement in the social field and led to the establishment of the Episcopal Commission on Social Action (1966) and the National Catholic Rural Congress (1967). (2) The Institute of Social Order, founded by Jesuits with headquarters in Manila, conducts sociological analysis and studies of social concern and promotes credit unions and social action training centres for priests and laymen. (3) The Free Farmers' Federation (FFF) is an organization independent of the hierarchy, founded in 1953 and still directed by a former dean of the law faculty at Ateneo University and adviser to the World Council of Laymen in Rome. In 1972 this group had nearly 200,000 members in 30 provinces of the country and an even larger number of sympathizers. Its purpose is to lead peasants, who form 75% of the population, to organize themselves and to become sufficiently educated to gain their proper place in society and to transform social structures to make this possible. The FFF is involved in 2 types of action: political action to bring before the public the rights of the peasant class; and legal action, providing aid in the form of lawyers in cases dealing with employee-employer relations. The FFF was the most radical of the various Catholic movements in the Philippines prior to the declaration of martial law. At present the FFF is badly divided, and prohibited in certain regions. (4) The Federation of Free Workers, founded in 1950 by a Jesuit priest, is the first national Catholic organization for the working class and does for workers what the FFF does for rural people. The FFW is not dependent upon the hierarchy. Directed by a layman and affiliated to the World Federation of Workers (Confédération Mondial des Travailleurs, CMT) with headquarters in Brussels, the FFW has experienced a spectacular development during recent years and had 64,000 members in 1972. (5) The National Federation of Sugar Workers (NFSW) was founded in 1971 and has been supported by several religious congregations and rural missionary sisters. (6) The National Secretariat for Social Action (NASSA) is an agency of the Episcopal Conference. (7) The Christian Life Community (CLC) is a student movement independent of the hierarchy, begun by a Jesuit priest. This group holds practical seminars on the important problems of the country, visits slums and richer suburbs and makes comparative studies of Marxism and Christianity. Between 1967 and 1970, 300,000 Manila youth attended these seminars, but the number of Catholic activists is still small. One CLC group has demonstrated openly against what it calls the medieval nature of the church. (8) The South East Asian Rural Social Leadership Institute (SEARSOLIN) was founded at Cagayan de Oro in 1966 by Jesuits.
Institutions of pastoral and higher religious studies are as follows: (1) Faculties or departments of theology in the Catholic University of the Philippines at Manila (OP), Ateneo de Manila University (SJ) and University of San Carlos in Cebu City (SVD); (2) the East Asian Pastoral Institute (EAPI), founded in Manila in 1953 by Jesuits under the name Institute for Mission Apologetics, which trains teachers in catechetics as well as regional and diocesan directors, is open to students from other countries in Asia and Oceania, and also plays a major role in pastoral and catechetical research in the Far East; (3) the Pius XII Catechetical Institute in Iloilo City, which offers courses in catechetics on the Asian level, together with a 4-year training programme.
In 1965 the hierarchy established the Mission Society of the Philippines based in Cebu City, a national society to recruit, train, send and support Filipino missionaries (priests, sisters, brothers and lay volunteers) for service outside the nation. In 1973 some 850 Filipino Catholics were serving abroad as missionaries, in Thailand, Indonesia, Brazil and other countries.
Educational statistics for 1970 were as follows: 1,893 Catholic schools with a total enrolment of 860,299 pupils. These included 280 kindergartens, 443 elementary schools, 772 high schools, and 231 at college level. There were also 11 universities: Royal and Pontifical University of Santo Tomas (Catholic University of the Philippines, founded in 1611, with 26,457 students, run by OP); Ateneo de Manila which became a university in 1959 (6,823 students, run by SJ); Adamson University (5,984, run by CM); Xavier University, founded in Cagayan de Oro City in 1958 (2,229, run by SJ); University of San Carlos, founded in Cebu City in 1595 and a university in 1948 (8,548, run by SVD); University of San Augustin, founded in 1904 in Iloilo City (run by OSA); University of Negros Occidental in Bacolod City (6,068, run by ORSA); Aquinas University of Legazpi, founded in Legazpi City in 1948 (3,285, run by OP); Divine Word University, founded in Tacloban City in 1929 (5,612, run by SVD); Notre Dame University in Cotabato City (3,112, run by OMI); and St Louis University, founded in Baguio City in 1963 (9,087 students, run by CICM). There is an Association of the Catholic Universities of the Philippines, which has its headquarters in Baguio City.
Medical action and welfare in 1968 included 135 hospitals and dispensaries, 2 leper colonies, 16 orphanages and 17 homes. Social, medical and educational services are supervised by Catholic Charities of the Archdiocese of Manila, founded in 1953, which is affiliated to Caritas Internationalis in Rome.
CHRISTIAN & MISSIONARY ALLIANCE CHURCHES. *Acronym.* CAMACOP. *Adult members.* Very rapid recent growth from 10,348 in 469 churches (1957) to 51,629 in 830 churches (1978).
CONSERVATIVE BAPTIST ASSOCIATION OF THE PHILIPPINES. *Adult members.* Rapid growth from 492 in 10 churches (1963) to 1,903 in 45 churches (1972), to 5,664 in 81 churches (1978).
PHILIPPINE BAPTIST MISSION. *Adult members.* Rapid growth from 2,211 in 14 churches (1957) to 14,492 in 164 organized churches (1970), to 33,879 in 522 churches (1978).
PHILIPPINE INDEPENDENT CHURCH. The membership figures in the table above (which refer to the year 1970) and those in this footnote are figures of affiliated members as reported by the office of the Obispado Maximo, Manila. They differ from, and are much larger than, the government census figures because (a) large numbers of PIC members report themselves in censuses as Católicos, and (b) a large number also are regarded as members by both the PIC and the Roman Catholic Church (including in Tables 1 and 2 under the category doubly-affiliated). *Membership.* There has been rapid growth from 1970 to (in 1976) 4,600,000 baptized members, 3,800,000 communicants, and 1,500,000 Easter communicants. *Dioceses* (1977). 30. *Parishes* (1977). 568, with 2,644 out-stations in the barrios (slums), and a total of 3,830 congregations. *Baptisms.* (1976) 192,000 infants, 600 adults. *Confirmations* (1976). 200,000, including Roman Catholics received. *Bishops* (1977). 46 active (30 diocesans, 7 suffragans, 2 coadjutors, 6 non-diocesan, 1 obispo maximo); all citizens. *Clergy* (1977). 568 parish priests, 18 deacons, 530 deaconesses; all citizens. *Lay workers* (1977). 2,400 men, 800 women. *Licensed lay readers* (1977). 350 men, 11 women. *Ordinands* (1977). 11.
UNITED CHURCH OF CHRIST IN THE PHILIPPINES. A 1948 union of United Evangelical Church of the Philippines (itself a 1929 union of Presbyterian, Congregational, and United Brethren Churches), Philippines Methodist Church, Evangelical Church in the Philippines (a 1944 union of various Evangelical churches).

# PITCAIRN ISLANDS

## SECULAR DATA

**STATE. Official name:** The Colony of the Pitcairn Islands.
**Flag** (shown above right): That of the UK (Britain).
**Area:** 48 sq.km. (18.5 sq.miles), including uninhabited islands Henderson, Ducie and Oeno. Agricultural land: 50.0%.
**Government:** British colony, since 1898 (1790 founded by Bounty mutineers).
**Official language:** English.

**Capital:** Adamstown.

**DEMOGRAPHY. Population:** 92 (census of XII.1971. For 1970–2000 (UN), see last row of Table 1). Population density (1975): 2/sq.km. (5/sq.mile). Under 15 years: 44%. Growth rate (1975–80): −5.8% per year, due to substantial emigration since 1950 to New Zealand. Household size: 4 persons.
**Major languages:** English.

**ETHNOLINGUISTIC GROUPS:** 98% Pitcairner (Euronesian)

(European/Polynesian).

**MONEY** (1977). **Monetary unit:** New Zealand dollar (= 100 cents); US$1 = NZ$1.07.
**National income per person:** US$2,500. Average annual family income: US$10,000.

**EDUCATION.** Adult literacy: 90%.

**COMMUNICATION** (per 1,000 people). Phones: 460.

### TABLE 1.   RELIGIOUS ADHERENTS IN THE PITCAIRN ISLANDS

| Year Name | 1900 Adherents | % | mid-1970 Adherents | % | Annual change, 1970–1980 Natural | Conversion | Total | Rate | mid-1975 Adherents | % | mid-1980 Adherents | % | 2000 Adherents | % |
|---|---|---|---|---|---|---|---|---|---|---|---|---|---|---|
| **Christians** | 150 | 100.0 | 90 | 100.0 | 0 | 0 | 0 | 0.00 | 90 | 100.0 | 90 | 100.0 | 100 | 100.0 |
| professing | 150 | 100.0 | 90 | 100.0 | 0 | 0 | 0 | 0.00 | 90 | 100.0 | 90 | 100.0 | 100 | 100.0 |
| Protestants | 150 | 100.0 | 90 | 100.0 | 0 | 0 | 0 | 0.00 | 90 | 100.0 | 90 | 100.0 | 100 | 100.0 |
| affiliated | 150 | 100.0 | 90 | 100.0 | 0 | 0 | 0 | 0.00 | 90 | 100.0 | 90 | 100.0 | 100 | 100.0 |
| total practising | 147 | 98 | 85 | 95 | 0 | 0 | 0 | 0.00 | 85 | 95 | 85 | 95 | 90 | 90 |
| non-practising | 3 | 2 | 5 | 5 | 0 | 0 | 0 | 0.00 | 5 | 5 | 5 | 5 | 10 | 10 |
| Protestants | 150 | 100.0 | 90 | 100.0 | 0 | 0 | 0 | 0.00 | 90 | 100.0 | 90 | 100.0 | 100 | 100.0 |
| **Country's population** | 150 | 100.0 | 90 | 100.0 | 0 | 0 | 0 | 0.00 | 90 | 100.0 | 90 | 100.0 | 100 | 100.0 |

COLUMNS, ROWS. For meanings and definitions, see Codebook (Part 6). Note that, by definition, total 'Christians' = professing + crypto-Christians, which also = affiliated + nominal Christians. Percentages may not always total exactly, due to rounding.

**NOTES ON RELIGIONS**
CHRISTIANS. Anglicans until 1887; since then, all Seventh-day Adventists.

**CHRISTIANITY.** Pitcairn Island was uninhabited when a party of mutineers from the ship *Bounty* with some Tahitians arrived to settle it in 1790. The leader of the group, John Adams, was a zealous Christian and helped to form a highly-disciplined Church of England community. In 1877 Seventh-day Adventist literature arrived from the USA which transformed the life of the island. Within a decade the Church of England had been supplanted, and the SDA Pitcairn Island Mission was organized in 1895. To this day Pitcairn remains completely Adventist in its religious allegiance. The single congregation in Adamstown is served by a resident pastor.

**CHURCH AND STATE.** All education was organized by the SDA Mission until 1948 when the New Zealand Department of Education sent its first schoolmaster to the island. The government makes secondary education available to Pitcairn residents in both Fiji and New Zealand.

*Left.* Librarian examines Bounty Bible, original copy used for strict theocratic government by John Adams and crew of British ship HMS Bounty after 1789 mutiny. *Above.* Bounty Bible on postage stamp.

'BOUNTY' BIBLE
PITCAIRN ISLANDS   40c

### TABLE 2.   ORGANIZED CHURCHES AND DENOMINATIONS IN THE PITCAIRN ISLANDS

| Official name 1 | Begun 2 | Type 3 | Counc 4 | Congs 5 | Adults 6 | Affiliated 7 | Names, notes, and other statistics (see Codebook) 8 |
|---|---|---|---|---|---|---|---|
| **Seventh-day Adventist Church** | 1895 | P Adv | x•••• | 1 | 64 | 90 | *PI Mission*, Central Pacific Union Mission. 95% SDA. In Adamstown. 3n,1t(64). |
| Total affiliated (mid-1970) | | | | 1 | 64 | 90 | Total denominations (1970) . . . 1. |
| Total affiliated (mid-1975) | | | | 1 | 64 | 90 | Total denominations (1975) . . . 1. |
| Total affiliated (mid-1980) | | | | 1 | 64 | 90 | Total denominations (1980) . . . 1. |

**NOTES ON TABLE ABOVE**
COLUMNS: for meanings and CODES (cols. 1, 3, 4, 8): see Codebook (Part 6). Column 1: **Boldface type** = church with over 10% of country's affiliated Christians.

**PEOPLES** (ethnolinguistic). Christians: 98% Euronesian (Pitcairner).

**COUNTRY-WIDE TOTALS**
EVANGELIZATION (see Part 5). 1900: 100%. 1970: 100%.

1980: 100%.
PERSONNEL. 3.
SCRIPTURE DISTRIBUTION (1975). Annual totals: 3 Bibles (subsidized), 10 NTs (subsidized).

---

# POLAND

## SECULAR DATA

**STATE. Official name:** The Polish People's Republic (Polska Rzeczpospolita Ludowa). Adjectives of nationality: Polish, a Pole.
**Flag** (shown above right): White stripe over red stripe.
**Area:** 312,677 sq.km. (120,725 sq.miles). Agricultural land: 61.6%.
**Government:** One-party Communist state, since 1947 (1918 Independence as republic, 1926 dictatorship).
**Legislature:** Sejm, 460 members.
**Official language:** Polish (*Polski*).
**Chief cities:** capital Warsaw 1,377,100 (1973), Lodz 777,800, Krakow 651,300, Wroclaw 557,200.
**Political divisions:** 17 Provinces (Voivodships, wojewodztwa) and 5 Cities of province status; divided into 314 Rural and 76 Urban Districts; and 3,251 Local Authorities.
**Armed forces** (1976): Total 290,000 regular (190,000 conscripts): army 204,000, navy 25,000, air force 61,000 (804 combat aircraft). Reserves: 505,000. Paramilitary forces: 430,000 (350,000 Citizens Militia).
**Foreign forces** (1973): 18,000 USSR troops (2 divisions).

**DEMOGRAPHY. Population:** 32,642,270 (census of 8.XII.1970. For 1970–2000 (UN), see last row of Table 1). Population density (1975): 108/sq.km. (280/sq.mile). Under 15 years: 34%. Growth rate (1975–80): 0.85% per year (births 1.76%, deaths −0.90%). Life expectancy (1975–80): 70.7 years. Household size: 3.4 persons.
**Major languages:** Polish, Ukrainian, Russian, Kashubian, Byelorussian, German, Yiddish, et alia.
**Urban dwellers** (1970): 51.0%. Urban growth rate (1950–70): 2.9% per year.
**Labour force:** 52%.
**Refugees** (1977): From abroad, none. Exiles abroad: 24,000 Polish (ethnic Germans) in Federal Republic of Germany as a result of 1975 West German/Polish treaty.
**Tourists** (1970): 1,889,000. (1974) 7,893,400.

**ETHNOLINGUISTIC GROUPS:** 97.4% Polish, 0.7% Ukrainian, 0.6% Kashubian (Pomeranian), 0.6% Byelorussian, 0.2% German, 0.2% Russian (including 18,000 USSR troops), 0.2% Gypsy, 0.1% Slovak, Lithuanian (10,000), Greek (10,000), Macedonian, Jewish (8,000).

**MONEY** (1977). **Monetary unit:** zloty (= 100 groszy); US$1 = Zl 19.92.
**National income per person:** US$2,000. Average annual family income: US$6,800.
**Inflation:** (1970–74) 1.6% per year (1975: consumer price index 115).
**Cost of living in capital** (1976): index 110 (Washington DC = 100). Daily cost of living: US$39.

**HEALTH.** Hospitals: 1,436 (254,894 beds). Doctors: 53,040. Blind: 21,523. Psychotics: 300,000.

**EDUCATION.** Adult literacy: (1950) 94%, (1970) 98%. Education rate: 63%. Schools: 23,796. Universities: 10.

**LITERATURE.** Annual new book titles (1973): 10,744. Periodicals: 3,265. Scientific journals: 750. Newspapers: 44 dailies, 42 non-daily.

**COMMUNICATION** (per 1,000 people). Phones: 71. Radios: 236. TV sets: 180. Daily newspaper circulation: 226 copies.

TABLE 1. RELIGIOUS ADHERENTS IN POLAND

| Year | 1900 | | mid-1970 | | Annual change, 1970–1980 | | | | mid-1975 | | mid-1980 | | 2000 | |
|---|---|---|---|---|---|---|---|---|---|---|---|---|---|---|
| *Name* | *Adherents* | *%* | *Adherents* | *%* | *Natural* | *Conversion* | *Total* | *Rate* | *Adherents* | *%* | *Adherents* | *%* | *Adherents* | *%* |
| **Christians** | **21,989,500** | **90.9** | **29,626,685** | **91.2** | **258,714** | **–27,812** | **230,902** | **0.75** | **30,795,400** | **91.0** | **31,935,700** | **90.4** | **35,673,000** | **89.5** |
| crypto-Christians | 0 | 0.0 | 2,026,685 | 6.2 | 19,906 | 53,796 | 73,702 | 3.11 | 2,369,400 | 7.0 | 2,763,700 | 7.8 | 4,361,000 | 10.9 |
| professing | 21,989,500 | 90.9 | 27,600,000 | 85.0 | 238,808 | –81,608 | 157,200 | 0.55 | 28,426,000 | 84.0 | 29,172,000 | 82.6 | 31,312,000 | 78.6 |
| Roman Catholics | 19,002,500 | 78.5 | 26,970,000 | 83.0 | 244,425 | –80,825 | 163,600 | 0.59 | 27,772,000 | 82.1 | 28,606,000 | 81.0 | 30,681,000 | 77.0 |
| Orthodox | 2,240,000 | 9.3 | 400,000 | 1.2 | 3,486 | –486 | 3,000 | 0.72 | 415,000 | 1.2 | 430,000 | 1.2 | 480,000 | 1.2 |
| Protestants | 747,000 | 3.1 | 150,000 | 0.5 | –9,800 | –200 | –10,000 | –6.41 | 156,000 | 0.5 | 50,000 | 0.1 | 56,000 | 0.1 |
| Catholics (non-Roman) | 0 | 0.0 | 80,000 | 0.2 | 697 | –97 | 600 | 0.75 | 83,000 | 0.2 | 86,000 | 0.2 | 95,000 | 0.2 |
| nominal | 606,000 | 2.5 | 0 | 0.0 | 0 | 0 | 0 | 0.00 | 0 | 0.0 | 0 | 0.0 | 0 | 0.0 |
| affiliated | 21,383,500 | 88.4 | 29,626,685 | 91.2 | 258,714 | –27,812 | 230,902 | 0.75 | 30,795,400 | 91.0 | 31,935,700 | 90.4 | 35,673,000 | 89.5 |
| total practising | 19,245,200 | *90* | 27,849,080 | *94* | 243,191 | –26,143 | 217,048 | 0.75 | 28,947,680 | *94* | 30,019,560 | *94* | 32,105,700 | *90* |
| non-practising | 2,138,300 | *10* | 1,777,600 | *6* | 15,523 | –1,669 | 13,854 | 0.75 | 1,847,720 | *6* | 1,916,140 | *6* | 3,567,300 | *10* |
| Roman Catholics | 18,656,500 | 77.1 | 28,783,085 | 88.6 | 264,160 | –27,598 | 236,562 | 0.79 | 29,915,400 | 88.4 | 31,148,700 | 88.2 | 34,825,000 | 87.4 |
| Catholic pentecostals | 0 | 0.0 | 0 | 0.0 | 25 | 1,475 | 1,500 | 50.00 | 3,000 | 0.0 | 15,000 | 0.0 | 70,000 | 0.2 |
| Orthodox | 2,020,000 | 8.3 | 532,500 | 1.6 | 4,662 | –112 | 4,550 | 0.82 | 555,000 | 1.6 | 578,000 | 1.6 | 598,000 | 1.5 |
| Protestants | 707,000 | 2.9 | 187,000 | 0.6 | –11,200 | –200 | –11,400 | –5.85 | 195,000 | 0.6 | 73,000 | 0.2 | 90,000 | 0.2 |
| Evangelicals | 110,000 | 0.5 | 130,000 | 0.4 | –7,869 | 669 | –7,200 | –5.26 | 137,000 | 0.4 | 58,000 | 0.2 | 80,000 | 0.2 |
| Catholics (non-Roman) | 0 | 0.0 | 101,100 | 0.3 | 882 | –92 | 790 | 0.75 | 105,000 | 0.3 | 109,000 | 0.3 | 120,000 | 0.3 |
| Marginal Protestants | 0 | 0.0 | 23,000 | 0.1 | 210 | 190 | 400 | 1.60 | 25,000 | 0.1 | 27,000 | 0.1 | 40,000 | 0.1 |
| Non-religious | 20,000 | 0.1 | 1,843,115 | 5.7 | 17,290 | 21,041 | 38,331 | 1.94 | 1,971,560 | 5.8 | 2,226,420 | 6.3 | 2 751,000 | 6.9 |
| Atheists | 5,000 | 0.0 | 974,200 | 3.0 | 8,813 | 6,767 | 15,580 | 1.49 | 1,049,100 | 3.1 | 1,130,000 | 3.2 | 1 395,000 | 3.5 |
| Jews | 2,180,000 | 9.0 | 8,000 | 0.0 | –700 | 0 | –700 | –28.33 | 3,000 | 0.0 | 1,000 | 0.0 | 0 | 0.0 |
| Muslims | 500 | 0.0 | 1,000 | 0.0 | 8 | 0 | 8 | 0.77 | 1,040 | 0.0 | 1,080 | 0.0 | 2,000 | 0.0 |
| Other religionists | 5,000 | 0.0 | 20,000 | 0.1 | 175 | 5 | 180 | 0.86 | 20,900 | 0.1 | 21,800 | 0.1 | 25,000 | 0.1 |
| **Country's population** | **24,200,000** | **100.0** | **32,473,000** | **100.0** | **284,300** | **0** | **284,300** | **0.84** | **33,841,000** | **100.0** | **35,316,000** | **100.0** | **39,846,000** | **100.0** |

COLUMNS, ROWS. For meanings and definitions, see Codebook (Part 6). Note that, by definition, total 'Christians' = professing + crypto-Christians, which also = affiliated + nominal Christians. Percentages may not always total exactly, due to rounding.
CENSUSES. **30.XI.1921** (within 1921 boundaries): 74.3% Roman Catholics (11.8% Greek Catholics), 11.1% Orthodox, 10.8% Jews, 3.7% Protestants, 0.1% Mariavites.
POLLS. Numerous public-opinion polls and social surveys with religion questions have been taken, including the following. Students in Warsaw (1958): 59.5% practising believers, 17.1% non-practising believers, 20.2% non-religious (indifferent to religion), 3.1% atheists (hostile to religion). 1959 (Polish Radio & TV): 78% Catholics, 21.8% non-religious and atheists. Youth in Warsaw (1960: 12.1% non-religious or hostile to religion. 1964 (nationwide; VC): 'Are you a practising religious believer?' —64% believe and practise, 24% believe but not practise, 7% not believe but some private practice (weddings), 4% neither believe nor practise, 1% opposed to all religions. Women in village of Nova Huta (1967): 51% attend mass every Sunday, 28% occasionally, 6% believe but not attend, 15% non-believers; and 51% of all children attend catechism regularly, 4% are brought up to be atheists.

NOTES ON RELIGIONS
ATHEISTS. Polish United Workers' Party (Communist; in power; pro-Soviet): membership (1970) 2,270,000; Communist voters (election of 19.III.1972) 21,854,481 (97.9% of all votes). Only about 15% of party members are estimated to be committed atheists, the rest being non-religious with a considerable number of professing (and many practising) Catholics also. In 1958, 7.4% of the population were agnostics, 2.3% indifferent to religion, 3.1% atheists opposed to all religion (Pawelczyunka). Atheists and non-religious in urban population, 1960: 39.9% highly-educated intelligentsia, 34.0% intelligentsia, 25% skilled workers, 17.8% unskilled workers. In 1964, 7% of city populations were non-believers, 2% in rural areas. In 1971 an atheistic body, the Society for the Propagation of Secular Culture, numbered 316,000 nominal members.
CATHOLIC PENTECOSTALS (or, Catholic charismatics). Totals (1975): at least 500 involved adults in 20 prayer groups, including loosely-structured temporary student groups, also hundreds of young Jesus people and Jesus revolutionaries; total charismatic community including children, 3,000. In October 1975, 400 attended a first Polish charismatic conference, in Lublin.
CRYPTO-CHRISTIANS. Christians affiliated to churches but not known as such to the state. Since there is relative, if controlled, religious freedom in Poland, there is no organized underground church related to the main Protestant or Catholic traditions. Crypto-Christians exist, however, in 2 forms: (1) unregistered or prohibited denominations including Jehovah's Witnesses, who have a strong underground organization; and (2) Catholics, often practising, who do not reveal their affiliation publicly or to the state. There is also a tiny handful of isolated radio believers.
JEWS. In 1939, 3,500,000 ,of whom the Nazi Third Reich exterminated 3,350,000. In 1963, 31,000, declining rapidly by emigration. In 1968, 18 congregations and 11 synagogues. There is also a small Karaite (Readers of the Scriptures) community, the Religious Karaite Union.
MUSLIMS. In 1968, 2 mosques, 6 religious communities, and 3 imams.
NOMINAL CHRISTIANS. Only before 1945.
NON-RELIGIOUS. Agnostics, indifferent to religion, including most Communist party members. In addition, there were in 1975 another 7.0% of the population whom the polls record as non-religious but who are affiliated to the churches and so are classified here as crypto-Christians.
OTHER RELIGIONISTS. Including young Polish adherents of Buddhism, Spiritists, Occultists, adherents of Yoga, about 100 Baha'is in 2 isolated centres, and also several thousand non-Christian Gypsies.
PRACTISING CHRISTIANS. Weekly church attendance is very high among Roman Catholics: about 64% of the population, which is 80% of all affiliated Catholics (see polls above). Weekly mass attendance in 1977: 77% in cities, 87% in rural areas. Annual attendance (once a year or more): about 94% of all affiliated Christians. *Pilgrims.* 300,000 pilgrims a year visit the Pauline monastery of Jasna Gora at Czestochowa to celebrate the feast of the Assumption, including vast numbers of young people. In October 1975, 3,000 pilgrims from Poland visited Rome for the Holy Year.
PROTESTANTS. Decline by emigration in 1975–76 of 125,000 Lutherans and Reformed of German origin, allowed to emigrate to West Germany after the Helsinki Accord.

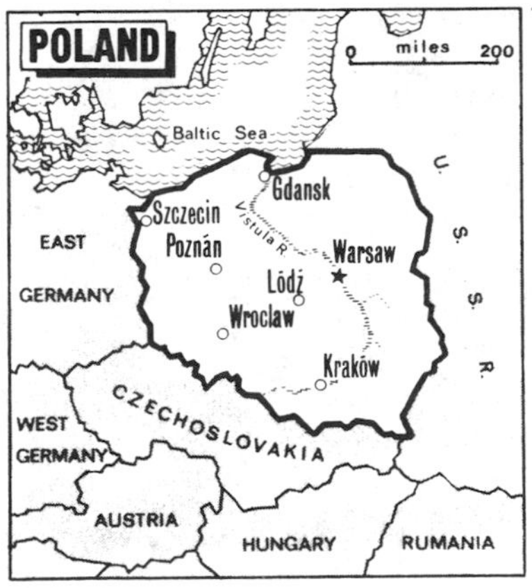


**NON-CHRISTIAN RELIGIONS. Judaism** consisted in 1939 of a large community of about 3.5 million Polish Jews. As a result of the World War II massacres which claimed 3 million victims, flight to the West and Russia, and post-war emigration to Israel, Jews were reduced to about 31,000 by 1963. Subsequently the anti-Zionist policy of the Polish government provoked even greater emigration, reducing the Jewish community to about 8,000 by 1970 and to almost nothing within the decade. Among the Jews, authority is centralized in the Union Congress Assembly in Warsaw. In 1968 there were 18 congregations, meeting in 11 synagogues and 19 other houses, plus communal baths, kosher bakeries and slaughter-houses.

**Islam** had 1,000 adherents in 1968, 3 imams, 2 mosques and 6 religious communities. The supreme authority for Islam in Poland is the Muslim College with a lay chairman.

**CHRISTIANITY.** In the year 966 the duke of Mieszka was converted to Christianity through his Christian wife, and in 968 the first bishopric was established in Poznan. Under Mieszka's son Boleslaw Chrobry who reigned until 1025, the power of both the kingdom and the church grew, and missionaries were sent out to other countries. German missionaries brought about much of the early development of Poland, and Boleslaw had to contend with German imperialistic designs. In AD 1000, however, Gniezno was made an independent archiepiscopal see with 3 suffragan bishoprics. After Boleslaw's death, a reaction set in against Christianity and foreign clergy and the country itself began to disintegrate. Some progress was made in restoring church-state relations during the next century, but Christianity in Poland for a long period failed to achieve the strength it had attained in western Europe. In 1364 the university of Kraków was established; and the pagan Lithuanian duke Jagiello became ruler of both Poland and Lithuania following his baptism in 1386. Once again the state took an interest in promoting the Christian faith, though Christianity in Poland seemed to owe as much to German missionary work and the eastward expansion of German settlers as to the conversion of the Polish rulers. The 15th century became known as the century of saints, and the 16th century was regarded as Poland's golden age with such men as Nicholas Copernicus among its scholars.

Lutheranism spread to Poland in 1518 and Poznan became the centre for those of the nobility who adopted this faith. Calvinism appeared in 1548, and exiled Moravians also began entering Poland. The result was the development of over 900 Protestant centres, with Protestants holding important posts in the government. A national church was requested by Roman Catholics but refused at the Council of Trent in 1564. Popular reaction against the Catholic Church accompanied similar dissatisfaction with royal authority. The Jagiello regime was finally overthrown in 1572, the throne became elective and a parliament was established. Shortly after, however, the Catholic Church was in 1587 given official recognition and Protestantism was restricted. Disputes continued among noblemen espousing the different faiths, and in 1772 Russia, Austria and Prussia took advantage of these internal conflicts and divided Polish territory among themselves. Catholic dioceses remained, though several had to operate without bishops for long periods. A certain amount of religious freedom existed in the territories annexed by Austria but greater repression was experienced in the Russian sector, and a number of bishops, priests and laymen were deported to Siberia.

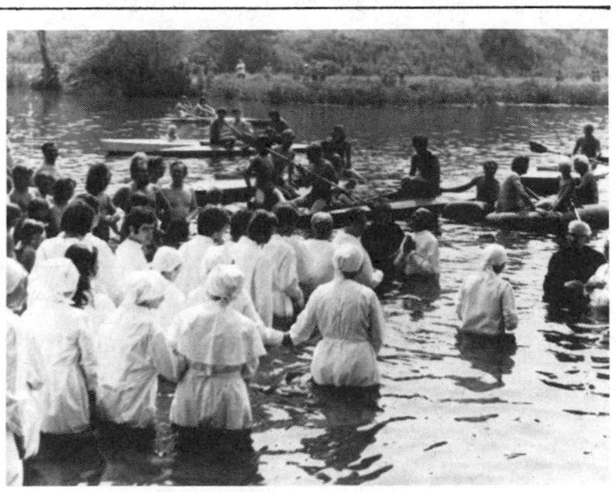
**United Evangelical Church of the Gospel.** Pentecostal catechumens enter river for mass believers' baptism (August 1974).

Following World War I, Poland became an independent nation once again. At the same time the influence of the Catholic Church was re-established and religious instruction required in all schools. During World War II the German Nazi regime liquidated 6 million Poles, half of them Jews, while Russia deported 1.7 million Poles. Since 1945 Poland has remained under a Communist regime.

CATHOLIC CHURCH. Since the creation of the Polish state in 966, the vigour and influence of Polish Catholicism have been closely linked with the fortunes of the Polish nation and people. The dismemberment of the nation in the 18th century again accentuated this link. It has been the church rather than the state which has traditionally served as the political and social focal point. Clergy, drawn from all levels of society, have played an active cultural and patriotic role. This fact is important in understanding the character of Polish Catholicism today. Although 6 bishops, 2,030 diocesan and religious priests, 127 seminarians, 173 brothers and 243 sisters were executed by the Nazis during World War II, the influence of the church since then has actually increased. This is due in no small part to the changes in the boundaries of Poland in 1945, when territory to the east was lost but territory to the west was gained. The shift in boundaries not only made Poland more homogeneous in nationality but also more uniform in religious profession.

Polish Catholicism is a popular and mass phenomenon based on a religiosity which believes that there is a kind of special link between God and the Polish people, a faith which is often blind and inflexible but which has resulted in a great attachment and fidelity to the church.

Today Catholics form the vast majority of the population and are served by a large and growing priesthood. There is little difference in religious practice from one social class to another. Religious traditions were developed among the working classes during the 19th century and new industrial centres have been populated by people from rural areas who brought their religious traditions with them. The percentage practising their religion, generally high in rural areas and reduced in the cities, remains much higher than in Western Europe. This is not uniform in all areas: religious practice is comparatively weak in industrial regions and areas with long-standing traditions of socialism such as Zaglebie, Dabrowskie, Lodz, and Warsaw as well as in several rural areas of the eastern part of the country, including the Lublin region. There are however industrial centres with strong traditional religious conviction, as in Upper Silesia, and yet others where religious conviction has shaped their evolution, as in Nowa Huta. Some new urban and industrial communities as yet have no churches including Swidnik K/Lublina, Nowy Krasnik, and Nowy Konin.

With regard to the special prestige of the cardinal-primate of Poland, Stefan Wyszynski, and his direction of the pastoral work of the church, criticism has come only from groups among the intelligentsia who charge that he has obstructed church reforms proposed by Vatican II. Open critism of the cardinal is however muted because of the possibility that such dissension might be exploited politically, and bring about schism within the church.

Councils or senates of priests exist in almost all dioceses. Members consist of those in charge of the different diocesan offices, who serve ex-officio, and also elected members representing various categories of priests including superiors, parish priests, vicars and chaplains in the armed forces. These senates in their meetings usually avoid major pastoral and theological problems in favour of practical problems such as relationships between parish priests and vicars, equalization of stipends and pensions for retired priests. At the end of 1975 diocesan synods, with lay representation, were held at Wloclawec, Poznan Kraków, Katowice, Warsaw and Gdansk. Themes have centred on the spiritualization of Catholic life. A national synod was being planned in 1976.

At the end of 1968 there were 13,276 Catholic church buildings in Poland compared with 7,257 churches and chapels in 1937, 984 of which were destroyed in World War II. Part of this increase was due to the acquisition of 3,297 churches in the former German territory ceded to Poland after the war. With regard to the number of priests, in 1937 this stood at 11,239, falling to 8,000 by the end of the war. In 1968 there were close to 18,000 priests. The number of priests in religious orders rose from 1,663 in 1937 to 4,487 at the end of 1968, and the number of sisters from 16,822 to 27,897 over the same period.

ORTHODOX CHURCH. The autocephalous Orthodox Church of Poland traces its origin back to the 10th century, with further development taking place after the union of Lithuania and Poland in the 14th century. When Poland was dismembered among its neighbours in 1772, its Orthodox church was united with the Orthodox Church of Russia, and this state of affairs continued until 1918. In 1925 the ecumenical patriarch of Constantinople recognized the autocephality of the Polish church, but the Russian church withheld agreement until 1948. Because of this lack of Russian recognition, the Polish government refused to accord it full status, and its members suffered discrimination prior to and during the war years. Before World War II the church had 10 bishops, 5 dioceses, about 2,000 parishes, 15 monasteries and around 4 million members. Its membership is now only 13% of its former size, part of this decrease being attributable to the church's past failures to involve itself in missionary activity of any kind. Clergy are trained at the Orthodox seminary and at the Orthodox Theological Department of the Christian Theology Academy. The latter institution

Catholic Church in Poland, Archdiocese of Krakow. *Above.* New church for Lenin Steelworks employees in Nowa Huta (New Foundry), finally completed despite massive bureaucratic opposition for 23 years. *Below.* Former Archbishop of Krakow returns to Warsaw as Pope John Paul II, June 1979.

is state-supported and jointly operated with various Protestant denominations.

PROTESTANT CHURCHES. Of the various Protestant denominations in Poland, only about a third are recognized by the government as churches. The rest are listed as religious organizations. Upper Silesia is the most Protestant part of the country.

The largest Protestant body has long been the Lutheran Church, although following the expulsion of Germans after World War II its membership was reduced by a third. Lutherans in the former German territory of west Poland have formed their own church as well as Poles outside the country who have established the Polish Lutheran Church in exile. Pastors are trained at the ecumenical Christian Theology Academy. After the Helsinki Accord, 125,000 Lutherans and Reformed of German origin were allowed to emigrate to West Germany in 1975–76.

The Reformed Church traces its origin to the entry of Calvinism into Poland in 1548. It is active in the ecumenical movement in the country.

The United Evangelical Church of the Gospel was created in 1947 by the amalgamation of 3 distinct denominations, with 2 more added in 1953: Union of Christian Evangelists, Free Christian Union, Committed Christian Union, Pentecostals and Church of Christ. Just under half of all members are Pentecostals. The church sponsors a home for the aged in Ostróda.

Three denominations with fraternal ties outside Poland were granted recognition after World War II: the Methodist, Adventist and Baptist churches. All are able to publish widely-circulated journals. Each has its headquarters in Warsaw; Methodists also operate an English-language school there.

The Epiphany Lay Missionary Movement has its seat in Poznan; the Free Union of Holy Scripture Seekers are centred in Kraków.

CATHOLIC (NON-ROMAN) CHURCHES. Several bodies have broken off from the Roman Catholic Church. In 1906 a schism took place in Poland known as the Old Catholic Mariavite Church, which has since its inception placed emphasis on moral renewal and the cult of the Virgin Mary (Mariavite=Imitator of Mary). From 1924 it was not regarded as genuinely Old Catholic and was excluded from the Union of Utrecht, but in 1973 it was once more accepted into the Old Catholic community. The church has founded a number of convents and also Plock seminary for training its clergy. In 1936 a further split from within this group produced the Catholic Mariavite Church.

A much larger schism originated in the USA in 1897 when the Polish National Catholic Church was founded as a protest against domination by German and Irish priests in Roman Catholic dioceses with large Polish Catholic majorities. The movement

150th Anniversary of Bible Society in Poland, 1966, in Polish Ecumenical Centre, hearing lecture by Bishop H. Hogsbro of Denmark.

spread to Poland following World War I and the church was officially recognized in 1922. The church is accepted as Old Catholic and belongs to the Union of Utrecht. There are now 4 dioceses in the USA, one in Canada, and 3 in Poland. Education for the priesthood is carried on at the Old Catholic Theological Department of the Christian Theology Academy.

**CHURCH AND STATE.** The constitution of 22 July 1952, Article 70, paragraph 1, 'guarantees freedom of conscience and religion to all citizens. The (Catholic) Church and other religious bodies may freely exercise their religious functions'. The same article proclaims the separation of church and state (paragraph 2), forbids citizens being prevented from taking part in religious activities or ceremonies (paragraph 1), and declares that it is punishable by law to 'abuse freedom of conscience and religion for ends contrary to the interests of the Popular Republic of Poland' (paragraph 3).

Relations between the Communist government emerging out of World War II and the Catholic Church have often been strained; but in spite of administrative difficulties, the Polish church has never experienced persecution comparable to that which has taken place in most other European Communist countries. Strongly nationalistic and retaining the loyalty of the great majority of the population, the Polish church has always been, and still remains, the principal representative of the churches with the state Bureau of Religious Affairs (Urzad do Spraw Wyznan). This bureau is under the president of the Council of Ministers, with headquarters at Warsaw and branches in each province *(voivodie)*. The authority and personality of cardinal Wyszynski has dominated almost the entire period since 1945. He has been spokesman for the churches before the Bureau since February 1949, whilst the state opposite number has changed several times. Since 1945, the principal sources of tension have been the status of the former German dioceses (finally settled in 1972), taxation of the church (a 1962 decree ordering listing of church property with a view to taxation was rescinded in 1972), religious education in public schools (suppressed in 1951, restored in 1956, suppressed again in 1961), and the construction of new church buildings.

Five important events in these relations between the Communist state and the Catholic Church may be noted. First was the unilateral denunciation by the state, on 14 September 1945, of the concordat of 1925 with the Holy See. Second was the failure of the government's attempt to create a national church which it could manipulate, and which was followed by the signing of an agreement between state and church on 14 April 1950, a compromise resulting in the government adopting a more conciliatory attitude and recognizing the pope as head of the church, with the church agreeing to support government foreign policies and to urge the Holy See to recognize Polish sovereignty over the former German territories in Oder-Neisse, Gdansk and east Prussia. This agreement provided the basis for the church to name residential bishops replacing the existing apostolic

administrators. The third event was the arrest of cardinal Wyszinski on 26 September 1953; and the fourth his release with numerous other priests in 1956 at the start of the Gomulka regime. Fifthly, a further agreement embodying a new modus vivendi was signed on 8 December 1956. Lastly, in May 1967 the Holy See appointed 4 apostolic administrators (ad nutum Sanctae Sedis) for the former German territories in the north and west and promoted them to titular bishops.

The most recent period has been characterized by the gradual solution of outstanding controversial matters. This new era began with the removal of Gomulka as Communist leader and his replacement by E. Gierek who attempted to bring about national unity by improving the social and economic disarray left by his predecessor. Several events have contributed to this. (1) In 1971 the beatification of the Franciscan priest Maximilian Kolbe, who died a martyr's death at the Auschwitz concentration camp, was celebrated as an event of national significance. (2) On 23 June 1971 the government transferred to the church property rights in the former German territory in the west and north. (3) At the beginning of 1972, it discontinued demanding the required listings of church property for tax purposes. (4) On 28 June 1973, after the West German treaty with Poland in which Germany recognized the Oder-Neisse boundary, the Holy See responded by appointing for the first time resident bishops in the former German areas and integrating them into existing Polish ecclesiastical provinces, with Wroclaw becoming a metropolitan see. Thus the situation in which since 1945 these regions had been under provisional administration attached to former German bishoprics finally came to an end. (5) In July 1974 the Polish government and the Holy See decided to establish permanent working contacts, in the form of a permanent Polish group in Rome officially attached to the Polish embassy in Italy and a similar group from the Holy See in Warsaw. This decision, generally interpreted as an important step towards the establishment of diplomatic relations, was preceded by numerous visits by representatives of the Holy See to Poland and Polish officials to the Vatican. The first of these was the 1967 visit and long stay in Poland by Msgr Casaroli, secretary of the Council for the Public Affairs of the Church. Although there were no immediate results, contacts were begun again in 1971. The decision of July 1974 is also important in the sense that it involved the Vatican officially in negotiations towards the normalization of relations between church and state in Poland. Until then only 2 parites had been active, the Polish state and the cardinal-primate of Poland.

Since 1971 the state has authorized the building of a number of new churches which the Catholic Church considers indispensable as a result of Poland's rapid urbanization. Earlier, such authorizations had almost always been refused. In the beginning of 1975 50 new churches were under construction and permission had been granted to initiate several others.

Although by 1973 church-state relations had greatly improved, there was still considerable tension due to the demands of cardinal Wysznski concerning

educational reform, which he considered 'to place youth in danger'. In mid-1975, however, it was clear that the church had more reason for satisfaction than discontent. By this time the principal concerns of the Polish episcopate had become: total freedom of association and meeting, since Catholic action groups were still non-existent; more authorizations to build new churches; recognition of the full rights of Polish Catholics in the life of the nation; and assurance that the educational system of the schools would respect the beliefs of all.

The Catholic Church receives no subsidy from the government, and relies solely on donations from its faithful, although it still owns some rural property. The agrarian reform of 1944 in fact resulted in the loss of no more than 50 hectares of Catholic property. The church and its institutions are not recognized as public bodies and are taxed in a way similar to private enterprises; but with the abolition of the compulsory annual listing, its taxes have been somewhat reduced. Nursery schools, primary schools and charitable institutions have now been taken over by government but the church continues to operate a few secondary schools, seminaries and theological faculties as well as the Catholic University of Lublin. Because of the separation of religion and schools, religious instruction is conducted in churches, chapels, and on parish and private premises. These catechetical centres, numbering about 18,200 in 1972, must be registered and submit to public education authorities annual reports of their activities, including numbers of hours of courses, numbers of children, but without having to name personnel involved. Furthermore, the Polish diet or parliament includes 3 small groups of Catholic deputies belonging to no party who are integrated into the National Committee of the Front for National Unity, the grouping of parties and political groups which implements programmes for the development of socialism.

It should also be noted that Poland is the only Communist state which permits Catholic military chaplains in its armed forces, the chief chaplain having the grade of colonel.

**INTERDENOMINATIONAL ORGANIZATIONS.** The Polish Ecumenical Council was formed in 1945, but it traces its tradition of co-operation back to the Sandomierz Accord of 1570 when Lutherans, Calvinists and Moravian Brethren began holding joint synods. The council consists of the 10 principal Old Catholic, Orthodox and Protestant bodies. The Christian Theological Academy in Warsaw is also a member. The council's aims are to develop an awareness of ecumenical, evangelistic and peace problems and to co-ordinate studies and pastoral work. It operates through 11 subsidiary regional bodies. A Joint Commission of the Polish Ecumenical Council and the Catholic Episcopal Commission for Ecumenism was formed in 1974.

**BROADCASTING.** The state radio permits Catholic broadcasts of church services on Sundays. From abroad, Protestant programmes in Polish are beamed in by Europe I (15 minutes on Saturdays) by TWR (Monaco; 45 minutes daily) and by Radio Luxembourg (15 minutes on Tuesdays). By a unique agreement with a Communist state, Pentecostal programmes are prepared by Poles in Poland for release over West European stations, on the understanding that no political matter intrudes. Radio Vatican beams in Catholic programmes in Polish for 5 hours 15 minutes a week.

**BIBLIOGRAPHY**
(Catholic Church in Poland: sociological studies) *Katoliczym Ludowu w Polsce: studia socjologiczne.* E. Ciupak. Warszawa: Wiedza Powszechna, 1973.
(Catholic encyclopedia) *Encyklopedia Katolicka.* Ed F. Gryglewicz et al. Lublin: Catholic University. Vols 1–12, 1973- (in progress).
(Contemporary Christianity in Poland) *Wspolczesne chrzescijanstwo w Polsce.* S. Markiewicz. Warszawa: Ksiazka i Wiedza, 1967.
*L'église catholique en Pologne.* P. Lenert. Paris: Centurion, 1962. 173p.
'Poland', J. Majka, in H Mol (ed), *Western religion* (The Hague: Mouton, 1972), p.403–425.
*Religious life in Poland.* J. Walicke. Warsaw: Interpress Publishers, 1970.
'Sociology of religion in Poland', *Social compass,* XV, 3–4 (1968).
'The character of Polish Catholicism', J. Majka, *Social compass,* XV, 3–4 (1968),185–208.
'The insoluble problem: church and state in Poland', L. Blir, *Religion in Communist lands,* I (May–June, 1973).
*Unser Weg: Vom Leben der Mitgliedkirchen des Polnischen Ökumenischen Rates.* J. Niewieczerzal. Warsaw: Polnische Ökumenische Rat, 1966. 225p.

TABLE 2. ORGANIZED CHURCHES AND DENOMINATIONS IN POLAND

| Official name 1 | Begun 2 | Type 3 | Counc 4 | Congs 5 | Adults 6 | Affiliated 7 | Names, notes, and other statistics (see Codebook) 8 |
|---|---|---|---|---|---|---|---|
| **Catholic Church in Poland** | c 950 | R Lat | B.B.R | 6,610 | 18,997,000 | 28,783,085 | *Kosció. Rzymsko-katolicki.* C=35+7+99. 26q,24s. 16731n,2390m,23865w,476200Yy. |
| M Gniezno | 1000 | R Lat | Bs | 304 | 618,400 | 937,028 | *Archidiecezja Gnieznienska.* Primatial see. 617 47 688 18005 |
| D Chelmno | 1243 | R Lat | Bs | 484 | 805,900 | 1,221,132 | *Diecezja Chelminska.* Traditional religiosity. 894 27 958 27597 |
| D Gdansk (Danzig) | 1925 | R Lat | Bs | 67 | 340,300 | 515,600 | Port, industry. Large pastoral activity. 232 15 211 8251 |
| D Koszalin-Kolobrzeg | 1972 | R Lat | Bs | 174 | 540,300 | 818,690 | Formed from D Berlin, PN Schneidemühl. 338 9 282 15023 |
| D Szczecin(Stettin)-Kamien | 1972 | R Lat | Bs | 145 | 559,000 | 847,000 | Detached from D Berlin. Northern port. 344 18 142 13771 |
| D Wloclawek (Wladislavia) | 996 | R Lat | Bs | 260 | 660,700 | 1,001,028 | Rural, being industrialized. Active practice. 584 122 677 20062 |
| M Kraków | 1000 | R Lat | Bs | 373 | 1,253,800 | 1,899,729 | Centre of national culture, strongly religious. 1585 820 2991 23505 |
| D Czestochowa | 1925 | R Lat | Bs | 251 | 870,000 | 1,318,000 | North rural, south dechristianized. Cult of Mary. 810 71 972 19028 |
| D Katowice | 1925 | R Lat | Bs | 325 | 1,056,000 | 1,600,000 | Working-class, religious. Protestant bloc in south. 869 97 1753 28429 |
| D Kielce | 1805 | R Lat | Bs | 286 | 592,700 | 898,074 | Industrial, becoming dechristianized. 600 0 518 15881 |
| D Tarnów | 1786 | R Lat | Bs | 356 | 754,800 | 1,143,600 | Many religious and priestly vocations. 1021 98 1332 22369 |
| M Warszawa (Warsaw) | 1798 | R Lat | Bs | 345 | 1,848,500 | 2,800,000 | Capital; attached to Gniezno. Dechristianization. 1441 400 2710 35158 |
| D Lódz | 1920 | R Lat | Bs | 152 | 825,000 | 1,250,000 | Socialist traditions. Shortage of priests. 480 43 683 19157 |
| D Lublin | 1805 | R Lat | Bs | 253 | 802,600 | 1,216,100 | Difficult pastorally, low religious practice. 777 55 1032 18252 |
| D Plock | 1075 | R Lat | Bs | 248 | 554,000 | 840,000 | Strongest area of Mariavite schismatics. 474 37 538 16901 |
| D Sandomierz | 1818 | R Lat | Bs | 271 | 776,000 | 1,175,000 | Industrial centres, becoming dechristianized.. 663 18 781 20939 |
| D Siedlce | 1818 | R Lat | Bs | 242 | 515,200 | 780,550 | East of Warsaw. Very active religious practice. 508 19 437 15080 |
| D Warmia | 1243 | R Lat | Bs | 297 | 759,000 | 1,150,000 | Rural. Ex East Prussia, with Polish settlers. 611 77 420 23179 |
| M Wroclaw (formerly Breslau) | 1000 | R Lat | Bs | 567 | 1,867,400 | 2,829,400 | 1972, parts added from D Meissen, AD Prague. 1227 70 2438 38809 |
| D Gorzów (formerly Landsberg) | 1972 | R Lat | Bs | 206 | 626,000 | 948,500 | Formed from Breslau, Berlin, Schneidemühl, Olomunek. 369 2 323 15524 |
| D Opole (formerly Oppeln) | 1972 | R Lat | Bs | 445 | 1,016,000 | 1,540,000 | Detached from M Breslau. Settlers from all Poland. 827 42 1765 25199 |
| AD Poznan | 968 | R Lat | Bs | 436 | 1,056,000 | 1,600,000 | Industrial and cultural centre. High practice. 1066 291 1933 27929 |
| AD in Bialystok (part of AD Vilna) | c1350 | R Lat | Bs | 60 | 187,000 | 283,348 | *Archidiecezja w Bialymstoku.* AD suppressed in 1945. 270 12 165 5000 |
| AD in Lubaczów (part of AD Lwów) | 1412 | R Lat | Bs | 28 | 51,300 | 77,734 | In AD Lvov (USSR) suppresed 1945. 76 0 59 1480 |
| D in Drohiczyn-on-Bug (D Pinsk) | 1925 | R Lat | Bs | 35 | 61,100 | 92,572 | In D Pinsk (White Russia) suppressed 1945. 78 0 57 1665 |
| Ch of Jesus C of Latter-day Saints | | M LdS | x.... | | 200 | 500 | *Mormons*, related to CJCLdS(Utah, USA). Neither recognized by state nor banned. |
| Churches of Christ | | P Dis | xv... | 21 | 1,000 | 2,000 | M=CCCC(Instrumental)(USA). Warsaw, Breslau and 10 other cities. Rapid growth. 2f. |
| Epiphany Lay Missionary Movement | | P ind | ..... | 87 | 1,700 | 3,000 | Lay movement linked to USA body. HQ Poznan. 87 houses of prayer, 274 elders. |
| Ev Ch of the Augsburg Confession in P | 1518 | P Lut | LWC.W | 368 | 95,000 | 120,000 | *Kosciól Ewangelicko-Augsburski w PRL.* 6 Dioceses. Germans. 107n,125b,1j,214t,1u. |
| Free Union of Holy Scripture Seekers | | P ind | ..... | 135 | 3,000 | 5,000 | Independents centred on Bible study. HQ Krakow. 320 preachers. |
| Indep Autonomous Roman Cath Parishes | 1962 | C CCa | ..... | 2 | 10,000 | 15,000 | Schisms ex RCC by 2 parishes: Wierzbica (11 villages, 9,000), & Kamionka Wielka. |
| Isolated radio churches | 1939 | P rad | ..... | 20 | 300 | 600 | Isolated believers in non-religious families. R=9600(SGA,TWR, Radio Vatican,&c). |
| Jehovah's Witnesses | 1905 | M Jeh | x.... | 790 | 12,162 | 20,000 | 1920, 700 attending meetings. Active witnessing under way by 1926. Underground. |
| Mariavite Ch of Ancient Catholic Rite | 1936 | C CCa | ....w | 27 | 3,000 | 4,000 | *Catholic Mariavite Ch.* Schism ex Old Catholic Mariavite Ch. HQ Felicjanow. 70n,24b. |
| Methodist Ch in the Polish Republic | 1922 | P Met | VvC.W | 52 | 4,233 | 12,000 | *Kosciól Metodystyczny.* Linked C&S Europe CC, UMC(USA). 5 Districts. 26n,1r(6000). |
| New Apostolic Church | | C CAp | x.... | | 300 | 500 | *Neo-Apostolic Association.* Bezirk Schweiz. World HQ Dortmund (FR Germany). Germans. |
| Old Catholic Church of Poland | 1946 | C CCa | ..... | | 500 | 1,000 | Schism ex RCC. Joined by Mariavite remnants. Links with NAORCC (USA). |
| Old Catholic Mariavite Ch of Poland | 1906 | C CCa | UWC.W | 59 | 15,000 | 24,000 | *Staro-Katolickiego Kościóla Mariawitów. Imitators of Mary.* 3 Dioceses. 39n,200w,1s. |
| Old Ritualist Church (Priestless) | 1634 | O OBe | ..... | 5 | 3,000 | 5,000 | *Philippians. Old Believers.* Schism ex Russian OC. HQ Wojnowo. 6-hour services. |
| Orthodox Church of Poland: | c 990 | O Pol | MWC.W | 300 | 330,000 | 527,000 | *Autokefaliczny Kosciól Prawoslawny.* 1939, 4 million. (1970) 216n,216b,1d,1e,1s,1u. |
| D Warszawa (Warsaw) & Bielsk | 1370 | O Pol | Mm | 120 | 130,000 | 207,000 | Mainly Ukrainians and Russians. 1 monastery for men (Jableczna). 94n (in 1977). |
| D Bialystok & Gdansk (Danzig) | | O Pol | Mb | 110 | 120,000 | 190,000 | North and northeast. Many White Russians (Byelorussians), Ukrainians, Russians. |
| D Lódz & Poznan | | O Pol | Ma | 40 | 50,000 | 80,000 | Centre of country, west of Warsaw. Byelorussians, Ukrainians. 16 priests in 1977. |
| D Wroclaw & Szczecin | | O Pol | Mb | 30 | 30,000 | 50,000 | Formerly Breslau and Stettin in Germany, now settled by Poles. 27 priests in 1977. |
| Polish Baptist Union | 1858 | P Bap | TvC.W | 121 | 4,000 | 8,000 | *Polski Kosciól Chrzescijan Baptystów.* 10,000 adults in 1939. Declining. 64n,1s. |
| Polish National Catholic Church | 1920 | C OCa | UWC.W | 96 | 30,000 | 56,600 | *Kosciól Polskokatolicki.* USA schism ex RCC. Dioc: Warsaw, Krakow,Wroclaw. 105n,1u. |
| Reformed Evangelical Church in Poland | 1548 | P Ref | RvC.W | 12 | 3,500 | 4,900 | *Kosciól Ewangelicko-Reformowany.* 1939–45, almost obliterated. Declining. 6n. |
| Seventh-day Adventist Church | 1912 | P Adv | x...w | 120 | 4,116 | 8,500 | *Kosciól Adwentystow Ds w Polsce. SDA, Polish UC.* 25n,75mw,1j,1s,120t(4801),189Y. |
| Union of Polish Brethren | | M Unt | I.... | | 300 | 500 | Unitarian tendencies. Links with Unitarian Universalist Association (USA). |
| United Evangelical Ch of the Gospel | 1909 | P Pe2 | ZPC.W | 269 | 10,000 | 20,000 | *Zjednoczony Kosciól Ewangeliczny.* 1947 5-church merger. 65% Pentecostals. 125n,1s. |
| Other Protestant denominations | | P | ..... | | 2,000 | 3,000 | Total about 15 others (see list below). |
| Other marginal Protestant bodies | | M | ..... | | 1,000 | 2,000 | Total about 10 others (see list below). |
| Other Orthodox churches | | O | ..... | | 200 | 500 | Isolated groups, including Armenian Apostolics (Gregorians). |
| **Total affiliated (mid-1970)** | | | | **9,180** | **19,531,511** | **29,626,685** | **Total denominations (1970) . . . 47.** |
| **Total affiliated (mid-1975)** | | | | **9,230** | **20,302,000** | **30,795,400** | **Total denominations (1975) . . . 48.** |
| **Total affiliated (mid-1980)** | | | | **9,280** | **21,053,700** | **31,935,700** | **Total denominations (1980) . . . 49.** |

NOTES ON TABLE ABOVE

COLUMNS: for meanings and CODES (cols. 1, 3, 4, 8): see Codebook (Part 6). Column 1: **Boldface type** = church with over 10% of country's affiliated Christians.

NATIONAL COUNCILS (Column 4, 5th letter).
- R = Polish Episcopal Conference (Konferencja Episkopatu Polski, KEP).
- W = Polish Ecumenical Council (Polska Rada Ekumeniczna, PRE).
- w = associate member of PRE.

*Local councils.* 11 subsidiary regional bodies of PRE.

OTHER PROTESTANT DENOMINATIONS. In addition to those listed in the table, there are around 15 others not recognized by the state as churches but as either registered religious associations, other associations, or unregistered. These include: Apostolic See in Jesus Christ, Association of Bible Students, Association for Christian Education, Ch of God, Ch of Sabbath-Day Christians in Poland, Ch of the Brethren (1946; 7 missionaries, USA), Communities of Non Confessional Christians, Disciples of Christ, Evangelical Association of Prayer, Exclusive Brethren (Kelly-Continental), Friends (Quakers), Mennonites.

OTHER MARGINAL PROTESTANT BODIES. These include: Amis de l'Homme 'Ange du Seigneur' (Friends of Man 'Angel of the Lord') Lay Movement (schism ex Jehovah's Witnesses), Ch of Christ Scientist, Divine See of the Lamb of the Apostles in the Spirit and the Truth of Alpha & Omega The Beginning and The End, Pan-Monistic Community, Rustres (Clowns or Louts).

**PEOPLES** (ethnolinguistic). Christians: 97.6% Polish, 0.7% Ukrainian, 0.6% Kashubian (Pomeranian), 0.6% Byelorussian, 0.2% German, 0.1% Gypsy, 0.1% Russian, 0.1% Slovak, Lithuanian, Greek, Macedonian.

**COUNTRY-WIDE TOTALS**

EVANGELIZATION (see Parts 5). 1900: 99%. 1970: 100%. 1980: 100%. *Mass evangelism.* 1978, visit by evangelist Billy Graham to 6 cities (25,000 attenders). *Radiophonic evangelism.* Annual listeners' letters (1975): 9,600 (7,200 SGA over TWR, about 2,000 Radio Vatican, 132 HCJB, et alia). About 4,500 listeners a year write for New Testaments or Bibles. *Literature evangelism.* There is widespread distribution from home to home.

FOREIGN MISSIONARIES AND PERSONNEL (nationals serving abroad) (1973). Total 1,476 Roman Catholics: 1,028 foreign missionaries (end of 1975) serving in 52 countries (265 in Brazil, 102 Canada, 91 Argentina, 79 Zambia, 44 Indonesia, 43 Australia, 36 Papua New Guinea, 32 Zaire, et alia), increasing from 877 (end of 1974), 826 (end of 1973) (597 priests, 45 brothers, 178 sisters, 6 lay) and 715 (in 1972); new missionaries per year 34 in 1970, 82 in 1973, 76 in 1974, 68 in 1975, 93 in 1976; also about 448 other personnel serving in Western Europe and USA but not officially regarded as missionaries. In addition, many personnel have fled as refugees or exiles; these are excluded here if they are no longer Polish citizens. In 1975, there were 23 Polish Jesuits serving in the USA, as well as many other Polish personnel.

FOREIGN MISSIONARIES AND PERSONNEL (aliens from abroad) (1973). Total 15. *From Western world.* About 15 Pro- testants (12 in 6 USA societies, 3 in 2 UK societies).

INSTITUTIONS (church-operated) (1973). Total 330, including 24 higher schools (10 minor seminaries), 220 charitable institutions, 10 religious communities, 5 research centres, 57 seminaries (50 RC, 4 Protestant, 2 Orthodox, 1 Catholic/non-Roman), 1 university.

PERIODICALS. About 75 titles, mostly Roman Catholic.

PERSONNEL. About 45,215 (45,200 national, 15 foreign).

RELIGIOUS LIBRARIES. About 76.

SCRIPTURE DISTRIBUTION (1975). Annual totals: 87,763 Bibles (1% free, 54% subsidized, 45% commercial), 34,616 NTs (3% free, 39% subsidized, 58% commercial), 78,261 UBS portions. *Translations completed.* Polish: portion in 1522, NT 1553, Bible 1561.

SERVICE AGENCIES. About 45, including CHSS, EES, KEP, KIK, PRE, SGA, SMSK, WLC(EHC).

ADDITIONAL DATA ON CHURCHES

CATHOLIC CHURCH IN POLAND. *Jurisdictions.* The list of jurisdictions shown in the table above represents a major change in Polish ecclesiastical administration agreed by the Vatican in 1972, harmonizing ecclesiastical frontiers with the de facto political frontiers existing since the end of World War II. The areas affected were not only the northern and western regions of Poland (formerly German territory), but also the southern regions along the Polish-Czechoslovak frontier where a 2-centuries-old anachronistic arrangement (since the Silesian wars) had placed several Polish deaneries under dioceses largely in Czechoslovakia. These adjustments in 1972 were also accompanied by a reorganization of ecclesiastical provinces within Poland proper. In the east and northeast, to the contrary, the situation remained unchanged: the USSR had overrun Polish territory in 1945, and had suppressed Catholic dioceses whose see cities it contained, but the Vatican had never accepted their suppression. The Diocese of Luck completely disappeared, and the only remnants were Polish parts of other dioceses which the Vatican continued to maintain (the last 3 in the table). The Eastern-rite jurisdictions of AD Lvov (Armenian), AD Lvov (Ukrainian) with its suffragans D Przemysl and D Stanislawów, and EA Lemkowszczyza (Byzantine), all disappeared completely although *Annuario Pontificio* continues to report them (1975). *Annual baptisms.* (1972) 99.6% infant, 0.4% adult. *Personnel.* All nationals. *Priests.* Increasing 1976 to 14,653 diocesan and 3,876 religious. New annual ordinations: 1969, 406 (256 diocesan, 150 religious); 1970, 381 (263 & 118); 1971, 480 (356 & 124); 1972, 604 (471 & 133); 1973, 557 (450 & 107); 1974, 638 (486 & 152). Growth of number of priests: 11,394 in 1937; 7,170 in 1944; 16,839 in 1964. In 1973 about half of all Polish priests were under 40 years of age. *Catholic charismatics* (1975). About 500 adults including religious personnel and students are active in over 20 prayer groups. *Seminaries.* Every archdiocese and diocese has its own major seminary except the AD in Lubaczów. In addition to these 24 diocesan seminaries there were, in 1973, 26 for religious priests (10 being in Krakow). *Seminarians.* (End of 1971) 4,088, (1972) 4,130, (1973) 4,174, (1974) 4,216 (3,091 diocesan, 1,125 religious), (1976) 4,705. *Religious personnel* (statistics at end of 1972). Priests: 35 congregations, with 7,000 professed. Brothers: 7 congregations for brothers only, with 230 professed. Sisters: 99 congregations, with 26,290 (24,999 professed in 87 congregations doing apostolic work, 1,291 professed in 12 contemplative congregations with 56 convents). These statistics are reconcilable with the totals in the table above since many brothers belong to congregations of priests, and many sisters are not attached to dioceses or communities. *Main orders and congregations.* Priests (congregations with over 350 in 1972): 848 SDB, 671 OFM, 666 OFMConv, 529 SJ, 362 SAC. Brothers (with over 25 professed): 79 OH, 45 Brothers Servants of the Virgin Mary, 34 Albertine Brothers of the Third Order of St Francis for service to the poor. Sisters (congregations with over 1,000 professed): 1,879 Daughters of Charity of St Vincent de Paul, 1,851 Sisters of St Elizabeth, 1,252 Servants of the Immaculate Virgin Mary of Starawies, 1,083 Daughters of Mary, 1,068 Servants of the Virgin Mary Immaculate.

*Catholic organizations.* Among the major national bodies are the Episcopal Conference of Poland (Konferencja Episkopatu Polski), a conference for men (Konferencja Przelozonych Wyzszych Zakonów Meskich w Polsce) and a conference for sisters (Konferencja Przelozonych Wyzszych Zenskich Institutow Zakonnych w Polsce). The 2 conferences of religious personnel began and continue to sponsor at Czestochowa a vocational centre (JOP) to enlighten public opinion and especially youth concerning the religious life and the requirements of the different religious communities. At Warsaw an inter-community course is offered to aid in the completion of training in temporary vows and preparation for the apostolate, and there is another course for brothers.

The Holy See has no diplomatic relations with Poland.

Polish lay Catholics are divided into 3 completely different movements which owe their origin to changes effected at the 8th plenary of the central committee of the unified Polish party in October 1956, the beginning of the Gomulka era, which opened the door to new possibilities for action in Catholic intellectual circles. Each of these 3 movements has its own orientation, but all are based on the desire to build a bridge between the Catholic Church and the regime. In the absence of other lay Catholic organizations these 3 associations play a major role in Poland. In order of ideological proximity to the Polish episcopate, these are: (a) Ruch 'Znak', (b) CHSS and (c) Pax.

(a) Ruch Znak (The Sign Movement) is a federation of associations and groups which collaborate on the basis of common general principles. Belonging to it are: (1) Catholic intellectual clubs (Klub Inteligencji Katolickiej) which were formed after October 1956. In 1972 there were 5, in the cities of Warsaw, Krakow, Poznan, Wroclaw and Torun, with 3,500 members, 1,500 being in Warsaw. They engage in training activities as well as social economic, moral and cultural studies, with special emphasis on discussion groups and publications. Each club is an autonomous association, but there is a co-ordinating secretariat in Warsaw. (2) The Social Institute of the Publication 'The Sign' Krakow (Spoleczny Instytut Wydawniczy Znak) was founded in 1957 by a group which edits the weekly *Tygodnik Powszechny* (The Universal Week). The institute produces a socio-cultural weekly with 40,000 circulation as well as the monthly *Znak* dedicated to theology, philosophy and cultural questions, with 7,000 circulation, and also about 10 books each year. (3) The monthly *Wiez* (The Bond), concerned with social problems, has been published in Warsaw since 1958, with a circulation of 6,000 and a resumé in French. It also publishes a collection of 3 or 4 books yearly. (4) The Centre of Information and Social Studies (Osrodek Dokumentacji i Studiów Spolecznych, ODiSS) was founded at Warsaw in 1967. It is related to the Catholic intellectual club of Warsaw and the Wiez group, and specializes in dialogue of the church with the contemporary world. It publishes *Chrzescijanin w Swiecie* (The Christian in the World) with 2,000 copies, a bi-monthly with a French summary, and one or 2 books a year. The Znak movement is undoubtedly the most influential of the

Polish Catholic groups. It is oriented towards the reforms of Vatican II. It sees its primary task as promoting the conciliar renewal of Polish Catholicism and assuring a Christian presence in the social thought of the country, stressing the training of Polish Catholics as both church members and active citizens. It influences directly many Catholic intellectual circles and some of the clergy who in turn influence large numbers of laity. It is represented politically by a parliamentary group (Kolo Znak, with 5 deputies), and keeps close contact with the Polish ecclesiastical hierarchy, who (as with the Lay Council in Rome) treat it as a semi-official organization of the Polish laity. It is a member of MIIC in Fribourg, Switzerland.

(b) The Christian and Social Association (Chrzescijanskie Stowarzyszenie Stoleczne, CHSS) was founded at Warsaw in 1957 and now has 14 regional affiliates. It is a social conciliar group heavily involved in politics, and publishes a popular weekly *Za i Przeciw* (The For and Against) with 50,000 copies, a monthly *Novum* with 1,500 copies, a bulletin of information (6 issues per year in English, French and German) and, irregularly, books. It manages its own enterprise Ars Christiana (devotional articles) which it sells in its own shops throughout Poland. Represented in parliament by 2 deputies, the CHSS has no official contact with the ecclesiastical hierarchy, and its social influence is limited.

(c) The Pax Association (Stowarzyszenie Pax) was formed in 1945 immediately following World War II by a group of Catholic laymen supported by government authorities. Known first by the title of its weekly magazine, *Dzis i Jutro* (Today and Tomorrow), this group adopted the name Pax (Peace) in 1947 and gradually built up a monopoly of influence prior to 1956, because of the changes and prohibitions which other Catholic intellectual groups suffered including the liquidation in 1948 of *Tygodnik Warszawski* (Warsaw Weekly), closure of Catholic student associations in 1949 and the disappearance of the weekly *Znak* (The Sign) in 1953. Some organizations of Catholic Action type, such as Catholic Youth (Katolickie Stowarzyszenie Mlodziezy) and Sodality of Mary (Sodalicja Marianska) were prohibited in 1949 also. Pax has its headquarters in Warsaw. Of all Catholic lay movements in Poland it is the organization which manifests the greatest political ambitions. It also has extensive means of influencing public opinion, including multiple branches and its own publishing body. Pax Publishing House (Instytut Wydawniczy Pax) produces 80 to 100 books per year, the only Catholic daily in the country *Slowo Powszechne* (The Public Word) with 100,000 circulation, a socio-cultural weekly *Kierunki* (Orientations) with 10,000 copies, a monthly *Zycie i Mysl* (Life and Thought) with 4,000 copies, as well as popular periodicals. Pax possesses also a centre for documentation and religious studies (Ostrodek Dokumentacji i Studiów Religijnych) and publishes a monthly review of the Polish Catholic press in 5 foreign languages. The association has popularized the ideals of Vatican II, but its actual influence in political circles is less than might be expected. It has attempted to convince both the Communist state of the importance of enlisting Catholics, and also the church of the importance of the socialist construction of Poland. In practice it has not realized this ambition and has tended to become a tool of the regime. Pax has a parliamentary representation of 5 deputies. It has no official contacts with the Catholic hierarchy, which from its side has continually warned the faithful of the dangers inherent in such an association.

All these 3 organizations are preoccupied with relations between church and government. In this sense they are very different from organizations in non-communist countries. At present they receive more recognition from the state than the church. A quite new type of Catholic organization, working within the church for its *aggiornamento*, is the Polish Centre for Conciliar Renewal — Veritas, Justicia, Caritas (Polskie Centrum Odnowy Soborowej — Veritas, Justicia, Caritas, PCOS-VIC). Founded in 1973 as an extension of the Conciliar Committee of the Polish Parish Clergy begun in 1962 which sporadically sent propositions to the Polish bishops and conciliar fathers at the time of Vatican II, the centre is independent of the ecclesiastical hierarchy and includes in its membership different groups of clergy and lay persons. Its purpose is to promote the conciliar renewal initiated by John XXIII in order to reform church structures and extend the application of its doctrines to contemporary thought without any break in historical continuity. Unlike the other 3 organizations, PCOS-VIC is not recognized by the state. It publishes a monthly periodical (*Ancora*) in 3 languages: Polish, English and French. The centre works from the assumption that conciliar renewal is blocked by the conservative forces of the church who want to minimize the inspiration of Vatican II.

Advanced pastoral and theological studies are available in several institutions. Bodies conferring academic degrees are the faculties of theology (Wydzial Teologiczny) and canon law (Wydzial Prawa Kanonicznego) of the Catholic University of Lublin. There are also faculties of theology, canon law and Christian philosophy at the Catholic Theological Academy of Warsaw (Akademia Teologii Katolickiej, ATK) which had 850 students in 1970–71. Created in 1954 by government following the suppression of the faculties of theology of the official universities of Krakow and Warsaw, the ATK possesses civil rather than ecclesiastical rights, and is supported by the state. There is also the Pontifical Faculty of Krakow. Other faculties which confer only licenciates are the Pontifical Faculties of Theology of Wroclaw and Poznan and the Higher School of Theology at Warsaw.

The Institute of Pastoral Theology (Instytut Teologii Pastoralnej) forms part of the Faculty of Theology of the Catholic University of Lublin but has its own autonomous programme. It was founded in 1958 and has been licensed since 1968 by the Vatican to confer higher degrees with ecclesiastical rights. Chairs of pastoral theology, catechesis, homiletics, liturgy and religious sociology are also maintained. The chair in religious sociology (Katedra Socjologii Religii) was established in 1960 and has been affiliated to FERES in Belgium, as is the Institute of Socio-Religious Research (Instytut Badan Socjalno-Religijny) at Ozanow Mazowiecki.

The Liturgical Institute of the Theological Faculty of Krakow (Instytut Liturgiczny Przy Wydziale Teologicznym w Krakowie) was founded in 1966 and carries on research in liturgical sciences. A missiological section, founded in 1968, sponsors a 5-year programme of studies in 4 parts: missionary theory, study of religions, socio-economic problems of development, and Polish problems.

The Missionary Commission of the Polish Episcopate (Komisja Episkopatu Polski do Spraw Misji Sekretariat Komisji) has its secretariat in Warsaw. It is governed in accordance with the missionary decree 'Ad Gentes' and the motu proprio 'Ecclesiae sanctae', with the aim of promoting and co-ordinating missionary activities in Poland and to stimulate and aid missionary vocations. The commission also plays the role of a national missionary council.

The Missionary Seminary of SVD Priests (Seminarium Misyjne Ksiezy Werbistow) is located at Pieniezno and is the most important missionary centre in Poland. Between 1965 and 1972 it provided more than 80 missionaries for foreign fields. It has the best missiological library in Poland.

Foreign missionary activity is exceptional for eastern Europe, and has experienced constant and important growth. Following World War II and the loss of many priests killed, and the need to provide priests for former German territories ceded to Poland, the sending of missionaries overseas was slow to regain momentum. Between 1945 and 1957 there were only 55 departures of Polish missionaries. During 1958–65 the number increased to 258, after which (1965) the government facilitated departures in part due to the request of the Indonesian government. Indeed, 20 Polish SVD priests left for Indonesia the same year. Nevertheless, 1971 is generally recognized as the year of 'liberalization' for missionary activity as revealed in these figures: 1970, 34 departures; 1971, 66; 1972, 54; 1973, 82; and 1974, 76. At the beginning of 1975 there were 877 Polish Catholic missionaries and at the end of 1975, 1,028 working in 52 countries in Africa, Asia, Latin America and Oceania. The principal missionary congregations in 1972 were Sisters of the Holy Family (Zgromadzenie Siòstr Misjonarek Sw Rodziny) founded in 1905, with 276 members in Poland and 4 in Zambia; Dominican Missionaries of Jesus and Mary (Zgromadzinie Siòstr Dominikanek Misjonarek Jezusa i Maryi) founded in 1932, with 33 members in Poland and 2 in Argentina; Society of Christ for Polish Emigrants, SCGR (Towarzystwo Chrystusowe Dla Wychodzców) founded in 1932, with 354 members in Poland, 38 in Argentina and Brazil and 9 in Australia; Servant Sisters of the BVM of the Immaculate Conception (Sluzebniczki Najswietszej Maryi Panny Ze Starej Wsi), founded in 1886 for social work, with 88 members in Poland and 19 in South Africa and Zambia. Male orders of foreign origin are the SVD (119 members), SDB (76), CM (40), SJ (32), OFMConv (28) and CSSR (27). Female congregations of foreign origin are the Franciscan Missionaries of Mary (45 members), Servant Missionaries of the Holy Spirit (15), and Sisters of the Holy Family of Bordeaux (11 members in Lesotho).

Educational statistics for 1972 include 3 secondary schools for boys (500 students) sponsored by the Pax Association, 11 for girls (1,600 students), and 2 professional schools for girls (200 students), run by sisters. With regard to higher education, in addition to establishments for ecclesiastical studies, there is the Catholic University of Lublin (Katolicki Uniwersytet Lubelski, KUL), founded in 1918, with 2,324 students in 1970–71. It is the only Catholic institution for higher studies and the only private university in eastern Europe. The degrees conferred by this university are recognized by the state. The KUL is directed by an ad hoc episcopal commission and its budget is covered entirely by gifts from the Catholic community.

The Secretariat for Charitable Pastoral Work, at Krakow, functions as an agency of the Episcopal Commission and has secretaries in each diocese. The Caritas Committee also at Krakow, was founded in 1950 and since 1966 has been affiliated to Caritas Internationalis. There are 202 charitable institutions of different types, plus 21 auxiliary centres, with 15,000 residents in homes for the aged, infirm, and handicapped infants, supervised by some 5,000 qualified workers half of whom are sisters belonging to 48 different congregations. In addition, other sisters work as state employees in government hospitals.

EVANGELICAL CHURCH OF THE AUGSBURG CONFESSION IN POLAND. In 1975–76 most members, being Germans, were allowed after the Helsinki Accord to emigrate to West Germany. By 1977, membership had fallen to 79,500 (from 270,000 in 1946).

POLISH BAPTIST UNION. Often referred to as the Christian Baptists.

UNITED EVANGELICAL CHURCH OF THE GOSPEL. A merger in 1947, completed in 1953, of 5 bodies: Ch of Christ, Free Christian Union, Pentecostalists, Union of Christian Evangelists, Union of Determined Christians.

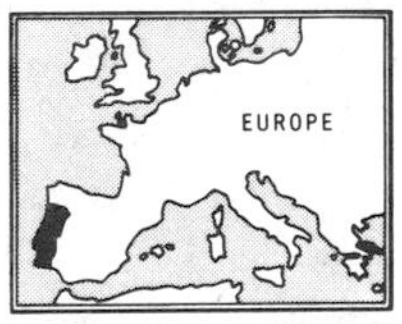


# PORTUGAL

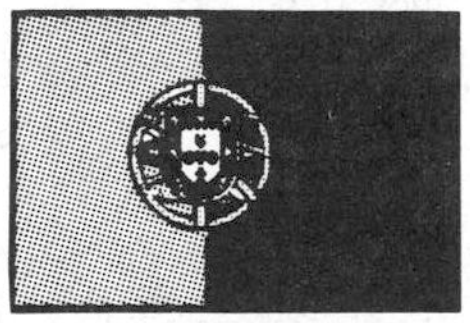

## SECULAR DATA

**STATE. Official name:** The Portuguese Republic (A República Portuguesa). Adjective of nationality: Portuguese.
**Flag** (shown above right): Green and red bars with national coat of arms.
**Area:** 92,082 sq.km. (35,553 sq.miles). Agricultural land: 46.9%.
**Government:** Parliamentary socialist republic, since 1976 (12th century independence as monarchy, 1910 republic, 1932 dictatorship, 1974 military junta).
**Legislature:** National Assembly, 263 seats.
**Official language:** Portuguese (*Português*).
**Chief cities:** capital Lisbon 1,611,890 (1972), Porto 1,314,790.
**Political divisions:** 18 Districts, 4 Islands.
**Armed forces** (1976): Total 59,800 regular: army 36,000, navy 13,800, air force 10,000 (46 combat aircraft). Paramilitary forces: 23,400.
**Foreign forces** (1973): 2,000 USA troops.

**DEMOGRAPHY. Population:** 8,568,703 (census of 15.XII.1970. For 1970–2000 (UN), see last row of Table 1). Population density (1975): 95/sq.km. (246/sq.mile). Under 15 years: 29%. Growth rate (1975–80): 0.44% per year (births 1.80%, deaths −1.01%, emigrants −0.35%). Life expectancy (1975–80): 69.3 years. Household size: 3.6 persons.
**Major languages:** Portuguese, Spanish, English.
**Urban dwellers** (1970): 37.2%. Urban growth rate (1950–70): 1.5% per year.
**Labour force:** 39%.
**Refugees** (1977): From abroad 750,000 (350,000 from Angola, 150,000 from Mozambique). Exiles abroad: over 100,000 Portuguese and Angolan refugees have moved on to Brazil.
**Tourists** (1971): 3,900,000. (1974) 2,621,802.

**ETHNOLINGUISTIC GROUPS:** 99.5% Portuguese, 0.3% alien (0.1% Spaniard, 0.1% British (8,000)), 0.2% Gypsy (20,000) Angolan, Mozambican, Brazilian, Caboverdian, Mestiço, North African Arab, Macao Chinese (250), Jewish, Timorese.

**MONEY** (1977). **Monetary unit:** escudo (= 100 centavos); US$1 = Esc 31.00.
**National income per person:** US$1,400. Average annual family income: US$5,040.
**Inflation:** (1970–74) 15.0% per year (1975: consumer price index 221), (1977) 32% per year, (1978) 29% per year.
**Cost of living in capital** (1976): index 106 (Washington DC=100) Daily cost of living: US$30.

**LITERATURE.** Annual new book titles (1973): 6,173. Periodicals: 900. Scientific journals: 250. Newspapers: 29 dailies, 686 non-daily.

**COMMUNICATION** (per 1,000 people). Phones: 111. Radios: 176. TV sets: 66. Daily newspaper circulation: 87 copies.

**HEALTH.** Hospitals: 577 (53,501 beds). Doctors: 8,972. Lepers: 3,390 (0.4 per 1,000). Blind: 8,225. Psychotics: 75,000. Drug addicts: 67,000.

**EDUCATION.** Adult literacy: (1950) 56%, (1970) 71%. Education rate: 46%. Schools: 16,406. Universities: 8.

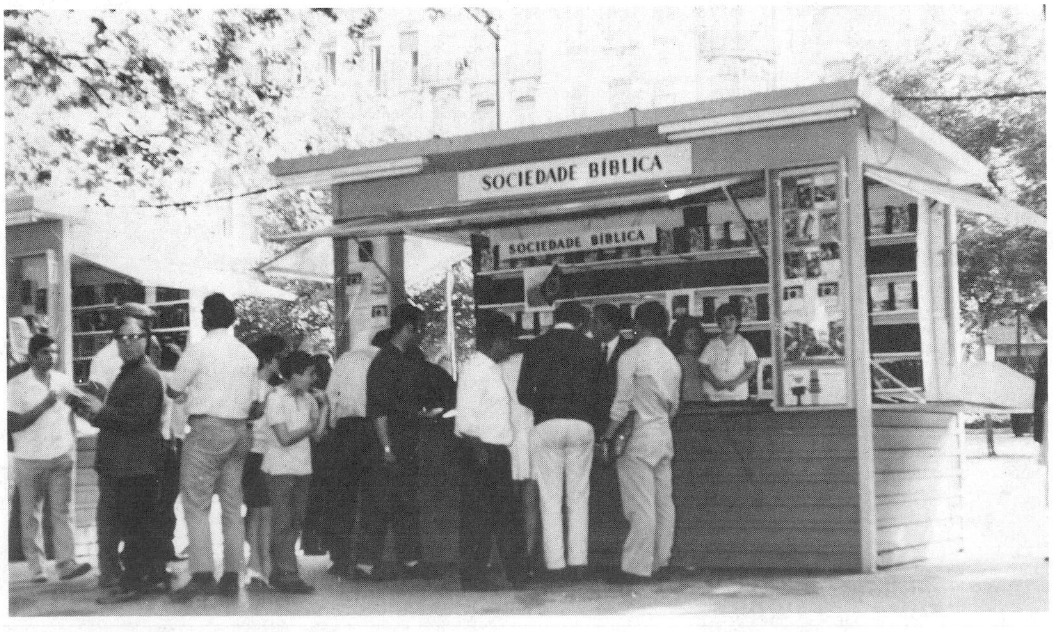

Bible Society stall at 40th Lisbon Book Fair, 1970.

TABLE 1. RELIGIOUS ADHERENTS IN PORTUGAL

| Year | 1900 | | mid-1970 | | Annual change, 1970–1980 | | | | mid-1975 | | mid-1980 | | 2000 | |
|---|---|---|---|---|---|---|---|---|---|---|---|---|---|---|
| *Name* | *Adherents* | *%* | *Adherents* | *%* | *Natural* | *Conversion* | *Total* | *Rate* | *Adherents* | *%* | *Adherents* | *%* | *Adherents* | *%* |
| **Christians** | **5,420,800** | **100.0** | **8,421,100** | **97.6** | **31,804** | **−20,224** | **11,580** | **0.14** | **8,470,000** | **96.7** | **8,536,900** | **95.3** | **8,921,500** | **90.0** |
| professing | 5,420,000 | 100.0 | 8,421,100 | 97.6 | 31,804 | −20,224 | 11,580 | 0.14 | 8,470,000 | 96.7 | 8,536,900 | 95.3 | 8,921,500 | 90.0 |
| Roman Catholics | 5,417,700 | 99.9 | 8,334,400 | 96.6 | 31,442 | −21,862 | 9,580 | 0.11 | 8,373,500 | 95.6 | 8,430,200 | 94.1 | 8,771,500 | 88.4 |
| Protestants | 2,000 | 0.0 | 56,700 | 0.7 | 240 | 1,260 | 1,500 | 2.34 | 64,000 | 0.7 | 71,700 | 0.8 | 99,000 | 1.0 |
| Marginal Protestants | 0 | 0.0 | 20,000 | 0.2 | 84 | 416 | 500 | 2.22 | 22,500 | 0.3 | 25,000 | 0.3 | 40,000 | 0.4 |
| Catholics (non-Roman) | 600 | 0.0 | 4,500 | 0.1 | 17 | −17 | 0 | 0.00 | 4,500 | 0.1 | 4,500 | 0.1 | 5,000 | 0.1 |
| Anglicans | 500 | 0.0 | 4,500 | 0.1 | 17 | −17 | 0 | 0.00 | 4,500 | 0.1 | 4,500 | 0.1 | 5,000 | 0.1 |
| Orthodox | 0 | 0.0 | 1,000 | 0.0 | 4 | −4 | 0 | 0.00 | 1,000 | 0.0 | 1,000 | 0.0 | 1,000 | 0.0 |
| nominal | 8,000 | 0.1 | 38,176 | 0.4 | 165 | 1,387 | 1,552 | 3.54 | 43,800 | 0.5 | 53,700 | 0.6 | 198,000 | 2.0 |
| affiliated | 5,412,800 | 99.8 | 8,382,924 | 97.2 | 31,639 | −21,611 | 10,028 | 0.12 | 8,426,200 | 96.2 | 8,483,200 | 94.7 | 8,723,500 | 88.0 |
| doubly-affiliated | −3,100 | −0.1 | −55,000 | −0.6 | −225 | −775 | −1,000 | 1.67 | −60,000 | −0.7 | −65,000 | −0.7 | −90,000 | −0.9 |
| total practising | 4,871,520 | *90* | 5,784,220 | *69* | 21,515 | −31,563 | −10,048 | −0.18 | 5,729,820 | *68* | 5,683,740 | *67* | 5,234,100 | *60* |
| non-practising | 541,280 | *10* | 2,598,700 | *31* | 10,124 | 9,952 | 20,076 | 0.74 | 2,696,380 | *32* | 2,799,460 | *33* | 3,489,400 | *40* |
| Roman Catholics | 5,412,800 | 99.8 | 8,349,224 | 96.8 | 31,494 | −22,486 | 9,008 | 0.11 | 8,387,600 | 95.7 | 8,439,300 | 94.2 | 8,660,500 | 87.3 |
| Catholic pentecostals | 0 | 0.0 | 0 | 0.0 | 11 | 789 | 800 | 26.67 | 3,000 | 0.0 | 8,000 | 0.1 | 60,000 | 0.6 |
| Protestants | 2,000 | 0.0 | 56,700 | 0.7 | 240 | 1,260 | 1,500 | 2.34 | 64,000 | 0.7 | 71,700 | 0.8 | 99,000 | 1.0 |
| Evangelicals | 1,500 | 0.0 | 48,000 | 0.6 | 203 | 1,097 | 1,300 | 2.40 | 54,200 | 0.6 | 61,000 | 0.7 | 85,000 | 0.9 |
| Marginal Protestants | | 0.0 | 20,000 | 0.2 | 84 | 416 | 500 | 2.22 | 22,500 | 0.3 | 25,000 | 0.3 | 40,000 | 0.4 |
| Catholics (non-Roman) | 600 | 0.0 | 4,500 | 0.1 | 17 | −17 | 0 | 0.00 | 4,500 | 0.1 | 4,500 | 0.1 | 5,000 | 0.1 |
| Anglicans | 500 | 0.0 | 4,500 | 0.1 | 17 | −17 | 0 | 0.00 | 4,500 | 0.1 | 4,500 | 0.1 | 5,000 | 0.1 |
| Third-World indigenous | 0 | 0.0 | 2,000 | 0.0 | 8 | 12 | 20 | 0.95 | 2,100 | 0.0 | 2,200 | 0.0 | 3,000 | 0.0 |
| Orthodox | 0 | 0.0 | 1,000 | 0.0 | 4 | −4 | 0 | 0.00 | 1,000 | 0.0 | 1,000 | 0.0 | 1,000 | 0.0 |
| Non-religious | 2 000 | 0.0 | 173,000 | 2.0 | 856 | 11,444 | 12,300 | 5.39 | 228,000 | 2.6 | 296,000 | 3.3 | 694,000 | 7.0 |
| Atheists | 0 | 0.0 | 30,000 | 0.3 | 225 | 8,775 | 9,000 | 15.00 | 60,000 | 0.7 | 120,000 | 1.3 | 298,000 | 3.0 |
| Baha'is | 0 | 0.0 | 1,800 | 0.0 | 7 | 13 | 20 | 1.05 | 1,900 | 0.0 | 2,000 | 0.0 | 2,500 | 0.0 |
| Jews | 200 | 0.0 | 1,300 | 0.0 | 5 | −5 | 0 | 0.00 | 1,300 | 0.0 | 1,300 | 0.0 | 1,000 | 0.0 |
| Muslims | 0 | 0.0 | 800 | 0.0 | 3 | −3 | 0 | 0.00 | 800 | 0.0 | 800 | 0.0 | 1,000 | 0.0 |
| **Country's population** | **5,423,000** | **100.0** | **8,628,000** | **100.0** | **32,900** | **0** | **32,900** | **0.38** | **8,762,000** | **100.0** | **8,957,000** | **100.0** | **9,918,000** | **100.0** |

COLUMNS, ROWS. For meanings and definitions, see Codebook (Part 6). Note that, by definition, total 'Christians' = professing + crypto-Christians, which also = affiliated + nominal Christians. Percentages may not always total exactly, due to rounding.
CENSUSES. **15.XII.1950:** 96.7% Roman Catholics, 2.6% non-religious, 0.7% other religionists. **15.XII.1960** (de jure): 97.9% Roman Catholics, 1.7% non-religious, 0.4% Protestants. **15.XII.1970:** 96.5% Roman Catholics, 2.4% non-religious and atheists, 0.5% Protestants, 0.5% other Christians (including some here termed Protestants), 1,300 Jews, 365 Muslims, 2,220 other non-Christians.
POLLS. February 1970: 95% Roman Catholics, 4% non-religious, under 1% Protestants.

NOTES ON RELIGIONS
ATHEISTS. Partido Communista Português (PCP) (banned and underground until 1974; pro-Soviet) and pro-Peking faction FAP: membership (1970) 1,000, (1973) 3,000, rapidly increasing after 1974 to 100,000; Communist voters (vote on constitution of 25.IV.1975) 26.38% of 5,665,707 total votes, with an increase of the total vote in the first free parliamentary election of April 1976 from 12.5% to 15%. Most Communist voters regard themselves also as Roman Catholics, and many are still practising Catholics.
BAHA'IS. Local spiritual assemblies: 1964, 9; 1973, 14.
CATHOLIC PENTECOSTALS (or, Catholic charismatics). In mid-1978, 1,500 people from all parts of Portugal attended the Second National Conference of the Charismatic Renewal, held at Vila Nova de Gaia, organized by prayer groups in the diocese of Porto, and supported by the bishops of Porto and Setubal.
DOUBLY-AFFILIATED. The term covers those affiliated to, or claimed by, both the Catholic Church and also another church: Evangelical (Protestant, marginal Protestant, Anglican, Third-World indigenous) or Catholic (non-Roman) or Orthodox; i.e. baptized Roman Catholics who have recently became Evangelicals or others. Because their statistics represent a duplication, they are shown in the table as a negative quantity (with a minus sign).
JEWS. With 2 synagogues in Lisbon and one in Oporto. There are also 100,000 Marranos (Crypto-Jews), whose ancestors adopted Catholicism under duress in and after 1497 but who still secretly keep the Passover and other Jewish practices. In northern Portugal they number up to 10% of all Catholics in some towns. In the table above, they are enumerated as Roman Catholics.
MUSLIMS. Originally from Pakistan, Mozambique, Guinea-Bissau, Timor, Macao and North Africa. A number are present illegally (hence unregistered in censuses). *Hajj pilgrims to Mecca.* (1970) 79; (1976) 8.
PRACTISING CHRISTIANS. Weekly mass attenders: in the south (with latifundia) 5% of Catholics. In Lisbon (1970; IPOPE), of all adults 2% attend mass more than twice a week, 24% once a week or fortnight, 18% from time to time, 23% rarely, 29% never or virtually never. *Pilgrims.* Around 400,000 pilgrims a year visit the shrine of the Virgin at Fátima. In 1951 pope Pius XII closed the Holy Year at Fátima in the presence of over a million, and in 1967 during the visit of pope Paul VI, one million pilgrims attended.
ROMAN CATHOLICS. Including 100,000 Marranos (Crypto-Jews, Anusim, New Christians, Conversos) who are baptized and outwardly-practising Catholics mainly in the north.

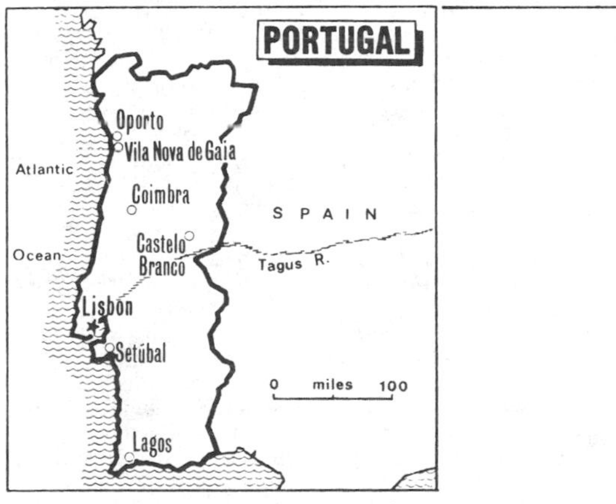


**NON-CHRISTIAN RELIGIONS. Baha'i** has a small and slowly-growing community of 1,900 people.

**Judaism** has a small but influential community centred primarily in Lisbon. After the Inquisition, their first synagogue was opened in 1813. There are at present about 1,300 Jews in Portugal, with 2 synagogues in Lisbon and one in Oporto. There are also 100,000 Marranos (Crypto-Jews), whose ancestors were forced to adopt Catholicism but who still keep Jewish practices.

**Islam** has about 800 followers in Portugal, coming originally from Pakistan, Mozambique, Guinea-Bissau, Timor and Macao. Portuguese Muslims are members of the Islamic Community of Lisbon (Comunidade Islámica de Lisboa) which was officially recognized in March 1968. One of its many objectives is to build the first mosque since the 15th century in Lisbon. The community publishes a quarterly, *O Islão*, which is the only periodical in Portuguese dealing with Islamic culture.

## CHRISTIANITY

CATHOLIC CHURCH. The Romans arrived in the western part of the Iberian peninsula in the second century. BC. Little is known of the introduction of Christianity other than that the Apostles James and Paul are said to have visited there. By the end of the second century AD, Christianity was firmly established. Visigoths from the north who were proponents of Arian Christianity entered the peninsula in the 5th century. The indigenous population eventually had Catholicism declared their state religion at the Third Council of Toledo in 589, but friction with the Goths continued. In the 6th and 7th centuries the church began to flourish only to be oppressed under the Moors, Muslim Arabs who defeated the Visigoths in 711. In 1095 Henry of Burgundy was granted part of western Iberia because of his success against the Moors, and his son declared it an independent nation in 1139. Conflicts continued with Moors and Castilians until 1385 when, under John I, Portugal's era of maritime expansion began. At this time many Jews who were suffering persecution in Spain fled to Portugal, but in 1497 all Jews in Portugal were compelled to accept Christian baptism or to leave the country. The notorious Inquisition was then introduced in order to detect those secretly practising the Jewish faith.

During the following century Portuguese explorers ranged extensively over the oceans; Bartholomeu Dias passed Africa's southern tip, Vasco da Gama sailed to India and Pedro Cabral discovered Brazil. Catholic missionaries usually accompanied such voyages. After a number of major discoveries by Portuguese and Spaniards, the Holy See issued a series of pronouncements the most important of which was the Demarcation Bull of 1493 which divided mission responsibilities across the world between Portugal and Spain, and under which Portugal was given authority over Africa and much of Asia and the East Indies, as well as, later, Brazil. The system known as the Patronato authorized civil authorities to make ecclesiastical appointments and to assume responsibility for the conversion of the heathen. In Africa the major mission was in the Congo; the first missionaries arrived in 1491, and more than a million Congolese were baptized within a century. Jesuits and Dominicans at the same time were beginning missions in Mozambique, and Francis Xavier and other Jesuits launched missions from Portuguese colonies in India and China, and many thousands were soon baptized. Portuguese missionary efforts, however, were often less successful than those of their Spanish counterparts. In many countries Portuguese Christianity later died out completely as a result of opposition from Asia's highly-developed cultures, Portugal's heavy involvement in the African slave trade, the decline of Portugal as a world power, and the decline of missionary fervour and recruiting at home.

From 1581 to 1640 Portugal itself came under the rule of Spain. Later in 1807 Napoleon entered Portugal and the royal family fled to Brazil whence the king returned in 1820. Political unrest continued during the 19th century, involving the church also. The Jesuits had been expelled from Portugal in 1759, and relations were broken with the Holy See between 1833 and 1841. Religious orders were suppressed in 1834. In 1857 a concordat concerning patronage privileges and responsibilities in the Orient was agreed upon with the Holy See. In 1910, the republic of Portugal was proclaimed, religious orders again suppressed, relations with the Holy See broken, the separation of church and state was declared, and the Catholic Church was disestablished. Following the Fátima appearances in 1917 a popular religious renewal took place, and in 1933 the church entered into a new alliance with Salazar's Estado Novo government. A further concordat with the Holy See in 1940 affirmed the separation of church and state but gave the church considerable autonomy in evangelization and education in overseas territories.

Portuguese Catholicism today still reflects the anti-clerical movement which accompanied the revolution of 1910. Isolated, living in the past and fearful of the modern world, such are the characteristics of Portuguese Catholicism which shared in its long and close relationship with the Salazar and Caetano regimes. Indeed the Catholic Church aided these regimes, from the foundation of the Estado Novo in 1933 until its fall in 1974, to suffocate every semblance of liberty or cultural and political innovattion. Exploited by Salazar in the name of anti-communism, even the spiritual movement resulting from the apparitions at Fátima in 1917 did no more than reinforce the conservatism of the Portuguese church.

The policy of the episcopate has always consisted, and still does consist, in attempting to create and maintain the cohesion and unity of Portuguese Catholics. Since the coup d'etat of 25 April 1974, the bishops have feared a repetition of the 1910 situation. Unquestionably, potential divisions have existed below the surface for a long time.

One such division is geographical, between North and South. The South is in many ways a dechristianized region, being earlier the fief of the regular clergy, who were driven out in 1834 and who preferred to install themselves in the ecclesiastical fortress of of the North. A region of large farms and industrial conglomerations such as Setubal, Portugal south of the Tagus has an extremely low percentage of Sunday church attendance and a very unfavourable ratio of priests to inhabitants: one to 4,500. On the other

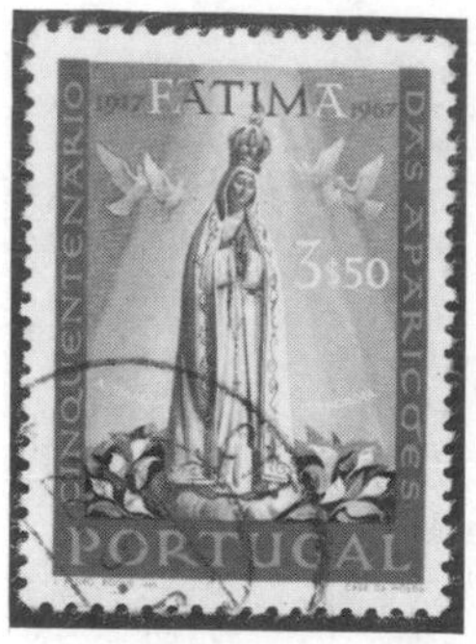


**Igreja Católica em Portugal.** 50th-anniversary postage stamp of Fátima, where half a million pilgrims a year visit.

hand, in the Centre and especially the North the church is powerful and firmly planted, with a priest for every 600 inhabitants. Weekly religious practice there is high and attains 100% in some villages, with clerical authority dominating the whole of life. Nevertheless, a factor bringing change is the large emigration of workers mostly from the North of Portugal, about a million of whom have made their way to other Western European countries, especially France. This has already affected recruitment to the priesthood, one of the traditions of the North.

A second divisive factor concerns the mentality of Portuguese Catholics. The mass of Portuguese, especially those of the rural areas of the Centre and North, practise a religion which is traditional, sociologically-conditioned and tainted with superstition and fatalism. This religiosity, far from being discouraged or corrected, has been encouraged by the hierarchy and indeed used to combat minority groups of priests and lay persons who are socially and politically involved. Thus during 1970–71 the following groups were suppressed: Pragma, a cultural co-operative founded in 1964; GEDOC, a movement of priests and lay persons engaged in social and ecclesial renewal; and CIDAC, a group of militant priests. Since 25 April 1974 the members of this 'parallel church' have been: (1) militants of certain Catholic Action movements who were earlier arrested and tortured by PIDE, the political police, and today are marginalized within the church by the disavowal of the hierarchy; and (2) Christians for Socialism, a movement founded in January 1975 which declares its desire to help detach the church from its position as a supporter of only the wealthy and conservative classes.

To all these problems can be added the crisis of the clergy, which is particularly serious in Portugal due to the recent large numbers of clergy leaving the priesthood. The diocese of Vila Real, with 70 married priests in 1974, holds unquestionably the record for this category of all the Catholic dioceses of Europe.

OTHER CHURCHES. Several of the first non-Catholic churches were built for citizens of other nations residing in Portugal, including German Lutherans (1763), Anglicans (1843) and Scottish Presbyterians (1871). These churches continue to function to the present day.

Early work with the Portuguese population during the 19th century was undertaken by missionaries from Great Britain and Brazil as well as by returned Portuguese emigrants. The first chapel was opened in 1838 by a returning Portuguese sent by the European Missionary Society. The first British missionary opened Brethren work in 1867 and by 1871 British Methodists were active in the north. A local Presbyterian church was also established in Lisbon in 1871 by another returned Portuguese. Baptists entered Portugal in 1888 and since then a number of different groups have been formed. Brazilian Baptist missionaries have been on the scene since 1908. Other early movements in Portugal were initiated by the Seventh-day Adventists and Assemblies of God.

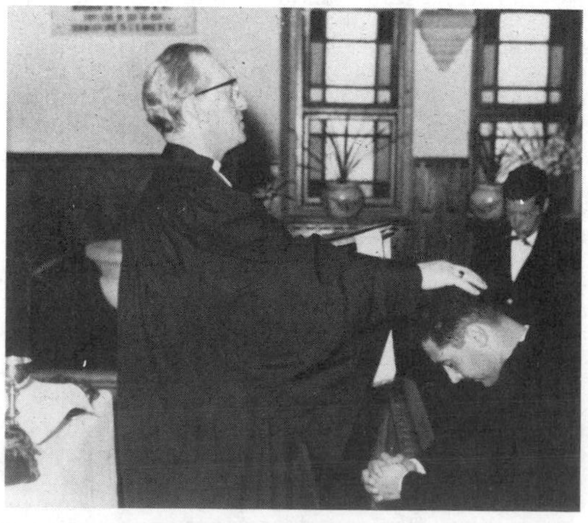

**Igreja Evangélica Metodista Portuguesa.** Confirmation service in Aleace taken by Rev. Albert Aspey.

The Lusitanian Church also owes its origin to the last century, being a schism from Catholicism by 11 Catholic priests in 1871. Its present bishop was consecrated by a Brazilian Episcopalian bishop in 1958, and the church has since 1980 been fully integrated into the Anglican Communion. Several other separatist bodies have been formed from the Methodist, Baptist and Pentecostal churches.

North American missionary influences began to make their presence felt around the time of World War II. The Evangelical Alliance Mission (TEAM) began in 1936, and United Presbyterians from the USA have lent support to local Presbyterianism since World War II, especially in the Carcavellos Seminary. Two new Baptist groups have also appeared, Conservative Baptists in 1946 to work with the Association of Portuguese Baptist Churches and more recently (1959) Southern Baptists who are under the Portuguese Baptist Convention.

While the Portuguese constitution guarantees freedom of religion and open opposition is minimal, Protestants have in fact been restricted in their public activities. The difficulties involved in obtaining official permission to own property and build churches have been important factors limiting church growth.

**CHURCH AND STATE.** Prior to the coup d'etat of 25 April 1974 the church-state situation was as follows. Section X of the constitution of 1933 (which is still largely although provisionally in effect) entitled 'Religious freedom and relations between the State and the Catholic Church and other religious bodies' contained 4 articles, 45–48. Of these the most important were the first 2: 'The State, recognizing its responsibilities before God and man assures freedom of worship and organization to those religious bodies whose doctrines are not contrary to the fundamental principles of the existing constitutional order, nor offend the social order or good morals, and whose worship respects the life, physical integrity and dignity of the person' (Article 45). 'The Roman Catholic Apostolic Religion is considered to be the traditional religion of the Portuguese nation. The Catholic Church possesses existence as a legal body. The principle regulating relations between the state and religious bodies is that of separation, without prejudice to the existence of concordats or agreements with the Holy See' (Article 46). A noteworthy paragraph stated: 'Portuguese Catholic missions in overseas provinces and training centres for their personnel shall be protected and aided by the State, both as institutions of education and social assistance and also as instruments of civilization'.

This legislation, already favourable to the Catholic Church, was made even more explicit by the concordat of 7 May 1940 consisting of 31 articles, the Missionary Agreement (Acordo Missionário) consisting of 21 articles annexed to the concordat, and the Missionary Statute (Estatuto Missionário) of 82 articles which became Law 31,207 on 5 April 1941.

The concordat stipulated that the appointment of bishops was subject to 'objections of a general political nature' which the Portuguese government might have against the candidates chosen by the Holy See (Article 10). The military service of priests was described as a 'religious presence given to the armed forces' (Articles 14 and 18), under which the church agreed to provide chaplains for the military, although this was not put into effect until the outbreak of the colonial wars in Africa (Decree 47,188 of September 1964). The church was free to own schools, which were put on a par with public schools and subsidized if they were located in missionary areas (Article 20). Education offered in public schools was to obey the principles of Christian doctrine and morals, since these are 'traditional principles in the country'; in consequence, the teaching of Catholic religion and morals was obligatory in public elementary and middle schools for all pupils whose parents did not request exemption (Article 21). The state recognized Catholic religious marriages as civil contracts and confirmed their indissoluble character (Articles 22 and 24), which gave rise to a dualism of marriage regulations since both secular marriage and secular divorce were authorized for non-Catholics. Missionary dioceses and jurisdictions were subsidized by the state (Article 27).

The Missionary Agreement and the Statute complemented each other, the second clarifying the first. (In the resume that follows, articles in the Agreement are identified by the letters MA and those in the Statute by MS). 'Portuguese Catholic missions are institutions of value from the imperial point of view, since they play an eminently civilizing role' (MS 2). In principle, all missionary personnel should be of Portuguese nationality (MS 15); at the request of bishops, however, the government may admit foreign junior personnel provided that they speak and write Portuguese fluently (MS 17). Bishops, vicars and prefects must however be Portuguese (MA 3) and their nomination must be approved by the Lisbon government (MA 7). Missionaries are not officials of the state (MA 17) and do not receive salaries from it, but they have the right to various privileges including exemption from taxes, travel expenses (MA 14), free medical care (MS 30) and a retirement pension. Moreover, 'as head of the missions of their respective dioceses' bishops, vicars and prefects have the right to an 'honourable salary' guaranteed by the Portuguese government (MA 12), equal to that of provincial governors (MS 19). Missionary organizations are subsidized by the governments of Metropolitan Portugal and of the colony (MA 9), and dioceses and missionary orders both in Portugal and in the colonies are exempt from taxes (MA 11). The education of native populations is placed entirely in the hands of missionary personnel (MS 66). The use of the Portuguese language is obligatory, except in the case of religious education where the local language is sanctioned (MA 16). This education is considered official and should be 'essentially nationalist' and obey the 'doctrinal orientation of the political constitution' (MS 68).

Portuguese religious legislation was further complemented by the Law on Religious Liberty of 22 July 1971, by which the way was opened for the state to officially recognize religious associations or organizations other than the Catholic Church, granting them also juridical personality (Article 9, paragraph 1). Recognition was secured by a church when it presented an application signed by at least 500 adult members (Article 9, paragraph 2). It could be refused or revoked by government if the latter considered the doctrine or activities of the organization to be contrary 'to the fundamental principles of constitutional order or to the interests of Portuguese sovereignty' (Article 8, paragraph 1). Only recognized religious bodies could build and operate places for worship (Article 17); they also had the right to hold meetings without previous authorization 'for community worship or for other specifically religious purposes'. At the time of formulation this statement was considered too restrictive by the more liberal members of parliament, because there was no clear definition of what was 'specifically religious', and also because the text restricted the understanding of religious life to acts of worship, without involvement in social action. Various amendments proposed by these members were all rejected so that the final text adopted was that presented by the government modified only by consideration of remarks made in an episcopal letter requesting that the unique position of the Catholic Church be even more strongly underlined.

Most Portuguese bishops did not provide open and whole-hearted support for the regime but nevertheless remained silent on political and social questions, especially those relating to colonial policy. An exception was the bishop of Porto, who was exiled from 1959 to 1969 and who demonstrated openness to the problems created by social injustice, emigration and the lack of fundamental liberties.

The first incident of open conflicts between Catholics and the government took place in 1955 at the time of a JOC congress. However, it was not until after 1958 that a tendency towards opposition, at the political as well as the ecclesiastical levels, began to make itself felt among militant Catholics and a small minority of the clergy. Anti-government hostility was especially pronounced within the ranks of Catholic Workers Action, which published 2 magazines, *Lar e Trabalho* (Home and Work) and *Voz do Trabalho* (Voice of Work), having a circulation of 44,000 copies in spite of the fact that the organization itself only had 8,000 members of whom 5,000 were women. A minority of the Portuguese Catholic intelligentsia attacked also the concordat especially because of the privileges given to the Catholic Church and because of Article 24 on divorce. To this the regime and hierarchy responded that Catholicism was not the religion of the state, that the clergy were not subsidized and that there was therefore no clericalism in Portugal. According to the former patriarch of Lisbon, who consistently supported the government in its policies, 'The concordat, is, as a document, a precursor and innovator which anticipated Vatican Council II' because it is a concordat of 'separation'. The new patriarch appointed in 1973 also assumed a position of support for the regime. The only exception to this was a declaration made in January 1973 in which he refused to dissociate himself entirely from a 'subversive' vigil for peace opposing the colonial war held by a group of Catholics in the Rato chapel on 30–31 December 1972. The vigil for peace had in fact been preceded by publication of a document criticizing the war, which originated from the Commission on Justice and Peace of the diocese of Porto, the only such commission existing in Portugal. However, when the Caetano regime continued its repression of such groups, the hierarchy maintained its silence.

It may be noted that relations between Portugal and the Vatican during this period were not devoid of paradox. The social encyclicals of pope John XXIII were censored in Portugal and in the colonies. The voyage of pope Paul VI to Bombay was boycotted by the Portuguese mass media because it followed so soon after the seizure of Goa by India. The audiences given by Paul VI in 1971 to leaders of African liberation movements from Mozambique, Angola and Guinea-Bissau also greatly irritated the Portuguese authorities. The latter, however, did not fail to exploit for political purposes the same pope's pilgrimage to Fatima in May 1967.

The church-state situation in Portugal has been significantly altered since the coup d'etat of 25 April 1974, when the ancient and close links between the former regime and the Portuguese church were broken and the army released from prison militant Christians (clergy and lay), communists, socialists and leftists.

The church has continued to be characterized by dualism, a conservative majority led by the hierarchy, with its strength in the North and most priests and faithful under its control, and a minority of priests and laity dedicated to the revolution.

The first reaction by the episcopate to the coup was a declaration published on 28 April, expressing the hope that the events would contribute to the well-being of Portuguese society, to the cause of justice, reconciliation and respect for all persons. The public statements of the hierarchy which followed were so reserved that one (issued on 5 May 1974) was widely interpreted as support for members of the hated and discredited PIDE.

In May 1974 a group of about a thousand Christians meeting in Lisbon demanded the removal of bishops and the apostolic nuncio who were known to be sympathetic to the former regime.

A year after the coup the Catholic Church was the only major institution to withhold its support from the Armed Forces Movement (MFA). At the time of the elections to the constituent assembly of 25 April 1975, the bishops warned Catholics not to vote for the Communist party. Indeed following the election, where the communists gained only 12% of the vote, Catholics attacked Communist party headquarters throughout the North and were instrumental in provoking in late 1975 the fall of premier Vasco Conçalves for his Marxist leanings.

From a juridical standpoint, the MFA promulgated in May 1974 a provisional constitution, maintaining temporarily those stipulations of the constitution of 1933 not in conflict with the principles of the MFA programme. The new regime did not denounce the concordat of 1940 but called for its revision. A partial agreement, called the 'Additional Protocol', was signed on 15 February 1975 between the Holy See and the Portuguese government which modified Article 24 allowing the courts to grant civil divorces for couples married in the church. The Missionary Agreement and Missionary Statute have become void by force of circumstance, at least as they relate to Portugal's former African colonies. On 31 December 1974, in signing the Indo-Portuguese Treaty of Reconciliation, Mario Soares, at that time Portugal's foreign minister, declared that the agreement requiring the Vatican to consult Lisbon before appointing religious authorities in Goa was 'obsolete'.

**INTERDENOMINATIONAL ORGANIZATIONS.** Co-operation among Protestants is carried on through the Portuguese Council of Christian Churches since 1974, and also through the following 13 organizations: (1) Portuguese Evangelical Alliance (Aliança Evangélica Portuguesa) with 2 sub-commissions, for northern and southern Portugal; (2) Portuguese Inter-Ecclesiastical Commission (Comissão Inter-Eclesiástica Portuguesa) composed of 3 members (Lusitanian, Methodist and Presbyterian churches); (3) Commission for Christian Literature (Comissão de Literatura Cristã); (4) Gypsy Evangelical Movement of Portugal (Movimento Evangélico Cigano de Portugal), which is de facto a denomination; (5) Beira-Vouga Convention (Convenção Beira-Vouga) founded in 1926 and modelled on the Keswick Convention of England; (6) Youth for Christ in Portugal (Moçidade para Cristo em Portugal); (7) Christian Businessmens' Movement (Movimento dos Homens Cristãos de Negóçios); (8) United Evangelical Women of Portugal (Senhoras Evangélicas Unidas de Portugal); (9) Women's Christian Union (União Cristã Feminina); (10) Evangelical Christian Medical Union (União Médica Cristã Evangélica); (11) Union of Sunday Schools of North Portugal (União das Escolas Dominicais do Norte de Portugal, UEDNOP) with Lusitanian, Methodist and Presbyterian membership; (12) Portuguese Union for Christian Endeavour (União Portuguesa de Esforço Cristão, UPEC) composed of Lusitanians and Methodists; and (13) Evangelical League for Missionary and Educational Action (Liga Evangélica de Accão Missionária e Educacional).

The Ecumenical Centre for Reconciliation (Centro Ecumenico Reconciliação), founded in 1969, provides opportunities for co-operation between the Protestant churches and YMCAs of Spain and Portugal. Participant members from Portugal are the Lusitanian, Methodist and Presbyterian churches. The Evangelical League for Missionary and Educational Action co-ordinates, on an ecumenical basis, the training of foreign missionaries studying the Portuguese language in Lisbon. The League also maintains an ecumenical hostel in the capital.

With regard to the Catholic Church, there is no specific commission for ecumenism under the Episcopal Conference. Ecumenical questions are handled by the Episcopal Commission for the Doctrine of the Faith and Social Communications.

**BROADCASTING.** All commercial stations accept religious programmes. In Lisbon there is one Catholic station Radio Renascença, inaugurated in 1936. Also in Lisbon, there is a secretariat for cinema and radio. There is as yet no national association of UNDA in Portugal. About 20 programmes a week are produced by Protestants (Adventists, Baptists, Bible Society, Brethren, Lutherans, Pentecostals). Pentecostals based in Stockholm operate IBRA over Radio Trans-Europe, reaching 52 countries in Eastern Europe, USSR and other continents. From overseas, HCJB (Ecuador), TWR (Bonaire) and Radio Vatican beam in Portuguese programmes.

## BIBLIOGRAPHY


*A situação religiosa de Portugal.* E. Moreira. Lisboa, 1937.

*Anuário Católico de Portugal, 1968.* Lisboa: Secretariado de Informação Religiosa, 1968.

*Atlas missionario português, 1964.* Ed A. da Silva Rego & E. dos Santos. Lisboa: Junta de Investigações do Ultramar e Centro de Estudos Históricos Ultramarinos, 1964.

*Crisóstomo Português.* E. Moreira. Lisboa, 1957.

*Os evangelicos portugueses e a lei.* E. Moreira. Lisboa, 1938.

'Portugal', A. Querido, in *Western religion*, ed H. Mol. The Hague: Mouton, 1972. 427–436.

*Prontuário de igrejas, organismos e obreiros evangélicos em Portugal.* Lisboa: Movimento Promotor de Evangelização, 1967. 176p.

*Vidas convergentes: história breve dos movimentos de reforma cristã em Portugal a partir do século XVIII.* E. Moreira. Lisboa: Junta Presbiteriana de Cooperação em Portugal, 1957. 409p.


TABLE 2. ORGANIZED CHURCHES AND DENOMINATIONS IN PORTUGAL

| Official name 1 | Begun 2 | Type 3 | Counc 4 | Congs 5 | Adults 6 | Affiliated 7 | Names, notes, and other statistics (see Codebook) 8 |
|---|---|---|---|---|---|---|---|
| Assembleias de Deus em Portugal | 1913 | P Pe2 | Z•••C | 250 | 7,500 | 24,000 | *Assemblies of God in Portugal.* M=AoG(UK). 35n,2x,G=6.4%pa,1j,200t,715Y,400z. |
| Assoc de Igrejas Batistas Portuguesas | c1930 | P Bap | xF••• | 19 | 1,000 | 2,000 | *AIBP. Assoc of Portuguese Baptist Chs.* Ex CBP. 1946, M=CBFMS(USA). 8n,2f,1s,W=60%. |
| Congregação Cristã em Portugal | | I pe2 | ••••• | 23 | 900 | 1,800 | *Christian Congregation in P.* Brazilians from church based on São Paulo. HQ Porto. |
| Convenção Batista Portuguesa | 1888 | P Bap | T•••C | 51 | 3,150 | 6,000 | *CBP. Portuguese Baptist Conv.* 1959, M=SBC(USA). SS=2336. 20n,6f,G=15%pa,1s,120Y. |
| Exército de Salvação | 1971 | P Sal | xwc•• | 2 | 50 | 100 | *Salvation Army, Portugal Command.* Recent beginnings in Porto and Lisbon. 2nx. |
| Igreja Adventista do Sétimo Dia | 1904 | P Adv | x•••• | 52 | 3,704 | 6,000 | *Seventh-day Adv,Port Mission,*SEurope UM. 14nx,G=2.8%pa,1j,1s,35t(3346),W=94%,438Y. |
| Igreja Anglicana (D Gibraltar) | 1656 | A plu | awc•• | 5 | 2,100 | 4,500 | English-speaking Anglican chaplaincies, including one on Madeira. 4x. |
| **Igreja Católica em Portugal:** | c 150 | R Lat | H•B•R | 4,312 | 5,927,900 | 8,349,224 | *Catholic Ch.* C=23+3+63. 6q,9s(312). 5166nx,1030m,6660w,156500Yy. |
| P Lisboa (Lisbon) | c 350 | R Lat | Hs | 372 | 1,530,700 | 2,156,179 | Industry, port, commerce, university. 1s(24),W=26%. 792 411 1913 24582 |
| D Angra | 1534 | R Lat | Hs | 150 | 205,400 | 289,296 | Azores. Fishing. Very traditional religiosity. 1s. 260 17 206 6812 |
| D Funchal | 1514 | R Lat | Hs | 102 | 174,200 | 245,420 | Madeira, 8 isles. Tourism. Traditional religiosity. 143 20 498 5897 |
| D Guarda | c 550 | R Lat | Hs | 360 | 231,700 | 301,000 | Mountains. Heavy emigration. Many vocations. 1s. 298 4 245 5901 |
| D Leiria | 1545 | R Lat | Hs | 67 | 134,000 | 189,000 | Rural. Major pilgrimage centre at Fátima (1917). 1s. 170 41 402 4489 |
| D Portalegre-Castelo Branco | 1550 | R Lat | Hs | 160 | 203,600 | 286,750 | Rural north, W=80%; urban and rural south, W=10%. 173 20 232 4510 |
| M Braga | c 350 | R Lat | Hs | 837 | 674,300 | 949,772 | Semi-industrial. Traditional religiosity. 1s,W=60%. 1079 204 685 20711 |
| D Aveiro | 1774 | R Lat | Hs | 95 | 166,000 | 233,750 | Heavy rural emigration, especially to France. 157 6 181 5138 |
| D Bragança & Miranda | 1545 | R Lat | Hs | 315 | 125,500 | 176,800 | Almost entirely rural and agricultural. 194 8 80 3700 |
| D Coimbra | c 550 | R Lat | Hs | 263 | 370,070 | 522,046 | Tourism, fishing, major university. 1s. 292 25 469 8920 |
| D Lamego | c1150 | R Lat | Hs | 222 | 124,000 | 174,000 | Impoverished, no industry. Mass emigration. 177 0 94 4560 |
| D Porto (Oporto) | c 350 | R Lat | Hs | 554 | 1,091,400 | 1,537,179 | Wine industry, commerce, university. 1s. 696 224 649 35000 |
| D Vila Real | 1922 | R Lat | Hs | 260 | 166,600 | 234,618 | Farms, sheep, wine, smoked meat. 70 married priests. 204 11 117 6312 |
| D Viseu | 572 | R Lat | Hs | 203 | 198,900 | 280,164 | Mountainous, poor agriculture. Heavy emigration. 1s. 222 7 179 5608 |
| M Evora | c 350 | R Lat | Hs | 166 | 206,000 | 290,000 | South. Old city, historic religious traditions. 1s. 166 30 581 5933 |
| D Beja | 1770 | R Lat | Hs | 115 | 156,000 | 220,000 | In south, landlordism (latifundia). Practice: W=5%. 67 2 70 4227 |
| D Fáro | 1577 | R Lat | Hs | 71 | 186,900 | 263,250 | Fishing, tourism. Few vocations. Practice: W=10%. 76 0 59 4200 |
| Igreja Evangélica Congregacional | | P Con | ••••C | 17 | 400 | 1,000 | *Congregational Ch.* Rejected 1952 merger with Presbyterian Ch. M=Brazil CC. 2n. |
| Igr Evangélica Luterana Portuguesa | 1763 | P Lut | ••••• | 2 | 70 | 100 | *Portuguese Ev Lutheran Ch. Igreja Alemã.* Germans. 1x,G=14.9%pa,W=63%,7Yy,10z. |
| Igr Evangélica Metodista Portuguesa | 1871 | P Met | VvC•d | 16 | 732 | 2,500 | *Methodist Ch.* 1964, applied to join WCC, rejected. 5n,1x,2f,G=2.4%pa,W=80%,18Yy,185z. |
| Igreja Evangélica Presbiteriana de P | 1838 | P Ref | RuC•d | 31 | 2,000 | 3,500 | *Ev Presbyterian Ch.* M=IPB(Brazil), UPUSA,PCUS. A=1952. 13n,1x,1H,24t(850),W=72%. |
| Igr Lusitana Católica Apostólica Ev | 1871 | C ReC | UuC•d | 18 | 1,500 | 4,500 | *Lusitanian Ch.* Schism ex Ch of Rome by 11 RC priests. 16n,2s,G=5.7%pa,W=45%,32Yy. |
| Igreja Ortodoxa Greca (D France) | 1949 | O Gre | Cwc•• | 1 | 500 | 1,000 | *Greek Orthodox Ch in Spain and Portugal.* Served from Madrid; HQ Paris. |
| Igrejas Aliança Evangélica | 1936 | P int | xM••C | 10 | 120 | 300 | M=Evangelical Alliance Mission(TEAM) (USA). HQ Lisbon. 2x,1m,7f,1k,1s,W=67%,31Y,5z. |
| Igrejas do Cristo | | P Dis | x•••• | 4 | 100 | 200 | *Churches of Christ.* M=CC(Non-Instrumental) (USA). Americans in Lisbon, Azores. |
| Igrejas Evangélicas dos Irmãos | 1867 | P CBr | x•••C | 120 | 4,000 | 8,000 | *Ev Chs of Brethren.* Plymouth (Open) Brethren. M=CMML(UK,USA). HQ Coimbra. 69m,17f. |
| Movimento Ev Cigano de Portugal | 1960 | P Pe2 | x•••• | 2 | 230 | 1,000 | *MECP. Gypsy Ev Movement.* Itinerant work among Gypsies. Porto. 1x,G=20.3%pa,W=61%. |
| Testemunhas de Jeová | 1925 | M Jeh | x•••• | 113 | 9,088 | 19,500 | *Jehovah's Witnesses.* 3 congs in Azores Is (c1945), 2 in Madeira (c1950). 1228Y. |
| Other Protestant denominations | | P | ••••• | | 1,000 | 2,000 | Total about 20 (see list below). |
| Other marginal Protestant bodies | 1976 | M | ••••• | | 200 | 500 | Including CJCLdS (Mormons from USA, widespread by 1979), Family of Love, et alia. |
| Other Third-World indigenous churches | | I | ••••• | | 100 | 200 | Including Unification Church (HSAUWC) among youth since 1976. |
| Doubly-affiliated (duplication) (1970) | | | | | –39,000 | –55,000 | Evangelicals who also are or were baptized Roman Catholics. |
| **Total affiliated (mid-1970)** | | | | **5,100** | **5,927,344** | **8,382,924** | **Total denominations (1970) . . . 38.** |
| **Total affiliated (mid-1975)** | | | | **5,150** | **5,957,900** | **8,426,200** | **Total denominations (1975) . . . 40.** |
| **Total affiliated (mid-1980)** | | | | **5,200** | **5,998,200** | **8,483,200** | **Total denominations (1980) . . . 42.** |

NOTES ON TABLE ABOVE
COLUMNS: for meanings and CODES (cols. 1, 3, 4, 8): see Codebook (Part 6). Column 1: **Boldface type** = church with over 10% of country's affiliated Christians.
NATIONAL COUNCILS (Column 4, 5th letter).
C = Aliança Evangélica Portuguesa (AEP) (Portuguese Evangelical Alliance).
d = Conselho Português de Igrejas Cristãs (COPIC) (Portuguese Council of Christian Churches, in working relationship with WCC), and also a member of Comissão Inter-Eclesiástica Portuguesa.
R = Conferência Episcopal Portuguesa da Metrópole (CEPM) (Portuguese Metropolitan Episcopal Conference.)
OTHER PROTESTANT DENOMINATIONS. These smaller bodies include: Apostolic Ch Missionary Movement (UK), Baptist Missionary Association of America (1954), Bible Christian Union (1966), Ch of Scotland (1871), Ch of the Nazarene (Madeira), Danske Sömandskirki (Marinheiros Dinamarqueses: Danish Seamen's Ch), European Missionary Fellowship, Igreja de Deus Pentecostal (Pentecostal Ch of God of America), Igreja de Deus (Ch of God, Cleveland), Igreja Ev Pentecostal, Igrejas Batistas Independentes, United Pentecostal Ch (1972), World Gospel Mission and USA military chaplaincies.

PEOPLES (ethnolinguistic). Christians: 99.5% Portuguese, 0.3% alien (0.1% Spaniard, 0.1% British), 0.2% Gypsy, Angolan, Mozambican, Brazilian, Caboverdian, Mestiço.

COUNTRY-WIDE TOTALS
EVANGELIZATION (see Part 5). 1900: 100%. 1970: 100%. 1980: 100%. *Mass evangelism.* Among recent campaigns: early 1960s, Lisbon crusade (70,000 attenders, 14,000 enquirers) lasting 3 weeks before being banned by government; 1969, Evangelism-in-Depth sponsored by Conservative Baptists; 1970, John Haggai 12-day crusade in Lisbon unhindered by government (8,000 attenders at closing meeting), also 1972 in Lisbon (63,000 attenders, 2,500 professions of faith, mostly by young men); 1976, 4 major evangelistic campaigns; 1977, Lisbon Evangelistic Crusade (Don Stellenberg; churches of Greater Lisbon; 900 decisions). *Radiophonic evangelism.* Radio Vatican, HCJB, TWR, ICI (75,000 active students), et alia.
FOREIGN MISSIONARIES AND PERSONNEL (nationals serving abroad) (1973). Total 4,219: 4,209 Roman Catholics (2,309 foreign missionaries (504 overseas missionary priests, 173 chaplains to emigrants, 1,351 missionary sisters, 192 lay brothers; including in Africa (1975) 386 priests, 152 lay brothers, 787 sisters) serving in Third-World countries, also about 1,900 other personnel serving the Portuguese diaspora in Western nations especially France, FR Germany, USA), about 10 Portestants.
FOREIGN MISSIONARIES AND PERSONNEL (aliens from abroad) (1973). Total 355. *From Western world.* 321: about 240 Roman Catholics, 77 Protestants (40 in 15 USA societies, 34 in 6 UK societies, 2 in 1 Canada society, 1 in 1 Netherlands society), 4 Anglicans from UK. *From Third World.* 34: about 20 Roman Catholics, 12 Protestants from Brazil and Puerto Rico, 2 Brazilian indigenous.
INSTITUTIONS (church-operated) (1973). Total 340, including 250 higher schools (65 minor seminaries), 40 medical centres (31 hospitals), 1 radio station, 7 religious communities, 5 research centres, 17 seminaries (9 RC, 8 Protestant), 1 university.
PERIODICALS. About 220 titles (40 Protestant).
PERSONNEL. About 13,455 (13,100 national, 355 foreign).
RELIGIOUS LIBRARIES. About 35.
SCRIPTURE DISTRIBUTION (1975). Annual totals: 50,403 Bibles (40% subsidized, 60% commercial), 44,696 NTs (7% free, 26% subsidized, 67% commercial), 54,788 UBS portions, 221,849 UBS selections. *Translations completed.* Portuguese: portion in 1505, NT 1681, Bible 1751.
SERVICE AGENCIES. About 130, including ACISJF, ACM (YMCA), AEP, CCC, CEF, CEPM, CNIR, COPIC, FNIRF, JAC, JCACP, JEC, JUC, LAC, LEC, LIAM, LIC, LOC, LOCF, LUC, MEC, MMM, MNEAF, NUCLEO, SPM, SU, UCP, UEDNOP, UMCE, WLC(EHC), YFC.

ADDITIONAL DATA ON CHURCHES
ASSEMBLEIAS DE DEUS EM PORTUGAL. By 1976, totals had increased to 300 congregations, 60 full-time pastors and evangelists, and 10,000 communicants.
IGREJA CATOLICA EM PORTUGAL. *New dioceses.* Created in 1975: D Santarém, D Setubal; created in 1977, D Viana do Castelo. *Annual baptisms.* (1972) 98.6% infant, 1.4% adult. *Personnel.* About 98% nationals, 2% expatriates. *Priests.* D Vila Real has the highest number of married priests (70) of any diocese in Europe. *Seminaries.* As a result of a serious crisis in vocations, the 15 major seminaries in 1968 had been regrouped by 1972 into 9 (Viseu and Porto being interdiocesan). Religious seminarians in 1972 numbered 242 (41 studying in Portugal, 67 abroad). *Main religious orders and congregations.* Priests (congregations with over 100 professed): 395 SJ, 326 OFM, 320 CSSp, 275 SDB, 191 SMP (of Portuguese origin), 112 CMF, 110 OSB, 108 IMC, 101 CM. Brothers: 147 OH. Sisters (congregations with over 300 professed): 1,419 Franciscan Nurses of the Immaculate Conception (of Portuguese origin), 771 Sisters of St Dorothea, 531 Franciscans of Our Lady of Victories (of Portuguese origin), 468 Sisters of the Sacred Heart of Mary, 387 Franciscans Missionaries of Our Lady, 367 Nurses of the Sacred Heart of Jesus, 328 Dominicans of St Catherine of Siena (of Portuguese origin), 309 Franciscans Missionaries of Mary.
*Catholic organizations.* The principal national bodies include the Portuguese Episcopal Conference (Conferência Episcopal Portuguesa, CEP); the National Conference of Religious Institutes (Conferência Nacional dos Institutos Religiosos, CNIR) for men; and the National Federation of Female Religious Institutes (Federação Nacional dos Institutos Religiosos Femininos, FNIRF) for sisters. For the armed forces, Portugal forms a military vicariate. There are no priests' councils. The Central Board for Portuguese Catholic Action (Junta Central da Acção Católica Portuguesa) co-ordinates the activities of several professional associations and the following specialized movements: Catholic Agrarian League (Liga Agraria Católica) which is active in the rural milieu among adults; Catholic School League (Liga Escolar Católica) among teachers; Catholic Workers League (Liga Operária Católica) among adult workers; Catholic University League (Liga Universitária Católica) among university adults; Catholic Independent League (Liga Independente Católica) which includes a wide variety of professional training in its membership; JAC, JEC, and JUC. Each of these movements has its equivalent for women. Also related to this central board are the secretariats of various other movements: National Corps of Scouts (Corpo Nacional de Escutas); Cursos de Cristandade (Cursillos); National Movement of Spirituality and Family Apostolate (Movimento Nacional de Espiritualidade e Apostolado Familiar); Better World Movement (Movimento Mundo Melhor); and Marian Congregations (Congregações Marianas).
The Holy See has diplomatic relations with Portugal and is represented to government and the Catholic hierarchy by a nuncio in Lisbon.
The international headquarters of the Blue Army of Our Lady of Fátima is found in Fátima, but there is also an international secretariat in Basel, Switzerland and the most active national organization is found in the USA. This traditionalist movement claims a world membership of 21.5 million in 110 countries, 5.3 million being in the USA.
The Portuguese Catholic University (Universidade Católica Portuguesa) was founded in Lisbon in 1968 and recognized by government in 1971. In 1972–73 it included a philosophical faculty run by Jesuits at Braga (Instituto Superior de Filosofia Beato Miguel de Carvalho), founded in 1967 and integrated into the university in 1968; a theological faculty opened in 1968 in Lisbon; and a faculty of social sciences (Escola de Ciências Socio-empresariais), founded at Lisbon in 1972.
The Catholic Culture Centres (Centros de Cultura Católica) cater for catechetical pastoralia among laymen in Lisbon. Founded in 1964, they provide an advanced course of 3 years plus in-service training in religious culture at Coimbra, Porto and Braga.
The Portuguese Society for Overseas Catholic Missions (Sociedade Portuguesa das Missões Católicas Ultramarinas, SPM) was founded in 1932 to serve the Portuguese colonies. It sponsors the Mission Seminary (Seminario das Missões) at Cucujaes, Porto. The League for the Intensification of Missionary Action (Liga Intensificadora da Acção Missionaria, LIAM) was founded in 1937 to promote the spirit of missionary action in Portugal.
In 1975 there were 422 Catholic schools in Portugal, 178 being secondary schools with 28,711 pupils in 1973. Jesuits, Salesians, Marists, Dominican Sisters and Sisters of St Dorothy operate a number of secondary schools. Some schools are in the hands of diocesan priests. Courses of advanced study are offered at the Higher Institute of Economics (Instituto Superior de Economia) at Évora and the Higher Institute of Applied Psychology (Instituto Superior de Psicologia) in Lisbon.
Caritas Portuguesa, known locally as the Union of Portuguese Charities (União de Caridade Portuguesa) was founded in 1945 upon government initiative and works under a constitution ratified by the Episcopal Conference in 1956. It co-ordinates the work of 73 charitable organizations spread throughout the country and the former colonies and engages in socio-economic research, training courses in social service, literacy, relief aid, vacation courses, assistance to emigrants both inside and outside Portugal and technical aid for voluntary workers. Since 1969 Caritas has distributed food provided by Catholic Relief Services of the USA. In 1972 the church operated 30 hospitals and sanatoria with 2,350 beds.

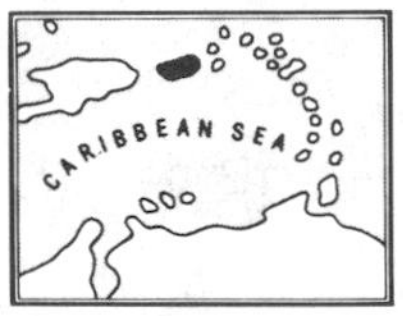


# PUERTO RICO

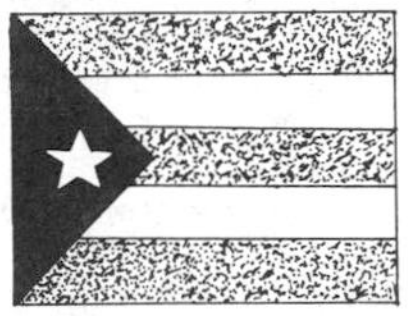

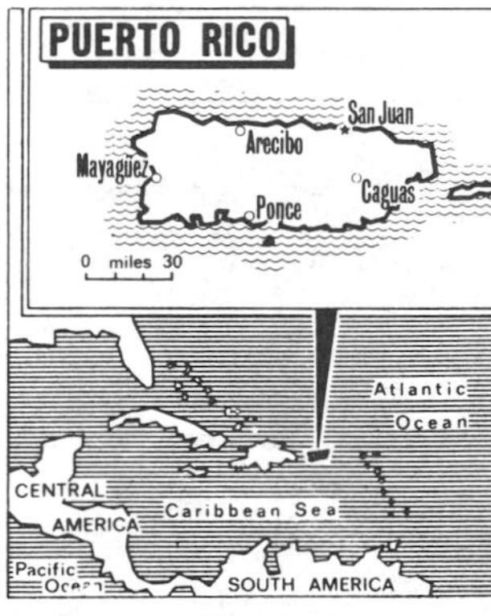


## SECULAR DATA

**STATE. Official name:** The Commonwealth of Puerto Rico (El Estado Libre Asociado de Puerto Rico).
**Flag** (shown above right): Three red and 2 white horizontal stripes, white star on blue triangle.
**Area:** 8,897 sq.km. (3,435 sq.miles). Agricultural land: 60.3%.
**Government:** Self-governing commonwealth in association with the USA, since 1952 (1492 Spanish possession, 1898 ceded to USA, 1917 US territory, 1952 commonwealth).
**Legislature:** Legislative Assembly: Senate, 27 members; House of Representatives, 51 members.
**Official languages:** Spanish (*Español*) and English.
**Chief cities:** capital San Juan 695,060, Ponce 158,980, Bayamon 156,190.
**Foreign forces** (1973): 7,000 USA troops.

**DEMOGRAPHY. Population:** 2,712,033 (census of 1.IV.1970. For 1970–2000 (UN), see last row of Table 1). Population density (1975): 326/sq.km. (845/sq.mile). Under 15 years: 43%. Growth rate (1975–80): 1.16% per year (births 2.14%, deaths −0.65%, emigrants −0.33%). Life expectancy (1975–80): 72.8 years. Household size: 4.0 persons.
**Major languages:** Spanish, English.
**Urban dwellers** (1970): 47.6%. Urban growth rate (1950–70): 2.1% per year.
**Labour force:** 29%.
**Refugees** (1977): About 5,000 from Haiti.
**Tourists** (1974): 1,441,000.

**ETHNOLINGUISTIC GROUPS:** 72.6% Puerto Rican White, 15.0% Black (African Negro), 10.0% Mulatto (Spanish/Black), 2.2% USA White, 0.1% Spaniard, 0.1% Jewish, Cuban, East Indian.

**MONEY** (1977). **Monetary unit:** US dollar (= 100 cents).
**National income per person:** US$2,300. Average annual family income: US$9,200.
**Inflation:** (1970–74) 8.5% per year.
**Cost of living in capital** (1976): Daily cost of living: US$42.

**HEALTH.** Hospitals: 131 (12,249 beds). Doctors: 3,346. Lepers: 1,380 (0.5 per 1,000). Blind: 4,500. Psychotics: 26,000.

**EDUCATION.** Adult literacy: (1950) 73%, (1970) 88%. Schools: 1,905. Universities 8.

**LITERATURE.** Periodicals: 147, Scientific journals: 45. Newspapers: 3 dailies, 12 non-daily.

**COMMUNICATION** (per 1,000 people). Phones: 152. Radios: 580. TV sets: 200. Daily newspaper circulation: 89 copies.

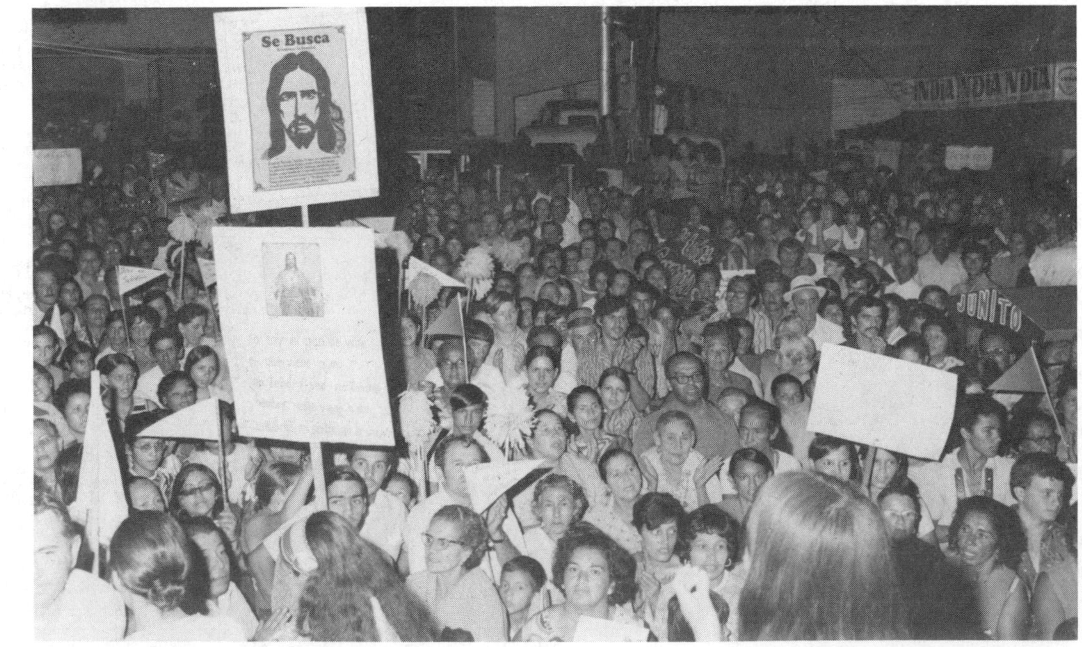


**Catholic pentecostals.** *Above.* 'Se Busca' ('Wanted!'). All-night praise and prayer meeting and procession in Orocovis, with 4,000 attenders.

*Facing page.* Charismatic healing by laying on of hands and prayer, at ECCLA III (Aguas Buenas, 1975).

TABLE 1.    RELIGIOUS ADHERENTS IN PUERTO RICO

| Year | 1900 | | mid-1970 | | Annual change, 1970–1980 | | | | mid-1975 | | mid-1980 | | 2000 | |
|---|---|---|---|---|---|---|---|---|---|---|---|---|---|---|
| *Name* | *Adherents* | *%* | *Adherents* | *%* | *Natural* | *Conversion* | *Total* | *Rate* | *Adherents* | *%* | *Adherents* | *%* | *Adherents* | *%* |
| Christians | 952,000 | 99.9 | 2,699,800 | 98.4 | 32,640 | −634 | 32,006 | 1.12 | 2,853,040 | 98.3 | 3,019,860 | 98.2 | 3,620,500 | 97.2 |
| professing | 952,000 | 99.9 | 2,699,800 | 98.4 | 32,640 | −634 | 32,006 | 1.12 | 2,853,040 | 98.3 | 3,019,860 | 98.2 | 3,620,500 | 97.2 |
| Roman Catholics | 951,200 | 99.8 | 2,527,800 | 92.2 | 30,498 | −1,787 | 28,711 | 1.08 | 2,665,810 | 91.9 | 2,814,910 | 91.5 | 3,342,200 | 89.8 |
| Evangelical Catholics | 700 | 0.1 | 157,914 | 5.8 | 1,977 | 1,208 | 3,185 | 1.84 | 172,830 | 6.0 | 189,770 | 6.2 | 266,600 | 7.2 |
| Spiritist Catholics | 19,000 | 2.0 | 100,000 | 3.6 | 1,196 | −96 | 1,100 | 1.05 | 104,500 | 3.6 | 111,000 | 3.6 | 149,000 | 4.0 |
| Protestants | 500 | 0.1 | 125,000 | 4.6 | 1,533 | 470 | 2,003 | 1.50 | 133,970 | 4.6 | 145,030 | 4.7 | 187,000 | 5.0 |
| Non-White indigenous | 0 | 0.0 | 30,000 | 1.1 | 398 | 602 | 1,000 | 2.87 | 34,800 | 1.2 | 40,000 | 1.3 | 59,600 | 1.6 |
| Marginal Protestants | 0 | 0.0 | 10,000 | 0.4 | 126 | 74 | 200 | 1.82 | 11,000 | 0.4 | 12,000 | 0.4 | 22,300 | 0.6 |
| Anglicans | 300 | 0.0 | 6,000 | 0.2 | 73 | 7 | 80 | 1.25 | 6,400 | 0.2 | 6,800 | 0.2 | 8,000 | 0.2 |
| Orthodox | 0 | 0.0 | 1,000 | 0.0 | 12 | 0 | 12 | 1.14 | 1,060 | 0.0 | 1,120 | 0.0 | 1,400 | 0.0 |
| nominal | 500 | 0.1 | 49,800 | 1.8 | 636 | 550 | 1,186 | 2.14 | 55,540 | 1.9 | 61,660 | 2.0 | 83,600 | 2.2 |
| affiliated | 951,500 | 99.8 | 2,650,000 | 96.6 | 32,004 | −1,184 | 30,820 | 1.10 | 2,797,500 | 96.4 | 2,958,200 | 96.2 | 3,536,900 | 95.0 |
| doubly-affiliated | −1,000 | −0.1 | −266,738 | −9.7 | −3,402 | −3,049 | −6,451 | 2.17 | −297,330 | −10.2 | −331,250 | −10.8 | −453,200 | −12.2 |
| total practising | 903,930 | 95 | 2,252,500 | 85 | 27,203 | −1,006 | 26,197 | 1.10 | 2,377,870 | 85 | 2,514,470 | 85 | 2,652,700 | 75 |
| non-practising | 47,570 | 5 | 397,500 | 15 | 4,801 | −178 | 4,623 | 1.10 | 419,630 | 15 | 443,730 | 15 | 884,200 | 25 |
| Roman Catholics | 950,000 | 99.7 | 2,585,824 | 94.3 | 31,275 | −497 | 30,778 | 1.12 | 2,733,700 | 94.2 | 2,893,600 | 94.1 | 3,443,800 | 92.5 |
| Catholic pentecostals | 0 | 0.0 | 2,000 | 0.1 | 458 | 7,342 | 7,800 | 19.50 | 40,000 | 1.0 | 80,000 | 2.0 | 400,000 | 8.1 |
| Protestants | 1,000 | 0.1 | 228,300 | 8.3 | 2,789 | 521 | 3,310 | 1.36 | 243,800 | 8.4 | 261,400 | 8.5 | 331,300 | 8.9 |
| Evangelicals | 800 | 0.1 | 183,000 | 6.7 | 2,290 | 1,240 | 3,530 | 1.76 | 200,200 | 6.9 | 218,300 | 7.1 | 297,800 | 8.0 |
| Non-White indigenous | 0 | 0.0 | 75,335 | 2.7 | 971 | 1,155 | 2,126 | 2.50 | 84,900 | 2.9 | 96,600 | 3.1 | 148,900 | 4.0 |
| Marginal Protestants | 0 | 0.0 | 15,557 | 0.6 | 229 | 675 | 904 | 4.52 | 20,000 | 0.7 | 24,600 | 0.8 | 44,700 | 1.2 |
| Anglicans | 500 | 0.1 | 9,722 | 0.4 | 118 | 10 | 128 | 1.24 | 10,300 | 0.4 | 11,000 | 0.4 | 18,600 | 0.5 |
| Orthodox | 0 | 0.0 | 1,000 | 0.0 | 12 | 1 | 13 | 1.21 | 1,070 | 0.0 | 1,130 | 0.0 | 1,400 | 0.0 |
| Catholics (non-Roman) | 0 | 0.0 | 1,000 | 0.0 | 12 | 0 | 12 | 1.14 | 1,060 | 0.0 | 1,120 | 0.0 | 1,400 | 0.0 |
| Non-religious | 0 | 0.0 | 29,000 | 1.1 | 382 | 558 | 940 | 2.81 | 33,500 | 1.2 | 38,400 | 1.2 | 71,500 | 1.9 |
| Atheists | 0 | 0.0 | 5,000 | 0.2 | 62 | 18 | 80 | 1.48 | 5,400 | 0.2 | 5,800 | 0.2 | 15,000 | 0.4 |
| Afro-American spiritists | 1,000 | 0.1 | 3,000 | 0.1 | 37 | 3 | 40 | 1.25 | 3,200 | 0.1 | 3,400 | 0.1 | 4,000 | 0.1 |
| Jews | 100 | 0.0 | 2,000 | 0.1 | 24 | 0 | 24 | 1.14 | 2,110 | 0.1 | 2,240 | 0.1 | 2,700 | 0.1 |
| Baha'is | 0 | 0.0 | 1,200 | 0.0 | 15 | 5 | 20 | 1.54 | 1,300 | 0.0 | 1,400 | 0.0 | 3,000 | 0.1 |
| Spiritists | 100 | 0.0 | 1,000 | 0.0 | 13 | 7 | 20 | 1.82 | 1,100 | 0.0 | 1,200 | 0.0 | 2,000 | 0.0 |
| Hindus | 0 | 0.0 | 1,000 | 0.0 | 12 | −2 | 10 | 0.95 | 1,050 | 0.0 | 1,100 | 0.0 | 1,300 | 0.0 |
| Other religionists | 0 | 0.0 | 1,000 | 0.0 | 15 | 45 | 60 | 4.62 | 1,300 | 0.0 | 1,600 | 0.1 | 3,000 | 0.1 |
| Country's population | 953,200 | 100.0 | 2,743,000 | 100.0 | 33,200 | 0 | 33,200 | 1.14 | 2,902,000 | 100.0 | 3,075,000 | 100.0 | 3,723,000 | 100.0 |

COLUMNS, ROWS. For meanings and definitions, see Code-book (Part 6). Note that, by definition, total 'Christians' = professing + crypto-Christians, which also = affiliated + nominal Christians. Percentages may not always total exactly, due to rounding.
CENSUSES. The religion question has not been asked.

**NOTES ON RELIGIONS**
AFRO-AMERICAN SPIRITISTS. Mostly Black and Mulatto immigrants from Cuba, including practitioners of Mayombe (based on Congolese traditional rites). There are also a number of Rastafarians (from Jamaica).
ATHEISTS. Partido Comunista Puertorriqueño (PCP) (legal; pro-Soviet): membership (1970) 100; Partido Socialista Puertorriqueño (PSP) (legal, independent on Sino-Soviet split): membership (1970) 18,000.
BAHA'IS. Growth from 1 local spiritual assembly (1964) to 8

(1973). In 1970 over 300 new believers were enrolled.
CATHOLIC PENTECOSTALS (or, Catholic charismatics). Totals (January 1974): 10,000 involved adults (over 15 years old) in over 100 prayer groups, rising to 15,000 in 200 prayer groups by mid-year; total charismatic community including children (mid-1974), 30,000. On several occasions 7,000 or more have met for day-long prayer meetings. By 1976, 100 priests were in the movement, prayer groups had arisen in almost all Puerto Rican cities, and 14 retreat centres provided direction to the Renewal.
DOUBLY-AFFILIATED. The term covers those affiliated to, or claimed by, both the Catholic Church and also a church termed Evangélica by the state (Protestant, marginal Protestant, Anglican or Non-White indigenous) or other church, i..e baptized Catholics who have recently become Evangelicals or others. Because their statistics represent a duplication, they are shown in the table as a negative quantity (with a minus sign).

EVANGELICAL CATHOLICS. This term is used here to describe persons who are affiliated to churches termed by the state Evangélica (Protestant, marginal Protestant, Anglican or indigenous churches), but who in censuses or polls are regarded as, or profess publicly to be, Roman Catholics.
HINDUS. Immigrants from India, also converts to new sects including 200 in the Bengali movement, Sri Chinmoy Centre; and 1 centre of ISKCON (Hare Krishna).
OTHER RELIGIONISTS. Adherents of other Western religions and cults, including Rosicrucians (6 AMORC centres).
NON-WHITE INDIGENOUS. In 35 denominations in 1970 (see Table 2).
SPIRITIST CATHOLICS. Roman Catholics active in various forms of spiritism.
SPIRITISTS. Adherents of non-Christian forms of spiritism, which was begun in 1898.

## NON-CHRISTIAN RELIGIONS.

Spiritism in various forms exists among some whose ties to the Catholic Church have become tenuous or even non-existent. It involves the use of native herbs to cure illness and mediums to contact the dead and divine the cause and solution to problems. In remote villages where the existence of witches is believed in, bracelets (*asabache*) are placed on the arms of children to protect them from the evil eye (*mal del ojo*). There are also forms of Afro-American spiritism brought by immigrants from Cuba.

**Judaism** is represented by a small Jewish community concentrated for the most part in San Juan.

## CHRISTIANITY

CATHOLIC CHURCH. Columbus touched Puerto Rico in 1493, and in 1511 the first Catholic diocese in the New World was established there. At the end of the 17th century, smallpox killed 21 of the 25 priests on the island, and little further activity took place for a hundred years. The shortage of priests continued until the beginning of the Latin American wars of independence, when members of the hierarchy loyal to Spain fled from other South American countries and established themselves in Puerto Rico. The loyalty of the hierarchy to Spain again weakened the position of the church during the second half of the 19th century, when Puerto Ricans began their own search for independence. The first Protestants entered Puerto Rico in 1860, followed by Anglicans in 1872, but it was not until after the Spanish-American war that Protestantism made any appreciable impact on the scene. With the end of Spanish rule, the number of Catholic priests began to decline. In 1930 there were only 45 diocesan priests and the number did not return again to the 1910 level until 1955. A majority of Catholic priests continue to belong to missionary societies from the USA and Spain.

In Puerto Rico as with the rest of Latin America, Catholicism is very ancient, having arisen from the joint missionary and colonizing zeal of Spanish monarchism. But, unlike Latin America, Puerto Rico has become the battleground between 2 distinct cultural traditions, Hispanic and North American. Whatever elements may be common to both due to modernization, the fact is that each has a separate symbolic existence in the island.

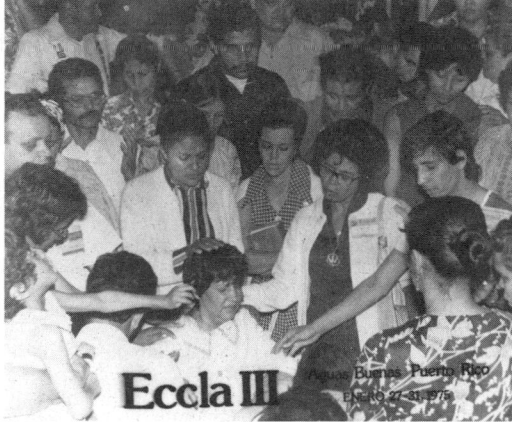

**Catholic pentecostals.** Healing in progress.

The Catholic Church as an institution or structure has been particularly sensitive to these traditions. Historically, in the Hispanic tradition the church is the unilateral arbiter of the religio-temporal identities of mankind. While temporal and religious goods are differentiated, the latter are by definition the superior ones. In the relationship between church and state, the latter must be beholden to the former. In the North American historical experience, on the other hand, Catholicism was and still is considered as a foreign, retardative element within the social milieu of Protestant libertarianism. The Catholic Church has had to adapt to that milieu or risk the stigma of disloyalty and unpatriotism. Thus, it is beholden to the state to the extent that the latter is protective or non-antagonistic to its interests and prerogatives.

In both traditions, the result has been a symbiotic relationship between church and state structures. This relationship has been galling to clergy in search of an image of relevance. In the 1974 episcopal view of the church situation in Puerto Rico 'Panorama of the Catholic Church in Puerto Rico since the Synod of Bishops 1971', one finds an oft-repeated theme of clerical desertion: priests who have abandoned their ministry are 'excessively lax in the discharge of their sacred obligations'; they 'provoke confrontation with

the ecclesiastical structure'. One also notes the paternalism of the hierarchy in the suggestion that ex-priests be returned to the lay apostolate 'once they overcome their emotional crisis'. Enthusiasm for the priestly vocation is widely lacking among Puerto Ricans, even at the hierarchical level. Under both the Spanish and American colonial regimes, Puerto Rican clergy never stood out in number or quality. In 1960, at the height of the American episcopate in the island, there were relatively fewer native clergy (one Puerto Rican among 9 clergy) than in 1897 near the end of Spanish rule, when one out of 5 clergy was Puerto Rican. By 1974 all Catholic bishops were native-born. While most Catholic movements or groups are conservatively oriented and take their cue directly from the Catholic hierarchy, a certain number of these (Juventud Obrera Cristiana, Juventud Estudiantil Cristiana, Juventud Universitaria Católica, Jornadas de Juventud, and segments of Cursillo de Cristiandad), together with their clerical sympathizers and mentors, have moved to active involvement in and for the cause of socio-political liberation in Puerto Rico. The reaction of church authorities has been either to withdraw recognition or to impose sanctions. Liberal and separatist clerics were forced out of their parishes and a number abandoned the ministry altogether, while others organized the Association of Priests (Associación Puertorriqueña de Sacerdotes) in Rio Pedras in 1972, which remained in 1975 the only Catholic organization wholly and openly in favour of political independence and socialism for Puerto Rico.

PROTESTANT CHURCHES. Puerto Rico was included among other former Spanish territories in the 1898 comity agreement among American Protestant churches, determining the location of their work after the Spanish-American war. The next year (1899) saw the arrival of 5 denominations (Baptists, Disciples, Lutherans, Presbyterians and United Brethren), followed by Methodists in 1900 and Adventists in 1909. Of these, Methodists and Adventists have built up the largest constituencies. Both have given considerable attention to schools, and Adventists also maintain important medical work. Adventist missionaries make up 26% of all foreign Protestant church workers on the island at the present time. The Baptist Convention of Puerto Rico, which is related historically to northern American Baptists in the USA, has also achieved a significant membership.

Presbyterians are strongest in western Puerto Rico, beginning there with a small group which had first been introduced to independent worship by an English trader of Reformed faith in 1860. In 1904 they opened one of the finest hospitals on the island and in 1919 contributed the first president to the new interdenominational Evangelical seminary. Although Lutheran membership remains small, Lutherans are responsible for administering Puerto Rico's main Protestant bookstore. In 1931 the United Evangelical Church was formed by a merger of 3 denominations: United Brethren, Christian Church and Congregational Church. Although the purpose of the merger was to build a strong united church, growth has been slow due in part to internal dissension over questions not resolved prior to union. The Disciples considered joining the UEC in 1933 but decided against it and remain an independent body.

Pentecostalism entered the island in 1916 with the return of Puerto Ricans who had come under the influence of the Assemblies of God while seeking work in Hawaii; and the Pentecostal Church of God is now the island's largest denomination outside Roman Catholicism. The church is fully self-supporting and maintains missionaries in Spain, Portugal and 9 other Latin American countries. Other Pentecostal groups include the Church of God (Cleveland), Church of God of Prophecy, International Church of the Foursquare Gospel, and United Pentecostal Church.

Protestantism has been able to penetrate all levels of social, economic and political life, both rural and urban, more completely in Puerto Rico than in any other Latin American country; and largely as a result of their schools, Protestants are now widely represented in the professions, business and government.

OTHER CHURCHES. Four years after Spain decreed religious tolerance 1868, the the English bishop of Antigua received permisssion to build the first Anglican church in Puerto Rico, at Ponce. Responsibility for Anglican work was transferred to the Episcopal Church in the USA in 1901. In 1923 the independent Church of Jesus, founded in 1902, merged with it, and although membership remains small, the Episcopal Church maintains a strong educational and medical programme.

A large number of indigenous churches have emerged in Puerto Rico, principally out of Pentecostalism. The most successful have been the Missionary Church of Christ, Defenders of the Faith Church, Pentecostal Church of Jesus Christ, and the Church of Christ in the Antilles. Jehovah's Witnesses also have experienced significant growth.

**CHURCH AND STATE.** In Puerto Rico, church and state are regarded as separate, mutually independent entities. The definitive legal commitment for this view is set forth in the constitution of the Commonwealth of Puerto Rico of 1952. Article II, section 3 of that constitution states that 'No law shall be made respecting an establishment of religion or prohibiting the free exercise thereof. There shall be complete separation of Church and State'.

Except for the second statement, the religion clause quoted above is a replica of that found in the first amendment to the federal constitution of the USA. In fact, statutory non-establishment and religious freedom were introduced into Puerto Rico with the transfer of sovereign rights over the island from Spain to the USA. Article X of the Treaty of Paris of 1898, which ended the Spanish-American War and provided among other items for such transfer, reads thus: 'The inhabitants of the territories over which Spain relinquishes or cedes her sovereignty shall be secure in the free exercise of their religion'. The prescription proscribing any establishment, which is the other of 2 co-ordinate or parallel aspects of the separation principle within the USA's historical tradition of church-state relationships, was implicit in the USA's acquisition of that sovereignty. It was later incorporated explicitly in the Jones Law of 1917 which the USA Congress passed to provide a framework of government for Puerto Rico. The law also included specific clauses to ensure that separation be an actual fact in a colony which was predominantly Roman Catholic and where the Spanish notion of the oneness of church and state had been deeply rooted. The separation guarantees (paragraphs 18 and 19 of Article II) were worded thus: 'That... the free exercise and enjoyment of religious profession and worship without discrimination or preference shall forever be allowed and that no political or religious tests other than an oath to support the constitution of the United States and the laws of Puerto Rico shall be required as a qualification to any office or public trust under the government of Puerto Rico'; also 'That no public money or property shall ever be appropriated, applied, donated, used, directly or indirectly, for the use, benefit, or support of any sect, church, denomination, sectarian institution, or association, or system of religion, or for the use, benefit, or support of any priest, preacher, minister, or other religious teacher or dignitary as such'.

The law, however, was unable to prevent church and state in Puerto Rico from becoming entangled in each other's domain. Relations between the two were further complicated by the presence of Protestants from the USA. From the beginning of American rule in the island, the Catholic Church fought a losing battle concerning the public schools which it criticized for their secularism and for depriving Catholics of their right to religious and moral instruction. The Catholic community was also critical of American Protestant evangelism and culturalism and

**Iglesia Metodista Unida.** Methodist Church at Jayuya.

the influence of Protestants both outside and inside the political community. Divorce was implanted within a few years after the advent of the Americans, while all attempts to provide moral instruction in the public schools proved fruitless.

In 1937, the Catholic conscience was outraged by the passage of so-called neo-Malthusian or eugenic laws by the island's legislature. Ostensibly to fight over-population and its negative influence on the social economy, these laws allowed and facilitated birth control, particularly in the form of sterilization of the deranged, lunatics, mentally retarded, epileptics, alcoholics, drug addicts, and also persons 'whose state of economic penury or bad conditions of life do not allow them to attend to the rearing and education of their children'. Official Catholic opposition to the laws was put in moral terms, as contravening the sacred procreative end of matrimony. In November 1974 and May 1975, the Catholic bishops twice condemned the government's massive birth control programme, including the sterilization of women, which they stated was not, as its sponsors officially claimed, entirely voluntary.

In 1942, under the new political leadership of the Populares, a law was passed recognizing, for all legal purposes, children born out of wedlock. By 1960, differences between church and state had been compounded not only by questions of the public schools and population control but also by personality conflicts between the Catholic hierarchy who were USA nationals and a vociferous native political leadership. The conflict came to a head when local political leader Muñoz Marín refused to yield on his party's commitment to institutionalized family planning and the Catholic hierarchy countered by hastily creating a Catholic party. This party failed to win a single seat in the island's legislature, while Marín's party, the Populares, received the largest electoral support ever. Four years later in 1964, the 2 USA bishops who had led the fight against Marín were recalled.

Since then the Puerto Rican bishops who have taken over the island's dioceses have avoided politics, particularly the issue of status for the island vis-a-vis the USA. At present, the main alternatives are defined as statehood, independence and some form of commonwealth. Critics of the hierarchy, among them separatist Catholics, suggest that the present Catholic withdrawal from politics is proof of its alliance with the economic power structure of the island which, in turn, is seen as an extension of that on the mainland. In recent years, clergy and sisters who have given up their vocations have been mostly separatists or sympathizers with the independence movement.

Since the churches are regarded in law as nonprofit, private, corporate bodies, church income and property are tax-exempt, and donations to them are tax-deductible (Law number 74, 1 January 1924). The idea of such concessions, interpreted in some quarters as subsidies to organized religion, originated in the USA where they came into law in 1916 and 1917. In 1947, the decision of the United States Supreme Court on the case of Everson vs Board of Education allowed state aid in the form of transportation to children of sectarian schools. The influence of this decision is seen in Section 5 of the Bill of Rights of the Puerto Rican constitution which, while providing for 'a system of free and wholly non-sectarian public instruction', does not forbid the state from 'furnishing to any child noneducational services established by law for the protection or welfare of children'. Thus, Catholic schools, like those of other religious groups, receive government aid in the form of transportation, lunches, dental service, scholarships, textbooks, and other services. In the island's budget approved by the Puerto Rican legislature in 1973, the sum of US$125,000 was destined as a grant to private schools, almost all of which were Catholic.

Of the religious denominations found on the island, all but the Catholic Church are registered in the archives of the Department of Justice. This fact derives from the legal attitude taken with regard to the nature of the island's Roman Catholic Church. Some maintain that the Catholic Church is 'a juridical-sovereign ecclesiastical body', with a public right to enter into a pact on an equal footing with the state, and that this view was affirmed in canon law and was the basis of the concordats of the 19th century between the Vatican and the Spanish monarchy. It is further claimed that this is compensation from the people of Puerto Rico and the government of the USA for property which allegedly had been lost to and remained unrestored to Spain at the time of the assumption of government by the USA.

**INTERDENOMINATIONAL ORGANIZATIONS.** The Evangelical Council of Puerto Rico (Concilio Evangélico de Puerto Rico) was begun in 1954 on the foundations laid earlier by the Evangelical Union in 1905 and the Association of Evangelical Churches of Puerto Rico in 1930. Full members include Baptists, Brethren, Disciples, Mennonites, Methodists, Presbyterians, Salvation Army and United Evangelicals.

The Catholic Episcopal Conference maintains a Commission for Ecumenism.

The Evangelical Seminary of Puerto Rico is sponsored by 10 denominations and serves 12 countries. It also works closely with the Episcopal Seminary of the Caribbean and the Catholic Theological Faculty at the Central University of Bayamon. Co-operative activities of these 3 seminaries (especially the first 2) include joint faculty meetings and sharing of faculty and library facilities.

**BROADCASTING.** On Sundays free radio and TV time is given to Christian programmes. The CEPR produces a weekly 30-minute TV programme. A Protestant mission, Calvary Evangelistic Mission, operates a missionary radio station WIVV which started in 1956. Situated on Vieques Island, WIVV broadcasts 18 hours daily to a million people living on 35 islands. HCJB-TV, formerly in Ecuador, now operates from here, and TWR has applied for a radio station also. The Catholic University of Puerto Rico also operates a station, WEUC.

For Catholics, Puerto Rico is a member of UNDA.

**BIBLIOGRAPHY**

*A consideration of some factors involved in the development of church planning in Puerto Rico*. R. Morales-Alamo. Thesis, Butler University Indianapolis (IN), 1964.

*Economic aspects of church development: a study of the policies and procedures of the major Protestant groups in Puerto Rico from 18971–957*. M. Saenz. Thesis, University of Pensylvania, Philadelphia (PA), 1961.

*Puerto Rico: iglesia y sociedad, 1969–1971*. A. Parilla-Bonilla. Sondeos No. 84, Cuernavaca (Mexico): CIDOC, 1971. 550p.

*Puerto Rico para Cristo: a history of the progress of the Evangelical missions on the island of Puerto Rico*. D.T. Moore. Sondeos No. 43, Cuernavaca (Mexico): CIDOC, 1969. 332p.

'Showcase for God: a study of Evangelical church growth in Puerto Rico', E.E. Carver. Thesis, Fuller Theological Seminary, Pasadena (CA), 1972. 254p.

TABLE 2. ORGANIZED CHURCHES AND DENOMINATIONS IN PUERTO RICO

| Official name 1 | Begun 2 | Type 3 | Counc 4 | Congs 5 | Adults 6 | Affiliated 7 | Names, notes, and other statistics (see Codebook) 8 |
|---|---|---|---|---|---|---|---|
| Asamblea des Iglesias Cristianas | 1940 | I pen | x.... | 58 | 2,500 | 5,000 | *Assembly of Christian Churches.* Begun 1939 by Puerto Ricans in New York, ex LACC. |
| Asambleas de Dios | 1957 | P Pe2 | ZF... | 35 | 1,560 | 3,000 | *Assemblies of God.* M=AoG(USA), until 1956 working with Iglesia de Dios Pente. 1p. |
| Convención Bautista de Puerto Rico | 1899 | P Bap | T.u.N | 48 | 9,000 | 20,000 | *Baptist Convention of PR.* 1899, M=ABHMS(USA). 4f,G=5.9%pa,1u. |
| Ejército de Salvación | 1961 | P Sal | xwu.N | 3 | 200 | 500 | *Salvation Army, PR Region,* USA Eastern Territory. San Juan. 1 emergency home. 1s. |
| Hermanos Libres | | P CBr | x.... | 5 | 250 | 500 | *Christian Brethren. Plymouth (Open) Brethren. Gospel Halls.* M=CMML(USA,UK). 10f. |
| Iglesia Adventista del Séptimo Día | 1901 | P Adv | x.... | 143 | 12,957 | 25,000 | *Seventh-day Adv, East/West PR Confs.* 26nx,195mw,72f,1H,2r,1s,150t(9339),1479Y. |
| Iglesia Alianza Cristiana y Misionera | 1900 | P Hol | xF... | 30 | 3,510 | 7,000 | *Christian & Missionary Alliance Ch.* M=CMA(USA). HQ Magnolia Gardens. 36m,1s. |
| **Iglesia Católica en Puerto Rico:** | 1509 | R Lat | B.L.R | 516 | 1,473,900 | 2,585,824 | *Catholic Ch in Puerto Rico.* C=24+3+75. 2q,2s. 716nx,124m,1664w,53739Yy. |
| M San Juan de Puerto Rico | 1511 | R Lat | Bs | 232 | 584,300 | 1,025,000 | Northeast quarter of island. Capital. 1s. 309 60 971 18968 |
| D Aracibo | 1960 | R Lat | Bs | 53 | 299,100 | 524,819 | Northwest. Bishop a leader of Charismatic Renewal. 122 29 126 8099 |
| D Caguas | 1964 | R Lat | Bs | 35 | 285,000 | 500,000 | Southeast, also Vieques islands (8,100), Culebra (700). 119 10 87 13436 |
| D Ponce | 1924 | R Lat | Bs | 196 | 305,500 | 536,005 | Southwest quarter of island. Charismatics strong. 166 25 480 13236 |
| Iglesia de Cristo en las Antillas | 1933 | I pen | ..... | 31 | 2,100 | 7,100 | *Ch of Christ in Antilles.* Mission to New York (USA). 24n,1x,G=19%pa,1s(76),150Y. |
| Iglesia de Cristo Misionera | 1934 | I pen | ..... | 56 | 5,100 | 10,000 | *Missionary Ch of Christ.* Until 1938 Iglesia de Cristo en las Antillas. |
| Iglesia de Dios | 1939 | I pen | ..... | 75 | 3,300 | 7,000 | *Ch of God.* Begun by 9 Puerto Ricans in east, expanded to west, SW, NE, SE. |
| Iglesia de Dios de la Profecía | 1938 | P Pe3 | Z.... | 25 | 700 | 2,000 | *Ch of God of Prophecy.* Ex CoG (Cleveland). HQ Rio Piedras. M=CGP(USA). 2f. |
| Iglesia de Dios Pentecostal | 1916 | P Pe2 | ZF... | 207 | 30,000 | 60,000 | *Pentecostal Ch of God.* Begun by Puerto Rican Catholics. M=AoG(USA). G=15%pa,1s. |
| Iglesia de Dios (Anderson) | 1966 | P Hol | x.... | 3 | 43 | 100 | *Ch of God.* M=CoG(Anderson) (USA). HQ Caguas, San José. 1 school. 1n,2f,W=50%. |
| Iglesia de Dios (Cleveland) | 1944 | P Pe3 | ZF... | 100 | 6,377 | 20,000 | M=CoG(Cleveland) (USA). Before 1944, Iglesia Roca de Salvación et al. 144n,4f,1p. |
| Iglesia de JC de los Santos de los UD | | M LdS | x.... | | 200 | 507 | *Ch of JC of Latter-day Saints. Mormons.* M=CJCLdS(USA). About 20 missionaries. |
| Iglesia de la Biblia Abierta | 1958 | P Pe2 | ZF... | 1 | 55 | 200 | *Open Bible Chs.* M=OBSC(USA). Classical Pentecostals. HQ Rio Piedras. 2f,1j. |
| Iglesia de los Hermanos | 1942 | P Dun | x.u.N | | 500 | 1,000 | M=Church of the Brethren(USA). Small mission of German Baptist origins. 5f. |
| Iglesia Defensores de la Fe | 1931 | I pen | xT... | 60 | 4,300 | 9,000 | *Defenders of the Faith Ch.* Missions to Dominican Republic. HQ Santurce. 1s. |
| Iglesia del Evangelio Cuadrangular | 1930 | P Pe2 | ZF... | 9 | 252 | 1,000 | M=Internat Ch of the Foursquare Gospel (USA). HQ Ponce. 14nm,2f,1p(11),W=56%,26Y. |
| Iglesia del Nazareno | 1943 | P Hol | xF... | 21 | 1,043 | 3,000 | *PR Distrito Nazareno.* M=Ch of the Nazarene (USA). 13n,9m,8f,G=4.7%pa,1s,20t(2565). |
| Iglesia Discípulos de Cristo | 1899 | P Dis | x.u.N | 110 | 9,065 | 15,000 | *Christian (Disciples) Convention of PR.* M=UCMS(USA). 1u. |
| Iglesia Episcopal: D Puerto Rico | 1872 | A Cen | aw.R. | 35 | 4,119 | 9,722 | *Episcopal Ch.* In PECUSA, Prov IX. 95% nationals. 35n,12x,1H,1s,W=25%,29Y,414y. |
| Iglesia Evangélica Unida de PR | 1899 | P uni | ..u.N | 92 | 6,000 | 12,000 | *United Ch of PR.* 1931 union of UBC, Christian Ch, Congregationalists. Static. 1u. |
| Iglesia Luterana Puertorriqueña | 1899 | P Lut | L.M.. | 21 | 4,000 | 8,000 | Caribbean Synod, Lutheran Ch in America. Main Protestant book distributor. 25n. |
| Iglesia Menonita | 1945 | P Men | G.u.N | 14 | 685 | 2,000 | *Puerto Rico Mennonite Conference.* M=MCNA(USA). Non-Germans. 9f,1H,2r,1s. |
| Iglesia Metodista Unida | 1900 | P Met | Vwu.N | 61 | 15,274 | 25,000 | *PR Provisional Annual Conference, United Methodist Ch*(USA). 58n,1r,1u. |
| Iglesia Mita | 1942 | I mar | ..... | | 2,000 | 5,000 | Messianic schism ex AoG, female founder Mita as incarnation of Holy Spirit. |
| Iglesia Nueva Apostólica | | C CAp | x.... | | 500 | 1,000 | *New Apostolic Ch,* USA Bezirk (District). M=NAC(Germany); world HQ Dortmund. |
| Iglesia Ortodoxa | | O Ara | Cwo.. | | 500 | 1,000 | Under Antiochian Orth Ch (USA) and P Antioch, E America. Lebanese, Syrian Arabs. |
| Iglesia Pentecostal de Jesucristo | 1938 | I pen | ..... | 45 | 4,400 | 9,000 | *Pentecostal Ch of Jesus Christ.* Ex Iglesia de Dios Pentecostal, in south & east. |
| Iglesia Pentecostal Unida | 1962 | P Pe1 | x.... | 10 | 375 | 1,000 | *United Pentecostal Ch. Jesus Only Church.* Unitarians. M=UPC(USA). 8n,4f,2p(22). |
| Iglesia Presbiteriana | 1860 | P Ref | ..u.N | 60 | 7,000 | 10,000 | *Presbytery of Puerto Rico.* M=UPUSA. Mostly around Mayagüez. 1H,1u |
| Iglesia Wesleyana | 1952 | I Hol | VF... | 9 | 385 | 735 | 1959 merger indigenous Tabernáculos de Dios. M=PHC,WC(USA). 5n,4x,19f,G=4%pa,1s. |
| Iglesias de Cristo | 1953 | P Dis | x.... | 20 | 488 | 1,000 | *Churches of Christ.* M=CC(Non-Instrumental) (USA). In cities. 16f,G=31%pa,1s. |
| Misión Bautista | 1956 | P Bap | T.... | 7 | 1,400 | 3,000 | M=Southern Baptist Convention (Home Mission Board) (USA). 14f,642Y. |
| Samaria Iglesia Evangélica | 1941 | I pen | ..... | 25 | 795 | 1,500 | *Samarian Ev Ch.* Begun Río Grande, ex Baptist Ch. Mission in New York state (USA). |
| Santa Iglesia Católica Apost Ortodoxa | 1961 | I CCa | .v... | 3 | 500 | 1,000 | *Holy Orth Cath Apost Ch.* Ex RCC, aided by Polish NCC(USA). 1968 applied to WCC. 1s. |
| Sociedad de la Ciencia Cristiana | | M Sci | x.... | 1 | 30 | 50 | *Christian Science.* First Ch of Christ, Scientist, San Juan. M=CCS(Boston,USA). |
| Testigos de Jehová | c1930 | M Jeh | x.... | 126 | 8,511 | 14,700 | *Jehovah's Witnesses. Watch Tower.* Active witnessing by 1932. G=16%pa,786Y. |
| Other Non-White indigenous churches | | I pen | ..... | | 10,000 | 20,000 | Total about 26 (see list below), almost all pentecostal. |
| Other Protestant denominations | | P | ..... | | 4,000 | 8,000 | Total about 25 (see list below). |
| Other marginal Protestant bodies | | M | ..... | | 100 | 300 | Incl: Unitarian Fellowship of San Juan, Unity School of Christianity (2 churches). |
| Doubly-affiliated (duplication) (1970) | | | | | –152,000 | –266,738 | Evangelicals who also are or were baptized Roman Catholics. |
| **Total affiliated (mid-1970)** | | | | **2,410** | **1,485,974** | **2,650,000** | **Total denominations (1970) . . . 89.** |
| **Total affiliated (mid-1975)** | | | | **2,500** | **1,564,400** | **2,797,500** | **Total denominations (1975) . . . 95.** |
| **Total affiliated (mid-1980)** | | | | **2,600** | **1,654,300** | **2,958,200** | **Total denominations (1980) . . . 101.** |

NOTES ON TABLE ABOVE
COLUMNS: for meanings and CODES (cols. 1, 3, 4, 8): see Codebook (Part 6). Column 1: **Boldface type** = church with over 10% of country's affiliated Christians.
NATIONAL COUNCILS (Column 4, 5th letter).
N = Concilio Evangélico de Puerto Rico (CEPR)/Evangelical Council of Puerto Rico.
R = Conferencia Episcopal Puertorriqueña (CEP)/Puerto Rico Episcopal Conference.
OTHER NON-WHITE INDIGENOUS CHURCHES. These bodies, begun by Puerto Ricans and Blacks, are almost all pentecostal, and include: Asamblea Cristiana, Concilio Iglesia de Dios Apostólica, Iglesia Cristiana de Nazareth, Iglesia de Cristo Séptimo Día, Iglesia de Dios Hebreos, Iglesia de Dios Primitiva, Iglesia de Dios Sacrificada, Iglesia de Dios Singular, Iglesia Ev de Avivamiento, Iglesia Ev del Buen Pastor, Iglesia Mensajeros de Cristo, Iglesia Monte Sión, Iglesia Pentecostal del Nazareno, Iglesia Refugio de Sión.
OTHER PROTESTANT DENOMINATIONS. These include: Baptist Bible Fellowship International (1955), Baptist International Missions, Baptist Mid-Missions (1959), Bethany Fellowship Missions (1965), Children of God International, Christian Reformed Ch (1967), Conservative Baptist Home Mission Society (1958; 5 churches), Exclusive Brethren (Kelly-Continental), Fellowship of Independent Missions (1968), Go-Ye Fellowship, Grace Mission (1961), Independent Assemblies of God, International Gospel League (1961), International Pentecostal Assemblies (1962), National Fellowship of Brethren Chs (1959), Reformed Baptists (USA; 1 church), Union Churches (in 2 cities), United Missionary Fellowship (1968) (merger of Pioneer Bible Mission, United Faith Mission), Wisconsin Ev Lutheran Synod (1963), World Gospel Crusades (1969), World-Wide Missions (1962). There are also military chaplaincies for the USA armed forces.
UNITING CHURCHES. Negotiations for organic union were under way in 1974 between: Iglesia Evangélica Unida de PR, Iglesia Metodista Unida.

**PEOPLES** (ethnolinguistic). Christians: 72.7% Puerto Rican White, 15.0% Black, 10.0% Mulatto, 2.2% USA White 0.1% Spaniard, Cuban, East Indian.

**COUNTRY-WIDE TOTALS**
EVANGELIZATION (see Part 5). 1900: 100%. 1970: 100%. 1980: 100%. *Mass evangelism.* Among recent campaigns: 1966, Southern Baptist crusades; 1967, Billy Graham 8-day crusade in San Juan (105,700 attenders, 4,355 enquirers) and Rally in Ponce (7,500/325); 1968, American Baptist and Southern Baptist crusades; 1971, Every Creature Crusades (World Gospel Crusades) reaching over half a million homes.
FOREIGN MISSIONARIES AND PERSONNEL (nationals serving abroad (1973). Total 615 in 20 countries: about 520 Roman Catholics in 13 countries (especially USA), about 70 Protestants (mainly Pentecostals) in 16 countries (especially USA), 25 Puerto Rican indigenous in Argentina, Dominican Republic, Spain, USA, Venezuela et alia.
FOREIGN MISSIONARIES AND PERSONNEL (aliens from abroad) (1973). Total 1,978. *From Western world.* 1,538: 1,230 Roman Catholics, 265 Protestants (258 in 34 USA societies, 5 in 1 Canada society, 2 in 1 UK society), about 30 marginal Protestants (20 Mormons from USA), 12 Anglicans in 1 USA society, 1 Orthodox. *From Third World.* 440: 420 Roman Catholics from other Latin American and Caribbean countries, about 10 Protestants, 10 Non-White indigenous from Caribbean and Mexico.
INSTITUTIONS (church-operated) (1973). Total 130, including 70 higher schools, 16 medical centres (hospitals), 2 radio stations, 1 religious community, 21 seminaries (13 Protestant, 4 RC, 3 indigenous, 1 Anglican), 1 university.
PERIODICALS. About 35 titles.
PERSONNEL. About 3,488 (1,510 national, 1,978 foreign).
RELIGIOUS LIBRARIES. About 25.
SCRIPTURE DISTRIBUTION (1975). Annual totals: 81,774 Bibles (6% free, 69% subsidized, 24% commercial), 191,341 NTs (75% free, 20% subsidized, 4% commercial), 144,453 UBS portions, 2,857,850 UBS selections.
SERVICE AGENCIES. About 50, including ACISJF, CCCI, CEF, CEM(WIVV), CEP, CEPR, COR, CORPORI, CRS, EDM, HCJB-TV, JAC, JUC, MBI, MCS, SU, TWR, UNELAM, YWCA.

**ADDITIONAL DATA ON CHURCHES**
IGLESIA CATOLICA EN PUERTO RICO. *New diocese.* In 1976, the diocese of Mayagüez was created. *Annual baptisms.* (1972) 96.2% infant, 3.8% adult. *Priests.* 263 secular, 453 religious. A majority of priests are missionaries from the USA or Spain. *Male religious.* Total including contemplatives (1970) 599, of whom 8% nationals, 6% from other Latin American nations, 86% from Europe and North America. *Sisters.* 38% nationals, 22% from other Latin American nations, 40% from Europe and North America. *Catholic charismatics.* The Charismatic Renewal expanded very rapidly throughout the island after 1970 with 15,000 adults receiving the charismatic experience from 1971–74, including 100 priests, and being active in over 100 prayer groups. *Catholic organizations.* The Episcopal Conference of Puerto Rico (Conferencia Episcopal Puertorriqueña, CEP) has its headquarters in San Juan. There are 2 conferences of religious personnel, Conferencia de Religiosos de Puerto Rico, for men, and Conferencia de Religiosas de Puerto Rico, for women. There are no official pastoral or presbyteral councils, nor any co-ordinating organization for the lay apostolate. The principal lay movements are Cursillos de Cristiandad, Juventud de Acción Católica, Caballeros de Colón (Knights of Columbus), Hijas Católicas de América, Sociedad de Santo Nombre (Holy Name Society), Legión de María, Hijas de María, and Club Serra.
The Holy See has no diplomatic relations with Puerto Rico. It is represented to the Catholic hierarchy by an apostolate delegate who serves also as nuncio to the Dominican Republic.
Other institutions and organizations are active. For theology and pastoralia, there are 2 theological faculties, one in the Catholic University in Ponce (Facultad de Teología, Universidad Católica de Puerto Rico) and one in the Central University of Bayamon, both being staffed by foreigners who are mostly Spaniards. There is also a Pastoral Institute (Instituto de Pastoral) in Santurce. In the cultural and social fields, the Intercultural Communication Institute (Instituto Intercultural para Communicaciones, formerly Larrain Institute), was begun at Ponce in 1957. Founded by Ivan Illich, it might well have been the precursor of CIDOC in Cuernavaca (Mexico), but its original objective of inter-American intercommunication has since disappeared. At present, it operates as the special summer school of the Catholic University of Puerto Rico to give courses to North American priests and men and women religious personnel working among the large numbers of Puerto Rican and Latin American immigrants to the United States. The Centro Social Juan XXIII in San Juan is a non-official organization involved in research in the social-economic and socio-political fields.
Educational work in 1973 included 5 pre-primary (60 pupils), 100 primary (47,596) and 59 secondary schools (14,580). The Universidad Católica de Puerto Rico founded in Ponce in 1948 and canonically erected in 1972 has 7,140 students. There is also a college for women in Santurce. Medical and social service institutions in 1971 included 10 general hospitals (1,068 beds), 3 special hospitals (250 beds), 9 homes for invalids for or the aged (1,433 beds) and 5 homes for children (225 children).
IGLESIA DE DIOS PENTECOSTAL. Though begun by Puerto Ricans, the church remained in the Protestant tradition affiliated to the Assemblies of God (USA) until 1956. In 1969 the church supported 16 foreign missionaries in Spain, Portugal and other countries.

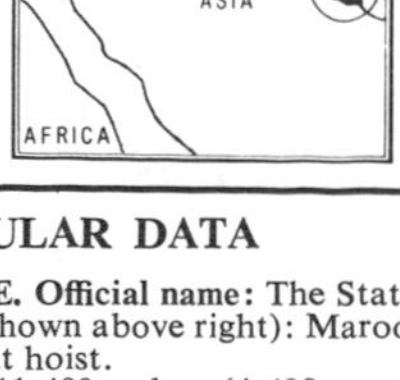


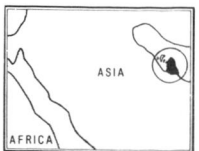

# QATAR

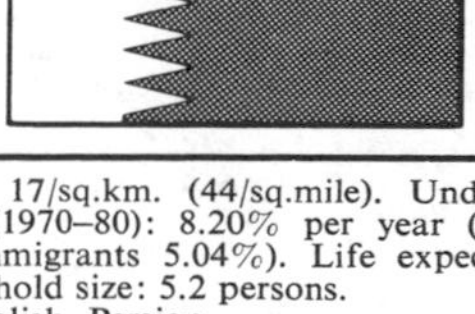

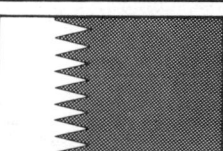

## SECULAR DATA

**STATE. Official name:** The State of Qatar (Dawlat Qatar).
**Flag** (shown above right): Maroon field with broad white serrated band at hoist.
**Area:** 11,400 sq.km. (4,400 sq.miles). Agricultural land: 4.7%.
**Government:** Absolute monarchy (1916 British protectorate, 1971 Independence as emirate).
**Official language:** Arabic.
**Capital:** Doha 140,000 (1974).
**Armed forces** (1976): Total 2,200 regular army (6 combat aircraft).

**DEMOGRAPHY. Population:** 100,000 (estimate of 1.VII.1969. For 1970–2000 including immigrants, see last row of Table 1). Population density (1975): 17/sq.km. (44/sq.mile). Under 15 years: 44%. Growth rate (1970–80): 8.20% per year (births 4.85%, deaths –1.69%, immigrants 5.04%). Life expectancy (1975–80): 49.5 years. Household size: 5.2 persons.
**Major languages:** Arabic, English, Persian.
**Urban dwellers** (1970): 69.4%. Urban growth rate (1950–70): 6.5% per year.

**Labour force:** 44%.

**ETHNOLINGUISTIC GROUPS:** 82% Arab (47% alien Palestinian & Lebanese & Syrian, 35% Qatari), 11% Black African (Bantu), 2% Persian, 2% Indian (Malayali, Tamil), 1.3% British (1,400), 1.0% USA White, 0.5% other European, Armenian, Sudanese.

**MONEY** (1977). **Monetary unit:** Qatar riyal (= 100 dirhams); US$1 = QR 4.03.
**National income per person:** US$12,500. Average annual family income: US$65,000.
**Cost of living in capital** (1976): Daily cost of living: US$90.

**HEALTH.** Hospitals: 5 (682 beds). Doctors: 105. Blind: 200. Psychotics: 900.

**EDUCATION.** Adult literacy: 20%. Education rate: 76%. Schools: 90.

**LITERATURE.** Annual new book titles (1973): 88. Periodicals: 3. Newspapers: 3 non-daily.

**COMMUNICATION** (per 1,000 people). Phones: 179. Radios: 350. TV sets: 302. Daily newspaper circulation: 149 copies.

## TABLE 1.　RELIGIOUS ADHERENTS IN QATAR

| Year | 1900 | | mid-1970 | | Annual change, 1970–1980 | | | | mid-1975 | | mid-1980 | | 2000 | |
|---|---|---|---|---|---|---|---|---|---|---|---|---|---|---|
| Name | Adherents | % | Adherents | % | Natural | Conversion | Total | Rate | Adherents | % | Adherents | % | Adherents | % |
| Muslims | 17,930 | 99.6 | 104,870 | 95.3 | 14,548 | −77 | 14,471 | 7.90 | 183,140 | 93.9 | 249,580 | 92.4 | 349,000 | 87.2 |
| Christians | 70 | 0.4 | 4,730 | 4.3 | 1,056 | 71 | 1,127 | 11.27 | 10,000 | 5.1 | 16,000 | 5.9 | 40,000 | 10.0 |
| crypto-Christians | 70 | 0.4 | 2,030 | 1.8 | 446 | 71 | 517 | 11.75 | 4,400 | 2.3 | 7,200 | 2.7 | 18,000 | 4.5 |
| professing | 0 | 0.0 | 2,700 | 2.4 | 610 | 0 | 610 | 10.89 | 5,600 | 2.9 | 8,800 | 3.3 | 22,000 | 5.5 |
| Protestants | 0 | 0.0 | 1,000 | 0.9 | 150 | 0 | 150 | 8.33 | 1,800 | 0.9 | 2,500 | 0.9 | 5,000 | 1.3 |
| Anglicans | 0 | 0.0 | 600 | 0.5 | 50 | 0 | 50 | 6.25 | 800 | 0.4 | 1,100 | 0.4 | 3,000 | 0.8 |
| Roman Catholics | 0 | 0.0 | 600 | 0.5 | 260 | 0 | 260 | 15.29 | 1,700 | 0.9 | 3,200 | 1.2 | 10,000 | 2.5 |
| Orthodox | 0 | 0.0 | 500 | 0.5 | 150 | 0 | 150 | 11.54 | 1,300 | 0.7 | 2,000 | 0.7 | 4,000 | 1.0 |
| affiliated | 70 | 0.4 | 4,730 | 4.3 | 1,056 | 71 | 1,127 | 11.27 | 10,000 | 5.1 | 16,000 | 5.9 | 40,000 | 10.0 |
| total practising | 63 | 90 | 3,780 | 80 | 845 | 57 | 902 | 11.27 | 8,000 | 80 | 12,800 | 80 | 28,000 | 70 |
| non-practising | 7 | 10 | 950 | 20 | 211 | 14 | 225 | 11.25 | 2,000 | 20 | 3,200 | 20 | 12,000 | 30 |
| Orthodox | 0 | 0.0 | 1,500 | 1.4 | 418 | 2 | 420 | 11.05 | 3,800 | 1.9 | 5,700 | 2.1 | 11,000 | 2.8 |
| Protestants | 0 | 0.0 | 1,400 | 1.3 | 200 | 10 | 210 | 8.40 | 2,500 | 1.3 | 3,500 | 1.3 | 7,000 | 1.8 |
| Evangelicals | 0 | 0.0 | 400 | 0.4 | 52 | 8 | 60 | 8.57 | 700 | 0.4 | 1,000 | 0.4 | 2,000 | 0.5 |
| Anglicans | 20 | 0.1 | 700 | 0.6 | 69 | 1 | 70 | 7.00 | 1,000 | 0.5 | 1,400 | 0.5 | 4,000 | 1.0 |
| Roman Catholics | 50 | 0.3 | 680 | 0.6 | 312 | 10 | 322 | 16.10 | 2,000 | 1.0 | 3,900 | 1.4 | 12,000 | 3.0 |
| Asian indigenous | 0 | 0.0 | 450 | 0.4 | 57 | 48 | 105 | 15.00 | 700 | 0.4 | 1,500 | 0.6 | 6,000 | 1.5 |
| Baha'is | 0 | 0.0 | 300 | 0.3 | 11 | 1 | 12 | 3.33 | 360 | 0.2 | 420 | 0.2 | 2,000 | 0.5 |
| Non-religious | 0 | 0.0 | 100 | 0.1 | 85 | 5 | 90 | 18.00 | 500 | 0.3 | 1,000 | 0.4 | 3,000 | 0.8 |
| Hindus | 0 | 0.0 | 0 | 0.0 | 300 | 0 | 300 | 30.00 | 1,000 | 0.5 | 3,000 | 1.1 | 6,000 | 1.5 |
| Country's population | 18,000 | 100.0 | 110,000 | 100.0 | 16,000 | 0 | 16,000 | 8.20 | 195,000 | 100.0 | 270,000 | 100.0 | 400,000 | 100.0 |

**COLUMNS, ROWS.** For meanings and definitions, see Codebook (Part 6). Note that, by definition, total 'Christians' = professing + crypto-Christians, which also = affiliated + nominal Christians. Percentages may not always total exactly, due to rounding.

**NOTES ON RELIGIONS**
**ASIAN INDIGENOUS.** Indians from the Mar Thoma Syrian Church, et alia; also Arab isolated radio believers (see Table 2).
**BAHA'IS.** Growth from 1 local spiritual assembly (1964) to 3

(1973).
**CHRISTIANS.** The rapid increase from 1970 is due to immigration of Arab, Indian and other Asian Christians.
**COUNTRY'S POPULATION.** The population has grown very rapidly since 1970 through the arrival of large numbers of immigrant workers. The column 'Natural change' includes this immigration, for all rows in the table also.
**CRYPTO-CHRISTIANS.** Mainly immigrant Arab Christians whom the state regards as Muslims, together with Arab isolated radio believers.

**HINDUS.** Indians arriving in the massive influx after 1970.
**MUSLIMS.** Indigenous Qataris are Sunnis (primarily Wahhabis), with a small number of Shias; Arabs (Qatari and expatriate), with some Indians and Iranians. *Hajj pilgrims to Mecca.* (1970) 1,392; (1975) 974; (1976) 847.
**NON-RELIGIOUS.** Mainly Europeans.
**PROFESSING CHRISTIANS.** Although no census of religion has been held, the state regards Europeans as professing Christians and either ignores or does not recognize most Arab Christians.

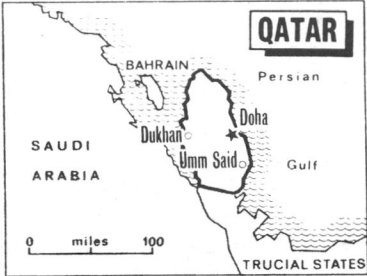

**NON-CHRISTIAN RELIGIONS. Islam** in Qatar as in Saudi Arabia is represented for the most part by Sunnis, primarily Wahhabis, although there are also a small number of Shias.

**Baha'i** has a few followers in 3 local spiritual assemblies.

## CHRISTIANITY

Christianity established itself in the Arabian Peninsula during the early centuries, with a hierarchy established in northwest Arabia before AD 244, but was completely eclipsed by Islam in the 7th century.
**CATHOLIC CHURCH.** The first Catholic of modern times returned to Aden in 1841, and by 1889 the whole of the peninsula was included in the vicariate of Arabia, which is now administered from Abu Dhabi. Qatar is served by one USA Capuchin priest based in Doha. In 1972 there were 680 Catholics, all expatriates including Arabs, but no Catholic institutions nor religious congregations.
**OTHER CHURCHES.** There are practically no indigenous professing Christians in Qatar, but a large interdenominational Christian expatriate community exists composed of Westerners (Anglicans, Episcopalians, Scottish Presbyterians, Lutherans, et alii), Indians (Syrian Orthodox, Mar Thoma Church, Church of South India) and Arabs from Palestine and Lebanon. Worship services are led by chaplains of the Arabian American Oil Company. Resident Christians also receive periodic visits from Anglican chaplains stationed at Abu Dhabi (United Arab

Emirates), and there are 2 organized Brethren congregations.

**CHURCH AND STATE.** Qatar came under British protection during the 19th century, largely through Britain's attempt to bring to an end the slave trade in the Gulf. Previously the country was a tribal patriarchal society under the firm control of the amir as chief of state, but a constitutional government was accepted when Independence was declared in 1970. The provisional constitution of 27 April 1970 makes Islam the official religion of the state and the source of its system of law, in addition to guaranteeing fundamental democratic rights for all. Govern-

ment departments are gradually being developed to meet social and economic needs as they arise. Although any attempt at proselytism is prohibited, expatriate Christians are free to organize and publicize their worship services; and clergy can enter and travel in the country without impediment. Thus far permission has not been given to construct church buildings, but this remains a hope of Qatar's Christian community.

**BROADCASTING.** No Christian broadcasting is permitted. From abroad, Christian programmes in Arabic can be easily heard over the international station FEBA (Seychelles).

**Muslims.** Grand Mosque (foreground) and royal palace (left), Doha.

## TABLE 2.　ORGANIZED CHURCHES AND DENOMINATIONS IN QATAR

| Official name 1 | Begun 2 | Type 3 | Counc 4 | Congs 5 | Adults 6 | Affiliated 7 | Names, notes, and other statistics (see Codebook) 8 |
|---|---|---|---|---|---|---|---|
| Anglican Church (D Cyprus & the Gulf) | 1916 | A plu | aw... | 2 | 200 | 700 | In Episcopal Ch in Jerusalem & ME. In Doha, Dukhan. Europeans, Indians, Arabs. |
| Catholic Church (VA Arabia) | c1880 | R Lat | P..L. | | 400 | 680 | All expatriates (including Arab Catholics). One Capuchin priest in Doha. |
| Christian Brethren | c1960 | P CBr | x.... | 2 | 100 | 200 | *Plymouth Brethren. Open Brethren. Gospel Halls.* Indians, British. |
| Isolated radio churches | c1950 | I rad | ..... | | 50 | 150 | Isolated Arab radio believers, mostly aged 12–25, through RVOG,FEBA,RVatican,ICI. |
| Other Orthodox churches | c1950 | O | ..... | | 800 | 1,500 | Expatriate Arabs (Greek, Syrian, Coptic), Indians (Syrian), Armenians, et alii. |
| Other Protestant denominations | 1940 | P | ..... | | 800 | 1,200 | Ch of Scotland, Free Ch (UK), USA, Lutherans, CSI (Indian), et al. House groups. |
| Other indigenous churches | c1965 | I | ..... | | 100 | 300 | Mostly Indians from Mar Thoma Syrian Ch. House groups; also at Anglican services. |
| Total affiliated (mid-1970) | | | | 20 | 2,450 | 4,730 | Total denominations (1970) . . . 19. |
| Total affiliated (mid-1975) | | | | 25 | 5,170 | 10,000 | Total denominations (1975) . . . 24. |
| Total affiliated (mid-1980) | | | | 40 | 8,300 | 16,000 | Total denominations (1980) . . . 34. |

## NOTES ON TABLE ABOVE

**COLUMNS:** for meanings and CODES (cols. 1, 3, 4, 8): see Codebook (Part 6). Column 1: **Boldface type** = church with over 10% of country's affiliated Christians. The data in the first 8 rows above refer to the situation in 1970. For 1970–80, see Table 1.

**PEOPLES** (ethnolinguistic). Christians (1970): 44% Arab (Palestinian, Lebanese, Syrian, Egyptian, Qatari), 19% British, 15% South Indian (Malayali, Tamil), 13% USA White, 7% other European, 2% Black, Armenian.

**COUNTRY-WIDE TOTALS**
**EVANGELIZATION** (see Part 5). 1900: 2%. 1970: 35%. 1980: 45%. *Radiophonic evangelism.* RVOG, TWR, FEBA, Radio Vatican, ICI, et alia.
**FOREIGN MISSIONARIES AND PERSONNEL** (aliens from abroad) (1973). Total 3. *From Western world.* 2 Roman Catholics. *From Third World.* 1 Orthodox from India.
**PERSONNEL** (1973). 3 (foreign).

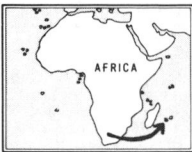

# REUNION

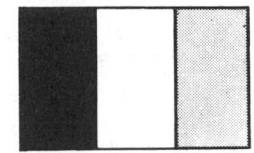

## SECULAR DATA

**STATE. Official name:** The Department of Reunion (Le Département de la Réunion). Unofficial name: Bourbon.
**Flag** (shown above right): That of France.
**Area:** 2,512 sq.km. (969 sq.miles). Agricultural land: 26.2%.
**Government:** Overseas department of France, since 1946 (1638 French possession).
**Legislature:** General Council, 36 members.
**Official language:** French (*Français*).
**Chief cities:** capital Saint-Denis 85,444 (1967), Saint-Paul 43,186.
**Political divisions:** 24 Communes.
**Foreign forces** (1973): French troops 4,000, decreasing to 2,000 by 1978.

**DEMOGRAPHY. Population:** 416,525 (census of 16.X.1967.

For 1970–2000 (UN), see last row of Table 1). Population density (1975): 199/sq.km. (517/sq.mile). Under 15 years: 44%. Growth rate (1975–80): 1.80% per year (births 2.55%, deaths −0.75%). Life expectancy (1975–80): 64.8 years. Household size: 4.9 persons.
**Major languages:** French, French Creole, Chinese, Swahili, Gujarati, Malayalam, Malagasy.
**Urban dwellers** (1970): 27.3%. Urban growth rate (1950–70): 3.0% per year.
**Labour force:** 26%.

**ETHNOLINGUISTIC GROUPS:** 91.0% Creole (Mulatto, Eurasian) (French/Black/Asiatic), 3% Chinese, 2.9% Swahili, 1.4% Indian (Gujarati, Malabari), 1.4% Malagasy, Pakistani, French.

**MONEY.** (1977). Monetary unit: French franc (= 100 centimes);

US$1 = Fr 5.00.
**National income per person:** US$1,200. Average annual family income: US$5,880.
**Inflation:** (1970–74) 10.0% per year.
**Cost of living in capital** (1976): Daily cost of living: US$27.

**HEALTH.** Hospitals: 22 (3,369 beds). Doctors: 224, Lepers: 1,000 (2.0 per 1,000). Blind: 1,000. Psychotics: 3,500.

**EDUCATION.** Adult literacy: (1954) 39%, (1975) 63%. Education rate: 80%. Schools: 439.

**LITERATURE.** Newspapers: 2 dailies, 11 non-daily.

**COMMUNICATION** (per 1,000 people). Phones: 34. Radios: 145. TV sets: 48. Daily newspaper circulation: 59 copies.

**TABLE 1.  RELIGIOUS ADHERENTS IN REUNION**

| Year | 1900 | | mid-1970 | | Annual change, 1970–1980 | | | | mid-1975 | | mid-1980 | | 2000 | |
|---|---|---|---|---|---|---|---|---|---|---|---|---|---|---|
| Name | Adherents | % | Adherents | % | Natural | Conversion | Total | Rate | Adherents | % | Adherents | % | Adherents | % |
| **Christians** | **90,000** | **52.0** | **431,300** | **96.5** | **9,763** | **137** | **9,900** | **2.04** | **484,300** | **96.7** | **530,300** | **96.8** | **697,500** | **95.3** |
| professing | 90,000 | 52.0 | 431,300 | 96.5 | 9,763 | 137 | 9,900 | 2.04 | 484,300 | 96.7 | 530,300 | 96.8 | 697,500 | 95.3 |
| **Roman Catholics** | 90,000 | 52.0 | 429,300 | 96.0 | 9,717 | 113 | 9,830 | 2.04 | 482,000 | 96.2 | 527,600 | 96.3 | 692,400 | 94.6 |
| Evangelical Catholics | 0 | 0.0 | 1,200 | 0.3 | 34 | 66 | 100 | 5.88 | 1,700 | 0.3 | 2,200 | 0.4 | 3,700 | 0.5 |
| Protestants | 0 | 0.0 | 2,000 | 0.4 | 46 | 24 | 70 | 3.04 | 2,300 | 0.5 | 2,700 | 0.5 | 5,100 | 0.7 |
| nominal | 30,000 | 17.3 | 1,072 | 0.2 | 38 | 65 | 103 | 5.41 | 1,900 | 0.4 | 2,100 | 0.4 | 15,300 | 2.1 |
| affiliated | 60,000 | 34.7 | 430,228 | 96.2 | 9,725 | 72 | 9,797 | 2.03 | 482,400 | 96.3 | 528,200 | 96.4 | 682,200 | 93.2 |
| total practising | 48,000 | 80 | 301,160 | 70 | 6,807 | 51 | 6,858 | 2.03 | 337,680 | 70 | 369,740 | 70 | 443,430 | 65 |
| non-practising | 12,000 | 20 | 129,070 | 30 | 2,918 | 21 | 2,939 | 2.03 | 144,720 | 30 | 158,460 | 30 | 238,770 | 35 |
| **Roman Catholics** | 50,000 | 34.7 | 427,028 | 95.5 | 9,645 | −18 | 9,627 | 2.01 | 478,400 | 95.5 | 523,300 | 95.5 | 673,400 | 92.0 |
| Protestants | 0 | 0.0 | 2,200 | 0.0 | 54 | 56 | 110 | 4.07 | 2,700 | 0.5 | 3,300 | 0.7 | 5,800 | 0.8 |
| Evangelicals | 0 | 0.0 | 1,300 | 0.3 | 32 | 38 | 70 | 4.38 | 1,600 | 0.3 | 2,000 | 0.4 | 3,600 | 0.5 |
| Marginal Protestants | 0 | 0.0 | 1,000 | 0.2 | 26 | 34 | 60 | 4.61 | 1,300 | 0.3 | 1,600 | 0.3 | 3,000 | 0.4 |
| Muslims | 20,000 | 11.6 | 10,900 | 2.4 | 231 | −131 | 100 | 0.88 | 11,400 | 2.3 | 11,900 | 2.2 | 13,000 | 1.8 |
| Baha'is | 0 | 0.0 | 1,200 | 0.3 | 30 | 30 | 60 | 4.00 | 1,500 | 0.3 | 1,800 | 0.3 | 3,700 | 0.5 |
| Tribal religionists | 53,000 | 30.6 | 1,000 | 0.2 | 16 | −56 | −40 | −5.00 | 800 | 0.2 | 600 | 0.1 | 0 | 0.0 |
| Hindus | 10,000 | 5.8 | 1,000 | 0.2 | 20 | −20 | 0 | 0.00 | 1,000 | 0.2 | 1,000 | 0.2 | 1,000 | 0.1 |
| Non-religious | 0 | 0.0 | 1,000 | 0.2 | 26 | 34 | 60 | 4.61 | 1,300 | 0.3 | 1,600 | 0.3 | 14,600 | 2.0 |
| Atheists | 0 | 0.0 | 500 | 0.1 | 12 | 8 | 20 | 3.33 | 600 | 0.1 | 700 | 0.1 | 2,000 | 0.3 |
| Other religionists | 0 | 0.0 | 100 | 0.0 | 2 | −2 | 0 | 0.00 | 100 | 0.0 | 100 | 0.0 | 200 | 0.0 |
| **Country's population** | **173,000** | **100.0** | **447,000** | **100.0** | **10,100** | **0** | **10,100** | **2.02** | **501,000** | **100.0** | **548,000** | **100.0** | **732,000** | **100.0** |

**COLUMNS. ROWS.** For meanings and definitions, see Codebook (Part 6). Note that, by definition, total 'Christians' = professing + crypto-Christians, which also = affiliated + nominal Christians. Percentages may not always total exactly, due to rounding.
**CENSUSES.** The religion question has not been asked.

## NOTES ON RELIGIONS

**ATHEISTS.** Reunion Communist Party (PCR) (legal): membership (1970) 800; Communist voters (1968 election) 25% of all votes.
**BAHA'IS.** Growth from 1 local spiritual assembly (1964) to 13 (1973).
**CHRISTIANS.** Including many expatriate French military and civilians.
**COUNTRY'S POPULATION.** This has increased from 1,200 (French settlers, Malagasy, Métis, Portuguese) in the year 1715, to 61,000 in 1789, to 225,000 in 1946. In 1848, 60,000 Black slaves were emancipated. Since 1945, there has been substantial emigration to France and Madagascar because of increasing unemployment and pressure on the land.
**HINDUS.** Indians, brought in temporarily as indentured labourers after 1848 emancipation of slaves.
**MUSLIMS.** Mainly Swahili (Bantu) with some Pakistanis and Indians; mostly Sunnis.
**NON-RELIGIOUS.** Including many French military and civilians.
**OTHER RELIGIONISTS.** Including Rosicrucians (1 AMORC centre).
**PRACTISING CHRISTIANS.** At Easter 1961, 140,000 Catholics took communion (49% of eligible Catholics).
**ROMAN CATHOLICS.** In 1900, 50,000 Catholics and many catechumens among freed slaves and their descendants.
**TRIBAL RELIGIONISTS.** From 1848 onwards, large numbers of Bantu and Malagasy freed slaves remained animist in religion, gradually being catechized and baptized by the Catholic Church, but with many remaining only nominal Christians.

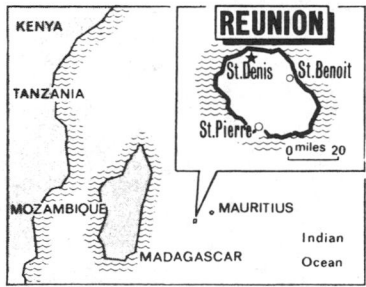

**NON-CHRISTIAN RELIGIONS. Islam** in 1972 made up 2.4% of the population, mainly Swahili with some Indo-Pakistanis.

## CHRISTIANITY

**CATHOLIC CHURCH.** Initial contacts were made at the beginning of colonization in 1653, and the island was afterwards served by visiting priests and sometimes by ships' chaplains. In 1712 a Lazarist was appointed prefect. The modern era of Catholic missions in Eastern Africa was intiated in 1817 by the arrival in Reunion of sisters of the Congregation of St Joseph of Cluny, and from here the evangelization of the East African coast was begun. The territory was placed under Holy Ghost priests in 1917. The diocese was divided into 12 deaneries, plus a Chinese mission founded in 1951 which is served by 2 Chinese secular priests. Reunion is overwhelmingly Catholic. The diocese covers the whole island but also works closely with other nearby islands including Mauritius. In 1970–71, as a result of political pressures many progressivist Catholic priests were forced to leave the island. In 1974 there were 48 priests native to Reunion, 5 from Mauritius, 64 from France and 10 from other European coutries.

**OTHER CHURCHES.** Seventh-day Adventist work is small but growing. Begun in 1936, there are at present 19 congregations. The Africa Evangelical Fellowship (South Africa) has opened work, also Assemblies of God (France) and the Reformed Church. Jehovah's Witnesses have 8 congregations.

**CHURCH AND STATE.** Since Reunion is a French overseas territory, separation of church and state, and freedom of religion, are guaranteed as in metropolitan France.

## BIBLIOGRAPHY
*Annuaire ecclésiastique du Diocèse de la Réunion, 1971.* Saint-Denis, Réunion: Évêché, 1971.

**Eglise Catholique, Diocèse de la Réunion.** *Right.* Extravagantly baroque parish church at Sainte-Anne.

TABLE 2. ORGANIZED CHURCHES AND DENOMINATIONS IN REUNION

| Official name 1 | Begun 2 | Type 3 | Counc 4 | Congs 5 | Adults 6 | Affiliated 7 | Names, notes, and other statistics (see Codebook) 8 |
|---|---|---|---|---|---|---|---|
| Assemblées de Dieu | c1960 | P Pe2 | Z.... | 10 | 300 | 800 | *Assemblies of God.* M=Assemblées de Dieu (France). Centres throughout the island. |
| Eglise Adventiste du Septième Jour | 1936 | P Adv | x.... | 19 | 497 | 1,000 | *Seventh-day Adv, Reunion Mission,* Indian Ocean UM. 11n,6m,12t(670),W=80%,104Y. |
| **Eglise Catholique: D La Réunion** | 1653 | R Lat | Pz..r | 70 | 239,100 | 427,028 | *Catholic Ch. French,* 13,000 Chinese. C=4+3+13. 43n,78x,50m,513w,P=49%,13580Yy. |
| Eglise Evangélique de la Réunion | 1970 | P int | xM... | 4 | 125 | 200 | *Evangelical Ch of Reunion.* M=Africa Evangelical Fellowship (SAGM). 1m,3f. |
| Eglise Réformée de la Réunion | | P Ref | ..... | 1 | 100 | 200 | *Reformed Ch of Reunion.* Chaplaincy to military and civil French. In St-Denis. |
| Témoins de Jéhovah | c1955 | M Jeh | x.... | 8 | 354 | 1,000 | *Jehovah's Witnesses. Watch Tower. IBSA.* Active witnessing under way by 1960. 27Y. |
| **Total affiliated (mid-1970)** | | | | **112** | **240,476** | **430,228** | **Total denominations (1970) . . . 7.** |
| **Total affiliated (mid-1975)** | | | | **115** | **269,600** | **482,400** | **Total denominations (1975) . . . 7.** |
| **Total affiliated (mid-1980)** | | | | **118** | **295,200** | **528,200** | **Total denominations (1980) . . . 8.** |

NOTES ON TABLE ABOVE
COLUMNS: for meanings and CODES (cols. 1, 3, 4, 8): see Codebook (Part 6). Column 1: **Boldface type** = church with over 10% of country's affiliated Christians.
NATIONAL COUNCILS (Column 4, 5th letter).
r = attached to Conférence Episcopale de France (CEF) (Episcopal Conference of France).

PEOPLES (ethnolinguistic). Christians: 94.4% Creole (Mulatto, Eurasian), 3% Chinese, 0.7% Malagasy, 0.4% South Indian (Malabari), French.

COUNTRY-WIDE TOTALS
EVANGELIZATION (see Part 5). 1900: 48%. 1970: 100%. 1980: 100%.
FOREIGN MISSIONARIES AND PERSONNEL (nationals serving abroad) (1973). Total about 5 Roman Catholics in Madagascar and France.
FOREIGN MISSIONARIES AND PERSONNEL (aliens from abroad) (1973). Total 272. *From Western world.* 252: 250 Roman Catholics, 2 Protestants in 1 France society. *From Third World.* About 20, mainly Roman Catholic Chinese and others from Mauritius and Madagascar.

INSTITUTIONS (church-operated) (1973). Total 20, including 9 higher schools, 5 medical centres (3 hospitals), 2 religious communities.
PERIODICALS. 2 titles.
PERSONNEL. About 2,610 (2,338 national, 272 foreign).
RELIGIOUS LIBRARIES. 2.
SCRIPTURE DISTRIBUTION (1975). Annual totals: 7,300 Bibles (86% subsidized, 14% commercial), 5,700 NTs (91% subsidized, 9% commercial), 37,500 UBS portions.
SERVICE AGENCIES. About 18, including ACF, ACGF, ACI, APECA, AREP, CEF, CV/AV, JOC/F, UOSR.

ADDITIONAL DATA ON CHURCHES
EGLISE ADVENTISTE DU SEPTIEME JOUR. For some years there has been considerable emigration of members to metropolitan France.
EGLISE CATHOLIQUE. Alternate name, D Saint-Denis de la Réunion. *Catechumens.* (1959) 75; (1961) 42; (1963) 30. *Annual baptisms.* (1972) 99.7% infant, 0.3% adult. *Priests.* (1974) 129: 48 Reunionese (46 secular, 2 religious), 5 Mauritians (4 secular), 64 metropolitan French (16 secular, 48 religious), 2 Chinese (secular), 10 other Europeans (2 secular, 8 religious). *Sisters.* 382 Réunionnaises. *Seminarians.* 15 (8 in France). *Catechists.* Total (1970) 1,893. Served by a pastoral catechetical team. *Indigenous religious congregations.* Sisters: Filles de Marie de St-Denis (begun 1848, 192 professed in 1970). *Main foreign congregations.* Priests: CSSp. Brothers: FSC. Sisters: St-Joseph de Cluny. *Catholic organizations.* The diocese is attached to the Episcopal Conference of France (Conférence Episcopale de France). There is no association of religious personnel, but a presbyteral council has been formed. The principal lay movements are ACGF, ACI, Légion de Marie (91 praesidia), ACF, Scouts, JOC/F and CV/AV.
The Holy See has no diplomatic relations with Reunion. It is represented to the Catholic hierarchy by an apostolic delegate based in Tananarive, Madagascar.
The Catholic school programme is co-ordinated by the Diocesan Service for Catholic Education. In 1973 there were 33 primary schools (9,037 pupils) and 9 secondary schools (2,338 pupils), in addition to the APECA Centre of Apprenticeship (Plaine des Cafres), which provides professional training. The Union of Reunionese Social Works (UOSR) co-ordinates medical and social activities. In 1971 there were 3 hospitals, 2 clinics and various other centres for medical care run by sisters. Secours Catholique is responsible for relief work.

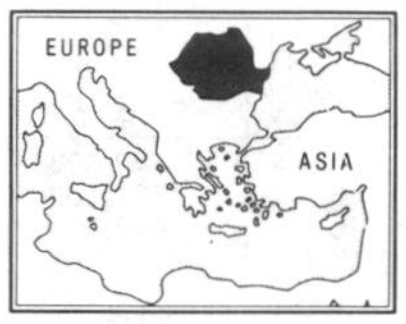


# ROMANIA

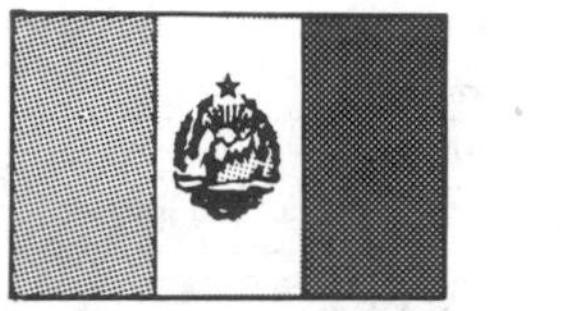

## SECULAR DATA

**STATE. Official name:** The Socialist Republic of Romania (Republica Socialistă România). Older orthography: Rumania. Adjective of nationality: Romanian.
**Flag** (shown above right): Blue, yellow, and red bars, with national coat of arms in centre.
**Area:** 237,500 sq.km. (91,699 sq.miles). Agricultural land: 62.9%.
**Government:** One-party Communist state, since 1947 (1504 in Ottoman empire, 1861 Independence, 1881 constitutional monarchy, 1938 fascist dictatorship, 1947 People's Republic).
**Legislature:** Grand National Assembly, 465 members.
**Official languages:** Romanian (*Romăneste*); also Hungarian (*Magyar*) in Transylvania.
**Chief cities:** capital Bucharest 1,528,560 (1973), Cluj 222,490, Brașov 263,160, Timisoara 204,690, Iasi 202,050.
**Political divisions:** 40 Districts (judet); 236 Towns (oras), 2,706 Local Authorities (comune).
**Armed forces** (1976): Total 181,000 regular (100,000 conscripts): army 145,000, navy 11,000, air force 25,000. Reserves: 545,500. Paramilitary forces: 530,000 (500,000 Militia).

**DEMOGRAPHY. Population:** 19,103,163 (census of 15.III.1966 For 1970–2000 (UN), see last row of Table 1). Population density (1975): 89/sq.km. (231/sq.mile). Under 15 years: 28%. Growth rate (1975–80): 0.81% per year (births 1.82%, deaths −1.01%). Life expectancy (1975–80): 68.7 years. Household size: 3.2 persons.
**Major languages:** Romanian, Hungarian, German, Romany, Yiddish, Turkish, Ukrainian, Serbo-Croatian, Russian, Slovak, Bulgarian, Czech, Greek, Armenian.
**Urban dwellers** (1970): 41.7%. Urban growth rate (1950–70): 3.1% per year.
**Labour force:** 48%.
**Refugees** (1977): From abroad, none. Exiles abroad: 12,000 Romanian Jews to Israel from 1973–76.
**Tourists** (1974): 3,825,252.

**ETHNOLINGUISTIC GROUPS:** 84.0% Romanian, 8.5% Hungarian, 3.1% Gypsy, 2.0% German (Saxon, Swabian), 0.5% Jewish, 0.5% Turkish, 0.3% Ukrainian (60,000), 0.3% Serbian (60,000), 0.2% Russian, 0.1% Tatar (21,000), 0.1% Slovak, 0.1% Armenian, 0.1% Bulgar (13,000), 0.1% Czech (12,000), 0.1% Greek (12,000), Polish, Croat.

**MONEY** (1977). **Monetary unit:** leu (plural lei) (= 100 bani); US$1 = Lei 12.00.
**National income per person:** US$1,200. Average annual family income: US$3,840.
**Inflation:** (1970–74) 0.7% per year, (1973: consumer price index 102).
**Cost of living in capital** (1976): Daily cost of living: US$50.

**HEALTH.** Hospitals: 608 (179,402 beds). Doctors: 24,720. Lepers: 4,000 (0.2 per 1,000). Blind: 15,918. Psychotics: 190,000. Criminals: 102,180.

**EDUCATION.** Adult literacy: (1956) 89%, (1975) 98%. Education rate: 53%. Schools: 14,899. Universities: 5.

**LITERATURE.** Annual new book titles (1973): 10,100. Periodicals: 635. Scientific journals: 170. Newspapers: 58 dailies, 17 non-daily.

**COMMUNICATION** (per 1,000 people). Phones: 43. Radios: 148. TV sets: 103. Daily newspaper circulation: 174 copies.

TABLE 1. RELIGIOUS ADHERENTS IN ROMANIA

| Year | 1900 | | mid-1970 | | Annual change, 1970–1980 | | | | mid-1975 | | mid-1980 | | 2000 | |
|---|---|---|---|---|---|---|---|---|---|---|---|---|---|---|
| *Name* | *Adherents* | *%* | *Adherents* | *%* | *Natural* | *Conversion* | *Total* | *Rate* | *Adherents* | *%* | *Adherents* | *%* | *Adherents* | *%* |
| **Christians** | **10,384,000** | **94.4** | **16,840,000** | **83.2** | **150,077** | **−16,817** | **133,260** | **0.76** | **17,530,800** | **82.8** | **18,172,600** | **82.4** | **20,837,000** | **80.9** |
| crypo-Christians | 0 | 0.0 | 1,620,000 | 8.0 | 15,409 | 21,091 | 36,500 | 2.03 | 1,800,000 | 8.5 | 1,985,000 | 9.0 | 2,580,000 | 10.0 |
| professing | 10,384,000 | 94.4 | 15,220,000 | 75.2 | 134,668 | −37,908 | 96,760 | 0.61 | 15,730,800 | 74.3 | 16,187,600 | 73.4 | 18,257,000 | 70.9 |
| Orthodox | 10,065,000 | 91.5 | 13,000,000 | 64.2 | 115,150 | −32,390 | 82,760 | 0.61 | 13,450,800 | 63.5 | 13,827,600 | 62.7 | 15,604,000 | 60.6 |
| Protestants | 154,000 | 1.4 | 1,210,000 | 6.0 | 10,615 | −3,615 | 7,000 | 0.56 | 1,240,000 | 5.9 | 1,280,000 | 5.8 | 1,442,000 | 5.6 |
| Roman Catholics | 165,000 | 1.5 | 1,010,000 | 5.0 | 8,903 | −1,903 | 7,000 | 0.67 | 1,040,000 | 4.9 | 1,080,000 | 4.9 | 1,211,000 | 4.7 |
| nominal | 330,000 | 3.0 | 0 | 0.0 | 0 | 0 | 0 | 0.00 | 0 | 0.0 | 0 | 0.0 | 0 | 0.0 |
| affiliated | 10,054,000 | 91.4 | 16,840,000 | 83.2 | 150,077 | −16,817 | 133,260 | 0.76 | 17,530,800 | 82.8 | 18,172,600 | 82.4 | 20,837,000 | 80.9 |
| doubly-affiliated | 0 | 0.0 | −2,236,312 | −11.0 | −19,578 | 9,409 | −10,169 | 0.44 | −2,287,000 | −10.8 | −2,338,000 | −10.8 | −2,576,000 | −10.0 |
| total practising | 9,551,000 | *95* | 15,492,800 | *92* | 138,071 | −15,472 | 122,599 | 0.76 | 16,128,340 | *92* | 16,718,790 | *92* | 17,711,500 | *85* |
| non-practising | 503,000 | *5* | 1,347,200 | *8* | 12,006 | −1,345 | 10,661 | 0.76 | 1,402,460 | *8* | 1,453,810 | *8* | 3,125,500 | *15* |
| Orthodox | 9,702,000 | 88.2 | 16,184,000 | 79.9 | 153,963 | −22,529 | 121,434 | 0.72 | 16,816,570 | 79.3 | 17,398,340 | 78.9 | 19,858,500 | 77.1 |
| Orthodox pentecostals | 0 | 0.0 | 0 | 0.0 | 9 | 191 | 200 | 20.00 | 1,000 | 0.0 | 2,000 | 0.0 | 50,000 | 0.2 |
| Protestants | 143,000 | 1.3 | 1,563,211 | 7.7 | 13,954 | −1,275 | 12,679 | 0.78 | 1,630,000 | 7.7 | 1,690,000 | 7.7 | 1,932,000 | 7.5 |
| Evangelicals | 121,000 | 1.1 | 1,417,000 | 7.0 | 12,872 | 4,238 | 17,110 | 1.14 | 1,503,600 | 7.1 | 1,588,100 | 7.2 | 1,855,000 | 7.2 |
| Neo-pentecostals | 0 | 0.0 | 5,000 | 0.0 | 86 | 1,414 | 1,500 | 15.00 | 10,000 | 0.0 | 20,000 | 0.1 | 100,000 | 0.4 |
| Roman Catholics | 152,000 | 1.4 | 1,268,901 | 6.3 | 11,215 | −2,105 | 9,110 | 0.70 | 1,310,000 | 6.2 | 1,360,000 | 6.2 | 1,571,000 | 6.1 |
| Marginal Protestants | 57,000 | 0.5 | 59,000 | 0.3 | 514 | −314 | 200 | 0.33 | 60,000 | 0.3 | 61,000 | 0.3 | 50,000 | 0.2 |
| Catholics (non-Roman) | 0 | 0.0 | 1,000 | 0.0 | 9 | −3 | 6 | 0.58 | 1,030 | 0.0 | 1,060 | 0.0 | 1,200 | 0.0 |
| Anglicans | 0 | 0.0 | 200 | 0.0 | 0 | 0 | 0 | 0.00 | 200 | 0.0 | 200 | 0.0 | 300 | 0.0 |
| Non-religious | 22,000 | 0.2 | 1,695,000 | 8.4 | 16,242 | 12,758 | 29,000 | 1.57 | 1,842,000 | 8.7 | 1,985,000 | 9.0 | 2,627,000 | 10.2 |
| Atheists | 6,000 | 0.1 | 1,356,000 | 6.7 | 12,328 | 4,272 | 16,600 | 1.15 | 1,440,000 | 6.8 | 1,552,000 | 6.9 | 1,880,000 | 7.3 |
| Muslims | 91,000 | 0.8 | 250,000 | 1.2 | 2,226 | −226 | 2,000 | 0.77 | 260,000 | 1.2 | 270,000 | 1.2 | 300,000 | 1.2 |
| Jews | 496,000 | 4.5 | 100,000 | 0.5 | 400 | 0 | 400 | 0.39 | 102,000 | 0.5 | 104,000 | 0.5 | 110,000 | 0.4 |
| Other religionists | 1,000 | 0.0 | 3,000 | 0.0 | 27 | 13 | 40 | 1.25 | 3,200 | 0.0 | 3,400 | 0.0 | 4,000 | 0.0 |
| **Country's population** | **11,000,000** | **100.0** | **20,244,000** | **100.0** | **181,300** | **0** | **181,300** | **0.86** | **21,178,000** | **100.0** | **22,057,000** | **100.0** | **25,758,000** | **100.0** |

COLUMNS, ROWS. For meanings and definitions, see Codebook (Part 6). Note that, by definition, total 'Christians' = professing + crypto-Christians, which also = affiliated + nominal Christians. Percentages may not always total exactly, due to rounding.
CENSUSES. XII.1899 (excluding Transylvania and northern parts of Romania): 91.5% Orthodox, 4.5% Jews, 2.9% Roman Catholics and Protestants, 0.8% Muslims, 0.4% other religionists. Subsequent censuses have not included the religion question.

NOTES ON RELIGIONS
ATHEISTS. Romanian Communist Party (in power; independent over Sino-Soviet dispute): membership (1970) 2,260,000, growing slightly faster than population growth. Of Communist party members, only around 15% are estimated to be committed and dedicatedly anti-religious atheists, the rest being non-religious with a considerable minority of professing Christians (Orthodox) also.
CRYPTO-CHRISTIANS. This bloc, usually referred to as the underground church, consists of 3 different kinds of believers: (1) unorganized individuals who are not professing Christians but who are affiliated to the legal churches; (2) members of unrecognized or illegal denominations including Greek Catholics who have refused to accept the liquidation of their church in 1948; and (3) a handful of isolated radio believers.
DOUBLY-AFFILIATED. The majority of all Protestants and Roman Catholics (especially Uniates) are also counted or claimed as members by the Romanian Orthodox Church, mostly in sensitive areas where it would be unwise to attempt to clarify the situation by detailed enumeration.
JEWS. Decline from 500,000 in 1939. In 1973, there were 70 communities with 130 synagogues under a chief rabbi. Under 25% have Yiddish as their mother tongue.
MUSLIMS. In 1899, Muslims were almost all in Constanta department and made up 37% of its population then. In 1975, they were more spread across the country, and consisted of Turks (all Turks being Hanafite Sunnis), Gypsies, Tatars, Bulgars, and others, who are now mainly Romanian nationals, with a mufti in Constanta.
NEO-PENTECOSTALS. By 1972, charismatics within the historic non-Pentecostal Protestant denominations were becoming widespread.
NOMINAL CHRISTIANS. Only before 1947.
NON-RELIGIOUS. Agnostics, indifferent to religion, including most Communist party members. In addition to this total, there

are another 8.0% of the population who are regarded by state and society as non-religious but who are affiliated to the churches and so are classified here as crypto-Christians.
OTHER RELIGIONISTS. Including about 100 Baha'is in 1 centre.
PRACTISING CHRISTIANS. Around 70% of Orthodox members attend church at some time or other weekly, and 90% at least once a year. Protestant services are crowded almost everywhere.
PROTESTANTS. Many thousands of adults are baptized into Protestant churches each year; in 1973, at least 18,000 (9,000 Baptists, 5,000 Pentecostals, 4,000 Open Brethren), which is considerably larger than natural population increase among the Protestant community. Revival is also spreading rapidly among the Gypsy population, with packed church services. In the column 'Conversion change' above, however, these figures are hidden by the gradual numerical erosion of Protestantism as a whole since the Communist regime began.

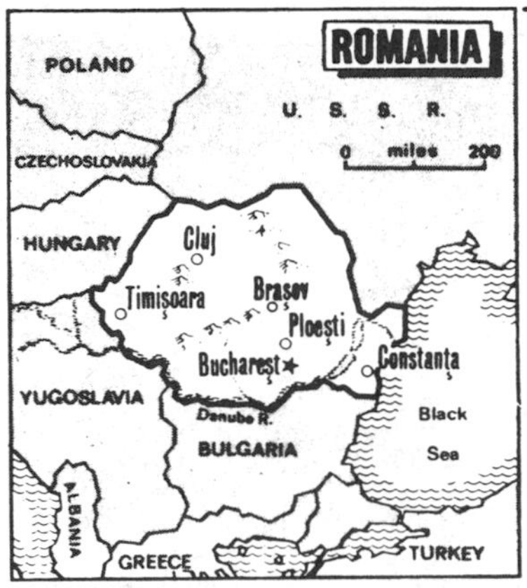


**NON-CHRISTIAN RELIGIONS. Islam** is composed largely of Turks who are now Romanian nationals. As in Bulgaria, Muslims constitute an ethnic, cultural and religious minority of relatively limited significance, underestimated and neglected. Several Muslim communities have been formed in Dobruja on the Black Sea coast, and there is a mufti at Constanta.

**Judaism** before World War II numbered around half a million Jews and formed a very dynamic minority in Moldavia, especially at Iasi and Czenovitz, and in Transylvania in the region of Maramures. These numbers were drastically reduced by the Nazi massacres of 1940–44, but today Judaism continues to be important, although the flexible foreign policy adopted by the Ceaucesçu regime has made possible large-scale emigration to Israel. By the end of 1972 the flow of emigrants seemed to be terminating, with remaining Jews practising their strongly-traditional Talmudic religion freely under the care of a grand rabbi in Bucharest. In 1973, there were 70 Jewish communities worshipping in 130 synagogues, with a Jewish population of 100,000. Conditions for the Jewish community in Romania are among the best in the Communist world.

**CHRISTIANITY.** Historically, Romania emerged out of the Roman province of Dacia established by the emperor Trajan in the 2nd century. Overrun by Goths, Huns, Avars, Slavs, Mongols and Bulgars in the following centuries, it remained basically a wedge of Latin culture between Slavs to the west and Mongols to the east. In the 10th century it became known as Walachia, and declared itself an independent principality in 1290. A second Romanian state, Moldavia, was established in 1363 to the north of Walachia, with the creation of Transylvania to the west following in 1526 as this part of Europe came under Turkish control. As the Turks were pushed back beginning in the 17th century, the peoples in this area found themselves driven back and forth between the armies of Austria, Hungary, Romania and Russia, and this has been true of the modern period as well.

The life of the Christian church among Romanians reflects this turbulent history. Tradition holds that the first apostles, including Andrew, brought the Christian message to the Romanian peoples living on the shores of the Black Sea, and Christianity certainly existed there in strength by the beginning of the 3rd century. Romanians were among the martyrs of the emperor Diocletian's persecution of 303. At first the liturgy was in Latin, but the formation of a Bulgarian state to the south and the introduction of a Slavic liturgy by Methodius and Constantine strongly influenced the Romanian people and drew them into the orbit of Constantinople. Catholic Hungarian and Polish immigrants during the 13th century, followed by Dominican missionaries brought about little change. The first Romanian metropolitan sees were created soon after the establishment of Wallachia and Moldavia, ultimately coming directly under the patriarch of Constantinople as the latter grew in authority in all areas under Turkish rule. When the Turks began to retreat along bordering territories, the Orthodox churches in these areas found themselves subjected to religious pressures from new conquerors: Austria, Hungary and Russia. Thus many of the Orthodox churches in Transylvania, which was captured by Austria and the Hapsburgs in 1688, became Uniate churches under Rome through Jesuit efforts. By 1733 there were in Transylvania 2,294 Uniate priests as opposed to 458 Orthodox priests and in 1750, 569,000 Romanian Uniates as contrasted with only 25,000 Orthodox. Calvinism was also introduced into Transylvania during the 16th and 17th centuries during the influence of Hungary, while both countries were still under Turkish rule. Those who remained Orthodox in these annexed areas were placed under regional patriarchs, and autocephalous patriarchates were declared in the 19th century as the Balkan nations struggled for their independence. The Uniate churches consistently resisted the introduction of Latin in their liturgy; and in 1862 the Orthodox churches, resentful of Greek domination, replaced the Greek liturgy with a liturgy in the Romanian language. At the Congress of Paris in 1856, Moldavia and Walachia achieved virtual independence from Turkish rule. The Romanian Orthodox Church then declared itself autocephalous in 1865 and was recognized as such by Constantinople in 1885.

ORTHODOX CHURCH. Following the establishment of new boundaries for Romania after World War I, the patriarchate of Bucharest was created in 1925 when the 2 Romanian metropolitanates of Walachia and Moldavia were united. Since 1965, the Orthodox Church has lived in a political situation which has benefitted it more than the other churches. Its present vitality is incontestable, with its seminaries now having 3 times as many candidates as there are pastoral vacancies. Participation of the faithful in the sacraments and in regular public worship is significant and becomes massive at Easter. Equally impressive is the religious life of educated youth in the cities and also of the working classes. In 1969, 100,000 copies of the Bible in Romanian were printed. The national Orthodox Church administers its own property, lands, presses and factories producing religious articles, operates a few minor seminaries, and produces 9 religious journals and a large number of books each year. Religious personnel previously expelled were allowed to return to their monasteries in 1967, but the number of monks continues to decline.

The Romanian Orthodox Church in 1971 consisted of 5 metropolitanates divided into 12 dioceses and 106 deaneries with 8,185 parishes, 2,847 annexes and 11,722 worship places served by 8,600 priests. Monastic foundations numbered 114, of which 57 were monasteries (30 for men and 27 for women) and 20 monastic annexes. The total number of religious personnel was 2,068, 575 being monks and 1,493 nuns. By 1975 monasteries and sketes totalled 122, with 540 monks and 1,433 nuns. In 1971 there were 312 ordinations to the priesthood and 205 new sanctuaries consecrated. The educational level of the clergy is exceptionally high: 6,174 have theological diplomas, 2,147 seminary diplomas, 57 doctorates in theology, and 49 others expect to receive doctoral degrees shortly; 157 have not yet completed their studies. The 2 theological institutes of Bucharest and Sibiu matriculated respectively 398 and 627 students in 1970–71. At the same time the seminary at Cluj had an enrolment of 246 students.

Other smaller Orthodox bodies in Romania include the Armenian, Bulgarian, Ancient Orthodox (Old Believers), Greek, Russian, Serbian and Ukrainian Orthodox churches.

CATHOLIC CHURCH. Officially all present-day Catholics are of the Latin rite only. Although there are several thousand German and Moldavian Catholics dispersed throughout the south of Transylvania and in Bucharest, the majority of Romanian Catholics belong to the Hungarian minority and live in Transylvania, a region formally part of the Austro-Hungarian empire until 1919. The Hungarian language is predominant in the Catholic Church, and the church's fortunes are intimately bound up with those of this Hungarian minority. At the beginning of 1975, there were 3 Latin-rite bishops in Romania but only 2, bishop Aaron Marton of Alba Julia and his coadjutor bishop Antonio Jakab, were recognized by the Romanian government and allowed to ordain an approved number of priests and visit parishes for confirmations. In spite of the fact that he was consecrated bishop in Rome in the presence of members of the Romanian embassy to Italy, bishop Peter Plesca, who acts as ordinary in the vacant see of Iasi, has been refused all government recognition. The 3 other Latin sees are vacant. Bishop Marton, who in 1974 was already over 90 years of age and was widely revered by the faithful, had long adopted a passive attitude towards the authorities of the country, characterized by prudence as well as a clear refusal to collaborate with the regime. Freed in 1967 after 18 years in prison, he was granted permission to visit Rome in 1969, and in that year the government adopted a more liberal policy in its relations with the Catholic Church. In spite of some arrests of Hungarian priests in 1970, it can be said that the Latin church enjoys freedom of worship within the limits normal under an Eastern European Communist regime. Some believe that the Orthodox Church has been instrumental in helping to create these improved relations between government and the Catholic Church.

As a result of its isolated situation, Romanian Catholicism tends to be introverted, concentrating its energy on survival and on interior spirituality. Apart from private visits by priests from Hungary and other countries Catholics are completely cut off from the outside world. The only impact of Vatican II has been in the language of the liturgy and in a new edition of the missal, in which all feasts of Hungarian saints have been removed. Catholic organizations are notable by their absence. However, the Status of Transylvania (Erdélyi Stàtus) is an old institution which continues to function as a pastoral council bringing together clergy and laity, but its activities are limited. Places of worship are well cared for, due to government subsidies, and the 2 Catholic seminaries do not lack for vocations. Franciscans, the only religious order permitted, live in the convent of Csiksomlyo and maintain it as a lay pilgrimage centre. Catholic schools have been suppressed, except for a minor seminary at Cluj which can take 100 pupils each year. There is a home for aged priests at Dès.

The Byzantine-rite Uniate Catholic church has fared much worse. These are Catholics of Hungarian origin who live in Transylvania. In 1698 the Orthodox Church of Transylvania proclaimed its union with Rome, a few years after the principality came under Austrian domination. At the instigation of the Orthodox, they were declared in 1919 a national church with a status next in importance to that of the Orthodox Church. However in December 1948 the church was formally declared by the new Communist regime to have voluntarily dissolved itself and to have rejoined the Orthodox Church. Although the latter accepts this thesis of 'auto-dissolution', the Uniate church was in fact forcibly suppressed. A synod was held at Cluj in October 1948 attended by 36 of the 1,818 Uniate priests, who ignored the local bishop's excommunication and, claiming to represent some 1,800 parishes and 1.6 million Uniates, decided on reunion with the Orthodox Church. At the time of its suppression, the Uniate church had a metropolitan see, Fagaras and Alba Julia founded in 1721, and 4 suffragan dioceses: Cluj-Cherla, Lugoj, Maramures, and Oradea Mare. All these were forced into the Orthodox metropolitanate of Transylvania. Several hundred priests and laity were imprisoned, and the 6 bishops died in prison, the last being Msgr Juliu Hossu in 1970. An emissary from Rome, Msgr Gerald O'Hara, consecrated other bishops; but these were arrested and later sent to monasteries from which they were only permitted to depart after promising that they would exercise no episcopal function. A vast number of the faithful still continue to consider themselves attached to Rome. In 1975 these were estimated to number around 900,000, with several hundred priests ministering clandestinely.

PROTESTANT CHURCHES. The largest body is the Reformed Church of Romania (Biserica Reformata), which came into being in 1554 as the result of the work of Pierre Melius. Attached to the Hungarian Reformed church in 1881, it did not become autonomous again until after World War I, and most of its members still belong to the Hungarian minority in Romania. Lutheranism was introduced in 1519 and spread rapidly among Germans in Transylvania while it was under Turkish control. When Transylvania came under Austrian rule in 1691, the Lutherans were persecuted by the Hapsburg regime, although harassment gradually lessened over the next century. After World War I, the German Lutherans of Bessarabia were annexed again to Romania and united with those of Transylvania to form the Evangelical Protestant Church in Romania of the Augsburg Confession (Biserica Protestanta Evangelica din Romania dupa Confeiunea dela Ausburg). After World War II, Bessarabia was taken again from Romania, the Lutheran Church losing these Lutherans as well as the German Lutherans of Transylvania who were forced into exile at the same time. Lutheran Hungarians had earlier formed their own church (Biserica Lutherana Ungara din Romania) after World War I.

The first Baptist community was established in Bucharest in 1856 among the German community, but there were no Romanian members until the beginning of the 20th century. The number increased greatly with the annexation of Transylvania and Bessarabia by Romania in 1918. A seminary was built in 1920, but between 1930 and 1944 the church was subject to state persecution. During World War II the Baptist Church was dissolved by the Nazis. In 1945 the Baptist Convention of Romania was established, but the church suffered persecution again after 1947. Today Baptists are found mostly among the Romanians of Walachia. They are increasing in number and their church is officially recognized by the government. Considerable numbers

are asking for baptism after hearing the gospel on foreign radio broadcasts. Adventists have been at work in Romania since 1911 and have built up a sizeable community organized into 4 conferences: Bacau, Bucharest, Cluj and Sibiu. Pentecostals began in 1922 and now have over 200,000 members with very many small communities scattered throughout Moldavia and Walachia.

Following the creation of the Popular Republic after World War II, all Protestant churches were cut off from the West, especially the bonds that they had maintained over the years with Germany and the Netherlands. Much cultural, linguistic and political pressure was brought to bear, particularly upon the Hungarian minority. However, since the recent liberalization of governmental policies, contacts with other countries have been re-established.

Since 1972 a large people movement to faith in Christ has taken place among the Gypsies, with thousands converted. There are also a few hundred Jewish Christians dating from the Norwegian Lutheran Church's 300 Jewish converts in the 1930s and 1940s.

MARGINAL CHURCHES. The Unitarian Church has an ancient history in Romania. Followers of Michael Servet and successors to the alleged Arian heresy in their negation of the doctrines of the Trinity and the divinity of Jesus, the Unitarians were established in Transylvania in 1566 under the protect-

ion of the Hungarian nobility. Their ancient historic quarrels with Calvinists have long since receded into the background. Sustaining itself more on past tradition than on any ecumenical spirit, the Unitarian Church today has become a vehicle of local cultural values but without any great external influence.

CHURCH AND STATE. Before 1948 the Orthodox Church was often closely allied with the state. In fact, around 1930 the Orthodox patriarch was also prime minister, and the head of the government's Department of Cults was another Orthodox bishop. From 1940–44 the German Nazi regime dissolved the Baptist and Pentecostal churches. Consequently, Communist rule from 1948, with its removal of religious privilege or discrimination, has greatly benefitted the Protestant churches.

During the past 25 years the Romanian government has changed its constitution 4 times, but the statements regarding freedom of worship have undergone no modification. Article 30 of the constitution of 1969 affirms that everyone is free to hold or not to hold a religious belief. Freedom of conscience and worship is guaranteed. The organization and internal functioning of religious groups is unhampered, but their finances are regulated by law. The same article adds that schools are separated from churches, the only church-administered schools permitted being those 'especially aimed at the training of ministers of the

**Romanian Orthodox Church.** *Right.* Packed believers standing inside Sibiu Cathedral, Archdiocese of Alba-Julia & Sibiu. *Above.* Former Patriarch Justinian (left) addresses crowd on October 27 Feast of St Demeter of Basarabov. *Below.* Orthodox monastery with chapel. *Below right.* Family of believers in front of parish church in Moldavia.

**Pentecostal Churches in the PRR**. *Above*. Sunday morning congregation of 1,500 members in small village on border with USSR. The presence of police informers in all such congregations is always assumed. *Right*. Executive Council of the Pentecostal Churches in the PRR, 1974.

denomination', which covers both major and minor seminaries.

The state office of religious affairs, the Department of Cults (Departamentul Cultelor), maintains surveillance over the churches and their worship, which is more strict in the case of Catholics than in the case of others. The organization Priests for Peace is less structured here than in other Communist countries. The government pays one-third of the salaries of all clergy and the entire salaries of seminary teachers, including those of Catholic seminaries. Seminarians are not subject to military service. A system of Sunday schools operates without hindrance in church buildings, and churches organize themselves freely. As an apparent gesture of reconciliation towards the churches, the government recently allocated a sum worth US$ 10 million for the renovation of churches.

Relations between government and churches must be understood in the light of both nationalism and also the government's position as a Communist state relatively independent of the USSR and other Eastern European countries. President Ceaucescu has acknowledged that among Romania's 20 million population at least 15 million are Orthodox and that it is necessary to be able to rely on the Orthodox Church in the development of its politically independent course as well as in the construction of socialism. In a certain sense, this also holds true for the non-Orthodox churches, though these are frequently seen as foreign minorities. The development of church-state relations must be evaluated and interpreted as a function of official policies towards these minorities. These tended to stiffen after 1948, for the purpose of protecting 'national unity' and 'Romanianism'. Thus the autonomous Magyar region, created in 1952 and remodelled in 1960, was suppressed in 1967. The religious life of the minorities is resented to the degree that it cannot be identified with national cultural aspirations. It still happens that some Magyar communities may be sent a Romanian priest or pastor ignorant of their language, while the same situation may take place in Romanian communities.

Relations between church and state have clearly improved since the end of 1965 when Nicolas Ceaucescu came to power. Previously, the churches had gone through a period of persecution and irritations much longer in duration than that of any other Eastern European country. The harassment which began in 1948 for the Catholic Church and in 1949 for the Orthodox Church continued until 1965. The period of most intense persecution was 1958–60, with the imprisonment of priests and laymen including the then Orthodox patriarch Justinian. Since the end of 1970, pressure has been relaxed under the direct influence of Ceaucescu who has entered into an

amicable and personal relationship with the heads of the different churches. Religious tolerance exists although within fairly narrow limits. The president requires that members of the Communist party (in which there are a number of Christians) and of its youth organization remain apart from religious offices, but he himself carried out his father's wishes to have a religious burial. On 28 February 1968, Ceaucescu invited the heads of the different churches to Bucharest and thanked them for their help in building socialism in Romania. In their turn, the Orthodox, Lutheran, Unitarian, Serbian Orthodox, Baptist and Jewish leaders gave the president an assurance of their loyalty and devotion. The single exception was the Catholic bishop Marton, who limited himself to wishes for good fortune and health.

The government passed a law in April 1974 prohibiting the reception or distribution of imported literature, including Bibles; and in July, Vasile Rascol, a Bucharest Pentecostal layman, was arrested and sentenced to 2 years in prison for being in possession of such Bibles and distributing them. Christians appealed against the sentence stating that it infringed Romania's constitution and the UN Declaration of Human Rights and that in fact thousands of Christian believers are guilty of the same offence. The judge accepted the appeal and quashed the sentence, although the security police refused to release Rascol from prison. A prominent Baptist theologian, Iosif Ton, has also been harassed for his writings, although not imprisoned.

In February 1975, Msgr Luigi Poggi, apostolic nuncio for special assignments of the Holy See, visited Romania for the first time to begin a dialogue with the regime. In April 1975, the Romanian National Assembly adopted a law requiring all those holding cultural or artistic treasures (individuals, cultural organizations and churches) to declare them before the Central Commission for National Cultural Treasures, which would in turn decide those objects to become state property with indemnity. Those items not commandeered at once were to be submitted for periodic examination and could be taken later if not maintained in a satisfactory condition. Objects of concern to the churches include works of art, manuscripts, rare books and other items used in worship. Before the adoption of the law the archives of parishes under the jurisdiction of the Reformed bishop of Nagyvarat had been confiscated by state officials, after inventory; and so the measures decided by the Assembly were interpreted as a deliberate policy to deprive national minorities of their historic past. To this has now been added another measure, namely the prohibition, applicable to priests and pastors and to them alone, from accepting gifts, property or foreign currency, whether from outside

or inside the country, without special authorization from the Department of Cults.

In March 1977, a major earthquake struck eastern and south-centre Romania killing and inflicting massive property damage estimated at over 50 million US dollars for the Orthodox Church alone. Among Church buildings destroyed were 38 Orthodox churches (with 500 others severely damaged and 1,117 partly damaged); 36 Adventist churches, 14 Reformed, 13 Brethren, 9 Baptist, and 6 Lutheran were virtually demolished. Three Orthodox seminaries the 800-student Orthodox Theological Institute in Bucharest, and the Baptist seminary there were all likewise demolished. The catastrophe afforded new opportunities for church-state co-operation.

**INTERDENOMINATIONAL ORGANIZATIONS.** Relations between the Orthodox and Romania's other religious bodies have improved markedly since 1965. Twice yearly the Orthodox patriarch organizes meetings between theologians of different denominations. Patriarch Justinian established a personal relationship with the Catholic bishop of Alba Julia and permitted Catholics to use the Orthodox press for their publications. Nevertheless Orthodox-Catholic relations continue strained due to the unresolved problem of the Catholic Uniates.

**BROADCASTING.** No religious broadcasting is permitted over the state Radiodifuziunea si Televiziunea Romana. From abroad, Protestant programmes in Romanian are beamed in by TWR (Monaco) for 2 hours 30 minutes a week and Catholic programmes in Romanian by Radio Vatican for one hour 45 minutes a week.

**BIBLIOGRAPHY**
'Despre Inochentie si Inochentism', H.H. Stahl, in *Archiva pentru Stiinta si Reforma Sociala*, X (1932), 175–182. (Socio-psychological study of a new religious cult in Romania).
'Romanian Baptists and the State', A. Scarfe, *Religion in Communist lands*, 4, 2 (Summer, 1976), 14–20.
'The Evangelical wing of the Orthodox Church in Romania', A. Scarfe, *Religion in Communist lands*, III, 6 (Nov–Dec, 1975), 15–19.
'The present situation of the Baptist Church in Romania', I. Ton, *Religion in Communist lands: supplementary paper No. 1* (November, 1973), 18p.
*The Romanian Orthodox Church*. 2nd edition. Bucharest: Orthodox Missionary Institute, 1968. 92p.
'The Romanian Orthodox Church today', M. Villiers, *Religion in Communist lands*, I, 3 (May–June, 1973), 4–7.
'Zur Situation der Christlichen Kirchen in Rumanien', *Herder Korrespondenz*, XXV, 7 (1971), 321–5.

TABLE 2. ORGANIZED CHURCHES AND DENOMINATIONS IN ROMANIA

| Official name 1 | Begun 2 | Type 3 | Counc 4 | Congs 5 | Adults 6 | Affiliated 7 | Names, notes, and other statistics (see Codebook) 8 |
|---|---|---|---|---|---|---|---|
| Armenian Apostolic Church: D Bucuresti | | O Arm | Rwc.K | 15 | 7,000 | 10,000 | *Gregorians*. Under C Echmiadzin (USSR). Covers Romania. Armenian emigres. |
| Baptist Union of Romania | 1856 | P Bap | Tv..K | 1,300 | 130,000 | 250,000 | *Uniunea Comunitatilor Crestine Baptiste din RPR*. Walachia. 200n,1s,W=90%,12000Y. |
| Burgarian Orthodox Church | | O Sla | Mwc.. | 2 | 1,000 | 2,000 | *Balgarskata Pravoslavna Crkva*. Parishes in Bucharest and Galati. Under P Sofia. |
| Catholic Church in Romania: | c1000 | R Lat | B.B.S | 662 | 914,000 | 1,268,901 | *Biserica Catolica Romana*. Long struggle with ROC. C=1+0+0. 2s. 919n,24000Yy. |
| M Bucuresti (Bucharest) | 1883 | R Lat | Bs | 24 | 59,700 | 82,902 | *Arch-Episcopia Bucuresti*. Diaspora Catholics: Moldavia, Walachia. 51 650 |
| D Alba Julia | c1150 | R Lat | Bs | 253 | 328,000 | 455,000 | *Episcopia Alba Julia. Gyulafehérvàri Egyhàzmegye*. 13m,19w,1s. 323 9581 |
| D Iasi | 1884 | R Lat | Bs | 104 | 150,300 | 208,999 | In Moldavia, on USSR border. 1s(Romanian-speaking). 153 6285 |
| D Satu Mare & Oradea Mare | 1077 | R Lat | bs | 121 | 146,000 | 202,000 | *Szatmàr-Nagyvàradi Egyhàzmegye* (in Hungarian). Closed since 1949. 240 3000 |
| D Timisoara | 1930 | R Lat | Bs | 160 | 230,000 | 320,000 | *Temesvàri Egyhàzmegye* (in Hungarian). Hungarians, Germans, et al. 152 4488 |
| Christian Brethren (Ch of the Gospel) | 1903 | P CBr | x...K | 350 | 50,000 | 120,000 | *Uniunea Cultului Crestin dupa Evanghelie din RSR*. Ex ROC. 2 factions, now united. |
| Church of England (J Fulham) | 1841 | A Cen | awc.. | 3 | 100 | 200 | Anglican chaplaincy, Bucharest. Official relations with Orthodox patriarchate. |
| Ev Church of the Augsburg Confession | 1519 | P Lut | LWC.K | 250 | 132,000 | 184,000 | *Biserica Ev dupa Confeiunea dela Augsburg*. German-speaking, Saxon origin. 222n. |
| Ev Lutheran Synodal Presbyterial Ch | 1886 | P Lut | LW..K | | 23,000 | 32,000 | *Biserica Ev Sinodo-presbiteriala* (Augsburg Confession). Hungarian-speaking. |
| Gypsy Evangelical Movement | | P Pe2 | x.... | | 500 | 1,000 | Nomadic caravan communities. 100% Gypsies. Aid from M=GGMS(Switzerland). |
| Isolated radio churches | c1955 | P rad | ..... | | 200 | 500 | Isolated radio believers in non-religious families. R=7900(RMS,HCJB,RVatican). |
| Jehovah's Witnesses | 1911 | M Jeh | x.... | 389 | 2,612 | 4,000 | Active witnessing by 1926. Prohibited, underground; 10-year prison sentences. |
| New Apostolic Church | | C CAp | x.... | | 500 | 1,000 | In Canada Bezirk, *NAK*. World headquarters in Dortmund (FR Germany). Underground. |
| Old Ritualist Ch of Ancient Orth Chr | c1800 | O OBe | x...K | | 40,000 | 60,000 | Chr=Christians. Ex Russian OC. Under Old Believers AD Moscow. In southeast. |
| Pentecostal Churches in the PRR | 1922 | P Pe2 | Z...K | 1,750 | 101,000 | 200,000 | *Biserica Pentecostala lui Dumnezeu Apostolica/Apostolic CoG*. 200n,G=4%pa,1s(15). |
| Reformed Church of Romania | 1554 | P Ref | RWC.K | 740 | 500,000 | 693,511 | *Biserica Reformata din Romania*. Mostly Transylvania. Hungarians. 783n,1090mw,1s. |
| **Romanian Orthodox Ch, P Bucuresti:** | c 100 | O Rum | CWC.K | 11,722 | 11,500,000 | 16,000,000 | *ROC. Biserica Ortodoxa Romana*. 8627m,8185b,122de(575m,1493w),1j,P=90%,9s,W=70%. |
| Metropolitanate of Ungrovlahia: | 1359 | O Rum | Cp | 4,052 | 3,982,000 | 5,530,000 | Province of Oungro-Walachia (formerly Muntenia), with 3 dioceses. HQ Bucharest. |
| AD Bucuresti (Bucharest) | | O Rum | Cp | 1,942 | 1,908,000 | 2,650,000 | Capital. In city, 228 parish churches with 405 priests and 16 deacons. 2s(454). |
| D Buzau | c1550 | O Rum | Cb | 940 | 922,000 | 1,280,000 | HQ Buzau. One minor seminary in Buzau. 1977: episcopal vicar dismissed by state. |
| D Dunarea de Jos (Lower Danube) | c1850 | O Rum | Cb | 1,170 | 1,152,000 | 1,600,000 | Lower Danube along USSR border. HQ Galati. Ancient monastery of Cocosu-Dobrogea. |
| Metropolitanate of Moldavia-Suceava: | 1401 | O Rum | Cm | 1,960 | 1,922,000 | 2,670,000 | Province of Moldavia and Suceava, with 2 dioceses. HQ Jassy (26 km from USSR). |
| AD Iasi (Jassy) | | O Rum | Ca | 1,010 | 986,000 | 1,370,000 | Along USSR border. HQ Jassy. Courses on church buildings and church art. |
| D Roman & Husi | c1450 | O Rum | Cb | 950 | 936,000 | 1,300,000 | In Moldavia, northeast Romania. HQ Roman. Repairing of churches widespread. |
| Metropol of Transilvania (Ardeal): | | O Rum | Cm | 3,210 | 3,133,000 | 4,380,000 | Province of Transylvania. 1948, 1,560,000 Catholic Uniates forcibly re-absorbed. |
| AD Alba-Julia & Sibiu | 1599 | O Rum | Ca | 1,330 | 1,280,000 | 1,800,000 | HQ Sibiu. Theological institute in Sibiu, 780 students. Very active press; 1j. |
| D Oradea | | O Rum | Cb | 1,010 | 990,000 | 1,380,000 | Northwest, along Hungary border. HQ Oradea. Repairs to churches under way. |
| D Vad, Fleac & Cluj | | O Rum | Cb | 870 | 863,000 | 1,200,000 | North centre of country. HQ Cluj. 589 parishes, 570 priests, 1s(246) at Cluj. |
| Metropolitanate of Oltenia: | 1370 | O Rum | Cm | 1,630 | 1,606,000 | 2,230,000 | Province of Oltenia (formerly Severin), with 2 dioceses. HQ Craiova. |
| AD Craiova | | O Rum | Ca | 820 | 807,000 | 1,120,000 | Southern plains, west of Bucharest. HQ Craiova. One minor theological seminary. |
| D Ramnic & Arges | c1550 | O Rum | Cb | 810 | 799,000 | 1,110,000 | South of Transylvanian Alps (Southern Carpathians). HQ Rimnicul Vilcea. 1s. |
| Metropolitanate of the Banat | | O Rum | Cm | 870 | 857,000 | 1,190,000 | Province of the Banat, with 2 dioceses. HQ Timisoara. Very active press; 1j. |
| AD Timisoara & Caransebes | | O Rum | Ca | 580 | 574,000 | 797,000 | West (Yugoslavia border). HQ Timisoara. One minor seminary in Caransebes. |
| D Arad-Ienopolei & Halmagiului | | O Rum | Cb | 290 | 283,000 | 393,000 | Extreme west of Romania, on border with Hungary. HQ Arad. |
| Russian Orthodox Church | | O Sla | Mwc.. | | 1,000 | 2,000 | Under jurisdiction of P Moscow. Russian expatriates, almost all in Bucharest. |
| Serbian Orthodox Church: D Timisoara | 1864 | O Ser | Cwc.. | 52 | 36,000 | 50,000 | Under jurisdiction of P Belgrade. No bishop permitted. 47n,4d, |
| Seventh-day Adventist Church | 1911 | P Adv | x...K | 512 | 40,864 | 80,000 | *Cultul Adventist de Ziua Saptea. Romanian UC*. 4 Confs. 172n,53mw,1s,512t(52857). |
| SDA Church, Reform Movement | | P Adv | x.... | | 100 | 200 | Schism ex SDAs. HQ Charlottenlund, Denmark. Not officially recognized. |
| Unitarian Churches in Romania | 1566 | M Unt | I...K | 162 | 40,000 | 55,000 | *Unitariani*. In Transylvania. Bishop, 8 Districts. HQ Cluj. Links with UUA(USA). 1s. |
| Other Orthodox churches | | O | ..... | | 45,000 | 60,000 | Including: Greek Orthodox Ch, Ukrainian Orthodox Ch. |
| Other Protestant denominations | | P | ..... | | 1,000 | 2,000 | About 10 smaller groupings, including Exclusive Brethren (Kelly-Continental). |
| Doubly-affiliated (duplication) (1970) | | | | | –1,610,100 | –2,236,312 | Protestants and Catholics also counted or claimed as members by Orthodox Church., |
| **Total affiliated (mid-1970)** | | | | **18,250** | **11,955,776** | **16,840,000** | **Total denominations (1970) . . .** 34. |
| **Total affiliated (mid-1975)** | | | | **18,500** | **12,446,200** | **17,530,800** | **Total denominations (1975) . . .** 35. |
| **Total affiliated (mid-1980)** | | | | **18,750** | **12,901,900** | **18,172,600** | **Total denominations (1980) . . .** 36. |

NOTES ON TABLE ABOVE
COLUMNS: for meanings and CODES (cols. 1, 3, 4, 8): see Codebook (Part 6). Column 1: **Boldface type** = church with over 10% of country's affiliated Christians.
NATIONAL COUNCILS (Column 4, 5th letter).
K = Romanian Council of Churches (unofficial; since 1974; all recognized churches, plus Jews and Muslims).
S = Romanian Catholic Episcopal Conference (unofficial), also member of Romanian Council of Churches.

PEOPLES (ethnolinguistic). Christians: 86.8% Romanian, 8.5% Hungarian, 2.0% German, 1.5% Gypsy, 0.3% Ukrainian, 0.2% Serbian, 0.2% Russian, 0.1% Slovak, 0.1% Bulgar, 0.1% Czech, 0.1% Greek, 0.1% Armenian, Polish, Croat, Jewish (200).

COUNTRY-WIDE TOTALS
EVANGELIZATION (see Part 5). 1900: 100%. 1970: 100%. 1980: 100%. *Radiophonic evangelism*. Annual listeners' letters (1975): 7,900 Romanian Missionary Society (USA), TWR, HCJB, Radio Vatican, et alia.
FOREIGN MISSIONARIES AND PERSONNEL (nationals serving abroad) (1973). Total 107 Orthodox, (about 40 priests, 60 monks, some bishops and nuns) in 17 countries.
FOREIGN MISSIONARIES AND PERSONNEL (from abroad) (1973). Total 30. *From Communist world*. About 30 Orthodox (aliens from Yugoslavia, USSR and Bulgaria).
INSTITUTIONS (church-operated) (1973). Total 205, including 1 press, 182 religious communities, 18 seminaries (9 Orthodox, 6 Protestant, 2 RC, 1 marginal Protestant).
PERIODICALS. About 21 titles (12 Orthodox).
PERSONNEL. About 14,530 (14,500 national, 30 foreign).
RELIGIOUS LIBRARIES. About 200.
SCRIPTURE DISTRIBUTION (1975). Annual totals: 55,000 Bibles (9% free, 91% subsidized), 61,000 NTs (2% free, 98% subsidized), 2,000 UBS portions. *Translations completed*. Portion: 2 languages since 1561. NT: Rumanian in 1648, Bible in 1688.
SERVICE AGENCIES. About 20, including 2 or 3 clandestine.

ADDITIONAL DATA ON CHURCHES
BAPTIST UNION OF ROMANIA. Divided into 6 Associations. *Baptized members*. Increasing from 130,000 (1970) to 160,000 (1976). *Conversions*. Annual baptisms have increased from 12,000 in 1970 to 20,000 a year since 1972.
CATHOLIC CHURCH IN ROMANIA. D Alba Julia is also termed (in Romanian) Episcopia Ardeal, or (in Hungarian Erdélyi Egyhàzmegye; it was one of the oldest dioceses of the ancient kingdom of Hungary, and now covers the whole of Transylvania. *Suppressed dioceses*. In 1948, 6 Eastern-rite (Uniate) jurisdictions with 1,562,979 Catholics in 1,794 parishes, which had been under the Church of Rome since 1698, were suppressed by the state and forcibly reunited with the Romanian Orthodox Church. They were: M Fagaras & Alba Julia, D Cluj-Gherla, D Lugoj, D Maramures, D Oradea Mare, and O Romania (Armenians). *Annuario Pontificio* still lists them each year as Catholic dioceses (1975), since around 900,000 still regard themselves as Uniates, though shown in this table as Orthodox. *Annual baptisms*. (1972) 99.9% infant, 0.1% adult. *Personnel*. All nationals. *Seminaries*. Romanian-speaking at Iasi, and Hungarian-speaking at Alba Julia. *Religious orders and congregations*. The only organized one present is OFM (priests). There are also a few SJ priests.
ROMANIAN ORTHODOX CHURCH. The church was finally recognized as autocephalous by the Ecumenical Patriarchate in 1885, and became a patriarchate in 1925. The church is organized in 5 metropolitanates or ecclesiastical provinces, whose boundaries coincide with political boundaries. These are divided into 12 territorial dioceses (whose boundaries do not coincide with political boundaries), 107 deaneries, and 8,185 parishes with 2,847 parish annexes; there are also 49 cathedrals, 123 monastery churches and 246 chapels. *New church buildings*. In 1971, 20 new churches were opened in 4 months: 5 in AD Bucharest, 4 in AD Iasi, 7 in D Oradea, 3 elsewhere in M Ardeal. *Congregations and members*. The church does not keep detailed statistics by diocese, and the figures in columns 5, 6 and 7 are general-order estimates based on the few diocesan statistics published, on the population census of 1.VII.1969, and on the fact that new parishes are formed with a minimum requirement of 500 Orthodox families in urban areas and 400 families in rural areas, which gives an average size of about 2,000 faithful per parish. *Bishops*. Total (1974) 19. *Priests*. Of the total of 8,627 in 1974, 56 had doctorates in theology and 40 were in process of obtaining them, 6,227 had a degree in theology, 2,226 a seminary diploma, and 127 had not yet completed their studies. With all other kinds of clergy including those abroad, the Patriarchate's total of priests in 1975 was over 11,000. *Ordinations*. (1976) About 420 new priests. (1977) About 430. *Seminarians* (1975). 454 in Bucharest, 780 in Sibiu, and 1,597 in minor seminaries. By 1977, those at Bucharest and Sibiu totalled over 1,400. Total all seminarians and theological students, over 3,200. *Religious personnel*. Numbers increased from the 1970 figures in the table above to (in 1975) 540 monks and 1,443 nuns (total inhabitants over 2,200) in 62 monasteries, 28 hermitages, and 15 dependencies (total monasteries and sketes 122). *Evangelical movements*. Since 1918 there has been an influential evangelical wing in the ROC influenced by Western Protestantism, led by the priests T. Popescu in the 1920s and J. Trifa in the 1930s. Both were defrocked and excommunicated. Followers of the former joined the Church of the Gospel (Christian Brethren), but those of the latter remained within the ROC under the name The Lord's Army; although suppressed by force by the state with many members fined and imprisoned in the mid-1950s, the Army survives today within the ROC as a substantial and growing minority, though still unrecognized by church or state. Members number some 300,000 Orthodox, including priests.

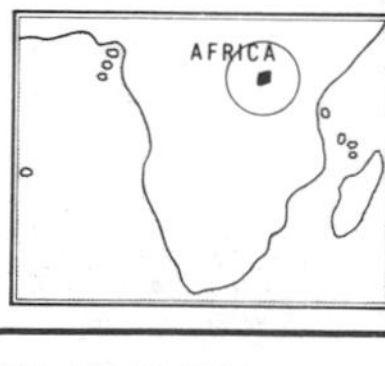


# RWANDA

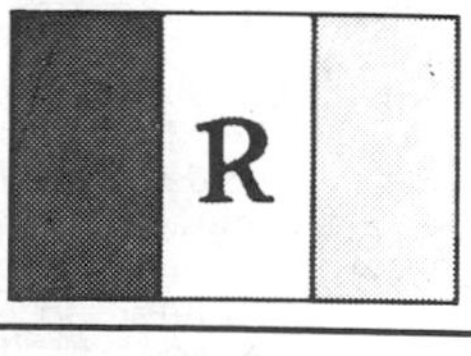


## SECULAR DATA

**STATE. Official name:** The Rwandese Republic (Republika ylu Rwanda/La République Rwandaise). Adjective of nationality: Rwandese (rwandais).
**Flag** (shown above right): Bars of red, yellow, and green, with black R in centre.
**Area:** 26,338 sq.km (10,169 sq.miles). Agricultural land: 64.1%.
**Government:** Republic under military rule, since 1973 (c1500 kingdom, 1899 in colony of German East Africa, 1918 Belgium mandated territory, 1961 Independence as republic proclaimed).
**Legislature:** National Assembly, 47 members.
**Official languages:** Kinyarwanda, French (*Français*).
**Capital:** Kigali 54,400 (1970).
**Political divisions:** 10 Prefectures, 144 Communes.
**Armed forces** (1976): Total 3,750 regular army. Paramilitary forces: 1,200.

**DEMOGRAPHY. Population:** 3,572,550 (census of V–XI.1970. For 1970–2000 (UN), see last row of Table 1). Population density (1975): 159/sq.km. (413/sq.mile). Under 15 years: 45%. Growth rate (1975–80): 2.94% per year (births 5.13%, deaths –2.19%). Life expectancy (1975–80): 43.5 years. Household size: 4.9 persons.
**Major languages:** Ruanda (Kinyarwanda), French, Rundi (Kirundi), Swahili, Hima, and others.
**Urban dwellers** (1970): 3.0%. Urban growth rate (1950–70): 2.1% per year.
**Labour force:** 53%.
**Refugees** (1977): 7,400 from Burundi (1973: 40,000 Hutus from Burundi). Exiles abroad: 164,800 Rwandans (78,000 in Uganda, 48,500 in Burundi, 24,300 in Zaire, 14,000 in Tanzania).

**ETHNOLINGUISTIC GROUPS:** 92.7% Ruanda (88% Hutu, 4% Tutsi), 4.9% Rundi, 1.8% Twa Pygmy, Belgian, French, Swahili, Indo-Pakistani, Arab.

**MONEY** (1977). **Monetary unit:** Rwanda franc (= 100 centimes); US$1 = RwFr 92.00.
**National income per person:** US$70. Average annual family income: US$343.
**Inflation:** (1970–74) 10.4% per year (1975: consumer price index 204).
**Cost of living in capital** (1976): index 138 (Washington DC = 100). Daily cost of living: US$42.

**HEALTH.** Hospitals: 175 (5,380 beds). Doctors: 71. Lepers: 42,000 (10.0 per 1,000). Blind: 12,000. Psychotics: 29,000.

**EDUCATION.** Adult literacy: (1962) 16%. Education rate: 40%. Schools: 2,013. Universities: 1.

**LITERATURE.** Annual new book titles (1972): 13. Periodicals: 20.

**COMMUNICATION** (per 1,000 people). Phones: 1. Radios: 8.

TABLE 1.   RELIGIOUS ADHERENTS IN RWANDA

| Year | 1900 | | mid-1970 | | Annual change, 1970–1980 | | | | mid-1975 | | mid-1980 | | 2000 | |
|---|---|---|---|---|---|---|---|---|---|---|---|---|---|---|
| *Name* | *Adherents* | *%* | *Adherents* | *%* | *Natural* | *Conversion* | *Total* | *Rate* | *Adherents* | *%* | *Adherents* | *%* | *Adherents* | *%* |
| Christians | 0 | 0.0 | 2,283,600 | 62.1 | 80,648 | 46,092 | 126,740 | 4.44 | 2,856,000 | 68.0 | 3,551,000 | 73.0 | 7,400,000 | 85.0 |
| professing | 0 | 0.0 | 2,283,600 | 62.1 | 80,648 | 46,092 | 126,740 | 4.44 | 2,856,000 | 68.0 | 3,551,000 | 73.0 | 7,400,000 | 85.0 |
| Roman Catholics | 0 | 0.0 | 1,738,600 | 47.3 | 61,283 | 35,171 | 96,454 | 4.44 | 2,170,230 | 51.7 | 2,703,140 | 55.6 | 5,629,100 | 64.7 |
| Protestants | 0 | 0.0 | 364,000 | 9.9 | 12,928 | 7,102 | 20,030 | 4.38 | 457,800 | 10.9 | 564,300 | 11.6 | 1,175,400 | 13.5 |
| Anglicans | 0 | 0.0 | 180,000 | 4.9 | 6,404 | 3,816 | 10,220 | 4.51 | 226,800 | 5.4 | 282,200 | 5.8 | 592,100 | 6.8 |
| African indigenous | 0 | 0.0 | 500 | 0.0 | 17 | 3 | 20 | 3.33 | 600 | 0.0 | 700 | 0.0 | 2,000 | 0.0 |
| Orthodox | 0 | 0.0 | 500 | 0.0 | 16 | 0 | 16 | 2.81 | 570 | 0.0 | 660 | 0.0 | 1,400 | 0.0 |
| nominal | 0 | 0.0 | 96,580 | 2.6 | 3,558 | 3,764 | 7,322 | 5.81 | 126,000 | 3.0 | 169,800 | 3.5 | 434,000 | 5.0 |
| affiliated | 0 | 0.0 | 2,187,020 | 59.4 | 77,090 | 42,328 | 119,418 | 4.37 | 2,730,000 | 65.0 | 3,381,200 | 69.5 | 6,966,000 | 80.0 |
| total practising | 0 | 0 | 1,858,970 | 85 | 65,526 | 35,979 | 101,505 | 4.37 | 2,320,500 | 85 | 2,874,020 | 85 | 5,572,800 | 80 |
| non-practising | 0 | 0 | 328,050 | 15 | 11,564 | 6,349 | 17,913 | 4.37 | 409,500 | 15 | 507,180 | 15 | 1,393,200 | 20 |
| Roman Catholics | 0 | 0.0 | 1,684,095 | 45.8 | 59,263 | 32,454 | 91,717 | 4.37 | 2,098,690 | 50.0 | 2,601,260 | 53.5 | 5,351,300 | 61.5 |
| Catholic pentecostals | 0 | 0.0 | 0 | 0.0 | 11 | 289 | 300 | 75.00 | 400 | 0.0 | 3,000 | 0.1 | 60,000 | 0.7 |
| Protestants | 0 | 0.0 | 339,926 | 9.2 | 12,097 | 6,450 | 18,547 | 4.33 | 428,400 | 10.2 | 525,600 | 10.8 | 1,088,400 | 12.5 |
| Evangelicals | 0 | 0.0 | 298,000 | 8.1 | 10,792 | 7,568 | 18,360 | 4.80 | 382,200 | 9.1 | 481,600 | 9.9 | 1,045,000 | 12.0 |
| Anglicans | 0 | 0.0 | 161,899 | 4.4 | 5,693 | 3,417 | 9,110 | 4.52 | 201,600 | 4.8 | 253,000 | 5.2 | 522,400 | 6.0 |
| Evangelicals | 0 | 0.0 | 161,000 | 4.4 | 5,665 | 3,435 | 9,100 | 4.54 | 200,600 | 4.8 | 252,000 | 5.2 | 520,000 | 6.0 |
| African indigenous | 0 | 0.0 | 500 | 0.0 | 17 | 3 | 20 | 3.33 | 600 | 0.0 | 700 | 0.0 | 2,000 | 0.0 |
| Orthodox | 0 | 0.0 | 500 | 0.0 | 16 | 0 | 16 | 2.81 | 570 | 0.0 | 660 | 0.0 | 1,400 | 0.0 |
| Marginal Protestants | 0 | 0.0 | 100 | 0.0 | 4 | 4 | 8 | 5.71 | 140 | 0.0 | 180 | 0.0 | 500 | 0.0 |
| Tribal religionists | 1,068,000 | 99.8 | 1,076,900 | 29.3 | 27,571 | −46,741 | −19,170 | −1.96 | 976,360 | 23.2 | 885,200 | 18.2 | 501,000 | 5.8 |
| Muslims | 2,000 | 0.2 | 312,000 | 8.5 | 10,166 | 634 | 10,800 | 3.00 | 360,000 | 8.6 | 420,000 | 8.6 | 784,000 | 9.0 |
| Baha'is | 0 | 0.0 | 5,500 | 0.1 | 183 | 17 | 200 | 3.08 | 6,500 | 0.2 | 7,500 | 0.2 | 20,000 | 0.2 |
| Hindus | 0 | 0.0 | 1,000 | 0.0 | 32 | −2 | 30 | 2.63 | 1,140 | 0.0 | 1,300 | 0.0 | 2,000 | 0.0 |
| Country's population | 1,070,000 | 100.0 | 3,679,000 | 100.0 | 118,600 | 0 | 118,600 | 2.82 | 4,200,000 | 100.0 | 4,865,000 | 100.0 | 8,707,000 | 10.00 |

COLUMNS, ROWS. For meanings and definitions, see Codebook (Part 6). Note that, by definition, total 'Christians' = professing + crypto–Christians, which also = affiliated + nominal Christians. Percentages may not always total exactly, due to rounding.
CENSUSES. No religion question was asked until introduced in 1970. 5.XI.1970: 47.3% Roman Catholics, 29.4% tribal religionists and others, 14.8% Protestants and Anglicans, 8.5% Muslims.

NOTES ON RELIGIONS
AFRICAN INDIGENOUS. In one immigrant denomination in 1970 (see Table 2); two by 1975.
BAHA'IS. Rapid growth to 37 local spiritual assemblies by 1973, assisted by immigrant Ugandan Baha'is.
CATHOLIC PENTECOSTALS (or, Catholic charismatics). Totals (mid–1975): 150 involved adults, in majority Rwandans, with many religious personnel; total charismatic community including children, 400, increasing rapidly.
COUNTRY'S POPULATION. After Independence in 1962, 150,000 Watutsi were slaughtered or fled abroad.
MUSLIMS. In 1970, Asian (Indo-Pakistani), Arab and Swahili merchants numbered 19,826, including 200 Shias. There are also many Africans (all Sunnis), Rwandese, also Ugandans, Tanza-

nians, Sudanese and others. Swahili is spoken in Arab and Arab-influenced town districts. There has been a steady stream of conversions of Rwandese to Islam over the years.
PRACTISING CHRISTIANS. Regular church attenders (1971): 70% of all Roman Catholics, 90% of all Protestants and Anglicans. Annual attenders: about 85% of all Christians.
TRIBAL RELIGIONISTS. Animists (also called Imanists or worshippers of the supreme being Imana), including the Twa pygmies (Gesera; 30,000), who are 90% animist. There is also the ancestor cult; a public initiation rite sacred to the hero Ryangombe king of the Imandwa (30 powerful spirits); and the cult of Nyabingi (a female spirit).

NON-CHRISTIAN RELIGIONS. **African traditional religions** are practised by a minority of the Hutu and Tutsi and the majority of the Twa, only 10% of the latter having become Christian. Among the Banyarwanda God is known as Imana. He is basically good but occasionally creates unsuccessfully, at which times he is identified as Ruremakwaci. The spirits of the dead (Bazimu) inhabit the underworld ruled by Nyamuzinda. The ancestral cult is aimed at appeasing the Bazimu who are mostly conceived of as malevolent. A particularly important group owes allegiance to Ryangombe who was once human. After death, Ryangombe's initiates (Imandwa) are believed to inhabit a paradise called Karisimbi. Ryangombe is Imana's servant and the intermediary between his initiates and God. His living followers are protected from harm by the deceased Imandwa. A more recent spirit-possession cult is that of the female deity Nyabingi, who while living was a Karagwe queen named Kitami.

**Islam** has long been present in several small Indo-Pakistani, Arab and Swahili merchant communities, numbering around 20,000 by 1970 mostly in the cities of Kigali and Butare. There are also large numbers of Rwandese Muslims, also Ugandans, Tanzanians, Sudanese and others, almost all Sunnis.

## CHRISTIANITY

CATHOLIC CHURCH. White Fathers from the vicariate of Victoria Nyanza visited Ruanda as early as 1889 but the first permanent missions were not established until 1900. In 1912 the vicariate of the Kivu was erected including Ruanda and Burundi (then Urundi), and 10 years later (1922) Ruanda became a vicariate in its own right. The first Ruanda priests were ordained in 1917. The Catholic Church grew rapidly during the 1930s and by the beginning of World War II had 300,000 members. In 1952 the first Ruanda bishop was consecrated, with the archdiocese of Kabgayi formed in 1959.

The success of the Catholic Church's missionary endeavour is evident in the fact that today more than half the population claims to be Catholic. The church's strength is its rural parish structure composed of branch establishments (chapels, schools) which are divided into elementary groups of Christians (*inama*). Each group consists of approximately 30 families and elects its own chief (*mukuru*) who, together with the catechists, form a liaison between the families and the visiting priest.

PROTESTANT CHURCHES. The first Protestants were Lutherans of the Bethel Mission who crossed the border from Tanzania in 1907 and built a station prior to World War I. All German missionaries were expelled in May 1916, and Belgium refused to allow them to return after the war. American Adventists came in 1919 although they were unable to establish themselves prior to 1921. Nevertheless, progress was rapid thereafter, and the Adventist community is now second in size only to the Catholic Church.

In 1921 the Belgian Society of Protestant Missions in the Congo, the missionary arm of the Reformed Church of Belgium, took over responsibility for part

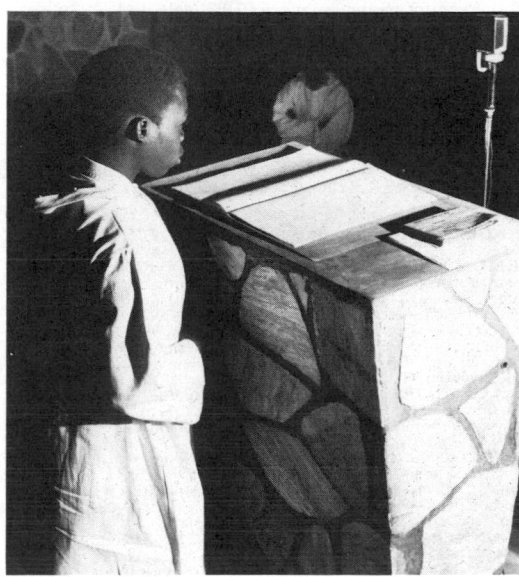

**Eglise Catholique au Rwanda.** *Left.* Packed Sunday mass in Kigali, Archdiocese of Kigali. *Above.* A youth reads Sunday Epistle, in Rutongo church.

of the work of the Bethel Mission, helping to form the Presbyterian Church of Rwanda which became autonomous in 1959. Other Protestant groups in the pre-World War II period were American Free Methodists in 1935, Danish Baptists in 1938 and Swedish Pentecostals in 1940. Newer missions have been established by the Friends, Brethren and Conservative Baptists since 1960, but all remain small. Except for the Adventists who are found in all parts of the country, Protestantism is for the most part characterized by a regional orientation: Free Methodists in southwest Rwanda, Pentecostals near Gisenyi, Baptists south of Butare and Presbyterians near Kigali.

ANGLICAN CHURCH. In 1920 an extensive medical and evangelistic programme was begun by the Ruanda Mission (CMS), of Low Church Evangelical background. Together with the indigenous Revival Movement (Balokole, or Saved Ones) since 1927, CMS has contributed towards making the Anglican church the third largest Christian community in the country. The Rwanda church is part of the Church of the Province of Burundi, Rwanda & Zaire, which had 7 dioceses in 1980.

**CHURCH AND STATE.** The constitution of 24 November 1962 began in its Preamble: 'The National Assembly, Entrusting in Almighty God, . . .'. In Title 1, Article 3, the state declares that 'It respects all religions'. The constitution has since been suspended under military rule; but while awaiting the promulgation of a new one, Articles 37–39 from 1962 relating to religion, remain in vigour. The preamble to the 1962 constitution invokes confidence in the All-Powerfulness of God. Article 37 guarantees to all liberty of conscience, free profession and practice of religion. Article 38 permits the establishment of religious institutions and communities who administer their affairs autonomously. Communist propaganda and activity are forbidden in Article 39.

**Eglise Anglicane du Rwanda.** 'Yesu naamara' ('Jesus Satisfies'): Brethren preaching in 4 languages (Chiga, Ganda, Ruanda, English) at mass convention of 10,000 members of East African Revival (begun in 1927 in Ruanda).

Despite some friction regarding education, relations between the churches and the state remain friendly. The Catholic Church is very strong and the churches play an important role in social action. The official University of Butare was created in 1964 served by Canadian Dominican priests.

**INTERDENOMINATIONAL ORGANIZATIONS.** The Protestant Council of Rwanda was established in 1935. Anglicans, Baptists, Free Methodists and Presbyterians, are full members, with the following maintaining an associate member status: Friends, Pentecostals and the Taizé Community. Adventists co-operate in Bible translation work. The brothers of Taizé and Benedictine priests of Gihindamuyaga form the Ecumenical Fraternity of Kigali which organizes regular meetings between Catholics, Anglicans and Protestants, with SDAs as observers.

**BROADCASTING.** The Radiodiffusion de la République Rwandaise has a regular Christian broadcasting schedule, giving the Protestant Council of Rwanda two 30-minute programmes and nearly 3 hours weekly for the Catholics. In Gitarama there is a radio school Université Radiophonique de Gitarama (URG) founded in 1963 and mainly concerned with educating rural people. It has a radio production studio and its programmes are transmitted by Radio Kigali. Recently it started a Centre Rural Agricole et de Formation Artisanale de Gitarama (CRAFAG). For Catholics, Rwanda is registered as a member of UNDA. From abroad, French programmes were heard over RVOG (Ethiopia) until its 1977 closure.

## BIBLIOGRAPHY

*Annuaire ecclésiastique, Burundi et Rwanda, 1970–71*. Bujumbura, Burundi: SECOREB, 1971.
*Burundi et Rwanda 1964–1968: plan quinquennal de développement*. Usumbura: COREB, 1963. 160p.
*Church and revolution in Rwanda*. I. & J. Linden. London: Brill, 1977. 320p.
'De la religion subie au modernisme refusé: théophagie, ancêtres clandestins et résistance populaire au Rwandais', C. Vidal, *Archives de sciences sociales des religions*, 35 (1974), 63–90.
'Indifférence religieuse et neo-paganisme au Ruanda', S. Bushayija, *Rythmes du monde*, IX, 1 (1961), 58–67.
*La philosophie bantu-rwandaise de l'être*. A. Kagame. Bruxelles: Académie Royale des Sciences Coloniales, 1956.
'Le culte de Nyabingi (Rwanda)', M. Pauwels, *Anthropos* (Freiburg), XLVI, 3–4 (1951), 337–357.
'Mythe et société féodale: le culte de Kubandwa dans le Rwanda traditionnel', L. de Heusch, *Archives de sociologie des religions*, 9, 18 (July–Dec, 1964), 133–146.
*Road to revival: the story of the Ruanda Mission*. A.C. Stanley Smith. London: Church Missionary Society, 1946. 116p.
'Rwanda: strength and weakness of the centre of Africa', *Pro Mundi Vita* (Brussels), 6 (1965).
'The kingdom of Ruanda', J.J. Maquet, in D. Forde (ed), *African worlds* (London: Oxford, 1954), p. 164–189.
*Théologie et pastorale au Rwanda et au Burundi*, VII, 1 (January, 1967), 1–60.

TABLE 2. ORGANIZED CHURCHES AND DENOMINATIONS IN RWANDA

| Official name 1 | Begun 2 | Type 3 | Counc 4 | Congs 5 | Adults 6 | Affiliated 7 | Names, notes, and other statistics (see Codebook) 8 |
|---|---|---|---|---|---|---|---|
| Assemblée des Frères | 1961 | P CBr | ••••• | 1 | 50 | 100 | *Assembly of Brethren, Open Brethren*. From Zaire via Burundi; 1961 in Kigali. 1k. |
| Assoc des Eglises Baptistes du Rwanda | c1965 | P Bap | xF••• | 27 | 1,249 | 2,000 | *Assoc of Baptist Chs of Rwanda*. 1972 M=Conservative Baptist FMS(USA). 32m,2f,354Y. |
| Eglise Adventiste du Septième Jour | 1919 | P Adv | x•••• | 461 | 87,839 | 200,000 | *Seventh-day Adv, N,E,S,W, Rwanda Fields*. 132nx,17f,1H,2h,1s,806t(185000),12688Y. |
| Eglise Anglicane du Rwanda | 1920 | A Low | AwAVK | 1,228 | 69,111 | 161,899 | *EAR*. In CURBZ. 1976, 2 Dioceses. M=RCMS(UK). 35n,5x,30f,3H,1s,W=50%,14050Y,3697y. |
| **Eglise Catholique au Rwanda:** | 1889 | R Lat | P•S•P | 160 | 926,200 | 1,684,095 | *Catholic Ch*. C=6+8+29. 5p,3s(99),289343z. 142n,245x,264m,766w,P=71%,110587Yy. |
| M Kabgayi (1976, M Kigali formed) | 1912 | R Lat | Pwf | 24 | 215,300 | 391,533 | Weekend exodus problem. 80% Hutu, 19% Tutsi. 22 91 107 160 68 28589 |
| D Butare | 1961 | R Lat | Ps | 22 | 268,000 | 487,191 | Intellectual and religious hub. M=WF,OSB. 1s. 38 74 66 313 74 31213 |
| D Kibungo | 1968 | R Lat | Ps | 8 | 72,200 | 131,364 | Formed out of M Kabgayi. M=WF. 64 alien RCs. 10 14 16 42 78 8740 |
| D Nyundo | 1952 | R Lat | Ps | 90 | 190,900 | 347,056 | In west. M=WF. 383 expatriate Catholics. 1s. 56 21 56 163 71 21614 |
| D Ruhengeri | 1960 | R Lat | Ps | 16 | 179,800 | 326,951 | Densely populated. 90%Hutu, 9% Tutsi. M=WF. 16 45 19 88 69 20431 |
| Eglise Ev Calvaire d'Afrique du Rwanda | c1971 | I pe2 | ••••• | 22 | 150 | 400 | *Calvary Ev Ch of Africa in Rwanda. Ev Fraternity*. M=PEFA, AIM (Kenya). HQ Gisenyi. 4n. |
| Eglise Kimbanguiste | c1965 | I pen | xwi•• | 2 | 50 | 100 | *Ch of Christ on Earth through Prophet Simon Kimbangu*. |
| Eglise Libre Méthodiste au Rwanda | 1935 | P Hol | VF••K | 87 | 7,500 | 10,000 | *ELMR. Free Methodist Ch*. M=FMC(USA). 11n,3x,94m,15f,G=10%,1H,3h,1s,62t(2933),747Y. |
| Eglise Orthodoxe (AD Afrique Centrale) | 1958 | O Gre | Cw••• | 2 | 300 | 500 | *Orthodox Ch*. Parish of Bujumbura. Under Greek P Alexandria. Mostly Greeks. |
| Eglise Presbytérienne au Rwanda | 1907 | P Ref | R•A•K | 33 | 5,012 | 21,293 | *EPR. Presb Ch*. M=BCMC(Belgium),RCN(Neth). A=1959. 95% Hutu, 5%Tutsi. 16n,1H,2h,1u. |
| Eglises de Pentecôte | 1940 | P Pe2 | Z•••k | 413 | 30,484 | 85,000 | *ADEEP. Chs of Pentecost*. M=SFM(Sweden). 91% Hutu. 45n,9x,369m,W=90%,7515Y,2225z. |
| Mission Evangélique des Amis | c1950 | P Qua | QF••k | | 200 | 500 | M=Friends Africa Gospel Mission(Kansas YM,USA). In Burundi Quarterly Meeting. |
| Témoins de Jéhovah | c1965 | M Jeh | x•••• | 1 | 15 | 100 | *Jehovah's Witnesses. Watch Tower*. In 1973, 5,150 hours of witnessing put in. 5Y. |
| Union des Eglises Baptistes du Rwanda | 1938 | P Bap | T•A•K | 183 | 13,811 | 21,033 | *UEBR*. M=Danish,Finnish BMs, SBC (USA). 11n,2x,94m,G=30%pa,1p,1u,W=90%,3893Y,4804z. |
| **Total affiliated (mid-1970)** | | | | **2,620** | **1,141,971** | **2,187,020** | **Total denominations (1970) . . . 13.** |
| **Total affiliated (mid-1975)** | | | | **3,000** | **1,425,500** | **2,730,000** | **Total denominations (1975) . . . 14.** |
| **Total affiliated (mid-1980)** | | | | **3,400** | **1,765,500** | **3,381,200** | **Total denominations (1980) . . . 16.** |

**NOTES ON TABLE ABOVE**
COLUMNS: for meanings and CODES (cols. 1, 3, 4, 8): see Codebook (Part 5). Column 1: **Boldface type** = church with over 10% of country's affiliated Christians.
NATIONAL COUNCILS (Column 4, 5th letter).
K = Conseil Protestant du Rwanda (CPR) (Protestant Council of Rwanda).
k = associate member of CPR.
P = Conférence des Ordinaires du Rwanda et du Burundi (COREB) (Bishops' Conference of Rwanda & Burundi).

**PEOPLES** (ethnolinguistic). Christians: 94.3% Ruanda (90% Hutu, 4% Tutsi), 4.9% Rundi, 0.2% Twa Pygmy, Belgian, French.

**COUNTRY-WIDE TOTALS**
EVANGELIZATION (see Part 5). 1900: 0%. 1970: 95%. 1980: 98%.
FOREIGN MISSIONARIES AND PERSONNEL (nationals serving abroad) (1973). Total about 70 Roman Catholics in Burundi, Kenya, Niger, Tanzania, Uganda and Zaire.
FOREIGN MISSIONARIES AND PERSONNEL (aliens from abroad) (1973). Total 867. *From Western world*. 796: 647 Roman Catholics, 119 Protestants (37 in 3 USA societies, 30 in 1 Sweden society, 20 in 1 Belgium society, 9 in 1 Denmark society, 9 in 3 UK societies, 7 in 1 Switzerland society, 5 in 1 Netherlands society, 2 in 1 Finland society), 30 Anglicans in 2 UK societies. *From Communist world*. 17 Roman Catholics from Poland. *From Third World*. 54: about 50 Roman Catholics from Zaire, Uganda et alia, 2 Anglicans, 2 Protestants.
INSTITUTIONS (church-operated) (1973). Total 145, including 65 higher schools (7 minor seminaries), 55 medical centres (8 hospitals), 10 religious communities, 7 seminaries (3 RC, 3 Protestant, 1 Anglican).
PERIODICALS. About 12 titles (3 ADEEP).
PERSONNEL. About 4,605 (3,738 national, 867 foreign).
RELIGIOUS LIBRARIES. About 17.
SCRIPTURE DISTRIBUTION (1975). Annual totals: 9,000 Bibles (78% subsidized, 22% commercial), 6,000 NTs (83% subsidized, 17% commercial), 30,000 UBS portions. *Translations completed*. In Kinyarwanda: portion 1914, NT 1931, Bible 1954.
SERVICE AGENCIES. About 38, including AEC, COREB, COSUMA, CPR, GBUAF, JAC, JAC/F, JOC/F, LSC, MFC, SNEC, SU, USMR.

**ADDITIONAL DATA ON CHURCHES**
EGLISE ANGLICANE DU RWANDA. Until 1976 the church formed the Diocese of Rwanda in the Church of Uganda, Rwanda, Burundi and Boga-Zaire. From 1976 it divided into 2 dioceses of similar size, D Butare (21 parishes, 25 clergy, 430 catechists, 11 missionaries) and D Kigali (24 parishes, 36 clergy, 600 catechists, 9 missionaries), prior to the formation of a new French-speaking Anglican province covering Rwanda, Burundi and Zaire. *Schools* (1977). 4 secondary, 75 primary, 3 technical.
EGLISE CATHOLIQUE AU RWANDA. *New dioceses*. In 1976, a new metropolitan archdiocese of Kigali was set up, and Kabgayi was reduced to diocese and restricted in area. *Catechumens*. (1959) 266,472; (1961) 238,584; (1963) 315,463; (1968) 445,889; (1971) 407,119; (1973) 289,343. *Annual baptisms*. (1972) 56.5% infant, 43.5% adult. *Growth*. Expansion has been phenomenal since 1930; from 1965–75 it was still averaging a rate of 6% per year. *National priests*. By 1977, local Rwandan priests numbered 219 (208 diocesan, 11 religious), of whom 18 were serving abroad and another 18 studying abroad. The first ordinations were in 1917. In 1969, 40% of Rwandan priests were over 60 years of age. *Brothers*. Of whom 154 nationals. *Sisters*. Of whom 474 nationals. *Catholic charismatics*. From beginnings in 1974 in a White Sisters' convent in Kabgayi, the renewal has grown to group prayer meetings at the national level to involve 150 regularly by mid-1975. *Seminarians*. 99, rising to (1972) 127, all secular. *Catechists*. Total (1970) 2,178, of whom 230 had diplomas. There are 4 diocesan training schools, and one interdiocesan in Kabgayi. *Indigenous religious congregations*. Brothers: 127 Bayozefiti (Brothers of Joseph, begun 1928). Sisters: 322 Benebikira (Daughters of the Virgin, begun 1919), 33 Biseramariya (Sisters of Mary, begun 1956). *Main foreign orders and congregations*. Priests: WF, SJ, SDB, OP, OSB. Brothers: FSC. Sisters: Sisters of the Assumption, White Sisters, Bernadines, Penitents of St Francis of Opbrakel, Little Sisters of Jesus, Benedictines, Carmelites.
*Catholic organizations*. The Conference of the Bishops of Rwanda and Burundi (Conférence des Ordinaires du Rwanda et du Burundi, COREB), which has its headquarters in Rwanda, and is a member of SECAM, provides common services for both countries, including sponsorship of the Centre for Liturgica and Catechetical Pastoralia, Theological Service and the African Catechetical Institute. There are no pastoral or presbyteral councils, but religious personnel are organized into 2 associations the Conference of Male Major Superiors (Conférence des Supérieurs Majeurs, COSUMA) and the Union of Female Major Superiors (Union des Supérieures Majeures). The principal lay movements are: Xaveri (10,027 members), JOC/F (6,004), JAC/F (477), Mouvement Familial (1,241), Equipes Enseignantes, Légion de Marie (17,493) and Ligue du Sacre Coeur (17,434).

The Holy See has diplomatic relations with Rwanda and is represented to government and the Catholic hierarchy by a nuncio in Kigali.

In 1971, Catholic schools catered for 60% of Rwanda's primary pupils, with a further 30% in Anglican and Protestant schools and 10% in state schools. In 1973, there were 1,042 Catholic elementary schools (213,866 pupils) and 57 secondary schools (6,069 pupils), these secondary schools being either Catholic institutions or official schools placed under the responsibility of a religious congregation. Religious personnel also work in the interdenominational state-sponsored Rilima school which was established to serve refugees from Burundi. Catholic medical work in 1971 included 2 hospitals at Kabgayi and Mibirizi, 38 dispensaries and maternities, 46 nutritional centres and units specializing in the fight against kwashiorkor, 5 service institutions to care for ambulatory leprosy cases, one home for lepers and a psychiatric centre. Religious personnel also serve 4 state dispensaries and maternities. The social sector consisted of 38 social centres, 5 orphanages, 4 homes for the aged, 3 centres for the handicapped and 2 hostels for girls. An extensive literacy programme has been initiated, including an attempt at providing a basic education (reading, arithmetic, hygiene, agriculture, civic education) for non-school children. In 1971, 187,178 children were involved, 76,670 being boys and 110,508 girls. Other institutions include the Cultural Centre of St Michael at Kigali, a bureau of architecture, and numerous co-operatives in the fields of nutrition, sewing, construction and cattle breeding. Caritas-Rwanda, which is affiliated with Caritas Internationalis in Rome, is active; and there is also an Office for Migrants in Kigali.

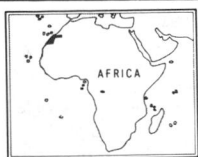

# SAHARA

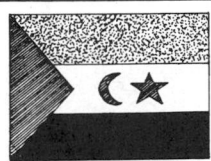

## SECULAR DATA

**STATE. Official name:** (1) The Sahara Arab Democratic Republic (Al-Jumhuriyah as-Sahra al-Arabiyah ad-Dimuqratiyah). (2) Area annexed by Morocco and Mauritania.
**Flag** (shown above right, that of Polisario): Stripes of green, white, and black, with red triangle on hoist, and red crescent and star on white band.
**Area:** 266,000 sq.km. (102,703 sq.miles). Agricultural land: 18.8%.
**Government:** (1) Socialist republic (Polisario Front, supported by Algeria, Communist nations and leftist African countries). (2) Part of Morocco and Mauritania, annexed 1976 (1860 Spanish colony of Spanish West Africa, 1958 province of Spanish Sahara, 1976 Independence proclaimed, 1976 absorbed by Morocco and Mauritania).
**Official language:** Arabic.
**Capital:** El Aaiun 24,520 (1970).

**Political divisions** (1975): 3 Districts.
**Armed forces** (1977): Polisario Front.
**Foreign forces** (1977): Occupying troops from Morocco and Mauritania.

**DEMOGRAPHY. Population:** 76,425 (census of 31.XII.1970. For 1970–2000 (UN), see last row of Table 1). Population density (1975): 0.4/sq.km. (0.9/sq.mile). Under 15 years: 43%. Growth rate (1975–80): 1.01% per year. Household size: 5.2 persons.
**Major languages:** Arabic (Hassaniyah), Spanish.
**Urban dwellers** (1970): 32.0%. Urban growth rate (1950–70): 8.9% per year.
**Refugees** (1977): From abroad, none. Exiles abroad: 20,000 in Algeria.
**Tourists** (1971): 21,163.

**ETHNOLINGUISTIC GROUPS:** (1970) 65.4% Saharan Arab (Reguibat, Izarguien, Ouled Delim, Ouled Tedrarin, Arosien),

34.6% Spanish (Spaniard) (18.2% civilian, 16.4% military). (1976) 99.9% Arab.

**MONEY** (1977). **Monetary unit:** Spanish, Moroccan, Mauritanian and Algerian currency.
**National income per person:** US$900. Average annual family income: US$4,680.

**HEALTH.** Hospitals: 6 (258 beds). Doctors: 53. Lepers: 50 (0.5 per 1,000). Blind: 1,000. Psychotics: 800.

**EDUCATION.** Adult literacy: 10%. Schools: 23.

**LITERATURE.** Periodicals: 2. Newspapers: 1 non-daily.

**COMMUNICATION** (per 1,000 people). Radios: 130. TV sets: 17.

### TABLE 1. RELIGIOUS ADHERENTS IN SAHARA

| Year | 1900 | | mid-1970 | | Annual change, 1970–1980 | | | | mid-1975 | | mid-1980 | | 2000 | |
|---|---|---|---|---|---|---|---|---|---|---|---|---|---|---|
| Name | Adherents | % | Adherents | % | Natural | Conversion | Total | Rate | Adherents | % | Adherents | % | Adherents | % |
| Muslims | 14,900 | 99.3 | 59,600 | 65.3 | 640 | 0 | 640 | 1.02 | 63,000 | 66.3 | 66,000 | 99.7 | 82,000 | 99.5 |
| Christians | 100 | 0.7 | 31,600 | 34.6 | −3,150 | 0 | −3,150 | −9.88 | 31,890 | 33.6 | 100 | 0.2 | 200 | 0.2 |
| professing | 100 | 0.7 | 31,600 | 34.6 | −3,150 | 0 | −3,150 | −9.88 | 31,890 | 33.6 | 100 | 0.2 | 200 | 0.2 |
| Roman Catholics | 100 | 0.7 | 31,600 | 34.6 | −3,150 | 0 | −3,150 | −9.88 | 31,890 | 33.6 | 100 | 0.2 | 200 | 0.2 |
| nominal | 0 | 0.0 | 1,600 | 1.8 | −160 | 0 | −160 | −10.00 | 1,600 | 1.7 | 0 | 0.0 | 0 | 0.0 |
| affiliated | 100 | 0.7 | 30,000 | 32.8 | −2,990 | 0 | −2,990 | −9.87 | 30,290 | 31.9 | 100 | 0.2 | 200 | 0.2 |
| total practising | 70 | 70 | 21,000 | 70 | −2,091 | 0 | −2,091 | −9.86 | 21,200 | 70 | 90 | 90 | 140 | 70 |
| non-practising | 30 | 30 | 9,000 | 30 | −899 | 0 | −899 | −9.89 | 9,090 | 30 | 10 | 10 | 60 | 30 |
| Roman Catholics | 100 | 0.7 | 30,000 | 32.8 | −2,990 | 0 | −2,990 | −9.87 | 30,290 | 31.9 | 100 | 0.2 | 200 | 0.2 |
| Baha'is | 0 | 0.0 | 100 | 0.1 | 0 | 0 | 0 | 0.00 | 110 | 0.1 | 100 | 0.2 | 200 | 0.2 |
| Country's population | 15,000 | 100.0 | 91,300 | 100.0 | −2,510 | 0 | −2,510 | −2.64 | 95,000 | 100.0 | 66,200 | 100.0 | 82,400 | 100.0 |

**COLUMNS, ROWS.** For meanings and definitions, see Codebook (Part 6). Note that, by definition, total 'Christians' = professing + crypto-Christians, which also = affiliated + nominal Christians. Percentages may not always total exactly, due to rounding.
**CENSUSES. 31.XII.1963:** 79.2% Muslims (Arabs), 20.8% Roman Catholics (Spanish civilians). **31.XII.1970:** 78.2% Muslims (59,777 Arabs), 21.8% Roman Catholics (16,648 Spanish civilians). In addition, there were in 1970–75 around

15,000 Spanish military, not included in the census.

**NOTES ON RELIGIONS**
**BAHA'IS.** In 1973, in 3 isolated groups (1 in Rio de Oro).
**COUNTRY'S POPULATION.** The total for mid-1970 in the table is composed of 59,700 Arabs, 16,600 Spanish civilians, and 15,000 Spanish military. The same 3 groups were present in 1975 and are included in the mid-1975 total; but all Spanish military then left in January 1976, together with Spanish civilians, and the

1980 figure is of Arabs alone (including Moroccans and Mauritanians) with only a small handful of Europeans. The annual change figures are averaged over the decade 1970–1980.
**MUSLIMS.** Sunnis (of the Malikite rite), largely nomadic Arabs.
**NOMINAL CHRISTIANS.** Spanish civilians and (up to 1975) military.
**ROMAN CATHOLICS.** All Spanish; in 1970 and 1975, civilian and military; in 1980 a few civilians only.

**NON-CHRISTIAN RELIGIONS. Islam** is the principal religion, and virtually the entire indigenous population is Muslim. Most are Sunnis of the Malikite rite.

**CHRISTIANITY.** The Christian faith was known first around the end of the second century, but all traces were eradicated during the years of Muslim rule.
**CATHOLIC CHURCH.** Spain first came into contact with the territory as early as 1476, but no protectorate was proclaimed until 1885 and no extensive Spanish settlement was begun until well into the 20th century. A Catholic prefecture was erected in 1954, confided to Oblates of Mary Immaculate with help from Salesian Sisters of the Sacred Heart of Jesus. Except for 11 indigenous wives of Spanish settlers who have become Catholics, the Catholic population is confined to the European (mostly Spanish) community, which has tended to diminish since Spain relinquished its authority over the colony in 1976. There are 6 parishes: 3 in Aaiun, one at Bucraa, one at Villa Cisneros and one at Güera.
**PROTESTANT CHURCHES.** Seventh-day Adventists from Spain have attempted to open work in Spanish Sahara, but by 1972 had not been successful.

**CHURCH AND STATE.** Prior to the withdrawal of Spain in 1976, the concordat of the Spanish state with the Holy See was not considered applicable to the Muslim population of Spanish Sahara, and the government gave due respect to Muslim laws, customs and practices. The legal system was a combination of

Christian themes occasionally appeared on Sahara postage stamps under Spanish rule in Spanish West Africa (of which Ifni was a part, from 1946-58): (left): Church of Santa Cruze del Mar (1960). (right) Seville Cathedral (1963).

Spanish civil law and customary law. Spanish courts were responsible for the handling of Spanish interests, while communal concerns of the indigenous population come under the jurisdiction of the Muslim court system with its source in the Quran. With the de facto division of the territory in 1976, the North is governed by Moroccan legislation and the South by Mauritania.

### TABLE 2. ORGANIZED CHURCHES AND DENOMINATIONS IN SAHARA

| Official name 1 | Begun 2 | Type 3 | Counc 4 | Congs 5 | Adults 6 | Affiliated 7 | Names, notes, and other statistics (see Codebook) 8 |
|---|---|---|---|---|---|---|---|
| Iglesia Católica: PA Sahara | 1476 | R Lat | P...r | 6 | 24,000 | 30,000 | *Catholic Ch.* M=OMI. 50% military. 2 schools(185). C=1+0+1. 9x,1m,19w,3h,P=48%,267Yy. |
| **Total affiliated (mid-1970)** | | | | 6 | 24,000 | 30,000 | Total denominations (1970) . . . 1. |
| **Total affiliated (mid-1975)** | | | | 6 | 24,230 | 30,290 | Total denominations (1975) . . . 1. |
| **Total affiliated (mid-1980)** | | | | 1 | 80 | 100 | Total denominations (1980) . . . 1. |

**NOTES ON TABLE ABOVE**
**COLUMNS:** for meanings and CODES (cols. 1, 3, 4, 8): see Codebook (Part 6). Column 1: **Boldface type** = church with over 10% of country's affiliated Christians.
**NATIONAL COUNCILS** (Column 4, 5th letter).
r = attached to Conferencia Episcopal Española (CEE) (Spanish Episcopal Conference).

**PEOPLES** (ethnolinguistic). Christians: 99.9% Spanish (Spaniard).

**COUNTRY-WIDE TOTALS**
**EVANGELIZATION** (see Part 5). 1900: 4%. 1970: 49%. 1980: 10%.
**FOREIGN MISSIONARIES AND PERSONNEL** (aliens from abroad) (1973). Total 29. *From Western world.* 29 Roman

Catholics.
**INSTITUTIONS** (church-operated) (1973). Total 4.
**PERIODICALS.** 1 title.
**PERSONNEL.** 29 in 1973 (all foreign).

**ADDITIONAL DATA ON CHURCHES**
**IGLESIA CATOLICA.** From 1631 the territory was under a Franciscan mission, then under VA Morocco, then under D Canary Islands, and eventually (1954) became PA Spanish Sahara & Ifni, until in 1969 Ifni was detached from the prefecture when the territory was ceded by Spain to Morocco. *Catholics.* The totals above refer to the year 1970 and include (1) 15,168 Catholics on the records of the civilian prefecture, all Spaniards except for 11 natives married to Spaniards, and (2) about 15,000 Catholics in the Spanish military. Both civilians and military left in 1975. *Congregations* (column 5). 3 parishes or chapels in

El Aaiun; one in Bucraa (phosphate industry) in Seguiet el Hamra, in the north; one in Villa Cisneros, and one at Güera (fishing region) in Rio de Oro, in the south. *Annual baptisms.* (1972) 100% infants, no adults. *Priests and religious personnel.* All Spanish. Transient military chaplains not included. *Religious congregations.* Priests: OMI (Spanish province). Sisters: Salesians of the Sacred Heart of Jesus.
*Catholic organizations.* Until 1976, the prefecture was attached to the Conferencia Episcopal Española (Spanish Episcopal Conference). Religious personnel were included in the corresponding Spanish organizations.
Until 1976, the Holy See had diplomatic relations with Spain and was represented to government and the Catholic hierarchy by a nuncio residing in Madrid.
The church sponsors 2 schools and 3 hospitals.

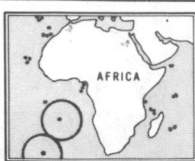

# ST. HELENA

## SECULAR DATA

**STATE. Official name:** The Crown Colony of St Helena.
**Flag** (shown above right): British Blue Ensign with shield of the Colony in the fly.
**Area:** 122 sq.km. (47 sq.miles). Agricultural land: 12.9%.
**Government:** Crown colony of the United Kingdom, since 1834 (1633 Dutch possession, 1661 British colony).
**Legislature:** Legislative Council, 15 members.
**Official language:** English.
**Capital:** Jamestown 1,475 (1966).
**Armed forces** (1976): None. Paramilitary police force, 24.

**DEMOGRAPHY. Population:** 5,310 (census of 24.VII.1966. For 1970–2000 (UN), see last row of Table 1). Population density (1975): 55/sq.km (142/sq.mile). Under 15 years: 42%. Growth rate (1975–80): 0.75% per year. Household size: 4.5 persons.
**Major languages:** English.
**Labour force:** 25%.

**ETHNOLINGUISTIC GROUPS:** 80% St Helena White (British/Chinese/African/Malay/seamen), 20% alien White (USA,UK).

**MONEY** (1977). **Monetary unit:** UK pound (= 100 new pence); US$1 = UK£0.585.

**National income per person:** US$600. Average annual family income: US$2,700.

**HEALTH. Hospitals:** 2 (68 beds). Doctors: 3. Blind: 12.

**EDUCATION.** Adult literacy: (1956) 95%, (1966) 98%. Schools: 8.

**LITERATURE.** Periodicals: 3.

**COMMUNICATION** (per 1,000 people). Phones: 23. Radios: 120.

### TABLE 1. RELIGIOUS ADHERENTS IN ST HELENA

| Year | 1900 | | mid-1970 | | Annual change, 1970–1980 | | | | mid-1975 | | mid-1980 | | 2000 | |
|---|---|---|---|---|---|---|---|---|---|---|---|---|---|---|
| Name | Adherents | % | Adherents | % | Natural | Conversion | Total | Rate | Adherents | % | Adherents | % | Adherents | % |
| Christians | 3,000 | 100.0 | 6,470 | 99.5 | 38 | −3 | 35 | 0.53 | 6,640 | 99.2 | 6,820 | 99.1 | 6,870 | 98.1 |
| professing | 3,000 | 100.0 | 6,470 | 99.5 | 38 | −3 | 35 | 0.53 | 6,640 | 99.2 | 6,820 | 99.1 | 6,870 | 98.1 |
| Anglicans | 2,970 | 99.0 | 5,880 | 90.5 | 34 | −4 | 30 | 0.50 | 6,030 | 90.2 | 6,185 | 89.9 | 6,210 | 88.7 |
| Protestants | 30 | 1.0 | 420 | 6.5 | 2 | −4 | −2 | −0.49 | 410 | 6.1 | 400 | 5.8 | 350 | 5.0 |
| Marginal Protestants | 0 | 0.0 | 140 | 2.1 | 1 | 4 | 5 | 2.81 | 160 | 2.4 | 185 | 2.7 | 240 | 3.4 |
| Roman Catholics | 0 | 0.0 | 30 | 0.5 | 1 | 1 | 2 | 5.00 | 40 | 0.6 | 50 | 0.7 | 70 | 1.0 |
| nominal | 0 | 0.0 | 780 | 12.0 | 5 | 14 | 19 | 2.13 | 870 | 13.0 | 965 | 14.0 | 1,260 | 18.0 |
| affiliated | 3,000 | 100.0 | 5,690 | 87.5 | 33 | −17 | 16 | 0.28 | 5,770 | 86.3 | 5,855 | 85.1 | 5,610 | 80.1 |
| total practising | 2,850 | 95 | 4,550 | 80 | 26 | −13 | 13 | 0.29 | 4,615 | 80 | 4,685 | 80 | 4,210 | 75 |
| non-practising | 150 | 5 | 1,140 | 20 | 7 | −4 | 3 | 0.26 | 1,155 | 20 | 1,170 | 20 | 1,400 | 25 |
| Anglicans | 2,970 | 99.0 | 5,200 | 80.0 | 30 | −14 | 16 | 0.31 | 5,280 | 78.9 | 5,365 | 78.0 | 5,110 | 73.0 |
| Protestants | 30 | 1.0 | 360 | 5.5 | 2 | −7 | −5 | −1.49 | 335 | 5.0 | 310 | 4.5 | 240 | 3.4 |
| Marginal Protestants | 0 | 0.0 | 100 | 1.5 | 1 | 2 | 3 | 2.61 | 115 | 1.7 | 130 | 1.9 | 190 | 2.7 |
| Roman Catholics | 0 | 0.0 | 30 | 0.5 | 0 | 2 | 2 | 5.00 | 40 | 0.6 | 50 | 0.7 | 70 | 1.0 |
| Baha'is | 0 | 0.0 | 20 | 0.3 | 0 | 1 | 1 | 4.00 | 25 | 0.4 | 30 | 0.4 | 50 | 0.7 |
| Non-religious | 0 | 0.0 | 10 | 0.2 | 0 | 2 | 2 | 8.00 | 25 | 0.4 | 30 | 0.4 | 80 | 1.1 |
| Country's population | 3,000 | 100.0 | 6,500 | 100.0 | 38 | 0 | 38 | 0.57 | 6,690 | 100.0 | 6,880 | 100.0 | 7,000 | 100.0 |

**COLUMNS, ROWS.** For meanings and definitions, see Codebook (Part 6). Note that, by definition, total 'Christians' = professing + crypto-Christians, which also = affiliated + nominal Christians. Percentages may not always total exactly, due to rounding.
**CENSUSES.** 27.X.1946: 99.8% Christians. 21.X.1956: 90.9%

Anglicans, 7.6% Protestants (2.9% Baptists, 2.7% Salvation Army, 1.8% SD Adventists), 1.2% marginal Protestants (Jehovah's Witnesses), 0.3% Roman Catholics. 24.VII.1966: 90.6% Anglicans, 6.7% Protestants (2.8% Baptists, 2.4% Salvation Army, 1.3% SD Adventists), 1.9% marginal Protestants (Jehovah's Witnesses), 0.5% Roman Catholics.

**NOTES ON RELIGIONS**
BAHA'IS. In one isolated centre.
NON-RELIGIOUS. Expatriate Whites.

## CHRISTIANITY

**ANGLICAN CHURCH.** Residents of the islands are mostly Anglicans. The colony is covered by 2 dioceses, St Helena and Cape Town; the former is responsible for the islands of St Helena and Ascension, while the latter has jurisdiction over Tristan da Cunha island. Both dioceses belong to the Church of the Province of Southern Africa.

In 1966 St Helena island by itself was 94% Anglican, and the total population 91% Anglican. There are 12 well-attended Anglican churches spread throughout the island of St Helena and one on Ascension.

**OTHER CHURCHES.** Baptist, Salvation Army, Seventh-day Adventist and Catholic churches are found at Jamestown, and there is a congregation of Jehovah's Witnesses at Levelwood. A Catholic priest took up residence on St Helena in 1958, with annual trips to Ascension after 1965. St Helena belongs to the Catholic archdiocese of Cape Town, South Africa. Occasional visits by Catholic clergy are also made from Cape Town to Tristan da Cunha.

**CHURCH AND STATE.** The Anglican Church has a special relationship to the colonial government dating back to the establishment of the diocesan see by the British sovereign. The original church ordinances enshrined in colonial law are still valid. Other religions are required to register their buildings only for official marriage purposes.

**INTERDENOMINATIONAL ORGANIZATIONS.** The Anglican bishop has attempted to form a Christian council, but there has been disagreement regarding membership. The Baptists refused to join without the Adventists, who were in turn opposed by a number of Anglican clergy.

**Anglican Church, Diocese of St Helena.** Cathedral Church of St Paul.

### TABLE 2. ORGANIZED CHURCHES AND DENOMINATIONS IN ST HELENA

| Official name 1 | Begun 2 | Type 3 | Counc 4 | Congs 5 | Adults 6 | Affiliated 7 | Names, notes, and other statistics (see Codebook) 8 |
|---|---|---|---|---|---|---|---|
| **Anglican Church:** | 1851 | A ACa | AwaV. | 16 | 4,200 | 5,200 | In Church of the Province of Southern Africa (CPSA). M=USPG(UK). 4f. |
| D Cape Town | c1968 | A ACa | a | 1 | 200 | 250 | Tristan da Cunha island. Part of D Cape Town, in CPSA. 90% Anglican. |
| D St Helena | 1859 | A ACa | A | 15 | 4,000 | 4,950 | Covers St Helena, Ascension. In CPSA. 1,200 expatriates. 1n,4x,W=30%,4Y,151y. |
| Baptist Church | | P Bap | ••••• | 1 | 80 | 120 | Congregation in Jamestown. Links with Baptist Union of South Africa. |
| Catholic Church (M Cape Town) | 1958 | R Lat | P.S.. | 1 | 20 | 30 | *Sacred Heart Church*, Jamestown, under M Cape Town. 1 resident priest since 1958. |
| Jehovah's Witnesses | c1930 | M Jeh | x..... | 1 | 63 | 100 | Active witnessing under way by 1973. Congregation in Levelwood, St Helena. 12Y. |
| Salvation Army | 1884 | P Sal | xwa.. | 1 | 80 | 120 | Attached to South Africa Territory. Congregation in Jamestown. |
| Seventh-day Adventist Church | 1933 | P Adv | x.... | 1 | 50 | 70 | SDA, Good Hope Conference, South African Union Conf. Congregation in Jamestown. |
| Other Protestant denominations | | P | ••••• | | 20 | 50 | Including: Presbyterian Ch, Two-by-Two Mission (South Africa). |
| **Total affiliated (mid-1970)** | | | | 24 | 4,513 | 5,690 | Total denominations (1970) . . . 9. |
| **Total affiliated (mid-1975)** | | | | 24 | 4,580 | 5,770 | Total denominations (1975) . . . 9. |
| **Total affiliated (mid-1980)** | | | | 25 | 4,640 | 5,855 | Total denominations (1980) . . . 9. |

**NOTES ON TABLE ABOVE**
**COLUMNS:** for meanings and CODES (cols. 1, 3, 4, 8): see Codebook (Part 6). Column 1: **Boldface type** = church with over 10% of country's affiliated Christians.

**PEOPLES** (ethnolinguistic). Christians: 80% St Helena White (mixed race), 20% alien White (USA, UK).

**COUNTRY-WIDE TOTALS**
EVANGELIZATION (see Part 5). 1900: 100%. 1970: 100%. 1980: 100%.
FOREIGN MISSIONARIES AND PERSONNEL (aliens from abroad) (1973). Total 10. *From Western world.* 5: 4 Anglicans in 1 UK society, 1 Roman Catholic. *From Third World.* 5: about 3 Anglicans from South Africa, 2 Protestants in 1 South Africa

society.
PERIODICALS. 2 titles.
PERSONNEL. About 13 (3 national, 10 foreign).
SCRIPTURE DISTRIBUTION (1975). Annual totals: 20 Bibles (subsidized), 50 NTs (subsidized).
SERVICE AGENCIES. 2.

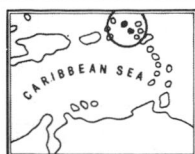

# ST. KITTS-NEVIS

## SECULAR DATA

**STATE. Official name:** The State of St Christopher, Nevis and Anguilla.
**Flag** (shown above right): Green, yellow, and blue vertical bands, black 3-branched palm tree.
**Area:** 269 sq.km. (104 sq.miles). Agricultural land: 41.7%.
**Government:** Republic, formerly self-governing state in association with the United Kingdom (Britain) since 1967 (1623 British colony).
**Legislature:** Unicameral.
**Official language:** English.
**Chief cities:** capital Basseterre 15,730 (1960), Charlestown 1,530.

**DEMOGRAPHY. Population:** 64,000 (census of 7.IV.1970, including Anguilla. For 1970–2000 (UN), see last row of Table 1). Population density (1975): 222/sq.km. (576/sq.mile). Under 15 years: 43%. Growth rate (1975–80): 0.27% per year (births 2.87%, deaths −0.68%, emigrants −1.92%). Life expectancy (1975–80): 69.1 years. Household size: 4.4 persons.
**Major languages:** English, Hindi.
**Urban dwellers** (1970): 27.8%. Urban growth rate (1950–70): 2.8% per year.
**Labour force:** 48.6%.
**Tourists** (1973): 14,900.

**ETHNOLINGUISTIC GROUPS:** 90.5% Black (Negro), 5.0% Mulatto, 3.0% Indo-Pakistani, 1.5% White.

**MONEY** (1977). Monetary unit: East Caribbean dollar (= 100 cents); US$1 = EC$2.70.

**National income per person:** US$480. Average annual family income: US$2,112.
**Inflation:** (1970–74) 4.8% per year.
**Cost of living in capital** (1976): Daily cost of living: US$31.

**HEALTH. Hospitals:** 5 (364 beds). Doctors: 18. Lepers: 95 (1.6 per 1,000). Criminals: 2,486.

**EDUCATION. Adult literacy:** (1946) 81%, (1960) 88%. Schools: 51.

**LITERATURE. Periodicals:** 10. Newspapers: 2 dailies.

**COMMUNICATION** (per 1,000 people). Phones: 28. Daily newspaper circulation: 15 copies.

TABLE 1.  RELIGIOUS ADHERENTS IN ST KITTS-NEVIS

| Year | 1900 | | mid-1970 | | Annual change, 1970–1980 | | | | mid-1975 | | mid-1980 | | 2000 | |
|---|---|---|---|---|---|---|---|---|---|---|---|---|---|---|
| Name | Adherents | % | Adherents | % | Natural | Conversion | Total | Rate | Adherents | % | Adherents | % | Adherents | % |
| Christians | 42,300 | 100.0 | 58,430 | 99.2 | 278 | 0 | 278 | 0.47 | 59,320 | 99.2 | 61,210 | 99.2 | 62,130 | 98.0 |
| professing | 42,300 | 100.0 | 58,430 | 99.2 | 278 | 0 | 278 | 0.47 | 59,320 | 99.2 | 61,210 | 99.2 | 62,130 | 98.0 |
| Protestants | 26,440 | 62.5 | 30,350 | 51.5 | 144 | −3 | 141 | 0.46 | 30,795 | 51.5 | 31,760 | 51.5 | 31,380 | 49.5 |
| Anglicans | 13,530 | 32.0 | 21,470 | 36.5 | 103 | 2 | 105 | 0.48 | 21,800 | 36.5 | 22,520 | 36.5 | 21,870 | 34.5 |
| Roman Catholics | 2,330 | 5.5 | 4,810 | 8.2 | 23 | 2 | 25 | 0.51 | 4,900 | 8.2 | 5,060 | 8.2 | 5,710 | 9.0 |
| Black indigenous | 0 | 0.0 | 1,500 | 2.5 | 7 | −1 | 6 | 0.39 | 1,520 | 2.5 | 1,560 | 2.5 | 2,540 | 4.0 |
| Marginal Protestants | 0 | 0.0 | 300 | 0.5 | 1 | 0 | 1 | 0.33 | 305 | 0.5 | 310 | 0.5 | 630 | 1.0 |
| nominal | 3,300 | 7.8 | 8,355 | 14.2 | 41 | 37 | 78 | 0.90 | 8,670 | 14.5 | 9,140 | 14.8 | 10,140 | 16.0 |
| affiliated | 39,000 | 92.2 | 50,075 | 85.0 | 237 | −37 | 200 | 0.39 | 50,650 | 84.7 | 52,070 | 84.4 | 51,990 | 82.0 |
| total practising | 35,100 | 90 | 40,060 | 80 | 190 | −30 | 160 | 0.39 | 40,520 | 80 | 41,660 | 80 | 36,390 | 70 |
| non-practising | 3,900 | 10 | 10,015 | 20 | 47 | −7 | 40 | 0.39 | 10,130 | 20 | 10,410 | 20 | 15,600 | 30 |
| Protestants | 25,000 | 59.1 | 25,575 | 43.4 | 121 | −75 | 46 | 0.18 | 25,595 | 42.8 | 26,030 | 42.2 | 25,680 | 40.5 |
| Evangelicals | 20,700 | 48.9 | 15,500 | 26.3 | 74 | −54 | 20 | 0.13 | 15,600 | 26.1 | 15,700 | 25.4 | 16,000 | 25.2 |
| Anglicans | 12,000 | 28.4 | 17,500 | 29.7 | 83 | −1 | 82 | 0.46 | 17,750 | 29.7 | 18,320 | 29.7 | 17,120 | 27.0 |
| Roman Catholics | 2,000 | 4.7 | 4,000 | 6.8 | 19 | 13 | 32 | 0.77 | 4,130 | 6.9 | 4,320 | 7.0 | 4,760 | 7.5 |
| Black indigenous | 0 | 0.0 | 2,700 | 4.6 | 13 | 26 | 39 | 1.36 | 2,870 | 4.8 | 3,090 | 5.0 | 3,800 | 6.0 |
| Marginal Protestants | 0 | 0.0 | 300 | 0.5 | 1 | 0 | 1 | 0.33 | 305 | 0.5 | 310 | 0.5 | 630 | 1.0 |
| Baha'is | 0 | 0.0 | 200 | 0.3 | 1 | 1 | 2 | 0.95 | 210 | 0.3 | 220 | 0.4 | 300 | 0.5 |
| Non-religious | 0 | 0.0 | 60 | 0.1 | 0 | 0 | 0 | 0.00 | 60 | 0.1 | 60 | 0.1 | 640 | 1.0 |
| Other religionists | 0 | 0.0 | 210 | 0.4 | 1 | −1 | 0 | 0.00 | 210 | 0.4 | 210 | 0.3 | 330 | 0.5 |
| Country's population | 42,300 | 100.0 | 58,900 | 100.0 | 280 | 0 | 280 | 0.47 | 59,800 | 100.0 | 61,700 | 100.0 | 63,400 | 100.0 |

**COLUMNS, ROWS.** For meanings and definitions, see Codebook (Part 6). Note that, by definition, total 'Christians' = professing + crypto-Christians, which also = affiliated + nominal Christians. Percentages may not always total exactly, due to rounding.
**CENSUSES. 1844** (St Kitts). 67.4% Protestants (43.9% Methodists, 23.5% Moravians), 32.2% Anglicans, 0.3% Roman Catholics.

**4.IV.1881** (St Kitts): 65.3% Protestants (45.9% Methodists, 19.3% Moravians), 29.2% Anglicans, 5.5% Roman Catholics.
**7.IV.1960** (St Kitts-Nevis; de jure): 54.4% Protestants (34.7% Methodists, 10.6% Moravians, 3.4% Pilgrim Holiness Church, 1.7% SDAs), 36.5% Anglicans, 8.1% Roman Catholics, 0.7% non-Christian religionists, 0.3% marginal Protestants, 0.1% non-religious.

**NOTES ON RELIGIONS**
**BAHA'IS.** In 2 local spiritual assemblies (1973).
**BLACK INDIGENOUS.** In 6 denominations in 1970 (see Table 2).
**OTHER RELIGIONISTS.** Mainly Muslims and Afro-American spiritists, including a number of Rastafarians (from Jamaica).

**NON-CHRISTIAN RELIGIONS. Bahai's** has a small work with 2 local spiritual assemblies.

## CHRISTIANITY

**PROTESTANT CHURCHES.** The first Protestants in St Kitts were Moravians, in 1777, followed by the Methodist Thomas Coke and 2 others a decade later. Nevis was reached by Methodists in 1787. The respective strength of these 2 oldest and largest Protestant churches is reversed when one compares St Kitts-Nevis with Antigua. On Antigua the Moravian community is twice as large as that of the Methodists, whereas Methodists are 3 times as numerous as Moravians in St Kitts-Nevis. Of the other churches on the islands, most of which have been established by conservative American missionary societies in the present century, the largest is the Wesleyan Church.

**ANGLICAN CHURCH.** The Anglican Church is the original church of the islands, its first chaplains coming from England to serve the European settler community in the 17th century. The Leeward Islands were transferred from the bishopric of London to that of Barbados in 1824, and the archdeaconry of Antigua (including St Kitts-Nevis) was formed in the same year. The archdeaconry was elevated to a diocese in 1842 and since 1883 has been an integral part of the Church of the Province of the West Indies. Anglicans are not as strong in St Kitts-Nevis as in Antigua or Montserrat, but they are still the largest single denomination.

**CATHOLIC CHURCH.** Catholicism is not strong in any of the Leeward Islands. St Kitts-Nevis forms part of the diocese of Saint John's in Antigua, which was detached from the diocese of Roseau, Dominica in 1971. On St Kitts in 1974 there were 3 parishes served by 4 Redemptorist priests, one mission station and several sisters (Canadian

**Anglican Church.** Priest of Diocese of Antigua with young people in village of Cayon, St Kitts.

Daughters of Jesus) working in 3 Catholic schools and a non-Catholic general hospital. Nevis Island has one parish with a resident Redemptorist priest, in addition to Daughters of Jesus nuns who are engaged in hospital work.

INDIGENOUS CHURCHES. There are at least 6 denominations indigenous to the islands begun by Blacks, of which the best-known are the Spiritual Baptists. Several have spread by emigration to Britain and North America.

CHURCH AND STATE. St Kitts-Nevis is a secular state, associated with Great Britain, which assures complete freedom of religion for all. Churches are not obliged to register with government, but permission must be granted for new denominations to begin work in the islands. Such permission is not difficult to obtain, and recognized bodies may be licensed to perform marriages. Through the auspices of the Christian Council of St Kitts, the churches are now compiling a syllabus for religious teaching in state schools. There is no separate government ministry or department dealing with religion.

INTERDENOMINATIONAL ORGANIZATIONS. The Christian Council of St Kitts has in its member-

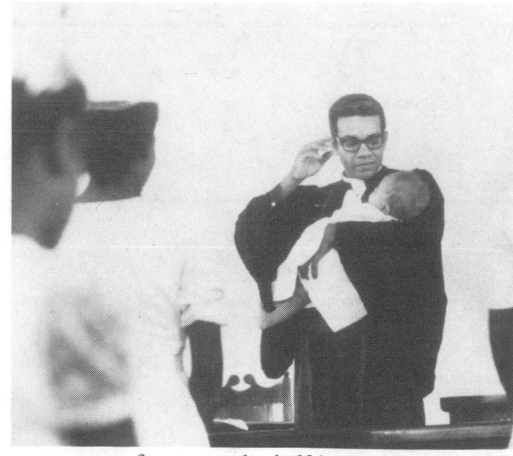

**Methodist Church in the Caribbean & The Americas.** *Above.* 1967 postage stamps commemorating Methodist founders John and Charles Wesley and Thomas Coke. *Right.* Minister baptizes infant in a St Kitts church.

ship Anglican, Catholic, Methodist and Moravian churches and the Salvation Army. The first 3 bodies, plus the Wesleyan Church and the Red Cross, are also members of the Co-ordinating Council for Social Action of Nevis.

BROADCASTING. The government station Radio ZIZ accepts religious programmes, Protestant ones for 4 hours 30 minutes from Mondays to Saturdays and one hour 15 minutes on Sundays, Catholic programmes for one and a half hours from Mondays to Saturdays and half an hour on Sundays. Most of the Protestant programmes are produced locally. From abroad, Protestant programmes can easily be heard over international stations, also from Radio PJ2 (St Maarten) and WIVV (Puerto Rico).

TABLE 2.   ORGANIZED CHURCHES AND DENOMINATIONS IN ST KITTS-NEVIS

| Official name 1 | Begun 2 | Type 3 | Counc 4 | Congs 5 | Adults 6 | Affiliated 7 | Names, notes, and other statistics (see Codebook) 8 |
|---|---|---|---|---|---|---|---|
| **Anglican Church (D Antigua)** | 1623 | A ACa | avHRC | | 9,000 | 17,500 | *CPWI.* In Ch of Province of WIndies. M=USPG. 95% West Indians (90% Black). W=58%. |
| Antioch Baptist Church | 1963 | I Bap | .T.... | 6 | 90 | 1,500 | Baptist body founded by Blacks. HQ Basseterre. 2n,G=20.7%pa,W=99%,3Y,20z. |
| Catholic Church (D Saint John's) | 1861 | R Lat | P.NHC | 13 | 2,800 | 4,000 | In D Saint John's (Antigua). Assisted by CSSR priests. 5nx,8w,200Yy. |
| Christian Brethren | | P CBr | x.... | 7 | 400 | 600 | *Open Brethren. Gospel Halls.* M=CMML(UK,USA,Bermuda). 1 group on Nevis. 7f. |
| Church of God of Prophecy | | P Pe3 | Z.... | 7 | 540 | 1,000 | M=CGP(USA). Holiness Pentecostals (3-stage). Split in USA ex CoG (Cleveland). |
| Church of God (Anderson) | 1946 | P Hol | x.... | 5 | 253 | 513 | *General Assembly of the CoG (St Kitts).* M=CoG(Anderson) (USA). 3n,2f,W=99%. |
| Church of God (Cleveland) | 1943 | P Pe3 | ZF... | 8 | 464 | 900 | M=CoG(Cleveland) (USA). St Kitts: 5 churches. Nevis: 2 churches, 1 mission. 7n. |
| Jehovah's Witnesses | c1940 | H Jeh | x.... | 5 | 157 | 300 | *Watch Tower. IBSA.* Active witnessing under way by 1942. HQ Sandy Point. 5Y. |
| **Methodist Ch in Caribbean & Americas** | 1787 | P Met | VwH.C | 30 | 6,000 | 12,000 | In MCCA (1967), Leeward Islands District. M=MMS(UK). HQ Basseterre. 5n,1x,1f. |
| Moravian Church | 1777 | P Mor | xvH.C | 4 | 1,210 | 4,045 | *St Kitts Conference,* Eastern West Indies Province, Unity of Brethren. W=44%,94Y. |
| Salvation Army | | P Sal | xvH.C | 1 | 50 | 70 | In Caribbean & CAmerica Territory (HQ Jamaica). In Basseterre. |
| Seventh-day Adventist Church | | P Adv | x.... | | 908 | 1,300 | *SDA,* East Caribbean Conference, Caribbean Union Conference. HQ Basseterre. |
| Wesleyan Church | 1902 | P Hol | VP.,C | 19 | 663 | 2,647 | *Pilgrim Holiness Ch.* M=WC(USA). HQ Basseterre. 10n,2x,2f,G=2.8%pa,W=31%,33Y,20z. |
| Other Protestant denominations | | P | ..... | | 1,300 | 2,500 | Total about 15 bodies (see list below). |
| Other Black indigenous churches | | I | ..... | | 700 | 1,200 | Total over 6 (see list below). |
| **Total affiliated (mid-1970)** | | | | 220 | 24,535 | 50,075 | Total denominations (1970) . . . 35. |
| **Total affiliated (mid-1975)** | | | | 240 | 24,820 | 50,650 | Total denominations (1975) . . . 36. |
| **Total affiliated (mid-1980)** | | | | 260 | 25,510 | 52,070 | Total denominations (1980) . . . 37. |

**NOTES ON TABLE ABOVE**
COLUMNS: for meanings and CODES (cols. 1, 3, 4, 8): see Codebook (Part 6). Column 1: **Boldface type** = church with over 10% of country's affiliated Christians.
NATIONAL COUNCILS (Column 4, 5th letter).
C = Christian Council of St Kitts, and/or Co-ordinating Council for Social Action of Nevis.
*Other national councils.* St Kitts Evangelical Association.
OTHER PROTESTANT DENOMINATIONS. These numerous smaller bodies include: Baptist Ch, Chs of Christ, Exclusive Brethren (Kelly-Continental), Missionary Ch, Pentecostal Assemblies of the West Indies (many emigrants to UK).
OTHER BLACK INDIGENOUS CHURCHES. These include:

Assemblies of the First-Born, Ch of the Apostolic Faith, Evangelical Faith Ch, International Ministerial Council, Spiritual Baptist Churches. Several now have branches in Britain due to emigration of their members.

PEOPLES (ethnolinguistic). Christians: 93.0% Black, 5.0% Mulatto, 1.5% White (British), East Indian.

COUNTRY-WIDE TOTALS
EVANGELIZATION (see Part 5). 1900: 100%. 1970: 100%. 1980: 100%.
FOREIGN MISSIONARIES AND PERSONNEL (nationals serving abroad) (1973). Total about 2 Black indigenous in UK.

FOREIGN MISSIONARIES AND PERSONNEL (aliens from abroad) (1973). Total 28. *From Western world.* 23: 13 Protestants (7 in 6 USA societies, 4 in 2 UK societies, 2 in 1 Canada society), about 10 Roman Catholics. *From Third World.* About 5 Protestants (3 from Trinidad & Tobago, 2 Brethren from Bermuda).
PERIODICALS. About 6 titles.
PERSONNEL. About 74 (46 national, 28 foreign).
SCRIPTURE DISTRIBUTION (1975). Annual totals: 270 Bibles (subsidized), 300 NTs (subsidized), 300 UBS portions, 12,100 UBS selections.
SERVICE AGENCIES. About 8, including SPCK, YMCA, YWCA.

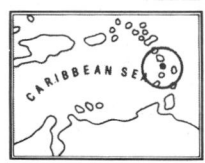

# ST.LUCIA

## SECULAR DATA

**STATE. Official name:** The State of St Lucia.
**Flag** (shown above right): Blue field, centred isosceles triangle in black, gold and white.
**Area:** 616 sq.km. (238 sq.miles). Agricultural land: 38.7%.
**Government:** Republic, formerly self-governing state in association with the United Kingdom (Britain) since 1967 (1814 British colony, Independence 1979).
**Legislature:** Unicameral.
**Official language:** English.
**Capital:** Castries 45,000.

**DEMOGRAPHY. Population:** 99,806 (census of 7.IV.1970. For 1970–2000 (UN), see last row of Table 1). Population density (1975): 175/sq.km. (454/sq.mile). Under 15 years: 47%. Growth rate (1975–80): 1.21% per year (births 3.35%, deaths −0.77%, emigrants −1.37%). Life expectancy (1975–80): 67.4 years. Household size: 4.4 persons.
**Major languages:** English, French patois, Dominican Creole, Hindi.
**Urban dwellers** (1970): 60%. Urban growth rate (1950–70): 2.8% per year.
**Labour force:** 36.4%.
**Tourists** (1964): 17,716. (1973) 45,800. (1974) 51,816.

**ETHNOLINGUISTIC GROUPS:** 50.3% Black (Negro), 45.4% Mulatto, 3.0% Indo-Pakistani, 1.2% White.

**MONEY** (1977). **Monetary unit:** East Caribbean dollar (= 100 cents); US$1 = EC$2.70.
**National income per person:** US$500. Average annual family income: US$2,200.
**Inflation:** (1970–74) 10.0% per year.
**Cost of living in capital** (1976): Daily cost of living: US$31.

**HEALTH. Hospitals:** 6 (512 beds). **Doctors:** 28. **Lepers:** 55 (0.5 per 1,000). **Blind:** 200.

**EDUCATION. Adult** literacy: (1946) 52%. Schools: 87 (74 primary, 12 secondary).

**LITERATURE.** Periodicals: 8. Newspapers: 4 non-daily.

**COMMUNICATION** (per 1,000 people). Phones: 55. Radios: 405. TV sets: 23.

**Catholic Church, Archdiocese of Castries.** Town and parish church of Soufrière at foot of Pitons mountains.

TABLE 1. RELIGIOUS ADHERENTS IN ST LUCIA

| Year | 1900 | | mid-1970 | | Annual change, 1970–1980 | | | | mid-1975 | | mid-1980 | | 2000 | |
|---|---|---|---|---|---|---|---|---|---|---|---|---|---|---|
| *Name* | *Adherents* | *%* | *Adherents* | *%* | *Natural* | *Conversion* | *Total* | *Rate* | *Adherents* | *%* | *Adherents* | *%* | *Adherents* | *%* |
| **Christians** | **48,670** | **97.7** | **99,330** | **98.3** | **1,371** | **−78** | **1,293** | **1.22** | **105,800** | **98.0** | **112,260** | **97.6** | **126,100** | **97.0** |
| professing | 48,670 | 97.7 | 99,330 | 98.3 | 1,371 | −78 | 1,293 | 1.22 | 105,800 | 98.0 | 112,260 | 97.6 | 126,100 | 97.0 |
| Roman Catholics | 40,970 | 82.3 | 90,350 | 89.5 | 1,244 | −126 | 1,118 | 1.16 | 95,950 | 88.8 | 101,530 | 88.3 | 112,630 | 86.6 |
| Evangelical Catholics | 0 | 0.0 | 1,850 | 1.8 | 27 | 20 | 47 | 2.29 | 2,050 | 1.9 | 2,320 | 2.0 | 2,740 | 2.1 |
| Protestants | 1,730 | 3.5 | 5,350 | 5.3 | 80 | 87 | 167 | 2.71 | 6,160 | 5.7 | 7,020 | 6.1 | 9,620 | 7.3 |
| Anglicans | 5,970 | 12.0 | 3,430 | 3.4 | 44 | −42 | 2 | 0.06 | 3,460 | 3.2 | 3,450 | 3.0 | 3,250 | 2.5 |
| Marginal Protestants | 0 | 0.0 | 200 | 0.2 | 3 | 3 | 6 | 2.61 | 230 | 0.2 | 260 | 0.2 | 600 | 0.5 |
| affiliated | 48,670 | 97.7 | 99,330 | 98.3 | 1,371 | −78 | 1,293 | 1.22 | 105,800 | 98.0 | 112,260 | 97.6 | 126,100 | 97.0 |
| disaffiliated | 0 | 0.0 | −1,500 | −1.5 | −26 | −74 | −100 | 5.00 | −2,000 | −1.9 | −2,500 | −2.2 | −3,500 | −2.7 |
| doubly-affiliated | 0 | 0.0 | −2,510 | −2.5 | −39 | −60 | −99 | 3.30 | −3,000 | −2.8 | −3,500 | −3.0 | −5.000 | −3.8 |
| total practising | 43,800 | *90* | 79,460 | *80* | 1,097 | −62 | 1,035 | 1.22 | 84,640 | *80* | 89,810 | *80* | 94,570 | *75* |
| non-practising | 4,870 | *10* | 19,870 | *20* | 274 | −16 | 258 | 1.22 | 21,160 | *20* | 22,450 | *20* | 31,530 | *25* |
| Roman Catholics | 40,970 | 82.3 | 92,510 | 91.6 | 1,282 | −12 | 1,270 | 1.28 | 98,900 | 91.6 | 105,210 | 91.5 | 118,390 | 91.1 |
| Catholic pentecostals | 0 | 0.0 | 0 | 0.0 | 5 | 95 | 100 | 25.00 | 400 | 0.4 | 1,000 | 0.9 | 6,000 | 4.6 |
| Protestants | 1,730 | 3.5 | 6,280 | 6.2 | 89 | 42 | 131 | 1.90 | 6,900 | 6.4 | 7,590 | 6.6 | 9,620 | 7.4 |
| Evangelicals | 1,500 | 3.0 | 4,500 | 4.5 | 66 | 44 | 110 | 2.16 | 5,100 | 4.7 | 5,600 | 4.9 | 7,800 | 6.0 |
| Anglicans | 5,970 | 12.0 | 3,000 | 3.0 | 42 | 3 | 45 | 1.39 | 3,240 | 3.0 | 3,450 | 3.0 | 3,250 | 2.5 |
| Black indigenous | 0 | 0.0 | 1,250 | 1.2 | 18 | 18 | 36 | 2.57 | 1,400 | 1.3 | 1,610 | 1.4 | 2,340 | 1.8 |
| Marginal Protestants | 0 | 0.0 | 300 | 0.3 | 5 | 5 | 10 | 2.78 | 360 | 0.3 | 400 | 0.3 | 1,000 | 0.8 |
| Afro-American spiritists | 0 | 0.0 | 1,500 | 1.5 | 26 | 74 | 100 | 5.00 | 2,000 | 1.9 | 2,500 | 2.2 | 3,500 | 2.7 |
| Baha'is | 0 | 0.0 | 170 | 0.2 | 3 | 4 | 7 | 3.50 | 200 | 0.2 | 240 | 0.2 | 400 | 0.3 |
| Hindus | 970 | 1.9 | 0 | 0.0 | 0 | 0 | 0 | 0.00 | 0 | 0.0 | 0 | 0.0 | 0 | 0.0 |
| Muslims | 160 | 0.3 | 0 | 0.0 | 0 | 0 | 0 | 0.00 | 0 | 0.0 | 0 | 0.0 | 0 | 0.0 |
| **Country's population** | **49,800** | **100.0** | **101,000** | **100.0** | **1,400** | **0** | **1,400** | **1.30** | **108,000** | **100.0** | **115,000** | **100.0** | **130,000** | **100.0** |

COLUMNS, ROWS. For meanings and definitions, see Codebook (Part 6). Note that, by definition, total 'Christians' = professing + crypto-Christians, which also = affiliated + nominal Christians. Percentages may not always total exactly, due to rounding.

CENSUSES. **1901** Census of the British Empire (as in 1900 column above, adjusted), **7.IV.1960:** 92.5% Roman Catholics, 3.8% Anglicans, 3.6% Protestants (1.8% SD Adventists), 0.1% marginal Protestants. **7.IV.1970:** 90.5% Roman Catholics, 5.3% Protestants (2.4% SD Adventists), 3.4% Anglicans, 0.6% non-Christians, 0.2% marginal Protestants. This census took no account of Catholics who had become Rastafarians.

NOTES ON RELIGIONS

AFRO-AMERICAN SPIRITISTS. For some years there has been a growing movement among the poorer Black Catholics, youths in particular, to turn to the Ras Tafari Movement from Jamaica (here classified as one manifestation of Afro-American spiritism) and to become Rastas themselves. From being delinquents known as 'wharf rats', these youths have become productive craftsmen living communally. Unlike Jamaican Rastas, St Lucian Rastas do not hold repatriation to Ethiopia or Africa as an ideal, but regard Africa as being wherever they live. Other cults include Kele (Shango).

BAHA'IS. In 2 local spiritual assemblies (1973).

BLACK INDIGENOUS. In about 5 denominations in 1970 (see Table 2).

CATHOLIC PENTECOSTALS (or, Catholic charismatics). Totals (mid-1975): 200 involved adults (over 15 years) in 2 prayer groups; total charismatic community including children, 400.

DISAFFILIATED. This term is used here to describe youths and other Black persons who, although baptized Roman Catholics and therefore regarded by the Catholic Church as still affiliated to it (and hence enumerated in Table 2 as such), have recently withdrawn or disaffiliated themselves from it and have become Rastafarians (Rastas). Because their statistics represent a duplication, they are shown in the table above as a negative quantity (with a minus sign).

DOUBLY-AFFILIATED. The term covers those affiliated to, or claimed by, both the Catholic Church and also a church regarded as Evangelical by state or society (Protestant, Anglican, Black indigenous, marginal Protestant), i.e. baptized Catholics who have recently become Evangelicals or others. Because their statistics represent a duplication, they are shown in the table as a negative quantity (with a minus sign).

EVANGELICAL CATHOLICS. This term is used here to describe persons who are affiliated to churches regarded by the state or society as Evangelical ( Protestant, Anglican, marginal Protestant or Black indigenous churches), but who in censuses or polls are regarded individually by state and society as, or who profess to be, Roman Catholics.

**NON-CHRISTIAN RELIGIONS. Rastafarianism,** an Afro-American cult from Jamaica, has made many converts from among unemployed young Blacks, particularly delinquents known as 'wharf rats'. Now trained as craftsmen, they live communally and stress development, thrift schemes, literacy and so on.

**Baha'i** has a small but growing following, with 2 assemblies in 1973.

## CHRISTIANITY

CATHOLIC CHURCH. Catholicism gained an early foothold in 1719 under the French, and this has never been relinquished. The archdiocese of Castries is today entrusted to the French FMI. St Lucia is also served by Presentation Brothers and 3 congregations of sisters: St Joseph of Cluny, Sisters of the Sorrowful Mother and Corpus Christi Carmelites. The composition of the Catholic community is approximately 50% Negroes of African origin, 46% mixed race, 3% East Indians and 1% Whites.

OTHER CHURCHES. Anglicans form the largest of the non-Catholic churches and are part of the diocese of the Windward Islands, in the Church of the Province of the West Indies. The diocese was created in 1878, the Windward Islands having been previously part of the diocese of Barbados. Seventh-day Adventists, who organized the East Caribbean Conference including St Lucia in 1926, greatly outnumber the older Methodist (1809) and Moravian churches; but the fastest growth in recent years has been experienced by the Evangelical Church of the West Indies and an independent Black pentecostal group with ties to Barbados and the USA, the United Holy Church of America. Other smaller denominations include Baptist Mid-Missions, Church of God (Cleveland) and the Orthodox Baptist Church.

Many postage stamps portray the story of Christ: (left) the Crucifixion, by Raphael, and (right) 'Noli me tangere (Do not touch me)', by Titian (Easter 1968).

**CHURCH AND STATE.** Although the state is secular, the government gives annual grants to the Roman Catholic, Anglican and Methodist churches. Except for a vocational school for girls, all Catholic schools receive government aid.

**INTERDENOMINATIONAL ORGANIZATIONS.** There is an Inter-Church Council, with Catholic membership, whose purpose is to create good relations between the churches, to prepare joint services, to organize social work including feeding programmes and to promote common interests in education, the family, and other areas of concern.

**BROADCASTING.** The government Windward Islands Broadcasting Service which also serves Grenada, Dominica and St Vincent, transmits religious programmes from Mondays to Saturdays (Protestants 3 hours, Catholics one hour) and on Sundays (Protestants and Catholics 30 minutes each). Radio Caraibes broadcasts religious programmes each Sunday morning in French and English; and St Lucia Television Service relays programmes from Barbados.

## BIBLIOGRAPHY


*A history of the Roman Catholic Church in St Lucia*. C. Gachet. Port of Spain (Trinidad): Key Publications, c1976.

'The Kele (Chango) cult in St Lucia', G.E. Simpson, *Caribbean studies*, 13 (October, 1973), 110–116.


TABLE 2. ORGANIZED CHURCHES AND DENOMINATIONS IN ST LUCIA

| Official name 1 | Begun 2 | Type 3 | Counc 4 | Congs 5 | Adults 6 | Affiliated 7 | Names, notes, and other statistics (see Codebook) 8 |
|---|---|---|---|---|---|---|---|
| Anglican Church (D Windward Is) | | A ACa | awMRC | | 1,500 | 3,000 | In Ch of Prov of West Indies. 90% Black. Decline from 5,980 in 1900. 1f,W=20%. |
| Baptist Mid-Missions | 1946 | P Bap | x.... | | 200 | 400 | M=Baptist Mid-Missions(USA). Regular Baptists. Fundamentalists. 9f. |
| **Catholic Church: M Castries** | 1719 | R Lat | PxNMC | 21 | 49,000 | 92,510 | Island 92% Catholic. 3% East Indian, 1% White. C=2+1+3. 5n,27x,6m,38w,P=45%,3545Yy. |
| Christian Brethren | | P CBr | x.... | 2 | 100 | 200 | *Open Brethren. Plymouth Brethren. Gospel Halls.* 2 missionaries from UK. |
| Christian Brethren (Executive) | | P EBr | x.... | 4 | 200 | 400 | *Exclusive (Plymouth) Brethren.* Group: Kelly-Continental. |
| Church of God (Cleveland) | 1940 | P Pe3 | ZF... | 2 | 100 | 200 | M=CoG(Cleveland) (USA). Holiness Pentecostals (3-stage). 1 church, 1 mission. 1n. |
| Evangelical Church of the West Indies | 1949 | P int | xM... | 5 | 700 | 1,200 | M=WIM(USA). Island base for evangelism in Windward Islands. 1 school. 7f. |
| Jehovah's Witnesses | 1953 | M Jeh | x.... | 4 | 190 | 300 | *Watch Tower. International Bible Students Association.* Rapid growth. 24Y. |
| Methodist Ch in Caribbean & Americas | 1809 | P Met | VwM.C | 3 | 375 | 600 | *MCCA*, South Caribbean Dist. Begun from Dominica. Decline (1,400 in 1900). 2x,17y. |
| Moravian Church | c1850 | P Mor | xwM.. | | 100 | 200 | Eastern West Indies Province, Unity of Brethren. Blacks. In 1900, 130 Moravians. |
| Orthodox Baptist Church | | I Bap | ..... | | 100 | 250 | Independent Baptist congregations. Also in Trinidad and Tobago. Blacks. |
| Pentecostal Assemblies of the W Indies | | P Pe2 | ZF... | 1 | 30 | 50 | M=PAoC(Canada). Classical Pentecostals (2-stage). Emigration to UK. 1f. |
| Salvation Army | | P Sal | xwM.. | 1 | 20 | 30 | In Barbados Division, Caribbean & CAmerica Territory (HQ Jamaica). HQ Castries. |
| Seventh-day Adventist Church | 1926 | P Adv | x.... | | 1,893 | 2,500 | *SDA*, East Caribbean Conference, Caribbean Union Conference. 1r(SDA Academy). |
| United Holy Church of America | c1965 | I pe3 | x.... | 2 | 200 | 400 | *UHCA*, Barbados District. M=UHCA(USA Black pentecostals). Begun from Barbados. |
| Other Black indigenous churches | | I pen | ..... | | 200 | 600 | Several bodies including Spiritual Baptists (Shouters, Shakers). |
| Other Protestant denominations | | P | ..... | | 200 | 500 | Total about 5, including Bible Missionary Church, Church of the Nazarene, Streams of Power. |
| Doubly-affiliated (duplication) (1970) | | | | | −1,300 | −2,510 | Evangelicals and others who also are or were baptized Roman Catholics. |
| Disaffiliated (duplication) (1970) | | | | | −800 | −1,500 | Baptized Catholics, mostly Black youths, who have recently become Rastafarians. |
| **Total affiliated (mid-1970)** | | | | **105** | **53,008** | **99,330** | **Total denominations (1970) . . . 20.** |
| **Total affiliated (mid-1975)** | | | | **125** | **56,460** | **105,800** | **Total denominations (1975) . . . 21.** |
| **Total affiliated (mid-1980)** | | | | **145** | **59,910** | **112,260** | **Total denominations (1980) . . . 22.** |

NOTES ON TABLE ABOVE

COLUMNS: for meanings and CODES (cols. 1, 3, 4, 8): see Codebook (Part 6). Column 1: **Boldface type** = church with over 10% of country's affiliated Christians.

NATIONAL COUNCILS (Column 4, 5th letter).
C = St Lucia Inter-Church Council.

**PEOPLES** (ethnolinguistic). Christians: 50.5% Black, 45.5% Mulatto, 2.7% East Indian, 1.2% White (British).

**COUNTRY-WIDE TOTALS**
EVANGELIZATION (see Part 5). 1900: 100%. 1970: 100%. 1980: 100%. *Mass evangelism*. In 1975 the Evangelistic Association, Pentecostal Assemblies of the West Indies, conducted a large crusade.
FOREIGN MISSIONARIES AND PERSONNEL (aliens from abroad) (1973). Total 96. *From Western world*. 86: 65 Roman Catholics, 20 Protestants (17 in 4 USA societies, 2 in 1 UK society, 1 in 1 Canada society), 1 Anglican in 1 Canada society. *From Third World*. About 10, mainly Roman Catholics from Trinidad & Tobago.
INSTITUTIONS (church-operated) (1973). Total 7, including 4 higher schools, 1 hospital.
PERIODICALS. About 7 titles.
PERSONNEL. About 161 (65 national, 96 foreign).
SCRIPTURE DISTRIBUTION (1975). Annual totals: 1,550

Bibles (13% free, 81% subsidized, 6% commercial), 2,400 NTs (subsidized), 3,600 UBS portions, 700 UBS selections.
SERVICE AGENCIES. About 13, including CLC, CYO.

**ADDITIONAL DATA ON CHURCHES**
CATHOLIC CHURCH. The diocese was erected in 1956 as a suffragan of M Port of Spain (Trinidad), entrusted to French FMI; in 1974 it became an archdiocese with 3 suffragan dioceses: Roseau (Dominica), Saint George's in Grenada, and Saint John's (Antigua). *Catholics*. 50% Blacks, 45% Mulatto (mixed race), 3% East Indians, 1% Whites. *Annual baptisms*. (1972) 99.9% infant, 0.1% adult. *Priests*. Nationals: 4 diocesan, 1 religious. Expatriates: 25 French and 2 Canadians, all religious *Brothers*. All expatriates. *Sisters*. A few indigenous sisters. *Catechists*. (1974) Over 50. *Foreign religious congregations*. Priests: 25 FMI, 2 SFM. Brothers: 6 Presentation Brothers. Sisters: 22 St Joseph of Cluny, 9 Sisters of the Sorrowful Mother, 7 Corpus Christi Carmelites.
*Catholic organizations*. St Lucia belongs to the Antilles Episcopal

Conference (AEC) with its headquarters in Kingston, Jamaica, and through it is a member of CELAM. Religious personnel are represented on the Conference of Major Superiors of the Antilles, which belongs to CLAR and also has its seat in Jamaica. A Council of Priests and a Pastoral Council have been formed, the latter consisting of 7 priests, 8 laymen, one sister and one brother. Lay groups include the Catholic Youth Organization, Catholic Scouts and Guides, Legion of Mary, St Vincent de Paul, and Ladies of Charity.
The Holy See has no diplomatic relations with St Lucia. It is represented to the Catholic hierarchy by an apostolic delegate based in Port-au-Prince, Haiti.
Institutions in 1974 included 57 primary schools (25,100 pupils), 2 secondary schools (541 students), one senior school and one vocational school for girls, one hospital (100 beds), one home for the aged (75 residents), one day nursery (50 children) and one Ozanam shelter for the destitute (12 beds).

# St. Pierre & Miquelon

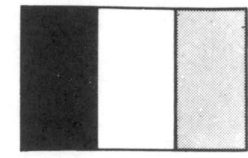

## SECULAR DATA

**STATE. Official name:** The Department of St Pierre and Miquelon (Le Département des Iles Saint-Pierre et Miquelon).
**Flag** (shown above right): That of France.
**Area:** 242 sq.km. (93 sq.miles). Description: 8 islands. Agricultural land: 12.5%.
**Government:** Overseas department of France, since 1975 (1535 French possession, 1946 overseas territory).
**Legislature:** General Council, 14 members.
**Official language:** French (*Français*).
**Capital:** St-Pierre 4,287.

**DEMOGRAPHY. Population:** 5,840 (census of 18.II.1974. For 1970–2000 (UN), see last row of Table 1). Population density (1975): 23/sq.km. (59/sq.mile). Under 15 years: 32%. Growth rate (1975–80): 0.0% per year. Household size: 4.1 persons.
**Major language:** French.
**Labour force:** 36%.
**Tourists** (1969): 7,200.

**ETHNOLINGUISTIC GROUPS:** 99.5% French (French/Basque origin).

**MONEY** (1977). **Monetary unit:** French franc (= 100 centimes);

US$1 = Fr 5.00.
**National income per person:** US$4,000. Average annual family income: US$16,400.

**HEALTH. Hospitals:** 2 (95 beds). Doctors: 5.

**EDUCATION. Adult literacy:** (1967) 99%. Schools: 8.

**COMMUNICATION** (per 1,000 people). Phones: 245. Radios: 350. TV sets: 280.

TABLE 1.    RELIGIOUS ADHERENTS IN ST PIERRE & MIQUELON

| Year | 1900 | | mid-1970 | | Annual change, 1970–1980 | | | | mid-1975 | | mid-1980 | | 2000 | |
|---|---|---|---|---|---|---|---|---|---|---|---|---|---|---|
| Name | Adherents | % | Adherents | % | Natural | Conversion | Total | Rate | Adherents | % | Adherents | % | Adherents | % |
| Christians | 6,500 | 100.0 | 5,450 | 99.1 | 0 | −2 | −2 | −0.04 | 5,440 | 98.9 | 5,430 | 98.7 | 5,900 | 98.3 |
| professing | 6,500 | 100.0 | 5,450 | 99.1 | 0 | −2 | −2 | −0.04 | 5,440 | 98.9 | 5,430 | 98.7 | 5,900 | 98.3 |
| Roman Catholics | 6,500 | 100.0 | 5,400 | 98.2 | 0 | −2 | −2 | −0.04 | 5,390 | 98.0 | 5,380 | 97.8 | 5,800 | 96.7 |
| Protestants | 0 | 0.0 | 50 | 0.9 | 0 | 0 | 0 | 0.00 | 50 | 0.9 | 50 | 0.9 | 100 | 1.7 |
| nominal | 1,200 | 18.5 | 67 | 1.2 | 0 | 3 | 3 | 4.16 | 80 | 1.5 | 100 | 1.8 | 180 | 3.0 |
| affiliated | 5,300 | 81.5 | 5,383 | 97.9 | 0 | −5 | −5 | −0.10 | 5,360 | 97.4 | 5,330 | 96.9 | 5,720 | 95.3 |
| total practising | 5,247 | 99 | 5,275 | 98 | 0 | −5 | −5 | −0.10 | 5,250 | 98 | 5,220 | 98 | 5,150 | 90 |
| non-practising | 53 | 1 | 108 | 2 | 0 | 0 | 0 | 0.00 | 110 | 2 | 110 | 2 | 570 | 10 |
| Roman Catholics | 5,300 | 81.5 | 5,383 | 97.9 | 0 | −5 | −5 | −0.10 | 5,360 | 97.4 | 5,330 | 96.9 | 5,720 | 95.2 |
| Baha'is | 0 | 0.0 | 50 | 0.9 | 0 | 2 | 2 | 3.33 | 60 | 1.1 | 70 | 1.3 | 100 | 1.7 |
| Country's population | 6,500 | 100.0 | 5,500 | 100.0 | 0 | 0 | 0 | 0.00 | 5,500 | 100.0 | 5,500 | 100.0 | 6,000 | 100.0 |

COLUMNS, ROWS. For meanings and definitions, see Codebook (Part 6). Note that, by definition, total 'Christians' = professing + crypto-Christians, which also = affiliated +

nominal Christians. Percentages may not always total exactly, due to rounding.
CENSUSES. **20.IV.1962:** 99.0% Roman Catholics, 1.0% Protestants.

NOTES ON RELIGIONS
PROTESTANTS. Individuals unaffiliated to churches.

**CHRISTIANITY.** Catholic work was begun in 1689, and this remains the only church on the islands. The vicariate covers the whole territory and is attached, with consultative voice, to the Episcopal Conference of France. The islands are served by 7 Holy Ghost priests (5 French, one Canadian, one Spanish), together with St Joseph de Cluny sisters.

**CHURCH AND STATE.** Legal statutes relating to the church are the same as for metropolitan France.

**Eglise Catholique: VA Iles S-P & M.** Postage stamps illustrating the main church buildings.

TABLE 2.    ORGANIZED CHURCHES AND DENOMINATIONS IN ST PIERRE & MIQUELON

| Official name 1 | Begun 2 | Type 3 | Counc 4 | Congs 5 | Adults 6 | Affiliated 7 | Names, notes, and other statistics (see Codebook) 8 |
|---|---|---|---|---|---|---|---|
| **Eglise Catholique: VA Iles S-P & M** | 1689 | R Lat | P...r | 2 | 3,000 | 5,383 | Territory is 98% Catholic. M=CSSp. 4 schools. C=1+0+1. 7x,1m,18w,P=95%,131y. |
| Total affiliated (mid-1970) | | | | 2 | 3,383 | 5,383 | Total denominations (1970) . . . 1. |
| Total affiliated (mid-1975) | | | | 2 | 2,990 | 5,360 | Total denominations (1975) . . . 1. |
| Total affiliated (mid-1980) | | | | 2 | 2,970 | 5,330 | Total denominations (1980) . . . 1. |

**NOTES ON TABLE ABOVE**
COLUMNS: for meanings and CODES (cols. 1, 3, 4, 8): see Codebook (Part 6). Column 1: **Boldface type** = church with over 10% of country's affiliated Christians.
NATIONAL COUNCILS (Column 4, 5th letter).
   r = consultative member, Conférence Episcopale de France (CEF) (Episcopal Conference of France).

**PEOPLES** (ethnolinguistic). Christians: 99.5% French.

**COUNTRY-WIDE TOTALS**
EVANGELIZATION (see Part 5). 1900: 100%. 1970: 100%. 1980: 100%. *Literature evangelism*. By 1975, Every Home Crusade had completed evangelistic coverage of literature to all households.

FOREIGN MISSIONARIES AND PERSONNEL (aliens from abroad) (1973). Total 26. *From Western world*. 26 Roman Catholics.
INSTITUTIONS (church-operated) (1973). Total 2 higher schools.
PERIODICALS. 1 title.
PERSONNEL. 28 (2 national, 26 foreign).
SCRIPTURE DISTRIBUTION (1975). Annual totals: 20 Bibles (subsidized), 20 NTs (commercial).
SERVICE AGENCIES. About 5, including CEF, CV/AV.

**ADDITIONAL DATA ON CHURCHES**
EGLISE CATHOLIQUE. *Annual baptisms*. (1972) 100% infants, no adults. *Priests*. 5 metropolitan French, 1 Canadian,

1 Spanish (chaplain to seamen). *Sisters*. Metropolitan French (born in France). *Indigenous religious congregations*. None. *Foreign congregations*. Priests: CSSp. Sisters: St-Joseph de Cluny. *Catholic organizations*. The diocese is attached, with consultative voice, to the Episcopal Conference of France (Conférence Episcopale de France). There are no presbyteral or pastoral councils, nor associations of religious personnel. The principal lay movements are Scouts and CV/AV, the latter with 320 children.
The Holy See has no diplomatic relations with the territory. It is represented to the Catholic hierarchy by an apostolic delegate based in Ottawa, Canada.
The church supervises 4 schools, 2 centres for sailors, a hostel and an orphanage.

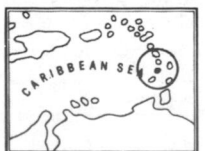

# ST. VINCENT

## SECULAR DATA

**STATE. Official name:** The State of St Vincent.
**Flag** (shown above right): Blue, yellow, green and white bars, with

Arms of St Vincent with motto 'Pax et Justitia'.
**Area:** 388 sq.km. (150 sq.miles). Agricultural land: 55.9%.
**Government:** Republic, formerly self-governing state in association with the United Kingdom (Britain) since 1969 (1783 British

colony, 1979 Independence).
**Legislature:** Bicameral.
**Official language:** English.
**Capital:** Kingstown 4,308 (1960).

**DEMOGRAPHY. Population:** 89,129 (census of 7.IV.1970. For 1970–2000 (UN), see last row of Table 1). Population density (1975): 241/sq.km. (624/sq.mile). Under 15 years: 47%. Growth rate (1975–80): 1.01% per year (births 3.35%, deaths −0.77%, emigrants −1.57%). Life expectancy (1975–80): 67.4 years. Household size: 4.4 persons.
**Major languages:** English, Hindi.
**Urban dwellers** (1970): 35%. Urban growth rate (1950–70): 2.8% per year.
**Labour force:** 32%.
**Tourists** (1973): 16,600.

**ETHNOLINGUISTIC GROUPS:** 65.5% Black (African Negro), 19.9% Mulatto, 5.5% Indo-Pakistani (East Indian), 3.5% White (British, European, USA), 2.0% Amerindian (Carib), Spaniard, French, Portuguese, Mestizo, Latin American White, Syrian Arab.

**MONEY** (1977). **Monetary unit:** East Caribbean dollar (= 100 cents); US$1 = EC$2.70.
**National income per person:** US$250. Average annual family income: US$1,100.
**Cost of living in capital** (1976): Daily cost of living: US$32.

**HEALTH.** Hospitals: 8 (529 beds). Doctors: 16. Lepers: 54 (0.6 per 1,000). Blind: 100.

**EDUCATION.** Adult literacy: (1946) 76%, (1970) 80%. Schools: 60 (58 primary).

**COMMUNICATION** (per 1,000 people). Phones: 45.

TABLE 1.  RELIGIOUS ADHERENTS IN ST VINCENT

| Year | 1900 | | mid-1970 | | Annual change, 1970–1980 | | | | mid-1975 | | mid-1980 | | 2000 | |
| Name | Adherents | % | Adherents | % | Natural | Conversion | Total | Rate | Adherents | % | Adherents | % | Adherents | % |
|---|---|---|---|---|---|---|---|---|---|---|---|---|---|---|
| **Christians** | 47,000 | 98.8 | 86,200 | 96.9 | 871 | −26 | 845 | 0.93 | 90,460 | 96.7 | 94,650 | 96.6 | 103,800 | 95.2 |
| professing | 47,000 | 98.9 | 86,200 | 96.9 | 871 | −26 | 845 | 0.93 | 90,460 | 96.7 | 94,650 | 96.6 | 103,800 | 95.2 |
| Anglicans | 37,490 | 78.9 | 36,110 | 40.6 | 342 | −425 | −83 | −0.23 | 35,500 | 38.0 | 35,280 | 36.0 | 32,700 | 30.0 |
| Protestants | 7,130 | 15.0 | 34,700 | 39.0 | 361 | 135 | 496 | 1.32 | 37,510 | 40.1 | 39,660 | 40.5 | 44,000 | 40.4 |
| Roman Catholics | 2,380 | 5.0 | 14,690 | 16.5 | 161 | 261 | 422 | 2.53 | 16,700 | 17.9 | 18,910 | 19.3 | 25,600 | 23.5 |
| Black indigenous | 0 | 0.0 | 500 | 0.6 | 5 | 1 | 6 | 1.13 | 530 | 0.6 | 560 | 0.6 | 1,000 | 0.9 |
| Marginal Protestants | 0 | 0.0 | 200 | 0.2 | 2 | 2 | 4 | 1.82 | 220 | 0.2 | 240 | 0.2 | 500 | 0.5 |
| nominal | 4,750 | 10.0 | 23,070 | 25.9 | 237 | 51 | 288 | 1.17 | 24,560 | 26.3 | 25,950 | 26.5 | 29,700 | 27.2 |
| affiliated | 42,250 | 88.9 | 63,130 | 70.9 | 634 | −77 | 557 | 0.85 | 65,900 | 70.5 | 68,700 | 70.1 | 74,100 | 68.0 |
| total practising | 38,020 | 90 | 50,500 | 80 | 507 | −61 | 446 | 0.85 | 52,720 | 80 | 54,960 | 80 | 51,870 | 70 |
| non-practising | 4,230 | 10 | 12,630 | 20 | 127 | −16 | 111 | 0.84 | 13,180 | 20 | 13,740 | 20 | 22,230 | 30 |
| Anglicans | 35,500 | 74.7 | 30,000 | 33.7 | 282 | −428 | −146 | −0.50 | 29,280 | 31.3 | 28,540 | 29.1 | 19,300 | 17.7 |
| Protestants | 4,750 | 10.0 | 17,500 | 19.7 | 180 | 60 | 240 | 1.28 | 18,700 | 20.0 | 19,900 | 20.3 | 27,200 | 25.0 |
| Evangelicals | 3,800 | 8.0 | 10,600 | 11.9 | 109 | 41 | 150 | 1.33 | 11,300 | 12.1 | 12,100 | 12.3 | 16,600 | 15.2 |
| Roman Catholics | 1,900 | 4.0 | 14,330 | 16.1 | 158 | 261 | 419 | 2.55 | 16,400 | 17.5 | 18,520 | 18.9 | 25,100 | 23.0 |
| Catholic pentecostals | 0 | 0.0 | 0 | 0.0 | 2 | 38 | 40 | 20.00 | 200 | 0.2 | 400 | 0.4 | 2,000 | 1.8 |
| Black indigenous | 100 | 0.2 | 1,100 | 1.2 | 12 | 28 | 40 | 3.08 | 1,300 | 1.4 | 1,500 | 1.5 | 2,000 | 1.8 |
| Marginal Protestants | 0 | 0.0 | 200 | 0.2 | 2 | 2 | 4 | 1.82 | 220 | 0.2 | 240 | 0.2 | 500 | 0.5 |
| Afro-American spiritists | 500 | 1.0 | 1,800 | 2.0 | 18 | −2 | 16 | 0.86 | 1,870 | 2.0 | 1,960 | 2.0 | 2,000 | 1.8 |
| Baha'is | 0 | 0.0 | 600 | 0.7 | 7 | 13 | 20 | 2.86 | 700 | 0.7 | 800 | 0.8 | 1,000 | 0.9 |
| Non-religious | 0 | 0.0 | 400 | 0.4 | 4 | 15 | 19 | 4.04 | 470 | 0.5 | 590 | 0.6 | 2,200 | 2.0 |
| **Country's population** | 47,500 | 100.0 | 89,000 | 100.0 | 900 | 0 | 900 | 0.96 | 93,500 | 100.0 | 98,000 | 100.0 | 109,000 | 100.0 |

**COLUMNS, ROWS.** For meanings and definitions, see Codebook (Part 6). Note that, by definition, total 'Christians' = professing + crypto-Christians, which also = affiliated + nominal Christians. Percentages may not always total exactly, due to rounding.
**CENSUSES.** 7.IV.1960: 47.4% Anglicans, 40.6% Protestants (33.4% Methodists), 11.1% Roman Catholics, 0.5% Black indigenous (393 Spiritual Baptists), 0.3% non-religious, 0.1% marginal Protestants.

**NOTES ON RELIGIONS**
AFRO-AMERICAN SPIRITISTS. There are centres of Shango (Yoruba syncretism), including Obeah and other spirit-possession cults. There are also many Rastofarians (from Jamaica).
BAHA'IS. Growth of local spiritual assemblies: 1964, none; 1973, 6 (2 on Grenadines). Converts include Carib Indians.
BLACK INDIGENOUS. In 2 denominations in 1970 (see Table 2).
CATHOLIC PENTECOSTALS (or, Catholic charismatics).

Totals (mid-1975): 100 involved adults (over 15 years) in 3 prayer groups; total charismatic community including children, 200.
NOMINAL CHRISTIANS. As in several other Caribbean countries, there are large numbers of persons professing in government censuses to be Anglicans, Methodists or other Protestants, but who have no church affiliation.

**Anglican Church, Diocese of the Windward Islands.** *Above.* A series of government postage stamps commemorating Diocesan Centenary in 1977.
**Methodist Church in the Caribbean & The Americas.** *Right.* Kingstown Church.

**NON-CHRISTIAN RELIGIONS. Afro-American spiritism** is followed by a small number of persons of African descent.

**Baha'i** has a number of followers, mostly former Hindus and Muslims among East Indians.

## CHRISTIANITY
ANGLICAN CHURCH. Anglicanism has an ancient history in St Vincent dating back to the end of the 17th century and is still the principal church of the island. St Vincent belongs to the diocese of the Windward Islands, in the Church of the Province of the West Indies. The church is about 90% Black.
PROTESTANT CHURCHES. The Methodist Church, which first came to St Vincent in 1787, is the main Protestant body and has nearly twice the membership of all other Protestant groups put together. Of some 14 smaller mostly American-based Protestant denominations begun in the present century, the largest are the Seventh-day Adventists and the Brethren.
CATHOLIC CHURCH. The territory of St Vincent belongs to the diocese of Bridgetown-Kingstown which is based on and includes Barbados. Catholicism has never gained a strong foothold in

these islands, making up less than 18% of the population of St Vincent and 4% on Barbados. In 1974, St Vincent had 4 Catholic parishes of which one was the co-cathedral of Kingstown, 13 stations, 7 SFM priests, 5 FSC brothers and 13 sisters (7 St Joseph of Cluny and 6 Corpus Christi Carmelites).

CHURCH AND STATE. St Vincent was granted home rule in 1969, 2 years after the other 3 islands of the Windward group. No special status is accorded to the Anglican Church in spite of its strength and its traditional relationship to the British Crown.

INTERDENOMINATIONAL ORGANIZATIONS. The Christian Council of St Vincent was founded in 1969 with 4 member bodies: Anglican, Catholic and Methodist churches, and Salvation Army. The council works in close co-operation with the World Council of Churches; and in fact membership is restricted to churches who are members of the WCC, or whose parent bodies are, with the exception of the Catholic Church. Nevertheless, membership in the council's 5 commissions (ecumenism, family life, social action, communications, and youth) is open to denominations which have no WCC affiliation.

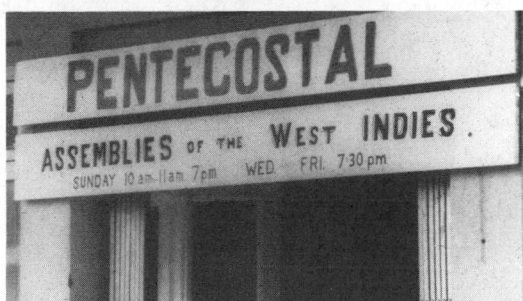

**Pentecostal Assemblies of the West Indies.** Noticeboard with times of regular services. Many St Vincent Pentecostals have emigrated to Britain.

BROADCASTING. The government-sponsored Windward Islands Broadcasting Service in Grenada has a relay station at St Vincent and transmits both Protestant and Catholic programmes for one hour daily.

**BIBLIOGRAPHY**
'Spirit-possession belief and trance behavior in two fundamentalist groups in St Vincent', J.H. Henney, in F.D. Goodman et al., *Trance, healing and hallucination* (New York: Wiley, 1974), p. 6–111.
'The Shakers of St Vincent: a stable religion', J.H. Henney, in E. Bourguignon, *Religion, altered states of consciousness, and social change* (Columbus: Ohio State University Press, 1971).

TABLE 2. ORGANIZED CHURCHES AND DENOMINATIONS IN ST VINCENT

| Official name 1 | Begun 2 | Type 3 | Counc 4 | Congs 5 | Adults 6 | Affiliated 7 | Names, notes, and other statistics (see Codebook) 8 |
|---|---|---|---|---|---|---|---|
| **Anglican Church: D Windward Isles** | c1700 | A ACa | AwMRK | 30 | 6,000 | 30,000 | 1878, Diocese in CPWI. M=USPG(UK). 95% WIndian(90% Black). 8n,12x,12f,W=20%,1265y. |
| Baptist Churches | 1947 | P Bap | x.... | | 300 | 600 | M=Baptist Mid-Missions (USA). Regular Baptists. Links with St Lucia. 8f,1s. |
| **Catholic Ch (D Bridgetown-Kingstown)** | | R Lat | P.NMK | 4 | 7,600 | 14,330 | In D Bridgetown-Kingstown (Barbados). C=1+1+2. 7x(SFM),5m(FSC),12w,1H,3r,500Yy. |
| Christian Brethren | | P CBr | x.... | 7 | 700 | 1,500 | *Gospel Halls. Plymouth Brethren* (Open). M=CMML(UK,USA). 2f. |
| Christian Brethren (Exclusive) | | P EBr | x.... | 4 | 200 | 400 | *Exclusive* (*Plymouth*) *Brethren*. Group: Kelly-Continental. |
| Christian Pilgrim Church of St Vincent | | I ind | ..... | | 200 | 500 | Indigenous Black church led by bishop. HQ Georgetown. |
| Church of God of Prophecy | | P Pe3 | Z.... | 1 | 25 | 100 | M=CGP(USA). Holiness Pentecostals. Schism in USA from CoG (Cleveland). |
| Church of God (Cleveland) | 1940 | P Pe3 | ZF... | 17 | 292 | 600 | M=CoG(Cleveland) (USA). Holiness Pentecostals. 11 churches, 6 missions. 13n. |
| Churches of Christ | | P Dis | x.... | 8 | 50 | 100 | M=CC(Non-Instrumental) (USA). In most larger towns. Independent congregations. |
| Evangelical Church of the West Indies | 1952 | P int | xM... | 9 | 400 | 600 | M=West Indies Mission(USA). Linked to WIM branches elsewhere in Caribbean. 3m,4f. |
| Jehovah's Witnesses | 1932 | M Jeh | x.... | 4 | 139 | 200 | *Watch Tower. IBSA*. Including Beguia Island (1956). 7Y. |
| **Methodist Ch in Caribbean & Americas** | 1787 | P Met | VwM.K | 24 | 3,650 | 10,000 | In MCCA, South Caribbean District. M=MMS(UK). 72% women. 4n,G=–0.8%pa,518y. |
| Pentecostal Assemblies of the W Indies | | P Pe2 | Z.... | | 300 | 500 | Formerly M=PAoC(Canada). Classical Pentecostals (2-stage). Emigration to UK. |
| Salvation Army | | P Sal | xwM.K | | 100 | 200 | In Caribbean & CAmerica Territory (HQ Jamaica). HQ Kingstown. |
| Seventh-day Adventist Church | | P Adv | x.... | | 1,000 | 2,000 | *SDA*, South Caribbean Conference, Caribbean UC. Increasing; many East Indians. 2r. |
| Spiritual Baptist Churches | c1860 | I pen | ..... | | 300 | 600 | *Shouters*, *Shakers*. Banned 1913–65. White robes, vestments, RC ritual, Obeah. Bishop. |
| Wesleyan Church | | P Hol | VF... | 3 | 317 | 500 | Before 1968 merger, M=Pilgrim Holiness Ch(USA). Holiness doctrines. |
| Other Protestant denominations | | P | ..... | 5 | 200 | 400 | Bible Missionary Ch, Ch of God (Anderson), Presbyterian Ch, Streams of Power(1965). |
| **Total affiliated (mid-1970)** | | | | **160** | **21,773** | **63,130** | **Total denominations (1970) . . . 20.** |
| **Total affiliated (mid-1975)** | | | | **170** | **22,730** | **65,900** | **Total denominations (1975) . . . 20.** |
| **Total affiliated (mid-1980)** | | | | **180** | **23,690** | **68,700** | **Total denominations (1980) . . . 21.** |

**NOTES ON TABLE ABOVE**
COLUMNS: for meanings and CODES (cols. 1, 3, 4, 8): see Codebook (Part 6). Column 1: **Boldface type** = church with over 10% of country's affiliated Christians.
NATIONAL COUNCILS (Column 4, 5th letter).
K = Christian Council of St Vincent (CCSV).

**PEOPLES** (ethnolinguistic). Christians: 69.0% Black, 21.0% Mulatto, 3.5% White (British), 2.0% Amerindian (Carib), 1.5% East Indian, 1.0% Latin European (Spaniard, French, Portuguese), Latin American White.

**COUNTRY-WIDE TOTALS**
EVANGELIZATION (see Part 5). 1900: 100%. 1970: 100%. 1980: 100%. *Mass evangelism*. In 1975 the Evangelistic Association, Pentecostal Assemblies of the West Indies, conducted a large crusade.
FOREIGN MISSIONARIES AND PERSONNEL (aliens from abroad) (1973). Total 55. *From Western world*. 30: about 15 Roman Catholics, 14 Protestants (12 in 4 USA societies, 1 in 1 Canada society, 1 in 1 UK society), 1 Anglican in 1 Canada society. *From Third World*. 25: about 12 Roman Catholics, about 11 Anglicans, some Protestants.
INSTITUTIONS (church-operated) (1973). Total 6, including 3 higher schools, 1 hospital, 1 seminary (Protestant).
PERIODICALS. About 4 titles.
PERSONNEL. About 90 (35 national, 55 foreign).
RELIGIOUS LIBRARIES. 1.
SCRIPTURE DISTRIBUTION (1975). Annual totals: 2,000 Bibles (50% free, 50% subsidized), 1,000 NTs (90% subsidized, 10% commercial), 1,900 UBS portions, 2,700 UBS selections.
SERVICE AGENCIES. About 7, including CCSV, CTA, SPCK, YMCA, YWCA.

**ADDITIONAL DATA ON CHURCHES**
CATHOLIC CHURCH. *Catholic organizations*. In 1974 the church was responsible for 2 primary schools with 1,000 pupils, 3 secondary schools with 755 students, a hospital for infants and a day nursery.

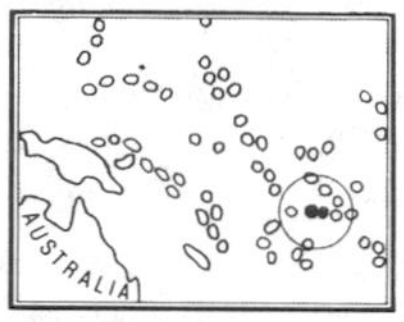


# SAMOA

## SECULAR DATA

**STATE. Official name:** The Independent State of Western Samoa (Malotuto'atasi o Samoa i Sisifo). Since 1977 the official UN-adopted shortened name has been: Samoa. Adjective of nationality: Samoan.
**Flag** (shown above right): Red field with blue rectangle in upper hoist corner; 5 white stars representing Southern Cross.
**Area:** 2,842 sq.km. (1,097 sq.miles). Agricultural land: 24.3%.
**Government:** Constitutional monarchy, since 1889 (1800 rival chiefdoms, 1900 German protectorate, 1919 New Zealand mandated territory, 1946 UN trusteeship, 1962 Independence).
**Legislature:** Legislative Assembly, 47 members.
**Official languages:** Samoan and English.
**Capital:** Apia 29,000 (1970).

**DEMOGRAPHY. Population:** 146,627 (census of 3.XI.1971 For 1970–2000 (UN), see last row of Table 1). Population density (1975): 58/sq.km. (149/sq.mile). Under 15 years: 48%. Growth rate (1975–80): 3.28% per year (births 4.11%, deaths –0.79%, emigrants –0.08%). Life expectancy (1975–80): 60.3 years. Household size: 6.2 persons.
**Major languages:** Samoan, English, Chinese.
**Urban dwellers** (1970): 24.0%. Urban growth rate (1950–70): 5.6% per year.
**Labour force:** 26%.
**Tourists** (1969): 14,584. (1975) 40,000.

**ETHNOLINGUISTIC GROUPS:** 88.9% Samoan, 10.1% Euronesian (European/Polynesian) (part-Samoan) (European Chinese/under 75% Samoan), 0.6% European (740), 0.3% other Pacific islander, 0.1% Chinese, Maori.

**MONEY** (1977). **Monetary unit:** Western Samoan tala (= 100 sene); US$1 = WS$0.80.
**National income per person:** US$280. Average annual family income: US$1,736.
**Inflation:** (1970–74) 12.0% per year (1975: consumer price index 170).
**Cost of living in capital** (1976): Daily cost of living: US$31.

**HEALTH.** Hospitals: 15 (655 beds). Doctors: 45. Lepers: 900 (5.5 per 1,000).

**EDUCATION.** Adult literacy: (1951) 86%, (1971) 98%. Education rate: 69%. Schools: 173.

**LITERATURE.** Periodicals: 25. Newspapers: 3 non-daily.

**COMMUNICATION** (per 1,000 people). Phones: 17. Radios: 338. TV sets: 0.5. Daily newspaper circulation: 1 copy.

TABLE 1. RELIGIOUS ADHERENTS IN WESTERN SAMOA

| Year | 1900 | | mid-1970 | | Annual change, 1970–1980 | | | | mid-1975 | | mid-1980 | | 2000 | |
|---|---|---|---|---|---|---|---|---|---|---|---|---|---|---|
| *Name* | *Adherents* | *%* | *Adherents* | *%* | *Natural* | *Conversion* | *Total* | *Rate* | *Adherents* | *%* | *Adherents* | *%* | *Adherents* | *%* |
| **Christians** | **32,800** | **100.0** | **139,200** | **98.7** | **5,219** | **–69** | **5,150** | **3.19** | **161,500** | **98.5** | **190,700** | **98.3** | **338,100** | **98.0** |
| professing | 32,800 | 100.0 | 139,200 | 98.7 | 5,219 | –69 | 5,150 | 3.19 | 161,500 | 98.5 | 190,700 | 98.3 | 338,100 | 98.0 |
| Protestants | 29,470 | 89.8 | 96,410 | 68.4 | 3,602 | –138 | 3,464 | 3.11 | 111,450 | 68.0 | 131,050 | 67.6 | 266,400 | 65.6 |
| Roman Catholics | 3,000 | 9.1 | 30,880 | 21.9 | 1,144 | –102 | 1,042 | 2.94 | 35,400 | 21.6 | 41,300 | 21.3 | 70,700 | 20.5 |
| Marginal Protestants | 330 | 1.0 | 10,860 | 7.7 | 433 | 171 | 604 | 4.51 | 13,400 | 8.2 | 16,900 | 8.7 | 36,900 | 10.7 |
| Polynesian indigenous | 0 | 0.0 | 700 | 0.5 | 27 | 3 | 30 | 3.53 | 850 | 0.5 | 1,000 | 0.5 | 3,500 | 1.0 |
| Anglicans | 0 | 0.0 | 350 | 0.2 | 13 | –3 | 10 | 2.50 | 400 | 0.2 | 450 | 0.2 | 600 | 0.2 |
| nominal | 600 | 1.8 | 3,983 | 2.8 | 165 | 97 | 262 | 5.13 | 5,100 | 3.1 | 6,600 | 3.4 | 15,900 | 4.6 |
| affiliated | 32,200 | 98.2 | 135,217 | 95.9 | 5,054 | –166 | 4,888 | 3.12 | 156,400 | 95.4 | 184,100 | 94.9 | 322,200 | 93.4 |
| total practising | 31,880 | *99* | 133,870 | *99* | 5,004 | –165 | 4,839 | 3.12 | 154,840 | *99* | 182,260 | *99* | 289,980 | *90* |
| non-practising | 320 | *1* | 1,350 | *1* | 50 | –1 | 49 | 3.14 | 1,560 | *1* | 1,840 | *1* | 32,220 | *10* |
| Protestants | 28,770 | 87.7 | 82,500 | 58.5 | 3,033 | –408 | 2,625 | 2.80 | 93,850 | 57.2 | 108,750 | 56.1 | 177,000 | 51.3 |
| Evangelicals | 24,600 | 75.0 | 21,100 | 15.0 | 788 | –28 | 760 | 3.11 | 24,400 | 14.9 | 28,700 | 14.8 | 49,700 | 14.4 |
| Roman Catholics | 3,000 | 9.1 | 29,830 | 21.2 | 1,108 | –91 | 1,017 | 2.96 | 34,300 | 20.9 | 40,000 | 20.6 | 67,300 | 19.5 |
| Marginal Protestants | 330 | 1.0 | 21,737 | 15.4 | 869 | 337 | 1,206 | 4.48 | 26,900 | 16.4 | 33,800 | 17.4 | 73,800 | 21.4 |
| Polynesian indigenous | 100 | 0.3 | 800 | 0.6 | 31 | –1 | 30 | 3.16 | 950 | 0.6 | 1,100 | 0.6 | 3,500 | 1.0 |
| Anglicans | 0 | 0.0 | 350 | 0.2 | 13 | –3 | 10 | 2.50 | 400 | 0.2 | 450 | 0.2 | 600 | 0.2 |
| Baha'is | 0 | 0.0 | 1,800 | 1.3 | 81 | 69 | 150 | 6.00 | 2,500 | 1.5 | 3,300 | 1.7 | 6,900 | 2.0 |
| **Country's population** | **32,800** | **100.0** | **141,000** | **100.0** | **5,300** | **0** | **5,300** | **3.23** | **164,000** | **100.0** | **194,000** | **100.0** | **345,000** | **100.0** |

COLUMNS, ROWS. For meanings and definitions, see Codebook (Part 6). Note that, by definition, total 'Christians' = professing + crypto-Christians, which also = affiliated + nominal Christians. Percentages may not always total exactly, due to rounding.
CENSUSES. **25.IX.1945:** 75.3% Protestants, 20.5% Roman Catholics, 4.2% marginal Protestants. **25.IX.1951:** 74.8% Protestants, 20.8% Roman Catholics, 4.4% marginal Protestants. **25.IX.1956:** 98.4% Christians, 1.6% other religionists. **25.IX.1961:** 71.3% Protestants (53.6% Congregationalists, 16.0% Methodists, 1.3% SD Adventists), 21.6% Roman Catholics, 6.3% marginal Protestants (Mormons), 0.5% Polynesian indigenous (Congregational Ch), 0.3% Anglicans. **21.XI.1966:** 69.1% Protestants (52.1% Congregationalists, 15.4% Methodists, 1.6% SD Adventists), 22.2% Roman Catholics, 7.2% marginal Protestants (Mormons), 0.5% Polynesian indigenous, 0.3% Anglicans, 0.8% other religionists. **3.XI.1971:** 69.4% Protestants (51.0% Congregationalists, 15.7% Methodists, 1.7% SD Adventists), 21.8% Roman Catholics, 7.8% marginal Protestants (Mormons), 0.2% Anglicans, 0.5% other religionists.

**NOTES ON RELIGIONS**
BAHA'IS. Rapid growth from 8 local spiritual assemblies (1964) to 26 (1973). In 1973, the malietoa (king) of Samoa announced his conversion to the Baha'i faith. In 1980, the world's 7th Baha'i Temple was under construction in Apia.
MARGINAL PROTESTANTS. In the 1971 census, 7.8% of the population professed to be Mormons; however, in 1970 the Mormon mission claimed to have 21,537 adherents (15.3% of the population). It is clear therefore that, due to the exceptionally large Mormon missionary force and the extremely rapid growth in numbers of adherents, many persons who profess to be Congregationalists or Methodists in censuses have in fact joined and are still joining the Mormons.
POLYNESIAN INDIGENOUS. In 3 denominations in 1970 (see Table 2).

**NON-CHRISTIAN RELIGIONS. Baha'i** has a rapidly-growing community of recent origin. In 1973, the malietoa (king) announced his conversion to the Baha'i faith.

## CHRISTIANITY

PROTESTANT CHURCHES. The principal denomination is the Congregational Christian Church in Samoa, which owes its origin to the pioneer work of Tahitian teachers left by John Williams of the London Missionary Society in 1830. Williams and his Tahitian co-workers arrived at a particularly propitious time for the establishment of Christianity following a popular revolt against the despotic ruler Tamafaiga, who exercised the role of chief and high priest. Samoans not only accepted Christianity with enthusiasm but by 1840 had dedicated themselves to spreading the gospel to other South Sea islanders. They were in fact instrumental in taking Christianity to Tokelau, Niue, the Gilbert and Ellice Islands and the New Hebrides, and by 1972 over 210 Samoan Congregationalists had gone overseas as foreign missionaries. At present the Congregational Christian Church, which is autonomous, fully supports 6

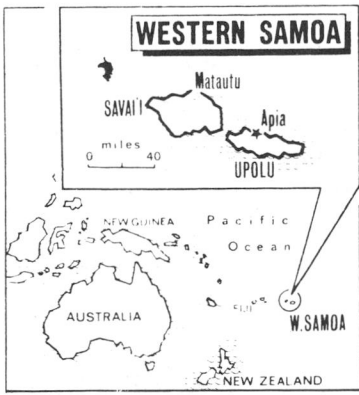

A series of postage stamps set illustrating (from top, left to right) Mormon Church, LMS church, RC Cathedral, SDA sanatorium.

Samoan missionary couples in Papua New Guinea and has another couple in training in Australia. Although the church has in recent years been losing ground to such rapidly-growing groups as Mormons, Pentecostals, and Adventists, the people of Samoa are still more than 50% Congregationalist.

Methodism was introduced through the ministry of a Samoan who was converted in 1827 and brought his new faith back home with him. British missionaries appeared in 1835 and the church later developed a special relationship with Australian Methodism. Seventh-day Adventists have built up a substantial following since their arrival in 1895 and continue to grow. Other groups include Assemblies of God, Brethren, Nazarenes, and the United Pentecostal Church.

Congregationalists, Methodists and Adventists are all heavily involved in education.

CATHOLIC CHURCH. The faith was first brought to Samoa by Wallisians (Uveans) from Wallis and Futuna Islands, now a completely Catholic territory. By 1966, Catholics numbered 22% of the population, a figure which has not altered significantly since the 1940s. The problem created by the lack of priests and the extensive area of the diocese has been resolved in part by the remarkable development of its system of catechists: 135 serving 23 parishes in 1974. In many cases several catechists and their families live together in communities. Although the diocese covers 3 different countries (Western Samoa, American Samoa and Tokelau Islands), Western Samoa is the most heavily populated and has the most priests: 34 out of 42 for the whole diocese in 1974, of which 9 were nationals.

MARGINAL CHURCHES. Mormons are numerous in Western Samoa as in other parts of Oceania and are engaged in an extensive educational programme. Their growth has been extraordinarily rapid; those professing in censuses to be Mormons rose from 4.2% in 1945 to 6.3% in 1961 and to 7.8% in 1971. However, the church itself claimed much larger numbers (15% by 1970), reflecting the large number of Congregationalists attending Mormon activities and becoming Mormons.

INDIGENOUS CHURCHES. There are 3 independent churches, Ponesi's Church (Congregat-

ional Church of Jesus Christ), an old split from the Congregational Church, and 2 small pentecostal groups, Makisua's Church (a schism from the Assemblies of God) and the Samoan Full Gospel Church.

CHURCH AND STATE. Western Samoa is a Christian state, as is indicated by the Preamble to the constitution of 28 October 1960: 'In the Holy Name of God, the Almighty, the Ever Loving: whereas sovereignty over the Universe belongs to the Omni-present God alone... Western Samoa (is) an Independent State based on Christian principles and Samoan custom and tradition.'

The constitution of January 1962 guarantees freedom of religion in Western Samoa. Although no government subsidies are provided, the churches operate numerous schools in close co-operation with the government Department of Education. Of 6 schools preparing students for New Zealand school

**Church of Jesus Christ of Latter-day Saints.** Two native Samoan girls, who serve as Mormon missionaries, at a Zone Conference near Apia, with some of the other 350 missionaries contributing to this church's massive growth in Samoa.

certificate level in 1966, 5 belonged to the churches, the sole government school being Samoa College. The latter institution, along with 3 mission schools, also provides sixth-form instruction leading to New Zealand university entrance.

Samoan culture and Christianity have become so intertwined that it is virtually impossible to separate them. Not only does almost the entire population claim to be Christian, but also in some villages non-churchgoing is regarded as anti-social and fines are still levied for failure to attend church services.

INTERDENOMINATIONAL ORGANIZATIONS. The Fellowship of Christian Churches in Samoa (FCCS) has recently been formed, with Anglican, Catholic, Congregational and Methodist churches as full members and Seventh-day Adventists as associates. A notable feature is the new atmosphere of cordial relations being developed between Protestants and Catholics. The Week of Prayer for Christian Unity is observed, and there is a joint quarterly meeting of the leaders of Congregational, Methodist and Catholic theological colleges. These 3 denominations are also participating in a Christian Action Committee, the result of a visit to Samoa by the Pacific Islands Christian Education Curriculum Team.

BROADCASTING. Daily morning devotionals and Sunday evening programmes are prepared by 6 churches in rotation for broadcast over the government radio station. For Catholics, an association grouping Samoa with Tonga, Wallis and Futuna and the Cook Islands is a member of UNDA.

**BIBLIOGRAPHY**
'The great Samoan awakening of 1839', A.G. Daws, *Journal of the Polynesian Society*, LXX, 3 (September, 1961), 326–337.
'The Joe Gimlet or Siovili cult: an episode in the religious history of early Samoa', in J.D. Freeman & W.R. Geddes (eds), *Anthropology in the South Seas* (New Plymouth, 1959), p.185–198.
'Two webs meet', chapter 4 in A.R. Tippett, *People movements in Southern Polynesia* (Chicago: Moody Press, 1971), p.111–136.

TABLE 2. ORGANIZED CHURCHES AND DENOMINATIONS IN WESTERN SAMOA

| Official name 1 | Begun 2 | Type 3 | Counc 4 | Congs 5 | Adults 6 | Affiliated 7 | Names, notes, and other statistics (see Codebook) 8 |
|---|---|---|---|---|---|---|---|
| Anglican Church (D Polynesia) | | A Hig | swpKC | 5 | 150 | 350 | Part of CPNZ. 57% European, 35% part-Samoan, 6% Samoan. 1x,W=40%,3Y,4y. |
| Assemblies of God in Samoa | 1928 | P Pe2 | ZF... | 31 | 2,608 | 3,000 | M=AoG(USA). Classical Pentecostals. Rapid expansion after 1970. HQ Apia. 52n,2f. |
| Catholic Ch: D Samoa & Tokelau (Apia) | 1845 | R Lat | PzPYC | 18 | 15,500 | 29,830 | 1957, suffragan of M Suva (Fiji). C=1+1+4. 9n,25x,26m,109w.P=78%,1p,1837Yy. |
| Christian Brethren | | P CBr | x.... | 3 | 150 | 300 | *Plymouth Brethren. Open Brethren. Gospel Halls.* |
| Ch of Jesus C of Latter-day Saints | 1888 | M LdS | x.... | | 15,000 | 21,537 | *Mormons.* M=CJCLdS(USA). 81% Samoans, 17% part-Samoans, 140 Whites. 350f,G=3.0%pa. |
| Church of the Nazarene | 1960 | P Hol | xF... | 3 | 100 | 300 | A home mission district of M=CoN(USA), still regarded as pioneer area. 4n,SS=350. |
| Congregational Christian Ch in Samoa | 1830 | P Con | RWP,C | 244 | 19,000 | 60,000 | *CCCS. Ekalesia Faapotopotoga Kerisiano i Samoa.* M=LMS/CWM(UK). 18n,3x,1s,W=95%. |
| Congregational Church of Jesus Christ | 1846 | I Con | .v... | | 300 | 600 | *Ponesi's Church. Ch of JC in Samoa.* Schism ex CCCS. Many now returned to CCCS. |
| Jehovah's Witnesses | 1938 | M Jeh | x.... | 1 | 109 | 200 | Placed under Australian branch in 1938. First active witnessing 1951. 17Y. |
| Makisua's Church | | I pen | ..... | | 50 | 100 | Schism ex Assemblies of God. Small Samoan indigenous pentecostal group. |
| Methodist Church of Samoa | 1827 | P Met | VuP,C | 103 | 9,424 | 15,000 | *Lotu Tonga/Ch of Tonga* (first workers Tongans). 161n,673m,3p,1s(34),W=93%,899Yy. |
| Samoan Full Gospel Church | c1965 | I pen | ..... | | 50 | 100 | Indigenous pentecostal body. Samoans. Branch also in American Samoa. |
| Seventh-day Adventist Church | 1895 | P Adv | x...c | 11 | 1,500 | 2,800 | *SDA, Samoa Mission.* Central Pacific UM. Rapid growth. 6nx,41mw,2r,54t(2755),188Y. |
| United Pentecostal Church | c1965 | P Pe1 | x.... | 15 | 395 | 600 | *Jesus Only Church.* M=UPC(USA). Unitarian Pentecostals. 5n,2f,1p(16). |
| Other Protestant denominations | | P | ..... | | 200 | 500 | Including Church of Christ, United Missionary Fellowship (1 church, 2 workers). |
| | | | | | | | |
| Total affiliated (mid-1970) | | | | 665 | 64,536 | 135,217 | Total denominations (1970) . . . 16. |
| Total affiliated (mid-1975) | | | | 740 | 74,600 | 156,400 | Total denominations (1975) . . . 18. |
| Total affiliated (mid-1980) | | | | 820 | 87,900 | 184,100 | Total denominations (1980) . . . 20. |

**NOTES ON TABLE ABOVE**
COLUMNS: for meanings and CODES (cols. 1, 3, 4, 8): see Codebook (Part 6). Column 1: **Boldface type** = church with over 10% of country's affiliated Christians.
NATIONAL COUNCILS (Column 4, 5th letter).
C = Fellowship of Christian Churches in Samoa (FCCS) (National Council of Christian Churches in Samoa).
c = related to FCCS.

PEOPLES (ethnolinguistic). Christians: 89.0% Samoan, 10.1% Euronesian, 0.6% European (White), 0.3% other Pacific islander,

Chinese, Maori.

COUNTRY-WIDE TOTALS
EVANGELIZATION (see Part 5). 1900: 100%. 1970: 100%. 1980: 100%. *Radiophonic evangelism.* FEBC, TWR, ICI (4,445 enrolments, 55 conversions reported), et alia.
FOREIGN MISSIONARIES AND PERSONNEL (nationals serving abroad) (1973). Total 162 in 18 countries: about 105 marginal Protestants (Mormons) in 11 countries, 57 Protestants in 13 countries. Over the years since 1839, over 210 Samoan Congregationalists have served overseas as foreign missionaries

to other islands.
FOREIGN MISSIONARIES AND PERSONNEL (aliens from abroad) (1973). Total 508. *From Western world.* 447: about 300 marginal Protestants (290 Mormons from USA, New Zealand et alia), about 140 Roman Catholics, 7 Protestants (5 in 1 Australia society, 2 in 1 USA society). *From Third World.* 61: about 40 marginal Protestants (Mormons) from Tonga, Philippines, Fiji et alia, about 20 Roman Catholics from Wallis & Futuna et alia, 1 Anglican. By 1975, 2 Protestants from Korea were also at work.
INSTITUTIONS (church-operated) (1973). Total 18, including 13 higher schools (1 minor seminary), 1 lay training centre,

2 seminaries (Protestant).
PERIODICALS. About 14 titles (including 6 SDA, 1 LdS).
PERSONNEL. About 1,624 (1,116 national, 508 foreign).
RELIGIOUS LIBRARIES. 3.
SCRIPTURE DISTRIBUTION (1975). Annual totals: 8,000 Bibles (subsidized), 1,200 NTs (92% subsidized, 8% commercial), 2,700 UBS portions, 16,700 UBS selections. *Translations completed.* Samoan: portion in 1836, NT 1846, Bible 1855.
SERVICE AGENCIES. About 12, including FCCS, SHSW, YWAM.

### ADDITIONAL DATA ON CHURCHES

CATHOLIC CHURCH. In Samoan: Lotu Katoliko, or Ekalesia Katoliko. Alternative names: Diocese (in Samoan, Puleaga) of Samoa and Tokelau, formerly D Apia until 1975. The diocese includes American Samoa and the Tokelau Islands. *Annual baptisms.* (1972) 85.7% infant, 14.3% adult. *Priests.* 5 diocesan,

29 religious. In 1968 the first indigenous bishop in Oceania was consecrated bishop of Apia. *Seminarians.* 9 diocesan, 3 religious; training in Suva (Fiji) and New Zealand. *Catechists.* Total (1971) 126, rising (1974) to 135. The catechist training school is at Moamoa on Upolu. *Foreign religious congregations.* Priests: SM. Brothers: Marist Brothers. Sisters: Missionary Sisters of the Society of Mary, Discalced Carmelite Nuns, Sisters of Our Lady of Nazareth, Sisters of Our Lady of the Missions.
*Catholic organizations.* The diocese is represented on the Episcopal Conference of the Pacific (CEPAC); and in 1970, a Senate of Priests was formed. The principal lay organizations are: Full-time Catechists Association (Fesoasoani Kotoliko), Laymen's Council (Fono Aofia), St Anne's Society of Catholic Mothers (Sagata Ana), Sacred Heart Society of Women (Finagalo Paia) and Legion of Mary (Autau a Maria).
The Holy See has no diplomatic relations with Western Samoa. It is represented to the Catholic hierarchy by the Apostolic

Delegation to New Zealand and the Islands of the Pacific, based on Wellington, New Zealand.
In 1973 the Catechetical School of Moamoa was selected by CEPAC as the training centre for permanent deacons for all the member dioceses of CEPAC.
The diocese of Apia supervises 18 primary and 6 secondary schools, 7 of which are staffed entirely by Samoan teachers, together with 10 homes for the aged. The church is also co-operating with government and the Food and Agriculture Organization (FAO) in a major socio-economic development plan for land reform.
CONGREGATIONAL|CHRISTIAN|CHURCH|IN|SAMOA. The church, which became autonomous in 1942 and received its present name in 1961, has long operated extensive foreign mission work in other territories overseas.

# SAN MARINO

## SECULAR DATA

STATE. Official name: The Most Serene Republic of San Marino (La Repubblica di San Marino). Adjective of nationality: Sanmarinese.
Flag (shown above right): White stripe over blue stripe with national coat of arms in centre.
Area: 61 sq.km. (23.6 sq.miles). Agricultural land: 16.7%.
Government: Parliamentary republic, since Independence recognized by the pope in 1631 (AD 301 founded as republic). Legislature: Grand and General Council, 60 members.
Official language: Italian (*Italiano*).

Capital: San Marino 5,223 (1973).

DEMOGRAPHY. Population: 12,100 (census of 28.IX.1947. For 1970–2000 (UN), see last row of Table 1). Some 20,000 citizens live abroad. Population density (1975): 328/sq.km. (849/sq.mile). Under 15 years: 25%. Growth rate (1975–80): 0.87% per year. Household size: 3.6 persons.
Major language: Italian.
Urban dwellers (1970): 92.4%.
Tourists (1970): 2,343,700. (1974): 2,202,113.

ETHNOLINGUISTIC GROUPS: 99.9% Italian.

MONEY (1977). Monetary unit: San Marino lira (= 100 centesimi); US$1 = SML 650.3.
National income per person: US$3,400. Average annual family income: US$12,240.

EDUCATION. Adult literacy: 100%. Education rate: 40%. Schools: 19.

LITERATURE. Periodicals: 8. Newspapers: 5 non-daily.

COMMUNICATION (per 1,000 people). Phones: 300. Radios: 196. TV sets: 126. Daily newspaper circulation: 350 copies.

### TABLE 1. RELIGIOUS ADHERENTS IN SAN MARINO

| Year<br>Name | 1900<br>Adherents | %  | mid-1970<br>Adherents | %  | Annual change, 1970–1980<br>Natural | Conversion | Total | Rate | mid-1975<br>Adherents | %  | mid-1980<br>Adherents | %  | 2000<br>Adherents | %  |
|---|---|---|---|---|---|---|---|---|---|---|---|---|---|---|
| Christians | 8,000 | 100.0 | 18,230 | 95.9 | 191 | −14 | 177 | 0.92 | 19,120 | 95.6 | 20,000 | 95.2 | 23,300 | 93.2 |
| professing | 8,000 | 100.0 | 18,230 | 95.9 | 191 | −14 | 177 | 0.92 | 19,120 | 95.6 | 20,000 | 95.2 | 23,300 | 93.2 |
| Roman Catholics | 8,000 | 100.0 | 18,230 | 95.9 | 191 | −14 | 177 | 0·92 | 19,120 | 95.6 | 20,000 | 95.2 | 23,300 | 93.2 |
| nominal | 0 | 0.0 | 200 | 1.1 | 3 | 13 | 16 | 5.71 | 280 | 1.4 | 360 | 1.7 | 800 | 3.2 |
| affiliated | 8,000 | 100.0 | 18,030 | 94.9 | 188 | −27 | 161 | 0.85 | 18,840 | 94.2 | 19,640 | 93.5 | 22,500 | 90.0 |
| total practising | 7,600 | 95 | 16,230 | 90 | 169 | −24 | 145 | 0.85 | 16,960 | 90 | 17,680 | 90 | 18,000 | 80 |
| non-practising | 400 | 5 | 1,800 | 10 | 19 | −3 | 16 | 0.85 | 1,880 | 10 | 1,960 | 10 | 4,500 | 20 |
| Roman Catholics | 8,000 | 100.0 | 18,000 | 94.7 | 188 | −30 | 158 | 0.84 | 18,800 | 94.0 | 19,580 | 93.2 | 22,300 | 89.2 |
| Marginal Protestants | 0 | 0.0 | 30 | 0.2 | 0 | 3 | 3 | 7.50 | 40 | 0.2 | 60 | 0.3 | 200 | 0.8 |
| Non-religious | 0 | 0.0 | 500 | 2.6 | 6 | 7 | 13 | 2.32 | 560 | 2.8 | 630 | 3.0 | 1,000 | 4.0 |
| Atheists | 0 | 0.0 | 200 | 1.1 | 2 | 5 | 7 | 2.92 | 240 | 1.2 | 270 | 1.3 | 500 | 2.0 |
| Baha'is | 0 | 0.0 | 70 | 0.4 | 1 | 2 | 3 | 3.75 | 80 | 0.4 | 100 | 0.5 | 200 | 0.8 |
| Country's population | 8,000 | 100.0 | 19,000 | 100.0 | 200 | 0 | 200 | 1.00 | 20,000 | 100.0 | 21,000 | 100.0 | 25,000 | 100.0 |

COLUMNS, ROWS. For meanings and definitions, see Codebook (Part 6). Note that, by definition, total 'Christians' = professing + crypto-Christians, which also = affiliated + nominal Christians. Percentages may not always total exactly,

due to rounding.

#### NOTES ON RELIGIONS
ATHEISTS. Partito Comunista di San Marino (PCSM): membership (1974) 1,000. Many members remain practising Catholics.

BAHA'IS. In 1 local spiritual assembly (1973).
PRACTISING CHRISTIANS. The table enumerates residents only. In addition, large numbers of the 2 million tourists annually attend churches in San Marino during their visits.

## CHRISTIANITY

CATHOLIC CHURCH. The history of the church goes back at least to AD 441 when a hermitage was built. Today, the Republic of San Marino is part of the 2 Italian dioceses of Montefeltro (Conciliar Region of Marche) and of Rimini (Conciliar Region of Romagna/Flaminia). The population is almost entirely Catholic. In 1972 there were 12 parishes, 8 in the diocese of Montefeltro and 4 in the diocese of Rimini. Male religious congregations include OFM (3 members), OFMCap (4), OFMConv (3) and OSM (2). Female religious congregations include Clarisses (19 contemplative sisters), Maestre Pie dell'Addolorata (16) and Figlie di Santa Anna.
OTHER CHURCHES. Jehovah's Witnesses are

**Chiesa Cattolica.** Basilica of San Marino. The church's history dates back to AD 441.

the only organized non-Catholic religious body in the republic. Beginning in the 1960s, the Witnesses have built up a small community. Another body is the Seventh-day Adventist Church which, although it has no organized work, has since 1933 regularly sent in colporteurs to distribute SDA publications.

CHURCH AND STATE. The law as it relates to

Many postage stamps carry Christian themes: here (at Christmas 1967) the Cimabue Crucifix in Florence.

religious matters is more customary than codified. There is no specific treaty between the Republic of San Marino and the Holy See. Religious marriages have civil significance because they are recorded in state registers. Non-Catholic religious bodies are free to practise their worship without the requirement of government registration.

### TABLE 2. ORGANIZED CHURCHES AND DENOMINATIONS IN SAN MARINO

| Official name<br>1 | Begun<br>2 | Type<br>3 | Counc<br>4 | Congs<br>5 | Adults<br>6 | Affiliated<br>7 | Names, notes, and other statistics (see Codebook)<br>8 |
|---|---|---|---|---|---|---|---|
| Chiesa Cattolica | 441 | R Lat | B,B.. | 12 | 12,000 | 18,000 | *Catholic Ch.* Parts in D Montefeltro and in D Rimini(Italy). C=4+0+3. 12nx,40w,1H. |
| Testimoni di Geova | c1965 | M Jeh | x.... | 1 | 25 | 30 | *Jehovah's Witnesses.* First activity 1969. 1971 Circuit Assembly: 1,749 present. 4Y. |
| Total affiliated (mid-1970) | | | | 13 | 12,025 | 18,030 | Total denominations (1970) . . . 2. |
| Total affiliated (mid-1975) | | | | 13 | 12,560 | 18,840 | Total denominations (1975) . . . 2. |
| Total affiliated (mid-1980) | | | | 13 | 13,100 | 19,640 | Total denominations (1980) . . . 2. |

**NOTES ON TABLE ABOVE**
COLUMNS: for meanings and CODES (cols. 1, 3, 4, 8): see Codebook, (Part 6). Column 1: **Boldface type** = church with over 10% of country's affiliated Christians.

PEOPLES (ethnolinguistic). Christians: 99.9% Italian.

**COUNTRY-WIDE TOTALS**
EVANGELIZATION (see Part 5). 1900: 100%. 1970: 100%. 1980: 100%.
FOREIGN MISSIONARIES AND PERSONNEL (aliens from abroad) (1973). Total 20. *From Western world.* About 20 Roman Catholics.
INSTITUTIONS (church-operated) (1973). Total 1 hospital.
PERIODICALS. 2 titles.

PERSONNEL. About 22 (2 national, 20 foreign).
SCRIPTURE DISTRIBUTION (1975). Annual totals: 60 Bibles (subsidized), 60 NTs (subsidized).

**ADDITIONAL DATA ON CHURCHES**
CATHOLIC CHURCH. *Catholic organizations.* In 1972 the church was responsible for 4 nursery schools (over 300 infants), one hospital and one home for the aged.

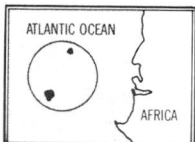

# São Tomé & Príncipe

## SECULAR DATA

STATE. Official name: The Democratic Republic of São Tomé and Príncipe (A República Democratica de São Tomé e Principe).
Flag (shown above right): Stripes of green, yellow, and green with red triangle at hoist; 2 black stars on centre yellow stripe.
Area: 964 sq.km. (372 sq.miles). Agricultural land: 32.3%.
Government: One-party socialist state, since 1975 (1470 Portuguese possession, 1951 overseas province of Portugal, 1975 Independence).
Official language: Portuguese (*Português*).
Capital: São Tomé 5,714 (1960).

DEMOGRAPHY. Population: 73,811 (census of 30.IX.1970). For 1970–2000 (UN), see last row of Table 1). Population density (1975): 83/sq.km. (215/sq.mile). Under 15 years: 40%. Growth rate (1975–80): 1.21% per year. Household size: 4.9 persons.
Major languages: Portuguese, Fang.
Urban dwellers (1970): 20.5%. Urban growth rate (1950–70): 1.3% per year.
Tourists: numerous.

ETHNOLINGUISTIC GROUPS: 90.9% Bantu (Fang), 7.1% Mestiço (Portuguese/Black), 1.9% White (Portuguese).

MONEY (1977). Monetary unit: São Tomé & Príncipe escudo (= 100 centavos); US$1 = STPEsc 25.41.
National income per person: US$400. Average annual family income: US$1,960.
Cost of living in capital (1976): Daily cost of living: US$32.

HEALTH. Hospitals: 54 (1,997 beds). Doctors: 17. Lepers: 120 (1.5 per 1,000). Blind: 200.

EDUCATION. Schools: 48.

LITERATURE. Newspapers: 2 non-daily.

COMMUNICATION (per 1,000 people). Phones: 8. Radios: 96.

TABLE 1.    RELIGIOUS ADHERENTS IN SAO TOME & PRINCIPE

| Year | 1900 | | mid-1970 | | Annual change, 1970–1980 | | | | mid-1975 | | mid-1980 | | 2000 | |
|---|---|---|---|---|---|---|---|---|---|---|---|---|---|---|
| Name | Adherents | % | Adherents | % | Natural | Conversion | Total | Rate | Adherents | % | Adherents | % | Adherents | % |
| **Christians** | 1,250 | 3.1 | 71,750 | 97.2 | 1,092 | 45 | 1,137 | 1.46 | 78,010 | 97.5 | 83,120 | 97.8 | 86,920 | 98.8 |
| professing | 1,250 | 3.1 | 71,750 | 97.2 | 1,092 | 45 | 1,137 | 1.46 | 78,010 | 97.5 | 83,120 | 97.8 | 86,920 | 98.8 |
| Roman Catholics | 1,250 | 3.1 | 68,050 | 92.2 | 1,034 | 14 | 1,048 | 1.42 | 73,850 | 92.3 | 78,530 | 92.4 | 81,460 | 92.6 |
| African indigenous | 0 | 0.0 | 2,200 | 3.0 | 35 | 17 | 52 | 2.10 | 2,480 | 3.1 | 2,720 | 3.2 | 3,170 | 3.6 |
| Protestants | 0 | 0.0 | 1,500 | 2.0 | 23 | 14 | 37 | 2.20 | 1,680 | 2.1 | 1,870 | 2.2 | 2,290 | 2.6 |
| nominal | 250 | 0.6 | 6,030 | 8.2 | 96 | 66 | 162 | 2.35 | 6,880 | 8.6 | 7,650 | 9.0 | 9,680 | 11.0 |
| affiliated | 1,000 | 2.5 | 65,720 | 89.0 | 996 | −21 | 975 | 1.37 | 71,130 | 88.9 | 75,470 | 88.8 | 77,240 | 87.8 |
| total practising | 900 | 90 | 52,580 | 80 | 797 | −17 | 780 | 1.37 | 56,900 | 80 | 60,380 | 80 | 54,070 | 70 |
| non-practising | 100 | 10 | 13,140 | 20 | 199 | −4 | 195 | 1.37 | 14,230 | 20 | 15,090 | 20 | 23,170 | 30 |
| Roman Catholics | 1,000 | 2.5 | 62,720 | 85.0 | 949 | −48 | 901 | 1.33 | 67,770 | 84.7 | 71,730 | 84.4 | 71,700 | 81.5 |
| African indigenous | 0 | 0.0 | 2,000 | 2.7 | 31 | 15 | 46 | 2.05 | 2,240 | 2.8 | 2,460 | 2.9 | 3,780 | 4.3 |
| Protestants | 0 | 0.0 | 1,000 | 1.3 | 16 | 12 | 28 | 2.50 | 1,120 | 1.4 | 1,280 | 1.5 | 1,760 | 2.0 |
| Evangelicals | 0 | 0.0 | 700 | 0.9 | 11 | 9 | 20 | 2.50 | 800 | 1.0 | 900 | 1.1 | 1,400 | 1.6 |
| Tribal religionists | 38,750 | 96.9 | 2,000 | 2.7 | 27 | −48 | −21 | −1.09 | 1,920 | 2.4 | 1,790 | 2.1 | 880 | 1.0 |
| Baha'is | 0 | 0.0 | 50 | 0.1 | 1 | 3 | 4 | 5.71 | 70 | 0.1 | 90 | 0.1 | 200 | 0.2 |
| Country's population | 40,000 | 100.0 | 73,800 | 100.0 | 1,120 | 0 | 1,120 | 1.40 | 80,000 | 100.0 | 85,000 | 100.0 | 88,000 | 100.0 |

COLUMNS, ROWS. For meanings and definitions, see Codebook (Part 6). Note that, by definition, total 'Christians' = professing + crypto-Christians, which also = affiliated + nominal Christians. Percentages may not always total exactly, due to rounding.

**NOTES ON RELIGIONS**
AFRICAN INDIGENOUS. In one denomination in 1970 (see Table 2).

TRIBAL RELIGIONISTS. Animists among the indigenous and immigrant Bantu population.

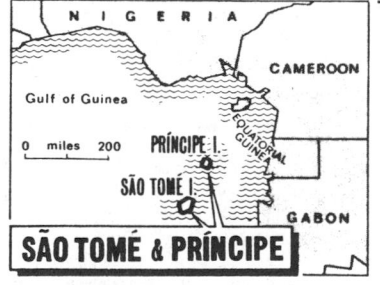

**NON-CHRISTIAN RELIGIONS. Traditional religions** have nearly disappeared, remaining mainly as a sub-stratum underlying the beliefs of professing Christians. In 1900, adherents of traditional religions were estimated at 97% of the population, falling to 17% by 1964 and to under 2.5% by 1975 as a result of Catholic evangelistic activity among immigrant Bantu.

## CHRISTIANITY

CATHOLIC CHURCH. From the end of the 15th century, São Tomé and Príncipe served as a strategic supply centre for the Portuguese exploration of southern Africa and the later trade route to India. Pope Paul III erected a diocese for the territory in 1534; at first it was attached to the ecclesiastical province of Funchal (Madeira); then it became a suffragan diocese of, successively, Lisbon, Baia de Todos-os-Santos (Brazil), Lisbon again, and finally Luanda in 1940. It was originally responsible for all islands from Cape Palmas to the Cape of Good Hope, but these were transferred to the new diocese of Angola and the Congo in 1596. There has been no resident bishop since 1816. The diocese has been administered since 1940 by the archbishop of Luanda through a vicar-general. Catholics made up 92% of the population in 1970.

From 1975, all Portuguese overseas territories, which were formerly under the Council for the Public Affairs of the Church, in Rome began to be transferred to Propaganda (SC for the Evangelization of Peoples).

OTHER CHURCHES. The Evangelical Church

Emergency relief supplies from international and Christian agencies being loaded in São Tomé for airfreighting to Eastern Nigeria at height of Biafran civil war in 1969.

was created entirely through indigenous efforts. The church was planted by an Angolan Christian exiled for penal servitude to São Tomé during the 1930s. The first scriptures and hymnbook were written down from memory. In 1957, an African Methodist missionary was sponsored by the Evangelical Alliance of Angola for work with indigenous Christians, and in 1960 another African missionary was sent from the Evangelical Church of Central Angola. Political conditions made further contacts between the 2 churches difficult. There were in 1975 2 congregations on São Tomé and one on Príncipe. In 1964 Protestants and African indigenous Christians numbered 4% of the population, with little change subsequently.

Portuguese Seventh-day Adventists first appeared on São Tomé in 1938, and in 1947 organized the St

Official postage stamps depicting (top) a Roman Catholic village church (1960), and (bottom) 1951 Exhibition of Missionary Art.

Thomas Island Mission as part of their Angola Union Mission. There are now 6 preaching places on São Tomé and one on Príncipe.

CHURCH AND STATE. Prior to 1974 relations between church and state were governed, as with all Portuguese overseas territories, by the 1940 concordat signed between the Portuguese government and the Holy See. São Tomé was for many years the penal colony for Angola, a fact which contributed to the spread of Protestantism.

## BIBLIOGRAPHY

*Atlas missionário português.* A. Rego & E. do Santos. Lisboa: Junta de Investigações do Ultramar, 1964. (Map of all mission stations on São Tomé and Princípe, history and statistics).
*Boletim eclesiástico de Angola e São Tomé.* Ano XXIII–XXIV. Luanda: Missões Católicas Portuguesas, 1965. 234p.

TABLE 2. ORGANIZED CHURCHES AND DENOMINATIONS IN SAO TOME & PRINCIPE

| Official name 1 | Begun 2 | Type 3 | Counc 4 | Congs 5 | Adults 6 | Affiliated 7 | Names, notes, and other statistics (see Codebook) 8 |
|---|---|---|---|---|---|---|---|
| Assembleias de Deus | | P Pe2 | ••••• | 6 | 140 | 500 | *Assemblies of God.* Local leadership; large 800-seat temple in city. |
| Igreja Adventista do Sétimo Dia | 1938 | P Adv | x•••• | 7 | 200 | 500 | *Seventh-day Adventists, St Thomas Island Mission*, Angola UM. 1x,7m,8t(495),30Y. |
| **Igreja Católica: D São Tomé & Príncipe** | 1534 | R Lat | H,S,P | 15 | 38,000 | 62,720 | *Catholic Ch.* Suffragan of M Luanda. 96% Catholic. C=1+0+2. 15x,2m,16w,1250Yy,580z. |
| Igreja Evangélica | c1935 | I int | ••••• | 3 | 1,000 | 2,000 | Begun by Angolan exiled to São Tomé. Later assisted by African Protestants. |
| **Total affiliated (mid-1970)** | | | | **31** | **39,340** | **65,720** | **Total denominations (1970) . . . 3.** |
| **Total affiliated (mid-1975)** | | | | **32** | **42,580** | **71,130** | **Total denominations (1975) . . . 3.** |
| **Total affiliated (mid-1980)** | | | | **33** | **45,180** | **75,470** | **Total denominations (1980) . . . 3.** |

NOTES ON TABLE ABOVE
COLUMNS: for meanings and CODES (cols. 1, 3, 4, 8): see Codebook, (Part 6). Column 1: **Boldface type** = church with over 10% of country's affiliated Christians.
NATIONAL COUNCILS (Column 4, 5th letter).
P = Conferência Episcopal de Angola e São Tomé (CEAST) (Episcopal Conference of Angola & São Tomé).

PEOPLES (ethnolinguistic). Christians: 90.9% Bantu (Fang), 7.1% Mestiço, 1.9% White (Portuguese).

COUNTRY-WIDE TOTALS
EVANGELIZATION (see Part 5). 1900: 14%. 1970: 100%. 1980: 100%.
FOREIGN MISSIONARIES AND PERSONNEL (aliens from abroad) (1973). Total 36. *From Western world.* 31: about 30 Roman Catholics, 1 Protestant in 1 USA society. *From Third World.* About 5 mainly Roman Catholics from Angola.
INSTITUTIONS (church-operated) (1973). Total 1 higher school.
PERIODICALS. 1 title.
PERSONNEL. About 46 (10 national, 36 foreign).
SCRIPTURE DISTRIBUTION (1975). Annual totals: 500 Bibles (subsidized), 300 NTs (commercial).
SERVICE AGENCIES. About 5, including CEAST.

ADDITIONAL DATA ON CHURCHES
IGREJA CATOLICA. Before 1977, the diocese (erected 1534) was a suffragan of M Luanda. From February 1977 it was made immediately subject to the Holy See. *Annual baptisms.* (1972) 98.5% infant, 1.5% adult. *Personnel.* Virtually all metropolitan Portuguese. No diocesan clergy. *Indigenous religious congregations.* None. *Foreign congregations.* Priests: CMF (Portuguese province). Sisters: Portuguese Franciscan Hospital Sisters, Canossians (Daughters of Charity, Italy). *Catholic organizations.* São Tomé and Príncipe are included in the Episcopal Conference of Angola and São Tomé (Conferência Episcopal de Angola e São Tomé, CEAST) with headquarters in Luanda, which is a member of SECAM. There is no presbyteral or pastoral council, nor organizations of religious personnel, but lay activity is carried on in the form of Catholic Action and pious associations.
Until 1975 the Holy See had diplomatic relations with Portugal. Since Independence the Holy See has been represented to the Catholic hierarchy by an apostolic delegate residing in Dakar.

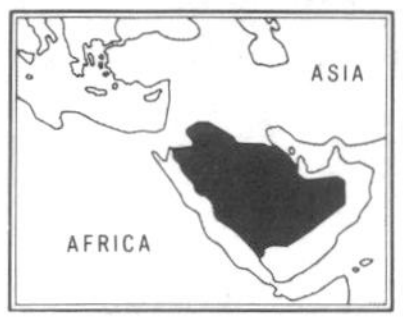


# SAUDI ARABIA

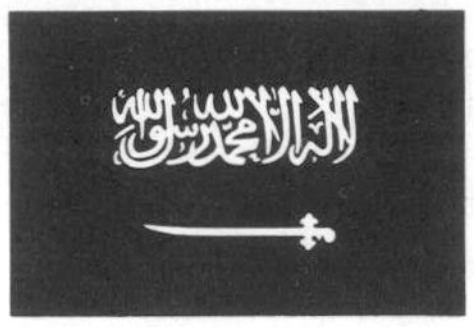

## SECULAR DATA

**STATE. Official name:** The Kingdom of Saudi Arabia (Al-Mamlakah al-Arabiyah as-Saudiyah). Adjective of nationality: Saudi Arabian, Saudi.
**Flag** (shown above right): Green, with inscription 'There is no god but Allah and Mohammed is His prophet' in white Arabic characters above white sword.
**Area:** 2,149,690 sq.km. (830,000 sq.miles). Agricultural land 39.9%.
**Government:** Absolute monarchy, since 1932 (7th century in Arab empire, c1500 under Ottoman empire, 1905 Nejd recaptured, 1927 Independence endorsed by Britain, 1932 unified Saudi Arabian Kingdom proclaimed).
**Legislature:** Council of Ministers, Legislative Assembly in Mecca.
**Official language:** Arabic.
**Chief cities:** capital Riyadh 225,000 (1965), Mecca 300,000, Jidda 194,000.
**Armed forces** (1976): Total 51,500 regular: army 40,000, navy 1,500, air force 10,000 (97 combat aircraft). Paramilitary forces: 26,500.
**Foreign forces** (1973): 250 USA troops.

**DEMOGRAPHY. Population:** 7,012,642 (census of 9–14.IX.1974. For 1970–2000 including immigrants, see last row of Table 1). Population density (1975): 4/sq.km (11/sq.mile). Under 15 years: 43%. Growth rate (1970–80): 3.49% per year (births 4.83%, deaths –1.82%, immigrants 0.48%). Life expectancy (1975–80): 47.8 years. Household size: 5.2 persons.
**Major languages:** Arabic, Persian, Hindi, Chinese, English, Korean, Turkish, Indonesian, Mahri, Shakari, and numerous smaller languages.
**Urban dwellers** (1970): 23.6%. Urban growth rate (1950–70): 6.5% per year.
**Labour force:** 28%.
**Refugees:** Rapid increase of Palestinians to (1974) 200,000.

**ETHNOLINGUISTIC GROUPS:** (1970) 97.0% Arab (over 60 Saudi tribes including Bedouin nomad (300,000), 20.0% Yemeni, 0.3% Palestinian (20,000), Egyptian, Jordanian, Lebanese, Syrian), 1.2% Black African (Bantu), 0.7% Persian, 0.5% Indo-Pakistani, 0.4% Chinese (30,000), 0.2% USA (rising to 30,000 by 1977), Indonesian, British (3,800), Italian, Korean, Turkish, Sudanese, Somali, Baluchi, Malay, Mahra (Australoid Veddoids speaking Semitic languages), Shahara, & other smaller groups. From 1975–80, the state development plan encouraged 500,000 more immigrant foreign workers (Arabs, Pakistanis, 20,000 Koreans, et alii).

**MONEY** (1977). **Monetary unit:** Saudi riyal (= 20 quirsh = 100 hallalas); US$1 = SAR 3.55.
**National incomr per person:** US$3,700. Average annual family income: US$19,240.
**Inflation:** (1970–74) 40% per year (1975 consumer price index 229).
**Cost of living in capital** (1976): index 123 (Washington DC=100). Daily cost of living: US$31.

**HEALTH.** Hospitals: 71 (9,136 beds). Doctors: 2,000. Lepers: 960 (0.1 per 1,000). Blind: 230,000. Psychotics: 65,000. Criminals: 3,000.

**EDUCATION.** Adult literacy: (1962) 3%, (1970) 10%. Education rate: 20%. Schools: 2,467. Universities: 3.

**LITERATURE.** Annual new book titles (1973): 82. Periodicals: 10. Newspapers: 7 dailies, 5 non-daily.

**COMMUNICATION** (per 1,000 people). Phones: 1. Radios: 11. TV sets: 2. Daily newspaper circulation: 7 copies.

TABLE 1. RELIGIOUS ADHERENTS IN SAUDI ARABIA

| Year | 1900 | | mid-1970 | | Annual change, 1970–1980 | | | | mid-1975 | | mid-1980 | | 2000 | |
|---|---|---|---|---|---|---|---|---|---|---|---|---|---|---|
| *Name* | *Adherents* | % | *Adherents* | % | *Natural* | *Conversion* | *Total* | *Rate* | *Adherents* | % | *Adherents* | % | *Adherents* | % |
| Muslims | 2,729,950 | 100.0 | 7,684,700 | 99.3 | 309,182 | –852 | 308,330 | 3.44 | 8,964,900 | 99.1 | 10,768,000 | 98.8 | 20,107,000 | 98.1 |
| **Christians** | **50** | **0.0** | **24,900** | **0.3** | **5,800** | **610** | **6,410** | **13.08** | **49,000** | **0.5** | **89,000** | **0.8** | **307,000** | **1.5** |
| crypto-Christians | 50 | 0.0 | 16,900 | 0.2 | 4,100 | 610 | 4,710 | 13.85 | 34,000 | 0.4 | 64,000 | 0.6 | 227,000 | 1.1 |
| professing | 0 | 0.0 | 8,000 | 0.1 | 1,700 | 0 | 1,700 | 11.33 | 15,000 | 0.2 | 25,000 | 0.2 | 80,000 | 0.4 |
| Protestants | 0 | 0.0 | 6,000 | 0.1 | 400 | 0 | 400 | 5.00 | 8,000 | 0.1 | 10,000 | 0.1 | 20,000 | 0.1 |
| Roman Catholics | 0 | 0.0 | 2,000 | 0.0 | 800 | 0 | 800 | 16.00 | 5,000 | 0.1 | 10,000 | 0.1 | 40,000 | 0.2 |
| Orthodox | 0 | 0.0 | 0 | 0.0 | 500 | 0 | 500 | 25.00 | 2,000 | 0.0 | 5,000 | 0.0 | 20,000 | 0.1 |
| affiliated | 50 | 0.0 | 24,900 | 0.3 | 5,800 | 610 | 6,410 | 13.08 | 49,000 | 0.5 | 89,000 | 0.8 | 307,000 | 1.5 |
| total practising | 45 | *90* | 22,410 | *90* | 5,220 | 549 | 5,769 | 13.08 | 44,100 | *90* | 80,100 | *90* | 245,600 | *80* |
| non-practising | 5 | *10* | 2,490 | *10* | 580 | 61 | 641 | 13.08 | 4,900 | *10* | ·8,900 | *10* | 61,400 | *20* |
| Arab indigenous | 0 | 0.0 | 11,300 | 0.1 | 800 | 570 | 1,370 | 7.61 | 18,000 | 0.2 | 25,000 | 0.2 | 90,000 | 0.4 |
| Protestants | 0 | 0.0 | 6,950 | 0.1 | 1,280 | 0 | 1,280 | 10.80 | 11,850 | 0.1 | 19,750 | 0.2 | 49,000 | 0.2 |
| Evangelicals | 0 | 0.0 | 2,200 | 0.0 | 450 | 30 | 480 | 12.00 | 4,000 | 0.0 | 7,000 | 0.0 | 17,500 | 0.0 |
| Roman Catholics | 50 | 0.0 | 2,600 | 0.0 | 2,210 | 30 | 2,240 | 22.40 | 10,000 | 0.1 | 25,000 | 0.2 | 80,000 | 0.4 |
| Orthodox | 0 | 0.0 | 2,000 | 0.0 | 1,300 | 0 | 1,300 | 21.67 | 6,000 | 0.1 | 15,000 | 0.1 | 81,000 | 0.4 |
| Anglicans | 0 | 0.0 | 2,000 | 0.0 | 200 | 0 | 200 | 6.67 | 3,000 | 0.0 | 4,000 | 0.0 | 6,000 | 0.0 |
| Marginal Protestants | 0 | 0.0 | 50 | 0.0 | 10 | 10 | 20 | 13.33 | 150 | 0.0 | 250 | 0.0 | 1,000 | 0.0 |
| Non-religious | 0 | 0.0 | 20,000 | 0.2 | 748 | 252 | 1,000 | 4.00 | 25,000 | 0.3 | 30,000 | 0.3 | 70,000 | 0.3 |
| Buddhists | 0 | 0.0 | 5,000 | 0.1 | 5 | –5 | 0 | 0.00 | 5,000 | 0.1 | 5,000 | 0.0 | 3,000 | 0.0 |
| Chinese folk-religionists | 0 | 0.0 | 4,000 | 0.1 | –80 | –20 | –100 | –2.86 | 3,500 | 0.0 | 3,000 | 0.0 | 2,000 | 0.0 |
| Hindus | 0 | 0.0 | 1,000 | 0.0 | 305 | –5 | 300 | 15.00 | 2,000 | 0.0 | 4,000 | 0.0 | 8,000 | 0.0 |
| Baha'is | 0 | 0.0 | 400 | 0.0 | 40 | 20 | 60 | 10.00 | 600 | 0.0 | 1,000 | 0.0 | 3,000 | 0.0 |
| **Country's population** | **2,730,000** | **100.0** | **7,740,000** | **100.0** | **316,000** | **0** | **316,000** | **3.49** | **9,050,000** | **100.0** | **10,900,000** | **100.0** | **20,500,000** | **100.0** |

COLUMNS, ROWS. For meanings and definitions, see Codebook (Part 6). Note that, by definition, total 'Christians' = professing + crypto-Christians, which also = affiliated + nominal Christians. Percentages may not always total exactly, due to rounding.

NOTES ON RELIGIONS
ARAB INDIGENOUS. Small indigenous congregations and groups of 2 kinds (see Table 2): among immigrant Christian Arabs, and isolated radio believers.
BAHA'IS. Slow growth from 2 local spiritual assemblies in 1962 (Riyadh, Fahahil) with 5 other groups, to 4 local spiritual assemblies (1973); then considerable immigration.
BUDDHISTS. Chinese.
CHRISTIANS. Rapid growth since 1970, and especially 1975, is due to high immigration rate from Arab churches abroad, especially Palestine and Lebanon.
COUNTRY'S POPULATION. The totals shown from 1975 onwards include the 500,000 immigrant foreign workers called for by the 1975–80 second national development plan. By 1975 there were nearly 2 million Yemenis (mostly male labourers, without their families) and 200,000 Palestinians. By 1977 this influx had included a vast additional number of Arabs (100,000 Yemenis, 50,000 Lebanese, 50,000 Palestinians) and Pakistanis (over 50,000), 30,000 Chinese, 20,000 Koreans, 20,000 Indians, et alii. The column 'Natural change' in the table above includes the average annual immigration for 1970–80 for this row and all other rows.
CRYPTO-CHRISTIANS. Arabs. In general the state regards Europeans as the only Christians and either ignores or does not recognize Arab Christians.
HINDUS. Expatriates from India.
MUSLIMS. Almost all Sunnis (of the Shafiite rite dominant in the Hejaz and Asir, and Wahhabi (Hanbalite) reform movement in Nejd and Eastern Province, with a few Hanafite, Malikite, and other Hanbalite minorities); and also 130,000 Shias (Ismailis, known as Qarmatian schismatics, particularly Jafaris in the east, Makramis in southern Asir, and Zaydis near Mecca). Immigrant workers were initially restricted to persons from Pakistan (Sunnis) and 700,000 from North Yemen (Zaydi Shias), with Palestinians, a few Indians, Iranians, Indonesians and Turks. After 1975 Muslims were immigrating from many other countries, including 20,000 Chinese Muslims. *Hajj pilgrims to Mecca.* In 1912, these numbered 300,000; from 1920–40, the total averaged 70,000 a year (225,000 in 1927 of whom 90,662 from abroad), falling to 9,024 from abroad in 1940; 23,863 in 1941, rising to 99,069 in 1949, 164,072 in 1954, then to the following totals present during the 7-day Hajj in November-December each year: (1965), 294,118 from abroad, (1966) 316,226 from abroad, (1967) 318,507 from abroad, (1968) 692,784 total (318,000 from Saudi Arabia, 374,784 from abroad), (1969) 406,295 from abroad, (1970) 1,079,760 (648,490 from Saudi Arabia, 431,270 from abroad; of the total, 67.9% were men and 32.1% women), (1971) 1,042,027 total (562,688 from SA, 479,339 from abroad), (1972) 1,216,951 total (571,769 from SA, 645,182 from abroad), (1973) 1,122,545 (514,790 from SA, 607,755 from abroad), (1974) 1,484,975 total (566,188 from Saudi Arabia, 918,777 from abroad), (1975) 1,557,867 total (306,159 Saudis and 357,135 non-Saudis from SA, 894,573 from abroad), (1976) 1,456,432 total (302,303 Saudis and 435,089 non-Saudis from SA, 719,040 from abroad), (1977) 1,627,589 total (392,129 Saudis and 496,141 non- Saudis resident in SA, 739,319 from abroad), (1978) 1,899,420 total (400,179 Saudis and 669,005 non-Saudis resident in SA, 830,236 from abroad). These figures indicate a sharp annual rise to 1974 followed since 1974 by a gradual decline in numbers. These official statistics are divided up by immediate country of origin or departure (not by citizenship), and are reproduced in this Encyclopedia for each country under most countries' Tables 1, footnote MUSLIMS. In addition to the official Hajj period in November-December, in 1976 over a million other pilgrims came to Mecca at other times of the year. The Ministry of Hajj's target by 1980 was to make arrangements for at least 5 million pilgrims a year.
NON-RELIGIOUS. Europeans, Chinese and other expatriates.
ORTHODOX. Many expatriate Arabs (Greek, Syrian, Coptic Orthodox), with some Indians (Syrian Orthodox) and Armenians. Most are unknown to or ignored by the state.
PROTESTANTS. In 1970, the great majority were USA Whites

and British; by 1975 large numbers of Arab Protestants were arriving as immigrant workers.
ROMAN CATHOLICS. In 1973 Jeddah had one Catholic church, and Catholic activity among European expatriates there and at Dhahran was tolerated but not officially recognized. After 1975 Catholic immigrants, mostly Arabs, became numerous, but official church structures (parishes) lagged a long way behind in the interests of caution.

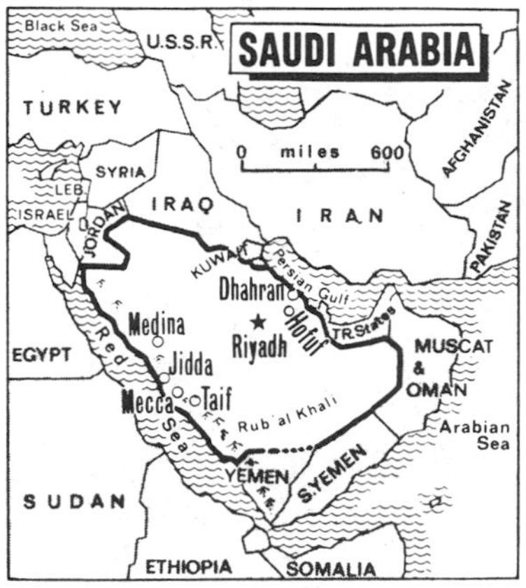


**NON-CHRISTIAN RELIGIONS. Islam** is the religion of 99% of the population. Muslims are mostly Sunnis; the Shafiite rite is dominant in the Hejaz and Asir while the Wahhabi reform movement is more important in Nejd and Eastern Province. There have always been a few Hanafite and Malikite minorities, such as at the Hofuf Oasis. In Ahsa the majority are semi-Wahhabite Hanbalites, but there also exist 60,000 Ismailis, known here as Qarmatian schismatics. Wahhabism, the Sunni sect which dominates the country, is a puritan reform movement and is intimately bound up with Saudi royalty. The Hejaz, where the holy places of Islam are located, has been increasingly closed to non-Muslims. It has become an extension of Haram, the holy land, where one comes to accomplish the Hajj, the obligatory pilgrimage of all Muslims.

Arabia is the heart of the Muslim world, Mecca and Medina being the 2 principal holy cities of Islam. The great mosque of Mecca, where the Kaaba is found, has been enlarged and now holds 300,000 people. The annual pilgrimage to Mecca attracts a growing number of foreign Muslims: 9,024 in 1940; 164,072 in 1954; 918,777 in 1974, falling to 719,040 in 1976. This increase now poses massive organizational problems for the pilgrimage only lasts 7 days.

Saudi Arabia is the headquarters for 2 of Islam's most important international organizations. (1) The Muslim World League (Rabita Al-Alam Al-Islami), founded in Mecca in 1963, is the major Muslim religious organization in the world. Its purposes are to propagate the message of Islam, to make known its teaching and doctrine and to strengthen the unity of the Muslim world. The members of its Constituent Council are chosen from among Islam's most eminent religious and cultural personalities. The League also maintains offices in a number of non-Muslim countries or countries where Islam is a minority, notably the USA (New York), Switzerland (Geneva), Denmark (Copenhagen), Nigeria, Madagascar and Thailand. In 1975 the League decided to found a World Muslim Missionary Organization and to concern itself more actively with the Muslim diaspora.

(2) The Islamic Conference, with headquarters in Jeddah, is the major Muslim political organization in the world, whose 38 member states in 1975 were as follows: Afghanistan, Algeria, Bangladesh, Bahrain, Cameroon, Chad, Egypt, Gabon, Gambia, Guinea, Guinea Bissau, Indonesia, Iran, Jordan, Kuwait, Lebanon, Libya, Malaysia, Mali, Mauritania, Morocco, Niger, Oman, Pakistan, Qatar, Saudi Arabia, Senegal, Sierra Leone, Somalia, Sudan, Syria, Tunisia, Turkey, Uganda, United Arab Emirates, Upper Volta, Yemen Arab Republic, Democratic Yemen. Its purpose is to foster solidarity and co-operation between member states. Beyond its secretary general, there is a Conference of Monarchs, consisting of heads of state and government, and a Conference of the Ministers of Foreign Affairs. In 1952 the Islamic Conference created an international Islamic press agency (IINA), with headquarters in Kuala Lumpur, Malaysia, to aid efforts in maintaining the activities of Islamic cultural centres in non-Muslim countries.

Since about 1950, Saudi Arabia has developed a vast network of teaching and religious training institutions, of which a number are open to foreigners. Of special importance are the following: (1) the Islamic University of Medina, founded in 1961, whose purpose is essentially missionary and which has admitted since its foundation students from more than 70 countries of Asia, Africa, Europe and North America; (2) Faculty of the Sharia and Islamic Studies in Mecca, which is part of the King Abdul Aziz University of Jeddah, founded in 1967; (3) Higher Institute of the Judiciary, founded in Riyadh in 1965, which trains judges with specialized competence in the diverse Islamic Sharia law rules; and (4) Islamic Jurisprudence College (or Sharia College), founded in Mecca in 1949, which trains teachers in religious and Arabic language subjects, as well as judges and missionaries. All of these institutions are self-governing or under the control of the Ministry of Education. In addition there are 2 other colleges in Riyadh and institutes in 34 different cities and towns of Saudi Arabia, under the control of the General Presidency for Institutes and colleges, the first of these institutes being founded in 1950. Plans were also announced in February 1976 for some 2 dozen Muslim organizations to co-operate in the construction of a powerful radio station in Mecca, called The Voice of Islam, to counter the influence of Christian radio programmes in Africa.

**CHRISTIANITY.** According to tradition, the Apostle Bartholomew was the first missionary to Arabia. Christianity was firmly established by AD 525, but in the 7th century it was completely vanquished by Islam.

PROTESTANT CHURCHES. Protestant work was begun in Aden as early as 1885 and carried on after 1890 in several countries of the Persian gulf by Samuel Zwemer of the American Arabian Mission. Missions have never been permitted in Saudi Arabia, however. In 1970, there were 2 small congregations of Brethren and a Church of Christ group in Dhahran, all serving expatriates, together with a large number of house groups. Since 1970, however, the situation has been dramatically altered by the enormous influx of several hundred thousand immigrant workers from many lands. A significant proportion of these have been Arab Protestants from Lebanon, Syria and Palestine, followed later by Indian Protestants, Korean Protestants and others. In 1978, a house-church in Dhahran was formed for 60 Urdu-speaking Pakistanis.

CATHOLIC CHURCH. The first Catholic of the modern era was a Servite priest who arrived in Aden in 1841. Aden was included in the vicariate of Galla in Africa in 1851, becoming a separate prefecture in 1854 and a vicariate in 1888. The vicariate of Arabia, to which Saudi Arabia belongs, was formed in 1889 and is now administered from Abu Dhabi. Saudi Arabia in 1974 was served by 3 American Capuchins based in Dhahran. In 1970 there were only some 2,600 Catholics, mostly Americans or foreign Arabs working for the ARAMCO oil company. Since 1970, there has been a large influx of Arab and other Catholics from many lands.

OTHER CHURCHES. Because of severely anti-Christian measures, prohibitions and social pressures in the past, there now exist large numbers of Arabs, expatriate and citizen, who have either entered as immigrants holding privately to Christian beliefs, or have become Christians through house groups or through radio programmes, all of whom prefer to remain as secret believers.

**CHURCH AND STATE.** The king of Saudi Arabia is also the imam or spiritual leader of all Muslim believers. He holds all power: executive, legislative, judicial and religious. In addition, at the pan-Islamic level he benefits from the prestige accorded Saudi Arabia because the Muslim holy places Mecca and Medina, of which he is the recognized guardian, are located there and because of the pilgrims they attract. Indeed each year on the day following the Aïd El Kebir (feast on the Sacrifices), the king washes the interior of the Kaaba and changes the cloth of black brocade which envelops it. He is the only person allowed to enter the shrine.

The supreme law of the land is the Sharia, Islamic religious law. Although in recent years civic administrative courts have been set up, the religious tribunals continue to retain a virtual monopoly over judicial decisions. The highest office is held by the grand mufti, supreme judge and head of the department of Sharia affairs. There exists, in addition, a Ministry of Pilgrimage and Religious Trusts, concerned with the welfare of pilgrims in such matters as food, transportation and medical services, in addition to the construction and upkeep of mosques, the safeguarding of archeological ruins of religious interest, and the promotion of tourism.

All religions other than Islam are prohibited. Christian worship services are held for foreign personnel, but it is important to stress that these meetings are completely private. Although tacitly tolerated by Saudi authorities, they are not officially recognized, nor is the presence of non-Muslim clergy within Arabia officially admitted.

The faithful practice of Islam is encouraged by rewards, such as the edict of November 1954 offering US$200 for every Muslim able to repeat the Quran by heart, as well as by enforcement and surveillance on the part of the authorities. One of the most feared of government agencies is the corps of Mujahidun, in ancient times known as the Ikhwans. The Mujahidun make up the personal militia of the king, and are especially charged with maintaining public respect for the morals and the practice of Muslim rituals according to the principle of Wahhabism. They are also used on occasion in the suppression of strikes. Ancient Quranic punishments have been carried over in modernized form, such as the surgical severing of the hand of a thief.

The policy of the king, in general, is to maintain an equilibrium between the Ulama, Muslim theologians who are traditionally conservative, and the new bourgeoisie, whose influence is slowly growing.

**BROADCASTING.** No Christian broadcasting is allowed. Foreign Christian programmes in Arabic can however be heard over the international stations FEBA (Seychelles), TWR (Monaco) for 4 hours a week, and Radio Vatican for 3 hours 30 minutes a week.

The Voice of Islam, a powerful radio station at Mecca, is now being planned, involving over 25 Muslim broadcasting organizations.

**BIBLIOGRAPHY**


'Basic statistics on Hajj'. Hajj Research Centre, King Abdulaziz University, Jeddah, 1978. 18p.
*Pilgrimage to Mecca.* M. Amin. London: Visnews, 1977. 256p. (Pictorial description of Hajj of 1975 and 1976).


TABLE 2. ORGANIZED CHURCHES AND DENOMINATIONS IN SAUDI ARABIA

| Official name 1 | Begun 2 | Type 3 | Counc 4 | Congs 5 | Adults 6 | Affiliated 7 | Names, notes, and other statistics (see Codebook) 8 |
|---|---|---|---|---|---|---|---|
| Anglican Church (D Cyprus & the Gulf) | | A plu | aw... | 2 | 1,000 | 2,000 | In Episcopal Church of Jerusalem & the Middle East. Mostly British expatriates. |
| **Catholic Church (VA Arabia)** | 1875 | R Lat | P..L. | | 1,500 | 2,600 | All expatriates: ARAMCO Americans, Arabs. 3x(USA) in Dhahran. Rapid immigration. |
| Christian Brethren | | P CBr | x.... | 2 | 100 | 200 | *Plymouth Brethren. Open Brethren. Gospel Halls.* Also M=RSMT. All expatriates. |
| Church of Christ | | P Dis | x.... | 1 | 30 | 50 | M=Churches of Christ(Non-Instrumental) (USA). In Dhahran. Mainly Americans. |
| **Isolated radio churches** | c1950 | I rad | ..... | 200 | 4,000 | 8,300 | Isolated Arab believers, mostly aged 12–25. R=350(TWR,RVOG,RV,FEBA),T=2000(ICI). |
| Unitarian Fellowship of Dhahran | c1960 | M Unt | I.... | 1 | 30 | 50 | Small fellowship of expatriate Whites. In 1964, 33 members, 56 total community. |
| Other Protestant denominations | 1938 | P | ..... | | 3,970 | 6,700 | USA and European Protestants (ARAMCO, etc), CSI (India), Arabs. House churches. |
| Other Arab indigenous churches | c1965 | I ind | ..... | | 1,000 | 3,000 | Small interdenominational house groups, begun by immigrant Arab Christians. |
| Other Orthodox churches | c1965 | O | ..... | | 1,500 | 2,000 | Expatriate Arabs (Greek, Syrian, Coptic), Indians (Syrian). Private meetings. |
| **Total affiliated (mid-1970)** | | | | 320 | 13,130 | 24,900 | **Total denominations (1970) . . . 15.** |
| **Total affiliated (mid-1975)** | | | | 400 | 25,800 | 49,000 | **Total denominations (1975) . . . 20.** |
| **Total affiliated (mid-1980)** | | | | 500 | 46,900 | 89,000 | **Total denominations (1980) . . . 30.** |

*Concluded on page 606*

PILGRIMAGE TO MECCA. The following 9 photographs illustrate this Encyclopedia's statistics of pilgrims of all kinds (Christian, Muslim, Hindu, et alia) by describing the major Islamic annual event, the 7-day Hajj to Mecca, birthplace of Muhammed, in the month of Dhu al-Hijjah (in 1978, November). This pilgrimage is the last of the 5 Pillars (or absolute requirements) of Islam prescribed by the Quran, and is usually only performed once a lifetime by all Muslims who are able to afford it. Statistics of total pilgrims each year from 1912-1976 are given under Table 1 above, and for every country in the footnote MUSLIMS under its Table 1.

1.  Signpost on road to Mecca: no non-Muslims are permitted within the Haram, a sacred area 20 miles long by 6 miles wide with Mecca in its middle.
2.  Logistics and progress of the Hajj, with its up to 2 million pilgrims at one time, are controlled by the governor, the Emir of Mecca (right) flying overhead by helicopter. Hajj control is now handled by an all-Arabic computer with 200 TV monitor screens. The government Ministry of Hajj is planning for 5 million pilgrims a year by 1980.
3.  The Emir's helicopter passes over the Mount of Mercy swarming with pilgrims, as he monitors the whole vast tented area accommodating 2 million pilgrims on the bare Arafat plain.
4.  In the heart of the Sacred City of Mecca (normal population 376,000 in 35,000 houses covering 10 square miles) is Al-Masjid al-Haram, the Great or Sacred Mosque, covering an area of 1,724,032 square feet. At its right is the long al-Mas'a (Place of Running) within which pilgrims run 7 times.
5.  Every available spot both within the Mosque and outside is crowded during prayers with (as here) 1.2 million worshippers in sacred robes (ihram). The inner courtyard holds over 500,000 worshippers at once, with a further 700,000 outside.

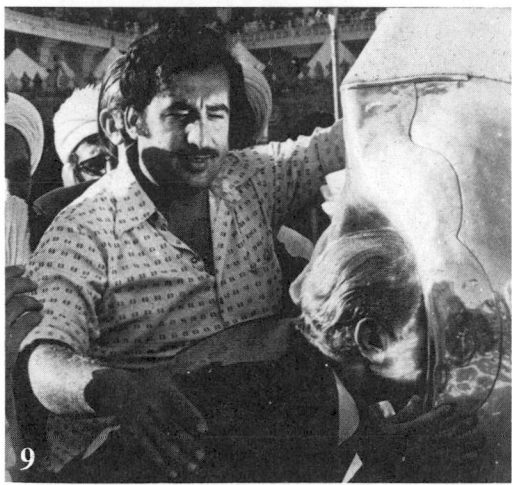

6. At the centre of the inner courtyard is the Ka'bah (or Kaaba), the most sacred area in the entire Muslim world, the House of God first built by Abraham, and the physical axis of the Muslim world towards which 500 million Muslims world-wide face for prayer 5 times a day.

7. Worshippers individually circle the Kaaba 7 times, and this Tawaf or circling (3 times running, 4 times slowly, starting from and kissing the Black Stone each time) can be clearly seen in photographs taken at night (below). Not without reason, this area round the Kaaba with its running and jostling day and night (stopping only when prayers are said) has been called the most dangerous spot in Arabia.

8. The Kaaba is a structure of grey stone and marble, 45 feet high, cubical in shape, its 4 corners roughly aligned with the cardinal points of the compass, with one door and with an interior empty except for 3 pillars and suspended lamps. It is covered each year with a magnificent newly-woven covering of black silk brocade, the Kiswah, weighing 2.2 tons, on which are embroidered verses from the Quran in gold thread. At the southeastern corner (bottom right) is its focal point, the Black Stone (Hajar al-Aswad).

9. The climax. On each of his 7 circuits the devout pilgrim places his head inside the protective silver sheath to kiss or touch the Hajar al-Aswad, a simple 12-inch polished Black Stone placed there, according to tradition, by the Prophet Muhammed himself.

PEOPLES (ethnolinguistic). Christians (1970): 60.5% Arab (49% alien (Palestinian, Lebanese, Egyptian), 11% Saudi), 28.3% USA White, 7.4% British, 2.0% Italian and other European, 1.6% Indian, Armenian, Chinese. After 1975, in addition Christians included over 2,000 Koreans, also Pakistanis et alii.

COUNTRY-WIDE TOTALS
EVANGELIZATION (see Part 5). 1900: 3%. 1970: 18%. 1980:

32%. *Radiophonic evangelism.* TWR, FEBA, RVOG, RSB, ICI, Radio Vatican, et alia.
FOREIGN MISSIONARIES AND PERSONNEL (aliens from abroad) (1973). Total 13. *From Western world.* 3 Roman Catholics from USA. *From Third World.* About 10, mostly Roman Catholic Arabs from Lebanon, Palestine et alia.
PERSONNEL (1973). About 13 (foreign).

# SENEGAL

## SECULAR DATA

**STATE.** Official name: The Republic of Senegal (La République du Sénégal). Adjective of nationality: Senegalese (sénégalais).
Flag (shown above right): Bars of green, gold, and red, with centered green star.
Area: 196,192 sq.km. (75,750 sq.miles). Agricultural land: 40.8%.
Government: One-party republic, since 1962 (1857 French possession, 1960 Independence as republic).
Legislature: National Assembly, 100 members.
Official language: French (*Français*).
Chief cities: capital Dakar 581,000 (1969), Kaolack 96,240, Thiès 90,460.
Armed forces (1976): Total 5,950 regular: army 5,500, navy 250, air force 200 (no combat aircraft). Paramilitary forces: 1,600.
Foreign forces (1973): 2,000 French troops; (1978) 1,300.

**DEMOGRAPHY. Population:** 3,620,047 (census of 1.V.1970-30.IV.1971. For 1970–2000 (UN), see last row of Table 1). Population density (1975): 23/sq.km. (58/sq.mile). Under 15

years: 42%. Growth rate (1975–80): 2.43% per year (births 4.72%, deaths −2.29%). Life expectancy (1975–80): 41.0 years. Household size: 4.9 persons.
Major languages: French, Wolof, Serer, Fulani, English, Tukulor, Diola, Mandingo, Bambara, and about 15 smaller languages.
Urban dwellers (1970): 26.0%. Urban growth rate (1950–70): 3.7% per year.
Labour force: 44%.
Refugees (1975): From abroad, 82,000 (from Guinea and Guinea-Bissau).
Tourists (1974): 124,730.

**ETHNOLINGUISTIC GROUPS:** 35% Wolof, 16% Serer, 14% Fulani (Peul), 9% Tukulor, 9% Diola (Jola), 7% Mandingo, 3% Guinean (refugees), 2% Bambara, 2% French (50,000), 1% Zenaga, 0.8% Cape Verdean, 0.5% Lebanese, 0.4% Tenda (Bassari), Soninke, Moor (Mauri), Bassari, Papel, Balante, Manjaco, Syrian, et alii.

**MONEY** (1977). Monetary unit: CFA franc (= 100 centimes);

US$1 = CFAF 250.00.
National income per person: US$290. Average annual family income: US$1,421.
Inflation: (1970–74) 7.8% per year, (1975) 31% per year (consumer price index 170).
Cost of living in capital (1976): index 149 (Washington DC=100). Daily cost of living: US$40.

HEALTH. Hospitals: 41 (5,453 beds). Doctors: 275. Lepers: 74,000 (16.7 per 1,000). Blind: 22,000. Psychotics: 35,000.

EDUCATION. Adult literacy: (1961) 6%. Education rate: 23%. Schools: 1,215. Universities: 1.

LITERATURE. Periodicals: 40. Newspapers: 1 daily.

COMMUNICATION (per 1,000 people). Phones: 7. Radios: 67. TV sets: 1. Daily newspaper circulation: 6 copies.

TABLE 1. RELIGIOUS ADHERENTS IN SENEGAL

| Year | 1900 | | mid-1970 | | Annual change, 1970–1980 | | | | mid-1975 | | mid-1980 | | 2000 | |
|---|---|---|---|---|---|---|---|---|---|---|---|---|---|---|
| Name | Adherents | % | Adherents | % | Natural | Conversion | Total | Rate | Adherents | % | Adherents | % | Adherents | % |
| Muslims | 699,600 | 70.0 | 3,532,000 | 90.0 | 96,310 | 4,527 | 100,837 | 2.52 | 3,998,980 | 90.5 | 4,540,370 | 91.0 | 7,599,000 | 93.0 |
| **Christians** | **18,400** | **1.8** | **224,500** | **5.7** | **6,083** | **30** | **6,113** | **2.42** | **252,570** | **5.7** | **285,630** | **5.7** | **473,600** | **5.8** |
| professing | 18,400 | 1.8 | 224,500 | 5.7 | 6,083 | 30 | 6,113 | 2.42 | 252,570 | 5.7 | 285,630 | 5.7 | 473,600 | 5.8 |
| Roman Catholics | 18,000 | 1.8 | 219,600 | 5.6 | 5,948 | 32 | 5,980 | 2.42 | 247,000 | 5.6 | 279,400 | 5.6 | 456,600 | 5.6 |
| Protestants | 400 | 0.0 | 4,300 | 0.1 | 117 | −7 | 110 | 2.27 | 4,850 | 0.1 | 5,400 | 0.1 | 14,000 | 0.2 |
| Marginal Protestants | 0 | 0.0 | 400 | 0.0 | 12 | 3 | 15 | 3.12 | 480 | 0.0 | 550 | 0.0 | 2,000 | 0.0 |
| Anglicans | 0 | 0.0 | 200 | 0.0 | 6 | 2 | 8 | 3.33 | 240 | 0.0 | 280 | 0.0 | 1,000 | 0.0 |
| nominal | 3,100 | 0.3 | 36,829 | 0.9 | 1,066 | 215 | 1,281 | 2.90 | 44,250 | 1.0 | 49,640 | 1.0 | 118,600 | 1.5 |
| affiliated | 15,300 | 1.5 | 187,671 | 4.8 | 5,017 | −185 | 4,832 | 2.32 | 208,320 | 4.7 | 235,990 | 4.7 | 355,000 | 4.3 |
| total practising | 14,530 | 95 | 150,140 | 80 | 4,014 | −149 | 3,865 | 2.32 | 166,660 | 80 | 188,790 | 80 | 248,500 | 70 |
| non-practising | 770 | 5 | 37,530 | 20 | 1,003 | −36 | 967 | 2.32 | 41,660 | 20 | 47,200 | 20 | 106,500 | 30 |
| Roman Catholics | 15,000 | 1.5 | 183,021 | 4.7 | 4,888 | −190 | 4,698 | 2.31 | 203,000 | 4.6 | 230,000 | 4.6 | 339,400 | 4.2 |
| Catholic pentecostals | 0 | 0.0 | 0 | 0.0 | 4 | 146 | 150 | 30.00 | 500 | 0.0 | 1,500 | 0.0 | 5,000 | 0.1 |
| Protestants | 300 | 0.0 | 4,150 | 0.1 | 114 | 1 | 115 | 2.44 | 4,720 | 0.1 | 5,300 | 0.1 | 13,000 | 0.2 |
| Evangelicals | 200 | 0.0 | 2,900 | 0.1 | 78 | 2 | 80 | 2.42 | 3,300 | 0.1 | 3,700 | 0.1 | 9,500 | 0.1 |
| Marginal Protestants | 0 | 0.0 | 400 | 0.0 | 12 | 3 | 15 | 3.12 | 480 | 0.0 | 550 | 0.0 | 2,000 | 0.0 |
| Anglicans | 0 | 0.0 | 100 | 0.0 | 3 | 1 | 4 | 3.33 | 120 | 0.0 | 140 | 0.0 | 600 | 0.0 |
| Tribal religionists | 282,000 | 28.2 | 166,000 | 4.2 | 3,938 | −4,578 | −640 | −0.39 | 163,500 | 3.7 | 159,600 | 3.2 | 72,400 | 0.9 |
| Baha'is | 0 | 0.0 | 2,400 | 0.1 | 67 | 13 | 80 | 2.86 | 2,800 | 0.1 | 3,200 | 0.1 | 25,000 | 0.3 |
| Other religionists | 0 | 0.0 | 100 | 0.0 | 2 | 8 | 10 | 6.67 | 150 | 0.0 | 200 | 0.0 | 1,000 | 0.0 |
| **Country's population** | **1,000,000** | **100.0** | **3,925,000** | **100.0** | **106,400** | **0** | **106,400** | **2.41** | **4,418,000** | **100.0** | **4,989,000** | **100.0** | **8,171,000** | **100.0** |

COLUMNS, ROWS. For meanings and definition, see Codebook (Part 6). Note that, by definition, total 'Christians' = professing + crypto-Christians, which also = affiliated + nominal Christians. Percentages may not always total exactly, due to rounding.
CENSUSES. IV.1960–VIII.1961 (de jure): 89.7% Muslims, 5.6% Roman Catholics, 4.6% tribal religionists, 0.06% Protestants.

NOTES ON RELIGIONS
AFFILIATED CHRISTIANS. Although numbers of conversions from paganism to Christianity are taking place each year, the nett total is negative because of losses from the churches to Islam, especially school children. In the Bignona region, 15,000 Catholics became Muslims from 1955–65.
ATHEISTS. None; only a small outlawed pro-Communist party, African Party of Independence (PAI); communist membership negligible.

BAHA'IS. From 1964, growth to 16 local spiritual assemblies (1973).
CATHOLIC PENTECOSTALS (or, Catholic charismatics). Totals (January 1975): 200 involved adults; total charismatic community including children, 400, increasing rapidly every month.
MUSLIMS. African Sunnis (of the Malikite rite). Islamic brotherhoods active (1957): Qadiriya with 304,000 members, the missionary order of Tijaniya with 1 million with one of its major Black African headquarters in Kaolack, Muridiya 423,000 (attaining overwhelming power during the 20th century), and 23,000 in others. Conversions to Islam are taking place among tribal religionists, particularly the Serer (420,000), who were entirely pagans up to 1870, resisted Islam through 2 brutal jihads against them, until 1900 when islamization began, remaining weak (due to resistance by the powerful Serer monarchy, tenacious fetishism and sacrificial religion) until 1950 when the traditional chieftainships disappeared; by 1972 the Serer had become 40%

Muslim. Half of the Diola, 100,000 or so, became Muslims from 1940–70. *Missionaries.* A number of Egyptian missionaries sent by Al-Azhar University (Cairo) are at work, with several big building projects. *Hajj pilgrims to Mecca.* (1970) 2,422; (1974) 3,403; (1975) 3,832; (1976) 4,148.
OTHER RELIGIONISTS. Including Rosicrucians (1 AMORC centre).
ROMAN CATHOLICS. Professing and affiliated Catholics rose rapidly in numbers from 1865 to 1960, creating a large nominal fringe of professing but not affiliated Catholics. In 1960, however, the rate abruptly fell, and affiliated Catholics have been growing at a rate less than the population increase, and the proportion of Catholics to population has gradually declined from 4.9% in 1960 to 4.7% in 1970.
TRIBAL RELIGIONISTS. Animists, usually strongly resistant to Islam, mainly among the Serer (still 34% traditionalist in 1972) and Diola (20%).

**NON-CHRISTIAN RELIGIONS. Islam** with its strength concentrated in the north (among the Wolofs) and east (among the Fulani) is the dominant religion of Senegal, with 90% of the population. Several brotherhoods are active: Qadiriya from Morocco

with 300,000 members, the first to arrive; Tijaniya also from Morocco with one million members, many of its adherents having come from Qadiriya; and Muridiya with over 400,000 members whose headquarters is Touba. The Murid chiefs control about 50% of Senegal's peanut production through a feudal system. The conservatism and sectarianism of the Qadiriya and Tijaniya marabouts (called Serigue among the Wolofs and Tierno among the Fulani) has provoked a movement of resistance by youth and intellectuals centred in the Union Culturelle Musulmane, begun in 1953. Arabic is widely spoken, encouraged by the civil authorities. A chair of Muslim languages and civilizations and an Islamic Institute exist at the University of Dakar. The West African regional office of the World Muslim Congress (headquarters in Pakistan) is found at Kaolack.
**African traditional religions** retain their vitality especially among the Diola of Casamance and the Serer of Sine-Salcum. Among the latter, God (Rog) is recognized as creator and is invoked in time of war. Nevertheless, appeal is made more often to departed ancestors who possess men, animals and inanimate objects. For the Diola, ancestral veneration, directly by a separated priestly class, is also more widely

practised than the worship of God (Emit). The Diola Felup believe in the existence of a satanic being, Buso, who epitomizes evil.

**CHRISTIANITY**
CATHOLIC CHURCH. The coast of Senegal was explored by Portuguese in 1445, providing the first Christian contacts with the local population. In 1486 the Senegalese chief Behemoi was baptized in Lisbon, and by 1490 the first religious establishments were set up in the region of Ziguinchor. The diocese of Funchal, including Senegal, was created in 1514, and although a prefecture of St Louis was erected in 1779, work was sporadic prior to the arrival of St Joseph of Cluny sisters in 1819. Three Senegalese priests were ordained in 1840, and Holy Ghost priests arrived in 1845. The vicariate of The Two Guineas was formed in 1847, becoming the vicariate of Senegambia in 1863 and of Dakar in 1936. The hierarchy was established in 1955, Dakar becoming an archdiocese, and its first African archbishop was consecrated in 1962. In 1970, the church was served by 43 national and 168 expatriate priests. In 1972 the bishop in Senegal decided that all dioceses should have African priests, since the preceding year 3 dioceses had only

**Muslims.** *Left.* Serer converts to Islam at daily prayers outside their homestead, in region of Kaolack. *Above.* Inside Grand Mosque of Dakar.

expatriate clergy. Following this decision, newly-ordained Senegalese priests were to consider themselves as 'national' rather than 'diocesan' priests.

Christians, as is the case also with traditionalists, are found mostly among the Serer and Diola in southwestern Senegal, with many living in the region of Dakar.

PROTESTANT CHURCHES. The Protestant Church of Dakar, whose membership is about 60% European, is the result of the activity of the Paris Mission as early as 1863 and is one of the 2 largest Protestant churches. The Worldwide Evangelization Crusade from Britain arrived in 1935, and since World War II a number of small conservative missions, mostly from the USA, have taken up work in the country. The most successful of these new arrivals have been the Assemblies of God, who have done extensive evangelism through radio broadcasts.

CHURCH AND STATE. According to the constitution of March 1963, modified by the constitutional law of 26 February 1970, the republic is secular, assuring equality for all citizens and freedom of religion (Title I, Article 1). Freedom of conscience, and the profession and free practice of religion, are guaranteed to all; and institutions and religious communities not under state control may regulate and administer their affairs in an autonomous

manner (Title II, Article 49). Private confessional education is subsidized provided it follows the government programme, and religious instruction is given in state schools.

The government encourages the various churches and religious groups, without discrimination to play a positive role in development, manifesting an understanding of the importance of the spiritual dimension of life. Although Senegal is 90% Muslim it has been led since Independence by a Catholic president, Leopold Sedar Senghor. In 1962 he imprisoned the Muslim prime minister, Mamadou Dia, and several other Muslim collaborators, because of their socialistic tendencies, but this provoked no religious animosity. The Muslim marabouts, especially the Murids, contribute significantly to a maintenance of the social status quo.

INTERDENOMINATIONAL ORGANIZATIONS. The Evangelical Fellowship of Senegal (Fraternité Evangélique du Sénégal) has in its membership most of the Evangelical groups working in Senegal at the present time. Among Protestant bodies, the principal non-members are the Protestant Church of Dakar and the Seventh-day Adventists.

BROADCASTING. The government Radiodiffusion du Sénégal accepts religious broadcasting. The

Assemblies of God Mission has two 15-minute programmes a week and two 5 minute spots on Radio Dakar. At their studio, 14 programmes a week are produced in French, Bambara, Wolof, Diola and Bassari. The Catholic Church produces for radio Dakar a 15-minute French programme on Thursdays and a Sunday mass, as well as Sunday broadcasts in Wolof and Serer. Other Catholic programmes are produced for local stations: Radio St Louis, Radio Kaolack and Radio Ziguinchor. The Reformed Church of Sengal is allotted the same amount of time and number of programmes as the Catholics. The church also provides programming facilities to Conservative Baptists and the Worldwide Evangelization Crusade, who sponsor Voix de l'Evangile (Voice of the Gospel) on Radio Dakar. From abroad, ELWA (Liberia) can be easily heard. For Catholics, UNDA is represented by a national association.

### BIBLIOGRAPHY
*Annuaire catholique du Sénégal pour l'année 1972.* Dakar: Archevêché de Dakar, 1972. (Annual).
*La chrétienté africaine de Dakar.* V. Martin. Dakar: Fraternité St Dominique, 1964.
'Lat-Dyor, Damel du Kayor (1842–86) et l'Islamisation des Wolofs du Sénégal', V. Monteil, in I.M. Lewis (ed), *Islam in tropical Africa* (London: Oxford, 1966), p.342–49.
*Spotlight on Senegal.* B. MacIndoe. London: Worldwide Evangelization Crusade.

TABLE 2.    ORGANIZED CHURCHES AND DENOMINATIONS IN SENEGAL

| Official name 1 | Begun 2 | Type 3 | Counc 4 | Congs 5 | Adults 6 | Affiliated 7 | Names, notes, and other statistics (see Codebook) 8 | | | | | | |
|---|---|---|---|---|---|---|---|---|---|---|---|---|---|
| Assemblées de Dieu | 1956 | P Pe2 | ZPG.E | 29 | 768 | 1,500 | *Assemblies of God.* M = AoG(USA). Polygamists baptized. 17n,15f,1h,1r,1s(14),40Y. | | | | | | |
| Eglise Adventiste du Septième Jour | 1952 | P Adv | x.... | 2 | 84 | 200 | *SDA, Seventh-day Adventists, Senegal Mission.* HQ Dakar. 1nx,20mw,1h,1r,3t(158),23Y. | | | | | | |
| Egl Anglicane (D Gambia & Rio Pongas) | | A ACa | avaV. | 1 | 60 | 100 | In CPWA. St Peter's Anglican congregation, Dakar. All expatriates. | | | | | | |
| Eglise Catholique au Sénégal: | 1445 | R Lat | P,SFP | 57 | 106,200 | 183,021 | *Catholic Ch.* 45% Serer. C = 10+4+29. 1p,1s(18). | 43n,168x,119m,482w,P = 71%,7654Yy. | | | | | |
| M   Dakar | 1863 | R Lat | Pa | 27 | 58,800 | 101,450 | 65% Serer,20% White,10% Cape Verdean,5%Wolof. | 12 | 85 | 59 | 236 | 70 | 3751 |
| D   Kaolack | 1957 | R Lat | Pmac | 10 | 4,800 | 8,236 | 90% Serer, 4% Diola, 3% Wolof, 1% Bassari. | 0 | 21 | 7 | 40 | 77 | 278 |
| D   Saint-Louis du Sénégal | 1763 | R Lat | Pcaap | 7 | 1,000 | 1,726 | 99% Muslim. Serer, Manjak, Diola, Europeans. | 0 | 12 | 9 | 12 | 66 | 72 |
| D   Thiès | 1969 | R Lat | Pa | 8 | 12,300 | 21,171 | Regions of Thiès and Diourbel. | 10 | 11 | 23 | 64 | 70 | 895 |
| D   Ziguinchor | 1939 | R Lat | Pa | 4 | 29,000 | 49,908 | 1970, Niaguis-Boffa mission: Guinea-B refugees. | 21 | 31 | 20 | 119 | 71 | 2596 |
| PA Tambacounda | 1970 | R Lat | Pcaap | 1 | 300 | 530 | Bassari. Many Guinea (Conakry) refugees. | 0 | 8 | 1 | 11 | 77 | 62 |
| Eglise Protestante du Sénégal | 1863 | P Ref | R,A,. | 1 | 300 | 1,500 | *Prot Ch of Dakar.* 1863, M = PEMS(France). 60% White, 40% Black. 1x(Malagasy),30Yy. | | | | | | |
| Mission Baptiste du Sénégal | 1961 | P Bap | xPG,E | 2 | 20 | 100 | M = Conservative Baptist Foreign Mission Soc(USA). Work among Wolof. 1 school. 14f. | | | | | | |
| Mission Ev de l'Afrique Occidentale | 1935 | P int | xPG,E | 6 | 50 | 200 | M = Worldwide Evangelization Crusade(UK,USA). HQ Ziguinchor & Saint-Louis. 17f,1p. | | | | | | |
| Mission Mondiale Unie | 1955 | P int | xPG,E | 2 | 20 | 250 | M = United World Mission(USA). Centre Evangélique, Dakar. Orphanage, radio. 18f. | | | | | | |
| Témoins de Jéhovah | c1930 | M Jeh | x.... | 3 | 207 | 400 | *Jehovah's Witnesses.* Watch Tower. HQ Dakar. Active witnessing by 1932. 41Y. | | | | | | |
| Other Protestant denominations | | P | ..G.E | | 200 | 400 | Total about 8 (see list below). | | | | | | |
| Total affiliated (mid-1970) | | | | 115 | 107,909 | 187,671 | Total denominations (1970) . . . 17. | | | | | | |
| Total affiliated (mid-1975) | | | | 120 | 119,800 | 208,320 | Total denominations (1975) . . . 18. | | | | | | |
| Total affiliated (mid-1980) | | | | 125 | 135,700 | 235,990 | Total denominations (1980) . . . 20. | | | | | | |

**NOTES ON TABLE ABOVE**
COLUMNS: for meanings and CODES (cols. 1, 3, 4, 8): see Codebook (Part 6). Column 1: **Boldface type** = church with over 10% of country's affiliated Christians.
NATIONAL COUNCILS (Column 4, 5th letter).
  E = Fraternité Evangélique du Sénégal (FES) (Evangelical Fellowship of Senegal).
  P = Conférence Episcopale de Sénégal-Mauritanie (CESM) (Episcopal Conference of Senegal & Mauritania).
OTHER PROTESTANT DENOMINATIONS. These, most of which are members of FES, include: Action Biblique, Christian Brethren (UK), Ch of the Nazarene, Mission Evangélique Indépendante, Mission Luthérienne Finlandaise, New Tribes Mission (1955; 10 missionaries), Southern Baptist Convention

(1969), World-Wide Missions (1965).

PEOPLES (ethnolinguistic). Christians: 44% Serer, 23% French, 14% Diola, 8% Cape Verdean, 4% Wolof, 3% Lebanese, 3% alien African (Ivorian, Dahomean, Togolese, Malian), 0.5% Bassari, Papel, Balante, Manjaco.

COUNTRY-WIDE TOTALS
EVANGELIZATION (see Part 5). 1900: 14%. 1970: 42%. 1980: 50%. *Mass evangelism.* Early 1960s, Conservative Baptist street campaigns and outdoor film shows in Thiès. *Radiophonic evangelism.* RSB, ICI (1,364 enrolments, 476 active).
FOREIGN MISSIONARIES AND PERSONNEL (nationals serving abroad) (1973). Total about 70 Roman Catholics in

Benin, France, Gambia, Ivory Coast, Mali et alia.
FOREIGN MISSIONARIES AND PERSONNEL (aliens from abroad) (1973). Total 753. *From Western world.* 731: about 640 Roman Catholics, 91 Protestants (65 in 4 USA societies, 17 in 2 UK societies, 6 in 2 Australia societies, 3 in 2 New Zealand societies). *From Third World.* 22: about 20 Roman Catholics, 2 Protestants from Madagascar and Cameroon.
INSTITUTIONS (church-operated) (1973). Total 110, including 40 higher schools (5 minor seminaries), 50 medical centres, 6 religious communities, 2 seminaries (1 RC, 1 Protestant).
PERIODICALS. About 14 titles.
PERSONNEL. About 1,869 (1,116 national, 753 foreign).
RELIGIOUS LIBRARIES. 8.
SCRIPTURE DISTRIBUTION (1975). Annual totals: 2,000

Bibles (65% subsidized, 35% commercial), 9,000 NTs (44% free, 44% subsidized, 11% commercial), 15,500 UBS portions, 8,600 UBS selections. *Translations completed.* Portion: 2 languages (in 1873, 1961).
SERVICE AGENCIES. About 35, including ACO, CESM, CIMADE, CV/AV, FES, GBUAF, JAC, JAC/F, JEC, JOC/F, SCS, SU, UJCRS, YWCA.

### ADDITIONAL DATA ON CHURCHES
EGLISE CATHOLIQUE AU SENEGAL. *Catechumens.* (1959) 7,935; (1961) 10,083; (1963) 15,481; (1971) 9,434, divided among the 6 jurisdictions in the order shown (and included in column 7), as follows: 3845, 1381, 31, 680, 3497, 0. *Annual baptisms.* (1972) 79.2% infant, 20.8% adult. *National priests.* The first 3 Senegalese were ordained in 1840, with 70 others subsequently. Nowadays no vocations come from the cities or towns even though 53 priests work in Dakar alone with its total of 20% of the population. *Total priests.* 54 secular, 157 regular (1971). *Brothers.* 21 nationals, 98 expatriates. *Sisters.* 96 nationals, 386 expatriates. *Catholic charismatics* (January 1975). About 200 involved adults in 10 predominantly Catholic prayer groups. The Catholic Charismatic Renewal began in 1973 in Casamance through nuns and brothers from Europe. *Catechists.* Total (1971) 916, of whom

108 were in Dakar. *Indigenous religious congregations.* Brothers: 26 Frères Missionnaires de St-Joseph (begun 1925). Sisters: 50 Filles du S-C de Marie (begun 1858). *Main foreign orders and congregations.* Priests: CSSp, MSCl, OSB. Brothers: S-C de Granby (Canada) et St-Gabriel. Sisters: Filles du S-C de Marie, Immaculée Conception de Castres, St-Joseph de Cluny, Présentation de Marie de Bourg, Franciscaines Missionnaires de Marie, St-Charles d'Angers, Bénédictines, Carmélites.
*Catholic organizations.* The Episcopal Conference of Senegal and Mauritania (Conférence Episcopale de Sénégal-Mauritanie), with headquarters in Dakar, is a member of the Inter-Territorial Episcopal Conference of Francophone West Africa and of SECAM. There are no national presbyteral or pastoral councils. Religious personnel have representation in the Conférence des Supérieurs Majeurs des Instituts Masculins du Sénégal, and the 'Anima Una' Union des Supérieures Majeures des Congrégations Autochtones d'Afrique de l'Ouest Francophone, in Bamako, Mali.

The National Bureau of Catholic Works (Direction Nationale des Oeuvres Catholiques) co-ordinates the activities of national organizations of the lay apostolate, the principal movements being CV/AV (3,000 members), JEC (2,000), JOC/F (500 militants), JAC/F (34 groups), Scouts and Guides, Légion de Marie

(43 praesidia), ACO (12 teams), plus teacher teams.
The Holy See has diplomatic relations with Senegal and is represented to government and the Catholic hierarchy by a pro-nuncio in Dakar, who serves also as pro-nuncio in Upper Volta and Niger and apostolic delegate to Guinea-Bissau, Mali and Mauritania.

Since 1947 (except for the period 1972–74 for financial reasons), the influential Catholic weekly *Afrique nouvelle*, serving all of francophone West Africa, has been published in Dakar.

In 1971 the Catholic Church provided direction for 96 primary schools (24,540 pupils); 27 first-cycle secondary schools (5,745); 5 second-cycle secondary schools (790); and 16 technical schools (1,560). In the medical sector in 1970 there were 40 dispensaries (1 million annual consultations), several of which provide care to lepers. Catholic sisters also work in the 10 principal public hospitals, 7 state dispensaries and the leprosarium of the Dakar hospital. Regarding social service, several congregations of sisters are involved in literacy and the education of women. Other groups active in the social sector are JAC and Catholic Relief (Secours Catholique), the latter in well-drilling and agriculture. Misereor participates in 2 rural development projects at Bambey and Fatick.

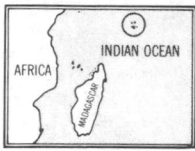

# SEYCHELLES

## SECULAR DATA

STATE. Official name: The Republic of Seychelles (La République des Seychelles). Adjective of nationality: a Seychellois (seychellois).
Flag (shown above right): White St Andrew's cross; blue triangles at top and bottom; red triangle at hoist and fly.
Area: 376 sq.km. (145 sq.miles). Description: 92 islands and islets. Agricultural land: 13.2%.
Government: Parliamentary republic, since 1976 (1768 French colony, 1794 British possession, 1903 British crown colony, 1970 sef-government, 1976 Independence).
Legislature: Legislative Assembly, 19 members.
Official languages: English and French (*Français*).
Capital: Victoria 13,736 (1971).
Armed forces (1976): Paramilitary police forces: 300.

DEMOGRAPHY. Population: 52,650 (census of 5.V.1971. For 1970–2000 (UN), see last row of Table 1). Population density (1975): 157/sq.km. (406/sq.mile). Under 15 years: 44%. Growth rate (1975–80): 2.24% per year. Household size: 4.7 persons.
Major languages: English, French, French Creole, Gujarati, Tamil, Chinese.
Urban dwellers (1970): 30.0%. Urban growth rate (1950–70): 2.1% per year.
Labour force: 38%.
Tourists (1973): 19,464.

ETHNOLINGUISTIC GROUPS: 95.7% Creole (Mulatto) (French/Black), 1.9% French, 1.0% British, 0.9% Indo-Pakistani (0.4% Gujarati, 0.2% Tamil), 0.5% Chinese, Swahili, other Bantu.

MONEY (1977). Monetary unit: Seychelles rupee (= 100 cents);

US$1 = SRs 7.60
National income per person: US$450. Average annual family income: US$2,115.
Inflation: (1975) consumer price index 238.
Cost of living in capital (1976): Daily cost of living: US$33.

HEALTH. Hospitals: 8 (348 beds). Doctors: 16. Lepers: 50 (0.8 per 1,000). Blind: 150. Psychotics: 450.

EDUCATION. Adult literacy: (1947) 26%, (1971) 58%. Schools: 35.

LITERATURE. Periodicals: 3. Newspapers: 2 dailies, 3 non-daily.

COMMUNICATION (per 1,000 people). Phones: 45. Radios: 136. Daily newspaper circulation: 55 copies.

TABLE 1.    RELIGIOUS ADHERENTS IN SEYCHELLES

| Year | 1900 | | mid-1970 | | Annual change, 1970–1980 | | | | mid-1975 | | mid-1980 | | 2000 | |
|---|---|---|---|---|---|---|---|---|---|---|---|---|---|---|
| Name | Adherents | % | Adherents | % | Natural | Conversion | Total | Rate | Adherents | % | Adherents | % | Adherents | % |
| **Christians** | **18,700** | **97.1** | **51,100** | **98.3** | **1,373** | **−27** | **1,346** | **2.33** | **57,840** | **98.0** | **64,560** | **97.8** | **98,010** | **96.1** |
| professing | 18,700 | 97.1 | 51,100 | 98.3 | 1,373 | −27 | 1,346 | 2.33 | 57,840 | 98.0 | 64,560 | 97.8 | 98,010 | 96.1 |
| Roman Catholics | 16,060 | 83.4 | 46,800 | 90.0 | 1,255 | −40 | 1,215 | 2.30 | 52,880 | 89.6 | 58,950 | 89.3 | 89,030 | 87.3 |
| Anglicans | 2,530 | 13.1 | 3,950 | 7.6 | 105 | −12 | 93 | 2.10 | 4,420 | 7.5 | 4,880 | 7.4 | 7,140 | 7.0 |
| Marginal Protestants | 0 | 0.0 | 200 | 0.4 | 7 | 13 | 20 | 6.67 | 300 | 0.5 | 400 | 0.6 | 1,020 | 1.0 |
| Protestants | 110 | 0.6 | 150 | 0.3 | 6 | 12 | 18 | 7.50 | 240 | 0.4 | 330 | 0.5 | 820 | 0.8 |
| nominal | 200 | 1.0 | 850 | 1.6 | 27 | 35 | 62 | 5.49 | 1,130 | 1.9 | 1,470 | 2.2 | 2,950 | 2.9 |
| affiliated | 18,500 | 96.1 | 50,250 | 96.6 | 1,346 | −62 | 1,284 | 2.26 | 56,710 | 96.1 | 63,090 | 95.6 | 95,060 | 93.2 |
| total practising | 14,800 | 80 | 30,150 | 60 | 808 | −38 | 770 | 2.26 | 34,030 | 60 | 37,850 | 60 | 95,040 | 60 |
| non-practising | 3,700 | 20 | 20,100 | 40 | 538 | −24 | 514 | 2.27 | 22,680 | 40 | 25,240 | 40 | 57,040 | 60 |
| Roman Catholics | 17,000 | 88.3 | 46,000 | 88.5 | 1,231 | −63 | 1,168 | 2.25 | 51,860 | 87.9 | 57,680 | 87.4 | 86,700 | 85.0 |
| Anglicans | 1,500 | 7.8 | 3,900 | 7.5 | 104 | −12 | 92 | 2.11 | 4,370 | 7.4 | 4,820 | 7.3 | 6,830 | 6.7 |
| Protestants | 0 | 0.0 | 250 | 0.5 | 7 | 1 | 8 | 2.67 | 300 | 0.5 | 330 | 0.5 | 820 | 0.8 |
| Evangelicals | 0 | 0.0 | 100 | 0.2 | 3 | 5 | 8 | 5.71 | 140 | 0.2 | 180 | 0.3 | 400 | 0.4 |
| Marginal Protestants | 0 | 0.0 | 100 | 0.2 | 4 | 12 | 16 | 8.89 | 180 | 0.3 | 260 | 0.4 | 710 | 0.7 |
| Hindus | 390 | 2.0 | 310 | 0.6 | 8 | 0 | 8 | 2.37 | 350 | 0.6 | 390 | 0.6 | 820 | 0.8 |
| Non-religious | 30 | 0.2 | 190 | 0.4 | 8 | 26 | 34 | 9.71 | 350 | 0.6 | 530 | 0.8 | 2,040 | 2.0 |
| Muslims | 60 | 0.3 | 170 | 0.3 | 5 | −1 | 4 | 2.11 | 190 | 0.3 | 210 | 0.3 | 310 | 0.3 |
| Baha'is | 0 | 0.0 | 150 | 0.3 | 4 | 2 | 6 | 3.33 | 180 | 0.3 | 210 | 0.3 | 510 | 0.5 |
| Other religionists | 80 | 0.4 | 80 | 0.1 | 2 | 0 | 2 | 2.37 | 90 | 0.1 | 100 | 0.1 | 310 | 0.3 |
| **Country's population** | **19,260** | **100.0** | **52,000** | **100.0** | **1,400** | **0** | **1,400** | **2.37** | **59,000** | **100.0** | **66,000** | **100.0** | **102,000** | **100.0** |

COLUMNS, ROWS. For meanings and definitions, see Codebook (Part 6). Note that, by definition, total 'Christians' = professing + crypto-Christians, which also = affiliated + nominal Christians. Percentages may not always total exactly, due to rounding.
CENSUSES. 1901 Census of the British Empire: 83.4% Roman Catholics, 13.7% Anglicans and Protestants, 2.0% Hindus,

0.3% Muslims, 0.3% Chinese folk-religionists, 0.2% non-religious. 4.V.1960: 90.7% Roman Catholics, 7.8% Anglicans, 0.4% Hindus, 0.3% Protestants (0.3% SDAs), 0.3% Muslims, 0.1% Chinese folk-religionists, 0.1% Parsis, 0.1% Jains. 5.V.1971: 90.0% Roman Catholics, 7.6% Anglicans, 0.6% Hindus, 0.4% marginal Protestants (Jehovah's Witnesses), 0.4% non-religious, 0.3% Muslims, 0.3% Baha'is, 0.3% Protestants, 0.1% other religionists (Parsis, Jains, Chinese folk-religionists).

NOTES ON RELIGIONS
BAHA'IS. Growth from 1 local spiritual assembly (1964) to 8 (1973), and from 15 adherents in 1960 census to 156 in 1971 census. Since 1969, Baha'i teaching and singing over government radio has been permitted.
OTHER RELIGIONISTS. Parsis, Jains, Chinese folk-religionists.

### NON-CHRISTIAN RELIGIONS. Hinduism is
practised by Indian traders and other settlers, and **Islam** by Muslims of Asian extraction.
**Baha'i** has a small community, and there are also a few Parsis, Jains, and Chinese folk-religionists.

### CHRISTIANITY
CATHOLIC CHURCH. Catholics, whose origins date from 1770, make up 90% of the population of the Seychelles, and include Creoles, Europeans, Blacks (Bantu) and 280 Chinese. There are parishes with resident priests at Mahé, Praslin, and La Digue;

Postage stamps showing Anglican and Roman Catholic cathedrals and churches in Victoria, Bel Ombre and Praslin.

while other islands receive one or 2 pastoral visits each year, including the islands of the British Indian Ocean Territory. The diocese of Port Victoria is served by 7 national priests and 22 expatriates; and the first national bishop was consecrated in 1975. There is one indigenous congregation of nuns, the Sisters of St Elizabeth, which was formed in 1940.

ANGLICAN CHURCH. Anglican work began in 1843 and now exists on both Mahé and Praslin Islands, the population of the latter being one-third Anglican. The Anglican diocese of the Seychelles has been since 1975 part of the Church of the Province of the Indian Ocean. The church has established 9 schools.

OTHER CHURCHES. There are 2 Seventh-day Adventist congregations, one at Mahé and the other at Praslin. Adventists have been in the Seychelles since 1929.

**CHURCH AND STATE.** Relations are generally good in spite of continuing friction over the use of French by the Catholic Church. Since 1945 Catholic school personnel have been appointed and paid by government, with the church retaining control over appointments.

**INTERDENOMINATIONAL ORGANIZATIONS.** An Ecumenical Committee, composed of 3 Catholic and 2 Anglican members, was formed in April 1970.

**BROADCASTING.** The government Seychelles Broadcasting Service transmits religious programmes every Sunday, alternating weekly Sunday morning Catholic masses and Anglican services. There is also a 15-minute Sunday evening broadcast shared equally by Catholics and Anglicans.

In 1972 a new Protestant international station, the Far East Broadcasting Association (FEBA), the first all-British and Commonwealth missionary radio station, began operations, broadcasting to Africa, India, Pakistan and Sri Lanka.

For Catholics, Seychelles is registered as a member of UNDA.

**BIBLIOGRAPHY**
*Seychelles calling.* D. Winter. Woking, Surrey: FEBA, 1971. 35p. (Describes founding of FEBA).

Far East Broadcasting Association (FEBA), whose station was begun in 1972. *Above.* General view of masts and antennae. *Right.* Operator/programmer at work.

TABLE 2.  ORGANIZED CHURCHES AND DENOMINATIONS IN SEYCHELLES

| Official name 1 | Begun 2 | Type 3 | Counc 4 | Congs 5 | Adults 6 | Affiliated 7 | Names, notes, and other statistics (see Codebook) 8 |
|---|---|---|---|---|---|---|---|
| Anglican Church: D Seychelles | 1843 | A Hig | Aw.V. | 10 | 1,500 | 3,900 | In Ch of Province of the Indian Ocean. Until 1973 in D Mauritius. M=USPG. 4n,3x. |
| Catholic Church: D Port Victoria | 1770 | R Lat | pzSEr | 18 | 27,000 | 46,000 | *Eglise Catholique.* Mostly French-speaking. C=1+1+2. 7n,22x,11m,61w,P=39%,1684Yy. |
| Jehovah's Witnesses | c1960 | M Jeh | x.... | 1 | 12 | 100 | Congregation in Victoria, Mahé. Active witnessing under way by 1964. 2Y. |
| Seventh-day Adventist Church | 1929 | P Adv | x.... | 2 | 94 | 150 | *SDA, Seychelles Field,* East African Union. Mahé; recently Praslin. 2x,2t(83),9Y. |
| Other Protestant denominations | | P | ..... | | 50 | 100 | Including: International Christian Fellowship (UK). |
| Total affiliated (mid-1970) | | | | 33 | 28,656 | 50,250 | Total denominations (1970) . . . 6. |
| Total affiliated (mid-1975) | | | | 35 | 32,340 | 56,710 | Total denominations (1975) . . . 6. |
| Total affiliated (mid-1980) | | | | 37 | 35,980 | 63,090 | Total denominations (1980) . . . 8. |

**NOTES ON TABLE ABOVE**
COLUMNS: for meanings and CODES (cols. 1, 3, 4, 8): see Codebook, (Part 6). Column 1: **Bold face type** = church with over 10% of country's affiliated Christians.
NATIONAL COUNCILS (Column 4, 5th letter).
r = member, Kenya Episcopal Conference (KEC).

**PEOPLES** (ethnolinguistic). Christians: 96.6% Creole (Mulatto), 1.9% French, 1.0% British, 0.5% Chinese, Tamil, Black (Bantu).

**COUNTRY-WIDE TOTALS**
EVANGELIZATION (see Part 5). 1900: 100%. 1970: 100%. 1980: 100%.
FOREIGN MISSIONARIES AND PERSONNEL (aliens from abroad) (1973). Total 88. *From Western world.* 83: 45 Roman Catholics, 35 Protestants (32 in 2 UK societies, 3 in 3 Australia societies), 3 Anglicans in 1 UK society. *From Third World.* About 5 mostly Roman Catholics from Mauritius. After 1975 there were also Protestants from Singapore and elsewhere working with FEBA.
INSTITUTIONS (church-operated) (1973). Total 16, including about 12 higher schools, 1 medical centre, 1 radio station, 1 religious community.
PERIODICALS. 2 titles.
PERSONNEL. About 150 (62 national, 88 foreign).
RELIGIOUS LIBRARIES. 2.
SCRIPTURE DISTRIBUTION (1975). Annual totals: 2,000 Bibles (subsidized), 200 NTs (commercial). *Translations completed.* In Seychelles Creole: portion 1974.
SERVICE AGENCIES. About 14, including CV/AV, FEBA (24 missionaries), UCS/SCU, USTC.

**ADDITIONAL DATA ON CHURCHES**
CATHOLIC CHURCH. The jurisdiction was erected in 1852. *Catholics.* Creoles, Europeans, Bantu and 280 Chinese. *Catechumens.* (1959) 3; (1961) 1; (1963) 21. *Annual baptisms.* (1972) 99.8% infant, 0.2% adult. *Brothers.* 1 national. *Sisters.* 48 nationals. *Catechists.* Total (1970) 2. *Indigenous religious congregations.* Soeurs de Ste-Elisabeth (begun 1940, 26 professed in 1970). *Foreign orders and congregations.* Priests: OFMCap (Swiss province). Brothers: Instruction Chrétienne. Sisters: St-Joseph de Cluny.
*Catholic organizations.* The diocese is attached to the Kenya Episcopal Conference (KEC). There is a Presbyteral Council composed of 8 Capuchins and 2 national secular priests. The principal lay movements are Happy Youth Club, CV/AV, Seychelles Christian Union and Christian Workers.
The Holy See has no diplomatic relations with the Seychelles. It is represented to the Catholic hierarchy by an apostolic delegate based in Nairobi, Kenya.
In 1976 the Catholic Church was responsible for 36 primary schools (10,379 pupils) and 19 secondary and other schools (3,769); one sanatorium annexed to the government hospital at Victoria where 3 sisters were at work; a training programme for nurses; 2 housing development societies; 2 orphanages (82 orphans); one home for elderly women; and numerous nurseries.

# SIERRA LEONE

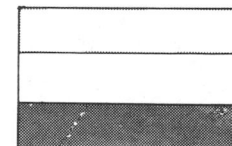

## SECULAR DATA

**STATE. Official name:** The Republic of Sierra Leone. Adjective of nationality: Sierra Leonean.
**Flag** (shown above right): Stripes of green (top), white and blue.
**Area:** 71,740 sq.km. (27,699 sq.miles). Agricultural land: 82.9%.
**Government:** One-party republic, since 1971 (1808 British colony and (1896) protectorate, 1961 Independence, 1967 military junta, 1971 republic).
**Legislature:** House of Representatives, 97 members.
**Official language:** English.
**Capital:** Freetown 214,440 (1974).
**Political divisions:** 3 Provinces, divided into 12 Districts, and 147 Chiefdoms.
**Armed forces** (1976): Total 2,145 regular army.

**DEMOGRAPHY. Population:** 2,729,479 (census of 8.XII.1974. For 1970–2000 (UN), see last row of Table 1). Population density (1975): 42/sq.km. (108/sq.mile). Under 15 years: 42%. Growth rate (1975–80): 2.57% per year (births 4.44%, deaths −1.87%). Life expectancy (1975–80): 46.0 years. Household size: 4.0 persons.
**Major languages:** English, Krio (Pidgin English), Mende, Temne, Mandingo, Koranko, Susu, Limba, Kono, Fulani, Loko, Kissi, and about 10 other languages.

**Urban dwellers** (1970): 13.9%. Urban growth rate (1950–70): 3.7% per year.
**Labour force:** 41%.
**Refugees** (1977): 5,000 from Lebanon.
**Tourists** (1974): 7,800.

**ETHNOLINGUISTIC GROUPS:** 30.9% Mende, 29.8% Temne, 9.8% Nuclear Mande (3.7% Koranko, 3.1% Susu, 2.3% Malinke, 0.7% Yalunka), 8.4% Limba, 4.8% Kono, 3.4% Sherbro, 3.1% Fulani, 2.9% Loko, 2.3% Kissi, 2.1% Creole (Krio), 0.8% Bullom, 0.4% Krim, 0.4% Vai, 0.2% Kru, 0.2% Asian (5,000), 0.2% Gola, 0.1% European (3,000), Lebanese Arab, & a number of smaller tribes.

**MONEY** (1977). **Monetary unit:** leone (= 100 cents); US$1 = L 1.21.
**National income per person:** US$210. Average annual family income: US$840.
**Inflation:** (1970–74) 5.8% per year, (1975) 20% per year (consumer price index 162).
**Cost of living in capital** (1976): index 125 (Washington DC=100). Daily cost of living: US$34.

**HEALTH. Hospitals:** 36 (2,458 beds). Doctors: 149. Lepers: 100,000 (33.5 per 1,000). Blind: 28,000. Psychotics: 21,000. Criminals: 5,000.

**EDUCATION.** Adult literacy: (1963) 7%. Education rate: 14%. Schools: 1,031. Universities: 1.

**LITERATURE.** Annual new book titles (1967): 73. Periodicals: 26. Newspapers: 5 dailies, 4 non-daily.

**COMMUNICATION** (per 1,000 people). Phones: 3. Radios: 21. TV sets: 2. Daily newspaper circulation: 17 copies.

TABLE 1.    RELIGIOUS ADHERENTS IN SIERRA LEONE

| Year | 1900 | | mid-1970 | | Annual change, 1970–1980 | | | | mid-1975 | | mid-1980 | | 2000 | |
|---|---|---|---|---|---|---|---|---|---|---|---|---|---|---|
| Name | Adherents | % | Adherents | % | Natural | Conversion | Total | Rate | Adherents | % | Adherents | % | Adherents | % |
| Tribal religionists | 876,600 | 85.4 | 1,419,950 | 53.7 | 39,354 | −6,634 | 32,720 | 2.08 | 1,569,420 | 52.6 | 1,747,150 | 51.5 | 2,651,200 | 46.4 |
| Muslims | 102,600 | 10.0 | 1,005,000 | 38.0 | 28,947 | 4,193 | 33,140 | 2.87 | 1,154,400 | 38.7 | 1,336,400 | 39.4 | 2,457,900 | 43.0 |
| Ahmadis | 0 | 0.0 | 5,000 | 0.2 | 176 | 224 | 400 | 5.71 | 7,000 | 0.2 | 9,000 | 0.3 | 30,000 | 0.5 |
| Christians | 46,800 | 4.6 | 216,800 | 8.2 | 6,432 | 2,418 | 8,850 | 3.45 | 256,500 | 8.5 | 305,300 | 9.0 | 600,200 | 10.5 |
| professing | 46,800 | 4.6 | 216,800 | 8.2 | 6,432 | 2,418 | 8,850 | 3.45 | 256,500 | 8.6 | 305,300 | 9.0 | 600,200 | 10.5 |
| Protestants | 20,000 | 1.9 | 112,500 | 4.3 | 3,365 | 1,325 | 4,690 | 3.49 | 134,200 | 4.5 | 159,400 | 4.7 | 314,400 | 5.5 |
| Roman Catholics | 3,000 | 0.3 | 52,900 | 2.0 | 1,570 | 600 | 2,170 | 3.47 | 62,600 | 2.1 | 74,600 | 2.2 | 142,900 | 2.5 |
| Anglicans | 23,500 | 2.3 | 31,700 | 1.2 | 891 | −35 | 856 | 2.41 | 35,540 | 1.2 | 40,260 | 1.2 | 58,900 | 1.0 |
| African indigenous | 300 | 0.0 | 17,000 | 0.6 | 524 | 486 | 1,010 | 4.83 | 20,900 | 0.7 | 27,100 | 0.8 | 75,000 | 1.3 |
| Marginal Protestants | 0 | 0.0 | 2,200 | 0.1 | 68 | 42 | 110 | 4.07 | 2,700 | 0.1 | 3,300 | 0.1 | 8,000 | 0.1 |
| Orthodox | 0 | 0.0 | 500 | 0.0 | 14 | 0 | 14 | 2.51 | 560 | 0.0 | 640 | 0.0 | 1,000 | 0.0 |
| nominal | 4,520 | 0.4 | 26,646 | 1.0 | 804 | 637 | 1,441 | 4.50 | 32,040 | 1.1 | 41,060 | 1.2 | 77,800 | 1.4 |
| affiliated | 42,280 | 4.1 | 190,154 | 7.2 | 5,628 | 1,781 | 7,409 | 3.30 | 224,460 | 7.5 | 264,240 | 7.8 | 522,400 | 9.1 |
| total practising | 33,820 | 80 | 133,110 | 70 | 3,940 | 1,247 | 5,187 | 3.30 | 157,120 | 70 | 184,970 | 70 | 339,600 | 65 |
| non-practising | 8,460 | 20 | 57,050 | 30 | 1,688 | 534 | 2,222 | 3.30 | 67,340 | 30 | 79,270 | 30 | 182,800 | 35 |
| Protestants | 19,000 | 1.8 | 99,187 | 3.8 | 2,916 | 736 | 3,652 | 3.14 | 116,300 | 3.9 | 135,700 | 4.0 | 262,900 | 4.6 |
| Evangelicals | 9,000 | 0.9 | 65,300 | 2.5 | 1,921 | 509 | 2,430 | 3.17 | 76,600 | 2.6 | 89,600 | 2.6 | 175,000 | 3.1 |
| Roman Catholics | 2,980 | 0.3 | 47,467 | 1.8 | 1,422 | 611 | 2,033 | 3.59 | 56,700 | 1.9 | 67,800 | 2.0 | 137,200 | 2.4 |
| Catholic pentecostals | 0 | 0.0 | 0 | 0.0 | 13 | 87 | 100 | 20.00 | 500 | 0.0 | 1,000 | 0.0 | 5,000 | 0.1 |
| Anglicans | 20,000 | 1.9 | 25,000 | 0.9 | 689 | −189 | 500 | 1.82 | 27,500 | 0.9 | 30,000 | 0.9 | 40,000 | 0.7 |
| Evangelicals | 17,000 | 1.7 | 20,000 | 0.8 | 564 | −64 | 500 | 2.22 | 22,500 | 0.8 | 25,000 | 0.7 | 32,000 | 0.6 |
| African indigenous | 300 | 0.0 | 16,000 | 0.6 | 524 | 586 | 1,110 | 5.31 | 20,900 | 0.7 | 27,100 | 0.8 | 74,300 | 1.3 |
| Marginal Protestants | 0 | 0.0 | 2,000 | 0.1 | 63 | 37 | 100 | 4.00 | 2,500 | 0.1 | 3,000 | 0.1 | 7,000 | 0.1 |
| Orthodox | 0 | 0.0 | 500 | 0.0 | 14 | 0 | 14 | 2.51 | 560 | 0.0 | 640 | 0.0 | 1,000 | 0.0 |
| Hindus | 0 | 0.0 | 1,400 | 0.1 | 40 | 0 | 40 | 2.51 | 1,580 | 0.1 | 1,800 | 0.1 | 3,000 | 0.1 |
| Baha'is | 0 | 0.0 | 750 | 0.0 | 24 | 16 | 40 | 4.21 | 950 | 0.0 | 1,150 | 0.0 | 2,700 | 0.0 |
| Other religionists | 0 | 0.0 | 100 | 0.0 | 3 | 7 | 10 | 6.67 | 150 | 0.0 | 200 | 0.0 | 1,000 | 0.0 |
| Country's population | 1,026,000 | 100.0 | 2,644,000 | 100.0 | 74,800 | 0 | 74,800 | 2.51 | 2,983,000 | 100.0 | 3,392,000 | 100.0 | 5,716,000 | 100.0 |

**COLUMNS, ROWS.** For meanings and definitions, see Codebook (Part 6). Note that, by definition, total 'Christians' = professing + crypto-Christians, which also = affiliated + nominal Christians. Percentages may not always total exactly, due to rounding.
**CENSUSES. 1891** (Colony only): 34.8% tribal religionists, 27.5% Anglicans, 27.1% Protestants, 9.9% Muslims, 0.8% Roman Catholics. **1901** (Colony): 31.4% tribal religionists, 29.2% Anglicans, 26.0% Protestants, 12.4% Muslims, 1.0% Roman Catholics, 0.4% African indigenous. **1911** (Colony): 32.5% tribal religionists, 25.0% Anglicans, 24.7% Protestants, 15.2% Muslims, 1.9% Roman Catholics, 0.6% African indigenous. **1921** (Colony): 32.7% tribal religionists, 23.7% Anglicans, 21.2% Protestants, 19.5% Muslims, 2.3% Roman Catholics, 0.6% African indigenous. **1931** (Colony): 28.8% tribal religionists, 26.3% Muslims, 21.4% Anglicans, 19.7% Protestants, 3.4% Roman Catholics, 0.4% African indigenous. **1931** (Protectorate): 86.5% tribal religionists, 11.6% Muslims, 1.9% Christians. **1931** (Colony and Protectorate): 83.4% tribal

religionists, 12.4% Muslims, 4.2% Christians. Subsequently the religion question was not asked.

**NOTES ON RELIGIONS**
**AFRICAN INDIGENOUS.** In 12 denominations in 1970 (see Table 2).
**AHMADIS.** Begun 1957; Qadianis from Pakistan, with missions in Freetown and Bo; 10% of adherents are in Temne country, 90% in Mende. An attempt to plant the mission in the diamond-mining Kono district had collapsed by 1959. The number of branches elsewhere grew from 25 in 1963 to 40 in 1970. There were also 17 primary schools in 1963, and a printing press and bookstore.
**BAHA'IS.** In 5 local spiritual assemblies (1973).
**CATHOLIC PENTECOSTALS** (or, Catholic charismatics). By 1975, the Catholic charismatic renewal was under way, with its centre in Port Loko.
**HINDUS.** Indian traders.
**MUSLIMS.** Almost all Sunnis (of the Malikite rite). Islamized

peoples: Bullom (80%), Fulbe, Koranko (30% Muslim), Krim (40%), Limba (35%), Loko (39%), Malinke, Mende (40%), Sherbro (40%), Susu (95%), Temne (30% in 1956, 60% by 1972), Vai (100%), Yalunka (60% Muslim). There is an Ahmadiya Mission (enumerated here as Muslims, though declared non-Muslim by Pakistan) in Bo and Freetown, and the Muslim Brotherhood (Ikhwan al-Muslimin) is active in Freetown. *Hajj pilgrims to Mecca.* (1970) 353; (1974) 504; (1975) 377; (1976) 319.
**OTHER RELIGIONISTS.** Including Rosicrucians (1 AMORC centre).
**ROMAN CATHOLICS.** In 1900 there were 2,400 indigenous baptized Catholics and 575 catechumens.
**TRIBAL RELIGIONISTS.** Animists, mainly among peoples in the east. Tribes with over 60% traditionalists in 1972: Kono (95% animist), Kissi (80%), Koranko (69%), Limba (60%), Loko (60%). Of the largest tribes, the Mende are 40% animist and the Temne 15%.

**Tribal religionists.** Kono wayside sacrificial stone. 95% of the Kono are traditionalists (pagans).

**NON-CHRISTIAN RELIGIONS. African traditional religions** are strongest in eastern Sierra Leone. The Kono remain 95% animist, the Kissi 80% and the Koranko 69%, while 60% of the Limba and Loko of the north central part of the country still follow their ancestral tribal religions. The Mende are 40% traditionalist, mostly concentrated in the east. The supreme being is identified as Kanu among the Limba and Kuru among the Temne. The Kono have 2 names for God, Meketa (Everlasting One) and Yataa (Omnipresent One), although the latter is more common today. Kono divinities include Dugbo (Mother Earth), the wife of Yataa; Kwigbe, who is believed to reside in a sacred stone at Gbamandu and provides aid to barren women; Nyalwe, a river spirit to whom animals are offered during initiation ceremonies; and Kaene, a river divinity who guides the affairs of chiefs' sons. Offerings are made to the ancestral spirits (Fuenu) at designated altars (*kotina*) throughout the region, and special ceremonies are performed periodically by priests (*kongoyasoenu*.) The departed ancestors are believed to serve as intermediaries between the living community and God. This is also true of the Mende who conceive of God (Ngewo) as a great chief and approach him most commonly through the recent dead (Kekeni). The Kekeni in turn petition the distant ancestors (Ndebla)

who pass the requests on to Ngewo. Both among the Kono and Mende there are strong beliefs in the efficacy of charms, medicine men, divination and the reality of witchcraft. Secret societies have increased in importance in recent years.
**Islam** is found principally in the north and west although the coastal peoples have also come under Muslim influence. The Susu, Vai and Bullom are predominantly Muslim, and Islam is also strong among the Yalunka and Temne. There has recently been an upsurge in conversions to Islam among the Mende. The Ahmadiya Mission has been active since 1957; adherents now are 90% Mende, 10% Temne.

**CHRISTIANITY.** Christianity has had its greatest success near the coast; however, only the Creoles are

**Ahmadis.** Students at the Ahmadiya Missionary School, Freetown.

fully christianized. The Mende and Temne have shown themselves partially responsive to the gospel, but the churches have made few converts among most of the other tribal peoples.

PROTESTANT CHURCHES. Protestantism came to Sierra Leone in 1785 with the arrival of Black settlers from Nova Scotia, who brought with them their own denominations. Methodist and Baptist churches and the Countess of Huntingdon's Connexion were established at that time. British Baptist missionaries entered in 1975, followed by British Methodists in 1796 and pioneers of the London, Edinburgh and Glasgow missionary societies in 1799. The first North Americans (1842) belonged to the American Missionary Association. United Brethren entered in 1850, but divided in 1889 into United Brethren and EUB factions. The merger of the EUB with American Methodists in the USA in 1968 produced the present United Methodist Church. Another Methodist group was the Wesleyan Church which came from the USA in 1889. The present century has witnessed the arrival of Seventh-day Adventists, Assemblies of God and many other smaller denominations.

The work of the various Protestant churches is widely spread throughout the country; and except among the northern Susu and the southeastern Vai, Christian work is carried on among all peoples. Assemblies of God, United Pentecostals, United Brethren and Missionary Church Association have grown little over the past quarter century. Wesleyan Methodists have shown greater gains although these have been spasmodic. Methodists grew rapidly from 1945 to 1955 followed by a period of decline from which they have been trying to recover. The most consistent and sustained progress has been recorded by United Methodists (formerly EUB) whose growth since 1955 has been spectacular. In the decade prior to 1955 they increased by only 40%, but the following decade showed a growth of more than 100%. Moreover the momentum has been sustained up to the present time. Whereas in 1962 they had slightly over 10,000 members and a total Christian community of 21,000, by 1971 they had 23,232 full and 4,080 preparatory members with a total Christian community of 40,000. Almost all Methodist bodies in Sierra Leone, Dahomey, Gambia, Ghana, Ivory Coast and Nigeria are linked in the Council of the Methodist Church in West Africa.

CATHOLIC CHURCH. Portuguese mariners first touched the coast of Sierra Leone in the 15th century and various unsuccessful attempts were made to open work during succeeding centuries. The vicariate of Sierra Leone was erected in 1858 and given to the Lyons Fathers, followed by Holy Ghost priests in 1860. Nevertheless, significant progress was not made until 1950 when the diocese of Freetown and Bo was erected and placed under the direct supervision of Propaganda. The first indigenous priest was ordained in 1939, but by 1970 there were still only 3 national priests as contrasted with 95 expatriates.

ANGLICAN CHURCH. Anglicans began work in 1804, but since the beginning attention has been

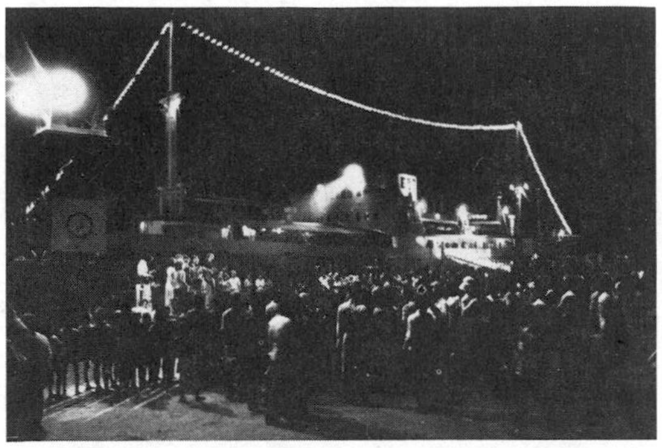

**Protestants.** Quayside rally at night in Freetown during visit of evangelistic ship MV Logos in February 1977.

focused on the Creole community with little concern for the surrounding tribal peoples. Numerically the church has barely increased at all since 1900.

INDIGENOUS CHURCHES. The West African Methodist Church was formed in 1844 when Africans were refused permission to preach in the Methodist Church founded by Nova Scotia settlers. For a period, missionaries were received from dissident British Methodist groups, but since Methodist union in Britain in 1932 this largely Creole Church has had no formal relations with any foreign denomination. In 1945, a schism from the EUB produced the God is Our Light Church which has close ties to Ghana, and the National Pentecostal Church split from the Assemblies of God in 1970. Outside influences from Blacks in the USA have formed the AMEC and the PAW churches, and the Church of the Lord (Aladura) has spread to Sierra Leone from Nigeria and Ghana.

**CHURCH AND STATE.** The constitution of April 1971 guarantees freedom of conscience, expression, assembly and association (Article 11). In 1971, parliament passed a resolution to the effect that all aid (technical, financial or otherwise, including all forms of food supplies, clothing and medical supplies) received from foreign governments and organizations should be channelled through the Sierra Leone government. Recognized Christian schools receive partial grants from the Ministry of Education. There is no ministry or governmental department in charge of religious matters. Churches are not obliged to register with government; but for purposes of Christian marriage, 'places of worship' and ministers must be registered.

**INTERDENOMINATIONAL ORGANIZATIONS.** Twelve denominations are full members of the United Christian Council of Sierra Leone (UCCSL), which was founded in 1924. The Church of the Lord (Aladura) is an affiliate member. The council's aims and functions are 'to restore the unity of the Church of Christ, preserve comity among the Churches and Missions, serve as spokesman of the Church on religious, educational, moral, social and such other matters as affect the Christian cause in Sierra Leone; and where necessary, to take joint action'. In addition

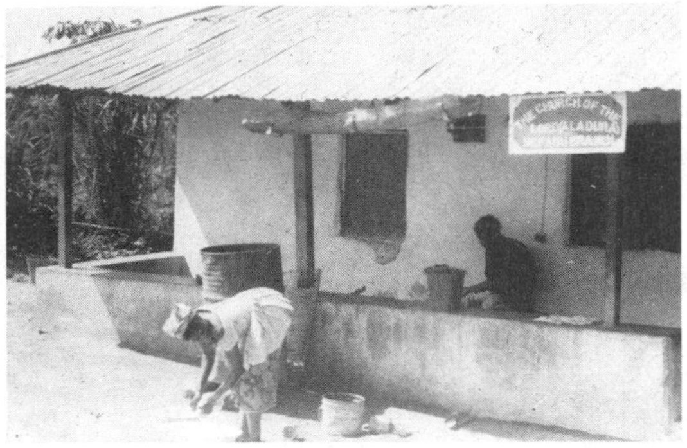

**Church of the Lord (Aladura).** Sefadu branch, among Kono tribe, of a Nigeria-based indigenous church with numerous foreign missions.

to its other activities the council manages 327 primary schools. The Sierra Leone Evangelical Fellowship (SLEF) has been formed more recently with 6 members, all also members of the UCCSL.

In 1973 at the insistence of the government, one of the 2 Catholic teacher training colleges was united with a Protestant one to form a state institution, the Normal School of Bo, which is open to all without religious distinction. The director in 1975 was a lay Protestant and the assistant director a Catholic priest. Religious instruction is given separately to Protestants and Catholics.

**BROADCASTING.** The government-owned Sierra Leone Broadcasting Service accepts both Protestant and Catholic programmes, including morning prayers, worship services, and special Christian events. From abroad, Christian programmes can easily be heard over ELWA (Liberia), and also over BBC (UK) daily. For Catholics, UNDA is represented by a national association.

In 1979, the Lutheran World Federation and WACC were considering Sierra Leone as a possible site for a successor radio station to RVOG (Ethiopia).

## BIBLIOGRAPHY


'Ahmadiyya in Sierra Leone', H. Fisher, *Sierra Leone bulletin of religion*, II, 1 (1960), 1–10.

'Ancestor worship', H. Sawyerr, *Sierra Leone bulletin of religion*, VI, 2 (December, 1964), 25–33.

*Centenary souvenir of Holy Ghost Fathers in Sierra Leone, 1864–1964*. Ed E. Hamelberg. Freetown: CSSp, n.d. (c1965). 136p.

*Church growth in Sierra Leone*. G.W. Olson. Grand Rapids, Michigan: Eerdmans, 1969. 222p.

*Deep Mende: religious interactions in a changing African rural society*. D. Reeck. London: Brill, 1976. 102p.

*Religion in an African society: a study of the religion of the Kono people of Sierra Leone in its social environment*. R.T. Parsons. Freetown, 1964.

'The Baptist churches in Sierra Leone', M. Banton, *Sierra Leone bulletin of religion*, V, 2 (December, 1963), 55–60.

*The Church of the United Brethren in Christ in Sierra Leone*. E.D. Cox. South Pasadena (CA): William Carey Library, 1970. 171p.

'The Martha Davies Confidential Benevolent Association', I.M. Ndanema, *Sierra Leone bulletin of religion*, III, 2 (1961), 64–67.

'The Mende in Sierra Leone', K.L. Little, in *African worlds* (London: Oxford, 1954), p.111–137.

*The springs of Mende belief and conduct*. W.T. Harris & H. Sawyerr. Freetown: Sierra Leone University Press, 1968.


TABLE 2. ORGANIZED CHURCHES AND DENOMINATIONS IN SIERRA LEONE

| Official name 1 | Begun 2 | Type 3 | Counc 4 | Congs 5 | Adults 6 | Affiliated 7 | Names, notes, and other statistics (see Codebook) 8 |
|---|---|---|---|---|---|---|---|
| African Methodist Episcopal Church | 1886 | I Met | Vw..N | 9 | 861 | 1,500 | M=AMEC(Black mission from USA). Creoles. 2 elementary schools. 6n,1x,6m,1r. |
| Assemblies of God | 1916 | P Pe2 | ZFG.a | 48 | 1,823 | 4,000 | M=AoG(UK,USA). 56% Limba, 19% Kissi, 9% Kru, 9% Loko. 6x,40m,16f,2s(33),156Y. |
| **Catholic Church in Sierra Leone:** | 1858 | R Lat | P.SGP | 222 | 27,500 | 47,467 | Slow growth. C=2+1+4. 3n,95x,10m,62w,P=43%,3199Yy. |
| M Freetown & Bo (1981: Bo separate) | 1858 | R Lat | Pcssp | 200 | 20,200 | 34,800 | Mainly Temne, Mende. 1,120 expatriates. 3 47 5 36 38 1900 |
| D Kenema | 1970 | R Lat | Pcssp | 10 | 3,600 | 6,322 | In southeast. Kono and other smaller tribes. 0 15 0 10 40 671 |
| D Makeni | 1952 | R Lat | Psx | 12 | 3,700 | 6,345 | 71% Temne, 11% Limba, 5% Mende, 3% Loko. 0 33 5 16 73 628 |
| Church of God of Prophecy | 1934 | P Pe3 | Z.... | 27 | 805 | 2,400 | M=CGP(USA). Members of Temne tribe at Port Loko and Magburaka. HQ Freetown. |
| Church of the Lord (Aladura) | 1947 | I pen | xwI.n | 26 | 300 | 1,000 | Aladura=Praying. Church from Nigeria, leaders Ghanaians. Mende, Kono, Creoles. |
| Churches of Christ | 1961 | P Dis | x.... | 40 | 600 | 1,000 | M=CC(Non-Instrumental) (USA). HQ Freetown. Creoles. 1 school. 12f,1s,63Y. |
| Countess of Huntingdon's Connexion | 1792 | P Con | ....N | 14 | 1,200 | 2,000 | Begun by Nova Scotia settlers. 1825, M=CHC; Sierra Leone Mission(UK). Creoles. |
| Free Gospel Church | 1920 | P Pe4 | ..... | 10 | 100 | 300 | M=FGC(HQ Turtle Creek,PA,USA). Pentecostals. 8m,4f,1h. |
| God is Our Light Church | 1945 | I pen | ..... | 30 | 700 | 1,500 | *GIOL*. Indigenous church ex EUB, controlled from Ghana. Anti-medicine. Kono, Mende. |
| Greek Orthodox P Alexandria (D Accra) | | O Gre | Cw... | | 300 | 500 | HQ Yaoundé (Cameroon). Under P Alexandria (Egypt). Lebanese, Greek traders. |
| Jehovah's Witnesses | 1923 | M Jeh | x.... | 35 | 1,002 | 2,000 | *Watch Tower*. First missionaries entered 1923. Strong among Temne in Makeni. 113Y. |
| **Methodist Church, Sierra Leone** | 1792 | P Met | VWA.N | 394 | 12,424 | 30,000 | *SL Conf*. M=MMS. 70% Creole,27% Mende,3% Kissi. 35n,12x,34f,1p,5r,W=60%,618Y,464y. |
| National Pentecostal Church | 1970 | I pen | ..... | 10 | 200 | 500 | Schism ex Assemblies of God. Sierra Leonian indigenous pentecostals. |
| Nigerian Baptist Convention | 1960 | P Bap | Twa.a | 7 | 67 | 600 | M=NBC(Nigeria). Work among Limba at Magburaka. 1x,4m,6f,W=45%,16Y,25z. |
| Open Bible Standard Churches | 1967 | P Pe2 | ZP... | 1 | 50 | 100 | M=OBSC(USA). Classical Pentecostals (2-stage). 4f. |
| Pentecostal Assemblies of the World | | I pel | xv... | | 500 | 1,000 | M=PAW(USA Blacks). Strong in Liberia (HQ Monrovia). 1967 enquiry re joining WCC. |
| Seventh-day Adventist Church | 1905 | P Adv | x.... | 69 | 2,738 | 4,854 | *Sierra Leone Mission*, WAfrican UM. 75% Mende, 25% Temne. 8n,3x,21f,1H,1p,2r,168Y. |
| Sierra Leone Baptist Union | 1785 | P Bap | ..G.a | 5 | 150 | 700 | Begun by Nova Scotians. M=EBMS. 75% Bassa, Creole. 3n,3x,7f,G=2.9%pa,1h,W=73%,9Y. |
| **Sierra Leone Church** | 1804 | A Low | AwAVN | 65 | 10,000 | 25,000 | *Diocese of SL*, in CPWA. M=CMS(UK). 82% Creole, 10% Mende, 5% Limba. 36n,2x,11f,1s. |
| Sierra Leone Missionary Church | 1945 | P Hol | xFG.a | 35 | 320 | 1,350 | *SLMC*. M=Missionary Church Assoc, now MC(USA). Koranko, Yalunka. 3n,7x,25f,3h,1p. |
| Sierra Leone Wesleyan Church | 1889 | P Hol | VFG.a | 228 | 3,314 | 5,383 | M=WC. Limba, Temne,Loko. 20 schools. 9n,8x,38m,37f,G=4.5%pa,1H,3h,1p,1s,W=65%,237Yy. |
| United Brethren in Christ | 1850 | P Hol | xFG.a | 136 | 2,391 | 4,000 | M=UBC(USA). Holiness body. Mende. 32 schools. 21n,4x,106m,33w,28f,1H,1s. |
| **United Methodist Church** | 1850 | P Met | VwA.N | 318 | 27,312 | 40,000 | Till 1968, EUB. SL Provisional CC,UMC(USA),EMK. Mende, Temne. 28n,6x,22f,1p. |
| United Pentecostal Church | c1960 | P Pel | x.G.E | 6 | 1,000 | 1,500 | *Jesus Only Ch*. M=UPC(USA). Unitarians. HQ Magburaka. 95% Temne, 5% Limba. |
| West African Methodist Church | 1844 | I Met | V...N | 25 | 6,081 | 10,000 | Ex Nova Scotia Methodists. A=1933. 83% Creole, 11% Kru, 5% Mende. 10n,1r,18Y,205y. |
| Other Protestant denominations | | P | ..... | | 500 | 1,000 | Total about 6, including: Calvary Baptist Ch, World-Wide Missions (1965). |
| Other African indigenous churches | | I | ..... | | 200 | 500 | Total 6: Christ Apostolic Ch (Nigeria; 1968), Ch of Salvation, Salvation Band, &c. |
| **Total affiliated (mid-1970)** | | | | **1,770** | **111,438** | **190,154** | **Total denominations (1970) . . . 37.** |
| **Total affiliated (mid-1975)** | | | | **2,080** | **131,500** | **224,460** | **Total denominations (1975) . . . 40.** |
| **Total affiliated (mid-1980)** | | | | **2,390** | **154,900** | **264,240** | **Total denominations (1980) . . . 43.** |

NOTES ON TABLE ABOVE
COLUMNS: for meanings and CODES (cols. 1, 3, 4, 8): see Codebook (Part 6). Column 1: **Boldface type** = church with over 10% of country's affiliated Christians.
NATIONAL COUNCILS (Column 4, 5th letter).
a = member of both UCCSL and SLEF.
E = Sierra Leone Evangelical Fellowship (SLEF).
N = United Christian Council of Sierra Leone (UCCSL).
n = associate member of UCCSL.
P = Inter-Territorial Episcopal Conference of the Gambia, Liberia & Sierra Leone.
*Other national or plurinational councils.* United Pentecostal Assemblies of the World in Liberia & Sierra Leone.

PEOPLES (ethnolinguistic). Christians: 29.0% Mende, 28.5% Creole (Krio), 27.5% Temne, 5.6% Limba, 3.4% Kono, 1.5% White (British, European), 1.5% Kissi, 0.8% Kru, 0.8% Loko, 0.5% Koranko, 0.3% Bassa, 0.3% Sherbro, 0.1% Greek, 0.1% Lebanese Arab, Gola, et alii.

COUNTRY-WIDE TOTALS
EVANGELIZATION (see Part 5). 1900: 18%. 1970: 71%. 1980: 76%. *Mass evangelism.* 1969–70, New Life for All campaign (5,000 nightly attenders in Makeni, with 1,100 enquirers after one week). *Radiophonic evangelism.* ELWA, ICI (1,405 active students).
FOREIGN MISSIONARIES AND PERSONNEL (nationals serving abroad) (1973). Total about 2 Anglicans in Nigeria.
FOREIGN MISSIONARIES AND PERSONNEL (aliens from abroad) (1973). Total 446. *From Western world.* 415: 238 Protestants (163 in 15 USA societies, 58 in 7 UK societies, 13 in 2 WGermany societies, 2 in 1 Finland society, 2 in 1 Canada society), 165 Roman Catholics, 11 Anglicans in 1 UK society, 1 Black indigenous from USA. *From Third World.* 31: about 13 African indigenous from Ghana, Nigeria and Liberia, about 10 Roman Catholics from Nigeria et alia, about 8 Protestants from Ghana and Nigeria.
INSTITUTIONS (church-operated) (1973). Total 80, including 40 higher schools, 25 medical centres, 6 seminaries (5 Protestant, 1 Anglican).
PERIODICALS. About 15 titles.
PERSONNEL. About 1,111 (665 national, 446 foreign).
RELIGIOUS LIBRARIES. About 8.
SCRIPTURE DISTRIBUTION (1975). Annual totals: 9,719 Bibles (6% free, 88% subsidized, 5% commercial), 21,639 NTs (72% free, 24% subsidized, 4% commercial), 17,825 UBS portions, 11,911 UBS selections. *Translations completed.* Portion: 6 languages since 1816. NT: 3 languages since 1868. Bible: Mende in 1959.
SERVICE AGENCIES. About 24, including BB, CLC, NLFA, SCM, SLEF, SU, UCCSL, WATI, YMCA, YWCA.

ADDITIONAL DATA ON CHURCHES
CATHOLIC CHURCH IN SIERRA LEONE. *Catechumens.* (1959) 20,007; (1961) 21,229; (1963) 24,970. *Annual baptisms.* (1972) 38.3% infant, 61.7% adult. *National priests.* The first Sierra Leonian priest was ordained in 1939. *Foreign priests.* In 1975, the bishop of Onitsha (Nigeria) loaned 3 priests to the diocese of Kenema for 3 years. *Brothers.* All expatriate. *Sisters.* Of whom 2 are Sierra Leonians. *Seminarians.* There being no national seminary, in 1971 the 9 seminarians were studying in Ghana and Nigeria, and since 1974 at the regional seminary in Liberia. *Catechists.* Total (1970) 245 part-time, mostly teaching in Catholic schools. *Indigenous religious congregations.* Sisters of the Most Pure Heart (Nigerian). *Foreign congregations.* Priests: CSSp, SX. Brothers: OH. Sisters: St-Joseph de Cluny, Holy Rosary, Blessed Sacrament (Mexico).
*Catholic organizations.* The Inter-Territorial Episcopal Conference of Liberia, Sierra Leone and the Gambia is a member of both SECAM and the Regional Episcopal Conference of Ghana, Liberia, Sierra Leone and the Gambia. The latter organization was founded in 1972 and has its headquarters in Freetown. There are no national presbyteral or pastoral councils, and no associations of religious personnel. The 2 most active lay apostolate movements are the Legion of Mary and the Society of St Vincent de Paul.
The Holy See has no diplomatic relations with Sierra Leone. It is represented to the Catholic hierarchy by an apostolic delegate who serves also as pro-nuncio in Liberia.
An important factor in recent Catholic growth has been its extensive school system, in 1973 numbering 412 primary schools (55,636 pupils) and 27 secondary schools (10,284), plus 2 teacher training colleges. Of the latter one has been united with a Protestant one to form a state institution. There are also 3 general hospitals, 1 leprosarium, various dispensaries and maternity hospitals. Catholic Relief Services are active in development projects, credit unions and co-operatives in addition to the distribution of clothing, educational and medical supplies.

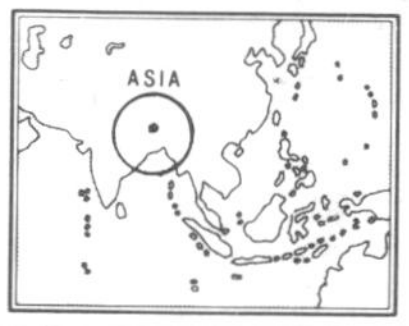


# SIKKIM

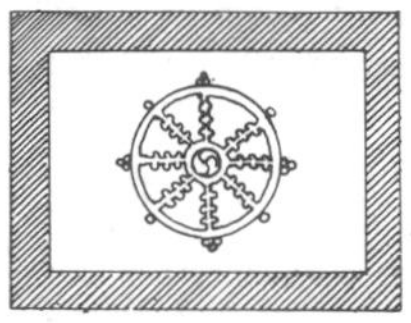

## SECULAR DATA

**STATE. Official name:** Sikkim (Denjong, = The Valley of Rice).
**Flag** (shown above right): Golden yellow wheel with 8 spokes, representing Buddha's eightfold path to Nirvana, on a white background with a red border.
**Area:** 7,107 sq.km. (2,744 sq.miles). Agricultural land: 10.5%.
**Government:** Territory under Indian control, since 1975 (14th century monarchy, 1839 British Protectorate, 1886 in British empire, 1947 Independence as absolute monarchy, 1974 constitutional monarchy, 1975 absorbed by India as its 22nd state).
**Official language:** English.
**Capital:** Gangtok 15,000.
**Political divisions** (1975): 4 Districts.
**Armed forces** (1976): Total 350 regular army. Paramilitary forces: police 400.
**Foreign forces** (1973): About 25,000 Indian troops.

**DEMOGRAPHY. Population:** 204,760 (census of 1.IV.1971. For 1970–2000 (UN), see last row of Table 1). Population density (1975): 35/sq.km. (91/sq.mile). Under 15 years: 42%. Growth rate (1975–80): 2.10% per year. Household size: 5.4 persons.
**Major languages:** Sikkimese, Bhotia (Dzongkha), Lepcha, Nepali, English, Bengali, Hindi, Bihari, Assamese, Punjabi, Newari, and several others.
**Urban dwellers** (1970): 6.3%. Urban growth rate (1950–70): 7.2% per year.
**Refugees** (1977): 3,600 Tibetans from China.
**Tourists:** numerous.

**ETHNOLINGUISTIC GROUPS:** 25% Kirati, 22% Nepali, 12% Lepcha, 10% Bengali, 9% Bhotia, 6% Tamang, 5.8% other Indian (Hindi, Bihari, Assamese, Punjabi), 3% Sherpa, 3% Newari, 3% Magar, 0.6% Sunwar, 0.6% Gurung, Tibetan.

**MONEY** (1977). **Monetary unit:** Indian rupee (= 100 paisa); US$1 = IRs 8.1.
**National income per person:** US$100. Average annual family income: US$540.

**HEALTH.** Hospitals: 5 (292 beds). Doctors: 22. Lepers: 1,290 (5.2 per 1,000). Blind: 1,300. Psychotics: 1,500.

**EDUCATION.** Schools: 191.

**COMMUNICATION** (per 1,000 people). Phones: 3.

TABLE 1. RELIGIOUS ADHERENTS IN SIKKIM

| Year | 1900 | | mid-1970 | | Annual change, 1970–1980 | | | | mid-1975 | | mid-1980 | | 2000 | |
|---|---|---|---|---|---|---|---|---|---|---|---|---|---|---|
| *Name* | *Adherents* | *%* | *Adherents* | *%* | *Natural* | *Conversion* | *Total* | *Rate* | *Adherents* | *%* | *Adherents* | *%* | *Adherents* | *%* |
| Hindus | 36,400 | 64.9 | 150,950 | 65.6 | 2,612 | –157 | 2,455 | 1.50 | 163,200 | 65.3 | 175,500 | 65.0 | 243,800 | 64.0 |
| Buddhists | 18,500 | 33.0 | 61,280 | 26.6 | 1,068 | 17 | 1,085 | 1.63 | 66,760 | 26.7 | 72,130 | 26.7 | 100,900 | 26.5 |
| Baha'is | 0 | 0.0 | 7,600 | 3.3 | 140 | 100 | 240 | 2.74 | 8,750 | 3.5 | 10,000 | 3.7 | 17,100 | 4.5 |
| **Christians** | **100** | **0.2** | **4,750** | **2.1** | **90** | **86** | **176** | **3.12** | **5,650** | **2.3** | **6,510** | **2.4** | **11,800** | **3.1** |
| crypto-Christians | 0 | 0.0 | 950 | 0.4 | 20 | 34 | 54 | 4.19 | 1,290 | 0.5 | 1,490 | 0.6 | 1,500 | 0.4 |
| professing | 100 | 0.2 | 3,800 | 1.7 | 70 | 52 | 122 | 2.80 | 4,360 | 1.7 | 5,020 | 1.9 | 10,300 | 2.7 |
| Protestants | 100 | 0.2 | 2,800 | 1.2 | 51 | 39 | 90 | 2.81 | 3,200 | 1.3 | 3,700 | 1.4 | 6,800 | 1.8 |
| Indian indigenous | 0 | 0.0 | 500 | 0.2 | 10 | 10 | 20 | 3.33 | 600 | 0.2 | 700 | 0.3 | 2,300 | 0.6 |
| Roman Catholics | 0 | 0.0 | 500 | 0.2 | 9 | 3 | 12 | 2.14 | 560 | 0.2 | 620 | 0.2 | 1,200 | 0.3 |
| affiliated | 100 | 0.2 | 4,750 | 2.1 | 90 | 86 | 176 | 3.12 | 5,650 | 2.3 | 6,510 | 2.4 | 11,800 | 3.1 |
| total practising | 90 | *90* | 3,800 | *80* | 72 | 69 | 141 | 3.12 | 4,520 | *80* | 5,210 | *80* | 8,260 | *70* |
| non-practising | 10 | *10* | 950 | *20* | 18 | 17 | 35 | 3.10 | 1,130 | *20* | 1,300 | *20* | 3,540 | *30* |
| Protestants | 100 | 0.2 | 3,500 | 1.5 | 62 | 18 | 80 | 2.05 | 3,900 | 1.6 | 4,300 | 1.6 | 7,000 | 1.8 |
| Evangelicals | 100 | 0.2 | 2,400 | 1.0 | 43 | 17 | 60 | 2.22 | 2,700 | 1.1 | 3,000 | 1.1 | 5,000 | 1.3 |
| Indian indigenous | 0 | 0.0 | 600 | 0.3 | 16 | 59 | 75 | 7.50 | 1,000 | 0.4 | 1,350 | 0.5 | 3,000 | 0.8 |
| Roman Catholics | 0 | 0.0 | 600 | 0.3 | 11 | 3 | 14 | 2.09 | 670 | 0.3 | 740 | 0.3 | 1,500 | 0.4 |
| Marginal Protestants | 0 | 0.0 | 50 | 0.0 | 1 | 6 | 7 | 8.75 | 80 | 0.0 | 120 | 0.0 | 300 | 0.1 |
| Tribal religionists | 1,100 | 2.0 | 2,300 | 1.0 | 36 | –46 | –10 | –0.44 | 2,250 | 0.9 | 2,200 | 0.8 | 1,900 | 0.5 |
| Muslims | 0 | 0.0 | 1,620 | 0.7 | 28 | 0 | 28 | 1.59 | 1,760 | 0.7 | 1,900 | 0.7 | 3,000 | 0.8 |
| Sikhs | 0 | 0.0 | 1,500 | 0.7 | 26 | 0 | 26 | 1.60 | 1,630 | 0.7 | 1,760 | 0.7 | 2,500 | 0.7 |
| **Country's population** | **56,100** | **100.0** | **230,000** | **100.0** | **4,000** | **0** | **4,000** | **1.60** | **250,000** | **100.0** | **270,000** | **100.0** | **381,000** | **100.0** |

COLUMNS, ROWS. For meanings and definitions, see Codebook (Part 6) Note that, by definition, total 'Christians' = professing + crypto-Christians, which also = affiliated + nominal Christians. Percentages may not always total exactly, due to rounding.
CENSUSES. **1911** (total population 87,920) 66.7%: Hindus (Brahmanic), 32.9% Buddhists, 0.3% Christians (285 persons, of whom 267 Indians, 14 Europeans, 4 Anglo-Indians), 0.1% Muslims (44 persons). **1.III.1951:** 71.1% Hindus, 28.6% Buddhists, 0.22% Christians (304 persons), 0.1% Muslims (also 19 Jains and 18 Sikhs). **1.III.1961:** 66.7% Hindus, 30.8% Buddhists, 1.74% Christians (2,813 persons), 0.7% Muslims (also 72 Sikhs, 19 Jains and 19 others).

NOTES ON RELIGIONS
BAHA'IS. Very rapid growth from 6 local spiritual assemblies (1964) to 76 (1973); mainly Indians, with intense Baha'i missionary activity.
BUDDHISTS. Mahayana, religion of Tibetans (formerly in the Rnying-mapa, a liberal Mahayana tendency in Tibet) and Lepchas, much syncretized with animism, Bon, Lamaism and Hinduism. There are also many recent Buddhist refugees from neighbouring territories. Sikkim has 67 Buddhist monasteries, and 3,000 lamas.
CHRISTIANS. The majority are Indians, either in the civilian administration or in the strong Indian military presence in Sikkim.
COUNTRY'S POPULATION. The totals for 1970–80 include an average of 25,000 Indian troops (1973) and many Indian civilian administrators.
HINDUS. Followers of a peculiarly Himalayan syncretistic variety of Hinduism, introduced in mid-19th century by large numbers of immigrants from India and Nepal.
INDIAN INDIGENOUS. In about 6 denominations or groupings in 1970 (see Table 2).
MUSLIMS. Sunnis, mainly Indian rural merchants, traders, butchers and bakers.
SIKHS. Punjabis serving in the Indian armed forces.
TRIBAL RELIGIONISTS. Animists among the Lepcha in the remotest valleys, following pre-Buddhist religion Bon.

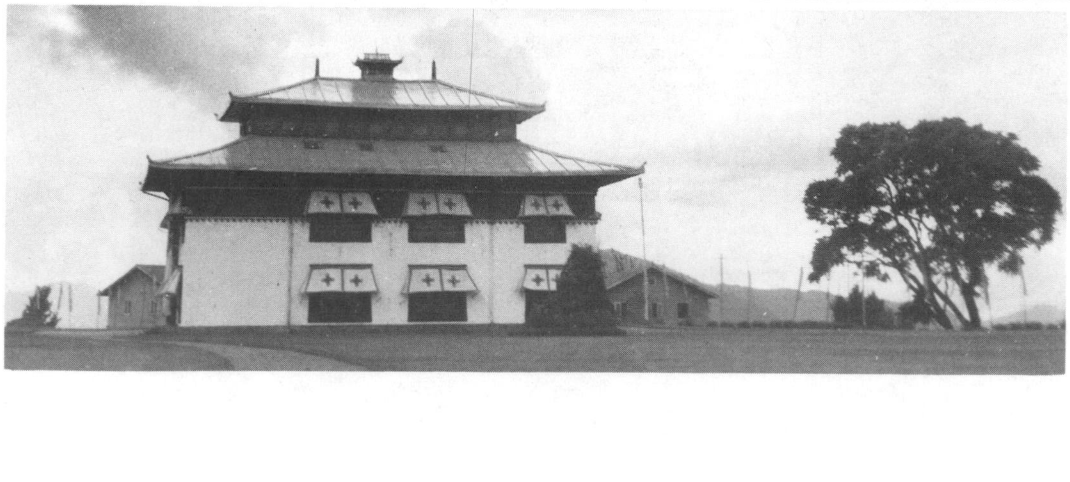

**Buddhists.** *Left.* 'The Light of Asia', king's monastery at Gangtok, most imposing in all Sikkim, with unsurpassed interior murals depicting life of the Buddha.

NON-CHRISTIAN RELIGIONS. **Hinduism** is the religion of the majority of the population, having been introduced in Himalayan form in the mid-19th century by large numbers of immigrants from Nepal and India. Some Nepalese castes, however, are Buddhists, and others worship a pantheon of both Hindu and Buddhist deities.

**Mahayana Buddhism** is the official religion, the religion of almost all Bhotias and Tibetans and of most indigenous Lepchas. The spiritual leader of the Karma-pa (Red Hat) Lama sect resides in Sikkim, in the monastery of Rumtek. The Namgyal Institute of Tibetology in Gangtok is a research centre for the study of Mahayana Buddhism and contains the

third-largest collection of Tibetan books in the world (exceeded only by the libraries in Peking and Leningrad).

**Baha'i** has a rapidly-growing and active community, originally in Gangtok and now with over 80 local spiritual assemblies.

**Traditional tribal religion** is found among some indigenous Lepchas.

**Islam** is represented in the merchant community of the rural markets and at Gangtok.

## CHRISTIANITY

**CATHOLIC CHURCH.** Sikkim forms part of the Catholic diocese of Darjeeling in India and consists of one parish with about 250 baptized Catholics and numerous other adherents. One half are resident Indian immigrants living mostly at Gangtok, and the other half are citizens located in 2 widely-separated centres. Citizen Catholics are approximately 50% of Hindu origin, mostly Nepalese, and 50% Lepchas. The 2 rural centres are Nepali-speaking congregations, while English and Hindi are used in Gangtok. In 1971 there were only 3 baptisms (infants). Personnel

consist of one Indian priest resident at Pakyong, 4 Indian nuns, 2 Indian seminary students working in the only Catholic school in the country (a middle school in Pakyong), and one halftime catechist. It was not until 1953 that a Catholic priest was permitted to take up residence in Sikkim. The first Catholic convent was opened at Pakyong in 1973, run by Sisters of St Joseph of Cluny. Local vocations include one Nepalese nun finishing her noviciate in India and one Lepcha studying in a minor seminary at Darjeeling.

**PROTESTANT CHURCHES.** Protestants entered Sikkim at the end of the 19th century, the Church of Scotland Mission in 1886 followed by the Finnish Alliance Mission among Tibetans in 1891. Scottish missionaries pioneered in elementary education and built a secondary school for girls in the capital. This work, with congregations in Gangtok and Tenni, is now part of the Church of North India. Free Church of Finland missionaries took over from the Alliance Mission in 1909 and later extended their activities into Bhutan and Nepal. In Sikkim they are located at Lachung, Luchen and Mangen. Their last missionary was killed in 1950. Protestants supervise 12 schools and 10 dispensaries in various parts of the country. There are also 2 small Adventist congregations in Sikkim. In the west of the country are many small local churches of Protestant origin, often begun by Indian Christians.

**OTHER CHURCHES.** A small indigenous congregation, brought to Sikkim by Brother Bakht Singh from Hyderabad, AP (India), is the Jehova Shammah Assembly. In addition there are several other small congregations in the west begun by Indian indigenous evangelists. Jehovah's Witnesses have also been active since 1970.

**CHURCH AND STATE.** Mahayana Buddhism (Great Vehicle) is the state religion, although in theory and in practice other religions are tolerated; Christian baptisms and open-air preaching face no difficulties. There are Hindu temples and at least one mosque as well as Catholic and Protestant churches

**Buddhists.** A Karma-pa (Red Hat, or Unreformed) lama. The spiritual leader of the Karma-pa sect resides in Sikkim, in the monastery of Rumtek.

in Gangtok. Western missionaries are restricted in Sikkim; they may enter and hold services for their faithful, but they are not given residence permits. On the other hand Indian Christians and evangelists are allowed free entry.

**BROADCASTING.** There are no radio or TV stations or government programmes in Sikkim. Christian programmes can be heard from abroad in Nepali, Hindi, Bengali and other languages.

TABLE 2. ORGANIZED CHURCHES AND DENOMINATIONS IN SIKKIM

| Official name 1 | Begun 2 | Type 3 | Counc 4 | Congs 5 | Adults 6 | Affiliated 7 | Names, notes, and other statistics (see Codebook) 8 |
|---|---|---|---|---|---|---|---|
| Assemblies (Jehova Shammah) | | I CBr | x.... | 1 | 50 | 100 | Nepali-speaking assembly in capital. Mostly Indians; Bakht Singh (HQ Hyderabad). |
| **Catholic Church (D Darjeeling)** | | R Lat | P.F.. | 3 | 300 | 600 | 50% Indians in Gangtok, 50% rural (25% Nepali, 25% Lepcha). 1x,1e,4w,3y. |
| **Church of North India (D Darjeeling)** | 1886 | P uni | Rwe.. | 10 | 500 | 2,500 | Large congregation in Gangtok; also Tenni. 1886, M=CSM(UK). 1 girls high school. |
| **Free Church of Finland Mission** | 1891 | P Con | K.... | 8 | 300 | 600 | M=Free Ch of Finland (Suomen Vapaakirkko). In Lachung, Luchen, Mangen. Tibetans. |
| Full Gospel Church | | I pe3 | ..... | 1 | 50 | 100 | Congregation in capital. Mostly Indian indigenous pentecostals. M=FFFM(Finland). |
| Jehovah's Witnesses | c1970 | M Jeh | x.... | 2 | 20 | 50 | *Watch Tower. IBSA.* First witnessing reported in 1970. Underground. 2Y. |
| Seventh-day Adventist Church | | P Adv | x.... | 2 | 50 | 100 | *SDA,* under Northern Union (India), Southern Asia Division. Mostly Indians. |
| **Other Protestant denominations** | | P | | 10 | 150 | 300 | Rural work by Indian Baptists and Pentecostals, also military chaplaincies. |
| Other Indian indigenous churches | | I | ..... | 8 | 180 | 400 | Several small congregations in west begun by Indian indigenous evangelists. |
| Total affiliated (mid-1970) | | | | 45 | 1,600 | 4,750 | Total denominations (1970) . . . 15. |
| Total affiliated (mid-1975) | | | | 48 | 1,780 | 5,650 | Total denominations (1975) . . . 16. |
| Total affiliated (mid-1980) | | | | 51 | 2,060 | 6,510 | Total denominations (1980) . . . 17. |

**NOTES ON TABLE ABOVE**
COLUMNS: for meanings and CODES (cols. 1, 3, 4, 8): see Codebook (Part 6). Column 1: **Boldface type** = church with over 10% of country's affiliated Christians.

PEOPLES (ethnolinguistic). Christians: about 64% Indian (Bengali, Hindi, Assamese, Bihari), 25% Tibetan-speaking, 5% Nepali, 5% Lepcha.

**COUNTRY-WIDE TOTALS**
EVANGELIZATION (see Part 5). 1900: 2%. 1970: 46%. 1980: 51%. *Literature evangelism.* Every Home Crusade (World Literature Crusade) with full-time WLC staff.
FOREIGN MISSIONARIES AND PERSONNEL (aliens from abroad) (1973). Total 13. *From Western world.* About 3 Protestants. *From Third World.* 10 (5 Roman Catholics, 3 Protestants) from India, 2 Indian indigenous.

INSTITUTIONS (church-operated) (1973). Total 13, including 1 higher school, 10 medical centres.
PERSONNEL. 13 (foreign).
SCRIPTURE DISTRIBUTION (1975). Annual totals: 200 NTs (free). *Translations completed.* Portion: Lepcha in 1845.
SERVICE AGENCIES. About 3, including WLC(EHC).

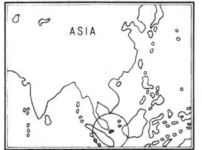

# SINGAPORE

## SECULAR DATA

**STATE. Official name:** The Republic of Singapore (Hsin-chia-po Kung-ho-kuo (Chinese)/Republik Singapura (Malay)/Singapore Kudiyarasu (Tamil)). Adjective of nationality: Singaporean.
**Flag** (shown above right): Red and white stripes, with white crescent and 5 white stars on red stripe.
**Area:** 581 sq.km. (224 sq.miles). Agricultural land: 15.5%.
**Government:** Parliamentary republic, since 1965 (1000 Sumatran colony, 1824 British possession, 1867 British crown colony, 1959 self-government, 1963 in Federation of Malaysia, 1965 Independence).
**Legislature:** Parliament (Legislative Assembly), 58 members.
**Official languages:** Malay (national language), Chinese (Mandarin), Tamil and English (language of administration).
**Capital:** Singapore.
**Armed forces** (1976): Total 31,000 regular: army 25,000, navy 3,000, air force 3,000 (97 combat aircraft). Reserves: 45,000. Paramilitary forces: 40,000.
**Foreign forces** (1973): 2,500 British (UK) marines and Royal Air Force, 1,000 Australian troops, 1,000 New Zealand troops.

**DEMOGRAPHY. Population:** 2,074,507 (census of 22.VI.1970. For 1970–2000 (UN), see last row of Table 1). Population density (1975): 3,869/sq.km. (10,021/sq.mile). Under 15 years: 43%. Growth rate (1975–80): 1.61% per year (births 2.14%, deaths

−0.53%). Life expectancy (1975–80): 70.8 years. Household size: 5.3 persons.
**Major languages:** Chinese (Fukienese/Hokkienese), English, Malay, Tamil, Malayalam, Punjabi, Hindi, Javanese.
**Urban dwellers** (1970): 80.8%. Urban growth rate (1950–70): 5.3% per year.
**Labour force:** 39%.
**Tourists** (1972): 783,015. (1974) 1,233,854.

**ETHNOLINGUISTIC GROUPS:** 74.2% Chinese (South Fukienese (Hokkien), Hainanese, Hoklo; 30% Amoy, 17% Teochew (from Swatow), 15% from Kwangtung), 15.0% Malay, 7.0% Indo-Pakistani (4.2% Tamil, Malayali, Punjabi, Hindustani, Kanarese), 2.2% Javanese, 1.0% Eurasian (20,000), 0.5% British, Batak, Sinhalese, Riau, Palembang, Buginese, Arab, USA, Jewish.

**MONEY** (1977). **Monetary unit:** Singapore dollar (= 100 cents); US$1 = S$2.45.
**National income per person:** US$2,200. Average annual family income: US$11,660.
**Inflation:** (1970–74) 12.6% per year, (1975: consumer price index 162).
**Cost of living in capital** (1976): index 122 (Washington DC=100). Daily cost of living: US$40.

**HEALTH.** Hospitals: 21 (8,251 beds). Doctors: 1,524. Lepers: 8,500 (3.8 per 1,000). Blind: 427. Psychotics: 20,000. Drug addicts: 12,000 (4,000 on morphine, 1,000 mandrax, 800 heroin). Criminals: 10,243.

**EDUCATION.** Adult literacy: (1970) 69%. Education rate: 84%. Schools: 548. Universities: 2.

**LITERATURE.** Annual new book titles (1973): 676. Periodicals: 167. Newspapers: 10 dailies, 3 non-daily.

**COMMUNICATION** (per 1,000 people). Phones: 114. Radios: 139. TV sets: 106. Daily newspaper circulation: 190 copies.

TABLE 1. RELIGIOUS ADHERENTS IN SINGAPORE

| Year | 1900 | | mid-1970 | | Annual change, 1970–1980 | | | | mid-1975 | | mid-1980 | | 2000 | |
|---|---|---|---|---|---|---|---|---|---|---|---|---|---|---|
| *Name* | *Adherents* | *%* | *Adherents* | *%* | *Natural* | *Conversion* | *Total* | *Rate* | *Adherents* | *%* | *Adherents* | *%* | *Adherents* | *%* |
| Chinese folk-religionists | 123,800 | 49.5 | 1,125,000 | 54.2 | 19,569 | –759 | 18,810 | 1.55 | 1,215,000 | 54.1 | 1,313,100 | 53.9 | 1,645,200 | 52.7 |
| Muslims | 55,000 | 22.0 | 373,000 | 18.0 | 6,407 | –1,307 | 5,100 | 1.28 | 397,900 | 17.7 | 424,000 | 17.4 | 506,400 | 16.2 |
| Ahmadis | 0 | 0.0 | 1,000 | 0.0 | 18 | 2 | 20 | 1.82 | 1,100 | 0.0 | 1,200 | 0.0 | 3,000 | 0.1 |
| Buddhists | 42,500 | 17.0 | 200,000 | 9.6 | 3,295 | –2,335 | 960 | 0.47 | 204,600 | 9.1 | 209,600 | 8.6 | 218,800 | 7.0 |
| **Christians** | **10.000** | **4.0** | **161,700** | **7.8** | **2,956** | **1,737** | **4,693** | **2.56** | **183,570** | **8.2** | **208,630** | **8.6** | **318,400** | **10.2** |
| professing | 10,000 | 4.0 | 161,700 | 7.8 | 2,956 | 1,737 | 4,693 | 2.56 | 183,570 | 8.2 | 208,630 | 8.6 | 318,400 | 10.2 |
| Roman Catholics | 5,500 | 2.2 | 90,000 | 4.3 | 1,629 | 821 | 2,450 | 2.42 | 101,160 | 4.5 | 114,500 | 4.7 | 171,900 | 5.5 |
| Protestants | 3,000 | 1.2 | 49,000 | 2.4 | 906 | 534 | 1,440 | 2.56 | 56,200 | 2.5 | 63,400 | 2.6 | 93,800 | 3.0 |
| Anglicans | 1,450 | 0.6 | 11,500 | 0.6 | 201 | –1 | 200 | 1.60 | 12,500 | 0.6 | 13,500 | 0.6 | 18,000 | 0.6 |
| Asian indigenous | 0 | 0.0 | 11,000 | 0.5 | 217 | 383 | 600 | 4.44 | 13,500 | 0.6 | 17,000 | 0.7 | 34,400 | 1.1 |
| Orthodox | 50 | 0.0 | 200 | 0.0 | 3 | 0 | 3 | 1.43 | 210 | 0.0 | 230 | 0.0 | 300 | 0.0 |
| nominal | 1,450 | 0.6 | 18,972 | 0.9 | 319 | –81 | 238 | 1.20 | 19,810 | 0.9 | 21,350 | 0.9 | 32,700 | 1.0 |
| affiliated | 8,550 | 3.4 | 142,728 | 6.9 | 2,637 | 1,818 | 4,455 | 2.72 | 163,760 | 7.3 | 187,280 | 7.7 | 285,700 | 9.1 |
| total practising | 7,700 | *90* | 99,910 | *70* | 1,846 | 1,273 | 3,119 | 2.72 | 114,630 | *70* | 131,100 | *70* | 199,990 | *70* |
| non-practising | 850 | *10* | 42,820 | *30* | 791 | 545 | 1,336 | 2.72 | 49,130 | *30* | 56,180 | *30* | 85,710 | *30* |
| Roman Catholics | 5,000 | 2.0 | 80,000 | 3.9 | 1,485 | 995 | 2,480 | 2.69 | 92,200 | 4.1 | 104,800 | 4.3 | 156,300 | 5.0 |
| Protestants | 2,500 | 1.0 | 42,376 | 2.0 | 760 | 362 | 1,122 | 2.38 | 47,200 | 2.1 | 53,600 | 2.2 | 78,100 | 2.5 |
| Evangelicals | 2,000 | 0.8 | 31,800 | 1.5 | 580 | 380 | 960 | 2.67 | 36,000 | 1.6 | 41,400 | 1.7 | 62,500 | 2.0 |
| Anglicans | 1,000 | 0.4 | 10,000 | 0.5 | 176 | 4 | 180 | 1.65 | 10,900 | 0.5 | 11,800 | 0.5 | 15,000 | 0.5 |
| Anglican pentecostals | 0 | 0.0 | 100 | 0.0 | 18 | 272 | 290 | 26.36 | 1,100 | 0.0 | 3,000 | 0.1 | 6,000 | 0.2 |
| Asian indigenous | 0 | 0.0 | 9,500 | 0.5 | 201 | 449 | 650 | 5.20 | 12,500 | 0.6 | 16,000 | 0.7 | 34,000 | 1.1 |
| Marginal Protestants | 0 | 0.0 | 650 | 0.0 | 12 | 8 | 20 | 2.67 | 750 | 0.0 | 850 | 0.0 | 2,000 | 0.1 |
| Orthodox | 50 | 0.0 | 202 | 0.0 | 3 | 0 | 3 | 1.43 | 210 | 0.0 | 230 | 0.0 | 300 | 0.0 |
| Hindus | 16,200 | 6.5 | 120,000 | 5.8 | 2,077 | –187 | 1,890 | 1.46 | 129,000 | 5.7 | 138,900 | 5.7 | 172,000 | 5.5 |
| Non-religious | 0 | 0.0 | 62,000 | 3.0 | 1,267 | 2,283 | 3,550 | 4.51 | 78,700 | 3.5 | 97,500 | 4.0 | 187,600 | 6.0 |
| Sikhs | 2,500 | 1.0 | 20,000 | 1.0 | 349 | 1 | 350 | 1.61 | 21,700 | 1.0 | 23,500 | 1.0 | 30,000 | 1.0 |
| New-Religionists | 0 | 0.0 | 10,000 | 0.5 | 209 | 391 | 600 | 4.62 | 13,000 | 0.6 | 16,000 | 0.7 | 34,000 | 1.1 |
| Atheists | 0 | 0.0 | 2,000 | 0.1 | 48 | 152 | 200 | 6.67 | 3,000 | 0.1 | 4,000 | 0.2 | 10,000 | 0.3 |
| Baha'is | 0 | 0.0 | 700 | 0.0 | 13 | 7 | 20 | 2.50 | 800 | 0.0 | 900 | 0.0 | 2,000 | 0.1 |
| Jews | 0 | 0.0 | 400 | 0.0 | 7 | 0 | 7 | 1.63 | 430 | 0.0 | 470 | 0.0 | 600 | 0.0 |
| Other religionists | 0 | 0.0 | 200 | 0.0 | 3 | 17 | 20 | 6.67 | 300 | 0.0 | 400 | 0.0 | 1,000 | 0.0 |
| **Country's population** | **250,000** | **100.0** | **2,075,000** | **100.0** | **36,200** | **0** | **36,200** | **1.61** | **2,248,000** | **100.0** | **2,437,000** | **100.0** | **3,126,000** | **100.0** |

COLUMNS, ROWS. For meanings and definitions, see Codebook (Part 6). Note that, by definition, total 'Christians' = professing + crypto-Christians, which also = affiliated + nominal Christians. Percentages may not always total exactly, due to rounding.
CENSUSES. The religion question has not been asked.

NOTES ON RELIGIONS
AHMADIS. Begun 1935; Qadianis (world HQ Rabwah, Pakistan).
ANGLICAN PENTECOSTALS (or, Anglican charismatics). The charismatic renewal, begun 1972, has centred on the Anglican cathedral, bishop's house and house churches, with the Anglican bishop as leader. By 1976, the Spiritual Renewal Fellowship also served a few hundred Protestants (Lutherans, Methodists) and also about 100 Catholic charismatics.
ANGLICANS. The Anglican proportion of the population remained unchanged from 1900 to 1970. A large part of its membership are expatriate British, and although in 1970 there were 117 adult baptisms and a growth rate of 3.2% per year, these gains were offset later in the decade by emigration of British expatriates and losses to other denominations.
ASIAN INDIGENOUS. Mostly Chinese indigenous with some Indian indigenous Christians; in about 26 denominations in 1970 (see Table 2).
ATHEISTS. Communist Party of Malaya (illegal; pro-Chinese): membership (1970) 200, all underground.
BAHA'IS. Growth from 1 local spiritual assembly (1964) to 5 (1973).
BUDDHISTS. Chinese adherents of Mahayana Buddhism; with Sinhalese (Ceylonese), and a Chinese minority, following Theravada Buddhism; the latter are assisted by a number of Theravada missionaries from Thailand who have established several temples in Singapore. Total temples (1971): over 75. Buddhists are gradually declining in proportion to the population as their children abandon the old beliefs and practices.
CHINESE FOLK-RELIGIONISTS. The bulk are followers in varying degrees of the popular amalgam of Buddhism, Taoism, Confucianism, the ancestor-cult and spiritism, with numerous temples and deities. There are a number of spirit-medium cults (Shenism).
HINDUS. Tamils and Malayalees from south India, with 31 temples. A Hindu sect, Ananda Marga (Path of Bliss), also has a following.
JEWS. With 2 synagogues.
MUSLIMS. Mostly Malays, also Indians, Pakistanis, Javanese, Arabs, Buginese, and several hundred Chinese Muslims; with a total of 83 masjids and saraus. There is also an Ahmadiya Mission (Qadianis; enumerated here as Muslims though declared non-Muslim by Pakistan). *Hajj pilgrims to Mecca.* (1974) 954; (1975) 1,152; (1976) 434.
NEW-RELIGIONISTS. Followers of various Chinese and Japanese syncretistic or salvationist New Religions, including the faith-healing Tao Yuan Organization (for Chinese only) and its related philanthropic association for non-members, the World Red Swastika Society (Singapore Association, begun 1936, membership falling from 1,331 in 1948 to 770 by 1970). Others are: T'ung-shan She (Fellowship of Goodness), universalistic in membership and attracting mainly middle-class Chinese, which was brought to Singapore in 1927; the Religion of the Void, which appeared in Singapore in 1900; Great Way of Former Heaven (Hsien-t'ien Ta Tao), a number of separate sects each with its own leader; and Soka Gakkai (Nichiren Shoshu) from Japan, with 1,700 adherents in Singapore in 1975.
NON-RELIGIOUS. Chinese, especially youths, who have abandoned their former folk-religious beliefs and practices.
OTHER RELIGIONISTS. Adherents of other Western religions and cults, including Rosicrucians (1 AMORC centre).
SIKHS. Punjabis; with 4 temples.

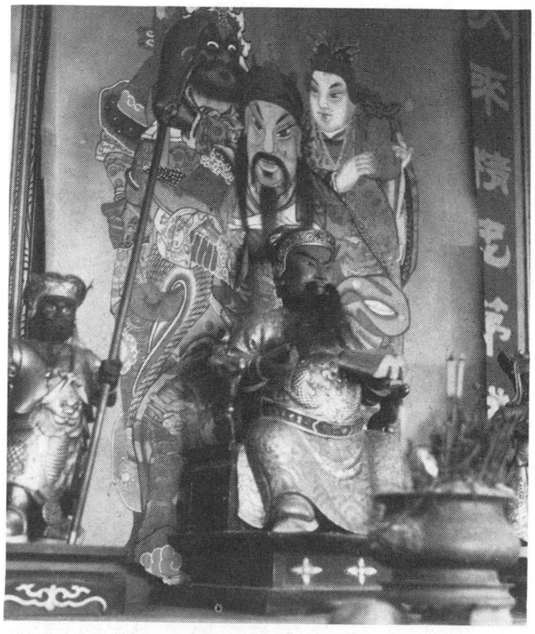

**Chinese folk-religionists.** Over half the population acknowledge Chinese gods as shown here in a Confucian temple in Singapore.

**NON-CHRISTIAN RELIGIONS. Buddhism** and **Chinese folk religion** are the most prevalent forms of religious expression in Singapore, involving rituals and moral regulations common to Chinese culture. There are about 200,000 Buddhists on the island in addition to over a million adherents of this Chinese popular religion, which is a syncretistic mixture of Buddhism, Taoism, Confucianism and traditional magical practices. The majority of the Buddhists in Singapore are Chinese and belong to the Mahayana school. A small Chinese minority and the Ceylonese majority follow the Theravada school. These 2 schools have been brought closer together by the co-ordinating activities of the Singapore Buddhist Federation, the Singapore Buddhist Sangha Organization and the Singapore Regional Centre of the World Fellowship of Buddhists.

**Islam** is found primarily among the Malays, Indians and Pakistanis. The Muslim population numbers 400,000, the second largest religious community in Singapore. The Muslim Religious Council (Majlis Ugama Islam), under the Ministry of Social Affairs, conducts and regulates the activities of the community under Islamic law.

**Hinduism** exists among the Tamils and Malayalees from South India. The Hindu population numbers over 100,000.

**Judaism** has 400 adherents who worship in 2 synagogues.

**CHRISTIANITY.** Although the majority of Singapore's churches are Chinese, Christianity is found among all the various ethnic groups on the island. The multiplicity of cultures and languages among Christians is a major problem; congregations worshipping in a single language may use Mandarin, Hokkien, Cantonese, Teochew, English, Malay, Tamil, Malayalam, Foochow, Hainan, Hakka, Hingwa, Matak, Punjabi or several others. Despite their close proximity, efforts to co-ordinate denominational activities in Singapore and Malaysia have been hampered by this linguistic diversity.

CATHOLIC CHURCH. The first Catholic priests arrived in Malacca following the conquest by the Portuguese in 1511. Francis Xavier came in 1545 and the diocese of Malacca was established in 1557. Catholic activity was suppressed by the Dutch in 1641 from which it was slow to recover. In 1819 there were only 12 Catholics in Singapore, but by 1831 membership had risen to 300. Singapore and Malaya became an independent vicariate in 1841, and Singapore was made the seat of the diocese of Malacca in 1888, and an archdiocese in 1953.

In December 1972, the metropolitan see of Singapore-Malacca covering Singapore and a part of West Malaysia was divided, one part being the area of the republic of Singapore which thus lost its metropolitan character. About 70% of the 80,000 Catholics in Singapore are Chinese. One relic of the Portuguese patronage system is the important Portuguese parish of Singapore which is part of the diocese of Macao and which consists of 9,000 Catholics with 4 priests from Portugal, Goa and Macao. The Apostolic Visitor for the Chinese of the Diaspora lives in Singapore and has responsibility for all Chinese communities throughout the world with the exception of Taiwan, Hong Kong and Macao. The visitor has the rank of bishop and his services are integrated into the archdiocese of Singapore. His work is to animate and co-ordinate the activities of some 700,000 Chinese Catholics scattered over the 6 continents. Its central bureau includes such services as the press, correspondence courses on religion, a library, catechesis, and social assistance.

PROTESTANT CHURCHES. Protestantism began with the Dutch conquest of Malaysia in 1641, but was confined to Europeans until the London Missionary Society sent its first missionary, a Presbyterian, to Malacca in 1814. Singapore was reached in 1819, and during the following decades the LMS, the American Board (ABCFM) and the Paris Mission (PEMS) contributed much to the development of education on the island. In 1841 the LMS church members numbered only 10, rising to 60 by 1843. In 1846 the LMS closed the mission in Singapore and transferred its work to China, but the church continued under indigenous leadership. Other Presby-

**Anglican Church, Diocese of Singapore.** Chinese funeral in Queenstown, with relatives of deceased wearing off-white hoods. According to Chinese tradition, an elaborate and costly funeral shows a family's honour for its dead.

terian missionaries appeared in 1850 and 1881, and by 1925 there were 800 Chinese members, primarily due to an influx of immigrants. Chinese immigrant congregations continued to use the name Church of Christ in China until 1949 when they became part of the Presbyterian Church in Singapore and Malaysia. The Presbyterian Church has 14 Chinese and 3 English congregations and is the fourth largest denomination on the island. Presbyterian schools have a large enrolment.

The first Methodist missionary arrived in Singapore from India in 1885. In 1888 Malaysia became a separate mission, and the first session of the Malaya Annual Conference was held in Singapore in 1893. Two conferences were formed in 1936, one English-speaking and one Chinese-speaking, and a Tamil Provisional Conference was added in 1968. The Malaysia and Singapore Methodist Church became autonomous in 1968 under its own local bishop and is the largest non-Catholic church in Singapore. From its beginning the Methodist Church emphasized education, and now has 7 educational institutions with 18,000 students. Church membership more than doubled between 1940 and 1960 in both the English and Chinese conferences. During the 1960s, adult members in the former increased by 25%, and in the latter by 50%.

The work of Brethren Assemblies was opened in 1856 by 2 independent couples. Chinese Baptist immigrants came to Singapore in 1905, worshipping at first in the Presbyterian Church, but in 1937 the first independent Baptist service was conducted. Since 1950 Southern Baptist missionaries from the USA had been at work with the church. Assemblies of God entered in 1933 and now have 14 congregations; they form one of the most rapidly-growing denominations in Singapore at present.

Other Protestant bodies include Adventists, Evangelical Free Church, Lutherans, and Salvation Army.

In 1970, the proportion of Protestant congregations speaking each of the various languages was as follows: 52% used English, 18% Mandarin, 9% Hokkien, 6% Cantonese, 5% Tamil, 3% Teochew, 2% Malay, 1% or under Foochow, Hakka, Hainan, Punjabi, Malayalam and several others.

ANGLICAN CHURCH. Anglicanism, the third largest denomination after Catholicism and Methodism, entered Singapore with the appointment of an Anglican chaplain by the East India Company in 1826 to serve the European population. Missionary activity began in 1856 based on the first Singapore Anglican church, St Andrew's Church Mission, which worked in collaboration with SPG missionaries from England. During the next 50 years work was carried out in the Hokkien, Tamil, Malay and Cantonese languages. The first bishop was appointed for Singapore as a separate diocese in 1909. In 1966

the first local bishop was consecrated with Singapore becoming a diocese separate from Malaysia in 1970. Since 1968 the bishop has been the leader of a rapidly-growing charismatic renewal among Anglicans, centred on the cathedral.

INDIGENOUS CHURCHES. Numerous small independent churches, mostly Chinese, are active in Singapore. The first was the True Jesus Church which dates from 1927, but the majority were established after the Christian exodus from China in 1949. A Ceylonese group using Tamil, the Ceylon Pentecostal Church of Malaya, was founded in 1936.

ORTHODOX CHURCH. There are 2 congregations, one of the Orthodox Syrian Church in Singapore, and one for Armenians related to Echmiadzin (USSR).

CHURCH AND STATE. Singapore is a secular state and its constitution of 1966 has little to say about religion. Religious minorities are protected in Article 89:1, in the following words: 'It shall be the responsibility of the government constantly to care for the interests of the racial and religious minorities in Singapore'. Islam is referred to in Article 6:2 which states that the legislature shall by law make provision for regulating Muslim religious affairs and for constituting a council to advise the president in matters relating to the Muslim religion. At the end of 1971, Jehovah's Witnesses were prohibited by the government on the grounds that they constitute a danger to 'public welfare and good order'.

Christians have been commended by the prime minister for their interest in politics; 15 members of parliament out of 69 (22%) are Christians.

INTERDENOMINATIONAL ORGANIZATIONS. The Council of Churches of Malaysia and Singapore was created in 1948, the result of shared experiences of expatriate church leaders in prison camps during World War II. Its headquarters were in Singapore until it divided in 1975 into 2 separate councils, one in each nation. Its membership includes 9 churches and 4 agencies, and it represents 23% of Singapore's Christian community. Affiliated to the Singapore Regional Council are a Student Centre, Churches' Counselling Service, Singapore Urban Industrial Mission Board (SUIM), Singapore Churches' Conference Centre, Community Study Centre and a Radio/TV Broadcasting Committee. The Counselling Service has a staff of 5 under the management of a board including Anglicans, Methodists, Lutherans and Presbyterians; it now includes a 24-hour telephone counselling ministry. SUIM was set up in 1969 to pioneer community work in 2 large housing estates and a satellite town being built by government. Lutherans sponsor one housing unit on an ecumenical basis; Catholics and other Protestants co-operate in the other. The Institute for the Study of Religions and Society in Singapore and Malaysia, founded in 1968, is engaged in research on local religion and the social impact of industrialization, urbanization and secularization. Activities include studies in rural and urban development of manpower and resources, folk religions, and local cultural patterns. Theological colleges (Trinity College, Singapore Bible College, and the Discipleship Training Centre) are ecumenical in character. There is also an Inter-Religious Organizations Council, a private body recognized by government.

The headquarters of the Christian Conference of Asia (CCA, formerly EACC) were moved in 1973 from Bangkok (Thailand) to Singapore. Begun in 1959, the conference by 1973 had 78 member denominations and 16 member councils of churches, representing over 40 million Christians in 17 nations.

BROADCASTING. The government Radio Singapore gives churches 45 minutes each on Sunday. From abroad, Christian programmes in Chinese, Malay and English can easily be heard over FEBC (Manila), which has a production studio in Singapore. For Catholics, Malaysia/Singapore is a member of UNDA.

BIBLIOGRAPHY
*A handbook of churches and Christian organizations in Singapore.* J.Y.K. Wong. Singapore: Study Group for Church Growth and Evangelism, 1971. 69p.
'A study of the contemporary Protestant Christian ministry in Singapore'. P.S.K. Tow. Thesis, Trinity Evangelical Divinity School (USA), 1973. 244p.
'Chinese religious festivals in Singapore', C.H. Ming, *Annual publication of the China Society* (Singapore), 1949.
*Chinese spirit-medium cults in Singapore.* A.J.A. Elliot. London: London School of Economics, 1955.
*Chinese temples of Singapore.* A.K. Tong. Singapore: Nanfong Commercial Publishing Bureau, 1949.
*Conversions à Singapour: contribution à une sociologie de la mutation socio-religieuse.* P. Lopez de Ceballas. Paris: Ecole Pratique des Hautes Etudes, 1974.

**True Jesus Church.** 1st Theological Seminar for Singapore, Malaysia & India, 1973, seated in front of Singapore church.

*Directory of Singapore churches.* Ed L.N. Capen. Singapore: Council of Churches of Malaysia and Singapore, 1969. 43p.
*Directory of urban industrial mission projects in the EACC area, 1970.* Singapore: Stamford College Press, 1970.
*Guide to Chinese Catholic diaspora, 1971.* Singapore: Singapore Catholic Central Bureau, 1971.
'Singapore, Malaysia and Brunei: the church in a racial melting pot', J.R. Fleming, in G.H. Anderson (ed), *Christ and crisis in southeast Asia* (New York: Friendship Press, 1968).
'Singapore: the urban church in the midst of rapid social change', J.Y.K. Wong. Thesis, Fuller Theological Seminary, Pasadena (CA), 1972. 285p.
'The emergence and social function of Chinese religious associations in Singapore', M. Topley, *Comparative studies in society and history*, III (1960–61), 289–314.
*The kingdom and the country.* R.Nyce. Singapore: Institute for the Study of Religions and Society, 1970. 100p.
Urbanisation and church growth in Singapore'. J.Y.K. Wong. Singapore: Graduates Christian Fellowship, 1971.

TABLE 2. ORGANIZED CHURCHES AND DENOMINATIONS IN SINGAPORE

| Official name 1 | Begun 2 | Type 3 | Counc 4 | Congs 5 | Adults 6 | Affiliated 7 | Names, notes, and other statistics (see Codebook) 8 |
|---|---|---|---|---|---|---|---|
| Anglican Church: D Singapore | 1826 | A Cen | awEAW | 20 | 5,014 | 10,000 | Language 60% English,34% Chinese,6% Tamil. 14n,16x,G=3.2%pa,1u (5),W=50%,117Y,150y. |
| Apostolic Church of Singapore | 1961 | I pen | ..... | 5 | 120 | 200 | South Indians. Malayalam, Hokkien, English. 1n,1x,G=29.9%pa,W=59%,13Y,11z. |
| Armenian Apostolic Church | c1850 | O Arm | Ew... | 1 | 50 | 100 | *Ch of St Gregory the Illuminator.* Few services, but still legally registered. |
| Assemblies of God | 1933 | P Pe2 | ZF... | 14 | 2,000 | 4,000 | *Elim Ch.* M=AoG(USA). One of fastest-growing bodies. 36n,10x,6f,G=15%pa,1p,33z. |
| Batak Christian Protestant Church | 1948 | P Lut | Lwe.. | 1 | 125 | 200 | *Independent Lutheran Ch. Huria Kristen Batak Protestan. HKBP.* Bataks (Indonesia). |
| Bible Church | 1958 | I ind | ..... | 4 | 90 | 300 | Begun by Singaporeans. Till 1964, Sunday Bible School (SBS). Help from M=OMF. |
| Bible Presbyterian Ch of S & Malaysia | 1950 | I Ref | .TT.T | 20 | 1,250 | 2,000 | Schism from Chinese Christian Ch. Sponsors Malaysia Christian Pioneer Mission. |
| **Catholic Church: AD Singapore** | 1511 | R Lat | pzF.P | 27 | 45,000 | 80,000 | *Gereja Katolik.* 70% Chinese. C=5+3+7. 37n,54x,13m,85w,P=50%,1p,1300Y,2200y. |
| Christian Assembly | 1935 | I ind | ..... | 1 | 420 | 1,000 | Independent congregation, Services in English, Mandarin, Hokkien. In Singapore 9. |
| Christian Brethren Assemblies | 1856 | P CBr | x.... | 16 | 2,500 | 5,000 | *Gospel Halls.* Congs: 8 English,4 Hokkien,3 Malay,1 Cantonese. 18m,3f,W=69%,180Y. |
| Chr Nationals Evangelism Commission | 1951 | P int | xF... | 8 | 250 | 550 | *CNEC. Keristen Nasionals Pengar Injil.* 5 schools. 2n,3x,G=38%pa, 1s,W=65%. |
| Church of Christ of Malaya | 1949 | I ind | ..... | 1 | 250 | 400 | Independent church with work in Malaysia also. Services in Hakka, Mandarin. |
| Church of Christ, Scientist | | M Sci | x.... | 1 | 20 | 50 | *Christian Science.* M=CCS(Boston USA). Singapore Society, in Singapore 10. |
| Church of Jesus C of Latter-day Saints | | M LdS | x.... | | 50 | 100 | *Mormons.* M=CJCLdS(USA). Mainly USA expatriates. In Singapore 10. |
| Church of Singapore | 1963 | I pen | ..... | 1 | 355 | 700 | Chinese charismatics, ex Brethren. House church. By 1978, 1,000 baptized. W=50%. |
| Churches of Christ | 1956 | P Dis | x.... | 10 | 700 | 1,500 | M=CC(Non-Instrumental) (USA). English, Mandarin, Cantonese services. 1p. |
| Evangelical Free Ch of Malaysia & S | 1957 | P Con | KF... | 3 | 150 | 300 | M=EFC of Canada. 2 organized churches; preaching points in Malaysia. 4f. |
| Ev Lutheran Ch in Malaysia & S | c1950 | P Lut | ....W | 2 | 67 | 109 | Mission from Tamil ELC(India) to Tamils. 1961, M=SKM(Sweden). G=0.4%pa,12Yy. |
| Evangelize China Fellowship | 1951 | I int | x.... | 1 | 50 | 100 | Begun in China by a Chinese. M=ECF(HQ,USA). HQ Singapore 13. 3f. |
| Fishermen of Christ Church | 1957 | I ind | ..... | 2 | 170 | 300 | Indigenous church. Services in Mandarin and English. Located in Singapore 1 & 7. |
| Jehovah's Witnesses | 1912 | M Jeh | x.... | 4 | 255 | 300 | *Watch Tower. IBSA.* Small but active group, in Singapore 9 & 11. Banned 1971. 37Y. |
| Lutheran Church in Malaysia & S | 1966 | P Lut | L...W | 5 | 452 | 800 | *Ma Sin Tsue Dtuk Tsau Sin Yi Whei.* M=ULCA(now LCA) (USA). Chinese, Indians. 15f,1u. |
| Malaysia-Singapore Baptist Convention | 1937 | P Bap | T.... | 14 | 1,506 | 3,000 | Begun by Chinese from South China. 1950, M=SBC(USA). 2 schools. 6n,20f,64Y. |
| Mar Thoma Syrian Church in Singapore | 1936 | I ReO | xwe.W | 1 | 350 | 600 | In D Bahya Kerala (Outside Kerala). Malayali Indians. Declining. 1n,2x,W=60%,10Yy. |
| **Methodist Church in Singapore** | 1885 | P Met | VuE.W | 25 | 8,626 | 15,000 | M=UMC(USA), 13f/MMS(UK)2f. A=1968. Confs: Engl, Chinese,Tamil. G=2.6%pa,7r(1800),1u. |
| Orthodox Syrian Church in Singapore | 1958 | O SyM | Dwe.W | 1 | 50 | 102 | In Diocese of Bahya Keralam (Outside Kerala). Syrians from South India. 1b. |
| Pentecostal Church of Malaya | 1936 | I pe2 | Z.... | 1 | 200 | 400 | *CPM.* M=Ceylon Pentecostal Mission(Sri Lanka). Tamil-speaking. In Singapore 12. |
| Pentecostal Evangelical Churches | 1957 | P Pe2 | Z.... | 7 | 600 | 1,000 | *Glad Tidings Free Pente Ch.* M=FFFM(Finland),GTMS(Canada). 1n,G=14%pa,W=42%,34Y,15z. |
| Presbyterian Church in Singapore | 1819 | P Ref | R...W | 20 | 4,144 | 5,817 | *Chinese Christian Ch.* Autonomous 1975. M=LMS,PCE. 12n,5x,G=3.3%pa,1u,W=43%,198Yy. |
| Presbytery of Malaysia & Singapore | 1851 | P Ref | Rw..W | 1 | 50 | 100 | *Presbyterian Ch of England.* Chaplaincy for British expatriates. |
| Salvation Army | 1935 | P Sal | xwE.W | 6 | 500 | 1,000 | *Kiu Se Kun* (Amoy), *Kau Shai Kwan* (Cantonese). *S & Malaysia Command.* 20n,1s. |
| Seventh-day Adventist Church | 1904 | P Adv | x.... | 4 | 1,806 | 3,000 | *Gereja Masehi Advent Hari Ketujah.* In Malaya Miss, Southeast Asia UM. 65f,1H,1j,4r. |
| True Jesus Church | 1927 | I pe1 | x.... | 9 | 900 | 1,500 | *Gereja Isa Benar Abadi.* Chinese; begun 1917 in China. Services in Mandarin. |
| Other Chinese indigenous churches | | I | ..... | | 1,000 | 2,000 | Total about 15 (see list below). |
| Other Protestant denominations | | P | ..... | | 500 | 1,000 | Total about 12 (see list below). |
| Other marginal Protestant bodies | | M | ..... | | 100 | 200 | Including Asia HQ of Branhamites (Local Believers, End Time Believers) from USA. |
| **Total affiliated (mid-1970)** | | | | **280** | **79,670** | **142,728** | **Total denominations (1970) . . . 59.** |
| **Total affiliated (mid-1975)** | | | | **310** | **91,400** | **163,760** | **Total denominations (1975) . . . 64.** |
| **Total affiliated (mid-1980)** | | | | **390** | **104,500** | **187,280** | **Total denominations (1980) . . . 69.** |

**NOTES ON TABLE ABOVE**
COLUMNS: for meanings and CODES (cols. 1, 3, 4, 8): see Codebook (Part 6). Column 1: **Boldface type** = church with over 10% of country's affiliated Christians.
NATIONAL COUNCILS (Column 4, 5th letter).
P = Catholic Bishops' Conference of Malaysia-Singapore.
T = Malaysia Council of Christian Churches (Singapore & Malaysia).
W = National Council of Churches of Singapore (until 1975 'of Malaysia & Singapore').
OTHER CHINESE INDIGENOUS CHURCHES. There are numerous independent congregations, as well as groupings. These include: Ch of God in Singapore, Free Christian Ch, Jehovah True God Ch, Jesus Saves Mission (1964), Revival Centre Ch (1953), Singapore Ch (Independent).
OTHER PROTESTANT DENOMINATIONS. Including Baptist Bible Fellowship International (1968), Ch of the Nazarene (1972), Overseas Missionary Fellowship (1951; 31 missionaries, but not church-planting), Religious Society of Friends (Quakers) (1958), Voice of China & Asia Missionary Society, Worldwide Evangelization Crusade, World-Wide Missions (1961).
UNITING CHURCHES. Negotiations for organic union were under way in 1974 between: Anglican Ch in M & S, Ev Lutheran Ch in M & S, Mar Thoma Syrian Ch in M, Presbyterian Ch in S & M.

**PEOPLES** (ethnolinguistic). Christians: about 72.0% Chinese (25% Mandarin, 20% Hokkien, 14% Cantonese, 8% Teochew, 2% Foochow, 1% Hainan (Li), 1% Hakka), 10.5% Eurasian, 7.0% British, 6.0% Tamil, 3.0% Malayali, 1.0% Malay, 0.2% Batak, 0.2% Armenian, Sinhalese, USA, Kanarese.

**COUNTRY-WIDE TOTALS**
EVANGELIZATION (see Part 5). 1900: 21%. 1970: 85%. 1980: 91%. *Mass evangelism.* Among recent campaigns and events: 1960, founding of indigenous Tamil Evangelistic Crusade, with periodic mass meetings; 1964, 1965 and 1966, Asian Evangelistic Crusades; 1968, Asia/South Pacific Congress on Evangelism; 1969, Grady Wilson revival meeting (46,000 attenders); 1969, Morris Cerullo's 'Christ is the Answer' healing campaign; 1977 Here's Life Singapore (CCCI) (71,841 contacted, 25,504 heard presentation, 9,104 decisions); April 1978, Congress on Evangelism for Malaysia and Singapore (COEMAS); November 1978, Asian Leadership Conference on Evangelism (ALCOE); December 1978, 1–week Billy Graham crusade (337,000 attenders, 19,600 decisions of which 80% were under 30 years of age and 65% were first-time commitments). *Radiophonic evangelism.* Annual listeners' letters (1975): 2,400 FEBC. Bible correspondence courses: ICI (10,000 enrolments, 2,000 active, 500 conversions reported), Roman Catholic, CLC. *Literature evangelism.* Every Home Crusade in 1976 completed its second nationwide coverage (visitation of every home with literature).
FOREIGN MISSIONARIES AND PERSONNEL (nationals serving abroad) (1973). Total 12: about 10 Protestants and 2 Roman Catholics in Japan, Malaysia, Thailand, Indonesia, Philippines, China (Taiwan), New Zealand and USA. By 1976, the number of Protestant missionaries sent out by OMF and Asia Evangelistic Fellowship, based in Singapore, had increased to 61; many, however, were nationals of other nations than Singapore.
FOREIGN MISSIONARIES AND PERSONNEL (aliens from abroad) (1973). Total 462. *From Western world.* 395: 251 Protestants (173 in 23 USA societies, 37 in 6 UK societies, 13 in 6 Australia societies, 15 in 5 New Zealand societies, 8 in 3 Canada societies, 3 in 1 Finland society, 2 in 1 Sweden society), 125 Roman Catholics, 19 Anglicans (13 in 3 UK societies, 4 in 1 New Zealand society, 2 in 1 Australia society). *From Third World.* 67: about 40 Roman Catholics, 15 Protestants from India, Indonesia, Japan, Korea, Hong Kong, Philippines, South Africa, Taiwan, et alia, about 9 Asian indigenous from Taiwan, India (2 Mar Thoma priests) and Indonesia, 2 Anglicans, 1 Orthodox from India.
INSTITUTIONS (church-operated) (1973). Total 55, including 32 higher schools, 3 medical centres, 2 research centres, 2 study centres, 6 seminaries (Protestant).
PERIODICALS. About 25 titles (3 SDA).
PERSONNEL. About 702 (240 national, 462 foreign).
RELIGIOUS LIBRARIES. About 10.
SCRIPTURE DISTRIBUTION (1975). Annual totals: 15,000 Bibles (7% free, 93% subsidized), 144,900 NTs (85% free, 14% subsidized, 1% commercial), 162,157 UBS portions, 1,387,113 UBS selections.
SERVICE AGENCIES. About 60, including CCA, CCCI, CCEA(CCSEA), CEF, CFSM, COFAE, CRS-USCC, CSS, CWL, FEBC, FECCC, IFES, JOCI, MTS, OC, SCM, SPCK, SU, TAP, WLC(EHC), YCS, YCW, YFC, YMCA, YWAM, YWCA.

**ADDITIONAL DATA ON CHURCHES**
ANGLICAN CHURCH. *Growth.* As a result of the charismatic renewal, 10 new congregations were founded from 1974–78. *Lay personnel.* (1977) 6 lay workers (3 women), 65 lay readers (2 women). *Seminarians* (1977). 5.
CATHOLIC CHURCH. The ancient diocese of Malacca-Singapore, founded 1557, was divided in 1972. The statistics refer only to Singapore. *Catholics.* Includes 71,000 Catholics in AD Singapore, also institutions and services dependent on the Military Vicariate (Vicariatus Castrensis), and also 9,000 Catholics in the Portuguese parish dependent on D Macau. *Annual baptisms.* (1972) 71.0% infant, 29.0% adult. *Priests.* Nationals: 29 local (28 secular, 1 CSSR), and 8 secular Chinese born in China. Expatriates: 25 MEP, 11 CSSR, 5 CICM, 5 OFM, 4 SSCC, 4 SJ. *Brothers and sisters.* 75% local, 25% expatriate. *Seminarians.* 15, trained in Malaysia. *Catechists.* Total about 20. *Indigenous religious congregations.* None. *Foreign orders and congregations.* Priests: MEP, CICM, CSSR, SJ, OFM, SSCC. Brothers: FSC, PFM, Brothers of St Gabriel. Sisters: Sisters of the Holy Infant Jesus, Canossian Daughters of Charity, Little Sisters of the Poor, Carmelites, Good Shepherd Sisters, Franciscan Sisters of the Divine Motherhood, Franciscan Missionaries of Mary.
*Catholic organizations.* Most Catholic organizations co-ordinate their work in Singapore with that in Malaysia, although Singapore is alone in having a Senate of Priests. The Catholic Bishops' Conference Malaysia-Singapore has its seat in Miri, East Malaysia. The Superiors' Conference of Malaysia and Singapore concerns itself with the activities of religious men, while the Association of Major Superiors of Women does the same for sisters. Lay organizations include the Joyful Vanguard (children), YCW, YCS, Catholic Students' Society (university students), Catholic Women's League, Christian Family and Social Movement, Legion of Mary, and Society of St Vincent de Paul.
The Holy See has no diplomatic relations with either Singapore or Malaysia. It is represented to the Catholic hierarchy by the Apostolic Delegation to Laos, Malaysia and Singapore, with its headquarters in Bangkok. The apostolic delegate also serves as pro-nuncio in Thailand.
The Asia secretariat for JOC International is found in Singapore.
In 1972 there were 36 Catholic schools (34,000 pupils) and one Catholic general hospital with 300 beds.

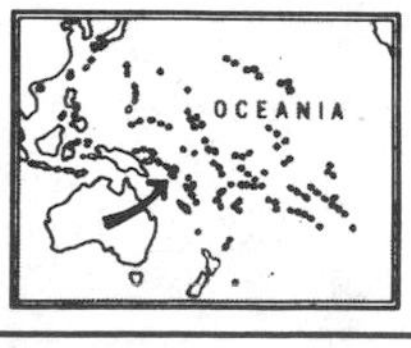


# SOLOMON ISLANDS

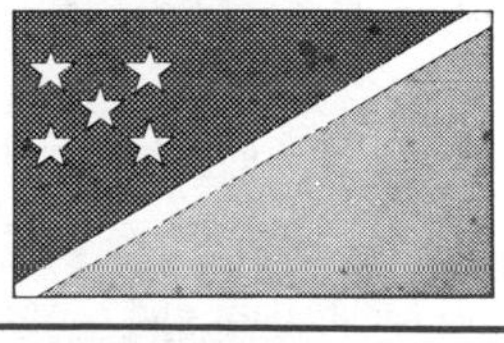

## SECULAR DATA

**STATE. Official name:** The Solomon Islands (until 1978, The British Solomon Islands Protectorate, BSIP).
**Flag** (shown above right): Two triangles with 5 stars.
**Area:** 28,446 sq.km. (10,983 sq.miles). Agricultural land: 6.8%.
**Government:** Parliamentary state (constitutional monarchy), since 1978 (1893 British protectorate, 1975 self-government, 1978 Independence).
**Legislature:** Governing Council, 27 members.
**Official language:** English.
**Capital:** Honiara 11,190.
**Armed forces** (1976): British.

**DEMOGRAPHY. Population:** 160,998 (census of 7.II.1970. For 1970–2000 (UN), see last row of Table 1). Population density (1975): 7/sq.km. (17/sq.mile). Under 15 years: 42%. Growth rate (1975–80): 2.89% per year (births 4.02%, deaths −1.17%, immigrants 0.04%). Life expectancy (1975–80): 55.9 years. Household size: 5.1 persons.
**Major languages:** English, Pidgin English (Neo-Melanesian), Bambatana, Bugotu, Roviana, Nggela, Vaturanga, and about 85 other vernacular languages.
**Urban dwellers** (1970): 6.9%. Urban growth rate (1950–70): 12.0% per year.
**Tourists** (1970): 3,392. (1973) 4,677. (1977) 7,359.

**ETHNOLINGUISTIC GROUPS:** 92.7% Solomoni Melanesian (Bambatana, Bugotu, Kerebuto, Kwaio, Kwara'ae, Lau, Maringe, Nggela, Roviana, Sa'a, To'abaita, Vaturanga, & 55 other languages), 4.0% Solomoni Polynesian (Nukuria, Pilheri, Rennellese, Sikaiana, Taku, Tikopian), 1.5% Gilbertese (Micronesian) (2,360), 0.8% European (1,280), 0.4% Solomoni Papuan, 0.4% Chinese (580), 0.1% Fijian, 0.1% Euronesian, Savo, Malo, Nanggu, Nea, Nooli, et alii.

**MONEY** (1977). **Monetary unit:** Australian dollar (= 100 cents); US$1 = A$0.94.
**National income per person:** US$290. Average annual family income: US$1,479.
**Inflation:** (1970–74) 3.2% per year.
**Cost of living in capital** (1976): Daily cost of living: US$34.

**HEALTH.** Hospitals: 73 (1,413 beds). Doctors: 38. Lepers:

1,700 (9.1 per 1,000). Blind: 370. Psychotics: 1,300. Criminals: 1,430.

**EDUCATION.** Adult literacy: 70%. Schools: 405 (399 primary).

**LITERATURE.** Periodicals: 10. Newspapers: 5 non-daily.

**COMMUNICATION** (per 1,000 people). Phones: 8. Radios: 69.

TABLE 1.   RELIGIOUS ADHERENTS IN THE SOLOMON ISLANDS

| Year | 1900 | | mid-1970 | | Annual change, 1970–1980 | | | | mid-1975 | | mid-1980 | | 2000 | |
|---|---|---|---|---|---|---|---|---|---|---|---|---|---|---|
| Name | Adherents | % | Adherents | % | Natural | Conversion | Total | Rate | Adherents | % | Adherents | % | Adherents | % |
| Christians | 15,400 | 20.5 | 154,250 | 94.6 | 5,031 | 130 | 5,161 | 2.91 | 177,520 | 94.9 | 205,860 | 95.3 | 354,300 | 96.0 |
| professing | 15,400 | 20.5 | 154,250 | 94.6 | 5,031 | 130 | 5,161 | 2.91 | 177,520 | 94.9 | 205,860 | 95.3 | 354,300 | 96.0 |
| Protestants | 0 | 0.0 | 61,200 | 37.6 | 1,999 | 46 | 2,045 | 2.90 | 70,550 | 37.7 | 81,650 | 37.8 | 139,500 | 37.8 |
| Anglicans | 15,000 | 20.0 | 54,570 | 33.5 | 1,776 | 25 | 1,801 | 2.87 | 62,650 | 33.5 | 72,580 | 33.6 | 124,000 | 33.6 |
| Roman Catholics | 400 | 0.5 | 30,880 | 18.9 | 1,007 | 31 | 1,038 | 2.92 | 35,530 | 19.0 | 41,260 | 19.1 | 71,200 | 19.3 |
| Melanesian indigenous | 0 | 0.0 | 4,600 | 2.8 | 148 | −3 | 145 | 2.77 | 5,240 | 2.8 | 6,050 | 2.8 | 10,700 | 2.9 |
| Marginal Protestants | 0 | 0.0 | 3,000 | 1.8 | 101 | 31 | 132 | 3.72 | 3,550 | 1.9 | 4,320 | 2.0 | 8,900 | 2.4 |
| nominal | 3,000 | 4.0 | 18,770 | 11.5 | 608 | −15 | 593 | 2.76 | 21,450 | 11.5 | 24,700 | 11.4 | 45,900 | 12.4 |
| affiliated | 12,400 | 16.5 | 135,480 | 83.1 | 4,423 | 145 | 4,568 | 2.93 | 156,070 | 83.5 | 181,160 | 83.9 | 308,400 | 83.6 |
| total practising | 12,030 | 97 | 126,000 | 93 | 4,113 | 135 | 4,248 | 2.93 | 145,140 | 93 | 168,480 | 93 | 262,150 | 85 |
| non-practising | 370 | 3 | 9,480 | 7 | 310 | 10 | 320 | 2.93 | 10,930 | 7 | 12,680 | 7 | 46,300 | 15 |
| Anglicans | 12,000 | 16.0 | 50,000 | 30.7 | 1,633 | 47 | 1,680 | 2.92 | 57,600 | 30.8 | 66,800 | 30.9 | 112,900 | 30.6 |
| Protestants | 0 | 0.0 | 47,128 | 28.9 | 1,537 | 36 | 1,573 | 2.90 | 54,230 | 29.0 | 62,860 | 29.1 | 106,300 | 28.8 |
| Evangelicals | 0 | 0.0 | 39,500 | 24.2 | 1,292 | 68 | 1,360 | 2.98 | 45,600 | 24.4 | 53,100 | 24.6 | 94,100 | 25.5 |
| Roman Catholics | 400 | 0.5 | 30,828 | 18.9 | 1,006 | 32 | 1,038 | 2.92 | 35,500 | 19.0 | 41,200 | 19.1 | 70,100 | 19.0 |
| Melanesian indigenous | 0 | 0.0 | 4,578 | 2.8 | 148 | −6 | 142 | 2.71 | 5,240 | 2.8 | 6,000 | 2.8 | 10,600 | 2.9 |
| Marginal Protestants | 0 | 0.0 | 2,946 | 1.8 | 99 | 36 | 135 | 3.87 | 3,500 | 1.9 | 4,300 | 2.0 | 8,500 | 2.3 |
| Tribal religionists | 59,600 | 79.5 | 7,750 | 4.8 | 233 | −144 | 89 | 1.08 | 8,230 | 4.4 | 8,640 | 4.0 | 9,200 | 2.5 |
| Baha'is | 0 | 0.0 | 400 | 0.2 | 17 | 23 | 40 | 6.67 | 600 | 0.3 | 800 | 0.4 | 3,000 | 0.8 |
| Non-religious | 0 | 0.0 | 300 | 0.2 | 10 | 0 | 10 | 2.83 | 350 | 0.2 | 400 | 0.2 | 2,000 | 0.5 |
| Other religionists | 0 | 0.0 | 300 | 0.2 | 9 | −9 | 0 | 0.00 | 300 | 0.2 | 300 | 0.1 | 500 | 0.1 |
| Country's population | 75,000 | 100.0 | 163,000 | 100.0 | 5,300 | 0 | 5,300 | 2.83 | 187,000 | 100.0 | 216,000 | 100.0 | 369,000 | 100.0 |

**COLUMNS, ROWS.** For meanings and definitions, see Codebook (Part 6). Note that, by definition, total 'Christians' = professing + crypto-Christians, which also = affiliated + nominal Christians. Percentages may not always total exactly, due to rounding.
**CENSUSES.** 1.XI.1959 (non-representative sample census): 48% Protestants (27% South Sea Ev Mission, 14% Methodists, 7% SDAs), 34% Anglicans, 14% Roman Catholics, 4% tribal religionists. 9.II.1970: 37.6% Protestants (17.2% SSEC, 11.2% United Church, 9.2% SDAs), 33.5% Anglicans, 18.9% Roman Catholics, 4.8% tribal religionists (called in census 'heathen'),

2.8% Solomoni indigenous (Christian Fellowship Church), 1.8% marginal Protestants (Jehovah's Witnesses), 0.2% non-religious, 0.2% Baha'is, 0.2% other religionists.

**NOTES ON RELIGIONS**
BAHA'IS. Since beginning in 1954, there has been rapid growth from 8 local spiritual assemblies (1964) to 50 (1973).
MELANESIAN INDIGENOUS. In 5 denominations in 1970 (see Table 2).
NON-RELIGIOUS. Expatriates, mostly Europeans and Chinese in the towns.
OTHER RELIGIONISTS. Hindus, Buddhists, and a group of

people from Malaita.
PRACTISING CHRISTIANS. Weekly attendance for all churches except the Roman Catholic ranges from 75% to 90% (average 85%); annual Easter practice is 70%, with 15% more attending annually at other times. For Catholics, annual Easter practice is 70%, with 15% more attending annually at other times.
TRIBAL RELIGIONISTS. Animists, or adherents of custom (customary beliefs); 7,000 on Malaita mostly in the bush, and about 500 on Guadalcanal. This category, in both past and present, also covers the over 12 distinct non-Christian cargo cults (movements of revitalization based on traditional religion).

---

**NON-CHRISTIAN RELIGIONS.** Traditional tribal religions recognize the existence of a supreme being called Banara on Vella Lavella, Banara la'ata on Choiseul, and Koevasi (who is female) on Guadalcanal. Although active in creation, the supreme being is little recognized and seldom worshipped. Attention is focused instead on departed ancestors and free spirits which were never human, as well as *mana* the impersonal power which pervades all things and may be manipulated for good or evil purposes. The desire for mana is the explanation for many of the customs of the islanders such as the collection of skulls and cannibalism. Mana is also fundamental for understanding sorcery, the anti-social side of magic, which is widely believed in. Other spirits are Nanama (those possessed of special power), Ndave (warrior spirits), Vi'ona (female snake spirits), Vaurangga (shark spirits), and clan spirits; the general term for spirits is Anggalo. Movements of revitalization based on traditional religion have been numerous; by 1973 a total of over 12 distinct cargo cults had arisen in the Solomons.

**CHRISTIANITY**
PROTESTANT CHURCHES. There are 4 Protestant churches in the islands which together make up 38% of the population (1970). Nearly half of all Protestants (17% of the population) belong to the South Sea Evangelical Church, which owes its origin to the evangelization of Solomon Islands sugar plantation workers in Queensland (Australia) as early as 1882. SSEM missionaries from Australia first arrived in Malaita in 1904. The church is found mainly on Malaita, Guadalcanal, San Cristobal, Rennell and Bellona. The United Church is a union of Methodists and Congregationalists; it is found in all parts of the Solomons but is strongest in the

western islands. Seventh-day Adventists (9%) are concentrated on New Georgia, Guadalcanal and Malaita, and are also present on Rennell and Bellona.
Protestants sponsor 170 primary schools and 3 secondary schools, 4 hospitals, one maternity hospital, 9 clinics, a vocational training school, and various development projects and publications.
ANGLICAN CHURCH. Anglicans belong since 1975 to the province of Melanesia, previously a missionary diocese of the Church of the Province of New Zealand and now with 3 dioceses and a fourth for the New Hebrides. In 1970 they were the largest single religious body, with 34% of the population. The church is strongest in the eastern islands: Santa Isabel, Malaita, Guadalcanal and San Cristobal. Anglicans and Roman Catholics pioneered in education at the end of the 19th century; the first government school was not begun until after World War I. There are 100 Anglican primary schools, a secondary school and a teacher-training college; a number of church schools are now being handed

over to the government. Medical and social service institutions include 2 hospitals, one clinic, a leprosarium, and several community development centres.
CATHOLIC CHURCH. The first Catholics were Marist priests in 1845, but the mission later had to be abandoned. Begun again, a prefecture was established in 1897 and elevated to a vicariate in 1912. Since 1966 the church has been organized into 2 jurisdictions, the diocese of Gizo in the western Solomons and the diocese of Honiara in the southern islands. Catholics in 1970 formed 19% of the population of the islands.
INDIGENOUS CHURCHES. The largest indigenous movement is the Christian Fellowship Church, also known as Etoism after its founder-messiah Silas Eto. It was the result of a schism on New Georgia from the former Methodist Church during 1959–61. Members number 2.4% of the population of the islands. They operate 11 primary schools.

Passion Play enacted by combined churches of Honiara, at Easter 1966.

**CHURCH AND STATE.** Guadalcanal was first discovered in 1568, but it was not considered an important island by Europeans during several subsequent centuries. The British declared a protectorate over the islands in 1893. There is no established church in the territory, and freedom of religion is protected. Since World War II a number of religio-political bodies (notably the Pokokogoro Cult, Marching Rule, and Hahalis Welfare Movement) have come into conflict with the government over the question of native rule. Internal self-rule was granted in November 1975, with full independence following in 1978.

**INTERDENOMINATIONAL ORGANIZATIONS.** The Solomon Islands Christian Association was formed in 1967 with Anglican, Catholic and United churches as members. The Solomon Islands Region of the United Church also belongs to the Melanesian Council of Churches (which covers Papua New Guinea and the Solomon Islands). The South Sea Evangelical Church is a member of the Evangelical

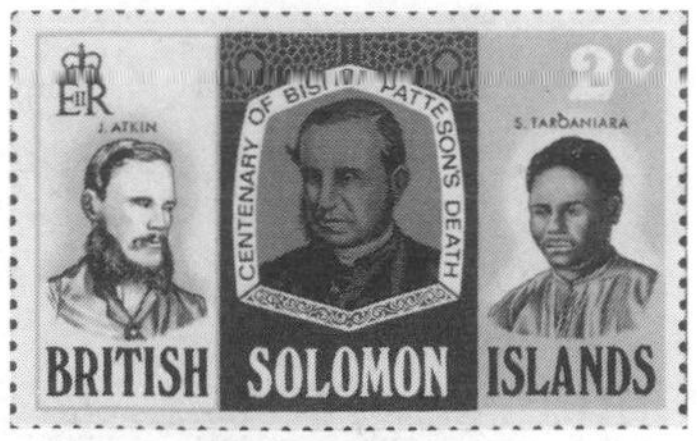


**Church of Melanesia.** Government postage stamp commemorating centenary of Bishop Patteson's martyrdom in 1871.

Alliance of Papua New Guinea and the Solomon Islands, and also an observer member of SICA.

**BROADCASTING.** Time over government radio is shared between all the churches, and on Sundays there is a 15-minute devotional, 30 minutes of hymns and a 15-minute news programme. Each weekday morning there is a 5-minute devotional. The Christian Broadcasting Service in Banz (Papua New Guinea), produces material for broadcasting in the Solomon Islands. For Catholics, the Solomon Islands is a member of UNDA.

**BIBLIOGRAPHY**

'Catholic missions in the Solomon Islands'. H.M. Laracy. Dissertation, Australia National University, Canberra, 1970.
'Crisis and mass conversion on Rennell Island in 1938', T, Monberg, *Journal of the Polynesian Society*, 71, 2 (1962), 145-150.
'Protestant missions in the Solomon Islands, 1849–1942'. D.L. Hilliard. Dissertation, Australia National University, Canberra, 1965.
*Romance of Rennell Island*. N. Deck. Westchester, IL (USA): Good News Publishers, 1963. 64p. (Work of SSEM. Condensed from *South from Guadalcanal*, Zondervan).
'Silas Eto of New Georgia', E. Tuza, in G.W. Trompf, ed. *Prophets of Melanesia* (Port Morsby, 1977), p. 108ff.
*Solomon Islands Christianity: a study in growth and obstruction*. A.R. Tippett. New York: Friendship Press, 1967. 407p.
'The Remnant Church: a separatist church'. M. Mailiu. Christian Leaders' Training College, Banz, WHP, Papua New Guinea.
*The story of the Solomons*. C.E. Fox. Honiara: Diocese of Melanesia Press, 1967.
*The United Church in Papua, New Guinea and the Solomon Islands: the development of an indigenous church*. R.G. Williams. Rabaul: Trinity Press, 1972. 320p.

TABLE 2. ORGANIZED CHURCHES AND DENOMINATIONS IN THE SOLOMON ISLANDS

| Official name 1 | Begun 2 | Type 3 | Counc 4 | Congs 5 | Adults 6 | Affiliated 7 | Names, notes, and other statistics (see Codebook) 8 |
|---|---|---|---|---|---|---|---|
| Assemblies of God | 1970 | P Pe2 | ZF... | 9 | 500 | 700 | M=AoG(USA). Honiara, Malaita. Rapid growth. 10n. |
| **Catholic Church in the Solomon Is:** | 1845 | R Lat | Px..Q | 38 | 17,900 | 30,828 | 1844 mission failed. 3.5% Gilbertese. C=2+1+3. 1s. 6n,36x,20m,142w,P=70%,1408Yy. |
| D Gizo | 1959 | R Lat | Pop | 5 | 2,000 | 3,474 | Northwest. Suffragan of M Rabaul. 80 expatriates. 1 6 2 10 81 163 |
| D Honiara | 1897 | R Lat | Psm2 | 33 | 15,900 | 27,354 | Suffragan of M Rabaul. 60 expatriates. 5 30 18 132 69 1245 |
| Christian Fellowship Church | 1960 | I pen | ..... | 26 | 2,000 | 3,878 | *Etoism* (followers of prophet Eto). Schism ex Methodist Ch on New Georgia. W=90%. |
| **Church of Melanesia** | 1848 | A ACa | AWPKK | 607 | 40,000 | 50,000 | 91% Melanesian, 8% Polynesian. 114n,12x,150m,50w,3H,18h,3p,1s(44),W=75%,80Y,2000y. |
| Jehovah's Witnesses | c1950 | M Jeh | x.... | 13 | 601 | 2,946 | *Watch Tower. IBSA*. Active witnessing under way by 1953. W=90%,54Y. |
| Pentecostal Church | 1970 | I pen | ..... | | 100 | 200 | Small indigenous body begun by an Anglican islander. In eastern Solomons. |
| Remnant Church | 1954 | I pen | ..... | | 200 | 300 | Only survivor of several schisms ex SSEC. 2 special villages on Malaita: Heaven, and Radefasu. |
| **Seventh-day Adventist Church** | 1914 | P Adv | x.p.. | 141 | 7,609 | 13,700 | *SDA.Missions:EasternSI,Western SI,Malaita*.19n,2x,4H,5h,1r,142t(10791),W=75%,436Y. |
| Solomons Baptist Association | c1970 | P Bap | x.... | 6 | 100 | 300 | *ABA*. M=American Baptist Association (USA). Regular and independent Baptists. 6nm. |
| **South Sea Evangelical Church** | 1904 | P int | xH..a | 365 | 12,900 | 20,000 | *SSEC*. M=SSEM(Australia). Malaita, Guadalcanal. 273mw,1H,9p,1s,W=90%,600Y,680z. |
| United Church in PNG & the SI | 1902 | P uni | VWP.K | 139 | 6,189 | 12,428 | *SI Region*.Methodist till 1968 union with LMS Papua. 13n,8x,4H,4h,1r,96t(4162),W=80%. |
| Other Melanesian indigenous churches | | I mar | ..... | | 100 | 200 | Remnants of cargo cults with Christian elements and christianized congregations. |
| **Total affiliated (mid-1970)** | | | | **1,400** | **88,199** | **135,480** | **Total denominations (1970) . . . 15.** |
| **Total affiliated (mid-1975)** | | | | **1,500** | **101,600** | **156,070** | **Total denominations (1975) . . . 16.** |
| **Total affiliated (mid-1980)** | | | | **1,600** | **117,900** | **181,160** | **Total denominations (1980) . . . 18.** |

**NOTES ON TABLE ABOVE**
**COLUMNS: for meanings and CODES (cols. 1, 3, 4, 8): see Codebook (Part 6). Column 1: Boldface type = churches with over 10% of country's affiliated Christians.**
NATIONAL COUNCILS (Column 4, 5th letter).
a = member of EASPI, also observer member of SICA.
E = Evangelical Alliance of the South Pacific Islands (EASPI) (all members are in Papua New Guinea except SSEC).
K = Solomon Islands Christian Association (SICA) (member of Pacific Conference of Churches).
Q = Bishops' Conference of Papua New Guinea and the Solomon Islands, also member of SICA.
*Other national councils*. The Solomon Islands Region, United Church, also belongs to the Melanesian Council of Churches.
UNITING CHURCHES. Negotiations for organic union were under way in 1974 between: Ch of the Province of Melanesia, United Ch in PNG & SI.

**PEOPLES** (ethnolinguistic). Christians: 92.9% Melanesian, 4.0% Polynesian, 1.5% Gilbertese (Micronesian), 0.8% European, 0.4% Solomoni Papuan, 0.2% Chinese, 0.1% Fijian, 0.1% Euronesian.

**COUNTRY-WIDE TOTALS**
EVANGELIZATION (see Part 5). 1900: 24%. 1970: 100%. 1980: 100%. *Mass evangelism*. 1965, campaigns in Honiara and Auki (George Francis, Crusade of Christ in Australia, sponsored by SSEC), also in 1967 Honiara, Auki, Onepusu, Malu'u; 1970, Maori evangelist Muri Thompson (New Zealand, sponsored by SSEC) crusades on Guadalcanal, Russell Islands, Rennell and Bellona, San Cristobal, Malaita; 1970, Pentecostal and Adventist campaigns; 1971, 2 Anglican campaigns (Honiara cathedral, Reef Islands); 1977, Ralph Bell campaign 'Solomons for Christ Crusade' (73,000 attenders, over 6,500 decisions). *Radiophonic evangelism*. ICI (275 active students).
FOREIGN MISSIONARIES AND PERSONNEL (nationals serving abroad) (1973). Total 45 in Fiji, Indonesia, Malaysia, New Hebrides, North Solomons, Papua New Guinea: 26 Protestants, 14 Anglicans, 5 Roman Catholics. Over the years, over 140 Solomon Islanders have served overseas as foreign missionaries.
FOREIGN MISSIONARIES AND PERSONNEL (aliens from abroad) (1973). Total 320. *From Western world*. 280: 118 Protestants (97 in 3 Australia societies, 18 in 3 New Zealand societies, 2 in 1 UK society, 1 in 1 WGermany society), 112 Roman Catholics, 50 Anglicans (20 in 2 Australia societies, 16 in 1 NZ society, 13 in 5 UK societies, 1 in 1 Canada society). *From Third World*. 40 (Protestants, Anglicans, Roman Catholics) from Fiji, Tonga, Hong Kong et alia.
INSTITUTIONS (church-operated) (1973). Total 53, including 6 higher schools, 40 medical centres (22 hospitals), 2 religious communities, 3 seminaries (1 RC, 1 Anglican, 1 Protestant).
PERIODICALS. About 8 titles.
PERSONNEL. About 1,331 (1,011 national, 320 foreign).
RELIGIOUS LIBRARIES. About 5.
SCRIPTURE DISTRIBUTION (1975). Annual totals: 2,500 Bibles (20% free, 80% subsidized), 9,200 NTs (46% free, 54% subsidized), 5,000 UBS portions, 10,000 UBS selections. *Translations completed*. Portion: 18 languages since 1879. NT: 10 languages since 1910. Bible: Marovo in 1956.
SERVICE AGENCIES. About 9, including CEF, EASPI, SICA, SPAC.

**ADDITIONAL DATA ON CHURCHES**
CATHOLIC CHURCH IN THE SOLOMON IS. The 2 dioceses are suffragans of M Rabaul (Papua New Guinea). D Gizo comprises these islands: Treasury, Shortland, Choiseul (Varese-speaking), Santa Isabel, New Georgia, Vella Lavella, their dependencies, and Lord Howe Island. D Honiara comprises the islands of Guadalcanal, Malaita, San Cristobal, Rennell, and dependencies. *Catechumens*. In 1973, D Honiara had 98 catechumens. *Annual baptisms*. (1972) 94.8% infant, 5.2% adult. *Priests*. 36 religious, 6 diocesan. *Brothers*. 6 local. *Sisters*. At least 80 local. *Catechists*. Total (1973) 261. *Indigenous religious congregations*. Sisters: Daughters of Mary Immaculate (in D Honiara; 1972, 79 professed). *Foreign religious orders and congregations*. Priests: SM, OP. Brothers: PFM. Sisters: Dominican Sisters of Australia, Missionary Sisters of the Society of Mary. *Catholic organizations*. The Bishops' Conference of Papua New Guinea and the Solomon Islands has its headquarters in Port Moresby, Papua. Organizations of religious personnel are the Association of Religious Superiors for men, and the National Conference of Major Women Superiors. The National Presbyteral Council, a consultative group meeting monthly with members elected by the priests of the 5 principal islands, was founded in 1968. The Pastoral Council of the Church in the Solomon Islands was founded in 1969 and meets twice yearly. It consists of 35 members, mostly lay delegates elected by the parishes, in addition to one elected member for each group of religious, including native priests, foreign priests and so on.
The Holy See has no diplomatic relations with the Solomon Islands. It is represented to the Catholic hierarchy by an apostolic delegate based in Sydney, Australia.
The Catholic Church operates 75 schools, 10 hospitals and one leprosarium. The schools include (1973) 73 primary (3,148 pupils) and 2 secondary schools (182 pupils).
CHURCH OF MELANESIA. Also called Church of the Province of Melanesia. The diocese of Melanesia, founded in 1861, was a missionary diocese of the Church of the Province of New Zealand until the Province of Melanesia was created in 1975. There are 4 dioceses in the Solomon Islands: D Central Melanesia covers all BSIP except islands under D Malaita and D Ysabel; D Malaita covers Malaita, Sikaiana, and Ontong Java: D Temotu; and D Ysabel covers Gela, Savo, Russells, and Gizo. The Province has a fifth diocese, D New Hebrides. *Home missionaries*. Over 1,000 indigenous brothers in the Melanesian Brotherhood have pioneered work in non-Christian areas on Malaita, Guadalcanal and the Santa Cruz islands. In 1973, there were 110 Melanesian Brothers and 30 novices in the Solomons, New Hebrides, Fiji and New Guinea (HQ Tabalia, Guadalcanal). *Other religious personnel*. 5 Friars of St Francis, 5 Sisters of the Church. *Other personnel* (1975). About 1,782 lay readers and catechists (men), 40 women. *Schools* (1973). 83 junior primary, 17 senior primary boarding, 1 secondary boarding school, 1 teacher-training college, 1 nurses' training school. *Medical centres*. 1 hospital, 2 leprosaria, 18 clinics and dispensaries.
UNITED CHURCH IN PAPUA NEW GUINEA AND THE SI. *Areas:* mainly New Georgia, Choiseul (strongest membership in UC) and western islands. *Languages*. Roviana is widely spoken, also Babatana on Choiseul, Pidgin and English. *Expatriate ministers*. Including 2 Papuans, 2 Fijians, 2 Tongans, 2 New Zealand Whites. One bishop and the moderator in 1975 were Solomonis.

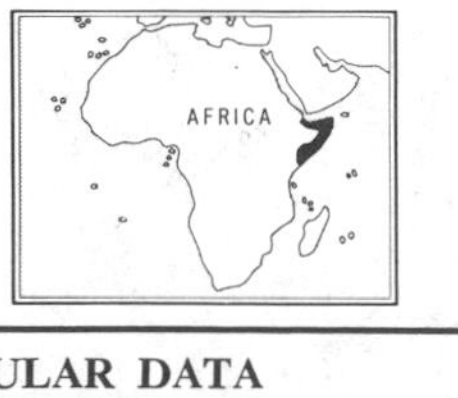


# SOMALIA

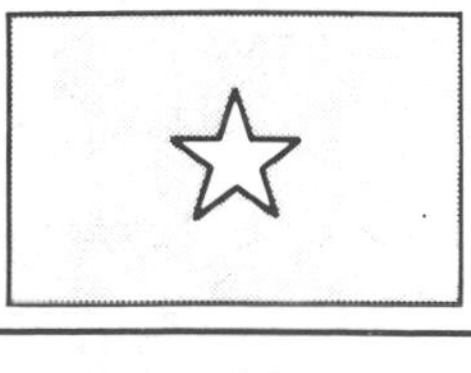

## SECULAR DATA

**STATE. Official name:** The Somali Democratic Republic (Jamhuuriyadda Somalida ee Dimugraadiga ah/Jamhuriyadda Dimoqraadiga Soomaaliya/Al-Jumhouriya As-Somaliya Al-Democradia). Adjective of nationality: Somali.
**Flag** (shown above right): Light blue field with centred white star.
**Area:** 637,657 sq.km. (246,201 sq.miles). Agricultural land: 46.9%.
**Government:** One-party socialist state, since 1970 (1884 British protectorate in north and 1889 Italian in south, 1960 Independence as republic, 1969 leftist military junta).
**Official languages:** Somali (*Somalinya*) (national language), Arabic, Italian (*Italiano*), and English.
**Capital:** Mogadiscio 230,000 (1972).
**Political divisions:** 8 Regions.
**Armed forces** (1976): Total 25,000 regular: army 22,000, navy 300, air force 2,700 (66 combat aircraft). Paramilitary forces: 3,000.
**Foreign forces:** USSR military and advisors: (1973) 600, (1975) 3,600, (1977) 6,000, then expelled.

**DEMOGRAPHY. Population:** 2,941,000 (estimate of 1.VII.1972. For 1970–2000 (UN), see last row of Table 1). Population density (1975): 5/sq.km. (13/sq.mile). Under 15 years: 44%. Growth rate (1975–80): 2.83% per year (births 4.83%, deaths −2.00%). Life expectancy (1975–80): 43.5 years. Household size: 4.9 persons.
**Major languages:** Somali, Arabic, Italian, English, Bantu, Russian, Afar (Danakil), and others.
**Urban dwellers** (1970): 20.2%. Urban growth rate (1950–70): 3.1% per year.
**Labour force:** 39%.
**Refugees:** About 500,000 (1977), rising to 1.5 million (1980).

**ETHNOLINGUISTIC GROUPS:** 95.0% Somali (76% Darod, with Ishaak, Hawiya, Dir, 19% Sab), 2.9% Bantu (80,000) (Gosha, Shebelle, Bajun, Swahili), 1.5% Arab (42,000) (1.1% Yemeni), 0.2% Italian (with other European) (6,000), 0.1% Asian (Indo-Pakistani et alii), 0.1% USSR military (3,600 in 1975), Amhara, Eritrean, Baluchi, Boni.

**MONEY** (1977). **Monetary unit:** Somali shilling (= 100 centesimi); US$1 = SoSh 6.23.
**National income per person:** US$110. Average annual family income: US$539.
**Inflation:** (1970–74) 5.0% per year, (1975: consumer price index 148).
**Cost of living in capital** (1976): index 122 (Washington DC = 100). Daily cost of living: US$27.

**HEALTH.** Hospitals: 15 (4,882 beds). Doctors: 193: Lepers. 5,000 (1.6 per 1,000). Blind: 10,000. Pyschotics: 25,000.

**EDUCATION.** Adult literacy: (1962) 2%, (1972) 5%, with compulsory literacy campaigns aiming for 70% by 1980. Education rate: 4%. Schools: 243. Universities: 1.

**LITERATURE.** Annual new book titles (1965): 17. Periodicals: 3. Newspapers: 2 dailies, 2 non-daily.

**COMMUNICATION** (per 1,000 people). Phones: 2. Radios: 22. Daily newspaper circulation: 1 copy.

TABLE 1. RELIGIOUS ADHERENTS IN SOMALIA

| Year | 1900 | | mid-1970 | | Annual change, 1970–1980 | | | | mid-1975 | | mid-1980 | | 2000 | |
|---|---|---|---|---|---|---|---|---|---|---|---|---|---|---|
| *Name* | *Adherents* | *%* | *Adherents* | *%* | *Natural* | *Conversion* | *Total* | *Rate* | *Adherents* | *%* | *Adherents* | *%* | *Adherents* | *%* |
| Muslims | 809,400 | 99.9 | 2,780,290 | 99.7 | 86,323 | –34 | 86,289 | 2.72 | 3,161,950 | 99.7 | 3,643,180 | 99.8 | 6,526,200 | 99.7 |
| **Christians** | **600** | **0.1** | **4,010** | **0.1** | –176 | **2** | **–174** | **–7.13** | **2,440** | **0.1** | **2,270** | **0.1** | **3,600** | **0.1** |
| crypto-Christians | 50 | 0.0 | 1,210 | 0.0 | 44 | 2 | 46 | 3.19 | 1,440 | 0.0 | 1,670 | 0.0 | 2,900 | 0.0 |
| professing | 550 | 0.1 | 2,800 | 0.1 | –220 | 0 | –220 | –22.00 | 1,000 | 0.0 | 600 | 0.0 | 700 | 0.0 |
| Roman Catholics | 550 | 0.1 | 2,800 | 0.1 | –220 | 0 | –220 | –22.00 | 1,000 | 0.0 | 600 | 0.0 | 700 | 0.0 |
| affiliated | 600 | 0.1 | 4,010 | 0.1 | –176 | 2 | –174 | –7.13 | 2,440 | 0.1 | 2,270 | 0.1 | 3,600 | 0.1 |
| total practising | 540 | *90* | 3,210 | *80* | –141 | 2 | –139 | –7.13 | 1,950 | *80* | 1,820 | *80* | 2,500 | *70* |
| non-practising | 60 | *10* | 800 | *20* | –35 | 0 | –35 | –7.14 | 490 | *20* | 450 | *20* | 1,080 | *30* |
| Roman Catholics | 600 | 0.1 | 3,300 | 0.1 | –200 | 0 | –200 | –12.50 | 1,600 | 0.1 | 1,300 | 0.0 | 1,400 | 0.0 |
| Protestants | 0 | 0.0 | 550 | 0.0 | 18 | 2 | 20 | 3.08 | 650 | 0.0 | 750 | 0.0 | 1,100 | 0.0 |
| Evangelicals | 0 | 0.0 | 550 | 0.0 | 18 | 2 | 20 | 3.08 | 650 | 0.0 | 750 | 0.0 | 1,100 | 0.0 |
| Anglicans | 0 | 0.0 | 100 | 0.0 | 4 | –4 | 0 | 0.00 | 100 | 0.0 | 100 | 0.0 | 100 | 0.0 |
| Somali indigenous | 0 | 0.0 | 60 | 0.0 | 2 | 4 | 6 | 6.67 | 90 | 0.0 | 120 | 0.0 | 1,000 | 0.0 |
| Non-religious | 0 | 0.0 | 2,500 | 0.1 | 82 | 18 | 100 | 3.33 | 3,000 | 0.1 | 3,500 | 0.1 | 8,000 | 0.1 |
| Atheists | 0 | 0.0 | 1,000 | 0.0 | 33 | 7 | 40 | 3.33 | 1,200 | 0.0 | 1,400 | 0.0 | 3,000 | 0.0 |
| Baha'is | 0 | 0.0 | 700 | 0.0 | 23 | 7 | 30 | 3.53 | 850 | 0.0 | 1,000 | 0.0 | 2,000 | 0.0 |
| Hindus | 0 | 0.0 | 500 | 0.0 | 15 | 0 | 15 | 2.72 | 560 | 0.0 | 650 | 0.0 | 1,200 | 0.0 |
| **Country's population** | **810,000** | **100.0** | **2,789,000** | **100.0** | **86,300** | **0** | **86,300** | **2.72** | **3,170,000** | **100.0** | **3,652,000** | **100.0** | **6,544,000** | **100.** |

COLUMNS, ROWS. For meanings and definitions, see Codebook (Part 6). Note that, by definition, total 'Christians' = professing + crypto-Christians, which also = affiliated + nominal Christians. Percentages may not always total exactly, due to rounding.
CENSUSES. The religion question has not been asked.

NOTES ON RELIGIONS
ATHEISTS. A few Marxist intellectuals; also 600 USSR military advisers (1973). In 1976 was formed the Somali (Communist) Socialist Revolutionary Party.
BAHA'IS. Begun 1955. Growth from 1 local spiritual assembly (1964) to 5 (1973). Previously there was a large Middle Eastern presence, mainly Persians, but the last were expelled in 1975, leaving only Somali Baha'is. However, there is now a strong community of Somalis, including in 1976 one cabinet minister.
CRYPTO-CHRISTIANS. Unorganized individual Somalis (nationals) in the recognized churches, also isolated radio believers; in addition, Arab Christians have been sent from Lebanon as teachers.
HINDUS. Expatriate Indians, including many teachers and persons in government service; there are also a handful of Sikhs.
MUSLIMS. All Sunnis (of Shafiite rite south of the Horn, with many Hanafite north of it). There are also about 1,000 Shias (Indo-Pakistanis and other Asians). *Missionaries.* There is a large Egyptian mission sent from Al-Azhar University (Cairo). *Hajj pilgrims to Mecca.* (1970) 19; (1974) 3,767; (1975) 3,112; (1976) 7,508. Under the military regime Muslim institutions have been undercut, resulting in a revival of religion including greater attendance at Friday prayers.
NON-RELIGIOUS. Italians, French, Russians and other European expatriates, with a growing number of Somali intellectuals. Most of the younger Italians entering for government service are non-religious.
PRACTISING CHRISTIANS. Practice is very high for almost all Somali Christians. Of the 800 Somali Catholics in 1975, 300 took communion at the 1975 Christmas midnight mass in Mogadishu cathedral. Expatriates have much lower attendance.
PROFESSING CHRISTIANS. The only Christians the state recognizes are expatriates (mainly Italians).
PROTESTANTS. In 1970, numerous expatriates (mostly USA missionaries); by 1976, missionaries had been expelled and Protestants were almost all Somalis.
ROMAN CATHOLICS. The rapid decline from 1970 onwards is due to emigration of Italians. The column 'Natural change' for affiliated Roman Catholics therefore includes biological increase in the Catholic community (72 persons a year), minus emigration (242 persons a year), making the nett decrease shown, –170 persons a year.
SOMALI INDIGENOUS. Somali crypto-Christians scattered across the country who are isolated radio believers unrelated to existing denominations.

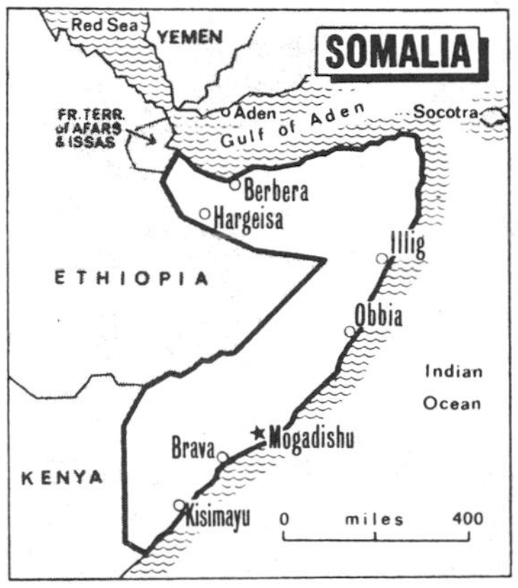


**NON-CHRISTIAN RELIGIONS. Islam** is the official religion. Somalis are virtually 100% Muslims and are all Sunnis of the Shafiite rite south of the Horn, with many of the Hanafite rite north of it. There are also about 1,000 Shias who are Indo-Pakistanis and other Asians. Despite the growing disaffection concerning religious practice among the youth in the cities, Islam continues to dominate the scene in every sphere of life. The Islamic Assembly in Mogadishu serves also as the regional office for East Africa of the World Muslim Congress, which has international headquarters in Pakistan.

**Hinduism** exists among the few Indians living in Mogadishu, Brava and Kismayu, who work in technical assistance programmes and others attached to the Indian diplomatic mission.

**CHRISTIANITY**

CATHOLIC CHURCH. Missionaries of the Catholic Church have been in Somalia since 1881, but throughout this period members have been predominantly foreigners, with only 500 Somali Catholics by 1969. The majority are still Italians working under 2-year assistance contracts, since those who resided permanently in Somalia during the colonial period have now almost all left because of the policy of Somalization in employment. Because of this predominantly expatriate character, the Catholic community has been decreasing rapidly in recent years. Deprived in its traditional missionary role by the government's prohibition of evangelistic activity, the Catholic Church has nevertheless carried on social and charitable work in service to the nation. Prior to 1972, the church was served by a bishop (who died unexpectedly in January 1973), 23 priests, 4 brothers and 85 sisters. Its 16 schools were frequented almost exclusively by Muslim pupils and contained nearly 10% of the total enrolment in the country. The church also sponsored 12 classes of lower secondary level and 6 technical schools, training young people in mechanical and electrical engineering, printing, sewing, tailoring, tanning, shoemaking, secretarial work, accounting and translation work. In addition there were 12 Catholic dispensaries, one leprosarium, 11 orphanages, one boarding school for girls, an Association of Somali Youth in which children needing social assistance were registered, and a home for the poor which provided meals and care for the sick.

On 21 October 1972, the government passed a law nationalizing church property (schools, charitable institutions, printing presses, some churches and other buildings), which has profoundly modified the situation of the Catholic Church. A number of priests and sisters then left the country since the institutions they worked in had been nationalized. By May 1975 there remained only 7 priests and 2 brothers, all Franciscans from the province of Lombardy in Italy, 7 of whom were resident in Mogadishu, with one each at Marka and Kismayu, the latter serving also Jilib. There were also 62 Consolata sisters from Turin, Italy, 44 in Mogadishu, and others being at Afgoi, Marka, Kismayu and Jilib. In addition there were 5 Catholic lay associates.

The Catholic community by 1975 had been reduced to about 1,600 persons: 1,050 Italians, 50 diplomats and their families from various countries, 30 Indians, the rest being Somalis dispersed in various parts of the country. Catholic sisters work mostly in state hospitals and social centres, with a few in pastoral work. Seven mission stations were closed following nationalization, but at Mogadishu the government has not touched the church's property. Thus the cathedral and another church, parish houses and 2 small schools for Somali infants remain under church control. At Afgoi, Marka, Kismayu and Jilib also Catholics have either total or partial control of their church buildings and parish houses. The English Capuchins, who remained at Hargeysa (ex-British Somaliland) after this part of Somali territory was included in the vicariate of Mogadiscio (1971), were expelled following nationalization. However, the chapel and parish house at Hargeysa continue at the disposition of the Catholic Church, and the small community of 20 European and Indian Catholics there is visited twice yearly, at Christmas and Easter, by a priest who remains for about 3 weeks each time. It appears that the government is willing to accept more sisters for work in government hospitals and social centres but not priests for chaplaincy duties or work with Catholic communities. As of May 1976 there had not yet been any move to expel all Catholic personnel from Somalia.

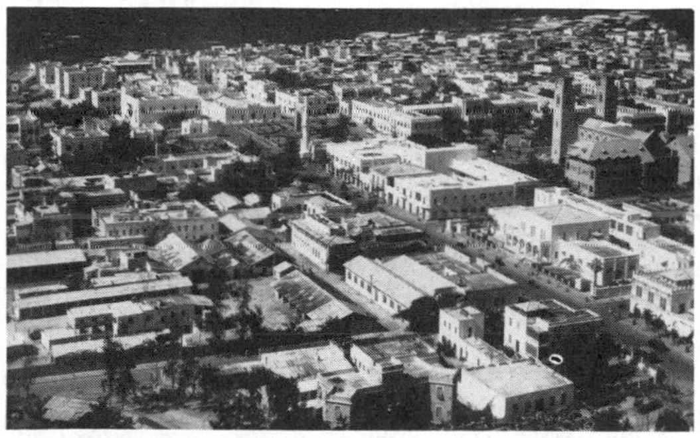
Catholic Church, Diocese of Mogadishu. Centre of old city, with mosques and (middle right) Catholic cathedral (also used for Protestant services).

PROTESTANT CHURCHES. Protestantism in Somalia dates from the year 1898 when Swedish Lutheran missionaries began work in what is today southern Somalia. There they developed an educational, medical and agricultural programme, in addition to evangelistic outreach and the baptism of some 350 Christians by 1935. These latter were mostly Bantu-speaking former slaves, with a few Somalis among them. Italy assumed control of the area after World War I and in 1935 expelled all the Lutheran missionaries. Some indigenous Christians lapsed while others moved to Kenya, and only a few of those remaining in Somalia continued to retain a Christian commitment.

Protestantism was revived following World War II with the arrival of Mennonites in 1953 and the Sudan Interior Mission (SIM) in 1954, both having worked earlier in Ethiopia. As with the Catholics, Protestant activity has been largely confined to social service. When in 1963 the teaching of Islam was made compulsory for all schools, the SIM terminated its educational system, although it continued to operate adult English classes and a medical programme consisting of 3 dispensaries and a hospital until 1972, and in 1971 produced the Somali translation of the New Testament. Following the nationalization of church property in 1972, SIM missionaries were withdrawn except for 3 who continued until 1974 to offer Bible classes on an informal person-to-person basis and to run the European Sunday school in Mogadishu.

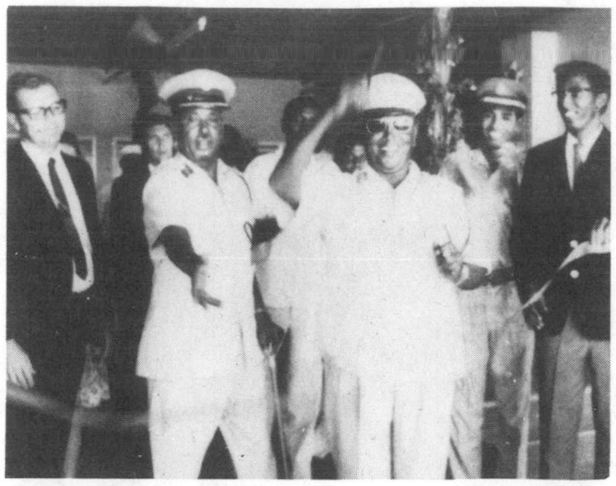

**Somalia Mennonite Mission.** Government officials including District Commissioner (centre) open new Mennonite secondary school in 1972; 8 months later it was nationalized without warning.

Until 1972 the Mennonites with 35 missionaries operated 6 schools (a secondary, 2 intermediate and and 3 adult schools), a community development centre, a bookstore and a hospital at Jamana including nurses' training. During 1973–76 Mennonite missionaries worked under government auspices in their former posts as well as other government institutions. In July 1975 the first Somali was ordained as a minister.

In May 1976 the Ministry of Education suddenly terminated the teaching contracts of the remaining 10 Mennonite missionaries who then had to leave the country, and no expatriate Protestant missionaries remained in Somalia. However, small groups of Somali Christians formerly associated with Mennonite and SIM work, continue to meet and worship together using Somali songs and hymns in Johar, Mahadday, Jamama, Kismayu and several other centres, in addition to holding regular weekly services in the Catholic cathedral in Mogadishu.

ANGLICAN CHURCH. A small Anglican community, consisting mostly of expatriates, exists at Mogadishu. The church has been organized by lay persons, there being no resident clergy. Periodic chaplaincy services were until recently provided by a priest from Addis Ababa, but this is no longer possible, although Anglicans from 1976 have run the English-language Sunday school. The Anglican group, which meets in a private home, is regarded as attached to the Episcopal Church in Jerusalem and the Middle East.

**CHURCH AND STATE.** The military government in power since 21 October 1969 suspended the constitution of 1 July 1960, but government practice concerning religion has remained unchanged. The old constitution proclaimed Islam to be the state religion (Article 1, paragraph 3) and guaranteed liberty of conscience and worship (Article 29), while at the same time requiring Muslim citizens to follow the general principles of Islam (Article 30). Classes in Islam were obligatory for Muslim students in primary and secondary schools, both in public and private education (Article 35, paragraph 6), although the latter was not enforced in Christian mission schools until 1963. Freedom of education was recognized and private schools could obtain the same status as public schools although no state subsidies were available to them (Article 35, paragraphs 3–5).

The law of 21 October 1972 nationalizing church property affected all Mennonite property and most Catholic property. On 11 January 1975 the Somali government decided to revise its laws to eliminate all discrimination between men and women, which led ultra-conservative Muslims to declare the decision a 'sacrilege' and begin agitation against it. When 10 ulemas were shot on 23rd January, the head of state declared that Islam had come to modify and improve the society of its time and not to freeze injustices and defects. In May 1976 the last Protestant foreign missionaries were expelled.

The Ministry of Grace, Justice, and Religious Affairs (Ministerio di Grazia, Ciustizia ed Affari Religiosi) deals with questions of Islamic legislation and is responsible for sanctioning mixed marriages. The churches are accepted by the government provided that they abstain from any form of proselytism meaning direct and public evanglistic activity.

**BROADCASTING.** No Christian broadcasting is allowed by the government, which invokes the clause in the Somali constitution which reads 'It shall not be permissible to spread or propagandize any religions other than the true religion of Islam'. Christian programmes in Somali, however, were begun in 1974 over FEBA (Seychelles), and its 15-minute programmes 4 nights a week can easily be heard.

**BIBLIOGRAPHY**


*A pastoral democracy*. I.M. Lewis. London: Oxford University Press, 1961.

'A study of Mennonite presence and church development in Somalia from 1950 through 1970'. D.W. Shenk. Dissertation, New York University, 1972. 412p.

'Conformity and contrast in Somali Islam', I.M. Lewis, in Lewis (ed), *Islam in tropical Africa* (London: Oxford University Press, 1966), p.253–267.

*Peoples of the Horn: Somali, Afar and Saho*. I.M. Lewis. London: International African Institute, 1955. (Sections on religion).

*Sons of Adam: stories of Somalia*. O. Eby. Scottdale, Pennsylvania: Herald Press, 1970.

'Sufism in Somaliland: a study in tribal Islam', I.M. Lewis, *Bulletin of the School of Oriental and African Studies* (London) XVII (1955), 581–602, and XVIII (1956), 145–160.


TABLE 2. ORGANIZED CHURCHES AND DENOMINATIONS IN SOMALIA

| Official name 1 | Begun 2 | Type 3 | Counc 4 | Congs 5 | Adults 6 | Affiliated 7 | Names, notes, and other statistics (see Codebook) 8 |
|---|---|---|---|---|---|---|---|
| Anglican Church (D Egypt, L & NA) | | A Can | aw.U. | 2 | 30 | 100 | Under Epis Ch in Jerusalem & Middle East. UK expatriates at Mogadishu, Hargeysa. |
| **Catholic Church: D Mogadishu** | 1881 | R Lat | PxSL. | 13 | 1,800 | 3,300 | *Chiesa Cattolica Romana*. 1975: 800 Somalis. C=1+0+1. 19x,6m,94w,P=26%,6Y,22y,150z. |
| Isolated radio churches | 1973 | I rad | ..... | | 20 | 60 | Isolated radio believers, mostly youths aged 12–25. 4 FEBA programmes weekly. |
| Somalia Believers Fellowship | 1954 | P int | xM... | 4 | 75 | 250 | *SBF*. M=SIM(USA). Abandoned schools 1963. 25f(until withdrew 1974),2H,3h,3i. |
| Somalia Mennonite Mission | 1953 | P Men | G.... | 10 | 200 | 300 | Formerly, M=EMBMC(Mennonite)(USA). 1n,30f(until 1976 expulsion),1H,3i,4r. |
| **Total affiliated (mid-1970)** | | | | **33** | **2,125** | **4,010** | **Total denominations (1970) . . . 5.** |
| **Total affiliated (mid-1975)** | | | | **37** | **1,290** | **2,440** | **Total denominations (1975) . . . 5.** |
| **Total affiliated (mid-1980)** | | | | **41** | **1,200** | **2,270** | **Total denominations (1980) . . . 5.** |

NOTES ON TABLE ABOVE
COLUMNS: for meanings and CODES (cols. 1, 3, 4, 8): see Codebook (Part 6). Column 1: **Boldface type** = church with over 10% of country's affiliated Christians.

PEOPLES (ethnolinguistic). Christians: (1970) 69% Italian (and other Latin), 25% Somali, 3% British, 2% USA, 1% Bantu (ex-slave), Amhara, Eritrean, Arab. (1976) 62% Somali, 33% Italian (and other Latin), 4% British, 1% Bantu, USA, Amhara, Eritrean, Arab.

COUNTRY-WIDE TOTALS
EVANGELIZATION (see Part 5). 1900: 1%. 1970: 18%. 1980: 22%. *Radiophonic evangelism*. From 1973 FEBA (Seychelles), with by 1976 four 15-minute programmes weekly.
FOREIGN MISSIONARIES AND PERSONNEL (aliens from abroad) (1973). Total 206. *From Western world*. 186: 119 Roman Catholics, 67 Protestants (55 in 6 USA societies, 8 in 1 Australia society, 2 in 1 WGermany society, 2 in 1 UK society). *From Third World*. About 20, mostly Roman Catholics, with some Protestants (Palestinian Arab teachers from Lebanon).
INSTITUTIONS (church-operated) (1973). Total 26, including 4 higher schools, 20 medical centres (4 hospitals).
PERIODICALS. 1 title.
PERSONNEL. About 219 in 1973 (13 national, 206 foreign).
SCRIPTURE DISTRIBUTION (1975). Annual totals: 20 Bibles (subsidized), 30 NTs (subsidized), 180 UBS portions, 170 UBS selections. *Translations completed*. In Somali: portion 1935, NT 1972, Bible 1977 (translation completed).
SERVICE AGENCIES. 5 including MCC.

ADDITIONAL DATA ON CHURCHES
CATHOLIC CHURCH. Until 1975, the diocese was a vicariate. *Catholics*. The statistics in columns 5–7 above refer to the situation in 1970. By 1975 Catholics had decreased to about 1,600 (50% Italians, 50% Somalis, a few Eritreans and other Europeans). Indigenous Somali Catholics increased from 500 in 1969 to 800 in 1975. *Annual baptisms*. (1972) 76% infant, 24% adult. *Personnel*. All expatriates. As shown above in column 8, in 1970 there were 19 priests, 6 brothers and 94 sisters; in 1973, 23 priests, 4 brothers and 85 sisters; and by mid-1975, 7 priests and 62 sisters. No Somali had become a priest by 1977. *Sisters*. All expatriates. *Catechists*. Total (1969) 12. *Indigenous religious congregations*. None. *Foreign orders and congregations*. Priests: OFM. Sisters: Consolata (Italy).
*Catholic organizations*. The diocese is part of the Conference of Latin Bishops of the Arab Regions (CELRA) with its headquarters in East Jerusalem. There is a Pastoral and a Presbyteral Council but no organization for religious personnel.
The Holy See has no diplomatic relations with Somalia. It is represented to the Catholic hierarchy by an apostolic delegate based in Khartoum, Sudan.

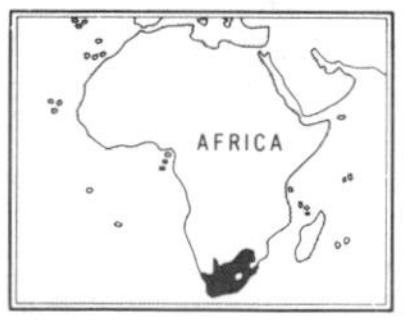


# SOUTH AFRICA

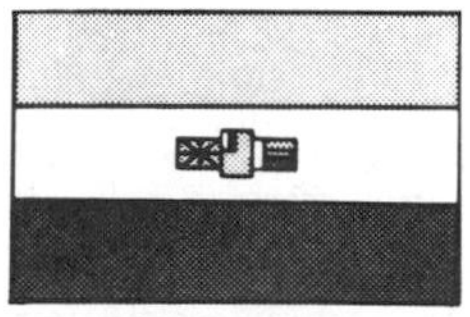

## SECULAR DATA

STATE. **Official name:** The Republic of South Africa (Republiek van Suid-Afrika). Adjective of nationality: South African.
**Flag** (shown above right): Orange, white, and blue stripes; in centre, replicas of Union Jack, old flag of Orange Free State, an old Transvaal Vierkleur (4-colour).
**Area:** 1,221,037 sq.km. (471,445 sq.miles). Agricultural land: 79.0%.
**Government:** Parliamentary republic, since 1961 (1652 Dutch settlement, 1814 British colony, 1910 Union of South Africa, 1934 Independence as constitutional monarchy, 1961 republic).
**Legislature:** Parliament: Senate, 54 members; House of Assembly, 171 members.
**Official languages:** Afrikaans and English.
**Chief cities:** legislative capital Cape Town 1,096,600, administrative capital Pretoria 561,700, judicial Bloemfontein 180,180, Johannesburg 1,432,640, Soweto 1,400,000, Durban 843,330.
**Political divisions:** 4 Provinces: Cape of Good Hope, Natal, Orange Free State, Transvaal; and 10 Bantustans (13% of nation's land area, all but one self-governing by 1974; each followed here by name of dominant tribe, area, and population in 1970): Bophutha-Tswana (Tswana; 14,500 sq.miles; 880,000; Independence 1977), Gazankulu (Shangaan/Tsonga; 2,600 sq.miles; 269,000), KwaZulu (Zulu; self-governing territory, 1977; 12,100 sq.miles; 2,115,000), Lebowa (North Sotho: North Ndebele, Pedi; 8,500 sq.miles; 1,089,000). Qwaqwa (South Sotho; 200 sq.miles; 26,000, South Ndebele (Southern Ndebele; 309 sq.miles; 160,000, with 450,000 living in other areas), Swazi (Swazi; 800 sq.miles; 118,000) Transkei (Xhosa; 15,830 sq.miles; 1,743,000; Independence 1976), Venda (Venda; 2,300 sq.miles; 269,000; Independence after 1977), Ciskei (Xhosa; 3,500 sq.miles; 529,000). In 1970, 7 million Bantu lived in the Bantustan areas, and 8 million in White areas. In 1973, agreement was reached on a Black federation of all Bantustans.
**Armed forces** (1976): Total 130,000 regular (35,400 conscripts): officially-released figures = army 38,000, navy 5,000, air force 8,500 (625 combat aircraft). Reserves: 173,500. Paramilitary forces: 90,000 Commandos. Total all militarily-trained personnel: 450,000.

**DEMOGRAPHY. Population:** 21,448,169 (census of 6.V.1970. For 1970–2000 (UN), see last row of Table 1). Population density (1975): 20/sq.km. (52/sq.mile). Under 15 years: 40%. Growth rate (1975–80): 2.92% per year (births 4.31%, deaths –1.39%). Immigration: in 1976, 20,000 British. Life expectancy (1975–80): 54.0 years. Household size: 5.1 persons.
**Major languages:** Afrikaans, English, Zulu, Xhosa, Tswana (Setswana), Pedi (Sepedi), Sotho (Sesotho), Tsonga, Swazi (siSwati), Venda, Chewa (Chichewa), Portuguese, Greek, Tamil, Hindi, Telugu, Gujarati, German, and 25 smaller languages.
**Urban dwellers** (1970): 50.5%. Urban growth rate (1950–70): 3.2% per year.
**Labour force:** 36%.
**Refugees** (1977): 4,700 from Angola. Exiles abroad: about 4,000 South African Blacks in Botswana, Lesotho, Swaziland et alia.
**Tourists** (1971): 459,500. (1976) 638,000.

**ETHNOLINGUISTIC GROUPS:** 70.2% Bantu [18.8% Zulu, 18.3% Xhosa, 7.8% Tswana, 7.5% Pedi, 6.3% Sotho, 3.0% Tsonga, 2.2% Swazi, 1.7% Venda, 0.5% Lesothan (100,000), 0.4% Malawian migrant labour (80,000), with many smaller peoples], 16.8% White (9.1% Afrikaner, 5.5% British, 1.9% Portuguese, German, French, 0.2% Greek, & other European), 9.4% Coloured (including Griqua, Baster), 2.9% Indo-Pakistani (1.2% Tamil, 0.8% Hindi, 0.3% Telugu, 0.3% Gujarati, 0.2% Urdu, 0.1% Mauritian), 0.6% Jewish, Chinese (9,000), Makua: Hottentot, Malay, Gypsy, et alii. Total migrant workers (1973), 300,000 from Lesotho, Swaziland, Botswana, Rhodesia, Malawi, Mozambique.

**MONEY** (1977). **Monetary unit:** rand (= 100 cents); US$1 = R 0.87.
**National income per person:** US$1,150. Average annual family income: US$5,865.
**Inflation:** (1970–74) 8.3% per year, (1975) 13% per year (consumer price index 166).
**Cost of living in capital** (1976): index 105 (Washington DC = 100). Daily cost of living: US$33.

**HEALTH.** Hospitals: 711 (87,905 beds). Doctors: 11,309. Lepers: 20,000 (0.8 per 1,000). Blind: 62,000. Psychotics: 210,000.

**EDUCATION.** Adult literacy: (1960) 57% Education rate: 28%. Schools: 15,615. Universities: 16.

**LITERATURE.** Annual new book titles (1973): 2,673. Periodicals: 900. Scientific journals: 295. Newspapers: 22 dailies, 160 non-daily.

**COMMUNICATION** (per 1,000 people). Phones: 75. Radios: 102. TV sets: 11. Daily newspaper circulation: 40 copies.

TABLE 1. RELIGIOUS ADHERENTS IN SOUTH AFRICA

| Year | 1900 | | mid-1970 | | Annual change, 1970–1980 | | | | mid-1975 | | mid-1980 | | 2000 | |
|---|---|---|---|---|---|---|---|---|---|---|---|---|---|---|
| *Name* | *Adherents* | *%* | *Adherents* | *%* | *Natural* | *Conversion* | *Total* | *Rate* | *Adherents* | *%* | *Adherents* | *%* | *Adherents* | *%* |
| **Christians** | **1,992,200** | **40.7** | **16,598,000** | **77.2** | **549,982** | **50,028** | **600,010** | **3.11** | **19,286,500** | **78.2** | **22,598,100** | **79.2** | **40,710,000** | **81.5** |
| professing | 1,992,200 | 40.7 | 16,598,000 | 77.2 | 549,982 | 50,028 | 600,010 | 3.11 | 19,286,500 | 78.2 | 22,598,100 | 79.2 | 40,710,000 | 81.5 |
| Protestants | 1,604,500 | 32.7 | 8,376,100 | 39.0 | 262,879 | 881 | 263,760 | 2.76 | 9,569,200 | 38.8 | 11,013,700 | 38.6 | 18,482,000 | 37.0 |
| Non-White indigenous | 15,000 | 0.3 | 4,300,000 | 20.0 | 157,113 | 47,867 | 194,980 | 3.78 | 5,158,900 | 20.9 | 6,249,800 | 21.9 | 12,737,000 | 25.5 |
| Roman Catholics | 70,000 | 1.4 | 1,870,500 | 8.7 | 76,110 | 25,020 | 101,130 | 4.36 | 2,318,300 | 9.4 | 2,881,800 | 10.1 | 5,994,000 | 12.0 |
| Anglicans | 300,000 | 6.1 | 1,695,500 | 7.9 | 52,045 | –24,715 | 27,330 | 1.50 | 1,825,100 | 7.4 | 1,968,800 | 6.9 | 2,498,000 | 5.0 |
| Catholics (non-Roman) | 0 | 0.0 | 240,000 | 1.1 | 7,985 | 815 | 8,800 | 3.14 | 280,000 | 1.1 | 328,000 | 1.1 | 649,000 | 1.3 |
| Marginal Protestants | 1,000 | 0.0 | 90,000 | 0.4 | 3,080 | 720 | 3,800 | 3.52 | 108,000 | 0.4 | 128,000 | 0.4 | 300,000 | 0.6 |
| Orthodox | 1,700 | 0.0 | 25,900 | 0.1 | 770 | –560 | 210 | 0.78 | 27,000 | 0.1 | 28,000 | 0.1 | 50,000 | 0.1 |
| nominal | 688,500 | 14.1 | 3,754,370 | 17.5 | 126,593 | 25,830 | 152,423 | 3.43 | 4,439,300 | 18.0 | 5,278,600 | 18.5 | 8,991,000 | 18.0 |
| affiliated | 1,303,700 | 26.6 | 12,843,630 | 59.7 | 423,389 | 24,198 | 447,587 | 3.01 | 14,847,200 | 60.2 | 17,319,500 | 60.7 | 31,719,000 | 63.5 |
| total practising | 1,173,330 | *90* | 10,403,340 | *81* | 342,945 | 19,601 | 362,546 | 3.01 | 12,026,230 | *81* | 14,028,800 | *81* | 24,741,000 | *78* |
| non-practising | 130,370 | *10* | 2,440,290 | *19* | 80,444 | 4,597 | 85,041 | 3.01 | 2,820,970 | *19* | 3,290,700 | *19* | 6,978,000 | *22* |
| Protestants | 1,027,000 | 21.0 | 5,557,303 | 25.8 | 173,877 | –13,747 | 160,130 | 2.55 | 6,272,800 | 25.4 | 7,158,600 | 25.1 | 12,295,000 | 24.6 |
| Evangelicals | 910,000 | 18.6 | 4,285,000 | 19.9 | 134,676 | –6,786 | 127,890 | 2.63 | 4,858,600 | 19.7 | 5,563,900 | 19.5 | 9,890,000 | 19.8 |
| Neo-pentecostals | 0 | 0.0 | 0 | 0.0 | 570 | 3,430 | 4,000 | 20.00 | 20,000 | 0.1 | 40,000 | 0.1 | 100,000 | 0.2 |
| Non-White indigenous | 15,000 | 0.3 | 4,080,415 | 19.0 | 139,956 | 45,492 | 185,448 | 3.78 | 4,907,900 | 19.9 | 5,934,900 | 20.8 | 11,988,000 | 24.0 |
| Roman Catholics | 53,000 | 1.1 | 1,588,674 | 7.4 | 60,550 | 20,283 | 80,833 | 4.15 | 1,948,000 | 7.9 | 2,397,000 | 8.4 | 4,995,000 | 10.0 |
| Catholic pentecostals | 0 | 0.0 | 0 | 0.0 | 29 | 471 | 500 | 50.00 | 1,000 | 0.0 | 5,000 | 0.0 | 30,000 | 0.1 |
| Anglicans | 206,500 | 4.2 | 1,295,946 | 6.0 | 37,984 | –30,479 | 7,505 | 0.56 | 1,332,000 | 5.4 | 1,371,000 | 4.8 | 1,501,000 | 3.0 |
| Evangelicals | 39,000 | 0.8 | 125,000 | 0.6 | 3,793 | –2,023 | 1,770 | 1.33 | 133,000 | 0.5 | 142,700 | 0.5 | 150,000 | 0.3 |
| Anglican pentecostals | 0 | 0.0 | 1,000 | 0.0 | 855 | 5,045 | 5,900 | 19.67 | 30,000 | 0.1 | 60,000 | 0.2 | 100,000 | 0.2 |
| Catholics (non-Roman) | 0 | 0.0 | 210,000 | 1.0 | 7,200 | 1,800 | 9,000 | 3.56 | 252,500 | 1.0 | 300,000 | 1.0 | 600,000 | 1.2 |
| Marginal Protestants | 700 | 0.0 | 81,292 | 0.4 | 2,852 | 1,019 | 3,871 | 3.87 | 100,000 | 0.4 | 120,000 | 0.4 | 280,000 | 0.6 |
| Orthodox | 1,500 | 0.0 | 30,000 | 0.1 | 970 | –170 | 800 | 2.35 | 34,000 | 0.1 | 38,000 | 0.1 | 60,000 | 0.1 |
| Tribal religionists | 2,793,000 | 57.0 | 3,889,210 | 18.1 | 119,475 | –54,956 | 64,519 | 1.54 | 4,189,700 | 17.0 | 4,534,400 | 15.9 | 6,519,000 | 13.1 |
| Hindus | 50,000 | 1.0 | 433,100 | 2.0 | 13,916 | –726 | 13,190 | 2.70 | 488,000 | 2.0 | 565,000 | 2.0 | 990,000 | 2.0 |
| Muslims | 30,000 | 0.6 | 269,900 | 1.3 | 8,983 | 227 | 9,210 | 2.92 | 315,000 | 1.3 | 362,000 | 1.3 | 597,000 | 1.2 |
| Ahmadis | 0 | 0.0 | 3,000 | 0.0 | 114 | 86 | 200 | 5.00 | 4,000 | 0.0 | 5,000 | 0.0 | 13,000 | 0.0 |
| Non-religious | 2,000 | 0.0 | 150,000 | 0.7 | 5,703 | 5,297 | 11,000 | 5.50 | 200,000 | 0.8 | 260,000 | 0.9 | 750,000 | 1.5 |
| Jews | 30,000 | 0.6 | 119,600 | 0.6 | 3,881 | –81 | 3,800 | 2.79 | 136,100 | 0.6 | 157,600 | 0.6 | 276,000 | 0.6 |
| Baha'is | 0 | 0.0 | 15,300 | 0.1 | 542 | 228 | 770 | 4.05 | 19,000 | 0.1 | 23,000 | 0.1 | 50,000 | 0.1 |
| Atheists | 0 | 0.0 | 5,000 | 0.0 | 171 | 29 | 200 | 3.33 | 6,000 | 0.0 | 7,000 | 0.0 | 20,000 | 0.0 |
| Sikhs | 200 | 0.0 | 4,000 | 0.0 | 131 | –1 | 130 | 2.83 | 4,600 | 0.0 | 5,300 | 0.0 | 10,000 | 0.0 |
| Spiritists | 1,000 | 0.0 | 2,000 | 0.0 | 66 | –6 | 60 | 2.61 | 2,300 | 0.0 | 2,600 | 0.0 | 4,000 | 0.0 |
| Buddhists | 100 | 0.0 | 2,250 | 0.0 | 71 | –26 | 45 | 1.80 | 2,500 | 0.0 | 2,700 | 0.0 | 3,000 | 0.0 |
| Chinese folk-religionists | 500 | 0.0 | 1,640 | 0.0 | 51 | –15 | 36 | 2.00 | 1,800 | 0.0 | 2,000 | 0.0 | 2,000 | 0.0 |
| Other religionists | 1,000 | 0.0 | 10,000 | 0.0 | 328 | 2 | 330 | 2.87 | 11,500 | 0.0 | 13,300 | 0.0 | 20,000 | 0.0 |
| **Country's population** | **4,900,000** | **100.0** | **21,500,000** | **100.0** | **703,300** | **0** | **703,300** | **2.85** | **24,663,000** | **100.0** | **28,533,000** | **100.0** | **49,951,000** | **100.0** |

COLUMNS, ROWS. For meanings and definitions, see Codebook (Part 6). Note that, by definition, total 'Christians = professing + crypto-Christians, which also = affiliated + nominal Christians. Percentages may not always total exactly, due to rounding.

CENSUSES. **1911**: 50.7% tribal religionists, 34.7% Protestants (15.0% NGK/NHK/GK, 10.0% Methodists, 3.3% Lutherans, 3.1% Congregationalists, 2.2% Presbyterians, 0.4% Moravians), 8.9% Anglicans, 1.9% Hindus, 1.5% Roman Catholics, 0.8% Jews, 0.8% Muslims, 0.7% Non-White indigenous Christians. (Total Christians in 1911, 45.7%). **1921**: 45.1% tribal religionists 37.5% Protestants (16.1% NGK/NHK/GK, 12.0% Methodists, 3.8% Lutherans and Moravians, 2.8% Presbyterians, 2.3% Congregationalists), 10.3% Anglicans, 2.1% Roman Catholics, 1.6% Hindus, 1.4% Non-White indigenous Christians, 0.9% Jews, 0.7% Muslims, 0.2% Buddhists, 0.2% non-religious (Whites). (Total Christians in 1921, 51.3%). **7.V.1946**: 40.6% Protestants (16.1% NGK/NHK/GK, 11.1% Methodists, 4.1% Lutherans and Moravians, 2.3% Apostolic Faith Mission (Pentecostals), 2.2% Presbyterians, 2.0% Congregationalists), 33.5% tribal religionists, 9.8% Anglicans, 7.0% Non-White indigenous Christians, 4.8% Roman Catholics, 1.6% Hindus, 1.0% Muslims, 0.9% Jews, 0.3% non-religious (Whites). (Total Christians in 1946, 62.4%). **6.IX.1960**: 39.4% Protestants (16.6% NGK/NHK/GK, 10.7% Methodists, 4.1% Lutherans, 2.0% Presbyterians, 1.8% Congregationalists, 1.2% Apostolic Faith Mission), 22.0% tribal religionists, 17.5% Non-White indigenous Christians, 8.8% Anglicans, 6.8% Roman Catholics, 2.1% Hindus, 1.2% Muslims, 0.8% Catholics (non-Roman), 0.7% Jews, 0.4% non-religious (Whites), 0.1% Orthodox, 0.1% marginal Protestants. (Total Christians in 1960, 73.5%). **6.V.1970**: 39.0% Protestants (15.7% NGK/NHK/GK, 10.6% Methodists, 4.4% Lutherans, 2.7% Presbyterians, 1.8% Congregationalists, 1.0% Apostolic Faith Mission), 20.0% Non-White indigenous Christians, 18.1% tribal religionists, 8.7% Roman Catholics, 7.9% Anglicans, 2.0% Hindus, 1.2% Muslims, 1.1% Catholics (non-Roman), 0.7% non-religious (Whites, Coloureds), 0.6% Jews, 0.4% marginal Protestants, 0.1% Orthodox, 0.1% other religionists. (Total Christians in 1970, 77.2%). Note: the 1970 census was incomplete in that a total of 4,349,525 Bantu were incompletely classified (No religion, no church 3,945,976; Unspecified 324,345; Other religious (non-Christian) 59,729; Object to state 19,475). It is generally agreed that whilst most of these were animists (traditional religionists,) a small proportion actually belonged to indigenous churches. The 1970 percentages just given represent this modification of the census totals. Several categories, including 'pagan' have not been consistently or satisfactorily defined or employed throughout the series of censuses since 1911.

POLLS. A number have been taken on religion. Some results concerning religious practice are given below.

## NOTES ON RELIGIONS

AHMADIS. Begun 1946; Qadianis (HQ Rabwah, Pakistan). There is extensive missionary propaganda among orthodox Muslims and Black Christians.

ANGLICAN PENTECOSTALS (or, Anglican charismatics). Total involved adults (1975) around 15,000 of all races; total charismatic community including children, 30,000, increasing rapidly. In August 1977, 2,300 leaders of the charismatic renewal, from 13 denominations, held their first national conference, in Johannesburg.

ATHEISTS. South African Communist Party (SACP) (banned 1950; pro-Soviet): membership (1970) 100. There are also many humanists.

BAHA'IS. Entered before 1921. Recent growth from 28 local spiritual assemblies (1964) to 85 (1973) including 17 in Zululand.

BUDDHISTS. Chinese (494 Asian, 201 White, 152 Coloured) and 1,407 Bantu (Zulu and Xhosa).

CATHOLIC PENTECOSTALS (or, Catholic charismatics). Total (mid-1975) about 500 involved adults; total charismatic community including children, 1,000.

CHINESE FOLK-RELIGIONISTS. Confucians among the 9,000 Chinese in 1970, also 467 Confucians classified as Bantu.

CHRISTIANS. The steady increase in percentage of Christians from 1900 (40.7%) to 1960 (73.5%) began to fall off after 1960, due to increasing resistance to conversion by traditional religionists (pagans); marked decreases in work among pagans by all churches except Roman Catholics, Bantu indigenous, Dutch Reformed and Pentecostal bodies; and a growing reluctance to call themselves Christians on the part of young radical urban blacks.

EVANGELICALS. The English term is used here as understood within the churches, and covers the following 4 groupings: (1) all persons affiliated to all Protestant denominations which are Conservative Evangelical in theology and emphasis, (2) Evangelicals within the non-Evangelical or conciliar Protestant denominations usually affiliated to the Ecumenical Movement, (3) a few Fundamentalists, and (4) Anglican Evangelicals.

HINDUS. In addition to Indian immigrants from India and their descendants, there were (in 1970) 1,157 Bantu Hindus (half being Zulus), 1,053 Coloured and 603 Whites. Since 1970 there have been numerous non-Asian converts to Hindu sects including (in 1973) 5,000 adults who have 'taken knowledge' in the Divine Light Mission led by Guru Maharaj Ji. Hare Krishna (ISKCON) has 2 centres.

JEWS. The first Jews arrived with the earliest Portuguese. A community was organized at Cape Town in 1841. By 1950 there were 200 middle-class communities, mostly in larger cities and with their own synagogues.

MUSLIMS. 49.6% Cape Coloureds (Malays, Afrikaans-speaking) 46.7% Asians (Indians and Pakistanis, speaking Gujarati and Urdu respectively, traders in Transvaal and Natal) and 3.3% (8,896) Blacks (1970) of whom half were migrant labourers from Mozambique; also 945 Whites. In 1938, Muslims numbered 111,000 (69,000 Indians, 42,000 Malays) with 100 mosques and 90 imams. Muslims are all Sunnis except for a few Shias and a mosque in Pretoria. There are also Ahmadis (Qadianis; enumerated here as Muslims although declared non-Muslim by Pakistan). *Hajj pilgrims to Mecca.* (1970) 1,951; (1974) 2,015; (1975) 1,815; (1976) 1,265.

NEO-PENTECOSTALS. Although charismatics in the non-Pentecostal denominations were strongest in the Anglican CPSA, charismatics in organized groups within non-Pentecostal Protestant denominations numbered in 1975 around 10,000 adults (total charismatic community including children, 20,000). These came mainly from English-speaking churches, Presbyterian, Methodist and others; but from 1974 onwards several hundred ministers and seminarians of the NGK, and several thousand laity, became increasingly involved. There are also numbers of young people in the Jesus Movement, mostly Whites.

NON-RELIGIOUS. 70% Whites, 30% Coloured, some Chinese.

NON-WHITE INDIGENOUS. In over 3,040 African and Coloured denominations in 1970 (see Table 2). Professing adherents at the various censuses have always been considerably higher than those listed under the official classification 'Bantu separatist churches' because many have been classified under other categories. In the 1946 census for the Bantu population, in addition to 3,244,264 adherents of the main-line Western-related denominations, there were 753,891 classified under 'Native separatist churches' (9.6% of the Bantu, 6.6% of the total population and a further 52,694 under 'Various Christian sects' (0.7% of Bantu, 0.5% of total); a majority of these latter were also in indigenous churches. In the 1960 census for the Bantu population, in addition to 4,521,295 in Western-related denominations, there were 2,313,309 classified under Bantu separatist churches (21.2% of Bantu, 14.6% of total) and a further 584,048 under 'Other Christians' (5.3% of Bantu, 3.7% of total), a majority in indigenous churches. In the 1970 census for the Bantu population, in addition to 6 million in Western-related denominations, there were 2,716,019 listed under Bantu separatist or Christian churches (17.7% of Bantu, 12.7% of total), and a further 361,763 under 'Other Christian churches' (2.4% of Bantu, 1.7% of total); also, a small proportion of the 4,349,525 Bantu incompletely classified were probably in indigenous churches. In addition, in 1970 there were about 100,000 Coloureds (0.5% of population) in indigenous churches. It is probable therefore that our category of professing Non-White indigenous Christians numbered about 7.0% of the total population in 1946, about 17.5% in 1960, and in 1970 about 19.5% (Bantu) + 0.5% (Coloured) = 20.0%. *Conversions.* The Bantu and other indigenous churches are winning converts from tribal religions far more rapidly than are any other religious bodies; the total shown in the table (47,867 per year) is greater than the total for Roman Catholics, Protestants and Anglicans combined.

OTHER RELIGIONISTS. Adherents of other non-Christian religions and cults. Rosicrucians (AMORC) have 6 Lodges and centres.

PRACTISING CHRISTIANS. Roman Catholics: Easter practice 47% (1969). Anglicans: Easter practice about 40%. Protestants: about 40% attend church weekly, 65% monthly, 85% at least once annually. 80% of DRC Whites and 85% of DRC Blacks go to church once a month at least. Indigenous churches: about 80% weekly, 95% at least once annually. Other miscellaneous polls: White married women in Johannesburg (1957): 38% attended church often, 46% seldom, 16% never (NGK/NHK: 57% often, 37% seldom, 6% never; Anglican/Methodist: 33% often, 48% seldom, 19% never; Roman Catholic: 54% often, 33% seldom, 13% never). White adults in King William's Town (1965): 38% weekly, 27% monthly only, 16% sometimes, 10% never. Youths aged 16–24 (1973; South African Broadcasting Corporation): 40% attended church every Sunday. *Pilgrimages.* Among the largest is the Easter pilgrimage to Morija City (42 km east of Pietersburg, Northern Transvaal) by 40,000 Bantu of the Zion Christian Church, using over 300 buses (1973), and wearing khaki uniforms for men and multi-coloured ones for women.

ROMAN CATHOLICS. In 1900, 49,593 baptized (all races), about 3,000 catechumens. By 1970, annual increase was very considerable, due to (a) relatively high natural increase, (b) conversions from tribal religion, and (c) heavy immigration from Latin Europe.

SPIRITISTS. Whites. The number has remained at under 2,000 since 1900.

TRIBAL RELIGIONISTS. The percentage of animists in the nation decreased from 50.7% in 1911 to 18.1% in 1970. In the latter census, the percentage animist of each of 8 major tribes was as follows: Venda 70.9%, Shangaan 54.9%, Pedi 53.2%, Zulu 31.2%, Xhosa 28.3%, Swazi 25.3%, Sotho 12.0%, Tswana 9.6%. Since 1945 there has been a resurgence of ancestor-veneration among the Bantu. Although the 1960 percentage has been acknowledged by the state department of statistics to be too low due to 11% underenumeration of Africans then (underenumeration being only 4.2% in the 1970 census), the rapid decline of animism is evident. After 1960, however, the rate of conversion of pagans to Christianity declined appreciably to the figures for 1970–80 shown in the table, with the large majority of pagan converts joining indigenous churches because of their widespread healing ministries.

**NON-CHRISTIAN RELIGIONS. Traditional religions** continue to retain the allegiance of 17% of the population, the highest proportion being among the Venda who are 70% traditionalists. Traditional thought combines an emphasis on magical practices with ancestral veneration, in addition to belief in the supreme being who is known by various names: Unkulunkulu (Zulu), Thixo (Xhosa), Utixo (Hottentots), Tilo (Tsonga), Khuzwane (Lovedu) and

Raluvhimba (Venda). A distinctive feature of Lovedu traditional religion is the role played by the divine queen who must be without physical weakness and who eventually commits ritual suicide by poison before the young male initiates emerge from her reign's fourth circumcision school. She is especially responsible for rain-making, calling to her aid her own divinity, the royal rain-medicines and the royal ancestral spirits. The supreme being is not involved. Also important is the belief in the power of medicine men (*lelopo*), diviners (*mugome*), witchcraft (*vuloi*) and taboo (*hu-ila*), as well as a female fertility cult (Vyali-Vuhwera) involving the use of 4 sacred drums (*digoma*). A number of spirit-possession cults have also spread to South Africa from neighbouring Zimbabwe. The Molombo cult among the Venda owes its origin to the period following World War I and continues active. Possession is by ancestors and not by animal spirits as with the Shona or alien spirits among the Tsonga; and this is true also for the Lovedu. The older Zulu ancestral-possession cult called Ukuthwasa has now given way to the Amandiki cult in which foreign spirits play a key role.

**Hinduism** is confined almost entirely to the Asian community, with in 1970, 603 Whites, 1,053 Coloureds and 1,157 Bantu. Hindus make up 2% of the population. Although many Hindus are being converted to Christianity, a fair number of non-Hindu Whites and other non-Asians have been converted to the Divine Light Mission.

**Islam** is found mostly among the Urdu- and Gujarati-speaking peoples of Indian descent, settled mainly in Natal. There is also an Afrikaans-speaking Muslim community known as Cape Malays, of Asiatic origin but now mixed with other races resulting in their being officially classed as Coloured. A few African workers, immigrants from Mozambique, are also Muslims. Islam is active and has made some headway among urbanized Africans through the Islamic Bureau, based on Athlone, Cape, which promotes systematic missionary endeavour with South African. Muslims form 1.3% of the population.

**Judaism** is represented by a prosperous middle-class community found almost exclusively in the larger cities, in particular Cape Town and Johannesburg, and to a lesser extent Durban and elsewhere. Jewish immigration dates from the end of the 19th century and has been especially large from Eastern Europe. The first synagogue was built in Cape Town in 1862, some 20 years after the establishment of the first Jewish community in the city and country (1841). The South African Jewish Board of Deputies, established in 1912, officially represents the interests of the Jewish community. Jews make up 0.6% of the population.

**CHRISTIANITY.** Bartholomew Diaz rounded the Cape of Good Hope in 1488, but because of the hostile attitude of the Hottentots no efforts were made to settle. The first European settlers were the Dutch in 1652, and for some years church attention centred on securing clergy for them rather than for missions to Africans. The first missionary to the Hottentots was George Schmidt, sent by Moravians in 1737.

Britain gained control of the Cape in 1795, and in 1799 the London Missionary Society founded Bethelsdorp near the southeast coast. Because of dissatisfaction with British rule and the abolition of slavery in 1833, Boer settlers trekked north to the Orange Free State, Natal and the Transvaal between 1835 and 1848, leading to wars with the Zulus, Matabele and other Bantu states. In 1843 Britain gained control of Natal; and after the discovery of gold and diamonds, it annexed the Orange Free State in 1871 and the Transvaal in 1877. The Boers fought to regain their independence in 1899 but lost to the British in 1902. In 1910 the 4 states became the Union of South Africa and in 1948 Dutch Afrikaners gained control of the government and began to legalize their apartheid policies, with support from the Dutch Reformed Church.

Christianity has made steady progress since the last century, and by 1970 77% of the population were professing Christians, including 93% of Whites, 90% of Coloureds, 70% of Blacks and 8% of Asians. Almost all Afrikaners belong to one of the Dutch Reformed churches or the Apostolic Faith Mission. Most English-speaking Europeans are members of the Anglican, Methodist, Presbyterian or Catholic churches, living mainly in Natal and the east coast. Although 90% of the Coloureds speak Afrikaans, only 31% are Dutch Reformed, 43% belonging to English-speaking churches. Among the Blacks, independent churches claim the allegiance of 18%, and 52% remain attached to the historical mission churches. In 1970, when 70% of the population of South Africa consisted of Blacks, the following figures represented the Black membership percentages of the main-line denominations: Lutherans 85%, Methodists 79%, Catholics 72%, Anglicans 57%, Congregationalists 55% and Dutch Reformed (NGK) 30%.

**PROTESTANT CHURCHES.** The Dutch Reformed Church (Nederduitse Gereformeerde Kerk, NGK) began in 1652 upon the arrival of the first settlers from Holland. The needs of the indigenous peoples were largely ignored until the end of the 18th century. In 1824 a committee on missions was appointed and in 1836 the first missionary to Blacks was commissioned. In the latter half of the 19th century several stations were built as well as a missionary training school, and the work was extended northward. Between 1853 and 1866, 5 schisms took place within the NGK. The Nederduits Hervormde Kerk (NHK) was founded in the Transvaal in 1853, separating due to their opposition to native missions, and their desire for complete independence from British control. The Gereformeerde Kerk was formed in 1859 mostly over doctrinal questions, especially alleged Methodist influences in the mother church. The 3 other separations were largely regional in nature and resulted in the formation of churches in Natal, Transvaal and the Orange Free State. In 1963 these 3 regional churches, plus a fourth which was founded later in South West Africa, re-united with the original mother church in Cape Town to form the General Synod NGK. The members of all these churches are of European descent but their missions have resulted in the creation of separate Black, Coloured and Indian churches as well. The General Synod NGK plus its mission churches are associated together in the Federal Council of the Dutch Reformed Churches. The Dutch Reformed, in all their various branches, are the principal church tradition in South Africa, with 15.6% of the population (but only 6.2% of the Bantu) in 1970.

In 1806 Methodist soldiers stationed in Cape Colony built a small chapel near Table Mountain for their meetings, thus initiating the Methodist presence in South Africa. The first Methodist missionary arrived from Great Britain in 1816, working in the southeast, followed by others who built a series of stations along the eastern coast. Today the Methodists have the largest Bantu membership (11.1% of the African population) and form the second largest church tradition in the republic with

**Tribal religionists.** Zulu traditional religious figurine. The total number of adherents of tribal religions in South Africa has nearly doubled since 1900, is over 4.4 million now, and is still increasing by some 64,000 a year.

**Dutch Reformed Church (Mother Church).** Largest General Synodal Session of the Whites-only NGK ever held, with 900 Afrikaner delegates (October 1973); *above*, last session of old Cape Synod. At its October 1978 General Synod the NGK again rejected any merger or umbrella synod with its Non-White daughter churches.

**Non-White indigenous churches.** Over 5 million Blacks and Non-Whites belong to over 3,100 indigenous denominations, growing by over 45,000 nett conversions a year. *Left.* Exorcism to drive out evil spirit, in Soweto. *Above.* Prayer before outdoor baptism in river. Sacred colours of Zionists' robes are white and blue (less frequently, white and green).

10.6% of the population in 1970.

The next largest church tradition in South Africa is Lutheranism. The Evangelical Lutheran Church owes its origin to the work of North American, German, Swedish and Norwegian societies during the 19th century. Lutherans numbered 4.4% of the population in 1970.

A Presbyterian church was formed in 1813 to serve Whites at the Cape, and the first Scottish Presbyterian of the Glasgow Missionary Society arrived in 1820, followed in subsequent years by several other Presbyterian societies. An outstanding product of this early influence has been the Lovedale school with its comprehensive educational and community development programmes. Out of this early work has also come 2 important denominations: the Bantu Presbyterian Church, which is entirely Black, and the Presbyterian Church of Southern Africa, which is 65% White. Union negotiations between these 2 bodies continue. Presbyterians now account for 2.7% of the population.

The London Missionary Society entered the Cape in 1799 and produced in the early years some of Africa's best-known missionaries: Johannes Vanderkemp, Robert Moffat, John Philip and David Livingstone. Together with 3 other missions and churches, including the work originally begun in 1835 by the American Board among the Zulus of Natal, they merged in 1967 to form the United Congregational Church of Southern Africa. In 1970, 1.8% of the population were Congregationalists.

The Apostolic Faith Mission is a Pentecostal body founded in 1908. This church and other similar but smaller denominations numbered 1.0% of the population in 1970. Its membership consists of substantial numbers of Blacks, Whites and Coloureds. It is the only denomination outside the Dutch Reformed churches to have made extensive inroads among the Afrikaans-speaking community.

Other Protestant groups include Assemblies of God, Baptists, Brethren, Full Gospel Church of God, Moravians, Nazarenes, Salvation Army, Seventh-day Adventists and a large number of smaller denominations.

INDIGENOUS CHURCHES. South Africa has the greatest proliferation of separatist churches of any country in the world. Separatist movements initiated by African churchmen began near the end

of the 19th century. By 1904, 3 large denominations with 25,000 followers were in existence, growing to 130 bodies in 1925, 1,300 bodies in 1946 with one million adherents, 2,000 bodies in the 1950s with 1.5 million followers, and over 3,000 bodies with 4 million adherents in 1970. In 1970 independents numbered 18.4% of the Bantu and 12.9% of the total population. The first bodies were identified with the Ethiopian movement emphasizing African independence, but with churches patterned after the established bodies from which they seceded. Later, the Zionist movement grew which was more pentecostal in nature, emphasizing healing and spiritual experience and drawing more freely from elements found in traditional religions. This was often accompanied by the appearance of charismatic semi-messianic figures to whom special powers were attributed. While independent churches are found throughout the continent, South Africa has been a more fertile seed bed for their growth than any other African state. Various efforts have been made to bring them together through local Bantu ministers' associations and theological correspondence courses, but more schisms than unions continue to take place each year. The largest bodies today (with 1970 statistics) are the Zion Christian Church (600,000), Nazarite Baptist Church (430,000), Assemblies of God (Back to God) (430,000), Presbyterian Church of Africa (300,000) and St John's Apostolic Faith Mission (300,000). Blacks from the USA have also played an important role on the South African scene, the most important of several Black American denominations being the African Methodist Episcopal Church (300,000).

CATHOLIC CHURCH. Catholicism was late in establishing itself in South Africa, although the first Catholic church was built by Portuguese at Mossel Bay (Natal) as early as 1501. Six Jesuits visited the Cape in 1685, but permission to celebrate mass was denied. The first priests were not allowed to settle until 1805, and regular work was not begun until 1820. A vicariate was erected in 1837 and by 1850 two additional vicariates had been added. Also in 1850, Missionary Sisters of the Assumption built the first convent at Grahamstown. Freedom of worship for Catholics was officially guaranteed throughout the whole country in 1870, and in 1922 the Holy See appointed its first apostolic delegate to South Africa. The hierarchy was established in

1951 and the first Black bishop consecrated in 1953. In 1970, priests included 98 Blacks, 28 Coloureds and Indians, 187 White South Africans and 906 expatriates. At the same time 25% of all sisters were Blacks, 4% Coloureds and 71% Europeans. There are at present 4 archdioceses, 17 dioceses and 5 other jurisdictions. In 1970 Catholics formed 8.7% of the total population and 8.8% of the Bantu population.

ANGLICAN CHURCH. Although Anglicans regularly met in a Dutch Reformed church in Cape Town after 1806, Church of England missions did not begin until the arrival of the first SPG missionary in 1821; and the most active phase followed the appointment of the first Anglican bishop in 1847. In 1870 a dissident Evangelical group separated to form the Church of England in South Africa. The main Anglican body today is the Church of the Province of Southern Africa with 11 dioceses. In 1970 Anglicans were 7.9% of the population, and 6.2% of the Bantu.

CHURCH AND STATE. The constitution of 31 May 1961, known as the Constitutional Law of the Republic of South Africa, contains no declaration of either individual or collective rights, a notable omission among 20th-century constitutions in other countries. Its preamble states: 'In humble submission to Almighty God, who controls the destinies of nations and the history of peoples, who gathered our forefathers together from many lands and gave them this land for their own, who has guided them from generation to generation, and who has wondrously delivered them from the dangers that beset them, we, who are here in Parliament assembled...'. The invocation of God reappears in the oaths of office taken by the president of the republic, cabinet ministers and parliamentarians (Articles 12, 20 and 52). Article 2 affirms that 'The people of the Republic of South Africa recognize the sovereignty and help of Almighty God'.

The Dutch Reformed churches in general support the government's policy of apartheid (racial segregation) and have frequently sought scriptural or theological justification for it. While accepting the general principles of apartheid, synodal declarations since 1948 have regularly called upon the political authorities to respect human dignity. In 1961 the NGK withdrew from the World Council of Churches after the WCC-sponsored Cottesloe consultation following the Sharpeville massacre in 1960, which condemned apartheid. The Dutch Reformed churches defend the idea that the historic role of the Afrikaner people is to protect Christian civilization from anti-Christian forces, in particular Communism. Nevertheless, the unity of these churches has been severely shaken in recent times. An ultra-conservative right wing continues to influence the government, while an active left wing grouped around the Christian Institute of South Africa has broken away radically from the theory and practice of apartheid. In April 1978, the NGK severed relations with the Netherlands Reformed Church (Holland) over the latter's support of African liberation movements.

Certain Pentecostal groups have adopted a strong pro-government attitude, but the English-speaking churches are for the most part officially opposed to apartheid, although their protestations are generally addressed in measured tones. In 1968 the South African Council of Churches published a 'Message to the people of South Africa', describing the policy of apartheid as anti-Christian. It was signed by 78 South African theologians and called on the faithful also to sign it. Only 1,800 did so, of which 600 were ecclesiastics of various confessions. In 1970 when the WCC decided to allocate its first sum of US$ 200,000 to 19 anti-racist organizations throughout the world, for humanitarian work, the South African churches criticized the implied support thus given to terrorism. Among the beneficiaries that year was the African National Congress of South Africa and several liberation movements in Rhodesia and the Portuguese colonies. Nevertheless, no church followed the prime minister when he attempted to intimidate them into leaving the WCC under pain of sanctions. On the other hand African clergy and laity accuse the English-speaking churches of practising an apartheid of their own. Thus, the Catholic Church, which is 72% Black (Bantu) and tolerates no racial segregation in its churches, is still reproached for having had only one African bishop (an auxiliary) appointed by 1972 and only 3 by 1975. Catholics are also accused of appointing Black priests to rural parishes of secondary importance. Africans are increasingly vociferous in exerting their rights, and there is a growing Black Theology movement among many Black churchmen. In 1971 the SACC elected as president a Non-White, the leader of the Federation of Evangelical Lutheran Churches in Southern Africa, and a Coloured man was elected a full-time executive of the United Congregational Church. During the same year, the SACC and the Christian Institute published the SPROCAS reports (Study Project on Christianity in an Apartheid Society) setting out the implications of apartheid for Christians in South Africa.

Church-state conflicts have increased considerably in recent years. In January 1971, the prime minister denied that any confrontation between state and churches was developing, and stated that although there were then 1,440 foreign religious workers in the republic, over the previous 10 years actions had been brought against only 25 of them. In 1972 however, the Christian Institute published details of 408 instances of state action against churchmen as churchmen (with also one Jew and 3 Muslims) between 1920 and 1972, not including 100 Jehovah's Witnesses convicted as conscientious objectors. The first instance in 1920 was the Bullhoek Massacre which took the lives of 163 African Israelites, but all other confrontations have taken place since 1955. In 1971 there were 31 cases, mainly refusals of re-entry or residence permits, withdrawals of passports, police raids, restrictions, bannings, deportations and imprisonments. In 1972, the Ministry of Immigration announced that the only foreign priests to be allowed entry in future would be those cleared of any suspicion of subversive activity. In addition, immigration visas would be refused to all professing atheists. During recent years the repression has become more acute for the leaders of the Christian Institute, due especially to the activities of the Schlebusch Commission in its investigation of anti-apartheid movements. In 1973 the SACC decided to pay the court appeal costs of a dozen persons, including members of the Christian Institute, who refused to testify before the commission. In 1974 a high official of the World Council of Churches was declared 'undesirable' by the minister of the Interior of the South African government because of aid furnished by the WCC to liberation movements. Arbitrary measures involving exile and expulsion have also been used against pastors and priests, an example being the refusal to allow the former national Catholic chaplain of JOC to re-enter the country in 1972.

Three other regulations from earlier periods directly affect church affairs. The Natives Urban Areas Act, Section 7, requires both municipal and government permission for the erection of churches in White residential areas if mainly for non-Whites. Only twice so far has this regulation been invoked, once against Methodists and once against Congregationalists. Secondly, the so-called 'church clause' of the Native Laws Amendment Act (1957) empowers the government to prohibit African church attendance in White areas where such attendance would be regarded as a nuisance, provided alternative facilities exist and municipal authorities concur. This clause has not yet been invoked. Thirdly, the Bantu Education Act (1953) provides for the transfer of all African schools to state control. Churches may, at their own expense, maintain private church schools for Africans at the discretion of the state and provided the state syllabus is followed. Church schools for the other races are not subject to such control.

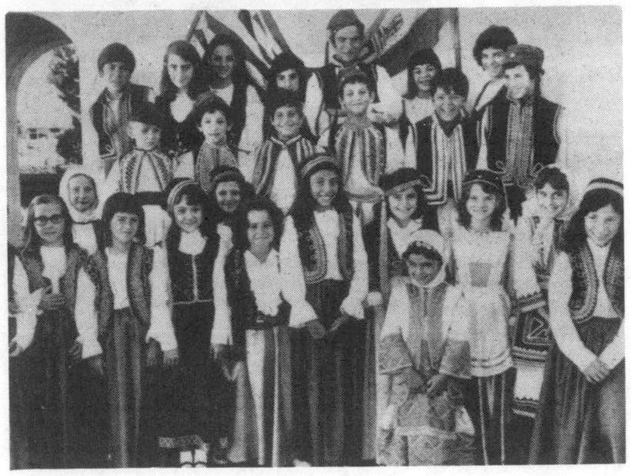

**Greek Orthodox Church.** Greek youngsters, in Greek national dress, in Port Elizabeth Orthodox Church, 1974.

In 1978, the government announced a new policy through which churches may opt to open their doors to all races without hindrance.

Churches do not have to register with government, although the mass of small indigenous churches are not recognized and so cannot be granted land for building. From 1925–65 the government had machinery for the recognition of churches, but of the 81 recognised by 1965 only 11 were indigenous churches. None of the over 2,500 Zionist denominations were ever recognized.

Ecclesiastical marriage officers must be registered, and marriages are invalid unless solemnized by a registered officer. There are no state subsidies for churches, but the state subsidizes church hospitals and institutions for the handicapped in various degrees.

**INTERDENOMINATIONAL ORGANIZATIONS.** The South African Council of Churches (SACC) was established in 1936, building on the foundation of the South African General Missionary Conference begun in 1904. In addition to the Dutch Reformed churches which no longer belong, the Baptist Union has recently withdrawn and the Salvation Army shows signs of doing the same. The critical attitude of the SACC towards apartheid, as well as its continued association with the WCC and the AACC, are factors contributing to its controversial situation.

The following 14 sub-regional and local councils are affiliated to the SACC and work closely with it: Bloemfontein, Bophutatswana homeland, Border, Goldfields and Kroonstad, Kimberley, Natal, North Natal, Northern Transvaal, Pietermaritzburg, Port Elizabeth, Transkei, Western Province, Witwatersrand and Zululand.

Numerous attempts have been made to form associations of Black independent churches, the most important of which are the African Independent Churches Association (AICA), Federation of Non-White Pentecostal and Apostolic Missionary Churches in Africa, Reformed Independent Churches Association (RICA), Assembly of Zionist and Apostolic Churches, African Independent Churches Movement (AICM), and Association of Pentecostal Ministers of South Africa.

On the Catholic side, the South African Bishops' Conference sponsors a Commission for Ecumenism and Afrikaans Affairs.

Two commissions have been formed for dialogue between the churches. The Church Unity Commission involves the Anglican, Presbyterian, Congregational and Methodist churches, looking towards a possible merger after 1976. There is also a commission responsible for official discussions between the Anglican and Catholic churches, including also a joint monthly magazine in Afrikaans and joint pastoral action in prisons.

Six ecumenical institutes and centres are in operation. The Christian Institute of Southern Africa is an unofficial radical body engaged in race relations, action against apartheid, and dialogue with African independent churches. It was established in 1963 by NGK members but has now become interdenominational and its staff includes Catholics and independents. The Ecumenical Research Unit was founded in 1970 as a joint undertaking of the Catholic Bishops' Conference, SACC and the Anglican Church, and studies pastoral and missiological problems. The Edendale Lay Ecumenical Centre is the only lay academy in South Africa initiated by Blacks to develop Black leadership and Black initiative. Founded in 1965 by an African pastor of the Methodist Church, it is a member of the SACC, runs an independent programme, and is now the base for IDAMASA, the Interdenominational African Ministers' Association of Southern Africa. Other important ecumenical institutions include the Wilgespruit Fellowship Centre, which is interdenominational; Emmaus House (formerly Stellenbosch Ecumenical Centre) founded in 1967, sponsored by an interdenominational committee and run by the Catholic Dominicans; and Koinonia Conference Centre.

Two co-operative theological ventures are the Federal Theological Seminary at Alice and the Association of Southern African Theological Institutions.

An organization working for better relations between religions, notably Christians and Jews, is the Spiritual Unity of Nations (SUN), in Somerset West, an international association with its headquarters in South Africa.

**BROADCASTING.** The South African Broadcasting Corporation and Radio RSA (External) both accept religious programmes. At Stellenbosch there are Protestant recording studios operated by Christian Action by Radio in Africa (CARA) and by Lutheran Production. A short-wave radios programme in Zulu is operated by the Africa Evangelical Fellowship; produced in the Christian Radio Fellowship studios near Johannesburg, programmes are then sent to Trans World Radio in Swaziland, where they are transmitted back to South Africa. RVOG (Ethiopia) also operated a similar service until its closure in 1977. For Catholics, South Africa is registered as a member of UNDA. A Sunday mass is broadcast live from the cathedral and a separate service for Black people from tape over Radio Bantu. The churches are taking advantage of the new opportunities offered by TV, which was initiated in South Africa during 1975.

## BIBLIOGRAPHY


*A history of Christian missions in South Africa.* J.C. du Plessis. London: Longmans, Green, 1911. 494p.

*Bantu prophets in South Africa.* B.G.M. Sundkler. London: Lutterworth, Oxford, 1948 (revised edition, 1961, 381p).

*Bishops and prophets in a Black city: African independent churches in Soweto, Johannesburg.* M. West. Cape Town: David Philip, 1975. 225p. (On 900 indigenous churches in Soweto).

*Calvary now.* R.A. Reeves. London: SCM Press, 1965.

*Chiefs and gods: religious and social elements in the south eastern Bantu kingship.* O. Pettersson. Lund: Gleerup, 1953. 405p.

*Christianity and Xhosa tradition: Belief and ritual among Xhosa-speaking Christians.* B.A. Pauw. London: Oxford, 1975. 390p.

*Councils in the ecumenical movement in South Africa, 1904-1975.* D. Thomas. Braamfontein: SAAC, 1979 .

*Eingeborenenkirchen in Süd- und Südwestafrika.* K. Schlosser. Kiel: W.G. Mühlau, 1958. 355p.

*Pentecostal penetration into the Indian community in metropolitan Durban, South Africa.* G.C. Oosthuizen. Leiden: Brill, 1975. 356p.

*Recent developments in the South African mission field.* G.B.A. Gerdener. Cape Town: NG Kerk-Uitgewers, 1958. 286p.

*Religion in a Tswana chiefdom.* B.A. Pauw. London: Oxford University Press, 1960.

'Sociology and anthropology of religion in South Africa', *Social compass*, XIX ,1 (1972).

'South Africa', E. Higgins, in H. Mol (ed), *Western religion* (The Hague: Mouton, 1972) p.437–458.

*Supplement to the Catholic directory of Southern Africa 1971–1972.* Cape Town: Salesian Press, 1972.

*The Catholic Church is South Africa, from its origins to the present day.* E.W. Brown. London: Burns & Oates, 1960. 384p.

*The Catholic directory of southern Africa, 1971.* Cape Town: Salesian Press, 1971.

'The Lovedu of the Transvaal', J.D. Krige & E.J. Krige, in D. Forde (ed), *African worlds* (London: Oxford University Press 1954), p.55–82.

*The planting of the churches in South Africa.* J.M. Sales. Grand Rapids: Eerdmans, 1971. 170p.

*The theology of a South African messiah: an analysis of the hymnal of the Church of the Nazirites.* G.C. Oosthuizen. Leiden: Brill, 1967.

*Zulu Zion and some Swazi Zionists.* B. Sundkler. London: Oxford University Press, 1976. 337p.

TABLE 2. ORGANIZED CHURCHES AND DENOMINATIONS IN SOUTH AFRICA

| Official name 1 | Begun 2 | Type 3 | Counc 4 | Congs 5 | Adults 6 | Affiliated 7 | Names, notes, and other statistics (see Codebook) 8 |
|---|---|---|---|---|---|---|---|
| Africa Evangelical Church | 1889 | P int | xM••• | 178 | 2,905 | 8,367 | M=AEF (formerly SAGM). Bantu in Natal, Transvaal, Transkei. 12n,48f,1H,1h,2s. |
| African Assemblies of God (Back to God) | 1943 | I pe2 | x•••• | 200 | 200,000 | 430,000 | Rapidly-expanding Nicholas Bhengu pentecostal movement. 1959,exAoG(USA). Xhosa, Zulu. 200n. |
| African Catholic Church | 1947 | I Ang | ••••W | 49 | 30,000 | 54,000 | Ex CPSA. Dioceses: Vereeniging, Pretoria, Reitz OFS, Cape. Sotho, Xhosa. 37n. |
| African Congregational Church | 1917 | I Con | ••••• | | 45,000 | 70,000 | Zulu church, schism ex ABCFM. Steady growth since origin, despite schisms. |
| African Gospel Church | 1947 | I pen | ••••• | | 20,000 | 50,000 | Schism ex Full Gospel Ch of God. Strong in Natal, Cape; Zulu, also Xhosa. |
| African Methodist Episcopal Church | 1892 | I Met | Vw••W | 2,000 | 100,000 | 300,000 | Ex Wesleyan Meth Ch; 1894, affiliated to AMEC(USA), 15th Episcopal Dist. 2f,1j,1s. |
| African Orthodox Ch in the Rep of SA | 1924 | I ARo | ••••W | 20 | 5,000 | 10,000 | *AOC*. Split ex African Ch. Link with USA Black body, severed 1960. 4 Dioceses. 50n. |
| Apostle Miracle Church of South Africa | 1929 | I pen | ••••I | 17 | 1,840 | 2,428 | *Kereke ea MBM*. 45% Sotho, 26% Tswana, 21% Zulu. Declining, 8n,20m,30w,10Y,62z. |
| Apostles & Christian Brethren Ch of SA | 1922 | I pen | ••••I | 11 | 6,000 | 10,000 | Ex AFM. Bantu pentecostals. 80% Northern Sotho. 47n,160m,240w,20Y. |
| Apostolic Church (Apostle Unity) | 1949 | C CAp | x•••• | 20 | 2,000 | 5,000 | 1949, 1957 schisms ex New Apostolic Ch. In VAC (Switzerland); 6 nations. |
| Apostolic Faith Mission of S Africa | 1908 | P Pe2 | Z•••• | 500 | 102,000 | 200,000 | *Apostoliese Geloof Sending*.Ex DRC. 57% Black, 33% White, 9% Coloured. 167n,1j. |
| Apostolic Holy Zion Mission of SA | 1932 | I pen | ••••y | 17 | 1,050 | 3,200 | Bantu pentecostals. Healing. 52% Zulu, 48% Sotho. Growing. 15n,7m,7w,17Y,56z. |
| Assemblies of God in S & Central Africa | 1910 | P Pe2 | ZF••• | 95 | 5,791 | 21,676 | M=AoG(UK,USA). Schisms: AoG(1950), Internat AoG(1964). 80n,51f,1j,3s(88). |
| Bantu Bethlehem Ch of Zion in SA | | I pen | ••••I | | 20,000 | 50,000 | Bantu pentecostals. Healing church. Members Bantu, Coloured, Indians. |
| Bantu Evangelical Church | 1889 | P int | xM••• | 309 | 9,581 | 17,000 | M=TEAM(formerly Scandinavia Alliance M). 2 schools. HQ Durban. 112f,1H,3h,5s. |
| Bantu Methodist Church | 1932 | I Met | ••••• | | 5,000 | 10,000 | *Donkey Church* (named after church's symbol). Ex MCSA. Strong women's Manyanos. |
| Bantu New Christian Cath Apostolic Ch | 1917 | I CCa | ••••I | 72 | 1,564 | 3,726 | Ex Roman Catholic Ch. 54% Xhosa, 27% Sotho, 11% Zulu, 8% Coloured. 16n,200m,182Y. |
| Bantu Presbyterian Ch of South Africa | 1820 | P Ref | RWA•W | 1,070 | 43,134 | 66,543 | M=CSM(UK). A=1923. HQ Umtata. 65% Xhosa,23% Zulu,12% Sotho. 49n,5x,12f,SS=11251. |
| Baptist Union of South Africa | 1820 | P Bap | T•••f | 1,110 | 53,400 | 170,000 | *BUSA. Bantu Bapt Conv*, Mahon M(SABMS). 29% English, 17% Zulu, 14% Xhosa. 297n. |
| Calvinist Protestant Ch of South Africa | 1950 | I Ref | ••••• | 14 | 3,000 | 6,000 | Coloured schism ex DR Mission Ch. Cape Peninsula, and Namaqualand. |
| **Catholic Church in South Africa:** | 1501 | R Lat | PzSSw | 905 | 953,200 | 1,588,674 | 72% Bantu, 16% Wh, 10% Col. C=32+7+74. 1q,2s. 126n,1093x,531m,4777w,P=47%,77869Yy. |
| M Bloemfontein | 1951 | R Lat | Pomi | 136 | 31,100 | 51,750 | 94% Bantu (Sotho), 5% White, 1% Coloured. 2 24 19 74 60 3671 |
| D Bethlehem | 1948 | R Lat | Pcssp | 9 | 24,800 | 41,261 | Rural. 82% Sotho, 16% Zulu, 1% White. 0 28 5 35 48 1439 |
| D Keimoes | 1885 | R Lat | Posfs | 37 | 20,800 | 34,642 | Rural. 98% Coloured, 2% White. 4 28 11 52 43 2173 |
| D Kimberley | 1886 | R Lat | Pomi | 5 | 31,900 | 53,217 | Urban. 90% Tswana, 6% Coloured, 4% White. 3 33 30 83 38 3981 |
| D Kroonstad (Bisdom Kroonstad) | 1923 | R Lat | Pop | 19 | 34,100 | 56,875 | Only Afrikaans-title diocese. 90% Bantu. 0 19 11 79 44 2953 |
| M Cape Town | 1847 | R Lat | Ps | 50 | 60,800 | 101,356 | 54% Coloured, 40% White, 6% Bantu. 6 136 71 505 51 4452 |
| D Aliwal | 1923 | R Lat | Pscj | 18 | 16,500 | 27,430 | 64% Xhosa, 28% Sotho, 6% Col, 2% White. 4 27 6 158 68 1130 |
| D De Aar | 1953 | R Lat | Pscj | 12 | 4,400 | 7,404 | 53% Col, 33% Xhosa, 10% Sotho, 4% White. 2 10 1 20 29 353 |
| D Oudtshoorn | 1874 | R Lat | Psac | 23 | 6,600 | 11,050 | Rural. 75% Coloured, 14% White, 10% Bantu. 2 27 5 127 94 671 |
| D Port Elizabeth | 1847 | R Lat | Ps | 31 | 35,800 | 59,730 | 41% Col, 33% White, 20% Xhosa, 2% Indian. 6 70 25 531 60 2716 |
| D Queenstown | 1938 | R Lat | Psac | 79 | 15,200 | 25,302 | 83% Bantu (Xhosa), 9% Coloured, 8% White. 5 35 16 127 83 2078 |
| M Durban | 1850 | R Lat | Pomi | 67 | 91,700 | 152,820 | 62% Zulu, 18% White, 13% Coloured, 6% Tamil. 20 115 38 611 52 8755 |
| D Eshowe | 1921 | R Lat | Posb | 28 | 29,300 | 48,829 | 93% Zulu, 4% White, 2% Coloured. 4 40 33 220 42 3504 |
| D Kokstad | 1935 | R Lat | Pofm | 13 | 23,600 | 39,399 | 65% Xhosa, 28% Sotho, 6% Coloured, 1% White. 1 22 4 83 52 1582 |
| D Mariannhill | 1921 | R Lat | Pcmm | 43 | 120,400 | 200,621 | Rural. 98% Zulu, 1% Coloured, 1% White. 18 58 62 523 34 7676 |
| D Umtata | 1930 | R Lat | Pcmm | 21 | 26,700 | 44,581 | 52% Sotho, 17% Pondo, 14% Hlubi, 12% Tembu. 4 27 9 186 45 2515 |
| D Umzimkulu | 1954 | R Lat | Ps | 59 | 32,600 | 54,343 | 97% Zulu, 2% White, 1% Coloured. 16 10 7 102 61 1565 |
| M Pretoria | 1948 | R Lat | Ps | 39 | 45,500 | 75,904 | 28% Tswana, 19% Pedi, 18% White, 15% Zulu. 8 82 28 288 35 4194 |
| D Johannesburg | 1886 | R Lat | Ps | 52 | 165,300 | 275,265 | Industrialized. Mines, migrant labour. 12 160 72 749 37 8770 |
| D Louis Trichardt-Tzaneen | 1962 | R Lat | Pmsc | 17 | 14,300 | 23,794 | 94% Sotho/Venda/Tsonga, 5% White, Malawians. 1 25 0 27 51 2130 |
| D Lydenburg-Witbank | 1923 | R Lat | Pmfsc | 22 | 29,500 | 49,200 | 45% Zulu, 27% Pedi, 18% Shangaan, 9% White. 3 41 20 95 74 2750 |
| AN Pietersburg | 1910 | R Lat | Posb | 11 | 29,700 | 49,546 | 67% Pedi, 16% Ndebele, 14% Tswana, 2% White. 4 20 31 97 67 2315 |
| PA Ingwavuma | 1962 | R Lat | Posm | 60 | 5,900 | 9,835 | 52% Zulu, 26% Swazi, 18% Tsonga, 2% White. 0 13 5 18 81 420 |
| PA Rustenburg | 1971 | R Lat | Pcssr | 1 | 6,000 | 10,000 | Formerly part of M Pretoria. 0 12 4 43 35 870 |
| PA Volksrust | 1958 | R Lat | Pofm | 11 | 21,800 | 36,353 | 81% Zulu, 9% Sotho, 6% White, 2% Coloured. 1 19 3 123 45 1827 |
| PA Western Transvaal (D Klerksdorp) | 1965 | R Lat | Pomi | 42 | 28,900 | 48,167 | Urban. 89% Bantu, 8% White, 2% Coloured. 0 24 19 62 28 3379 |
| Christadelphian Ecclesias | 1900 | P Ade | x•••• | 8 | 500 | 800 | *Christadelphian Auxiliary Lecturing Society of SA*. 8 ecclesias (churches). |
| Christian Apostolic Faith Ch in Zion | 1942 | I pen | ••••• | | 3,000 | 13,000 | *AmahlokoHloko*. Healing. Zulu, Sotho, Shangaan pentecostals. 20n,20m,60w,500Y. |
| Christian Assemblies | 1931 | I pen | ••••• | 40 | 10,000 | 40,000 | *Christen Gemeente*. 80% Coloured. N&W Cape, Natal, also SWA. 28n(14 Coloured). |
| Christian Bantu Apostolic Ch in Zion | 1966 | I pen | ••••J | 6 | 1,700 | 2,000 | *Isonto Labantu Abanga-Makrestu Asepostoli yama Zion*. 65% Zulu, 35% Sotho. 9n,343Y. |
| Christian Brethren | 1850 | P CBr | x•••• | 178 | 5,530 | 17,500 | *SAEv&M Trust*. M=CMML(UK,USA). 52% White, 35% Zulu, 6% Xhosa. 25m,44f,W=81%,236Y |
| Christian Nat Apost Ch in Zion of SA | 1940 | I pen | ••••y | 22 | 2,624 | 3,792 | Very large turnover of members joining and leaving. Zulu, Sotho. 19n,10m,9w,16Y. |
| Church of Christ | 1910 | I pen | ••••• | 1,000 | 50,000 | 120,000 | *Ibandla lika Kristu. Bp Limba's Ch. Sigxabhayi*. Pt Elizabeth. Xhosa, all bearded. |
| Church of Christ Mission | 1906 | P Dis | x•••• | 150 | 9,500 | 15,000 | Formerly African Christian MS. Bantu members; linked with CCCC(USA). 46f. |
| Church of Christ, Scientist | | M Sci | x•••• | 28 | 3,000 | 4,500 | *Christian Science*. M=CCS(USA). 79% White, 17% Bantu. 51 practitioners(7m,43w). |
| Church of England in South Africa | 1870 | A sEv | J•••• | 170 | 30,000 | 60,000 | *Ch of Sobantu* (Colenso). Evangelical. Churches: 150 Zulu, 17 White, 2 Coloured. |
| Church of God in Christ | | I pe3 | Z•••• | 20 | 2,000 | 4,000 | M=CoGiC(Black mission from USA). Mission across border in Botswana also; 2 bishops. |
| Ch of Jesus C of Latter-day Saints | 1853 | M LdS | x•••• | | 3,000 | 6,092 | *Mormons*. M=CJCLdS(Utah,USA). 78% White, 18% Bantu, 3% Coloured. 200f,G=1.8%pa. |
| Church of the Holy Ghost/Spirit | 1916 | I pen | ••••• | | 5,500 | 10,000 | Ch *of the Canaanites/Nzuza's Ch.* Zionist, exclusivist. Bus company. HQ Hammersdale. |
| Church of the Light | 1910 | I pen | ••••• | | 4,500 | 10,000 | *Ibandla loku Kanya. Cekwane's Ch.* Zionists; colour red. HQ Himeville, Drakensberg. |
| Church of the Nazarene | 1910 | P Hol | xF••• | 268 | 6,154 | 21,861 | M=CoN. Fields: European, Coloured, Indian, 2 Bantu. 140n,24x,84f,2H,9h,1s(35). |
| Ch of the Province of Southern Africa: | 1806 | A Hig | AWAVW | 3,706 | 327,436 | 1,235,946 | CPSA. 56% Black, 24% White. 511b,18de,18H,96h,12r,4s(81). 647n,180x,9373Y,38100y. |
| D Cape Town (Bisdom Kaapstad) | 1847 | A ACa | A | 164 | 33,019 | 267,000 | 56% White, 37% Xhosa, 7% Coloured. 1H,P=58%. 89 47 1000 8000 |
| D Bloemfontein | 1863 | A Hig | A | 236 | 12,572 | 43,000 | 83% Bantu, 16% White, 1% Coloured. P=51%. 40 8 662 2579 |
| D George | 1911 | A Cen | A | 230 | 40,402 | 55,000 | 86% Coloured, 8% Xhosa, 6% White. P=44%. 14 10 139 1886 |
| D Grahamstown | 1853 | A plu | A | 230 | 30,889 | 51,100 | 68% Xhosa (Order of Ethiopia), 27% White. P=33%,W=16%. 47 32 697 1598 |
| D Johannesburg | 1922 | A Hig | A | 324 | 72,000 | 398,500 | Urban. 62% Bantu, 31% White, 7% Coloured. W=54%. 125 22 1709 7067 |
| D Kimberley & Kuruman | 1911 | A Hig | A | 218 | 6,000 | 15,970 | 46% Tswana, 38% Coloured, 9% White, 7% Xhosa. 1H,W=30%. 23 8 240 1880 |
| D Natal | 1853 | A Hig | A | 380 | 24,790 | 100,000 | 82% White, 18% Zulu. M=SSM. 2H,P=78%,W=28%. 106 5 892 3137 |
| D Port Elizabeth | 1970 | A plu | A | 94 | 16,512 | 30,000 | 34% Xhosa, 34% English, 23% Col, 8% Afrikaner. P=33%. 24 18 451 1855 |
| D Pretoria | 1878 | A ACa | A | 678 | 17,000 | 60,000 | 48% Bantu, 48% White, 4% Coloured. 1H,P=44%,W=40%. 48 12 455 1452 |
| D St John's (Kaffraria) | 1873 | A Hig | A | 878 | 63,030 | 155,376 | 83% Xhosa, 14% Sotho, 2% English. 7H,P=40%,1s,W=38%. 88 7 2237 5335 |
| D Zululand | 1870 | A Hig | A | 274 | 11,222 | 60,000 | KwaZulu. 91% Zulu, 7% English, 1% Afrikaner. 2H,P=72%. 43 11 891 2556 |
| Churches of Christ | 1900 | P Dis | x•••• | 80 | 2,000 | 5,000 | *Gemeente van Christus*. 1920, M=CCCC(Instrumental)(USA). Whites only. 46f. |
| Churches of Christ (Non-Instrumental) | 1949 | P Dis | x•••• | 20 | 1,000 | 2,000 | M=CC(Non-Instrumental) (USA). Splits ex Disciples of Christ (UCMS). 19f,2s. |
| Coptic Orthodox Church | 1949 | O Cop | Nwa•• | | 5,000 | 10,000 | Mission under Coptic P Cairo begun 1949. Contact lost after diplomatic break. |
| Dutch Reformed Church in SA (NHK) | 1804 | P Ref | R•••• | 250 | 105,062 | 175,239 | *Nederduitsch Hervormde Kerk van Africa*. Ex NGK. 87% White. In WCC 1948–61. 173n. |
| Elim Church | | P Pe2 | ZG••• | | 450 | 2,800 | M=Elim Foursquare Gospel Alliance(UK), Elim(Denmark). HQ Witbank, Transvaal. 10f. |
| Emmanuel Wesleyan Church | 1900 | P Hol | ••••• | 329 | 4,494 | 7,000 | *Southern Africa Field*. Wesleyan doctrines. 31n,15x,G=5.8%pa,2p,W=10%,531Y,188z. |
| Ethiopian Catholic Ch of South Africa | c1890 | I pen | ••••I | 175 | 18,819 | 25,000 | Indigenous body. Recognition by president Krüger in 1896. Xhosa, Sotho members. |
| Ev Lutheran Church in Southern Africa: | | P Lut | LW•JW | 1,846 | 262,392 | 385,963 | *ELCSA*. Affiliated Lutherans are under 50% of all professing Lutherans. 95% Bantu. 4s. |
| Cape/Orange Diocese | 1834 | P Lut | LW•JW | 207 | 21,170 | 42,039 | M=BMW(Berlin). Members Coloured, subsistence farmers, diamond workers. 46n,18f, |
| Indian parishes | | P Lut | •••J• | 4 | 150 | 286 | Indians only. M=HN(Germany). 1n,2m,2f. |
| South-Eastern Diocese | 1844 | P Lut | LWAJW | 482 | 60,000 | 106,856 | M=ALC(USA),BMW,SKM(Sweden),Hermannsburg,Norwegian. HQ Mapumulo. 95% Zulu. 130f,1s. |
| Transvaal Diocese(& Central Diocese) | 1861 | P Lut | LWAJW | 694 | 100,072 | 119,467 | M=BMW. Sotho. A=1962. HQ Pietersburg. 1975,Central Diocese formed. 90n,34f. |
| Western Diocese | 1857 | P Lut | LW•JW | 459 | 81,000 | 117,315 | *Kereke ya Luthere ya Efangele mo Afrika kwa Borwa*. M=HM. 42n,56f,1s(23),5021Yy. |
| **Federal Council of Dutch Ref Chs in SA:** | 1652 | P Ref | F•••• | 3,955 | 1,103,000 | 2,142,000 | *Federale Raad van Nederduitse Gereformeende Kerke. NGK*. A family of churches. 9x. |
| General Synod DRC (Mother Church) | 1652 | P Ref | F•••• | 1,067 | 799,876 | 1,200,000 | *Algemeene Sinode NGK (Moederkerk)*. Whites only. 1963 union of 6 Synods. 1200n,4s. |
| DR Mission Church (Coloured) | 1799 | P Ref | F•••w | 874 | 135,280 | 340,000 | *NG Sendingkerk van SA*. Coloured only (Afrikaans-speaking). 133n(100 Whites),1s. |
| Indian Reformed Church in Africa | 1947 | P Ref | F•••w | 14 | 416 | 2,000 | Indians only (90% Tamil, 7% Telugu). 9 ministers (1 Indian, 8 European). |
| DRC in Africa (Bantu Church) | 1859 | P Ref | F•••W | 2,000 | 167,428 | 600,000 | *NGKA. Algemeene Sinode NGK in Afrika*(*Bantoe Kerk*). 6 Synods. Blacks. 700n,180x,4s. |
| Free Church of Scotland | 1908 | P Ref | JG••• | | 3,000 | 10,000 | M=FCSFMB(UK). HQ King William's Town. Districts: Transkei, Pirie, Burnshill. Xhosa. |
| Free Evangelical Lutheran Synod in SA | 1890 | P Lut | •••J• | 16 | 1,000 | 3,000 | *FELS*. Schism from Hermannsburg Synod. Conservative German-speaking farmers. Declining. |
| Free Methodist Church in South Africa | 1885 | P Hol | VF••• | 63 | 2,000 | 4,000 | M=FMC(USA). HQ Izingolweni, Natal. 2 schools. 14nx,30f,G=0.8%pa,1H,2h,2s,738z. |
| Free Protestant Unitarian Church of SA | 1867 | M Unt | I•••• | 2 | 200 | 300 | In General Assembly of Unitarian & Free Christian Chs(UK). Cape Town, Joburg. 1n. |
| Full Gospel Ch of God in Southern A | 1910 | P Pe3 | Zq••• | 1,167 | 89,000 | 141,000 | 1951, M=CoG(Cleveland). Vast Indian work. 1955, applied to WCC. 1215n,10x,1j,4s. |
| Greater World Chr Spiritualist League | | M Spi | x•••• | 2 | 200 | 400 | Chr=Christian. Christian spiritists. In Foreshore and Oranjezicht (Cape Town). |
| Greek Orthodox Church (P Alexandria) | 1907 | O Gre | Cw••• | 20 | 6,600 | 20,000 | Dioceses: Kabe Elpis (Cape), Ioannopolis (Johannesburg). Under Cairo. Greeks. 13n. |
| Hanoverian Ev Luth Free Ch Mission | 1890 | P Lut | ••••• | 85 | 11,323 | 23,351 | Ex Hermannsburg after schism in German Hanover state church. Zulu, Tswana. 35f. |
| Holy Apostolic Ch in Christ Mission | | I pen | ••••• | | 2,000 | 5,000 | In Pietermaritzburg (Natal). Assisted by Ev Lutheran Ch in SA. Pastors 59n. |
| Indian Christian Church | | P int | xM••• | 22 | 777 | 1,590 | M=Africa Evangelical Fellowship (formerly SAGM). Indians only; south coast. |
| International Assemblies of God | 1964 | P Pe2 | Z•••E | 82 | 1,660 | 5,000 | Left AoG in SA for closer links with AoG(USA). 65n,30x,G=27.1%pa,5s,200Y,100z. |
| Internat Ch of the Foursquare Gospel | 1929 | P Pe2 | ZF••• | 88 | 4,573 | 10,000 | M=ICFG(USA,Los Angeles). HQ Willowvale, Transkei. 127nm,4f,1p(19),W=84%,84Y. |
| International Pentecostal Assemblies | 1964 | P Pe2 | ••••• | 20 | 121 | 220 | *IPA*. Schism ex Assemblies of God. Main language Northern Sotho. HQ Pietersburg. 1f. |
| Jehovah's Witnesses | c1895 | M Jeh | x•••• | 452 | 23,527 | 50,000 | *Watch Tower*. Literature disseminated 1907 by JBooth. HQ Elandsfontein. 1j,2163Y. |
| Latter Rain Assemblies of SA | c1927 | P Pe4 | x•••• | | 2,000 | 5,000 | *Spate Reën Gemeenten/Blourokkies*(Blue-clothed women). White. Huge church in Benoni. |
| Lutheran Church in Southern Africa | 1892 | P Lut | •••J• | 121 | 15,000 | 22,378 | Zulu/Tswana. Related to FELS. M=MELFC(Bleckmar). Tvl, Natal, Botswana. 22n,25f. |
| Methodist Church of South Africa | 1806 | P Met | VWA•W | 6,795 | 373,675 | 942,505 | British origin. 77% Black, 17% White, 5% Coloured. 650n,4H,1j,5r,2s(60),2400t,2u. |
| Moravian Ch, Eastern Cape Province | 1828 | P Mor | LWAJW | 115 | 13,461 | 29,073 | Xhosa and Coloured members. HQ Cedarville. New Transkei work begun. 13n,3x,7f,1s. |
| Moravian Ch, Western Cape Province | 1737 | P Mor | LWAJW | 58 | 15,568 | 41,587 | *Evangeliese Broederkerk*. 1737 Schmidt among Hottentots. 99% Cape Coloured. 12f,1s. |
| National Baptist Ch of South Africa | | I Bap | ••••W | 100 | 25,000 | 50,000 | Begun and assisted by M=NBCUSA(Black Americans). 1974 joined SAACC. 120n. |
| National Tembu Church | 1884 | I ind | ••••• | | 2,000 | 5,000 | Founded by Nehemiah Tile, first indigenous Black theologian, ex Methodists. |
| Native Independent Congregational Ch | 1885 | I Con | ••••• | | 500 | 1,000 | Largest indigenous body out of the 19 among Tlhaping tribe. Ex LMS. |
| Nazarite Baptist Church | 1910 | I pen | ••••• | | 200,000 | 430,000 | *Ama-Nazaretha*, founded by Isaiah Shembe. Zulus. Holy city Ekuphakameni. HQ Inanda. |
| New Apostolic Church | 1903 | C CAp | x•••• | 1,000 | 110,000 | 200,000 | *Niuwe Apostolisch Kerk*. Begun by German immigrants. World HQ Dortmund (Germany). |
| New Church of Southern Africa | 1912 | M Swe | x•••• | 121 | 15,309 | 20,000 | M=Gen Conf NC(UK). 1961 merged with Ethiopian Cath Ch in Zion; declining. 5n. |
| New World Apostolic Church in Zion | 1944 | I pen | ••••I | 8 | 1,053 | 1,269 | *Niue Wereld Apostoliesie Kerk*. Bantu pentecostals. 99% Sotho. 12n,4m,7w,48Y. |
| Norwegian Free Evangelical Mission | 1914 | P Pe2 | Z•••• | | 1,000 | 2,000 | M=NPY(Norway). Classical Pentecostals (2-stage). Mostly Zulus. HQ Eshowe. |

*Continued overleaf*

*Table 2–continued*

| Official name 1 | Begun 2 | Type 3 | Counc 4 | Congs 5 | Adults 6 | Affiliated 7 | Names, notes, and other statistics (see Codebook) 8 |
|---|---|---|---|---|---|---|---|
| Old Apostolic Church | | C CAp | x.... | | 2,000 | 5,000 | White mission, split (in UK) ex Catholic Apostolic Ch. Mission in Kitwe (Zambia). |
| Pentecostal Assemblies of God | 1908 | P Pe2 | ZF... | 198 | 20,000 | 60,000 | *PAG.* 1915 M=PAoC(Canada). Co-operates with AoG (Nicholas Bhengu). 238n,14x,1s(22). |
| Pentecostal Holiness Ch in S Africa | 1913 | P Pe3 | ZF... | 371 | 23,552 | 40,000 | Widespread throughout Southern Africa. M=PHC(USA). 40n,18x,900m,32f,1h,1s. |
| People's Church of Africa | 1922 | I Con | ..... | 10 | 5,000 | 10,000 | *Volkskerk van Afrika.* Coloured schism ex Cong Union of SA, Cape Province. |
| Phillipian Church of South Africa | | I ind | ..... | | 2,000 | 5,000 | In Natal based on Durban. Assisted by Ev Lutheran Ch in SA. Pastors 69n. |
| Presbyterian Church of Africa | 1898 | I Ref | R.A.b | 266 | 150,000 | 300,000 | *African Presbyterian Ch.* Zulu schism ex UFCSM(UK). Declining. SS=86000,8000z. |
| Presbyterian Church of Southern Africa | 1829 | P Ref | RWA.W | 660 | 65,000 | 122,000 | *PCSA.* Constituted 1897. 65%White. Union talks with Bantu Presb Ch. 170n,1u. |
| Reformed Baptist Church | 1903 | P Bap | ..... | | 1,000 | 2,000 | M=Reformed Bapt M of Canada(1966, merged with Wesleyan Ch). Natal. 4n,9f,1p. |
| Reformed Church in South Africa | 1859 | P Ref | J.... | 390 | 82,198 | 140,303 | *GKSA. Gereformeerde Kerk. Doppers.* Conservative schism ex NGK. 72% White. 236n. |
| Reformed Covenant Church of Christ | 1966 | I Ref | ....I | | 1,000 | 4,000 | Indigenous body. In Bloemfontein and OFS. Xhosa, Zulu, Tswana, Sotho. 7n,300Y. |
| Religious Society of Friends in SA | c1770 | P Qua | Q...W | 5 | 150 | 300 | *Quakers.* Part of Southern Africa Yearly Meeting (SA,Rhod,Bots,Zamb,Malawi) (1948). |
| St John's Apostolic Faith Mission | c1940 | I pen | x.... | | 150,000 | 300,000 | Begun ex AFM by person healed by Mother Mokutudu Nku. Swazi, Botswana branches. |
| St John's Mission | 1911 | I Ang | ....I | | 19,261 | 30,000 | Founded in Umtata, ex Anglicans. HQ Meadowlands. 7 bishops incl 2 for Transkei and Swaziland. |
| St Paul's Apostolic Church of SA | 1944 | I pen | ....I | 32 | 2,000 | 2,500 | HQ Middleburg (Transvaal). Healing pentecostals. Expanding. 12n,50m,30w,100Y. |
| Salvation Army of South Africa | 1883 | P Sal | xwA.W | 375 | 33,900 | 50,000 | *Heilsleër. Impi yo Sindiso* (Zulu). 3 White divisions, 7 Bantu. 281nx,5H,1j,2s. |
| Scandinavian Independent Baptist Union | 1892 | P Bap | x.... | | 2,200 | 4,000 | *SIBU.* Natal Zululand. Now amalgamated with Norwegian Mission Union (1889). 32fm. |
| Self-Supporting Rhenish Church | | I Lut | ..... | 10 | 200 | 500 | Coloured split ex Lutherans in Cape Town; links with similar Nama Hottentot bodies. |
| Seventh-day Adventist Church | 1887 | P Adv | x.... | 291 | 22,289 | 50,000 | *SAfrican UC*(White,Coloured), *SUnion*(Black). 93n,8f,1H,5h,1j,8r,538t,(36691),2046Y. |
| Swazi Christian Ch in Zion of SA | 1962 | I ind | .v..I | 16 | 6,008 | 10,000 | Split ex mother church in Swaziland. 1966, applied to join WCC. HQ Moroka (Joburg). |
| Swedish Alliance Mission | 1901 | P ind | x.... | | 16,000 | 19,000 | M=SAM(Sweden). Transvaal. HQ Cleveland(Joburg). Branches Swaziland, Rhodesia. 59m. |
| Swedish Holiness Union Mission | 1890 | P Hol | x.... | 245 | 6,022 | 19,089 | M=Swedish Zulu Mission. Bothas Hill. 30n,12x,39f,G=2%pa,1H,1h,14i,1j,1s,W=60%,419Y. |
| Tsonga Presbyterian Church | 1875 | P Ref | R.A.W | 337 | 15,000 | 20,000 | *TPC.* M=Swiss Mission. A=1962. Miners from Mozambique (Tsonga, Ronga). 16n,9x,3H. |
| Union Public Christian Apos Ch in Zion | 1945 | I pen | ....I | 47 | 3,615 | 5,000 | *Ensimbini.* HQ Mozodo, Johannesburg. Swazi, Zulu, Xhosa. 32n,4m,6w,70Y. |
| United Apostolic Faith Church | 1912 | P Pe2 | x.... | 350 | 20,000 | 40,000 | M=UAFC(UK). British-Israelite Pentecostals. HQ Pretoria. Mission to Malawi. 1s. |
| United Church of Ethiopia South Africa | | I ind | ..... | | 2,000 | 5,000 | Zulu church based on Durban. Assisted by Ev Luth Ch in SA. 13 circuits. 24n. |
| United Church of the OFS Goldfields | 1954 | P uni | ....W | 22 | 663 | 3,298 | Autonomous church formed by LEC (Lesotho) & UCCSA; Sotho miners. M=PEMS(France). |
| United Congr Ch of Southern Africa | 1799 | P Con | RWA.W | 2,660 | 100,479 | 210,000 | *UCCSA.* 1967 union CUSA,CCA,UCMS,LMS. 50% Coloured, 40% Bantu, 10% White. 180n,1u. |
| United Evangelical Lutheran Ch of SA | c1850 | P Lut | L..Jw | 70 | 10,000 | 24,000 | *UELCSA.* 4 German-speaking White synods (Cape, Hermannsburg, Transvaal, SWA). |
| United Free Church of Scotland | 1931 | P Ref | Rw... | | 2,195 | 4,500 | M=UFCSM(UK). Stations from Lovedale into Natal. Links with Bantu Presbyterian Ch. |
| United Methodist Church | 1898 | P Met | Vwa.W | 30 | 1,000 | 2,360 | *SE Conference,* UMC(USA). Work among miners only, mainly Mozambicans (Tshwa). 9f. |
| United Pentecostal Church | 1948 | P Pel | x.... | 200 | 18,000 | 40,000 | *Jesus Only Church.* M=UPC(USA). Indians around Durban; fast growth. 100n,4f. |
| Wesleyan Church | 1893 | P Hol | VF... | 231 | 5,664 | 7,000 | Formerly M=Pilgrim Holiness M, now WC(USA). Growing. 12 schools. 431m,30f,2h,2s. |
| Zion Apostolic Church of South Africa | 1911 | I pen | ..... | 44 | 22,035 | 30,000 | *ZAC.* Ex AFM. HQ Lethabong (Transvaal). Sotho, Zulu, Xhosa, Venda. 20n,15m,215Y. |
| Zion Apostolic in Jerusalem Church | 1925 | I pen | ....I | 20 | 4,450 | 6,000 | Indigenous pentecostals. Healing church. Members all Zulu. 17n,18m,18w,20Y. |
| Zion Christian Church | 1914 | I pen | x.... | | 300,000 | 600,000 | *ZCC. Lekganyane's Ch.* Largest IC in SA. Ex AFM. Colours green, yellow. Pedi, &c. |
| Zion Church in South Africa | | I pen | ....I | | 20,000 | 40,000 | Opposes Christian Institute control over AICA. Aim: a Black United Ch of SA. |
| Zion City Apostolic Ch of South Africa | 1923 | I pen | ....J | 31 | 2,504 | 3,000 | Ex Christian Apostolic Ch in Zion. 52% Venda, 20% Tsonga, 16% Xhosa. 8n,31m,200Y. |
| Zion Mission Church of South Africa | 1922 | I pen | .v... | 693 | 5,000 | 20,000 | Members mainly Zulu, Swazi, Xhosa. HQ Phirima, Johannesburg. 230n,15x. |
| Zulu Congregational Church | 1896 | I Con | ..... | | 50,000 | 100,000 | Zulu schism ex ABCFM(USA). 12 circuits. Numerous schisms over the years. 26n. |
| Zulu Jerusalem Church in South Africa | c1970 | I uni | ..... | | 25,000 | 50,000 | De facto merger of many Zionist bodies, paralleling political union KwaZulu. |
| Other Bantu indigenous churches | | I | ..... | | 370,739 | 850,000 | Total around 3,000 more bodies (see below), most with under 50 adults each. |
| Other Protestant denominations | | P | ..... | | 100,000 | 200,000 | Total about 100 (see list below). |
| **Total affiliated (mid-1970)** | | | | **59,500** | **6,185,797** | **12,843,630** | **Total denominations (1970) . . . 3,210.** |
| **Total affiliated (mid-1975)** | | | | **67,000** | **7,150,700** | **14,847,200** | **Total denominations (1975) . . . 3,350.** |
| **Total affiliated (mid-1980)** | | | | **76,000** | **8,341,500** | **17,319,500** | **Total denominations (1980) . . . 3,500.** |

NOTES ON TABLE ABOVE

COLUMNS: for meanings, and CODES (cols. 1, 3, 4, 8): see Codebook, (Part 6). Column 1: **Boldface type** = church with over 10% of country's affiliated Christians.

NATIONAL COUNCILS (Column 4, 5th letter).

- b = member of AICA and also of SACC.
- f = formerly a member of SACC (withdrew 1976).
- I = African Independent Churches Association (AICA); 478 member denominations, but mainly smaller Ethiopian ones; 1970, affiliated member organization of SACC.
- J = Federation of Non-White Pentecostal & Apostolic Missionary Churches in Africa (Federasie Pinkster Sending Kerke in SA); begun 1961, 8 branches across SA and Rhodesia, 20,000 members; now affiliated member organization of SACC.
- W = South African Council of Churches (SACC).
- w = observer member of SACC.
- y = Reformed Independent Churches Association (RICA); formed with Afrikaner help as rival to AICA; 600 member churches; member of SACC.

*Other national councils.* African Independent Churches' Ecumenical Movement (applied to join WCC; rejected). African Independent Churches Movement (split ex AICA in 1973; 460 small member churches). African Ministers' Independent Churches Association (begun 1934, mainly Zulu; Ethiopian and Zionist). Apostolic Ministers Association of Southern Africa (about 100 Zulu churches). Assembly of Zionist & Apostolic Churches/Apostolic and Zionist Assembly of South Africa (AZASA) (established 1965 by IDAMASA; more success than AICA in recruiting larger indigenous churches; 180 Zionist bodies in 1967, linked to SACC). Association of Evangelicals of South Africa (AESA) (Southern Africa Evangelical Council) (affiliated to WEF and AEAM). Association of Pentecostal Ministers of South Africa (Black; 20 churches; member of SACC). Bantu Independent Churches Union of South Africa (1937). Bantu United Ministers' Association (c1940; 250 independent churches). Bureau of Bantu Churches (begun 1962 in Durban, claiming 500 churches). Federation of Bantu Churches in South Africa (1943; 750 churches by 1959). Federation of Evangelical Lutheran Churches in Southern Africa (FELCSA), linking ELCSA, UELCSA, UELCSWA, Moravian Ch. Pentecostal Mission Churches Association (PMCA) (begun 1947; over 400 Zionist and Apostolic churches). South African Council of Christian Churches (SACCC) (affiliated to ICCC; no member churches in 1973). United Churches of Christ (1929). Zion Combination Churches in South Africa (1957; 28 Zionist churches).

*Local councils.* 14 regional councils are affiliated to SACC.

OTHER BANTU INDIGENOUS CHURCHES. The table above lists 40 of the better-known larger or more visible bodies. The membership of the 5 largest has been estimated from their annual sales of hymnbooks. South Africa has the greatest proliferation of separatist churches in the world. Beginning with the first secession in 1872, the total distinct denominations rose to 15 in 1906, 30 (1913), 65 (1918), 130 (1926), 293 (1932), 600 (1939), 800 (1948), 1,286 (1955), 2,100 (1958), 2,200 (1960) and to about 3,000 in 1970. For a listing, see B.G.M. Sundkler 1960: 354–374. *Membership.* The larger urban bodies are multi-tribal with members from the whole range of tribes working in the cities, but many rural and smaller bodies come from a single tribe. A number of these include in their title the name of their dominant tribe, thus: African Bavenda Ch, Lutheran Bapedi Ch of South Africa (1890), South African BaRolong Ch, Zion Apostolic Swazi Ch of South Africa (1918), Zulu Congregational Baptist Ch (2,000 members).

OTHER PROTESTANT DENOMINATIONS. These smaller bodies include: African Evangelistic Mission (1910; in mine compounds), Associated Gospel Chs, Brethren in Christ, Christian Catholic Ch (1903), Ch of God of Prophecy (1967; 89 churches by 1975), Cooneyites (Go-Preachers), Ev Bible Ch (Canada, 1955), Exclusive Brethren (Raven-Taylor group), Free Baptist Ch, Igreja de Deus (Portuguese Pentecostals), Igreja Evangélica Portuguesa (serving Protestants among the 600,000 Portuguese in South Africa), Independent Assemblies of God, Metropolitan Church Association (1930), New Protestant Ch (c1958 ex DRC; Afrikaners), Pentecostal Protestant Ch (Pinkster Protestantse Kerk; c1963 ex AFMSA protesting political involvement), Protestant United Ch, Reconstituted DRC (Hervormde Nederduitse Gereformeerde Kerk, 1940; Afrikaners), Salem Mission, Swedish Free Mission, World Missions (1959). There are also a large number of Protestant groups begun by Whites among the Bantu.

UNITING CHURCHES. In 1979, 3 separate sets of negotiations for organic union were under way, as follows: (1) Church Unity Commission (CUC), provisionally towards the United Church in Southern Africa: Bantu Presbyterian Ch (withdrew in 1976), Ch of the Province of SA, Methodist Ch of SA, Presbyterian Ch of SA (withdrew in 1976), Tsonga Presbyterian Ch, United Congregational Ch of SA. (2) United Presbyterian Ch of Southern Africa: Bantu Presbyterian Ch, Presbyterian Ch of SA, Tsonga Presbyterian Ch. (3) United Lutheran Ch in South Africa: German Ev Lutheran Churches of Cape, Transvaal, SW Africa; other Lutheran churches. In 1976, the 3 indigenous church federations AICA, AICM and RICA agreed to federate as a first step towards total unity.

PEOPLES (ethnolinguistic). Christians: 65.8% Bantu (18.7% Xhosa, 18.5% Zulu, 9.3% Tswana, 7.7% Sotho (0.5% alien from Lesotho), 4.5% Pedi, 2.2% Swazi, 1.8% Shangaan (Tsonga), 0.6% Venda, 3.5% other Bantu (Malawian, Mozambican, et alii)), 22.1% White (11.7% Afrikaner, 7.0% British, 2.4% Portuguese, 0.8% German, French, 0.1% Greek and other European), 11.2% Coloured, 0.4% Asian (Indian), Hottentot, Chinese (2,400), Gypsy.

COUNTRY-WIDE TOTALS

EVANGELIZATION (see Part 5). 1900: 52%. 1970: 100%. 1980: 100%. *Mass evangelism.* Among many recent campaigns by African Enterprise and others: 1973, Billy Graham interracial meetings in Durban and Johannesburg (60,000 attenders, 6,000 enquirers); 1973, South African Congress on Evangelism (Durban); 1978, Here's Life Benoni (CCCI); July 1979, South African Christian Leadership Assembly (SACLA). *Radiophonic evangelism.* Annual listeners' letters (1975): 900 TWR, 90 RVOG, 36 HCJB, Radio Vatican, FEBC. Bible correspondence courses: numerous, including ICI (8,639 enrolments, 1,776 active).

FOREIGN MISSIONARIES AND PERSONNEL (nationals serving abroad) (1973). Total 1,180: 730 Protestants in 30 countries (90% White, 10% Black; 282 DRC, 78 SDA, 75 Meth Ch of SA) (increase from 560 in 1963), about 180 African indigenous serving in 8 neighbouring countries, about 110 Anglicans (65% White, 35% Black) in 17 countries (including UK, USA, Canada, Australia, NZ, South America), about 100 Roman Catholics serving in 8 countries, about 30 marginal Protestants (Jehovah's Witnesses), about 10 Catholics (non-Roman).

FOREIGN MISSIONARIES AND PERSONNEL (aliens from abroad) (1973). Total 6,507. *From Western world.* 6,279: about 4,400 Roman Catholics (Whites born outside South Africa, including 1,089 from Ireland), 1,385 Protestants (547 in 44 USA societies, 380 in 8 WGermany societies, 178 in 18 UK societies, 161 in 5 Sweden societies, 33 in 2 Switzerland societies, 31 in 4 Canada societies, 27 in 4 Australia societies, 16 in 2 Norway societies, 4 in 2 Netherlands societies, 4 in 1 Denmark society, 3 in 2 Finland societies, 1 in 1 New Zealand society), 227 Anglicans (224 in 13 UK societies, 2 in 1 USA society, 1 in 1 New Zealand society), about 220 marginal Protestants (200 Mormons, 20 Jehovah's Witnesses) from USA, about 40 Catholics (non-Roman) mainly from Germany, 5 Black indigenous from USA, about 2 Orthodox from Greece. *From Communist world.* 25 Roman Catholics (20 from Poland, others from Yugoslavia). *From Third World.* 203 (about 100 Roman Catholics, 58 African indigenous, 40 Protestants, 5 Anglicans) from neighbouring countries and also Malawi, India et alia.

INSTITUTIONS (church-operated) (1973). Total 850, including 5 ecumenical centres, over 300 higher schools (10 minor seminaries), 380 medical centres (90 hospitals), 10 presses, 25 religious communities, 9 research centres, about 70 seminaries (54 Protestant, 6 African indigenous, 4 Anglican, 3 RC), 15 study centres.

PERIODICALS. About 240 titles (150 Protestant (21 SDA, 15 Pentecostal), 12 Anglican, numerous Bantu indigenous).

PERSONNEL. About 29,142 (22,635 national, 6,507 foreign.)

RELIGIOUS LIBRARIES. About 150.

SCRIPTURE DISTRIBUTION (1975). Annual totals: 738,400 Bibles (95% subsidized, 5% commercial), 582,800 NTs (18% free, 74% subsidized, 8% commercial), 610,000 UBS portions, 180,000 UBS selections. *Translations completed.* Portion: 6 languages since 1830. NT: 7 languages since 1840. Bible: 6 languages since 1857.

SERVICE AGENCIES. About 160, including AE, AICA, AICM, ASATI, CARA, CARE, CATF, CCCI, CWL, DM, ECM, IDAMASA, IHCF, LEMIK, LIFE, MAF, MEMA, MTS, NCFS, OM, PTL, RICA, SACBC, SACC, SACP, SGM, SPCK, SU, TWR, UCM,WVI, YCS, YCW, YMCA, YWCA.

ADDITIONAL DATA ON CHURCHES

CATHOLIC CHURCH IN SOUTH AFRICA. In Afrikaans, Roomse Katolieke Kerk. *New diocese.* In 1978 PA Western Transvaal became D Klerksdorp, suffragan to M Pretoria. *Catholics.* Including 2,125 Chinese in 1975. *Councils.* 8 dioceses are individually members of local ecumenical Christian councils. *Catechemens.* Totals: (1959) 40,027; (1961) 42,636; (1963) 54,438; (1970) 64,474, divided as follows among the 26 dioceses in 1971 in the order shown (and included in column 7 above): 1550, 4652, 229, 1743, 2875; 421, 1485, 681, 321, 1711, 1610; 2820, 4292, 1608, 4134, 4515, 559; 4803, 3792, 5500, 6200, 1496; 1377, 1607, 1353, 4747. *Annual baptisms.* (1972) 74.7% infant, 25.3% adult. *Bishops.* In early 1975 a third Black bishop was appointed (of Eshowe). *Priests.* The codes and totals shown in the Catholic sub-table above are: 126n (nationals, here excluding Whites) = 98 Africans, 28 Coloureds and Indians; 1093x (expatriates, here including White citizens) = 187 Whites born in South Africa, 906 Whites born outside South Africa. *Sisters.* 71% European (82% being in provinces of Cape Town and Durban), 25% African (over 70% being in ecclesiastical province of Durban), 4% Coloured (70% being in ecclesiastical province of Cape Town). *Catholic charismatics* (January 1975). About 340 involved adults (90% lay, 10% religious) in 7 organized prayer groups in the Catholic Charismatic Renewal. *Major seminaries.* Total 3: Hammanskraal (Black), Pretoria (White), Athlone (Coloured). *Seminarians* (1972). 66 secular, 55 religious. *Catechists.* Total (1970) 2,935. *Catechist training schools.* Total 6. *Indigenous (Black) religious congregations.* Brothers: Franciscan Familiar of St Joseph (FFJ, begun 1923, Mariannhill). Sisters: 300 Daughters of St Francis of Assisi (begun 1922), 79 Benedictine Sisters of Zululand (begun 1933), 38 Handmaids of Christ the King (begun 1932), 24 Daughters of the Immaculate Heart of Mary (begun 1949), 19 Companions of St Angela (begun 1955), Missionary Sisters of the Sacred Heart, Sisters of St Brigid, Congregation of Our Lady Mother of Divine Love, Dominican Sisters of Montebello, Servite Sisters of Zululand, Sisters of Ladysmith (Natal). *White religious congregations.* Priests: CMM (Missionaries of Mariannhill, begun 1920); the other 31 male congregations originated in Europe. Brothers: FSC, SC. Sisters: total 63 congregations.

*Catholic organizations.* The Southern African Catholic Bishops' Conference, SACBC (Beraadsliggaam van die Suid-Afrikaanse Katolieke Biskoppe) is a member of SECAM. It covers the dioceses of the republic of South Africa and also Botswana, Namibia, and Swaziland. Since February 1972, Lesotho has been independent of the SACBC and has had its own bishops' conference. Two bodies serve religious personnel: the Conference of Clerical Religious Superiors in Southern Africa; and the Association of Women Religious. For the armed forces, South Africa forms a military vicariate. The Southern African Council of Priests (SACP), which received episcopal sanction in 1971, is an advisory body and includes representatives of all dioceses in Botwana, Namibia, South Africa and Swaziland (but not Lesotho). Membership is on the basis of 2 priests per 50 in each ecclesiastical jurisdiction with a minimum of 2 priests, even if there are less than 50 in a diocese. In 1969, the archdiocese of

Durban held a diocesan synod.

There are 2 lay co-ordinating bodies. The constitution for the Southern African Council of Catholic Laity, provisionally set up in September 1970, was approved by the bishops in February 1972. The second body, the Commission for the Lay Apostolate, co-ordinates the activities of a number of lay associations, the most important being YCW (fully multiracial), Christian Life Group (apostolic and social work), Legion of Mary, Knights of da Gama (men's fraternal), Catholic Women's League (mainly White), Women of St Anne (mainly African), St Vincent de Paul, Men of the Sacred Heart (mainly African), Kobe Association (intellectual circles), Boy Scouts, YCS, Chiro, National Catholic Federation of Students, and The Grail.

The Holy See has no diplomatic relations with the republic of South Africa. It is represented to the Catholic hierarchy by the apostolic delegate to South Africa and Namibia, who also serves as pro-nuncio to Botswana, Lesotho and Swaziland, with residence in Pretoria.

Other organizations include Catholic Action for Racial Education (CARE), which is an active unofficial group working for improved racial relations, and the Missiological Research and Training Institute, founded in 1966 at Lumku, Queenstown, which provides courses in languages, anthropology, music, customs, law and catechetics.

The church has since its beginning been heavily involved in education and social service. In 1970 there were 592 schools for Africans (99,424 pupils), 115 schools for Coloureds (32,994), 168 schools for Whites (43,575) and 9 schools for Asians, in addition to 577 Asian and Coloured pupils in the diocese of Johannesburg and not counted above. In 1973 the total of all Catholic schools was 577 primary (125,007 pupils) and 170 secondary (22,419). Medical and welfare institutions in 1970 were 48 hospitals, 129 dispensaries, 40 orphanages (15 for Coloureds, 13 for Africans and 12 for Europeans) and 76 other institutions for the deaf, aged, juvenile delinquents and handicapped persons. The Catholic Church co-operates with the Inter-Church Aid Division of the South African Council of Churches and has on several occasions played a leading role in combating problems created by the government's homelands resettlement schemes for Africans.

CHURCH OF THE PROVINCE OF SOUTHERN AFRICA. *Membership.* 55.9% Bantu, 23.9% White (23.6% British, 0.3% Afrikaner), 19.9% Coloured, 0.4% Asian. *Order.* The Order of Ethiopia began in 1900 when the indigenous Ethiopian Church joined the Anglican Church. In 1908 the Order had 3,500 members and in 1975 about 50,000 members across the Republic, most being Xhosa, and most living in the diocese of Grahamstown. *Missions.* In addition to British and USA missionaries, in D St John's the Old Catholic Church in the Netherlands supports St Paul's Mission, Transkei. *Charismatics.* A charismatic (pentecostal) renewal began in 1970, which by 1975 was strongest in the dioceses of Zululand (including among Black priests), Grahamstown (mainly since 1973) and Cape Town, involving around 10% of all clergy, 3 of the younger bishops (Cape Town, Port Elizabeth, Pretoria) and some 15,000 adults of all races (though in majority Whites). *Lay workers* (1977). 50 men, 150 women. *Licensed lay ministers* (1977). 4,000 men, 700 women. *Seminarians* (1977). 95.

DUTCH REFORMED CHURCH IN SOUTH AFRICA. The NHK began in 1804 as a body distinct from its parent body, the Netherlands Reformed Church but under the Classis of Amsterdam. After 1836, 3 independent republics in South Africa had it as the established state church. In 1853 it broke relations with the NGK and has since been a separate denomination.

EVANGELICAL LUTHERAN CHURCH IN SOUTHERN AFRICA. In Afrikaans = Evangeliese Lutherse Kerk in Suidelike Afrika. Organized as an autonomous church in 1975. *New diocese.* Central Diocese (45,000 members in 1977) created out of Transvaal Diocese, comprising the urban areas of Johannesburg, Pretoria, Soweto. *Growth.* Increasing by 1977 to 455,909 members.

FULL GOSPEL CHURCH OF GOD IN SOUTHERN AFRICA. *Growth.* By 1978, there were 184,824 members and adherents.

MORAVIAN CHURCH. Western Province = Evangeliese Broederkerk in die WKP. Eastern Province = I-Cawa yama-Moravi emphumalanga kumzantsi Afrika (in Xhosa).

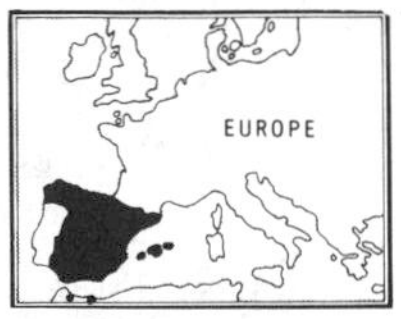


# SPAIN

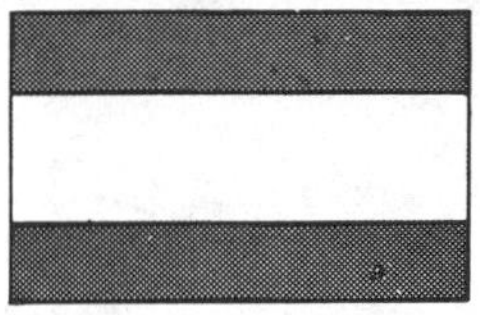

## SECULAR DATA

**STATE. Official name:** The Spanish State (El Estado Español) Adjective of nationality: Spanish, a Spaniard (español).
**Flag** (shown above right): Wide yellow stripe in centre with narrow red stripes at top and bottom, with coat of arms in centre.
**Area:** 504,782 sq.km. (194,897 sq.miles). Agricultural land: 63.5%.
**Government:** Constitutional monarchy, since 1975 (15th century monarchy and empire, 1923 dictatorship, 1931 republic, 1938 dictatorship, 1975 monarchy).
**Legislature:** Cortès, 561 members; replaced 1977 by bicameral parliament.
**Official language:** Spanish (*Español*).
**Chief cities:** capital Madrid 3,146,070 (1970), Barcelona 1,745,140, Valencia 653,690, Seville 548,070.
**Political divisions:** 50 Provinces, with 8,655 Municipalities.
**Armed forces** (1976): Total 302,300 regular (213,400 conscripts): army 220,000, navy 46,600, air force 35,700 (205 combat aircraft). Paramilitary forces: 65,000 Guardia Civil.
**Foreign forces** (1973): 9,000 USA troops.
**Dependencies** (Overseas Areas): Balearic Islands, Canary Islands, Ceuta and Melilla (Spanish North Africa).

**DEMOGRAPHY. Population:** 33,956,376 (census of 31.XII.1970. For 1970–2000 (UN), see last row of Table 1). Population density (1975): 70/sq.km. (18/sq.mile). Under 15 years: 27%. Growth rate (1975–80): 0.98% per year (births 1.93%, deaths −0.86%, emigrants −0.09%). Life expectancy (1975–80): 72.8 years. Household size: 3.6 persons.
**Major languages:** Spanish, Catalan, Galician, Basque, Romany, Portuguese, French, English, and several others.
**Urban dwellers** (1970): 60.9%. Urban growth rate (1950–70): 2.3% per year.
**Labour force:** 38%.
**Refugees** (1977): 14,390 from Cuba. Exiles abroad: 56,000 Spaniards in France.
**Tourists** (1972): 32,500,000. (1974) 30,343,000.

**ETHNOLINGUISTIC GROUPS:** 72.8% Spanish (Spaniard), 16.4% Catalan, 8.2% Galician, 2.3% Basque, 0.1% pure Gypsy, 0.1% Portuguese, 0.1% British (28,000), USA White, French, German, Jewish, Latin American White & Mestizo, Chinese (650), et alii.

**MONEY** (1977). **Monetary unit:** peseta (= 100 céntimos); US$1 = Ptas 68.00.
**National income per person:** US$1,800. Average annual family income: US$6,480.
**Inflation:** (1970–74) 10.9% per year, (1975: consumer price index 192); (1977) 30%.
**Cost of living in capital** (1976): index 116 (Washington DC=100). Daily cost of living: US$37.

**HEALTH.** Hospitals: 1,459 (151,044 beds). Doctors: 49,256. Lepers: 5,190 (0.1 per 1,000). Blind: 30,000. Psychotics: 350,000. Criminals: 31,167.

**EDUCATION.** Adult literacy: (1950) 82%, (1970) 90%. Education rate: 46%. Schools: 36,500. Universities: 19.

**LITERATURE.** Annual new book titles (1973): 23,608. Periodicals: 4,192. Scientific journals: 320. Newspapers: 115 dailies, 121 non-daily.

**COMMUNICATION** (per 1,000 people). Phones: 182. Radios: 214. TV sets: 164. Daily newspaper circulation: 98 copies.

TABLE 1. RELIGIOUS ADHERENTS IN SPAIN

| Year | 1900 | | mid-1970 | | Annual change, 1970–1980 | | | | mid-1975 | | mid-1980 | | 2000 | |
|---|---|---|---|---|---|---|---|---|---|---|---|---|---|---|
| *Name* | *Adherents* | *%* | *Adherents* | *%* | *Natural* | *Conversion* | *Total* | *Rate* | *Adherents* | *%* | *Adherents* | *%* | *Adherents* | *%* |
| **Christians** | **18,797,000** | **100.0** | **32,851,600** | **97.7** | **332,498** | **–24,388** | **308,110** | **0.90** | **34,360,700** | **97.4** | **35,932,700** | **97.0** | **42,155,000** | **94.4** |
| professing | 18,797,000 | 100.0 | 32,851,600 | 97.7 | 332,498 | –24,388 | 308,110 | 0.90 | 34,360,700 | 97.4 | 35,932,700 | 97.0 | 42,155,000 | 94.4 |
| Roman Catholics | 18,797,000 | 100.0 | 32,818,600 | 97.6 | 332,163 | –24,433 | 307,730 | 0.90 | 34,326,050 | 97.3 | 35,895,900 | 96.9 | 42,105,300 | 94.3 |
| Evangelical Catholics | 8,000 | 0.0 | 128,105 | 0.4 | 1,454 | 3,516 | 4,970 | 3.31 | 150,220 | 0.4 | 177,810 | 0.5 | 329,800 | 0.7 |
| Protestants | 0 | 0.0 | 30,000 | 0.1 | 305 | 45 | 350 | 1.11 | 31,500 | 0.1 | 33,500 | 0.1 | 45,000 | 0.1 |
| Orthodox | 0 | 0.0 | 2,000 | 0.0 | 20 | 0 | 20 | 0.95 | 2,100 | 0.0 | 2,200 | 0.0 | 2,700 | 0.0 |
| Anglicans | 0 | 0.0 | 1,000 | 0.0 | 10 | 0 | 10 | 0.95 | 1,050 | 0.0 | 1,100 | 0.0 | 2,000 | 0.0 |
| affiliated | 18,797,000 | 100.0 | 32,851,600 | 97.7 | 332,498 | –24,388 | 308.110 | 0.90 | 34,360,700 | 97.4 | 35,932,700 | 97.0 | 42,155,000 | 9.44 |
| disaffiliated | –2,000 | 0.0 | –595,567 | –1.8 | –6,428 | –12,996 | –19,424 | 2.92 | –664,270 | –19.0 | –789,810 | –2.1 | –1,099,100 | –2.5 |
| doubly-affiliated | –8,300 | 0.0 | –130,000 | –0.4 | –1,355 | –645 | –2,000 | 1.43 | –140,000 | –0.4 | –150,000 | –0.4 | –200,000 | –0.4 |
| total practising | 18,421,060 | *98* | 31,866,050 | *97* | 322,523 | –23,656 | 298,867 | 0.90 | 33,329,880 | *97* | 34,854,720 | *97* | 35,831,800 | *85* |
| non-practising | 375,940 | *2* | 985,550 | *3* | 9,975 | –732 | 9,243 | 0.90 | 1,030,820 | *3* | 1,077,980 | *3* | 6,323,200 | *15* |
| Roman Catholics | 18,799,000 | 100.0 | 33,414,062 | 99.4 | 338,472 | –14,308 | 324,164 | 0.93 | 34,978,000 | 99.2 | 36,655,700 | 99.0 | 43,071,800 | 96.5 |
| Catholic pentecostals | 0 | 0.0 | 1,000 | 0.0 | 48 | 852 | 900 | 18.00 | 5,000 | 0.0 | 10,000 | 0.0 | 100,000 | 0.2 |
| Protestants | 7,000 | 0.0 | 105,090 | 0.3 | 1,210 | 3,281 | 4,491 | 3.59 | 125,000 | 0.4 | 150,000 | 0.0 | 267,800 | 0.6 |
| Evangelicals | 6,500 | 0.0 | 93,000 | 0.3 | 1,094 | 3,306 | 4,400 | 3.89 | 113,000 | 0.3 | 137,000 | 0.4 | 250,000 | 0.6 |
| Neo-pentecostals | 0 | 0.0 | 1,500 | 0.0 | 39 | 611 | 650 | 16.25 | 4,000 | 0.0 | 8,000 | 0.0 | 20,000 | 0.0 |
| Marginal Protestants | 0 | 0.0 | 40,915 | 0.1 | 426 | 282 | 708 | 1.61 | 44,000 | 0.1 | 48,000 | 10.1 | 90,000 | 0.2 |
| Anglicans | 1,000 | 0.0 | 12,000 | 0.0 | 122 | –2 | 120 | 0.95 | 12,600 | 0.0 | 13,200 | 0.0 | 16,000 | 0.0 |
| Catholics (non-Roman) | 300 | 0.0 | 2,000 | 0.0 | 20 | 0 | 20 | 0.95 | 2,100 | 0.0 | 2,200 | 0.0 | 2,800 | 0.0 |
| Orthodox | 0 | 0.0 | 2,000 | 0.0 | 20 | 0 | 20 | 0.95 | 2,100 | 0.0 | 2,200 | 0.0 | 2,700 | 0.0 |
| Latin American indigenous | 0 | 0.0 | 1,100 | 0.0 | 11 | 0 | 11 | 0.94 | 1,170 | 0.0 | 1,210 | 0.0 | 3,000 | 0.0 |
| Non-religious | 2,000 | 0.0 | 605,000 | 1.8 | 6,822 | 14,178 | 21,000 | 2.98 | 705,000 | 2.0 | 815,000 | 2.2 | 1,785,000 | 4.0 |
| Atheists | 0 | 0.0 | 140,000 | 0.4 | 1,703 | 10,197 | 11,900 | 6.76 | 176,000 | 0.5 | 259,000 | 0.7 | 670,000 | 1.5 |
| Jews | 0 | 0.0 | 8,500 | 0.0 | 86 | –6 | 80 | 0.90 | 8,900 | 0.0 | 9,300 | 0.0 | 11,000 | 0.0 |
| Muslims | 1,000 | 0.0 | 5,000 | 0.0 | 50 | 0 | 50 | 0.96 | 5,200 | 0.0 | 5,500 | 0.0 | 7,000 | 0.0 |
| Ahmadis | 0 | 0.0 | 600 | 0.0 | 7 | 13 | 20 | 2.86 | 700 | 0.0 | 800 | 0.0 | 1,500 | 0.0 |
| Baha'is | 0 | 0.0 | 3,900 | 0.0 | 41 | 19 | 60 | 1.43 | 4,200 | 0.0 | 4,500 | 0.0 | 6,000 | 0.0 |
| **Country's population** | **18,800,000** | **100.0** | **33,614,000** | **100.0** | **341,200** | **0** | **341,200** | **0.97** | **35,260,000** | **100.0** | **37,026,000** | **100.0** | **44,634,000** | **100.0** |

COLUMNS, ROWS. For meanings and definitions, see Codebook (Part 6). Note that, by definition, total 'Christians' = professing + crypto-Christians, which also = affiliated + nominal Christians. Percentages may not always total exactly, due to rounding.

POLLS. January 1965 (IOP): 'What is your religion?': 98% Roman Catholics, 2% non-religious and atheists. February 1970: 98% Roman Catholics, 2% non-religious and atheists. 1975 (Asociación Evangélica Española): of young people, 82% said people need a religious faith, 16% denied this.

### NOTES ON RELIGIONS

AFFILIATED. By adding up diocesan totals in *Annuario Pontificio* (as is done in Table 2 below), it may be seen that (as is shown in the table above) the Roman Catholic Church in the 1960s and 1970s claimed 99.4% of the total population as affiliated members on the grounds that that number were, or had once been, baptized Catholics and were still on the church's rolls. However, as elaborated below, in 1975 about 140,000 were also Evangelicals or other Christians and so were doubly-affiliated, and over 660,000 regarded themselves as having disaffiliated completely from Christianity and were now non-religious (agnostics) or atheists. Subtracting these 2 groups from the aggregate totals claimed by the churches produces the figures on the line 'affiliated', i.e. 34.36 million distinct individuals in 1975.

AFFILIATED PROTESTANTS. Including over 20,000 expatriates (USA civilian and military, British, et alia).

AHMADIS. Begun 1946; Qadianis, based on Rabwah (Pakistan).

ATHEISTS. Partido Comunista de España (PCE) (illegal until 1977; independent in Sino-Soviet dispute): membership (1970) 5,000, (1974) 20,000, (1975) 70,000 militants. Communist voters in trade union elections: 250,000, in underground "workers' commissions" (illegal trade unions). In 1976 the Communist vote was estimated to be 12% of the electorate; in the election of 15.VI.1977, the PCE won only 9% of the total vote and 5.4% of seats in parliament.

BAHA'IS. Local spiritual assemblies: 1964, 14; 1973, 26 (5 in Canary Islands).

CATHOLIC PENTECOSTALS (or, Catholic charismatics). Totals (1975): 3,000 involved adults (over 15 years old) in 50 organized prayer groups; total charismatic community including children, 5,000. The First National Conference for the Charismatic Renewal in Spain was held in Madrid in July 1977, with 1,700 attenders (including 70 priests).

COUNTRY'S POPULATION. This table for Spain excludes the population of Spanish North Africa, treated here as a separate territory, with 165,000 in 1970.

DISAFFILIATED. This term is used here to describe dechristianized persons who, although baptized Roman Catholics and therefore regarded by the Catholic Church as still affiliated to it (and hence enumerated in Table 2 as such), have recently disaffiliated themselves completely from Christianity and now profess (for example in polls) to be either non-religious (agnostics) or atheists. Because their statistics represent a duplication, they are shown in the table above as a negative quantity (with a minus sign). Although in polls non-religious persons and atheists, number over 4% in urban areas, many Catholic dioceses continue to claim virtually the entire population; the archdiocese of Madrid, for instance, reported in *AP 1974* a total population of 4,052,324 within its borders, out of whom 4,023,000 were baptized Catholics (99.3%). The table above incorporates all of these data and interpretations.

DOUBLY-AFFILIATED. The great majority of non-Catholic Christians are also baptized Roman Catholics or are counted as affiliated by the Catholic dioceses they live in. Our term covers persons affiliated to, or claimed by, both the Catholic Church and also an Evangelical, Protestant, Anglican, indigenous, Catholic (non-Roman) or Orthodox church. Because their statistics represent a duplication, they are shown in the table as a negative quantity (with a minus sign). It is in fact not uncommon for people to attend a Protestant church for some time before becoming a member, if ever.

EVANGELICAL CATHOLICS. Although religious liberty was proclaimed in 1967, virtually all non-Catholic Christians are still regarded by the state as Roman Catholics. Our term describes persons who are affiliated to churches termed by the state Evangélica (Protestant, Anglican, Latin American indigenous, or marginal Protestant churches), but who in polls are regarded by state and society as, or who profess to be, Roman Catholics.

JEWS. Sefardic; in 7 communities. There were no Jews in Spain from their expulsion in 1492 until the 1920s in Barcelona and

refugees during World War II. There are also 200,000 Marranos (Crypto-Jews, Anusim, Conversos, New Christians) whose ancestors adopted Catholicism under duress in and after 1492 and who secretly keep up the Passover and Jewish practices; in the table above, they are enumerated as Roman Catholics.
LATIN AMERICAN INDIGENOUS. In about 8 denominations from 5 countries in 1970 (see Table 2).
MUSLIMS. Mostly in Madrid, in 2 associations including Ahmadiya (enumerated here under Muslims although declared non-Muslim by Pakistan). *Hajj pilgrims to Mecca.* (1970) 32; (1974) 196; (1975) 1; (1976) 4.
NEO-PENTECOSTALS. Charismatics in the non-Pentecostal

Protestant denominations, who are involved in scores of ecumenical pentecostal prayer meetings especially in Madrid and Barcelona.
PRACTISING CHRISTIANS. January 1965 (IFOP): 'How regularly do you practise your religion?': 25% very regularly, 57% with certain regularity, 15% with little regularity, 3% do not practise. June 1966 (Steinmetz Institute; urban females): 'When did you last go to church?': 78% within past 7 days, 6% within past 14 days, 13% over 2 weeks ago, 3% seldom or never. 1975 (Asociación Evangélica Española), church attendance: more than once a week 14% of under 30s, 19% of over 30s; once a week (same 2 age groups) 36% and 38%; once a month

9% and 7%; less than once a month 41% and 36%. 1976: 23.3% practise frequently, 45.1% sometimes, 21.2% rarely, 10.4% never. 1977: 48% of all adult Spaniards consider themselves regularly practising Catholics. *Pilgrims.* Basilica of Montserrat Abbey, Catalonia: 1.3 million a year (1973), 15,000 daily in summer.
PROTESTANTS. Protestant work began in 1835; by 1874, there were 1,840 Protestants (Evangelicals) and 360 churches.
ROMAN CATHOLICS. Including 200,000 Marranos (Crypto-Jews, Anusim, Conversos, New Christians) who are baptized and outwardly-practising Catholics, but who also follow Jewish rites.

## NON-CHRISTIAN RELIGIONS.

**Judaism** is adhered to by only a few thousand Jews in the country. The first synagogue constructed in Spain since the 15th century was inaugurated in Madrid in December 1968. On that occasion, the minister of Justice published a decree officially revoking the edict of 1492 with which queen Isabella had banned all Jews. By June 1973, 7 Jewish communities had been registered with the Ministry of Justice, located in Madrid, Malaga, Barcelona, Alicante, Valencia, Tenerife (Canary Islands), Palma de Majorque (Baleares); and 2 others in Ceuta and Melilla, in Spanish North Africa. There are still also some 200,000 Marranos or Crypto-Jews, baptized Catholics whose ancestors were forcibly converted to Catholicism and who still observe the Passover and other Jewish rites.

**Islam,** once the ruling power in the middle ages, is today reduced to a small number of Muslims living for the most part in Madrid and other university cities. By June 1973, 4 associations had been officially registered. Two of these were in Spain proper: the Ahmadiya Mission of Islam in Spain (Misión Ahmadia del Islam en España) and the Muslim Association in Spain (Asociación Musulmana en España), both in Madrid; 2 more are in Spanish North Africa. There is also an Islamic centre at Granada, and the Egyptian government has established in Madrid an Egyptian Institute of Islamic Studies (Instituto Egipcio de Estudios Islámicos).

**Baha'i** adherents were estimated in 1961 to number not more than 195, but by 1973 they had grown to 4,000 in 26 local spiritual assemblies.

## CHRISTIANITY.

During the first century the Apostle Paul is believed to have brought Spain the Christian message. Christianity was already well-established when the invading Arian Visigoths overran the Iberian peninsula in 409. The Arians were then converted to Catholicism which was declared the state religion at Toledo in 589.

In the 8th century Spain came under the control of Muslim Berbers from north Africa, and Spanish Islam achieved its highest development in the 10th century. The gradual reconquest by Christians took on the dimensions of a crusade. In 1085 the king of Castille and Leon took the title of Ruler of All Hispania, but the last Muslim stronghold in Spain, Granada, did not fall until 1492. The allocation of large areas of land to military orders and noble families during this period resulted in the feudalistic latifundia socio-economic pattern that characterized parts of Spain during subsequent centuries. Great missionary orders began to emerge in the 12th century, and a century later religious military orders came into being as well as numerous universities. By the 16th century Spain had entered its golden age. Leading in the discovery of new lands across the world, Spain acquired a vast overseas empire and great wealth and developed the strongest army in Europe. The colonies became the arena of a new foreign missionary thrust, while the Catholic Church at home was busy with the Counter Reformation and Inquisition. The latter was intended at first to force Spanish Jews and Moors to decide either to become Christians or to leave Spain, and it effectively prevented the growth of

religious or political movements outside the established church.

As Spain's power began to decline, the crown increasingly intervened in the affairs of the church. A concordat officially recognizing the system of royal patronage was concluded in 1753, and Jesuits were expelled from Spain and all Spanish territories in 1767. Most of the Spanish empire was lost during the next century.

During the 19th century, Catholic clergy came increasingly under attack from proponents of greater freedom of thought and action. In 1868 religious tolerance for non-Catholics was granted for the first time. Spanish Christians exiled to Gibraltar then returned to openly assist clandestine Protestant groups, and Protestantism began to develop gradually.

**CATHOLIC CHURCH.** During the past 20 years, the church has experienced a significant change, from being a conventional to an optional Catholicism. The first type, also called national Catholicism, goes back to the 6th century. After a short period under the anti-clerical republic from 1931 to 1939 including the civil war of 1936–39, the Franco government renewed the tradition of national Catholicism, mingled with a new religious ideology and national mystique.

The second type of Catholicism, optional, can be traced to the 1950s when the first Catholic workers' dispute took place denouncing existing working conditions as anti-Christian. About 1956 the church began to appear as 2 distinct overlapping churches, one being traditional and politically conservative, the other progressive and opposed to the national-Catholic image. The so-called second church was given a new impetus by Vatican II and has also been benefitted by the recent episcopal appointments of the Holy See. This new type of Catholicism, based more on personal faith than on the traditional cultural context of the Spanish people, began to prevail decisively in March 1972 when the conciliar bishops became a majority in the Spanish Episcopal Conference for the first time. From this constantly changing situation have emerged several new initiatives involving both clergy and laity, 3 of which will be mentioned here.

The first innovative movement consists of local communities centred on the liturgy. Their strength is in urban areas; in 1972 there were about 70 of these in Barcelona alone. They engage in periodical eucharistic celebrations, usually presided over by a priest, during which they jointly agree to undertake some socio-political prophetic task. The hierarchy's permission is never asked. As a general rule, the bishops do not intervene, although the meetings

appear to reject the institutional church. Some bishops even give private encouragement.

Secondly, there are the New Communities. These are groups more or less structured and existing along the lines of the parish concept and rarely in conflict with it, but seeking to reshape the old anachronistic parish system. At Cordoba, the bishop decided not to create new parishes in the new suburban areas, but instead left the task to priests and laity.

A third important initiative has come with the establishment of the synod of the diocese of Seville. The first session began in 1970 and brought together 900 persons, 50% being lay and 50% priests and religious. An important group of young priests insisted then that the work be carried out on a strictly objective basis. The synod continued through 1971, building on the results of an extensive survey, as well as on conclusions reached by the Bishops-Priests Joint Assembly. In 1972, 3,000 persons of all social strata participated in the synod in small discussion groups, and their concrete proposals were combined in a document to be submitted to the vote in the next plenary assembly.

In the sociographic domain, nothing has been done on a national level concerning a survey of the practice of religion. A study published in 1971 by the National Secretariat for the Clergy revealed a great difference between the dioceses of the north and of the south in the distribution of clergy. Thus more than three-fourths of the dioceses in the northern half of the country are well served with one priest for less than 1,000 persons, while in the south no diocese has less than 1,000 and in more than 60% one priest serves more than 2,000. Moreover, the crisis in vocations has become more serious in recent years. While there were 5,211 major seminarians in 1970, in 1973 this had fallen to 3,014. The annual number of ordinations averaged 1,000 between 1952 and 1962, but in 1972 this was down to 395. Nevertheless, of all the countries of the world Spain continues to have the largest number of contemplative sisters (19,221 in 1968) and cloistered convents (929 in 1973).

**PROTESTANT CHURCHES.** As with Islam and Judaism, following the institution of the Inquisition in 1492 Protestantism was outlawed in Spain. This remained true until 1868, when for the first time an article proclaiming religious tolerance was written into the constitution. This in turn became obsolete a century later in 1967, with the passage of the Law concerning Religious Liberty.

Attempts at Protestant activity prior to 1868 were met with severe penalties. Plymouth Brethren from England began holding house meetings in 1836, and

**Iglesia Católica en España.** Palma Cathedral and Almudaina palace, in Diocese of Mallorca (Majorca)

in 1845 the Spaniard Francisco de Paula Ruet, influenced by Waldensians in Italy, began preaching in Barcelona but was exiled to Gibraltar. Others were converted in Gibraltar, and some were sent to England for theological study. From Gibraltar a clandestine evangelistic outreach was begun in Spain, the first sizeable organized Protestant groups being formed in Granada and Malaga in 1863. Out of this early work and following the proclamation of religious toleration in 1868, grew the Spanish Evangelical Church, now the fourth largest Protestant church in the country. In 1880 a division took place in which the Spanish Reformed Episcopal Church was established, with special links to the Anglican Church of Ireland.

The 2 principal Protestant denominations, the Brethren and Baptist Union, also owe their origin to this period. The former is the result of the missionary activity of British Plymouth Brethren. The latter joins together work initiated by American Baptists in 1869, followed by Swedish Baptists in 1881 and Southern Baptists in 1921. In addition there are several smaller independent Baptist churches. Seventh-day Adventists appeared in 1903 and in 1928 Swedish missionaries founded the Pentecostal Church of Spain. Other Pentecostal groups followed, including the Assemblies of God in 1930 and the Church of God (Cleveland) in 1937. Since World War II a large number of small missions have flooded into the country, mostly from the USA. After 1970, Pentecostalism began to spread rapidly.

Protestants today are dispersed widely throughout the country, with their most important centres in the border areas as opposed to the interior, with the exception of urban concentrations in Barcelona and Madrid. Recruitment of members is carried on for the most part among urban marginal social strata, especially workers, small employers and newcomers from the rural areas and villages. Conversion to Protestantism in Spain can be partly explained by marginality and anomie, which also explains the pietistic and conservative spirituality of Spanish Protestants. Exceptions, however, may be found among Protestants of the second or third generation, belonging to the middle class and having experienced a certain amount of social mobility. Traditionally, Spanish Protestantism has been a social movement centred on opposition to traditional Catholicism. As a result, the renewal of Catholicism, as seen in Vatican II as well as in recent ecumenical tendencies, in addition to the passage of the Law concerning Religious Liberty in 1967, have plunged Protestantism into a profound identity crisis. The institutional consequences of this have expressed themselves in the stagnation of older denominations and even a decline in membership. This can also be observed in the increase of recently-arrived marginal groups, including Jehovah's Witnesses.

MARGINAL CHURCHES. Jehovah's Witnesses are the largest non-Catholic denomination in Spain. Their growth to 40,000 today is all the more startling in light of the fact that they were an illegal body prior to 1967.

OTHER CHURCHES. There are about 2,000 Greek Orthodox in Spain, of whom 600 are in Madrid. The church is under the Ecumenical Patriarchate of Constantinople. In June 1973 the first Greek Orthodox church building was consecrated in Madrid. The Anglican community, of 12,000 including British residents and chaplaincies, is attached to the diocese of Gibraltar.

CHURCH AND STATE. The relationship between church and state, especially that between the Catholic Church and the Spanish government, can best be seen by an examination of 3 fundamental legislative texts (Concordat of 1953, Organic Law of 1967, and Law concerning Religious Liberty of 1967), together with a discussion of the compromises and conflicts between the 2 powers in general and more particularly the disputes concerning the revision of the concordat.

The concordat of 1953 was completed under the pontificate of Pius XII after more than 4 years of negotiations. This replaced the concordat of 1851 which had been abrogated by the republic in 1931. Drawn up to regulate reciprocal relations 'conforming to the Law of God and to the Catholic tradition of the Spanish nation' (Introduction), the new concordat began with the following affirmation: 'The Catholic, Apostolic and Roman religion, being the only religion of the Spanish nation, enjoys rights and prerogatives which are its due conforming to Divine and Canon Law' (Article I).

Advantages to the state include the right to intervene in the alteration of ecclesiastical jurisdictions

**Iglesia Católica on España.** *Above.* Over one million Catholics including former head of state General Franco at open-air solemn pontifical mass celebrated by papal legate Cardinal Tedeschini in Plaza de Pío XII, Barce-

(Article IX); and the head of state's right to intervene in the naming of residential or coadjutor archbishops and bishops (Article VII, referring back to the Accord signed on 7 June 1941 between the Holy See and the Spanish government). At the time of the preliminary negotiations, the head of state, general Franco, was inclined to soften this 'privilege of presentation' of bishops. Nevertheless, at the time of signing the 2 parties accepted the stricter form agreed on in 1941. The present system is as follows. The Spanish Ministry of Foreign Affairs and the papal nuncio prepare jointly a list of 6 candidates, from among whom the pope chooses 3 listing them in order of preference. From these the head of state selects one, which is usually but not necessarily the first on the papal list; this candidate is then officially named. The Holy See retains the right to appoint, without consultation, apostolic administrators with full jurisdiction over vacant dioceses. Up to the present this right has rarely been exercised.

Advantages to the Catholic Church (36 are listed) reflect the government's recognition of its character as a 'perfect society' (Article II.1) and its juridical personality (Article IV.1). The Church receives financial advantages (Article XIX), the government giving massive annual subsidies (about US$ 110 million in 1973) which are however variable depending on general economic conditions. This aid includes the salaries of archbishops, bishops, vicars generals, cathedral and college chaplains and parish clergy, as well as subsidies for seminaries, Catholic universities, the maintenance of worship, the construction and maintenance of parish churches, and religious orders, congregations and ecclesiastical institutes dedicated to missionary activities. Article XX lists 10 types of tax exemption, and Article XV states that priests and religious personnel are exempt from military service, while Article XVI prohibits their prosecution before the courts without the agreement of their bishops. Articles XXIII and XXIV provide for government recognition of the civil nature of religious marriages as well as decisions of ecclesiastical tribunals on separation and annulment. In matters of education, the teaching of the Catholic religion is obligatory in all educational institutions including universities, except when dispensation is accorded to children of non-Catholics on the request of their father or legal guardian. The church has the right to censor all educational programmes (Article XXVI).

The church's own publications are however exempt from all interference by the state. Public services including radio and television are required

lona. *Below.* Hooded laymen carry crosses in Holy Week Silence Procession parade through streets in Seville, Archdiocese of Seville.

to reserve adequate time for the exposition and defence of 'religious truth'; and priests and religious personnel are assigned to this work in agreement with the local bishop (Article XXIX).

The Organic Law of the State (Ley Organica del Estado) of January 1967 had as its purpose the modification and completion of the collection of constitutional texts of the Spanish nation. Its dispositions regarding church-state relations are in 2 categories: those concerned with the church's involvement in the institutions of highest power (head of state, government, Cortès, National Council and Council of the Realm); and those concerned with modifications in matters relating to religious liberty. The Organic Law stipulates that the head of state must 'profess the Catholic religion' (additional disposition IV, Article 9). Concerning the Cortès, which until 1977 consisted of a single chamber composed of elected members as well as members appointed by the head of state, the law specifies that the head of state may appoint members of the ecclesiastical hierarchy (additional disposition III, Article 2). At the end of 1972 there were 3 prelates serving as members of the Cortès. Although theoretically they serve as individuals without involving the entire Catholic hierarchy in responsibility for their actions, public opinion generally takes it as evidence of direct co-operation between the Catholic Church, or at least certain sections of it, and the regime in power. The Council of the Realm, which includes representatives of such large bodies as the clergy, army and university, has played an important role in the matter of succession. The clergy are to be represented on it by 'the oldest and most elevated in the hierarchical echelon among the prelate deputies to the Cortès' (additional disposition IV, Article 4). Along with the president of the Cortès and the commander of the army, this prelate also participates in the Council of Regency which exercises the powers of the head of state during an interregnum and names his successor.

other than those which stem from fidelity to the law, from respect for the Catholic religion which is the religion of the Spanish nation, and for other religious denominations; and from morality, peace and the co-existence of the legitimate rights of others as well as the demands of public order' (Article 2). It is forbidden for anyone who has been ordained *in sacris* or has been placed under the solemn vow of chastity in the Catholic Church to contract a marriage without having received canonical dispensation (Article 6.2). Finally, 'The legal recognition in Spain of non-Catholic religious confessions may be requested on the basis of their constitutions as confessional associations'. They may thereby obtain juridical personality by registration in a register (Article 14) held by the Ministry of Justice (Article 36). Within this Ministry, there is a Commission for Religious Liberty (Commisión de Libertad Religiosa, Ministerio de Justícia) in which 194 non-Catholic religious associations were registered as of June 1973, with 4 others having been dissolved since their registration.

for the purpose of christianizing the intellectual and leadership milieux. Widespread now across the world, it is especially important in Spain where a number of its members occupy key posts in publishing, universities, business and government. In October 1969, Opus Dei members were accorded more positions in the higher echelons of the government, but many of these were lost during the cabinet reshuffle of June 1973, when Opus Dei retained only a single ministry. Opposition to Opus Dei has in fact appeared not only from the extreme right but also from the conciliar wing of the church, who suspected the organization of plotting to seize political and economic control of Spanish life after Franco.

The most important recent examples of tension between church and state are as follows. (1) A position was adopted in 1970 by the Commission of the Social Apostolate of the Episcopal Conference condemning the government's trades union draft bill. (2) A joint pastoral letter was issued by the bishops of San Sebastian and Santander in December 1970, demanding that 7 revolutionary Basque militants (at that time being judged by a military tribunal) be be brought before a civil court. (3) In June 1971 one of the principal representatives of the conciliar wing was appointed apostolic administrator and head of the archdiocese of Madrid. Taking advantage of one of the loopholes of the concordat, the Vatican justified its choice according to the conciliar decree, *Christus Dominus*, which 'for exceptionally grave reasons' authorizes the alteration of those procedures expressly provided for in a concordat for the nomination of bishops. The same person has since become cardinal-archbishop of Madrid and president of the Episcopal Conference. (4) In September 1971 the first Bishops-Priests Joint Assembly adopted resolutions requesting the separation of church and state. (5) In March 1972 a new composition for the Episcopal Conference was announced in which the Holy See, taking advantage of the concordat's silence on the matter, freely named a number of young auxiliary bishops. (6) In January 1973 the Episcopal Conference adopted a document entitled 'The Church and the Political Community'. In the part concerned with 'relations between church and state', the document details those provisions which, in the eyes of the bishops, should be removed from the concordat of 1953: the religious character of the Spanish state, the state's privilege of naming bishops, the favoured treatment accorded priests and bishops before the law and the presence of prelates in the highest institutions of the state. The bishops wanted religious freedom maintained in education and state economic aid, but they wanted this extended to other religious confessions also. In spite of a number of ambiguities, such as that concerning economic aid which the church receives from the state and which is here presented as a right rather than a privilege, this document bears witness to an important change in the thought of the Spanish Catholic Church. (7) In September 1973, the Ministry of Education and Science decided to appoint teachers of religion directly and to choose religious text books itself, conceding to the church only the right of veto. Some bishops considered this decision to be unilateral and contrary to the concordat. (8) A growing number of priests have been imprisoned on political grounds in a special prison at Zamora and increasingly more frequent and heavy fines are meted out to priests and even sisters, principally in working-class areas, Catalonia and Basque country, for their homilies and other allegedly subversive activities, such as participation in public demonstrations. The review *Vida nueva* of 8 March 1975 calculated the fines of priests for their alleged subversive homilies at more than 11 million pesetas in 3 years, divided among 108 penalized persons, several of whom had been fined 2 or 3 times. Individual fines ranged between 5,000 and 500,000 pesetas. (9) At the funeral of admiral Carrero Blanco, the prime minister assassinated in Madrid at the end of 1973, the Catholic right wing insulted the archbishop of Madrid and publicly threatened to kill him together with other so-called 'red' bishops; for its part the hierarchy throughout the country made a strong protest against the assassination. (10) The heightening of the repression in Basque country has caused numerous conflicts with the church. The bishop of Bilbao, Msgr Anoveros, and one of his close collaborators were confined under house arrest for a period during 1974, and the government attempted without success to exile the bishop from the country. He was reproached for having approved the reading in all churches of his diocese of a homily entitled 'Christianity, message of liberation for the peoples', which the government considered to be in favour of

**Iglesia Evangélica Española.** A Congregation of the Spanish Evangelical Church ready for open-air witness.

With regard to religious liberty, additional disposition I of the Organic Law modifies Article 6 of the Charter of the Spaniards (Fuero de los Españoles), the fundamental law promulgated in 1945, which is henceforth given the following wording: 'The profession and practice of the Catholic religion, which is that of the Spanish State, is officially protected. The State assumes responsibility for the protection of religious liberty which is guaranteed by an effective juridical guardianship, assuring at the same time the maintenance of morality and public order'. This modification was made following the publication of the Declaration on Religious Freedom by Vatican Council II, and its application is found in the Law regulating the Exercise of Civil Rights in Relation to Religious Liberty (Ley de Regulación del Ejercicio del Derecho Civil a la Libertad Religiosa), better known under its abridged title Law concerning Religious Liberty (Ley de Libertad Religiosa). This law was also brought into being by external pressures from the USA. It affirms that 'The Spanish State recognizes the right of religious liberty founded on the dignity of the human person' and excludes all coercion in this regard (Article 1.1). Nevertheless, 'the exercise of the right of religious liberty' is 'conceived according to Catholic doctrine' and 'must in every case be compatible with the religion of the Spanish State as it is proclaimed in its fundamental laws' (Article 1.3). Other limitations are as follows: 'The right of religious liberty shall not have limitations

Most of the registered associations are Christian, or of Christian inspiration. Among the most important denominations, only the Spanish Evangelical Church (IEE) had not yet requested registration by June 1973. The law was poorly received by both Catholics and non-Catholics. The principal objection was the gap which exists between the spirit and letter of the conciliar texts of Vatican II, which describe religious freedom as an inalienable right of individuals and groups, and the confessional nature of the affirmations of the Spanish government. In fact, the original draft of the law developed by the previous minister for Foreign Affairs, before consultation with other government officials, was much more liberal than the present version.

The recent profound changes in the Spanish church have had significant repercussions on its relationship with the state. Unconditional collaboration between the church and the Franco regime and its successor, that of king Juan Carlos, no longer exists, nor does the earlier interpretation of the civil war of 1936–39 as the fruit of a religious crusade against atheists and communists. With the aid of Vatican II, calls for a revision of the concordat have been increasingly heard since 1965. In the sphere of church-state relations, promises are frequently denounced and conflicts appear. Of special significance has been the rise of Opus Dei to a position of influence. This group, whose full name is Sacerdotal Society of the Holy Cross and Work of God, was founded in 1928

Basque separation and thus an attack on national unity. In 1975 a number of priests were among the persons arrested following the proclamation of martial law in Basque country. (11) In February 1975 an amnesty petition for political prisoners, prepared by the church's National Commission of Justice and Peace and supported by 160,000 signatures (including those of 2,000 army officers) and various religious organizations, was finally presented after hesitation to the head of state by cardinal Tarancon.

After Franco's death in November 1975, the government requested a new accord with the Holy See, and in July 1976 a revision of the concordat was signed, under which the Spanish ruler can no longer nominate or veto the nomination of Spain's bishops, and Catholic clergy are no longer immune from civil prosecution. Unrevised portions of the concordat remain in effect, with Spain therefore still officially a Catholic nation. The introduction to the 8 protocols of the new concordat taking note of a 'transformation' in Spanish society. Future revisions of the concordat are juridically within the exclusive competence of the Holy See and the Spanish government. In principle both are in agreement that any further concordat should contain no doctrinal declaration nor privileges that could be considered religiously discriminatory. Nevertheless, as the Holy See takes full control of the selection of bishops, the Spanish government will increasingly suppress all economic aid to the church. Meanwhile, a growing segment of public opinion rejects the very idea of any kind of concordat.

In 1978, Parliament and a popular referendum ratified a new constitution under which Spain no longer has an official religion (Article 16). Discrimination over burial places and restrictions on the establishment of new churches were ended, and religious freedom, freedom of marriage and freedom to change one's religious beliefs are now upheld. The Roman Catholic Church still has a leading role, however: 'The public authorities will keep in mind the religious beliefs of the Spanish society and will maintain co-operation with the Catholic Church and the other confessions'.

## INTERDENOMINATIONAL ORGANIZATIONS.

Several Protestant organizations exist to promote co-operation in the Evangelical community. The Spanish Evangelical Alliance maintains an advisory committee of 20 church leaders, who meet annually to discuss matters of mutual interest. The Spanish Evangelical Council, consisting of 5 denominations, also provides opportunities for exchange of information and consideration of joint problems. Other co-operative bodies are: (1) the Spanish Evangelical Press and Publishing Association, which is dedicated to improving the quality and effectiveness of Christian journalism; (2) the Evangelical Foreign Missions Consultation Committee, which serves as an information agency on policies of missions working in Spain; and (3) the Evangelical Service of Legal Assistance, formerly the Commission of Evangelical Defence, which works towards achieving more equitable laws relating to religion and provides legal counsel and representation before the government.

Several churches have ecumenical secretariats, including the Spanish Evangelical Church and the Spanish Reformed Episcopal Church; and the National Secretariat of Ecumenism (Secretariado Nacional de Ecumenismo) of the Catholic Episcopal Conference has ecumenical commissions in 55 dioceses.

Catholics also sponsor institutes for ecumenical studies. The John XXIII Ecumenical Institute (Instituto Ecuménico Juan XXIII) at the Pontifical University of Salamanca, begun in 1962, is dedicated to study and action, oriented specifically towards spiritual, doctrinal and pastoral ecumenism on the national and international levels. It arranges programmes of studies, meetings, conferences and seminars. The Work of Eastern Christianity and Centre for Eastern Studies (Obra del Oriente Cristiano y Centro de Estudios Orientales), begun in Madrid in 1944, offers a varied programme of studies, leadership training and conferences. It conducts scientific studies relating to problems encountered by churches in eastern Europe.

There are 2 independent interdenominational centres: the Ecumenical Centre in Barcelona, which is concerned particularly with relations between Catholics and Protestants and of which the majority of members are lay; and the Interconfessional Ecumenical Centre (Centro Ecuménico Interconfessional) in Valencia, which is devoted to spiritual and pastoral ecumenism and includes members of the Catholic, Baptist and Reformed Episcopal Churches. In addition, 3 Catholic diocesan centres are located in Cordoba, Bilbao and Gran Canaria. Finally, Missionaries of Unity, founded in Madrid in 1962, is a Catholic centre oriented towards spirituality and ecumenical activities. It infuses ecumenical ideas among Catholics through a teaching programme, correspondence courses, interdenominational meetings, dialogue, pilgrimages and ecumenical prayers.

On the inter-religious level, Judeo-Christian Friendship (Amistad Judeo-Cristiana) in Madrid, which belongs to the Sisters of Notre Dame of Sion, maintains a documentation bureau for relations between Christians and Jews. In September 1974 Amistad Islamo-Cristiana, which has a specialized library in Madrid, organized jointly with the Hispano-Arab Institute of Culture (a state institution) Cordoba's first Islamo-Christian international congress. The Spanish government also created in Madrid in 1961 an institution for the study of Sefardic Judaism, the Instituto 'Arias Montano' de Estudios Hebraicos Sefardies y Oriente Proximo, which studies Sefardic communities in their diversity and as found in different countries. A Secretariat for Non-Believers (Secretariado para non-Creyentes) was created by the Catholic Episcopal Conference in 1974.

## BROADCASTING.

All commercial stations accept religious programmes. Since 1959 the government has permitted the Catholic Church to operate a chain of 45 radio stations (one in each of the 45 dioceses) in a chain Cadena de Ondas Populares Españolas (COPE), with a central station located in Madrid. Programmes reach 24% of the national listening audience. In 1970 a Catholic priest began a service using the telephone number of the government Radio Nacional de España for one hour every day. This service started a radio programme called Extension 293 once a week over national radio. Several Catholic stations carry on systematic courses for mass education, especially in the south. In Las Palmas de Gran Canaria, Radio ECCA (Emisora Cultural Canaria) gives lessons in general culture, English, music and accounting. In 1969, 19,850 students were following these courses. For Catholics, Spain is a member of UNDA. Protestants were by 1974 still not permitted to broadcast in Spain. They do however produce tapes locally for foreign stations. From abroad, Trans World Radio (Monaco) broadcast 8 hours 15 minutes a week of Protestant programmes in Spanish, and Radio Vatican transmits in Spanish for 3 hours 30 minutes a week.

## BIBLIOGRAPHY


*Analisis sociologico del catolicismo español*. R. Duocastella et alia. Barcelona: ISPA, 1967.

*Anuario evangélico español, 1973*. Madrid: Tipografía Artistica, 1973. 272p.

*Guia de la Iglesia en España, 1970*. Madrid: Oficina General de Información y Estadística de la Iglesia, 1970.

*Las confesiones no católicas de España*. R. Saladrigas. Barcelona: Ediciones Peninsula, 1971.

*L'église et le pouvoir en Espagne*. J.F. Nadinot. Paris: M. Th. Génin, 1973.

*Los Protestantes espanoles*. J. Estruch. Barcelona: Nova Terra, 1968. 230p.

'Problematica de los colegios de la Iglesia en España'. R. Duocastella. Madrid: ISPA, 1969. 20p. (Duplicated).

*Protestants in modern Spain: a struggle for religious pluralism*. D.G. Vought. South Pasadena (CA): William Carey Library, 1973.

*Realidades socio-religiosas de España*. J.M. Vasquez. Madrid: Editorial Nacional, 1967.

'Spain', P. Almerich, in H. Mol (ed), *Western religions* (The Hague: Mouton: 1972), p.459–477.


TABLE 2. ORGANIZED CHURCHES AND DENOMINATIONS IN SPAIN

| Official name 1 | Begun 2 | Type 3 | Counc 4 | Congs 5 | Adults 6 | Affiliated 7 | Names, notes, and other statistics (see Codebook) 8 |
|---|---|---|---|---|---|---|---|
| Asambleas de Dios de España | 1930 | P Pe2 | ZF... | 35 | 625 | 1,500 | *ADE. Assemblies of God of Spain*. M=AoG(UK,USA). Well-organized. 25n,21f,1s(7). |
| Asambleas de Hermanos en Cristo | | P EBr | x.... | 4 | 100 | 300 | *AHC. Darbistas (Darbyites). Plymouth Brethren* (Exclusive). In Barcelona, Palma. |
| Asambleas Pentecostales de España | 1959 | P Pen | ..... | 7 | 43 | 100 | *APE. Pentecostal Assemblies of Spain*. Aid from USA. 1n,7x,G=5%pa,1s,W=50%,13Y. |
| Asoc de Igl Ev Bautistas Indep de E | | P Bap | ..... | 5 | 200 | 500 | *AIEBI. Assoc of Independent Baptist Chs*. Split ex UEBE. M=Strict Baptists(UK). 1s. |
| Asociación Ev Bautista Española | | P Bap | ..... | 4 | 150 | 300 | *Spanish Ev Baptist Association*. Small grouping of independent Baptists. |
| Comunidad de Iglesias Evangélicas | | P ind | x.... | 5 | 150 | 300 | *Community of Independent Chs*. M=World-Wide Missions(USA). In Torre Molinos. |
| Comunión Bautista Independiente | | P Bap | xF... | 7 | 200 | 400 | *CBI. Indep Baptist Communion. Canary Is Gospel Mission*. Ex UEBE. M=CBFMS(USA). |
| Congregaciones Ev Neotestamentarias | | P int | x.... | 6 | 200 | 400 | *Unión Misionara Neotestamentaria. New Testament Congs*. M=NTMU(UK). HQ Granada. |
| Federación de Iglesias Ev Indep de E | 1953 | P Con | KM..C | 55 | 2,362 | 4,090 | *FIEIDE. Federation of Independent Ev Chs*. M=TEAM(USA). In northeast. 27n,11f,1s. |
| Iglesia Anglicana (D Gibraltar) | 1850 | A plu | awc.. | 14 | 4,700 | 12,000 | *Comunidad Anglicana. Ch of England*. CCCS chaplaincies; 3 in Canary Is. 8x. |
| Iglesia Apostólica de España | | P PeA | Z.... | 2 | 40 | 200 | *IAE. Apostolic Ch of Spain*. M=Apostolic Ch(Germany). 1 congregation in Cordoba. 1n. |
| **Igesia Católica en España:** | c 63 | R Lat | B.B.R | 21,223 | 24,393,700 | 33,414,062 | *Catholic Ch in Spain*. C=62+9+244. 114q,48s. 35006n,10372m,82619w,618423Yy. |
| M Burgos | 1075 | R Lat | Bs | 998 | 260,100 | 356,360 | *Archdiócesis de Burgos*. No diocesan councils. 867 374 1701 5569 |
| D Bilbao | 1949 | R Lat | Bs | 281 | 742,600 | 1,017,245 | *Diócesis de Bilbao*. Basque country. D=pc(23,0,0) 1337 523 3340 21501 |
| D Osma-Soria | c1150 | R Lat | Bs | 447 | 80,800 | 110,745 | No diocesan pastoral or priests' council. 255 16 330 1305 |
| D Palencia | c 250 | R Lat | Bs | 468 | 150,000 | 205,000 | Diocesan councils: D=pc(6,6,23),PC(23,2). 539 258 1076 2113 |
| D Vitoria | 1861 | R Lat | Bs | 421 | 153,700 | 210,500 | In north, in Basque country. Guerrillas active. 505 284 1160 4155 |
| M Granada | c 250 | R Lat | Bs | 249 | 410,000 | 561,645 | In extreme south; Sierra Nevada. HQ Granada. 565 319 2054 13154 |
| D Almería | 1492 | R Lat | Bs | 215 | 271,600 | 372,059 | Diocesan priests' council being formed. 195 35 525 7519 |
| D Cartagena | c 90 | R Lat | Bs | 270 | 606,000 | 830,000 | In southeast. HQ Murcia. D=pc(0,6,20). 476 117 1358 19919 |
| D Guadix | c 90 | R Lat | Bs | 110 | 102,000 | 140,000 | Mountainous area northeast of Granada. 95 3 214 2643 |
| D Jaén | c 650 | R Lat | Bs | 189 | 847,000 | 667,101 | No diocesan pastoral or priests' council. 381 65 1305 13408 |
| D Málaga | c 350 | R Lat | Bs | 367 | 540,000 | 740,000 | Also 70,000 in Melilla (NAfrica). D=pc(3,2,10). 402 80 1740 25000 |
| M Oviedo | 811 | R Lat | Bs | 939 | 763,000 | 1,045,000 | On northwestern coastline. D=pc(0,8,19). 948 232 1860 16089 |
| D Astorga | 747 | R Lat | Bs | 655 | 250,900 | 343,655 | South of Cordillera Cantabrica. D=pc(3,4,12). 515 21 543 4891 |
| D León | c 350 | R Lat | Bs | 744 | 234,000 | 321,000 | South of Cordillera Cantabrica. 743 221 1064 5678 |
| D Santander | 1754 | R Lat | Bs | 609 | 344,100 | 471,362 | Northwest coastline, west of Bilbao. 742 182 1243 8442 |
| M Pamplona (& D Tudela) | c 450 | R Lat | Bs | 636 | 332,600 | 455,570 | Up to northwest Pyrenees. D=pc(0,4,48). 1402 550 2786 8324 |
| D Calahorra &laCalzada-Logroño | c 450 | R Lat | Bs | 281 | 175,300 | 240,209 | South of Pamplona. HQ Calahorra. D=pc(0,7,18). 421 166 929 3980 |
| D Jaca | 1063 | R Lat | Bs | 178 | 35,700 | 48,868 | In Pyrenees area. D=pc(0,4,12). 122 7 107 572 |
| D San Sebastián | 1949 | R Lat | Bs | 200 | 460,000 | 630,000 | Basque country, near France border. D=pc(10,3,16). 1151 564 3040 12334 |
| M Santiago de Compostela | c 850 | R Lat | Bs | 1,036 | 879,100 | 1,204,300 | Extreme northwest of country. D=pc(0,6,58). 1575 112 1397 22935 |
| D Lugo | c 150 | R Lat | Bs | 678 | 234,200 | 320,815 | Inland diocese in northwest corner. 770 38 488 3989 |
| D Mondoñedo-Ferrol | 1114 | R Lat | Bs | 421 | 254,800 | 349,000 | Extreme northwestern point of Spain. D=pc(4,2,15). 388 10 510 3000 |
| D Orense | c 450 | R Lat | Bs | 737 | 312,900 | 428,586 | Inland northwestern diocese. D=pc(6,6,28). 746 50 492 2175 |
| D Túy-Vigo | c 550 | R Lat | Bs | 272 | 285,000 | 390,000 | Coastal diocese bordering on northern Portugal. 370 96 718 8117 |
| M Sevilla (Seville) | c 250 | R Lat | Bs | 289 | 1,262,200 | 1,729,105 | Southwest. D=pc,PC(with lay minority), Synod. 1001 363 3824 39983 |
| D Badajoz | 1255 | R Lat | Bs | 216 | 426,900 | 584,853 | Southwest, bordering on Portugal. D=pc. 429 68 955 10913 |
| D Cádiz & Ceuta | 1241 | R Lat | Bs | 85 | 365,000 | 500,000 | Also 80,000 in Ceuta (NAfrica). D=pc(113,22). 260 65 1060 12000 |
| D Cordoba | c 250 | R Lat | Bs | 192 | 568,700 | 779,120 | North of Cordillera Penibética. D=pc(5,3,26). 597 70 450 4125 |
| D Huelva | 1953 | R Lat | Bs | 160 | 295,900 | 405,300 | Extreme southwest, bordering sea and Portugal. 207 22 426 7502 |
| D Islas Canarias | 1406 | R Lat | Bs | 162 | 421,000 | 576,700 | Diocesan priests' council being formed. 297 32 647 11591 |
| D San Cristóbal (Tenerife) | 1819 | R Lat | Bs | 230 | 405,400 | 555,325 | *D San Cristóbal de La Laguna*. D=pc(elected). 315 65 940 13302 |

*Continued overleaf*

*Table 2–continued*

| Official name 1 | Begun 2 | Type 3 | Counc 4 | Congs 5 | Adults 6 | Affiliated 7 | Names, notes, and other statistics (see Codebook) 8 | | | | |
|---|---|---|---|---|---|---|---|---|---|---|---|
| M Tarragona | c 90 | R Lat | Bs | 190 | 183,000 | 250,000 | Catalonia. on northeast coast. D=pc(3,3,14). | 266 | 86 | 749 | 5023 |
| D Gerona | c 90 | R Lat | Bs | 403 | 282,100 | 386,400 | Catalonia. D=pc(1,4,12). | 478 | 113 | 1095 | 5954 |
| D Lérida | c 450 | R Lat | Bs | 228 | 188,300 | 257,931 | Catalonia. Presbyteral Commission (elected). | 231 | 45 | 538 | 4120 |
| D Solsona | 1593 | R Lat | Bs | 214 | 94,400 | 129,290 | Catalonia. D=pc(5,7,6), PC. | 213 | 12 | 403 | 1804 |
| D Tortosa | c 350 | R Lat | Bs | 140 | 166,000 | 227,000 | Catalonia. No diocesan councils. | 204 | 9 | 442 | 2323 |
| D Urgel | c 350 | R Lat | Bs | 407 | 105,000 | 143,895 | Catalonia. Also includes Andorra. D=pc(3,4,13). | 238 | 50 | 344 | 1950 |
| D Vich | c 450 | R Lat | Bs | 260 | 223,800 | 306,600 | Inland diocese in Catalonia. D=pc. | 400 | 102 | 1300 | 4352 |
| M Toledo | c 90 | R Lat | Bs | 245 | 408,000 | 558,960 | See of primate of Spain. D=pc(10,4,29). | 450 | 53 | 1290 | 8054 |
| D Coria-Cáceres | 1142 | R Lat | Bs | 150 | 179,000 | 245,202 | On Portugal border. HQ Coria. | 219 | 9 | 396 | 4159 |
| D Cuenca | 1183 | R Lat | Bs | 337 | 178,700 | 244,796 | East centre of country. | 304 | 6 | 408 | 4400 |
| D Plasencia | 1189 | R Lat | Bs | 195 | 237,000 | 325,000 | Astride Sierra de Gredos. D=pc(2,2,21). | 277 | 55 | 654 | 4139 |
| D Sigüenza-Guadalajara | 589 | R Lat | Bs | 420 | 116,800 | 159,960 | HQ Sigüenza. D=pc(6,1,4). | 280 | 185 | 300 | 1760 |
| M Valencia | 1238 | R Lat | Bs | 617 | 1,364,300 | 1,868,905 | No diocesan pastoral or priests' council. | 1565 | 419 | 4565 | 37248 |
| D Albacete | 1949 | R Lat | Bs | 196 | 249,400 | 341,660 | No diocesan pastoral or priests' council. | 219 | 14 | 482 | 6555 |
| D Ibiza | 1782 | R Lat | Bs | 24 | 37,600 | 51,500 | Ibiza island in Balearic Islands. D=pc(0,2,11). | 50 | 2 | 74 | 1414 |
| D Mallorca (Majorca) | c 450 | R Lat | Bs | 163 | 306,400 | 419,800 | Balearic Islands. HQ Palma. D=pc. | 572 | 185 | 2065 | 8836 |
| D Menorca (Minorca) | c 450 | R Lat | Bs | 60 | 37,500 | 51,370 | Balearic Is. HQ Ciudadela. No diocesan councils. | 61 | 10 | 115 | 1071 |
| D Orihuela-Alicante | 1564 | R Lat | Bs | 185 | 453,000 | 620,000 | On mainland south of Valencia. D=pc(0,5,25). | 403 | 41 | 1118 | 17582 |
| D Segorbe-Castellón de la Plana | c 550 | R Lat | Bs | 148 | 239,300 | 327,861 | On mainland north of Valencia. D=pc(3,0,16). | 256 | 67 | 668 | 3368 |
| M Valladolid | 1595 | R Lat | Bs | 313 | 285,000 | 390,000 | West central Spain. D=pc(1,13,13). | 756 | 292 | 1111 | 13276 |
| D Avila | c1050 | R Lat | Bs | 253 | 150,600 | 206,320 | North of Sierra de Gredos. D=pc(0,5,13). | 304 | 33 | 763 | 2602 |
| D Ciudad Rodrigo | c 350 | R Lat | Bs | 119 | 47,500 | 65,083 | Along Portugal border. D=pc(0,0,14). | 115 | 0 | 127 | 814 |
| D Salamanca | c 950 | R Lat | Bs | 333 | 213,000 | 291,744 | Up to Portugal border. D=pc(5,0,3),PC(6,1). | 731 | 488 | 1353 | 2112 |
| D Segovia | c 550 | R Lat | Bs | 297 | 118,800 | 162,700 | North of Madrid and Sierra de Guadarama. | 312 | 38 | 498 | 3150 |
| D Zamora | c 950 | R Lat | Bs | 270 | 147,200 | 201,648 | Along northern Portugal border. D=pc,PC(27,15). | 356 | 83 | 745 | 1813 |
| M Zaragoza | c 450 | R Lat | Bs | 283 | 550,600 | 754,228 | In central northeast Spain. D=pc(0,5,10),PC(14,0). | 744 | 277 | 2052 | 10000 |
| D Barbastro | 1100 | R Lat | Bs | 172 | 25,800 | 35,365 | Among Pyrenees up to France. D=pc(1,3,10). | 88 | 8 | 84 | 574 |
| D Huesca | 533 | R Lat | Bs | 189 | 61,500 | 84,250 | Up to foothills of Pyrenees. D=pc(0,3,13). | 167 | 20 | 335 | 1110 |
| D Tarazona | c 450 | R Lat | Bs | 147 | 80,700 | 110,532 | No diocesan pastoral or priests' council. | 175 | 5 | 399 | 1212 |
| D Teruel & Albarracín | 1172 | R Lat | Bs | 252 | 81,600 | 111,769 | HQ Teruel. D=pc(5,3,19),PC(26,6). | 238 | 25 | 289 | 1338 |
| AD Madrid-Alcalá | 1884 | R Lat | bs | 657 | 2,765,200 | 3,787,902 | 1972: 9 Episcopal Vicariates. D=pc(0,7,24). | 3346 | 1580 | 12320 | 106059 |
| AD Barcelona | c 350 | R Lat | hs | 437 | 2,336,000 | 3,200,000 | Includes monastery of Montserrat. D=PC(10,0). | 2057 | 992 | 6503 | 25580 |
| RN Ciudad Real | 1875 | R Lat | hs | 184 | 370,100 | 506,968 | Spanish military orders. D=pc(0,9,17),PC(5,0). | 315 | 60 | 752 | 8443 |
| Iglesia Cristiana Adventista del 7 Día | 1903 | P Adv | x.... | 34 | 3,069 | 7,000 | *SDA. Seventh-day Adventists, Spanish Ch*, SEuropean UM. 21nx,1j,1s,34t(3114),337Y. | | | | |
| Iglesia Cristiana Ev de Pentecostés | | P Pen | ..... | 2 | 70 | 200 | *Ev Christian Church of Pentecost*. Small charismatic group. HQ Alicante. | | | | |
| Iglesia de Dios de España | 1937 | P Pe3 | ZF... | 5 | 70 | 200 | *IDE. Ch of God.* M=CoG(Cleveland)(USA). Begun by Spanish convert from New York. 6n. | | | | |
| Iglesia de Dios Pentecostal | 1963 | P Pe2 | Z.... | 15 | 200 | 2,200 | *IDP. Pentecostal Ch of God.* M=PCG(Puerto Rico,USA). Madrid. 4n,2x,1p,W=25%,56Y,68z. | | | | |
| Iglesia de JC de los Santos de los UD | | M LdS | x.... | 11 | 400 | 815 | UD=Ultimos Dias. *Ch of JC of Latter-day Saints. Mormons.* M=CJCLdS(USA). HQ Madrid. | | | | |
| Iglesia El Buen Pastor | | I pel | ..... | 2 | 50 | 100 | *Ch of the Good Shepherd.* Pentecostals from Mexico (schism ex Aaronistas). | | | | |
| Iglesia Española Reformada Episcopal | 1880 | C Pro | UuC.C | 15 | 700 | 1,000 | *IERE. Spanish Reformed Episcopal Ch.* Ex IEE. 1894, Anglican succession. 10n,1u. | | | | |
| Iglesia Evangélica Española | 1863 | P Ref | RWC.C | 105 | 2,073 | 10,000 | *IEE. Spanish Ev Ch.* 1880, episcopal section (IERE) broke off. 45n,1f,1u(8). | | | | |
| Iglesia Evangélica Filadelfia | | P Pe2 | ..... | 40 | 6,000 | 25,000 | *Philadelphia Ch. Misión Ev Gitana. Movement of Spanish Gypsies.* 21n,150m,G=6%pa. | | | | |
| Iglesia Evangélica Pentecostal de E | 1928 | P Pe2 | Z.... | 6 | 200 | 500 | *Pentecostal Ch of Spain.* Oldest Pentecostal group in Spain. M=SFM(Sweden). | | | | |
| Iglesia Nueva Apostólica | | C CAp | x.... | | 500 | 1,000 | *New Apostolic Ch*, in Switzerland District (Bezirk Schweiz). HQ Dortmund (Germany). | | | | |
| Iglesia Ortodoxa Griega en España | 1949 | O Gre | Cwc.. | 3 | 1,000 | 2,000 | *Spanish Greek Orthodox Ch.* Under Constantinople & D France. Greeks, Russians. 1x. | | | | |
| Iglesias de Cristo en España | 1964 | P Dis | x.... | 25 | 500 | 1,000 | *Chs of Christ.* M=CC(Non-Instrumental)(USA). USA servicemen. 12n,1k,1s,W=60%,100Y. | | | | |
| Iglesias del Nuevo Testamento | | P CBr | x.... | 10 | 300 | 500 | *Chs of the New Testament. Plymouth Brethren.* Open, liberal (women may minister). | | | | |
| Iglesias Evangélicas de Hermanos | 1836 | P CBr | x...C | 95 | 6,000 | 15,000 | *IEH. Assemblies of Brethren* (Open). M=CMML(UK,USA). Extreme northwest. 120m,12f. | | | | |
| Misión Evangélica Española | 1913 | P ind | .G... | 20 | 250 | 400 | *Spanish Gospel Mission.* M=SGM(UK). Valdepeñas. Declining due to emigration. 6n,30Y. | | | | |
| Sociedad de la Ciencia Cristiana | | M Sci | x.... | 3 | 50 | 100 | *Ch of Christ, Scientist/Christian Science.* M=CCS. Madrid, Palma (Majorca). 1m,3w. | | | | |
| Testigos de Jehová | 1919 | M Jeh | x.... | 144 | 14,531 | 39,500 | *Jehovah's Witnesses. IBSA.* Legalized 1967. 240 in prison. 800n,G=4%pa,2005Y. | | | | |
| Unión Evangélica Bautista Española | 1869 | P Bap | T...C | 127 | 6,147 | 15,000 | *UEBE. Spanish Ev Baptist Union.* 1921, M=SBC(USA). East coast. 51n,31f,1k,1s,250Y. | | | | |
| Other Protestant denominations | | P | ..... | 300 | 10,000 | 20,000 | Total about 110 (see list below), mostly very small groups. | | | | |
| Other Latin American indigenous chs | | I | ..... | | 500 | 1,000 | From Mexico, Puerto Rico, Chile, Colombia, and other Spanish-speaking countries. | | | | |
| Other marginal Protestant bodies | | M | ..... | | 100 | 500 | Smaller groups and cults, including Horpenites (from Saxony, Germany). | | | | |
| Doubly-affiliated (duplication)(1970) | | | | | –94,900 | –130,000 | Evangelicals and others who also are or were baptized Roman Catholics. | | | | |
| Disaffiliated (duplication)(1970) | | | | | –434,800 | –595,567 | Baptized Catholics now completely disaffiliated agnostics or atheists. | | | | |
| **Total affiliated (mid-1970)** | | | | **22,370** | **23,925,480** | **32,851,600** | **Total denominations (1970) . . . 144.** | | | | |
| **Total affiliated (mid-1975)** | | | | **23,000** | **25,024,500** | **34,360,700** | **Total denominations (1975) . . . 148.** | | | | |
| **Total affiliated (mid-1980)** | | | | **23,700** | **26,169,400** | **35,932,700** | **Total denominations (1980) . . . 152.** | | | | |

NOTES ON TABLE ABOVE
COLUMNS: for meanings and CODES (cols. 1, 3, 4, 8): see Codebook (Part 6). Column 1: **Boldface type** = church with over 10% of country's affiliated Christians.
NATIONAL COUNCILS (Column 4, 5th letter).
C = Consejo Evangélico Español (CEE) (Spanish Evangelical Council).
R = Conferencia Episcopal Española (CEE) (Spanish Episcopal Conference).
*Other national councils.* Alianza Evangélica Española (Spanish Evangelical Alliance) (affiliated to EEA and WEF).
OTHER PROTESTANT DENOMINATIONS. These include about 30 denominations proper, over 50 independent congregations, about 24 foreign congregations catering for civilian expatriates from other European countries and churches (11 German-speaking, 6 Dutch-speaking, 3 Swiss Reformed, 2 English-speaking (Baptist), 1 Danish, 1 Norwegian), foreign congregations catering for USA expatriate civilians, and USA military chaplaincies among the 9,000 USA servicemen and their dependants. Denominations with some local membership include (names are given in Spanish unless better known in English): Association of Baptists for World Evangelism (1968), Baptist International Missions (1964), Bible Christian Union, Central American Mission (1971, 12 missionaries), Children of God International (Barcelona), Ejército de Salvación (Salvation Army, 1971), Federación Ev Bautista Española (Barcelona), Gospel Missionary Union (1967), Iglesia Bautista Bíblica, Iglesia de la Biblia Abierta (1969; M=Open Bible Standard Chs, USA), Iglesia Ev Pentecostal de Madrid, Iglesia Ev Pentecostal Salem, Iglesia Pentecostal Unida de España, Iglesia Reformada de la Santísima Trinidad, Iglesia Reformada Presbiteriana, Oriental Missionary Society (1972), Reformed Baptists (USA), SDA Movement of Reform, Sociedad de Amigos Cuáqueros (Society of Friends, Quakers), Spanish Pioneer Mission (1930), Swedish Church Mission, United World Mission (1946), West Indies Mission (1970, in Canary Islands), World Baptist Fellowship (1959), Worldwide Evangelization Crusade (1936, in Canary Islands).

**PEOPLES** (ethnolinguistic). Christians: 72.8% Spanish (Spaniard), 16.4% Catalan, 8.2% Galician, 2.3% Basque, 0.1% Gypsy, 0.1% Portuguese, 0.1% British, USA White, French, German, Latin American White & Mestizo, Chinese (200).

COUNTRY-WIDE TOTALS
EVANGELIZATION (see Part 5). 1900: 100%. 1970: 100%. 1980: 100%. *Mass evangelism.* Among recent campaigns and events: 1972–73, 238 Southern Baptists from Texas (USA) conducted 8-day crusades in 17 Spanish cities (sponsored by the Spanish Evangelical Baptist Union, UEBE; 300 enquirers); June 1974, Iberian Congress on Evangelism, Madrid; 1978, Here's Life Barcelona (CCCI). *Radiophonic evangelism.* Annual listeners' letters (1975) about 5,000 Radio Vatican, 1,840 TWR, 149 HCJB, et alia. Bible correspondence courses: many agencies, including ICI (10,163 enrolments). *Literature evangelism.* 1976, first nationwide Every Home Crusade coverage.
FOREIGN MISSIONARIES AND PERSONNEL (nationals serving abroad) (1972). Total 27,901: 27,881 Roman Catholics (22,181 foreign missionaries (1,064 secular priests, 8,795 religious priests and brothers, 11,981 sisters, 341 lay) serving in Third-World countries, and about 5,700 other personnel in Western nations especially Italy, France, FR Germany, USA, Portugal, Belgium, 106 in Switzerland, et alia), about 10 Protestants, about 10 marginal Protestants (Jehovah's Witnesses).
FOREIGN MISSIONARIES AND PERSONNEL (aliens from abroad) (1973). Total 1,638. *From Western world.* 1,293: about 1,000 Roman Catholics, 284 Protestants (204 in 37 USA societies, 57 in 12 UK societies, 6 in 2 Netherlands societies, 4 in 1 Finland society, 4 in 1 Sweden society, 3 in 1 Canada society, 3 in 1 Australia society, 2 in 1 Norway society, 1 in 1 New Zealand society), 8 Anglicans in 3 UK societies, 1 Orthodox. *From Third World.* 345: about 280 Roman Catholics mainly from Bolivia and other Latin American countries, about 40 Non-White indigenous (20 from Colombia, others from Mexico, Puerto Rico and other Latin American countries), about 25 Protestants from Colombia, Puerto Rico, Argentina, South Africa, et alia.
INSTITUTIONS (church-operated) (1973). Total 4,100, including 2,760 higher schools (283 minor seminaries), about 1,000 social service/welfare/medical centres, 46 radios stations, 33 religious communities, 25 research centres, 171 seminaries (162 RC, 9 Protestant), 4 universities.
PERIDICALS. About 910 titles (850 RC).
PERSONNEL. About 129,838 (128,200 national, 1,638 foreign).
RELIGIOUS LIBRARIES. About 300.
SCRIPTURE DISTRIBUTION (1975). Annual totals: 915,346 Bibles (2% subsidized, 98% commercial), 1,158,268 NTs (29% free, 2% subsidized, 69% commercial), 66,721 UBS portions, 106,960 UBS selections. *Translations completed.* Portion: 8 languages since 1514. NT: 2 languages since 1543. Bible: 3 languages since 1553.
SERVICE AGENCIES. About 300, including ACASE, ACISJF, ACJ(YMCA), AEE, AMS, BICE, CCCI, CCEM, CECADE, CEE, CEF, CET, CLC, CONFER, COPE, FCME, FECUN, FEDAAS, FERE, HOAC/F, HOAC/M, ICIA, IEME, IFES, JOC, MFC, OCASHA, OCSHA, OM, PPC, PPP, PSSP, PTL, SEMINCI, SIPE, SU, TWR, UNAS, WLC(EHC), WVI, YWAM.

ADDITIONAL DATA ON CHURCHES
IGLESIA CATOLICA EN ESPANA. *Annual baptisms.* (1972) 99.8% infant, 0.2% adult. *Diocesan councils.* Column 8 shows (after the code D=) the extent to which dioceses have followed the requirements of Vatican II by creating functioning priests' councils (pc), pastoral councils (PC), and diocesan synods, with priestly, religious and lay representatives (showing the situation in 1970; see full explanation of code on p. ). *Personnel.* About 99% nationals, 1% expatriates. *Catholic charismatics* (January 1974). 500 adults including a number of religious personnel are active in 10 prayer groups in the Charismatic Renewal. By 1976 there was at least one prayer group in almost every diocese. *Seminaries.* Up to 1965, each of the 64 dioceses had its own major seminary covering both philosophy and theology; by 1973 regrouping had reduced the number to 48, these being based either on towns with university faculties of theology (Salamanca, Granada, Barcelona, Madrid) or those with a regional centre for ecclesiastical studies (Centro Regional de Estudios Eclesiásticos: Valencia, Seville, Zaragosa). A similar regrouping has taken place for study houses of religious orders and congregations, reduced by 1973 to 114. In certain dioceses groups of priests have opened informal training houses for young potential ordinands, in opposition to the established seminaries. *Seminarians.* Decline from 5,211 in 1970 to 3,014 in 1973. *Major religions orders and congregations* (1972). Priests (congregations with over 500 members including novices and students): 3,009 SJ, 2,467 SDB, 1,437 OFM, 1,084 CMF, 1,066 OP, 1,022 SP, 843 OFMCap, 807 AA, 803 OCD, 704 SMI, 637 Religious of St Vincent de Paul, 533 ORSA. Brothers (congregations with over 150 members): 1,891 FSC, 1,618 PFM, 541 OH, 359 SC, 190 FICP. Sisters (congregations with over 1,250 members): 10,928 Hijas de la Caridad de San Vicente de Paúl, 2,626 Carmelitas de la Caridad, 2,419 Caridad de Santa Ana, 2,187 Hermanitas de los Ancianos de Desamparados, 1,716 Compañia de Maria, 1,574 Esclavas del Sagrado Corazón, 1,488 Servas de Maria, 1,482 Dominicas de la Anunciata, 1,323 Mercedarias de la Caridad. The total of all congregations of sisters founded in Spain is 135. *Catholic organizations.* The Spanish Episcopal Conference (Conferencia Episcopal Española, CEE) is not dividedinto regional pastoral zones except for the region covered by the Episcopal Conference of Catalonia (Conferencia Episcopal Tarraconense, CET). This conference, with its headquarters in Barcelona, has developed significantly since 1967 and has its own statutes, commissions and secretariats. In addition, the following 3 ecclesiastical provinces and regions co-ordinate their own pastoral activities, without being constituted as episcopal conferences: St James of Compostelle (Santiago de Compostela) which is preparing a provincial synod; Douro (Duero) for the dioceses of Old Castille with headquarters at Valladolid; and Andalusia which groups 9 dioceses in Andalusia and that of Cartagena with headquarters at Seville. The bishops of the Basque and Navarra area, although belonging to different ecclesiastical provinces, meet frequently to deal with questions common to the region.

Associations for religious personnel include the Spanish Conference of Male Religious (Conferencia Española de Religiosos, CONFER) with regional conferences in Catalonia, Basque-Navarra, Andalusia, Valencia, Castille-Galicia-Madrid, and the Spanish Conference of Sisters (Conferencia Española de Religiosas). For the armed forces, Spain forms a military vicariate.

There is no national priests' organization, nor a national pastoral council. However, a Bishops-Priests Joint Assembly (Asamblea Conjunta de Obispos y Sacerdotes) met in Madrid in September 1971. With 2 years of preparation by a national clergy secretariat including a vast sociological enquiry touching 80% of the priests in 60 of Spain's 64 dioceses, the assembly brought together 247 participants with right to vote, the majority being priests. Only the Basque and Catalan provinces failed to send their elected delegates. The assembly had as its theme 'The Church and the World in Today's Spain' and 56 of 60 final recommendations were adopted with the necessary two-thirds majority. The assembly dealt with such questions as the separation of church and state, political injustice, the priestly ministry and the pastoral action of the church.

The National Union of the Secular Apostolate (Unión Nacional de Apostolado Seglar, UNAS) united, in 1972, 91 associations of the lay apostolate. Some important organizations are not members of UNAS such as Scouts and Cursillos de Cristiandad (Christian Study Courses). Catholic Action retains a formal structure directed by the National Board of Spanish Catholic Action (Junta Nacional de AC Española) with branches for men, women, boys and girls. However, many movements have detached themselves from Catholic Action (especially JOC and men's HOAC) and only the women's branches remain effective. The principal movements of the lay apostolate (some belonging to UNAS, some to Catholic Action and some autonomous) are: (1) Spanish Union of Professional Brotherhoods (Unión Española de Hermandades Profesionales) and Movement of Working Brotherhoods (Movimiento de las Hermandades del Trabajo) which include both those in the liberal professions and also workers, with 107,000 members in two-thirds of the dioceses in 1971; (2) Cursillos de Cristiandad, which is a branch of the international movement, with 54,000 Spanish members in 1971 as contrasted with 175,000 in 1966; (3) Workers Brotherhood of Male Catholic Action (Hermandad Obrera de Acción Católica Masculina, HOAC masculina) which is the Spanish equivalent of Workers' Catholic Action, and counts 10,000 active 'militants' and 25,000 'adherents'; (4) Feminine HOAC (HOAC Feminina); (5) Male and Female JOC which is more radical than HOAC (its publication, *Juventud Obrera*, is banned), with about 10,000 members; (6) Christian Family Movement (Movimiento Familiar Cristiano) which is inspired by Catholic Action but does not separate the sexes; and (7) Scouts and Guides. The total membership of Catholic lay organizations was estimated to be about 400,000 in 1971.

The Holy See has diplomatic relations with Spain and is represented to government and the Catholic hierarchy by a nuncio in Madrid.

No international Catholic organizations have their headquarters in Spain, with the possible exception of the worldwide Cursillos de Cristiandad movement (Christian Study Courses), which although it has no world secretariat, originated in Palma de Majorca in 1949. The movement organizes weekends called cursillos during which the conversion of participants is anticipated, and which is followed by a programme called post-cursillo. Its methods of training, its bourgeois participants and the secrecy surrounding the movement are contrary to the church's conciliar trend and make the movement one of the main supporters of religious and political conservatism.

Considering the conciliar evolution in the Spanish church, unofficial opinion groups tend to display conservative tendencies. The progressivist groups are usually located within the body of official, authorized institutions. The clandestine movement of Christians for Socialism appeared for the first time in January 1973 at a secret meeting in Avila, with more than 200 Christians from all over Spain in attendance. The Spanish Priestly Fraternity (Hermandad Sacerdotal Española) in Madrid is an association of conservative priests and brothers, originating in Vich, Catalonia, in 1968. It holds annual congresses, is registered as an association in its own right, and is a member of the Union of Professional Brothers (Unión de Hermandades Profesionales). The Fraternity claimed to represent 6,000 Spanish priests in 1971. It is not recognized by the episcopate although it receives important support from within it. Another grouping is called International Priestly Study Days, organized in Saragosa in 1972, which brings together some 2,000 priests from all parts of Spain and such other countries as France, West Germany and Italy.

Conservative movements among the laity are numerous although rarely explicit or formally organized. Only 3 organizations have fixed headquarters: (1) the Alliance for the Persecuted Church (Alianza del Credo por la Iglesia Persequida) from Barcelona, which is an organization recognized by the church and dependent upon the episcopate; (2) the National Catholic Confederation of Heads of Families (Confederación Católica Nacional de Padres de Familia), an organization also recognized and dependent upon the episcopate, created in Madrid in 1932 for the defence of religious schools threatened by the laws of the republic, which declined after 1940 but was revived during 1968–69, and has become a conservative faction in Catholic Action; and (3) the Centre for Information and Orientation (Centro de Información y Orientación), which became active in Madrid in 1970. In most instances, conservative movements are clandestine, disavowing episcopal authority but benefitting sometimes from tacit government and police protection. The best known clandestine movement is the Guerrillas of Christ the King (Guerillas de Cristo Rey, sometimes also Guerilleros de Cristo Rey). The Guerilleros first made themselves known in 1969 in Rome, supporting a tract directed against the Second European Assembly of Priests. Their main actions, such as attacks on so-called progressivist parishes, have taken place mostly in Madrid and in the north. Another group of organizations are the diverse traditional Carlist political associations which are known primarily for their religious conservatism. In addition, there are a large number of conservative journals and periodicals.

Several institutions dealing with research and socio-religious problems are active. The General Church Office of Religious Sociology and Statistics (Oficina General de Sociología Religiosa y Estadística de la Iglesia) in Madrid is directly under the secretariat of the Spanish episcopate. The Institute of Applied Sociology (ISPA) is an independent centre in Barcelona. The Institute of Applied Sociology in Madrid (ISAMA) was begun in 1955 under the name of Barriada y Vida and changed its name in 1968; it is an autonomous centre begun by a Dominican priest. The 'Social Ferment' Institute of Social Studies, in Madrid, was started in 1929 under the name of Centre of Social Studies and is now a private Jesuit institution. The Catholic Institute of Social Studies, of Barcelona, is under the local archbishop and has ties with the university faculty of theology. There are also various university institutes including the Leo XIII Social Institute (Marid) (Instituto Social Leon XIII) under the Pontifical University of Salamanca, and the Institute of Social Sciences (Instituto de Ciencias Sociales) (Bilbao) under the University of Deusto specializing inter alia in industrial social psychology. Another important centre is the Faith and Secularism Institute (Instituto Fe y Secularidad, FEYSEC), an autonomous institution begun by Jesuits in Madrid in 1968, which is related to the Pontifical University of Comillas, conducts studies on secularization and atheism and promotes dialogue between Christians and non-believers. Finally there are the Institute of Theology founded in Barcelona in 1972, the Institute of Advanced Training in Religious Sciences (Instituto de Formación Superior en Ciencias Religiosas) at the University of Deusto, the Institute of Advanced Religious Culture (Instituto de Cultura Religiosa Superior) in Madrid catering particularly for militants in apostolic movements, the Centre for University Studies in Madrid, Instituto Juan XXIII de Pedagogía Sacerdotal in Madrid and the Liturgical Pastoral Centre (Centro de Pastoral Litúrgical) at the Benedictine monastery of Montserrat, near Barcelona, for liturgical and biblical studies and a notable centre of Catalan culture.

For pastoral and theological training, the following ecclesiastical faculties may be mentioned: the Theological Faculty of Barcelona, a Jesuit institution; the Faculty of Sacred Theology of the University of Deusto under Jesuits; the Theological Faculty of the North (Facultad Teológica del Norte); the Faculties of Sacred Theology, Canon Law and Philosophy (Facultades de Sagrada Teología, de Derecho Canónico y de Filosofía) of the Pontifical University of Comillas (Madrid) under Jesuits; the Faculty of Theology and Canon Law of the University of Navarra in Pamplona under Opus Dei; and the Faculties of Theology and Canon Law of the Pontifical University of Salamanca, under the Episcopal Conference. There exist also 6 diocesan seminaries providing theological courses (León, Madrid, Oviedo, Sigüenza, Valencia and Saragosa), which are affiliated with university faculties; and 8 faculties of theology and 6 of philosophy reserved for members of religious orders and congregations (SJ, OP, SDB, CMF, OSA). Two other seminaries exist at Valladolid, serving English priests (Colegio Inglese) and Scottish seminarians (Real Colegio de Escoceses, Royal Scots College). The latter, founded in Madrid in 1627 and transferred to Valladolid in 1771, had 26 students in 1972. The Advanced Institute of Pastoral Work (Instituto Superior de Pastoral), founded in Madrid in 1955, is under the Pontifical University of Salamanca and has departments of evangelization, catechesis and liturgy. There is also a Centre of Pastoral Studies, founded in Barcelona in 1968, which is affiliated to the Episcopal Conference of Catalonia and is engaged in research, teaching and provides a pastoral documentation service.

Foreign missionary activity is co-ordinated by the following bodies. The Episcopal Commission for Missions and Co-operation (Comisión Episcopal de Misiones y Cooperación) is an official organ of the Episcopal Conference. It shares with CECADE (Episcopal Commission for Diocesan Apostolic Co-operation for Foreign Missions) a common secretariat which includes numerous departments and services. Secular priests are sent out by diocesan missionary delegations or secretariats and by the Work of Hispanoamerican Sacerdotal Co-operation (Obra de Cooperación Sacerdotal Hispanoamericana, OCSHA) which was begun in Madrid in 1948 to promote and channel at the national level the sending of priests to Latin America. Numerous agencies exist for sending secular personnel, in particular the Work of Hispanoamerican Lay Apostolic Co-operation (Obra de Cooperación Apostólica Seglar Hispanoamericana, OCASHA) and the Association of Lay Missionary Action (Asociación de Misionerismo Seglar, AMS) begun in 1947. There are also numerous other missionary associations. In Madrid, the Centre for Missionary Training (Centro de Formación Misionera) prepares candidates, and the Raymond Lull Spanish School of Medicine for Missionaries (Escuela Española de Medicina para Misioneros Raimundo Lulio) in Madrid offers a diploma in Medicine recognized by both academic and civil authorities. The Centre for Information, Documentation and Sociology (Centro de Información Documentación, y Sociología) in Madrid is especially involved in research regarding Latin America; and another group concerned about missionary activity is Semanas Españolas de Misionología in Burgos. The Department of Spanish Missiology (Departmento de Misionología Española) of the Higher Council for Scientific Research studies the history of Spanish missions, especially in Latin America. In 1972 there were 2,047 officially-sent Spanish Catholic foreign missionaries (priests, brothers, sisters, lay) serving in Africa, 15,502 in Latin America, 957 in Asia, and 235 in Oceania; together with at least 3,440 others. Of these, 1,064 were secular priests, 8,795 men religious. 11,981 sisters, and 341 lay workers. The numbers serving with the principal male missionary bodies in 1972 were: 687 OFM, 545 ORSA, 500 OP, 466 AA, 420 OFMCap, 310 CP, 288 SJ, 262 SP and 380 PFM (brothers).

All schools in Spain are regarded as Catholic since Catholism is the state religion; the only exceptions are certain small schools recently begun under the Law of Religious Freedom. There are nevertheless 3 different types of school: state schools; Catholic schools operated by dioceses, religious congregations or secular institutes; and private schools run through private initiative. In 1972 the Catholic Church operated 2,804 kindergartens (271,873 children), 4,119 primary schools (880,207 pupils), and 2,370 general, technical or pfofessional secondary schools (541,496). In addition there were in 1971 5,733 students in Catholic universitiee and 1,824 in higher technical schools. In 1970–71, 60% of the student population at all levels were in state schools, 24% (1,649,953 students) were in Catholic schools, and 16% were in private schools. Catholic universities include the Pontifical University of Salamanca, founded in 1940 and dependent on the episcopate, and the Pontifical University of Comillas, founded in Madrid in 1904 by Jesuits, which has only an ecclesiastical faculty. Two more are church-related: the University of Deusto founded in Bilbao by Jesuits about 1890, and the University of Navarra of Pamplona which was canonically erected in 1960 and is dependent on Opus Dei. A Church Journalism School (Escuela de Periodismo de la Iglesia) was founded in Madrid in 1960 and is dependent on the Episcopal Conference.

The church's programme of social service is largely co-ordinated and promoted by Caritas Spain (Caritas Española), founded in 1942, and is involved in relief distribution, social action and development. Caritas is dependent on the Episcopal Commission for Caritative and Social Action and has sections in all 64 dioceses as well as 12,000 parish commissions. It is a member of Caritas Internationalis, in Rome. In addition there are a large number of other social service organizations.

IGLESIA EVANGELICA FILADELFIA. A mass charismatic movement involving 25,000 Spanish Gypsies, who itinerate ceaselessly in evangelism.

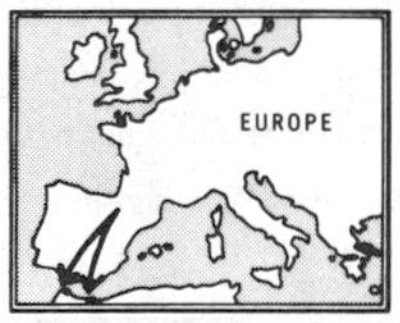


# Spanish North Africa

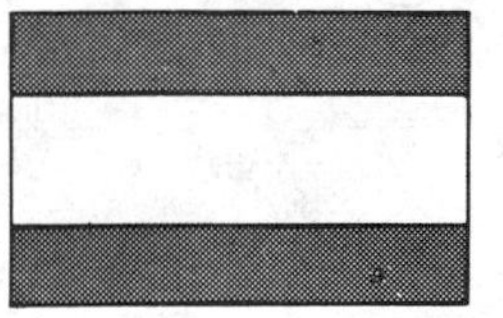

## SECULAR DATA

**STATE. Official name:** Spanish North Africa (Africa del Norte Español). This name was listed as a separate non-sovereign country by the United Nations until 1973 after which the areas were included under 'Spain'.
**Flag** (shown above right): That of Spain.
**Area:** 31 sq. km. (12 sq. miles). Description: 5 plazas (enclaves or fortified towns) in Morocco. Agricultural land: 0.0%.
**Government:** Overseas areas with special relationship to Spain, governed as parts of 2 provinces (1415 Portuguese possession, then Spanish: 1496 Melilla, 1580 Ceuta).
**Official language:** Spanish (*Español*).
**Chief cities:** Ceuta 67,187 (1970), Melilla 64,942.
**Foreign forces** (1976): 19,000 Spanish troops (Ceuta 9,000, Melilla 10,000).

**DEMOGRAPHY. Population:** 152,768 (census of 31.XII.1960. For 1970–2000 (UN), see last row of Table 1). Population density (1975): 5,581/sq. km. (14,454/sq. mile). Under 15 years: 44%. Household size: 4.5 persons.
**Major languages:** Spanish, Arabic.

**ETHNOLINGUISTIC GROUPS:** 90.3% Spanish (Spaniard), 6.5% Arab, 3.2% Maghreb Jewish.

**MONEY** (1977). **Monetary unit:** Spanish peseta (=100 céntimos); US$1=Ptas 68.00.
**National income per person:** US$2,000. Average annual family income: US$9,000.

TABLE 1. RELIGIOUS ADHERENTS IN SPANISH NORTH AFRICA

| Year | 1900 | | mid-1970 | | Annual change, 1970–1980 | | | | mid-1975 | | mid-1980 | | 2000 | |
|---|---|---|---|---|---|---|---|---|---|---|---|---|---|---|
| *Name* | *Adherents* | *%* | *Adherents* | *%* | *Natural* | *Conversion* | *Total* | *Rate* | *Adherents* | *%* | *Adherents* | *%* | *Adherents* | *%* |
| **Christians** | **20,970** | **90.0** | **149,000** | **90.3** | **1,660** | **0** | **1,660** | **1.06** | **156,400** | **90.4** | **165,600** | **90.5** | **263,900** | **91.0** |
| professing | 20,970 | 90.0 | 149,000 | 90.3 | 1,660 | 0 | 1,660 | 1.06 | 156,400 | 90.4 | 165,600 | 90.5 | 263,900 | 91.0 |
| Roman Catholics | 20,970 | 90.0 | 149,000 | 90.3 | 1,660 | 0 | 1,660 | 1.06 | 156,400 | 90.4 | 165,600 | 90.5 | 263,900 | 91.0 |
| Evangelical Catholics | 0 | 0.0 | 300 | 0.2 | 4 | 0 | 4 | 1.25 | 320 | 0.2 | 340 | 0.2 | 700 | 0.2 |
| nominal | 470 | 2.0 | 8,650 | 5.2 | 132 | 63 | 195 | 2.05 | 9,500 | 5.5 | 10,600 | 5.8 | 20,300 | 7.0 |
| affiliated | 20,500 | 88.0 | 140,350 | 85.1 | 1,528 | −63 | 1,465 | 1.00 | 146,900 | 84.9 | 155,000 | 84.7 | 243,600 | 84.0 |
| total practising | 19,475 | *95* | 126,310 | *90* | 1,375 | −56 | 1,319 | 1.00 | 132,210 | *90* | 139,500 | *90* | 194,880 | *80* |
| non-practising | 1,025 | *5* | 14,040 | *10* | 153 | −7 | 146 | 1.00 | 14,690 | *10* | 15,500 | *10* | 48,720 | *20* |
| Roman Catholics | 20,500 | 88.0 | 140,000 | 84.8 | 1,524 | −63 | 1,461 | 1.00 | 146,530 | 84.7 | 154,610 | 84.5 | 242,700 | 83.7 |
| Protestants | 0 | 0.0 | 350 | 0.2 | 4 | 0 | 4 | 1.08 | 370 | 0.2 | 390 | 0.2 | 900 | 0.3 |
| Evangelicals | 0 | 0.0 | 300 | 0.2 | 4 | 0 | 4 | 1.25 | 320 | 0.2 | 340 | 0.2 | 700 | 0.2 |
| Muslims | 930 | 4.0 | 10,600 | 6.4 | 156 | 0 | 156 | 1.38 | 11,300 | 6.5 | 12,160 | 6.6 | 20,100 | 6.9 |
| Jews | 1,400 | 6.0 | 5,300 | 3.2 | −16 | 0 | −16 | −0.31 | 5,200 | 3.0 | 5,140 | 2.8 | 5,800 | 2.0 |
| Baha'is | 0 | 0.0 | 100 | 0.1 | 0 | 0 | 0 | 0.00 | 100 | 0.1 | 100 | 0.1 | 200 | 0.1 |
| **Country's population** | **23,300** | **100.0** | **165,000** | **100.0** | **1,800** | **0** | **1,800** | **1.04** | **173,000** | **100.0** | **183,000** | **100.0** | **290,000** | **100.0** |

COLUMNS, ROWS. For meanings and definitions, see Codebook (Part 6). Note that, by definition, total 'Christians' = professing + crypto-Christians, which also = affiliated + nominal Christians. Percentages may not always total exactly, due to rounding.

NOTES ON RELIGIONS

BAHA'IS. Begun about 1955. In 1962 there were in the former Spanish Morocco 4 local spiritual assemblies and 6 groups, including an assembly in Ceuta and a group in Melilla.

EVANGELICAL CATHOLICS. Protestants affiliated to Protestant churches, but regarded by state and society as, or who profess to be, Roman Catholics.

JEWS. In 2 registered communities (Ceuta, Melilla). The total under the column 'Natural change' includes loss by emigration.

MUSLIMS. Arabs (Sunnis), in 2 registered associations. The

total under the column 'Natural change' includes immigration. Their mosques are dependent on the Habous of Tetouan.

ROMAN CATHOLICS. In 1900, there were 12,900 Catholics in Ceuta.

**NON-CHRISTIAN RELIGIONS. Islam** is the religion of 6% of the population of the 2 cities of Ceuta and Melilla, who are Arabs. Mosques are dependent on the Habous of Tetouan. Muslim schools are staffed by Moroccan teachers from Rabat who also provide religious instruction. There are 2 officially registered bodies: the Muslim Association of Melilla (Asociación Musulmana de Melilla), and the Zania Musulmana de Mohamadia Mahoma, in Ceuta

## CHRISTIANITY

CATHOLIC CHURCH. Arab Muslims gained control of North Africa at the end of the 7th century, and with the aid of Berbers they succeeded in conquering the Iberian peninsula itself soon afterwards. However by the end of the 15th century all Muslims had been driven out of Spain. The expansive Spanish and Portuguese Catholic regimes continued their conquest of ports along the coast of North Africa, with the sparsely-populated interior remaining in the hands of the nomadic Muslim Berbers. Ceuta was taken by the Portuguese in 1415 but passed to Spain in 1580, Melilla having already been conquered by Spain in 1496. In 1704, Our Lady of Africa church was built at Ceuta on the site of a former mosque. Although Morocco obtained its independence from France and Spain in 1956, Ceuta and Melilla have continued as possessions of Spain. Almost all the Spanish residents of the 2 cities are Catholics.

Ceuta is part of the Catholic diocese of Cadiz in Spain, and Melilla is in the diocese of Malaga, also in Spain. In 1958 there were in Ceuta 5 parishes, one archpriest, 9 priests, one congregation of brothers (AA) and 3 congregations of sisters; at the same time Melilla had 8 parishes, one archpriest, 13 priests, 3 congregations of brothers and 3 of sisters. There has been little change in this situation since 1958, except that by 1972 there were only 2 congregations of brothers in Melilla. In 1970 Ceuta and Melilla each had one designated and 2 elected representatives in the priests' senates of their respective dioceses.

PROTESTANT CHURCHES. Seventh-day Adventists include Ceuta and Melilla in the sphere of influence of their Spanish Church, but there are no organized Adventist churches in either city. The Church of God has one congregation in Ceuta, whereas Spanish Baptists and the Church of Christ have concentrated their attention in Melilla. All Protestant groups are small.

CHURCH AND STATE. Relations between church and state are the same as in metropolitan Spain.

TABLE 2.    ORGANIZED CHURCHES AND DENOMINATIONS IN SPANISH NORTH AFRICA

| Official name 1 | Begun 2 | Type 3 | Counc 4 | Congs 5 | Adults 6 | Affiliated 7 | Names, notes, and other statistics (see Codebook) 8 |
|---|---|---|---|---|---|---|---|
| Iglesia Católica (D Cádiz, D Málaga) | c 400 | R Lat | B.B.r | 13 | 100,000 | 140,000 | Ceuta is in D Cádiz (M=AA), Melilla in D Málaga (M=OFMCap,FSC). C=2+2+3. 24x. |
| Iglesia Cristiana Adventista del 7 Dia | | P Adv | x.... | | 50 | 100 | SDA. Unorganized Seventh-day Adventists, part of Spanish Church, SEuropean UM. |
| Iglesia de Cristo en Melilla | c1965 | P Dis | x.... | 2 | 50 | 100 | Ch of Christ in Melilla. Related to CC(Non-Instrumental) in Spain and USA. 1n. |
| Iglesia de Dios de España | | P Pe3 | Z.... | 1 | 20 | 50 | IDE. Church of God of Spain. M=IDE(Spain). 1 church in Ceuta. 1n. |
| Unión Evangélica Bautista Española | | P Bap | T.... | 1 | 30 | 100 | UEBE. Spanish Ev Baptist Union. M=UEBE(Spain),SBC(USA). Church in Melilla. |
| **Total affiliated (mid-1970)** | | | | 18 | 100,150 | 140,350 | Total denominations (1970) . . . 5. |
| **Total affiliated (mid-1975)** | | | | 18 | 105,800 | 146,900 | Total denominations (1975) . . . 5. |
| **Total affiliated (mid-1980)** | | | | 19 | 110,600 | 155,000 | Total denominations (1980) . . . 6. |

**NOTES ON TABLE ABOVE**
COLUMNS: for meanings and CODES (cols. 1, 3, 4, 8): see Codebook (Part 6). Column 1: **Boldface type** = church with over 10% of country's affiliated Christians.
NATIONAL COUNCILS (Column 4, 5th letter).
 r = Conferencia Episcopal Española (CEE) (Spanish Episcopal Conference).

PEOPLES (ethnolinguistic). Christians: 99.9% Spanish (Spaniard).

**COUNTRY-WIDE TOTALS**
EVANGELIZATION (see Part 5). 1900: 97%. 1970: 100%. 1980: 100%.
FOREIGN MISSIONARIES AND PERSONNEL (aliens from abroad) (1973). Total 52. From Western world. 52: About 50 Roman Catholics, about 2 Protestants.
INSTITUTIONS (church-operated) (1973). Total 2.
PERSONNEL. About 56 (4 national, 52 foreign).
SCRIPURE DISTRIBUTION (1975). Annual totals: 1,700 Bibles (commercial), 1,730 NTs (commercial).
SERVICE AGENCIES. About 5.

**ADDITIONAL DATA ON CHURCHES**
IGLESIA CATOLICA. Ceuta depends on D Cádiz & Ceuta (in Spain), and Melilla on D Málaga. Catholics. Virtually all Spaniards. Councils (column 4). In 1970, Ceuta and Melilla each had 2 elected representatives, and one nominated, on the priests' councils of their respective dioceses. Parishes (column 5). Ceuta 5, Melilla 8. Personnel. There has been practically no change since 1958, when there were in Ceuta one archpriest, 9 priests, one religious congregation for men (AA) and 3 for sisters; and in Melilla one archpriest, 13 priests, 3 religious orders or congregations for men (including OFMCap, FSC) and 3 for sisters.

# SRI LANKA

**Buddhists.** Recumbent Buddha in Asokaramya Temple, Colombo.

## SECULAR DATA

**STATE. Official name:** The Republic of Sri Lanka (Janarajaya) (Sri Lanka=Great and Beautiful Island). Unofficial name: Ceylon (former name), until 1972. Shortened forms of name: Sihala (Sinhalese), Ilam (Tamil). Adjective of nationality: Sri Lankan.
**Flag** (shown above right): Yellow border around maroon rectangle with yellow finials in each corner; yellow sword-carrying lion in centre; green and orange bars at hoist.
**Area:** 65,610 sq. km. (25,332 sq. miles). Agricultural land: 36.9%.
**Government:** Parliamentary socialist republic, since 1972 (6th century BC monarchy, 1505 Portuguese settlement, c1650 Dutch, 1802 British colony, 1948 Independence as British dominion of Ceylon, 1972 socialist republic).
**Legislature:** National State Assembly, 157 members.
**Official language:** Sinhalese (Sinhala).
**Chief cities:** capital Colombo 618,000 (1973), Dehiwala-Mount Lavinia 136,000, Jaffna 112,000.
**Political divisions:** (1963) 9 Provinces. (1975) 22 Districts; 12 Municipalities, 39 Urban Councils, 85 Town Councils, 542 Village Committees.
**Armed forces** (1976): Total 13,600 regular: army 8,900, navy 2,400, air force 2,300 (5 combat aircraft). Reserves: 13,100. Paramilitary forces: 16,300.
**Foreign forces** (1973): 100 USSR military advisors.

**DEMOGRAPHY. Population:** 12,711,143 (census of 9.X.1971. For 1970–2000 (UN), see last row of Table 1). Population density (1975): 213/sq. km. (552/sq. mile). Under 15 years: 42%. Growth rate (1975–80): 2.01% per year (births 2.59%, deaths -0.58%). Life expectancy (1975–80): 69.3 years. Household size: 5.4 persons.
**Major languages:** Sinhalese, English, Tamil, Punjabi, Malay, Dutch, Chinese, and others.
**Urban dwellers** (1970): 19.9%. Urban growth rate (1950–70): 3.9% per year.
**Labour force:** 35%.
**Refugees:** Internally displaced: 30,000 Tamils.
**Tourists** (1974): 85,011.

**ETHNOLINGUISTIC GROUPS:** 70.5% Sinhalese (42.2% Low Country, 28.8% Kandyan), 21.6% Tamil (11.0% Ceylonese, 10.6% Indian), 6.6% Moor (Muslim; Tamil-speaking) (6.3% Ceylonese, 0.3% Indian), 0.5% Punjabi (including Pakistani), 0.4% Burgher (Dutch/Portuguese/Asian) & Eurasian, 0.3% Malay, 0.1% European, Chinese (1,200), Arab, Vedda Aborigine (700).

**MONEY** (1977). Monetary unit: Sri Lanka rupee (=100 cents); US$1=SLRs 8.88.
**National income per person:** US$220. Average annual family income: US$1,188.
**Inflation:** (1970–74) 7.7% per year, (1975: consumer price index 145).
**Cost of living in capital** (1976): index 106 (Washington DC=100). Daily cost of living: US$18.

**HEALTH.** Hospitals: 457 (39,505 beds). Doctors: 2,120. Lepers: 10,300 (0.7 per 1,1000). Blind: 65,000. Psychotics: 110,000.

**EDUCATION.** Adult literacy: (1971) 78%. Education rate: 82%. Schools: 9,502. Universities: 4.

**LITERATURE.** Annual new book titles (1973): 1,502. Periodicals: 338. Scientific journals: 20. Newspapers: 25 dailies, 120 non-daily.

**COMMUNICATION** (per 1,000 people). Phones: 5. Radios: 39. Daily newspaper circulation: 42 copies.

TABLE 1. RELIGIOUS ADHERENTS IN SRI LANKA

| Year | 1900 | | mid-1970 | | Annual change, 1970–1980 | | | | mid-1975 | | mid-1980 | | 2000 | |
|---|---|---|---|---|---|---|---|---|---|---|---|---|---|---|
| *Name* | *Adherents* | *%* | *Adherents* | *%* | *Natural* | *Conversion* | *Total* | *Rate* | *Adherents* | *%* | *Adherents* | *%* | *Adherents* | *%* |
| Buddhists | 2,115,051 | 59.2 | 8,277,575 | 66.1 | 212,807 | −5,545 | 207,262 | 2.23 | 9,301,700 | 66.5 | 10,350,200 | 66.9 | 14,554,000 | 68.5 |
| Hindus | 828,000 | 23.2 | 2,177,000 | 17.4 | 30,740 | −1,000 | 29,740 | 1.27 | 2,335,700 | 16.7 | 2,474,400 | 16.0 | 2,817,000 | 13.2 |
| **Christians** | **378,859** | **10.6** | **1,083,125** | **8.7** | **25,083** | **−5,035** | **20,048** | **1.69** | **1,188,800** | **8.5** | **1,283,600** | **8.3** | **1,707,000** | **8.0** |
| crypto-Christians | 24,059 | 0.7 | 98,125 | 0.8 | 2,361 | 187 | 2,548 | 2.28 | 111,900 | 0.8 | 123,600 | 0.8 | 205,000 | 1.0 |
| professing | 352,800 | 9.9 | 985,000 | 7.9 | 22,722 | −5,222 | 17,500 | 1.62 | 1,076,900 | 7.7 | 1,160,000 | 7.5 | 1,502,000 | 7.0 |
| Roman Catholics | 289,100 | 8.1 | 879,000 | 7.0 | 20,390 | −3,790 | 16,600 | 1.72 | 966,400 | 6.9 | 1,045,000 | 6.8 | 1,387,000 | 6.5 |
| Protestants | 31,200 | 0.9 | 57,000 | 0.5 | 1,224 | −1,024 | 200 | 0.34 | 58,000 | 0.4 | 59,000 | 0.4 | 63,000 | 0.3 |
| Anglicans | 32,500 | 0.9 | 44,000 | 0.4 | 992 | −392 | 600 | 1.28 | 47,000 | 0.3 | 50,000 | 0.3 | 45,000 | 0.2 |
| Asian indigenous | 1,720 | 0.0 | 5,000 | 0.0 | 116 | −16 | 100 | 1.82 | 5,500 | 0.0 | 6,000 | 0.0 | 7,000 | 0.0 |
| affiliated | 378,859 | 10.6 | 1,083,125 | 8.7 | 25,083 | −5,035 | 20,048 | 1.69 | 1,188,800 | 8.5 | 1,283,600 | 8.3 | 1,707,000 | 8.0 |
| total practising | 359,920 | *95* | 931,490 | *86* | 21,321 | −6,647 | 14,674 | 1.45 | 1,010,480 | *85* | 1,078,220 | *84* | 1,365,600 | *80* |
| non-practising | 18,940 | *5* | 151,640 | *14* | 3,762 | 1,612 | 5,374 | 3.01 | 178,320 | *15* | 205,380 | *16* | 341,400 | *20* |
| Roman Catholics | 295,859 | 8.3 | 954,175 | 7.6 | 22,101 | −4,468 | 17,633 | 1.68 | 1,047,450 | 7.5 | 1,130,500 | 7.3 | 1,523,800 | 7.1 |
| Catholic pentecostals | 0 | 0.0 | 0 | 0.0 | 320 | 3,180 | 3,500 | 23.33 | 15,000 | 0.1 | 35,000 | 0.2 | 90,000 | 0.4 |
| Protestants | 40,000 | 1.1 | 65,250 | 0.5 | 1,477 | −502 | 975 | 1.39 | 70,000 | 0.5 | 75,000 | 0.5 | 85,000 | 0.4 |
| Evangelicals | 20,000 | 0.6 | 35,600 | 0.3 | 838 | −8 | 830 | 2.09 | 39,700 | 0.3 | 43,900 | 0.3 | 60,000 | 0.3 |
| Anglicans | 41,000 | 1.1 | 46,200 | 0.4 | 1,076 | −196 | 880 | 1.72 | 51,000 | 0.4 | 55,000 | 0.4 | 65,000 | 0.3 |
| Asian indigenous | 2,000 | 0.1 | 15,900 | 0.1 | 390 | 120 | 510 | 2.76 | 18,500 | 0.1 | 21,000 | 0.1 | 30,000 | 0.1 |
| Catholics (non-Roman) | 0 | 0.0 | 1,000 | 0.0 | 24 | 6 | 30 | 2.61 | 1,150 | 0.0 | 1,300 | 0.0 | 2,000 | 0.0 |
| Marginal Protestants | 0 | 0.0 | 600 | 0.0 | 15 | 5 | 20 | 2.86 | 700 | 0.0 | 800 | 0.0 | 1,200 | 0.0 |
| Muslims | 245,000 | 6.9 | 867,000 | 7.0 | 22,950 | 800 | 23,750 | 2.39 | 993,000 | 7.1 | 1,113,500 | 7.2 | 1,622,000 | 7.6 |
| Ahmadis | 0 | 0.0 | 1,000 | 0.0 | 24 | 6 | 30 | 2.61 | 1,150 | 0.0 | 1,300 | 0.0 | 2,000 | 0.0 |
| Non-religious | 0 | 0.0 | 50,000 | 0.4 | 2,068 | 8,432 | 10,500 | 10.71 | 98,000 | 0.7 | 155,000 | 1.0 | 427,000 | 2.0 |
| Sikhs | 4,000 | 0.1 | 25,000 | 0.2 | 591 | 9 | 600 | 2.14 | 28,000 | 0.2 | 31,000 | 0.2 | 40 000 | 0.2 |
| Atheists | 0 | 0.0 | 16,000 | 0.1 | 633 | 2,267 | 2,900 | 9.67 | 30,000 | 0.2 | 45,000 | 0.3 | 150,000 | 0.7 |
| Baha'is | 0 | 0.0 | 6,700 | 0.1 | 173 | 127 | 300 | 3.66 | 8,200 | 0.1 | 9,700 | 0.1 | 20,000 | 0.1 |
| Parsis | 500 | 0.0 | 1,800 | 0.0 | 40 | −20 | 20 | 1.05 | 1,900 | 0.0 | 2,000 | 0.0 | 2,000 | 0.0 |
| Chinese folk-religionists | 0 | 0.0 | 500 | 0.0 | 11 | −11 | 0 | 0.00 | 500 | 0.0 | 500 | 0.0 | 0 | 0.0 |
| Tribal religionists | 1,990 | 0.1 | 300 | 0.0 | 4 | −24 | −20 | −10.00 | 200 | 0.0 | 100 | 0.0 | 0 | 0.0 |
| **Country's population** | **3,573,400** | **100.0** | **12,514,000** | **100.0** | **295,100** | **0** | **295,100** | **2.11** | **13,986,000** | **100.0** | **15,465,000** | **100.0** | **21,339,000** | **100.0** |

COLUMNS, ROWS. For meanings and definitions, see Codebook (Part 6). Note that, by definition, total 'Christians' = professing + crypto-Christians, which also = affiliated + nominal Christians. Percentages may not always total exactly, due to rounding.
CENSUSES. **1881**: 61.5% Buddhists, 21.5% Hindus, 9.7% Christians, 7.2% Muslims. **1891**: 62.4% Buddhists, 20.5% Hindus, 10.0% Christians, 7.0% Muslims. **1901** (including 3,650 British and other foreign military personnel): 60.0% Buddhists, 23.2% Hindus, 9.9% Christians (8.1% Roman Catholics, 0.9% Anglicans, 0.8% Protestants), 6.9% Muslims. **1911**: 60.3% Buddhists, 22.9% Hindus, 10.0% Christians, 6.9% Muslims. **1921**: 61.6% Buddhists, 21.8% Hindus, 9.9% Christians, 6.7% Muslims. **1931**: 61.6% Buddhists, 22.0% Hindus, 9.8% Christians, 6.7% Muslims. **19.III.1946** (excluding 36,606 non-resident military and shipping personnel): 64.5% Buddhists, 19.8% Hindus, 9.1% Christians, 6.6% Muslims. **20.III.1953**: 64.3% Buddhists, 19.9% Hindus, 8.9% Christians (7.5% Roman Catholics, 0.6% Anglicans, 0.3% Methodists), 6.7% Muslims, 0.1% other religionists. **8.VII.1963**: 66.3% Buddhists, 18.4% Hindus, 8.3% Christians (7.2% Roman Catholics, 1.1% Protestants & Anglicans), 6.9% Muslims.

NOTES ON RELIGIONS
AHMADIS. Qadianis from Pakistan, begun 1951, now with 2 mosques.
ASIAN INDIGENOUS. In the 1901 census, 1,718 persons were reported as Independent Catholics; these belonged to the Independent Catholic Church of Ceylon, Goa and India (an 1866 schism of Latin-rite Catholics opposing Propaganda in Rome; obtained Jacobite (Antioch) succession of bishops; defunct 1950, though a few families still left in 1976). In 1970, this category was made up of about 9 denominations (see Table 2), mainly indigenous pencostals and isolated radio believers from both the Sinhalese and Tamil language groups.
ATHEISTS. 2 parties: Communist Party of Sri Lanka (pro-Soviet) 3,000 members, Communist Party of Sri Lanka/Marxist-Leninist (pro-Chinese) 1,000 members, both legal; Communist voters (election of 27.V.1970) 169,199 (3% of all votes). Also present are 100 USSR military advisers (1973). In the 1953 census, persons calling themselves freethinkers numbered 1,750, and agnostics 865.
BAHA'IS. Rapid growth from 8 local spiritual assemblies (1964) to 45 (1973).
BUDDHISTS. Theravada (or Hinayana, Little Vehicle); Sinhalese, also about 500 Chinese. There are 6,000 temples or monasteries, 17,000 monks (bhikkus) and 14,000 novices. A number of organized full-time Buddhist missionaries are active, e.g. at Colombo airport, in various cities of India through the Maha Bodhi Society of Ceylon, and through the Buddhist Training Centre for Missionaries.
CATHOLIC PENTECOSTALS (or, Catholic charismatics). The Catholic Charismatic Renewal began in 1971 and spread through retreats and prayer groups. In 1975, over 9,000 adults attended a charismatic rally. In early 1977, there were 70 Sinhalese-speaking and over 10 English-speaking prayer groups for adults, and over 100 for young people aged 7–12 years; and over 12,000 adults were active in the renewal, known locally as the Apostolate of Renewal, supported by the cardinal archbishop and several bishops; total charismatic community including children in 1977, 25,000. Members operate a farm to raise funds. There was in 1977 a considerable drop-out rate due to absence of follow-up and shortage of Sinhalese Bibles and literature.
CHRISTIANS. In 1722, Protestants numbered 424,392 (21% of the population of the island) through forced conversion by the Dutch Reformed Church. In 1801 the total of all Christians was 430,000 or 18% of the total population (342,000 Protestants registered as affiliated to the Dutch Reformed Church (recognized by the British in 1802 as the established church of the country) and its schools, 85,000 Roman Catholics, a few Anglicans). By 1810 under British rule and neglect, a massive defection was under way, almost all Protestants eventually returning to Buddhism or Hinduism. Subsequently the percentage of Christians in Ceylon increased slightly up to 1911, then declined gradually with each decade up to the present, when a small number are still emigrating (especially Protestant Burghers) but considerably larger numbers are being converted back to Buddhism.
COUNTRY'S POPULATION. By agreement in 1964 between Ceylon and India, 700,000 Indian Tamils, all aliens, were to be repatriated to India over a 15-year period, with up to 300,000 to be offered Ceylonese citizenship. By 1972 only 73,000 had in fact returned, but in 1973 the rate was increased to nearly 10,000 a month.
CRYPTO-CHRISTIANS. Christians affiliated to churches, but not known as such to the state because not recorded in censuses, of 3 kinds: (a) those in recognized or legal churches, (b) members of clandestine bodies, and (c) isolated radio and correspondence course believers.
HINDUS. Tamils from South India, mainly resident in north and west Ceylon and in Colombo. Most are Shaivites. The proportion is rapidly delining due to the repatriation of Indian Tamils (aliens) to India, at a peak rate in 1973 of 10,000 a month. The column 'Natural' above incorporates average emigration over 1970–80. Sects include the Ramarkrishna Order (5 centres). A neo-Hindu movement, the Theosophical Society in 1974 had 8 Lodges with 75 members.
MUSLIMS. Moors (Ceylonese and Indian) and Malays of the coast; mostly Sunnis (of the Shafiite rite) with some Shias south of Colombo. There is also an Ahmadiya Mission in Colombo (Qadianis; enumerated here as Muslims though declared non-Muslim by Pakistan) *Hajj prigrims to Mecca.* (1970) 152; (1976) 126.
PARSIS. Zoroastrians, originally from India (Bombay) and Persia.
PRACTISING CHRISTIANS. (1969) 41% of all eligible Catholics attend mass every Sunday (men 35%, women 45%, girls 50%, boys 39%). Weekly practice is however declining gradually.
PROFESSING CHRISTIANS. Professing Christians gradually rose to a peak of 10.0% by 1911, then gradually declined each subsequent decade (see censuses above). Although they are less than 8.0% of the total population, Christians form 48.4% of the population in Chilaw, 40.2% in Mannar, 28.6% in Puttalam, and 20.7% in Colombo district; elsewhere they form a small minority.
SIKHS. Punjabis from India.
TRIBAL RELIGIONISTS. Animistic Veddas, Sinhalese-speaking, still retain a widely-practised ancestral cult. The Vedda free ancestral spirits (Yakas) are controlled through emotional dances by shaman priests (*kapurala*). There has been a gradual change in Vedda population from 3,971 in 1901 (when 50% were reported as animists, 36% Hindus, 12% Buddhists, and 2% Christians) to 5,300 in 1911 and to 800 in 1964.

NON-CHRISTIAN RELIGIONS. **Theravada or Hinayana Buddhism** was introduced during the 3rd century BC, and is practised by a majority of the Sinhalese, accounting for about 67% of the population. Oppressed by Portuguese domination from 1505 on, then by the Dutch, and finally by the British up to 1948, Buddhism has for more than a century been seeking to create a modern renewal movement that will bring back its privileged and unique position of ancient times. The attempt to form a unified nationalist and social purpose is centered around 3 principal organizations: the Maha Bodhi Society of Ceylon, founded in 1891; Colombo Young Men's Association, founded in 1898; and the All Ceylon Buddhist Congress, founded in 1918. Displaying a certain anti-Christian bias, this movement has obtained control of a large number of public schools, formerly for the most part Christian, and has begun to provide them with Buddhist religious education.

Monasticism is well developed, with 6,000 monasteries, about 17,000 monks (bhikkus) and 14,000 novices, who apart from their religious vocation often serve as teachers. Lately there has been a decrease in religious vocations due primarily to the fact that, because of existing social inequality, religious leaders have increasingly stressed the importance of social action and development, as well as modernization and scientific education. On the other hand, the missionary spirit developed by the Maha Bodhi Society and the Buddhist Training Centre for Missionaries as well as other less important missionary societies, is one of the most active and astute of Asia. Numerous missions and some of the best exegetes of the Pali Canon are sent to the West.

In rural areas, Buddhism is tainted with shamanism and Hinduism against which the struggle, aided by public authorities, progresses slowly. From a geographical standpoint, Buddhism in Sri Lanka has its strength in the centre, south and west.

**Hinduism** is found mostly among Tamils who constitute approximately 22% of the population. The first Tamils came from southern India to northern Ceylon about 300 BC, but others were brought as labourers by the British during the last century. They are now spread throughout the island, with their greatest concentration in the north and east, notably in Colombo and on the great tea plantations.

**Islam** is the religion of 7% of the population, mostly Moors and Malays of the coast, with pockets in the interior in the region of Kandy. Major Muslim organizations include the Sri Lanka Assembly of Muslim Youth in Colombo and the Islamic Study Circle in Bandarawela.

CHRISTIANITY. According to tradition, Sri Lanka was first evangelized in the early days of the Christian era by the Apostle Thomas. In AD 537 a Nestorian Christian visitor reported the presence of many converts and churches. In more recent times, 3 different forms of Christianity have made their appearance under the 3 successive colonial powers. The Portuguese arriving in 1505 introduced Catholicism; the Dutch brought in Reformed Christianity 150 years later; and the British introduced Anglicanism during the 19th century. Most Christians live on the west coast. They make up 30% of Colombo's population and include Sinhalese, Tamils and Burghers. The latter, who are descendants of the Dutch and Portuguse colonists are of Western culture and almost entirely Christian; but they are diminishing in numbers through emigration. Of the over one million Christians, 88% are Catholics, most being descendants of converts from Portuguese times. The second largest denomination is the Anglican Church. Conversions to the churches are almost non-existent, and they are often critizised as complacent and indifferent to mission.

CATHOLIC CHURCH. Catholicism was introduced during the Portuguese era from 1505-1656. Although many Catholics later joined the Reformed Church during the Dutch regime, most returned to Catholicism under British rule 150 years afterwards. Church attendance remains high; a nation-wide survey in 1969 reported that 41% of Catholics eligible to attend mass did so each Sunday. Attendance varied from 29% in the diocese of Chilaw to 58% in the diocese of Jaffna. The relatively high percentages are notable because the Sunday chosen for the survey was during the period following the proclamation of the Buddhist Poya Day as the nation's official day of rest. In 1970, about 82% of all priests and 93% of all sisters were nationals. Vocations also are high.

A synod was held in November 1966 in the diocese of Kandy with active participation lay of persons, sisters and brothers. A provincial synod took place in 1971, but it was a canonical synod without lay participation. Nevertheless, the synod was preceded by a Pastoral Convention in 1968 where lay persons were represented.

PROTESTANT CHURCHES. The Dutch Reformed Church, now Presbytery of Ceylon, dates back to 1642. It is made up mostly of Burghers, and at one time it numbered 20,000 families; but its membership has been vastly reduced from 424,000 in 1722 to 3,000 by 1970, and continues to decrease due to emigration.

In 1804 the London Missionary Society began its first mission in Ceylon. In 1812, through the influence of William Carey, the Baptist Missionary Society opened work. The resulting Baptist church is now

autonomous but has only a small membership which continues to depend on outside financial assistance. British Methodists entered Ceylon in 1814; their church became independent in 1964. In 1967 it reported a membership loss of 3% over the previous year, nor has growth recovered much. American Congregationalists, the only mission from the USA in the earlier days, in 1816 opened an educational centre among the Tamils on the Jaffna peninsula; and in 1823 they founded Jaffna College, the first in Asia to offer modern higher education in English. In 1947 the Congregational Church in Ceylon became the Jaffna diocese of the Church of South India. Congregationalists, Methodists, Baptists and Presbyterians as well as Anglicans are all involved in the negotiations leading to a united Church of Lanka. In addition, there are also a few Pentecostal churches.

ANGLICAN CHURCH. The first Anglican services were held in 1796. The Church Missionary Society sent the first group of Anglican clergy to Ceylon in 1818, 2 years after Britain had wrested the island from the Dutch. Work began at Kandy, which had just come for the first time under European control. Many Dutch Reformed Christians became Anglicans, and other centres across Ceylon were opened within the next few years. Anglican institutions in 1973 included 6 colleges, 2 middle schools, and 2 teacher training colleges. Anglicans have grown more rapidly that most Protestant churches, and until 1970 formed part of the Church of India, Pakistan, Burma and Ceylon (CIPBC); now they form the 2 dioceses of the Church of Ceylon. The Anglican Church is involved in discussions for the formation of a united Church of Lanka.

INDIGENOUS CHURCHES. There has long been a handful of dissident or independent bodies in Ceylon. The first was the secession from Rome in 1866 of the Independent Catholic Church of Ceylon, Goa and India, who consisted of 5,000 Latin-rite Catholics who opposed Propaganda in Rome and then obtained Syrian Orthodox (Antioch) episcopal succession; they finally submitted to Rome in 1950 and remnants were deported to India. Other bodies include pentecostal and Reformed schisms.

CHURCH AND STATE. The constitution of 23 May 1972 stipulates in chapter II, article 6, that 'In the Republic of Sri Lanka, Buddhism, the religion of the majority of the citizens, will be accorded a place appropriate to it and, in consequence, the duty of the State will be to protect and favour it, at the same time assuring all religions of the rights guaranteed in Article 18, 1d'. This latter article specifies that these rights include 'the freedom to have or to adopt the religion or belief of one's own choice as well as the freedom, individually or in groups, in public or in private, to manifest one's religion or belief by worship, observance, practice and education'. Article 16, which lists the 'principles of action of the State', affirms in section 9 that 'The State will strive to create the economic and social climate necessary for permitting people of all faiths to make their religious

**Buddhists.** *Top.* Massive stupa Ruvanvalisaya at Anuradhapura. *Above.* Temple of the Tooth of Lord Buddha (Dalada Maligawa), Kandy.

principles a living reality'.

Land belonging to Buddhist temples, the result of royal endowments, is exempt from taxes, as well as certain properties of other religious groups in their capacity as charitable organizations.

During the colonial period and until 1961, the Christian churches enjoyed a privileged position because of their schools, the appointment of Christians as government functionaries, and the support they provided for the United National Party, which was the conservative party in control from 1947 to 1956 and which maintained in power a Westernized group owing its origin to colonialism. After 1956, under the first Bandaranaike government, Buddhism received considerable official support although it was not raised to the rank of state religion until 1972. The Ministry of Religious and Cultural Affairs (Sanskruthika Amathyansaya), created in 1956, has become an organization catering for the revival and protection of Buddhism. In 1961 the government nationalized without compensation all privately subsidized schools including the Catholic Church's 724 schools with 253,000 pupils; but it left the churches free to conduct schools without public financial aid. In 1961, in the same manner, religious personnel serving as nurses in state hospitals were dismissed. Also in 1956, the teaching of religion was made compulsory in all schools, in each case the religion to be taught being that of the parents.

After the seizure of the schools, the Catholic Church continued to support the UNP, prohibiting the faithful from voting for other parties. This direct intervention in politics did not cease until after the elections of 1970. During the events of 1971, especially the youth revolution, the majority of Catholics did not participate, although the movement found sympathizers among Catholic youth. The churches as a whole, as with the other institutions of the country, did not become involved. Nevertheless, after having pledged their moral support to the government, Protestant authorities through the National Christian Council, and Catholics through the cardinal-archbishop of Colombo, sent to the government in 1972 a memorandum requesting the revision of 2 proposed laws, 'Commissions of Criminal Justice' and the 'Amendment Bill', which were judged to be excessively repressive.

In 1966 Sunday was abolished as a day of rest and was replaced by Poya, a day of special significance to Buddhists. In 1972, however, Sunday was restored to its former position.

In late 1975, church union between Anglicans, Methodists, Presbyterians, CSI and Baptists was finally ready, and the united Church of Lanka was to be inaugurated on 16 November 1975, the bishops having been already elected. Shortly beforehand, the country's supreme court pronounced the proposed basis of union to be in conflict with the constitution of the country, enforcing abandonment of the inauguration and an indefinite delay in the creation of the new church.

INTERDENOMINATIONAL ORGANIZATIONS. The National Christian Council of Sri Lanka was founded in 1923. Its relative lack of activities and activism tends to reflect the absence of a dynamic witness which characterizes individual churches. It maintains the Study Centre for Religion and Society, founded by Methodists, but makes little use of its work or facilities. The interdenominational Christian Institute for the Study of Religion and Society, founded in 1959 and related to that in Bangalore, South India carries on studies of the sociological character of the churches and society, especially in the Tamil region of the island. Another co-operative organization is the Sodepax Sri Lanka Committee.

Concerning interreligious dialogue, the Congress of Religions, begun in 1961 for 'service to the nation through religious harmony', gives as its goal the promotion of mutual understanding and the creation of social services with a spiritual emphasis, such as the Leprosy Association of Sri Lanka. It was also responsible for the creation of the Inter-Religions Council, composed of Buddhist, Hindu, Christian (Anglican, Presbyterian, Catholic and Methodist), Muslim, Jewish and Zoroastrian leaders. The Council of Religions Batticaloa consists of the various religious leaders of the town of Batticaloa and is neither a regional nor a national organization. Buddhist-Christian study groups are also active at the Vidyodaya Buddhist university.

BROADCASTING. In 1955, the Audio-Visual Aids Department of the National Christian Council of

India began a half-hour programme over Radio Ceylon, which reached India as well; however, in 1957, the government discontinued religious broadcasting. Lutheran Hour programmes being transmitted over Radio Ceylon were then changed to FEBC, Manila. Sri Lanka has recently allowed religious broadcasting again over government radio, and these programmes (including those prepared by WEC from UK) are increasingly popular. Programmes from abroad can also be heard from FEBC (Manila), and FEBA (Seychelles). Programmes for FEBA in Sinhalese and Tamil are prepared by the popular studio Back to the Bible, in Colombo. For Catholics, Sri Lanka is a member of UNDA. Catholic programmes are at present prepared in the studios of the Sri Lanka Broadcasting Corporation, but a Catholic sound recording studio is under construction.

In 1978, Trans World Radio (TWR) completed at Puttalam a new superpower 400,000-watt medium-wave installation in Sri Lanka, for daily programmes in several Indian and other languages.

## BIBLIOGRAPHY


*A history of the Diocese of Colombo*. Ed F.L. Beven. Calcutta: Times of Ceylon, 1946. 426p. (Anglican).

*Buddhism in Ceylon and studies on religious syncretism in Buddhist countries*. H. Bechert. London: Brill, 1978. 360p.

*Ceylon church history*. W.L.A.D. Peter. Colombo: Catholic Press, 1963.

'Ceylon', *Pro Mundi Vita* (Brussels), 3 (1964).

*National Catholic directory of Sri Lanka, 1978*. Ed J.B.C. Anandappa. Colombo: Archbishop's House, 1978. 520p.

*Religion and ideology in Sri Lanka*. F. Houtart. Bangalore: TPI (and Colombo: Hansa), 1974.

'Sociology and anthropology of religion in Sri Lanka', *Social compass*, XX, 2 (1973).


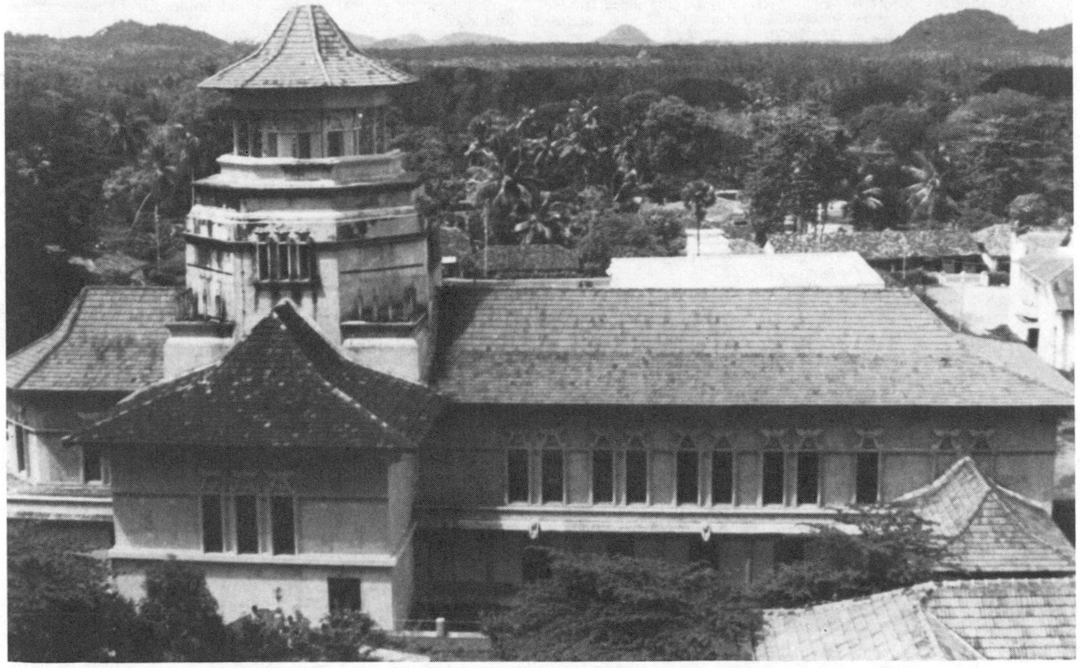

**Church of Ceylon, Diocese of Kurunagala.** Anglican cathedral at Kurunagala (Kandy), incorporating Sinhalese and Buddhist architectural features.

TABLE 2. ORGANIZED CHURCHES AND DENOMINATIONS IN SRI LANKA

| Official name 1 | Begun 2 | Type 3 | Counc 4 | Congs 5 | Adults 6 | Affiliated 7 | Names, notes, and other statistics (see Codebook) 8 |
|---|---|---|---|---|---|---|---|
| Assemblies of God in Sri Lanka | 1925 | P Pe2 | ZF... | 14 | 1,350 | 3,000 | M=AoG(USA). Originated from AoG in South India. HQ Colombo 7. 32n,2s(27). |
| **Catholic Church in Sri Lanka:** | 1517 | R Lat | P.F.R | 339 | 553,400 | 954,175 | *Romanu Katolike Sabhava*. C=7+6+24,1p,3q,1s,W=41%. 595nx,432m,2361w,P=76%,23953Yy. |
| M Colombo | 1845 | R Lat | Ps | 87 | 285,400 | 492,106 | Catholics: 30% city of Colombo; & fishermen. 231 215 1225 79 11883 |
| D Chilaw | 1939 | R Lat | Ps | 48 | 117,900 | 203,281 | Catholics mainly in fishing villages. W=29%. 82 16 212 70 5099 |
| D Galle | 1893 | R Lat | Ps | 105 | 16,800 | 29,000 | Sinhalese fishermen; Tamil tea estate workers. 50 7 178 65 701 |
| D Jaffna | 1845 | R Lat | Ps | 51 | 78,400 | 135,131 | Tamil fishermen, except near Anuradhapura. W=58%. 91 27 408 73 3495 |
| D Kandy | 1883 | R Lat | Ps | 21 | 33,600 | 58,000 | Scattered tea estate Tamils; Kandy, Sinhalese. 82 128 253 94 1760 |
| D Trincomalee-Batticaloa | 1893 | R Lat | Ps | 27 | 21,300 | 36,657 | Tamil fishing villagers, Sinhalese colonists. 59 39 85 70 1015 |
| Ceylon Pentecostal Mission | 1923 | I pe2 | Z.... | 53 | 5,000 | 10,000 | Communal property. M=FFFM(Finland). Tamils. 10n,G=4.6%pa,1p(9),W=80%,175Y,100z. |
| Christian Brethren | | P CBr | x.... | 1 | 50 | 100 | *Plymouth Brethren*, *Open Brethren*. Small group meeting in Colombo 4. |
| Church of Ceylon: | 1796 | A Hig | AWE.W | 155 | 30,500 | 46,200 | *Lanka Sabhawa*. Until 1910, in CIPBC. In 1900, 32,500 Anglicans. 104n,5x,197Y,993y. |
| D Colombo | 1845 | A Hig | A | 127 | 25,000 | 38,400 | M=CMS. 49% Sinhalese, 38% Tamil, 11% Burgher, 1% White. 1u(17). 80 4 164 778 |
| D Kurunagala | 1950 | A Hig | A | 28 | 5,500 | 7,800 | Centre of island. Decreasing. 1d,1e,4r,W=48%. 24 1 33 215 |
| Church of Scotland | | P Ref | Rwc.W | 1 | 50 | 100 | Single congregation in Colombo, supported by Ch of Scotland, Overseas Council. |
| Church of South India: D Jaffna | 1816 | P uni | .we.W | 31 | 5,525 | 20,000 | Congregationalist. M=UCBWM. Tamils. HQ Vaddukoddai. 80n,2f,W=61%,24Y,85y,61z. |
| Isolated radio churches | 1952 | I rad | ..... | 90 | 1,800 | 3,600 | Radio believers, mainly aged 12–25. R=4400(WEC,FEBA),T=8000(EHC,VOP,TEAM,ICI). |
| Jehovah's Witnesses | 1910 | M Jeh | x.... | 9 | 315 | 600 | *Watch Tower*. *IBSA*. Active witnessing under way by 1926. HQ Colombo 3. 39Y. |
| Lanka Christian Mission | 1908 | I int | ....w | 5 | 300 | 500 | M=India Christian Mission, based in Eluru, Andhra Pradesh (India). 2f. |
| Methodist Church of Ceylon | 1814 | P Met | VWE.W | 141 | 14,227 | 25,504 | Autonomous conf 1964. M=MMS(UK),VEM. 46n,6x,G=1.8%pa,2r(2400),1u,W=46%,472Yy,136z |
| New Apostolic Church | c1970 | C CAp | x.... | | 500 | 1,000 | In Canada Bezirk, *NAK*. World HQ Dortmund (FR Germany). Rapid growth as in India. |
| Presbytery of Ceylon | 1642 | P Ref | F...W | 17 | 1,800 | 3,000 | *Dutch Ref*. 40% Burgher, 30% Sinhalese,18% Tamil. Emigrating. 8n,G=–5.9%pa,1s,30Yy. |
| Presbytery of Lanka | 1953 | I Ref | R...W | 8 | 250 | 800 | Schism ex DRC (Presbytery of Ceylon). Rapidly declining. 1n,1x,W=46%,9Yy,10z. |
| Salvation Army | 1883 | P Sal | xwF.W | 195 | 3,727 | 5,000 | *Galavima Hamudava. Sri Lanka Terr*. 1 Division, 5 Districts. 100n,8x,G=1.1%pa,1s. |
| Seventh-day Adventist Church | 1920 | P Adv | x.... | 20 | 1,629 | 3,000 | *SDA, Sri Lanka Union*. 9n,2x,89mw,12f,G=8.0%pa,1H,1j,1s,25t(1303),W=75%,164Y,100z. |
| Sri Lanka Baptist Union | 1812 | P Bap | Tv..W | | 1,622 | 2,500 | *SL Baptist Sangamaya*. M=BMS(UK). Decline from 3,309 Baptists in 1900. 9f,1u. |
| Sri Lanka Lutheran Church Council | 1924 | P Lut | L.... | 18 | 226 | 546 | M=IELC(India),LC Missouri Synod(USA); in tea estates of Nuwara Eliya. 3f,5t(145),52Yy. |
| Swedish Pentecostal Mission | 1948 | P Pe2 | Z.... | 10 | 300 | 500 | *Svenska Fria Mission*. M=SFM(Sweden). HQ Colombo 6, also Nugegoda. 10f. |
| United Pentecostal Church | | P Pe1 | x.... | 12 | 403 | 1,000 | *Jesus Only Church*. M=UPC(USA). Unitarian Pentecostals. HQ Dehiwala. 6n,5m. |
| Other Protestant denominations | | P | ..... | | 500 | 1,000 | Total about 10 (see list below). |
| Other indigenous churches | | I pen | ..... | | 500 | 1,000 | Total about 5, including: Zion Pentecostal Ch, and pentecostal bodies from India. |
| **Total affiliated (mid-1970)** | | | | **1,180** | **623,974** | **1,083,125** | **Total denominations (1970) . . . 34.** |
| **Total affiliated (mid-1975)** | | | | **1,220** | **684,800** | **1,188,800** | **Total denominations (1975) . . . 37.** |
| **Total affiliated (mid-1980)** | | | | **1,270** | **739,500** | **1,283,600** | **Total denominations (1980) . . . 40.** |

NOTES ON TABLE ABOVE

COLUMNS: for meanings and CODES (Cols 1, 3, 4, 8): see Codebook (Part 6). Column 1: **Boldface type** = church with over 10% of country's affiliated Christians.

NATIONAL COUNCILS (Column 4, 5th letter).

R = Bishops' Conference of Sri Lanka (BCSL) (Lanka Raja Guru Sammelanaya).

W = National Christian Council of Sri Lanka (NCCSL).

w = associated with NCCSL.

*Other national councils*. Evangelical Alliance of Sri Lanka (EASL) (members individuals, congregations and agencies; affiliated to WEF).

OTHER PROTESTANT DENOMINATIONS. These include: Christian Fellowship Centre, Christian Inland Mission (Christian Enquiries), Christian Nationals Evangelism Commission (1972), Ch of Christ (Non-Instrumental), Evangelical Alliance Mission (TEAM) (1955), World-Wide Missions (1963).

UNITING CHURCHES. Negotiations for organic union were under way in 1980, under the name Church of Lanka (Lanka Sabhava), between: Ch of Ceylon (Anglican), Ch of South India (D Jaffna), Methodist Ch of Ceylon, Presbytery of Lanka, Sri Lanka Baptist Sangamaya. In November 1975 the envisaged union had been indefinitely abandoned due to legal action.

**PEOPLES** (ethnolinguistic). Christians: 70.0% Tamil, 24.0% Sinhalese, 4.1% Burgher & Eurasian, 0.9% European (White), Vedda Aborigine, Chinese (40).

**COUNTRY-WIDE TOTALS**

EVANGELIZATION (see Part 5). 1900: 30%. 1970: 48%. 1980: 55%. *Mass evangelism*. 1972, Morris Cerullo charismatic campaign (140,000 attenders, 80% Buddhists); 1978, Here's Life Colombo (CCCI; 3,500 evangelized, 2,050 decisions). *Radiophonic evangelism*. Annual listeners' letters (1975): about 4,400 (2,600 WEC, 1,100 FEBA, et alia). Bible correspondence courses: EHC, VOP, TEAM, ICI, et alia.

FOREIGN MISSIONARIES AND PERSONNEL (nationals serving abroad) (1973). Total 90 in Australia, France, India, Kenya, Malaysia, Nigeria, Pakistan, UK, USA et alia: 36 Sinhalese and Tamil indigenous, 30 Roman Catholics, 20 Anglicans, 4 Protestants.

FOREIGN MISSIONARIES AND PERSONNEL (aliens from abroad) (1973). Total 350. *From Western world*. 298: about 230 Roman Catholics, 63 Protestants (29 in 5 UK societies, 19 in 15 USA societies, 10 in 1 Sweden society, 4 in 2 WGermany, societies, 1 in 1 Canada society), 5 Anglicans in 3 UK societies. *From Communist world*. 2 Roman Catholics from Poland. *From Third World*. 50: about 32 Roman Catholics from India, 14 Protestants from India and Japan, 4 Indian indigenous.

INSTITUTIONS (church-operated) (1973). Total 130, including 70 higher schools (11 minor seminaries), 20 medical centres, 9 religious communities, 3 research centres, 11 seminaries (7 Protestant, 4 RC), 1 university.

PERIODICALS. About 70 titles (3 Anglican, 3 SDA, 2 Salvation Army).

PERSONNEL. About 4,513 (4,163 national, 350 foreign).

RELIGIOUS LIBRARIES. About 25.

SCRIPTURE DISTRIBUTION (1975). Annual totals: 4,127 Bibles (4% free, 89% subsidized, 7% commercial), 24,954 NTs (62% free, 33% subsidized, 4% commercial), 87,447 UBS portions, 270,900 UBS selections. *Translations completed*. Portion: 3 languages since 1739. NT: 3 languages since 1776. Bible: Sinhala in 1823.

SERVICE AGENCIES. About 45, including BCSL, CCCI, CEF, CLC, CLS, CWF, CWM, EASL, FABC, MTS, NCCSL, SCM, SEDEC, SLBS, SODEPAX, SU, WLC(EHC), YCW, YFC, YMCA, YWCA.

ADDITIONAL DATA ON CHURCHES

CATHOLIC CHURCH IN SRI LANKA. M Colombo = Kolombe Agre Raja Guru Padaviya; D Chilaw = Halavata Raja Guru Padaviya; D Galle = Galle Raja Guru Padaviya; D Kandy = Nuvara Raja Guru Padaviya. *New jurisdictions*. In 1972, D Badulla was formed out of D Kandy; in 1975, PA Anuradhapura was created. *Catechumens*. (1959) 1,247; (1961) 1,052; (1963) 1,035. *Annual baptisms*. (1972) 93.2% infant, 6.8% adult. *Priests*. In 1970, about 82% nationals, 18% expatriates (most of the latter being from 40 to 70 years old). *Sisters*. About 93% nationals, 7% expatriates (including 75 Asians). In addition to the statistics in the table, there are other contemplative sisters. *Catholic charismatics* (1977). Over 12,000 involved adults in 200 prayer groups, including many priests and religious, and several bishops including the bishop of Chilaw. *Seminarians* (1972). 130 secular, 117 religious. *Catechists*. Totals (1970): 36 pastoral workers, 60 full-time catechists, 400 part-time. *Indigenous religious congregations*. Brothers: 48 Brothers of St Joseph (begun 1964). Sisters: 111 Congregation of the Sisters of the Holy Angels (begun 1903). *Main foreign orders and congregations*. Priests (with over 50 members): OMI, SJ, OSB Sylvestrins. Brothers (with over 50): FSC, PFM, Brothers of St Vincent de Paul. Sisters (with over 100 members): 586 Sisters of the Holy Family, 205 Apostolic Carmel, 157 Franciscan Missionaries of Mary, 141 Sisters of Charity of Jesus.

*Catholic organizations*. The Bishops' Conference of Sri Lanka (Lanka Raja Guru Sammelanaya) is a member of FABC. No national presbyteral or pastoral councils have been formed. The Ceylon Conference of Major Religious Superiors, Brothers' Subsection, has its secretariat in Bangalore, India. Lay organizations include the Catholic Union, YCW, Legion of Mary and St. Vincent de Paul Society.

The Holy See had no diplomatic relations with Sri Lanka until 1976, when relations were set up and a pro-nuncio resident in Colombo was appointed.

The office of the Social Communications of the FABC is found in Sri Lanka. Catholic institutions at Kandy include the Social and

Economic Development Centre (SEDEC), an organization sponsored by the episcopate which is a member of CIDSE in Belgium; and the Satyodaya Encounter and Social Research Centre. There is also a National Pastoral Institute.

The Catholic Church by 1973 had retained influence in 44 primary and 40 secondary schools, and had 20 schools unsubsidized by the state serving 25,000 students of whom 75% were Catholic. Further nationalizations of church schools occurred in 1976. The Church operates 17 professional training schools, 3 social service training centres, and Aquinas University College in Colombo. There are 6 Catholic dispensaries and clinics, 24 orphanages with 2,000 children, and 8 homes for the handicapped and aged.

CHURCH OF CEYLON. In Sinhalese: Lanka Sabhawa. Since 1970, composed of 2 Dioceses formerly in the Church of India, Pakistan, Burma & Ceylon, left over after that church entered the union churches in India (CNI) and Pakistan. *Personnel* (1977). 110 priests (1 expatriate), 22 lay workers (4 women), 21 lay readers (1 woman). Seminarians 7.

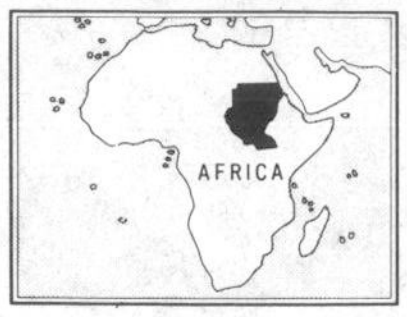


# SUDAN

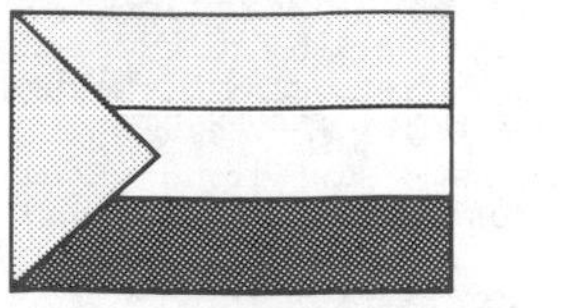

## SECULAR DATA

**STATE. Official name:** The Democratic Republic of the Sudan (Jumhuriyat as-Sudan ad-Dimuqratiyah). Adjective of nationality: Sudanese.
**Flag (shown above right):** Green triangle: red, white, and black stripes.
**Area:** 2,505,813 sq. km. (967,500 sq. miles). Agricultural land: 12.4%.
**Government:** One-party republic, since 1971 (1820 Ottoman rule, 1885 independent theocratic Mahdist state, 1899 Anglo-Egyptian condominium, 1956 Independence as republic, 1958 military junta, 1964 civilian rule, 1969 military junta, 1971 one-party republic).
**Legislature:** People's Assembly, 250 members.
**Official language:** Arabic (spoken by 51%).
**Chief cities:** capital Khartoum 261,840 (1971), Omdurman 258,530, Khartoum North 127,670, Port Sudan 110,090.
**Political divisions:** 9 Provinces, 84 Local Government Areas.
**Armed forces** (1976): Total 52,600 regular: army 50,000, navy 600, air force 2,000 (50 combat aircraft). Paramilitary forces: 3,500.
**Foreign forces** (1973): 500 USSR military advisers.

**DEMOGRAPHY. Population:** 14,171,732 (census of 3.IV.1973. For 1970–2000 (UN), see last row of Table 1). Population density (1975): 7/sq. km. (19/sq. mile). Under 15 years: 44%. Growth rate (1975–80): 3.18% per year (births 4.75%, deaths –1.57%). Life expectancy (1975–80): 51.1 years.
Household size: 5.2 persons.
**Major languages:** Arabic, English, Dinka, Nuer, Bari, Shilluk, Azande, Beja, Nuba, Nubian Hausa, Fur and over 130 minor languages.
**Urban dwellers** (1970): 10.0%. Urban growth rate (1950–70): 4.2% per year.
**Labour force:** 32%.
**Refugees** (1977): 91,000 from Ethiopia, rising (1978) to 200,000. Exiles abroad: 11,000 Sudanese in Ethiopia. By 1975 most of the 500,000 refugees from the civil war in the South had returned.

**ETHNOLINGUISTIC GROUPS:** 46.0% Sudanese Arab (Gaaliin, Guhayna, Jamala, Kababish, Kawahla, Messiria, Selim, Shaiqiya, et alii), 25.5% Nilotic (11% Dinka, 5% Nuer, 2.6% Bari, 2% Shilluk, 1.5% Latuka, 0.7% Murle, 0.4% Anuak, 0.1% Acholi, Fajulu, Kakwa, Toposa, Jie, Didinga), 5.6% Azande (with Moru-Mangbetu, Fertit, Madi), 5.6% Nuba (1.9% Koalib, Talodi, Tumtum, Kadugli, Heliban), 5.0% Beja, 3.6% other Sudanic (Ndogo, et alii), 3% West African (1.7% Fulani, 0.8% Kanuri, 0.5% Hausa), 2.2% Fur, 2.0% Nubian, 1% Fung (Prenilote) (Ingessana, Gule, Berta, Koma, Uduk), 0.2% Egyptian, Indo-Pakistani (3,500), Greek (2,000), Syrian, Galla, Jewish, Armenian, & numerous smaller tribes.

**MONEY** (1977). **Monetary unit:** Sudanese pound (=100 piastres =1,000 millièmes); US$1 = S£0.40.
**National income per person:** US$190. Average annual family income: US$988.
**Inflation:** (1970–74) 13.7% per year, (1975) 24% per year (consumer price index 170).
**Cost of living in capital** (1976): index 119 (Washington DC = 100). Daily cost of living: US$35.

**Health.** Hospitals: 122 (15,391 beds). Doctors: 1,263. Lepers: 100,000 (5.5 per 1,000). Blind: 110,000. Psychotics: 140,000. Criminals: 60,000.

**EDUCATION.** Adult literacy: (1956) 12%, (1966) 15%. Education rate: 61%. Schools: 4,530. Universities: 2.

**LITERATURE.** Annual new book titles (1973): 104. Periodicals: 30. Newspapers: 22 dailies, 12 non-daily.

**COMMUNICATION** (per 1,000 people). Phones: 3. Radios: 80. TV sets: 4. Daily newspaper circulation: 8 copies.

TABLE 1. RELIGIOUS ADHERENTS IN THE SUDAN

| Year | 1900 | | mid-1970 | | Annual change, 1970–1980 | | | | mid-1975 | | mid-1980 | | 2000 | |
|---|---|---|---|---|---|---|---|---|---|---|---|---|---|---|
| *Name* | *Adherents* | *%* | *Adherents* | *%* | *Natural* | *Conversion* | *Total* | *Rate* | *Adherents* | *%* | *Adherents* | *%* | *Adherents* | *%* |
| Muslims | 3,390,000 | 62.0 | 11,140,000 | 71.0 | 412,207 | 37,493 | 449,700 | 3.42 | 13,153,000 | 72.0 | 15,637,000 | 73.0 | 30,012,000 | 77.0 |
| Tribal religionists | 2,077,400 | 38.0 | 3,258,652 | 20.8 | 107,211 | –75,176 | 32,035 | 0.94 | 3,421,000 | 18.7 | 3,579,000 | 16.7 | 3,545,000 | 9.1 |
| **Christians** | **2,375** | **0.0** | **1,165,798** | **7.4** | **47,239** | **30,111** | **77,350** | **5.13** | **1,507,370** | **8.3** | **1,939,300** | **9.1** | **4,488,000** | **11.5** |
| crypto-Christians | 1,155 | 0.0 | 270,798 | 1.7 | 12,531 | 16,009 | 28,540 | 7.14 | 399,870 | 2.2 | 556,200 | 2.6 | 1,343,000 | 3.4 |
| professing | 1,220 | 0.0 | 895,000 | 5.7 | 34,708 | 14,102 | 48,810 | 4.41 | 1,107,500 | 6.1 | 1,383,100 | 6.5 | 3,145,000 | 8.1 |
| Roman Catholics | 200 | 0.0 | 605,000 | 3.8 | 23,473 | 10,277 | 33,750 | 4.51 | 749,000 | 4.1 | 942,500 | 4.4 | 2,144,000 | 5.5 |
| Anglicans | 20 | 0.0 | 250,000 | 1.6 | 9,746 | 3,814 | 13,560 | 4.36 | 311,000 | 1.7 | 385,600 | 1.8 | 896,000 | 2.3 |
| Orthodox | 1,000 | 0.0 | 30,000 | 0.2 | 1,097 | –97 | 1,000 | 2.86 | 35,000 | 0.2 | 40,000 | 0.2 | 75,000 | 0.2 |
| Protestants | 0 | 0.0 | 10,000 | 0.1 | 392 | 108 | 500 | 4.00 | 12,500 | 0.1 | 15,000 | 0.1 | 30,000 | 0.1 |
| affiliated | 2,375 | 0.0 | 1,165,798 | 7.4 | 47,239 | 30,111 | 77,350 | 5.13 | 1,507,370 | 8.3 | 1,939,300 | 9.1 | 4,488,000 | 11.5 |
| total practising | 2,260 | *95* | 990,930 | *85* | 40,153 | 25,594 | 65,747 | 5.13 | 1,281,260 | *85* | 1,648,400 | *85* | 3,590,400 | *80* |
| non-practising | 120 | *5* | 174,870 | *15* | 7,086 | 4,517 | 11,603 | 5.13 | 226,110 | *15* | 290,900 | *15* | 897,600 | *20* |
| Roman Catholics | 345 | 0.0 | 687,768 | 4.4 | 28,586 | 22,157 | 50,743 | 5.56 | 912,170 | 5.0 | 1,195,200 | 5.6 | 2,768,000 | 7.1 |
| Anglicans | 30 | 0.0 | 300,000 | 1.9 | 12,022 | 7,248 | 19,270 | 5.02 | 383,600 | 2.1 | 492,700 | 2.3 | 1,208,000 | 3.1 |
| Evangelicals | 30 | 0.0 | 300,000 | 1.9 | 12,022 | 7,248 | 19,270 | 5.02 | 383,600 | 2.1 | 492,700 | 2.3 | 1,200,000 | 3.1 |
| Orthodox | 2,000 | 0.0 | 107,200 | 0.7 | 3,917 | 163 | 4,080 | 3.26 | 125,000 | 0.7 | 148,000 | 0.7 | 275,000 | 0.7 |
| Protestants | 0 | 0.0 | 65,030 | 0.4 | 2,476 | 421 | 2,897 | 3.67 | 79,000 | 0.4 | 94,000 | 0.4 | 210,000 | 0.5 |
| Evangelicals | 0 | 0.0 | 63,000 | 0.4 | 2,397 | 413 | 2,810 | 3.67 | 76,500 | 0.4 | 91,100 | 0.4 | 203,000 | 0.5 |
| African indigenous | 0 | 0.0 | 5,600 | 0.0 | 229 | 111 | 340 | 4.66 | 7,300 | 0.0 | 9,000 | 0.0 | 25,000 | 0.1 |
| Marginal Protestants | 0 | 0.0 | 200 | 0.0 | 9 | 11 | 20 | 6.67 | 300 | 0.0 | 400 | 0.0 | 2,000 | 0.0 |
| Non-religious | 0 | 0.0 | 100,000 | 0.6 | 4,575 | 6,825 | 11,400 | 7.81 | 146,000 | 0.8 | 214,000 | 1.0 | 780,000 | 2.0 |
| Atheists | 0 | 0.0 | 30,000 | 0.2 | 1,254 | 746 | 2,000 | 5.00 | 40,000 | 0.2 | 50,000 | 0.2 | 150,000 | 0.4 |
| Baha'is | 125 | 0.0 | 500 | 0.0 | 19 | 1 | 20 | 3.33 | 600 | 0.0 | 700 | 0.0 | 2,000 | 0.0 |
| Jews | 100 | 0.0 | 50 | 0.0 | –5 | 0 | –5 | –16.67 | 30 | 0.0 | 0 | 0.0 | 0 | 0.0 |
| **Country's population** | **5,470,000** | **100.0** | **15,695,000** | **100.0** | **572,500** | **0** | **572,500** | **3.13** | **18,268,000** | **100.0** | **21,420,000** | **100.0** | **38,977,000** | **100.0** |

COLUMNS, ROWS. For meanings and definitions, see Codebook (Part 6). Note that, by definition, total 'Christians' = professing + crypto-Christians, which also = affiliated + nominal Christians. Percentages may not always total exactly, due to rounding.
CENSUSES. The religion question has never been asked.

NOTES ON RELIGIONS
AFRICAN INDIGENOUS. In 3 small groupings in 1970 (see Table 2).
ANGLICANS. Anglican growth has been extremely rapid because the CMS mission worked among the responsive Nilo-Hamitic and non-Nilotic tribes. The Azande were the first to respond in large numbers, then the Bari, Moru, Kuku and Moro (Nuba mountains).
ATHEISTS. Sudan Communist Party (SCP) (suppressed 1971); pro-Soviet): membership (1970) 10,000 active, and about 10,000 sympathizers. The party has changed over the years from being strongly anti-religious at its founding to formal recognition of Allah and the practice of prayer by members. Also present have been 500 USSR military advisers (1973), finally evicted in 1977.
BAHA'IS. First entered the Sudan before 1892. No growth; only 4 local spiritual assemblies in both 1964 and 1973.
COUNTRY'S POPULATION. During the civil war of 1963–72, an estimated one million persons in the South were killed or died of starvation or attrition, over 500,000 during the 3 years 1963–66. A large proportion of these were Christians.
CRYPTO-CHRISTIANS. Christians affiliated to churches but unknown as such to the state or to society at large.
MUSLIMS. Sunnis (mostly of the Malikite rite with some Shafiites). Sufi religious orders are strong in the Sudan; there are strong-based brotherhoods especially Khatimiya (Mirghaniya) with 1,000,000 followers and Ansar (Madhiya) with 3,000,000 (mostly small farmers and nomadic herdsmen, and including 200,000 armed tribesmen and 200,000 other militants), both suppressed after the Ansar revolt of 1970; other brotherhoods include Qadariya, Sammaniya, Idrisiya, Senusiya, Ismailiya, Shadhiliya and Tijaniya. The practice of Islam is widespread, Ramadan is generally observed, and many go on the hajj to Mecca. There are also about 3,500 Asians (Indo-Pakistanis and others). The spread of Islam has resulted in the islamization of tribes on the Ethiopian border, and major advances in the Darfur area among the Dadjo, Guimr, Tama, Masalit and Fur tribes, and in the Nuba mountains through the operating of schools. The Ahmadiya Mission (from Pakistan) has attempted work but is prohibited as heretical. *Missionaries*. There are a number of Egyptian missionaries sent by Al-Azhar University (Cairo), and also Egyptian and Sudanese missionaries of the Muslim Brotherhood (working in the Nuba Mountains and elsewhere). *Hajj pilgrims to Mecca*. (1968) 18,035; (1969) 20,495; (1970) 14,865; (1971) 29,004; (1972) 29,506; (1973) 33,222; (1974) 42,084; (1975) 24,209; (1976) 41,652.
PRACTISING CHRISTIANS. Catholics: in the north, Sunday mass attendance by Catholics fell from 40% of all Catholics in 1960 to 28% in 1970, then rose again by 1975. Anglicans: weekly church attendance 75% for tribal vernacular services, 45% for services in English or Arabic.
PROTESTANTS. Growth has been very slow because Protestant missions have worked only among the highly-resistant nomadic Nilotic peoples (Dinka, Nuer, Shilluk, et alia).
ROMAN CATHOLICS. In the year 1910, there were 1,344 Catholics (65% Whites).
TRIBAL RELIGIONISTS. Animists in the South (with a few peoples in the North), especially among tribes which over the last 100 years have resisted Christianity as well as Islam. Tribes over 60% traditionalist (animist) in 1972: Didinga (99%), Ingessana (99%), Meban (99%), Murle (99%), Nuer (99%), Topotha (99%), Anuak (95%), Dinka (95%), Lotuka (90%), Uduk (85%), Shilluk (75%), Koalib (70%), Krongo (70%).

**NON-CHRISTIAN RELIGIONS. Islam** is the professed religion of 72% of the population and has almost the complete allegiance of the peoples of the North. Muslims are Sunnis, mostly of the Malikite rite although some are Shafiites. Especially in the rural areas, Sudanese Islam is characterized by strong brotherhoods called tariqas, at the head of which are holy men (sheikhs or walis) who dictate the ritual and ascetic rules to be followed by their disciples. During the 20th century 2 tariqas have grown to national significance: the one-million-strong Khatmiya or Mirghaniya established in the 18th century and implanted to the north and east of Khartoum; and the 3-million-strong Ansar or Mahdiya, a xenophobic and eschatological movement founded by Muhammed al-Mahdi Ahmed in 1881, with its strength to the south and southwest of the capital. Since 1940 these 2 brotherhoods have played a significant role in national life, each supporting its own political party. Following the installation of a socialist regime in 1970 the Khatmiya and Ansar have been severely suppressed, the latter's structure being virtually eliminated following an armed revolt in April 1970. A similar fate befell those members of the intelligentsia professing atheism and Communism in July 1971. The cause of Islam is aided by the College of Arabic and Islamic studies founded at

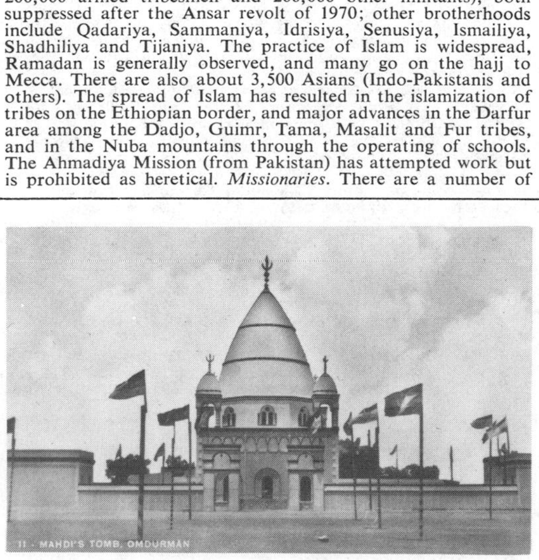


**Muslims.** *Left.* Mahdi's Tomb, Omdurman. Today the Mahdi's party (Ansar or Mahdiya) is still strong, with 3 million farmers and herdsmen as followers, despite government's crushing of 1970 Ansar revolt.

**Tribal religionists.** Animists number 3.5 million, still gradually increasing in numbers. *Left*. Azande witchdoctor conducts Avuré (Sorcerer's Dance). *Right*. A traditional spirit hut.

Omdurman in 1912.

**Traditional religions** retain the allegiance of 19% of the population and are still a significant force in the South. Those tribes which have been especially resistant to the claims of both Islam and Christianity include the following: Anuak, Didinga, Dinka, Ingessana, Koalib, Krongo, Topotha, Lotaka, Meban, Murle, Nuer, Shilluk and Uduk. Unlike other Nilotic peoples, the Shilluk are distinguished by their concept of divine kingship. The king (*reth*) is part of the royal clan founded by Nyikang, the first Shilluk king. Shrines and priests of Nyikang, the principal cult of the Shilluk, are found in various parts of the country, and spirit possession by Nyikang is a distinctive feature of the cult. While Nyikang is believed to care for the Shilluk people as a whole, the needs of smaller groups are covered through offerings by clan heads to their own ancestral spirits. There is no cult for the direct worship of God, Juok being approached primarily through the kings and Nyikang. Names for God of other Sudanese peoples include Mboli (among the Azande and Makaraka), Ngun (Bari, Fajulu), Tamukujen (Didinga), Nhialic (Dinka) and Kwoth (Nuer).

**CHRISTIANITY.** Coptic Christians were in Nubia by the 4th century. The first Melkite missionaries were sent by the emperor Justinian in AD 543; but the emperor's wife, Theodora, favouring the Monophysites, also sent her representative, Julian, who succeeded in converting the king of Nobatae. Monophysitism held sway in Nubia until about AD 1000 when a Nubian bishop introduced the Orthodox Melkite (Greek) tradition, provoking a split between the church in Nubia and the Copts in Egypt. Although Christianity continued to flourish up to the 14th century, Islam increasingly gained ascendency and ultimately extinguished all Christian presence in Nubia. The modern era of Catholic missions began in 1842, with the creation of the vicariate of Central Africa at Khartoum in 1846. Franciscans took charge of the vicariate in 1861, and in 1872 it was confided to the Verona Fathers under D. Comboni, their founder. The church was virtually destroyed during the Mahdist insurrection in 1881 but was begun again in 1898. Anglicans appeared the following year (1899) followed by other Protestant and Orthodox groups at and after the turn of the century.

**CATHOLIC CHURCH.** The Catholic Church is the largest Christian body in the Sudan, having grown from 250 in 1898 to 40,000 in 1930, 78,000 in 1949 and over 600,000 including catechumens by 1970. The church is divided into 7 ecclesiastical territories, but its strength is concentrated in the South. Many southern churches and all seminaries were destroyed during the civil war of the early 1960s, but rebuilding has been rapid since 1971. Minor seminaries were opened in Wau in 1968 and a major seminary at Juba in 1971. The first ordination of Sudanese priests was in 1944 and the first Sudanese bishop was consecrated in 1955.

Since 1972, following the Addis Ababa peace accord of 28 February putting an end to 17 years of civil war, and the granting of autonomy within the framework of national unity to southern Sudan (3 March), the Catholic Church has been able to re-organize its work. Pope Paul VI announced on 12 December 1972 the official institution of the hierarchy in the country, there being previous to that only vicariates and prefectures. There are now 2 archdioceses, Khartoum for the north and Juba for the south. The numerical size of the church has been underestimated in the past due to the constant movement of the population and the continuing return of refugees from both the exterior and interior of the country.

Sudanese clergy are mostly secular. Foreign priests are all Combonians, except for 3 Indian Jesuits who entered in 1971. All the bishops except the archbishop of Khartoum were Sudanese in 1975.

Few expatriate missionaries have received permission to work in the south. In 1964, 228 were expelled: 118 Verona priests, 12 Mill Hill priests and 98 Verona sisters.

One of the main tasks of the Sudanese episcopate at the present time is to stimulate the development of indigenous vocations. Members of local congregations have re-entered their original dioceses, although some sisters remain temporarily in Uganda awaiting the return of all the refugees. A new major seminary was opened at Bussere in the diocese of Wau in 1973.

**ANGLICAN CHURCH.** The CMS opened the first Anglican station at Omdurman in 1899 and from there an extensive work was developed in the southern region, making Anglicanism today the second largest Christian community in the Sudan. Until 1974 the Episcopal Church in the Sudan was under the Jerusalem Archbishopric; in 1976 it became autonomous as the Province of the Episcopal Church of the Sudan, with 4 dioceses.

**ORTHODOX CHURCHES.** Three Oriental Orthodox churches, all Monophysite in tradition, are found in the Sudan: Copts, who are Sudanese of Egyptian origin and form the largest of the Orthodox denominations; Ethiopians, who have only been organized as a religious community since 1965; and Armenians, a small group in Khartoum without a resident priest.

Eastern Orthodoxy is represented by the diocese of Nubia of the Greek Orthodox Patriarchate of Alexandria, with a resident archbishop and 14 parishes, although membership has declined significantly since 1950.

These various Orthodox bodies are largely self-contained ethnic groups, existing in the north and catering for their own members, with little impact on the wider community.

**PROTESTANT CHURCHES.** Six Protestant churches are at work in Sudan, including 2 groups of Presbyterians, both of which are related to the United Presbyterian Church in the USA. The Evangelical Church in the Sudan is composed of northern Sudanese of Egyptian origin, whereas the Church of Christ in the Upper Nile consists of southern indigenous peoples. The other Protestant churches are all active in the south and are the result of the outreach of 3 faith missions: the African Inland Mission,

**Catholic Church in the Sudan.** Easter communicants during mass movement in 1940. Catholics have grown phenomenally from 250 in 1898 to 40,000 in 1930 to over 1.0 million in 1978.

**Province of the Episcopal Church of the Sudan.** Kakwa-speaking Anglican Revivalists (Balokole) in their weekly after-church meeting, outside Yei church. On left, a home-made megaphone. *Inset.* Anglican cathedral in Khartoum, requisitioned by government in 1971 'as a security risk'.

the Sudan Interior Mission and the former Sudan United Mission. All missionaries attached to the southern churches were expelled during the 1960s, but most returned after 1973.

**CHURCH AND STATE.** During the Anglo-Egyptian Condominium, all churches were officially recognized. In the Self Government Statute of 1953, section 5(2), religious freedom was guaranteed in the following words: 'All persons shall enjoy freedom of conscience, and the right freely to profess their religion, subject only to such conditions relating to morality, public order or health as may be imposed by law'. This same section was repeated verbatim in the Sudan Transitional Constitution of 1956, and in the amended Transitional Constitution of 1964. The Republic Order No. 1 issued after the coup in May 1969 suspended the constitution but made no statement regarding religious freedom; it was therefore assumed that the previous provision was still valid.

The new constitution of 12 April 1973 begins in its Preamble with these words: 'In the name of God, the Compassionate, the Merciful, the creator of peoples and grantor of freedoms'; and the Preamble terminates with a reference to 'the will of God and his favour'. Part I, Article 9 states that 'The Islamic Law and custom shall be main sources of legislation. Personal matters of non-Muslims shall be governed by their personal laws'. Part II, Chapter 1, Article 15 expresses the view that the family, which is 'the foundation of society', should be 'guided by religion, morals and citizenship'. A key section of the constitution relating to religion is Article 16: '(a) In the Democratic Republic of the Sudan Islam is the religion and the society shall be guided by Islam being the religion of the majority of its people and the State shall endeavour to express its values. (b) Christianity is the religion (sic) in the Democratic Republic of the Sudan, being professed by a large number of its citizens who are guided by Christianity and the State shall endeavour to express its values. (c) Heavenly religions and the noble aspects of spiritual beliefs shall not be insulted or held in contempt. (d) The State shall treat followers of religions and noble spiritual beliefs without discrimination as to the rights and freedoms guaranteed to them as citizens by this Constitution. The State shall not impose any restrictions on citizens or communities on the grounds of religious faith. (e) The abuse of religious and noble spiritual beliefs for political exploitation is forbidden. Any act which is intended or is likely to promote

feelings of hatred, enmity or discord among religious communities shall be contrary to this Constitution and punishable by law.' Article 22 calls for the guidance of youth 'on the basis of religion and morals'; and Article 38 affirms that Sudanese are 'equal before the courts' and 'have equal rights and duties, irrespective of origin, race, locality, sex, language or religion'. Finally, Article 47 states: 'Freedom of belief, prayer and performance of religious practices, without infringement of public order or morals, is guaranteed'.

In practice, however, Christians have in the past been severely discriminated against. Under the Missionary Societies Act of 1962, section 3, it has been illegal for any church or 'missionary society' to perform in the Sudan 'any missionary act except in accordance with the terms of the licence granted by the Council of Ministers'; and although often applied for, licences were not issued. The provisions of the Missionary Societies Act, however, were never enforced in the North and are now in disuse in all parts of the country.

Since Independence in 1956, a number of administrative measures have been felt to be restrictive of church activities. The main sources of concern have been: the prohibition against increasing the number of foreign missionaries above the quota existing in 1956, the refusal to permit any expansion of the school system beyond its 1956 level, bureaucratic difficulties since 1958 in obtaining replacements for missionaries leaving the country permanently and in receiving permits to build churches and other church institutions, restrictions on the travel of all foreigners inside the country beginning in 1967, and the suspension of church-owned periodicals through the nationalization of the press in 1970. Relations between churches and government, which became very tense after the nationalization of all 295 mission schools in the South in 1957 and again after the expulsion of all foreign missionaries from the South in 1963-64, later showed a gradual improvement. These relations were indirectly affected by the fluctuating situation of the guerrilla movement in the South and also by relief and press campaigns abroad in favour of Sudanese refugees. Since 1955, accusations levelled against churches or church organizations, and fanned by the mass media, have created an atmosphere of suspicion around Christians in general and churchmen in particular.

On the other hand, there have also been numerous gestures of appreciation by the government, such as

the establishment in 1966 of a Catholic minor seminary at Khartoum, the 1968 decision providing for the secondment of a number of teachers from government elementary schools to be trained for teaching Christianity in the same schools, the creation of an Office for Christian Education (Maktab Taftish deen al Maseeh) in the Ministry of Education in 1969, the establishment at the same time in Khartoum of a Catholic apostolic delegation for the Red Sea countries which was elevated to the rank of an apostolic nunciature in 1972, the granting of permission in 1971 to 5 Indian Jesuits to enter the country for the purpose of opening a new major seminary at Juba, and other personal favours to churches and churchmen. The teaching of the Christian religion to Christian pupils in government elementary schools was approved in principle in 1968, and church buildings have been exempt from taxation.

During the summer of 1971, the WCC and the AACC, with the approval of the Sudanese government, acted as intermediaries between Khartoum and the South Sudan Liberation Movement (political arm of the Anya Nya guerrillas) with a view to ending the hostilities between them. The discussions took place in Addis Ababa, Ethiopia, and led to an agreement which was signed on 28 February 1972 by the 2 sides, as well as by the 3 delegates of the WCC and the AACC acting as witnesses. The main features of the agreement deal with the termination of the conflict, the reintegration of the guerrillas into Sudanese life, and the establishment of new political structures granting a large measure of self-government to the 3 Southern provinces grouped together into a single region. At the beginning of 1974, at the request of the missionaries, the Khartoum authorities facilitated the education of Christian students in state schools by providing a school in the capital where they could meet to receive religious instruction. In spite of all these gestures, however, in 1977 there was still widespread discontent across the South based on the conviction that government had not honoured the 1972 agreement, especially with regard to complete religious liberty and religious rights.

There is no government ministry dealing solely with religion, and there is no obligation that churches formally register with the government. The Ministry of the Interior is responsible for supervising the activities of churches and their foreign personnel. Minor educational matters are handled through the Office for Christian Education. The Sudan Council of Churches makes official approaches in the name of all its member Christian denominations, although questions concerning the Catholic Church are mainly dealt with between the government and the apostolic pro-nuncio.

**INTERDENOMINATIONAL ORGANIZATIONS.** The Sudan Council of Churches was established in 1965, being the successor to the Northern Sudan Christian Council. At present its membership includes 8 churches covering a wide Christian spectrum: Catholic, Orthodox, Anglican and Protestant, although the more conservative faith missions are not members. The council represents the churches before government, stimulates co-operation between churches, promotes observance of the Week of Christian Unity and co-ordinates the occasional diffusion of Christian programmes on Radio Sudan. It has been instrumental in obtaining Catholic recognition of non-Catholic baptism, and since the 1972 Addis Ababa agreement it has begun important relief and reconstruction work in the South. The council is affiliated with the NECC and the AACC. Four offices of the various denominations are especially charged with ecumenical relations and activities: the Sudan Catholic Information Office (SCIO), secretariat of Clergy House (Anglican), Christian Literature Centre (Presbyterian) and Coptic archbishopric.

**BROADCASTING.** Radio Omdurman (Broadcasting Service of the Democratic Republic of the Sudan) carries Muslim religious broadcasts in Arabic, and in principle accepts both Protestant and Catholic broadcasts also, and regular programmes are in fact transmitted weekly. The Sudan Council of Churches has a special body, the Interfaith Radio Committee. In December 1976 the SCC opened its own ecumenical radio station in Juba, sponsored by WACC and LWF. From abroad, Christian programmes in Arabic can be heard over international stations including ELWA (Liberia).

## BIBLIOGRAPHY

*A pilgrim church's progress.* O. Allison. London: Church Missionary Society, 1966. (By the Anglican bishop).
'A study of shamanism in the Nuba mountains', S.F. Nadel, *Journal of the Royal Anthropological Institute* LXXVI (1946), 25–37).
*Ambassadors by the Nile.* W.B. Anderson. London: USCL, 1963. 47p.
*Directory of the Christian churches in the Sudan, 1967.* Khartoum: Sudan Council of Churches, 1967. 45p.
*Divinity and experience: the religion of the Dinka.* G. Lienhardt. Oxford: Clarendon, 1961.
'Guinea and the Sudan'. Special note, *Pro Mundi Vita* (Brussels), 2 (1968).
*Islam in the Sudan.* J.S. Trimingham. London: Oxford, 1949.
*Mahdism and the Egyptian Sudan.* Wingate. London, 1967.
*Nuer religion.* E.E. Evans-Pritchard. Oxford: Clarendon, 1956. 335p.
'Some aspects of the spread of Islam in the Nuba mountains', R.C. Stevenson, in I.M. Lewis (ed), *Islam in tropical Africa* (London: Oxford, 1966), p. 208–232.
*The divine kingship of the Shilluk of the Nilotic Sudan.* E.E. Evans-Pritchard. Cambridge: University Press, 1948.
*The last of the Nuba.* L. Riefenstahl. London: Collins, 1976. 208p, mostly colour photographs. (On the Mesakin, an unevangelized people).
*The Mahdist state in the Sudan, 1881–1898.* P.M. Holt. London: Oxford, 1958.
*The people of Kau.* L. Riefenstahl. London: Collins, 1976. 224p, mostly colour photographs. (On the unevangelized Kau Nuba or South-East Nuba).
'The unreached people of Kau', D.B. Barrett, in C.P. Wagner & E.R. Dayton (eds), *Unreached peoples 1979.* Elgin, IL: David C. Cook, 1978).
*Through fire and water: 10 critical years in the life of the Church in the Southern Sudan, 1964–1974.* O Allison. London: Church Missionary Society, 1976. 110p. (By retired Anglican bishop).
'Two Nuba religions: an essay in comparison', S.F. Nadel, *American anthropologist*, LVII (1955), 661–679.


TABLE 2. ORGANIZED CHURCHES AND DENOMINATIONS IN THE SUDAN

| Official name 1 | Begun 2 | Type 3 | Counc 4 | Congs 5 | Adults 6 | Affiliated 7 | Names, notes, and other statistics (see Codebook) 8 |
|---|---|---|---|---|---|---|---|
| African Inland Church | 1936 | P int | xM..C | 5 | 250 | 1,000 | M=AIM(USA). Among Madi, Lotuka, Acholi. Obliterated in civil war. By 1977, 2f. |
| Armenian Apostolic Church (D Egypt) | c1900 | O Arm | Ew..K | 1 | 250 | 400 | Armenian residents, in north only. Under jurisdiction of AD Cairo. No priest. |
| **Catholic Church in the Sudan:** | 1842 | R Lat | P.SWS | 81 | 385,000 | 687,768 | *Catholikiyya.* 950 Greek Catholics. C=1+2+3. 3p,1s(39). 126nx,30m,188w,8829Yy |
| M Juba | 1927 | R Lat | Ps | 19 | 196,000 | 350,000 | In 1960, annual growth=15%. 1s(re-opened 1971). 29 5 21 2837 |
| D Malakal | 1933 | R Lat | Ps | 10 | 12,000 | 21,221 | In south, from Nile to Ethiopia. Shilluk, Nuer, Anuak. 9 0 5 793 |
| D Rumbek | 1955 | R Lat | Ps | 6 | 17,000 | 30,190 | Extreme south. Dinka. Life totally disrupted before 1970. 8 0 0 103 |
| D Tombora (PA Mopoi till 1974) | 1949 | R Lat | Ps | 9 | 79,000 | 140,694 | Azande. In 1960, G=25%pa. M=FSCJ. 1230z. 11 2 9 1134 |
| D Wau | 1913 | R Lat | Ps | 16 | 46,000 | 82,763 | 50% Jur, 20% Balanda, 15% Ndogo, 5% Dinka. 1s(1973). 12 8 11 1763 |
| M Khartoum | 1913 | R Lat | Pfscj | 13 | 30,000 | 54,250 | North. Mostly southerners. 1p,890z. 46 12 121 1719 |
| D El Obeid | 1960 | R Lat | Pfscj | 8 | 5,000 | 8,650 | North, southwest of Khartoum. 2p,650z. 11 3 21 480 |
| Church in the East Central Sudan | 1937 | P int | xM..C | 14 | 1,150 | 1,500 | *CECS. Ev Ch of Eastern Sudan.* M=SIM(USA,UK). Uduk, Meban, Shilluk. 2n, 5m,5f,1p. |
| Church of Christ in the Upper Nile | 1900 | P Ref | RuANK | 43 | 3,000 | 7,000 | *Presb Ch in Sudan.* M=UPUSA, expelled 1964–73. A=1956. Shilluk, Nuer. 8n,1f,1p. |
| Coptic Orthodox Church in the Sudan: | c 350 | O Cop | NwaNk | 25 | 52,000 | 90,000 | Under P Cairo. In Northern cities and towns; 800 Blacks, 1 Black priest. 2n,26x,8r. |
| D Khartoum & the South | 1947 | O Cop | Na | 14 | 27,000 | 50,000 | Archbishop and 14 priests. 3 churches in Khartoum, others scattered across country. |
| D Omdurman & the North | 1947 | O Cop | Na | 11 | 25,000 | 40,000 | Archbishop and 12 priests. Mostly Egyptians in Omdurman and along Nile river. |
| Episcopal Praisers | 1957 | I Ang | ..... | | 100 | 300 | *Tore (Trumpeters).* Strivers. Revivalists among Kakwa, Kuku, split ex Anglicans. |
| Eternal Life Church | 1977 | I pe2 | ..... | 2 | 200 | 500 | Split ex Episcopal Ch over healing campaigns. M=PEFA (Kenya). HQ Juba. 2n. |
| Ethiopian Orthodox Ch in the Sudan | 1965 | O Eth | Nwa.K | | 10,000 | 15,000 | Eritrean and Ethiopian refugees, across North and in NE. 1 primary school. 3x. |
| Evangelical Church in the Sudan | 1900 | P Ref | ...NK | 8 | 600 | 1,500 | *Injili Church.* In North. Sudanese Arabs of Egyptian origin. M=UPUSA. 6n,1k,1p,4r. |
| Evangelical Revival Church | 1970 | I pen | ..... | 10 | 300 | 800 | Moru revivalists. Split ex Episcopal Ch after veto on traditional Moru music. |
| Greek Orth P Alexandria: D Nubia | c1000 | O Ara | Cw.NK | 14 | 1,000 | 1,800 | *D Nubia & Ptolemais.* Greeks, Cypriots. Decline from 5,000 in 1950. Bishop,5x,1r. |
| Isolated radio churches | c1960 | I rad | ..... | 80 | 1,800 | 4,000 | Isolated Arab radio believers, mainly aged 12–25. R=400(TWR,RVOG&c),T=1000(ICI). |
| Jehovah's Witnesses | c1945 | M Jeh | x.... | 1 | 48 | 200 | *Watch Tower.* First active witnessing 1950. No recent baptisms; underground. |
| **Province of the Epis Ch of the Sudan** | 1899 | A Eva | AWAUK | 650 | 100,000 | 300,000 | 4 Dioceses. M=CMS(UK),BCMS. Bari, Azande, Moru. 91n,2x,500m,14f,1h,2r,20000Yy. |
| Sudanese Church of Christ | 1907 | P ind | ....C | 96 | 12,018 | 53,000 | In Nuba Mountains. 1920–62, M=SUM(UK,Australia). Koalib, Moro, Otoro. |
| Seventh-day Adventist Church | 1953 | P Adv | x.... | 1 | 20 | 30 | *SDA, Sudan Station,* Middle East Division. Small expatriate group in Khartoum. |
| Other Protestant denominations | | P | ..... | | 500 | 1,000 | Including Baptists, Churches of Christ (CMF), and others in the South. |
| **Total affiliated (mid-1970)** | | | | **1,040** | **568,236** | **1,165,798** | **Total denominations (1970) . . . 20.** |
| **Total affiliated (mid-1975)** | | | | **1,250** | **734,700** | **1,507,370** | **Total denominations (1975) . . . 21.** |
| **Total affiliated (mid-1980)** | | | | **1,460** | **945,200** | **1,939,300** | **Total denominations (1980) . . . 23.** |

**NOTES ON TABLE ABOVE**
COLUMNS: for meanings and CODES (cols. 1, 3, 4, 8): see Codebook (Part 6). Column 1: **Boldface type** = church with over 10% of country's affiliated Christians.
NATIONAL COUNCILS (Column 4, 5th letter).
- C = Association of Evangelical Christians of the Sudan (begun 1973).
- K = Sudan Council of Churches (SCC) (Maglis al Kanayis fi Sudan).
- k = formerly full member of SCC, withdrew temporarily in 1976.
- S = Sudan Episcopal Conference (SEC), also member of SCC.

PEOPLES (ethnolinguistic). Christians: about 56% Sudanic (20% Azande, 10% Moru-Mangbetu, 5.3% Nuba (1.7% Koalib, 1.5% Moro, 1.2% Otoro, 0.3% Shwai, 0.3% Labu, 0.2% Heiban, Krongo), 3% Madi, 18% Ndongo and other Sudanic), 35% Nilotic (10% Dinka, 5% Bari, 3% Shilluk, 3% Nuer, 0.2% Anuak, 13.8% other Nilotic (Acholi, Fajulu, Jur, Kakwa, Koma, Kuku, Latuka, Murle, Mondari, Padang, Pari, Prenilote, Topotha, Uduk)), 7% Arab (Egyptian, some Sudanese, 0.2% Syrian), 0.5% Amhara, 0.2% Greek, Idio, Mundu, Banda, Mittu, Balanda, Meban, Armenian, Nyimang, Temein, et alii.

**COUNTRY-WIDE TOTALS**
EVANGELIZATION (see Part 5). 1900: 8%. 1970: 30%. 1980: 35%. *Mass evangelism.* 1978, Here's Life Khartoum (CCCI). *Radiophonic evangelism.* TWR (370 listeners' letters a year), RVOG, ELWA, Radio Vatican, ICI, et alia.
FOREIGN MISSIONARIES AND PERSONNEL (nationals serving abroad) (1973) Totals 60: about 55 Roman Catholics and 5 Anglicans in Central African Republic, Uganda, Zaire et alia.
FOREIGN MISSIONARIES AND PERSONNEL (aliens from from abroad) (1973). Total 283. *From Western world.* 246: about 180 Roman Catholics, 52 Protestants (18 in 7 USA societies, 9 in 2 Switzerland societies, 9 in 3 Australia societies, 9 in 3 New Zealand societies, 4 in 3 WGermany societies, 3 in 2 Canada societies), 14 Anglicans (13 in 1 UK society, 1 in 1 USA society). Although all Protestant and Anglican missionaries were expelled in 1964, many missions had been allowed back by 1976. In 1977 these included AIM, CMS, SIM, UPUSA. *From Third World.* 37: 18 Orthodox from Egypt and Ethiopia, about 15 Roman Catholics mainly from India, 2 Protestants (AICMB from Kenya), 2 Anglicans.
INSTITUTIONS (church-operated) (1973). Total 60, including about 30 higher schools, 20 medical centres, 1 religious community, 4 seminaries (2 RC, 1 Protestant, 1 Orthodox).
PERIODICALS. About 12 titles.
PERSONNEL. About 1,843 in 1973 (1,560 national, 283 foreign).
RELIGIOUS LIBRARIES. 5.
SCRIPTURE DISTRIBUTION (1975). Annual totals: 1,860 Bibles (subsidized), 7,706 NTs (subsidized), 80,231 UBS portions, 88,486 UBS selections. *Translations completed.* Portion: 21 languages since 1905. NT: 13 languages since 1940.
SERVICE AGENCIES. About 27, including ACROSS, AICMB, CCCI, CWS, LWR, MAF, MAP, MCC, RSMT, SCC, SCIO, SEC, SFM, SNEM, WVI.

**ADDITIONAL DATA ON CHURCHES**
CATHOLIC CHURCH IN THE SUDAN. The civil war of 1964–72 began at a point when the Catholic Church was expanding in the south at a phenomenal rate. In 1960, growth was 15% per year in VA Juba and 25% per year in PA Mopoi, and the same a couple of years later in the other jurisdictions. A massive exodus of refugees began in 1961. In 1964, just before the expulsion of missionaries, the Catholic Church in the south numbered 401,000 baptized (Juba 215,000, Mopoi 88,000, Wau 63,000, Rumbek 25,000, Malakal 10,000); 30 Sudanese priests (first ordination 1944); and 90 seminarians. *Situation in 1970. North.* In the 2 northern vicariates, 80,000 Catholics from the south had taken refuge and opened various schools and facilities. Khartoum also has small Melkite (begun 1915, under P Antioch), Maronite (begun 1932, under P Antioch), Coptic and Armenian communities. Institutions in 1970: 30 schools (9,371 Sudanese pupils, half Muslims); 1 clinic; sisters in Omdurman hospital. *South.* Although numerous churches and all seminaries were destroyed in 1964–65, the situation has rapidly returned to normal. Since 1968 minor seminaries have been organized in VA Wau. Before 1972 most Catholics and two-thirds of the Sudanese clergy were refugees in neighbouring countries. After 1971 numbers of expatriates were again allowed into the south. *Annual baptisms.* (1972) 58.1% infant, 41.9% adult. *Priests.* After 1970 the number of Sudanese priests increased annually with new ordinations. *Brothers.* 17 Sudanese, 6 expatriates (in north only). *Sisters.* 56 Sudanese, 138 expatriates (in north only). *Seminaries.* Juba, re-established 1971; and Bussere (D Wau), opened 1973. *Catechists.* Total (1974) about 750 (Khartoum 46, El Obeid 49, Tombora 337, Wau 35). *Indigenous religious congregations.* Brothers: 3 Brothers of St Martin of Porres (D Juba; rising by 1978 to 27 professed, 14 novices, 42 aspirants), 10 St Josph's Brothers (begun 1954, D Wau). Sisters: 37 Sisters of the Sacred Heart (begun 1951, D Juba), 13 Nazareth Sisters of Wau (begun 1955), Sisters of Our Lady of Victories (begun 1960, PA Mopoi, all in exile in 1970). *Foreign congregations* (in 1970 only in the north). Priests: FSCJ. Sisters: Combonians (Pie Madri della Nigrizia). *New dioceses.* In November 1974, the 5 vicariates and 2 prefectures were elevated to be 2 metropolitan sees with 5 suffragan dioceses, as shown in the table above.
*Catholic organizations.* The Sudan Episcopal Conference (SEC) is an associate member of the Conference of Latin Bishops in the Arab Regions with headquarters in East Jerusalem, and a member of SECAM. There are no national presbyteral or pastoral councils, nor associations of religious personnel; but the following lay organizations are active: Legion of Mary, St Vincent de Paul St Anne League, St Augustine Society and Catholic Action.
The Holy See has diplomatic relations with the Sudan and is represented to government and the Catholic hierarchy by a pro-nuncio based in Khartoum.
The church supervises 6 primary and 2 secondary schools, 4 professional workshops, 4 social centres for home science and 3 orphanages. Catholic education is co-ordinated by the Diocesan Secretariat for Catholic Education, while social service work is supervised by Catholic Aid.
CHURCH OF CHRIST IN THE UPPER NILE. Rapid expansion from (1972) 52 small churches to (1978) 106 churches in 13 parishes with 44,800 adherents.
COPTIC ORTHODOX CHURCH IN THE SUDAN. *Churches.* (1977) 3 in Khartoum with 6 priests; others in Omdurman, El Obeid, Nuba Mountains (Kadugli, et alia), Sennar, and along the Nile. *Members.* Most are 4th- or 5th-generation immigrants from Upper Egypt, now Sudanese citizens. *Priests.* Mostly Egyptian citizens, and mostly monks, but with 1 Black priest and 800 Black members.
PROVINCE OF THE EPISCOPAL CHURCH OF THE SUDAN. Also known as the Episcopal Church in the Sudan. Formally inaugurated as an autonomous province within the Anglican Communion in October 1976, with 4 dioceses: Juba, Omdurman, Rumbek, Yambio; with 4 bishops and 114 clergy. *Membership.* 46% Bari, 40% Azande, 8% Moru, 3% Dinka. 3% Nuba. *Priests.* Growth by 1977 to 190 (2 expatriate). *Lay readers* (1977). 140 men, 84 women. *Seminarians.* 15.
SUDANESE CHURCH OF CHRIST. From 1920–62, the Sudan United Mission worked in the Nuba Mountains, building on earlier foundations. Until 1970 the church was known as the Church of Christ in the Nuba Mountains. *Districts.* (1978) 4 Districts: Kalib (5 main church centres, 39 churches), Heiban (3 centres, 21 churches), Southern Nuba Mountains (3 centres, 36 churches), Northern (everywhere outside Nuba Mountains; no churches, but 1,000 persons under instruction). *Baptized.* Membership, through adult baptism, has strict requirements. Total baptized (1920–1978) 2,568, of whom about 200 have subsequently died. *Non-baptized adults.* 9,450 adherents and catechumens (about 3,000). *Bible school.* In Omdurman, with 10 students. *Theological students.* 3 in Bukuru, Jos (Northern Nigeria).

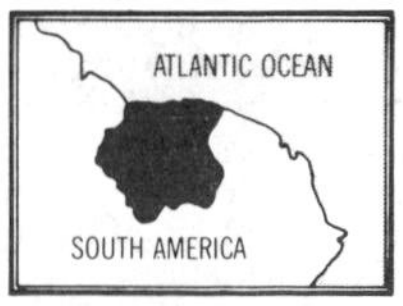


# SURINAME

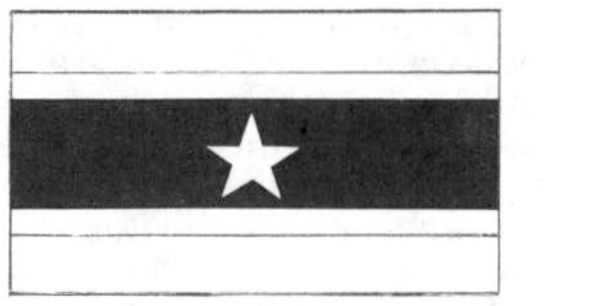

## SECULAR DATA

**STATE. Official name:** The Republic of Suriname (Surinam). Earlier name: Dutch Guiana. Adjective of nationality: Surinamese.
**Flag** (shown above right): Stripes of green, white, red, white, and green with yellow star in centre.
**Area:** 163,265 sq.km. (63,037 sq.miles). Agricultural land: 0.3%.
**Government:** Parliamentary state, since 1975 (1651 British settlement, 1667 Dutch colony, 1815 Dutch Guiana, 1954 autonomous territory of the Netherlands, 1975 Independence).
**Legislature:** Parliament (Staten), 39 members.
**Official language:** Dutch (*Nederlands-Vlaams*).
**Capital:** Paramaribo 182,100 (1964).
**Political divisions** (1974): 9 Districts.

**DEMOGRAPHY. Population:** 384,903 (census of 31.XII.1971. For 1970–2000 (UN), see last row of Table 1). Population density (1975): 3/sq.km. (7/sq.mile). Under 15 years: 48%. Growth rate (1975–80): 3.05% per year (births 4.19%, deaths −0.65%, emigrants −0.49%). Life expectancy (1975–80): 67.2 years. Household size: 4.1 persons.
**Major languages:** Dutch, English, Sranang Tongo (Sranan) (Surinamese), Hindustani, Javanese, Chinese, Arawak, Carib, Arabic, and 10 smaller languages.
**Urban dwellers** (1970): 37.8%. Urban growth rate (1950–70): 3.5% per year.
**Labour force:** 28%.
**Tourists** (1970): 17,462.

**ETHNOLINGUISTIC GROUPS:** 37.7% Creole (African Negro/White), 31.0% Indian (Hindustani; decreasing to under 15% by 1976), 14.0% Javanese, 11.0% Bush Negro, 2.0% Chinese (8,000) (Hakka, some Cantonese), 2.0% Amerindian (7,400) (Arawak, Carib, Trio, Waiyana, Akuliyo), 1.4% White (mainly Dutch, including Jewish), 0.9% Syro-Lebanese.

**MONEY** (1977). **Monetary unit:** Surinam guilder or florin (= 100 cents); US$1 = SFls 1.77.
**National income per person:** US$830. Average annual family income: US$3,403.
**Inflation:** (1970–74) 5.3% per year (1975: consumer price index 154).
**Cost of living in capital** (1976): index 122 (Washington DC=100).
Daily cost of living: US$43.

**HEALTH.** Hospitals: 16 (1,910 beds). Doctors: 180. Lepers: 3,600 (8.5 per 1,000). Blind: 1,300. Psychotics: 3,300.

**EDUCATION.** Adult literacy: (1964) 84%. Education rate: 80%. Schools: 584. Universities: 1.

**LITERATURE.** Periodicals: 10. Newspapers: 6 dailies.

**COMMUNICATION** (per 1,000 people). Phones: 31. Radios: 250. TV sets: 76. Daily newspaper circulation: 57 copies.

TABLE 1. RELIGIOUS ADHERENTS IN SURINAM

| Year | 1900 | | mid-1970 | | Annual change, 1970–1980 | | | | mid-1975 | | mid-1980 | | 2000 | |
|---|---|---|---|---|---|---|---|---|---|---|---|---|---|---|
| *Name* | *Adherents* | % | *Adherents* | % | *Natural* | *Conversion* | *Total* | *Rate* | *Adherents* | % | *Adherents* | % | *Adherents* | % |
| **Christians** | **35,100** | **46.2** | **187,000** | **50.4** | **14,491** | **2,654** | **17,145** | **6.64** | **258,300** | **61.2** | **358,450** | **73.0** | **679,700** | **75.2** |
| professing | 35,100 | 46.2 | 187,000 | 50.4 | 14,491 | 2,654 | 17,145 | 6.64 | 258,300 | 61.2 | 358,450 | 73.0 | 679,700 | 75.2 |
| Protestants | 16,000 | 21.1 | 96,500 | 26.0 | 7,294 | 1,021 | 8,315 | 6.40 | 130,000 | 30.8 | 179,650 | 36.6 | 341,600 | 37.8 |
| Roman Catholics | 19,000 | 25.0 | 89,000 | 24.0 | 7,102 | 1,678 | 8,780 | 6.94 | 126,600 | 30.0 | 176,800 | 36.0 | 334,500 | 37.0 |
| Anglicans | 100 | 0.1 | 1,500 | 0.4 | 95 | −45 | 50 | 2.94 | 1,700 | 0.4 | 2,000 | 0.4 | 3,600 | 0.4 |
| nominal | 2,000 | 2.6 | 29,721 | 8.0 | 1,986 | −638 | 1,348 | 3.81 | 35,400 | 8.4 | 43,200 | 8.8 | 94,900 | 10.5 |
| affiliated | 33,100 | 43.5 | 157,279 | 42.4 | 12,505 | 3,292 | 15,797 | 7.09 | 222,900 | 52.8 | 315,250 | 64.2 | 584,800 | 64.7 |
| total practising | 28,130 | *85* | 110,100 | *70* | 8,753 | 2,304 | 11,057 | 7.09 | 156,030 | *70* | 220,670 | *70* | 380,100 | *65* |
| non-practising | 4,970 | *15* | 47,180 | *30* | 3,752 | 988 | 4,740 | 7.09 | 66,870 | *30* | 94,580 | *30* | 204,700 | *35* |
| Roman Catholics | 18,000 | 23.7 | 80,000 | 21.5 | 6,631 | 2,059 | 8,690 | 7.35 | 118,200 | 28.0 | 166,900 | 34.0 | 316,400 | 35.0 |
| Protestants | 15,000 | 19.7 | 74,429 | 20.1 | 5,723 | 1,284 | 7,007 | 6.91 | 101,350 | 24.0 | 144,500 | 29.4 | 260,700 | 28.8 |
| Evangelicals | 12,000 | 15.8 | 19,000 | 5.1 | 1,547 | 283 | 1,830 | 6.68 | 27,400 | 6.5 | 37,300 | 7.6 | 72,300 | 8.0 |
| Anglicans | 100 | 0.1 | 1,000 | 0.3 | 65 | −35 | 30 | 2.61 | 1,150 | 0.3 | 1,300 | 0.3 | 2,600 | 0.3 |
| Marginal Protestants | 0 | 0.0 | 1,000 | 0.3 | 30 | 10 | 40 | 3.33 | 1,200 | 0.3 | 1,400 | 0.3 | 3,000 | 0.3 |
| Non-White indigenous | 0 | 0.0 | 800 | 0.2 | 53 | −23 | 30 | 3.16 | 950 | 0.2 | 1,100 | 0.2 | 2,000 | 0.2 |
| Catholics (non-Roman) | 0 | 0.0 | 50 | 0.0 | 3 | −3 | 0 | 0.00 | 50 | 0.0 | 50 | 0.0 | 100 | 0.0 |
| Muslims | 7,600 | 10.0 | 78,000 | 21.0 | −1,300 | −120 | −1,420 | −1.98 | 71,700 | 17.0 | 63,800 | 13.0 | 108,500 | 12.0 |
| Ahmadis | 0 | 0.0 | 2,000 | 0.5 | 50 | 30 | 80 | 3.33 | 2,400 | 0.6 | 2,800 | 0.6 | 6,000 | 0.7 |
| Hindus | 20,100 | 26.4 | 60,000 | 16.2 | −4,000 | −1,000 | −5,000 | −12.50 | 40,000 | 9.5 | 10,000 | 2.0 | 16,000 | 1.8 |
| Tribal religionists | 10,640 | 14.0 | 26,000 | 7.0 | 1,563 | −1,163 | 400 | 1.43 | 28,000 | 6.6 | 30,000 | 6.1 | 45,000 | 5.0 |
| Afro-American spiritists | 1,500 | 2.0 | 11,000 | 3.0 | 700 | −400 | 300 | 2.40 | 12,500 | 3.0 | 14,000 | 2.9 | 20,000 | 2.2 |
| Non-religious | 0 | 0.0 | 3,650 | 1.0 | 274 | 41 | 315 | 6.49 | 4,850 | 1.1 | 6,800 | 1.4 | 17,000 | 1.9 |
| Baha'is | 0 | 0.0 | 3,000 | 0.8 | 150 | 50 | 200 | 5.00 | 4,000 | 0.9 | 5,000 | 1.0 | 13,000 | 1.4 |
| Buddhists | 460 | 0.6 | 1,000 | 0.3 | 61 | −41 | 20 | 1.82 | 1,100 | 0.3 | 1,200 | 0.2 | 1,500 | 0.2 |
| Jews | 200 | 0.3 | 650 | 0.2 | 20 | 0 | 20 | 2.67 | 750 | 0.2 | 850 | 0.2 | 1,500 | 0.2 |
| Chinese folk-religionists | 400 | 0.5 | 600 | 0.2 | 36 | −26 | 10 | 1.54 | 650 | 0.2 | 700 | 0.1 | 800 | 0.1 |
| Other religionists | 0 | 0.0 | 100 | 0.0 | 5 | 5 | 10 | 6.67 | 150 | 0.0 | 200 | 0.0 | 1,000 | 0.1 |
| **Country's population** | **76,000** | **100.0** | **371,000** | **100.0** | **12,000** | **0** | **12,000** | **2.84** | **422,000** | **100.0** | **491,000** | **100.0** | **904,000** | **100.0** |

COLUMNS, ROWS. For meanings and definitions, see Codebook (Part 6). Note that, by definition, total 'Christians' = professing + crypto-Christians, which also = affiliated + nominal Christians. Percentages may not always total exactly, due to rounding.
CENSUSES. Percentages have fluctuated considerably from year to year due to continuous immigration and emigration. **1960:** 26.1% Protestants, 25.2% Muslims, 24.5% Hindus, 20.9% Roman Catholics, 2.2% tribal religionists, 0.9% Chinese folk-religionists and Buddhists, 0.2% Jews. **1961:** 25.7% Protestants, 24.7% Hindus, 24.5% Muslims, 21.6% Roman Catholics, 2.4% tribal religionists, 0.8% Chinese folk-religionists and Buddhists, 0.3% Jews. **1962:** 24.9% Protestants, 24.3% Hindus, 23.2% Muslims, 21.3% Roman Catholics, 5.3% tribal religionists, 0.8% Chinese folk-religionists and Buddhists, 0.2% Jews. **31.III.1964:** 27.0% Hindus, 25.0% Protestants, 21.9% Roman Catholics, 19.7% Muslims, 5.6% tribal religionists, 0.8% other religionists.

**NOTES ON RELIGIONS**
AFRO-AMERICAN SPIRITISTS. Bush Negroes follow Winti and other cults derived from Ashanti religion (from Ghana). There are also many followers of Vodoun and Obeah.
AHMADIS. Begun 1956; Qadianis (world HQ Rabwah, Pakistan).
BAHA'IS. Rapid growth in local spiritual assemblies, from none in 1964, to 23 in 1973. Converts from Hinduism and Islam.
BUDDHISTS. Chinese, first arriving as contract workers after 1863, then staying on as shopkeepers in rural areas.
COUNTRY'S POPULATION. Before 1960, the annual rate of growth had reached a high peak of 4.34% per year. Due to the heavy emigration to the Netherlands during 1964–75 it fell to 2.57% per year (1970–75), then after Independence in 1975 increased again with a rate of 3.45% per year being anticipated for 1980–85.
HINDUS. Hindustani-speaking East Indians (mainly small farmers), with 2 branches: Arya Dewaker (orthodox), and Sanathan Dharm (modernizing). Steadily-increasing emigration (62,700 from 1964–71, and a total of 80,000 from 1965–75) culminated in an exodus of 12,000 a month in 1975 to the Netherlands before Independence, leaving only a small Hindu minority. In the column 'Natural change', this emigration is included, averaged over the decade 1970–80.
JEWS. Two communities, Dutch and Portuguese, originally refugees in 1639 from persecution in Brazil.
MUSLIMS. In 3 groups: Javanese (Shafiite Sunnis) from Indonesia who form 14% of the population, mainly as small farmers; East Indians (Hindustanis); and Syro-Lebanese. There is also an Ahmadiya Mission (enumerated here although declared non-Muslim by Pakistan).
NON-WHITE INDIGENOUS. In about 3 Black and Amerindian groups in 1970 (see Table 2).
OTHER RELIGIONISTS. Including Rosicrucians (1 AMORC centre).
TRIBAL RELIGIONISTS. Shamanism is practised among pagan Bush Negroes (Heiden-Bosnegers, 16,875 in the 1964 census) and among many of the 7,400 lowland or jungle Amerindians, especially among the Caribs and in the interior.

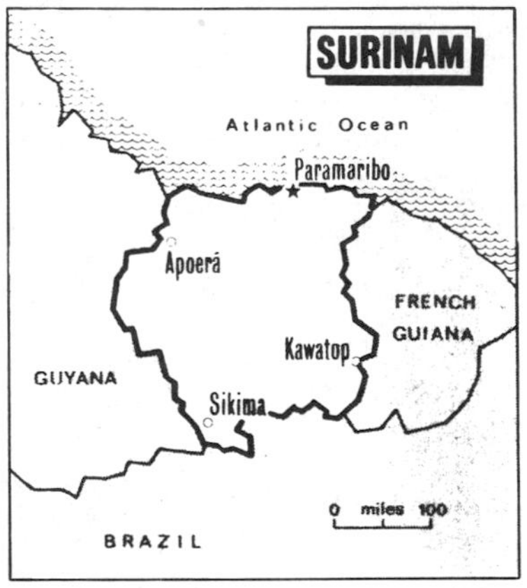


**NON-CHRISTIAN RELIGIONS. Islam** is represented by the Surinam Muslim Association (Surinaamse Islamitisch-Vereniging), with its seat at Paramaribo. Muslims are Javanese, East Indians, and Syro-Lebanese.

**Hinduism** is found in 2 branches: Arya Dewaker, an orthodox group which maintains the caste system; and Sanathan Dharm, a group with modernizing tendencies under Western influence, which has abandoned the caste system. Vast numbers of Hindus have emigrated since 1964, chiefly to the Netherlands.

**Traditional tribal religions** of shamanistic type are still practised by Bush Negroes and jungle Amerindians.

**Judaism** exists among 2 European groups, the Portuguese Israelite Community (Portuguees-Israëlitische Gemeente) and the Dutch Israelite Community (Nederlands-Israëlitische Gemeente).

## CHRISTIANITY

CATHOLIC CHURCH. Although Catholic priests resided briefly in Surinam during 1683-86 and 1786–93, work of a permanent nature was not begun until 1817. At that time a prefecture was established which was elevated to vicariate in 1852. Redemptorists and Oblates (OMI) arrived in 1865 and devoted themselves to the development of schools and charitable institutions, in addition to parish activity. The diocese of Paramaribo, which covers the whole of Surinam, was erected in 1958.

The Roman Catholic Church covers most ethnic groups; 60% are of mixed race. More than 80% of Amerindians have received Catholic baptism. The majority of the faithful (65%) live in the capital where, according to sociological studies made in 1965, Sunday practice averaged 16%.

PROTESTANT CHURCHES. The most significant Protestant work has been carried on by Moravians who established their first congregation in 1735. The EBGS is considered by many to be the national church of Surinam, with the majority of Bush Negroes and numbers of Mestizos belonging to it. The Dutch Reformed and Lutheran churches were also formed in the 18th century. The former consists almost exclusively of Dutch settlers, while the latter counts in its membership a substantial Creole community. Twentieth-century arrivals since World War I include the Wesleyan Church, Salvation Army, Assemblies of God and Seventh-day Adventists, with several other North American missions arriving after World War II.

OTHER CHURCHES. Anglicans have been represented in Surinam since the 19th century. Surinam belongs to the diocese of Guyana of the Church of the Province of the West Indies. The African Methodist Episcopal Church also joins administratively its work in Guyana and Surinam, through a single annual conference. In addition there is a small Old Catholic Church and an active Jehovah's Witnesses Community.

**CHURCH AND STATE.** Unlike the Netherlands, Surinam has no law regarding religious societies. Any group wishing to receive government subsidies must acquire juridical personality and register as such. The state gives salaries to all bishops and to Protestant pastors, as well as to teachers of religion and a certain number of Catholic priests. As far as is financially possible, public and private education are treated on equal terms, but the state does not help in the construction of private schools. Religious education can be included in the schedule of classes of a school. There is no ministry or ministerial department charged with religious affairs.

**INTERDENOMINATIONAL ORGANIZATIONS.** The Surinam Christian Council of Churches (Comité Christelijke Kerken), founded about 1960, includes in its membership the Moravian, Catholic, Dutch Reformed and Lutheran churches. It provides for mutual recognition of baptisms, settlement of difficulties concerning mixed marriages, exchanges of preachers, and other matters of mutual concern. The Christian Pedagogical Institute (Christelijk Peadagogisch Institut), established in 1970, is responsible for the training of Christian teachers. This institute, which is a remarkable example of ecumenical collaboration in the domain of education, is under the direction of 2 bishops (Moravian and Roman Catholic). Classes on non-religious matters are held in common, while religious instruction is given by priests or pastors to each's own religious group.

**BROADCASTING.** The government Surinam Broadcasting Company accepts Protestant programmes for 2.5 hours from Mondays to Saturdays and for one and a half hours on Sundays; and Catholic programmes for one and a half hours Mondays to Saturdays and half an hour on Sundays. Almost all the Protestant programmes are locally produced. The 4 commercial stations all accept religious broadcasting. The TV network Surinaamse Televisie Stichting allows both Protestants and Catholics 10 minutes each from Monday to Saturday and all Protestant programmes are locally produced.

## BIBLIOGRAPHY

'Animism and Islam among the Javanese in Surinam', A. De Waal Malefijt, *Anthropological quarterly*, XXXVII, 3 (1964), 149–155.
'The Winti cult in the Para District', C.J. Wooding, *Caribbean studies*, 12 (April, 1972), 51–78.

**Catholic Church in Surinam.** Postage stamp set commemorating Centenary of Redemptorists.

**Evangelical Church of the West Indies.** *Left.* Sunday service with translation into 3 Amerindian tribal languages. *Above.* Conference bringing together 4 Amerindian tribes.

## TABLE 2. ORGANIZED CHURCHES AND DENOMINATIONS IN SURINAM

| Official name 1 | Begun 2 | Type 3 | Counc 4 | Congs 5 | Adults 6 | Affiliated 7 | Names, notes, and other statistics (see Codebook) 8 |
|---|---|---|---|---|---|---|---|
| African Methodist Episcopal Church | | I Met | VₐM₊₊ | | 200 | 300 | *Guyana-Surinam Annual Conf*, 16th Episcopal District. M=AMEC(USA). Blacks on coast. |
| Anglican Church (D Guyana) | c1840 | A ACa | aₐMR₊ | | 500 | 1,000 | Part of Church of the Province of the West Indies (CPWI). Mainly Black immigrants. |
| Assemblies of God | 1958 | P Pe2 | ZP₊₊₊ | 5 | 181 | 500 | M=AoG(USA). Classical Pentecostals (2-stage). 1n,4f. |
| Catholic Church: D Paramaribo | 1683 | R Lat | PₐNMC | 74 | 42,000 | 80,000 | *Rooms-Kath Kerk.* 3,360 Chinese. C=2+1+3. 3n,50x,35m,156w,P=46%,1p,W=16%,3561Yy. |
| Dutch Reformed Church | c1750 | P Ref | ₊₊₊₊C | 9 | 5,000 | 10,500 | *Nederlandse Hervormde Gemeente.* Dutch officials, settlers. No inland missions. 3x. |
| Evangelical Church of the West Indies | 1955 | P int | xM₊₊₊ | 9 | 500 | 1,000 | M=WIM(USA),IM,DTLM(USA), Surinam Interior Fellowship. Bush Negroes, Indians. 32f. |
| Evangelical Lutheran Church in Surinam | 1741 | P Lut | Iv₊₊C | 7 | 2,500 | 4,750 | *Evangelisch-Lutherse Gemeente.* Dutch Creoles. 1967 applied to join WCC. 1x,79Yy. |
| Evangelical Methodist Church in Guiana | 1956 | P Hol | ₊T₊₊₊ | 4 | 300 | 500 | Bible Methodists. Fundamentalists. M=EMC(USA). HQ Paramaribo. 2x,4f. |
| Jehovah's Witnesses | c1915 | M Jeh | x₊₊₊₊ | 10 | 586 | 1,000 | *Getuigen van Jehova. Watch Tower.* Active witnessing under way by 1929. 19Y. |
| Moravian Church in Surinam | 1735 | P Mor | xₐM₊C | 80 | 22,000 | 52,180 | *EBGS. Surinam Province/UoB.* M=ZZG,DLM. 50% Bush Negroes, 30% Javanese. 53nx,3H,1s. |
| Old Catholic Church | | C OCa | U₊₊₊₊ | 1 | 30 | 50 | Community of Dutch Old Catholics related to Church of Utrecht (Netherlands). |
| Salvation Army | 1926 | P Sal | xₐM₊₊ | | 200 | 500 | *SA, Surinam Region*, Caribbean & CAmerica Territory (HQ Kingston, Jamaica). |
| Seventh-day Adventist Church | 1945 | P Adv | x₊₊₊₊ | 9 | 744 | 2,000 | *SDA, Surinam Mission*, Caribbean Union Conference. 2nx,27mw,12t(648),113Y. |
| Wesleyan Church | c1920 | P Hol | VP₊₊₊ | 23 | 63 | 499 | *Pilgrim Holiness Ch.* M=WC(USA). Bush Negroes. 6n,1x,2f,G=6.5%pa,W=24%,13Y. |
| Other Protestant denominations | | P | ₊₊₊₊₊ | | 1,000 | 2,000 | Total about 8 (see list below). |
| Other indigenous churches | | I | ₊₊₊₊₊ | | 200 | 500 | Aramawali: Waiyana prophet Ridima (1963, ex WIM) who built skyboats, airstrip; &c. |
| **Total affiliated (mid-1970)** | | | | 270 | 76,004 | 157,279 | Total denominations (1970) . . . 24. |
| **Total affiliated (mid-1975)** | | | | 290 | 107,700 | 222,900 | Total denominations (1975) . . . 25. |
| **Total affiliated (mid-1980)** | | | | 310 | 152,300 | 315,250 | Total denominations (1980) . . . 26. |

### NOTES ON TABLE ABOVE
COLUMNS: for meanings and CODES (cols. 1, 3, 4, 8): see Codebook (Part 6). Column 1: **Boldface type** = church with over 10% of country's affiliated Christians.
NATIONAL COUNCILS (Column 4, 5th letter).
  C = Surinam Christian Council of Churches (Comité Christelijke Kerken, CCK); formerly Committee of Christian Churches in Surinam.
  *Other national councils.* Caribbean Council of Christian Churches (CCCC). Federation of Evangelical Churches.
OTHER PROTESTANT DENOMINATIONS. These include: Christian Reformed Ch, Free Evangelical (Baptist) Ch, International Missions (1961), Southern Baptist Convention (1971), Streams of Power, Verenigde Protestantse Gemeente (United Protestant Congregation), Walloon Ch (Waalse Gemeente).

PEOPLES (ethnolinguistic). Christians: 58.0% Creole (Dutch-speaking), 20.5% Bush Negro, 11.0% Javanese, 3.1% White (European, Dutch), 2.2% Chinese, 2% East Indian, 1.9% Amerindian (Arawak, Waiyana, Akuliyo, Trio), 0.5% Syro-Lebanese Arab.

### COUNTRY-WIDE TOTALS
EVANGELIZATION (see Part 5). 1900: 57%. 1970: 94%. 1980: 98%. *Radiophonic evangelism.* HCJB, TWR, ICI (1,004 enrolments), et alia.
FOREIGN MISSIONARIES AND PERSONNEL (nationals serving abroad) (1973). Total about 10 Roman Catholics and Protestants in Netherlands et alia.
FOREIGN MISSIONARIES AND PERSONNEL (aliens from abroad) (1973). Total 330. *From Western world.* 310: 211 Roman

Catholics, 99 Protestants (71 in 10 USA societies, 22 in 5 Netherlands societies, 4 in 1 Denmark society, 2 in 1 WGermany society). *From Third World.* 20: about 15 Roman Catholics from Colombia, Venezuela and Caribbean countries, about 5 Protestants from Trinidad & Tobago and Indonesia.
INSTITUTIONS (church-operated) (1973). Total 35, including about 20 higher schools, about 10 medical centres (1 hospital), 1 religious community, 1 seminary (Protestant).
PERIODICALS. 5 titles.
PERSONNEL. About 494 (164 national, 330 foreign).
RELIGIOUS LIBRARIES. 2.
SCRIPTURE DISTRIBUTION (1975). Annual totals: 1,064 Bibles (subsidized), 731 NTs (86% subsidized, 14% commercial), 40 UBS portions, 14,081 UBS selections. *Translations completed.* Portion: 3 languages since 1970. NT: Taki Taki in 1829.
SERVICE AGENCIES. About 24, including CCCC, CCK, CEF, IMF (Indonesia) KOB, MAF, PAS, PWO, WBT, YWCA.

### ADDITIONAL DATA ON CHURCHES
CATHOLIC CHURCH. Including (1966) 3,360 Chinese Catholics, rising to 5,500 by 1975. The diocese (in Dutch, Bisdom Paramaribo) is a suffragan of M Port of Spain (Trinidad). *Annual baptisms.* (1972) 93.2% infant, 6.8% adult. *Priests.* Expatriates: all Dutch except 1 Indian and 1 Chinese. *Brothers.* All Dutch. *Sisters.* 28 nationals. *Catechists.* Total (1970) 44. *Indigenous religious congregations.* 18 Dochters van Maria Onbevlekte Ontvanger, or Zusters van Paramaribo (Daughters of the Immaculate Conception of Mary, or Sisters of Paramaribo; begun 1932). *Foreign congregations.* Priests: CSSR, OMI. Brothers: Fraters van Tilburg (Brothers of Tilburg). Sisters: Sisters of the Third Order of St Francis of Oudenbosch, Sisters of Our Lady of

Mercy (Tilburg).
*Catholic organizations.* The diocese is part of the Antilles Episcopal Conference with its headquarters in Kingston, Jamaica. The Conference of Major Superiors of the Antilles groups together religious personnel, and a Priesters Raad (Presbyteral Council) is in the process of formation. The principal movements of the lay apostolate are the Katholieke Jeugdraad (Council of Catholic Youth), Catholic Boy Scouts and Girl Guides, Progressive Werknemers Organisatie (Progressive Workers Union), and Katholieke Onderwijzers Kring (Catholic Teachers' Circle).
The Holy See has no diplomatic relations with Surinam. It is represented to the Catholic hierarchy by an apostolic delegate based in Port-au-Prince, Haiti.
In 1974 the church sponsored 133 schools (124 primary schools with 25,104 pupils; 9 secondary schools with 3,899 students) co-ordinated by the Katholiek Onderwijs; one hospital with 240 beds; one organization for home health care; 2 homes for the elderly serving 140 persons; the Jepie Makandra, a mutual aid association for the unemployed and families in need; and the Association Father Ahlbrinck (Pater Ahlbrinckstichting), which provides social help, schools, technical training and health care for Bush Negroes and Amerindian forest peoples.
MORAVIAN CHURCH. Surinam Province, Unity of Brethren; in Dutch, Evangelische Broedergemeenschap Suriname (EBGS), or Hernhutters. The church has been supported by the ZZG (Zeist Mission Society, Netherlands) since 1793, and since 1914 by the Danish Lutheran Mission also. It became autonomous in 1963. In 1965 there were 107 workers (42 European), 46 mission stations, and over 50 schools with more than 20,000 pupils. *Emigration.* From 1965–75, about 7,000 Creoles and other members emigrated to the Netherlands.

# Svalbard & Jan Mayen Islands

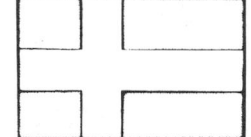

## SECULAR DATA

STATE. Official name: Svalbard and Jan Mayen Islands (Svalbard — Cold Coast). Alternative name: Spitzbergen.
Flag (shown above right): That of Norway.
Area: 62,422 sq.km. (24,101 sq.miles).
Government: Overseas area of Norway, since 1925 (1596 Dutch claim, 1920 Norwegian sovereignty, 1925 part of Norway).
Official language: Norwegian (*Norsk*).

DEMOGRAPHY. Population: 3,431 (census of 1.XI.1960. For 1970–2000 (UN), see last row of Table 1). Population density (1975): 0/sq.km. (0.1/sq.mile). Under 15 years: 26%. Household size: 3 persons.

Major languages: Norwegian, Russian.

ETHNOLINGUISTIC GROUPS: 64.9% Russian (military), 35.1% Norwegian.

MONEY (1977). Monetary unit: Norwegian krone (= 100 ore); US$1 = NKr 5.23.

### TABLE 1. RELIGIOUS ADHERENTS IN THE SVALBARD & JAN MAYEN ISLANDS

| Year / Name | 1900 Adherents | % | mid-1970 Adherents | % | Annual change, 1970–1980 Natural | Conversion | Total | Rate | mid-1975 Adherents | % | mid-1980 Adherents | % | 2000 Adherents | % |
|---|---|---|---|---|---|---|---|---|---|---|---|---|---|---|---|
| Non-religious | 20 | 4.0 | 2,000 | 57.1 | 0 | 17 | 17 | 0.81 | 2,100 | 60.0 | 2,170 | 62.0 | 2,450 | 70.0 |
| **Christians** | **480** | **96.0** | **1,500** | **42.9** | **0** | **−17** | **−17** | **−1.21** | **1,400** | **40.0** | **1,330** | **38.0** | **1,050** | **30.0** |
| professing | 480 | 96.0 | 1,500 | 42.9 | 0 | −17 | −17 | −1.21 | 1,400 | 40.0 | 1,330 | 38.0 | 1,050 | 30.0 |
| Protestants | 280 | 56.0 | 1,200 | 34.3 | 0 | −7 | −7 | −0.61 | 1,150 | 32.9 | 1,130 | 32.3 | 950 | 27.1 |
| Orthodox | 200 | 40.0 | 300 | 8.6 | 0 | −10 | −10 | −4.00 | 250 | 7.1 | 200 | 5.7 | 100 | 2.9 |
| nominal | 30 | 6.0 | 500 | 14.3 | 0 | 6 | 6 | 1.13 | 530 | 15.0 | 560 | 16.0 | 590 | 16.9 |
| affiliated | 450 | 90.0 | 1,000 | 28.6 | 0 | −23 | −23 | −2.64 | 870 | 25.0 | 770 | 22.0 | 460 | 13.1 |
| total practising | 360 | *80* | 700 | *70* | 0 | −16 | −16 | −2.62 | 610 | *70* | 540 | *70* | 480 | *60* |
| non-practising | 90 | *20* | 300 | *30* | 0 | −7 | −7 | −2.69 | 260 | *30* | 230 | *30* | 180 | *40* |
| Protestants | 450 | 90.0 | 1,000 | 28.6 | 0 | −23 | −23 | −2.64 | 870 | 25.0 | 770 | 22.0 | 460 | 13.1 |
| **Country's population** | **500** | **100.0** | **3,500** | **100.0** | **0** | **0** | **0** | **0.00** | **3,500** | **100.0** | **3,500** | **100.0** | **3,500** | **100.0** |

COLUMNS, ROWS. For meanings and definitions, see Codebook (Part 6). Note that, by definition, total 'Christians' = professing + crypto-Christians, which also = affiliated + nominal Christians. Percentages may not always total exactly,

due to rounding.
CHRISTIANS. About 1,200 Norwegian Lutherans (since 1611), and 300 Russian Orthodox (since 1715).
COUNTRY'S POPULATION. This changes seasonally; the

islands are inhabited during the winter season only; during the summer months, tourists arrive.
NON-RELIGIOUS. 98% Russians, 2% Norwegians.

**CHRISTIANITY.** Formal church activities are confined to the Church of Norway. Lutheran chaplains serve a population consisting of Norwegians on temporary assignment in the islands. They are numbered among Norwegian population statistics because they belong to the municipalities in Norway

in which they normally reside. The territory is theoretically also part of the Catholic vicariate of North Norway (Tromso), but there are few if any Catholics, no resident Catholic priest nor Catholic religious services.

**CHURCH AND STATE.** The Svalbard archipelago and Jan Mayen Island are dependencies of Norway and are subject to the same laws regarding church and state as exist in the mother country.

TABLE 2. ORGANIZED CHURCHES AND DENOMINATIONS IN THE SVALBARD & JAN MAYEN ISLANDS

| Official name 1 | Begun 2 | Type 3 | Counc 4 | Congs 5 | Adults 6 | Affiliated 7 | Names, notes, and other statistics (see Codebook) 8 |
|---|---|---|---|---|---|---|---|
| Church of Norway | | P Lut | Lwc.. | 1 | 700 | 1,000 | *Norske Kirke.* Occasional services for temporary Norwegian staff. |
| Total affiliated (mid-1970) | | | | 1 | 700 | 1,000 | Total denominations (1970) . . . 1. |
| Total affiliated (mid-1975) | | | | 1 | 600 | 870 | Total denominations (1975) . . . 1. |
| Total affiliated (mid-1980) | | | | 1 | 540 | 770 | Total denominations (1980) . . . 1. |

**NOTES ON TABLE ABOVE**
COLUMNS: for meanings and CODES (cols, 1, 3, 4, 8), see Codebook (Part 6). Column 1: **Boldface type** = church with over 10% of country's affiliated Christians.

PEOPLES (ethnolinguistic). Christians: 99% Norwegian.

**COUNTRY-WIDE TOTALS**
EVANGELIZATION (see Part 5). 1900: 100%. 1970: 100%. 1980: 100%.

FOREIGN MISSIONARIES AND PERSONNEL (aliens from abroad) (1973). Total 2. *From Western world.* About 2 Protestants from Norway.
PERSONNEL. 2 (foreign).

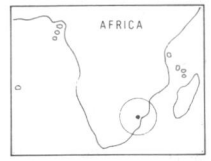

# SWAZILAND

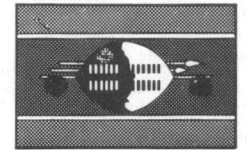

## SECULAR DATA

**STATE. Official name:** The Kingdom of Swaziland (Umbuso weSwatini). Unofficial name: Ngwane (traditional). Adjective of nationality: Swazi.
**Flag** (shown above right): Stripes of blue, yellow, red, yellow, and blue, with black and white Swazi shield of Emasotsha regiment in red stripe.
**Area:** 17,363 sq.km. (6,704 sq.miles). Agricultural land: 87.4%.
**Government:** Absolute monarchy, since 1973 (independent before 1890, 1894 South African protectorate, 1907 British protectorate, 1968 Independence as constitutional monarchy, 1973 absolute monarchy).
**Official languages:** siSwati (isiSwathi) and English.
**Chief cities:** administrative capital Mbabane 20,800 (1973), royal and legislative capital Lobamba, Manzini 16,000.
**Political divisions:** 4 Districts.

**DEMOGRAPHY. Population:** 374,697 (census of 24.V.1966.

For 1970–2000 (UN), see last row of Table 1). Population density (1975): 27/sq.km. (70/sq.mile). Under 15 years: 47%. Growth rate (1975–80): 2.98% per year (births 4.92%, deaths −1.94%). Life expectancy (1975–80): 46.0 years. Household size: 5.1 persons.
**Major languages:** Swazi (siSwati), English, Zulu, Afrikaans, Tsonga, Sotho (Sesotho), and a few others.
**Urban dwellers** (1970): 4.6%. Urban growth rate (1950–70): 11.5% per year.
**Labour force:** 46%.
**Refugees** (1977): 150,000 from South Africa.
**Tourists** (1973): 92,000. (1975) about 200,000 a year.

ETHNOLINGUISTIC GROUPS: 90.6% Swazi, 2.3% Zulu, 2.3% Tsonga, 1.4% Afrikaner, 1.0% Coloured, 0.8% English, 0.6% Nyasa, 0.5% Sotho, 0.1% Asian.

MONEY (1977). **Monetary unit:** emalangeni (= 100 cents); US$1 = E 0.87.

**National income per person:** US$340. Average annual family income: US$1,734.
**Inflation:** (1970–74) 12% per year (1975: consumer price index 157).
**Cost of living in capital** (1976): index 84 (Washington DC=100). Daily cost of living: US$32.

**HEALTH.** Hospitals: 28 (1,662 beds). Doctors: 64. Lepers: 4,670 (10.0 per 1,000). Blind: 1,000. Psychotics: 3,700.

**EDUCATION.** Adult literacy: (1946) 5%, (1966) 30%. Education rate: 35%. Schools: 395. Universities: 1.

**LITERATURE.** Periodicals: 30. Newspapers: 2 non-daily.

**COMMUNICATION** (per 1,000 people). Phones: 14. Radios: 115. Daily newspaper circulation: 17 copies.

TABLE 1. RELIGIOUS ADHERENTS IN SWAZILAND

| Year | 1900 | | mid-1970 | | Annual change, 1970–1980 | | | | mid-1975 | | mid-1980 | | 2000 | |
|---|---|---|---|---|---|---|---|---|---|---|---|---|---|---|
| Name | Adherents | % | Adherents | % | Natural | Conversion | Total | Rate | Adherents | % | Adherents | % | Adherents | % |
| Christians | 800 | 1.0 | 286,000 | 69.9 | 9,915 | 3,296 | 13,211 | 3.81 | 346,300 | 74.0 | 418,110 | 77.0 | 790,440 | 84.0 |
| professing | 800 | 1.0 | 286,000 | 69.9 | 9,915 | 3,296 | 13,211 | 3.81 | 346,300 | 74.0 | 418,110 | 77.0 | 790,440 | 84.0 |
| Protestants | 600 | 0.8 | 120,000 | 29.3 | 4,261 | 1,767 | 6,028 | 4.05 | 148,810 | 31.8 | 180,280 | 33.2 | 319,940 | 34.0 |
| African indigenous | 100 | 0.1 | 110,000 | 26.9 | 3,738 | 955 | 4,693 | 3.59 | 130,570 | 27.9 | 156,930 | 28.9 | 310,530 | 33.0 |
| Roman Catholics | 20 | 0.0 | 40,000 | 9.8 | 1,380 | 484 | 1,864 | 3.87 | 48,200 | 10.3 | 58,640 | 10.8 | 112,920 | 12.0 |
| Anglicans | 80 | 0.1 | 14,000 | 3.4 | 456 | −10 | 446 | 2.80 | 15,910 | 3.4 | 18,460 | 3.4 | 37,640 | 4.0 |
| Marginal Protestants | 0 | 0.0 | 2,000 | 0.5 | 80 | 100 | 180 | 6.41 | 2,810 | 0.6 | 3,800 | 0.7 | 9,410 | 1.0 |
| nominal | 120 | 0.1 | 84,397 | 20.6 | 2,987 | 1,008 | 3,995 | 3.83 | 104,340 | 22.3 | 124,350 | 22.9 | 165,620 | 17.6 |
| affiliated | 680 | 0.9 | 201,603 | 49.3 | 6,928 | 2,288 | 9,216 | 3.81 | 241,960 | 51.7 | 293,760 | 54.1 | 624,820 | 66.4 |
| total practising | 610 | 90 | 141,120 | 70 | 4,850 | 1,601 | 6,451 | 3.81 | 169,370 | 70 | 205,630 | 70 | 374,890 | 60 |
| non-practising | 70 | 10 | 60,480 | 30 | 2,078 | 687 | 2,765 | 3.81 | 72,590 | 30 | 88,130 | 30 | 249,930 | 40 |
| African indigenous | 100 | 0.1 | 85,900 | 21.0 | 2,948 | 951 | 3,899 | 3.79 | 102,970 | 22.0 | 124,890 | 23.0 | 263,480 | 28.0 |
| Protestants | 500 | 0.6 | 76,384 | 18.7 | 2,600 | 675 | 3,275 | 3.61 | 90,790 | 19.4 | 109,140 | 20.1 | 235,250 | 25.0 |
| Evangelicals | 400 | 0.5 | 60,900 | 14.9 | 2,070 | 540 | 2,610 | 3.61 | 72,300 | 15.4 | 87,000 | 16.0 | 190,000 | 20.2 |
| Roman Catholics | 0 | 0.0 | 33,984 | 8.3 | 1,179 | 473 | 1,652 | 4.01 | 41,180 | 8.8 | 50,500 | 9.3 | 98,800 | 10.5 |
| Anglicans | 80 | 0.1 | 3,635 | 0.9 | 134 | 100 | 234 | 5.00 | 4,680 | 1.0 | 5,970 | 1.1 | 18,820 | 2.0 |
| Marginal Protestants | 0 | 0.0 | 1,700 | 0.4 | 67 | 89 | 156 | 6.67 | 2,340 | 0.5 | 3,260 | 0.6 | 8,470 | 0.9 |
| Tribal religionists | 79,200 | 99.0 | 115,700 | 28.3 | 3,217 | −3,438 | −221 | −0.20 | 112,360 | 24.0 | 113,490 | 20.9 | 127,260 | 13.5 |
| Baha'is | 0 | 0.0 | 7,000 | 1.7 | 258 | 142 | 400 | 4.44 | 9,000 | 1.9 | 11,000 | 2.0 | 22,600 | 2.4 |
| Muslims | 0 | 0.0 | 300 | 0.1 | 10 | 0 | 10 | 2.94 | 340 | 0.1 | 400 | 0.1 | 700 | 0.1 |
| Country's population | 80,000 | 100.0 | 409,000 | 100.0 | 13,400 | 0 | 13,400 | 2.86 | 468,000 | 100.0 | 543,000 | 100.0 | 941,000 | 100.0 |

COLUMNS, ROWS. For meanings and definitions, see Codebook (Part 6). Note that, by definition, total 'Christians' = professing + crypto-Christians, which also = affiliated + nominal Christians. Percentages may not always total exactly, due to rounding.
CENSUSES. 3.V.1921: 91.5% tribal religionists, 8.5% Christians (6.3% Protestants, 1.5% Anglicans, 0.3% African indigenous, 0.3% Roman Catholics). 1936: 69.8% tribal religionists, 30.2% Christians (13.2% African indigenous, 11.5% Protestants (5.2% Methodists, 3.6% SDAs, 1.3% Lutherans), 2.8% Anglicans, 2.7% Roman Catholics). 7.V.1946: 62.8% tribal religionists, 37.2% Christians (22.8% Protestants, 8.8% African indigenous,

2.9% Roman Catholics, 2.7% Anglicans). **17.VII.1956:** this census gave 58,640 Zionists, 86,108 other Christians; altering the faulty total population figure to a correct one of 292,000, this gives 50.4% tribal religionists, 49.6% Christians (20.1% African indigenous). VII.1960 (sample survey of persons of 18 years or older): 55.4% Christians (22.6% Protestants, 21.4% African indigenous, 7.2% Roman Catholics, 4.2% Anglicans), 44.6% tribal religionists.

**NOTES ON RELIGIONS**
AFRICAN INDIGENOUS. In about 52 denominations in 1970 (see Table 2). Many are called Zionists (Emazioni), others

Apostolics (Emapostoli), still others have both names in their titles.
BAHA'IS. Very rapid growth from 8 local spiritual assemblies (1964) to 57 (1973). Around 1960, one of the first Baha'i primary schools in Africa was opened in Swaziland.
MUSLIMS. Mostly immigrants from the Comoro Islands and Mozambique-born Africans working in Swaziland. No conversions of Swazis to Islam are known to have taken place.
TRIBAL RELIGIONISTS. Traditional Swazi religious beliefs and practices remain very strong, the king and his family holding that allegiance to any specific Christian denomination is incompatible with their official positions.

**NON-CHRISTIAN RELIGIONS. Traditional religion** has steadily decreased the proportion of its adherents throughout the 20th century, though its influence and practice remain extremely strong. In former days the king exercised an even stronger religious function than today, and the prosperity of the nation was believed to be mystically dependent upon the strength, virility and general well-being of the ruler. His most important role was as rain-maker, a task shared by his mother, with the royal ancestors serving as intermediaries before the First Being, Umkhulumcandi. Spirit possession by ancestors is an ancient belief

among the Swazi, and around the middle of the 19th century possession by foreign and animal spirits became common. The more recent Mafefenyane possession cult (involving dancing, drumming and speaking in tongues, but not divination) was introduced from the Pedi to the west of Swaziland. The Mandzawe cult, on the other hand, includes divination.

## CHRISTIANITY
INDIGENOUS CHURCHES. Independent African churches have been an important factor in Swazi church life. Strong influences have been exerted from

the proliferation of indigenous churches in neighbouring South Africa, in addition to internal schism. The first secession occurred in the African Methodist Episcopal Church, itself a Black church from the USA, and the Independent Methodist Church was formed in 1906. The 1936 census listed 20 indigenous groups and a membership numbering 13% of the total population. By 1940 independents were estimated at half the Christian population. Although the proportional growth of indigenous to historic denominations has tended to diminish since World War II, they are still a significant force. Approximately 23% of the

SWAZILAND

MOZAMBIQUE

Transvaal

Havelock Mine

Lourenço Marques

✠ Mbabane

Manzini

Natal

Indian Ocean

0 miles 100

population today are members of independent churches. The largest of some 40 groups at present at work are the Christian Catholic Apostolic Holy Spirit Church in Zion and the Swazi Christian Church in Zion.

PROTESTANT CHURCHES. At the invitation of the Swazi king, Methodist missionaries came from South Africa to Mahamba in the southern region as early as 1825. Today Methodists form the largest of the Swazi Protestant churches. Other early attempts to evangelize the country, by Wesleyan and Hermannsburg missionaries in 1847 and 1860, ended in failure; but German Lutherans arrived in 1887 and in 1891 the South Africa General Mission was able to plant a permanent station at Bethany on the Great Usutu river, their first mission in southern Africa. This early SAGM work is now incorporated in the Africa Evangelical Church. Indeed the major Protestant denominations in Swaziland were established prior to World War I.

The various Protestant denominations now occupy the following areas: Methodists in southwestern, central and eastern Swaziland; Nazarenes in the northeast; Evangelical Lutherans north of Mbabane; Africa Evangelical Church south of Mbabane; Alliance Church in Western Swaziland, south of the Great Usutu river; Emmanuel Wesleyans south of Stegi; Evangelical Church of Swaziland, Free Evangelical Assemblies, and Free Gospel Mission in the south.

CATHOLIC CHURCH. In spite of a slow beginning, considerable progress has been made by Catholics over the past 50 years. The first missionaries of the Order of the Servants of Mary (OSM) arrived in 1913. The original mission was attached to the vicariate of Natal, but within 10 years (1923) a prefecture for Swaziland was created. By 1939 this was elevated to vicariate and became a suffragan diocese of Pretoria in 1961. The major growth of the church has come since World War II.

**CHURCH AND STATE.** The constitution of February 1968, which was repealed by king Sobhuza II in April 1973, provided for a constitutional monarchy and named the Ngwanyama as chief of state. Under the 1968 constitution, the king appointed a prime minister from among members of parliament who acted as head of government; the constitution also guaranteed freedom of religion.

In 1939 king Sobhuza I attempted, with limited success, to unite the country's various small independent churches into one national Swazi church. The name of this church was changed in 1944 to the United Christian Church of Africa, and the king continues to be considered its head. Many years ago the king gave the church land near the new parliament at Lobamba to build a cathedral, but the building remained unfinished until its opening at Easter 1979 as the National Swazi Church. At Easter time members of all Swazi indigenous churches gather at the king's home at Lobamba for preaching and prayer services, the king himself traditionally attending the Easter Monday meeting.

**INTERDENOMINATIONAL ORGANIZATIONS.** The Swaziland Missionary Conference was formed in 1911. Although it went through a period of inactivity, it was revived in 1929 and continues to meet regularly. The Swaziland Conference of Churches came into existence in 1965. Its membership is one of the broadest of any African interdenominational organization, including Catholic, Adventist and conservative Protestant representation. An association serving independent churches is the League of African Churches in Swaziland (LAC), founded in 1937. There is also an Association of Evangelicals of Swaziland.

At the end of 1976 the Catholic, Anglican, Mennonite, AME and Lutheran churches, with the United Christian Church of Africa, launched a new body intended to be an ecumenical council, the Council of Swaziland Churches (CSC). Members who were also in the SCC were expected to withdraw from it after a short period.

**BROADCASTING.** The Swaziland Conference of Churches arranges all Christian broadcasts over the government Radio Swaziland (Swaziland Broadcasting Service). There are 26 co-operating denominations, 10 of which are European churches with siSwati counterparts. Catholics are given 10% of all religious programmes in English and 6% of all siSwati programmes, which consists of three 4-minute spots a day and 2 church services on a Sunday. Trans World Radio has built a new international radio station, which began operations in 1975.

**BIBLIOGRAPHY**
*An African aristocracy: rank among the Swazi.* H. Kuper. London: Oxford University Press, 1947.
'The Church of Jericho, Swaziland'. A. Fogelquist. Dissertation, University of Uppsala, 1980.
'The Swazi reaction to missions', H. Kuper, *African studies* (Johannesburg), V, 3 (1946), 177–189.
*Zulu Zion and some Swazi Zionists.* B. Sundkler. London: Oxford University Press, 1976. 337p.

**African indigenous churches.** 10,000 worshippers (League of African Churches in Swaziland) at annual 3-day Easter Festival, Lobamba, 1976. *Left.* 4,000 Zionists at annual Good Friday service adjacent to Royal Kraal, Lobamba. *Right.* Zionists en route to Easter Sunday festival (Zionist colours: white and blue).

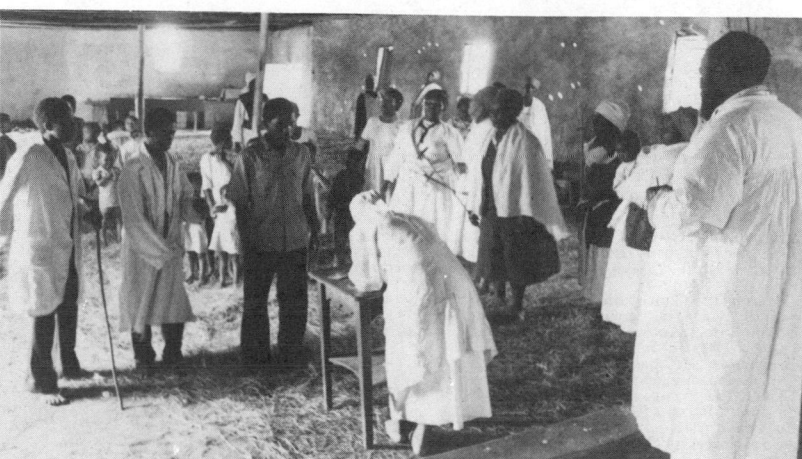

*Left.* National Swazi Church (building 1939-79) is officially opened by King Sobhuza II (left rear) in presence of 15,000 Independents together with the Anglican and Roman Catholic bishops, and the Baha'i head, on Easter Sunday 1979.

*Right.* **Swazi Christian Church in Zion of South Africa.** Church at Mbekelwini, with (right) Bishop Mncina, Vice-Chairman of League of African Churches in Swaziland.

TABLE 2. ORGANIZED CHURCHES AND DENOMINATIONS IN SWAZILAND

| Official name 1 | Begun 2 | Type 3 | Counc 4 | Congs 5 | Adults 6 | Affiliated 7 | Names, notes, and other statistics (see Codebook) 8 |
|---|---|---|---|---|---|---|---|
| Africa Evangelical Church | 1891 | P int | xM..k | 25 | 5,000 | 7,000 | M=AEF(formerly SAGM). HQ Mbabane. 3 main stations. Strong wor‹. 5nx,51m,5f. |
| African Methodist Episcopal Church | 1904 | I Met | Vw..Z | 9 | 2,000 | 5,000 | *Ikhushi*. Begun by Africans; later, M=AMEC(USA). Several schisms. 79% rural. |
| Alliance Church of Swaziland | 1915 | P ind | x...K | 55 | 1,200 | 3,000 | *Iswidi*. M=Swedish Alliance Mission. In west. 85% rural. 2n,13m,5f,W=60%,40Y. |
| Anglican Church: D Swaziland | 1881 | A ACa | AwaVd | 74 | 2,456 | 3,635 | *Isheshe*. 1968, diocese in CPSA. M=USPG. 500 whites. 11n,11x,P=75%,3r,104Y,508y. |
| Antioch Zionist Church | | I pen | ....I | | 1,000 | 3,500 | *Antioc*. Members 83% rural (46% Highveld, 15% Middleveld, 11% Lowveld), 17% urban. |
| Apostolic Faith Mission of SAfrica | | P Pe2 | Z...K | 10 | 2,000 | 5,000 | M=AFM(SA). Work in south. Members 95% rural (56% in Highveld), 5% urban. |
| Assemblies of God | | P Pe2 | Z...K | 12 | 600 | 1,000 | M=Assemblies of God(USA,UK). HQ Stegi. Under Swazi leadership. Strong in north. |
| Bantu Swedish Free Church | 1950 | I ind | ....K | 8 | 2,500 | 4,000 | Schism ex Swedish Aliance M. Swazi, Zulu, Malawians. 5n,20mw,W=40%,230Y,300y. |
| **Catholic Church: D Manzini** | 1913 | R Lat | P.SSd | 10 | 18,000 | 33,984 | *Roma*. M=SM. 7% White, 4% Coloured. C=2+0+4. 3n,29x,14m,120w,P=25%,1804Yy,684z. |
| Christian Apostolic Ch in Zion of SA | 1920 | I pen | ....I | 14 | 3,000 | 10,000 | *Eqiniswenisweni*. Mabilitsa's Zion. Middleveld, Highveld. 82% rural. HQ Alexandra, Joburg. |
| **Christian Cath Ap Holy Spirit Ch in Z** | 1913 | I pen | ....I | | 10,000 | 21,000 | Z=Zion. Nkonyane's Zion (HQ Natal). First Zionists in SAfr. 94% rural (Middleveld). |
| Church of the Nazarene | 1910 | P Hol | xF..K | 200 | 3,601 | 12,000 | *Ibandla LomNazarene*. M=CoN. 27n,4x,412mw,73f,1H,15h,1s(25),149t(9954),W=78%,104Y. |
| Damascus Church | | I ind | ....I | | 1,000 | 3,000 | *Damaseko-Damascus*. Strongest in Middleveld, some in Lowveld. 90% rural. |
| Dutch Reformed Church | | P Ref | F...K | 7 | 400 | 1,000 | *NGK*. 100 Afrikaners from Transvaal synod; recently, 5 Bantu congregations begun. |
| Dutch Reformed Church in Africa | | P Ref | R.... | 1 | 30 | 50 | *Nederduitsch Hervormde Kerk* (*NHK*); 1853 split ex NGK(SA). Afrikaners. |
| Emmanuel Wesleyan Church | 1903 | P Hol | VF..K | 20 | 500 | 1,000 | M=Wesleyan Ch(USA). 1968 merged with Pilgrim Holiness Ch(USA). No growth. 33mw,5f. |
| Evangelical Bible Church | | P int | xM..k | 3 | 200 | 500 | Members Coloured. M=TEAM(USA,SAfrica). In Manzini, Mbabane, Mhlotsheni. |
| Evangelical Church of Swaziland | 1892 | P int | xM..K | 110 | 5,000 | 15,000 | Formerly Bantu Ev Ch. M=TEAM(USA,SA),Norwegian Ev M(NLM). Swazi, Zulu. 15f,2p. |
| Evangelical Lutheran Ch (SE Diocese) | 1887 | P Lut | Lwa.d | 25 | 1,910 | 3,984 | *Luthela*. Formerly, M=Berlin MS; SKM. 71% rural. 3n,5x(4 being Zulu),11m,19Y,156y. |
| Free Evangelical Assemblies | 1909 | P Pe2 | Z...K | 17 | 1,000 | 3,000 | M=Norwegian Pentecostal Mission(NPY). Strong in south. 25% urban. 1H,2i,1p. |
| Free Gospel Mission | | P Pe2 | ....K | 3 | 50 | 100 | Schism led by Norwegian missionary ex Norwegian Ev Mission (NLM). HQ Nhlangano. |
| Full Gospel Ch of God in Southern A | | P Pe3 | ZF... | 7 | 700 | 1,500 | Branch of church in SA. M=Church of God(Cleveland)(USA). 5n,2f(Afrikaners). |
| Independent Methodist Ch of S Africa | 1904 | I Met | ..... | | 200 | 500 | Schism 1906 ex African Methodist Episcopal Ch. One of oldest indigenous bodies. |
| Jehovah's Witnesses | c1945 | M Jeh | x.... | 14 | 694 | 1,500 | *Watch Tower. IBSA*. Active witnessing under way by 1949. 1976: persecution. 32Y. |
| Jericho Christian Church in Zion | 1951 | I pen | ....I | 90 | 2,000 | 5,000 | *Jeliko-Jerico*. 52% Highveld, 17% Lobombo, 11% Lowveld, 10% Middleveld, 10% urban. |
| Methodist Church of South Africa | 1825 | P Met | Vwa.K | | 2,500 | 20,000 | *Weseli*. Re-begun c1895. English and African circuits. 36% Highveld, 23% urban. |
| Metropolitan Church Association | 1936 | P Hol | ....K | 8 | 100 | 200 | M=MCA(USA). 2 stations, HQ Sifuntaneni Halt, Manzini. Highveld and urban. 3f,1h. |
| Pentecostal Assemblies of Africa | | I pen | ....k | 6 | 200 | 400 | Schism ex Assemblies of God, led by African from Rhodesia. HQ Lomahasha. |
| Pentecostal Holiness Church | 1913 | P Pe3 | Z.... | 1 | 30 | 50 | M=PHC(USA), brought in by members from South Africa. Holiness Pentecostals. |
| St John's Apostolic Faith Church | 1951 | I pen | x...I | | 2,000 | 5,500 | *AbaPostoli. Ma Nku's Ch*. Sotho origin. HQ Joburg. 50% urban. Holy water ministry. |
| Seventh-day Adventist Church | 1920 | P Adv | x...K | 20 | 500 | 1,000 | *Isabatha. Swaziland Field*. 96% Swazi, some Whites. Rural. 3n,1x,11mw,18t(800),54Y. |
| Swazi Christian Ch in Zion of SA | 1937 | I pen | ....I | | 5,000 | 15,000 | Bp Mncina's church. One of the largest Zionist bodies. HQ Kwaluseni. 91% rural. |
| United Christian Church of Africa | 1939 | I Ang | ..A.Z | 35 | 2,000 | 3,000 | *Ibandla lama Krestu*. National Swazi Ch, attempt by king to unite all churches. 18n. |
| Other indigenous Zionist churches | c1917 | I pen | ....I | | 5,000 | 10,000 | Total about 40 (see list below), including many independent congregations. |
| Other Protestant denominations | | P | ..... | | 500 | 1,000 | Total about 10 (see list below). |
| Other marginal Protestant bodies | | M | ..... | | 100 | 200 | Including: New Church in Southern Africa. |
| **Total affiliated (mid-1970)** | | | | **1,210** | **82,971** | **201,603** | **Total denominations (1970) . . . 84.** |
| **Total affiliated (mid-1975)** | | | | **1,300** | **99,580** | **241,960** | **Total denominations (1975) . . . 87.** |
| **Total affiliated (mid-1980)** | | | | **1,400** | **120,900** | **293,760** | **Total denominations (1980) . . . 90.** |

NOTES ON TABLE ABOVE
COLUMNS: for meanings and CODES (cols. 1, 3, 4, 8): see Codebook (Part 6). Column 1: **Boldface type** = church with over 10% of country's affiliated Christians.
NATIONAL COUNCILS (Column 4, 5th letter).
- C = Council of Swaziland Churches (CSC) (set up at the end of 1976, with members expecting to pull out of SCC within a short time).
- d = member of both SCC and CSC.
- I = League of African Churches in Swaziland (LACS) or League of Swazi Independent Churches (Inhlangano yamabandla Enkolo Esizwe/Inkatsa yamabandla Enkolo ka Ngwane) (founded in 1937; mainly an Easter convention; at least 25 member churches).
- K = Swaziland Conference of Churches (SCC).
- k = not a member of SCC, but its related foreign mission is a member.
- Z = member of LACS, SCC and CSC.

*Other national councils*. Association of Evangelicals of Swaziland (member of AEAM). Federation Churches in Zion/Federation of Zion Churches in Africa/League of Zionist Churches.
OTHER INDIGENOUS ZIONIST CHURCHES. These are mostly Zionist splits from Nkonyane's Zion and the Swazi Christian Church in Zion, also branches of Zulu churches from the republic of South Africa. They include: African Congregational Ch (begun 1928), African Native Baptist Ch, African Zion Ch, Apostolic Ch of Christ, Assemblies of God (Nicholas Bhengu), Bantu Methodist Ch of SA (Donkey Church; begun 1935), Christian Apostolic Zulu Ch, Ch of Christ, Congregational Catholic Apostolic Ch (1931), Free Ev Assembly Independent Ch (Ebenezer; ex NPY), Holy Apostolic Ch in Christ (1924), Holy Spirit Apostolic Ch in Zion (EECHSACZ, or Tongo Tongo; ex Nkonyane's Zion), National Ch of Africa's Union (began 1932 ex Scandinavian Alliance Mission; member of LACS), Nazarite Baptist Ch (Shembeites) (1911), Nazarite Bible Ch (HQ South Africa), Pentecost East Star Jerusalem Ch in Sabbath, Swazi Christian Ch of the Kingdom of Swaziland in Zion (1956), United Ch of Ethiopian South Africa, Zion Apostolic Faith Mission (1912), Zion Apostolic Swazi Ch of South Africa (begun 1918 ex ZAC), Zion Christian Ch (Lekganyane) (1925), Zulu Apostolic Ch in Zion (1924 ex Nkonyane's Zion; member of LACS), Zulu Congregational Ch. Also, a USA Black mission is at work: National Baptist Convention USA (1971).
OTHER PROTESTANT DENOMINATIONS. Among these smaller bodies are the following: Chs of Christ (Non-Instrumental), Gereformeerde Kerk, Mennonite Committee in Swaziland (member of 1976 council, CSC), Norwegian Mission Union, Salvation Army, Swedish Zulu Mission, United Apostolic Faith Ch.

PEOPLES (ethnolinguistic). Christians: 89.9% Swazi, 2.2% Tsonga, 2.1% Zulu, 2.0% Afrikaner, 1.2% English & other European, 1.2% Coloured, 0.7% Nyasa, 0.6% Sotho.

COUNTRY-WIDE TOTALS
EVANGELIZATION (see Part 5). 1900: 12%. 1970: 100%. 1980: 100%. *Mass evangelism*. 1978, Here's Life Africa (CCCI pilot project) in Mbabane.
FOREIGN MISSIONARIES AND PERSONNEL (nationals serving abroad) (1973). Total 28: about 20 African indigenous in South Africa, 8 Protestants in Malawi, Nigeria and South Africa.
FOREIGN MISSIONARIES AND PERSONNEL (aliens from abroad) (1973). Total 433. *From Western world*. 278: 155 Protestants (87 in 7 USA societies, 37 in 4 Norway societies, 15 in 2 UK societies, 8 in 2 Sweden societies, 5 in 1 Australia society, 2 in 1 WGermany society, 1 in 1 Iceland society), 105 Roman Catholics, 18 Anglicans in 2 UK societies. *From Third World*. 155: 95 Protestants (71 in 8 South Africa societies), about 30 African indigenous from South Africa, about 20 Roman Catholics (16 from South Africa), about 10 Anglicans from South Africa et alia.
INSTITUTIONS (church-operated) (1973). Total 50, including 15 higher schools (1 minor seminary), about 30 medical centres (3 hospitals), 1 radio station, 1 religious community, 1 seminary (Protestant).
PERIODICALS. About 20 titles.
PERSONNEL. About 1,306 (873 national, 433 foreign).
RELIGIOUS LIBRARIES. 3.
SCRIPTURE DISTRIBUTION (1975). Annual totals: 5,300 Bibles (6% free, 94% subsidized), 5,000 NTs (50% free, 40% subsidized, 10% commercial), 2,000 UBS portions, 3,000 UBS selections. *Translations completed*. In siSwati (Swazi): portion 1976.
SERVICE AGENCIES. About 18, including AWR, CCCI, CEF, CRF, LACS, MAP, NLFA, SACBC, SCC, SU, TWR, YWCA.

ADDITIONAL DATA ON CHURCHES
CATHOLIC CHURCH. The diocese is a suffragan of M Pretoria. *Catholics*. 87% Bantu, 7% European, 4% Coloured. *Catechumens*. (1959) 901; (1961) 897; (1963) 793; (1969) 684. *Annual baptisms*. (1972) 64.6% infant, 35.4% adult. *Sisters*. 54 Africans, 66 Europeans. *Seminarians*. Total 11. *Catechists*. Total (1971) 43. *Indigenous religious congregations*. Sisters Servants of Mary of Swaziland. *Foreign orders and congregations*. Priests: OSM, SDB. Sisters: Dominican Sisters of Oakford, Sisters of Our Lady of Namur, Mantellate Sisters.
*Catholic organizations*. The diocese of Manzini is a member of the Southern Africa Catholic Bishops' Conference (SACBC) which in turn is a member of SECAM. Two associations serving religious personnel are the Conference of Clerical Religious Superiors in Southern Africa, and the Association of Women Religious, both based in South Africa.
The Holy See has diplomatic relations with Swaziland and is represented to government and the Catholic hierarchy by a pro-nuncio with residence in Pretoria, South Africa.
In 1973 there were 52 Catholic primary schools (12,151 pupils) and 8 secondary schools (2,378). In addition there was one hospital and an orphanage.
CHRISTIAN CATHOLIC APOSTOLIC HOLY SPIRIT CHURCH IN ZION. Also called Apostolic Holy Catholic Christian Church in Zion, and Libandla laka Masangane, this is the Swaziland branch of Nkonyane's Zion whose headquarters is in Charlestown, Natal. It was begun in South Africa in 1903 as the Christian Catholic Church, and renamed in 1908 to Christian Catholic Apostolic Church in Zion, and in 1922 to its present name.
CHURCH OF THE NAZARENE. This church's annual growth rate in 1972 was 5.1%pa.
UNITED CHRISTIAN CHURCH OF AFRICA. Founded at the instigation of king Sobhuza II in 1939 as the National Swazi (or Swazi National) Church (Libandla lelive), mostly from non-Zionist and mainly Methodist churches. In 1944 it was renamed with its present name, UCCA, again on the initiative of the king. It fostered the idea of a national Swazi cathedral at Lobamba, begun 1953.

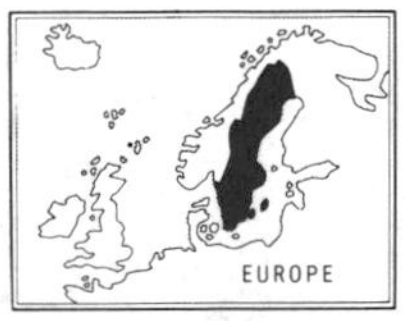


# SWEDEN

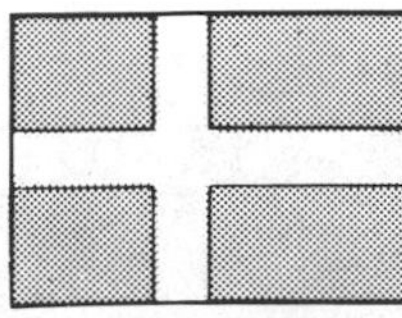

## SECULAR DATA

**STATE. Official name:** The Kingdom of Sweden (Konungariket Sverige). Adjectives of nationality: Swedish, a Swede.
**Flag** (shown above right): Light blue field with yellow cross.
**Area:** 449,750 sq. km. (173,732 sq. miles). Agricultural land: 8.3%.
**Government:** Constitutional monarchy, since 1718 (1397 united Scandinavian monarchy, 1523 independent kingdom, 1660 absolute monarchy, 1718 constitutional monarchy, 1917 parliamentary government).
**Legislature:** Riksdag, 350 members.
**Official language:** Swedish (*Svensk*).
**Chief cities:** capital Stockholm 1,349,890 (1973), Göteborg 685,700, Malmö 450,620, Uppsala 136,070.
**Political divisions:** 24 Counties (län); 278 Communes.
**Armed forces** (1976): Total 65,400 regular (49,300 conscripts): army 46,000, navy 11,200, air force 8,200, (550 combat aircraft). Reserves: 500,000.

**DEMOGRAPHY. Population:** 8,076,903 (census of I.XI.1970. For 1970–2000 (UN), see last row of Table 1). Population density (1975): 18/sq. km. (48/sq. mile). Under 15 years: 22%. Growth rate (1975–80): 0.61% per year (births 1.46%, deaths -1.10%, immigrants 0.25%). Life expectancy (1975–80): 73.4 years. Household size: 2.6 persons.
**Major languages:** Swedish, Finnish, Greek, Serbo-Croatian, German, Norwegian, Danish, English, Dutch, Estonian, Russian, Lapp, Romany, Italian, Romanian.
**Urban dwellers** (1970): 79.6%. Urban growth rate (1950–70): 1.6% per year.
**Labour force:** 49%.
**Refugees** (1977): From abroad, about 21,000 (20,000 from Eastern Europe, 200 from Chile).
**Tourists** (1974): about 7 million (710,216 from outside Norway, Denmark, Finland).

**ETHNOLINGUISTIC GROUPS:** 89.9% Swedish, 4.4% Finnish (350,000), 2.4% other migrant worker (203,000) (0.4% Greek, 0.4% Serbian, 0.2% Croatian, 0.1% Italian, Romanian, Syrian, other Arab, Turkish), 0.6% German, 0.6% Norwegian, 0.5% Danish, 0.5% Dutch, 0.3% Estonian 0.3% Eastern European refugee (20,000) (Russian, Latvian, Hungarian, et alii), 0.2% Jewish, 0.1% Lapp (10,000), 0.1% Gypsy (8,500), 0.1% British (5,000), French, USA (White & Black), Swiss, Tibetan, Assyrian (immigrants, beginning 1967; 9,000 by 1979). Total foreign immigrants by 1977: 750,000.

**MONEY** (1977). **Monetary unit:** Swedish krona (=100 ore); US$1=SKr 4.16.
**National income per person:** US$6,151. Average annual family income: US$15,993.
**Inflation:** (1970–74) 7.4% per year, (1975) 10% per year (consumer price index 156), (1977) 16% per year.
**Cost of living in capital** (1976): index 162 (Washington DC=100). Daily cost of living: US$47.

**HEALTH.** Hospitals: 721 (123,131 beds). Doctors: 11,920. Blind; 15,716. Psychotics: 95,000. Drug addicts; over 15,000 (10,000 on cannabis, 2,000 heroin). Criminals: 311,289.

**EDUCATION.** Adult literacy: 100%. Education rate: 56%. Schools: 4,800. Universities: 10.

**LITERATURE.** Annual new book titles (1973): 8,242. Periodicals: 4,100. Scientific journals: 710. Newspapers: 114 dailies, 53 non-daily.

**COMMUNICATION** (per 1,000 people). Phones: 612. Radios: 368. TV sets: 339. Daily newspaper circulation: 534 copies.

TABLE 1. RELIGIOUS ADHERENTS IN SWEDEN

| Year | 1900 | | mid-1970 | | Annual change, 1970–1980 | | | | mid-1975 | | mid-1980 | | 2000 | |
|---|---|---|---|---|---|---|---|---|---|---|---|---|---|---|
| *Name* | *Adherents* | *%* | *Adherents* | *%* | *Natural* | *Conversion* | *Total* | *Rate* | *Adherents* | *%* | *Adherents* | *%* | *Adherents* | *%* |
| **Christians** | **5,077,000** | **98.8** | **6,032,000** | **75.0** | **36,690** | **−33,990** | **2,700** | **0.04** | **6,047,600** | **72.9** | **6,059,000** | **70.9** | **5,854,700** | **62.3** |
| professing | 5,077,000 | 98.8 | 6,032,000 | 75.0 | 36,690 | −33,990 | 2,700 | 0.04 | 6,047,600 | 72.9 | 6,059,000 | 70.9 | 5,854,700 | 62.3 |
| Protestants | 5,073,700 | 98.8 | 5,819,000 | 72.3 | 31,470 | −36,050 | −4,580 | −0.08 | 5,795,800 | 69.9 | 5,773,200 | 67.6 | 5,390,700 | 57.4 |
| Roman Catholics | 2,500 | 0.0 | 95,000 | 1.2 | 2,440 | 20 | 2,460 | 2.28 | 107,800 | 1.3 | 119,600 | 1.4 | 118,000 | 2.0 |
| Orthodox | 100 | 0.0 | 70,000 | 0.9 | 2,410 | −10 | 2,400 | 2.90 | 82,900 | 1.0 | 94,000 | 1.1 | 131,000 | 1.4 |
| Marginal Protestants | 600 | 0.0 | 45,000 | 0.6 | 352 | 2,048 | 2,400 | 4.14 | 58,000 | 0.7 | 69,000 | 0.8 | 141,000 | 1.5 |
| Catholics (non-Roman) | 0 | 0.0 | 2,000 | 0.0 | 12 | −2 | 10 | 0.49 | 2,050 | 0.0 | 2,100 | 0.0 | 2,500 | 0.0 |
| Anglicans | 100 | 0.0 | 1,000 | 0.0 | 6 | 4 | 10 | 0.05 | 1,050 | 0.0 | 1,100 | 0.0 | 1,500 | 0.0 |
| affiliated | 5,077,000 | 98.8 | 6,032,000 | 75.0 | 36,690 | −33,990 | 2,700 | 0.04 | 6,047,600 | 72.9 | 6,059,000 | 70.9 | 5,854,700 | 62.3 |
| disaffiliated | −50,000 | −1.0 | −1,970,000 | −24.5 | −10,312 | 66,302 | 55,990 | −3.29 | −1,699,700 | −20.5 | −1,410,100 | −16.5 | 0 | −0.0 |
| doubly-affiliated | −280,000 | −5.4 | −896,435 | −11.1 | −5,030 | 17,763 | 12,733 | −1.54 | −829,100 | −10.0 | −769,100 | −9.0 | −90,000 | −1.0 |
| total practising | 4,569,300 | *90* | 4,825,600 | *80* | 27,517 | −85,947 | −58,430 | −1.29 | 4,535,700 | *75* | 4,241,300 | *70* | 3,512,800 | *60* |
| non-practising | 507,700 | *10* | 1,206,400 | *20* | 9,173 | 51,957 | 61,130 | 4.04 | 1,511,900 | *25* | 1,817,700 | *30* | 2,341,900 | *40* |
| Protestants | 5,404,070 | 105.2 | 8,744,311 | 108.7 | 48,185 | −119,780 | −71,595 | −0.85 | 8,397,780 | 101.3 | 8,028,360 | 93.9 | 5,555,600 | 59.2 |
| Evangelicals | 3,050,000 | 59.4 | 980,000 | 12.2 | 5,709 | −2,709 | 3,000 | 0.30 | 995,000 | 12.0 | 1,010,000 | 11.8 | 1,050,000 | 11.2 |
| Neo-pentecostals | 0 | 0.0 | 4,000 | 0.0 | 158 | 9,442 | 9,600 | 36.92 | 26,000 | 0.3 | 100,000 | 1.2 | 400,000 | 4.3 |
| Roman Catholics | 2,230 | 0.0 | 58,929 | 0.7 | 1,777 | 20 | 1,797 | 2.71 | 66,300 | 0.8 | 76,900 | 0.9 | 150,000 | 1.6 |
| Orthodox | 100 | 0.0 | 51,000 | 0.6 | 1,740 | 0 | 1,740 | 3.00 | 58,000 | 0.7 | 68,400 | 0.8 | 103,000 | 1.1 |
| Marginal Protestants | 500 | 0.0 | 39,695 | 0.5 | 302 | 1,709 | 2,011 | 4.05 | 49,700 | 0.6 | 59,800 | 0.7 | 131,000 | 1.4 |
| Anglicans | 100 | 0.0 | 3,000 | 0.0 | 19 | 1 | 20 | 0.65 | 3,100 | 0.0 | 3,200 | 0.0 | 3,500 | 0.0 |
| Catholics (non-Roman) | 0 | 0.0 | 1,500 | 0.0 | 9 | −5 | 4 | 0.26 | 1,520 | 0.0 | 1,540 | 0.0 | 1,600 | 0.0 |
| Non-religious | 50,000 | 1.0 | 1,187,000 | 14.8 | 7,451 | 19,149 | 26,600 | 2.02 | 1,318,000 | 15.9 | 1,453,000 | 17.0 | 2,028,000 | 21.6 |
| Atheists | 5,000 | 0.1 | 799,000 | 9.9 | 5,430 | 14,660 | 20,090 | 2.24 | 895,000 | 10.8 | 999,900 | 11.7 | 1,437,000 | 15.3 |
| Jews | 4,000 | 0.1 | 15,000 | 0.2 | 100 | −10 | 90 | 0.58 | 15,400 | 0.2 | 15,900 | 0.2 | 30,000 | 0.3 |
| Muslims | 0 | 0.0 | 2,450 | 0.0 | 575 | −20 | 555 | 9.25 | 6,000 | 0.1 | 8,000 | 0.1 | 16,000 | 0.2 |
| Ahmadis | 0 | 0.0 | 120 | 0.0 | 8 | 10 | 18 | 9.00 | 200 | 0.0 | 300 | 0.0 | 800 | 0.0 |
| Baha'is | 0 | 0.0 | 1,500 | 0.0 | 10 | 30 | 40 | 2.35 | 1,700 | 0.0 | 1,900 | 0.0 | 4,000 | 0.0 |
| Buddhists | 0 | 0.0 | 300 | 0.0 | 2 | −2 | 0 | 0.00 | 300 | 0.0 | 300 | 0.0 | 300 | 0.0 |
| Other religionists | 0 | 0.0 | 5,750 | 0.1 | 42 | 183 | 225 | 3.21 | 7,000 | 0.1 | 8,000 | 0.1 | 20,000 | 0.2 |
| **Country's population** | **5,136,000** | **100.0** | **8,043,000** | **100.0** | **50,300** | **0** | **50,300** | **0.61** | **8,291,000** | **100.0** | **8,546,000** | **100.0** | **9,390,000** | **100.0** |

COLUMNS, ROWS. For meanings and definitions, see Codebook (Part 6). Note that, by definition, total 'Christians' = professing +crypto-Christians, which also = affiliated + nominal Christians; and, total 'affiliated' = affiliated Roman Catholics + affiliated Protestants (+the other 4 major blocs), *minus* doubly-affiliated persons, *minus* disaffiliated persons. Percentages may not always total exactly, due to rounding.
CENSUSES. Sweden's censuses of religion have obtained membership figures direct from the churches themselves, hence have measured religious affiliation and not religious preference or profession as defined in this survey.
POLLS. Polls of religion are very numerous. *Preference*. Stockholm (1967): 25% regularly practising Christians, 21% deists (i.e. nominal Christians), 35% agnostics, 19% atheists. Alingsas, a country town in the west (1966): 54% Christians, 21% deists, 15% agnostics, 10% atheists. Elsewhere, atheists have been as high as 27% (northern town of Lulea), and agnostics 43% (country north and south of Stockholm). Polls of atheism, and of religious practice, are given below.

NOTES ON RELIGIONS
AFFILIATED PROTESTANTS. The totals for the years 1900–1975 are each over 100% because many Protestants are always counted by 2 denominations at once (see DOUBLY-AFFLIATED below). *Affiliation to the Church of Sweden* (1965, according to the church centre RIS): 98.25%; regionally, Stockholm city 97.00%, Stor-Stockholm 97.03%, Stor-Goteborg 97.08%, Malmo-Lund region 98.02%. These totals up to 1980 reflect the church's position as the state church, and include both doubly-affiliated Christians and a large number of agnostics and atheists (see DISAFFILIATED below).
AHMADIS. Begun 1960; HQ Goteborg. Qadianis from Pakistan (HQ Rabwah), with a few Swedish converts.
ATHEISTS. Many polls of atheists have been taken. A very conservative average estimate is that in 1970 10% of the population definitively called themselves atheists. Many of these are humanists, or are politically right-wing, but a large proportion are communists, members of the left party-communists (Vänsterpartiet Kommunisterna, VPK) (legal; split on Sino-Soviet dispute): membership (1970) 17,000, (1974) 15,000; Communist voters (election of IX.1944) 318,466 (10.5% of all votes), (election of 20.IX.1970, including supporters of KFML) 257,885 (5% of all votes), (IX.1973) 274,929 (5.3% of all votes). Among youths aged 18–24, in 1974 12% professed to be atheists and 41% to have no religious affiliation or interest (Gallup).
BAHA'IS Local spiritual assemblies: 1964, 4; 1973, 10.
BUDDHISTS. In 5 groups and institutions: Uppsala, Alingsas, Strömstad, and 2 Tibetan Buddhist centres (based on Copenhagen): Stockholm and Göteburg.
DISAFFILIATED. This term is used here to describe dechristianized persons who, although mostly baptized as Lutherans in the state church and therefore regarded by that church as still affiliated to it (and hence enumerated in Table 2 as such), have recently withdrawn or disaffiliated themselves completely from Christianity and now profess to be either non-religious (agnostics) or atheists (see polls above). Because their statistics represent a duplication, they are shown in the table above as a negative quantity (with a minus sign). With regard to our projections for 1975–2000, the assumption here is that the total of disaffiliated will drop gradually until the date for proposed disestablishment of the Church of Sweden (1983), after which, and certainly by the year 2000, this category will be reduced to zero since the Church of Sweden will then be counting its members more realistically by excluding those who have left to become agnostics or atheists, as well as those who have left to belong to the free churches.
DOUBLY-AFFILIATED. The term covers those affiliated to, or claimed by, both the state church and also another denomination, mostly baptized Lutherans who have recently joined another church but who retain their original membership also. Because their statistics represent a duplication, they are shown in the table as a negative quantity (with a minus sign). Membership of the free churches has risen from about 300,000 in 1900 (3% of the state church) to about 800,000 by 1970 (20% of the state church). Some 90% of all free church members retain state church membership and are regarded as members by the state church, which therefore enumerates them all as such. From the statistics in the table it is clear also that a sizeable number of the 210,000 professing Roman Catholics, Orthodox and marginal Protestants (2.6% of the population) are also being counted in state church's total.
JEWS. Present since 1774. In 8 congregations.
MUSLIMS. In 2 groups: earlier refugees, and more recent migrant workers (in 1970: 1,700 Turkish, 470 Moroccans, 140 Tunisians, 140 Algerians, Syrians) including by 1975, 3,000 Yugoslavs. All are Sunnis. Immigration has continued rapidly during the 1970s. There is also an Ahmadiya Mission (enumerated here under Muslims although declared non-Muslim by Pakistan).
NEO-PENTECOSTALS. The total (1975) includes 3,000 lay charismatics and 40 clergy within the state church in 200 organized prayer groups, about 5,000 in other non-Pentecostal Protestant denominations, and about 5,000 young Jesus People within these denominations (over 100 groups of them in Stockholm), giving a total of 13,000 involved adults, and a total charismatic community including children of 26,000 by mid-1975. In 1972, 10,000 charismatics (almost all neo-pentecostals) attended the ecumenical Charisma 72 for 5 days in Stockholm.
ORTHODOX. In the 1970s there has been considerable immigration, including about 2,000 Assyrians in 1977.
OTHER RELIGIONISTS. Adherents of other non-Christian religions and cults, including Theosophy (9 Lodges, 335 members), Rosicrucianism (6 Lodges in AMORC, 2 centres of Lectorium Rosicrucianum), ISKCON (Hare Krishna; 1 centre) and other Hindu sects including Ananda Marga; et alia.
PRACTISING CHRISTIANS. Weekly church attendance has declined from, in 1900, 17% of the entire population at state church Sunday morning services, and from 20% in 1948, to (1968) 6% of the population (3.5% attending state church, 2.5% attending free churches) (youths aged 18–24, also 6%). Monthly attendance is 28% of the whole population. May-June 1968 (SIFO): 9% weekly, 6% fortnightly, 4% every 3 weeks, 9% monthly, 33% once every 2 months, 39% less than annually or never. 1968 (Stockholm only): 41% were keen and practising members of the Church of Sweden, 35% were lapsed members. In addition to church attendance, 35% of the whole population regularly (monthly) listens to or views radio/TV church services. Radio services: 25% of population weekly. TV services: 35% regularly (monthly). Using the definitions of this Encyclopedia, this gives a total of Christians practising monthly of around 40% of the population, and annually-practising Christians around 60% of the population. Expressing this as a percentage of affiliated Christians, this gives annual practice of around 80%.
PROTESTANTS. A report of the Religionssociologiska Institutet i Stockholm ('Prediktion av samfundens medlemstal 1990', 16.5.1969), predicts, for the period 1968–1990, a drop in state church membership of nearly 50% (from a nominal 7.9 million in 1968 to a nominal 4.0 million by 1990); a drop of about 30% for most free churches including Pentecostals; a rise of nearly 100% for Jehovah's Witnesses and Mormons; and a rise of 130% for Roman Catholic and Orthodox churches. These trends are incorporated in the above table, with the massive drop in state church membership being interpreted as an increasingly realistic attitude on the part of the state church with regard to not counting as its members persons who are at present disaffiliated or doubly-affiliated.
ROMAN CATHOLICS. Only 62% of all Catholics are affiliated to parishes or known by name and address; the rest are recent immigrants unknown to the clergy. In the 1970s steady immigration has continued.

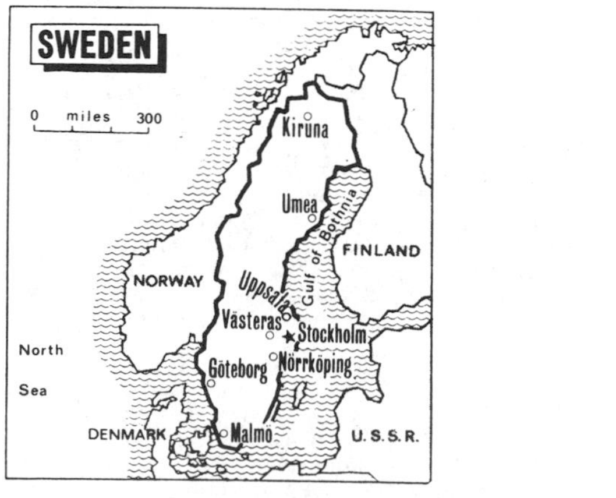


**NON-CHRISTIAN RELIGIONS. Judaism** has existed in Sweden for 2 centuries, the first Jews being authorized to settle, under strict control, in 1774. Emancipated in 1870, there are now about 15,000 Jews in the country, with orthodox and liberal synagogues in Stockholm, Göteborg and Malmö.

**Islam** has followers among earlier refugees and more recent migrant workers from Turkey, Morocco, Tunisia, Algeria, Syria and Yugoslavia.

**Buddhism** is represented by 5 groups and institutions: Bodhi in Uppsala, Buddhistiska Institutionen in Alingsas and Sällskapet för Buddhistisk Information in Strömstad; also Tibetan Buddhist centres in Stockholm and Göteborg.

**CHRISTIANITY.** Anskar, a French monk, made 2 visits to Sweden in the 9th century, the second time at the invitation of king Olaf. He brought many noblemen to the faith, but Christianity lapsed until the 10th century when the first English missionaries made their appearance. During the following century Christianity spread throughout the country, the first bishop being installed at Uppsala in 1164. King Gustav Vasa was the principal leader of the Swedish Reformation, resulting in the adoption of the Lutheran Confession in 1527. Though the former ecclesiastical structures and liturgy were not radically changed, identification with the national church contributed to the growth of a national self-awareness and an independent Swedish culture, making Sweden a dominant European power in the 17th century. In the 19th century a spiritual revival took place, which placed new emphasis on the New Testament as well as on pietism and lay preaching. Out of this revival denominationalism also appeared, with the first free church emerging from it in 1878. A number of Swedes belong both to the Church of Sweden and to free churches.

PROTESTANT CHURCHES. Anyone born a Swedish citizen is considered de facto a member of the Church of Sweden, in 1970 members being 98.7% of the total population. It is a folk church, closely linked to rural society, rooted in the history and tradition of the country, still tied to parochial structures inherited from the Middle Ages, and theologically inclusive of all wings of Christianity. The church has 13 dioceses and 2,563 parishes, and maintains 194 missionaries in Africa and Asia as well as missions for seamen in 24 ports. At the international level, the Church of Sweden has long been a leader in the ecumenical and confessional movements, and played a leading role in the founding of the Lutheran World Federation in 1947. There are 4 streams of churchmanship within the contemporary church: (1) the Young Church, which places emphasis on doctrinal freedom and the folk church concept; (2) the Old Church, uniting a strong Lutheran orthodoxy with the pastoral traditions of the Pietists; (3) the Low Church, representing at one time 10% but now only 1% of the clergy, noted for new forms of spontaneous worship; and (4) the High Church, to which about one third of the clergy adhere and which is strongly influenced by Anglicanism. The latter group seeks to promote liturgical revival and rediscovery of the catholicity of the church in Sweden. A strong bond exists between the Church of England and the Church of Sweden, symbolized

**Pentecostal Revival Movement of Sweden.** Annual week of tent revival meetings (Nyhemsveckan) in summer 1967, with thousands in attendance in massive tent.
**Church of Sweden.** *Left.* Youth demonstration past royal castle in Stockholm (right) en route to 1968 WCC Assembly in Uppsala. *Lower left.* In Uppsala Cathedral, 'Tree of Reconciliation' grows and expands, over a broken earth.

by their full intercommunion since 1922. Ordination of women has been permitted since 1959, and by 1963, 7 women had been ordained, although one third of the male clergy refused to co-operate with them; by 1978 this had risen to 235 women out of 3,200 active clergy (7%). At present 3% of the Swedish population attend the state church weekly, despite the fact that 80% have their children baptized and confirmed. The high proportion of church weddings among non-churchgoers indicates that church weddings serve more as a family than a religious ritual. The 98% of the population who retain official church membership assume also responsibility for the regular payment of church taxes.

The free churches in Sweden are distinguished by fervour and pietism, by their emphasis on church membership as a matter for personal decision, and and by the importance they place on independence from the state. In recent years their liturgy has been slowly returning to a more traditional form not greatly different from Lutheranism. The free churches form 10% of the population, the most significant of them being the Swedish Mission Covenant Church (Svenska Missionsförbundet) which was formed in 1878. This church and the smaller Swedish Alliance Mission (Svenska Alliansmission, 1853) are strongest in rural areas, whereas the Methodist Church is urban in character. The Methodist Church is in fact the oldest of Sweden's free churches. British

preachers were sent to Stockholm in 1826 to serve expatriate Methodists from the UK already there. A church was built in 1840; but because of opposition from the state church, the work came to an end in 1842. However, it was revived again by the conversion of a Swede in New York in 1850 who brought Methodism in its American connection back home with him. Another older free church is the Baptist Union of Sweden (Svenska Baptistsamfundet), founded in 1848. The Salvation Army is divided into an English branch (1882) and a much smaller Swedish branch. All of these churches have experienced a steady decline in membership since 1930; one of the causes has been the increasing urbanization. The Pentecostal movement (Pingströrelsen), which arose in 1907, expanded rapidly from 1930 to 1960 but since then has also experienced a decline in membership. Nevertheless, the Pentecostal Revival Movement of Sweden is now the largest Protestant denomination in the country. Other important Protestant churches are the Finnish Lutherans, Örebro Pentecostals and a number of smaller groups. Many of these free churches since the middle of the 19th century have sent missionaries to foreign fields, in particular to Africa, India and Japan. They are now responsible for 1,540 missionaries including 930 Pentecostals. The latter are also active in Latin America.

CATHOLIC CHURCH. From 1604 until 1873 no Swedish citizen was permitted to be a Catholic. Even today, despite its activism the Catholic Church remains on the fringe of Swedish society. The number of Catholics has increased due to the influx of immigrant workers and political refugees, especially Poles from 1945, Hungarians in 1956, Czechs and Slovaks in 1968, also Chileans and Brazilians more recently. There were 1,390 Catholics in 1890, 4,763 in 1930, and 27,416 in 1960. In 1969, of the 53,751 Catholics registered in parish records, 8,550 were Swedish, 5,067 had one Swedish parent, and 40,134 were recent immigrants. On 30 June 1973 there were approaching 70,000 affiliated Catholics of whom some 10,000 were Swedish. However, many immigrants have no contact with the church, and although exact enumeration is impossible since 1952 when government registers ceased to record immigrants' religion, it was estimated in 1970 that there were in fact about 95,000 Catholics. Of these, 15,000 were Croatians and Slovenes from Yugoslavia, 12,000 Germans and Austrians, 10,000 Italians, 6,000 Poles, 5,000 Spanish, 4,000 Hungarians, 2,000 Czechs and Slovaks, with many of the rest being Swedes. The hierarchy has attempted to provide pastoral services in the minorities' own languages, but it has also tried to contribute to their social integration by using the Swedish language at mass and in catechetical classes. The Catholic population is relatively young; between July 1969 and July 1970, there were 1,096 infant baptisms registered, but only 173 funerals. Since 1970 the number of baptisms and marriages has progressively decreased. In 1973 there were 101 priests (63 being religious priests and 38 secular priests), 10 of whom were of Swedish origin, and 209 sisters, 23 being Swedish. A survey conducted in Stockholm in November 1969 indicated that, of those required to attend mass weekly 26% did so.

Another survey conducted by the Institute of Religious Sociology in 1972 and covering all Christian denominations, showed that the Catholics had the highest percentage of Sunday attendance (19%), while the Lutheran Church was lowest (0.8%). The same survey indicated that only 1.9% of the inhabitants of Stockholm and its suburbs attend church on Sundays.

In 1977 Sweden, along with Scandinavia, was transferred from the jurisdiction of Propaganda (Rome) to that of the Congregation for Bishops.

OTHER CHURCHES. As a result of the influx of refugees during World War II, Orthodox churches increased considerably in numbers of affiliated to 10,000 faithful in 1960 and 51,000 in 1970, including Estonians, Finns, Greeks, Romanians, Russians, Serbs and Syrians. A group equal in size to the largest Orthodox community is that of the Jehovah's Witnesses. English-speaking Anglican chaplaincy services are also available.

**CHURCH AND STATE.** Relations between church and state are governed by the Ecclesiastical Law (Kyrkolag) of 1686, the constitution of 1809, amended most recently in 1961, and the Law of Religious Freedom (Religionsfrihetslag) of 1951. According to these, the Church of Sweden has a privileged position in relation to the state. The king, who is the supreme head of the church, names the archbishop and bishops on presentation by the Synod (Kyrkomöte) of 3 candidates for each vacancy. In principle, the freedom of the church is assured by the fact that the Synod can veto parliament's proposals concerning ecclesiastical matters. Membership in the Church of Sweden is acquired automatically at birth and not by baptism; but since 1951 an individual may request to be released from membership, whether or not he wishes to join another church. The state imposes a church tax; those who do not belong to the Church of Sweden pay only 40% of this, which covers the services performed by the Church of Sweden for the civil state. The state pays the Lutheran clergy who also are responsible for keeping state registers in addition to other municipal functions, State schools provide religious instruction, which is non-denominational and objective in nature. Teachers of religion are not required to belong to a church in order to qualify. The Church of Sweden, as all other churches, provides its own denominational instruction outside of school hours.

Religious and ecclesiastical affairs are under the jurisdiction of the Office for Ecclesiastical Affairs (Byran för Kykokamerale Fragor), of the Ministry of Education (Utbildningsdepartementet). If the minister of Education does not belong to the Church of Sweden, a minister without portfolio who is a member is put in charge of ecclesiastical affairs. The churches are not required to be registered, but clergy must receive official authorization to perform marriages recognized by the state. The opening of cloistered convents is also subject to royal authorization.

In 1958 a commission was appointed by government to investigate the question of relations between the state and the Church of Sweden. Its report was presented in March 1972, but parliament has not yet made a final decision on the matter. The report's recommendations called for the separation of the Church of Sweden and the state by 1 January 1983. From 1975 to 1982, civil state registration would be progressively transferred to the state, and in 1981–82 the bishops would hold their first independent assemblies. The Church of Sweden would keep all its property, but would then have to live on its own resources, except in areas becoming depopulated.

It was initially expected that parliament would decide the matter by 1974. However, in 1973 prime minister Olaf Palme stated that it would take several years to undertake any action in this realm. The reason for this is the hostility manifest in Lutheran Church circles concerning the proposals of the parliamentary committee. During a church-state conference at Malmö on 28 May 1974, the minister in charge of ecclesiastical affairs stated that a new document of 7,500 pages, with 900 questions and answers, would open a fresh discussion of the subject. The adoption of a new constitution in 1974 was to have been the occasion for introducing change in church-state relations; however, the ad hoc parliamentary committee thought it best not to be precipitous but to await a calmer atmosphere. Hence the new constitution, which was voted in 1974 and took effect on 1 January 1975, includes no modification in church-state relations over the constitution of 1809.

The government does not generally give subsidies to churches other than the Church of Sweden, nor to the few private schools existing in the country; but in an unusual gesture in 1971, parliament granted substantial financial aid to be shared among the Salvation Army, Baptist, Methodist, Orthodox and Catholic churches as well as with the Jewish and Muslim communities.

**INTERDENOMINATIONAL ORGANIZATIONS,** The Swedish churches have long been active in the ecumenical field. During World War I, archbishop Nathan Söderblom attempted to bring about a worldwide peace conference of all churches, which was later expanded to include other social and practical aspects of the Christian witness. As a result, an ecumenical conference on Life and Work took place in Stockholm in 1925, and in 1952 a Faith and Order conference in Lund. The Church of Sweden and the Swedish Mission Covenant Church joined the nascent World Council of Churches in 1939 and 1946 respectively, before its formal founding in 1948. The Swedish Ecumenical Council (Svenska Ekumeniska Nämnden) was established in 1932, building on foundations laid as early as 1915; and there are now about 75 local Christian councils with others in different stages of formation. The first national conference for local ecumenical councils was held in 1971. There is also a Swedish Free Church Council and a Swedish Missionary Council (Svenska Missionsradet). The latter was originally established in 1912 following the Edinburgh Conference of 1910 and was re-organized under its present name in 1920. The Stockholm Institute for the Sociology of Religion provides regular surveys of churches and evaluation of data in the field of religion. The Nordic Ecumenical Institute is an international body created in 1940 to provide a study and information centre for ecumenical and evangelistic activities in all northern European countries, including Norway, Sweden, Denmark, Finland and Iceland. The Swedish Ecumenical Committee for Development, Justice and Peace (SEKURF) is responsible for Sweden's Sodepax programme.

**BROADCASTING.** The state Sveriges Radio (Swedish Broadcasting Corporation) broadcasts morning and evening prayers on weekdays and on weekdays and on Sundays a Lutheran church service at 10 am. Stockholm is the headquarters of the world's largest Pentecostal broadcasting association, IBRA, begun in 1955, which produces programmes in 50 languages and buys 150 hours' time weekly on international stations (Radio Trans-Europe in Portugal and recently over facilities in Malta) for worldwide transmission to 70 countries. From abroad, a Protestant programme in Swedish is beamed in over Trans World Radio (Monaco) for 15 minutes on Thursday evenings, and a Catholic programme in Swedish over Radio Vatican for 15 minutes a week.

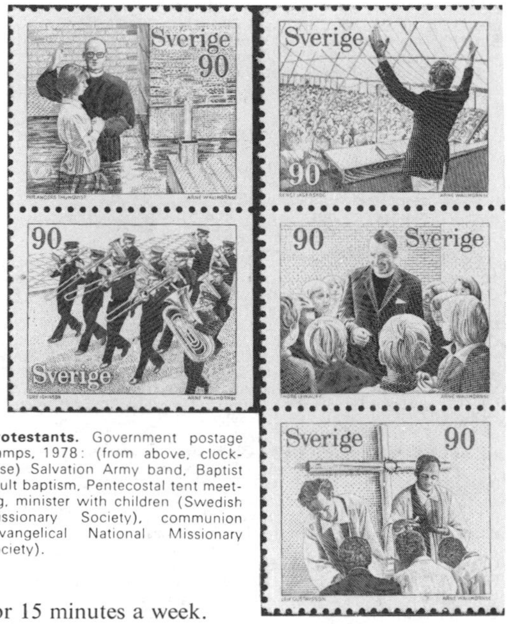


**Protestants.** Government postage stamps, 1978: (from above, clockwise) Salvation Army band, Baptist adult baptism, Pentecostal tent meeting, minister with children (Swedish Missionary Society), communion (Evangelical National Missionary Society).

## BIBLIOGRAPHY


*Catholicisme en Scandinavie.* M. de Paillerets. Paris: Spes, 1967.
*L'Eglise Suédoise: son histoire et son organisation.* R. Murray. Stockholm, 1970.
*Svensk missionsatlas.* Ed B. Sundkler & G. Sommarström. Stockholm: Svenska Institutet för Missionsforskning, n.d. (1957). 49p.
*Svenska Kyrkans Arsbok, 1970.* Stockholm: Verbum Kyrkliga Central-förlaget, 1970. 323p.
'Sweden', B. Gustafsson, in H. Mol (ed), *Western religion* (The Hague: Mouton, 1972), p.479–510.
'The church and secularized society: the Scandinavian experience', *Pro Mundi Vita* (Brussels), 29 (1969).
'The role of religion in modern Sweden', B. Gustafsson, *American behavioral scientist*, XVII, 6 (July-August, 1974), 175–186.


TABLE 2. ORGANIZED CHURCHES AND DENOMINATIONS IN SWEDEN

| Official name 1 | Begun 2 | Type 3 | Counc 4 | Congs 5 | Adults 6 | Affiliated 7 | Names, notes, and other statistics (see Codebook) 8 |
|---|---|---|---|---|---|---|---|
| Ancient Church of the East (P Tehran) | c1975 | O Nes | Yv... | | 500 | 1,000 | *Assyrian Ch. Nestorians.* Assyrian refugees from Lebanon and Cyprus wars. |
| Baptist Union of Sweden | 1848 | P Bap | TvX.z | 680 | 26,110 | 60,000 | *Svenska Baptistsamfundet.* Decline from 1940. 266n,G=−2.9%pa,1p,1s,W=60%,320Y,450z. |
| Catholic Church: D Stockholm | 1783 | R Lat | bzBQW | 29 | 46,000 | 58,929 | *Romersk-katolska Kyrkan.* 83% aliens. C=9+0+12. 8n,91x,5m,229w,W=26%,9Y,948y. |
| Christian Brethren | | P CBr | x.... | 2 | 100 | 200 | *Plymouth Brethren. Open Brethren. Gospel Halls.* Independent congregations. |
| Church of Christ, Scientist | 1905 | M Sci | x.... | 5 | 2,300 | 4,000 | *Kristen Vetenskap. Christian Science.* M=CCS(Mother Ch,Boston,USA). 1m,8w. |
| Church of England (J Fulham) | c1750 | A plu | awc.. | 6 | 1,000 | 3,000 | *Anglikanska Kyrkan.* Anglican (English) chaplaincies for 5,000 UK citizens. 2x. |
| Church of Jesus C of Latter-day Saints | 1853 | M LdS | x.... | 35 | 3,000 | 5,195 | *Jesu Kristi Kyrka av Sista Dagars Heliga.* Emigrating. 180f,G=5.1%pa,W=70%,260Yy. |
| **Church of Sweden:** | 829 | P Lut | LWX.a | 2,563 | 3,096,000 | 7,941,561 | *Svenska Kyrkan.* Attenders: annual 3,969,000; weekly 192,849. Priests: 2,601. |
| AD Uppsala | 1164 | P Lut | L | 216 | 228,000 | 584,992 | *Uppsala Arkestift.* 292,000 13,144 222 |
| D Göteborg | 1620 | P Lut | L | 284 | 389,000 | 998,267 | *Göteborgs Stift.* 499,000 33,833 307 |
| D Härnösand | 1647 | P Lut | L | 129 | 158,000 | 404,357 | *Härnösands Stift.* 202,000 10,408 163 |
| D Karlstad | 1647 | P Lut | L | 139 | 152,000 | 389,970 | *Karlstads Stift.* 195,000 10,888 148 |
| D Linköping | 1130 | P Lut | L | 213 | 197,000 | 506,224 | *Linköpings Stift.* 253,000 13,969 171 |
| D Lulea | 1904 | P Lut | L | 79 | 193,000 | 494,504 | *Lulea Stift.* 247,000 13,042 186 |
| D Lund | 1060 | P Lut | L | 441 | 434,000 | 1,113,301 | *Lunds Stift.* 557,000 21,835 363 |
| D Skara | 1014 | P Lut | L | 368 | 188,000 | 482,977 | *Skara Stift.* 241,000 20,002 192 |
| D Stockholm | 1942 | P Lut | L | 77 | 493,000 | 1,265,066 | *Stockholms Stift.* 632,000 10,222 260 |
| D Strängnäs | 1120 | P Lut | L | 149 | 197,000 | 505,594 | *Strängnäs Stift.* 253,000 8,741 160 |
| D Vasteras | 1120 | P Lut | L | 123 | 224,000 | 573,228 | *Vasteras Stift.* 287,000 10,994 176 |
| D Växjö | 1170 | P Lut | L | 253 | 222,000 | 569,050 | *Växjö Stift.* 284,000 23,268 215 |
| D Visby | 1570 | P Lut | L | 92 | 21,000 | 54,031 | *Visby Stift.* 27,000 2,504 38 |
| Churches of Christ | 1957 | P Dis | x.... | 2 | 50 | 100 | *Kristi Församling.* M=CC(Non-Instrumental)(USA). In Gothenburg, Stockholm. |
| Estonian Ev Lutheran Church in Exile | 1941 | P Lut | LWC.. | | 1,500 | 2,000 | *Eesti Evangeeliumi Luteri Usu Kirik.* Estonian USSR refugees. World HQ Stockholm. |
| Estonian Orthodox Church in Exile | c1945 | O Sla | C...w | 5 | 3,000 | 4,000 | Estonian refugees from USSR. Bishop and one large congregation in Stockholm. |
| Finnish Evangelical Lutheran Church | | P Lut | Lwc.. | 29 | 30,000 | 45,000 | *Finsksprakigt Lutherskt Församlingsarbete.* Serves 350,000 Finnish migrant workers. |
| Finnish Orthodox Church | 1958 | O Fin | Cwc.w | 10 | 3,000 | 4,000 | *Routsin Suomalainen Ortodoksinen Seurakunta.* Finns. Use Swedish churches. 1n,6Yy. |
| Free Baptist Union | 1872 | P Bap | x...C | 50 | 1,300 | 3,200 | *Fribaptistsämfundet. Scandinavian Independent Baptist Union.* In south. 20n. |
| Free Pentecostal Mission | 1930 | P Pe4 | ..... | | 200 | 500 | *Fria Pingstforsämlingen.* Schism from Filadelfia, Stockholm Ch(SFM). |
| Hungarian Protestant Congregations | 1957 | P LuR | ..... | 4 | 2,000 | 3,000 | *Ungerska Protestantiska Församlingen.* Hungarian refugees, Reformed and Lutheran. |
| Jehovah's Witnesses | 1899 | M Jeh | x.... | 232 | 12,401 | 27,000 | *Jehovas Vittnen. Watch Tower.* Active witnessing by 1926. HQ Jakobsberg. 826Y. |
| Latvian Ev Lutheran Church in Exile | 1945 | P Lut | Lwc.. | 12 | 1,592 | 4,500 | *Lettiska Evangelisk-Lutherska Kyrkan.* Latvian refugees. 7n,G=−1.6%pa,W=36%,5Yy. |
| Liberal Catholic Church | 1925 | C Lib | xV... | 5 | 100 | 300 | *Liberala Katolska Kyrkan.* M=LCC(UK). HQ Lindingö. 1968, applied to join WCC. |
| Maranatha Revival Church | 1959 | P Pe4 | x.... | | 10,000 | 15,000 | *Maranataväckelsen.* Radical schism ex Filadelfia Church. 3 factions. HQ Bromma. |
| Methodist Church in Sweden | 1826 | P Met | VwX.z | 178 | 8,994 | 25,000 | *Metodistkyrkan. Swedish Annual Conf*, NEurope CC, UMC(USA). 123n,G=−2.3%pa,1s,71Yy. |
| New Apostolic Church | 1898 | C CAp | x.... | | 500 | 1,000 | *Nyäpostoliska Kyrkan.* In Hamburg Bezirk; world HQ Dortmund (Germany). Germans. |
| New Church | 1887 | M Swe | x.... | 2 | 100 | 200 | *Nya Kyrkan. Swedenborgians. Stockholm Society*, and *Jönköping Circle.* |
| Örebro Mission Society | 1892 | P Pe2 | Z.D.x | 350 | 19,650 | 44,650 | *Örebro Missionsforening.* 1937 ex BUS. HQ Örebro. 165n,140m,G=0,2j,1s,W−33%,370Y. |
| Orthodox Church in Sweden: D Swedia | 1960 | O Gre | Cwc.w | 11 | 20,000 | 30,000 | *Grekisk-Ortodoxa Kyrkan. D Swedia & All Scandinavia*, & E Northern Lands. Greeks. 2x. |
| Pentecostal Revival Movement of Sweden | 1907 | P Pe2 | Z.D.a | 2,000 | 92,500 | 230,000 | *Pingstväckelsen i Sverige/Pingströrelsen/Filadelfia Ch.* SFM. 1200n,1j,1s,1300Y. |
| Religious Society of Friends | c1916 | P Qua | Q.... | 7 | 106 | 500 | *Vännernas Samfund i Sverige. Sweden Yearly Meeting* (1935). *Quakers.* HQ Stockholm. |
| Romanian Orthodox Church | c1970 | O Rum | Cwc.w | 1 | 500 | 1,000 | In Stockholm. Under jurisdiction of P Bucharest. Romanians. Migrant labourers. |
| Russian Orth Ch: D Western Europe | 1617 | O Sla | x...w | 1 | 500 | 1,000 | In Russian Orthodox Ch Outside of Russian (Paris). Bishop in Sweden. Convervative. |
| Salvation Army | 1882 | P Sal | xwx.a | 1,496 | 69,453 | 90,000 | *Frälsningsarmén. Sweden Territory.* Declining. 101 institutions,650n,G=−0.9%pa,1s. |
| Serbian Orthodox Church | 1972 | O Ser | Cwc.w | 1 | 4,500 | 9,000 | Under P Belgrade; bishop in England. Many Serbian migrant labourers. In Västeras. |
| Seventh-day Adventist Church | 1880 | P Adv | x.... | 68 | 3,800 | 7,200 | *Swed UC*(excl Finland Swedish Conf,Finland). 33n,G=0.2%pa,2H,1j,1p,1s(8),W=71%,111Y. |
| Swedish Alliance Mission | 1853 | P ind | x.D.x | 491 | 13,974 | 33,900 | *Svenska Alliansmissionen.* Only 23 churches have over 100 members. 170n,G=0.1%pa. |
| Swedish Holiness Union | 1886 | P Hol | x.D.x | 504 | 5,955 | 15,000 | *Helgelseförbundet/Covenant of Sanctification.* USA links. 163n,G=0.1%pa,1p,W=71%. |
| Swedish Mission Covenant Church | 1878 | P Con | xWX.z | 2,012 | 91,397 | 213,000 | *SMF. Svenska Missionsförbundet.* Revival ex state church. 623n,150m,31w,1s(107). |
| Swedish Religious Reform Society | | M Unt | I.... | | 200 | 300 | *Sveriges Religiosa Reformförbund.* Unitarians. Links with UUA(USA). HQ Skepptuna. |
| Swedish Salvation Army | 1905 | P Sal | ..D.x | 18 | 1,924 | 5,000 | *Svenska Frälsningsarmén.* 1905, rejected authority of international HQ, London. 25n. |
| Syrian Orthodox Church | 1970 | O Syr | Dw.Nw | 1 | 500 | 1,000 | Under (Jacobite) P Antioch (Damasqus). 200 families. Arabs. Migrant labourers. |
| Other Protestant denominations | | P | ..... | | 2,000 | 5,000 | Total about 30 (see list below). |
| Other marginal Protestant bodies | | M | ..... | | 1,000 | 3,000 | Total over 30 smaller marginal sects and cults. |
| Other Catholic (non-Roman) churches | | C | ..... | | 100 | 200 | Very small bodies including Cath Apost Ch(Irvingites)(Katolsk-apostoliska Kyrkan). |
| Doubly-affiliated (duplication)(1970) | | | | | −349,000 | −896,435 | 90% of all free church members including Pentecostals remain in state church. |
| Disaffiliated (duplication)(1970) | | | | | −768,000 | −1,970,000 | Baptized Lutherans now completely disaffiliated, professing agnostics or atheists. |
| **Total affiliated (mid-1970)** | | | | **11,050** | **2,460,806** | **6,032,000** | **Total denominations (1970) . . . 98.** |
| **Total affiliated (mid-1975)** | | | | **11,060** | **2,467,200** | **6,047,600** | **Total denominations (1975) . . . 107.** |
| **Total affiliated (mid-1980)** | | | | **11,070** | **2,471,800** | **6,059,000** | **Total denominations (1980) . . . 117.** |

NOTES ON TABLE ABOVE
COLUMNS: for meanings and CODES (cols. 1, 3, 4, 8): see Codebook (Part 6). Column 1: **Boldface type** = church with over 10% of country's affiliated Christians.
NATIONAL COUNCILS (Column 4, 5th letter).
a = member of both SEC and SEA.
C = Swedish Free Church Council (SFCC) (Sveriges Frikyrkorad).
d = member of both SFCC and SEC.
e = Swedish Evangelical Alliance (SEA) (Evangeliska Alliansens Svenska Avdelning) (affiliated to EEA but not to WEF).
W = Swedish Ecumenical Council (SEC) (Svenska Ekumeniska Nämnden).
w = associate member of SEC.
x = member of both SFCC and SEA.
z = member of both SFCC, SEC and SEA.
*Local councils.* About 75.
OTHER PROTESTANT DENOMINATIONS. There are about 30 additional smaller denominations, including: Apostolic Episcopal Ch (Apostoliska Episcopala Kyrkan), Apostolic Faith (Apostoliska Trons Mission), Children of God International, Christadelphians (Bröderna i Kristus), Christian Society, Ch of God (Anderson) (1 church), Ch of the Nazarene, Exclusive Brethren (Raven-Taylor), French Reformed Ch (Eglise Réformée de France: Fransk-Reformerta Församlingen), Gypsy Evangelical Movement (France, Switzerland), International Ch, Moravian Ch (Evangeliska Brödraförsamlingen), Worldwide Evangelization Crusade.

PEOPLES (ethnolinguistic). Christians: about 91% Swedish, 4% Finnish, 0.7% German, 0.7% Norwegian, 0.6% Danish, 0.6% Dutch, 0.5% Greek, 0.2% Croatian, 0.2% Serbian, 0.1% Lapp, 0.1% Italian, 0.1% Latvian, 0.1% Estonian, 0.1% Gypsy, 0.1% British, 0.1% Hungarian, Russian, Romanian, Syrian Arab, French, USA (White & Black), Swiss, Assyrian.

COUNTRY-WIDE TOTALS
EVANGELIZATION (see Part 5). 1900: 100%. 1970: 100%. 1980: 100%. *Mass evangelism.* Among recent campaigns: Billy Graham rally in 1955 in Gothenburg (26,000 attenders, 150 enquirers), and a 5-day crusade in January 1977 in Gothenburg (867 enquirers), and in 1978, Skandia '78 on radio/TV; 1979, Here's Life Uppsala (CCCI). *Radiophonic evangelism.* Annual listeners' letters (1975): 2,735 HCJB, 420 TWR, 74 RVOG, FEBC, Radio Vatican, IBRA, et alia.
FOREIGN MISSIONARIES AND PERSONNEL (nationals serving abroad) (1973). Total 1,846: 1,796 Protestants (increase from 1,541 in 1963, 1,571 in 1968, and 1,709 in 1972; including 930 Pentecostals in 18 societies in 50 countries, about 30 marginal Protestants (Jehovah's Witnesses), about 20 Roman Catholics in Scandinavia.
FOREIGN MISSIONARIES AND PERSONNEL (aliens from abroad) (1973). Total 594. *From Western world.* 545: 304 Roman Catholics including lay missionaries, about 200 marginal Protestants (170 Mormons from USA), 35 Protestants (24 in 8 USA societies, 5 in 3 UK societies, several Scandinavians), about 4 Orthodox, 2 Anglicans from UK. *From Communist world.* 46: about 43 Roman Catholics from Poland, 3 Orthodox from USSR and Yugoslavia. *From Third World.* About 3 Protestants.
INSTITUTIONS (church-operated) (1973). Total 60, including about 10 higher schools, 10 medical centres, 7 presses, 7 religious communities, 4 research centres, 7 seminaries (Protestant).
PERIODICALS. About 230 titles (10 Pentecostal, 5 Salvation Army, 3 SDA; including many missionary periodicals).
PERSONNEL. About 7,284 (6,690 national, 594 foreign).
RELIGIOUS LIBRARIES. About 40.
SCRIPTURE DISTRIBUTION (1975). Annual totals: 133,000 Bibles (98% subsidized, 2% commercial), 146,000 NTs (1% free, 98% subsidized, 1% commercial), 121,500 UBS portions. *Translations completed.* Portion: Lapp in 1648. NT: 2 languages since 1526. Bible: 2 languages since 1541.
SERVICE AGENCIES. About 90, including CCCI, CEF, EFS, FKG, FLOD, IASOT, IBRA, KATS, KFUK/KFUM(YMCA/YWCA), MBV, NEC, SEA, SEC, SEF, SEKURF, SFCC, SFM, SU, SUK, WBT, WTMA, YWAM.

ADDITIONAL DATA ON CHURCHES
CATHOLIC CHURCH. *Catholics.* The total 58,929 is of those enrolled on parish records in 1970, including 10,000 Swedish Catholics. In addition there are about 40,000 recent immigrants not on parish records (20,000 Croats, 18,000 Germanic peoples, 10,000 Italians). *Growth.* (1890) 1,390 Catholics, (1930) 4,763, (1960) 27,416, (1968) 52,365 (only 8,880 being Swedish). *Annual baptisms.* (1972) 99.1% infant, 0.9% adult. *Priests.* 34 secular, 65 religious. Growth (Swedish+expatriates): (1960) 8+55, (1965) 5+76, (1973) 10+91. From 1960–70, 7 Swedish priests were ordained. *Brothers.* 1 national. *Sisters.* 20 nationals, 3 Danish, 3 Norwegians, 203 non-Scandinavian (105 Germans, 43 Polish, 14 Italians, 14 French). *Main-religious orders and congregations.* Priests: SJ, OMI (American, Polish provinces), OP (French province), CP, SDB, OCD, OFM. *Sisters.* 60 Sisters of St Elizabeth, 32 Sisters of Our Lady, Sisters of Ste-Brigitte, Dominicans (2 orders), Franciscans, Sisters of St Joseph, Carmelites, Sisters of St Mary (2 orders).
*Catholic organizations.* The Diocese of Stockholm is represented on the Nordic (or Scandinavian) Episcopal Conference (Nordiske Bispekonferanse), with headquarters in Oslo, Norway. There are no national organizations of religious personnel, but there is a Priests' Council with 10 members elected from the diocesan clergy. Major lay movements include: Catholic Youth of Sweden (Sveriges Unga Katoliker, SUK), the central organization for all parish youth groups; Federation University Student Groups (KATS), with about 190 members; Studium Catholicum Sueciae, for Catholic intellectuals; Legion of Mary, with 125 members; and Scouts with around 260 members.
The Holy See has no diplomatic relations with Sweden. It is represented to the Catholic hierarchy by the apostolic delegation for Scandinavia based in Copenhagen, Denmark.
In 1970 there were 2 Catholic nursery schools (170 children) and 2 primary schools (290 pupils), but only 7% of those attending were Catholics. The church also sponsors 7 clinics, 2 homes for the aged and 6 orphanages. Caritas aids in the resettlement of immigrants.
CHURCH OF JESUS CHRIST OF LATTER-DAY SAINTS. Many Mormons are now emigrating to the USA.
CHURCH OF SWEDEN. All Swedish-born citizens belong by right to the state church, and hence church officials claimed in 1970 that 98% of the total Swedish population were affiliated to it, i.e. a church population, as shown in column 7 above, of 7,941,561. Of these a large number, around 13%, had been baptized as infants or had otherwise been regarded as Christians in childhood, but had now long been agnostics or atheists. Using the criterion of baptism, in 1970 some 85% of the total population had been baptized in the state church (88,568 during the year); however, of these at least 10% had recently withdrawn (in accordance with the 1951 and 1968 laws) and regarded themselves as no longer Christians (although the rate of formal withdrawal has recently become less, 3,000 each year or 0.3% per year). A further 15% still regarded themselves as members but had no connection with nor participation in church activities. This leaves 60% of the population who were in 1970 known as members by the church's parishes, of whom about four-fifths were annually practising. In the above table this situation is enumerated for the 13 dioceses; column 6 shows all adults affiliated to each diocese who are also practising members (at least annually); column 7 shows the total claimed church population for each diocese; and column 8 shows first ('annual attenders') the total practising church population of each diocese in 1970 (defined as all who attend once or more a year), and second ('weekly attenders') the total attending high mass every Sunday in its parishes (1958–68 figures). *Inner missions.* The largest mission within the state church is the National Evangelical Union (Evangeliska Fosterlandsstiftelsen, EFS). Membership in it declined from 40,000 in 1960 to 28,586 in 1969, and to 28,222 in 1970. There are also 20,000 Laestadians from the Finnish Laestadian revival movement. *Clergy.* In addition to parish priests as shown in column 8 above, there are numerous others. Total (1978) 3,200 active ministers, of whom 235 were women priests (7%). Women priests now serve in all 13 dioceses. *Seminaries.* One seminary, 3 Bible schools. In January 1978, 75 new clergy were ordained (22 being women).

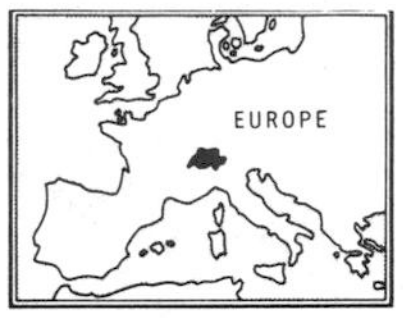


# SWITZERLAND

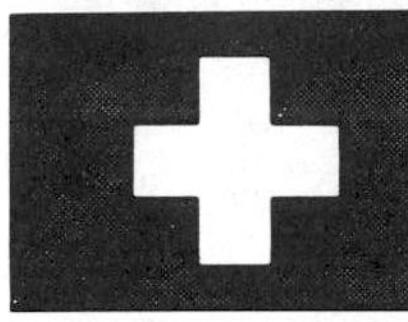

## SECULAR DATA

**STATE. Official name:** The Swiss Confederation (La Confédération Suisse/Schweizerische Eidgenossenschaft/Confederazione Svizzera). Shorter official names: Switzerland/Schweiz/Suisse/Svizzera. Adjective of nationality: Swiss (suisse).
**Flag** (shown above right): White cross on red field.
**Area:** 41,288 sq. km. (15,941 sq. miles). Agricultural land: 48.8%.
**Government:** Federal Republic, since 1848 (1291 Swiss confederation, 1499 independent, 1798 Helvetic Republic).
**Legistrature:** Parliament: Council of States (Stränderat), 44 members; National Council (Nationalrat), 200 members.
**Official Language:** German (*Deutsch*), French (*Français*), Italian (*Italiano*), and Romansh.
**Chief Cities:** Capital Bern 284,740, Zürich 719,320, Basel 381,450, Geneva 321,080, Lausanne 226,680.
**Political divisions:** 25 Cantons (6 being half-cantons). 19 are German-speaking, 5 French-speaking, 1 Italian-speaking. In 1974, a referendum decided to create a 26th canton, Jura (francophone), at some future date.
**Armed forces** (1976): Total 46,500 regular: army 37,500, air force 9,000 (345 combat aircraft). Reserves: 578,500.

**DEMOGRAPHY. Population:** 6,269,783 (census of 1.XII.1970. For 1970–2000 (UN), see last row of Table 1). Population density (1975): 158/sq. km. (410/sq. mile). Under 15 years: 24%. Growth rate (1975–80): 0.60% per year (births 1.40%, deaths -1.03%, immigrants 0.23%). Life expectancy (1975–80): 72.7 years. Household size: 2.9 persons.
**Major languages:** 64.9% German, 18.1% French, 11.9% Italian, 0.8% Romansh, Spanish, English, Turkish, Hungarian, Dutch, Czech, Greek.
**Urban dwellers** (1970): 58.4%. Urban growth rate (1950–70): 2.8% per year.
**Labour force:** 48%.
**Refugees** (1977): From abroad, 35,000 (about 33,000 from Eastern Europe, 1,000 Tibetans from China, 200 from Chile).
**Tourists** (1974): 6,221,776.

**ETHNOLINGUISTIC GROUPS:** 63.2% German Swiss, 18.1% Franco-Swiss, 7.2% Italian, 3.7% Italo-Swiss, 2.0% Spaniard, 1.6% German, 0.8% Romansh, 0.7% French, 0.5% Austrian, 0.5% British, 0.4% Jewish, 0.2% Turkish (11,300), 0.2% Hungarian, 0.2% Dutch, 0.2% Czech, 0.2% Greek, 0.1% Russian, 0.1% Romanian, Gypsy, USA, Arab (2,300), Scandinavian, other Slav, Chinese (1,320), et alii. Total aliens (1974): 18%.

**MONEY** (1977). **Monetary unit:** Swiss franc (=100 centimes or rappen); US$1=SFr 2.44.
**National income per person:** US$6,340. Average annual family income: US$18,386.
**Inflation:** (1970–74) 7.9% per year (1975: consumer price index 147), falling to 1.1% per year by 1977.
**Cost of living in capital** (1976): index 166 (Washington DC=100). Daily cost of living: US$48.

**HEALTH.** Hospitals: 438 (71,276 beds). Doctors: 10,625. Blind: 9,000. Psychotics: 65,000. Drug addicts: over 13,000.

**EDUCATION.** Adult literacy: 100%. Education rate: 53%. Schools: 4,000. Universities: 9.

**LITERATURE.** Annual new titles (1973): 7,942. Periodicals: 1,429. Scientific journals: 810. Newspapers 98 dailies, 173 non-daily.

**COMMUNICATION** (per 1,000 people). Phones: 561. Radios: 311. TV sets: 253. Daily newspaper circulation: 386 copies.

TABLE 1. RELIGIOUS ADHERENTS IN SWITZERLAND

| Year | 1900 | | mid-1970 | | Annual change, 1970–1980 | | | | mid-1975 | | mid-1980 | | 2000 | |
|---|---|---|---|---|---|---|---|---|---|---|---|---|---|---|
| *Name* | *Adherents* | *%* | *Adherents* | *%* | *Natural* | *Conversion* | *Total* | *Rate* | *Adherents* | *%* | *Adherents* | *%* | *Adherents* | *%* |
| **Christians** | **3,295,000** | **99.4** | **6,154,000** | **98.2** | **46,430** | **–5,930** | **40,500** | **0.63** | **6,391,400** | **97.8** | **6,559,000** | **97.4** | **6,797,400** | **92.3** |
| professing | 3,295,000 | 99.4 | 6,154,000 | 98.2 | 46,430 | –5,930 | 40,500 | 0.63 | 6,391,400 | 97.8 | 6,559,000 | 97.4 | 6,797,400 | 92.3 |
| Roman Catholics | 1,346,000 | 40.6 | 3,108,400 | 49.6 | 46,710 | –2,000 | 44,710 | 1.34 | 3,345,600 | 51.2 | 3,555,500 | 52.8 | 4,014,500 | 54.5 |
| Protestants | 1,916,000 | 57.8 | 2,941,800 | 47.0 | –1,160 | –3,940 | –5,100 | –0.17 | 2,937,700 | 45.0 | 2,890,800 | 42.9 | 2,646,800 | 35.9 |
| Catholics (non-Roman) | 34,000 | 1.0 | 51,200 | 0.8 | 400 | –20 | 380 | 0.72 | 53,000 | 0.8 | 55,000 | 0.8 | 52,000 | 0.7 |
| Orthodox | 1,000 | 0.0 | 21,000 | 0.3 | 160 | 0 | 160 | 0.73 | 21,800 | 0.3 | 22,600 | 0.3 | 37,000 | 0.5 |
| Marginal Protestants | 0 | 0.0 | 16,600 | 0.3 | 200 | 40 | 240 | 1.35 | 17,800 | 0.3 | 19,000 | 0.3 | 29,500 | 0.4 |
| Anglicans | 1,000 | 0.0 | 15,000 | 0.2 | 120 | –10 | 110 | 0.71 | 15,500 | 0.2 | 16,100 | 0.2 | 17,600 | 0.2 |
| nominal | 66,000 | 2.0 | 247,888 | 4.0 | 4,331 | 10,100 | 14,431 | 4.47 | 322,500 | 4.9 | 392,200 | 5.8 | 567,200 | 7.7 |
| affiliated | 3,229,000 | 97.4 | 5,906,112 | 94.2 | 42,099 | –16,030 | 26,069 | 0.43 | 6,068,900 | 92.9 | 6,166,800 | 91.6 | 6,230,200 | 84.6 |
| total practising | 2,906,100 | *90* | 4,902,070 | *83* | 34,520 | –25,216 | 9,304 | 0.19 | 4,976,500 | *82* | 4,995,110 | *81* | 4,361,140 | *70* |
| non-practising | 322,900 | *30* | 1,004,040 | *17* | 7,579 | 9,186 | 16,765 | 1.53 | 1,092,400 | *18* | 1,171,690 | *19* | 1,869,060 | *30* |
| Roman Catholics | 1,312,900 | 39.6 | 2,860,611 | 45.6 | 42,519 | –4,000 | 38,519 | 1.26 | 3,064,900 | 46.9 | 3,245,800 | 48.2 | 3,646,200 | 49.5 |
| Protestants | 1,873,600 | 56.5 | 2,824,781 | 45.1 | –2,138 | –13,000 | –15,138 | –0.55 | 2,770,800 | 42.4 | 2,673,400 | 39.7 | 2,283,500 | 31.0 |
| Evangelicals | 470,000 | 14.2 | 520,200 | 8.3 | –401 | 231 | –170 | –0.03 | 519,500 | 7.9 | 518,500 | 7.7 | 516,000 | 7.0 |
| Neo-pentecostals | 0 | 0.0 | 1,000 | 0.0 | 0 | 900 | 900 | 30.00 | 3,000 | 0.0 | 10,000 | 0.1 | 50,000 | 0.7 |
| Marginal Protestants | 1,000 | 0.0 | 134,652 | 2.1 | 1,025 | 1,000 | 2,025 | 1.41 | 143,800 | 2.2 | 154,900 | 2.3 | 191,500 | 2.6 |
| Catholics (non-Roman) | 40,000 | 1.2 | 55,068 | 0.9 | 423 | –20 | 403 | 0.71 | 57,100 | 0.9 | 59,100 | 0.9 | 60,000 | 0.8 |
| Orthodox | 1,000 | 0.0 | 21,000 | 0.3 | 160 | 0 | 160 | 0.73 | 21,800 | 0.3 | 22,600 | 0.3 | 37,000 | 0.5 |
| Anglicans | 500 | 0.0 | 10,000 | 0.2 | 110 | –10 | 100 | 0.95 | 10,500 | 0.2 | 11,000 | 0.2 | 12,000 | 0.2 |
| Non-religious | 5,700 | 0.2 | 46,800 | 0.7 | 0 | 4,440 | 4,440 | 6.42 | 69,200 | 1.1 | 91,200 | 1.4 | 365,000 | 5.0 |
| Jews | 13,000 | 0.4 | 20,700 | 0.3 | 150 | 0 | 150 | 0.70 | 21,500 | 0.3 | 22,200 | 0.3 | 25,000 | 0.3 |
| Atheists | 1,000 | 0.0 | 20,000 | 0.3 | 0 | 1,370 | 1,370 | 5.25 | 26,100 | 0.4 | 33,700 | 0.5 | 147,000 | 2.0 |
| Muslims | 400 | 0.0 | 16,400 | 0.3 | 120 | 0 | 120 | 0.71 | 17,000 | 0.3 | 17,600 | 0.3 | 20,000 | 0.3 |
| Ahmadis | 0 | 0.0 | 200 | 0.0 | 0 | 10 | 10 | 4.00 | 250 | 0.0 | 300 | 0.0 | 1,000 | 0.0 |
| Baha'is | 0 | 0.0 | 3,100 | 0.0 | 0 | 40 | 40 | 1.21 | 3,300 | 0.1 | 3,500 | 0.1 | 4,000 | 0.1 |
| Hindus | 0 | 0.0 | 2,000 | 0.0 | 0 | 40 | 40 | 1.82 | 2,200 | 0.0 | 2,400 | 0.0 | 3,000 | 0.0 |
| Buddhists | 0 | 0.0 | 2,000 | 0.0 | 0 | 0 | 0 | 0.00 | 2,000 | 0.0 | 2,000 | 0.0 | 1,600 | 0.0 |
| Other religionists | 300 | 0.0 | 2,000 | 0.0 | 0 | 40 | 40 | 1.82 | 2,200 | 0.0 | 2,400 | 0.0 | 3,000 | 0.0 |
| **Country's population** | **3,315,400** | **100.0** | **6,267,000** | **100.0** | **46,700** | **0** | **46,700** | **0.71** | **6,535,000** | **100.0** | **6,734,000** | **100.0** | **7,366,000** | **100.0** |

COLUMNS, ROWS. For meanings and definitions, see Codebook (Part 6). Note that, by definition, total 'Christians' = professing + crypto-Christians, which also = affiliated + nominal Christians. Percentages may not always total exactly, due to rounding.
CENSUSES. (Held every 10 years since 1860). **1860:** 58.9% Protestants, 40.7% Roman Catholics, 0.2% Jews, 0.2% non-religious and other religionists. **1900:** 57.8% Protestants 40.6% Roman Catholics, 1.0% Old Catholics (non-Roman), 0.4% Jews, 0.2% non-religious and other religionists. **1910:** 56.1% Protestants, 41.5% Roman Catholics, 1.0% Old Catholics, 0.9% non-religious and other religionists, 0.5% Jews. **1920:** 57.5% Protestants, 39.9% Roman Catholics, 1.1% non-religious and other religionists, 1.0% Old Catholics, 0.5% Jews. **1930:** 57.3% Protestants, 40.1% Roman Catholics, 1.3% non-religious and other religionists, 0.9% Old Catholics, 0.4% Jews. **1941:** 57.6% Protestants, 40.4% Roman Catholics, 0.8% non-religious and other religionists, 0.7% Old Catholics, 0.5% Jews. **1.XII.1950** (de jure): 56.3% Protestants, 41.6% Roman Catholics, 1.1% non-religious and atheists and other religionists, 0.6% Old Catholics (non-Roman), 0.4% Jews. **1.XII.1960** (de jure): 52.7% Protestants, 45.4% Roman Catholics, 0.8% non-religious and atheists and other religionists, 0.5% Old Catholics, 0.4% Jews, 0.1% Orthodox. **1.XII.1970:** 49.6% Roman Catholics, 47.0% Protestants, 1.1% non-religious and atheists, 0.8% Catholics (non-Roman) (0.5% New Apostolics, 0.3% Old Catholics), 0.3% Orthodox, 0.3% marginal Protestants, 0.3% Jews, 0.3% Muslims, 0.2% Anglicans, 0.1% other religionists.

NOTES ON RELIGIONS
AHMADIS. Qadianis, based on Rabwah (Pakistan), with

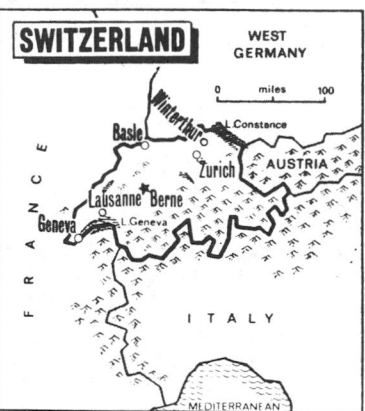

**NON-CHRISTIAN RELIGIONS. Judaism** increased slightly in numbers from 1930 to 1970 (17,973 to 20,744), but the proportion of Jews in the total population decreased over the same period from 0.4% to 0.3%. This is true of both the Jewish citizen (Swiss national) population (9,803 and 0.3% in 1930; 11,977 and 0.2% in 1970) and Jewish expatriate population (8,170 and 2.3% of all expatriates in 1930; 8,767 and 0.8% of expatriates in 1970). Jews are strongest in urban centres: Geneva (1.3% of the population), Basel (0.9%), Zürich (0.6%), Vaud (0.5%) and Bern (0.1%). The Union of Swiss Jewish Communities, in Zürich, included in 1970 groups in over 22 cities. Switzerland is the headquarters of the very important World Jewish Congress, founded in Geneva in 1936, whose purposes are to assure the survival of the Jewish people, to reinforce their unity and to co-ordinate the work of the European offices of the American Jewish Joint Distribution Committee.

**Islam** is represented by Turkish migrant workers, and by the Ahmadiya Mission of Islam in Zürich.

**Baha'i** has followers in over 16 local spiritual assemblies, with headquarters in Bern.

**Hinduism** is represented by the Krishnamurti Friends of Switzerland (Krishnamurti-Freunde der Schweiz) in Novaggio; the Vedantic Centre (Centre Védantique) in Geneva, which disseminates the thought of Sri Ramakrishna and commentaries on the Gita; and a recent sect, the Divine Light Centre (Divine Light Zentrum) in Winterthur.

**Buddhism** has only about 2,000 followers in the country, including 500 Tibetan refugees after the annexation of their country by China in 1950. Nevertheless, Switzerland plays an important role in Buddhist studies through its universities, the review *Cahiers Bouddhistes* and the Zürich Buddhist library. It is also in Switzerland that several important Buddhist centres serving Europe are found: (1) the Tibet Institute of Rikon, near Zürich, where the Dalai Lama has assigned many Gelukpa and Sakyapa lamas and which maintains an important specialized library, a centre for oral instruction, a periodical *Opuscula Tibetana* and relations with the universities of Zürich, Götingen and Giessen; and (2) the European Institute for Buddhist Studies, in Geneva, which emphasizes (though not exclusively) Japanese Jôdo-Shinshû and facilitates its spread to francophone countries. There exist also numerous local Buddhist groups which are attempting to federate into a Buddhist Community of Switzerland. This in turn is

mostly Swiss converts; mosque in Zürich, opened in 1963.
ATHEISTS. Parti Suisse du Travail (PST): membership (1970, 1974) 3,000 members, and 2 extreme leftist factions: Partie Populaire Suisse (PPS), Organisation des Communistes de Suisse (OCS/ML); Communist voters (election of X.1947) 49,353 (5.1% of all votes), (30.X.1971) 50,831 (2.7% of all votes). 71% of all communists, and of Communist voters, are from French-speaking cantons. Among youths aged 18–24, a 1974 poll found 4% professing to be atheists (Gallup).
BAHA'IS. Entered before 1921. Local spiritual assemblies: 1964, 12; 1973, 16. HQ Bern.
BUDDHISTS. Initially, 500 refugees from Tibet after the 1950 occupation by China; and also about 1,200 Chinese. There are several important centres of Buddhist studies.
COUNTRY'S POPULATION. There has been substantial immigration of foreign workers since 1930, mainly Roman Catholics from Mediterranean countries. In 1970–80 most of the annual natural increase was due to immigration. The column 'Natural change' above incorporates both immigration and biological increase figures, and shows the division of the total among the various religions and blocs.
HINDUS. Ramakrishna Mission, and numerous young Swiss converts to the Divine Light Mission, ISKCON (Hare Krishna), Ananda Marga, and a few other groups. A neo-Hindu movement, the Theosophical Society, in 1975 had 8 Lodges with 240 members.
JEWS. 42% expatriates; urban, in over 22 cities. Co-ordinated through the Union of Swiss Jewish Communities (Zürich).
MARGINAL PROTESTANTS. The totals professing to belong to this category in the 1970 census (e.g. 1,980 Mormons) are much smaller than those claimed as affiliated by these marginal churches themselves (e.g. 5,652 Mormons). Many marginal

bodies prefer to operate clandestinely or in total anonymity.
MUSLIMS. 2 distinct groups: Turkish migrant workers since 1960 (11,300 in 1970), and Arab workers (2,300), all being Sunnis; and since 1948 the Ahmadiya Mission (Qadianis) (enumerated here under Muslims, though declared non-Muslim by Pakistan) based on Zürich.
NEO-PENTECOSTALS (1974). Charismatics within the non-Pentecostal Protestant denominations, in the French-speaking Reformed churches (12 pastors involved) and German-speaking (3 pastors). There are also a number of youths in the Jesus Movement.
OTHER RELIGIONISTS. Adherents of numerous smaller religions and cults, including Rosicrucians (10 AMORC centres).
PRACTISING CHRISTIANS. May–June 1968 (Isopublic, Gallup): church attenders 30% of population weekly, 11% fortnightly, 8% once every 3 weeks, 11% once monthly, 18% once every 2 months, 22% less than annually, or never. On our definition, therefore, annual practice = 78% of the population = 83% of all affiliated Christians. Zürich area: 20% attend regularly, 33% from time to time, 29% seldom, 16% never, 2% non-religious. 1974: of youths aged 18–24, 18% attend church weekly (Gallup). *Pilgrims*. In the year 1900, 150,000 pilgrims a year were visiting the Marian shrine of the Black Virgin at Einsiedeln, still today the largest and most famous Swiss pilgrimage centre.
ROMAN CATHOLICS. The increase in proportion over the decades has been due to (1) higher Roman Catholic fertility than Protestant fertility and (2) the much larger influx of Roman Catholic foreign workers. Expatriate Roman Catholics increased from 202,445 professing in the census of 1950, to 464,553 in 1960, and to 864,666 in 1970 (an immigration rate of 40,000 a year).

expected to be a member of the Buddhist Community of Europe, which is also still in the process of formation.

**CHRISTIANITY.** The Christian faith was originally brought to Switzerland from Gaul and Italy by merchants, soldiers and slaves who passed along the imperial highway of Helvetia. The abbey of St Maurice was built in 300, followed by the abbey of Romainmôtiers in 400. From Ireland, Colomban's mission profoundly influenced the christianization of the country through the foundation of the abbey of St Gall in 613. In the 12th century more monasteries were added through the Cistercian reform, including at Einsiedeln, while a mystic movement centred in mendicant orders came into being a hundred years later.

In 1519 Zwingli began to preach the 'pure Gospel' at Zürich, but soon found himself in conflict with Anabaptists as well as Catholics. Efforts to establish the Catholics by force were successful at Baden in 1526, but the Reform movement continued to spread at St Gall, Bern, Basel and Schaffhouse. Fighting broke out between the Defensive Alliance consisting of the Reformed cantons, and the Christian Union consisting of the Catholic cantons under Ferdinand of Austria; and Zwingli himself was killed in the second battle of Kappel. Catholics were victorious again in 1531; but the Reform movement aided by Bern freed itself from the Catholic dukes of Savoy. In 1536 Calvin established a Christian community in Geneva. Fribourg became the pivot of Catholicism in the western part of the country, and the Counter

Reformation emerged under the influence of Charles Borromeo and Francis de Sales.

Catholic-Protestant rivalry contained to characterize Swiss political and religious life during succeeding centuries. It is only in relatively recent years that an ecumenical spirit has begun to manifest itself.

Catholicism has since 1970 become the majority religion of Switzerland. In 1930 there were 2,330,303 Protestants, forming 57.3% of the population, compared with 1,629,043 Catholics (40.1%). Between 1930 and 1970 Protestants continued to increase in absolute numbers to 2,991,694, but proportionally they decreased to 47.0% of the population. During the same period Catholics grew to 3,096,654, or 49.6% of the population. This rapid growth is due in part to immigration patterns, especially the large influx of expatriate workers from the Roman Catholic Mediterranean countries. The Swiss citizen population remains in majority Protestant (55%, as against 43% for Catholics), whereas the expatriate population is overwhelmingly Catholic (80%, as against 12.7% for Protestants).

These population movements have resulted in an increasing mixture of the Protestant and Catholic communities. Hence the traditionally Protestant cities of Bern, Vaud, Zürich and Basel are becoming increasingly Catholic, and the traditionally Catholic cities of Valais, Tessin and Fribourg increasingly Protestant. This is also true of the cantons themselves.

CATHOLIC CHURCH. In Switzerland each Catholic diocese is directly dependent on the Holy See in Rome, there being no metropolitan archbishopric and no ecclesiastical province. Vatican II

The Cross over Switzerland: a parish church in Saanen.

**Katholische Kirche in der Schweiz, Abtei Nullius Maria Einsiedeln.** The Abbey Church, built 1719-35, is a major pilgrimage centre. *Above.* Baroque interior of Abbey Church. *Right.* 3-dimensional tableau in circular Panorama of the Crucifixion.

has been the source of a much greater collaboration between the dioceses, which is especially apparent in the Episcopal Conference. It is still time to say, however, that the secretariat of this conference is very limited in its organization and function.

Catholic life in Switzerland has been greatly influenced in recent years by the Swiss Catholic Synod. In preparation since 1969, it opened in November 1972 and was expected to continue for 3 or 4 years. It has consisted of 4 sessions each year, 2 at the diocesan level and 2 interdiocesan. The role of the interdiocesan assemblies has been to co-ordinate the work of the diocesan assemblies. Planned in the beginning as simultaneous and co-ordinated meetings of diocesan synodal assemblies according to a federalist procedure, the synod became genuinely national. This began during the second session in June 1973, when the diocesan assemblies recognized their inability to handle some of the subjects submitted to them, including legislation on mixed marriages and abortion. Wishing to benefit from wider contacts, a single national synodal meeting met at Bern in September 1973. Such questions as Sunday attendance, confirmation of children and intercommunion were left to the interdiocesan assemblies. Each diocesan assembly consisted of between 160 and 200 delegates, half being priests and religious personnel and half laity. Proportional representation was guaranteed as follows: of the lay delegates, at least one-third were women, one-fifth youth between 16 and 25 years of age and one-seventh foreign labourers; of the other delegates two-thirds were priests, one-sixth brothers and one-sixth sisters. Diocesan bishops named 10% of the lay delegates as well as 10% of the priests and religious, but all other delegates were chosen by their peers.

The average age of the lay delegates was 33 years in Chur, 36 in Sion and 36 in Lausanne, Fribourg and Geneva. In this last diocese, as well as in Lugano, the president of the synodal presidium of the synod was a layman, although everywhere else a priest. Direction and co-ordination were under a central secretariat and an interdiocesan preparatory commission which included 2 non-Catholic counsellors. The synod was preceded by an extensive inquiry by the bishops, with 335,000 responses received. These were sorted into 12 general themes for study, including doctrinal, pastoral and social subjects of national and international significance. For each of these themes, 12 preparatory commissions were established in each diocese. Great freedom of expression characterizes the synods, though they are only consultative with the last word being left to the hierarchy.

Although there are no worker priests in Switzerland in the strict sense of the word, there exist different types of experimental ministries: Workers' Soul Care (Arbeiterseelsorger) in Ennetbaden, founded about 1940, with 12 'pastors to workers'; Church and Industry Swiss Catholic Work Team (Schweizerische Katholishe Arbeitsgemeinschaft 'Kirche und Industrie'), begun in 1969, with 12 priests and laymen who study the problems of workers in industry and provide interconfessional training for pastors already at work with local groups; and Industrial Seminar with Workshop Experience for Theological Students (Industrieseminar mit Betribsprakticum für Theologiestudenten), formed in 1970.

PROTESTANT CHURCHES. The principal body is the Federation of the Protestant Churches of Switzerland, which consists of 18 cantonal Reformed churches, with the Free Church of Geneva and the Evangelical Methodist Church. Each cantonal church is autonomous, there being no single or unified Swiss Reformed Church. Their legal status varies. Some have concordat relationships with the state, some are state churches, while others are entirely independent. They also display a surprising diversity in liturgy and constitution. However, most maintain synods and synodal councils which exercise legislative and executive functions for their member congregations. Zwinglian influences have been predominant in the German-speaking region, whereas Calvinism has been more important in the French areas. However, spiritual unity is maintained through the acceptance by most cantonal churches of the Helvetic Confession of 1566. The first attempt to unite the cantonal churches was made through the formation of the Conference of Swiss Churches in 1858, and in 1920 the present Federation was established, consisting at first only of Reformed churches until the Free and Methodist churches were added. There is some question as to whether this is a church or a federation of churches as its name seems to imply. It is in fact both in the sense that its constituent bodies maintain their independence but delegate part of their authority to the federation and its council. It is through the Federation, and not as individual churches, that representation in supranational or ecumenical bodies is usually carried on, including membership in the WCC and WARC.

The Salvation Army, Lutherans, Adventists, Mennonites and a host of smaller denominations are also active. Pentecostalism has not been very successful in Switzerland, although some 25 distinct bodies have been identified. The largest is the Swiss Pentecostal Mission.

MARGINAL CHURCHES. The Friends of Man is a group founded in 1919 by Alexandre Freytag, who was baptized in a Reformed church but later was converted to Adventism and then to Jehovah's Witnesses in 1898. A schism in 1947 by Bernand Sayerce, formerly a Catholic, produced the Sayerce branch of the Friends of Man.

Jehovah's Witnesses have been in Switzerland since the end of the last century, but the majority of their faithful have been lost to the Friends of Man. Small groups of Christian Scientists and Mormons also exist, the latter having one of their 15 world temples in Switzerland.

CATHOLIC (NON-ROMAN) CHURCHES. Several movements out of the Church of Rome have been active in Switzerland since the last century. Until recently the most important was the Christian Catholic Church, a schism from Catholicism in Bern in 1872 resulting from the papal infallibility dogma of Vatican I. Membership has declined from 37,307 (0.9% of the population) in 1930 to 20,268 (0.3%) in 1970.

The Catholic Apostolic Church spread from England to Switzerland about 1850, but it has been rapidly losing members in recent years. On the other hand, a schism from the above, the New Apostolic Church, is growing rapidly and has now surpassed the Christian Catholic Church in size.

**CHURCH AND STATE.** Switzerland being a confederation, it is the responsibility of the federal government to assure religious liberty and peace between the religions, and to legislate for each of its 25 cantons or semi-cantons on matters concerning relations with the churches.

The federal constitution, established 29 May 1874 but often modified subsequently, begins with a religious affirmation: 'In the name of Almighty God, the Swiss Confederation. . . has adopted the following Federal Constitution.' It then guarantees freedom

**Eglises Réformées.** International Monument to the Reformation, Geneva: from left, Farel, Calvin, Beza, Knox.

of conscience and belief (Article 49.1) as well as freedom of worship (Article 50.1). Additional provisos are included concerning the exercise of religious freedom (Article 49.2-6), such as the fixing of 16 years of age as the limit of parental authority for the religious education of children (Article 49.3). Religious conflicts of the past were responsible for the article stipulating that 'The cantons and the confederation may take necessary measures to maintain public order and peace between members of different religious communities' (Article 50.2). Recourse to the government is possible in cases of disputes concerning the creation of or divisions between religious communities (Article 50.3). Originally the establishment or modification of bishoprics was submitted for approval to the confederation (Article 50.4); but in June 1972, the Council of States (the federal legislative assembly elected by the cantonal assemblies) accepted a motion from the National Council (the federal legislative assembly elected by direct popular suffrage) tending to abrogate this article. Article 51 on the suppression of the Jesuits, and Article 52 prohibiting the re-establishment of convents and suppressed religious orders, were abrogated on 20 May 1973 by a referendum, with 790,799 voting for and 648,959 against. Introduced into the constitution following the war of Sonderbund in the middle of the 19th century in which Catholics and Protestants opposed each other, these articles had already fallen into disuse before the voting of May 1973. In fact there were about 80 Jesuits openly living in Switzerland at the time. Nevertheless, their official abrogation permitted the Helvetic Confederation to ratify the European Declaration of the Rights of Man. In addition, 2 other restrictive constitutional provisions are still being discussed: Article 75 declaring church officials ineligible for the National Council, and Article 25 forbidding the ritual slaughter of animals by orthodox Jews.

According to the federal constitution, cantons may freely determine their own relationships with the churches. Separation of church and state is followed by Geneva and Neuchâtel, although in an incomplete manner (Cantonal Constitution of Geneva Article 166, and Neuchâtel Article 71). Any religious community may establish itself, under federal civil law, without having to be registered. In addition there is a system of public ecclesiastical sovereignty. The Catholic and Reformed churches are officially recognized by the constitution or legislation of all cantons, with the exception of Basel-City (Reformed Church only) and Tessin (Catholic Church only). Previously the Catholic Church was also the state church in Valais, but this was abolished by a referendum held on 17 March 1974. The Christian Catholic Church is juridically recognized in the cantons of Zürich, Bern, Luzern, Soleure Bâle, St Gall and Argovie. Public ecclesiastical sovereignty varies from full religious liberty existing in certain cantons to the establishment of national churches in others. The financial situation also varies according to different juridical situations, cantons with a strong Reformed tradition commonly making state funds available to the churches. Religious education is generally included in the curriculum of schools; and if not, the school building may be used by churches for religious instruction. In 1973 a Swiss pressure group was set up to seek, through a referendum, a constitutional amendment requiring the complete separation of church and state.

State departments of religion exist in a few cantons. More generally the cantonal department of the Interior or of Justice handles ecclesiastical matters when they arise. Where federal regulations are involved, matters are then dealt with by the federal Department of Justice and the police.

**INTERDENOMINATIONAL ORGANIZATIONS.** The headquarters of many international interconfessional bodies are in Switzerland, as well as those of several national interdenominational bodies. A few of the major ones are described below.

WORLD COUNCIL OF CHURCHES. The WCC has its secretariat in Geneva. It was inaugurated in 1948, based on a decision made in 1938 to combine the 2 movements Faith and Order, and Life and Work, to facilitate the co-operative work of churches throughout the world. In 1961 the International Missionary Council was also amalgamated with the WCC. The WCC's principal policy-making bodies are the General Assembly, which has met 5 times since its foundation (Amsterdam 1948, Evanston 1954, New Delhi 1961, Uppsala 1968 and Nairobi 1975), and the Central Committee, which meets

yearly. WCC membership is open to those churches which 'confess the Lord Jesus Christ as God and Saviour according to the Scriptures and therefore seek to fulfil together their common calling to the glory of the one God, Father, Son and Holy Spirit'. Other criteria such as size and stability are taken into consideration in assessing membership qualifications. In mid-1974 there were 260 Protestant, Orthodox, Anglican, Old Catholic and Independent member churches in 90 countries. Most of the historical Orthodox churches are now members, and at the Uppsala Assembly nearly twice as many Third-World churches were represented as at Amsterdam. The World Council was re-organized in 1971 into 3 Programme Units: Faith and Witness, Justice and Service, Education and Communication. Included in Faith and Witness are 2 commissions (Commission on Faith and Order, Commission on World Mission and Evangelism, CWME) and several agencies: Department on Church and Society, Dialogue with Men of Living Faiths and Ideologies, Christian Medical Commission, Agency for Christian Literature Development, and Theological Education Fund (TEF). Justice and Service is divided into 6 branches: Commission on Inter-Church Aid, Refugee and World Service, Ecumenical Church Loan Fund (ECLoF), Commission of the Churches on International Affairs (CCIA), Commission on the Churches' Participation in Development, Advisory Committee on Technical Services, and Ecumenical Programme to Combat Racism. Education and Communication carries on its work through 3 Staff Working Groups (Renewal, Education, Communication) and an office for Relations with Regional and National Councils. In addition there are sections dealing with Finance and Central Services and Periodicals. The Ecumenical Institute of Bossey and Special Study Portfolios are under the direct supervision of the General Secretariat; the former was founded by the WCC in 1946 as a centre for study and research as well as being a place of encounter between Christianity and the modern world. Courses are also offered for students at the nearby University of Geneva leading to academic certificates.

SODEPAX. The Committee for the Study of the Problems of Society, Development and Peace, commonly known as SODEPAX, was founded in Geneva in 1968. This is a joint organization of the WCC and the Justice and Peace Pontifical Commission of the Vatican, with the general secretary a Catholic and the associate general secretary a Protestant. Between 1968 and 1970 SODEPAX organized a series of conferences, including 2 on World Co-operation for Development at Beirut in 1968 and Montreal in 1969 and the interreligious conference on peace at Kyoto (Japan) in 1970, as well as consultations at Driebergen (Netherlands) in 1970 on Church, Communications and Development, and at Baden (Austria) on Christian Preoccupation for Peace. In 1970 conferences were also organized on the interests of under-developed countries and on international monetary reform, as well as ones dealing with the second decade of development. Altogether these meetings have produced a large number of reports, as well as contributing to the creation of co-operative ecumenical organizations dedicated to development and peace in several countries; including among others Australia, Canada, Hong Kong, Indonesia, Japan, Lesotho, Malawi, Papua New Guinea, South Korea, Sri Lanka, Sweden, Switzerland and Uruguay. In 1971, the 2 promoting organizations decided to limit the activities of SODEPAX which, with a reduced secratariat, has been devoting its attention to the promotion of education. In 1975 SODEPAX was given a new mandate by the WCC and the Vatican, for an additional 3-year period, until the end of 1978.

YMCA. The interconfessional World Alliance of Young Men's Christian Associations (YMCA) was founded in 1855 and has its headquarters in Geneva.

INTERNATIONAL CHRISTIAN YOUTH EXCHANGE. This was begun in Geneva in 1946 as an independent movement which however works closely with the WCC and national and regional youth movements. Its purpose is to promote exchange visits between youth of different denominations and countries as a means of training them for undertaking Christian action concerning justice and peace in the world.

CHRISTIAN COUNCILS. The Working Community of the Christian Churches in Switzerland is an official organization begun in 1971, consisting of the Reformed, Catholic, Old Catholic, Methodist and Baptist churches, as well as the Salvation Army. Its purposes are to foster ecumenical dialogue and

**Eglises Réformées.** Bern Cathedral (Munster), with 'Last Judgement' over main doors.

collaboration and to promote common interests in public life. The Swiss Missionary Council (Schweizerischer Evangelischer Missionsrat/Conseil Suisse des Missions Evangéliques), founded in 1944, provides opportunities for interdenominational contacts between the various Protestant groups, and there are also co-operative unions of missionary societies serving respectively the German-speaking and French-speaking churches. Swiss Protestant Inter-church Aid (Entraide Protestante Suisse aux Eglises de l'Etranger et aux Réfugiés, EPER) is similarly involved in joint relief and development projects. Catholic ecumenical concerns are co-ordinated by the Commission for Ecumenism of the Catholic Episcopal Conference.

OTHER ORGANIZATIONS. The Commission for Dialogue between the Reformed Churches and the Roman Catholic Church was formed in 1966 by the Federation of Swiss Protestant Churches and the Catholic Bishops' Conference. Its Secretariat is located at the Institute of Ecumenical Studies of the University of Fribourg. The Commission for Dialogue between the Roman Catholic Church and Christian Catholic Church was begun in 1966 by the Synodal Council of the latter and the Catholic Bishops'

Common prayer at WCC's Ecumenical Centre, Geneva, during visit of Pope Paul VI in June 1969.

Conference. It provides for mutual aid in liturgical and pastoral matters.

The Swiss Evangelical Alliance (Schweizerische Evangelische Allianz) is not an association of churches but of individuals dedicated to the promotion of evangelization, prayer, Bible study and Christian fellowship.

Switzerland and the Third World is a commission of the Swiss churches begun in 1970. Its purpose is to stimulate public conscientization concerning development and peace in conformity with the WCC's Church and Society stance and the Catholic encyclical 'Populorum progressio'. It functions as a Swiss SODEPAX committee.

There is also a joint Commission for Pastoral Work among Mixed Families.

The Orthodox Centre of the Ecumenical Patriarchate, in Chambésy promotes contact and collaboration between autocephalous Orthodox churches, the organization of inter-Orthodox and ecumenical consultations, the collection of information on the life and activity of Orthodox churches throughout the world, and the establishment of a secretariat for a future Pan-Orthodox world meeting provisionally called the Great and Holy Council.

The Institute of Ecumenical Studies of the University of Fribourg, founded in 1964, is a research centre attached to the Faculty of Theology. It studies the common origins of diverse Christian peoples, analyses the causes of divergences and carries out research on ways of promoting reconciliation. Its archives include files on ecumenical theology, church life and hermeneutics. It conducts conferences, seminars, special courses and has a library that specializes in ecumenical literature, both Protestant and Orthodox, particularly of the 16th, 19th and 20th centuries.

The Protestant Study Centre, in Geneva, was founded in 1954 by the National Protestant Church of Geneva. It is concerned with the training of Christians, dialogue with the modern world and research required by the churches. It also conducts work projects, courses and conferences.

The John Knox Centre was founded in Geneva in 1953 by the Presbyterian Church of the USA and the National Protestant Church of Geneva. It serves as an international meeting-place for students and for conferences. Attached to it is an agency for the study of relations between the Third World and Europe.

Das Schweizerisch Ostkirchenwerk Catholica Unio, founded in Luzern in 1958, is a centre for Catholic action. The Catholica Unio movement in reality was begun in 1923, its purpose being to study and develop contacts between Catholics and Orthodox, without however today seeking for the return of the Orthodox to the Catholic Church. Approved by the Congregation for the Oriental Churches in Rome, the movement exists also in Austria, West Germany and Brazil.

Two organizations are dedicated to Jewish-Christian dialogue: The Church and the Jewish People, sponsored by the WCC in Geneva, and the Christlich-Jüdische Arbeitsgemeinschaft in der Schweiz/Amitié Judéo-Chrétienne en Suisse/Amicitia Ebraico-Cristiana Ticino, founded in Basel in 1946 with 2,000 members in 1971. With other religions there are as yet no formalized institutions, but such an organization is under study at the Faculty of Theology at the University of Fribourg.

**BROADCASTING.** The Swiss Broadcasting Corporation has regular Christian radio and TV programmes in its 3 language areas German, French and Italian. Equal treatment is given to Catholics and Protestants, and a smaller slot is reserved for Old Catholics. Radio broadcasts include a Catholic mass and a Protestant service each Sunday, plus a number of denominational programmes during the week. On TV there is a church service and a fortnightly magazine each for Catholics and Protestants. There is no commercial broadcasting in Switzerland.

The Federation of the Protestant Churches of Switzerland has a specialized co-ordinating committee on the mass media. The radio-TV section of the WCC Department of Communication, and the Broadcasting Service of the Lutheran World Federation, both of which are located in the Ecumenical Centre in Geneva, are active on an international level. They jointly produce a monthly news tape service, Intervox, English and French versions of which are distributed internationally. For Catholics, Switzerland is a member of UNDA.

## BIBLIOGRAPHY


*Agenda pastoral des églises protestantes de Suisse, 1970.* Basel: Verlag Friedrich Reinhardt, 1970. 332p.

*Handbuch der Reformierten Schweiz.* Zürich: EVZ Verlag, 1962. 573p.

*Handbuch die Kirchen, sonder Gruppen und religiosen Vereinigungen.* O. Eggenberger. Zürich: Evangelische Verlag, 1965.

*Kirche und Staat in der Schweiz.* U. Lampert. Freiburg, 1937. 2 vols.

*Les Eglises protestantes de la Suisse au siècle de l'oecuménisme et de l'entraide: 50 ans de Fédération 1920–1970.* A. Mobbs. Berne: Fédération des Eglises Protestantes de la Suisse, 1970. 117p.

'Switzerland', R.J. Campiche, in H. Mol (ed), *Western religion* (The Hague: Mouton, 1972), p.511–528.


TABLE 2. ORGANIZED CHURCHES AND DENOMINATIONS IN SWITZERLAND

| Official name 1 | Begun 2 | Type 3 | Counc 4 | Congs 5 | Adults 6 | Affiliated 7 | Names, notes, and other statistics (see Codebook) 8 |
|---|---|---|---|---|---|---|---|
| Altevangelisch-Taufgesinnte Gemeinden | 1614 | P Men | G•••C | 12 | 3,000 | 5,000 | *Mennonite Ch in Switzerland.* First begun 1614 in Zürich. HQ Emmental, Kanton Bern. |
| Amis de l'Homme (Freytag) | 1919 | M Jeh | x•••• | | 40,000 | 90,000 | *Friends of Man.* Schism ex Jehovah's Witnesses by A.Freytag. |
| Amis de l'Homme (Sayerce) | 1947 | M Jeh | x•••• | | 5,000 | 10,000 | *Friends of Man/Kingdom of God Ch.* Split ex Freytag by former Catholic B.Sayerce. |
| Assemblées de Dieu | 1967 | P Pe2 | ZF••• | 2 | 150 | 300 | *Assemblies of God.* Links with M=AoG(USA). Classical Pentecostals (2-stage). 2n,2f. |
| Assemblées des Frères Darbystes | 1838 | P EBr | x•••• | 45 | 2,500 | 5,000 | *Brethren* (Closed, some Open). Schisms ex Eglise Libre after visits by JNDarby. 2f. |
| Assoc Ev d'Egls Baptistes Françaises | 1890 | P Bap | TT••• | 9 | 545 | 1,500 | *Assoc of French-speaking Ev Bapt Chs.* Ex FEEBF(France). 2n,4x,G=3.0%pa,W=33%,10Y. |
| Biblische Glaubensgemeinde | 1951 | P Pe2 | ••••• | 8 | 200 | 400 | *Bible-Believing Congregations.* HQ Bern. Ex Volksmission Entschiedener Christen. |
| Brüdergemeine im Schweiz | | P Mor | xwc•• | 13 | 300 | 500 | European Continental Conf, Unity of Brethren. Moravians. In cities. HQ Birsfelden. |
| Bund der Baptistengemeinden in der S | 1849 | P Bap | T•C•d | 14 | 1,422 | 3,000 | *Baptist Union of Switzerland.* HQ Ruschlikon-Zürich. 1948, M=SBC(USA). 21f,1s. |
| Bund Freier Ev Gemeinden der Schweiz | 1824 | P Con | K•••C | 113 | 2,750 | 5,000 | *Federation of Free Evangelical Congregations in Switzerland.* HQ Steffisburg. 20n. |
| Chiese Evangeliche di lingua Italiana | | P Ref | ••••• | 5 | 500 | 1,000 | *ACELIS. Italian-speaking Ev Chs.* In Basel, Geneva, Chaux-de-Fonds, Renens, Zürich. |
| Christadelphianer | | P Ade | x•••• | 1 | 30 | 50 | *Christadelphian Bible Mission.* 1 ecclesia (church) in Leysin (Vaud). Pacifist. |
| Christengemeinschaft | 1911 | M Gno | x•••• | | 500 | 1,000 | *Sonnenwesen/Sun-Being. General Anthroposophical Society.* HQ Dornach (Basel). |
| Christkatholische Kirche der Schweiz | 1872 | C OCa | UW••K | 54 | 15,400 | 20,268 | *Christian Cath Ch, D Bern.* Schism ex Ch of Rome. Declining 5%pa. 45n,2x,1s,200Yy. |
| Deutsche Spätregenmission | | P Pe4 | x•••• | 2 | 100 | 200 | *Latter Rain Mission*, from South Africa and Germany. Revivalist Pentecostals. |
| Eglise Adventiste du Septième Jour | 1870 | P Adv | x•••• | 57 | 3,920 | 8,000 | *Seventh-day Adv, German* (55%) *& French* (45%) *Swiss Confs.* 31nx,93m,1H,1j,2r,133Y. |
| Eglise Anglicane au Suisse | 1552 | A plu | awc•• | 42 | 5,000 | 10,000 | *Ch of England.* D Gibraltar (south), J Fulham. Chaplaincies (19 seasonal). 11x. |
| Eglise Catholique Apostolique | c1850 | C CAp | x•••• | 16 | 200 | 300 | *Catholic Apostolic Ch. Irvingites.* Rapidly dwindling since death of last clergy. |
| Eglise de Dieu (Anderson) | | P Hol | x•••• | 4 | 70 | 100 | *Ch of God* (*Anderson*). M=CoG(Anderson)(USA). Holiness denomination. 2n. |
| E de JC des Saints des Derniers Jours | 1850 | M LdS | x•••• | | 3,400 | 5,652 | *Latter-day Saints.* Zollikofen: Mormon temple (only 15 in world). 70f,G=5%pa. |
| Eglise du Christ Scientiste | | M Sci | x•••• | 37 | 1,000 | 2,000 | *Ch of Christ, Scientist/Christliche Wissenschaft/Christian Science.* M=CCS. 8m,42w. |
| Eglise d'Ecosse | 1556 | P Ref | Rwc•• | 3 | 200 | 500 | *Ch of Scotland.* Scots in Geneva et alia. HQ Grand-Saconnex. 1x,W=52%,11Yy,2z. |
| Eglise Evangélique du Réveil | 1933 | P Pe2 | Z•••H | 10 | 1,000 | 2,000 | *Evangelische Kirke der Erweckung. Ev Ch of Revival.* HQ Geneva. M=AdD(France). 1s. |
| Eglise Ev Libre du Canton de Vaud | 1847 | P Ref | ••••K | | 1,000 | 3,000 | *Ev Free Ch of Vaud Canton.* Renewal movement ex Eglise Réformée Vaudoise. |
| Eglise Orthodoxe Romaine | | O Rum | Cwc•• | 3 | 3,000 | 5,000 | *Biserica Ortodoxa Romana.* Under P Bucharest. Geneva, Bern, Zürich. Romanians. 4x. |
| Eglise Orthodoxe Russe | | O Sla | Mwc•• | 4 | 1,000 | 3,000 | *Russian Orthodox Ch.* In jurisdiction of Moscow Patriarchate, and bishop of Zürich. |
| Eglise Orthodoxe Russe de Genève | | O Sla | x•••• | 13 | 500 | 2,000 | D Western Europe, Russian OC Outside of Russia (HQ,USA). Bishop in Netherlands. |
| Egls Evangéliques Espagnoles en Suisse | | P Ref | ••••• | 3 | 150 | 300 | *Spanish-speaking Ev Churches in S.* Basel, Geneva. Linked with cantonal churches. |
| Ev Gesellschaft des Kantons Bern | 1931 | P Ref | ••••C | 42 | ,2,000 | 4,000 | Renewal movement in Bern cantonal church; virtually a free church. G=–0.5%pa. |
| Ev-Lutherische Kirche im Schweiz & L | 1891 | P Lut | l•••• | 3 | 8,000 | 11,000 | *Assoc of Ev Luth Chs in S & Liechtenstein.* Includes ELC of Basel & NWSwitzerland. |
| **Fédération des Egls Prot de la Suisse:** | 1920 | P Ref | RWC•K | 1,582 | 2,065,150 | 2,714,331 | *FEPS. Schweizerischer Ev Kirchenbund* (*Swiss Federation of Prot Chs*). 1697n. |
| Eglise Evangélique Libre de Genève | 1849 | P Ref | R•••K | 4 | 500 | 1,000 | *Evangelical Free Ch of Geneva.* Geneva, Neuchâtel. 3n,26Yy. |
| Eglises Réformées cantonales: | c1520 | P Ref | Rwc•K | 1,248 | 2,046,300 | 2,692,500 | Independent cantonal churches. French=Calvinist,German-Zwinglian. 33022Yy. |
| Aargau (Argovie) | 1516 | P Ref | Rwc•K | 92 | 140,200 | 184,500 | L=G (German-speaking); includes *Eglise Française d'Argovie.* 2375 |
| Appenzell (AR & IR) | 1521 | P Ref | Rwc•K | 20 | 23,800 | 31,300 | G AR=Ausser Rhoden, HQ Herisau. IR=Diaspora, one parish. 378 |
| Basel-Land (Bâle-Campagne) | 1517 | P Ref | Rwc•K | 41 | 80,900 | 106,400 | G Basel-Landschaft. Basel rural area. 4 Deaneries (Dekanat). 1353 |
| Basel-Stadt (Bâle-Ville) | 1517 | P Ref | Rwc•K | 14 | 84,600 | 111,300 | G *Ev-Ref Kirche des Kantons Basel-Stadt.* Basel city. 2s. 828 |
| Bern (Berne) | 1520 | P Ref | Rwc•K | 285 | 540,000 | 702,500 | G Parishes: 250 German, 35 French (Egl Réf Ev du Canton de B). 1s. 10226 |
| Freiburg (Fribourg) | 1803 | P Ref | Rwc•K | 11 | 16,500 | 21,700 | G *Freiburgische Reformierte Kirche.* 1 French parish. 301 |
| Genève, Eglise Nationale Prot de | 1532 | P Ref | Rwc•K | 44 | 86,300 | 113,600 | F *Nat Prot Ch of G. Genfer Landskirche* (1 German parish). W=7%,1s. 757 |
| Glarus (Glaris) | 1520 | P Ref | Rwc•K | 16 | 14,500 | 19,100 | G *Glarnerische Kirche.* HQ Glarus. 25n. 253 |
| Graubünden (Grisons) | 1521 | P Ref | Rwc•K | 86 | 51,000 | 67,000 | G *Ev-Rhätische Landeskirche des Cantons Gr.* 7 Districts(Colloquen). 1135 |
| Neuchâtel (Neuenburg) | 1530 | P Ref | Rwc•K | 57 | 67,000 | 88,200 | F *Eglise Neuchâteloise.* 6 French Districts, 4 German parishes. 1s. 911 |
| St Gallen (Saint-Gall) | 1524 | P Ref | Rwc•K | 64 | 91,300 | 120,200 | G *Ev Kirche des Kantons St Gallen.* 3 Church Districts(Kirchenbezirk). 1669 |
| Schaffhausen (Schaffhouse) | 1529 | P Ref | Rwc•K | 32 | 32,000 | 42,100 | G German, with 1 French-speaking church in Schaffhausen. 544 |
| Solothurn (Soleure) | 1529 | P Ref | Rwc•K | 33 | 23,000 | 30,200 | G *Ev-Reformierte Kirche im Kanton Solothurn.* HQ Däniken. 390 |
| Thurgau (Thurgovie) | 1528 | P Ref | Rwc•K | 57 | 68,900 | 90,600 | G *Ev-Reformierte Kirche des Kantons Thurgau.* 3 Chapters (Kapitel). 1306 |
| Vaud (Waadt) | 1526 | P Ref | Rwc•K | 157 | 212,400 | 297,500 | F *Eglise Ev Réformée Vaudoise.* 6 Districts (Arrondissements). 1s. 2916 |
| Valais (Wallis) | 1815 | P Ref | Rwc•K | 11 | 6,200 | 8,200 | F *Eglise Réformée Evangélique du Valais.* 90 |
| Zürich | 1521 | P Ref | Rwc•K | 178 | 451,200 | 583,800 | G *Ev-Reformierte Kirche des Kantons Zürich.* 11 Districts(Bezirk). 1s. 6603 |
| Zentralschweiz & Tessin (Diaspora) | 1520 | P Ref | Rwc•K | 50 | 56,500 | 74,300 | G In 6 RC cantons: Luzern, Zug, Schwyz, Iri, Tessin, Unterwald. 866 |
| Evangelisch-Methodistische Kirche | c1830 | P Met | VwC•d | 330 | 18,350 | 20,831 | *Methodist Ch* (including EUB). In C&S Europe CC, UMC(USA). 115n,2f,2H,W=65%,230Yy. |
| Fraternité Chrétienne | c1950 | P Pe2 | ••••• | 5 | 100 | 300 | *Christian Brotherhood.* HQ Yverdon. Healing ministry to the handicapped and sick. |
| Freie Christengemeinden der Schweiz | 1920 | P Pe2 | ••••H | 27 | 700 | 2,000 | *Free Christian Assemblies.* HQ Kappel. 1962, split in 3 groups. Africa mission. 10n. |
| Freie Pfingstgemeinde | | P Pe2 | ••••• | 3 | 100 | 200 | *Free Pentecostal Assemblies.* HQ Neuhausen. Split ex Swiss Pentecostal Mission. |
| Gemeinde Christi | 1955 | P Dis | x•••• | 7 | 140 | 300 | *Churches of Christ.* M=CC(Non-Instrumental)(USA). In all largest cities. 9f. |
| Gemeinde Entschiedener Christen | | P Pe2 | ••••H | 5 | 100 | 300 | *Community of Definite Christians.* 2-stage Pentecostals. In Basel, Zürich. |
| Gemeinde für Urchristentum | 1919 | P PeA | Z•••H | 82 | 1,500 | 2,000 | *Apostolic Ch.* Works with Apostolic European Council. Hierarchical. 18n,2x,1j,1p. |
| Gemeinde Gottes (Cleveland) | | P Pe3 | ZF••• | 3 | 100 | 300 | *Ch of God.* M=CoG(Cleveland)(USA). HQ Rorschach/SG. 5n,8f,1p. |
| Gemeinschaft Evangelisch-Taufgesinnter | 1832 | P Hol | x•••• | 35 | 1,000 | 2,000 | *Apostolic Christian Church* (*Nazarean*). Spread 1847 to USA; also 16 nations. |
| Griechisch-Orth Kirche (D Österreich) | | O Gre | Cwc•• | 4 | 7,000 | 10,000 | *Greek Orthodox Ch.* Part of D Austria, under EP Constantinople. Greeks. |
| Heilsarmee (Armée du Salut) | 1882 | P Sal | xwc•d | 150 | 15,000 | 30,000 | *Salvation Army, S & Austria Territory.* 300 officers, 39 institutions. HQ Bern. 1s. |
| **Katholische Kirche in der Schweiz:** | c 200 | R Lat | b•B•S | 1,792 | 2,174,100 | 2,860,611 | *Eglise Catholique. Catholic Ch.* C=27+2+50. 2q,4s,10Y. 4430nx,648m,9595w,65200y. |
| D Basel (Bâle) | 740 | R Lat | bs | 524 | 836,000 | 1,100,000 | *Bistum Basel.* 6 Pastoral Regions (1 French). 1s. L=G,1283 130 3200 30000 |
| D Chur (Coira, Cuera) | 451 | R Lat | bs | 422 | 422,100 | 555,360 | *Uestgiu da Cuera.* 16 Deaneries (1 Italian). 1s. G 789 160 900 14143 |
| D Lausanne, Genève & Fribourg | c 350 | R Lat | bs | 287 | 412,000 | 542,000 | *Diocèse de LGF.* In west. HQ Fribourg. 2s. F 930 180 2100 8669 |
| D Lugano | 1888 | R Lat | bs | 261 | 167,450 | 220,313 | *Diocesi di Lugano.* In south, adjoining Italy. I 366 20 1061 3500 |
| D Sankt Gallen (Saint-Gall) | 1823 | R Lat | bs | 141 | 178,200 | 234,497 | *Bistum SG.* Northeast of country, adjoining Bodensee. G 445 35 1321 5292 |
| D Sion (Sitten) | 381 | R Lat | bs | 150 | 155,000 | 204,000 | *Diocèse de Sion* (*Bistum Sitten*). Illegal seminary. F 442 67 991 3500 |
| AN Maria Einsiedeln | 934 | R Lat | bosb | 1 | 350 | 455 | *Abtei Nullius Unserer Lieben Frau.* Pilgrimages. G 61 45 0 0 |
| AN Saint-Maurice | 344 | R Lat | bs | 6 | 3,000 | 3,986 | *Abbaye St-Maurice d'Aganne.* Valais. Under Holy See. F 114 11 22 66 |
| Kirche Schwedens (AD Uppsala) | c1962 | P Lut | Lwc•• | 5 | 1,000 | 2,000 | *Ch of Sweden* (*Overseas*). Swedes in Bern, Geneva, Lausanne, Lugano, Zürich. |
| Neuapostolische Kirche | c1870 | C CAp | x•••• | 230 | 20,000 | 32,000 | *New Apostolic Ch.* 1954, 2 Swiss Apostles deposed by Chief Apostle in Germany. |

*Continued opposite*

*Table 2–continued*

| Official name 1 | Begun 2 | Type 3 | Counc 4 | Congs 5 | Adults 6 | Affiliated 7 | Names, notes, and other statistics (see Codebook) 8 |
|---|---|---|---|---|---|---|---|
| Pilgermission St-Chrischona | 1840 | P ind | x...C | 60 | 2,000 | 5,000 | Based on St-Chrischona, near Basel. Communities in Alsace, Germany, Ethiopia. |
| Religiöse Gesellschaft der Freunde | 1934 | P Qua | Q.... | 7 | 126 | 200 | *Société Religieuse des Amis/Switzerland Yearly Meeting/RS Friends*. G=1.3%pa,W=66%. |
| Schweizerische Pfingstmission | 1920 | P Pe2 | Z...H | 108 | 3,172 | 6,000 | *SPM. Swiss Pentecostal Mission*. HQ Zürich. Foreign missions: 5 fields. 25n, 366Y. |
| Schweizerischer Verein für Freies C | | M Unt | I.... | 50 | 2,000 | 5,000 | C=Christentum. *Free Christian Union*. Unitarians. M=UUA(USA). Zürich,St-Gall. |
| Strome der Kraft | | P Pe3 | ..... | 20 | 300 | 500 | *Rivers of Power*. Ben Hoekendijk Evangelistic Campaigns (Holland). HQ Schaffhausen. |
| Témoins de Jéhovah | 1891 | M Jeh | x.... | 156 | 8,017 | 15,000 | *Zeugen Jehovas. Jehovah's Witnesses*. Activity begun 1927. 1j(74 languages),673Y. |
| Vereinigung Apostolischer Christen | 1954 | C CAp | x.... | 25 | 1,000 | 2,000 | *VAC. Union of Apostolic Christians*. Union of splits ex New Apost Ch. In 6 nations. |
| Volksmission Entschiedener Christen | 1934 | P Pe2 | x...H | 10 | 200 | 500 | *People's Mission of Definite Christians*. 2-stage Pentecostals. HQ Aarburg. 1j. |
| Other Protestant denominations | | P | ..... | | 4,000 | 8,000 | Total about 40 (see list below). |
| Other marginal Protestant bodies | | M | ..... | | 2,500 | 6,000 | Total over 20 (see list below) |
| Other Orthodox churches | | O | ..... | | 500 | 1,000 | Incl: Armenian Apostolic Ch, Syrian OC (100 Arab families), Ukrainian OC (Sobornopravna). |
| Other Catholic (non-Roman) churches | | C | ..... | | 300 | 500 | Total about 30 (see list below), including 20 under bishops-at-large. |
| **Total affiliated (mid-1970)** | | | | **5,620** | **4,412,942** | **5,906,112** | **Total denominations (1970) . . . 141.** |
| **Total affiliated (mid-1975)** | | | | **5,650** | **4,534,600** | **6,068,900** | **Total denominations (1975) . . . 145.** |
| **Total affiliated (mid-1980)** | | | | **5,680** | **4,607,700** | **6,166,800** | **Total denominations (1980) . . . 149.** |

**NOTES ON TABLE ABOVE**
COLUMNS: for meanings and CODES (cols. 1, 3, 4, 8): see Codebook (Part 6). Column 1: **Boldface type** = church with over 10% of country's affiliated Christians. *Language*. Names in column 1 are given in either German, French, or Italian, depending on which is the major usage.
NATIONAL COUNCILS (Column 4, 5th letter).
C = Verband Unabhängiger Evangelischer Kirchen und Korperschaften der Schweiz (Aarauer Verband).
d = member of both ACKS and Aarauer Verband.
H = Bund Pfingstlicher Gemeinden (Federation of Pentecostal Churches), begun 1961.
K = Arbeitsgemeinschaft Christlicher Kirchen in der Schweiz (ACKS)/Commission de Travail des Eglises Chrétiennes en Suisse (Working Community of the Christian Churches in Switzerland).
S = Conférence des Evêques Suisses/Schweizerische Bischofskonferenz/Conferenza die Vescovi Svizzeri (Conference of Swiss Bishops), also member of ACKS.
*Other national councils*. Schweizerische Evangelische Allianz (SEA) (Swiss Evangelical Alliance) (affiliated to EEA and WEF; members not churches but individuals).
OTHER PROTESTANT DENOMINATIONS. Among the large number of other smaller denominations are the following: Amis du Réveil, Bible Christian Union (1954), Children of God International, Christian Ch of North America (Italian Christian Churches of North Europe, CCINE; Pentecostal), Ch of the Kingdom of God (Geneva 1920), Ch of the Nazarene, Communauté des Chrétiens, Dutch Reformed Congregations, Eglises Vaudoises d'Italie en Suisse, Elim Missionary Assemblies (USA, 1956), Evangelical Lutheran Ch of Geneva (founded 1707), Ev Lutheran Ch in Bern, Fribourg & Neuchâtel (1,700 members; begun 1951), Exclusive Brethren (Raven-Taylor, and Kelly-Continental) (nicknamed Mômires, Bigots), Gemeinde der Christen Ecclesia (Zürich), Glaubensheim Bethel, Gospel Missionary Union (USA, 1962), Gypsy Gospel Mission of Switzerland (1913), Hungarian Reformed Congregations, International Protestant Ch of Zürich, Mission de l'Evangile, Mission Populaire Ev de France, Pentecôtistes Libres, Presbyterian Ch (Lausanne), World-Wide Missions (USA), 1969; also several other independent Lutheran groups.
OTHER MARGINAL PROTESTANT BODIES. There is a large number of small cults and sects, including: Eglise Chrétienne Universelle (Témoins du Christ Revenu), Gralsbewegung (HQ Vomperberg, Tyrol), New Church (Swedenborgians) (3 churches, 107 members), Temple de l'Arc-en-Ciel (British-Israelite) (Lausanne).
OTHER CATHOLIC (NON-ROMAN) CHURCHES. These include: Antoinists (from Belgium and France), Eglise Apostolique Primitive, Eglise Catholique Apostolique des Frères Philadelphie, Eglise Catholique Libérale, Eglise Mariavite; and about 20 miniscule episcopal churches under bishops-at-large (episcopi vagantes) (see names in table at end of Part 9).

**PEOPLES** (ethnolinguistic). Christians: 63.6% German Swiss, 18.3% Franco-Swiss, 7.2% Italian, 3.7% Italo-Swiss, 2.0% Spaniard, 1.6% German, 0.8% Romansh, 0.7% French, 0.5% Austrian, 0.5% British, 0.2% Greek, 0.2% Hungarian, 0.2% Dutch, 0.2% Czech, 0.1% Romanian, 0.1% Russian, USA White, Gypsy, Scandinavian, other Slav, Chinese (40).

**COUNTRY-WIDE TOTALS**
EVANGELIZATION (see Part 5). 1900: 100%. 1970: 100%. 1980: 100%. *Mass evangelism*. Among many recent campaigns: Billy Graham crusades and rallies 1955 in Zürich and Geneva (90,000 attenders, 8,000 enquirers), in 1960 in Bern, Zürich, Basel and Lausanne (168,000 attenders, 7,559 enquirers), also Euro '70 TV crusade in Geneva and Freiburg televised from Dortmund, Germany; July 1974, International Congress on World Evangelization (ICOWE) in Lausanne; May 1978, Anton Achulte campaign; December 1979, Mission '80 (Lausanne). *Radiophonic evangelism*. HCJB, TWR, Radio Vatican (since 1939), RVOG, ICI, et alia.
FOREIGN MISSIONARIES AND PERSONNEL (nationals serving abroad) (1972). Total 2,808: 2,303 Roman Catholics (1,803 foreign missionaries (706 priests, 176 brothers, 680 sisters, 241 lay) serving in Third-World countries, and about 500 other personnel serving in Western nations), 465 Protestants (decrease from 579 in 1963) (including 60 Pentecostals) in 40 countries, about 30 marginal Protestants (Jehovah's Witnesses, Mormons), about 10 Catholics (non-Roman).
FOREIGN MISSIONARIES AND PERSONNEL (aliens from abroad) (1973). Total 1,074. *From Western world*. 961: about 750 Roman Catholics (440 from Italy (145 priests, 295 sisters), 110 from Spain), about 100 marginal Protestants (65 Mormons from USA), 90 Protestants (66 in 20 USA societies, 18 in 4 UK societies, 6 from France), 11 Anglicans in 2 UK societies, about 8 Catholics (non-Roman), about 2 Orthodox. *Fom Communist world*. 33: 25 Roman Catholics (8 priests from Yugoslavia, 6 priests from Hungary, 6 priests from Czechoslovakia, 1 priest from Poland), about 8 Orthodox from Romania and USSR. *From Third World*. 80: about 70 Roman Catholics, 10 Protestants from Africa, Japan, Indonesia, India, Korea, et alia.
INSTITUTIONS (church-operated) (1973). Total 190, including 55 higher schools, 10 medical centres, 25 religious communities, 20 research centres, 19 seminaries (12 Protestant, 6 RC, 1 Catholic/non-Roman), 20 study centres.
PERIODICALS. About 220 titles (10 Orthodox, 10 SDA, 7 Pentecostal, 6 LdS, 3 Old Catholic).
PERSONNEL. About 17,574 (16,500 national, 1,074 foreign).
RELIGIOUS LIBRARIES. About 150.
SCRIPTURE DISTRIBUTION (1975). Annual totals: 57,020 Bibles (12% subsidized, 88% commercial), 88,511 NTs (11% free, 49% subsidized, 40% commercial), 38,000 UBS portions, 104,000 UBS selections. *Translations completed*. Portion: 3 languages since 1562. NT: 2 languages since 1560. Bible: 2 languages since 1679.
SERVICE AGENCIES. About 480, including ACEL, ACGH, ACISJF, ACKS, ACO, ACTS, AFI, AME, BICE, CAJ, CCCI, CCCS, CCEE, CCIA, CCRT, CEC, CES, CICM, CIRIC, CJA, CNG, CRAL, CRS-USCC, CSS, CWME, DICARWS, DWME, EKLoF, EPD, EPER, EPS, FSSPX, IBO, ICMC, ICVA, ICYE, IDAC, IFES, IKUE, IMPL, JOC, JRC, KAB, KIPA, KLS, LWF, MBI, MIEC, MIIC, OM, ROEG, RKZ, RPS, SAFE, SAKES, SCSB, SEA, SEFAI, SEMR, SES, SIAC, SIEIC SIESC, SIIAEC, SIJC, SIQS, SJWB, SKAF, SKF, SKJB, SKJV, SKLW, SKV, SMB, SODEPAX, SOG, SPP, SSS, SSV, SU, SZM, TEF, TKL-KGK, TWR, UCF, UCIP, UCJG (YMCA/CVJM), USC, USM, USMSR, UVA, VBG, VKLS, WARC, WCC, WCCE, WLC(EHC), WSCF, YFC, YWAM, YWCA.

**ADDITIONAL DATA ON CHURCHES**
EGLISE ANGLICANE AU SUISSE. Church of England work dates from 1552 in Geneva, and 1818 in Lansanne.
EGLISE CATHOLIQUE AU SUISSE. *Languages*. The first sub-column in column 8 gives the first language of each jurisdiction (L = G, German; F, French; I, Italian). Several use more than one language; thus Basel uses also French, Chur uses also Italian and Rheto-romansch (Grisons), and Sion uses also German. *Jurisdictions*. The ecclesiastical organization of the church parallels that of the secular cantons which are autonomous. There is no ecclesiastical province, and all dioceses depend directly on Rome. Each canton has its own Catholic legal entity. In addition to the Conference of Swiss Bishops covering the whole country, there is a Conférence Centrale Catholique Romaine des Eglises Nationales (Romisch-Katholische Zentralkonferenz der Landeskirchen, RKZ) dealing with organizational and financial matters in 11 German-speaking cantons (Aargau, Basel-Land, Basel-Stadt, Bern, Graubünden, Luzern, St-Gallen, Schaffhausen, Solothurn, Thurgau, Zürich). *Annual baptisms*. (1972) 100% infants, only 10 adults. *Personnel*. About 90% nationals, 10% expatriates. *Catholic charismatics* (January 1974). 250 adults including a number of religious personnel are active in 7 organized prayer groups in the Charismatic Renewal. *Seminaries*. There is a theological faculty at Luzern, a theological high school at Chur, and a major seminary at Fribourg. In D Sion there is also at Ecône a reactionary French-language seminary founded by a French archbishop, Marcel Lefebvre, but formally condemned by the French episcopate, which adheres to conservative pre-Vatican-II training for the priesthood. *Religious orders and congregations*. Of the 30 or so congregations of sisters, 10 have their mother house in French-speaking Switzerland, the rest in German-speaking Switzerland or abroad. Priests (with more than 100 members in 1970): 780 OFMCap, 548 OSB, 389 SMB, 197 SJ, 169 CSSR, 130 WF (PB), 128 CSSp, 128 Canons Regular of St-Maurice, 107 OP. Brothers: 61 Barmherzige Brüder von Mariahilf, 36 PFM. Sisters (1972): 8,000 Schwestern von Ingebohl, 3,000 Schwestern von Menzingen, 1,000 Schwestern von der Gottlichen Vorsehung von Baldegg, 500 Dominikanerinnen von Ilanz, 350 Schwestern von Heiligkreuz (Cham, OSB).
*Catholic organizations*. The Swiss Bishops' Conference (Schweizerische Bischofskonferenz/Conférence des Evêques Suisses/Conferenza dei Vescovi Svizzeri) has its headquarters in Geneva. Associations of religious personnel include the Vereinigung der Höhern Ordensobern der Schweiz/Union des Supérieurs Majeurs Religieux de Suisse (USM) for men; and the Vereinigung Höherer Oberinnen Ordensgemeinschaften der Deutschensprachigen Schweiz, and the Union des Supérieures Majeures de Suisse Romande (USMSR), for sisters. There is no national pastoral council. Lay activities of the 3 ethnic regions of Switzerland are organized autonomously, but they are co-ordinated at the national level by the Comité National de l'Apostolat de Laïcs. All movements in French-speaking Switzerland are co-ordinated by the Communauté Romande de l'Apostolat des Laïcs (CRAL), founded in 1958. The principal movements of the Swiss lay apostolate are: Katholische Arbeitnehmer-Bewegung, Schweizerischer Verband Marianischer Kongregation (about 20,000 single women in 350 parishes), Schweizerischer Katholischer Volksverein, Action Catholique Générale des Hommes, Schweizerischer Katholischer Frauenbund, Action Catholique Ouvrière, Christliche Arbeitjugen (CAJ), JOC (in French and Italian-speaking Switzerland), Jeunesse Rurale Catholique, Schweizerischer Studentenverein (SSV), Société des Etudiants Suisses, Schweizerischer Katholischer Jugen-Verband (SKJV). Associated with this latter organization are: Schweizerischer Jungwachtbund (SJWB) for children, Schweizerische Kirchlich Jugen-Bewegung (SKJB), for youth, and Mädchenverband Bläuring for girls, Scouts and Guides in all 3 regions.

The Holy See has unilateral diplomatic relations with Switzerland and is represented by a nuncio in Geneva; there is however no Swiss embassy at the Vatican.

International organizations having their headquarters in Switzerland include the following: (1) The Conférence des Organisations Internationales Catholiques has its Permanent secretariat and an information centre in Switzerland but its permanent secretary resides in Belgium. (2) The Secrétariat du Conseil des Conférences Episcopales Européennes (CCEE), in Chur, was previously an informal liaision group of European bishops which in 1971 became an official body charged with promoting the co-operation of European episcopates without however possessing juridical power over them. Episcopal conferences and isolated dioceses are members. The CCEE organized symposia at Noordwijkerhout (Netherlands) in 1967, Chur in 1969 and conferences at Rome in 1971, Leitershofen (West Germany) in 1973 and Rome again in 1975. (3) The Commission Internationale Catholique pour les Migrations (CICM) was founded in Geneva in 1951, and co-ordinates Catholic activities in aid of migrants and refugees in co-operation with Caritas Internationalis in Rome and the National Catholic Welfare Conference in Washington, USA. In 1971 member organizations were found in 38 countries, with regional offices in Egypt, Turkey and Greece. (4) The Union Catholique Internationale de la Presse (UCIP), which was recently transferred from France to Switzerland, unites 5 international federations: International Federation of Catholic Journalists, International Federation of Catholic Dailies and Periodicals, International Federation of Catholic Press Agencies. International Federation of the Church Press (diocesan), and International Catholic Association of Teachers and Researchers in the Sciences and Techniques of Information. (5) The Bureau International Catholique de l'Enfance (BICE), founded in Geneva in 1947, is dedicated to the promotion and protection of childrens' interests. It carries on its work through 12 permanent commissions and counts 80 member organizations in 23 countries. (6) The Mouvement International des Etudiants Catholiques (MIEC) founded in Fribourg in 1921, co-ordinates, aids and represents its member organizations working with university students, especially in their relations with international organizations. Regional secretariats are located in Peru for Latin America and in Hong Kong for Asia. Specialized secretariats include the Secrétariat International des Elèves Ingénieurs Catholiques (SIEIC) in Paris and Brussels. In 1972 MIEC counted 75 member organizations or associates. (7) The Mouvement International des Intellectuels Catholiques (MIIC), founded in Fribourg in 1947, co-ordinates, organizes and represents Catholic intellectuals in the international community. Regional secretariats exist in Paraguay, USA and Hong Kong. Professional secretariats have also been formed for artists (SIAC) and teachers (SIESC) in the Netherlands, engineers (SIIAEC) and scientists (SIQS) in France, and judges (SIJC) in Italy. In 1970, 99 national organizations were members or associates. (8) The Association Catholique Internationale des Services de la Jeunesse Féminine (ACISJF) founded in Fribourg in 1897, is dedicated to aiding single working girls through the establishment of homes, clubs, restaurants, and other social services. It works in 64 countries on 5 continents. (9) The Alliance International Jeanne d'Arc founded in London in 1911 under the name Catholic Women's Suffrage Society and located at Geneva under its new name since 1931, is dedicated to advancing the rights of women for the benefit of country and church. Since Vatican II it has worked for the full participation of women in the church. In 1972 it had affiliated bodies in 24 countries on 5 continents. (10) The Auxiliaires Féminines Internationales (AFI), founded in Belgium in 1937 with its headquarters now in Geneva, is dedicated to the development of cross-cultural contacts in both Third-World and industrialized countries. In 1972 it had international and interracial teams in 30 countries. (11) The Fédération Internationale Una Voce, founded in Rome in 1966 and now located at Clarens, is a non-official association dedicated to the restoration of the liturgy 'in conformity to the tradition of the Church' (Mass of Pius X) and the defence of Latin, the Gregorian Chant, and sacred music. In 1972 it grouped together 18 national associations on 4 continents. (12) The International Union of Catholic Esperantists (Internacia Katholika Unuigo Esperantista, IKUE), founded in Paris in 1910 with its headquarters now in Switzerland (Zêrchersmâhle), is a member of the Universal Association of Esperanto and publishes a monthly journal in Esperanto. In 1972 it was in existence in 28 countries and had 12 national branches and 1,200 individual members. (13) The Blue Army of Our Lady of Fatima, founded in Basel in 1947, is a traditionalist organization with emphasis on prayer and offerings. Its strength is in the USA, and another important centre is found at Fatima, Portugal. The Blue Army claims 21.5 million members in 110 countries.

Concerning progressivist opinion groups, it is important to note that the international secretariat for Collectif de Genève is found in Switzerland. The Collectif was formed following the International Assembly of Christians in Revolution for the Future of Man, held in Lyons, France, in November 1973, an assembly organized by Exchanges et Dialogue of France and the November 7 Movement of Italy in continuity with the international assemblies of 'Militant Priests' in Rome (1969) and 'Critical Christians' in Amsterdam (1970). The Collectif, in liaison with a certain number of militant Christian groups, is now attempting to enlarge the base of its representation and to put into action the perspectives of the Lyons assembly. It is represented in 10 Western European countries.

Among other Swiss Catholic opinion groups may be mentioned the following: (1) The Solidaritätsgruppen, whose secretariat was established in 1969, are composed of progressivist priests and laymen. Active ecumenically but composed principally of Catholics, they numbered 10 communities in 1972. (2) Communione e Liberazione, founded in 1968 with 200 members in 1971, and Dialoghi, founded in 1953 with 50 members in 1971, are also progressivist groups. The first is limited to Italian-speaking students, while the second is concerned for the church and politics. (3) Una Voce Helvetica (UVA), founded in 1966, is a militant traditionalist movement, dedicated to the restoration of the religious, intellectual and artistic traditions of the church, such as the conservation of the Latin liturgy. (4) The Fraternité Sacerdotale St Pie X, founded in 1969 at Fribourg and then transferred to Ecône, serves as support for the illegal traditionalist major seminary, Séminaire St Pie X, which was founded at Ecône in 1971 by Msgr Marcel Lefebvre, former bishop of Dakar now without a residential see. The seminary trains priests who are opposed to the conciliar movement and who insist on the use of Latin and the mass of Pius X. At first the seminary received some support from Rome but was finally disowned in May 1974. Although all the episcopates of francophone Europe have stated that they will not accept these students in the ranks of their clergy this is the only seminary in Western Europe that has so many applicants that it is forced to turn students away even after enlarging its facilities. At the time of the Roman disavowal, there were more than 200 seminarians, of whom two-thirds were French. In the Swiss canton of Valais and beyond, the fraternity exercises an important influence and attracts hundreds of faithful who refuse to accept the aggiornamento of the church.

A number of organizations are engaged in research and social action. (1) The Kirchensoziologische Forschung und Beratung

(KFB), founded in Zürich in 1967, engages in analysis and planning of the work of the Swiss churches. (2) The Schweizerisches Pastoralsoziologisches Institut (SPI), in St Gallen, is involved in pastoral planning studies for the diocese of St Gallen and socio-religious investigations concerning priests and Swiss male congregations. Its documentation and archival centre serves also as the headquarters of the secretariat for pastoral planning of the Swiss Episcopal Commission, as well as being the headquarters of the Swiss Association of Sociologists of Religion. (3) The Bildungsrat der Schweizer Katholiken has an office dealing with cultural affairs in Luzern and unites the presidents of Catholic educational institutions with the Schweizerische Katholische Arbeitsgemeinschaft für Elternschulung (SAKES), at St Gallen since 1956, which promotes adult education, and the Schweizerisches Soziales Seminar (SSS) at Luzern since 1960, which is a federation of local social seminars for training adults. (4) The Schweizerische Katholische Arbeitsgemeinschaft für Fremdarbeiter (SKAF)/Communauté de Travail Catholique Suisse pour les Travailleurs Etrangers, founded at Luzern in 1965, is concerned with the pastoral, human, social and political problems of foreigners and engages in research and action projects to that end. It is dependent on the Episcopal Commission for Foreigners. (5) The Katholische Arbeitnehmer Bewegung der Schweiz (KAB), founded in Zürich in 1899, is dedicated to cultural, social and economic development, 'the flowering of the whole man' through education and joint activities. It had 21,000 members in 330 local sections in 1971. (6) Fastenopfer der Schweizer Katholischen/Action de Carême des Catholiques Suisses, founded in Luzern in 1962, provides aid to underdeveloped countries and to missions, as well as helping to finance the Swiss church. It is a member of CIDSE. (7) Interteam, founded in Luzern in 1964 for German Switzerland, and Frères sans Frontières, founded in Fribourg in 1959 for French and Italian Switzerland, recruit and train laymen with special professional and human skills for service in the Third World. By 1972 the 2 organizations had 280 volunteers at work in various parts of the world.

Pastoral and religious training is provided by several institutions. (1) The Faculté de Théologie Catholique of the University of Fribourg is run by Dominicans. (2) The Liturgisches Institut of Zürich and the Katechetisches Institut of Luzern are dependent on the Episcopal Conference. They edit liturgical books, study the sacraments and train catechists. (3) The Interdiozesane Vereinigung (TKL-KGK) in Zürich, makes available theological studies for laymen. (4) The Inländische Mission/Missions Intérieures collects funds to aid isolated Catholic parishes in Protestant countries, especially those in high mountain areas. (5) The Institut für Weltanschauliche Fragen, founded by Jesuits in Zürich in 1932 under the name Apologetisches Institut, edits the journal *Orientierung* which deals with theological, philosophical and cultural questions. Its members collaborate also with different journals and radio-TV stations. (6) The Ecole de la Foi, founded in Fribourg in 1969, provides biblical, theological and missionary training for future lay and religious evangelists. In 1971 it had 80 students from 4 continents. (7) The Schweizer Seelsorgezentrum, in Olten, serves as the Swiss information centre for pastoralia. (8) The Katholische Internationale Press-Agentur (KIPA) in Fribourg and the Centre International de Reportages et d'Information Culturelle (CIRIC) are Catholic press and photo-press agencies. In 1975 the latter produced 200,000 photos and 60,000 slides.

The principal organization for the co-ordination of missionary action is the Schweizerischer Katholischer Missionsrat/Conseil Missionnaire Catholique Suisse, founded in Fribourg in 1963. An arm of the Episcopal Conference, it represents 90 different institutions, organizations and works. Studies and services are provided by the Institut d'Etudes Missionnaires of the University of Fribourg, and by Sonolux, a centre in Fribourg which prepares and distributes audio-visual materials in collaboration with 24 catechetical and pastoral centres throughout the world.

The principal Swiss missionary communities are the Schweizerische Missionsgesellschaft Bethlehem (SMB); the Verein der Schweizer-Missions-Franziskanerinnen; the Lehrschwestern vom Heiligen Kreuz; the Schwestern von der Gottlichen Vorsehung; the Barmherzige Schwestern vom Heiligen Kreuz; in addition to Fidei Donum, OFMCap, WF(PB), CSSp, and Bénédictins-Missionnaires d'Uznach. Missionary statistics for 1972 list 706 priests, 176 brothers, 680 sisters and 241 lay volunteers.

Educational statistics for 1968 give 40,000 students in 240 Catholic private boarding schools, of which 22 are colleges recognized by the canton or confederation. There are no Catholic universities.

With regard to medical and social service, Caritas Switzerland (Schweizerischer Caritasverband/Union Suisse de Charité/Unione Svizzera di Carità), in Luzern since 1901, has 14 regional affiliates which provide aid to the aged, orphans, prisoners, alcoholics, handicapped and foreigners.

EGLISES REFORMEES CANTONALES (KANTONALE REFORMIERTE KIRCHEN). The 18 cantonal churches are each autonomous and independent, with its own relationship to the secular canton. In the 1970 population census, the Protestant population was divided among these 18 regions, in the order shown in the table, as follows (with a total of 2,991,694): 205002, 34816, 118192, 123718, 789497, 24084, 126195, 21186, 74391, 97993, 133557, 46772, 33603, 100638, 310608, 9092, 659814, 82536. A large number of these persons however, around 10%, do not belong to the cantonal churches but to other Protestant denominations, as shown. For the purposes of the table, therefore, affiliated memberships of the cantonal churches are here assumed to be 90% of these census figures. The figures in column 5 are of organized parishes. *Languages*. The first single letter in column 8 indicates the main or official language used: G = German, F = French.

FEDERATION DES EGLISES PROTESTANTES DE LA SUISSE/Schweizerischer Evangelischer Kirchenbund (Federation of the Protestant Churches of Switzerland). Additional members outside Switzerland are the Swiss Reformed churches of Barcelona, Buenos Aires, Florence, Genoa, Johannesburg, London, Marseilles, Milan, Misiones (Argentina), Naples, Rio de Janeiro, São Paulo (Brazil).

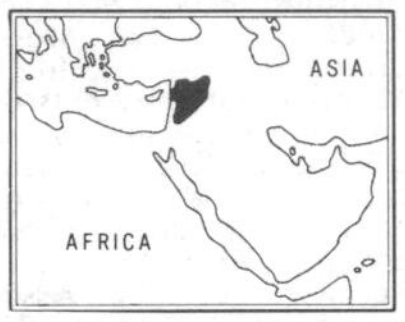


# SYRIA

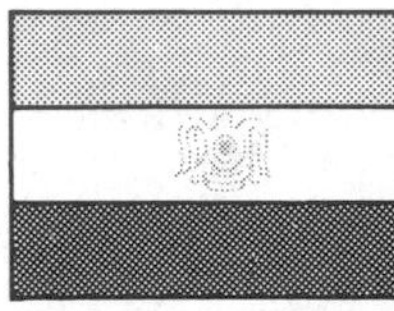

## SECULAR DATA

**STATE. Official name:** The Syrian Arab Republic (Al-Jumhuriyah al-Arabiyah as-Suriyah). Adjective of nationality: Syrian.
**Flag** (shown above right): Red, white, and black stripes, with hawk in centre stripe.
**Area:** 185,180 sq. km. (71,498 sq.miles). Agricultural land: 67.1%.
**Government:** Socialist republic, since 1973 (1516 under Ottoman empire, 1920 French mandated territory, 1946 Independence as republic, 1958–61 in United Arab Republic (with Egypt), 1968, military junta).
**Legislature:** People's Assembly, 186 members.
**Official language:** Arabic.
**Chief cities:** capital Damascus 923,250, Aleppo 639,430, Homs 215,420.
**Political divisions:** 13 Districts (mohafazets).
**Armed forces** (1976): Total 227,000 regular: army 200,000, navy 2,000, air force 25,000 (440 combat aircraft). Reserves: 102,500. Paramilitary forces: 9,500.
**Foreign forces** (1973): 1,100 USSR military technicians.

**DEMOGRAPHY. Population:** 6,304,685 (census of 23.IX.1970. For 1970–2000 (UN), see last row of Table 1). Population density (1975): 39/sq. km. (102/sq. mile). Under 15 years: 44%. Growth rate (1975–80): 3.24% per year (births 4.56%, deaths -1.33%). Life expectancy (1975–80): 56.5 years. Household size: 5.9 persons.
**Major languages:** Arabic, Kurdish, French, Armenian, Turkoman, Circassian, Chaldean (Aramaic), and others.

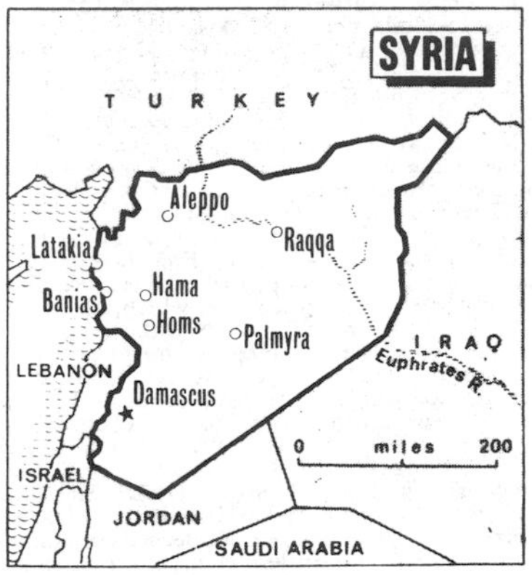


**Urban dwellers** (1970): 43.7%. Urban growth rate (1950–70): 4.0% per year.
**Labour force:** 27%.
**Refugees** (1977): 434,042 (250,000 from Lebanon, 184,042 Palestinians under UNRWA).
**Tourists** (1973): 454,766.

**ETHNOLINGUISTIC GROUPS:** 88.8% Arab (7% Bedouin, 2.9% Palestinian (180,000)), 6.3% Kurdish, 2.8% Armenian, 0.6% Turkmen, 0.5% Circassian, 0.5% Assrian, 0.2% Gypsy, 0.1% Jewish (4,000), 0.1% Turkish, USSR military (1,100), French, Persian, Greek.

**MONEY** (1977). **Monetary unit:** Syrian pound (=100 piastres); US$1 = Sy£3.90.
**National income per person:** US$530. Average annual family income: US$3,127.
**Inflation:** (1970–74) 9.9% per year, (1975) 16% per year (consumer price index 189).
**Cost of living in capital** (1976): index 93 (Washington DC=100). Daily cost of living: US$30.

**HEALTH.** Hospitals: 89 (6,854 beds). Doctors: 1,914. Lepers: 2,600 (0.4 per 1,000). Blind: 12,000. Psychotics: 65,000.

**EDUCATION.** Adult literacy: (1960) 35%, (1970) 40%. Education rate: 61%S chools: 6,446. Universities: 2.

**LITERATURE.** Annual new book titles (1972): 459. Periodicals: 55. Newspapers: 5 dailies, 12 non-daily.

**COMMUNICATION** (per 1,000 people). Phones: 21. Radios: 374. TV sets: 22. Daily newspaper circulation: 9 copies.

TABLE 1. RELIGIOUS ADHERENTS IN SYRIA

| Year | 1900 | | mid-1970 | | Annual change, 1970–1980 | | | | mid-1975 | | mid-1980 | | 2000 | |
|---|---|---|---|---|---|---|---|---|---|---|---|---|---|---|
| *Name* | *Adherents* | *%* | *Adherents* | *%* | *Natural* | *Conversion* | *Total* | *Rate* | *Adherents* | *%* | *Adherents* | *%* | *Adherents* | *%* |
| Muslims | 1,453,900 | 83.1 | 5,559,744 | 89.0 | 210,834 | –2,223 | 208,611 | 3.22 | 6,480,000 | 89.3 | 7,645,850 | 89.6 | 14,267,500 | 90.2 |
| Druzes | 52,500 | 3.0 | 185,000 | 3.0 | 6,820 | –20 | 6,800 | 3.16 | 215,000 | 3.0 | 253,000 | 3.0 | 470,000 | 3.0 |
| Yazidis | 5,000 | 0.3 | 10,000 | 0.2 | 366 | –6 | 360 | 3.10 | 11,600 | 0.2 | 13,600 | 0.2 | 20,000 | 0.1 |
| Ahmadis | 0 | 0.0 | 300 | 0.0 | 13 | 7 | 20 | 5.00 | 400 | 0.0 | 500 | 0.0 | 1,000 | 0.0 |
| **Christians** | **274,000** | **15.7** | **621,156** | **9.9** | **15,312** | **–1,023** | **14,289** | **2.08** | **686,500** | **9.4** | **764,050** | **8.9** | **1,107,700** | **7.0** |
| crypto-Christians | 94,000 | 5.4 | 246,156 | 3.9 | 7,832 | –423 | 7,409 | 2.65 | 279,500 | 3.8 | 320,250 | 3.7 | 460,600 | 2.9 |
| professing | 180,000 | 10.3 | 375,000 | 6.0 | 7,480 | –600 | 6,880 | 1.69 | 407,000 | 5.6 | 443,800 | 5.2 | 647,100 | 4.1 |
| Orthodox | 142,000 | 8.1 | 250,000 | 4.0 | 4,420 | –400 | 4,020 | 1.50 | 268,600 | 3.7 | 290,200 | 3.4 | 411,400 | 2.6 |
| Roman Catholics | 38,000 | 2.2 | 112,000 | 1.8 | 2,650 | –190 | 2,460 | 1.99 | 123,400 | 1.7 | 136,600 | 1.6 | 205,700 | 1.3 |
| Protestants | 0 | 0.0 | 13,000 | 0.2 | 410 | –10 | 400 | 2.67 | 15,000 | 0.2 | 17,000 | 0.2 | 30,000 | 0.2 |
| affiliated | 274,000 | 15.7 | 621,156 | 9.9 | 15,312 | –1,023 | 14,289 | 2.08 | 686,500 | 9.4 | 764,050 | 8.9 | 1,107,700 | 7.0 |
| total practising | 246,600 | *90* | 496,930 | *80* | 12,250 | –819 | 11,431 | 2.08 | 549,200 | *80* | 611,240 | *80* | 775,390 | *70* |
| non-practising | 27,400 | *10* | 124,230 | *20* | 3,062 | –204 | 2,858 | 2.08 | 137,300 | *20* | 152,810 | *20* | 332,310 | *30* |
| Orthodox | 218,000 | 12.5 | 412,648 | 6.6 | 9,100 | –855 | 8,245 | 1.83 | 450,000 | 6.2 | 495,100 | 5.8 | 671,100 | 4.2 |
| Roman Catholics | 55,000 | 3.1 | 179,468 | 2.9 | 5,400 | –297 | 5,103 | 2.51 | 203,200 | 2.8 | 230,500 | 2.7 | 364,000 | 2.3 |
| Protestants | 1,000 | 0.1 | 21,890 | 0.3 | 521 | –10 | 511 | 2.13 | 24,000 | 0.3 | 27,000 | 0.3 | 45,000 | 0.3 |
| Evangelicals | 800 | 0.0 | 11,700 | 0.2 | 282 | 28 | 310 | 2.38 | 13,000 | 0.2 | 14,800 | 0.2 | 26,000 | 0.2 |
| Non-White indigenous | 0 | 0.0 | 6,500 | 0.1 | 268 | 132 | 400 | 4.71 | 8,500 | 0.1 | 10,500 | 0.1 | 25,000 | 0.2 |
| Marginal Protestants | 0 | 0.0 | 600 | 0.0 | 23 | 7 | 30 | 4.00 | 750 | 0.0 | 900 | 0.0 | 2,500 | 0.0 |
| Anglicans | 0 | 0.0 | 50 | 0.0 | 0 | 0 | 0 | 0.00 | 50 | 0.0 | 50 | 0.0 | 100 | 0.0 |
| Non-religious | 0 | 0.0 | 50,000 | 0.8 | 2,289 | 2,951 | 5,240 | 7.22 | 72,600 | 1.0 | 102,400 | 1.2 | 395,600 | 2.5 |
| Atheists | 0 | 0.0 | 12,000 | 0.2 | 505 | 295 | 800 | 5.00 | 16,000 | 0.2 | 20,000 | 0.2 | 50,000 | 0.3 |
| Jews | 22,000 | 1.3 | 4,000 | 0.1 | –40 | 0 | –40 | –1.05 | 3,800 | 0.1 | 3,600 | 0.0 | 3,000 | 0.0 |
| Baha'is | 100 | 0.0 | 100 | 0.0 | 0 | 0 | 0 | 0.00 | 100 | 0.0 | 100 | 0.0 | 200 | 0.0 |
| **Country's population** | **1,750,000** | **100.0** | **6,247,000** | **100.0** | **228,900** | **0** | **228,900** | **3.15** | **7,259,000** | **100.0** | **8,536,000** | **100.0** | **15,824,000** | **100.0** |

COLUMNS, ROWS. For meanings and definitions, see Codebook (Part 6). Note that, by definition, total 'Christians' = professing + crypto-Christians, which also = affiliated + nominal Christians. Percentages may not always total exactly, due to rounding.
CENSUSES. **1944** (government estimate): 81.7% Muslims, 10.1% Orthodox (4.8% Greek, 3.6% Armenian, 1.4% Syrian, 0.3% Nestorian), 3.6% Roman Catholics, 3.0% Druzes, 1.0% Jews, 0.4% Protestants. **1949** (estimate): 81.8% Muslims, 9.9% Orthodox (4.8% Greek, 3.4% Armenian, 1.4% Syrian, 0.3% Nestorian), 3.6% Roman Catholics, 3.0% Druzes, 1.0% Jews, 0.4% Protestants. **20.IX.1960**: 91.6% Muslims, 8.3% Christians (361,064 persons), 0.1% Jews (5,067 persons).

NOTES ON RELIGIONS
ATHEISTS. Communist Party of Syria (CPS) (proscribed; split over Sino-Soviet dispute): membership (1970) 3,000. Also present are 1,100 USSR military advisers (1973).
BAHA'IS. First entered Syria before 1892. Ever since, Baha'is have been subjected to severe persecution by Muslim and government authorities.
DRUZES. An 11th-century Muslim Shia Ismaili schism with Christian and Jewish elements. Mainly in the south in Djebel Druze.
JEWS. Arabic-speaking Sefardis. Decline from 1.0% of the population in 1944 by emigration to Israel.
MUSLIMS. Orthodox Muslims are 85% Sunnis, 13% Alawites or Nusayris (Shias, Latakia province), 1.2% Ismailis, and other Shia sects (0.5%). There are also the heterodox or syncretistic Druzes and Yazidis, and a small Ahmadiya community in Damascus (begun 1924), all of which are enumerated here under Muslims. *Hajj pilgrims to Mecca*. (1968) 14,521; (1969) 22,383; (1970) 42,339; (1971) 27,045; (1972) 31,777; (1973) 10,448; (1974) 31,583; (1975) 31,209; (1976) 24,446.
NON-WHITE INDIGENOUS. Isolated Arab radio and correspondence course believers, also one Assyrian schism (see Table 2).
ORTHODOX. The majority are Greek Orthodox and Syrian Orthodox. In 1905, there were about 15,000 Armenian Apostolics (2,000 in the diocese of Damascus or Sham); after 1915, vast numbers immigrated as refugees from Turkey, but subsequently

about 100,000 Orthodox have emigrated from Syria to Lebanon in recent years.

**PROFESSING CHRISTIANS.** There has been very considerable and continuous emigration after 1944 (when Christians were 14.1% of the population) to 1949 (13.9%), 1960 (8.3%), and 1970 (6.0%).

YAZIDIS (Yezidis, Devil Worshippers). A 12th-century Muslim syncretistic religion; enumerated here under Muslims. Around Taziral, Aleppo, and in the extreme northeast in Djebel Sinjar.

**Muslims.** Omayad Mosque in Damascus, built in AD 715, traditional repository of the head of John the Baptist (revered as an Islamic prophet).

**NON-CHRISTIAN RELIGIONS. Islam** is the main religion of Syria and makes up 89% of the population. Muslims conquered the country in AD 636, and between 660 and 750 Damascus was the centre of the vast Umayyad empire. In later centuries Syria was ruled by Egyptian Mamelukes, Asian Mongols and Ottoman Turks. Most Muslims today are Sunnis, although there are also Alawites, Ismailis and several other smaller Shia sects. Alawites form at least 11% of the population and are centered in the province of Latakia. Ismailis, 1% of the population, have their strength in the Salamiya district.

**Druzes** are a sect begun in the 11th century when their founder, Darasi, identified Egyptian caliph al-Hakim as the incarnation of Allah. They represent a mixture of Jewish, Christian and Muslim elements. Their community exceeds 200,000 found mostly in the southern area of Djebel Druze.

**Yazidi religion** is a complex mixture of ideas taken from many religions (Islam, Judaism, Manachaeism, Zoroastrianism, Nestorianism), although Muslim thought is predominant. It was founded in the 12th century by Shaikh Adi, who was regarded as the incarnation of the fallen angel Malak Ta'us. Yezidis consist of some 12,000 living at Aleppo in the northern part of Djebel Sinjar.

**Judaism** has suffered from emigration to Israel since World War II, but a small Arabic-speaking Sefardic community remains.

**CHRISTIANITY.** In Syria, Christianity antedates the Apostle Paul who was converted on his way to Damascus; and after the fall of Jerusalem in AD 70, Antioch became the Christian centre of the eastern half of the Roman empire. Antioch's theologians played a leading role in the controversies concerning the nature of Christ in the early centuries, with Nestorians and Jacobites becoming increasingly separated from the rest of the church following the Council of Chalcedon in 451. Catholic Uniate churches began to emerge as early as 1181, the Maronites coming fully under the authority of Rome in 1516. Periodic movements among branches of Eastern-rite churches from the 16th to the 18th centuries resulted in the creation of more Uniate churches, including the Chaldean, Armenian, Greek Melkite and Syrian Catholic churches, although the Greek Orthodox church has remained the largest Christian denomination in the country. Christians increased in number when Armenians fled into Syria from massacres in Turkey and Iraq, but in recent years Christians have been migrating to other parts of the world.

Protestant missionaries began exploratory missions in the 19th century, seeking Jewish and Muslim converts, but most of their members have in fact come from other Christian churches. This has made them suspect to both Muslims and Eastern-rite Christians, as well as to the govenment which has been apprehensive of any kind of European intervention.

Until recent years, Syrian Christian communities were composed mostly of peasants. In the urban milieux they formed part of the commercial and industrial bourgeoisie and the liberal professions, in addition to being artisans and skilled workers. Whether rural or urban, they remained attached to their ancient religious traditions, fervent but withdrawn from society in closed and close-knit communities.

Independence in 1943 and the evolution of Syrian society since 1963 have changed this situation. The majority of the socio-professional categories continue, but the old bourgeoisie has been partially broken up or has emigrated, many going to Lebanon; and a new class of young adults from the peasant, artisan and semi-proletarian classes are coming to the fore. Many of these have technical or university training, while the army and government include important and often influential numbers of Christians. The result is that today Christians are integrating themselves more into the main stream of society, whose tendency is in the general direction of secularization. The rural exodus is helping to create a new social mixture and a socio-cultural development which may well contribute to the wider introduction of Christianity into Syrian life.

The recovery by Syria of a part of the Golan Heights, following the signing of the disengagement agreement by Syrian and Israeli armed forces on 31 May 1974, has had no effect on the size of the Christian community since the Syrian population of the area had taken refuge in the interior of the country. Before leaving, Israelis completely destroyed the city of Kuneitra, pillaging churches and mosques, including the Orthodox cathedral. Only the Catholic church remained intact, due undoubtedly to the international political position of the Holy See.

In summary, it can be stated that the influence of Western Christianity, especially Latin and European, has been strongly felt since 1890 especially due to the large part its schools have played in training an intellectual elite. At present the Christian minority is characterized by: (1) the traditionalism and conservatism of its past ecclesiastical structures mixed with a practical ecumenism which seeks to break down the rigid barriers between Catholics and Orthodox; (2) a new approach to the reformist wing of the Muslim community which is more liberal and tolerant; and (3) a movement towards social and political awareness which has introduced a quality of dynamism and modernism into Christian institutions.

**ORTHODOX CHURCHES.** The Greek Orthodox form the most deeply-rooted Christian community in the country, and the best-adapted to its recent evolution. It is Greek only in its Byzantine traditions, since its liturgy is in Arabic and its membership and leaders are Arabs. It is historically the mother church of the Jacobites, who broke away in the 6th century, and the Greek Catholics (Melkites) who separated in the 16th century. There are 2 monasteries (Our Lady of Saidnaya near Damascus, and St Georges, in the Valley of the Christians between Homs and Latakia) which are places of pilgrimage visited by many since medieval times. The patriarch lives in Damascus and is assisted in the governing of the church by the synod of bishops and a mixed commission of laymen and clergy. The lay element has often had a decisive influence in episcopal elections and especially in the administration of church property (Wakfs). The church maintains good relations with the other autocephalous Orthodox churches, particularly with the Moscow Patriarchate. The latter gave its support in 1898 to the proposal that the patriarch of Antioch should be a native Syrian rather than a Greek. The church's strength is in the western half of the country near Aleppo, Homs and Latakia. The Movement of Orthodox Youth is especially active, as in Lebanon.

The Armenian Orthodox are the third largest Christian community in Syria, after the Greek Orthodox and Catholic churches. Monophysite in tradition, they are administratively related to the catholicate of Cilicia (Sis) at Antelias in Lebanon. Nearly half their membership is found in the city of Aleppo where they form the largest Christian community.

The Syrian Orthodox or Jacobites are also of the Monophysite tradition. Most are found in the extreme northeast in the Qamishli area across the Turkish border from Tour Abdin where are located their

**Syrian Orthodox Patriarchate of Antioch.** Patriarch Mar Ignatius Yacoub III (right) reads the Gospel at service of ordination for a monk, 1973.

ancient monastic institutions, Deir-el-Zeferan and Deir Gabriel. There is also a large membership at Aleppo and Homs. The patriarchal see, which has jurisdiction over such foreign communities as the Syrian Malankaras in Kerala, India and the Syrian Orthodox in America, was moved from Homs to Damascus in 1954. A new faculty of theology is being planned for Bikfaïa, Lebanon.

The Assyrian Church of the East consists of a small community found in eastern Syria. Assyrians are stronger in Iraq and Iran than in Syria.

**CATHOLIC CHURCH.** Six different Catholic rites exist in Syria, in order of size: Greek Catholic (Melkite), Armenian, Syrian, Maronite, Latin and Chaldean.

Melkites are the predominant Catholic group in the country due to their leadership, tradition and institutions. The Melkite patriarch has his residence at Damascus, but his jurisdiction goes beyond the limits of the patriarchate of Antioch since he has held also for more than a century the titles and jurisdiction of the patriarchates of Jerusalem and Alexandria. He also has jurisdiction over Melkite districts erected in 1971–72 in America and in other parts of the diaspora. On the whole the Melkite clergy observe the Byzantine tradition. Married clergy are in charge of rural parishes, while diocesan clergy are celibate. The latter and also religious personnel are generally well-educated, including some highly-trained elites, and concerned to meet the needs of Melkite society which is considered conservative in the domain of religion. Their major strength is in Aleppo. The establishment of a Melkite major seminary in Syria is seen as a priority.

Armenians form a strong ethnic minority who fled to Syria during the Turkish massacres of 1894–96 and 1917–21. They are the strongest Catholic community in Aleppo.

Syrian Catholics are found mostly in Djéziré in the extreme northeast, as well as in Aleppo, Homs and Damascus, the latter with no more than 200 families. An active lay movement, Institut Jésus Ouvrier, is centred in Aleppo.

Maronites are concentrated in the west. Their principal centre is Aleppo which lies near the traditional home of St Maron from whom they derive their name. However, Maronites are few in Syria as compared with neighbouring Lebanon.

Latin Catholics live in western Syria with nearly half their membership in Aleppo where the vicar apostolic has his residence. Aleppo has been a centre of Latin influence since the 13th century when it played an important role in the Crusades. Some 25 Franciscan priests are at work in Syria.

Chaldeans are strongest in eastern Syria, in addition to some 1,500 in Aleppo and 500 in Damascus.

Co-ordination and collaboration between these 6 rites exist at both the national and local levels in such cities as Damascus and Aleppo where Catholic bishops of different rites meet together regularly. Specialized Catholic Action youth movements have not been successful, possibly because of their Western origin. It is to be noted also that youth groups were suppressed in 1964 after the Baathist regime came to power. Some of the most important of existing inter-rite organizations are those concerned with catechetics. These have taken on a special significance since the seizure and closing of Catholic schools when they did not conform to government edicts in 1967. At Damascus there exists a centre for advanced religious training, run by Lazarists and called the St Paul Centre. Numerous other centres are active where laymen, especially youth, collaborate with clergy and religious personnel in teaching the catechism to children of different school levels. Such centres, attached to the Catechism Society, are found in Damascus, Homs, Latakia and especially at Aleppo. Another group at Damascus and Aleppo called 'The Flame' mobilizes the generosity of city Christians to help poor rural parishes.

PROTESTANT CHURCHES. The first Protestant to explore mission work in Syria was a member of the London Jews' Society in 1822. The American Board (ABCFM) began work in Beirut in 1823, moving to Syria in 1848. In 1879 it transferred its work to the Presbyterian Church in the USA. Other early groups were the North American Reformed Presbyterian Mission and the Danish Mission to the Orient. During the 1940s these 3 joined together to form the autonomous National Evangelical Synod of Syria and Lebanon, which is Presbyterian in polity. It is now declining rapidly by emigration.

The Union of Armenian Evangelical Churches is strong in the north where Armenian refugees from Turkey fled after World War I. The Armenian Union and National Evangelical Synod together form the bulk of the Protestant population which is about 25,000.

The CMA from the USA arrived in 1921, followed by Nazarene missionaries and a number of other groups later. All foreign missionaries were expelled in 1963, but small churches continue under Syrian leadership. Two CMA congregations are known to exist in Homs and Damascus. Several expelled mission groups maintain contact with Syria from Beirut, which has long been the central headquarters of the Christian churches in the Middle East.

**CHURCH AND STATE.** Until the beginning of 1973, Syria was officially a Muslim state, but the new regime then inaugurated instituted by general Hafez El-Assad in November 1970 has sought to divorce the state from any religious commitment. In fact, the new constitution of March 1973 envisages Islam as the religion of the head of state only, and no longer the religion of the state itself. This resulted in religious riots in some towns in February and April 1973, just before a referendum to ratify the constitution. Since the end of the French mandate (1920–45), Christians have always advocated just such a constitutional change which would recognize Islam as the religion of the majority of the population but not the official religion of the state. Christian churches and socio-religious communities are legally recognized and designated by the state as juridical personalities with definite rights and privileges. The Ministry of Religious Foundations (Wizarat Al-Awkaf) is nominally occupied with the management of religious properties, but in actuality is involved in all that relates to religious personnel, worship and Muslim politics in the country.

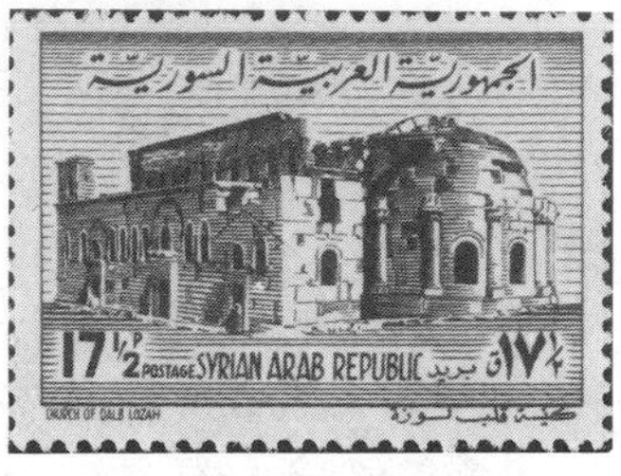

**Syrian Orthodox Patriarchate of Antioch.** Church of Qalb Lozah.

Freedom of religion, sanctioned by law, does in fact exist. Solemn processions are authorized during the course of the year, and the construction of new religious buildings encounters no legal obstacle.

Private religious schools, which had been placed under the direct control of the Ministry of National Education in 1967, were restored to their owners following a decision of the supreme administrative court in December 1974. Except for Catholics, the different religious communities, Christian and Muslim, had accepted the 1967 decision as final. It was thus a Catholic appeal which produced the definitive court decision of 1974, recognizing the private character of all religious schools. From November 1970 on, the government attempted to soften its position by extending to all Syrian citizens the right to establish private schools, a measure which was used by Catholics to open a certain number of allegedly new schools.

Another mark of the liberalism of the state and Islam in Syria is the law, especially evident in the proceedings of the Court of Appeal, which allows minor children when they come of age to change their religion if they were only considered Muslim because of the conversion of their fathers. Normally Islamic law prohibits converts and their minor children, who are automatically considered Muslims, from changing their religion, and minor children continue to be considered Muslims after they come of age.

The churches themselves are not subsidized, nor do they receive any material assistance from the state. Nevertheless, church communities do have certain administrative and jurisdictional rights, since Islam recognizes them as 'civil and religious nations' within the larger Muslim society. Thus, churches may keep registers of baptisms and marriages, and their official certificates have public recognition. The state accepts as valid only those marriages formally solemnized by a church according to its established procedures. Church tribunals in each community have competence in that which relates to the religious aspects of matrimonial contracts and mixed marriages, such as the care of children. Real estate (Wakfs) belonging to places of worship or to patriarchates has the same exemptions and privileges as that of Muslim communities.

No church enjoys privileges at the expense of others, but those which are the most deeply-rooted in the country and which have broken their ties with former colonial regimes are in fact favoured; and their missionary, social and cultural activities are not hindered. In actuality, Christians are well represented at all levels of public life, such as in administration, army and liberal professions. Greek Orthodox political thinkers, intelligentsia and middle classes have often been a determining factor in decisions concerning the destiny of the country. Between 1925 and 1945, the thought of Antoun Saadeh, founder of the Syrian Popular Party (PPS), and since 1950 that of another Orthodox, Michel Aflak, ideological pioneer of the Baathist party, have played an important role in the political and national evolution of Syria and Lebanon as well as that of other Arab countries in the Middle East.

**INTERDENOMINATIONAL ORGANIZATIONS.** The Middle East Council of Churches, founded in Beirut in 1927, includes 6 Syrian churches in its membership. Since 1948 the council has been active in Palestinian refugee work and has received considerable assistance from the WCC and CWS.

The Greek Orthodox and Greek Catholic patriarchates each have an ecumenical commission. The Catholic Commission founded in 1968 is under the annual Melkite synod. Although no permanent organizations for ecumenical co-ordination or collaboration exist, in 1967 experts named by all the hierarchies at government request prepared a single manual of Christian religious education consisting of several volumes, which was accepted by the Ministry of Education for examinations in government schools. In 1972 a liturgical congress took place between Greek Catholics and Greek Orthodox, as an experiment and without publicity. The visit of the Syrian Orthodox patriarch Jacob III to pope Paul VI in Rome in 1971, followed by a visit by cardinal Willebrands as papal representative to Damascus in 1972, has had a profound effect in Syria. The Rome meeting resulted in the joint signing of a Declaration of Doctrinal Order.

**BROADCASTING.** No Christian broadcasts are allowed. Foreign Christian programmes in Arabic can however easily be heard from TWR (Monaco) for 4 hours a week, ELWA (Liberia), over CBC (Cyprus), FEBA (Seychelles), and Radio Vatican for 3 hours 30 minutes a week.

**BIBLIOGRAPHY**


(*History of the Syrian church of Antioch*). Parts I–II. S.J. Tuma (Patriarch of Antioch). Beirut, 1953–57 (in Arabic).

'Religion', chapter 11 in *US Army area handbook for Syria* (Washington, DC: US Government Printing Office, 1965), p. 123–141.


TABLE 2. ORGANIZED CHURCHES AND DENOMINATIONS IN SYRIA

| Official name 1 | Begun | Type 3 | Counc 4 | Congs 5 | Adults 6 | Affiliated 7 | Names, notes, and other statistics (see Codebook) 8 |
|---|---|---|---|---|---|---|---|
| Ancient Church of the East: D Hassaké | 1933 | O Nes | Yw... | | 11,000 | 20,000 | *Assyrian Ch. Nestorians.* 1933 mass refugees from Iraq; in Khabur Valley. 5nx. |
| **Armenian Apostolic Ch (C Cilicia):** | c1440 | O Arm | Sw.N. | 22 | 62,500 | 111,648 | *Gregorians.* Under jurisdiction of C Sis (Lebanon). Half members in Aleppo. |
| AD Dimashq (Damascus) | | O Arm | Sa | 10 | 31,400 | 56,000 | Armenians are the main non-Arab Christian community in the capital. |
| AD Halab (Aleppo) | | O Arm | Sa | 12 | 31,100 | 55,648 | Northern Syria. Largest Christian community in city of Aleppo. |
| Armenian Ev Spiritual Brethren | 1920 | P CBr | x.... | 1 | 50 | 200 | *Holiness Brethren.* Ex other Armenian churches. 25 Armenian families in Aleppo. |
| Assemblies of God | | P Pe2 | Z.... | 1 | 35 | 100 | M=AoG(USA). Small mission in Classical Pentecostal (2-stage) tradition. |
| Bible Preaching Church | 1962 | P ind | x.... | | 400 | 800 | M=World-Wide Missions(USA). Evangelicals, with links in Pasadena, CA (USA). |
| **Catholic Church in Syria:** | 295 | R LEr | O...R | 189 | 100,500 | 179,468 | *Al-Kanissa al-Kathoulikiah.* Six rites. C=7+1+18. 3q. 223nx,14m,249w,2503Yy. |
| P Cilicia (*Armenians*) (VP Syria) | 1742 | R Arm | Os | 1 | 1,500 | 2,600 | *Patriarchal Vicariate*, in Damascus. Patriarch in Beirut. 1 2 0 33 |
| M Bostra & Hauran (*Melkite*) | 1687 | R Mel | Os | 31 | 9,400 | 16,800 | *Al Rounn al-Malakioun al-Kathoulik.* Growth since 1960. 23 0 10 372 |
| M Dimashq (Damascus)(*Syrian*) | 1633 | R Syr | Os | 4 | 1,900 | 3,350 | *Al-Sourian al-Kathoulik.* Under P Antioch (Lebanon). 5 0 0 62 |
| M Dimashq (Damascus)(*Melkite*) | 1709 | R Mel | Os | 18 | 19,600 | 35,000 | Patriarchal diocese, P Antioch & All the East. Growing. 20 0 30 450 |
| M Halab (Aleppo)(*Melkite*) | c 350 | R Mel | Os | 7 | 8,400 | 15,000 | Numerical decline. 7 schools until 1967. 19 1 27 154 |
| M Hims (Homs)(*Syrian*) | 1678 | R Syr | Os | 12 | 3,400 | 6,000 | *M Homs-Emesa, Hama & Nabk.* Growing. 6 schools until 1967. 12 0 0 182 |
| M Hims (Homs)(*Melkite*) | 1849 | R Mel | Os | 17 | 8,700 | 15,600 | Restored 1849. M Homs, Hama & Jabrud. Rapid growth. 17 0 24 200 |

*Continued opposite*

*Table 2–continued*

| Official name 1 | Begun 2 | Type 3 | Counc 4 | Congs 5 | Adults 6 | Affiliated 7 | Names, notes, and other statistics (see Codebook) 8 |
|---|---|---|---|---|---|---|---|
| AD Al-Ladhiqiyah (Latakia)(*Melkite*) | 1961 | R Mel | Os | 20 | 6,700 | 12,000 | *AD Laodicea of Syria*. Numerical growth. 15 1 17 50 |
| AD Dimashq (Damascus)(*Maronite*) | 1527 | R Mar | Os | 1 | 1,100 | 2,002 | *Al-Mawarinah*. In P Antioch (Lebanon). 1 0 0 51 |
| AD Halab (*Maronite*) | c1650 | R Mar | Os | 4 | 1,900 | 3,420 | D Beroea. 2 schools, closed 1967. 7 0 0 40 |
| AD Halab (Aleppo)(*Syrian*) | 1695 | R Syr | Os | 3 | 4,800 | 8,500 | Gradual numerical growth. 4 schools until 1967. 5 0 0 58 |
| AD Halab (Aleppo)(*Armenian*) | 1710 | R Arm | Os | 9 | 9,000 | 16,000 | *Al-'rman al-Kathoulik*. Under P Cilicia (Lebanon). 13 0 12 150 |
| AD Hassaké-Nisibi (*Syrian*) | 1957 | R Syr | Os | 8 | 2,000 | 3,596 | In northeast. 5 schools until 1967. Declining. 9 0 2 105 |
| D Halab (*Chaldean*) | 1957 | R Cha | Os | 8 | 5,000 | 9,000 | *Al-Kaldan*. Under P Babilonia. From Iraq since 1920. 16 0 0 100 |
| D Kamechlié (*Armenian*) | 1954 | R Arm | Os | 7 | 1,600 | 2,900 | Qameshliyeh. In northeast, on Turkish frontier. 5 0 0 81 |
| AA Al-Ladhiqiyah (*Maronite*) (1977,D) | 1954 | R Mar | Os | 30 | 8,800 | 15,700 | Laodicea of Syria. Parishes of D Tripoli (Lebanon). 21 1 18 305 |
| VA Halab (*Latin*) | 1762 | R Lat | Os | 9 | 6,700 | 12,000 | *Al-Latinn*. Half in Aleppo, growing. Many projects. M=OFM. 35 11 109 143 |
| Church of God (Anderson) | | P Hol | x...C | 2 | 200 | 500 | M=CoG(Anderson)(USA). Holiness denomination. |
| Church of God (Cleveland) | | P Pe3 | ZF... | 1 | 50 | 100 | M=CoG(Cleveland)(USA). Small Holiness Pentecostal (3-stage) body. |
| Church of the East | | I Nes | ..... | | 500 | 1,000 | Assyrian schism (anti-party) from patriarchate in Iraq. Refugees. 2x. |
| Epis Ch in Jerusalem & ME(D Jerusalem) | | A Low | aw.NC | 1 | 30 | 50 | Formerly in Jerusalem Archbishopric. Arabs, with Arab bishop in Jerusalem. |
| Evangelical Church in Damascus | | P Ref | ..... | 1 | 200 | 500 | Congregation in Damascus; 1950s, refused to join National Evangelical Synod. |
| Evangelical Church of the Nazarene | 1920 | P Hol | xF..C | 7 | 132 | 640 | *Kniset Innasari Il Injiliyeh*. M=CoN(USA). Declining in numbers. 13m,11t(500). |
| **Greek Orth Patriarchate of Antioch:** | 30 | O Ara | CW.N. | 127 | 112,000 | 200,000 | Members Arabs, liturgy Arabic. Strongest in the west. 123n,5d,2e,P=60%,W=10%. |
| AD Dimashq (Damascus) | | O Ara | Cp | 50 | 34,000 | 60,000 | P Antioch is main bastion of Greek Orthodox in Middle East. 50n,5d(75 monks). |
| D Al-Ladhiqiyah (Latakia) | | O Ara | Cm | 23 | 22,000 | 40,000 | North coast. Most deeply-embedded of all Christian communities in Syria. 20n. |
| D Halab (Aleppo)(Beroa) | | O Ara | Cm | 10 | 11,000 | 20,000 | *Diocese of Beroa & Alexandretta* (Iskendarun, Turkey). In northwest. 10n. |
| D Hamah (Epiphania) | | O Ara | Cm | 18 | 17,000 | 30,000 | North central Syria. HQ Hamah, 50 km north of Hims. 18 parish priests. |
| D Hims (Homs, Emessa) | | O Ara | Cm | 16 | 17,000 | 30,000 | Central Syria. HQ Archevêché Grec-Orthodoxe, Hims. 16 parish priests. |
| D Vostro (Bostra, Soueida) | | O Ara | Cm | 10 | 11,000 | 20,000 | South. HQ Archevêché Grec-Orthodoxe, Soueida (As-Suwayda). 9 parish priests. |
| Isolated radio churches | c1950 | I rad | ..... | 160 | 3,000 | 5,500 | Arab radio believers, mainly aged 12-25. R=500(TWR,RVOG,&c),T=30000(ICI,GMU). |
| Jehovah's Witnesses | c1920 | M Jeh | x.... | 5 | 153 | 600 | *Témoins de Jéhovah. Watch Tower*. Active witnessing under way by 1926. 2Y. |
| National Ev Christian Alliance Church | 1921 | P Hol | x...C | 8 | 200 | 2,000 | M=CMA(USA). A=1956. Damascus, Homs, other towns. Growing 8%pa. 3n,W=50%,8Y,15z. |
| National Ev Synod of Syria & Lebanon | 1823 | P Ref | RW.NC | 27 | 1,675 | 10,000 | Scattered. Decline by emigration, G=–5.2%pa. M=ABCFM/UCBWM. 8n,1H,W=57%,47Yy,66z. |
| Seventh-day Adventist Church | 1890 | P Adv | x...C | 1 | 20 | 50 | *SDA, Syria Station*, East Mediterranean Field, Middle East Union. In Damascus. |
| **Syrian Orth Patriarchate of Antioch:** | 30 | O Syr | DW.N. | | 45,000 | 81,000 | *Jacobites*. Members mainly in northeast on Turkish border. HQ Damascus. W=10%. |
| AD Dimashq (Damascus) | | O Syr | Dp | | 14,000 | 26,000 | Patriarchal diocese. 1919–57, patriarch resided at Homs. Heavy emigration. |
| D Al-Hasakah (Hassaké) | | O Syr | Dm | | 25,000 | 45,000 | Strongest concentration of members in Qamishli area, in extreme northeast corner. |
| D Halab (Aleppo) | | O Syr | Dm | | 3,000 | 5,000 | Northwest Syria. Contacts with, and support for, Syrian Orthodox in Turkey. |
| D Hims (Homs) | | O Syr | Dm | | 3,000 | 5,000 | Formerly patriarchal seat until 1957. Central Syria, north of Damascus. |
| Union of Armenian Ev Chs in Near East | 1918 | P Con | Rw.NC | 12 | 3,000 | 6,000 | Armenian refugees from 1914–18 Turkey massacres. World HQ Beirut. 9 schools,1H. |
| Other Protestant denominations | | P | ..... | | 500 | 1,000 | Total about 7 (see list below). |
| **Total affiliated (mid-1970)** | | | | **780** | **341,145** | **621,156** | **Total denominations (1970) . . . 27.** |
| **Total affiliated (mid-1975)** | | | | **790** | **377,000** | **686,500** | **Total denominations (1975) . . . 27.** |
| **Total affiliated (mid-1980)** | | | | **800** | **419,600** | **764,050** | **Total denominations (1980) . . . 28.** |

NOTES ON TABLE ABOVE
COLUMNS: for meanings and CODES (cols. 1, 3, 4, 8): see Codebook (Part 6). Column 1: **Boldface type** = church with over 10% of country's affiliated Christians.
NATIONAL COUNCILS (Column 4, 5th letter).
C = Counseil Supérieur des Eglises Evangéliques de Syrie et du Liban (Supreme Council of Evangelical Churches of Syria and Lebanon).
R = Assemblée de la Hiérarchie Catholique en Syrie (Assembly of Bishops in the Syrian Arab Republic); inter-rite.
OTHER PROTESTANT DENOMINATIONS. These small bodies include: Chs of Christ (Christian Chs), Ev Baptist Missions (1957), Mennonite Ch (1923), Religious Society of Friends (1869), World-Wide Missions (1962).
UNITING CHURCHES. Negotiations for organic union were under way in 1974 between: Episcopal Ch, National Ev Synod of Syria & Lebanon.

PEOPLES (ethnolinguistic). Christians: 72.2% Arab (Syrian, Palestinian, Lebanese, Jordanian), 22.8% Armenian, 4.9% Assyrian, French, Greek, Gypsy.

COUNTRY-WIDE TOTALS
EVANGELIZATION (see Part 5). 1900: 42%. 1970: 48%. 1980: 57%. *Radiophonic evangelism*. TWR, Radio Vatican, ICI, et alia.
FOREIGN MISSIONARIES AND PERSONNEL (nationals serving abroad) (1973). Total 96 in 15 countries: 60 Orthodox in 14 countries, 36 Roman Catholics in 3 countries.
FOREIGN MISSIONARIES AND PERSONNEL (aliens from abroad) (1973). Total 111. *From Western world*. 80: about 70 Roman Catholics, 10 Protestants in 8 USA societies. *From Communist world*. 1 Roman Catholic from Poland. *From Third World*. 30: about 16 Orthodox from Lebanon, Iraq et alia, about 10 Roman Catholics from Lebanon, about 4 Protestants.
INSTITUTIONS (church-operated) (1973). Total 35, including about 15 higher schools (6 minor seminaries), 10 medical centres.
PERIODICALS. About 30 titles.
PERSONNEL. About 801 (690 national, 111 foreign).
SCRIPTURE DISTRIBUTION (1975). Annual totals: 581 Bibles (subsidized), 1,153 NTs (subsidized), 3,761 UBS portions, 46,266 UBS selections. *Translations completed*. Modern Western Armenian: NT 1825, Bible 1853.
SERVICE AGENCIES. About 29, including AHCS/ACHS, CEF, CELRA, CCCI, CEEC, LWR, OCSC.

ADDITIONAL DATA ON CHURCHES
CATHOLIC CHURCH IN SYRIA. *Annual baptisms*. (1972) 99.6% infant, 0.4% adult. *Seminarians*. Training is in Syria, Lebanon or Rome. Total: 29, all religious. *Religious orders and congregations*. Priests: (Melkites) Missionnaires de St-Paul, Ordre Basilien Salvatorien; (Latins) OFM, SJ, CM, SDB, OFMCap. Brothers: (Latins) PFM. Sisters: (Melkites) Soeurs de la Charité de Besançon, Perpétuel Secours, Alépines, Chouérites, Petites Soeurs de Jésus, Bon Service; (Armenians) Immaculée Conception; (Chaldeans) Soeurs Chaldéennes; (Maronites) St-Famille; (Latins) Franciscaines Missionnaires de Marie, Filles de la Charité, Carmel St-Joseph, Carmélites, Salésiennes, SS Coeurs (oriental congregation with 486 in Lebanon and 60 in Syria), St-Joseph de l'Apparition, Soeurs Franciscaines d'Egypte, Soeurs Franciscaines de la Croix (the latter of Lebanese origin).
*Catholic organizations*. No national episcopal conference exists, but there is an inter-rite Assembly which was founded in 1967 and meets twice yearly. This is primarily consultative, leaving the bishops free to put into effect the decisions of their own patriarchal synods. The Latin vicar apostolic of Aleppo is a member of the Conference of Latin Bishops in the Arab Regions (CELRA) in East Jerusalem. There are no national associations for religious personnel or priests, although Syria's Melkite priests are represented in the Congress of Melkite Priests which meets in Lebanon. For the laity, the Legion of Mary is used as a confraternity in support of local parishes, and has developed greatly in Damascus. The Conferences of St Vincent de Paul, recognized for their public service, have been able to continue their activities Scouts and Guides are active in Damascus, and exist under different names at Aleppo and other centres. Groups of students, called university parish and numerous other informal groups, work among youth.
The Holy See has diplomatic relations with Syria and is represented to government and the Catholic hierarchy by a pronuncio in Damascus.
As for those Catholic schools which were left open in 1967 or later received permission to open in 1973, there were then 5 of Syrian rite, 4 Melkite, 3 Armenian, 3 Latin and one of Chaldean rite. Following a government decision of December 1974, the 92 Catholic schools nationalized or closed in 1967 were returned to their owners, 6 religious congregations and secular clergy.
In the area of charitable activities, Al-Kalimat Social Works (Oeuvres Sociales Al-Kalimat), founded in Aleppo in 1929 and officially recognized by the Syrian government in 1938, is affiliated with Caritas International in Rome. This organization operates a hospital considered to be the most modern in the country, and a home for the aged for 116 inmates. Altogether in 1972 there were 5 hospitals (3 at Aleppo and 2 at Damascus), 4 orphanages (3 at Aleppo and one at Damascus) and one home for the aged. There are operated by either Greek Melkite or Latin religious personnel.

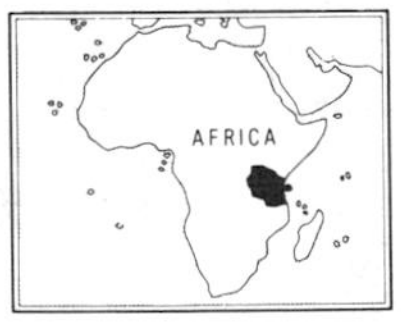


# TANZANIA

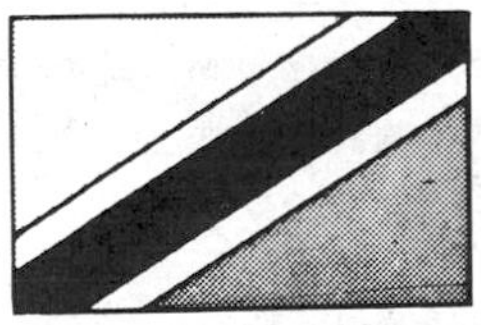

## SECULAR DATA

**STATE. Official name:** The United Republic of Tanzania (Jamhuri ya Mwungano wa Tanzania). Adjective of nationality: Tanzanian.
**Flag.** (shown above right): Green triangle (upper left) and blue triangle (lower right) separated by diagonal gold-bordered black stripe.
**Area:** 945,087 sq. km. (364,900 sq. miles). Agricultural land: 54.7%.
**Government:** One-party socialist republic, since 1961 (1890 British protectorate (Zanzibar) and German protectorate (Tanganyika), 1918 British mandated territory, 1961 Independence, 1964 Tanganyika and Zanzibar united).
**Legislature:** National Assembly, 217 members.
**Official languages:** Swahili (*Kiswahili*), also English.
**Chief cities:** capital Dar es Salaam 343,910 (1970), Zanzibar 57,920. After 1982 the new capital will be Dodoma (1967) population, 18,000).
**Political divisions:** 22 Regions (Tanganyika 18, Zanzibar 4). By 1974, 6,900 ujamaa (socialist collective) villages with 9 million population had been begun.
**Armed forces** (1976): Total 14,600 regular: army 13,000, navy 600, air force 1,000 (33 combat aircraft). Paramilitary force: 35,000 Citizen's Militia.

**DEMOGRAPHY. Population:** 12,313,469 (census of 26.VIII.1967. For 1970–2000 (UN), see last row of Table 1). Population density (1975): 16/sq. km. (42/sq. mile). Under 15 years: 44%. Growth rate (1975–80): 3.13% per year (births 4.93%, deaths -1.80%). Life expectancy (1975–80): 47.0 years. Household size: 4.4 persons.
**Major languages:** Swahili, English, Sukuma, Nyamwezi, Hehe, Makonde, Chagga, Haya, Ha, Gogo, Nyakysua, Sambaa, Arabic, Luguru, Chinese, and over 110 other tribal languages.
**Urban dwellers** (1970): 6.3%. Urban growth rate (1950–70): 5.8% per year.

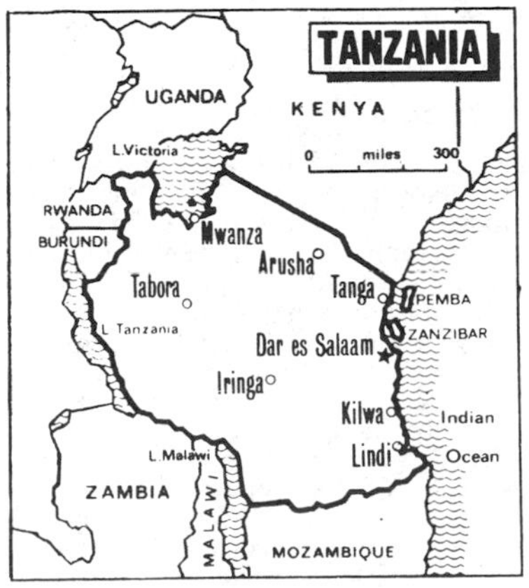


**Labour force:** 44%.
**Refugees** (1977): 124,500 (110,005 from Burundi, 14,000 from Rwanda, also Mozambique, Uganda and Zimbabwe).
**Tourists** (1972): 490,000. (1973) 120,000.

**ETHNOLINGUISTIC GROUPS:** 13.0% Sukuma, 9% Rufiji cluster (3.1% Hehe, 2.1% Bena, 0.8% Pogoro, 0.3% Sagara), 5% Rukwa cluster (1.4% Fipa, 0.7% Safwa, Iwa), 4.1% Makonde, 3.7% Chagga, 3.5% Haya, 3.5% Nyamwezi, 3.3% Ha, 3.1% Gogo, 2.6% Nyakyusa, 2.3% Shambala (Sambaa), 2.3% Zanzibari (with Swahili, Arab), 2.2% Luguru, 2.1% Turu, 2.0% Zaramo, 2.0% Southern Cushitic (1.7% Iraqw, Mbulu), 1.8% Yao, 1.6% Zigula, 1.6% Pare, 1.6% Iramba, 1.5% Mwera, 1.4% Tutsi (Rundi, Ruanda), 1.4% Makua, 1.3% Rangi, 1.3% Jita, 1.1% Luo, 1.1% Kuria, 1.0% Ngindo, 1.0% Kaguru, 0.9% Nguni, 0.9% Pangwa, 0.8% Arusha, 0.7% Maasai, 0.7% Indo-Pakistani, 0.5% Nyasa, 0.4% Zinza, 0.4% Meru, 0.3% Sandawe, 0.3% Zanaki, 0.3% Digo, 0.2% British, 0.1% other European, 0.1% Chinese (20,000), 0.1% Somali, other Bantu (about 6%), Bemba, Comorian, Greek Cypriot, Kindiga, Dorobo, Jewish, Cuban (500 civilian), et alii. British Asians declined from 50,000 in 1968 to 8,000 by 1977.

**MONEY** (1977). **Monetary unit:** Tanzania shilling (=100 cents= 0.05 Tanzanian pounds); US$1=TSh 8.31.
**National income per person:** US$150. Average annual family income: US$660.
**Inflation:** (1970–74) 12.4% per year, (1975) 26% per year (consumer price index 186).
**Cost of living in capital** (1976): index 118 (Washington DC=100). Daily cost of living: US$34.

**HEALTH.** Hospitals: 1,144 (17,515 beds). Doctors: 537. Lepers: 120,000 (7.8 per 1,000). Blind (1974): 40,000. Psychotics: 110,000.

**EDUCATION.** Adult literacy: (1967) 28%. Education rate: 23%. Schools: 4,891. Universities: 1.

**LITERATURE.** Annual new book titles (1972): 123. Periodicals: 55. Newspapers: 3 dailies, 23 non-daily.

**COMMUNICATION** (per 1,000 people). Phones: 4. Radios: 16. TV sets: 1. Daily newspaper circulation: 5 copies.

TABLE 1. RELIGIOUS ADHERENTS IN TANZANIA

| Year | 1900 | | mid-1970 | | Annual change, 1970–1980 | | | | mid-1975 | | mid-1980 | | 2000 | |
|---|---|---|---|---|---|---|---|---|---|---|---|---|---|---|
| *Name* | *Adherents* | *%* | *Adherents* | *%* | *Natural* | *Conversion* | *Total* | *Rate* | *Adherents* | *%* | *Adherents* | *%* | *Adherents* | *%* |
| **Christians** | **92,000** | **2.4** | **4,778,000** | **36.0** | **191,160** | **125,340** | **316,500** | **5.13** | **6,175,200** | **40.0** | **7,943,000** | **44.0** | **18,044,000** | **53.0** |
| professing | 92,000 | 2.4 | 4,778,000 | 36.0 | 191,160 | 125,340 | 316,500 | 5.13 | 6,175,200 | 40.0 | 7,943,000 | 44.0 | 18,044,000 | 53.0 |
| Roman Catholics | 70,000 | 1.8 | 3,069,900 | 23.1 | 122,338 | 79,742 | 202,080 | 5.11 | 3,952,000 | 25.6 | 5,090,700 | 28.2 | 11,643,000 | 34.2 |
| Protestants | 15,000 | 0.4 | 1,221,100 | 9.2 | 48,902 | 31,748 | 80,650 | 5.11 | 1,579,700 | 10.2 | 2,027,600 | 11.2 | 4,507,000 | 13.2 |
| Anglicans | 7,000 | 0.2 | 438,000 | 3.3 | 17,682 | 10,728 | 28,410 | 4.97 | 571,200 | 3.7 | 722,100 | 4.0 | 1,600,000 | 4.7 |
| African indigenous | 0 | 0.0 | 40,000 | 0.3 | 1,913 | 3,117 | 5,030 | 8.14 | 61,800 | 0.4 | 90,300 | 0.5 | 272,000 | 0.8 |
| Orthodox | 0 | 0.0 | 9,000 | 0.1 | 325 | 5 | 330 | 3.14 | 10,500 | 0.1 | 12,300 | 0.1 | 22,000 | 0.1 |
| nominal | 14,600 | 0.4 | 453,375 | 3.4 | 18,639 | 15,463 | 34,102 | 5.66 | 602,100 | 3.9 | 794,400 | 4.4 | 2,043,000 | 6.0 |
| affiliated | 77,400 | 2.0 | 4,324,625 | 32.6 | 172,521 | 109,877 | 282,398 | 5.07 | 5,573,100 | 36.1 | 7,148,600 | 39.6 | 16,001,000 | 47.0 |
| total practising | 73,530 | *95* | 3,892,160 | *90* | 155,269 | 98,889 | 254,158 | 5.07 | 5,015,790 | *90* | 6,433,740 | *90* | 13,601,000 | *85* |
| non-practising | 3,870 | *5* | 432,460 | *10* | 17,252 | 10,988 | 28,240 | 5.07 | 557,310 | *10* | 714,860 | *10* | 2,400,000 | *15* |
| Roman Catholics | 62,400 | 1.6 | 2,806,662 | 21.1 | 111,826 | 69,618 | 181,444 | 5.02 | 3,612,400 | 23.4 | 4,621,100 | 25.6 | 10,316,000 | 30.3 |
| Protestants | 10,000 | 0.3 | 1,072,728 | 8.1 | 43,010 | 28,427 | 71,437 | 5.14 | 1,389,400 | 9.0 | 1,787,100 | 9.9 | 3,946,000 | 11.6 |
| Evangelicals | 9,000 | 0.2 | 982,000 | 7.4 | 40,140 | 31,350 | 71,490 | 5.51 | 1,296,700 | 8.4 | 1,696,900 | 9.4 | 3,847,000 | 11.3 |
| Anglicans | 5,000 | 0.1 | 386,095 | 2.9 | 15,292 | 9,279 | 24,571 | 4.97 | 494,000 | 3.2 | 631,800 | 3.5 | 1,430,000 | 4.2 |
| Evangelicals | 500 | 0.0 | 164,000 | 1.2 | 6,501 | 4,099 | 10,600 | 5.05 | 210,000 | 1.4 | 270,000 | 1.5 | 620,000 | 1.8 |
| Anglican pentecostals | 0 | 0.0 | 0 | 0.0 | 31 | 169 | 200 | 20.00 | 1,000 | 0.0 | 2,000 | 0.0 | 20,000 | 0.1 |
| African indigenous | 0 | 0.0 | 46,140 | 0.3 | 1,913 | 2,502 | 4,416 | 7.15 | 61,800 | 0.4 | 90,300 | 0.5 | 272,000 | 0.8 |
| Orthodox | 0 | 0.0 | 9,000 | 0.1 | 325 | 5 | 330 | 3.14 | 10,500 | 0.1 | 12,300 | 0.1 | 22,000 | 0.1 |
| Marginal Protestants | 0 | 0.0 | 4,000 | 0.0 | 155 | 45 | 200 | 4.00 | 5,000 | 0.0 | 6,000 | 0.0 | 15,000 | 0.0 |
| Tribal religionists | 3,439,900 | 90.5 | 4,227,000 | 31.8 | 131,668 | –142,840 | –11,172 | –0.26 | 4,220,390 | 27.3 | 4,115,280 | 22.8 | 3,822,800 | 11.2 |
| Muslims | 266,000 | 7.0 | 4,181,000 | 31.5 | 152,923 | 15,667 | 168,590 | 3.41 | 4,940,000 | 32.0 | 5,866,900 | 32.5 | 11,916,000 | 35.0 |
| Ahmadis | 0 | 0.0 | 6,700 | 0.1 | 248 | 22 | 270 | 3.38 | 8,000 | 0.1 | 9,400 | 0.1 | 25,000 | 0.1 |
| Baha'is | 0 | 0.0 | 41,000 | 0.3 | 1,548 | 352 | 1,900 | 3.80 | 50,000 | 0.3 | 60,000 | 0.3 | 130,000 | 0.4 |
| Hindus | 2,000 | 0.1 | 21,000 | 0.2 | –180 | –20 | –200 | –1.00 | 20,000 | 0.1 | 19,000 | 0.1 | 10,000 | 0.0 |
| Non-religious | 0 | 0.0 | 18,000 | 0.1 | 774 | 1,426 | 2,200 | 8.80 | 25,000 | 0.2 | 40,000 | 0.2 | 100,000 | 0.3 |
| Atheists | 0 | 0.0 | 3,000 | 0.0 | 124 | 76 | 200 | 5.00 | 4,000 | 0.0 | 5,000 | 0.0 | 20,000 | 0.1 |
| Sikhs | 0 | 0.0 | 3,000 | 0.0 | –100 | 0 | –100 | –4.00 | 2,500 | 0.0 | 2,000 | 0.0 | 1,000 | 0.0 |
| Jains | 100 | 0.0 | 800 | 0.0 | –20 | 0 | –20 | –2.86 | 700 | 0.0 | 600 | 0.0 | 1,000 | 0.0 |
| Jews | 0 | 0.0 | 100 | 0.0 | 3 | –1 | 2 | 1.82 | 110 | 0.0 | 120 | 0.0 | 200 | 0.0 |
| Parsis | 0 | 0.0 | 100 | 0.0 | 0 | 0 | 0 | 0.00 | 100 | 0.0 | 100 | 0.0 | 0 | 0.0 |
| **Country's population** | **3,800,000** | **100.0** | **13,273,000** | **100.0** | **477,900** | **0** | **477,900** | **3.10** | **15,438,000** | **100.0** | **18,052,000** | **100.0** | **34,045,000** | **100.0** |

COLUMNS, ROWS. For meanings and definitions, see Codebook (Part 6). Note that, by definition, total 'Christians' = professing + crypto-Christians, which also = affiliated + nominal Christians. Percentages may not always total exactly, due to rounding.
CENSUSES. **1931** (Tanganyika; non-Africans): 52.5% Muslims, 24.3% Christians, 19.0% Hindus, 1.9% Sikhs, 0.1% Jains, 0.1% Parsis. **1931** (Zanzibar): 95.2% Muslims (83.4% Sunnis, 8.5% Ibadis, 1.4% Ismailis, 0.9% Ithna-Asharis, 0.8% Bohoras, 0.2% other Shias), 1.5% Hindus, 1.4% tribal religionists, 1.1% Roman Catholics, 0.7% Protestants, 0.1% Parsis. **25.II.1948** (Tanganyika; Africans): 57.5% tribal religionists, 24.9% Muslims, 17.6% Christians. **1948** (Tanganyika; non-Africans): 54.5% Muslims (22.1% Ismailis, 8.3% Sunnis, 6.0% Ibadis, 5.7% Ithna-Asharis, 5.6% Hanafites), 22.3% Hindus, 19.3% Christians (7.4% Roman Catholics, 6.2% Anglicans), 2.5% Sikhs, 0.6% Jains, 0.1% Parsis. **1948** (Zanzibar): 94.8% Muslims, 2.1% Christians, 1.6% Hindus, 1.3% tribal religionists, 0.1% Jains, 0.1% Parsis. **1957** (Tanganyika; Africans): 44.2% tribal religionists, 30.9% Muslims, 24.9% Christians (17.1% Roman Catholics, 7.8% Protestants and Anglicans). **1957** (Tanganyika; non-Africans): 49.2% Muslims, 23.7% Hindus, 22.4% Christians, 3.5% Sikhs, 0.7% Jains, 0.1% Parsis. **1957** (Tanganyika; all races): 43.6% tribal religionists, 31.1% Muslims, 24.9% Christians, 0.3% Hindus. **20.II.1957** (Tanganyika and Zanzibar; all races): 42.2% tribal religionists, 33.2% Muslims, 24.2% Christians, 0.4% Hindus. **27.VIII.1967** (heads of households only): 36.2% tribal religionists ('local belief'), 31.6% Christians, 31.4% Muslims, 0.8% Hindus, Baha'is and other religionists. **27.VIII.1967** (mainland only): 37.3% tribal religionists, 32.4% Christians, 29.5% Muslims, 0.8% Hindus and other religionists. **27.VIII.1967** (Zanzibar): 95.5% Muslims, 2.9% Christians (9,877 persons), 1.0% Hindus and other world-religionists, 0.6% tribal religionists. Since pagan heads of households are one generation older than their children, and since the % Christian is higher among children due to education in Christian schools, adjusted figures for the whole population in 1967 are: 34.3% tribal religionists, 33.5% Christians, 31.4% Muslims, 0.8% Hindus and other religionists.

NOTES ON RELIGIONS
AFRICAN INDIGENOUS. In 40 denominations in 1970 (see Table 2).
AHMADIS. Begun 1934; Qadianis, with work in Dar es Salaam, Rufiji (Utete), Lindi and Tabora, and about 40 other branches. Most Asian followers emigrated after 1963, leaving mainly African followers.
ATHEISTS. Mainly intellectuals, gradually increasing in numbers in the 1970s; also a large number of expatriate technicians from the People's Republic of China.
BAHA'IS. Growth from 66 local spiritual assemblies (1964) to 211 (1973). As with Uganda and Kenya, the work is deeply entrenched in certain African tribes.
HINDUS. Numbers are declining by emigration through the gradual repatriation of Hindus who are citizens of the UK (Britain).
MUSLIMS. Conversions to Islam on a large scale began around 1880 and were especially numerous from 1910–30. The most important wave of mass conversions followed the collapse of German rule in 1917. *Regions.* Zanzibar is 95.0% Muslim, Tanganyika (mainland) 21.0% Muslim. *Communities.* Africans are Shafiite Sunnis, and there are also 12,000 Shias, about 70,000 Arabs, other Sunnis and 6,000 Ibadis on Zanzibar. Indians and Pakistanis are mainly Shias (30,000 Ismailis (90% Tanzania citizens), Ithna-Asharis, 7,000 Bohoras, also Sunnis). There is also an Ahmadiya Mission (enumerated here under Muslims though declared non-Muslim by Pakistan). *Missionaries.* There are numerous Egyptian doctors and others sent by Al-Azhar University (Cairo), with many clinics in Tanzania. *Hajj pilgrims to Mecca.* (1970) under 50; (1974) 645; (1975) 580; (1976) 591. *Conversions to Islam.* Islamization is still proceeding among several tribes, although the rate of conversion has slowed appreciably since Independence in 1961. Today many pagan schoolchildren leave school as Muslims. In 1970, about 100 Christians a year were becoming Muslims (often Ahmadis). The Shia Ithna-Ashari community operate the Bilal Muslim Mission in Arusha, Dar es Salaam and elsewhere, and claim several hundred converts from Christianity. *Conversions from Islam.* About 1,000 Muslims a year were becoming Christians in 1970, including 550 Digo, 150 Pare, 80 Zigula, 50 Zaramo, and others from 10 other tribes. Of these, 67% became Anglicans, 26% Lutherans, and 6% Roman Catholics. *Islamized tribes.* The Makonde (550,000 in Tanzania and 300,000 in Mozambique) are typical of the numerous islamized tribes; they have been 90% Muslims since their mass conversion in 1910–20 but still retain intact most of their traditional animism, with a bare minimum of Muslim customs. Similarly, the Zaramo (296,000) are 95% Muslim but are still strong animists in practice. Other largely Muslim tribes: Luguru (89%), Mwera (79%), Rangi (90%), Sambaa (65%), Yao (85%), Zigula (92%).
NON-RELIGIOUS. Chinese technicians from People's Republic of China.
PRACTISING CHRISTIANS. Urban areas (1970): 69% of all affiliated Christians attend church weekly, 15% more than once monthly. Dar es Salaam (1970): 30% of Christians attend weekly, 30% occasionally. Before migrating to cities, 76.5% of all Christians attended church every Sunday, and 12.5% more than once monthly.
ROMAN CATHOLICS. In the year 1900, there were 29,400 indigenous baptized Catholics, and 33,000 catechumens.
SIKHS. Declining by emigration.
TRIBAL RELIGIONISTS. Animists. Tribes with over 60% traditionalists in 1972; Dorobo (99% animist), Barabaig (98%), Safwa (97%), Maasai (95%), Sonjo (95%), Arusha (88%), Iraqw (83%), Burungi (80%), Sukuma (1,770,000; 80%), Turu (79%), Zinza (75%), Gogo (70%), Nyakyusa (69%), Kindiga (Hadza) (60%), Nyamwezi (60%).

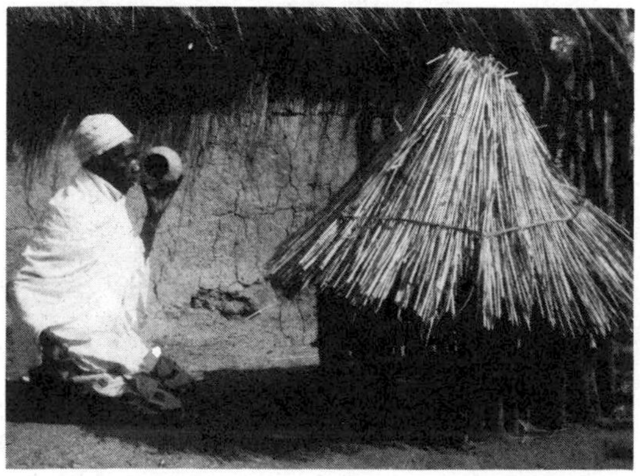

**Tribal religionists.** Kutimbana (private prayer to ancestors): a pagan chief of the Kimbu (who are 25% pagan), wearing white cloth and hat, spits offering of *impemba* (white maize flour and water) from gourd before empty *ichanga* (ancestor spirit hut), makes petition, ends with formula 'Ilyuva liwine' (God has seen it).

**NON-CHRISTIAN RELIGIONS: Traditional religions,** usually based on animism, were followed by 32% of the population in 1970, declining by just under 1% per year. The greatest number is found among the Sukuma whose 1.8 million members remain 80% traditionalist. Other large ethnic groups with a high proportion of traditionalists are the Nyamwezi (total population 590,000 in 1972; 60% traditionalist), Gogo (480,000; 70%), Nyakyusa (355,000; 69%), Turu (316,000; 79%), Iraqw (218,000; 83%), Arusha (110,000; 88%), Safwa (102,000; 97%), and Maasai (100,000; 95%). The Zinza, Barabaig, Burungi, Sonjo and Dorobo are smaller tribes over 75% traditionalist. The idea that natural phenomena are manifestations of God is a common idea, resulting in the use of the same word for God and the sun among several Tanzanian peoples: Ruva (Chagga), Iruva (Meru), Nguruvi (Safw) and Riob (Sonjo). For the Maasai, En-Kai means rain and sky as well as God, and the word Engai for God is also found among the Arusha. Mulungu, Mlungu and Murungu are common names for the supreme being found among the Bena, Bondei, Luguru, Sukuma and Turu; while other names include Kyala (among the Nyakyusa), Kyumbi (Pare), Ishwanga (Haya) and Isewahanga (Zinza). In addition to belief in a supreme being, there is still considerable emphasis on the veneration of ancestor spirits (Masamva among the Sukuma), amulets (*mnigi*), diviners (*bafumo*), as well as the evil activities of the sorcerer (*nogi*). The ancient Shetani spirit-possession cults, which owe their origin to the Muslim coastal towns, have made an impact on the Zaramo, Kaguru, Nguu and Pare peoples. Among the Zaramo, the alien Shetani spirits have been absorbed into the traditional cult of the departed, a common belief being that they are no longer independent but are now under the control of the ancestors. This is also happening with the Jini, a new group of coastal spirits.

**Islam** is the professed religion of 32% of the population. Islam is strongest on the coast and along the traditional caravan route through Tabora to Ujiji on Lake Tanganyika. The Zaramo (95%), Makonde (90%) and Yao (85%) are overwhelmingly Muslim; and Islam has also made substantial inroads among the Shambala (65%), Matumbi (50%), Kwere (33%), and Nyamwezi (25%). Muslims are mainly Sunnis of the Shafiite rite, although there are some Ismailis and Ibadites. A major Islamic co-ordinating agency with government recognition is the National Muslim Council of Tanzania (Bakwata).

**Baha'i** and **Hinduism** both have sizeable followings.

## CHRISTIANITY

CATHOLIC CHURCH. Although Portuguese Catholic priests attempted to found a church in Tanganyika in the 16th century, Christian influence was never significant and the eclipse of Portugal as a maritime power resulted in the disintegration of the church by the end of the 17th century. A new beginning was made in 1860 when 3 secular priests moved to Zanzibar from the island of Reunion. They were joined in 1863 by Holy Ghost priests who founded Bagamoyo on the mainland in 1868. Originally a freed-slave settlement, Bagamoyo became the base for evangelistic activity in the interior including the thrust of White Fathers towards Uganda in 1878. Benedictines of St Ottilien of Bavaria appeared in 1887 after Tanganyika had become a German colony. These were followed after World War I by Consolata priests (1920), Capuchins (1921), Passionists (1933), Pallotines (1940), Rosminians (1945), Maryknoll priests (1946), Salvatorians (1955) and more recently Camillian priests, Priests of the Precious Blood and Jesuits. Missionary sisters, brothers and laymen have also made significant contributions. Even more important has been the role of Tanzanian priests, brothers, sisters and catechists. Tanzanian sisters now greatly outnumber missionary sisters. The church is organized into 2 provinces under national leadership.

**Ahmadis.** Village in Pangale, Unyanyembe, of African converts to Ahmadiya with Pakistani missionary (centre, with white turban), 1958.

The Seminar Study Year (SSY) of 1969 proved to be a milestone in the tanzanization of the Catholic Church. Parish discussions on the state of the church were followed in December 1969 by a general meeting, called unofficially a pastoral council. Although council members were only one-third Africans, with little lay representation, the African voice dominated the discussions, contributing to a new understanding of the problems of ecclesiastical life. Subsequent to the Arusha Declaration of 1967, Catholics have played leading roles in church renewal and development.

PROTESTANT CHURCHES. The Evangelical Lutheran Church in Tanzania, the largest Protestant church in the country, was created in 1963 through the union of 7 dioceses and synods originally initiated by several distinct German, American and Scandinavian societies beginning at the end of the 19th century. German missions entered soon after Germany assumed control of the country. The first was Berlin Mission III which arrived in Zanzibar in 1886 and moved to the mainland the following year. Next were the Bethel and Leipzig Missions in 1889 and 1893, and Berlin Mission I in 1901. German missionaries were forced out during World War I, and American Lutherans were asked to provide support. The Augustana Lutheran Church of America responded by sending personnel in 1922, followed by Swedish Lutherans in 1939. The National Lutheran Council of America assumed responsibility for the work following the exodus of German missionaries once again during World War II, and after the war, aid was also received from the Lutheran churches of Finland, Denmark and Norway. In 1969 the church sponsored 2 medical assistants' training centres, one school of nursing, 14 hospitals, 64 dispensaries, one leprosarium, 3 orphanages, and also a school for the blind, a mental institution, a trade school and farm centre.

In 1891 German Moravians took over the work pioneered by the LMS in 1879. The United Free Church of Scotland provided interim assistance at the time of World War I until 1926 when the German Moravian missionaries were able to return. In World War II German Moravian missionaries were replaced by British Moravians. Today Tanzania's Moravians, who are concentrated in the west and southwest, form the largest Moravian provinces in the world. The Moravians sponsor 4 hospitals and 5 dispensaries.

The area east of Lake Victoria is served by the Adventist, Mennonite and Africa Inland churches. German Adventists first appeared in 1903, followed by the Africa Inland Mission in 1908 and American Mennonites in 1934. These churches sponsor 3 hospitals, 21 dispensaries and one leprosarium.

Pentecostals from Sweden, Canada and the USA have been at work since the 1930s and have built up a sizeable Pentecostal community. Other groups include the Baptist Convention of Tanzania, Salvation Army, Church of God, and Churches of Christ.

Prior to the government takeover of schools in 1969, there were 790 Protestant primary schools, 10 secondary schools and 2 teacher training colleges.

ANGLICAN CHURCH. Anglicans form the third-largest church in Tanzania, following Catholics and Lutherans. Four different foreign missionary societies have been active. The UMCA was the first Anglican society beginning on Zanzibar in 1864 and moving to the mainland in 1875. The High Church UMCA and SPG joined together in 1965 to form the USPG. Evangelical Anglicans arrived to work among the Gogo in 1878 through the CMS from Britain, Australia and later New Zealand, followed still later by the Low-church BCMS. In 1970 the Church of the Province of East Africa was divided into separate jurisdictions for Kenya and Tanzania. The present Church of the Province of Tanzania has 9 dioceses in 1977. In 1969 there were 17 hospitals, 22 dispensaries and one leprosarium. The church's 101 primary schools, 5 secondary schools and 3 teacher training colleges were taken over by government in 1969.

INDIGENOUS CHURCHES. Tanzania is characterized by the relative absence of independent churches. Indeed the most important indigenous groups, such as Maria Legio, Nomiya Luo and the Church of Christ in Africa, have spread into Tanzania from nearby Kenya. The largest body indigenous to Tanzania itself has been the Church of the Holy Spirit which was the result of a schism among the Haya in 1953. Most of its members subsequently returned to the Lutheran church. In 1956, 2 Gogo Anglican clergy seceded to form the Tanzania African Church. Reduced from 40 congregations at its height to 14, it applied for membership in the AACC in 1966 as the Tanzania African Church. Several small schisms have taken place among the Nyakyusa of southwestern Tanzania following World War I, but none has become significant.

CHURCH AND STATE. The interim constitution of July 1965 is devoted entirely to the constitutional arrangements resulting from the unification of Tanganyika with Zanzibar. Annexed to it, under the title 'First Schedule', is the constitution of the Tanganyika African National Union (TANU), Tanganyika's only political party (renamed in 1976 CCM, Chama cha Mapinduzi/Party of the Revolution), which includes among its principal aims the following: 'To safeguard the inherent dignity of the individual in accordance with the Universal Declaration of Human Rights', and 'to see that the Government gives equal opportunity to all men and women irrespective of race, religion or status'. (Article 2, Preamble). This text is also reproduced without change in the Arusha Declaration of 1967 which serves as the charter for Tanzania socialism. Church and state are separate in Tanzania, the churches being considered as voluntary agencies invited by the state to collaborate in the development of the country. The position was clearly stated by president Nyerere in December 1973: 'Tanzania has no religion,

**African Greek Orthodox Church.** Church in Moshi, Diocese of Eirenopolis.

**Church of the Province of Tanzania.** On 1960 visit to Dodoma Cathedral (DCT), Archbishop Fisher of Canterbury and other bishops preach in open air.

Muslim/Christian joint funeral. Lutheran, Anglican, Catholic (Maryknoll) and other Christian clergy (robed) officiate together with sheikhs and other

Muslims (with hands palms upwards in prayer) at mass burial in Kaloleni Cemetery, Arusha, of 17 unidentified victims of a bus accident in 1969.

church union discussions were carried on between Lutherans, Anglicans, Moravians, Presbyterians and Methodists of Tanzania and Kenya; but these broke down in 1968.

The Catholic Church sponsors an Episcopal Commission for Ecumenism, and relations between Catholics and Protestants are cordial. The Dar es Salaam Committee of Churches includes Catholics; the education secretaries of the various churches meet regularly; the Tanzania Christian Medical Association is completely ecumenical; religious broadcasting over Radio Tanzania is regulated by a joint committee; and Bible distribution is carried on co-operatively. In addition, joint worship services are widely held at Christmas and Easter and during the Week of Prayer for Christian Unity.

**BROADCASTING.** The government Radio Tanzania gives one hour 30 minutes of radio time weekly to Catholic, Protestant and Muslim programmes, and also accepts cultural and educational material produced by church groups. Christian programmes are prepared by the Christian Council of Tanzania in the Radio Tanzania studio, the Lutheran Radio Centre at Moshi (2 programmes daily), a new IBRA (Pentecostal) studio, and a Catholic studio at Dar es Salaam. From abroad Protestant programmes in Swahili (also prepared in Moshi) were transmitted from RVOG (Ethiopia) until its closure in 1977. Other stations heard are FEBA (Seychelles) and Radio CORDAC (Burundi). For Catholics, UNDA is represented by a national association.

**BIBLIOGRAPHY**
*Catholic directory of Eastern Africa, 1977–79.* Tabora: TMP Book Department, 1977. 258p. (Earlier editions: 1959, 1965, 1968, 1971, 1974–76).
*Christian Council of Tanzania directory, 1972.* Dar es Salaam: Christian Council, 1972. 31p.
*Church, clan and the world.* J. M. Kibira. Studia Missionalia Upsaliensia XXI. Uppsala: Almqvist & Wiksell, 1974. 128p. (By Lutheran bishop of NW Tanganyika).
'Church, mission and state relations in pre- and post-independent Tanzania'. L.W. Swartz. Occasional Paper 19, Syracuse University Program of Eastern African Studies, 1967.
*Communal rituals of the Nyakyusa.* M. Wilson. London: Oxford, 1959. 228p.
*Eglise et socialisme en Tanzanie.* B. Joinet. Nos. 39–40. Paris: Centre Lebret, 1976.
*German missionaries in Tanganyika, 1891–1941.* M. Wright. Oxford: Clarendon, 1971. 249p.
'Kamcape: an anti-sorcery movement in southwest Tanzania', *Africa*, XXXVIII, 1 (1968), 1–15.
*Lutherische Kirche Tanzania: Ein Handbuch.* Ed G. Mellinghoff & J. Kiwovele. Erlanger Taschenbücher Band 39. Erlangen: Ev-Lutherische Mission, 1976. 393p. (33 essays).
*Missions on a colonial frontier west of Lake Victoria: evangelical missions in north-west Tanganyika to 1932.* C.J. Hellberg. Lund: Gleerup, 1965. 256p.
'Seminar study year 1969: the Church in Tanzania today'. Special notes, *Pro Mundi Vita* (Brussels), 13 (1970).
'Significance of the Arusha Declaration as seen in teachings and practices of the Christian Church in Tanzania today'. Z. Gunda. Thesis, Lutheran School of Theology at Chicago (USA), 1971.
*Socialisme et église en Tanzanie.* S. Urfer. Paris: IDOC-France, 1975.
'Sociological factors in the contact of the Gogo of central Tanzania with Islam', P.J.A. Rigby, in I.M. Lewis (ed), *Islam in Tropical Africa* (London: Oxford, 1966), p. 268–295.
*The Lutheran Church on the coast of Tanzania, 1887–1914, with special reference to the ELCT Synod of Uzaramo–Uluguru.* S. von Sicard. London: Brill, 1970. 260p.
'The spirit possession cults and their social setting in a Zaramo coastal community'. M.-L. Swartz. Vol 3, Proceedings of Social Science Conference, Dar es Salaam, 1968.
*Transition in African beliefs, traditional religion and Christian change: a study in Sukumaland, Tanzania, East Africa.* R.E.S. Tanner. Maryknoll, NY: Maryknoll Publications, 1967.

the Party has no religion, the Government has no religion, but most Tanzanians are religious people and the Party and the Government guarantee to each citizen the freedom to choose his own religion'.

Since the Christian churches have exercised an important historical responsibility in education and medical service, problems in church-state relations are situated primarily in these areas. Except for about 10 free schools mostly serving foreigners, all private schools were nationalized in 1969, although their administration has remained for the most part unchanged, since previously also they had been subsidized by government. In the realm of medical service, conflicts have arisen over the subsidizing of salaries of personnel in church medical institutions.

The CCM requires the churches to become more involved in the formation and organization of ujamaa (brotherhood) villages, communal villages which are the basis of Tanzanian socialism. A part of the clergy has been reticent, because of the resistance of local populations in some areas and from fear of being used for political purposes; whereas others, including bishops, have collaborated in these initiatives. Numerous seminars have been organized between

leaders of CCM and the churches.

In August 1975, 2 Muslim sects were banned by government, the Sunni Jamat and United Cutchi Sunni Muslim Jamat, in an apparent attempt to avoid conflict between them and the National Muslim Council of Tanzania (Bakwata) which has government support. At the same time 2 other Muslim groups in the West Lake Region, the Shaffi 'R.A.' Ijumaa and Adhuhuri, were ordered to desist from all activities for failure to fulfil official registration requirements.

**INTERDENOMINATIONAL ORGANIZATIONS.**
The Tanganyika Missionary Council, formed in 1936, was the predecessor of the present Christian Council of Tanzania (CCT). Full members include Lutherans, Anglicans, Moravians, Baptists, Mennonites, AIC, Salvation Army and Friends, while Adventists and Assemblies of God are consultative members. Tanganyika Christian Refugee Service is separately organized, operated by the Lutheran World Federation in consultation with the CCT. Two conservative missions joined the Evangelical Fellowship of East Africa, re-organized later as the Tanzania Evangelical Fellowship. During the 1960s

**TABLE 2.    ORGANIZED CHURCHES AND DENOMINATIONS IN TANZANIA**

| Official name 1 | Begun 2 | Type 3 | Counc 4 | Congs 5 | Adults 6 | Affiliated 7 | Names, notes, and other statistics (see Codebook) 8 | | | | | | |
|---|---|---|---|---|---|---|---|---|---|---|---|---|---|
| Africa Inland Church | 1908 | P int | xM..K | 461 | 50,000 | 80,000 | *AIC.* 1887 M=CMS;1908 AIM,AMB. 80% Sukuma, 15% Jita. 60n,25x,73f,1H,10h,1j,8k,2p. | | | | | | |
| African Apostolic Ch of Johane Masowe | 1964 | I peA | x.... | 2 | 700 | 1,500 | *Gospel of God Ch. Vapostori (Apostles).* Shona body from Rhodesia. In Dar, Arusha. | | | | | | |
| African Brotherhood Church | 1960 | I ind | xva.K | 4 | 200 | 340 | M=ABC(Kenya). Kamba migrants from Kenya; HQ Kibauni. In 1960: 178 Christians. | | | | | | |
| African Greek Orth Ch (D Eirenopolis) | | O Grc | Cv... | 8 | 5,000 | 9,000 | Under Greek P Alexandria. HQ Nairobi. Kikuyu, Greeks, Cypriot farmers. 1h,1000z. | | | | | | |
| African Israel Church Nineveh | c1960 | I pen | .w... | | 4,000 | 8,000 | M=AICN(Kenya). Luo migrants from Kenya (HQ Nineveh, Kisumu); also Luhya members. | | | | | | |
| African Methodist Episcopal Church | 1933 | I Met | Vw... | 5 | 500 | 1,000 | *AMEC.* Begun in Ufipa by Zambians. 1945, branches poened in Mbeya, Tukuyu, Kyela. | | | | | | |
| African National/International Church | 1932 | I Ref | | | 500 | 1,000 | *ANC.* Schism in Nyasaland ex CCAP. 90% Nyakyusa. Polygamists. HQ Rungwe. | | | | | | |
| Baptist Convention of Tanzania | 1956 | P Bap | T...K | 289 | 14,227 | 20,000 | M=BMEA(SBC,USA). 59% Nyakyusa. 1 school. 2n,21x,58f,1H,4h,1p,1s,2000Y. | | | | | | |
| Bible Church | 1957 | P CBr | x.... | 70 | 350 | 1,000 | M=CMML(Germany). 50% Ngoni, 25% Makua, 20% Makonde. 3n,10x,22f,1H,3h,1p,48Y. | | | | | | |
| **Catholic Church in Tanzania:** | 1449 | R Lat | P,,SRR | 689 | 1,571,800 | 2,806,662 | *Kanisa Katoliki.* C=13+4+39. 12p,4s(389). | 518n,818x,363m,2888w,P=44%,117979Yy. | | | | | |
| M  Dar es Salaam | 1887 | R Lat | Ps | 17 | 39,900 | 71,287 | *Jimbo Kuu la D.* Catholics up-country tribes. | 4 | 26 | 5 | 68 | 25 | 4192 |
| D  Arusha | 1963 | R Lat | Pcssp | 12 | 11,100 | 19,770 | 72% Chagga, 11% Kikuyu, 4% Sonjo, 2% Arusha. | 4 | 18 | 2 | 10 | 42 | 1960 |
| D  Dodoma | 1935 | R Lat | Pcp | 25 | 69,200 | 123,630 | 24% Sandawe, 16% Gogo, 15% Hehe, 14% Rangi. | 13 | 38 | 12 | 209 | 51 | 5578 |
| D  Iringa | 1922 | R Lat | Pimc | 35 | 116,200 | 207,554 | 70% Hehe, 16% Bena, 8% Kinga, 6% Sangu. | 24 | 49 | 41 | 270 | 31 | 4176 |
| D  Mahenge | 1964 | R Lat | Ps | 27 | 51,000 | 91,072 | 56% Pogoro, 17% Bena, 14% Ndamba, Mbunga. | 18 | 38 | 56 | 114 | 39 | 5089 |
| D  Mbulu | 1943 | R Lat | Psac | 19 | 37,200 | 66,452 | 40% Turu, 30% Iraqw, 10% Goroa, 6% Mbugwe. | 9 | 10 | 4 | 90 | 35 | 4276 |
| D  Morogoro | 1906 | R Lat | Ps | 76 | 106,500 | 190,201 | 62% Luguru, 23% Sagara, 10% Nguru, 5% Kwere. | 35 | 56 | 12 | 181 | 33 | 6385 |
| D  Moshi | 1910 | R Lat | Ps | 25 | 178,100 | 318,024 | 90% Chagga, 2% Pare, Haya, Luo. 1s. | 58 | 28 | 8 | 447 | 30 | 10385 |
| D  Mtwara (formerly AN Ndanda) | 1931 | R Lat | Ps | 25 | 38,800 | 69,206 | 58% Mwera, 23% Makonde, 18% Makua. M=OSB. | 15 | 58 | 40 | 93 | 49 | 4229 |
| D  Nachingwea | 1963 | R Lat | Psda | 37 | 21,300 | 37,983 | 52% Makua, 25% Yao, 18% Mwera, 3% Ndonde. | 4 | 25 | 14 | 19 | 47 | 1575 |
| D  Njombe | 1968 | R Lat | Posb | 93 | 65,300 | 116,605 | 28% Ngoni, 27% Matengo, 12% Bena, 10% Pangwa. | 16 | 37 | 15 | 58 | 40 | 4955 |
| D  Singida | 1972 | R Lat | Ps | | 38,100 | 68,094 | *Jimbo la Singida.* 50% Turu, 30% Iramba. | 5 | 10 | 1 | 17 | 40 | 2389 |
| D  Songea (Peramiho) | 1927 | R Lat | Ps | 43 | 124,900 | 223,058 | Until 1969, AN Peramiho. M=OSB. 1p,1s. | 65 | 58 | 86 | 281 | 65 | 9602 |
| D  Tanga | 1950 | R Lat | Ps | 16 | 29,700 | 52,952 | *Jimbo la Tanga.* Shambaa, Bondei, Ngoni, 1p. | 6 | 33 | 5 | 121 | 40 | 4636 |
| M  Tabora | 1886 | R Lat | Ps | 23 | 47,400 | 84,589 | 84% Nyamwezi, 8% Fipa, 5% Sumbwa, 2% Ha. 1s. | 37 | 40 | 10 | 106 | 47 | 4799 |
| D  Bukoba | 1951 | R Lat | Ps | 35 | 124,600 | 222,500 | 85% Haya, 5% Subi, 5% Ruanda, 3% Ganda. 1s. | 75 | 20 | 9 | 357 | 36 | 9240 |
| D  Kigoma | 1946 | R Lat | Ps | 14 | 48,200 | 86,065 | 95% Ha, 5% Congolese. 1p. | 4 | 43 | 6 | 53 | 66 | 4060 |

*Continued opposite*

*Table 2–continued*

| Official name 1 | Begun 2 | Type 3 | Counc 4 | Congs 5 | Adults 6 | Affiliated 7 | Names, notes, and other statistics (see Codebook) 8 |
|---|---|---|---|---|---|---|---|
| D Mbeya | 1932 | R Lat | Ps | 18 | 39,500 | 70,483 | 40% Safwa, 22% Nyakyusa, 17% Lambya. 1p. 8 39 2 43 46 3799 |
| D Musoma | 1950 | R Lat | Ps | 18 | 60,200 | 107,501 | 36% Luo, 21% Kwaya, 13% Kuria, 6% Jita. 1p. 6 28 4 42 32 3796 |
| D Mwanza | 1929 | R Lat | Ps | 25 | 81,900 | 146,312 | 66% Sukuma, 29% Kerewe, 3% Zinza, 2% Kara. 36 57 16 93 51 6356 |
| D Rulenge | 1960 | R Lat | Ps | 14 | 70,900 | 126,667 | 49% Haya, 24% Zinza, 22% Hangaza. 17 26 5 86 52 4535 |
| D Shinyanga | 1950 | R Lat | Pmm | 20 | 29,200 | 52,198 | 98% Sukuma. Workers in Mwadui mine. 7 31 6 17 32 1616 |
| D Sumbawanga (Karema) | 1946 | R Lat | Ps | 26 | 131,000 | 233,856 | 65% Fipa, 4% Bende, 1% Lungu. 2p. 44 36 4 84 73 9124 |
| PA Same (1977, D Same) | 1963 | R Lat | Pcasp | 37 | 9,900 | 17,603 | 99% Pare. Many missions; no pagans left. 5 14 0 25 54 957 |
| AA Zanzibar & Pemba | 1964 | R Lat | Ps | 9 | 1,700 | 3,000 | 2 islands. First mission 1449. Formerly M=CS. 3 0 0 4 51 270 |
| Christian Brethren | 1951 | P CBr | x.... | 4 | 100 | 500 | M=CMML(UK), Works with Bible Church. In towns. HQ Dar es Salaam. 18f,1H. |
| Christian Revival Meeting Group | c1968 | I ind | .T.T. | 15 | 1,200 | 3,000 | *Revivalist Churches*. Group of revivalists. Many ex Anglicans. HQ Mwanza. 3n. |
| Christian Witness Church | c1968 | I Ang | ..... | 5 | 120 | 300 | *Mashaidi wa Ukristo*. Schism ex Anglicans, Geita. 30% Sukuma. 1n,3m,W=50%,17Y,28y. |
| Church of Christ in Africa | 1957 | I Ang | xT.T. | | 1,000 | 3,000 | *Area Diocese of Musoma. JoHera*(*People of Love*). M=CCA(Kenya), Luo schism ex CMS. |
| Church of God | 1951 | P Pe3 | ZP... | 31 | 230 | 600 | M=Ch of God (Cleveland)(USA). Begun by immigrants from Zambia, Malawi. 1n. |
| Church of God in East Africa | 1958 | P Hol | x.... | 31 | 2,500 | 5,000 | *CGEA*. M=CoG(Anderson)(USA). Migrants from large Kenya CoG church. 29n,4f,1s,W=50%. |
| Church of JC the Light of the World | 1967 | I Ang | ..... | | 1,000 | 2,000 | *Kujitawala* (*Independence*). *Neukirchner Uhuru Ch.* Ha schism ex Anglicans in west. |
| Church of the Holy Spirit | 1953 | I Lut | .T... | | 1,000 | 2,000 | Balokole (Revival) split ex ELCT(NW Diocese), Bukoba. 99% Haya. 1962, 50% returned. |
| Church of the Province of Tanzania: | 1864 | A plu | AWAVK | 2,167 | 158,100 | 386,095 | *CPT. Kanisa la Jimbo la Tanzania* (*KJT*). 160f,3s(55). 305n,43x,8629Y,16200y. |
| D Central Tanganyika | 1927 | A Eva | A | 1,068 | 28,025 | 92,470 | *DCT*. M=CMS,NKM. 85% Gogo. 60f,2H,1h,1j,1s(26),W=83%. 86 11 3514 4247 |
| D Dar es Salaam | 1965 | A ACa | A | 23 | 5,000 | 10,000 | Capital. M=USPG,MTS. 50% Gogo migrants. 1s,P=43%,W=18%. 12 5 6 360 |
| D Masasi | 1926 | A ACa | A | 182 | 25,000 | 50,000 | M=USPG. 65% Makua, 25% Makonde, 10% Yao. 1H,3h,1s,W=40%. 37 6 500 2000 |
| D Morogoro | 1965 | A Eva | A | 261 | 11,505 | 26,619 | Rural. M=BCMS,CMS. 90% Kaguru. 250m,12f,1H,1p,W=50% 30 3 1678 1615 |
| D Ruvuma | 1971 | A ACa | A | 75 | 22,000 | 50,000 | Rural, town. M=USPG. Many refugees. 48m,1H,W=60%,600z. 19 2 900 2400 |
| D South-West Tanzania | 1952 | A ACa | A | 160 | 38,000 | 60,000 | M=USPG. Mozambican refugees: 4,000 Anglicans. 1h,W=70%. 28 5 100 1000 |
| D Victoria Nyanza | 1963 | A Eva | A | 174 | 9,625 | 25,828 | M=CMS. 53% Hangaza, 18% Sukuma. 1H, 1p,1974z. 31 5 881 1356 |
| D Western Tanganyika | 1966 | A Eva | A | 130 | 6,445 | 19,178 | 2 towns. M=CMS,NKM. 90% Ha. 21f,2H,1p(20). 1967 schism. 28 3 484 871 |
| D Zanzibar & Tanga | 1892 | A ACa | A | 94 | 12,500 | 52,000 | M=USPG.35% Zigua,30% Bondei,25% Sambaa.3H,P=80%,W=25% 34 3 566 1945 |
| Church of the Watch Tower | 1919 | I Jeh | x.... | 10 | 500 | 1,000 | Ex Jehovah's Witnesses. Entered Ufipa from NRhodesia. Anti-state. Declining. |
| Churches of Christ | | P Dis | x.... | 75 | 2,000 | 4,000 | M=CC(Non-Instrumental)(USA). Independents. Southern Highlands. 40n,12f,1H,1i. |
| **Evangelical Lutheran Ch in Tanzania:** | 1886 | P Lut | LWA.K | 2,912 | 274,843 | 592,342 | *ELCT. KKKT*(Swahili). A=1963. M=TAC. 1641m,1s(126),W=75%. 314n,47x,7500Y,28500y. |
| S Arusha Synod | 1973 | P Lut | L | 12 | 10,000 | 22,000 | Formed out of Northern Diocese. Arusha, Maasai, 5f. 15 |
| S Central Synod | 1926 | P Lut | L | 218 | 19,500 | 34,100 | 53% Iramba, 28% Turu. 20f,1H,14h,1p,W=60%. 30 4 1155 1940 |
| S Eastern & Coastal Synod | 1887 | P Lut | L | 90 | 10,820 | 16,000 | 70% up-country tribes, 30% Zaramo. Muslim area. 2h,W=70%. 11 5 280 845 |
| S Mbulu Synod | 1938 | P Lut | L | 56 | 2,783 | 7,454 | M=EFS,NLM. 80% Iraqw. 5m,20f,1H,2h,1040z. 5 3 207 576 |
| D Northeastern Diocese | 1891 | P Lut | L | 210 | 29,510 | 50,350 | M=Bethel MS. 90% Shambala. 60m,13f,3H,7h,1j. 35 3 400 1500 |
| D Northern Diocese | 1893 | P Lut | L | 1,200 | 98,830 | 229,200 | 57% Chagga, 16% Pare, 14% Meru. 515m,5H,20h,1p,1s,W=63%. 110 10 2155 11851 |
| D Northwestern Diocese | 1910 | P Lut | L | 264 | 37,900 | 88,897 | M=Ch of Sweden M, VEM. 95% Haya. 34f,2H,6h,1p. 65 8 1109 3605 |
| S Southern Synod | 1891 | P Lut | L | 862 | 65,500 | 144,341 | M=BMW. 40% Nyakyusa,39% Bena,20% Hehe. 830m,57f,4H,13h,1p. 58 14 2162 8152 |
| Gospel Furthering Fellowship | 1935 | P int | .M... | 6 | 108 | 300 | M=GFF(USA). Schism ex AIM by missionaries. Mbugwe, Fiome. 1n,1x,7m,1p,28z. |
| Jehovah's Witnesses | 1919 | M Jeh | x.... | 33 | 1,271 | 4,000 | First apostles entered Ufipa in 1919 from Zambia. Banned from 1966. 92y. |
| Last Church of God & His Christ | 1929 | I Ref | ..... | | 2,000 | 5,000 | *BaNgemela* (*Ngemela's Ch*). Nyakyusa. Polygamy, communal life. HQ Rungwe. |
| Manchira Monthly Meeting | | P Qua | Q...K | 11 | 210 | 500 | Musoma area. Friends (Quakers). Immigrant Luhya from Nyanza (Kenya). 1n. |
| Maria Legio of Africa | 1963 | I CCa | x.... | | 1,000 | 3,000 | M=MLA(Kenya). Luo immigrants from Kenya schism ex Roman Catholic Church, D Kisii. |
| Moravian Church | 1879 | P Mor | xwA.K | 250 | 51,800 | 99,500 | 2 Provinces: *Western*(Nyamwezi), *Southern*(Nyakyusa). M=MBG. 72n,5x,21f,4H,5h,1s. |
| Nomiya Luo Church | 1929 | I Ang | x.... | 10 | 1,000 | 2,000 | Nomiya=God gave me His Word. M=NLC(Kenya). Luo immigrants in Musoma area. |
| Pemba Yearly Meeting of Friends | 1897 | P Qua | Q.... | 5 | 225 | 400 | On Pemba Island. 1897 Industrial Mission (UK); 1916, Yearly Meeting. 1n,4m,1p. |
| Pentecostal Assemblies of God | 1955 | P Pe2 | ZP... | 110 | 5,000 | 15,000 | *PAG*. M=PAoC(Canada). Lake Victoria area. Members Mbugwe, Fiome. 80n,8x,8f. |
| Pentecostal Churches in Tanzania | 1932 | P Pe2 | Z.... | 261 | 18,850 | 40,000 | *PCSAT*.M=SFM,NPY,FFFM. 50% Ha,40% Nyamwezi. 14n,20x,360m,150f,1H,13h,2p,2679Y,2232z. |
| Pente Evangelistic Fellowship of Africa | 1953 | P Pe2 | ZG... | 155 | 10,000 | 20,000 | *PEFA*. M=Elim FGA(UK),IPA(USA). North. 20 churches closed 1973 in ujamaa resettling. |
| Pente Holiness Association Mission | c1938 | P Pe3 | Z.... | 104 | 25,000 | 35,000 | M=PHC(Zambia). Until 1945 M=PHC(USA). Southern Highlands. Nyakyusa. 33n,25m. |
| Presbyterian Church of East Africa | | P Ref | Rwa.K | 3 | 335 | 450 | *PCEA*(Kenya). Main church in Dar es Salaam. 70% Malawians; some Whites. 1n,1x. |
| Salvation Army | 1933 | P Sal | xwa.K | 27 | 2,490 | 8,682 | *Jeshi la Wokovu. Tanzania Division.* HQ Dar es Salaam. 25n,5x,20m. |
| Seventh-day Adventist Church | 1903 | P Adv | x...k | 557 | 26,149 | 105,000 | *Tanzania Union*. 3 aircraft. 81n,6x,12f,1H,21h,3j,1r,1s,571t(44416),W=88%,1418Y. |
| Tanganyika Mennonite Church | 1934 | P Men | G...K | 222 | 8,993 | 24,454 | *TMC*. M=EMBMC. 35% Luo,30% Jita,30% Kuria. 24n,1x,22f,1H,5h,1j,1p,1r,1s,W=75%,650Y. |
| Tanzania African Church | 1956 | I Ang | .T.T. | 14 | 1,000 | 3,000 | *TAC*. Schism ex Anglican DCT. 70% Gogo, 30% Nyamwezi. 1966, tried to join AACC. |
| Tanzania Assemblies of God | 1930 | P Pe2 | ZP..k | 113 | 4,772 | 15,000 | *TAG*. M=AoG(USA). Classical Pentecostals. Arusha, Moshi, Mbeya. 114n,17f,2s(76). |
| Other African indigenous churches | | I | ..... | | 5,000 | 10,000 | Total about 25 (see list below), especially from Kenya, Malawi, Zaire, Zambia. |
| Other Protestant denominations | | P | ..... | | 2,000 | 5,000 | Total about 7 (see list below). |
| **Total affiliated (mid-1970)** | | | | **9,100** | **2,257,073** | **4,324,625** | **Total denominations (1970) . . . 71.** |
| **Total affiliated (mid-1975)** | | | | **10,500** | **2,908,700** | **5,573,100** | **Total denominations (1975) . . . 77.** |
| **Total affiliated (mid-1980)** | | | | **11,900** | **3,730,900** | **7,148,600** | **Total denominations (1980) . . . 83.** |

**NOTES ON TABLE ABOVE**

COLUMNS: for meanings and CODES (cols. 1, 3, 4, 8): see Codebook (Part 6). Column 1: **Boldface type** = church with over 10% of country's affiliated Christians.

NATIONAL COUNCILS (Column 4, 5th letter).

K = Christian Council of Tanzania (CCT) (Jumuiya ya Makanisa ya Tanzania).

k = consultative member of CCT.

R = Tanzania Episcopal Conference (TEC).

*Other national councils*. Tanzania Evangelical Fellowship (in process of formation in 1976; to be affiliated to AEAM).

OTHER AFRICAN INDIGENOUS CHURCHES. Although there are very few Tanzanian-founded bodies, numerous bodies from Kenya, Malawi, Rhodesia, Zaire and Zambia have churches in Tanzania. The total includes: African Catholic Ch, Chief Mavuta's Ch, Christ the Light of the Universe (Kristo Mwanga wa Ulimwengu; ex Anglicans, HQ Kasulu; banned in 1977), Ch of Jesus Christ (HQ Sumbawanga; Fipa tribe; member of ICCC), Deliverance Ch (Kenya), Dini ya Bapali (Polygamous Ch, or Malakite Ch; from Uganda 1924), Eglise Kimbanguiste (EJCSK, Zaire), Episcopal Ch of Africa (Luos from Kenya), Holy Ghost Ch of the Cross, Lyimo's Ch, Nomiya Luo Sabbath (from Kenya). In 1975, a Korean movement, Holy Spirit Association for the Unification of World Christianity, sent 3 evangelists (a German, a Japanese and one English) but they were imprisoned and deported.

OTHER PROTESTANT DENOMINATIONS. These include: Christian Ch in East Africa, Independent Assemblies of God, Swedish Holiness Union Mission (2 congregations), World-Wide Missions (1965).

OTHER MARGINAL PROTESTANT BODIES. Branhamites (Local Believers, End Time Believers) from USA.

UNITING CHURCHES. Negotiations for organic union were under way in 1980 between: Ch of the Province of Tanzania, Ev Lutheran Ch in Tanzania, Moravian Ch (negotiations on East Africa-wide basis began 1961, broke down 1965 and 1968, Kenya churches left after 1970).

**PEOPLES** (ethnolinguistic). Christians: about 10.0% Chagga, 8.0% Haya, 6.0% Sukuma, 4.8% Hehe, 4.0% Nyakyusa, 3.6% Fipa, 3.0% Ha, 3.0% Bena, 2.9% Luguru, 2.5% Shambala (Sambaa), 2.1% Gogo, 1.8% Turu, 1.7% Luo, 1.6% Makua, 1.5% Nyamwezi, 1.4% Pare (Asu), 1.2% Pogoro, 1.1% Mwera, 1.0% Ngoni, 1.0% Kerewe, 1.0% Hangaza, 0.9% Sagara, 0.9% Iramba, 0.8% Zinza, 0.7% Makonde, 0.7% Sandawe, 0.7% Matengo, 0.7% Meru, 0.7% European (White), 0.6% Iraqw, 0.6% Bende, 0.6% Kimbu, 0.6% Kaguru, 0.6% Bondei, 0.6% Jita, 0.5% Kwaya, 0.5% Kuria, 0.4% Nguru (Nguu), 0.4% Rangi, 0.4% Kinga, 0.4% Zigua (Zigula), 0.3% Yao, 0.3% Pangwa, 0.3% Lambya, 0.3% Sangu, 0.3% Ndamba, 0.2% Kikuyu, 0.2% Arusha, 0.2% Matumbi, 0.2% Safwa, 0.2% Kwere, 0.1% Mbugwe, 0.1% Goroa, 0.1% Lungu, 0.1% Kara, 0.1% Zaramo, 0.1% Maasai, 0.1% Luhya, 0.1% Greek Cypriot, Zairian, Malawian, Zambian, Kenyan, Ruanda, Ganda, Subi, Mbunga, Indian; & also (members of small tribes) about 10% other Tanganyika Bantu, 4% other Interlacustrine Bantu, 4% other Bantu.

COUNTRY-WIDE TOTALS

EVANGELIZATION (see Part 5). 1900: 19%. 1970: 80%. 1980: 88%. *Mass evangelism*. Among recent campaigns: 1960, Billy Graham 2-day crusade in Moshi (40,000 attenders, 5,211 enquirers); annual Lutheran campaign in Dar es Salaam; annual Anglican campaign in Morogoro. *Radiophonic evangelism*. RVOG, FEBA, ICI (45,000 active students, 600 conversions reported), et alia. *Literature evangelism*. Every Home Crusade coverage 1974, second coverage of all homes 1976; 230,000 booklets a month delivered, with 6,001 decision cards a month returned.

FOREIGN MISSIONARIES AND PERSONNEL (nationals serving abroad) (1973). Total 100: 92 Roman Catholics and 8 Protestants in WGermany, Kenya, Sudan and Zaire.

FOREIGN MISSIONARIES AND PERSONNEL (aliens from abroad) (1973). Total 2,971. *From Western world*. 2,833: 1,837 Roman Catholics, 834 Protestants (243 in 22 USA societies, 178 in 12 WGermany societies, 153 in 5 Sweden societies, 77 in 4 Denmark societies, 50 in 2 Norway societies, 46 in 3 Finland societies, 42 in 7 UK societies, 17 in 3 Canada societies, 10 in 1 Australia society, 8 in 2 Netherlands societies, 7 in 2 New Zealand societies, 3 in 1 Switzerland society). 160 Anglicans (86 in 8 UK societies, 52 in 1 Australia society, 21 in 1 New Zealand society, 1 in 1 USA society), about 2 Orthodox. *From Communist world*. About 26 Roman Catholics (22 from Poland, 4 Yugoslavia). *From Third World*. 112: about 70 Roman Catholics from India et alia, about 30 African indigenous from Kenya, Zambia, Malawi, Rhodesia and Zaire, 10 Protestants (including from Singapore) and 2 Anglicans.

INSTITUTIONS (church-operated) (1973). Total 440, including about 70 higher schools (18 minor seminaries; others state-managed), 300 medical centres, 10 presses, 22 religious communities, 1 research centre, 16 seminaries (9 Protestant, 4 RC, 3 Anglican), 10 study centres.

PERIODICALS. About 60 titles (10 Anglican).

PERSONNEL. About 17,381 (14,410 national, 2,971 foreign).

RELIGIOUS LIBRARIES. About 60.

SCRIPTURE DISTRIBUTION (1975). Annual totals: 37,340 Bibles (95% subsidized, 5% commercial), 54,659 NTs (98% subsidized, 2% commercial), 316,876 UBS portions, 1,616,602 UBS selections. *Translations completed*. Portion: 27 languages since 1868. NT: 18 languages since 1879. Bible: 4 languages since 1891.

SERVICE AGENCIES. About 75, including AEATC. BWKT, CCT, CRS, CTP, IBRA, LWR, MAF, MAP, NLFA, PCSAT, RVOG, SU, TAC, TEC, TYCS, UMAWATA, WLC(EHC), WUCW, YMCA, YWCA.

**ADDITIONAL DATA ON CHURCHES**

CATHOLIC CHURCH IN TANZANIA. In Swahili, Kanisa Katoliki katika Tanzania. *Catechumens*. Totals: (1959) 188,051; (1961) 201,512; (1963) 217,395; (1967) 150,737; (1972) 118,723, divided as follows among the 25 dioceses in the order shown (and included in column 7): 1287, 1596, 4000, 4580, 1337, 5176, 1342, 3090, 5623, 434, 3107, 15318, 3058, 830,5089, 2500, 16763, 5102, 2608, 16000, 4620, 8782, 5731, 750, 0. *Annual baptisms*. (1972) 75.8% infant, 24.2% adult. *Expatriate priests*. Mainly from: Netherlands, West Germany, USA, Switzerland, Italy, Canada, Ireland. *Brothers*. 109 Tanzanians, 254 expatriates. *Sisters*. 2,123 Tanzanians, 765 expatriates. *Seminarians* (1972). 389, all secular. *Catechists*. Total (1972) 6,560, a number being part-time. *Indigenous religious congregations*. Brothers: Immaculate Heart (1 member in 1972), Apostles of Jesus (in D Moshi). Sisters (12 congregations): 227 Our Lady of Kilimanjaro Sisters (begun 1931; Moshi), 209 Bathereza (St Teresa Sisters, begun 1932; Bukoba), 159 Daughters of the Blessed Virgin (begun 1933; Tabora), 150 Sisters of St Gemma Galgani (begun 1945; Dodoma), 143 Missionary Sisters of St Teresa of the Child Jesus (begun 1931; Iringa), 137 Sisters of St Agnes (begun 1938; Songea), 93 Immaculate Heart of Mary Sisters (begun 1936; Morogoro), 44 Sisters of Divine Providence (begun 1941; Dar es Salaam), Immaculate Sisters of Africa (begun 1953; Musoma), Benedictine Sisters of Our Lady Help of Christians (begun 1948; Mtwara), Sisters of Holy Mary Queen of Africa (begun 1907; Sumbawanga), Sisters of Our Lady of Usambara (begun 1953; Tanga). *Main foreign orders and congregations*. Priests (with over 50 members): 344 WF, 269 OSB, 104 CSSp, 151 OFMCap, 79 IMC. 74 MM. Brothers: FSC, FICP, Mercy Brothers. Sisters: White Sisters. Benedictines, Consolata Sisters, Maryknoll Sisters, Verona Sisters, Salvatorians, Medical Missionaries of Mary, Franciscans, Precious Blood, Divine Providence.

*Catholic organizations*. The Tanzania Episcopal Conference (TEC) is a member of AMECEA and SECAM. Religious personnel are organized into the Association of Religious Superiors in Tanzania, for priests and brothers, and the Association of Women Religious Superiors of Tanzania, for sisters. The Association of Diocesan Priests of Tanzania (UMAWATA) was founded in 1971 and has received the bishops' approval for its statutes. There are no official pastoral councils, but the Seminar Study Year of 1969 served a similar purpose. The Council of Catholic Laity in Tanzania (Baraza la Waumini Katoliki Tanzania) co-ordinates the efforts of local lay councils from village to national levels. It is a meeting point for dialogue of the following lay apostolate organizations: World Union of Catholic Women, Tanzania Youth Christian Students, St Vincent de Paul Society (2,500 members in 1968), Third Order of St Francis (2,502 members in 1968), and Legion of Mary.

The Holy See has diplomatic relations with Tanzania and is represented to government and the Catholic hierarchy by a pronuncio in Dar es Salaam.

Other institutes and organizations include the Tanzania Pastoral Research Institute (TAPRI), founded in 1964 as the Bukumbi Pastoral Institute under the Episcopal Conference; Nyegezi Social Training Centre, founded in Mwanza in 1961; Kipalapala Pastoral Centre, founded by White Fathers in Tabora in 1963; Maryknoll Mission Language School in Musoma; Sisters' Training in Lushoto. Caritas Tanzania was founded in 1970 in Dar es Salaam and operates 7 community centres for rural development, 4 social literacy centres, 5 domestic science centres, 120 dispensaries and numerous credit unions. Development projects are integrated with government programmes, and charitable activities including orphanages are operated by the Society of St Vincent de Paul in co-operation with Catholic Relief Services.

All schools were taken over by government in 1969. Catholic education in 1966 had been responsible for 1,378 primary schools, 19 secondary schools and 9 teacher training colleges. In 1973 Catholic influence in education was still strong enough for the

church to report 57 primary schools (3,772 pupils) and 40 secondary (7,489).
CHURCH OF THE PROVINCE OF TANZANIA. *East African Revival.* Members of the Revival (Balakole, Saved Ones) are in majority Anglicans, and numbered in 1975 around 30,000 committed adults, or a total community of about 90,000. *New diocese.* One was expected to be formed in 1978–79. *Personnel* (1977). 417 priests (23 expatriate), 28 deacons, 1,650 lay workers, 30 seminarians.
EVANGELICAL LUTHERAN CHURCH IN TANZANIA. In Swahili, Kanisa la Kiinjili la Kilutheri Tanzania (KKKT). Northern Diocese=Dayosisi ya Kaskazini. Central Synod= Sinodi ya Kati. *Membership.* By 1975, members had increased to 775,768. *New dioceses.* (1) Diocese of Pare, formed in 1974 out of Northern Diocese; (2) Ulanga/Kilombero Synod (Malinye, Ikafara); (3) in 1977, Konde Synod. *Church growth.* Statistics in the table above are for 1970. By 1975, the figures for congregations/adults/affiliated had increased to: Arusha 120/17,646/37,470; Central 279/21,403/64,209; Eastern-Coastal 36/19,777/26,835; Mbulu 60/4,343/9,717; Northeastern 217/23,625/49,428; Northern 405/103,422/234,707; Northwestern 266/32,186/99,197; Pare 84/20,005/43,480; Southern 758/85,613/189,440; Ulanga/Kilombero Synod with 6,000 adults and 18,000 affiliated. Total affiliated: (1970) 592,342; (1975) 772,484; (1977) over 800,000. The ELCT also counts as a constitutent part the Kenya Synod (in 1975, 17/2,061/3,284), located in Kenya. *Supporting missions* (1970). The work of the following 17 missions is co-ordinated by the Lutheran Coordination Service (East Africa) in Hamburg (Germany) and TAC, Tanzania Assistance Committee: American Lutheran Ch, Berlin Missionary Society, Breklum Mission Society, Christoffel-Blindermission, Ch of Sweden Mission, Danish Lutheran Mission, Danish Missionary Society, Ev Lutheran Ch in Bavaria (Neuendettelsau), Finnish Missionary Society, Leipzig Mission, Lutheran Ch in America, Lutheran Ch of the Netherlands, Norwegian Lutheran Mission, Norwegian Missionary Society, Swedish Ev Mission Society (EFS), United Ev Lutheran Ch of Germany, United Ev Mission. *Institutions.* 16 hospitals, 49 health centres, 3 technical schools, 3 secondary schools, increasing by 1975 to 18 hospitals and 68 dispensaries.
PENTECOSTAL ASSEMBLIES OF GOD. *Growth.* Assemblies increased in number from 60 in 1967 to 160 in 1975, even though 55 congregations of Kenya immigrants disappeared when the latter were repatriated to Kenya.

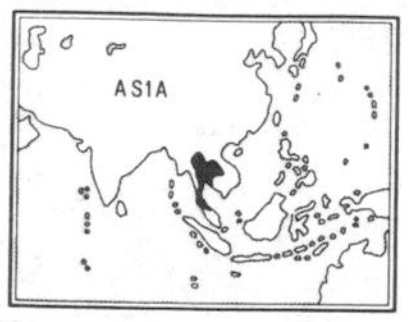


# THAILAND

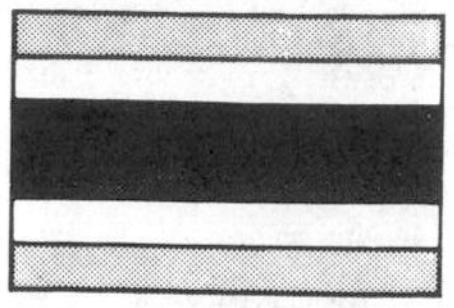

## SECULAR DATA

**STATE. Official name:** The Kingdom of Thailand (Prathet Thai/Muang-Thai). Adjective of nationality: Thai.
**Flag** (shown above right): Red, white, blue (double width), white, and red stripes.
**Area:** 514,000 sq.km. (198,457 sq.miles). Agricultural land: 28.0%.
**Government:** Constitutional monarchy controlled by military junta, since 1957 (13th century kingdom, 1939 name changed from Siam to Thailand, 1957 military junta, 1974 democratic constitution, 1976 military junta).
**Legislature:** Administrative Reform Council, 24 members (military junta).
**Official language:** Thai.
**Chief cities:** capital Bangkok 1,867,300 (1970), Thonburi 627,990.
**Political divisions:** 71 Provinces (changwad), divided into 509 Districts (amphur), 27 Sub-Districts (king amphur), 5,036 Communes (tambon), 44,606 Villages (mooban).
**Armed forces** (1976): Total 210,000 regular: army 141,000, navy 27,000, air force 42,000 (179 combat aircraft). Reserves: 350,000. Paramilitary forces: 66,000.
**Foreign forces** (1973): 45,000 USA troops (reduced to 250 by 1976).

**DEMOGRAPHY. Population:** 34,397,374 (census of 1.IV.1970. For 1970–2000 (UN), see last row of Table 1). Population density (1975): 82/sq.km. (212/sq.mile). Under 15 years: 45%. Growth rate (1975–80): 3.23% per year (births 4.16%, deaths −0.93%). Life expectancy (1975–80): 60.3 years. Household size: 5.8 persons.
**Major languages:** Thai, English, Lao, Chinese, Malay, Khmer, Vietnamese, and 40 smaller languages.
**Urban dwellers** (1970): 14.8%. Urban growth rate (1950–70): 4.8% per year.
**Labour force:** 47%.
**Refugees** (1977): From abroad 73,100 (52,900 from Laos, 18,600 from Cambodia, 1,600 from Viet Nam), rising to 92,398 (76,143 from Laos).
**Tourists** (1974): 1,107,392.

**ETHNOLINGUISTIC GROUPS:** 79.0% Thai (55.0% Siamese (Khon-Tai), 23.9% Lao), 11.6% Chinese (Hainanese, Hakka, Hoklo, South Fukienese, Swatow; 0.9% alien), 3.5% Malay, 1.3% Khmer, 1.3% Kui (Soai), 0.6% Sui, 0.4% Karen, 0.4% Phutai, 0.3% Mon, 0.3% Lu, 0.2% Khmu, 0.2% Shan, 0.2% Indian, 0.1% USA (in 1970, 45,000 military, declining by 1976 to 4,200 civilians), 0.1% Vietnamese (45,000), 0.1% Phuteng, Burmese, Ho, Senoi, Semang, Lawa, Chao Nam (Sea-dwellers), Miao (Meo, Mhong), Yao, Lahu, Lisu, European (6,100) (British, Australian, New Zealander), Eurasian, Jewish, et alii.

**MONEY** (1977). **Monetary unit:** baht (= 100 satang); US$1 = Bt 20.15.
**National income per person:** US$308. Average annual family income: US$1,786.
**Inflation:** (1970–74) 9.9% per year (1975: consumer price index 160).
**Cost of living in capital** (1976): index 103 (Washington DC=100). Daily cost of living: US$42.

**HEALTH.** Hospitals: 542 (40,781 beds). Doctors: 4,313. Lepers: 390,000 (10.5 per 1,000). Blind: 210,000. Psychotics: 320,000. Drug addicts: 450,000 (mainly opium, with 50,000 on heroin).

**EDUCATION.** Adult literacy: (1947) 52%, (1970) 79%. Education rate: 57%. Schools (1965): 25,965. Universities: 7.

**LITERATURE.** Annual new book titles (1973): 2,255. Periodicals: 868. Scientific journals: 50. Newspapers: 38 dailies, 22 non-daily.

**COMMUNICATION** (per 1,000 people). Phones: 7. Radios: 76. TV sets: 7. Daily newspaper circulation: 21 copies.

TABLE 1. RELIGIOUS ADHERENTS IN THAILAND

| Year | 1900 | | mid-1970 | | Annual change, 1970–1980 | | | | mid-1975 | | mid-1980 | | 2000 | |
|---|---|---|---|---|---|---|---|---|---|---|---|---|---|---|
| *Name* | *Adherents* | *%* | *Adherents* | *%* | *Natural* | *Conversion* | *Total* | *Rate* | *Adherents* | *%* | *Adherents* | *%* | *Adherents* | *%* |
| Buddhists | 5,487,850 | 90.8 | 32,933,000 | 92.1 | 1,264,401 | −1,448 | 1,262,953 | 3.26 | 38,767,080 | 92.1 | 45,562,530 | 92.1 | 78,752,900 | 92.0 |
| Muslims | 90,000 | 1.5 | 1,395,000 | 3.9 | 53,551 | −51 | 53,500 | 3.26 | 1,642,000 | 3.9 | 1,930,000 | 3.9 | 3,300,000 | 3.9 |
| Chinese folk-religionists | 240,000 | 4.0 | 640,000 | 1.8 | 23,351 | −8,151 | 15,200 | 2.12 | 716,000 | 1.7 | 792,000 | 1.6 | 1,027,000 | 1.2 |
| **Christians** | **35,150** | **0.6** | **338,874** | **0.9** | **13,986** | **4,267** | **18,253** | **4.26** | **428,850** | **1.0** | **521,400** | **1.1** | **973,000** | **1.1** |
| crypto-Christians | 12,150 | 0.2 | 135,874 | 0.4 | 6,094 | 4,059 | 10,153 | 5.43 | 186,850 | 0.4 | 237,400 | 0.5 | 473,000 | 0.5 |
| professing | 23,000 | 0.4 | 203,000 | 0.6 | 7,892 | 208 | 8,100 | 3.35 | 242,000 | 0.6 | 284,000 | 0.6 | 500,000 | 0.6 |
| Roman Catholics | 20,000 | 0.3 | 135,000 | 0.4 | 5,218 | 82 | 5,300 | 3.31 | 160,000 | 0.4 | 188,000 | 0.4 | 330,000 | 0.4 |
| Protestants | 3,000 | 0.0 | 68,000 | 0.2 | 2,674 | 126 | 2,800 | 3.41 | 82,000 | 0.2 | 96,000 | 0.2 | 170,000 | 0.2 |
| affiliated | 35,150 | 0.6 | 338,874 | 0.9 | 13,986 | 4,267 | 18,253 | 4.26 | 428,850 | 1.0 | 521,400 | 1.1 | 973,000 | 1.1 |
| total practising | 31,630 | *90* | 274,490 | *81* | 11,329 | 3,455 | 14,784 | 4.26 | 347,370 | *81* | 422,330 | *81* | 729,750 | *75* |
| non-practising | 3,520 | *10* | 64,380 | *19* | 2,657 | 812 | 3,469 | 4.26 | 81,480 | *19* | 99,070 | *19* | 243,250 | *25* |
| Roman Catholics | 30,000 | 0.5 | 153,831 | 0.4 | 6,131 | 786 | 6,917 | 3.68 | 188,000 | 0.4 | 223,000 | 0.5 | 395,000 | 0.5 |
| Catholic pentecostals | 0 | 0.0 | 0 | 0.0 | 33 | 267 | 300 | 30.00 | 1,000 | 0.0 | 3,000 | 0.0 | 20,000 | 0.0 |
| Protestants | 5,000 | 0.1 | 95,965 | 0.3 | 4,011 | 1,393 | 5,404 | 4.39 | 123,000 | 0.3 | 150,000 | 0.3 | 270,000 | 0.3 |
| Evangelicals | 4,300 | 0.1 | 81,000 | 0.2 | 3,391 | 1,309 | 4,700 | 4.52 | 104,000 | 0.2 | 128,000 | 0.3 | 240,000 | 0.3 |
| Asian indigenous | 0 | 0.0 | 86,700 | 0.2 | 3,751 | 2,079 | 5,830 | 5.07 | 115,000 | 0.3 | 145,000 | 0.3 | 300,000 | 0.3 |
| Marginal Protestants | 50 | 0.0 | 1,678 | 0.0 | 65 | 7 | 72 | 3.61 | 2,000 | 0.0 | 2,400 | 0.0 | 6,000 | 0.0 |
| Anglicans | 100 | 0.0 | 700 | 0.0 | 28 | 2 | 30 | 3.53 | 850 | 0.0 | 1,000 | 0.0 | 2,000 | 0.0 |
| Tribal religionists | 180,000 | 3.0 | 250,000 | 0.7 | 8,806 | −4,806 | 4,000 | 1.48 | 270,000 | 0.6 | 290,000 | 0.6 | 320,000 | 0.4 |
| Non-religious | 0 | 0.0 | 80,000 | 0.2 | 4,109 | 7,691 | 11,800 | 9.37 | 126,000 | 0.3 | 198,000 | 0.4 | 856,000 | 1.0 |
| Hindus | 6,000 | 0.1 | 60,000 | 0.2 | 2,316 | −16 | 2,300 | 3.24 | 71,000 | 0.2 | 83,000 | 0.2 | 140,000 | 0.2 |
| Atheists | 0 | 0.0 | 30,000 | 0.1 | 1,631 | 2,369 | 4,000 | 8.00 | 50,000 | 0.1 | 70,000 | 0.1 | 200,000 | 0.2 |
| Sikhs | 1,000 | 0.0 | 10,000 | 0.0 | 305 | −5 | 300 | 2.61 | 11,500 | 0.0 | 13,000 | 0.0 | 22,000 | 0.0 |
| Baha'is | 0 | 0.0 | 6,460 | 0.0 | 267 | 87 | 354 | 4.32 | 8,200 | 0.0 | 10,000 | 0.0 | 20,000 | 0.0 |
| New-Religionists | 0 | 0.0 | 1,600 | 0.0 | 75 | 65 | 140 | 6.09 | 2,300 | 0.0 | 3,000 | 0.0 | 7,000 | 0.0 |
| Jews | 0 | 0.0 | 66 | 0.0 | 2 | −2 | 0 | 0.00 | 70 | 0.0 | 70 | 0.0 | 100 | 0.0 |
| **Country's population** | **6,040,000** | **100.0** | **35,745,000** | **100.0** | **1,372,800** | **0** | **1,372,800** | **3.26** | **42,093,000** | **100.0** | **49,473,000** | **100.0** | **85,618,000** | **100.0** |

COLUMNS, ROWS. For meanings and definitions, see Codebook (Part 6). Note that, by definition, total 'Christians' = professing + crypto-Christians, which also = affiliated + nominal Christian. Percentages may not always total exactly, due to rounding.
CENSUSES. **1937** (Thai year 2480): 95.1% Buddhists and Chinese folk-religionists, 4.3% Muslims, 0.5% Christians, 0.1% others. **23.V.1947** (Thai year 2490): 94.1% Buddhists, 3.8% Muslims, 1.6% Chinese folk-religionists, 0.5% Christians. **25.IV.1960:** 93.6% Buddhists, 3.9% Muslims, 1.8% Chinese folk-religionists, 0.6% Christians, 0.1% tribal religionists. **1966:** 93.6% Buddhists. **1.IV.1970** (excluding unenumerated hill peoples): 93.6% Buddhists, 3.9% Muslims, 1.8% Chinese folk-religionists, 0.6% Christians (195,300 persons), 0.2% Hindus and Sikhs.

NOTES ON RELIGIONS
AFFILIATED PROTESTANTS. Among recent conversions to Thai churches have been several hundred Buddhists, including monks and nuns through the ministry of CCCI. The total of of Protestants for 1970–75 includes many USA military and civilian expatriates among the 45,000 USA troops and their dependants (1973) until their departure by 1976.
ASIAN INDIGENOUS. Chinese and Thai indigenous churches, in about 6 denominations in 1970, the vast majority being isolated radio and Bible correspondence course believers (see Table 2).
ATHEISTS. Communist Party of Thailand (CPT) (prohibited since 1952; clandestine; pro-Chinese): membership (1970) 1,000 (mostly Chinese), and 5,500 rural insurgents (ethnic Thai and hill tribes) in so-called liberated areas in northern mountains; also 1,800 Malaysia-oriented communist terrorists in border regions in south Thailand.
BAHA'IS. Growth from 22 local spiritual assemblies (1964) to 43 (1973). Tribal converts include Yao, Manser, Yaw, Khon Muang.
BUDDHISTS. Theravada (or Hinayana, Lesser Vehicle), in 2 religious orders: Thommayutt and Mohanikay. In 1966 the Thai Sangha reported 23,700 monasteries (temples), with 173,126 monks and 88,251 novices as inmates, with a supreme patriarch governing the whole community of monks. There were also 6,634 Nak-Dharma religious schools with 14,474 monk-teachers, 615 Pali schools with 1,964 monk-teachers, and 2 Buddhist universities. Peoples: Thai, Chinese, Vietnamese, Khmer.
CRYPTO-CHRISTIANS. Christians affiliated to churches but not known as such to the state or society, or in censuses, of 2 kinds: (1) secret believers in the known churches, and (2) isolated radio and Bible correspondence course believers.
HINDUS. Of 3 kinds: (1) 4,000 Brahmin families, astrologers, who almost always direct and perform royal and official ceremonies, blending their rites with those of Buddhism; (2) large numbers of Indian merchants and traders, speaking various languages of India, concentrated in the central region chiefly around Bangkok; and (3) adherents of newer Hindu sects including Ananda Marga.
MUSLIMS. Sunnis (of the Shafiite rite); Malays (islamized here since the 14th century) and others in the extreme south. Muslims form about 85% of the one million inhabitants of the southern peninsula. There are 1,400 mosques. *Hajj pilgrims to Mecca.* (1970) 4,981; (1975) 654; (1976) 192.
NEW-RELIGIONISTS. Adherents of Soka Gakkai (Japan), Cao Dai (Viet-Nam), and Chinese syncretistic New Religions.
NON-RELIGIOUS. Including many foreigners (especially European, Chinese, USA military), Thai communist sympathizers, et alii.
PRACTISING CHRISTIANS. *Roman Catholics.* Sunday mass attendance varies from 30% to 60%. Easter communicants: in rural areas 68%. *Protestants.* Weekly practice is over 50%.
ROMAN CATHOLICS. In the year 1900, 22,480 baptized Catholics, and 44 schools with 3,020 children.
SIKHS. In central region, mainly in and around Bangkok; Punjabis from India.
TRIBAL RELIGIONISTS. Animists among the Montagrards and other tribes: Akha, Kui, Lisu, Lu, Meo (29,000), Pwo Karen, Sgaw Karen, Tin (25,000), Yao (20,000).

**NON-CHRISTIAN RELIGIONS. Theravada Buddhism** (also called Hinayana or Lesser Vehicle) is the official religion of Thailand and the religion of the great majority of the population, with more than 24,000 temples and 200,000 monks. The number of persons in monasteries fluctuates because of the traditional requirement that each adolescent should sometime spend 6 months to 2 years in residence in a monastery. It is in Thailand that the movement for the renewal of Buddhism is most accepted. This movement is part of the programme of the great universities of Mahâmakuta na Mahâchulalongkorn which steer monks towards social service to the lay community and prepare students for teaching posts in the provinces. Monks in the provinces are supposed to follow where possible a social education course at the Phra Kiihiwuttho Centre in Chonburi, a suburb of Bangkok. Of importance also is the movement towards a deep renewal of monastic and religious life under the influence of Bhikkhu (monk) Buddhadâsa, the head of the Wat Mahadhatu monastery in Chaiya, south Thailand, who has attempted to create a degree of uniformity in Buddhist doctrine by mixing traditional Theravada with aspects from

**Buddhists.** *Left.* Temple of Dawn (Wat Aroon), Bangkok. *Below.* Temples in Wat Pho, Bangkok. *Above.* 70-foot Standing Buddha.

Mahayana. His disciple, Khun Sunya Dhammasakti, president of the most important lay group, spreads his doctrine among the populace.

Bangkok is the central headquarters of the World Fellowship of Buddhists (WFB), founded in Sri Lanka in 1950, which works for peace and the well-being of peoples through following Buddha's teaching principles, and which has regional centres in 34 countries of Asia, America, Europe and Oceania. Thailand also serves as the centre for Theravada in its mission of conciliation between the various orientations of Buddhism.

**Islam** is Thailand's second largest religion. Mostly Sunnis of the Shafiite rite, Muslims are found in the south where they are the predominant group, and include almost the entire Malay population as well as others. The region of Bangkok-Thonburi has about 100 of the country's 1,400 mosques. A National Council of Muslims in Thailand was established in 1945, and provincial councils exist in areas of heavy Muslim population. Quranic schools (*pondoks*) are also numerous.

**Confucianism** maintains its importance among the Chinese, who place special emphasis on the ancestor cult. Usually termed Chinese folk-religionists, Confucianists are usually also adherents of Mahayana Buddhism (Great Vehicle).

**Hinduism** and **Sikhism** are religions professed by immigrants from India, the majority of whom are artisans and merchants in the larger cities.

**Traditional tribal religions** still exist among the Montagnard peoples, the Karen, Meo, Tin and Yao. The supreme being among the Karen is called Y'wa; although they have been strongly influenced by Christianity, many remain animists.

**CHRISTIANITY.** Although citizens, Thailand's Christians are often considered foreigners due to their ethnic origin. Most Catholics are Vietnamese and Chinese with a growing number of Montagnards. Protestantism is strongest among Chinese and has also made recent gains among Montagnards. Christianity's inability to penetrate the Hinayana Buddhist world contributes to the conviction that a Thai cannot become a Christian without abandoning the Thai community. On the other hand, its success with Montagnard peoples shows that it appeals to animists. Numerous Christians are found among North Vietnamese refugees, but it has not been easy to integrate them into local communities.

CATHOLIC CHURCH. In 1554, 2 Dominican priests took up positions as chaplains to Portuguese soldiers attached to the king of Siam and were instrumental in the conversion of some 1,500 Thais. Franciscans entered in 1583 followed by Jesuits in 1606, and the vicariate of Siam was erected in 1673. The 18th century was characterized by a series of violent persecutions which left only a few Christians, but more progress has been made subsequently. The first Thai bishop was consecrated in 1945.

Catholics are found in all parts of the country but their greatest concentration is in the central and northeastern areas. Catholic rural communities are often regrouped in so-called Christian villages. Socially and economically the Catholic milieu is humble, even poor, especially in the countryside. At Bangkok, on the other hand, all social levels are represented, with a majority in the merchant classes.

The first Catholic monastery in Thailand was founded in 1970 at Nongri. It attempts to be typically Thai in mentality and customs and has sought contacts with Buddhist monasteries.

PROTESTANT CHURCHES. Missionaries of the Netherlands and London societies (NZG and LMS) arrived in 1828, followed by representatives of the American Board in 1831, American Baptists who

opened work among the Chinese in 1833 and American Presbyterians in 1840, the latter being the principal force at work among the Thai. In 1934 the Presbyterians united with the Baptists, Disciples of Christ and Lutherans of the Marburger Mission (the latter 2 having begun work later) to form the Church of Christ in Thailand (CCT). This is now the largest Protestant church in the country and is composed of Thai, Chinese and Karen congregations. In 1957 all missions were integrated into the church and missionaries have since been received from India, Japan, Korea, Indonesia and the Philippines, as well as Europe and North America. In addition to its theological seminary at Chieng Mai, the church sponsors 37 primary and 5 secondary schools, 5 hospitals, 32 dispensaries, a mobile clinic, a rehabilitation institute, an agricultural farm and an adult literacy department.

Numerous other Protestant denominations are now active including Seventh-day Adventists, who have a large hospital in Bangkok and a smaller one at Haadyai; Evangelical Gospel Church related to the CMA; and the Karen Baptists who originally came from Burma. None however has been so successful as the United Pentecostal Church which has since World War II built up a community of 20,000 largely at the expense of other churches. Some missions owe their presence to the stationing of USA troops in Thailand.

**CHURCH AND STATE.** The constitution of June 1968 was suspended by the military junta's Revolutionary Committee in October 1971. Nevertheless, it is unlikely that the next constitution will differ fundamentally from it in its approach to religion. According to the 1968 constitution, Buddhism is the state religion; the king must profess and defend the Buddhist faith (Chapter II, section 6); 'Everyone, notwithstanding his birth and religion, has an equal right to the protection of the Constitution' (Chapter III, section 24); there is full liberty to profess 'every religion, sect and religious belief' and to participate in the worship which is related to it; and protection is assumed against any act of the state which would violate the exercise of this freedom (Chapter III, section 26).

Buddhist influence is often utilized by the political rulers to reinforce national unity and to thai-ize the non-Thai peoples. The state legislates on questions of religious organization by passing laws for the Buddhist community such as those of 1902, 1941 and

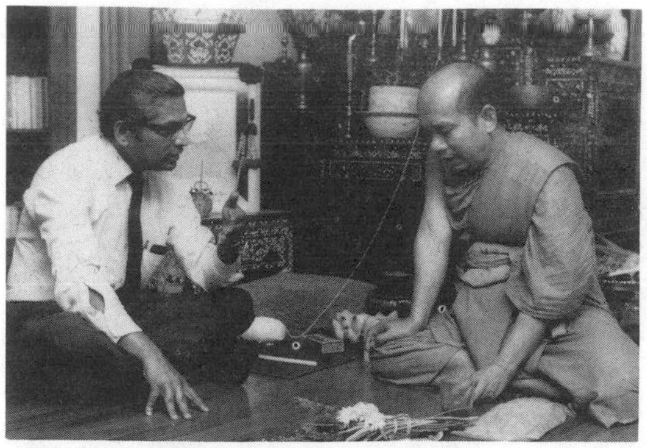

Christian/Buddhist dialogue. Monk in Buddhist temple in Bangkok converses with (left) Dr Stanley Samartha of WCC.

1962. The latter, promulgated in October 1962, strengthened considerably the central direction of the Buddhist organization (known as the Buddhist Church), placing full power of decision in the hands of the supreme partriarch then Somdet Phrasangkharaat) who appoints the members of his council (the Council of Elders, or Mahaatheerasamaakom).

Religious matters come within the jurisdiction of the Department of Religious Affairs (Kromkarn Satsana), which forms part of the Ministry of Education. Its director-general is also secretary-general, ex-officio, of the Council of Elders of the Buddhist Church. This department organizes every year, in consultation with the churches, a 'National Day of the Religions', when by means of posters, conferences, displays and films, all religions have the opportunity of publicizing their aims and activities. Religious toleration is a reality in Thailand. Although more symbolic than real, the Department of Religious Affairs provides subsidies to the different religious groups based on size of membership. Moreover, the state exempts churches from direct taxation except for property tax. Private confessional schools which receive less than 100 bahts per student per term or trimester may request financial aid from the Ministry of Education for their teachers' salaries.

State and private schools are subject to similar control. Religious instruction is authorized in schools, but it must be given outside regular school hours, even in confessional schools.

Special Islamic judges (Dato Yuttitham, or kadis) are provided for the administration of justice in predominantly Muslim areas, namely the south. A kadi sits with 2 trial judges in order to administer Islamic laws in civil cases involving questions of family or inheritance where all parties concerned are Muslims. In such cases the kadi's interpretation is final.

**INTERDENOMINATIONAL ORGANIZATIONS.** The Church of Christ in Thailand was formed in 1934 as the Thai United Church, a union of members of the Siam National Christian Council begun in 1930. Protestant ecumenical contacts are now centred in the supra-national Christian Conference of Asia (CCA). Catholic-Protestant co-operation is evident in the Asian Ecumenical Conference on Health. The Evangelical Fellowship of Thailand has a membership of 27 foreign missions, 11 Thai bodies, and 100 individual congregations.

With regard to interreligious relations, 2 organizations are active. (1) The Asian Religious and Cultural Forum on Development (ARCFOD), founded in 1972, unites the representatives of 5 religions (Christianity, Buddhism, Shinto, Islam and Hinduism) in 6 Asian countries: Japan, Philippines, Malaysia, Sri Lanka, India and Thailand. National committees exist in each of these countries, with a central organization in Bangkok. The principal purpose is to provide an interreligious forum to discuss problems of development and to decide what type of co-operative action the religions can take in a given country. (2) The National Interreligious Committee to Promote Sane Morals, which includes representatives of all the major religions of Thailand, was created through the initiative of the Council for Social Works of Thailand, with the king as patron. Its aim is to sensitize the conscience of the population concerning moral values.

**BROADCASTING.** Most commercial stations broadcast Protestant programmes daily, and a weekly 15-minute programme of Catholic news is heard over radio station VOR.POR.TOR.705. From abroad, Christian programmes can easily be heard from FEBC (Manila), who broadcast in many languages, until recently South East Asia Radio Voice (SEARV, Manila) in Thai, and Radio Veritas (Catholic) also from Manila. There are 5 studios in Bangkok preparing Christian programmes. These include FEBC, Christian Conference of Asia, Finnish and Swedish Free Missions (Pentecostal), and Southern Baptists who prepare programmes for TV as well for an hour a week. At Chiengmai, the Voice of Peace prepares programmes for release on FEBC (Manila). Altogether in 1973 about 220 Protestant programmes a week (75 hours) were being broadcast over 34 radio stations in Thailand. In Nakhon

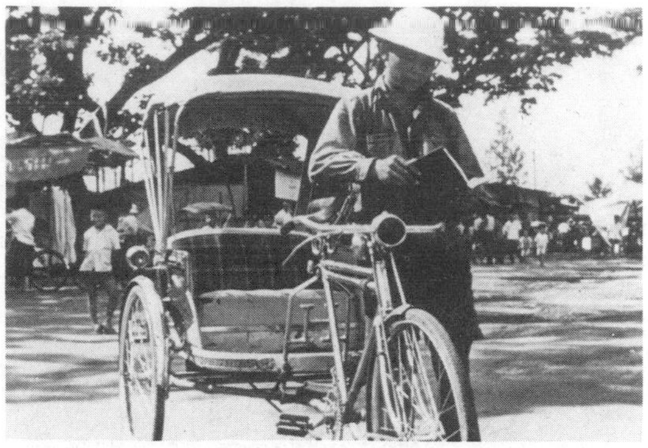

Distribution or sales of the Bible are brisk—in 1975, 9,515 Bibles, 175,478 New Testaments, 384,921 portions.

Ratchasima, there is a centre operated by Catholics, National Catholic Office for Radio and TV, which has a recording studio. Programmes are transmitted daily through Radio Veritas in Manila, and daily on Radio Yan-Khroh locally. These programmes are of a socio-cultural nature. For Catholics, Thailand is a member of UNDA.

## BIBLIOGRAPHY


*Annual report of religious activities for 1967.* Bangkok: Ministry of Education, 1967. (Annual).
*Buddhism and the spirit cults in northeast Thailand.* S.J. Tambiah. Cambridge: Cambridge University Press, 1970.
*Buddhism in transition.* D. Swearer. Philadelphia (PA): Westminster, 1970.
*Catholic directory of Thailand, 1967.* Bangkok: Xavier Hall, 1967.
*Chinese churches in Thailand.* C.E. Blanford. Bangkok: Suribayan Publishers, 1975. 272p.
*Christian directory to Thailand, Vietnam, Laos, Khmer Republic and Malaysia, 1974.* Bangkok, 1974.
*Description du royaume Thai ou Siam.* 2 vols. J.B. Pallegoix. Paris, 1854.
*Ecole, mission et l'église de demain.* M. Fiévet. Paris: Cerf, 1969.
'Growth study in North Thailand'. J.E. Hudspith. Thesis, Fuller Theological Seminary, Pasadena (CA), 1969. 363p. (Among 9 tribes).
*Guide to Christian work in Thailand.* Bangkok: Church of Christ in Thailand, n.d. 29p.
*History of Protestant work in Thailand, 1828–1958.* K.E. Wells. Bangkok: Church of Christ in Thailand, 1958. 213p.
*Monks and magic: an analysis of religious ceremonies in central Thailand.* B.J. Terwiel. Scandinavian Institute of Asian Studies. Leiden: Brill, 1978 (2nd rev. edition). 310p.
'Syncretistic rural Thai Buddhism'. J.W. Gustafson. Thesis, Fuller Theological Seminary, Pasadena (CA), 1970. 272p.
'Thailand in transition: the church in a Buddhist country', *Pro Mundi Vita* (Brussels), 48 (1973).
*The role of Thailand in world Buddhism.* R.A. Gard. Bangkok: World Fellowship of Buddhists, 1971.
'The unfinished mission in Thailand', S. Kim. Dissertation, Fuller Theological Seminary, Pasadena (CA), 1974.
*1978 Thailand Christian directory.* Bangkok: S. Chaviwan, PO Box 1405, Bangkok, 1978. 82p.


TABLE 2. ORGANIZED CHURCHES AND DENOMINATIONS IN THAILAND

| Official name 1 | Begun 2 | Type 3 | Counc 4 | Congs 5 | Adults 6 | Affiliated 7 | Names, notes, and other statistics (see Codebook) 8 |
|---|---|---|---|---|---|---|---|
| Anglican Church (D Singapore) | 1894 | A Cen | aweAE | 4 | 300 | 700 | *Christ Church*, Bangkok. 1903, M=SPG(UK). 99% expatriates (UK,USA). W=40%. |
| Assembly Hall Church | | I CBr | x.... | 1 | 50 | 200 | *Little Flock.* Chinese indigenous body begun mainland China 1926. In south. |
| **Catholic Church in Thailand:** | 1554 | R Lat | P.F.R | 229 | 84,600 | 153,831 | *Phrasatsanachakr Roman Khatholik.*C=9+2+20. 129n,185x,189m,1065w,P=61%,1704Y,5085y. |
| M Bangkok | 1841 | R Lat | Ps | 40 | 25,800 | 46,915 | Rapid industrializing. Most RCs Chinese. 35 32 134 476 46 462 1358 |
| D Chanthaburi | 1944 | R Lat | Ps | 35 | 12,400 | 22,522 | Vietnamese(in SE),Thai-Lao(NE),Chinese. 43 8 24 201 75 152 399 |
| D Chiang Mai | 1955 | R Lat | Pscj | 29 | 3,400 | 6,144 | Rural. RCs Karien elephant breeders. 1 24 10 29 65 163 255 |
| D Nakhon Sawan | 1967 | R Lat | Pmep | 33 | 2,600 | 4,732 | Rural plains, mountains. Non-Thai tribes. 0 18 4 21 62 79 124 |
| D Ratchaburi | 1934 | R Lat | Ps | 12 | 7,700 | 14,061 | All rural; rice, plantations. RCs Chinese. 21 11 8 55 75 73 365 |
| D Surat Thani | 1969 | R Lat | Psdb | 24 | 2,400 | 4,341 | Muslims (Malays) strong. RCs Chinese. 2 26 0 33 75 57 107 |
| M Tharé & Nonseng | 1950 | R Lat | Ps | 13 | 15,100 | 27,432 | RCs Thai-Lao; 2,100 Vietnamese refugees. 21 9 0 75 60 347 1306 |
| D Nakhon Ratchasima | 1965 | R Lat | Pmep | 10 | 1,900 | 3,369 | Many migrants to Bangkok. RCs Thai-Lao. 0 10 4 21 61 97 174 |
| D Ubon Ratchathani | 1953 | R Lat | Pmep | 16 | 7,800 | 14,265 | Rural. RCs Thai-Lao. 310 aliens. 4 19 3 130 66 107 566 |
| D Udon Thani | 1953 | R Lat | Pcssr | 17 | 5,500 | 10,050 | Rural, impoverished. Most RCs Vietnamese. 2 28 2 24 68 167 431 |
| Christian Brethren | c1885 | P CBr | x...E | 5 | 300 | 600 | M=CMML(UK,Australia,NZ). Pentecostal. Chinese. Work in south, Sea Gypsies. 19f. |
| Chr Nationals Evangelism Commission | 1955 | P int | xF..E | 6 | 125 | 190 | *CNEC. Chung Hui Chuan Do Hwei.* Begun China 1942. 2 schools. G=23%pa,W=60%. |
| **Church of Christ in Thailand** | 1828 | P uni | RWE.N | 269 | 21,794 | 40,000 | *CCT.*65% Thai, 25%Chinese,5% Karen. 48n,16x,150f,G=2.1%pa,6H,33h,3k,2p,5r,2s,2089Yy. |
| Church of Christ, Scientist | | M Sci | x.... | 1 | 20 | 100 | *Christian Science.* M=CCS(Boston,USA). Bangkok Society. Many Americans. |
| Ch of Jesus C of Latter-day Saints | 1854 | M LdS | x.... | | 300 | 578 | *Mormons.* M=CJCLdS(Utah,USA). Mainly USA military. Missionaries imprisoned 1972. |
| Churches of Christ | 1949 | P Dis | x.... | 10 | 200 | 400 | M=CCCC(USA). Mountain tribes (Yao); USA military personnel. 16f,G=0,1h,W=75%,20Y. |
| Churches of Christ (Non-Instrumental) | 1957 | P Dis | x.... | 30 | 1,000 | 2,000 | M=CC(Non-Instrumental)(USA). Mainly USA military personnel. 1 school. 19f. |
| Evangelical Gospel Church of Thailand | 1929 | P Hol | xF..E | 123 | 2,576 | 6,000 | M=CMA. Thais, 160 aliens. Losses to UPC. 11n,70f,G=2.3%pa,1h,2p(63),W=86%,131Y. |
| Grace Baptist Church | 1964 | P Bap | xT..E | 8 | 35 | 100 | M=Philippine ABWE(Filipinos). Thai, Chinese. Expanding. 1x,5f,W=90%,7Y,3z. |
| **Isolated radio churches** | 1952 | I rad | ..... | 2,000 | 40,000 | 86,000 | Isolated Thais and Chinese, mainly aged 12–25. R=16000(FEBC),T=166000(FEBC,ICI,&c). |
| Jehovah's Witnesses | 1936 | M Jeh | x.... | 18 | 423 | 1,000 | *Watch Tower. IBSA.* First pioneer 1936. HQ Bangkok 11. 29Y. |
| Karen Baptist Convention of Thailand | 1880 | P Bap | Twe.N | 30 | 2,000 | 4,000 | Begun by M=BBC(Burma); 1952, ABFMS(USA). Karen, Mon. Loose affiliation in CCT. |
| Lutheran Church in Thailand | | P Lut | ....E | 1 | 50 | 100 | *Lutheran Church Center.* Bangkok. M=Lutheran Council in USA. Mainly expatriates. |
| New Tribes Mission | 1951 | P int | x...E | 6 | 330 | 475 | M=NTM(USA). HQ Kanchanaburi. Lawa & other tribes. 1 school. 12n,20f,1h,W=60%,60Y. |
| Overseas Missionary Fellowship | 1951 | P int | xM..E | 65 | 500 | 2,000 | M=OMF. Lisu,Thai,Malay. Believers 50% lepers. 20x,227f,G=5.7%pa,3H,2p,W=50%,105Y. |
| Seventh-day Adventist Church | 1918 | P Adv | x.... | 17 | 1,948 | 4,000 | *Thailand M*, SE Asia UM. 4n,5x,62f,G=7.5%pa,3H,3h,1j,6p,1s,17t(1586),W=59%,174Y. |
| Thai Full Gospel Church | 1948 | P Pe2 | ZF..E | 30 | 1,000 | 3,000 | *Assemblies of God.* M=FFFM,SFM(Sweden),PAoC. 13n,9x,50f,G=7.0%pa,1s(12),W=65%,50Y. |
| Thailand Baptist Churches Association | 1949 | P Bap | T...E | 51 | 1,252 | 2,000 | M=SBC(USA). 25% Thai, 10% Chinese. 16n,2x,69f,G=6.0%pa,1H,8h,1s,W=40%,96Y,146z. |
| True Jesus Church | 1956 | I pe1 | x.... | 2 | 100 | 200 | *Chen Ye-su Chiao Hui.* Chinese body begun on mainland China in 1917. |
| United Pentecostal Church of Thailand | c1945 | P Pe1 | x.... | 95 | 10,000 | 20,000 | *Jesus Only Church.* M=UPC(USA). Many ex Gospel Church of T(CMA). 95n,45m,5000Y. |
| Worldwide Evangelization Crusade | 1947 | P int | xF..E | 32 | 400 | 800 | M=WEC(UK,USA,Germany). North. HQ Tak (Raheng). 20x,45f,G=14.9%pa,6h,W=75%,75Y |
| World-Wide Missions of Thailand | 1965 | P ind | x.... | | 150 | 300 | M=World-Wide Missions(USA). Evangelicals with base in Pasadena, CA (USA). |
| Other Protestant denominations | | P | ..... | | 5,000 | 10,000 | Total about 12 (see list below). |
| Other indigenous churches | | I | ..... | | 100 | 300 | Total about 3, Chinese and Thai, including: Evangelize China Fellowship (1958). |
| **Total affiliated (mid-1970)** | | | | 3,180 | 174,553 | 338,874 | **Total denominations (1970) . . . 39.** |
| **Total affiliated (mid-1975)** | | | | 3,980 | 220,900 | 428,850 | **Total denominations (1975) . . . 42.** |
| **Total affiliated (mid-1980)** | | | | 4,900 | 268,600 | 521,400 | **Total denominations (1980) . . . 45.** |

**NOTES ON TABLE ABOVE**

COLUMNS: for meanings and CODES (cols. 1, 3, 4, 8): see Codebook (Part 6). Column 1: **Boldface type** = church with over 10% of country's affiliated Christians.

NATIONAL COUNCILS (Column 4, 5th letter).
E = Evangelical Fellowship of Thailand (EFT) (United Christian Fellowship).
N = Council of the Church of Christ and Affiliated Missions in Thailand (CCT) (formerly National Council of Churches in Thailand).
R = Episcopal Conference of Thailand (ECT) (Sapa Sangkharat Heng Prathet Thai).

OTHER PROTESTANT DENOMINATIONS. These include: Children of God International (USA), Ch of God of Prophecy (1968), Ch of God in Thailand (Cleveland) (USA), Ev Covenant Ch of America (1971), General Conference Mennonite Ch (1967); also USA military chaplaincies among the 45,000 USA servicemen present until 1976.

PEOPLES (ethnolinguistic). Christians (1970): 38.0% Chinese (South Fukienese, Hoklo, Swatow), 26.0% Thai (Khon-Thai), 15.0% Lao (Thai Lao), 8.0% USA (7.2% White, 0.8% Black), 6.5% Vietnamese, 2.9% Hill tribe, 2.0% Karen, 1.0% Lisu, 0.2% British, 0.1% Yao, Miao (Meo, Mhong), Phutai, Lu, Indian, Eurasian.

COUNTRY-WIDE TOTALS
EVANGELIZATION (see Part 5). 1900: 18%. 1970: 47%. 1980: 57%. *Mass evangelism.* 1968, Operation Mobilization formed prayer cells throughout country and regional interdenominational evangelistic committees; 1970, Indonesian team campaign; 1970, All Thailand Congress on Evangelism, followed by numerous in-depth evangelistic campaigns; 1978, Toward New Life rallies (40,000 attenders, 1,100 decisions); 1978, Here's Life Bangkok (CCCI). *Radiophonic evangelism.* Annual listeners' letters (1975): 15,927 FEBC, et alia. Bible correspondence courses: 166,000 enrolments (12,238 ICI, 8,200 Lamp of Thailand (begun 1961), 3,207 FEBC, et alia). *Literature evangelism.* From January to June 1975, Every Home Crusade delivered 1,254,800 booklets to homes. The first nationwide EHC coverage, named Operation Torch, was completed in March 1977 with 95% saturation achieved (5,975,998 homes reached, 38,037 written responses for Christ recorded). The remaining 5% included the militarily inaccessible Laos and Cambodia border areas.
FOREIGN MISSIONARIES AND PERSONNEL (nationals serving abroad) (1973). Total 15: about 10 Protestants (CCT, Thai Overseas Missionary Society, CMA) in Burma, Laos and Malaysia, 5 Roman Catholics.
FOREIGN MISSIONARIES AND PERSONNEL (aliens from abroad) (1973). Total 1,333. *From Western world.* 1,195: 745 Protestants (398 in 27 USA soceties, 127 in 5 UK societies, 51 in 8 Australia societies, 38 in 9 New Zealand societies, 36 in 2 Canada societies, 34 in 4 WGermany societies, 19 in 1 Finland society, 15 in 2 Sweden societies, 13 in 2 Denmark societies, 9 in 1 Norway society, 5 in 3 Netherlands societies), about 450 Roman Catholics. *From Communist world.* About 4 Roman Catholics from Yugoslavia. *From Third World.* 134: about 95 Protestants from 13 Asian countries and South Africa, about 35 Roman Catholics from Philippines et alia, about 4 Chinese indigenous from Taiwan.
INSTITUTIONS (church-operated) (1973). Total 230, including 120 higher schools (8 minor seminaries), about 80 medical centres (20 hospitals), 7 religious communities, 6 seminaries (5 Protestant, 1 RC).
PERIODICALS. About 20 titles.
PERSONNEL. About 3,203 (1,870 national, 1,333 foreign).
RELIGIOUS LIBRARIES. About 15.
SCRIPTURE DISTRIBUTION (1975). Annual totals: 9,515 Bibles (30% free, 59% subsidized, 11% commercial), 175,478 NTs (80% free, 17% subsidized, 3% commercial), 384,921 UBS portions, 2,664,046 UBS selections. *Translations completed.* Portion: 6 languages since 1834. NT: 4 languages since 1843. Bible: 2 languages since 1883.
SERVICE AGENCIES. About 90, including ARCFOD, AREC(FIAMC), B-RAVA, CBCT, CCA(EACC), CCCI, CCT, CCTD, CECT, CEF, CLC, CTAT, ECCE, ECT, EFT, FEBC, LBI, MCS, SCM, SU, TCGC, TOMS, WLC(EHC), WVI, YFC, YMCA, YWAM, YWCA.

ADDITIONAL DATA ON CHURCHES
CATHOLIC CHURCH IN THAILAND *Catholics.* Including (1966) 39,384 Chinese (mainly traders), increasing to about 70,000 by 1975. *Catechumens.* (1959) 2,417; (1961) 3,962; (1963) 3,737. *Annual baptisms.* (1972) 76.3% infant, 23.7% adult. *Priests.* The first national was ordained in 1880. *Sisters.* In D Udon Thani, 120 of the 130 sisters were nationals in 1970. *Seminaries.* In 1972 the Major Seminary of Thailand was opened in Samphran (M Bangkok), as the first seminary in the country, with 92 seminarians. *Catechists.* Total (1972) 425 (92 full-time, 214 part-time, 119 occasional). Training is provided at 3 catechists' schools. *Indigenous religious congregations.* Sisters: 151 Daughters of the Holy Cross (begun 1803), 119 Servants of Mary (begun 1961), 72 Lovers of the Cross (begun 1924), 54 Auxiliaries of the Immaculate Heart of Mary (begun 1937), Daughters of the Queenship of Mary, Sisters of the Sacred Heart. *Main foreign congregations.* Priests (with over 20 members): CSSR, MEP, SDB, Prêtres du S-C de Bétharram. Brothers (with over 20): FSC, Brothers of St Gabriel. Sisters (with over 50): Carmelites, Sisters of St Paul de Chartres, Ursulines.
*Catholic organizations.* The Episcopal Conference of Thailand (Sapa Sangkharat Heng Prathet Thai), which is a member of FABC in Hong Kong, has its headquarters in Bangkok, along with 2 organizations for religious personnel: Association of Major Religious Superiors of Men in Thailand, and Association of Major Religious Superiors of Women in Thailand. There are no national presbyteral or pastoral councils. The principal national lay movements are the Legion of Mary (10,000 members of which 3,000 are active); Society of St Vincent de Paul; and the University Students Catholic Centre (450 members divided into 12 sections) in Bangkok.
The Holy See has diplomatic relations with Thailand and is represented to government and the Catholic hierarchy by a pro-nuncio in Bangkok.
The Catholic Education Council in 1973 supervised 138 primary schools (88,343 pupils) and 102 secondary (42,135). These provide facilities for 2% and 14% of the total number of students in their respective categories. In its programme of social and medical service, the church has 6 hospitals, 15 dispensaries, 3 leprosaria, 8 homes for the aged and 8 homes for children. The principal agency for socio-economic development is the Catholic Council of Thailand for Development (CCTD) (in Thai: Sapha Khatholik Heng Pratet Thai Phua Karn Phrathana), which was founded in 1971 and has as its executive organ the National Catholic Centre. The CCTD is best described as a federation of Catholic organizations concerned with social and economic development, and serves as the co-ordinating body of the Catholic Church in this domain. It is a member of CIDSE in Belgium and Caritas Internationalis in Italy. Credit unions were launched in Thailand during 1966–67 by a priest; but although they are still dependent on priests and related to the CCTD, the CCTD itself is tending now to pass out of clerical control and become a national movement with Buddhist and Protestant participation. Among established projects of particular interest may be mentioned the St Joseph Centre for Social Assistance at Ban Pong, Ratchaburi; 4 centres for professional training in the diocese of Chiang Mai; a centre for adult instruction in the diocese of Ubon Ratchathani; and a Youth Town in the diocese of Udon Thani.
CHURCH OF CHRIST IN THAILAND. In Thai, = Sapah Krischak Nai Prathet Thai (Council of the Church in Thailand). The Thai Church is a 1934 union of Presbyterians (about 80%), Baptists and Disciples. It includes members of the International Church Congregations (Bangkok and Chiang Mai), and Maitri Chit (Friendly Mind) Chinese Baptist Church (the oldest Protestant church for Chinese in the world, begun 1837). Co-operating missions: work was begun by LMS and NZG (in 1828), ABCFM (1831), ABFMS (1833), US Presbyterians (1840), UCMS (Disciples, 1903), and now also supported by the Marburger Mission (Lutherans, 1953), Church of South India, UCCJ (Kyodan, Japan), Presbyterian Church of Korea, Presbyterian Church of Australia, UCCP (Philippines), PCNZ (New Zealand), UCA (Australia), ICU (Japan), TLM (Australia), LCA (USA), KIM (Korea), et alia. In 1976 a new presbytery was added consisting of lepers and ex-lepers, with other such isolated persons. *Growth.* By 1978, communicant membership had increased to 31,154 in 191 organized churches with 93 other worshipping groups.

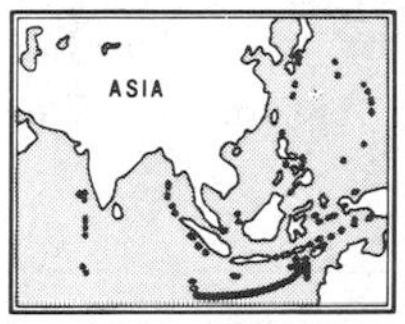


# TIMOR

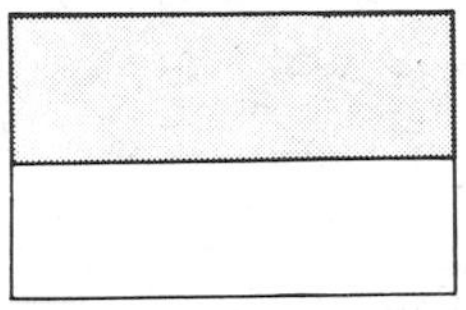

## SECULAR DATA

**STATE. Official name:** Timor (East Timor).
**Flag** (shown above right) (1977): That of Indonesia.
**Area:** 14,925 sq.km. (5,762 sq.miles). Agricultural land: 15.4%.
**Government:** Independent territory annexed by Indonesia, since 1976 (1586 Portuguese colony, 1896 Portuguese province, 1975 civil war and Independence declared, 1976 annexed by Indonesia as its 27th province).
**Official language** (1975): Portuguese (*Português*). (1977) Indonesian (*Bahasa Indonesia*).
**Capital:** Dili 52,160 (1960).
**Foreign forces** (1975): Portuguese. (1977) Indonesian.

**DEMOGRAPHY. Population:** 610,500 (census of 15.XII.1970. For 1970–2000 (UN), see last row of Table 1). Population density (1975): 45/sq.km. (117/sq.mile). Under 15 years: 41%. Growth rate (1975–80): 2.31% per year (births 4.41%, deaths −2.10%). Life expectancy (1975–80): 42.5 years. Household size: 5.1 persons.
**Major languages:** Timorese, Indonesian, Portuguese, Chinese, and 15 smaller languages.
**Urban dwellers** (1970): 11.1%. Urban growth rate (1950–70): 2.6% per year.
**Labour force:** 31%.
**Refugees** 1977): From abroad, none. Exiles abroad: 40,000 Timorese in 1976 fled to Indonesia.
**Tourists** (1972): 12,800.

**ETHNOLINGUISTIC GROUPS:** 97.5% East Timorese Indonesian [40.4% Tetum (Belu), 17.3% Mambai, 11.5% Macassai, 11.5% Mare (Bunak), 9.6% Tokode, 6.7% Dagada, Quemaque, Vaiqueno, Galoli], 1.6% Chinese (10,000), 0.4% Portuguese, 0.3% West Timorese Indonesian, 0.2% Euronesian (Eurasian).

**MONEY** (1977). **Monetary unit:** Portuguese escudo, Indonesian rupiah.
**National income per person:** US$140. Average annual family income: US$714.

**HEALTH.** Hospitals: 74 (1,590 beds). Doctors: 24. Lepers: 680 (1.0 per 1,000).

**EDUCATION.** Adult literacy: 30%. Schools: 342.

**LITERATURE.** Periodicals: 3. Newspapers: 2 non-daily.

**COMMUNICATION** (per 1,000 people). Phones: 1.5. Radios: 6.

TABLE 1. RELIGIOUS ADHERENTS IN TIMOR

| Year | 1900 | | mid-1970 | | Annual change, 1970–1980 | | | | mid-1975 | | mid-1980 | | 2000 | |
|---|---|---|---|---|---|---|---|---|---|---|---|---|---|---|
| *Name* | *Adherents* | *%* | *Adherents* | *%* | *Natural* | *Conversion* | *Total* | *Rate* | *Adherents* | *%* | *Adherents* | *%* | *Adherents* | *%* |
| Tribal religionists | 324,200 | 87.6 | 395,594 | 65.5 | 9,411 | −4,130 | 5,281 | 1.26 | 420,150 | 62.5 | 448,400 | 59.4 | 588,100 | 51.4 |
| **Christians** | **45,000** | **12.2** | **198,206** | **32.8** | **5,406** | **4,153** | **9,559** | **3.97** | **240,600** | **35.8** | **293,800** | **38.9** | **532,400** | **46.5** |
| crypto-Christians | 5,000 | 1.4 | 43,806 | 7.2 | 1,224 | 1,277 | 2,501 | 4.59 | 54,470 | 8.1 | 68,820 | 9.1 | 96,200 | 8.4 |
| professing | 40,000 | 10.8 | 154,400 | 25.6 | 4,182 | 2,876 | 7,058 | 3.79 | 186,130 | 27.7 | 224,980 | 29.8 | 436,200 | 38.1 |
| Roman Catholics | 40,000 | 10.8 | 151,650 | 25.1 | 4,091 | 2,714 | 6,805 | 3.74 | 182,100 | 27.1 | 219,700 | 29.1 | 423,600 | 37.0 |
| Protestants | 0 | 0.0 | 2,750 | 0.5 | 91 | 162 | 253 | 6.28 | 4,030 | 0.6 | 5,280 | 0.7 | 12,600 | 1.1 |
| affiliated | 45,000 | 12.2 | 198,206 | 32.8 | 5,406 | 4,153 | 9,559 | 3.97 | 240,600 | 35.8 | 293,800 | 38.9 | 532,400 | 46.5 |
| total practising | 40,500 | *90* | 138,750 | *70* | 3,784 | 2,907 | 6,691 | 3.97 | 168,420 | *70* | 205,660 | *70* | 319,440 | *60* |
| non-practising | 4,500 | *10* | 59,460 | *30* | 1,622 | 1,246 | 2,868 | 3.97 | 72,180 | *30* | 88,140 | *30* | 212,960 | *40* |
| Roman Catholics | 45,000 | 12.2 | 194,206 | 32.1 | 5,285 | 3,994 | 9,279 | 3.95 | 235,200 | 35.0 | 287,000 | 38.0 | 515,200 | 45.0 |
| Protestants | 0 | 0.0 | 4,000 | 0.7 | 121 | 159 | 280 | 5.19 | 5,400 | 0.8 | 6,800 | 0.9 | 17,200 | 1.5 |
| Evangelicals | 0 | 0.0 | 3,700 | 0.6 | 114 | 166 | 280 | 5.49 | 5,100 | 0.8 | 6,500 | 0.9 | 16,000 | 1.4 |
| Buddhists | 0 | 0.0 | 6,000 | 1.0 | 146 | −46 | 100 | 1.54 | 6,500 | 1.0 | 7,000 | 0.9 | 9,000 | 0.8 |
| Chinese folk-religionists | 0 | 0.0 | 3,000 | 0.5 | 67 | −67 | 0 | 0.00 | 3,000 | 0.4 | 3,000 | 0.4 | 2,000 | 0.2 |
| Muslims | 800 | 0.2 | 1,000 | 0.2 | 64 | 86 | 150 | 10.00 | 1,500 | 0.2 | 2,500 | 0.3 | 11,500 | 1.0 |
| Baha'is | 0 | 0.0 | 200 | 0.0 | 6 | 4 | 11 | 4.00 | 250 | 0.0 | 300 | 0.0 | 2,000 | 0.2 |
| **Country's population** | **370,000** | **100.0** | **604,000** | **100.0** | **15,100** | **0** | **15,100** | **2.25** | **672,000** | **100.0** | **755,000** | **100.0** | **1,145,000** | **100.0** |

COLUMNS, ROWS. For meanings and definitions, see Codebook (Part 6). Note that, by definition, total 'Christians' = professing + crypto-Christians, which also = affiliated + nominal Christians. Percentages may not always total exactly, due to rounding.
CENSUSES. **15.XII.1970:** 74.2% tribal religionists, 25.1% Roman Catholics, 0.5% Protestants, 0.1% Muslims.

NOTES ON RELIGIONS
BAHA'IS. Begun 1958. Growth from 1 local spiritual assembly (1964) to 3 (1973), assisted by Australian Baha'i missionaries.
BUDDHISTS. Chinese.
COUNTRY'S POPULATION. During the fighting of 1975–76 before annexation by Indonesia, about 60,000 East Timorese were killed and 100,000 imprisoned. In 1977, control was still being contested between Indonesian troops who held most towns and the revolutionary independence front Fretelin in control of the mountainous hinterland.
CRYPTO-CHRISTIANS. Persons affiliated to the churches are considerably more numerous than those professing to be Christians in censuses. These crypto-Christians are mostly interior tribesmen and others from societies hostile or opposed to conversion to Christianity.
MUSLIMS. Indonesian traders among coastal peoples, and subsequent converts; Sunnis (of the Shafiite rite). Muslims are few also in western (Indonesian) Timor (East Nusa Tenggara Timur), which in 1972 was 60.1% Protestant, 29.1% Roman Catholic, 7.2% tribal religionist (animist), 3.5% Muslim, 0.1% Hindu and Buddhist. After the 1976 takeover of Timor by Indonesia, the number of Muslims increased rapidly by immigration as well as by conversions from among pagans. The column above, 'Natural change', incorporates this immigration.
TRIBAL RELIGIONISTS. Animists and ancestor-venerators among interior tribes, especially the Akit, Batin, Benua, Bunaque, Dagadá, Galoli, Kubu, Lubu, Macassai, Mambai, Quemaque, Tetum, Tocodé, Utan, and Vaiqueno.

**NON-CHRISTIAN RELIGIONS. Traditional tribal religions** centred in ancestor veneration, continue to be the main religions of the largely illiterate interior tribes: the Tetum, Mambai, Macassai, Bunaque, Dagadá, Tocodé, Galoli, Quemaque, Vaiqueno and others.

**Islam** has won a few converts among the coastal peoples, having been introduced by Indonesian traders.

## CHRISTIANITY

CATHOLIC CHURCH. Portugal and Christianity first made contact with Timor in 1511, and by 1561 the principal ruler of the island had been converted to Christianity. Early missionary activity was carried on by Dominicans, but their work was decimated by the Dutch in 1754. A new beginning was made after the arrival of priests of the Oblates of Mary Immacu-

PORTUGUESE TIMOR

late in 1816, and in 1881 the Catholic population numbered 40,000. Originally part of the diocese of Macao, Dili was made a suffragan diocese of Goa in 1940. Growth has been especially rapid since the mid-1950s, as revealed by the following figures of baptized Catholics: 66,790 in 1956, 91,332 in 1961 and 179,911 in 1970.

PROTESTANT CHURCHES. There were no large-scale organized Protestant churches in Portuguese Timor. There is a small work of the Assemblies of God, and also work carried on by members of the strong Protestant churches in west Timor and adjacent islands. The Worldwide Evangelization Crusade has been attempting unsuccessfully to enter Timor since 1961. In 1975, there were some 2,000 Protestants on the island of Ataúro, 25 km from the mainland, with one pastor.

**CHURCH AND STATE,** Until 1975 church-state relations were covered by Portugal's concordat of 1940 with the Vatican, which applied to Timor as to

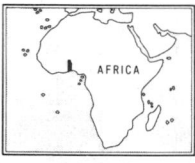

**Protestants.** Many persons from Eastern as well as Western Timor (Indonesia) attended in May 1976 this vast evangelistic rally at Kupang under auspices of Indonesian Missionary Fellowship with evangelists

Petrus Octavianus (right) and Stanley Mooneyham (second from right). **Roman Catholics.** *Inset.* Postage stamp showing early Franciscan missionaries catechising on Timor, 1572.

all other overseas Portuguese territories as long as Portugal was in control. However, during 1976 Indonesia formally announced its takeover of Timor,

after which the church-state relations existent in Indonesia began to be applied.

TABLE 2.    ORGANIZED CHURCHES AND DENOMINATIONS IN TIMOR

| Official name 1 | Begun 2 | Type 3 | Counc 4 | Congs 5 | Adults 6 | Affiliated 7 | Names, notes, and other statistics (see Codebook) 8 |
|---|---|---|---|---|---|---|---|
| Assembléias de Deus | | P Pe2 | ••••• | | 1,000 | 2,000 | *Assemblies of God.* Considerable expansion. Links with AoG (Portugal, Indonesia). |
| **Igreja Católica: D Dili** | 1511 | R Lat | Ns... | 15 | 114,600 | 194,206 | *Catholic Ch.* Suffragan of P Goa. C=2+0+2. 46nx,5m,45w,4314Y,5993y,14295z. |
| Other Protestant denominations | | P | ••••• | | 1,000 | 2,000 | Mostly Indonesian nationals from western Timor, including from M=GMIT. |
| **Total affiliated (mid-1970)** | | | | 70 | 116,600 | 198,206 | Total denominations (1970) . . . 4. |
| **Total affiliated (mid-1975)** | | | | 80 | 141,500 | 240,600 | Total denominations (1975) . . . 5. |
| **Total affiliated (mid-1980)** | | | | 90 | 172,800 | 293,800 | Total denominations (1980) . . . 6. |

**NOTES ON TABLE ABOVE**
COLUMNS: for meanings and CODES (cols. 1, 3, 4, 8): see Codebook (Part 6). Column 1: **Boldface type** = church with over 10% of country's affiliated Christians.

**PEOPLES** (ethnolinguistic). Christians · (1974): 97.0% East Timorese Indonesian (Tetum, Mambai, Macassai, Mare, Tokode, Dagada), 1.2% Portuguese, 0.7% alien Indonesian, 0.6% Euronesian (Eurasian), 0.3% Chinese.

**COUNTRY-WIDE TOTALS**
EVANGELIZATION (see Part 5). 1900: 21%. 1970: 42%. 1980:

50%.
FOREIGN MISSIONARIES AND PERSONNEL (aliens from abroad) (1973). Total 62. *From Western world.* 50 Roman Catholics. *From Third World.* 12: about 8 Roman Catholics from Macao and Indonesia, 4 Protestants from Indonesia.
INSTITUTIONS (church operated) (1973). Total 10, including 6 higher schools (2 minor seminaries).
PERIODICALS. 2 titles.
PERSONNEL. About 143 (81 national, 62 foreign).
SERVICE AGENCIES. 3.

**ADDITIONAL DATA ON CHURCHES**
IGREJA CATOLICA. The diocese dates from 1940· *Annual baptisms.* (1972) 57.9% infant, 42.1% adult. *Priests.* 36 secular, 10 religious. *Catechists.* Total (1973) 41. *Indigenous religious congregations.* None. *Foreign religious orders and congregations.* Priests: SJ, SDB. Sisters: Canossians, Dominicans.
*Catholic organizations.* There is no episcopal conference and no organization for religious personnel, although a presbyteral council has been formed.
Until 1975 the Holy See had diplomatic relations with the territory when under Portugal and was represented to government and the Catholic hierarchy by a nuncio residing in Lisbon.

# TOGO

**SECULAR DATA**

**STATE. Official name:** The Togolese Republic (La République Togolaise). Adjective of nationality: Togolese (togolais).
**Flag** (shown above right): Green and yellow stripes, with white star centred in red square at upper hoist corner.
**Area:** 56,000 sq. km. (21,622 sq. miles). Agricultural land: 44.4%.
**Government:** One-party military dictatorship, since 1967 (1885 German colony, 1922 French mandated territory, 1946 UN trusteeship, 1960 Independence, 1963 military junta, 1967 military dictatorship).
**Official language:** French (*Français*).
**Capital:** Lomé 148,440 (1970).
**Political divisions:** 19 Districts.
**Armed forces** (1976): Total 2,250 regular army, also air force. Paramilitary forces: 1,200.

**DEMOGRAPHY. Population:** 1,950,646 (census of 1.III–30.IV.1970. For 1970–2000 (UN), see last row of Table 1). Population density (1975): 40/sq. km. (104/sq. mile). Under 15 years: 45%. Growth rate (1975–80): 2.88% per year (births 4.97%, deaths −2.10%). Life expectancy (1975–80): 43.5 years. Household size: 4.9 persons.
**Major languages:** French, Ewe, Fon, Kabre, Moba, Tem, Akposo, Gurma, Yoruba, Hausa, Twi, and over 30 other tribal languages.
**Urban dwellers** (1970): 13.3%. Urban growth rate (1950–70): 6.7% per year.
**Labour force:** 41%.
**Refugees** (1977): From abroad, none. Exiles abroad: about 7,000 Togolese in Ghana and Benin.
**Tourists** (1974): 24,100.

**Eglise Catholique au Togo.** One of the 500 Catholic catechists in Togo.

**ETHNOLINGUISTIC GROUPS:** 44% Ewe cluster (21% Ewe, 10% Fon, 5% Mina (Popo), Adja), 24% Kabre cluster (14% Kabre, 0.7% Mossi, Losso, Lamba, Tamberma, Logba), 7% Moba (with Konkomba, Ngangan), 7% Kotokoli (Tem) (with Bassari, Tchamba), 5% Central Togolese (Akposo, Akebu, Adele, Buem), 5% Gurma, 3% Yoruba (Ana, Egba, Nago), 2% Hausa, 1% Chokossi, 1% Akan, 0.7% Fulani, Somba, French.

**MONEY** (1977). Monetary unit: CFA franc (=100 centimes); US$1=CFAF 250.00.
**National income per person:** US$230. Average annual family income: US$1,127.
**Inflation:** (1970–74) 7.6% per year, (1975) 18% per year (consumer price index 164).
**Cost of living in capital** (1976): index 143 (Washington DC=100). Daily cost of living: US$32.

**HEALTH. Hospitals:** 26 (3,075 beds). Doctors: 100. Lepers: 54,000 (24.0 per 1,000). Blind: 9,000. Psychotics: 18,000.

**EDUCATION.** Adult literacy:(1970)16%. Education rate: 37%. Schools: 983. Universities: 1.

**LITERATURE.** Periodicals: 20. Newspapers: 3 dailies.

**COMMUNICATION** (per 1,000 people). Phones: 3. Radios: 24. Daily newspaper circulation: 6 copies.

TABLE 1.    RELIGIOUS ADHERENTS IN TOGO

| Year / Name | 1900 Adherents | % | mid-1970 Adherents | % | Annual change, 1970–1980 Natural | Conversion | Total | Rate | mid-1975 Adherents | % | mid-1980 Adherents | % | 2000 Adherents | % |
|---|---|---|---|---|---|---|---|---|---|---|---|---|---|---|
| Tribal religionists | 447,000 | 95.1 | 1,102,260 | 56.2 | 32,442 | −23,848 | 8,594 | 0.75 | 1,146,650 | 51.0 | 1,188,200 | 45.8 | 1,169,000 | 25.2 |
| **Christians** | **4,000** | **0.8** | **595,840** | **30.4** | **21,434** | **15,032** | **36,466** | **4.81** | **757,600** | **33.7** | **960,500** | **37.0** | **2,320,000** | **50.0** |
| professing | 4,000 | 0.8 | 595,840 | 30.4 | 21,434 | 15,032 | 36,466 | 4.81 | 757,600 | 33.7 | 960,500 | 37.0 | 2,320,000 | 50.0 |
| Roman Catholics | 2,500 | 0.5 | 460,520 | 23.5 | 16,791 | 13,217 | 30,008 | 5.06 | 593,500 | 26.4 | 760,600 | 29.3 | 1,907,000 | 41.1 |
| Protestants | 1,500 | 0.3 | 109,760 | 5.6 | 3,624 | 450 | 4,074 | 3.18 | 128,100 | 5.7 | 150,500 | 5.8 | 283,000 | 6.1 |
| African indigenous | 0 | 0.0 | 21,560 | 1.1 | 849 | 1,135 | 1,984 | 6.61 | 30,000 | 1.3 | 41,400 | 1.6 | 111,000 | 2.4 |
| Marginal Protestants | 0 | 0.0 | 4,000 | 0.2 | 170 | 230 | 400 | 6.67 | 6,000 | 0.3 | 8,000 | 0.3 | 19,000 | 0.4 |
| nominal | 670 | 0.1 | 80,182 | 4.1 | 2,524 | −932 | 1,592 | 1.78 | 89,200 | 4.0 | 96,100 | 3.7 | 172,000 | 3.7 |
| affiliated | 3,330 | 0.7 | 515,658 | 26.3 | 18,910 | 15,964 | 34,874 | 5.22 | 668,400 | 29.7 | 864,400 | 33.3 | 2,148,000 | 46.3 |
| total practising | 3,000 | 90 | 386,740 | 75 | 14,183 | 11,973 | 26,156 | 5.22 | 501,300 | 75 | 648,300 | 75 | 1,503,600 | 70 |
| non-practising | 330 | 10 | 128,920 | 25 | 4,727 | 3,991 | 8,718 | 5.22 | 167,100 | 25 | 216,100 | 25 | 644,400 | 30 |
| Roman Catholics | 2,130 | 0.4 | 427,594 | 21.8 | 15,838 | 14,092 | 29,930 | 5.35 | 559,800 | 24.9 | 726,900 | 28.0 | 1,847,000 | 39.8 |
| Protestants | 1,200 | 0.3 | 71,700 | 3.6 | 2,354 | 336 | 2,690 | 3.23 | 83,200 | 3.7 | 98,600 | 3.8 | 190,000 | 4.1 |
| Evangelicals | 1,000 | 0.2 | 38,000 | 1.9 | 1,273 | 377 | 1,650 | 3.67 | 45,000 | 2.0 | 54,500 | 2.1 | 107,000 | 2.3 |
| African indigenous | 0 | 0.0 | 13,364 | 0.7 | 571 | 1,213 | 1,784 | 8.83 | 20,200 | 0.9 | 31,200 | 1.2 | 93,000 | 2.0 |
| Marginal Protestants | 0 | 0.0 | 3,000 | 0.2 | 147 | 323 | 470 | 9.04 | 5,200 | 0.2 | 7,700 | 0.3 | 18,000 | 0.4 |
| Muslims | 19,000 | 4.0 | 258,700 | 13.2 | 9,602 | 8,658 | 18,260 | 5.38 | 339,400 | 15.1 | 441,300 | 17.0 | 1,114,000 | 24.0 |
| Ahmadis | 0 | 0.0 | 500 | 0.0 | 20 | 20 | 40 | 5.71 | 700 | 0.0 | 900 | 0.0 | 3,000 | 0.1 |
| Baha'is | 0 | 0.0 | 2,100 | 0.1 | 69 | 1 | 70 | 2.86 | 2,450 | 0.1 | 2,800 | 0.1 | 14,000 | 0.3 |
| Non-religious | 0 | 0.0 | 500 | 0.0 | 28 | 122 | 150 | 15.00 | 1,000 | 0.0 | 2,000 | 0.1 | 20,000 | 0.4 |
| Other religionists | 0 | 0.0 | 600 | 0.0 | 25 | 35 | 60 | 6.67 | 900 | 0.0 | 1,200 | 0.0 | 3,000 | 0.1 |
| Country's population | 470,000 | 100.0 | 1,960,000 | 100.0 | 63,600 | 0 | 63,600 | 2.83 | 2,248,000 | 100.0 | 2,596,000 | 100.0 | 4,640,000 | 100.0 |

COLUMNS, ROWS. For meanings and definitions, see Codebook (Part 6). Note that, by definition, total 'Christians' = professing + crypto-Christians, which also = affiliated + nominal Christians. Percentages may not always total exactly, due to rounding.
CENSUSES. XI.1958-XII.1960: 67.0% tribal religionists, 24.2% Christians (17.7% Roman Catholics, 6.5% Protestants), 8.8% Muslims. I.III–30.IV.1970: 56.3% tribal religionists, 30.4% Christians (23.5% Roman Catholics, 6.9% Protestants, African indigenous and marginal Protestants), 13.2% Muslims. This latter census uses the term 'traditionalists' to cover tribal religionists.

NOTES ON RELIGIONS
AFRICAN INDIGENOUS. In about 29 denominations in 1970 (see Table 2).

AHMADIS. Begun 1960; Qadianis (HQ Rabwah, Pakistan). Many Ghanaians, also Yoruba.
BAHA'IS. Begun 1955. Growth to 11 local spiritual assemblies by 1973.
MUSLIMS. All Sunnis (of the Malikite rite); in the north, especially among the Chakossi (48%), Chamba (95%), Fulani (Fula, Peulh, 84%), Hausa, Mande, Mossi (59%), Nago (Egba, Yoruba; 72%), Tamberma (60%) and Tem (Kotokoli; 74%). There is a small Ahmadiya Mission (enumerated here although declared non-Muslim by Pakistan). *Hajj pilgrims to Mecca.* (1970) 111; (1976) 95. *Conversions.* Islam has spread rapidly among pagan peoples in the north, the proportion of Muslims in the country rising from 8.8% in 1960 to 13.2% in 1970. There are numerous schools staffed by Arab teachers.
OTHER RELIGIONISTS. Including Rosicrucians (11 AMORC centres).

PROTESTANTS. The 1900 statistics refer to the situation only in the territory which forms present-day Togo. At that time the main Protestant work (the Bremen Mission) was in western German Togoland (Ho) which is now in Ghana.
ROMAN CATHOLICS. In 1900, there were 1,331 baptized Catholics and 800 catechumens.
TRIBAL RELIGIONISTS. Animists. Tribal religion is still extremely strong. Tribes with over 70% traditionalists in 1972: N'Gangan (96%), Lamba (93%), Konkomba (92%), Gurma (90%), Moba (88%), Wachi (88%), Kabre (85%), Kpessi (84%), Bassari (80%), Adele (79%), Kebu (75%), Naudeba (Losso; 75%). There are several fetishist initiation convents, but the ones which still draw the biggest numbers of Togolese are those in Benin and Ghana.

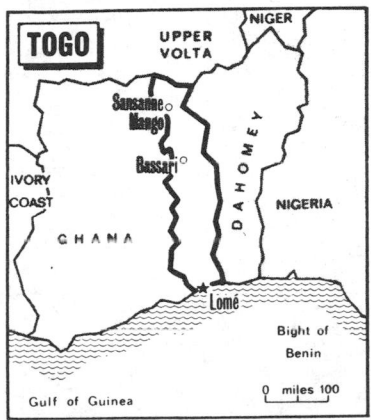

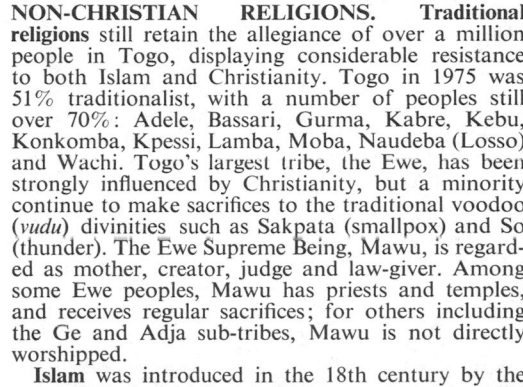

**NON-CHRISTIAN RELIGIONS. Traditional religions** still retain the allegiance of over a million people in Togo, displaying considerable resistance to both Islam and Christianity. Togo in 1975 was 51% traditionalist, with a number of peoples still over 70%: Adele, Bassari, Gurma, Kebu, Konkomba, Kpessi, Lamba, Moba, Naudeba (Losso) and Wachi. Togo's largest tribe, the Ewe, has been strongly influenced by Christianity, but a minority continue to make sacrifices to the traditional voodoo (*vudu*) divinities such as Sakpata (smallpox) and So (thunder). The Ewe Supreme Being, Mawu, is regarded as mother, creator, judge and law-giver. Among some Ewe peoples, Mawu has priests and temples, and receives regular sacrifices; for others including the Ge and Adja sub-tribes, Mawu is not directly worshipped.

**Islam** was introduced in the 18th century by the warrior Chakossi tribe, and its expansion was aided by German colonial policy. Sokodé can be considered the historic capital of Islam in Togo, the first mosque being built there in 1820. All Togolese Muslims are Sunnis of the Malikite rite. Although generally localized in the north, they are also numerous in the southern cities. Islam has the allegiance of a majority of the Chamba, Mossi, Nagot, Fulani, Tamberma and Tem (Kotokoli). The Muslim Union of Togo (Union Musulmane du Togo) was formed in late 1973 and is involved especially in a struggle against deviant marabouts and unorthodox brotherhoods. Mosques of permanent construction are at present being built throughout the country, as are Quranic schools staffed by Arab teachers.

**CHRISTIANITY**
CATHOLIC CHURCH. The area was visited by Roman Catholic priests considerably earlier than the first mission stations were established, in 1871 at Agoué and 1886 by the Society of African Missions, from Lyons, France. Togo was declared a prefecture

**Tribal religionists.** *Right.* Traditionalist funeral and burial among the 100,000 Bassari animists, who are still 80% pagans. Note corpse and bearers sprinkled with whitewash; and gun at right. *Above.* Spirit offerings made by Bassari animists.

in 1892 and a vicariate in 1914 under SVD priests; but Lyons Fathers returned in 1918 after German missionaries were forced to leave the country. They are still the principal foreign religious society. The first Togolese priest was ordained in 1930 and by 1962 Togo had an African archbishop. The church is strongest in the south, since up-country missions were not authorized by German authorities until 1913.

PROTESTANT CHURCHES. The earliest Protestants in what is now Togo were immigrants or local men trained in Christian schools on the Gold Coast. In Anecho by 1870, the ruling Lawson clan were strong Methodists. A Methodist catechist, an African from Lagos, was appointed to Anecho in 1876, and the first Methodist European missionary in 1880. In 1893 the Bremen Mission opened their Lomé station. At the beginning of World War I all German missionaries were expelled from the area, which helped to create self-reliance among indigenous Christians, a sense which was not lost when aid was later received from the Paris Mission and the UCBWM. The autonomous Evangelical Church of Togo (EET) is the largest Protestant body in the country and carries on extensive educational and social work as well: (1970) 65 primary (72 by 1976) and 2 secondary schools, a hospital and clinics, social and literacy centres, 4 hostels, a professional training programme and 3 agricultural centres.

The Methodist Church, related to British Methodism, is still confined largely to the coastal area around Anecho. The second largest Protestant denomination today is the Assemblies of God who entered Togo in 1937 and opened the first Protestant stations in the north in 1940. Other groups making their appearance more recently are Seventh-day Adventists and Southern Baptists. The latter came to Lomé at the request of indigenous Baptists who were first evangelized by Nigerian traders. Methodists have one secondary and 7 primary schools, and Adventists and Assemblies of God each have 2 schools.

INDIGENOUS CHURCHES. The Apostles Revelation Society began in Ghana in 1939 as a schism from the Ewe (now Evangelical) Presbyterian Church led by prophet Wovenu; it then entered Togo the following year. In 1951 the Apostolic Church of Togo was founded, and has spread to Benin, although a split during the mid 1950s resulted in the creation of a new body, the Pentecostal Apostolic Church. Other indigenous bodies include the White Cross Society, Heavenly Christianity Church, Sacred Order of Deliverance, Cherubim and Seraphim, and Church of the Lord (Aladura). The latter 2 are also widely dispersed across other countries of West Africa.

**Eglise de Pentecôte Apostolique.** A small Ewe indigenous church, one of 30 indigenous denominations in Togo, banned by regime in 1978 and so driven underground.

**CHURCH AND STATE.** The military regime which came to power in 1967 suspended the constitution of May 1963, although its general principles relative to the government attitude towards religion continue to be respected. According to that constitution, the Togolese republic is described as secular. The state 'respects all creeds' (Article 1) and assures all citizens of equality before the law without distinction of religion. Freedom of conscience and religion are guaranteed to all (Article 17). Religious institutions and communities 'have the right to develop without impediment in conformity with current laws and regulations' (Article 17), for their educational role is fully recognized (Article 16). 'Private and confessional schools may be opened with the authorization of and under the control of the State' (Article 16). Substantial financial grants in aid to Catholic and Protestant confessional schools were authorized in October 1970. Despite this, the Protestant role in education has markedly decreased during the 20th century. In the year 1912, there were 181 Catholic schools, 156 EET schools and 7 Methodist schools out of a total of 347 for Togo. By 1976, EET schools had dropped in number to 72 primary and one secondary school, whilst Catholic schools had risen to 236 primary and 29 secondary. In 1975 only 24,140 pupils (8% of the national total) were in Protestant schools.

In 1978, the People's Party of Togo (RPT) banned 20 religious bodies including Jehovah's Witnesses and various indigenous pentecostal churches, on the grounds that sects were proliferating alarmingly. The only bodies permitted to continue were the Roman Catholic and Protestant churches, Assemblies of God, Seventh-day Adventists and the Baptist Church of Togo; and also Islam.

**INTERDENOMINATIONAL ORGANIZATIONS.** There is no Christian council in Togo. In the field of ecumenical studies, both Catholic and Protestant clergy and laity (especially OSB priests) co-operate in the South Togo Cultural and Religious Research Group (Groupe de Recherches Culturelles et Religieuses dans le Sud Togo, or GREST), with headquarters at the monastery of Dzoghégan near Palimé, which began its activities in 1967 with a study of the ancestor cult and is now engaged on cultural and ecumenical research.

**BROADCASTING.** The government Radiodiffusion du Togo treats Catholics and Protestants equally, giving each a one-hour church service on Sundays, plus daily prayers alternating between the 2 groups and some additional output. For Catholics, UNDA is represented by a national association.

**BIBLIOGRAPHY**

*A church between colonial powers: a study of the church in Togo.* H.W. Debrunner. London: Lutterworth, 1965. 366p. (On the Evangelical Church of Togo).

TABLE 2. ORGANIZED CHURCHES AND DENOMINATIONS IN TOGO

| Official name 1 | Begun 2 | Type 3 | Counc 4 | Congs 5 | Adults 6 | Affiliated 7 | Names, notes, and other statistics (see Codebook) 8 |
|---|---|---|---|---|---|---|---|
| Assemblées de Dieu | 1921 | P Pe2 | ZF... | 70 | 3,014 | 5,000 | *Assemblies of God.* M=AoG(USA). North: Bassari, Moba. 2 schools. 26n,14f,1p,1s(30). |
| Association Baptiste Togolaise | c1950 | P Bap | T.... | 12 | 720 | 1,500 | *Togo Baptist Assoc.* Begun by Nigerian traders. M=NBC,SBC. HQ Lomé. 2n,11f,1p,80Y. |
| Chérubin et Séraphin du Mont Zion du T | 1964 | I peA | x...I | 8 | 262 | 364 | *Ordre Sacré des C&S.* M=C&S Mt Zion(Nigeria). 83% Ewe;Mina. 1n,7m,9w,W=70%,38Y,12y. |
| Eglise Adventiste du Septième Jour | 1964 | P Adv | x.... | 1 | 46 | 200 | *Seventh-day Adventists, Togo–Dahomey Mission*, WAfrican UM. Lomé. 1nx,2f,5t,20Y. |
| Eglise Apostolique du Togo et Bénin | 1951 | I peA | x.I.I | 13 | 3,000 | 5,000 | *Apostolic Ch. Divine Healers Temple. Praisers.* Ewe. Across south & Benin. Banned 1978. |
| **Eglise Catholique au Togo:** | 1871 | R Lat | P.SFR | 55 | 235,200 | 427,594 | *Catholic Ch in Togo.* C=4+5+15. 2p,27096z. 87n,53x,35m,257w,P=34%,15509Yy. |
| M Lomé | 1892 | R Lat | Ps | 24 | 160,200 | 291,060 | Capital. Coastal area, plateau. Ewe, Mina, Popo. 41 25 20 163 23 8993 |
| D Atakpamé | 1964 | R Lat | Ps | 9 | 43,200 | 78,605 | Plateau region. 443 alien RCs. Akposo, Egba. 19 5 0 31 59 3175 |
| D Dapango | 1960 | R Lat | Pofm | 7 | 4,000 | 7,300 | In north. 35% Moba, 35% Gurma, 28% Kabre. 1p. 1 20 7 28 52 519 |
| D Sokodé | 1937 | R Lat | Ps | 15 | 27,800 | 50,629 | Central and La Kara regions. Kabre, Bassari. 1p. 26 3 8 35 58 2822 |
| Eglise de la Guérison Divine du Togo | c1960 | I pe3 | x.I.. | | 500 | 1,000 | *Togo Mawu me Doyo Ha. Divine Healer's Ch of Togo. The Lord is There Temple.* M=DHC (Ghana). |
| Eglise de Pentecôte Apostolique | c1955 | I peA | ....I | 3 | 150 | 300 | *Pentecostal Apostolic Ch.* Ex Eglise Apostolique opposing TLOsborn(USA) aid. Ewe. |
| Eglise du Christ | 1962 | I pen | ....I | 5 | 250 | 500 | *Church of Christ.* Begun in Lomé by an Ewe pastor. Work in Ghana also. Ewe, Mina. |
| Eglise du Christanisme Céleste | 1963 | I peA | x.I.I | 5 | 600 | 1,000 | *Heavenly Christianity Church.* HQ Porto Novo (Benin). Mina, Ewe, Yoruba, Gun. Banned 1978. |
| Eglise du Pentecôte du Togo | c1950 | P PeA | ZG... | 147 | 3,000 | 5,000 | *Ch of Pentecost in Togo.* M=CoP(Ghana), EMS(UK). Banned 1978, doors cemented up. |
| Eglise du Seigneur (Aladura) | 1960 | I pen | xwI.I | 9 | 300 | 600 | *Church of the Lord (Aladura) (Praying).* M=CLA(Nigeria). HQ Lomé. Ewe, Mina, Yoruba. |
| **Eglise Evangélique du Togo** | 1893 | P Ref | .WA.. | 326 | 13,000 | 56,000 | *EET. Ev Ch of Togo.* 1893, M=NBM; PEMS,UCC,UCBWM. 57% Ewe. 37n,5x,36f,1H,2h,1p,2r. |
| Eglise Prot Méthodiste au Togo | c1860 | P Met | VWA.. | 17 | 1,997 | 4,000 | *Meth Ch.* M=MMS(UK). 95% Mina. Many Togolese elite. 2n,1x,1p,1r,1s,41Y,202y,157z. |
| Ordre Sacré de Déliverance | 1968 | I pen | ....I | 1 | 50 | 100 | *Sacred Order of Deliverance.* Founded locally by an Ewe. HQ Lomé. Ewe, Mina. |
| Société de la Croix Blanche | | I pen | ..... | 8 | 1,000 | 2,000 | *White Cross Society. Atitso Gaxie Habobo. EP Healing Group.* Ex EPC(Ghana). Ewe. |
| Société Révélation Apostolique | 1940 | I pen | x...I | 3 | 300 | 500 | *Apostolowo Fe Dedefia Habobo.* M=Apostles Revelation Society (Ghana). Ewe. Banned 1978. |
| Témoins de Jéhovah | c1945 | M Jeh | x.... | 27 | 1,779 | 3,000 | *Jehovah's Witnesses.* Active witnessing by 1949. Akposo et alii. Banned 1978. 248Y. |
| Other African indigenous churches | | I | ..... | | 1,000 | 2,000 | Total about 18 (see list below), mostly Ghanaians or from Nigeria. |
| **Total affiliated (mid-1970)** | | | | **765** | **266,168** | **515,658** | **Total denominations (1970) . . . 36.** |
| **Total affiliated (mid-1975)** | | | | **800** | **345,000** | **668,400** | **Total denominations (1975) . . . 42.** |
| **Total affiliated (mid-1980)** | | | | **840** | **446,200** | **864,400** | **Total denominations (1980) . . . 48.** |

**NOTES ON TABLE ABOVE**

COLUMNS: for meanings and CODES (cols. 1, 2, 4, 8): see Codebook (Part 6). Column 1: **Boldface type** = church with over 10% of country's affiliated Christians.

NATIONAL COUNCILS (Column 4, 5th letter).
- I = Association des Eglises Chrétiennes (AEC) (Association of Christian Churches).
- R = Conférence Episcopale du Togo (CET) (Episcopal Conference of Togo).

OTHER AFRICAN INDIGENOUS CHURCHES. A number of other Ghanaian and Nigerian bodies have followers in Togo. Among the total are: African Faith Tabernacle Ch, Army of the Cross of Christ Ch (MDCC) (from Ghana, among the Fante; 94 members), Bethlehem Revival Ch, Eglise du Christ Apostolique (Christ Apostolic Church from Nigeria).

**PEOPLES** (ethnolinguistic). Christians: about 58.0% Ewe cluster (48.0% Ewe, 5.0% Mina, 4.6% Fon & Adja), 12.2% Akposo, 7.6% Kabre, 4.8% Naudeba (Losso), 3.9% Yoruba (Ana, Egba, Nago), 3.9% Bassari, 1.7% Moba, 1.4% Kotokoli (Tem), 1.0% Akebu, 1.0% Ghanaian (Akan), 0.5% Gurma, Chakossi, European (French).

**COUNTRY-WIDE TOTALS**

EVANGELIZATION (see Part 5). 1900: 11%. 1970: 66%. 1980: 70%. *Radiophonic evangelism.* ELWA, RVOG, ICI (2,500 enrolments, 900 active), et alia.

FOREIGN MISSIONARIES AND PERSONNEL (nationals serving abroad) (1973). Total 38: about 32 Roman Catholics, 4 African indigenous and 2 Protestants in Benin, Ghana, Niger, Nigeria and Upper Volta.

FOREIGN MISSIONARIES AND PERSONNEL (aliens from abroad) (1973). Total 316. *From Western world.* 231: 185 Roman Catholics, 46 Protestants (33 in 5 USA societies, 5 in 1 WGermany society, 4 in 1 Switzerland society, 4 in 1 France society). *From Communist world.* About 8 Roman Catholics (4 from Poland, 4 Yugoslavia). *From Third world.* 77: about 35 African indigenous from Ghana, Benin and Nigeria, about 22 Protestants mainly from Ghana, about 20 Roman Catholics mainly from Ghana.

INSTITUTIONS (church-operated) (1973). Total 60, including 37 higher schools (5 minor seminaries), about 10 medical centres, 2 religious communities, 1 research centre, 2 seminaries (Protestant).

PERIODICALS. About 10 titles (4 RC).

PERSONNEL. About 1,166 (850 national, 316 foreign).

RELIGIOUS LIBRARIES. 5.

SCRIPTURE DISTRIBUTION (1975). Annual totals: 1,650 Bibles (subsidized), 5,500 NTs (91% subsidized, 9% commercial), 3,200 UBS portions, 17,600 UBS selections. *Translations completed.* Portion: 3 languages since 1920. NT: Mina in 1962.

SERVICE AGENCIES. About 32, including ACF, AEC, ASTOVOCT, CCAC, CET, CV/AV, GBUAF, GREST, JAC, JAC/F, JEC/F, JOC/F, LWR, SCAD, SCM, UCJF(YWCA), UCJG(YMCA), WBT, YWAM.

**ADDITIONAL DATA ON CHURCHES**

EGLISE CATHOLIQUE AU TOGO. *Catechumens.* (1959) 24,295; (1961) 29,364; (1963) 22,227; (1971) 27,096. In 1970 they numbered 26,733, divided as follows among the 4 dioceses, in order (and included in column 7): 16186, 4590, 1738, 4219. *Annual baptisms.* (1972) 74.0% infant, 26.0% adult. *Priests.* The first Togolese was ordained in 1930. *Brothers.* 9 Togolese, 26 expatriates. *Sisters.* 131 Togolese, 126 expatriates. *Seminarians* (1972). 43, all secular. *Catechists.* Total (1970) about 500. *Indigenous religious congregations.* Brothers: St-Jean Baptiste, Disciples de Jésus. Sisters: 62 Soeurs de N-D de l'Eglise (begun 1952). *Foreign orders and congregations.* Priests: SMA, OFM, FSCJ, OSB. Brothers: OM, FSC. Sisters (with over 20 professed): 49 N-D des Apôtres, 23 Providence de St-André-de-Peltre. *Catholic organizations.* The Episcopal Conference of Togo (Conférence Episcopale du Togo) is a member of SECAM and of the Inter-Territorial Conference of Francophone West Africa. There are no national presbyteral or pastoral councils. Male religious personnel are represented in the Union des Supérieurs Majeurs des Congrégations Autochtones d'Afrique de l'Ouest Francophone, and sisters in the 'Anima Una' Union des Supérieures Majeures, both with headquarters in Bamako, Mali. The Comité des Coordination des Mouvements des Jeunes (CCAC) co-ordinates the activities of such youth groups as JOC/F, JEC/F, JAC/F (265 groups with 4,500 members), CV/AV, Scouts and Guides. Adult movements include Action Catholique des Foyers, Equipes Chrétiennes de la Fonction Publique, and Légion de Marie.

The Holy See has no diplomatic relations with Togo. It is represented to the Catholic hierarchy by an apostolic delegate based in Abijan, Ivory Coast.

The Catholic Church is responsible for 40% of Togo's educational system, in 1970 operating 196 primary schools (rising to 236 by 1973) and 29 secondary (6 being colleges). There is also a professional school and a large experimental farm and training

centre called the Civil and Agricultural Society of Dzoghegan (Société Civile et Agricole de Dzoghégan, SCAD).
EGLISE EVANGELIQUE DU TOGO. Work was begun in 1893 by the North German Mission (Bremen); with World War I

it was transferred to the Paris Mission; and since 1946 has been assisted by what is now the UCC (UCBWM) (USA). *Membership.* 57% Ewe (including 7% Adja), 37% Akposo, 4% Kabre, 3% Akebu.

EGLISE PROTESTANTE METHODISTE AU TOGO. Until 1979 named Eglise Protestante Méthodiste au Bénin-Togo.

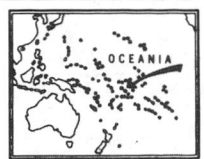

# TOKELAU ISLANDS

## SECULAR DATA

**STATE. Official name:** The Territory Overseas of the Tokelau Islands.
**Flag** (shown above right): That of New Zealand.
**Area:** 10 sq.km. (4 sq.miles). Description: 3 atolls. Agricultural land: 0.0%.
**Government:** Territory overseas of New Zealand, since 1949 (1925 New Zealand possession).
**Official language:** English.

**DEMOGRAPHY. Population:** 1,599 (census of 21.II.1972. For 1970–2000 (UN), see last row of Table 1). Population density (1975): 165/sq.km. (427/sq.mile). Under 15 years: 44%. Growth rate (1975–80): −2.2% per year (mainly emigration). Life expectancy (1975–80): 60.3 years. Household size: 5.8 persons.
**Major languages:** English, Tokelauan, Samoan.
**Labour force:** 22%.

**ETHNOLINGUISTIC GROUPS:** 99% Tokelauan (Polynesian, with some Portuguese elements), 1% Samoan.

**MONEY** (1977). **Monetary unit:** New Zealand dollar (= 100 cents); US$1 = NZ$1.07.
**National income per person:** US$400. Average annual family income: US$2,320.

**HEALTH.** Hospitals: 1.

**EDUCATION.** Adult literacy: (1951) 97%. Education rate: 80%. Schools: 3.

### TABLE 1. RELIGIOUS ADHERENTS IN THE TOKELAU ISLANDS

| Year | 1900 | | mid-1970 | | Annual change, 1970–1980 | | | | mid-1975 | | mid-1980 | | 2000 | |
| Name | Adherents | % | Adherents | % | Natural | Conversion | Total | Rate | Adherents | % | Adherents | % | Adherents | % |
|---|---|---|---|---|---|---|---|---|---|---|---|---|---|---|
| **Christians** | 900 | 100.0 | 1,640 | 96.5 | −10 | −2 | −12 | −0.76 | 1,580 | 95.8 | 1,520 | 95.0 | 1,800 | 90.0 |
| professing | 900 | 100.0 | 1,640 | 96.5 | −10 | −2 | −12 | −0.76 | 1,580 | 95.8 | 1,520 | 95.0 | 1,800 | 90.0 |
| Protestants | 900 | 100.0 | 1,130 | 66.5 | −7 | 6 | −1 | −0.09 | 1,150 | 69.7 | 1,120 | 70.0 | 1,300 | 65.0 |
| Roman Catholics | 0 | 0.0 | 510 | 30.0 | −3 | −8 | −11 | −2.56 | 430 | 26.1 | 400 | 25.0 | 500 | 25.0 |
| nominal | 0 | 0.0 | 240 | 14.1 | −2 | 4 | 2 | 0.80 | 250 | 15.1 | 260 | 16.3 | 400 | 20.0 |
| affiliated | 900 | 100.0 | 1,400 | 82.4 | −8 | −6 | −14 | −1.05 | 1,330 | 80.6 | 1,260 | 78.8 | 1,400 | 70.0 |
| total practising | 860 | 96 | 1,320 | 94 | −8 | −6 | −14 | −1.12 | 1,250 | 94 | 1,180 | 94 | 1,120 | 80 |
| non-practising | 40 | 4 | 80 | 6 | 0 | 0 | 0 | 0.00 | 80 | 6 | 80 | 6 | 280 | 20 |
| Protestants | 900 | 100.0 | 1,000 | 58.8 | −6 | −4 | −10 | −1.05 | 950 | 57.6 | 900 | 56.3 | 950 | 47.5 |
| Roman Catholics | 0 | 0.0 | 400 | 23.5 | −2 | −2 | −4 | −1.05 | 380 | 23.0 | 360 | 22.5 | 450 | 22.5 |
| **Baha'is** | 0 | 0.0 | 60 | 3.5 | 0 | 2 | 2 | 2.86 | 70 | 4.2 | 80 | 5.0 | 200 | 10.0 |
| **Country's population** | 900 | 100.0 | 1,700 | 100.0 | −10 | 0 | −10 | −0.61 | 1,650 | 100.0 | 1,600 | 100.0 | 2,000 | 100.0 |

**COLUMNS, ROWS.** For meanings and definitions, see Codebook (Part 6). Note that, by definition, total 'Christians' = professing + crypto-Christians, which also = affiliated + nominal Christians. Percentages may not always total exactly, due to rounding.
**CENSUSES. 25.IX.1945:** 66.9% Protestants, 33.1% Roman Catholics. **25.IX.1951** (indigenous population only): 63.2% Protestants, 36.3% Roman Catholics, 0.4% other religionists.

**25.IX.1961:** 62.9% Protestants (LMS), 37.0% Roman Catholics. **21.II.1972:** 70.2% Protestants (LMS), 28.3% Roman Catholics, 1.4% other religionists.

**NOTES ON RELIGIONS**
**COUNTRY'S POPULATION.** After 1960, the population fell from 1,870 (1961) to 1,832 (1968), 1,687 (1970) and to 1,599 in 1972, due to 700 Tokelauans being encouraged to emigrate for

resettlement in the North Island of New Zealand; in 1970 emigration was continuing at the rate of 100 persons a year, considerably larger than the natural (biological) population increase. The column 'Natural change' above shows the average annual natural increase (biological plus migration) from 1970–80.
**ROMAN CATHOLICS.** Though Catholics were present in numbers as immigrants long before 1946, mission work was not organized until that year.

Two of the numerous postage stamps with Christian themes: Nativity, in 1969 and 1970.

**NON-CHRISTIAN RELIGIONS. Baha'i** has a small work in the islands. No other religions exist, the original traditional Polynesian religions having disappeared over the past 2 centuries.

**CHRISTIANITY.** Only 2 churches exist in the islands, the Church in Tokelau and the Catholic Church. The former is congregationalist in polity and owes its origin to the evangelistic outreach of the London Missionary Society from 1861. Congregationalists in 1972 made up 70% of the population, and Catholics 28%. The inhabitants of Atafu Island are Protestants while Nukunono Island is entirely Catholic. Both denominations are present on Fakaofo Island. Catholic administration places the Tokelau Islands in the diocese of Apia in Western Samoa. There are 2 Catholic parishes, the one on Nukunono Island

being administered by a priest, while the other on Fakaofo Island is served by a full-time catechist with the faculties of a deacon. There have been no brothers or sisters since 1969, but a convent exists and the bishop of Apia was expected in 1974 to send 2 sisters to occupy it within a short time.

**CHURCH AND STATE.** Atafu Island was first sighted by British seamen in 1765, followed by Nukunono in 1791 and Fakaofo in 1835. A British protectorate was proclaimed over the 3 atolls in 1877, and in 1925 the islands became territories of New Zealand. Freedom of religion has never been an issue and since 1926 has been guaranteed by New Zealand's constitution.

### TABLE 2. ORGANIZED CHURCHES AND DENOMINATIONS IN THE TOKELAU ISLANDS

| Official name 1 | Begun 2 | Type 3 | Counc 4 | Congs 5 | Adults 6 | Affiliated 7 | Names, notes, and other statistics (see Codebook) 8 |
|---|---|---|---|---|---|---|---|
| **Catholic Church (D Samoa & Tokelau)** | 1946 | R Lat | P.,FY. | 1 | 200 | 400 | In D Apia, WSamoa. All Nukunono, part Fakaofo. M=SM2. School, 196 pupils. 1x,P=78%. |
| **Congregational Christian Ch in Samoa** | 1861 | P Con | Rwp.. | 6 | 400 | 1,000 | *Church in Tokelau.* M=LMS(UK),CCCS(Samoa). Atafu, part Fakaofo. 40mw,W=95%,24y. |
| Total affiliated (mid-1970) | | | | 7 | 600 | 1,400 | Total denominations (1970) . . . 2. |
| Total affiliated (mid-1975) | | | | 7 | 570 | 1,330 | Total denominations (1975) . . . 2. |
| Total affiliated (mid-1980) | | | | 8 | 540 | 1,260 | Total denominations (1980) . . . 2. |

**NOTES ON TABLE ABOVE**
**COLUMNS:** for meanings and CODES (cols. 1, 3, 4, 8): see Codebook (Part 6). Column 1: **Boldface type** = church with over 10% of country's affiliated Christians.

**PEOPLES** (ethnolinguistic). Christians: 99% Tokelauan, 1% Samoan.

**COUNTRY-WIDE TOTALS**
**EVANGELIZATION** (see Part 5). 1900: 100%. 1970: 100%. 1980: 100%.
**FOREIGN MISSIONARIES AND PERSONNEL** (aliens from abroad) (1973). Total 3. *From Western world.* 1 Roman Catholic. *From Third World.* About 2 Protestants from Samoa.
**PERIODICALS.** 1 title.

**PERSONNEL.** About 43 (40 national, 3 foreign).
**SCRIPTURE DISTRIBUTION** (1975). Annual totals: 20 Bibles (subsidized), 20 NTs (subsidized).

**ADDITIONAL DATA ON CHURCHES**
**CATHOLIC CHURCH.** *Catholic organizations.* The church operates a school at Nukunono.

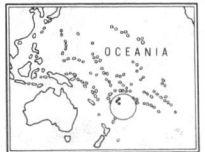

# TONGA

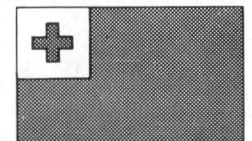

## SECULAR DATA

**STATE. Official name:** The Kingdom of Tonga (Pule'anga Tonga). **Unofficial name:** The Friendly Islands. **Adjective of nationality:** Tongan.
**Flag** (shown above right): Red field with red cross on white square in upper hoist corner.
**Area:** 699 sq.km. (270 sq.miles). Description: 169 islands and islets. Agricultual land: 82.9%.
**Government:** Constitutional monarchy, since 1862 (c1000 absolute monarchy, 1862 constitutional monarchy, 1900 British protect-

orate, 1970 Independence).
**Legislature:** Legislative Assembly, 23 members.
**Official language:** Tongan.
**Capital:** Nuku'alofa 25,000.
**Armed forces** (1976): a small standing army.

**DEMOGRAPHY. Population:** 77,429 (census of 30.XI.1966. For 1970–2000 (UN), see last row of Table 1). Population density (1975): 144/sq.km. (374/sq.mile). Under 15 years: 48%. Growth rate (1975–80): 3.27% per year (births 4.11%, deaths −0.91%, immigrants 0.07%). Household size: 6.9 persons.

**Major languages:** Tongan, English.
**Urban dwellers** (1970): 21.8%. Urban growth rate (1950–70): 3.8% per year.
**Labour force:** 24%.
**Tourists** (1966): 16,000. (1970) 36,000.

**ETHNOLINGUISTIC GROUPS:** 98.3% Tongan, 0.7% Euronesian or part-Tongan (Tongan/European) (510), 0.5% European (400) (0.3% Anglo-Australian, 0.2% British), 0.4% other Pacific islander, 0.1% Chinese, Maori.

**MONEY** (1977). **Monetary unit:** Tongan pa'anga (= 100 seniti); US$1 = P 0.97.
**National income per person:** US$250. Average annual family income: US$1,725.
**Inflation:** (1970–74) 10.8% per year (1975: consumer price index 180).

**Cost of living in capital** (1976): Daily cost of living: US$25.

**HEALTH.** Hospitals: 7 (254 beds). Doctors: 30. Lepers: 200 (2.0 per 1,000).

**EDUCATION.** Adult literacy: (1976) 100%. Education rate:

100%. Schools: 181.

**LITERATURE.** Periodicals: 15. Newspapers: 1 non-daily.

**COMMUNICATION** (per 1,000 people). Phones: 12. Radios: 99.

TABLE 1.   RELIGIOUS ADHERENTS IN TONGA

| Year / Name | 1900 Adherents | % | mid-1970 Adherents | % | Annual change, 1970–1980 Natural | Conversion | Total | Rate | mid-1975 Adherents | % | mid-1980 Adherents | % | 2000 Adherents | % |
|---|---|---|---|---|---|---|---|---|---|---|---|---|---|---|
| **Christians** | 20,000 | 100.0 | 84,870 | 98.7 | 3,253 | −13 | 3,240 | 3.25 | 99,570 | 98.6 | 117,270 | 98.5 | 208,550 | 98.4 |
| professing | 20,000 | 100.0 | 84,870 | 98.7 | 3,253 | −13 | 3,240 | 3.25 | 99,570 | 98.6 | 117,270 | 98.5 | 208,550 | 98.4 |
| Protestants | 3,100 | 15.5 | 44,150 | 51.3 | 1,702 | 62 | 1,764 | 3.39 | 52,100 | 51.6 | 61,790 | 51.9 | 108,210 | 51.0 |
| Polynesian indigenous | 16,400 | 82.0 | 18,580 | 21.6 | 647 | −411 | 236 | 1.19 | 19,800 | 19.6 | 20,940 | 17.6 | 25,440 | 12.0 |
| Roman Catholics | 500 | 2.5 | 14,400 | 16.7 | 572 | 121 | 693 | 3.96 | 17,500 | 17.3 | 21,330 | 17.9 | 42,460 | 20.0 |
| Marginal Protestants | 0 | 0.0 | 6,880 | 8.0 | 297 | 205 | 502 | 5.52 | 9,090 | 9.0 | 11,900 | 10.0 | 29,680 | 14.0 |
| Anglicans | 0 | 0.0 | 860 | 1.0 | 35 | 10 | 45 | 4.17 | 1,080 | 1.1 | 1,310 | 1.1 | 2,760 | 1.3 |
| nominal | 80 | 0.4 | 745 | 0.9 | 36 | 49 | 85 | 7.77 | 1,100 | 1.1 | 1,600 | 1.3 | 5,030 | 2.4 |
| affiliated | 19,920 | 99.6 | 84,125 | 97.8 | 3,217 | −62 | 3,155 | 3.20 | 98,470 | 97.5 | 115,670 | 97.2 | 203,520 | 96.0 |
| total practising | 18,920 | 95 | 71,510 | 85 | 2,735 | −53 | 2,682 | 3.20 | 83,700 | 85 | 98,320 | 85 | 162,820 | 80 |
| non-practising | 1,000 | 5 | 12,620 | 15 | 482 | −9 | 473 | 3.20 | 14,770 | 15 | 17,350 | 15 | 40,700 | 20 |
| Protestants | 3,080 | 15.4 | 38,891 | 45.2 | 1,486 | −33 | 1,453 | 3.19 | 45,480 | 45.0 | 53,420 | 44.9 | 88,580 | 41.8 |
| Evangelicals | 2,600 | 13.0 | 21,000 | 24.4 | 807 | 23 | 830 | 3.36 | 24,700 | 24.5 | 29,300 | 24.6 | 52,600 | 24.8 |
| Marginal Protestants | 0 | 0.0 | 15,992 | 18.6 | 653 | 248 | 901 | 4.50 | 20,000 | 19.8 | 25,000 | 21.0 | 48,800 | 23.0 |
| Roman Catholics | 480 | 2.4 | 14,342 | 16.7 | 570 | 126 | 696 | 3.99 | 17,440 | 17.3 | 21,300 | 17.9 | 42,400 | 20.0 |
| Polynesian indigenous | 16,360 | 81.8 | 14,100 | 16.4 | 475 | −409 | 66 | 0.45 | 14,540 | 14.4 | 14,760 | 12.4 | 21,200 | 10.0 |
| Anglicans | 0 | 0.0 | 800 | 0.9 | 33 | 6 | 39 | 3.86 | 1,010 | 1.0 | 1,190 | 1.0 | 2,540 | 1.2 |
| **Baha'is** | 0 | 0.0 | 1,100 | 1.3 | 46 | 14 | 60 | 4.29 | 1,400 | 1.4 | 1,700 | 1.4 | 3,400 | 1.6 |
| **Hindus** | 0 | 0.0 | 30 | 0.0 | 1 | −1 | 0 | 0.00 | 30 | 0.0 | 30 | 0.0 | 50 | 0.0 |
| **Country's population** | 20,000 | 100.0 | 86,000 | 100.0 | 3,300 | 0 | 3,300 | 3.27 | 101,000 | 100.0 | 119,000 | 100.0 | 212,000 | 100.0 |

**COLUMNS, ROWS.** For meanings and definitions, see Codebook (Part 6). Note that, by definition, total 'Christians' = professing + crypto-Christians, which also = affiliated + nominal Christians. Percentages may not always exactly, due to rounding.
**CENSUSES. 26–27.IX.1956:** 51.1% Protestants (49.6% Free Wesleyans, 1.5% SD Adventists), 27.7% Polynesian indigenous (17.6% Free Ch of Tonga, 9.9% Ch of Tonga), 14.8% Roman Catholics, 5.2% marginal Protestants (Mormons), 0.9% Anglicans, 0.3% other religionists. **30.XI.1966:** 52.0% Protestants (49.9% Free Wesleyans, 1.8% SD Adventists), 23.4% Polynesian indigenous (14.3% Free Ch of Tonga, 9.0% Ch of Tonga), 16.0%

Roman Catholics, 7.3% marginal Protestants (Mormons), 1.0% Anglicans, 0.3% Baha'is.

**NOTES ON RELIGIONS**
**BAHA'IS.** Growth from 6 local spiritual assemblies (1964) to 13 (1973).
**COUNTRY'S POPULATION.** Emigration: (1969) 1,700, (1970) 2,220, (1972) 5,840, (1973) 6,870; in 1973, 4,870 to New Zealand, 680 to Fiji, 480 to USA, 370 to American Samoa, 140 to Australia.
**HINDUS.** Indians.
**MARGINAL PROTESTANTS.** Professing Mormons grew from 2,925 (5.2% of the population) in the 1956 census to 5,519 (7.3%)

in the 1966 census. However, affiliated Mormons known to the church itself have been far more numerous: in 1930, 1,185; (1940) 1,777; (1950) 2,820; (1960) 5,160; (1965) 8,560; (1967) 10,835; (1970) 14,355; (1971) 15,842. This has been due to a vast and continuing influx of persons professing in censuses to be Methodists into the new Mormon churches and schools. In 1975 there were 3 stakes of Zion (dioceses) for Tonga. Although the growth rate of affiliated Mormons rose as high as 10% per year in 1970, it then rapidly fell to its average of 4.5% per year for the decade 1970–80.
**POLYNESIAN INDIGENOUS.** In 3 denominations in 1970 (see Table 2), the first dating from the year 1885.

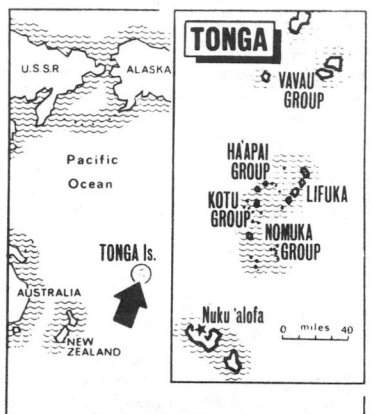

## NON-CHRISTIAN RELIGIONS. Baha'i has a growing community of followers.

## CHRISTIANITY
PROTESTANT AND INDIGENOUS CHURCHES. Pioneers of the London Missionary Society reached Tonga as early as 1797, but local opposition forced their withdrawal after 3 missionaries were massacred in 1799. A further unsuccessful attempt was made in 1822 by Wesleyan missionaries, but after 1825 a permanent work resulted. Evangelization centred on the conversion of chiefs who in turn led their peoples into the church. When Taufa'ahau (later George Tupou I) became king of Tonga in 1845, Christianity became the dominant religion, and by 1853 all Tongans were Christians, at least in name. Methodists today are divided into 4 denominations. The main body is the Free Wesleyan Church, the original mission-controlled parent body. In 1885, however, in a desire for local autonomy led by the

king and his prime minister (previously a Methodist missionary), an independent body, the Wesleyan Free Church, was founded by the king in opposition to the original church and mission and all Christians were ordered to join it on pain of persecution. For 4 decades the 2 churches were bitter rivals. An attempt by the monarch to unite the 2 groups in 1924 brought together 4,000 old Wesleyans with 12,000 Free Wesleyans while another 6,000 Free Wesleyans refused, preferring to continue as the separate body, renamed the Free Church of Tonga. This latter church has been declining rapidly in influence since then, especially since the 1950s, and has experienced 2 further schisms: the Church of Tonga in 1929, and the much smaller Church of the Red Coats in 1962. Tonga is still predominantly Methodist, although Methodists are tending to lose their proportionate place in the population to the rapidly-growing Assemblies of God, Adventists, Catholics and Mormons. Since 1829, many Tongan Methodists have

**Anglican Church.** *Above.* 'Welcome!' Tongans greet foreign visitors with old tribal dances, after which everybody enters church building for Evensong.

**Free Wesleyan Church of Tonga.** *Right.* The 1967 Coronation of His Majesty King Taufa'ahau Tupou IV, performed by Free Wesleyan Church at hands of its President with Rev. C.F. Gribble, President-General, Methodist Church of Australasia.

served overseas as foreign missionaries to other islands.

CATHOLIC CHURCH. A Catholic missionary tried unsuccessfully to enter Tonga in 1837. Marist Fathers also suffered persecution after their arrival in 1842, but religious freedom was proclaimed in a treaty between Tonga and France in 1855. The first Tongan priest was ordained in 1933. The vicariate of Tonga was erected in 1937 and became a diocese in 1966. The Catholic population continues to grow.

MARGINAL CHURCHES. Mormons have recently become the fastest-growing denomination in Tonga, mostly at the expense of Methodists. With a very large number of Mormon missionaries from the USA, they have launched an aggressive programme of building 40 new churches a year and are attracting large numbers through their extensive school system. Their annual building expenditure in 1970, at US$1.25 million, was over one quarter the size of the total state budget. A small Jehovah's Witness community exists also.

**CHURCH AND STATE.** The Tongan state specifies its religious conviction in its constitution of 1 January 1967, Part I, Declaration of Rights, Article 1: 'Since it appears to be the will of God that man should be free as He has made all men of one blood...'. Constitutionally, the Tongan monarch is the head of the Free Wesleyan Church of Tonga and ratifies the annual appointment of the church's elected president. The Free Wesleyan Church enjoys a special position because of its majority status and the prominence given to the royal family within its membership. From earliest days the monarchs have played an active role. The 19th-century kings were the principal forces contributing to the christianization of the islands. In 1885 king Tupou I was a prime mover in the separation of the Free Church from its parent body, the Wesleyan Church; and in 1924, the queen, recognized as the 'chief member' of the Free Church, was involved in the attempt to heal the breach between the 2 churches.

Tonga is one of the few countries of the world where the observance of Sunday as a day of rest receives special mention in the constitution: 'The Sabbath Day shall be sacred in Tonga for ever and it shall not be lawful to do work or play games or trade on the Sabbath. And any agreement made or documents witnessed on this day shall be counted void and not recognized by the Government' (Article 6).

The churches continue to be heavily involved in education; in 1976 the Free Wesleyan Church managed 30 primary schools (2,794 pupils), 18 secondary schools (3,740), and an agricultural college (46 students) as well as its seminary with 71 students. There is no state aid to any church institutions in Tonga.

**BROADCASTING.** The government Tonga Broadcasting Commission allows all churches to broadcast, giving time in proportion to the numerical size of each denomination. Catholics thus are given one free hour every seventh week. In addition Catholics buy an extra half hour weekly and Protestants an extra one and a half hours weekly. For Catholics, an association grouping Tonga with Samoa, Wallis and Futuna and the Cook Islands is a member of UNDA.

## BIBLIOGRAPHY

'The Tongan web', chapter 3 in A.R. Tippett, *People movements in Southern Polynesia* (Chicago: Moody Press, 1971), p.76–110.

TABLE 2. ORGANIZED CHURCHES AND DENOMINATIONS IN TONGA

| Official name<br>1 | Begun<br>2 | Type<br>3 | Counc<br>4 | Congs<br>5 | Adults<br>6 | Affiliated<br>7 | Names, notes, and other statistics (see Codebook)<br>8 |
|---|---|---|---|---|---|---|---|
| Anglican Church (D Polynesia) | 1902 | A Hig | awpKK | 8 | 400 | 800 | In Ch of the Province of New Zealand. 80% Tongan. 3n,W=21%,3Y,31y. |
| Assemblies of God of Tonga | c1930 | P Pe2 | ZF... | 62 | 500 | 1,250 | 1965, M=AoG(USA). Rapid growth. Many nominal Methodists. 65n,2x,2f,W=75%,100Y. |
| **Catholic Church: D Tonga** | 1837 | R Lat | pzPYK | 13 | 7,500 | 14,342 | VA Tonga erected 1937. M=SM. 86 aliens. C=1+0+1. 8n,10x,2m,75w,P=65%,914Yy. |
| Christian Brethren | c1960 | P CBr | x.... | 1 | 50 | 100 | *Plymouth Brethren. Open Brethren. Gospel Hall.* Independent congregation. |
| Church of God & the People of Tonga | 1962 | I Met | ..... | 2 | 50 | 100 | *Church of the Red Coats.* Indigenous schism ex Free Church of Tonga. |
| **Ch of Jesus C of Latter-Day Saints** | 1916 | M LdS | x.... | | 9,000 | 15,842 | *Mormons* (USA). 40 new churches a year, also schools. 250f,G=9.9%pa, 1r(1200). |
| Church of Tonga | 1929 | I Met | ..P.K | | 3,600 | 6,000 | Large indigenous schism ex Free Church of Tonga. Methodist polity. |
| Churches of Christ | c1955 | P Dis | x.... | 2 | 100 | 200 | M=Churches of Christ(Non-Instrumental) (USA). In Nuku'alofa. Independents. 1f. |
| Free Church of Tonga | 1885 | I Met | ....k | | 5,700 | 8,000 | Schism of 82% ex Wesleyan Ch, led by king. 1967, prophetess movement. Declining. |
| **Free Wesleyan Church of Tonga** | 1822 | P Met | VWP.K | 180 | 10,154 | 35,641 | *FWCT. Siasi Vesiliana Tauataina o Tonga.* 114n,3x,92mw,G=0,1p,8r,1s,W=55%,870Yy. |
| Jehovah's Witnesses | c1937 | M Jeh | x.... | 1 | 50 | 150 | *Watch Tower. IBSA.* Active witnessing in 1937, reported from 1963 onwards. 2y. |
| Seventh-day Adventist Church | 1895 | P Adv | x...k | 10 | 1,484 | 1,700 | *Tonga Mission*, Central Pacific UM. Organized 1921. 10nx,25mw,1s,25t(1200),28Y. |
| **Total affiliated (mid-1970)** | | | | **680** | **38,588** | **84,125** | **Total denominations (1970) . . . 12.** |
| **Total affiliated (mid-1975)** | | | | **880** | **45,170** | **98,470** | **Total denominations (1975) . . . 13.** |
| **Total affiliated (mid-1980)** | | | | **1,090** | **53,060** | **115,670** | **Total denominations (1980) . . . 14.** |

NOTES ON TABLE ABOVE

COLUMNS: for meanings and CODES (cols. 1, 3, 4, 8): see Codebook (Part 6). Column 1: **Boldface type** = church with over 10% of country's affiliated Christians.

NATIONAL COUNCILS (Column 4, 5th letter).

K = Tonga Council of Churches (TCC) (1973; formerly Inter-Church Committee, formed 1968).

k = fraternal member of TCC.

PEOPLES (ethnolinguistic). Christians: 98.4% Tongan, 0.7% Euronesian, 0.5% European (White), 0.4% other Pacific islander (Samoan, et alii), Chinese, Maori.

COUNTRY-WIDE TOTALS

EVANGELIZATION (see Part 5). 1900: 100%. 1970: 100%. 1980: 100%. *Mass evangelism.* 1966, Good News Crusade sponsored by Assemblies of God; 1969, 4-day Billy Graham crusade led by A.A. Haqq (12,000 attenders, 500 enquirers).

FOREIGN MISSIONARIES AND PERSONNEL (nationals serving abroad) (1973). Total 28: about 24 Protestants and 4 marginal Protestants (Mormons) in Australia, Niue, Northern Solomons, Papua New Guinea, Samoa, Solomon Islands.

FOREIGN MISSIONARIES AND PERSONNEL (aliens from abroad) (1973). Total 320. *From Western world.* 260: about 200 marginal Protestants (Mormons from USA), 45 Roman Catholics, 15 Protestants (10 in 1 Australia society, 5 in 3 USA societies). *From Third World.* 60: about 50 marginal Protestants (Mormons from Samoa et alia), 6 Protestants, about 4 Roman Catholics.

INSTITUTIONS (church-operated) (1973). Total 25, including 20 higher schools, 2 seminaries (Protestant).

PERIODICALS. About 8 titles.

PERSONNEL. About 787 (467 national, 320 foreign).

RELIGIOUS LIBRARIES. 2.

SCRIPTURE DISTRIBUTION (1975). Annual totals: 2,550 Bibles (98% subsidized, 2% commercial), 500 NTs (20% subsidized, 80% commercial), 400 UBS portions, 1,300 UBS selections. *Translations completed.* Tongan: portion in 1844, NT 1849, Bible 1862.

SERVICE AGENCIES. About 6.

ADDITIONAL DATA ON CHURCHES

CATHOLIC CHURCH. Catholic missions began in 1842 with the erection of VA Central Oceania (VA Tonga Island, 1937). Statistics exclude Niue Island, which formed part of the diocese until 1972. *Annual baptisms.* (1972) 87.9% infant, 12.1% adult. *Brothers.* Both Tongans. *Sisters.* 40 Tongans, 35 expatriates. *Catechists.* Total (1974) 87. *Foreign religious congregations.* Priests: SM. Sisters: Missionary Sisters of the Society of Mary *Catholic organizations.* The bishop of Tonga is a member of the Episcopal Conference of the Pacific (CEPAC) with its seat in Suva, Fiji, and there is a Senate of Priests on the islands.

The Holy See has no diplomatic relations with Tonga. It is represented to the Catholic hierarchy by the apostolic delegation to New Zealand and the Islands of the Pacific, based on Wellington, New Zealand.

In 1970 the church sponsored 14 primary schools (2,840 pupils), 3 middle schools (220 pupils) and 2 high schools (850 pupils). An agricultural training farm and an adult education programme have also been launched, and the church has begun a conscientization campaign to prepare the way for the creation of credit unions.

FREE WESLEYAN CHURCH OF TONGA. Alternate name, Methodist Church in Tonga. The church, the original Methodist work on Tonga, was also since 1924 the Tonga Conference of the Methodist Church of Australasia until its autonomy in 1976. It has long had a major work in education in Tonga. For some years now, it has experienced heavy numerical losses, especially of school pupils, to the Mormon mission. *Seminarians.* 73.

# TRANSKEI

## SECULAR DATA

**STATE. Official name:** The Republic of the Transkei. Adjective of nationality: Transkeian.
**Flag** (shown above right): Stripes of red (top), white, and green.
**Area:** 43,190 sq.km. (16,675 sq.miles).
**Government:** Parliamentary republic, since 1976 (1872 annexed by Britain, 1930 United Transkeian Territories, 1963 self-government as Bantustan within South Africa, 1976 Independence).
**Legislature:** National Assembly, 150 members (75 tribal chiefs, 75 elected members).
**Official language:** Xhosa.
**Capital:** Umtata 24,805 (1970; in 1960, 12,221; in 1951, 9,185).
**Political divisions:** 26 Districts.
**Armed forces** (1976): Regular army (White officers).

**DEMOGRAPHY. Population:** 1,743,000 (census of 6.V.1970; increasing from 1,439,195 in 1960 census, and 1,300,920 in 1951 census). In addition, 1.5 million Xhosas living outside Transkei in 1976 lost South African citizenship and became citizens of Transkei. Population density (1975): 50/sq.km. (129/sq.mile). Under 15 years: 60%. Growth rate (1975–80): 6.5% per year (births 4.5%, deaths −1.5%, immigrants 3.5%). Since 1960, there has been massive forced resettlement of Bantu considered economically useless from White areas of South Africa, estimated at 300,000 a year into all Bantustans, and 80,000 a year into Transkei. After Independence in 1976, however, 50,000 fled from Transkei into Ciskei. Life expectancy (1975–80): 46 years. Household size: 5.1 persons.
**Major languages:** Xhosa, English, Afrikaans, Sotho.
**Urban dwellers** (1970): 3.6% (3.2% in 1960, 3.1% in 1951). Urban growth rate (1950–70): 1.0% per year.
**Labour force:** 35%; unemployment 25%.

**Tribal religionists.** Traditional customs and belief are still held by 30% of the Xhosa.

**ETHNOLINGUISTIC GROUPS:** 97.0% Bantu (92.0% Xhosa (including Pondo (Mpondo), Mpondomise, Tembu, Bomvana), 3.0% Sotho, 1.0% Zulu (Fingo)), 2.0% White (Afrikaner, English), 1.0% Coloured, Indian.

**MONEY** (1977). **Monetary unit:** SA rand (= 100 cents); US$1 = R 0.87.
**National income per person** (1974): US$97, declining gradually since 1950 due to forced population influx. Average annual family income: US$495.
**Inflation:** (1970–74) 13% per year (1975: consumer price index 166).
**Cost of living in capital** (1976): index 80 (Washington DC=100). Daily cost of living: US$18.

**HEALTH.** Hospitals: 22.

**EDUCATION.** Adult literacy: 40%. Education rate: 30%.

**COMMUNICATION** (per 1,000 people). Phones: 3. Radios: 20.

*Note.* The Republic of the Transkei has not been recognized outside South Africa as an independent republic, but is regarded instead as still an integral part of South Africa. For this reason its religious statistics are included in this survey in South Africa. Details of the Transkei's religions and denominations are given here in Table 1 below, but its figures, being duplicated by inclusion also in South Africa's Tables 1 and 2, should not be used when compiling continental or global totals.

All other Bantustans are described under South Africa.

TABLE 1.    RELIGIOUS ADHERENTS IN THE TRANSKEI

| Year | 1900 | | mid-1970 | | Annual change, 1970–1980 | | | | mid-1975 | | mid-1980 | | 2000 | |
|---|---|---|---|---|---|---|---|---|---|---|---|---|---|---|
| Name | Adherents | % | Adherents | % | Natural | Conversion | Total | Rate | Adherents | % | Adherents | % | Adherents | % |
| Christians | 59,700 | 19.9 | 1,199,700 | 68.8 | 52,537 | 2,493 | 55,030 | 3.89 | 1,413,700 | 69.4 | 1,750,000 | 70.0 | 3,285,000 | 73.0 |
| professing | 59,700 | 19.9 | 1,199,700 | 68.8 | 52,537 | 2,493 | 55,030 | 3.89 | 1,413,700 | 69.4 | 1,750,000 | 70.0 | 3,285,000 | 73.0 |
| Protestants | 45,000 | 15.0 | 575,200 | 33.0 | 25,100 | 800 | 25,900 | 3.83 | 675,400 | 33.2 | 834,200 | 33.4 | 1,495,500 | 33.2 |
| Black indigenous | 1,500 | 0.5 | 357,300 | 20.5 | 15,898 | 2,122 | 18,020 | 4.21 | 427,800 | 21.0 | 537,500 | 21.5 | 1,125,000 | 25.0 |
| Anglicans | 12,000 | 4.0 | 170,800 | 9.8 | 7,269 | −849 | 6,420 | 3.28 | 195,600 | 9.6 | 235,000 | 9.4 | 382,500 | 8.5 |
| Roman Catholics | 1,200 | 0.4 | 92,400 | 5.3 | 4,088 | 422 | 4,510 | 4.10 | 110,000 | 5.4 | 137,500 | 5.5 | 270,000 | 6.0 |
| Marginal Protestants | 0 | 0.0 | 4,000 | 0.2 | 182 | −2 | 180 | 3.67 | 4,900 | 0.2 | 5,800 | 0.2 | 12,000 | 0.3 |
| nominal | 15,000 | 5.0 | 175,400 | 10.1 | 7,797 | 1,163 | 8,960 | 4.27 | 209,800 | 10.3 | 265,000 | 10.6 | 540,000 | 12.0 |
| affiliated | 44,700 | 14.9 | 1,024,300 | 58.8 | 44,740 | 1,330 | 46,070 | 3.83 | 1,203,900 | 59.1 | 1,485,000 | 59.4 | 2,745,000 | 61.0 |
| total practising | 42,460 | 95 | 870,660 | 85 | 38,029 | 1,130 | 39,159 | 3.83 | 1,023,310 | 85 | 1,262,250 | 85 | 2,196,000 | 80 |
| non-practising | 2,240 | 5 | 153,640 | 15 | 6,711 | 200 | 6,911 | 3.83 | 180,590 | 15 | 222,750 | 15 | 549,000 | 20 |
| Protestants | 32,100 | 10.7 | 439,200 | 25.2 | 18,994 | −434 | 18,560 | 3.63 | 511,100 | 25.1 | 624,800 | 25.0 | 1,070,000 | 23.8 |
| Evangelicals | 25,600 | 8.5 | 296,300 | 17.0 | 12,790 | −420 | 12,370 | 3.59 | 344,200 | 16.9 | 420,000 | 16.8 | 720,000 | 16.0 |
| Black indigenous | 1,200 | 0.4 | 339,900 | 19.5 | 15,140 | 2,120 | 17,260 | 4.24 | 407,400 | 20.0 | 512,500 | 20.5 | 1,080,000 | 24.0 |
| Anglicans | 10,500 | 3.5 | 158,000 | 9.1 | 6,737 | −787 | 5,950 | 3.28 | 181,300 | 8.9 | 217,500 | 8.7 | 337,500 | 7.5 |
| Roman Catholics | 900 | 0.3 | 83,700 | 4.8 | 3,709 | 421 | 4,130 | 4.14 | 99,800 | 4.9 | 125,000 | 5.0 | 247,500 | 5.5 |
| Marginal Protestants | 0 | 0.0 | 3,500 | 0.2 | 160 | 10 | 170 | 3.95 | 4,300 | 0.2 | 5,200 | 0.2 | 10,000 | 0.3 |
| Tribal religionists | 240,300 | 80.1 | 535,300 | 30.7 | 22,795 | −2,515 | 20,280 | 3.31 | 613,400 | 30.1 | 738,100 | 29.5 | 1,186,000 | 26.3 |
| Hindus | 0 | 0.0 | 3,500 | 0.2 | 156 | −6 | 150 | 3.57 | 4,200 | 0.2 | 5,000 | 0.2 | 9,000 | 0.2 |
| Non-religious | 0 | 0.0 | 2,500 | 0.1 | 119 | 21 | 140 | 4.38 | 3,200 | 0.2 | 3,900 | 0.2 | 12,000 | 0.3 |
| Other religionists | 0 | 0.0 | 2,000 | 0.1 | 93 | 7 | 100 | 4.00 | 2,500 | 0.1 | 3,000 | 0.1 | 8,000 | 0.2 |
| Country's population | 300,000 | 100.0 | 1,743,000 | 100.0 | 75,700 | 0 | 75,700 | 3.72 | 2,037,000 | 100.0 | 2,500,000 | 100.0 | 4,500,000 | 100.0 |

COLUMNS, ROWS. For meanings and definitions, see Code-book (Part 6). Note that, by definition, total 'Christians' = professing + crypto-Christians, which also = affiliated + nominal Christians. Percentages may not always total exactly, due to rounding.
CENSUSES. 6.V.1970: figures as in table above.

NOTES ON RELIGIONS
ANGLICANS. (1) The Church of the Province of South Africa (CPSA) has the diocese of St Johns, formed 1873, which is coterminous with the Transkei, and was the first Anglican diocese to appoint an African bishop. Membership: 83% Xhosa, 14% Sotho, 2% English, 1% Coloured, plus 100 Afrikaans-speaking. (2) The Church of England in South Africa (Church of Sobantu), unrelated to the CPSA, has work in Transkei also.
BLACK INDIGENOUS. There is a large number of Bantu separatist denominations, numbering well over 200. One of the best-known, begun in 1910, is Ibandla lika-Krestu (The Church of Christ; Bishop Limba's Church, ex-Methodist; Sigxabhayi; the National Church/iNkonzo we Siswe) with 120,000 members mostly Xhosa in the Transkei and outside. Other bodies, mostly

Xhosa in the Transkei, include: African Catholic Ch, African Gospel Ch, Assemblies of God (Back to God) (Bhengu), Bantu Methodist Ch, Bantu New Christian Catholic Apostolic Ch (54% Xhosa), Bantu Ngqika-Ntsikana Ch, Ch of Christ for the Union of the Bantu and Protection of Bantu Customs, Ethiopian Catholic Ch of SA, Ethiopian Ch of Christ, National Tembu Ch, Ntsikana Memorial Ch, Presbyterian Ch of Africa, Reformed Covenant Ch of Christ, St John's Mission, Zion Apostolic Ch of South Africa. Details of these churches may be found in South Africa's Table 2.
COUNTRY'S POPULATION. After 1975, there was increasingly heavy immigration as Xhosa old people and others considered economically useless by the South African government were forcibly removed from South African cities and resettled in the Transkei.
HINDUS. Indians, mostly traders.
MARGINAL PROTESTANTS. Jehovah's Witnesses, Mormons, Christian Scientists.
NON-RELIGIOUS. Whites.
PROTESTANTS. First mission station 1828. In the 1970 census, Protestant groupings (with total percentage of the population

professing adherence) were: Methodist 24.9%, Presbyterian 4.2%, Lutheran 1.4%, Dutch Reformed 1.1%, Congregationalist 0.9%, Apostolic Faith Mission 0.2%, others 0.3%. The total of about 40 Protestant denominations includes: Africa Evangelical Ch, Bantu Presbyterian Ch of SA (65% Xhosa), Baptist Union of SA, Christian Brethren, Dutch Reformed, Evangelical Ch (AEF), Free Ch of Scotland, International Ch of the Foursquare Gospel, Methodists, Moravians, Pentecostals (all varieties; about 100,000), Pilgrim Holiness (Wesleyan), Presbyterian Ch of SA, Salvation Army, Seventh-day Adventists, United Congregationalists. Total foreign missionaries at work: about 500. Details of these churches may be found in South Africa's Table 2.
ROMAN CATHOLICS. The Transkei is covered by the diocese of Umtata and part of the dioceses of Kokstad, Queenstown and Umzimkulu, although the boundaries rarely coincide with those of the Republic of the Transkei.
TRIBAL RELIGIONISTS. Traditional religion (animism) is still strong and widely-practised among the Xhosa, Pondo and Tembu.

NON-CHRISTIAN RELIGIONS. Traditional religion, animistic in form, is still extremely strong and is widely practised among the Xhosa, Pondo, Tembu and other tribes. Ancestral veneration and magical practices are emphasized, as well as belief in the supreme being Thixo (Xhosa).

Hinduism is present among Indians who are mostly traders in the towns.

CHRISTIANITY. The first Protestant mission station was begun in 1828, and Protestantism has grown steadily over the years. Anglican work centres on the diocese of St Johns, founded in 1873. Roman Catholics are found in the diocese of Umtata and parts of the dioceses of Kokstad and Umzimkula.

The fastest-growing churches are, however, the African indigenous or Bantu separatist churches, of which well over 200 exist in the Transkei.

CHURCH AND STATE. The whole history of the churches in the Transkei has taken in the context of law and church-state relations in the republic of South Africa, and this situation has been little changed since independence. Certain liberal denominations in the republic, however, denounced independence as meaningless, and in 1978 the regime banned the Methodist Church of South Africa because of its clergy's opposition, and its ties with the World Council of Churches. In consequence, a schism from the MCSA took place, replacing it with

the Methodist Church of the Transkei with government approval.

INTERDENOMINATIONAL ORGANIZATIONS. The Transkei Council of Churches has for some time operated as a sub-regional or local council affiliated to the South Africa Council of Churches, with the same membership.

BIBLIOGRAPHY
'A separatist church: Ibandla lika-Krestu', L. Mqotsi & N. Mkele, African studies, V, 2 (June, 1946), 124ff.
Bantu prophets in South Africa. B.G.M. Sundkler. London: Lutterworth, Oxford, 1948 and 1961. 381p.

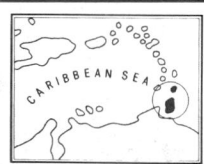

# TRINIDAD & TOBAGO

## SECULAR DATA

STATE. Official name: The Republic of Trinidad and Tobago.
Flag (shown above right): Red field crossed diagonally by white-bordered black stripe.
Area: 5,128 sq.km. (1,980 sq.miles). Agricultural land: 32.7%.
Government: Parliamentary republic, since 1976 (1498 Spanish possession, 1802 British crown colony of Trinidad, 1889 colony with Tobago, 1958–61 in West Indies Federation, 1962 Independence as parliamentary constitutional monarchy, 1976 republic).
Legislature: Parliament: Senate, 24 members; House of Representatives, 36 members.
Official language: English.
Capital: Port of Spain 67,870 (1970).
Armed forces (1976): Total 800 regular army. Paramilitary police force 2,600.

DEMOGRAPHY. Population: 945,210 (census of 7.IV.1970. For 1970–2000 (UN), see last row of Table 1). Population density (1975): 197/sq.km. (510/sq.mile). Under 15 years: 43%. Growth rate (1975–80): 1.03% per year (births 2.32%, deaths −0.58%, emigrants −0.71%). Life expectancy (1975–80): 70.8 years. Household size: 4.4 persons.
Major languages: English, Spanish, Hindi, Chinese, Portuguese, Arabic, Arawak.
Urban dwellers (1970): 50.3%. Urban growth rate (1950–70): 5.9% per year.
Labour force: 33%.
Tourists (1974): 324,740.

ETHNOLINGUISTIC GROUPS: 42.0% Black (African Negro), 36.5% East Indian (from North India), 16.3% Mulatto, 3.1% Chinese (30,000) (1.5% Cantonese, 1.5% Hakka), 1.9% White (16,000) (English, Spaniard, North American, French, Portuguese, German), 0.2% Syro-Lebanese (1,600), Jewish, Arawak.

MONEY (1977). Monetary unit: dollar (= 100 cents); US$1 = TT$2.40.

Continued opposite

Hindus. New Hindu temple in Port of Spain. Hindus in Trinidad are mostly East Indians and are 69% Sanatanists (idol-worshippers).

National income per person: US$1,400. Average annual family income: US$6,160.
Inflation: (1970–74) 12.2% per year, (1975) 17% per year (consumer price index 199).
Cost of living in capital (1976): index 97 (Washington DC=100). Daily cost of living: US$35.

HEALTH. Hospitals: 28 (5,839 beds). Doctors: 441. Lepers: 2,400 (2.4 per 1,000). Blind: 1,300. Psychotics: 8,000. Criminals: 16,210.

EDUCATION. Adult literacy: (1946) 74%, (1970) 92%. Education rate: 77%. Schools: 713 (601 primary, 112 secondary).

Universities: 1.

LITERATURE. Newspapers: 3 dailies, 2 non-daily.

COMMUNICATION (per 1,000 people). Phones: 63. Radios: 276. TV sets: 79. Daily newspaper circulation: 134 copies.

TABLE 1.    RELIGIOUS ADHERENTS IN TRINIDAD AND TOBAGO

| Year | 1900 | | mid-1970 | | Annual change, 1970–1980 | | | | mid-1975 | | mid-1980 | | 2000 | |
| Name | Adherents | % | Adherents | % | Natural | Conversion | Total | Rate | Adherents | % | Adherents | % | Adherents | % |
|---|---|---|---|---|---|---|---|---|---|---|---|---|---|---|
| **Christians** | 193,300 | 70.6 | 640,600 | 67.1 | 7,136 | −826 | 6,310 | 0.94 | 672,950 | 66.7 | 703,700 | 66.3 | 831,700 | 65.0 |
| professing | 193,300 | 70.6 | 640,600 | 67.1 | 7,136 | −826 | 6,310 | 0.94 | 672,950 | 66.7 | 703,700 | 66.3 | 831,700 | 65.0 |
| Roman Catholics | 89,200 | 32.6 | 339,700 | 35.6 | 3,820 | 230 | 4,050 | 1.12 | 360,200 | 35.7 | 380,200 | 35.8 | 467,200 | 36.5 |
| Spiritist Catholics | 13,700 | 5.0 | 19,100 | 20.0 | 214 | −4 | 210 | 1.04 | 20,200 | 2.0 | 21,200 | 2.0 | 12,800 | 1.0 |
| Anglicans | 74,900 | 27.4 | 172,600 | 18.1 | 1,862 | −1,322 | 540 | 0.31 | 175,750 | 17.4 | 178,000 | 16.8 | 181,700 | 14.2 |
| Protestants | 29,200 | 10.7 | 117,300 | 12.3 | 1,327 | 213 | 1,540 | 1.23 | 125,100 | 12.4 | 132,700 | 12.5 | 163,800 | 12.8 |
| Marginal Protestants | 0 | 0.0 | 6,000 | 0.6 | 69 | 31 | 100 | 1.54 | 6,500 | 0.6 | 7,000 | 0.7 | 10,200 | 0.8 |
| Black indigenous | 0 | 0.0 | 4,000 | 0.4 | 46 | 14 | 60 | 1.40 | 4,300 | 0.4 | 4,600 | 0.4 | 6,400 | 0.5 |
| Orthodox | 0 | 0.0 | 1,000 | 0.1 | 12 | 8 | 20 | 1.82 | 1,100 | 0.1 | 1,200 | 0.1 | 1,500 | 0.1 |
| nominal | 2,700 | 1.0 | 9,879 | 1.0 | 124 | 348 | 472 | 4.04 | 11,700 | 1.2 | 14,600 | 1.4 | 38,500 | 3.0 |
| affiliated | 190,600 | 69.6 | 630,721 | 66.0 | 7,012 | −1,174 | 5,838 | 0.88 | 661,250 | 65.5 | 689,100 | 64.9 | 793,200 | 62.0 |
| doubly-affiliated | 0 | 0.0 | −29,800 | −3.1 | −394 | −1,196 | −1,590 | 4.28 | −37,150 | −3.7 | −45,700 | −4.3 | −78,500 | −6.1 |
| total practising | 171,540 | 90 | 504,580 | 80 | 5,610 | −940 | 4,670 | 0.88 | 529,000 | 80 | 551,280 | 80 | 594,900 | 75 |
| non-practising | 19,060 | 10 | 126,140 | 20 | 1,402 | −234 | 1,168 | 0.88 | 132,250 | 20 | 137,820 | 20 | 198,300 | 25 |
| Roman Catholics | 88,700 | 32.4 | 363,000 | 38.0 | 4,119 | 1,001 | 5,120 | 1.32 | 388,400 | 38.5 | 414,200 | 39.0 | 512,000 | 40.0 |
| Catholic pentecostals | 0 | 0.0 | 0 | 0.0 | 85 | 1,415 | 1,500 | 18.75 | 8,000 | 0.8 | 15,000 | 1.4 | 70,000 | 5.5 |
| Anglicans | 73,100 | 26.7 | 150,000 | 15.7 | 1,594 | −1,724 | −130 | −0.09 | 150,300 | 14.9 | 148,700 | 14.0 | 137,000 | 10.7 |
| Protestants | 27,400 | 10.0 | 126,021 | 13.2 | 1,433 | 405 | 1,838 | 1.36 | 135,200 | 13.4 | 144,400 | 13.6 | 179,200 | 14.0 |
| Evangelicals | 25,000 | 9.1 | 95,000 | 9.9 | 1,080 | 360 | 1,440 | 1.41 | 101,900 | 10.1 | 109,400 | 10.3 | 139,500 | 10.9 |
| Black indigenous | 1,400 | 0.5 | 12,200 | 1.3 | 149 | 231 | 380 | 2.70 | 14,100 | 1.4 | 16,000 | 1.5 | 25,600 | 2.0 |
| Marginal Protestants | 0 | 0.0 | 5,200 | 0.5 | 64 | 96 | 160 | 2.67 | 6,000 | 0.6 | 6,800 | 0.7 | 12,800 | 1.0 |
| Orthodox | 0 | 0.0 | 4,100 | 0.4 | 47 | 13 | 60 | 1.36 | 4,400 | 0.4 | 4,700 | 0.4 | 5,100 | 0.4 |
| **Hindus** | 68,900 | 25.2 | 235,900 | 24.7 | 2,659 | 621 | 3,280 | 1.30 | 252,000 | 25.0 | 268,700 | 25.3 | 333,000 | 26.0 |
| **Muslims** | 10,450 | 3.8 | 60,200 | 6.3 | 685 | 195 | 880 | 1.36 | 64,600 | 6.4 | 69,000 | 6.5 | 90,000 | 7.0 |
| Ahmadis | 0 | 0.0 | 1,000 | 0.1 | 12 | 8 | 20 | 1.82 | 1,100 | 0.1 | 1,200 | 0.1 | 2,000 | 0.2 |
| **Baha'is** | 0 | 0.0 | 6,000 | 0.6 | 74 | 126 | 200 | 2.86 | 7,000 | 0.7 | 8,000 | 0.8 | 13,000 | 1.0 |
| **Afro-American spiritists** | 770 | 0.3 | 4,000 | 0.4 | 43 | −23 | 20 | 0.49 | 4,100 | 0.4 | 4,200 | 0.4 | 2,000 | 0.2 |
| **Chinese folk-religionists** | 200 | 0.1 | 4,000 | 0.4 | 40 | −80 | −40 | −1.05 | 3,800 | 0.4 | 3,600 | 0.3 | 3,000 | 0.2 |
| **Buddhists** | 180 | 0.1 | 2,000 | 0.2 | 21 | −21 | 0 | 0.00 | 2,000 | 0.2 | 2,000 | 0.2 | 2,000 | 0.1 |
| **Non-religious** | 0 | 0.0 | 1,000 | 0.1 | 12 | 8 | 20 | 1.82 | 1,100 | 0.1 | 1,200 | 0.1 | 4,000 | 0.3 |
| **Jews** | 0 | 0.0 | 300 | 0.0 | 20 | 0 | 20 | 5.00 | 400 | 0.0 | 500 | 0.0 | 1,000 | 0.1 |
| **Other religionists** | 0 | 0.0 | 1,000 | 0.1 | 10 | 0 | 10 | 0.95 | 1,050 | 0.1 | 1,100 | 0.1 | 1,300 | 0.1 |
| **Country's population** | 273,800 | 100.0 | 955,000 | 100.0 | 10,700 | 0 | 10,700 | 1.06 | 1,009,000 | 100.0 | 1,062,000 | 100.0 | 1,280,000 | 100.0 |

COLUMNS, ROWS. For meanings and definitions, see Codebook (Part 6). Note that, by definition, total 'Christians' = professing + crypto-Christians, which also = affiliated + nominal Christians. Percentages may not always total exactly, due to rounding.
CENSUSES. First census, 1851 (Trinidad only, population 68,600): 63.6% Roman Catholics, 23.7% Anglicans, 6.1% Protestants, 3.9% Hindus, 1.5% Muslims, 1.2% other non-Christians. 1891 (Trinidad & Tobago): 33.8% Roman Catholics 25.5% Hindus, 25.5% Anglicans, 10.9% Protestants, 4.0% Muslims, 0.2% Buddhists. 21.IV.1901: 32.6% Roman Catholics, 27.4% Anglicans, 25.2% Hindus, 3.8% Muslims, 0.2% non-religious, 0.1% Buddhists. 9.IV.1946: 34.5% Roman Catholics, 24.3% Anglicans, 22.7% Hindus, 11.9% Protestants (3.6% Presbyterians, 2.5% Wesleyan Methodists, 2.2% Baptists, 1.3% Moravians, 1.2% SDAs), 5.8% Muslims, 0.5% non-religious, 0.1% marginal Protestants, 0.1% Jews, 0.1% other religionists. 7.IV.1960: 36.2% Roman Catholics, 23.0% Hindus (15.8% Sanatanists, 0.1% Arya Samajists), 21.1% Anglicans, 12.6% Protestants (3.9% Presbyterians, 2.3% Methodists, 1.5% SDAs, 1.4% Baptists, 0.9% Moravians), 6.0% Muslims, 0.5% marginal Protestants, 0.5% non-religious, 0.4% Black indigenous (3,644 Spiritual Baptists), 0.1% Orthodox. 7.IV.1970: 35.6% Roman Catholics, 24.7% Hindus, 18.1% Anglicans, 12.3%

Protestants (4.2% Presbyterians, 1.8% SDAs, 1.7% Methodists, 0.7% Moravians), 6.3% Muslims, 3.0% others. In censuses, Baha'is are usually enumerated as Muslims or Hindus, or 'Others'.

NOTES ON RELIGIONS
AFRO-AMERICAN SPIRITISTS. Non-Christian adherents of Afro-Caribbean cults. There are numerous centres of Shango (Yoruba syncretism), led in the main by men only; also Obeah and other spirit-possession cults. In addition, there are numerous Rastafarians (from Jamaica), and young Blacks especially are joining.
AHMADIS. Begun 1950; Qadianis (world HQ Rabwah, Pakistan) Mission in Calcutta Settlement.
BAHA'IS. Rapid growth from 1 local spiritual assembly (1964) to 60 (1973). Many are East Indians, formerly Hindus or Muslims. From 1971 weekly radio programmes have been broadcast.
BLACK INDIGENOUS. In about 13 denominations in 1970 (see Table 2).
BUDDHISTS. Chinese.
CATHOLIC PENTECOSTALS (or, Catholic charismatics). Begun 1971 by 2 nuns. Totals (mid-1975); 4,000 involved adults (over 15 years old) in 55 prayer groups; total charismatic community including children, 8,000; (January 1977) over 4,000 adults in 120 prayer groups; over 7,000 attenders at second National

Rally, Port of Spain.
DOUBLY-AFFILIATED. The term covers those affiliated to, or claimed by, both the Roman Catholic Church and also the Anglican Church or a Protestant, marginal Protestant or indigenous church, i.e. persons who have recently changed their denominational allegiance without withdrawing from their original churches. Because their statistics represent a duplication, they are shown in the table as a negative quantity (with a minus sign).
HINDUS. Mostly Indians who are 69% Sanatanists (idol-worshippers) and 0.6% Arya Samajists. The Divine Light Mission is also at work; and 1 centre of ISKCON (Hare Krishna).
MUSLIMS. Indo-Pakistanis, with some Syro-Lebanese Arabs. There is also an Ahmadiya Mission (Qadianis; enumerated here under Muslims although declared non-Muslim by Pakistan). Mosques. Over 60.
NON-RELIGIOUS. Mainly Chinese youth who have abandoned their family religion.
OTHER RELIGIONISTS. Adherents of smaller religions and cults, including Rosicrucians (1 AMORC centre).
SPIRITIST CATHOLICS. Roman Catholics involved in organized spiritism and spirit-possession cults (Shango, Obeah, et alia).

TRINIDAD & TOBAGO

**NON-CHRISTIAN RELIGIONS. Hinduism** is the principal non-Christian religion in Trinidad and Tobago, followed by 22% of the population. Most Hindus belong to the Sanatan Dharma Maha-Sabha, other organizations being the Vighna Hindu Parishad, Kabir Panthi, Divine Life Society and Arya Prithindi Sabha.

**Islam** is the religion of 6% of the population. As with Hindus, Muslims are Indo-Pakistanis who came to work on the islands' plantations between 1845 and 1917. Four important Muslim organizations are the Anjuman Sunnatul Jamat Association, a Sunni group in San Fernando; the Islamic Missionaries Guild of the Caribbean and South America, in Port of Spain; Tackveeyatul Islamic Association; and the Trinidad Muslim League.

**Muslims.** Mosque on outskirts of Port of Spain. Muslims in Trinidad are Indo-Pakistanis and Arabs, who are Sunnis with some Ahmadis and others.

**Afro-American spiritism** is composed of several syncretistic religions based on African cults including the Yoruba cult of Shango, and has been evolved over the last 2 centuries.

## CHRISTIANITY

CATHOLIC CHURCH. The islands were discovered by Columbus in 1498. The first 2 Dominican missionaries, who arrived in Trinidad in 1513, were subsequently killed; but Carmelites, Capuchins and Jesuits soon followed, nominally under the jurisdiction of the vicariate of London. Spain offered free land grants in 1783 which attracted many non-Spanish settlers, especially French. Britain took over Trinidad in 1797, but the status of the church was little changed, and the government continued to subsidize clergy. In 1818 a vicariate was established at Trinidad which included British Guiana and the Antilles as far as Puerto Rico. In 1850 Port of Spain became an archdiocese, composed of the islands of Dominica, St Lucia, St Vincent, Barbados, Trinidad and Tobago, Grenada and the Grenadines. In 1968, a Trinidadian was appointed archbishop. Most of the clergy are members of European religious orders, especially from Ireland, with others from England and France. Catholicism is strongest in urban areas and among the Negro, White and mixed races; it has had little success among East Indians. The church has an overseas interest: some Trinidadian Holy Ghost priests are involved in missionary activity in the diocese of Concepción, Paraguay.

ANGLICAN CHURCH. Although the Anglican Church had become well established in the West Indies during the 18th century, by 1836 there was still only one clergyman in Trinidad. Missionaries of the SPG arrived that year, followed soon after by members of the CMS. Special attention was given to educational work among Negro freed slaves, and similar educational efforts were initiated for indentured workers arriving from India. In 1845 the colonial government divided Trinidad into 17 Anglican parishes and also began subsidizing Anglican clergy. When the Church of England was disestablished in the West Indies, Trinidad became an independent diocese, and it now belongs to the Church of the Province of the West Indies.

PROTESTANT CHURCHES. Moravian missionaries arrived in the islands in 1783, but the church has remained small in membership. British Methodists entered in 1795, devoting their attention primarily to the large Negro population. The 2 most important Protestant denominations today trace their history to Canadian missionary outreach. The Presbyterian Church in Trinidad and Grenada owes its origin principally to the initiative in 1868 of a Nova Scotian clergyman of the Canadian Presbyterian Church, who was concerned about conditions among the newly-arriving indentured workers from India. Schools were organized with financial help from plantation owners and later from government. This church, which is 95% East Indians, maintains a continuing close relationship with the United Church of Canada. The other important Canadian influence has been Pentecostal and has resulted in the establish-

ment of the Pentecostal Assemblies of the West Indies. Seventh-day Adventists and the Baptist Union also have a strong work in the islands. The latter was begun by the Baptist Missionary Society from Great Britain in 1815 and is now supported by Southern Baptists from the USA.

Christian Brethren, Nazarenes, New Testament Church of God, Open Bible Standard Churches and a number of smaller Protestant groups are also active.

INDIGENOUS CHURCHES. The main Black independent churches are the several different bodies of Spiritual Baptists, who came into existence around 1860. The influence of Blacks from the USA has also been strong and has resulted in the establishment of the African Methodist Episcopal Church, Church of God in Christ and the United Holy Church of America.

ORTHODOX CHURCHES. Orthodoxy is represented by the Greek and Ethiopian Orthodox churches, the latter with 16 congregations in 1970.

**CHURCH AND STATE.** Section 3 of the 1962 constitution identifies the state as religious: 'The People of Trinidad and Tobago have affirmed that the nation is founded on principles that acknowledge the supremacy of God, faith..., endowed by their Creator'.

There has not always been religious freedom for all churches, however. In 1917, the colony's Legislative Council passed the Shouters Prohibition Ordinance an attempt to end charismatic practices, prohibiting the Spiritual Baptists from holding worship services or funerals, or having buildings. In fact, this body of Christians merely went underground until they successfully forced the repeal of the legislation in 1949.

Article 1 of the constitution of 22 January 1974 now guarantees 'freedom of conscience, of expression and of assembly and association', and these guarantees are made even more explicit as related to freedom of religion in Article 9, including the freedom to change one's religion and to propagate it. Article 9 also makes provision for the establishment of confessional schools and the teaching of religion in them, provided that no one is required to receive such instruction against his will.

Several churches, specifically Catholics and Anglicans, receive subsidies from the government, an apparent relic of the Spanish days when clergy were paid by the state. As stated in the constitution, churches are allowed to operate private schools, provided these schools meet the physical and educational requirements of the government and are registered with the Ministry of Education. Religious instruction is permitted in both government and private schools. Buildings for churches and schools are exempt from taxation, but the property on which churches and schools are constructed is taxed. Churches are not required to register with the government; but if they wish to own property in the name of the church or denomination, they must be incorporated and consequently registered. There is no ministry in charge of religious affairs, although priests and ministers must receive permission from

**Anglican Church, Diocese of Trinidad & Tobago.** Bishop William James Hughes (1962-72) confirms new church members.

the Ministry of Home Affairs in order to perform marriages.

**INTERDENOMINATIONAL ORGANIZATIONS.** The Christian Council of Trinidad and Tobago (CCTT) was formed in 1966, including the large Roman Catholic and Anglican churches, as well as 9 other members and associated bodies. A Federal Council of Evangelical Churches of Trinidad and Tobago also exists, begun about 1940, now named the Trinidad and Tobago Council of Evangelical Churches. Indigenous bodies are united in the National Spiritual Baptist Council of Churches.

St Andrew's Theological College, formerly training Indians for the Presbyterian ministry, now offers interdenominational training for lay leadership, with several confessions represented on its staff. An ecumenically-sponsored programme is offered at Christ College to provide vocational training to boys in the area, and an Institute for Social and Religious Action is being set up in the Ecumenical Centre at the University of Trinidad.

Concerning relations between the various religions, the Inter-Religious Organisation of Trinidad and Tobago (IRO) was formed in 1970 and held its first elections in 1972. Full members are 10 Christian

**National Spiritual Baptist Council of Churches.** Begun about 1860. Spiritual Baptists are also nicknamed Shouters or Shakers, and were banned from 1917-51 under British rule. *Left.* New Spiritual Baptist church building in Gonzales, with foundation stone commemorating its laying by Prime Minister Eric Williams. *Right.* Spiritual Baptists in same church 'dancing, trumping and labouring for the Holy Ghost' counter-clockwise around centre post (centre of the world, 'axis to heaven'), seeking to be Spirit-possessed.

denominations (AMEC, Anglican, Catholic, Methodist, Salvation Army, Ethiopian Orthodox and 4 indigenous groups: West Indies Spiritual Baptist Churches, Mount Horeb Pentecostal Church, Unity Faith Healing Church, and National Spiritual Baptist Council of Churches), 5 Hindu bodies (Arya Prithindi Sabha, Divine Light Society, Kabir Panthi, Sanatan Dharma Maha-Sabha, Vishna Hindu Parishad), and 4 Muslim bodies (Anjuman Sunnar-ul-Jamaat Association, Islamic Missionary League, Tackveeyatul Islamic Association, Trinidad Muslim League). In 1976 the secretary was the Catholic archbishop of Port of Spain, a Trinidadian.

**BROADCASTING.** The government station GIO has Protestant programmes for 3 hours on Sundays and Catholic programmes for 30 minutes. A third of Protestant programmes are produced locally. The commercial station Radio Trinidad (Voice of the Caribbean) has Protestant programmes for one hour from Mondays to Saturdays and 2 hours 20 minutes on Sundays. Catholics get half an hour on Sundays only. Half of all Protestant programmes are produced locally. For Catholics, UNDA is represented by a national association.

## BIBLIOGRAPHY


'The acculturative process in Trinidadian Shango', G.E. Simpson, *Anthropological quarterly*, XXXVII (1964), 16–27.

'The Shango cult in Nigeria and in Trinidad', G.E. Simpson, *American Anthropologist*, LXIV, 2 (1963), 1204–1219.

'The Shango cult in Trinidad', G.E. Simpson, Caribbean Monograph Series No. 2 (Institute of Caribbean Studies, University of Puerto Rico), 1965.


TABLE 2. ORGANIZED CHURCHES AND DENOMINATIONS IN TRINIDAD & TOBAGO

| Official name 1 | Begun 2 | Type 3 | Counc 4 | Congs 5 | Adults 6 | Affiliated 7 | Names, notes, and other statistics (see Codebook) 8 |
|---|---|---|---|---|---|---|---|
| African Methodist Episcopal Church | | I Met | VwM.a | | 400 | 1,000 | Windward Is Annual Conference, 16th Episcopal District. M=AMEC(USA Blacks). |
| **Anglican Ch: D Trinidad & Tobago** | 1797 | A Hig | AwMRN | 80 | 29,000 | 150,000 | In CPWI. 80% Black, 10% White, 5% Indian (Asian). 27n,11x,P=61%,5r,3800Yy. |
| Assembly of God | 1946 | I pen | ..... | 5 | 400 | 1,000 | Indigenous pentecostal group begun by taxi driver at Piarco Village, Trinidad. |
| Baptist Union of Trinidad & Tobago | 1815 | P Bap | T.H.a | 25 | 6,000 | 10,000 | Begun by military settlers. 1962, M=SBC; BMS. 13n,6x,10f,G=3.7%pa,W=39Y,37%,250z. |
| **Catholic Church: M Port of Spain** | 1513 | R Lat | PzNMN | 60 | 207,000 | 363,000 | 4 suffragan dioceses elsewhere. C=3+1+6. 38n,100x,25m,280w,2H,28r,1s(14),9923Yy. |
| Christadelphian Ecclesias | | P Ade | x.... | 3 | 60 | 100 | *Christadelphian Bible Mission* (*CBM*). 3 ecclesias (churches) HQ Birmingham (UK). |
| Christian Brethren | c1915 | P CBr | x.... | 24 | 1,300 | 2,600 | *Plymouth Brethren. Gospel Halls. Open Brethren.* M=CMML(UK). 6f. |
| Christian Brethren (Exclusive) | | P EBr | x.... | 10 | 600 | 1,200 | *Exclusive* (Closed) *Plymouth Brethren.* Groups: Ames, Kelly-Continental. |
| Church of Christ, Scientist | | M Sci | x.... | 2 | 100 | 200 | *Christian Science.* M=CCS(Boston,USA). Port of Spain. 1m. |
| Church of God in Christ | | I pe3 | Z.... | | 50 | 200 | M=CoGiC(USA Black pentecostals). Small body loosely supported from Memphis (USA). |
| Church of God of Prophecy | 1954 | P Pe3 | Z.... | 8 | 500 | 1,000 | M=CGP(USA). Split in USA ex CoG (Cleveland). Holiness Pentecotals. |
| Church of God (Anderson) | 1906 | P Hol | x.H.L | 28 | 800 | 1,500 | *General Assembly of the CoG* (*T&T*). M=CoG(Anderson) (USA). 12n,2f,1s,W6=2%. |
| Church of Scotland | | P Ref | Rwc.a | 2 | 50 | 100 | M=CSM(UK), continuing separate from Presbyterian Ch in Trinidad & Grenada. |
| Church of the Nazarene | 1926 | P Hol | xFH.L | 24 | 758 | 3,500 | M=CoN(USA). HQ Port of Spain. 9n,6x,12m,17f,G=6.2%pa,1s(8),35t(3350),W=80%,88Y,56z. |
| Churches of Christ | | P Dis | x.... | 8 | 400 | 1,000 | M=CC(Non-Instrumental)( USA). In San Fernando, Papira. Rapidly growing. |
| Episcopal Orth Ch (Greek Communion) | c1920 | I Lib | x.... | | 500 | 1,000 | Black. Schism ex AOC(USA). HQ Bridgetown(Barbados), but founded first in Trinidad. |
| Ethiopian Orthodox Church:D Trinidad | c1970 | O Eth | Nwa.n | 16 | 3,000 | 4,000 | *EOC.* Under P Addis Ababa (Ethiopia). Blacks. Parallel missions in Jamaica, Guyana. |
| Evangelical Church of the West Indies | 1951 | P int | xM... | 20 | 500 | 1,000 | M=TEAM,WIM(USA). Radio station. Work began at Blanchisseuse (north coast). 22f,1s. |
| Greek Orthodox Church | | O Gre | Cw... | 1 | 50 | 100 | Congregation under Greek Orthodox Archdiocese of North and South America (USA). |
| Jehovah's Witnesses | 1912 | M Jeh | x.... | 40 | 2,305 | 5,000 | Branch 1921. Active witnessing by 1926; 1932 to Tobago (now 2 churches). 231Y. |
| Lutheran Church in America | 1964 | P Lut | LwM.N | 1 | 50 | 150 | Caribbean Synod. M=LCA(USA). 1964 arrival despite FCEC disapproval. 1m,2f. |
| Methodist Ch in Caribbean & Americas | 1795 | P Met | VwM.a | 30 | 4,728 | 9,000 | In MCCA, South Caribbean District. 3 Circuits. M=MMS(UK). 7n,1x,G=15%pa,IY,239y. |
| Moravian Church | 1783 | P Mor | xwM.a | 10 | 1,525 | 4,985 | Eastern WI Province. Decline from 6,320 in 1900, 7,152 in 1946. 2f,1u,W=46%,119Yy. |
| National Ev Spiritual Baptist Ch | c1860 | I pen | ....I | | 1,500 | 3,000 | *Shouters.* Banned 1917–51. Cathedral in Gonzales. Many former RCs and Anglicans. |
| New Testament Church of God | 1940 | P Pe3 | ZF... | 43 | 1,231 | 3,000 | M=CoG(Cleveland) (USA). 1956 joined by Christian General Assembly (1950). 28n,2f,1s. |
| Open Bible Standard Churches | 1953 | P Pe2 | ZF... | 66 | 5,000 | 7,000 | M=NPY(Norway). Mainly Tobago. Radio station. 14n,5x,7f,G=8.9%pa,1k,2p,1s,400Y,75z. |
| Orthodox Baptist Churches | | I Bap | ..... | | 1,500 | 2,000 | Independent Baptist congregations. Also in St Lucia. Mainly Blacks. |
| Pentecostal Assemblies of the WIndies | 1926 | P Pe2 | ZF... | 131 | 15,500 | 30,000 | M=PAoC (Canada). A=1953. Mainly Trinidad. 49n,3x,3f,G=5.3%pa,1s,W=60%,625Y,200z. |
| Presbyterian Ch in Trinidad & Grenada | 1968 | P Ref | RWM.a | 116 | 6,000 | 30,000 | M=PCC(Canada). 95% Hindi-speaking East Indians. San Fernando. 15n,4x,7w,7r,1u(6). |
| Salvation Army | 1901 | P Sal | xwM.a | | 200 | 400 | *SA*, *Trinidad Division*, Caribbean& CAmerica Terr (HQ Kingston). HQ Port of Spain. |
| Seventh-day Adventist Church | 1893 | P Adv | x.... | | 6,000 | 13,000 | *SDA*, South Caribbean Conference, Caribbean Union Conference. 1 plane. 1H,3h,5r,1s. |
| United Holy Church of America | c1960 | I pe3 | x.H.L | 8 | 500 | 1,000 | M=UHCA(USA) Black pentecostals. Spread from Barbados. HQ Laventille. One bishop. |
| Wesleyan Church | 1911 | P Hol | VFH.L | | 930 | 1,486 | M=Pilgrim Holiness Ch, now WC(USA). HQ St Joseph. 10n,G=1.8%pa,W=35%,61Y,23z. |
| West Indies Spiritual Baptist Churches | c1860 | I pen | ....I | 16 | 1,000 | 2,000 | *Shouters*, *Shakers*. Banned 1917–51. White robes, vestments, RC ritual, Obeah; bishop. |
| Other Protestant denominations | | P | ..... | | 2,000 | 5,000 | Total about 25 (see list below). |
| Other Black indigenous churches | | I | ..... | | 500 | 1,000 | Total about 10 (see list below). |
| Doubly-affiliated (duplication) (1970) | | | | | −13,600 | −29,800 | Protestants and others who also are, or were, baptized Anglicans or Roman Catholics. |
| **Total affiliated (mid-1970)** | | | | **1,120** | **288,337** | **630,721** | **Total denominations (1970) . . .** **67.** |
| **Total affiliated (mid-1975)** | | | | **1,170** | **302,200** | **661,250** | **Total denominations (1975) . . .** **69.** |
| **Total affiliated (mid-1980)** | | | | **1,220** | **314,900** | **689,100** | **Total denominations (1980) . . .** **71.** |

NOTES ON TABLE ABOVE

COLUMNS: for meanings and CODES (cols. 1, 3, 4, 8): see Codebook (Part 6). Column 1: **Boldface type** = church with over 10% of country's affiliated Christians.

NATIONAL COUNCILS (Column 4, 5th letter).

a = full or associate member of both CCTT and TTCEC.

I = National Spiritual Baptist Council of Churches.

L = Trinidad & Tobago Council of Evangelical Churches (TTCEC) (Trinidad and Tobago Evangelical Council of Churches; Federal Council of Evangelical Churches of Trinidad and Tobago, FCEC).

N = full member of Christian Council of Trinidad and Tobago (CCTT).

n = associate member of CCTT.

*Other national councils.* Ecumenical Commission of Tobago (Catholic Church, Salvation Army, et alia). Inter-Religious Organisation of Trinidad and Tobago (IRO) (members: 10 Christian denominations, 5 Hindu bodies, 4 Muslim bodies).

*Local councils.* Commission for Tobago Affairs (Anglican, Methodist, Moravian, RC, Salvation Army).

OTHER PROTESTANT DENOMINATIONS. Other smaller bodies include: Assemblies of God, Bethany Fellowship Missions (1970), Evangelical Orthodox Assembly of the Western Hemisphere, International Ch of the Foursquare Gospel, International Pentecostal Assemblies, Pentecostal Ch of God in Trinidad (PCG of America), Streams of Power, Trinidad Mennonite Mission (1971), United Ch of Canada Mission (1868), World-Wide Missions (1968).

OTHER BLACK INDIGENOUS CHURCHES. These include several other different varieties of Spiritual Baptists, also Mount Horeb Pentecostal Ch, Unity Faith Healing Ch, and others; the Ch of the Lord (Aladura) from Nigeria; and a few churches of 2 USA Black bodies: the American Catholic Ch, Archdiocese of New York; and Bible Way Churches of Our Lord Jesus Christ World Wide.

PEOPLES (ethnolinguistic). Christians: 59.0% Black, 22.0% Mulatto, 14.0% East Indian (Hindi- and English-speaking), 2.5% White (British, Spaniard, Portuguese, French, German, USA), 2.3% Chinese, Syro-Lebanese Arab.

COUNTRY-WIDE TOTALS

EVANGELIZATION (see Part 5). 1900: 95%. 1970: 100%. 1980: 100%. *Mass evangelism.* In 1975, the Evangelistic Association, Pentecostal Assemblies of the West Indies, held a 4-week crusade in San Fernando, resulting in 70 baptisms. *Radiophonic evangelism.* HCJB, TWR, ICI (300 active students) et alia.

FOREIGN MISSIONARIES AND PERSONNEL (nationals serving abroad) (1973). Total 85 in 13 countries: about 33 Roman Catholics (5 in Paraguay), 22 Anglicans, 18 Black indigenous, 12 Protestants.

FOREIGN MISSIONARIES AND PERSONNEL (aliens from abroad) (1973). Total 366. *From Western world.* 320: about 160 Roman Catholics, 143 Protestants (88 in 22 USA societies, 29 in 4 UK societies, 19 in 2 Canada societies, 7 in 1 Norway society), 17 Anglicans in 2 UK societies. *From Third World.* 46: about 30 Roman Catholics, 6 Protestants, 4 Anglicans, 4 Black indigenous from Jamaica et alia, 2 Orthodox from Ethiopia.

INSTITUTIONS (church-operated) (1973). Total 80, including 50 higher schools, about 12 medical centres (4 hospitals), 1 religious community, 9 seminaries (8 Protestant, 1 RC).

PERIODICALS. About 20 titles.

PERSONNEL. About 876 (510 national, 366 foreign).

RELIGIOUS LIBRARIES. About 10.

SCRIPTURE DISTRIBUTION (1975). Annual totals: 8,000 Bibles (13% free, 86% subsidized, 1% commercial), 42,700 NTs (85% free, 14% subsidized), 14,800 UBS portions, 145,100 UBS selections.

SERVICE AGENCIES. About 30, including CCJCA, CCTT, CEF, CEG, CFM, CLC, CTA, CTATT, CYO, FCEC, IRO, SCM, SPCK, SSF, TEC, YMCA, YWCA.

ADDITIONAL DATA ON CHURCHES

CATHOLIC CHURCH. Until 1974 the archdiocese had 8 suffragan sees in other nations: Bridgetown-Kingstown (Barbados, St Vincent), Castries (St Lucia), Georgetown (Guyana), Paramaribo (Surinam), Roseau (Dominica), St George's in Grenada, St John's in Antigua, Willemstad (Netherlands Antilles). In 1974, Castries became an archdiocese with as suffragans the 5th, 6th and 7th of these. *Catholics.* Including (1966) 15,000 Chinese. *Annual baptisms.* (1972) 79.8% infant, 20.2% adult. *Priests.* Nationals: 19 diocesan, 31 religious. Expatriates: 2 diocesan, 86 religious. *Brothers.* 15 nationals, 10 expatriates. *Sisters.* 200 nationals, 80 expatriates. *Foreign religious orders and congregations.* Priests: OP, CSSp, OSB. Brothers: Presentation Brothers (Ireland). Sisters: 65 Corpus Christi Carmelites, 42 Dominican Sisters of the Congregation of St Catherine of Siena, Sisters of St Joseph of Cluny, 28 Sisters of the Holy Faith of Dublin, 21 Second Order of St Dominic, 8 Sisters of the Sorrowful Mother.

*Catholic organizations.* The archdiocese is a member of the Antilles Episcopal Conference (AEC), with its headquarters in Kingston, Jamaica, and through it is a member of CELAM. Religious personnel are represented on the Conference of Major Superiors of the Antilles, which belongs to CLAR and also has its seat in Kingston. A Council of Priests for the archdiocese was formed in 1968.

Lay organizations for Catholic Action in 1970 included the following: Catholic Youth Organization (1,200 members), Catholic Teachers' Association (21,000), Catholic Evidence Guild, Christian Family Movement, Catholic Scouts and Guides, Legion of Mary, Society of St Vincent de Paul (460 members) and Children of Mary. The total 1970 membership of those involved in Catholic Action was 28,750 members.

The Holy See had no diplomatic relations with Trinidad and Tobago until these were set up in 1978. It is represented to government and the Catholic hierarchy by a pro-nuncio in Trinidad.

Catholic institutions in 1974 were: 134 elementary schools (68,800 pupils), 31 secondary schools (15,000), 1 teacher training college, 1 vocational school, 3 hospitals, 2 orphanages (about 70 children), 8 homes for the aged and invalids (240 residents), and 7 other charitable institutions (79 residents). The Catholic Church has also been involved in the establishment of credit unions and co-operatives.

METHODIST CHURCH IN THE CARIBBEAN AND THE AMERICAS. The church has declined from 11,000 members in the year 1900.

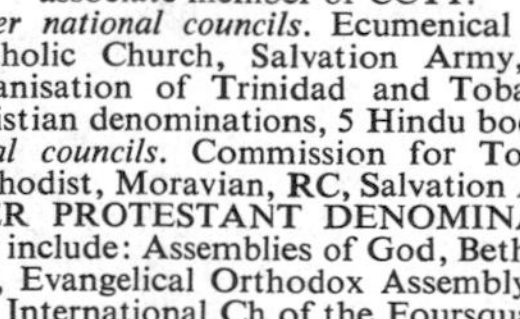

# TUNISIA

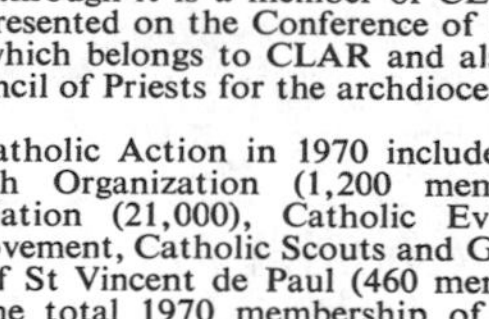

## SECULAR DATA

**STATE. Official name:** The Republic of Tunisia (Al-Jumhuriyah at-Tunisiyah). Adjective of nationality: Tunisian (tunisien).
**Flag** (shown above right): Red field with white circle containing red crescent and star.
**Area:** 163,610 sq.km. (63,378 sq.miles). Agricultural land: 46.5%.
**Government:** One-party republic, since 1957 (1574 Turkish province, 1883 French protectorate, 1956 Independence as monarchy, 1957 republic).
**Legislature:** National Assembly, 101 members.
**Official language:** Arabic.
**Chief cities:** capital Tunis 647,640 (1966), Sfax 215,840, Bizerta 95,020, Sousse 82,670.
**Political divisions:** 15 Governorates (gouvernorats).
**Armed forces** (1976): Total 20,000 regular (13,000 conscripts): army 16,000, navy 2,000, air force 2,000 (20 combat aircraft). Paramilitary forces: 9,000.

**DEMOGRAPHY. Population:** 4,533,351 (census of 3.V.1966. For 1970–2000 (UN), see last row of Table 1). Population density (1975): 35/sq.km (91/sq.mile). Under 15 years: 44%. Growth rate (1975–80): 2.65% per year (births 4.10%, deaths −1.26% emigrants −0.19%). Life expectancy (1975–80): 56.6 years. Household size: 5.1 persons.
**Major languages:** Arabic, French, Berber (Tmagourt-Sened-Jerba), Italian, Maltese.
**Urban dwellers** (1970): 43.5%. Urban growth rate (1950–70): 3.5% per year.
**Labour force:** 25%.

Tourists (1972): 780,350. (1974) 716,003.

**ETHNOLINGUISTIC GROUPS:** 95.5% Tunisian Arab, 2.4% Algerian Arab, 1.5% Oasis Berber, 0.2% French (12,000), 0.2% Maghreb Jewish (12,000), 0.1% Italian (5,000), 0.1% Maltese (4,000), Greek, Byelorussian, British, USA.

**MONEY** (1977). Monetary unit: Tunisian dinar (= 1,000 millimes); US$1 = TD 0.430.
**National income per person:** US$607. Average annual family income: US$3,096.
**Inflation:** (1970–74) 4.2% per year, (1975) 10% per year (consumer price index 136); (1977) 35%.
**Cost of living in capital** (1976): index 141 (Washington DC=100). Daily cost of living: US$35.

**HEALTH.** Hospitals: 90 (12,721 beds). Doctors: 1,004. Lepers: 9,000 (1.6 per 1,000). Blind: 25,000. Psychotics: 50,000. Criminals: 37,808.

**EDUCATION.** Adult literacy: (1956) 16%, (1975) 38%. Education rate: 44%. Schools: 2,214. Universities: 1.

**LITERATURE.** Annual new book titles (1971): 82. Periodicals: 60. Scientific journals: 15. Newspapers: 4 dailies, 6 non-daily.

**COMMUNICATION** (per 1,000 people). Phones: 18. Radios: 74. TV sets: 15. Daily newspaper circulation: 28 copies.

### TABLE 1.    RELIGIOUS ADHERENTS IN TUNISIA

| Year | 1900 | | mid-1970 | | Annual change, 1970–1980 | | | | mid-1975 | | mid-1980 | | 2000 | |
|---|---|---|---|---|---|---|---|---|---|---|---|---|---|---|
| Name | Adherents | % | Adherents | % | Natural | Conversion | Total | Rate | Adherents | % | Adherents | % | Adherents | % |
| Muslims | 1,399,900 | 87.5 | 5,087,320 | 99.0 | 143,664 | −84 | 143,580 | 2.52 | 5,703,720 | 99.2 | 6,523,120 | 99.4 | 10,806,000 | 99.6 |
| **Christians** | **120,000** | **7.5** | **33,280** | **0.6** | **−1,094** | **42** | **−1,052** | **−3.82** | **27,520** | **0.5** | **22,760** | **0.3** | **27,000** | **0.2** |
| crypto-Christians | 1,100 | 0.1 | 15,280 | 0.3 | −204 | 52 | −152 | −1.05 | 14,520 | 0.3 | 13,760 | 0.2 | 22,100 | 0.2 |
| professing | 119,000 | 7.4 | 18,000 | 0.3 | −890 | −10 | −900 | −6.92 | 13,000 | 0.2 | 9,000 | 0.1 | 4,900 | 0.0 |
| Roman Catholics | 119,000 | 7.4 | 17,400 | 0.3 | −890 | −10 | −900 | −7.26 | 12,400 | 0.2 | 8,400 | 0.1 | 4,000 | 0.0 |
| Protestants | 0 | 0.0 | 400 | 0.0 | 0 | 0 | 0 | 0.00 | 400 | 0.0 | 400 | 0.0 | 600 | 0.0 |
| Orthodox | 0 | 0.0 | 200 | 0.0 | 0 | 0 | 0 | 0.00 | 200 | 0.0 | 200 | 0.0 | 300 | 0.0 |
| affiliated | 120,100 | 7.5 | 33,280 | 0.6 | −1,094 | 42 | −1,052 | −3.82 | 27,520 | 0.5 | 22,760 | 0.3 | 27,000 | 0.2 |
| total practising | 96,080 | 80 | 23,300 | 70 | −766 | 29 | −737 | −3.83 | 19,260 | 70 | 15,930 | 70 | 16,200 | 60 |
| non-practising | 24,020 | 20 | 9,980 | 30 | −328 | 13 | −315 | −3.81 | 8,260 | 30 | 6,830 | 30 | 10,800 | 40 |
| Roman Catholics | 120,000 | 7.5 | 25,000 | 0.5 | −1,035 | 5 | −1,300 | −7.22 | 18,000 | 0.3 | 12,000 | 0.2 | 5,000 | 0.0 |
| Arab indigenous | 0 | 0.0 | 7,100 | 0.1 | 206 | 34 | 240 | 2.89 | 8,300 | 0.1 | 9,500 | 0.1 | 20,000 | 0.2 |
| Protestants | 50 | 0.0 | 630 | 0.0 | 4 | 2 | 6 | 0.91 | 660 | 0.0 | 690 | 0.0 | 1,000 | 0.0 |
| Evangelicals | 20 | 0.0 | 350 | 0.0 | 2 | 2 | 4 | 1.08 | 370 | 0.0 | 390 | 0.0 | 600 | 0.0 |
| Orthodox | 0 | 0.0 | 250 | 0.0 | 0 | 0 | 0 | 0.00 | 250 | 0.0 | 250 | 0.0 | 300 | 0.0 |
| Anglicans | 50 | 0.0 | 150 | 0.0 | 0 | 0 | 0 | 0.00 | 150 | 0.0 | 150 | 0.0 | 200 | 0.0 |
| Marginal Protestants | 0 | 0.0 | 150 | 0.0 | 1 | 1 | 2 | 1.25 | 160 | 0.0 | 170 | 0.0 | 500 | 0.0 |
| Jews | 80,000 | 5.0 | 12,000 | 0.2 | −300 | 0 | −300 | −2.86 | 10,500 | 0.2 | 9,000 | 0.1 | 5,000 | 0.0 |
| Non-religious | 0 | 0.0 | 3,000 | 0.1 | 87 | 13 | 100 | 2.86 | 3,500 | 0.1 | 4,000 | 0.1 | 10,000 | 0.1 |
| Atheists | 0 | 0.0 | 1,000 | 0.0 | 32 | 28 | 60 | 4.62 | 1,300 | 0.0 | 1,600 | 0.0 | 4,000 | 0.0 |
| Baha'is | 0 | 0.0 | 400 | 0.0 | 11 | 1 | 12 | 2.61 | 460 | 0.0 | 520 | 0.0 | 1,000 | 0.0 |
| **Country's population** | **1,600,000** | **100.0** | **5,137,000** | **100.0** | **142,400** | **0** | **142,400** | **2.48** | **5,747,000** | **100.0** | **6,561,000** | **100.0** | **10,853,000** | **100.0** |

**COLUMNS, ROWS.** For meanings and definitions, see Code-book (Part 6). Note that, by definition, total 'Christians' = professing + crypto-Christians, which also = affiliated + nominal Christians. Percentages may not always total exactly, due to rounding.
**CENSUSES. 1.XI.1946:** 90.4% Muslims, 7.4% Christians & others, 2.2% Jews. **1.II.1956:** 92.1% Muslims, 6.4% Christians (250,000), 1.5% Jews (57,792 persons).

### NOTES ON RELIGIONS
**ARAB INDIGENOUS.** Mostly isolated radio believers (see Table 2).
**ATHEISTS.** Tunisian Communist Party (TCP) (banned 1963; pro-Soviet): membership (1970) 100. Also, up to 1,000 communist technicians from Communist nations including China are at work in Tunisia. There have been in addition numerous atheists among the French and Italian communities.
**BAHA'IS.** Growth from 1 local spiritual assembly (1964) to 3 (1973).
**CHRISTIANS.** Declining annually by emigration of Catholics, also of individuals and families from most other Christian bodies.
**CRYPTO-CHRISTIANS.** Christians unrecognized by the state and society, mainly Arabs (Tunisian and expatriate church members, and Tunisian isolated radio believers).
**JEWS.** Maghreb Jews, declining rapidly due to emigration to Israel and France. In 1956, there were 57,840 Tunisian Jews; from 1956–70, some 100,000 Jews (French, Italian and others as well as Tunisian) left Tunisia, with only 10% remaining.
**MUSLIMS.** Mainly Sunnis (of the Malikite rite), with an Ibadi (Kharijite) minority of 40,000 on Djerba island; Arabs (Tunisian and expatriate), also Berbers. *Hajj pilgrims to Mecca.* (1970) 4,407; (1974) 10,785; (1975) 7,673; (1976) 7,538. *Surveys.* University students' self-description: 10% very religious, 45% rather religious, 31% slightly religious, 13% not religious; 42% practise fast of Ramadan strictly, 17% most of time, 12% when required to, 26% rarely, 1% never. *Missionaries.* There are a number of Egyptians sent by Al-Azhar University (Cairo).
**NON-RELIGIOUS.** French.
**ROMAN CATHOLICS.** In the year 1900, all Italians and other Europeans, except 350 indigenous Tunisian (Arab) Catholics. In 1970, French, Italians, Maltese. Baptized Catholics have declined drastically by emigration recently, from 280,000 (1954) to 70,000 (1959), 25,000 (1970), and to 20,000 (1973).

### NON-CHRISTIAN RELIGIONS.
**Islam** is the official and preponderant religion of the country. Muslims are principally Sunnis of the Malikite rite. A Kharijite minority is found on the island of Djerba. Kairouan, a holy city and place of pilgrimage, is famous as an Islamic centre.

**Judaism** has declined massively in numbers over the past 15 years. Between 1965 and 1968 more than 50,000 Tunisian Jews departed from the country, leaving only a small Jewish remnant.

### CHRISTIANITY
**CATHOLIC CHURCH.** Christianity was implanted near the end of the 1st century and suffered the first of many persecutions in AD 180. In the 4th century the church was rent by the Donatist schism, and 3 centuries later Islam swept across North Africa. Nevertheless, although the loss of Christians to Islam and by emigration to Europe was enormous, the church continued to exist for another 300 years. The last contacts between the Roman pope and a bishop of Carthage took place in 1076. A new venture was launched by Franciscans and Dominicans in Tunis in the early part of the 13th century and by Capuchins and Lazarists in the 17th century. A prefecture was erected in 1650 which became a vicariate in 1843, Catholic membership consisting almost entirely of foreigners. The archbishop of Carthage was re-established in 1884 under cardinal Lavigerie, served by White Fathers, but Independence in 1957 brought about a mass exodus of Europeans (from 280,000 in 1954 to 25,000 in 1970) and consequent diminution of Catholic influence.

Catholics are an ethnically and socially heterogeneous community, consisting mostly of French expatriates. The Catholic Church was served in 1970 by 83 expatriate priests (all White Fathers), 21 brothers and 350 sisters. There are no indigenous priests or religious personnel.

**OTHER CHURCHES.** Through the Church's Ministry among the Jews, Anglicans began work in Tunis as early as 1829; but the first Protestants, the North Africa Mission, did not arrive until 1881. The latter began an extensive and popular Bible correspondence course in 1962 which reached 20,000 Muslims before being banned by government. The course office has now been transferred to Marseilles, France; but the NAM continues to work in Tunisia as well.

Three North American missions entered prior to World War I, namely Adventists, Methodists and Pentecostals; and French Reformed and Brethren congregations have also been formed to serve the expatriate community. Methodists carry on some kindergarten and youth camp activities; but the Protestant churches all remain small, having a limited influence both in numbers and in social work. Greek and Russian Orthodox also have organized congregations in Tunisia.

**CHURCH AND STATE.** The constitution of the Tunisian republic (1 June 1959) proclaims that Islam is the state religion (Article 1), stipulates that the chief of state must be a Muslim (Article 37), guarantees freedom of conscience and protects the free exercise of worship.

Since national Independence, modernizing tendencies at the heart of Tunisian Islam as represented by the intelligentsia and the Neo-Dastur party are gaining ground over against traditional groups associated with the mosques and the Al-Zituna University. The Code of Personal Status, proclaimed by government on 13 August 1956 contributes to the improvement of the status of women by guaranteeing the juridical equality of both spouses, although this new interpretation of Islamic law has not been accepted by certain Islamic religious groups. The educational measures of 1958 integrated all secondary schools and post-secondary studies at Al-Zituna into a single system of state education.

The juridical situation of the Catholic Church, the principal Christian confession in Tunisia, is regulated by the modus vivendi concluded on 10 July 1964 between the Tunisian government and the Holy See. According to the terms of this agreement, the Catholic Church is given juridical personality, and a Catholic pro-nuncio is nominated by the Holy See after secret consultation with the Tunisian government. The church ceded to the government, without request for compensation, all but 5 of its places of worship and all but one of its landed properties. Educational and medical institutions belonging to the various religious associations or societies are authorized to exercise their activities. Established chapels in these institut-

**Muslims.** Great Mosque in Kairouan, a renowned holy city and pilgrimage centre.

ions and certain private homes (if they have received authorization), may serve as places of worship. In case of need, the government may also assign other places for Catholic worship.

Since this agreement, the government interprets it in a liberal way. It also shows an attitude of tolerant neutrality with regard to other Christian confessions in the country. The Ministry of Foreign Affairs (Wizarat al-Umuri al-Kharjiya) is responsible for all questions relating to Christianity.

**INTERDENOMINATIONAL ORGANIZATIONS.** An Inter-Church Council composed of Anglican, Greek Orthodox, Russian Orthodox, Methodist and Reformed Churches was organized in 1964. A Catholic priest participates in its programme of social service and aid to refugees. In similar vein, a Protestant pastor serves on the Catholic Pastoral Council. The Service Oecuménique en Tunisie operates the Association pour le Développement et l'Animation Rurale (ASDEAR) based in Tunis.

With regard to interreligious relations, an important Islamic-Christian colloquium was held in Tunisia in November 1974 on the initiative of the Centre for Studies and Economic and Social Research (Centre d'Etudes et de Recherches Economiques et Sociales) of the University of Tunisia and the Hammamet International Cultural Centre (Centre Culturel International de Hammamet).

**Eglise Méthodiste en Afrique du Nord.** Arab girl in Tunis explains Bible verse on blackboard.

**BROADCASTING.** No Christian broadcasting is permitted. Foreign Christian programmes in Arabic can however easily be heard on the international stations ELWA (Liberia), TWR (Monaco) for 4 hours a week, and Radio Vatican for 3 hours 30 minutes a week. Radio School of the Bible runs Bible correspondence courses from France, which are beamed into North Africa. The programmes are in French, English, and Arabic. Each month over 3,000 test papers are sent out, and about 2,000 are returned to be corrected.

**BIBLIOGRAPHY**

*Baal, Christ and Mohammed: religion and revolution in North Africa.* J.K. Cooley. New York: Holt, Rinehart & Winston, 1965. 369p.
*Ordo et annuaire de la prélature de Tunis pour l'année 1970.* Tunis: Prelature, 1970.

TABLE 2. ORGANIZED CHURCHES AND DENOMINATIONS IN TUNISIA

| Official name 1 | Begun 2 | Type 3 | Counc 4 | Congs 5 | Adults 6 | Affiliated 7 | Names, notes, and other statistics (see Codebook) 8 |
|---|---|---|---|---|---|---|---|
| Eglise Anglicane (D Egypt) | 1829 | A Cen | aw.UC | 1 | 100 | 150 | In Episcopal Ch in Jerusalem & Middle East. St George's Ch, Tunis. M=CMJ(UK). 1x. |
| **Eglise Catholique: PN Tunis** | 1219 | R Lat | bxSH. | 23 | 14,000 | 25,000 | *Catholic Ch.* Formerly AD Carthage. M=WF. Europeans. C=4+1+15. 83x,21m,350w,162Yy. |
| Eglise Méthodiste en Afrique du Nord | 1908 | P Met | Vw.NC | 1 | 20 | 30 | *Methodist Ch in North Africa.* In NA Annual Conference, related to UMC(USA). 4f. |
| Eglise Orthodoxe Grecque: D Carthage | | O Ara | Cw.NC | 3 | 100 | 200 | *St George*, Tunis. Under P Alexandria. Decline from 10,000 Greeks before 1959. |
| Eglise Orthodoxe Russe | 1917 | O Sla | ....C | 1 | 25 | 50 | *Ch of the Resurrection*, Tunis. White Russian exiles, independent of P Moscow. |
| Eglise Pentecôtiste | 1911 | P Pe3 | Z.... | 1 | 70 | 100 | 1947, M=CoG(Cleveland) (USA). Formerly, Assemblea di Dio (Italian Tunisians). |
| Eglise Réformée en Tunisie | | P Ref | ....C | 4 | 70 | 200 | *Reformed Ch in Tunisia.* Serves French Protestants in Tunis, Bizerta, Sfax. 1x. |
| **Eglises radiophoniques isolées** | | I rad | ..... | 160 | 3,400 | 6,900 | Isolated Arab believers, mostly aged 12–25. R=420,T=52000(NAM,ICI,GMU,&c). |
| Frères Larges | | I CBr | x.... | 2 | 100 | 200 | *Christian (Plymouth, Open) Brethren.* Fluctuating small indigenous fellowship. |
| Mission Adventiste du Septième Jour | 1905 | P Adv | x.... | 3 | 50 | 100 | *SDA. Seventh-day Adventists*, in North African Mission, Euro-Africa Division. |
| Mission d'Afrique du Nord | 1881 | P int | xMg.. | 2 | 50 | 100 | *NAM.* First and only Protestant Tunisians. Mail courses; banned 1963. 2x,11f,1j. |
| Témoins de Jéhovah | c1950 | M Jeh | x.... | 1 | 42 | 150 | *Jehovah's Witnesses.* Active witnessing under way by 1950. No baptisms in 1971. |
| Other Protestant denominations | | P | ..... | | 30 | 100 | Including Children of God International (USA, Europe: drug addict ministry). |
| **Total affiliated (mid-1970)** | | | | **212** | **18,057** | **33,280** | **Total denominations (1970) . . . 15.** |
| **Total affiliated (mid-1975)** | | | | **220** | **14,900** | **27,520** | **Total denominations (1975) . . . 15.** |
| **Total affiliated (mid-1980)** | | | | **240** | **12,300** | **22,760** | **Total denominations (1980) . . . 16.** |

**NOTES ON TABLE ABOVE**
COLUMNS: for meanings and CODES (cols. 1, 3, 4 8): see, Codebook (Part 6). Column 1: **Boldface type** = church with over 10% of country's affiliated Christians.
NATIONAL COUNCILS (Column 4, 5th letter).
C = Inter-Church Council of Tunisia.

**PEOPLES** (ethnolinguistic). Christians (1970): 41.0% Arab, 30.5% French, 15.0% Italian, 12.5% Maltese, 0.6% Greek, 0.2% Byelorussian, British, USA.

**COUNTRY-WIDE TOTALS**
EVANGELIZATION (see Part 5). 1900: 18%. 1970: 25%. 1980: 31%. *Radiophonic evangelism.* TWR (270 listeners' letters a year), RSB, ELWA, FEBA, Radio Vatican. Bible correspondence courses: 52,000 enrolments (30,000 NAM/RSB, 20,000 ICI, 2,000 GMU).
FOREIGN MISSIONARIES AND PERSONNEL (aliens from abroad) (1973). Total 462. *From Western world.* 450: about 420 Roman Catholics, 29 Protestants (15 in 2 USA societies, 9 in 1 UK society, 2 in 1 Sweden society, 2 in 1 Switzerland society, 1 in 1 France society), 1 Anglican in 1 UK society. *From Communist world.* About 2 Roman Catholics from Yugoslavia. *From Third World.* About 10: mostly Roman Catholic Arabs and 2 Protestants (Baptists).
INSTITUTIONS (church-operated) (1973). Total 40, including 16 higher schools, about 20 medical centres, 2 research centres.
PERIODICALS. 1 title.
PERSONNEL. About 487 (25 national, 462 foreign).
RELIGIOUS LIBRARIES. 2.
SCRIPTURE DISTRIBUTION (1975). Annual totals: 100 Bibles (20% free, 80% subsidized), 70 NTs (71% free, 29% subsidized), 10 UBS portions. *Translations completed.* Portion: 2 languages (in 1897, 1911).
SERVICE AGENCIES. About 18, including ACGF, ACGH, ACI, ACO, ASDEAR, BMJ, CCCS, UDCT.

**ADDITIONAL DATA ON CHURCHES**
EGLISE CATHOLIQUE. In Arabic, al-Kanissa al-Katholikia. The present jurisdiction was erected in 1884 as AD Carthage and became a prelature in 1964. *Catholics.* The total has declined drastically by repatriation of French and Italians, from 280,000 in 1954, to 70,000 in 1959, to 25,000 in 1970, and thereafter by around 3,000 less each year. *Annual baptisms.* (1972) 97.1% infant, 2.9% adult. *Priests.* 37 out of the 83 are in parish work. Average age of priests is 50–55 years. *Indigenous religious congregations.* None. *Foreign religious congregations.* Priests: WF. Brothers: FSC. Sisters: Missionaries of Our Lady of Africa (White Sisters), St Joseph of the Apparition.
*Catholic organizations.* The Episcopal Conference of North Africa (Conférence Episcopale d'Afrique du Nord) has its headquarters in Algiers. There is one association of female religious personnel, the Union des Congrégations Féminines en Tunisie (UDCT). A Pastoral Council has been formed consisting of 50% lay members, 30% priests and 20% religious personnel together with one Protestant pastor. The principal lay movements are: ACI, ACO, ACGF, ACGH, Légion de Marie and the university parish.

The Holy See has diplomatic relations with Tunisia and is represented to government and the Catholic hierarchy by a pro-nuncio based in Algiers.

The Catholic Church carries on an extensive educational, medical and cultural programme. In 1970, the schools of the prelature contained 12,000 pupils, mostly in primary schools and with some in professional training. By 1973 these had declined to 21 primary schools (6,736 pupils) and 16 secondary (2,845). In 1970 there were 100 students in apprenticeship centres and 220 in the school of agriculture at Thibar, which belongs to government but is directed by White Fathers. A total of 38 religious sisters work in Catholic medical institutions (one clinic and numerous dispensaries) while 42 others and 3 priests are active in state hospitals and social services. On the cultural level, the Institute of Arab Literature (Institut des Belles Lettres Arabes, IBLA), founded in 1928 by White Fathers, carries on scientific studies in Islam and specializes in dialogue and training missionaries destined for Muslim countries.

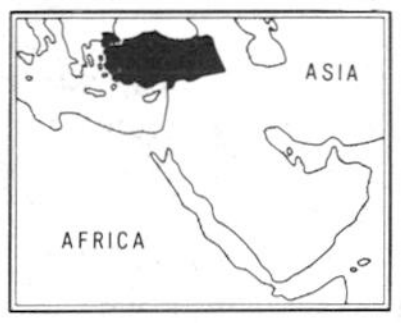


# TURKEY

## SECULAR DATA

**STATE. Official name:** The Republic of Turkey (Türkiye Cumhuriyeti). Adjectives of nationality: Turkish, a Turk.
**Flag** (shown above right): White star and crescent on red field.
**Area:** 780,576 sq. km. (301,382 sq. miles). Agricultural land: 71.1%.
**Government:** Parliamentary republic, since 1923 (1453 Turkish Ottoman Empire, 1923 republic, 1960 military junta, 1961 republic, 1980 military junta).
**Legislature:** Grand National Assembly: Senate, 185 members; National Assembly, 450 members.
**Official language:** Turkish (*Türkce*).
**Chief cities:** capital Ankara 1,553,900 (1973), Istanbul 3,135,350, Izmir 819,280, Bursa 426,570, Adana 383,050.
**Political divisions:** 67 Provinces (Il).
**Armed forces** (1976): Total 480,000 regular (257,000 conscripts): army 375,000, navy, 40,000, air force 45,000 (370 combat aircraft). Reserves: 825,000. Paramilitary forces: 75,000 gendarmerie.
**Foreign forces** (1973): 7,000 USA troops (10,000 including dependants; decline from 1966, 27,000 including dependants; and 1971, 15,000 including dependants). (1976) 1,200 USA troops.

**DEMOGRAPHY. Population:** 35,666,549 (census of 25.X.1970. For 1970–2000 (UN), see last row of Table 1). Population density (1975): 51/sq. km. (132/sq. mile.) Under 15 years: 41%. Growth rate (1975–80): 2.58% per year (births 3.81%, deaths –1.13%, emigrants –0.10%). Life expectancy (1975–80): 59.2 years. Household size: 5.1 persons.

**Major languages:** Turkish (spoken by 98%; Osmanli), Kurdish, Arabic, French, German, English, Turkoman, Circassian, Armenian, Greek, Georgian, Ladino, Chinese, Chaldean, Abkhazi, Laze and numerous others.

**Urban dwellers** (1970): 36.9%. Urban growth rate (1950–70): 4.7% per year.
**Labour force:** 45%. Over a million Turkish workers and dependants reside in Western Europe, mainly Germany.
**Refugees** (1977): From abroad, about 1,000.
**Tourists** (1974): 1,110,298.

**ETHNOLINGUISTIC GROUPS:** 90.0% Turkish, 6.9% Kurdish, 1.2% Arab, 0.3% Turkmen, 0.3% Armenian, 0.2% Circassian (Cherkess), 0.2% Greek, 0.2% Georgian, 0.1% Laze, 0.1% Bulgar, 0.1% Jewish, 0.1% Chinese (24,000), 0.1% Karapapakh, 0.1% Bosnian, 0.1% USA (military & civilian; 28,000 in 1970), Spanish Jew (Ladino) (9,100), Serbian (7,000), French (5,000), German (5,000), Italian (4,000), British, Assyrian, Gypsy, Tatar, Persian, Albanian, Spaniard, & a number of smaller peoples.

**MONEY** (1977). **Monetary unit:** Turkish lira (=100 kurus or piastres,=4,000 paras); US$1=TL 16.50.
**National income per person:** US$750. Average annual family income: US$3,825.
**Inflation:** (1970–74) 14.6% per year, (1975) 20% per year (consumer price index 265), (1978) 38% per year, (1979) 70% per year.
**Cost of living in capital** (1976): index 102 (Washington DC=100). Daily cost of living: US$34.

**HEALTH.** Hospitals: 768 (75,529 beds). Doctors: 17,365. Lepers: 30,000 (0.8 per 1,000). Blind: 38,178. Psychotics: 330,000.

Drug addicts: very few.

**EDUCATION.** Adult literacy: (1950) 32%, (1975) 60%. Education rate: 49%. Schools: 41,733 (39,268 primary, 2,465 secondary). Universities: 5.

**LITERATURE.** Annual new book titles (1973): 7,479. Periodicals: 1,301. Scientific journals: 90. Newspapers: 433 dailies, 645 non-daily.

**COMMUNICATION** (per 1,000 people). Phones: 22. Radios: 106. TV sets: 7. Daily newspaper circulation: 41 copies.

TABLE 1. RELIGIOUS ADHERENTS IN TURKEY

| Year | 1900 | | mid-1970 | | Annual change, 1970–1980 | | | | mid-1975 | | mid-1980 | | 2000 | |
|---|---|---|---|---|---|---|---|---|---|---|---|---|---|---|
| *Name* | *Adherents* | *%* | *Adherents* | *%* | *Natural* | *Conversion* | *Total* | *Rate* | *Adherents* | *%* | *Adherents* | *%* | *Adherents* | *%* |
| Muslims | 10,978,370 | 77.3 | 34,862,515 | 99.0 | 1,016,103 | −474 | 1,015,629 | 2.57 | 39,524,900 | 99.1 | 45,018,800 | 99.2 | 72,109,000 | 99.3 |
| **Christians** | **3,091,530** | **21.8** | **263,785** | **0.7** | **−1,953** | **−16** | **−1,969** | **−0.77** | **254,200** | **0.6** | **244,100** | **0.5** | **195,000** | **0.3** |
| crypto-Christians | 476,530 | 3.4 | 65,585 | 0.2 | 451 | 80 | 531 | 0.77 | 68,950 | 0.2 | 70,900 | 0.2 | 63,000 | 0.1 |
| professing | 2,615,000 | 18.4 | 198,200 | 0.6 | −2,404 | −96 | −2,500 | −1.35 | 185,250 | 0.5 | 173,200 | 0.4 | 132,000 | 0.2 |
| Orthodox | 2,500,000 | 17.6 | 145,000 | 0.4 | −2,900 | −100 | −3,000 | −2.31 | 130,000 | 0.3 | 130,000 | 0.3 | 55,000 | 0.1 |
| Roman Catholics | 60,000 | 0.4 | 29,900 | 0.1 | 900 | 10 | 910 | 2.68 | 34,000 | 0.1 | 39,000 | 0.1 | 60,000 | 0.1 |
| Protestants | 50,000 | 0.4 | 21,000 | 0.1 | −410 | 10 | −400 | −2.11 | 19,000 | 0.0 | 17,000 | 0.0 | 14,000 | 0.0 |
| Anglicans | 5,000 | 0.0 | 2,000 | 0.0 | 0 | 0 | 0 | 0.00 | 2,000 | 0.0 | 2,000 | 0.0 | 3,000 | 0.0 |
| Turkish indigenous | 0 | 0.0 | 300 | 0.0 | 6 | −16 | −10 | −4.00 | 250 | 0.0 | 200 | 0.0 | 0 | 0.0 |
| nominal | 1,000 | 0.0 | 10,000 | 0.0 | 390 | 10 | 400 | 3.33 | 12,000 | 0.0 | 14,000 | 0.0 | 20,000 | 0.0 |
| affiliated | 3,090,530 | 21.8 | 253,785 | 0.7 | −2,343 | −26 | −2,369 | −0.98 | 242,200 | 0.6 | 230,100 | 0.5 | 175,000 | 0.2 |
| total practising | 2,936,000 | *95* | 228,410 | *90* | −2,109 | −23 | −2,132 | −0.98 | 217,980 | *90* | 207,090 | *90* | 140,000 | *80* |
| non-practising | 154,530 | *5* | 25,380 | *10* | −234 | −3 | −237 | −0.98 | 24,220 | *10* | 23,010 | *10* | 35,000 | *20* |
| Orthodox | 2,950,000 | 20.8 | 193,500 | 0.5 | −3,050 | −100 | −3,150 | −1.77 | 178,000 | 0.4 | 162,000 | 0.3 | 80,000 | 0.1 |
| Protestants | 60,000 | 0.4 | 27,940 | 0.1 | −404 | 10 | −394 | −1.52 | 26,000 | 0.1 | 24,000 | 0.1 | 20,000 | 0.0 |
| Evangelicals | 45,000 | 0.3 | 10,300 | 0.0 | −149 | −1 | −150 | −1.56 | 9,600 | 0.0 | 8,800 | 0.0 | 7,000 | 0.0 |
| Roman Catholics | 74,500 | 0.5 | 26,937 | 0.1 | 1,004 | 2 | 1,006 | 3.14 | 32,000 | 0.1 | 37,000 | 0.1 | 60,000 | 0.1 |
| Turkish indigenous | 0 | 0.0 | 2,300 | 0.0 | 74 | 46 | 120 | 4.14 | 2,900 | 0.0 | 3,500 | 0.0 | 8,000 | 0.0 |
| Anglicans | 6,000 | 0.0 | 2,000 | 0.0 | 0 | 0 | 0 | 0.00 | 2,000 | 0.0 | 2,000 | 0.0 | 3,000 | 0.0 |
| Marginal Protestants | 30 | 0.0 | 1,108 | 0.0 | 33 | 16 | 49 | 3.78 | 1,300 | 0.0 | 1,600 | 0.0 | 4,000 | 0.0 |
| Jews | 80,000 | 0.6 | 37,000 | 0.1 | −3,000 | 0 | −3,000 | −13.64 | 22,000 | 0.1 | 7,000 | 0.0 | 1,000 | 0.0 |
| Non-religious | 0 | 0.0 | 30,000 | 0.1 | 1,016 | 984 | 2,000 | 5.00 | 40,000 | 0.1 | 50,000 | 0.1 | 200,000 | 0.3 |
| Shamanists | 50,000 | 0.4 | 15,000 | 0.0 | 356 | −556 | −200 | −1.43 | 14,000 | 0.0 | 13,000 | 0.0 | 10,000 | 0.0 |
| Atheists | 0 | 0.0 | 10,000 | 0.0 | 356 | 444 | 800 | 5.71 | 14,000 | 0.0 | 18,000 | 0.0 | 60,000 | 0.1 |
| Buddhists | 0 | 0.0 | 5,000 | 0.0 | 50 | −150 | −100 | −2.22 | 4,500 | 0.0 | 4,000 | 0.0 | 2,000 | 0.0 |
| Chinese folk-religionists | 0 | 0.0 | 5,000 | 0.0 | 60 | −260 | −200 | −5.00 | 4,000 | 0.0 | 3,000 | 0.0 | 1,000 | 0.0 |
| Baha'is | 100 | 0.0 | 3,700 | 0.0 | 112 | 28 | 140 | 3.18 | 4,400 | 0.0 | 5,100 | 0.0 | 10,000 | 0.0 |
| **Country's population** | **14,200,000** | **100.0** | **35,232,000** | **100.0** | **1,013,100** | **0** | **1,013,100** | **2.54** | **39,882,000** | **100.0** | **45,363,000** | **100.0** | **72,588,000** | **100.0** |

COLUMNS, ROWS. For meanings and definitions, see Codebook (Part 6). Note that, by definition, total 'Christians' = professing + crypto-Christians, which also = affiliated + nominal Christians. Percentages may not always total exactly, due to rounding.
CENSUSES. **21.X.1945:** 98.4% Muslims, 1.1% Christians (0.9% Orthodox, 0.1% Roman Catholics), 0.4% Jews, 0.1% other religionists. **23.X.1955:** 98.9% Muslims, 0.9% Christians, 0.2% Jews. **23.X.1960:** 99.0% Muslims, 0.79% Christians (0.64% Orthodox, 0.09% Roman Catholics, 0.06% Protestants), 0.16% Jews. **24.X.1965:** 99.2% Muslims, 0.68% Christians (0.5% Orthodox, 0.09% Roman Catholics, 0.07% Protestants), 0.12% Jews. These censuses have all included expatriates, both civilians and USA military personnel.

NOTES ON RELIGIONS
AFFILIATED PROTESTANTS. Mainly expatriate civilians and USA military. Protestants who are also Turkish citizens are found mainly in Istanbul, but with small communities of Syriac origin in Kurdish country in southeast Anatolia, and a few families in Iskenderun.
ANGLICANS. In 1865, an Armenian Apostolic archbishop at Gaziantep and congregations in 7 cities seceded to Anglicanism (Jerusalem Archbishopric). They were dispersed in the Armenian massacres of World War I, and today Anglicans are only expatriate UK and USA personnel.
ATHEISTS. Communist Party of Turkey (Türkiye Komünist Partisi, TKP) (illegal since 1925; pro-Soviet), also a Marxist group, the Turkish Workers' Party (TIS); membership (1970) 1,500, (1974) 2,000; Communist voters for TIS, (1965) 276,000, (1969) 244,000.
BAHA'IS. First entered Turkey before 1892. Recent growth from 12 local spiritual assemblies (1964) to 25 (1973).
CRYPTO-CHRISTIANS. Turkish subjects who prefer not to reveal their Christian affiliation in government censuses.
JEWS. Turkish Jews are almost all Sefardis, declining by emigration to Israel since 1948.
MUSLIMS. Almost all Sunnis (of the Hanafite rite), with a 15% Shia minority (including Alevis or Alawites in Cilicia) among the Kurds and in Izmir, Taurus, northeast and east; also some Yazidis around Diyarbakir, and several semi-Muslim shamanistic sects (Tahtacis, Ahl-el Hak) (here enumerated also with Muslims). *Mosques.* 43,000. *Hajj pilgrims to Mecca.* (1968) 41,998; (1969) 56,578; (1970) 13,269; (1971) 23,922; (1972) 27,235; (1973) 36,258; (1974) 106,045; (1975) 136,115; (1976) 137,291.
NOMINAL CHRISTIANS. Expatriate Catholics (from Italy, France) and Protestants (USA) who profess to be Christians in censuses but have not affiliated themselves to any church.
NON-RELIGIOUS. Europeans and many of the 25,000 Chinese (in 1975), but also including a growing number of Turkish intellectuals and others.
ORTHODOX. In 1900, there were 1,350,000 Greek Orthodox and 1,600,000 Armenian Apostolics. In 1915, the Turkish state attempted to deport the 1,750,000 Armenians; at least 600,000 were massacred and 600,000 deported, leaving 550,000 in Turkey, of whom the vast majority have subsequently emigrated. In 1923, 1,500,000 Greek Orthodox resident in Turkey (Anatolia and Thrace) including the 50,000 Karamanlis (Turkish-language Orthodox) were forcibly repatriated to Greece in exchange for 400,000 Muslim Turks resident in Greece. In 1965–75, steady and rapid emigration of Armenians, Syrians and (more rapidly) of Greeks was still taking place each year, at an average rate (for affiliated Orthodox) of 7,570 emigrants a year, offset by natural (biological) increase of 4,520 a year to give a nett decline including a few defections, of 3,150 a year (as shown above).
PROFESSING CHRISTIANS. The total relative to the population has declined by emigration from 1.1% in 1945 to 0.68% in 1965.
PROFESSING PROTESTANTS. The total includes (as do government censuses) a large number of expatriate English-speaking Protestants among the 2,600 British civilians, 12,300 USA civilians and their dependants, 7,000 USA military with about 5,000 dependants in 1971. The large USA military presence fell from 27,000 including dependants in 1966 to 15,000 in 1971 and to 10,000 in 1972.
ROMAN CATHOLICS. In 1970, largely expatriate Italians, French, Germans, et alia. In 1905 there were 58,500 Armenian Catholics alone, apart from Latin and other Eastern-rite Catholics.
SHAMANISTS. Traditional religions are still practised by a number of peoples resistant to Islam and Christianity.
TURKISH INDIGENOUS. In 5 denominations or groupings in 1970 (see Table 2). Only the Turkish Orthodox Church is recognized or acknowledged by the state.

**NON-CHRISTIAN RELIGIONS. Islam** came to Turkey at the end of the 10th century, and today Muslims form 99% of the entire population. The great majority are Sunnis of the Hanafite rite, as is also the official organization of Islam in Turkey. A minority of Shias (Alevis), especially among the Kurds, are dispersed in different regions of the country, but they are unorganized and, because government censuses do not count members of this rite, there are no accurate statistics. A few small sects such as the Tahtacis and Ahl-el Hak are separatists (semi-Muslim, semi-shamanistic), but it is difficult to determine their number, for officially they pass as Muslim. The efforts of Mustafa Kemal Ataturk to modernize Turkey after the fall of the Ottoman Empire led him to challenge the control exerted by Muslim religious leaders over political and public life in the country. Nevertheless, the reforms of those days seem to have had only a limited effect, particularly in rural areas. The rigid divorce of religion from the state began to ease after the death of Ataturk in 1938. Especially since 1950, the state has taken measures to relax its militant secularization, without renouncing its principle of the separation of civil and religious powers. Measures favourable to Islam, including multiplication of mosques, establishment of a more structured Islamic organization, re-introduction of Islamic education in primary schools in 1949 and in secondary schools in 1956 after being suppressed since before World War II, have all been inspired in part by the desire to provide a strong front in the face of atheistic Communism, in addition to the conviction that lack of religious education has favoured multiplication of sects and increase of superstitious practices. These measures have, however, not been considered adequate by some Islamic preachers of the extreme right. Education for Islamic teachers and imams has been undertaken by the Ankara Faculty of Theology (Ilâhiyat Fakültesi) and 5 higher institutes of Islamic studies (Yüksek Islâm Enstitüsü), particularly at Istanbul since 1959 and Konya since 1962, as well as by 114 schools for imams and preachers. Eight primary schools for imams were opened in 1949. All these establishments are under the Ministry of Education rather than the Presidency of Religious Affairs.

**Judaism** was already present at the beginning of the Christian era, as indicated by the communities in Asia Minor visited by the Apostle Paul. A new influx came from Spain following the anti-Jewish edict of 1492. Turkish Jews are almost all Sefardis, consisting of a community of 38,267 in 1965, whose number is diminishing because of emigration to Israel. In 1965, 30,700 lived in Istanbul and 4,030 in Smyrna (Izmir), with smaller groups in Ankara, Canakkale (ancient Troy), Bursa and elsewhere. All are under the jurisdiction of the Great Rabbi who resides at Istanbul.

**Shamanism** still prevails among a number of Turkish peoples who have been resistant to Islam and Christianity. In addition to ancestor veneration, emphasis is placed on an extensive pantheon of divinities headed by Yulgen (formerly called Tengri) who resides in the sky. Evil is centred in the figure of Erlik, Yulgen's arch-opponent.

**CHRISTIANITY.** In the first century the Apostle Paul brought the gospel to Asia Minor, transforming it into a centre for the establishment and dissemination of the Christian faith. According to tradition the Apostle Andrew preached in Byzantium in AD 38 and ordained Stachys as bishop there. Many of the early ecumenical councils important in the shaping of doctrine were held in present-day Turkey. When Constantine moved the capital of the Roman empire to Constantinople in AD 330, its patriarch achieved a new status; but the split between the western and eastern churches began to widen, resulting ultimately in the Great Schism of 1054. Muslim invasions weakened the Orthodox hold over the people, and the Crusades did more harm than good to the Christian cause in Asia Minor. Islam's influence continued to grow during the period of the Ottoman empire.

At the beginning of World War I, Christians still made up a sizeable force of over 20% of the country. In 1914, Roman Catholics had 4 archdioceses, 16 dioceses, 2 vicariates and 2 missions sui juris. Between 1915 and 1917, however, over 600,000 Armenians and many Chaldeans were massacred by Turks, and over 600,000 more Armenians were deported. The subsequent massive exodus of the survivors and their emigration to other countries, followed in 1923 after the treaty of Lausanne by the forced exchange of 1.5 million Greek Orthodox from Anatolia in Turkey for Turkish Muslims in Greece, and later by slow but steady emigration, have reduced the number of Christians to a small minority. Today what remains of Christianity is found in only a few centres, divided among numerous denominations and rites, the majority being Oriental Orthodox. The 2 principal centres for Christianity are Istanbul and the southeastern part of the country (Upper Mesopotamia), other islands of relative importance being Ankara and Izmir. In addition there are small dispersed and isolated groups, often with neither priest nor church; but their members tend to migrate to the cities, especially Istanbul.

A main reason for the diminution of Christians in recent years has been their emigration to Syria and Lebanon and as labourers to European countries, particularly West Germany. Some villages in the southeast, especially those of the Syrian Jacobites, diminished by half between 1965 and the end of 1973. This exodus is not a uniquely Christian phenomenon, but their small numbers make it most strongly felt among Christians. Conversions to Islam are rare, more rare than in such countries as Egypt, but the

**Muslims.** Istanbul is renowned for its mosques. *Above.* Hagia/Santa Sophia (left, built AD 531-7, now a museum). Blue Mosque (right), and others. *Below.* Blue Mosque (Sultanahmet Camii).

children of mixed marriages invariably become Muslim.

Christians are generally considered aliens in the country, even if this is an unconscious feeling and their families have lived in Turkey for centuries. This is especially true for Latin Catholics, the majority of whom are descendants of immigrant families. Oriental Christians resent the fact that national life is based on the Muslim community and is frequently identified with it. This discrimination, although a reality in daily life, does not exist as far as legislation is concerned, since the state is secular and does not judge its citizens by their beliefs.

ORTHODOX CHURCHES. Orthodoxy is represented by a wide variety of traditions in Turkey. The ecumenical patriarch of Constantinople, who has a unique position of honour in Eastern Orthodoxy although without power to interfere in the affairs of other churches, has his see in Istanbul. In AD 1000 the partiarchate had under it some 624 dioceses, but its jurisdiction has been radically reduced since then, especially since the Greco-Turkish war of 1922 and the more recent anti-Greek riot of September 1955 when 60 of the patriarchate's 80 churches in Istanbul were sacked. Today the patriarch has oversight in Turkey, Crete, Mount Athos, Finland and over Greeks of the dispersion, mostly in North America. In Turkey itself there exist the Holy Synod, and 4 metropolitans with 89 clergy. The overwhelming majority of the faithful are found in Istanbul. In 1972 the patriarchate was responsible for 53 schools with 3,160 students. The renowned theological college at Halki was closed by government order in 1974.

Other Eastern Orthodox, not directly under the ecumenical patriarch, are Greek Orthodox Arabs related to the patriarchate of Antioch, with 5 congregations in southern Turkey; Bulgarian Orthodox, with 2 churches and an exarch at Istanbul, and a parish at Edirne; Russian Orthodox with a church in Istanbul; and Serbian Orthodox under the patriarchate of Belgrade.

Non-Chalcedonian Oriental Orthodox are divided into Armenian and Syro-Jacobite communities, and form the largest single Christian tradition in Turkey.

The Armenian patriarchate of Constantinople, with its see at Istanbul, is dependent on the Catholicate of Echmiadzin in Soviet Armenia. The faithful are concentrated in Istanbul, where 35 of the patriarchate's 44 parishes are located, although there are also

churches in Ankara, Kastamonu, Kayseri, Malatya, Sivas, Diyarbakir and Iskenderun. Educational and social service institutions include 2 orphanages (270 children) in Istanbul and some 40 schools with 7,500 students. Syrian Orthodox are found mostly in the southeast, their 2 dioceses of Mardin and Midyat stretching along the Syrian border; there are also groups at Istanbul and Ankara which are growing at present due to migration from the rural southeast. These are administratively related to the diocese of Mardin, the latter having jurisdiction over the entire country with the exception of Midyat. The Syrians are dependent on the patriarchate of Antioch with its see in Damascus.

In 1922 an attempt was made by Turkish nationals under the ecumenical patriarch to establish an autocephalous Turkish Orthodox Church, with the strong support of Mustafa Kemal and the government of Turkey. The expectation that it would be joined by the 50,000 Karamanlis (Turkish-language Orthodox) was frustrated when the latter were all deported to Greece in 1923. The resulting schism has continued ever since, but with decreasing support and numbers, though a large following is claimed among emigres in the USA.

CATHOLIC CHURCH. Catholics are divided among several rites: Latin, Armenian, Chaldean, Syrian and Byzantine. Most Latin Catholics live in Istanbul, Ankara, Izmir and their suburbs. There is also a parish at Mersin and another at Iskenderun, both within the vicariate of Istanbul, in addition to the parishes of Trabzon (Trébizonde) and Sumsun, in the mission sui juris of the Black Sea, and a few isolated groups scattered in other parts of the country. The faithful in Istanbul are largely descendants of families who immigrated from the west in the distant past and are all Turkish citizens. Those at Ankara are for the most part foreigners who reside there temporarily as civil servants, technicians or professionals. The same holds true for a number of other Catholics scattered about the country isolated from the services of a priest. Several languages are used in the liturgy: Latin, French, Italian, German, English and Turkish.

Armenian Catholics are concentrated in Istanbul and its suburbs (6,000), with some 2,300 living in Ankara, Malatya, Sivas, Diyarbakir and in small groups or isolated families throughout the country. All clergy are centred in Istanbul.

Most of the Chaldeans live in the southeast near the Iraqi border, although there is also a sizeable Chaldean Catholic community in Istanbul.

Syrian Catholics are found in both Istanbul and the southeast at Mardin or in neighbouring villages. Their small numbers notwithstanding, Catholics

**Ecumenical Patriarchate of Constantinople.** Former Ecumenical Patriarch, His All-Holiness Athenagoras I, meets with Holy Synod (bishops, seated) in Cathedral of St George, Istanbul, in 1967.

of the Byzantine rite are divided between the apostolic exarchate of Istanbul, which includes 75 Greek Catholics directly under Rome, and the patriarchal vicariate of Istanbul, which counts 450 Melkites, some in Istanbul and others in the southeast. The latter are directly under the Greek-Melkite patriarch of Antioch.

There are also a few Maronites, mostly in the south together with some Bulgarians and Georgians. They have no local hierarchy, clergy or places of worship, but usually attend churches of other Catholic rites.

OTHER CHURCHES. British Anglicans and German Lutherans each have parishes at Istanbul, Ankara and Izmir which cater exclusively for their expatriate communities; while the large numbers of USA military personnel are served by North American military chaplaincies, as well as through the Churches of Christ and the Union Church of Istanbul. The Union of Armenian Evangelical Churches, founded by American Board missionaries in the middle of the last century and with 60,000 faithful before 1914, continues to lose members through emigration. Other ethnic minority denominations are the Bulgarian Congregational and Greek Evangelical churches. A number of North American bodies (Seventh-day Adventists, Southern Baptists, World-Wide Missions, Mormons, Jehovah's Witnesses) have been active but with indifferent success.

**CHURCH AND STATE.** In contrast to almost all other Islamic countries, Turkey, although having a Muslim population of 99%, is officially a secular state (Article 2 of the constitution of 1961). After proclaiming a republic in 1923, Ataturk abolished Islam as the state religion 5 years later, replaced Islamic law with European law, and introduced secularization in 1928 and had it legalized in the constitution in 1937.

Article 12 of the constitution of 1961, which was revised in 1971, states that all citizens are 'equal before the law, without distinction of language, race, sex, political opinion, philosophical belief, religion or worship'. Article 19 states that 'Everyone has freedom of conscience and opinion and religious faith. Religious prayers, rites, and ceremonies may be freely practised as long as they are not incompatible with public order or public morals or with laws promulgated to this effect. No one may be restrained from taking part in religious prayers, rites and ceremonies nor from declaring his religious beliefs and opinions. No one may be critized for his religious beliefs and opinions. Religious education is dependent on the desire of each person or legal representative in the case of minors. No one may exploit religion or religious sentiments or those things considered sacred by a religion, or abuse them in such a manner that they are used to exert personal or political influence on the social, economic, political or juridical order of the state. Those who contravene this interdiction or incite others to do so are liable to punishment before the law.' Finally, Article 20 guarantees freedom of thought and conviction, and freedom of 'diffusing them by written or spoken word, by pictures or other means'. Nevertheless, 163 of the Turkish criminal code states that proselytism is prohibited.

Despite the secular character of the Turkish state and the unstructured nature of Islam (which usually has no hierarchy nor organization comparable to that of Christian churches), supreme authority for Islam in Turkey has, since the abolition of the Caliphate on 3 March 1924, been vested in the Presidency or Office of Religious Affairs (Diyanet Isleri Baskanligi), which is attached directly to the Presidency of the Council with its seat at Ankara. Law 633 of 22 June 1965, which constitutes the latest reorganization of this body, lists its purpose as follows: 'To direct the affairs pertaining to the beliefs of the Muslim religion and to the foundations of worship and morals; to enlighten the population on the subject of religion and to administer places of worship' (Article 1). The supreme authority is the president of religious affairs (Diyanet Isleri Boskani) who is named and removed from office by the president of the Republic. Under him in each province or department (*vilayet*) is a mufti; these now number 67. At a still lower level, each ward (*ilce*) has a mufti of second rank (now numbering 572), under

**Greek Orthodox Patriarchate of Antioch, Diocese of Tarsus & Adana.** Orthodox Arab priest in his parish church in Antioch.

whom are imams for each locality in the district. The Presidency of Religious Affairs publishes numerous religious works, including 2 journals (a monthly and a weekly) both of which are called *Diyanet*. It also sends delegations of imams and teachers to other countries, especially Germany, to provide for the care of Turkish migrant workers. The salaries of such Muslim functionaries as muftis and imams are paid from the state budget.

Non-Muslim religious communities are not subject to the Presidency of Religious Affairs. Thus deprived of public or private juridical personality, they are reduced to 'juridically amorphous gatherings of individuals' with the old Ottoman millet system having been abolished for these communities, although not completely so for Muslims. Concerning Christian communities, a distinction is made between the churches of 'minorities', those consisting of Turkish citizens, and those falling under special conditions given to certain foreign institutions as defined in the 1923 Treaty of Lausanne, which paved the way for the independence of Turkey and abolished the so-called Capitulations. Freedom of action for the first group is guaranteed by Articles 38–44 of the Treaty of Lausanne. Local churches of minorities are subject in every way to the legislation of the country, and their clergy must be of Turkish nationality. In the eyes of the Turkish state, the most important of these minority churches, the Ecumenical Patriarchate of Constantinople (called by the Turkish Republic the 'Patriarchate of Istanbul'), is no more than a Turkish national institution whose jurisdiction extends over all Turkish citizens of the Greek Orthodox religion. It is subject to legal control and must limit itself to purely religious activities. For this reason its publishing house was suppressed in 1964, and the finances of the properties of the Monastery of St George (the patriarchate) are audited. The paradox of this sociologically Greek but legally Turkish patriarchate, whose patriarch and clergy are of Turkish nationality, is evident when one compares the attitude of both Turkey and Greece towards it. Turkey recognizes it only as having an exclusively religious character, uniquely at the national level, while a foreign power, Greece, refers to the same body in its own constitution.

As far as French, Italian and English religious, educational and medical institutions are concerned, their existence in Turkey in 1914 was officially recognized in letters annexed to the Treaty of Lausanne. Thus they may continue their work as at that time, although in actuality a large number no longer exist. Nevertheless, it is legal for those still active to have foreign priests, superiors and teachers.

Christian clergy are not paid by the state. They are usually provided for by their respective communities through the vakif or foundations administered by a committee of laymen of the community, under the supervision (sometimes interference) of the civil authorities. It is for this reason that clergy or pastors of Christian communities are not considered to be the heads of their communities by the civil authorities, who recognize instead the presidents of these committees of laymen.

According to Law 1778 of 25 March 1931, no foreigner may teach Turkish citizens in primary schools. Since that time all foreign schools (except those catering entirely for foreign students), including religious schools run by Western religious congregations, have been only at the college or secondary level.

**INTERDENOMINATIONAL ORGANIZATIONS.** No organization or structured group dedicated to ecumenical matters exists, with the exception of the Commission for Ecumenical Affairs of the Latin vicariate of Istanbul, which is official but largely inactive. A Library for Ecumenical Questions was created in 1969 by the Greek Catholic exarchate of Istanbul but was forced to close in 1973. An unofficial Protestant union of congregations also exists.

**BROADCASTING.** The government-owned Turkish Radio-Television Corporation permits no Christian broadcasting. There are no Christian recording studios either, and no Turkish Christians with the necessary competence. From abroad, however, Christian programmes in Turkish (prepared by Armenians) can be heard over the international station TWR (Monaco) which beams in programmes 6 times a week, and IBRA twice a week.

## BIBLIOGRAPHY


*A brief history of American Board schools in Turkey*. E.W. Putney, Istanbul: Nesriyat Dairesi, 1964. 11p.

'An autocephalous Turkish Orthodox Church', X. Jacob, *Eastern churches review*, III, 1 (1970), 59–71.

'Le giurisdizioni delle chiese cristiane sul territorio della Republica Turca', L.A. Missir, *Il diritto ecclesiastico*, LXXVIII, 3–4 (1967), 346–352.

'Lo statuto dei beni ecclesiastici in Turchia', L.A. Missir. Contribution à la XXXIX Semaine de Missiologie de Louvain, Namur, 24–28 août 1969, p.31–51.

'Religion and culture', chapter XII in B. Lewis, *The emergence of modern Turkey* (London: Oxford, 1961), p. 395–418 et seq.

*The development of secularism in Turkey*. N. Berkes. Montreal, 1964.


TABLE 2. ORGANIZED CHURCHES AND DENOMINATIONS IN TURKEY

| Official name 1 | Begun 2 | Type 3 | Counc 4 | Congs 5 | Adults 6 | Affiliated 7 | Names, notes, and other statistics (see Codebook) 8 |
|---|---|---|---|---|---|---|---|
| Ancient Church of the East (P Tehran) | 500 | O Nes | Yw••• | | 300 | 1,000 | *Nestorians*. Assyrian massacre remnants. A few families in southeast. No clergy. |
| **Armenian Apostolic P of Constantinople** | c 400 | O Arm | Ew••• | 44 | 47,000 | 80,000 | *Armeni Patrikhanesi*. 45 dioceses till 1915 massacres. 41n,1H,1s,W=10%,900Yy. |
| Baptist Church | | P Bap | T•••• | 1 | 60 | 100 | *Galatian Baptist Church*, Ankara. English-language. Expatriates, USA workers. 1x. |
| Bulgarian Congregational Church | c1900 | P Con | ••••• | 5 | 500 | 1,000 | *Soborna Congrezanska Crkva*. Bulgarians, now citizens, in west. Aid, M=CCCI(USA). |
| Bulgarian Orthodox Church: E Turkey | 1870 | O Sla | Mwc•• | 3 | 1,000 | 2,200 | *Bulgar Eksarhanesi*. Under P Sofia. Bulgarians in western Turkey, now citizens. 1n. |
| **Catholic Church in Turkey:** | 1198 | R LEr | O•••R | 71 | 15,790 | 26,937 | *Katolik Kilisesi*. Italians, French, &c. Growing. C=9+1+8. 25n,51x,56m,189w,575Yy. |
| M Izmir (Smyrna) (*Latin*) | 1322 | R Lat | Os | 12 | 1,600 | 2,650 | Latin metropolitan see 1322, 1818. 3 schools. 1H. 0 15 12 20 32 |
| AD Diarbekir (Amida) (*Chaldean*) | 1553 | R Cha | Os | 22 | 4,700 | 8,000 | In P Babylon. Destroyed 1918, restored 1966; growing. 6 0 0 0 475 |
| AD Istanbul (*Armenian*) | 1830 | R Arm | Os | 10 | 4,900 | 8,300 | *P Cilicia*. 14 dioceses destroyed 1915. 7 schools. 1H. 10 0 0 14 32 |
| D Mardin & Amida (*Syrian*) | 1888 | R Syr | Os | 4 | 700 | 1,300 | *Patriarchal Vicariate*, P Antioch. 1972 titular bishopric. 3 0 0 0 0 |
| EA Istanbul (*Byzantine*) | 1911 | R Byz | Os | 1 | 50 | 82 | Byzantine-rite Catholics across Turkey. Rapid decline. 1 0 0 0 0 |
| VA Istanbul (*Latin*) | 1742 | R Lat | Os | 20 | 3,500 | 6,000 | All aliens. 10,900 in 1955, decreasing. 17 schools. 5H. 4 34 43 155 36 |
| m Trabzon (*Latin*) | 1895 | R Lat | Os | 2 | 90 | 155 | Previously PA until 1896. 3 churches. M=OFMCap. 0 2 1 0 0 |
| VP Turkey (*Melkite*) | | R Mel | Os | | 250 | 450 | *Melkit Katolikler*. Rapid decline. HQ Istanbul. 1 0 0 0 0 |
| Christian Brethren | 1900 | P CBr | x•••• | 2 | 100 | 200 | *Plymouth Brethren. Open Brethren*. Initial work among Armenians. M=CMML(UK,USA). 4f. |
| Church of England (D Gibraltar) | 1598 | A plu | awc•• | 5 | 500 | 2,000 | 1865 Armenian Apostolic schism to Anglicanism. Now only UK, USA expatriates. 2x. |
| Ch of Jesus C of Latter-day Saints | 1884 | M LdS | x•••• | | 200 | 308 | *Mormons*. M=CJCLdS(Utah,USA). Former Armenian work; now mainly USA expatriates. |
| Churches of Christ | | P Dis | x•••• | 10 | 1,000 | 3,000 | M=CC(Non-Instrumental)(USA). USA personnel on military and air force bases. |

*Continued opposite*

*Table 2–continued*

| Official name 1 | Begun 2 | Type 3 | Counc 4 | Congs 5 | Adults 6 | Affiliated 7 | Names, notes, and other statistics (see Codebook) 8 |
|---|---|---|---|---|---|---|---|
| **Ecumenical Patr of Constantinople:** | c 38 | O Gre | CWC•• | 88 | 39,000 | 65,000 | *Rum Ortodoks Patrikhanesi.* 70% citizen Greeks; emigration 9%pa. 89n,P=95%,1s,W=30%. |
| AD Constantinople | | O Gre | Cp | 58 | 18,000 | 30,000 | Mostly Greeks. 8 auxiliary bishops, 35 pilgrimage centres. 58n,8d,6r. |
| D Chalcedon | | O Gre | Cm | 10 | 5,000 | 9,000 | Greeks. 1 auxiliary bishop. HQ Kadiköy. 7 schools, 6 welfare associations. 10n. |
| D Derkos | | O Gre | Cm | 5 | 4,000 | 6,000 | Bogaziçi. Bosphorus. Greeks. 2 welfare associations, 3 educational unions. 5n. |
| D Imbross & Tenedos (Bozcaada) | | O Gre | Cm | 11 | 8,000 | 14,000 | *Rum Ortodoks Imroz Metropoliti.* 2 islands in Dardanelles. HQ Imroz Adasi. 11n. |
| D Prinkipos (Prinkiponnisa) | | O Gre | Cm | 4 | 4,000 | 6,000 | *Rum Ortodoks Adalar Metropoliti.* HQ Büyükada, Istanbul. 2 welfare bodies. 5n. |
| Followers of Jesus | | I ind | ••••• | | 500 | 1,000 | *Jesusists.* Muslims who accept Jesus but reject name Christian. Around Gaziantep. |
| German Protestant Church | 1843 | P Lut | ••••• | 3 | 800 | 1,500 | *Deutsch Ev Gemeinde in der Turkei.* Germans in Istanbul, Izmir, Ankara. 1x,1H,8y. |
| Greek Evangelical Church | 1888 | P Ref | Rwc•C | 1 | 100 | 200 | Greek Protestants, related to main body in Greece. In Istanbul. 1n,W=40%,3y,4z. |
| Greek Orth P Ant: D Tarsus & Adana | c 33 | O Ara | Cw•N• | 5 | 1,200 | 2,000 | Arabic churches in southern Turkey: HQ Mersin; Antioch, Alexandretta. 2n,1H. |
| Isolated radio churches | c1960 | I rad | ••••• | | 100 | 200 | Isolated radio believers, mostly aged 12–25, scattered over country. T=1000(ICI). |
| Jehovah's Witnesses | 1933 | M Jeh | x•••• | 10 | 300 | 800 | Turkish converts from Islam. Istanbul, Ankara, southeast. Persecution. |
| Operation Mobilisation | 1963 | P ind | x•••• | 8 | 50 | 100 | M=OM(UK). Literature evangelism, small churches in Ankara et alia. Ship MV Logos. |
| Pentecostal Churches | | I pen | ••••• | | 100 | 300 | *Pentakostçu.* Turkish indigenous pentecostals. Underground. |
| Protestant Churches | | I Ref | ••••• | 5 | 300 | 500 | Immigrants in Tarsus-Antakya region. Origins with M=UPUSA and other missions. |
| Religious Society of Friends | 1957 | P Qua | Q•••• | 1 | 15 | 40 | Small Quaker meeting in Istanbul. Little connection with Quakers abroad. |
| Russian Orthodox Church | | O Sla | Mwc•• | 1 | 200 | 300 | *Russkaya Pravoslavnaya Tserkov.* One church in Istanbul. Russian emigres. 1x. |
| Serbian Orthodox Church | | O Ser | Cwc•• | | 2,000 | 3,000 | Under P Belgrade. Serbian immigrants and transients from Yugoslavia. |
| Seventh-day Adventist Church | 1889 | P Adv | x•••• | 5 | 100 | 200 | *SDA, Turkey Station*, East Mediterranean Field, Middle East Union. In Istanbul. |
| Southern Baptist Convention | 1966 | P Bap | T•••• | 1 | 55 | 100 | M=SBC(USA). In Ankara for brief time, with worship services. 2f,9Y. |
| **Syrian Orth Patriarchate of Antioch** | c 33 | O Syr | Dw•N• | 72 | 18,000 | 30,000 | *Süryani Kadim Kilisesi.* D Mardin, D Midyat. 65n,5d,1e(8),G=–4%pa,1900Yy. |
| Turkish Orthodox Church: P Istanbul | 1922 | I ReO | xv••• | 3 | 50 | 300 | *Müstakil Türk Ortodoks Kilisesi.* State-aided schism. 1954 applied to WCC. In USA. |
| Union Church of Istanbul | | P com | ••••C | 1 | 50 | 200 | Dutch chapel (in Netherlands embassy). English-speaking, interdenominational. |
| Union of Armenian Ev Chs in Near East | 1819 | P Con | Rw•NC | 4 | 220 | 800 | M=UCBWM. 1914, 60,000; 50% massacred. Emigration. 63f,G=–6%pa,1H,1h,1j,3r,3s,W=80%. |
| World-Wide Missions | 1961 | P ind | x•••• | | 250 | 500 | M=World-Wide Missions(USA). Evangelicals with links in Pasadena, CA (USA). |
| Other Protestant denominations | | P | ••••• | | 5,000 | 20,000 | Expatriates (USA, UK, German, Dutch), also NATO and USA military chaplaincies. |
| Other Orthodox churches | | O | ••••• | | 6,000 | 10,000 | Mainly Georgian Orthodox remnants (ex USSR) among the 60,000 Georgians. |
| **Total affiliated (mid-1970)** | | | | **610** | **140,840** | **253,785** | **Total denominations (1970) . . . 33.** |
| **Total affiliated (mid-1975)** | | | | **613** | **134,400** | **242,200** | **Total denominations (1975) . . . 34.** |
| **Total affiliated (mid-1980)** | | | | **616** | **127,700** | **230,100** | **Total denominations (1980) . . . 35.** |

NOTES ON TABLE ABOVE
COLUMNS: for meanings and CODES (cols. 1, 3, 4, 8): see Codebook (Part 6). Column 1: **Boldface type** = church with over 10% of country's affiliated Christians.
NATIONAL COUNCILS (Column 4, 5th letter).
C = Union of Evangelical Churches (UEC) (unofficial grouping of congregations and UCBWM in Istanbul; begun 1965).
R = Episcopal Conference of Turkey (begun 1978).
SUPPRESSED DIOCESES. During 1915–18, of the 1,750,000 Turkish Armenians, 600,000 were massacred and 600,000 deported, resulting in the destruction of 45 Armenian Apostolic dioceses and 14 Armenian Catholic ones. The Chaldean Catholic dioceses of Mardin and Siirt were also destroyed at the same time.
OTHER CATHOLIC (NON-ROMAN) CHURCHES. The New Apostolic Ch (Germany) maintains a small work, under the Wiesbaden Bezirk (District).

**PEOPLES** (ethnolinguistic). Christians: 35.1% Armenian, 25.3% Greek, 13.1% Arab, 9.0% USA, 3.5% Assyrian, 3.4% Latin European (French, Italian, Spaniard), 3.2% Turkish (8,200), 2.4% Georgian, 1.5% German, 1.2% Serbian, 1.2% Bulgar, 1.0% British, 0.1% Russian, Dutch, Albanian, Chinese.

COUNTRY-WIDE TOTALS
EVANGELIZATION (see Part 5). 1900: 46%, 1970: 20%, 1980: 26%. *Mass evangelism.* Mass literature distribution programmes: by Operation Mobilisation, and in 1969 by Plymouth Brethren. *Radiophonic evangelism.* TWR, HCJB, RSB, ICI et alia. Bible correspondence courses: begun 1965; 585 applicants in 1977.
FOREIGN MISSIONARIES AND PERSONNEL (nationals serving abroad) (1973). Total about 10 Orthodox.
FOREIGN MISSIONARIES AND PERSONNEL (aliens from abroad) (1973). Total 345. *From Western world.* 341: about 240 Roman Catholics, 79 Protestants (67 in 4 USA societies, 10 in 1 WGermany society, 2 in 1 UK society), about 20 Orthodox, 2 Anglicans from UK. *From Communist world.* About 2 Orthodox from USSR and Yugoslavia. *From Third World.* About 2 Orthodox from Syria.
INSTITUTIONS (church-operated) (1973). Total 43, including 15 higher schools (1 minor seminary), 20 medical centres (11 hospitals), 1 press, 5 seminaries (3 Protestant, 2 Orthodox).
PERIODICALS. About 13 titles (5 Orthodox).
PERSONNEL. About 675 (330 national, 345 foreign).
RELIGIOUS LIBRARIES. About 7.
SCRIPTURE DISTRIBUTION (1975). Annual totals: 1,927 Bibles (5% free, 95% subsidized), 2,741 NTs (18% free, 82% subsidized), 7,933 UBS portions, 43,172 UBS selections. *Translations completed.* Portion: 2 languages since 1782. NT: 2 languages since 1819. Bible: Turkish in 1827.
SERVICE AGENCIES. About 17, including ACISJF, ICMC, OK, OM, UEC, YMCA, YWCA.

ADDITIONAL DATA ON CHURCHES
CATHOLIC CHURCH IN TURKEY. *Catholics.* Including a majority of expatriates (Italians, French, Germans, Dutch, Spanish, USA). *Rites.* Names for the 5 rites are: Ermeni Katolikler (Armenians) in Arsipiskoposluk Instanbul (AD Instanbul), Keldani Katolikler (Chaldeans), Melkit Katolikler (Melkites), Suryani Katolikler (Syrians), and Latinler (Latins). *Annual baptisms.* (1972) 99.8% infant, 0.2% adult. *Priests.* Armenian: 4 secular, 6 regular (all citizens). Chaldean: 6 secular (nationals). Melkite: none except the 2 heads of jurisdictions. Latin: 4 secular (nationals), 51 regular (49 being expatriates). *Brothers.* All Latins, and all expatriates. *Sisters.* Latin: 5 nationals, 170 expatriates. *Armenian religious congregations* (1973). Priests: 3 Méchitaristes de Venise, 3 Méchitaristes de Vienne. Sisters: 14 Sisters of the Immaculate Conception. *Latin religious orders and congregations.* Priests (with over 10 members in 1973): 18 OFMCap, 16 CM. Brothers: 28 FSC. Sisters (with over 10 in 1973): 86 Daughters of Charity, 38 Sisters of the Immaculate Conception (Ivrea), 17 Little Sisters of the Poor, 15 Sisters of Our Lady of Zion.
*Catholic organizations.* The Episcopal Conference of Turkey was set up experimentally by the Holy See in 1978. There are no pastoral or presbyteral councils or organizations of religious personnel. The Latin vicariate of Istanbul sponsors a Commission for Catholic Action, but the only movement of the lay apostolate is the Friends of the Poor.

The Holy See has had diplomatic relations with Turkey since 1960 and is represented by a pro-nuncio based in Ankara.

Latin Catholic schools number 15, from pre-primary to secondary level, while Armenian Catholics sponsor 7 schools: one pre-primary with 150 children, 3 primary with 590 pupils and 3 secondary with 1,175 students.

Religious personnel of the Latin rite operate 6 hospitals, 2 homes for the aged and one orphanage. The Friends of the Poor, with branches in several Istanbul parishes, fulfils somewhat the same function as the societies of St Vincent de Paul in the West. Armenian Catholics are responsible for a hospital and home for the aged in Istanbul.

An affiliate of the USA-based Catholic Relief Services is established in the country and, as with other similar Latin or Armenian Catholic social welfare institutions, serves mostly Muslims.
CHURCH OF ENGLAND. Anglican chaplaincy work dates from 1598 in Constantinople, and 1634 in Smyrna (Izmir).
ECUMENICAL PATRIARCHATE OF CONSTANTINOPLE. In Greek, Oikumenikon Patriarcheion. All priests and the 10 bishops are Turkish citizens.
SYRIAN ORTHODOX PATRIARCHATE OF ANTIOCH. Jacobites. There are 2 dioceses remaining: Mardin, and Midyat.

# Turks & Caicos Islands

## SECULAR DATA

**STATE. Official name:** The Crown Colony of the Turks and Caicos Islands.
**Flag** (shown above right): British Blue Ensign with shield of the Colony in the fly.
**Area:** 430 sq.km. (166 sq.miles). Description: Over 30 small islands (cays). Agricultural land: 2.3%.
**Government:** Crown colony of the United Kingdom, since 1962 (1678 under Bermuda and Jamaica).
**Legislature:** State Council, 16 members.
**Official language:** English.
**Capital:** Cockburn Town (Grand Turk) 2,339.

**DEMOGRAPHY. Population:** 5,558 (census of 29.X.1970. For 1970–2000 (UN), see last row of Table 1). Population density (1975): 13/sq.km. (33/sq.mile). Under 15 years: 43%. Growth rate (1975–80): 0.0% per year (births 2.87%, deaths –0.68%, emigrants –2.19%). Life expectancy (1975–80): 69.1 years. Household size: 4.4 persons.
**Major language:** English.
**Labour force:** 37%.
**Tourists** (1972): 4,670.

**ETHNOLINGUISTIC GROUPS:** 77.0% Black (African Negro), 17.3% Mulatto (Black/White), 5.7% White (4.3% USA (250), 1.3% European (80)).

**MONEY** (1977). **Monetary unit:** US dollar (= 100 cents).
**National income per person:** US$600. Average annual family income: US$2,640.
**Cost of living in capital** (1976): Daily cost of living: US$26.

**HEALTH.** Hospitals: 2 (28 beds). Doctors: 2.

**EDUCATION.** Adult literacy: (1954) 89%, (1960) 91%. Schools: 17.

**LITERATURE.** Newspapers: 1 non-daily.

**COMMUNICATION** (per 1,000 people). Phones: 82. Radios: 511.

TABLE 1. RELIGIOUS ADHERENTS IN THE TURKS & CAICOS ISLANDS

| Year | 1900 | | mid-1970 | | Annual change, 1970–1980 | | | | mid-1975 | | mid-1980 | | 2000 | |
|---|---|---|---|---|---|---|---|---|---|---|---|---|---|---|
| *Name* | *Adherents* | *%* | *Adherents* | *%* | *Natural* | *Conversion* | *Total* | *Rate* | *Adherents* | *%* | *Adherents* | *%* | *Adherents* | *%* |
| **Christians** | **5,100** | **100.0** | **5,530** | **99.5** | 0 | –2 | –2 | –0.04 | **5,520** | **99.3** | **5,510** | **99.1** | **5,900** | **98.3** |
| professing | 5,100 | 100.0 | 5,530 | 99.5 | 0 | –2 | –2 | –0.04 | 5,520 | 99.3 | 5,510 | 99.1 | 5,900 | 98.3 |
| Protestants | 2,300 | 45.1 | 4,265 | 76.7 | –1 | 0 | –1 | –0.02 | 4,235 | 76.2 | 4,255 | 76.5 | 4,400 | 73.3 |
| Anglicans | 2,800 | 54.9 | 1,160 | 20.9 | –14 | –2 | –16 | –1.51 | 1,060 | 19.1 | 1,000 | 18.0 | 1,000 | 16.7 |
| Roman Catholics | 0 | 0.0 | 105 | 1.9 | 15 | 0 | 15 | 6.67 | 225 | 4.0 | 255 | 4.6 | 500 | 8.3 |
| nominal | 100 | 2.0 | 250 | 4.5 | 2 | –2 | 0 | 0.00 | 250 | 4.5 | 250 | 4.5 | 500 | 8.3 |
| affiliated | 5,000 | 98.0 | 5,280 | 95.0 | –2 | 0 | –2 | –0.04 | 5,270 | 94.8 | 5,260 | 94.6 | 5,400 | 90.0 |
| total practising | 4,500 | *90* | 4,220 | *80* | –1 | 0 | –1 | –0.02 | 4,220 | *80* | 4,210 | *80* | 3,800 | *70* |
| non-practising | 500 | *10* | 1,060 | *20* | –1 | 0 | –1 | –0.10 | 1,050 | *20* | 1,050 | *20* | 1,600 | *30* |
| Protestants | 2,250 | 44.1 | 3,850 | 69.2 | –5 | 0 | –5 | –0.13 | 3,810 | 68.5 | 3,800 | 68.3 | 3,500 | 58.3 |
| Evangelicals | 2,000 | 39.2 | 3,200 | 57.5 | –4 | 6 | 2 | 0.06 | 3,210 | 57.7 | 3,220 | 57.9 | 3,200 | 53.3 |
| Anglicans | 2,750 | 53.9 | 1,000 | 18.0 | –12 | –2 | –14 | –1.56 | 900 | 16.2 | 860 | 15.5 | 900 | 15.0 |
| Black indigenous | 0 | 0.0 | 300 | 5.4 | 0 | 0 | 0 | 0.00 | 300 | 5.4 | 300 | 5.4 | 500 | 8.3 |
| Roman Catholics | 0 | 0.0 | 100 | 1.8 | 15 | 0 | 15 | 6.82 | 220 | 3.9 | 250 | 4.5 | 400 | 6.7 |
| Marginal Protestants | 0 | 0.0 | 30 | 0.5 | 0 | 2 | 2 | 5.00 | 40 | 0.7 | 50 | 0.9 | 100 | 1.7 |
| Baha'is | 0 | 0.0 | 30 | 0.5 | 0 | 2 | 2 | 5.00 | 40 | 0.7 | 50 | 0.9 | 100 | 1.7 |
| **Country's population** | **5,100** | **100.0** | **5,560** | **100.0** | **0** | **0** | **0** | **0.00** | **5,560** | **100.0** | **5,560** | **100.0** | **6,000** | **100.0** |

COLUMNS, ROWS. For meanings and definitions, see Codebook (Part 6). Note that, by definition, total 'Christians' = professing + crypto-Christians, which also = affiliated + nominal Christians. Percentages may not always total exactly, due to rounding.

CENSUSES. 7.IV.1960 (de jure): 79.1% Protestants (44.2% Baptists, 25.1% Methodists, 6.5% Ch of God), 20.5% Anglicans, 0.4% Roman Catholics (25 persons). 29.X.1970: 76.7% Protestants (42.4% Baptists, 22.7% Methodists), 20.9% Anglicans, 1.9% Roman Catholics (106 persons), 0.5% other religionists.

NOTES ON RELIGIONS
BLACK INDIGENOUS. In about 4 small groupings in 1970 (see Table 2).
MIGRATION. All figures in the column 'Natural change' represent nett immigration (plus) or emigration (minus).

## CHRISTIANITY

PROTESTANT CHURCHES. Baptists are the principal denomination on the island, as in the nearby Bahamas. Most are related to the Jamaica Baptist Union, dating from the middle of the last century, although there is also a small Baptist Bible Church.

Methodists have maintained their position as the second largest denomination, although their proportion of the population decreased during the decade 1960–70. Methodist work began in the nearby Bahamas and spread to Turks and Caicos about the turn of the century.

Two American Pentecostal missions are active, the Church of God of Prophecy which has work at Grand Turk, Bottle Creek, Salt Cay, Kew and Blue Hills; and the Church of God (Cleveland) with a congregation on Grand Turk known as the New Testament Church of God. Small Christian Brethren and Adventist communities also exist.

ANGLICAN CHURCH. Anglicans opened work in the islands during the 18th century and represent the third largest denomination, with 20% of the

Christian themes occur on numerous postage stamps: here (Easter 1970), a series on the Crucifixion by Dürer.

population. The church belongs to the diocese of Nassau and the Bahamas, in the Church of the Province of the West Indies.

CATHOLIC CHURCH. Although still a very small minority, the Catholic community has been growing due to immigration, from 25 people in the census of 1960 to 106 in 1970, and to 210 baptized Catholics and 10 children receiving instruction in 1973. The Turks and Caicos islands belong to the diocese of Nassau and are served by an OCD priest who resides on Grand Turk.

CHURCH AND STATE. The islands were uninhabited when discovered by Ponce de León in 1512 and remained so until 1678 when salt was first extracted for use in Bermuda. Administered from Jamaica until 1962, Turks and Caicos are now governed by an administrator appointed by the British sovereign. There are no church-operated schools or medical institutions in the islands. Freedom of religion is guaranteed, but there is no established church.

INTERDENOMINATIONAL ORGANIZATIONS. On the initiative of the Anglican vicar on Grand Turk, informal discussions have begun regarding the formation of a Christian council.

### TABLE 2.   ORGANIZED CHURCHES AND DENOMINATIONS IN THE TURKS & CAICOS ISLANDS

| Official name 1 | Begun 2 | Type 3 | Counc 4 | Congs 5 | Adults 6 | Affiliated 7 | Names, notes, and other statistics (see Codebook) 8 |
|---|---|---|---|---|---|---|---|
| Anglican Church (D Nassau & B) | c1750 | A ACa | avMRC | 3 | 400 | 1,000 | In Ch of the Province of the West Indies, D Nassau and the Bahamas. On Grand Turk. |
| Baptist Bible Church | | P Bap | x.... | 1 | 20 | 50 | Related to BBFI (USA). Small congregation on Grand Turk. Fundamentalists. |
| Catholic Church (D Nassau) | | R Lat | PxNMC | 1 | 70 | 100 | Part of D Nassau (Bahamas). One OCD priest, residing on Grand Turk. |
| Christian Brethren | | P EBr | x.... | 1 | 50 | 100 | *Exclusive (Closed) Brethren. Plymouth Brethren.* Group: Kelly-Continental. |
| Church of God in Christ | | I pe3 | Z.... | 1 | 50 | 100 | M=CoGiC(Black mission from USA) on Grand Turk. Based in neighbouring Jamaica. |
| Church of God of Prophecy | 1932 | P Pe3 | Z.... | 5 | 200 | 300 | M=CGP(USA). Holiness Pentecostals. Split in USA ex CoG(Cleveland). |
| Jamaica Baptist Union | c1849 | P Bap | T.M.C | 13 | 1,000 | 2,000 | Part of Jamaica Baptist Union, M=SBC(USA). On Grand Turk. |
| Jehovah's Witnesses | c1958 | M Jeh | x.... | 1 | 10 | 30 | *Watch Tower. International Bible Students Association.* Witnessing since 1959. |
| Methodist Ch in Caribbean & Americas | c1800 | P Met | VvM.C | | 500 | 1,000 | Part of Bahamas District, MCCA. On Grand Turk. In. |
| New Testament Church of God | 1922 | P Pe3 | ZF... | 1 | 48 | 300 | M=CoG(Cleveland)(USA). Holiness Pentecostals. Congregation on Grand Turk. 1n. |
| Seventh-day Adventist Church | 1964 | P Adv | x.... | 3 | 57 | 100 | *SDA, T&CI Mission,* WIndies Union Conference. HQ Grand Turk. 1nx,6mw,1r,3t(179),5Y. |
| Other Black indigenous churches | | I pen | ..... | | 100 | 200 | Small groupings, including Spiritual Baptists (Shouters) et alia. |
| Total affiliated (mid-1970) | | | | 45 | 2,605 | 5,280 | Total denominations (1970) . . . 14. |
| Total affiliated (mid-1975) | | | | 47 | 2,600 | 5,270 | Total denominations (1975) . . . 14. |
| Total affiliated (mid-1980) | | | | 49 | 2,590 | 5,260 | Total denominations (1980) . . . 15. |

### NOTES ON TABLE ABOVE
COLUMNS: for meanings and CODES (cols. 1, 3, 4, 8): see Codebook (Part 6). Column 1: Boldface type = church with over 10% of country's affiliated Christians.
NATIONAL COUNCILS (Column 4, 5th letter).
C = Turks & Caicos Inter-Church Committee (TCICC).

PEOPLES (ethnolinguistic). Christians: 77.0% Black, 17.3% Mulatto, 5.7% White (4.3% USA, 1.3% European).

COUNTRY-WIDE TOTALS
EVANGELIZATION (see Part 5). 1900: 100%. 1970: 100%. 1980: 100%.
FOREIGN MISSIONARIES AND PERSONNEL (aliens from abroad) (1973). Total 7. *From Western world.* 4: 3 Protestants in 2 USA societies, 1 Roman Catholic. *From Third World.* 3 Protestants from Jamaica.

INSTITUTIONS (church-operated) (1973). Total higher school.
PERIODICALS. 2 titles.
PERSONNEL. About 17 (10 national, 7 foreign).
SCRIPTURE DISTRIBUTION (1975). Annual totals: 20 Bibles (subsidized), 20 NTs (subsidized).
SERVICE AGENCIES. About 3.

---

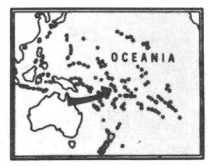

# TUVALU

## SECULAR DATA

STATE. Official name: The State of Tuvalu. Earlier name: Ellice Islands.
Flag (shown above right): Blue with British Union Jack at upper hoist corner; nine golden stars placed in the same relation as the nine principal islands of Tuvalu.
Area: 24 sq.km. (9.5 sq.miles). Agricultural land: 0.0%.
Government: Parliamentary state, since 1978 (1892 British protectorate of Ellice Islands with Gilbert Islands, 1916 British crown colony of Gilbert & Ellice Islands, 1976 secession as separate colony, 1978 Independence).
Official language: English.
Capital: Fongafela, Funafuti (826 persons).

DEMOGRAPHY. Population: 7,100 (estimate of mid-1975. For 1970–2000 (UN), see last row of Table 1). Population density (1975): 273/sq.km. (710/sq.mile). Under 15 years: 44%. Growth rate (1975–80): 2.94% per year (births 3.49%, deaths −0.79, immigrants 0.24%). Life expectancy (1975–80): 63.8 years. Household size: 6.0 persons.
Major languages: English, Tuvaluan (Ellice, Samoan), Gilbertese.
Urban dwellers (1970): 10%. Urban growth rate (1950–70): 10% per year.
Labour force: 25%.

ETHNOLINGUISTIC GROUPS: 97.0% Ellice Islander (Polynesian), 1.0% Gilbertese (Micronesian), 1.0% Euronesian, 1.0% European (White), Chinese.

MONEY (1977). Monetary unit: Australian dollar (= 100 cents); US$1 = A$0.94.
National income per person: US$270. Average annual family income: US$1,620.
Cost of living in capital (1976): Daily cost of living: US$32.

HEALTH. Hospitals: 2.

EDUCATION. Adult literacy: 95%. Schools: 10.

COMMUNICATION (per 1,000 people). Phones: 5. Radios: 200.

### TABLE 1.   RELIGIOUS ADHERENTS IN TUVALU (Ellice Islands)

| Year | 1900 | | mid-1970 | | Annual change, 1970–1980 | | | | mid-1975 | | mid-1980 | | 2000 | |
|---|---|---|---|---|---|---|---|---|---|---|---|---|---|---|
| Name | Adherents | % | Adherents | % | Natural | Conversion | Total | Rate | Adherents | % | Adherents | % | Adherents | % |
| Christians | 2,500 | 100.0 | 5,800 | 96.7 | 220 | −10 | 210 | 3.09 | 6,800 | 95.8 | 7,900 | 95.2 | 12,200 | 93.8 |
| professing | 2,500 | 100.0 | 5,800 | 96.7 | 220 | −10 | 210 | 3.09 | 6,800 | 95.8 | 7,900 | 95.2 | 12,200 | 93.8 |
| Protestants | 2,500 | 100.0 | 5,700 | 95.0 | 216 | −14 | 202 | 3.03 | 6,660 | 93.8 | 7,720 | 93.0 | 11,800 | 90.8 |
| Roman Catholics | 0 | 0.0 | 100 | 1.7 | 4 | 4 | 8 | 5.71 | 140 | 2.0 | 180 | 2.2 | 400 | 3.1 |
| nominal | 0 | 0.0 | 0 | 0.0 | 0 | 0 | 0 | 0.00 | 0 | 0.0 | 0 | 0.0 | 260 | 2.0 |
| affiliated | 2,500 | 100.0 | 5,800 | 96.7 | 220 | −10 | 210 | 3.09 | 6,800 | 95.8 | 7,900 | 95.2 | 11,940 | 91.8 |
| total practising | 2,250 | 90 | 4,640 | 80 | 176 | −8 | 168 | 3.09 | 5,440 | 80 | 6,320 | 80 | 8,360 | 70 |
| non-practising | 250 | 10 | 1,160 | 20 | 44 | −2 | 42 | 3.09 | 1,360 | 20 | 1,580 | 20 | 3,580 | 30 |
| Protestants | 2,500 | 100.0 | 5,700 | 95.0 | 216 | −14 | 202 | 3.03 | 6,660 | 93.8 | 7,720 | 93.0 | 11,540 | 88.8 |
| Evangelicals | 600 | 24.0 | 900 | 15.0 | 35 | 0 | 35 | 3.24 | 1,070 | 15.1 | 1,250 | 15.1 | 2,080 | 16.0 |
| Roman Catholics | 0 | 0.0 | 100 | 1.7 | 4 | 4 | 8 | 5.71 | 140 | 2.0 | 180 | 2.2 | 400 | 3.1 |
| Baha'is | 0 | 0.0 | 200 | 3.3 | 10 | 10 | 20 | 6.67 | 300 | 4.2 | 400 | 4.8 | 800 | 6.2 |
| Country's population | 2,500 | 100.0 | 6,000 | 100.0 | 230 | 0 | 230 | 3.24 | 7,100 | 100.0 | 8,300 | 100.0 | 13,000 | 100.0 |

COLUMNS, ROW. For meanings and definitions, see Codebook (Part 6). Note that, by definition, total 'Christians' = professing + crypto-Christians, which also = affiliated + nominal Christians. Percentages may not always total exactly, due to rounding.
CENSUSES. In the 1963 and 1968 censuses, the question on religion was asked. Combined results are given under Table 1 for the Gilbert Islands.

NOTES ON RELIGIONS
BAHA'IS. In 1969 a small section of land was leased by Baha'is on Funafuti, an atoll of 30 islets. Converts are former Congregationalists.

**NON-CHRISTIAN RELIGIONS. Baha'i** has recently been making converts in Tuvalu from among Congregationalists.

## CHRISTIANITY

PROTESTANT CHURCHES. In 1861 Congregationalist pastors from Samoa began preaching in the Ellice Islands, aided after 1870 by J.S. White of the London Missionary Society. By the year 1900 the whole population was Congregationalist. For many years the LMS served a united church of the Gilbert and Ellice Islands, but as a result of ethnic tensions separate churches for the 2 groups were formed in 1968. Adventists have had a small work for over 20 years.

CATHOLIC CHURCH. There is only a small Catholic community. In 1972 only one lay brother was at work, located in Nanumea.

**CHURCH AND STATE.** Until 1964, Catholics were unable to open work in the Ellice Islands, these having been declared until then a 'closed district' in which only Protestants were allowed to work. Although Catholics are now legally permitted in Tuvalu, local anti-Catholic sentiment prevents the building of Catholic churches on most islands.

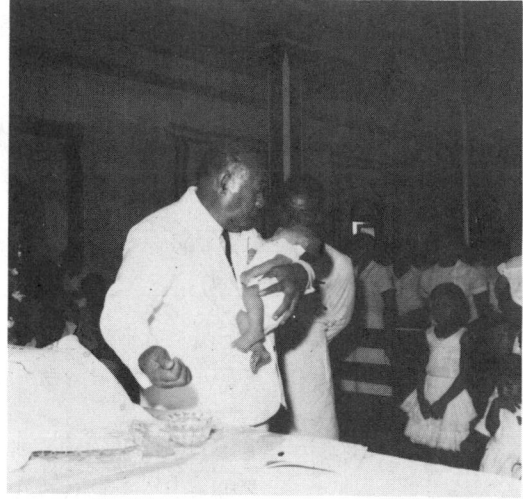

**Tuvalu Church.** Formerly Ellice Islands Church. *Above.* Baptism of an infant. *Right.* Church at Funafuti.

Postage stamps illustrating (left) New Testament translation and (right) the largest church buildings.

TABLE 2.    ORGANIZED CHURCHES AND DENOMINATIONS IN TUVALU (Ellice Islands)

| Official name 1 | Begun 2 | Type 3 | Counc 4 | Congs 5 | Adults 6 | Affiliated 7 | Names, notes, and other statistics (see Codebook) 8 |
|---|---|---|---|---|---|---|---|
| Catholic Ch: D Tarawa, Nauru&Funafuti | 1964 | R Lat | P.PT. | 2 | 60 | 100 | Closed to RC missions until 1964. On Nanumea, spread from Gilbert Is. 1 brother. |
| Seventh-day Adventist Church | 1955 | P Adv | x.... | 1 | 50 | 70 | *SDA, G&EI Mission.* Central Pacific Union Mission. Begun from Abemama (Gilbert Is). |
| Tuvalu Church | 1861 | P Con | ..P.. | 13 | 2,560 | 5,630 | *Ekalesia Elise.* M=LMS, now CWM(UK). A=1968. 12n,7m,4w,1f,G=2.1%pa,1p,W=75%,110y. |
| Total affiliated (mid-1970) | | | | 16 | 2,670 | 5,800 | Total denominations (1970) . . . 3. |
| Total affiliated (mid-1975) | | | | 18 | 3,130 | 6,800 | Total denominations (1975) . . . 3. |
| Total affiliated (mid-1980) | | | | 20 | 3,640 | 7,900 | Total denominations (1980) . . . 3. |

**NOTES ON TABLE ABOVE**
COLUMNS: for meanings and CODES (cols. 1, 3, 4, 8): see Codebook (Part 6). Column 1: **Boldface type** = church with over 10% of country's affiliated Christians.

**PEOPLES** (ethnolinguistic). Christians: 97.0% Ellice Islander (Polynesian), 1.0% Gilbertese (Micronesian), 1.0% European (White), Chinese.

**COUNTRY-WIDE TOTALS**
EVANGELIZATION (see Part 5). 1900: 100%. 1970: 100%. 1980: 100%.
FOREIGN MISSIONARIES AND PERSONNEL (aliens from abroad) (1973). Total 3. *From Western world.* 2. *From Third World* 1.
INSTITUTIONS (church-operated) (1973). Total 1.
PERIODICALS. 2.
PERSONNEL. About 28 (25 national, 3 foreign).

SCRIPTURE DISTRIBUTION (1975). Annual totals: about 100 Bibles (subsidized), 100 NTs (subsidized). *Translations completed.* Ellice: portion in 1969.

**ADDITIONAL DATA ON CHURCHES**
TUVALU CHURCH. Ekalesia Elise (Ellice Islands Church) or Ekalesia Tuvalu. There are 2 Districts. *Origin.* The church was begun in 1861 through the work of Samoan pastors of the LMS.

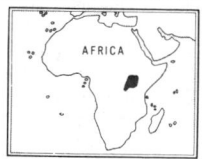

# UGANDA

## SECULAR DATA

**STATE. Official name:** The Republic of Uganda. Adjective of nationality: Ugandan.
**Flag** (shown above right): Black, yellow, and red stripes, with crested crane on white circle in centre.
**Area:** 236,036 sq. km. (91,134 sq. miles). Agricultural land: 42.9%.
**Government:** Parliamentary democracy, since 1979 (c1500 several kingdoms, 1894 British protectorate, 1962 Independence as federal state, 1966 one-party republic, 1971 military dictatorship).
**Official language:** English.
**Capital:** Kampala 330,700 (1969).
**Political divisions** (1975): 4 Regions, divided into 17 Districts.
**Armed forces** (1976): Total 21,000 regular: army 20,000, air force 1,000 (21 combat aircraft).
**Foreign forces** (1977): 2,000 Cubans, about 1,000 Palestinian and Libyan Arabs, 1,000 Russians.

**DEMOGRAPHY. Population:** 9,548,847 (census of 18.VIII.1969. For 1970–2000 (UN), see last row of Table 1). Population density (1975): 48/sq. km. (125/sq. mile). Under 15 years: 43%. Growth rate (1975–80): 3.05% per year (births 4.47%, deaths −1.43%). Life expectancy (1975–80): 52.5 years. Household size: 4.9 persons.
**Major languages:** English, Ganda (Luganda), Swahili, Nkole, Teso, Soga, Kiga (Ruchiga), Ruanda, Lango, Acholi, Gisu, Lugbara, Toro, Nyoro, Arabic, and over 45 other tribal languages.
**Urban dwellers** (1970): 9.5%. Urban growth rate (1950–70): 7.7% per year.
**Labour force:** 39%.
**Refugees** (1977): 78,000 from Rwanda and Zaire. Exiles abroad: 260,000 Ugandans (50,000 Asians expelled 1972 (29,000 taken by UK, 8,000 by Kenya, 8,000 India/Pakistan, 2,000 North America,

**Catholic Church in Uganda.** Visit of Pope Paul VI to Kampala in August 1969. *Right.* Concelebrated mass on Kololo Hill with consecration of 12 African bishops, in presence of congregation of 20,000.

rest by Europe), 200,000 Africans 1972–76 and 10,000 Africans in early 1977, all mainly or initially to Kenya).
**Tourists** (1974): 10,296.

**ETHNOLINGUISTIC GROUPS:** 16.3% Ganda, 8.1% Nkole, 8.1% Teso, 7.8% Soga, 7.1% Kiga, 5.9% Ruanda, 5.6% Lango (singular; plural Langi), 5.1% Gisu, 4.4% Acholi, 3.7% Lugbara, 3.3% Toro, 2.9% Nyoro, 2.2% Rundi, 2.1% Luhya (1.4% Nyore, 0.7% Samia), 2.0% Karamojong, 1.9% Alur, 1.7% Konjo, 1.6% Padhola, 1.3% Kenyan (1.0% Luo, Kikuyu), 1.2% Madi, 1.0% Indo-Pakistani (80,000, until expelled 1972), 1.0% Kumam, 0.6% Kakwa, 0.6% Sabei, 0.5% Amba, 0.3% Suk, 0.1% European (9,500), 0.1% Goanese, Twa & Efe Pygmy (3,000), Dodoth, Jie, Labwor, Topotha, Haya, Teuso, Kongo, Swahili, Palestinian Arab, Libyan Arab, Yemen & other Arab, Sudanese, Cuban (2,000), & a number of smaller tribes.

**MONEY** (1977). **Monetary unit:** Uganda shilling (=100 cents); US $1 = USh 8.31.
**National income per person:** US$190. Average annual family income: US$931.
**Inflation:** (1970–74) 23.6% per year (1975: consumer price index 293).
**Cost of living in capital** (1976): Daily cost of living: US$38.

**HEALTH.** Hospitals: 328 (15,294 beds). Doctors: 305. Lepers: 120,000 (10.6 per 1,000). Blind: 209,000. Psychotics: 110,000. Criminals: 20,000.

**EDUCATION.** Adult literacy: (1959) 25%, (1962) 35%. Education rate: 33%. Schools: 2,937. Universities 1.

**LITERATURE.** Annual new book titles (1971): 205. Periodicals: 30. Newspapers: 7 dailies.

**COMMUNICATION** (per 1,000 people). Phones: 3. Radios: 26. TV sets: 1. Daily newspaper circulation: 7 copies.

TABLE 1. RELIGIOUS ADHERENTS IN UGANDA

| Year | 1900 | | mid-1970 | | Annual change, 1970–1980 | | | | mid-1975 | | mid-1980 | | 2000 | |
|---|---|---|---|---|---|---|---|---|---|---|---|---|---|---|
| *Name* | *Adherents* | *%* | *Adherents* | *%* | *Natural* | *Conversion* | *Total* | *Rate* | *Adherents* | *%* | *Adherents* | *%* | *Adherents* | *%* |
| **Christians** | **180,000** | **6.8** | **6,766,000** | **69.0** | **258,060** | **100,640** | **358,700** | **4.27** | **8,400,000** | **74.0** | **10,353,000** | **78.3** | **20,417,900** | **84.5** |
| professing | 180,000 | 6.8 | 6,766,000 | 69.0 | 258,060 | 100,640 | 358,700 | 4.27 | 8,400,000 | 74.0 | 10,353,000 | 78.3 | 20,417,900 | 84.5 |
| Roman Catholics | 100,000 | 3.8 | 4,315,000 | 44.0 | 163,926 | 60,374 | 224,300 | 4.20 | 5,335,900 | 47.0 | 6,558,000 | 49.6 | 12,804,800 | 53.0 |
| Anglicans | 80,000 | 3.0 | 2,252,000 | 23.0 | 86,208 | 34,892 | 121,100 | 4.32 | 2,806,100 | 24.7 | 3,463,000 | 26.2 | 6,761,800 | 28.0 |
| Protestants | 0 | 0.0 | 150,000 | 1.5 | 5,929 | 4,171 | 10,100 | 5 23 | 193,000 | 1.7 | 251,000 | 1.9 | 652,300 | 2.7 |
| African indigenous | 0 | 0.0 | 38,000 | 0.4 | 1,598 | 1,202 | 2,800 | 5.38 | 52,000 | 0.5 | 66,000 | 0.5 | 169,000 | 0.7 |
| Orthodox | 0 | 0.0 | 11,000 | 0.1 | 399 | 1 | 400 | 3.08 | 13,000 | 0.1 | 15,000 | 0.1 | 30,000 | 0.1 |
| nominal | 50,000 | 1.9 | 1,747,644 | 17.8 | 68,291 | 35,815 | 104,106 | 4.68 | 2,222,900 | 19.6 | 2,788,700 | 21.1 | 4,783,900 | 19.8 |
| affiliated | 130,000 | 4.9 | 5,018,356 | 51.2 | 189,769 | 64,825 | 254,594 | 4.12 | 6,177,100 | 54.4 | 7,564,300 | 57.2 | 15,634,000 | 64.7 |
| total practising | 125,000 | *96* | 3,512,850 | *70* | 132,838 | 45,378 | 178,216 | 4.12 | 4,323,970 | *70* | 5,295,010 | *70* | 10,162,100 | *65* |
| non-practising | 5,000 | *4* | 1,505,510 | *30* | 56,931 | 19,447 | 76,378 | 4.12 | 1,853,130 | *30* | 2,269,290 | *30* | 5,471,900 | *35* |
| Roman Catholics | 70,000 | 2.6 | 3,434,988 | 35.0 | 129,048 | 36,503 | 165,551 | 3.94 | 4,200,600 | 37.0 | 5,090,500 | 38.5 | 9,905,600 | 41.0 |
| Catholic pentecostals | 0 | 0.0 | 0 | 0.0 | 60 | 540 | 600 | 30.00 | 2,000 | 0.0 | 6,000 | 0.0 | 80,000 | 0.3 |
| Anglicans | 60,000 | 2.3 | 1,393,951 | 14.2 | 53,016 | 21,789 | 74,805 | 4.33 | 1,725,700 | 15.2 | 2,142,000 | 16.2 | 4,832,000 | 20.0 |
| Evangelicals | 60,000 | 2.3 | 1,390,000 | 14.2 | 52,841 | 21,859 | 74,700 | 4.34 | 1,720,000 | 15.2 | 2,137,000 | 16.2 | 4,825,000 | 20.0 |
| Anglican pentecostals | 0 | 0.0 | 500 | 0.0 | 61 | 389 | 450 | 22.50 | 2,000 | 0.0 | 5,000 | 0.0 | 60,000 | 0.2 |
| Protestants | 0 | 0.0 | 111,917 | 1.1 | 4,534 | 4,104 | 8,638 | 5.85 | 147,600 | 1.3 | 198,300 | 1.5 | 555,700 | 2.3 |
| Evangelicals | 0 | 0.0 | 107,000 | 1.1 | 4,362 | 4,138 | 8,500 | 5.99 | 142,000 | 1.3 | 192,000 | 1.5 | 540,000 | 2.2 |
| African indigenous | 0 | 0.0 | 67,200 | 0.7 | 2,790 | 2,390 | 5,180 | 5.70 | 90,800 | 0.8 | 119,000 | 0.9 | 314,100 | 1.3 |
| Orthodox | 0 | 0.0 | 10,000 | 0.1 | 369 | 31 | 400 | 3.33 | 12,000 | 0.1 | 14,000 | 0.1 | 25,000 | 0.1 |
| Marginal Protestants | 0 | 0.0 | 300 | 0.0 | 12 | 8 | 20 | 5.00 | 400 | 0.0 | 500 | 0.0 | 1,600 | 0.0 |
| Tribal religionists | 2,416,700 | 91.2 | 2,152,300 | 21.9 | 60,297 | −109,427 | −49,130 | −2.50 | 1,962,700 | 17.3 | 1,661,000 | 12.6 | 1,208,000 | 5.0 |
| Muslims | 53,000 | 2.0 | 588,400 | 6.0 | 21,972 | 6,458 | 28,430 | 3.98 | 715,200 | 6.3 | 872,700 | 6.6 | 1,787,800 | 7.4 |
| Ahmadis | 0 | 0.0 | 3,000 | 0.0 | 111 | 29 | 140 | 3.78 | 3,700 | 0.0 | 4,400 | 0.0 | 10,000 | 0.0 |
| Baha'is | 0 | 0.0 | 226,000 | 2.3 | 8,372 | 2,088 | 10,460 | 3.84 | 272,500 | 2.4 | 330,600 | 2.5 | 724,800 | 3.0 |
| Hindus | 300 | 0.0 | 65,000 | 0.7 | −6,500 | 0 | −6,500 | −20.00 | 0 | 0.0 | 0 | 0.0 | 0 | 0.0 |
| Sikhs | 0 | 0.0 | 5,700 | 0.1 | −570 | 0 | −570 | −20.00 | 0 | 0.0 | 0 | 0.0 | 0 | 0.0 |
| Jains | 0 | 0.0 | 1,000 | 0.0 | −100 | 0 | −100 | −20.00 | 0 | 0.0 | 0 | 0.0 | 0 | 0.0 |
| Non-religious | 0 | 0.0 | 1,000 | 0.0 | 61 | 239 | 300 | 15.00 | 2,000 | 0.0 | 4,000 | 0.0 | 20,000 | 0.1 |
| Jews | 0 | 0.0 | 500 | 0.0 | 18 | 2 | 20 | 3.33 | 600 | 0.0 | 700 | 0.0 | 1,500 | 0.0 |
| Parsis | 0 | 0.0 | 100 | 0.0 | −10 | 0 | −10 | −20.00 | 0 | 0.0 | 0 | 0.0 | 0 | 0.0 |
| **Country's population** | **2,650,000** | **100.0** | **9,806,000** | **100.0** | **341,600** | **0** | **341,600** | **3.01** | **11,353,000** | **100.0** | **13,222,000** | **100.0** | **24,160,000** | **100.0** |

COLUMNS, ROWS. For meanings and definitions, see Codebook (Part 6). Note that, by definition, total 'Christians' = professing + crypto-Christians, which also = affiliated + nominal Christians. Percentages may not always total exactly, due to rounding.
CENSUSES. **1911**: 82.2% tribal religionists, 8.1% Roman Catholics, 7.1% Anglicans, 2.6% Muslims. Buganda: **42.7%** Christians (23.5% Roman Catholics, 19.2% Anglicans). **1921** (Africans only): 76.8% tribal religionists, 8.7% Anglicans, 8.3% Roman Catholics, 3.2% Muslims, 3.0% African indigenous (KOAB Malakites). **1931** (all races): 71.9% tribal religionists, 11.5% Roman Catholics, 11.1% Anglicans, 3.6% Muslims, 1.6% African indigenous (KOAB), 0.2% Hindus. **18-19.VIII.1959**: (all races): 36.9% tribal religionists, 32.2% Roman Catholics, 24.6% Anglicans, 5.4% Muslims, 0.7% Hindus, 0.1% Sikhs. The religion question was not asked in subsequent censuses.

NOTES ON RELIGIONS
AFRICAN INDIGENOUS. In 1970 there were about 23 indigenous denominations (see Table 2). The first movement, the KOAB (Katonda Omu Ainza Byona: Society of the One Almighty God) or Bamalaki (People of Malaki, Malakite Church), began in 1914 and had 91,740 Ganda adherents in 1921, 56,952 in 1930 and declined to 1,000 by 1966.
AHMADIS. Introduced around 1946, organized in 1956, by Qadianis from Pakistan, with HQ in Jinja and a mosque built there in 1959 by Pakistani missionaries. Most Asian followers emigrated after 1963 or were expelled in 1972, leaving only African followers (including many Soga and Ganda formerly nominal Christians or Muslims).
ANGLICANS. In the year 1896, there were 6,905 baptized Anglicans, and 2,591 catechumens, with 57,380 readers or enquirers; in 1902, 35,897 baptized; by 1912, 83,200. At this early period, readers (still mostly pagans) and enquirers were over twice as numerous as baptized Anglicans.
BAHA'IS. Mostly Africans, especially around Mount Elgon; all Asian Baha'is were expelled 1972. In 1955, there were 900 believers in 100 centres, then rapid growth took place from 671 local spiritual assemblies (1964) to 1,507 (1973). One of the world's 7 Baha'i temples is in Kampala. In September 1977, Baha'i was banned by the government.
CATHOLIC PENTECOSTALS (or, Catholic charismatics). Totals (mid-1975): about 1,000 adults, or 2,000 total charismatic community including children.
COUNTRY'S POPULATION. From 1971–78 over 300,000 Ugandans (mostly Christians) were killed by the Amin regime, including 20,000 soldiers and several thousand police, and over 250,000 others fled to exile in Kenya and elsewhere (including, in 1972, the 50,000 Asians expelled). The column 'Annual change' in the table above spreads this mass killing and emigration over the decade 1970–80 and gives average annual figures over the decade.
HINDUS. Indians, almost all expelled in 1972.
JEWS. A congregation of African Jews (Bayudaya) with a synagogue exists in Mbale, begun in 1926 by a Muganda (a former Anglican and Malakite) without external Jewish influence. From a peak of 2,000 followers in 1928, numbers subsequently declined to 350 in 1962, rising to 500 by 1968 when the state of Israel was in favour with the Obote regime. In September 1977, they were declared banned by the Amin regime.
MUSLIMS. Islam was introduced to Buganda from 1844 onwards. African Muslims are all Sunnis (of the Shafiite rite, with Sudanese (Nubians) of the Malikite rite in Arua and West Nile). The main Muslim areas are Madi (36% Muslim in 1959), Busoga (13%) and West Nile (9%). Before their mass expulsion in 1972 Asian Muslims numbered 11,000 Ismailis, 4,000 Ithna-Asharis, also Bohoras and Memons (all with no African members). There is also an Ahmadiya Mission (enumerated here as Muslims, though declared non-Muslim by Pakistan). Islamization still proceeds among Bantu tribes in several areas, including Toro, but only slowly. Since 1972 the Amin regime has produced numerous professed conversions in the armed forces, but the overall total remains small as shown in the column 'Conversion' above. At the same time, steady numbers of Muslims are being converted to the Catholic and Anglican churches. *Missionaries*. By 1977, there were numerous Egyptian missionaries at work sent by Al-Azhar University (Cairo). *Hajj Pilgrims to Mecca*. (1970) 940; (1974) 3,107; (1975) 3,031; (1976) 2,491.
NON-RELIGIOUS. Mainly European expatriates.
ROMAN CATHOLICS. In the year 1903, there were 106,234 indigenous baptized Catholics (60,000 in Buganda) in the 2 vicariates of North Nyanza (White Fathers) and Upper Nile (Mill Hill Mission), covering the present-day territory of Uganda. At this period, enquirers, interested persons (still pagans) and catechumens were nearly twice as numerous as baptized Catholics.
SIKHS. Indians, all expelled in 1972.
TRIBAL RELIGIONISTS. Animists, mainly among the Pokot (Suk) (83%), Jie (80%), Niporen (80%), and Karamojong (60%).

**NON-CHRISTIAN RELIGIONS. Traditional religions** are followed by a rapidly-decreasing minority of most of Uganda's peoples. Among these animists are a majority of the Paranilotic Jie (80%), Karamojong (60%) and Pokot (83%). The Ganda, Uganda's largest tribe, still have numerous traditionalists who revere a complex pantheon of more than 40 divinities (Balubaale) who act as intermediaries between the supreme being Katonda and his people. Katonda's wife is Nalwanga and his chief minister Mukasa. The oldest of the divinities is Wanga, Mukasa's grandfather; while his brother, Kibuka, and father, Mususi, are appealed to respectively in time of war and earthquake. Other divinities are responsible for such matters as childbirth, plague, hunting, agriculture and death. A less-developed system is found among the Bahima and Bunyoro. Both identify God as Ruhanga (Creator). Among the Bahima, Ruhanga's son Rugaba distributes good and evil and his son Kazoba is responsible for providence. The same functions are performed in Bunyoro by Ruhanga's brothers, Nkya and Kakya. Spirit-possession cults in Uganda include the Cwezi and Embandwa in Bunyoro and the Yakan cult of the Alur and Lugbara.

**Islam** was first brought to Uganda in the mid-19th century by Arab traders from the coast. They achieved considerable influence at the court of the Kabaka of Buganda, particularly under Mutesa I, and a good number of the Ganda became Muslims. One factor in the spread of Islam throughout Uganda was the use made by the British colonial power of Muslims as low-ranking officials and interpreters. Islam was also brought into Uganda from the north by Sudanese troops who came with Emin Pasha and were then allowed to settle in the country. These Sudanese (known, incorrectly, as Nubians) are numerous in West Nile although pockets of them also survive in Bombo, Jinja and Entebbe. African Muslims are all Sunnis. Previous to the expulsion and flight of Asians

**Muslims.** Kibuli Mosque (Sunni), Kampala.

in 1972 there were 11,000 Ismailis, 4,000 Ithna-Asharis and smaller numbers of Bohoras and Memons. These sects had hardly any African members. Ahmadiya, whose first missionary came to Uganda in 1946, claim to number about 4,000 today. African Muslims divided on the death of their leader Mbogo in 1921, one group following Badru Kakungulu, while the other group refused to recognize him. A third sect was formed in 1947. The National Association for the Advancement of Muslims (NAAM) has been formed to bring all these groups together and produced a constitution in 1970 which purports to be

**Baha'is.** First Baha'i House of Worship (Temple) in Africa, on a hill in Kampala. Baha'i has, in Uganda, one of its strongest mission fields.

evident. The first Ugandan priests were ordained in 1913; the first East African bishop was consecrated in 1939. A local sisterhood, the novitiate for the Bannabikira, was opened in 1908, and today there are numerous indigenous congregations of priests, brothers and sisters.

The visit of pope Paul VI to Uganda in 1969, at which time he canonized 22 of the Catholic Namugongo martyrs, was an event of great significance and a sign of the importance which the Vatican attaches to this church.

ANGLICAN CHURCH. The Anglican Church accounts for over 25% of Uganda's population. As with Catholics, growth has been rapid and there has been sustained momentum through the years. By 1914 baptized members numbered 98,477, increasing three-fold over the next 2 decades to 301,000 in 1936. Today there are 2 million baptized Anglicans, with many new converts every year. The first Ugandan clergy were ordained in 1893, and the first African bishop and archbishop were appointed respectively in 1947 and 1966. The CMS has since 1877 been the principal foreign missionary society, augmented since 1918 by the African Inland Mission in the diocese of Madi and West Nile, and since 1929 by the BCMS among the Karamojong. The Ugandan church also has produced missionaries, the most famous being Apolo Kivebulaya who pioneered among the pygmies of Congo's Ituri forest as early as 1897. In 1961 the Church of Uganda, Rwanda and Burundi became an independent province in the Anglican Communion. A great stimulus to Anglican growth has come from the East African Revival (Balokole, Saved Ones) which began in Ruanda in 1927 and continues to make its influence widely felt.

PROTESTANT CHURCHES. Seventh-day Adventists began work in 1926, the Salvation Army in 1931, and the Pentecostal Assemblies of Canada in 1935. By 1970 another 13 denominations had entered and begun work.

INDIGENOUS CHURCHES. In 1914 a sizeable schism occurred among the Ganda members of the Anglican Church, the KOAB or Society of the One Almighty God. By 1921 membership had grown to one third of the whole Anglican Church; but after 1940 the movement collapsed. The East African Revival has been responsible for 2 schisms: one, from the AIM in 1955, known among local Kakwa and Okefu tribesmen as Trumpeters or Praisers; and the other from the Anglicans in 1967 among the Acholi, called the Chosen Evangelical Revival. At least 14 independent churches have spread to Uganda from neighbouring Kenya, including the African Israel Church Nineveh, Church of Christ in Africa and Maria Legio of Africa.

ORTHODOX CHURCH. The African Greek Orthodox Church began as an indigenous split from the Anglicans (CMS) in 1929, but succeeded in gaining admittance to the Greek Orthodox communion in 1946. Dissatisfaction with inadequacies of Greek Orthodox assistance provoked a further split in 1957, and later in 1966 the formation of the African Orthodox Autonomous Church South of the Sahara.

**African Greek Orthodox Church.** *Above.* Cathedral, with a Soga priest. *Below.* Founder, and eventually Bishop, Reuben S.S.M. Spartas.

for all Muslims in Uganda. Islam took on a new aggressiveness after the accession of Idi Amin to the presidency.

**Baha'i** has in Uganda one of its strongest mission fields, with over 1,500 local spiritual assemblies and one of the world's 7 Baha'i temples in Kampala. In 1977, it was declared banned by the Amin regime.

**Hinduism,** which before 1972 had temples in Kampala and many towns, has virtually disappeared with the exodus of Asians.

CHRISTIANITY. One of the most vigorous examples of Christianity existing anywhere in Africa is found in Uganda, Christian witness there being largely concentrated in 2 churches, Catholic and Anglican. The pioneers were Anglicans who responded to Stanley's call for missionaries after visiting Kabaka Mutesa in 1875. The first resident evangelist was an African, Dallington Maftaa, a UMCA Anglican freed slave from Nyasaland, whom Stanley left behind to teach the Bible to the Kabaka. This he did for 2 years until the arrival of the first CMS missionaries in 1877. They were followed some months later by the first Catholic missionaries. The early history of Uganda involves a complex interaction of political and religious forces, with Catholics, Anglicans, and Muslims all playing a role. One of the results was the martyrdom of between 200 and 300 Catholic and Anglican African Christians at Namugongo during 1885-86.

CATHOLIC CHURCH. Catholicism was introduced into Uganda in 1879 when White Fathers reached the court of Kabaka Mutesa. They were joined in 1895 by Mill Hill priests, who assumed responsibility for eastern Uganda, and by Mill Hill sisters in 1902. These efforts proved successful from the beginning, and by 1912 there were 136,204 baptized Catholics in the 2 vicariates. In 1936 Catholic membership had grown to 477,000, 13% of the total population. Today the church has over 4 million baptized members and over 48% of the population professing to be Catholics. Impulses towards the early development of an indigenous clergy were also

CHURCH AND STATE. The constitution of 8 September 1967 establishes, in Articles 16 and 20, freedom of conscience and religion, the right to manifest and propagate one's religion, as well as the unconstitutionality of all discriminatory acts, includ-

ing those for religious reasons. After general Idi Amin, a Muslim Nubian of the Kakwa tribe, seized power, a wave of killings began. A Department of Religious Affairs within the office of the President was created in 1971 to facilitate surveillance of the churches. In early 1972 Amin intervened in a leadership dispute which threatened to divide the Anglican Church, refusing to allow the dioceses of West Buganda and Namirembe to secede from the rest of

**Catholic Church in Uganda.** *Above.* Anglican Archbishop Sabiti, with Pope Paul on his right, prays at Anglican Martyrs' sanctuary at Namugongo. *Right.* Sisters Scholasticate from Diocese of Jinja on television with traditional musical instruments (rattles, harps, etc), 1969.

the church. In late 1972, Amin expelled 58 missionaries from the country, 55 of whom were Catholics. The break in relations with Israel in 1972, followed by Uganda's increasingly friendly contacts with the Muslim countries of North Africa and the Middle East, particularly Libya, resulted in a growing aggressiveness on the part of Muslims.

In June 1973 Amin accused 28 Christian denominations and organizations of subversive activities and later banned them from the country. As a result, some groups were brought under the wing of the Anglican Church, while others went underground.

By 1976 the Amin government had been widely recognized internationally as a lawless regime. Killings were continuing to such an extent that around 400,000 Christians had either been killed by the regime's death squads since 1971, or had disappeared without trace, or had fled the country. In August 1976, therefore, Catholic and Muslim leaders sent a joint memorandum documenting these charges to Amin demanding an end to the killings. In February 1977 the Anglican bishops sent a further demand. Whereupon the Anglican archbishop Janani Luwum, was summoned to the president's office and was murdered apparently by Amin himself. Five further Anglican bishops on the death list managed to flee the country, and the missionary bishop of Karamoja was deported. Other victims included the Muslim chief Kadhi of Uganda. Documents then became available indicating that the regime intended to murder all leading Anglicans in government or positions of influence, and also every male in the Acholi and Lango tribes. A number of Pentecostal pastors in these 2 tribes were killed, and the 2 Anglican dioceses of Northern Uganda and Lango ceased to have any overt administration and went underground. Meanwhile, widespread charismatic revival among youth gathered momentum across Northern Uganda; and international outrage over Luwum's death became massive.

In September 1977, the regime announced the banning of 27 religious organizations for alleged subversion, including Baha'i, Salvation Army, Seventh-day Adventists, Southern Baptists, and a number of indigenous churches. Three months later, Friday was decreed a national day of rest in addition to Sunday.

**INTERDENOMINATIONAL ORGANIZATIONS.** The Uganda Joint Christian Council, with Anglican, Catholic and Orthodox membership, was founded in 1963 to provide for joint participation in education, social and medical work, press, radio and television, and to further ecumenical relations in the country. There is also the Uganda Association of Evangelicals, linking 4 denominations.

**BROADCASTING.** The government Radio Uganda provides 8 hours of religious broadcasting monthly, made up largely of 15-minute programmes shared equally by Catholics and Anglicans. From abroad, Protestant programmes can easily be heard over international stations including Radio Cordac (Burundi). For Catholics, UNDA is represented by a national association.

## BIBLIOGRAPHY


'Abamalaki in Buganda, 1914–1919', F.B. Welbourn, *Uganda journal* (Kampala), XXI, 2 (September, 1957), 150–161.

*A century of Christianity in Uganda, 1877–1977: a historical appraisal of the development of the Uganda Church over the last one hundred years.* Ed A.D.T. Tuma & P. Mutibwa. Nairobi: Uzima Press, 1978. 189p. (History of the Anglican Church).

'A congregation of African Jews in the heart of Uganda', A. Oded, *Dini na mila*, III, 1 (May, 1968), 7–11.

*A dictionary of Christianity in Uganda.* Ed. L. Pirouet. Kampala: Makerere University College, 1969. 86p. (Mimeographed).

*A short history of the Vicariate of the Upper Nile, Uganda.* J. Biermans. Kampala, 1920. (By one of the first Catholic bishops).

*Black evangelists: the spread of Christianity in Uganda, 1891–1914.* L. Pirouet. London: R. Collings, 1978. 255p.

*Building a Ugandan Church.* A.D.T. Tuma. Nairobi: East African Literature Bureau, 1978. 200p.

*Catholic directory of Eastern Africa 1977–1979.* Tabora (Tanzania): TMP Book Department, 1977. 258p. (Earlier editions 1959, 1965, 1968, 1971, 1974–76).

*Church planting in Uganda: a comparative study.* G. Van Rheenen. South Pasadena, CA: William Carey Library, 1976. 153p.

*East African rebels: a study of some independent churches.* F.B. Welbourn. London: SCM, 1961.

*Lugbara religion: ritual and authority among an East African people.* J. Middleton. London: Oxford University Press, 1960. 276p.

*Men without God? a study of the impact of the Christian message in the North of Uganda.* J.K. Russell. London: Highway Press, 1966. 96p. (By the Anglican bishop).

*Revival: an enquiry.* M.A.C. Warren. London: SCM, 1954. 123p. (On the Balokole or East African Revival).

*So abundant a harvest.* Y. Tourigny. London: Darton, Longman & Todd, 1978. 224p. (Centenary volume for Catholic Church in Uganda).

'The ghost cult in Bunyoro', J.H.M. Beattie, *Ethnology*, III, 2 (April, 1964), 127–151.

*The growth of the church in Buganda.* J.V. Taylor. London: SCM, 1958. 288p.

'The introduction and growth of Christianity in Busoga, 1891–1940, with particular reference to the roles of the Basoga clergymen, catechists and chiefs'. T. Tuma. Dissertation, University of London (SOAS), 1973. 392p.

'The Yakan or Allah water cult among the Lugbara', J. Middleton, *Journal of the Royal Anthropological Institute*, XCIII, 1 (Jan–June, 1963), 80–108.

*Uganda and the Mill Hill Fathers.* H.P. Gale. London: Macmillan, 1959.

'Witchcraft and sorcery in Lugbara', in J. Middleton & E.H, Winter (eds), *Witchcraft and sorcery in East Africa* (London: Routledge & Kegan Paul, 1963), p.257–275.


TABLE 2. ORGANIZED CHURCHES AND DENOMINATIONS IN UGANDA

| Official name 1 | Begun 2 | Type 3 | Counc 4 | Congs 5 | Adults 6 | Affiliated 7 | Names, notes, and other statistics (see Codebook) 8 |
|---|---|---|---|---|---|---|---|
| African Brotherhood Church | c1960 | I ind | xva.. | | 500 | 1,000 | *ABC, Uganda Pastorate.* M=ABC(Kenya). Kamba immigrants, et alii. |
| African Greek Orth Ch (D Eirenopolis) | 1929 | O Gre | Cw..K | 50 | 6,000 | 10,000 | *AGOC.* Under Greek P Alexandria. Schism ex CMS over paternalism. Ganda, Langi. 2x. |
| African Israel Church Nineveh | c1960 | I pen | .v... | | 21,000 | 32,000 | M=AICN(Kenya). Brought by workers of Mowlem contractors. Luo,Luhya. Banned 1977. |
| African Orthodox Autonomous Ch SS | 1966 | I ReO | ..... | 2 | 500 | 1,000 | SS=South of the Sahara. Schism ex AGOC protesting Greek paternalism. Banned 1977. |
| Association of Baptist Churches | 1961 | P Bap | xFG.G | 40 | 1,000 | 2,000 | M=CBFMS(USA). Ganda. 12f; missionaries expelled 1973. HQ Masaka. |
| Baptist Church of Uganda | 1962 | P Bap | T.... | 140 | 3,600 | 7,000 | M=Bapt Miss of EAfrica(Southern Baptists, USA). Banned 1977. 80n,24f,6p,1s,1711Y. |
| **Catholic Church in Uganda:** | 1879 | R Lat | P.SES | 277 | 1,957,900 | 3,434,988 | *Eklezia Enkatoliki.* C=6+3+17. 11p,4s(254). 312n,544x,310m,2004w,P=31%,151794Yy. |
| M Kampala (Rubaga) | 1894 | R Lat | Ps | 60 | 369,400 | 648,070 | 70% Ganda, 5% Ruanda, 5% Rundi, Goans. 1s. 93 96 68 502 35 22437 |
| D Arua | 1958 | R Lat | Pfscj | 28 | 220,400 | 386,680 | 42% Lugbara, 38% Alur, 18% Madi, 2% Kakwa. 26 51 56 121 28 20573 |
| D Fort Portal | 1961 | R Lat | Pcsc | 11 | 103,900 | 182,300 | 68% Toro, 13% Konjo, 8% Amba, 6% Kiga. 10 44 15 128 67 9087 |
| D Gulu | 1923 | R Lat | Ps | 15 | 158,200 | 277,489 | 90% Acholi, 1p. 17,000 Sudanese (1972). 9 29 37 149 18 10697 |
| D Hoima | 1965 | R Lat | Ps | 11 | 80,010 | 140,600 | 98% Nyoro (only tribe living in diocese). 18 19 0 56 18 8100 |
| D Jinja | 1966 | R Lat | Pmhm | 18 | 89,600 | 157,198 | In east. 98% Soga, 2% Samia (Luhya). 1p. 5 32 8 421 30 4226 |
| D Kabale | 1966 | R Lat | Ps | 16 | 136,500 | 239,424 | In extreme west. 85% Kiga, 15% Ruanda. 1p. 17 33 0 76 42 10474 |
| D Lira | 1968 | R Lat | Ps | 15 | 103,400 | 181,470 | 90% Lango. First parish 1930. 1p. 4 49 11 37 17 10456 |
| D Masaka | 1939 | R Lat | Ps | 28 | 198,300 | 347,821 | 80% Ganda, 10% Haya, 10% Ruanda. 1p,1s. 83 23 73 324 33 15765 |
| D Mbarara | 1934 | R Lat | Ps | 16 | 133,000 | 233,304 | 78% Nkole, 8% Kiga, 8% Ruanda. 1p. 17 49 13 147 45 6670 |
| D Moroto | 1965 | R Lat | Pfscj | 13 | 56,000 | 98,288 | 55% Karamojong, 20% Jie, 10% Topotha. 0 33 9 28 23 10379 |
| D Tororo | 1894 | R Lat | Ps | 46 | 309,100 | 542,344 | 60% Teso, 15% Gisu, 10% Sabei, 10% Luo. 1p. 30 86 20 147 21 22930 |
| Chosen Evangelical Revival | 1949 | I Ang | ..... | | 500 | 1,000 | *CER. Lwak Ayera (Chosen Ones):. Trumpeters.* Revival schism ex CURBZ. Acholi, Alur. |
| Church of Christ in Africa | c1960 | I Ang | xT.T. | | 3,000 | 5,000 | *Area Diocese of Tororo.* One of 8 Dioceses of M=CCA(Kenya). 80% Luo. Banned 1977. |
| Church of God in East Africa | 1969 | P Hol | x.... | | 2,000 | 4,000 | Luhya from M=CGEA(Kenya), aided by M=CoG(Anderson) (USA). Kampala, rural areas. 2f. |
| **Church of Uganda:** | 1875 | A Eva | AWAVK | 6,536 | 306,355 | 1,383,951 | *CURBZ.* M=CMS,RCMS,AIM(UK). 142f,8H,1j,7p(170),1s(175). 647n,28x,82517Y,33984y. |
| D Kampala | 1972 | A Eva | A | 16 | 3,000 | 5,000 | Metropolitan archiepiscopal see, in capital. 9 2 100 300 |
| D Ankole (1976 divided into E,W) | 1960 | A Low | A | 848 | 44,740 | 200,270 | Rural. 75% Nkole, 10% Ruanda (refugees). 907m,W=25%. 49 1 22073 14664 |
| D Bukedi | 1972 | A Low | A | 400 | 20,000 | 100,000 | Bukedi District, divided from D Mbale. Bakedi tribe. 20 0 5620 1181 |
| D Bunyoro-Kitara | 1972 | A Eva | A | 200 | 15,000 | 60,000 | Bunyoro District, divided from D Ruwenzori. Nyoro. 20 0 2000 1000 |
| D Busoga (Jinja) | 1972 | A Eva | A | 600 | 20,000 | 100,000 | Separated from D Namirembe. Soga. Church crop schemes. 30 0 2000 1000 |
| D Kigezi | 1967 | A Low | A | 780 | 50,000 | 200,000 | Rural, mountainous. M=RCMS(UK). Chiga. W=25%. 52 3 5000 2000 |
| D Madi & West Nile | 1969 | A Low | A | 420 | 12,500 | 30,000 | 1918, M=AIM(UK). Lugbara, Alur, Kakwa. 7f,2H,2h,1s,W=60%. 60 3 1500 1500 |
| D Mbale | 1961 | A Low | A | 229 | 25,000 | 120,000 | 1972, D Bukedi divided off. Now Gisu, Sabei. W=30%. 97 0 10800 2397 |
| D Namirembe | 1960 | A Cen | A | 990 | 30,000 | 160,000 | 1971 secession attempt. Ganda. 1H,W=40%. 101 5 19055 4640 |
| D Northern Uganda (1975, divided) | 1961 | A Eva | A | 400 | 50,000 | 150,000 | Acholi, Lango. 1970: 20,000 Sudan, Zaire refugees. W=12%. 58 7 2500 2500 |
| D Ruwenzori | 1960 | A Eva | A | 789 | 14,590 | 120,000 | Toro tribe. Many Congolese refugees. 750m. 62 3 4063 1350 |
| D Soroti (1975, divided) | 1961 | A Eva | A | 389 | 7,797 | 92,604 | M=CMS,BCMS. 1975, D Karamoja formed. 80% Teso. 25f,2H. 40 3 4046 472 |
| D West Buganda (1977, divided) | 1960 | A Eva | A | 475 | 13,728 | 46,077 | Rural. 1961–71, in schism opposing archbishop. W=14%. 49 1 3760 980 |
| Deliverance Church | 1962 | I pe4 | x.... | 5 | 500 | 1,000 | Split ex PAG. 1969 spread to Kenya (YCAF). Kampala. Youths. Banned 1977. |
| Eastern Orthodox Church | 1957 | I ReO | ..... | 1 | 100 | 200 | Schism ex AGOC by disaffected African Orthodox priest. Ganda. |
| Elim Pentecostal Fellowship of Uganda | 1962 | P Pe2 | ZGG.G | 500 | 10,000 | 30,000 | *PEFA.* 1962, M=EMA,IPA(USA). Widespread. Kampala, in north. Banned 1973. 12f,1s. |
| Episcopal Church in the Sudan | 1964 | A Low | aw... | | 5,000 | 10,000 | 1966: 120,000 refugees, 2 bishops, 30 priests from Sudan. Most returned by 1974. |
| Full Gospel Churches of Uganda | 1959 | P Pe2 | x.G.G | 100 | 2,000 | 6,000 | *Mungu Mwema* (*God is Good*). M=Glad Tidings Miss Soc (Canada). Banned 1977. 16f,1p. |
| Israel Anglican Church | 1948 | I mar | ..... | | 1,000 | 2,000 | *Dini ya Msambwa* (*Religion of the Ancestral Spirits*). 1967, Gisu resurgence. |
| Jehovah's Witnesses | 1935 | M Jeh | x.... | 2 | 128 | 300 | *IBSA.* 1935, literature distributed by missionaries. Banned 1973. 17f,18Y. |
| Maria Legio of Africa | | I CCa | x.... | | 2,000 | 5,000 | M=MLA(Kenya), large schism ex Roman Catholic Church. 90% Luo. Banned 1973. |
| Pentecostal Assemblies of God | 1935 | P Pe2 | ZFG.G | 265 | 15,000 | 40,000 | *PAG.* M=PAoC. 40% Teso, 15% Gisu, 15% Luhya. Banned 1973. 117n,9x,11f,1s(100),685Y. |
| Presbyterian Church of East Africa | | P Ref | Rwa.. | | 500 | 1,000 | *PCEA*(Kenya). Chaplaincy to expatriates (Kikuyu, Scottish) in Kampala. Banned 1977. |
| Religious Society of Friends | 1955 | P Qua | Q.... | 20 | 140 | 600 | East Africa Yearly Meeting. 30% Luhya from EAYM(Kenya). Banned 1973. W=85%. |
| Salvation Army | 1931 | P Sla | xwa.. | | 1,210 | 2,017 | *Jeshi la Wokovu. Uganda Div.* 40% Gisu, 20% Kenyans, 15% Soga, 10% Bakedi. Banned 1977. |
| Seventh-day Adventist Church | 1926 | P Adv | x.... | 300 | 9,387 | 18,000 | 50% Ganda, 21% Konjo. Banned 1977. 31n,1x,26f,1H,3h,1s,393t(15785),W=75%,1313Y. |
| Society of the One Almighty God | 1914 | I Ang | ..... | | 500 | 1,000 | *KOAB. Bamalaki. Malakite Ch.* 1914, schism of 92,000 ex CMS. Almost extinct. |
| United Pentecostal Fellowship | 1969 | I pe2 | ..... | | 1,000 | 2,000 | Split ex PEFA (Elim) among Toro, supported by Swedish and Finnish Pentecostals. |
| World-Wide Missions | 1962 | P ind | x.... | | 150 | 300 | M=World-Wide Missions(USA). Evangelicals linked with Pasadena, CA (USA). |
| Other African indigenous churches | | I | ..... | | 8,000 | 16,000 | Total about 24 (see below), including 15 immigrant bodies from Kenya and Zaire. |
| Other Protestant denominations | | P | ..... | | 500 | 1,000 | Total about 5 (see list below). |
| **Total affiliated (mid-1970)** | | | | **8,860** | **2,359,470** | **5,018,356** | **Total denominations (1970) . . . 56.** |
| **Total affiliated (mid-1975)** | | | | **10,400** | **2,904,300** | **6,177,100** | **Total denominations (1975) . . . 61.** |
| **Total affiliated (mid-1980)** | | | | **12,100** | **3,556,500** | **7,564,300** | **Total denominations (1980) . . . 66.** |

**NOTES ON TABLE ABOVE**

COLUMNS: for meanings and CODES (cols. 1, 3, 4, 8): see Codebook (Part 6) Column 1: **Boldface type** = church with over 10% of country's affiliated Christians.

NATIONAL COUNCILS (Column 4, 5th letter).

G = Uganda Association of Evangelicals (formerly, Evangelical Fellowship of Uganda).

K = Uganda Joint Christian Council (UJCC).

S = Uganda Episcopal Conference (UEC), also member of UJCC.

OTHER AFRICAN INDIGENOUS CHURCHES. Immigrant bodies from Kenya, in addition to those in table, are about 13, including: African Ch of the Holy Spirit, African Divine Ch (banned 1977), Apostolic Faith of Africa, Holy Ch of Kenya/Uganda, Holy Ghost Ch of East Africa (banned 1977), Lost Israelites of Kenya, Miracle Revival Fellowship Pentecostal Ch (claiming 15,000 adherents in Uganda), Nomiya Luo Ch. In addition, there are about 12 other groups, including: Apostolic Ch of Christ, Apostolic Ch of East Africa, Church of Christ in the World (Ugandan pentecostal), Church of Jesus the Messiah (in Luganda: Kanisa ya Isa Mesia; banned 1977), Eglise Kimbanguiste (EJCSK) from Zaire, Gospel of God (Vapostori, Apostles, from Rhodesia), Redeemed Ch of Uganda (leader from Ghana; banned 1977), Wide World Miracle Ch (banned 1977).

OTHER PROTESTANT DENOMINATIONS. These smaller groups include: Reformed Episcopal Ch (USA; 1956; working with AIM and CURBZ), Uganda Ch of Christ (Non-Instrumental) (banned 1973), United Pentecostal Ch (banned 1973).

OTHER MARGINAL PROTESTANT BODIES. Branhamites (Local Believers, End Time Believers) from USA.

**PEOPLES** (ethnolinguistic). Christians: 19.7% Ganda, 8.8% Teso (2.0% Bakedi, 0.6% Kumam), 8.7% Chiga (Kiga), 6.9% Acholi, 6.7% Nkole, 6.5% Toro, 5.2% Soga, 4.6% Lango, 4.0% Nyoro, 3.8% Gisu, 3.5% Lugbara, 3.1% Alur, 2.8% Ruanda, 2.2% Luhya, 1.8% Rundi, 1.7% Luo, 1.4% Madi, 1.4% Sabei, 1.2% Karamojong, 0.8% Padhola, 0.7% Haya, 0.6% Konjo, 0.6% Sudanese, 0.4% Jie, 0.3% Amba, 0.3% Kakwa, 0.2% Goanese, 0.2% Topotha, 0.1% Kikuyu, 0.1% European (White), 0.1% Teuso, 0.1% Labwor, 0.1% Pokot (Suk).

## COUNTRY-WIDE TOTALS

EVANGELIZATION (see Part 5). 1900: 24%. 1970: 94%. 1980: 98%. *Mass evangelism.* Mainly since 1935 through the East African Revival Movement (Balokole) and its large conventions. *Radiophonic evangelism.* TWR, RVOG, Radio Cordac, Radio Vatican, et alia.

FOREIGN MISSIONARIES AND PERSONNEL (nationals serving abroad) (1973). Total 128 in Burundi, Canada, Kenya, Rhodesia, Rwanda, Sudan, Tanzania, UK, USA, and Zaire: about 110 Roman Catholics, 12 Anglicans, 6 African indigenous.

FOREIGN MISSIONARIES AND PERSONNEL (aliens from abroad) (1973). Total 1,566. *From Western world.* 1,465: 1,160 Roman Catholics, 143 Anglicans (136 in 6 UK societies, 4 in 2 USA societies, 3 in 1 Canada society), 142 Protestants (94 in 13 USA societies, 29 in 2 Canada societies, 10 in 3 UK societies, 5 in 2 Australia societies, 4 in 2 WGermany societies), 17 marginal Protestants (Jehovah's Witnesses), 3 Orthodox from Greece. By 1975, North American missionaries had fallen to 28. *From Communist world.* About 7 Roman Catholics (4 from Yugoslavia, 3 Poland). *From Third World.* 94: about 60 Roman Catholics from Kenya, Sudan, Zaire, et alia, about 30 African indigenous mostly from Kenya, 2 Anglicans, 2 Protestants.

INSTITUTIONS (church-operated) (1973). Total 230, including about 100 higher schools (13 minor seminaries; rest state-controlled), 100 medical centres (31 hospitals), 3 presses, 13 religious communities, 2 research centres, 9 seminaries (4 RC, 4 Protestant, 1 Anglican).

PERIODICALS. About 28 titles (13 RC, 8 Anglican, 2 SDA).

PERSONNEL. About 13,616 (12,050 national, 1,566 foreign).

RELIGIOUS LIBRARIES. About 28.

SCRIPTURE DISTRIBUTION (1975). Annual totals: 52,048 Bibles (8% free, 88% subsidized, 4% commercial), 79,284 NTs (29% free, 70% subsidized, 1% commercial), 455,474 UBS portions, 372,621 UBS selections. *Translations completed.* Portion: 13 languages since 1887. NT: 7 languages since 1893. Bible: 4 languages since 1896.

SERVICE AGENCIES. About 59, including AE, ARU, BB, CCCI, CEF, COMSIU, CRS, MAP, NCCW, NCLA, SU, UCPA, UEC, UJCC, WGC, YCS, YCW, YMCA, YWCA.

## ADDITIONAL DATA ON CHURCHES

CATHOLIC CHURCH IN UGANDA. Name, Eklezia Enkatoliki mu Uganda (a combination of Luganda and Greek). *Catechumens.* (1959) 71,842; (1961) 132,168; (1963) 122,517. The total reported in 1969 was 74,342, divided as follows among the 12 dioceses in order (and included in column 7): 51000, 5000, 11000, 3456, 2000, 926, 12397, 3457, 3454, 8304, 4421, 14827. *Annual baptisms.* (1972) 76.7% infant, 23.3% adult. *National priests.* The 2 first Ugandan priests were ordained in 1913 (the first Africans ordained in the modern era). In 1939 Masaka became the first modern African vicariate (and in 1953 diocese) to receive an African bishop; it is now the most africanized of the Uganda dioceses. *Brothers.* Including 157 Ugandans. *Sisters.* Including 1,533 Ugandans. *Seminaries.* Including Katigondo (philosophy), Gaba (theology). There are also Sudanese seminarians in them. *Seminarians.* (1972) 254, all secular. *Catechists.* Total (1970) about 4,000, mostly part-time. Training is in 7 diocesan or interdiocesan and 4 regional schools. *Indigenous religious congregations.* Priests: Apostles of Jesus (1968), Religious African Missionary Congregation (begun 1968; 2 priests, 17 theologians, novices and postulants, 154 aspirants from 6 African countries). Brothers: Bannakaroli (Brothers of St Charles Lwanga, begun 1927), Marian Brothers. Sisters: 700 Bannabikira (Daughters of the Virgin, begun 1910), 189 Our Lady of Good Counsel (begun 1937), 165 Little Sisters Regular Third Order of St Francis of Assisi (begun 1923, 36 in Kenya), 130 Banyatereza (Daughters of St Theresa, begun 1940), 97 Little Sisters of Mary Immaculate (begun 1942), 80 Immaculate Heart of Mary (begun 1948), Maria Reparatrix, Perpetual Adoration (begun 1960). *Sudanese congregation.* 26 Sisters of the Sacred Heart (begun Juba 1950, moved to Arua, Uganda, 1963). *Main foreign congregations.* Priests: FSCJ, MHM, CSC. Brothers: FICP, SC. Sisters: Our Lady of Africa, Verona Sisters, Sacred Heart, Franciscan Missionary Sisters for Africa.

*Catholic organizations.* The Uganda Episcopal Conference (UEC) is a member of AMECEA and of SECAM. Religious personnel are represented by the Conference of Major Superiors in Uganda (COMSIU) for men, and the Association of Religious Personnel of Uganda (Associatio Religiosarum Ugandae, ARU) for sisters. There are no national presbyteral or pastoral councils. The National Council of the Lay Apostolate and its secretariat co-ordinate iay activities, the principal lay movements being YCS, YCW, Catholic Boy Scouts and Girl Guides, Legion of Mary, National Committee of Catholic Women, Parents' Association, Catholic Teachers Guild, St Vincent de Paul, Child Welfare Society and Catholic Women's Clubs. For the armed forces, Uganda forms a military vicariate.

The Holy See has diplomatic relations with Uganda and is represented to government and the Catholic hierarchy by a pro-nuncio in Kampala.

Catholic schools in 1973 numbered 1,495 primary (197,125 pupils) and 78 secondary (14,216). The Obote government had earlier assumed responsibility for the administration of all schools, but the degree of integration of former church schools into the public educational system varies according to the level involved. In practice, the church link is still retained.

The Catholic medical programme is extensive, with 20 hospitals (3,212 beds), 4 leprosaria, 24 dispensaries, 24 maternities, 8 baby nutrition centres, 3 homes for polio victims and 2 schools for blind children. There are also homes for the aged, and the Comboni Charity Fund which provides secondary school scholarships for refugees. Each diocese has a co-operative movement, a credit union and a loan fund. The Catholic Church is involved in severalextensive agricultural projects, such as the Mugalibe Tea and Dairy Schemes, the Buswale Agricultural Scheme, and the Agricultural and Animal Husbandry School in Tororo.

CHURCH OF UGANDA. Full name: Church of Uganda, Rwanda, Burundi and Boga-Zaire (the latter being a diocese in the republic of Zaire), until 1980. Diocese of Mbale = Ubulabirizi bwa Mbale. *Early dioceses.* The first diocese, formed in 1884, was Eastern Equatorial Africa, which included also Kenya and Tanganyika. From it the diocese of Uganda was formed in 1897, and in turn the diocese of the Upper Nile in 1926. In 1960–61 these 2 dioceses were divided into several dioceses as shown in columns 1–2 above. *New dioceses.* In addition to the 1970–72 situation depicted in the table above, D Lango was subsequently formed out of D Northern Uganda; in 1975 D Karamoja was formed out of D Soroti; in 1976, D Ankole was divided into East and West; in 1977 D Singo-Buweekula was formed out of D West Buganda; and further new dioceses were envisaged for 1978 onwards. *Bishops.* In 1976, there were 15 diocesan bishops in Uganda, and 3 assistant bishops. *Clergy.* In 1976, there were 757 clergy including 40 archdeacons. *East African Revival.* Members of the Revival, the Balokole (Saved Ones), are mostly Anglicans, and numbered in 1975 about 150,000 committed adult members, with a total community of about 450,000 (about half being in Kigezi and Ankole), divided among 3 rival factions. *Lay workers* (1977). 5,000 men, 200 women. *Lay readers* (1977). 1,000 men, 50 women. *Seminarians* (1977). 350.

SEVENTH-DAY ADVENTIST CHURCH. Uganda Field (organized 1927), in the SDA East African Union.

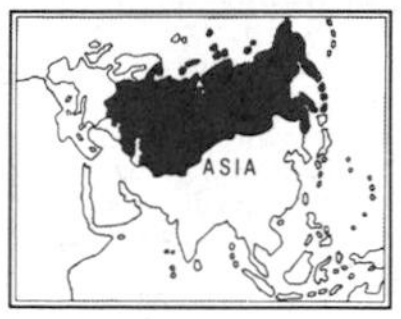


# USSR

## SECULAR DATA

**STATE. Official name:** The Union of Soviet Socialist Republics, USSR (Soyuz Sovetskikh Sotsialisticheskikh Respublik, SSSR). Unofficial name: The Soviet Union. Adjectives of nationality: Soviet; also Ukrainian, Byelorussian.

**Flag** (shown above right): Red field with gold hammer and sickle below gold-bordered star in upper hoist corner.

**Area:** 22,402,200 sq. km. (8,649,539 sq. miles). Agricultural land: 27.1%.

**Government:** One-party Communist state, since 1917 (1547 empire, 1905 constitutional monarchy, 1917 Bolshevik revolution).

**Legislature:** Supreme Soviet: Soviet of the Union, 767 members; Soviet of Nationalities, 750 members.

**Official language:** Russian (*Russki*). Each republic also uses its own language as co-official.

**Chief cities:** capital Moscow 7,528,000 (1974), Leningrad 4,243,000, Kiev 1,887,000, Tashkent 1,552,000, Baku 1,359,000, Kharkov 1,330,000, Gorki 1,260,000, Novosibirsk 1,243,000.

**Political divisions:** 15 Republics, divided into 130 Territories and Regions (including 20 Autonomous Republics, 8 Autonomous Regions, 10 National Areas), divided into 2,970 Districts (41,049 Rural Districts), 1,978 Towns, and 3,542 Urban Settlements.

**Armed forces** (1976): Total 3,650,000 regular (excluding 750,000 uniformed civilians): strategic nuclear forces 925,000 (2,650 combat aircraft), army 1,825,000, navy 450,000 (645 combat aircraft), air force 450,000 (5,350 combat aircraft). Reserves: up to 25 million. Paramilitary forces: 350,000 (175,000 KGB border guards, 175,000 MVD security troops), also 9 million DOSAAF part-time military training organization.

**DEMOGRAPHY. Population:** 262,085,000 (census of 15.I.1979. For 1970–2000 (UN), see last row of Table 1). Population density (1975): 11/sq. km. (29/sq. mile). Under 15 years: 31%. Growth rate (1975–80): 1.00% per year (births 1.84%, deaths –0.84%). Life expectancy (1975–80): 70.9 years. Household size: 3.7 persons.

**Major languages:** Russian (spoken by 76% of population), Ukrainian, Uzbek, Byelorussian, Tatar, Kazakh, Armenian, Azerbaijani, Georgian, Moldavian, Lithuanian, and over 120 other main languages (Soviet Academy of Sciences); 65 being literary.

**Urban dwellers** (1970): 57.1%. Urban growth rate (1950–70): 3.3% per year.

**Labour force:** 48%.

**Refugees** (1977): 60,000 from People's Republic of China. Exiles abroad: 110,634 (71,634 Jews to USA from 1973-76, 10,000 to Israel from 1973–76, 17,000 citizens to France, 12,000 ethnic Germans to FRG). A further 150,000 Jews are awaiting exit visas.

**Tourists** (1960): 712,000. (1970) 2,059,000. (1974) 3,446,933.

ETHNOLINGUISTIC GROUPS: (1970) 53.1% Russian, 16.9% Ukrainian (0.2% Ruthenian) 3.8% Uzbek, 3.7% Byelorussian, 2.5% Tatar, 2.2% Kazakh, 1.8% Azerbaijani (Azeri), 1.5% Armenian, 1.3% Georgian, 1.2% Jewish, 1.1% Moldavian, 1.1% Lithuanian, 0.9% Tadzhik, 0.8% German, 0.7% Chuvash, 0.7% Polish, 0.6% Mordvin, 0.6% Latvian, 0.6% Kirgiz, 0.6% Turkmen, 0.5% Bashkir, 0.5% Dagestani (0.2% Avar, 0.1% Dargin, 0.1% Lezgin, Tabasaran), 0.4% Estonian, 0.3% Udmurt, 0.3% Chechen, 0.2% Bulgar, 0.2% Mari, 0.2% Komi, 0.2% Ossetian, 0.2% Circassian, 0.2% Gypsy, 0.1% Korean (360,000), 0.1% Ingush, 0.1% Greek, 0.1% Gagauz, 0.1% Karelian, 0.1% Romanian, 0.1% Buryat, 0.1% Hungarian, 0.1% Yakut, 0.1% Kara-Kalpak, 0.1% Uighur, Finnish (100,000), Kurdish, Kalmyk, Paleoasiatic (Aboriginal Siberian) (40,000), Samoyed (40,000), Eskimo, Czech, Slovak, Assyrian, Lapp, Persian, Tat, Chinese, Dungan, Baluchi, & a large number of smaller peoples. Since 1970, relative size of ethnic Muslim peoples has increased markedly due to higher fertility, as shown in the 1979 census thus: (1979) 52.4% Russian, 16.2% Ukrainian (0.2% Ruthenian), 4.8% Uzbek, 3.6% Byelorussian, 2.5% Kazakh, 2.4% Tatar, 2.1% Azerbaijani (Azeri), 1.6% Armenian, 1.4% Georgian, 1.1% Moldavian, 1.1% Tadzhik, 1.1% Lithuanian, 0.8% Turkmen, 0.7% German, 0.7% Kirgiz, 0.7% Jewish, 0.7% Chuvash, 0.6% Dagestani, 0.5% Latvian, 0.5% Bashkir, 0.5% Mordvin, 0.4% Polish, 0.4% Estonian, 0.3% Chechen, 0.3% Udmurt, 0.2% Mari, 0.2% Ossetian, 0.2% Komi, 0.1% Korean, 0.1% Bulgar, 0.1% Buryat, 0.1% Greek, 0.1% Yakut, 0.1% Circassian, 0.1% Kara-Kalpak, 0.1% Uighur, 0.1% Gypsy, 0.1% Ingush, 0.1% Gagauz, 0.1% Hungarian, 0.1% Tuvinian, 0.1% Karelian, 0.1% Kalmyk, et alii.

**MONEY** (1977). **Monetary unit:** rouble (=100 kopeks); **US$1** = Rub 0.754.

**National income per person:** US$2,010. Average annual family income: US$7,437.

**Inflation:** (1970–74) small.

**Cost of living in capital** (1976): index 136 (Washington DC = 100). Daily cost of living: US$46.

HEALTH. Hospitals: 25,400 (2,793,000 beds). Doctors: 634,600.

*Continued overleaf*

TABLE 1. RELIGIOUS ADHERENTS IN THE USSR

| Year | 1900 | | mid-1970 | | Annual change, 1970–1980 | | | | mid-1975 | | mid-1980 | | 2000 | |
|---|---|---|---|---|---|---|---|---|---|---|---|---|---|---|
| *Name* | *Adherents* | *%* | *Adherents* | *%* | *Natural* | *Conversion* | *Total* | *Rate* | *Adherents* | *%* | *Adherents* | *%* | *Adherents* | *%* |
| **Christians** | **104,993,000** | **83.6** | **86,012,300** | **35.4** | **907,238** | **164,182** | **1,071,420** | **1.17** | **91,285,000** | **35.8** | **96,726,500** | **36.1** | **118,101,000** | **37.5** |
| crypto-Christians | 0 | 0.0 | 23,511,300 | 9.7 | 257,060 | 225,760 | 482,820 | 1.87 | 25,865,000 | 10.1 | 28,339,500 | 10.6 | 39,658,000 | 12.6 |
| professing | 104,993,000 | 83.6 | 62,501,000 | 25.7 | 650,178 | –61,578 | 588,600 | 0.90 | 65,420,000 | 25.6 | 68,387,000 | 25.5 | 78,443,000 | 24.9 |
| Orthodox | 91,188,000 | 72.6 | 55,000,000 | 22.7 | 572,846 | –40,246 | 532,600 | 0.92 | 57,639,000 | 22.6 | 60,326,000 | 22.5 | 69,306,000 | 22.0 |
| Protestants | 2,213,000 | 1.8 | 4,000,000 | 1.6 | 41,245 | –11,245 | 30,000 | 0.72 | 4,150,000 | 1.6 | 4,300,000 | 1.6 | 5,355,000 | 1.7 |
| Roman Catholics | 11,588,000 | 9.2 | 3,500,000 | 1.4 | 36,077 | –10,077 | 26,000 | 0.72 | 3,630,000 | 1.4 | 3,760,000 | 1.4 | 3,780,000 | 1.2 |
| Anglicans | 4,000 | 0.0 | 1,000 | 0.0 | 10 | –10 | 0 | 0.00 | 1,000 | 0.0 | 1,000 | 0.0 | 2,000 | 0.0 |
| nominal | 7,991,000 | 6.4 | 0 | 0.0 | 0 | 0 | 0 | 0.00 | 0 | 0.0 | 0 | 0.0 | 0 | 0.0 |
| affiliated | 97,002,000 | 77.2 | 86,012,300 | 35.4 | 907,238 | 164,182 | 1,071,420 | 1.17 | 91,285,000 | 35.8 | 96,726,500 | 36.1 | 118,101,000 | 37.5 |
| total practising | 87,301,800 | *90* | 64,509,220 | *75* | 689,500 | 307,518 | 997,018 | 1.44 | 69,376,600 | *76* | 74,479,400 | *77* | 94,480,800 | *80* |
| non-practising | 9,700,200 | *10* | 21,503,080 | *25* | 217,738 | –143,336 | 74,402 | 0.34 | 21,908,400 | *24* | 22,247,100 | *23* | 23,620,200 | *20* |
| Orthodox | 85,000,000 | 67.6 | 75,174,000 | 31.0 | 790,828 | 110,572 | 901,400 | 1.13 | 79,572,000 | 31.2 | 84,188,000 | 31.4 | 102,384,000 | 32.5 |
| Orthodox pentecostals | 0 | 0.0 | 10,000 | 0.0 | 497 | 8,503 | 9,000 | 18.00 | 50,000 | 0.0 | 100,000 | 0.0 | 400,000 | 0.1 |
| Protestants | 2,000,000 | 1.6 | 6,434,300 | 2.7 | 70,971 | 63,099 | 134,070 | 1.88 | 7,141,000 | 2.8 | 7,775,000 | 2.9 | 10,396,000 | 3.3 |
| Evangelicals | 1,800,000 | 1.4 | 6,306,000 | 2.6 | 69,551 | 61,849 | 131,400 | 1.88 | 6,998,000 | 2.7 | 7,620,000 | 2.8 | 10,188,000 | 3.2 |
| Roman Catholics | 10,000,000 | 8.0 | 4,393,500 | 1.8 | 45,320 | –9,670 | 35,650 | 0.78 | 4,560,000 | 1.8 | 4,750,000 | 1.8 | 5,300,000 | 1.7 |
| Marginal Protestants | 0 | 0.0 | 10,000 | 0.0 | 114 | 186 | 300 | 2.61 | 11,500 | 0.0 | 13,000 | 0.0 | 20,000 | 0.0 |
| Anglicans | 2,000 | 0.0 | 500 | 0.0 | 5 | –5 | 0 | 0.00 | 500 | 0.0 | 500 | 0.0 | 1,000 | 0.0 |
| Non-religious | 200,000 | 0.2 | 68,151,700 | 29.1 | 740,645 | 235,575 | 976,220 | 1.35 | 72,770,700 | 28.5 | 77,913,900 | 29.1 | 96,257,000 | 30.6 |
| Atheists | 49,800 | 0.0 | 56,500,000 | 23.3 | 575,381 | –300,081 | 275,300 | 0.48 | 57,894,000 | 22.7 | 59,253,000 | 22.1 | 62,060,000 | 19.7 |
| Muslims | 14,013,000 | 11.2 | 28,000,000 | 11.5 | 288,952 | –59,252 | 229,700 | 0.79 | 29,074,000 | 11.4 | 30,297,000 | 11.3 | 34,653,000 | 11.0 |
| Yazidis | 14,000 | 0.0 | 12,000 | 0.0 | –10 | –50 | –60 | –0.51 | 11,700 | 0.0 | 11,400 | 0.0 | 10,000 | 0.0 |
| Jews | 5,263,000 | 4.2 | 3,000,000 | 1.2 | 13,000 | –1,000 | 12,000 | 0.39 | 3,060,000 | 1.2 | 3,120,000 | 1.2 | 3,300,000 | 1.0 |
| Karaites | 12,900 | 0.0 | 5,500 | 0.0 | –40 | 0 | –40 | –0.75 | 5,300 | 0.0 | 5,100 | 0.0 | 5,400 | 0.0 |
| Shamanists | 700,000 | 0.5 | 600,000 | 0.2 | 4,969 | –24,969 | –20,000 | –4.00 | 500,000 | 0.2 | 400,000 | 0.1 | 300,000 | 0.1 |
| Buddhists | 437,000 | 0.3 | 500,000 | 0.2 | 4,472 | –14,472 | –10,000 | –2.22 | 450,000 | 0.2 | 400,000 | 0.1 | 350,000 | 0.1 |
| Baha'is | 200 | 0.0 | 4,000 | 0.0 | 43 | 17 | 60 | 1.40 | 4,300 | 0.0 | 4,600 | 0.0 | 6,000 | 0.0 |
| **Country's population** | **125,656,000** | **100.0** | **242,768,000** | **100.0** | **2,534,700** | **0** | **2,534,700** | **0.99** | **255,038,000** | **100.0** | **268,115,000** | **100.0** | **315,027,000** | **100.0** |

SECULAR DATA *concluded.*
Lepers: 12,000. Blind: 350,000. Psychotics: 2,300,000. Prisoners (1979): 10 million (10,000 political, 1,000 religious) in 1,000 labour camps and jails.

**EDUCATION.** Adult literacy: (1959) 98%, (1970) 100%. Education rate: 65%. Schools: 181,000. Universities: 58.

**LITERATURE.** Annual new book titles (1973): 80,196. Periodicals: 5,618. Scientific journals: 2,100. Newspapers: 647 dailies, 7,216 non-daily.

**COMMUNICATION** (per 1,000 people). Phones: 62. Radios: 442. TV sets: 197. Daily newspaper circulation: 347 copies.

**FOOTNOTES TO TABLE 1.**

COLUMNS, ROWS. For meanings and definitions, see Codebook (Part 6). Note that, by definition, total 'Christians' = professing + crypto-Christians, which also = affiliated + nominal Christians. Percentages may not always total exactly, due to rounding.

NOTE ON BOUNDARIES. The figures for 1900 refer to territory within the present boundaries of the USSR. In 1900 within the empire 80% of Estonia and 56% of Latvia were Lutherans, and most of Lithuania and western Byelorussia were Roman Catholics. Finland (excluded from the table above) was within the empire until 1917, as was part of Poland until 1918.

CENSUSES. **28.1.1897** (First General Census of the Empire, within 1897 boundaries including Finland): 72.0% Orthodox (69.3% Russian Orthodox (87,123,604 persons; including Ukrainian, Georgian), 1.8% Old Believers and other schismatics (2,204,596), 0.9% Armenian Apostolics (1,179,241)), 11.1% Muslims, 9.1% Roman Catholics, 4.2% Jews (including Karaites), 2.9% Protestants (3,572,653 Lutherans, 85,400 Reformed, 66,564 Mennonites, 38,139 Baptists), 0.4% shamanists, 0.3% Buddhists. After adjusting boundaries to include only territory within the USSR in 1975, these percentages for the year 1900 become as shown in the first column of figures in the table. Some observers consider that around the year 1900 Orthodox dissenters and sectarians numbered up to 25 million, but here they are treated as revolts within Orthodoxy. In the **1937** census, the government included a question on religion; the results were suppressed and never published, but 33% of the urban population and 67% of the rural population were said to have called themselves 'believers' (i.e. in any religion), making 56% for the whole of the USSR; in 1945, it was said to be 50% for the entire Red Army. No subsequent census has enumerated religion. The figures for 1970 above give a total of 38.8% professing believers of all kinds (in any religion), which indicates both the long-term gradual erosion of professing belief caused by state hostility, and also the conservative nature of the estimates in this table.

**NOTES ON RELIGIONS**

AFFILIATED CHRISTIANS. In 1970, our adjective 'affiliated' refers (as elsewhere in this Encyclopedia) to Christians known to the churches (for the Orthodox, known as baptized), and does not refer merely to persons inscribed on congregational rolls in accordance with state law since these rolls are meaningless because limited by state law to a maximum of 20 persons per congregation. Affiliation statistics are not officially collected, compiled or published in the USSR, hence the 1970 figures in this table must be regarded only as rough estimates based on piecemeal documentation (the methodology is described in Table 2 below under ADDITIONAL DATA ON CHURCHES).

ATHEISTS. There is a long history of militant atheism in the USSR, from the League of Militant Godless (1925–41; 3 million members by 1930, 5 million in 50,000 local groups by 1935), Groups of Godless Youth, and the All-Union Society for the Dissemination of Scientific and Political Knowledge (founded in 1947), to the ongoing massive atheistic campaigns from 1964 onwards, symbolized in the contemporary journal *Nauka i Religia* (*Science and religion*, circulation 140,000), university departments and specialized schools of atheism (in a dozen universities) and, at the more popular level, the Museums of Atheism in Leningrad and from 1966 in Vilnius. Each year, there are still millions of atheistic lectures, exhibitions, film shows, etc, and several thousand new book titles a year are published in millions of copies. In Byelorussia alone, in 1965 there were 5,500 atheist lecturers and political instructors at work, together with 1,400 propagandists and 23,000 workers called agitators (who conduct individual work with believers). It is widely agreed by analysts and observers, however, that Marxist ideology and militant atheism as a pseudo-religion or quasi-religion in the USSR has been at an end since the 1950s, and that only a small minority among CPSU members even pretends to take Marxist ideology seriously. Most of what passes for 'scientific atheism' is very crude, a mere repetition of 18th- and 19th-century arguments. Nevertheless, it is possible to emunerate those holding this ideology even if in attenuated form. Atheists and anti-religious persons, defined in this Encyclopedia as those avowedly opposed to religion, were estimated at 56.5 million in 1970 by totalling membership of the CPSU (14.0 million party members and candidates, over 18 years (rising to 17 million members by 1980): 40% workers, 15% collective farmers, 45% engineers/scientists/teachers/bureaucrats/etc), Komsomol (VLKSM; All-Union Leninist Communist League of Youth, preparing people for party membership; over 28 million members, including 8 million aged 14 to 18; 160 newspapers with 64 million circulation), Pioneers (All-Union Lenin Pioneer Organization; militantly atheistic; 20 million members aged 10–15, increasing to 25 million by 1975), and Octoberists (14.5 million children aged 7–9). Distribution of CPSU membership by republics is shown in the table in the text below. Surveys of religion and atheism by Soviet scientists indicate that the proportion of atheists in the population declines gradually with age; it approaches 90% for the 16–19 years age-group but then falls evenly to around 20% for the over-70 age-group.

BAHA'IS. In about 12 isolated groups; Persians and others. Baha'i entered before 1892 into Armenia, Azerbaijan, Georgia and Turkmenistan. The latter had the first of Baha'i's 7 temples until it was demolished in 1963. There has been severe persecution in 1928, 1938 and subsequently.

BUDDHISTS. Mahayana (Buryats, Kalymyks, and other Mongols; also Tuvinians, and a minority of the 360,000 Koreans), with Tantrayana in parts of Siberia. Active lamas number about 300. Two Buddhist monasteries were still open in 1976 (Ivolga near Ulan-Ude, Aga near Chita). Since 1960 many converts have arisen in European Russia, Estonia and Lithuania.

CHRISTIANS. *Conversions*. In the column 'Conversion', the figures are very rough estimates intended to give only the general order of magnitude of conversions to or defections from the various groupings. What seems most likely to be happening (1970–80) in all the churches is that (1) a large number of the children of believers (the demographic increase shown) are baptized (Orthodox) or dedicated in church (Baptists) but then grow up apart from the faith of their parents as a result of the state's anti-religious attitudes, especially the prohibition of religious education and church attendance for children between the ages of 3 and 18; but also that (2) a large number of such persons have merely hidden their religiosity while children, and at a later stage in their lives are converted back to active Christianity. In addition, there are large numbers of decisions for Christ among youth at evangelistic gatherings (10,000 decisions being reported in Siberia alone for 1971, especially in forest meetings). The figures in this column are each the nett total of conversions minus defections; where the figure is negative, defections outnumber conversions. *Future projections*. As in all countries with massive Christian populations, the future growth or expansion of the churches (as measured by totals of affiliated Christians) depends primarily on internal factors (the churches' own inner dynamic, quality of life, sense of mission, and so on), and only secondarily does it depend on external factors (state hostility, persecution, secularism, and so on). This means that recent trends in the totals of affiliated Christians over the last 2 or 3 decades, as measured in the table above by natural increase and conversion increase, are relatively stable and likely to continue, and so may legitimately be projected into the near future. Future state attitudes to religion will influence primarily not totals of affiliated Christians, but totals of professing Christians and crypto-Christians; if the state becomes more tolerant, professing Christians will increase in numbers and crypto-Christians will decrease; but if the state becomes more virulently anti-Christian, professing Christians will decrease in number and crypto-Christians will increase. In other words, the churches in themselves (as measured by the number of affiliated Christians) will continue to grow with a certain measure of autonomy; if state pressure then increases, millions more will simply go underground and hide their activities from the state and society. In the USSR, future state attitudes and policies towards religion are unpredictable; hence our percentages above for professing and crypto-Christians over the period 1980–2000 must be regarded only as one set of possible development, being projections based on current trends.

COUNTRY'S POPULATION. During World War II, around 18,000,000 USSR military and civilians were killed.

CRYPTO-CHRISTIANS. The term in this USSR context refers to 5 quite different groups, who in aggregate are popularly referred to as the underground church, clandestine church, catacomb church, church of silence, or church of the martyrs. (1) The first are unorganized masses of affiliated (baptized) Christians known individually to the legal churches (especially the Russian Orthodox Church) but who remain unknown to (or regarded as non-religious by) the state through their non-profession and non-practice, irregular practice or secret practice. In 1970 these secret believers were mainly young persons and students preparing for future careers, and also the younger middle-aged classes and professionals. The total is expected to decrease with time as Christians become more accepted as citizens with guaranteed rights. (2) There are several millions of Christians, especially Ukrainian Catholics, Jehovah's Witnesses and other sects, who have over the decades been imprisoned en masse, deported to Siberia, or otherwise scattered and dispersed in labour camps or in exile mostly across Siberia. Few are counted as Christians by the state, but many remain believing and witnessing Christians and are remembered as such by families and friends in their home churches. (3) There are several unregistered denominations (the best-known being the CCECB), and numerous unregistered congregations in legal denominations, which are forced to remain illegal and to operate underground by the state's refusal to register them despite repeated requests. (4) There are a number of totally and deliberately clandestine bodies, namely the over 40 highly-organized illegal underground churches, with centrally-organized nation-wide networks of believers totalling in 1970 well over half a million adherents (see Table 2). Lastly (5) there are scattered across the entire Soviet Union several hundred thousand organized and unorganized isolated radio believers (see Table 2).

JEWS. Declined from 5.26 million in 1900 to 3.02 million in 1939, with 1.30 million massacred during 1941–45. In the 1970 official Soviet census, 2,151,000 Jews were recorded, but Western experts estimated the real figure at 3.0 million, the other 849,000 being either crypto-Jews unwilling to reveal their religion to the state, or secularized non-religious Jews. Of the total in 1970, around 500,000 adults were practising Jews (25%). By 1969, an average of 12,000 Jews a year were emigrating to Israel; in 1972 emigration increased to 35,500 and in 1973 to 34,750, falling to 30,500 in 1978 making an annual average of about 17,000 during the 1970s, which figure is then deducted from Jewish annual population increase of about 30,000 to arrive at the figure for 1970–80 in the column 'Natural change' above (13,000). Since 1917, over 3,000 synagogues have been boarded up, knocked down or desecrated; in 1970, only 60 remained open in the whole of the USSR, and in 1975 only 50.

KARAITES (Readers of the Scriptures). An 8th-century AD Jewish sect similar to the Sadducees, rejecting Jewish Talmudic oral tradition. Badly treated under Soviet rule, they have declined by emigration, mostly to Israel and Poland, from 10,000 in 1917, and 8,300 in 1926, to 5,900 in 1959.

MUSLIMS. *Muslim political entities*. There are 6 Muslim nations or peoples with their own republics (SSRs): Azeris (Azerbaijan), Kazakhs (Kazakhstan), Kirgiz (Kirgizia), Tadzhiks (Tadzhikstan), Turkmen (Turkmenistan), and Uzbeks (Uzbekistan); there are also 9 Muslim ASSRs and 4 AOs (autonomous regions). *Ethnic Muslims*. The total population of these Muslim SSRs, ASSRs and AOs was 49,700,000 in the 1970 census. Of these residents, 15,470,000 were ethnically non-Muslims (mainly Russian, Ukrainian and Byelorussian immigrants), leaving 34,230,000 ethnic Muslims in the Muslim regions and a grand total of 35,400,000 including those in non-Muslim republics and areas. Proportionate to the whole population, ethnic Muslims are increasing markedly due to higher fertility and birth rate, from 11.6% of the population (1959 census) to 14.6% (1970 census) to 15.6% by 1977, with projected estimates for AD 2000 running from 22% to as high as 31%. *Professing Muslims*. Of the ethnic Muslims, about 82% (28 million) in 1974 professed to be or regarded themselves individually as religious Muslims, the rest being professedly atheists or non-religious. In order of adhesion to Islam, the main peoples involved are Turkmen (95% professing Muslims), Tadzhik (90%), Tatar (85%), Bashkir (80%), Azeri (80%), Uzbek (80%), Kazakh (70%), and Kirgiz (only 45%). The proportions of non-believers are increasing due to intensive anti-religious campaigns in Soviet Central Asia dating back up to 60 years in some areas. Among recent scientific polls, 21% of all Chechens declared themselves atheists and 63% Muslim believers (1974); Dagestanis 46% Muslim believers (1974); and Kara-Kalpaks 22% atheists and 78% Muslim believers (1972). *Practice*. Of these 28 million professing Muslims, a very high proportion (90%) practise their faith regularly. Circumcision is virtually universal for Muslims, and Ramadan, religious marriages and burials in Muslim cemeteries are widely observed even by atheists. *Schools*. Most Muslims are Sunnis (of the Hanafite rite, with a few Shafiites in Dagestan and Armenia), with some 3 million Shia Twelvers in Azerbaijan, 100,000 Ismailis in Pamir, and a few extremist or syncretistic sects, including Yazidis in Armenia and the Caucasus. The following peoples are Sunnis: Uzbeks, Tatars, Kazakhs, Tadzhiks, Turkmen, Bashkirs, Kirgiz, Chechens, Circassians, Kara-Kalpaks, Ingush, Uighurs, Karachai, Balkars, Turks, Dungans, Abaza, Arabs and Baluchis. Shia peoples are: Azerbaijanis (Azeris), Talyshi, Kurds, Tats and Persians. *Official Islam*. Officially-tolerated Islam operates under 4 ineffective Muftiats or Spiritual Directorates with resident muftis (at Tashkent, Ufa, Baku, and Buinaksk in Dagestan) with under 1,000 registered imams. *Clandestine or 'Parallel' Islam*. There are several million militant Muslims who belong to unofficial, clandestine, highly-structured, tightly-disciplined, ultra-conservative Sufi tariqas (brotherhoods, secret societies, in particular Naqshebandiya and Qadiriya) hostile to Communism and to russification, immune to persecution, and who exist and are increasing in numbers in all parts of the USSR. *Evolution*. In 1912, there were in the Russian Empire 16.3 million Muslims and 24,321 Muslim communities, with 26,279 mosques. As a result of a violent, vicious, brutal and protracted anti-Islamic campaign since 1928, by 1978 there were in the USSR only 300 registered mosques left, but there were also around 2,000 other unregistered (illegal) district or branch mosques, another 8,000 known unregistered groups and innumerable other clandestine mosques and bodies. Moscow has about 100,000 Muslims, and Leningrad 40,000. The Quran was published in Russian in 1963. *Hajj pilgrims to Mecca*. (1976) 23. Due to the impossibility of obtaining permission to visit Mecca, millions of Muslims go on pilgrimages to shrines in North Caucasus et alia.

NOMINAL CHRISTIANS. Only before the 1917 revolution. Subsequently, due to the radical polarization of believers and non-believers produced by state hostility to religion, virtually all professing Christians have been affiliated to churches (through baptism), and most have also been practising Christians; unlike almost all other nations with over 40 million Christians, the USSR had no bloc of nominal Christians professing openly to be believers but not affiliated to churches.

NON-RELIGIOUS. Agnostics, indifferent to both religion and atheism, including large numbers of government officials. In addition to the 29.1% shown in the table (for 1980), there is a further 10.6% of the population who are regarded as non-religious by state and society but who are affiliated to churches and so are classified as crypto-Christians.

ORTHODOX PENTECOSTALS (or, Orthodox charismatics). There has been a long charismatic or pentecostal tradition in Russian Orthodoxy. Large movements within Orthodoxy have often gone into schism, and other schismatic bodies have become charismatic when subjected to intense persecution by the Soviet regime (True Orthodox Christians, et alia). Before 1965, individual Orthodox who became charismatic or pentecostalist usually left the ROC and joined the AUCECB or other Pentecostal denominations. Since 1970, however, the tendency has been to remain within the ROC, where in 1975 a large but completely unorganized number of charismatics and charismatic house groups exist, mostly underground, and often in contact with local Pentecostal congregations. A fair number of Orthodox priests are known to have had charismatic experience. In addition, there are thousands of unorganized Jesus movement youths and Jesus revolutionaries.

PRACTISING CHRISTIANS. Since around 1963 the participation of children (under 18 years) in public worship has been prohibited for all denominations, so denominational figures of attendance refer only to adults. Statistics of practising Orthodox are derived from the known sales of votive candles bought and lit on entering a church (12 tons in 1959, 18 tons in 1961). In 1961 on joining the WCC the ROC officially stated it had 30 million regular weekly adult worshippers (35 million by 1970, 40 million by 1975), which implies for 1970 at least 50 million adults practising once a year or more. Catholic and Protestant affiliated figures represent practising members even more than Orthodox. In addition, some 20 million listen regularly to Protestant radio broadcasts from abroad (12 million to TWR programmes). When to these figures are added believers' children who, though legally prohibited from church services since 1963, may nevertheless be practising Christians, the approximate total in the table above of 64 million (in 1970) is arrived at. It should also be remembered that a large number of other affiliated Christians are not included in this total because for one reason or another they are unable to practise openly. Independent confirmation of the general order of magnitude of church attendance comes from periodic statements by various Soviet government officials to the effect that between 10% and 15% of the population of the USSR (30 million adults) attend religious services. *Pilgrims*. Before 1917, there were numerous pilgrimage centres; Kiev alone recorded 1,200,000 pilgrims during 1886. Since 1917 pilgrimages have taken on the character of legitimate acts of defiance against atheistic communism, and vast numbers visit the ancient shrines yearly.

PROFESSING CHRISTIANS (known to the state). The state has access to numerous scientific surveys and reports on the numbers of Christians. In 1967 the Institute of Scientific Atheism (Academy of Social Sciences, CPSU Central Committee) estimated the number of Christian believers of all denominations at 15% of the population in towns and cities and 30% in western rural areas; and regularly-practising adult believers at 12% of the entire population.

PROTESTANTS. As shown in Table 2, the totals include (in 1970) 1,590,000 isolated radio believers scattered across the country, namely that portion of the total listening community for all religious radio broadcasts into the Soviet Union (Protestant, Catholic, BBC and other secular stations, and also a number of clandestine stations within the USSR) who for a variety of reasons (mainly geographical) remain isolated from the organized denominations. The methodology for this computation is given near the end of Part 3.

ROMAN CATHOLICS. The massive numerical decline from 1900–1975 is due to (1) forced mass conversions of Uniates and other Catholics to Orthodoxy, (2) heavy emigration, and (3) sustained and continuous state persecution against Catholic hierarchy, priests and laity.

SHAMANISTS. Shamanism and tribal religion remain widespread among numerous peoples and tribes of northern Russia and Siberia, including the Chukchi, Tungus and Samoyed peoples. Likewise, the suppression of Christianity and the destruction of churches after 1918 in the Caucasus caused widespread revivals of traditional shamanistic religion, especially in the inaccessible mountainous regions of Southern Ossetia, Khevsuria and Svanetia (Georgia).

YAZIDIS (Yezidis, Devil-Worshippers). A 12th-century Muslim syncretistic religion, enumerated here under Muslims; Kurds speaking Kurmandji, dispersed across Armenia and Georgia. Decline from 14,500 in 1926 census.

**Russian Orthodox Church.** *Above.* Close-up of believers at open-air service in Zagorsk. Some 28% of all congregations such as this are secret believers (crypto-Christians, as defined here). A smaller percentage (averaging 0.3%) are KGB informants or operatives, usually easily detectable by hats or other non-religious attitudes. *Below.* End of service in Uspensky Cathedral (Assumption), built 1559-1585, inside grounds of Troitse-Sergieva Lavra (Monastery of the Holy Trinity, founded 1337), Zagorsk. Note absence of under-18s, whose attendance or instruction is prohibited by law.

**NON-CHRISTIAN RELIGIONS. Atheism** is the official ideology of the Soviet regime and has had a strong influence on Russian life and thought. A quarter of the population now profess to be active or militant atheists and another 30% are agnostics or non-religious. Members of the Communist Party of the Soviet Union and others militantly opposed to religion form a larger than average percentage of the population in the RSFSR and the Georgian SSR, and smaller than average in the other 13 republics, as the table below shows.

**Islam** is the professed religion of 11% of the population. The confrontation of the Slavic Russian and Muslim worlds is ancient. When Moscow entered modern history powerful Muslim kingdoms were camped at her doors, first the Great Bulgars of the Volga and then the Mongols of the Golden Horde. Ottoman domination was extended very late from Bessarabia to the Caucasus and over the peoples of Turkey and Central Asia, most of whom then came under the Russian empire during the 19th century. Since the 1917 revolution, the Soviets have given Muslims a certain nominal autonomy. Six Muslim national groups or peoples belong to the USSR:

Azerbaijan (Azeris) in the Caucasus, Kazakhstan (Kazakhs), Turkmenistan (Turkmen), Tadzhikistan (Tadzhiks), Uzbekistan (Uzbeks) and Kirgizia in Central Asia. There are 9 Muslim autonomous republics (ASSRs) as well as 4 Muslim autonomous regions. The Soviet attitude towards them has varied greatly since 1917, with periods of severe repression followed by a measure of toleration. A profound shift in Muslim social structure has been the result.

A large majority of the 30 million Muslims are Sunnis, practically all of the Hanafite rite, except for a few Shafiites in Dagestan and Armenia. There is also an important Shia minority of Twelvers in Azerbaijan (2,275,000 in 1939), 100,000 Ismailis in Pamir, and some extremist sects. There is at least one theological institute, at Bukhara. Administratively, Sunni Islam is divided into 3 centres, namely those of (1) Muslims belonging to the European part of the USSR and Siberia with headquarters at Ufa in Bashkiria; (2) Muslims of central Asia and Kazakhstan with headquarters at Tashkent in Uzbekistan; and (3) Muslims of Dagestan and the northern Caucasus with headquarters at Buinaksk, in Dagestan. Shia Islam has established its centre for Muslims of the

### MEMBERSHIP IN COMMUNIST PARTY OF THE SOVIET UNION BY REPUBLICS, 1966-1975

| Republic | Population | Ethnic % | CPSU, 1966 | CPSU, 1970 | % of CPSU | % of republic | Komsomol | Trade unionists |
|---|---|---|---|---|---|---|---|---|
| | 1 | 2 | 3 | 4 | 5 | 6 | 7 | 8 |
| Armenian SSR | 2,493,000 | 88.6 | 114,535 | 130,000 | 0.9 | 7.3 | 225,000 | 818,000 |
| Azerbaijan SSR | 5,111,000 | 73.8 | 221,694 | 241,000 | 1.8 | 6.9 | 432,000 | 1,242,000 |
| Byelorussian SSR | 9,003,000 | 81.0 | 359,595 | 420,000 | 3.0 | 6.4 | 990,000 | 3,100,000 |
| Estonian SSR | 1,357,000 | 68.2 | 61,722 | 70,000 | 0.5 | 7.2 | 107,738 | 618,000 |
| Georgian SSR | 4,688,000 | 66.8 | 265,730 | 290,000 | 2.2 | 9.0 | 500,000 | 1,700,000 |
| Kazakh SSR | 12,850,000 | 32.4 | 498,065 | 515,000 | 4.1 | 6.2 | 1,100,000 | 4,900,000 |
| Kirgiz SSR | 2,933,000 | 43.8 | 95,291 | 105,000 | 0.8 | 5.2 | 210,000 | 790,000 |
| Latvian SSR | 2,365,000 | 56.8 | 107,353 | 122,000 | 0.9 | 7.2 | 205,500 | 1,130,000 |
| Lithuanian SSR | 3,129,000 | 80.1 | 99,379 | 120,000 | 0.8 | 5.0 | 271,000 | 1,185,500 |
| Moldavian SSR | 3,572,000 | 64.6 | 99,024 | 110,500 | 0.8 | 4.4 | 301,000 | 980,000 |
| Russian SFSR | 130,090,000 | 82.8 | 7,676,003 | 8,300,000 | 63.2 | 9.4 | 16,700,000 | 55,367,600 |
| Tadzhik SSR | 2,900,000 | 56.2 | 76,001 | 89,000 | 0.6 | 4.2 | 198,000 | 520,000 |
| Turkmen SSR | 2,158,000 | 65.6 | 62,679 | 68,000 | 0.5 | 4.6 | 120,000 | 400,000 |
| Ukrainian SSR | 47,136,000 | 74.9 | 2,044,191 | 2,200,000 | 16.8 | 6.9 | 4,705,000 | 18,000,000 |
| Uzbek SSR | 11,963,000 | 64.7 | 353,841 | 400,000 | 2.9 | 4.7 | 1,000,000 | 2,605,000 |
| USSR | 241,748,000 | — | 12,135,103 | 13,190,500 | 100.0 | 8.0 | 27,064,738 | 93,356,100 |

*Definitions of columns 1–8.*
1. Total population figures from 15.I.1970 census.
2. Proportion of republic's population who belong to the main ethnic group as named in the title of the republic (Armenians, Azerbaijanis etc).
3. 1966 party membership (excluding candidates) reported in CPSU handbook, 1 January 1967. Candidate members then numbered 549,030. *Growth of membership.* This has increased from 80,000 in April 1917 and 240,000 in July 1917, to 611,978 (1920), 1,088,000 (1925), 2,477,666 (1939), 6,882,145 (1952), 7,215,505 (1956), 8,239,000 (1959), 13,810,089 plus 645,232 candidates (April 1971), to a total of 14.7 million by December 1972, and to 16 million by 1980.
4. 1970 party membership, projected from earlier years.
5. CPSU members in republic in 1975 as % of total CPSU membership.
6. CPSU members in republic in 1975 as % of adult population over 18 years (=65% total population) in each republic and (last line) in the USSR.
7. Members of Komsomol (All-Union Leninist Communist League of Youth, or VLKSM) in 1970.
8. Members of trade unions, 1970 (under All-Union Trade Union Congress).

Transcaucasus at Baku.

**Judaism** had 2.1 million adherents in the 1970 census (probably 3 million including secularized Jews) as contrasted with 5.2 million in the Russian empire in 1897, 3,020,000 in 1939, and 1,850,000 in 1945. About 1,300,000 were massacred during World War II. The Jewish community is divided into 2 groups: (1) Western Jews, for the most part coming from Germany in the 17th and 18th centuries, found in Moscow, the Ukraine and Byelorussia, as well as in the RSFSR; and (2) Eastern Jews who are ancient inhabitants of the Crimea, Georgia and central Asia. Of note also is the small Jewish sect of Karaites in Lithuania, the Crimea and the Ukraine, and a series of half-Christian half-Jewish sects which have sprung from Russian Orthodoxy or Protestant denominations but have been strongly influenced by Judaism. Although recognized officially, Judaism has lost nearly all means of cultural expression, and there are only 50 synagogues open in the whole of the USSR. Even before the Israeli-Arab war of 1967 but especially since then, Soviet authorities have shown increasing hostility towards the Jewish community.

A numerus clausus is applied to Jews in such professions as diplomacy, the army, and in universities and specialized institutes. The Jewish request to be regarded as another nationality (as contrasted with citizenship) has been refused, although it has

wishing to emigrate to Israel: 1968–70, 4,300 visas; 1971, 14,000; 1972, 32,500; 1973, 34,900; and January-September 1974, 17,000.

**Shamanism** is still widely practised by the Chukchi, Tungus and Samoyed peoples of Siberia who believe in the existence of ancestral and free nature spirits, divinities of fire and the sun, and a supreme being who resides in the sky. In remote areas of Georgia also there have been revivals of pre-Christian religion. In some areas the organization of hereditary magician-priests represents a high degree of sophistication.

**Buddhism** is officially recognized, though it also

after; and by the 3rd century there were churches in the Crimea.

ORTHODOX CHURCHES: (1) LEGAL (state-recognized).

Orthodoxy was introduced into Russia in AD 988, and a Russian Orthodox patriarchate was instituted in 1589, after which the church called itself the Third Rome. During subsequent years relations between the Orthodox Church and the ruling authorities were close; thus from 1613–33 Filaret served as patriarch while his son Michael ruled as the first Romanov tsar. In 1700 patriarch Adrian opposed a number of

*Above.* Russian Orthodox bishops process in Zagorsk.

**Armenian Apostolic Church.** *Top right.* Crowd of 42,000 on 26 September 1976 standing in front of Echmiadzin Cathedral (built AD 303) for 7-yearly 4-hour-long Blessing of the Holy Chrism, in presence of 20

bishops including the Patriarchs of Russia, Georgia, and Malabar, Cardinal Willebrands, and Anglican Bishop of London. *Above.* Closeup of above bishops, led by Catholicos Vasken I (centre). *Left.* Baptism of young believer

by Armenian priest using newly-blessed chrism. In the USSR, Armenian baptisms each year number at least 5,000 adults and 15,000 infants; the total for all churches is about 90,000 adults and 600,000 infants each year.

been authorized for other nationalities of the USSR (a Latvian for example can obtain Russian nationality). These and other measures contribute towards the development of the idea that Soviet Jews are second-class citizens. The severe and often bloody anti-semitism which Soviet Jews have suffered in Russia explains the desire of many to emigrate to Israel, whose economic and cultural success are also important attractions. In addition Soviet authorities have often shown a tendency to confuse anti-Zionism and anti-semitism and have thus contributed to the development of a sense of insecurity in the minority Jewish community. Having first refused all emigration visas to Israel, the government then modified its attitude and for a period imposed on emigrants who had completed higher studies the payment of large sums as reimbursement for training received. Dutch authorities, who since 1967 have looked after the interests of Israel in the USSR, were able to obtain the following numbers of visas for Russian Jews

has a long history of repression since 1917. From 1933–38, all 120 Buddhist monasteries were destroyed or closed. Buddhists are principally Mongols, divided into different communities: Buryats in the Buryat autonomous republic where the headquarters of the Central Buddhist Office is located, Kalmyks located before 1941 in the Lower Volga but now widely dispersed, and Mongols of Chita region. There are other groups in eastern and central Asia including Koreans who numbered 180,000 in 1939. As part of the general renaissance of religion in the USSR, since 1960 many young converts have arisen in European Russian, Estonia and Lithuania.

**CHRISTIANITY.** The first Christians in all probability were Armenians, converted according to tradition by the Apostle Thaddeus a few years after the Day of Pentecost. The nation of Armenia became the first in the ancient world to accept Christianity as its state religion; Georgia also was christianized soon

reforms instituted by Peter the Great, and as a result the patriarchate was abolished. Peter established a synod in 1721 composed of bishops and a tsar-appointed ober-procurator. From 1721–1917 the tsar ruled the church through the synod. From March 1917 with the abdication of tsar Nicholas II the relationship between church and state was terminated. During the provisional government in August 1917 a church council was convoked and the patriarchate re-established. From 1925 to 1944 there was no patriarch, but at the end of World War II a patriarch was appointed once again as part of Stalin's rapprochement with the church. The 87 million Russian Orthodox in 1914 (65% of the population) had fallen by 1970 to 70 million (29%) due to decades of repression and harassment. The total number of open, active or registered churches declined from 80,792 in 1913 to 39,000 in 1925, and to only 1,000 in 1939; rising to 16,000 in 1945, to 20,000 by 1957, declining again to 5,100 by 1973; thus illustrating the severity of state repression at the various periods. Likewise, the total of monks and nuns fell from 94,629 in 1913 to around 5,000 today, all indicative of continuing remorseless state pressure against all forms of religion. Nevertheless, the Russian Orthodox Church has survived as a formidable Christian force, retains a vast reservoir of spirituality and courage, and in many areas is generating powerful new renewal movements.

The Armenian Apostolic Church is usually termed Monophysite because of the absence of representatives from Armenia at the Council of Chalcedon in 451, but Armenian theologians reject the term. The head of the church is the catholicos of Echmiadzin, who has jurisdiction over Armenian Orthodox in Soviet Armenia and throughout the diaspora. In 1956 a large number outside the USSR accused him of complicity with the Soviet Communist regime and transferred their allegiance to the rival Armenian catholicos of Sis at Antelias, Lebanon. The church is a uniquely national one, and even today its leaders claim 'All Armenians are Christians'. The number of recognized parishes in the USSR fell drastically from 1,446 in 1917 to 89 by 1954, but this has not affected the fervour of Christian spirituality and practice. The monastery at Echmiadzin plays a leading administrative role, and the church was able to open a theological institute in 1945 which by 1960 had 40 students. In 1962 the church became a member of the World Council of Churches, and in 1969 it was represented at the Zagorsk Peace Conference. By 1977 it was clear that a sizeable spiritual revival was sweeping through the church.

The Old Believers went into schism from the Russian Orthodox Church in the 17th century in opposition to liturgical reform, and eventually splintered into 3 main groups: Beglopopovtsy (Church of Fugitive Priests), who form the smallest group with only 17 parishes governed by the arch-bishop of Novozybkov; Popovtsy (Priestists, or Old Ritualist Church of the Belokrinitsa Concord) who have about 300 churches in 5 dioceses concentrated in Russia, the Ukraine and Byelorussia, administered under the archbishopric of Moscow; and Bespopovtsy (Priestless) existing in 6 sub-groups with 46 further divisions.

The Georgian Orthodox Church is mainly found in the mountainous area between the Caucasus and the Armenian plateau to the east of the Black Sea. It is one of the most ancient churches of Christendom; missionary activity began in Georgia in the era of Constantine, although one tradition links the church with the apostle Andrew. From the 1917 figures of 2,455 parishes in 15 dioceses, there are at present only 80 officially-recognized churches. Again, the 1970s have witnessed a revival of church-going particularly churches packed with young people.

ORTHODOX CHURCHES: (2) UNDER-GROUND (illegal, unrecognized).

All of the above-mentioned Orthodox bodies are recognized by the Soviet regime; there are, however, in addition at least 34 unregistered, illegal and highly-clandestine Orthodox denominations, churches, sects and other dissenting bodies with at least 576,000 members in 1970, which are (with their Protestant and Catholic counterparts) popularly known in the Western world as the underground church, the catacomb church, the church of silence, or the church of the martyrs. All totally reject the Soviet regime and all churches which collaborate with it. Some, in particular the True Orthodox Church, adhere steadfastly to conservative Russian Orthodoxy in theology, liturgy, ritual and church government. Others, unable to get priestly ministrations, are operated by lay leadership networks. These churches steadily increase their influence, often aided by nation-wide clandestine administrative networks, and there is no shortage of young recruits to their ranks.

Orthodox dissenting bodies and sub-Orthodox sects are also widespread.

Several groups of Spiritual Christians have sprung up out of the Orthodox milieu, rejecting Orthodox ritual. The Khlysty (Whippers), who had a vast geographical spread under the tsars, preserve most faithfully the traditions of the original sect formed in the 17th century. Further schisms have produced the New Israelites, Brethren of Christ (also called Skoptsy or Castrated Ones), Dukhobors (Spirit-Wrestlers), and Molokans (Milkdrinkers) who were a million strong in 1917. All are highly clandestine and operate underground.

PROTESTANT CHURCHES. The Union of Evangelical Christians-Baptists (AUCECB) was formed in 1944 as a union of Baptists (who originated in 1841) and Evangelical Christians (Brethren,

Stundists, from around 1870). Several Pentecostal groups joined in 1945 and 1947, some of whom later left, and some Mennonites have been members since 1963. The church is stongest in the Ukraine, Baltic states and the Far East. Large numbers attend without seeking membership through adult baptism. During 1960–65 a schism resulted from the government anti-religious campaign leading to the formation of the Council of Churches of Evangelical Christians-Baptists, although this latter group has been consistently refused legal recognition and has remained critical of state atheistic policies. Its leaders

**Union of Evangelical Christians-Baptists.** *Top.* Packed women's service inside Baptist church in Tiflis, Georgian SSR. Again, note absence of children under 18 who are prohibited by law at worship services.

*Bottom.* Outdoors congregation in Siberia. The text reads: 'Young men, you are strong' (1 John 2.14).

are under constant harassment, with many imprisonments.

Lutherans are concentrated in the Baltic states, particularly Latvia and Estonia, where recognized Lutheran denominations exist. Until recently there were only 2 official Lutheran congregations outside these states (Tselinograd and Karaganda, both in Kazakhstan), despite the fact that Lutherans are found in other parts, particularly Siberia. Many continue to worship as clandestine groups, while several congregations have obtained registration. The Lutheran Church of Russia was dissolved in 1938.

The Reformed Church of Russia which began in the 17th century has been suppressed since 1917. Subsequently, territorial acquisition has brought within the Soviet Union other Reformed bodies, namely the churches of Carpatho-Ukraine, Lithuania

and Latvia.

Mennonites exist both within the AUCECB and outside. They first emigrated to Russian in the 18th century, mostly from Germany, but there has been considerable emigration out of Russia over the last hundred years, largely to the Americas. Many Old Mennonites exist in Asiatic Russia where they were forcibly resettled after World War II.

The Pentecostal movement began spreading in Russia during the 1920s. In 1944, 400 of the 700 known Pentecostal congregations (called Christians of Evangelical Faith) joined the AUCECB. By 1970, however, there were more Pentecostals outside the AUCECB than inside, though forced to operate clandestinely and underground.

About 80 other Protestant denominations exist, mostly underground.

CATHOLIC CHURCH. There are over 4.5 million Roman Catholics in the USSR, concentrated primarily in Lithuania, western Ukraine and western Byelorussia. Outside these areas, in 1973 there were only 5 registered churches, served by priests of Baltic origin: one in Leningrad, one in Moscow (St Louis of the French), one in Odessa, one in Frunze and one in Tiflis in Georgia. Since the Stalin-Roosevelt accord of 1933 an American priest has resided permanently in Moscow to minister to diplomats and their families, a deceptive gesture which hides the desperate lack of pastoral care for Catholics across the whole of the

USSR.

In the entire Soviet Union there is no Catholic diocese with a legally-recognized residential bishop. Many have been executed or killed since 1940. In 1971 there were only 5 titular bishops, apostolic administrators or their auxiliaries. During 1972 one new bishop was consecrated. There is no central leadership and virtually no official contact with the Vatican. Nevertheless, in May 1971 for the first time 3 Lithuanian bishops were given permission to travel together to Rome. The only active dioceses are in Latvia and Lithuania, from which bodies Catholics were represented at the 1969 Zagorsk Peace Conference.

The situation in 1971 in the 6 areas of Catholic concentration was as follows. (1) *Estonia* in 1938 had 6 churches, 3,000 Catholics, 15 priests and a bishop. Nothing is known of the fate of the bishop, who was arrested in 1941, nor of his priests. In 1971 only 2 churches were open, served by 2 Latvian priests. (2) *Latvia* in 1939 had 200 churches, 500,000 Catholics (25% of the population), 200 priests and 4 bishops. In 1971 there were 218 parishes, 340,000 faithful, over 6,000 baptisms, 134 secular and 13 regular priests, and one apostolic administrator not recognized by the authorities. (3) *Lithuania* in 1940 had 717 parishes, 330 other churches and chapels, 2,560,000 faithful (84% of the population), 1,450 priests, 10 archbishops and bishops, 4 major seminaries, 425 diocesan and 141 religious seminarians, a theological faculty, 37 monasteries and 85 convents. In 1971 there were 543 parishes, 2,010,000 faithful, 716 diocesan priests (many aged), 28 seminarians, a major seminary at Kaunas, and 21,188 annual baptisms. To the 6 ecclesiastical jurisdictions in Lithuania should be added the Soviet part of the archdiocese of Vilna, the other part of which has been in Poland since World War II. Although the town of Vilna is situated in the USSR, the diocese is not recognized by the Soviet authorities. Under Lithuania, there are 6 bishops, all appointed by pope Paul VI: an apostolic administrator and his auxiliary coadjutor at Kaunas, 2 bishops at Telsiai, and in 1974 the pope appointed 2 other apostolic administrators for Panevezys and Vilkaviskis. In 1955-57, Pius XII had appointed 2 bishops but one was not allowed to exercise his functions, and the other was never recognized by the authorities. Until recently the seminary was restricted to 30 students and was inadequate, this being a cause of protest in letters from Lithuanian clergy. An atheistic article published in May 1970 testifies to a wide range of unofficial Catholic protest writing as yet unknown in the West, and in December 1971 and January 1972, 17,000 Lithuanian Catholics addressed a memorandum concerning the anti-religious policies of the government to the Communist Party general secretary, L. Brezhnev, with a copy to the secretary general of the United Nations, as a result of which severe reprisals were taken. On 14th May 1972, a young Kaunas Catholic 20 years of age, Romanus Kelanta, burned himself to death to protest against these encroachments on religious freedom. Four days later demonstrations broke out in the streets of the second largest city of Lithuania. After this, the situation improved: priests received permission to hold retreats and pastoral meetings and the bishop was allowed to join in with them. In 1974 there were about 50 students at the Kaunas seminary and some 15 at Riga in Estonia. In 1974 for the first time since World War II an international Catholic organization,

the Executive Committee of the Berlin Conference of Catholic Christians from European States, with headquarters in East Germany, was allowed to gather in a Baltic country and hence in the USSR. This delegation was able to meet the bishop of Vilnius and other Lithuanian priests and concelebrated mass with them. (4) *Western Byelorussia* has a strong concentration of Latin-rite Catholics, but no bishops. The secretary of the Council for the Public Affairs of the Church (Rome) attempted to raise the issue with the Soviet authorities in February 1971, but without success. The number of priests in Byelorussia is thought to be about 80, serving a hundred parishes. (5) *The Western Ukraine* had, in 1971, Latvian priests serving 14 Latin parishes, but the most important Catholic group is of Ukrainian Oriental-rite Catholics, called Uniates after the Union of Brest in 1596, and termed the Ukrainian Greek Catholic Church in the 20th century. In 1939, when the Polish Ukraine was annexed by the Soviets, there were 3,500,000 faithful, 2,500 priests and 8 bishops. In 1946 at a synod meeting in Lvov, government pressure was put on the Uniates to join the Russian Orthodox Church, although no Uniate bishop was in attendance. This forcible annexation by the Orthodox Church was followed by ruthless persecution of Uniate bishops, clergy, monks and laity. At present, all Uniate bishops and priests are dead, imprisoned or unrecognized. Metropolitan Slipyj was imprisoned in April 1945, but was released in 1963 and allowed to go to Rome. Despite the fact that the Uniate Church has been officially dead for a third of a century, the Soviet press still carries bitter articles about it, revealing widespread and continuing activity. At the end of 1968, bishop Velichkovsky was imprisoned for 3 years after he was discovered taking communion to the home of a sick person. Having served his term, he obtained a visa and went to Rome in February 1972. He had been consecrated secretly and had directed the Ukrainian church clandestinely before his arrest. In 1977 the Ukrainian Catholic Church was still by far the largest banned religious body in the USSR. (6) *The Subcarpathian Ukraine* in 1944 had 461,555 Ruthenian Catholics of the Byzantine rite, 281 parishes, 374 priests and some 10 convents. The Ruthenians, whose attachment to Rome goes back to the Union of Uzhorod in 1646, were forcibly absorbed by the Orthodox Church in 1949, by which time many priests had already fled. In 1939 the area also had 81,500 Latin-rite Catholics. In 1970 the Vatican located Mukachevo as a suffragan diocese of the archdiocese of Esztergom in Hungary, with only 3 parishes left, 3 diocesan priests, and only 1,800 Catholics. Large numbers of Catholics, mostly of Latin rite, are scattered widely dispersed across the entire RSFSR to Vladivostok.

**CHURCH AND STATE.** Article 124 of the constitution of 1936 stipulated that 'With the purpose of assuring the liberty of conscience of all citizens, the Church in the USSR is separated from the State and the school from the Church; all citizens enjoy the freedom to hold religious services and the freedom to engage in anti-religious propaganda.' The first Soviet constitution, that of Lenin in July 1918, had recognized equally the right of disseminating religious propaganda, but this was suppressed by constitutional changes effected under Stalin on 18 May 1929 which inter alia prohibited religious education for persons under 18 years old. The separation of church and state, and consequently church and school, rests ultimately

on a decree of 23 January 1918 which deprived the Orthodox Church of the privileged position which it enjoyed under the tsars. The law concerning religious associations of 8 April 1929 makes their registration obligatory (Articles 2, 5, 6). These communities should be composed of a minimum of 20 persons (Article 3) whose names must be submitted (Article 8). The civil authorities have a month in which to accept or refuse the registration; and in case of refusal, they are not required to divulge their reasons (Article 7); in practice, however, they often fail to comply with the former requirement. Clergy must also be registered before they can exercise their offices. Article 17 contains a number of prohibitions limiting the life of the church to worship services. In general, the law virtually ignores the church as a hierarchical organization.

After 1960 there was a hardening in the attitude of the state vis-a-vis the church. The dispositions of the penal code were modified on 27 June 1961, increasing the penalties for infractions of laws relating to religious activities. A new law concerning marriage and the family was passed containing passages which facilitate the practice already existent of removing children from believing parents.

The Council for Religious Affairs (Sovet po Delam Religii) is a governmental organization, part of the Council of Ministers of the USSR, and created in 1966 by the fusion of the Council for the Affairs of the Russian Orthodox Church with the Council for the Affairs of Religious Cults, the latter previously handling non-Orthodox matters. Operating without known legal statutes (at least until 1976), its powers are undefined but appear to be absolute. Its functionaries have tended to interpret the law of 1929 in a restrictive sense without any apparent legal basis. The registration of religious acts (baptism, marriage, extreme unction, communion of the sick) was made obligatory in 1958; and the number of members of religious associations is now limited to exactly 20, which excludes the major portion of believers from the economic and administrative life of their church. Effective administration is in the hands of a lay council of 3, over whose names the local Communist authorities have the right of veto.

There are increasing internal tensions in the Russian Orthodox Church concerning the allegiance given by the hierarchy to the state. Many faithful resent this continued support, given the hardening of the government's attitude towards the church in and since the 1960s. This uneasiness was typified in a published letter written in 1965 by 2 priests to the patriarch of Moscow. The state for its part has responded by increasing prosecution and imprisonment of priests and pastors, as well as the closing of seminaries and churches. In addition, it is widely known that there are police spies in every church service and in particular in most sanctuaries (among clergy and church officers). Paradoxically the separation of church and state is, by choice of the latter, far from being a reality. In November 1972 the archbishop of Novosibirsk, who had been demoted and transferred to the smaller diocese of Vologda, was relieved of all his functions by the patriarch. He was considered the chief partisan of a strict application of the separation of the 2 powers and had thus often been in conflict with the Council for Religious Affairs.

Some denominations, notably the Council of Churches of Evangelical Christians-Baptists, have repeatedly requested registration but this has been denied them. Lutherans have been similarly treated:

**Council of Churches of Evangelical Christians-Baptists.** This denomination is clandestine and is predominantly young people. *Above & right.* Illegal (unregistered) Baptists at mass baptismal service near Brest.

for the 1.8 million ethnic Germans in Kazakhstan, only 30 congregations have been registered. Others including the True Orthodox Christians, Pentecostals and the Catholic Uniates, have never been tolerated at all by the state, and in their turn have never wanted or requested registration from a state they consider to be the Antichrist. Consequently more than others they have suffered ruthless persecution, wholesale imprisonment of clergy and closure of worship centres.

From 1917–53, an estimated 60 million Soviet citizens were killed directly or indirectly as a result of the Bolshevik revolution (40% being executed or killed by communist officials), and a further 66 million were incarcerated in prisons or labour camps. At least half of these 2 totals were Christian believers, the great majority for alleged political offences. From 1953–56 most of the survivors were released. Even so in 1976 there were still 10,000 political and about 1,000 religious prisoners in Soviet jails, out of a total of 10 million prisoners in 1,000 labour camps and jails.

In 1976, a Soviet publication for official use only, *Legislation on religious cults*, was leaked to Western Europe. Printed in 1971 in a strictly-controlled and numbered edition of 21,000, it is a directive detailing secret Soviet laws on religion. Since 80% of all Soviet decrees remain unpublished, including those on religion, it is impossible for the churches to know what the laws are that the state demands that they obey. This secret publication explains the legal basis for many commonplace acts of religious persecution, and also helps in the assessment of the 1975 amendments to the 1929 Law on Religion.

**INTERDENOMINATIONAL ORGANIZATIONS.** International organizations are not permitted in the USSR, but 6 churches became members of the World Council of Churches between 1962–65. They and others were active participants in the 1969 Conference of Members of All Religions in the USSR for Co-operation and Peace among the Nations, held at Zagorsk, which is the nearest to an ecumenical council that the regime has permitted.

**BROADCASTING.** No religious broadcasting of any kind is permitted within the country. There are foreign international stations which beam in broadcasts daily or weekly. Protestant programmes are easily heard over Trans World Radio (Monaco), for a total of 14 hours a week (in Estonian one hour, Latvian one hour, Lithuanian 15 minutes, Russian 10 hours, Ukrainian one hour 45 minutes). Europe I also broadcasts Protestant material on Thursdays. Radio Vatican broadcasts each week for 10 hours 15 minutes (in Armenian 45 minutes, Latvian one hour, Lithuanian 2 hours, Russian 3.5 hours, White Ruthenian one hour 15 minutes, Ukrainian one hour 45 minutes). The religious broadcasts of the BBC (London) are also widely heard, with a regular audience of several million. The Pentecostal body IBRA broadcasts 90 minutes daily in Russian, from Radio Trans-Europe (in Lisbon), and FEBC (Manila) in Russian for 4 hours a day in 1976. There are several other programme-producing agencies including Mennonite Broadcasts (Harrisonburg, USA), and Word of Life Fellowship (USA). The total hours broadcast per week are around 250, and there is a known total listening community of around 20 million.

**BIBLIOGRAPHY**

*Christian religion in the Soviet Union: a sociological study*. C. Lane. London: Allen & Unwin, 1978. (Analysis of the vast corpus of data from Soviet sociologists since 1955).
*Christians in contemporary Russia*. N. Struve. London: Harvill Press, 1967.
*Church handbook for the USSR*. J. Innes (England). Duplicated. 1967–74; in progress. (Loose-leaf; descriptions and rough maps of locations of open church buildings throughout USSR).
*Communist Russia and the Russian Orthodox Church, 1943–1962*. W.B. Stroyen. Washington, DC: Catholic University of America, 1967. (P.117–143 gives texts of Soviet laws on religion).
*Kirchengeschichte Russlands der neuesten Zeit*. C.P. Johannes. 3 vols. München-Salzburg: Anton Pustet, 1965, 1966, 1969.
*Land of crosses: the Catholic Church in Lithuania today*. M.A. Bourdeaux. Devon: Augustine Press, 1978. 350p.
*L'Islam en Union Soviétique*. A. Bennigsen & C. Lemercier-Quelquejay. Paris: Payot, 1968.
*Opium of the people: the Christian religion in the USSR*. M.A. Bourdeaux. London: Faber, 1965. 244p.
*Patriarch and prophets: persecution of the Russian Orthodox Church today*. M.A. Bourdeaux. London: Macmillan, 1969.
(Problems of the history of religion and atheism) *Voprosy istorii religii i ateizma*. Academy of Sciences of USSR. 12 vols. Moscow: Academy Press, 1961.
*Religion and atheism in the USSR and Eastern Europe*. Ed B.R. Bociurkiw & J.W. Strong. London, 1975.
*Religion and the search for new ideals in the USSR*. W.C. Fletcher & A.J. Strover (eds). New York: Frederick A. Praeger, 1967.
*Religion in the Soviet Union*. W. Kolarz. London: Macmillan, 1961. 518p. (The most thorough overall study).
*Religious ferment in Russia: Protestant opposition to Soviet religious policy*. M.A. Bourdeaux. London: Macmillan, 1968. 255p.
*Religious minorities in the Soviet Union, 1960–73*. London: Minority Rights Group, 1977 (revised edition). 28p.
'Religious problems in Russia today', *Pro Mundi Vita* (Brussels), 58 (January, 1976), 1–32.
(Religious sectarianism and the present) *Religioznoye sektantstvo i sovremennost*. A.I. Klibanov. Moskva: Nauka, 1969. (Third volume of 3-vol history, 14th century to present).
'Sociology of religion in the USSR', *Social compass*, XXI, 2 (1974), 115–214. (7 articles).
*The Catholic Church, dissent and nationality in Soviet Lithuania*. V.S. Vardys. East European Monographs 43. London: Brill, 1978. 336p.
*The Russian Orthodox Church: organization, situation, activity*. Moscow: Orthodox Patriarchate, n.d. (c1960). (Official publication; very truncated historical section).
*The Russian Orthodox Church underground, 1917–1970*. W.C. Fletcher. London: OUP, 1971. (Detailed documentation on over 40 highly-organized clandestine movements).
*The Ukrainian Catholic Church 1945–1975*. Ed M. Labunka & L. Rudnytsky. Philadelphia (USA): St Sophia Religious Association, 1976. 162p. (18-page bibliography, also chronology from 1945–75).
'USSR', W.C. Fletcher, in H. Mol (ed), *Western religion* (The Hague: Mouton, 1972), p.565–586.
*Young Christians in Russia*. M.A. Bourdeaux & K. Murray. Lakeland, 1976. 156p.

TABLE 2. ORGANIZED CHURCHES AND DENOMINATIONS IN THE USSR

| Official name 1 | Begun 2 | Type 3 | Counc 4 | Congs 5 | Adults 6 | Affiliated 7 | Names, notes, and other statistics (see Codebook) 8 |
|---|---|---|---|---|---|---|---|
| Adventists of the True Remnant | c1920 | P Adv | ••••• | | 21,000 | 30,000 | *Adventisty Vernogo Ostatka*. SDA split, rejecting state interference. Underground. |
| Ancient Church of the East (P Tehran) | c 400 | O Nes | Yw... | | 10,000 | 22,000 | Syriac-speaking Assyrians in Armenia, Georgia; isolated, unorganized, attend ROC. |
| Anglican Ch (J North & Central Europe) | c1670 | A plu | awc.u | 3 | 200 | 500 | Chaplaincies in Kiev, Leningrad, Moscow. British expatriate personnel. |
| Apocalyptists | 1923 | P Apo | ••••• | | 1,000 | 2,000 | *Apokalipsisty*. Begun Vinnitsa by Catholic priest, spread to Far East; underground. |
| Armenian Apostolic Church: | c 35 | O Arm | EWc.u | 89 | 964,000 | 1,400,000 | *Gregorians*. National church of all Armenians. Schism 1956 (C Sis, Lebanon). 200n,6d,1s. |
| C Ararat (Yerevan) | 280 | O Arm | Ep | 33 | 517,000 | 750,000 | Diocese of catholicos, HQ Echmiadzin. 59% urban. 5d(30),1s(50),W=95%. |
| AD Georgia (Tbilisi)(Tiflis) | | O Arm | Ea | 14 | 220,000 | 320,000 | *AD Georgia & Imeritia*. Bishop in Tiflis. Most churches closed. 20n. |
| D Azerbaijan (Baku) | | O Arm | Eb | 28 | 131,000 | 190,000 | 50% urban. Includes Turkestan, Siberia. Half all churches closed since 1954. 32n. |
| D Nor-Nakhichevan & Russia | | O Arm | Eb | 7 | 28,000 | 40,000 | Caucasus to South Russia, Don area. 24% urban. 76% rural. Armenian diaspora. 8n. |
| D Shirak (Leninakan) | | O Arm | Eb | 5 | 48,000 | 70,000 | One of 5 dioceses open (in 1908, 18 suffragan dioceses, most now suppressed). 12n. |
| V Moskva | | O Arm | E | 2 | 20,000 | 30,000 | Armenians in Moscow and north Russia. One archimandrite. |
| Basic Link of Christ | 1957 | O Tru | ••••• | 100 | 1,000 | 3,000 | *Osnovnoe Zveno Khrista*. True Orthodox Christians in Crimea & Ukraine. Underground. |
| Brethren of Christ | 1765 | O sub | ••••• | | 20,000 | 50,000 | *Skoptsy* (*Castrated Ones*). *White Lambs*, Spiritual Christians. Danube delta. |
| Bulgarian Orthodox Church | | O Sla | Mwc.u | 1 | 500 | 1,000 | *Balgarskata Pravoslavna Crkva*. Bulgarians in Moscow; resident bishop of Kropunich. |
| Catholic Church in the USSR: | 1084 | R LEr | B...u | 1,000 | 3,030,000 | 4,393,500 | *Rimsko-Katolicheskaya Tserkov*. All in west USSR. No HQ. 2s. 1200n,1300mw,45000Yy. |
| M Kaunas (Lithuania) | 1417 | R Lat | Bs | 122 | 390,000 | 560,000 | 1971–2, massive protests by laity and priests. 1s(30). 190 420 5282 |
| D Kaisiadorys | 1926 | R Lat | Bs | 65 | 150,000 | 220,000 | Almost all children receive baptism. Attendance very high. 79 65 1972 |
| D Panevezys | 1926 | R Lat | Bs | 120 | 280,000 | 410,000 | No bishops; apostolic administrator. In 1944, 93% Catholic. 161 102 3489 |
| D Telsiai | 1926 | R Lat | Bs | 131 | 260,000 | 380,000 | 1947, bishop shot; replaced 1968, 2 churches burned down. 148 97 4171 |
| D Vilkaviskis | 1926 | R Lat | Bs | 94 | 240,000 | 350,000 | No bishop. Opposed by vast network of atheistic centres. 124 117 4981 |
| PN Klaipeda | 1926 | R Lat | Bs | 11 | 60,000 | 90,000 | Lithuanian port, formerly Memel. No bishop. 53% Catholic. 14 0 1290 |
| M Lvov (Lwow) | 1412 | R Lat | Bs | | 7,000 | 10,000 | Southwest Ukraine. Diocese is mostly in Poland; in 1935, 1,015,000 Catholics. |
| D Lutsk (Luck) | 1428 | R Lat | Bs | | 3,000 | 5,000 | NW Ukraine. Formerly Polish territory; in 1935, D Lutsk had 260,000 Catholics. |
| D Przemysl | 1375 | R Lat | Bs | | 3,000 | 5,000 | 1945, replaced by Orthodox D Drogobych (after 1959, Lvov). 100n. |
| M Mogilev | 1783 | R Lat | Bs | | 140,000 | 200,000 | Northern Russia; RSFSR from Murmansk-Urals. In 1910 diocese had 755,766 Catholics. |
| D Kamenets | c1350 | R Lat | Bs | | 70,000 | 100,000 | Podolia, western Ukraine. In 1910, diocese had 311,318 Catholics. |
| D Minsk | 1798 | R Lat | Bs | | 552,900 | 800,000 | Eastern White Russia. Closed. Byelorussian Catholics unregistered, illegal. 80n. |
| D Tiraspol | 1848 | R LEr | Bs | | 100,000 | 150,000 | Latins in Volga, Georgia, Crimea, Caucasus; 100,000 Armenian-rite across USSR. |
| D Zhitomir | 1321 | R Lat | Bs | | 70,000 | 100,000 | Volhynia. In 1910, diocese had 489,924 Catholics. Virtually suppressed. |
| M Riga (Latvia) | c1250 | R Lat | Bs | 178 | 180,000 | 260,000 | Unrecognized apostolic administrator. 4% Protestants. 134n,36m,11w,1s(15),5289Yy. |
| D Liepaja | 1937 | R Lat | Bs | 40 | 55,000 | 80,000 | Latvians. In 1944, diocese had 89,617 Catholics (15% of population). |
| M Vilnius (Wilno, Vilna) | 1388 | R Lat | Bs | | 35,000 | 50,000 | Part of D is in Poland. 1963, communists initiated secular rites; no success. |
| D Pinsk | 1925 | R Lat | Bs | 10 | 35,000 | 50,000 | Western Byelorussia. Part of diocese is in Poland. 75n,54w,1674Yy. |
| D Iasi | 1884 | R Lat | Bs | | 3,500 | 5,000 | Major part of diocese is in Romania. Rest suppressed; scattered believers only. |
| D Mukachevo (*Ruthenian-rite*) | 1646 | R Rut | Os | 3 | 1,200 | 1,800 | Ruthenians. Remnants of diocese forced in 1949 into Orthodox D Mukachevo. 3n,21Yy. |
| D Vladivostok | 1923 | R Lat | bs | | 300 | 500 | Southeastern RSFSR. Closed. A few underground Catholics are known to remain. |
| AA Estonia (Tallinn) | 1924 | R Lat | Bs | 4 | 1,700 | 2,500 | 1941, bishop disappeared with all 15 Estonian priests. 1972, 2 Latvian priests. |
| EA Russia (*Russian-rite*) | 1917 | R Rus | Os | | 2,000 | 3,000 | For all Russians of Byzantine rite. Suppressed, inactive. |
| VA Sibiria (Siberia) | 1921 | R Lat | Ps | | 300 | 500 | North & Central Asia. Closed. Scattered Catholics here and there. |
| PA Karafuto (Sakhalin) | 1932 | R Lat | Ps | | 100 | 200 | Formerly Japanese part of Sakhalin island, occupied by USSR since 1945. |
| Eastern-Rite Catholics (*Uniates*) | 1087 | R Ukr | Os | | 390,000 | 560,000 | 1945, 3.5 million forced into ROC; illegal, underground, active. 3 bishops,330n. |
| Christians of Evangelical Faith | 1921 | P Pe2 | ••••• | 600 | 80,000 | 320,000 | *CEF. Khristiane Evangel'skoy Very*. Underground. 65% of all CEF; rest are in AUCECB. |
| Christians of Zion | c1935 | P Pe4 | ••••• | 50 | 2,000 | 5,000 | *Khristiane Siona. Murashkovtsy* (founder Murashko). Polish Ukraine; across USSR. |
| Church of God | c1935 | P Pe3 | ••••• | 50 | 2,000 | 5 000 | *Tserkov Bozh'ya. Kirche Gottes*. Holiness Germans. Kazakhstan. Losses to CEF. |
| Council of Churches of Ev Chr-Baptists | 1961 | P Bap | ••••• | 1,000 | 45,000 | 150,000 | *STEKhB/CCECB/Initsiativniki*. Anti-state schism ex AUCECB. Viciously harassed. 1j. |
| Ev Christian Pentecostal Zionists | c1920 | P Pe2 | ••••• | 100 | 10,000 | 20,000 | *Evangel'skie Khristiane Pyatidesyatniki-Sionisty*. Ukraine; split ex CEF. 7th-day. |
| Ev Christians in the Apostolic Spirit | 1913 | P Pe1 | ••••• | 50 | 2,000 | 5,000 | First Russian Pentecostals. Foot-washing. 1947, loose union in AUCECB. |
| Evangelical Lutheran Ch of Estonia | c1250 | P Lut | LWC.u | 164 | 150,000 | 300,000 | 1940, 78% Estonians Lutheran. 1944, mass flight to Sweden, Americas. 125n,1s(25). |
| Evangelical Lutheran Church of Latvia | c1550 | P Lut | LWC.u | 240 | 200,000 | 350,000 | Declined from 1 million in 1938. 15 dioceses. 102 pastors,P=65%,1s(40),W=10%. |
| Evangelical Lutheran Ch of Lithuania | c1400 | P Lut | L...u | 27 | 10,000 | 20,000 | 1918, autonomous. 1938, 95 parishes. 1968, 7 pastors, 2 students. 1967 joined LWF. |
| Evangelical Reformed Ch of Lithuania | 1557 | P Ref | Rv..u | 12 | 5,000 | 10,000 | *Unitas Lithuanica*. After 1945, 70% of leaders formed exile church in USA. 3n. |
| Followers of Innocent | 1908 | O sub | ••••• | | 2,000 | 5,000 | *Innokentievtsy*. Founded by Orthodox monk. Extensively underground in Moldavia. |
| Followers of John | c1883 | O sub | ••••• | | 1,000 | 2,000 | *Ioannitsy*. Founder John Kronshtadtsky. Still active Ukraine, Voronezh, Krasnodar. |
| Georgian Orthodox Church | c 150 | O Geo | MW..u | 80 | 500,000 | 800,000 | 48% urban. 1917, 2,455 churches; almost all destroyed 1920–40. 105n,4e(16),1s(10). |
| C Mtskheta & Tbilisi (Tiflis) | c 350 | O Geo | Mp | 30 | 250,000 | 400,000 | 11 churches open in Tiflis. 40% of Georgians are Orthodox. 1e(50 nuns),1j,1s. |
| D Kutaisi & Gelenati | | O Geo | Mb | 15 | 100,000 | 150,000 | Western part of Georgia. One of present 15 dioceses (9 suppressed). |
| D Sukhumi & Abkhazia | | O Geo | Mb | 20 | 50,000 | 100,000 | Abkhaz ASSR. Abkhazis a traditionally Orthodox people 44% urban. Many Baptists. |
| D Urbnissi | c 500 | O Geo | Mb | 15 | 100,000 | 150,000 | Diocese also administered D Argveti and D Manglisi, both without bishops until 1974–76. |
| German Evangelical Lutheran Church | | P LuR | ••••• | 58 | 30,000 | 50,000 | Among 150,000 German-speaking farmers: Altai, Kirgizia, Kazakhstan. Unregistered. |
| Isolated radio churches | 1939 | P rad | ••••• | 39,750 | 1,100,000 | 1,590,000 | Isolated radio believers. R=6000(2800 SGA,415 HCJB,300 FEBC,60 TWR,RVatican,BBC,&c). |
| Jehovah's Witnesses | c1920 | M Jeh | x.... | | 5,000 | 10,000 | *Svideteli Iegovi*. Mass deportations 1948–51 to Siberia, Arctic. Strong in Ukraine. |
| Korean Methodist Church | 1937 | P Met | ••••• | | 500 | 1,000 | 1937: 1,500 Koreans transplanted from Far East to Central Asia; not heard of since. |
| Methodist Church of Estonia | 1907 | P Met | Vv..u | 14 | 2,300 | 4,000 | Only surviving organized Methodists in USSR. In NEurope CC, UMC(USA). 16n,G=4%pa. |
| New Israelites | c1900 | O sub | ••••• | | 2,000 | 5,000 | *Novy Izrail*. Spiritual Christians in Rostov region; many emigrated to Uruguay. |
| New-Christian Union | c1940 | O sub | ••••• | | 500 | 1,000 | In Krasnodar and Stavropol in 1950–51; descended from New Israelites. Illegal. |
| Old Ritualist Ancient Orth Christians | c1860 | O OBe | x...u | 17 | 150,000 | 200,000 | *AD Moscow. Beglopopovtsy* (*Ch of Fugitive Priests*). Ex Popovtsy. Volga,Siberia.18n. |

*Continued overleaf*

*Table 2–continued*

| Official name<br>1 | Begun<br>2 | Type<br>3 | Counc<br>4 | Congs<br>5 | Adults<br>6 | Affiliated<br>7 | Names, notes, and other statistics (see Codebook)<br>8 |
|---|---|---|---|---|---|---|---|
| Old Ritualist Ch Belokrinitsa Concord | 1666 | O OBe | x•••u | 300 | 700,000 | 1,000,000 | *AD Moscow. Raskolniki* (*Schismatics*), *Popovtsy* (*Priestists*). 5 Dioceses. 200n. |
| Old Ritualist Church (Priestless) | c1710 | O OBe | ••••u | 285 | 700,000 | 1,000,000 | *Bespopovtsy*. Old Believers. 46 factions (Pomortsy, &c). Baltic, Byelorussia. |
| Old Ritualist Runaways | c1770 | O OBe | ••••• | | 1,000 | 2,000 | *Beguny* (*Runners*), *Bezdenezhniki* (*Moneyless*). Totally reject Soviet state. Siberia. |
| Old Mennonites (Church Mennonites) | c1750 | P Men | ••••• | | 60,000 | 80,000 | German immigrants; forcibly resettled east and southeast of Urals. Unregistered. |
| Redeemed Israelites | c1930 | O sub | ••••• | | 500 | 1,000 | *Iskuplenny Izrail*. Founder Mother Mary; Spiritual Christians in Orenburg region. |
| Reformed Church in Carathpo-Ukraine | 1945 | P Ref | Rv••u | 90 | 50,000 | 120,000 | Until 1918 in Ref Ch of Hungary, till 1945 Ref Ch of Slovakia. Hungarians. 70n. |
| Reformed Church in Latvia | | P Ref | R•••• | 1 | 100 | 300 | Reduced drastically 1939–50, to 1 church shared with Lutherans and Brethren. 1n. |
| **Russian Orthodox Church:** | 988 | O Sla | MWC•u | 5,107 | 48,410,000 | 70,120,000 | *ROC. Russkaya Pravoslavnaya Tserkov*. 75 bishops. 14000n,60de(5000),1j,5s(1700). |
| P Moskva (Moscow) | 1325 | O Sla | Mp | 97 | 2,690,000 | 3,900,000 | Patriarchal diocese. 86% urban. 42 active churches in Moscow city. 6 bishops. 2s. |
| D Alma Ata & Kazakhstan | 1872 | O Sla | Mm | 45 | 1,350,000 | 1,950,000 | 51% urban. Includes D Semipalatinsk & Pavlodar (suppressed 1950). Ethnic Russians. |
| D Arkhangelsk & Kholmogory | 1682 | O Sla | Mb | 7 | 800,000 | 1,160,000 | 60% urban. Includes D Olonets & Pentrozavodsk. Only 3 churches left in Komi ASSR. |
| D Astrakhan & Enotaevka | 1609 | O Sla | Mb | 7 | 180,000 | 260,000 | 61% urban. Many Muslims. 1973, only 7 parishes open. Orthodox mostly Russians. |
| D Cheboksary & Chuvash | 1853 | O Sla | Mb | 35 | 250,000 | 370,000 | Chuvash ASSR. Traditionally Orthodox. Theological samizdat circulation. |
| D Chelyabinsk & Zlatoust | 1908 | O Sla | Mb | 15 | 680,000 | 990,000 | 78% urban. Vacant since 1961. Administered by D Sverdlovsk, then D Perm. |
| D Gorkiy & Arzamas | 1672 | O Sla | Ma | 10 | 770,000 | 1,110,000 | Nizhni Novgorod. 61% urban population get children baptized. 1968 protest to WCC. |
| D Irkutsk & Chita | 1727 | O Sla | Ma | 25 | 1,640,000 | 2,380,000 | 67% urban. East Siberia. Includes D Khabarovsk & D Vladivostok (suppressed 1958). |
| D Ivanovo & Kineshma | 1866 | O Sla | Ma | 30 | 280,000 | 400,000 | 75% urban. Regular harassment of believers of all denominations. |
| D Izhevsk & Udmurtia | 1657 | O Sla | Mb | 30 | 290,000 | 420,000 | Udmurt ASSR. Traditionally Orthodox. 57% urban. Under D Kazan. Many pagans still. |
| D Kalinin & Kashin | 1271 | O Sla | Mb | 35 | 350,000 | 510,000 | Formerly called D Tver. 57% urban. Determined state obstruction to all churches. |
| D Kaluga & Borovsk | 1789 | O Sla | Ma | 23 | 210,000 | 300,000 | 52% urban. 1965, archbishop in conflict with state and Holy Synod, dismissed. |
| D Kazan & Mari ASSR | 1555 | O Sla | Ma | 30 | 520,000 | 750,000 | Traditionally Orthodox. 50% urban. 1960, archbishop given 3 years' prison. |
| D Kirov & Slobodskoy | 1657 | O Sla | Ma | 35 | 360,000 | 520,000 | 55% urban. 1960, 40 chs closed, massive protests. Diocese solidly reform-minded. |
| D Kishinev & Moldavia | 1813 | O Sla | Ma | 300 | 1,040,000 | 1,500,000 | Bessarabia. Traditionally Orthodox. 32% urban. 300 active churches, few closed. |
| D Kostroma & Galich | 1744 | O Sla | Ma | 70 | 180,000 | 260,000 | 53% urban. Steady state pressure against all organized religion. |
| D Krasnodar & Kuban | 1842 | O Sla | Ma | 76 | 930,000 | 1,350,000 | 47% urban. 1959, 300 churches; 1971, reduced to 76 by unremitting state hostility. |
| D Kursk & Belgorod | 1667 | O Sla | Mb | 30 | 560,000 | 820,000 | 1667 D Belgorod founded; 1787 Kursk. Now 34% urban. Anti-religious state pressure. |
| D Kuybyshev & Syzran | 1850 | O Sla | Mb | 20 | 570,000 | 830,000 | Formerly called D Samara. 72% urban. Severe repression. |
| D Leningrad & Novgorod | 992 | O Sla | Mm | 60 | 1,260,000 | 1,830,000 | 85% urban. Includes D Velikiye Luki & Toropets (suppressed 1957). 1s,1225Y,12941y. |
| D Minsk & Byelorussia | 1793 | O Sla | Ma | 425 | 3,100,000 | 4,500,000 | White Russia. 43% urban. Includes D Grodno, D Pinsk. 1959, 900 churches open. 1d. |
| D Novosibirsk & Barnaul | 1908 | O Sla | Mb | 50 | 1,070,000 | 1,550,000 | 55% urban. Includes D Krasnoyarsk, suppressed 1948. 1972 bishop forced to retire. |
| D Omsk & Tyumen | 1895 | O Sla | Ma | 12 | 670,000 | 970,000 | Vast and important Siberian diocese. 52% urban. 1970 archbishop imprisoned. |
| D Orel & Bryansk | 1799 | O Sla | Mm | 50 | 520,000 | 750,000 | 44% urban. Vast samizdat circulation. Old Believers HQ. |
| D Orenburg & Buzuluk | 1799 | O Sla | Ma | 30 | 430,000 | 620,000 | Chkalov. 53% urban. Long local history of sub-Orthodox sectarianism. |
| D Penza & Saransk | 1799 | O Sla | Mb | 40 | 530,000 | 770,000 | 40% urban. Mordvinians, traditionally Orthodox. 1970, bishop dismissed. |
| D Perm & Solikamsk | 1383 | O Sla | Mb | 60 | 870,000 | 1,260,000 | Unremitting state obstruction. Perm cathedral closed 1960 on traffic-jam pretext. |
| D Pskov & Porkhov | 1589 | O Sla | Mm | 30 | 210,000 | 300,000 | 43% urban. Pskovo-Pechersky (Monastery of the Caves), 30,000 pilgrims regularly. |
| D Riga & Latvia | 1836 | O Sla | Ma | 90 | 350,000 | 500,000 | Before 1945, Latvian Orthodox Ch; 1972, well-organized Orthodox life. 62% urban. |
| D Rostov-on-Don&Novocherkassk | 1829 | O Sla | Mb | 70 | 790,000 | 1,150,000 | 63% urban. Systematic campaign against overt religion; trials, imprisonments. |
| D Ryazan & Kasimov | 1198 | O Sla | Mb | 20 | 290,000 | 420,000 | 47% urban. Vacant until bishop appointed 1973. Long history of IPKh activity. |
| D Saratov & Volgograd | 1828 | O Sla | Mb | 31 | 990,000 | 1,430,000 | Formerly Stalingrad. 65% urban. Steady state pressure against all denominations. |
| D Smolensk & Vyazma | 1137 | O Sla | Mb | 48 | 230,000 | 330,000 | 48% urban. 1965, diocese reported in chaotic disarray; bishop's reforms thwarted. |
| D Stavropol & Baku | 1842 | O Sla | Mb | 100 | 1,520,000 | 2,200,000 | Azerbaijan SSR. 48% urban. Unremitting government hostility and obstruction. |
| D Sverdlovsk & Kurgan | 1885 | O Sla | Mb | 21 | 1,120,000 | 1,620,000 | 73% urban. Severe repression. 1976 appeal to WCC to oust absentee bishop. |
| D Tallin & Estonia | 1842 | O Sla | Mm | 50 | 140,000 | 200,000 | 1923–45, Estonian Apostolic Orthodox Ch. 59% Estonian, 41% Russian. 65% urban. 1e. |
| D Tambov & Michurinsk | 1682 | O Sla | Ma | 25 | 310,000 | 450,000 | 39% urban. Regular circulation of samizdat theological literature. IPKh stronghold. |
| D Tashkent & Central Asia | 1871 | O Sla | Ma | 30 | 560,000 | 810,000 | 25% urban. New cathedral built after earthquake (only new one in USSR since 1917). |
| D Tula & Belev | 1799 | O Sla | Mm | 32 | 410,000 | 590,000 | 71% urban. Many Reform Baptists; severe persecution after 1969 Tula conference. |
| D Ufa & Sterlitamak | 1799 | O Sla | Ma | 20 | 520,000 | 750,000 | Bashkir ASSR. 48% urban. 1967 formerly imprisoned Kazan bishop appointed to Ufa. |
| D Ulyanovsk & Melekess | 1838 | O Sla | Mb | 15 | 260,000 | 370,000 | 52% urban. Vacant since 1959. 1965, administered by bishop of Kuybyshev. |
| D Vilnius & Lithuania | 1321 | O Sla | Mb | 43 | 70,000 | 100,000 | Lithuanian SSR. 50% urban. Many well-organized Old Believers (Raskolnisk), 1d. |
| D Vladimir & Suzdal | 1214 | O Sla | Ma | 30 | 310,000 | 450,000 | Monasteries built 11th and 12th centuries. Now 68% urban. |
| D Vologda & Velikiy Ustyug | 1472 | O Sla | Ma | 17 | 270,000 | 390,000 | 48% urban. Only 17 churches open. 1972, theologian bishop dismissed by Holy Synod. |
| D Voronezh & Lipetsk | 1682 | O Sla | Mb | 55 | 770,000 | 1,120,000 | 45% urban. Only 55 churches open. Continual state harrassment. IPKh stronghold. |
| D Yaroslavl & Rostov | 992 | O Sla | Mm | 83 | 300,000 | 430,000 | 70% urban. 83 churches open, 85 priests. One of stronger Orthodox areas in RSFSR. |
| Exarchate of the Ukraine: | 1918 | O Sla | Me | 2,650 | 16,890,000 | 24,480,000 | 1917–35, 1941–42 Ukrainian Autocephalous Orthodox Ch. 3 million former RC Uniates. |
| D Kiyev (Kiev) & Galitsiya | 991 | O Sla | Me | 220 | 1,720,000 | 2,500,000 | Diocese of exarch. 57% urban. 1959, 680 churches open; 1971, 220. 2 convents open. |
| D Chernigov & Nezhin | 992 | O Sla | Mb | 107 | 540,000 | 780,000 | 35% urban. 1961 bishop given 8 years prison. 1973 cathedral closed, bishop removed. |
| D Chernovtsy & Bukovina | 1945 | O Sla | Mb | 32 | 290,000 | 420,000 | Traditionally 95% Orthodox. Romanian Orth until forced into ROC 1945. 35% urban. |
| D Dnepropetrovsk & Zaporozhye | 1775 | O Sla | Mb | 100 | 1,770,000 | 2,560,000 | 73% urban. Vacant since 1965, administered as part of D Simferopol & Crimea. |
| D Ivano-Frankovsk & Kolomyya | 1946 | O Sla | Ma | 100 | 430,000 | 630,000 | Traditionally Orthodox. Uniate D Stanislav till 1946 forced into ROC. 31% urban. |
| D Kharkov & Bogodukhov | 1799 | O Sla | Ma | 100 | 970,000 | 1,410,000 | 1833 named Kharkov. 69% urban. Many illegal beatings-up and trials of believers. |
| D Khmelnitskiy & Kemenets-P | 1795 | O Sla | Mb | 60 | 560,000 | 810,000 | Kemenets-Podolskiy. 27% urban. Since 1966 administered as part of D Vinnitsa. |
| D Kirovograd & Nikolayev | 1837 | O Sla | Mb | 90 | 830,000 | 1,200,000 | 48% urban. Many former and present Uniate Roman Catholics in area. |
| D Lugansk & Donetsk | 1943 | O Sla | Mb | 40 | 2,630,000 | 3,820,000 | 80% workers, 86% urban. Vacant 1965; under D Odessa. 1,500 parishes, only 40 open. |
| D Lvov & Ternopol | 1946 | O Sla | Mm | 950 | 1,580,000 | 2,290,000 | Uniate D Lvov till 1946. Includes D Drogobych & Sambor. 1959, 1,300 churches open. |
| D Mukachevo & Uzhgorod | 1945 | O Sla | Ma | 400 | 360,000 | 530,000 | Zakarpat. RC Greek-Ruthenian diocese till forced into ROC in 1946. 30% urban. 1d. |
| D Odessa & Kherson | 1837 | O Sla | Mm | 90 | 1,180,000 | 1,710,000 | 1959, 400 churches open. Still open: Rozhdestvensky convent, Uspensky monastery. |
| D Poltava & Kremenchug | 1775 | O Sla | Mb | 59 | 590,000 | 850,000 | 40% urban. Theological materials circulate in typewritten samizdat form. |
| D Simferopol & Crimea | 1859 | O Sla | Mb | 12 | 630,000 | 910,000 | First Christian settlments AD 250. Now 63% urban. Cathedral re-opened 1965. |
| D Sumy & Akhtyrka | 1860 | O Sla | Mb | 50 | 520,000 | 750,000 | 44% urban. Vacant since 1959; 1964, under D Chernigov; 1973 bishop appointed. |
| D Vinnitsa & Bratslav | 1912 | O Sla | Ma | 80 | 740,000 | 1,070,000 | 25% urban. Many Protestants in area, also Uniates; systematic beatings-up reported. |
| D Volhynia & Rovno | 992 | O Sla | Ma | 100 | 990,000 | 1,430,000 | Lutsk. Traditionally 95% Orthodox. 30% urban. Strong religious life. 1e(Pochaev). |
| D Zhitomir & Ovruch | 1795 | O Sla | Ma | 60 | 560,000 | 810,000 | 35% urban. 1961 Ovruch Convent closed at gun-point. 1973 lay protests at closures. |
| Seventh-day Adventist Church | 1883 | P Adv | x•••u | 834 | 40,000 | 100,000 | *SDA*. Organized 1920. Strong in Ukraine, Siberia, Central Asia. 834t(46814),W=60%. |
| Seventh-day Christians | c1935 | P Adv | ••••• | | 1,000 | 2,000 | Schism ex SDAs on doctrinal issues. Suppressed, now active underground. |
| Spiritual Christians (Whippers) | c1650 | O sub | ••••• | | 1,000 | 2,000 | *Khlysty*. Vast spread under tsars; now smallest surviving Spiritual Christians. |
| Spiritual Christians-Milkdrinkers | c1765 | O sub | ••••u | | 35,000 | 50,000 | *Molokans*. Split ex Dukhobors; a million strong in 1917. Azerbaijan, Georgia, Asia. |
| Spirit-Wrestlers (Dukhobors) | c1650 | O sub | ••••• | 500 | 35,000 | 50,000 | Emigrations to Canada, then returns. Villages: Caucasus, Georgia, Siberia, CAsia. |
| True Orthodox Christian Wanderers | 1956 | O Tru | ••••• | 2,000 | 15,000 | 30,000 | *IPKh Stranniki*. First nationally-organized totally-clandestine body. Across USSR. |
| True Orthodox Christians | 1944 | O Tru | ••••• | 15,000 | 150,000 | 200,000 | *IPKh*. Vast underground network, immune to detection. No clergy. Across USSR. |
| True Orthodox Christians in Hiding | c1900 | O OBe | ••••• | | 2,000 | 5,000 | *Skrytniki*. Since 1926, network of Old Believer ascetic hermits in northern forests. |
| True Orthodox Church | 1927 | O Tru | ••••• | 1,000 | 10,000 | 20,000 | *IPTS. Istinno-Pravoslavnaya Tserkov*. Remnants of underground church smashed by KGB. |
| Union of Ev Christians-Baptists: | 1944 | P uni | TWC•u | 5,500 | 730,000 | 3,050,000 | *VSEKhB* (*AUCECB*). 31% German, 30% Russian, 20% Ukrainian. 5000n,32313m,3s,10000Y. |
| Baptists | 1841 | P Bap | T | 4,000 | 540,000 | 2,200,000 | Strong Ukraine; congregations throughout USSR. Losses to CCECB/STEKhB. 6000Y. |
| Christians of Evangelical Faith | 1921 | P Pe2 | • | 400 | 40,000 | 160,000 | *CEF. Pyatidesyatniki* (*Pentecostals*). Spread by mass migrations. Only 35% of all CEF. |
| Evangelical Christians | c1870 | P CBr | x | 1,000 | 110,000 | 630,000 | *Stundists*. 1928, 4 million in 3,219 congs; 1920–40 persecution; 1947 joined AUCECB. |
| Mennonite Brethren (New Mennonites) | c1750 | P Men | • | 100 | 40,000 | 60,000 | AUCECB 1963. German-speaking. Siberia, Frunze, Karaganda; rapid growth in Ukraine. |
| Other Orthodox dissenting bodies | | O sub | ••••• | 1,000 | 100,000 | 200,000 | Total about 20 (see list below), underground, organized, nationwide. |
| Other Pentecostal bodies | | P Pen | ••••• | 900 | 80,000 | 160,000 | Total over 40 underground bodies, including Ev Christians in the Apostles' Faith. |
| Other Protestant denominations | | P | ••••• | 300 | 30,000 | 60,000 | Total about 30 (see list below), all unregistered and mostly underground. |
| Other Orthodox churches | | O | ••••u | | 2,000 | 5,000 | Small congregations of immigrants from Eastern European countries. |
| **Total affiliated (mid-1970)** | | | | **78,200** | **57,499,600** | **86,012,300** | **Total denominations (1970) . . . 140.** |
| **Total affiliated (mid-1975)** | | | | **83,000** | **61,024,400** | **91,285,000** | **Total denominations (1975) . . . 146.** |
| **Total affiliated (mid-1980)** | | | | **87,900** | **64,662,100** | **96,726,500** | **Total denominations (1980) . . . 152.** |

NOTES ON TABLE ABOVE

COLUMNS: for meanings and CODES (cols. 1, 3, 4, 8): see Codebook (Part 6). Column 1: **Boldface type** = church with over 10% of country's affiliated Christians.

NATIONAL COUNCILS (Column 4, 5th letter).

- u = legally-registered or permitted bodies, participants in 1969 Conference of Members of All Religions in the USSR for Co-operation and Peace among the Nations (Zagorsk), and/or 1952 Zagorsk peace conference, and/or foreign chaplaincy churches.
- • = illegal unregistered prohibited bodies, underground, non-participants in 1969 Zagorsk conference.

OTHER ORTHODOX DISSENTING BODIES. Around the year 1900, Orthodox sects numbered several million adherents, reduced by incessant persecution to under half a million today, found in over 20 distinct bodies. In addition to those listed in the table above, they include: God's People, Churikovtsy (c1920, 4,000 near Leningrad), Fyodorovtsy, Imyaslavtsy (begun 1910 from Greece), Malevantsy (begun 1889), Old Israel (Stary Izrail), Postniki (Fasters), Righteous Brotherhood (Zion Tidings), Trezvenniki (Teetotallers) (begun 1900), True Orthodox Christians-Silent Ones (Molchalniki) (begun 1955; 70% women; vow of total silence), Undergrounders. Many clandestine underground groups are ideally suited to avoiding detection and even thrive on severe pressure from the regime. Many other bodies have been completely suppressed, including the Russian Greek Catholic Church (former Roman Catholic Uniates who seceded in 1917 with tsarist encouragement but were destroyed in 1923). Another schism, the Living Church movement of 1922 (also known as Church of the Regeneration, Free Labour Church, Renovationists, Revival Church, Union of Communities of the Ancient Apostolic Church, Union of Religious Communal Societies), controlled 50% of all Russia's parishes in 1923, 21% in 1927, declining further thereafter until its extinction in 1946.

OTHER PROTESTANT DENOMINATIONS. There are at least 30 smaller Protestant non-Pentecostal groups, mostly unregistered and operating underground, including the following: Blue Cross Society, Brethren of Holy Zion, Disciples of Christ, Holiness Baptists, Holiness Ev Christians, Old Christians, Sabbathizers, True and Free Seventh-day Adventists (1924 split; 3 groups: Caucasian, Western, Central; savagely persecuted), Zionists, et alii.

PEOPLES (ethnolinguistic). Christians: 45.4% Russian (Great Russian), 30.9% Ukrainian, 7.0% Byelorussian (White Russian), 2.6% Lithuanian, 1.8% Moldavian, 1.8% Armenian, 1.6% Polish, 1.4% Latvian, 1.3% German, 1.0% Georgian, 0.9% Mordvin, 0.6% Ruthenian, 0.5% Mari, 0.5% Estonian, 0.4% Chuvash, 0.4% Udmurt, 0.2% Bulgar, 0.2% Greek, 0.2% Ossetian, 0.2% Gagauz, 0.1% Gypsy, 0.1% Tatar (Kryashen), 0.1% Yakut, 0.1% Karelian, 0.1% Romanian, 0.1% Korean, 0.1% Finnish, 0.1% Bashkir, 0.1% Komi, 0.1% Hungarian, Khakassian, Altai (Oirot), Assyrian, Czech, Slovak, Vepsian, Shorian, Lapp, Evenki, Buryat, Abkhazian, Itelmen, Eskimo.

COUNTRY-WIDE TOTALS

EVANGELIZATION (see Part 5). 1900: 97%. 1970: 64%. 1980: 71%. *Radiophonic evangelism.* A vast number of agencies and stations beam programmes into the USSR. Only a small number of listeners' letters escape censorship and reach Western Europe or the USA, including (in 1974) 2,800 SGA, 415 HCJB, 300 FEBC, Radio Vatican, RVOG, IBRA, et alia. SGA, TWR and other agencies however report large crowds of listeners attend their meetings when their personnel visit the USSR.

FOREIGN MISSIONARIES AND PERSONNEL (nationals serving abroad) (1973). Total 157 Orthodox (14 bishops, 88 priests, 55 monks and nuns) in 28 countries. The Moscow Patriarchate of the ROC had, in 1970, 13 bishops from the USSR posted to serve in exarchates abroad, with their staffs. The Armenian Catholicate of Echmiadzin likewise had a few personnel abroad. In addition, excluded here, there are countless personnel who have fled or been deported over the years and who are now citizens of other countries.

FOREIGN MISSIONARIES AND PERSONNEL (aliens from abroad) (1973). Total 30. *From Western world.* 20: about 10 Protestants, 5 Orthodox, 3 Roman Catholics, 2 Anglicans. *From Communist world.* About 10 Orthodox.

INSTITUTIONS (church-operated) (1973). Total 80, including 25 monasteries (legal), about 7 presses (most illegal), 14 (legal) seminaries (7 Orthodox, 5 Protestant, 2 RC); the total includes quite a number of other clandestine institutions.

PERIODICALS. About 70 titles. Officially-sanctioned or legal

publications number around 25 (15 Russian, Armenian and Georgian Orthodox; 10 Protestant). Illegal or clandestine regular publications in samizdat total at least 20 (including several True Orthodox, 3 Baptist and 1 Lithuanian Roman Catholic). In addition, however, at least 600 illegal Christian samizdat documents including irregular serials are produced and circulated each year (70% Baptist, 25% Orthodox; from 1 to 80 pages in length; 30% mimeographed, 60% typed with carbon copies, 5–10% handwritten; being personal letters, news of Christians and Christian activity, teaching, records of persecution, documentation of house searches, arrests, trials ,fines and imprisonments. Among these latter, there are at least 25 which appear from time to time as serials and are therefore considered here as periodicals. PERSONNEL. About 60,730 (60,700 national, 30 foreign). RELIGIOUS LIBRARIES. About 72.
SCRIPTURE DISTRIBUTION (1975). Annual totals: 64,000 Bibles (83% free, 16% subsidized, 1% commercial), 146,000 NTs (81% free, 19% subsidized), 2,000 UBS portions. *Translations completed.* Portion: 46 languages since 1491. NT: 17 languages since 1580. Bible: 8 languages since 1581.
SERVICE AGENCIES. About 120 (20 legal, about 100 illegal or clandestine).

## ADDITIONAL DATA ON CHURCHES

ARMENIAN APOSTOLIC CHURCH. Founded, according to tradition, by the Apostle Thaddeus in AD 35. By 1975 a widespread religious revival was under way in the church in Armenia. Baptisms had increased four-fold, with many communists bringing their children to be baptized. In many areas 70% of all Armenians were said to be baptized, with over 95% in rural areas. 1974 figures: 5,000 baptisms and 200 marriages a year in Echmiadzin, 3,000 baptisms a year at Ghegard monastery. Half of all Armenians are said to attend church. *Monasteries.* Only 6 survive, with about 30 monks.
CATHOLIC CHURCH IN THE USSR. *Eastern-rite Catholics (Uniates).* The Ukrainian Greek Catholic Church (nowadays known as the Ukrainian Catholic Church), which dates from the Union of Brest in 1596, was viciously repressed in the 1930s under Stalin, experienced a spontaneous widespread mass revival during the Nazi occupation from 1941–44, was suppressed by the USSR in 1946 and forcibly annexed to the Moscow Patriarchate, but still in 1977 is in existence as by far the largest banned religious group in the USSR. In the above table most of the 3.5 million adherents are shown under the Russian Orthodox dioceses where, de facto, they exist today, but a majority still regard themselves as loyal Uniates. Over half a million still refuse to attend Orthodox churches and instead continue Uniate practice in the so-called Catacomb Church underground, served by 3 illegal Catholic bishops and 330 priests, with a large number of newly-trained younger priests regularly joining them. Since 1968, Uniate activities in the Western Ukraine have intensified markedly. There is also an apocalyptic and nationalistic Neo-Uniate movement known as Pokutnyky (Penitents) dating from the 1950s which has broken away from the Catacomb Church, which totally repudiates the Soviet regime, and which has been subjected to ruthless persecution by the administration and the police.
COUNCIL OF CHURCHES OF EVANGELICAL CHRISTIANS-BAPTISTS. In Russian: Sovet Tserkvei Yevangelskikh Khristian-Baptistov (STEKhB); also known as Initsiativniki (Action Group) or Reform Baptists. The CCECB, originating in 1961 as a protest against AUCECB accommodation to state restrictions and severely persecuted thereafter, was formally organized in 1964. To some extent it has been also an anti-Pentecostal protest movement. In 1975 it was still an underground movement, with 200 leaders and numerous members imprisoned. Members are predominantly young people.
EVANGELICAL CHRISTIANS IN THE APOSTOLIC SPIRIT. Evangel'skie Khristiane v Dukhe Apostol'skom.
EVANGELICAL LUTHERAN CHURCH OF ESTONIA. Eesti Evangeeliumi Luteriusu Kirik.
EVANGELICAL LUTHERAN CHURCH OF LATVIA. Latvijas Evangeliská Luteriská Baznica. In 1976, 11 new pastors were ordained, graduates of Riga theological institute.
EVANGELICAL LUTHERAN CHURCH OF LITHUANIA. Lietuvos Evangeliku Liuteronu Baznycia.
GEORGIAN ORTHODOX CHURCH. In the 1970s a religious revival amongst the younger generation of Georgians, with packed churches at Eastertide, provoked a major Soviet government attack on the church and a massive attempt to subvert and discredit the hierarchy, infiltrate its leadership with KGB agents, and stimulate substantial ecclesiastical corruption implicating the patriarch David V and another bishop.
ISOLATED RADIO CHURCHES. Isolated radio believers are that portion of the total listening community for all religious radio broadcasts in and into the Soviet Union (a total audience of about 20 million) who are believers but who through geographical remoteness or other causes remain isolated from the organized

churches and denominations. The formula from which these totals have been computed is derived at the end of Part 3. There are many known cases across the USSR of isolated radio cells of this nature in which members have been converted to the Christian faith entirely through radio.
RUSSIAN ORTHODOX CHURCH (ROC). *Pre-Revolution situation.* The number of churches (omitting chapels) was 15,761 in 1722, and increased to 35,775 in 1850, and to 45,037 in 1890. In 1913 the 87,123,604 Orthodox reported by the Holy Synod were found in 73 dioceses, with 163 active bishops, 51,105 parish clergy, 80,792 churches (54,174 parish churches, 25,593 chapels (mostly cemeteries), 1,025 monasteries and convents), 94,629 monks and nuns, 4 ecclesiastical academies, 57 seminaries, 185 minor seminaries, 37,528 parish schools, 291 hospitals, 1,113 hospices, and 34,497 parish libraries. *Revolution.* Immediately after the Revolution, 10,000 priests, monks and nuns were arrested, and executed in 1922. *Situation in 1939.* After 22 years of severe persecution and especially the purges of 1937–39, only about 1,000 churches remained open throughout the USSR, mostly in the Ukraine (estimates vary from 1,000 down to only 100), with only 4 active diocesan bishops and a few hundred priests. *Present names of dioceses.* Diocesan boundaries are required by the state to be co-terminous with political boundaries. Dioceses are named after 2 cities, the first being usually the chief city of the political region, the second the see city or a smaller city of historical ecclesiastical importance. *Diocese of Minsk & Byelorussia.* Before 1945, the church in the White Russian SSR was known as the Byelorussian Autocephalous Orthodox Church. *Diocese of Lugansk & Donetsk.* The cities were formerly called Voroshilovgrad & Stalino. *Bishops.* In column 4, 2nd. letter, the relative importance of a diocese to the Holy Synod in mid-1973 may be approximately assessed by the rank of its diocesan bishop at the time, in the following descending order: p = patriarch, e = exarch, m = metropolitan, a = archbishop, b = bishop. Bishops are transferred from diocese to diocese frequently as part of the continual struggle between church and state. Average tenure is under one year. In mid-1973, 6 dioceses were vacant (with no bishops). *Closed dioceses.* A fair number of traditional dioceses have been closed or suppressed since 1917; in addition to those shown in column 8 as now part of other dioceses, these include Blagoveschenk, Drogobych & Sambor (now in Lvov), Kamchatka, Tobolsk, Tomsk, Yakutsk. *Closed and open churches.* The number of churches open to Orthodox worship has fluctuated since the 1917 Revolution in proportion to the severity of state opposition, pressure and persecution. The 80,792 churches active in 1913 were reduced to 39,000 in 1925, then drastically after the Great Purges to 1,000 in 1939; but as a result of World War II vast numbers were allowed to re-open, rising from 16,000 in 1945 to reach a peak of about 20,000 by 1957, of which perhaps 10,000 were legally registered. From 1959–63, however, a carefully-orchestrated though illegal state programme of mass closures was enforced; there were few closings in western territories which in 1939 had not been in the USSR; more in those territories which had at one time been lost to the Germans during 1941–44; but the severest closures were enforced in the rest of the Soviet Union which had never been under German occupation. By 1962 the total had fallen to 11,500; by 1964, to 10,000. Although violent harassment declined after 1964, by 1966 this systematic policy had reduced the number of registered and open churches to 7,500, and by 1973 to around 5,107 as shown in column 5 above; in 1975 the process was still continuing. One result is intensive use of church buildings; often an Orthodox church has 2 liturgies a day 7 days a week. *Orthodox population.* The figures in columns 6 and 7 above are estimates derived from numerous pieces of information, which may be summarized as follows. (1) The percentage of ethnic Russians who get their children baptized in the ROC is known from polls to vary widely (e.g. 19% in Leningrad City (registered only, excluding unregistered baptisms); 60% in a working-class district of Moscow; 61% in the industrial city of Gorkiy; 70% in the district of Ryazan) and probably averages 40%; this means that, on a conservative estimate and allowing for large-scale defections from organized religion, around 30% of all Russians are affiliated (by baptism) to the ROC, and around 20% are active members. By comparison, 80% of all Armenians receive baptism in the Armenian Apostolic Church; and in Lithuania 81% of all children receive Roman Catholic baptism. (2) In the Ukraine and Byelorussia, baptisms average 50%, around 50% are affiliated, and around 30% are active. Church life is especially strong in the west; most villages between Lvov and Uzhgorod have a functioning church. (3) The total population of each diocese in 1970 is known from the Soviet census of 15.I.1970, since diocesan boundaries must be co-terminous with political boundaries; and hence the numbers of ethnic Russians, Ukrainians and Byelorussians in each diocese are known. (4) Combining these figures and percentages, the figures for affiliated were then calculated as shown in column 7. These estimates are more conservative than the detailed analysis by diocese of churches and Orthodox Christians contained in the

2 articles by G.A. Rahr, 'Combien d'Orthodoxes y a-t-il en Russie?' (*Catacombes*, February 1973, p.6, 12), and 'Combien d'églises y a-t-il en Russie?' (*Catacombes*, January 1974, p.6, 8). *Monasteries.* By 1976 there were only 10 monasteries and 15 convents legally remaining open in the entire USSR, all Orthodox. However, there is a large number of illegal or clandestine ones, especially of the True Orthodox and other underground bodies.
TRUE ORTHODOX CHRISTIAN WANDERERS. In response to massive state repressive pressure, this IPKh variant with Old Believer roots has become the first nationally-organized totally-clandestine religious movement, its high geographical mobility and flexibility rendering it impervious to detection. Found across Siberia, the Far North, Central Asia, and in many major cities, it is totally opposed to the state and alienated from society, and has centrally-controlled networks of secret schools, seminaries and academies, home monasteries, convents, periodicals, underground publishing houses, shortwave radio transmitters emitting regular broadcasts, and vast numbers of physically subterranean cells. Its clandestine skills include secret codes, cyphers, couriers, recognition signals, non-existent decoys, extensive use of hand-copying, chain letters, charismatic utterances and prophecies, and nationwide communication and distribution networks.
TRUE ORTHODOX CHRISTIANS. In Russian: Istinno-Pravoslavnye Khristiane (IPKh). Begun originally in 1944 in Ryazan, Tambov and Voronezh, this vast, diffuse, clandestine, underground network of believers rejecting all compromise with the secular state and society resulted partially from the gradual suppression of the more organized True Orthodox Church (IPTS), and up to 1956 was spread unwittingly by the state as a result of 30 years of mass arrests,deportations and imprisonment throughout the Arkhipelag GULag (Chief Administration of Corrective Labour Camps). It is unorganized, mobile, immune to detection or attack, monastic, apocalyptic, charismatic, and mainly rural; its congregations average 10 adults each up to a maximum of 15. It rejects the Soviet state, society, the Moscow Patriarchate, infant baptism, the priesthood and the episcopate. Many members are youths formerly in Konsomol.
TRUE ORTHODOX CHURCH. Successor to the Josephite schism begun by an Orthodox metropolitan of Leningrad, the IPTS expanded rapidly from 1942 to number several millions by 1948, in a highly-organized, socially-alienated, mainly urban, clandestine network, duplicating institutional and liturgical Orthodoxy (of conservative pre-Revolution type, with monastic and apocalyptic emphases) and rejecting the legal Russian Orthodox Church. At one time it had numerous sub-groups, including Leontevtsy, Mikhailovtsy, Podgornovtsy, Agapitovtsy, Iovtsy, Solianovtsy. Increasing police surveillance finally suppressed the IPTS as a mass movement by about 1960, when many of its members joined the less-organized True Orthodox Christians (IPKh).
UNION OF EVANGELICAL CHRISTIANS-BAPTISTS. In Russian, Vsesoyuzny Sovet Yevangelskikh Khristian-Baptistov, VSEKhB (All-Union Council of Evangelical Christians-Baptists, AUCECB). Founded in 1944, the Union became part of an attempt by the state to drive all Protestant streams into a single body to obtain closer state control. *Churches.* Over half of the 5,400 registered congregations in 1959 were forcibly closed during the purge of 1959–63, the total falling to 2,000 by 1965; about 5% have subsequently been legally re-opened but many others operate without registration. From 1960–70, over 50 new churches were opened in one part of the Ukraine alone. *Growth.* Adult members in 1914 numbered 97,000 Baptists and 8,472 Evangelical Christians; 250,000 in 1922; 350,000 in 1947; 512,000 in 1954. 44 new congregations (with 2,446 members) are known to have been registered in 1975, 105 (51 Pentecostal, 51 Baptist, 3 Mennonite) from 1973–75, and over 50 in 1976 (20 in the Ukraine). *Baptisms.* No exact central records are kept, but officials reported 6,185 baptisms of new adult members in 1975; in addition, 436 followers of the CCECB and 846 CEF (Christians of Evangelical Faith) left to join the AUCECB. In 1975–76, there were over 13,000 baptisms. Most converts come from the working class. In Odessa, there are about 1,000 baptisms of adult Baptists each year. Before baptism there is a trial period of 12 months and a comprehensive examination of Bible knowledge. *Pentecostals* (Christians of Evangelical Faith, CEF). Begun in 1921 in Odessa sponsored by the Assemblies of God (USA); 1924, Union in Odessa region, 1925 Ukrainian Union, 1927 a National Union with about 20,000 CEF in 350 congregations in the Soviet Union; 1939, 20,000 CEF in Polish USSR; also Moldavia, Baltic states; 1944, 400 of the 700 known CEF congregations joined AUCECB; 1945, Polish movement (Chrzescijane Wiary Ewangelicznej) in western Ukraine and Byelorussia, distinct from CEF, joined AUCECB; 1970, CEF largest Pentecostal body in the USSR, but more outside AUCECB, underground, than inside; 1971, 20 underground CEF congregations registered independent of AUCECB. *Baptists.* The work in Russia began in 1867. Total now includes 9,000 baptized members in Estonia (begun 1877), 7,000 in Latvia (begun 1860), 400 in Lithuania (begun 1841).

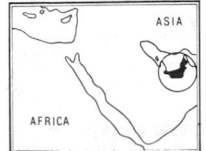

# UNITED ARAB EMIRATES

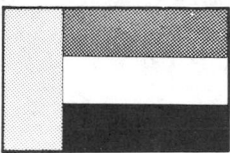

## SECULAR DATA

STATE. Official name: The United Arab Emirates (Ittihad al-Imarat al-Arabiyah).
Flag (shown above right): Red bar at hoist; stripes of green, white, and black.
Area: 83,600 sq.km. (32,278 sq.miles). Agricultural land: 2.5%.
Government: Confederation of monarchies, since 1971 (c1500 Portuguese rule, 1853 British protectorate of the Trucial States, 1971 Independence).
Legislature: National Assembly, 40 members.
Official language: Arabic.
Chief cities: capital Abu Dhabi 85,000, Dubai 60,000, Sharjah 19,200.
Political divisions: 7 Arab Sheikhdoms (Abu Dhabi, Ajman, Al Fujayrah, Dubai, Ras al Khaymah, Sharjah, Umm al Qaywayn).
Armed forces (1976): Total 21,400 regular: army 18,800, navy 800, air force 1,800 (38 combat aircraft).

DEMOGRAPHY. Population (excluding immigrant workers): 179,126 (census of 15.III–16.IV.1968. For 1970–2000 including immigrants, see last row of Table 1). Population density (1975): 3/sq.km. (7/sq.mile). Under 15 years: 44%. Growth rate (1970–80): 3.33% per year (births 4.85%, deaths −1.69%, immigrants

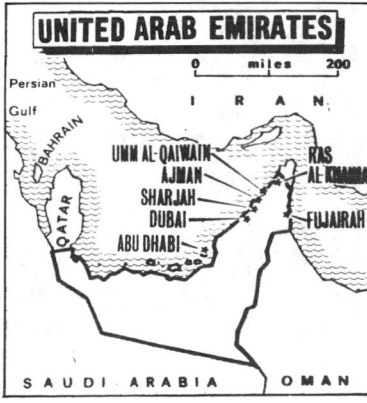

0.17%). Life expectancy (1975–80): 49.5 years. Household size: 5.2 persons.
Major languages: Arabic, Persian, English, Hindi, Baluchi, Urdu, Shihuh, and others.
Urban dwellers (1970): 52.1%. Urban growth rate (1950–70): 6.1% per year.
Refugees (1977): 50,000 from Lebanon; 4,000 Palestinians, Iraqis and Iranians.

ETHNOLINGUISTIC GROUPS: 80% alien (mostly Arab; also 5.0% Somali, 1.3% USA White, 0.8% British (2,300), other European, Palestinian, Japanese, Indian, Baluchi, 0.7% Gypsy (2,000), Pakistani, Persian, Syrian, Lebanese, Jordanian, Egyptian, Sudanese), 20% national (10% nomadic Arab, 10% sedentary Arab; including 3% Shihuh cave-dweller, also Black African).

MONEY (1977). Monetary unit: UAE dirham (= 100 fils); US$1 = UAEDh 3.95.
National income per person: US$16,000. Average annual family income: US$83,200.
Inflation: (1975): consumer price index 135).
Cost of living in capital (1976): index 141 (Washington DC=100). Daily cost of living: US$80.

**HEALTH.** Doctors: 211. Lepers: 15. Blind: 400. Pyschotics: 1,800.

**EDUCATION.** Adult literacy: (1968) 21%. Education rate: 22%. Schools: 147.

**COMMUNICATION** (per 1,000 people). Phones: 124. Radios: 145. TV sets: 46. Daily newspaper circulation: 25 copies.

TABLE 1.    RELIGIOUS ADHERENTS IN THE UNITED ARAB EMIRATES

| Year | 1900 | | mid-1970 | | Annual change, 1970–1980 | | | | mid-1975 | | mid-1980 | | 2000 | |
|---|---|---|---|---|---|---|---|---|---|---|---|---|---|---|
| Name | Adherents | % | Adherents | % | Natural | Conversion | Total | Rate | Adherents | % | Adherents | % | Adherents | % |
| Muslims | 49,950 | 99.9 | 286,230 | 95.4 | 11,295 | −44 | 11 251 | 3.28 | 342,690 | 95.2 | 398,740 | 94.9 | 653,000 | 93.3 |
| Christians | 50 | 0.1 | 10,270 | 3.4 | 533 | 36 | 569 | 4.39 | 12,960 | 3.6 | 15,960 | 3.8 | 31,500 | 4.5 |
| crypto-Christians | 50 | 0.1 | 6,370 | 2.1 | 429 | 36 | 465 | 5 43 | 8,560 | 2.4 | 11,020 | 2.6 | 14,000 | 2.0 |
| professing | 0 | 0.0 | 3,900 | 1.3 | 104 | 0 | 104 | 2.36 | 4,400 | 1.2 | 4,940 | 1.2 | 17,500 | 2.5 |
| Roman Catholics | 0 | 0.0 | 1,500 | 0.5 | 32 | 0 | 32 | 1.93 | 1,660 | 0.5 | 1,820 | 0.4 | 5,600 | 0.8 |
| Anglicans | 0 | 0.0 | 900 | 0.3 | 27 | 0 | 27 | 2.62 | 1,030 | 0.3 | 1,170 | 0.3 | 2,000 | 0.3 |
| Protestants | 0 | 0.0 | 900 | 0.3 | 26 | 0 | 26 | 2.25 | 1,020 | 0.3 | 1,160 | 0.3 | 6,500 | 0.9 |
| Orthodox | 0 | 0.0 | 400 | 0.1 | 14 | 0 | 14 | 2.98 | 470 | 0.1 | 540 | 0.1 | 3,000 | 0.4 |
| Asian indigenous | 0 | 0.0 | 200 | 0.1 | 5 | 0 | 5 | 2.27 | 220 | 0.1 | 250 | 0.1 | 400 | 0.1 |
| affiliated | 50 | 0.1 | 10,270 | 3.4 | 533 | 36 | 569 | 4.39 | 12,960 | 3.6 | 15,960 | 3.8 | 31,500 | 4.5 |
| total practising | 45 | 90 | 8,220 | 80 | 426 | 29 | 455 | 4.39 | 10,370 | 80 | 12,770 | 80 | 22,050 | 70 |
| non-practising | 5 | 10 | 2,050 | 20 | 107 | 7 | 114 | 4.40 | 2,590 | 20 | 3,190 | 20 | 9,450 | 30 |
| Roman Catholics | 30 | 0.1 | 2,400 | 0.8 | 170 | 10 | 180 | 5.62 | 3,200 | 0.9 | 4,200 | 1.0 | 9,100 | 1.3 |
| Anglicans | 20 | 0.0 | 1,700 | 0.6 | 37 | 1 | 38 | 2.01 | 1,890 | 0.5 | 2,080 | 0.5 | 3,300 | 0.5 |
| Protestants | 0 | 0.0 | 3,200 | 1.1 | 138 | 20 | 158 | 3.95 | 4,000 | 1.1 | 4,780 | 1.1 | 8,600 | 1.2 |
| Evangelicals | 0 | 0.0 | 1,800 | 0.6 | 70 | 20 | 90 | 3.91 | 2,300 | 0.6 | 2,700 | 0.6 | 5,000 | 0.7 |
| Orthodox | 0 | 0.0 | 2,500 | 0.8 | 170 | 0 | 170 | 5.17 | 3,290 | 0.9 | 4,200 | 1.0 | 8,600 | 1.2 |
| Asian indigenous | 0 | 0.0 | 470 | 0.2 | 18 | 5 | 23 | 3.97 | 580 | 0.2 | 700 | 0.2 | 1,900 | 0.3 |
| Non-religious | 0 | 0.0 | 1,500 | 0.5 | 103 | 7 | 110 | 5.50 | 2,000 | 0.6 | 2,600 | 0.6 | 9,500 | 1.4 |
| Hindus | 0 | 0.0 | 1,000 | 0.3 | 32 | −2 | 30 | 2.61 | 1,150 | 0.3 | 1,300 | 0.3 | 3,000 | 0.4 |
| Baha'is | 0 | 0.0 | 1,000 | 0.3 | 37 | 3 | 40 | 3.33 | 1,200 | 0.3 | 1,400 | 0.3 | 3,000 | 0.4 |
| Country's population | 50,000 | 100.0 | 300,000 | 100.0 | 12,000 | 0 | 12,000 | 3.33 | 360,000 | 100.0 | 420,000 | 100.0 | 700,000 | 100.0 |

**COLUMNS, ROWS.** For meanings and definitions, see Codebook (Part 6). Note that, by definition, total 'Christians' = professing + crypto-Christians, which also = affiliated + nominal Christians. Percentages may not always total exactly, due to rounding.
CENSUSES. 15.III–16.IV.1968 (home population excluding foreign workers): 96.0% Muslims, 2.1% Christians, 1.9% other religionists.

**NOTES ON RELIGIONS**
ASIAN INDIGENOUS. South Indian and Arab indigenous congregations, in 2 groupings in 1970 (see Table 2).
BAHA'IS. Growth from 6 local spiritual assemblies (1964) to 10 (1973).
COUNTRY'S POPULATION. 80% expatriates (from India, Pakistan, Iran, Syria, Lebanon, Jordan, Egypt, Europe, USA). About 10% of nationals are nomads. The figures in the last row of the table include all categories of resident immigrant worker.
CRYPTO-CHRISTIANS. Many Arabs are known to the churches as believers, though regarded as Muslims by the state or in censuses. During the 1970s the state tended to ignore the large number of expatriate Arab Christians who were entering as immigrant workers, and regarded them also as Muslims. There is also a growing number of isolated radio believers. The column 'Natural change' above includes nett immigration for all rows.
HINDUS. Expatriate Indians.
MUSLIMS. Nationals are mostly Sunnis of various rites, with a small Shia minority. There are also expatriate Muslims from all schools and sects. *Hajj pilgrims to Mecca.* (1970) 2,164; (1976) 4,196.
NON-RELIGIOUS. Europeans, Japanese and other expatriates.

**Muslims.** *Top.* Most rulers are Sunnis.
**Anglicans.** *Bottom.* Holy Trinity Church, Abu Dubai.

**NON-CHRISTIAN RELIGIONS. Islam** is the majority religion, most Muslims (nationals and expatriates) being Sunnis belonging to various rites. A small Shia minority also exists.

**Hinduism** is the religion of many expatriate Indians working in the oilfields.

**CHRISTIANITY**
CATHOLIC CHURCH. The vicariate of Arabia was erected in Aden in 1889, building on work begun by a Servite priest as early as 1841. After its expulsion from South Yemen in 1974, the vicariate's headquarters were transferred to Abu Dhabi, although, given changes in the government attitude towards Christians, the future of the vicariate in the United Arab Emirates remains uncertain. In recent years, the vicariate has shown steady growth due to the increase in foreign Christians in the various Gulf countries. In 1973 the vicariate included 12,060 faithful, 11 parishes and 15 chapels, 8 schools, 17 religious priests and 41 sisters, with 283 baptisms during the year. In 1972, Catholics in the Emirates numbered 2,400 in 2 parishes, each served by a resident priest. The parish of Abu Dhabi was founded in 1964 and the other, Dubai, in 1967.

OTHER CHURCHES. St Andrew's Church in Abu Dhabi is the centre for the Anglican chaplaincy of Qatar, Muscat and Oman and the United Arab Emirates, in the Anglican diocese of Cyprus and the Gulf. Another Anglican priest has recently been installed at Dubai to cover the northern Emirates and Muscat.

Syrian Orthodox clergy have been present in the Emirates for a number of years serving the expatriate Arab and Indian Syrian community.

Protestant groups include the Reformed Presbyterian Church Evangelical Synod, Plymouth Brethren, Independent Presbyterians and the Evangelical Alliance Mission (TEAM). At the request of the ruler, the latter mission opened a hospital in 1960 at the Buraimi oasis in the southeastern part of the country. Permission was given at the same time to preach and teach the Bible, but this is no longer possible.

CHURCH AND STATE. According to the provisional constitution of the United Arab Emirates, 'Islam shall be the official religion of the Union', the Islamic Sharia (Law) is the main source of legislation and Arabic is the official language of the union (Article 7). The union is 'an Islamic and Arab society... the Supreme and Omnipotent Creator... may Allah, our best Protector and Defender, grant us success'. All persons are equal before the law, without distinction due to race, religious belief or social status (Article 25). Freedom to exercise religious worship is guaranteed in accordance with established customs, provided that it does not conflict with public policy or violate public morals (Article 32).

Prior to April 1975, there was little anti-Christian sentiment in the United Arab Emirates. The various rulers not only permitted the building of churches but also provided land for them, and in some cases were present at their opening ceremonies and provided free electrical power for their air-conditioning as is done with mosques. The rulers welcomed personal visits by Anglican, Syrian Orthodox and Catholic priests as well as the various North American missionaries resident in the country. Christians were able to work openly and freely.

In April 1975, however, the sheikdoms comprising the federation agreed to forbid in their territories all missionary or proselytizing activities by non-Muslims. The Abu Dhabi Ministry of Justice now fines or imprisons anyone found contravening the new ruling. This hardening of attitude towards Christians is similar to that experienced in other Arab states in recent years.

BROADCASTING. No Christian broadcasting is permitted. From abroad, Christian programmes in Arabic can easily be heard over international stations including FEBA (Seychelles).

Many postage stamps, especially those issued by individual emirates before 1972, have carried Christian themes; here, the 14 Stations of the Cross, with the Ascension added.

TABLE 2. ORGANIZED CHURCHES AND DENOMINATIONS IN THE UNITED ARAB EMIRATES

| Official name 1 | Begun 2 | Type 3 | Counc 4 | Congs 5 | Adults 6 | Affiliated 7 | Names, notes, and other statistics (see Codebook) 8 |
|---|---|---|---|---|---|---|---|
| **Anglican Church (D Cyprus & the Gulf)** | | A plu | av••• | 2 | 800 | 1,700 | Chaplaincy, in Episcopal Ch in Jerusalem & ME. Abu Dhabi, Dubai. Expatriates. 2x. |
| **Catholic Church (VA Arabia)** | 1964 | R Lat | P••L• | 2 | 1,800 | 2,400 | Expatriates (including Arab Catholics). 2x,2b(Abu Dhabi, Dubai), 1r(580). |
| Christian Brethren | | P CBr | x•••• | 2 | 100 | 200 | *Plymouth (Open) Brethren. Gospel Halls.* Indians, few Arabs; in Abu Dhabi, Dubai. |
| Evangelical Alliance Mission | 1960 | P int | xM••• | 4 | 500 | 1,000 | M=TEAM(USA), MECO (MEGM/USA). Clinic in Al-Buraymi oasis. 22f,1H,1h,1k. |
| Isolated radio churches | c1950 | I rad | ••••• | 10 | 100 | 270 | Isolated Arab radio believers: pupils and students aged 12–25. T=2000(ICI,&c). |
| Mar Thoma Syrian Ch (D Bahya Kerala) | | I ReO | xwe•• | 1 | 100 | 200 | In Diocese of Outside Kerala. South Indian Malayalis in Abu Dhabi, Dubai. 2x. |
| Orthodox Syrian Church of the East | | O Syr | Dw••• | | 200 | 500 | In D Bahya Kerala. South Indians from Kerala, under Catholicate of the East. |
| Other Orthodox churches | c1965 | O | ••••• | | 1,500 | 2,000 | Expatriate Arabs (Greek, Syrian, Coptic Orthodox). House meetings. |
| Other Protestant denominations | | P | ••••• | | 1,000 | 2,000 | IBPFM (1942), Reformed Presb Ch Ev Synod. USA Protestants, some Arabs. 4f,1H,1h. |
| **Total affiliated (mid-1970)** | | | | 45 | 6,100 | 10,270 | **Total denominations (1970) . . . 14.** |
| **Total affiliated (mid-1975)** | | | | 50 | 7,700 | 12,960 | **Total denominations (1975) . . . 19.** |
| **Total affiliated (mid-1980)** | | | | 55 | 9,500 | 15,960 | **Total denominations (1980) . . . 26.** |

NOTES ON TABLE ABOVE
COLUMNS: for meanings and CODES (cols. 1, 3, 4, 8): see Codebook (Part 6). Column 1: **Boldface type** = church with over 10% of country's affiliated Christians. The data in the first 10 rows above refer to the situation in 1970. For 1970–80, see Table 1.

PEOPLES (ethnolinguistic). Christians (1970): 46.0% Arab (41% alien (Palestinian, Syrian, Lebanese, Jordanian, Egyptian), 5% citizen), 30.2% USA White, 13.6% British, 8.3% South Indian (Malayali), 1.9% other European (German, French, Italian), Pakistani (Punjabi, Sindhi).

COUNTRY-WIDE TOTALS
EVANGELIZATION (see Part 5). 1900: 1%. 1970: 58%. 1980: 66%. *Radiophonic evangelism.* TWR, RVOG, FEBA, Radio Vatican, ICI et alia.
FOREIGN MISSIONARIES AND PERSONNEL (aliens from abroad) (1973). Total 74. *From Western world.* 42: 35 Protestants (23 in 3 USA societies, 4 in 1 Canada society, 4 in 1 UK society, 2 in 1 Netherlands society, 2 in 1 New Zealand society), 5 Roman Catholics, 2 Anglicans from UK. *From Third World.* 32: 29 Roman Catholics (15 from Iraq, 10 Lebanon, 4 India), 2 Indian indigenous, 1 Orthodox.
INSTITUTIONS (church-operated) (1973). Total 5, including 1 higher school, 3 medical centres.
PERIODICALS. 2 titles.
PERSONNEL. 74 (all foreign).
SERVICE AGENCIES. About 6, including MAP, WEC.

ADDITIONAL DATA ON CHURCHES
CATHOLIC CHURCH. *Catholic organizations.* There are 3 schools: in Dubai, St Mary's High School under Capuchins (580 boys and girls); and, in Abu Dhabi, Rosary School (Arabic; 450 pupils) and St Joseph's Primary School (English; 56 pupils).

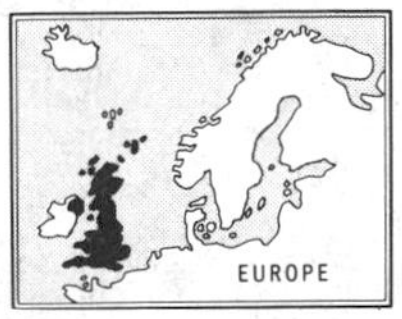


# UK of Great Britain & Northern Ireland

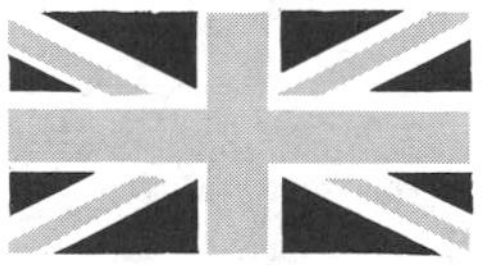

## SECULAR DATA

**STATE. Official name:** The United Kingdom of Great Britain and Northern Ireland (UK). Unofficial name: Britain. Adjective of nationality: British.
**Flag** (shown above right): Union Jack: red-on-white crosses of St George of England and St Patrick of Ireland, and white-on-blue cross of St Andrew of Scotland.
**Area:** 244,044 sq.km. (94,227 sq.miles). Agricultural land: 76.4%.
**Government:** Parliamentary constitutional monarchy, since 1690 (c500 kingdoms, 1215 parliamentary monarchy, 1649 commonwealth, 1660 monarchy, 1690 constitutional monarchy, 1801 United Kingdom formed).
**Legislature:** Parliament: House of Lords, 1,075 members; House of Commons, 635 members.
**Official language:** English.
**Chief cities:** capital London 7,281,080 (1973), Manchester 2,389,260, Birmingham 2,358,980, Leeds 1,735,700, Glasgow 1,727,620, Liverpool 1,226,310.
**Political divisions:** 4 Countries: (1) England: 38 Non-Metropolitan Counties, Greater London Metropolitan Area, 5 Metropolitan Counties; subdivided into 310 Districts, and again into 10,000 Parishes and 500 Areas. (2) Wales: 8 Non-Metropolitan Counties, 37 Districts, 1,000 Communities. (3) Scotland: 9 Regions, 3 Island Areas; divided into 53 Districts. (4) Northern Ireland: 8 Counties and County Boroughs. England, Wales and Scotland together constitute Great Britain.
**Armed forces** (1976): Total 344,150 regular (14,700 women): army 177,600, navy 76,350, air force 90,200 (450 combat aircraft). Reserves: 237,300.
**Foreign forces** (1973): 21,000 USA troops plus 10,000 US Air Force personnel.
**Dependencies:** Anguilla, Antigua, Belize, Bermuda, British Antarctic Territory, British Indian Ocean Territory, British Virgin Islands, Brunei, Cayman Islands, Channel Islands, Dominica, Falkland Islands, Gibraltar, Hong Kong, Isle of Man, Montserrat, Pitcairn Islands, St Helena, St Kitts-Nevis, St Lucia, St Vincent, Turks & Caicos Islands.

**DEMOGRAPHY. Population:** 55,506,131 (census of 25.IV.1971. For 1970–2000 (UN), see last row of Table 1). Population density (1975): 231/sq.km. (599/sq.mile). Under 15 years: 23%. Growth rate (1975–80): 0.38% per year (births 1.65%, deaths −1.18%, emigrants −0.09%). Life expectancy (1975–80): 72.8 years. Household size 3.3 persons.
**Major languages:** English, Irish, Welsh (26% in Wales), French, Italian, Greek, Polish, Gaelic, Punjabi, Gurajati, Bengali, Chinese (Cantonese), German, Arabic, Ukrainian, Russian, Romany, Spanish, Maltese.
**Urban dwellers** (1970): 80.7%. Urban growth rate (1950–70): 0.7% per year.
**Labour force:** 46%.
**Refugees** (1977): From abroad 40,000 (30,000 Asians from Uganda, 10,000 from Lebanon). (1979) 15,000 from Viet Nam.
**Tourists** (1970): 6,730,000. (1974) 7,935,000.

**ETHNOLINGUISTIC GROUPS:** (1970) 78.5% English, 9.5% Scottish, 2.4% Irish (including 0.1% Irish Traveller (50,000)), 1.9% Welsh, 1.8% Ulster Irish, 1.5% West Indian Black (Jamaican, et alii), 1.4% Indo-Pakistani (0.6% Punjabi, 0.4% Gujarati, 0.3% Bengali, Kashmiri, Tamil & other South Indian, Pathan), 0.8% Jewish, 0.4% Greek Cypriot, 0.2% Polish (130,000), 0.2% Italian (96,000), 0.2% USA White (87,000), 0.2% Gaelic, 0.2% Chinese (100,000) (Cantonese), 0.1% Australian (62,000), 0.1% German, 0.1% French, 0.1% West African Black (50,000) (Nigerian, Ghanaian, et alii), 0.1% Arab (including Palestinian (7,000)), 0.1% Ukrainian (55,000), 0.1% Russian, Gypsy (27,000), Hungarian (18,000), USA Black, Dutch, Austrian, Afrikaner, Serbian, Armenian, Latvian, Estonian, Byelorussian, Romanian, Spaniard, Goan (10,000), Maltese, Assyrian (7,000), Korean, et alii. (1980) Percentages as above, with the following changes: 77.6% English, 2.2% Indo-Pakistani (0.8% Punjabi, 0.5% Gujarati, 0.5% Bengali).

**MONEY** (1977). **Monetary unit:** pound (= 100 new pence); US$1 = £0.592 (operational rate of exchange).
**National income per person:** US$3,094. Average annual family income: US$10,210.
**Inflation:** (1970–74) 10.4% per year, (1975) 15% per year (consumer price index 206), (1976) 26% per year, (1977) 17% per year, (1978) 9.1% per year, (1980) 22% per year.
**Cost of living in capital** (1976): index 113 (Washington DC=100). Daily cost of living: US$39.

**HEALTH.** Hospitals: 2,900 (525,870 beds). Doctors: 72,049. Lepers: 360. Blind (1968): 116,414. Psychotics: 560,000. Criminals: 378,530.

**EDUCATION.** Adult literacy (1980): 95%. Education rate: 63%. Schools: 29,086 (23,000 primary, 550 middle). Universities: 50.

**LITERATURE.** Annual new book titles (1973): 35,177. Periodicals: 15,000. Scientific journals: 2,090. Newspapers: 109 dailies, 581 non-daily.

**COMMUNICATION** (per 1,000 people). Phones: 363. Radios: 680. TV sets: 311. Daily newspaper circulation: 530 copies.

TABLE 1. RELIGIOUS ADHERENTS IN THE UNITED KINGDOM OF GREAT BRITAIN & NORTHERN IRELAND

| Year | 1900 | | mid-1970 | | Annual change, 1970–1980 | | | | mid-1975 | | mid-1980 | | 2000 | |
|---|---|---|---|---|---|---|---|---|---|---|---|---|---|---|
| *Name* | *Adherents* | *%* | *Adherents* | *%* | *Natural* | *Conversion* | *Total* | *Rate* | *Adherents* | *%* | *Adherents* | *%* | *Adherents* | *%* |
| **Christians** | **37,125,000** | **97.4** | **49,298,000** | **88.8** | **168,118** | **−101,518** | **66,600** | **0.13** | **49,604,000** | **87.9** | **49,964,000** | **86.9** | **51,182,000** | **81.5** |
| professing | 37,125,000 | 97.4 | 49,298,000 | 88.8 | 168,118 | −101,518 | 66,600 | 0.13 | 49,604,000 | 87.9 | 49,964,000 | 86.9 | 51,182,000 | 81.5 |
| Anglicans | 25,100,000 | 65.9 | 31,624,000 | 57.0 | 109,007 | −4,307 | 104,700 | 0.32 | 32,163,000 | 57.0 | 32,671,000 | 56.8 | 33,909,000 | 54.0 |
| Protestants | 9,475,000 | 24.9 | 9,432,000 | 17.0 | 30,597 | −110,997 | −80,400 | −0.89 | 9,028,000 | 16.0 | 8,628,000 | 15.0 | 7,535,000 | 12.0 |
| Roman Catholics | 2,530,000 | 6.6 | 7,212,000 | 13.0 | 24,860 | 7,440 | 32,300 | 0.44 | 7,335,000 | 13.0 | 7,535,000 | 13.1 | 8,352,000 | 13.3 |
| Marginal Protestants | 12,000 | 0.0 | 550,000 | 1.0 | 2,000 | 6,300 | 8,300 | 1.41 | 590,000 | 1.0 | 633,000 | 1.1 | 816,000 | 1 3 |
| Orthodox | 2,000 | 0.0 | 360,000 | 0.6 | 1,244 | 256 | 1,500 | 0.41 | 367,000 | 0.6 | 375,000 | 0.6 | 420,000 | 0.7 |
| Third-World indigenous | 0 | 0.0 | 80,000 | 0.1 | 285 | 515 | 800 | 0.95 | 84,000 | 0.1 | 88,000 | 0.2 | 120,000 | 0.2 |
| Catholics (non-Roman) | 6,000 | 0.0 | 40,000 | 0.1 | 125 | −725 | −600 | −1.62 | 37,000 | 0.1 | 34,000 | 0.1 | 30,000 | 0.0 |
| nominal | 998,600 | 2.6 | 5,406,777 | 9.7 | 22,165 | 208,037 | 230,202 | 3.52 | 6,539,800 | 11.6 | 7,708,800 | 13.4 | 9,587,000 | 15.3 |
| affiliated | 36,126,400 | 94.8 | 43,891,223 | 79.1 | 145,953 | −309,555 | −163,602 | −0.38 | 43,064,200 | 76.3 | 42,255,200 | 73.5 | 41,595,000 | 66.2 |
| total practising | 30,707,440 | *85* | 28,369,700 | *65* | 91,950 | −351,353 | −259,403 | −0.96 | 27,130,450 | *63* | 25,775,670 | *61* | 23,293,200 | *56* |
| non-practising | 5,418,960 | *15* | 15,521,520 | *35* | 54,003 | 41,798 | 95,801 | 0.60 | 15,933,750 | *37* | 16,479,530 | *39* | 18,301,800 | *44* |
| Anglicans | 24,536,400 | 64.4 | 29,063,241 | 52.4 | 97,725 | −139,649 | −41,924 | −0.15 | 28,834,000 | 51.1 | 28,644,000 | 49.8 | 28,257,000 | 45.0 |
| Evangelicals | 12,954,000 | 34.0 | 7,556,000 | 13.6 | 27,365 | 76,335 | 103,700 | 1.28 | 8,074,000 | 14.3 | 8,593,000 | 14.9 | 10,675,000 | 17.0 |
| Anglican pentecostals | 0 | 0.0 | 60,000 | 0.1 | 1,017 | 52,983 | 54,000 | 18.00 | 300,000 | 0.5 | 600,000 | 1.0 | 1,200,000 | 1.9 |
| Protestants | 9,144,000 | 24.0 | 8,357,343 | 15.1 | 26,582 | −131,816 | −105,234 | −1.34 | 7,843,000 | 13.9 | 7,305,000 | 12.7 | 6,405,000 | 10.2 |
| Evangelicals | 5,715,000 | 15.0 | 2,164,000 | 3.9 | 7,650 | 11,750 | 19,400 | 0.86 | 2,257,000 | 4.0 | 2,358,000 | 4.1 | 2,826,000 | 4.5 |
| Neo-pentecostals | 0 | 0.0 | 20,000 | 0.0 | 305 | 17,695 | 18,000 | 20.00 | 90,000 | 0.2 | 200,000 | 0.3 | 400,000 | 0.6 |
| Roman Catholics | 2,429,000 | 6.4 | 5,543,431 | 10.0 | 18,359 | −43,502 | −25,143 | −0.46 | 5,417,000 | 9.6 | 5,292,000 | 9.2 | 5,651,000 | 9.0 |
| Catholic pentecostals | 0 | 0.0 | 2,000 | 0.0 | 41 | 2,259 | 2,300 | 19.17 | 12,000 | 0.0 | 25,000 | 0.0 | 100,000 | 0.2 |
| Marginal Protestants | 10,000 | 0.0 | 480,888 | 0.9 | 1,745 | 5,166 | 6,911 | 1.34 | 515,000 | 0.9 | 550,000 | 1.0 | 754,000 | 1.2 |
| Orthodox | 2,000 | 0.0 | 351,100 | 0.6 | 1,213 | 177 | 1,390 | 0.39 | 358,000 | 0.6 | 365,000 | 0.6 | 400,000 | 0.6 |
| Third-World indigenous | 0 | 0.0 | 74,470 | 0.1 | 262 | 311 | 573 | 0.74 | 77,300 | 0.1 | 80,200 | 0.1 | 110,000 | 0.2 |
| Catholics (non-Roman) | 5,000 | 0.0 | 20,750 | 0.0 | 67 | −242 | −175 | −0.88 | 19,900 | 0.0 | 19,000 | 0.0 | 18,000 | 0.0 |
| Non-religious | 720,000 | 1.9 | 4,248,400 | 7.7 | 6,500 | 73,100 | 79,600 | 1.73 | 4,610,900 | 8.2 | 5,044,400 | 8.8 | 7,819,000 | 12.5 |
| Jews | 235,000 | 0.6 | 450,000 | 0.8 | 1,620 | −20 | 1,600 | 0.35 | 458,000 | 0.8 | 466,000 | 0.8 | 505,000 | 0.8 |
| Muslims | 0 | 0.0 | 635,000 | 1.1 | 14,400 | 5,100 | 19,500 | 2.67 | 730,000 | 1.3 | 830,000 | 1.4 | 1,130,000 | 1.8 |
| Ahmadis | 0 | 0.0 | 8,000 | 0.0 | 140 | 60 | 200 | 2.22 | 9,000 | 0.0 | 10,000 | 0.0 | 15,000 | 0.0 |
| Atheists | 10,000 | 0.0 | 300,000 | 0.5 | 1,149 | 9,151 | 10,300 | 3.04 | 339,000 | 0.6 | 403,000 | 0.7 | 942,000 | 1.5 |
| Hindus | 0 | 0.0 | 220,000 | 0.4 | 10,423 | 5,577 | 16,000 | 5.33 | 300,000 | 0.5 | 380,000 | 0.7 | 560,000 | 0.9 |
| Sikhs | 0 | 0.0 | 200,000 | 0.4 | 1,050 | −50 | 1,000 | 0.49 | 205,000 | 0.4 | 210,000 | 0.4 | 310,000 | 0.5 |
| Buddhists | 0 | 0.0 | 30,000 | 0.1 | 303 | 8,797 | 9,100 | 11.30 | 80,500 | 0.1 | 121,000 | 0.2 | 230,000 | 0.4 |
| Spiritists | 10,000 | 0.0 | 20,000 | 0.0 | 64 | −264 | −200 | −1.05 | 19,000 | 0.0 | 18,000 | 0.0 | 16,000 | 0.0 |
| Chinese folk-religionists | 0 | 0.0 | 15,000 | 0.0 | 47 | −247 | −200 | −1.43 | 14,000 | 0.0 | 13,000 | 0.0 | 10,000 | 0.0 |
| Baha'is | 0 | 0.0 | 13,600 | 0.0 | 50 | 150 | 200 | 1.37 | 14,600 | 0.0 | 15,600 | 0.0 | 25,000 | 0.0 |
| Other religionists | 0 | 0.0 | 50,000 | 0.1 | 176 | 244 | 400 | 0.77 | 52,000 | 0.1 | 54,000 | 0.1 | 65,000 | 0.1 |
| **Country's population** | **38,100,000** | **100.0** | **55,480,000** | **100.0** | **203,900** | **0** | **203,900** | **0.36** | **56,427,000** | **100.0** | **57,519,000** | **100.0** | **62,794,000** | **100.0** |

COLUMNS, ROWS. For meanings and definitions, see Codebook (Part 6). Note that, by definition, total 'Christians' = professing + crypto-Christians, which also = affiliated + nominal Christians. Percentages may not always total exactly, due to rounding.
CENSUSES. The question on religious profession has never been asked in government censuses of the whole of Great Britain. *England and Wales*. The only national census of religion in England and Wales was taken on Sunday, **30.III.1851**. A total of 10,896,066 attendances was recorded, by (since 50% went twice) 7,261,032 individuals (3,526,900 Anglicans, 3,478,500 Protestants (Free Churches), 255,600 Roman Catholics). Since Sunday-school children were excluded, and since at that time about 30% of the population (then 16.9 million) were under 15 years old, this means that 61.4% of the total adult population were weekly Sunday attenders. Assuming that weekly attendance was 90% for Protestants but only 50% for Anglicans and Catholics, and that nominal Christians were less than 1%, this gives the following proportions for both professing and affiliated Christians in England and Wales in 1851: 62.0% Anglicans, 33.0% Protestants, 5.0% Roman Catholics; and also a figure of about 90% for annually practising Christians as defined in this Encyclopedia. *Northern Ireland* (Ulster). **8.IV.1951**: 65.0% Anglicans & Protestants, 34.4% Roman Catholics, 0.5% non-religious, 0.1% Jews. **23.IV.1961**: 39.7% Protestants, 35.6% Roman Catholics, 24.7% Anglicans.
POLLS. Religion questions have been asked in secular polls for 40 years or more (mainly Gallup, Great Britain). Most cover only Great Britain (GB) and exclude Northern Ireland, so have been adjusted to represent the entire UK before entering in the table above. All polls figures refer to total adult population rather than to Christians only, unless specified otherwise. *Religious profession (adherence, preference)*. 1970 (GB): 58% Anglicans, 12% Roman Catholics, 8% Nonconformists (including 7% Methodist), 8% Church of Scotland, 8% non-religious and atheists, 5% other Christians (including 2% Baptists). Sept/Oct 1974 (GB): 58% Anglicans, 11% Roman Catholics, 9.3% non-religious and atheists, 7% Church of Scotland, 6.3% Nonconformists (Free Churches), 6.6% other Christians and other religionists. Inclusion of Northern Ireland changes the proportions, for the UK in 1970, to: 57% Anglicans, 17% Protestants, 13% Roman Catholics. *Profession trends* (Gallup polls 1939–70; GB). Anglicans: decline 62%–58%. Roman Catholics: increase 9%–12%. Protestants: decline 25%–17%. Non-religious: increase 4%–8%, sometimes 9%. 1970–75: Anglicans, virtually no change; Roman Catholics, Church of Scotland, Nonconformists, all slight decline. *Regional variations* (1964). England: 69% Anglicans, 14% Protestants, 10% Roman Catholics, 5% non-religious and atheists. Wales: 45% Anglicans, 40% Protestants (Nonconformists), 6% Roman Catholics, 4% non-religious and atheists. Scotland: 73% Protestants (67% Church of Scotland), 16% Roman Catholics, 5% non-religious and atheists, 3% Anglicans. Northern Ireland: 38% Protestants (30% Presbyterians, 5% Methodists), 36% Roman Catholics, 25% Anglicans, 2% non-religious. *Practice*. Polls of church attendance are given below under PRACTISING CHRISTIANS. *Charismatic renewal*. 1977 in England (*Catholic Herald*): 82% had heard of the renewal, 17% had not; 17% approved, 26% did not, 39% undecided; 21% had attended a prayer meeting.

## NOTES ON RELIGIONS

AHMADIS. The Ahmadiya mission from Qadian, India, was opened in London in 1913; by 1975 there were Qadiani branches in 17 other cities and towns, with 2,000 practising adults and a total of 9,000 adherents; mostly immigrants from Pakistan and East African Asians. The smaller Lahori sect had a mosque at Woking, closed by 1975.
ANGLICAN PENTECOSTALS (or, Anglican charismatics). The charismatic renewal in the Church of England began in a parish in Sunderland in 1907, then lapsed until it recommenced in 1962. Total involved adults (January 1975) around 130,000 in prayer groups within some 1,000 Church of England parishes (1,500 congregations), including around 1,500 clergy; total charismatic community including children, 300,000, increasing rapidly. Also included are a large number of young Jesus People who remain Anglicans. By 1979, over 3,500 clergy were involved.
ATHEISTS. Communist Party of Great Britain (CPGB) (legal; pro-Soviet): membership (1970) 29,000, (1974) 28,000; Communist voters (election of 1922) 52,000, (election of VII.1945) 102,780 (4% of all votes), (18.VI.1970) 37,996 (0.1% of all votes), (III.1974) 32,741 (0.1%). In the 30 major trade unions, 150 of the 900 senior posts (17%) are held by communists or their open sympathizers. In the UK, communists are mainly in London, Glasgow and south Wales. There have been numerous polls taken concerning irreligion. In 1959 at Cambridge University, 21% of students were agnostics. In 1961 at Oxford University, 23% declared themselves agnostics and 11% atheists, humanists or rationalists. In 1962 at the University of London, 17% declared themselves atheists (London School of Economics 40%). In a 1973 Gallup poll of youths aged 18–24 years, 2% professed to be atheists, and 32% to have no affiliation or interest in religion. There is also the Secular Movement with working-class membership which supports militant atheism. British Humanists declined from 4,000 in 1970 to under 3,000 a year later.
BAHA'IS. Entered Britain in 1905. Recent growth from 49 local spiritual assemblies in 1964 to 91 in 1973 (England 69, Scotland 11, Wales 6, Northern Ireland 5) and 434 other isolated centres and groups.
BUDDHISTS. In 1970 about 50% Chinese, 50% from Sri Lanka, also Thai monks, and Tibetans in Wales. After 1970, however, there were massive numbers of British converts during 1971–77, including at least 20,000 men who became bhikkus (monks). By 1977 all Buddhists were 50% followers of Tibetan Buddhism, 25% of Theravada, and 25% of Zen; with 12 main Buddhist centres, 45 affiliated groups, and 12 priests.
CATHOLIC PENTECOSTALS (or, Catholic charismatics). Totals (January 1974): 5,000 involved adults (over 15 years old) in over 50 prayer groups; total charismatic community including children, 10,000. 1977 polls in England indicated 82% of the population were aware of the Charismatic Renewal; and 41% of all Catholics claimed to have attended a charismatic meeting. At Easter 1978, 450 diocesan and religious priests held a charismatic conference in Manchester.
COUNTRY'S POPULATION. Regional totals in the 25 April 1971 census of UK (excluding Channel Islands and Isle of Man): England 45,879,670 (82.87%), Scotland 5,223,600 (9.44%), Wales 2,724,275 (4.92%), Northern Ireland 1,536,065 (2.77%). The first 3 regions constitute Great Britain. *Indo-Pakistanis*. The totals have risen from 10,000 in 1955 to 100,000 by 1960 to 720,000 by 1970, to over 1.2 million by 1980.
EVANGELICALS. This category as used in the churches covers the following 4 groupings, in order of size: (1) Anglican Evangelicals, i.e. Evangelicals affiliated to Anglican churches, mostly in the Church of England and the Church of Ireland, with a few (4,600) in Anglican free or dissident churches; (2) Conservative Evangelicals, here enumerated as all persons affiliated to Protestant denominations which are Conservative Evangelical in theology and emphasis; (3) Conciliar Evangelicals, namely Evangelicals within non-Evangelical or conciliar Protestant denominations usually within the Ecumenical Movement; and (4) Fundamentalists, being all persons affiliated to Protestant denominations of fundamentalist theology, usually linked with the ICCC or other fundamentalist councils. The definition as used here does not include Black indigenous church members. *Anglican Evangelicals*. After the Evangelical Revival from 1739 onwards, by 1800 about 5% of all clergy and a higher percentage of the laity in the Church of England were avowed Evangelicals; by 1853, 41% of all clergy were High Church, 21% Broad Church, and 38% Low Church (W.J. Conybeare); the latter then rose rapidly until by 1900 around 53% were Evangelicals or Low Churchmen of one kind or another. After the year 1900, the proportion of Evangelicals in the Church of England (including the large proportion of Low Churchmen) declined rapidly to around 20% by 1948, but since 1950 a gradual numerical resurgence has been underway, especially during the 1970s, accompanied by a spiritual, theological and ecclesiological renewal, and stimulated to a considerable extent by the Anglican charismatic renewal, of whose members a majority in England are Evangelicals. By 1977 it had become clear that the Church of England as a whole was steadily assuming a distinctly Evangelical character. (a) *Parishes*. In 1975, of the Church of England's 14,400 parishes, 14% regarded themselves as High Church in churchmanship, 48% as Central or Broad Church (or non-Evangelical), 34% as Evangelical (of whom 21% were Conservative Evangelical or Low Church Evangelical), and 4% as Low Church but not Evangelical. With regard to foreign mission support, 58% of all parishes in 1977 supported USPG (High/Central; 21% also supporting CMS), 51% supported CMS (Evangelical; 21% also supporting USPG, and 12% also SAMS, BCMS or RCMS), 15% supported SAMS, 5% BCMS and 4% Ruanda CMS (the latter 3, Conservative Evangelical); these figures total to over 100% because, as indicated, many parishes support 2 or more of these major societies. (b) *Clergy*. With regard to clergy, in 1977 some 35% of the Church of England's 17,500 active clergy regarded themselves as Evangelicals (16% Conservative Evangelicals). (The results of our present survey gave Evangelical clergy as from 25% to 40% depending on the exact definition followed). By 1975 the formerly-strong Liberal Evangelicals, as represented by clergy in the Anglican Evangelical Group Movement, had virtually disappeared. These percentages had all increased considerably over the preceeding 25 years; and in 1977, 45% of all ordinands for the Church of England were in training in the 6 Evangelical theological colleges, and about 25% of newly-ordained clergy were Conservative Evangelicals. (c) *Laity*. With regard to the laity, around 28% regarded themselves as Evangelicals in 1975, rising gradually each year from around 20% in 1948. (The results of our present survey gave lay Evangelicals as from 25% to 35% depending on the exact definition followed). As can be seen from the column 'Conversion' above, over half of the annual increase in Evangelicals comes from the increase in Anglican pentecostals. (d) *Anglican Evangelical organizations and conferences*. These include: AEGM, BCMS, CEEC (Church of England Evangelical Council), Climbers, CMJ, CMS, CPAS, Church Society, CWN, CYFA (Church Youth Fellowship Association; 494 groups), Diocesan Evangelical Fellowships, Eclectics, ECOC, Explorers, FEC, FECOF, Islington Clerical Conference, Lee Abbey, NEAC (National Evangelical Anglican Congress, 1977), Pathfinders, RCMS, SAMS, SEAC (Senior Evangelical Anglican Clergy Conference), Simeon's Trustees.
HINDUS. Originally Indian immigrants, the vast majority Gujaratis from central and southern Gujarat, mostly of the Vaisya (merchant) caste; in 1970, about 130,000 born in India, rest born in UK. The column 'Natural change' above consists of biological increase annually and new immigrants each year. Unlike Muslims and Sikhs, Hindus have not built or opened more than a handful of orthodox temples in the UK because of the prohibition of such activity outside India. The total includes a number of sects: 30,000 followers of the Swaminarayan Hindu Mission, the Ramakrishna Mission, Eckankar, Auroville International, Meher Baba Association (Oceanic Limited), and several sects with widespread White followings and annual White converts: Divine Light Mission (DLM), begun in India in 1960 and in England in 1971 (8,000 adult followers of Guru Maharaj Ji in 31 centres in the UK by 1973); 3,000 members of Hare Krishna (International Society for Krishna Consciousness, ISKCON), which reached the UK in 1968 and had 3 temples by 1973; Spiritual Regeneration Movement (SRM) or Transcendental Meditation, a yoga therapy introduced around 1965 (350 qualified teachers in 1977, 65 centres, 75,000 meditators); 1,000 adherents (170 committed disciples) of the Bengali movement Sri Chimnoy Centre; Ananda Marga; et alia. The Theosophical Society, a neo-Hindu movement, in 1975 had 80 Lodges with 2,570 members.
JEWS. 77% belong to the United Synagogue (Orthodox), 8% Liberal, 7% Reform, 8% no synagogue. There are 350 synagogues in Britain. Over half of all Jews live in the London area. Attendance at synagogue (NOP 1970): of all Jews, 26% attend weekly, 6% fortnightly, 8% monthly, 19% quarterly, 20% less often, 21% never. Liberal and Reform Jews attend less regularly than United.
MUSLIMS. Over 80% are immigrants since 1950 from Pakistan and other British Commonwealth Muslim countries and areas with their dependants. The 1971 census enumerated about 220,000 born overseas in Muslim areas, with about 110,000 children born in the UK. The column 'Natural change' above consists of biological increase annually and new immigrants each year. In 1971 the majority of Muslims were Sunnis from Pakistan (including Bengalis from Bangladesh), with about 100,000 Sunnis from India (mainly Gujaratis), around 40,000 Arabs and Middle Easterners (including 5,000 Moroccans), 20,000 Turkish Cypriots (Sunnis), 20,000 from Malaysia, 20,000 from East Africa, 10,000 from West Africa, 10,000 Ismaili Shias, 2,000 Yemenis, 1,000 Somalis, 10,000 Eritreans, some Shias, and 8,000 in the Ahmadiya Mission. *Muslim temporary residents* (excluded from Table 1). (1980) 500,000. *Mosques*. (1980) About 1,200. *Quranic schools*. (1980) 5,000. *Hajj pilgrims to Mecca*. (1974) 1,254; (1976) 757.
NEO-PENTECOSTALS. Charismatics in organized groups who remain within non-Pentecostal Protestant denominations numbered in 1974 around 40,000 adults (or, total charismatic community including children, 80,000) including many young Jesus People. These figures exclude movements which have left, or been excommunicated from, their parent bodies, who are then enumerated as separate Pentecostal denominations in Table 2.
NON-RELIGIOUS. Among these are followers of the over 91 humanist groups, most affiliated to one of the national bodies.
OTHER RELIGIONISTS. There is a large number of smaller non-Christian religious groupings. These include 10,000 militant supporters of Moral Re-Armament (MRA) with 100,000 sympathizers or adherents most of whom belong to Christian churches; about 30,000 practising self-styled witches who practise occultism and black magic in England; many adherents of African, Asian and Afro-American non-Christian and syncretistic religions, including non-Christian Rastafarians from Jamaica; 1,200 adherents of Soka Gakkai (Nichiren Shoshu) from Japan, in 1975; Rosicrucians (AMORC with 16 Lodges and centres, also Lectorium Rosicrucianum and other orders); Druidism and Neo-Paganism; Atlanteans and followers of other New Age cults; and other groupings. Some of the 1 million Freemasons in the British Isles practise it as a non-Christian religion, although most are either professing or nominal Anglicans or Protestants, or non-religious.
PRACTISING CHRISTIANS. *Church attendance*. 1938 (GB; Gallup): 27% regularly, 41% occasionally, 17% for weddings only, 15% never. December 1947 (GB): 20% weekly, 10% fortnightly, 30% often, 40% seldom. February 1957 (GB): 28% once a month or more, 18% occasionally, 4% Christmas and Easter only, 11% special family occasions only, 7 radio/TV services only, 32% seldom or never. March 1960 (GB): 23% weekly, 6% fortnightly only, 13% monthly only, 21% annually only, 37% seldom or never. April 1968 (GB): 23% once a month or more, 20% occasionally, 3% Christmas and Easter only, 11% special family occasions only, 4% radio/TV services only, 39% seldom or never. 1969 (GB): 28% on Christmas Day, 72% not. October 1970 (GB): 20% weekly. 1977: 18% weekly. 1979 (Marplan): 16% weekly, 23% monthly, 30% quarterly. 1970 (GB): 30% on Christmas Day, 70% not. 1968 (Northern Ireland): 57% weekly (Anglicans 41%, Roman Catholics 92%, Presbyterians 37%, Methodists 42%), 91% (total) annually (Anglicans 88%, Roman Catholics 99%, Presbyterians 88%, Methodists 90%). 1964 (England): Of the 23% who attend church weekly, 45% are Anglicans, 33% Protestants, 22% Roman Catholics. *Anglican/Protestant church attendance* (GB; NOP 1970). Of all professing Anglicans and Protestants, 10% attend weekly, 4% fortnightly, 7% monthly, 21% 3–12 times a year, 32% less often, 25% never. *Anglican/Protestant communion attendance* (GB; NOP 1970). Of all professing Anglicans and Protestants, 3% take Holy Communion weekly, 2% fortnightly, 6% monthly, 8% 3–12 times a year, 18% less often (once or twice a year), 63% never. *Anglican/Protestant Easter and Christmas attendance* (GB; NOP 1970). Of all professing Anglicans and Protestants, 32% attend special services at Easter each year regularly, 13% sometimes, 54% never; and 41% attend special services at Christmas each year regularly, 13% sometimes, 45% never. *Roman Catholic attendance* (GB; NOP 1970). Of all professing Catholics, 4% attend mass daily, 59% weekly, 4% fortnightly, 8% monthly, 7% 3–12 times a year, 11% less often (once or twice a year), 7% never. *RC communion attendance* (GB; NOP 1970). Of all professing Catholics, 3% take communion daily, 25% weekly, 7% fortnightly, 19% monthly, 14% 3–12 times a year, 18% less often, 13% never. *RC Easter and Christmas attendance* (GB; NOP 1970). Of all professing Catholics, 73% attend special services at Easter each year regularly, 7% sometimes, 19% never; and 79% attend special services at Christmas each year regularly, 5% sometimes, 15% never. *Easter and Christmas practice*. Attendance on these feast days is, statistically, not an important part of practice in Britain, being less than for harvest festivals, carol services and war remembrance services. In the polls listed above, only 30% of the population attend on Christmas Day, and only 4% attend only at Christmas and Easter. Likewise, Anglican communicants at these festivals are only a small fraction of all Anglican attenders. For this reason, the low figures for Easter communions published annually in the *Church of England year book* give a misleadingly low (though technically correct) picture of Anglican practice; for although Easter communicants are only 20% of affiliated Anglicans, and weekly attendance only 16%, the polls indicate that the total of Anglican annual attenders is 63%. *Attendance trends* (GB). Annual attenders in GB have thus fallen from 68% of the total population in 1938, 60% in 1947, 57% in 1957, and to 50% in 1968, i.e. an average loss of 0.6% of the total population of GB each year (351,000 per year in 1975), somewhat offset by natural increase. In northern Ireland there has been little or no annual change in the figure of 91%. The annual nett decline in practising Christians in the UK in 1975 is about 259,000. *Radio/TV services*. Weekly participation in Sunday services (1966): BBC, 24% of the population; ITV (Independent Television, now IBA), 18%. *Children*. 61% of all parents in GB encourage their children to attend weekly Sunday school (NOP 1970). *Summary*. The polls listed above indicate that, in 1970, 20% of the population of GB and 57% in Northern Ireland attended church weekly; and the total annual attenders (all attending services of public worship at least once a year, including 4% over radio/TV (largely the elderly, sick and disabled), but excluding 11% attending only for family occasions) was 50% in GB (26,971,600 persons) and 91% in Northern Ireland (1,398,100 persons), making a total of 28,369,700 practising Christians, in the UK in 1970. However, 11.2% of the UK in 1970 were non-Christians, and only 79.1% of the UK were affiliated Christians. Therefore, using this Encyclopedia's definition of practising Christians (annually practising Christians as a % of affiliated Christians), annual religious practice in 1970 in the UK was 65%. By the same reasoning, weekly attendance for the UK was 26% of affiliated Christians.
ROMAN CATHOLICS. Annual converts (adult baptisms) have declined (as a % of all Catholics) from 1911–75: there were 7,700 in 1911, a peak of 13,735 in 1959, a plateau of 12,000 from 1960–62, then a decline to 3,897 in 1972. Nominal Catholics (alienated to the extent of not using church offices for baptisms, marriages or funerals) increased from 4% of all professing Catholics in 1958 to 23% in 1970 and to 27% by 1975. In England, the Roman Catholic Church recognizes that it is out of touch with around 30% of all Catholics, who are either unknown to the church and clergy, or lapsed, or non-practising, or practising elsewhere.
SIKHS. Immigrants from India; Punjabis, mainly from 2 districts in the Punjab: Jullundur and Hoshiarpur. There are over 38 temples in the British Isles. In the 1970s there was still a small annual immigration (included in the column 'Natural change' above).
SPIRITISTS. Non-Christian adherents of several varieties of specifically non-Christian Spiritism and mediumistic religions, which nevertheless hold some basic Christian tenets and assign a leading role to Christ, and hence also claim numerous Christian adherents; including White Eagle Lodge (begun 1936; 3,000 adult members by 1980, in 120 groups in UK, USA, Netherlands, Sweden, Norway, Switzerland and over 30 other countries; HQ at White Temple, Liss, UK).
THIRD-WORLD INDIGENOUS. In about 108 distinct denominations in 1970 (see Table 2), increasing each year. In addition, there are a large number of other Black and Black-led churches with dominant West Indian membership which are not classified here as Third-World indigenous because they are part of, or affiliated to, White Protestant churches based in the USA or the UK; the largest are the New Testament Church of God, Seventh-day Adventist Church, Church of God of Prophecy, Moravian Church, Church of God Fellowship (Welsh Latter Rain Movement), Seventh Day Baptist Church, United Pentecostal Church, et alia, with over 60,000 affiliated Black members.

**Church of England.** Governing body, 1976: General Synod, addressed by the monarch, Queen Elizabeth II, as Head of the Church of England.

**NON-CHRISTIAN RELIGIONS. Judaism** has had a long history as the largest of the religious communities outside Christendom in the UK. Jews first came to England during the Norman conquest, but a 13th-century edict by Edward I resulted in their expulsion. The present Anglo-Jewish community, one of the largest in Europe, dates from 1656 and is composed of 2 branches, Ashkenazi (originally from Germany and eastern Europe) and Sefardi (from Spain and Portugal), both divided into Orthodox and Reformed schools of thought. About 90% of all practising Jews are Orthodox, the chief rabbi being the head of the Ashkenazis, the principal group, and the haham the leader of the Sefardis. Reformed Judaism began in 1840 and was succeeded by the liberal Jewish movement in 1901. There are at present some 350 synagogues in the UK, and recent years have witnessed a growth in Jewish schools which now cater for 20% of all Jewish children.

International Jewish organizations with their headquarters in London include the World Sefardi Federation, World Union of Jewish Students, World Zionist organization, Institute of Jewish Affairs, Conference of European Rabbis, and Jewish Colonization Association.

Among the many national Jewish organizations may be mentioned the following: the Chief Rabbinate, Reform Synagogues of Great Britain, Union of Liberal and Progressive Synagogues, Central Council for Jewish Social Service, Federation of Jewish Relief Organizations, Jewish Agency for Israel, Zionist Federation of Great Britain and Ireland, Federation of Women Zionists of Great Britain and Ireland, Central Council for Jewish Religious Education, Institute of Jewish Studies, Association for Jewish Youth, Hillel Foundation, Inter-University Jewish Federation of Great Britain and Ireland, Association of Jewish Women's Organizations in the United Kingdom, and League of Jewish Women.

**Islam** has the largest following among Asian religions in Britain due to immigration, amounting to 0.9% of the population in 1975. The Central Mosque and Islamic Cultural Centre in London serve as headquarters for the orthodox Muslim community, while mosques and centres also exist in Liverpool, Manchester, Cardiff, Bradford and other cities. The majority are Sunnis but several Shia sects are also present, together with (since 1913) a vigorous Ahmadiya community of 9,000. An international Muslim organization with its headquarters in London is the Islamic Council of Europe. Three national organizations based in London are the Union of Muslim Organizations of UK and Eire, Islamic Cultural Centre, and Muslim Students Society; while the Islamic Foundation has its centre in Leicester.

**Hinduism** has the next largest following, 0.4% of the population in 1975. Due to Hindu custom when outside India no temples have been built and hardly any opened in Britain, the exception being the East London Hindu Centre which opened a temple in London in 1970. In addition to traditional Hindu sects, there are many White converts to new sects of which the largest are the Divine Light Mission (8,000), the Hare Krishna movement (3,000), and the Spiritual Regeneration Movement (TM).

**Sikhism** amounted to 0.4% of the population in 1975, and 38 new Sikh temples have been built or acquired in London, Birmingham and elsewhere.

**Buddhism** has a long history in the UK going back to the 19th century, although there were only about 30,000 adherents in the country in 1970. The Buddhist Society, founded in London in 1924, maintains a shrine room and one of Europe's finest Buddhist libraries, and includes as members most of Buddhism's numerous local associations, in Aberdeen, Devon, Dover, and Edinburgh, to cite only a few. These groups are often small but very active and characterized by independence with regard to the variety of Buddhist practices. More recently Tibetan schools have established centres of meditation, and the Theravada school of Thailand has opened a temple (Buddhapadipa Temple) in East Sheen, London which is much used for daily meditation. The Buddhist Society belongs to the Buddhist Community of Europe, based in France, which is in the process of formation. Since 1971, massive numbers of British converts have been won, including 20,000 men who have become bhikkus (monks).

**CHRISTIANITY.** The definitive introduction of Christianity into Britain may be put at around the end of the first century, the first church according to tradition having been erected at Glastonbury in AD 61. In AD 314, 3 English bishops attended the Council of Arles in France. From about 350 the Celtic church in Britain was cut off from the rest of Christendom, finally becoming absorbed by the church of the Romans during 632–777. In 563, Columba left Ireland to found a monastery at Iona (Scotland), and Augustine was sent by the Roman pope in 596 to England, which had become a virtually heathen country again; he became the first bishop of Canterbury. During the next century Wilfred and Theodore of Tarsus completed the evangelization of England and the organization of the British church, and Willibrord and Boniface were sent out as missionaries to Holland, Germany and Denmark. Norwegian and Swedish kings educated in England in their turn introduced Christianity to their own countries before the year 1000. British kings and nobles were involved in the Crusades during the 13th century, and universities and mendicant orders were developed during this period of the Middle Ages. The 14th and 15th centuries were a time of secular disillusionment and religious dissatisfaction with current Christian practices, voiced by John Wycliffe and the Lollards, who stressed the importance of the Bible, the practice of poverty and personal spirituality.

Britain severed its relationship with Rome during the 16th century, the Church of England becoming autonomous through Henry VIII's Supremacy Act of 1534, making the British monarch head of the church. In 1534 the English Bible was placed in all parish churches. Persecution of Catholics was widespread under Edward VI (1549–53), and of Protestants under Mary (1553–58). In 1560 the Church of Scotland was reformed. Congregationalists arose in 1580, and the next century saw the rise of Baptists and Friends.

Reaction against nonconformists set in under Charles II, with the passage of the Uniformity Act of 1662 through which 2,000 clergymen were displaced because of their refusal to accept the Book of Common Prayer. During this period foreign missionary activity was begun by the Society for the Propagation of the Gospel in New England in 1649, the Society for the Promotion of Christian Knowledge in 1698 and the Society for the Propagation of the Gospel in Foreign Parts in 1701.

The most notable development of the 18th century was the Wesleyan Revival and the formation of the Methodist Church which also helped to spark a renewal of interest in missions and the creation of new bodies: Baptist Missionary Society in 1792, London Missionary Society in 1795, Scottish and Glasgow Missionary Societies in 1796, Church Missionary Society in 1799 and British and Foreign Bible Society in 1804. The 19th century was characterized not only by the creation of many new Protestant denominations, including the Brethren and Salvation Army, but also by a new tolerance towards Roman Catholicism. Civil rights were restored to Roman Catholics in 1829, and thousands of Irish Catholics migrated to Britain following the potato famine of 1846. The Roman Catholic hierarchy was restored in England in 1850, Scotland following suit in 1878. The Oxford Movement, with attention focused on reunion with Rome, resulted in a number of prominent Anglicans becoming Roman Catholics. The 20th century has witnessed the arrival of new holiness and pentecostal groups and the growth of secularism, accompanied by a massive numerical decline of Anglican and main-line Protestant churches.

**ANGLICAN CHURCHES.** The major tradition in the United Kingdom is that of the Anglican Communion, which exists as 4 distinct churches corresponding to the main geographical divisions of England, Wales, Scotland and Ireland. These churches go back to the earliest days of Christianity in Britain, as their claimed dates of origin (given in Table 2 below) attest. The smaller of these churches will be briefly described first.

The Episcopal Church in Scotland is the smallest of the 4 and the most uniformly in the High Church tradition of churchmanship (including both Prayer Book Catholic and Anglo-Catholic). In 1970 it had 335 parishes divided into 7 dioceses with a total baptized community of just under 90,000, declining annually in size. The church is governed by the Episcopal Synod, Consultative Council on Church Legislation, and Representative Church Council. The former consists of 2 chambers of bishops and clergy while the latter 2 include also the laity. Anglican strength in Scotland is concentrated in the east, northeast and Perthshire, its membership being upper middle class with a large number of landed aristocrats.

The Church of Ireland consists of 2 provinces, Dublin and Armagh, Dublin being entirely in the republic of Ireland while Armagh is mostly in Ulster (Northern Ireland). The church in Eire, which has a baptized community of less than 100,000, is traditionally Low Church (also Evangelical) in ritual. It continues to lose members by emigration to the north whose 481 parishes in 5 dioceses have over 300,000 Anglicans. The General Synod consists of a House of Bishops and a House of Representatives, the latter composed of both clergy and laity.

The Church in Wales, with 1,450 parishes in 6 dioceses and a baptized community of about one million, is in the High Church tradition. Its dioceses are co-terminous with the geographical boundaries of Wales and Monmouthshire (now Gwent). Central legislative functions are carried out by the Governing Body consisting of bishops, clergy and laity, with financial and administrative control exercised by the church's Representative Body.

In terms of membership and significance, the Church of England is the major Anglican church in the world. It is divided into 2 provinces, Canterbury and York, with 14,400 parishes in 43 dioceses and a baptized community of nearly 28 million. The archbishop of Canterbury is the primate of all England and is also recognized as the leader and focus of unity for the entire world-wide Anglican Communion.

Although the Anglican Church is omnipresent in England, there is a considerable geographical variation in its strength. Anglicans play a more important role in rural areas with small populations that in urban areas. Carlisle and Hereford, which have the lowest population densities of all English dioceses, manifest also the highest church-going. Allegiance is lowest in the urban areas of London, Birmingham, northeast Midlands and the Potteries; whereas Anglican influence is greatest in the West (West Midlands, West Country except for Cornwall, and the northwest generally), East Anglia, Lincolnshire, Oxford and portions of the southern coastal region.

Anglicanism in England represents a wide diversity of traditions of churchmanship existing within the one church without serious conflict. The major traditions and their respective emphases are: Low Church, sometimes called Conservative Evangelical (emphasizing conservative theology and simplicity of faith and ritual), Evangelical (the importance of the Bible, evangelism, holy communion, and foreign missions), Central or Broad Church (Prayer Book worship, liberal theology), High Church or Prayer Book Catholic and Anglo-Catholic (accepting much of Roman Catholic ritual and dogma but without the supremacy of the pope). Many parishes in England follow predominantly one or other of these traditions. At the diocesan level, the traditions are far more intermingled, although individual bishops may be known as Evangelicals or High Churchmen. However, it is possible to distinguish traditions sufficiently to say that of the 43 English dioceses and their bishops, 2 tend to have a Low Church emphasis, 3 Evangelical, 12 Central or Broad Church, 7 High Church, and one Anglo-Catholic, with 18 of pluralistic traditions. In a 1970 poll, 14% of Anglicans in Great Britain described themselves as of High Churchmanship, 70% of Low (including Central) churchmanship, and 16% of no particular views on the subject. Evangelicals numbered 10 million laity and 5,000 clergy in 1975.

The Church of England was the originator of the worldwide Anglican Communion, and is still the largest of its 25 autonomous member Churches and 6 non-autonomous churches, with in 1977 a total of 40 ecclesiastical provinces and 390 dioceses in 120 countries. Since 1867 the bishops of the entire Communion have met in Lambeth Palace, London, for the 10-yearly Lambeth Conferences. At the 1968 Conference, a body representative of laity and clergy as well as bishops was formed, the Anglican Consultative Council with headquarters in London, which has around 50 delegates and meets biennially.

Although most Anglican Churches overseas are now autonomous, there are still several detached dioceses (in Asia, Bermuda and the Falkland Islands) which come under the metropolitical jurisdiction of the archbishop of Canterbury. Also, Anglican chaplaincies have existed in Europe since the Reformation, and in 1970 the diocese of Gibraltar (covering southern Europe) was extended to cover the jurisdiction of North & Central Europe, under the combined name Anglican Church in Europe.

PROTESTANT CHURCHES. The principal Protestant tradition in the United Kingdom is Presbyterianism, the main bodies being the Church of Scotland, Presbyterian Church in Ireland, Presbyterian Church of Wales, and United Reformed Church, the latter resulting from a 1972 merger of the Presbyterian and Congregational churches in England. A number of smaller Presbyterian denominations are also active, particularly in Scotland: Free Church of Scotland, Free Presbyterian Church of Scotland, Reformed Presbyterian Church of Scotland

**Church of England.** *Above.* Governing body, 1969: Convocations of Canterbury and York, in Church House, Westminster, voting on Anglican-Methodist reunion scheme. *Below left.* On steps of St Paul's Cathedral,

City of London, 10,000 marchers supporting CND (Campaign for Nuclear Disarmament) demonstrate, addressed by (*right*) pacifist Canon L.J. Collins of St Paul's.

and United Free Church of Scotland. The Church of Scotland is the largest and most significant body in the Reformed tradition, with 3,000 parishes divided into 12 synods and 59 presbyteries and a Christian community of 2,500,000. Tracing its history back through the Scottish Reformation of 1560 to the 4th century, the Church of Scotland was re-united in 1929 with the United Free Church, which came into existence in 1900 following schisms in 1843 and 1893. The church's central legislative body is the General Assembly, and the administrative offices of the church include departments termed General Interests, Finance, Church and Ministry, Publicity and Publication, Education, Social and Moral Welfare, in addition to the Overseas Council, Home Board Women's Guild and Deaconess Board.

Methodism is the second most important Protestant tradition, owing its origin to the 18th-century Wesleyan revival. Five Methodist denominations exist: the Free Methodist Church, Wesleyan Reform Union, Independent Methodist Connexion, Methodist Church in Ireland, and Methodist Church of Great Britain, the latter being by far the largest with nearly 10,000 churches and chapels grouped in about 1,600 areas called circuits and a Christian community of 2 million. The result of a merger in 1932 of United, Primitive and Wesleyan Methodists, the present Methodist Church of Great Britain has its strength in the southwestern counties of Cornwall and Devon, the Isle of Wight, the eastern counties of Yorkshire and Lincolnshire and the northern counties of Cumberland, Durham and Northumberland.

Baptists first came to England as immigrants from Holland at the beginning of the 16th century, but the emergence of the General Baptists (moderates rejecting Calvinism) as an organized movement did not take place until 1611. A stricter Calvinistic Particular Baptist group began to form after 1633, followed by a new body, the General Baptists of the New Connexion in 1770. By 1813 the first attempt had been made to form a Baptist Union. At the present time the Baptist tradition in the United Kingdom is organized into 4 different unions with some overlapping of membership, plus about 500 unaffiliated churches. There are also small groups of Seventh-day and Strict Baptists. The largest body is the Baptist Union of Great Britain and Ireland which includes also 43% of the member churches of the Baptist Union of Wales and Monmouthshire (Gwent) and 10 parishes of the Baptist Union of Scotland, the Baptist Union of Ireland being entirely separate. Baptists are strongest in the counties north of London, in the area of the Bristol Channel and to a lesser extent in the southeast. Few are found in northern England.

The Salvation Army owes its origin to William Booth, a minister of the Methodist New Connexion, who began work in east London in 1865. Booth's Christian Revival Association, later called the Christian Mission, continued to develop and spread; in 1878 the name was changed to the Salvation Army and it became a world-wide movement. At the present time there are 17,000 corps and outposts throughout the world, of which 1,100 serve a Christian community of 500,000 in the United Kingdom. The Salvation Army is noted for its vast proliferation of social service activities, as well as for its evangelistic work.

The Brethren movement was begun in Dublin through an Anglican clergyman, John Darby, in 1827 and in Britain also in 1828. An early important centre was at Plymouth, England (1831) from which the popular name Plymouth Brethren was derived, although this name has never been accepted by the membership. In 1848 a conservative faction split off to form the Exclusive or Closed Brethren, and in 1889 another schism among the Open Brethren produced the Churches of God in the British Isles and Overseas.

Congregationalists, dating from the Reformation period, formed about 70% of the membership of the United Reformed Church at its inauguration in 1972. Other Congregational groups include the Union of Welsh Independents, Congregational Union of Scotland and the Congregational Union of Ireland.

Pentecostals have not been particularly successful among the British. The largest denominations are the Assemblies of God, Elim Pentecostal Church and the Apostolic Church.

Other small but active groups include Adventists, Disciples, Lutherans, Moravians, Quakers and several holiness churches.

CATHOLIC CHURCH. Several Catholic dioceses in Britain go back to the early centuries, as their claimed dates of origin (given in Table 2 below)

**Anglican pentecostals.** Charismatic renewal service in Cathedral of the Holy Spirit, Diocese of Guildford. Charismatics in the Church of England numbered 450,000 in 1978.

attest: 4th century in Ireland, 5th century in Scotland, 7th century in England and Wales. These 3 churches will now be considered separately. (1) *England and Wales.* During the reign of Henry VIII, through Acts passed by the Reformation Parliament of 1530–36 papal authority over the Church of England was formally repudiated, and the established Church of England continued as an institution separate from Rome. For almost 3 centuries, with one short break during the reign of Mary Tudor (1553–58), Catholics who maintained allegiance to the pope were penalized in a variety of ways. The Roman Catholic population gradually dwindled until by the middle of the 18th century it was restricted to a number of upper-class and aristocratic families and a small minority of farmers living mainly in the north of England. In 1767, Roman Catholics in England and Wales numbered 80,000.

From the last part of the 18th century and throughout the 19th century the Roman Catholic population increased considerably, largely due to the influx of immigrants from Ireland who came to England and Wales seeking employment. From 70,000 in 1780 (0.9% of the total population of England and Wales), Catholics increased to 580,000 in 1840 (4%) and to 2,500,000 in 1880 (8%). Most of the Irish settled in the rapidly developing urban areas, and by 1850 their numbers were sufficient to warrant the re-establishment of the Roman Catholic hierarchy, which was now possible after the Catholic Emancipation Act of 1829 which finally removed almost all the disabilities under which Roman Catholics had suffered. Subsequently the Roman Catholic Church in England and Wales developed until by 1975 it consisted of 5 provinces and 19 dioceses.

In 1975 the impact of Irish immigration was still being strongly felt. It is this which accounts for the geographical division of the Catholic Church in England into 2 parts, the large western cities including Liverpool on the one hand and the London conurbation on the other, the latter representing the most important concentration of English Catholics although always less than one third of the population. The majority of Catholic priests in Great Britain

**Catholic Church in England and Wales.** Roman Catholic churches overlap, parallel, or duplicate Anglican churches almost everywhere; above, Anglican neo-Gothic Liverpool Cathedral (4th largest cathedral in world) dominates skyline of Liverpool (left), but so does Roman Catholic ultramodern circular Metropolitan Cathedral of Archdiocese of Liverpool (centre). In May 1980 the latter hosted the 5-day National Pastoral Congress of England & Wales, with 2,100 elected delegates.

continue to be Irish immigrants, with only a few English and Welsh clergy. Between 1965 and 1970, 209 priests were ordained in Ireland for service in the dioceses of Great Britain.

For many years after 1850 the Roman Catholic urban population remained isolated; since 1950, however, this isolation has been breaking down and Catholics are increasingly becoming more socially mobile and more easily assimilated within the wider society.

One major field of activity since the re-establishment of the hierarchy is that of education. Considerable effort has been put into building up a very wide-ranging system of schools for all age groups. In this the church has received, for most of the 20th century, financial support from the state. At the present time the state provides 80% of the capital cost of building schools and colleges and accepts responsibility for maintenance of buildings and payment of teachers' salaries.

Ecclesiastically, the Catholic Church in England and Wales has always been considered highly traditionalist, and has yet to involve itself in renewal. This was the conclusion of a recent report jointly produced by the episcopal and priests' conferences, entitled 'The Church in the Year 2000', which proposed a complete restructuring of all dioceses. In July 1974 the episcopal conference published a proposal for the dismantling of the present 19 dioceses and the creation of 37 dioceses, each with a population serving from 80,000 to 200,000 Catholics, and whose boundaries would coincide with those of the civil administration. After discussion with priests and laity, the plan was to be submitted to the Holy See for approval.

(2) *Scotland*. On 24 August 1560 there came into force legislation enacted by the Scottish parliament under which the Catholic religion and papal authority were abolished, celebration of mass declared illegal and Protestantism established as the state religion. But as the events of the next 3 centuries were to show, the Presbyterian reformation in Scotland was never complete. Catholicism survived in the southwest and northeast, the highlands and the islands; and Episcopalianism also continued active in the northeast. Nevertheless, by the end of the 18th century Catholicism in Scotland was at its lowest ebb. Apart from general religious persecution since the reformation, the attachment of the Catholic Church to the fortunes of the Stuart family brought inevitable repression after the failure of the rebellions of 1715 and 1745. To add further to their suffering, the beginning of the highland clearances in the second half of the 18th century forced many Catholics to leave Scotland or to join the highland regiments which were then being formed for service in foreign wars. By the year 1800 the Catholic population of Scotland numbered only about 30,000, less than 2% of the total population then.

The 19th century however witnessed a dramatic increase in the number of Catholics in Scotland. The prime cause of this was firstly immigration from Ireland caused first by the failure of the Irish rebellion of 1798, and secondly massive immigration after the failure of the Irish potato crops in 1845 and succeeding years. In 1851 Catholics numbered 145,860 (5% of the population), and in 1878 the Catholic hierarchy was restored. Irish immigration continued for the rest of the 19th century, although by 1908 it had been reduced to insignificant numbers. By 1973, the Catholic population numbered 822,000 (16% of the population), consisting mainly of a small core of highland Catholics and a very large number of third-, fourth-, and fifth-generation descendants of 19th-century Irish immigrants. Since the end of World War II in 1945, immigration of English, Polish, Ukrainian and German Catholics has increased significantly.

About 70% of the Scottish Catholic population live in the ecclesiastical province of Glasgow. For many years Scotland was dependent on a continuing supply of young Irish priests to staff its parishes; and as recently as 1940 half of all new ordinands were Irish. This is no longer the case; with the exception of a very small number of Irish-born priests who for family reasons wish to work in Scotland, all ordinands to the priesthood now are Scottish-born. In a 1959 survey, it was estimated that 25% of all adult church members in Scotland were Catholics, and that 63% of Catholic adults attended mass every Sunday. Subsequently these figures have not altered markedly.

Socially, one of the most liberalizing influences in the development of the Catholic community in Scotland was the enactment of the Education (Scotland) Act of 1918. This both relieved an economically depressed community from the burden of maintaining its parochial school system, and also opened to it opportunities for higher education.

Ecclesiastically, the Scottish Catholic community is conservative and has been little affected by the spirit of Vatican II. This is especially true of Glasgow and the western part of the country. Aberdeen and northeastern Scotland on the other hand display a style of Catholicism which is more open and tolerant.

(3) *Northern Ireland*. The Catholic Church in Ulster is the largest single denomination, although Catholics form only one-third of the population. There is in reality only one church for the whole of Ireland served by one episcopal conference located in Eire. The archdiocese of Armagh is found entirely in Ulster as is its suffragan diocese of Down & Connor. The other dioceses of Clogher, Derry and Dromore cover parts of both Ulster and Eire.

MARGINAL CHURCHES. The main para-Christian or marginal Protestant churches in the UK include Spiritualists, Jehovah's Witnesses, Mormons, Christian Scientists, Unitarians and Swedenborgians. Those registering the most significant gains in recent years are the Mormons and Jehovah's Witnesses.

ORTHODOX AND OTHER CATHOLIC CHURCHES. Orthodox churches in the UK include the Armenian, Assyrian, Byelorussian, Bulgarian, Coptic, Estonian, Greek, Polish, Romanian, Russian (3 groups), Serbian, Syrian and Ukrainian churches. The Greek Orthodox Archdiocese for Western Europe, under the Ecumenical Patriarchate of Constantinople, has its headquarters in London. Catholic (non-Roman) churches include the Catholic Apostolic Church, English Catholic Church, Liberal Catholic Church, New Apostolic Church, Old Catholic Church of England and Old Roman Catholic Church (English Rite). Over the last century there has also been in England a proliferation of bishops-at-large (episcopi vagantes) as the heads of autocephalous Catholic churches most of which have very small lay memberships.

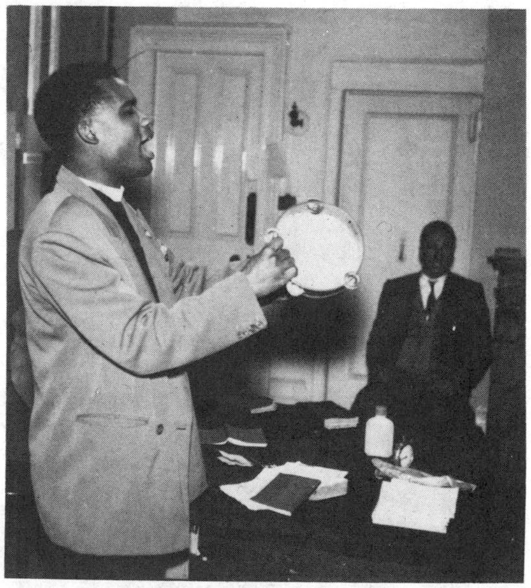

**Third-World indigenous churches.** Over 120 Black and Non-White indigenous denominations exist, most having immigrated from Africa, Asia or West Indies. *Above.* Black pentecostal pastor.

THIRD-WORLD INDIGENOUS CHURCHES. There are over 108 predominantly Black denominations in the UK, most of which were brought to Britain by immigrants from the West Indies, especially Jamaicans and Guyanans. Most average 1,000 members each. Some of these are entirely independent, while others maintain ties with mother churches in the USA and the Caribbean. The largest of these is the First United Church of Jesus Christ (Apostolic) from Jamaica. Several West African indigenous churches are also active, the most important being the Church of the Lord (Aladura) and the Church of the Cherubim and Seraphim, both based in Nigeria.

**CHURCH AND STATE.** The British constitution has never been formulated as a single written document. The rules governing Britain's political institutions are found in several areas: in written laws known as statutes or acts of Parliament, in judicial decisions interpreting both these laws and also common law, and in unwritten but definitive conventions. In all of these, the part played by religion and ecclesiastical authorities is considerable.

There are 2 established or state churches in the UK. The Church of England is the established church in England, and the Church of Scotland (Presbyterian) is established in Scotland; and the sovereign is the head of both. The Church of Ireland and the Church in Wales, both Anglican, were disestablished respectively by the Irish Church Act of 1869 and the Welsh Church Acts of 1914 and 1919.

The close relations of the Church of England with the state date back to the 6th century. A millenium later in the reign of Henry VIII, by various acts of Parliament between 1532 and 1534 the church repudiated papal jurisdiction and separated itself from Rome. The former position was temporarily restored under Mary I, a Roman Catholic, but the legislation of Henry VIII was reinstated by the Act of Supremacy in 1558, the first year of the reign of Elizabeth I.

In the UK, the British sovereign is the supreme governor of the church under God, and during the coronation service is crowned by the archbishop of Canterbury. Parliament has authority to pass legislation on church affairs, such as sanction for the Book of Common Prayer which was authorized by the Act of Uniformity in 1662. Since 1965 the church may authorize services that do not conform to the 1662 pattern. Through the Submission of the Clergy Act of 1533, the ancient Convocations of Canterbury and York received permission to pass canons subject to certain restrictions, and by the Church of England (Assembly) Powers Act of 1919 the then newly-created Church Assembly was given authority to pass measures having the force of acts of Parliament and the right to repeal or amend them. Measures required the simple assent of both Houses of Parliament but could not be amended by them; they also required the royal assent. The Synodical Government Measure of 1969 substituted the General Synod for the Church Assembly, and this body now passes both measures and canons.

According to the Appointment of Bishops Act of 1533, diocesan bishops are chosen by the sovereign on the advice of the prime minister after careful consultation with the church. In 1974, General Synod voted that the decisive voice should be that of the church, and more acceptable procedures were evolved which came into operation in 1977. The 26 senior bishops are entitled to sit as members in the House of Lords. A recognized system of ecclesiastical courts was formed through the Ecclesiastical Jurisdiction Measure of 1963. Incumbents (clergy in charge of parishes) have a pastoral relationship with their parishioners, and marriages conducted by the church are recognized in their own right.

The Church of Scotland also dates from early times, being reformed in 1560–67 at which time it also separated from the Church of Rome. In 1592 the church was recognized as Presbyterian and became self-governing except that secular courts have always been recognized as having jurisdiction in matters of property and civil rights. The General Assembly is the governing body. The main purpose of the Church of Scotland Act of 1921, which has appended to it declaratory articles setting out the position of the church, was to reunite the church following the schism of 1843 over the question of lay patronage, subsequently abolished.

The other churches and denominations in the UK have no special links with the state but the major Protestant denominations are governed by constitutions defined and promulgated by themselves which have been ratified by private acts of Parliament. The Toleration Act of 1688 largely freed Protestant nonconformists from disabilities, and none now exist. Roman Catholics were in the past subject to penal legislation, and a few traces of little importance still survive. Churches are not registered as such, but church buildings of non-established churches may be registered under the Places of Worship Registration Act of 1855, from which certain financial advantages are derived.

Religious affairs are handled for the state by various government ministries depending upon the particular subject in question, the Home Office being the principal ministry involved. Clergy are not paid by the state unless specifically in its employ, as is the case with chaplains to the armed forces and prisons, and all hospital chaplains. A clergyman may claim a reduction of half the land rate on his residence. There is also a tax reduction in respect of money used for the maintenance, heating, lighting and cleaning of his residence and for meeting the expenses of his office. Church buildings are free of taxation and also from certain restrictions under the Town and Country

Planning Acts. Church buildings in use generally receive no financial support from the state, but a contribution is made for historic buildings no longer required for worship.

Under the Education Act (England and Wales) of 1944, schools and colleges of education for teacher training may be formed by church bodies. All maintenance costs, including staff salaries, are paid from public funds, as well as 80% of capital expenditures. In Scotland with its quite different educational system, the religious issue in the schools was settled by the (Scottish) Education Act of 1918, which accepted the principle of denominational schools and established a broadly-based national system of primary, secondary and further education leading to higher study. The effect of this was to relieve the churches of the financial burden of maintaining their own parochial schools through the assumption of responsibility by government for administrative control and financial upkeep of church schools. For their part, the churches were granted specific safeguards concerning the belief and character of the teachers appointed to their schools and also given control of the religious instruction taught in them.

A major source of contention within the UK is the long-drawn-out sectarian conflict or civil war in Northern Ireland. This has not been merely a church-state problem or even a Protestant-Catholic issue, since there are many political, social and economic factors involved. Nevertheless, this is clearly an area where religion has become the focus of unrest within the body politic.

**INTERDENOMINATIONAL ORGANIZATIONS.** The British Council of Churches (BCC) was founded in 1942, uniting the Council on the Christian Faith and the Common Life (1937), the Commission of the Churches for International Friendship and Social Responsibility (1937) and the British Section of the World Conference on Faith and Order. Member churches in 1975 include 12 denominations in England, 5 in Scotland and 3 each in Ireland and Wales. In 1977, new members included the first Black church, the Holy Order of Cherubim & Seraphim Church, and also the Congregational Federation and the Russian Orthodox Church (under Moscow). Associate members are the Friends and Unitarians, and the Catholic Churches in England and Wales and in Scotland are consultant observers. Whether the Catholic Church will eventually join the council has been a major question since October 1972 when the Catholic Episcopal Conference of England and Wales decided to submit the idea for consideration to its various pastoral and presbyteral councils and episcopal commissions. In the same year the BCC adopted a resolution assuring the Catholic Church that whenever it presents its request for membership, this request 'will be positively and sympathetically received'. In 1974, however, the Catholic bishops decided to withdraw, principally due to a possible divergence of view on such ethical questions as abortion, divorce and contraception. The Scottish Episcopal Conference had already made a similar decision in 1973. Nevertheless, the Catholic Church already belongs to most of the main city councils of churches including Sheffield, Liverpool and Bristol, as well as to 73% of the 720 local councils of churches in the UK which are associated councils of the British Council of Churches.

Two other sub-national or local councils are the Scottish Churches' Council, founded in 1964 with 9 member churches, and the Council of Churches for Wales (Cyngor Eglwysi Cymru), with 8 member and 3 observer churches, which was formed in 1955 building on the work begun in 1930 by the Committee for Mutual Co-operation and Understanding between Christian Communions in Wales, and which has over 60 affiliated local councils of churches.

The Conference for World Mission (CFWM), known up to 1978 as the Conference of Missionary Societies in Great Britain and Ireland (CBMS), was founded in 1912 as an association of organizations dedicated to the propagation of the gospel overseas in partnership with churches in other lands. In 1975 it had 33 full member societies, with 18 others in associate relationship. The Conference is affiliated to CWME/WCC and works in association with the BCC. The Sodepax programme for England comes under the Churches' Action for World Development.

Other Anglican and Protestant interdenominational councils and societies include the British and Foreign Bible Society (BFBS, formed in 1804), Evangelical Alliance of Great Britain (1846), Free Church Federal Council, National Christian Education Council (1803), and the United Society for Christian Literature

(USCL, 1799). There are also a number of smaller interdenominational councils of churches.

The 2 Catholic episcopal conferences (England and Wales; Scotland) each sponsor an ecumenical commission. In September, 1972, the Catholic Church of England and Wales and the Catholic Church of Scotland, for the first time officially participated to the full extent in a Church Leaders Conference at Birmingham, thus bringing together all the major Christian denominations of the UK.

studies relating to Christianity include: (1) Scottish Institute of Missionary Studies in Aberdeen, with members belonging to several Scottish university departments and centres and other Christian bodies, which fosters the study of Christian missions; (2) Society for African Church History, founded in Freetown, Sierra Leone, in 1962 and now centred in Aberdeen, with individual and institutional members in 23 African countries, 14 European countries, plus Canada, USA, India, Taiwan and Australia;

God answered prayer at Dunkirk; God answers prayer today'. Ecumenical waterborne procession of witness on river Thames passes Battersea power station, south London.

In addition to 2 international commissions which are of particular interest in Great Britain (Anglican/Roman Catholic and Methodist/Roman Catholic), there are several national joint working groups between Anglicans and Protestants on the one hand and Catholics on the other: (1) the Joint Commission between the Church of England and Catholic Church in England (began 1971); (2) English Roman Catholic/Methodist Committee (began 1968, reorganized 1972); (3) British Council of Churches/Roman Catholic Joint Working Group (begun 1967); (4) Church in Wales (Anglican)/Roman Catholic Church Joint Working Group (begun 1971); and (5) the Roman Catholic/Church of Scotland Joint Commission on Marriage. Two other dialogues are in process of formation: Church of Scotland/Roman Catholic Church, and Baptist Union of Scotland/Roman Catholic Church.

A council of Black or Black-led churches was formed in 1977, the Afro-West Indian United Council of Churches (or, Afro-Caribbean United Church Council), but with as members only 9 Black denominations out of the 110 Third-World and a dozen Protestant Black churches.

International associations based in the UK are very numerous, and include: (1) the World Association for Christian Communication (WACC), founded in London in 1963, which provides for co-operation concerning all means of communication and organizes every 2 years with UNDA in Switzerland the International Christian Television Festival; (2) the Ecumenical Satellite Commission (ECUSAT), founded in London in 1970, which was created jointly by Catholics (UNDA and UCIP in Switzerland; OCIC in Belgium) and Protestants (WACC) for the purpose of informing the churches concerning communications by satellite and to place the latter at the service of man in a Christian perspective; (3) the International Ecumenical Fellowship, founded in London in 1952 and reorganized in 1967, an interdenominational international association of Christians who, by prayer, study and action, aim to foster the visible unity of all Christians; and (4) International Hebrew Christian Alliance (IHCA), founded in London in 1925 and now located in Ramsgate, Kent, with national branches in 13 countries on 5 continents, whose purpose is to unite Christians of Jewish background who recognize their origin but remain Christian and continue to bear Christian witness within the Jewish community.

Non-denominational associations of religious

and (3) Society for the Study of the New Testament (Studiorum Novi Testamenti Societus, SNTS), founded in Old Aberdeen in 1938, a scholarly society which in 1973 had more than 600 members in 29 countries on 5 continents.

A very large number of national ecumenical associations and centres for dialogue and co-operation exist. Among the major ones are the following: Audenshaw Foundation (1964) for educational experimentation; Blaendulais Ecumenical Centre (1958); Church Union (1859) to promote the Catholic cause within the Anglican Communion; Ecumenical Centre of the Westminster Archdiocese; Society of St John Chrysostom (1929), for Catholic/Orthodox understanding, Vita et Pax Foundation for Unity (1925); St George House, Windsor Castle (1966); Farnecombe Community (1965), a community of Anglican and Methodist sisters; Ecumenical Society of the Blessed Virgin Mary (1969); Fellowship of St Alban and St Sergius (1928) for understanding between Western and Eastern Churches; Lee Abbey; Scottish Churches House (1961); Skelmersdale Ecumenical Centre (1973, Anglican/Methodist/Baptist/United Reformed); Spode House, Hawkesyard Priory (1953); Portsmouth Diocesan Pastoral Centre (Catholic); Wood Hall Pastoral and Ecumenical Centre (1966); Father Bernard Delany Ecumenical Centre (1969); Christian Unity Centre of Charlton; and London Ecumenical Centre (1965).

Several national and international organizations in Britain are dedicated to the promotion of inter-religious dialogue. International bodies with head-quarters in London include: (1) World Congress of Faiths (WCF), founded in London in 1936 with its membership composed of individuals and branches in 25 countries, whose aim is to promote a spirit of fellowship among mankind through religion and to awaken and develop a world loyalty while allowing complete freedom for the diversity of men, nations and faiths; (2) Standing Conference of Jews, Christians and Muslims in Europe (JCM), founded in London in 1971 with local branches in West Berlin (West Germany) and the Netherlands (in addition to a local British branch), which seeks to promote respect for the theological, political and national differences of the 3 religions, to remove misunderstanding between them and to enlarge common areas of religious awareness; (3) International Council of Christians and Jews, with its international secretariat in London and some 12 branches throughout the world (including a local

British affiliate known as the Council of Christians and Jews), whose purposes are to establish dialogue between Christians and Jews on the basis of religious and human concerns, to promote freedom of conscience and respect for the convictions and rights of others, and to work for the abolition of discrimination from which Judaism has suffered; and (4) World Spiritual Council, founded in Ashford, Kent in 1946, with autonomous national branches in 4 countries (Denmark, France, Holland and UK) and individual members in other countries, which seeks to establish contacts between all the great religions, as well as esoteric schools, artists and writers.

National London-based Catholic organizations dealing with Christian-Jewish relations are the Study Centre for Christian-Jewish Relations, and the Commission to Implement the Vatican Declaration on the Jews, both of which are sponsored by the Sisters of Our Lady of Zion.

The International Association for the History of Religions (IAHR), founded in Bailrigg, Lancaster in 1950, is a non-denominational organization devoted to the scholarly study of the history of religions and related disciplines: psychology of religion, sociology of religion and phenomenology of religion. Member groups exist in Canada, England, France, Germany, Holland, Hungary, Israel, Italy, Japan, Norway, Poland, South Korea, Sweden and the USA, and congresses have been held in Rome (1955), Tokyo (1958), Marburg (1960), Claremont, California (1965) and Stockholm (1970). Publications include *Numen* (International review for the history of religions) and the *International bibliography of the history of religions.*

**BROADCASTING.** There are 2 main broadcasting networks in the UK, the British Broadcasting Corporation (BBC) which is an independent body created by royal charter and operated under a licence from the Minister of Posts and Telecommunications, and the Independent Broadcasting Authority (IBA) which is a commercial operation. Other smaller stations are Radio Manx (Isle of Man), which is heard in England, and Radio Clyde (Scotland). The BBC has a Religious Broadcasting Department responsible for a wide variety of religious programmes, both for radio at home and overseas and for TV. The aims of religious broadcasting in the UK are stated to be: (1) to sustain and deepen the faith of committed Christians, and (2) to establish effective communication with those who regard the Christian faith as irrelevant. Many programmes are planned with the latter audience in mind. It is agreed policy that strict denominational representation should be subordinate to the requirements of successful religious broadcasting. On matters of policy the BBC is advised by a representative Central Religious Advisory Committee (CRAC), which also acts as adviser to the IBA. There are 4 radio stations: Radio 1 (Popular Music), Radio 2, Radio 3, and Radio 4. Radio 2 (Light) and Radio 4 (Home Service) are the main channels for religious programmes, mainly short daily services, late epilogues, and special Sunday programmes. There is a certain amount of regional variation, especially in Northern Ireland, Scotland and Wales. BBC Scotland (part of Radio 4) devotes 28 minutes each day to items of religious interest. In 1973 Scotland's first commercial station, Radio Clyde, began operation; it includes spots given by local ministers. Radio Manx also broadcasts religious programmes. Local radio, which is in the experimental stage under the BBC, has no mandate for religious broadcasting, but it does accept occasional epilogues. Altogether, in 1974 the BBC and IBA were spending about £4 million a year on religious broadcasting over radio and TV.

Religious broadcasting by the IBA includes TV programmes carried by the entire network, on Sundays and late-night 5 or 10-minute programmes transmitted in various parts of the country on weeknights. Sunday programmes include a morning service, and 2 or 3 other programmes in the closed period (5.15-7.25 pm). Under section 9(2) (a) of the Television Act (1964), the Authority is required to arrange for the assistance of a committee representative of the main streams of religious thought to advise it on religious broadcasting; for this purpose the Authority adopted as adviser the BBC's CRAC, although in day-to-day affairs decisions are delegated to the IBA's own panel of religious advisers.

There are many recording studios. In Hatch End (Middlesex) there is the Catholic Radio and TV Centre, responsible for all Catholic radio and TV in Great Britain, and in Bushey (Herts) the Churches' Television and Radio Centre for the Anglican and other churches.

From overseas, a vast number of programmes in English are beamed to the UK, including 3 hours 30 minutes a week from Radio Vatican and 24 hours 45 minutes a week from Trans World Radio (Monaco). For Catholics, England/Wales and Scotland are members of UNDA.

## BIBLIOGRAPHY

*A history of the Church in Wales.* Ed D. Walker. Penarth: Church in Wales Publications, 1976.
*A history of the Jews in England.* C. Roth. London: Brill, 1978 (3rd edition). 328p.
*A sociology of English religion.* D. Martin. London: Heinemann, 1967. 158p.
'Aspects of the Roman Catholic Church in England', *Pro Mundi Vita* (Brussels), 70 (January–February, 1978), 1–36.
'Black Christian communities in Britain, with special reference to the Birmingham area'. R. Gerloff. Dissertation, University of Birmingham (UK), 1978. (Research in progress; much of the data on Black churches in Table 2 below was provided by Dr Gerloff).
*Catholic directory of England and Wales, 1975.* London: Associated Catholic Newspapers, 1975. (1970 edition: 808p).
*Catholicism in England: portrait of a minority, its culture and tradition.* D. Mathew. London: Eyre & Spottiswoode, 1955.
*Church and society in England, 1770–1970: a historical study.* E.R. Norman. Oxford: Clarendon, 1976. 507p. (With full bibliography).
*Church and state: report of the Archbishops' Commission.* London: Church Information Office, 1970. 120p.
*Churches and churchgoers: patterns of church growth in the British Isles since 1700.* R. Currie, A. Gilbert & L. Horsley. Oxford: Clarendon, 1977. 244p. (Statistical time series for major denominations).
*Conflict and Christianity in Northern Ireland: an illustrated documentation.* B. Mawhinney & R. Wells. London: Lion Publishing, 1975.
*Crockford's clerical directory, 1977.* London: Oxford University Press, 1977. (Bibliographical details of all Anglican clergy. Biennial).
*Disestablishment in Ireland and Wales.* P.M.H. Bell. London: SPCK, 1969. 400p.
*Facts and figures about the Church of England: No. 3.* Ed R.F. Neuss. London: Church Information Office, 1965. 96p.
*God's people: West Indian Pentecostal sects in England.* M.J.C. Calley. London: Oxford University Press, 1965. (Describes 13 sects).
'Great Britain: England', D. Martin, in H. Mol (ed), *Western religion* (The Hague: Mouton, 1972), p.229–247.
'Great Britain: Scotland', J. Highet, in H. Mol (ed), *Western religion* (The Hague: Mouton, 1972), p.249–269.
*History of the Church of Scotland, beginning the Year of Our Lord 203, and continued to the end of the reign of King James VI.* J. Spottiswood. London, 1847–51. London: Brill, 1978. 3 vols.
*Le Catholicisme contemporain en Grand Brétagne.* J. Dingle. Paris: Spes, 1967.
*Local councils of churches today: an interim report.* London: British Council of Churches, 1971. 117p.
*Patterns of sectarianism: organisation and ideology in social and religious movements.* Ed B.R. Wilson. London: Heinemann, 1967. 416p. (Detailed studies of 9 British sects).
'Religion', R. Currie & A. Gilbert, in A.H. Halsey (ed), *Trends in British society since 1900* (London: Macmillan, 1972), p.407–447.
*Religion and society in industrial England: church, chapel, and social change, 1740–1914.* A.D. Gilbert. London: Longmans, 1975. (Statistical sociology).
*The bitter harvest: church and state in Northern Irelana.* A.J. Menendez. Washington: R.B. Luce, 1973.
*The British: their identity and their religion.* D. Jenkins. London: SCM, 1975. 200p.
*The British churches today.* K. Slack. 2nd rev.ed. London: SCM, 1970. 144p.
*The Celtic Churches: a history, AD 200–1200.* J.T. McNeill. Chicago: University of Chicago, 1974. 290p.
*The Church of England year book 1978.* London: Church Information Office, 1978. 430p. (Annual).
*The Church of England, 1815–1948: a documentary history.* Ed R.P. Flindall. London: SPCK, 1972. 512p.
*The Church of England, 1900–1965.* R. Lloyd. London: SCM, 1966. 623p.
*The Church of Scotland year-book 1974.* Glasgow: Department of Publicity and Publication, 1974. 430p. (Annual).
*The deployment and payment of the clergy.* L. Paul. London: Church Information Office, 1964. 311p. (Church of England).
*The geography of religion in England.* J.D. Gay. London: Duckworth, 1971. 334p.
*The Scottish churches: a review of their state 400 years after the Reformation.* J. Highet. London: Skeffington, 1960. 224p.
*UK Protestant missions handbook:* Vol 1, *Overseas;* Vol 2, *Home.* P. Brierley. London: EAGB, 1977 & 1978. 80p and 56p.

TABLE 2. ORGANIZED CHURCHES AND DENOMINATIONS IN THE UNITED KINGDOM OF GREAT BRITAIN & NORTHERN IRELAND

| Official name 1 | Begun 2 | Type 3 | Counc 4 | Congs 5 | Adults 6 | Affiliated 7 | Names, notes, and other statistics (see Codebook) 8 |
|---|---|---|---|---|---|---|---|
| African Methodist Episcopal Church | 1966 | I Met | Vw..I | 1 | 120 | 220 | In 16th Episcopal District, AMEC (USA). WIndians. London N7. New style ministries. |
| African Methodist Episcopal Zion Ch | c1960 | I Met | Vw... | 30 | 2,200 | 3,500 | In 1st Epis Dist, AMEZC(USA). In UK, pentecostal. Jamaicans, Guyana Asians. 11nx. |
| Aladura International Ch, UK & Overseas | 1970 | I peA | x.I.J | 1 | 300 | 500 | Nigerians, Ghanaians, West Indians. 95% students. M=C&S(Ibadan). London SW18. 7x. |
| Ancient Assyrian Church of the East | c1930 | O Nes | Yw... | 1 | 500 | 1,000 | *Holy Apostolic & Cath Ch of the East.* Nestorians. 200 Assyrian refugee families. |
| Anglo-West-Indian Assembly | 1962 | I pe2 | x.... | 2 | 85 | 250 | *Ev Reformed Ch.* From Montserrat, St Kitts, Jamaica, ex PAoWI. HQ London E5. 2nx. |
| Apostolic Church of God | 1973 | I pe1 | ..... | 4 | 100 | 200 | Jamaican pentecostals, schism ex PAW. M=Highway Ch of Christ of AF(USA). 4nx. |
| Apostolic Church of Great Britain | 1904 | P PeA | Z...H | 230 | 20,000 | 40,000 | Formed 1916. HQ SWales. Centralized hierarchy of apostles, prophets. 85n,1j,1s. |
| Apostolic Church of Jesus Christ | c1960 | I pen | ..... | 20 | 2,000 | 4,000 | West Indian Blacks. Third-largest West Indian immigrant church. 60% women. |
| Armenian Apostolic Church: D England | c1850 | O Arm | Ewc.. | 20 | 12,000 | 20,000 | *Gregorians.* Under C Echmiadzin (USSR). London, Manchester. 700 families. 2 bishops. |
| Assemblies of God in GB & Ireland | c1912 | P Pe2 | ZG..H | 584 | 30,000 | 70,000 | Originally Pentecostal Missionary Union, until 1924. HQ Nottingham. 617n,1s. |
| Assemblies of the First-Born | 1961 | I pe2 | ..... | 10 | 500 | 1,200 | From St Kitts & Jamaica (HQ Kingston). HQ London SW8. Became pentecostals in UK. |
| Baptist Church of God | 1972 | I pe3 | ..... | 5 | 130 | 350 | Jamaicans. Link with British Free Baptists, now pentecostal. HQ London NW10. 8nx. |
| Baptist Churches in GB & Ireland: | 1607 | P Bap | ..... | 3,227 | 259,000 | 700,000 | 4 overlapping Unions with common statistics. Includes 500 unaffiliated churches. |
| Baptist Union of GB & Ireland | 1611 | P Bap | TWC.W | 2,177 | 210,646 | 600,000 | *BUGBI* (1812). General & Particular Baptists. 2090n,G=−1.9%pa,7s(162),W=65%,4000Y. |
| Baptist Union of Ireland | 1648 | P Bap | ..... | 75 | 6,600 | 19,000 | Not in BUGBI. 7 more churches in Republic of Ireland. 50n,1s(31),W=41%,400Y. |
| Baptist Union of Scotland | 1750 | P Bap | Tv..W | 166 | 17,000 | 60,000 | Not in BUGBI (except 10 churches). Member of WCC 1948–55. 130n,1x,1s(25),415Y. |
| Baptist Un of Wales&Monmouthshire | 1649 | P Bap | .w... | 693 | 51,272 | 150,000 | *Undeb Bedyddwyr Cymru* (1866). 43% in BUGBI. 80% Welsh. 216n,G=−3.1%pa,2s(33),W=68%. |
| Unaffiliated churches | c1800 | P Bap | ..... | 500 | 10,000 | 20,000 | *Calvinistic Particular Baptists, Ev Free, Gospel Standard,* and *Old Baptists.* |
| Bible Church of God | 1964 | I pe3 | x.... | 3 | 100 | 300 | Jamaicans. M=CoG World HQ(Alabama,USA). 2 bishops: Birmingham, Nottingham. |
| Bible Pattern Church Fellowship | 1940 | P Pe2 | ..... | | 1,200 | 2,000 | Split ex Elim Foursquare Gospel Alliance by founder GJeffreys. British-Israelite. |
| Bible Way Churches of Our Lord JC WW | 1958 | I pe1 | x.... | 16 | 1,000 | 2,000 | WW=World Wide. West Indians. M=BWCOLJCWW(USA). HQ London SE13. Bishop,18n. |
| Bulgarian Orthodox Church | | O Sla | Mwc.. | | 1,000 | 1,600 | *Balgarskata Pravoslavna Crkva.* Under P Sofia. Bulgarians. No full-time priest. |
| Byelorussian Autocephalic Orthodox Ch | c1945 | O Sla | x.... | 2 | 1,000 | 1,500 | Refugees; White Russian church begun AD 1291. HQ Brooklyn(USA). Linked Polish OC. 2n. |
| Calvary Church of God in Christ | 1952 | I pe3 | Z...I | 50 | 3,000 | 5,000 | First Jamaican pentecostals. M=CoGiC(USA Blacks). HQ London. Bishop, 28nx,20m,15w. |
| Catholic Apostolic Church | 1832 | C CAp | x.... | 6 | 5,000 | 8,000 | *Irvingites.* Early pentecostals. No clergy left; 59 churches closed; almost extinct. |
| Catholic Church in England & Wales: | c 678 | R LEr | B.B.s | 3,070 | 3,182,000 | 4,132,905 | C=55+12+352. P=75%,5s,W=43%. 50% Irish; 7% converts. 6371nx,1187m,16590w,115619Yy. |
| M Birmingham | 1850 | R Lat | Bs | 232 | 267,200 | 347,500 | Catholics mostly Irish in industry. Few rural. 1s. 571 71 1395 10211 |
| D Clifton | 1850 | R Lat | Bs | 97 | 77,000 | 100,000 | Mostly in Bristol; scattered rural Catholics. 138 35 600 2302 |
| D Shrewsbury | 1850 | R Lat | Bs | 109 | 148,000 | 192,000 | Cheshire, Shrops, part Lancs, Derby. Largely rural. 246 69 372 4873 |
| M Cardiff | 1850 | R Lat | Bs | 138 | 79,700 | 103,476 | *Eglwys Catholig Rufeinig.* Mainly Irish; and French. 196 8 341 5590 |
| D Menevia | 1898 | R Lat | Bs | 133 | 30,300 | 39,410 | Central and north Wales. HQ Wrexham. Rural. 176 12 451 1018 |
| M Liverpool | 1850 | R Lat | Bs | 228 | 397,000 | 515,644 | Seaport. Mainly Irish in city, industries. 663 76 960 13004 |
| D Hexham & Newcastle | 1850 | R Lat | Bs | 187 | 213,900 | 277,742 | Diocese AD 678. Northumberland, Durham. 1s(Ushaw). 380 35 545 5778 |
| D Lancaster | 1924 | R Lat | Bs | 109 | 99,800 | 129,688 | Cumbria, and Lancs south to Preston. Largely rural. 250 8 416 2716 |
| D Leeds | 1878 | R Lat | Bs | 185 | 202,300 | 262,753 | West Yorks. Catholics in industry and mining areas. 375 10 775 6275 |
| D Middlesbrough | 1878 | R Lat | Bs | 89 | 66,100 | 85,832 | North Yorks, Humberside. Mostly in Middlesbrough. 231 27 278 2333 |
| D Salford | 1850 | R Lat | Bs | 212 | 276,200 | 358,684 | Salford, Blackburn. Urban manufacturing areas. 537 91 751 10416 |
| M Southwark | 1850 | R Lat | Bs | 170 | 281,000 | 364,900 | London south of Thames, and Kent. RCs urban. 1s. 528 80 1400 9314 |
| D Arundel & Brighton | 1965 | R Lat | Bs | 115 | 105,000 | 136,000 | Sussex, Surrey. HQ Hove. Densely urban. 1s. 418 64 1471 3191 |
| D Plymouth | 1850 | R Lat | Bs | 87 | 41,800 | 54,349 | Cornwall, Devon, Dorset. Seaports, thin rural RCs. 197 15 720 2599 |
| D Portsmouth | 1882 | R Lat | Bs | 114 | 113,800 | 147,813 | Berks, Hants, IoW, Channel Is. Catholics urban. 320 93 1028 3849 |
| M Westminster | 1850 | R Lat | Bs | 282 | 373,200 | 484,680 | Primatial see. London north of Thames. 180e,1s(81). 341 400 3150 18160 |
| D Brentwood | 1917 | R Lat | Bs | 153 | 134,900 | 175,170 | East London, Essex. Catholics mainly urban. 208 24 694 4700 |
| D Northampton | 1850 | R Lat | Bs | 284 | 140,600 | 182,597 | Beds,Bucks,Cambs,Northants,Norfolk,Suffolk. Rural. 264 14 736 5026 |

*Continued opposite*

*Table 2–continued*

| Official name 1 | Begun 2 | Type 3 | Counc 4 | Congs 5 | Adults 6 | Affiliated 7 | Names, notes, and other statistics (see Codebook) 8 |
|---|---|---|---|---|---|---|---|
| D Nottingham | 1850 | R Lat | Bs | 125 | 115,200 | 149,667 | Derby, Leics, Lincoln, Notts. Catholics in cities. 332 52 501 4264 |
| EA Great Britain (*Ukrainian*) | 1957 | R Ukr | Os | 51 | 19,000 | 25,000 | *Ukrainian Catholic Exarchate in GB*. HQ London. 18 3 6 107 |
| Catholic Church in Ireland: | c 350 | R Lat | B.B.R | 195 | 453,600 | 588,410 | In Ulster. 82% of Church is in Eire. C=34+11+104. 835nx, 337m, 1483w, 16970Yy. |
| M Armagh | 445 | R Lat | Bs | 57 | 114,600 | 148,820 | All in Ulster. HQ Armagh, Northern Ireland. 270 118 613 4391 |
| D Clogher | 454 | R Lat | Bs | 20 | 31,000 | 40,000 | Other half of diocese is in Eire. HQ Monaghan(Eire). 70 11 130 800 |
| D Derry | 1158 | R Lat | Bs | 30 | 77,000 | 100,000 | 25% of diocese is in Eire. HQ Londonderry, NI. 100 13 170 3000 |
| D Down & Connor | c 470 | R Lat | Bs | 73 | 200,000 | 259,590 | All in Ulster. HQ Belfast. 1970–78 violence. 335 165 420 7779 |
| D Dromore | 514 | R Lat | Bs | 15 | 31,000 | 40,000 | 30% of diocese is in Eire. HQ Newry, NI. 60 30 150 1000 |
| Catholic Church in Scotland: | c 400 | R Lat | B.B.s | 451 | 633,000 | 822,116 | Hierarchy restored 1878. Many Irish. C=22+4+51. 2s. 1204nx, 176m, 1307w, 18378Yy |
| M Glasgow | 1878 | R Lat | Bs | 103 | 245,000 | 318,000 | D in 6th century. Glasgow, Dumbarton. Irish. 1s. 370 56 360 6027 |
| D Motherwell | 1947 | R Lat | Bs | 68 | 137,700 | 178,800 | Lanarkshire. Catholics 30% of total population. 185 3 102 4165 |
| D Paisley | 1947 | R Lat | Bs | 32 | 63,700 | 82,700 | Renfrewshire. Catholics 23% of total population. 97 4 133 2019 |
| M St Andrews & Edinburgh | 1878 | R Lat | Bs | 102 | 95,600 | 124,200 | D in 10th century. Berwick to St Andrews. 1s. 264 35 378 3170 |
| D Aberdeen | 1878 | R Lat | Bs | 40 | 8,000 | 10,347 | D AD 1125, vacant 1577–1878. Orkneys, Shetlands. 78 25 76 408 |
| D Argyll & the Isles | 1878 | R Lat | Bs | 24 | 9,000 | 11,769 | D AD 1200, vacant 1579–1878. HQ Oban. 32 0 40 350 |
| D Dunkeld | 1878 | R Lat | Bs | 38 | 40,400 | 52,700 | Created AD 1115, restored 1878. HQ Dundee. 76 17 96 1099 |
| D Galloway | 1878 | R Lat | Bs | 44 | 33,600 | 43,600 | D in 4th century. Southwest. HQ Ayr. 102 36 122 1140 |
| Catholic Tridentine Church | 1976 | C CCa | x.... | | 1,000 | 2,000 | Ex Ch of Rome, supporting archbishop Lefebvre (Latin mass, &c). Also in USA, NZ, et alia. |
| Children of God International | c1967 | P Apo | xv... | | 1,000 | 2,000 | Apocalyptic youth group from USA, living in communes. In 60 countries. HQ Bromley. |
| Christ Apostolic Church | 1974 | I peA | x.I.. | 2 | 50 | 150 | *Bethel*. Nigerians. M=CAC(Ibadan,Nigeria). HQ London N8. |
| Christadelpian Ecclesias | c1848 | P Ade | x.... | 342 | 14,000 | 30,000 | *Birmingham Central Basis of Fellowship*. 342 ecclesias. Pacifist. Declining. |
| Christian Brethren (Exclusive, Closed) | 1848 | P EBr | x.... | 900 | 50,000 | 100,000 | *Kelly-Continental; Continuing Tunbridge Wells; Raven-Taylor; Glanton. Darbyites.* |
| Christian Brethren (Open) | 1828 | P CBr | x.... | 1,800 | 100,000 | 240,000 | 1831, Plymouth Brethren. 25% in Scotland. Missions abroad (CMML). 181m. |
| Christian Community, The (1685) | 1685 | P int | ..... | 33 | 208 | 332 | Founded by French Huguenot refugees. Social and hospital services. W=30%,11Y. |
| Church in Wales: | c 300 | A Hig | AWC.W | 1,620 | 350,000 | 1,000,000 | *Eglwys yng Nghymru*. State church until 1920. P=47%,2s(50),1000Y. 893n,14000y. |
| D Bangor | 550 | A Hig | A | 243 | 36,000 | 103,000 | Welsh: 60% first language, 20% some, 20% none. P=44%,W=22%,80Y. 106 1134 |
| D Llandaff | 550 | A Hig | A | 313 | 77,000 | 220,000 | Industrial (coal, steel). Declining 5% pa. P=43%,3r,1s(40). 124 3000 |
| D Monmouth | 1921 | A Hig | A | 236 | 40,000 | 114,000 | Declining 3% pa. 50% rural; industrializing, new town Cwmban. P=43%. 150 1200 |
| D St Asaph | 560 | A Cen | A | 296 | 69,000 | 197,000 | Rural depopulation and industrialization. 80% Welsh-speaking. 1s. 149 3000 |
| D St Davids | 601 | A plu | A | 303 | 91,000 | 260,000 | Largely rural; coal, oil, tourism. 80% Welsh-speaking. 3r,1s. 237 4000 |
| D Swansea & Brecon | 1923 | A Cen | A | 229 | 37,000 | 106,000 | Largely rural (Brecon), industrial area (Gower). P=44%,177Y. 127 1661 |
| Church of Christ, Scientist | 1896 | M Sci | x.... | 301 | 25,000 | 50,000 | *Christian Science*. HQ Mother Church, Boston, USA. 431 practitioners. |
| **Church of England:** | 100 | A plu | AWC.W | 17,611 | 9,648,000 | 27,659,000 | Reformed 1558. 100x,308m,2358w,23s(950). 17465n,P=20%,W=16%,9013Y,389100y. |
| Province of Canterbury: | 597 | A plu | A | 13,171 | 6,526,000 | 17,836,000 | SEngland. Confirmees declining at 7% pa. 13002 21 17 7090 254571 |
| D Canterbury | 597 | A Cen | A | 397 | 262,000 | 613,000 | Archdeaconries: 2 rural, 1 urban. 1s. 459 19 17 305 8918 |
| D Bath & Wells | 909 | A Hig | A | 621 | 286,000 | 436,000 | Confirmees declining since 1965 at 7% pa. 520 20 15 277 5998 |
| D Birmingham | 1905 | A plu | A | 262 | 150,000 | 838,000 | Mainly urban, vast new housing estates. 2s. 337 21 22 185 11513 |
| D Bristol | 1542 | A plu | A | 217 | 116,000 | 427,000 | Urban. Confirmees: 2,195(1966), 1,718(1969).2s. 280 26 22 141 5873 |
| D Chelmsford | 1914 | A Eva | A | 658 | 324,000 | 1,313,000 | Urban, suburban; vast housing estates. 498b. 659 21 20 469 18031 |
| D Chichester | 1075 | A plu | A | 564 | 371,000 | 680,000 | Rapid population growth in new towns. 1s. 736 23 18 313 9347 |
| D Coventry | 1918 | A plu | A | 260 | 148,000 | 506,000 | 75% urban. Cathedral ministry to secular life. 273 19 17 147 6957 |
| D Derby | 1927 | A plu | A | 377 | 186,000 | 646,000 | Industry, mining, housing estates, villages. 306 19 15 176 8880 |
| D Ely | 1109 | A plu | A | 373 | 132,000 | 296,000 | Mainly rural. Confirmations 1,400 a year. 2s. 351 19 17 127 4063 |
| D Exeter | 1050 | A ACa | A | 644 | 323,000 | 515,000 | Rural, 494 parishes. Agriculture, tourism. 662 22 16 242 7080 |
| D Gloucester | 1540 | A Hig | A | 432 | 137,000 | 364,000 | Confirmees declining since 1965 at 8% pa. 1s. 357 27 21 173 5007 |
| D Guildford | 1927 | A plu | A | 230 | 187,000 | 535,000 | Confirmees: 3,296 (1966), 2,644 (1969). 320 24 20 204 7358 |
| D Hereford | 676 | A plu | A | 473 | 166,000 | 204,000 | Rural. Confirmees: 1,639 (1966), 1,344 (1969). 208 15 9 78 3037 |
| D Leicester | 1926 | A plu | A | 322 | 144,000 | 418,000 | Diocese existed 7–8th centuries. 50% urban. 277 21 17 476 6501 |
| D Lichfield | 664 | A Cen | A | 684 | 365,000 | 1,581,000 | Large industrial areas, vast overspill areas. 575 22 17 149 21734 |
| D Lincoln | 1072 | A Hig | A | 730 | 224,000 | 638,000 | Mainly rural. 42 deaneries, 505 parishes. 1s. 450 18 15 166 8767 |
| D London | 180 | A plu | A | 562 | 424,000 | 1,327,000 | Refounded 604. Urban, north of Thames. 1012 20 19 876 22328 |
| D Norwich | 1091 | A Low | A | 691 | 182,000 | 439,000 | Formerly D Thetford. Rural. Many abbeys. 464 21 18 145 6296 |
| D Oxford | 1542 | A plu | A | 865 | 359,000 | 1,052,000 | Rapid industrialization; university. 12de,4s. 886 22 18 384 14458 |
| D Peterborough | 1541 | A plu | A | 390 | 150,000 | 329,000 | Partly rural, Corby new town development. 300 20 17 164 4520 |
| D Portsmouth | 1927 | A plu | A | 185 | 121,000 | 331,000 | Rapid urbanization. Tourism, Navy. 223 24 20 174 5136 |
| D Rochester | 604 | A plu | A | 272 | 233,000 | 752,000 | 30% urban, 30% suburban. Many new churches. 2s. 395 19 18 296 11745 |
| D Salisbury | 1078 | A Cen | A | 641 | 260,000 | 443,000 | Rural, Poole harbour. Many ancient churches. 1s. 519 19 15 222 6282 |
| D Southwark | 1905 | A plu | A | 381 | 347,000 | 953,000 | London south of Thames. Industrial mission. 1s. 677 18 17 362 13093 |
| D St Albans | 1887 | A Cen | A | 440 | 270,000 | 699,000 | Vast population & housing explosion (5% pa). 461 24 18 250 10000 |
| D St Edmundsbury & Ipswich | 1914 | A Low | A | 495 | 171,000 | 305,000 | Mainly rural. 500 West Indians. 146 schools. 333 18 15 151 4196 |
| D Truro | 1876 | A Hig | A | 312 | 113,000 | 197,000 | Rural. Cornwall is 25% Methodist, 50% Anglican. 246 23 19 104 2766 |
| D Winchester | 662 | A Cen | A | 392 | 226,000 | 566,000 | Rural. In addition, covers Channel Islands. 434 22 17 219 8733 |
| D Worcester | 679 | A Hig | A | 301 | 149,000 | 433,000 | 180 parishes. Confirmees declining at 9% pa. 260 20 16 115 5954 |
| Province of York: | 735 | A plu | A | 4,440 | 3,122,000 | 9,823,000 | NEngland. Confirmees declining at 6% pa. 4463 20 15 1923 134490 |
| D York | 625 | A plu | A | 672 | 280,000 | 869,000 | 3 large urban areas, rest rural. 4 bishops. 481 21 15 116 12485 |
| D Blackburn | 1926 | A Eva | A | 323 | 293,000 | 656,000 | Industrial, rural, and residential areas. 382 25 16 174 9015 |
| D Bradford | 1920 | A Cen | A | 185 | 106,000 | 351,000 | Some Anglicans among huge Pakistani influx. 205 20 18 136 4818 |
| D Carlisle | 1133 | A Hig | A | 362 | 192,000 | 374,000 | Major problem building new churches required. 308 20 13 65 5133 |
| D Chester | 1541 | A Cen | A | 411 | 325,000 | 980,000 | Formed 1541 out of diocese of Lichfield. 387 21 16 156 13463 |
| D Durham | 995 | A Cen | A | 347 | 367,000 | 1,048,000 | 60% urban. Confirmees: 4,445(1966), 3,892(1969). 401 15 12 60 14406 |
| D Liverpool | 880 | A Eva | A | 260 | 340,000 | 1,050,000 | Includes 250 West Indians. City 40% Catholic. 375 19 15 300 13000 |
| D Manchester | 1848 | A Cen | A | 450 | 415,000 | 1,265,000 | Densely-populated city. 250 church schools. 498 18 13 215 17382 |
| D Newcastle | 1882 | A plu | A | 254 | 148,000 | 475,000 | Seaport, many ethnic groups. High unemployment. 254 24 18 48 6533 |
| D Ripon | 1836 | A Hig | A | 281 | 162,000 | 448,000 | First founded 650. Leeds city and rural areas. 271 19 16 109 6162 |
| D Sheffield | 1914 | A Cen | A | 254 | 177,000 | 944,000 | Heavy industry (coal,steel). Industrial Mission. 264 15 14 62 12970 |
| D Southwell | 1884 | A Cen | A | 341 | 134,000 | 631,000 | Rural, coal-mining in Sherwood Forest. 300 22 21 311 8667 |
| D Wakefield | 1888 | A Cen | A | 300 | 183,000 | 732,000 | 90% urban industrial (textiles, coal). 303 18 15 155 10064 |
| Church of God Fellowship | 1967 | I pe3 | ..... | 8 | 136 | 400 | From Barbados,Grenada, Jamaica. Broke with NTCoG(UK). 1 overseer,5nx,7m,6 deacons. |
| Ch of God Fellowship in GB World Wide | 1943 | P Pe4 | ..... | 7 | 200 | 500 | *Welsh Latter Rain movement*. 4 West Indian congregations. HQ. Trethomas. |
| Church of God in Christ Pentecostal | 1948 | I pe3 | Z.... | 11 | 1,500 | 5,000 | Begun by Black USA troops. M=CoGiC,1st British Jurisd. HQ Luton. Bishop,13nx,21w. |
| Church of God of Prophecy | 1952 | P Pe3 | Z...I | 100 | 3,200 | 17,000 | Jamaicans; 4 White, 2 Greek congs. M=CGP(USA). 269nx,64m,1f,3p,84t. |
| Church of God Pentecostal | 1958 | I pe3 | ..... | | 1,000 | 2,000 | Barbados, Jamaica, some White. M=CoG(Huntsville,USA). HQ East Ham. 4 bishops,29nx. |
| Church of God Seventh-day | c1963 | I pen | ..... | 6 | 200 | 500 | Jamaicans. M=CoGSD(Denver,USA). Sabbatarians, now pentecostal. HQ SNorwood. 4nx. |
| Church of God (Anderson) | 1900 | P Hol | x...I | 5 | 150 | 350 | M=CoG(Anderson) (USA). Anti-Pentecostal. 50% Black. Belfast, London, Liverpool. 1n. |
| Church of God (UK) | 1958 | I pe3 | ..... | 4 | 200 | 300 | From Antigua, Barbados, Jamaica; some Whites. HQ London E7. 2 bishops. 10n,18m. |
| Church of Ireland: | c 350 | A Low | AWc.W | 481 | 100,697 | 313,196 | *Province of Armagh* only (of its 8 dioceses, 3 wholly in Eire, 3 partly). 397n. |
| D Armagh | 444 | A Low | A | 103 | 15,000 | 45,000 | Southern tip of diocese is in Eire. Rural, 4 towns. 1970–78 violence. 68 |
| D Clogher | 1128 | A Eva | A | 55 | 3,697 | 15,953 | Other 10% of diocese is in Eire. Rural, west of Armagh. W=30%. 38 |
| D Connor | 506 | A Low | A | 140 | 40,000 | 130,000 | Part of UDs Down, Connor & Dromore 1451–1944. Vast new housing estates. 130 |
| UDs Derry & Raphoe | 950 | A Eva | A | 66 | 17,000 | 28,243 | Western 20% of diocese is in Eire. Urban and rural, in extreme northwest. 44 |
| UDs Down & Dromore | 580 | A Cen | A | 117 | 25,000 | 94,000 | County Down. Belfast being formed into new diocese. W=25%(rural 35%). 117 |
| Church of Jesus C of Latter-day Saints | 1837 | M LdS | x.... | 460 | 50,000 | 70,138 | *Mormons* (HQ Utah, USA). Temple SLondon. Growing, 3.7%pa. 1600f,W=66%,5115Yy,17675z. |
| Ch of Our Lord JC of the Apost Faith | 1964 | I pel | ..... | 5 | 250 | 400 | WIndians. Link with Greater Refuge Temple, NY (USA). HQ London SW16. Bishop,4n,15m. |
| Church of Scotland | 397 | P Ref | RWC.W | 3,000 | 1,156,211 | 2,500,000 | Established 1560. 12 Synods. Declining 2.1%pa. 1782n,6p,4s(160),35371Yy. |
| Church of the First-Born | 1959 | I ind | x.... | 4 | 200 | 500 | From Barbados & Jamaica (HQ Kingston). Branches in USA, Canada. HQ Birmingham 23. |
| Church of the Living God | 1962 | I pel | ..... | | 1,000 | 2,000 | West Indian church brought by Black immigrants. Split ex Victorious Ch of God. |
| Church of the Lord (Aladura) | 1964 | I pen | xwI.. | 10 | 850 | 1,600 | Nigerians, Ghanaians; Yoruba elites. M=CLA(Lagos). London SW4. Several UK schisms. |
| Church of the Nazarene | 1906 | P Hol | xFD.E | 100 | 7,926 | 10,000 | M=CoN(USA). Ex Congr U of Scotland. Joined by IHM, Calvary Holiness Ch. 1963n,1s. |
| Churches of Christ in GB & Ireland | 1842 | P Dis | xW..W | 101 | 4,719 | 10,000 | *Disciples of Christ*. *Campbellites*. Ex Ch of Scotland. 26n,200m,G=–6%pa,1s,48Y. |
| Churches of Christ (Non-Instrumental) | 1945 | P Dis | x.... | 70 | 3,200 | 6,000 | M=CC(Non-Instrumental)(USA). Rapid growth. 55 churches in England. 44f,1s. |
| Chs of God in the British I & Overseas | 1889 | P EBr | x.... | 88 | 5,000 | 10,000 | *Luxmore Needed Truth, Green Pastures* (=periodicals). Ex Open Brethren. 250m. |
| Congregational Federation | 1831 | P Con | ....W | 260 | 10,000 | 18,000 | Group of churches rejecting 1972 merger in United Reformed Church. 62n,206m. |
| Congregational Union of Ireland | c1600 | P Con | R.... | 30 | 1,800 | 5,360 | Union formed 1829. Declining. HQ Greenisland, Newtonabbey. 11n,W=70%,3617z. |
| Congregational Union of Scotland | 1795 | P Con | RW..W | 119 | 25,284 | 49,626 | 1795, ex Ch of Scotland; 1812, Union. Declining 3.4%pa. 105n,1s(5),W=35%,1263Yy. |
| Cooneyites (Go-Preachers) | 1894 | P ind | x.... | | 5,000 | 10,000 | *Two by Twos*. In NI. Itinerants, also in USA, Australia, South Africa. No books. |
| Coptic Orthodox Church | c1965 | O Cop | Nwa.. | 4 | 2,650 | 4,300 | Parishes: Kensington, Holborn. Under P Alexandria (Egypt). Egyptians. 1x. |
| Countess of Huntingdon's Connexion | 1777 | P Con | ..D.E | 31 | 877 | 2,000 | Schism ex CofE. Many congs also in United Ref Ch. Declining 3.2%pa. 12n,W=60%. |
| Divine Prayer Society 1944 | 1960 | I pen | ..... | 2 | 150 | 400 | *Ch of Family of God & JC*(HQ Accra). Ghanaians, WIndians. Ex Aladura. Northampton. 8nx. |
| Eden Revival Church | 1972 | I pen | xv... | 2 | 100 | 200 | Split ex Ch of Universal Prayer Fellowship. M=EFC(Accra,Ghana). HQ London SE27. |
| Elim Pentecostal Church | 1915 | P Pe2 | Z...H | 310 | 21,000 | 45,000 | *Elim Foursquare Gospel Alliance*. Schisms 1939–42. 209n,G=0,1j,1s(60),W=99%. |
| Emmanuel Holiness Church | 1916 | P Hol | ..... | 10 | 350 | 1,000 | Holiness denomination. HQ Birkenhead. Mission in Morocco, Sahara. 13n,1j,1p,1s. |
| English Episcopal Church | 1947 | A sEv | ..... | | 500 | 1,000 | *Ch of England (Ev)*. Ex Ev Ch of England. Use 1662 BCP. HQ Acton. West Indians. |
| Episcopal Church in Scotland: | 397 | A Hig | AWc.W | 335 | 49,540 | 86,351 | *Scottish Episcopal Church*. Disestablished 1689. G=–2.2%pa,1s,25Y. 291n,1787y. |
| UD Aberdeen & Orkney | 1073 | A ACa | A | 48 | 5,163 | 8,334 | One city, 5 towns. Includes Shetland Is. Numerical decline 3% pa. 31 200 |
| UD Argyll & the Isles | 1079 | A Hig | A | 26 | 1,419 | 2,132 | United diocese 1819. Rural. Long-term depopulation. W=30%. 18 38 |
| D Brechin | 1153 | A Hig | A | 29 | 5,553 | 8,989 | Rural depopulation, expanding city (Dundee) and estates. 1x,W=20%. 26 190 |
| D Edinburgh | 1633 | A plu | A | 65 | 12,550 | 23,096 | City, suburban and rural. Widely scattered. 1r,W=26%. 82 487 |
| UD Glasgow & Galloway | 430 | A plu | A | 80 | 16,160 | 28,950 | Mainly urban industrial; new towns around Glasgow. W=40%. 74 537 |
| UD Moray, Ross, & Caithness | 1110 | A ACa | A | 34 | 2,414 | 4,174 | Rural; atomic plant and other industry. Some Gaelic spoken. P=98%. 24 106 |
| UD St Andrews, Dunkeld, Dunblane | 809 | A ACa | A | 53 | 6,281 | 10,676 | Medieval dioceses united in 1837. HQ Perth (in D St Andrews). 1r. 36 229 |
| Estonian Apostolic Orth Ch in Exile | c1950 | O Sla | C.... | 4 | 2,000 | 4,000 | One London parish. Estonian refugees. Under archbishop of Great Britain & Sweden. |

*Continued overleaf*

*Table 2–continued*

| Official name<br>1 | Begun<br>2 | Type<br>3 | Counc<br>4 | Congs<br>5 | Adults<br>6 | Affiliated<br>7 | Names, notes, and other statistics (see Codebook)<br>8 |
|---|---|---|---|---|---|---|---|
| Estonian Ev Lutheran Church in Exile | 1944 | P Lut | LwC.. | 46 | 3,000 | 5,000 | Refugees from Estonia after 1940. Independent of ELCE(USSR). World HQ Stockholm. |
| Eternal Sacred Order of Morning Star | 1971 | I peA | ....I | 3 | 100 | 200 | . . . *& St Michael Star Fountain of Life Mount Zion*. Ex Holy Order of C&S. Nigerians. |
| Ethiopian Orthodox Ch (P Addis Ababa) | c1970 | O Eth | Nwa.. | 3 | 550 | 1,200 | London, Birmingham. Under bishop of New York. Jamaicans, other West Indians. |
| Evangelical Church of England | 1922 | A sEv | ..... | 12 | 250 | 500 | Ex CofE opposing Anglo-Catholicism. Archbishop in Ferrette succession. Lancashire. |
| Ev Fellowship of Congregational Chs | 1967 | P Con | ....C | 108 | 4,465 | 10,000 | *Ev Congregational Ch*. Group of congs rejecting 1972 merger in United Reformed Ch. |
| Evangelical Lutheran Ch of England | 1896 | P Lut | x.... | 16 | 833 | 1,197 | Confessional Lutheranism. M=LC Missouri S(USA). 1n,13x,G=8.3%pa,1s(5),W=48%,29y. |
| Evangelical Presbyterian Church of NI | 1927 | P Ref | J...C | 50 | 3,000 | 5,000 | *Irish Evangelical Ch*. Independent congregations in and around Belfast, NIreland. |
| Fellowship of Independent Ev Churches | 1922 | P ind | ....C | 400 | 22,000 | 30,000 | *FIEC*. *Peculiar People* (Essex). Growing as new autonomous congregations join. 400n. |
| First United Ch of JC (Apostolic) | 1956 | I pel | ..... | 35 | 5,000 | 10,000 | Jamaicans. Former Bethel Apost/Shilo Ch. M=FUCJCA(USA). HQ Birmingham 20. 61nx,56m. |
| Free Church of England | 1844 | A sEv | x.D.E | 34 | 2,539 | 3,194 | *Reformed Episcopal Ch*. Linked REC(USA). 2 Dioceses. Declining. 33n(5 bishops), 38m. |
| Free Church of Scotland | 1843 | P Ref | JGD.x | 175 | 6,000 | 21,000 | *Wee Frees*. Ex Ch of Scotland. 1900, most joined United Free C of S. 130n,1s. |
| Free Methodist Church in the UK | 1959 | P Hol | VFD.E | 17 | 545 | 2,500 | Small branches in Wigan and Belfast. M=FMC(USA). Expanding. 14n,3p,W=48%,65Y,50z. |
| Free Presbyterian Church of Scotland | 1893 | P Ref | ..... | 68 | 1,000 | 4,500 | Ex Free Ch of Scotland. Presbyteries: Northern, Western, Southern, Outer Is. 36n. |
| Free Presbyterian Church of Ulster | 1951 | P Ref | .TT.T | 40 | 10,000 | 35,000 | Fundamentalist body, rejecting religious or political rapprochement with Catholics. |
| Free Protestant Episcopal Church | 1897 | C ARo | x.... | 40 | 1,000 | 3,000 | Healing. Bishops. Branches: USA, Canada, West Indies, West Africa. HQ Tottenham. |
| General Church of the New Jerusalem | 1890 | M Swe | x.... | 2 | 180 | 250 | *Swedenborgian Church*. Split ex New Church. 2 Societies: Colchester, London. 3n. |
| Greater World Chr Spiritualist League | 1852 | M Spi | x.... | 219 | 20,000 | 30,000 | 1931, *GWCSL*. *GW Sanctuary*. Specifically Christian body of spiritualists. Urban. |
| Greek Orthodox Ch: AD Thyateira & GB | 1815 | O Gre | Cwc.W | 55 | 149,500 | 219,000 | Under EP Constantinople. 90% Greek Cypriots. 4 bishops. 20n,41x,2d,1e,1600Yy. |
| Gypsy Evangelical Movement | | P Pe2 | x.... | | 200 | 1,000 | 100% Gypsies, run by Gypsies. Nomadic caravan communities. M=GGMS(Switzerland). |
| Healing Ch of God in Christ UK | 1964 | I pe2 | ..... | 2 | 70 | 150 | Ex Ch of God in Christ Pentecostal. West Indians. HQ Forest Gate,E7. Bishop,4nx. |
| Holy Order of Cherubim & Seraphim Ch | 1965 | I peA | xvI.W | 0 | 2,000 | 3,000 | HQ Nigeria. Largest African body in UK. Rapid growth. Yoruba, WIndians. 60% men. |
| House-Church Movement/Restoration | 1974 | P Pe4 | x.... | 200 | 10,000 | 20,000 | Ch of the Great Shepherd/Pyramid Church. M=CGM(USA). Strong Yorks, West Country. 20m. |
| Independent Methodist Connexion | 1805 | P Met | .v..W | 143 | 6,957 | 16,000 | NWEngland. HQ Loughborough. Seatings 40000. Declining 5% pa. 235n,140t(8000). |
| International City Mission | 1961 | I pen | x.... | 9 | 300 | 700 | Barbados, Jamaica (HQ Kingston); some Whites. Also in USA. Women bishops. 4nx,4f. |
| International Evangelistic Fellowship | c1960 | I pe3 | ..... | 4 | 500 | 1,000 | West Indian immigrants. Link with Swedish Pentecostals. HQ London SE24.1n. |
| International Ministerial Association | 1965 | I pel | ..... | 15 | 600 | 900 | Independent congregations of Jamaica Apostolics. M=IMA(Houston,USA). 15nx. |
| Internat Ministerial Council of GB | 1974 | I pel | ..... | 11 | 700 | 1,200 | From St Kitts,Guyana,India,Jamaica(Apostolics).Ecumenical. HQ London N19. 10nx,1p. |
| Jamaica WI Hackney Pente Apostolic Ch | 1968 | I pel | ....I | 8 | 600 | 1,000 | WI=West Indies, Jamaican Apostolics. 22 congregations in WI. HQ London E8. 4n. |
| Jehovah's Witnesses | 1881 | M Jeh | x.... | 895 | 64,361 | 200,000 | Missionaries 1881, branch office 1900. HQ Brooklyn, USA. Growing at 4%pa. 5177Y. |
| Latvian Ev Lutheran Church in Exile | 1946 | P Lut | Lwc.. | 42 | 2,300 | 5,500 | *Latvijas Evangeliska Luteriska Baznica*. Refugees from USSR. 7n,G=0.9%pa.21Yy,55z. |
| Liberal Catholic Church | 1915 | C Lib | xv... | 21 | 995 | 1,250 | Split ex ORCC. HQ London. 1965, applied to WCC, rejected. 28n,2x,W=45%,31Yy,43z. |
| Life & Light Fellowship | 1966 | I pen | ..... | 2 | 103 | 250 | Jamaicans. Large healing crusades. Mission to Jamaica. HQ Handsworth. 3nx,3m. |
| London City Mission | 1835 | P int | ..... | 60 | 3,000 | 5,000 | One of 50 city missions begun by DNasmith. LCM: 150 missionaries, 60 mission halls. |
| Lutheran Council of Great Britain | 1669 | P Lut | l...W | 165 | 12,500 | 16,500 | Joint Lutheran ministry to refugees, immigrants and diaspora congregations. 47nx. |
| Manchester City Mission | | P int | ..... | 16 | 1,000 | 2,000 | Second largest city mission. 20 missionaries and deaconesses, 16 mission halls. |
| Methodist Church in Ireland | 1795 | P Met | VWc.W | 230 | 28,089 | 70,000 | Northern Ireland (8,000 others in Republic). 235n,328pp,G=–1.4%pa,1s,W=76%,1000Yy. |
| Methodist Church of Great Britain | 1795 | P Met | VWC.W | 9,948 | 651,139 | 2,000,000 | 1795, ex CofE. 34 Districts. Declining 1.8%pa. 4167n,20652pp,1p,4s(141),43423Yy. |
| Moravian Church in GB & Ireland | 1737 | P Mor | xWX.a | 40 | 3,212 | 7,000 | *British Province*.Unity of Brethren. 5 Districts. Since 1961, 15% WIndians. 30n,17m. |
| New Apostolic Church | | C CAp | x.... | | 1,000 | 2,000 | *NAC*, Canada Bezirk (District). Ex Catholic Apost Ch. World HQ Dortmund (Germany). |
| New Church | 1783 | M Swe | xv... | 65 | 3,685 | 7,500 | *General Conference of the New Church*. *Swedenborgian Ch*. Overseas missions. 36n,1s. |
| New Testament Assembly (England) | 1966 | I pe3 | ..... | 8 | 150 | 400 | Jamaicans; Grenada, Trinidad, et al. Black. HQ Leyton,E10. Social work, 8nx,14m. |
| New Testament Church of God | 1951 | P Pe3 | ZF..i | 90 | 11,000 | 22,000 | Jamaicans, few Irish. M=CoG(Cleveland). HQ Handsworth. 160n,G=15%pa,1p,W=60%,1323Y. |
| Non-Subscribing Presb Ch of Ireland | 1725 | P Ref | I.... | 39 | 6,500 | 8,500 | Unitarian tendencies. Linked to General Assembly, UFCC. 20n,W=30%,100Yy,800z. |
| Old Roman Catholic Ch (English Rite) | 1950 | C CCa | ..... | 12 | 1,000 | 1,500 | Schism ex ORCC. 1963, large USA branch of 65,000 added (HQ Chicago). |
| Order of the Cross | 1904 | M The | x.... | 41 | 1,500 | 3,000 | Theosophical. In England, Scotland, Wales, Ulster. Sacramentalist, vegetarian. 5 nations. |
| Orthodox Syrian Ch of the East | c1970 | O SyM | Dwe.. | | 1,000 | 2,000 | Immigrants from Kerala (South India), around Southall, Middlesex. |
| Pentecostal Assemblies of the World | 1969 | I pel | x.... | 4 | 300 | 500 | From St Kitts, Grenada, Jamaica. Ex FUCJCA. M=PAW,UPC(USA). HQ Battersea. 3nx. |
| Pentecostal Church of God | 1956 | I pen | ..... | 8 | 400 | 1,000 | Trinidad,Jamaica. 3 Districts. Missions: Nigeria, India. HQ Islington. 2 bishops,6n. |
| Pentecostal Holiness Church | | P Pe3 | ZF... | 7 | 143 | 500 | *PHC*, *British Conference*. Holiness Pentecostals. HQ Bristol 6. M=PHC(USA). 14n. |
| Pilgrim Wesleyan Holiness Church | 1958 | P Hol | V...I | 20 | 466 | 1,600 | Blacks from Barbados,St Kitts,Trinidad,Jamaica.M=WC(USA). HQ Birmingham. 19n,36m. |
| Polish Orthodox Church Abroad | c1940 | O Pol | Cw... | 5 | 15,000 | 20,000 | 5 parishes. Resettled Polish army refugees after 1940. Under GOC AD Thyateira. 7n. |
| Polish Reformed Church in Exile | c1940 | P Ref | .T... | 3 | 1,000 | 2,000 | Refugees from Polish church obliterated in World War II. 1956, M=IBPFM(USA). |
| Presbyterian Church in Ireland | 1610 | P Ref | RW..W | 566 | 142,498 | 396,216 | 19 Presbyteries in NI. 475n,G=–1%pa,P=70%,2s(41),750t(70688),W=40%,6789Yy. |
| Presbyterian Church of Wales | 1735 | P Ref | RW..W | 1,327 | 110,155 | 145,309 | *Eglwys Bresbyteraidd Cymru*. *Calvinistic Meth Ch*. HQ Brecon. 368n,G=–3.2%pa,1s,601Yy. |
| Process Church of the Final Judgement | 1960 | M Apo | xv... | | 5,000 | 10,000 | *Processeans*. Free shops, kitchens, food handouts. HQ London. 1972 applied to WCC. |
| Ras Tafari Melchizedek Orthodox Ch | 1960 | I mar | x.... | 4 | 500 | 2,000 | Ras Tafari=Haile Selassie of Ethiopia. Radical WIndian Black youths, some Whites. |
| Reformed Presbyterian Ch of Ireland | 1763 | P Ref | J...C | 48 | 3,250 | 8,000 | *RPC*. *Covenanters*. HQ Belfast. 30n,G=–0.1%pa,1s(6),W=90%,90Yy,100z. |
| Reformed Presbyterian Ch of Scotland | 1743 | P Ref | J.... | 5 | 605 | 800 | *RPC*. *Modern Covenanters*. *Joint Reformed Presbyteries of Edinburgh & Glasgow*. 4n. |
| Religious Society of Friends | 1652 | P Qua | Q...w | 435 | 18,855 | 30,600 | *London Yearly Meeting*. *Quakers*. In Wales: *Cymdeithas y Cyfeillion*. Declining. 1s. |
| Religious Soc of Friends in Ireland | 1654 | P Qua | Qv... | 20 | 1,300 | 2,500 | *Ulster Quarterly Meeting*, Ireland Yearly Meeting (established 1669). Emigration. |
| Reorganized Ch of JC of L-d Saints | | M LdS | xv... | | 500 | 1,700 | Schism in USA ex CJCLdS (Utah Mormons). Birmingham 13, Leicester, Gloucester. |
| Resurrected Church of God | 1967 | I pen | ..... | 6 | 100 | 250 | Jamaicans. M=Resurrected CoG(Philadelphia,USA) (Black). HQ Wolverhampton. 6nx. |
| Romanian Orthodox Church | c1955 | O Rum | Cwc.. | 1 | 1,500 | 2,500 | *Biserica Ortodoxa Romana*. Under P Bucharest. Romanian immigrants, 400 families. 1x. |
| Russian Orth Ch: PE Western Europe | 1500 | O Sla | Mwc.W | 5 | 4,000 | 6,000 | Under P Moscow. Russians, also some UK converts. 1 charismatic parish. 8nx,1d(5). |
| Russian Orthodox Church in Exile | c1950 | O Sla | x.... | 7 | 15,000 | 20,000 | *D Great Britain*, *ROC Outside of Russia* (HQ New York). Ultra-conservative. 1e(6). |
| Salvation Army | 1865 | P Sla | xWC.W | 1,100 | 255,000 | 500,000 | *SA*, *British Territory*, *Scotland Territory*. 31 Divisions. 2200n,2j,2s. |
| Serbian Orthodox Church | c1960 | O Ser | ..... | 1 | 500 | 1,000 | Schismatic diocese under Libertyville(USA) opposing P Belgrade. Strong in Bradford. |
| Serbian Orth Ch: D WEurope, Australia | 1952 | O Ser | Cwc.. | 20 | 8,000 | 17,000 | Under jurisdiction of P Belgrade. Serbian immigrants after 1945. 4 parishes. 7x. |
| Seventh Day Baptist Church | 1617 | P Bap | Tw... | 3 | 57 | 200 | In SDBC(USA). Began 1617 in UK, brought back 1966 by Jamaicans. HQ London N19. 4nx. |
| Seventh-day Adventist Church | 1878 | P Adv | x...W | 153 | 12,313 | 25,000 | *British Union Conf*. 55% Blacks(Jamaicans,&c). 99nx,409mw,1H,1j,2r,188t(12330),563Y. |
| Shilo Pentecostal Fellowship (UK) | 1965 | I pe2 | ..... | 8 | 200 | 500 | From Trinidad,Montserrat, Grenada (work of PAoC); few Whites. HQ London E8. 5n,1p. |
| Shilo United Ch of Christ (Apostolic) | 1958 | I pel | ....I | 5 | 165 | 400 | From Jamaica,Trinidad,Barbados. Link, Int Ministerial Council of GB. 9nx,10mw,1p. |
| Spiritualist Association of GB | 1872 | M Spi | ..... | | 7,000 | 10,000 | Originally Marylebone Spiritualist Association, till 1960. Psychic research. Urban. |
| Spiritualists National Union | 1891 | M Spi | ..... | 473 | 17,769 | 30,000 | *SNU*. Former Spiritualists Nat Federation. Includes non-Christian spiritists. Urban. |
| Strict & Particular Baptist Churches | 1620 | P Bap | .T..C | 700 | 8,000 | 20,000 | *National Strict Baptist Assembly*. 3 regional Associations. Not in BUGBI. 74n. |
| Triumphant Church of God | 1959 | I Pe3 | ..... | 6 | 300 | 700 | From Jamaica,Montserrat. Split ex CGP. Mission in USA. HQ West Bromwich. 4nx,8m. |
| True Jesus Church | c1965 | I pel | x.... | 3 | 300 | 500 | *TJC*, World Conference (HQ Taiwan). Chinese. 3 halls: London, Edinburgh, Newcastle. |
| Ukrainian Autocephalic Orthodox Ch | 1947 | O Sla | X.... | 35 | 20,000 | 30,000 | *Sobornopravna* (*Democratic*). Linked to UOC (USA). Ukrainian refugees, 1945. 12n. |
| Unaffiliated fundamentalist chapels | | P sin | ..... | 2,500 | 250,000 | 500,000 | Large de facto grouping. Expanding. Healing, foreign missions. 2000n. |
| Union of Evangelical Churches | 1838 | P ind | ..D.x | 27 | 800 | 2,000 | Independent congregations in East London and Essex. 56n,28m(local preachers). |
| Union of Welsh Independents | 1639 | P Con | .W..W | 761 | 89,000 | 140,000 | *Undeb yr Annibynwyr Cymraeg* (1871). Welsh-speaking only. 235n,101m,G=–2%pa,2s. |
| Unitarian & Free Christian Churches | 1645 | M Unt | Iv..w | 330 | 22,000 | 40,000 | *General Assembly of UFCC*. Unitarians. 1928 merger. Declining. 223n,2s. |
| United Apostolic Faith Church | c1910 | P Pe2 | x...H | | 5,000 | 10,000 | Pentecostals with British-Israel doctrines. HQ London N8. Missions in SAfrica. |
| United Church of God | 1963 | I pe3 | ..... | 3 | 104 | 300 | Jamaica,Barbados. Ex NTCoG. M=Un Holiness Ch of Faith in Christ(USA Blacks). 1n,3m. |
| United Free Church of Scotland | 1900 | P Ref | RW..W | 94 | 16,223 | 19,753 | 1929, majority rejoined Ch of Scotland. 5 Presbyteries. 77n,G=–3.7%pa,1u,346Yy. |
| United Holy Church of God | 1961 | I pe3 | x.... | 9 | 250 | 650 | Jamaicans. M=UHCA(NJ,USA). 2 British Districts, HQ Paddington. 2 bishops,10nx. |
| United Pentecostal Church | c1960 | P Pel | x.... | 15 | 900 | 2,000 | *Jesus Only Ch*. Jamaicans. M=UPC,PAW(USA). Also in Europe. HQ London SW2. 10n,4f. |
| United Pentecostal Church of God | 1974 | I pe2 | ..... | 3 | 60 | 150 | Mainly Jamaicans. Split ex Triumphant Ch of God. HQ Birmingham 21. 1n. |
| United Reformed Church | 1662 | P Ref | RWc.W | 3,056 | 222,049 | 350,000 | 1972 union Congr Ch in E&W(74%),Presb CofE(26%). 12 Provs. 2080n,G=–3.4%pa,6s,1u. |
| Universal Church of God | 1965 | I Hol | ..... | 6 | 200 | 400 | Mainly Jamaicans. Split ex CoG (Anderson)(USA). Anti-pentecostal. HQ Aston. 6nx. |
| Universal Pentecostal Church | c1965 | I pe2 | Z.... | 20 | 1,000 | 2,000 | M=Ceylon Pente Mission. Sri Lanka Tamil immigrants. London, Midlands, Wales, York. |
| Universal Pente Ch (Ghana & Overseas) | 1973 | I peA | ..... | 2 | 100 | 150 | Ex Ch of the Lord (Battersea). Ghanaians, Sierra Leonians, WIndians. London SE13. |
| Universal Prayer Fellowship | 1965 | I pen | ..... | | 300 | 1,000 | West African transients & students. Collective healing prayer, fasting, dreams. |
| Victorious Church of God | c1965 | I pe3 | ..... | | 1,000 | 2,000 | Black (West Indian) pentecostal immigrants. Schism ex Ch of God in Christ. |
| Wesleyan Reform Union | 1849 | P Met | V.D.a | 156 | 5,100 | 12,000 | Expelled ex British Wesleyan Methodism. Midlands, North. 22n,237m,G=–2.8%pa. |
| Worldwide Church of God | 1953 | M BrI | x.... | 150 | 15,000 | 20,000 | *WCG*. *Radio Church of God*. Radio, TV, literature ministries. HQ Pasadena, CA(USA). |
| World-Wide Missions | 1967 | P ind | x.... | | 950 | 2,000 | M=World-Wide Missions(USA). Evangelicals based on Pasadena, CA(USA). |
| Other Protestant denominations | | P | ..... | | 10,000 | 20,000 | Total over 100 (see list below). |
| Other Third-World indigenous churches | | I | ..... | 150 | 5,500 | 12,200 | Total over 80 (see list below), mainly West Indians and West Africans. |
| Other city missions | c1830 | P int | ..... | 200 | 5,000 | 10,000 | In: Bristol, Chester, Edinburgh, Glasgow, Leeds, Liverpool, York & 40 other cities. |
| Other marginal Protestant bodies | | M | ..... | | 4,500 | 8,300 | Total about 30 bodies (see list below), and many independent congregations. |
| Other Catholic (non-Roman) churches | | C | ..... | | 1,000 | 3,000 | Total about 50 (see list below), including about 35 under bishops-at-large. |
| **Total affiliated (mid-1970)** | | | | **63,200** | **18,603,618** | **43,891,223** | **Total denominations (1970) . . . 470.** |
| **Total affiliated (mid-1975)** | | | | **63,400** | **18,253,100** | **43,064,200** | **Total denominations (1975) . . . 500.** |
| **Total affiliated (mid-1980)** | | | | **63,600** | **17,910,200** | **42,255,200** | **Total denominations (1980) . . . 530.** |

NOTES ON TABLE ABOVE

COLUMNS: for meanings and CODES (cols. 1, 3, 4, 8): see Codebook (Part 6). Column 1: **Boldface type** = church with over 10% of country's affiliated Christians.

NATIONAL COUNCILS (Column 4, 5th letter).

- a = member of both BCC & EAGB.
- C = British Evangelical Council (BEC).
- E = Evangelical Alliance of Great Britain (EAGB) (other members not shown in table: Assemblies of God in GB & I, Elim Pentecostal Ch).
- H = British Pentecostal Fellowship (begun 1948).
- I = Afro-West Indian United Council of Churches (Afro-Caribbean United Church Council) (begun 1977).
- i = member of I (preceding line) and also of H.
- J = Council of African & Allied Churches in the UK (begun 1979; 20 churches).
- R = Episcopal Conference of Ireland (ECI).
- s = Bishops' Conference of England & Wales (or Bishops' Conference of Scotland), also consultant member of BCC.
- T = British Council of Protestant Christian Churches.
- W = British Council of Churches (BCC).
- w = associate member of BCC, or (Seventh-day Adventist Church) observer member.
- x = member of both EAGB and BEC.

*Other national councils*. Council of Churches for Wales (Cyngor Eglwysi Cymru) = Baptist Union of GB & I, Baptist Union of Wales, Ch in Wales, Chs of Christ (observer), Methodist Ch, Presbyterian Ch of Wales, Religious Society of Friends (observer), Roman Catholic Ch (Consultant observer), Salvation Army, Union of Welsh Independents, United Reformed Ch. Free Church Federal Council (FCFC) = Baptist Union of GB & I, Churches of Christ in GB & I, Congregational Federation, Countess of Huntingdon's Connexion, Free Ch of England, Independent Methodist Connexion, Methodist Ch in GB, Moravian Ch, Presbyterian Ch of Wales, Salvation Army (joined 1974), Union of Welsh Independents, United Reformed Ch, Wesleyan Reform Union. Irish Council of Churches (ICC) = Ch of Ireland, Methodist Ch in Ireland, Moravian Ch, Non-Subscribing Presbyterian Ch of Ireland, Presbyterian Ch in Ireland, Religious Society of Friends, Salvation Army. Scottish Churches Council (SCC) = Baptist Union of Scotland, Churches of Christ, Ch of Scotland, Congregational Union of Scotland, Episcopal Ch in Scotland, Methodist Ch in Scotland, Religious Society of Friends, Salvation Army, United Free Ch of Scotland.

*Other local councils*. The BCC has some 720 local (county,

city, town or regional) Christian councils, or councils of churches, affiliated to it (some linked also with CCW, SCC or ICC). The EAGB has 46 area fellowships affiliated to it.

TRADITION (Column 3). *Types of Anglican churchmanship.* Almost all of the 61 Anglican dioceses in the UK have parish churches of every tradition of churchmanship, from Anglo-Catholic to Low Church, although former clearcut divisions are disappearing and the issue is increasingly seen as unimportant or even irrelevant. Nevertheless a descriptive typology is still possible and useful. In a 1970 public-opinion poll (NOP), Anglicans in Great Britain described themselves as: 14% High Church, 70% Low (including Central) Church, 16% no particular views. These percentages apply to the entire church, which is 99.9% laity; for clergy, the proportions are different. The type of Anglican churchmanship recorded here in column 3 gives each diocese's self-description, as seen from the diocesan office, of the main emphasis or predominant tradition of churchmanship found in the diocese. The *Church of Ireland* is traditionally Low Church in ritual, the *Episcopal Church in Scotland* is traditionally Anglo-Catholic, and the *Church in Wales* is High Church (Prayer Book Catholic). In the *Church of England* itself, these traditions are far more pluralistic or mixed, and it is often impossible to state a dominant tradition; the code above therefore gives only an impressionistic view of the major tradition in the diocese, as seen from the diocesan office, sometimes following the churchmanship or emphases of the incumbent bishops during 1970–75.

OTHER PROTESTANT DENOMINATIONS. In addition to the denominations listed in the table, there are a large number of smaller groups (many from the USA since 1970), including the following: Apostolic Faith Church, Armenian Ev Ch (1 congregation at Bromley), Berean Forward Movement, Bible Fellowship Union (ex Jehovah's Witnesses), Calvary Holiness Ch (HQ Glamorgan), Calvinistic Independent Ch, Christian Israelite Ch, Ch of Denmark (begun 1689), Ch of Finland, Ch of Norway, Ch of Sweden (begun 1710), Chs of Christ (Instrumental) (1958), Crown Covenanters Society, Dutch Reformed Ch (begun 1550), Ev Movement of Wales, Evangelistic Association, Evangelization Society, Free Presbyterian Ch of England, Free Salvationist Mission, Frichley Friends (schism ex Quakers), Gospels Halls (a large number of independent congregations across GB and NIreland), Greek Evangelical Ch (begun 1960), Hebrew Christian Movement, Hutterian Brethren (Wheathill Bruderhof, Salop), Independent Baptists, Independent Ch of God, Independent Holiness Ch, Independent Jesus Name, International Laymen's Bible Fellowship, Italian Christian Chs of North Europe (CCINE; Pentecostal), Italian Pentecostal Ch (1969), Kingdom Revival Crusade, Maranatha Convention, Mennonite Ch, Netherlands Reformed Ch, Old Baptist Union (begun 1880), Original Scottish Succession, Pentecostal Ch of the West Indies, Pillar of Fire (USA; 1922; holiness body with 2 churches), Polish Ev Lutheran Ch in Exile (6 pastors), Primitive Baptists, Railway Mission, Reformed Ch of France (begun 1550), Slavic & Baltic Missionary Society, Society of Dependants (1850 Loxwood, Sussex; Cogglers, Cokelers; 100 left), Spanish Evangelical Ch (1961), Swiss Reformed Ch. There are also USA military chaplaincies in addition to those already listed in the table above.

OTHER THIRD-WORLD INDIGENOUS CHURCHES. Numerous other Third-world immigrant groups have established branches of their home churches in the UK. Most were begun by West Indian Blacks, some by Indians, Sinhalese or Koreans, and some by Africans (including Nigerians who have begun Aladura (Praying) churches). These additional bodies numbered over 80 by 1976 and included the following, all of which are operated by West Indian Blacks unless another nation is indicated here in parentheses: African Orthodox Ch (USA Blacks), All Nations Ch of God, Apostolic Churches (several independent Jesus-Only pentecostal congregations in West Bromwich, Stafford, &c, from Apostolic movement in Jamaica; including Apostolic Church of God in Christ), Army of the Cross of Christ Ch (MDCC, from Ghana; church in London), Asian Ch of Jesus Christ (Pakistani and West Indian pentecostals; HQ Ilford), Bethel Apostolic Ch, Bible Truth Ch of God (HQ Brixton), Bible Way Pentecostal Ch, Celestial Ch of Christ (2 churches; from Benin and Nigeria), Cherubim & Seraphim Society (Nigeria; begun 1974; 110 members in 1976), Ch of God Assembly (begun 1974), Ch of God Holiness (Jamaicans, 2 congregations), Ch of God (Holiness) (Jamaicans, HQ Handsworth), Ch of Jesus (Jamaica), Ch of the Lord (Battersea) (Ghanaians), Ch of Universal Prayer Fellowship (1968 ex CLA (Nigeria); Ghanaians, Nigerians, Sierra Leonians), Deeper Last Day World Vision (Ev Ch of God), Emmanuel Ch of God, Emmanuel Pentecostal Faith Ch of God, Evangelical Touring Harmonizing Ch (HQ Peckham), Father Divine Peace Mission Movement (USA Blacks), Gospel of God Ch (Apostles of Johane Masowe, from Rhodesia/Zimbabwe), Holy Spirit Association for Unification of World Christianity (from South Korea; by 1976, 3,000 adherents in 20 communities), Holy Tabernacle of Christ Jesus, Latter Rain Outpouring Revival, Mount Carmel Ch of God (HQ Brixton), Mount Olivet Spiritual Baptist Ch, Mount Zion Sanctuary Assembly Seventh-day (Jamaicans, HQ Croydon), New Covenant Ch of God (HQ Brixton), People's Christian Fellowship, Recruit for Christ Evangelistic Crusade, Redeemed Ch of Christ (1968; ex Holy Order of C&S; Nigerians, Ghanaians, West Indians), Refuge Ch of God (1961; Jamaican pentecostals), Sacred Chrubim and Seraphim (Nigeria), Seventh Ch of Melchizedek (1975), Seventh Day Pentecostal Ch (Jamaica), Spiritual Baptist Ch (Trinidad), Universal Ch of the Lord (1975), Voice of Prophecy Ch; and at least 50 other Black denominations (1977). There are also numerous single congregations of revivalist type, including Miracle Ministry Mission (London E7), Miracle Revival Fellowship (London E17), Ressurrection Revival Ministry (London E7).

OTHER MARGINAL PROTESTANT BODIES. Among the many small marginal bodies are the following: Bible Students (ex Jehovah's Witnesses), Branhamites (End Time Local Believers), British-Israel World Federation, Christian Science Parent Ch (c1920 split), Christian Spiritualist Ch, Ch of Scientology, Ch of the Good Shepherd (Chelsea; Spaxtonites; healing of animals), Divine Science Federation International (1 church), General Anthroposophical Society (Christian Community Ch), Goshen Fellowship (ex Jehovah's Witnesses), Maranatha Convention (ex Jehovah's Witnesses), Millennial Dawn Association, New Jerusalem Fellowship (ex British Israelites), New Thought, Olive Branch Ch, Progressive Spiritualist Ch, Religious Science Ch, United Ch of Religious Science (3 churches), Unity School of Christianity. Among the numerous independent congregations are around 180 unaffiliated spiritualist churches.

OTHER CATHOLIC (NON-ROMAN) CHURCHES. Miniscule unrecognized episcopal churches begun by bishops-at-large (episcopi vagantes) number over 30. In addition there are another 15 or so larger autocephalous Catholic churches, including: Ancient British Ch, Ancient Catholic Ch, English Catholic Ch, Free Catholic Ch, Old Holy Catholic Ch, Old Roman Catholic Ch, Polish Mariavite Ch, Reformed Catholic Ch (Utrecht Confession). For details of all these bodies, see table in Part 9. There are also other cults stemming from Roman Catholicism, including Antoinists (from Belgium and France). The totals given above exclude numerous other such bodies which were in existence earlier but are now defunct.

UNITING CHURCHES. In 1980, 6 separate sets of negotiations for organic union were under way, between the following groups of churches: (1) Church of England, Methodist Ch (talks broke down 1972). (2) Ch of England, Ch of Scotland, Episcopal Ch in Scotland, United Reformed Ch. (3) Churches of Christ in GB & Ireland, United Reformed Ch (talks broke down 1977, rebegan 1979). (4) Church in Wales, Methodist Ch, Presbyterian Ch of Wales, United Reformed Ch. (5) Baptist Union of Wales, Methodist Ch, Presbyterian Ch of Wales, Union of Welsh Independents, United Reformed Ch. (6) Ch of Ireland, Methodist Ch in Ireland, Presbyterian Ch in Ireland.

In 1976, the Churches' Unity Commission (CUC) was formed, with 8 churches, becoming in 1978 the Churches' Council for Covenanting (Baptist Union, BCC, Chs of Christ, Ch of England, Congregational Federation, Covenanting Chs in Wales, Free Ch Federal Council, Lutheran Council, Methodist Ch, Moravian Ch, Roman Catholic Ch, United Reformed Ch).

**PEOPLES** (ethnolinguistic). Christians: 80.5% English, 9.6% Scottish, 2.4% Irish (0.1% Irish Traveller), 2.2% Welsh, 1.8% Ulster Irish, 1.5% West Indian Black (Jamaican, et alii), 0.5% Greek Cypriot, 0.2% Polish, 0.2% Italian, 0.2% USA White, 0.2% Scottish Gaelic, 0.1% Australian, 0.1% Ukrainian, 0.1% Russian, 0.1% German, 0.1% French, Hungarian, Armenian, Dutch, Austrian, Afrikaner, Spaniard, Maltese, USA Black, Nigerian (Black, Yoruba), Chinese, Arab, South Indian (Tamil), Serbian, Latvian, Gypsy, Estonian, Byelorussian, Romanian, Pakistani, Korean, Ghanaian, Goan, Assyrian et alii.

**COUNTRY-WIDE TOTALS**

EVANGELIZATION (see Part 5). 1900: 100%. 1970: 100%. 1980: 100%. *Mass evangelism.* Among the very large number of recent campaigns: 1954, Billy Graham 3-month Harringay Crusade (2,047,333 attenders, 38,447 enquirers), 1955 All-Scotland Crusade (Billy Graham), Glasgow (2,647,365/52,253), London Crusade (450,000/23,806), 1961 Billy Graham 3-week crusade at Manchester (416,500 attenders, 17,769 enquirers), with landline relays (400,000/6,000) and one-day visits to Glasgow (40,000/600) and Belfast (55,000/900), also in 1966 for 32-day crusade in London (955,368/39,592), also in 1967 a 9-day All-Britain (London) crusade (1,006,254/34,367), and in 1970 in Chatham and Swansea the Euro '70 TV Crusade from Dortmund (Germany); 1963, Oral Roberts campaign in Newport, South Wales; 1965, 1967, Christian Film Festivals at Bromley, Kent; 1969–71, Assemblies of God evangelist Melvin Banks crusades in Spalding (6,000/700), Wigan (20,000/2,250), Clapton (10,000/1,000), Bristol (10,000/800), and subsequently elsewhere (with 12,000 adult decisions for Christ over 5-year period); 1969, 'Face the Facts' Arthur Rose Summer Tent Crusade; 1967–71, Capernwray Missionary Fellowship outreach in Manchester; 1972, 27-church campaign in Perth, Scotland; Easter 1974, POWER organized by Evangelical Alliance of GB; 1977, Luis Palau 1-month Wales crusade (60,000 attenders, 1,500 decisions); 1979, Here's Life Southampton (CCCI). *Radiophonic evangelism.* Annual listeners' letters (1975): 70,100 TWR, 1,274 HCJB, about 1,000 Radio Vatican, RVOG, IBRA, et alia. There are also many Bible correspondence course agencies.

FOREIGN MISSIONARIES AND PERSONNEL (nationals serving abroad) (1973). Total 10,288: 4,900 Protestants in over 160 societies, 2,590 Anglicans (720 clergy and 940 lay in 17 societies and 12 religious orders, and about 930 other clergy not in Anglican societies), 2,488 Roman Catholics (1,588 foreign missionaries (622 priests, 53 brothers, 413 sisters, 500 lay) serving in Third-World countries, and about 900 other personnel serving in Western nations), 230 marginal Protestants (140 Jehovah's Witnesses, about 40 Mormons), about 80 Black indigenous (in Jamaican and other missions to Nigeria, India, et alia).

FOREIGN MISSIONARIES AND PERSONNEL (aliens from abroad) (1973). Total 5,740. *From Western world.* 5,164: about 2,900 Roman Catholics, 1,800 marginal Protestants (1,600 Mormons mostly from USA, about 30 Jehovah's Witnesses), 282 Anglicans (about 170 clergy from USA, Canada, Australia, NZ, Ireland), 152 Protestants (139 in 32 USA societies, 6 in 3 Canada societies, 4 in 4 New Zealand societies, 2 in 1 Netherlands society, 1 in 1 WGermany society), about 20 Black indigenous from USA, about 8 Orthodox, about 2 Catholics (non-Roman) from USA. *From Communist world.* 93: about 74 Roman Catholics from Poland, Yugoslavia and Hungary, about 19 Orthodox priests and monks from Romania, USSR and Yugoslavia. *From Third World.* 483: about 210 Black and Third-World indigenous (116 from Jamaica, 40 Nigeria, 12 Ghana, India, Sri Lanka, Korea, China (Taiwan), Hong Kong and 6 other West Indian countries), about 100 Roman Catholics (35 from India), about 50 Anglicans (30 clergy from Africa, Asia, West Indies), 50 Protestants (mostly from West Indies), about 43 Orthodox from Cyprus, India and Egypt, about 30 marginal Protestants.

INSTITUTIONS (church-operated) (1973). Total 2,200, including about 20 ecumenical centres, about 1,500 higher schools, 80 lay training centres, about 130 medical centres (90 hospitals), over 20 presses, 150 religious communities, 60 research centres, 110 seminaries (60 Protestant, 26 Anglican, 15 RC, 3 marginal Protestant).

PERIODICALS. About 1,400 titles (including 200 Anglican, 180 Protestant (35 Pentecostal, 15 Quaker, 9 SDA), 150 RC, 40 marginal Protestant (5 LdS, 2 Unitarian, etc), 30 Black indigenous, 30 Catholic (non-Roman), 10 Orthodox; 400 non- or inter-denominational; including 220 foreign mission society periodicals). About 600 of these titles are listed in *Newsaper press directory*, *Willings press guide*, and *Guide to current British periodicals;* the *Church of England yearbook* and other denominational directories list several hundreds more.

PERSONNEL. About 107,340 (101,600 national, 5,740 foreign).

RELIGIOUS LIBRARIES. About. 480.

SCRIPTURE DISTRIBUTION (1975). Annual totals: 1,834,409 Bibles (2% free, 18% subsidized, 80% commercial), 2,037,322 NTs (53% free, 12% subsidized, 35% commercial), 1,130,000 UBS portions, 2,300,000 UBS selections. *Translations completed.* Portion: 27 languages or dialects since 1567. NT: 4 languages since 1526. Bible: 3 languages since 1535.

SERVICE AGENCIES. About 1,300 (mostly Anglican and Protestant, with 110 Roman Catholic), including ACC, ACCM, ACISJF, ACLD, ACP, AEGM, AID, AYPA, BB, BCC, BCMS, BEC, BFBS, BICE, BMMF, BMS, BPF, BRF, BWA, CA, CAFOD, CCCI, CCCS, CCIA, CCW, CEC, CEEC, CEF, CEMS, CESSAC, CFWM(CBMS), CIIR, CIOEW, CITC, CLC, CMA, CMAC, CMJ, CMML, CMS, CORAT, CPAS, CPSS, CR, CRAC, CRM, CRSL, CSC, CSCU, CSM, CSSM, CTS, CU, CUS, CWL, CWM(CCWM/LMS), CWN, CYC, CYFA, EAGB, ECI, ECM, ECOC, ECUSAT, EFAC, EMA, EUSA, FCFC, FEC, FECOF, FOR, FSC, FWCC, GFS, LAHR, IAMS, IBRA, ICC, ICF, ICGS, ICMA, ICTF, IEF, IFES, IHCA, ISCF, JEM, LCM, LDOS, MAF, MCU, MHM, MMA, MMS, MU, NBCW, NCEC, NCF, NCLA, NCP, NCSW, NCYA, NMCEW, NTMU, NYLC, OCU, OM, PTL, RADIUS, RBMU, RCMS, RSCM, RTS, SAMS, SASRA, SCA, SCC, SEAC, SGM, SIAC, SIL, SNTS, SPCK, SSJE, SSM, SU, SUM, TWR, UBS, UCCF(IVF), UCM, UMCA, USCL, WACC, WAMRAC, WCCE, WCF, WEC, WRMF, WWCTU, YCW, YFC, YMCA, YWAM, YWCA, ZEM. The total includes 430 Protestant book suppliers and 120 book distributors.

**ADDITIONAL DATA ON CHURCHES**

CATHOLIC CHURCH. There are 3 distinct and separate churches: England & Wales; Scotland; Ireland. *New dioceses.* 1976, D East Anglia; 1980, D Hallam (South Yorkshire). *Annual baptisms.* (1972) 95.8% infant, 4.2% adult. *Personnel.* About 90% nationals, 10% expatriates. *Priests.* In addition to those on diocesan staffs shown in the table above, there are numerous others. Totals in England and Wales have declined gradually from 7,911 in 1966 (5,096 diocesan, 2,791 religious, 24 bishops) to 7,562 in 1972 (4,955/2,580/27) and to 7,202 in 1977 (4,751/2,420/31). *Ordinations* (England). (1946) 189, (1956) 236, (1966) 172, (1976) 118 (72 diocesan, 40 religious). *Seminaries.* In addition to 6 secular and 9 religious seminaries in Great Britain, there are in Europe 4 English colleges (Lisbon, Valladolid, and 2 in Rome) and 2 Scottish colleges (Valladolid, Rome). *Religious orders and congregations.* England & Wales: of the 352 congregations of women, 280 are active and 72 contemplative. *Priests.* Including 104 Polish and 62 foreign chaplains to foreign immigrants; also many other foreign priests. *Religious priests* (1961 figures). 590 OSB, 516 SJ, 254 SDB, 236 OFM, 188 OP. *Catholic charismatics* (January 1974). 5,000 adults including many religious personnel are active in over 50 organized prayer groups in the Charismatic Renewal. In a 1977 Catholic Herald/Gallup Poll, 41% of all Catholics in Britain claimed to have attended charismatic meetings.

*Catholic organizations.* The United Kingdom is served by 3 Catholic episcopal conferences: the Bishops' Conference of England and Wales, Bishops' Conference of Scotland and the Episcopal Conference of Ireland, the latter located in Eire. There is a Council of Major Religious Superiors of England and Wales, and the Council of Major Superiors of Scotland, both serving men and women, while Northern Ireland is included in the Conference of Major Religious Superiors based in Eire. For the armed forces, Great Britain forms a military vicariate.

Lay activities in England and Wales are co-ordinated by the National Council for the Lay Apostolate, the National Board of Catholic Women, and the National Catholic Youth Association; with the same functions carried on in Scotland by the National Council for the Lay Apostolate in Scotland, Scottish National Council of Catholic Women's League and Catholic Youth Council. Associations include the Legion of Mary, Young Christian Workers, Catholic Students Council, Catholic University Societies, League of Christ the King, Catholic Guide Advisory Council, Scottish Catholic Guiders' Advisory Committee, Catholic Scout Advisory Council, Knights of St Columba, Catholic Women's League, Union of Catholic Mothers, Catholic Union, Catholic Marriage Advisory Council, Society of St Vincent de Paul, Ladies of Charity, St Louise de Marillac Association, The Grail, Serra Club, and many others.

Diplomatic relations between the UK and the Holy See have been partially established. The UK appoints a British ambassador to the Holy See; the Vatican, however, appoints not a nuncio but an apostolic delegate. Northern Ireland is included in the Nunciature of Dublin in Eire, and the apostolic delegate to Great Britain serves Gibraltar as well.

Of progressivist movements, the most important in England and Wales is the Catholic Renewal Movement, founded in Slough (Bucks) in 1969, which is composed of laymen and some priests. Its aim is 'to promote the renewal of the Catholic Church in the spirit of Vatican II, and in particular the sharing of responsibility within the church and the pursuit of truth and justice'. It sponsors conferences, working parties, special projects and publications, and in 1970 had 1,000 active members and 4,000 sympathizers divided in 60 groups in most of the main towns of England and Wales. Other progressivist movements are the Pastoral Development Group (PDG), founded in Dartford (Kent) in 1968 with 30 active members in 1970, which seeks to assist the church by fostering through research and publication the development of theological ideas related to pastoral problems; Priest's Forum, with 150 members in 1970; and ONE for Christian Renewal, founded in London in 1970 with 1,000 members, which is oriented towards an ecumenical stance.

Traditionalist movements include: the Pro Fide Movement, founded in South Croydon (Surrey) in 1971, which is a lay movement to defend the 'authentic teaching of the church' against the assaults of neo-modernism; the Catholic Priests' Association founded in Polegate (Sussex) in 1971, which speaks for 1,000 Catholic priests united for the defence of the moral and doctrinal tradition of Catholicism; and the Latin Mass Society of England and Wales, established in London as an affiliate of the Una Voce International Federation of Clarens (Switzerland), which unlike the above organizations has official episcopal sanction.

Scottish branches of both progressivist and traditionalist movements are the Scottish Renewal Group, founded in Glasgow in 1970; and the Pro Fide Movement, founded in Ayrshire in 1973 and the Una Voce Scottish Branch in Edinburgh.

Several institutions dealing with research and socio-religious problems are active. The Catholic Institute for International Relations (CIIR), founded in London in 1939 under the name Sword of the Spirit with its new name dating from 1966, is a centre for information and education on international questions, particularly those relating to world poverty and race relations. The Catholic Fund for Overseas Development (CAFOD) in London is a member of CIDSE in Belgium and assists projects sponsored by Catholic dioceses and missionaries which are designed to overcome hunger and poverty overseas. Other Catholic organizations chiefly concerned with overseas development are Catholic Overseas Appointments in London which recruits and appoints educational, medical and other qualified personnel for developing countries; Ad Lucem, training persons taking up work overseas; and the Catholic Women's League. In addition, Catholic People's Weeks, Parkstone (Dorset )is an association of priests and lay persons which organizes residential courses for adult education. In Scotland the official Catholic organization for providing overseas aid is the Scottish Catholic International Aid Fund in Aberdeen.

For pastoral and theological training, the following institutions have been established: Heythrop College, a theological school founded in London in 1964, which became by royal charter of 14 May 1971 a school in the Faculty of Theology of the University of London; the Institute of Religious Education Corpus Christi College, founded in London in 1956, for training specialists in catechetics; and the National Catechetical Centre, in London, which coordinates all catechetical work in England and Wales. Three organizations are active in the liturgical and biblical fields: the Church Music Association, in London; the Catholic Biblical Association in Allen Hall, Ware (Herts); and the Society of St Gregory, in Bristol, which encourages active participation in the liturgy. Scottish religious education centres for catechetical studies are located in Glasgow, Motherwell and Ayrshire, the

Glasgow centre also containing the Vigilanti Audio-Visual Library. The Scottish Catholic Historical Association in Glasgow has since its foundation in 1950 established an international reputation for its work, which is published in a twice-yearly journal *Innes Review*.

Catholic foreign missionary activity is co-ordinated by the National Missionary Council of England and Wales, with its Mission Secretariat in London. Agencies providing aid to foreign missions include CAFOD, mentioned above, and the Volunteer Missionary Movement, in London, which recruits Fidei Donum priests for 3-year terms of service overseas. The Missionary Institute, founded in London in 1968, provides a degree course for priests of most of the male missionary congregations, and a diploma course for sisters and lay personnel.

In 1972, Catholic missionaries from the UK numbered 622 priests, 53 brothers, 413 sisters and 500 lay missionaries. The main missionary congregations founded in England and Wales, with 1972 statistics, are: St Joseph's Society for Foreign Missions (commonly called Mill Hill Missionaries, MHM), a clerical congregation founded in 1866 with 1,200 members, serving in 12 countries of Africa, Asia and South America; Franciscan Missionary Sisters, founded in 1883 with 350 members serving in Kenya, East Malaysia, Peru and Chile; and Franciscan Missionary Sisters of the Divine Motherhood, founded in 1947, serving in Africa and the Far East. Other important missionary congregations include for men, WF, CSSp, SMA, FSCJ, SVD and SJ; and for women, White Sisters, Medical Mission Sisters, Franciscan Missionaries of Mary, Servants of the Holy Spirit and Missionary Sisters of Verona. Missionary activity from Scotland is co-ordinated by the Scottish National Council of the Pontifical Society for the Propagation of the Faith in Glasgow. There are no missionary congregations native to Scotland, but congregations recruiting personnel include for men, MHM, WF, SPS, FSCJ, CSSp and SX; and for women, Franciscan Missionary Sisters for Africa and Franciscan Missionaries of Mary.

Educational activities are co-ordinated by the Catholic Education Council, with the following statistics recorded in 1972: 5 pre-primary schools (ages under 5 years) with 189 pupils; 2,222 primary schools (including pre-primary pupils educated in primary schools) with 525,139 pupils; 784 secondary schools with 367,562 pupils; 47 special schools with 3,378 pupils; 15 higher education institutes (teacher training colleges, and students aged 18 or over) with 10,782 students. In January 1971, the Catholic school system (excluding higher education) in England and Wales therefore numbered 896,268 pupils, which was 10.2% of the 8,812,347 pupils in the whole school system in England and Wales excluding higher education. Catholic schools have thus expanded very rapidly from 394,000 pupils in 1950 to about 700,000 in 1960 and to nearly 900,000 in 1971. By 1977, numbers had stabilized to 889,438 pupils (368,000 in secondary schools) in 3,070 schools.

Scottish Catholic schools are co-ordinated by the Catholic Education Commission and in 1972 numbered 350 primary schools with 139,026 pupils and 82 secondary schools with 64,564 pupils, the great majority being in the west central region surrounding Glasgow.

Social service statistics for England and Wales in 1972 included 77 Catholic hospitals (general hospitals, maternities, nursing homes and convalescent homes), 14 homes for the mentally handicapped, 68 homes for the aged, 70 residential hostels, 27 holiday or rest homes, 17 diocesan children's societies and 156 children's homes (71 mixed homes, 5 boys' homes, 6 girls' homes, 15 residential nurseries, 20 special schools and special homes, 11 schools and homes for physically handicapped children, 19 hostels, 8 training homes for girls and one probation hostel for boys). The following associations are also active: Catholic Women's League, Relief and Refugee Committee, founded in London in 1942 and affiliated to Caritas Internationalis; Society of St Vincent de Paul, founded in London in 1935 and also affiliated to Caritas, which serves the poor, hospitals and prisons; Aged Poor Society, in London; Catholic Handicapped Children's Society, in Stanley (Durham); Catholic Housing Aid Society, in London; Catholic Needlework Guild, in Wincanton (Somerset) which provides clothing and assistance for the poor; Catholic Prisoners' Social Service, in London; International Catholic Girls Society, in London; Ladies of Charity and Companions of St Vincent, in London; St Joseph's Hospice Association, in Liverpool, which serves the incurably sick and destitute: and St Vincent's Family Housing Association Ltd, providing flats and houses for the needy. Social services for Scotland in 1972 included 3 general hospitals and maternities; 3 hospitals for handicapped; one child guidance clinic; 5 hostels for boys, women or girls; one asylum for the deaf, mute and blind; 2 homes for the mentally retarded; 6 homes (girls, chronically ill, invalids, convalescents); one hostel; and one orphanage. Social service associations include the Catholic Adoption Society (Edinburgh) St Margaret of Scotland Adoption Society (Glasgow). St Vincent de Paul Society (Glasgow) and Catholic Social Service Centre, (Edinburgh). The National Council for Social Welfare in Glasgow co-ordinates the work of child adoption societies and the Child Welfare Office.

CHURCH IN WALES. *Clergy*. The total had fallen to 817 priests by 1977, with 32 deacons and 5 deaconesses. *Lay readers* (1977). 440 men, 14 women. *Seminarians* (1977). 61.

CHURCH OF ENGLAND. The 43 dioceses in the 2 Provinces of Canterbury and York are autonomous and self-governing. These dioceses have within them 58 suffragan sees with suffragan bishops. The dioceses are sub-divided into 105 archdeaconries, 784 rural deaneries, with (in 1970) 14,422 parishes (each with one parish church, but with a total of 17,636 parochial churches, chapels and cathedrals) combined into 11,162 parochial livings (9,898 occupied, 1,264 vacant, in 1969). These figures barely change from year to year; in 1963 they were 14,421 parishes (with 17,896 parochial churches, chapels and cathedrals) combined in 11,436 parochial livings (10,376 occupied, 1,060 vacant). *Seating accommodation*. Seats in all parochial churches, chapels and cathedrals have declined slightly due to closures from 54 million in 1963. *Membership*. In 1968 there were 1,974,844 Easter communicants, or 20.3% of all confirmed persons in England. Members of church electoral rolls (habitually attending adults over 17 resident in parish, not necessarily confirmed) numbered 2,636,412. *Weekly Sunday attendance*. In 1968 this was 1,605,670 persons including clergy, choir, adults and children (but not infants), or 16% of all confirmed persons. Weekly communicants numbered 672,000 or 7% of all confirmed persons. *Government*. A synodical system of church government was introduced in 1970; the General Synod of the Church of England meeting 3 times a year, consists of the Convocations of Canterbury and York joined together in a House of Bishops, a House of Clergy and a House of Laity (total 555 members). *Decline in church commitment, 1900–1973*. There has been a steady fall in numbers. *Clergy* (bishops, priests, deacons, including non-parochial part-time and 1,300 fully-retired) declined from 23,670 (1901) to 19,950 (1969). From 1967–77, total clergy declined by 200 each year, and incumbents by 100 each year. *Ordinations*. (1946) 427, (1956) 757, (1966) 633, (1974) 393, (1976) 281. *Authorized lay workers* (1975). Men: 181 Church Army captains, 146 in religious communities. Women: 139 Church Army sisters, 117 deaconesses, 298 lay workers, 202 social workers, 1,475 members of religious communities. *Licenced lay readers* (part-time; 1975). 6,215 men, 322 women. *Annual infant baptisms* declined from (in 1901) 578,018 or 65.8% of all live births in England, to (in 1968) 381,447 or 49.0% of all live births, to 347,167 (46.6% of live births) in 1970, and to 297,580 in 1973. *Easter communicants* have fallen from 2,317,000 in 1922 (8.9% of the population over 14) to 2,004,000 in 1950 (6.2%), to 1,974,844 in 1968 (5.6% of the population over 14, or 20.3% of all eligible, i.e. confirmed persons), to 1,813,892 in 1970 (5.1% of the population, 19.1% of all confirmed), and to 1,684,110 in 1973 (18.1% of all confirmed). However, as explained in Table 1 (footnote PRACTISING CHRISTIANS), Easter communicants are only a small part of Anglican annual attenders whom polls show to be 63% of all affiliated (baptized) Anglicans. The same is true of Christmas communicants, who numbered 1,689,236 in 1970. *Annual confirmations* declined from (in 1911) 244,030 or 4.3% of all young persons aged 12–20 in England, to 167,000 in 1956, to (in 1969) 116,631 or 1.7% of young persons, to 100,227 in 1973, and to 96,543 in 1975. The fall from 140,134 in 1966 to 1969 represents an average decrease of 7%pa. A few dioceses now confirm children at the age of 10 years, though for most the usual age is 15 or over. *Sunday-school enrolment* fell from 2,333,000 children on registers in 1901 (30% of all children ages 3–14), to 1,039,000 in 1960 (13% all children). *Armed services*. In 1970 there were 320 Anglican chaplains in the 3 services, including 141 in the Army, 80 in the Royal Air Force and 70 in the Royal Navy. The British Army (192,000) is 68% Anglican, 17% Roman Catholic, 7% Methodist. The churches maintain 275 garrison chapels (from church buildings to temporary huts) and 223 Army chaplains (141 Anglican, 32 RC, 21 Church of Scotland). In 1968 there were 1,104 Anglican persons confirmed. Easter communicants in Army services in 1969 numbered 8,406 (but most of the Army would be at home attending Easter parish services). In the Royal Navy in 1968 there were 341 Anglican confirmations and 3,473 Easter communicants. In the Royal Air Force in 1968, 522 persons were confirmed, and in 1969 there were 4,581 Easter communicants. *Anglican charismatics* (January 1975). The charismatic or neo-pentecostal renewal within the Church of England, first begun in 1907 in Sunderland, took root in 1962 and has since operated firmly within existing parish and diocesan structures, mainly through parish prayer groups, parish communes, and interdenominational conferences for clergy and laity (Fountain Trust). By 1975 it had become widespread and influential, with about 7% of all Anglican clergy identifying themselves as charismatics (from all schools of churchmanship including Anglo-Catholics and Evangelicals), around 53% of clergy uncommitted but generally favourable and open to the movement (of whom 20% were actively knowledgeable about it), 30% suspicious, and 10% opposed. Of the Church's 17,000 congregations, 6% (around 1,000) had one or more charismatic prayer groups; and around 4% were being described as charismatic parishes, this varying from 5% in the north (dioceses such as Blackburn, Newcastle and Sheffield) to 3% in the south (dioceses such as Bath & Wells, Bristol, Chelmsford, Guildford and Southwark). These groups contained a total of persons in some way involved numbering around 5% of all electoral roll members (130,000 adults, or 300,000 total charismatic community including children). In 1975, all totals were rapidly growing. However, since the charismatic movement recognizes itself to be only a part of a wider spiritual renewal in the Church of England, no formal membership is recognized nor are prayer groups officially enumerated or listed.

*Anglican organizations*. The Anglican Communion worldwide is not centrally controlled or organized, but London is the headquarters of the 2 major Anglican advisory and consultative organizations. (1) The Lambeth Conference is a 10-yearly meeting of all Anglican bishops across the world, convened at the invitation of the archbishop of Canterbury. The first was held in London in 1867, then on average every 10 years subsequently. Numbers of bishops present: (1867) 76, (1878) 100, (1888) 145, (1897) 194, (1908) 242 (preceded by a Pan-Anglican Congress with 7,000 delegates), (1920) 252, (1930) 307, (1948) 329, (1958) 310, (1968, the first to which assistant bishops were invited) 459, and (1978) about 420. (2) The Anglican Consultative Council (ACC) was brought into being by the 1968 Lambeth Conference and has held meetings at Limuru, Kenya (1971), Dublin (1973) and Trinidad (1976). It is a small body of about 55 representatives of all Anglican Churches and includes bishops, clergy and laity.

The major organizations serving the Church of England are as follows. The central legislative body of the Church of England is the General Synod which consists of the Convocations of Canterbury and York united in a House of Bishops and a House of Clergy, with a House of Laity elected by lay members of deanery synods of the Provinces of Canterbury and York. The Central Board of Finance provides administrative funds for the General Synod, Convocations, boards and councils, in addition to loan services for church schools, personnel grants and grants-in-aid for other bodies including the Lambeth Conference, Anglican Consultative Council and Central Readers' Board.

Advisory committees and permanent commissions of the General Synod include: (1) Advisory Council for the Church's Ministry (ACCM), responsible for the forms and training of the accredited ministry, ordained and lay; (2) Board of Education, which promotes and supervises the general educational work of the church including publications; (3) Board for Mission and Unity, which provides for consultation between the foreign missionary societies and is responsible for ecumenical and evangelistic activities; (4) Board for Social Responsibility, which co-ordinates the thought and action of the church in matters relating to family, social and industrial life; (5) Church Information Office, including press, radio/TV, enquiries, publishing and bookshop services; (6) Legal Advisory Commission, which counsels all organizations of the church on legal matters; (7) Council for Places of Worship, advising the church on the construction and care of church buildings; (8) Council for the Deaf, which promotes physical and spiritual work on behalf of the deaf; (9) Hospital Chaplaincies Council; and (10) Prison Chaplaincies Council (until disbanded in 1976).

Other boards, councils and commissions include: (1) Church Commissioners for England, which handles investments, pays clergy and pension stipends, provides housing for clergy and discharges other administrative functions; (2) Central Readers' Conference (formerly Board), which promotes the ministry of lay readers throughout the country; (3) National Society for Promoting Religious Education, for the advancement of religious education through grants to church schools and colleges; (4) Archbishop of Canterbury's Counsellors on Foreign Relations, who advise the archbishop on relations between Anglicans and other Christians in the light of general political, social and economic conditions; (5) Liturgical Commission, preparing forms for worship services and exchanging information on liturgical matters with other churches; (6) Doctrinal Commission, which advises the House of Bishops and the General Synod on questions of faith; (7) Archbishop's Council on Evangelism, which encourages local churches in their mission of presenting the gospel to the world; (8) Corporation of Church House, which runs the headquarters offices of the Church of England; and (9) Pensions Board, responsible for pensions of clergy, widows and dependants, and other church workers.

The Church of England has 14 recognized foreign missionary societies. In alphabetical order these are: (1) Bible Churchmen's Missionary Society (BCMS), founded in 1922 by Conservative Evangelicals; (2) Church Army, begun 1882, with some 400 captains and sisters engaged in evangelistic and social welfare work throughout the country and overseas; (3) Church Missionary Society (CMS), founded in 1799, an Evangelical society with 434 missionaries serving in 74 dioceses in 27 countries of Africa, Asia, South America and Australia; (4) Church's Ministry among the Jews (CMJ), begun 1809; (5) Commonwealth and Continental Church Society (CCCS), begun 1823, providing clergy and teachers for service to British residents abroad; (6) Jerusalem and the East Mission (JEM), begun 1888, providing support to the Episcopal Church in Jerusalem and the Middle East; (7) Korean Mission, begun 1889, high church; (8) Melanesian Mission, begun 1849, high church; (9) Missions to Seamen, begun 1856, serving seamen at home and overseas; (10) Mothers' Union (MU), founded in 1876 to strengthen marriage and family life; (11) New Guinea Mission, begun 1891, high church; (12) Ruanda Mission CMS, founded 1921, Conservative Evangelical; (13) South American Missionary Society (SAMS), begun 1844, Conservative Evangelical; and (14) United Society for the Propagation of the Gospel, a 1965 merger of the high church SPG (begun 1701) and the UMCA (begun 1857), with the Cambridge Mission to Delhi (1877) joining in 1968, which sponsors 550 missionaries in 70 dioceses in 40 countries.

Other church agencies include 25 diocesan associations which raise funds in aid of overseas dioceses; 12 men's and 47 women's religious orders and communities; and a proliferation of other organizations catering for specialized needs and interests.

In education, the Church of England was responsible in 1963 for 6,813 church primary schools (33% of the total number in the country with 716,910 pupils or 18% of the total) and 233 secondary schools (4%, with 78,490 or 3% of all pupils), employing 30,075 full-time teachers. In 1973, Church of England and Church in Wales schools of all kinds numbered over 6,300, classifiable under several heads: (1) 5,908 maintained schools within the diocesan pattern operated by civil local education authorities (5,680 primary with 842,803 pupils and 228 secondary with 98,617 pupils), these being sub-divided into 2,446 aided schools (i.e. with a 2:1 majority of church-appointed foundation managers) (2,301 primary with 368,849 pupils and 145 secondary with 67,452 pupils) and 3,462 controlled schools (i.e. with a 1:2 minority of church-appointed foundation managers) (3,379 primary with 473,954 pupils and 83 secondary with 31,165 pupils); (2) a number of maintained schools outside the diocesan pattern but with Church of England trustees (termed Christian Faith schools); (3) 90 direct-grant grammar schools (out of a total of 173) with Church of England trustees; and (4) a large number of independent schools including 50 Church of England public schools, of which the best known are the 28 Woodard Schools. Church schools of the Church in Wales were few in number being 98 primary and 3 secondary. In 1973, of the 8 million pupils in all maintained schools in England and Wales nearly one million were in Anglican schools, several of which were new middle and comprehensive schools.

Sixty per cent of all Anglican aided schools are found in 7 dioceses: Blackburn, Liverpool, London, Manchester, Oxford, Salisbury and Southwark; the other 40% are spread around the remaining 42 dioceses of England and Wales. Most dioceses have at least one secondary school, and the largest numbers are in the dioceses of Blackburn, London, Manchester and Southwark. There are also 25 church teacher-training colleges of education of Anglican foundation (2 for men, 4 for women, 19 co-educational). The major Anglican society for advancing religious education in schools of all kinds is the National Society for Promoting Religious Education, with secretaries in most dioceses, which is especially concerned with church schools.

CHURCH OF SCOTLAND. The church is sub-divided into 12 Synods in Scotland and 59 Presbyteries. In 1970 there were 1,156,211 communicants on church rolls. During the year there were 81,138 removals (death, departure or removal) and 57,015 admissions (profession or arrival), making a nett decrease of 24,123 (2.1% pa). There were 35,371 baptisms in the year, 49,807 elders, 220,873 Sunday-school pupils and 30,606 teachers, and 46,850 Bible class pupils. The total of communicants has remained almost unchanged each year since 1901 when they numbered 1,163,594. *Nominal adherents*. Persons professing but not affiliated are numerous. Whereas persons affiliated to the Church of Scotland in GB numbered around 2.5 million in 1970, in 1970 those professing to belong numbered 67% (in polls) in Scotland (3.5 million), or 8% in GB (4.3 million) (see POLLS under Table 1). *Church attendance*. 1963: 39% at least once a month, 27% more at least once a year. *Neo-pentecostals*. The charismatic renewal was growing rapidly in 1975, with around 10,000 adults involved. The movement is served by Scottish Churches Renewal.

EPISCOPAL CHURCH IN SCOTLAND. *Licensed lay readers* (1977). 91 men, 3 women. *Seminarians* (1977). 25.

HOUSE CHURCH MOVEMENT/RESTORATION. A new paradenomination forming itself as Restoration out of the Charismatic Renewal within the mainline Protestant and Anglican churches; also known as the Shepherding Movement or Church of the Great Shepherd, because of its strict pastoral oversight, or The Pyramid Church because of its rigid hierarchical structure of apostles (shepherds). A majority of members are former Anglicans or Plymouth Brethren. The parallel movement in the USA is Christian Growth Ministries. Work is expanding in several overseas countries, including in Africa.

METHODIST CHURCH OF GREAT BRITAIN. In Wales: Eglwys Fethodistaidd. Formed in 1932 as a union of several Methodist bodies. The church is governed by a single Conference meeting annually, and is divided into 34 Districts covering England, Wales and Scotland. *Affiliated membership*. (1978) 516,798 members, and 1,370,515 adherents (non-members) on the Community Roll. *Sunday attenders*. 1978 (adults; Sunday morning and evening): 463,000. *Nominal adherents*. Nominal Methodists (professing but not affiliated) in Great Britain are very numerous. Whereas affiliated in GB numbered around 2 million in 1970, in 1963 and 1970 professing Methodists numbered 7% (in polls) or 3.7 million (see POLLS under Table 1). *Sunday-school scholars*. (1966) 476,436 (1974) 461,917. *Decline*. Membership fell gradually from 838,019 in 1932 to 601,068 in 1973, to 557,249 in 1975, and to 516,798 in 1978; and Sunday-school scholars from 1,297,953 in 1932 to 461,917 in 1974, and to 204,942 in 1978. *Ministers*. Decline from 4,357 in 1932 to 3,955 by 1973, to 3,635 by 1978. *Churches*. Decline to 8,310 by 1978. *Local preachers*. Decline from 34,948 in 1932 to 20,652 by 1973. *Teachers and leaders*. (part-time) 73,000.

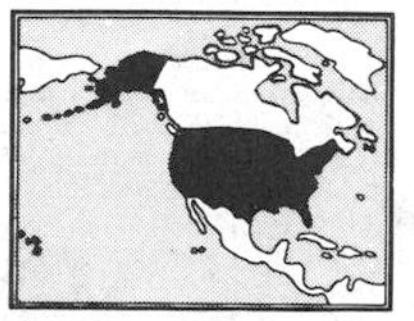

# UNITED STATES OF AMERICA

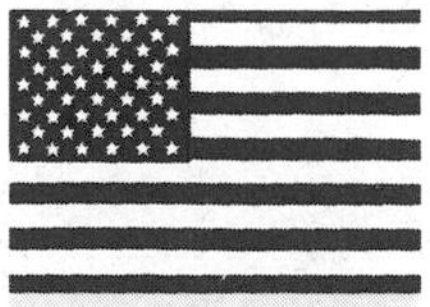

## SECULAR DATA

**STATE. Official name:** The United States of America. Adjective of nationality: American.
**Flag** (shown above right): Seven red and 6 white alternating stripes; blue canton with 50 white 5-pointed stars, one for each state.
**Area:** 9,363,123 sq.km. (3,615,122 sq.miles). Agricultural land: 45.6%.
**Government:** Federal republic, since 1776 (1620 settlement followed by British, Spanish, French, Dutch and Swedish colonies; 1763 British colony dominant; 1776 Independence).
**Legislature:** Congress: Senate, 100 members; House of Representatives, 435 members.
**Official language:** English (Spanish is co-official in New Mexico).
**Chief cities:** capital Washington DC 2,861,120 (1970), New York 11,571,900 (SMSA 9,944,000), Chicago SMSA 6,978,950, Los Angeles SMSA 7,032,080, Philadelphia SMSA 4,817,910, Detroit SMSA 4,489,000, Boston SMSA 3,417,000, San Francisco SMSA 3,109,520, Washington SMSA 2,999,000. (SMSA = Standard Metropolitan Statistical Area).
**Political divisions:** 50 States and the District of Columbia, divided into 3,054 Counties, divided (1967) into 18,048 Municipalities, 17,105 Townships, 21,782 School Districts, 21,264 Special Districts (total 81,248 units).
**Armed forces** (1976): Total 2,086,700 regular (including 110,500 women): strategic nuclear forces (453 bombers in Strategic Air Command, 331 interceptors), army 782,000, marine corps 196,000, navy 524,600, air force 584,100 (4,500 combat aircraft). Reserves: 874,500.
**Dependencies:** American Samoa, Canton & Enderbury Islands, Guam, Johnston Island, Midway Islands, Pacific Islands, Panama Canal Zone, Puerto Rico, US Virgin Islands, Wake Island.

**DEMOGRAPHY. Population:** 203,235,298 (census of 1.IV.1970. For 1970–2000 (UN), see last row of Table 1). Population density (1975): 23/sq.km. (59/sq.mile). Under 15 years: 31%. Growth rate (1975–80): 0.93% per year (births 1.72%, deaths −0.97%, immigrants 0.18%). Life expectancy (1975–80): 71.6 years. Household size: 3.1 persons.
**Major languages:** English, Spanish, German, Italian, Polish, Irish, French, Yiddish, Navajo, Cherokee, Sioux, Hindi, Swedish, Japanese, Norwegian, Hungarian, Chinese, Dutch, Czech, Slovak, Russian, Greek, Portuguese, Filipino, Korean, Vietnamese. In addition there are over 250 other languages spoken. Amerindian languages number 200 (or 360 including dialects).
**Urban dwellers** (1970): 74.1%. Urban growth rate (1950–70): 2.2% per year.
**Labour force:** 43%.
**Refugees** (1977): From abroad 872,789 (655,980 Cubans, 127,766 Vietnamese, 50,000 Haitians, 10,566 Laotians, 10,000 USSR Jews, 6,326 Cambodians, 5,000 Lebanese, et alii). (1979): 210,000 Indo-Chinese refugees settled.
**Tourists** (1970): 13,167,000. (1974) 14,123,000.

**ETHNOLINGUISTIC GROUPS:** There are 3 major groups: USA White (assimilated, of numerous ethnic origins but now with English as mother tongue), USA Black (Negro), and Hispanic (Mexican, Latin American or Spanish origin, all Spanish-speaking). Percentages of these 3 groups have varied from 1970–80 due to massive Hispanic immigration, both legal and illegal, reaching 1 million annually by 1978, as follows. (1970) 66.3% USA White (including 1.0% assimilated Hispanic), 11.1% USA Black, 5.5% unassimilated Hispanic. (1980) 62.8% USA White (1.2% assimilated Hispanic), 11.7% Black, 8.2% unassimilated Hispanic. **1980 composition** (in detail): 62.8% USA White (assimilated; English mother-tongue) [ethnic origin: 41.7% Anglo-Saxon (20.0% British, 11.0% German, 5.0% Anglo-Canadian, 3.0% Scandinavian, 1.9% Dutch, 0.7% Austrian, et alii), 8.5% Irish, 7% Latin Mediterranean (2.3% Italian, 1.7% French, 1.0% French-Canadian, 0.4% Portuguese, 0.1% Romanian, et alii), 3% Slavic (1.2% Polish, 0.9% Russian, 0.2% Ukrainian, 0.2% Czech, 0.2% Slovak, 0.1% Ruthenian, Serbo-Croatian, Bulgar), 1.2% Hispanic Latin American (mainly Mexican), 0.9% Greek, 0.2% Armenian, 0.2% Gypsy, 0.1% Arab, Hungarian, Lithuanian, Latvian, Estonian, Albanian, Welsh, Latin American White, Chinese, Japanese & 100 other groups], 11.7% USA Black (Negro; genetically 80% African Negro/20% White, 8.2% unassimilated Hispanic (2.9% Mexican expatriate, 2.9% USA Mestizo (Spanish-speaking; Chicano; citizen of native USA parentage), 0.8% Puerto Rican White, 0.3% Cuban (0.15% expatriate), 0.1% Spaniard, 1.2% other Latin American Mestizo & White expatriate including Bolivian (100,000)), 3.0% Jewish (2.0% German Jew, 0.8% Yiddish), 2.5% German, 2.0% Italian, 1.2% Polish, 1.0% Irish, 0.9% French, 0.5% Austrian, 0.4% British, 0.4% Anglo-Canadian, 0.4% French-Canadian, 0.4% USA Amerindian (including 0.1% part-Indian; largest tribes Navajo (96,700), Cherokee (66,200), Sioux (47,800), Chippewa (42,000), Pueblo (31,000); & 150 other tribes), 0.4% Indo-Pakistani, 0.3% Swedish, 0.3% Japanese, 0.3% Norwegian, 0.3% Hungarian, 0.3% Chinese (Mandarin, Cantonese, Fukienese), 0.2% Dutch, 0.2% Czech, 0.2% Slovak, 0.2% Lithuanian, 0.2% Ruthenian, 0.2% Russian, 0.2% Greek, 0.2% Portuguese, 0.2% Filipino (0.1% Tagalog, 0.1% Ilocan), 0.1% Serbo-Croatian, 0.1% Ukrainian, 0.1% Armenian, 0.1% Finnish, 0.1% Hawaiian (Polynesian), 0.1% Arab, 0.1% Korean (250,000 by 1978), 0.1% Vietnamese (200,000 by 1978), Romanian, Bulgar, Albanian, Byelorussian, Thai, Gypsy (80,000), Caboverdian (Cape Verdean), Eskimo (39,000), & over 70 other groups. All the above groups are 95–100% USA citizens except for groups described as 'expatriate', who are 100% aliens. *Hispanics.* The proportion has increased markedly from 6.5% in 1970 (2.0% Mexican expatriate, 2.0% USA Mestızo (Chicano), 0.7% Puerto Rican, 0.3% Cuban, 0.1% Spaniard, 0.4% other Latin American expatriate, 1.0% assimilated Hispanic), to 9.4% in 1980 as detailed above (8.2% unassimilated Hispanic, 1.2% assimiliated Hispanic). Of this 9.4% in 1980, 5.6% were legal residents, and 3.8% illegal (8.5 million, mostly Mexicans).

**MONEY** (1977). **Monetary unit:** US dollar (= 100 cents).
**National income per person:** US$5,941. Average annual family income: US$18,417.
**Inflation:** (1970–74) 6.2% per year (1975: consumer price index 145), (1977) 6.6% per year.
**Cost of living in capital** (1976): index 100 (Washington DC = 100). Daily cost of living: US$48.

**HEALTH.** Hospitals: 7,678 (1,507,988 beds). Doctors: 333,299. Lepers: 950 (Hawaii 560). Blind (1974): 482,850. Psychotics: 2,100,000. Alcoholics: 4,700,000. Drug addicts: over 700,000 (500,000 on heroin; 36 million have tried cananbis, 4 million cocaine). Criminals (1971): 6,626,100 arrested (1,301,400 for serious crimes).

**EDUCATION.** Adult literacy: (1950) 97%, (1969) 99% (increase from 95% in 1930). Education rate: 78%. Schools: 107,700 (78,100 elementary (14,100 non-public), 29,600 secondary (3,600 non-public)). Universities and colleges: 2,665 (1,182 public, 1,483 non-public).

**LITERATURE.** Annual new book titles (1973): 83,724. Periodicals: 28,500. Scientific journals: 6,100. Newspapers: 1,761 dailies, 9,490 non-daily.

**COMMUNICATION** (per 1,000 people). Phones: 677. Radios: 1,752. TV sets: 549. Daily newspaper circulation: 297 copies.

TABLE 1. RELIGIOUS ADHERENTS IN THE UNITED STATES OF AMERICA

| Year | 1900 | | mid-1970 | | Annual change, 1970–1980 | | | | mid-1975 | | mid-1980 | | 2000 | |
|---|---|---|---|---|---|---|---|---|---|---|---|---|---|---|
| *Name* | *Adherents* | % | *Adherents* | % | *Natural* | *Conversion* | *Total* | *Rate* | *Adherents* | % | *Adherents* | % | *Adherents* | % |
| **Christians** | **73,270,200** | **96.4** | **186,121,000** | **90.8** | **1,718,200** | **−595,900** | **1,122,300** | **0.59** | **191,176,500** | **89.4** | **197,344,000** | **88.0** | **226,563,000** | **85.7** |
| professing | 73,270,200 | 96.4 | 186,121,000 | 90.8 | 1,718,200 | −595,900 | 1,122,300 | 0.59 | 191,176,500 | 89.4 | 197,344,000 | 88.0 | 226,563,000 | 85.7 |
| Protestants | 49,540,200 | 65.2 | 94,701,000 | 46.2 | 818,400 | −1,331,800 | −513,400 | −0.56 | 91,739,400 | 42.9 | 89,567,000 | 40.0 | 90,434,000 | 34.2 |
| Roman Catholics | 13,000,000 | 17.1 | 53,268,000 | 26.0 | 541,000 | 850,000 | 1,391,000 | 2.31 | 60,192,700 | 28.1 | 67,178,000 | 30.0 | 87,785,000 | 33.2 |
| Black/Non-White indigenous | 6,080,000 | 8.0 | 20,356,000 | 9.9 | 195,500 | −57,000 | 138,500 | 0.66 | 20,965,000 | 9.8 | 21,741,000 | 9.7 | 25,385,000 | 9.6 |
| Marginal Protestants | 1,000,000 | 1.3 | 6,600,000 | 3.2 | 65,300 | 81,580 | 146,880 | 2.02 | 7,273,400 | 3.4 | 8,068,800 | 3.6 | 11,370,000 | 4.3 |
| Anglicans | 3,000,000 | 3.9 | 6,146,000 | 3.0 | 51,300 | −127,980 | −76,680 | −1.33 | 5,776,000 | 2.7 | 5,379,200 | 2.4 | 5,289,000 | 2.0 |
| Orthodox | 500,000 | 0.7 | 4,500,000 | 2.2 | 42,200 | −2,200 | 40,000 | 0.85 | 4,700,000 | 2.2 | 4,900,000 | 2.2 | 5,800,000 | 2.2 |
| Catholics (non-Roman) | 150,000 | 0.2 | 550,000 | 0.3 | 4,500 | −8,500 | −4,000 | −0.75 | 530,000 | 0.2 | 510,000 | 0.2 | 500,000 | 0.2 |
| nominal | 18,845,200 | 24.8 | 32,920,376 | 16.1 | 308,000 | 42,562 | 350,562 | 1.03 | 34,124,500 | 16.0 | 36,426,000 | 16.2 | 47,360,000 | 17.9 |
| affiliated | 54,425,000 | 71.6 | 153,200,624 | 74.8 | 1,410,200 | −638,462 | 771,738 | 0.49 | 157,052,000 | 73.4 | 160,918,000 | 71.8 | 179,203,000 | 67.8 |
| total practising | 51,703,750 | *95* | 137,880,560 | *90* | 1,255,100 | −882,372 | 372,728 | 0.27 | 139,776,280 | *89* | 141,607,840 | *88* | 152,322,600 | *85* |
| non-practising | 2,721,250 | *5* | 15,320,060 | *10* | 155,100 | 243,910 | 399,010 | 2.31 | 17,275,720 | *11* | 19,310,160 | *12* | 26,880,400 | *15* |
| Protestants | 35,000,000 | 46.1 | 70,653,087 | 34.5 | 649,500 | −299,809 | 349,691 | 0.48 | 72,401,000 | 33.8 | 74,150,000 | 33.1 | 80,122,000 | 30.3 |
| Evangelicals | 26,598,000 | 35.0 | 50,688,600 | 24.7 | 489,370 | 336,470 | 825,840 | 1.51 | 54,550,900 | 25.5 | 58,947,000 | 26.3 | 74,040,000 | 28.0 |
| Neo-pentecostals | 0 | 0.0 | 600,000 | 0.3 | 8,980 | 71,020 | 80,000 | 8.00 | 1,000,000 | 0.5 | 1,400,000 | 0.6 | 3,000,000 | 1.1 |
| Roman Catholics | 10,775,000 | 14.2 | 48,390,990 | 23.6 | 440,500 | −320,499 | 120,001 | 0.24 | 48,991,000 | 22.9 | 49,591,000 | 22.1 | 54,200,000 | 20.5 |
| Catholic pentecostals | 0 | 0.0 | 200,000 | 0.1 | 10,800 | 169,200 | 180,000 | 15.00 | 1,200,000 | 0.6 | 2,000,000 | 0.9 | 4,230,000 | 1.6 |
| Black/Non-White indigenous | 5,750,000 | 7.6 | 19,678,819 | 9.6 | 184,500 | −23,082 | 161,418 | 0.79 | 20,485,000 | 9.6 | 21,293,000 | 9.5 | 24,856,000 | 9.4 |
| Black Evangelicals | 5,320,000 | 7.0 | 13,551,000 | 6.6 | 129,090 | 39,910 | 169,000 | 1.18 | 14,333,000 | 6.7 | 15,241,000 | 6.8 | 18,775,000 | 7.1 |
| Black neo-pentecostals | 0 | 0.0 | 400,000 | 0.2 | 6,500 | 23,500 | 30,000 | 5.45 | 550,000 | 0.3 | 700,000 | 0.3 | 1,600,000 | 0.6 |
| Marginal Protestants | 800,000 | 1.1 | 6,384,315 | 3.1 | 64,000 | 85,569 | 149,569 | 2.10 | 7,130,000 | 3.3 | 7,880,000 | 3.5 | 10,842,000 | 4.1 |
| Orthodox | 400,000 | 0.5 | 4,387,325 | 2.1 | 40,800 | −9,532 | 31,268 | 0.69 | 4,540,000 | 2.1 | 4,700,000 | 2.1 | 5,550,000 | 2.1 |
| Orthodox pentecostals | 0 | 0.0 | 2,000 | 0.0 | 90 | 1,710 | 1,800 | 18.00 | 10,000 | 0.0 | 20,000 | 0.0 | 100,000 | 0.0 |
| Anglicans | 1,600,000 | 2.1 | 3,234,277 | 1.6 | 26,800 | −64,828 | −38,028 | −1.25 | 3,044,000 | 1.4 | 2,854,000 | 1.3 | 3,173,000 | 1.2 |
| Evangelicals | 150,000 | 0.2 | 485,000 | 0.2 | 4,490 | 1,010 | 5,500 | 1.08 | 510,000 | 0.2 | 540,000 | 0.2 | 700,000 | 0.3 |
| Anglican pentecostals | 0 | 0.0 | 40,000 | 0.0 | 880 | 15,120 | 16,000 | 16.00 | 100,000 | 0.0 | 200,000 | 0.1 | 400,000 | 0.2 |
| Catholics (non-Roman) | 100,000 | 0.1 | 471,811 | 0.2 | 4,100 | −6,281 | −2,181 | −0.47 | 461,000 | 0.2 | 450,000 | 0.2 | 460,000 | 0.2 |
| Non-religious | 1,000,000 | 1.3 | 9,900,000 | 4.8 | 87,700 | 414,000 | 501,700 | 4.05 | 12,380,000 | 5.8 | 14,917,000 | 6.7 | 22,127,000 | 8.4 |
| Jews | 1,500,000 | 2.0 | 6,700,000 | 3.3 | 62,900 | −7,000 | 55,900 | 0.80 | 6,979,500 | 3.3 | 7,259,000 | 3.2 | 8,197,000 | 3.1 |
| Muslims | 10,000 | 0.0 | 800,000 | 0.4 | 37,800 | 70,500 | 108,300 | 8.02 | 1,350,000 | 0.6 | 1,883,000 | 0.8 | 3,173,000 | 1.2 |
| Black Muslims | 0 | 0.0 | 200,000 | 0.1 | 4,500 | 55,500 | 60,000 | 12.00 | 500,000 | 0.2 | 800,000 | 0.3 | 1,700,000 | 0.6 |
| Ahmadis | 0 | 0.0 | 4,000 | 0.0 | 40 | 60 | 100 | 2.22 | 4,500 | 0.0 | 5,000 | 0.0 | 10,000 | 0.0 |
| Atheists | 1,000 | 0.0 | 200,000 | 0.1 | 2,700 | 17,300 | 20,000 | 6.67 | 300,000 | 0.1 | 400,000 | 0.2 | 950,000 | 0.4 |
| Buddhists | 30,000 | 0.0 | 200,000 | 0.1 | 1,900 | −3,900 | −2,000 | −1.05 | 190,000 | 0.1 | 180,000 | 0.1 | 130,000 | 0.0 |
| Baha'is | 2,800 | 0.0 | 138,000 | 0.1 | 1,600 | 5,600 | 7,200 | 4.14 | 174,000 | 0.1 | 210,000 | 0.1 | 350,000 | 0.1 |
| New-Religionists | 0 | 0.0 | 110,000 | 0.0 | 4,000 | 55,000 | 59,000 | 14.75 | 400,000 | 0.2 | 700,000 | 0.3 | 1,100,000 | 0.4 |
| Hindus | 1,000 | 0.0 | 100,000 | 0.0 | 2,700 | 37,300 | 40,000 | 13.33 | 300,000 | 0.1 | 500,000 | 0.2 | 700,000 | 0.3 |
| Chinese folk-religionists | 70,000 | 0.1 | 90,000 | 0.0 | 800 | −800 | 0 | 0.00 | 90,000 | 0.0 | 90,000 | 0.0 | 60,000 | 0.0 |
| Tribal religionists | 100,000 | 0.1 | 70,000 | 0.0 | 600 | −1,600 | −1,000 | −1.54 | 65,000 | 0.0 | 60,000 | 0.0 | 30,000 | 0.0 |
| Other religionists | 10,000 | 0.0 | 450,000 | 0.2 | 4,500 | 9,500 | 14,000 | 2.69 | 520,000 | 0.2 | 590,000 | 0.3 | 1,050,000 | 0.4 |
| **Country's population** | **75,995,000** | **100.0** | **204,879,000** | **100.0** | **1,925,400** | **0** | **1,925,400** | **0.90** | **213,925,000** | **100.0** | **224,133,000** | **100.0** | **264,430,000** | **100.0** |

COLUMNS, ROWS. For meanings and definitions, see Codebook (Part 6). Note that, by definition, total 'Christians' = professing + crypto-Christians, which also = affiliated + nominal Christians. Percentages may not always total exactly, due to rounding. *Natural change.* The column of this name above includes both biological increase (with certain groups including Roman Catholic and Blacks having higher fertility than the national average) and also nett immigration increase (with certain non-Christian religions in particular having higher immigration rates than the national average.
CENSUSES. No question on religious adherence (profession) has ever been included in the decennial US censuses. However, enumerators collected statistics direct from churches during the censuses of 1850, 1860, 1870, 1880 and 1890; and in 1906, 1916, 1926 and 1936, the US Bureau of the Census conducted a Census of Religious Bodies; since the membership statistics thus obtained came direct from church bodies themselves they therefore measured not what we here term professing Christians but what we term affiliated Christians. *Statistics for 1900.* Our estimates for the year 1900 in the table above are based on the government enumerations of 1890 and 1906, modified by the methodology evolved in this survey. *Recent statistics.* In 1957, the US Bureau of the Census took a sample survey of religious profession of adults (of 14 years and older), which showed: 66.8% Protestants (including Episcopalians, Black church adherents, and marginal Protestants) (19.9% Baptists, 14.1% Methodists, 7.1% Lutherans, 5.6% Presbyterians, 20.1% others), 25.9% Roman Catholics, 3.3% Jews, 2.7% non-religious, 1.3% Orthodox, Old Catholics, other Christians and other religionists.
POLLS. A very large number of questions on religious adherence (religious preference or profession) have been asked since 1935 in public-opinion polls with nation-wide samples (Gallup, NORC, Harris, et alia). Those up to 1964 are summarized in H.G. Erskine, 'The polls: organized religion', *Public opinion quarterly*, XXIX (1965), 326–337. Subsequent to 1955, the Gallup Opinion Index (AIPO) has taken regular polls, published in *Special report on religion* (February, 1969), *Religion in America* (1971, 1975, 1977–78), et alia; there are also data from NORC, Harris, et alia. The polls figures for the period 1950–60 are virtually identical with the US Bureau of the Census 1957 sample survey. Around 1965, polls indicated that the religious profession of the population stood at 64% Protestants (including Black church adherents, and marginal Protestants; subdivided into 21% Baptists, 14% Methodists, 7% Lutherans, 6% Presbyterians, but excluding Episcopalians), 26% Roman Catholics, 3% Anglicans (Episcopalians), 3% Jews, about 3% non-religious, and the remainder Orthodox and others. (Note: polls figures are always given rounded to the nearest integer). Thereafter, there was a shift to (1970) 61% Protestants & Blacks, 26% Roman Catholics, 5% non-religious and atheists, 3% Episcopalians, 3% Jews; and (1980) 55% Protestants & Blacks (26% Baptists, 9% Methodists,

6% Lutherans, 5% Presbyterians), 30% Roman Catholics, 7% non-religious and atheists, 3% Episcopalians, 3% Jews (AIPO). *Church membership.* Persons claiming to be church members (i.e. affiliated) have fallen from 77% in 1936 to 73% (1965) to 71% (1975) and to 69% (1979) (*Religion in America 1979-80*, p.37). *Active or practising church members.* Persons so claiming, 56% of adult population in 1976 (AIPO). *Pentecostal-charismatics* (1980 Christianity Today/Gallup poll). (a) *Self-identification, preference, profession:* 19% of all USA adults over 17 years (29 million) consider themselves to be Pentecostal or charismatic Christians, or to be more related to this tradition than to any other, or to have belonged to it in the past (3.1% being Classical Pentecostals affiliated to the Pentecostal denominations, 5.4% professing to be Roman Catholic charismatics, and 9.6% professing to be neo-Pentecostals (two-thirds Whites, one-third Blacks)): this 19% represents the total population influenced by Pentecostalism and the charismatic movement; though 77% of them are affiliated to churches, and 49% of them attend church weekly, only 19% of them all are regularly and actively involved in charismatic prayer groups or ministries (tongues-speaking, healing, etc). (b) *Tongues-speaking* as a criterion: only one-sixth of this 19%, or 3.6% of the adult population (5 million adults) have actually spoken in tongues (86% of these being Protestant, 14% RC). (c) *Active or practising charismatics:* from 1976-80 (AIPO/PRRC), about the same number, namely 3% of the adult population, were actively involved regularly in Pentecostal-charismatic activities. *Classical Pentecostals.* Of the 7 million members of Classical Pentecostal denominations (including Black pentecostals) in the USA in 1980, studies show that only 30% to 50% speak in tongues, and only 50%-60% are charismatically active on a regular basis. *Total active Pentecostal-charismatics.* From these figures, we deduce a total regularly-active Pentecostal-charismatic community including children of 3.5% of the USA total population in 1980, i.e. 7,800,000, made up as follows: (1) 3,400,000 Classical Pentecostals (50% of all members of Pentecostal and Black pentecostal denominations); and (2) 4,400,000 active charismatics in the non-Pentecostal denominations, defined as and restricted here to active charismatic-oriented persons and groups usually or predominantly made up of active tongues-speakers or tongues-emphasizers who stress or recognize as their norm the charismatic ministries (prayer groups/tongues/prophecy/interpretation/healing); and made up of 2,000,000 active Catholic pentecostals, 1,400,000 active Protestant neo-pentecostals (mostly Whites), 700,000 active Black neo-pentecostals, 200,000 active Anglican pentecostals, and a few others. *Non-traditional religious movements.* A 1976 Gallup poll found 12% of American adults engaged in these movements: 4% in TM (Transcendental Meditation), 3% in Yoga, 2% in the charismatic movement (3 million persons), 2% in mysticism, 1% in Eastern religions. *Unchurched persons.* A major Gallup poll on this subject was conducted in April 1978; its data and findings are reported below in the footnote NOMINAL CHRISTIANS.

## NOTES ON RELIGIONS

AHMADIS. Ahmadiya (Qadianis, from Pakistan) has had its USA HQ in Washington since its beginning in 1921. Followers are US Blacks with some Pakistani immigrants. From 1975, there have been 5 Pakistani missionaries in the USA.

ANGLICAN PENTECOSTALS (or, Episcopalian charismatics). The pentecostal or charismatic renewal within the non-Pentecostal denominations in the USA began in 1960 within the Protestant Episcopal Church. By 1973 it involved 30,000 adults (60,000 total community) in 1,500 prayer groups, including over 1,100 clergy and several bishops, the totals increasing rapidly (to 3,200 clergy by 1977). These figures include Episcopalian youth involved in the Jesus Movement (Jesus People).

ATHEISTS. Communist Party of the USA (CPUSA) (legal, pro-Soviet): membership (1970) 14,000; about 7 splinter groups including pro-Chinese Progressive Labour Party (PLP), WWP, MLCP, SWP, ACFI: total membership about 3,000. Polls occasionally enumerate declared atheists: in universities (1960) 1%; among youths aged 18–24 (1974) 1%.

BAHA'IS. Entered USA soon after 1892. Rapid growth from 350 local spiritual assemblies (1964) to 928 (1973); many young White adherents. One of the world's 7 Baha'i Houses of Worship (temples) is at Wilmette, Chicago. From 1970–72 in South Carolina, nearly 20,000 rural Blacks were claimed to have joined as converts. In 1970 there were 23,879 regularly-active adult Baha'is in the USA excluding Alaska and Hawaii, with an annual increase of 3,219 members. The statistics on this line in the table refer to total adherents including children, and also include the largest of several minor schisms from Baha'i, the Orthodox Abha World Faith begun in 1960 by an American, Charles Mason Remey, who claimed to be the Second Guardian of the Faith. It also has a handful of followers in Pakistan and elsewhere.

BLACK MUSLIMS. Officially termed the World Community of Al-Islam in the West (America), or (before 1977) the Nation of Islam; also called Bilalians. Begun 1913 as Moorish Science Temples; 1930 Temple of Islam; 1959, 30,000; 1961, 69 USA temples and 100,000 followers; 1975, claimed a total community of 500,000 US Blacks, 300,000 being militants, in 80 temples, with 50,000 new converts a year mostly nominally-Christian Blacks. By the end of 1976 over 235 mosques had been set up, daily radio broadcasts of Quranic verses and teachings were under way, and the movement was being realigned with orthodox Quranic Islam.

BLACK/NON-WHITE INDIGENOUS or (more fully) BLACK/NON-WHITE/THIRD-WORLD INDIGENOUS CHRISTIANS, i.e. persons in churches indigenous to the Black/Non-White population or to the Third World (see extended definition and discussion in Part 3). *Statistics for 1900.* These are based on those reported for the year 1906 by the US Bureau of the Census, when those reporting numbered 29,547 all-Negro congregations (18,359 Baptist, 11,188 Methodist) with 3,166,393 communicant members (2,296,683 Baptists, 869,710 Methodists); the total community of Negro independent churches then was about 6 million including children, infants and adherents. Since in the year 1900 the USA had a Negro population of 8,834,000 (11.6% of the total population), this indicates that persons affiliated to Negro independent churches in 1900 numbered around 5,650,000 or 64% of all Negroes. Another type of indigenous church at that period was the Native American Church with around 100,000 Indians (about 40% of the 237,200 American Indians then). In sum, as Table 2 below indicates, there were in the year 1900 about 20 Black independent denominations in existence (7 Methodist, 7 pentecostal, 3 Baptist, 1 Reformed) and 6 American Indian denominations. *Statistics for 1970.* In the year 1970, this bloc's 19,678,819 affiliated adherents in the USA consisted of over 200 distinct and separate denominations (as detailed in Table 2 below) in 4 distinct groups: (1) 18,929,019 in US Black churches (including 2,753,090 Black pentecostals), (2) 482,000 in American Indian churches, (3) 184,000 in Hispanic (Spanish-speaking; Spanish American and Latin American) churches, and (4) 83,800 in other immigrant Third-World indigenous churches.

BLACK NEO-PENTECOSTALS. Active charismatics (more traditionally, 'sanctified' Black/Negro/Coloured persons) in the non-pentecostal Black denominations (NBCUSA, NBCA, AMEC, AMEZC, CMEC, PBC, et alia). About 6 million others call themselves charismatics but are not actively involved.

BUDDHISTS. This category here covers only orthodox Buddhism, excluding the Japanese New Religions (Soka Gakkai et alia, listed here under NEW-RELIGIONISTS). Buddhists are Japanese and Chinese, with White converts; including 121,000 in Hawaii, 2,000 adherents of Zen in 12 centres, and 1,000 Kalmyk Tartar Buddhists in New Jersey. There are also several Lamaist temples, built with government grants from China (Taiwan), for Mongolians resident in the USA; and adherents of over 40 other Buddhist sects. In the year 1900, Buddhists included most of the 24,326 Japanese in the USA and some of the 89,863 Chinese. From 1960 onwards, large numbers of Buddhists began to be converted to the Japanese New Religions, especially to Nichiren Shoshu (Soka Gakkai). In particular, the organized Buddhist Churches of America (founded 1899; representing the Jodo Shinshu sect of Buddhism in the USA) reported a rapid decline in membership over the period 1970–74, from 100,000 with 101 priests in 1970, to 60,000 with 86 priests in 1974.

CATHOLIC PENTECOSTALS (or, Catholic charismatics). Since its beginning at Duquesne University in 1967, the Catholic Charismatic Renewal (CCR) in the USA grew rapidly to involve 200,000 charismatic or neo-pentecostal adult Catholics by 1972, and 500,000 (these being adults over 15 with a definite commitment to Christ) by 1974, rising to around 670,000 by mid-1976, and including a score of bishops and 3 cardinals, in 1,800 prayer groups. Most members are 20–40 years old. These statistics do not include children or infants; if the children of members are included the totals should be at least doubled, giving in 1974 a Catholic charismatic community of 1 million in the USA, rising to 1.2 million in 1975. All these totals include Catholic youth involved in the Jesus Movement (Jesus People). In addition to these committed members shown in the table, there were in 1977 a further one million or more sympathizing Catholics involved or less involved than those with full commitment. By 1980, 8 million adult Catholics were identifying themselves as charismatics, though not all actively involved. The future numerical expansion of the active movement shown in the table above is only one possible projection based on current trends.

CHINESE FOLK-RELIGIONISTS. Chinese in the USA increased from 34,933 in 1860, to 89,863 in 1900, to 435,062 in 1970. Initially the majority practised Chinese folk religion, with some Buddhists; now only a decreasing minority practise either.

COUNTRY'S POPULATION. The column 'Natural increase' includes both biological increase (births minus deaths each year) and also migration increase (in 1970, a total of 373,000 immigrants into the USA, rising to a million a year, including illegal immigrants, by 1980). Major refugee migrations to the USA since 1950 include 40,000 Hungarians, 600,000 Cubans and 130,000 Indo-chinese.

EVANGELICALS. In the table above, there are 3 separate rows termed Evangelicals, indicating that in the USA the term is used to cover 3 groupings, Protestant Evangelicals, Black Evangelicals and Anglican (Episcopalian) Evangelicals. There is a history of polls on this subject. In a 1955 poll (Opinion Research Corporation) of Protestant and Episcopalian clergymen, 35% stated that they were Fundamentalist, 39% Conservative or Conservative Evangelical, and 26% Neo-orthodox or Liberal. A 1970 poll found that about 42 million adults in the USA (30%) said they were Evangelicals, found primarily in the Protestant and Black denominations. A 1976 poll (AIPO) gave the following percentages for evangelicals (with a small 'e') in various church traditions: 42% of all Baptists, 39% of Lutherans, 28% of Methodists, 22% of Presbyterians, 25% of Episcopalians, and 60% of all Black Christians. AIPO's definition included Roman Catholics who term themselves evangelicals, whereas our definition of Evangelicals here refers (more correctly) only to Protestants, Anglicans and Non-White indigenous Christians.

In 1970 our table above indicates that in all denominations these together totalled 64,724,600 Evangelicals (31.6% of the total population), increasing by 1975 to 69,393,900 (32.4%). The 3 groupings we use in our table are defined, and may be further subdivided, as follows (with 1970 statistics added). (1) *Protestant Evangelicals* (50.7 million or 24.7% in 1970) from a movement within the Protestant churches, and consist of 3 major subdivisions: (a) Conservative Evangelicals (26 million in 1970), sometimes also called non-Conciliar Evangelicals, or Neo-Evangelicals, or Neo-Fundamentalists, enumerated here in 2 groups: (i) the total communities, including children, affiliated to institutionalized Conservative Evangelicalism, i.e. to the NAE (4.1 million) or the WEF (6.1 million in the USA), and (ii) the total communities affiliated to all other Conservative Evangelical denominations which are not aligned with the NAE or WEF (19 million in the USA), of which the largest are the Southern Baptist Convention (14.2 million in 1970; approximately 95% Evangelical, 5% Liberal), Churches of Christ (Non-Instrumental) (4.0 million), and Lutheran Church—Missouri Synod (3.0 million), together with a mass of smaller denominations and isolated congregations; (b) Conciliar Evangelicals (19 million in 1970), sometimes called ecumenical Evangelicals but who usually call themselves simply Evangelicals, who remain within and are affiliated to Protestant denominations not regarded as entirely Conservative Evangelical but which are instead within the Ecumenical Movement affiliated to the NCCCUSA and/or the WCC (e.g. American Baptist Churches in the USA, who are about 50% Evangelicals); and (c) Fundamentalists (20 million in 1970), moderate or extreme, enumerated here as the total communities of Protestant denomination of fundamentalist doctrine and emphasis, in several cases affiliated to the ACCC, ACAC or ICCC. Secondly, (2) *Black Evangelicals* (13.6 million or 6.6% in 1970) are affiliated members of Black denominations in the USA who regard themselves as Evangelicals or part of the Conservative Evangelical movement; the largest denominational group is that in the NBCUSA (itself 6.4 million) which is the most conservative of the 3 largest Black Baptist denominations. Thirdly, (3) *Anglican Evangelicals* (485,000 in 1970) are those within the Episcopal Church in the USA, together with members of several Anglican Evangelical bodies, shown in Table 2 below, which have split from ECUSA. *Experience of new birth.* Traditionally this emphasis, together with literal belief in the Bible and personal evangelism, have been regarded as the hallmarks of Evangelicalism, but by 1976 they were also characterizing large sections of non-Evangelical and non-Protestant denominations. In a 1976 Gallup poll, 34% of all Americans (nearly 50 million over age 18; 48% of all Protestants, 18% of all Catholics) said they had had a 'born-again' experience, a turning-point where they committed themselves to Jesus Christ; 38% of Americans are biblical fundamentalists, believing the Bible 'literally, word for word'; and, 47% of the population (58% of all Protestants) said they had done personal witnessing (encouraging others to believe in Christ or to accept him as Saviour). A large number of all these persons are not Evangelicals nor Protestants but are Episcopalians or Roman Catholics, especially Catholic pentecostals and other charismatics.

HINDUS. These include (1975) about 30,000 Hindu immigrants from India, and also large numbers of American devotees of about 60 neo-Hindu or new Hindu sects: 50,000 adult Americans (by 1973) who have 'taken knowledge' in the Divine Light Mission (DLM) led by Guru Maharaj Ji since its introduction in 1971; about 10,000 followers of ISKCON (International Society for Krishna Consciousness, or the Hare Krishna Movement) introduced in 1965, with 28 centres and 6 farms by 1975; about 2,000 adherents (with 500 committed disciples) of the Bengali movement Sri Chinmoy Centre; 7,000 followers of messiah Meher Baba; 67 centres of the Self-Realization Fellowship (150 centres worldwide); 20 satsang societies of Eckankar (500,000 followers worldwide); 11 Sri Aurobindo Society centres; 2,000 in the Ramakrishna Mission; Ananda Marga (Path of Bliss); the neo-Hindu movement the Theosophical Society in America (in 1975, 93 Lodges with 5,280 members); et alia. There is also a movement with Hindu origins which claims to be a philosophy but not a religion: the Science of Creative Intelligence (SCI) with about 80,000 adult meditators (with 500,000 followers in other religions also) following Transcendental Meditation (TM, introduced about 1963), with over 4,000 teachers; on the world scene it has 1.3 million meditators and 10,000 teachers, mainly in the USA, UK, Germany and Switzerland.

JEWS. Growth: beginning in 1654 with 23 Portuguese Sefardi Jews in New Amsterdam; 3,000 in 1776, 15,000 (1840); then waves of Ashkenazi immigration from Germany in the 1840s and 1850s; 200,000 (1858, 1,500,000 (1900), 4,200,000 (1928), 3,868,000 professing Jews of 14 years and over (3.27% of the entire population) in 1957 survey (US Bureau of the Census); 5,500,000 affiliated to 3,990 synagogues and congregations in 1964, 6,115,000 affiliated to 5,000 congregations in 1972, with 6,400 rabbis (5,100 in charge of congregations). The statistics on this line in the table refer to professing Jews (including both those affiliated to synagogues and those not affiliated). *Divisions.* 28% Orthodox (in congregations with 1 million active members), 42% Conservative (1.5 million), 30% Reform (1.1 million). *Weekly attendance at synagogues.* This declined gradually from 27% of all Jews in 1955 to 25% in 1963, to 19% in 1973, and to 16% in 1974. *Race.* The great majority of USA Jews are White, but about 250,000 are Black, of 5 kinds: (1) Blacks in White Jewish synagogues; (2) Black Jews: 38,000 in the Church of God and Saints of Christ (classified in this Encyclopedia as a Christian rather than a Jewish body), and Church of God (Black Jews); (3) 150,000 Black Hebrews, followers of conservative Orthodox Judaism; (4) Falashas (Black Jews) from Ethiopia; and (5) many thousands of Black Israelites (Original Hebrew Israelite Nation), many of whom have emigrated to Israel. *Organizations.* There are over 220 national Jewish organizations in the USA. *Periodicals.* There are over 210 Jewish periodicals and newspapers in 43 states. *Conversions from Judaism.* Since 1965 an estimated 30,000 American Jews have become Christians (survey by Jews for Jesus Organization); by 1972, about 6,500 young Jews were converting to Christianity each year. There are about 10,000 in Hebrew-Christian bodies, 100,000 Jews (including children and infants) belong to the main USA Protestant denominations, and a further large number prefer to remain as witnesses to Jesus within their own synagogues and communities. In addition to conversions to Christianity, there is a small number of Jews each year who abandon religion and regard themselves as non-religious.

MARGINAL PROTESTANTS. In about 330 denominations in 1970 (see Table 2). Many have grown very rapidly since 1900; e.g. Mormons from 268,331 (1900) to 393,437 (1910), 526,032 (437,500 in the USA) (1920), 672,488 (541,900 in the USA) (1930), 862,664 (670,500 in the USA) (1940), 1,111,314 (926,700 in the USA) (1950), 1,693,180 (1,422,700 in the USA) (1960), 2,930,810 (2,016,800 in the USA) (1970), and to 3,321,556 in 1973. In 1906 also there were 70,542 adult Unitarians, 64,158 Universalists, and 85,717 Christian Scientists (the latter rising to 268,915 in 1936). The annual growth rates for 1970 or 1965–75 are given in Table 2, column 8. Unitarian Universalists are declining; Mormons, Jehovah's Witnesses, Worldwide Church of God and other newer bodies are increasing rapidly.

MUSLIMS. There are 3 groupings. (1) Orthodox (mainly Sunni) Muslims: their number has increased greatly since 1900 with the immigration of Middle East Arabs (300,000 by 1970), Turks (24,000), Persians (24,000), Albanians (8,000), Malays (6,000), and other Muslim peoples, making a total of over 800,000 by 1975; (2) the World Community of Islam in the West (America) (before 1977 called the Nation of Islam), or Black Muslims, or Bilalians; and (3) Ahmadiya. These last 2 are enumerated here under Muslims although Black Muslims are regarded as heretical by the bulk of Islam, and Ahmadis have been declared non-Muslim by Pakistan. *Hajj pilgrims to Mecca.* (1970) 84; (1974) 136; (1975) 354; (1976) 80.

NEO-PENTECOSTALS. Charismatics active in the organized charismatic renewal who remain within non-Pentecostal Protestant denominations numbered in 1973 around 305,000 adults (or total charismatic community including children, 610,000) in around 5,000 prayer groups, the adults being distributed approximately as follows: 30,000 Baptists (including 10,000 Southern Baptists), 110,000 Lutherans, 45,000 Methodists, 40,000 Presbyterians and Reformed, and at least 80,000 in other Protestant denominations including 1,000 SDAs; and these totals were rapidly growing. In addition, youth in these denominations who were involved in the Jesus Movement (Jesus People) were estimated in 1972 at considerably over 200,000 in over 5,000 communes and communities. Allowing for overlapping involvements, this makes a total Neo-pentecostal community of about 800,000 in 1973 rising to around one million by 1975. By 1977, most large denominations had sizeable charismatic followings (e.g. American Baptist Churches in the USA, with over 100,000), and most had each its own denominational charismatic organization for fellowship and services. The number of priests and clergy involved averages 10–15% of all clergy in each denomination. By 1977 the renewal was still largely White, on non-Black, with very few participants from the Black churches (AMEC, AMEZC, NBCA, NBCUSA, et alia) and little contact with the Black pentecostal churches in the USA. In 1980, some 6 million more called themselves charismatics though not actively involved.

NEW-RELIGIONISTS. Several of the Japanese syncretistic New Religions (or, new religious movements) have branches in the USA; of these the largest is Nichiern Shoshu of America (NSA) (True Church of Nichiren), known in Japan as Soka Gakkai (Value Creation Society). Begun in Los Angeles in 1960 with 300 Japanese members, the USA branch had 30,000 by 1967; and in 1972, NSA claimed 100,000 households, with 300,000 members (70% non-Asians; including 28,800 in Hawaii) and 60,000 Americans (mostly young Whites) were undergoing *shakubuku* (aggressive-conversion process) each year. Among the smaller Japanese bodies are the Sect of the Dancing Goddess (Tensho Kotai Jingu Kyo) in Hawaii, and the Church of Perfect Liberty (PL Kyodan) with 5,000 US adherents mainly in southern California (50% Japanese, 25% White, 15% Black, 10% Spanish-

American; 6 churches, 15 missions); also Tenrikyo (2,000 members, 99% Japanese, in 60 churches and missions in the USA), Seicho no Iye (7,000 in the USA, 98% Japanese), and Sekai Kyusei Kyo (Church of World Messianity; 3,500 in USA, half in Hawaii; 35% Japanese). By 1975, there were other New Religions also from Korea, Viet Nam, Indonesia (including 2,000 followers in 70 cities of Subud, founded 1925 in Indonesia) and the Chinese diaspora.

NOMINAL CHRISTIANS. Defined in this Encyclopedia as: Persons professing in polls to be Christians, but not affiliated to churches, i.e. not church members; unaffiliated or unchurched; Christians not, or no longer, attached to organized Christianity, or who have rejected the institutional churches whilst retaining Christian beliefs and values. In the USA, these nominal Christians are mainly Protestants (chiefly Methodists, Baptists, Presbyterians, Lutherans). In the early days of the USA republic, up to as late as 1900, large numbers of professing Christians, especially recent immigrants, remained uncontacted by, and hence unaffiliated to, the various denominations. By the 1970s, large numbers of nominal Christians were involved in occult religions (see note on OTHER RELIGIONISTS below).

A full statistical study of this category in the USA has been provided by Gallup International in their poll 'The unchurched American' (June 1978), whose main finding was: 'A majority of American adults who for one reason or another have rejected the institutional church still adhere to most traditional Christian beliefs and values'. Gallup's definition of the category 'unchurched' is considerably more inclusive than this Encyclopedia's as given above, being defined by Gallup as 'those who are not members of a church or synagogue or have not attended a worship service (apart from weddings or funerals) during the past six months' (yielding in April 1978 a total of 41% of all adult Americans, or 61 million adults, or 90 million Americans of all ages including children). Gallup's definition covers, and is equivalent to, the following categories described in this Encyclopedia (with January 1978 percentages of total population as shown in this Table 1 above): (1) nominal Christians (16.1%), (2) non-practising Christians (8.1%), (3) practising Christians who are annual attenders only (i.e. attending public worship less often than once every 2 months; 6.5%), (4) nominal Jews, non-practising Jews, and Jewish once-annually attenders (1.6%), (5) all atheists and agnostics and other non-religious persons (6.7%), and (6) adherents of all other non-Christians religions, religious movements, cults and philosophies (1.9%). Most persons in categories (5) and (6) have, of course, never been church members of any kind, and so they ought not, strictly speaking, to be termed 'unchurched'. Altogether, these 6 categories of ours add up to 40.9% of the total population or 89.6 million Americans, which is almost identical to the Gallup totals.

Among Gallup's findings were the following. (a) Demographically, the unchurched were more likely to be young, single or divorced, and male; mobile; 55% professed to be Protestants and 18% Catholics. (b) There is a remarkably small degree of difference in basic Christian beliefs between churched and unchurched. Many unchurched were 'very religious', with 25% of them reporting a significant 'born-again' experience; 43% of them were providing their children with religious and moral training at home and in school; 68% believed in the resurrection of Christ, 64% in his deity, 73% in the Bible as the inspired Word of God. (c) Reasons given for rejecting the institutional church represent a severe indictment of organized religion's sincerity and relevance in the modern world. (d) 90% of the unchurched (as well as 70% of all churched) believed that 'One can be a good Christian or Jew and still not attend church or synagogue'.

NON-RELIGIOUS. Persons professing no religion, or agnostics, have increased gradually over recent years. In the 1950s, persons who were not Protestant, Catholic or Jew but who had another religion or no religion averaged under 3% in all polls. In the 1957 survey (US Bureau of the Census), those with no religion numbered 2.7%. In the 1960s, those with no religion averaged 3–4%. From 1970–75, those with no formal religion or religious preference rose from 5% to 6%, of whom at least 3% regarded themselves as definitely non-believers, the rest being indifferent to religion (*Religion in America 1975*, Gallup).

ORTHODOX PENTECOSTALS (or, Orthodox charismatics). The charismatic renewal within the Orthodox churches began in 1968 in the Greek Orthodox Archdiocese. By 1973 it involved over 30 Greek parishes with 12 priests and 2,000 lay adults, also 2 Antiochian priests, some in the OCA, some Ukrainian Orthodox, and 3 priests in ROCOR. The movement was in 1975 encountering considerable church opposition, in contrast to its Catholic, Protestant and Episcopalian counterparts.

OTHER RELIGIONISTS. This term covers only committed non-Christian members of a large number of smaller bodies, including the following: (1) a host of non-Christian or part-Christian or syncretistic movements begun in the USA, including non-Christian Spiritism, Rosicrucianism (AMORC, begun 1915 and now with 91 Lodges; 2 centres of Lectorium Rosicrucianum; and over 8 other bodies), Neo-Paganism, Druidism, Psychiana, Mighty I Am (at one time claiming 350,000), Church Universal and Triumphant (Summit International; 1958 split from I Am; 80 centres, also 6 overseas countries especially Ghana), Arcane School, Astara Foundation, Satanic Church (15,000), First Church of Voodoo (Tennessee) and other occult, psychical and magical bodies, together with a large number of persons experimenting with Eastern mysticism; (2) immigrant Asian religions including 43,500 Shintoists in Hawaii, Parsis, 5,000 Indian Sikhs and several thousand White Americans in the quasi-Sikh Healthy-Happy-Holy Organization (3HO) (110 ashrams in the USA, Canada and overseas in 1977), et alia (in 1970 new immigrants from Asia numbered 91,059; in 1972, 115,978); and (3) immigrant religions from elsewhere, including Afro-American spiritists (Santeria from Cuba, with centres in Miami and many northern cities among immigrant Cubans with some US Black followers; Vodoun; over 7,000 Rastafarians (from Jamaica and West Indies islands) in New York, many allegedly with criminal records; et alii). In addition to these committed non-Christian members, it is estimated that some 10 million Americans dabble in the occult arts (witchcraft, black masses, orgies), of whom at least 6 million are devotees or part-time adherents of some sect or cult; and a further 15 million (mostly nominal Christians) are sympathetic and interested onlookers. The 10,000 registered astrologers in the USA claim 40 million customers a year. Another quasi-religious movement is Freemasonry, an international male brotherhood which is the largest worldwide secret society and which affirms belief in the Supreme Being and reveres the Bible as the Volume of the Sacred Law. Of the USA's 4 million Freemasons, some practice it as a non-Christian religion, although most are either professing or nominal Protestants, or non-religious.

PRACTISING CHRISTIANS. There has been since 1939 a large number of USA-wide polls recording weekly, monthly and once-yearly church attendance (those up to 1964 are listed in H.G. Erskine, 'The polls: church attendance', *Public opinion quarterly*, XXVIII (1964), 671–9; see also detailed reports of Gallup (AIPO), Roper, Harris, et alia). *Weekly attendance.* Taken together, these indicate that for the whole adult population attendance on a normal Sunday (not Easter or Christmas) rose from 36% in 1942 to a peak of 49% in 1955, and 48% in 1960, after which it has declined steadily to 42% in 1970 and remained constant at 40% for 1971, 1972, 1973, 1974 and 1975, and rose to 42% in 1976. It must be noted that, on our definition, '40% of the whole population' means that 53% of all affiliated Christians are weekly attenders. Seasonally, attendance is highest during the year in February, March and April. *Mid-week attendance.* In a 1975 poll, 20% of all adults stated that during that week they had participated in religious activities other than church services, i.e. prayer group meetings, Bible study classes, et alia. *Monthly attendance.* Those going to church once a month or more averaged 57% of the total population in 1943, 58% in 1944, 62% in 1960 and 68% in 1963, falling to about 64% in 1970. *Active attenders.* In 1976, 68% of the adult population stated that they were church members, and 56% claimed active membership (AIPO). *Once-yearly attendance.* Those attending church (or synagogue/mosque/temple) at least once a year, including those attending only on special family occasions, averaged 82% of the total population during the period 1960–70. A typical poll, May–June 1968 (Gallup): church (including synagogue/mosque/temple) attenders 41% of population weekly, 11% fortnightly, 5% once every 3 weeks, 7% once monthly, 18% once every 2 months, 18% less than annually, or never. Using our present definitions (excluding those who only attend church on special family occasions, but including the elderly, infirm and sick who listen to services over radio), this means that annually-practising Christians in 1970 were about 67% of the total population. *Practising Christians.* All these preceding attendance polls percentages apply to the total adult population of the USA. In this Encyclopedia, however, it is pointed out that the children and infants of practising Christians can also be active attenders and should therefore also be enumerated; hence the adult percentages here can fairly be extended to apply to the entire population. Moreover, according to our interpretation, Christian practice should always be expressed as a percentage not of a nations' total population but of its affiliated Christians only, who in the USA in 1970 numbered 74.8% of the total population. On this definition, then, Christian practice around 1970 was as follows: weekly attenders, 53%; monthly attenders, 80%; attenders at public worship once a year or more (the definition here of 'practising Christians'), 90%. This latter is the figure used for 1970 in the table above, from which the absolute numbers have been computed. *Protestant practice* (AIPO). Weekly attendance on the part of professing (not affiliated) Protestants (this term, in polls, covering also Episcopalians, marginal Protestants, and Black church adherents) rose gradually from 33% in 1950 to 38% in 1964, and 39% in 1967, subsequently remaining at 37% from 1971–74 (Lutherans 43%, Baptists 39%, Methodists 38%, Presbyterians 34%, Episcopalians 29%), then rising in 1976 to 40%. *Catholic practice* (AIPO). Weekly attendance on the part of professing (not affiliated) Roman Catholics has declined gradually from 78% in 1954, to 71% in 1964, 65% in 1968, 56% in 1972, to 55% in 1973 and 50% in 1974, rising again to 55% in 1976. These findings indicate that the decline in weekly churchgoing in the USA from 1964–73 is a Catholic, not a Protestant, phenomenon. Once-yearly attendance moreover has declined far less noticeably.

PROTESTANTS. This term in almost all polls, and to the US Bureau of the Census (1957 et alia), includes also Episcopalians (Anglicans), marginal Protestants, and members of Black and Third-World indigenous churches. In our present survey, we exclude these latter 3 blocs from our definition of Protestants. *Losses and gains.* The column in the table 'Total annual change' indicates a nett loss by conversion of 299,800 affiliated Protestants every year during the period 1970–80, offset and hidden by a larger natural (biological and immigration) increase. This nett loss itself masks great variations among denominations: Methodists, Presbyterians and Lutherans are losing vast numbers of members each year, whilst other traditions, mainly Pentecostals, are gaining them. The exact annual growth or decline figures for 1970 or the period 1965–75 are given for many denominations in Table 2, column 8. The most rapid nett losses have been experienced by the United Presbyterian Church in the USA, whose total annual change averaged −2.3% per year, with a peak of −3.5% per year in 1973.

ROMAN CATHOLICS. The proportions of professing and affiliated Catholics in the USA have increased since 1900, and are still increasing, due to both immigration (especially of Puerto Ricans, whose immigration is restricted by no quota) and higher natural fertility of Catholic families. Conversions, which have declined in number recently, are mostly due to mixed marriages. *Growth.* By 1977 Catholics had increased to 49,325,752, with an annual increase of 443,880 after several years of annual decreases.

TRIBAL RELIGIONISTS. American Indians in the USA declined in numbers from 850,000 in the 16th century to 237,196 in 1900, at which time nearly half still followed Indian traditional or shamanistic religion. In 1970, they had increased again to 792,730 in 150 tribes, of whom about 9% professed to be traditionalists and 91% Christians.

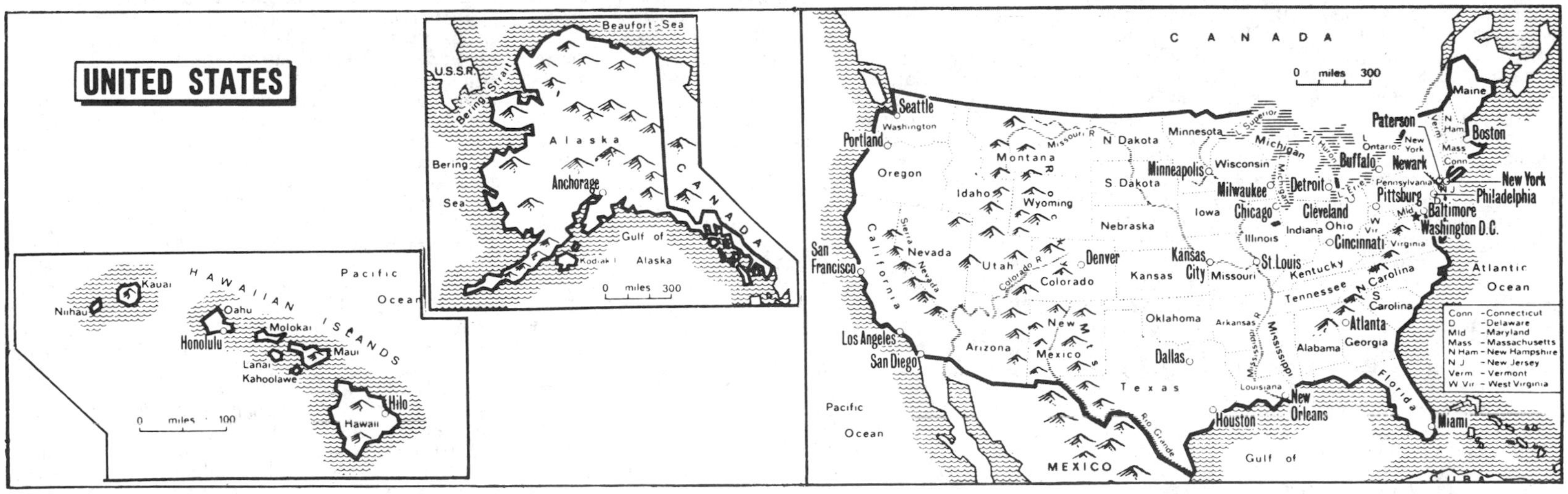


**NON-CHRISTIAN RELIGIONS. Judaism** is a major force in American life. The Jewish community, numbering over 6 million, constitutes the largest concentration of Jews in the world, twice the number of Jews in Israel and also in the USSR, and accounts for nearly half of world Jewry. Despite their small numbers relative to the general population, Jews hold generally high status as one of the so-called 3 major religions in the USA, namely Protestant, Catholic, Jew, these being regarded as the 'triple melting pot' through which the American identity is realized. Even though the Jewish community is only 3% of the total population, both as a group and individually it plays significant roles in such spheres of American life as religion, education, cultural activities and national urban politics.

The Jews have their greatest numerical population strength in the metropolitan centres of the USA (over 3.7 million in 10 cities), although since World War II there has been a pronounced move to the suburbs. In recent years, there has been a gradual decline in numbers owing to a low fertility rate (2.1%), and a rise in intermarriage, estimated nationally at 40%.

The American Synagogue includes 3 major branches: Orthodox (28% of all Jews), Conservative (42%), and Reform (30%). Each of these Jewish denominations has its own national rabbinic body and lay congregational group. The Orthodox groups are the Rabbinical Council of America and the Union of Orthodox Jewish Congregations; the Conservative are the Rabbinical Assembly and the United Synagogue of America; and the Reform are the Central Conference of American Rabbis and the Union of American Hebrew Congregations (750 temples). These groups are member agencies of the Synagogue Council of America, founded in New York City in 1926, which co-ordinates common activity in social, interreligious and international affairs. There are other Jewish religious bodies which are not members of the Synagogue Council, including the Union of Orthodox Rabbis, the Agudas Israel, and Young Israel. In most local Jewish communities there exist also interdenominational rabbinic associations.

Orthodox Jews observe Jewish religious traditions based on the commandments (*mitzwot*) contained in the Torah, the Five Books of Moses, in accordance with the interpretations of the rabbinic codes which guide the religious practices and ethical behaviour of Jews in their daily conduct. Reform Jews are so called because they have reformed many of the traditional rituals and ceremonies, believing that the forms of religion which reflect particular historic or cultural situations should change as life itself changes. Conservative Jews are the centre movement in American Judaism, appearing sometimes to lean closer to the Orthodox; at other times, they resemble Reform Jews. Within Conservative Judaism there exists the Reconstructionist schools of thought which have sought to rebuild Judaism as a natural religion

**Black Muslims.** USA Black women of the World Community of Al-Islam in the West/America listen to former leader Elijah Muhammad.

in order to make it relevant to contemporary rational and scientific thought. Almost 3,000 of the 4,000 American synagogues are identifiable as Orthodox, although no more than 720 are formally affiliated with the national body, the Union of Orthodox Jewish Congregations. Affiliated with Conservative Judaism are 832 congregations. Reform or Liberal Judaism reports 698 synagogues or temples.

The 3 branches of Judaism maintain their own seminaries for the training of rabbis. The major Orthodox seminary is at Yeshiva University in New York City. Conservative Judaism's seminary is the Jewish Theological Seminary, also in New York. The Reform Seminary has 2 branches: the Jewish Institute of Religion in New York City, and Hebrew Union College in Cincinnati. In recent years each group has developed west coast branches in Los Angeles. The Reconstructionist movement has also opened a rabbinical school in Philadelphia. There are a number of less prominent Orthodox talmudic schools (*yeshivas*) in various parts of the USA. The Lubavitcher Hasidic movement has demonstrated a remarkable vitality in its religious outreach to American Jewry through its headquarters in the Williamsburgh section of New York.

The most impressive evidence of the expansion of religious life among the Jews of America is to be seen in increased enrolment in every type of synagogue school. There are an estimated 544,468 children attending some 2,727 Jewish schools of various types in which they receive some form of Jewish education.

Another recent development is the growth of Jewish study programmes on secular colleges and university campuses which now number some 200 chairs of Jewish studies or lecture courses in Judaica. This is in part due to the large number of Jewish students on the university scene, estimated to be about 400,000 or 80% of all Jews of college age.

In contrast to Christian church-centred groups, the Jewish community carries out much of its work in social welfare, education and community relations through specialized agencies which are not under the

auspices of synagogues. Among the more important of these may be mentioned the following: Council of Jewish Federations and Welfare Funds, National Jewish Welfare Board, American Association for Jewish Education, Jewish Publication Society, American Jewish Committee, American Jewish Congress, National Jewish Community Relations Advisory Council, National Council of Jewish Women, and B'nai B'rith (including its Hillel Foundation and Anti-Defamation League).

**Islam** has grown appreciably since large numbers of Muslims began arriving in the USA in the 1860s. Although no US Bureau of the Census growth statistics are available, Muslim officials estimate that in 1975 approximately 400,000 orthodox Sunni Muslims reside in North America, mostly in the USA. Immigrants have come from all over the world. At present, 76% of their descendants and later immigrants are of Middle Eastern heritage (Arabs), 17% Far Eastern and 7% European. Muslims live in all states but are most numerous in the Detroit-Dearborn area. Except in Dearborn, where there are about 7,000 Muslims, they do not reside in any one area of a city.

Islam is of special significance for Black Americans. As they relate to Islam, Blacks fall into 2 categories: those who follow historical Islam, associate with Tolamic mosques, and openly protest the use of the name Muslim by the Nation of Islam; and secondly, the followers of the the Nation of Islam itself, known as Black Muslims or Bilalians, who are regarded as heretical by Sunnis.

Several important Islamic organizations are active. The Federation of Islamic Associations of the United States and Canada (FIA), was founded in Cohasset (MA) in 1952, and received support from Al-Azhar, Egypt's religious university. The Muslim Students Association of the United States and Canada (MSA), in Gary (IN), has a membership of about 10,000 students from foreign countries studying at 130 colleges and universities in North America. The Islamic Center and Mosque, founded in Washington, DC, in 1952, sponsors public lectures and publishes material on Islam.

**Buddhism** as a movement in the USA is as rich as it is scattered over the country. Its greatest success has been in Hawaii and in California among the large number of residents there of Japanese ancestry. Its major organization which has recently celebrated its 75th anniversary is the Buddhist Churches of America, with headquarters in San Francisco, which is predominantly Jôdo-shinshû but seeks unity among the various schools of Buddhism in the USA. Three major institutions have an international reputation. (1) The College of Oriental Studies, in Los Angeles, is devoted to the study of Buddhist philosophy (Indian, Tibetan, Chinese and Japanese traditions), Zen and its origins and comparative religions, and arranges exchanges of staff and students with several Far Eastern counterparts. Affiliated with the college is the Buddhist Meditation Center

which promotes Tibetan, Sesshins Zen, Yoga, and Tai-chi-shuan meditation. (2) The Institute of Buddhist Studies, established in Berkeley, California by the Japanese community in the USA, is dedicated to the task of teaching Buddhism both academically and practically through an emphasis on intensive meditation. Served by a predominantly Japanese faculty, comparative studies are made of other religions and Buddhism's various schools, with special stress on Jôdo-shinshû Amidism. (3) A number of centres for Zen have been opened including the Zen Center, founded in San Francisco in 1959; and the Zen Mountain Center, Zenshinji Monastery, in Carmel Valley, Tassajara, California, founded in 1967. In addition to these there are several centres of Tibetan Lamaism, including Vajra Datu Karma Dzong, in Boulder, Colorado, which has 33 branches; Lamaist Buddhist Monastery, in Farmington, New Jersey; and Tail of the Tiger Buddhist Community in Barnet, Vermont.

**Other religions** found in the USA are Baha'i, Hinduism, American Indian tribal religion and a wide variety of small groups representing most of the world's religious traditions.

## CHRISTIANITY

**PROTESTANT CHURCHES.** Protestantism continues to constitute the Christian majority in the USA, although its proportional place in the population has steadily diminished during the present century, from 65% in 1900 to about 46% in 1970, due primarily to the growth of Catholicism by immigration.

**Baptists** form the principal Protestant tradition at the present time, a position held by Methodists in 1900. The American Baptist Churches in the USA, the largest of the northern Baptist denominations, look to Roger Williams as the founder of the country's first Baptist church, in Providence, Rhode Island in 1639. For a century and a half work was confined entirely to local communities, and after the Revolutionary War, associations were formed in several states; but the first national body (the Northern Baptist Convention) was not created until 1907. The name was changed to the American Baptist Convention in 1950 and to its present name in 1972.

The largest Baptist church in America is the Southern Baptist Convention, which came into being in 1845 in reaction to the refusal of the American Baptist Foreign Mission Society, with headquarters in Boston, to accept slave-owners as missionaries. Southern Baptists immediately established a strong central administration, a factor which has contributed to their extraordinary growth over the past century. Conventions now exist in 31 states, and there are a large number of denominational organizations. Of special note are their impressive Sunday school programme in the USA and extensive overseas missionary work, the latter with 2,564 workers in 70 countries in 1972. Unlike many large Protestant denominations, Southern Baptist numerical growth has shown few signs of decreasing in recent years.

Schisms and the creation of new Baptist denominations have taken place almost since the beginning, these including the National Association of Free Will Baptists in 1701, General Association of General Baptists in 1714, Primitive Baptists about 1830 and Baptist General Conference in 1852; and the present century has witnessed the formation of several large fundamentalist groups: the American Baptist Association in 1905, Conservative Baptist Association of America in 1947, Baptist Missionary Association of America in 1950, and Baptist Bible Fellowship International also in 1950. In addition to these larger bodies, all with communities over 100,000, there are many small Baptist denominations and independent congregations.

**Methodists** constitute the second largest Protestant tradition in the USA; but unlike the Baptists, the overwhelming majority are found in one denomination, the United Methodist Church. A number of other Methodist groups exist but they are for the most part small. Although John and Charles Wesley worked in Georgia as early as 1736, the first Methodist society in the New World was not formed until 1766, with the Methodist Episcopal Church itself being organized in 1784. During the 19th century schisms took their toll, the Methodist Protestant Church seceding in 1830 over the question of episcopal authority and the whole southern branch of the church in 1845 over slavery. Nevertheless these 3 bodies united once again in 1939 to form The Methodist Church, and a further merger with the Evangelical United Brethren Church in 1968 has produced the present United Methodist Church. The Church is organized into 5 jurisdictional and 81 annual conferences (including Puerto Rico) and 45 episcopal areas. The United Methodist Church is about equal in size with the Southern Baptist Convention, the difference being that the former has experienced annual decreases in adherents in recent years, while the latter has continued to grow in membership.

Other Methodist denominations exist which have broken with the main denomination in order to re-emphasize the Wesleyan doctrine of sanctification, and which now form part of the 2-million strong American holiness movement, including the Wesleyan Church and the Free Methodist Church, founded respectively in 1843 and 1860.

Other important bodies in the holiness movement include the Church of God (Anderson), Christian and Missionary Alliance, and Church of the Nazarene.

*Lutherans* from Germany first came to New York in 1623 and were known to have organized a congregation there by 1649. Other European immigrants followed; but the first synod, called the Ministerium of Pennsylvania, was not assembled until 1748. A general synod was held in 1820.

Most of these early synods remained independent until 1918 when they merged to form the United Lutheran Church. In 1962 the Lutheran Church of America was created by a merger of the United Lutheran Church with the Swedish-speaking Augustana Lutheran Church (founded in 1860), Finnish Evangelical Lutheran Church (1890) and the American Evangelical Lutheran Church (1872), the latter working particularly among Danish immigrants. The Lutheran Church of America is now the largest Lutheran denomination in the USA. It is divided into 31 synods, each consisting of several regions.

Almost equal in size with the above is the Lutheran Church—Missouri Synod which was founded in Missouri by German immigrants from Saxony who joined with others in 1847 to form the German Evangelical Lutheran Synod of Missouri, Ohio and Other States. This church has been noted for its doctrinal conservatism but has in recent years been rent by division over alleged liberalism in its principal theological school, Concordia Seminary.

The American Lutheran Church came into being in 1960 through the union of 3 denominations: a church of the same name (American Lutheran Church), which was German in background and traced its history to 1818; the United Evangelical Lutheran Church, founded by Danes in 1896; and the Evangelical Lutheran Church, which consisted mostly of Norwegians. A further merger in 1963 also brought in the Lutheran Free Church, another Norwegian body.

Among a number of other smaller Lutheran denominations, the most important is the Wisconsin Evangelical Lutheran Synod.

*Disciples of Christ* form a relatively recent tradition in American Protestantism. In the early part of the 19th century, 2 separate groups concerned for Christian unity arose among Presbyterians in Kentucky and Pennsylvania. The Kentucky group called themselves 'Disciples' while the Pennsylvania group were identified simply as 'Christians'. In 1832 they joined together to form the Christian Church (Disciples of Christ). This church, whose supreme body at the national level is a general assembly, is divided into 39 regions.

Two massive schisms have taken place among the Disciples since the founding of their church. The first was a conservative split which took place about 1870 and resulted in the creation of the Churches of Christ, a denomination which is commonly described by the adjective Non-Instrumental for its refusal to allow the use of organs or musical instruments during worship services. This body is completely congregational in structure, with no hierarchical or centralized organization, and maintains an extensive missionary work throughout the world. It is also one of the fastest-growing denominations in the USA at the present time.

The second major schism came about 1935 and produced the Christian Churches and Churches of Christ, which is usually described as Instrumental because it permits musical instruments in worship.

*Presbyterians* and *Reformed* constitute another major tradition, the former being the term for those of British origin (Scots and Irish), and the latter for those of Continental origin, mainly Dutch. In North America the Presbyterian wing is by far the most significant.

The United Presbyterian Church in the USA, the largest of all these groups, was formed in 1958 from a union of the Presbyterian Church in the USA and the United Presbyterian Church of North America.

The former was first organized in 1706, whereas the latter was itself the result of a merger of the Associate Presbyterian Church and the Associate Reformed Presbyterian Church in 1858. The church is today organized into congregations, presbyteries and synods, questions of national significance being handled by the annual general assembly, the general council and the judicial commission.

Presbyterianism, as was true of many American denominations, suffered from the North-South conflict over slavery which ended finally in the Civil War of 1861–65. Out of this period came 2 splits of southern synods and presbyteries within the Presbyterian Church in the USA, the first in 1857 and the second in 1861. These 2 southern groups in turn united in 1865 to form the Presbyterian Church in the US.

The 2 principal Reformed denominations are the Reformed Church in America, founded by Dutch settlers to New York in 1628, and the Christian Reformed Church, a schism from the former which took place in Michigan in 1837 over questions of discipline and doctrine.

*Pentecostals* in the USA form a dynamic tradition which grew out of the 19th-century American holiness movement, adding to its teaching an emphasis on the baptism of the Holy Spirit, faith healing, and the exercise of charismatic gifts. Several bodies including the Pentecostal Holiness Church, founded in 1898, continue to retain both emphases in their titles or in their teaching, and the first Pentecostal body in the USA, the Church of God (Cleveland), was at one point actually the Holiness Church. The latter began as a study and fellowship group in Cleveland, Tennessee in 1886, and a key event in its development took place in 1903 when A.J. Tomlinson, who had previously worked for the American Bible Society, joined its ranks, becoming moderator in 1909. The church has shown great vitality in its growth during the present century. In 1923 Tomlinson was removed from office and withdrew to form a separate Pentecostal body which adopted the name Church of God of Prophecy in 1953.

The largest Pentecostal body in the USA with mainly White members at the present time is the Assemblies of God, which dates its beginnings to 1906, although its founding meeting did not take place until 1914. Its churches, although entirely self-governing, are organized into 47 districts and include every state.

and have always had their strength in New England. In 1959 they entered on a major merger with the Evangelical and Reformed Church, a German Calvinistic body, which was itself the result of a union in 1934 of the Evangelical Synod of North America dating back to 1840, and the Reformed Church in the US begun by Germans in Pennsylvania as early as 1730. The resulting United Church of Christ, which at union was 64% Congregationalists and 36% E & R, represents an attempt to blend Congregationalism and Presbyterianism. Although local churches have full autonomy, there are area associations, regional conferences and the general synod at the national level which play an important role.

A still more ambitious union scheme is the Consultation on Church Union which was begun in 1962 and proposes to unite in one church 9 churches: Disciples, Episcopalian, Methodist (4 groups, including 3 Black Methodist denominations), Presbyterian (2) and the United Church of Christ.

*Other Protestants* exist in a great variety of traditions, many of them with very significant constituencies. Among the more important of these are the Seventh-day Adventist Church, founded in 1844, with 9 unions in the USA; the Salvation Army, which entered in 1880 and now has 38 USA divisions; several Brethren (German Baptist or Dunker) groups; 5 Quaker bodies, the earliest going back to 1656;

and a large number of Mennonite groups from as early as 1683.

Lastly, there are over 2,000 single independent congregations unaffiliated with any particular Protestant tradition, some of which have up to 8,000 members each. Altogether they total around a million adherents.

CATHOLIC CHURCH. Catholic history in the USA dates from the first Spanish missions to Indians in 1526, and the year 1565 when the first permanent Catholic community was established at St Augustine,

**Catholic Church in the USA.** Largest single denomination in the country, the church was heavily charismatic in 1978 (over 8 million professing to be Catholic pentecostals). *Above.* Processional of charismatic priests and bishops during mass, Notre Dame stadium, South Bend, 1973. *Top.* 'The Spirit of Jesus among us', theme of massive conventions and rallies.

One of the most notable of America's Pentecostal denominations is the International Church of the Foursquare Gospel, which grew out of the revival meetings of Aimée Semple McPherson in Los Angeles, beginning in 1918.

Other important bodies include the United Pentecostal Church (1914) and the Pentecostal Church of God of America (1919).

*Congregationalists* have had a variegated history. They first came to the USA with the pilgrims in 1620

Florida. Maryland became a Catholic colony in 1634, but it was not until the adoption of the American constitution in 1787 that Catholics received full religious liberty. The first Catholic diocese was erected in Baltimore in 1789, becoming an archdiocese in 1808. The USA had its first cardinal appointed from Rome in 1875. By 1975, there were over 48 million Catholics in 32 archdioceses and 134 dioceses in the USA. Jurisdictions with over 2 million Catholics each include Chicago and Boston, joined in 1975 by Los Angeles; and 6 others had over a million each in 1975.

In addition to English-speaking White Americans, the 2 major ethnic groups within the US Catholic Church are about 9 million Spanish-speaking Catholics and 855,193 Black Catholics, in 1973. Signs that these 2 latter groups are beginning to come into their own include the appointment of a 40-year-old Mexican-American priest as archbishop of Santa Fé, New Mexico, and the continued growth and vitality of the National Office for Black Catholics (NOBC), founded in 1970. The NOBC maintains close ties with the National Conference of Catholic Bishops and is funded by annual collections sponsored by the bishops in their dioceses. The NOBC has sponsored studies and seminars to improve the work of the church among Black Catholics, foster pride in their heritage, promote vocations among Blacks, and to assist those of all races and backgrounds to relate more effectively to the Black community. For the Spanish-speaking community, a similar function is performed by the Mexican American Cultural Centre in San Antonio, Texas. In 1974, the USCC Division for the Spanish-speaking, which was formerly a part of the Department of Social Development and World Peace, was upgraded to the status of a secretariat within the USCC.

Historically, the Catholic community in the USA has lived until recent years in a certain isolation from attitudes and values prevailing in the larger American society. It remained separate and homogeneous so that in a host of different ways, from the trivial to the essential, the distinctiveness of Catholic beliefs, values and practices was affirmed and reinforced.

This state of affairs has changed markedly and with increasing rapidity since the end of Vatican Council II. An important question now is whether Catholics in the USA are more influenced by the church or by secular society. Many would say that for a large number of Catholics, the influence of secular society, for good as well as ill, counts more heavily than the influence of the church.

As a result, the Catholic Church in the USA has many of the same problems as the rest of organized religion. Polarization and ferment are widespread in the church, not least in religious life. The shortage of vocations to the priesthood and religious life remains a serious problem. The reaffirmation

**National Baptist Convention of America.** 97th Annual Session, September 1977 in New Orleans. Largest grouping of the nation's 21 million followers of over 200 Black, Non-White and Amerindian indigenous denominations, the 3 major Black Baptist denominations have over 10 million Black members.

of clerical celibacy by the 1971 Synod of Bishops in Rome reduced confrontation on that issue, yet departures from the active ministry continue at a very high rate. Further, weekly attendance at mass has dropped from 78% of all Catholics in 1954 to 50% by 1974, and monthly confession from 37% in 1963 to 17% by 1974.

On the other hand, there are now many signs that a profound spiritual renewal is taking place among American Catholics. Centres and movements for the study and practice of spirituality among priests, religious and laity are springing up in many places. Over half a million adult Catholics including large numbers of religious personnel and several bishops are involved and active in the pentecostal Catholic Charismatic Renewal. Spiritually-oriented movements for married couples are attracting increasing numbers. After a period of transition, liturgical reforms are now widely accepted and working well. Parish and diocesan councils have spread extensively and involved more people than ever before in the exercise of shared responsibility. Many priests and religious, after a period of uncertainty and confusion, manifest renewed dedication to the mission of the church. Lastly, there is widespread interest in the future of religious education, highlighted by the bishops' collective pastoral 'To teach as Jesus did' in 1972, the document 'Basic teachings for Catholic religious education' in 1973, and the bishops' plan for a national catechetical directory.

BLACK/INDIAN/THIRD-WORLD CHURCHES. Some 21 million US Blacks, American Indians, Spanish-Americans and immigrants from Third-World countries belong to churches indigenous to their own communities, separate from, unsupported by and uncontrolled by White denominations.

*Black churches.* Although Blacks are found in most of the major USA denominations, with the largest numbers in the Roman Catholic Church

(855,000) and the United Methodist Church (500,000), the majority of all USA Blacks are members of over 140 separate Black denominations which have split either from predominantly White or White-controlled denominations or from other Black groups over the past 2 centuries.

The majority of American Blacks are Baptists. The first independent Black Baptist congregation was formed in 1773, at Silver Bluff near Augusta, Georgia, although it was not until 1836 that an association of Black Baptists was organized, the Providence Baptist Association of Ohio. The first national body established was in 1880, called the Foreign Mission Baptist Convention. Others followed: the American National Baptist Convention in 1886 and the Baptist National Educational Convention in 1893, both of which joined the Foreign Mission Baptist Convention to form the National Baptist Convention of America in 1895. In 1915 a major dissension occurred from which emerged 2 churches, the National Baptist Convention USA, and the National Baptist Convention of America. These remain the largest Black denominations in the USA. A further schism from the NBCUSA produced the Progressive National Baptist Convention in 1961. Another very large denomination is the National Primitive Baptist Convention. In addition, there are many small Black Baptist denominations and independent congregations.

The second largest church tradition claiming the allegiance of Blacks is Methodism. A first group of Black dissidents appeared in Philadelphia in 1787 and in 1816 officially organized the African Methodist Episcopal Church. Another group began in New York City in 1796 and eventually grew to be known as the African Methodist Episcopal Zion Church. A third important body, the Coloured (now Christian) Methodist Episcopal Church, was formed in 1870 as a schism from the Methodist Episcopal Church South. The AME, AME Zion and CME churches are all now involved in church union negotiations among themselves, as well as being members of COCU, the Consultation on Church Union. Many small Black Methodist churches are also active.

Pentecostalism has had a wide appeal among Blacks. The largest body is the Church of God in Christ, which was begun in 1895 through a Baptist interested in 'the doctrine of entire sanctification through the outpourings of the Holy Spirit'. A major schism from this body in 1969 produced the Church of God in Christ International. Other important Black pentecostal denominations are the Pentcostal Assemblies of the World (1914), United Holy Church of America (1886) and a host of smaller churches and individual congregations. The Black pentecostal community in the USA, which has little contact with either White Pentecostals or the Neo-pentecostal (charismatic) movement among Whites, numbered over 2.7 million adherents in 1970.

*American Indian churches.* A small number of churches begun by, and indigenous to, American Indians have come into being during the past century, some 19 separate groups being in existence in 1970. The largest is the Native American Church of North America, dating from 1870, which is now found among almost all American Indian tribes. Because of its incorporation of Indian traditional religious concepts and practices including use of the drug peyote, it is regarded by most other American churches as only marginally Christian. The Navajo Native American Church, formed around the turn of the century has an estimated 60% of all Navajos in the USA. The oldest independent Indian group is the Narraganset Indian Church organized in Charlestown, Rhode Island, in 1741. Another early group was the Yaqui Church which, although now very small, traces its origin to Jesuit work in Arizona during the later half of the 18th century.

*Hispanic churches.* In addition to USA Black and American Indian churches, there are several churches, begun in the USA by, and indigenous to, the Spanish-speaking community of USA nationality, especially among those of Puerto Rican and Mexican origin.

*Third-World indigenous churches.* All of the above bodies are indigenous to the USA. Over and above them, however, there are a large and growing number of Third-World indigenous bodies, i.e. originating in the Third World among Non-White peoples, which have been introduced into the USA by immigrant adherents from Africa, Asia, the Caribbean, Latin America and Oceania. The greatest impact thus far has been made by Spanish-speaking groups from Latin America and Puerto Rico, the largest of these being the Spanish wing of the Assemblies of God and the Apostolic Assembly, both of which have entered

**Church of God in Christ.** Black pentecostals (in USA pentecostal denominations) totalled 3.2 million by 1978. Largest of all USA pentecostal churches is the Church of God in Christ, whose Bishop B.R. Stewart (above) is seen celebrating a Black rock star's marriage in New York's Madison Square before 23,000 fans.

the USA from Mexico. New denominations introduced from Africa include the African Apostolic Church of Johane Maranke from Zimbabwe, the Kimbanguist Church from Zaire and the Church of the Lord (Aladura) from West Africa. The Church of the First-Born and the International City have both come from Jamaica, while the True Jesus Church and the Church of Christ (Iglesia ni Cristo) owe their beginnings respectively to China and the Philippines. More than 40 such churches existed in the USA in 1970; and although most are still small, they will undoubtedly grow in numbers over the next decade or two.

ORTHODOX CHURCHES. *Eastern Orthodoxy* in the USA represents a phenomenon of great variety and complexity. Churches of the Byzantine and Slavic traditions consist of more than 20 separate churches, the largest single denomination being the Greek Orthodox Archdiocese of North and South America. Although a Greek community was founded in New Smyrna, Florida as early as 1767, the first church in New Orleans, was not organized until 1864. The archdiocese itself was established in 1921 with headquarters in New York City. This church, which is part of the Ecumenical Patriarchate of Constantinople, suffered 3 or 4 minor schisms by Old Calendrist bodies following the acceptance of the new Gregorian calendar in 1924.

In 1792, 8 Russian Orthodox missionary monks arrived in Kodiak, Alaska, where they built their base and first church; and by 1794 they had baptized 25,000 Eskimos. Alaska remained part of Russia until 1867. Russian Orthodoxy at present is represented by 3 bodies in the USA, of which the Orthodox Church in America (OCA) has the longest history (1792) and the greatest number of adherents. Originally known as the Russian Orthodox Greek Catholic Church of America, it was granted autocephalous status by the Moscow Patriarchate in 1970 and adopted its new name in the same year. The Romanian Orthodox Episcopate and the Albanian Orthodox Archdiocese, founded respectively in 1904 and 1908, are at present under the canonical jurisdiction of the OCA. Two other smaller denominations which have entered the USA in the present century are the Russian Orthodox Church in the Americas, an exarchate of the Moscow Patriarchate, and the Russian Orthodox Church Outside of Russia. The latter is strongly opposed to the Moscow Patriarchate because of its collaboration with the Soviet communist regime.

A large number of Orthodox bodies have been formed by other ethnic immigrant groups from Eastern Europe, and these are today often divided into 2 distinct rival bodies (as are each the Albanian, Bulgarian, Romanian, and Serbian) or even 3 (as is the Ukrainian). In addition there are Byelorussian, Estonian, Finnish, Hungarian, Macedonian and Carpatho-Russian bodies. Two rival groups related to the Patriarchate of Antioch in Syria are also active. An attempt in 1932 to unite all Eastern Orthodox in America into one church produced yet another denomination, the American Holy Orthodox Catholic Eastern Church.

The most important organization providing for contacts between the various Eastern Orthodox groups is the Standing Conference of Canonical Orthodox Bishops in the Americas, with 11 member churches.

*Oriental Orthodoxy* has a following of 577,000. Of the 5 non-Chalcedonian churches in the USA, the largest are the Armenian Church of North America, and the Armenian Apostolic Church of America. The former, begun in 1889, owes allegiance to the Catholicate of Echmiadzin in Soviet Armenia, while the latter, which split from it in 1933, is now related to the Catholicate of Cilicia (Sis) at Antelias in Lebanon.

The Syrian Orthodox Church (Jacobite) was introduced into North America in 1895. Forming part of the Patriarchate of Antioch with headquarters in Damascus, Syria, the archdiocese of the USA and Canada is based in Hackensack, New Jersey. Two other small Monophysite groups are the Ethiopian and Coptic Orthodox churches which entered the USA with immigrants in 1959 and 1960.

*Nestorians.* The Nestorian branch of Christianity, the Ancient Church of the East, has been present in the USA since 1907, and has the name Holy Apostolic and Catholic Church of the East. Its patriarchate was moved from Iraq to San Francisco in 1940; there are 10,000 faithful.

MARGINAL CHURCHES. Several large churches exist on the periphery of American Protestantism which are not properly termed Protestant because they do not accept mainline Protestant christocentric orthodoxy. In this survey they are called, for want of a better term, marginal Protestant bodies.

*Mormons.* The Church of Jesus Christ of Latter-day Saints, better known as Mormonism, traces its history to visions of its founder, Joseph Smith, at Fayette, New York in 1830. Severely persecuted everywhere, the Mormons ultimately settled in Utah where they built up a large religious community under the leadership of Brigham Young. Mormonism has 2 orders of priests, the higher priesthood of Melchizedek and the lesser priesthood of Aaron. Church organization is highly centralized, including the First Presidency, which is the supreme executive and legislative body of the church, and the Council of the Twelve Apostles, which carries out the directives of the First Presidency and ordains ministers. The geographical districts of the church are called stakes and local congregations, wards. Mormons are responsible for an extensive educational and social service programme and are heavily involved in missionary work. In addition to full-time missionaries, some 4,000 youth are sent out yearly in pairs to spend a 2-year short-term service in propagating Mormonism throughout the world. The result has

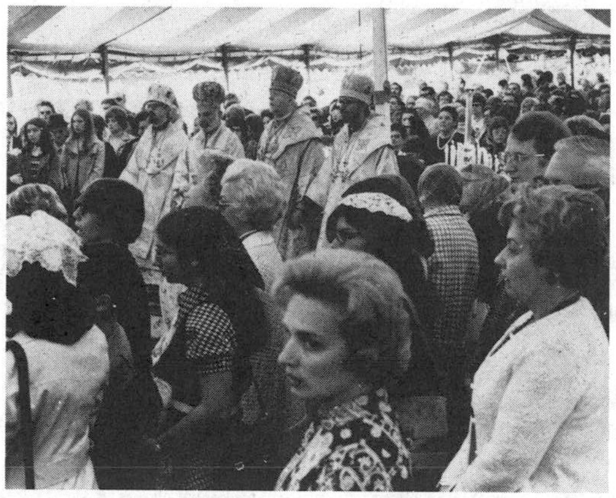

**Orthodox Church in America.** Metropolitan Ireney (third bishop from left), head of Russian-origin million-member OCA, concelebrates with Bishop Elias of Patriarchate of Antioch (second bishop from left) and 2 other hierarchs during 1974 Orthodox Education Day at St Vladimir's Seminary.

been vast expansion on all other continents except Africa, due to the Mormon refusal to open its priesthood to Blacks, a problem which has also hindered Mormon work among Blacks in the USA.

Since 1831 at least 89 schismatic offshoots have split from the mother LDS church, while retaining essential Mormon beliefs and practices. The largest is the Reorganized Church of Jesus Christ of Latter-day Saints; others are known as Temple Lot, Bickertonites and Strangites.

*Jehovah's Witnesses* came into being through the work of Charles Taze Russell, a Congregationalist who was influenced by Adventism in 1870. Russell organized his first congregation in Pittsburg in 1872 and registered his first incorporated society in 1884. Until the name Jehovah's Witnesses was adopted in 1931, adherents were known as Russellites, Millenial Dawnists and International Bible Students. At present the organization is based on 3 USA corporations, the Watch Tower Bible and Tract Society of Pennsylvania, Watchtower Bible and Tract Society of New York and the International Bible Students Association. Congregations meet in kingdom halls and are grouped into circuits and districts, there being 31 districts in the USA. There is no separate clergy; all members are ministers and are expected to give personal witness and distribute literature from door to door, resulting in a massive voluntary missionary enterprise technically known as publishing, with members being called publishers. As with the Mormons, a sizeable number of schisms have broken from Jehovah's Witnesses through the years, several in a mainline Protestant direction, including the Laymen's Home Missionary Movement (1918), Churches of the Kingdom of God, Greek Bible Students, and Converted Jehovah's Witnesses.

*Christian Science.* The Church of Christ, Scientist was founded at Boston in 1879, by Mary Baker Eddy, whose own personal experience of healing in 1866 led to the founding of a worldwide movement centred on spiritual healing. The denomination retains its headquarters in Boston, where the First Church of Christ, Scientist is still universally regarded as the Mother Church. The Christian Science Board of Directors in Boston is the supreme administrative body of the church. In addition to Sunday and week-day services, local churches maintain reading rooms and an extensive literature distribution programme. Key congregational leaders are known as readers, teachers and practitioners, the latter bearing special responsibility for healing.

*Unitarianism.* Universalists organized their first church in 1778, and Unitarians in 1796. In 1961 they joined to form the Unitarian Universalist Association. The strength of the movement has been in New England and Boston remains the national headquarters, but membership is declining.

*Spiritism* or Spiritualism has a wide appeal in the USA and is organized into many separate groups, the largest being the International General Assembly of Spiritualists formed in 1936.

A host of over 300 smaller marginal Protestant bodies of all kinds are also active in the USA. Many of them have expanded overseas during the 20th century.

Schisms in a Protestant, or mainline Christian, direction have taken place over the years from most other major bodies as well as from Mormons and Jehovah's Witnesses. In 1973, the largest USA congregation of Unity School of Christianity (in Los Angeles, with 5,000 members) became pentecostal and broke from Unity; and there have been numerous other such cases.

ANGLICAN CHURCH. Sir Francis Drake touched the shores of California in 1578, claiming the New World for the British queen and the Church of England, but it was not until the foundation of the Virginia colony in 1607 that Anglicans began evangelistic work in America. Anglicanism nearly came to an end at the time of the Revolutionary War, with many of its clergy fleeing to England or Canada. Nevertheless, the period after 1783 was a time of rebuilding, and the constitution of the newly-created Protestant Episcopal Church in the USA was adopted in 1789. Although the church was spared the divisions which rent many Protestant denominations at the time of the Civil War, it has experienced several minor schisms since the formation of the Reformed Episcopal Church in 1873. The Episcopal Church is now in 1974 organized into 8 ecclesiastical provinces in the USA (with Province IX covering Latin American work) and 92 dioceses, with a further diocese being created in 1975.

CATHOLIC (NON-ROMAN) CHURCHES. A large number of at least 60 distinct and separate bodies exist in the USA which claim to be Catholic and which cannot properly be called either Roman Catholic, Protestant, Anglican, or Orthodox. Of these, by far the largest is the Polish National Catholic Church in America. This church was formed in Scranton, Pennsylvania in 1897 after a conflict going back many years between immigrant Polish Catholics and the Irish-dominated hierarchy in parts of the Roman Catholic Church in the USA. The first synod of the church took place in 1904 and in 1907 the first bishop was consecrated by 3 Old Catholic bishops in Utrecht, Holland. Several other smaller denominations are also in the Old Catholic tradition related to Utrecht, but most of the others are not recognized by Utrecht. About 30 of these bodies are miniscule episcopal churches under bishops-at-large with very small followings.

**CHURCH AND STATE.** In the early years of settlement most states recognized an official church. In 1609, the Church of England was established by law in Virginia, with a statute of 1610 providing for compulsory church attendance. This Anglican establishment was later extended to other colonies: lower New York in 1693, Maryland in 1702, South Carolina in 1706, North Carolina in 1711, Georgia in 1758, and ultimately Pennsylvania, Delaware and New Jersey as well. On the other hand strong anti-Anglican feelings in New England brought by the Pilgrims contributed to the establishment of the Congregational Church as the official religion in Massachusetts and Connecticut. In 1632 Maryland was created as a home for Catholics, and many of the first Catholic immigrants settled there. However, after 1689 Protestants were in control and succeeded in passing laws discriminating against Catholics. Indeed in this early period a strong anti-Catholic bias existed everywhere except in Rhode Island and Pennsylvania.

The desire for religious freedom, accompanied by resentment against Anglicanism because of its ties to Great Britain, was a dominant factor in the religious situation during 1776–89 and resulted in the disestablishment of the Church of England in the southern and middle colonies from 1776–90 and also of Congregationalism in New England (1818 in Connecticut, 1833 in Massachusetts). An important impulse towards that end came from the first federal constitution of 1789 which gave clear expression to the idea of the separation of church and state which had been growing since before the Revolutionary War. Since the formulation of the US constitution in 1787, therefore, the United States has been clearly defined as a secular state in which church and state are legally separated. The constitution makes no reference to God (except for George Washington's signature 'In the Year of our Lord 1787'), nor to the state as believing in God, although in 1954 Congress added the words 'under God' to the Pledge of Allegiance.

From a legal standpoint the past 25 years have seen a number of important Supreme Court decisions that have further clarified the nature of the separation of church and state in America. The intent of the 16-word constitutional requirement 'Congress shall make no law respecting an establishment of religion or prohibiting the free exercise thereof' (First Amendment, 1791) has always been ambiguous and has needed clarification as the emotional post-1945 issues of abortion, prayer in public schools, taxation of church-owned property, an appointment to the Vatican by a president, and birth-control issues and devices dispensed by public agencies have been considered.

religious authorities by adjusting the schedule of public events to sectarian needs, it follows the best of our traditions. For it then respects the religious nature of our people and accommodates the public service to their spiritual needs. To hold that it may not would be to find in the Constitution a requirement that the government show a callous indifference to religious groups. That would be preferring those who believe in no religion over those who do believe.'
(4) Burstyn v. Wilson (1952) declared the censorship of films, in this case 'The Miracle' by Roberto Rossellini, under the guise of sacrilege and blasphemy to be both vague and unconstitutional. (5) Torcaso v. Watkins (1961) affirmed that the state of Maryland could not require of public office holders 'a declaration of belief in the existence of God' and that even this minimal statement was a religious test invading the appellant's freedom and was thus unenforceable. (6) Engel v. Vitale (1962) banned the use of official state-sanctioned prayers in public school. The particular case in question was that of the New York State Board of Regent's prayer: 'Almighty God, we acknowledge our dependence upon Thee, and we beg Thy blessings upon us, our parents, our teachers and our country.' A storm of protest followed this decision, and there is sentiment in both Houses of Congress for a constitutional amendment which would allow prayer in school. (7) Pennsylvania v. Schempp (1963) held that the reading of Bible verses

fixed star in our constitutional constellation, it is that no official, high or petty, can prescribe what shall be orthodox in politics, nationalism, religion, or other matters of opinion or force citizens to confess by word or act their faith therein.'
(9) Welsh v. United States (1970) liberalized and legalized a new basis for conscientious objection to war and exemption from military service. Hitherto, belief in a supreme being was necessary. Afterwards, a deeply-held and morally-consistent repugnance to war and the taking of life was deemed acceptable. (10) Walz v. Tax Commission of New York (1970) denied that the tax-exempt status of church property constituted an 'establishment' of religion' and continued such exemption as long as such property was for religious use exclusively. Noting that many municipal governments are hard-pressed for revenue, some churches have recently made token gifts for such public services as police and fire protection. (11) Sloan v. Lemon (1973) and Committee for Public Education and Religious Liberty v. Nyquist (1973) were 2 significant decisions in the long and continuing controversy over providing significant state aid to parochial schools. In the former judgement, a Pennsylvania statute providing for reimbursement of tuition paid by parents who send their children to non-public schools was declared unconstitutional under the establishment clause. In the latter, a New York case, repair grants and highly-complicated tuition reimbursement arrangements to parents of students in parochial schools in low-income areas were judged contrary to the First Amendment. (12) Miller v. California (1973) in a close 5–4 decision allowed states and/or their local communities to take punitive action against those who produce, sell, exhibit or display works 'which appeal to the prurient interest in sex, which portray sexual conduct in a patently offensive way and which taken as a whole, do not have serious literary, artistic, political or scientific value'. Chief justice Warren Burger wrote:
'It is neither realistic nor constitutionally sound to read the First Amendment as requiring that the people of Maine or Mississippi accept the public depiction of conduct found tolerable in Las Vegas or New York City.'
The minority opinion claimed that the decision would not relieve the court of 'the awesome task' of making case-by-case decisions and thus would be unworkable. Their position seemed to be substantiated in the first test case of the above Miller decision, Jenkins v. Georgia (1974), when the court overturned a state's decision that the film 'Carnal Knowledge' was pornographic and obscene. (13) Wheeler v. Barrera (1974) decided that educationally-deprived non-public-school children should have equitable treatment regarding the distribution of federal funds in aid of special programmes for the disadvantaged. The court affirmed that the federal statute (Title I) did not obligate the state to provide on-the-premises instruction in non-public schools (as prohibited by the Missouri Constitution) and that state and local officials had various other options available in order to comply with the requirement of comparable services to all schools. (14) Roe v. Wade (1973), perhaps the most important decision of the past decade, found the court in a 7–2 decision drafting national guide lines that broadly liberalized abortion laws. Only during the last 10 weeks of pregnancy, the period during which the foetus is judged to be capable of surviving if born, can a state prohibit abortion. The majority decision rejected the view that a foetus becomes a 'person' upon conception, while the dissenting opinion called the decision 'an exercise of raw judicial power' that values 'the convenience of the pregnant mother more than the continued existence and development of the life or potential life which she carries'. The Catholic hierarchy together with some conservative Protestant churches bitterly attacked the decision and have been instrumental in founding politically-powerful Right to Life groups whose aim is the defeat of abortion-on-demand politicians and the passage of a constitutional amendment prohibiting abortion. The issue is a divisive one that will traumatize the body politic for some time into the future and will probably retard the ecumenical movement.

In terms of common practice and general trends regarding the future, there is no governmental ministry of religious affairs, nor are churches obligated to register with the government, nor is this situation likely to change. There are no diplomatic relations between the United States and the Holy See, although president Nixon appointed a personal representative to the Vatican as president Franklin D. Roosevelt had done before him.

**Native American Church of North America.** Contemporary Navajo peyote ritual session, declared legal by US Supreme Court in 1961 because 'The NAC is a legitimate church entitled to the protection of the First Amendment. Drummer (left) accompanies chanter (centre), while Road Chief (officiating priest, right) guides ceremony. The NAC has 23 Chapters and over 400,000 members.

Important Supreme Court cases treating church-state issues since 1947 include the following fourteen. (1) Everson v. Board of Education (1947) upheld state policies extending auxiliary services (health care, lunches, text-books, bus transportation) for students attending parochial schools under the 'general welfare' clause of the constitution. Protestants were generally shocked by this decision believing that it would ultimately lead to full public support of Catholic Parochial education. Thus, a year later Protestants and Other Americans United for Separation of Church and State (POAU) was founded, supported mainly by Baptist, Unitarian, and independent Protestant groups, to protect the separation of church and state. (2) McCollum v. Board of Education (1948) declared that 'released time' programmes of religious instruction by church-sponsored teachers on public school property were unconstitutional. (3) Zorach v. Clauson (1952) modified the McCollum decision, allowing school boards to provide for religious instruction if this was done off public school premises. Justice Douglas summarized the matter in an oft-quoted statement:
'We are a religious people whose institutions presuppose a Supreme Being. . . When the state encourages religious instruction or cooperates with

without comment or interpretation was unconstitutional, because for some the exercise had a devotional and religious character. (8) McGowan v. Maryland (1961) invalidated a state's so-called 'blue laws' relating to required closure of certain businesses on Sundays. Other decisions during the past decade have extended civil and religious freedom. Black Muslim prisoners have been given access to religious literature, services and pastoral visitation; Seventh-day Adventists and Orthodox Jews have had their job security protected when they abstain from Saturday work; and Jehovah's Witnesses have been exempted from securing licences to sell their literature and may restrain from the public school flag-salute and Pledge of Allegiance. In the latter case (West Virginia School Board of Education v. Barnette, 1943), justice Jackson stated in a widely-quoted passage:
'To believe that patriotism will not flourish if patriotic ceremonies are voluntary and spontaneous instead of a compulsory routine is to make an unflattering estimate of the appeal of our institutions to free minds. We can have intellectual individualism and the rich cultural diversities that we owe to exceptional minds only at the price of occasional eccentricity and abnormal attitudes. . . If there is any

During the past 2 decades a great deal of the residual anti-Catholic sentiment among Protestant Americans has been dissipated by such diverse movements as the election in 1960 of the first Catholic president of the United States, John F. Kennedy; the increasing Americanization of the Catholic Church; the diminution of Catholicism's siege mentality; increasing self-criticism by Catholic clergy and laity; the wide acceptance of 'Good Pope' John XXIII; and Vatican II's decrees on Ecumenism and Religious Freedom and the new interreligious dialogue they have created. Moreover, many Protestants are turning away from the POAU's separationism because of its anti-Catholic bias, as well as its pietism and lack of social policy with respect to war, race, and economic and political issues.

The post-World War II trend of American Protestantism may be described as transformationist with regard to church-state relations. This position applies a theocentric principle (the sovereignty of God) to church-state theory and practice, and is committed to a prophetic church, a strong social ethic and a realistic view of sin. Transformationism neither advocates a unity of church and state nor their complete separation, but an intermediate position. It avoids a negative separationism that leads to increased secularization of culture and irresponsibility in politics; yet it guards against preferential privilege for any one church whereby the independent stance necessary for prophetic criticism of the state is lost and injustice is done to non-preferred religious bodies. Thus what is being sought is a new kind of 'creative co-operation' or 'benevolent neutrality' between church and state.

## INTERDENOMINATIONAL ORGANIZATIONS

*National and local councils of churches.* The major national co-ordinating body is the National Council of the Churches of Christ in the USA (NCCCUSA), founded in New York City in 1950, growing out of the earlier Federal Council of the Churches of Christ in North America (1908). Member denominations number 32, including most of America's largest Protestant, Orthodox and Black churches. Notable by their absence are the Roman Catholic Church and the Southern Baptist Convention. However, Catholic interest in ecumenism, which is co-ordinated by the Bishop's Committee for Ecumenical and Interreligious Affairs of the NCCB, is strong. In 1969 a joint Catholic—NCCC commission was appointed to investigate the possibility of eventual Catholic membership in the council. The work of the NCCC is carried out through 3 divisions (Church and Society, Education and Ministry, Overseas Ministry), 4 commissions and 3 offices.

With the exception of Alabama and Mississippi, every state in the USA has its own council or conference of churches, interchurch or interfaith association or agency; and several states have more than one. In addition there are a vast number of city-wide councils. The Catholic Church holds membership in 15 state councils of churches and more than 50 metropolitan ecumenical agencies (1974).

Other national inter-denominational co-ordinating bodies include the National Association of Evangelicals (NAE), National Black (formerly Negro) Evangelical Association (NBEA, NNEA), Associated Gospel Churches (representing fundamentalist denominations with over 3.5 million members), Pan-Indian Ecumenical Association, American Council of Christian Churches, Christian Holiness Association, Council of Japanese American Christian Churches in North America and National Fraternal Council of Churches.

*International bodies* with headquarters in the USA include: International Association of Women Ministers; International Christian Youth Exchange; International Ministerial Federation; and World's Christian Endeavor Union.

International ecumenical organizations with branches in the USA include: Ecumenical Satellite Commission (which is concerned for press, cinema, radio and TV), United States Conference for the World Council of Churches, North American Office of the World Student Christian Federation.

*National service agencies* include the American Bible Society, American Tract Society, Associated Church Press, Christian Ministry in the National Parks, Church Women United, Evangelical Press Association, General Commission on Chaplains and Armed Forces Personnel, National Association of Christian Schools, National Association of Ecumenical Staff, National Council of YMCAs, National Interreligious Service Board for Conscientious Objectors, North American Academy of Ecumenists,

Religion in American Life (which attempts to reach the American public through advertising), Religion Newswriters Association, Religious Public Relations Council, and YWCA of the USA.

*Confessional councils.* National and international confessional councils and federations with their world headquarters in the USA, serving one ecclesiastical confession, include the Baptist World Alliance, Lutheran Council in the USA, Mennonite World Conference, North American Baptist Fellowship, Pentecostal Fellowship of North America, Standing Conference of the Canonical Orthodox Bishops in the Americas, World Convention of Churches of Christ (Disciples) and World Methodist Council.

Other international bodies with branches but not world headquarters in the USA include: Friends World Committee for Consultation, Lutheran World Federation, Pentecostal World Conference and World Alliance of Reformed Churches, the latter serving Presbyterians and Congregationalists.

*Union negotiations.* Four sets of negotiations towards organic church union were under way in 1976, as follows: (1) the 3 principal denominations of Black Methodists: AMEC, AMEZC, and CMEC; (2) Orthodox Presbyterian and Reformed Presbyterian (Evangelical Synod) churches; (3) Presbyterian Church in the US and United Presbyterian Church in the USA; and (4) the Consultation on Church Union (COCU), which proposes to unite 9 major US Protestant and Black denominations: AMEC, AME ZionC, CMEC, Disciples, Episcopalians, Southern Presbyterians, United Presbyterians, United Methodists and United Church of Christ.

*Dialogue consultation.* A significant number of other conversations are in progress sponsored by churches and confessional families nationally. These include joint dialogue between Lutherans and Anglicans, Anglicans and Orthodox, Lutherans and Orthodox, and 8 consultations in which Catholics are involved. Concerning these latter, joint dialogue is being carried on between the Catholic episcopal conference (Bishops' Committee for Ecumenical and Interreligious Affairs) and the following: American Baptist Convention (Division of Cooperative Christianity; first meeting held in April, 1967); Christian Church (Disciples of Christ) (Council of Christian Unity; March, 1967); Episcopal Church (Joint Commission on Ecumenical Relations; begun June, 1965), Lutheran churches (USA National Committee of the Lutheran World Federation; March, 1965); United Methodist Church; June, 1966; Orthodox churches (Standing Conference of Canonical Orthodox Bishops of America; September, 1969); Presbyterian-Reformed churches (North American Council of the World Alliance of Reformed churches; July, 1965); and Southern Baptists (Department of Interfaith Witness; May 1969). These continuing consultations aim through dialogue to investigate points at issue which have been factors in the separation of churches, with the hope of achieving a deeper and broader agreement among Christians.

*Theological education.* A major future of the current North American ecumenical scene is the growth of clusters and consortia of theological schools, involving Protestant, Catholic, Orthodox and Anglican institutions. The 1974 *Directory of the American Association of Theological Schools* lists 16 in the USA (14 in 1973), the most important being the Chicago Cluster of Theological Schools, California Graduate Theological Union, Washington Theological Consortium, and Boston Theological Institute. These co-operative enterprises differ greatly in emphasis but involve cross-registration, joint planning and the development of a common network of library facilities. Some follow a practice of exchanging teaching staff and others conduct joint research programmes.

*Study and research.* Many societies and associations dedicated to the scientific study of religion on an ecumenical basis have been formed, the most important of which belong to the Council on the Study of Religion. Members of the council in 1975 included the following: American Academy of Religion, American Society of Christian Ethics, American Society of Church History, American Society of Missiology, American Theological Library Association, Catholic Biblical Association, Catholic Theological Society of America, College Theological Society, Society of Biblical Literature, Society for the Scientific Study of Religions, and Religious Education Association.

Other academic institutions giving special attention to ecumenical study and research are: (1) the Ecumenical Continuing Education Centre, founded at Yale University in 1967, which links the Yale

Religious Ministry, United Ministries in Higher Education at Yale, New Haven and Connecticut Councils of Churches, includes on its board of directors Protestants, Catholics and Orthodox, and provides opportunities for pastors and lay persons to engage in study programmes in a university setting; (2) the Ecumenical Institute, founded in Chicago in 1954, which is a Division of the Church Federation of Greater Chicago and provides a research, study and training centre for religious renewal on an ecumenical basis focusing on the needs of the local congregation; (3) the Ecumenical Institute of Religious Studies, founded in Worcester, Massachusetts in 1967, which is run by Catholic Assumptionists; (4) Graymoor Ecumenical Institute, founded in Garrison, New York in 1967, which is operated by Catholic Friars of the Atonement under an interdenominational board, with its research, study and action centre dedicated to the search for a Christian response to social and religious issues facing American life; and to ecumenical and interreligious dialogue; (5) the Institute for Advanced Religious Studies, founded at the University of Notre Dame in Indiana in 1966, which explores the conveyance of religion with other fields of study and concentrates on the relationship of Christianity to the non-Christian world; (6) the Institute for Ecumenical and Cultural Research, founded at St John's University in Collegeville, Minnesota in 1967, which though centred in a Catholic university is independently incorporated, having a predominantly Protestant board of directors, and which offers research facilities to individual scholars studying the problems of ecumenism broadly conceived; (7) John XXIII Institute for Eastern Christian Studies, founded at Fordham University in New York City in 1971, which is a Catholic institute emphasizing Orthodox-Catholic relations and the study of the Eastern tradition of Christianity; and (8) Institute for Thomistic and Ecumenical Studies, founded by the Dominican Province of the Holy Name in Berkeley, California in 1966, which provides facilities for competent scholars to pursue post-doctoral studies related to ecumenism.

*Ecumenical action.* Centres and agencies for ecumenical action include: (1) Berkeley Center for Human Interaction, founded in Berkeley, California in 1966, which sponsors intensive small-group conferences and programmes; (2) Christians Associated for Relationships with Eastern Europe (CAREE), in Elgin, Illinois, which aims to foster good relations with Christians in Eastern Europe especially through the Christian Peace Conference, to promote Christian-Marxist dialogue and to work for international peace and justice; (3) Cooperation in Development (CODEL), founded in New York City in 1969, an inter-faith consortium which co-ordinates the work of member Christian service and mission groups in the areas of hunger, health and housing; (4) the Ecumenical Institute, founded at Wake Forest University in Winston Salem, NC, in 1968, which is a Southern Baptist centre offering resources for conferences, study and dialogue; (5) the Ecumenical Institute, founded in Merrimac, Massachusetts in 1964, which emphasizes the renewal of the local congregation; (6) the Gustav Weigel Society, founded at Wesley Theological Seminary in Washington, DC in 1966, which promotes spiritual ecumenism through retreats for pastors and lay persons; (7) John XXIII Ecumenical Center, founded in Paoli, Pennsylvania in 1969, which is an independent and interdenominational institution seeking to enlist all men in the common worship of God and service of their neighbour; (8) John LaFarge Institute, founded by Jesuits in New York City in 1964, which promotes ecumenical and interracial activities and holds conferences; (9) LAOS, in Washington, DC, which is an ecumenical agency for training and recruiting volunteers with professional skills for work in developing countries and in areas of need in the USA; (10) Laymen's Academy for Ecumenical Studies, founded in Amherst, Massachusetts in 1961, which emphasizes Catholic-Protestant and Black-White relations, in addition to lay theological education; (11) Packard Manse Ecumenical Center, founded in Stoughton in Massachusetts, 1947, which is dedicated to social ecumenism at the local level; and (12) the World Center for Liturgical Studies, founded in Boyton Beach, Florida in 1965, which sponsors conferences and provides study facilities for the continuing education of church leaders with special emphasis on pastoral and liturgical areas of the ministry.

*Jewish-Christian relations.* The major concern of inter-religious dialogue in the USA is Jewish-Christian relations, and a number of Christian, Jewish and joint organizations have been formed to improve contacts between Christians and Jews.

Joint organizations include: (1) Interreligious Committee of General Secretaries, founded in 1968, which enables the executive officers of the NCCCUSA, USCC and the Synagogue Council of America to collaborate in matters of mutual interest; (2) National Conference of Christians and Jews (NCCJ), founded in New York City in 1928, which is a member of the international Council of Christians and Jews in London, and seeks to combat religious and social prejudice through its 70 regional offices, its sponsorship of Religious News Service (RNS), and its promotion of an annual Brotherhood Committment Week; (3) World Conference of Religion for Peace (WCRP), established as a permanent interreligious body in 1971 following the first world conference on religion and peace in Kyoto, Japan in 1970, which includes members of all the principal world faiths in sharing insights and promoting common action for peace, justice and mutual understanding; (4) US Interreligious Committee on Peace (USICOP), founded in Washington, DC in 1964, which works in close co-operation with WCRP in promoting peace issues and action among the entire spectrum of religious groups in the USA; and (5) Inter-met (Interfaith Association in Metropolitan Theological Education), founded in Washington, DC in 1969, which is an interfaith (Protestant, Catholic, Jewish) organization seeking to develop a metropolitan-wide system of theological training for continuing education and to effect a better structure of education for congregational ministries.

Specifically-Christian institutions and organizations include: (1) Office for Jewish-Christian Relations of the NCCCUSA, organized in New York City in 1974, which disseminates information and encourages meetings and action programmes involving the 2 communities; (2) Ecumenical and Interreligious Affairs Committee of the NCCB, founded in Washington, DC in 1964, which is concerned for relations among Christians and Christianity and secularism, as well as inter-faith dialogue through its separate Secretariat for Catholic-Jewish Relations; (3) Saint-Meinrad School of Theology, in St Meinrad, Indiana, which stresses Jewish studies and is engaged in co-operative ventures with several Jewish agencies; (4) Boston College, which offers courses in Jewish-Christian relations; (5) Institute of Judeo-Christian Studies, a Catholic institute founded at Seton Hall University, New Jersey, in 1951; (6) Centre for Judaic Studies, founded by the Graduate Theological Union in Berkeley, California; (7) Philo Institute, founded at McCormick Theological Seminary in Chicago in 1971, which studies Judaism's influence on early Christianity and publishes *Studia Philonica*; (8) Israel Study Group, attached to the NCCCUSA in New York City; and (9) Christians Concerned about Israel, in Philadelphia.

Jewish institutions and organizations include: (1) Synagogue Council of America, in New York City, which relates mainly to the executives of the NCCCUSA and USCC and has little substantive programming; (2) Jewish Institute of Religion at Hebrew Union College, in Cincinnati, Ohio, which offers doctoral studies in Rabbinic Judaism to Christian ministers; (3) Dropsie University, in Philadelphia, which also provides advanced Jewish studies by Christians; (4) Jewish Theological Seminary, in New York City, which conducts institutes on social studies for Christian and Jewish clergy, seminary students and academicians; (5) Interreligious Affairs Department of the American Jewish Committee, in New York City, which conducts colloquia, institutes, seminars and dialogues with Catholic, Protestant, Orthodox, Evangelical and Black groups in the USA; (6) Anti-Defamation League of B'nai B'rith in New York City, which specializes in studies and programmes combatting anti-Semitism, conducts conferences with Christian leaders and publishes materials on Jewish-Christian relations; (7) Jewish Chautauqua Studies of the Union of American Hebrew Congregations, in New York City, which produces films and audio-visual aids and provides Jewish lectures to seminaries and college campuses; and (8) Centre of Interreligious Research, in Chicago, which is a small group of university and seminary staff seeking to organize systematic research on an interreligious basis.

**BROADCASTING.** Because there is no state monopoly of broadcasting, in 1971 some 7,235 medium-wave radio broadcasting stations had been licensed in the USA (93% commercial; 4,494 AM, 2,339 FM, 592 educational FM; 246 being of 10 kW or over in strength). Call signs beginning with W are assigned to stations east of the Mississippi, K to those west. Of these stations over 700 are owned or operated by churches, Catholic dioceses or colleges, or local groups of Protestant businessmen. Many Christian stations are FM ones abandoned before 1965 when FM appeared to be a failure, which were then bought up cheaply and are now used for religious programmes specializing in good conservative religious music. Range is usually 10–30 miles, covering a town or city with suburbs. In 1945 the National Religious Broadcasters (NRB) (an affiliate of the NAE) was organized to co-ordinate evangelical broadcasting; by 1977 its 850 members (85% of the USA's religious producers and broadcasters) and 325 affiliated stations handled 85% of all Protestant religious broadcasts in the USA and 75% in the world. In 1975–78, new Christian radio stations were being formed in the USA at a rate of one per week. By 1980, Evangelicals owned and operated 40 TV stations.

Similarly in 1971 there were 1,021 TV broadcasting stations in the USA (802 commercial, 219 educational); among these were 8 Protestant stations, about 10 stations run by Catholic dioceses and several run by Catholic universities specilizing in instructional TV. Many other Catholic colleges and universitites have closed-circuit TV systems. For Catholics, the USA is a member of UNDA.

There is a vast number of Catholic and Protestant studios producing programmes for which time is bought on commercial stations. One of the largest bodies is the Lutheran Hour, a worldwide enterprise of the Lutheran Church—Missouri Synod, based in St Louis, which broadcasts in 41 languages over 1,400 stations to over 125 nations.

There are several USA-based religious broadcasting companies which operate radio stations and services across the world; these include the Far East Broadcasting Company (California), Trans World Radio (New Jersey), and World Radio Missionary Fellowship (Florida). The Billy Graham Evangelistic Association has recently applied for a licence to build a one-million-watt station in Hawaii.

From abroad, Radio Vatican beams programmes in English to the USA for one hour 45 minutes a week.

## BIBLIOGRAPHY

Although the literature on religions in the USA is immense, we offer here a selection of the major descriptive and analytical works. In addition, almost every denomination has its own yearbook or directory; a selection of 20 of these are listed here in the Topical Directory, part 13.

*A bibliography of Black Methodism*. J.G. Melton. Evanston: Institute for the Study of American Religion, 1970. 45p.

*A directory of religious bodies in the United States*. J.G. Melton. New York: Garland, 1977. 305p. (1,200 Christian denominations and non-Christian groups).

*A directory of religious organizations in the United States*. J.G. Melton. London: E.J. Brill, 1977. 553p.

*A history of the Catholic Church in the United States*. T.T. McAvoy. South Bend, IN: University of Notre Dame Press, 1969. 504p.

*A history of the churches in the United States and Canada*. R.T. Handy. Oxford History of the Christian Church. Oxford: Oxford University Press, 1977. 486p.

*A religious history of the American people*. S.E. Ahlstrom. New Haven: Yale University Press, 1972. 1,158p.

*An encyclopedia of religious groups in the United States*. J.G. Melton. Wilmington, NC: Consortium Books, 1977. 4 vols. (Describes 1,200 denominations/primary religious groups, including non-Christian ones).

*Aspects sociologiques du Catholicisme américain: vie urbaine et institutions religieuses*. F. Houtart. Paris: Editions Ouvrières, 1957. 340p.

'Black Pentecostal Concept: interpretations and variations', W.J. Hollenweger, *Concept* (Geneva), 30 (June 1970), 1–68. (Documentation on 33 USA Black pentecostal churches).

*Church and State in the United States*. A.P. Stokes. New York: Harper & Brothers, 1964. 3 vols.

*Churches & church membership in the United States: an enumeration by region, state and county*. Eds D.W. Johnson, P.R. Picard, B. Quinn. Washington, DC: Glenmary Research Center, 1971. 237p.

*Contemporary Catholicism in the United States*. Ed P. Gleason. South Bend, IN: University of Notre Dame Press, 1969.

*Handbook of American Orthodoxy, 1972*. New York: Forward Movement Publications, 1972. 191p.

*Handbook of denominations in the United States: their history, doctrines, organization, present status*. F.S. Mead. 5th edition. Nashville, TN: Abingdon, 1970. 265p.

*Handbook of the National Council of the Churches of Christ in the USA*. New York: NCCCUSA, 1967, 1968, 1969.

*Historical atlas of religion in America*. E.S. Gaustad. New York: Harper & Row, 1962.

*Mission handbook: North American Protestant ministries overseas*. Ed E.R. Dayton. Monrovia, CA: MARC, 1973. 645p. (Triennial).

'New religious movements in the USA', *Social compass* (Louvain), XXI, 3 (1974), 223–360. (10 essays).

*Official Catholic directory*. New York: P.J. Kenedy & Sons, 1978. 1,608p. (Annual; first issue 1817; 63 categories of current statistics).

*Official guide to Catholic educational institutions and religious communities in the US, 1972–73*. Ed Doris B. Gray. Washington, DC: US Catholic Conference, 1972.

'Old and new religions among North American Indians: missiological impressions and reflections', H.W. Turner, *Missiology* (South Pasadena, USA), I, 2, April 1973, 47–66.

*Parishes and clergy of the Orthodox and other Eastern Churches in North and South America, together with the parishes and clergy of the Polish National Catholic Church, 1970–71*. New York: Episcopal Church in the USA, 1971. 208p. (Illustrated).

*Profiles in belief: the religious bodies of the USA and Canada*. Vol 1: *Roman Catholic, Old Catholic and Eastern Orthodox*. A.C. Piepkorn. New York: Harper & Row, 1977. (7 volumes projected).

*Religion in America: the Gallup Opinion Index, 1977–78*. Report No. 145. Princeton, NJ: Gallup International, 1977. 119p. (Also 1975, 1973, 1971 and earlier editions).

*Religion in the United States: a concise introduction to 53 denominations and groups*. B.Y. Landis. New York: Barnes & Noble, 1965. 120p.

'Religion reported by the civilian population of the United States: March 1957', US Bureau of the Census, *Current population reports*, 2 February 1958, Series P-20 No. 79. (A sample survey of 100,000 persons).

*Religious and spiritual groups in modern America*. R.S. Ellwood, Jr. Englewood Cliffs, NJ: Prentice-Hall, 1973p. 334p. (Contemporary sects and cults).

*Religious movements in contemporary America*. Ed I.I. Zaretsky & M.P. Leone. Princeton: Princeton University Press, 1974. 837p. (On marginal religious movements. Bibliography of 1,100 items).

*The American Holiness movement: a bibliographic introduction*. D.W. Dayton. Wilmore, KY: B.L. Fisher Library (Asbury Theological Seminary), 1971.

*The American Pentecostal movement: a bibliographical essay*. D.W. Faupel. Wilmore, KY: B.L. Fisher Library (Asbury Theological Seminary), 1972. 56p.

*The Black Muslims in America*. C.E. Lincoln. Boston: Beacon Press, 1961. 276p.

*The history and philosophy of the metaphysical movements in America*. J.S. Judah. Philadelphia: Westminster Press, 1967. 317p.

*The Latter-day Saints: the Mormons yesterday and today*. R. Mullen. Garden City, NY: Doubleday, 1966. 316p.

*The Native American Christian community: a directory of Indian, Aleut and Eskimo churches*. R. Pierce Beaver. Monrovia (CA): MARC, 1979. 395p.

*The Negro Church in America*. E.F. Frazier. New York: Schocken Books, 1964. 92p.

*The Peyote religion*. J.S. Slotkin. Glencoe, IL: Free Press, 1956. (American Indian religion).

*The Protestant Churches of America*. J.A. Hardon. New York: Doubleday, 1969. 439p.

*The religious dimension in Hispanic Los Angeles: a Protestant case study*. C.L. Holland. South Pasadena, CA: William Carey Library, 1974. 541p. (Churches among 3.5 million Spanish-speaking Mexican Americans in California).

*The small sects in America*. E.T. Clark. New York: Abingdon Press, 1937, 1949. 256p. (Study of 300 sects).

*The state of the churches in the USA, 1973: as shown in their own official yearbooks*. Sun City, AZ: Ecumenism Research Agency. (Listing of USA denominational yearbooks, minutes, reports, published on microfilm).

*Why Conservative churches are growing: a study in sociology of religion*. D.M. Kelley. New York: Harper & Row, 1972. 184p.

*Yearbook of American and Canadian Churches, 1980*. Ed C.H. Jacquet, Jr. New York: NCCCUSA & Abingdon Press, 1979. 282p. (Annual since 1916).

TABLE 2. ORGANIZED CHURCHES AND DENOMINATIONS IN THE UNITED STATES OF AMERICA

| Official name 1 | Begun 2 | Type 3 | Counc 4 | Congs 5 | Adults 6 | Affiliated 7 | Names, notes, and other statistics (see Codebook) 8 |
|---|---|---|---|---|---|---|---|
| Advent Christian Church | 1854 | P Adv | xF... | 394 | 30,713 | 40,000 | *General Conf of America*. 31 Confs. 493n,G=0.7%pa,2j,2s(70),360t(24481),W=68%. |
| African Methodist Episcopal Church | 1787 | I Met | VW..b | 6,000 | 1,100,000 | 1,529,000 | *AMEC*. 99% Black. 13 Districts in USA. Missions in Africa, West Indies. 7089n,17r. |
| African Methodist Episcopal Zion Ch | 1796 | I Met | VW..b | 4,500 | 940,000 | 1,307,000 | *AMEZC*. Black. 10 bishops in Americas, Europe, 2 in Africa. 5500n,G=–3%pa,1j,6r. |
| African Orthodox Church | 1919 | I ARo | x...J | 24 | 4,000 | 6,000 | *AOC*. Schism ex PECUSA. West Indian Blacks. HQ New York. Many overseas fields. 50n. |
| African Union First Coloured MP Church | 1866 | I Met | ..... | 41 | 3,000 | 5,000 | MP=Methodist Protestant. Black members. Schism ex Methodist Episcopal Ch. 48n. |
| Albanian Orth Archdiocese in America | 1908 | O Alb | M.o.. | 20 | 46,000 | 62,000 | Albanian refugees. Linked to Orthodox Ch in America. 23n,13t(1375),W=66%. |
| Albanian Orthodox Diocese of America | 1950 | O Alb | C.O.. | 10 | 1,500 | 5,150 | Albanian refugees. Rapid growth through mixed marriages. 4n,G=4.6%pa,W=57%,25Yy. |
| Alleghany Wesleyan Meth Connection | 1843 | P Hol | ..... | 114 | 2,900 | 9,089 | Original Wesleyan conference in area. Mostly in eastern USA. 150n,G=0,W=68%. |
| Amana Church Society | 1842 | M ind | ..... | 7 | 735 | 1,500 | 1714, Community of True Inspiration (Germany). Moved to Amana (Faithfulness), Iowa. |
| American Baptist Association | 1905 | P Bap | xT... | 3,321 | 86,900 | 1,300,000 | *ABA*. *Landmarkers*. Regular Baptists. Mainly south. 3368n,G=5%pa,2s,3336t(450000). |
| American Baptist Churches in the USA | 1639 | P Bap | TW..W | 6,035 | 1,412,000 | 2,100,000 | Formerly American Baptist Convention. 8222n,G=–0.4%pa,9s(1090),W=34%,3456Y. |
| American Carpatho-Russian OGC Church | 1891 | O Sla | C.O.. | 71 | 74,000 | 106,900 | OGC=Orthodox Greek Cath. Former Uniates from USSR. 67n,G=0.7%pa,1s(19),56t(5098). |
| American Catholic Ch (Syro-Antiochian) | 1915 | C CCa | ..... | 5 | 1,031 | 1,500 | *Assyrian Jacobite Apost Ch*. Monophysite. Orders from Syrian P Antioch. 9n,1t(37). |

*Continued opposite*

*Table 2–continued*

| Official name 1 | Begun 2 | Type 3 | Counc 4 | Congs 5 | Adults 6 | Affiliated 7 | Names, notes, and other statistics (see Codebook) 8 |
|---|---|---|---|---|---|---|---|
| American Catholic Church, AD New York | 1927 | I ARo | ..... | 18 | 3,435 | 4,369 | Black. Schism ex AOC. Old Catholic; Jacobite orders through Vilatte. 16t(450). |
| American Episcopal Church | 1968 | A sEv | ..... | 11 | 650 | 1,000 | Schism ex PECUSA. Eastern and southern USA. Whites. 7n,1s(2),W=70%. |
| American Ev Christian Churches | 1944 | P ind | ..... | 83 | 12,763 | 20,000 | *AECC. Community Churches. American Bible Chs. Ev Christian Chs.* HQ Chicago. 164n. |
| American Holy Orth Cath Apost E Ch | 1932 | I ARo | ..... | 30 | 3,000 | 5,000 | E=Eastern. Schism ex AOC (Black). Greek rite. Attempt to unite all Orthodox. 35n. |
| American Lutheran Church | 1818 | P Lut | LW... | 4,822 | 1,775,059 | 2,543,293 | 1960 union ELC/Norw,ALC/German,UELC/Danish. 6103n,G=–0.7%pa,3s(842),W=43%,56028Yy |
| American Orthodox Catholic Church | 1961 | O ReO | .v... | | 1,000 | 2,000 | *AOCC.* Rival groups, White (Russian) and Black. Continual mergers, fresh schisms. |
| American Orth Cath Ch (AD N&S Am) | 1964 | O ReO | xv... | 37 | 10,000 | 14,000 | Ex Ukrainian Orth Ch of USA. 8 bishops. US Virgin Islands France, Zaire, Nigeria. |
| American Rescue Workers | 1896 | P ind | ..... | 46 | 5,410 | 10,000 | Home missionary society, military organization. HQ Philadelphia. 53n,36t(9226). |
| Anglican Catholic Ch in North America | 1977 | A smi | x.... | 160 | 5,000 | 10,000 | *ACC*, previously *ACNA*. Schism ex ECUSA protesting ordination of women. 4 Dioceses. |
| Anglican Orthodox Ch of North America | 1963 | A sEv | xT... | 38 | 2,000 | 4,000 | Split ex PECUSA in NCarolina. Anglican Orthodox Communion in 10 nations. 19n,35t. |
| Antiochian Orth Archdiocese of Toledo | 1935 | O Ara | .v..W | 25 | 20,000 | 30,000 | In communion with Greek P Antioch. 95% Arab origin. 26n,6x,12t,W=50%,250Yy. |
| Antiochian Orth Christian ADNew York | c1920 | O Ara | CWO.W | 92 | 76,000 | 110,000 | Formerly Syrian Antiochian Orth AD NY & NA. Under Greek P Antioch. 110n,G=–1.4%pa. |
| Apostolic Assembly of the Faith in JC | 1911 | I pel | x.... | 195 | 24,000 | 50,000 | *Asamblea Apostólica de la Fe en CJ.* M=Iglesia AFCJ(Mexico). In 6 states. 195n. |
| Apostolic Christian Church (Nazarean) | 1907 | P Hol | x.... | 43 | 2,347 | 4,000 | Split ex ACCA protesting use of German. In IL, OH, 17 nations. 147n,39t(1575). |
| Apostolic Christian Church of America | 1847 | P Hol | x.... | 75 | 9,160 | 15,000 | *ACCA.* Swiss origin. Pacifist (a peace church), holiness emphasis. 273n,77t(8950). |
| Apostolic Episcopal Church | 1925 | C ARo | x.... | 20 | 1,000 | 3,000 | *Holy Eastern Cath & Apostolic Orth Ch.* Ex PECUSA. Chaldean rite. In 5 nations. |
| Apostolic Faith Church | 1923 | P Pe3 | ..... | 8 | 500 | 1,000 | *Jesus Coming Soon Church.* Holiness Pentecostals (3-stage). 4n,W=50%,120Y. |
| Apostolic Faith Mission | 1900 | P Pe3 | x.... | 44 | 4,835 | 7,000 | *AFM Portland*, Oregon. 65% White, 35% Black. 75n,44t(6600),W=75%,120Y. |
| Apostolic Lutheran Church of America | 1872 | P Lut | xv... | 82 | 6,994 | 16,000 | *ALCA. Church of Laestadius.* Finnish-speaking; in Midwest. White. In 4 nations. 65n. |
| Apostolic Overcoming Holy Ch of God | 1916 | I pel | ..... | 300 | 30,000 | 75,000 | Black pentecostals. Ex Methodists. Foot-washing, liturgical dance. 350n,1j. |
| Armenian Apostolic Church of America | 1933 | O Arm | Sw.N. | 34 | 100,000 | 150,000 | *Gregorians.* 1933 split ex Echmiadzin; 1957, under C Cilicia. 28nx,G=0,29t,500Yy. |
| Armenian Church of North America | 1889 | O Arm | Ewc.W | 65 | 200,000 | 372,000 | *D California, D NAmerica.* Under C Echmiadzin. 60% all US Armenians. 71n,90t(8000). |
| Armenian Ev Spiritual Brethren | c1925 | P CBr | x.... | 4 | 1,000 | 2,000 | Schism ex Armenian Evangelical Union. Plymouth Brethren and Holiness doctrines. |
| Armenian Ev Union of Churches | c1920 | P Con | Rw... | 40 | 10,000 | 20,000 | Eastern US, California. Armenian refugees after 1915; also in Middle East. |
| Assemblies of God | 1906 | P Pe2 | ZF.XE | 8,799 | 679,813 | 1,500,000 | *General Conference.* 95% White. 12037n,G=2.7%pa,1j,4r,13s,9200t(1078332),20864Y. |
| Assemblies of God (Spanish) | c1915 | I pe2 | ..... | 300 | 30,000 | 70,000 | *Asambleas de Dios.* Spanish-speaking pentecostals (California Mexicans, et al). |
| Assemblies of the Lord Jesus Christ | 1952 | P Pel | ..... | 300 | 25,000 | 60,000 | Apostolic. Mainly in eastern and southern USA. HQ Memphis (Tennessee). 300n. |
| Assembly Hall Churches | 1961 | I EBr | x.... | 40 | 2,000 | 4,000 | *Local Chs. Little Flock.* Begun China 1926. HQ Los Angeles. 60% White, 33% Chinese. |
| Assembly of Christian Churches | 1939 | I pen | x.... | 100 | 4,000 | 10,000 | *Asamblea de Igl Cristianas.* Split ex LACCC. Mostly Puerto Ricans. HQ Brooklyn (NY). |
| Associate Reformed Presbyterian Church | 1782 | P Ref | F.... | 150 | 28,443 | 34,625 | *ARPC, Gen Synod. Covenanters.* SE USA. 142n,G=0.8%pa,1s,141t(17109),W=50%,553Yy. |
| Associated Brotherhood of Christians | 1915 | P Pel | x.... | 100 | 2,500 | 6,000 | Jesus Only schism ex Assemblies of God. Pacifists. HQ Hot Springs (AR). |
| Associated Churches of God | 1974 | P BrI | ..... | 50 | 5,000 | 10,000 | Schism ex Worldwide Ch of God rejecting multiple tithing. HQ Washington DC. 40n. |
| Associated Gospel Churches | 1939 | P Met | .t..t | 25 | 1,000 | 3,000 | Formerly ABFA, ex Meth Prot Ch. Also agency serving 3 million fundamentalists. |
| Association of Evangelical Lutheran Chs | 1976 | P Lut | Lv... | 300 | 100,000 | 150,000 | *AELC.* Liberal schism ex LCMS (Missouri). 5 Regional Synods. ELIM,1s. HQ St Louis. |
| Assoc of Free Lutheran Congregations | 1897 | P Lut | ..... | 120 | 6,300 | 10,000 | Lutheran Free Ch rejecting 1963 ALC merger. Norwegian origin. 78n,G=2%pa,1p(20),1s. |
| Association of Independent Methodists | c1965 | P Met | ..... | 25 | 3,200 | 5,000 | Conservative schism ex United Methodist Church. In Alabama, Mississippi, Tennessee. |
| Assyrian Church of the East (P Tehran) | 1907 | O Nes | YW... | 12 | 7,000 | 10,000 | *Holy Apostolic & Cath Ch of the East. Nestorians.* From Iran, Iraq, Lebanon. 39n. |
| Autocephalous Greek Orthodox Ch | c1924 | O OCd | c.... | 4 | 1,000 | 2,000 | Split ex GOC rejecting New (Gregorian) Calendar. Parishes: Newark, Memphis (TN). |
| Baptist Bible Fellowship International | 1950 | P Bap | x.... | 2,200 | 600,000 | 1,200,000 | *BBFI.* Ex SBC et alia. 1.7 million by 1976. Whites. In 48 countries. G=6%pa,1s. |
| Baptist General Conference | 1852 | P Bap | TF..E | 681 | 103,955 | 130,000 | Early Swedes, most now non-Swedish. 1032n,G=3.6%pa,1p,1s,681t(119192),W=80%,4182Y. |
| Baptist Missionary Assoc of America | 1950 | P Bap | x.... | 1,508 | 187,246 | 230,000 | NA Bapt Assoc to 1968. Regular Baptist. 3000n,G=0,5p,3s,1408t(107406),W=60%,9431Y. |
| Beachy Amish Mennonite Church | 1927 | P Men | G.... | 62 | 3,688 | 8,000 | Ex Old Order Amish MC. Amish Mennonite Aid. 103n(& 35 bishops, 25 deacons). |
| Berean Fundamental Churches | 1934 | P Bap | ..... | 52 | 2,718 | 4,500 | Conservative theology. Most midwest, Colorado. HQ Nebraska. 45n,G=9%pa,50t(4466). |
| Bethel Baptist Assembly | 1934 | P Bap | ..... | 25 | 4,000 | 6,000 | *Bethel Ministerial Association.* Mainly Indiana (begun Evansville). 105n,25t(5500). |
| Bethesda Missionary Temple | 1934 | P ind | ..... | 6 | 2,450 | 3,000 | Independent churches. National radio ministry. 8n,W=83%,300Y,425z. |
| Bible Methodist Church | 1929 | P Hol | ..... | 20 | 1,000 | 2,000 | *Bible Methodist Connection of Tennessee.* HQ Knoxville. 37n,G=0,5p,W=60%,50Yy. |
| Bible Presbyterian Church | 1938 | P Ref | xT..T | 69 | 5,000 | 8,000 | Fundamentalist schism ex Orthodox Presbyterian Ch. ICCC base. HQ Collingswood(NJ). |
| Bible Protestant Church | 1939 | P Hol | .T..T | 52 | 2,549 | 3,186 | Schism ex Methodist Protestant Ch, rejecting merger. HQ Linwood (NJ). 60n,1s,145Yy. |
| Bible Way Churches of Our Lord JC WW | 1951 | I pel | x...J | 350 | 30,000 | 42,000 | WW=World Wide. Black pentecostals. Ex COLJCAF. 360n,G=10%pa,4p,W=95%,1000Y. |
| Brethren Church (Ashland, Ohio) | 1881 | P Dun | xF..E | 120 | 16,937 | 35,000 | Ex CoBrethren; 1939, NFBC (Grace) secedes. 130n,G=–1.1%pa,1s,119t(12377),W=58%. |
| Brethren in Christ Church | 1778 | P Men | GF..E | 155 | 9,145 | 19,000 | Known as River Brethren until 1863. In Ohio,PA,WV,MD. 325n,G=2.5%pa,155t(17729). |
| Bulgarian Eastern Orthodox Church | 1907 | O Sla | MwO.. | 23 | 60,000 | 86,000 | *D N&S America & Australia.* Under P Sofia. Dioceses; New York, Akron, Detroit. 13nx. |
| Byelorussian Autocephalic Orthodox Ch | 1948 | O Sla | x.... | 5 | 10,000 | 20,000 | Refugees from White Russian church begun in AD 1291. 4 bishops (1 in Canada). |
| Calvary Grace Church of Faith | 1954 | P ind | ..... | 78 | 10,000 | 20,000 | Independent White group, one of many similar loosely-structured denominations. 120n. |
| Calvary Pentecostal Church | 1931 | P Pe2 | ..... | 22 | 8,000 | 15,000 | White. Begun in Olympia (WA) by group of ministers. Missions in Brazil, India. |
| Cathedral of Tomorrow | 1952 | P tel | ..... | 2 | 6,000 | 20,000 | In Akron. On 534 TV stations to 20 million in 15 countries. Staff 150. Pentecostal. |
| Catholic Apostolic Church | 1851 | C CAp | x.... | 2 | 1,700 | 2,500 | *Irvingites*, from UK. Millenarian, 12-fold apostleship. No clergy, rapid decline. |
| **Catholic Church in the USA:** | 1526 | R LEr | B...R | 18,259 | 33,387,100 | 48,390,990 | ST, RE, 57421nx,9740m,146914w,836H,2075r, 75s, 79012Y,1054933y. C=127+27+430.W=60% |
| M Anchorage | 1966 | R Lat | Bs | 16 | 21,100 | 30,588 | AK XII 36 4 25 2 0 0 77 449 |
| D Fairbanks | 1894 | R Lat | Psj | 24 | 9,100 | 13,241 | AK XII 39 7 28 0 2 0 18 297 |
| D Juneau | 1931 | R Lat | Bs | 7 | 2,500 | 3,707 | AK XII 15 0 12 1 0 0 8 109 |
| M Atlanta | 1956 | R Lat | Bs | 36 | 41,000 | 59,452 | GA IV 155 25 159 4 3 0 325 1622 |
| D Charleston | 1820 | R Lat | Bs | 65 | 32,200 | 46,752 | SC IV 140 29 254 5 4 0 299 1318 |
| D Charlotte | 1971 | R Lat | Bs | 50 | 23,600 | 34,208 | NC IV 68 1 233 4 4 0 183 877 |
| D Raleigh | 1924 | R Lat | Bs | 57 | 24,300 | 35,220 | NC IV 91 0 153 1 0 0 176 1201 |
| D Savannah | 1850 | R Lat | Bs | 42 | 24,700 | 35,850 | GA IV 114 8 214 3 5 0 245 1090 |
| M Baltimore | 1789 | R Lat | Bs | 143 | 287,500 | 416,622 | MD IV 819 132 2455 9 33 3 905 9802 |
| D Richmond | 1820 | R Lat | Bs | 120 | 172,100 | 249,453 | VA IV 350 29 800 7 20 0 802 6792 |
| D Wheeling-Charleston | 1850 | R Lat | Bs | 100 | 66,700 | 96,621 | WV IV 201 15 552 8 13 1 469 1958 |
| D Wilmington | 1868 | R Lat | Bs | 53 | 79,400 | 115,036 | DE IV 202 30 412 1 11 0 153 2823 |
| M Boston | 1808 | R Lat | Bs | 401 | 1,392,600 | 2,018,034 | MA I 2573 203 5664 11 75 4 508 30840 |
| D Burlington | 1853 | R Lat | Bs | 103 | 99,500 | 144,239 | VT I 256 20 498 1 8 0 229 3528 |
| D Fall River | 1904 | R Lat | Bs | 112 | 210,000 | 305,000 | MA I 432 45 828 2 9 0 104 6289 |
| D Manchester | 1884 | R Lat | Bs | 126 | 181,600 | 263,233 | NH I 417 83 1166 3 12 0 189 6173 |
| D Portland | 1853 | R Lat | Bs | 140 | 187,300 | 271,428 | ME I 345 41 1129 7 8 0 444 5922 |
| D Springfield in Massachusetts | 1870 | R Lat | Bs | 136 | 264,300 | 383,052 | MA I 348 30 1073 4 10 0 190 7325 |
| D Worcester | 1950 | R Lat | Bs | 131 | 237,100 | 343,585 | MA I 512 125 990 2 15 0 136 6452 |
| M Chicago | 1843 | R Lat | Bs | 452 | 1,722,400 | 2,496,300 | IL VII 2175 458 8067 23 82 2 2623 45467 |
| D Belleville | 1887 | R Lat | Bs | 130 | 79,500 | 115,250 | IL VII 229 36 605 8 7 0 392 2431 |
| D Joliet in Illinois | 1948 | R Lat | Bs | 109 | 222,000 | 322,000 | IL VII 393 125 1028 2 12 0 421 6648 |
| D Peoria | 1875 | R Lat | Bs | 170 | 148,300 | 214,968 | IL VII 382 19 833 12 10 0 792 4831 |
| D Rockford | 1908 | R Lat | Bs | 97 | 141,900 | 205,609 | IL VII 276 29 470 5 9 0 452 4449 |
| D Springfield in Illinois | 1853 | R Lat | Bs | 143 | 126,000 | 182,674 | IL VII 307 47 1002 12 13 0 644 3475 |
| M Cincinnati | 1821 | R Lat | Bs | 259 | 365,200 | 529,220 | OH VI 852 328 2451 11 33 2 1128 10021 |
| D Cleveland | 1847 | R Lat | Bs | 236 | 607,000 | 879,771 | OH VI 914 168 2984 9 34 2 1486 17795 |
| D Columbus | 1868 | R Lat | Bs | 105 | 123,000 | 178,000 | OH VI 339 4 842 7 16 2 793 4247 |
| D Steubenville | 1944 | R Lat | Bs | 73 | 38,400 | 55,600 | OH VI 195 20 237 2 6 2 384 1308 |
| D Toledo | 1910 | R Lat | Bs | 142 | 227,000 | 328,977 | OH VI 400 17 1439 7 21 0 917 7838 |
| D Youngstown | 1943 | R Lat | Bs | 117 | 215,800 | 312,708 | OH VI 342 58 631 3 7 0 599 5787 |
| M Denver | 1887 | R Lat | Bs | 117 | 206,200 | 298,784 | CO VI 340 34 864 7 14 2 799 7487 |
| D Cheyenne | 1887 | R Lat | Bs | 39 | 31,000 | 45,000 | WY VIII 71 2 100 1 1 0 164 1314 |
| D Pueblo | 1941 | R Lat | Bs | 60 | 72,600 | 105,197 | CO VIII 165 13 231 6 3 0 148 2854 |
| M Detroit | 1833 | R Lat | Bs | 327 | 1,117,200 | 1,619,081 | MI VI 1297 159 3600 11 61 4 1975 29504 |
| D Gaylord | 1971 | R Lat | Bs | 58 | 45,000 | 66,000 | MI VI 77 2 130 4 5 0 204 1688 |
| D Grand Rapids | 1822 | R Lat | Bs | 81 | 101,900 | 147,672 | MI VI 210 0 712 2 8 0 564 3619 |
| D Kalamazoo | 1971 | R Lat | Bs | 45 | 57,600 | 83,416 | MI VI 80 16 311 3 4 0 368 1943 |
| D Lansing | 1937 | R Lat | Bs | 83 | 127,200 | 184,309 | MI VI 213 30 482 5 9 0 699 5073 |
| D Marquette | 1857 | R Lat | Bs | 92 | 69,200 | 100,359 | MI VI 166 2 231 5 0 0 191 2162 |
| D Saginaw | 1938 | R Lat | Bs | 102 | 108,700 | 157,560 | MI VI 184 2 249 2 5 0 433 4353 |
| M Dubuque | 1837 | R Lat | Bs | 201 | 158,800 | 230,215 | IA IX 512 89 1721 13 18 1 581 5193 |
| D Davenport | 1881 | R Lat | Bs | 119 | 74,800 | 108,365 | IA IX 235 6 540 9 12 1 349 2729 |
| D Des Moines | 1911 | R Lat | Bs | 93 | 55,700 | 80,786 | IA IX 142 0 253 3 3 0 407 2043 |
| D Sioux City | 1902 | R Lat | Bs | 141 | 73,400 | 106,378 | IA IX 226 1 428 6 12 0 369 2398 |
| M Hartford | 1843 | R Lat | Bs | 217 | 556,800 | 806,902 | CT I 750 94 1629 4 21 0 362 16122 |
| D Bridgeport | 1953 | R Lat | Bs | 82 | 222,500 | 322,500 | CT I 375 31 733 2 15 0 142 6018 |
| D Norwich | 1953 | R Lat | Bs | 70 | 135,500 | 196,384 | CT I 211 41 385 0 9 0 115 3572 |
| D Providence | 1872 | R Lat | Bs | 154 | 414,400 | 600,595 | RI I 603 144 1555 3 20 1 290 9804 |
| M Indianapolis | 1834 | R Lat | Bs | 164 | 144,500 | 209,412 | IN VII 436 89 2342 3 16 2 809 4885 |
| D Evansville | 1944 | R Lat | Bs | 74 | 58,700 | 85,074 | IN VII 148 11 615 3 7 0 229 1823 |
| D Fort Wayne-South Bend | 1857 | R Lat | Bs | 81 | 107,400 | 155,624 | IN VII 447 200 868 5 14 0 481 3385 |
| D Gary | 1956 | R Lct | Bs | 87 | 127,600 | 184,876 | IN VII 232 42 415 5 6 0 389 3881 |
| D Lafayette in Indiana | 1944 | R Lat | Bs | 56 | 57,500 | 83,383 | IN VII 164 15 206 5 4 0 379 1920 |
| M Kansas City in Kansas | 1877 | R Lat | Bs | 96 | 95,500 | 138,350 | KS IX 286 25 964 5 11 0 502 3142 |
| D Dodge City | 1951 | R Lat | Bs | 49 | 23,000 | 33,408 | KS IX 75 1 208 4 1 0 125 748 |
| D Salina | 1887 | R Lat | Bs | 99 | 38,500 | 55,776 | KS IX 135 5 462 6 8 0 238 1358 |
| D Wichita | 1887 | R Lat | Bs | 96 | 60,900 | 88,202 | KS IX 193 10 528 7 5 0 448 2087 |
| M Los Angeles | 1922 | R Lat | Bs | 324 | 1,236,400 | 1,791,932 | CA XI 1404 334 3168 23 75 1 2757 61570 |
| D Fresno | 1967 | R Lat | Bs | 84 | 185,000 | 268,145 | CA XI 167 21 251 5 3 0 347 8390 |
| D Monterey in California | 1850 | R Lat | Bs | 43 | 65,000 | 95,000 | CA XI 117 33 220 2 3 0 156 2663 |
| D San Diego | 1936 | R Lat | Bs | 164 | 353,600 | 512,412 | CA XI 502 22 829 4 12 1 823 13527 |
| M Louisville | 1808 | R Lat | Bs | 124 | 133,100 | 192,861 | KY V 406 139 1253 5 17 0 451 4168 |
| D Covington | 1853 | R Lat | Bs | 83 | 71,400 | 103,500 | KY V 215 16 1123 10 16 2 244 2093 |
| D Memphis | 1970 | R Lat | Bs | 27 | 26,900 | 39,006 | TN V 70 62 175 3 6 0 301 918 |

*State.* The first sub-column in column 8, headed ST, gives the standard 2-letter zip code of the civil state within which each diocese is located, and over which its jurisdiction extends either in whole or in part. Ecclesiastical boundaries do not usually follow civil boundaries exactly, although in the main this is the case. All dioceses but 5 are each located entirely within a single state; and 11 dioceses are each co-terminous with a single state. The 2 letters US indicate that a jurisdiction extends over the whole of the USA.

*Region.* The second sub-column, headed RE, gives the ecclesiastical region of which the diocese is a part. The whole USA territory (with US territories abroad) was divided originally into 3 ecclesiastical regions, which by 1972 had been increased to 12. These geographical regions provide more local consultation and discussion than is possible in the NCCB with its 300 participants. The regions act somewhat after the manner of the *circuli minores* employed in Rome at the Synod of Bishops. The regions cover civil states as follows (using the zip code abbreviations for states):

*Region I.* CT, MA, ME, NH, RI, VT.
*Region II.* NY.
*Region III.* NJ, PA.
*Region IV.* DC, DE, FL, GA, MD, DC, SC, VA, WV (also US Virgin Islands).
*Region V.* AL, AR, KY, LA, MS, TN.
*Region VI.* MI, OH.
*Region VII.* IL, IN, WI.
*Region VIII.* CO, MN,

*Continued overleaf*

*Table 2–continued*

| Official name 1 | Begun 2 | Type 3 | Counc 4 | Congs 5 | Adults 6 | Affiliated 7 | Names, notes, and other statistics (see Codebook) 8 |
|---|---|---|---|---|---|---|---|
| D Nashville | 1837 | R Lat | Bs | 46 | 37,000 | 53,558 | TN V 99 26 49 4 6 0 556 1215 |
| D Owensboro | 1937 | R Lat | Bs | 72 | 33,400 | 48,412 | KY V 88 5 583 2 6 0 195 1081 |
| M Miami | 1958 | R Lat | Bs | 115 | 393,000 | 569,543 | FL IV 452 65 761 21 1 1 606 10752 |
| D Orlando | 1968 | R Lat | Bs | 54 | 94,500 | 136,957 | FL IV 106 0 175 3 5 0 385 2307 |
| D Saint Augustine | 1770 | R Lat | Bs | 70 | 53,000 | 76,828 | FL IV 113 0 163 2 3 0 395 2101 |
| D Saint Petersburg | 1968 | R Lat | Bs | 70 | 106,700 | 154,628 | FL IV 208 36 357 4 9 0 437 3219 |
| M Milwaukee | 1843 | R Lat | Bs | 265 | 480,300 | 696,090 | WI VII 1195 227 4082 20 23 1 1002 14760 |
| D Green Bay | 1868 | R Lat | Bs | 193 | 218,800 | 317,102 | WI VII 520 96 1167 8 13 0 405 6709 |
| D La Crosse | 1868 | R Lat | Bs | 178 | 138,000 | 200,023 | WI VII 359 33 1055 8 10 0 474 4566 |
| D Madison | 1945 | R Lat | Bs | 112 | 134,600 | 195,132 | WI VII 254 16 826 6 4 0 492 3799 |
| D Superior | 1905 | R Lat | Bs | 88 | 58,100 | 84,272 | WI VII 139 0 729 7 2 0 174 1850 |
| M Munhall (*Ruthenian*)(1977, Pittsb) | 1924 | R Rut | Os | 77 | 103,000 | 150,000 | PA III 93 5 166 0 0 0 200 1400 |
| D Parma (*Ruthenian*) | 1969 | R Rut | Os | 46 | 19,200 | 27,847 | OH VI 58 0 51 0 1 0 39 554 |
| D Passaic (*Ruthenian*) | 1963 | R Rut | Os | 79 | 69,000 | 99,968 | NJ III 94 3 50 0 0 0 33 787 |
| M New Orleans | 1793 | R Lat | Bs | 163 | 460,000 | 666,702 | LA V 605 178 1500 4 36 1 619 12934 |
| D Alexandria-Shreveport | 1853 | R Lat | Bs | 86 | 50,700 | 73,451 | LA V 184 15 282 7 8 0 313 1765 |
| D Baton Rouge | 1961 | R Lat | Bs | 65 | 100,400 | 145,529 | LA V 149 26 207 4 8 0 318 3859 |
| D Birmingham, USA | 1969 | R Lat | Bs | 57 | 28,400 | 41,202 | AL V 135 19 276 2 4 0 313 927 |
| D Lafayette | 1918 | R Lat | Bs | 151 | 272,600 | 395,035 | LA V 293 37 421 2 19 0 350 9565 |
| D Mobile | 1829 | R Lat | Bs | 66 | 31,100 | 45,016 | AL V 173 22 326 8 5 0 366 1164 |
| D Natchez-Jackson(1977,DJackson) | 1837 | R Lat | Bs | 105 | 58,300 | 84,554 | MS V 210 61 358 3 13 0 398 2066 |
| M New York | 1808 | R Lat | Bs | 406 | 1,242,000 | 1,800,000 | NY II 2158 1010 7729 17 96 1 4000 48750 |
| D Albany | 1847 | R Lat | Bs | 211 | 292,700 | 424,219 | NY II 454 125 1881 7 23 1 372 9291 |
| D Brooklyn | 1853 | R Lat | Bs | 229 | 1,026,300 | 1,487,360 | NY II 1374 487 3388 5 41 1 600 37341 |
| D Buffalo | 1847 | R Lat | Bs | 282 | 642,800 | 931,623 | NY II 1208 97 2877 16 44 2 609 13563 |
| D Ogdensburg | 1872 | R Lat | Bs | 122 | 118,300 | 171,536 | NY II 249 34 506 3 7 1 240 3908 |
| D Rochester | 1868 | R Lat | Bs | 160 | 218,600 | 316,790 | NY II 498 58 1238 4 9 2 634 8682 |
| D Rockville Center | 1957 | R Lat | Bs | 127 | 669,000 | 969,611 | NY II 519 105 2257 4 18 1 319 22575 |
| D Syracuse | 1886 | R Lat | Bs | 169 | 284,000 | 411,523 | NY II 512 49 970 4 20 0 457 9605 |
| M Newark | 1853 | R Lat | Bs | 253 | 1,175,300 | 1,703,356 | NJ III 1327 255 2919 9 56 1 719 24586 |
| D Camden | 1937 | R Lat | Bs | 123 | 220,800 | 319,984 | NJ III 458 19 754 1 14 0 411 7923 |
| D Paterson | 1937 | R Lat | Bs | 102 | 212,500 | 308,042 | NJ III 501 66 1279 7 22 0 199 7812 |
| D Trenton | 1881 | R Lat | Bs | 194 | 503,500 | 729,727 | NJ III 483 53 1629 3 23 0 508 15987 |
| M Oklahoma City | 1905 | R Lat | Bs | 70 | 45,300 | 65,715 | OK X 164 16 328 7 4 0 400 2100 |
| D Little Rock | 1843 | R Lat | Bs | 79 | 38,000 | 55,025 | AR V 181 54 606 11 7 0 280 1190 |
| D Tulsa | 1972 | R Lat | Bs | 52 | 35,100 | 50,893 | OK X 100 10 235 3 2 0 236 733 |
| M Omaha | 1885 | R Lat | Bs | 139 | 137,300 | 199,045 | NE IX 407 48 1103 10 24 0 662 4456 |
| D Grand Island | 1912 | R Lat | Bs | 56 | 35,300 | 51,169 | NE IX 87 0 178 6 7 0 213 1237 |
| D Lincoln | 1887 | R Lat | Bs | 136 | 41,400 | 59,956 | NE IX 157 14 231 2 6 0 312 1390 |
| M Philadelphia | 1808 | R Lat | Bs | 316 | 937,700 | 1,359,012 | PA III 1706 271 6407 16 62 1 2025 28025 |
| D Allentown | 1961 | R Lat | Bs | 151 | 176,900 | 256,443 | PA III 419 42 1085 3 12 0 349 6036 |
| D Altoona-Johnstown | 1901 | R Lat | Bs | 120 | 101,500 | 147,069 | PA III 252 28 499 2 5 0 296 2964 |
| D Erie | 1853 | R Lat | Bs | 126 | 147,200 | 213,286 | PA III 340 13 952 6 15 1 409 4465 |
| D Greensburg | 1951 | R Lat | Bs | 116 | 151,800 | 220,043 | PA III 293 18 475 1 6 0 330 3485 |
| D Harrisburg | 1868 | R Lat | Bs | 102 | 131,300 | 190,252 | PA III 247 21 998 2 11 0 397 4027 |
| D Pittsburgh | 1843 | R Lat | Bs | 320 | 635,600 | 921,148 | PA III 863 100 3030 7 47 2 809 17047 |
| D Scranton | 1868 | R Lat | Bs | 239 | 245,700 | 356,056 | PA III 551 13 1351 6 17 1 316 6465 |
| M Philadelphia (*Ukrainian*) | 1924 | R Ukr | Os | 101 | 115,300 | 167,085 | PA III 134 0 152 0 2 0 48 962 |
| D Saint Nicholas of Chicago (*Ukr*) | 1961 | R Ukr | Os | 28 | 20,600 | 29,893 | IL VII 47 0 21 0 1 0 31 349 |
| D Stamford (*Ukrainian*) | 1956 | R Ukr | Os | 57 | 60,500 | 87,700 | CT I 93 16 71 0 5 0 10 399 |
| M Portland in Oregon | 1846 | R Lat | Bs | 119 | 129,800 | 188,061 | OR XII 330 83 1043 6 14 1 738 4432 |
| D Baker | 1903 | R Lat | Bs | 31 | 16,400 | 23,818 | OR XII 55 0 106 4 1 0 111 596 |
| D Boise City | 1893 | R Lat | Bs | 66 | 40,800 | 59,117 | ID XII 112 2 201 8 2 0 406 1869 |
| D Great Falls | 1904 | R Lat | Bs | 72 | 46,900 | 67,916 | MT XII 141 5 272 4 7 0 179 1640 |
| D Helena | 1884 | R Lat | Bs | 57 | 48,600 | 70,500 | MT XII 154 11 172 6 6 0 151 1545 |
| M Saint Louis | 1826 | R Lat | Bs | 248 | 357,300 | 517,870 | MO IX 1095 95 2926 12 45 2 1237 10251 |
| D Jefferson City | 1956 | R Lat | Bs | 83 | 45,000 | 66,000 | MO IX 158 8 243 3 2 0 346 1523 |
| D Kansas City-Saint Joseph's | 1880 | R Lat | Bs | 94 | 87,400 | 126,695 | MO IX 393 43 748 4 13 2 577 2968 |
| D Springfield-Cape Girardeau | 1956 | R Lat | Bs | 59 | 27,900 | 40,462 | MO IX 107 9 211 7 3 0 218 815 |
| M Saint Paul & Minneapolis | 1850 | R Lat | Bs | 218 | 374,000 | 541,958 | MN VIII 598 73 1673 8 19 2 1093 13852 |
| D Bismarck | 1909 | R Lat | Bs | 83 | 50,300 | 72,968 | ND VIII 159 19 393 6 8 0 167 1694 |
| D Crookston | 1909 | R Lat | Bs | 51 | 26,600 | 38,591 | MN VIII 76 3 320 5 2 0 99 942 |
| D Duluth | 1889 | R Lat | Bs | 86 | 68,500 | 99,318 | MN VIII 143 2 311 4 2 0 228 2345 |
| D Fargo | 1889 | R Lat | Bs | 116 | 68,200 | 98,858 | ND VIII 178 8 456 13 3 0 252 2168 |
| D New Ulm | 1957 | R Lat | Bs | 86 | 48,100 | 69,673 | MN VIII 127 0 195 4 4 0 149 1536 |
| D Rapid City | 1902 | R Lat | Bs | 51 | 25,000 | 36,000 | SD VIII 108 12 104 2 3 0 179 1212 |
| D Saint Cloud | 1889 | R Lat | Bs | 146 | 100,300 | 145,347 | MN VIII 337 80 1420 6 8 0 289 3210 |
| D Sioux Falls | 1889 | R Lat | Bs | 126 | 69,800 | 99,673 | SD VIII 211 30 516 12 7 0 300 2237 |
| D Winona | 1889 | R Lat | Bs | 131 | 81,700 | 118,393 | MN VIII 215 32 896 5 9 1 420 2830 |
| M San Antonio | 1874 | R Lat | Bs | 152 | 368,000 | 533,382 | TX X 416 188 1705 7 22 2 408 15423 |
| D Amarillo | 1926 | R Lat | Bs | 56 | 44,500 | 64,571 | TX X 95 0 120 2 3 0 176 2943 |
| D Austin | 1947 | R Lat | Bs | 81 | 95,400 | 138,221 | TX X 159 52 180 7 3 0 342 3121 |
| D Beaumont | 1947 | R Lat | Bs | 33 | 62,900 | 91,200 | TX X 81 2 142 2 2 0 266 1806 |
| D Brownsville | 1965 | R Lat | Bs | 57 | 182,300 | 264,186 | TX X 109 16 183 1 2 0 83 9238 |
| D Corpus Christi | 1912 | R Lat | Bs | 72 | 124,200 | 180,060 | TX X 149 18 328 3 5 0 149 8473 |
| D Dallas | 1890 | R Lat | Bs | 52 | 77,300 | 111,984 | TX X 201 17 432 4 8 2 425 4433 |
| D Fort Worth | 1969 | R Lat | Bs | 47 | 46,300 | 67,076 | TX X 93 16 200 2 3 0 272 2256 |
| D Galveston-Houston | 1847 | R Lat | Bs | 117 | 221,000 | 320,300 | TX X 343 14 597 5 12 2 953 10556 |
| D San Angelo | 1961 | R Lat | Bs | 42 | 43,000 | 62,340 | TX X 71 0 52 1 1 0 111 2417 |
| M San Francisco | 1853 | R Lat | Bs | 151 | 571,300 | 827,950 | CA XI 852 156 1636 7 35 2 1555 15003 |
| D Honolulu (Hawaii) | 1941 | R Lat | Bs | 66 | 149,400 | 216,500 | HA XI 160 89 387 2 9 0 273 5754 |
| D Oakland | 1962 | R Lat | Bs | 82 | 228,900 | 331,700 | CA XI 360 162 775 3 13 0 1232 7889 |
| D Reno-Las Vegas | 1931 | R Lat | Bs | 38 | 60,000 | 87,000 | NV XI 94 14 138 2 2 0 155 1650 |
| D Sacramento | 1886 | R Lat | Bs | 89 | 156,000 | 226,028 | CA XI 273 56 408 6 10 0 482 5107 |
| D Salt Lake City | 1891 | R Lat | Bs | 36 | 34,900 | 50,581 | UT XI 85 19 147 2 3 0 198 1561 |
| D Santa Rosa | 1962 | R Lat | Bs | 36 | 44,300 | 64,169 | CA XI 114 32 186 4 6 0 220 1697 |
| D Stockton | 1962 | R Lat | Bs | 31 | 64,100 | 92,964 | CA XI 98 7 102 1 2 0 210 2663 |
| M Santa Fe | 1850 | R Lat | Bs | 90 | 184,400 | 267,231 | NM X 233 151 415 7 6 2 238 7807 |
| D El Paso | 1914 | R Lat | Bs | 71 | 138,400 | 200,664 | TX X 185 23 374 2 5 0 122 10592 |
| D Gallup | 1939 | R Lat | Bs | 43 | 47,200 | 68,481 | MN X 74 19 136 2 1 0 598 1371 |
| D Phoenix | 1969 | R Lat | Bs | 57 | 145,700 | 211,131 | AZ X 192 22 330 1 9 0 317 6526 |
| D Tucson | 1897 | R Lat | Bs | 54 | 120,600 | 174,757 | AZ X 147 10 384 4 3 0 220 5173 |
| M Seattle | 1907 | R Lat | Bs | 126 | 232,200 | 336,475 | WA XII 402 36 799 10 16 2 1001 6819 |
| D Spokane | 1913 | R Lat | Bs | 57 | 49,700 | 71,967 | WA XII 198 8 519 7 6 1 306 1685 |
| D Yakima | 1951 | R Lat | Bs | 38 | 34,800 | 50,384 | WA XII 79 1 62 2 1 0 193 1351 |
| M Washington DC | 1939 | R Lat | Bs | 123 | 267,200 | 387,220 | DC IV 1153 378 781 4 36 2 1123 9727 |
| D St Maron of Brooklyn (*Maronite*) | 1966 | R Mar | os | 43 | 105,200 | 152,407 | US – 55 0 5 0 0 0 16 438 |
| EA Boston (*Melkite*) (1976, Eparchy) | 1966 | R Mel | Os | 24 | 14,000 | 20,000 | US – 45 0 0 0 0 0 25 406 |
| AN Mary Help of Christians-Belmont | 1910 | R Lat | bosb | 1 | 400 | 571 | NC IV 48 10 0 0 1 0 5 32 |
| MV United States of America | 1957 | R LEr | Bs | 1,040 | 1,373,100 | 1,990,000 | US – 2392 0 0 0 0 0 3008 27020 |
| Children of God International | 1965 | P Apo | xv... | 60 | 3,000 | 5,000 | *COG. Teens for Christ.* 800 Colonies,80 countries. 267 million letters distributed. |
| Christ Catholic Ch of America & Europe | 1965 | C OCa | ..... | 4 | 471 | 1,000 | *D Boston.* Old Catholic. Aims at total comprehensiveness. 5n,2t(75),W=42%,92Yy. |
| Christ Orth Cath Exarchate of Americas | 1959 | C CCa | ..... | 15 | 3,500 | 5,513 | Byelorussian origins. 1959 merger Old Catholic and Orthodox. 21n,G=–6%pa,3x,W=47%. |
| Christadelphian Ecclesias | 1844 | P Ade | x.... | 850 | 15,800 | 22,000 | *Brothers of Christ.* No central organization or clergy. Pacifist, adventist. |
| Christian & Missionary Alliance | 1881 | P Hol | xF..E | 1,376 | 88,962 | 150,000 | *C&MA.* 18 districts in USA. 1340n,G=3%pa,5p(85),3s,1085t(141924),W=66%,5133Y. |
| Christian Brethren (Exclusive) | 1870 | P EBr | x.... | 300 | 7,000 | 20,000 | *Assemblies. Plymouth Brethren* I/III/IV/V/VI/VII/VIII (separate groups). White. |
| Christian Brethren (Open) | c1880 | P CBr | x.... | 820 | 42,000 | 80,000 | *Plymouth Brethren II. Brethren Assemblies.* G=4.8%pa,2p,1s,700t(33000),W=90%. |
| Christian Catholic Church | 1896 | P Con | x.... | 6 | 1,555 | 3,000 | In church-planned Zion City (IL). Healing. 2 Navajo Indian churches. In 7 nations. |
| Christian Church of North America | 1904 | P Pe2 | xF..E | 110 | 8,500 | 11,800 | *CCNA. General Council.* 1948, union of Italian Chr Ch NA, Italian Pente AoG. 134n,W=33%. |
| Christian Church (Disciples of Christ) | 1809 | P Dis | xW..W | 3,863 | 1,391,210 | 1,641,628 | Liberal wing, Restoration Movement. Schisms. 6886n,G=–6.5%pa,4s(348),W=39%,24481Y. |
| Christian Churches & Chs of Christ | c1935 | P Dis | x.... | 5,901 | 1,024,734 | 1,500,000 | *Church of Christ* (*Instrumental*). Schism ex Disciples. 7312n,40s,6012t(1243445). |
| Christian Congregation | 1887 | P Hol | ..... | 263 | 50,801 | 100,000 | Non-credal body in rural, mountainous and neglected areas in NC. 265n,252t(33355). |
| Christian Growth Ministries | 1973 | P Pe4 | x.... | 2,000 | 50,000 | 100,000 | *CGM.* Charismatic paradenomination, stressing authority, shepherding. HQ Florida. |
| Christian Methodist Episcopal Church | 1870 | I Met | VW..b | 2,598 | 466,718 | 600,000 | Black members ex Methodist Episcopal Ch South; Coloured MEC until 1956. 2259n,5s. |
| Christian Nation Church, USA | 1895 | P Hol | ..... | 16 | 3,300 | 5,000 | Begun by independent 'equality evangelists' in Indiana. Declining. 29n,11t(2000). |
| Christian Reformed Church | 1837 | P Ref | JF... | 763 | 154,276 | 285,628 | Ex RCA. Some Dutch churches. 999n,G=0.6%pa,1p,1s(183),601t(69240),W=98%,5733Yy. |
| Christian Union of America | 1864 | P Con | ....E | 113 | 5,956 | 11,000 | Origins in revivals of 1860s. Central USA. 96n,G=0.4%pa,1p,108t(10055),W=69%. |
| Christ's Sanctified Holy Church | 1892 | I pe3 | ..... | 30 | 800 | 2,000 | Black pentecostals. Schism ex CME Church. East, southeast USA. 30n,W=62%,200z. |
| Church of Christ | 1968 | I ind | x.... | 5 | 500 | 1,000 | *INC. Iglesia ni Cristo* (Manalista)(HQ Manila). Filipinos in Hawaii & California. |
| Church of Christ (Holiness) USA | 1894 | I pe3 | ..... | 159 | 9,289 | 20,000 | Black pentecostals. Foot-washing, episcopal church order. 76n,1j,1s. |

ND, SD, WI.
*Region IX.* IA, KS, MO, NE.
*Region X.* AZ, MN, OK, TX.
*Region XI.* CA, HA, NV, UT (also Guam and USTT Pacific Islands/ Micronesia).
*Region XII.* AK, ID, MT, OR, WA.

*New dioceses.* In 1974, D Arlington was created (a suffragan of M Baltimore); in 1975, D Pensacola-Tallahassee; and in 1976, D Orange in California. In 1977 AN Belmont Abbey became part of D Charlotte; and D Biloxi and D Houma-Thibodaux were created; 1978, D San Bernardino, (RCs 65% Hispanic).

*Colleges and schools.* The total of 2,075 (1972) consists of: 260 Catholics colleges and universities, 1,086 diocesan and parochial high schools, and 729 private hgh schools.

*Seminaries.* In 1972, there were 439 seminaries for all types of clergy, including major, minor, secular and religious seminaries; of these, were novitiates, 94 high schools, 135 colleges, 103 theologates, 14 major seminaries, 14 minor seminaries. Those for major seminarians of the diocesan clergy only, numbered 75 in 1972 (declining a year later to 68), as shown in the adjacent column (39 colleges, 27 theologates, 9 major seminaries); and major seminaries for religious clergy numbered 107 in 1973.

*Continued opposite*

*Table 2–continued*

| Official name 1 | Begun 2 | Type 3 | Counc 4 | Congs 5 | Adults 6 | Affiliated 7 | Names, notes, and other statistics (see Codebook) 8 |
|---|---|---|---|---|---|---|---|
| Church of Christ (Temple Lot) | 1852 | M LdS | ..... | 32 | 2,400 | 3,000 | Schism ex LdS(Utah). Some Maya Indian members, Yucatan, Mexico. 5 splits. 188n. |
| Church of Christ, Scientist | 1879 | M Sci | x.... | 2,430 | 475,000 | 1,000,000 | *Christian Science*. Healing ministry. HQ Mother Church, Boston. Decline 2%pa. 5848n. |
| Church of God & Saints of Christ | 1896 | I Jew | x.... | 217 | 38,217 | 50,000 | *Black Jews* (Jewish observances). Black members. Also Africa, West Indies. |
| Church of God by Faith | 1914 | P Pen | ..... | 135 | 5,300 | 10,000 | In eastern and southeastern USA (FL, GA, AL, SC, MD, NJ, NY). One bishop. 155n. |
| Church of God founded by Jesus Christ | | I pen | ..... | 37 | 1,000 | 2,000 | Black pentecostals. HQ Salisbury (North Carolina). |
| Church of God in Christ | 1895 | I pe3 | Z...J | 7,000 | 500,000 | 1,600,000 | Black. Largest pentecostal church in USA. HQ Memphis (Tennessee). 5000n,1j,1p,1s. |
| Church of God in Christ International | 1969 | I pe3 | x.... | 1,041 | 250,000 | 501,000 | Black. Schism ex Ch of God in Christ by 14 bishops. 18 US dioceses. 1465n,984t. |
| Church of God in Christ, Mennonite | 1859 | P Men | G.... | 38 | 6,543 | 10,000 | Schism ex Mennonite Ch, Ohio. Also Canada, Mexico, Nigeria, Haiti, Brazil. 86n. |
| Church of God of Prophecy | 1923 | P Pe3 | Z.... | 1,600 | 53,988 | 120,000 | *All Nations Flag Ch*. Ex CoG(Cleveland). 1487n,35x,G=4.5%pa,1j,18p,1s,12436Y. |
| Church of God of the Apostolic Faith | 1913 | P Pen | ..... | 29 | 1,000 | 1,600 | HQ Pharr (Texas). Mission and seminary in Mexico. White Pentecostals. 50n. |
| Church of God (Abrahamic Faith) | 1800 | P Ade | x.... | 127 | 8,500 | 11,500 | *Gen Conf*. Christadelphians. Formerly Chs of God in Christ Jesus. 110n,G=4%pa,1s. |
| Church of God (Anderson) | 1880 | P Hol | x.... | 2,282 | 150,198 | 390,000 | Movement calling all to church union. 2793n,G=1.6%pa,1j,1p,4s,2000t(238692),W=80%. |
| Church of God (Cleveland) | 1886 | P Pe3 | ZF.XE | 4,024 | 272,276 | 600,000 | First US Pentecostal body. 95% White. In 107 countries. 7359n,G=4.9%pa,1j,3p,1s,5266t(478984). |
| Church of God (Mountain Assembly) | 1906 | P Pe3 | ...X. | 102 | 3,500 | 10,000 | Schism ex Baptists. HQ Jellico (Tennessee). 136n,G=3.1%pa,1j,W=50%,160Y. |
| Church of God (Queen's Village) | 1943 | P Pe3 | x.... | 2,025 | 75,890 | 105,000 | Ex CoG(Cleveland); HA Tomlinson visits worldwide as King of Nations. G=0.4%pa. |
| Church of God (Seventh-day) | 1865 | P Adv | ..... | 7 | 2,000 | 5,000 | HQ Salem (West Virginia). Reorganized 1933. Schism: Radio Church of God. 9n. |
| Church of God (Seventh-day)(Denver) | 1900 | P Adv | x.... | 56 | 5,500 | 10,000 | A faction maintains CoG (Seventh-day) World HQ, in Jerusalem (Israel). 76n,1j. |
| Church of Illumination | 1908 | M Gno | ..... | 14 | 9,000 | 12,500 | Attempt to harmonize all philosophy and religion. Members by correspondence. 60n. |
| Church of Jesus C of Latter-day Saints | 1830 | M LdS | x.... | 5,112 | 1,797,584 | 2,185,810 | *Mormons*. HQ Utah. Also 700,000 overseas. 17272n,G=2.9%pa,4663t(2023287),91237Y. |
| Ch of Our Lord JC of Apostolic Faith | 1919 | I pel | x...J | 200 | 45,000 | 60,000 | Black pentecostals. Missions: WAfrica, WIndies, Philippines. 320n,1H,1p,1s,2362Y. |
| Church of Our Lord JC (Bickertonites) | 1862 | M LdS | x.... | 42 | 1,000 | 4,200 | *Bickerton Organization*. Ex CJCLdS (Mormons). In 5 nations. 215n,G=0.6%pa,50t(4125). |
| Church of the Brethren | 1719 | P Dun | xW..W | 1,124 | 181,183 | 252,000 | 1708, German pietist origins. Declining. 2011n,G=-1.1%pa,1s,1034t(82079),W=51%,4784Y. |
| Church of the Christian Crusade | 1948 | P ind | ..... | | 10,000 | 25,000 | *Christian Echoes Ministry*. HQ Tulsa. Fundamentalist, anti-Communist, White. |
| Church of the Living God | 1889 | I pe3 | ..... | 165 | 8,000 | 15,000 | *CWFF. Christian Workers for Fellowship*. Black. Freemasonry doctrine. 165n. |
| Ch of the Living God (Pillar & G of T) | 1925 | I pe3 | ..... | 107 | 2,350 | 5,000 | GofT=Ground of Truth. Black pentecostals, split ex Ch of the Living God. |
| Ch of the Lutheran Brethren of America | 1900 | P Lut | x.... | 81 | 5,042 | 10,000 | Members formerly United Norwegians. Upper Midwest. 70n,G=9.3%pa,1p,1s(20),W=89%. |
| Church of the Lutheran Confession | 1959 | P Lut | x.... | 72 | 6,637 | 9,449 | *CLC*. Schism ex Synodical Conference over practice. 60n,G=2.4%pa,1p,1s(8),280Yy. |
| Church of the Nazarene | 1907 | P Hol | xF... | 4,659 | 384,596 | 885,038 | *International Ch of the Nazarene*. 6976n,G=2.4%pa,1j,7s,4806t(868911),W=49%,25644Y. |
| Church of the Universal Truth | 1969 | M The | ..... | 19 | 876 | 1,210 | Small marginal Christian body with metaphysical dogmas. 5n,W=68%,96Yy. |
| Churches of Christ in Christian Union | 1909 | P Hol | xF..E | 264 | 8,741 | 20,000 | Wesleyan doctrine. East, southwest. 362n,G=2.4%pa,1j,1p,1s,231t(16623). |
| Churches of Christ (Non-Instrumental) | c1870 | P Dis | x.... | 17,500 | 2,500,000 | 4,000,000 | Conservative anti-organ split ex Disciples. 10% Black. 10000n,G=6.1%pa,22s,130000Y. |
| Churches of God in North America, GE | 1830 | P Ref | x...t | 352 | 35,905 | 50,000 | *GE=General Eldership*. Begun in 19th-century revival. 353n,G=-0.1%pa,1s. |
| Churches of God (Holiness) | 1890 | I pe3 | x.... | 32 | 25,600 | 35,000 | Black pentecostals. Missions in Caribbean. Footwashing practised. HQ Atlanta. 29n. |
| Conference of Fundamental Churches | | P ind | ....T | | 4,000 | 6,000 | Grouping of independent fundamentalist congregations. White. |
| Congregational Christian Churches | 1955 | P Con | ..... | 327 | 85,000 | 150,000 | *National Assoc of CCC*. North-central, NE USA. 35% Black. 391n,326t(30000),W=33%. |
| Congregational Holiness Church | 1921 | P Pe3 | x..X. | 168 | 5,000 | 7,377 | Schism ex Pentecostal Holiness Ch. Southern states. 302n,G=-1.6%pa,1j,W=54%,378Y. |
| Congregational Methodist Church | 1852 | P Hol | .T..T | 223 | 15,000 | 25,000 | Schism ex Methodist Episcopal Church. HQ Dallas. College in Tehuacana, TX. 1p. |
| Conservative Baptist Assoc of America | 1947 | P Bap | xF... | 1,143 | 300,000 | 450,000 | No central organization. World missions: CBHMS, CBFMS. 2s,5253Y. |
| Conservative Congr Christian Conf | 1935 | P Con | ....E | 119 | 17,328 | 30,000 | *CCCC*. Schism ex Congr Christian Chs. 196n,G=10%pa,6p,4s(16),117t(14169),W=73%. |
| Conservative Mennonite Conference | 1910 | P Men | G.... | 99 | 6,853 | 10,000 | Accepts Dortrecht Confession of faith. 121n(and 43 bishops),G=1.0%pa,1p,W=90%. |
| Converted Jehovah's Witnesses | | P Jeh | ..... | | 5,000 | 10,000 | One of many schisms ex Jehovah's Witnesses in a Protestant direction. |
| Cooneyites (Tramp-Preachers) | c1910 | P ind | x.... | | 50,000 | 100,000 | *Go-Preachers*. In west. Irish itinerants, also in Europe, Australia. |
| Coptic Orthodox Church (P Alexandria) | 1964 | O Cop | NwaNW | 24 | 22,000 | 43,000 | Egyptian immigrants. By 1977, 50,000 across USA; visit by Cairo pope. 5n,14x. |
| Creek Independent Indian Baptist Chs | c1910 | I Bap | ....I | 54 | 2,000 | 5,000 | Creek Indians. Chain of 54 churches in Oklahoma. Annual Bible school. |
| Cumberland Presbyterian Church | 1810 | P Ref | R.... | 901 | 57,147 | 92,025 | *CPC*. White (Blacks belong to Second Cumberland PC). 717n,G=0,1s,880t(57726). |
| Czechoslovak Hussite Church | c1950 | C ReC | Iwc.. | 2 | 500 | 1,000 | *Ceskoslovenska Cirkev*. Large 1920 schism ex Ch of Rome in Prague. 500 in New York. |
| Damascus Christian Church | 1939 | I pen | x.... | 12 | 925 | 2 000 | Spanish-speaking churches in New York City (HQ Bronx). Puerto Ricans. |
| Divine Science Federation International | 1888 | M Sci | i.... | 50 | 5,000 | 10 000 | Metaphysical (New Thought). In INTA. Christ Method of Healing. HQ Denver. 30mw,1s. |
| Duck River & Kindred Assoc of Baptists | 1825 | P Bap | ..... | 81 | 8,492 | 13,000 | Calvinistic schism. 5 associations, in 4 southern states. White. 128n. |
| Elim Assemblies | 1924 | P Pe2 | Z..XE | 70 | 5,000 | 10,000 | *EMA. Elim Missionary Assemblies, Elim Ministerial Fellowship*. 200n,1s,70t. |
| Emmanuel Holiness Church | 1953 | P Pe3 | ...X. | 56 | 1,200 | 6,000 | Schism ex Pentecostal Fire Baptised Holiness Ch. Southern US. Mission in Mexico. |
| Episcopal Church in the USA | 1578 | A plu | AW.RW | 7,135 | 2,139,053 | 3,196,277 | *PECUSA*. 8 US Provinces, 92 Dioceses. 11272n,G=-1.3%pa,14s,W=29%,6370Y,62814y. |
| Estonian Evangelical Lutheran Church | 1941 | P Lut | LWC.. | 24 | 8,655 | 12,000 | *Eesti Evangeeliumi Luteri Usu Kirik*. Refugees from USSR. World HQ Stockholm. 27n. |
| Estonian Orthodox Church in Exile | c1940 | O Sla | C.... | 4 | 700 | 1,000 | Refugees from USSR. Parishes: Los Angeles (HQ),San Francisco,Chicago,NY,Canada. |
| Ethiopian Orthodox Church in the USA | 1959 | O Eth | Nwa.. | 8 | 1,100 | 2,000 | Under P Addis Ababa (Ethiopia). Mostly US Blacks. 1n(Black),2x(Ethiopians). |
| Evangelical Baptist Churches | 1935 | P Pe3 | ..... | 31 | 2,200 | 3,000 | *General Conference*. Formerly Ch of the Full Gospel, ex Free Will Baptists. 37n,1s. |
| Evangelical Christian Churches | 1966 | P ind | ..... | 83 | 12,763 | 20,000 | Grouping of independent congregations, based on Fontana (California). 164n. |
| Evangelical Church of North America | 1968 | P Hol | ....E | 112 | 9,197 | 14,500 | Former EUB congregations rejecting 1968 merger with UMC. 104n,6s(20),W=58%,415Y. |
| Evangelical Congregational Church | 1922 | P Hol | xF..E | 167 | 29,652 | 40,000 | Former East Pennsylvania Conf. East USA. 210n,G=-0.1%pa,1s,159t(28311),W=54%,657Y. |
| Evangelical Covenant Church of America | 1885 | P Con | K.... | 541 | 68,764 | 100,000 | 19th-century pietist revivals (Sweden). 669n,G=1.0%pa,1p,1s(68),500t(66194),2761Y. |
| Evangelical Free Church of America | 1884 | P Con | KF..E | 562 | 70,490 | 100,000 | Swedish immigrants, joined by Norwegian and Danish denominations. Rapid growth.1s. |
| Evangelical Friends Alliance | 1965 | P Qua | QF..E | 254 | 23,683 | 40,000 | *EFA, Association of Ev Friends*. 4 *YMs: Ev Friends Ch, Kansas, Rocky M, Northwest*. |
| Ev Luth Ch in America (Eielsen Synod) | 1846 | P Lut | ..... | 3 | 1,000 | 1,500 | Norwegians (first synod in USA). Declining. Mostly Minnesota and Wisconsin. 1n. |
| Evangelical Lutheran Synod | 1917 | P Lut | ..... | 100 | 11,030 | 15,663 | Norwegian groups rejecting 1917 merger. Decline. Upper Midwest. 81n,1s,79t(4381). |
| Ev Mennonite Brethren Conference | 1873 | P Men | G...E | 32 | 3,753 | 6,500 | 1873 immigrants from Russia. In Canada, SAmerica. 37n,G=1.6%pa,33t(4854),W=92%. |
| Evangelical Mennonite Church | 1865 | P Men | GF..E | 20 | 3,040 | 5,200 | Formerly, Defenseless Mennonite Ch. Ex Amish. 67n,G=2.5%pa,W=80%,115Y. |
| Evangelical Methodist Ch in America | 1946 | P Hol | xF..E | 144 | 10,150 | 17,000 | Protest against theological liberalism. HQ Altoona (PA). 257n,G=1.7%pa,W=63%,577Yy. |
| Father Divine Peace Mission Movement | 1919 | I mar | x.... | | 5,000 | 10,000 | Formerly 1 million followers. 1965 death of founder. 95% Black. In 13 nations. |
| First Congregational Methodist Church | 1852 | P Hol | ..... | 100 | 6,457 | 10,000 | Schism ex Methodist Episcopal Ch South. In southern states. 50n,657Yy. |
| Founding Church of Scientology | 1955 | M Sci | x.... | 100 | 16,000 | 20,000 | Dianetics. Psychoanalytic spirituality. 3 million influenced. 500n,1p,1s,W=67%. |
| Free Christian Zion Church of Christ | 1905 | I pe3 | ..... | 742 | 22,260 | 30,000 | Black pentecostals. Split ex AMEZC & Nat Bapt Conv USA. Relief programmes. 340n. |
| Free Gospel Church | 1916 | P Pen | ...X. | 12 | 1,000 | 2,000 | Small Pentecostal denomination. Rigid membership standards. 20n,1s. |
| Free Methodist Church of North America | 1860 | P Hol | VF..E | 1,132 | 135,096 | 225,000 | 3 *General Conferences: NAmerica*, Egypt, Japan. 700n,G=1.0%pa,1j,1s(59),W=58%. |
| Friends General Conference | 1656 | P Qua | QW... | 350 | 32,645 | 50,000 | *FGC*. Organized 1900. 9 YMs in USA (4 also in FUM), including Philadelphia, NY. |
| Friends United Meeting | 1902 | P Qua | QW..W | 517 | 69,205 | 100,000 | *FUM. Five Years Meeting*. 26% all world's Quakers. 11 YMs in USA. 548n,412t(36299). |
| Friends Yearly Meetings (unaffiliated) | | P Qua | Q.... | 60 | 5,536 | 8,000 | 6 *YMs. Alaska, Central, Missouri Valley, Oregon, Pacific, Southern Appalachian*. |
| Full Gospel Mission in Hawaii | 1936 | I pe2 | ..... | 18 | 1,200 | 2,000 | 1936 founded in Hawaii, linked with M=ICFG(Los Angeles). All Filipinos. 1s. |
| General Assoc of General Baptists | 1714 | P Bap | TF... | 854 | 64,890 | 100,000 | Organized 1870. Mid-central, SW USA. 1115n,G=1.0%pa,1j,1s,854t(80500),W=80%,500Y. |
| General Assoc of Regular Baptist Chs | 1932 | P Bap | xt..t | 1,400 | 197,056 | 300,000 | *GARBC*. Anti-modernist, ex Amer Bapt Conv. 1976: 1,528 churches. G=3%pa,6s,10445Y. |
| General Church of the New Jerusalem | 1897 | M Swe | x.... | 33 | 2,112 | 1,940 | *New Ch*. Swedenborgian. Schism ex General Conv of NJ. 31n,G=1.4%pa,7s,W=25%,120Yy. |
| General Conference Mennonite Church | 1860 | P Men | G.... | 187 | 35,536 | 49,105 | *GCMC*. Large membership in Canada and South America. 314n,G=-0.3%pa,1s,192t(31809). |
| General Convention, Swedenborgian Ch | 1792 | M Swe | x...W | 60 | 3,000 | 10,000 | *New Church*. 1817, General Convention of the New Jerusalem. 66n,G=-1.1%pa,1s(5). |
| God's Missionary Church | 1935 | P Met | ..... | 39 | 593 | 2,000 | High membership standards. Eastern, southern USA. 41n,1p,W=98%,1483z. |
| Grace Gospel Fellowship | 1939 | P ind | .F... | 35 | 2,400 | 10,000 | Ultra-dispensationalist. Teaches Holy Spirit baptism. HQ Grand Rapids. 62n,1s. |
| Greek Evangelical Church | c1960 | P Ref | Rwc.. | 10 | 600 | 1,000 | *Hellenike Evangelike Ekklesia*. Immigrants from GEC (Greece). HQ Boston. |
| Greek Orthodox AD of N & S America | 1864 | O Gre | CwO.W | 500 | 1,300,000 | 1,900,000 | AD, 1922. In EP Constantinople. 585n,P=77%,14r,1s(120),709t(64471),W=30%,12650Yy. |
| Handsome Lake (Long House) Religion | 1800 | I mar | ..... | | 2,000 | 4,000 | Seneca Iroquois Indians, NY. Oldest continuing prophet movement in world. |
| Hebrew-Christian communities | 1894 | P Jew | x.... | 25 | 5,000 | 10,000 | M=American Board of Missions to Jews. 100,000 converts in other denominations also. |
| Hellenic Orthodox Church of America | 1924 | O OCd | c.... | 2 | 500 | 1,000 | Schism ex Greek Orthodox AD rejecting New (Gregorian) Calendar. Astoria (LI). |
| Holiness Christian Church | 1882 | P Hol | ..... | 46 | 1,132 | 5,900 | White. Rigid membership requirements. In mid-Atlantic states. 44n,G=5.4%pa,W=36%. |
| Holiness Methodist Churches | 1900 | P Hol | x.... | 26 | 2,000 | 3,000 | Two bodies: N Carolina, N Dakota. Grew out of Northwestern Holiness Assoc. 1s. |
| Holy Ukrainian Autocephalic OC Exile | 1951 | O Sla | C.O.. | 15 | 3,300 | 4,800 | OC=Orthodox Ch in. Schism ex Ukrainian Orth Ch in the USA. 1 bishop,24n. |
| Hopi Independent Indian Churches | 1946 | I ind | ....I | 10 | 500 | 1,000 | Several Hopi churches in Arizona. Ex Mennonites. One centre in Hotevilla. |
| House of God, Ch of the Living God | 1889 | I pen | ..... | 102 | 2,500 | 3,000 | *Pillar & Ground of the Truth*. Black pentecostals. Freemason origin. 200n,1p,24Y. |
| Hungarian Reformed Church in America | 1891 | P Ref | RW..W | 27 | 7,000 | 11,250 | Immigrants from Ref Ch of Hungary, 1924 refusal to join E&RC (now UCC). 34n. |
| Hutterian Brethren | 1874 | P Men | x.... | 200 | 6,322 | 8,800 | Origin from Jacob Hutter (c1550). Mid-west. Majority in Canada. White. 20h. |
| Independent AME Church | 1907 | I Met | ..... | 12 | 1,000 | 2,000 | Schism ex African Methodist Episcopal Church in Jacksonville (Florida). Black. |
| Independent Assemblies of God | 1911 | P Pe4 | ..... | 136 | 7,000 | 20,000 | *Philadelphia churches*. Scandinavians, linked with Swedish Pentecostalism. 367n. |
| Independent Bible Baptist Missions | 1949 | P Bap | xT..T | | 10,000 | 30,000 | Independent fundamentalist Baptist churches with strong overseas missions. 1s. |
| Indep Fundamental Chs of America | 1930 | P ind | .t..t | 900 | 100,000 | 210,000 | *IFCA*. Organized to safeguard fundamentalist doctrine. 2131n,1p,4s,904t(203812). |
| Independent Spiritualist Association | 1924 | M Spi | ..... | 100 | 5,000 | 10,000 | *ISA*. Schism ex NSA. Rapid growth, now schisms. 700 mediums, healers, missioners. |
| Indian Shaker Church | 1883 | I mar | ....I | 22 | 2,000 | 5,000 | Yakima Reservation. Shuffle dance. 1960s upsurge among young Indians, NCalifornia. |
| Internat Ass of Religious Science Chs | 1948 | M Sci | x.... | 40 | 4,000 | 10,000 | *IARSC*. Schism ex Ch of Religious Science, rejecting authority of mother church. |
| Internat Ch of the Foursquare Gospel | 1918 | P Pe2 | ZF.XE | 741 | 89,215 | 200,000 | *ICFG*. HQ Angelus Temple, Los Angeles. 90% White. 2690n,1s(LIFE Bible Coll),11603Y. |
| International Evangelism | 1959 | P ind | ..... | 105 | 5,000 | 8,000 | *IEC*. Independent White grouping. Autonomous congregations. 150n,1p,1s,W=80%,100Y. |
| Internat Gen Assembly of Spiritualists | 1936 | M Spi | ..... | 209 | 110,000 | 164,072 | Overall organization to sponsor new spiritualist churches. 221n. |
| International Pentecostal Ch of Christ | 1914 | P Pe3 | x..XE | 98 | 11,209 | 33,500 | 1976 merger of IPA, PCC. In 11 states; missions 13 countries. 246n,2s,95t(15501). |
| International Pentecostal Holiness Ch | 1898 | P Pe3 | ZF.XE | 1,341 | 72,696 | 250,000 | *IPHC*. White. 3-body merger. Worldwide. 41 periodicals. 2422n,G=2.0%pa,1j,4p,2s,W=60%. |
| Jehovah's Witnesses | 1872 | M Jeh | x.... | 5,730 | 421,205 | 1,000,000 | *IBSA. Watch Tower*. World HQ Brooklyn. In USA, 22% Blacks. 25740n,G=3.7%pa,40814Y. |
| Latin American Council of Chr Chs | 1923 | I pen | ..... | 105 | 4,200 | 20,000 | *LACCC. Concilio Latino-Americana de Igls Cr*. Begun by Mexicans, ex AoG. 50% Texas. |
| Latvian Ev Lutheran Church in Exile | 1946 | P Lut | Lw... | 69 | 16,744 | 20,000 | *Latvijas Ev Lut Baznica*. Latvian refugees from USSR. 84n,G=-0.3%pa,W=30%,197Yy. |
| Liberal Catholic Church | 1947 | C Lib | ..... | 21 | 2,000 | 4,000 | *LCC*(California). Split ex LCC in Christian direction. 5 bishops,62n,W=35%,110Yy. |
| Liberal Cath Ch, Order of St Germain | 1969 | C Lib | ..... | 7 | 1,822 | 3,000 | In Texas, Colorado, Oklahoma, California. 22n,5p(58),W=50%,79Yy. |
| Light of the World Church | c1950 | I pel | x.... | | 1,000 | 2,000 | *Iglesia La Luz del Mundo* (*Aaronistas*). Pentecostals from Mexico, in California. |
| Lithuanian National Cath Ch in America | 1914 | C OCa | U.... | 4 | 2,500 | 4,000 | Old Catholics from USSR. Under jurisdiction of Polish NCC of America. 4n. |
| Lutheran Church in America | 1623 | P Lut | LW..W | 5,813 | 2,187,162 | 3,228,939 | *LCA*. 1962 merger ULCA/Augustana ELC/AELC/FELC. 7329n,G=-0.8%pa,9s,W=43%,62755Yy. |
| Lutheran Church—Missouri Synod | 1847 | P Lut | x.... | 6,474 | 1,822,569 | 2,895,668 | German origin. 1976 schism: AELC. 7041n,G=0,16s(1041),5552t(815522),W=45%,94363Yy. |
| Lutheran Churches of the Reformation | 1964 | P Lut | ..... | 31 | 5,009 | 6,273 | Split ex LCMS to establish confessional Lutheranism. HQ Detroit. 31n,31t(1950). |
| Mar Thoma Syrian Church of Malabar | | I ReO | xWE.. | | 1,000 | 2,000 | Immigrant Malayalam-speaking Syrians from South India, with own clergy. |
| Mennonite Brethren Ch of N America | 1876 | P Men | GF..E | 160 | 14,767 | 20,000 | *General Conference*. 1860 schism in Ukraine. 1960, joined by Krimmer MBC. 173n,1s. |
| Mennonite Church of North America | 1683 | P Men | G.... | 1,181 | 89,505 | 120,000 | German. Regions II–IV(I in Canada). 2236n,G=1.4%pa,1p,3s,967t(110475),W=80%,2845Y. |
| Mennonites (unaffiliated) | c1800 | P Men | ..... | 87 | 4,425 | 8,000 | Scattered Amish and other groups unrelated to any Mennonite denomination. |
| Midwest Congr Christian Fellowship | 1958 | P Con | ....E | 31 | 5,000 | 8,000 | Grouping of independent White congregations. HQ Union City (Indiana). |

*Continued overleaf*

*Table 2–continued*

| Official name<br>1 | Begun<br>2 | Type<br>3 | Counc<br>4 | Congs<br>5 | Adults<br>6 | Affiliated<br>7 | Names, notes, and other statistics (see Codebook)<br>8 |
|---|---|---|---|---|---|---|---|
| Missionary Church | 1889 | P Hol | xF••E | 354 | 21,250 | 38,000 | 1969 union Missionary Ch Assoc, United Miss Ch. 489n,G=1.6%pa,1j,1s,W=66%,1333Y. |
| Missionary Methodist Ch of America | 1913 | P Hol | ••••• | 17 | 1,002 | 1,330 | Schism ex Wesleyan Methodist Church. Mainly North Carolina. 29n,W=24%,38Yy. |
| Moravian Church in America | 1734 | P Mor | xW••W | 161 | 60,574 | 100,000 | 3 *Provs* (*Northern,Southern,Alaska*), Unity of Brethren. 136n,G=–1.3%pa,4r,1s(14). |
| Mount Tabor Assoc of Regular Baptists | 1890 | P Bap | ••••• | 7 | 860 | 1,200 | Independent fundamentalist grouping. In Indiana and Illinois. White. 8n,W=50%,30Y. |
| Narraganset Indian Church | 1741 | I ind | ••••I | 1 | 500 | 1,000 | In RI. Oldest Indian independent ch in USA. Focus for large Indian annual meetings. |
| National Assoc of Free Will Baptists | 1701 | P Bap | xF••• | 2,250 | 190,000 | 280,000 | Ex ABC. Whites. 1972, left NAE. 3669n,G=1.3%pa,3s(250),2200t(181000),W=60%,3500Y. |
| National Baptist Convention of America | 1773 | I Bap | TW••W | 15,200 | 2,700,000 | 3,300,000 | *NBC*. Part of first major Black Baptist body; NBCUSA split off in 1915. 28574n,1s. |
| National Baptist Convention, USA | 1773 | I Bap | TW••b | 30,200 | 5,500,000 | 6,426,000 | *NBC*. 1915 split, incorporated as body separate from NBC America. Black. 27500n,1s. |
| National Baptist Ev LSS Assembly USA | 1937 | I Bap | ••••• | 264 | 57,674 | 70,000 | LSS=Life & Soul Saving. Black. Begun 1921, under NBC until 1937 split. 137n. |
| National Council of Community Churches | 1946 | P Con | •W••W | 185 | 125,000 | 200,000 | Formerly Int Council of Community Chs. 50% Black. Links with UCC. 1974 joined WCC. |
| Nat David Spiritual Temple of Christ | 1932 | I pe2 | ••••• | 66 | 40,815 | 60,000 | Black. Ex Baptist Missionary Ch; founder archbishop David Short. 1j,1s. |
| National Fellowship of Brethren Chs | 1939 | P Dun | xF••• | 237 | 33,239 | 50,000 | *NFBC* (*Grace*)(*Winona Lake*). Ex Ashland. 404n,G=2.6%pa,1s,226t(40326),W=86%,2275Y. |
| National Primitive Baptist Convention | 1865 | I Bap | ••••• | 2,198 | 1,645,000 | 2,007,000 | Black. Formerly Colored Primitive Baptists. HQ Tallahassee (FL). 597n,2150t(32200). |
| National Spiritual Alliance of the USA | 1913 | M Spi | ••••• | 34 | 3,230 | 5,000 | Schism ex NSA. Social, literary, educational, music activity. 56n. |
| National Spiritualist Assoc of Chs | 1893 | M Spi | x•••• | 204 | 5,811 | 8,000 | *NSA*. Main orthodox spiritualist body. Provides spiritism's literature. 163n,1s. |
| Native American Ch of North America | 1870 | I mar | x•••I | | 150,000 | 400,000 | *NAC*. 23 Chapters. Among all US Indian tribes. Strict ethics; peyote eating. |
| Navajo Native American Church | c1900 | I mar | ••••I | | 20,000 | 60,000 | 60% of all Navajo Indians. Linked with NAC. One of many Navajo indigenous bodies. |
| Neo-American Church | 1903 | P ind | ••••• | 31 | 3,850 | 10,000 | Begun by plains settlers in Oklahoma. Declining. 73n,1p,1s(18),W=25%. |
| Neo-American Church of California | c1960 | M Gno | •v••• | | 6,000 | 8,000 | Syncretistic body mainly in California, with chief priest. Hippies et alii. |
| Netherlands Reformed Congregations | 1865 | P Ref | ••••• | 22 | 3,255 | 7,319 | Immigrants from Holland. HQ Grand Rapids (Michigan). 4n,G=3.7%pa,120Yy. |
| New Apostolic Church of North America | 1863 | C CAp | x•••• | 262 | 21,765 | 30,000 | World organization based on Chief Apostle in Dortmund (Germany). 383n,262t(7186). |
| North American Baptist General Conf | 1840 | P Bap | TF••• | 243 | 38,000 | 60,000 | German Baptist immigrants in 19th century. 423n,G=0.7%pa,1s,332t(55815),1910Y. |
| North American Catholic Church | 1958 | C CCa | ••••• | 25 | 800 | 1,290 | Ex original NAORCC. Declining. HQ Brooklyn. Under bishops-at-large. |
| North American Old Roman Catholic Ch | 1912 | C CCa | ••••• | 121 | 40,000 | 60,098 | *NAORCC*. Ex RCC. Italians, Poles, Lithuanians. 111n,3s(53),33t,230Yy. |
| Old Calendar Greek Orthodox Church | 1924 | O OCd | c•••• | 12 | 2,000 | 3,000 | *Authentic Orth Ch* (200,000 in Greece). Schism rejecting New (Gregorian) Calendar. |
| Old German Baptist Brethren | 1881 | P Dun | ••••• | 54 | 4,225 | 8,000 | *Old Order Dunkers*. Schism ex Church of the Brethren. White. 130n. |
| Old Order & Wisler Mennonite Church | 1872 | P Men | G•••• | 35 | 7,000 | 10,000 | *Pleasant View Mennonite Church*. Indiana, Ohio, PA, VA. Also in Canada. 101n,125Y. |
| Old Order Amish Mennonite Church | 1720 | P Men | G•••• | 325 | 23,075 | 32,000 | Amish immigrants 1720–40. Iowa. Not centralized. Worship in homes. 1497n,1j. |
| Old Ritualist Church (Priestless) | 1952 | O OBe | ••••• | 5 | 500 | 1,000 | *Old Believers*. *Bespopovsty*. Ex Russian OC, refugees from Turkey, 1952. 1n,1j. |
| Old Roman Catholic Apostolic Church | c1965 | C CCa | ••••• | | 1,500 | 2,500 | Italians, ex Ch of Rome. New York state. Bishop consecrated in Vilatte succession. |
| Old Roman Catholic Ch (English Rite) | 1963 | C CCa | ••••• | 186 | 40,000 | 65,128 | *Veteris Romanae Catholicae Ecclesiae, US Province*. Declining. 214n,1s(14),W=60%. |
| Open Bible Standard Churches | 1919 | P Pe2 | ZF•XE | 275 | 25,000 | 35,000 | In part a 1932 schism ex ICFG against founder. 725n,G=0,1j,3s(250),275t,W=83%. |
| Original Church of God | 1886 | P Pe3 | ••••• | 75 | 20,000 | 30,000 | Schism ex CoG (Cleveland). White. Mainly east, south-central USA. 150n,40t(129). |
| Orthodox Church in America | 1792 | O Sla | MWO•W | 435 | 680,000 | 960,000 | *OCA*. Formerly Russian Orth Gk-Cath Ch. A=1970. 7 US dioceses. 440n,33x,2s(150). |
| Orthodox Presbyterian Church | 1936 | P Ref | Jt••t | 116 | 9,400 | 14,300 | Anti-modernism schism by 100 ministers ex Presbyterian Ch in USA. 190n,G=–1.3%pa. |
| Pentecostal Assemblies of the World | 1914 | I pe1 | x•••• | 550 | 45,000 | 60,000 | Black pentecostals. Missions in Caribbean, India, Israel, Nigeria. 600n,1j,1s. |
| Pentecostal Church of God in America | 1919 | P Pe2 | Z•••E | 900 | 119,000 | 180,000 | White. HQ Joplin (MO). 46 missionaries in 20 countries. 1325n,1j,2p,2r. |
| Pentecostal Free Will Baptist Church | 1919 | P Pe3 | •••X• | 176 | 13,500 | 20,000 | Schism ex Free Will Baptists. Mostly east coast. 221n,G=2.1%pa,2p,1s(75),W=60%. |
| Philippine Independent Church | 1959 | I ReC | Uwe•• | 10 | 700 | 2,000 | *PIC*. *Iglesia Filipina Independiente*(HQ Manila). Filipinos in Hawaii. M=PECUSA. 3x. |
| Pillar of Fire | 1901 | P Hol | x•••• | 61 | 5,100 | 7,000 | Until 1917, Pentecostal Union. Missions: Liberia, UK. 2 radio stations. 4p,2r,2s. |
| Polish National Catholic Ch of America | 1897 | C OCa | UW••W | 162 | 196,000 | 272,082 | *PNCC*. Poles, ex Irish-dominated USA RC dioceses. Aids Lithuanian Nat CC. 151n,1s. |
| Presbyterian Church in America | 1973 | P Ref | xF••• | 370 | 41,232 | 75,000 | *PCA*. 1973, National Presb Ch. Conservative schism ex PCUS, in south. White. 260n. |
| Presbyterian Church in the US | 1706 | P Ref | RW••W | 3,788 | 878,600 | 1,220,000 | *PCUS*. Mainly in South. Missions in 9 nations. 1973, 8% lost in schism. 4595n,4s. |
| Primitive Advent Christian Church | c1930 | P Adv | ••••• | 10 | 600 | 1,000 | Schism ex Advent CC. HQ Sissonville (West Virginia). 15n,G=1.8%pa,W=50%,25Y. |
| Primitive Baptists | c1830 | P Bap | ••••• | 2,085 | 72,000 | 100,000 | *Old School Baptists*. 4 factions: Absolute, Absoluter, Conditionalist, Progressive. |
| Primitive Methodist Church, USA | 1829 | P Hol | VF••E | 83 | 12,805 | 20,000 | Missions in Guatemala and other countries. 59n,G=–0.5%pa,W=61%. |
| Process Church of the Final Judgement | 1966 | M Apo | xv••• | | 5,000 | 10,000 | Begun 1960 in UK. Chicago, New Orleans, Cambridge, NY. 1972, applied to join WCC. |
| Progressive National Baptist Convention | 1961 | I Bap | TW••W | 655 | 521,692 | 636,000 | *PNBC*. Black. Schism ex NBCUSA, over elections. 863n. Share NBC seminary. |
| Progressive Spiritual Church | 1907 | M Spi | ••••• | 21 | 11,347 | 20,000 | Spiritualist body with benevolent, social, literary and psychical activities. |
| Protestant Conference (Lutheran) | 1926 | P Lut | ••••• | 7 | 1,600 | 2,600 | Begun by 45 pastors suspended from Wisconsin ELS. 15n,G=2.2%pa,7t(600),W=40%,50Yy. |
| Protestant Reformed Chs in America | 1926 | P Ref | ••••• | 19 | 1,677 | 3,187 | Schism ex Christian Reformed Church. Mainly Mid-West. HQ Oak Lawn (IL). 17n,1s. |
| Reformed Baptists | c1680 | P Bap | ••••• | 200 | 5,000 | 10,000 | *Particular Baptists*. Calvinistic (Philadelphia Confession). Independent; no HQ. |
| Reformed Cath Ch (Utrecht Confession) | c1950 | C ARo | x•••• | 20 | 1,000 | 2,200 | Schism in UK ex Old Cath Ev Ch of God. HQ Los Angeles. Bishops in UK, France, FRG. |
| Reformed Church in America | 1628 | P Ref | RW••W | 923 | 224,170 | 367,606 | *RCA*. Begun by Dutch settlers. 1307n,G=–0.6%pa,2s(170),905t(127359),W=80%,7071Yy. |
| Reformed Church in the United States | 1934 | P Ref | ••••• | 25 | 3,043 | 4,038 | Churches rejecting 1934 merger. North central. 25n,G=3.0%pa,24t(807),W=90%,76Yy. |
| Reformed Episcopal Church | 1873 | A sEv | xv••• | 65 | 7,018 | 11,000 | Ex PECUSA led by asst bishop of Kentucky. 54% Black. 95n,1p,1s(10),W=75%,240Yy. |
| Reformed Mennonite Church | 1812 | P Men | G•••• | 12 | 553 | 1,000 | Pacifist. White. In Pennyslvania. Members also in Canada. 21n. |
| Reformed Methodist Union Episcopal Ch | 1885 | I Met | ••••• | 20 | 5,000 | 8,000 | Black. Schism ex AME Church. HQ Charleston (NC). Bishops since 1899. 21n. |
| Reformed Presbyterian Ch of North A | 1743 | P Ref | JF••E | 71 | 4,328 | 7,500 | *Covenanters*. Synod 1798. 7 Presbyteries. 91n,G=–0.8%pa,1r,1s(12),W=67%,174Yy. |
| Reformed Presbyterian Ch, Ev Synod | 1774 | P Ref | x•••t | 129 | 14,027 | 17,400 | 1965 union Ev Presb Ch, RPC in NA. Scots. 310n,10x,G=4.7%pa,1s(50),W=75%,351Yy. |
| Reformed Zion Union Apostolic Church | 1869 | I Met | ••••• | 50 | 9,000 | 16,000 | Black. Schism ex AME Zion Church. HQ South Hill (Virginia). 23n. |
| Religious S of Friends (Conservative) | c1845 | P Qua | Q•••• | 26 | 1,870 | 3,000 | S=Society. Wilburites. 3 Yearly Meetings: Iowa, North Carolina, Ohio. White. |
| Reorganized Ch of JC of L-d Saints | 1860 | M LdS | xv••• | 1,025 | 152,670 | 202,675 | Ex Mormons, over legal succession. In 28 nations. 13720n,G=1.0%pa,1H,1s,4871Yy. |
| Romanian Orth Episcopate of America | 1904 | O Rum | MW••• | 45 | 30,000 | 50,000 | Schism rejecting P Bucharest. Now under Orth Ch in America. 50n,G=0,39t(1693). |
| Romanian Orth Missionary Episcopate | 1929 | O Rum | CwO•• | 5 | 3,000 | 5,000 | Bishop of N and S America & Canada; in communion with P Bucharest (Romania). |
| Russian Orth Ch in the Americas, PE | c1950 | O Sla | MwO•W | 41 | 30,000 | 50,000 | *Patriarchal Exarchate* of P. Moscow. Parishes now joining Orthodox Ch in A. 65nx. |
| Russian Orthodox Ch Outside of Russia | 1920 | O Sla | x•••• | 81 | 40,000 | 55,000 | *ROCOR*. 1950 world HQ moved to New York. 5 Dioceses. Ultra-conservative. 168n,1d,1s. |
| St Joseph's Indian Reform Church | | I ind | ••••I | | 500 | 1,000 | Apache Reservation, Mescalero (NM). Linked to Apache ceremonial grounds, dances. |
| Salvation Army | 1880 | P Sal | xw••• | 1,176 | 74,967 | 392,299 | *Territories: Central*, *Eastern*, *Southern*, *Western*. 38 Divs. 3735n,G=1.8%pa,33H,4s. |
| Schwenkfelder Church in the USA | 1782 | P Lut | ••••• | 5 | 1,000 | 2,250 | German Silesian immigrants. In Philadelphia only; disappeared in Europe. 9n,1r. |
| Second Cumberland Presbyterian Church | 1869 | I Ref | R•••• | 149 | 6,355 | 15,000 | Black. Formerly Coloured Cumberland PC; related to Cumberland PC (Whites). 125n. |
| Seminole Independent Indian Church | c1950 | I Bap | ••••I | 5 | 500 | 1,000 | Seminole Indians, split ex Southern Baptists, Florida. No ministers. |
| Separate Baptists in Christ | 1695 | P Bap | ••••• | 84 | 7,496 | 11,000 | Early refugees from England. Completely independent, rejecting mergers. 106n. |
| Serbian Orth Ch in the USA & Canada | 1894 | O Ser | CwO•W | 52 | 65,000 | 150,000 | 3 *Dioceses* under P Belgrade: *Mid-West*, *Western*, *Eastern America* & *Canada*. 64nx. |
| Serbian Orthodox Diocese | 1963 | O Ser | ••••• | 3 | 2,000 | 3,000 | Schismatic diocese, HQ Libertyville, led by bishop Dionysie, opposing P Belgrade. |
| Seventh Day Baptist General Conference | 1671 | P Bap | TW••f | 70 | 5,331 | 8,000 | Immigrants from England. 1973, left NCCC. 81n,G=–1.5%pa,1s,47t(2837),W=56%,79Y. |
| Seventh-day Adventist Church | 1844 | P Adv | x•••• | 3,218 | 420,419 | 700,000 | *SDA*. 9 *Unions*. 18% Black. 3365n,G=3.1%pa,42H,5j,88r,3s,3315t(375031),W=88%,24575Y. |
| Slovak National Catholic Ch in America | | C OCa | U•••• | 4 | 2,000 | 3,000 | Old Catholics from Czechoslovakia. Under jurisdiction of Polish NCC of America. |
| Social Brethren | 1867 | P int | ••••• | 32 | 1,685 | 3,000 | Group in Illinois with Baptist and Methodist customs. 42n,30t. |
| Southern Baptist Convention | 1845 | P Bap | T•••• | 34,360 | 11,629,880 | 14,200,000 | *SBC*. 1845 ex North. 99% White. 31000n,G=1.6%pa,2H,6s,33435t(7138741),W=39%,409659Y. |
| Southern Methodist Church | 1939 | P Met | •T••T | 172 | 9,917 | 20,000 | White. Ex Meth Epis Ch South rejecting 1939 merger. HQ Orangeburg. 63n,150t(9630). |
| Spanish Christian Churches | | I pe3 | ••••• | 240 | 18,500 | 30,000 | Linked, Latin American Council of Chs. Spanish-speaking Puerto Ricans, Mexicans. |
| Spiritual Science Church | 1923 | M Spi | ••••• | 50 | 20,000 | 50,000 | *Ecclesiastical Council*. Spiritualists ex Christian Science. Mainly NY state. 40n. |
| Spiritualist Episcopal Church | 1941 | M Spi | ••••• | 50 | 3,000 | 5,000 | Schism ex ISA. Liturgical services, healing. 1956, serious schism. |
| Synod of Evangelical Lutheran Churches | 1902 | P Lut | ••••• | 63 | 10,000 | 21,500 | Slovak Lutherans, conservative theology. Since 1971 under LC Missouri Synod. White. |
| Syrian Orth P Antioch: AD USA &Canada | 1895 | O Syr | Dw••W | 8 | 25,000 | 50,000 | Under Syrian Orthodox P Antioch. HQ Hackensack (NJ). Syrians. 14nx,10t(530). |
| The Way International | 1953 | P Pen | ••••• | 20 | 15,000 | 30,000 | Ex Jesus Revolution. HQ New Knoxville. 3000 WOW (Word over World) workers. 50n,1s. |
| Tioga River Christian Conference | 1931 | P Con | •T••T | | 1,500 | 3,000 | Group rejecting Congregational-Christian merger of 1931. White. New York state. |
| Triumph the Church & KoG in Christ | 1902 | I pe3 | ••••• | 498 | 44,835 | 55,090 | KoG=Kingdom of God. Black pentecostals. Pacifists. 1375n,495t(51777). |
| Turkish Orthodox Church in America | 1924 | I ReO | xv••• | 20 | 10,000 | 14,800 | 1922 schism in Turkey ex EP Constantinople; under own P Istanbul. 26n,14t(2216). |
| Ukrainian Evangelical Baptist Conv | 1945 | P Bap | •T••T | 25 | 3,000 | 4,500 | USSR refugees. 6 radio programmes (2 to USSR). HQ Chester (PA). 20n,1p,W=80%,50Y. |
| Ukrainian Orthodox Church of America | 1928 | O Sla | C•O•W | 24 | 30,000 | 45,000 | *UOCA* (*Ecumenical Patriarchate*). Canonical, recognized by Constantinople. 52n. |
| Ukrainian Orthodox Church of the USA | 1919 | O Sla | X•••• | 107 | 60,000 | 87,475 | Disputed succession. Dioceses: 3 USA; 3 Canada; Brazil; Germany; Australia. 131n. |
| Ukrainian Orthodox Ch (Sobornopravna) | 1947 | O Sla | X•••• | 4 | 1,000 | 2,000 | *UOC* (*Democratic*). Ukrainians. HQ Chicago; also a bishop for Europe (Geneva). 12n. |
| Unification Church of America | c1956 | I mar | xv••• | 120 | 10,000 | 30,000 | M=HSAUWC(Korea). Many Whites. 1973 applied to WCC. 1976, 700 deported (Asians). |
| Union American Methodist Episcopal Ch | 1805 | I Met | ••••• | 256 | 15,000 | 27,560 | Black. One of first Negro independent Methodist churches. 276n. |
| Unitarian Universalist Association | 1778 | M Unt | I•••• | 1,025 | 162,645 | 265,408 | 1961 merger of Unitarian Ch, Universalist Chs. Declining. 886n,G=–1.4%pa,2s(150). |
| United Baptist Church | 1787 | P Bap | ••••• | 568 | 63,641 | 100,000 | Merger of Separate & Regular Baptists. White. In southeast USA. 1100n. |
| United Brethren in Christ | 1767 | P Hol | xF••E | 296 | 24,544 | 40,000 | Arose from 1760s revival in Pennsylvania & Maryland. HQ Huntington (IN). 197n,1s. |
| United Church of Christ | 1620 | P uni | RW••W | 6,688 | 1,928,674 | 2,680,000 | *UCC*. 1957 union E&R, Congreg Christian Chs. 1% Black. 9378n,G=–1.6%pa, 13s(918). |
| United Church of Religious Science | 1917 | M Sci | i•••• | 93 | 10,000 | 20,000 | Metaphysical (New Thought, mental science). Healing crusades, literature. 156mw. |
| United Free Will Baptist Church | 1901 | I Bap | ••••• | 836 | 100,000 | 122,000 | *UFWBC* (*Colored*). Black members, in NC, GA, FL, MS, LA, TX. HQ Kingston (NC). 915n. |
| United Fundamentalist Church | 1939 | P Pe2 | ••••• | 300 | 10,000 | 20,000 | White Pentecostals (2-stage type). HQ Flagstaff (Arizona). |
| United Holy Church of America | 1886 | I pe3 | x•••• | 470 | 50,000 | 70,000 | Black pentecostals. 1976, schism. Missions: Liberia, SAfrica, Trinidad, UK. 400n. |
| United House of Prayer for All People | 1919 | I pe3 | ••••• | 300 | 30,000 | 50,000 | Black pentecostals. Founder Bishop (Daddy) Grace, died 1960. |
| United Liberal Catholic Ch of the USA | 1917 | C Lib | xv••• | 30 | 1,500 | 2,000 | UK origin ex Old Roman Cath Ch. Theosophical. HQ London (UK). 84n,W=30%,100Yy. |
| United Methodist Church | 1766 | P Met | VW••W | 39,626 | 10,334,521 | 14,353,000 | *UMC*. 1968, EUB merger. 96% White, 4% Black. 81 Confs. 34974n,G=–1.4%pa,13s,W=36%. |
| United Old Catholic Church | 1964 | C OCa | ••••• | 35 | 2,644 | 3,000 | Attempt to unite all Old Catholic factions. 1 monastery. 28n,2s(8),W=73%,73Yy. |
| United Pentecostal Church | 1914 | P Pe1 | x•••• | 2,300 | 250,000 | 450,000 | 1945 union Pente Assemblies of JC, Pente Ch. White. 4800n,G=2.6%pa,1j,8p,8s. |
| United Presbyterian Church in the USA | 1706 | P Ref | RW••W | 8,610 | 2,906,147 | 3,546,941 | *UPUSA*. 16 Synods. 99% White, 1% Black. 13451n,G=–2.3%pa,8s,8760t(1203488),W=34%. |
| United States (USA) Episcopal Church | 1976 | A sAC | ••••• | 50 | 7,000 | 10,000 | Schism ex PECUSA protesting ordination of women priests. Formerly Anglicans United. |
| United Zion Church | 1855 | P Pen | ••••• | 17 | 854 | 1,500 | Mainly in Pennsylvania. 22n,G=–0.2%pa,13t(1327),W=86%,35Y. |
| Unity of the Brethren | c1880 | P Mor | x•••• | 32 | 6,142 | 10,000 | *Unitas Fratrum*. Until 1962, Ev Unity of Czech-Moravian Brethren. In Texas. White. |
| Unity School of Christianity | 1887 | M Sci | i•••• | 315 | 50,000 | 150,000 | Major schism ex Christian Science. 1.5 million world subscribers. 700 workers. |
| Universal Fellowship of MCCs | 1968 | P ind | x•••• | 64 | 19,000 | 30,000 | *UFMCC*. MCCs=Metropolitan Community Chs. Gay/homosexual. In 8 nations. 100n,W=69%. |
| Universal Spiritualist Association | 1956 | M Spi | ••••• | 26 | 2,000 | 4,000 | Schism ex Spiritualist Episcopal Church by its founder. In 10 US states. |
| Voice of the Nazarene Assoc of ICs | 1955 | P Hol | •T••• | 23 | 1,500 | 4,000 | ICs=Independent Churches. Grouping of fundamentalist holiness congregations. 45Y. |
| Volunteers of America | 1896 | P Sal | ••••• | 219 | 20,000 | 32,760 | Social welfare agency run on military lines. Extensive ministry in prisons. 432n. |
| Wesleyan Church | 1843 | P Hol | VF••E | 1,898 | 71,433 | 120,000 | 1968 union Pilgrim Holiness, Wesleyan Meth Chs. In 30 nations. 2925n,G=0.6%pa,2s. |
| Wesleyan Holiness Assoc of Churches | 1960 | P Hol | ••••• | 67 | 2,000 | 4,000 | Association stressing sanctification and rejecting Wesleyan mergers. 112n,67t. |
| Wisconsin Evangelical Lutheran Synod | 1850 | P Lut | x•••• | 967 | 271,117 | 381,321 | *WELS*. Prussian origin. In Luth Synodical Conf. 957n,25x,G=0.9%pa,1s(225),8018Yy. |
| World Baptist Fellowship | 1928 | P Bap | xT••T | | 2,000 | 5,000 | *WBF*. Fundamentalist mission body (20 nations) with affiliated churches in USA. 1s. |

*Continued opposite*

*Table 2–continued*

| Official name 1 | Begun 2 | Type 3 | Counc 4 | Congs 5 | Adults 6 | Affiliated 7 | Names, notes, and other statistics (see Codebook) 8 |
|---|---|---|---|---|---|---|---|
| Worldwide Church of God | 1930 | M BrI | x.... | 350 | 85,000 | 200,000 | *Radio Ch of God*. Ex CoG(SD). Extensive radio, TV. Schisms 1974. 400n,G=17%pa,W=97%. |
| Yaqui Church | 1769 | I mar | ..... | 10 | 500 | 2,000 | Yaqui Indians in Arizona. 1760, abandoned by Jesuits in NW Mexico. Easter dramas. |
| Zion Evangelistic Fellowship | | P Pe2 | ..... | 96 | 10,000 | 20,000 | Grouping of Pentecostals; little contact with other Pentecostals. |
| Other independent single congregations | | P sin | ..... | 2,000 | 500,000 | 1,000,000 | In over 100 de facto groupings; including Moody Bible Institute (8,000 members). |
| Other marginal Protestant bodies | | M | ..... | 10,000 | 500,000 | 1,000,000 | Total about 300 (see list below). |
| Other Protestant denominations | | P | ..... | 2,800 | 133,145 | 274,000 | Total about 500 (see list below). including over 40 White Pentecostal bodies. |
| Other Black indigenous churches | | I | ..... | | 49,000 | 98,000 | Total over 200 (see list below), and also many independent congregations. |
| Other Third-World indigenous churches | | I | ..... | 500 | 14,000 | 28,000 | Total over 30 (see list below). |
| Other Catholic (non-Roman) churches | | C | ..... | | 3,000 | 5,000 | Total about 40 (see below), including 30 small churches under bishops-at-large. |
| Other Orthodox churches | | O | ..... | | 2,000 | 4,000 | Total about 20 smaller bodies (see list below). |
| Other Amerindian indigenous churches | | I | ..... | | 1,000 | 2,000 | Total about 110 (see list below), begun among North American Indians, mostly Navajo. |
| Other Anglican denominations | | A | ..... | | 1,000 | 2,000 | Total about 10 (see list below), mostly recent schisms ex PECUSA. |
| **Total affiliated (mid-1970)** | | | | **362,200** | **106,307,266** | **153,200,624** | **Total denominations (1970) . . . 1,680.** |
| **Total affiliated (mid-1975)** | | | | **370,400** | **108,979,600** | **157,052,000** | **Total denominations (1975) . . . 1,860.** |
| **Total affiliated (mid-1980)** | | | | **385,000** | **111,662,300** | **160,918,000** | **Total denominations (1980) . . . 2,050.** |

NOTES ON TABLE ABOVE

COLUMNS: for meanings and CODES (cols. 1,3,4,8): see Codebook (Part 6). Column 1: **Boldface type** = church with over 10% of country's affiliated Christians.

NATIONAL COUNCILS (Column 4, 5th letter).

- b = member of both NCCCUSA and NFCC.
- E = National Association of Evangelicals (NAE) (and linked body, National Black (formerly Negro) Evangelical Association, NBEA).
- I = Pan-Indian Ecumenical Association of the USA and Canada (annual conferences: 1970 Cree Reservation, Montana, 1971 Stony Reserve, Alberta).
- J = National Fraternal Council of Churches (NFCC) (Black: began 1929).
- R = National Conference of Catholic Bishops (NCCB).
- T = American Christian Action Council (ACAC) (affiliated to ICCC).
- t = American Council of Christian Churches (ACCC) (affiliated to ICCC until withdrawal in 1968), including 6 bodies formerly in ACCC, now withdrawn; in addition, ACCC has as members 8 of the 12 bodies still in ICCC ACAC.
- W = National Council of the Churches of Christ in the USA (NCCCUSA) (constituent bodies).

*Other national councils*. Anglican Episcopal Council of Churches (formed 1975). Associated Gospel Churches (service agency for 3-million strong fundamentalist denominations). Christian Holiness Association (CHA) (Wesleyan-Arminian bodies; before 1971, National Holiness Association, NHA). Christian Hope Indian Eskimo Fellowship (CHIEF) (for native Amerindian groups in North and South America). Council of Japanese American Christian Churches in North America. Inter-church Holiness Convention (IHC). Lutheran Council in the USA (members ALC, LCA, LCMS). National Conference of Independent Catholic and Orthodox Jurisdictions. National Federation of Pentecostal Churches (Black). North American Baptist Fellowship. North American Presbyterian and Reformed Council (NAPARC) (begun 1975 with 6 member denominations: CRC, OPC, RPCES, RPCNA, PCA, ARPC).

*Local councils*. Over 50 state councils of churches linked with NCCCUSA, also many hundreds of metropolitan and city councils.

OTHER MARGINAL PROTESTANT BODIES. The table includes all known larger marginal Protestant bodies. In addition, there is a vast proliferation of smaller bodies, many being schisms, in a more orthodox or christocentric direction, out of the 3 major bodies (Church of Christ Scientist, Jehovah's Witnesses, Mormons). Among these are the following better-known bodies: American Prophetic League, Anthroposophical Society in America (Christian Community Ch), Aquarian Brotherhood of Christ, Assembly of Yahvah, Associated Bible Students, Believerism (Balanced Life), Branhamites (Local Church, End Time Local Believers, Spoken Word Believers; HQ Jeffersonville, IN), Brotherhood of the Followers of the Present Jesus, Christ Temple Ch of Personal Experience, Christ Truth League (member of INTA), Christ Unity Science Ch, Christ's True Ch & School of Wisdom, Ch of God International (1978 schism ex Worldwide Ch of God by founder's son), Ch of Jesus Christ (Cutlerites), Ch of Jesus Christ of Latter-day Saints (Strangites) (300), Ch of Light, Ch of the Awakening (1958; pharmacological (peyote, mescaline); 400 Whites; now illegal), Ch of the Firstborn of the Fulness of Times (ex Mormons; polygamous fundamentalists), Ch of the Healing Christ, Ch of the Lord Jesus Christ (Ishi Temple), Ch of the One, Ch of the Truth (member of INTA), Cosmopolitan Churches of Prayer (Spiritual), Dawn Bible Students Association (ex JWs), Ev Ch of Christ Scientist, Fellowship of the Order of Christian Mystics, First Christian (Essene) Ch, Good Samaritan Ch of Truth, Greek Bible Students, Home of Truth (member of INTA), Institute of Religious Science and Philosophy, ISMAS (a Christian psychic group in California), Laymen's Home Missionary Movement (1918 split ex Jehovah's Witnesses), New Age Bible Centre, Order of the Cross (3 centres), Philanthropic Assembly (Chs of the Kingdom of God; in Europe, Amis de l'Homme; split ex Jehovah's Witnesses), Primitive Ch of Christ Scientist, Purgatorial Society, Servants of Yah (ex Jehovah's Witnesses), Spiritual Frontiers Fellowship, Stand Fast Bible Students, Twentieth Century Ch of God (ex Worldwide Ch of God), United Society of Believers in Christ's Second Appearing (Shakers), Universal Life Ch (claims 2 million mail-order followers in USA; enquiry re membership made to WCC), Warriors for Faith & Truth (Horpenites; from Saxony, Germany). In addition to these organized denominations, there are large numbers of independent congregations including 130 metaphysical groupings affiliated to INTA.

OTHER PROTESTANT DENOMINATIONS. The table includes known denominations with 1,000 adherents or more. There is however a vast number of smaller Protestant denominations down to bodies with only a handful of members and congregations. New US-founded bodies come into existence every year; also, many large churches elsewhere in the world start congregations in the USA as their members immigrate (e.g. in 1976 the Korean Presbyterian Ch in the USA was organized). The following list gives 91 of the 500 or more smaller Protestant (White) denominations in 1973, with in parentheses date of origin, total affiliated, etc: Albigensian Ch, American World Patriarchates (1961), Anchor Bay Evangelistic Association, Apostolic Ch, Apostolic Christian Ch of Jesus Christ, Apostolic Methodist Ch, Associate Presbyterian Ch of North America, Back to the Bible Way, Berean Fellowship International, Bethel Pentecostal Temple (Seattle), Bible Fellowship Ch (Mennonite), Bible Missionary Chs, Carolina Evangelistic Association, Ch of Christian Liberty (begun 1969; 400), Ch of Eternal Life, Ch of God as Organized by Christ, Ch of God (Apostolic) (600), Ch of God (Bishop Poteat), Ch of God (Greenville), Ch of God Holiness (HQ Overland Park, Kansas), Ch of God (New Dunkards), Ch of Jesus Christ, Ch of Liberty, Ch of the Awakening, Ch of the Blessed Hope, Ch of the Full Gospel (300), Ch of the Gospel (100), Ch of the New Birth, Ch of the Revelation (750), Ch Which is Christ's Body, Christian Believers Conference, Churches of God in the British Isles & Overseas (5 churches), Concordia Lutheran Conference (1945 split ex LCMS; 6 churches), Conference of Fundamental Chs, Cumberland Methodist Ch, Eglise Ev Française, Ev Ch of Christ, Followers of Jesus (ex Roman Catholic Ch; 600 members in 1969), Free Pentecostal Ch, Free Reformed Ch of North America (2 churches, 575 members), Free Will Baptist Ch of the Pentecostal Faith, Full Gospel Grace Fellowship (1954), Fundamental Conference of America, Fundamental Methodist Ch, General Six-Principle Baptists, Gospel Lighthouse Ch (Dallas, Texas), Gospel Mission Corps, Gypsy Ev Movement (France), House of David (900), Independent Baptist Bible Mission, Independent Baptist Ch of America, Independent Pentecostal Assemblies, International Conference of Calvary Tabernacles (member of ICCC), International Deliverance Chs (Pentecostal), International Evangelical Ch (Pentecostal; member of WCC), Israel Gospel Ch, Jesus Ch, Justified Ch of God, Latter Rain Movement, Lithuanian Reformed Ch in Exile (1968 applied to join WCC), Methodist Protestant Ch (member of ICCC), Militant Fundamental Bible Chs, Miracle Revival Fellowship (1951), Mount Calvary Holy Ch of America, New Bethel Ch of God in Christ Pentecostal, New Congregational Methodist Ch, New Covenant Apostolic Order (NCAO, begun 1970; led by former Campus Crusade (CCCI) leaders named apostles stressing authority and congregational discipline; 2,000 members, all Whites, no pastors; 1978, 25% secede), New Testament Association of Independent Baptist Chs, Orthodox Baptists, Orthodox Lutheran Conference (1955), Pentecostal Ev Ch of God, People's Christian Ch, People's Methodist Chs, People's Mission Ch, People's Temple (founded 1956; de facto ex Disciples of Christ; 90% USA Black; 1974 exodus to Jonestown in Guyana jungle; 1978 mass suicide-murder there of 912 followers), Reformed Cumberland Presbyterian Ch, Reformed New Congregational Methodist Ch, Remnant Ch, Seventh Day Baptists (German), Stauffer Mennonite Ch, True Ch of Jesus Christ (mail-order body), True Dutch Reformed Ch, Two-Seed-in-the-Spirit Predestinarian Baptists, Union of Messianic Jewish Congregations (1979; 19 congregations), United Christian Ch (400; member of ICCC), United Ev Chs (1961), United Indian Missions, United Seventh-day Brethren, United Wesleyan Methodist Ch of America (550), Universal World Ch, Waldensian Ch in America, Weaver Mennonite Ch, Welsh Calvinistic Methodist Ch.

OTHER BLACK INDIGENOUS CHURCHES. In addition to the US Black bodies listed in the table, there are a very large number of independent single congregations; and also around 100 smaller Black denominations, including: African Orthodox Ch of New York & Massachusetts (1938 schism ex AOC), African Universal Ch (begun 1927; pentecostal; missionaries to Ghana), Apostolic Ch of Jesus Christ (Jesus Only pentecostals), Black Christian Nationalist Ch (1972, ex United Ch of Christ), Black Unitarian Universalist Ch (Black Humanist Fellowship; not yet separate from UUA), Ch of God (Mother Horn), Fire-Baptized Holiness Ch (998), Free Ch of God in Christ, Fundamental Baptist Fellowship Association (1962), Glorified Ch of God, Holiness Ch of God (begun 1920), Holsteen Ch of God, House of Faith, House of the Lord, Kodesh Ch of Immanuel (582), Latter House of the Lord for All People, Mount Carmel Holy Ch of the Lord Jesus (HQ Camden, NJ), Mount Sinai Holy Ch of America (begun 1924; in 18 states, 3 nations; women bishops), Pentecostal Fire-Baptized Ch of the Americas, Pentecostal Fire-Baptized Holiness Ch, School of the Prophets (a Father-Only organization), Sought-out Ch of God in Christ, United Christian Evangelistic Association (formerly United Ch of Jesus Christ for All People; ex Bible Way Ch; 'Science of Living', 'Mind Science'; daily radio programme over 270 stations, also TV, from United Palace and Science of Living Institute, New York City; claims one million Blacks), Victory Way Free Ch of God True Holiness USA (in 6 Mid-West states). There are also several miniscule episcopal churches under bishops-at-large (episcopi vagantes).

OTHER THIRD-WORLD INDIGENOUS CHURCHES. There are an increasing number of immigrant indigenous churches from Africa, Asia, Latin America and the Caribbean, usually established in the USA by their immigrant followers. In addition to the 12 listed in the table, the over 30 others include: African Apostolic Ch of Johane Maranke (from Rhodesia), Ceylon Pentecostal Mission, Ch of the First-Born (from Jamaica), Ch of the Gospel of Jesus Christ (in Hawaii), Ch of the Lord (Aladura) (1968, from Nigeria), Defenders of the Faith (Puerto Rico; 1923), Filipino Assemblies of the First Born (1933), Gideon's Evangelistic Band (Mexico), Iglesia Ev Pentecostal de Chile (1 church in New York), International City Mission (Jamaica), Kimbanguist Ch (EJCSK, from Zaire; US Blacks), Prince of Peace (Kealiiokamalu; in Hawaii), True Jesus Ch (Chinese, begun 1930 in Honolulu; 148 baptized in 3 churches and 1 preaching hall, in California and Hawaii), True Jesus Mission of the Latter Rain (in Hawaii). There is also a Nestorian schism from Iraq, the American Assyrian Apostolic Ch (c1950 schism ex Ancient Ch of the East; HQ Chicago).

OTHER CATHOLIC (NON-ROMAN) CHURCHES. The total includes around 30 miniscule unrecognized episcopal churches under bishops-at-large (episcopi vagantes) (for names, see part 9); this total excludes numerous other such bodies in existence earlier but now defunct. Among other autocephalous Catholic churches with larger followings are: American Orthdox Missionary Ch, Byzantine American Ch, Free Protestant Episcopal Ch (Ecumenical Church Foundation) (12 congregations, several bishops), Holy Orthodox Ch in America (Eastern Catholic & Apostolic), Independent Episcopal Ch of the USA and Canada, International Liberal Catholic Ch, Old Catholic Ch in America, Polish Mariavite Ch. For details of all these bodies see table at end of part 9. There are also several cults stemming from Roman Catholicism, including Antoinists (from France and Belgium).

OTHER ORTHODOX CHURCHES. There are several smaller bodies, including: Alexandrian Orthodox Ch in America (Russians, Ukrainians; Blacks), Assyrian Ch of the East (Mar Addai's faction), Autocephalous Slavonic Orthodox Ch in Exile, Bulgarian Orthodox Diocese of America (under ROCOR), Finnish Orthodox Ch (1955), Hungarian Orthodox Greek Catholic Ch, Macedonian Orthodox Ch (1961), Molokan Christian Ch (1905; Russians), 2 Romanian Orthodox independent parishes.

OTHER AMERINDIAN INDIGENOUS CHURCHES. Since their first contact with Whites in North America, American Indians have produced over 100 distinguishable new religious movements (1740–1975); among them many have had distinctively Christian elements, and of these some 20 still existed in 1975. In addition to the 10 American Indian churches listed in the table, there are about 100 other small Indian bodies or single Indian congregations, including: American Indian Ch Independent (Chicago), American Indian Ev Ch (1956; pentecostal), Apache Pentecostal Ch (San Carlos Reservation), First Born Ch of Christ (begun 1914 at Redrock, Oklahoma), Miccosukee Independent Indian Ch (Florida, ex Southern Baptist Mission), Mohave Mission Ch, Pima Independent Ch, San Carlos Apache Independent Ch. Several of these bodies support the Southwest Indian Bible Conference, with its grounds in Prescott, Arizona. The majority however are found in Navajoland.

OTHER ANGLICAN DENOMINATIONS. There are a number of other secessions from the Episcopal Church in the USA (PECUSA), which still regard themselves as authentically Anglican in tradition. These include: Anglican Ch of America (1968), Anglican Episcopal Ch of North America (c1972), Episcopal Ch (Evangelical), United Episcopal Ch (1973), these 4 belonging to the Anglican Episcopal Council of Churches (1975); also Old Episcopal Ch (c1960), Southern Episcopal Ch (1953). In addition, there are numerous other formerly Anglican (Episcopalian) schisms which regard themselves as no longer Anglican but now belonging to another tradition, either Catholic (non-Roman), Orthodox or Protestant.

UNITING CHURCHES. At least 5 separate sets of major negotiations for organic union were under way in 1980: (1) Church of Christ Uniting (COCU): AME Ch, AME Zion Ch, CME Ch, Christian Church (Disciples of Christ), Episcopal Ch in the USA, National Council of Community Churches, Presbyterian Ch in the US, United Ch of Christ, United Methodist Ch, United Presbyterian Ch in the USA (latter withdrew in 1972, and rejoined in 1973). (2) AME Ch, AME Zion Ch, CME Ch. (3) Orthodox Presbyterian Ch, Reformed Presbyterian Ch (Evangelical Synod). (4) Presbyterian Ch in the US, United Presbyterian Ch USA. (5) Wesleyan Evangelical Ch: Free Methodist Ch, Wesleyan Ch (past negotiations 1907–15 and 1943–55 broke down).

PEOPLES (ethnolinguistic). Note: The following figures, in accordance with our ethnolinguistic definition and classification (see Part 4), refer to mother tongue and not simply to ethnic group into which people were born. The present size of the corresponding cultural minorities (e.g. Russians, Armenians, Ukrainians) may be 2 or 3 times larger than those who still speak the mother tongue (as in their ethnic churches in the USA) because many have now become English-speaking. Percentages of the 3 major races have changed noticeably from 1970 to 1980, because of massive immigration of Hispanics, in the following manner. Christians (1970): 70.3% USA White, 11.1% USA Black, 5.5% unassimilated Hispanic. (1980): 66.6% USA White, 11.9% USA Black, 8.2% unassimilated Hispanic. *1980 composition* (in detail). Christians: 66.6% USA White (English-speaking), 11.9% USA Black (Negro), 8.2% unassimilated Hispanic (2.9% Mexican expatriate, 2.9% USA Mestizo (Chicano), 0.8% Puerto Rican White, 0.3% Cuban, 0.1% Spaniard), 2.5% German, 2.0% Italian, 1.2% Polish, 1.0% Irish, 0.9% French, 0.5% Austrian, 0.4% USA Amerindian (0.1% part-Indian), 0.4% British, 0.4% Anglo-Canadian, 0.4% French-Canadian, 0.3% Swedish, 0.3% Norwegian, 0.2% Dutch, 0.2% Czech, 0.2% Slovak, 0.2% Hungarian, 0.2% Ruthenian (Carpatho-Russian), 0.2% Russian, 0.2% Greek, 0.2% Lithuanian, 0.2% Portuguese, 0.2% Filipino (0.1% Tagalog, 0.1% Ilocan), 0.1% Armenian, 0.1% Serbo-Croatian, 0.1% Finnish, 0.1% Ukrainian, 0.1% Jewish, 0.1% Hawaiian (Polynesian), 0.1% Chinese (100,000), 0.1% Japanese, 0.1% Korean, Bolivian, Gypsy, Arab, Byelorussian, Latvian, Assyrian, Romanian, Bulgar, Albanian, Vietnamese, Latin American White, Eskimo, and over 160 other groups.

COUNTRY-WIDE TOTALS

EVANGELIZATION (see Part 5). 1900: 100%. 1970: 100%. 1980: 100%. *Mass evangelism*. The USA has several thousands of full-time or professional evangelists at local, regional and national levels, the most renowned being Billy Graham whose appeals for commitment to Christ produced, from 1947–75, 1.5 million enquirers (professions of faith, decisions for Christ). His USA crusades (averaging one week) and rallies (1 or 2 days only) each year included the following (places, in time order, with total attenders, and total enquirers or decisions for Christ): *1947*. October: Grand Rapids, MI (6,000 attenders, 500 enquirers). November: Charlotte, NC (42,000/1,200). *1948*. Augusta and Modesto (69,000/2,200). *1949*. Miami, Baltimore, Altoona, Los Angeles (441,000/5,700). *1950*. Boston, Columbia, New England, Portland, Minneapolis, Atlanta (1,757,000/43,700). *1951*. Southern states, Fort Worth, Shreveport, Memphis, Seattle, Hollywood, Greensboro, Raleigh (2,006,550/33,892). *1952*. Washington DC, Houston, Jackson, Pittsburgh, Albuquerque, et alia (1,695,330/32,722). *1953*. Florida, Chattanooga, St Louis, Dallas, West Texas, Syracuse, Detroit, Asheville (1,892,030/31,103). *1954* (first year of crusades outside USA). West Coast, Nashville, New Orleans (1,058,800/16,649). *1955*. Nil: all crusades abroad. *1956*. Richmond, Oklahoma City, Louisville (1,255,249/20,227). *1957*. New York City (2,397,400/61,148). *1958*. 8 crusades and rallies (1,482,712/59,241). *1959*. Little Rock, Wheaton, Indianapolis (479,127/13,570). *1960*. Washington DC, New York City (182,500/6,110). *1961*. 18

crusades and rallies (1,370,552/37,492). *1962.* 7 crusades and rallies (1,048,600/29,098). *1963.* Los Angeles (910,445/36,487). *1964.* 12 crusades and rallies (1,165,120/54,298). *1965.* 12 crusades and rallies (901,015/34,394). *1966.* Greenville, SC (269,200/7,311). *1967.* Kansas City (363,500/11,380). *1968.* Portland, San Antonio, Pittsburgh (605,397/24,690). *1969.* New York City, Anaheim (618,000/31,183). *1970.* Knoxville, New York City, Baton Rouge (888,500/27,404). *1971.* Lexington, Chicago, Oakland, Irving (1,127,400/48,489). *1972.* Charlotte, Birmingham, Cleveland (817,840/34,105). *1973.* Atlanta, Minneapolis, Raleigh, St Louis (1,046,750/42,637). *1974.* Phoenix, Hollywood, Hampton and Norfolk (456,654/17,658). *1975.* Albuquerque, Jackson, Lubbock (675,400/23,063). *1976.* Seattle, Williamsburg, San Diego, Pontiac (1,073,568/42,904). *1977.* Cincinnati. *1978.* Memphis, TN. By the end of 1976, Billy Graham had preached in 29 years to face-to-face audiences worldwide of 50,780,505 in 229 crusades lasting 374 weeks, resulting in 1,526,729 enquirers (decisions) (3.0%). Billy Graham film ministries: 'The Restless Ones' released 1965 had been shown in 2,400 US cities by 1973 (5 million attenders, 370,000 decisions for Christ); 'For Pete's Sake', released 1966, in 667 cities (1.5 million attenders, 68,000 decisions). Nation-wide interdenominational campaigns and events have included: Explo '72 (including 3 CCCI telecasts watched by 30 million each with 11,000 decisions for Christ); KEY 73 (involving many denominations including 50% of all United Methodist congregations). The first US Congress on Evangelism, with 4,600 delegates, was held in Minneapolis in 1969; a similar one in 1970, CLADE, focussed on the Spanish-speaking population. Most denominations also engage in mass or large-scale personal and house-to-house evangelism, as exemplified by the only denomination that keeps exact statistics on the subject, Jehovah's Witnesses, who in 1974 in the USA had 472,662 peak publishers (door-to-door visitors) conducting 281,337 house Bible studies, conducting 34,208,792 return visits and spending 78,806,678 man-hours. Other recent campaigns by other bodies: 1970–71, 'Passover' evangelistic film televised by American Board of Missions to the Jews for 12 USA cities (audience one million Jews, 3% responding afterwards by letter); 1976–77, Here's Life America (CCCI), numerically the largest and densest evangelistic campaign in American history, reaching 10 million homes through 14,000 involved churches and 300,000 trained persons in 220 major cities (89% of total population, with at least 870,000 decisions for Christ recorded); in addition, radio and TV decisions were unrecorded; one TV special was seen by 50 million in its 240 showings. *Radiophonic evangelism.* There are a vast number of stations and agencies. Annual listeners' letters received from USA listeners by overseas stations (1975): 10,540 HCJB, several thousand Radio Vatican, 1,960 TWR, 843 FEBC, 213 RVOG, et alia. Bible correspondence courses: over 3 million Protestant enrolments (including SDA/VOP rising from annual enrolments of 365,000 in 1971 to 510,400 in 1973) and a million Roman Catholic enrolments in numerous courses. Regular audiences for Christian radio/TV programmes: (1977) 125 million adults (85% of the USA).

FOREIGN MISSIONARIES AND PERSONNEL (nationals serving abroad) (1973). Total 57,212: 32,400 Protestants (increase from 23,600 in 1963, and 31,700 in 1969) (about 8,400 under EFMA, 7,000 under IFMA), 12,229 marginal Protestants (10,600 Mormons, about 1,000 Jehovah's Witnesses), 11,990 Roman Catholics (7,690 foreign missionaries from over 200 agencies in 110 Third-World countries (decline from 9,655 in 1968), and about 4,300 other personnel serving in Western nations), 220 Orthodox (over 130 priests in 17 countries), 190 Black indigenous (US Blacks from about 13 denominations), 173 Anglicans (Episcopalians) (decline from 351 in 1963, and 279 in 1965), about 10 Catholics (non-Roman). In addition and not included in this enumeration of foreign missionaries) there is a large and rapidly-growing number of short-term personnel mostly young people serving for 3–6 months, or well under 2 years), both Roman Catholic, Protestant and other. For Protestant, the total of these short-term personnel rose from 580 in 1965 to 3,959 in 1970, and to over 8,000 in 1975.

FOREIGN MISSIONARIES AND PERSONNEL (aliens from abroad) (1973). Total 16,746. *From Western world.* 14,534: about 9,000 Roman Catholics (from Ireland, Italy, et alia; including 92 Jesuits from Western Europe), about 5,042 Protestants from Canada and Europe (including 50 in 10 UK societies, 3 in 3 New Zealand societies), about 220 Anglicans from UK, Canada et alia, about 220 marginal Protestants (about 200 Mormons from Canada and Europe), about 30 Orthodox from Greece et alia, about 22 Catholics (non-Roman). In addition, a large number of short-term independent missionaries from many countries are temporarily at work in the USA. *From Communist world.* 127: about 82 Roman Catholics from Poland, Yugoslavia and Hungary, about 40 Orthodox from 5 countries, 5 Cuban indigenous from Cuba. In addition to these personnel legally serving abroad, there are large numbers of personnel who are Eastern European exiles or refugees, most of whom are in process of obtaining USA citizenship. In 1975 there were 73 Jesuits from Eastern Europe serving in the USA. *From Third World.* 2,085: about 1,500 Roman Catholics from India, Japan, Mexico, Philippines, Puerto Rico, et alia (including 98 Jesuits), 200 Protestants from Africa, Asia, Mexico, et alia, about 180 Third-World indigenous from Chile, Japan, Korea, Mexico, Nigeria, Philippines, Puerto Rico, Rhodesia, Sri Lanka, Taiwan, West Indies, et alia, 100 marginal Protestants (mostly Mormons), 81 Orthodox from 10 countries, 24 Anglicans from South Africa et alia.

INSTITUTIONS (church-operated) (1973). Total 6,900, including (1975) about 50 ecumenical centres, 3,000 higher schools (1,950 Roman Catholic including 127 minor seminaries and 141 nurses training schools), 1,000 hospitals (761 RC), 200 lay training centres, 100 presses, over 700 radio stations, 300 religious communities, 150 research centres, 610 seminaries (345 Protestant including 50 interdenominational or undenominational or united, 182 RC, 20 marginal Protestant, 16 Anglican, 8 Catholic/non-Roman, 6 Orthodox, 2 Non-White indigenous), 18 TV stations, 690 universities and colleges (430 Protestant, 251 RC).

PERIODICALS. About 5,430 titles. This total may be divided and subdivided in various ways, as follows. (1) *Contents:* about 1,000 academic or scholarly (religion and theology), 4,400 non-academic or popular (information, news, teaching). (2) *Home or abroad:* about 700 focus on foreign missions or the world outside the USA, and 4,700 on the USA situation or affairs. (3) *Professional associations:* about 450 relate to the Catholic Press Association, 200 to Associated Church Press, 200 to Evangelical Press Association; of the remainder, a few are attached to other associations but most remain unattached. (4) *Denominations:* (a) 3,730 denominational, of which 1,900 Protestant (350 Pentecostal, 100 UMC, 90 SDA, 50 SBC, 42 LCMS, 38 Quaker, 28 CCCC, and about 500 other denominations with 1, 2, 3, or more periodicals), 1,100 Roman Catholic (national, diocesan, missionary, religious, scholarly, charismatic, et alia), 400 marginal Protestant (40 LdS, Christian Science), 130 Episcopalian (Anglican) (35 national, 85 diocesan), 100 Orthodox (35 Greek Orthodox, 8 OCA, 4 ROCOR), 80 Black/Third-World indigenous (18 AMEC/AMEZC/CMEC, 8 CoGiC), 20 Catholic (non-Roman) (5 New Apostolic, 2 PNCC, 1 NAORCC, 1 Christ Catholic, 1 LCC); of which over 650 are put out by denominational foreign mission societies; (b) 1,700 interdenominational or non-denominational (service agencies, academic journals, et alia). Documentation on about 1,700 of these 5,430 titles may be found in 'Religious publications', *Ayer directory of publications* (annual); *Standard periodical directory;* 'Religions and theology' in *Ulrich's international periodical directory* (annual); et alia; in addition, denominational listings will be found in most denominations' annual yearbooks. Christian and religious periodicals, on our definition, therefore numbered in 1973 about 13% of the 40,000 or so periodicals of all kinds published in the USA (of which about 12,000 were newspapers (1,761 dailies), 10,000 monthlies and the rest weeklies, bi-weeklies, quarterlies, etc).

PERSONNEL. About 691,746 (about 675,000 national, 16,746 foreign).

RELIGIOUS LIBRARIES. About 2,700.

SCRIPTURE DISTRIBUTION (1975). Annual totals: 16,637,991 Bibles (5% free, 4% subsidized, 91% commercial), 25,257,476 NTs (24% free, 11% subsidized, 66% commercial), 4,992,055 UBS portions, 101,116,329 UBS selections. *Translations completed.* Portion: 30 languages since 1655. NT: 12 languages since 1661. Bible: 3 languages since 1663.

SERVICE AGENCIES. About 2,300 (mostly Protestant, with 180 Roman Catholic, some Orthodox, Anglican, etc), including AATS, ABS, ABWE, ACAC, ACCC, ACMC, AEM, AIM, AMHC, ASA, ASCE, ASE, AST, BGEA, BMM, BMMF, CAMEO, CARF, CBA, CBFMS, CBHMS, CBN, CCCA, CCF, CCCI, CCICA, CCMA, CCUA, CCWL, CEF, CFM, CHA, CICOP, CLC, CMF, CMMB, CMML, CMSM, COCU, CODEL, CPA, CRF, CROP, CRS-USCC, CSCW, CTSA, CUF, CYO, ECF, EFMA, ELO, EMIS, FCA, FEBC, FOR, GCP, GMU, ICB, ICCFM, ICYE, IDUM, IFES, IFMA, IMRA, IVCF, JARS, LCWR, LIFE, LMH, MAP, MCA, MECCA, MM, MTS, MUST, NAE, NARB, NASCC, NAWR, NBCCC, NBEA(NNEA), NBLCC, NBSA, NBSC, NCAN, NCCA, NCCB, NCCC, NCCCUSA, NCCIJ, NCCJ, NCCL, NCCM, NCEA, NCF, NCWU, NFPC, NOBC, NRB, NSFC, NSVC, NTM, OM, OPF, OSFO, PAO, PFNA, PTL, RES, RNA, SBL, SCLC, SIL, SIM, SPFM, SSSR, SU, TEAM, TFP, UBS, UCBWM, UFM, UMCOR, USCC, USCMC, USICOP, VBS, VISA, WBT, WCEU, WEF, WGM, WLSM, WMC, WSCF, WVI, YCM(YCW), YCS, YFCI, YMCA, YWAM, YWCA.

ADDITIONAL DATA ON CHURCHES

AMERICAN BAPTIST CHURCHES IN THE USA. *Neo-pentecostals.* In 1973 the charismatic renewal within the ABC involved over 600 ministers (7%) and 20,000 lay adults, co-ordinated by the American Baptist Charismatic Fellowship (founded 1968).

AMERICAN LUTHERAN CHURCH. Organized in 1960 to unite the American Lutheran Ch (ALC) of German origin, Ev Lutheran Ch (ELC) of Norwegian origin, and United Ev Lutheran Ch (UELC) of Danish origin; joined in 1963 by the Lutheran Free Ch (LFC). *Theology.* More conservative than the Lutheran Church in America (LCA).

ASSEMBLIES OF GOD. *Membership.* Increase from 679,813 in 1970 to 785,348 in 1974. *Conversions.* 344,642 (including children) in 2-year period 1973–75.

CATHOLIC CHURCH IN THE USA. *Hispanic (Spanish-speaking) Catholics.* Increase from 20% of all RCs in 1970 to 25% in 1980, due to immigration legal and illegal. *Black (Negro) Catholics.* The total has risen from 80,000 (in 1890) to 100,000 (1900), 280,000 (1940), 400,000 (1950), 653,217 (1961), and to 855,193 (1973) in 636 predominantly Black parishes (plus individual Blacks in many White parishes), with 3 Black bishops, 190 Black priests (127 secular, 63 religious in SVD, SSJ, CSSp) and 40 pastors, 171 brothers, 30 deacons, 714 Black sisters in, inter alia, 4 Black congregations (286 Holy Family Sisters (founded 1842), 262 Oblate Sisters of Providence (1892), 47 Franciscan Handmaids (1917), 10 Blessed Sacrament). There are 369 schools in Black communities, with 106,221 pupils. US Black personnel serving overseas include 2 priests in Ghana and New Guinea, a brother in Honduras, and 22 sisters in Bahamas, Costa Rica, Honduras, Uganda and Zambia. Dioceses with most Black Catholics (in order): Lafayette (83,709, or 21% of all Catholics), Chicago (80,000; 3%), Washington DC (76,120; 19%), New Orleans (75,280; 11%), New York (57,500; 3%), Philadelphia, Galveston, Los Angeles, Baltimore, Brooklyn. *Parishes.* Total (1977) 18,572. *Annual baptisms.* (1972, all races) 93.0% infant, 7.0% adult. Annual baptisms declined annually from 1962 to 884,925 infants a year in 1976 (decrease of 10,067 over previous year) and 79,627 adults. *Personnel* (all races; bishops, priests, brothers, sisters). About 95% nationals, 5% expatriates. *Priests.* (1975) 36,005 diocesan, 22,904 religious; (1977) 58,301. *Brothers.* Declining from peak of 12,539 in 1967 to 8,745 by 1977. *Sisters.* Declining from peak of 176,671 in 1967 to 130,804 by 1977. *Catholic charismatics* (or Catholic pentecostals). Total adults involved in the Catholic Charismatic Renewal (CCR) (January 1974): 500,000 adults including large numbers of religious personnel, and about 3,000 priests (5% of total priests), in 1,800 prayer groups (see footnote under Table 1), co-ordinated by the Catholic Charismatic Renewal Service Committee (founded 1970). Dioceses with strong charismatic movements: Birmingham, Boston, Chicago, Detroit, Grand Rapids (1 bishop involved), Hartford, Los Angeles, New Orleans, New Ulm (new bishop in 1976 a charismatic), Philadelphia, Rochester, St Louis (Missouri; 27% of all priests were involved in 1976).

*Catholic organizations.* In the USA, there are 2 national Catholic conferences which are related in membership and authority but distinct in nature, purpose and function. Both have their headquarters in the same building in Washington, DC. The distinction in name between them serves to highlight the fact that through them the bishops fulfill 2 separate and distinct responsibilities. (1) The National Conference of Catholic Bishops (NCCB), established in its present form in 1966, is the successor of the Annual Meeting of the Bishops of the United States, founded in 1919. Like other episcopal conferences throughout the world, the NCCB is a strictly ecclesiastical and canonical body in and through which the bishops act together as pastors of the church. The NCCB operates through a number of committees whose task is to prepare materials for the decision and action of the bishops assembled as a conference. The NCCB is divided into geographical regions to provide for more effective consultation and discussion, there being 12 regions in 1972. (2) The United States Catholic Conference (USCC), was founded in 1967 to take the place of the National Catholic Welfare Conference of 1923, which was itself formed in 1917 under the name National Catholic War Council. Sponsored by the NCCB, the USCC is a civil corporation and an agency in and through which the bishops collaborate with other members of the church (priests, religious and lay persons) in areas where voluntary collective action on an interdiocesan and national basis can be of benefit to the church and society. The USCC serves as the operational secretariat and service agency of the NCCB and is thus the action arm of the Catholic Church on the national level. The offices of the NCCB also serve as offices of the USCC, and the same general secretary is responsible for administering both organizations.

The USCC maintains liaison with the National Association of State Catholic Conferences, which in 1973 was responsible for co-ordinating the activities of 29 conferences, each being the local counterpart of the USCC. The objectives of these conferences are 'to develop and sponsor co-operative programmes designed to cope with pastoral and common-welfare needs, and to represent the dioceses before governmental bodies, the public and in the private sectors'. The USCC itself is organized into 3 departments: (1) Department of Education, with divisions for elementary and secondary education, higher education, religious education, family life, and youth activities; (2) Department of Social Development and World Peace, with divisions for chaplains services, health affairs, justice and peace, rural life, and urban affairs, in addition to liaison with agencies for Latin America, migration and refugee services; and (3) Department of Communication, with divisions for public information, film and broadcasting, and the National Catholic News Service.

Working in close association with the USCC are the National Council of Catholic Laity, National Catholic Community Serivice, Campaign for Human Development, and Catholic Relief Services.

There are in the USA several associations of religious personnel. For men, 2 are active: Conference of Major Superiors of Mens' Institutes of the USA (CMSM), founded in 1960, which is divided into 6 regional chapters; and National Association of Religious Brothers, founded in 1972. For women, 8 may be mentioned: (1) Leadership Conference of Women Religious in the United States of America (LCWR), first formed in 1956 with its name changed in 1971, which promotes the spiritual and apostolic welfare of the sisterhoods of the USA and is organized in 15 regional committees; (2) National Coalition of American Nuns (NCAN), founded in 1968 with a membership of 2,000 sisters in 1972, which defends the rights of all women and especially women religious from undue interference by male clerics; (3) National Sisters Vocation Conference (NSVC), with over 1,200 members in 1972, representing not only the USA but other countries as well, whose aim is to deepen the understanding of the role of women, especially women religious, in the church, through service in the vocational apostolate; (4) National Sister Formation Conference (NSFC), founded in 1954 and since 1970 independent of the LCWR with which it had been affiliated, which is divided into 15 geographical regions and whose aim is to serve congregations of women religious in their efforts to develop a life permeated with the love of God and man; (5) National Association of Women Religious (NAWR), founded in 1970, whose membership (including individuals and groups) consists of nearly half the total of all sisters in the USA and whose main goal is to challenge women religious to communicate a valid concept of the role of consecrated celibate women in the church today; (6) Association of Contemplative Sisters, founded in 1969, to provide a vehicle of communication and collaboration among contemplatives in the USA and English-speaking Canada, whose membership (which is on an individual, not a community basis) includes over 1,000 sisters representing more than half of the 170 contemplative communities and every contemplative tradition in the USA; (7) Las Hermanas, founded in 1971, which is a national organization of Hispanic women religious including also sisters who are not of Hispanic origin but are working for the welfare of or are related to Spanish-speaking people in the USA; and (8) National Black Sisters' Conference (NBSC), founded in 1968 as a national organization of Black sisters (including also a few White sisters working in Black communities and some former Black sisters who have left their communities) from (in 1972) 123 religious congregations in the USA and its territories, which collaborates with the National Office for Black Catholics and other organizations of Black Catholics, with the aim of developing Black vocations to religious life in the unique contemporary Black life-style, working for a redistribution of Black sisters and participating in the liberation of Black people.

Plans to establish a national pastoral council, formulated between 1970 and 1974 by a committee formed from the US Catholic Bishops' Advisory Council, were cancelled in 1974. The Advisory Council, created by the NCCB and the USCC, is composed of 60 members, all elected by their peers, including 12 laymen, 12 laywomen, 6 bishops, 6 priests, 6 religious men and women and 18 other members.

For priests, there is no official national presbyteral council, but the independently-organized National Federation of Priests' Councils (NFPC), founded in Chicago in 1966, represents the majority of all USA priests. Its officers meet annually with a liaison committee of the NCCB and seek to represent local councils of priests, both senates (official organizations initiated by diocesan bishops) and associations (independent organizations established by priests themselves within a diocese). In the NFPC membership is by council only, not individuals. In 1972 the NFPC had a membership of 127 councils organized in 27 provinces, which parallel approximately the ecclesiastical provinces, representing 30,000 priests. Of the 127 councils, 96 were senates, 27 associations (only one association from a diocese being allowed to affiliate with the federation) and 4 religious congregations; and they represented 115 out of the 152 dioceses in the continental USA. Black priests are represented through the National Black Catholic Clergy Caucus (NBCCC), founded in 1968; and the National Black Seminarians Association (NBSA) was formed in 1970.

Organizations of the lay apostolate may be divided into those for youth and those for adults. The principal co-ordinating and service agency for the former is the Division of Youth Activities, a division of the Department of Education within the USCC. Member organizations of the division are the National CYO Federation and the National Catholic Camping Association. The division collaborates with the US Youth Council and international youth organizations. Catholicism's main organizations for youth and young adults are: Catholic Youth Organization (CYO), the official parish-centred body organized in each diocese; Boy Scouts and Girl Scouts in the Catholic Church (where the USCC Division of Youth Activities works in co-operation with the Boy Scouts of America and with the Girl Scouts of the USA in promoting Catholic principles); Camp Fire Girls (up to 6 years of age; over 600,000 members); St Dominic Savio Classroom Club (from the later years of elementary school to high school); Forest Rangers (about 40,000 members in the USA and Canada); Columbian Squires (junior branch of Knights of Columbus); Junior Catholic Daughters of America (4,500 members from 11 to 18 years of age); Junior Daughters of Isabella (10 to 22 years of age); National Catholic Forensic League (school-centred); Catholic Central Youth Union of America (youth branch of the Catholic Central Union of America); Young Christian Students (YCS) (3,000 students in high school); Black Christian Students (BCS) (a separate organization which split from the YCS but maintains liaison with it); Young Christian Movement (YCM) (formerly Young Christian Workers, YCW).

The principal co-ordinating and service agency for adults is the National Council of Catholic Laity (NCCL), a USCC-related agency established in 1971 by 60 lay organizations representing

20 million members, under the auspices of the NCCW and the NCCM. In 1974, some 15,000 local and national lay organizations (10,000 related to women) were represented in the NCCL, which serves to co-ordinate and represent US lay persons, as well as to intensify missionary activity of Catholic laity. General goals are threefold: the renewal of the church, challenge to the social order and concern for the future of the world. NCCL provides services and leadership training institutes for individuals, parish, pastoral councils, diocesan and archidiocesan organizations and also for state and national organizations. The 2 parent associations of the NCCL, the National Council of Catholic Women (NCCW) with more than 10,000 affiliated local and national organizations, and the National Council of Catholic Men (NCCM), with more than 9,000 affiliated organizations, are autonomous federations retaining their own identity, although their members also form the membership of the NCCL. The National Secretariat of the NCCL also serves the NCCM and NCCW.

The principal organizations for laymen are: Knights of Columbus; Catholic Knights of America (a fraternal insurance society, with 90,000 members); Catholic Order of Foresters (180,000 members in the USA and Canada); and Catholic Central Union of America (one of the oldest lay organizations in the USA, to develop Christian principles in personal, social, and civic life; about 20,000 members).

The principal organizations for lay women are: Catholic Daughters of America (over 200,000 members); Daughters of Isabella (over 120,000 members); National Catholic Women's Union (female branch of the Catholic Central Union of America; about 28,000 members).

The principal organizations serving families are: the Division of Family Life of the USCC, which co-ordinates the activities of family life directors in some 139 dioceses; Christian Family Movement (CFM); and Cana Conferences. The latter, which serves married couples (Pre-Cana also being available for engaged couples), is organized in many dioceses, although the movement is autonomous in each diocese and has no central headquarters.

Other non-specialized spirituality movements are: Apostleship of Prayer, Christian Life Communities (formerly Sodalities of Our Lady), Cursillo Movement (Cursillos de Cristiandad, with headquarters in Spain), Group 7 (USA home mission apostolate), Holy Name Society, Legion of Mary, Serra Clubs, numerous archconfreries and other movements.

The Black laity are represented through the National Black Lay Catholic Conference (NBLCC), founded in 1970.

The Holy See has no diplomatic relations with the USA, but since 1893 has been represented to the Catholic hierarchy by an apostolic delegate based in Washington, DC, who serves also as apostolic delegate to Guam, the Caroline and Marshall Islands and the British and US Virgin Islands. Two American presidents, F.D. Roosevelt and R.M. Nixon, appointed personal representatives to the Vatican.

International Catholic organizations with headquarters in the USA include: International Confederation of Christian Family Movements (ICCFM), founded in Montevideo, in 1947 and later moved to Caracas and finally to Chicago, which is dedicated to strengthening marriages and families and counted as members in 1974 some 180,000 couples in 50 countries, mostly in Latin America; Serra International, founded in Chicago in 1935, with 12,500 lay members in 3,600 clubs in more than 20 countries in 1974, which fosters vocations to the priesthood and trains Catholic lay leadership; and World Union of Catholic Philosophical Societies, founded in Washington, DC in 1948, and affiliated to OIC in Belgium, with 1,500 members in some 20 countries in 1974, which facilitates relations between societies and represents them before international philosophical organizations.

Concerning opinion groups, in the USA 2 categories of organizations have arisen outside of the hierarchically-initiated federations, associations and movements. The first category has 2 main organizations. The Catholic Traditionalist Movement, founded in Waterbury (NY) in 1964 espouses the theological position that the English canon of the mass is not valid; it is usually considered outside the communion of faith. Citizens United for Faith (CUF), a conservative group founded in New Rochelle in 1968 'in response to the Vatican II call to the laity to assume their proper place in the Church', with 12,500 members in all 50 states and Canada, rejects the term traditionalist because they see themselves as entirely within the communion of the Catholic Church. CUF is a member of the international conservative federation Pro Fide et Ecclesia in France. Other small traditional movements are Una Voce America, and the American Society for the Defense of Tradition, Family and Property. The latter, centred in Little Neck (NY), has the same name and purposes as the TFP in Brazil.

The second category includes the progressivist usually called liberal organizations. Five may be noted. (1) The National Association of Laity (NAL) recently held their 8th annual meeting and voted to stay in existence, which had been in doubt. It is independent of official church ties and characterizes itself as 'the loyal opposition'. With only 100 dues-paying members, they nevertheless have a large mailing list of 3,000 and 30 official affiliated groups. (2) The Catholic Worker Movement, founded in New York City in 1933, publishes *The Catholic Worker*, 9 times a year. Differing from the hierarchy in their radical promotion of pacifism and their espousal of radical decentralization of the political order, they encourage credit unions, co-operatives, unions of workers and mutual aid. (3) The Judean society is growing rapidly. Founded in 1952 at Mt View (CA) to seek a revision of canon law relating to divorce, it seeks to offer divorced women 'friendship, encouragement and spiritual renewal' and to find ways to 'preserve Christian marriage in America'. Under that umbrella are over 40 unauthorized groups such as Women Alone in Youngstown (OH), Divorced Women in Tucson (AZ) and New Life in Wilmington (DE). (4) A group of Catholic homosexual men have formed an organization called Dignity, with 32 chapters in the USA, one in Canada and 4 in Australia where it is called Acceptance. Founded in Boston in 1969, they now have 3,000 members and publish a national monthly newsletter. (5) In 1973, a group of married priests formed an organization called Federation of Christian Ministry, which is an outgrowth of an earlier group called Society of Priests for a Free Ministry (SPFM), founded in 1967. It publishes a monthly newsletter, called *Diaspora*. An ad hoc support group in the Chicago area has arisen for FCM, called CORPUS, which is made up of about 500 clergy.

The following organizations are involved in research and socio-religious action. (1) The Department of Social Development and World Peace of the USCC in Washington, DC, is the official co-ordinating body of the church in justice and peace affairs and seeks to assist all the church's agencies to implement the social doctrines of the Catholic Church. (2) The Center for Applied Research in the Apostolate (CARA), founded in Washington, DC, in 1965 and affiliated to FERES in Belgium, is involved in planning, programming and strategy development in the service of the church's social and religious mission in the modern world, at home and overseas. (3) The Paulist Institute for Religious Research was founded in Washington, DC, in 1959. (4) The Cambridge Center for Social Studies formerly called the Institute of Social Order was founded by Jesuits in Cambridge (MA). (5) The Association for Social-Economics (ASE) formerly called the Catholic Economic Association (CEA) was founded at Marquette University, Milwaukee (WI) in 1941. (6) Campaign for Human Development, founded in Washington, DC, by the NCCB in 1969, is a national education information and development programme to inform the people of USA about the facts of poverty and to assist the poor of America through self-help projects.(7) The National Catholic Rural Life Conference, founded in Des Moines (IA) in 1923 and now under the sponsorship of the Division of Rural Life of USCC, works for the spiritual and material welfare of rural families, in co-operation with almost 100 officially-appointed diocesan rural life directors. (8) The Glenmary Research Center, founded in Washington, DC, by the Glenmary Missioners in 1966, helps to serve the research needs of the Catholic Church in small towns and rural America. (9) The National Center for Urban Ethnic Affairs, founded in Washington, DC, in 1971. (10) The National Catholic Conference for Interracial Justice (NCCIJ) was formed in Chicago in 1961 out of the Catholic Interracial Council movement, as an independent lay agency recognized by the church. (11) The Catholic Interracial Council of New York, was founded in 1934 and publishes the *Interracial review* quarterly. (12) Friendship House, founded in Chicago in 1938 engages in ethnic and prison-reform studies. (13) The Division of Migration and Refugee Services of the USCC works in co-operation with volunteer agencies at the national and diocesan levels on all matters concerning immigration and migration, especially remedial legislation. Three branch offices are located in New York City, El Paso (TX), and San Francisco. Another branch, Cuban Refugee Emergency Centre, is located in Miami and cares for the largest percentage of Cuban refugees of any organization in the USA. Its services are also co-ordinated with the National Catholic Resettlement Council in New York City. (14) In addition to the above agencies, departments of religious sociology have been formed in 8 Catholic colleges and universities.

National associations and societies dedicated to specialized areas of theological study are as follows: (1) Catholic Theological Society of America, founded in Mundelein (IL) in 1946, which is the largest Catholic theological society in the world; (2) Canon Law Society of America, founded in Hartford (CT) in 1939, which promotes research and study in canon law and has been in the forefront of canonical renewal since 1963; (3) Catholic Biblical Association of America, founded in Washington, DC, in 1936, which publishes the *Catholic Biblical quarterly;* (4) Association for the Sociology of Religion (formerly the American Catholic Sociological Society), founded in Los Angeles in 1938, which publishes *Sociological analysis;* (5) Liturgical Conference, in Washington, DC, which sponsors education, research and publication programmes; (6) American Catholic Philosophical Association, founded in Washington, DC, in 1926; (7) American Catholic Historical Association, founded in Washington, DC, in 1919; and (8) Church Music Association of America, which has its headquarters in Milwaukee (WI).

Pontifical theological faculties and institutes include: the School of Sacred Theology (founded in Washington, DC, in 1889); Dominican House of Studies (Washington, DC; 1897; only for the OP); School of Divinity, St Louis University (St Louis (MO); 1897); School of Theology, St Mary's Seminary and University (Baltimore (MD); 1822); Jesuit School of Theology at Berkeley (Berkeley (CA); member of the Graduate Theological Union); Bellarmine School of Theology (Chicago; 1934; SJ); Woodstock College (New York City; 1869; SJ); and Pontifical College Josephinum (Worthington (OH); 1888).

Almost all Catholic universities and many Catholic colleges, in addition to non-pontifical Catholic seminaries, maintain departments of theology or religious studies. Of these the most important are: Aquinas Institute of Theology (Dubuque (IA); 1950); Department of Theology, University of Notre Dame (Notre Dame (IN)); Department of Theology, Fordham University (New York City); Department of Theology, Marquette University (Milwaukee); Franciscan School of Theology (Berkeley (CA); 1901); Catholic Theological Union at Chicago (1968); and St Meinrad School of Theology (St Meinrad (ID)).

In 1974 there were 104 diocesan seminaries (11,223 seminarians) and 269 religious seminaries or novitiates and scholasticates (6,579 seminarians), these figures being 5 fewer diocesan seminaries than in 1974, with 542 less seminarians, and 24 fewer religious seminaries, with 1,004 less seminarians.

The most important of the rapidly-growing number of pastoral institutes and centres of pastoral study and research are: (1) Mexican American Cultural Centre, founded in 1971; (2) School of Applied Theology, founded in Berkeley (CA), in 1960, which is affiliated with the Graduate Theological Union; (3) Pastoral Institute of Spirituality and Continuing Education, founded in St Paul (MN) in 1975; (4) Office of Pastoral Research, founded in New York City in 1971; (5) Woodstock Theological Center, founded in Washington, DC, in 1974; (6) Vatican II Institute for Clergy Education, founded in Menlo Park (CA) in 1973; (7) Center for Pastoral Studies of the Catholic University of America, founded in Washington, DC, in 1969; (8) Pastoral Theological Program of the University of Notre Dame, in Notre Dame (IN); and (9) Catholic Committee on Urban Ministry, in Notre Dame (IN). In addition to the above-mentioned and other pastoral institutes and centres of pastoral study and research, there is also the National Organization of Continual Education for Priests, which was founded in 1972 and in many cases serves as a pastoral institute and centre of pastoral study for priests involved in the active ministry.

Organizations and institutes dedicated to the study and promotion of the liturgy and church music include: (1) US Bishops' Liturgical Committee in Washington, DC, which is sponsored by the NCCB and is the principal co-ordinating agency of the church in liturgical matters; (2) Murphy Center for Liturgical Research, founded at University of Notre Dame (IN) in 1971; (3) Composers' Forum for Catholic Worship, founded at Sugar Creek (MO) in 1970, which is a research centre for the creation of new music for worship and furnishes a framework whereby liturgists, musicians and experts of various disciplines may work together; and (4) Gregorian Institute of America, founded in Chicago in 1940.

The principal co-ordinating agency for the support of Catholic missionary activity outside the USA is the United States Catholic Missionary Council, founded in Washington, DC, in 1969 with the approval of NCCB. The main organizations furnishing aid to missions are: (1) 3 pontifical societies; Society for the Propagation of the Faith in New York City, Holy Childhood Association in Pittsburgh (PA), and Catholic Near East Welfare Association in New York City; (2) Latin America Bureau, in Washington, DC, the executive office of the Division for Latin America (founded in 1960) inside the USCC International Affairs Department which aims to assist the spiritual and material endeavours of the people of Latin America, and which established in 1963 the Catholic Inter-American Cooperation Program (CICOP) as the instrumental body to educate North Americans to the realities of Latin America; and (3) Catholic Relief Services (CRS/USCC), founded in New York City in 1943, which is a member of Caritas Internationalis in Rome and CIDSE in Brussels. A separately-incorporated organization of the USCC, CRS is the official overseas aid and development agency of American Catholics. Originally created for the purpose of assisting war victims throughout the world, CRS today is the world's largest voluntary overseas aid agency. It conducts relief, welfare and self-help programmes in areas of need in 80 countries, giving priority to community development, credit unions, co-operatives, leadership training and nutrition education, with a special emphasis on projects aimed at developing local agriculture. Overseas regional offices are located in Geneva, Rome and Nairobi; and local offices have been opened in 64 foreign countries.

The main organizations for sending lay personnel to Third-World countries to assist Catholic missions are (with 1973 statistics): Catholic Medical Mission Board, founded in New York City in 1928 (with 110 persons in 17 countries); Jesuit Volunteer Corps (93 in 7 countries); Catholic Relief Services (92 in 44 countries); and Lay Mission Helpers (52 in 12 countries and 8 in home missions in 1971). In total, there are some 40 sponsoring agencies, with a membership of more than 500 in overseas assignments.

Catholic mission study centres include: the Marianist Mission Institute (University of Dayton in Ohio), Duquesne University (Pittsburgh), African Studies Program (University of Notre Dame, IN), Maryknoll Institute (Maryknoll, NY), Chicago Cluster of Theological Schools (IL), Missions Colloquia of the Boston Theological Institute (Cambridge, MA), Summer Mission Institute (University of San Francisco) and School of Divinity (St Louis University, MO). There are also some 16 Catholic colleges and universities offering Latin American area studies, the most important being Fordham University, Catholic University of America, Marquette University, Boston College, Georgetown University, University of Notre Dame, University of Portland, St Louis University and University of San Diego.

The total number of USA Catholic citizens serving abroad as missionaries in 1972 was 7,659 persons (known to the US Catholic Mission Council), of whom 3,171 were religious priests and priests in missionary institutes (15.3% of all religious priests in the USA), 244 diocesan priests (0.7%), 634 brothers (2.1%), 3,127 sisters (3.3%), 97 seminarians and 376 lay helpers. These figures include a very small number of Catholic missionaries serving with Protestant sending agencies and an equally small number of Protestant and Jewish volunteers serving with Catholic agencies. Statistics by continents were as follows: 45% of the total missionary personnel were serving in Latin America and the Caribbean islands, 26% in Asia, 15% in Africa, 9.5% in Oceania, 3% in North America (Alaska, North Canada, Greenland) and 0.5% in Europe (mostly in Nordic countries). More than half of all USA Catholic missionaries were found in 11 of the 116 countries and territories: Philippines, 597; Peru, 548; Brazil, 533; Puerto Rico, 425; Japan, 355; Bolivia, 293; Tanzania, 241; New Guinea, 233; Chile, 217; Taiwan, 209; and Hawaii, 207.

Male missionary congregations founded in the USA include: (1) Maryknoll Missioners (MM) (Catholic Foreign Mission Society of America), a community of American secular priests and brothers, established in 1911 near New York City, with 713 members in 1972 in 17 mission fields, mostly in Tanzania, Japan, Taiwan, Bolivia, South Korea, Philippines, Chile and Guatemala; (2) Missionary Society of St James the Apostle, founded in 1958, with 65 members in Bolivia, Peru and Ecuador; (3) Franciscan Friars of the Atonement (SA), founded in 1889 at Graymoor, Garrison (NY) to promote Christian unity through ecumenical and missionary activity, with 22 priests and brothers in Japan and Brazil; and (4) Sons of Mary, Health of the Sick (FMSI), founded in 1952 for the education of nationals as nurse-catechists and doctor-catechists, with 6 professed priests and brothers in Peru.

Female missionary congregations founded in the USA include: (1) Maryknoll Sisters of St Dominic (MM), founded in New York City, with in 1972, 696 USA sisters (plus 85 non-citizens) in 22 different mission fields, especially in Hawaii, Philippines, Hong Kong, Tanzania, Chile and Bolivia; (2) Medical Mission Sisters (SCMM) (Society of Catholic Medical Missionaries), founded in Washington, DC, in 1925, with 92 USA sisters in 10 countries, principally in Ghana, Pakistan, India and Venezuela; (3) Daughters of Charity of St Vincent de Paul (DC), founded in 1809 in Emmetsburg (IA) to care for the sick and poor, with 66 members in mission countries, especially Bolivia, Puerto Rico and Japan; and (4) Franciscan Sisters of the Atonement (SA), founded in 1898, with 30 sisters in Japan, Brazil and Canada.

Other important missionary congregations (with their 1972 statistics of USA personnel serving abroad) include: (1) for men; SJ (702), OFM (267), SVD (205), CSSR (197), OMI (172), OFMCap (155) and OSB (106); and (2) for women; Franciscans (295), Sisters of St Joseph (157), Sisters of Mercy (137), Dominicans (119) and Marists (119). The major missionary lay volunteers include: Jesuit Volunteer Corps (82), Catholic Relief Services (74), Catholic Medical Mission Board (54), Lay Mission Helpers (40) and Fronteir Apostolate (27).

For the Catholic educational programme, the 2 principal co-ordinating agencies are: (1) the Department of Education of the USCC which conducts studies and seminars and provides leadership in such areas as elementary, secondary and higher education, religious education, family life and youth activities; and (2) the National Catholic Education Association (NCEA), a professional organization founded in Washington, DC, in 1904, with a present membership of 16,000 institutional and individual members, which seeks to stimulate and improve Catholic education and to make it better known and understood by the general population. The NCEA is a member of the Catholic International Education Office (OIEC) in Belgium.

In 1975 the Catholic Church in the USA was responsible for a total of 10,839 separate educational institutions, 170 fewer than reported in 1974. The total includes 251 colleges and universities, 995 diocesan and parish high schools, 681 private high schools, 8,199 parish elementary schools, 340 private elementary schools; the total also includes the 104 diocesan seminaries and 269 religious seminaries. There were in addition 110 protective institutions, with 9,231 youths in attendance. Full-time teaching staffs of all educational institutions under Catholic auspices decreased by 2,914 between 1974 and 1975 to a total of 171,797, comprising 6,974 priests, 434 scholastics, 3,512 brothers, 55,050 sisters and 104,827 lay teachers. The number of full-time pupils in Catholic elementary and high schools decreased by 109,885 from 1974–75. The 995 parish and diocesan high schools reported 590,494 pupils, an increase of 13,638; the 681 private high schools with 330,021 showed a decrease of 4,852 in one year. Pupils in 8,199 parish elementary schools numbered 2,535,406, or 123,646 fewer, while students in the 340 private elementary schools totalled 63,821, an increase of 4,975. In 1973, of the 262 Catholic universities, colleges, and junior colleges, about 65% were co-educational, 31% for women, and 4% for men.

The principal co-ordinating agency for the social service programme of the Catholic Church in the USA is the National

Conference of Catholic Charities (NCCC), founded in Washington, DC, in 1910, which is a member of Caritas Internationalis in Rome. The NCCC is a federation of independent Catholic social service agencies and institutions throughout the USA, including diocesan agencies, homes for the aged, day care centres, maternity homes and dependent children centres. Its membership in 1973 numbered 525 agencies and 300 institutions. Other important co-ordinating agencies are the Division of Health Affairs to the USCC, in Washington, DC; Catholic Hospital Association, founded in St Louis (MO) in 1915; Conference of Catholic Schools of Nursing, in St Louis (MO); National Federation of Catholic Physicians, in Milwaukee (WI); National Guild of Catholic Psychiatrists, in Washington, DC; and the Special Education Department of the National Catholic Educational Association, founded in St Louis (MO) in 1954. The main auxiliary agencies for Catholic social service work are, in addition to the diocesan directors of Catholic charities in each USA diocese, the following: Association of Ladies of Charity in each diocese, with 34,000 members in 1973; Society of St Vincent de Paul, in St Louis (MO), with about 36,000 members in 1973; National Christ Child Society, in Washington, DC, with about 10,000 adults and junior members in 1973, which cares for underprivileged children; American Federation of Catholic Workers for the Blind and Visually Handicapped, founded in Elyria (OH), in 1954, which is a federation of 14 independent agencies and of individuals; Xavier Society for the Blind, founded in New York City in 1900, which is a centre for publications and also maintains a circulating library; the Carroll Rehabilitation Centre for the Visually Impaired (formerly Catholic Guild for the Blind), in Newton (MA); and International Catholic Deaf Association, founded in Brooklyn (NY) in 1949, with more than 6,000 members, mostly in the USA.

CHRISTIAN BRETHREN (EXCLUSIVE). The roman numerals, chosen arbitrarily by the US Bureau of the Census, designate the following groups. All are schisms among Exclusive Brethren except II. Brethren I: Grant Brethren (1884). II: Open Brethren (no central organization, 450 domestic full-time workers, 400 foreign missionaries sent through CMML, USA). III: Continental Brethren (1890) uniting in 1926 with Kelly Brethren; now the largest worldwide Brethren communion. IV: Raven Brethren (1890), or Taylor Brethren. V: Continuing Tunbridge Wells Brethren (1909 ex III; largest Exclusive group in USA). VI: Glanton Brethren (1908, ex IV; in USA, absorbed by VIII since 1939). VII: ex I in 1928; 1953 united with III. VIII: Booth Brethren (1928 ex I). IX: Ames Brethren (1949 ex VIII). X: 1960 ex Taylor Brethren. A merger is taking place between Glanton, Booth and Kelly-Continental Brethren.

CHRISTIAN CHURCH (DISCIPLES OF CHRIST). Membership is 4% Black.

CHURCH OF GOD IN CHRIST. There are 109 ecclesiastical jurisdictions. Bible colleges exist in 80 cities. By 1975 the church claimed a total constituency of 3 million sympathizers in 4,676 organized churches, and overseas branches in 23 African and Caribbean countries. In the USA, largest state memberships are not in the South but in California, Texas, New York and the Midwest. *Headquarters.* The huge national headquarters under construction in downtown Memphis (The Saints Center) will have a 15,000-seat auditorium, a 2,000-car garage and other facilities.

CHURCH OF CHRIST, SCIENTIST. *Membership.* Declining. *Active membership* (1979). 220,000 adults, a decline of 100,000 from 1950, i.e. 1.6% per annum decline. *Churches.* From 1968–78, 257 branch churches and 97 storefront reading rooms were closed. *Teachers* (qualified to teach 2-week course on doctrine once a year). 500.

CHURCH OF JESUS CHRIST OF LATTER-DAY SAINTS. The Mormon church has a world membership (= all baptized persons, aged 8 and over, and all infants and children of baptized persons) of 3,227,000 (December 1972, rising to 3,389,909 by December 1974, 3.57 million a year later, and to over 4 million by 1978), divided into 632 geographical dioceses called stakes (537 in the USA) (rising to a total of 675 in December 1974), 30 of which were new stakes organized in 1972; and 113 Missions. Stakes are further subdivided into 4,365 parishes called wards (usually of 450 to 1,200 members), increasing by around 23 a year (to 4,756 in December 1974), with 7,554 congregations (1974). In 1972 membership increased by 137,000 (4.2% pa, of which 2.6% was natural increase). Baptisms for the dead and sealing of marriages take place in 12 Temples in the USA, and in 4 others in other nations. The church has an unpaid non-professional lay clergy; at the end of 1972 there were 403,601 Aaronic Priesthood bearers, and 383,335 Melchizedek Priesthood bearers. The church welfare programme in 1972 aided 102,900 persons (1974: 109,212) and placed 14,500 in remunerative employment. Over the years since 1831 there has been a total of at least 89 schismatic offshoots, most based on some claimed new revelation. *Missionaries.* In 1973, there were 17,501 full-time proselytizing missionaries (young persons on 2-year service, 95% US citizens) and 5,374 part-time missionaries, plus many health service missionaries, serving across the world (6,334 full-time serving in the USA itself). The total full-time has risen from 2,790 in 1952 to 11,768 in 1962, to 19,000 by December 1974, and to 25,000 in 47 countries by 1978. *Attendance* (world-wide, 1973). Weekly attendance at worship (Sacrament Meeting) 37% (49% for the age group 12–19 years). Annual attendance (once a year or more): over 90%. Weekly attendance at Sunday-school: 42% (60% for young people 12–19 years). *Congregations.* Total (world-wide) 7,554 (1974). *Converts.* 83,514 convert baptisms in 1971; 91,237 in 1972; 69,018 in 1974 (plus 47,234 children baptized, usually at age 8); 223,000 new members (168,000 from other religious backgrounds) in 1977. *Broadcasting.* The church operated several radio and TV stations in Utah, and 15 cable-TV services.

EPISCOPAL CHURCH IN THE USA. Officially termed the Protestant Episcopal Church in the USA (PECUSA), the church in the USA is divided into 8 Provinces with 92 dioceses, as follows: Province I (entitled New England), 7 dioceses; Province II (New York & New Jersey), 8 dioceses; Province III (Washington), 13 dioceses; Province IV (Sewanee), 18 dioceses; Province V (Mid-West), 13 dioceses; Province VI (Northwest), 8 dioceses; Province VII (Southwest), 11 dioceses; Province VIII (Pacific, including Alaska & Hawaii), 14 dioceses. Province IX (Caribbean) covers 11 Central American countries. In the USA, 14 non-self-supporting dioceses (formerly missionary districts until 1970) are funded through a board named Coalition 14. For names, statistics and details of all dioceses, see *Membership, manpower and money in the Anglican Communion* (London, 1973), and *The Episcopal Church Annual 1977* (New York, 1977). *New diocese* (1975). D San Diego, formed out of D Los Angeles. A further jurisdiction, the Navajoland Episcopal Church, was formed in 1977 to serve Navajo Indians. *Race.* About 2% Black in the USA. *Personnel* (1977). 144 bishops (home and abroad), 12,439 men priests and deacons, 95 women priests, 19,740 lay readers. *Seminarians* (1974). 669. *Charismatics.* The pentecostal renewal began in the Episcopal Church, as the first non-Pentecostal denomination to become involved in the USA, in 1959. By 1973 Episcopalian charismatics numbered 30,000 adults (including 1,100 involved clergy and several bishops) in 1,500 prayer groups, co-ordinated by the Episcopal Charismatic Fellowship (founded 1973). By 1976 the organizers were claiming 3,000 clergy and 21,000 lay members. *Other renewal agencies.* 15 other organizations emphasizing spiritual renewal have joined the ECF to form the alliance Pew-action, including the Bible Reading Fellowship, Brotherhood of St Andrew (4,500 members), Faith Alive, Fellowship of Witness, and the Order of St Luke the Physician.

GREEK ORTHODOX ARCHDIOCESE OF NORTH & SOUTH AMERICA. In Greek, Hellenike Orthodoxos Archiepiskope Boreiou kai Notiou Amerikes. The first Greek Orthodox immigrants settled in New Smyrna, Florida, in 1767; the first church was begun in 1864 by Greek merchants in New Orleans; 1892, New York and Chicago; large influxes of Greek immigrants 1890–1914; under Church of Greece until 1918; archdiocese founded 1921 under Ecumenical Patriarchate; now exarchate of the Ecumenical Patriarchate. The liturgical language has always been Greek; celebration of the liturgy in English was prohibited by the Patriarchate in 1970. The Archdiocese is divided into 12 Archdiocesan Districts, with a bishop over each: 1st, Middle Atlantic States (HQ New York) with 28% of all members; 2nd, Middle-Western States (Chicago) with 20% of all USA members; 3rd, New England States (Boston), 13%; 4th, Western States (San Francisco), 10%; 5th, Southern States (Charlotte, NC), 6%; 6th, Central States (Pittsburgh), 8%; 7th, Middle-Northern States (Detroit), 8%; 8th, South-Western States (Houston), 5%; 9th, Canada (Toronto); 10th, Argentina, Chile, Uruguay (Buenos Aires); 11th, Brazil, Bolivia, Paraguay, Peru (São Paulo); 12th, Mexico, Guatemala, Panama, Cuba, Venezuela, Ecuador, Colombia (Mexico City). *Growth.* Annual numerical increase 1.4%. *Charismatics.* A pentecostal renewal, meeting with strong church opposition, began in 1968 and by 1973 had involved 30 parishes in the USA, 12 clergy and 2,000 laity, co-ordinated by the Logos Foundation for Orthodox Awakening.

INTERNATIONAL CHURCH OF THE FOURSQUARE GOSPEL. *Annual growth* (1978). 269,065 converts; 40,300 water baptisms.

JEHOVAH'S WITNESSES. Self-designation Jehovah's Christian witnesses (with a small 'w'). *Districts.* The USA is divided into 31 Districts.

LUTHERAN CHURCH IN AMERICA. The largest Lutheran body in the USA, the LCA was formed in 1962 by a merger of the United Lutheran Ch in America (of German origin), Augustana Ev Lutheran Ch (Swedish), American Ev Lutheran Ch (Danish) and Finnish Ev Lutheran Ch. There are 31 synods. *Charismatics.* The neo-pentecostal renewal in the LCA numbered in 1973 some 10,000 adults in about 120 prayer groups. The Lutheran Co-ordinating Committee (founded 1973) serves charismatics in both the LCA, ALC, LC Missouri Synod, and also dissident Lutherans.

LUTHERAN CHURCH-MISSOURI SYNOD. A major clash from 1972 between conservatives and liberals produced in 1975 a threatened liberal schism (Lutheran Church in Mission, LCM) involving around 900 congregations, which resulted in the actual schism in 1976 of the Association of Evangelical Lutheran Churches (AELC).

ORTHODOX CHURCH IN AMERICA. The oldest Orthodox church in the USA was of Russian foundation and was considerably strengthened by influxes of Russian refugees after World Wars I and II. It was known as the Russian Orthodox Greek Catholic Church of America, until granted autocephalous status in 1970 by the patriarchate of Moscow. Celebration of the liturgy in English is now universal, in the USA. There are 7 dioceses in the USA; Alaska, Michigan, New England, New York, Philadelphia & Pennsylvania, Pittsburgh & West Virginia, San Francisco & Western United States; and 2 dioceses outside the USA (Canada, South America). *Membership.* 40% Ukrainians and Carpatho-Russians (Ruthenians) (mostly 3rd- or 4th-generation immigrants from Austria-Hungary, not Russia), 20% Romanians, 15% Russians, 8% Albanians, 7% Aleuts, Indians and Eskimos, and 10% USA White converts. *Priests.* 440 citizens, 33 expatriates (Canadian, Mexican, South American, or stateless). 15 OCA priests serve as chaplains in the US Armed Forces.

RUSSIAN ORTHODOX CHURCH OUTSIDE OF RUSSIA. Russian emigrés and exiles, ultra-conservative Orthodox, opposed to both the Moscow Patriarchate and the Soviet government; begun 1920 in Europe, HQ moved to New York in 1950. *Membership.* About 200,000 worldwide, in 13 Dioceses: Eastern America & New York (world HQ), Chicago & Detroit, Syracuse & Holy Trinity, Western America, Los Angeles & Southern California, Canada, Germany, Western Europe & Austria, Argentina, Brazil & Venezuela, Chile, Australia, Great Britain.

SOUTHERN BAPTIST CONVENTION. The Convention is 99% White (Black members number 75,000, with 120 Black ministers). A major problem of SBC statistics is that a large proportion of members are no longer resident in their original State Convention but have moved elsewhere. Thus in 1970 resident adult membership (over 9 years old) was only 8,451,769 out of a total of 11,629,880. The Convention is sub-divided into 31 State Conventions, with 1,192 Associations, and adult membership over 9 years (totalling 11,629,880) as follows: Alabama 843,840, Alaska 10,740, Arizona 70,190, Arkansas 349,724, California 253,016, Colorado 38,344, DC 37,818, Florida 647,239, Georgia 1,013,979, Hawaii 9,124, Illinois 191,359, Indiana 53,153, Kansas 54,779, Kentucky 670,631, Louisiana 474,474, Maryland 87,876, Michigan 34,522, Mississippi 536,667, Missouri 515,554, New Mexico 91,587, New York 10,348, North Carolina 1,023,147, Northern Plains 12,373, Northwest (formerly Oregon-Washington) 41,296, Ohio 90,735, Oklahoma 546,872, South Carolina 587,304, Tennessee 892,001, Texas 1,898,605, Utah-Idaho 9,118, Virginia 533,465. *Total affiliated.* The preceding figures are for adult baptized members. In practice however adult baptism is now administered between the ages 8–10 years, and sometimes as young as 6 years old. The preceding figures therefore refer to the age group over 9 years old. Since in the USA in 1970 children and infants aged 0–9 years formed 18.1% of the total population, those over 9 were 81.9%. Dividing adult members by 81.9% we arrive at an estimated total affiliated figure (column 7) of 14,200,000 in 1970. *Growth.* By 1974 these figures had grown to 34,734 places of worship with 12,515,842 full members. *Gains and losses.* (1977 SBC survey). In 1976, 39,000 persons joined the SBC from other religious bodies (79% mainline Protestant (34% Methodist, 12% Presbyterian, 4% Lutheran, 4% Assemblies of God), 14% Roman Catholic, 4% smaller Christian sects), and 46,000 left the SBC for other denominations (9% to small Christian sects). *Charismatics.* Although the Convention is not favourable to the Charismatic Renewal, about 300 ministers are known to be involved in it.

UKRAINIAN ORTHODOX CHURCH OF THE USA. In 1973, the UOCUSA joined the Ukrainian Greek-Orthodox Ch of Canada, and similar churches in Australia, Europe and Latin America, to form a new world union or communion with the name Ukrainian Orthodox Church of the Free World, claiming 3,000 parishes and 1.5 million faithful.

UNITED METHODIST CHURCH. The UMC is a world denomination composed in 1972 of a General Conference (the supreme law-making body, meeting every 4 years) with, overseas, 10 Central Conferences and one Provisional Central Conference, subdivided into 37 Annual Conferences, 8 Provisional Annual Conferences and 1 Mission (Yugoslavia); fraternal relations are also maintained with 21 affiliated autonomous churches which are outgrowths of UMC work but not part of its structure. In the USA, the UMC has 5 Jurisdictional Conferences (created in 1939 at the union of the Methodist Episcopal Church North, Methodist Episcopal Church South, Methodist Protestant Church; main function is to elect bishops), named North Central, Northeastern, South Central, Southeastern, and Western Jurisdictions; these are subdivided into 81 Annual Conferences (with Puerto Rico conference also attached to NE Jurisdiction) created from 1784 (Baltimore) onwards. For purposes of episcopal oversight, these 82 conferences are grouped into 45 Episcopal Areas each under a bishop. *Adult members.* Membership statistics (in column 6 above) refer to full members, who are over 14 years old, and also preparatory members (1,731,764 in 1971). *Total affiliated.* The figure for total community in column 7 above is derived by dividing the 1970 total of adult (full) members (10,334,521) by the proportion of adults over 14 in the total population (72%). In 1970 there were also 1,731,764 preparatory members, defined as follows. Almost all children of members are baptized as infants, whereupon they are termed preparatory members until they reach the age of 15 or so when they can become full members. However, large numbers of baptized children are not included on present rolls because their names were not transferred when their parents moved home. A better indicator of the total of Methodist children is derived from the figure 5,380,147 for church school membership in 1970; of these about 25% were full members and 75% were preparatory members and other, unregistered, children. This gives a total of Methodist children under 15 of 4,035,000, which is 28% of the total of 14,353,000 Methodist children and adults; this is exactly the same as the national percentage of children aged under 15 to the total population of the USA, 28% in 1970 (*Statistical yearbook of the US*, 1973, p.6). *Black members.* About 3.7% of all members are US Blacks (366,000 out of 9,893,000 full members in 1960). *Membership growth.* In 1970, 217,164 new members were received on confession of faith or restored, 285,633 were received by transfer, 534,084 were removed by transfer, and 116,510 were removed through death, making a nett decrease of 147,797 (a decline of 1.4%pa). The number of organized churches also declined by 1.1% in 1970. *Weekly church attenders.* In 1971 these were 3,765,800 members out of 10,622,173 (35%). *Sunday-schools.* Enrolment (all ages) in 1970 was 5,634,662 and weekly attendance 3,112,573 (55%). *Rolls.* It should be noted that the UMC (as with Methodism generally) is one of the strictest denominations in keeping membership rolls up-to-date, and members inactive for longer than 2 or 3 years are regularly removed from rolls. *Charismatics.* The neo-pentecostal renewal among Methodists began later than in the other major Protestant denominations. By 1973, 15% of all UMC ministers were involved (about 5,000), and also around 40,000 laity, in several hundred prayer groups. *Foreign missionaries.* The UMC's World Division, New York City, in 1974 supported 839 foreign missionaries: 90.5% were USA citizens (2.5% Black, Spanish-American or Asian-American), and 9.5% were expatriates (1.9% Third-World citizens, 1.8% Norwegians, 1.3% UK, 1.3% Swedish, 0.7% Germans, 0.6% Canadians).

UNITED PRESBYTERIAN CHURCH IN THE USA. The church was formed in 1958 through a merger of the United Presbyterian Church of North America (dating from 1858) and the Presbyterian Church in the USA (dating from 1706). In 1972 the entire church was restructured, and the 35 synods in the USA were reduced to 16. *Charismatics.* The neo-pentecostal renewal within the UPUSA involved, in 1973, some 2,000 ministers and 20,000 laity, co-ordinated by the Presbyterian Charismatic Communion (founded 1966, representing also the Presbyterian Church in the US). *Foreign missionaries abroad.* The total, once over 2,000, had declined by 1973 to 604.

WORLDWIDE CHURCH OF GOD. In 1975 church programmes were being broadcast over 237 radio and 131 TV stations in the USA and Canada, plus 23 international outlets. The church expects to use 2,000 radio stations by 1980. *Attendance.* At the October 1976 Feast of Tabernacles, 105,000 attended at 60 sites worldwide. *Periodical.* 'Plain truth' in 1977 had a world circulation of 2 million in 5 languages in 187 countries.

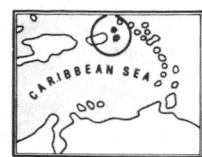

# United States Virgin Islands

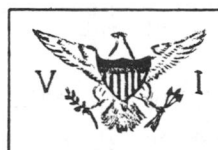

## SECULAR DATA

**STATE. Official name:** The Territory of the Virgin Islands of the United States.
**Flag** (shown above right): Golden American eagle with shield on white field; eagle between blue letters V and I.
**Area:** 344 sq.km. (133 sq.miles). **Description:** 53 islands and cays. Agricultural land: 44.1%.
**Government:** Self-governing unincorporated territory of the USA, since 1954 (1493 Spanish possession, 1716 Danish West Indies colony, 1917 US colony, 1954 under US Department of the Interior).
**Legislature:** Single-chambered Legislature, 15 senators.
**Official language:** English.
**Capital:** Charlotte Amalie 12,220 (1970).

**DEMOGRAPHY. Population:** 62,468 (census of 1.IV.1970. For 1970–2000 (UN), see last row of Table 1). Population density (1975): 192/sq.km. (497/sq.mile). Under 15 years: 43%. Growth rate (1975–80): 0.75% per year (births 2.87%, deaths −0.68%, emigrants −1.44%). Life expectancy (1975–80): 69.1 years. Household size: 4.4 persons.
**Major languages:** English, Spanish, French Creole, French.
**Urban dwellers** (1970): 56.1%. Urban growth rate (1950–70): 3.9% per year.
**Labour force:** 43%.
**Tourists** (1969): 1,107,000. (1973) 1,310,000.

**ETHNOLINGUISTIC GROUPS:** 62.3% Black (African Negro), 16.4% White (North American, European), 12.0% Puerto Rican, 9.0% Creole (French-speaking Black), 0.3% Jewish, East Indian.

**MONEY** (1977). Monetary unit: US dollar (=100 cents).
National income per person: US$3,600. Average annual family income: US$15,840.
**Cost of living in capital** (1976): Daily cost of living: US$40.

**HEALTH** Hospitals: 3 (248 beds). Doctors: 68. Lepers: 60 (0.9 per 1,000).

**EDUCATION.** Adult literacy: 95%. Schools: 39.

**LITERATURE.** Newspapers: 3 dailies, 2 non-daily.

**COMMUNICATION** (per 1,000 people). Phones: 350. Radios: 460. TV sets: 170. Daily newspaper circulation: 300 copies.

TABLE 1     RELIGIOUS ADHERENTS IN THE US VIRGIN ISLANDS

| Year / Name | 1900 Adherents | % | mid-1970 Adherents | % | Annual change, 1970–1980 Natural | Conversion | Total | Rate | mid-1975 Adherents | % | mid-1980 Adherents | % | 2000 Adherents | % |
|---|---|---|---|---|---|---|---|---|---|---|---|---|---|---|
| Christians | 30,500 | 100.0 | 61,400 | 98.2 | 589 | −19 | 570 | 0.88 | 64,750 | 98.1 | 67,100 | 98.0 | 73,790 | 97.1 |
| professing | 30,500 | 100.0 | 61,400 | 98.2 | 589 | −19 | 570 | 0.88 | 64,750 | 98.1 | 67,100 | 98.0 | 73,790 | 97.1 |
| Protestants | 15,250 | 50.0 | 26,300 | 42.1 | 252 | −22 | 230 | 0.83 | 27,690 | 42.0 | 28,600 | 41.8 | 31,000 | 40.9 |
| Roman Catholics | 6,100 | 20.0 | 20,000 | 32.0 | 197 | 103 | 300 | 1.39 | 21,650 | 32.8 | 23,000 | 33.6 | 27,460 | 36.1 |
| Anglicans | 9,150 | 30.0 | 11,900 | 19.0 | 109 | −109 | 0 | 0.00 | 12,010 | 18.2 | 11,900 | 17.4 | 11,000 | 14.5 |
| Black indigenous | 0 | 0.0 | 2,500 | 4.0 | 24 | 6 | 30 | 1.13 | 2,650 | 4.0 | 2,800 | 4.0 | 3,270 | 4.3 |
| Marginal Protestants | 0 | 0.0 | 700 | 1.1 | 7 | 3 | 10 | 1.33 | 750 | 1.1 | 800 | 1.2 | 1,060 | 1.4 |
| nominal | 1,000 | 3.3 | 5,964 | 9.5 | 60 | 64 | 124 | 1.87 | 6,600 | 10.0 | 7,200 | 10.5 | 9,100 | 12.0 |
| affiliated | 29,500 | 96.7 | 55,436 | 88.7 | 529 | −83 | 446 | 0.77 | 58,150 | 88.1 | 59,900 | 87.4 | 64,690 | 85.1 |
| total practising | 28,020 | 95 | 47,120 | 85 | 450 | −71 | 379 | 0.77 | 49,430 | 85 | 50,910 | 85 | 51,750 | 80 |
| non-practising | 1,480 | 5 | 8,320 | 15 | 79 | −12 | 67 | 0.77 | 8,720 | 15 | 8,990 | 15 | 12,940 | 20 |
| Protestants | 14,900 | 48.8 | 23,180 | 37.1 | 222 | −31 | 191 | 0.87 | 24,450 | 37.0 | 25,090 | 36.6 | 27,000 | 35.5 |
| Evangelicals | 12,200 | 40.0 | 15,900 | 25.4 | 152 | −22 | 130 | 0.78 | 16,700 | 25.3 | 17,200 | 25.1 | 19,000 | 25.0 |
| Roman Catholics | 6,000 | 19.7 | 18,870 | 30.2 | 184 | 69 | 253 | 1.25 | 20,200 | 30.7 | 21,400 | 31.2 | 25,080 | 33.0 |
| Catholic pentecostals | 0 | 0.0 | 0 | 0.0 | 5 | 195 | 200 | 40.00 | 500 | 0.8 | 2,000 | 2.9 | 4,000 | 5.3 |
| Anglicans | 8,600 | 28.2 | 9,686 | 15.5 | 87 | −131 | −44 | −0.46 | 9,570 | 14.5 | 9,250 | 13.5 | 7,600 | 10.0 |
| Black indigenous | 0 | 0.0 | 2,500 | 4.0 | 24 | 6 | 30 | 1.13 | 2,650 | 4.0 | 2,800 | 4.0 | 3,270 | 4.3 |
| Marginal Protestants | 0 | 0.0 | 700 | 1.1 | 7 | 3 | 10 | 1.33 | 750 | 1.1 | 800 | 1.2 | 1,060 | 1.4 |
| Orthodox | 0 | 0.0 | 500 | 0.8 | 5 | 1 | 6 | 1.13 | 530 | 0.8 | 560 | 0.8 | 680 | 0.9 |
| Non-religious | 0 | 0.0 | 600 | 1.0 | 6 | 16 | 22 | 3.10 | 710 | 1.1 | 820 | 1.2 | 1,520 | 2.0 |
| Baha'is | 0 | 0.0 | 300 | 0.5 | 3 | 3 | 6 | 1.82 | 330 | 0.5 | 360 | 0.5 | 460 | 0.6 |
| Jews | 0 | 0.0 | 200 | 0.3 | 2 | 0 | 2 | 0.95 | 210 | 0.3 | 220 | 0.3 | 230 | 0.3 |
| Country's population | 30,500 | 100.0 | 62,500 | 100.0 | 600 | 0 | 600 | 0.91 | 66,000 | 100.0 | 68,500 | 100.0 | 76,000 | 100.0 |

**COLUMNS, ROWS.** For meanings and definitions, see Codebook (Part 6). Note that, by definition, total 'Christians' = professing + crypto-Christians, which also = affiliated + nominal Christians. Percentages may not always total exactly, due to rounding.
**CENSUSES.** The religion question has not been asked.

**NOTES ON RELIGIONS**
**BAHA'IS.** In 3 local spiritual assemblies (1973).

**BLACK INDIGENOUS.** In about 6 denominations in 1970 (see Table 2).
**CATHOLIC PENTECOSTALS** (or, Catholic charismatics). The renewal became widespread in 1977, spread by citizens who had experienced renewal in Puerto Rico, with 2 large meetings in November 1977: one on St Thomas (300 attenders), and one on St Croix (700).
**COUNTRY'S POPULATION.** The actual population has increased from 1970–75 faster than is shown above, to 99,765

in 1975. However, consistent enumeration is complicated by the vast number of annual tourists (1,310,000 in 1973) many of whom stay on as residents. We therefore use above the de jure resident population figures for 1975 onwards as computed in *World population prospects, 1970–2000, as assessed in 1973* (New York: UN, 1975).

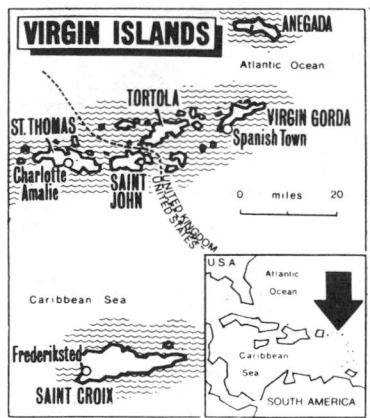

**NON-CHRISTIAN RELIGIONS. Baha'i** has a small community, in 3 local spiritual assemblies.
**Judaism** is also present, with about 200 Jews.

## CHRISTIANITY

**PROTESTANT CHURCHES.** Moravians sent their first missionaries to St Thomas in 1732, and the island was also visited by Zinzendorf in 1739, and Moravians remain the largest Protestant community on the islands. Lutherans arrived earlier (1666) and British Methodists later (1891), but the second most important Protestant denomination, the Church of God of Prophecy, a Pentecostal body, did not enter until 1926. Other active churches include Adventists, Baptists, Salvation Army and a large number of smaller groups mostly from the USA.

**CATHOLIC CHURCH.** There were 18,870 Catholics in the US Virgin Islands in 1970, consisting of either local inhabitants or Puerto Ricans and Americans. There are 3 parishes served by Redemp-

**Methodist Church in the Caribbean & The Americas.** Christchurch Methodist Church, St Thomas.

torist priests, who also make periodic visits to the British Virgin Islands, and 2 congregations of sisters: missionary Sisters of the Immaculate Heart of Mary, and Sisters of Charity. St Thomas is the seat of the prelature of the Virgin Islands, a suffragan of the archdiocese of Washington DC (USA).

ANGLICAN CHURCH. The Church of England began work in the Virgin Islands during the early part of the 18th century, and by 1848 one-third of the population was Anglican. Today the population is only 18% Anglican, a proportion slightly lower than that in the British Virgin Islands. In 1916 the mission was transferred to the Episcopal Church in the USA.

INDIGENOUS CHURCHES. Blacks and Puerto Ricans from the USA have been instrumental in the establishment of 6 denominations in the Virgin Islands, 2 being Methodist (AMEC and AME Zion) and 4 others being Pentecostal. No independent churches have arisen from within the territory.

**CHURCH AND STATE.** Freedom of religion is fully guaranteed, but a somewhat rigid separation of church and state is maintained as in all US overseas territories.

**INTERDENOMINATIONAL ORGANIZATIONS.** The St Thomas Inter-Church Council has 6 members: AME, Episcopal, Lutheran, Methodist, Moravian churches and the Salvation Army.

TABLE 2. ORGANIZED CHURCHES AND DENOMINATIONS IN THE US VIRGIN ISLANDS

| Official name 1 | Begun 2 | Type 3 | Counc 4 | Congs 5 | Adults 6 | Affiliated 7 | Names, notes, and other statistics (see Codebook) 8 |
|---|---|---|---|---|---|---|---|
| African Methodist Episcopal Church | | I Met | VwM.C | 5 | 900 | 1,200 | *Virgin Islands Annual Conference*, 16th Episcopal District. M=AMEC(USA Blacks). |
| African Methodist Episcopal Zion Ch | 1917 | I Met | Vw... | 1 | 400 | 600 | M=AMEZC(Black mission from USA). 1919, took over Coloured Methodist Episcopal work. |
| American Orth Cath Ch (AD N&S Am) | c1965 | O ReO | x.... | | 200 | 500 | Am=America. *D Virgin Islands*. Schism in USA ex Ukrainian Orthodox Ch of USA. |
| Baptist International Missions | 1964 | P Bap | x.... | | 500 | 1,000 | M=BIM(USA). Fundamentalist Baptists. One school. 14f,1s. |
| **Catholic Church: D Saint Thomas** | 1648 | R Lat | B...r | 6 | 10,800 | 18,870 | Suffragan M Washington. M=CSSR. Not in CELAM. C=1+0+2. 14nx,2m,28w,3r(484),1090Yy |
| Christian Brethren | | P CBr | x.... | 1 | 50 | 100 | *Plymouth Brethren. Open Brethren. Gospel Hall*. Small independent congregation. |
| Church of God Holiness | 1947 | P Hol | x.... | 8 | 100 | 200 | M=CGH(Overland Park, Kansas, USA). Wesleyan doctrines. 1 school. 5f. |
| Church of God of Prophecy | 1926 | P Pe3 | Z.... | 33 | 2,725 | 5,000 | M=CGP(USA). Holiness Pentecostals. Ex CoG (Cleveland). HQ St Thomas. 2f. |
| Church of God (Cleveland) | 1945 | P Pe3 | ZF... | 9 | 398 | 700 | M=CoG(Cleveland) (USA). St Thomas: 3 churches. St Croix: 1 church. 7n,2f,1p. |
| Church of the Nazarene | 1961 | P Hol | xF... | 3 | 66 | 330 | M=CoN(USA). Holiness denomination. Growing. 1n,2f,W=68%,13Y,7z. |
| Damascus Christian Church | | I pen | x.... | 2 | 100 | 200 | Spanish-speaking pentecostals, mostly Puerto Ricans. HQ Bronx (USA). |
| **Episcopal Church: D Virgin Islands** | c1700 | A ACa | aw.RC | 10 | 4,533 | 9,686 | 1963, extra-provincial missionary diocese of PECUSA. 14n, 1x,5f,W=36%,609Yy. |
| Jehovah's Witnesses | c1940 | M Jeh | x.... | 6 | 306 | 700 | *Watch Tower* (Brooklyn, New York). Active witnessing under way by 1947. 20Y. |
| Lutheran Church in America | 1664 | P Lut | L.M.C | 5 | 1,000 | 1,939 | In Caribbean Synod, LCA. M=LCA(USA). Lutheran Welfare Society (St Croix). |
| Methodist Ch in Caribbean & Americas | 1891 | P Met | VwM.C | 12 | 1,500 | 3,000 | In MCCA (1967 union), Leeward Islands District. M=MMS(UK). 2n,1x,1f. |
| Metropolitan Church Association | | P Hol | x.... | 3 | 100 | 300 | M=MCA(USA). Holiness denomination. HQ Christiansted, St Croix. |
| Moravian Church | 1732 | P Mor | xWM.C | 8 | 1,729 | 5,101 | *VI Conf*, Eastern WIndies Province. 1968 applied to WCC. 8f,G=0,9%pa,W=63%,209Yy. |
| Salvation Army | | P Sal | xwM.C | | 500 | 1,500 | *Virgin Islands Region*, Caribbean & CAmerica Territory (HQ Jamaica). HQ St Thomas. |
| Seventh-day Adventist Church | c1926 | P Adv | x.... | 13 | 600 | 1,500 | *SDA*, in East Caribbean Conference, Caribbean Union Conference. |
| United Methodist Church | | P Met | Vw... | 2 | 257 | 500 | In Puerto Rico Conference, UMC (USA). Only on St Croix. 1t(260),W=81%. |
| United Pentecostal Church | | P Pe1 | x.... | 5 | 220 | 500 | *Jesus Only Church*. Unitarian Pentecostals. M=UPC(USA). 4n. |
| Wesleyan Church | 1911 | P Hol | VF... | 6 | 256 | 510 | Until 1968 Pilgrim Holiness Ch (USA). 1 school. 4n,1f,G=2.9%pa,1j,1k,W=95%,11Y. |
| Other Protestant denominations | | P | ..... | | 500 | 1,000 | Total about 10 (see list below). |
| Other Non-White indigenous churches | | I | ..... | | 300 | 500 | Missions from USA, including Assembly of Christian Chs, Church of God in Christ. |
| **Total affiliated (mid-1970)** | | | | **186** | **28,040** | **55,436** | **Total denominations (1970) . . .** **35.** |
| **Total affiliated (mid-1975)** | | | | **200** | **29,410** | **58,150** | **Total denominations (1975) . . .** **37.** |
| **Total affiliated (mid-1980)** | | | | **215** | **30,300** | **59,900** | **Total denominations (1980) . . .** **39.** |

**NOTES ON TABLE ABOVE**
COLUMNS: for meanings and CODES (cols. 1, 3, 4, 8): see Codebook (Part 6). Column 1: **Boldface type** = church with over 10% of country's affiliated Christians.
NATIONAL COUNCILS (Column 4, 5th letter).
C = St Thomas Inter-Church Council.
r = member, National Conference of Catholic Bishops, USA (NCCB).
OTHER PROTESTANT DENOMINATIONS. There are numerous groups from the USA, including: Apostolic Faith Mission, Baptist Bible Fellowship International (1972), Bethany Fellowship Missions (1966), Christian Mission, Dutch Reformed Ch, Reformed Ch in America.

**PEOPLES** (ethnolingustic). Christians: 62.6% Black (English-speaking), 16.4% White (North American, European), 12.0% Puerto Rican, 9.0% Creole (French-speaking Black).

**COUNTRY-WIDE TOTALS**
EVANGELIZATION (see Part 5). 1900: 100%. 1970: 100%. 1980: 100%.
FOREIGN MISSIONARIES AND PERSONNEL (aliens from abroad)(1973). Total 91. *From Western world*. 84: 38 Protestants in 9 USA societies, about 35 Roman Catholics, about 6 Black indigenous from USA, 5 Anglicans in 1 USA society. *From Third World*. About 7 (4 Roman Catholics, 3 Protestants) from Puerto Rico.
INSTITUTIONS (church-operated)(1973). Total 10, including 2 higher schools, 3 medical centres, 1 press.
PERIODICALS. About 12 titles.
PERSONNEL. About 141 (50 national, 91 foreign).
SCRIPTURE DISTRIBUTION (1975). Annual totals: 1,400 Bibles (29% subsidized, 71% commercial), 3,400 NTs (12% free, 59% subsidized, 29% commercial), 1,240 UBS portions, 97,000 UBS selections.
SERVICE AGENCIES. About 10, including NCCB, WGC, YMCA, YWCA.

**ADDITIONAL DATA ON CHURCHES**
CATHOLIC CHURCH. Before 1977, PN Virgin Islands, changed in 1977 to D Saint Thomas. *Catholic organizations*. In 1970 the church was responsible for 3 schools with 1,993 primary and 484 secondary students.

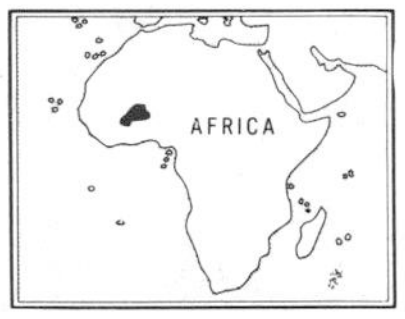


# UPPER VOLTA

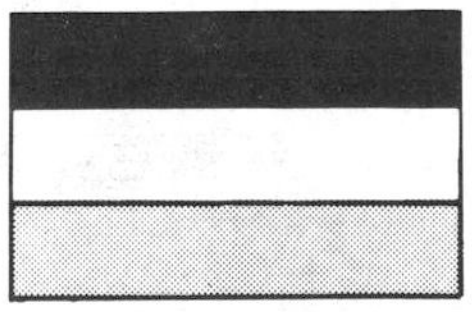

## SECULAR DATA

**State. Official name:** The Republic of the Upper Volta (La République de Haute-Volta). Adjective of nationality: voltaïque.
**Flag** (shown above right): Black, white, and red stripes.
**Area:** 274,200 sq.km. (105,869 sq.miles). Agricultural land: 69.8%.
**Government:** One-party republic under military rule, since 1974 (c1300 Mossi empire, 1896 French colony, 1958 autonomous territory, 1960 Independence as republic, 1966 military junta, 1970 republic, 1974 military junta).
**Official language:** French (*Français*).
**Capital:** Ouagadougou 110,000 (1966).
**Armed forces** (1976): Total 3,050 regular army. Paramilitary forces: 2,850.

**DEMOGRAPHY. Population:** 6,144,013 (census of 1–7.XII.1975. For 1970–2000 (UN), see last row of Table 1). Population density (1975): 22/sq.km. (57/sq.mile). Under 15 years: 42%. Growth rate (1975–80): 2.32% per year (births 4.79%, deaths –2.48%). Life expectancy (1975–80): 39.0 years. Household size: 4.9 persons.
**Major languages:** Mossi, French, Bobo, Senufo, Fulani, Grunshi, Lobi, Gurma, Busansi, Dogon, and 40 other tribal languages.
**Urban dwellers** (1970): 3.7%. Urban growth rate (1950–70): 4.9% per year.
**Labour force:** 56%.
**Tourists** (1974): 10,747.

**ETHNOLINGUISTIC GROUPS:** 44% Mossi (Mole, Moshi) (Yatenga, Tengkedogo), 15.5% Western Mande (7.3% Bobo, Barka, Samo), 7% Senufo (Sene, Siena, Minianka), 6% Grunshi (Kusasi, Kasena, Sissala, Nunuma), 6% Fulani, 5% Lobi (Dian, Gan, Dorossie, Birifor, Dagari), 5% Gurma, 5% Busansi (Bisa), 2.5% Soninke, 2.0% Songhai, 0.8% Karaboro (Tyefo), 0.8% Malinke, 0.2% Tuareg, 0.1% French (3,500), Dogon, Hausa, Yoruba, Ivorian, Dahomean, Togolese, & other smaller peoples.

**MONEY** (1977). **Monetary unit:** CFA franc (= 100 centimes); US$1 = CFAF 250.00.
**National income per person:** US$67. Average annual family income: US$328.
**Inflation:** (1970–74) 3.8% per year (1975: consumer price index 127).
**Cost of living in capital** (1976): index 149 (Washington DC=100). Daily cost of living: US$38.

**HEALTH.** Hospitals: 148 (4,675 beds). Doctors: 96. Lepers: 232,000 (38.5 per 1,000). Blind: 90,000. Psychotics: 48,000.

**EDUCATION.** Adult literacy: (1962) 2%, (1975) 11%. Education rate: 7%. Schools: 630.

**LITERATURE.** Periodicals: 13. Newspapers: 1 daily, 3 non-daily.

**COMMUNICATION** (per 1,000 people). Phones: 1. Radios: 16. TV sets: 1. Daily newspaper circulation: 0.4 copies.

TABLE 1. RELIGIOUS ADHERENTS IN THE UPPER VOLTA

| Year | 1900 | | mid-1970 | | Annual change, 1970–1980 | | | | mid-1975 | | mid-1980 | | 2000 | |
|---|---|---|---|---|---|---|---|---|---|---|---|---|---|---|
| *Name* | *Adherents* | *%* | *Adherents* | *%* | *Natural* | *Conversion* | *Total* | *Rate* | *Adherents* | *%* | *Adherents* | *%* | *Adherents* | *%* |
| Tribal religionists | 1,260,000 | 90.0 | 2,984,300 | 55.4 | 69,605 | –64,745 | 4,860 | 0.16 | 3,020,520 | 50.1 | 3,032,900 | 44.8 | 2,991,000 | 27.3 |
| Muslims | 140,000 | 10.0 | 1,884,000 | 35.0 | 54,199 | 48,701 | 102,900 | 4.38 | 2,352,000 | 39.0 | 2,913,000 | 43.0 | 6,033,000 | 55.0 |
| Ahmadis | 0 | 0.0 | 1,000 | 0.0 | 30 | 30 | 60 | 4.62 | 1,300 | 0.0 | 1,600 | 0.0 | 5,000 | 0.0 |
| **Christians** | **0** | **0.0** | **514,762** | **9.6** | **15,166** | **15,998** | **31,164** | **4.73** | **658,160** | **10.9** | **826,400** | **12.2** | **1,937,400** | **17.7** |
| crypto-Christians | 0 | 0.0 | 62,462 | 1.2 | 1,960 | 2,624 | 4,584 | 5.39 | 85,060 | 1.4 | 108,300 | 1.6 | 346,900 | 3.2 |
| professing | 0 | 0.0 | 452,300 | 8.4 | 13,206 | 13,374 | 26,580 | 4.64 | 573,100 | 9.5 | 718,100 | 10.6 | 1,590,500 | 14.5 |
| Roman Catholics | 0 | 0.0 | 376,900 | 7.0 | 11,121 | 12,159 | 23,280 | 4.82 | 482,600 | 8.0 | 609,700 | 9.0 | 1,371,100 | 12.5 |
| Protestants | 0 | 0.0 | 75,400 | 1.4 | 2,085 | 1,215 | 3,300 | 3.65 | 90,500 | 1.5 | 108,400 | 1.6 | 219,400 | 2.0 |
| affiliated | 0 | 0.0 | 514,762 | 9.6 | 15,166 | 15,998 | 31,164 | 4.73 | 658,160 | 10.9 | 826,400 | 12.2 | 1,937,400 | 17.7 |
| total practising | 0 | *0* | 432,400 | *84* | 12,740 | 13,438 | 26,178 | 4.74 | 552,850 | *84* | 694,180 | *84* | 1,549,900 | *80* |
| non-practising | 0 | *0* | 82,360 | *16* | 2,426 | 2,560 | 4,986 | 4.73 | 105,310 | *16* | 132,220 | *16* | 387,500 | *20* |
| Roman Catholics | 0 | 0.0 | 416,349 | 7.7 | 12,192 | 12,314 | 24,506 | 4.63 | 529,090 | 8.8 | 661,410 | 9.8 | 1,533,000 | 14.0 |
| Protestants | 0 | 0.0 | 95,263 | 1.8 | 2,880 | 3,594 | 6,474 | 5.18 | 125,000 | 2.1 | 160,000 | 2.4 | 394,900 | 3.6 |
| Evangelicals | 0 | 0.0 | 95,200 | 1.8 | 2,878 | 3,582 | 6,460 | 5.17 | 124,900 | 2.1 | 159,800 | 2.4 | 394,000 | 3.6 |
| African indigenous | 0 | 0.0 | 3,100 | 0.1 | 92 | 88 | 180 | 4.50 | 4,000 | 0.1 | 4,900 | 0.1 | 9,000 | 0.1 |
| Marginal Protestants | 0 | 0.0 | 50 | 0.0 | 2 | 2 | 4 | 5.71 | 70 | 0.0 | 90 | 0.0 | 500 | 0.0 |
| Non-religious | 0 | 0.0 | 500 | 0.0 | 16 | 24 | 40 | 5.71 | 700 | 0.0 | 900 | 0.0 | 4,000 | 0.0 |
| Baha'is | 0 | 0.0 | 338 | 0.0 | 11 | 15 | 26 | 5.57 | 470 | 0.0 | 600 | 0.0 | 3,000 | 0.0 |
| Other religionists | 0 | 0.0 | 100 | 0.0 | 3 | 7 | 10 | 6.67 | 150 | 0.0 | 200 | 0.0 | 600 | 0.0 |
| **Country's population** | **1,400,000** | **100.0** | **5,384,000** | **100.0** | **139,000** | **0** | **139,000** | **2.30** | **6,032,000** | **100.0** | **6,774,000** | **100.0** | **10,969,000** | **100.0** |

COLUMNS, ROWS. For meanings and definitions, see Codebook (Part 6). Note that, by definition, total 'Christians' = professing + crypto-Christians, which also = affiliated + nominal Christians. Percentages may not always total exactly, due to rounding.
CENSUSES. (Official estimates). VII.1958: 72.1% tribal religionists, 23.1% Muslims, 4.5% Roman Catholics, 0.23% Protestants (8,000 persons). 1960–61 (Ouagadougou only): 53.5% Muslims, 33.5% Roman Catholics, 11.0 tribal religionists, 1.2% Protestants. 1966 (UNDP estimates): 61.8% tribal religionists, 30.9% Muslims, 6.2% Roman Catholics, 1.1% Protestants. 1970 (Ouagadougou only): 59.5% Muslims, 35.5% Roman Catholics, 4.7% tribal religionists, 1.2% Protestants.

### NOTES ON RELIGIONS
AFRICAN INDIGENOUS. In about 9 denominations in 1970 (see Table 2).
AHMADIS. Qadianis (HQ Rabwah, Pakistan). The mission has encountered severe opposition from orthodox Muslims. There are some converts in the south made by Ahmadis from Ghana.
BAHA'IS. In 1973, in 3 local spiritual assemblies.

CRYPTO-CHRISTIANS. The number of professing Roman Catholics and Protestants known to the state and society through censuses, polls and surveys is appreciably less than those on the churches' records. Crypto-Christians, defined as affiliated but not professing, are probably deterred from profession by the growing numerical strength of Islam in all parts of the country.
MUSLIMS. Sunnis (of the Malikite rite): 45.2% Tijaniya, 22.1% Qadariya, 12.3 Hamaliya. Islamized peoples; Liptako (Fulani, entering from the north), Masina, Sia, Songhai, Udalan, Wala, Zerma, Diola traders from the north. *Conversions to Islam.* These increased rapidly in number after Independence in 1960, and from 1960–62 there was massive reorganization of Muslim propaganda and propagation, with nation-wide organization, weekly radio programmes reaching vast numbers of people, and a system of médersas (schools teaching Arabic). Conversions are taking place in 3 ways: (1) among tribal religionists, especially on their migration to cities; (2) as local or mass collective conversions of whole communities and villages due to marabouts practising healing; and (3) among the country's youths, 70% of whom work abroad as labourers and are islamized there (350,000 a year, or 7.3% of the population, leave to search for work in

the mines, plantations and towns of Ghana and Ivory Coast). There is also an Ahmadiya Mission (enumerated here as Muslims though declared non-Muslim by Pakistan), which makes a handful of converts each year. *Hajj pilgrims to Mecca.* (1970) 540; (1974) 1,576; (1975) 1,540; (1976) 1,809. *Mosques.* In Ouagadougou, there were 3 in 1952, rising to 47 in 1970.
NON-RELIGIOUS. Mainly French expatriate personnel, also a few national intellectuals.
OTHER RELIGIONISTS. Including Rosicrucians (2 AMORC centres).
PRACTISING CHRISTIANS. In 1974, there were 54,506 Sunday-attending Protestants (AdD 39,606, CMA 8,400, SIM 4,000, MEP 1,500, WEC 1,000).
TRIBAL RELIGIONISTS. Animists. Tribes with over 60% traditionalists in 1972: Lobi (98%), Minianka (93%), Komono (90%), Birifor (89%), Dorosie (85%), Lilse (81%), Nunuma (81%), Guin (80%), Dian (75%), Tusyan (75%), Wara (75%), Karaboro (73%), Deforo (70%), Samo (70%), Bobo (65%), Dagari (65%) Busansi (62%), Dafi (60%), Mossi (60%). There are smaller percentages also in most other tribes. The Mossi resisted Islam completely until around 1950.

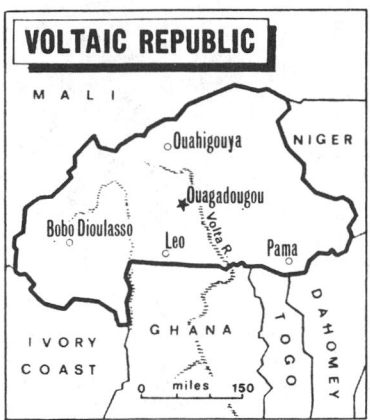

**VOLTAIC REPUBLIC**

### NON-CHRISTIAN RELIGIONS. Traditional religions
retain the allegiance of about half of the population. Ethnic groups which are more than 80% traditionalist include the following: Birifor 89%, Dorosie 85%, Komono 90%, Lilse 81%, Lobi 98%, Minianka 93%, and Nunuma 81%. Names for God include Winnam among the Mossi, Na'angmin among the Lodagaa and Amma among the Dogon.

Islam entered the Upper Volta during the 18th century, with the building of the first mosque in Ouagadougou and the installation of the first imam dating from the end of the century. Under French colonial rule Islam experienced harassment, persecution, imprisonments and executions. With Independence in 1960, Islam experienced a surge of conversions which has continued to the present day. Islam's greatest impact is felt in the large cities of Bobo Dioulasso and Ouagadougou and secondary commerical centres and villages situated along the main transportation arteries. The current migratory pattern of Upper Volta citizens to Ivory Coast for short periods is an important factor in islamization. Islam is spreading most rapidly among the urban masses, but rural areas are also affected. Almost

completely islamized peoples are the Liptako (Fulani), Masina, Sia, Songhai, Udalan, Wala and Zerma. Other tribes with more than 20% Muslims are the Bobo, Busansi, Dafi, Deforo, Dian, Grunshi, Guin, Gurma, Mossi, Samo, Tusyan and Wara. In 1962 Muslims established a national association, called the Muslim Community (Communauté Musulmane), which maintains contact with the wider world of Islam and with Muslim groups in neighbouring countries. Its purpose is to facilitate social, cultural and religious activities. A Committee for Muslim Youth (Comité pour la Jeunesse Musulmane) was formed in 1972.

### CHRISTIANITY
CATHOLIC CHURCH. White Fathers entered the Upper Volta in 1900 and established a mission at Ouagadougou the following year. The first baptisms were recorded in 1905 and were followed by severe persecution. In 1911 the work was strengthened by the arrival of White Sisters. The Grunshi were reached in 1912 and the Bobo and Samo in 1913. The vicariate of Ouagadougou was created in 1921 and became an archdiocese in 1955. An indigenous congregation of over 200 nuns, the Black Sisters of the Immaculate Conception, was formed in 1922, and the first indigenous priests were ordained in 1942. Catholicism is strongest among the Mossi, who make up half the population of the country and in 1970 were 11% Christian. Other groups among whom some progress had been made, with over 5% professing Catholics, are the Birifor, Bobo, Busansi, Dafi, Dagari, Dorosie, Gurma, Karaboro, Lilse, Nunuma and Tusyan. Catholics are growing rapidly in numbers, with over 12,000 converts each year from traditional religions.

Catholic laity are especially active through their organization, the Christian Community of Upper Volta (Communauté Chrétienne de Haute-Volta), which was first established in 1970. Recognized by the Episcopal Conference since 1971, Communauté Chrétienne is composed of local, diocesan and national representatives who assume diverse responsibilities

**Eglise Apostolique de Haute-Volta.** Headquarters building in Ouagadougou of first indigenous schismatic church, a split from AoG and CMA missions.

in the church and country. The association is officially recognized by the state.

PROTESTANT CHURCHES. The Protestant pioneers in the Upper Volta both in date of arrival and extent of activity have been the Assemblies of God. Begun in 1919 by North American Pentecostal missionaries and followed later by their counterparts from France, the Assemblies of God have grown to be the most important Protestant church in the country. The church has been characterized by extensive Sunday-school and publishing programmes as well as by widespread training of national leadership. A revival during a 4-year period in the 1960s resulted in a doubling of the Christian community. The church has been autonomous since 1955. Other groups include the churches supported by the CMA among the Bobo (1923), the SIM among the Gurma (1930), the WEC among the Lobi and Birifor (1937) and Canadian Pentecostals among the Nouna (1945).

INDIGENOUS CHURCHES. Separatist churches are not a significant factor in the Upper Volta church life. In 1958 there was only one small independent congregation in Ouagadougou, Temple Apostolique, which was joined in 1974 by 2 dissident congregations of the ECEHV among the Bobo. Called the Eglise Apostolique de Haute Volta, the group applied unsuccessfully to the WCC for membership in 1971.

CHURCH AND STATE. Until around 1950, the Mossi empire formed a large and powerful traditional religionist or animistic state which held islamization in check for several centuries. After Independence in 1960, the new state was proclaimed secular. The constitution of the second republic of the Upper Volta, adopted by referendum in 1970, guarantees 'the freedom of conscience, the profession and free practice of religion' (Article 14). 'The Republic assures equality before the law without distinction as to origin, race, sex, religion or political opinion. The Republic respects all creeds' (Article 21). The constitution was suspended on 8 February 1974 following a political crisis involving the military, but the rights affirmed in Articles 14 and 21 of the old constitution continued to be recognized and guaranteed, as with the other fundamental rights of man. The various dioceses, religious congregations and denominations have administrative councils which are recognized by government as 'private moral persons, invested with a juridical personality'. This recognition of juridical personality is based on Law 726/AP promulgated by a former French governor-general and dated 16 January 1939. Religious affairs are supervised by the Ministry of the Interior and Security.

### INTERDENOMINATIONAL ORGANIZATIONS.
The Federation of Evangelical Churches and Missions in the Upper Volta (Fédération des Eglises et Missions Evangéliques en Haute-Volta, FEME), formed in 1961, is a member of the Association of Evangelicals

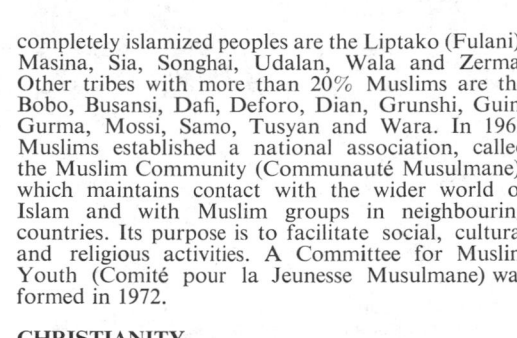

**Tribal religionists.** *Left.* Bobo dancers, masked to impersonate tribal ancestors. The Bobo are still 65% traditionalist (pagan animists).
**Muslims.** *Above.* At end of fast of Ramadan, Muslims in Ouagadougou celebrate with Feast of Idd. Every year there are some 49,000 converts to Islam across the nation.

**Eglise Catholique en Haute-Volta, Archdiocèse de Ouagadougou.** *Left.* Massed service in Ouagadougou. *Above.* Mossi Catholics after Sunday service in Dassouri.

of Africa and Madagascar, based in Nairobi (Kenya). FEME provides common representation before government and co-operative endeavour in relief and development projects. It was also responsible for the building of a student hostel in the capital, called the Foyer de Ouagadougou, during 1974.

**BROADCASTING.** The government Radiodiffusion-Télévision Voltaïque accepts both Catholic and Protestant programmes, and Catholics broadcast regularly on both radio and TV. Protestant recording studios are situated at Bobo Dioulasso (for the CMA), Koudougou and Ouagadougou. For Catholics, the Upper Volta is registered as a member of UNDA. From abroad, Protestant programmes can easily be heard over ELWA (Liberia).

## BIBLIOGRAPHY

'Christianity and Islam among the Mossi', E.P. Skinner, *American anthropologist*, LX, 6 (1958).

*Croyances religieuses et vie quotidienne: Islam et Christianisme à Ouagadougou.* R. Deniel. Recherches Voltaïques 14. Paris, Ouagadougou: CNRS/CVRS, 1970. 357p.
'Historique des missions protestantes en Haute-Volta avec un état de la formation actuelle des autochtones'. M. Vaillant. Thesis, Faculté Libre de Théologie Évangélique, Vaux-sur-Seine (France), 1975. 87p.
'Islam in Mossi society', E.P. Skinner, in I.M. Lewis (ed), *Islam in tropical Africa* (London: Oxford, 1966), p.350–373.
*Les Assemblées de Dieu en Haute-Volta: 50e anniversaire.* Ouagadougou: Assemblées de Dieu, 1971. 40p.
'L'Eglise catholique en Haute-Volta', B. Nouaille-Degorge, *Année africaine*, 1971, 361-380.

TABLE 2.   ORGANIZED CHURCHES AND DENOMINATIONS IN THE UPPER VOLTA

| Official name 1 | Begun 2 | Type 3 | Counc 4 | Congs 5 | Adults 6 | Affiliated 7 | Names, notes, and other statistics (see Codebook) 8 |
|---|---|---|---|---|---|---|---|
| **Assemblées de Dieu en Haute-Volta** | 1919 | P Pe2 | ZFG₂G | 900 | 32,076 | 80,000 | *Assemblies of God.* M=AoG(USA); 1947,AdD(France). A=1955. Mossi. 330n,22f,1j,1s(52). |
| Assoc des Eglises Evangéliques en H-V | 1930 | P int | xMG₂G | 34 | 550 | 3,500 | *AEHV. Assoc of Ev Chs.* M=ECWA(Nigeria),SIM(USA). A=1962. Gurma. 6n,22f,1H,4h,1s, |
| Eglise Apostolique de Haute-Volta | 1958 | I pen | .v.... | 3 | 800 | 1,500 | Schism ex AoG in Ouagadougou, also 1974 ex CMA. M=AC(Ghana). Applied to WCC 1971. |
| Eglise Baptiste de Haute-Volta | c1965 | P Bap | T.... | 2 | 100 | 200 | *Baptist Ch.* M=NBC(Nigeria). Yoruba. 1971, M=SBC(USA); correspondence courses. 11f. |
| **Eglise Catholique en Haute-Volta:** | 1900 | R Lat | P.SFP | 89 | 241,500 | 416,349 | *Catholic Ch in UV.* C=4+4+19. 8p,1s(57).               95n,295x,173m,570w,P=74%,21477Yy. |
| M   Ouagadougou | 1921 | R Lat | Ps | 14 | 61,200 | 105,460 | 95% Mossi. 23,554 catechumens. M=WF.           26    42    64    170      50      5669 |
| D   Bobo-Dioulasso | 1927 | R Lat | Pwf | 9 | 18,100 | 31,129 | Potentially rich agricultural land. 17 tribes.          11    64    51    132      93      1580 |
| D   Diébougou | 1968 | R Lat | Ps | 9 | 26,100 | 45,050 | 80% Mossi. Main tribe, Lobi, unevangelized.           16    20      7      29      93      1862 |
| D   Fada N'Gourma | 1959 | R Lat | Pcssr | 9 | 6,400 | 10,966 | 70% Mossi, 29% Gurma, 1% Fulani (Liptako).            4    21      4      60      75        526 |
| D   Kaya | 1969 | R Lat | Ps | 4 | 5,200 | 9,015 | Formed from M Ouagadougou, D Koupéla. Mossi.          2    11      1        9      97        481 |
| D   Koudougou | 1947 | R Lat | Ps | 11 | 42,100 | 72,591 | Small industrial town. Mossi, Grunsi. 26960z.            4    37    31      61      80      3232 |
| D   Koupéla | 1956 | R Lat | Ps | 11 | 30,500 | 52,584 | 90% Mossi, also Busansi and Kusasi.                    20    23      3      41      91      4445 |
| D   Nouna-Dédougou | 1947 | R Lat | Pwf | 14 | 32,900 | 56,784 | 33% Samo, 23% Bobo, 11% Pana, 7% Marka.             5    52      4      34      61      2544 |
| D   Ouahigouya | 1958 | R Lat | Ps | 8 | 19,000 | 32,770 | 96% Mossi, 4% Foulsé (Lilse). M=WF. 18034z.           7    25      8      34      82      1138 |
| Eglise Chrétienne Evangélique en H-V | 1923 | P Hol | xPG₂G | 106 | 2,696 | 5,563 | *ECEHV.* M=CMA. A=1964. 74% Bobo, 16% Samo. 26n,9x,37m,25f,2h,1s(12),W=55%,146Y. |
| Eglises Ev de Pentecôte en H-V | 1945 | P Pe1 | x₂G₂G | 40 | 500 | 2,000 | *MEP.* M=UVM(ACP,Canada). 64% Nouna, 11% Dian, 11% Sissala, 7% Birifor. 10n,18f,55Y. |
| Eglises radiophoniques isolées | c1960 | I rad | ..... | 40 | 500 | 1,100 | Isolated radio believers, mainly pupils and students aged 12–25. T=11000(ICI). |
| Mission Ev de l'Afrique Occidentale | 1931 | P int | xPG₂G | 20 | 600 | 2,000 | 1931, M=Qua Iboe; 1937, WEC(UK),WEK. Lobi, also Birifor, Dagari, Guin. 12f,1p. |
| Témoins de Jéhovah | c1960 | M Jeh | x..... | 2 | 30 | 50 | *Jehovah's Witnesses.* Active witnessing by 1962, then lapse until 1967. 6f. |
| Other Protestant denominations | | P | ..... | | 1,000 | 2,000 | Total about 4, including: SDA (USA; 1971), World-Wide Missions (1965). |
| Other African indigenous churches | | I | ..... | | 200 | 500 | About 7 churches from Ghana, Togo, Benin and Ivory Coast have missions at work. |
| **Total affiliated (mid-1970)** | | | | 1,270 | 280,552 | 514,762 | Total denominations (1970) . . .   19. |
| **Total affiliated (mid-1975)** | | | | 1,460 | 358,700 | 658,160 | Total denominations (1975) . . .   20. |
| **Total affiliated (mid-1980)** | | | | 1,650 | 450,400 | 826,400 | Total denominations (1980) . . .   21. |

**NOTES ON TABLE ABOVE**
COLUMNS: for meanings and CODES (cols. 1, 3, 4, 8): see Codebook (Part 6). Column 1: **Boldface type** = church with over 10% of country's affiliated Christians.
NATIONAL COUNCILS (Column 4, 5th letter).
   G  = Fédération des Eglises et Missions Evangéliques en Haute-Volta (FEME)(Federation/Association of Evangelical Churches and Missions in the Upper Volta).
   P  = Conférence Episcopale de Haute-Volta et Niger (CEHVN)(Episcopal Conference of the Upper Volta & Niger).

**PEOPLES** (ethnolinguistic). Christians: about 60.0% Mossi, 13.0% Bobo, 7.0% Dagari, 5.0% Grunshi (0.6% Kusasi, 0.2% Nunuma), 4.0% Busansi, 3.8% Samo, 2.0% Gurma, 1.2% Pana, 1.0% Lilse, 1.0% Birifor, 0.6% French, 0.2% Lobi, Ivorian, Dahomean, Togolese, Senufo, Dogon, et alii.

**COUNTRY-WIDE TOTALS**
EVANGELIZATION (see Part 5). 1900: 0%. 1970: 46%. 1980: 51%. *Radiophonic evangelism.* Christ Vous Appelle (Assemblées de Dieu, France), ICI (10,442 enrolments, 3,754 active, 49 conversions reported), et alia.
FOREIGN MISSIONARIES AND PERSONNEL (nationals serving abroad)(1973). Total about 56 Roman Catholics in France, Guinea, Ivory Coast, Mali and Niger.
FOREIGN MISSIONARIES AND PERSONNEL (aliens from abroad)(1973). Total 894. *From Western world.* 814: 687 Roman Catholics, 121 Protestants (80 in 7 USA societies, 18 in 2 Canada societies, 10 in 2 UK societies, 4 in 1 Netherlands society, 3 in 3 Australia societies, 2 in 1 France society, 2 in 2 New Zealand societies, 2 in 1 WGermany society), 6 marginal Protestants (Jehovah's Witnesses). *From Communist world.* 1 Roman Catholic from Poland. *From Third World.* 79: about 50 Roman Catholics from Togo, Ivory Coast, Benin, Ghana, Nigeria and Zaire, 15 Protestants from Benin, Ivory Coast and Nigeria, 14 indigenous from Ghana, Togo, Benin, Ivory Coast and Korea.

INSTITUTIONS (church-operated)(1973). Total 60, including 30 higher schools (8 minor seminaries), 15 medical centres, 2 presses, 4 religious communities, 2 research centres, 4 seminaries (3 Protestant, 1 RC).
PERIODICALS. About 9 titles.
PERSONNEL. About 3,574 (2,680 national, 894 foreign).
RELIGIOUS LIBRARIES. About 14.
SCRIPTURE DISTRIBUTION (1975). Annual totals: 900 Bibles (89% subsidized, 11% commercial), 10,000 NTs (subsidized), 4,300 UBS portions, 17,900 UBS selections. *Translations completed.* Portion: 6 languages since 1930. NT: 3 languages since 1939.
SERVICE AGENCIES. About 30, including ACRA, CEHVN, CF, CV/AV, FEME, GBUAF, ICI, JAC/F, JEC/F, MAP, MCC, NLFA, SIL, UNEC, WBT, WVI.

**ADDITIONAL DATA ON CHURCHES**
ASSEMBLEES DE DIEU EN HAUTE-VOLTA. By 1976 there were 1,030 assemblies, congregations and preaching points.
EGLISE CATHOLIQUE EN HAUTE-VOLTA. *Catholics.* 54% Mossi. *Catechumens.* (1963) 71,093. In 1971 there numbered 113,400, divided among the 9 dioceses in the order shown as follows (and included in column 7): 23554, 5885, 2941, 2615, 3802, 26960, 13231, 16378, 18034. In Ouahigouya in 1971, catechumens exceeded baptized Catholics in number. *Annual baptisms.* (1972) 61.0% infant, 39.0% adult (8,053). *National priests.* The first 3 nationals were ordained in 1942. Since then Koumi seminary had trained 108 others by 1971. Growth: 1942, 3; 1952, 23; 1962, 64; 1971, 95. *Brothers.* Including 82 nationals. *Sisters.* Including 269 nationals. *Seminarians.* In addition to the 57 nationals, the seminary also serves Niger, Mali and Guinea. *Catechists.* Total (1969) 1,855, working in 1,596 of the over 7,000 villages in the nation. *Indigenous religious congregations.* Sisters: 205 Soeurs de l'Immaculée-Conception (begun 1922), 64 Soeurs de l'Annonciation (begun 1948). There are no longer congregations of brothers since the 2 original ones merged into international ones. *Main foreign congregations.* Priests: WF (PB), CSSR.

Brothers: FSC, FSF. Sisters: Soeurs Missionnaires de N-D d'Afrique, Franciscaines Missionnaires de Marie, Soeurs de l'Assomption de Paris, Filles du Coeur de Marie de Paris.
*Catholic organizations.* The Episcopal Conference of the Upper Volta and Niger (Conférence Episcopale de Haute-Volta et Niger), with headquarters in Ouagadougou, is a member of the Inter-Territorial Episcopal Conference of Francophone West Africa, and of SECAM. Female religious personnel are represented on the 'Anima Una' Union des Supérieures Majeures des Congrégations Autochtones d'Afrique de l'Ouest Francophone, and male religious personnel in the Association des Supérieurs Majeurs des Instituts Masculins et Haute-Volta, both based in Bamako, Mali. There are no national presbyteral or pastoral councils. Lay activities are co-ordinated by the Secretariat of the Lay Apostolate (Secrétariat de l'Apostolat des Laïcs), the principal youth movements being JAC/F, JEC/F, CV/AV, Scouts and Guides; with ACRA, CF, Légion de Marie and Teacher Teams serving adults.

The Holy See has diplomatic relations with the Upper Volta and is represented to government and the Catholic hierarchy by a pro-nuncio based in Dakar, Senegal.

The Catholic Church turned over its 161 primary schools to government in 1969 but continues to direct, through the Union National de l'Enseignement Catholique (UNEC), 7 colleges for boys, 7 colleges for girls and 2 trade schools. In addition to a pediatric unit, 2 ophthalmological centres and 5 dispensaries, under direct supervision, there are numerous religious nurses working in state hospitals and dispensaries. Rural development is promoted by several Catholic Action movements (ACRA and JAC/F). Two centres are engaged in urban research and the training of personnel for programmes of social and economic development: Centre d'Etudes Economiques et Sociales d'Afrique Occidentale (CESAO) at Bobo Dioulasso and the Centre de Recherche et d'Action Sociale (CERAS) at Ouagodougou. Caritas Voltaïque, which is a member of Caritas Internationalis, is also active.

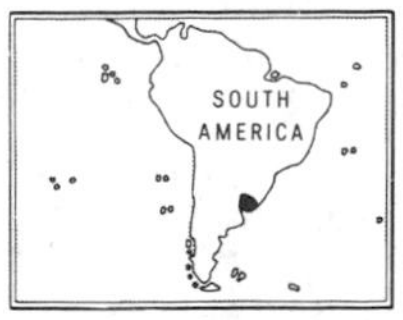


# URUGUAY

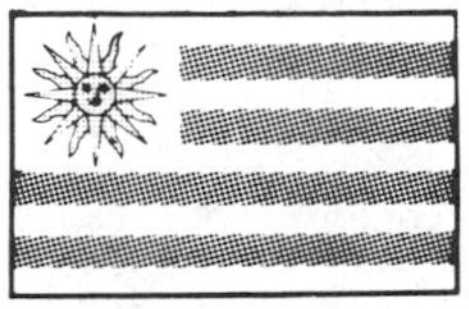

## SECULAR DATA

**STATE. Official name:** The Eastern Republic of Uruguay (La República Oriental del Uruguay). Adjective of nationality: Uruguayan (uruguayo).
**Flag** (shown above right): Blue stripes on white field, with golden sun in upper hoist corner.
**Area:** 177,508 sq.km (68,536 sq.miles). Agricultural land. 87.1%.
**Government:** Military junta, since 1973 (1624 Spanish settlement, 1820 part of Brazil, 1825 Independence as republic, 1973 military rule).
**Official language:** Spanish (*Español/Castellano*).
**Capital:** Montevideo 1,203,700 (1970).
**Political divisions:** 19 Departments.
**Armed forces** (1976): Total 23,000 regular: army 17,000, navy 4,000, air force 2,000 (14 combat aircraft). Reserves: 100,000. Paramilitary forces: 22,000.

**DEMOGRAPHY. Population:** 2,763,964 (census of 21.V.1975. For 1970–2000 (UN), see last row of Table 1). Population density (1975): 18/sq.km. (45/sq.mile). Under 15 years: 28%. Growth rate (1975–80): 0.97% per year (births 1.97%, deaths –0.95%, emigrants –0.05%). Life expectancy (1975–80): 70.2 years. Household size: 3.8 persons.
**Major languages:** Spanish, Italian, Galician, German, Portuguese, Russian, Greek, and others.
**Urban dwellers** (1970): 78.4%. Urban growth rate (1950–70): 3.0% per year.
**Labour force:** 38%.
**Refugees** (1977): None from abroad. Exiles abroad: over 800,000 have fled for political reasons or left for economic reasons, mainly to Argentina (by 1975, almost 500,000).
**Tourists** (1968): 604,189. (1974) 587,649.

**ETHNOLINGUISTIC GROUPS:** 85.9% Uruguayan White (Spanish/Italian origin), 3.0% Mestizo (Spanish/Amerindian), 2.6% Italian, 1.8% Jewish, 1.7% Mulatto (Negro/European) (50,000), 1.2% Galician, 0.9% German, 0.9% Brazilian, 0.9% Spaniard, 0.4% Russian, 0.4% Greek, 0.3% Black (African Negro)(10,000), Ukrainian, Armenian, Argentinian, Chilean, Polish, Czech, Slovak, Serbian, Croat, Bulgar, French, Basque, Amerindian, Assyrian.

**MONEY** (1977). **Monetary unit:** Uruguayan new peso (= 100 centésimos); US$1 = UrugN$4.00.
**National income per person:** US$1,150. Average annual family income: US$4,370.
**Inflation:** (1970–74) 66.1% per year (1975: consumer price index 1,409).
**Cost of living in capital** (1976): index 104 (Washington DC = 100). Daily cost of living: US$24.

**HEALTH.** Hospitals: 97 (15,107 beds). Doctors: 3,250. Lepers: 2,000 (0.6 per 1,000). Blind: 3,000. Psychotics: 30,000.

**EDUCATION.** Adult literacy: (1963) 90%, (1975) 94%. Education rate: 80%. Schools: 2,328. Universities: 1.

**LITERATURE.** Annual new book titles (1966): 266. Periodicals: 299. Scientific journals: 135. Newspapers: 54 dailies, 158 non-daily.

**COMMUNICATION** (per 1,000 people). Phones: 82. Radios: 507. TV sets: 102. Daily newspaper circulation: 267 copies.

TABLE 1. RELIGIOUS ADHERENTS IN URUGUAY

| Year | 1900 | | mid-1970 | | Annual change, 1970–1980 | | | | mid-1975 | | mid-1980 | | 2000 | |
|---|---|---|---|---|---|---|---|---|---|---|---|---|---|---|
| *Name* | *Adherents* | *%* | *Adherents* | *%* | *Natural* | *Conversion* | *Total* | *Rate* | *Adherents* | *%* | *Adherents* | *%* | *Adherents* | *%* |
| **Christians** | **574,700** | **62.8** | **1,902,600** | **64.4** | **19,596** | **–4,636** | **14,960** | **0.76** | **1,977,400** | **63.6** | **2,052,200** | **62.9** | **2,302,200** | **59.6** |
| professing | 574,700 | 62.8 | 1,902,600 | 64.4 | 19,596 | –4,636 | 14,960 | 0.76 | 1,977,400 | 63.6 | 2,052,200 | 62.9 | 2,302,200 | 59.6 |
| Roman Catholics | 560,000 | 61.2 | 1,802,600 | 61.0 | 18,554 | –4,614 | 13,940 | 0.74 | 1,872,300 | 60.2 | 1,942,000 | 59.5 | 2,169,700 | 56.2 |
| Evangelical Catholics | 0 | 0.0 | 26,306 | 0.9 | 293 | 357 | 650 | 2.20 | 29,500 | 0.9 | 32,800 | 1.0 | 47,500 | 1.2 |
| Protestants | 14,600 | 1.6 | 57,500 | 1.9 | 600 | 0 | 600 | 0.99 | 60,500 | 1.9 | 63,500 | 1.9 | 77,000 | 2.0 |
| Orthodox | 100 | 0.0 | 21,500 | 0.7 | 224 | –4 | 220 | 0.97 | 22,600 | 0.7 | 23,700 | 0.7 | 27,000 | 0.7 |
| Catholics (non-Roman) | 0 | 0.0 | 20,000 | 0.7 | 208 | –8 | 200 | 0.95 | 21,000 | 0.7 | 22,000 | 0.7 | 27,000 | 0.7 |
| Anglicans | 0 | 0.0 | 1,000 | 0.0 | 10 | –10 | 0 | 0.00 | 1,000 | 0.0 | 1,000 | 0.0 | 1,500 | 0.0 |
| affiliated | 574,700 | 62.8 | 1,902,600 | 64.4 | 19,596 | –4,636 | 14,960 | 0.76 | 1,977,400 | 63.6 | 2,052,200 | 62.9 | 2,302,200 | 59.6 |
| disaffiliated | –77,000 | –8.4 | –289,043 | –9.8 | –2,844 | 3,488 | 644 | –0.22 | –286,900 | –9.2 | –282,600 | –8.7 | –233,900 | –6.1 |
| doubly-affiliated | –1,000 | –0.1 | –50,000 | –1.7 | –545 | –455 | –1,000 | 1.82 | –55,000 | –1.8 | –60,000 | –1.8 | –75,000 | –1.9 |
| total practising | 459,760 | *80* | 1,331,820 | *70* | 13,717 | –3,245 | 10,472 | 0.76 | 1,384,180 | *70* | 1,436,540 | *70* | 1,381,300 | *60* |
| non-practising | 114,940 | *20* | 570,780 | *30* | 5,879 | –1,391 | 4,488 | 0.76 | 593,220 | *30* | 615,660 | *30* | 920,900 | *40* |
| Roman Catholics | 637,000 | 69.6 | 2,115,337 | 71.6 | 21,650 | –8,004 | 13,646 | 0.62 | 2,184,700 | 70.3 | 2,251,800 | 69.0 | 2,431,100 | 63.0 |
| Protestants | 14,600 | 1.6 | 57,553 | 1.9 | 600 | –5 | 595 | 0.98 | 60,500 | 1.9 | 63,500 | 1.9 | 77,000 | 2.0 |
| Evangelicals | 6,000 | 0.7 | 43,300 | 1.5 | 451 | –1 | 450 | 0.99 | 45,500 | 1.5 | 47,800 | 1.5 | 59,000 | 1.5 |
| Marginal Protestants | 0 | 0.0 | 23,553 | 0.8 | 263 | 332 | 595 | 2.24 | 26,500 | 0.9 | 29,500 | 0.9 | 42,500 | 1.1 |
| Orthodox | 100 | 0.0 | 21,500 | 0.7 | 224 | –4 | 220 | 0.97 | 22,600 | 0.7 | 23,700 | 0.7 | 27,000 | 0.7 |
| Catholics (non-Roman) | 1,000 | 0.1 | 20,000 | 0.7 | 208 | –8 | 200 | 0.95 | 21,000 | 0.7 | 22,000 | 0.7 | 27,000 | 0.7 |
| Non-White indigenous | 0 | 0.0 | 2,700 | 0.1 | 30 | 30 | 60 | 2.00 | 3,000 | 0.1 | 3,300 | 0.1 | 5,000 | 0.1 |
| Anglicans | 0 | 0.0 | 1,000 | 0.0 | 10 | –10 | 0 | 0.00 | 1,000 | 0.0 | 1,000 | 0.0 | 1,500 | 0.0 |
| Evangelicals | 0 | 0.0 | 500 | 0.0 | 5 | –5 | 0 | 0.00 | 500 | 0.0 | 500 | 0.0 | 700 | 0.0 |
| Non-religious | 339,880 | 37.1 | 906,700 | 30.7 | 9,603 | 3,097 | 12,700 | 1.31 | 969,100 | 31.2 | 1,033,700 | 31.7 | 1,310,700 | 33.9 |
| Atheists | 1,000 | 0.1 | 88,000 | 3.0 | 985 | 1,305 | 2,290 | 2.30 | 99,400 | 3.2 | 110,900 | 3.4 | 170,000 | 4.4 |
| Jews | 60 | 0.0 | 52,000 | 1.7 | 541 | –1 | 540 | 0.99 | 54,600 | 1.7 | 57,400 | 1.7 | 65,600 | 1.7 |
| Baha'is | 0 | 0.0 | 3,400 | 0.1 | 36 | 4 | 40 | 1.11 | 3,600 | 0.1 | 3,800 | 0.1 | 5,000 | 0.1 |
| Afro-American spiritists | 0 | 0.0 | 1,500 | 0.1 | 30 | 220 | 250 | 8.33 | 3,000 | 0.1 | 4,000 | 0.1 | 5,000 | 0.1 |
| Muslims | 60 | 0.0 | 300 | 0.0 | 3 | –3 | 0 | 0.00 | 300 | 0.0 | 300 | 0.0 | 500 | 0.0 |
| Other religionists | 0 | 0.0 | 500 | 0.0 | 6 | 14 | 20 | 3.33 | 600 | 0.0 | 700 | 0.0 | 2,000 | 0.1 |
| **Country's population** | **915,700** | **100.0** | **2,955,000** | **100.0** | **30,800** | **0** | **30,800** | **0.99** | **3,108,000** | **100.0** | **3,263,000** | **100.0** | **3,861,000** | **100.0** |

COLUMNS, ROWS. For meanings and definitions, see Codebook (Part 6). Note that, by definition, total 'Christians' = professing + crypto-Christians, which also = affiliated + nominal Christians. Percentages may not always total exactly, due to rounding.
CENSUSES. **1908** (all ages): 61.2% Roman Catholics, 37.1% non-religious (22.7% of no religion, 14.4% freethinkers), 1.6% Evangelicals (16,498 persons), 0.1% atheists. **1908** (adults only, over 14 years old): 70.0% Roman Catholics, 27.9% non-religious (20.6% freethinkers (126,425 adults)), 2.0% Evangelicals (12,232 adults), 0.1% atheists. **1963**: 62% Roman Catholics.
POLLS. Several with a religion question have been held by Gallup Uruguay. *Religious preference.* November 1970: 61% Catholics, 34% non-religious or atheists, 2% Protestants, 2% other religionists (Orthodox, New Apostolic, et alia), 1% Jews.

### NOTES ON RELIGIONS

AFRO-AMERICAN SPIRITISM. Afro-American non-Christian low spiritism among the 10,000 Blacks and 50,000 Mulattoes remained relatively unorganized and ineffective until 1973 when Umbanda was introduced from Brazil and began winning converts from among the lowest classes in the larger cities.
ATHEISTS. Uruguayan Communist Party (PCU) (legal; pro-Soviet): membership (1970) 22,000; Communist voters (election of 28.XI.1971) 89,291 (6% of all votes). Leftist terrorist groups (National Liberation Movement (MLN), Tupamaros) are numerous also.
BAHA'IS. Rapid growth from 3 local spiritual assemblies (1964) to 23 (1973).
DISAFFILIATED. This term is used here to describe persons who, although baptized Roman Catholics and therefore regarded by the Catholic Church as still affiliated to it (and hence enumerated as such), have recently disaffiliated themselves completely from Christianity and now profess in polls to be either non-religious (agnostics) or atheists. Because their statistics represent a duplication, they are shown in the table above as a negative quantity (with a minus sign).
DOUBLY-AFFILIATED. The term covers those affiliated to, or claimed by, both the Catholic Church and also a church termed Evangélica by the state (Protestant, marginal Protestant, Anglican, or Non-White indigenous) or other churches, i.e. baptized Catholics who have recently become Evanglicals or others. Because their statistics represent a duplication, they are shown in the table as a negative quantity (with a minus sign).
EVANGELICAL CATHOLICS. This term is used here to describe persons who are affiliated to churches termed by the state Evangélica (Protestant, Non-White indigenous, Anglican or marginal Protestant churches), but who are regarded by state and society as, or in polls profess publicly to be, Roman Catholics.
JEWS. In 6 synagogues. Jews immigrated in 3 major waves from Russia, Germany, Eastern Europe and the middle East.
NON-RELIGIOUS. There has been a longer history of large-scale non-religion in Uruguay than in any other Latin American nation, or than in most European nations. In the 1908 census, 37.2% professed to be *liberales*, i.e. non-religious (14.4% calling themselves freethinkers, the rest agnostics, pantheists, materialists, theosophists, evolutionists, and several other categories); in 1970, 34% called themselves non-religious or atheists. Among the numerous causative factors are a history of 19th-century anticlericalism, steady influx of non-religious Spaniards, Italians and French from Europe, early separation of church and state, diffusion of liberal and agnostic philosophies from Europe, and the presence of thousands of short-term residents from Argentina awaiting divorces under Uruguay's liberal laws.
NON-WHITE INDIGENOUS. In about 7 denominations in 1970 (see Table 2).
OTHER RELIGIONISTS. Adherents of smaller religions and cults, including Rosicrucians (1 AMORC centre).
PRACTISING CHRISTIANS. *Church attendance.* 1965: (Catholics) 10.4% weekly in all churches in Salto, Colonia and Canelones. 1968: weekly church attenders (in cities only) 24% of whole population. November 1970: 18% attended church in previous 7 days.

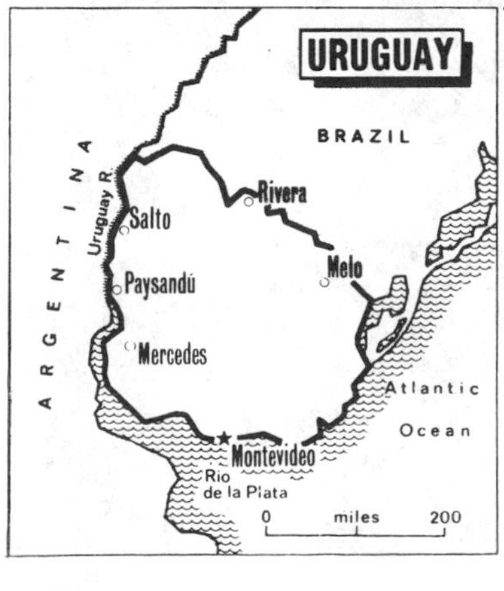


**NON-CHRISTIAN RELIGIONS. Non-religion** and **atheism** have had a longer history, and are numerically far stronger, in Uruguay than in any other South American nation. About 94% of Uruguay's population are Europeans or of European origin mostly coming originally from Spain, Italy and France, who brought with them those countries' anticlericalism and opposition to state-related Catholicism. There were only small numbers of Indian inhabitants when Spanish settlement was begun, and the last were exterminated in 1832. The high literacy rate, large urban middle class and early separation of church and state (formalized in 1916) all contributed to a further reduction in Catholic influence and to the creation of a substantial group by the year 1900 claiming to be freethinkers, agnostics or atheists; and this situation has continued relatively unchanged to the present day. Uruguay is in fact the least Catholic and least Christian of any Latin American Spanish- or Portuguese-speaking country.

**Judaism** has increased in size in the 20th century, to over 55,000 adherents today.

**Baha'i** has grown rapidly since 1964, from 3 local spiritual assemblies then to 23 by 1973.

**Umbanda,** a syncretistic Afro-Brazilian religion, was introduced from Brazil during 1973–74 and has already begun to make inroads among the lower classes of the large cities. At the end of 1974 a survey in Montevideo showed the existence of some 40 *terreiros* (cult centres). The sudden appearance and vogue of Umbanda are undoubtedly a reaction to Uruguay's desperate political and economic stituation. Umbanda's ceremonies are conducted in Portuguese.

### CHRISTIANITY

CATHOLIC CHURCH. Franciscan and Jesuit missionaries arrived in 1616, and the Jesuits were soon involved in developing communal villages among the Indians. These were later destroyed following the expulsion of Jesuits from Uruguay in 1767. In 1726 Montevideo became a Catholic parish under the see of Buenos Aires. A diocese was established in 1878 which became an archdiocese in 1897.

In contrast with its early preoccupation with evangelization only, the church has in recent years turned its attention towards problems of development in urban ghettos. This change, begun in 1957 at the time of the restructuring of Catholic Action into specialized movements, was carried further due to the influence of Medellín and the papal encyclical 'Populorum progressio' which focused attention on the needs of society and contributed to the polarization of leftist and rightist wings in the church. The hierarchy itself is deeply divided, but the progressivist wing prevails, as seen in the collective pastoral letter on social problems of 1967, and various pastoral letters by the archbishop of Montevideo on the state of the country (1968), and the church and politics (1970). At the level of internal church organization, new initiatives have been taken towards increasing the role of the laity in certain dioceses, through lay and parish groups. A survey carried out on a Sunday in May 1965 in all the churches of Salto province (population 60,000) showed that only 10.4% of Catholics over 7 years of age attended mass weekly. Of those over 20 years of age, 7.6% attended (10.9% for women and only 4.4% for men). A study was also made at the same time in the towns of Colonia and Canelones with similar results.

PROTESTANT CHURCHES. North American Methodists were the first to assign a missionary to Uruguay, in 1838. Due to continued civil war and revolutions the mission was closed, but re-opened again in 1878. Methodism has produced some of the most able leaders in Uruguay and also in all Latin America, but the church itself remains small.

The Waldensian Church began with the arrival of Italians in 1856, the first pastor being appointed in 1877. It is the second largest Protestant church, and many of its congregations are under the pastoral care of laymen. Other important groups which became established during the last century are German Lutherans, Salvation Army and Seventh-day Adventists.

Southern Baptists entered Montevideo from Argentina in 1911. With few missionaries in the early days, progress was slow until recently. Seven Pentecostal churches are at work and have made an important impact on the country. The largest numerical increases have been recorded by the Assemblies of God and the Church of God (Cleveland). A number of smaller denominations are also present.

OTHER CHURCHES. The largest denomination outside Catholicism is the New Apostolic Church, found mainly among recent German immigrants. Other groups of importance are Mormons, Greek and Russian Orthodox, and Jehovah's Witnesses.

Anglicans also have a small community with 3 urban congregations.

CHURCH AND STATE. The juridical status of the Catholic Church has not been modified since 1916, when the church was formally separated from the state. Since then the church has been free to name its own bishops. The constitution of 15 February 1967

'Las Buenas Nuevas' (Good News). On Bible Society's stand at international trade fair, 2 girls sell modern gospel translations to sceptics.

stipulates in Chapter III, Article 5: 'All religions are authorized in Uruguay. The State supports no religion whatever. It recognizes the right of the Catholic Church to ownership of all temples'. The same article regulates, to the advantage of the Catholic Church, the question of ownership of religious buildings built with government funds. Also, 'buildings dedicated for worship by the diverse religions' are declared exempt from all taxes.

During the first part of the 20th century, progressive ideas exemplified by the statesman José Batlle y Ordoñez were translated into a campaign against alleged obscurantism in the church, resulting in anticlerical laws and, in 1909, prohibition of religious instruction in public schools. The Catholic Church then went on the defensive, developing a network of organizations parallel to those of the state: schools, agricultural unions, savings and loan centres, banks and other economic and social institutions. Of this whole network only the Catholic schools remain today, and they now collaborate with the state.

After a short period of peaceful co-existence between church and state, tension arose again, this time between a church critical of the capitalist system (especially after Medellín and 'Populorum progressio') and a government becoming increasingly conservative. The new conflict between church and state has manifested itself in different ways: episcopal declarations on social and economic matters, arrests of priests suspected of encouraging revolutionary movements, and police searches of churches and convents. During this period, the episcopate was more involved than in merely making public declarat-

ions. As one example, in June 1972 the archbishop of Montevideo accompanied by 2 other prelates took part in the public funeral of 8 communist workers killed by the armed forces.

After the fascist military coup of 27 June 1973, the Catholic episcopate and the Federation of Evangelical Churches published separate protests. As in other parts of South America, the repression of alleged subversive activities has affected both non-Catholics and Catholics, including priests, sisters and lay militants. Pastor Emilio Castro, of the CWME/WCC, and Msgr Mendiharat bishop of Salto, went into exile. Among others, the government suspended at the end of 1974 the official organ of the Waldensian Church, *Mensajero Valdense*, which provoked a conflict between the WCC and government, the latter claiming that the former 'invariably favours Marxist subversion on the five continents'. Ironically the Waldensian Church in the River Plate is not a member of the WCC.

A more direct conflict with the Catholic Church has been provoked by the government's decision to restrict the autonomy of confessional teaching centres, accused of fomenting 'Marxist conscientization'. The Catholic episcopate, though divided into conservative and progressivist factions, has unanimously opposed the government plan which it insists is unconstitutional. In May 1975 the government suppressed the important Catholic journal *Vispera*, whose influence has spread far beyond the borders of Uruguay.

INTERDENOMINATIONAL ORGANIZATIONS. The Federation of Evangelical Churches of Uruguay (Federación de Iglesias Evangélicas del Uruguay, FIEU) has 8 full members and 2 associate members. It was founded in 1956 as the successor to the Uruguay Committee of the Confederation of Evangelical Churches of the River Plate, which held its first meeting in 1939. The council is affiliated to the Commission on World Mission and Evangelism, World Council of Churches, and also to 2 regional organizations: the Latin American Christian Education Council (Comisión Evangélica Latinoamericana de Educación Cristiana, CELADEC), and UNELAM (Movimiento pro Unidad Evangélica Latinoamericana). The latter body has its headquarters in Montevideo. The Evangelical Institute of Montevideo was opened by Lutherans in 1966 and includes on its staff Catholic as well as Protestant theologians. A Sodepax-type organization is also active.

Concerning interreligious relations, the Judeo-Christian Brotherhood (Confraternidad Judeo-Cristiana) was formed in 1964 and devotes itself to cultural initiatives and the organization of theological symposia concerning problems of common interest.

BROADCASTING. Commercial radio and TV stations all accept religious broadcasting, and on many there are both Catholic and Protestant programmes for an hour a week or more. Although the

Luis Palau 23-day Campaign in 6 cities (1978), carried over 31 radio and 2 TV stations, with 101,000 attenders and 8,000 decisions for Christ. *Above.* A capacity audience hears gospel in Montevideo. *Right.* At close, 10% flock forward as enquirers, seekers, or having decided for Christ.

Catholic Church owns no radio or TV stations, there are 2 Catholic radio/TV production studios in Montevideo: Asociación pro Emisiones Culturales (APEC), founded in 1963, and Servicio de Radio y TV which is part of the Officina Nacional de Medios de Comunicación Social. For Catholics, Uruguay is a member of UNDA.

There are several Protestant studios. The Waldensian Church has a studio where programmes are produced, including Bible correspondence courses. The Federation of Evangelical Churches of Uruguay has sponsored a 5-minute daily programme on local radio and pastors speak on various subjects on TV.

## BIBLIOGRAPHY


*Guia de la Iglesia Uruguaya.* Montevideo: Curia Eclesiástica de Montevideo, 1971.

*La religión en Uruguay.* C.M. Rama. Montevideo: Nuestro Tiempo, 1964.


TABLE 2. ORGANIZED CHURCHES AND DENOMINATIONS IN URUGUAY

| Official name 1 | Begun 2 | Type 3 | Counc 4 | Congs 5 | Adults 6 | Affiliated 7 | Names, notes, and other statistics (see Codebook) 8 |
|---|---|---|---|---|---|---|---|
| Alianza Cristiana y Misionera del U | 1960 | P Hol | x•••• | 4 | 217 | 900 | M=Christian & Miss Alliance(USA), begun from Argentina. 2x,G=19.2%pa,W=74%,75Y. |
| Asambleas de Dios (Sueca) | 1938 | P Pe2 | Z•••• | 15 | 1,700 | 3,000 | *Assemblies of God (Swedish).* M=SFM(Sweden), FFFM(Finland). Classical Pentecostals. |
| Asambleas de Dios (USA) | 1944 | P Pe2 | ZF••• | 161 | 5,213 | 10,000 | *Assemblies of God.* M=AoG(USA). Classical Pentecostals (2-stage). 75n,8f,1s(28). |
| Congregación Ev Luterana (Misurí) | 1935 | P Lut | x•••• | 2 | 100 | 142 | *San Pablo* (Montevideo). 1942, M=LC Missouri Synod(USA). Montevideo, Paysandú. |
| Convención Evangélica Bautista del U | 1911 | P Bap | T•••• | 65 | 1,995 | 3,500 | *Ev Baptist Convention.* M=SBC(USA). 27n,4x,22f,G=4.1%pa,4h,1s(12),W=38%,294Y,185z. |
| Ejército de Salvación | 1890 | P Sal | xwu•N | 10 | 1,000 | 2,000 | *Salvation Army, Uruguay & Argentina Littoral District*, SAmerica East Territory. |
| Iglesia Adventista del Séptimo Día | 1895 | P Adv | x•••• | 29 | 3,281 | 6,000 | *Seventh-day Adventists, Uruguay M*, Austral UC. 8n,1x,50mw,26f,G=4.4%pa,1r,267Y. |
| Iglesia Anglicana (D Argentina & ESA) | | A Eva | aw•C• | 3 | 100 | 1,000 | *Anglican Ch.* ESA=Eastern South America. Urban. Uruguayans of UK origin. 1x,W=30%. |
| Iglesia Apostólica Armenia: D Uruguay | | O Arm | Ewc•• | 1 | 200 | 500 | *Armenian Apostolic Ch. Gregorians.* Under jurisdiction of C Echmiadzin (USSR). 2nx. |
| Iglesia Bautista Libre | 1962 | P Bap | xF••• | 5 | 210 | 500 | *Free Will Baptist Ch.* M=NAFWB(USA). HQ Rivera (Brazil border). 1n,5f. |
| Iglesia Bautista Nacional | 1965 | I Bap | Tw••• | | 100 | 200 | M=National Baptist Convention USA. Blacks, assisting Uruguayan Baptists. |
| **Iglesia Católica en el Uruguay:** | 1616 | R Lat | BzL•R | 216 | 1,524,000 | 2,115,337 | *Catholic Ch in Uruguay.* C=34+1+51. 1s,W=18%. 633nx,262m,2044w,43340Yy. |
| M Montevideo | 1878 | R Lat | Bs | 75 | 655,000 | 910,000 | 1968: 10,000 laity mobilized in parish groups. 1s. 366 200 1300 19700 |
| D Canelones | 1961 | R Lat | Bs | 33 | 177,000 | 245,565 | Northeast of capital. Low religious practice: W=10%. 58 20 217 4395 |
| D Florida | 1897 | R Lat | Bs | 16 | 72,000 | 100,000 | Central area of Uruguay: hilly, lakes. 28 8 95 1796 |
| D Maldonato-Punta del Este | 1966 | R Lat | Bs | 11 | 65,000 | 90,100 | Southeast coastal area. HQ Maldonado. 16 7 66 1993 |
| D Melo | 1955 | R Lat | Bs | 12 | 58,000 | 80,000 | Northeast part of country, bordering on Brazil. 26 1 63 1953 |
| D Mercedes | 1960 | R Lat | Bs | 18 | 99,000 | 137,572 | Same name as Argentina diocese across River Plate. 37 3 62 1248 |
| D Minas | 1960 | R Lat | Bs | 8 | 50,000 | 69,000 | Inland southeastern area of country. 17 4 25 1418 |
| D Salto | 1897 | R Lat | Bs | 15 | 171,000 | 238,000 | Very scattered. Numerous wealthy landowners. W=10%. 44 7 81 5737 |
| D San José de Mayo | 1955 | R Lat | Bs | 14 | 76,000 | 105,100 | Coast area west of Montevideo. 15 11 54 2471 |
| D Tacuarembó | 1960 | R Lat | Bs | 14 | 101,000 | 140,000 | Centre north of country, adjoining Brazil. 26 1 81 2629 |
| Iglesia de Dios de la Profecía | 1957 | P Pe3 | Z•••• | 6 | 110 | 300 | *Ch of God of Prophecy.* M=CGP(USA). Holiness Pentecostals; ex CoG(Cleveland). 2f. |
| Iglesia de Dios (Cleveland) | 1940 | P Pe3 | ZF••• | 34 | 2,000 | 4,500 | *Ch of God.* M=CoG(Cleveland) (USA). Begun by laymen from Argentina. 22n,1p. |
| Iglesia de JC de los Santos de los UD | c1942 | M LdS | x•••• | | 12,000 | 16,053 | *Ch of JC of Latter-day Saints. Mormons.* M=CJCLdS(USA). 300f,G=6.4%pa. |
| Iglesia del Evangelio Cuadrangular | | P Pe2 | ZF••• | 1 | 75 | 300 | *International Ch of the Foursquare Gospel.* M=ICGF(USA). 1962, mission withdrew. |
| Iglesia del Nazareno | 1949 | P Hol | xF••n | 10 | 293 | 1,000 | *Nazarenes.* M=CoN(USA). 4n,3x,7m,6f,G=13.4%pa,1s(12),14t(878),W=90%,42Y,62z. |
| Iglesia Evangélica Armenia | 1930 | P Con | ••u•N | | 200 | 300 | *Armenian Ev Ch.* 1965, M=Armenian Missionary Association of America. Refugees. |
| Iglesia Evangélica del Río de la Plata | 1860 | P LuR | •wu•N | | 1,600 | 4,400 | *La Plata Ev Ch. Igl Ev Alemana.* 1899 union German diaspora congs (10% Reformed). |
| Iglesia Evangélica Menonita | 1966 | P Men | GFu•N | 4 | 150 | 306 | *Mennonite Ch.* M=MBCNA(USA). Germans,Poles,Russians. 2n,1x,4f,G=6%pa,2p,W=21%,19Y. |
| Iglesia Evangélica Metodista en el U | 1838 | P Met | Vuu•N | 47 | 2,730 | 6,000 | *Ev Methodist Ch of U.* A=1968. M=UMC(USA). 12n,2x,2f,G=25%pa,2r,2s,20t,W=20%. |
| Iglesia Ev Pentecostal de Chile | c1950 | I pe2 | x•••• | 3 | 600 | 1,500 | *Ev Pentecostal Ch of Chile.* Indigenous mission from Chile. Chilean Mestizos. |
| Igl Ev Valdense del Río de la Plata | 1856 | P Wal | R•u•N | 23 | 4,878 | 7,945 | *Waldensian Ch in River Plate.* Italian immigrants. Strong youth movement. 17n,1u. |
| Iglesia Menonita | 1956 | P Men | G•••n | 10 | 600 | 1,300 | M=GCMC(USA). Germans,Poles,Russians; re-emigrating. 22n,4x,G=–2.6%pa,1s,W=15%,28Y. |
| Iglesia Nueva Apostólica | | C CAp | x•••• | 100 | 15,000 | 20,000 | *NAC. New Apostolic Ch.* Many German immigrants. World HQ Dortmund (Germany). |
| Iglesia Ortodoxa Griega | | O Gre | Cwo•• | 5 | 7,000 | 10,000 | Part of 10th Archidiocesan District, Greek Orthodox AD of N&SAmerica. Greeks. |
| Iglesia Ortodoxa Russa (D Argentina) | | O Sla | x•••• | 1 | 500 | 1,000 | Russian Orth Ch Outside of Russia. M=ROCOR (New York, USA). Conservative Russians. |
| Iglesia Ortodoxa Russa (P Moscú) | | O Sla | Mwo•• | | 4,500 | 8,000 | *Russian Orthodox Church.* Under P Moscow. Russian emigres after 2 World Wars. |
| Iglesia Ortodoxa Ucrania | | O Sla | X•••• | | 500 | 1,000 | *Ukrainian Autocephalous Orthodox Ch.* M=UOCUSA. Ukrainian refugees from USSR. |
| Iglesia Pentecostal Unida | 1956 | P Pel | x•••• | 7 | 207 | 500 | *United Pentecostal Ch. Jesus Only Church.* M=UPC(USA). Unitarians. 2n,4f,2p(70). |
| Iglesia Reformada Ungara del Uruguay | c1956 | P Ref | ••u•N | | 300 | 500 | *Hungarian Reformed Ch of Uruguay.* Refugees from Hungary from 1956 and later. |
| Iglesias Cristianas Evangélicas | | P CBr | x•••• | 20 | 700 | 1,500 | *Ev Christian Churches. Plymouth (Open) Brethren.* M=CMML(NZ,UK,USA). 9f. |
| Misión de la Igl Luterana en América | 1948 | P Lut | l•u•N | 2 | 100 | 160 | 1952, M=Lutheran Church in America (USA). In Rivera. Begun from Argentina. 2f. |
| Nuevos Israelitas | | O sub | ••••• | | 500 | 1,000 | *New Israelites. Novy Izrail.* Russian Spiritual Christians from Rostov region, USSR. |
| Sociedad de la Ciencia Cristiana | | M Sci | x•••• | 4 | 200 | 500 | *Ch of Christ, Scientist. Christian Science.* M=CCS(Boston,USA). Montevideo. 6w. |
| Testigos de Jehovà | 1923 | M Jeh | x•••• | 62 | 3,370 | 7,000 | *Jehovah's Witnesses.* Watch Tower. Active witnessing under way by 1940. 405Y. |
| Unión Misionera Neotestamentaria | | P int | x•••• | | 200 | 500 | M=New Testament Miss Union(UK,USA). Strong in Paraguay, Argentina, Brazil. 2f. |
| Other Protestant denominations | | P | ••••• | | 1,000 | 2,000 | Total about 15 (see list below). |
| Other Non-White indigenous churches | | I pen | ••••• | | 500 | 1,000 | Total about 5 (see list below). |
| Doubly-affiliated (duplication) (1970) | | | | | –36,000 | –50,000 | Evangelicals who also are or were baptized Roman Catholics. |
| Disaffiliated (duplication) (1970) | | | | | –208,100 | –289,043 | Baptized Catholics now completely disaffiliated agnostics or atheists. |
| **Total affiliated (mid-1970)** | | | | **1,040** | **1,353,829** | **1,902,600** | **Total denominations (1970) . . . 55.** |
| **Total affiliated (mid-1975)** | | | | **1,050** | **1,407,100** | **1,977,400** | **Total denominations (1975) . . . 58.** |
| **Total affiliated (mid-1980)** | | | | **1,360** | **1,460,300** | **2,052,200** | **Total denominations (1980) . . . 61.** |

NOTES ON TABLE ABOVE

COLUMNS: for meanings and CODES (cols. 1, 3, 4, 8): see Codebook (Part 6). Column 1: **Boldface type** = church with over 10% of country's affiliated Christians.

NATIONAL COUNCILS (Column 4, 5th letter).

- N = Federación de Iglesias Evangélicas del Uruguay (FIEU) (Federation of Evangelical Churches of Uruguay).
- n = affiliate member of FIEU.
- R = Conferencia Episcopal del Uruguay (CEU)(Uruguay Episcopal Conference).

OTHER PROTESTANT DENOMINATIONS. These include: Apostolic Christian Ch (Nazarean), Baptist Bible Fellowship International (1959), Baptist Missionary Association of America (1965), Baptist World Mission (1964), Christian Ch of North America, Ch of God (Seventh-day), Ch of Scotland, Chs of Christ (Non-Instrumental), Ev Mission to Uruguay (Baptist), Gospel Mission of South America (1971), Independent Bible Baptist Missions (1950), Slavic Gospel Association, Uruguayan Evangelistic Mission, Worldwide Evangelization Crusade.

OTHER NON-WHITE INDIGENOUS CHURCHES. These consist of small groups from the strong indigenous pentecostal bodies in Brazil, Argentina and Chile. They include: Iglesia Pentecostal Independiente, Misión Iglesia Pentecostal (from Chile).

UNITING CHURCHES. Negotiations for organic union were under way in 1974 between: Iglesia Ev Metodista en el U, Iglesia Ev Valdense del Río de la Plata, plus 2 Argentina bodies (Iglesia Ev Metodista Argentina, Iglesia Ev Valdense), plus Iglesia Discípulos de Cristo del Paraguay.

**PEOPLES** (ethnolinguistic). Christians: 87.3% Uruguayan White, 3.0% Mestizo, 2.6% Italian, 1.7% Mulatto, 1.2% Galician, 1.1% German, 0.9% Brazilian, 0.9% Spaniard, 0.5% Russian, 0.5% Greek, 0.3% Black, Argentinian, Ukrainian, Armenian, Chilean, Polish, Czech, Slovak, Serbian, Croat, Bulgar, French, Basque, Amerindian, Assyrian.

## COUNTRY-WIDE TOTALS

EVANGELIZATION (see Part 5). 1900: 90%. 1970: 100%. 1980: 100%. *Mass evangelism.* Among recent campaigns: 1962, Billy Graham 8-day crusade in Montevideo; 1965–66, Pocket Testament League 6-month campaign (2 evangelistic teams, holding 400 meetings, disseminating 250,000 copies of Gospel of John, enrolling 6,000 in a Bible correspondence course); 1978, Luis Palau 23-day Crusade (101,000 attenders, 31 radio and 2 TV stations, 8,000 professions of faith (70% non-church members). *Radiophonic evangelism.* HCJB, FEBC, Radio Vatican, PTL (6,000 enrolments), ICI (615 enrolments), et alia.

FOREIGN MISSIONARIES AND PERSONNEL (nationals serving abroad)(1973). Total 369 in Argentina, Bolivia, Brazil, Paraguay et alia: about 350 Roman Catholics, 15 Protestants, 4 marginal Protestants.

FOREIGN MISSIONARIES AND PERSONNEL (aliens from abroad)(1973). Total 1,975. *From Western world.* 1,441: 950 Roman Catholics, about 320 marginal Protestants (280 Mormons from USA), 168 Protestants (132 in 27 USA societies, 10 in 1 Sweden society, 8 in 1 Finland society, 8 in 3 UK societies, 4 in 1 Canada society, 4 in 1 New Zealand society, 2 in 1 WGermany society), about 2 Orthodox, 1 Anglican. *From Communist world.* 8: about 7 Roman Catholics (4 from Yugoslavia, 3 Poland), 1 Orthodox. *From Third World.* 526: 490 Roman Catholics from other Latin American countries, about 25 Protestants, about 6 Latin American indigenous from Chile, Argentina and Brazil, about 5 Catholics (non-Roman).

INSTITUTIONS (church-operated)(1973). Total 130, including 95 higher schools (2 minor seminaries), 10 medical centres, 1 religious community, 7 research centres, 8 seminaries (7 Protestant, 1 RC), 3 study centres.

PERIODICALS. About 40 titles (25 RC, 6 SDA, 2 LdS).

PERSONNEL. About 3,785 (1,810 national, 1,975 foreign).

RELIGIOUS LIBRARIES. About 20.

SCRIPTURE DISTRIBUTION (1975). Annual totals: 15,490 Bibles (68% subsidized, 32% commercial), 45,392 NTs (57% free, 32% subsidized, 11% commercial), 120,988 UBS portions, 830,923 UBS selections.

SERVICE AGENCIES. About 68, including ACF(YWCA), ACI, APEC, CAJC(YMCA), CCCI, CCF, CEF, CEU, CIEF, CLC, FIEU, FRU, ICUI, INEL, IPRU, JAC, JEC, MCU, MEC, MFC, MIEC, MIJARC, MOAC, SGA, UCLAP, ULAJE, UNDA-AL, UNEC, WEC, WLC(EHC).

## ADDITIONAL DATA ON CHURCHES

IGLESIA CATOLICA EN EL URUGUAY. *Catholics.* Figures mostly from *AP 1970*, where M Montevideo reported 910,000 Catholics out of a population of 1,300,000 (70%). Since then numbers have increased rapidly. *Annual baptisms.* (1972) 95.2% infant, 4.8% adult. *Male religious personnel.* (1970) 693. Of all religious priests and brothers in 1970, 64% were nationals, 3% were from other Latin American countries, and 33% were from other continents (mainly Italians, Germans, French). *Sisters.* In 1970, 43% were nationals, 23% were from other Latin American countries, and 34% were from other continents (mainly Spanish, Italians and French).

*Catholic organizations.* The Uruguay Episcopal Conference (Conferencia Episcopal del Uruguay, CEU) is a member of CELAM. There is one organization for all (male and female) religious personnel, the Federation of Religious Personnel of Uruguay (Federación de Religiosos del Uruguay, FRU) which is a member of CLAR. The National Bureau of Priests (Mesa Nacional de Presbíteros) was founded in 1971, with one elected priest per diocese and 2 for the archdiocese; it collaborates closely with the CEU. Lay organizations include the following: JEC dealing with secondary education, Catholic University Movement (Movimiento Católico Universitario, MCU), Workers' Movement for Catholic Action (Movimiento Obrero de Acción Católica, MOAC), ACI, JAC and MFC.

The Holy See has diplomatic relations with Uruguay, and is represented to government and the Catholic hierarchy by the Apostolic Nunciature of Uruguay, with a nuncio in Montevideo.

Latin American secretariats for international organizations based in Uruguay are: International Catholic Association for Broadcasting and Television (UNDA-AL), with international headquarters in Fribourg, Switzerland; Latin American Union of the Catholic Press (UCLAP), which is the Latin American sub-secretariat of the Catholic International Union of the Press (UCIP), with headquarters in Geneva; and the Latin American secretariat for the International Movement of Farming Youth and Catholic Peasants (MIJARC), with headquarters in Louvain, Belgium.

Uruguayan groups and organizations involved in research and socio-religious action are: National Centre of Religious Sociology (Centro Nacional de Sociología Religiosa), operated by the episcopate and engaged in research on the priesthood; Centre for Investigation and Social Action (Centro de Investigación y Acción Social, CIAS), a Jesuit institution involved in theological research concerning social and cultural affairs; Centre for Religious Studies (Centre de Estudios Religiosos, CER), another Jesuit institution separate from CIAS but located at the same address, whose activities were temporarily suspended in 1972 due to lack of funds; Institute for Socio-Economic Development in Uruguay (Instituto de Promoción Económico-social del Uruguay, IPRU), which raises funds for development, trains social service leaders and furnishes technical assistance to national projects; Economia Humana, a socio-economic research team which carried on studies of the family in Montevideo in 1956 and in rural Uruguay in 1966; and Centre for Family Investigations and Studies (Centro de Investigaciones y Estudios Familiares, CIEF), which was founded in Lima at the general assembly of the Christian Family Movement in 1964 and began operations in Montevideo in 1966.

Institutions of pastoral and religious education are: Theological Institute of Uruguay (Instituto Teológico del Uruguay) which trains priests, brothers, sisters and laity; Centro Pedro Fabro, founded by Jesuits in Montevideo as a centre for theological reflection; Philosophical Institute of Uruguay; National Institute of Liturgical Studies (Instituto Nacional de Estudios Litúrgicos, INEL), founded by the Episcopal Conference in 1972 to provide for research and extension courses at the parish level; and Superior Institute for Adult Education (Instituto Superior de Catequesis de Adultos) which is involved in training programmes, research and publication.

The National Union of Catholic Education (Unión Nacional de Educación Católica, UNEC) sponsors 220 primary schools (70,640 pupils) and 90 secondary schools (23,883). Caritas Uruguaya has 2 programmes: Emmaus, which involves visitation and social aid in slum areas of Montevideo; and Castores de Emmaus, which constructs housing in urban slums and rural areas.

# VANUATU

## SECULAR DATA

**STATE. Official name:** The Republic (formerly Anglo-French Condominium) of Vanuatu/New Hebrides (Les Nouvelles-Hébrides).
**Flag** (shown above right): British Union flag, and French tricolour, until 1980; thereafter, national flag as shown.
**Area:** 14,763 sq.km. (5,700 sq.miles). **Description:** Over 70 volcanic islands. Agricultural land: 8.1%.
**Government:** State, formerly Anglo-French condominium, since 1906 (1887 joint Franco-British commission, 1980 Independence).
**Official languages:** Bislama, French (*Français*) and English.
**Capital:**.Vila (Efate) 13,294 (1973).
**Armed forces** (1976): French, British.

**DEMOGRAPHY. Population:** 77,988 (census of 28.V.1967. For 1970–2000 (UN), see last row of Table 1). Population density

(1975): 7/sq.km. (17/sq.mile). Under 15 years: 42%. Growth rate (1975–80): 2.74% per year (births 4.02%, deaths −1.17%, emigrants −0.11%). Life expectancy (1975–80): 55.9 years. Household size: 5.0 persons.
**Major languages:** French, English, Bislama (Pidgin English), Melanesian, Uvean, Vietnamese, Gilbertese, and about 110 other languages.
**Urban dwellers** (1970): 12.0%. Urban growth rate (1950–70): 2.8% per year.
**Labour force:** 45%.
**Tourists** (1968): 3,260. (1971) 16,000.

**ETHNOLINGUISTIC GROUPS:** 91.8% Melanesian (Mota, Nguna-Tongoa, Tanna, et alii), 3.8% French (3,000), 1.6% Polynesian (0.7% Wallisian (Uvean) (500), Tahitian), 1.1% British (890), 0.5% Vietnamese (360), 0.5% Gilbertese (370),

0.4% Fijian (350), 0.2% Chinese (150).

**MONEY** (1977). **Monetary unit:** New Hebridean franc (= 100 centimes); US$1 = NHFr 81.00.
**National income per person:** US$600. Average annual family income: US$3,000.
**Cost of living in capital** (1976): Daily cost of living: US$38.

**HEALTH.** Hospitals: 38 (891 beds). Doctors: 25. Lepers: 370 (3.9 per 1,000).

**EDUCATION.** Adult literacy: 60%. Schools: 274.

**LITERATURE.** Periodicals: 10. Newspapers: 9 non-daily.

**COMMUNICATION** (per 1,000 people). Phones: 9. Radios: 120.

TABLE 1.  RELIGIOUS ADHERENTS IN VANUATU (NEW HEBRIDES)

| Year | 1900 | | mid-1970 | | Annual change, 1970–1980 | | | | mid-1975 | | mid-1980 | | 2000 | |
| --- | --- | --- | --- | --- | --- | --- | --- | --- | --- | --- | --- | --- | --- | --- |
| Name | Adherents | % | Adherents | % | Natural | Conversion | Total | Rate | Adherents | % | Adherents | % | Adherents | % |
| Christians | 14,500 | 32.2 | 77,100 | 91.8 | 2,524 | 283 | 2,807 | 3.13 | 89,750 | 93.5 | 105,170 | 94.7 | 182,820 | 96.2 |
| professing | 14,500 | 32.2 | 77,100 | 91.8 | 2,524 | 283 | 2,807 | 3.13 | 89,750 | 93.5 | 105,170 | 94.7 | 182,820 | 96.2 |
| Protestants | 8,000 | 17.8 | 43,900 | 52.3 | 1,450 | 227 | 1,677 | 3.25 | 51,550 | 53.7 | 60,670 | 54.6 | 112,120 | 59.0 |
| Roman Catholics | 4,500 | 10.0 | 13,700 | 16.3 | 447 | 63 | 510 | 3.21 | 15,900 | 16.6 | 18,800 | 16.9 | 32,700 | 17.2 |
| Anglicans | 2,000 | 4.4 | 12,100 | 14.4 | 394 | 36 | 430 | 3.07 | 14,000 | 14.6 | 16,400 | 14.8 | 28,500 | 15.0 |
| Melanesian indigenous | 0 | 0.0 | 7,400 | 8.8 | 233 | −43 | 190 | 2.29 | 8,300 | 8.6 | 9,300 | 8.4 | 9,500 | 5.0 |
| nominal | 1,700 | 3.8 | 6,291 | 7.5 | 213 | 107 | 320 | 4.22 | 7,590 | 7.9 | 9,490 | 8.5 | 18,720 | 9.8 |
| affiliated | 12,800 | 28.4 | 70,809 | 84.3 | 2,311 | 176 | 487 | 3.03 | 82,160 | 85.6 | 95,680 | 86.2 | 164,100 | 86.4 |
| total practising | 12,160 | 95 | 63,020 | 89 | 2,057 | 157 | 2,214 | 3.03 | 73,120 | 89 | 85,160 | 89 | 131,280 | 80 |
| non-practising | 640 | 5 | 7,790 | 11 | 254 | 19 | 273 | 3.02 | 9,040 | 11 | 10,500 | 11 | 32,820 | 20 |
| Protestants | 7,000 | 15.6 | 40,200 | 47.9 | 1,317 | 123 | 1,440 | 3.08 | 46,800 | 48.8 | 54,600 | 49.2 | 99,200 | 52.2 |
| Evangelicals | 6,500 | 14.4 | 13,000 | 15.5 | 428 | 62 | 490 | 3.22 | 15,200 | 15.8 | 17,900 | 16.1 | 33,200 | 17.5 |
| Roman Catholics | 4,000 | 8.9 | 13,169 | 15.7 | 433 | 60 | 493 | 3.20 | 15,400 | 16.0 | 18,100 | 16.3 | 31,300 | 16.5 |
| Anglicans | 1,800 | 4.0 | 10,000 | 11.9 | 326 | 34 | 360 | 3.10 | 11,600 | 12.1 | 13,600 | 12.3 | 23,700 | 12.5 |
| Melanesian indigenous | 0 | 0.0 | 7,400 | 8.8 | 233 | −43 | 190 | 2.29 | 8,300 | 8.6 | 9,300 | 8.4 | 9,500 | 5.0 |
| Marginal Protestants | 0 | 0.0 | 40 | 0.0 | 2 | 2 | 4 | 6.67 | 60 | 0.0 | 80 | 0.0 | 400 | 0.2 |
| Tribal religionists | 30,500 | 67.8 | 6,530 | 7.8 | 163 | −286 | −123 | −2.12 | 5,800 | 6.0 | 5,300 | 4.8 | 5,700 | 3.0 |
| Non-religious | 0 | 0.0 | 200 | 0.2 | 7 | 3 | 10 | 4.00 | 250 | 0.3 | 300 | 0.3 | 1,000 | 0.5 |
| Baha'is | 0 | 0.0 | 100 | 0.1 | 4 | 2 | 6 | 4.62 | 130 | 0.1 | 160 | 0.1 | 400 | 0.2 |
| Buddhists | 0 | 0.0 | 70 | 0.1 | 2 | −2 | 0 | 0.00 | 70 | 0.1 | 70 | 0.1 | 80 | 0.0 |
| Country's population | 45,100 | 100.0 | 84,000 | 100.0 | 2,700 | 0 | 2,700 | 2.81 | 96,000 | 100.0 | 111,000 | 100.0 | 190,000 | 100.0 |

**COLUMNS, ROWS.** For meanings and definitions, see Codebook (Part 6). Note that, by definition, total 'Christians' = professing + crypto-Christians, which also = affiliated + nominal Christians. Percentages may not always total exactly, due to rounding.
**CENSUSES. 28.V.1967:** 52.2% Protestants (40.0% Presbyterians, 5.7% SD Adventists, 5.1% Churches of Christ), 16.1% Roman Catholics, 14.3% Anglicans, 8.8% Melanesian indigenous (6.0% John Frum cults, 1.6% French Protestant), 8.5% tribal religionists, 0.1% other religionists.

**NOTES ON RELIGIONS**
**BAHA'IS.** Begun 1953. Growth from 1 local spiritual assembly (1964) to 4 (1973).

**BUDDHISTS.** North Vietnamese (Tonkinese), and a few Chinese.
**MELANESIAN INDIGENOUS.** Two distinct groupings: (a) indigenous churches of main-line Christian type (Eglise Libre, and other congregations), and (b) those cargo cults, particularly the 3 John Frum factions, of anti-mission type which have broken off from Western mission-related churches. Although rejecting much of Christianity, these latter protest movements retain enough Christian elements for them to be classified as here, as part of the worldwide complex of anti-Western indigenous churches and movemen's.
**NON-RELIGIOUS.** Mainly French.
**ROMAN CATHOLICS.** In 1900, 1,000 baptized Catholics, 3,000 catechumens.
**TRIBAL RELIGIONISTS.** Animists (termed followers of

Custom) are still numerous on Aniwa (61.7% of the population in 1967), and are significant minorities on Santo (18.6%) and Vao (11.7%). Many have been non-Christian adherents of cargo cults. On Tanna (population 10,976 in 1967), however, of the 78.8% of the population recorded in the census as followers of Custom, only about half were persons retaining their traditional animism in unbroken continuity over the years; the other half were ex-Presbyterians (with some ex-Catholics and ex-SDAs) who rejected the missions from 1935 onwards and still remain followers of the John Frum cargo cults, which are enumerated in this survey as Melanesian indigenous churches. The rest of the Tanna population in 1967 were 14.8% Presbyterians, 3.0% Roman Catholics, and 2.8% SDAs.

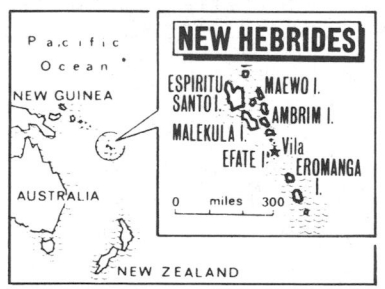

## NON-CHRISTIAN RELIGIONS. Traditional religion, popularly known in the New Hebrides as Custom, was the professed faith of over 8% of the population in 1967. Followers of Custom are predominant on Tanna and Aniwa while significant minorities are also found on Santo and Vao. By 1973 a total of over 8 distinct cargo cults had arisen in the New Hebrides.
**Baha'i** had 4 local spiritual assemblies in 1973.

## CHRISTIANITY
**PROTESTANT CHURCHES.** The first missionary to the New Hebrides was John Williams of the London Missionary Society who was martyred on the island of Eromanga in 1839. Presbyterians from Nova Scotia in Canada arrived in 1848 and were later followed by others from Scotland, Australia and New Zealand. The Presbyterian Church is the principal denomination of the islands, and has been autonomous since 1948. In 1967 the population identified itself as 40% Presbyterian. Presbyterians are almost entirely absent from the Torres and Banks Islands of the north, but they form the majority on most of

the other islands with the exception of Tanna (Tana) and Aniwa (where Custom predominates) and the Malekula offshore islands of Vao, Atchin and Wala. In 1970 the church had responsibility for 148 schools and 2 hospitals.

Adventists (5.7% of the population in 1967) have

been active since 1912. They are scattered throughout the islands and form about half the population of Aore, Atchin and Buninga. They are also well represented in Vao and Wala. The Churches of Christ (5.1% in 1967) are assisted by the Australian Churches of Christ Mission. They are strong in Aoba, Maewo

**Presbyterian Church of New Hebrides.** A congregation on Tanna leaves church on Sunday. Presbyterians on Tanna numbered 90% of the population until mass defections from 1940-45 to the John Frum cult; now they number only 15%.

**Church of Melanesia, Diocese of Vanuatu.** An Anglican priest vested for the Eucharist.

and Pentecost as well as on some of the Santo offshore islands including Tutuba and Malo where they form respectively 42% and 16% of the population. The Apostolic Church came to the New Hebrides from Australia in 1945. Apostolics are largely restricted to Aoba where they account for 10% of the population. The Assemblies of God have been represented at Vila on Efate Island by a Fijian pastor since 1967, and the small Independent Presbytery Mission from Australia has one congregation on Malekula Island.

CATHOLIC CHURCH. Although the first Catholic missionaries arrived in Eromanga as early as 1839, systematic evangelization did not begin until 1887. A prefecture was established in 1901, becoming a vicariate in 1904. The first national priest was ordained in 1955. Catholics are predominant on the islands of Vao, Atchin and Wala, and the church's 17 resident priests are distributed on the following islands: Efate 3, Malekula 3, Ambrym 2, Pentecost 3, Espiritu Santo 3, Aoba 1, and Tanna 2. Catholics were 16.1% of the population in 1967.

ANGLICAN CHURCH. Anglican missionaries arrived from New Zealand in 1848 and concentrated

their attention on the northern islands. The Banks and Torres islanders are today almost exclusively Anglican, and in Aoba, Maewo and Pentecost about half the combined populations also are Anglicans. Elsewhere their numbers are negligible. The Diocese of New Hebrides is part of the Church of the Province of Melanesia, formed in 1975 and based on Honiara, Solomon Islands.

INDIGENOUS CHURCHES. The John Frum cargo cults, of which there are 3 distinct factions, began from 1935 and still have followers. The movement was begun on Tanna Island among large numbers of Presbyterians and grew in strength after the arrival of North American military personnel with their extensive material possessions during Word War II. As with other cargo cults, the principal belief of the faithful concerns the predicted arrival of mythical figure John Frum (Frum=Broom), whom would sweep away all Whites and would bring great wealth to the local population. Although many members have been former Presbyterians, the movement has adopted a number of nativistic elements and has often taken an anti-missionary, anti-government stance.

The Free Church was founded through the missionary activity of an indigenous group from New Caledonia which split from the Evangelical Church of New Caledonia and the Loyalty Islands. Although their official title is the Free Church, they are locally known as the French Protestant Church. They are found mainly on Atchin and Wala, although there are small groups on Santo and Malekula as well. Another body, the Voice of Daniel, was formed in 1932 as the result of a schism from the Anglican Church on Pentecost Island.

CHURCH AND STATE. The first European to set eyes on the islands was a Spanish navigator in 1606, with Captain James Cook making a more thorough exploration in 1774. Sandalwood was discovered at Port Resolution in 1825 which stimulated European trade and settlement, mostly French and British. A decline in the supply of sandalwood prompted some traders to turn to labour recruitment (popularly called blackbirding) for the cotton plantations of Fiji and the cotton and sugar plantations of Queensland. Missionary protest at the abuses of blackbirding forced the passage of the Pacific Islanders Protection Bill by the British parliament in 1872. A joint French-British condominium was declared in 1906, with full guarantees for the free practice of religion.

Until 1980, the territory was secular in its attitude to religion. In 1979 in preparation for Independence, however, the new constitution affirmed the Christian faith: 'We the people of the New Hebrides proclaim the establishment of the United and Free Republic of the New Hebrides, founded on traditional Melanesian values, faith in God and Christian principles'.

INTERDENOMINATIONAL ORGANIZATIONS. The New Hebrides Christian Council was founded in 1967 and includes as full members Anglican, Catholic and Presbyterian churches, and the Churches of Christ. The Adventist and Apostolic churches are observer members. The council co-ordinates joint activities in literature translation, religious broadcasting and an interdenominational chapel in the new central hospital.

**John Frum cargo cults.** At Sulphur Bay, cargo cult centre on Tanna island, an adherent ('missionary') performs cultus in front of red-painted image of mythical cult founder John Frum, red-painted crosses, and red-painted aircraft, which symbolizes imminent arrival of cargo (cars, machines, clothes, utensils, etc). Adherents number 79% of Tanna's population.

BROADCASTING. Although the government station Radio Vila offers free time to the churches for religious broadcasts, no Protestant or Catholic programmes have been produced in recent years. For Catholics, an association grouping New Hebrides with New Caledonia is a member of UNDA.

## BIBLIOGRAPHY

'Culture contact and the John Frum movements on Tanna, New Hebrides', J. Guiart, *Southwestern journal of anthropology*, 12 (1956), 105–116. (Review from 1774 to 1955).
'John Frum movement in Tanna', J. Guiart, *Oceania*, 22 (1951), 165–75.
'Les missions dans la Pacifique', *Journal de la Société des Océanistes*, XXV, 25 (December, 1969).
'Les mouvements de John Frum et de Tieka: deux faits sociaux totaux aux Nouvelles-Hébrides', P. Martin, *Le monde non-chrétien*, 43–44 (July–Dec, 1957), 225–265.
*Misi Gete: John Geddie, pioneer missionary to the New Hebrides.* Ed R.S. Miller. Launceston (Australia): Presbyterian Church of Tasmania, 1975.
'Naked cult in central west Santo', J.G. Miller, *Journal of the Polynesian Society*, 57, 4 (1948), 330–341.
'The movements in the New Hebrides', in P. Worsley, *The trumpet shall sound: a study of cargo cults in Melanesia* (New York: Schocken, 1968), p.146–169.

TABLE 2. ORGANIZED CHURCHES AND DENOMINATIONS IN VANUATU (NEW HEBRIDES)

| Official name 1 | Begun 2 | Type 3 | Counc 4 | Congs 5 | Adults 6 | Affiliated 7 | Names, notes, and other statistics (see Codebook) 8 |
|---|---|---|---|---|---|---|---|
| Apostolic Church | 1945 | P PeA | Z...k | 2 | 500 | 800 | M=Apostolic Ch of Australia & NZ,ACMM(UK). On Aoba, with a few on Santo and Malo. |
| Assemblies of God | 1968 | P Pe2 | ZF... | 17 | 629 | 1,000 | M=AoG(USA). Classical Pentecostals (2-stage). Fijian pastor in Vila from 1967. 6n. |
| Catholic Church: D Port Vila | 1839 | R Lat | P.PYK | 15 | 7,600 | 13,169 | Suffragan, M Nouméa. M=SM2. 23% aliens. C=1+1+2. 3n,23x,4m,89w,P=79%,402Yy,100z. |
| Church of Melanesia: D Vanuatu | 1848 | A ACa | AwpKK | 82 | 7,000 | 10,000 | HQ Honiara. Formerly in CPNZ. Includes New Caledonia. 20m,10w,W=75%,20Y,500y. |
| Churches of Christ in Vanuatu | 1903 | P Dis | x.P.K | | 2,000 | 3,900 | Begun by deported Kanakas. M=Australian Churches of Christ Mission. On Aoba. 16f. |
| Free Church | | I Ref | ..... | | 800 | 1,200 | *Eglise Libre. French Protestant Church.* Mission of schism ex EENC(New Caledonia). |
| Independent Presbytery Mission | c1968 | P Ref | ..... | 1 | 100 | 200 | Centre on Malekula. Schism in Australia ex Presbyterian Ch of Australia. 1f. |
| Jehovah's Witnesses | 1933 | M Jeh | x.... | 1 | 19 | 40 | *Watch Tower. IBSA.* Placed under Australian branch 1933. |
| John Frum cargo cults | c1935 | I mar | ..... | | 1,600 | 4,000 | Frum=Broom. 3 cults on Tanna, ex Presbyterians. Red crosses, flags. HQ Sulphur Bay. |
| Nagriamel (Palm Tree) Church of Christ | 1967 | I mar | ..... | 1 | 400 | 1,000 | Linked to land reappropriation movement. Ex Chs of Christ. HQ Fanafo, SW Santo. 2n. |
| Presbyterian Ch of Vanuatu | 1848 | P Ref | RWP.K | 220 | 8,616 | 30,000 | M=PCs of Australia, NZ, Canada; FCS(UK). A=1948. 33n,9x,G=0.4%pa,2H,1p(6),822Yy. |
| Seventh-day Adventist Church | 1912 | P Adv | x...k | 28 | 2,619 | 4,300 | *SDA, NH Mission,* Central Pacific Union Mission. 7nx,91mw,1H,1s,53t(3100),131Y. |
| Voice of Daniel | 1932 | I Ang | ..... | | 80 | 200 | *Silon Daniel.* Vision by Anglican lay reader Daniel Tambe. In Raga, Pentecost. |
| Other Melanesian indigenous churches | | I mar | ..... | | 500 | 1,000 | Several of the 8 cargo cults have produced christianized congregations. |
| **Total affiliated (mid-1970)** | | | | **510** | **32,463** | **70,809** | Total denominations (1970) . . . **15.** |
| **Total affiliated (mid-1975)** | | | | **540** | **37,700** | **82,160** | Total denominations (1975) . . . **16.** |
| **Total affiliated (mid-1980)** | | | | **570** | **43,900** | **95,680** | Total denominations (1980) . . . **17.** |

## NOTES ON TABLE ABOVE

COLUMNS: for meanings and CODES (cols. 1, 3, 4, 8): see Codebook, (Part 6). Column 1: **Boldface type** = church with over 10% of country's affiliated Christians.
NATIONAL COUNCILS (Column 4, 5th letter).
K = Vanuatu Christian Council (VCC).
k = observer member of VCC.
*Local councils.* Santo Community Project Committee.

**PEOPLES** (ethnolinguistic). Christians: 90.2% Melanesian (Mota, Nguna-Tongoa, Tanna, et alii), 4.5% French, 2.0% Polynesian (0.8% Wallisian), 1.2% British, 0.9% Solomoni, 0.6% Gilbertese, 0.3% Vietnamese, 0.3% Fijian, Samoan, Tongan, Chinese.

**COUNTRY-WIDE TOTALS**
EVANGELIZATION (see Part 5). 1900: 39%. 1970: 100%. 1980: 100%. *Mass evangelism.* 1969, Presbyterian campaign in the northern islands, with other denominations collaborating. *Radiophonic evangelism.* ICI (1,015 enrolments, 840 active students).

FOREIGN MISSIONARIES AND PERSONNEL (nationals serving abroad) (1973). Total 2 Protestants in Australia and New Caledonia.
FOREIGN MISSIONARIES AND PERSONNEL (aliens from abroad) (1973). Total 200. *From Western world.* 182: 88 Roman Catholics, 76 Protestants (57 in 3 Australia societies, 18 in 2 New Zealand societies, 1 in 1 USA society), 18 Anglicans (10 in 2 Australia societies, 8 in 4 UK societies). *From Third World.* 18: 7 Roman Catholics from New Caledonia and Wallis & Futuna, 5 Protestants, 4 Melanesian indigenous from New Caledonia, 2 Anglicans.
INSTITUTIONS (church-operated) (1973). Total 15, including 10 medical centres, 1 seminary (Protestant).
PERIODICALS. 6 titles.
PERSONNEL. About 425 (225 national, 200 foreign).
RELIGIOUS LIBRARIES. 2.
SCRIPTURE DISTRIBUTION (1975). Annual totals: 1,000 Bibles (subsidized), 2,100 NTs (95% subsidized, 5% commercial), 7,900 UBS portions, 22,200 UBS selections. *Translations completed.* Portion: 35 languages since 1853. NT: 10 languages

since 1863. Bibles: 3 languages since 1879.
SERVICE AGENCIES. About 8, including CV/AV, NHCC.

**ADDITIONAL DATA ON CHURCHES**
CATHOLIC CHURCH. *Annual baptisms.* (1972) 86.5% infant, 13.5% adult. *Priests.* Indigenous clergy are Marists; the first was ordained in 1955. *Brothers.* Frères du Sacré-Coeur. *Sisters.* 61 expatriates all of Soeurs Missionnaires de la Société de Marie, 28 indigenous attached to Petites Filles de Marie (local congregation founded in 1911, also covering New Caledonia). *Catechists.* Total (1969) 25.
*Catholic organizations.* New Hebrides is a member of the Bishops' Conference of the Pacific (Conférence des Evêques du Pacifique, CEPAC) with its headquarters in Fiji. Lay organizations include scouts, guides and CV/AV.
The Holy See is represented in New Hebrides by the Apostolic Delegation for New Zealand and the Pacific Islands with its seat in Wellington, New Zealand.
The Catholic Church has established a number of schools and dispensaries, and sisters serve in French government hospitals.

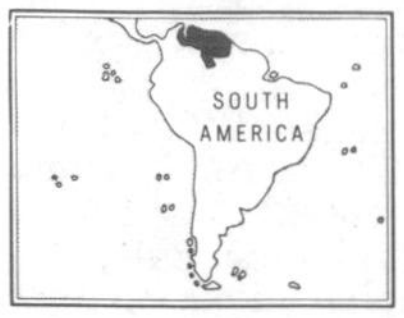


# VENEZUELA

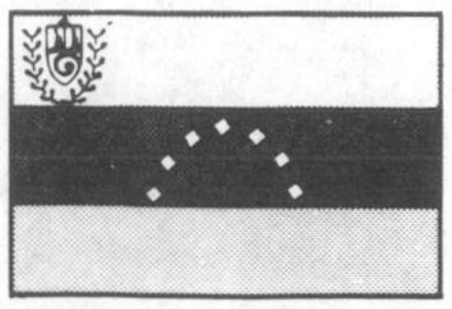

## SECULAR DATA

**STATE. Official name:** The Republic of Venezuela (La República de Venezuela). Adjective of nationality: Venezuelan (venezolano). **Flag** (shown above right): Yellow, blue, and red stripes, with 7 white stars in semicircle in centre, national coat of arms in upper hoist corner.
**Area:** 912,050 sq.km. (352,145 sq.miles). Agricultural land: 24.2%.
**Government:** Republic, since 1958 (1567 Spanish rule, 1811 Independence declared, several dictatorships, 1935 military junta, 1945 republic, 1948 military junta, 1958 republic).
**Legislature:** Congress: Senate, 55 members; Chamber of Deputies, 214 members.
**Official language:** Spanish (*Español/Castellano*).
**Chief cities:** capital Caracas 2,175,400 (1971), Maracaibo 651,570, Barquisimeto 330,820.
**Political divisions:** 20 States (divided into 156 Districts and 613 Municipalities), 2 Federal Territories (7 Departments), 1 Federal District (2 Departments, 2 Parishes), and Federal Dependencies (72 islands in the Antilles).
**Armed forces** (1976): Total 42,000 regular: army 28,000, navy 8,000, air force 6,000 (100 combat aircraft). Paramilitary forces: 10,000 National Guard.

**DEMOGRAPHY. Population:** 10,721,522 (census of 2.XI.1971. For 1970–2000 (UN), see last row of Table 1). Population density (1975): 13/sq.km. (35/sq.mile). Under 15 years: 45%. Growth rate (1975–80): 2.92% per year (births 3.56%, deaths –0.65%). Life expectancy (1975–80): 66.4 years. Household size: 5.3 persons.
**Major languages:** Spanish, Italian, English, Portuguese, Arawak, Carib, Guajiro, Chinese, and 30 smaller languages.
**Urban dwellers** (1970): 68.4%. Urban growth rate (1950–70): 5.7% per year.
**Labour force:** 31%.
**Refugees** (1977): About 10,000 from Chile.
**Tourists** (1971): 144,085. (1973) 284,603.

**ETHNOLINGUISTIC GROUPS:** 64.0% Mestizo (Spanish/Indian), 20.0% Venezuelan White, 10.0% Black (African Negro), 2.8% Amerindian (23 tribes, 296,000)(0.7% Carib, Guajiro (Arahuaco)(52,000), Bari (Motilone), Yanomamo), 1.3% Italian, 0.7% Colombian White, 0.4% Portuguese, 0.3% Cuban White, 0.3% Spaniard, 0.1% Chinese (10,000), 0.1% Jewish, Zambo (Amerindian/Negro), USA White, British, German, Polish, Basque, French, Catalonian. Total aliens: 6.1%.

**MONEY** (1977). **Monetary unit:** bolívar (= 100 céntimos); US$1 = Bs 4.28.
**National income per person:** US$2,048. Average annual family income: US$10,854.
**Inflation:** (1970–74) 4.7% per year (1975: consumer price index 138).
**Cost of living in capital** (1976: index 133 (Washington DC=100). Daily cost of living: US$45.

**HEALTH.** Hospitals: 340 (32,893 beds). Doctors: 11,222. Lepers: 25,000 (2.0 per 1,000). Blind: 18,000. Psychotics: 110,000. Criminals: 80,000.

**EDUCATION.** Adult literacy: (1950) 52%, (1971) 76%: Education rate: 71%. Schools: 10,591. Universities: 8.

**LITERATURE.** Periodicals: 500. Scientific journals: 90. Newspapers: 42 dailies, 21 non-daily.

**COMMUNICATION** (per 1,000 people). Phones: 45. Radios: 182. TV sets: 88. Daily newspaper circulation: 93 copies.

TABLE 1. RELIGIOUS ADHERENTS IN VENEZUELA

| Year | 1900 | | mid-1970 | | Annual change, 1970–1980 | | | | mid-1975 | | mid-1980 | | 2000 | |
|---|---|---|---|---|---|---|---|---|---|---|---|---|---|---|
| *Name* | *Adherents* | *%* | *Adherents* | *%* | *Natural* | *Conversion* | *Total* | *Rate* | *Adherents* | *%* | *Adherents* | *%* | *Adherents* | *%* |
| **Christians** | **2,297,700** | **93.0** | **10,155,100** | **96.2** | **343,886** | **804** | **344,690** | **2.93** | **11,747,900** | **96.2** | **13,602,000** | **96.2** | **22,310,000** | **94.7** |
| professing | 2,297,700 | 93.0 | 10,155,100 | 96.2 | 343,886 | 804 | 344,690 | 2.93 | 11,747,900 | 96.2 | 13,602,000 | 96.2 | 22,310,000 | 94.7 |
| Roman Catholics | 2,294,300 | 92.9 | 10,013,100 | 94.8 | 338,877 | 83 | 338,960 | 2.93 | 11,576,800 | 94.8 | 13,402,700 | 94.8 | 21,930,000 | 93.1 |
| Spiritist Catholics | 50,000 | 2.0 | 300,000 | 2.8 | 10,128 | –128 | 10,000 | 2.89 | 346,000 | 2.8 | 400,000 | 2.8 | 635,000 | 2.7 |
| Evangelical Catholics | 2,200 | 0.1 | 140,742 | 1.3 | 5,226 | 4,239 | 9,465 | 5.30 | 178,550 | 1.5 | 235,400 | 1.7 | 541,000 | 2.3 |
| Christo-pagans | 25,000 | 1.0 | 80,000 | 0.8 | 2,693 | –93 | 2,600 | 2.83 | 92,000 | 0.8 | 106,000 | 0.7 | 118,000 | 0.5 |
| Protestants | 3,400 | 0.1 | 99,000 | 0.9 | 3,513 | 587 | 4,100 | 3.42 | 120,000 | 1.0 | 140,000 | 1.0 | 259,000 | 1.1 |
| Venezuelan indigenous | 0 | 0.0 | 30,000 | 0.3 | 1,054 | 146 | 1,200 | 3.33 | 36,000 | 0.3 | 42,000 | 0.3 | 94,000 | 0.4 |
| Orthodox | 0 | 0.0 | 12,000 | 0.1 | 410 | –10 | 400 | 2.86 | 14,000 | 0.1 | 16,000 | 0.1 | 25,000 | 0.1 |
| Anglicans | 0 | 0.0 | 1,000 | 0.0 | 32 | –2 | 30 | 2.73 | 1,100 | 0.0 | 1,300 | 0.0 | 2,000 | 0.0 |
| nominal | 50,000 | 2.0 | 305,804 | 2.9 | 10,714 | 2,506 | 13,220 | 3.61 | 366,000 | 3.0 | 438,000 | 3.1 | 824,000 | 3.5 |
| affiliated | 2,247,700 | 91.0 | 9,849,296 | 93.3 | 333,172 | –1,702 | 331,470 | 2.91 | 11,381,900 | 93.2 | 13,164,000 | 93.1 | 21,486,000 | 91.2 |
| doubly-affiliated | –5,000 | –0.2 | –210,000 | –2.0 | –7,493 | –2,607 | –10,100 | 3.95 | –256,000 | –2.1 | –311,000 | –2.2 | –589,000 | –2.5 |
| total practising | 1,910,540 | *85* | 6,894,510 | *70* | 233,220 | –1,191 | 232,029 | 2.91 | 7,967,330 | *70* | 9,214,800 | *70* | 12,891,600 | *60* |
| non-practising | 337,160 | *15* | 2,954,790 | *30* | 99,952 | –511 | 99,441 | 2.91 | 3,414,570 | *30* | 3,949,200 | *30* | 8,594,400 | *40* |
| Roman Catholics | 2,247,100 | 91.0 | 9,775,054 | 92.6 | 330,384 | –4,029 | 326,355 | 2.89 | 11,286,650 | 92.4 | 13,038,600 | 92.2 | 21,151,000 | 89.8 |
| Catholic pentecostals | 0 | 0.0 | 200 | 0.0 | 585 | 7,395 | 7,980 | 39.90 | 20,000 | 0.2 | 80,000 | 0.6 | 500,000 | 2.1 |
| Protestants | 5,000 | 0.2 | 148,220 | 1.4 | 5,363 | 2,425 | 7,788 | 4.25 | 183,200 | 1.5 | 226,100 | 1.6 | 471,000 | 2.0 |
| Evangelicals | 4,500 | 0.2 | 128,000 | 1.2 | 4,631 | 2,109 | 6,740 | 4.26 | 158,200 | 1.3 | 195,400 | 1.4 | 410,000 | 1.7 |
| Venezuelan indigenous | 500 | 0.0 | 99,715 | 0.9 | 3,574 | 2,054 | 5,628 | 4.61 | 122,100 | 1.0 | 156,000 | 1.1 | 353,000 | 1.5 |
| Marginal Protestants | 0 | 0.0 | 21,667 | 0.2 | 849 | 484 | 1,333 | 4.60 | 29,000 | 0.2 | 35,000 | 0.2 | 70,000 | 0.3 |
| Orthodox | 0 | 0.0 | 12,300 | 0.1 | 421 | –1 | 420 | 2.92 | 14,400 | 0.1 | 16,500 | 0.1 | 26,000 | 0.1 |
| Catholics (non-Roman) | 0 | 0.0 | 1,200 | 0.0 | 35 | –35 | 0 | 0.00 | 1,200 | 0.0 | 1,200 | 0.0 | 2,000 | 0.0 |
| Anglicans | 100 | 0.0 | 1,140 | 0.0 | 39 | 7 | 46 | 3.41 | 1,350 | 0.0 | 1,600 | 0.0 | 2,000 | 0.0 |
| Tribal religionists | 123,000 | 5.0 | 200,000 | 1.9 | 6,427 | –5,227 | 1,200 | 0.58 | 207,600 | 1.7 | 212,000 | 1.5 | 235,000 | 1.0 |
| Afro-American spiritists | 49,000 | 2.0 | 100,000 | 0.9 | 3,220 | –1,020 | 2,200 | 2.00 | 110,000 | 0.9 | 122,000 | 0.9 | 165,000 | 0.7 |
| Non-religious | 0 | 0.0 | 49,000 | 0.5 | 2,458 | 5,202 | 7,660 | 9.14 | 83,800 | 0.7 | 125,600 | 0.9 | 702,000 | 3.0 |
| Baha'is | 0 | 0.0 | 24,900 | 0.2 | 878 | 132 | 1,010 | 3.37 | 30,000 | 0.2 | 35,000 | 0.2 | 65,000 | 0.3 |
| Jews | 300 | 0.0 | 12,000 | 0.1 | 0 | 0 | 0 | 0.00 | 12,000 | 0.1 | 12,000 | 0.1 | 15,000 | 0.1 |
| Atheists | 0 | 0.0 | 10,000 | 0.1 | 410 | 390 | 800 | 5.71 | 14,000 | 0.1 | 18,000 | 0.1 | 50,000 | 0.2 |
| Chinese folk-religionists | 0 | 0.0 | 5,000 | 0.0 | 132 | –232 | –100 | –2.22 | 4,500 | 0.0 | 4,000 | 0.0 | 3,000 | 0.0 |
| Buddhists | 0 | 0.0 | 2,000 | 0.0 | 59 | –59 | 0 | 0.00 | 2,000 | 0.0 | 2,000 | 0.0 | 2,000 | 0.0 |
| Other religionists | 0 | 0.0 | 1,000 | 0.0 | 30 | 10 | 40 | 3.33 | 1,200 | 0.0 | 1,400 | 0.0 | 5,000 | 0.0 |
| **Country's population** | **2,470,000** | **100.0** | **10,559,000** | **100.0** | **357,500** | **0** | **357,500** | **2.93** | **12,213,000** | **100.0** | **14,134,000** | **100.0** | **23,552,000** | **100.0** |

COLUMNS, ROWS. For meanings and definitions, see Codebook (Part 6). Note that, by definition, total Christians' = professing + crypto-Christians, which also = affiliated + nominal Christians. Percentages may not always total exactly, due to rounding.
CENSUSES. **1891** (excluding jungle Indians): 95.6% Roman Catholics, 0.1% Protestants (3,361 persons), 4.3% other religionists (including 247 Jews). The religion question has not been asked subsequently.

### NOTES ON RELIGIONS

AFRO-AMERICAN SPIRITISTS. The term describes non-Catholic and non-Christian adherents of the Culto Aborigen de Maria Lionza (Aboriginal Cult of Maria Lionza), which syncretizes African, Caribbean, Amerindian and Catholic religious elements. Each year in Holy Week, 30,000 make the pilgrimage to pray to the goddess Maria Lionza. There are also other cults including Shango (a Yoruba survival), and some Rastafarians (from Jamaica).
ATHEISTS. Parties: Communist Party of Venezuela (PCV; pro-Soviet) with 4,000 members, Movement of the Revolutionary Left (MIR), Union for Advancement (UPA), Movement to Socialism (MAS) with 5,000 members (all legal); Communist voters (election of 1.XII.1968) 103,368 (3% of all votes).
BAHA'IS. Rapid growth from 6 local spiritual assemblies (1964) to 166 (1973), especially among coastal Blacks and Guajiro Indians; over 1,000 Guajiro were enrolled as converts in May 1970 alone.
BUDDHISTS. Chinese.
CATHOLIC PENTECOSTALS (or, Catholic charismatics). Totals (January 1974): 1,000 involved adults (over 15 years old) including many priests, nuns and a bishop in 30 prayer groups, rising by 1975 to 6,000 in 190 groups; total charismatic community including children (1975), 20,000. In January 1976, over 25,000 persons attended the First National Charismatic Encounter in Barquisimeto, led by the Catholic archbishop (a charismatic) and 3 other bishops. In January 1977, ECCLA V was held in Caracas; at its conclusion, 30,000 attended a charismatic National Day of Prayer.
CHRISTO-PAGANS. Amerindians whose syncretistic folk-Catholicism combines 17th-century Spanish Catholicism with their own traditional animism, concepts and world-views.
DOUBLY-AFFILIATED. The term covers those affiliated to, or claimed by, the Catholic Church and also a church termed Evangélica by the state (Protestant, Venezuelan indigenous, Anglican, or marginal Protestant) or other church, i.e. baptized Catholics who have recently become Evanglicals or others. Because their statistics represent a duplication, they are shown in the table as a negative quantity (with a minus sign).
EVANGELICAL CATHOLICS. This term is used here to describe persons who are affiliated to churches termed by the state Evangélica (Protestant, Venezuelan indigenous, Anglican or marginal Protestant churches), but who are regarded by state and society as, or who profess publicly also to be, Roman Catholics.
JEWS. There are 2 groups. The Sefardis (originally from Spain) are the oldest, located mainly in the west (Coro area) and east. The Ashkenazis (originally from Eastern Europe) arrived after World War II from 1945 onwards.
OTHER RELIGIONISTS. Adherents of other non-Christian religions and syncretistic cults, including Muslims and Rosicrucians (AMORC, 17 Lodges and centres).
PRACTISING CHRISTIANS. Weekly mass attenders: in Caracas (1954) 12.7% of all Catholics, Barquisimeto (1964) 8.7%, Estado Monagas (1970) 16.0%.
SPIRITIST CATHOLICS. Roman Catholics involved regularly with the Aboriginal Cult of Maria Lionza, and other non-Christian cults.
TRIBAL RELIGIONISTS. Of the 296,000 pure tribal lowland or jungle Amerindians (including 52,000 Guajiros) in 1970, a high proportion are still animists and shamanists, including among the Chibcha, Arawak and Carib families.
VENEZUELAN INDIGENOUS. In about 33 denominations in 1970 (see Table 2).

**NON-CHRISTIAN RELIGIONS. Traditional Indian religions** remain influential among peoples of the Chibcha, Arawak and Carib families found mostly in the southern part of the country. The Yanamamö ('the fierce people'), saddling the Venezuela-Brazil border, have a population of 10,000 living in 125 villages. A violent, aggressive people living in a chronic state of warfare, they are one of the least-acculturated tribes left in all of South America. Their cosmology includes belief in the powers of medicine men or shamans (*shabori*), spirits (Yai) and a divinity called Wadawadariwa (Son of Thunder).

**Afro-American spiritism** is evident in the Maria Lionza cult which is a syncretistic movement composed of diverse African, Caribbean, Amerindian and Catholic elements. Central to its worship is the veneration of Maria Lionza, goddess of water and vegetation, who is associated by the populace with the Virgin Mary and popular Catholic saints, as well as with the Cacique Indians who resisted Spanish penetration at the Conquest, historical personages such as Negro Miguel (instigator of an uprising among the slaves) and even the nation's founding father Simon Bolivar. Maria Lionza is particularly venerated in the mountains of Sorte in Yaracuy state in the northwest, and also in rural and urban chapels and sanctuaries. Followers are drawn from all social classes, and include many nominal Catholics. The cult requires mediums or *bancos* who also supervise services and rituals. An attempt at unification of the various Maria Lionza groups was made in 1968 when the society was legalized under the name Aboriginal Cult of Maria Lionza (Culto Aborigen de Maria Lionza) with headquarters in Caracas.

**Baha'i** has grown phenomenally since 1964, from 6 local spiritual assemblies then to 166 by 1973. Coastal Blacks and Guajiro Indians have been most responsive.

**Judaism** is represented by 2 groups. Sefardi Jews originated in Spain and are the oldest Jewish community in Venezuela. They are most prevalent in the west and east. At Coro is located the oldest Jewish cemetery in Latin America. The second group are Ashkenazi Jews who came from central and eastern

Europe at the end of World War II.

## CHRISTIANITY

CATHOLIC CHURCH. Dominican and Franciscan priests arrived in the northeastern part of the country in 1513 and opened cocoa, coffee and sugar plantations as well as training the Indian population in stock-raising. Between 1658 and 1758, Capuchins founded 100 stations in the plains around Caracas, while Jesuits were opening missions along the Orinoco river. Much of this work was later destroyed before and during the wars of independence. A diocese of Caracas was established in 1637, becoming a metropolitan see in 1803.

Although Venezuela has been traditionally Catholic for centuries, a 1970 survey in 2 regions of the country demonstrated that 78% of the religious activities of the populace could only be explained or justified by them in terms of habit (as opposed to reason or personal conviction). Venezuela has an especially acute problem due to the failure to attract indigenous vocations to the priesthood. In 1960 only 18% of its priests were nationals, most of the rest being Spanish. However, more success has been achieved in recruiting Venezuelan sisters, 43% of the total being of local origin. An attempt at solving the problem of scarcity of priests is an experiment with 'parish curates' which was initiated in the slums of Caracas in 1969. These are sisters who have received 3 months' special training and who carry on pastoral work directly under the bishop in co-operation with priests. Since 1969 the dioceses of Barquisimeto, Cumana and Maracay have adopted a similar plan for rural areas and mission territories.

PROTESTANT CHURCHES. Although agents of the British and Foreign Bible Society visited Caracas in 1819, it was not until 1883 that the Brethren were able to organize a permanent congregation. The main thrust of Brethren activity came after 1910, and this is now one of the major Protestant denominations of Venezuela. Presbyterian missionaries from the USA arrived in 1897, but despite their extensive involvement in the development of institutions, the growth of the Iglesia Presbyteriana itself has been slow.

In 1898 an independent missionary couple opened work which was taken over in 1920 by the Evangelical Free Church Association (EFCA) and is now organized under the name Iglesias Evangélicas Libres de Venezuela. This church works closely with the Organización Venezolana de Iglesias Cristianas Evangélicas (OVICE), which was established through the missionary outreach of the Evangelical Alliance Mission (TEAM) in 1906. These 2 groups jointly founded the United Evangelical Seminary in 1969. TEAM built a press in 1907 and began publishing an evangelical newspaper, *La Estrella de la Manana* (Morning Star), which reaches every Latin American country.

Seventh-day Adventists appeared in 1910, and 8 years later the Orinoco River Mission entered eastern Venezuela, the latter work at present being included in the Asociación de Iglesias Evangélicas del Oriente.

The Assemblies of God, the first Pentecostal church to arrive and the country's largest Protestant denomination, came to Venezuela in 1916. They have experienced rapid growth in recent years aided by a network of Bible institutes, and recent evangelistic activity among the Guajiro Indians has produced many new members. The United Pentecostal Church and the International Church of the Foursquare Gospel have also built up important constituencies since the early 1950s.

Two Baptist denominations, related to Southern

**Afro-American spiritists.** *Above.* Folkloric event in May in town in Venezuelan Andes, combining elements of Catholicism, town saint's day, spiritism, and the Aboriginal Cult of Maria Lionza goddess of water and vegetation.

**Iglesia Católica en Venezuela.** *Below.* 'I am the Way, the Truth and the Life'. Massive statue of Christ in town of San Juan de los Morros, southwest of Caracas.

Baptists and Baptist Mid-Missions, are active; and the New Tribes Mission has created Christian communities among the Guaica, Maquiritare and Piaroa Indians. A host of other small mostly USA-based groups are also present.

INDIGENOUS CHURCHES. Venezuela has a significant number of churches begun solely by nationals. The earliest is the Alleluia Church, dating back over one hundred years. The largest, although it has suffered losses from recent schisms, is the Iglesias Nativas Venezolanas de Apure, commonly known as Bethel Church.

Most of Venezuela's indigenous churches are pentecostal in theology and worship. Some, such as the Iglesia Ebenezer and the Unión Evangélica Pentecostal Venezolana, both formed during the latter 1950s, rival the larger Protestant churches in membership; while many others are small denominations or independent single congregations.

OTHER CHURCHES. The first non-Catholic group to work in Venezuela were Anglicans, who began chaplaincy service for British nationals as early as 1832. The small Iglesia Anglicana de Venezuela was for long part of the diocese of Trinidad and Tobago of the Church of the Province of the West Indies, and in 1976 became a separate diocese. Six Orthodox churches are present, the largest being the Greek and Ukrainian churches. All are related to Orthodox bodies in the USA.

Jehovah's Witnesses, with a community of 20,000, have been in Venezuela since 1936.

**CHURCH AND STATE.** The constitution of 23 January 1961 invokes in its Preamble 'the protection of God Almighty', and then prohibits all discrimination based on religious belief (Article 16) and guarantees freedom of conscience and religion, specifying that 'Religious belief and practice may not be invoked either to avoid obeying the law or to prevent anyone from exercising his rights' (Article 65). Relations between the state and the Catholic Church, which have in the past been severely strained, are now regulated by a Bilateral Agreement drawn up in March 1964 between the Holy See and the government of Venezuela. It replaces the law of patronage (Ley de Patronato), voted in 1824 and ratified in 1830 at the time of the separation of Venezuela from Colombia. This law extended to the republican regime privileges originally granted to the Spanish crown, but in recent times these have had only limited significance. According to the 1964 Agreement, the government recognizes that the Holy See and the Catholic Church have legal status and guarantees their right to undertake work. The church informs the government in confidence of the names of candidates to fill episcopal vacancies prior to publication, in order that any 'objections of a general political character' may be discussed before the appointments are made public. Candidates for the episcopacy must be Venezuelan nationals, with the exception of nominees for missionary jurisdictions dependent on the Congregation for the Evangelization of Peoples in Rome. The state for its part pledges financial assistance to bishops, vicars general and cathedral canons, as well as aid towards the construction and maintenance of churches and seminaries. The rights of Catholic lay associations are also recognized, and bishops may request entry visas for foreign ecclesiastical personnel. Successive governments up to the present have accorded appreciable economic aid to churches and denominations in the country. Religious personnel receive no remuneration from the state, with the exception of dignitaries as noted above; and there is no general plan of subsidies agreed to by either state or church. Those grants which the state does make are given for specific projects or causes in special circumstances. Thus Catholic education recently received a subsidy to provide salary increases for lay teachers.

Ecclesiastical matters are the concern of the Department of Religion and Indian Affairs (Dirección de Cultos y Asuntos Indígenas) under the Ministry of Justice. This department is administratively responsible for keeping an up-to-date ecclesiastical catalogue (Nomenclador Eclesiástico) of buildings and religious personnel of the different churches and denominations, although in 1973 this was still incomplete. In addition, the department co-ordinates the state's activities concerning the Indian population with those of other involved agencies, particularly Catholic organizations to which the state is bound by the Law Concerning Missions (Ley de Misiones) of 1915. This law has only 8 clauses and refers to the Indian population from a strictly civil point of view, with the aim of incorporating them more fully into settled existence and into national life. Its application is entrusted to missionaries, in that the law permits the government to make contracts with religious orders concerning territories placed in their care. The Law Concerning Missions has not been reviewed since its promulgation, but recent legislation such as that on agrarian reform, which affects Indians as well as others, tends to reflect a new spirit. Thus Indians are no longer considered as second-class citizens, and there are no longer special privileges for missionaries.

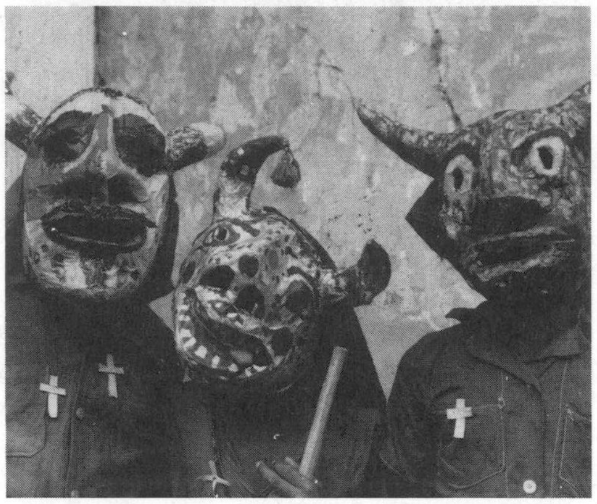

**Spiritist Catholics.** Los Diablos Danzantes (Dancing Devils) of San Francisco de Yare, Estado Miranda, on festival of Corpus Christi.

The Catholic Church is not formally linked to the state. However, the church often justifies its decisions and warnings on social matters by reference to the need to strengthen the functioning of democratic institutions which did not exist prior to 1958. The government, for its part, proclaims the importance of these institutions, while calling to mind from time to time the memory of recent dictatorships as an argument for them, in the same way that the church does. The Christian Socialist Party (COPEI) founded in 1946 and a Christian trade union (CODESA) begun in 1958 both owe their existence to Catholic initiative. These organizations, officially and through individual members, try to maintain their own identity as separate institutions, but they are not always successful. The political sympathies of the clergy are divided, and there is little to distinguish them at the popular level where church, state and Catholic political party tend to be seen as one.

**INTERDENOMINATIONAL ORGANIZATIONS.** The Venezuela Council of Churches (Consejo Evangélico de Venezuela) was organized in 1967, uniting most Protestant churches and missions in the country. It has no wider external affiliations. There is also a small English-speaking group, Ministerium, begun in 1965 and bringing together some 30 clergy and pastors of the main churches, as well as one Jewish rabbi, for monthly study meetings and social action projects. Catholic organizations responsible for ecumenism are the Secretariat for the Faith (Secretariado de la Fe), the executive arm of the Episcopal Conference's Commission on Faith, Morals and Ecumenism; and in Caracas, there is an Archdiocesan Commission on Ecumenism (Comisión Arquidiocesana de Ecumenismo).

**BROADCASTING.** All commercial radio stations accept religious programmes. There are 3 Catholic radio stations. In Caracas, the Servicio de Comunicación Social (SERCOS), begun by the Universidad Católica Andrés Bello produces radio programmes which are offered to stations and also to Catholic groups in charge of radio. There is also a national institution for radio schools, Acción Cultural Popular Venezolana (ACPOVEN), begun in 1961 under the name Escuelas Radiofónicas de Tovar. ACPOVEN has a radio station with, in 1970, 500 radio schools and 6,000 students. It has studios in Tovar and Caracas. In Acarigua, the commercial Radio Acarigua also has Catholic radio schools. For Catholics, Venezuela is a member of UNDA.

The Evangelical Alliance Mission in the Netherlands Antilles, off the coast of Venezuela, beams in programmes. The production and distribution centre of the Lutheran Hour in Spanish, Cristo para Todas Las Naciones, whose programmes are broadcast in many Latin American countries, is located in Caracas; and several other groups including Southern Baptists have production studios.

## BIBLIOGRAPHY


'A history of the Presbyterian Church in Venezuala'. C.A. Phillips. Caracas, 1958.

*Directorio de la Iglesia Católica en Venezuela, 1972–1973*. Caracas: CISOR, 1973.

*La Iglesia en Venezuela y Ecuador*. I. Alonso, et al. Fribourg: FERES, 1962.

*Maria Lionza, mito y culto venezolano*. A. Pollak-Eltz. Caracas: Instituto de Investigaciones Historicas, 1972.

'Venezuela', *Pro Mundi Vita* (Brussels), 14 (1966).

*Venezuela survey report: potential for revolutionary church growth*. A.E. Johnson. Fort Washington, Pennyslvania: Worldwide Evangelization Crusade, n.d. (c1967). 60p.


TABLE 2. ORGANIZED CHURCHES AND DENOMINATIONS IN VENEZUELA

| Official name 1 | Begun 2 | Type 3 | Counc 4 | Congs 5 | Adults 6 | Affiliated 7 | Names, notes, and other statistics (see Codebook) 8 |
|---|---|---|---|---|---|---|---|
| Asambleas de Dios en Venezuela | 1916 | P Pe2 | ZF... | 213 | 12,499 | 25,000 | *Assemblies of God*. M=AoG(USA). Losses to schism in 1957. 147n,13f,1s(27). |
| Asoc de Iglesias Bautistas Bíblicas | 1958 | P Bap | x.... | 4 | 100 | 200 | *Association of Baptist Bible Churches*. M=BBFI(USA). HQ Maracay, Aragua. 8f. |
| Asoc de Iglesias Evangélicas de V | | I ind | ..... | 8 | 200 | 400 | *Association of Evangelical Churches of Venezuela*. HQ Puerto Ordaz, Edo Bolivar. |
| Asoc de Iglesias Ev del Oriente | 1918 | P int | .M..C | 163 | 4,000 | 13,000 | *ASIGEO. Chs of East*. M=Orinoco River M. 5n,25x,47f,G=2.4%pa,1k,1s(20),W=61%,450Y. |
| Asoc de Iglesias Pentecostales Peniel | | I pen | ..... | 64 | 2,000 | 5,000 | *AIPP. Peniel Pentecostal Association*. Indigenous. HQ Caripito, Monagas. |
| Asociación de Igls Pente Peniel Libre | | I pen | ..... | 57 | 2,000 | 5,000 | *Free Peniel Pentecostal Association*. Schism ex AIPP. HQ San Juan de los Morros. |
| Asoc Evangelistica Peniel El que Vive | | I pen | ..... | 3 | 100 | 200 | *Peniel Pentecost Association 'He who lives'*. Indigenous pentecostals. HQ Caracas. |
| Centro Evangélico Pentecostal | 1964 | I pen | Z.... | 2 | 100 | 215 | *Pente Ev Centre*. Members Trinidad Blacks, Italians. Rapid growth. 1x,W=90%,2Y. |
| Consejo Luterano de Venezuela | 1949 | P Lut | L...C | 17 | 2,500 | 3,000 | *Luth Council*. Begun by LWF for large German influx. 3n,4x,6f,G=5.7%pa,W=10%,54Yy. |
| Convención Nacional Bautista de V | 1945 | P Bap | T...C | 70 | 1,833 | 6,000 | *National Baptist Convention of V*. M=SBC(USA). 30n,4x,33f,1k,1s(17),W=33%,209Y. |
| Hermanos Unidos | 1883 | P CBr | x.... | 106 | 8,000 | 20,000 | *United Brethren*. Formerly M=Canadian Brethren, CMML,UB(Scotland). 5n,20x,57m,1j. |
| Iglesia Adventista de Séptimo Día | 1910 | P Adv | x.... | 66 | 8,573 | 20,000 | *Seventh-day Adventists, E&W Venez Missions*. 24nx,145mw,6f,1h,2r,112t(9530),697Y. |
| Iglesia Alleluia | c1870 | I mar | ..... | | 500 | 1,000 | *Hallelujah Church*, based in Guyana. Macushi and other tribes straddling border. |
| Iglesia Anglicana de Venezuela | 1832 | A Hig | aw.J. | 10 | 339 | 1,140 | 1976, Anglican *D Venezuela*, Ch of Prov of West Indies. 1n,3x,3f,G=3.1%pa,W=80%,18Yy. |
| Igl Apostólica Venezolana y Misionera | | I pen | ..... | 9 | 307 | 1,000 | *Venezuela Apostolic Missionary Ch*. HQ Instituto de Hebron, Caracas. |
| Iglesia Armenia de Venezuela | 1910 | O Arm | Ew... | 5 | 200 | 300 | *Armenian Apostolic Ch of V. Gregorians*. Armenian immigrants since 1910. |
| Iglesia Católica Apostólica Venezolana | 1946 | I CCa | ..... | 20 | 1,000 | 2,000 | Schism ex Rome by 33 RC priests. M=ICAB(Brazil),Free Cath Ch in Germany. Caracas. |
| **Iglesia Católica en Venezuela:** | 1513 | R Lat | B.L.R | 844 | 5,376,000 | 9,775,054 | *Catholic Church*. C=31+3+78. 1q,5s(101),W=10%. 2284nx,562m, 960w,277002Yy. |
| M Barquisimeto | 1863 | R Lat | Bs | 66 | 322,000 | 585,000 | Area=Lara state. Both bishops are charismatics. W=9%. 145 17 207 18355 |
| D Guanare | 1954 | R Lat | Bs | 25 | 161,400 | 293,500 | Area=Portuguesa state, in west. 31 1 25 9125 |
| D San Felipe | 1966 | R Lat | Bs | 23 | 129,100 | 234,740 | Area=Yaracuy state, in northwest. 49 4 50 3554 |
| M Caracas | 1637 | R Lat | Bs | 87 | 990,500 | 1,800,000 | Huge urban area (2.2 million population). W=13%. 722 278 1646 35689 |
| D Calabozo | 1863 | R Lat | Bs | 37 | 195,500 | 355,500 | In Guárico state south of Caracas. 49 0 55 10890 |
| D La Guaira | 1970 | R Lat | Bs | 13 | 99,700 | 181,200 | Coastal area of federal district. 30 0 52 4764 |
| D Los Teques | 1965 | R Lat | Bs | 36 | 192,500 | 350,025 | Covers most of Miranda state. 153 121 174 15160 |
| D Maracay | 1958 | R Lat | Bs | 34 | 218,200 | 396,641 | City of Maracay (193,000) with sizeable rural area. 81 19 148 13676 |
| D Valencia en Venezuela | 1922 | R Lat | Bs | 58 | 324,000 | 590,000 | 1974, elevated as M Valencia en Venezuela. 119 10 168 19000 |
| PN San Fernando de Apure | 1954 | R Lat | Bop | 17 | 88,000 | 160,000 | Apure state. M=OP(Indian work). 1974, Diocese. 27 4 33 4069 |

*Continued opposite*

*Table 2–continued*

| Official name 1 | Begun 2 | Type 3 | Counc 4 | Congs 5 | Adults 6 | Affiliated 7 | Names, notes, and other statistics (see Codebook) 8 |
|---|---|---|---|---|---|---|---|
| M Ciudad Bolívar | 1790 | R Lat | Bs | 28 | 171,000 | 310,000 | Vast area across Venezuela (Guyana to Colombia). 67 7 90 7616 |
| D Barcelona | 1954 | R Lat | Bs | 40 | 207,000 | 377,000 | Area = Anzoátegui state, down to river Orinoco. 61 1 114 4731 |
| D Cumaná | 1922 | R Lat | Bs | 32 | 264,000 | 480 000 | Area = Sucre state in northeast, with islands. 47 1 59 6774 |
| D Margarita | 1969 | R Lat | Bs | 12 | 69,000 | 125,000 | Recently-formed diocese. HQ La Asunción. 23 1 37 3381 |
| D Maturín | 1958 | R Lat | Bs | 16 | 167,000 | 304,000 | Area = Monagas state. W = 16%. 21 0 30 5540 |
| M Maracaibo | 1897 | R Lat | Bs | 45 | 440,000 | 800,000 | Major oil-producing area, with Maracaibo (690,000). 183 38 387 23318 |
| D Cabimas | 1965 | R Lat | Bs | 21 | 198,000 | 360,000 | Bishop a leader in ECCLA (Charismatic Renewal in LA). 27 0 32 8964 |
| D Coro | 1922 | R Lat | Bs | 39 | 240,300 | 436,982 | First founded 1531. Covers Falcón state. 71 21 56 19052 |
| M Mérida | 1777 | R Lat | Bs | 53 | 187,100 | 340,136 | Area = Mérida state, in west. W = 41%. 91 14 152 16771 |
| D Barinas | 1965 | R Lat | Bs | 20 | 133,400 | 242,500 | Area = Barinas state, north of river Apure. 27 0 13 6776 |
| D San Cristóbal de Venezuela | 1922 | R Lat | Bs | 47 | 283,000 | 514,000 | Area = Tachira state, in extreme southwest. 118 2 275 17707 |
| D Trujillo | 1957 | R Lat | Bs | 53 | 212,000 | 386,000 | Small diocese in area, east of Lago de Maracaibo. 79 0 85 15900 |
| VA Caroní | 1922 | R Lat | Pofmc | 5 | 6,700 | 12,150 | In SE. Indians: Pemone, Taurepane, Arekuna. P = 10%. 11 2 18 593 |
| VA Machiques | 1943 | R Lat | Pofmc | 13 | 49,000 | 90,000 | 30 tribes: Motilone, Goajiro, Yupa, Paraujano. P = 13%. 17 18 19 3243 |
| VA Puerto Ayacucho | 1932 | R Lat | Psdb | 19 | 8,000 | 15,000 | Indians: Maco, Piaroa, Waica, Maquiritare. P = 23%. 12 9 12 1297 |
| VA Tucupita | 1954 | R Lat | Pofmc | 5 | 19,600 | 35,680 | Area = Delta Amacuro state. Guarauno Indians. P = 11%. 15 4 23 1057 |
| Iglesia Católica Liberal | | C Lib | xv... | 1 | 100 | 200 | *Liberal Catholic Ch.* St Martin, Caracas. HQ London (UK). 1965 applied to join WCC. |
| Iglesia de Cristo, Scientista | | M Sci | x.... | 3 | 100 | 200 | *Ch of Christ, Scientist. Christian Science.* M = CCS(Boston,USA). Caracas. 1w. |
| Iglesia de Dios Pentecostal | | P Pe2 | Z.... | 15 | 300 | 1,000 | *Pentecostal Ch of God.* M = PCG(Puerto Rico,USA). Classical Pentecostals. HQ Caracas. |
| Iglesia de Jesucristo de los SUD | 1966 | M LdS | x.... | 7 | 100 | 1,467 | *Ch of Jesus of Latter-day Saints. Mormons.* M = CJCLdS(USA). |
| Iglesia del Evangelio Cuadrangular | 1952 | P Pe2 | ZF... | 37 | 653 | 5,000 | *Int Ch of Foursquare Gospel.* M = ICFG(USA). In Tachira. 21nm,2f,1p(18),W = 77%,146Y. |
| Iglesia Ebenezer | 1958 | I pen | ..... | | 6,000 | 20,000 | *Ebenezer Church.* 1958 A.A.Allen faith-healing campaigns. 1,000 lost in schism. 1s. |
| Iglesia Evangélica Emmanuel | | I pen | ..... | | 1,000 | 2,000 | *Emmanuel Evangelical Church.* Indigenous Venezuelan pentecostals. |
| Iglesia Ev Pentecostal de Las Acacias | 1954 | I pen | ..... | 10 | 242 | 700 | *Pentecostal Ev Ch of Las Acacias.* Indigenous. 1x,G = 5.9%pa,W = 28%,30Y,15z. |
| Iglesia Independiente de Venezuela | | I ind | ..... | | 360 | 1,000 | *Independent Church of Venezuela.* Indigenous Venezuelans in independent groups. |
| Iglesia Nueva Apostólica | | C CAp | x.... | | 500 | 1,000 | *New Apostolic Ch.* In Canada Bezirk. Germans. World HQ Dortmund (Germany). |
| Iglesia Ortodoxa Griega | | O Gre | Cwo.. | 4 | 3,000 | 6,000 | In 12th Archidiocesan District, Greek Orthodox AD of N&S America. Greeks, Arabs. |
| Iglesia Ortodoxa Romana | | O Rum | Cwo.. | 1 | 300 | 500 | *Romanian Orthodox Ch*, SS Constantine & Helen, Caracas. In RO Miss Epis (USA). 1x. |
| Iglesia Ortodoxa Russa | | O Sla | Mwo.. | 3 | 500 | 1,000 | *Russian Orthodox Ch.* In D SAmerica, Orthodox Ch in America (USA). Russians. 1x. |
| I Ortodoxa Russa (D Caracas & V) | | O Sla | x.... | 7 | 300 | 500 | *Russian Orthodox Ch Outside of Russia.* M = ROCOR(USA). Ultra-conservative Russians. |
| Iglesia Ortodoxa Ucrania | | O Sla | X.... | | 2,500 | 4,000 | Branch of Ukrainian Orthodox Ch in the USA. Ukrainian refugees from USSR. |
| Iglesia Pentecostal Unida de V | 1954 | P Pel | x.... | 70 | 5,550 | 10,000 | *Jesus Only Ch.* M = UPC(USA). In 14 states. 42n,4x,6f,G = 18.5%pa,1p(50),W = 99%,800Y. |
| Iglesia Presbiteriana de Venezuela | 1897 | P Ref | RvU.C | 24 | 973 | 5,000 | *Presb Ch.* M = UPUSA. Widespread institutions. 8n,3x,6f,G = 2.7%pa,W = 36%,87Yy,134z. |
| Igls Bautistas de Delta, Monagas y G | 1924 | P Bap | x...C | 50 | 1,000 | 3,000 | G = Guayana. *Conferencia de IBDMG.* Baptist Chs in D,M,G. M = BMM(USA). 1n,5x,13f. |
| Iglesias de La Cruzada Mundial Ev | 1954 | P int | xF... | 17 | 140 | 750 | *Worldwide Ev C.* M = WEC(USA,UK). Many lost in split. 1x,6f,G = 7.0%pa,2k,1p,W = 47%,45Y. |
| Iglesias de la Misión Mundo Unido | 1924 | P int | xF... | 17 | 340 | 1,200 | *Asoc Ev de IMMU.* Since 1947, M = UWM(USA). 4n,3x,8f,G = 5%pa,1s(4),W = 70%,26Y. |
| Iglesias Ev Indep y Nacionales de V | | I ind | ....C | 32 | 1,000 | 3,000 | *Organización Venezolana de IEINV. National & Independent Chs of V.* HQ Maturín. |
| Iglesias Ev Libres de Venezuela | 1898 | P Con | xF..C | 51 | 1,093 | 3,620 | *Asoc de IELV.* 1920, M = EFCA; also VIM till 1949. 8n,10x,61f,G = 6.5%pa,1p,1s,234Y. |
| Iglesias Luteranas en Venezuela | 1951 | P Lut | x...C | 14 | 383 | 1,250 | *Conf of LCs.* M = LC Missouri S(USA). 2n,5x,3m,G = 4.1%pa,1s(7),10t(705),W = 30%,17Yy. |
| Iglesias Nativas Venezolanas de Apure | 1925 | I ind | ..... | 150 | 15,000 | 30,000 | *Native Chs in Apure State. Bethel Ch.* Lay founder Arístides Díaz. Many losses. |
| Iglesias Pente El Buen Samaritano | | I pen | ..... | 12 | 300 | 1,000 | *Good Samaritan Pentecostal Association.* Indigenous pentecostals. HQ Caracas. |
| Iglesias Pentecostales Emmaus | | I pen | ..... | 7 | 300 | 1,000 | *Emmaus Pentecostal Chs.* Venezuelan indigenous pentecostals. HQ Antimano, Caracas. 1p. |
| Iglesias Pentecostales Juan 3.16 | | I pen | ..... | 7 | 200 | 400 | *John 3.16 Pentecostal Churches.* Indigenous. HQ Barquisimeto. |
| Iglesias radiofónicas solitarias | 1959 | I rad | ..... | 50 | 700 | 1,500 | Isolated radio believers in jungles, mainly youths. R = 6500. BCCs: WEC,TEAM,&c. |
| Iglesias Unidas Hebrón | | I ind | ..... | 5 | 100 | 200 | *Hebron United Churches.* Indigenous groups around San Fernando de Apure. |
| Igreja Presbiteriana do Brasil | | P Ref | R.u.. | | 1,000 | 2,000 | *Presbyterian Ch of Brazil.* Immigrant Brazilians from large church in Brazil. |
| Misión Evangélica Venezuela | 1965 | P Pen | ..... | 8 | 600 | 1,200 | *Venezuela Evangelical Mission.* Mainly in Bolivar state. 10n,G = 32%pa,W = 76%,70Y,60z. |
| Misión Nuevas Tribus de Venezuela | 1946 | P int | x.... | 100 | 3,000 | 7,000 | M = NTM(USA). Indians: Maquiritare, Piaroa, Guaica. 61f,G = 8.4%pa,1h,1j,W = 80%,400Y. |
| Organización Venezolana de Igls Cri Ev | 1906 | P int | xM..C | 160 | 4,000 | 10,000 | *OVICE. Organiz of Ev Chr Chs of V.* M = TEAM(USA). Many schisms. 7n,16x,95f,1j,2s. |
| Testigos de Jehová | 1936 | M Jeh | x.... | 123 | 8,170 | 20,000 | *Jehovah's Witnesses. Watch Tower.* Active witnessing under way by 1940. 979Y. |
| Unión Cristiana Libre | 1964 | I pen | ....C | 9 | 160 | 300 | *Free Christian Union.* Indigenous. HQ Barquisimeto. 1n,G = 14.9%pa,W = 45%,18Y,16z. |
| Unión Evangelistica Mundial | | I pen | ..... | 6 | 429 | 800 | *World Evangelistic Union.* Indigenous pentecostals. HQ Puerto La Cruz, Anzoátegui. |
| Unión Ev Pentecostal Venezolana | 1957 | I pe2 | ..U.C | 100 | 5,000 | 10,000 | *Venezuela Ev Pentecostal Union.* Schism ex AoG. 6n,4f(from Puerto Rico),1p. |
| Unión Misionera Evangélica | 1967 | I ind | ..... | 63 | 1,550 | 7,000 | *Evangelical Missionary Union.* Indigenous grouping. 5n,G = 40%pa,W = 90%,60Y,200z. |
| Other indigenous pentecostal churches | | I pen | ..... | 100 | 3,000 | 6,000 | Total about 10 pentecostal groupings begun by Venezuelans (Mestizos and Blacks). |
| Other English-language congregations | | P com | ..... | 15 | 3,000 | 5,000 | Union Ch of Eastern V, United Christian Ch of Caracas, et al. USA expatriates. |
| Other Protestant denominations | | P | ..... | 100 | 2,000 | 5,000 | Total about 15 (see list below). Many independent congregations. |
| Doubly-affiliated (duplication)(1970) | | | | | –115,500 | –210,000 | Evangelicals who also are or were baptized Roman Catholics. |
| **Total affiliated (mid-1970)** | | | | **3,240** | **5,379,694** | **9,849,296** | **Total denominations (1970) . . . 88.** |
| **Total affiliated (mid-1975)** | | | | **3,500** | **6,216,800** | **11,381,900** | **Total denominations (1975) . . . 93.** |
| **Total affiliated (mid-1980)** | | | | **3,900** | **7,190,200** | **13,164,000** | **Total denominations (1980) . . . 98.** |

NOTES ON TABLE ABOVE
COLUMNS: for meanings and CODES (cols. 1, 3, 4, 8): see Codebook (Part 6). Column 1: **Boldface type** = church with over 10% of country's affiliated Christians.
NATIONAL COUNCILS (Column 4, 5th letter).
C = Consejo Evangélico de Venezuela (CEV) (Venezuela Council of Churches).
R = Conferencia Episcopal Venezolana (CEV)(Venezuela Episcopal Conference).
*Other national councils.* Alianza de Evangélicos (Alliance of Evangelicals).
OTHER PROTESTANT DENOMINATIONS. These include: Children of God International (in Caracas), Christian Ch of North America (Italian), Ch of God (Cleveland), Ch of God of Prophecy (1968), Chs of Christ (Instrumental) (1970), Chs of Christ (Non-Instrumental), South America Mission (1972), World-Wide Missions (1964).

PEOPLES (ethnolingustic). Christians: 65.5% Mestizo, 20.4% Venezuelan White, 9.5% Black, 1.3% Italian, 0.8% Amerindian (Guajiro, Bari, et alii), 0.7% Colombian White, 0.4% Portuguese, 0.3% Cuban White, 0.3% Spaniard, Zambo, USA White, British, German, Polish, Basque, French, Catalonian, Chinese (2,500).

COUNTRY-WIDE TOTALS
EVANGELIZATION (see Part 5). 1900: 97%. 1970: 99%. 1980: 99%. *Mass evangelism.* Among recent campaigns: 1962, Billy Graham crusades in Caracas and Maracaibo, and 1967 Billy Graham associates crusades in 3 cities; 1964, Evangelism-in-Depth (478 local Protestant churches from 30 denominations, 300,000 homes visited, 3,724 prayer cells formed, 17,791 professions of faith); 1978, Here's Life Valencia (CCCI). *Radiophonic evangelism.* Annual listeners' letters (1975): about 6,000 TWR, 310 HCJB, 81 FEBC, TEAM, WEC, Radio Vatican et alia.
FOREIGN MISSIONARIES AND PERSONNEL (nationals serving abroad)(1973). Total about 480 Roman Catholics in Costa Rica, Colombia, Kenya, Puerto Rico, Spain, Surinam, USA et alia.
FOREIGN MISSIONARIES AND PERSONNEL (aliens from abroad)(1973). Total 4,520. *From Western world.* 3,707: 3,253 Roman Catholics, 449 Protestants (408 in 30 USA societies, 23 in 2 Canada societies, 10 in 2 UK societies, 5 in 3 Australia societies, 3 in 3 New Zealand societies), 3 Anglicans in 1 Canada society, 2 Orthodox. *From Communist world.* 21: 19 Roman Catholics from Poland, 2 Orthodox. *From Third World.* 792: about 750 Roman Catholics from other Latin American countries, about 30 Non-White indigenous from Puerto Rico, Trinidad & Tobago, Jamaica, Brazil et alia, about 10 Protestants from 5 countries, 2 Anglicans.
INSTITUTIONS (church-operated)(1973). Total 370, including 310 higher schools (12 minor seminaries), 10 medical centres, 5 presses, 4 radio stations, 1 religious community, 10 research centres, 18 seminaries (10 Protestant, 6 RC, 1 indigenous), 1 university.
PERIODICALS. About 45 titles.
PERSONNEL. About 8,150 (3,630 national, 4,520 foreign).
RELIGIOUS LIBRARIES. About 44.
SCRIPTURE DISTRIBUTION (1975). Annual totals: 105,333 Bibles (43% subsidized, 57% commercial), 501,216 NTs (76% free, 10% subsidized, 14% commercial), 757,819 UBS portions, 4,212,732 UBS selections. *Translations completed.* Portion: 4 languages since 1948. NT: 3 languages since 1959.
SERVICE AGENCIES. About 78, including ACPOVEN, APEP, AVEC, CCCI, CCVM, CEF, CEV, CLAT(CLAST), CLC, CNAL, CONVER, CUSIC, FERVE, FIHC, IBO, INVICA JCFV, JCV, JOC, MAF, MEC, MFC, SERCOS, SU, TFP, UHC, UMAC, WLC(EHC).

ADDITIONAL DATA ON CHURCHES
IGLESIA CATOLICA EN VENEZUELA. Including 2,500 Chinese (1975). *New dioceses* (since 1972). In 1974 D Valencia became M Valencia, with as suffragans D Maracay and a new diocese D San Carlos de Venezuela. *Annual baptisms.* (1972) 98.1% infant, 1.9% adult. *Priests.* Of the 2,284 priests, 1,014 were diocesan and 1,270 religious (1972). In 1970, 82% were expatriates (mostly Spanish), 18% Venezuelan nationals (this latter is one of the lowest percentages for national priests in Latin America). Expatriate priests made up 70% of all diocesan clergy and 80% of all regular clergy. *Male religious.* 1,706 (1970). *Sisters.* In addition to those shown above, there were 197 others of unspecified residence. Of the total, 43% were Venezuelan nationals, 16% nationals of other Latin American countries, and 41% expatriates from outside the continent. *Catholic charismatics* (end of 1974). 6,000 adults including many religious personnel are active in 190 organized prayer groups in the Charismatic Renewal. *Seminaries.* One interdiocesan and one for adult vocations in Caracas, and one in D San Cristobal. *Catechists.* Total (1974) about 120, in jurisdictions under Propaganda. *Religious orders and congregations.* Priests (congregations with over 75 members in 1972): 224 SDB, 231 SJ, 97 OFMCap, 76 OP. Brothers (over 75): 156 FSC. Sisters (over 100): 282 Hermanitas de los Pobres de Maiquetia (of Venezuelan origin), 250 HH de la Caridad de Sta Ana, 216 HH Salesianas, 167 Dominicas Venezolanas (of Venezuelan origin), 152 Franciscanas del Sgdo Corazón de Jesús (of Venezuelan origin), 142 Misioneras Hijas de la Sgda Familia de Nazareth, 131 Hermanas del Sto Angel de la Guarda, 129 HH de San José de Tarbes, 123 HH Agustinas Recoletas del Corazón de Jesús, 120 Esclavas de Cristo Rey, 120 Hermanas Misioneras del Divino Maestro, 107 Capuchinas de la Sagrada Familia. *Catholic organizations.* The Venezuela Episcopal Conference (Conferencia Episcopal Venezolana, CEV) is a member of CELAM. There are 2 national organizations of religious personnel: Venezuela Conference of Male Religious (Conferencia Venezolana de Religiosos, CONVER) and the Federation of Sisters of Venezuela (Federación de Religiosas de Venezuela, FERVE). Both are members of CLAR, and they are related to one another through the Joint Secretariat of Male and Female Religious (Secretariado Conjunto de Religiosos y Religiosas). There are no national pastoral or priests' councils.

Lay movements are co-ordinated by the National Council of the Lay Apostolate (Consejo Nacional de Apostolado Laico), founded in 1974, and include: Christian Study Courses (Cursillos de Cristiandad, providing 1,250 cursillos between 1959 and 1970); Legion of Mary (Legión de Maria, with 1,121 praesidia and 14,030 active members in 1969); Christian Family Movement (Movimiento Familiar Cristiano, MFC, with 42 teams in 1970); Union of Catholic Men (Unión de Hombres Católicos); Union of Women for Catholic Action (Unión de Mujeres de Acción Católica, UMAC); JOC; Venezuela Catholic Youth (Juventud Católica Venezolana, JCV); and Venezuelan Catholic Girls (Juventud Católica Feminina Venezolana, JCFV).

The Holy See has diplomatic relations with Venezuela, and is represented to government and the Catholic hierarchy by the Apostolic Nunciature of Venezuela, with a nuncio in Caracas.

Latin American organizations established in Venezuela include the following: Latin American Federation of Workers (CALAT), which until 1971 was confessional in nature and was called the Latin American Federation of Christian Trade Unions (CLAST); Latin American Office for Christian Study Courses (Oficina Latinoamericana de Cursillos de Cristiandad), founded in 1968, with headquarters in Venezuela for the period 1972–76; International Federation of Catholic Men (FIHC), a regional office for the Rome-based organization; and the Secretariado Regional Latinoamericano de los Companeros Constructores (International Bouworde, IBO), founded in 1966 with its international headquarters in Belgium.

Concerning opinion groups, the Venezuelan Nucleus for the Defence of Tradition, Family and Property (Nucleo Venezolano de Defensa de la Tradición, Familia y Proprietad) is active in Caracas.

Venezuelan groups and organizations involved in research and socio-religious action are: Centre for Research in the Social (Sciences Centro de Investigaciones en Ciencias Sociales. CISOR), chosen in 1966 by the Episcopal Confernce as the technical organ for religious statistics; Gumilla Centre (Centro Gumilla), founded by Jesuits in 1968, for the study of the social doctrine of the church and to run a national programme of savings and credit co-operatives. In 1970 there were 78 co-operatives, 22,329 members, and a savings bank with substantial funds making 4 million loans. There are also: Caritas Homes Institute (Instituto de Viviendas Caritas, INVICA), which supervises family dwelling co-operatives) and Youth in Action (Jóvenes de Acción), a Christian youth movement founded in 1965 with 3,500 student members.

Institutions of pastoral and religious education are: Interdiocesan Seminary of Caracas (Seminario Interdiocesano de Caracas), affiliated to the Xaverian Pontifical University (Pontficia Universidad Javeriana) of Bogotá, Colombia; Centre for Religious Studies (Centro de Estudios Religiosos), an organ of FERVE founded in 1970, which is part of the Theological Faculty of the Xaverian University; Institute of Theological Studies (Instituto de Estudios Teológicos) of the Andrés Bello Catholic University, reorganized in 1973; National Pastoral Institute (Instituto Nacional de Pastoral); and Eastern Venezuela Pastoral Institute (Instituto Venezolano Oriental de Pastoral de Conjunto), founded in 1972.

Organizations for missionary action are the Venezuela Institute of Indian Languages (Instituto Venezolano de Lenguas Indigenas); and La Salle Foundation for Natural Sciences (Fundación La Salle de Ciencias Naturales), begun in 1957 for applied research in total national development, which has 2 specialized institutes mainly active in Bolivar state: Caribbean Institute of Anthropology and Sociology (Instituto Caribe de Antropologia y Sociologia, ICAS), begun in 1962 for the study of Indian peoples and modern rural life; and since 1966 the Centre for Indian Development (Centro de Desarrollo Indigena, CEDI), whose studies attempt to create self-governing and self-supporting Indian communities, and which has developed an extensive programme of experimental Indian farms.

Educational affairs are co-ordinated by the Venezuela Association for Catholic Education (Asociación Venezolana de Educación Católica, AVEC), grouping all Catholic private institutions. Of these, 69% are run by religious orders. Statistics for 1970 included 226,916 pupils, 9.4% of all in the nation. There were 287 pre-primary schools (19,787 pupils), 567 primary schools (150,260), 230 secondary schools (43,605), 29 teacher-training colleges (3,595), 44 technical schools (4,716), and one university (Andrés Bello Catholic University) with 4,953 students. This latter institution was founded in 1953 by the episcopate, and is run by Jesuits with faculties and institutes of law, engineering, education, journalism, arts, philosophy, psychology, theology, social sciences, economics and administration.

There are 2 important initiatives in adult education. The Faith and Joy Association (Fe y Alegria) was founded in Venezuela in 1955 and has since spread throughout Latin America. In 1972 its programme, under Jesuit direction, included 52 schools with 30,000 students. A second body is the Association for Promoting Adult Education (Asociación de Promoción de la Educación Popular, APEP), founded in 1964, which by 1969 was operating 56 junior trade schools affiliated with Catholic primary and secondary schools.

Caritas Venezolana has been at work in Venezuela since 1958, and in the interior since 1961. Another charitable organization, the Society of St Vincent de Paul (Sociedad de San Vicente de Paul), was begun in 1885 and by 1971 had 45 societies in the interior and 18 in Caracas.

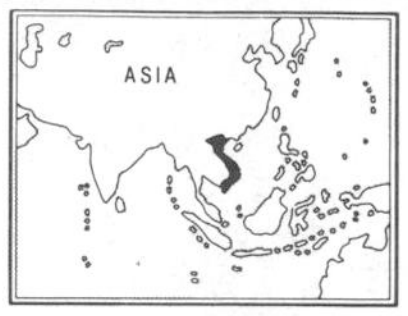


# VIET NAM

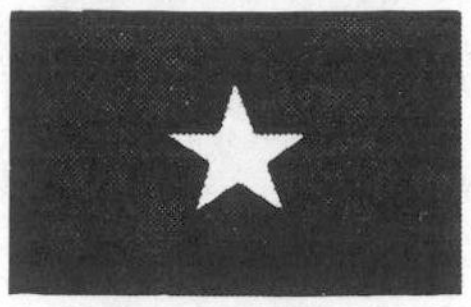

## SECULAR DATA

**STATE. Official name:** The Socialist Republic of Viet Nam. Names (and spellings) before 1976: (1) North: The Democratic Republic of Vietnam (Viet-Nam Dan-Chu Cong-Hoa); (2) South: The Republic of Vietnam (Viet Nam' Cong Hoa). Adjective of nationality: Vietnamese (vietnamien). In the pages that follow, the spellings used for 'Viet Nam' in English proper names follow the differing usages of the organizations themselves.
**Flag** (shown above right): Gold star centred on red field (North Viet-Nam's flag before 1976).
**Area:** 329,556 sq.km. (128,401 sq.miles). Agricultural land: 31.2%.
**Government:** One-party Communist state, since 1976 (Chinese rule until 939, 1471 unified empire, 1859 French conquest, 1867 South a colony, 1884 French protectorate over North and South, 1945 Independence declared by Ho Chi Minh, 1965 USA military involvement, 1975 South conquered by North, 1976 unification).
**Legislature:** National Assembly, 492 members.
**Official language:** Vietnamese.
**Chief cities:** capital Hanoi 414,620 (1973), Ho Chi Minh City (Saigon) 1,825,300, Danang 492,200, Nhatrang 216,230.
**Armed forces** (1976): Total 615,000 regular: army 600,000, navy 3,000, air force 12,000 (198 combat aircraft). Paramilitary forces: 1,550,000 (1,500,000 Armed Militia).
**Foreign forces** (North) 1973: 1,000 USSR military advisers, 20,000 PR China military advisers; (South) 1968: 536,000 USA troops. 1974: 250 USA troops only.

**DEMOGRAPHY. Population:** 43,451,000 (estimate for mid-1975. For 1970–2000 (UN), see last row of Table 1). Population density (1975): 132/sq.km. (341/sq.mile). Under 15 years: 36%. Growth rate (1975–80): 2.25% per year (births 4.05%, deaths –1.80%). Life expectancy (1975–80): 47.6 years. Household size: 6.2 persons.
**Major languages:** Vietnamese, French, Chinese, Thai, Muong, Khmer, Montagnard, English, and 60 others.
**Urban dwellers** (1970): 20.6%. Urban growth rate (1950–70): 5.5% per year.
**Labour force:** 52%.
**Refugees** (1977): From abroad, none. Internally displaced: 2,700,000 (decline from 1974 total of 4,500,000). Exiles abroad: 156,433 Vietnamese (127,766 in USA, 13,000 in France, 6,275 in Canada, 2,600 'boat people', 2,347 in Belgium, others in Malaysia, Philippines, Thailand). (1979): 240,000 Chinese in exile in China.
**Tourists** (1973): 79,219.

**ETHNOLINGUISTIC GROUPS:** (1970) 84.2% Vietnamese, 4.1% Tai, 3.2% Chinese, 3.0% Montagnard, 1.4% Muong, 1.4% Khmer, 0.7% Miao, 0.7% USA White, 0.6% Yao, 0.2% USA Black, USSR military, French, British, Filipino, Korean. (Mid–1975) 85.1% Vietnamese, 4.1% Tai, 3.1% Chinese, 2.9% Montagnard, 1.4% Muong, 1.4% Khmer, 0.7% Miao, 0.6% Yao, et alii.
**North:** 86.0% Vietnamese (Kinh), 7.5% Tai (3.2% Tay (Tho), 2.4% Thai, 1.9% Nung & Giai), 2.6% Muong, 1.3% Miao, 1.1% Yao, 0.7% Chinese (174,000), USSR military (1,000), et alii.
**South** (1970): 82.4% Vietnamese, 6.5% Montagnard (Highlander) (1.3% Jarai, 1.0% Rhade, 0.8% Bahnar, 0.7% Hre, 0.7% Sedang, 0.3% Mnong, 0.3% Ma, 0.3% Cham, 0.3% Raglai), 6.1% Chinese (1,100,000), 3.0% Khmer, 1.9% USA military (1.5% White, 0.4% Black)(in 1970; reducing to zero by 1975), French, British, Filipino, Korean, et alii.

**MONEY** (1977). **Monetary unit:** dong (= 10 chao = 100 sau); US$1 = D 2.4.
**National income per person:** US$130. Average annual family income: US$806.
**Inflation:** (1970–74) 35.0%.
**Cost of living in capital** (1976): Daily cost of living: Hanoi US$43, Saigon US$23.

**HEALTH.** Hospitals: 2,100 (50,000 beds). Doctors: 3,900. Lepers: 160,500 (3.7 per 1,000). Blind: 200,000. Psychotics: 390,000. Criminals (1972): 60,000.

**EDUCATION.** Adult literacy: (1960) North, 65%; (1970) whole country, 50%. Education rate: 60%. Schools: 20,406 (South 9,413, North 10,993). Universities: 6.

**LITERATURE.** Annual new book titles (1972): 729. Periodicals: 149. Scientific journals: 30. Newspapers: 56 dailies, 90 non-daily.

**COMMUNICATION** (per 1,000 people). Phones: 1. Radios: 70. TV sets: 15. Daily newspaper circulation: 37 copies.

TABLE 1. RELIGIOUS ADHERENTS IN VIET NAM (North & South)

| Year | 1900 | | mid-1970 | | Annual change, 1970–1980 | | | | mid-1975 | | mid-1980 | | 2000 | |
|---|---|---|---|---|---|---|---|---|---|---|---|---|---|---|
| *Name* | *Adherents* | *%* | *Adherents* | *%* | *Natural* | *Conversion* | *Total* | *Rate* | *Adherents* | *%* | *Adherents* | *%* | *Adherents* | *%* |
| Buddhists | 7,623,000 | 69.3 | 22,611,423 | 57.8 | 571,212 | –143,354 | 427,858 | 1.74 | 24,573,900 | 56.5 | 26,890,000 | 55.3 | 37,978,000 | 50.1 |
| New-Religionists | 0 | 0.0 | 4,500,000 | 11.5 | 109,575 | –5,175 | 104,400 | 2.09 | 4,997,000 | 11.5 | 5,544,000 | 11.4 | 7,580,000 | 10.0 |
| Non-religious | 0 | 0.0 | 4,200,000 | 10.7 | 121,921 | 138,979 | 260,900 | 4.69 | 5,560,000 | 12.8 | 6,809,000 | 14.0 | 14,402,000 | 19.0 |
| **Christians** | **900,000** | **8.2** | **3,264,577** | **8.3** | **41,109** | **–4,867** | **36,242** | **1.12** | **3,244,100** | **7.5** | **3,627,000** | **7.4** | **5,793,000** | **7.6** |
| crypto-Christians | 300,000 | 2.7 | 1,118,577 | 2.9 | 50,509 | 1,133 | 51,642 | 3.64 | 1,417,100 | 3.3 | 1,635,000 | 3.4 | 2,773,000 | 3.7 |
| professing | 600,000 | 5.5 | 2,146,000 | 5.5 | –9,400 | –6,000 | –15,400 | –0.84 | 1,827,000 | 4.2 | 1,992,000 | 4.1 | 3,020,000 | 4.0 |
| Roman Catholics | 600,000 | 5.5 | 1,950,000 | 5.0 | –800 | –4,500 | –5,300 | –0.30 | 1,740,000 | 4.0 | 1,897,000 | 3.9 | 2,810,000 | 3.8 |
| Protestants | 0 | 0.0 | 196,000 | 0.5 | –8,600 | –1,500 | –10,100 | –11.61 | 87,000 | 0.2 | 95,000 | 0.2 | 140,000 | 0.2 |
| affiliated | 900,000 | 8.2 | 3,264,577 | 8.3 | 41,109 | –4,867 | 36,242 | 1.12 | 3,244,100 | 7.5 | 3,627,000 | 7.4 | 5,793,000 | 7.6 |
| total practising | 855,000 | *95* | 2,938,120 | *90* | 34,943 | –38,595 | –3,652 | –0.13 | 2,757,480 | *85* | 2,901,600 | *80* | 4,055,000 | *70* |
| non-practising | 45,000 | *5* | 326,460 | *10* | 6,166 | 33,728 | 39,894 | 8.20 | 486,620 | *15* | 725,400 | *20* | 1,738,000 | *30* |
| Roman Catholics | 900,000 | 8.2 | 2,899,354 | 7.4 | 55,465 | –5,000 | 50,465 | 1.66 | 3,042,000 | 7.0 | 3,404,000 | 7.0 | 5,458,000 | 7.2 |
| Protestants | 0 | 0.0 | 324,696 | 0.8 | –14,570 | –900 | –15,470 | –9.67 | 160,000 | 0.4 | 170,000 | 0.3 | 220,000 | 0.3 |
| Evangelicals | 0 | 0.0 | 220,000 | 0.6 | –4,500 | –700 | –5,200 | –3.29 | 158,000 | 0.4 | 168,000 | 0.3 | 215,000 | 0.3 |
| Vietnamese indigenous | 0 | 0.0 | 31,000 | 0.1 | 857 | 1,043 | 1,900 | 4.86 | 39,100 | 0.1 | 50,000 | 0.1 | 110,000 | 0.1 |
| Marginal Protestants | 0 | 0.0 | 7,327 | 0.0 | –433 | 0 | –433 | –21.64 | 2,000 | 0.0 | 3,000 | 0.0 | 5,000 | 0.0 |
| Anglicans | 0 | 0.0 | 2,200 | 0.0 | –210 | –10 | –220 | –22.00 | 1,000 | 0.0 | 0 | 0.0 | 0 | 0.0 |
| Tribal religionists | 2,200,000 | 20.0 | 1,960,000 | 5.0 | 43,812 | –35,512 | 8,300 | 0.41 | 1,998,000 | 4.6 | 2,043,000 | 4.2 | 2,274,000 | 3.0 |
| Atheists | 0 | 0.0 | 1,080,000 | 2.8 | 33,353 | 77,547 | 110,900 | 7.29 | 1,521,000 | 3.5 | 2,189,000 | 4.5 | 6,164,000 | 8.1 |
| Chinese folk-religionists | 200,000 | 1.8 | 900,000 | 2.3 | 19,998 | –27,398 | –7,400 | –0.81 | 912,000 | 2.1 | 826,000 | 1.7 | 750,000 | 1.0 |
| Muslims | 77,000 | 0.7 | 390,000 | 1.0 | 9,620 | –20 | 9,600 | 2.21 | 435,000 | 1.0 | 486,000 | 1.0 | 531,000 | 0.7 |
| Baha'is | 0 | 0.0 | 200,000 | 0.5 | 2,200 | –200 | 2,000 | 0.95 | 210,000 | 0.5 | 220,000 | 0.5 | 330,000 | 0.4 |
| **Country's population** | **11,000,000** | **100.0** | **39,106,000** | **100.0** | **952,800** | **0** | **952,800** | **2.19** | **43,451,000** | **100.0** | **48,634,000** | **100.0** | **75,802,000** | **100.0** |

COLUMNS, ROWS. For meanings and definitions, see Codebook (Part 6). Note that, by definition, total 'Christians' = professing + crypto-Christians, which also = affiliated + nominal Christians. Percentages may not always total exactly, due to rounding.
CENSUSES. The religion question has not been asked in the major official censuses, but occasional surveys have been made. **1958** (urban survey of South Viet-Nam only, covering Saigon, Cantho, Dalat, Giadinh, Hue, Nhatrang): 52.4% Buddhists, 31.6% tribal religionists and non-religious, 14.2% Roman Catholics, 1.7% other religionists. **1962** (Saigon city): 73.7% Buddhists, 13.6% tribal religionists and non-religious, 11.1% Roman Catholics, 1.6% other religionists.

### NOTES ON RELIGIONS

AFFILIATED PROTESTANTS. In the South in 1970, 50% were Vietnamese nationals, and 50% USA military and civilians, with a few Koreans and Filipinos. After 1972, with the withdrawal of over 160,000 USA Protestants, virtually all remaining Protestants were Vietnamese.
ATHEISTS. (a) *North.* Vietnam Lao Dong (Workers') Party (in power; neutral over Sino-Soviet dispute): membership (1970) 1,100,000. Of Communist party members, around 20% are estimated to be committed atheists, the rest being non-religious with a considerable minority of professing religionists (Buddhists, some Christians). (b) *South.* The Communist party based in Hanoi was outlawed in the South from 1955 and had only unorganized members until 1975.
BAHA'IS. Begun 1954 almost entirely in the South; very rapid growth to 3,000 Baha'is by 1962, then to 195 local spiritual assemblies (1964), 602 (1971) with 116,088 adult members, and 659 (1973) with 972 other isolated centres or groups.
BUDDHISTS. Although most Vietnamese are regarded as Buddhists, Vietnamese religion is in reality a folk religion merging local folklore, animism, the ancestor cult and multiple village spirit cults and rites, together with Mahayana Buddhism, Confucianism and Taoism (in Viet Nam, the latter is a system of magic with a cult of sorcerers, practitioners and diviners). Buddhism in Viet Nam is divided into 16 sects. Active Buddhists in the South numbered about 3.1 million Vietnamese in 1970 (mainly Mahayana, with some Hinayana influence from Laos and Cambodia), 1 million Cambodians (Hinayana; arrived 1880; in 10 delta provinces; 20,000 monks, no nuns), and about 400,000 Chinese (Mahayana, with priests and temples separate from the Vietnamese). In 1963, Northern and Southern Buddhists united to form a body unique in world Buddhism, the Unified Buddhist Church (HQ Vietnam Quoc Tu/National Pagoda of Vietnam). The most important sect is Thien (Japanese, Zen) Buddhism, which in 1975 had 12,000 monks and 4,000 temples in Viet Nam. Another sect very popular with the masses is Amidism or the Pure Land School.
CHRISTIANS. In the South, before 1965, and after 1974, almost all were Vietnamese nationals; between these dates the totals include members of the USA armed forces (which built up to a peak of 541,500 in March 1969, fell to 343,700 by 1970, then to zero by 1972), also Korean, Filipino and other military, and USA civilians. *Emigration.* The column 'Natural change' is negative for most Christian blocs because it includes the massive emigration of 1970–75 (first USA military, then Vietnamese), averaged over the decade 1970–80.
COUNTRY'S POPULATION. The table includes the 343,700 USA troops in the country in 1970, this total then falling to zero by 1975. The column 'Natural change' includes the massive emigrations (mainly Christian) culminating in 1975, and averages these losses over the decade 1970–80. During the war of 1961–75, an estimated 250,000 South Vietnamese soldiers were killed and 1,400,000 civilians suffered casualties.
CRYPTO-CHRISTIANS. Christians affiliated to churches but unknown as such to either state, society or Buddhist authorities; including from 1952 many thousands of isolated radio believers in both North and South. Before 1975 in the North, and after 1975 in the South increasingly, many were Vietnamese unwilling to acknowledge their faith publicly before the Communist regime.
MUSLIMS. Sunnis; especially found among the Cham (Cham-Malay) minority, along the Mekong river. Organized by the Cham and Vietnam Muslim Association, Saigon. *Hajj pilgrims to Mecca.* In 1970, 71 Muslims from South Viet-Nam performed the hajj.
NEW-RELIGIONISTS. There are 2 major religio-political millenarian sects, both located mainly in Mekong delta: (1) Cao Dai, or the Cao Daist Missionary Church (Dai Dao Tam Ky Pho Do/Doctrine of the Third Revelation of God, or Third Amnesty for Sins) which was begun in 1919 to create an acceptable syncretism of the First Revelation (ancestor-worship, Taoism, Judaism, Buddhism), and the Second Revelation (Confucianism, Christianity, Islam), with Vietnamese culture, values and spiritism; its HQ is at Tay Ninh, 70 miles northwest of Saigon; there are 8 Cao Dai sub-divisions, sects or denominations, with a total of around 2.8 million adherents, ruled by a pope, 6 cardinals, 36 archbishops, 72 bishops, 3,000 priests, and monks and nuns; (2) Hoa Hao, a reformist variant of Hinayana Buddhism founded in 1936 to seek a purer Buddhism, which claims 1.5 million followers. Other sects include Binh Xuyen, Tien Thien, and Coconut Palm Religion (5,000 members, syncretizing Buddhism and Christianity).
NON-RELIGIOUS. Mostly secularized former Buddhists and Vietnamese folk-religionists in the North since 1945.
PRACTISING CHRISTIANS. In the South, regular (weekly) practice was very high up to 1975, averaging 80%. In the North, 85% attend Sunday mass weekly.
ROMAN CATHOLICS. Baptized Catholics have grown from 130,000 in 1639 (80,000 in North, 50,000 in South) to 270,000 in 1658, 320,000 in 1802, 420,000 in 1840, 600,000 in 1885, and 708,000 in 1890, with 70,000 converts recorded in the year 1890. In the last decade, Catholics were almost all Vietnamese nationals, with (1965–1972) about 70,000 USA military personnel in the South.
TRIBAL RELIGIONISTS. Animists properly so called, particularly among the Montagnard tribes mainly in the South, including Chrau (population 15,000), Bahnar, Loven, Mnong, Sedang, Jarai, Raglai, Rhade. The largest number in a Catholic diocese are 620,000 in D Kontum. In addition, many ethnic Vietnamese have been, and still are, more correctly described as animists than as Buddhists.
VIETNAMESE INDIGENOUS. In 1970, in 2 groupings in the North and 8 denominations in the South (see Table 2); Vietnamese and Chinese.

## NON-CHRISTIAN RELIGIONS. Buddhism has

long been the religion of the majority. Introduced in
the 2nd century AD, principally in the North,
Mahayana (Great Vehicle) grew significantly between
the 11th and 16th centuries, after which it experienced decline. In 1930 a Buddhist assembly met in Hué
for the purpose of integrating the 2 streams (Great
Vehicle and Small Vehicle) and forming a renewed
Buddhism, which in 1963 became formalized as the
Unified Buddhist Church. At the summit of leadership
was the supreme patriarchate (Tang Thong) and
below it 2 assemblies, one of which was the Committee
of the Supreme Patriarchate (Thuong Hoa) handling
doctrinal questions while the other (Vien Hoa Dao)
was more administrative.

Following the division of the country, Buddhists
became more active politically, especially in their
opposition to Catholic dominance. In the North,
prior to 1954 the majority of the population had
regarded itself as Buddhist, although many did not
attend pagoda services and most continued to observe
Confucian ancestral rites. Subsequently, the Communist government radio on occasion gave publicity
to Buddhist celebrations in Hanoi. Nevertheless,
subtle pressures were often used against those who
engaged in religious activity, and many pagodas and
temples were destroyed or taken over for secular
uses. The Unified Buddhist Association of Viet Nam
expressed its sympathy for and worked in co-operation
with the Communist regime.

In the South, in 1958 Buddhists experienced
difficulties with the Diem regime and openly protested
against privileges being accorded to Catholics.
Government harassment of them in turn created more
conflicts, provoking the self-immolation of monks.
Among Buddhists, 2 opposing tendencies emerged,
a minority movement in favour of the government
and represented by an anti-communist group of
Buddhist refugees from the North (about 200,000 in
1954) led by Thich Tam Chau, and the majority
who were opposed to the government and led by
Thich Tri Quang of the An Quang pagoda. In 1966
a Buddhist attempt to overthrow the Thieu-Ky
government in favour of free elections and a representative government was followed by severe repression.
While opposing direct political intervention, Tri
Quang presented Buddhism as the political conscience
of the nation. During the latter years of the war,
Buddhism represented the anti-American and anti-
communist lower middle class. After the Paris
Agreement, they became more active, proposing that
Buddhism could serve as a mediating force for
reconciliation in the country.

Vietnamese popular and folk religion continues
to exert an important influence on the life of the
people, although its communal aspects are much less
significant than previously. It is a syncretistic mixture
of Buddhism, Confucianism and Taoism combined
with magic, fortune-telling, astrology, geomancy and
ancestral veneration, although the majority of its
adherents are regarded simply as Buddhists. Diviners,
medicine men and other occult specialists retain their
importance. Many families have had their own
temples, with altars for the ancestors, sometimes with
other altars dedicated to the Buddha and such lesser
divinities as the god of the hearth. Communal
worship has traditionally been centred around the
village temple (*dinh*) where offerings are made

**New-Religionists: Cao Daist Missionary Church.** *Top.* Entrance to
Holy City at Tay Ninh near Cambodian border, with above gate 'The
Doctrine of the Third Revelation of God'. *Centre left.* A family in front of
twin-towered Holy See Great Divine Temple, built 1933-41. *Centre right.*
Cao Daist priests on steps of Temple. *Bottom.* Celebrants of Cao Daist mass
inside Temple facing altar and Divine Eye (women on left, men on right, as
always).

especially during the planting and harvesting seasons to the guardian spirit of the village and the divinity of the soil. Many of these temples have now been destroyed, but house altars are still used, not uncommonly with the photograph of Ho Chi Minh found displayed around those of the family ancestors.

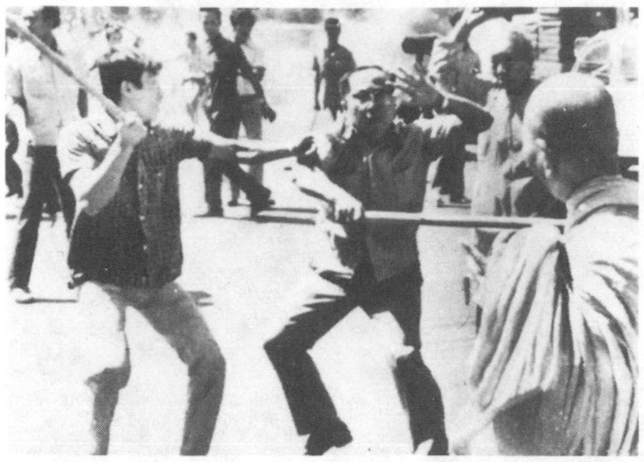

**Buddhists.** Two nuns (right) assaulted by stick-wielding plainclothes police in Saigon during January 1975 anti-government demonstrations.

**New Religions** syncretizing Buddhism and other world religions, which are in reality religio-political millenarian sects, have sizeable followings in the South. The largest is the Cao Daist Missionary Church (Doctrine of the Third Revelation of God), founded in the South in 1919 by Le Van Trung. It is a syncretistic faith involving a mixture of popular Buddhism, Confucian ethics, the ancestral cult and a Catholic-type organization. It has about 2.8 million members, mostly found in the Mekong Delta along the Cambodian frontier. The second pope, Pham Long Tac, allied himself with the Japanese against the French during World War II and continued to support the emperor Bao Dai. The hostility of the Diem regime resulted in the exile of Pham Long Tac to Phnom Penh, where he died in 1956 and many Cao Dai followers were massacred in Cambodia under the Lon Nol regime. Cao Dai has its Holy See at Tay Ninh. Another religio-political sect, Hoa Hao, is a reformist Buddhist sect founded in 1939 at Hoa Hao, dedicated to the attainment of a better life with the end of foreign domination. It has about 1.5 million adherents, mostly in the Mekong Delta. The Diem regime persecuted them viciously and at the end of the Thieu period military operations were being mounted against their militia. Their headquarters are at Cai San, in An-giang Province. Another recent syncretistic sect is the Coconut Palm Religion (Religion du Cocotier) founded on Mekong island during the 1950s by Nguyen Thanh Nam, an engineer, as a reaction against modernization. The founder was arrested several times by Ngo Dinh Diem. The movement still has several thousand followers. And there are several other such sects.

**Animism,** with its emphasis on the ancestral cult and protection against evil spirits, forms a foundation for the practical religious life of much of the population and is the basic religion of the ethnic minorities of the high plateaux, who number about 2.5 million.

**Confucianism** was introduced from China in the 11th century by the upper class and continues to co-exist with popular Buddhism. **Taoism,** also coming from China, is mixed with popular animistic religion as well as Buddhism. The 2 together compose Chinese folk religion, followed by a majority of Chinese in Viet Nam.

**Islam** exists among the Cham minority and is represented by the Cham and Vietnam Muslim Association in Saigon.

**CHRISTIANITY.** The first missionaries were Franciscans from the Phillippines in 1580, followed by Jesuits in 1615. Two Jesuits, Francesco Busomi and Alexandre de Rhodes, advocated a policy of adaptation to traditional culture, and the latter with the help of Vietnamese catechists invented the present alphabet. By 1639 there were 80,000 Catholics in the North and 50,000 in the South; and the viceroy of Kuang-Si, a convert, protected Catholicism. Christianity suffered its first persecution in 1645. In 1659 Propaganda in Rome, in opposition to the Patroado, created 2 vicariates (North and South), but without fixed residence because of persecution by the Confucian emperors. The year 1668 saw the ordination of 4 Vietnamese priests and the following year the formation of an indigenous female congregation: Lovers of the Cross. In 1678 Msgr Pallu, founder of the Missions Etrangères de Paris, called for the consecration of 6 Vietnamese bishops, but this was rejected by Rome. In 1679 Spanish Dominicans of the Province of Manila were made responsible for the Red River Delta of the North, while the South, Laos and Cambodia were given to the MEP. New persecutions appeared in 1698, and in 1789 Msgr Pierre Pigneaux de Behaine requested the intervention of French troops. In 1825 the emperor Minh Mang prohibited the entry of foreign missionaries. French interventions for the liberation of missionaries took place in 1843 and 1847, resulting in strong reaction against the Catholic minority. The Edict of Tu Du in 1851 resulted in the death of 115 priests and 90,000 faithful. The French imposed religious liberty in 1882 and 2 years later declared a protectorate over the territory. Thus the religious argument served as the pretext for colonial domination. The first Vietnamese Catholic bishop was consecrated at Phat Diem in the North in 1933. Catholic Christianity has experienced numerous persecutions, with a total of 130,000 martyrs across the years.

CATHOLIC CHURCH. The Catholic Church of North Viet-Nam has managed to maintain its relationship with Rome intact from 1954–75, for unlike the situation in China the government did not succeed in creating an autonomous Catholic Church opposed to Rome, except for a handful of 15 priests who in 1955 and 1963 at government instigation renounced the Vatican and formed a Patriotic Catholic Church, of which little has subsequently been heard. A high proportion of the faithful, around 85%, attend Sunday mass each week, and those Sundays when a priest is unable to come, parishioners meet for prayer. There is extensive use of traditional conservative Catholic devotions: rosary, perpetual adoration, invocation of saints and Our Lady of Fatima (the latter serving also as an expression of opposition to Communism), processions and pilgrimages. Catechetical sessions are held before and after mass in the churches as well as in homes. There is a catechist in every parish who organizes public prayers. The liturgy is celebrated in Vietnamese, but European chants are also used; during mass the priest keeps his back to the people. The theology of Vietnamese Catholicism remains traditionalist, based on old manuals with little influence from the perspectives of Vatican II.

In the North in 1954 the Catholic population was 1,395,000, served by 1,133 priests. Of these 560,500 (808 priests) emigrated south, leaving 834,500 Catholics and 325 priests in North Viet Nam in 1955. Since 1955 the Catholic Church has been growing there at the rate of 2% per year. There were in 1974 about 350 diocesan priests, after approximately 100 ordinations since 1954: 40 in Vinh, 30 in Buichu, 10 in Thai-Binh and less than 10 each for Hung-Hoa and Haiphong. In 1954 the average age of clergy was 52, a figure which had become even higher by 1974. Concerning male religious personnel, there are now only about 10 Cistercians and a few Redemptorists. In all, some 350 sisters are active in catechesis, dispensaries and social work: Lovers of the Cross (mother house at Lieu Thuy) working in the dioceses of Phat Diem, Hung-Hoa, Vinh and Hanoi (about 300); Dominicans at Buichu; Sisters of the Holy Rosary of Trung Linh; Sisters of the Visitation (mother house at Lien Thuy); and Sisters of St Paul of Chartres (about 10).

In the South, Catholicism is essentially rural, being found for the most part in villages which are completely or largely Catholic. It continues to appear foreign, being opposed to the traditional ancestral cult, dominated until 1975 by foreign clergy, and until the fall of the Thieu regime supported by colonial powers with privileges and power granted by the administration. Living in ghettos (converted clans or villages or converts gathered together because of persecution), Catholicism often provokes hostility. Catholics were not strongly involved in the struggle for independence. In 1945 a Catholic group calling for the formation of a truly Vietnamese church was suppressed by the hierarchy, and soon afterwards the church as with the country itself was divided into northern and southern parts.

Prior to 1975, Sunday church attendance in the South averaged 80%. Popular Catholicism was strongly disciplined, clergy being authoritarian and devotion firm. Religion was a factor in social identification and played an important protective role in South Vietnamese society. Six years after Vatican II there was still no complete translation of the conciliar documents. Vocations were numerous and favoured by the social situation. Catholicism was highly institutionalized, especially after 1955 due mostly to foreign aid. Parish structure was strong, with good lay participation. There were many schools and social service institutions. Among refugees from the North, the clergy's control was strong and for a long time parishes were organized into family groups for the anti-communist struggle, although these tended to disappear with the birth of a new generation following the exodus from the North.

After the unification of Viet Nam in 1976, the church began to face the vast problems involved in unifying itself also.

PROTESTANT CHURCHES. The first and by far the largest Protestant church has been the Evangelical Church of Viet-Nam. Although 2 CMA missionaries visited the North from China in 1895, it was not until 1911 that permission was granted by the French authorities to begin a mission at Da Nang. Success was almost immediate and included influential members of the community. In 1927 the CMA granted the church autonomy, and 2 years later governmental restrictions on the expansion of the church were withdrawn. Work among tribal peoples (especially the Raday and Koho) of the south-central highlands was initiated in 1934. Theological training has been provided by the Bible and Theological Institute in Nhatrang which offered a degree programme after 1969; and Bible institutes have also been active at Dalat and Ban Me Thuot.

Although Seventh-day Adventists began work in 1929, no new Protestant group appeared prior to the fall of Dien Bien Phu in 1954.

In the North, there has been only one active Protestant denomination, the Evangelical Church of North Viet-Nam (begun by the CMA). The church is served by 26 pastors, and most congregations hold evangelistic meetings on Thursdays in addition to 2 Sunday worship services. Conversions continue and membership training classes of 6 to 8 months' duration are organized. Protestant pastors serve on a full-time basis and receive their salaries from their own local congregations. The church's seminary was closed briefly because of the destruction caused by the American bombing, but it was re-opened in 1973. In 1972 contacts were made with the National Council of Churches of Christ in the USA, at which time Vietnamese Protestant leaders expressed criticism of America's role in the war. Similar contacts were made with the World Council of Churches in 1973, which resulted in the initiation of aid grants by the WCC to the church.

In the South, in addition to churches and foreign missions, a number of other church-related agencies entered during the 1950s. In 1973 there were 23 foreign missions and agencies in the South with total foreign personnel of 276. Eighteen other foreign missions and agencies provided support but no personnel.

As a result of the fall of the Thieu regime in 1975, organized Protestant churches and agencies were largely dispersed and many Protestants were evacuated as refugees out of Viet Nam. Several hundred pastors of the Evangelical Church (CMA) left in this way.

INDIGENOUS CHURCHES. A total of 10 small indigenous groupings have been begun by Vietnamese Christians independently of Western foreign missions. Three small independent denominations formed during the 1960s were the Church of Christ (which consisted entirely of Filipinos), Church of God, and Vietnam Christ's Church, the latter being a schism from the Evangelical Church in 1964.

**CHURCH AND STATE.** Relations between church and state in Viet Nam can best be studied by describing their history separately in the North and in the South, and since unification in 1976.

A. *North Viet-Nam.* Relations have followed the vicissitudes of the country's political history, and may be reviewed under 5 main periods. (1) The first period is that of the war with France, from the end of World War II until the end of the colonial war (1945–54). On 19 August 1945 Ho Chi Minh declared independence in the presence of 3 of the 4 Vietnamese Catholic bishops, the fourth failing to arrive only due to lack of transport. The 4 bishops sent a letter to pope Pius XII and Catholics throughout the world requesting support for this declaration. Bishop Le Huu Tu of Phat Diem was appointed a member of the Supreme Council and Ho Chi Minh addressed a Christmas message to Catholics. However, in the same year the Catholic Federation, an anti-communist movement, was founded, whose president was later executed for aiding the French expeditionary forces. The bishop of Phat Diem then broke with Ho Chi Minh, blaming him for the Fontainebleau agreement and demanding total independence.

In 1946, admiral Thierry d'Argenlieu (a priest of the Discalced Carmelite order) was appointed commandant of the French expeditionary forces. He bombarded Haiphong and proclaimed the autonomy of Cochin China (the southern third of South Viet-Nam), as a republic separate from Viet-Nam. Seeking Catholic support, he presented himself as the defender of Christian civilization. In 1947, 29 Catholics were executed by partisans of the Viet Minh for political reasons, an action which caused the authorities to declare the incompatibility between the faith and adherents to the Viet Minh. Bishop Le Huu Tu formed Catholic militias in the dioceses of Phat Diem and Buichu, who were armed by the French to fight against the Viet Minh. The result was atrocities on both sides, massacres, tortures and burning of villages. Appointed as forces for self-defence and joining with the French in the fight against Ho Chi Minh, the militias were led by a priest, Hoang Quynh, and numerous priests held the rank of commanders.

At the end of 1950, general de Lattre de Tassigny was named governor-general. Going first to Rome where he was received by Pius XII, he requested the appointment of an apostolic delegate to Hanoi and the condemnation of Communism by the Vietnamese episcopate. Pius XII blessed 'the French army which defends Christian civilization in Viet-Nam', and the apostolic delegate in Bangkok was appointed to Hanoi. On 9 November 1951, following a plenary meeting of the episcopate in Hanoi, a declaration was issued from the episcopate calling to mind the condemnation of Communism by the Holy Office (1 July 1949) and the excommunication of those belonging to the Communist party. The declaration added that Catholics should do nothing to aid the rise of communists to power (which in fact meant the prohibition of Catholic participation in the resistance) and affirmed that the social reforms of communists were nothing but a manoeuvre and their patriotism a mask. Priests were therefore forced to abandon their involvement in the resistance which in turn undermined Catholic collaboration in the nationalist movement. In May 1954, Dien Bien Phu fell to the Viet Minh, causing the end of French involvement in Indochina.

(2) The second period covers the Geneva Agreement and the exodus of Catholics from the North (1954–55). The Agreement made provision for an armistice line along the 17th parallel, the withdrawal of troops from both sides of the line, a choice for the populace of living in the North or the South, and the organization of elections 2 years after the signing of the agreement. Following that, about 1,500 persons emigrated north while some 870,000 went south. Among the latter there were between 10 and 20 thousand persons belonging to the middle classes, 100,000 soldiers and their families recruited by the French, 200,000 Buddhists and 560,000 Catholics. These emigrants included 40% of the total Catholic population in the North (1.39 million at that time), 71% of all priests (808 out of 1,133) and 6 bishops out of 10.

The reasons for this exodus were diverse. First there were those who had actively opposed the Viet Minh, which was true of a large number of clergy. Others fled to escape an anti-religious Communism. Intensive propaganda was initiated urging Catholic villagers to emigrate south. An American grant of US$ 93 million was provided to help resettle refugees in the South, and the American Seventh Fleet furnished ships for the exodus. Practically all Catholic religious congregations left the North and all the seminaries except that in the diocese of Vinh. The attitude of the bishops differed from diocese to diocese. Phat Diem and Buichu were particularly compromised and lost 85% of their clergy and 50% of their faithful. In Haiphong 8 priests out of 79 left for the South; while at Vinh, where the bishop (a Frenchman) requested the clergy to remain, more than 65% did so, including all seminarians. In Hanoi, despite the opposition of the Vietnamese archbishop, nearly 70% of the clergy emigrated. In Hung-Hoa, the bishop remained with 90% of the faithful and 60% of the clergy.

(3) The third period includes the beginning of military intervention by the USA (1955–64). Following the exodus, Rome progressively appointed Vietnamese to all new episcopal posts; but after the fighting measures were taken against any who had fought with the French. Accounts were settled especially with Catholics and many priests who had participated in the militia were arrested and punished. Churches were occupied and local cadres acting without authority from above attacked Catholics. The agrarian reform of 1953 was extended to all

parts in 1955 and included the confiscation of all productive land owned by the church except that necessary for the maintenance of worship and the clergy. Since every diocese and a large number of the parishes possessed land (in 1931 Catholic missions had owned 5.5% of all land), the bishops protested. In certain cases peasants seized mission property and utilized the agrarian reform as a pretext for settling past grievances, provoking strong counter-measures by the central authorities who then dismissed local agrarian reform leaders responsible for abuse of Catholics, freed imprisoned priests, restored illegally-confiscated property and made reparations.

In April 1955 a meeting was held in Hanoi of 55 priests and 300 lay persons to reorganize the liaison committees which functioned during the struggle against the French under the slogan 'Love God and country'. This was then condemned from Rome by the cardinal prefect of Propaganda. On 14 June 1955 the regime promulgated its Decree on Religious Liberty. Because of the excesses of the Agrarian Reform, the Catholics of Than-Hoa and the provinces of Nghe An and Ha Tinh (diocese of Vinh) revolted in 1956. This in turn was followed by a number of restrictive measures during 1957–58: suppression of

**Evangelical Church of Viet-Nam.** Believers emerging from worship service in Hanoi, 1977.

the St Teresa publishing house, expulsion of missionaries, imprisonment of the pro-vicar of Hanoi and the Cathedral pastor. In 1958 the premier Pham Van Dong called for a meeting with the bishops, but they refused on the grounds that church property had not been restored. At the end of 1959 the apostolic delegate was ordered to leave Hanoi, and the following year the government refused to authorize an episcopal consecration, the candidate being considered too reactionary. The seminaries were closed when the bishops refused to accept government control of them. Then in 1962 in a discourse to cadres of the Front, Ho Chi Minh declared that Catholics were seeking religious liberty which should be guaranteed to them. For a long time Catholics refused to enter rural co-operatives as a result of the episcopal declaration of 1951. Moreover, the bishops were not permitted to participate in Vatican Council II since the government feared they would thereby establish contacts with the South.

(4) The fourth period is that of the American war (1964–73). The intensification of the war in the North, and especially American bombing, caused a change of attitude in the Catholic population and rallied them to the government, in spite of reticence on the part of clergy and hierarchy. Some suggested that the bombing was a punishment from heaven against communists. Several movements came to the fore, one among Catholic families displaying

anti-Americanism for national salvation and another involving the enlistment of Catholic youth in the army. Several Catholics, including 3 priests, were elected to the national assembly and important posts were occupied by Catholics, including president of the Red Cross and military commands. In 1970, 70 priests and several thousand faithful wrote to American Catholics to explain the reasons for the suffering of the Vietnamese. The monthly journal of the Hoc Tap Party, *Etudes*, published an article concerning believers which denounced prejudice against them, affirmed that adherence to a creed is a democratic liberty which should not be interfered with, insisted that religion should not be used to propagate doubt, and affirmed that religions are able to evolve. A delegation of 3 Catholics (2 being priests) visited the Assembly of Christians Concerned for the Vietnamese, Laotian and Cambodian Peoples, in Paris. In 1971, 3 bishops were consecrated in Hanoi and the bishop of Vinh was received by the premier. The 2 others were given responsibilities in the militia. For the first time the episcopate was able to meet together. During the same year, a meeting of the National Liaison Committee of Patriotic and Peace-Loving Catholics was held which affirmed its

support for the regime's politics and the connection between faith and social involvement, denouncing at the same time the church's compromises with feudal and capitalist regimes which caused it to deviate from its evangelical perspectives. A delegation was also sent to the Quebec Assembly of Concerned Christians. In 1972 pope Paul VI received Xuan Thuy, the North Vietnamese negotiator at the Paris peace talks. Meanwhile in the aerial bombardment of the North, 500 churches had been destroyed and one bishop killed.

(5) The last of the 5 periods, 1973–75, followed the Paris agreement and was characterized by the visits of various North Vietnamese delegations, including religious leaders, to the West; and the provision of aid by Western-based religious organizations for the reconstruction of the country. An example of the former was the delegation to the Assembly of Concerned Christians at Turin in 1973, while examples of the latter were the rebuilding of the Hai Duong hospital by the World Council of Churches, in addition to aid provided by CIDSE and Caritas. The cathedral of Vinh was rebuilt with government help. The regime continued to demand that the Holy See acknowledge that the declaration of 1951 no longer corresponded to reality. The church still continued to be suspicious of the government, except for those clergy who had earlier rallied to its cause. For its part the government also was suspicious

of religious authorities because of past support given to the Saigon regime in the South. Progress towards reconciliation was however being made. In 1974 the auxiliary bishop of Hanoi participated in the Synod of Bishops at Rome and was received by the premier after his return. During Christmas 1974, the North Vietnamese Information Agency (AVI) emphasized the contribution played by Catholics in the war, especially the role of youth.

With regard to formal church-state relations, the attitude of government to religions has been determined by Decree 234 signed by the president of the Republic on 14 June 1955, whose first article is reproduced in Article 26 of the constitution of 1959. The following items are covered in the various articles of the decree: freedom of belief and worship (Article 1); equality of the rights of ministers and faithful with other citizens (Article 2); publication of literature provided it does not contravene the laws of the republic (Article 4); the right to open schools for the training of ministers (Article 5); protection by law of churches and pagodas (Article 6); provision of sufficient property for churches, pagodas and temples to make possible worship services and for the maintenance of religious personnel (Article 10); exemption of bishops, priests and monks from classification as land-owners (Article 11); reduction of the agricultural tax on property (Article 12); assurance that the civil authorities will not intervene in the internal affairs of the religions, and for Catholics acceptance of relations with the Holy See as an internal matter (Article 13); and the assurance of respect and protection of the freedom of belief and worship by governmental authorities (Article 15).

The Agrarian Reform law of 1953 provided for the confiscation of the property of expatriates who had collaborated with the colonial regime, including missionaries, especially Spanish priests. Nevertheless, Article 25 affirmed: 'Catholic and Protestant missions and Buddhist congregations may be authorized to retain a part of their land and rice fields for worship and the maintenance of priests and monks'.

The Committee for Religious Questions in the Office of the Council Presidency (Ban Ton Giao Phu Thu Tuong) has been the official government organ responsible for relations with the religions, control of the application of legislation concerning religious freedom, authorization of meetings including that of the bishops in 1971, importation of products used in worship including wine for mass, reconstruction of churches destroyed in the war, and other similar matters.

B. *South Viet-Nam.* Under the Diem regime, Decree 9 regulated relations between the state and the religions, providing for separation of state and religion, and freedom of worship. No official organ was ever created to formalize these relations. The constitution of 1 April 1967 established in Article 9 that the state 'respects and guarantees the freedom of belief, freedom of religious propagation and freedom of worship of all citizens, provided that these liberties do not prejudice the interests of the State, security and public order and are not contrary to good morals'. The same article added: 'The State recognizes no religion as the state religion'. Article 4 stated: 'Every act of propaganda or support in favour of communist doctrine is formally prohibited'. At the same time, strong Catholic protests were evoked because the constitution replaced the Catholic term God Almighty (Dieu Tout-puissant) by the traditional 'supreme being' (Thieng Lieng; Etre Suprême).

In August 1962, 2 years after its formation, the Front for National Liberation (FNL, FLN) published a declaration affirming that 'Freedom of thought, worship, opinion and organization are guaranteed to all citizens, political parties, mass organizations, religions and nationalities' (Article 6). Successive political programmes of the FNL and its successor, the Provisional Revolutionary Government (PRG), repeated these declarations.

On 18 July 1973, the fundamental stipulations proposed by the PRG for the re-organization of South Viet-Nam included the following: Article 16 '1. Freedom of belief and worship is to be respected and guaranteed; 2. All religions are free to exercise their religious activities in the 2 zones under the control respectively of the 2 South Vietnamese parties'; Article 17 'Equality between all religions is guaranteed, as well as that between believers and non-believers'; Article 18 '1. Pagodas, churches, Cao Dai holy places and temples are to be respected; 2. The right to ownership of properties of pagodas, churches, Cao Dai holy places etc... is to be protected'. On 3 April 1975, the PRG appealed to all Vietnamese without distinction of ethnic group or confession to participate in the reconstruction of the country. On the same day the PRG broadcast over North Viet-Nam Radio '10 Commandments' which they intended to see applied in liberated zones south of the 17th parallel, of which number 2 stated that the PRG recognized the 'equality of the sexes, freedom of conscience and worship, affirming the equality of all religions'.

The Catholic Church exercised an important influence between 1954 and 1975. The contribution of the 560,000 Catholic refugees from the North was of considerable significance for the regime of president Diem, himself a Catholic. The proportion of Catholics in the South increased by more than 100%, to form about 10% of the total population. Those from the North were used especially in reinforcing the regime: in the army, administration, police, special troops, recruitment of spies and saboteurs sent to the North. The brother of Diem was appointed archbishop of Hué, after having attempted in vain to be appointed to Saigon. Msgr Pham Ngoc Chi, formerly co-ordinator of the exodus from the North, was named bishop of Da-Nang. The Catholics from the North, a disciplined group under the direction of their clergy, settled around Saigon, near the demilitarized zone and also to some extent in the high plateaux. Prior to the Communist take-over in 1975, they received an important amount of international aid, and because of this, they achieved a relatively high economic status. The government favoured the church with privileges and subsidies and also showed its support symbolically by providing military escorts for certain bishops, collaboration in the organization of the Marian Year in 1958, aid to the cult of Our Lady of Fatima and so on. All of this contributed to mass conversions into the church, including that of the future president Thieu. The Saigon regime was recognized by the Holy See, and in 1960 a pastoral letter was circulated reminding the faithful of the Vatican's condemnation of Communism in 1951 and appealing for vigilance.

Between 1955 and the fall of Diem in 1963, the principal Catholic political movement was the Can Lao Nhan Vi (Personalization of Work), directed by Diem's younger brother, and whose spiritual leader was another Diem brother. After 1963, the movement was dissolved and the Dai Doan Ket (Great Union) was formed, under the direction of the priest Hoang Quynh, former commander-in-chief of the Catholic militia of the bishop of Phat Diem. This latter movement advocated military victory but progressively lost its strength. Following the Tet offensive from 1968, the Can Lao Nhan Vi was reorganized under the leadership of Msgr Nguyen Van Thuan, a nephew of Diem. With ties to Taiwan and the Philippines, it set as its purpose the elimination of Communism and retained a certain influence in the centre of the country until the fall of the Thieu regime in 1975.

The Catholic opposition remained for a long time the work of a small minority, with no political influence. Under Diem, 2 priests were arrested and several others expelled. The episcopate generally supported the regime and spoke only in very vague and theoretical terms about the need for peace (January 1968). In 1969, the archbishop of Saigon and the bishop of Dan-Nang travelled to Paris to make contact with the 4 delegations to the preparatory conference. The mission failed, but in 1970 a letter consisting of 7 propositions was sent to the 4 delegations. In 1971, following the declaration of the bishops of Asia, a pastoral letter was circulated expressing concern for the poor and criticizing the privileged.

In 1970, 50% of the seats in the National Assembly, 60% in the Senate and the presidency of the 2 chambers were held by Catholics. More than 50% of senior officers in the army and police were Catholics. In 1973 a large number of Catholics were active in 3 parties: Dan Chu (Democratic Party), the party of president Thieu; Con Hoa (Republican Party); and Tu Do (Liberty Party), a conservative tendency opposed to Thieu. After the Paris Agreement a more moderate attitude grew progressively; but the minority of the Catholic Left remained weak, composed of intellectuals, a few priests, and the leaders of JOC and JEC, many of whom were arrested.

During the 20 years following Dien Bien Phu, the Catholic community thus became very influential in the South and formed an important part of the new bourgeoisie supporting the Thieu regime. For a long time peace was considered as a work of subversion, and the Catholic Church was used to support the regime in power. In 1974 devotion to Our Lady of Fatima was celebrated in Saigon by the episcopate and the government. Cardinal Spellman of New York addressed the American military in Viet Nam as 'soldiers of Christ' and 'defenders of Christian civilization'. In 1958 the Marian sanctuary of La Vang in the demilitarized zone was made a national basilica as a bastion against Communism. The church became materially powerful; vast churches were built and financially lucrative properties obtained including a bank. A Cistercian monastery was built with the help of the army. The Thieu regime, as with that of Diem, did not hesitate to use the Catholics in its opposition to Buddhists and Cao Daists.

On the international level, the Holy See intervened on numerous occasions to state the case for peace. In 1965 pope Paul VI wrote to the political leaders of the USSR, China, USA and North Viet-Nam, and in 1969 he told American congressmen that the US should not abandon aid to 'a weak people who merit assistance to defend their right to self-determination'. He insisted that the South Vietnamese bishops should declare themselves for peace. Numerous Catholic movements condemned the war. Cardinal Lercaro who condemned American intervention was asked to resign. The pope received president Thieu after the Paris Agreement and intervened in favour of political prisoners.

In January 1974 the episcopate issued a declaration requesting of both North and South freedom for political prisoners, re-establishment of political liberties, possibility of visits by the International Red Cross, resumption of mail service between North and South, and reunion of families. The same declaration asked the North for freedom of conscience for believers, re-opening of seminaries, liberty for the ministry, and contacts with the Holy See and the episcopate of the South; while from the South it called for an end to corruption and the advancement of the working class. The PRG was ignored. In June 1974, 300 priests held a demonstration denouncing corruption and social injustice. Opposition grew in Catholic circles, even among Rightists, culminating in the fall of Thieu in 1975.

C. *Since unification.* After the collapse of the Thieu regime on 30 April 1975, the hierarchy made no move to evacuate Catholics and all bishops remained in their dioceses, a policy agreed on by the Episcopal Conference in January 1975. This represented a radically different position from that of 1954. In 1975, the bishops of Hué and Kontum, absent from their dioceses at the time of the revolutionary offensive, returned immediately to their posts. A new bishop was consecrated at Ban Me Thuot following the arrival of revolutionary forces in that city. The archbishop of Hué published a pastoral letter to all the faithful of central Viet Nam, in which he expressed his joy at the recovery of peace and his willingness to co-operate loyally with the PRG. A few weeks after the end of hostilities and soon after the expulsion of the apostolic delegate, the archbishop of Saigon affirmed that Catholics had not been interfered with and that North Vietnamese soldiers were attending church services. During this period, the PRG disseminated widely their instructions of 18 July 1973 relative to religions and religious belief. Some foreign missionaries left voluntarily, while others were asked to leave; still others were provisionally permitted to remain.

In July 1975 a meeting was held in Saigon between the new revolutionary authorities and Catholic leaders, bringing together 600 priests, sisters and lay persons. The archbishop of Saigon offered to place at the disposition of the new government all Catholic confessional schools.

During November 1975 delegations from the North and South met in Saigon to discuss the question of the unification of the country. Among the 50 conference members in attendance were 4 representatives of the Buddhist Church, 2 Catholic priests and one Protestant minister.

As of December 1975 the nationalization of schools was progressing, a new Catholic journal *Cong-Jiao Va Dan Toc* (Catholics of the Nation) had been launched and a Catholic agency established to cater for development, artisan training, urban and rural co-operatives.

By August 1976, however, the church's freedom of movement was being increasingly curtailed and even repressed, hundreds of Vietnamese Catholic priests were being arrested and others harassed throughout the South, and the last foreign missionaries were expelled.

**INTERDENOMINATIONAL ORGANIZATIONS.** Relief and rehabilitation have been the focus of co-operative work in Viet Nam since World War II, the most significant agency being Viet-Nam Christian Service, created in 1966 as a joint venture of the Mennonite Central Committee, Church World Service and the Lutheran World Federation. For Conservative Evangelical bodies, the World Relief Commission of the USA-based National Association of Evangelicals has been active. The Evangelical Fellowship of Viet-Nam was also active up to 1975.

Inter-religious dialogue has been sponsored by the Council of Religions in Saigon, which serves as an organ of contact between Buddhism, Cao Dai, Hoa Hao, Catholicism and Protestantism.

**BROADCASTING.** In the South prior to 1975, Catholics and Protestants were given time on national and local radio and TV stations for religious broadcasts. In Saigon, Southern Baptists had a studio preparing programmes in Vietnamese for release over local government and military radio and TV stations. The Catholic Centre in Saigon, Television Service Centre for Community Development of Education in South Viet-Nam, had TV production studios. An experiment was taking place in 30 pilot towns to provide health education by means of TV. A series of 25 programmes were sent out once a week on the national TV network and in 1970 reached 85% of the population. For Catholics, Viet Nam was formerly a member of UNDA. From Korea, the Christian Broadcasting System regularly prepared programmes for Korean military personnel in South Viet-Nam which were then broadcast on local stations.

In the North, no religious broadcasting has been allowed over the government Voice of Viet-Nam or Radio Liberation. However, from abroad, FEBC (Manila) can be heard very clearly in Viet-Nam, in many languages, as well as Radio Veritas (Catholic, Manila).

## BIBLIOGRAPHY


'A short history of the Evangelical Church of Vietnam'. Le Hoang Phu. Dissertation, New York University, 1972.
*By life and by death.* J.C. Hefley. Grand Rapids, Michigan: Zondervan, 1969.
*Caodai spiritism: a study of religion in Vietnamese society.* V.L. Oliver. Studies in the History of Religions, XXXIV. Leiden: Brill, 1976. 145p.
*Catholiques et Bouddhistes au Vietnam.* P. Gheddo. Paris: Alsatia, 1969. 422p.
'Eglise Catholique au Vietnam: des chrétiens du Viet Nam relisent l'histoire de leur Eglise', T.T. Tinh, *Foi et développement* (Paris) 31 (November, 1975), 1–4.
*Histoire et philosophie du Cao-Daisme.* G. Gobron. Paris, 1948.
'Les Catholiques au Vietnam-Nord', J. Vogel, *Information catholique internationel* (Paris), 422 (December, 1972), 12–16, 25–27.
*Minority groups in the Republic of Vietnam.* Ed J. Shrock. Washington, DC: American University, Cultural Information Analysis Center, 1966.
*Protestant directory of churches, missions and organizations in South Vietnam.* Ed R.E. Reimer. Saigon: Office of Missionary Information, 1973. 50p.
*The bamboo cross.* H.E. Dowdy. New York: Harper and Row, 1964.
*The cross and the bo-tree.* P. Gheddo. New York: Sheed and Ward, 1970.
'The political-religious sects of Vietnam', B.B. Fall, *Pacific affairs*, XXVIII, 3 (September, 1955), 235–253.
'The Protestant movement in Vietnam', R.E. Reimer. Thesis, Fuller Theological Seminary, Pasadena (CA), 1972. 320p.
*The religions of South Vietnam in faith and fact.* Washington, DC. Department of the Navy, 1967.
*Viet-Nam Cong-Giao Niên-Gian, 1964/Annuaire catholique du Vietnam.* Saigon, 1964.
*Vietnam: the Christian, the gospel, the church.* Philadelphia: United Presbyterian Church in the USA, 1967.
'Vietnam: the long road to religious oppression', P. O'Connor, *Religion and Communism* (Keston, Kent, October, 1976), 4.
*Vietnam: the lotus in the sea of fire.* T.N. Hanh. London: SCM, 1967. 128p.


TABLE 2. ORGANIZED CHURCHES AND DENOMINATIONS IN VIET NAM

| Official name<br>1 | Begun<br>2 | Type<br>3 | Counc<br>4 | Congs<br>5 | Adults<br>6 | Affiliated<br>7 | Names, notes, and other statistics (see Codebook)<br>8 |
|---|---|---|---|---|---|---|---|
| | | | | | | | (a) *North Viet-Nam, 1970* |
| **Catholic Church in North Viet-Nam:** | 1580 | R Lat | P...C | 626 | 703,900 | 1,100,000 | *Cong Giao.* C=2+0+5. 1s,W=85%. 1954–5 exodus: 560,500;808n,1970:315n,351w. |
| M Hanoi | 1678 | R Lat | Ps | 112 | 130,700 | 204,300 | Severe losses in bombings. Urban. 6% RC. 1s. 60,000 115 51 13 |
| D Bac Ninh | 1883 | R Lat | Ps | 48 | 30,300 | 47,400 | Industrial complex of Thai Nguyen. 1.7% RC. 38,000 56 7 24 |
| D Buichu | 1848 | R Lat | Ps | 117 | 139,200 | 217,500 | Red river delta. 1954, 34% RC; 1955, 19%. 150,000 170 30 90 |
| D Haiphon (Haiphong) | 1678 | R Lat | Ps | 61 | 46,400 | 72,500 | Port, coastal, mining. 3.6% RC. Few clergy. 65,000 79 8 4 |
| D Hung-Hoa | 1895 | R Lat | Ps | 23 | 59,100 | 92,300 | Plateaus, China-Laos; Diem Bien Phu area. 4% RC. 6,000 23 32 34 |
| D Langson & Caobang | 1913 | R Lat | Ps | 11 | 2,100 | 3,300 | On China frontier. Scattered population, 0.7% RC. 2,500 13 4 7 |
| D Phat Diem | 1901 | R Lat | Ps | 61 | 49,800 | 77,800 | Delta. 1950s, anti-communist RC militias. 13% RC. 80,000 144 26 39 |
| D Thai-Binh | 1936 | R Lat | Ps | 14 | 74,200 | 116,000 | Red river delta. 1954, 10% RC; 1955, 5%. 80,000 79 14 26 |
| D Than-Hoa | 1932 | R Lat | Ps | 44 | 39,700 | 62,000 | 1950s, scene of heavy RC/communist battles. 3% RC. 22,000 62 26 50 |
| D Vinh | 1846 | R Lat | Ps | 135 | 132,400 | 206,900 | Mountainous, poor. Worst-bombed diocese. 8% RC. 57,000 67 117 64 |
| Evangelical Church of North Viet-Nam | 1911 | P Hol | x...C | 100 | 10,000 | 20,000 | *Hoi Tin Lanh* (*Good News Society*). Formerly M=CMA(USA). Widespread. 26n,1s. |
| Isolated radio churches | 1952 | I rad | ..... | | 3,000 | 5,000 | Isolated radio believers across North. |
| Patriotic Catholic Ch in N Viet-Nam | 1955 | I CCa | ..... | 15 | 5,000 | 10,000 | 1955, 1963 state-aided attempts ex RCC. Vatican renounced. 15 priests. Declining. |
| **Total affiliated (mid-1970)** | | | | **840** | **721,900** | **1,135,000** | **Total denominations (1970) . . . 4.** |
| | | | | | | | (b) *South Viet-Nam, 1970* |
| Anglican Church (D Singapore) | | A Cen | aweA. | 3 | 1,150 | 2,200 | *Mekong Missionary District.* 60% USA including military, 40% British. W=27%. |
| Assemblies of God | 1972 | P Pe2 | ZF... | 23 | 100 | 200 | M=AoG(USA). Small group of Classical Pentecostal congregations. 6f. |
| **Catholic Church in South Viet-Nam:** | c1530 | R Lat | P.F.R | 1,365 | 1,169,600 | 1,799,354 | *Cong Giao.* C=11+10+12. 5q,6s(1043),W=80%. 1924nx,1291m,6475w,P=89%,84781Yy. |
| M Ho Chi Minh City (Saigon) | 1844 | R Lat | Ps | 229 | 309,300 | 475,695 | 1975: 3.2 million population, 16% Catholic. 494 512 2042 95 23701 |
| D Cantho | 1955 | R Lat | Ps | 51 | 52,300 | 80,431 | Rice-growing Mekong delta. 63,400 Caodaists. 93 16 312 76 4582 |
| D Dalat | 1960 | R Lat | Ps | 111 | 50,500 | 77,687 | High plateaus, tribes. Many schools, convents. 153 169 483 91 5508 |
| D Long-Xuyen | 1960 | R Lat | Ps | 61 | 69,100 | 106,377 | Near Cambodia. Mostly refugees from North. 108 8 200 95 3990 |
| D My-Tho | 1960 | R Lat | Ps | 91 | 39,800 | 61,188 | In Mekong delta; area southwest of Saigon. 65 0 165 95 3436 |
| D Phu-Cuong | 1965 | R Lat | Ps | 66 | 41,700 | 64,208 | Area north of Saigon in mountainous region. 61 0 56 78 2482 |
| D Vinh-Long | 1938 | R Lat | Ps | 51 | 51,700 | 79,613 | Mekong. 204,800 Caodaists, 90,700 Hoa Hao. 123 60 567 77 4372 |
| D Xuan-Loc | 1965 | R Lat | Ps | 147 | 196,700 | 302,611 | NE of Saigon. RCs all refugees from North. 210 164 808 80 11195 |
| M Hué | 1850 | R Lat | Ps | 67 | 54,600 | 83,988 | Northern coast. Ancient imperial capital. 163 91 742 78 3239 |
| D Ban Mê Thuôt | 1967 | R Lat | Ps | 38 | 30,100 | 46,338 | High plateau. Tribes. RCs all from North. 63 20 49 80 2175 |
| D Da-Nang | 1963 | R Lat | Ps | 37 | 72,300 | 111,216 | Coastal area, heavily damaged during war. 76 5 392 95 5132 |
| D Kontum | 1932 | R Lat | Pmep | 239 | 51,200 | 78,772 | Many tribes. 620,000 animists. 68 7 105 90 5875 |
| D Nhatrang | 1957 | R Lat | Ps | 131 | 88,400 | 136,000 | Coast near Dalat. Heavy fighting 1970–75. 158 102 337 95 5778 |
| D Qui-Nhon | 1659 | R Lat | Ps | 46 | 61,900 | 95,230 | Coastal area between Nhatrang and Danang. 89 137 217 95 3316 |
| Church of Christ | c1967 | I ind | x.... | | 100 | 300 | *INC. Iglesia ni Cristo* (Manalista), HQ Quezon (Philippines). Filipinos. |
| Church of God | 1968 | I ind | ..... | 5 | 61 | 100 | Small group of indigenous Vietnamese independent congregations. |
| Ch of Jesus C of Latter-day Saints | | M LdS | x.... | | 4,000 | 7,027 | *Mormons.* M=CJCLdS(Utah,USA). Many USA personnel and military till 1975 evacuation. |
| Churches of Christ (Non-Instrumental) | 1963 | P Dis | x.... | 6 | 100 | 200 | M=CC(Non-Instrumental) (USA). Until 1972 many USA personnel on military bases. 4f. |
| Evangelical Church of Viet-Nam | 1911 | P Hol | xF..E | 490 | 45,287 | 127,505 | *ECVN. Hoi-thanh Tin-lanh VN.* M=CMA. 344n,83f,G=4%pa,2H,46h,6p,4s(135),3600Y,19062z. |
| Isolated radio churches | 1952 | I rad | ..... | 190 | 3,800 | 7,600 | Radio believers in mountains, mostly youths and students. R=4500,T=39000(ICI). |
| Jehovah's Witnesses | 1936 | M Jeh | x.... | 2 | 68 | 300 | *Watch Tower. IBSA.* Active witnessing under way by 1957. Underground. 12Y. |
| Mennonite Church of Viet-Nam | 1957 | P Men | G...E | 1 | 145 | 300 | M=EMBMC(USA). Aid and relief. 1 school. 1n,4x,14f,G=30%pa,1h,1p,W=30%,22Y,3z. |
| Seventh-day Adventist Church | 1929 | P Adv | x.... | 21 | 2,758 | 5,000 | *SDA Mission in Vietnam. Vietnam Mission.* 8nx,105mw,15f,1H,1j,1r,24t(2877),459Y. |
| Vietnam Christ's Church | 1964 | I Hol | .v... | 7 | 3,000 | 5,000 | *Co-Doc-Giao. Viet-Nam Inland Mission.* Ex CMA. 1969 applied to join WCC. 3n,34m,2h. |
| Viet-Nam Baptist Mission | 1959 | P Bap | T.... | 31 | 1,173 | 5,000 | M=SBC(USA). Expanding until 1975. 4 schools. 14n,39f,1h,1s,235Y. |
| United World Mission | 1956 | P int | xF..E | 37 | 2,613 | 14,491 | M=UWM(USA). Among 14 Montagnard tribes. Leprosarium, 2 orphanages. 7f,1s. |
| USA military chaplaincies | 1961 | P int | x.... | | 80,000 | 150,000 | Chaplaincies to armed forces (USA, Australia, et alia) from 1961 till 1972 exodus. |
| Other indigenous churches | | I ind | ..... | 16 | 2,000 | 3,000 | Chinese Christian Assemblies, Spiritual Food Ch, and other Chinese bodies. |
| Other Protestant denominations | | P | ..... | 30 | 1,000 | 2,000 | Total about 15 (see list below); including 8 expatriate congregations. |
| **Total affiliated (mid-1970)** | | | | **2,580** | **1,316,955** | **2,129,577** | **Total denominations (1970) . . . 33.** |
| | | | | | | | (c) *North and South Viet-Nam combined, 1970–80* |
| **Total affiliated (mid-1970)** | | | | **3,420** | **2,038,855** | **3,264,577** | **Total denominations (1970) . . . 37.** |
| **Total affiliated (mid-1975)** | | | | **3,600** | **2,026,100** | **3,244,100** | **Total denominations (1975) . . . 42.** |
| **Total affiliated (mid-1980)** | | | | **3,700** | **2,265,200** | **3,627,000** | **Total denominations (1980) . . . 34.** |

NOTES ON TABLE ABOVE

COLUMNS for meanings and CODES (cols. 1, 3, 4, 8): see Codebook (Part 6). Column 1: **Boldface type** = church with over 10% of country's affiliated Christians.

NATIONAL COUNCILS (Column 4, 5th letter).

C = Vietnamese Association of Churches (government-sponsored in North before 1970).

E = Evangelical Fellowship of Viet-Nam (FEV)(Hoi Tin Lanh Tong Cong Vietnam), before 1975 in South only.

R = Conférence Episcopale du Viêtnam (CEV)(Episcopal Conference of Viet-Nam).

*Other national councils.* National Liaison Committee of Patriotic and Peace-Loving Catholics (government-organized in North before 1970).

OTHER PROTESTANT DENOMINATIONS. These, mainly from the USA, operated in the South only, until 1975, and included: Baptist Bible Fellowship International (1971), Baptist International Missions (1971), Bethany Fellowship Missions (1969), Christ-Bearers (Christusträger, WGermany), Ch of the Brethren (1965), Chs of Christ (Instrumental)(1972), Eglise Réformée de France, International Protestant Ch, Overseas Missionary Fellowship (1960), United Korean Ch in Viet-Nam, Worldwide Evangelization Crusade (1956), World-Wide Missions (1963).

PEOPLES (ethnolinguistic). Christians (a) *North.* (1970) About 88% Vietnamese, 7% Tai, 3% Muong, 1% Chinese. (b) *South.* (1970) 73.2% Vietnamese, 16.6% Montagnard (Highland tribal), 9.5% USA military and civilian (8.5% White, 1.0% Black), 0.7% Chinese, French, British, Anglo-Australian, Filipino, Korean. (1975) 80.8% Vietnamese, 18.4% Montagnard, 0.8% Chinese. (c) *North and South.* (1970) 78.2% Vietnamese, 10.8% Montagnard, 5.5% USA White, 2.4% Tai, 1.0% Muong, 0.8% Chinese, 0.7% USA Black, French, British, Anglo-Australian, Filipino, Korean. (Mid-1975) 83.2% Vietnamese, 12.0% Montagnard, 2.4% Tai, 1.0% Muong, 0.9 Chinese.

COUNTRY-WIDE TOTALS

EVANGELIZATION (see Part 5). 1900: 27%. 1970: 58%. 1980: 61%. *Mass evangelism.* Among recent campaigns: 1967, Oral Roberts visit; 1969, widespread campaign 'Evangelism Deep and Wide'; 1972, extensive campaigns in southern districts of Evangelical Church of Viet-Nam. *Radiophonic evangelism.* FEBC (4,107 listeners' letters in 1975; in 1976, 2.5 broadcast hours per day in Vietnamese), ICI (39,000 enrolments, 22,000 active students in 1975), et alia.

FOREIGN MISSIONARIES AND PERSONNEL (nationals serving abroad, from South Viet-Nam only)(1973). Total 360 in France, Cambodia, Laos, New Caledonia, Thailand, USA et alia: about 340 Roman Catholics, about 20 Protestants. After 1975 no more missionaries could officially leave.

FOREIGN MISSIONARIES AND PERSONNEL (aliens received from abroad, by South Viet-Nam only)(1973). Total 806. *From Western world.* 731: about 420 Roman Catholics, 311 Protestants (289 in 27 USA societies, 6 in 2 WGermany societies, 5 in 1 Norway society, 5 in 2 UK societies, 4 in 4 Australia societies, 1 in 1 Switzerland society, 1 in 1 New Zealand society). *From Third World.* 75: about 50 Roman Catholics, about 15 Protestants from Hong Kong and Korea, about 10 Asian indigenous from Philippines, Taiwan, Korea and Hong Kong. In 1975 the majority of all foreign missionaries left and no more were allowed in.

INSTITUTIONS (church-operated)(1973). Total 730 all in the South, including 310 higher schools (29 minor seminaries), 350 medical centres (54 hospitals), 43 religious communities, 17 seminaries (11 RC, 6 Protestant), 2 universities.

PERIODICALS. About 30 titles in the South in 1975 (including 15 RC).

PERSONNEL. (a) *North* (1973). 707 nationals. (b) *South* (1973). About 12,935 (12,129 national, 806 foreign). (c) *Viet-Nam* (1973). 13,642 (12,836 national, 806 foreign); (1976) About 12,300 (all nationals: in the South, 2,300 priests, 1,000 brothers, 6,000 sisters, 2,000 catechists; in the North, 300 priests and 700 sisters).

RELIGIOUS LIBRARIES. About 65.

SCRIPTURE DISTRIBUTION (1975). Annual totals: 20,912 Bibles (24% free, 66% subsidized, 10% commercial), 104,983

NTs (59% free, 40% subsidized, 1% commercial), 879,501 UBS portions, 1,578,572 UBS selections. *Translations completed.* Portion: 21 languages since 1890. NT: 4 languages since 1914. Bible: Vietnamese in 1916.
SERVICE AGENCIES. About 62, including CCCI, CECVN, CEV, COREV, CWS, EFV, ICRA, JAC, JEC, JIC, JOC, LWR, MCC, MTC, OC, OMI, ONEC, PTL, SIL, SU, THDL, VMS, WBT, WLC(EHC), WVI, YMCA, YWCA.

ADDITIONAL DATA ON CHURCHES
CATHOLIC CHURCH IN NORTH VIET-NAM. The number of Catholics has fluctuated greatly due to population movements. At the time of the Geneva Agreement in 1954, about 40% of all Catholics in the north, about 560,500 persons, fled to the south with 808 priests (71% of the total in 1954); this exodus is divided by diocese in the first 2 sub-columns of column 8 above. The heavy Catholic losses subsequently of members and buildings in bombings, warfare and emigration have been offset by population expansion and new construction. *Places of worship.* The numbers in 1963 were (for the 10 dioceses, in the order shown): 478, 236, 432, 316, 356, 14, 282, 536, 176, 650. Total: 3,476. *Personnel.* All nationals. *Priests* (1970). About 315, divided by diocese as shown in third sub-column, column 8. *Sisters* (1970). About 351, divided by diocese as shown in last sub-column of column 8.
*Catholic organizations.* Before unification there was no episcopal conference, the only meeting of bishops having taken place in 1971 on the occasion of the consecration of 3 new bishops. Individual Vietnamese bishops have received extensive powers from Rome. There are no associations of religious personnel, nor pastoral or presbyteral councils. Indeed few Catholic organizations of any sort are active, although there is an Association of Catholic Youth (Thanh Niem Cong Ciao) which is organized at the diocesan and parish levels and forms part of the government's National Council of Youth. It engages in both religious and social activities and was involved in civil defence during the recent war. Catholic girls also work in day nurseries and kindergartens.

Another important organization is the National Liaison Committee of Patriotic and Peace-Loving Catholics of Viet-Nam, which consists of a permanent council in Hanoi (with a priest president and a layman as vice-president) and is also organized at the regional (North, South, Centre) and provincial levels. During the period of French rule, a Catholic minority (about 10,000, of whom some 15 were priests) were involved in anti-colonial activities and organized in each administrative and military zone a Liaison Committee of Patriotic Catholics. Following the episcopal declaration of 1951 the majority continued to collaborate with the Viet Minh, believing the episcopal condemnation to be illegitimate. In 1955 they formed a national committee and today about two-thirds of all priests have joined these committees at various levels. After the American bombing began, their number increased. The hierarchy remained suspicious, considering this a Communist instrument to destroy religion, but they have not condemned it officially. The functions of the committee are to print the liturgy, publish the texts of Vatican II and others from Rome, edit the monthly journal *Chinh Nghia* (Just Cause) and other publications; manufacture communion hosts and import wine for mass; and organize meetings on social questions. The committee is integrated into the official government co-ordinating agency, Front de la Patrie.

Before 1954 each of the 10 dioceses had a minor seminary, and there were 5 major seminaries: (1) Hanoi, which was directed by Sulpicians, with seminarians from Hanoi and Hung-Hoa plus a few others; (2) Nam Dinh, a pontifical seminary directed by Spanish Dominicans serving the dioceses of Haiphong, Thai-Binh, Bac Ninh and Langson; (3) Phu Nhoc, which served the diocese of Phat Diem and whose seminarians were involved in the fight against the Viet Minh; (4) Buichu, which was founded in 1936 but joined to Hanoi in 1952; and (5) Xa Doai, which catered for the diocese of Vinh. Religious personnel also had training centres: Spanish Dominicans at Thai-Binh; Redemptorists at Thai Ha Ap; Franciscans at Vinh; Dominicans of Lyons at Hanoi; plus other centres for Benedictines, Cistercians and a few congregations of brothers. With the exodus South came the departure of all seminarians and staff except in the diocese of Vinh; and this was the same for religious personnel. The Vinh seminary continued to function until 1972 when it was abandoned because of the bombing. The bishop of Buichu then trained his own seminarians himself. Some training was also given at Hanoi until 1960 and this was begun again for 9 seminarians in 1973. A few priests were also trained at Hung Hoa.

Officially, ministerial training is authorized. The regulations laid down for minor seminaries require that they follow the official programme of secondary studies until the 10th year. Several were opened in 1955 but closed by the bishops in 1960, conditions being considered unacceptable. For major seminaries the following stipulations are in force: no anti-patriotic teaching, respect for non-Christians, and respect for the laws of the state. Certain manuals were banned by the civil authorities, including one concerning private property in divine law. Also a list of all candidates must be submitted for approval to government. Except at Vinh, the bishops have not agreed to these conditions. Seminarians are exempt from military service, and several privately-trained priests have failed to obtain government recognition as ordained clergy.

The Holy See has had no diplomatic relations with North Viet-Nam.
CATHOLIC CHURCH IN SOUTH VIET-NAM. *New diocese.* Created in 1975: D Phan-Thiêt, suffragan of Saigon. *Catholics.* Including (1966) 9,338 Chinese, rising to 12,000 by 1975. *Catechumens.* (1959) 97,407; (1961) 111,324; (1963) 110,990. *Annual baptisms.* (1972) 90.1% infant, 9.9% adult. *Personnel* (1973). About 95% nationals, 5% expatriates. *Priests* (1972). 1,924, including 176 expatriates, 366 religious. *Sisters* (1972). Including 150 expatriates. *Seminaries* (1973). 6. *Seminarians* (1972). 877 secular, 166 religious. (1976) About 1,000. *Catechists* (1972). 2,369. *Indigenous religious congregations.* 9 local congregations for brothers, and 25 for sisters, 15 of the latter being named Lovers of the Cross (Amantes de la Croix, first founded in 1670 and since spread at the diocesan level). *Foreign orders and congregations.* Priests: SOC, OSB, OP, OFM, OH, SJ, CSSR, SDB, MEP. Brothers: FSC, Little Brothers of Jesus. Sisters: St-Paul de Chartres, Providence de Portieux, Franciscans and others.
*Catholic organizations.* Prior to 1975, the Episcopal Conference of Viet-Nam (CEV) has had its headquarters in Saigon. Organizations of religious personnel were the Union of Male Major Superiors, and the Union of Female Major Superiors, but there were no priests' or pastoral councils. Several lay groups were active. Until 1970 when it was dissolved, one movement brought together Catholic refugees from the North for the struggle against Communism: Forces of the Great Union (Luc Luong Dai Doan Ket). Other lay movements were the Crusaders (for children); Legion of Mary, JOC, JEC, JAC and JIC (all of which were specialized movements of Catholic Action and whose chaplains were often arrested before 1975); Pax Romana and the Blue Army of Fatima, the latter being an anti-Communist and anti-progressivist group.

The Holy See has had no diplomatic relations with South Viet-Nam but was represented to the Catholic hierarchy by an apostolic delegate based in Saigon.

Training institutions included a pastoral centre for marriage preparation maintained by Jesuits; theological faculties at Dalat and Saigon; and major seminaries at Saigon, Vinh-Long, Long-Xuyen, Hué, Da-Nang and 2 at Dalat.

For home missions, the Vietnamese Missionary Society, founded by the episcopate in 1972, brought together priests, religious personnel and laity for the evangelization of tribal peoples, especially in the area of the high plateaux.

Th Catholic educational programme was co-ordinated by the Association of Christian Schools in Viet-Nam, founded in 1964. In 1970 there were 1,030 Catholic primary schools (355,765 pupils, of whom 97,347 were non-Catholics); 226 secondary schools (153,928 students, of whom 70,101 were non-Catholics); and 2 Catholic universities at Dalat and Saigon. In 1972 there were 41 Catholic hospitals (7,000 beds), 240 dispensaries and 9 leprosaria. Caritas Viet-Nam, a member of Caritas Internationalis, was organized on the national level in 1965 to respond to the problems posed by war and refugees. Catholic Relief Services working in co-operation with the USA government, provided large amounts of aid, especially food. In 1973, after the Paris Agreement, the bishops formed a national development organization (Committee of Co-operation for Rehabilitation in Viet-Nam, COREV) for channelling international aid. Agricultural development projects were co-ordinated by a social secretariat in Saigon, and the Catholic Church also gave attention to providing care for the large number of orphans created by the war. In 1974 there were 85 orphanages, 366 nurseries, and 29 homes for the aged.
EVANGELICAL CHURCH OF VIET-NAM. Full name: Hoi-thanh Tin-lanh Viet-Nam. *Membership.* In 1975, 40% tribal. *Schools.* Over 80, until nationalized in 1975.

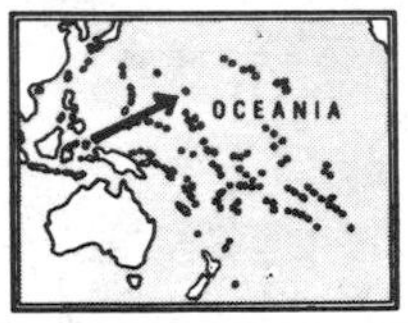


# WAKE ISLAND

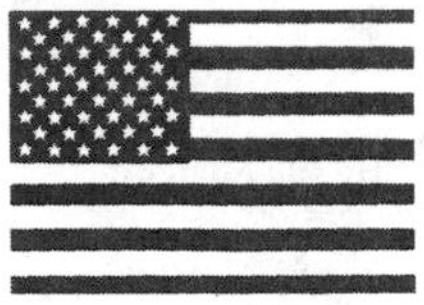

## SECULAR DATA

**STATE. Official name:** Wake Island. Earlier names: Halcyon Island, Helsion Island.
**Flag** (shown above right): That of the USA.
**Area:** 8 sq.km. (3 sq.miles). Description: 3 coral islets. Agricultural land: 0.0%.
**Government:** Island dependency (unincorporated territory) of the USA, since 1899 (1899 claimed by USA, 1941–45 Japanese rule).
**Official language:** English.
**Armed forces** (1973): 1,600 USA troops.

**DEMOGRAPHY. Population:** 1,647 (census of 1.IV.1970. For 1970–2000 (UN), see last row of Table 1). Population density (1975): 200/sq.km. (518/sq.mile). Under 15 years: 44%. Growth rate (1975–80): 0% per year (births 3.49%, deaths –0.79%, emigrants –2.70%). Life expectancy (1975–80): 63.8 years. Household size: 5.0 persons.
**Major languages:** English.

**ETHNOLINGUISTIC GROUPS:** 99% USA (military & civilian) (90% White, 9% Black).

**MONEY** (1977). **Monetary unit:** US dollar (= 100 cents). **National income per person:** US$4,000. Average annual family income: US$20,000.

**EDUCATION.** Adult literacy: 100%.

**COMMUNICATION** (per 1,000 people). Phones: 200.

TABLE 1. RELIGIOUS ADHERENTS IN WAKE ISLAND

| Year | 1900 | | mid-1970 | | Annual change, 1970–1980 | | | | mid-1975 | | mid-1980 | | 2000 | |
|---|---|---|---|---|---|---|---|---|---|---|---|---|---|---|
| *Name* | *Adherents* | *%* | *Adherents* | *%* | *Natural* | *Conversion* | *Total* | *Rate* | *Adherents* | *%* | *Adherents* | *%* | *Adherents* | *%* |
| **Christians** | **50** | **50.0** | **1,400** | **87.5** | **0** | **0** | **0** | **0.00** | **1,400** | **87.5** | **1,400** | **87.5** | **1,200** | **60.0** |
| professing | 50 | 50.0 | 1,400 | 87.5 | 0 | 0 | 0 | 0.00 | 1,400 | 87.5 | 1,400 | 87.5 | 1,200 | 60.0 |
| Protestants | 30 | 30.0 | 800 | 50.0 | 0 | 0 | 0 | 0.00 | 800 | 50.0 | 800 | 50.0 | 800 | 40.0 |
| Roman Catholics | 20 | 20.0 | 600 | 37.5 | 0 | 0 | 0 | 0.00 | 600 | 37.5 | 600 | 37.5 | 400 | 20.0 |
| nominal | 50 | 50.0 | 400 | 25.0 | 0 | 0 | 0 | 0.00 | 400 | 25.0 | 400 | 25.0 | 400 | 20.0 |
| affiliated | 0 | 0.0 | 1,000 | 62.5 | 0 | 0 | 0 | 0.00 | 1,000 | 62.5 | 1,000 | 62.5 | 800 | 40.0 |
| total practising | 0 | *0* | 800 | *80* | 0 | 0 | 0 | 0.00 | 800 | *80* | 800 | *80* | 400 | *50* |
| non-practising | 0 | *0* | 200 | *20* | 0 | 0 | 0 | 0.00 | 200 | *20* | 200 | *20* | 400 | *50* |
| Protestants | 0 | 0.0 | 500 | 31.3 | 0 | 0 | 0 | 0.00 | 500 | 31.3 | 500 | 31.3 | 400 | 20.0 |
| Roman Catholics | 0 | 0.0 | 500 | 31.3 | 0 | 0 | 0 | 0.00 | 500 | 31.3 | 500 | 31.3 | 400 | 20.0 |
| Other religionists | 50 | 50.0 | 200 | 12.5 | 0 | 0 | 0 | 0.00 | 200 | 12.5 | 200 | 12.5 | 800 | 40.0 |
| **Country's population** | **100** | **100.0** | **1,600** | **100.0** | **0** | **0** | **0** | **0.00** | **1,600** | **100.0** | **1,600** | **100.0** | **2,000** | **100.0** |

COLUMNS, ROWS. For meanings and definitions, see Codebook (Part 6). Note that, by definition, total 'Christians' = professing + crypto-Christians, which also = affiliated + nominal Christians. Percentages may not always total exactly, due to rounding.

NOTES ON RELIGIONS
CHRISTIANS. Mostly USA military and technical personnel.
OTHER RELIGIONISTS. Unorganized adherents of various non-Christian religions, serving in the armed forces.

**CHRISTIANITY.** Protestant and Catholic chaplains serving with the USA armed forces are active in organizing worship services for military personnel and other residents of the island. There are no other parishes apart from this military establishment. Wake Island is part of the Catholic diocese of Agaña in Guam.

**CHURCH AND STATE.** The island was annexed by the USA in 1899, and administrative jurisdiction is under the USA's Federal Aviation Administration. Although in theory church and state are separate in USA overseas territories, Protestant and Catholic chaplains serving Wake Island are government appointees paid through the USA military budget.

TABLE 2. ORGANIZED CHURCHES AND DENOMINATIONS IN WAKE ISLAND

| Official name 1 | Begun 2 | Type 3 | Counc 4 | Congs 5 | Adults 6 | Affiliated 7 | Names, notes, and other statistics (see Codebook) 8 |
|---|---|---|---|---|---|---|---|
| Catholic Church (D Agaña) | 1948 | R Lat | P.... | 1 | 300 | 500 | Under D Agaña (Guam). Temporary USA personnel. 1 OFM military chaplain. |
| Protestant military chaplaincies | c1930 | P uni | ..... | 3 | 300 | 500 | US Armed Forces chaplaincies, served by US military chaplains. |
| Total affiliated (mid-1970) | | | | 4 | 600 | 1,000 | Total denominations (1970) . . . 2. |
| Total affiliated (mid-1975) | | | | 4 | 600 | 1,000 | Total denominations (1975) . . . 2. |
| Total affiliated (mid-1980) | | | | 4 | 600 | 1,000 | Total denominations (1980) . . . 2. |

PEOPLES (ethnolinguistic). Christians: 99% USA military & civilian (90% White, 9% Black).

COUNTRY-WIDE TOTALS
EVANGELIZATION (see Part 5). 1900: 90%. 1970: 100%.

1980: 100%.
FOREIGN MISSIONARIES AND PERSONNEL (aliens from abroad)(1973). Total 2. *From Western world.* 2 (1 Roman Catholic, 1 Protestant) from USA.
PERSONNEL. About 2 (foreign).

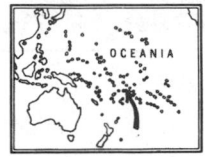

# Wallis & Futuna Islands

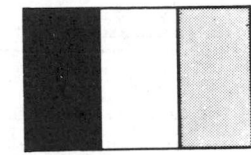

## SECULAR DATA

STATE. Official name: The Territory of the Wallis and Futuna Islands (Le Territoire de Wallis et Futuna).
Flag (shown above right): That of France.
Area: 200 sq.km. (77 sq.miles).
Government: Overseas territory of France, since 1961 (kingdoms under French advisers, 1887 French protectorate).
Legislature: Territorial Council, 6 members.
Official language: French (*Français*).
Capital: Mata Uta.
Armed forces (1976): French.

DEMOGRAPHY. Population: 8,546 (census of III.1969. For 1970–2000 (UN), see last row of Table 1). Population density (1975): 45/sq.km. (117/sq.mile). Under 15 years: 48%. Growth rate (1975–80): 0.0% per year (births 4.11%, deaths −0.91%, emigrants −3.20%). Life expectancy (1975–80): 60.3 years.
Household size: 5.8 persons.
Major languages: French, Uvean, Futunan.

ETHNOLINGUISTIC GROUPS: 66.5% Uvean, 31.9% Futunan (Polynesian), 0.9% French (75), 0.7% other White (European).

MONEY (1977). Monetary unit: CFP franc (= 100 centimes);

US$1 = CFPF 91.00.
National income per person: US$300. Average annual family income: US$1,740.
Cost of living in capital (1976): Daily cost of living: US$27.

HEALTH. Hospitals: 5 (108 beds). Doctors: 3. Lepers: 11 (1.2 per 1,000).

EDUCATION. Adult literacy: 95%.

COMMUNICATION (per 1,000 people). Phones: 53.

TABLE 1. RELIGIOUS ADHERENTS IN THE WALLIS & FUTUNA ISLANDS

| Year | 1900 | | mid-1970 | | Annual change, 1970–1980 | | | | mid-1975 | | mid-1980 | | 2000 | |
|---|---|---|---|---|---|---|---|---|---|---|---|---|---|---|
| Name | Adherents | % | Adherents | % | Natural | Conversion | Total | Rate | Adherents | % | Adherents | % | Adherents | % |
| Christians | 1,600 | 80.0 | 8,900 | 98.9 | 0 | 0 | 0 | 0.00 | 8,900 | 98.9 | 8,900 | 98.9 | 8,730 | 97.0 |
| professing | 1,600 | 80.0 | 8,900 | 98.9 | 0 | 0 | 0 | 0.00 | 8,900 | 98.9 | 8,900 | 98.9 | 8,730 | 97.0 |
| Roman Catholics | 1,600 | 80.0 | 8,900 | 98.9 | 0 | 0 | 0 | 0.00 | 8,900 | 98.9 | 8,900 | 98.9 | 8,730 | 97.0 |
| nominal | 100 | 5.0 | 538 | 6.0 | 0 | 0 | 0 | 0.00 | 540 | 6.0 | 540 | 6.0 | 630 | 7.0 |
| affiliated | 1,500 | 75.0 | 8,362 | 92.9 | 0 | 0 | 0 | 0.00 | 8,360 | 92.9 | 8,360 | 92.9 | 8,100 | 90.0 |
| total practising | 1,485 | 99 | 8,278 | 99 | 0 | 0 | 0 | 0.00 | 8,280 | 99 | 8,280 | 99 | 6,480 | 80 |
| non-practising | 15 | 1 | 84 | 1 | 0 | 0 | 0 | 0.00 | 80 | 1 | 80 | 1 | 1,620 | 20 |
| Roman Catholics | 1,500 | 75.0 | 8,362 | 92.9 | 0 | 0 | 0 | 0.00 | 8,360 | 92.9 | 8,360 | 92.9 | 8,100 | 90.0 |
| Other religionists | 400 | 20.0 | 100 | 1.1 | 0 | 0 | 0 | 0.00 | 100 | 1.1 | 100 | 1.1 | 270 | 3.0 |
| Country's population | 2,000 | 100.0 | 9,000 | 100.0 | 0 | 0 | 0 | 0.00 | 9,000 | 100.0 | 9,000 | 100.0 | 9,000 | 100.0 |

COLUMNS, ROWS. For meanings and definitions, see Codebook (Part 6). Note that, by definition, total 'Christians' = professing + crypto-Christians, which also = affiliated + nominal Christians. Percentages may not always total exactly, due to rounding.
CENSUSES. The religion question has not been asked.

COUNTRY'S POPULATION. The figures on the bottom line of the table are averages, since the population fluctuates considerably between 7,000 and 10,000 due to short-term labour migration of young men to New Caledonia (where 5,984 Wallis & Futuna Islanders lived in 1970, rising to 10,000 by 1976) and New Hebrides (500 in 1970).

OTHER RELIGIONISTS. Unorganized expatriates who are adherents of non-Christian religions including Baha'i, and a small number of traditional (tribal) religionists indigenous to the islands.

NON-CHRISTIAN RELIGIONS. Traditional pre-Christian religion has a few remnant adherents, and there are a few other non-Christian religionists.

CHRISTIANITY. Virtually the entire population has become Catholic, and Catholicism is the only organized denomination represented in the islands. A Marist priest established the first mission on Wallis in 1836, and there are now stations at Matautu, Malaetoli, and Lano. Futuna was reached later and is served by mission centres at Sigave and Alo. In 1972 the bishop, a Frenchman, resided at Lano; while his auxiliary, a national, was stationed in Futuna. However, in 1974 the European bishop withdrew and was replaced by his indigenous auxiliary. During the 1960s the last French bishop effected an aggiornamento (renewal) preparing for the departure of French clergy and sisters in order to leave the islands to national workers. Indigenous vocations have been successful, the first national priests being ordained as early as 1886. There were in 1974, 8 national priests in the islands (plus 4 more serving as missionaries in other parts of Oceania) as contrasted with only 2 expatriate priests and indigenous brothers and sisters are equally well represented.

**Eglise Catholique, Diocèse de Wallis et Futuna.** Government postage stamps commemorating 1836 arrival of first French missionaries.

CHURCH AND STATE. An agreement was signed in July 1969 between the bishop and the French government recognizing Catholic education, the only education existent, as the quasi-official educational system of the territory. At the same time provision was made for subsidizing it. As is true with other French overseas departments and territories but unlike France itself, there is no real separation of church and state. Until 1970 the Catholic bishop

bore the title 'co-prince' of the kingdom. The king and the mission, with the acquiescence of the French civil authorities, until recently formed a veritable theocracy, where for example failure to attend mass was punishable by fine of a pig.

BROADCASTING. For Catholics, an association grouping Wallis and Futuna with Samoa, Tonga and the Cook Islands is a member of UNDA.

TABLE 2. ORGANIZED CHURCHES AND DENOMINATIONS IN THE WALLIS & FUTUNA ISLANDS

| Official name 1 | Begun 2 | Type 3 | Counc 4 | Congs 5 | Adults 6 | Affiliated 7 | Names, notes, and other statistics (see Codebook) 8 |
|---|---|---|---|---|---|---|---|
| **Eglise Catholique: D Wallis & Futuna** | 1836 | R Lat | PzPY. | 5 | 4,300 | 8,362 | Suffragan, M Nouméa. M=SM2. 135 Whites. 99% Catholic. 8n,4x,8m,63w,1H,P=99%,372Yy. |
| Total affiliated (mid-1970) | | | | 5 | 4,300 | 8,362 | Total denominations (1970) . . . 1. |
| Total affiliated (mid-1975) | | | | 5 | 4,300 | 8,360 | Total denominations (1975) . . . 1. |
| Total affiliated (mid-1980) | | | | 5 | 4,300 | 8,360 | Total denominations (1980) . . . 1. |

PEOPLES (ethnolinguistic). Christians: 66.8% Wallisian (Uvean), 32.1% Futunan, 0.6% French, 0.5% other White (European).

COUNTRY-WIDE TOTALS
EVANGELIZATION (see Part 5). 1900: 98%. 1970: 100%. 1980: 100%.
FOREIGN MISSIONARIES AND PERSONNEL (nationals serving abroad)(1973). Total about 16 Roman Catholics in New Caledonia, New Hebrides, Solomon Islands, Tonga, Western Samoa et alia.
FOREIGN MISSIONARIES AND PERSONNEL (aliens from abroad)(1973).Total 22. *From Western world.* 18 Roman Catholics. *From Third World.* About 4 Roman Catholics.
INSTITUTIONS (church-operated)(1973). Total 2, a school and a hospital.
PERIODICALS. 1 title.
PERSONNEL. 83 (61 national, 22 foreign).
SCRIPTURE DISTRIBUTION (1975). Annual totals: 50 Bibles (commercial), 100 NTs (commercial). *Translations completed.* Wallisian: portion in 1971.
SERVICE AGENCIES. 6, including ACH.

ADDITIONAL DATA ON CHURCHES
EGLISE CATHOLIQUE. *Annual baptisms.* (1972) 100% infants, no adults. *Priests.* The first national (Wallisian) priests were ordained in 1886. In 1973 they numbered 12 (7 diocesan, 5 religious), but 4 were serving elsewhere (2 in New Caledonia, 1 in Samoa, 1 in New Hebrides). *Brothers.* 7 Wallisians, 1 ex-

patriate. *Sisters.* 46 nationals, 17 expatriates. *Religious congregations.* Priests: SM2. Brothers: PFM. Sisters: Soeurs Missionnaires de la Société de Marie.
*Catholic organizations.* The Diocese of Wallis and Futuna is a member of the Bishops' Conference of the Pacific (Conférence des Evêques du Pacifique, CEPAC) with its seat in Fiji. An association of priests, called the Presbyteral Council (Conseil Presbytéral), has been formed, and there are several active lay organizations: Third Order of Mary (Tiers Ordre de Marie), Legion of Mary (Légion de Marie), and Catholic Action for Men (Action Catholique des Hommes).
The Holy See is represented to the hierarchy by the Apostolic Delegation for New Zealand and the Pacific Islands based in Wellington, New Zealand.
In 1972 the church was responsible for 11 schools with 2,500 pupils and one hospital.

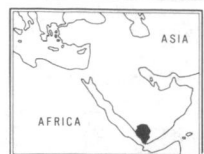

# YEMEN, North

## SECULAR DATA

**STATE. Official name:** The Yemen Arab Republic (Al-Jumhuriyah al-Arabiyah al-Yamaniyah). Unofficial name: North Yemen. Adjectives of nationality: Yemeni, a Yemenite.
**Flag** (shown above right): Red, white, and black stripes, green star.
**Area:** 195,000 sq.km. (75,290 sq.miles). Agricultural land: 42.3%.
**Government:** Military junta, since 1974 (885 Rassid dynasty, 1517 Turkish rule, 1918 imamate (monarchy), 1962 republican military coup, 1970 republic, 1974 military rule).
**Official language:** Arabic.
**Chief cities:** capital Sana 120,000 (1970), Taiz 40,000, Hodeida 40,000.
**Armed forces** (1976): Total 39,000 regular: army 37,000, navy 500, air force 1,500 (28 combat aircraft). Paramilitary forces: 20,000 tribal levies.
**Foreign forces** (1973): 200 USSR military advisers.

**DEMOGRAPHY. Population:** 5,237,893 (census of 13.I.1975. For 1970–2000 (UN), see last row of Table 1). Population density (1975): 34/sq.km. (89/sq.mile). Under 15 years: 43%. Growth rate (1975–80): 2.99% per year (births 4.83%, deaths −1.85%). Life expectancy (1975–80): 47.3 years. Household size: 5.2 persons.
**Major languages:** Arabic, Somali, Hindi, Persian, and numerous other languages.
**Urban dwellers** (1970): 5.8%. Urban growth rate (1950–70): 7.4% per year.
**Labour force:** 29%. About 1,200,000 Yemenis live abroad as labourers, mostly in Saudi Arabia.

**ETHNOLINGUISTIC GROUPS:** 98.4% Arab (in 25 tribes) & Arabized Black, 1.1% Somali, 0.2% Indo-Pakistani, 0.2% Persian, Jewish, British, USA, Latin European, Sudanese.

**MONEY** (1977). **Monetary unit:** Yemen rial (= 100 fils); US$1 = YR 4.55.

**National income per person:** US$140. Average annual family income: US$728.
**Inflation:** (1975: consumer price index 187).
**Cost of living in capital** (1976): index 121 (Washington DC=100). Daily cost of living: US$43.

**HEALTH.** Hospitals: 37 (4,200 beds). Doctors: 245. Lepers: 1,200 (0.2 per 1,000). Blind: 260,000. Psychotics: 40,000.

**EDUCATION.** Adult literacy: (1962) 2%, (1975) 20%. Education rate: 5%. Schools: 1,237.

**LITERATURE.** Newspapers: 3 dailies, 1 non-daily.

**COMMUNICATION** (per 1,000 people). Phones: 1. Radios: 40. Daily newspaper circulation: 10 copies.

### TABLE 1. RELIGIOUS ADHERENTS IN NORTH YEMEN

| Year | 1900 | | mid-1970 | | Annual change, 1970–1980 | | | | mid-1975 | | mid-1980 | | 2000 | |
| Name | Adherents | % | Adherents | % | Natural | Conversion | Total | Rate | Adherents | % | Adherents | % | Adherents | % |
|---|---|---|---|---|---|---|---|---|---|---|---|---|---|---|
| Muslims | 1,970,000 | 98.5 | 5,764,543 | 100.0 | 197,377 | −20 | 197,357 | 2.96 | 6,665,370 | 100.0 | 7,738,110 | 100.0 | 13,743,300 | 100.0 |
| Christians | 0 | 0.0 | 1,357 | 0.0 | 41 | 6 | 47 | 2.99 | 1,580 | 0.0 | 1,830 | 0.0 | 4,700 | 0.0 |
| crypto-Christians | 0 | 0.0 | 1,357 | 0.0 | 41 | 6 | 47 | 2.99 | 1,580 | 0.0 | 1,830 | 0.0 | 4,700 | 0.0 |
| affiliated | 0 | 0.0 | 1,357 | 0.0 | 41 | 6 | 47 | 2.99 | 1,580 | 0.0 | 1,830 | 0.0 | 4,700 | 0.0 |
| total practising | 0 | 0 | 1,086 | 80 | 33 | 4 | 37 | 2.97 | 1,260 | 80 | 1,460 | 80 | 3,290 | 70 |
| non-practising | 0 | 0 | 271 | 20 | 8 | 2 | 10 | 3.09 | 320 | 20 | 370 | 20 | 1,410 | 30 |
| Arab indigenous | 0 | 0.0 | 1,100 | 0.0 | 35 | 5 | 40 | 3.08 | 1,300 | 0.0 | 1,500 | 0.0 | 4,000 | 0.0 |
| Anglicans | 0 | 0.0 | 90 | 0.0 | 1 | 0 | 1 | 1.11 | 90 | 0.0 | 100 | 0.0 | 200 | 0.0 |
| Roman Catholics | 0 | 0.0 | 87 | 0.0 | 2 | 1 | 3 | 3.30 | 100 | 0.0 | 120 | 0.0 | 300 | 0.0 |
| Protestants | 0 | 0.0 | 80 | 0.0 | 3 | 0 | 3 | 3.33 | 90 | 0.0 | 110 | 0.0 | 200 | 0.0 |
| Evangelicals | 0 | 0.0 | 80 | 0.0 | 3 | 0 | 3 | 3.33 | 90 | 0.0 | 110 | 0.0 | 200 | 0.0 |
| Jews | 30,000 | 1.5 | 500 | 0.0 | −40 | 0 | −40 | −13.33 | 300 | 0.0 | 100 | 0.0 | 0 | 0.0 |
| Non-religious | 0 | 0.0 | 300 | 0.0 | 11 | 9 | 20 | 5.26 | 380 | 0.0 | 500 | 0.0 | 3,000 | 0.0 |
| Baha'is | 0 | 0.0 | 200 | 0.0 | 7 | 3 | 10 | 4.17 | 240 | 0.0 | 300 | 0.0 | 1,000 | 0.0 |
| Atheists | 0 | 0.0 | 100 | 0.0 | 4 | 2 | 6 | 4.62 | 130 | 0.0 | 160 | 0.0 | 1,000 | 0.0 |
| Country's population | 2,000,000 | 100.0 | 5,767,000 | 100.0 | 197,400 | 0 | 197,400 | 2.96 | 6,668,000 | 100.0 | 7,741,000 | 100.0 | 13,753,000 | 100.0 |

**COLUMNS, ROWS.** For meanings and definitions, see Codebook (Part 6). Note that, by definition, total 'Christians' = professing + crypto-Christians, which also = affiliated + nominal Christians. Percentages may not always total exactly, due to rounding.
**CENSUSES.** The religion question has not been asked in censuses.

## NOTES ON RELIGIONS
**ARAB INDIGENOUS.** Isolated Yemeni and other Arab radio

believers (see Table 2).
**ATHEISTS.** A small Communist party exists; membership negligible. Also present have been 200 USSR military advisers (1973).
**BAHA'IS.** Local spiritual assemblies: 1964, none; 1973, 2.
**CRYPTO-CHRISTIANS.** Unorganized individual nationals in recognized churches. In addition, for some years Yemen has had a number of Palestinian Arab Christians from Lebanon teaching in schools.

**JEWS.** In 1948–51, over 50,000 Yemeni Jews emigrated to Israel. In the 1970s the last remnants also were emigrating.
**MUSLIMS.** 3 distinct groups: 55% Zaydis (a rural Shia sect), 40% urban-dwelling Sunnis (of the Shafiite rite), 5% Ishmaelites (Ismailis). *Hajj pilgrims to Mecca.* (Including South Yemenis, about 10% of the whole); (1968) 31,489; (1969) 54,658; (1970) 50,269; (1971) 60,358; (1972) 60,250; (1973) 54,082; (1974) 75,557; North Yemen only (1975) 113,899; (1976) 61,110.

**Muslims.** Mullah (in window) hands down answers to petitions presented to him by crowd.

**Catholic Church.** In Taiz, Indian missionary nun (from Mother Teresa's Missionary Sisters of Charity) treats some of the over 1,000 Muslim lepers.

**NON-CHRISTIAN RELIGIONS. Islam** is the religion of all Yemeni nationals since the emigration of more than 50,000 Jews to Israel during 1948–51. Muslims are divided into 2 principal groups: Zaydis, a Shia sect, in the north, centre and west; Sunnis of the Shafiite rite in the south and southwest; and a few Ismailis. The ancient royal family are Zaydis.

**CHRISTIANITY.** In its early history, Yemen was identified with the ancient biblical kingdom of Sheba. Over the centuries, it was the scene of a series of conflicts between Egyptians, Turks and Arabians, as well as its own contesting imams. Christians are known to have flourished in North Yemen beginning around AD 500, but all were wiped out by Muslims within 2 centuries.
**CATHOLIC CHURCH.** Yemen is part of the vicariate of Arabia with headquarters in Abu Dhabi since 1974, having earlier been centred in Aden. The first Catholic priest, a Servite, entered Aden in 1841 and the prefecture of Aden was formed in

1854, becoming a vicariate in 1888. The vicariate was extended to cover all of Arabia in 1889.

A priest lived briefly in Hodeida towards the end of the last century, and another took up residence in 1963 for a few years in order to serve the Italian embassy and the European community.

In 1972 there were 87 baptized Catholics, all foreigners, served by Capuchins from Aden, who who were unable to obtain permission to reside in

North Yemen. In early 1973 the authorities officially invited Mother Teresa's Missionaries of Charity from India to take charge of a home for the aged and helpless built in the suburbs of Hodeida, and the first 5 sisters arrived in the country in August. The invitation was made through the USA-based Catholic Relief Services (CRS/USCC) which has been assisting Yemen since 1970. CRS was requested at the same time to seek personnel for other medical and educational posts, especially those financed by CRS and CONCERN, the latter being an Irish Catholic organization providing development assistance. A French White Father, a medical doctor by profession, also entered in 1973 for work at Sana hospital.

Although not allowed to engage in proselytism, by 1975 there were 3 White Fathers and 20 sisters resident in Yemen. In addition to their house at Hodeida, the Missionaries of Charity opened another in Taiz in 1974 and a third house, in Sana, in 1975.

PROTESTANT CHURCHES. At the invitation of the Ministry of Health, the Southern Baptist mission opened a clinic in Taiz in 1964 and another in Jibla in 1968. The Baptists have had a staff of 15 missionaries all engaged in medical work, including surgery at their main hospital. The Red Sea Team (RSMT) entered Yemen in 1969 after persistent efforts. It also operates a clinic at Yarim in co-operation with government. There are a few Yemeni secret believers. A Lebanese Arab Baptist pastor built up a congregation of 12 believing men in Taiz before being expelled in 1974 and has since been replaced by another short-term Arab pastor.

CHURCH AND STATE. According to the constitution of December 1970, Islam is the state religion, and the Sharia (Islamic law) is the basis of all legislation. The constitution was suspended following the coup d'etat of 13 June 1974, but the religious situation

Royalist postage stamps (1969) commemorating Christian themes: (left) The Presentation of Jesus in the Temple, (right) St George's 'Dragon Miracle'.

remains unaltered. In April 1975 the Yemen Arab Republic granted the 'right of return' to Jews who emigrated to Israel after the founding of the Jewish state in 1948.

BROADCASTING. No Christian broadcasts are permitted. Christian programmes in Arabic can however be heard on the international stations, FEBA (Seychelles), TWR (Monaco), ELWA (Liberia), and Radio Vatican. For a long time, Yemen audiences also had Coptic Orthodox broadcasts in Arabic from Addis Ababa.

TABLE 2. ORGANIZED CHURCHES AND DENOMINATIONS IN NORTH YEMEN

| Official name 1 | Begun 2 | Type 3 | Counc 4 | Congs 5 | Adults 6 | Affiliated 7 | Names, notes, and other statistics (see Codebook) 8 |
|---|---|---|---|---|---|---|---|
| Anglican Church (D Cyprus & the Gulf) | | A Cen | av... | 1 | 30 | 90 | In ECJME. Expatriates, among the 160 UK personnel working in Yemen. Also M=CMS. |
| Baptist Church | 1964 | P Bap | T.... | 3 | 20 | 50 | M=Southern Baptist Convention(USA). Temporary Lebanese Arab pastors. 15f,1H. |
| Catholic Church (VA Arabia) | 1963 | R Lat | P..L. | 1 | 50 | 87 | 3 WF priests, 20 sisters (13 White Sisters, 7 Missionaries of Charity; 7 Indian). |
| Isolated radio churches | c1960 | I rad | ..... | 30 | 500 | 1,100 | Isolated Arab radio believers (mostly pupils, students), via TWR, RVOG, ICI, &c. |
| Red Sea Team | 1968 | P int | xG... | 1 | 20 | 30 | M=RSMT(UK,USA). Isolated local believers and adherents. 7f,1h(Yarim). |
| Total affiliated (mid-1970) | | | | 36 | 620 | 1,357 | Total denominations (1970) . . . 5. |
| Total affiliated (mid-1975) | | | | 40 | 720 | 1,580 | Total denominations (1975) . . . 5. |
| Total affiliated (mid-1980) | | | | 45 | 840 | 1,830 | Total denominations (1980) . . . 6. |

NOTES ON TABLE ABOVE
COLUMNS: for meanings and CODES (cols. 1, 3, 4, 8): see Codebook (Part 6). Column 1: **Boldface type** = church with over 10% of country's affiliated Christians.

PEOPLES (ethnolinguistic). Christians: about 53% Arab (31% alien (Palestinian, Lebanese), 22% Yemeni), 27% British, 13% USA and other European, 6% Indian.

COUNTRY-WIDE TOTALS
EVANGELIZATION (see Part 5). 1900: 0%. 1970: 12%. 1980: 14%. *Radiophonic evangelism*. TWR, RVOG, ICI, et alia.
FOREIGN MISSIONARIES AND PERSONNEL (aliens from abroad)(1973). Total 66. *From Western world*. 49: 33 Protestants (15 in 2 USA societies, 11 in 2 UK societies, 7 in 1 Netherlands society), 16 Roman Catholics. *From Third World*. 17: about 10 Protestants (Palestinian Arab teachers from Lebanon), 7 Roman

Catholics from India.
INSTITUTIONS (church-operated)(1973). Total 2 medical centres.
PERSONNEL. 66 (foreign).
SERVICE AGENCIES. 4, including CONCERN, CRS-USCC, MC.

---

# YEMEN, South

## SECULAR DATA

STATE. **Official name**: The People's Democratic Republic of Yemen (Al-Jumhuriyah al-Yemen ad-Dimuqratiyah ash-Shabiyah). Official shortened name: Democratic Yemen. Unofficial name: Southern Yemen, South Yemen.
**Flag** (shown above right): Red, white, and black stripes with light blue triangle containing red star at hoist.
**Area**: 287,683 sq.km. (111,075 sq.miles). Agricultural land: 32.7%.
**Government**: One-party Marxist republic, since 1969 (885 North Yemeni control, 1839 British rule in Aden, 1962 Federation of South Arabia (17 sultanates), 1967 Independence as republic, 1969 Marxist regime).
**Official language**: Arabic.
**Capital**: Aden (Madinat As-Shaab/Al Ittihad) 285,370 (1973).
**Armed forces** (1976): Total 21,300 regular: army 19,000, navy 300, air force 2,000 (27 combat aircraft). Paramilitary forces: 1,500.
**Foreign forces** (1973): 300 USSR military advisers, and (1978) 1,000 Cubans.

DEMOGRAPHY. **Population**: 1,590,275 (census of 14.V.1973. For 1970–2000 (UN), see last row of Table 1). Population density (1975): 6/sq.km. (15/sq.mile). Under 15 years: 43%. Growth rate (1975–80): 2.99% per year (births 4.83%, deaths –1.85%). Life expectancy (1975–80): 47.3 years. Household size: 5.2 persons.
**Major languages**: Arabic, English, Hindi, Somali, Malay, Russian, Persian, Mahari (Mahri), Kharawi, Harsusi, Botahari, Sokotri, and numerous others.
**Urban dwellers** (1970): 28.8%. Urban growth rate (1950-70) 5.2% per year.
**Labour force**: 24%.

ETHNOLINGUISTIC GROUPS: 92.9% Arab (in over 1,300 tribes: Abdali, Aqrabi, Socotran, Yafa, &c, including Mahra and other non-Mediterranean Semitic-speaking Australoid Veddoid), 2.5% Indo-Pakistani, 2.2% Somali, 1.2% Black African (Bantu), 0.2% Jewish, 0.2% Malay, 0.1% USSR military (2,000 by 1975), 0.1% Persian, Sudanese, Cuban, East German.

MONEY (1977). **Monetary unit**: Yemeni dinar (= 1,000 fils); US$1 = YD£0.343.
**National income per person**: US$150. Average annual family income: US$780.
**Inflation**: (1970–74) 12.4% per year (1975: consumer price index 171).
**Cost of living in capital** (1976): Daily cost of living: US$31.

HEALTH. Hospitals: 17 (1,222 beds). Doctors: 117. Lepers: 400 (0.2 per 1,000). Blind: 33,000. Psychotics: 12,000.

EDUCATION. Adult literacy: (1962) 3%, (1975) 20%. Education rate: 22%. Schools: 961.

LITERATURE. Periodicals: 5. Newspapers: 3 dailies, 2 non-daily.

COMMUNICATION (per 1,000 people). Phones: 6. Radios: 90. TV sets: 20. Daily newspaper circulation: 1 copy.

TABLE 1. RELIGIOUS ADHERENTS IN SOUTH YEMEN

| Year | 1900 | | mid-1970 | | Annual change, 1970–1980 | | | | mid-1975 | | mid-1980 | | 2000 | |
|---|---|---|---|---|---|---|---|---|---|---|---|---|---|---|
| Name | Adherents | % | Adherents | % | Natural | Conversion | Total | Rate | Adherents | % | Adherents | % | Adherents | % |
| Muslims | 518,850 | 97.9 | 1,427,860 | 99.4 | 49,127 | –63 | 49,064 | 2.97 | 1,651,180 | 99.5 | 1,918,500 | 99.5 | 3,408,700 | 99.5 |
| Ahmadis | 0 | 0.0 | 200 | 0.0 | 9 | 9 | 18 | 6.21 | 290 | 0.0 | 380 | 0.0 | 1,000 | 0.0 |
| Hindus | 2,800 | 0.5 | 4,000 | 0.3 | 0 | 0 | 0 | 0.00 | 4,000 | 0.2 | 4,000 | 0.2 | 3,000 | 0.1 |
| Non-religious | 0 | 0.0 | 1,500 | 0.1 | 59 | 41 | 100 | 5.00 | 2,000 | 0.1 | 2,500 | 0.1 | 7,000 | 0.2 |
| Jews | 3,100 | 0.6 | 800 | 0.1 | –20 | 0 | –20 | –2.86 | 700 | 0.0 | 600 | 0.0 | 500 | 0.0 |
| Christians | 4,500 | 0.8 | 740 | 0.1 | 18 | 10 | 28 | 3.18 | 880 | 0.1 | 1,020 | 0.1 | 2,300 | 0.1 |
| crypto-Christians | 0 | 0.0 | 740 | 0.1 | 18 | 10 | 28 | 3.18 | 880 | 0.1 | 1,020 | 0.1 | 2,300 | 0.1 |
| professing | 4,500 | 0.8 | 0 | 0.0 | 0 | 0 | 0 | 0.00 | 0 | 0.0 | 0 | 0.0 | 0 | 0.0 |
| Protestants | 2,000 | 0.4 | 0 | 0.0 | 0 | 0 | 0 | 0.00 | 0 | 0.0 | 0 | 0.0 | 0 | 0.0 |
| Anglicans | 2,000 | 0.4 | 0 | 0.0 | 0 | 0 | 0 | 0.00 | 0 | 0.0 | 0 | 0.0 | 0 | 0.0 |
| Roman Catholics | 500 | 0.1 | 0 | 0.0 | 0 | 0 | 0 | 0.00 | 0 | 0.0 | 0 | 0.0 | 0 | 0.0 |
| affiliated | 4,500 | 0.8 | 740 | 0.1 | 18 | 10 | 28 | 3.18 | 880 | 0.1 | 1,020 | 0.1 | 2,300 | 0.1 |
| total practising | 3,150 | 70 | 590 | 80 | 14 | 9 | 23 | 3.29 | 700 | 80 | 820 | 80 | 1,610 | 70 |
| non-practising | 1,350 | 30 | 150 | 20 | 4 | 1 | 5 | 2.78 | 180 | 20 | 200 | 20 | 690 | 30 |
| Arab indigenous | 0 | 0.0 | 300 | 0.0 | 12 | 8 | 20 | 5.00 | 400 | 0.0 | 500 | 0.0 | 1,500 | 0.0 |
| Protestants | 2,000 | 0.4 | 240 | 0.0 | 5 | 1 | 6 | 2.22 | 270 | 0.0 | 300 | 0.0 | 500 | 0.0 |
| Evangelicals | 400 | 0.1 | 190 | 0.0 | 4 | 2 | 6 | 2.73 | 220 | 0.0 | 250 | 0.0 | 400 | 0.0 |
| Roman Catholics | 500 | 0.1 | 120 | 0.0 | 1 | 1 | 2 | 1.54 | 130 | 0.0 | 140 | 0.0 | 200 | 0.0 |
| Anglicans | 2,000 | 0.4 | 80 | 0.0 | 0 | 0 | 0 | 0.00 | 80 | 0.0 | 80 | 0.0 | 100 | 0.0 |
| Parsis | 350 | 0.1 | 600 | 0.0 | 0 | 0 | 0 | 0.00 | 600 | 0.0 | 600 | 0.0 | 500 | 0.0 |
| Atheists | 0 | 0.0 | 300 | 0.0 | 12 | 8 | 20 | 5.00 | 400 | 0.0 | 500 | 0.0 | 2,000 | 0.1 |
| Baha'is | 0 | 0.0 | 100 | 0.0 | 4 | 4 | 8 | 5.71 | 140 | 0.0 | 180 | 0.0 | 500 | 0.0 |
| Other religionists | 400 | 0.1 | 100 | 0.0 | 0 | 0 | 0 | 0.00 | 100 | 0.0 | 100 | 0.0 | 500 | 0.0 |
| Country's population | 530,000 | 100.0 | 1,436,000 | 100.0 | 49,200 | 0 | 49,200 | 2.96 | 1,660,000 | 100.0 | 1,928,000 | 100.0 | 3,425,000 | 100.0 |

COLUMNS, ROWS. For meanings and definitions, see Codebook (Part 6). Note that, by definition, total 'Christians' = professing + crypto-Christians, which also = affiliated + nominal Christians. Percentages may not always total exactly, due to rounding.
CENSUSES. **1901** Census of the British Empire (Aden, total population 43,974): 76.4% Muslims, 9.0% Christians (3,969 persons), 7.0% Jews, 6.2% Hindus, 0.7% Parsis, 0.4% Jains, 0.2% Buddhists, 0.2% Sikhs. **8.II.1955** (Aden Colony, excluding Perim: population 138,441): 91.3% Muslims, 4.0% Christians (total 5,580), 3.5% Hindus, 0.6% Jews, 0.4% Parsis.

## NOTES ON RELIGIONS
AHMADIS. Since 1946, there has been a small Ahmadiya community in Aden (Qadianis; HQ Rabwah, Pakistan).
ARAB INDIGENOUS. Isolated Yemeni and other Arab radio believers (see Table 2).
ATHEISTS. A few intellectuals; also 300 USSR military advisers (1973) increasing to 2,000 by 1975.
BAHA'IS. In 1 local spiritual assembly (1964, 1973).
CHRISTIANS. Since they are not recognised by the state, all Christians exist as crypto-Christians whose presence is tolerated or ignored. Before 1967, Aden used to have thousands of South Indian Protestants teaching in its schools; though these all went

at Independence in 1967, a number of Palestinian Arab Christians from Lebanon have replaced them. Although most Christians are expatriate Arabs, Indians and Europeans, there is a small number of Yemeni believers in the main churches.
MUSLIMS. Mostly Sunnis (of the Shafiite rite), with several thousand Ismailis and other Shias, also Ahmadis (the latter enumerated here under Muslims, though declared non-Muslim by Pakistan). *Hajj pilgrims to Mecca.* (1970) 2,103; (1975) 5,508; (1976) 7,792.
OTHER RELIGIONISTS. In 1901, these included 166 Jains, 75 Buddhists, 71 Sikhs.

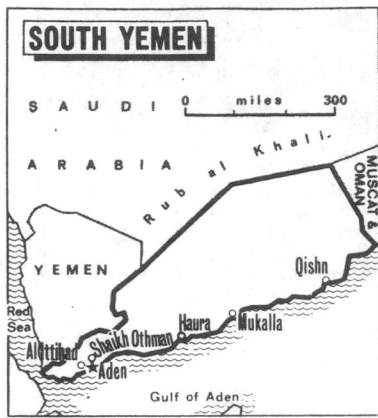

Aden: Post Office Bay and Steamer Point, with church building.

## NON-CHRISTIAN RELIGIONS. Islam is the
religion of the Arab population. Most Muslims are Sunnis of the Shafiite rite, although there are several thousand Ismailis and other Shias, and a handful of Ahmadis.

**CHRISTIANITY.** Christians existed in the 4th century and a church was built then on the site of Aden. Nestorian Christians also existed then on Socotra island, which remained a bishopric for over a thousand years. All traces of Christianity on the mainland, however, were eradicated with the coming of Islam.
CATHOLIC CHURCH. A Servite priest arrived in Aden in 1841, and a decade later the territory became part of the Vicariate of the Galla in Africa. In 1854 the prefecture of Aden was established, elevated to vicariate in 1888. The following year it was extended to cover the whole peninsula and renamed. Kuwait was detached in 1953, and in 1971 former British Somaliland was placed under Mogadishu. Aden was the headquarters of the vicariate of Arabia from the time of its establishment in 1889 until 1974 when its base was transferred to Abu Dhabi in the United Arab Emirates.
In 1972 the vicariate apostolic of Arabia had on its rolls 7,817 baptized members, all foreigners, most of whom were Indian, British, American and Italian, with a growing number of Arabs. Of these 6,980 were of the Latin rite and 877 of Eastern rites. The vicariate included 7 parishes; 15 Italian, American and Indian priests; 32 Italian sisters and a smaller number of Palestinian religious, the Rosary Sisters of Jerusalem, who arrived at the end of 1971.
In Democratic Yemen itself there were only 120 baptized Catholics in 1972 as contrasted with 9,640 in 1961. All were foreigners working in the republic. The virtual disappearance of the Catholic community during this period was due to the departure of the

British and the decline of the port of Aden following the closure of the Suez Canal. There were 4 parishes, 6 priests who also served Yemen and 22 Italian Verona Sisters. The sisters were primarily engaged in educational activities.
In 1973 private schools were nationalized and all missionaries expelled, except for 2 priests who received permission to remain in order to serve the foreign Catholic community. By 1975 no church

**Muslims.** Farmer reads Quran.

buildings had yet been confiscated.
OTHER CHURCHES. The British captured the port of Aden in 1839 and new importance was attached to it after the opening of the Suez Canal in 1869. These events had their effect on the religious situation. Anglican chaplains were soon in evidence to serve the British community and an Anglican parish still exists under the Episcopal Church in Jerusalem and the Middle East. The first Protestant missionary to the Muslims of the Arabian Peninsula was Ian Keith-Falconer, son of a Scottish earl, who opened a mission centre at Sheikh Othman in 1885. Following his death 2 years later, the Church of Scotland took over his work, where they have maintained a hospital for more than 80 years. In 1961 the Church of Scotland united with the Danish Mission to form the Church of South Arabia, which today has a small congregation supervised by an ordained pastor, all of whom are nationals. Other missions to enter Aden in recent years have been the Sudan Interior Mission, Evangelical Alliance Mission (TEAM) and the Red Sea Mission Team. During the civil war in 1965 all missionaries were withdrawn; and although several were able to return in 1968, they were forced out again by government order in 1973.

**CHURCH AND STATE.** The only Arab country to proclaim itself Marxist-Leninist, Democratic Yemen is also the only one to formally proclaim itself a secular state. The constitution restricts itself to an affirmation that 'The State shall safeguard the Arab and Islamic legacy' (Part I, Article 31).

**BROADCASTING.** No Christian broadcasting is allowed, but foreign programmes in Arabic can be heard over FEBA (Seychelles), TWR (Monaco), and Radio Vatican.

TABLE 2.   ORGANIZED CHURCHES AND DENOMINATIONS IN SOUTH YEMEN

| Official name 1 | Begun 2 | Type 3 | Counc 4 | Congs 5 | Adults 6 | Affiliated 7 | Names, notes, and other statistics (see Codebook) 8 |
|---|---|---|---|---|---|---|---|
| Anglican Church (D Cyprus & the Gulf) | | A Cen | aw... | 1 | 20 | 80 | Part of Episcopal Ch in Jerusalem & the Middle East. All expatriates. |
| Catholic Church: VA Arabia | 1841 | R Lat | P...L.. | 4 | 100 | 120 | Decline from 9,640 RCs in 1961; all aliens. 1973: 4x,13w,2r(1483); 1974, only 2x. |
| Christian Brethren | | P CBr | x.... | 2 | 50 | 100 | *Gospel Halls.* Indigenous congregations similar to Plymouth (Open) Brethren. |
| Church of South Arabia | 1885 | P uni | ..... | 2 | 50 | 100 | 1961 union of Ch of Scotland Mission, Ch of Denmark Mission. 1n,1f,1H,15Yy. |
| Isolated radio churches | c1960 | I rad | ..... | 8 | 100 | 300 | Isolated Arab radio believers (mainly pupils, students), via TWR, RVOG, ICI, &c. |
| Red Sea Team | 1952 | P int | xG... | 1 | 10 | 20 | M=RSMT(UK,USA). Isolated local believers, adherents and transients. |
| Other Protestant denominations | | P | ..... | 3 | 10 | 20 | Including: Evangelical Alliance Mission (TEAM), Sudan Interior Mission (8f). |
| Total affiliated (mid-1970) | | | | 21 | 340 | 740 | Total denominations (1970) . . . 9. |
| Total affiliated (mid-1975) | | | | 21 | 400 | 880 | Total denominations (1975) . . . 9. |
| Total affiliated (mid-1980) | | | | 22 | 470 | 1,020 | Total denominations (1980) . . . 10. |

## NOTES ON TABLE ABOVE
COLUMNS: for meanings and CODES (cols. 1, 3, 4, 8): see Codebook (Part 6). Column 1: **Boldface type** = church with over 10% of country's affiliated Christians.

PEOPLES (ethnolinguistic). Christians: about 69% Arab (Palestinian, Yemeni, Lebanese, et alii), 16% Latin European, 12% British, 2% Indian.

COUNTRY-WIDE TOTALS
EVANGELIZATION (see Part 5). 1900: 7%. 1970: 25%. 1980: 29%. *Radiophonic evangelism.* TWR, RVOG, ICI, et alia.
FOREIGN MISSIONARIES AND PERSONNEL (aliens from

abroad)(1973). Total 68. *From Western world.* 38: 21 Protestants (8 in 2 USA societies, 7 in 1 Australia society, 4 in 1 WGermany society, 2 in 2 UK societies), 17 Roman Catholics. *From Third World.* 30: about 20 Roman Catholics from India and Palestine, 10 Protestants (Palestinian Arab teachers from Lebanon).
INSTITUTIONS (church-operated)(1973). Total 4 (up to 1973: 3 higher schools, 1 medical centre).
PERSONNEL. 68 (all foreign) in 1973.
SCRIPTURE DISTRIBUTION (1975). Nil. *Translations Completed.* Portion: Sokotri in 1902, Mehri in 1902.
SERVICE AGENCIES. 1.

ADDITIONAL DATA ON CHURCHES
CATHOLIC CHURCH. In the whole VA Arabia in 1970 (7 nations, HQ Aden), there were 7,857 Catholics (90% Latin-rite Indians, British, North Americans, Italians, 10% Eastern-rite), 7 parishes, 15 priests (Italian & American OFMCap), 32 sisters (Pie Madri della Nigrizia, Verona), a dozen Rosary Sisters (Palestinians), 7 schools (4,350 pupils). By 1975 (HQ Abu Dhabi, UAE), there were 12,060 Catholics, 11 parishes, 15 churches, 17 priests, and 61 sisters (12 Verona, 15 Iraqi, 10 Lebanese, 13 White Sisters, 11 Indians).
*Catholic organizations.* In 1973 the Catholic Church operated 5 elementary schools (1,802 pupils) and 3 secondary schools (331 pupils). Sisters were involved in the training of young women and social service of a general nature.

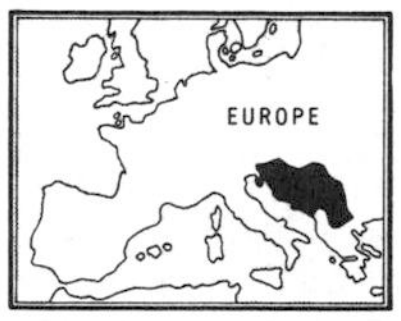


# YUGOSLAVIA

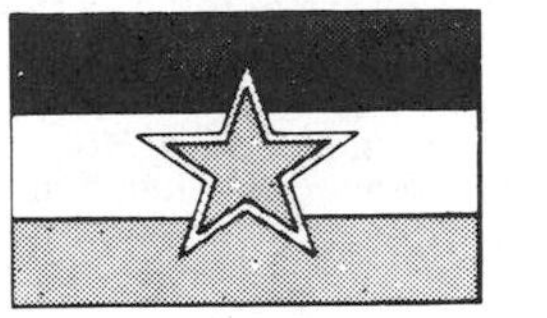

## SECULAR DATA

**STATE. Official name:** The Socialist Federal Republic of Yugoslavia (Socijalisticka Federativna Republika Jugoslavija, SFRJ). Adjective of nationality: Yugoslav.
**Flag** (shown above right): Stripes of blue, white, and red, with centred red star outlined in gold.
**Area:** 255,804 sq.km. (98,766 sq.miles). Agricultural land: 56.4%.
**Government:** One-party Communist republic, since 1945 (1918 united kingdom, 1921 absolute monarchy, 1941-45 German rule, 1945 republic).
**Legislature:** Assembly: Federal Chamber, 220 delegates; Chamber of the Republics and Provinces, 88 delegates.
**Official languages:** Serbo-Croatian (*Srp, Hrvat*), Macedonian, Slovene. Serbian is written in Cyrillic characters, Croat in Latin.
**Chief cities:** capital Belgrade 1,204,270 (1971), Zagreb 566,220, Skopje 312,980, Sarajevo 271,130, Ljubljana 213,300.
**Political divisions:** 6 Republics (Bosnia-Herzegovina, Crna Gora (Montenegro), Croatia, Macedonia, Serbia, Slovenia), 2 Autonomous Provinces within Serbia (Kosovo, Vojvodina).
**Armed forces** (1976): Total 250,000 regular (155,000 conscripts): Army 200,000, navy 20,000, air force 30,000 (350 combat aircraft). Reserves and paramilitary forces: 1,414,000.

**DEMOGRAPHY. Population:** 20,522,972 (census of 31.III.1971. For 1970–2000 (UN), see last row of Table 1). Population density (1975): 83/sq.km. (216/sq.mile). Under 15 years: 31%. Growth rate (1975–80): 0.90% per year (births 1.83%, deaths –0.94%). Life expectancy (1975–80): 68.5 years. Household size: 3.8 persons.
**Major languages:** Serbo-Croatian, Slovenian, Macedonian, Hungarian, Albanian, Bosnian, Montenegrin, Turkish, Romany, Italian, German, Slovak, Bulgarian, Greek.
**Urban dwellers** (1970): 36.8%. Urban growth rate (1950–70): 5.0% per year.
**Labour Force:** 43%.
**Refugees** (1977): About 26,000 from Albania.
**Tourists** (1960): 873,000. (1971) 5,238,000. (1974) 5,457,688. Arrivals at borders, including excursionists (1970): 28 million.

**ETHNOLINGUISTIC GROUPS:** 38.7% Serbian, 21.1% Croatian, 8.4% Bosnian, 8.2% Slovene, 6.4% Albanian, 5.8% Macedonian, 3.5% Gypsy, 2.5% Montenegrin, 2.3% Magyar (Hungarian), 0.6% Turkish, 0.4% Slovak, 0.4% Aromanian, 0.4% German, 0.3% Bulgar, 0.3% Romanian, 0.2% Italian, 0.1% Ruthenian, 0.1% Czech, Polish, Austrian, Greek, Jewish, Ukrainian, Russian.

**MONEY** (1977). **Monetary unit:** Yugoslav new dinar (= 100 paras); US$1 = ND 18.35.
**National income per person:** US$1,140. Average annual family income: US$4,332.
**Inflation:** (1970–74) 18.3% per year (1975: consumer price index 260).
**Cost of living in capital** (1976): index 95 (Washington DC = 100). Daily cost of living: US$35.

**HEALTH.** Hospitals: 490 (122,106 beds). Doctors: 23,147. Lepers: 60. Blind: 23,000. Psychotics: 210,000. Drug addicts: 900.

**EDUCATION.** Adult literacy: (1953) 73%, (1971) 83%. Education rate: 77%. Schools: 13,761. Universities: 7.

**LITERATURE.** Annual new book titles (1973): 10,110. Periodicals: 1,436. Scientific journals: 400. Newspapers: 25 dailies, 1,493 non-daily.

**COMMUNICATION** (per 1,000 people). Phones: 54. Radios: 192. TV sets: 131. Daily newspaper circulation: 89 copies.

TABLE 1. RELIGIOUS ADHERENTS IN YUGOSLAVIA

| Year | 1900 | | mid-1970 | | Annual change, 1970–1980 | | | | mid-1975 | | mid-1980 | | 2000 | |
|---|---|---|---|---|---|---|---|---|---|---|---|---|---|---|
| *Name* | *Adherents* | *%* | *Adherents* | *%* | *Natural* | *Conversion* | *Total* | *Rate* | *Adherents* | *%* | *Adherents* | *%* | *Adherents* | *%* |
| **Christians** | **8,254,000** | **88.2** | **15,296,004** | **75.1** | **142,630** | **–46,770** | **95,860** | **0.61** | **15,773,600** | **74.0** | **16,254,600** | **72.9** | **17,550,500** | **68.4** |
| crypto-Christians | 0 | 0.0 | 1,861,004 | 9.1 | 19,714 | 47,066 | 66,780 | 3.06 | 2,180,200 | 10.2 | 2,528,800 | 11.3 | 3,480,500 | 13.6 |
| professing | 8,254,000 | 88.2 | 13,435,000 | 66.0 | 122,916 | –93,836 | 29,080 | 0.21 | 13,593,400 | 63.8 | 13,725,800 | 61.6 | 14,070,000 | 54.8 |
| Orthodox | 4,295,000 | 45.9 | 7,537,000 | 37.0 | 69,020 | –51,220 | 17,800 | 0.23 | 7,633,000 | 35.8 | 7,715,000 | 34.6 | 7,696,000 | 30.0 |
| Roman Catholics | 3,800,000 | 40.6 | 5,704,000 | 28.0 | 52,057 | –42,657 | 9,400 | 0.16 | 5,757,000 | 27.0 | 5,798,000 | 26.0 | 6,157,000 | 24.0 |
| Protestants | 159,000 | 1.7 | 183,000 | 0.9 | 1,736 | 64 | 1,800 | 0.94 | 192,000 | 0.9 | 201,000 | 0.9 | 205,000 | 0.8 |
| Catholics (non-Roman) | 0 | 0.0 | 11,000 | 0.1 | 103 | –23 | 80 | 0.70 | 11,400 | 0.1 | 11,800 | 0.1 | 12,000 | 0.0 |
| nominal | 468,000 | 5.0 | 0 | 0.0 | 0 | 0 | 0 | 0.00 | 0 | 0.0 | 0 | 0.0 | 0 | 0 0 |
| affiliated | 7,786,000 | 83.2 | 15,296,004 | 75.1 | 142,630 | –46,770 | 95,860 | 0.61 | 15,773,600 | 74.0 | 16,254,600 | 72.9 | 17,550,500 | 68.4 |
| total practising | 7,007,400 | *90* | 11,472,000 | *75* | 106,972 | –35,077 | 71,895 | 0.61 | 11,830,200 | *75* | 12,190,950 | *75* | 12,285,300 | *70* |
| non-practising | 778,600 | *10* | 3,824,000 | *25* | 35,658 | –11,693 | 23,965 | 0.61 | 3,943,400 | *25* | 4,063,650 | *25* | 5,265,200 | *30* |
| Orthodox | 4,014,000 | 42.9 | 8,119,075 | 39.8 | 75,580 | –26,787 | 48,793 | 0.58 | 8,358,000 | 39.2 | 8,607,000 | 38.6 | 9,286,000 | 36.2 |
| Roman Catholics | 3,594,000 | 38.4 | 6,960,723 | 34.2 | 64,973 | –20,745 | 44,228 | 0.62 | 7,185,500 | 33.7 | 7,403,000 | 33.2 | 8,004,000 | 31.2 |
| Catholic pentecostals | 0 | 0.0 | 0 | 0.0 | 4 | 196 | 200 | 50.00 | 400 | 0.0 | 2,000 | 0.0 | 20,000 | 0.1 |
| Protestants | 178,000 | 1.9 | 194,606 | 1.0 | 1,872 | 667 | 2,539 | 1.23 | 207,000 | 1.0 | 220,000 | 1.0 | 231,000 | 0.9 |
| Evangelicals | 40,000 | 0.4 | 116,000 | 0.6 | 1,117 | 423 | 1,540 | 1.25 | 123,500 | 0.6 | 131,400 | 0.6 | 140,000 | 0.5 |
| Catholics (non-Roman) | 0 | 0.0 | 14,200 | 0.1 | 133 | –33 | 100 | 0.68 | 14,700 | 0.1 | 15,200 | 0.1 | 16,000 | 0.1 |
| Marginal Protestants | 0 | 0.0 | 7,000 | 0.0 | 72 | 128 | 200 | 2.50 | 8,000 | 0.0 | 9,000 | 0.0 | 13,000 | 0.1 |
| Anglicans | 0 | 0.0 | 400 | 0.0 | 0 | 0 | 0 | 0.00 | 400 | 0.0 | 400 | 0.0 | 500 | 0.0 |
| Muslims | 1,048,000 | 11.2 | 2,241,000 | 11.0 | 20,636 | –12,836 | 7,800 | 0.34 | 2,281,000 | 10.7 | 2,319,000 | 10.4 | 2,360,000 | 9.2 |
| Non religious | 5,000 | 0.1 | 1,591,496 | 7.8 | 17,330 | 47,550 | 64,880 | 3.39 | 1,914,600 | 9.0 | 2,243,300 | 10.1 | 3,720,500 | 14.5 |
| Atheists | 3,000 | 0.0 | 1,230,000 | 6.0 | 12,144 | 12,056 | 24,200 | 1.80 | 1,343,000 | 6.3 | 1,472,000 | 6.6 | 2,001,000 | 7.8 |
| Jews | 50,000 | 0.5 | 7,500 | 0.0 | 60 | 0 | 60 | 0.77 | 7,800 | 0.0 | 8,100 | 0.0 | 9,000 | 0.0 |
| Other religionists | 0 | 0.0 | 2,000 | 0.0 | 0 | 0 | 0 | 0.00 | 2,000 | 0.0 | 2,000 | 0.0 | 4,000 | 0.0 |
| **Country's population** | **9,360,000** | **100.0** | **20,371,000** | **100.0** | **192,800** | **0** | **192,800** | **0.90** | **21,322,000** | **100.0** | **22,299,000** | **100.0** | **25,653,000** | **100.0** |

COLUMNS, ROWS. For meanings and definitions, see Codebook (Part 6). Note that, by definition, total 'Christians' = professing + crypto-Christians, which also = affiliated + nominal Christians. Percentages may not always total exactly, due to rounding.
CENSUSES. **31.I.1921:** 46.8% Orthodox, 39.8% Roman Catholics (0.4% Greek Catholics), 10.9% Muslims, 1.8% Protestants, 0.5% Jews, 0.2% other religionists. **1928:** 47.3% Orthodox, 38.6% Roman Catholics (0.3% Greek Catholics), 11.5% Muslims, 2.0% Protestants, 0.6% Jews. **1931:** 48.7% Orthodox, 37.9% Roman Catholics, 11.2% Muslims, 1.7% Protestants, 0.5% Jews. **31.III.1953** (de jure): 41.3% Orthodox, 31.7% Roman Catholics, 13.3% termed 'atheists' (i.e. non-religious as well as atheists), 12.3% Muslims, 0.9% Protestants (157,702 persons), 0.4% 'other Christians' (other Protestants, Old Catholics, marginal Protestants; 61,274 persons), 0.015% Jews (2,565 persons).
POLLS. A number covering religion have been taken. Some results for practice are given below.

NOTES ON RELIGIONS
ATHEISTS. League of Communists of Yugoslavia (LCY) (in power; independent over Sino-Soviet dispute): membership (1970) 1,025,476 (29% workers). Of Communist party members, around 30% are estimated to be committed atheists, the rest being non-religious with a small minority of professing Christians. In 1960, of university students in Sarajevo, 52% declared themselves to be atheists.
CATHOLIC PENTECOSTALS (or, Catholic charismatics). The charismatic renewal began in 1975 through a Yugoslav priest returning from Rome, with prayer groups in Jelsa (diocese of Hvar) and Zagreb university before the end of 1975. By 1977 several hundred clergy, nuns and seminarians were involved.
CRYPTO-CHRISTIANS. Christians affiliated to churches but not known as such to the state, of 3 kinds: (1) unorganized individuals in the legal churches, (2) members of the many illegal or underground churches, and (3) isolated radio believers.
JEWS. Decline from 80,000 in 1925 due to mass murders under Nazi rule. In 1970, 36 communities, with a League of Jewish Communities based in Belgrade.
MUSLIMS. Sunnis (of the Hanafite rite), in about 2,250 mosques, with 1,588 imams. Sarajevo is considered as the Muslim capital and is where the Supreme Council of Islam is situated. The Bosnians are mainly Muslim (since the days of their conquest by Turkey); there are also many Albanians, Serbs, Turks, Gypsies and others. *Hajj pilgrims to Mecca.* (1970) 2,211; (1974) 1,845; (1975) 1,048; (1976) 855.
NOMINAL CHRISTIANS. Before 1939 only.
NON-RELIGIOUS. Agnostics, indifferent to religion, including most Communist party members. In addition, there are another 10% of the population whom the polls record as non-religious but who are affiliated to churches and so are classified here as crypto-Christians.
OTHER RELIGIONISTS. Adherents of several non-Christian religions or cults, including about 200 Baha'is in 6 isolated centres.
PRACTISING CHRISTIANS. June 1966 (Steinmetz Institute: urban females): 'When did you last go to church?' – 4% within past 7 days, 4% within past 14 days, 13% over 2 weeks ago, 79% seldom or never go. 1969, in Zagreb: 48.9% of whole population profess to be Christian believers; 10.5% attend church regularly, 27.8% from time to time, 13.4% only on church festivals.
PROFESSING CHRISTIANS. As can be seen from the censuses recorded above, the proportion of Orthodox in the country increased gradually from 1921–31 and up to 1939, then has since fallen more rapidly under the Nazi and Communist regimes; and the proportion (%) of Roman Catholics declined gradually from the 1920s and more recently under Communism.

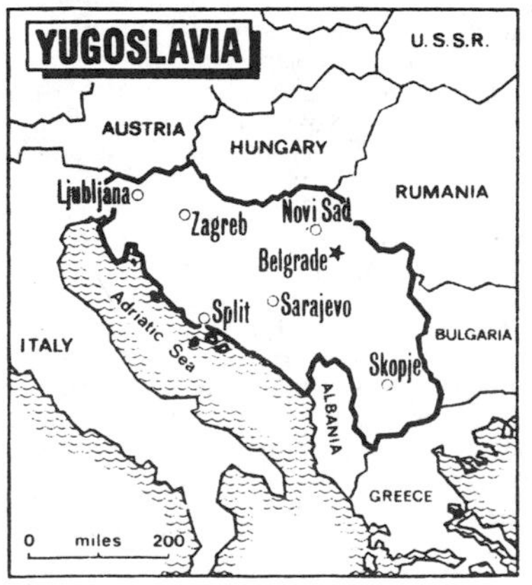


**NON-CHRISTIAN RELIGIONS. Islam** is one of the principal religious communities of Yugoslavia. Islamization began in the 14th century and was pursued through the Turkish conquest of 1459 and the subsequent settlement of Turkish nomadic tribes and military colonies. Following the Muslim conquest, part of the peasant class, especially in Bosnia, and the Croatian and Bogomil (Cathari) feudal classes converted to Islam. At the present time, the Supreme Assembly (Vrhovni Sabor) with headquarters at Sarajevo (Islamska Zajednica) is the highest authority of the Federal Republic's Muslim community. At the head of its executive organ is the reis-ul-ulema who serves as Islam's supreme religious chief. At the regional level there are 4 assemblies: at Sarajevo for the republics of Bosnia-Herzegovina, Croatia and Slovenia; at Pristina (in Kossovo) for Serbia; at Titograd for Montenegro; and at Skopje for Macedonia. In the whole country, there were in 1970 some 2,250 mosques, 378 chapels (*mesdzide*), 1,573 imams and 15 principal imams. The Muslim community possesses 2 schools for training religious officials, at Sarajevo and Pristina, with a total of 396 students; and a faculty of theology is being built in Sarajevo.

**Judaism** has an ancient history in Yugoslavia. Before World War II there were 76,000 resident Jews, of which some 60,000 died in concentration camps run by Nazis and their local collaborators. After the war about 8,000 emigrated to Israel. Today, Yugoslavia's Jews are organized into 36 communities, united through the League of Jewish Communities of Yugoslavia, which was founded in 1919. There are no professional religious officials, the work of rabbis being done by the laity.

**CHRISTIANITY.** The first Christians arrived in Dalmatia and Illyricum near the end of the Apostle Paul's ministry, being probably converted Jews of the Diaspora. Organized Christianity came to Yugoslavia from both Rome and Constantinople by the middle of the 4th century, and the influence of Byzantium grew in the 9th century through the missionary activity of Cyril and Methodius who translated the liturgy into the national language of the people. In 1054 the Great Schism separated the peoples on religious lines, creating divisions which continue until today. At the same time the autocephalous Orthodox archdiocese of Ohrid was erected in southern Macedonia. A desire for greater autonomy stimulated the formation of an independent Serbian Orthodox Church in 1219 which continued its ties with the ecumenical patriarch, but in 1346 the Serbian archiepiscopate was raised to a patriarchate at Pec to the dismay of Constantinople. The Turks favoured the rival archiepiscopate of Ohrid over the Pec patriarchate, suppressing the latter completely between 1463 and 1557. The 16th century saw the

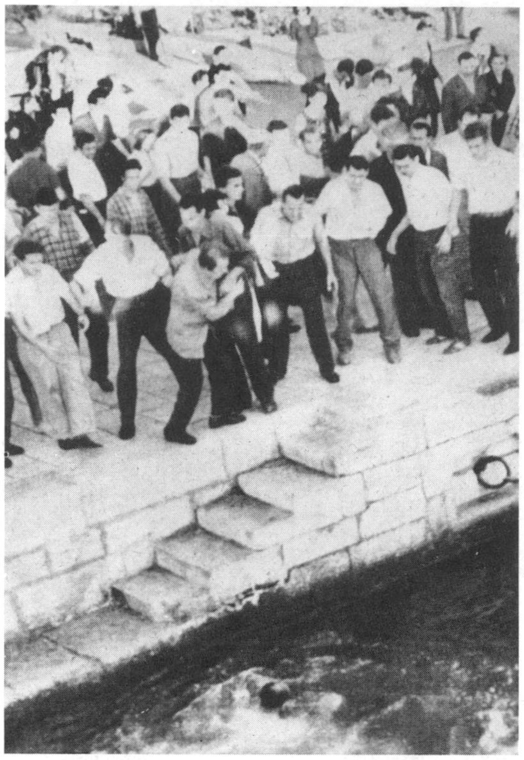

**Atheists.** Hostile anti-religious mob throw Roman Catholic priest into river in Croatia.

rise of Protestantism, Lutheranism from Germany and Calvinism from Switzerland, although the Counter Reformation prevented Protestants from gaining a major foothold. During the same period (1557) the Pec patriarchate was re-established and continued to function until 1766, when the ecumenical patriarch succeeded in having it revoked by edict of the sultan. In 1611 the first Uniates of the Byzantine rite passed over to the Roman Catholic Church. The Orthodox drive to free itself from the control of Constantinople resulted in 1832 in the granting of internal autonomy to the Serbian Orthodox Church, with the right to elect metropolitans and bishops, followed by the proclamation of complete autocephality and the election of its own patriarch in 1920. The latter half of the 19th century also witnessed the arrival of a number of new Protestant denominations. Yugoslavia's major denominations at the present time are the Orthodox and Catholic churches, Orthodoxy having its strength in the east and centre (Serbia, Macedonia, Montenegro and part of Bosnia) while Catholicism is concentrated in the west (Slovenia, Croatia and to a lesser extent Bosnia).

ORTHODOX CHURCHES. Prior to World War I, Serbian Orthodox were divided into 3 autocephalous churches nominally under the patriarch of Constantinople: in Serbia, Montenegro and Dalmatia, and Austro-Hungary. The political unity achieved after the war stimulated efforts to unify the church; and the united Serbian Orthodox Church was formed in 1919, followed by the institution of the Serbian patriarchate in 1920.

The Serbian Orthodox Church has usually been considered the dominant church of the country. Although never the official state church, prior to World War II it was the church of the ruling dynasty and was widely acknowledged to be the traditional church of the people. The patriarch sat on the royal council, and many Orthodox priests were members of the national assembly. Orthodox holidays took precedence, and parliamentary oaths were celebrated according to Orthodox rites. In addition, the church owned large estates and received important subsidies for its schools and the salaries of its leaders. In Montenegro priests were recognized and paid as civil servants. All of these privileges were swept away by the Communist regime after World War II. Nevertheless, the Serbian Orthodox Church continues to exert an important influence in the country.

The patriarch as head of the church is archbishop of Pec and metropolitan of Belgrade-Karlovci, with his see in Belgrade; and the bishops of the eparchies of Dabar-Bosnia, Montenegro-Coastland and Zagreb also bear the title of metropolitan. Eparchies outside Yugoslavia include those of Eastern America and Canada (with see in Cleveland, Ohio, USA); Mid-West America (Chicago, Illinois, USA); Western America (Alhambra, California, USA); Western Europe and Australia (London, England); Budim (Szentendre, Hungary); and Timisoara (Romania).

The church's main legislative and administrative organs are: (1) the Holy Archiepiscopal Council, composed of the patriarch and all diocesan bishops, which is the supreme legislative and juridical authority; (2) the Holy Archiepiscopal Synod, composed of the patriarch and 4 diocesan bishops, which is the supreme executive authority; (3) the High Ecclesiastical Tribunal, composed of 3 bishops, which is the church's highest court (although appeals may be made to the Holy Archiepiscopal Council); (4) the Patriarchal Council; and (5) the Patriarchal Administrative Board. Each eparchy or diocese in turn, in addition to its bishop, has an Eparchy Ecclesiastical Court, Eparchy Council and Eparchy Administrative Board.

The Serbian Orthodox Church has 81 monasteries, 72 convents (82 till recently), 3,368 churches and chapels, 1,731 parish halls and 2,404 organized parishes, 769 of the latter being at present without priests. In addition, there are 4 secondary-level seminaries with 613 students and 48 teachers, one secondary-level monastic school with 34 students and 4 teachers, and a post-secondary theological faculty in Belgrade with 120 students and 11 lecturers.

A striking feature of the church's life is the large variety of church newspapers and journals. These include *Pravoslavlje* (The Orthodox Creed), *Glasnik* (The Messenger), *Pravoslavni Misionar* (The Orthodox Missionary), *Svetosavsko Zvonce* (The Bell of St Sava), *Bogoslovlje* (Divinity), *Vesnik* (The Messenger), *Pravoslavna Misao* (Orthodox Thought) and *Teoloski Pogledi* (Theological Views).

The Macedonian Orthodox Church, which was integrated into the Serbian Orthodox Church in 1919, declared itself autocephalous in 1967. The movement towards independence began to grow following World War II and received a new impulse from the 1958 national church council in Ohrid, at which time it was decided to re-establish the ancient archiepiscopal see of Ohrid. The original constitution of the Macedonian Orthodox Church, while proclaiming autonomy, recognized the Serbian Orthodox patriarch as its own also. However, dissatisfaction with this state of affairs continued to grow resulting in full independence in 1967. The head of the church is the archbishop, with his see in Skopje. The principal ecclesiastical organizations are the Holy Archiepiscopal Synod, Archiepiscopal National Church Assembly and Administrative Council, Archiepiscopal Juridical Church Council, and Archiepiscopal Educational Church Council; and similar organizations are duplicated at diocesan level. Theological training is provided at the St Kliment Ohridski school in Skopje with 92 students. In addition to its 953 churches and chapels, the church maintains 86 monasteries.

Other Orthodox bodies in Yugoslavia include the Romanian Orthodox Church with 30 parishes in the northeast, Russian Orthodox Church with one parish in Belgrade, and sizeable Albanian Orthodox and Bulgarian Orthodox communities.

CATHOLIC CHURCH. Yugoslav Catholicism does not present a uniform outward appearance. In Slovenia it has been under Austrian influence, while on the Dalmatian coast Venetian influence is predominant (although there exists also a secular tradition of resistance by priests against Italian control). In Croatia proper secular nationalism plays a major role. The east and south of the country have only 3 dioceses and an apostolic administration. Thus in the republics of Serbia and Macedonia, it is possible to speak of Catholics of the diaspora, given the fact that they consist mostly of small minority groups of largely Croatian background. One of the most important of these communities is the 5,000 inhabitants of the little town of Janjevo, in the autonomous province of Kossovo (diocese of Skopje), who are all Catholics descended from Croatian immigrants of 6 centuries ago. Nevertheless 80% of the Catholics of the diocese of Skopje are Albanians. Other Albanians living dispersed in numerous Yugoslavian towns have generally remained faithful to both their Christian and Albanian traditions. Croatian emigrants to foreign countries, especially West Germany, make up about 65% of all Yugoslav emigrants and are assisted by several Catholic missions which maintain contact with the Episcopal Conference of Yugoslavia. Of note also are the Byzantine-rite Catholics, descendants of Orthodox, who emigrated to Croatia in the 16th century and passed over to the Roman Catholic Church in 1611.

It is difficult to say to what extent Christians in general, and Catholics in particular, have retained their religious convictions. In 1953, 86% of the total population claimed to be believers, but religious sentiment has undoubtedly been decreasing since 1945. A survey conducted in 1969 in the essentially Catholic industrialized and urban region of Zagreb showed that only 48.9% of the population professed Christian belief, 10.5% went regularly to church, 27.8% went from time to time and 13.4% went only on feast days. Religious sentiment and practice are higher among Catholics than Orthodox. The level of belief and religious practice also varies according to sex (being higher among women), profession (farmers, housewives and artisans being more religious) and education (being strongest among the less well-educated). A public opinion poll conducted in Slovenia in 1968 showed one-third of the population as traditional believers, one-third as nonconformist believers and one-third as unbelievers.

Concerning vocations to the priesthood, Yugoslavia was until 1972 better served than many other countries, although a significant decrease in seminary enrolment has been in evidence since the beginning of the 1972 year. For the year 1972–73, there were 250 new candidates for the priesthood throughout the country; whereas a few years before, this number represented the total of candidates for the archdiocese of Zagreb alone. An official survey of superiors of male religious orders revealed that on 1 January 1974 there were 2,898 male religious personnel (compared with 2,928 on 1 March 1973), of whom 1,756 were priests, 329 brothers, 137 novices and 676 candidates, theology students and students in Catholic secondary schools. The inquiry shows a decrease of 157 candidates as compared with the previous year. In 1973 there were 7,960 sisters, 416 more than in 1969, and 271 novices.

In general one can say that Vatican II has split the Catholic community, with ecclesiastics now divided into progressivist and conservative wings. The episcopate remains for the most part traditionalist and protective of its authority, in part due to conservatism, partly from fear of Communism, as well as from anxiety that the church will lack the necessary cohesion to face any new period of tension with the state.

OTHER CHURCHES. The principal Protestant tradition is Lutheranism, which began during the 16th-century Reformation but later suffered severe persecution in the Counter Reformation. The period of tolerance proclaimed by the Austro-Hungarian emperor Joseph II permitted the re-establishment of Lutheran communities which remained largely under the Hungarian Evangelical Church until World War I. In 1918 the Evangelical Church of Yugoslavia came into existence, comprising all but Slovak Lutherans, and this was re-named the German Evangelical Church in Yugoslavia in 1933. Lutheran unity disintegrated during World War II, and the churches were reconstituted as separate entities after 1945. Lutherans are today divided into 4 separate ethnic denominations: (1) the Slovak Evangelical Christian Church, centred in Novi Sad among descendants of immigrant farmers from Slovakia, whose supreme administrative and legislative authority is vested in a synod of 96 members, chaired jointly by a bishop and a lay-president, and whose theological students are trained in Czechoslovakia and West Germany; (2) the Evangelical Christian Church in Slovenia, with its headquarters in Lendava and the majority of its parishes in the Prekmurje region, which served as a Lutheran refuge during the Counter Reformation; (3) the Evangelical Church in Croatia, Bosnia and Herzegovina and Vojvodina, with its see at Zagreb; and (4) the Evangelical Church in Serbia, centred in Subotica, which is composed mostly of Hungarians.

The Reformed Christian Church in Yugoslavia also owes its origin to the Reformation, when Calvinism gained a foothold among Croatians and

Hungarians in Baranja and Slavonia. Disbanded under Turkish rule, the church was re-established under the Austro-Hungarian empire as part of the Reformed Church of Hungary. Autonomy was proclaimed in 1920 when Yugoslavia was created as a separate state. The Reformed community is still mostly of Hungarian background. The church is organized into 3 seniorates (Backa, Banat, and Baranja-Slavonia) each composed of several parishes. The supreme legislative body is the synod with 2 presidents (a bishop and a layman), with the synodal council acting ad interim. Clergy are educated abroad in Austria and Hungary.

Of the many new Protestant denominations established over the past hundred years, the most successful has been the Christian Adventist Church. Adventists began work in Banat, Backa, Slovenia, Bosnia and Croatia shortly after the turn of the century, forming their first community in Belgrade, Serbia in 1909 and Prilep, Macedonia in 1923. The church is now organized into 4 districts, with its central headquarters in Belgrade. Educational institutions include a higher divinity school in Rakovica near Belgrade, with 70 students, and a secondary religious school at Marusevac near Varazdin, with 120 students.

Many Pentecostal bodies are active, the largest being the Church of God in Yugoslavia; and there are also a number of other small Protestant denominations: Brethren, Baptists, Nazarenes, Methodists and others.

Reform movements out of Roman Catholicism began in 1919 resulting in the formation of the Croatian Old Catholic Church by 1923 which joined the Utrecht Union of Old Catholic Churches. Prior to World War II internal conflicts produced a division between the Croatian Old Catholic Church and the Croatian National Old Catholic Church. A series of further schisms from the former resulted in the creation of Old Catholic churches in Slovenia in 1946, in Serbia and Vojvodina in 1954, and in Bosnia and Herzegovina in 1965. In 1954 the Union of Old Catholic Churches in Yugoslavia was formed in Belgrade to provide a degree of unity for the divided churches, although only 3 of the 5 denominations have joined: Croatian Nationals, Serbians and Slovenians. There are no Old Catholic religious schools in Yugoslavia, clergy being trained in Switzerland and Germany.

**CHURCH AND STATE.** The constitution of Yugoslavia promulgated on 21 February 1974 proclaims equality of rights and duties for all citizens without any discrimination especially due to religion (Article 154). Article 174, which is devoted to religious questions, stipulates: 'The manifestation of religion is free; it is the personal affair of each individual. Religious communities are separate from the State; they are free as far as the exercise of religious affairs and worship are concerned. Religious communities may establish confessional schools only for the training of priests. It is anti-constitutional to abuse religion and religious activities by using them for political purposes. The social community may accord material aid to religious communities. Religious communities may have, within the limits fixed by the law, a right of ownership over property.' These 2 articles have been reproduced without change from the previous constitutions.

Religious communities may constitute themselves without other impediments than those specified in the laws of the state. Each republic and each commune possess a commission for relations with religious communities, whose purpose is to co-ordinate relations between the state and the institutionalized churches, but without interfering in their life. In Belgrade there also exists a commission of the federal government for relations with religious communities (Komisija Saveznog Izvrsnog Vijeca za Odnose s Vjerskim Zajednicama).

In fact religious communities enjoy a liberty which is rare among East European regimes, and their relationships with the state may be considered as normalized. The specific character of Yugoslav independent socialism, which is clearly distinguished from Stalinist dogmatic socialism, contributes considerably to this situation. In these conditions dialogue is possible not only between churches and state but also between Marxists and Christians, especially in Croatia. The first public dialogue, between a Marxist philosopher and a Jesuit, took place at Zagreb in March 1967. At the University of Zagreb, Catholic and Orthodox ecclesiastics sponsor conferences on atheism and religion; and a more formal dialogue involving the International Conference of Religious Sociology (based in France), the Zagreb Institute of

**Serbian Orthodox Church.** *Top right.* Vikentije Prodanov, Patriarch from 1950-58. *Above.* German Djorich, Patriarch from 1958. *Right.* One of the 200 monasteries in Serbia.

Social Research and the 'Christian Present' Catholic Centre was held at Opatija in September 1971. There exist many other similar encounters, of special note being the publication in 1971 of the book *Religions in Yugoslavia*, written by Orthodox, Catholic, Protestant, Muslim and Marxist contributors.

One of the fundamental principles of the statutes concerning religious communities in the Yugoslav socialist regime is the depoliticization of the churches (which may speak in the name of their members only concerning strictly religious questions) and the politicization of the faithful in terms of their being responsible citizens. In the implementation of this principle, there has been opposition on the part of conservatives, whether laity or hierarchy, of Marxist politicians wishing to institute the principle of atheism in the state. There is therefore a real tendency to make use of the churches and the faith, as well as atheism, for political ends. The churches' freedom of activity depends also on internal movements affecting the socialist state, whether conservative or progressivist. In affirming the principle of independence, progressivists tend to avoid distinctions between Christians and non-Christians.

The situation has obviously not remained static

**Pentecostal Churches of Christ in Yugoslavia.** Group of baptism candidates in village church, with their pastor.

throughout the whole period of Communist rule. One can in fact distinguish 4 successive phases. The first, from 1945 to 1950, was characterized by opposition and serious tension between the 2 powers, due principally to the policy of agrarian reform, nationalization and suppression of former privileges. Those most affected were the Catholic Church and the Islamic community. Beginning in 1950, a period of transition ensued during which, although anti-religious campaigns continued (especially in 1952 and

1957–58 against Catholics), there was a progressive improvement of relationships between government and Orthodox and Muslims. Following the promotion to the cardinalate of Msgr Stepinac, accused by the regime of collaboration with the Ustachis (those seeking the creation of an independent Croatian state) during World War II, Yugoslavia broke off diplomatic relations with the Vatican in 1952. A law concerning religious communities was adopted in 1953 which took up again and considered more fully various matters in the constitution of 1946, thereby providing an opportunity for the state to show that it had a positive attitude towards religion. This law of 1953 expired in 1970 and religious affairs have now been relegated to the competence of the republics. However, all the republics are not agreed that a religious law is necessary.

The third period began during the 1960s, and became much more evident after 1967, leading to a phase of normalization. It was characterized especially by improvement of relations between the state and the Catholic Church, facilitated by the death of cardinal Stepinac in 1960 and the Vatican's change of attitude towards questions of peace, the Third World and Communism. A protocol was signed between the Holy See and Yugoslavia in 1966 which gave official recognition to the socialist system of government and repudiated the use of religion for political purposes. This was followed in 1970 by the visit of president Tito to the Vatican and by the re-establishment of diplomatic relations, making Yugoslavia and Cuba the only Communist countries maintaining official relations with the Vatican.

The fourth phase, one characterized by a hardening of attitude on the part of the authorities, dates from 1972. The 'Take charge' campaign launched in 1971 by the Communist League, which was centred on the purification of party leadership in several republics (Croatia in 1971, Serbia and Slovenia in 1972), as well as the battle against nationalism and liberalism, has not spared the religious milieu, either Orthodox or Catholic. While in no sense returning to the systematic persecution of the earlier period, repression continues to express itself concretely through seizures of newspapers, imprisonment of priests and laity and loss of jobs of teachers known for their religious convictions. Party leaders criticize the church for having taken advantage of the 'euphoria of nationalism and liberalism' to mix in purely political matters, and this also creates fear among the faithful, in some cases leading to conflict. The hierarchies of the Catholic and Serbian Orthodox churches have made known their views through direct representation to the authorities in power.

**INTERDENOMINATIONAL ORGANIZATIONS.** The Ecumenical Council of Churches in Yugoslavia was formed in 1968 and counts in its membership the 3 Yugoslav churches belonging as full members to the WCC (Serbian Orthodox, Lutheran, Reformed) and 3 others. There is also a loose Federation of Protestant churches; and the Catholic Episcopal Conference maintains a Commission for Ecumenism. Catholic/Serbian Orthodox relations are still difficult, due to the unresolved problem of the Uniate churches, but in 1976 the situation was gradually improving.

**BROADCASTING.** The government Jugoslovenska Radiotelevizija permits the broadcasting of occasional Orthodox and Catholic church services. From abroad, Protestant programmes are beamed in over Europe I in Serbo-Croatian for 15 minutes on Wednesdays, and by TWR (Monaco) for one hour 15 minutes a week in Serbo-Croatian and 15 minutes in Serbian on Saturdays. Radio Vatican beams in Catholic programmes in Croatian and Slovenian, each for one hour 45 minutes a week.

## BIBLIOGRAPHY


'Church-state relations in Yugoslavia since 1967', S. Alexander, *Religion in Communist lands*, IV, 1 (1976), 18–27.
(General survey of the Catholic Church in Yugoslavia) *Opci sematizam katolicka crkve u Jugoslaviji, cerkerv Jugoslaviji, 1974*. Zagreb: Biskupska konferencija Jugoslavije, 1975. 1,166p. (Parts in Croat, Slovenian, Latin, English, French, German).
(History of the Serbian Orthodox Church) *Istoria srpske pravoslavne Crkve*. D. Slijepvecic. 2 vols. München, 1962, 1966.
'La situación religiosa en Yugoslavia', G. Canders, *Revista de estudios politicos* (Madrid), CLXI (1968), 259–67.
'Recent developments in church-state relations in Yugoslavia', C. Criic, *Religion in Communist lands*, I, 1 (March-April, 1973), 6–8.
'Religion et opinions chez les étudiants de l'Université Sarajevo', J. Fisera & A. Fiamengo, *Archives de sociologie des religions*, XII (1961), 145–155.
*Religions in Yugoslavia*. Ed Z. Frid. Zagreb: Binoza, 1971. 170p.
*The position of the Church in Yugoslavia*. R. Vidic. Belgrade: Izdavac, 1962.
(The Serbian Orthodox Church, 1219–1969) *Srpska pravoslavna Crkve, 1219–1969*. Beograd: Patriarchate, 1969.
(The Serbian Orthodox Church 1920–1970) *Srpska Pravoslavna Crkva 1920–1970*. Belgrade: Holy Episcopal Synod, 1971. 539p.
'Yugoslavia', A. Fiamengo, in *Western religion* (The Hague: Mouton, 1972), 587–599.
'Yugoslavie aujourd'hui: une église entre l'est et l'ouest', *Information catholique internationale* (Paris), 400 (January, 1972), 7–15.


TABLE 2. ORGANIZED CHURCHES AND DENOMINATIONS IN YUGOSLAVIA

| Official name 1 | Begun 2 | Type 3 | Counc 4 | Congs 5 | Adults 6 | Affiliated 7 | Names, notes, and other statistics (see Codebook) 8 |
|---|---|---|---|---|---|---|---|
| Albanian Orthodox Church | | O Alb | ••••• | 5 | 3,000 | 5,000 | Related to suppressed church in Albania. 2 villages in Macedonia, et alia. |
| Bulgarian Orthodox Church | | O Sla | Mwc•• | | 10,000 | 15,000 | *Balgarskata Pravoslavna Crkva*. Under P Sofia. Bulgarian residents. |
| **Catholic Church in Yugoslavia:** | c 250 | R LEr | B•B•R | 2,840 | 4,802,900 | 6,960,723 | *Rimokatolicka Crkva*. C=16+0+32. 2p,4q,8s. 3971n,1052m,6806w,94537Yy. |
| M Ljubljana | 1461 | R Lat | Bs | 342 | 455,400 | 660,000 | *Nadskopija Ljubljana*. Church language: Slovenian. 1s. 493 154 623 10041 |
| D Maribor | 1228 | R Lat | Bs | 274 | 493,200 | 714,925 | *Skofija Maribor*. Slovenia. Slovenian-speaking. 379 19 146 10756 |
| M Rijeka-Senj | c 350 | R Lat | Bs | 184 | 296,700 | 430,000 | *Nadbiskupija Rijeka-Senj*. Croatia. Croatian. 1s. 147 30 275 2258 |
| D Krk | 900 | R Lat | Bs | 51 | 23,500 | 34,000 | *Biskupija Krk*. Croatia (Dalmatia). Croatian. 70 7 112 270 |
| D Porec & Pula | c 250 | R Lat | Bs | 128 | 103,100 | 149,455 | Croatia (Istria). Croatian and Italian. 108 3 87 1580 |
| M Split-Makarska | c 250 | R Lat | Bs | 174 | 220,800 | 320,000 | Croatia (Dalmatia). Croatian. HQ Split. 1s. 291 51 519 5243 |
| D Dubrovnik (Ragusa) | 990 | R Lat | Bs | 65 | 50,400 | 73,000 | Croatia (Dalmatia). Croatian. 113 75 252 931 |
| D Hvar | c1150 | R Lat | Bs | 43 | 22,800 | 33,000 | Croatia (Dalmatia). Croatian. 62 2 110 339 |
| D Kotor | c 950 | R Lat | Bs | 28 | 7,800 | 11,356 | Montenegro. Croatian, Montenegrin. 20 0 128 121 |
| D Sibenik | 1298 | R Lat | Bs | 71 | 97,200 | 140,853 | Croatia (Dalmatia). Croatian. 86 4 134 1375 |
| M Vrhbosna (Sarajevo) | c 650 | R Lat | Ps | 114 | 308,900 | 447,748 | Bosnia-Herzegovina. Croatian. HQ Sarajevo. 339 85 364 10005 |
| D Banja Luka | 1881 | R Lat | Ps | 38 | 147,200 | 213,261 | Bosnia-Herzegovina. Croatian. P=59%. 64 1 193 2815 |
| D Mostar-Duvno | c 550 | R Lat | Ps | 69 | 139,400 | 202,000 | Bosnia-Herzegovina. Croatian. High practice: P=97%. 145 90 158 3645 |
| D Skopje-Prizren | c 350 | R Lat | Ps | 19 | 33,000 | 48,000 | Macedonia. Croatian, Macedonian, Albanian. HQ Skopje. 29 0 167 2036 |
| M Zagreb | 1093 | R Lat | Bs | 419 | 1,311,000 | 1,900,000 | Croatia. Croatian. Major RC centre in Yugoslavia. 1s. 792 483 1645 23237 |
| D Djakovo & Srem | c 350 | R Lat | Bs | 157 | 345,000 | 500,000 | Bosnia. Croatian. HQ Djakovo. 1s. 224 15 650 7622 |
| D Krizevci (*Byzantine*) | 1777 | R Byz | Os | 53 | 40,500 | 58,643 | For whole of Yugoslavia. 1s(Zagreb). 63 2 115 702 |
| AD Bar | c 850 | R Lat | ps | 18 | 13,800 | 19,994 | *Nadbiskupija Bar*. Montenegro. Croat, Albanian. P=92%. 18 3 70 850 |
| AD Beograd (Belgrade) | c 850 | R Lat | bs | 15 | 24,900 | 36,043 | Serbia. Serbian. 5 parishes in the capital. W=10%. 33 3 347 184 |
| AD Zadar | c 350 | R Lat | bs | 116 | 96,200 | 139,370 | Croatia (Dalmatia). Croatian. 113 4 151 1510 |
| D Subotica | 1968 | R Lat | bs | 165 | 276,000 | 400,000 | Serbia (Vojvodina). Croatian and Hungarian. 100 7 266 4369 |
| AA Banat | 1923 | R Lat | Bs | 32 | 79,400 | 115,000 | Serbia. Croatian, Hungarian, Slovenian. HQ Zrenjanin. 40 2 91 1049 |
| AA Koper & Gorizia | c1945 | R Lat | Bs | 204 | 146,300 | 212,000 | Yugoslav part of M Gorizia (HQ in Italy). Slovenes. 185 10 140 2587 |
| AA Pazin (Trieste) | c1945 | R Lat | Bs | 61 | 70,400 | 102,075 | Yugoslav part of D Trieste (HQ in Italy). Croats. 57 2 63 1012 |
| Christian Adventist Ch in Yugoslavia | 1909 | P Adv | x•••• | 273 | 10,360 | 20,000 | *Adventisticka Crkva. Seventh-day Adventists, Yugoslavian UC*. 53n,1r,1s(70),354Y. |
| Christian Nazarene Community | 1871 | P Hol | x•••• | 150 | 2,000 | 5,000 | From Hungary. Severe persecution up to 1920. Vojvodina; HQ Novi Sad. Declining. |
| Church of Christ | | P Dis | x•••• | 1 | 30 | 50 | Link with M=CC(Non-Instrumental)(USA). In Zagreb. Independent congregation. |
| Church of England (D Gibraltar) | c1850 | A plu | awc•• | 2 | 200 | 400 | English-speaking expatriates in Belgrade, Zagreb. Good relations with Serbian OC. |
| Church of God in Yugoslavia | | P Pen | ••••• | 24 | 4,000 | 9,000 | *Crkva Bozja u SFRJ*. HQ Vinkovci. Many north of Belgrade; Croatia, Macedonia. |
| Ch of the Spirit (Foot-washing) | c1930 | P Pe1 | ••••• | 80 | 2,500 | 7,000 | *Kristova Duhovna Crkva 'Nogoprani'*. HQ Vrdnik. Baptism in name of Jesus only |
| Ch of the Spirit (Infant-baptizing) | c1930 | P Pe2 | •v••• | 50 | 2,000 | 5,000 | *Kristova Duhovna Crkva 'Malkrsteni'*. HQ Subotica. Indigenous Pentecostal church. |
| Ch of United Brethren in Christ in Y | c1900 | P LuR | Rwc•• | 24 | 1,000 | 3,000 | *Ceskobratrska Církev Ev*. Slovaks: 71% Serbia, 21% Croatia, 8% Slovenia. HQ Zagreb. |
| Croatian Old Catholic Church | 1923 | C OCa | ••••• | 3 | 2,000 | 5,000 | Split ex Ch of Rome. Separate from other 4 Old Catholic bodies. 4 priests. |
| Evangelical Christian Ch in Slovenia | 1540 | P Lut | L•••W | 33 | 10,000 | 25,170 | *Evangelicanska-Krscanska Cerkev AV v SR Sloveniji*. A=1945. HQ Lendava. 13n,21m,P=30%. |
| Ev Church in Croatia, Bosnia & H, & V | c1750 | P Lut | LvC•W | 18 | 2,000 | 5,000 | *Ev Crkva u SR Hrvatskoj SR Bosni i Hercegovini i AP Vojvodini*. German remnant. 11n. |
| Evangelical Church in PR of Serbia | c1800 | P Lut | l•••• | 9 | 3,000 | 6,000 | *Ev Crkva u NR Srbiji*. A=1945. Diaspora Hungarian farmers. 1967, joined SECC. 2n,4m. |
| Free Brethren Congregations | c1905 | P CBr | xv••• | 25 | 3,500 | 10,000 | *Slobodna Braca*. 2 rival groups, Open and Closed. 1952, applied to join WCC. |
| Isolated radio churches | c1950 | P rad | ••••• | | 200 | 500 | Isolated radio believers in non-religious families across nation, mostly aged 12–25. |
| Macedonian Orthodox Church: | c 60 | O Sla | cv••• | 953 | 818,000 | 1,200,000 | *Makedonska Pravoslavna Crkva*. Slavs. 1967, schism ex SOC. 334n,86d(80mw),1s(92). |
| M Skopje | c1250 | O Sla | cm | 333 | 276,000 | 400,000 | Part of old diocese is in Serbian Orthodox Church. 1s(92) in Dracevo (Skopje). |
| D Debar-Kicevo | c1000 | O Sla | cb | 150 | 133,000 | 200,000 | Area of Autonomous Church of Macedonia. AD 1000. HQ Ohrid, cradle of Slav Orthodoxy. |
| D Palagonia | | O Sla | cb | 80 | 69,000 | 100,000 | On border Yugoslavia and Greece. Bishop appointed for armed services in area. |
| D Prespa-Bitola | 1018 | O Sla | cb | 150 | 133,000 | 200,000 | Originally called Pelagonia, then (to 1959) Ochrid-Bitola. HQ Bitola. |
| D Zletovo-Strumica | c1350 | O Sla | cb | 240 | 207,000 | 300,000 | HQ Stip. 5,000 Roman Catholics of Macedonian ethnic sub-rite in this area. |
| Methodist Church in Yugoslavia | c1890 | P Met | Vwc•W | 40 | 1,611 | 4,000 | *Metodisticka Crkva. Provisional Annual Conf*. C&S Europe Central C, UMC(USA). 6n. |
| Old Catholic Ch in Bosnia&Herzegovina | 1965 | C OCa | ••••• | 1 | 500 | 1,000 | Founded separate from other 4 Old Catholic churches; outside Union of OCC in Y. |
| Pentecostal Churches of Christ in Y | c1910 | P Pe2 | Z•••• | 100 | 2,373 | 5,000 | *Kristova Pentekostna Crkva*. Till 1954, Religious Ch of Christ. German. 54n,1s(18). |
| Reformed Christian Ch in Yugoslavia | c1550 | P Ref | RWC•W | 135 | 10,000 | 26,716 | *Református Keresztyén Egyház*. Scattered diaspora Hungarians. A=1920. 26n,1s. |
| Romanian Orthodox Church | | O Rum | Cwc•• | 30 | 5,000 | 10,000 | *Biserica Ortodoxa Romana*. Under P Bucharest. In northeast. HQ Vojvodina. 30nx. |
| Russian Orthodox Church | | O Sla | Mwc•• | 1 | 1,000 | 3,000 | Parish in Belgrade. Under jurisdiction of P Moscow. Russians, Ukrainians. |
| **Serbian Orthodox Church:** | c 150 | O Ser | CWc•W | 2,404 | 4,751,400 | 6,886,075 | *Srpska Pravoslavna Crkva*. P since 1346. 1j,6s. 1421n,70d(200),82e(658),87616Yy. |
| P Beograd (Belgrade) & Karlovci | c 350 | O Ser | Cp | 87 | 150,400 | 217,994 | Patriarchal D. 1725, union P Karlovci, 2s(292). 72 1 2 4 46 4692 |
| M Dabar-Bosnia | 1219 | O Ser | Cm | 63 | 127,900 | 185,370 | HQ Sarajevo (Muslim centre of country). 43 1 1 2 5 4504 |
| M Montenegro & Coastland | 1219 | O Ser | Cm | 184 | 154,200 | 223,491 | Autocephalous till 1920. HQ Cetinje. 1s(34). 17 20 17 1 5 571 |
| M Zagreb | 1930 | O Ser | Cm | 44 | 49,700 | 72,000 | Covers Croatia and Slovenia. HQ Zagreb. 18 1 2 1 1 536 |
| D Backa | c1550 | O Ser | Cb | 101 | 240,700 | 349,000 | HQ Novi Sad, northwest of Belgrade. 78 2 4 0 0 2209 |
| D Banat | 1931 | O Ser | Cb | 132 | 316,000 | 458,000 | HQ Vrsac, on border with Romania. 98 1 0 3 11 3604 |
| D Banja Luka | 1900 | O Ser | Cb | 123 | 253,800 | 367,672 | In Bosnia. HQ Banja Luka. Strong Muslim area. 61 1 4 2 13 8662 |
| D Branicevo | c 350 | O Ser | Cb | 127 | 330,000 | 478,280 | HQ Pozarevac, southeast of Belgrade. 102 2 18 9 119 5107 |
| D Dalmacija (Dalmatia) | 1808 | O Ser | Cb | 80 | 149,000 | 216,000 | HQ Split. 1s(144) in Krka monastery. Croat area. 39 3 5 0 0 4915 |
| D Gornji Karlovac | 1695 | O Ser | Cb | 144 | 207,000 | 300,000 | In Croatia. HQ Karlovac, southwest of Zagreb. 25 0 2 1 4 1832 |
| D Nis | c 250 | O Ser | Cb | 276 | 594,000 | 860,803 | *Pravoslavne Eparhije Niske*. HQ Nis. 166 4 20 72 72 8750 |
| D Raska-Prizren | c1150 | O Ser | Cb | 66 | 176,200 | 255,363 | Present name from 1789. HQ Prizren. 1s(129). 31 4 11 7 27 4766 |
| D Sabac-Valjevo | 1831 | O Ser | Cb | 145 | 330,200 | 478,518 | HQ Sabac; area west of Belgrade. 112 4 22 5 35 7720 |
| D Skopje (part only) | c1250 | O Ser | Cb | 51 | 137,200 | 198,829 | Half old diocese is now in Macedonian Orth Ch. 40 3 2 0 0 3060 |
| D Slavonija | c1550 | O Ser | Cb | 78 | 84,000 | 121,732 | Croatia. HQ Pakrac, small town to the east. 38 1 2 2 6 1268 |
| D Srem | 1947 | O Ser | Cb | 142 | 139,100 | 201,576 | HQ Sremski Karlovci. 1s(168). 93 3 8 6 25 2931 |
| D Sumadija (Shumadia) | 1947 | O Ser | Cb | 154 | 374,000 | 542,093 | HQ Kragujevac, SE of Belgrade. Serb heartland. 132 4 23 5 88 5274 |
| D Timok | 1833 | O Ser | Cb | 89 | 212,800 | 308,401 | HQ Zajecar, northeast of Nis on Bulgaria border. 39 2 6 5 13 2148 |
| D Zahumlje-Herzegovina | 1219 | O Ser | Cb | 46 | 40,500 | 58,679 | In Bosnia. Old diocese of Hum. HQ Mostar. 19 2 1 3 11 1226 |
| D Zica | 1219 | O Ser | Cb | 179 | 408,700 | 592,274 | D created by St Sava. 1972, bishop imprisoned. 150 9 44 11 159 7880 |
| D Zvornik-Tuzla | c1550 | O Ser | Cb | 93 | 276,000 | 400,000 | In Bosnia. HQ Tuzla. Many Muslims in area. 48 2 6 1 18 5971 |
| Slovak Evangelical Christian Church | c1680 | P Lut | LWC•W | 39 | 30,000 | 53,170 | *Slovacká ev-kr AV Cirkev*. Rural emigrants from Slovakia, c1800; A=1918. 20n,P=30%. |
| Union of Baptist Churches in Y | 1875 | P Bap | T•••• | 116 | 3,400 | 7,000 | *Savez Baptisticka Crkva u SFRJ. Baptist Union* (1923). 23n,G=–2.8%pa,1s(10),100Y. |
| Union of Old Catholic Churches in Y: | 1954 | C OCa | U•••• | 15 | 4,000 | 8,000 | Begun to united all OCs, but 2 of the 5 remain outside. HQ Belgrade. Declining. |
| Croatian National Old Catholic Ch | 1933 | C OCa | Uv••• | 8 | 2,000 | 4,000 | Split ex Croatian Old Catholic Ch. Bishop, 4 priests. 1398, tried to join WCC. |
| Old Catholic Church in Slovenia | 1946 | C OCa | Uv••• | 4 | 1,000 | 2,000 | Schism ex Croatian OCC. HQ Ljubljana. 1 bishop. 1952, applied to join WCC. 3n. |
| Old Cath Ch of Serbia & Vojvodina | 1954 | C OCa | U•••• | 3 | 1,000 | 2,000 | Separately founded. One vicar administrator. 3 priests. |
| United Jehovah's Witnesses in Y | 1925 | M Jeh | x•••• | 104 | 3,000 | 7,000 | *Verska Zajednica Jehovinih Svedoka*. HQ Zagreb. Scriptures from Bible Society. |
| Other Protestant denominations | | P | ••••• | | 2,000 | 3,000 | Total about 40 (see list below), mainly incognito or underground bodies. |
| Other Catholic (non-Roman) churches | | C | ••••• | | 100 | 200 | Including: Liberal Catholic Ch, New Apostolic Ch (Germany), underground. |
| **Total affiliated (mid-1970)** | | | | **7,640** | **10,491,074** | **15,296,004** | **Total denominations (1970) . . . 69.** |
| **Total affiliated (mid-1975)** | | | | **7,680** | **10,818,600** | **15,773,600** | **Total denominations (1975) . . . 70.** |
| **Total affiliated (mid-1980)** | | | | **7,720** | **11,148,500** | **16,254,600** | **Total denominations (1980) . . . 71.** |

NOTES ON TABLE ABOVE

COLUMNS: for meanings and CODES (cols. 1, 3, 4, 8): see Codebook (Part 6). Column 1: **Boldface type** = church with over 10% of country's affiliated Christians.

NATIONAL COUNCILS (Column 4, 5th letter).

R = Yugoslav Bishops' Conference (YBC)(Viskupska Konferencija Jugoslavije).

W = Ecumenical Council of Churches in Yugoslavia (ECCY) (Ekumenski Savet Crkava u Jugoslaviji).

*Other national councils*. There is also a loosely-organized Federation of Protestant Churches.

OTHER PROTESTANT DENOMINATIONS. These are mostly of Yugoslav origin rather than foreign, have 100 or less members, include many Pentecostal bodies, and prefer to remain incognito or underground. They include: Christ's Religious Ch of the Gospel Brethren (HQ Belgrade), Ch of God (Cleveland) (USA) (23 churches, 376 adults), Ch of the Latter Rain (HQ Osijek), Divine Ch of the Seventh Day (HQ Glozan, Novi Sad), Free Catholic Ch (HQ Zagreb), Jesus Christ Divine Ch of the Holy (HQ Zagreb), Gypsy Evangelical Movement (France), Religious Community Esotorial University (HQ Zagreb), Salvation Army (began 1933, missionaries long since withdrawn), Seventh-day Adventist Reform Movement (HQ Belgrade), Spiritual Ch of Christ.

**PEOPLES** (ethnolinguistic). Christians: 47.0% Serbian, 26.3% Croatian, 10.8% Slovene, 7.6% Macedonian, 2.0% Albanian

(Shiptar), 2.0% Hungarian, 1.5% Gypsy, 1.3% Montenegrin, 0.4% German, 0.4% Slovak, 0.2% Italian, 0.1% Bulgar, 0.1% Romanian, 0.1% Aromanian, 0.1% Ruthenian, Czech, Polish, Austrian, Greek, Ukrainian, Russian.

COUNTRY-WIDE TOTALS
EVANGELIZATION (see Part 5). 1900: 100%. 1970: 94%. 1980: 98%. *Mass evangelism.* On July 8–9, 1967, Billy Graham was permitted to hold 2 mass rallies in Belgrade (7,500 attenders, 250 enquirers); in 1970, Zagreb was the centre for the Euro '70 TV Crusade, televised from Dortmund (Germany), with attenders from across Yugoslavia and Hungary. *Radiophonic evangelism.* Radio Vatican (Croatian, Slovene), TWR (600 listeners' letters a year), et alia.
FOREIGN MISSIONARIES AND PERSONNEL (nationals serving abroad)(1974). Total 652 in 59 countries: 526 Roman Catholics (266 foreign missionaries (50% Slovenes, 49% Croats; 95 religious priests, 21 diocesan priests, 4 brothers, 127 sisters, 19 lay) serving in 45 mostly Third-World countries, and about 260 other personnel serving in Western nations but not officially regarded as missionaries), 126 Orthodox (102 bishops and priests, 24 monks) serving in 22 countries.
FOREIGN MISSIONARIES AND PERSONNEL (aliens from abroad)(1973). Total 379. *From Western world.* 365: about 350 Roman Catholics, 15 Protestants (6 in 5 USA societies, 3 in 1 UK society, 2 in 1 Canada society, other Europeans). *From Communist world.* About 14 Orthodox from Bulgaria, Romania and USSR.
INSTITUTIONS (church-operated)(1973). Total 310, including 30 higher schools (18 minor seminaries), 2 lay training centres, 250 monasteries, 2 presses, 1 research centre, 23 seminaries (12 RC, 7 Orthodox, 4 Protestant).
PERIODICALS. About 120 titles (including 72 RC, 24 Protestant (8 SDA), 15 Orthodox, 4 Jehovah's Witnesses, 2 Old Catholic).
PERSONNEL. About 14,979 (14,600 national, 379 foreign).
RELIGIOUS LIBRARIES. About 280.
SCRIPTURE DISTRIBUTION (1975). Annual totals: 72,444 Bibles (17% subsidized, 83% commercial), 24,027 NTs (17% subsidized, 83% commercial), 60,000 UBS portions. *Translations completed.* Portion: 4 languages since 1555. NT: 4 languages since 1563. Bible: 2 languages since 1584.
SERVICE AGENCIES. About 40, including AKSA, BFBS, CKS, ECCY, ECM, NMC, SGA, UVRPJ, VIJECE-VRP, VKJ(YBC).

ADDITIONAL DATA ON CHURCHES
CATHOLIC CHURCH IN YUGOSLAVIA. The first place name in column 8 gives the republic, the next name(s) the church language(s) in use. Croatian is used in the Catholic Church throughout Yugoslavia; Slovenian also is used in Slovenia, and there are other languages in use as shown. *Dioceses.* Detailed statistics are kept. M Ljubljana (1975) had 90,000 children in primary schools, of whom 70% were receiving religious instruction and 51% attending mass regularly. *New dioceses.* (1977) D Koper. *Annual baptisms.* (1972) 99.0% infant, 1.0% adult. *Personnel.* About 97% nationals, 3% expatriates. The figures given in the table above are for personnel in dioceses; in addition, there are numbers of contemplative monks and nuns. *Seminaries.* There are Catholic theological faculties at Ljubljana for Slovenia with a section at Maribor; and at Zagreb for the rest of the country; major seminaries in 3 dioceses. Jesuits have a philosophical and theological institute at Zagreb, and Franciscans have 3 seminaries with a philosophy school at Rijeka. *Catechists.* The great majority are sisters, although lay persons also may attend the 2 catechetical institutes at Ljubljana and Zagreb. *Main religious orders and congregations* (1972). Priests (with over 90 professed each): 1,180 OFM, 211 SJ, 178 SDB, 95 OP, 93 OFMConv. Sisters (with over 180 professed each): 1,584 Soeurs de la Charité de St-Vincent de Paul, 900 Soeurs du Tiers Ordre de St-François de l'Immaculée Conception, 700 Ste-Croix du Tiers Ordre de St François, 260 Adoratrices du Précieux Sang de Jésus, 183 Moniales de Ste-Ursule.
*Catholic organizations.* Official organizations include the Episcopal Conference of Yugoslavia or Yugoslav Bishops' Conference (Viskupska Konferencija Jugoslavije), Superior Council of Male Religious Personnel (Vijece Visih Redovnickih Poglavara, VIJECE-VRP) and the Union of Female Major Superiors in Yugoslavia (Unija Visih Redovnickih Poglavarica Jugoslavije). There are no pastoral or presbyteral councils. All organizations for the lay apostolate were prohibited in 1945. The Episcopal Conference maintains a Commission for the Lay Apostolate, but it has little importance.
The Holy See has diplomatic relations with Yugoslavia and is represented to government and the Catholic hierarchy by a pro-nuncio in Belgrade.
Among the more important Catholic organizations active in Yugoslavia are the following. (1) The 'Present Christian' Centre (Centar Krscanska Sadasnjost), in Zagreb, was created after Vatican II and erected canonically in 1968. A self-governing institution but placed under the general control of the archdiocese of Zagreb, the centre brings together representatives from many different Christian groups as well as persons claiming no religious affiliation and intellectuals from diverse disciplines. It initiates dialogue with Marxists and the contemporary world in Yugoslavia in addition to its promotion of ecumenical encounters and discussions concerning the relationship of church and society in Croatia. The centre is involved in publications and other activities concerning liturgical, familial, catechetical, pastoral and theological renewal; and is responsible for founding and operating the AKSA press agency. It is perhaps best known for its bimonthly *Glas Koncila/The Voice of the Council*, printed in 130,000 copies, which has contributed to the centre's reputation both in Yugoslavia and abroad as being one of the most important institutions for conciliar renewal in the world. The editorial board of Glas Koncila also produces *Mali Koncil* (Little Council) for youth and is responsbile for organizing the Catechism Olympic throughout Yugoslavia. (2) The Croatian Literary Society of St Cyril and St Methodius (HKD sv Cirila i Metoda), in Zagreb, was founded in 1868 as the Society of St Jerome and renamed in 1946. It is a lay institution under the control of the archdiocese of Zagreb which provides a meeting place for laity and publishes popular catechisms and prayer books. (3) The Istrian Literary Society of St Cyril and St Methodius (Istarsko Knjizevno Drustvo sv Cirila i Metoda) was founded in Pazin in 1893 under the name Druzba sv Cirila i Metoda, and during the Italian occupation assisted the Croatian clergy in Istria in the opposition to Italy. (4) The Druzina (Family), in Ljubljana, is a publishing house for the Slovenian language which produces also a weekly magazine, *Druzina*, with a distribution of 123,000 copies. (5) The Episcopal Centre for Socio-Pastoral Research (Skofijski svet za Pastoralno Socioloska Raziskovanjo, SPSS) was founded in 1959 in Maribor. (6) The National Missionary Council, founded in Sarajevo in 1971, co-ordinates and stimulates missionary initiatives of the Yugoslav Catholic Church in its relationship with younger churches overseas. Missionary statistics for 1975 listed 95 religious priests, 21 diocesan priests, 4 theological students, 127 sisters and 19 lay persons, serving in 45 mostly Third-World countries. Of these 52 were at work in Asia, 97 in South America, 14 in North America, 92 in Africa and 7 in Oceania.
Regarding educational institutions, the Yugoslav constitution stipulates that confessional schools are restricted to those catering for the training of church personnel. These are of 2 types: (1) theological faculties, diocesan seminaries and training centres for religious congregations; and (2) secondary schools preparing students for advanced theological and pastoral training, including 13 establishments for future secular priests, 9 for male religious personnel and one for sisters and their novices.
The liaison office between the Yugoslav Episcopal Conference and Caritas Internationalis (Viskupska Konferencija Jugoslavije, Ured zu Vezu sa Caritas Internationalis), in Zagreb, promotes charitable activities for the Catholic Church in Yugoslavia, including one home for unmarried mothers, 2 homes for the care of babies, an adoption agency and a programme of assistance for the handicapped. The office serves also as a channel to aid the wider church in cases of natural catastrophe, such as the earthquakes of Banja Luka and Skopje.
MACEDONIAN ORTHODOX CHURCH. The church was originally autonomous around AD 1000. After 1920 it became part of the Serbian Orthodox Church, was permitted to become autonomous in 1959, but then in 1967 with state support seized its own autocephality. It remains unrecognized as canonical by any other Orthodox church (1974). There are branches in the USA, Canada, and Australia, under one inclusive diocese.
PENTECOSTAL CHURCHES OF CHRIST IN YUGOSLAVIA. Originally among Germans, now mainly in Croatia and Slovenia, with a few assemblies in Serbia. The Romanian-speaking Branch has 13 assemblies (1976), mainly in villages northeast of Belgrade; in 1976 the Branch had over 70 adult baptisms.
SERBIAN ORTHODOX CHURCH. The church became autocephalous in 1219 and a patriarchate in 1346. The patriarchate (Srpska Patrijarsija) has one archbishopric (Belgrade), and the rest are eparchies (D), except the 3 jurisdictions (M) which are styled metropolia, which were independent churches before the union of 1920. In 1969 the dioceses were divided into 145 vicariates or ecclesiastical districts, and these into 1,990 congregations (these latter being composed of one or more parishes; e.g. in Belgrade one congregation is composed of 60 parishes). *Parishes.* 769 are vacant (temporarily served by priests of other parishes); 28 have no supply priests at all. 126 parishes have monks as parish priests. *Church buildings* (parish, monastery, also chapels). From 1945–70, the church built 181 churches and renovated 840; built 150 chapels and renovated 126; and built 8 monasteries and 450 presbyteries. Total parish churches, chapels and monasteries in 1969: 3,368. During that year, 272 were constructed or renovated. *Statistics* (Columns 5, 7 and 8). Figures published (duplicated) by Patriarchate for 1969. *Monasteries.* The total in 1975 was 81 monasteries, 72 convents. *Priests.* In 1970, 103 ordinations a year. *Monks.* 200 in monasteries, plus 74 others (1 working in Patriarchate). *Nuns.* There has been a rapid increase from 73 in 1924, to 286 in 1941, and to 658 in 1969, originating in a colony of Russian nuns who settled after 1917. *Seminarians.* Theological students in Belgrade number 120 in the Theological Faculty, and 172 in St Sava's Seminary. The total for the whole church is 5 seminaries with 620 students. *Weddings.* Church weddings 10,816 a year (1969). *Funerals.* Church funerals 53,356 a year (1969). *Sunday-school children.* 7,121 enrolled (regarded as unsatisfactorily low).

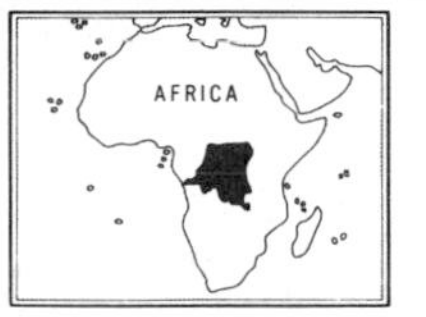


# ZAIRE

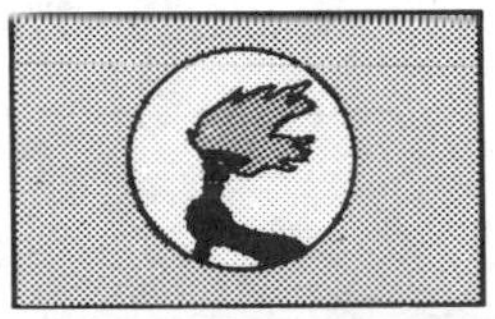

## SECULAR DATA

**STATE. Official name:** The Republic of Zaire (La République du Zaïre). Earlier name (till 1971): Congo-Kinshasa. Adjective of nationality: Zairian (zaïrois).
**Flag** (shown above right): Green field with yellow circle in centre showing arm carrying torch.
**Area:** 2,345,409 sq.km. (905,568 sq.miles). Agricultural land: 13.9%.
**Government:** One-party republic, since 1971 (15th-century kingdom of the Congo, 1885 Congo Free State (absolute monarchy), 1908 Belgian Congo colony, 1960 Independence as republic, 1965 military dictatorship, 1971 parliamentary republic).
**Legislature:** National Assembly, 420 members.
**Official language:** French (*Français*).
**Chief cities:** capital Kinshasa 2,008,350 (1974), Kananga (Luluabourg) 601,240, Lubumbashi 403,620.
**Armed forces** (1976): Total 43,400 regular: army 40,000, navy 400, air force 3,000 (40 combat aircraft). Paramilitary forces: 20,000.

**DEMOGRAPHY. Population:** 12,768,706 (census of II.1958. For 1970–2000 (UN), see last row of Table 1). Population density (1975): 10/sq.km. (27/sq.mile). Under 15 years: 42%. Growth rate (1975–80): 2.65% per year (births 4.49%, deaths –1.85%). Life expectancy (1975–80): 46.0 years. Household size: 4.9 persons.
**Major languages:** Ngala (Lingala), Kongo (Kikongo), Swahili, French, Luba (Tshiluba), Mongo, Azande, and over 450 other tribal languages.
**Urban dwellers** (1970): 16.2%. Urban growth rate (1950–70): 7.4% per year.
**Labour force:** 37%.
**Refugees** (1977): From abroad 298,300 (250,000 from Angola, 24,300 from Rwanda, 24,000 from Burundi). The 75,000 from the Sudan had returned by 1974. Exiles abroad: about 40,000 Zairians in various countries. (1978) Total refugees in Zaire, including internally-displaced: 1 million.
**Tourists** (1974): 93,682.

**ETHNOLINGUISTIC GROUPS:** 36% Central Bantu (Kongo, Kuba, Kunda, Lala, 1% Luimbe, Ndembu, 1% Pende, Sakata, Yaka, Yanzi), 16% Mongo (Kasai Luba), 12% Luba (Katanga Luba, Lunda, Songye, Yeke), 12% Equatorial Bantu (Babwa, Bati, Binza, Bira, Budu, Kumu, Lengola, Lokele, Mbae, Ndoko, Ngala, Rega, Songola), 9% Kivu (Furiiru, Havu, Hunde, Nyanga, Ruanda, Rundi, Shi, Yira), 7% Azande (with Alur, Amba, Lugbara, Mangbetu, Mamvu-Mangatu), 6% Ngbandi (with

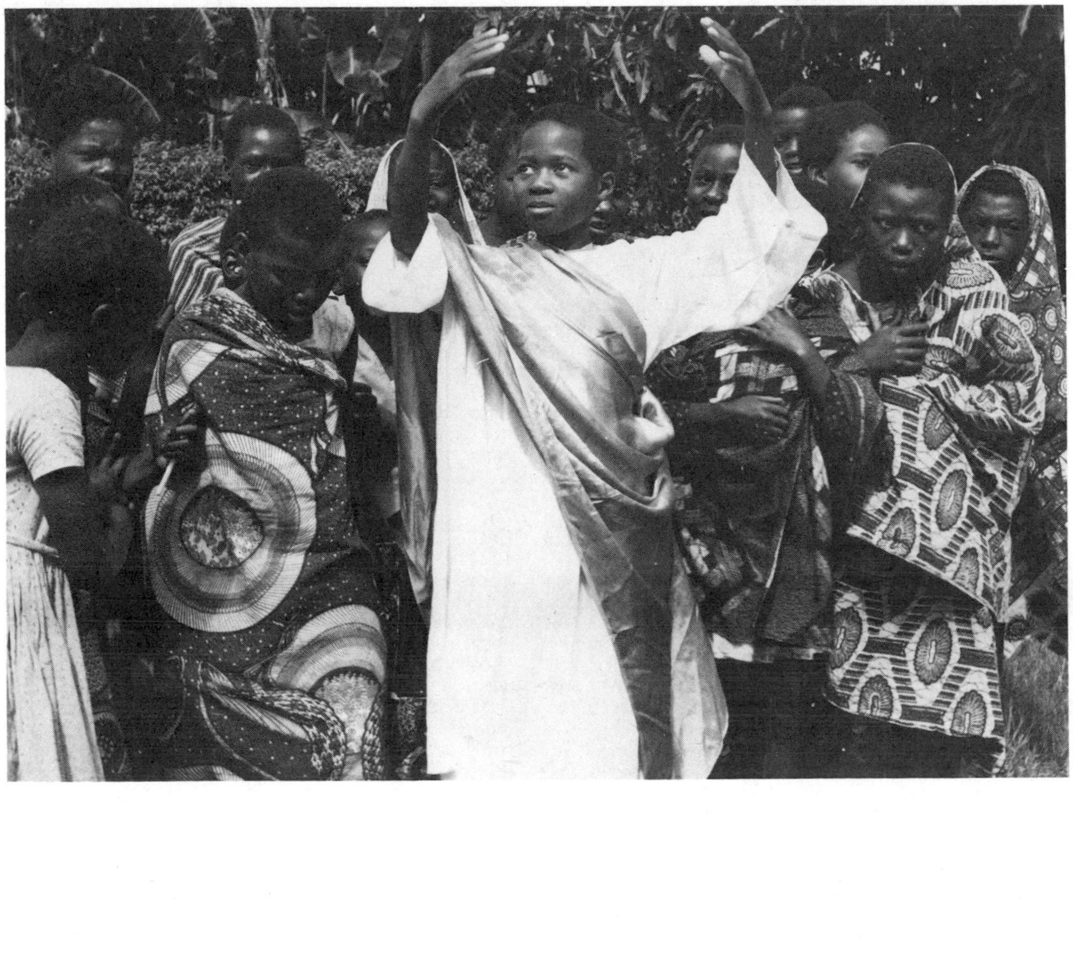

**Eglise Catholique au Zaïre.** Young Catholics enact Bible scenes.

Ngbaka, Mbandja), 1% Teke, 0.5% Pygmy, Swahili, Arab, Belgian, Greek, USA, Angolan, French, Jewish, & a large number of smaller tribes.

**MONEY** (1977). **Monetary unit:** zaire (= 100 makuta = 10,000 sengi); US$1 = Z 0.86.
**National income per person:** US$126. Average annual family income: US$617.

**Inflation:** (1970–74) 16.4% per year (1975: consumer price index 358), (1978) 75% per year.
**Cost of living in capital** (1976): index 164 (Washington DC=100). Daily cost of living: US$60.

**HEALTH.** Hospitals: 1,386 (67,624 beds). Doctors: 818. Lepers: 522,000 (21.3 per 1,000). Blind: 73,000. Psychotics: 200,000. Criminals: 50,000.

**EDUCATION.** Adult literacy: (1961) 31%. Education rate: 54%. Schools: 5,324. Universities: 3.

**LITERATURE.** Periodicals: 100. Newspapers: 13 dailies, 11 non-daily.

**COMMUNICATION** (per 1,000 people). Phones: 2. Radios: 4. TV sets: 0.3. Daily newspaper circulation: 9 copies.

TABLE 1. RELIGIOUS ADHERENTS IN ZAIRE

| Year | 1900 | | mid-1970 | | Annual change, 1970–1980 | | | | mid-1975 | | mid-1980 | | 2000 | |
|---|---|---|---|---|---|---|---|---|---|---|---|---|---|---|
| *Name* | *Adherents* | *%* | *Adherents* | *%* | *Natural* | *Conversion* | *Total* | *Rate* | *Adherents* | *%* | *Adherents* | *%* | *Adherents* | *%* |
| **Christians** | **124,650** | **1.4** | **19,537,000** | **90.3** | **587,384** | **100,380** | **687,764** | **3.02** | **22,778,110** | **93.0** | **26,414,640** | **94.5** | **47,957,800** | **97.0** |
| professing | 124,650 | 1.4 | 19,537,000 | 90.3 | 587,384 | 100,380 | 687,764 | 3.02 | 22,778,110 | 93.0 | 26,414,640 | 94.5 | 47,957,800 | 97.0 |
| Roman Catholics | 74,600 | 0.8 | 9,986,000 | 46.2 | 300,524 | 53,076 | 353,600 | 3.03 | 11,654,000 | 47.6 | 13,522,000 | 48.4 | 24,551,000 | 49.6 |
| Protestants | 50,000 | 0.6 | 6,044,000 | 27.9 | 180,580 | 25,630 | 206,210 | 2.94 | 7,002,700 | 28.6 | 8,106,100 | 29.0 | 14,538,300 | 29.4 |
| African indigenous | 0 | 0.0 | 3,500,000 | 16.2 | 106,073 | 21,677 | 127,750 | 3.11 | 4,113,390 | 16.8 | 4,777,500 | 17.1 | 8,848,500 | 17.9 |
| Orthodox | 50 | 0.0 | 7,000 | 0.0 | 207 | −3 | 204 | 2.54 | 8,020 | 0.0 | 9,040 | 0.0 | 20,000 | 0.0 |
| nominal | 0 | 0.0 | 649,603 | 3.0 | 20,018 | 3,381 | 23,399 | 3.01 | 776,280 | 3.2 | 883,590 | 3.2 | 1,462,200 | 3.0 |
| affiliated | 124,650 | 1.4 | 18,887,397 | 87.3 | 567,366 | 96,999 | 664,365 | 3.02 | 22,001,830 | 89.9 | 25,531,050 | 91.3 | 46,495,600 | 94.0 |
| total practising | 112,180 | *90* | 14,543,300 | *77* | 436,872 | 74,689 | 511,561 | 3.02 | 16,941,410 | *77* | 19,658,910 | *77* | 32,546,900 | *70* |
| non-practising | 12,470 | *10* | 4,344,100 | *23* | 138,494 | 22,310 | 152,804 | 3.02 | 5,060,420 | *23* | 5,872,140 | *23* | 13,948,700 | *30* |
| Roman Catholics | 74,600 | 0.8 | 9,940,873 | 45.9 | 298,652 | 51,752 | 350,404 | 3.03 | 11,581,400 | 47.3 | 13,444,910 | 48.1 | 24,473,300 | 49.5 |
| Catholic pentecostals | 0 | 0.0 | 0 | 0.0 | 77 | 923 | 1,000 | 33.33 | 3,000 | 0.0 | 10,000 | 0.0 | 70,000 | 0.1 |
| Protestants | 50,000 | 0.6 | 4,744,780 | 21.9 | 142,603 | 24,919 | 167,522 | 3.03 | 5,530,000 | 22.6 | 6,420,000 | 23.0 | 11,470,300 | 23.2 |
| Evangelicals | 48,000 | 0.5 | 3,350,000 | 15.5 | 100,828 | 18,172 | 119,000 | 3.04 | 3,910,000 | 16.0 | 4,540,000 | 16.2 | 8,200,000 | 16.6 |
| African indigenous | 0 | 0.0 | 4,164,744 | 19.2 | 125,017 | 20,343 | 145,360 | 3.00 | 4,848,030 | 19.8 | 5,618,350 | 20.1 | 10,432,000 | 21.1 |
| Marginal Protestants | 0 | 0.0 | 30,000 | 0.1 | 887 | −12 | 875 | 2.55 | 34,380 | 0.1 | 38,750 | 0.1 | 100,000 | 0.2 |
| Orthodox | 50 | 0.0 | 7,000 | 0.0 | 207 | −3 | 204 | 2.54 | 8,020 | 0.0 | 9,040 | 0.0 | 20,000 | 0.0 |
| Tribal religionists | 8,865,350 | 98.1 | 1,666,000 | 7.7 | 31,007 | −102,065 | −71,058 | −5.91 | 1,202,420 | 4.9 | 955,420 | 3.4 | 357,700 | 0.7 |
| Muslims | 50,000 | 0.5 | 300,000 | 1.4 | 8,897 | 103 | 9,000 | 2.61 | 345,000 | 1.4 | 390,000 | 1.4 | 700,000 | 1.4 |
| Baha'is | 0 | 0.0 | 128,000 | 0.6 | 3,868 | 1,332 | 5,200 | 3.47 | 150,000 | 0.6 | 180,000 | 0.6 | 396,000 | 0.8 |
| Non-religious | 0 | 0.0 | 5,000 | 0.0 | 180 | 220 | 400 | 5.71 | 7,000 | 0.0 | 9,000 | 0.0 | 30,000 | 0.1 |
| Hindus | 0 | 0.0 | 1,000 | 0.0 | 28 | −8 | 20 | 1.82 | 1,100 | 0.0 | 1,200 | 0.0 | 2,000 | 0.0 |
| Jews | 0 | 0.0 | 500 | 0.0 | 15 | −1 | 14 | 2.46 | 570 | 0.0 | 640 | 0.0 | 1,500 | 0.0 |
| Other religionists | 0 | 0.0 | 500 | 0.0 | 21 | 39 | 60 | 7.50 | 800 | 0.0 | 1,100 | 0.0 | 5,000 | 0.0 |
| **Country's population** | **9,040,000** | **100.0** | **21,638,000** | **100.0** | **631,400** | **0** | **631,400** | **2.58** | **24,485,000** | **100.0** | **27,952,000** | **100.0** | **49,450,000** | **100.0** |

COLUMNS, ROWS. For meanings and definitions, see Codebook (Part 6). Note that, by definition, total "Christians" = professing + crypto-Christians, which also = affiliated + nominal Christians. Percentages may not always total exactly, due to rounding.
CENSUSES. No question on religion has been asked in government censuses. However, before 1960 government statistics were collected of affiliated Roman Catholics including catechumens, as follows, which indicate the extremely rapid expansion of Catholics in those days: 1936, 20.6% Roman Catholics; 1937, 20.9%; 1954, 32.6%; 1955, 33.5%; 1958, 39.0%; 1959, 39.9%.

NOTES ON RELIGIONS
AFRICAN INDIGENOUS. In about 520 denominations in 1970 (see Table 2). The totals from 1970 onwards exclude the 13 indigenous churches with 440,500 adherents (in 1970; rising to 38 churches by 1977) which have joined the Eglise du Christ au Zaire, here classified as a Protestant body.
BAHA'IS. In a 1963 mass movement, 20,000 Africans became members; there has been subsequent very rapid growth from 223 local spiritual assemblies (1964) to 858 (1973).
HINDUS. Indian traders.
JEWS. One main community, in Lubumbashi, with 1 synagogue; decline from 1,377 Jews in 1961.
MUSLIMS. All African Muslims are Sunnis (Shafiite); there are also Arabs from Oman and Zanzibar who are Sunnis (mainly Shafiite), Pakistanis and Indians, about 1,000 Shia (Indians), and 20,000 West African Senegalese traders in the Qadiriya and Tijaniya orders. Waves of conversion to Islam took place in 1925–27 and 1932–35. A 1957 survey indicated 115,500 Muslims, but allowing for heavy underenumeration the actual figure then was 200,000. Since 1960 there has been substantial immigration of Muslims from East and West Africa. *Missionaries.* There are a number of Egyptian missionaries sent by Al-Azhar University (Cairo). *Hajj pilgrims to Mecca.* (1970) 7 persons; (1976) 158.
NON-RELIGIOUS. Mostly European expatriates, with some Zairean intellectuals.
OTHER RELIGIONISTS. Adherents of smaller religions and cults, including Rosicrucians (3 AMORC centres).
PRACTISING CHRISTIANS. Weekly mass attendance (Catholics): in 1959, 16.9% of all eligible Catholics. Easter communicants in 1970, 41% of all eligible Catholics. This figure is much lower than the total annual attenders because of difficulties of distance, travel and insufficiency of Easter services. Annual practice is therefore about 70% for Roman Catholics, about 80% for Protestants, and about 90% for indigenous churches, making an average of 77% for all affiliated Christians.
PROFESSING CHRISTIANS. The state in 1975 only recognized 4 Christians bodies: Roman Catholic, ECZ (Protestant), EJCSK, and Greek Orthodox. Others were officially illegal and unknown to the state.
PROTESTANTS. The totals of the ECZ from 1970 onwards include not only the 39 Protestant communities but also 13 African indigenous churches (in 1970) with 440,500 adherents and (rising by 1977 to 38 indigenous denominations), also the Anglican church with 100,000 adherents (1970) and 2 dioceses (from 1976 on).
ROMAN CATHOLICS. In the year 1900, there were 30,777 baptized (2,600 being Europeans), and 43,830 catechumens.
TRIBAL RELIGIONISTS. Animists, and adherents of witchcraft eradication cults and other traditionalist sects. Tribes with over 60% traditionalists in 1972: Mbuti Pygmies (90% animists), Bira (77%), Songomeno (75%), Bembe (73%), Hunde (66%), Kela (66%), Rega (66%), Azande (64%), Shila (64%), Budu (63%), Kuba (62%), Central Twa Pygmies (60%), Tabwa (60%).

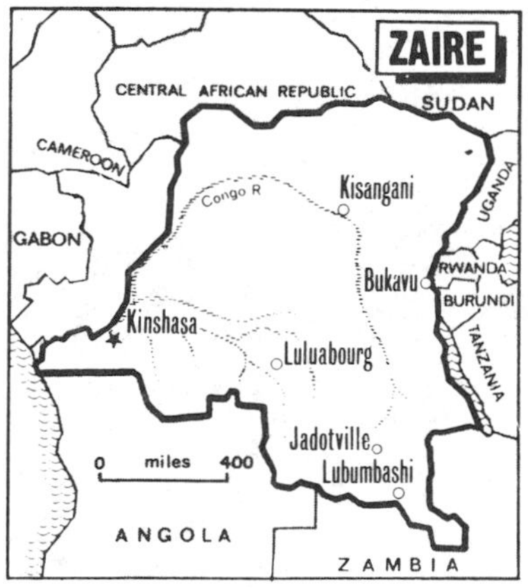


**NON-CHRISTIAN RELIGIONS. Traditional African religions** are practised everywhere, but they are strongest among the Azande, Bira, Budu, Central Twa Pygmies, Hunde, Kela, Kuba, Mbuti Pygmies, Rega, Shila, Songomeno and Tabwa. Tribal religions are characterized by magical practices, ancestral veneration and belief in a supreme being who is known under different names: Akongo (among the Ngombe), Arebati (Mbuti), Djakomba (Bachwa and Nkundo), Leza (Baluba), Nceme (Kuba), Njambi (Lole), Nzambi (Bakongo and Lunda), and Shungu (Tetela). Movements for the renewal of traditional religions, with a strong emphasis on witchcraft eradication, have played a significant role, especially among the Bakongo. Some have used Christian elements, but their tendency has been traditionalist. A movement known as Kiyoka (Burning) swept through northern Angola and Lower Zaire in the late 19th century, and more recent sects of similar type are Mvungism, Tonsi and Dieudonné. Eastern Zaire was also affected by the Mchape (Medicine) movement which began in Nyasaland in 1930 and subsequently spread to neighbouring countries.

**Islam** exists primarily in the Maniema, especially in the area of Kasongo, and in northern Shaba, with a small group in northeastern Zaire. Zairian Muslims are descendants of those converted in the 19th century. They are Sunnis, but their beliefs and practices display the continued influence of traditional religions. Other Muslim groups are composed of Arabs originating from Oman and Zanzibar (mostly Shafiite Sunnis), Pakistanis and Indians (mostly Ismailis), and some West African Blacks mostly belonging to the Qadiriya and Tijaniya brotherhoods.

**Baha'i** has spread rapidly since 20,000 Africans were converted in a 1963 mass movement. From 220 local spiritual assemblies then, the total had grown by 1973 to 858 assemblies.

**CHRISTIANITY.** Christianity reached Zaire in 1482 with the arrival of the Portuguese explorer, Diogo Cão. Early contacts were made with the Congo king, and Congolese were taken to Portugal for study. The first missionary party, which arrived in 1491, consisted of Franciscans, Dominicans, Canons of St John the Evangelist and secular priests; and before long they had baptized the king and built a large stone church at the royal capital (in present-day northern Angola), which they renamed San Salvador. Between 1506 and 1543 one of the most remarkable Christians of African history, Afonso I, ruled the Congo kingdom. His son Henry studied in Portugal and was the first Black African to be appointed a Catholic bishop, in 1518. He returned to Congo in 1521 where he served until his death in 1534. Afonso hoped that Henry would be replaced by another Congolese and that San Salvador would become the episcopal see for all Guinea. However, neither of these wishes were fulfilled. The island of São Tomé was chosen as the see for Guinea, Congo and the southwestern coast as far as the Cape of Good Hope, and the Portuguese dean of the royal chapel in Lisbon was named bishop. The growth of the Portuguese slave trade became an increasingly negative factor sapping the vitality of the Christian movement; and after Luanda was established in the latter half of the 16th century, attention was diverted to the area south of San Salvador. A revival of Catholic activity among the Bakongo took place in the 17th century. A prefecture of the Congo was erected in 1640 and placed under the care of Italian Capuchins, although this soon declined. When the modern era dawned, with the arrival of Holy Ghost priests at Boma in 1865, and Baptist missionaries at San Salvador in 1878, there was little left of the church which had flourished there nearly 400 years before.

CATHOLIC CHURCH. The Catholic Church enjoyed a privileged status during the colonial period. From the creation of the Congo Free State in 1885, the Belgian king Leopold II controlled placement of missionaries who in return received large concessions in the form of property, subsidies, the right to fulfill certain state functions and a virtual monopoly over education and medical service. When Belgium assumed control of the colony in 1908, the 'trinity of power' (colonial administration; missions, especially Catholics; and the business world) continued to exercise their respective roles. For political reasons Leopold II had obtained agreement from the Vatican that the evangelization of Congo should be an essentially Belgian affair and that only 'Belgian national missions' (those having their headquarters in Belgium, directed by Belgians and counting a fixed number of Belgians among their missionaries to Congo) should be involved. Protestant missions were placed at a severe disadvantage, and the colonial regime did not hestitate to serve as secular arm for the Catholic Church. A new climate was eventually produced by the concession of land to national missions (due to Protestant criticism), the extension of subsidies to Protestant schools in 1946 and the opening of state schools in 1954. In 1956 through the publication of a document entitled 'Declaration of the Bishops of Belgian Congo and Ruanda-Urundi', the Catholic Church took a position in opposition to the status quo by denouncing the injustices of the colonial regime, proclaiming the legitimacy of Congolese political emancipation, criticizing the paternalism and unfair salary scales of commercial enterprises and urging Christians to join labour unions for redress of their grievances. This political reorientation assisted the church to retain its dominant position after Independence in 1960 as well as during the period of disintegration from 1960–65. Anti-clericalism began to manifest itself among the elite, and 200 national and expatriate priests, brothers and sisters were killed during the disturbances. Under the Mobutu regime a determined attempt to reduce the church's power has been made. Nevertheless, the Catholic Church continues to play a significant role in the country and carries on important educational, medical, philanthropic and social services.

In 1973 Catholics formed about 47% of the population. Catholics exceed 50% in the dioceses of Boma, Kikwit, Kisantu and Popokabaka, southwest and southeast of Kinshasa; the dioceses of Lisala and Mbandaka in the northwest; the dioceses of Mahagi, Bunia, Butembo-Beni in the northeast; and the diocese of Sakania in southeastern Shaba. These regions contain only 18% of Zaire's area and 23% of its population, but they contain 35% of the total number of Catholics. In contrast, there are dioceses with Catholics less than 20% of the population, especially the dioceses of Bokungu-Ikala, Uvira, Kongolo and Kole. These regions cover 39% of the national territory and 31% of the total population but only 20% of all Catholics.

The major problems in the eyes of Catholic bishops is the lack of religious depth among the Catholic masses. Much thought and pastoral activity has been dedicated to this in recent years, of special note being cardinal Malula's 1973 proposal that beginning in September 1974 responsibility for parishes and places of worship in his diocese would be given to laymen who would continue their secular jobs but would receive systematic training, whilst clergy would be concentrated at central points. The plan was put into operation in January 1975 when 8 parishes situated in rapid-growth communes were placed in the care of lay 'guides' (*bakambi*). This proposal was designed to africanize the archdiocese as effectively as the local secular administration which had long been entirely in African hands. Another attempt at the africanization of Christian life, both older and more original, is the charismatic movement known as Jamaa (Family, in Swahili) begun by a Belgian missionary Placide Tempels among workers in Katanga (Shaba) in 1954. Most of its 20,000 members are married laymen between 30 and 40 years of age who are peasants or workers with limited formal education. The movement, now spread throughout Zaire, has brought a renewal of Christian life through emphasis on spiritual conversion, church attendance, the deepening of religious experience, the ideals of Christian marriage, and the practising of brotherhood and community. Some Jamaa groups have deviated beyond the recognized limits of faith and morals, resulting in episcopal intervention, and a few have become in effect separatist bodies.

PROTESTANT CHURCHES. There has been since 1970 only one recognized Protestant church, the Eglise du Christ au Zaire, ECZ (Church of Christ in Zaire), which was formed at the March 1970 assembly of the Congo Protestant Council. The union is unique in that the assembly vote which was not unanimous was taken as definitive without reference back to its member churches. During 1970 and 1971, 8 member churches led by the Methodist Church refused to accept the Council's decision and attempted to withdraw from the united body, and founded in February 1971 a new one known as the Council of Protestant Churches of the Congo (CEPCO, later CEPZA). However, they were unable to obtain government recognition and were forced by government to return to the ECZ.

The ECZ member churches are known officially as Communities (Communautés). In 1974, they numbered 53; in 1977, some 30 new Communities, mostly indigenous prophet-type splits from existing Communities, were admitted as full members. The ECZ has permitted them all to maintain their previous ecclesiastical traditions, structures and fraternal ties with churches outside Zaire, building its unity principally through national co-ordination. The church thus displays more internal diversity than perhaps any other united church in the world. The principal communities represent Baptist, Disciples, Methodist, Pentecostal and Presbyterian traditions, plus the work of the interdenominational Africa Inland Mission.

British Baptist missionaries were the first Protestants to arrive, in 1878, and built a series of stations following the course of the Zaire river. This work is now combined in the Baptist Community of the River Zaire. The Baptist Community of West Zaire, which includes the Lower Zaire area with an area east of Kinshasa, was begun by American Baptists. The Baptist Communities of Bandundu and the Lower Uele owe their origin to Scandinavian Baptists, the former being Swedish and the latter Norwegian. Baptist Mid-Missions have been active east and north of Kikwit and Conservative Baptists in Goma.

American Southern Presbyterians reached Luebo in 1891 and have concentrated their attention on the Kasai with headquarters at Kananga. The Disciples of Christ, which also arrived prior to the turn of the century, took over American Baptist work at Bolenge near Mbandaka in 1899.

The African Inland Mission opened its first

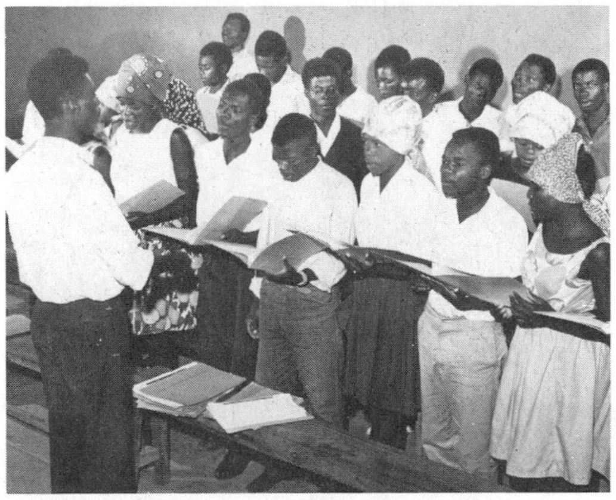

**Communauté Méthodiste au Zaïre.** Church choir in Mulungwishi, among Sanga tribe.

station at Kasengu in 1912 and built up an important work in northeastern Zaire. This church maintains fraternal ties with sister denominations in East Africa.

Methodists of both the northern and southern churches in the USA began work in 1913; and although united in 1939, they continue to exist as 2 communities within the ECZ. Free Methodists from Burundi have opened new stations in the region north of Kalemie since Independence.

Pentecostals have come from the UK, the USA and Scandinavia. The British Pentecostals of the Congo Evangelistic Mission initiated a strong work in northern Shaba in 1915 which is now known as the Pentecostal Community of Zaire, while the British Assemblies of God have been active at Kalemie since 1918. The Assemblies of God from the USA began work in Isiro, also in 1918, and have since spread to other parts of the country including Kinshasa, the Kinshasa group being an autonomous body. Norwegian and Swedish Pentecostals have been concentrated in the Bukavu area.

Other important communities are those which have sprung from the Christian Brethren in Shaba and the northeast, Christian and Missionary Alliance in Boma, Congo Balolo Mission (RBMU) in Basankusu, Covenant Church in Gemena, Heart of Africa Mission in Isiro, Mennonite groups in Kikwit and Tshikapa, Salvation Army in Kinshasa and the Lower Zaire, Seventh-day Adventists in Shaba, Swedish Covenant Mission in Lower Zaire and the Unevangelized Fields Mission in Kisangani.

Member communities of the ECZ have always been heavily involved in education and social service. In 1971–72 there were 1,195 recognized and subsidized primary schools (625,941 pupils, 16,500 teachers); and 253 secondary schools (42,986 students, 2,131 teachers including 681 expatriates). Adding non-subsidized schools, this gave a total of primary pupils exceeding one million. Medical institutions at the same time included 56 hospitals, 57 maternities and 275 dispensaries. A number of agricultural and animal husbandry projects have also been established at Kinshasa, Kimpese, Bolenge, Ikango, Gemena, Likati, Kajiji, Nyanga, Kikwit, Kama, Lwambo, Mwanza, Mbuji-Mayi, Kananga, Sandoa and Ndesha. In addition attention is given to literacy, technical training and public health.

On the national level these various activities are co-ordinated by the Bureau de l'Enseignement Protestant (BEP) and Entr'aide Protestante. The latter organization provides aid and relief for the needy and operates a central pharmacy.

Refugees in Zaire from Angola since 1960 numbered over 600,000 in 1973, of whom over 60% were Protestants. These had been accommodated in ECZ churches with some uneasiness for several years, and disaffection among the Angolans over their relative unimportance in church life came to a head in November 1973 when a provisional commission was formed in Kinshasa with the aim of establishing a United Church of Christ of Angola (Eglise du Christ Unie de l'Angola, EUA), bringing together almost all Angolan Protestant refugees. The following groups were represented on this commission: Eglise Baptiste de l'Angola (EBA), Eglise Evangélique de l'Angola (EEA), Eglise Méthodiste de l'Angola (EMA), Eglise Evangélique du Nord de l'Angola (EENA), Eglise Assemblée de Dieu de Pentecôte (EADP), Association des Chrétiens Angolais (ASCA, later renamed Eglise Luthérienne d'Angola), and Association des Salutistes Angolais (ASA).

INDIGENOUS CHURCHES. The largest independent church in Zaire and indeed in all of Africa is the Church of Jesus Christ on Earth through the Prophet Simon Kimbangu (EJCSK). The EJCSK also has the distinction of being one of the 4 Christian churches recognized by the government of Zaire (the others being the Catholic Church, ECZ and Greek Orthodox Church) and the first African indigenous church to be received into full membership of the WCC (1969). The church was founded by a Baptist catechist Simon Kimbangu from the Bakongo of Lower Zaire. Kimbangu began an extensive preaching and healing ministry in 1921 which attracted immense crowds. This alarmed the Belgian authorities who feared the movement as potentially a political insurrection. Kimbangu was brought to trial and condemned to death, a sentence which was later reduced to life imprisonment. The prophet was exiled to Shaba where he died 30 years later in 1951. The reaction of the mission churches to Kimbanguism was mixed but generally negative. Catholic priests uniformly opposed it while Protestant missionaries varied from outright opposition to seeing it as a genuine spiritual revival. Following the prophet's exile in 1921, the movement suffered severe persecution. Many were exiled, thus inadvertently contributing to the spread of Kimbanguism throughout the country; and the movement in Lower Zaire went underground. Because of the absence of centralized leadership, the movement splintered into a number of factions some of which took on syncretistic elements. In the mid-1950s the 3 sons of the prophet began to openly reorganize the church, and in 1959 the EJCSK was officially recognized by the Belgian authorities. The growth of the denomination has accelerated considerably since Independence in 1960. Some groups which claim to be Kimbanguist remain outside the EJCSK, but the tendency is towards reabsorption, especially since government recognition is confined to the one church. The EJCSK has an extensive educational, medical and social service programme, including an agricultural demonstration farm near Kinshasa; it also has a large seminary in Kinshasa.

By 1970 over 500 other indigenous churches had arisen in Zaire. In 1971 a large number which had previously held *personnalité civile* were deprived of legal existence when the government restricted its official recognition to only 4 Christian denominations (Greek Orthodox in 1972). Several joined the ECZ to legalize their existence. Of the other bodies, which remain unrecognized but active, the most important are the African Apostolic Church of Johane Maranke, which spread to Zaire from Rhodesia and is found mostly in Shaba and the Kasai, and the Church of Jesus Christ on Earth through the Holy Spirit, which has its strength in Kananga.

**CHURCH AND STATE.** The revolutionary constitution of 24 June 1967 begins by an acknowledgement of God in its Preamble: 'We, the Congolese people. . . conscious of our responsibilities before God, the nation and Africa. . .' It then stipulates in Article 10: 'Everyone has the right to freedom of thought, conscience and religion. In the Republic, there is no state religion. Everyone has the right to manifest his religion or his convictions, alone or in common, in public or private, by worship, teaching, practice, performance of rites and living a religious life, provided that public order and good morals are not infringed.' The first article of Law 71–012 elaborates that 'teaching' here is understood as the teaching of religion. Further, Article 13 states: '(Religious education) is provided for the education of youth by the national teaching service'. This 'includes public as well as recognized primary schools which are controlled by public authority and regulated

Greek Orthodox Church, Islamic Community, Jewish Community and the Baha'i Assembly. The first 3 were recognized in Article 11 of Law 71–012; Muslims, Jews and Greek Orthodox were added to the list in March 1972, and Baha'i on 9 June 1972. During March 1972 the government banned the Council of the Protestant Churches in Zaire (CEPZA). On 29 April 1972 the Ministry of Justice then published an appendix to Law 71–012 listing 76 Protestant communities recognized as members of the ECZ. The list was, however, disputed by the ECZ, and the number was reduced to 53 by Law 73–013 of 14 February 1973, the 23 excluding churches allegedly being bodies under expatriate control supported with foreign funds.

Until 1975 the teaching of religion or non-confessional ethics was obligatory in all primary and secondary schools of the national educational system, the choice of courses being left to the discretion of parents or students themselves if of age. In fact, religious education was often confined to the primary level and sometimes ignored completely, depending upon the local headmaster. At the secondary level, this course was given most often by priests, pastors, brothers, sisters or laymen trained in the various institutes of religious sciences. Since only institutes attached to universities are recognized by the state, those trained in non-recognized institutes had to possess another pedagogical diploma. The national Catholic educational system was responsible for the majority of primary and secondary schools, while the Protestant Education Office (BEP) of the ECZ, earlier the Congo Protestant Council, catered for Protestant schools.

In reality the constitution is of only secondary importance in the Zairian political edifice since the promotion of the Popular Revolutionary Movement (Mouvement Populaire de la Révolution, MPR) to the rank of 'supreme institution of the Republic', to which all other institutions including religious associations must be subordinate. This was made official by a constitutional revision in 1970. Founded in 1967 by president Mobutu, the MPR has become the country's sole political party, to which every Zairian is obliged to belong. Its charter is known as the Manifesto of N'Sele (a place in Kinshasa). Every 'church or sect' has 'the obligation to inculcate in its members a civic spirit conforming to the principles (of this Manifesto)' (Law 71–012, Article 9), which should be given in all educational establishments, including theological faculties. Beginning in December 1971 MPR doctrine was augmented by the key concept of Zairian authenticity, which soon became the official

**Eglise Kimbanguiste** (EJCSK). *Top left.* Founder Simon Kimbangu (1889–1951), in prison where he died. *Above.* Kimbangu's mausoleum at Nkamba-Jerusalem, with pillars of vast 10,000-seat temple under construction since 1975. *Right.* His son, Son Eminence Joseph Ku Ntima Diangienda (born 1918), Chef Spirituel, EJCSK, during foundation stone-laying for theological seminary, 1973. *Below right.* Largest EJCSK church, at Matete-Kinshasa; outside, overflow crowd for communion service. *Top right.* Open air Holy Communion service; Europeans are seminary staff.

by statutes fixed by law... National teaching establishments, working in collaboration with interested religious authorities, guarantee to minors whose parents request it and to students of age who also request it, an education which corresponds to their religious convictions. Private schools may be opened when they have fulfilled the requirements fixed by the law'. Moreover, according to Articles 3 and 5, any act of racial, ethnic or religious discrimination is prohibited, particularly in relation to educational material and access to public services.

The practice of religion is regulated by Law 71–012 of 31 December 1971 which stipulates that 'No church or religious sect may be constituted except in the form of a non-profit association with juridical personality. No one may preach any religion publicly unless he is a member of a church or religious sect having juridical personality' (Article 2). Only citizens may found new churches; expatriates may only represent their bodies whilst in Zaire. No one is permitted to be a 'founder' of a church or religious sect, or a 'representative' of a foreign church or sect, unless he fulfils the following conditions: to be of sane mind, of irreproachable conduct, of at least 40 years of age, to have had no prison sentence of over 5 months duration, to have a licenciate or doctoral degree in theology or another document attesting that he has completed a 4-year theological course in a local or foreign theological school, and to possess funds held in a Zairian bank account totalling not less than 100,000 zaires. Moreover, any would-be founder, who must be a citizen, must not previously have exercised the functions of pastor or priest in any

other church nor have left another church as a dissident. Any representative of a foreign church must have already exercised his functions for at least 10 years (Articles 4 and 5). Requests for the granting of juridical personality must be presented to the Ministry of Justice (Article 7).

Seven religious bodies had succeeded in obtaining juridical personality in Zaire by 1973, thus being the only recognized groups as far as the government was concerned. They were the Catholic Church, Church of Christ in Zaire (ECZ), Kimbanguist Church (EJCSK),

ideology of the regime. 'Return to authenticity' is an affirmation of and claim to cultural independence and national uniqueness which signifies also a rejection of foreign ideologies and interventions. From the religious point of view, return to authenticity implies the recognition of the God of the ancestors without however excluding the new religions and implies the complete zairization of all religious expression. With this is combined an affimation of the secularity of the state, separation of church and state, and a refusal to give privileges to religious denominations.

The application of this new doctrine has struck at the autonomy of all religious groups by its assumption of unified support for president and party, which implies that religious authorities are merely peripheral. For the Catholic Church this has resulted in serious conflict with the state, because of Catholicism's strength in Zaire, because of its relationship to the Holy See regarded as a foreign state, and because of its open attempt to retain freedom of movement to fulfil its prophetic and critical role in society, a role which it has reaffirmed on many occasions. It is possible to cite in this regard several homilies given by cardinal Malula, including one demanding a more inclusive justice, and another on living conditions of workers and an end to 'anarchic improvisation' in government policy-making; the latter homily was given in the presence of president Mobutu and the Belgian king on the occasion of the 10th anniversary of Independence, 29 June 1970. Among other actions contributing to the conflict may be mentioned an editorial in the Catholic Weekly *Afrique chrétienne* (12 January 1972) criticizing certain aspects of the ideology of authenticity. The authorities at first attributed the article to cardinal Malula, but he in fact neither wrote it nor read it prior to publication; and its author, an expatriate, was ultimately expelled from the country. Also of importance was the working document for the episcopate's 11th plenary assembly (28 February to 5 March 1972), entitled 'The Church in the service of the Zairian nation' and based on the theological doctrine of the 2 powers, the temporal power related to the state and the spiritual power related to the church. All of these provoked reaction on the part of government.

The evolution of the application of the politics of authenticity as it relates to religion may be summarized in the following 15 stages or sequences. (1) In August 1971 the 3 existing universitities, Lovanium University of Kinshasa (Catholic), the Official University of Lubumbashi (State), and the Free University of Kisangani (Protestant) were suppressed and amalgamated in the National University Zaire (UNAZA), with 3 campuses under direct government control. Catholic and Protestant theological faculties continued to function autonomously, one at Kinshasa and the other at Kisangani, but their integration in UNAZA was anticipated. The former rector of Lovanium was named rector of UNAZA. (2) In December 1971 the MPR demanded that MPR youth (JMPR) be introduced into the John XXIII Major Seminary in Kinshasa, which the episcopate promptly refused. This was then followed by the authenticity campaign and the promulgation of Law 71–012 regulating religious practice. (3) Between January and May 1972 there was sharp conflict between Mobutu and the political bureau of MPR on one side, and cardinal Malula on the other. The cardinal was expelled from his residence which was built, according to the MPR on property owned by the MPR, and on 24 January the John XXIII seminary was closed. On 12 February the cardinal left for Rome at the invitation of the pope. On 15 May, following intense negotiations, Mobutu authorized the cardinal's return, which took place on 28 June. (4) In February 1972 the churches were placed under surveillance by members of the JMPR in order to 'denounce subversive actions' by priests in any form, including prayers for the cardinal. On 16 February a directive was issued requiring that all infants born after this date be baptized with only Zairian (African) names. (5) On 7 March 1972 the political bureau of the MPR decided to install JMPR committees in all major and minor seminaries throughout the country. Because of Article 10 of the constitution which affirms that the republic recognizes no state religion, the political bureau decided that no government representatives would be permitted to participate in any religious ceremony in an official capacity. Every priest permitting the use of foreign names would henceforth be subject to penal servitude of from 6 months to 5 years. In the meantime, on 17 February, Rome had published a new baptismal rite for the entire church, giving parents entire liberty to choose the names of their children. (6) On 11 March 1972 the Belgian general secretary of the Episcopal Conference was expelled from Zaire, and numerous other foreign missionaries were also expelled during this period. On 17 April the John XXIII seminary was reopened after the quarrel over the implantation of JMPR agents in seminaries and training centres for religious personnel was resolved by a compromise which made provision for such installation but reduced considerably its practical effects. On 19th March, in answer to the presidential decree on 31 December 1971 abolishing as national holidays specifically Catholic celebrations which fell on week days, Rome accorded to the Zairian episcopate the right to celebrate the feasts of Ascension, Assumption and All Saints on the nearest Sundays. (7) On 29 November 1972 all confessional youth organizations (Catholic, Protestant and Kimbanguist) were suppressed, and the JMPR became the only authorized youth organization in the country. The law validating this decision was published in January 1973. (8) On 8 February 1973, 31 Catholic, Protestant and Kimbanguist press agencies were suspended, except in cases where the state commissioner for National Orientation made an exception, as he did on 7 May for the journal *Cahiers des religions africaines* 'because the journal makes a scientific contribution of the first order to the development of the country, within the framework of the specialized institutions of UNAZA'. On 9 February there was a violent press campaign against the Vatican concerning the 'dollars affair', funds provided by the Vatican for the university chaplaincy. On 12 February the Catholic bishops were forbidden to meet in assembly which meant the virtual dissolution of the Episcopal Conference, the provincial conferences and the general secretariat of the episcopate, although the technical services of the Episcopal Conference including the Office of Catholic Education continued to function. On 14 February the number of recognized Protestant communities forming part of the Church of Christ in Zaire was reduced from 76 to 53. On 22 February the Catholic apostolic nuncio left Zaire after the government refused to recognize him as dean of the diplomatic corps, on the grounds that the Zairian ambassador to the Holy See was not accorded an equivalent status. (10) On 24 April 1973 all church meetings beyond those of worship services were prohibited, an action which strengthened the monopoly of MPR and JMPR over meetings in Zaire. (11) On 4 May 1973 a decision was made to refuse further recognition of 'the existence of any church on university campus property' because of the secularity of the state. In fact existing chapels continue open, but it is forbidden to construct new ones. At the same time it was decided to establish 3 theological faculties within UNAZA, with a Protestant faculty joining that of the Catholics in Kinshasa and the creation of a new Kimbanguist faculty. By the beginning of 1974 this latter body had not yet come into existence due to the difficulties encountered by the Kimbanguists in raising their standards to university level. Also in May 1973 military chaplains were suppressed and military chapels closed. (12) On 24 June 1973 president Mobutu declared that the quarrel with the Catholic Church was ended; and in July the pope named a pro-nuncio to Zaire since he would no longer be dean of the diplomatic corps. This was followed by the relaxation of the prohibition against church meetings with the exception of those of the Catholic Episcopal Conference. The president affirmed that authorization for the latter would be granted as long as it did not infringe on the prerogatives of the state; and in 1974 provisional authorization was granted. (13) On 26 June 1974 the political office of the MPR ruled that in future Christmas would no longer be a public holiday, a decision which the head of the ECZ declared to be acceptable since it was relevant only to Christians. Nevertheless, there has been widespread opposition to this at the grass roots, with heavy attendance noted at Christmas services since then. (14) In December 1974 the Catholic, Protestant and Kimbanguist theological faculties were detached from the National University of Zaire (UNAZA). The 3 faculties were thus made independent and responsible for their own funding. (15) On 1 January 1975 all systems of education, including confessional schools (80% of all public schools), were suppressed and their property nationalized by the state. Religion courses in primary and secondary schools were eliminated and replaced by 'a course in civic, political training and Zairian traditional ethics'. About the same time, Catholic minor seminaries were taken over by government and opened to all, with minor seminarians becoming subject for the first time to the obligatory national civic service programme for secondary school graduates. In addition, crucifixes and religious pictures were removed from schools, hospitals and other public places and replaced by pictures of the head of state.

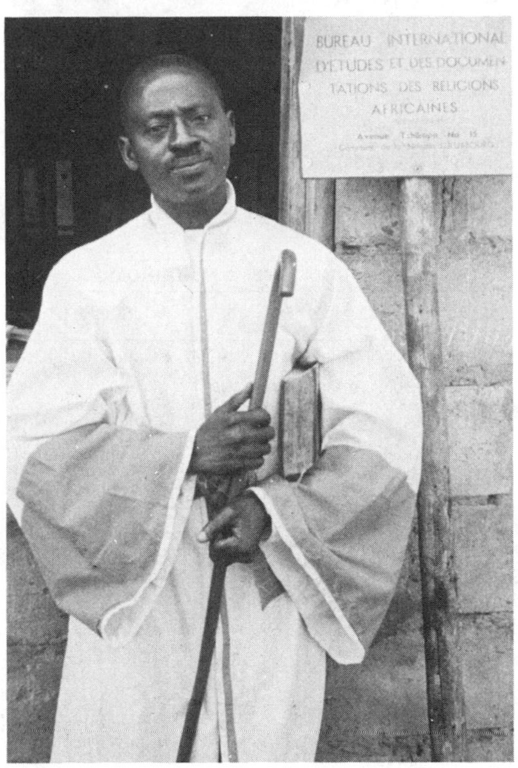


**COSSEUJCA.** Apostle Marc Kadima, founder of this 1965 Luluabourg federation of 30 indigenous denominations, vested with yellow-sleeved white robe, with staff and Tshiluba Bible.

It should be mentioned that, in a country as vast as Zaire, these various measures are subject to local conditions and inter-personal relations between civilian and ecclesiastical authorities. Some clergy and laity believed that certain measures taken recently by the government reflect the thought of a group which is neither Catholic nor Christian. Within the MPR itself, there is an increasingly evident tendency towards a form of state messianism. On 4 December 1974, the state commissioner in charge of political affairs and the co-ordination of party activities declared: 'The MPR should be considered as a church whose religion is authenticity and its founder as a messiah. Mobutu has come in the name of the ancestors and sent by them. He should be considered as our prophet'.

Despite this rapid growth of anti-Christian measures, however, it is clear that the churches are flourishing as never before. Banned or illegal churches, especially indigenous ones, simply carry on worship and evangelism as before, or continue underground; and the ban on religious instruction in schools grew ineffectual. As one result, at the end of 1976 the government dramatically reversed its position and announced that the administration of public primary and secondary schools would now be returned to the churches, a decision involving over 3 million pupils, 80,000 teachers and a budget of 20% of the total national budget. A probable reason for this action was the unexpectedly high cost of running a state education system, and the widespread moral regression in schools since nationalization.

In a second major reversal of policy, in 1978 president Mobutu (a practising Catholic) reauthorized religious broadcasting, banned since 1972, and gave radio and TV time once more to Catholics, Protestants, Kimbanguists and Muslims.

**INTERDENOMINATIONAL ORGANIZATIONS.** The Congo Protestant Council (Conseil Protestant du Congo, CPC) was formed in 1924 , reorganized in 1955, and in March 1970 was replaced by the Church of Christ in Congo, later the ECZ. Although ecumenism has been suspect in many Protestant circles, attempts to found other councils have been vetoed by government. Among councils banned in 1972 were: CEPZA, AEZ (Evangelical Alliance of Zaire/Alliance Evangélique du Zaire), and COSSEUJCA (Supreme Council of Priests for the United Church of Jesus Christ in Africa), an association of independent churches. On the Catholic side, the Episcopal Conference sponsors a Secretariat for Unity which is responsible for ecumenical relations between Catholics and Zaire's other churches.

There are no joint Catholic-Protestant organizations, but there is co-operative work. At Boende an ecumenical hospital has been opened under joint sponsorship. The Bible Society of Zaire (SBZ), with Catholic participation, is at work on a common translation of the Bible into the Lomongo, Kituba and Lingala languages.

**BROADCASTING.** The government La Voix du Zaire and Radiodiffusion Télévision Nationale did not broadcast regular Christian programmes from the end of 1972 until the ban was lifted in 1978. Previously, Catholics, Protestants and Kimbanguists had regular outputs on both radio and TV. The change was part of the restructuring of the country in line with the government's policy of authenticity. In 1963, the Catholic Church established a major programme production studio. To begin with, this was called STAR (African Radio Technical Service) and then TELESTAR combining both radio and TV production in its main centre in Kinshasa and in several regional studios. This project later became ecumenical, with the inclusion of Protestants, producing over 20 hours of programmes (with emphasis on cultural and educational programmes rather than religious ones) weekly for national radio and TV. In line with government policy, TELESTAR was nationalized in February 1973 and renamed RENAPEC, though it retained the same staff and programmes. For Catholics, Zaire is registered as a member of UNDA.

## BIBLIOGRAPHY


*Actes de la VIIe assemblée plénière de l'Episcopat du Congo, 1967.* Kinshasa: Secrétariat Général de l'Episcopat, *1969.*

*Annuire de l'église du Congo, 1969.* Kinshasa: Centre de Recherches Sociologiques, Service des Statistiques, 1969. 17p. (1974–75 edition, 600p).

'Church and authenticity in Zaire', Special note, *Pro Mundi Vita* (Brussels), 39 (1975), 1–32.

'Congo-Kinshasa 1969', *Pro Mundi Vita* (Brussels), 32 (1970).

*English-speaking missions in the Congo Independent State.* R.M. Slade. Brussels: Duculot, 1959.

*Histoire du Protestantisme au Congo.* E.M. Braekman. Bruxelles: Eclaireurs Unionistes, 1961. 300p.

'Introduction de l'influence de l'Islam au Congo', P. Ceulemans, in I.M. Lewis (ed), *Islam in tropical Africa* (London: Oxford, 1966), p. 174–192.

*Kimbangu: an African prophet and his church.* M.-L. Martin. Oxford: Blackwell, 1975. 198p.

*Kitawala: Ursprung, Ausbreitung und Religion der Watch-Tower-Bewegung in Zentralafrika.* H.J. Greschat. Marburg: Elwert Verlag, 1967.

'Le mouvement "Jamaa" au Katanga', T. Theuws, *Rythmes du Monde*, VIII, 1 (1960), 201–212.

'Les églises congolaises et la construction nationale', G. Bernard, in *Sociologie de la construction nationale des les nouveaux états* (Bruxelles: Institut de Sociologie, 1968).

*Messianic popular movements in the Lower Congo.* E. Andersson. Uppsala: Almquist & Wiksells, 1958. 287p.

*Midday in missions: Zaire 1977.* D.A. MacGavran & N.G. Riddle.

*Protestant missions in Congo, 1878–1969.* J.R. Crawford. Kinshasa: Librairie Evangélique du Congo, n.d. (c1970). 26p.

'Sectes dans l'est du Congo ex-Belge', in *Devant les sectes non-chrétiennes* (Louvain: Desclée de Brouwer, 1961).

*The Church of Christ in Zaire: a handbook of Protestant missions, churches and communities, 1878–1978.* C. Irvine, ed. Indianapolis, IN: Disciples of Christ, 1978. 161p.

*The Jamaa and the Church: a Bantu Catholic movement in Zaire.* W. de Craemer. Leiden: Brill, 1977. 212p.

*Un rayon d'espoir: évangélisation dans les Eglises Africaines Indépendantes.* Luntadila Ndala Za Fwa, EJCSK. Kinshasa: CEDI, 1975. 82p.

*Witchcraft, oracles and magic among the Azande.* E.E. Evans-Pritchard. Oxford: Clarendon, 1937. 558p.

'Zaire's super-church', R.L. Niklaus, *Christianity today*, XVI, 14 (April 1972), 4–10.


TABLE 2. ORGANIZED CHURCHES AND DENOMINATIONS IN ZAIRE

| Official name 1 | Begun 2 | Type 3 | Counc 4 | Congs 5 | Adults 6 | Affiliated 7 | Names, notes, and other statistics (see Codebook) 8 |
|---|---|---|---|---|---|---|---|
| Eglise Apostolique Africaine de JM | 1953 | I peA | x...I | 500 | 50,000 | 100,000 | *AACJM. Bapostolo.* M=African Apostolic Ch of Johane Maranke (Rhodesia). Kasai. |
| Eglise Apostolique Unie en Afrique | 1971 | I pen | .v... | 300 | 43,000 | 80,000 | *EAUA. United Apost Ch.* Also Brazzaville. 1973 applied to WCC. 42n,475m,2H,42h,2p. |
| **Eglise Catholique au Zaire:** | 1482 | R Lat | P.S.R | 1,682 | 5,765,700 | 9,940,873 | *Catholic Ch.* C=37+23+162. 11p,1q,9s(472). 596n,2190x,1117m,4290w,P=41%,384158Yy. |
| M Bukavu | 1929 | R Lat | Ps | 17 | 211,000 | 363,800 | Catholics 90% Bashi; Bahavu, refugees. 24 86 66 208 48 16803 |
| D Butembo-Beni | 1934 | R Lat | Ps | 82 | 348,900 | 601,504 | Ruwenzori. 90% Nande (Konjo); Bira, Lese. 21 38 59 214 31 16126 |
| D Goma | 1959 | R Lat | Ps | 14 | 157,800 | 272,150 | 70% Ruanda, 20% Nande; Hunde. Tourism. 15 61 30 80 82 13102 |
| D Kasongo | 1952 | R Lat | Ps | 14 | 72,000 | 124,200 | Rega, Zimba, Bangu-Bangu. 15% Muslim. 2 40 19 39 51 6150 |
| D Kindu | 1956 | R Lat | Ps | 15 | 41,600 | 71,793 | Tetela, Songola, Langa. Rural medical aid. 5 28 8 35 71 2751 |
| D Uvira | 1962 | R Lat | Psx | 11 | 40,900 | 70,482 | Vira, Fuleru, Bembe, Bwari, Hutu refugees. 6 33 10 24 58 3405 |
| M Kananga (Luluabourg) | 1904 | R Lat | Ps | 14 | 325,900 | 561,902 | 80% Lulua, 14% Bakwaluntu, 5% Babindi. 11 95 47 176 42 26539 |
| D Kabinda | 1953 | R Lat | Ps | 14 | 77,900 | 134,384 | 80% Songe; Tetela, Luba. Lusambo schools. 9 26 24 49 70 8773 |
| D Kole | 1951 | R Lat | Psscc | 16 | 13,200 | 22,792 | Kela, Tetela, Songomeno. No sisters. 0 18 5 0 38 2107 |
| D Luebo | 1959 | R Lat | Ps | 18 | 171,200 | 295,100 | 55% Lulua, 10% Luba, 9% Pende, 9% Chokwe. 6 25 9 67 25 9923 |
| D Luiza | 1967 | R Lat | Ps | 9 | 121,300 | 209,200 | 55% Basalampasu, 30% Mbagani, 15% Ambala. 3 27 11 6 40 11555 |
| D Mbuji-Mayi | 1966 | R Lat | Ps | 37 | 234,300 | 403,900 | 85% Luba, refugees from 1960 tribal wars. 44 43 36 213 40 10000 |
| D Mweka | 1953 | R Lat | Psj | 8 | 33,000 | 56,947 | 37% Kuba, 30% Luba, 17% Lulua. Art trade. 0 18 10 16 47 2259 |
| D Tshumbé | 1936 | R Lat | Ps | 14 | 54,800 | 94,482 | 70% Tetela, Nkutshu, Twa pygmies. 10 20 22 64 10 3234 |
| M Kinshasa | 1886 | R Lat | Ps | 45 | 419,300 | 722,854 | 200 tribes. 65% Kongo, 10% Yaka, 10% Ngala. 46 224 103 337 33 31488 |
| D Boma | 1934 | R Lat | Ps | 3 | 220,700 | 380,510 | 80% Yombe, 15% Kongo, 5% Woyo. 23 69 33 158 40 13251 |
| D Idiofa | 1937 | R Lat | Ps | 24 | 121,500 | 209,490 | 45% Dzing, 39% Bunda. 1964 Simba rising. 18 56 8 45 52 7203 |
| D Inongo | 1953 | R Lat | Ps | 11 | 78,100 | 134,575 | Many tribes. 55% Ekonda, 45% Sakata. 9 41 5 45 38 6220 |
| D Kenge | 1957 | R Lat | Ps | 120 | 74,200 | 127,918 | 45% Yanzi, 20% Yaka, 12% Mbala, 10% Suku. 5 57 26 85 34 6462 |
| D Kikwit | 1903 | R Lat | Ps | 16 | 359,800 | 620,326 | Suku, Chokwe, Pende, Kwese, Mbala, Lunda. 29 112 91 290 40 23382 |
| D Kisantu | 1931 | R Lat | Ps | 14 | 138,800 | 239,300 | 90% Kongo (Ntandu, Ndibu, Manianga). 45 59 46 196 40 7000 |
| D Matadi | 1911 | R Lat | Ps | 31 | 230,100 | 396,753 | 84% Kongo, 16% Sundi, Angolan refugees. 27 47 37 108 44 3000 |
| D Popokabaka | 1961 | R Lat | Ps | 15 | 113,000 | 194,784 | 95% Yaka, 5% Suku, Chokwe, Lunda and Holo. 4 58 22 127 40 7892 |
| M Kisangani (Stanleyville) | 1904 | R Lat | Ps | 27 | 145,300 | 250,200 | Small tribes: 8% Soko, 8% Kumu, 7% Ndaka. 10 37 29 64 24 5649 |
| D Bondo | 1926 | R Lat | Ps | 431 | 53,500 | 92,191 | Ancient Zande kingdom. Bandia, Kare. 12 14 5 19 38 3983 |
| D Bunia | 1922 | R Lat | Ps | 16 | 198,500 | 342,319 | 45% Lendu, 35% Bahema, 15% Bira, pygmies. 15 56 43 222 68 11909 |
| D Buta | 1911 | R Lat | Ps | 16 | 65,700 | 113,303 | Babwa, Makere, Bati. 1964 Simba massacres. 11 12 14 54 47 6158 |
| D Doruma-Dungu | 1958 | R Lat | Ps | 10 | 56,800 | 98,000 | 70% Azande, 30% Abarambo, Amadi. 7 23 22 32 40 4668 |
| D Isangi | 1951 | R Lat | Ps | 10 | 26,300 | 45,375 | 47% Ngandu, 30% Topoke, 13% Lokele. 0 19 3 19 40 2019 |
| D Isiro-Niangara | 1911 | R Lat | Ps | 19 | 138,200 | 238,350 | 40% Logo, 30% Azande, 20% Mangbetu. 14 48 15 88 59 14859 |
| D Mahagi-Nioka | 1962 | R Lat | Ps | 15 | 242,200 | 417,618 | 45% Alur, 35% Lugbara; Logo, Lendu. 27 26 22 107 28 14786 |
| D Wamba | 1949 | R Lat | Pscj | 75 | 41,900 | 72,195 | 30% Budu, 30% Lika, 30% Ndaka, 10% Lese. 3 14 3 12 28 3321 |
| M Lubumbashi (Elizabethville) | 1910 | R Lat | Ps | 52 | 151,000 | 260,426 | Shaba. 50% Sanga, 10% Lamba. 1,556 Orthodox. 46 109 49 259 38 10200 |
| D Kalemie-Kirungu (Baudouinville) | 1887 | R Lat | Ps | 16 | 73,700 | 126,989 | 42% Tabwa, 26% Hemba, 18% Luba-Hemba. 13 36 30 75 25 3260 |
| D Kamina | 1948 | R Lat | Ps | 7 | 53,200 | 91,711 | 38% Lunda, 15% Luba, 13% Chokwe, Swahili. 2 26 4 49 42 3379 |
| D Kilwa-Kasenga | 1948 | R Lat | Ps | 12 | 18,000 | 31,116 | 60% Shila, 20% Luba, 20% Zela, Tabwa. 2 15 3 30 48 1701 |
| D Kolwezi | 1971 | R Lat | Ps | 28 | 69,600 | 120,000 | Copper mines, Angola-Zambia border. 9 53 15 162 42 5828 |
| D Kongolo | 1911 | R Lat | Ps | 11 | 31,300 | 54,000 | Tembo, Songe, Buye. 1962 massacre 21 CSSp. 9 20 1 38 36 2889 |
| D Manono | 1971 | R Lat | Ps | 14 | 43,500 | 75,004 | Formed from Kongolo and Kalemie dioceses. 7 21 0 15 40 3684 |
| D Sakania-Kipushi | 1925 | R Lat | Ps | 12 | 44,700 | 77,033 | 45% Lamba, 16% Kaonde, 14% Lala, 12% Aushi. 2 62 20 41 53 3912 |
| M Mbandaka-Bikoro | 1924 | R Lat | Ps | 21 | 82,500 | 142,305 | 70% Mongo, 20% Nkundo, Mbole, Kutu. 3 59 17 130 28 2601 |
| D Basankusu | 1926 | R Lat | Ps | 15 | 46,500 | 80,197 | 36% Ngombe, 33% Ngandu, 31% Mongo. 4 42 7 22 35 4736 |
| D Bikoro (1975, in M Mbandaka) | 1931 | R Lat | Ps | 167 | 19,100 | 32,924 | Few people. 70% Etumba; Ekonda, Twa, Teke. 1 25 11 34 36 2069 |
| D Bokungu-Ikela | 1961 | R Lat | Ps | 10 | 17,300 | 29,848 | Rain-forest. Boyela, Lalia, Yasayama. 0 19 4 28 42 1611 |
| D Budjala | 1964 | R Lat | Ps | 16 | 107,900 | 186,090 | 25% each Bwaka, Banza, Ngbandi, Ngala. 9 45 10 53 40 8678 |
| D Lisala | 1919 | R Lat | Ps | 21 | 164,600 | 283,800 | 40% Ngombe, 35% Budja; Mongo, Ngbandi. 15 53 40 64 40 9300 |
| D Lolo | 1937 | R Lat | Ps | 74 | 24,400 | 41,983 | 80% Budja; Babango, Babwa, Ngbaka. 2 16 7 20 30 2655 |
| D Molegbe | 1911 | R Lat | Ps | 25 | 190,700 | 328,750 | Near CAR, Congo. Ngbaka, Banda, Mbanza. 11 59 16 71 40 11678 |
| Eglise Chrétienne Ev en Afrique | 1959 | I Bap | .T..T | 52 | 15,000 | 30,000 | *ECEA. Ev Christian Ch in Africa.* Ex Eglise de la Conscience Chrétienne. 120n. |
| Eglise de Dieu | 1966 | P Pe3 | ZF... | 29 | 5,163 | 10,000 | Former link with M=Church of God(Cleveland)(USA). 27 churches, 2 missions. 19n. |
| **EdeJC sur la Terre par le Prophète SK** | 1921 | I pen | xWi.N | 8,000 | 2,000,000 | 3,500,000 | *EJCSK. Ch of Christ on Earth thru Prophet Simon Kimbangu.* 1H,1s(82),W=44%,36747Y. |
| EdeJC sur la Terre par le St-Esprit | 1951 | I pen | .v... | 90 | 32,191 | 110,069 | *Ch of JC on Earth thru Holy Spirit.* Healings. 85% Luba. 100n,5000m,W=98%,2778Y. |
| Eglise de la Foi par Messie JC | 1954 | I CCa | .v..I | | 5,000 | 9,000 | *EFMJC. Ch of Faith thru Messiah JC.* Ex RCC. Aim: 'Love they neighbour'. Lulua,Luba. |
| Eglise des Noirs en Afrique Centrale | 1939 | I Sal | ....I | | 15,000 | 20,000 | *ENAC.* Founder-patriarch Simon Mpadi. Persecuted 21 years. 90% Kongo, 10% Chokwe. |
| Eglise Dieu-Donné au Zaire | 1945 | I mar | .v..I | | 12,000 | 20,000 | Syncretistic body among Teke, also Yaka. HQ Ngaba, Kinshasa. 1971 applied to WCC. |
| **Eglise du Christ au Zaire:** | 1924 | P uni | ....K | 19,540 | 1,519,499 | 4,728,280 | *ECZ. Ch of Christ in Z.* 1924, CPC; 1970, united ch. 2538n,10044m,1710f,180000z. |
| Co Anglicane du Zaire: D Boga-Zaire | 1895 | A Eva | AwaVK | 400 | 30,000 | 100,000 | *CAZ.* In CURBZ. M=CMS. HQ Bunia. Many Independents joining. 35n,3x,W=80%,848Y,255y. |
| Co Armée du Salut | 1934 | P Sal | xwA.K | 386 | 8,415 | 31,000 | *CAS. SA, Z Terr. Basolda na Kobikisa.* 70% Kongo. 150n,25x,8h,12r,1s,W=83%,275Y. |
| Co Assemblée de Dieu au Zaire-K | 1922 | P Pe2 | ZFG.a | 70 | 26,094 | 75,000 | *CADZ. Assembly of God in Zaire in Kinshasa.* Autonomous body. M=AoG(USA). 62n,10f. |
| Co Assemblée des Frères Ev au Z | 1923 | P CBr | x.G.a | 94 | 6,840 | 12,000 | *CAFEZA. Assembly of Brethren.* M=Emmanuel M(CMML,USA). Nyankunde. 52n,31f,1H,1j. |
| Co Assemblées de Dieu à l Est du Z | 1918 | P Pe2 | ZG..K | 220 | 4,409 | 10,780 | *CADEZA.*M=UPMGBI(AoG)(UK). HQKalemie.59% Bembe,31% Buye. 29n,2f,1H,W=73%, 302Y. |
| Co Assemblées de Frères au Shaba | 1961 | I CBr | xv..K | 120 | 4,358 | 25,000 | *CAFS*(formerly AFK). *Christian Brethren.* Ex CFCG. Lamba. 1968, applied to WCC. 57n. |
| Co Assoc des Egls Ev de la Lulonga | 1878 | P int | xGG.a | 468 | 33,450 | 75,000 | *CADELU. Ev Chs of the Lulonga.* M=Congo Balolo M(RBMU) (UK). HQ Basankusu. 67n,9f,2H. |
| Co Assoc des Frères en Christ au Z | 1931 | I CBr | ....K | 20 | 573 | 3,000 | *CM.* Mambasa. Split ex Emmanuel Mission. HQ Dibaya-Lubwe (Ituri). 5n,1f. |
| Co Baptiste au Kivu | 1928 | P Bap | xFg.a | 592 | 32,753 | 60,000 | *CBK*(formerly AEBK,EPBK). 1928,UAM;1946,M=CBFMS. HQ Goma. 100n,59f,1H,10h,2s,3663Y. |
| Co BaptAutonome entreWamba-Bakali | 1949 | I Bap | ....K | 15 | 1,940 | 7,500 | *CBAWB. Autonomous Baptists in WB.* Ex CEBB(Swedish Baptists). HQ Bandundu. 15n, |
| Co Baptiste du Bas-Uélé | 1918 | P Bap | ....K | 219 | 16,000 | 35,000 | *CBBU*(formerly EBBU). Lower Uélé. M=Norwegian Baptist Mission. HQ Bondo. 38n,15f. |
| Co Baptiste du Fleuve Zaire | 1878 | P Bap | T.A.K | 600 | 60,000 | 450,000 | *CBFZ.* Merger of 4 regions, M=BMS(UK). 50n,4x,97f,4s,W=73%,2460Y. |
| Co Baptiste du Zaire-Ouest | 1878 | P Bap | T...K | 700 | 100,000 | 450,000 | *CBZO*(formerly EBCO). *Bapt Ch of WZ.* 1884,M=ABFMS;CBOMB. 34n,110f,7H,33h,7369Y. |
| Co Baptiste Mission du Sud-Kwango | 1961 | P Bap | ....K | 15 | 833 | 12,000 | *CBMSK. Baptist Mission of SKwango.* M=Independent Baptist M(USA). Mainly Yaka. 4n. |
| Co Centrale du Christ en Afrique | 1956 | I Met | .T..K | 19 | 3,000 | 7,500 | *CCCA. Central Comm of Christ in A.* Ex Methodists. HQ Lubumbashi. Lunda, Bemba. 3n. |
| Co Coopération Evangélique au Zaire | 1965 | I pen | ....K | 10 | 2,633 | 8,000 | *CCEZ.* Ex CEBB(SBM). M=Coop Ev Mondiale (France). HQ Feshi (Bandundu). 4n,10f. |
| Co des Assemblées de Dieu au Zaire | 1918 | P Pe2 | ZFG.a | 270 | 16,019 | 50,000 | *CADZ*(formerly EADC). *Assemblies of God.* M=AoG(USA). HQ Isiro. 81n,9f,3h,2s(130). |
| Co des Disciples du Christ au Zaire | 1897 | P Dis | xWA.K | 841 | 198,568 | 650,000 | *CDCZ*(DCC). *Disciples of Christ.* 1899, M=UCMS. HQ Mbandaka. 65n,22f,5H,13h,1s. |
| Co des Eglises Baptistes de Bandundu | 1892 | P Bap | ....K | 192 | 18,812 | 50,000 | *CEBB* or *CBB*(formerly EB du Maindombe). M=SBM(Sweden). HQ Semendwa. 55n,39f. |
| Co des Eglises Bapt Indépendantes Ev | 1932 | P Bap | x...K | 226 | 10,592 | 25,000 | *CEBIE* (formerly AEBI). *Independent Baptist Chs.* 1953, M=BMM. HQ Kikwit. 35n,13f. |
| Co des Egls Chrétiennes en Afrique | 1948 | P Dis | x...K | 45 | 2,830 | 8,000 | *CECA. Community of Christian Chs in Africa.* M=ACM(CCCC) (USA). HQ Bukavu. 65n,13f. |
| Co des Eglises de Grace au Zaire | 1939 | P int | xFg.a | 152 | 5,538 | 20,000 | *CEGZ*(formerly MEM). *Chs of Grace in Z.* M=Maniema M(GM) (USA). HQ Bukavu. 69n,15f. |
| Co des Eglises de Pentecôte | 1921 | P Pe2 | Z...K | 700 | 46,785 | 200,000 | *CEP.* M=SFM. HQ Bukavu. 43% Bafulero, 31% Hunde. 194n,3x,49f,2H,1j,1s(47),7001Y. |
| Co des E des Frères Mennonites au Z | 1912 | P Men | GFG.a | 140 | 10,180 | 16,000 | *CEFMZ*(AEFMC). *Mennonite Brethren.* M=AMBM. HQ Kikwit. 50n,4x,43f,2H,2h,W=50%,350Y. |
| Co des Eglises Libres du Zaire | 1922 | P Pe2 | Z...K | 265 | 27,536 | 75,000 | *CELZA. Free Chs of Z.* M=NPY. Bukavu. 59% Bashi,30% Rega. 43n,6x,30f,1p,W=85%,3040Y. |
| Co des Fidèles Protestants | 1957 | I Bap | ....K | 141 | 8,000 | 15,000 | *CFP. Mission of Protestant Faithful.* Schism ex NBM. HQ Bondo. 80% Azande. 16n. |
| Co des Frères en Christ Garenganze | 1886 | P CBr | x...K | 355 | 10,200 | 31,000 | *CFCG. Garenganze Brethren in Christ.* M=GEM(CMML) (UK). HQ Lubumbashi. 155n,15f. |
| Co du Christ Lumière du St-Esprit | 1931 | I pen | .WA.K | 350 | 60,000 | 150,000 | *CL. Community of Light.* Schism ex EJCSK. 95% Luba. 300 schools. 160n. |
| Co Episcopale Baptiste Africaine | 1956 | I pen | .uA.K | 224 | 54,949 | 80,000 | *CEBA* (formerly EPROBA). *African Episcopal Baptist Ch.* Ex CEM. HQ Manono. 57n,1f. |
| Co Ev au Centre de l'Afrique | 1912 | P int | xMg.a | 1,140 | 63,047 | 300,000 | *CECA*(CCZO,EVACO). *Central Africa Ch.* M=AIM. HQ Bunia. 210n,115f,5H,19h,4s,4000Y. |
| Co Evangélique Beréenne au Zaire | 1938 | P int | .MG.a | 80 | 20,000 | 60,000 | *CEBZ*(formerly EEBC). *Berean Ch in Z.* M=BAMS(USA). HQ Shabunda (Kivu). 44n,19f. |

*Continued opposite*

*Table 2—continued*

| Official name 1 | Begun 2 | Type 3 | Counc 4 | Congs 5 | Adults 6 | Affiliated 7 | Names, notes, and other statistics (see Codebook) 8 |
|---|---|---|---|---|---|---|---|
| Co Evangélique de l'Alliance au Z | 1884 | P Hol | xPG.a | 856 | 23,343 | 60,000 | CEAZ (formerly EEAC). *Ch of Alliance in Z.* M=CMA(USA). HQ Boma. 106n,30f,1H,6h,1s. |
| Co Evangélique de Pentecôte au Shaba | | I pen | ....K | 180 | 18,014 | 50,000 | CEPS. *Ch of Pentecost in Shaba.* Related to CEM. HQ Lubumbashi. 152n. |
| Co Ev des Adventistes du 7e Jour | 1919 | P Adv | x...K | 300 | 30,287 | 70,000 | *Seventh-day Adv, Zaire U.* 2 planes. 141n,5x,26f,1H,9h,1r,1s,507t(56191),W=77%,3452Y. |
| Co Ev du Christ au Coeur d'Afrique | 1913 | P int | xGG.a | 550 | 52,201 | 110,000 | CECCA. *Heart of Africa Ch.* M=HAM(WEC) (UK). HQ Isiro. 157n,28f,1H,12h,1j,2s,690Y. |
| Co Evangélique du Christ en Ubangi | 1922 | P Con | xPG.a | 235 | 13,385 | 75,000 | CECU(MEU,ECU). *Ch of Christ in U.* M=EFCA(USA). HQ Gemena. 29n,53f,1H,1h,2s. |
| Co Evangélique du Haut-Zaïre | 1931 | P int | xMG.a | 370 | 21,600 | 40,000 | CEHZ. *Ev Ch of Upper Zaire.* M=UFM(UK). HQ Kisangani. 12n,26f,1H,9h,4s. |
| Co Evangélique du Kwango | 1952 | P ind | ....K | 206 | 6,700 | 20,000 | CEK(formerly EEK). *Ch of Kwango.* M=MEB(Ev M Among the Bayaka) (Switz). 16n,15f. |
| Co Evangélique du Zaïre | 1881 | P Con | .WA.K | 192 | 30,064 | 75,000 | CEZ(formerly EE de Manianga-Matadi,EEMM). M=SMF(Sweden). HQ Luozi. 141n,44f. |
| Co Evangélique en Ubandi-Mongala | 1937 | I Con | ....K | 410 | 34,011 | 70,000 | CEUM. *Ev Ch in U-M.* Ex CECU(EFCA), supported by M=ECCA(USA). HQ Gemena. 50n,50f. |
| Co Ev Mennonite du Sud-Kasaï | 1960 | I Men | ....K | 40 | 3,200 | 9,000 | CEMSK. Split ex Congo Inland Mission, now reconciled. HQ Mbuji-Mayi. 20n. |
| Co Evangélique Zaïroise | 1927 | P Bap | ....K | 72 | 4,537 | 12,000 | CEZ(AEBI). M=ZGM/CGM,BIM(USA). Badinga, Mbunda. 43n,1x,3f,2p,1s,W=58%,1601Y. |
| Co Libre de Maniema-Kivu | 1922 | P Pen | ....K | 85 | 10,065 | 20,000 | CLMK(formerly ELMK). *Free Ch of the Maniema.* M=ESAM(USA). HQ Shabunda. 59n,25f,3s. |
| Co Libre Méthodiste au Zaïre-Est | 1962 | P Hol | VFg.K | 166 | 11,438 | 30,000 | CLMZ(ELMCE). M=FMC(USA). 91% Bembe, 6% Ruanda. 81n,1x,12m,5f,1h,1s,W=99%,489Y. |
| Co Méthodiste au Sud-Zaïre | 1885 | P Met | VwA.K | 2,430 | 42,326 | 100,000 | CMSZ. *North Shaba & Southern Zaire Confs,* Africa CC, UMC(USA). 107n,35f,1H,1s(70). |
| Co Méthodiste au Zaïre Centrale | 1913 | P Met | VwA.K | 936 | 71,614 | 150,000 | CMZC. In Africa Central Conf, UMC(USA). HQ Kananga. 95% Tetela. 142n,43f,1H,431t. |
| Co Mennonite au Zaïre | 1896 | P Men | GW.,K | 290 | 38,200 | 110,000 | CMZ(formerly EMC). M=Congo Inland Mission(GCMC) (USA). HQ Chikapa. 195n,81f,5H,2s. |
| Co Pentecôtiste au Zaïre | 1915 | P Pe2 | ZGG.a | 600 | 54,371 | 180,000 | CPZ(EPCO). *Pentecostal Ch in Z.* M=CEM(ZEM) (UK). HQ Kamina. 611n,1j,33f,1p. |
| Co Presbytérienne au Zaïre | 1889 | P Ref | RWA.K | 2,013 | 120,000 | 300,000 | CPZa (formerly EPC). *Presbyterian Ch in Z.* M=APCM(PCUS). HQ Kananga. 225n,89f,1s. |
| Co Presbytérienne de Kinshasa | 1955 | P Ref | ..A.K | 15 | 8,413 | 20,000 | CPK(formerly EPK). *Presbyterian Ch in K.* M=APCM(PCUS). 17n,7f. |
| Co Protestante du Shaba | 1954 | I Met | .T..K | 15 | 2,609 | 8,000 | CPS(formerly EPROKAT). *Prot Ch in Shaba.* Ex Methodist. M=CBMEC(Belgium). Luba. 6n. |
| Co Région de Sankuru | 1897 | P EBr | x....K | 75 | 6,384 | 20,000 | CRS. M=North Kasai M(Westcott, North Sankuru). Glanton Brethren. HQ Kole. 31n,8f. |
| Co Union des Egls Baptistes du Kwilu | 1953 | I Bap | ....K | 35 | 2,383 | 7,500 | CUEBK. Baptist Churches of Kwilu. Split ex BMM. HQ Kikwit. 35n,8f. |
| Autres Communautés | | I | ....K | 400 | 30,000 | 100,000 | Other Communities, admitted to ECZ, including 30 in 1977. |
| Eglise du Christ Unie de l'Angola | 1973 | I uni | .v... | 100 | 50,000 | 100,000 | ECUA. United Ch of Christ of Angola. Ex ECZ by Angolans. 85% Kongo, 10% Kimbundu. |
| Eglise du Zaïre Sankuru à Kondji | 1936 | P int | .v... | 11 | 525 | 1,500 | Formerly M=Africa Evangelistic Band(UK,SAfrica). Pilgrims. HQ Kasai-Orientale. |
| Eglise Evangélique Africaine | 1959 | I CBr | .T..T | 35 | 6,000 | 10,000 | Schism ex Garenganze. In Zambia, Central Africa Ch(ex CMML). Lamba, Bemba, Yeke. |
| Eglise Evangélique du Haut-Uélé | 1960 | I ind | ..G.G | 48 | 5,082 | 10,000 | Formerly ECC(Gamba). Schism of all Mayogo ex HAM(WEC). 90% Mayogo. 180Y,635z. |
| Eglise Evangélique Zaïroise au Mayombe | 1962 | I Hol | .T..T | | 2,000 | 5,000 | APROCO (Assoc Prot du Congo). Schism of 50% ex M=CMA(USA), mostly returned. |
| Eglise Kitawala | 1923 | I Jeh | ....I | | 30,000 | 50,000 | *Ch of the Watchtower.* Ex Jehovah's Witnesses. 1950s, ruthlessly suppressed. In NE. |
| Eglise Lumpa | 1964 | I mar | ..... | | 5,000 | 10,500 | 'Church which itinerates abroad'. Refugees from church crushed by Zambia military. |
| Eglise Orthodoxe: AD Afrique Centrale | 1958 | O Gre | Cw... | 6 | 3,900 | 6,800 | Under P Alexandria. Greeks. 1958, HQ Lubumbashi; 1962, Bujumbura(Burundi). 3x,6f. |
| Eglise Sabbatique du Saint-Esprit | 1954 | I pen | .v... | 48 | 2,365 | 7,175 | ESSE. *Sabbatical Church of the Holy Spirit.* 70% Luba, 20% Chokwe. 53n,W=99%,289Y. |
| Eglise Unie du Saint-Esprit | 1965 | I pen | .v..I | 77 | 20,000 | 50,000 | EUSE. *United Holy Spirit Ch.* 6 Eccles Provs in Kasai, Shaba. 1974 applied to WCC. |
| Eglise Union du Septième Jour | 1961 | I Adv | ....I | 7 | 1,500 | 3,000 | Union 7th-day Ch. Schism ex SDAs. Members Bemba, Lamba, Lunda. |
| Témoins de Jéhovah | c1940 | M Jeh | x.... | 229 | 14,042 | 30,000 | *Jehovah's Witnesses.* 1970, briefly forced into ECZ. 1973, 240 in prison. 1486Y. |
| Other African indigenous churches | | I | ..... | | 20,000 | 50,000 | Total about 500 (see list below), including many small local groupings. |
| Other Protestant denominations | | P | ..... | | 2,000 | 5,000 | Total about 10 (see list below). |
| Other Orthodox churches | | O | ..... | | 100 | 200 | Total 2 bodies (see below): Eglise Orth Copte, Eglise Orth Catholique Américaine. |
| **Total affiliated (mid-1970)** | | | | 33,100 | 9,625,067 | 18,887,397 | **Total denominations (1970)** . . . 530. |
| **Total affiliated (mid-1975)** | | | | 37,000 | 11,212,200 | 22,001,830 | **Total denominations (1975)** . . . 540. |
| **Total affiliated (mid-1980)** | | | | 41,000 | 13,010,700 | 25,531,050 | **Total denominations (1980)** . . . 550. |

## NOTES ON TABLE ABOVE

**COLUMNS:** for meanings and CODES (cols. 1, 3, 4, 8): see Codebook (Part 6). Column 1: Boldface type = church with over 10% of country's affiliated Christians.
NATIONAL COUNCILS (Column 4, 5th letter).
a = member of ECZ, also of AEZ.
G = Alliance Evangélique du Zaïre (AEZ) (Alliance of Zaïre), declared illegal 1970.
I = Conseil Supérieur des Sacrificateurs pour les Eglises-Unies de Jésus-Christ en Afrique (COSSEUJCA) (Supreme Council of Priests for the United Churches of Jesus Christ in Africa); 28 member churches in 1967, 40 in 1969 when applied to join WCC; illegal after 1970; 1977, most joined ECZ.
K = Eglise du Christ au Zaïre (ECZ)(Church of Christ in Zaire), formerly 1924-71 CPC (Conseil Protestant du Congo).
N = Eglise de Jésus-Christ sur la Terre par le Prophète Simon Kimbangu (affiliated to CWME of WCC).
R = Conférence Episcopale du Zaïre (CEZ)(Episcopal Conference of Zaire).
T = Zaire Council of ICCC (10 member churches).
*Other national councils.* Conseil des Eglises Protestantes du Congo/Zaïre (CEPCO/CEPZA): this attempt in 1971 to form an evangelical council outside the ECZ supported by various churches including Methodists and Assemblies of God (USA) was banned by government in 1972. Conseil des Eglises Libres du Congo (CONELCO): founded by 16 indigenous churches before 1970 ban.
OTHER AFRICAN INDIGENOUS CHURCHES. In 1968, of the total of over 500 distinct African independent churches, about 200 were in process of obtaining government registration or had already obtained it. With the new law of 1970 all were ordered either to be suppressed or to join the Church of Christ in Zaire. In practice, by 1977 only a few had so joined, including 2 separatist movements which rejoined their parent bodies (CEBK, a large Nande schism in 1960 of 9,000 members ex CBFMS; and CEBI, a schism ex BMM with HQ Mangai). A number of other indigenous churches are still trying to join, and due to the impossibilities of communicating and enforcing the law the rest exist as formerly, more or less tolerated or ignored. Among these other unregistered indigenous churches are the 17 shown in the table, and the following smaller bodies: Apostolic Ch of Johane Masowe (Gospel of God, 1972 from Zimbabwe; 1,000 adult followers), Children of God of the Uganda Martyrs (Bena Nzambi wa BaMartyre ya Baganda), Eglise Chrétienne en Afrique (Eglise de la Conscience Chrétienne), Eglise de Dieu de Nos Ancêtres (Nzambi wa Bankambue, Bena Luhemba; 1956), Eglise de Digne (Fwanda, St Immanuel; ex RCC), Eglise de Notre Seigneur Jésus-Christ dans le Monde, Eglise de Pentecôte, Eglise de Pentecôte Zaïroise Universelle, Eglise Don de Dieu, Eglise du Christ Roi (ex RCC), Eglise du St-Esprit au Zaïre (ESEZA; Eglise Malembe, begun 1942 in Kasai), Eglise Ev Branche Indigène, Eglise Ev Kukebakeba (Church which Seeks People), Eglise Protection et Vérité du Christ (ex RCC), Eglise Ste Sara (1960, ex RCC: 10,000 members), Eglise Universelle (1965; marginal body begun by Eglise Chrétienne Universelle, from Paris, France; messianic healer Georges Roux), Followers of the Archangel Michael (Bena Michel), Katete (super-Jamaa), Maria Legio of Africa (from Kenya), Union Chrétienne de la Charité (1965 philanthropic movement partly within existing churches). There is also in Shaba a small work of the USA black mission, African Methodist Episcopal Ch, begun in 1957 by Africans from Northern Rhodesia.
OTHER PROTESTANT DENOMINATIONS. Although all Protestant missions are required to operate through the Church of Christ in Zaire, there are also a few other smaller missions with adherents who have only a very loose relation to it. These include: Africa Christian Mission (1964: USA Churches of Christ), Baptist Bible Fellowship International (1957), Christian Nationals' Evangelism Commission 1969), Exclusive Brethren (Booth group; in NE Zaire), Luanza Mission (1884, now counted with CFCG in ECZ), Reformed Episcopal Ch (USA; 1951; works in CECA/AIM), World-Wide Missions (1963).
OTHER ORTHODOX CHURCHES. (1) An Orthodox body related to episcopi vagantes (bishops-at-large) operates a mission field in Zaire: Eglise Orthodoxe Catholique Américaine, a branch of the American Orthodox Catholic Church (a USA Ukrainian schism). (2) The Coptic Orthodox Patriarchate of Alexandria (Egypt) has 25 families in Zaire (1978).

OTHER MARGINAL BODIES. These include: Ch of Jesus Christ of Latter-day Saints (Mormons).
UNITING CHURCHES. (1) In 1970 all Protestant and indigenous churches (except the EJCSK) were ordered united in the Church of Christ in Zaire, by government decree. No further negotiations for organic union are at present contemplated. (2) As a result of dissatisfaction with their minor roles for 12 years in the ECZ, many of the 300,000 Protestant Angolan refugees in Lower Zaire announced the creation in October 1973 of a united church for all Angolan refugees, the Eglise du Christ Unie de l'Angola (ECUA) which would unite Angolans at the time loosely in the ECZ but regarding themselves as members (with monthly Portuguese or Angolan-language services) of the following 7 unrecognized churches of Angolans in Zaire: Eglise Baptiste de l'Angola (EBA, related to BMS work in Angola), Eglise Evangélique de l'Angola (EEA, related to Igreja Evangélica de Angola and M=CBOMB,Canada), Eglise Méthodiste Unie de l'Angola (EMA, related to Igreja Metodista Unida), Eglise Evangélique du Nord de l'Angola (EENA, related to Igreja Evangélica do Norte de Angola), Eglise des Assemblées de Dieu de Pentecôte (EADP, Angolans who have become pentecostals since coming to Zaire), Eglise Luthérienne d'Angola (ELA, until 1973 known as Association des Chrétiens Angolais (ASCA), a loose organization of members from a variety of other Protestant bodies in Angola), and Association des Salutistes Angolais (ASA; Angolans who have joined Salvation Army while in Zaire. The Eglise Méthodiste Unie de l'Angola had previously in 1971 applied to join the WCC giving a full report of its activities and statistics.

PEOPLES (ethnolinguistic). Christians: about 41.0% Central Bantu (Kongo, Kunda, Ndembu, Yaka, Yanzi), 1.0% Pende, 1.0% Luimbe), 18.0% Mongo, 13.6% Luba, 11.0% Equatorial Bantu (Babwa, Bira, Kumu, Ngala, et alii), 10.0% Kivu (Interlacustrine), 3.0% Ngbandi & other Sudanic, 1.0% Azande, 0.8% Teke, 0.6% Moru-Mangbetu, 0.1% Pygmy, Yeke, Lunda, Binza, et alii.

COUNTRY-WIDE TOTALS
EVANGELIZATION (see Part 5). 1900: 17%. 1970: 98%. 1980: 100%. *Mass evangelism.* Among many recent campaigns: 1966-69, 'Christ for All' (Christ pour Tous) campaign (similar to Latin American Evangelism-in-Depth concept, and New Life for All movement of Nigeria), with mass meetings addressed by numerous expatriate evangelists; evangelist Makanzu of the ECZ visited northeastern Zaire (27 rallies, 10,500 professions of faith); also crusades of T.L. Osborn; 1976, AIM teams across northeastern Zaire, reaching over 50,000. *Radiophonic evangelism.* RVOG (205 listeners' letters a year), Radio Cordac, Radio Vatican, ICI 8,401 enrolments, 3,413 active students, 427 conversions reported), et alia.
FOREIGN MISSIONARIES AND PERSONNEL (nationals serving abroad)(1973). Total 438 in 18 countries: about 380 Roman Catholics in 13 countries, about 43 African indigenous in 9 countries, about 10 Protestants in Sudan, Kenya, Gabon et alia, about 5 marginal Protestants (Jehovah's Witnesses).
FOREIGN MISSIONARIES AND PERSONNEL (aliens from abroad)(1973). Total 8,985. *From Western world.* 8,568: about 6,800 Roman Catholics, 1,756 Protestants (1,066 in 42 USA societies, 230 in 9 UK societies, 213 in 3 Sweden societies, 85 in 3 Norway societies, 60 in 7 Switzerland societies, 53 in 6 Canada societies, 15 in 6 Australia societies, 11 in 5 New Zealand societies, 7 in 2 Denmark societies, 7 in 2 Netherlands societies, 5 in 1 Belgium society, 4 in 2 WGermany societies), 6 Orthodox from Greece, 4 Anglicans (3 in 1 UK society, 1 in 1 USA society). By 1975 North American Protestant missionaries had fallen to 817. *From Communist world.* 47 Roman Catholics(32 from Poland, 15 from Yugoslavia). *From Third World.* 372: about 300 Roman Catholics from 20 countries in Africa, Asia and Latin America, about 50 Protestants from 20 countries including Japan (and 6 in 2 South Africa societies), about 20 African indigenous from Angola, Congo, Rhodesia, Zambia et alia, 2 Anglicans.
INSTITUTIONS (church-operated)(1973). Total 2,050, including (1973) 10 ecumenical centres, 1,050 higher schools (34 minor seminaries), 860 medical centres (150 hospitals), 6 presses, 50 religious communities, 8 research centres, 50 seminaries (36 Protestant, 10 RC, 2 African indigenous), 2 universities. In 1975, all schools and colleges including minor seminaries were nationalized; in 1977 they were returned to the churches.
PERIODICALS. About 80 titles (30 RC ,25 Protestant). In 1960

there were over 85 RC periodicals, mostly missionary publications of which 30 were in Congolese languages, but most were subsequently suppressed.
PERSONNEL. About 44,985 (36,000 national, 8,985 foreign).
RELIGIOUS LIBRARIES. About 130.
SCRIPTURE DISTRIBUTION (1975). Annual totals: 54,000 Bibles (72% subsidized, 28% commercial), 79,000 NTs (68% subsidized, 32% commercial), 52,719 UBS portions, 406,151 UBS selections. *Translations completed.* Portion: 61 languages since 1886. NT: 30 languages since 1893. Bible: 13 languages since 1916.
SERVICE AGENCIES. About 95, including AEZ, AICSJF, AIX, ASUMA, BEC, BOM, CEF, CEPZA, CEZ, CFM, COSSEUJCA, DIA, GBUAF, IME, JAC, JAC/F, JOCI, LEZA, MAF, MAP, MCC, MFC, NLFA, RENAPEC, SBZ, SICA, SRAM-OIEC, STAR, SU, UECZ, UMH, USUMA, YMCA, YWCA.

ADDITIONAL DATA ON CHURCHES
EGLISE CATHOLIQUE AU ZAIRE. *Catechumens.* Totals: (1959) 604,663; (1961) 587,602; (1969) 379,957, divided as follows among the 48 dioceses of 1971 in the order shown (and included in column 7 above): 18500, 11000, 42000, 9200, 8100, 4650, 14000, 6092, 1550, 5100, 8700, 3000, 4300, 4582, 4854, 2500, 9390, 2000, 3820, 9462, 732, 6753, 10000; 2200, 2860, 42000, 10145, 18000, 3222, 12000, 13100, 2700, 7000, 12268, 5452, 1969, 5000, 4300, 5000, 3000; 4354, 1900, 2589, 3463, 11000, 3800, 1700, 8750. *Annual baptisms.* (1972) 55.7% infant, 44.3% adult (168,125). *National priests.* 91% secular, 9% religious. In addition to the 596 shown in the table, there were in 1970 about 125 others. 1977 totals: 675 diocesan, 44 religious. *Expatriate priests.* In 1970 almost all religious, with a few Fidei Donum secular priests; almost all Belgian until recent influx of personnel from Yugoslavia, Poland, Spain, South America. 1977 totals: 1,803 religious, 117 diocesan. *Bishops.* In 1972, of the 53 bishops (including coadjutors and auxiliaries) 36 were Zairois, 17 expatriate. *Brothers.* In addition to the 1,117 expatriates shown in the table, in 1970 there were 509 Zairois brothers. 1977 totals: 455 Zairians, 577 foreign. *Sisters.* Including about 1,452 Zairians in 1970. 1977 totals: 1,888 Zairians (1,265 in 27 local congregations), 2,221 foreign. Including contemplatives the total of all sisters is around 5,000. *Seminarians.* (1972) 433 secular, 39 religious. (1977) 497 diocesan in 10 seminaries; (1978) 11 seminaries. *Catechists.* Total (1970) about 12,000. Most of these are heads of rural communities. There are 500 head catechists. The tendency is not to open more than 11 special schools for catechists; but to train workers in situ or in short-term courses. *Indigenous religious congregations.* The totals by 1974 were 13 diocesan congregations of brothers, and 28 of sisters. Brothers (professed, in 1972): members of ASUMA: 86 Joséphites de Kikwit, 68 Servites du Rédempteur (Bunia, founded 1936), 48 Assomption (Beni), 48 St-Joseph de Kisantu, 34 Servites de Jésus-Prêtre (Bukavu, founded 1930), 22 St-Joseph de Mbuji-Mayi, 16 St-Joseph de Kananga, 15 de la Passion (Tshumbe); plus 5 embryonic congregations not members of ASUMA: Zairois Augustins (Doruma), N-D des Apôtres (Kasongo), St-Joseph de Boma, St-Joseph de Boyange (Lisala), St-Joseph de Molegbe. Sisters: 216 Soeurs Servantes de Jésus (Bunia, founded 1937), 168 Petites Soeurs de la Présentation (Beni), 109 Filles de Marie Reine des Apôtres (Bukavu, 1933), 75 Dominicaines Zaïroises de Niangara (1943), 63 Soeurs de Ste-Marie de Kisantu (1940), 62 Soeurs du Coeur Immaculé de la Bienheureuse Vierge Marie (Kananga, 1940), 59 Soeurs de Marie du Kwango (Kikwit, 1937), 48 Soeurs de Ste-Thérèse de l'Enfant Jésus (Mbuji-Mayi), 47 Soeurs de la Ste-Famille (Wamba, 1936); and 15 other local congregations. *Main foreign orders and congregations.* Priests (with over 100 professed): 677 CICM, 352 SJ, 310 WF, 145 SDB, 109 OFM. Brothers (over 50 professed): 103 FSC, 81 PFM. Sisters (over 100 professed): 298 Soeurs de la Charité de Jésus et de Marie, 276 Franciscaines Missionnaires de Marie, 210 Soeurs Missionnaires du Coeur Immaculé de Marie, 129 Soeurs de Marie de Pittem, 114 Missionnaires de N-D d'Afrique (White Sisters). *Indigenous movements.* The largest African movement, remaining within the church without schism, is the Jamaa or Yamaa (Family) charismatic movement begun in Katanga in 1945 and by 1970 widespread with over 20,000 members.
*Catholic organizations.* The Episcopal Conference of Zaire (Conférence Episcopale du Zaïre) is a member of SECAM. Because of the size and diversity of the country, there are 6 provincial conferences. The Episcopal Conference and all meetings

of bishops were suspended by the government in February 1973, but their technical agencies continued to function; and in 1974 the Conference was allowed to meet again on a provisional basis. Two agencies for religious personnel are the Assemblée des Supérieurs Majeurs (ASUMA) and the Union des Supérieures Majeures (USUMA). There are no priests' or pastoral councils. Lay organizations include the Christian Family Movement in Kinshasa, the Xaveri and Jamaa movements and other pious associations throughout the country.

The Holy See has diplomatic relations with Zaire and is represented to government and the Catholic heirarchy by a pronuncio in Kinshasa.

International Catholic agencies with headquarters in Zaire include the Aumônerie Internationale Xavéri in Bukavu, and the Kinshasa-based Secrétariat Régional pour l'Afrique et Madagascar (SRAM) of the Office International de l'Enseignement Catholique (OIEC) based on Brussels. The former is a youth movement founded in Bukavu in 1952 whose aim is 'to awaken and aid youth in the development of their African personalities, enabling them to be firm in their Christian faith and involved in their own local situation'. By 1974 the Xaveri movement counted nearly 200,000 active participants, including a number of Protestants. Although now existing in 13 African countries and one in Asia, this no longer functions as a distinct movement in Zaire but recommends that members involve themselves individually in the national youth organization (JMPR) and provide it with spiritual support. Prior to the suppression of confessional youth movements in Zaire, the Panafrican Secretariat of JOC International had its headquarters in Kinshasa. This secretariat is now without fixed residence.

Centres for research or socio-religious action include the following: (1) Centre de Recherches Sociologiques, founded in Kinshasa in 1962, which is attached to the Episcopal Conference and studies the structures, attitudes and mentality of individuals, groups and organizations within the Zairian church; (2) Bureau pour le Développement, founded in Kinshasa in 1967 as the executive organ of the Episcopal Commission for Development, which initiates and co-ordinates integral development projects throughout the country (numbering 172 in 1971); (3) Centre d'Etudes pour l'Action Sociale (CEPAS), founded by Jesuits in Kinshasa in 1965, for research and agricultural development training; (4) Centre d'Etudes Ethnologiques de Bandundu (CEEB) founded by the SVD, which publishes anthropological and linguistic works and organizes ethno-pastoral seminars; and (5) Centre Pédagogique Ntu (Ntu = Humanity), founded in Goma in 1963, for linguistic research on the role of the major Zairian languages in cultural renaissance.

Pastoral and religious training is carried on at the following institutions: (1) Faculté de Théologie Catholique, founded at Lovanium University in 1957, integrated into the National University of Zaire (UNAZA) in 1973, but detached from the latter in 1974, which includes a theology department, the Institut Supérieur de Sciences Religieuses, and the Centre d'Etudes des Religions Africaines (CERA), and which organizes every year a theological week with wide participation; (2) Centre d'Etudes Pastorales (CEP), in Kinshasa, for pastoral, catechetical and liturgical training; (3) Centre de Formation Socio-Pastorale (CENFO), founded in Kinshasa in 1966 under the National Episcopal Commission for the Clergy, which provides refresher courses in ecclesiology, socio-economic problems, general pastoralia and Zairian languages for those with at least 3 years of experience in Africa; and (4) catechetical centres in Lubumbashi and Kananga. In addition the Agencie de Presse DIA (Documentation Information Africaines), founded in Kinshasa in 1956, provides a daily press bulletin for all African countries as well as most Western countries and part of Asia.

Until 1975 the Bureau de l'Enseignement Catholique (BEC), in Kinshasa, co-ordinated the educational programme of the church, which in 1970–71 enrolled 1,901,307 primary pupils (of whom 739,568 were girls) in 42,720 classes (in 1973, in 4,802 schools), and 140,662 secondary or post-primary pupils (in 1973 in 701 secondary schools), including those in technical and professional schools.

The Bureau des Oeuvres Médicales, attached to the Episcopal Conference in Kinshasa, co-ordinated in 1973 the activities of 983 brothers and sisters (of whom 19 were doctors) working in 423 medical institutions (262 Catholic, 125 state and 36 private). Of the 262 Catholic institutions in 1973, there were 29 hospitals, one clinic, 172 out-patient maternities, 32 dispensaries, 4 itine rant dispensaries, 8 maternities, one sanatorium-maternity, one sanatorium, 3 health centres, 2 centres for re-education and one leprosarium. There were also 31 Catholic schools of nursing and midwifery.

Social services are co-ordinated by Caritas-Zaire, founded in 1960 to educate Christian opinion towards active participation in development. Organized at parish and diocesan levels as well as on a national basis, Caritas also provides relief for the needy, scholarships and funds in aid of co-operatives, and operates a central pharmacy.

EGLISE DE JESUS-CHRIST SUR LA TERRE PAR LE PROPHETE SIMON KIMBANGU. The Eglise Kimbanguiste is an independent body with charismatic features arising out of a 1921 revival at Nkamba. From 1921–57, 37,000 heads of families (over 100,000 persons) were exiled by the Belgians to over 30 concentration camps across the country. Large numbers of independent branches sprang up during its 40 years' existence as an underground church persecuted by the Belgian authorities, and even by 1974 many of its branches were still independent of the Chef Spirituel, the founder's son, in Kinshasa. Certain of its separatist churches have recently rejoined, including Eglise des Deux Témoins. *Regions.* 9 administrative Regions in Zaire, and others in 7 other nations. *Congregations.* Most groups have no building but worship on open-air sites. *Membership.* Members grew rapidly from 1 million in 1959 to 2 million adults by 1970. Members are found throughout the country, but are particularly strong in Lower Zaire. They are strong among the Kongo. Ngala, Luba, Kuba, Chokwe, Mongo, Lunda, and Pygmy tribes in the northeast. Several thousand Angolan refugees are members. *Spiritual retreats.* A large-scale revival beginning in 1972 has brought thousands of men and women to special retreats near Kinshasa. *Pilgrimages.* Vast numbers are involved: 2–7 April 1971, 350,000 at Nkamba. *Ministers.* No distinction is made between clergy and laymen. There are catechists (evangelists), deacons and deaconesses; these 3 groups are often responsible for running parishes. Elders have a very important role. *Seminarians* (1974). 82, from every region in Zaire; 4 from Angola, 3 from Congo-Brazzaville, also Zambia and Burundi. *Hospital.* In 1976 a 550-bed hospital in Kinshasa was under construction. *Dispensaries.* (1977) 200. *Foreign missionaries.* In 1972, there were 7 expatriate missionaries, all serving on the staff of the seminary in Kinshasa, sent by the following European bodies: Basel Mission, Moravian Mission, Apostolic Church, Dienst in Ubersee, Ev Landeskirche in Württemberg. *Baptism.* Baptism is practised, but without water; those initiated are regarded as baptized in the Holy Spirit. *Communicants.* Communion was not practised until the first celebration of 6 April 1971 when 350,000 Kimbanguists participated. It was now celebrated 3 times a year (Easter, Christmas, and on the feast of Kimbangu's death).

EGLISE DE JESUS-CHRIST SUR LA TERRE PAR LE SAINT-ESPRIT. One of the larger indigenous churches not related to the ECZ, also known as Eglise Spirituelle (Spiritual Church), or (in Luba) Ekelezia wa Yezu Kilisto pa Buloba mu Bulombodi bua Nyuma Muimpe. *Membership.* 85% Luba, 14% Swahili, 0.4% Bangala. In 1971 the geographical locations of members were as follows: 60% Kasai-Oriental, 25% Kasai-Occidental, 14% Lubumbashi. *Catechumens.* Total 7,409.

EGLISE DU CHRIST AU ZAIRE. *Anglicans.* In 1976, the Communauté Anglicane du Zaire (up till then the Diocese of Boga-Zaire in the Church of Uganda, Rwanda, Burundi and Boga-Zaire) was divided into 2 dioceses (D Boga, D Bukavu), prior to the formation of a new French-speaking Anglican province covering Zaire, Rwanda and Burundi. By 1977, membership had increased to 160,000 (D Boga 40,000, D Bukavu 120,000), parishes to 67, congregations to 700 (D Boga 200, D Bukavu 500), catechists to 750 (D Boga 200, D Bukavu 550), and clergy to 43 (D Boga 20, D Bukavu 23). In 1978 D Boga claimed the accession of an entire disaffected ECZ (Protestant) community in Kasai of 75 parishes with 294,000 members and 78 clergy. *Lutherans.* In 1976 the Evangelical Lutheran Community was legally recognized, with 800 members (HQ Kalemie) and 2 pastors (1 sent by ELCT, Tanzania). *Growth.* By 1978, the ECZ had 11,220 parishes, 2,500 ordained ministers, 2,830 primary and 300 secondary schools (total 1 million pupils), and 63 hospitals.

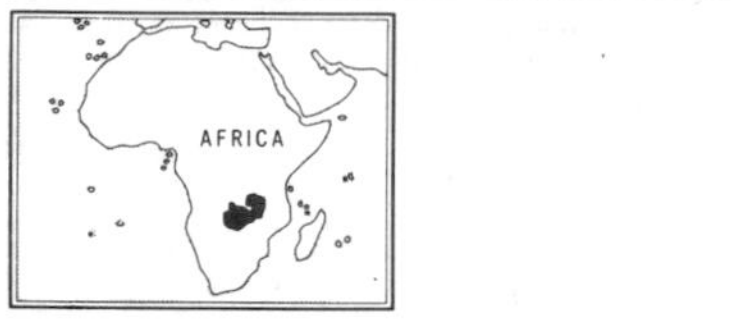


# ZAMBIA

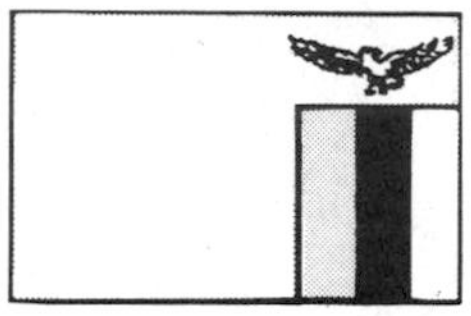

## SECULAR DATA

**STATE. Official name:** The Republic of Zambia. Adjective of nationality: Zambian.
**Flag** (shown above right): Green field with red, black, and orange bars on right surmounted by eagle.
**Area:** 752,614 sq.km. (290,586 sq.miles). Agricultural land: 46.5%.
**Government:** One-party republic, since 1972 (1888 British claims, 1924 British protectorate of Northern Rhodesia, 1953 in Federation of Rhodesia and Nyasaland, 1964 Independence, 1972 one-party republic).
**Legislature:** National Assembly, 136 members.
**Official language:** English.
**Chief cities:** capital Lusaka 347,900 (1972), Kitwe 290,100, Ndola 201,300, Chingola 181,500.
**Political divisions:** 8 Provinces.
**Armed forces** (1976): Total 7,800 regular: army 6,300, air force 1,500 (24 combat aircraft). Paramilitary forces: 2,500.

**DEMOGRAPHY. Population:** 4,056,995 (census of 22–30.VIII. 1969. For 1970–2000 (UN), see last row of Table 1). Population density (1975): 7/sq.km. (17/sq.mile). Under 15 years: 47%. Growth rate (1975–80): 3.14% per year (births 4.94%, deaths −1.81%). Life expectancy (1975–80): 47.0 years. Household size: 4.6 persons.
**Major languages:** English, Bemba, Tonga, Nyanja (Chichewa), Lunda, Lamba, Ila, Mambwe, Lozi, Ngoni, Afrikaans, Greek, Gujarati, Chinese, Shona, and over 30 other tribal languages.
**Urban dwellers** (1970): 23.6%. Urban growth rate (1950-70): 5.8% per year.
**Labour force:** 40%.
**Refugees** (1977): 60,000 from Angola, South Africa, Namibia, Zimbabwe.
**Tourists** (1974): 44,521.

**ETHNOLINGUISTIC GROUPS:** 37% Bemba cluster [15% Bemba (Bisa, Tabwa, Kunda, Senga), 8% Luapula (Lunda, Shila), 8% Lamba (Lala, Ambo), 7% Aushi (Ngumbo, Unga)], 19% Tonga cluster [12% Tonga, 4% Lenje (Sala, Soli), 2% Ila (Subia, Totela, Lumbu)], 12% Lunda cluster (9% Lunda-Luvale, Mbunda, Luchazi, Mashashe, Ndembu, Chokwe, 3% Kaonde), 11% Nyanja-speaking (Chewa, Nsenga, Chikunda), 8% Mambwe cluster [5% Mambwe (Lungu, Winamwange), 3% Tumbuka, Nkoya (Lambya)], 7% Lozi (Barotse) cluster (4% Luyana, 3% Lozi), 4% Ngoni (Mpezeni, Mombera), 1.2% White (43,000) (0.7% British, 0.4% Afrikaner, 0.1% Greek, Italian, Yugoslav), 0.3% Indian (Gujarati) (10,800), 0.2% Chinese, 0.1% Mulatto (Black/White) (4,000), Swahili, Shona, Jewish, & numerous smaller tribes. British Asians decreased from 12,000 in 1968 to 3,000 by 1977.

**MONEY** (1977). **Monetary unit:** kwacha (= 100 ngwee); US$1 = K 0.80.
**National income per person:** US$400. Average annual family income: US$1,840.
**Inflation:** (1970–74) 6.5% per year (1975: consumer price index 146).
**Cost of living in capital** (1976): index 126 (Washington DC = 100). Daily cost of living: US$39.

**HEALTH.** Hospitals: 540 (13,242 beds). Doctors: 307. Lepers: 30,000 (6.0 per 1,000). Blind: 38,000. Psychotics: 45,000. Criminals: 39,883.

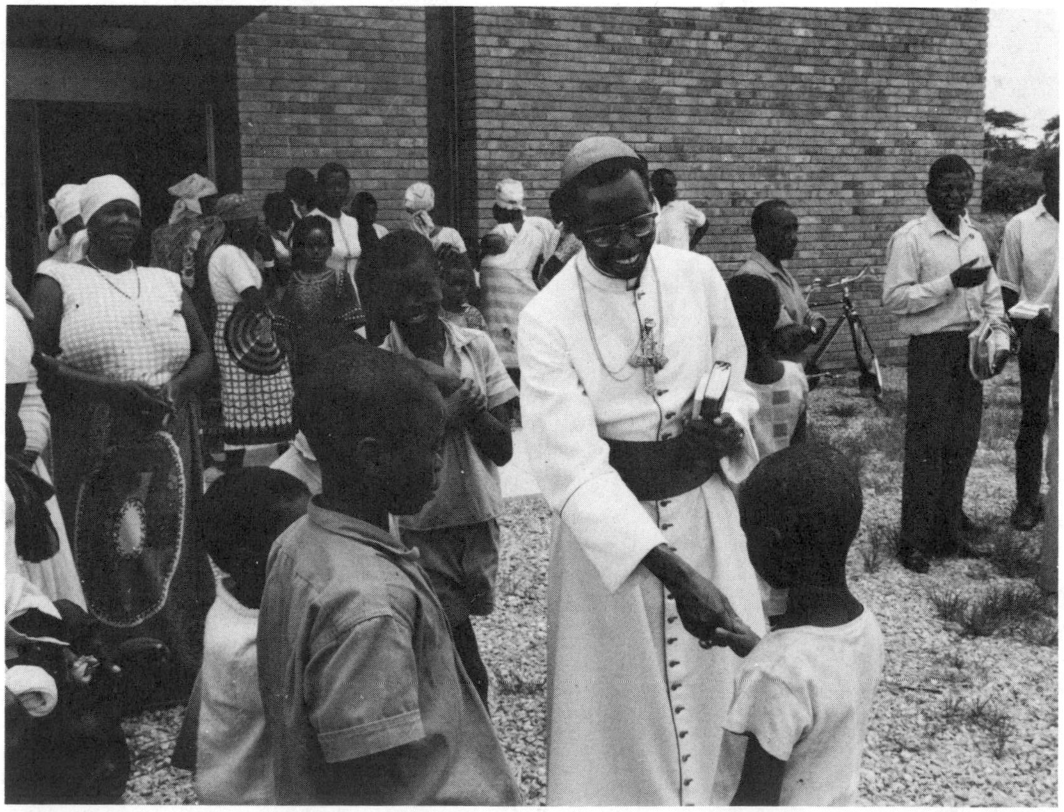

**Catholic Church in Zambia, Archdiocese of Lusaka.** Archbishop Emmanuel Milingo of Lusaka, leader of Zambia's Catholic pentecostals, greets congregation after mass in Lusaka Cathedral. After receiving a vision recently, he found he had charismatic gifts of healing and exorcism, which he then exercised widely; but in 1978 he was forbidden by the Vatican to continue exercising such gifts.

**EDUCATION.** Adult literacy: (1963) 41%, (1969) 47%. Education rate: 37%. Schools: 2,712 (2,598 primary, 114 secondary). Universities: 1.

**LITERATURE.** Annual new book titles (1965): 39. Periodicals: 80. Newspapers: 2 dailies, 12 non-daily.

**COMMUNICATION** (per 1,000 people). Phones: 12. Radios: 23. TV sets: 5. Daily newspaper circulation: 17 copies.

TABLE 1. RELIGIOUS ADHERENTS IN ZAMBIA

| Year | 1900 | | mid-1970 | | Annual change, 1970–1980 | | | | mid-1975 | | mid-1980 | | 2000 | |
|---|---|---|---|---|---|---|---|---|---|---|---|---|---|---|
| *Name* | *Adherents* | *%* | *Adherents* | *%* | *Natural* | *Conversion* | *Total* | *Rate* | *Adherents* | *%* | *Adherents* | *%* | *Adherents* | *%* |
| **Christians** | **2,000** | **0.3** | **2,786,000** | **64.9** | **108,093** | **36,257** | **144,350** | **4.20** | **3,435,730** | **68.4** | **4,229,500** | **72.0** | **9,678,270** | **83.7** |
| professing | 2,000 | 0.3 | 2,786,000 | 64.9 | 108,093 | 36,257 | 144,350 | 4.20 | 3,435,730 | 68.4 | 4,229,500 | 72.0 | 9,678,270 | 83.7 |
| Roman Catholics | 1,000 | 0.1 | 1,039,000 | 24.2 | 39,824 | 10,201 | 50,025 | 3.95 | 1,265,800 | 25.2 | 1,539,250 | 26.2 | 3,468,300 | 30.0 |
| Marginal Protestants | 0 | 0.0 | 740,000 | 17.2 | 27,908 | 4,737 | 32,645 | 3.68 | 887,060 | 17.7 | 1,066,450 | 18.2 | 2,498,320 | 21.6 |
| Protestants | 1,000 | 0.1 | 501,000 | 11.7 | 20,070 | 10,317 | 30,387 | 4.76 | 637,920 | 12.7 | 804,870 | 13.7 | 1,618,540 | 14.0 |
| African indigenous | 0 | 0.0 | 270,000 | 6.3 | 11,534 | 10,226 | 21,760 | 5.94 | 366,600 | 7.3 | 487,600 | 8.3 | 1,387,900 | 12.0 |
| Catholics (non-Roman) | 0 | 0.0 | 130,000 | 3.0 | 4,898 | 902 | 5,800 | 3.73 | 155,710 | 3.1 | 188,000 | 3.2 | 404,630 | 3.5 |
| Anglicans | 0 | 0.0 | 100,000 | 2.3 | 3,635 | –123 | 3,512 | 3.04 | 115,530 | 2.3 | 135,120 | 2.3 | 289,020 | 2.5 |
| Orthodox | 0 | 0.0 | 6,000 | 0.1 | 224 | –3 | 221 | 3.11 | 7,110 | 0.1 | 8,210 | 0.1 | 11,560 | 0.1 |
| nominal | 0 | 0.0 | 621,456 | 14.5 | 23,700 | 5,214 | 28,914 | 3.84 | 753,300 | 15.0 | 910,600 | 15.5 | 1,619,200 | 14.0 |
| affiliated | 2,000 | 0.3 | 2,164,544 | 50.4 | 84,393 | 31,043 | 115,436 | 4.30 | 2,682,430 | 53.4 | 3,318,900 | 56.5 | 8,059,070 | 69.7 |
| total practising | 1,900 | *95* | 1,731,630 | *80* | 67,515 | 24,834 | 92,349 | 4.30 | 2,145,940 | *80* | 2,655,120 | *80* | 5,641,350 | *70* |
| non-practising | 100 | *5* | 432,910 | *20* | 16,878 | 6,209 | 23,087 | 4.30 | 536,490 | *20* | 663,780 | *20* | 2,417,720 | *30* |
| Roman Catholics | 1,000 | 0.1 | 922,890 | 21.5 | 35,557 | 10,216 | 45,773 | 4.05 | 1,130,170 | 22.5 | 1,380,620 | 23.5 | 3,121,470 | 27.0 |
| Catholic pentecostals | 0 | 0.0 | 0 | 0.0 | 31 | 469 | 500 | 50.00 | 1,000 | 0.0 | 5,000 | 0.1 | 40,000 | 0.3 |
| Marginal Protestants | 0 | 0.0 | 452,100 | 10.5 | 17,383 | 4,970 | 22,353 | 4.04 | 552,530 | 11.0 | 675,630 | 11.5 | 1,734,150 | 15.0 |
| Protestants | 1,000 | 0.1 | 327,954 | 7.6 | 12,798 | 4,927 | 17,725 | 4.36 | 406,800 | 8.1 | 505,200 | 8.6 | 1,226,000 | 10.6 |
| Evangelicals | 800 | 0.1 | 233,000 | 5.4 | 9,123 | 3,777 | 12,900 | 4.45 | 290,000 | 5.8 | 362,000 | 6.2 | 880,000 | 7.6 |
| African indigenous | 0 | 0.0 | 250,900 | 5.8 | 10,744 | 9,996 | 20,740 | 6.07 | 341,500 | 6.8 | 458,300 | 7.8 | 1,330,100 | 11.5 |
| Catholics (non-Roman) | 0 | 0.0 | 120,050 | 2.8 | 4,583 | 992 | 5,575 | 3.83 | 145,670 | 2.9 | 176,250 | 3.0 | 381,510 | 3.3 |
| Anglicans | 0 | 0.0 | 85,000 | 2.0 | 3,161 | 89 | 3,250 | 3.24 | 100,460 | 2.0 | 117,500 | 2.0 | 254,340 | 2.2 |
| Anglican pentecostals | 0 | 0.0 | 0 | 0.0 | 3 | 47 | 50 | 50.00 | 100 | 0.0 | 500 | 0.0 | 5,000 | 0.0 |
| Orthodox | 0 | 0.0 | 5,200 | 0.1 | 167 | –147 | 20 | 0.38 | 5,300 | 0.1 | 5,400 | 0.1 | 11,500 | 0.1 |
| Tribal religionists | 748,000 | 99.7 | 1,467,200 | 34.2 | 48,309 | –36,459 | 11,850 | 0.77 | 1,535,470 | 30.6 | 1,585,700 | 27.0 | 1,758,730 | 15.2 |
| Muslims | 0 | 0.0 | 13,000 | 0.3 | 472 | –72 | 400 | 2.67 | 15,000 | 0.3 | 17,000 | 0.3 | 35,000 | 0.3 |
| Baha'is | 0 | 0.0 | 10,300 | 0.2 | 409 | 161 | 570 | 4.38 | 13,000 | 0.3 | 16,000 | 0.3 | 37,000 | 0.3 |
| Non-religious | 0 | 0.0 | 10,000 | 0.2 | 409 | 191 | 600 | 4.62 | 13,000 | 0.3 | 16,000 | 0.3 | 40,000 | 0.3 |
| Hindus | 0 | 0.0 | 7,700 | 0.2 | 283 | –53 | 230 | 2.55 | 9,000 | 0.2 | 10,000 | 0.2 | 16,000 | 0.1 |
| Jews | 0 | 0.0 | 800 | 0.0 | 25 | –25 | 0 | 0.00 | 800 | 0.0 | 800 | 0.0 | 1,000 | 0.0 |
| **Country's population** | **750,000** | **100.0** | **4,295,000** | **100.0** | **158,000** | **0** | **158,000** | **3.15** | **5,022,000** | **100.0** | **5,875,000** | **100.0** | **11,566,000** | **100.0** |

COLUMNS, ROWS. For meanings and definitions, see Codebook (Part 6). Note that, by definition, total 'Christians' = professing + crypto-Christians, which also = affiliated + nominal Christians. Percentages may not always total exactly, due to rounding.
CENSUSES. None have enumerated religion for Africans; censuses have been taken for non-Africans only. **15.X.1946** (Europeans): 20,815 Christians (15,199 Protestants and Anglicans, 5,283 Roman Catholics, 134 Orthodox, 199 others), 656 Jews, 229 non-religious and agnostics, 83 other religionists. **15.X.1946** (Coloured): 552 Christians (294 Protestants, 258 Roman Catholics), 37 non-religious, 18 Muslims, 73 other religionists. **15.X.1946** (Asiatics): 768 Hindus, 330 Muslims, 18 other religionists. **8.V.1951** (Europeans): 33,571 Christians, 766 Jews, 2,742 other religionists. **8.V.1951** (Coloured): 839 Christians, 74 Muslims, 77 non-religious, 80 other religionists. **8.V.1951** (Asiatics): 1,658 Hindus, 837 Muslims, 12 others. **8.V.1956** (non-Africans): 62,236 Christians, 3,763 Hindus, 2,878 non-religious, 1,724 Muslims, 974 Jews, 729 other religionists (28 Spiritists). **26.IX.1961** (non-Africans): 65,280 Christians, 5,490 Hindus, 3,820 non-religious, 2,390 Muslims, 850 Jews, 6,530 other religionists.

NOTES ON RELIGIONS
AFRICAN INDIGENOUS. In about 70 denominations in 1970 (see Table 2).
ANGLICAN PENTECOSTALS (or, Anglican charismatics). The renewal began about 1975, linked with the Catholic Charismatic Renewal also.
BAHA'IS. Rapid growth from 19 local spiritual assemblies (1964) to 69 (1973); in 1970 there were 3,250 adult believers.
CATHOLIC PENTECOSTALS (or, Catholic charismatics). The Catholic Charismatic Renewal was not formally organized by 1975, but many charismatics existed including the archbishop of Lusaka who was widely known as a charismatic healer. The First Inter-Diocesan Conference on the Charismatic Renewal was held in Lusaka in mid-1978, with 200 attenders including the archbishop, 20 priests and 45 sisters.
HINDUS. 70% of all Indians in Zambia (Gujaratis).
MARGINAL PROTESTANTS. Jehovah's Witnesses have grown rapidly since their arrival in 1911. By 1943 there were 2,784 active adult publishers; by 1948 peak publishers were 11,606; by 1959, 28,000 active publishers with a total community of 79,500 African and 5,000 European adherents; by 1963, 30,728 peak publishers; and by 1973, 52,339 peak publishers, over 130,000 adult members, 194,133 adult attenders at the annual Memorial services, a total affiliated community of over 500,000. It is estimated that at least one in every 4 adult Zambians (25%) has been involved in Jehovah's Witnesses (Watch Tower) at some time in his life, either as member or strong sympathizer or regular attender at meetings, i.e. a total professing or self-identifying community including children and infants of around 1,070,000 in 1970. Of these, 50,000 are in independent Watchtower groups (not under Jehovah's Witnesses). At least 280,000 have left the main body and are now affiliated with or adherents of other churches, but it also has successfully won back many from independent Watchtower. This leaves around 740,000 still professing some relation to Jehovah's Witnesses (in 1970).
MUSLIMS. About 3,000 Indo-Pakistanis, and African Muslims (Sunnis, of the Shafiite rite) from neighbouring countries. *Hajj pilgrims to Mecca.* (1976) 4 persons.
NON-RELIGIOUS. Mainly Chinese technicians from People's Republic of China, also Europeans.
PRACTISING CHRISTIANS. A survey in 1972 by Mindolo Ecumenical Centre obtained a total of 382,690 adult weekly church attenders of all denominations (85,800 Roman Catholics, 56,996 Jehovah's Witnesses, 50,000 New Apostolic Church, 27,000 AME Church, 20,000 CMML, 15,500 UCZ, 13,500 SDAs, 13,000 African Gospel Church, et alia).
TRIBAL RELIGIONISTS. Although tribal religions are also known as traditional religions, they are far from static; since the beginning of colonial times they have embodied and still embody a vast and continuing amount of non-Christian religious innovation, primarily in the form of possession healing movements. It is estimated that over 15% of the modern Zambian population (including numerous Christians) adhere to and are active in the many such movements. Peoples with over 60% traditionalists in 1972: Mashi Bushmen (99% animist), Subia (70%), Luvale (65%). Most other tribes have sizeable numbers of animists also.

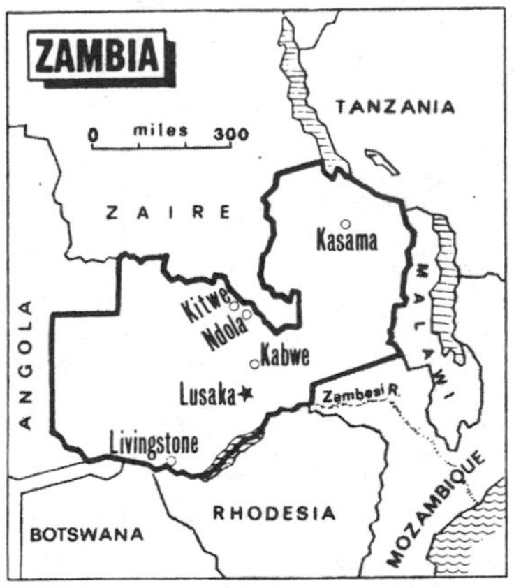


NON-CHRISTIAN RELIGIONS. **Traditional African religions** are based on belief in a supreme being called Lesa or Mulungu, in ancestor veneration, and in the practice of magic and witchcraft. They are especially strong in the rural areas. Some 30% of the population are still traditionalists, numbering over 60% in the Luvale, Mashi and Subia tribes. As with all African tribal religions, these are far from static; over the last century they have embodied a vast and continuing amount of non-Christian religious innovation. Spirit-possession healing movements or cults known by various names are common among Zambian peoples: **Baami** (among the Ila), **Wamowa** and **Awayambo** (Lamba), **Wamukamwami** (Lenji), **Bamoba** and **Baciwila** (Ambo), **Muba** (Lozi), **Mahamba** (Luvale, Luchazi), **Ihamba** (Ndembu) and **Ngulu** (Bemba). Zambia has been the meeting place of 2 spirit-possession movements owing their origin to the last century: the Mashave possession cults of the Shona moving northward, and the eastward movement of the Mahamba cults from Angola. The Mchape (Medicine) witchcraft eradication movement which began in Nyasaland in 1930 also spread to Northern Rhodesia.

**Islam** and **Hinduism** have small communities restricted to urban areas and largely composed of Asians. Islam has had little success in appealing to the African population.

**Baha'i** has a growing following among Africans, local spiritual assemblies increasing from 19 in 1964 to 69 in 1973.

## CHRISTIANITY

CATHOLIC CHURCH. Early contacts were made in the 18th century by Portuguese priests. In 1879 the Jesuit Zambezi Mission arrived, and in 1882 Jesuits went to Barotseland; but these attempts all failed. Catholicism came to Zambia definitively with the arrival of the first White Fathers in 1891. The Kasama mission was opened in 1913 and another at Lusaka in 1927, and in 1935 the Episcopal Conference of Northern Rhodesia was founded. The hierarchy was established in 1959 and the first African bishop consecrated in 1963. The Zambian church is divided into 2 archdioceses, Kasama (with 2 suffragan dioceses) and Lusaka (with 4 suffragan dioceses), plus the prefecture of Solwezi. Indigenous vocations have progressed slowly, there being in 1971 only 63 Zambian priests as contrasted with 380 expatriates, 12 Zambians of 189 brothers and 159 Zambians of 600 sisters. In addition to White Fathers, others active include Franciscans, Capuchins, Jesuits, Sacred Heart Brothers and Franciscan and Divine Motherhood Sisters. There are also 5 local congregations of sisters.

MARGINAL CHURCHES. Jehovah's Christian witnesses, as they term themselves and are correctly termed, first entered Northern Rhodesia from Nyasaland in 1911, and have had extraordinary success since, and massive influence on Zambia. Over 25% of the population or one million Zambians are estimated to have been involved in Jehovah's Witnesses at one time or another in their lives, either as members or regular attenders or strong sympathizers. Of these, large numbers have subsequently defected to join Catholic, Protestant or African separatist churches. Each year around 200,000 adults are present at the Memorial of Christ's Death held in April. The large headquarters at Bethel, Kitwe, contains massive archives. At various times in their history, governments have acted against the Witnesses, and all foreign missionaries were deported in 1969.

PROTESTANT CHURCHES. David Livingstone of the LMS journeyed through Zambia on his way to Luanda as early as 1853, and abortive attempts to open work were made by the LMS in 1859 and the Paris Mission in 1878. The first permanent Christians arrived in 1884 and the first permanent Paris Mission station was established in 1885. The LMS, Scottish Presbyterians and British Methodists soon followed, and in 1965 the churches created through the activity of these 4 missions joined together to form the United Church of Zambia. This is now the country's largest Protestant denomination. Three other early arrivals have constituencies of similar size: the Reformed Church, Christian Brethren and Seventh-day Adventists. Other early and important groups include the Churches of Christ and the Evangelical Church, the latter being related to the Africa Evangelical Fellowship. Some 45 different Protestant denominations are active in Zambia.

Although all primary schools now belong to the state, the Protestant churches continue to operate 10 private secondary schools and are tending to concentrate more of their resources on new educational approaches to teaching religion in the schools.

In 1974 Protestants operated 30 hospitals (including 8 leprosaria), 13 dispensaries, one clinic, one rural health centre, home for the aged, and through the Zambia Christian refugee service, an extensive programme of aid to refugees.

INDIGENOUS CHURCHES. There are about 70 active African indigenous churches at the present time. Many of these have been brought to Zambia from other countries: South Africa, Malawi,

Zimbabwe and Zaire. Zimbabwe has been the principal source, but the AME Church, a Black denomination from the USA, has the largest constituency. Of groups indigenous to Zambia, the best-known has been the Lumpa Church founded by Alice Lenshina in 1954. By 1958 this church had a total community of 100,000, but it later clashed with the Zambian government and was banned in 1965. Other independent denominations have been formed through schisms within the Brethren, Catholic, Reformed and United churches.

OTHER CHURCHES. Anglican pioneers of the UMCA entered Zambia in 1909. The church is divided into 3 dioceses and has been part of the Church of the Province of Central Africa since 1965. In 1974 Anglicans were responsible for 4 hospitals.

One of Zambia's largest denominations is the New Apostolic Church, with world headquarters in Dortmund (Germany), which is in the Catholic Apostolic tradition with over a million followers across the world. Outside Germany itself, the Zambia community is their second largest, after that in South Africa.

Orthodoxy is represented by several small Greek and Syrian Orthodox congregations.

**CHURCH AND STATE.** The 1964 constitution, Article 13, guarantees freedom of conscience. Article 14.1 specifies that this includes for everyone 'freedom of thought and religion, freedom to change his religion or belief, and freedom, either alone or in community with others, and both in public and in private, to manifest and propagate his religion or belief in worship, teaching, practice and observance'. The constitution defines in Article 14.3 what is meant by freedom of religious teaching; and from a practical standpoint there is an extensive religious education programme in Zambia's schools, in which both government and churches are involved.

The Protection of Fundamental Rights Rule, 1969 (Statutory Instrument No 156 of 1969) allows citizens to introduce petitions at the High Court when they consider their individual liberties endangered. The Education Act in almost the same terms provides for grant-aided and private schools run by church agencies, and the same freedom is allowed for denominationally-run hospitals and other medical institutions.

In 1965 the Lumpa Church was banned on security grounds, after clashes with government troops took 700 lives. Jehovah's Witnesses encountered serious persecution from supporters of the ruling United National Independence Party in Luapula province in 1969 when they refused to vote or take part in political life. Many worship halls were seized or burned and about 1,000 Witnesses fled, some to nearby Zaire. Although missionaries attached to Jehovah's Witnesses were expelled in 1969, Zambian Witnesses are allowed to continue their activities despite the conflict of authority between their views and those of the state. Freedom of conscience and religion is a reality for all other churches.

There is no ministry or governmental department in charge of religious affairs. Churches are required to register with the government's registrar of societies.

In 1974 the government nationalized all confessional primary schools, although secondary schools remain under the control of the churches.

**INTERDENOMINATIONAL ORGANIZATIONS.** A number of councils and associations are actively promoting interdenominational co-operations, including: (1) Christian Council of Zambia (CCZ) which was founded in 1945 and now has 13 member churches following the withdrawal of Seventh-day Adventists and the Wesleyan Church in 1974 in protest over the AACC's support of liberation movements; (2) Evangelical Fellowship of Zambia

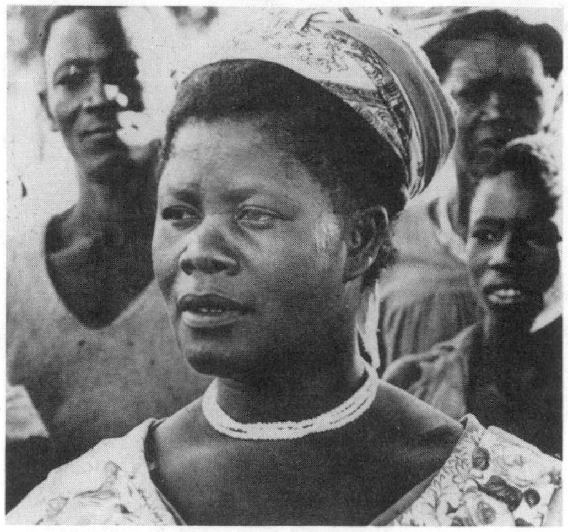

**Lumpa (Visible Salvation) Church.** Founded by (*above*) prophetess Alice Lenshina (= Regina, Queen) in 1954, banned 1965 (with 700 killed). At the time of her death in 1978 she was still in detention. *Below.* Signboard at headquarters.

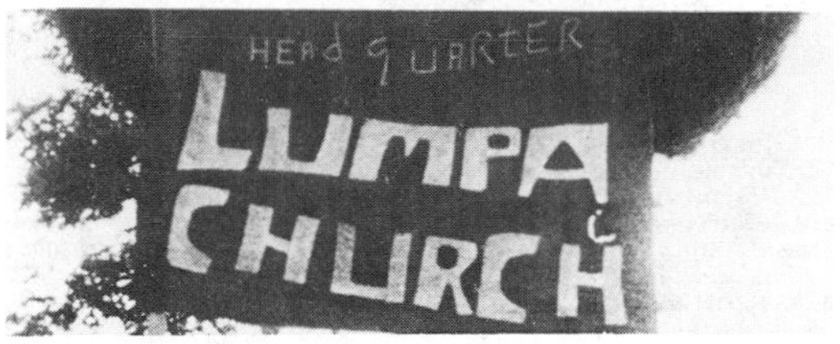


(EFZ), with 15 member churches, which is related to the Association of Evangelicals of Africa and Madagascar; and (3) Association of Independent Churches (AIC), with about 10 members, which provides for fellowship between indigenous churches. Catholic concern for ecumenism is fostered through the Catholic Ecumenical Commission.

The most representative council of all has been the Zambia Christian Commission for Development (ZCCD), which flourished particularly around 1973 with 30 member churches including the Roman Catholic Church and indigenous denominations also. After many conferences and widespread activity up to 1974, its role declined although it was still in existence in 1977.

Co-operation is also maintained through the work of several other bodies. The Mindolo Ecumenical Foundation, founded in 1958 is a social ecumenism centre affiliated with the CCZ and has a board of governors including Catholic and government representatives. It offers programmes for training, study, consultation and worship, at the service of the whole Zambian community and that of neighbouring countries, placing its emphasis on what the churches can bring to a society in rapid social change. The Mindolo Foundation serves also as the Sodepax agency in Zambia and is a member of the Regional Sodepax Programme MEND, with headquarters in Malawi. The Churches Medical Association of Zambia (CMAZ), founded in 1970, co-ordinates all Christian medical work in the country. In 1974 its institutions included 59 hospitals (30 Protestant, 25 Catholic, 4 Anglican), 16 dispensaries (13 Protestant, 3 Catholic), 4 clinics (3 Catholic, one Protestant), and 4 rural health centres (3 Catholic, one Protestant).

**BROADCASTING.** The government Radio Zambia (Zambia Broadcasting Services) allows both Protestant and Catholic programmes, giving in 1970 some 2% of its radio time free to them. The ZBS has a religious department which produces 57 programmes in 8 different languages each week on an ecumenical basis, including prayers, morning and evening epilogues and church services, and broadcasts concerned with the promotion of adult education. The Religious Advisory Board of the CBS is composed of church and government representatives who meet periodically to plan and co-ordinate policy. The Christian Broadcasting Co-ordinating Committee also assists in promoting co-operation. In 1970 Catholics were broadcasting 76 hours each year (767 programmes in 7 African languages and in English). Five television programmes are produced in English. In Lusaka, Multimedia Zambia is a centre founded in 1970 for collaboration in radio and TV, operated jointly by the Christian Council of Zambia and the Zambia Episcopal Conference, which plays a unique role in the world of joint church action in mass media, including production units to make films and radio/TV programmes in English and Zambian languages, a visual media library, and a press and publicity office.

**BIBLIOGRAPHY**

*A short history of the AME Church in central Africa, 1900-1962.* J.L.C. Membe. Luanshya (Zambia), 1969.
'Acts of Jehovah's Witnesses in modern times in Zambia', in *1972 Yearbook of Jehovah's Witnesses* (Brooklyn, NY: Watch Tower Bible & Tract Society, 1971), p.234–254. (Detailed historical narrative covering 1911–71).
*An African church in transition: a case study on the Roman Catholic Church in Zambia.* F.J. Verstraelen. Leiden: Interuniversity Institute for Missiological and Ecumenical Research, 1975. 2 vols.
*Christian missionaries and the creation of Northern Rhodesia.* R. Rotberg. Princeton: Princeton University Press, 1965.
*Christians of the Copperbelt: the growth of the church in Northern Rhodesia.* J.V. Taylor & D.A. Lehmann. London: SCM, 1961. 308p.
'Churches and development: directory for Zambia'. C.Woodhall. Kitwe: Mindolo Ecumenical Foundation, 1971. 23p. (Mimeographed).
'L'église du Sacré-Coeur', L. Oger, *Notes et documents* (Rome: White Fathers), 51 (November, 1964), 421–430.
*Magic, divination and witchcraft among the Barotse of Northern Rhodesia.* B. Reynolds. Berkeley: University of California Press, 1963. 181p.
*Ndembu divination: its symbolism and techniques.* V.W. Turner. Manchester: Manchester University Press, 1961.
*Profile for victory: new proposals for missions in Zambia.* M.W. Randall. South Pasadena (CA): William Carey Library, 1970. 204p.
*The Korsten Basketmakers: a study of the Masowe Apostles, an indigenous African religious movement.* C.M. Dillon-Malone. Manchester: Manchester University Press, 1978. 169p. (A study in Zambia, also in South and East Africa).
*The drums of affliction: a study of religious process among the Ndembu of Zambia.* V.W. Turner. Oxford: Clarendon, 1968. 326p.
'The Lenshina movement of Northern Rhodesia', R. Rotberg, *Rhodes-Livingstone journal* (Lusaka), XXIX (June 1961), 63–78.
'The Lumpa Church of Alice Lenshina', A.D. Roberts, in R. Rotberg & A. Mazrui (eds), *Protest and power in Black Africa* (New York: Oxford University Press, 1970), p.513–568.
*The plateau Tonga of Northern Rhodesia: social and religious studies.* E. Colson. Manchester: Manchester University Press, 1962.
'The Watch Tower movement in south central Africa, 1908–1945'. S. Cross. Dissertation, Oxford University, 1973.
*Tonga Christianity.* S. Shewmaker. South Pasadena (CA): William Carey Library, 1971.

TABLE 2. ORGANIZED CHURCHES AND DENOMINATIONS IN ZAMBIA

| Official name 1 | Begun 2 | Type 3 | Counc 4 | Congs 5 | Adults 6 | Affiliated 7 | Names, notes, and other statistics (see Codebook) 8 |
|---|---|---|---|---|---|---|---|
| African Gospel Church | 1947 | I peA | x.... | 15 | 13,000 | 30,000 | *Basketmakers. Hosannas. Apostles of Johane Masowe.* Shona, some Ndebele. Sabbatarian. 1973,schism. |
| African Methodist Episcopal Church | 1929 | I Met | Vw..d | 400 | 50,000 | 70,000 | M=AMEC(USA Blacks). 17th Episcopal District. Many development projects. 88n,W=54%. |
| African National Church | | I Ref | ....C | | 5,000 | 10,000 | M=ANC(Malawi). Copperbelt, Northern, Central. Several attempts to join CCZ. |
| Anglican Church in Zambia: | 1909 | A ACa | AwAVd | 185 | 42,000 | 85,000 | 1910,D NRhodesia; 1965 in CPCA. M=USPG. 65f,G=0,4H,P=20%,1s. 38n,32x,1390Y,1380y. |
| D Central Zambia | 1971 | A ACa | A | 44 | 12,000 | 25,000 | Ndola to Malawi. 49% Lala, 24% Bemba, 20% White. 1H,P=20%. 9 6 310 180 |
| D Lusaka | 1971 | A ACa | A | 95 | 20,000 | 40,000 | West. 42% Nsenga, 20% Nyanja, 19% Tonga, 14% White. 18 17 550 660 |
| D Northern Zambia | 1971 | A ACa | A | 46 | 10,000 | 20,000 | Two separated areas. Copperbelt. 80% Bemba, 14% White. 11 9 530 540 |
| Apostles in Zion Church | | I pen | ....I | | 2,000 | 5,000 | Zionists. South African Bantu members, indigenous Black pentecostals. |
| Apostolic Church in Zambia | 1958 | P PeA | Z.... | 10 | 500 | 1,000 | M=Danish missionaries of Apostolic Church(Netherlands). Pentecostals. 5n,2x. |
| Apostolic Church of Christ | 1961 | I pen | ..... | 4 | 150 | 300 | Indigenous pentecostals. Begun in Bulawayo(Rhodesia), then later spread to Zambia. |
| Apostolic Church of Johane Maranke | 1952 | I peA | x.... | 10 | 1,000 | 2,000 | *AACJM.* Scattered members of large Shona church based on Umtali (Rhodesia). |
| Apostolic Church of Pentecost | 1954 | P Pel | x.... | 10 | 400 | 1,000 | Scattered groups in Copperbelt and Lusaka. M=ACP(Canada), but aid discontinued. |
| Apostolic Faith & Acts Church | 1965 | I pen | ....b | 4 | 700 | 1,500 | In Lusaka, Luanshya, Ndola and Kitwe. Originally from Bulawayo (Rhodesia). |
| Apostolic Faith Church | | I pen | ....b | 21 | 700 | 1,500 | No buildings; meetings in rooms, under trees. Link with AFC, Bournemouth(UK). |
| Apostolic Faith Holy Gospel Church | 1947 | I pen | ....b | 70 | 12,800 | 20,000 | From Rhodesia. Growing. Ndola,Lusaka,Livingstone. 4 community development centres. |
| Apostolic Faith Mission of Zambia | 1947 | P Pe2 | Z.... | 120 | 4,000 | 8,000 | M=AFM(SA),Velberter Mission(Germany). 5n,3x,9f,G=5.9%pa,1p,1s,W=75%,250Y. |
| Apostolic Faith Star Church | 1971 | I pen | ..... | 10 | 700 | 1,500 | New separatist group of Bantu indigenous pentecostals. HQ in Kitwe. |
| Apostolic Faith (Born Again) Church | | I pen | ....I | | 150 | 300 | Small group of Bantu indigenous pentecostals. In Ndola, Kitwe, Luanshya. |
| Baptist Mission of Zambia | 1959 | P Bap | T.G.z | 50 | 2,050 | 4,000 | M=SBC(USA). 62% Lamba. 18,000 in mail courses. 12n,12x,36f,1j,1s(11),W=88%,404Y. |
| Baptist Union of Central Africa | | P Bap | ..G.E | 20 | 1,350 | 3,000 | British Baptists. Lusaka and the Copperbelt. 12 Zambian pastors, 3 expatriate. |
| Brethren in Christ Church | 1906 | P Men | GPG.z | 59 | 1,535 | 6,300 | M=BiCC(USA). Southern Province. Tonga. 4n,8x,6m,50f,1H,3h,1s(5),W=90%,240Y. |

*Continued opposite*

*Table 2–continued*

| Official name 1 | Begun 2 | Type 3 | Counc 4 | Congs 5 | Adults 6 | Affiliated 7 | Names, notes, and other statistics (see Codebook) 8 |
|---|---|---|---|---|---|---|---|
| **Catholic Church in Zambia:** | 1889 | R Lat | P.SEV | 1,133 | 489,100 | 922,890 | C=6+4+15. 5p,1q,1s(55). 63n,380x,189m,600w,P=52%,59818Yy. |
| M Kasama | 1913 | R Lat | Ps | 187 | 90,800 | 171,264 | Language: 50% Bemba, 45% Bisa, 5% Lungu. 11 43 25 74 43 5899 |
| D Mansa (Fort Rosebery) | 1952 | R Lat | Ps | 229 | 73,700 | 138,996 | Rural. 42% Ngumbo, 39% Aushi, 15% Lunda. 7 36 9 38 38 15841 |
| D Mbala (Abercorn) | 1933 | R Lat | Pwf | 205 | 43,300 | 81,783 | Rural. 65% Bemba, 19% Lundu, 14% Bisa. 10 43 14 35 51 6525 |
| M Lusaka | 1927 | R Lat | Ps | 67 | 65,900 | 124,384 | Urban. 60% Bemba, 30% Nyanja. Refugee camp. 1s. 11 67 67 148 33 7225 |
| D Chipata (Fort Jameson) | 1937 | R Lat | Ps | 130 | 54,700 | 103,180 | Rural. 49% Chewa, 20% Nsenga, 19% Ngoni. Refugees. 10 38 10 36 50 3552 |
| D Livingstone | 1936 | R Lat | Pofmc | 116 | 35,200 | 66,394 | 74% Lozi, 5% Maleya, 4% Luvale. 2 refugee camps. 0 44 25 114 34 4208 |
| D Monze | 1962 | R Lat | Psj | 65 | 26,200 | 49,404 | 80% Tonga, 10% Bemba, 8% Nyanja, 5% Lozi. 3 55 20 74 72 3134 |
| D Ndola | 1938 | R Lat | Pofmv | 72 | 96,400 | 181,954 | Copperbelt. Mainly Bemba, Lamba, Ngoni. 8 40 8 74 86 12900 |
| PA Solwezi (1976, D) | 1959 | R Lat | Pofmv | 62 | 2,900 | 5,531 | Rural. 2 main languages: Kaonde, Ndembu. 3 14 11 7 72 534 |
| Catholic Church of the Sacred Heart | 1955 | I CCa | ..... | | 3,000 | 6,000 | *Bana ba Mutimu. Followers of Emilyo.* Split ex RCC. Bemba. 1960 banned. |
| Central Africa Church | 1959 | I CBr | ..... | 9 | 2,000 | 4,000 | Copperbelt. Ex CMML. Lamba, Luvale. 7,000 also in Zaire (Assemblées des Frères). |
| Central Africa Pioneer Mission | 1958 | P Pen | ..G.E | 1 | 200 | 400 | Single congregation in Lusaka served by one tentmaking Australian family. |
| Central Church of God | | I ind | ....I | | 100 | 200 | Indigenous body in Central Province. No buildings, meetings in open air. |
| Christian Brethren | 1897 | P CBr | x.G.E | 450 | 20,000 | 50,000 | *Open Brethren.* M=CMML(UK,USA,NZ,SA). Mainly Luvale tribe. 114f,7H,3h. |
| Christian Reformed Church | | P Ref | ..... | 1 | 32 | 50 | *Gereformeerde Kerk. Doppers (Baptizers).* White Afrikaners; church disbanding. |
| Christian Zion Church | | I pen | ..... | 6 | 200 | 500 | Central and Eastern provinces; no church buildings, meetings in open air. |
| Church of Central Africa Presbyterian | | P Ref | R.... | 3 | 500 | 1,000 | Migrants from CCAP (Malawi), who refused to join UCZ. Lusaka, Kitwe, Chingola. |
| Church of Christ, Scientist | | M Sci | x.... | 4 | 50 | 100 | *Christian Science.* M=CCS(Boston,USA). Whites. Lusaka, Ndola, Kitwe, Chingola. |
| Ch of JC on Earth thru the Prophet SK | 1968 | I pen | xwi.d | 9 | 2,500 | 5,000 | SK=Simon Kimbangu. M=EJCSK(Zaire). Copperbelt. Bemba-speaking ex-Congo Zambians. 9x. |
| Church of Our Lord Jesus Christ | | I ind | ..... | | 500 | 1,000 | Grouping of indigenous Bantu Christians in Northwestern Province. |
| Church of the Nazarene | 1958 | P Hol | xFG.z | 11 | 500 | 1,000 | M=CoN(USA). Lozi,Bemba,Tonga; half members in Lusaka. 1x,4m,4f,G=12%pa,W=92%,47z. |
| Churches of Christ (Instrumental) | 1962 | P Dis | x.G.E | 30 | 2,000 | 4,000 | M=Zambia Christian Mission,CCCC(USA). Ndola, Kitwe, Livingstone, Lusaka. 20f,4i. |
| Churches of Christ (Non-Instrumental) | 1910 | P Dis | x.G.E | 183 | 8,000 | 20,000 | Begun by Rhodesian evangelists. 1923, M=CC(USA). 1 school. 24m,31f,G=20%pa. |
| Commandments Church | 1968 | I pen | ..... | | 500 | 1,000 | *Malango Ch.* Ex UCZ, traditional medicine, no baptism except Holy Spirit. Bemba. |
| Dutch Reformed Ch (Mother Church) | 1904 | P Ref | F...d | 11 | 450 | 1,000 | *NGK (Moederkerk).* All White Afrikaners; rapid emigration. HQ Lusaka. W=80%,6y, |
| Dutch Reformed Church (Reformed) | | P Ref | J.... | | 50 | 100 | *Gereformeerde Kerk.* South African Whites, declining fast. Last minister left 1964. |
| Evangelical Church in Zambia | 1910 | P int | xMG.E | 340 | 7,000 | 20,000 | M=AEF(SAGM)(SA,USA,UK,&c). A=1962. Kaonde, Mbunda, Nkoya. 139f,2H,13h,2s. |
| Evangelical Healing Church of Christ | 1972 | I pen | ....C | 4 | 200 | 500 | One of several indigenous pentecostal churches from Zaire. HQ Kitwe. 2 pastors. |
| Full Gospel Church of God | 1946 | P Pe3 | ZFG.a | 165 | 5,020 | 10,000 | Begun from Rhodesia. M=CoG(Cleveland)(USA). Nutrition, poultry farm schemes. 37n. |
| Gospel Seventh-day Church of Zambia | | I Adv | ..... | | 3,000 | 6,000 | Small Adventist split mainly on Copperbelt and in Southern Province. |
| Greek Orth Archbishopric of Rhodesia | c1910 | O Gre | Cw... | 3 | 2,500 | 5,000 | Churches in Kitwe and Luanshya. Under P Alexandria. Members Greek settlers. 1x. |
| Holy Gospel Church | 1959 | I pen | ....I | 4 | 300 | 500 | Split ex Apostolic Faith Holy Gospel Church. Central Province. Local pentecostals. |
| Independent Brethren Assemblies | | I CBr | ..... | 3 | 500 | 1,000 | Secession ex CMML in Mufulira, Chingola, Solwezi. Independent congregations. |
| Independent Methodist Church | 1965 | I Met | ....C | 10 | 3,000 | 4,000 | Migrant Shona (ex USA Methodists), joined UCZ in 1965, then split. |
| Independent Watchtower | c1940 | I Jeh | ..... | 5 | 3,000 | 5,000 | Ex Jehovah's Witnesses. 4 collective co-operative villages. Luapula, Copperbelt. |
| **Jehovah's Witnesses** | 1911 | M Jeh | x.... | 916 | 130,000 | 450,000 | Massive influence. 1973: 194,133 at annual Memorial. HQ Bethel, Kitwe. 3797Y. |
| Lambaland Baptist Church | 1905 | P Bap | .HG.z | 85 | 2,000 | 4,000 | M=South African & Australian Baptists. Lamba. HQ Ndola. 7n,53m,10f,2H,1j. |
| Last Church of Christ | | I ind | ..... | | 1,000 | 2,000 | *Last Church of God. Convenanter Brethren.* Indigenous Bantu Christians. |
| Lumpa (Visible Salvation) Church | 1954 | I mar | ..... | | 10,000 | 20,000 | Led by Alice Lenshina; 1958, 100,000; 1965 banned; still active. Bemba, Senga. |
| Lutheran Church of Central Africa | 1953 | P Lut | x.... | 42 | 851 | 2,639 | M=Wisconsin ELS(USA). 45% Chewa, 23% Tonga, 19% Ila. 1n,6x,10f,1h,6p,W=51%,123Y,249y. |
| New Apostolic Church | c1915 | C CAp | x.... | 200 | 80,000 | 120,000 | *Zambia-Malawi Church District.* M=NAC(HQ Dortmund,Germany). Lozi, Bemba. 12n,4x. |
| Old Apostolic Church | 1963 | C CAp | x.... | 4 | 150 | 500 | Split (in UK) from Catholic Apostolic Ch. From South Africa. Kitwe. 4 priests. |
| Orthodox Syrian Church of India | c1965 | O Syr | Dwe.. | 1 | 60 | 200 | D Bahya Kerala. Indians from all over Copperbelt meet in Mindolo chapel. 1 priest. |
| Pentecostal Assemblies of God of Z | 1948 | P Pe2 | ZFG.E | 45 | 3,200 | 6,000 | *PAG.* 1955, M=PAoC(Canada),AoG(USA). Along railway. 6n,14x,20m,8f,1s(11). |
| Pentecostal Church of Zambia | 1962 | I pe1 | ....C | 2 | 30 | 100 | Split ex ACP(Canada). Central and Southern provinces. Unitarian pentecostals. 1n. |
| Pentecostal Free Churches | c1968 | P Pe4 | ....C | 4 | 400 | 1,000 | Split ex PAG, aided by Pentecostals from UK. Mufulira, Kitwe, Copperbelt. 4n. |
| Pentecostal Holiness Association | 1934 | P Pe3 | ZFG.E | 26 | 1,042 | 2,000 | M=PHC(USA). Copperbelt. Isoka; expansion to Tanzania, Malawi. 16n,4f,1s,W=75%,55Y. |
| Presbyterian Church in Zambia | c1955 | P Ref | Rwa.d | 6 | 1,300 | 3,000 | *PCSA. Presbytery of Zambia.* Expatriates (Malawi,UK,SAfrica). HQ Lusaka. 2n,1x. |
| Reformed Church in Zambia | 1899 | P Ref | F.A.d | 140 | 30,000 | 50,000 | *Eklesia wa Cikonzedwe m'Zambia.* M=DRC(SA). 90% Chewa. 22n,3x,6f,2H,1p,1s(6). |
| Religious Society of Friends | 1964 | P Qua | Q...d | 1 | 30 | 100 | 2 workers, 2 work camps (Kafue, Northern Province). Joined UCZ, later left. |
| Remnant Church of Israel | | I ind | ....C | 7 | 1,300 | 3,000 | Lusaka area. Bishop and 4 pastors. Attempting to join Christian Council of Zambia. |
| Salvation Army | 1924 | P Sal | xwA.d | 58 | 3,015 | 7,132 | *Nkondo ya Lufutuko. Zambia Command.* 99% Tonga. 34n,43x,G=1.5%pa,2H,1r,1s,W=79%,65Y. |
| Salvation Church | 1930 | I ind | ..... | 16 | 2,000 | 4,000 | *Worldwide Missionary Christian Fellowship.* Ex BiCC. Choma. No church buildings. |
| Scandinavian Independent Baptist Union | 1931 | P Bap | x.G.E | 40 | 2,000 | 4,000 | M=SIBU(Free Baptists, Sweden). Mpongwe area. HQ Luanshya. 14n,10f,1H,1h. |
| Seventh-day Adventist Church | 1905 | P Adv | x...C | 173 | 22,186 | 50,000 | *Zambia Field,* Zambesi Union. 58% Tonga, 34% Bemba. 23nx,36f,3H,1r,546t(49597),2816Y. |
| United Church of Zambia | 1884 | P uni | WWA.d | 800 | 39,330 | 52,351 | *UCZ.* 1958/65 unions M=PEMS,LMS,MMS,CSM. Lozi,Bemba. 57n,28x,87f,3H,7h,5r,1s,9160Yy. |
| Watchman Healing Mission | 1937 | I Jeh | ..... | | 4,000 | 30,000 | *Mhlonda, Bamulonda.* From Malawi. Collective villages. Big non-member attendances. |
| Wesleyan Church | 1890 | P Hol | VFG.a | 78 | 4,100 | 6,882 | 1890 M=Primitive Meth,now WC(USA),RBM(Canada). 8n,9x,39f,G=–5%pa,4H,1s,W=64%,184Y. |
| Other African indigenous churches | | I | ..... | | 7,000 | 15,000 | Total about 40 (see list below). |
| Other Protestant denominations | | P | ..... | | 4,000 | 8,000 | Total about 15 (see list below). |
| Other marginal Protestant bodies | | M | ..... | | 1,000 | 2,000 | Including: Worldwide Ch of God (Radio Ch of God, USA). Many European adherents. |
| **Total affiliated (mid-1970)** | | | | **6,620** | **1,042,231** | **2,164,544** | **Total denominations (1970) . . . 122.** |
| **Total affiliated (mid-1975)** | | | | **7,900** | **1,291,600** | **2,682,430** | **Total denominations (1975) . . . 127.** |
| **Total affiliated (mid-1980)** | | | | **9,200** | **1,598,100** | **3,318,900** | **Total denominations (1980) . . . 132.** |

NOTES ON TABLE ABOVE
COLUMNS: for meanings and CODES (cols. 1, 3, 4, 8): see Codebook (Part 6). Column 1: **Boldface type** = church with over 10% of country's affiliated Christians.
NATIONAL COUNCILS (Column 4, 5th letter). The pattern of membership (1974) is complex. Some churches belong to one organization only (code letters C, G, I), but most belong to the ZCCD and also to some other council. The Christian Council of Zambia (CCZ) is affiliated to CWME of WCC. In 1975, 2 members of the CCZ (SDAC, Wesleyan Ch) withdrew in protest against AACC support for liberation movements.

- a = member of EFZ and ZCCD.
- b = member of ZCCD and AIC.
- C = Zambia Christian Commission for Development (ZCCD) (very active in 1973).
- d = member of Christian Council of Zambia (CCZ) and ZCCD.
- E = Evangelical Fellowship of Zambia (EFZ).
- I = Association of Independent Churches (AIC) (Lusaka area).
- V = Zambia Episcopal Conference (ZEC), and member of ZCCD.
- z = member of ZCCD, CCZ, and EFZ.

*Other national councils.* Zambia Anglican Council (ZAC).
OTHER AFRICAN INDIGENOUS CHURCHES. These others include (with total adult members in brackets): African Apostolic Faith Mission (50), African Christian Gospel Ch (150), African Covenant Ch, African Doctors Ch (30), African Evangelical Ch (150), African Independent Holiness Ch (30), African Reformed Pentecost Ch, Amos Apostolic Ch (100), Black Mans' Ch (home groups), Christian Holiness Ch (30), Ethiopian Catholic Ch in Zion (from South Africa about 1910), Full Gospel African Ch (100), Israel Ch of God (member of ZCCD), Love (Kutemwa) Ch, Messengers Ch, Modern Ch of God, New African Christian Movement, Nzila movement (a Lozi religious healing movment), Zambia True Gospel Ch (20), Zion Africa Ch, Zion City Ch (200). Indigenous bodies from other countries include the Unification Church, from Korea.
OTHER PROTESTANT DENOMINATIONS. These include: Christian Church (Disciples of Christ) (1960; 2 missionaries), Christian Nationals Evangelism Commission (1972), Dorothea Mission, Elim Missionary Society (UK), Zambesi Mission.

PEOPLES (ethnolinguistic). Christians: about 56.0% Bemba cluster [35.4% Bemba (4.1% Bisa, Senga), 7.9% Aushi (2.7% Ngumbo, Unga), 6.0% Lamba (Lala), 3.0% Luapula (Lunda, Shila)], 15.0% Nyanja-speaking (Chewa, Nsenga, Ngoni), 8.0% Tonga cluster (7.0% Tonga, Lenje, Ila), 8.0% Lozi, 5.5% Lunda cluster (Lunda-Luvale, Mbunda, Luchazi, Ndembu, Kaonde), 3.5% Mambwe cluster (Mambwe, Tumbuka, Nkoya), 2.0% South African Bantu (Nguni), 1.4% White (0.8% British, 0.4% Afrikaner, 0.2% Greek), 0.3% Shona, 0.2% Mulatto, et alia.

COUNTRY-WIDE TOTALS
EVANGELIZATION (see Part 5). 1900: 4%. 1970: 95%. 1980: 100%. *Mass evangelism.* Among recent campaigns: 1960, Billy Graham 7-day crusade in Kitwe (28,000 attenders, 1,497 enquirers). *Radiophonic evangelism.* RVOG, FEBA, ICI, and numerous other agencies. *Literature evangelism.* In 1975, Every Home Crusade (EHC) began to see growing results reaching 4,000 written decisions for Christ every month.
FOREIGN MISSIONARIES AND PERSONNEL (nationals serving abroad) (1973). Total 168 in Canada, Malawi, Rhodesia, South Africa, Tanzania, Zaire et alia: about 100 marginal Protestants (Jehovah's Witnesses), about 30 Roman Catholics, 15 African indigenous, 13 Protestants, about 10 Catholics (non-Roman).
FOREIGN MISSIONARIES AND PERSONNEL (aliens from abroad) (1973). Total 2,001. *From Western world.* 1,753: about 990 Roman Catholics, 677 Protestants (360 in 23 USA societies, 181 in 9 UK societies, 64 in 4 Canada societies, 21 in 2 WGermany societies, 16 in 3 Australia societies, 10 in 1 New Zealand society, 10 in 1 Sweden society, 9 in 2 Switzerland societies, 4 in 1 France society, 2 in 1 Netherlands society), 65 Anglicans (63 in 8 UK societies, 2 in 1 USA society), about 20 Catholics (non-Roman), 1 Orthodox. *From Communist world.* 94 Roman Catholics (79 from Poland, 15 from Yugoslavia). *From Third World.* 154: 50 Protestants (39 in 10 South Africa societies, 1 PAoWI from West Indies), about 45 Roman Catholics, 30 African indigenous from 6 countries, about 20 marginal Protestants (Jehovah's Witnesses), about 8 Anglicans from Rhodesia, Malawi, South Africa, Jamaica et alia, 1 Orthodox.
INSTITUTIONS (church-operated) (1973). Total 190, including 4 ecumenical centres, about 60 higher schools (6 minor seminaries), 90 medical centres, 5 presses, 3 religious communities, 2 research centres, 17 seminaries (12 Protestant, 2 RC, 1 Anglican).
PERIODICALS. About 40 titles (including JWs, SDA, African indigenous).
PERSONNEL. About 3,866 (1,865 national, 2,001 foreign).
RELIGIOUS LIBRARIES. About 33.
SCRIPTURE DISTRIBUTION (1975). Annual totals: 29,689 Bibles (2% free, 91% subsidized, 7% commercial), 74,465 NTs (46% free, 49% subsidized, 5% commercial), 183,992 UBS portions, 352,878 UBS selections. *Translations completed.* Portion: 14 languages since 1893. NT: 11 languages since 1901. Bible: 4 languages since 1951.
SERVICE AGENCIES. About 78, including AEBICAM, AIC, AZCC, CCZ, CEF, CWC, CWS, EHC, EFZ, LWR, MAP, MCC, NCCW, NCLA, NLFA, RSAZ, SU, UNZACSO, USCL, WLC, YCS, YCW, YMCA, YWCA, ZAC, ZAS, ZCCD, ZEC, ZSCM.

ADDITIONAL DATA ON CHURCHES
CATHOLIC CHURCH IN ZAMBIA. *Catechumens.* Totals: (1959) 74,882; (1961) 83,774; (1963) 88,775; (1970) 69,351; and (1971) 67,485, divided as follows among the 9 dioceses in order (and included in column 7): 11264, 16182, 8542, 7144, 9528, 5648, 4772, 3905, 500. *Annual baptisms.* (1972) 67.0% infant, 33.0% adult. *Priests.* Increasing by 1975 to 449 (54 nationals). *Brothers.* Including 12 nationals. *Sisters.* Including 159 nationals. *Seminaries.* The Mpima Major Seminary, the first national one, was opened near Kabwe (in M Lusaka) in 1973. *Seminarians.* Total (1971) 26, (1975) 55. *Catechists.* Total (1971) 925. There are 5 catechetical schools. *Indigenous religious congregations.* Sisters: 47 Sisters of the Child Jesus (begun 1927), Little Sisters of St Francis (begun 1958), Handmaids of the BVM (begun 1960), Daughters of the Holy Spirit (begun 1973), Daughters of the Redeemer (begun 1973). *Main foreign orders and congregations.* Priests: WF, OFMCap, OFMConv, SJ. Brothers: SC. Sisters: Franciscan Missionaries, Missionary Sisters of the Divine Motherhood.
*Catholic organizations.* The Zambia Episcopal Conference (ZEC) is a member of AMECEA and of SECAM. The Religious Superiors Association of Zambia serves male religious personnel, while the Zambia Association of Sisterhoods is responsible for female religious. There is no national pastoral council but the Association of Zambian Catholic clergy has been formed recently. Co-ordinating agencies for lay activities are the National Council for the Lay Apostolate and the Secretariat for the Lay Apostolate. The main lay movements are YCS, YCW, Xaverians, Boy Scouts and Girl Guides, Legion of Mary, St Vincent de Paul and Catholic Women's League.
The Holy See has diplomatic relations with Zambia and is represented to government and the Catholic hierarchy by a pro-nuncio in Lusaka.
In 1973 the Catholic Church was responsible for 543 primary schools (123,082 pupils) and 31 secondary (10,641), with 443 students enrolled in 2 teacher training colleges. In 1974 the primary schools were nationalized, while 34 post-primary institutions remain under Catholic control.
Concerning medical and social action, in 1974 there were 25 hospitals (including 4 leprosy settlements), 3 dispensaries, 3 clinics, 3 rural health centres, 4 institutions for the handicapped, 11 mission orphanages, 14 homecraft centres, 50 credit unions and 12 savings co-operatives.
FULL GOSPEL CHURCH OF GOD. In 1978, 71 new churches were organized.
LUTHERAN CHURCH OF CENTRAL AFRICA. Initials LCCA. *Growth.* Increasing by 1977 to 4,845 members, in 93 congregations.
UNITED CHURCH OF ZAMBIA. *Missionaries from abroad* (1973). Total 87: 7 CSM, 6 CWM, 28 MMS, 4 PEMS, 38 UC-Canada, 4 UCBWM.
WATCHMAN HEALING MISSION. Also known as Church of the Watchtower, People of the Watchman (Bamulonda), or People of Jehovah and Michael. Begun in northern Nyasaland in 1910 as a mass revival among the Tonga, with 10,000 baptized by Elliott Kamwana, by the 1920s it had become the major separatist movement in Central Africa. Although it later collapsed in Malawi, it became organized in Northern Rhodesia after 1937 and still has very large non-member attendances in Zambia. Members live in collective villages (1,500 in each), and practise co-operative farming.

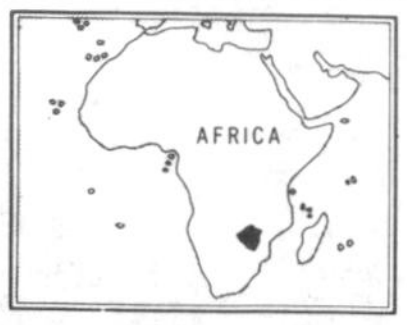


# ZIMBABWE

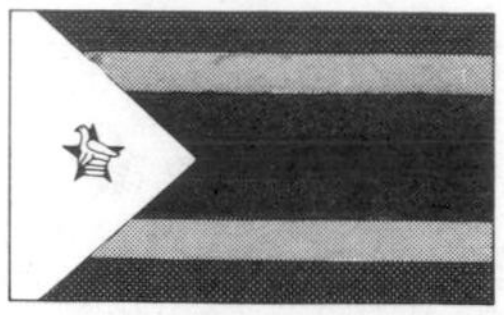

## SECULAR DATA

**STATE. Official name:** The Republic of Zimbabwe. Earlier name: The Colony of Southern Rhodesia. (1979) Zimbabwe/Rhodesia.
**Flag** (shown above right): Bird on red star in white triangle, 7 stripes of green, gold, red, black.
**Area:** 390,580 sq.km. (150,804 sq.miles). Agricultural land: 18.8%.
**Government:** Parliamentary republic, since 1980 (1890 British South Africa Company possession, 1923 British colony of Southern Rhodesia, self-governing colony, 1965 Independence declared by White regime, 1970 republic declared, 1980 Independence recognized).
**Legislature:** Senate, 23 members. House of Assembly, 66 members.
**Official language:** English.
**Chief cities:** capital Harare/Salisbury 502,000 (1973), Bulawayo 307,000.
**Armed forces** (1976): Total 9,200 regular (about 60% Black): army 7,900 (2,400 conscripts), air force 1,300 (44 combat aircraft). Reserves: 40,000 (Whites). Paramilitary forces: 44,000.

**DEMOGRAPHY. Population:** 5,099,344 (census of 21.IV–11.V.1969. For 1970–2000 (UN), see last row of Table 1). Population density (1975): 16/sq.km. (42/sq.mile). Under 15 years: 46%. Growth rate (1975–80): 3.55% per year (births 4.83%, deaths – 1.29%). Immigration: up to 1972, around 9,000 Europeans a year; by 1977, this had become emigration of about 12,000 Whites a year. Life expectancy (1975–80): 54.0 years. Household size: 5.0 persons.
**Major languages:** English, Shona, Ndebele, Tsonga, Venda, Tonga, Zulu, Afrikaans, Chewa (Chichewa), Pedi (Sepedi), Tswana (Setswana), Greek, Gujarati, Marathi, Portuguese, and about 15 smaller languages.
**Urban dwellers** (1970): 19.8%. Urban growth rate (1950–70): 7.3% per year.
**Labour force:** 34%.
**Refugees** (1977): None from abroad. Exiles abroad: 60,000 Zimbabweans in Mozambique, Tanzania and Zambia.
**Tourists** (1972): 351,689.

**ETHNOLINGUISTIC GROUPS:** 66.0% Shona (Kalanga, Karanga, Korekore, Manyika, Nambya, Ndau, Tawara, Zezuru), 16.0% Ndebele, 4.5% British, 3.5% Tsonga (Hlengwe, Shangaan), 2.9% Venda, 2.1% Tonga, 1.1% Afrikaner, 1.1% Chewa (Nyanja), 1.1% Pedi (Sotho), 1.0% Tswana, 0.3% Coloured (White/Black) (16,500), 0.2% Indo-Pakistani (9,200) (Gujarati, Marathi), 0.1% Greek, 0.1% Jewish, Swazi, Zulu, Lozi, Sena, Makua, Yao (Swahili), Bushman, Chinese (550), & a number of smaller tribes.

**MONEY** (1977). **Monetary unit:** Rhodesian dollar (= 100 cents); US$1 = R$0.57.
**National income per person:** US$500. Average annual family income: US$2,500.
**Inflation:** (1970–74) 3.9% per year (1975: consumer price index 132).
**Cost of living in capital** (1976): Daily cost of living: US$17.

**HEALTH.** Hospitals: 226 (17,753 beds). Doctors: 836. Lepers: 32,000 (5.1 per 1000). Blind: 15,000. Psychotics: 50,000.

**EDUCATION.** Adult literacy: (1962) 39%. Education rate: 57%. Schools (1965): 3,099. Universities: 1.

**LITERATURE.** Newspapers: 4 dailies.

**COMMUNICATION** (per 1,000 people). Phones: 27. Radios: 38. TV sets: 10. Daily newspaper circulation: 16 copies.

TABLE 1. RELIGIOUS ADHERENTS IN ZIMBABWE

| Year | 1900 | | mid-1970 | | Annual change, 1970–1980 | | | | mid-1975 | | mid-1980 | | 2000 | |
|---|---|---|---|---|---|---|---|---|---|---|---|---|---|---|
| *Name* | *Adherents* | *%* | *Adherents* | *%* | *Natural* | *Conversion* | *Total* | *Rate* | *Adherents* | *%* | *Adherents* | *%* | *Adherents* | *%* |
| **Christians** | **19,000** | **3.8** | **2,760,000** | **52.0** | **120,292** | **38,408** | **158,700** | **4.60** | **3,452,000** | **55.0** | **4,347,000** | **58.0** | **10,451,000** | **69.0** |
| professing | 19,000 | 3.8 | 2,760,000 | 52.0 | 120,292 | 38,408 | 158,700 | 4.60 | 3,452,000 | 55.0 | 4,347,000 | 58.0 | 10,451,000 | 69.0 |
| Protestants | 6,000 | 1.2 | 1,053,100 | 19.8 | 44,294 | 5,166 | 49,460 | 3.89 | 1,271,100 | 20.2 | 1,547,700 | 20.6 | 3,476,000 | 22.9 |
| Roman Catholics | 6,000 | 1.2 | 690,000 | 13.0 | 29,961 | 8,939 | 38,900 | 4.52 | 859,800 | 13.7 | 1,079,000 | 14.4 | 2,575,000 | 17.0 |
| African indigenous | 0 | 0.0 | 685,000 | 12.9 | 31,492 | 19,208 | 50,700 | 5.61 | 903,700 | 14.4 | 1,192,000 | 15.9 | 3,181,000 | 21.0 |
| Anglicans | 7,000 | 1.4 | 238,900 | 4.5 | 10,280 | 2,530 | 12,810 | 4.34 | 295,000 | 4.7 | 367,000 | 4.9 | 818,000 | 5.4 |
| Catholics (non-Roman) | 0 | 0.0 | 53,000 | 1.0 | 2,404 | 1,296 | 3,700 | 5.36 | 69,000 | 1.1 | 90,000 | 1.2 | 227,000 | 1.5 |
| Marginal Protestants | 0 | 0.0 | 32,000 | 0.6 | 1,533 | 1,267 | 2,800 | 6.36 | 44,000 | 0.7 | 60,000 | 0.8 | 151,000 | 1.0 |
| Orthodox | 0 | 0.0 | 8,000 | 0.2 | 328 | 2 | 330 | 3.51 | 9,400 | 0.2 | 11,300 | 0.2 | 23,000 | 0.2 |
| nominal | 3,000 | 0.6 | 624,957 | 11.8 | 27,345 | 9,079 | 36,424 | 4.64 | 784,700 | 12.5 | 989,200 | 13.2 | 2,272,000 | 15.0 |
| affiliated | 16,000 | 3.2 | 2,135,043 | 40.2 | 92,947 | 29,329 | 122,276 | 4.58 | 2,667,300 | 42.5 | 3,357,800 | 44.8 | 8,179,000 | 54.0 |
| total practising | 15,000 | *95* | 1,814,790 | *85* | 79,005 | 24,929 | 103,934 | 4.58 | 2,267,200 | *85* | 2,854,130 | *85* | 6,543,200 | *80* |
| non-practising | 800 | *5* | 320,260 | *15* | 13,942 | 4,400 | 18,342 | 4.58 | 400,100 | *15* | 503,670 | *15* | 1,635,800 | *20* |
| Protestants | 5,000 | 1.0 | 758,004 | 14.3 | 31,390 | 1,110 | 32,500 | 3.61 | 900,800 | 14.3 | 1,083,000 | 14.4 | 2,264,000 | 14.9 |
| Evangelicals | 4,000 | 0.8 | 541,000 | 10.2 | 22,476 | 1,224 | 23,700 | 3.67 | 645,000 | 10.3 | 778,000 | 10.4 | 1,630,000 | 10.8 |
| Neo-pentecostals | 0 | 0.0 | 0 | 0.0 | 28 | 472 | 500 | 62.50 | 800 | 0.0 | 5,000 | 0.1 | 30,000 | 0.2 |
| African indigenous | 0 | 0.0 | 586,500 | 11.0 | 26,902 | 16,378 | 43,280 | 5.61 | 772,000 | 12.3 | 1,019,300 | 13.6 | 2,878,000 | 19.0 |
| Roman Catholics | 5,000 | 1.0 | 556,789 | 10.5 | 24,274 | 7,737 | 32,011 | 4.60 | 696,600 | 11.1 | 876,900 | 11.7 | 2,121,000 | 14.0 |
| Catholic pentecostals | 0 | 0.0 | 0 | 0.0 | 14 | 186 | 200 | 50.00 | 400 | 0.0 | 2,000 | 0.0 | 40,000 | 0.3 |
| Anglicans | 6,000 | 1.2 | 153,600 | 2.9 | 6,551 | 1,319 | 7,870 | 4.19 | 188,000 | 3.0 | 232,300 | 3.1 | 530,000 | 3.5 |
| Anglican pentecostals | 0 | 0.0 | 0 | 0.0 | 35 | 165 | 200 | 20.00 | 1,000 | 0.0 | 2,000 | 0.0 | 20,000 | 0.1 |
| Catholics (non-Roman) | 0 | 0.0 | 40,000 | 0.8 | 1,969 | 1,531 | 3,500 | 6.19 | 56,500 | 0.9 | 75,000 | 1.0 | 212,000 | 1.4 |
| Marginal Protestants | 0 | 0.0 | 32,150 | 0.6 | 1,533 | 1,252 | 2,785 | 6.33 | 44,000 | 0.7 | 60,000 | 0.8 | 151,000 | 1.0 |
| Orthodox | 0 | 0.0 | 8,000 | 0.2 | 328 | 2 | 330 | 3.51 | 9,400 | 0.2 | 11,300 | 0.2 | 23,000 | 0.2 |
| Tribal religionists | 479,800 | 96.0 | 2,469,000 | 46.5 | 95,116 | –38,586 | 56,530 | 2.07 | 2,729,500 | 43.5 | 3,034,300 | 40.5 | 4,440,000 | 29.3 |
| Muslims | 1,000 | 0.2 | 50,000 | 0.9 | 2,056 | –56 | 2,000 | 3.39 | 59,000 | 0.9 | 70,000 | 0.9 | 140,000 | 0.9 |
| Baha'is | 0 | 0.0 | 9,700 | 0.2 | 418 | 62 | 480 | 4.00 | 12,000 | 0.2 | 14,500 | 0.2 | 45,000 | 0.3 |
| Non-religious | 0 | 0.0 | 8,000 | 0.2 | 348 | 152 | 500 | 5.00 | 10,000 | 0.2 | 13,000 | 0.2 | 40,000 | 0.3 |
| Jews | 200 | 0.0 | 5,200 | 0.1 | 213 | –3 | 210 | 3.44 | 6,100 | 0.1 | 7,300 | 0.1 | 14,000 | 0.1 |
| Hindus | 0 | 0.0 | 3,650 | 0.1 | 150 | –5 | 145 | 3.37 | 4,300 | 0.1 | 5,100 | 0.1 | 10,000 | 0.0 |
| Atheists | 0 | 0.0 | 1,000 | 0.0 | 45 | 15 | 60 | 4.62 | 1,300 | 0.0 | 1,600 | 0.0 | 4,000 | 0.0 |
| Spiritists | 0 | 0.0 | 300 | 0.0 | 12 | –2 | 10 | 2.86 | 350 | 0.0 | 400 | 0.0 | 600 | 0.0 |
| Other religionists | 0 | 0.0 | 1,150 | 0.0 | 50 | 15 | 65 | 4.48 | 1,450 | 0.0 | 1,800 | 0.0 | 2,400 | 0.0 |
| **Country's population** | **500,000** | **100.0** | **5,308,000** | **100.0** | **218,700** | **0** | **218,700** | **3.48** | **6,276,000** | **100.0** | **7,495,000** | **100.0** | **15,147,000** | **100.0** |

COLUMNS, ROWS. For meanings and definitions, see Codebook (Part 6). Note that, by definition, total 'Christians' = professing + crypto-Christians, which also = affiliated + nominal Christians. Percentages may not always total exactly, due to rounding.
CENSUSES. These have only been taken for the White and other non-African populations. **1936** (Europeans only; 55,450 persons): 42.9% Anglicans, 40.8% Protestants (17.8% Dutch Reformed, 11.4% Presbyterians, 8.9% Methodists), 8.5% Roman Catholics, 4.0% Jews 1.0% Greek Orthodox. **1941** (Europeans only; 68,950 persons): 43.3% Anglicans, 38.3% Protestants, 8.7% Roman Catholics, 4.7% Jews, 1.1% Greek Orthodox. **1946** (Europeans only; 82,406 persons): 37.9% Anglicans, 37.8% Protestants, 15.4% Roman Catholics, 4.2% Jews, 1.2% non-religious and atheists, 1.0% Greek Orthodox. **8.V.1956** (non-Africans): 170,612 Christians, 7,787 non-religious, 2,941 Jews, 1,379 Hindus, 1,097 Muslims, 567 other religionists. **26.IX.1961** (non-Africans): 209,700 Christians, 10,360 non-religious, 7,060 Jews, 3,310 Hindus, 3,100 Muslims, 4,970 other religionists. **1969** (Europeans, Asians and Coloureds only; 252,414 persons): 36.0% Protestants, 32.1% Anglicans, 14.0% Roman Catholics, 2.1% Jews, 2.0% non-religious and atheists, 1.6% Muslims, 1.5% Greek Orthodox, 1.4% Hindus.

NOTES ON RELIGIONS
AFRICAN INDIGENOUS. In about 120 denominations in 1970 (see Table 2). Although most converts come from tribal religion (paganism), a considerable number of Protestants, Anglicans and Roman Catholics join these churches each year.
ANGLICAN PENTECOSTALS (or, Anglican charismatics). The charismatic renewal began in 1973 and by 1977 was involving about 10 Anglican parishes, mainly White.
ATHEISTS. Europeans.
BAHA'IS. Growth from 13 local spiritual assemblies (1964) to 56 (1973). Including many Indians, formerly Hindus or Muslims.
HINDUS. Indians (Asians), with 23 Europeans and 39 Coloureds in 1969.
JEWS. The first pioneers arrived in 1869, followed by many from Eastern Europe. These are now congregations in Bulawayo, Gatooma, Que Que and Salisbury.
MUSLIMS. African Muslims from neighbouring countries especially Mozambique and Malawi (Makua, Yao, Swahili et alii)(Sunnis, of the Shafiite rite), also 3,350 Asian traders (Indians, Indo-Pakistanis) and 600 Coloured in 1969. *Hajj pilgrims to Mecca.* (1976) 12 persons.
NOMINAL CHRISTIANS. Africans who regard themselves as Christians having broken with traditional religion, but not yet initiated by the churches.
NON-RELIGIOUS. Europeans, with some Chinese. In the 1956 census of non-Africans, 7,176 (4.1% of all Whites) stated they were either non-religious, agnostics or atheists; in the 1969 census, the figure was 4,966 (2.0%).
OTHER RELIGIONISTS. Adherents of smaller religions and cults, including Rosicrucians (1 AMORC centre).
PRACTISING CHRISTIANS. The proportion is very high in Zimbabwe because almost all members of the indigenous churches are regularly practising, most being weekly attenders.
SPIRITISTS. Mostly Europeans, followers of non-Christian high spiritism.
TRIBAL RELIGIONISTS. Animists, adherents of traditional religions, especially among the Ndau (75% animist), and the Hiechware Bushmen (90%). All tribes however have numerous traditionalists still; and the largest, the Shona and Ndebele, are both still predominantly traditionalist and strongly resistant to Christianity. There are several highly-elaborate cults attended by vast crowds of many thousands, notably the Mwari cult in the Matopo hills where annually the voice of God is believed to be heard.

**NON-CHRISTIAN RELIGIONS. Traditional religions** are still practised by over 40% of the population. The eastern Ndau (75% traditionalist) and Hiechware Bushmen (90%) are the most resistant of the indigenous peoples to Christian influence. An unusual feature of Shona traditional religious practice is the Mwari cult of the Matopo Hills. Unlike many African traditional religions which picture God as remote, Mwari, the supreme being of the Shona, continues to speak to his people through the Rozvi priests at Matonjeni. His holy days (*chisi*) are observed at local cult shrines throughout Mashonaland where annual fees are collected and forwarded to Matonjeni as rain offerings to Mwari. Mwari's advice is also sought in times of national crisis. The Shona emphasis on God does not interfere with their traditional belief in the ancestors (Midzimu), for the latter are seen as intermediaries between man and God. Although the high God is not directly involved, the Korekore and Tawara peoples of the Mount Darwin district recognize the cults of Dzivaguru and Karuva as playing a role similar to that of Mwari at Matonjeni. Both were once human and Dzivaguru is said to have been the father of Karuva. The centre of both cults is the Chona chiefdom, and both spirits are renowned for their ability to produce rain. The Korekore also attach great significance to the role of lion spirits (Mhondoro) who are the spirits of chiefs ruling the area prior to the Korekore's arrival. The spirits have their abode in lions and speak through their recognized mediums. Spirit-possession cults among the southern Shona also have a long history. The Mashave are the most prevalent and have undergone gradual change from an earlier period when they were regarded as individual guardian spirits to a more recent identification of them as foreign spirits. The Ndebele have 4 spirit-possession types, the most important being the Amatshave. These are spirits of the previous inhabitants of the area and speak through their mediums in Shona.

**Islam** exists among African Muslims from neighbouring countries especially Malawi and Mozambique, and also among Asian traders and Coloureds.

**Baha'i** has grown rapidly among Africans, from 13 local spiritual assemblies in 1964 to 56 in 1973. There are also many Indian followers formerly Muslims or Hindus.

**Judaism** has an ancient history in Zimbabwe. Jewish pioneers from England arrived as early as 1869, followed by others from Eastern Europe. The first organized Jewish congregation, in Bulawayo, dates from 1849. Others are now found at Gatooma, Que Que and Salisbury, the latter with 2 groups including the only Sefardi congregation in the country. The principal co-ordinating agency for the Jewish community is the Central African Jewish Board of Deputies in Bulawayo.

**CHRISTIANITY.** The first Christian contact was made with the Shona by the Portuguese Jesuit Gonzalo da Silveira in 1561, and there were further efforts in the 1600s; but no permanent Catholic presence resulted until 1879. The pioneer Protestant missionary to Zimbabwe was Robert Moffat who received permission from the Ndebele chief Mziligazi to open a London Missionary Society station at Inyati in 1859. Several missions tried to follow in the footsteps of the LMS but were unsuccessful; and it was not until 1888 that new groups were able to commence work in the country.

White and Black Christians each have their distinctive image and form their own communities, largely separated from each other. White Christianity is urban and bears the imprint of the Whites' country of origin; England for Anglicans and Methodists, Ireland for Catholics, and South Africa for Dutch Reformed. It is plagued by marriage instability, the White community of Zimbabwe having the third highest divorce rate in the world (25%). Christianity has had little social relevance for White Christians. Black Christianity, on the other hand, is mainly rural, characterized by personalistic piety and conservative theology. The churches are predominantly African in membership, though many continue to remain under European leadership. Until 1973, all 5 Catholic bishops were White, as were also the 2 Anglican bishops then. Where church leaders have taken a liberal view on race relations, their ideas have been rejected by the majority of their White adherents; and there are also tensions within the ministry over the race issue. The great majority of African Christians are below the age of 30. The churches are numerically weakest among African men over 40, by far the most active and best-organized lay movement being that of married women.

PROTESTANT CHURCHES. The 2 decades after 1888 witnessed a rapid expansion of Protestantism and established patterns of church adherence which have largely continued until today. Zimbabwe is primarily a Protestant country, but there is no single predominant church. Rather there are a number of important churches, the largest of which owe their origin to the end of the last century and the early part of this century.

Methodism is represented by 2 major denominations, one related to British Methodism and the other to the USA's United Methodists. The former, arriving in 1890, has a substantial white constituency (16%); while the latter, which entered from Mozambique in 1896, is almost completely African. Other smaller bodies are the Free Methodist and Wesleyan churches. Taken as a whole, Methodists form the major Protestant church tradition in the country.

The Salvation Army, which has been at work since 1891, has the country's largest single Protestant community. The church is 90% Shona and is increasing in size at a phenomenal rate. Other rapidly growing churches with substantial growing constituencies are the African Reformed Church (Dutch Reformed) since 1891, and Seventh-day Adventists since 1894. A later arrival in 1903 was Swedish Lutherans who laid the foundation for the Evangelical Lutheran Church.

Several Presbyterian groups are active, including the Presbyterian Church of Southern Africa (begun 1896) composed mostly of White settlers, and the Church of Central Africa, Presbyterian (1912) consisting of Malawians.

The United Congregational Church is a product of early LMS work in 1859, while the United Church of Christ traces its history to the outreach of the American Board in 1893. The growth of both has been slow. The African Evangelical Church (formerly SAGM) dates from 1897.

British Baptists began work in 1917 but confined their activities to the European community; Southern Baptists from the USA came in 1950 and directed their attention to the African population.

Newer churches, representing for the most part North American Pentecostal and conservative groups, have as yet been unable to establish themselves as rapidly-growing denominations. Among these are the Pentecostal Assemblies of Canada, Assemblies of God, and Church of the Nazarene.

The Protestant churches have played a leading role in education, medicine and social service. Until 1970, 90% of all African students were educated in government-aided church schools.

CATHOLIC CHURCH. Growth has been substantial since the arrival of Catholic missionaries in 1879, and today the Salisbury archdiocese has 4 suffragan dioceses. In the 2 main cities of Salisbury and Bulawayo, the Catholic Church has been most closely associated with the White community, which exercises a strong influence on the clergy. On the other hand, clergy of the dioceses of Gwelo and Wankie, as well as German Jesuits in Salisbury, have long been known as progressivist and have been responsible for new impulses in the fields of liturgy and catechetics in recent years. Catholicism in Zimbabwe is characterized by strong lay activity.

Vocations to the priesthood remain a serious problem for the church. Less than 10% of Catholic priests are African, and the same holds true for brothers. African sisters, however, outnumber all others (695 Blacks out of 1,071). Undoubtedly one reason for the latter has been the establishment of 4 indigenous religious congregations: Little Children of Our Blessed Lady (formed in 1932), Sisters of the Child Jesus, Handmaids of Our Lady of Mount Carmel, and Servants of Mary the Queen. Until 1973 all Catholic bishops were Whites. The first Black bishop was consecrated in January 1973 and appointed as auxiliary bishop of Salisbury.

ANGLICAN CHURCH. The UMCA entered Zimbabwe in 1888 after receiving a grant of land from the British government. Beginning with the settler community, attention was later directed to the needs of the African population. At the present time Anglican work is divided into 2 dioceses, Mashonaland and Matebeleland, corresponding to the 2 major ethnic groups in the country. Anglicanism in Zimbabwe is part of the Church of the Province of Central Africa

INDIGENOUS CHURCHES. At the end of the last century, South African independent churchmen attempted to export their new faith to Zimbabwe but were prevented by government and mission hostility. However, Black American missionaries of the African Methodist Episcopal Church working in South Africa were able to obtain entrance in 1900. The first church indigenous to the country was established in 1906, and today there are more than 120 separate denominations with members from every tribe, several of which have very large constituencies. The African Apostolic Church of Johane Maranke, founded in 1932, is the largest with 260,000.

**CHURCH AND STATE.** Separation between church and state with freedom of conscience and religion were guaranteed in the illegal Smith regime's republican constitution of 1970, but freedom of expression, assembly and association were restricted through legal measures. Racial legislation brought churches into conflict with the government, especially since 1962. Between 1964 and 1971, 13 missionaries among whom was the head of the United Methodist Church, bishop Ralph Dodge, were expelled.

The constitution of 2 March 1970 began in its Dedication: 'The peoples of Rhodesia humbly acclaim the supremacy and omnipotence of Almighty God and acknowledge the ultimate direction by Him of the affairs of men'. However, it soon provoked direct confrontation between churches and state. The constitutional proposals were put before the mainly White electorate in June 1969, but were condemned by the 5 Catholic bishops as 'completely contrary to Christian teaching' in their pastoral letter of 5 June 1969, and by the heads of 9 Christian churches (including the Catholic bishops) as a 'potential tool of tyranny' in their statement of 6 June 1970. After this same republican constitution had come into force on 2 March 1970, the Catholic bishops threatened civil disobedience in their pastoral letter of 17 March 1970, a position which was supported in principle by the leaders of 16 Protestant churches in their joint statements of 18 April 1970. These leaders included those of the Salvation Army and the African branch of the Dutch Reformed Church, which have traditionally not spoken out on racial issues. The main argument of the churches

**Tribal religionists.** Traditionalists (pagans) number 2.9 million (1978), increasing by 56,000 a year. *Above.* Preparation for Mukwerere (rain ritual), with millet for sacrificial beer presented to ancestors by senior woman. *Below.* Burial dance by Hera (Zezuru) traditionalists.

centred around the new Land Tenure Act, which imposed severe limitations on the non-racial service of the churches. In essence, the Act divided Rhodesia into 2 areas, European and African, and thus introduced apartheid. Moreover, the Catholic bishops announced on 29 April 1970 that they would prefer to close all Catholic private schools (catering mainly for White children) than comply with the new Act which forbade Africans from attending those schools.

The Smith regime endeavoured to avoid a direct confrontation with the churches by amending those provisions of the Land Tenure Act which restricted the freedom of the churches, especially the requirement that churches register as 'voluntary associations' before being permitted to continue their multiracial work on 'mission land'. However, by a statement on 11 September 1970, the leaders of 11 churches rejected these amendments. The government made a further compromise with the churches, especially with the Catholic Church, when it proposed at the end of 1970 that Africans might continue to attend Catholic private schools located in European areas provided they constituted not more than 6% of the total enrolment of pupils. In February 1971 the Catholic bishops agreed to this condition on a temporary basis and 'under force majeure'. This compromise was heavily criticized within and outside Rhodesia and was partly attributed to the influence of an emissary sent by Rome, at the bishops' request.

In the sphere of public services to the African population, there is a tradition of close co-operation between churches and state, particularly in the fields of public health and education; and ministers of all churches retain the right of entry into schools for the purpose of teaching religion. Government

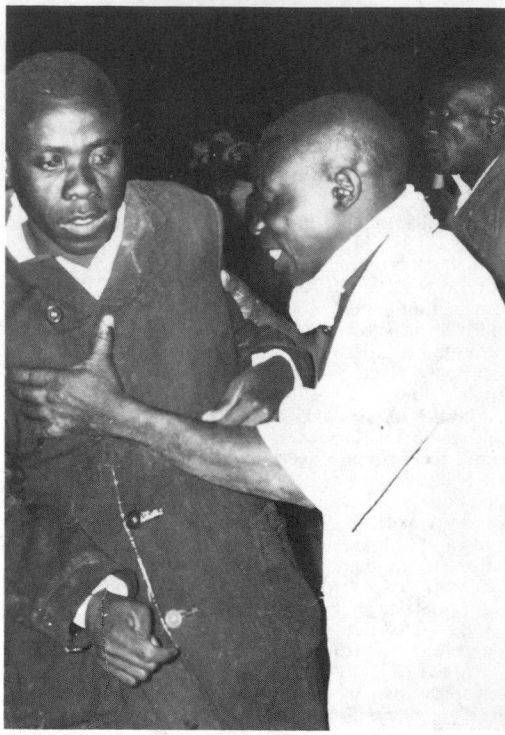

**African Apostolic Church of Johane Maranke** (AACJM). Largest of 130 indigenous denominations, the Vapostori (Apostles) have created new and striking forms. *Top left.* High Priest Abel Ngomberume, son of Johane Maranke, in Aaronic dress with 12-tribe breastplate. *Top right.* Liebauma prophets engaging in simultaneous audible prayer. *Above.* Healers in action (MRP=*Murapi*, Healer). *Right.* Zionist prophet of Mutendi's ZCC (right) detects and intercepts an unconfessed sinner (left) trying to enter sacred enclosure for holy communion.

## INTERDENOMINATIONAL ORGANIZATIONS.

The Christian Council of Rhodesia was founded in 1964. It has been active in race relations, taking positions which have been opposed by some Protestant churches. A larger organization, including also the Dutch Reformed Church, Salvation Army and several smaller conservative bodies, is the Rhodesian Christian Conference, which built on the foundations' first laid by the Southern Rhodesia Missionary Conference in 1903. A more conservative group is the Evangelical Fellowship of Zimbabwe which is a member of the Association of Evangelicals in Africa and Madagascar. The Episcopal Commission for Ecumenism represents the Zimbabwe Catholic Bishops' Conference in ecumenical relations. Epworth Theological College, sponsored by 5 denominations, illustrates Protestant ecumenism in theological education. Catholic-Protestant co-operation exists through the activities of the Ecumenical Adult Literacy Programme, Christian Publishers' Association, Christian Urban Programme and Ecumenical Arts Association. A non-church interracial body in Salisbury, Ranch House College, has played an important role in promoting ecumenical contacts.

In July 1972 the African Independent Churches Conference was formed, with 12 indigenous churches as founding members and 8 others considering membership.

## BROADCASTING.

The Zimbabwe Broadcasting Corporation transmits religious programmes prepared by the various churches. Nine churches rotate programmes on the English-language General Service, and 14 on the vernacular African Service. Their representatives form the Christian Broadcasting Committee begun in 1969 who meet periodically to plan and co-ordinate religious broadcasting. There is also some religious TV programming. From abroad, Christian programmes can be easily heard on several stations including Radio Cordac from Burundi. For Catholics, Zimbabwe is registered as a member of UNDA.

grants for the 75 church-run hospitals cover only a small portion of the cost; but schools, especially primary schools, until 1970 received grants for the total salaries of all teachers. After January 1971, the churches, with the exception of the Anglican diocese of Mashonaland and the Salvation Army, ceased to be responsible authorities for African primary education. They refused to co-operate further in this field because the government decreed that 5% of teachers' salaries should be contributed by African parents, who had already paid for the erection of school buildings, repairs and book fees. African primary schools were after this taken over 'ad interim' by the central government; but for financial reasons and to foster 'separate development' they were placed into the hands of local African authorities.

In 1971 the churches played a major role in influencing the outcome of the Pierce Commission inquiry and thus the decision of the British government to continue its refusal to recognize the minority government of Ian Smith. A key leader of the opposition at the time was bishop Abel Muzorewa, the head of both the United Methodist Church and the African National Council.

On 15 November 1974 the Catholic newspaper, *Moto*, was banned by vote of parliament.

By 1978 bishop Muzorewa was serving on a 4-man executive council with Smith, and a year later became prime minister. By mid-1978, over 40 White missionaries had been murdered by guerrillas.

In 1980 Robert Mugabe, a Marxist Socialist guerrilla leader, was elected to lead a new government and the independence of Zimbabwe was confirmed and recognized.

## BIBLIOGRAPHY

*African Apostles: ritual and conversion in the Church of John Maranke.* B. Jules–Rosette. Ithaca,NY: Cornell University Press, 1975. 302p.

*Catholic directory of Rhodesia, 1972.* Gwelo: Mambo Press, 1972. 75p.

'Christian missions and the British expansion in Southern Rhodesia, 1888–1923'. P. Hassing. Dissertation, American University, Washington DC (USA), 1970.

*Christianity and traditional religion in western Zimbabwe, 1859–1923.* N. Bhebe. Leiden: Brill, 1979. 208p.

*Missions in Southern Rhodesia.* P.S. King. Cape Town: Inyati Centenary Trust, 1959. 81p.

*Old and new in southern Shona independent churches.* M.L. Daneel. The Hague: Mouton. Vol 1: *Background and rise of the major movements*, 1971, 558p. Vol 2: *Church growth: causative factors and recruitment techniques*, 1974, 374p.

*Shona religion: with special reference to the Makorekore.* M. Gelfand. Cape Town: Juta & Co, 1962. 184 p.

'The early history of independency in Southern Rhodesia', T.O. Ranger, in W.N. Watt (ed), *Religion in Africa* (Edinburgh, 1964), p. 52–74. (Mimeographed).

*The God of the Matopo Hills: an essay on the Mwari cult of Rhodesia.* M.L. Daneel. The Hague: Mouton, 1969. 95p.

'The impact of Christianity on the political values of Africans in Rhodesia'. N.E. Thomas. Dissertation, Boston University (USA), 1968.

*The Korsten Basketmakers: a study of the Masowe Apostles, an indigenous African religious movement.* C.M. Dillon-Malone. Manchester: Manchester University Press, 1978, 169p.

*Zionism and faith healing in Rhodesia: aspects of African independent churches.* M.L. Daneel. The Hague: Mouton, 1970. 64p.

TABLE 2.    ORGANIZED CHURCHES AND DENOMINATIONS IN ZIMBABWE

| Official name 1 | Begun 2 | Type 3 | Counc 4 | Congs 5 | Adults 6 | Affiliated 7 | Names, notes, and other statistics (see Codebook) 8 |
|---|---|---|---|---|---|---|---|
| Africa Evangelical Church | 1897 | P int | xMG.E | 52 | 2,500 | 6,000 | M=SAGM(AEF).90%Ndau, near Mozambique.School.1n,3x,20f,G=7.5%pa,1h,1p,W=43%,175Y. |
| **African Apostolic Ch of Johane Maranke** | 1932 | I peA | x...I | 150 | 180,000 | 260,000 | AACJM. VaPostori (Apostles). Ex USA Methodists. Manyika, Zezuru; across Africa. |
| African Apost Ch St Simon & St Johane | 1963 | I peA | ..... | | 1,000 | 2,000 | Schism ex AACJM claiming succession after founder's death, by his cousin. Manyika. |
| African Congregational Church | 1930 | I Ref | ...I | | 8,000 | 15,000 | Chibarirwe (Born for us). Ex DRC. Returning Ndau labourers from South Africa. 6n. |
| African Free Presb Ch of Zimbabwe | 1953 | I Ref | ..... | | 1,000 | 2,000 | Schism ex FPCS protesting discrimination in use of mission transport. Shangaan. |
| African Full Gospel Church | 1923 | I pen | ..... | 2 | 200 | 500 | Begun by returning miners from Rand. 1947, split ex FGCoG(SA). Mainly Venda. |
| African Methodist Church in Zimbabwe | 1947 | I Met | .vA.d | | 3,000 | 5,000 | Schism ex UK Methodists. Ndebele. 1961, applied to WCC, rejected. HQ Selukwe. |
| African Methodist Episcopal Church | 1900 | I Met | Vv..d | 100 | 32,000 | 40,000 | AMEC, 17th Episcopal District. Ethiopian Church. Black mission from USA. Declining. |
| African Orthodox Church | 1924 | I ARo | x.... | 17 | 17,000 | 30,000 | M=AOC(USA). Ex Anglicans. Registered 1924; 1972 Rhodesian African bishop. Ndebele. |
| African Reformed Church in Zimbabwe | 1891 | P Ref | F.G.x | 607 | 36,109 | 60,000 | M=DRC(SA). HQ Morgenster. 60% Karanga, 30% Zezuru. 200f(1972),38f(1977);24n,10x,1s. |
| Alliance Church of Zimbabwe | | P ind | x.G.E | 6 | 200 | 500 | M=SAM(Sweden). HQ Bulawayo. HQ and main work in Transvaal, South Africa. 2f. |
| Anglican Church in Zimbabwe: | 1888 | A Hig | AwaVd | 1,159 | 73,275 | 153,000 | In CPCA, Ch of the Province of Central Africa. 103f,1s. |
| D    Mashonaland | 1891 | A Hig | A | 1,000 | 60,000 | 120,000 | East, northeast. 90% Shona, 10% White. M=USPG. P=26%,W=15%. |
| D    Matabeleland | 1953 | A Hig | A | 159 | 13,275 | 33,000 | West, southwest. 35% White, 31% Ndebele, 31% Shona. P=34%. |
| Anglican Orthodox Church of Zimbabwe | 1968 | A aEv | x.... | 4 | 175 | 300 | M=AOC(USA). Ex Anglican Ch. Whites. Fundamentalists opposing CPCA policies. 1n. |
| Apostolic Church | 1951 | P PeA | ZG... | 12 | 250 | 500 | Begun from South Africa. Largely Whites. M=ACCM(UK). HQ Chadcombe, Salisbury. 4f. |
| Apostolic Faith | | I pen | ..... | | 5,000 | 13,000 | Apostolic Faith (Portland). Some aid from M=AF(Portland,USA). Rapid growth. |
| Apostolic Faith Mission of SAfrica | 1918 | P Pe2 | Z... | 140 | 18,000 | 55,000 | AFMSA(Rhodesia). Shona-speaking. M=AFM(SA). 4% White. Static. HQ Bulawayo. 4f. |
| Assemblies of God African | 1965 | I pe2 | ..... | | 14,000 | 25,000 | AoG (Guti). Independent Black pentecostals. Growing very rapidly to 50,000 by 1978. |
| Assemblies of God in Zimbabwe | 1967 | P Pe2 | ZP... | 30 | 438 | 1,045 | M=AoG(USA,UK,SA). HQ Salisbury. Tent campaigns, up to 8,000 present. 7n,4f. |
| Assemblies of God (Back to God) | 1958 | I pe2 | x.... | | 3,000 | 6,000 | M=AoG (Nicholas Bhengu)(South Africa). Rapid expansion, some splits. Zulu et alii. |
| Baptist Convention of Zimbabwe | 1950 | P Bap | T...C | 151 | 5,064 | 14,000 | 1956, M=SBC(USA). 92% Zezuru, 8% Ndebele. 3 schools. 3n,52f,1H,17h,17h,1s,1040Y. |
| Baptist Union of Central Africa | 1917 | P Bap | ..G.x | 18 | 1,208 | 3,900 | BUCA. M=British & SA Baptists. Members Whites only. HQ Salisbury. |
| Bible Pattern Church | | I pen | ..... | | 1,000 | 2,000 | Independent Black pentecostals, split ex Elim Ch. Expanding. |
| Brethren in Christ Church in Africa | 1898 | P Men | GFG.x | 150 | 4,646 | 10,000 | M=BiCC(USA). A=1964. 98% Ndebele. 7n,55f,G=-2.1%pa,2H,1h,W=60%,260Y,2023z. |

*Continued opposite*

*Table 2–continued*

| Official name 1 | Begun 2 | Type 3 | Counc 4 | Congs 5 | Adults 6 | Affiliated 7 | Names, notes, and other statistics (see Codebook) 8 |
|---|---|---|---|---|---|---|---|
| **Catholic Church in Zimbabwe:** | 1561 | R Lat | P•SSs | 694 | 300,700 | 556,789 | 92% Black, 6% White. C=8+3+21. 1p,1s(64). 34n,341x,154m,1071w,P=51%,29893Yy. |
| M Salisbury | 1879 | R Lat | Psj | 48 | 114,200 | 211,495 | 85% Shona, 8% White (strong influence). 1s. 22 137 51 482 54 11913 |
| D Bulawayo | 1931 | R Lat | Pcmm | 48 | 37,600 | 69,596 | 52% Ndebere,24% Shona, 13% Kalanga,11% White. 1 46 20 204 44 2246 |
| D Gwelo | 1946 | R Lat | Psmb | 284 | 96,000 | 177,764 | 60% Karanga,20% Zezuru,10% Ndebele,2% White. 8 82 59 216 41 9894 |
| D Umtali | 1953 | R Lat | Pocar | 165 | 38,700 | 71,654 | 50% Manyika, 35% Hungwe, 12% Wesa, 2% White. 3 42 18 92 76 4200 |
| D Wankie | 1953 | R Lat | Psmi | 149 | 14,200 | 26,280 | 46% Shona, 33% Nambia, 14% Ndebele, 2% White. 0 34 8 77 43 1640 |
| Christadelphian Ecclesia | | P Ade | x•••• | 1 | 30 | 50 | *Christadelphian Bible Mission.* 1 ecclesia (church) in Salisbury. Pacifist. |
| Christian Brethren | c1903 | P CBr | x•••• | 20 | 3,000 | 5,000 | *Open.* Strong in south in Harding district. 1950, M=CMML(UK,USA,Australia). 23f. |
| Christian Marching Ch of Central Africa | 1954 | I Sal | ••••W | 30 | 1,200 | 3,000 | *CMC.* Ex Soldiers of God. 70% Zezuru, 30% Ndebele. 4n,G=20%pa,W=39%,60Y,150y,45z. |
| Ch of Central Africa, Presbyterian | 1912 | P Ref | J•••C | 150 | 6,350 | 18,000 | *CCAP, Salisbury Synod.* Malawians: 92% Chewa. 4n,4x,G=1.7%pa 1s,W=61%,371Y,568y. |
| Church of Christ, Scientist | | M Sci | x•••• | 3 | 200 | 370 | *Christian Science.* M=CCS(Boston,USA). 90% Whites. Decline from 1,500 in 1960. 6w. |
| Ch of England in SAfrica in Rhodesia | c1970 | A sEv | J•G•E | 3 | 100 | 300 | From SAfrica. Evangelicals opposing CPCA. Whites. Fort Victoria, Salisbury. |
| Ch of Jesus C of Latter-day Saints | | M LdS | x•••• | 1 | 200 | 280 | *Mormons.* M=CJCLdS(Utah,USA). All Whites. Based in Salisbury. |
| Church of the Nazarene | 1963 | P Hol | xFG•E | 11 | 1,536 | 2,000 | M=CoN(USA). Holiness denomination. HQ Salisbury. 2n,2x,4f,W=83%,75z. |
| Churches of Christ (NZ) | 1898 | P Dis | x•••d | 61 | 3,500 | 10,000 | M=Associated CCNZ. A=1943. HQ Dadaya. 90% Karanga, 10% Ndebele. 35 schools. 1H,2h. |
| Churches of Christ (Non-Instrumental) | 1921 | P Dis | x•••• | | 2,000 | 5,000 | M=CC(Non-Instrumental)(USA). Independent congregations. 1 school. 32f,2s. |
| Churches of Christ (USA) | 1896 | P Dis | x•••C | 200 | 2,000 | 14,000 | *Central African Christian Mission.* 1956, M=CCCC(Instrumental)(USA). Bulawayo. 87f. |
| Dutch Reformed Church (Mother Church) | | P Ref | F•••C | 10 | 9,000 | 17,000 | *NGK Moederkerk* (*Rhodesie*). Afrikaans-speaking Whites only. HQ Salisbury. 191Yy. |
| Elim Church | c1960 | P Pe2 | ZGG•E | 3 | 100 | 300 | M=Elim Foursquare Gospel Alliance (EMS,UK). Mozambique border. Schools. 14f,1H,191Y. |
| Evangelical Church of Zimbabwe | 1942 | P int | xMG•E | 95 | 2,500 | 6,000 | M=TEAM(USA,SA). 99% Korekore. HQ Hatfield. 2 schools. 15n,20x,82f,1H,7h,1s,161Y. |
| Evangelical Lutheran Ch in Zimbabwe | 1903 | P Lut | L••Jd | 220 | 20,000 | 42,039 | 2 Dioceses. M=SKM(Sweden). 66% Karanga. 24n,5x,4H,4h,1p,1u,W=67%,60Y,317y,3100z. |
| First Ethiopian Church | 1926 | I ind | ••••I | | 3,000 | 5,000 | 1910 founder joined church in South Africa, 1926 began in Rhodesia. Karanga. |
| Free Methodist Church | 1938 | P Hol | VFG•x | 87 | 2,303 | 6,000 | M=FMC(USA). 58% Karanga, 38% Hlengwe. 9n,3x,28f,G=−5.3%pa,1H,1h,1s(17),W=33%,100Y. |
| Free Presbyterian Church of Scotland | 1904 | P Ref | ••••• | 30 | 200 | 300 | M=FPCS(UK). Small mission from Scotland. Shangaan. Schools. 1H,1r. |
| Full Gospel Ch of God in Southern A | | P Pe3 | ZFG•E | 37 | 7,655 | 15,000 | Branch of South African body. M=CoG(Cleveland)(USA). 7% White. Static. 36n. |
| Gospel of God Church in Zimbabwe | 1932 | I peA | x•••• | 70 | 10,000 | 30,000 | *Basketmakers. Hosannas.* Ex Anglican Ch. Shona artisans. Missions in 11 countries. |
| Greek Orth Archbishopric of Zimbabwe | 1905 | O Gre | Cw••• | 4 | 5,000 | 8,000 | In P Alexandria. 4,000 Greek settlers from Greece, Egypt, Cyprus. 3x,W=20%,150y. |
| Independent African Church | 1942 | I Met | ••••W | | 1,100 | 5,000 | *Muchakata* (*Worshippers under trees*). Schism ex Methodists(USA). 80% Manyika. |
| Jehovah's Witnesses | c1910 | M Jeh | x•••• | 354 | 12,456 | 30,000 | Many active Witnesses from Zambia, Malawi, SAfrica. 94% African, 6% White. 684Y. |
| Mai Chaza Church | 1952 | I Met | ••••• | 153 | 3,585 | 50,000 | *Guta ra Jehovah* (*Cities of God*). Schism ex UK Methodists by Mother Chaza. Manyika. |
| Methodist Church in Zimbabwe | 1890 | P Met | VwA•d | 1,006 | 39,870 | 112,500 | M=MMS. 66% Zezuru, 16% White, 14% Ndebele. 49n,29x,340m,60f,G=5%pa,6r,1u,1191Y,4748y. |
| New Apostolic Church | c1910 | C CAp | x•••• | | 20,000 | 40,000 | *Rhodesia Church District.* Begun by Germans and Lozis. World HQ Dortmund (Germany). |
| Pentecostal Assemblies of God in Z | 1942 | P Pe2 | ZFG•E | 83 | 2,500 | 6,000 | *PAG.* M=PAoC(Canada). Southeast of country. HQ Salisbury. Static. 44n,10x,1p. |
| Pentecostal Holiness Church | 1950 | P Pe3 | ZF••• | 27 | 947 | 2,000 | M=PHC(USA). 26 African churches, 1 White church. Static. 27nm,4f,1s. |
| Presbyterian Church of Southern Africa | 1896 | P Ref | Rwa•d | 18 | 8,060 | 25,000 | *PCSA.* 2 Presbyteries. White settlers, some Ndebele. 21nx(16 Whites, 5 Africans). |
| Reformed True Methodist Church | 1964 | I Met | ••••• | | 500 | 2,000 | *RTMC.* Schism ex Methodist Ch; mainly Plumtree and Shabani. Declining. |
| Religious Society of Friends | c1920 | P Qua | Q•••d | 2 | 38 | 70 | *Central African General Mtg.* M=FSC(UK). 80% British. Salisbury, Bulawayo. W=70%. |
| Salvation Army, Zimbabwe Territory | 1891 | P Sal | xwA•d | 459 | 67,526 | 140,000 | *Hondo yo Ruponiso.* 90% Shona. 232n,105x,G=12%pa,2H,7h,5r,1s(24),W=64%,2873Y. |
| Seventh-day Adventist Church | 1894 | P Adv | x•••• | 180 | 28,346 | 50,000 | *Zambesi Union.* 69% Ndebele, 30% Shona. 44n,20x,38f,3h,4r,1s,703t(45611),W=90%,2694Y. |
| Soldiers of God | 1938 | I Sal | ••••• | 32 | 8,677 | 20,000 | *Soja we Mwari.* Ex Salvation Army. 50% Karanga, 20% Ndebele,20% Nyanja. 4n,84Y,66y. |
| United Apostolic Faith Church | 1920 | P Pe2 | x•••• | 145 | 3,000 | 5,000 | M=UAFC(SA,UK). HQ Pretoria. British-Israelite Pentecostals. 10% Whites. 20nx,1p. |
| United Church of Christ | 1892 | P uni | ••A•d | 77 | 1,185 | 4,300 | M=ABCFM, now UCBWM(USA). A=1963. 99% Ndau. Declining. 11n,17f,1u,W=65%,50Y,22y. |
| United Congr Ch of Southern Africa | 1859 | P Con | Rwa•d | 153 | 4,529 | 20,000 | *Zimbabwe Region, UCCSA.* 1859, M=LMS;CCWM. 95% Ndebele. 10n,5x,3h,W=20%,400Y. |
| United Methodist Church | 1896 | P Met | VwA•W | 365 | 38,934 | 90,000 | *Z Annual Conf, UMC.* 59% Manyika, 41% Zezuru. 54n,16x,93f,3H,W=35%,1368Y,6443y. |
| United Pentecostal Church | 1967 | P Pel | x•••• | 13 | 800 | 2,000 | *Jesus Only Church.* M=UPC(USA). Unitarian Pentecostals. 4n,1f,2p(37). |
| Wesleyan Church | 1888 | P Hol | VPG•E | 11 | 200 | 500 | Begun by M=WMMS(UK), then 1968 WC(USA). Holiness doctrines. 5 schools. 2f,1h. |
| Zion Apostolic Church | 1922 | I pen | ••••I | | 5,000 | 12,000 | *ZAC. Bishop Masuka's church.* Southeastern Zimbabwe. Karanga pentecostals. |
| Zion Apostolic Faith Mission | 1924 | I pen | ••••• | | 3,000 | 7,000 | *ZAFM. Bishop Shoko's church.* HQ Chibi Reserve. Southern part of country. |
| Zion Christian Church | 1923 | I pen | x•••I | | 21,000 | 25,000 | *ZCC.* Begun by Bishop Mutendi from South Africa. Holy cities. HQ Bikita. Karanga. |
| Ziwezano Church | c1960 | I Met | ••••W | | 1,000 | 3,000 | *Church of Wisdom.* Ex USA Methodists in Honde valley. Manyika. Industrial schools. |
| Other African indigenous churches | | I | ••••• | | 12,000 | 24,000 | Total about 100 (see list below). |
| Other Protestant denominations | | P | ••••• | | 4,300 | 9,000 | Total about 20 bodies (see list below). |
| Other marginal Protestant bodies | | M | ••••• | | 800 | 1,500 | Incl: Christian Spiritualist Ch (GWCSL, UK), Scientology. Whites. |
| **Total affiliated (mid-1970)** | | | | **8,940** | **1,067,992** | **2,135,043** | **Total denominations (1970) . . . 186.** |
| **Total affiliated (mid-1975)** | | | | **10,100** | **1,334,200** | **2,667,300** | **Total denominations (1975) . . . 206.** |
| **Total affiliated (mid-1980)** | | | | **11,300** | **1,679,600** | **3,357,800** | **Total denominations (1980) . . . 220.** |

NOTES ON TABLE ABOVE
COLUMNS: for meanings and CODES (cols. 1, 3, 4, 8): see Codebook (Part 6). Column 1: **Boldface type** = church with over 10% of country's affiliated Christians.
NATIONAL COUNCILS (Column 4, 5th letter).
- C = Rhodesia Christian Conference (RCC, or ZCC).
- d = member of both CCZ & RCC.
- E = Evangelical Fellowship of Rhodesia (EFR, or EFZ).
- I = African Independent Churches' Conference (AICC) (Fambidzano Yamakereke Avatema, = Cooperation of Churches of the Black People); about 15 members; 1973 application to Rhodesia Christian Conference as associate member.
- s = Rhodesia Catholic Bishops' Conference (RCBC), or Zimbabwe Catholic Bishops' Conference (ZCBC), and also associate member of CCZ.
- W = Christian Council of Zimbabwe (CCZ, former CCR).
- x = member of both EFR & RCC.

OTHER AFRICAN INDIGENOUS CHURCHES. Among the 100 smaller bodies are: African Catholic Ch (Ruponiso rwa Jesu, Moses Ch), African Ch of Israel, African Reformed Ch (ex African Cong Ch), African Zion Collar Church of Jesus ('Only the Bishop shall wear a clergical collar'; begun 1953), Apostolic Faith & Acts Ch, Apostolic Faith African, Apostolic Faith (Fort Victoria), Apostolic Followers, Apostolic Sabbath Ch of God, Assemblies of God (Lekuku), Central African Episcopal Ch, Ch of the Courageous Apostles, Ch of the Holy Cross, Evangelist Soldiers of God, Gospel of Christ Ch (Sande), Mashona United Independent Reformed Ch, National Baptist Assembly of Africa (Holy Trinity Ch; begun c1930 from Nyasaland), New Ch of Africa, Reformed Mai Chaza Ch, Smyrna & Crown of Life Mission, Swazi Christian Ch of SA, United African Apostolic Faith Ch of God, Zimbabwe Ch of the Orphans (c1960), Zion Apostolic Ch of Jesus, Zion Reformed Ch, Zion Sabbath Ch.
OTHER PROTESTANT DENOMINATIONS. Among the 20 are: Apostolic Ch of Pentecost of Canada (1951; 10 missionaries), Assemblies of God International, Cooneyites (Go-Preachers, from Ireland, UK, South Africa), Immanuel Ch (interdenomional), Nederduitsch Hervormde Kerk van Afrika, Pentecostal Ch in Malawi, Pentecostal Protestant Ch, Seventh Day Baptist Ch (113 members), Seventh-day Adventist Reform Movement, United Ev Churches (USA).
UNITING CHURCHES. Negotiations for organic union were under way in 1974, under the name United Church in Southern Africa, between: Anglican Dioceses of Mashonaland & Matabeleland, Methodist Ch in Rhodesia, Presbyterian Ch of SA, United Ch of Christ, United Congregational Ch of SA.

**PEOPLES** (ethnolinguistic). Christians: about 65.0% Shona (Kalanga, Karanga, Korekore, Manyika, Nambya, Ndau, Tawara, Zezuru), 13.0% Ndebele, 10.0% British (including Irish), 3.0% Tsonga, 2.5% Afrikaner, 1.2% Chewa (Nyanja), 1.0% Tonga, 1.0% Pedi (Sotho), 1.0% Tswana, 0.6% Coloured, 0.5% Venda, 0.4% Hlengwe, 0.2% Greek, Swazi, Zulu.

COUNTRY-WIDE TOTALS
EVANGELIZATION (see Part 5). 1900: 18%. 1970: 96%. 1980: 100%. *Mass evangelism.* February 1960, Billy Graham crusades in Bulawayo and Salisbury (78,000 attenders, 4,559 enquirers); 1970–71, New Life for All campaign; May 1976, national Congress on Evangelism in Context; September 1978, National African Christian Leadership Assembly (NACLA) in Salisbury. *Radiophonic evangelism.* TWR, FEBA, RVOG, ICI (3,631 enrolments, 2,703 active, 140 conversions reported).
FOREIGN MISSIONARIES AND PERSONNEL (nationals serving abroad)(1973). Total 96 in 8 countries: about 60 Rhodesian indigenous in Kenya, Malawi, Mozambique, South Africa, Tanzania, USA, Zaire and Zambia, 15 Protestants, about 10 Roman Catholics, about 5 marginal Protestants (Jehovah's Witnesses), 4 Catholics (non-Roman), 2 Anglicans.
FOREIGN MISSIONARIES AND PERSONNEL (aliens from abroad)(1973). Total 2,105. *From Western world.* 1,742: 850 Roman Catholics, 776 Protestants (504 in 30 USA societies, 179 in 11 UK societies, 41 in 2 Sweden societies, 32 in 4 Canada societies, 11 in 2 Norway societies, 3 in 3 New Zealand societies, 2 in 1 Finland society, 2 in 1 Switzerland society, 2 in 1 Australia society), 103 Anglicans (102 in 7 UK societies, 1 in 1 USA society), about 10 Catholics (non-Roman), 3 Orthodox from Greece. *From Communist world.* About 2 Roman Catholics from Yugoslavia. *From Third World.* 361: 246 Protestants (220 in 10 South Africa societies, others from Malawi, Zambia, Botswana), 50 African indigenous from South Africa, Malawi and Zambia, 48 Roman Catholics (11 from South Africa, 4 Uganda, 1 Malawi, 1 Zambia). 12 Anglicans from Malawi, South Africa et alia, about 5 Catholics (non-Roman).
INSTITUTIONS (church-operated)(1973). Total 360, including 95 higher schools (4 minor seminaries), 230 medical centres (75 hospitals), 6 religious communities, 1 research centre, 15 seminaries (12 Protestant, 1 RC, 1 Anglican, 1 African indigenous).
PERIODICALS. About 30 titles (including several African indigenous).
PERSONNEL. About 4,761 (2,656 national, 2,105 foreign).
RELIGIOUS LIBRARIES. About 25.
SCRIPTURE DISTRIBUTION (1975). Annual totals: 77,341 Bibles (1% free, 73% subsidized, 26% commercial), 64,712 NTs (51% free, 33% subsidized, 15% commercial), 77,592 UBS portions, 353,061 UBS selections. *Translations completed.* Portion: 7 languages since 1884. NT: 5 languages since 1884. Bible: 2 languages since 1949.
SERVICE AGENCIES. About 58, including AICC, CCR/CCZ, CEF, CMRSZ, CMSWRZ, CSSD, CWL, DM, EFR/EFZ, MAF, OC, RCBC/ZCBC, RCC/ZCC, RCCL,SCM, SGM, SU, UCRN, WLC(EHC), WVI, YMCA, YWAM, YWCA.

ADDITIONAL DATA ON CHURCHES
CATHOLIC CHURCH IN ZIMBABWE. *New jurisdiction* (created 1973). PA Sinoia, formed out of M Salisbury. *Catholics* (1970). 92% Africans, 6% Europeans: (total 33,700), 1.5% Coloured (total 8,500). *Catechumens.* Totals: (1959) 42,702 (1961) 44,258; (1963) 40,880; and (1970) 31,313 (294 being non-Africans), divided as follows among the 5 dioceses in the order shown (and included in column 7): 15700, 4000, 5000, 3113, 3500. *Annual baptisms.* (1972) 54.8% infant, 45.2% adult. *Priests.* National=indigenous, i.e. African and coloured. Expatriate= White. *Brothers.* Including 12 Africans in M Salisbury. *Sisters.* Including 695 Africans. *Catechists.* Total (1971) 646. *Indigenous religious congregations.* Sisters: 198 Little Children of Our Blessed Lady (begun 1932), 87 Sisters of the Child Jesus, 48 Handmaids of Our Lady of Mount Carmel (begun 1963), 24 Servants of Mary the Queen. *Main foreign orders and congregations.* Priests: SJ, CMM, SMB,OCarm, SMI. Sisters: Missionary Sisters of the Precious Blood, Dominican Sisters of the Most Sacred Heart of Jesus.
*Catholic organizations.* The Zimbabwe/Rhodesia Catholic Bishops' Conference is a member of SECAM. There is no national presbyteral or pastoral council but religious personnel are represented in the Conference of Major Religious Superiors of Zimbabwe, and the Conference of Major Superiors of Women Religious of Zimbabwe. The multi-racial Roman Catholic Council of the Laity consists of 3 delegates from each diocese and representatives of each lay apostolate organization which has a national body. The main national organizations are the Catholic Association (for African laity), Catholic Women's League (17 branches) and Society of St Vincent de Paul.

The Holy See had no diplomatic relations with Zimbabwe until these were established in 1980.

The principal organization for social action is the Commission on Social Service and Development, which is attached to the Catholic Secretariat and is a member of CIDSE in Belgium.

In 1970 there were 162,000 school pupils of all races, 49 hospitals, 96 dispensaries, 23 orphanages, 24 hostels, 13 credit unions and 67 savings clubs. The School of Social Work in Salisbury has been training leaders for urban community service since 1964. The Catholic communications centre and publishing house Mambo Press, which was founded in Gwelo in 1958, has made an important contribution in providing channels of mass communication for the African population. Prior to being banned in 1974, its newspaper *Moto* with a circulation of 41,500 in 1971 carried a special supplement edited by the Christian Council of Rhodesia.
EVANGELICAL LUTHERAN CHURCH IN ZIMBABWE= Kereke yeVangeri yaMaLutere mu Zimbabwe. Begun by the Church of Sweden Mission, the ELCZ became autonomous in 1962 and now has 2 Dioceses. *Membership.* 66% Karanga, 13% Ndebele, 10% Venda. In addition to the African work, there is also one German-speaking church, the Evangelical Lutheran Congregation of Rhodesia.
GOSPEL OF GOD CHURCH IN ZIMBABWE. *Names.* Originally, Vapostori (Apostles of Johane Masowe), later Apostolic Sabbath Church of God; after 1964, African Gospel Church; after 1973, Gospel of God Church. *Origin and history.* Founded in 1932 as a messianic movement under Johane Masowe (John of the Wilderness, John the Baptist, died 1973), the movement emigrated to Korsten, Port Elizabeth (South Africa) in 1947, until the 1,880 followers there were deported in 1962 to Rhodesia, finally settling as headquarters at Marrapodi, Lusaka (Zambia). Moving northwards in search of Jerusalem, Masowe moved in 1964 to Tanzania, then in 1967 to Nairobi (Kenya). Work in Ethiopia was opened around 1975. After Masowe's death in 1973, a major schism took place in Zambia between rebel Shona and loyalist Ndebele. *Missions.* In 1978 there were centres in 10 African countries and also in London (UK).

# PART 8
# STATISTICS
Global, continental and confessional statistical tables

*Beloved parish priests, pay attention, we beg you, to accurate and well-studied statistics.*
*They are a very important task in governing a parish.*
                              —John XXIII, Synod of the Diocese of Rome, 1960.

As explained at the beginning of Part 1, the Global Tables in Parts 1 and 8 form a series of 31 interconnected statistical tables. They are derived from the computerized World Christian Encyclopedia Database, which covers all nations, languages, ethnolinguistic groups, religions, blocs, traditions, denominations and Christian activities. Twelve shorter tables were given in Part 1. The remaining 19 tables given here are longer and more detailed. A complete listing of all 31 tables is found after the Table of Contents at the beginning of the book.

The exact method of computing the totals for 1975–85 in tables of affiliated Christians (organized Christianity) is slightly different to that in Global Tables 2, 4 et alia, and hence some very large figures may differ very slightly in their final 2 or 3 digits.

Most figures in these tables are given to the nearest 1,000, or 100 or 10. Many, however, are given to the last digit. This latter should not be taken as implying any bogus claim to precision or exactitude. The reason they are given to the last digit is in order that all totals and sub-totals should add up exactly, and be seen to add up exactly, without which their comprehensibility and credibility would be less satisfactory. When using or quoting all such individual figures, therefore, especially for publication elsewhere, the reader is advised to round them off to the nearest 100 or 1,000, 10,000 or 100,000, or even million, as may best serve his purpose.

These tables are built on precisely defined and exactly delimited definitions, which should be carefully examined when particular figures are wanted or are to be used or quoted elsewhere. In particular, our fundamental statistical distinction between 'global Christianity' (world total of all Christians of all categories) and 'global church membership' (world total of Christians affiliated to churches) should be borne in mind throughout.

Also to be remembered throughout is that all figures, especially those of change or changing situations, report *nett* totals of the categories concerned, i.e. births minus deaths, gains minus losses, immigrants minus emigrants, conversions minus defections, and so on.

## CONTENTS OF PART 8

Global Table 13.  WORLD POPULATION AND CHRISTIANS BY EXTENT OF DEMOCRATIC RULE, AD 1980.

The table tabulates world population and global Christianity by the varieties of democratic rule in 1980 in the world's 223 countries, i.e. by the extent to which all de facto political power is in the hands of the populace themselves. These data are given, tabulated for every country, in Global Table 31.

| Type of democratic rule | | Countries | Population, 1980 | | Christians, 1980 | |
|---|---|---|---|---|---|---|
| Code | Type of Country | | Total | % | Total | % |
| 1 | *multi-party states (de facto)* | | | | | |
| 1a | federal parliamentary republic/state/constitutional monarchy | 9 | 1,118,506,000 | 25.6 | 399,730,280 | 27.9 |
| 1b | parliamentary republic/state/constitutional monarchy | 55 | 531,845,500 | 12.2 | 345,223,070 | 24.1 |
| 1c | self-governing parliamentary state in association with another state | 5 | 429,700 | 0.0 | 420,640 | 0.0 |
| 2 | *one-party states (de jure or de facto)* | | | | | |
| 2d | ecclesiastical state | 1 | 6,000 | 0.0 | 6,000 | 0.0 |
| 2e | one-party republic/parliamentary state/constitutional monarchy/empire | 16 | 316,997,000 | 7.2 | 73,200,330 | 5.1 |
| 2f | one-party socialist or Marxist republic or state | 15 | 232,835,000 | 5.3 | 30,878,560 | 2.2 |
| 2g | one-party Communist republic or state | 18 | 1,395,633,000 | 31.9 | 218,542,000 | 15.3 |
| 3 | *no-party countries: dependencies* | | | | | |
| 3h | self-governing dependency, colony or territory | 19 | 5,427,500 | 0.1 | 5,140,820 | 0.4 |
| 3i | direct-rule dependency, colony or territory | 31 | 6,749,600 | 0.2 | 2,636,959 | 0.2 |
| 3j | condominium | 1 | 200 | 0.0 | 160 | 0.0 |
| 3k | colony under martial law | 0 | 0 | 0.0 | 0 | 0.0 |
| 3l | occupied territory with regime in exile | 1 | 1,653,000 | 0.0 | 76,450 | 0.0 |
| 3m | secessionist territory and regime | 1 | 101,500 | 0.0 | 100,290 | 0.0 |
| 3n | forcibly-annexed territory (in last 10 years) | 3 | 1,091,200 | 0.0 | 300,410 | 0.0 |
| 4 | *no-party countries: military rule* | | | | | |
| 4o | republic under martial law | 1 | 52,203,000 | 1.2 | 49,201,700 | 3.4 |
| 4p | republic under military rule | 9 | 269,058,000 | 6.2 | 171,849,040 | 12.0 |
| 4q | socialist or Marxist military rule | 5 | 93,737,000 | 2.1 | 35,538,010 | 2.5 |
| 4r | military junta | 13 | 225,460,000 | 5.2 | 66,276,000 | 4.6 |
| 5 | *no-party countries: dictatorships (autocracies)* | | | | | |
| 5s | absolute monarchy | 10 | 51,661,000 | 1.2 | 836,030 | 0.1 |
| 5t | no-party republic under authoritarian rule | 3 | 5,386,500 | 0.1 | 4,880,820 | 0.3 |
| 5u | republic under dictatorship | 2 | 40,506,000 | 0.9 | 14,421,100 | 1.0 |
| 5v | military dictatorship | 4 | 24,292,000 | 0.6 | 13,126,900 | 0.9 |
| 5w | absolute dictatorship, totalitarian rule | 1 | 339,000 | 0.0 | 300,950 | 0.0 |
| **GLOBAL TOTALS** | | 223 | 4,373,917,700 | 100.0 | 1,432,686,500 | 100.0 |

Global Table 14.  WORLD POPULATION AND CHRISTIANS BY POLITICAL FREEDOM, AD 1970-1980.

Political freedom is defined here as a nation's respect for human liberty, measured by the extent to which a country's population enjoys full political and civil rights, including human rights as defined in the United Nations' 1948 *Universal Declaration of Human Rights*. Our 3-fold typology below classifies countries by the extent to which they provide their populations with full individual and corporate freedom in civil and political rights (as assessed by the non-partisan Freedom House organization, New York). The first category below, coded 1 (see data for countries in column 10 of Global Table 31), covers societies with full civil and political rights; the second, basically-democratic societies but where numbers of political prisoners exist or large segments of society are denied these rights; the third, societies where massive or total suppression of these rights exists. A more detailed analysis can be obtained by using column 11 in Global Table 31, which is similar to the Political Freedom Index but scaled up to 100%.

| Political freedom | | Countries | Christians | | | | World population | | | |
|---|---|---|---|---|---|---|---|---|---|---|
| Code | Description | | 1970 | 1975 | 1980 | % | 1970 | 1975 | 1980 | % |
| 1 | Free | 74 | 533,601,700 | 548,716,300 | 566,112,100 | 39.5 | 759,456,800 | 804,413,500 | 852,660,000 | 19.5 |
| 2 | Partially-free | 81 | 391,413,500 | 451,436,200 | 521,044,100 | 36.4 | 1,251,778,500 | 1,420,757,900 | 1,616,949,500 | 37.0 |
| 3 | Not free | 68 | 291,564,200 | 316,628,300 | 345,530,300 | 24.1 | 1,598,799,300 | 1,741,540,000 | 1,904,308,200 | 43.5 |
| **GLOBAL TOTALS** | | 223 | 1,216,579,400 | 1,316,780,800 | 1,432,686,500 | 100.0 | 3,610,034,600 | 3,966,711,400 | 4,373,917,700 | 100.0 |

Global Table 15.   WORLD POPULATION AND CHRISTIANS BY STATE ATTITUDE TO RELIGION, AD 1900-1980.

The table is based on data for every country in columns 18-21
in Global Table 31. See Codebook (Part 6) and Methodology
(Part 3) for derivation and exact meanings of codes.

| | Year | 1900 | | | mid-1970 | | | mid-1975 | | | mid-1980 | | |
|---|---|---|---|---|---|---|---|---|---|---|---|---|---|
| | | Adherents | % | Countries | Adherents | % | Countries | Adherents | % | Countries | Adherents | % | Countries |
| **1. GLOBAL CHRISTIANITY** | | | | | | | | | | | | | |
| *State religion or philosophy* | *Code* | | | | | | | | | | | | |
| Atheistic | A | 0 | 0.0 | 0 | 193,311,407 | 15.9 | 17 | 210,624,930 | 16.0 | 23 | 254,103,210 | 17.7 | 30 |
| Secular | S | 106,446,410 | 19.1 | 78 | 436,036,258 | 35.8 | 92 | 474,370,826 | 36.0 | 93 | 516,253,159 | 36.0 | 92 |
| Religious | R | 451,609,922 | 80.9 | 145 | 587,231,756 | 48.3 | 114 | 631,785,095 | 48.0 | 107 | 662,330,150 | 46.2 | 101 |
| Adventist | RD | 150 | 0.0 | 1 | 90 | 0.0 | 1 | 90 | 0.0 | 1 | 90 | 0.0 | 1 |
| Anglican | RA | 37,515,430 | 6.7 | 7 | 49,929,970 | 4.1 | 7 | 50,218,360 | 3.8 | 6 | 50,372,720 | 3.5 | 5 |
| Buddhist | RB | 459,969 | 0.1 | 7 | 1,513,998 | 0.1 | 6 | 1,624,050 | 0.1 | 4 | 1,812,360 | 0.1 | 4 |
| Confucian | RG | 1,735,600 | 0.3 | 4 | 0 | 0.0 | 0 | 0 | 0.0 | 0 | 0 | 0.0 | 0 |
| Hindu | RH | 0 | 0.0 | 1 | 4,010 | 0.0 | 1 | 4,760 | 0.0 | 1 | 5,570 | 0.0 | 1 |
| Islamic | RI | 6,981,055 | 1.3 | 28 | 11,022,926 | 0.9 | 25 | 11,620,135 | 0.9 | 23 | 13,693,150 | 1.0 | 23 |
| Jewish | RJ | 0 | 0.0 | 0 | 72,150 | 0.0 | 1 | 78,600 | 0.0 | 1 | 85,100 | 0.0 | 1 |
| Lutheran | RL | 9,827,450 | 1.8 | 7 | 14,915,700 | 1.2 | 7 | 15,137,520 | 1.1 | 7 | 15,325,660 | 1.1 | 7 |
| Methodist | RM | 20,000 | 0.0 | 1 | 84,870 | 0.0 | 1 | 99,570 | 0.0 | 1 | 117,270 | 0.0 | 1 |
| Orthodox | RO | 120,917,000 | 21.7 | 4 | 22,216,000 | 1.8 | 2 | 24,380,790 | 1.9 | 2 | 8,911,400 | 0.6 | 1 |
| Reformed | RR | 553,150 | 0.1 | 2 | 0 | 0.0 | 0 | 0 | 0.0 | 0 | 0 | 0.0 | 0 |
| Roman Catholic | RC | 104,056,990 | 18.6 | 36 | 198,435,509 | 16.3 | 31 | 202,426,990 | 15.4 | 27 | 218,137,060 | 15.2 | 25 |
| Shinto | RS | 430,000 | 0.0 | 1 | 0 | 0.0 | 0 | 0 | 0.0 | 0 | 0 | 0.0 | 0 |
| Tribal religionist | RT | 8,250 | 0.0 | 7 | 0 | 0.0 | 0 | 0 | 0.0 | 0 | 0 | 0.0 | 0 |
| Christian (unspecified) | RX | 2,777,600 | 0.5 | 3 | 5,050,520 | 0.4 | 3 | 5,163,100 | 0.4 | 3 | 5,399,370 | 0.4 | 4 |
| Religious (unspecified) | R | 166,327,278 | 29.8 | 36 | 283,986,013 | 23.3 | 29 | 321,031,130 | 24.4 | 31 | 348,470,400 | 24.3 | 28 |
| **GLOBAL CHRISTIANITY** | | 558,056,332 | 100.0 | 223 | 1,216,579,421 | 100.0 | 223 | 1,316,780,851 | 100.0 | 223 | 1,432,686,519 | 100.0 | 223 |
| **2. WORLD POPULATION** | | | | | | | | | | | | | |
| *State religion or philosophy* | *Code* | | | | | | | | | | | | |
| Atheistic | A | 0 | 0.0 | 0 | 1,156,793,000 | 32.0 | 17 | 1,272,727,000 | 32.1 | 23 | 1,488,355,500 | 34.0 | 30 |
| Secular | S | 437,137,100 | 27.0 | 78 | 1,320,514,700 | 36.6 | 92 | 1,538,450,600 | 38.8 | 93 | 1,578,619,700 | 36.1 | 92 |
| Religious | R | 1,182,749,900 | 73.0 | 145 | 1,132,726,900 | 31.4 | 114 | 1,155,533,800 | 29.1 | 107 | 1,306,942,500 | 29.9 | 101 |
| Adventist | RD | 200 | 0.0 | 1 | 100 | 0.0 | 1 | 100 | 0.0 | 1 | 100 | 0.0 | 1 |
| Anglican | RA | 38,492,800 | 2.4 | 7 | 56,132,500 | 1.6 | 7 | 57,068,700 | 1.4 | 6 | 57,948,900 | 1.3 | 5 |
| Buddhist | RB | 14,497,500 | 0.9 | 7 | 59,556,000 | 1.6 | 6 | 57,502,000 | 1.4 | 4 | 66,535,000 | 1.5 | 4 |
| Confucian | RG | 486,900,000 | 30.1 | 4 | 0 | 0.0 | 0 | 0 | 0.0 | 0 | 0 | 0.0 | 0 |
| Hindu | RH | 4,430,000 | 0.3 | 1 | 11,232,000 | 0.3 | 1 | 12,572,000 | 0.3 | 1 | 14,231,000 | 0.3 | 1 |
| Islamic | RI | 71,691,000 | 4.4 | 28 | 306,480,000 | 8.5 | 25 | 269,055,000 | 6.8 | 23 | 375,980,000 | 8.6 | 23 |
| Jewish | RJ | 0 | 0.0 | 0 | 2,921,000 | 0.1 | 1 | 3,373,000 | 0.1 | 1 | 3,847,000 | 0.1 | 1 |
| Lutheran | RL | 9,911,700 | 0.6 | 7 | 17,145,500 | 0.5 | 7 | 17,640,500 | 0.4 | 7 | 18,106,500 | 0.4 | 7 |
| Methodist | RM | 20,000 | 0.0 | 1 | 86,000 | 0.0 | 1 | 101,000 | 0.0 | 1 | 119,000 | 0.0 | 1 |
| Orthodox | RO | 147,706,000 | 9.1 | 4 | 33,648,000 | 0.9 | 2 | 36,905,000 | 0.9 | 2 | 9,080,000 | 0.2 | 1 |
| Reformed | RR | 38,920,000 | 2.4 | 2 | 0 | 0.0 | 0 | 0 | 0.0 | 0 | 0 | 0.0 | 0 |
| Roman Catholic | RC | 121,491,100 | 7.5 | 36 | 215,116,000 | 6.0 | 31 | 214,768,700 | 5.4 | 27 | 233,372,200 | 5.3 | 25 |
| Shinto | RS | 44,825,000 | 2.8 | 1 | 0 | 0.0 | 0 | 0 | 0.0 | 0 | 0 | 0.0 | 0 |
| Tribal religionist | RT | 6,650,000 | 0.4 | 7 | 0 | 0.0 | 0 | 0 | 0.0 | 0 | 0 | 0.0 | 0 |
| Christian (uspecified) | RX | 3,054,800 | 0.2 | 3 | 6,270,000 | 0.2 | 3 | 6,524,000 | 0.2 | 3 | 6,930,000 | 0.2 | 4 |
| Religious (unspecified) | R | 194,139,800 | 12.0 | 36 | 424,139,000 | 11.7 | 29 | 480,022,800 | 12.1 | 31 | 520,792,800 | 11.9 | 28 |
| **WORLD POPULATION** | | 1,619,887,000 | 100.0 | 223 | 3,610,034,600 | 100.0 | 223 | 3,966,711,400 | 100.0 | 223 | 4,373,917,700 | 100.0 | 223 |

Global Table 16.   WORLD POPULATION AND CHRISTIANS BY RELIGIOUS LIBERTY OR PERSECUTION, AD 1970-1980.

1. Data for individual countries may be seen tabulated in column
22 of Global Table 31. See Codebook and Methodology for
derivation and exact meanings of codes or stages.
2. Note the major change from 1975-1980 due to the People's
Republic of China moving from stage 10 below in 1975 to
stage 9 in 1980.

| | | | Christians | | | | World population | | | |
|---|---|---|---|---|---|---|---|---|---|---|
| | *Religious liberty* | Countries | 1970 | 1975 | 1980 | % | 1970 | 1975 | 1980 | % |
| Stage | Definition | | | | | | | | | |
| 1 | state propagates Christianity | 1 | 4,950 | 5,500 | 6,000 | 0.0 | 5,000 | 5,500 | 6,000 | 0.0 |
| 2 | massive state subsidies to churches | 36 | 179,304,900 | 187,237,605 | 196,025,370 | 13.7 | 188,644,500 | 198,511,000 | 208,751,500 | 4.8 |
| 3 | limited state subsidies to churches | 37 | 260,832,795 | 281,253,395 | 305,048,385 | 21.3 | 462,136,700 | 511,444,000 | 568,142,800 | 13.0 |
| 4 | state subsidizes schools only | 37 | 255,585,187 | 267,399,460 | 281,394,970 | 19.6 | 443,613,000 | 479,451,000 | 525,490,500 | 12.0 |
| 5 | complete state non-interference | 33 | 32,566,517 | 38,194,821 | 45,112,904 | 3.1 | 683,200,400 | 764,437,400 | 857,118,900 | 19.6 |
| 6 | limited political restrictions | 24 | 126,138,496 | 147,283,450 | 172,021,350 | 12.0 | 203,016,500 | 230,204,500 | 261,977,500 | 6.0 |
| 7 | minorities discriminated against | 18 | 163,509,885 | 184,444,190 | 208,632,340 | 14.6 | 215,207,500 | 243,988,000 | 277,391,500 | 6.3 |
| 8 | state interference and obstruction | 25 | 98,453,160 | 105,346,970 | 113,197,910 | 7.9 | 331,903,000 | 369,248,000 | 412,548,000 | 9.4 |
| 9 | state hostility and prohibition | 9 | 97,866,901 | 103,397,560 | 110,927,990 | 7.7 | 306,994,000 | 327,167,000 | 1,239,865,000 | 28.3 |
| 10 | state suppression or eradication | 3 | 2,316,630 | 2,217,900 | 319,300 | 0.0 | 775,314,000 | 842,255,000 | 22,626,000 | 0.5 |
| **GLOBAL TOTALS** | | 223 | 1,216,579,421 | 1,316,780,851 | 1,432,686,519 | 100.0 | 3,610,034,600 | 3,966,711,400 | 4,373,917,700 | 100.0 |

Global Table 17.  WORLD POPULATION, CHRISTIANS, AND FULL-TIME PERSONNEL, BY STATUS OF FOREIGN MISSIONS, AD 1970-1980.

The data for every country may be seen tabulated in column 23 of Global Table 31. See Codebook and Methodology for derivation and exact meanings of codes. Note in particular the

codes:
M = received missionaries and personnel received per million population;
S = foreign missionaries and personnel sent out per million population;
T = total national and foreign personnel per million population.

| Country's situation Code | Status | Definition M=received, S=sent | Countries | Full-time Christian personnel | | | | Ratios | | | Christians | | | | World population | | | |
|---|---|---|---|---|---|---|---|---|---|---|---|---|---|---|---|---|---|---|
| | | | | Nationals | Received Aliens | Total | Sent | T | M | S | 1970 | 1975 | 1980 | % | 1970 | 1975 | 1980 | % |
| 1 | closed | M<8,S<8 | 25 | 107,176 | 416 | 107,592 | 385 | 89 | 0.3 | 0.3 | 143,459,055 | 149,328,351 | 155,543,904 | 10.9 | 1,126,718,100 | 1,213,753,600 | 1,306,316,100 | 29.9 |
| 2 | partially-closed | 8<M<40 | 24 | 236,804 | 18,043 | 254,847 | 7,157 | 203 | 14 | 6 | 95,358,992 | 105,240,500 | 116,985,920 | 8.2 | 1,113,389,500 | 1,255,886,000 | 1,425,404,500 | 32.6 |
| 3 | restricted | 40<M<100,S<40 | 18 | 223,527 | 16,245 | 239,772 | 1,758 | 788 | 53 | 6 | 66,943,771 | 67,142,590 | 78,821,780 | 5.5 | 275,450,000 | 304,331,000 | 336,963,000 | 7.7 |
| 4 | receiving | M>100,S<40 | 99 | 289,879 | 89,177 | 379,056 | 7,160 | 913 | 215 | 17 | 252,898,360 | 296,595,510 | 347,398,275 | 24.2 | 361,261,500 | 415,119,700 | 478,311,200 | 10.9 |
| 5 | receiving/sending | M>S>40 | 35 | 143,189 | 55,324 | 198,513 | 13,345 | 1,000 | 279 | 67 | 158,273,993 | 179,629,540 | 204,472,530 | 14.3 | 175,009,500 | 198,557,100 | 226,064,900 | 5.2 |
| 6 | sending | S>M,100>M>40 | 10 | 852,725 | 19,860 | 872,585 | 102,112 | 3,174 | 72 | 371 | 241,622,250 | 248,435,470 | 256,418,080 | 17.9 | 263,567,000 | 274,878,000 | 287,521,000 | 6.6 |
| 7 | sharing | S>M>100 | 12 | 827,049 | 48,698 | 875,747 | 115,846 | 2,879 | 160 | 381 | 258,023,000 | 270,408,890 | 273,046,030 | 19.1 | 294,639,000 | 304,186,000 | 313,337,000 | 7.2 |
| | GLOBAL TOTALS | | 223 | 2,680,349 | 247,763 | 2,928,112 | 247,763 | 676 | 62 | 62 | 1,216,579,421 | 1,316,780,851 | 1,432,686,519 | 100.0 | 3,610,034,600 | 3,966,711,400 | 4,373,917,700 | 100.0 |

Global Table 18.  CHRISTIANS ON 8 CONTINENTS AND IN 24 REGIONS, AD 1900-2000.

This table is an expanded version of Global Table 2 in Part 1, setting out, as variables, continents and regions as standardized by the United Nations, in the numerical order assigned to regions by the UN. The table is derived from the 223 Tables 1 presented in Part 7 for all countries. The term 'Christians' here means the grand total of all kinds of Christians (professing plus crypto-Christians, nominal plus affiliated Christians of all ecclesiastical traditions).

| Continent / Region Code Name | 1900 Adherents | % | mid-1970 Adherents | % | Annual change, 1970–1985 Natural | Conversion | Total | Rate | mid-1975 Adherents | % | mid-1980 Adherents | % | mid-1985 Adherents | % | 2000 Adherents | % | Countries (in 1980) |
|---|---|---|---|---|---|---|---|---|---|---|---|---|---|---|---|---|---|
| EAST ASIA | 2,179,350 | 0.4 | 12,668,243 | 1.0 | 276,181 | 359,622 | 635,803 | 4.04 | 15,727,850 | 1.2 | 19,026,270 | 1.3 | 22,324,690 | 1.4 | 32,337,300 | 1.6 | 8 |
| 1 China | 1,679,000 | 0.3 | 2,943,000 | 0.2 | 54,547 | -40,033 | 14,514 | 0.48 | 3,009,460 | 0.2 | 3,088,140 | 0.2 | 3,166,820 | 0.2 | 3,991,200 | 0.2 | 2 |
| 2 Japan | 430,000 | 0.1 | 3,100,000 | 0.3 | 39,645 | 2,995 | 42,640 | 1.28 | 3,333,600 | 0.3 | 3,526,400 | 0.2 | 3,719,200 | 0.2 | 5,317,000 | 0.3 | 1 |
| 3 Other East Asia | 70,350 | 0.0 | 6,625,243 | 0.5 | 181,989 | 396,660 | 578,649 | 6.17 | 9,384,790 | 0.7 | 12,411,730 | 0.9 | 15,438,670 | 1.0 | 23,029,100 | 1.1 | 5 |
| SOUTH ASIA | 16,920,469 | 3.0 | 78,124,616 | 6.4 | 2,645,668 | 447,043 | 3,092,711 | 3.35 | 92,188,835 | 7.0 | 109,051,740 | 7.6 | 125,914,645 | 8.1 | 192,264,050 | 9.5 | 37 |
| 4 Middle South Asia | 4,441,909 | 0.8 | 21,906,781 | 1.8 | 689,973 | 183,629 | 873,602 | 3.39 | 25,807,815 | 2.0 | 30,642,800 | 2.1 | 35,477,785 | 2.3 | 56,031,830 | 2.8 | 10 |
| 5 Eastern South Asia | 8,386,110 | 1.5 | 52,607,682 | 4.3 | 1,862,378 | 265,950 | 2,128,328 | 3.41 | 62,354,370 | 4.7 | 73,890,970 | 5.2 | 85,427,570 | 5.5 | 129,376,220 | 6.4 | 11 |
| 6 Western South Asia | 4,092,450 | 0.7 | 3,610,153 | 0.3 | 93,317 | -2,536 | 90,781 | 2.25 | 4,026,650 | 0.3 | 4,517,970 | 0.3 | 5,009,290 | 0.3 | 6,856,000 | 0.3 | 16 |
| EUROPE | 278,383,690 | 49.9 | 405,132,656 | 33.3 | 2,197,458 | -1,150,645 | 1,046,813 | 0.26 | 410,275,220 | 31.2 | 415,600,780 | 29.0 | 420,926,340 | 27.2 | 431,403,570 | 21.4 | 37 |
| 7 Western Europe | 91,057,820 | 16.3 | 134,722,030 | 11.1 | 557,688 | -309,455 | 248,233 | 0.18 | 136,032,335 | 10.3 | 137,204,360 | 9.6 | 138,376,385 | 8.9 | 135,886,390 | 6.7 | 9 |
| 8 Southern Europe | 68,466,060 | 12.3 | 114,430,314 | 9.4 | 780,849 | -493,754 | 287,095 | 0.25 | 115,771,205 | 8.8 | 117,301,260 | 8.2 | 118,831,315 | 7.7 | 125,015,110 | 6.2 | 11 |
| 9 Eastern Europe | 65,859,120 | 11.8 | 84,266,562 | 6.9 | 567,131 | -195,947 | 371,184 | 0.43 | 86,056,400 | 6.5 | 87,978,400 | 6.1 | 89,900,400 | 5.8 | 95,283,200 | 4.7 | 6 |
| 10 Northern Europe | 53,000,690 | 9.5 | 71,713,750 | 5.9 | 291,790 | -151,489 | 140,301 | 0.19 | 72,415,280 | 5.5 | 73,116,760 | 5.1 | 73,818,240 | 4.8 | 75,218,870 | 3.7 | 11 |
| USSR | 104,993,000 | 18.8 | 86,012,300 | 7.1 | 907,238 | 164,182 | 1,071,420 | 1.17 | 91,285,000 | 6.9 | 96,726,500 | 6.8 | 102,168,000 | 6.6 | 118,101,000 | 5.8 | 1 |
| 11 USSR | 104,993,000 | 18.8 | 86,012,300 | 7.1 | 907,238 | 164,182 | 1,071,420 | 1.17 | 91,285,000 | 6.9 | 96,726,500 | 6.8 | 102,168,000 | 6.6 | 118,101,000 | 5.8 | 1 |
| AFRICA | 9,938,448 | 1.8 | 142,962,732 | 11.8 | 4,586,648 | 1,466,149 | 6,052,797 | 3.55 | 170,702,570 | 13.0 | 203,490,710 | 14.2 | 236,278,850 | 15.3 | 393,326,210 | 19.5 | 59 |
| 12 Western Africa | 472,323 | 0.1 | 33,530,758 | 2.8 | 1,117,502 | 430,231 | 1,547,733 | 3.82 | 40,548,990 | 3.1 | 49,008,290 | 3.4 | 57,467,510 | 3.7 | 97,970,670 | 4.9 | 17 |
| 13 Eastern Africa | 4,515,830 | 0.8 | 51,793,301 | 4.3 | 1,797,000 | 708,818 | 2,505,818 | 3.96 | 63,245,450 | 4.8 | 76,851,480 | 5.4 | 90,457,510 | 5.8 | 157,217,180 | 7.8 | 19 |
| 14 Middle Africa | 193,350 | 0.0 | 31,128,507 | 2.6 | 882,004 | 236,816 | 1,118,820 | 3.08 | 36,374,710 | 2.8 | 42,316,510 | 3.0 | 48,259,230 | 3.1 | 76,577,820 | 3.8 | 9 |
| 15 Northern Africa | 2,700,645 | 0.5 | 7,865,066 | 0.6 | 184,607 | 23,043 | 207,650 | 2.34 | 8,861,710 | 0.7 | 9,941,570 | 0.7 | 11,021,430 | 0.7 | 15,901,600 | 0.8 | 8 |
| 16 Southern Africa | 2,056,300 | 0.4 | 18,645,100 | 1.5 | 605,535 | 67,241 | 672,776 | 3.10 | 21,671,710 | 1.6 | 25,372,860 | 1.8 | 29,073,490 | 1.9 | 45,658,940 | 2.3 | 6 |
| NORTHERN AMERICA | 78,811,810 | 14.1 | 206,443,460 | 17.0 | 2,008,880 | -669,881 | 1,338,999 | 0.63 | 212,429,330 | 16.1 | 219,833,450 | 15.3 | 227,237,570 | 14.7 | 253,589,450 | 12.6 | 5 |
| 17 Northern America | 78,811,810 | 14.1 | 206,443,460 | 17.0 | 2,008,880 | -669,881 | 1,338,999 | 0.63 | 212,429,330 | 16.1 | 219,833,450 | 15.3 | 227,237,570 | 14.7 | 253,589,450 | 12.6 | 5 |
| LATIN AMERICA | 62,002,115 | 11.1 | 267,383,563 | 22.0 | 8,419,292 | -291,821 | 8,127,471 | 2.66 | 305,111,950 | 23.2 | 348,658,275 | 24.3 | 392,204,600 | 25.3 | 571,157,820 | 28.3 | 47 |
| 18 Tropical South America | 29,948,800 | 5.4 | 148,910,080 | 12.2 | 4,982,383 | -153,764 | 4,828,619 | 2.82 | 171,377,910 | 13.0 | 197,196,270 | 13.8 | 223,014,630 | 14.4 | 325,949,650 | 16.1 | 10 |
| 19 Middle America (mainland) | 17,785,250 | 3.2 | 65,759,450 | 5.4 | 2,505,879 | -68,502 | 2,437,377 | 3.17 | 76,909,920 | 5.8 | 90,133,220 | 6.3 | 103,356,520 | 6.7 | 164,899,440 | 8.2 | 9 |
| 20 Temperate South America | 7,566,405 | 1.4 | 33,328,085 | 2.7 | 511,553 | -14,903 | 496,650 | 1.39 | 35,746,255 | 2.7 | 38,294,585 | 2.7 | 40,842,915 | 2.6 | 47,363,960 | 2.3 | 5 |
| 21 Caribbean | 6,701,660 | 1.2 | 19,385,948 | 1.6 | 419,477 | -54,652 | 364,825 | 1.73 | 21,077,865 | 1.6 | 23,034,200 | 1.6 | 24,990,535 | 1.6 | 32,944,770 | 1.6 | 23 |
| OCEANIA | 4,827,450 | 0.9 | 17,851,851 | 1.5 | 372,894 | -128,200 | 244,694 | 1.28 | 19,060,096 | 1.4 | 20,298,794 | 1.4 | 21,537,492 | 1.4 | 27,741,966 | 1.4 | 29 |
| 22 Australia & NZ | 4,442,430 | 0.8 | 14,349,930 | 1.2 | 270,327 | -135,117 | 135,210 | 0.90 | 15,045,890 | 1.1 | 15,702,030 | 1.1 | 16,358,170 | 1.1 | 20,201,190 | 1.0 | 2 |
| 23 Melanesia | 115,200 | 0.0 | 2,600,131 | 0.2 | 74,902 | 7,350 | 82,252 | 2.75 | 2,987,340 | 0.2 | 3,422,650 | 0.2 | 3,857,960 | 0.2 | 5,689,420 | 0.3 | 6 |
| 24 Micronesia & Polynesia | 269,820 | 0.0 | 901,790 | 0.1 | 27,665 | -433 | 27,232 | 2.65 | 1,026,866 | 0.1 | 1,174,114 | 0.1 | 1,321,362 | 0.1 | 1,851,356 | 0.1 | 21 |
| POLITICAL ALIGNMENT | | | | | | | | | | | | | | | | | |
| Western world | 470,991,120 | 84.4 | 526,141,240 | 43.2 | 3,761,782 | -1,706,852 | 2,054,930 | 0.38 | 535,703,030 | 40.7 | 546,690,540 | 38.2 | 557,678,050 | 36.0 | 592,155,430 | 29.3 | 35 |
| Communist world | 0 | 0.0 | 195,172,881 | 16.0 | 1,784,400 | 4,108,633 | 5,893,033 | 2.90 | 202,902,300 | 15.4 | 254,103,210 | 17.7 | 305,304,120 | 19.7 | 443,861,700 | 22.0 | 30 |
| Third World | 87,065,212 | 15.6 | 495,265,300 | 40.7 | 15,868,077 | -2,205,332 | 13,662,745 | 2.36 | 578,175,521 | 43.9 | 631,892,769 | 44.1 | 685,610,017 | 44.3 | 983,904,236 | 48.7 | 158 |
| DEVELOPMENT | | | | | | | | | | | | | | | | | |
| More developed world | 474,627,335 | 85.0 | 748,366,431 | 61.5 | 5,935,101 | -1,803,369 | 4,131,732 | 0.54 | 768,115,295 | 58.3 | 789,683,745 | 55.1 | 811,252,195 | 52.4 | 875,976,170 | 43.4 | 51 |
| Less developed world | 83,428,997 | 14.9 | 468,212,990 | 38.5 | 15,479,158 | 1,999,818 | 17,478,976 | 3.19 | 548,665,556 | 41.7 | 643,002,774 | 44.9 | 737,339,992 | 47.6 | 1,143,945,196 | 56.6 | 172 |
| GLOBAL CHRISTIANITY | 558,056,332 | 100.0 | 1,216,579,421 | 100.0 | 21,414,259 | 196,449 | 21,610,708 | 1.64 | 1,316,780,851 | 100.0 | 1,432,686,519 | 100.0 | 1,548,592,187 | 100.0 | 2,019,921,366 | 100.0 | 223 |

Global Table 19. WORLD POPULATION RANKED BY THE WORLD'S 76 OFFICIAL STATE LANGUAGES, AD 1980.

Global Table 20. CHRISTIANS RANKED BY THE WORLD'S 76 OFFICIAL STATE LANGUAGES, AD 1980.

1. The table gives the totals in 1980, ranked by magnitude, of all populations of countries for whom the languages shown are their official state languages (including official national languages) throughout their country. Data for individual countries are given, coded, in column 14 of Global Table 31. The full codes are given in the Codebook (Part 6).
2. Note that the table contains 1.2 billion duplications; several countries have 2, 3 or even 4 country-wide official languages, hence many populations have more than one official state language.

1. The table gives the totals ranked by magnitude, of total Christians in 1980 in countries for whom the languages shown are their official state languages (including official national languages) throughout their country.
2. Note that the table contains 307 million duplications, i.e. Christians who have more than one official state language.

| Language | | | | | Language | | | |
|---|---|---|---|---|---|---|---|---|
| Rank | Code | Name | Population | | Rank | Code | Name | Christians |
| 1 | E | English | 1,437,179,965 | | 1 | E | English | 515,851,490 |
| 2 | C | Chinese | 914,247,000 | | 2 | S | Spanish | 255,472,480 |
| 3 | H | Hindi | 694,309,000 | | 3 | F | French | 141,679,230 |
| 4 | R | Russian | 268,115,000 | | 4 | P | Portuguese | 138,388,910 |
| 5 | S | Spanish | 267,770,200 | | 5 | R | Russian | 96,726,500 |
| 6 | F | French | 207,944,670 | | 6 | G | German | 91,647,050 |
| 7 | A | Arabic | 169,688,000 | | 7 | I | Italian | 53,683,500 |
| 8 | P | Portuguese | 154,930,000 | | 8 | O | Filipino | 49,201,700 |
| 9 | X | Indonesian | 154,869,000 | | 9 | Y | Polish | 31,935,700 |
| 10 | J | Japanese | 117,546,000 | | 10 | H | Hindi | 27,078,000 |
| 11 | G | German | 103,827,200 | | 11 | M | Afrikaans | 23,364,050 |
| 12 | B | Bengali | 84,803,000 | | 12 | D | Dutch | 21,853,970 |
| 13 | U | Urdu | 82,952,000 | | 13 | S′ | Swahili | 19,395,200 |
| 14 | I | Italian | 63,074,000 | | 14 | R′ | Romanian | 18,172,600 |
| 15 | N | Persian | 60,530,000 | | 15 | L | Amharic | 17,967,000 |
| 16 | K | Korean | 55,370,000 | | 16 | q | Quechua | 17,364,000 |
| 17 | O | Filipino | 52,203,000 | | 17 | X | Indonesian | 17,363,700 |
| 18 | Z | Thai | 49,473,000 | | 18 | Q | Serbo-Croatian | 16,254,600 |
| 19 | V | Vietnamese | 48,634,000 | | 19 | M′ | Macedonian | 16,254,600 |
| 20 | T | Turkish | 46,077,000 | | 20 | W′ | Slovenian | 16,254,600 |
| 21 | Y | Polish | 35,316,000 | | 21 | A | Arabic | 13,484,870 |
| 22 | W | Burmese | 35,195,000 | | 22 | c | Czech | 12,098,800 |
| 23 | S′ | Swahili | 33,740,000 | | 23 | u′ | Slovak | 12,098,800 |
| 24 | L | Amharic | 31,522,000 | | 24 | K | Korean | 11,571,700 |
| 25 | M | Afrikaans | 29,328,000 | | 25 | s | Swedish | 10,484,500 |
| 26 | D | Dutch | 24,926,000 | | 26 | g | Greek | 9,476,370 |
| 27 | Q | Serbo-Croatian | 22,299,000 | | 27 | h | Hungarian | 8,919,600 |
| 28 | M′ | Macedonian | 22,299,000 | | 28 | r | Romansh | 6,559,000 |
| 29 | W′ | Slovenian | 22,299,000 | | 29 | b | Bulgarian | 5,853,300 |
| 30 | R′ | Romanian | 22,057,000 | | 30 | d | Danish | 4,957,200 |
| 31 | P′ | Pushtu | 22,038,000 | | 31 | m | Malagasy | 4,757,900 |
| 32 | q | Quechua | 17,711,000 | | 32 | f | Finnish | 4,425,500 |
| 33 | m′ | Malay | 16,595,000 | | 33 | C | Chinese | 4,097,170 |
| 34 | u | Sinhala | 15,465,000 | | 34 | j | Norwegian | 4,045,680 |
| 35 | c | Czech | 15,189,000 | | 35 | y | Rundi | 3,666,000 |
| 36 | u′ | Slovak | 15,189,000 | | 36 | V | Vietnamese | 3,627,000 |
| 37 | n | Nepali | 14,231,000 | | 37 | c′ | Chewa | 3,597,000 |
| 38 | s | Swedish | 13,234,000 | | 38 | r′ | Ruanda | 3,551,000 |
| 39 | h | Hungarian | 10,721,000 | | 39 | J | Japanese | 3,526,400 |
| 40 | g | Greek | 9,794,000 | | 40 | j | Irish | 3,280,700 |
| 41 | k | Khmer | 9,409,000 | | 41 | g′ | Guarani | 3,011,300 |
| 42 | m | Malagasy | 9,329,000 | | 42 | p | Pijin | 2,879,420 |
| 43 | b | Bulgarian | 9,075,000 | | 43 | W | Burmese | 1,970,900 |
| 44 | r | Romansh | 6,734,000 | | 44 | x | Sango | 1,693,400 |
| 45 | c′ | Chewa | 5,577,000 | | 45 | U | Urdu | 1,475,500 |
| 46 | d | Danish | 5,166,000 | | 46 | u | Sinhala | 1,283,600 |
| 47 | r′ | Ruanda | 4,865,000 | | 47 | w | Sotho | 1,191,500 |
| 48 | f | Finnish | 4,688,000 | | 48 | m′ | Malay | 1,083,270 |
| 49 | y | Rundi | 4,288,000 | | 49 | T | Turkish | 809,070 |
| 50 | j | Norwegian | 4,124,500 | | 50 | Z | Thai | 521,400 |
| 51 | e | Hebrew | 3,847,000 | | 51 | B | Bengali | 449,960 |
| 52 | l | Lao | 3,721,000 | | 52 | ö | Swazi | 418,110 |
| 53 | v | Somali | 3,652,000 | | 53 | ü | Tswana | 399,100 |
| 54 | i | Irish | 3,298,000 | | 54 | N | Persian | 342,640 |
| 55 | g′ | Guaraní | 3,062,000 | | 55 | ï | Maltese | 331,510 |
| 56 | p | Pijin | 2,980,500 | | 56 | ë | Luxemburgish | 325,670 |
| 57 | a | Albanian | 2,831,000 | | 57 | 5 | Icelandic | 222,830 |
| 58 | t | Tamil | 2,437,000 | | 58 | t | Tamil | 208,630 |
| 59 | x | Sango | 2,004,000 | | 59 | 8 | Samoan | 190,700 |
| 60 | o | Mongolian | 1,869,000 | | 60 | a | Albanian | 154,100 |
| 61 | z | Dzongkha | 1,327,000 | | 61 | 9 | Tongan | 117,270 |
| 62 | w | Sotho | 1,284,000 | | 62 | 1 | Bislama | 105,170 |
| 63 | ü | Tswana | 795,000 | | 63 | e | Hebrew | 85,100 |
| 64 | ö | Swazi | 543,000 | | 64 | l | Lao | 67,000 |
| 65 | ë | Luxemburgish | 345,000 | | 65 | 4 | Greenlandic | 61,200 |
| 66 | ï | Maltese | 335,000 | | 66 | k | Khmer | 56,000 |
| 67 | ä | Comorian | 298,500 | | 67 | 3 | Faeroese | 40,950 |
| 68 | 5 | Icelandic | 229,000 | | 68 | 2 | Catalan | 24,910 |
| 69 | 8 | Samoan | 194,000 | | 69 | P′ | Pushtu | 9,340 |
| 70 | 7 | Maldivian | 132,000 | | 70 | 6 | Latin | 6,000 |
| 71 | 9 | Tongan | 119,000 | | 71 | n | Nepali | 5,570 |
| 72 | 1 | Bislama | 111,000 | | 72 | o | Mongolian | 3,300 |
| 73 | 4 | Greenlandic | 62,000 | | 73 | v | Somali | 2,270 |
| 74 | 3 | Faeroese | 41,000 | | 74 | z | Dzongkha | 850 |
| 75 | 2 | Catalan | 25,000 | | 75 | ä | Comorian | 550 |
| 76 | 6 | Latin | 6,000 | | 76 | 7 | Maldivian | 170 |
| | Duplications | | −1,187,576,000 | | | Duplications | | −306,849,110 |
| | WORLD POPULATION | | 4,373,917,535 | | | GLOBAL CHRISTIANITY | | 1,432,686,520 |

Global Table 21. URBAN AND RURAL CHRISTIANS AND POPULATIONS ON 8 CONTINENTS, AD 1900-2000.

1. The table gives statistics of urban and rural dwellers, using United Nations' definitions of urbanized populations.
2. All percentages in this table are %s of the relevant continent's total population, except the last 6 lines which give percentages of the world population; and except for the column 'Rate' which gives annual increase.
3. Annual change is here divided into (a) natural increase (births minus deaths), (b) conversion increase (nett converts minus nett defections), and (c) transfer increase (nett immigration from rural areas to urban areas).
4. 'Rate' gives the rate of increase as percent per year.
5. The last column 'Cities' gives the number of cities in 1975 with over 100,000 population, and also over 1 million population.

| | 1900 | | mid-1970 | | Annual change, 1970–1985 | | | | | mid-1975 | | mid-1980 | | mid-1985 | | 2000 | | Cities, 1975 | |
|---|---|---|---|---|---|---|---|---|---|---|---|---|---|---|---|---|---|---|---|
| | *Adherents* | % | *Adherents* | % | *Natural* | *Conversion* | *Transfer* | *Total* | *Rate* | *Adherents* | % | *Adherents* | % | *Adherents* | % | *Adherents* | % | Over *100,000* | Over *1 million* |
| AFRICA | | | | | | | | | | | | | | | | | | 145 | 10 |
| Population | 107,854,260 | 100.0 | 351,800,770 | 100.0 | 10,905,648 | 0 | 0 | 10,905,648 | 2.72 | 401,322,860 | 100.0 | 460,857,250 | 100.0 | 520,381,640 | 100.0 | 813,390,700 | 100.0 | | |
| Urban population | 4,314,170 | 4.0 | 77,135,000 | 21.9 | 2,651,270 | 0 | 1,940,030 | 4,591,300 | 4.71 | 97,568,000 | 24.3 | 123,048,000 | 26.7 | 151,431,000 | 29.1 | 317,222,400 | 39.0 | | |
| Rural population | 103,540,090 | 96.0 | 274,665,770 | 78.1 | 8,254,378 | 0 | −1,940,030 | 6,314,348 | 2.08 | 303,764,860 | 75.7 | 337,809,250 | 73.3 | 368,950,640 | 70.9 | 496,168,300 | 61.0 | | |
| Christians | 9,938,448 | 9.2 | 142,962,732 | 40.6 | 4,586,648 | 1,466,149 | 0 | 6,052,797 | 3.55 | 170,702,570 | 42.5 | 203,490,710 | 44.2 | 236,278,850 | 45.4 | 393,326,210 | 48.4 | | |
| Urban Christians | 3,459,000 | 3.2 | 44,403,000 | 12.6 | 1,609,436 | 514,466 | 1,295,798 | 3,419,700 | 5.71 | 59,899,000 | 14.9 | 78,600,000 | 17.1 | 97,301,000 | 18.7 | 195,214,000 | 24.0 | | |
| Rural Christians | 6,479,448 | 6.0 | 98,559,732 | 28.0 | 2,977,212 | 951,683 | −1,295,798 | 2,633,097 | 2.38 | 110,803,570 | 27.6 | 124,890,710 | 27.1 | 138,977,850 | 26.7 | 198,112,210 | 24.4 | | |
| EAST ASIA | | | | | | | | | | | | | | | | | | 393 | 37 |
| Population | 532,691,000 | 100.0 | 926,422,000 | 100.0 | 16,046,500 | 0 | 0 | 16,046,500 | 1.60 | 1,004,979,000 | 100.0 | 1,086,887,000 | 100.0 | 1,168,795,000 | 100.0 | 1,373,242,000 | 100.0 | | |
| Urban population | 31,961,500 | 6.0 | 263,972,000 | 28.5 | 4,917,565 | 0 | 4,226,435 | 9,144,000 | 2.97 | 307,983,000 | 30.6 | 355,412,000 | 32.7 | 406,741,000 | 34.8 | 576,761,600 | 42.0 | | |
| Rural population | 500,729,500 | 94.0 | 662,450,000 | 71.5 | 11,128,935 | 0 | −4,226,435 | 6,902,500 | 0.99 | 696,996,000 | 69.4 | 731,475,000 | 67.3 | 762,054,000 | 65.2 | 796,480,400 | 58.0 | | |
| Christians | 2,179,350 | 0.4 | 12,668,243 | 1.4 | 276,181 | 359,622 | 0 | 635,803 | 4.04 | 15,727,850 | 1.6 | 19,026,270 | 1.8 | 22,324,690 | 1.9 | 32,337,300 | 2.4 | | |
| Urban Christians | 480,000 | 0.1 | 4,560,000 | 0.5 | 119,930 | 156,170 | 149,900 | 426,000 | 6.24 | 6,830,000 | 0.7 | 8,820,000 | 0.8 | 11,410,000 | 1.0 | 20,170,000 | 1.5 | | |
| Rural Christians | 1,699,350 | 0.3 | 8,108,243 | 0.9 | 156,251 | 203,452 | −149,900 | 209,803 | 2.36 | 8,897,850 | 0.9 | 10,206,270 | 0.9 | 10,914,690 | 0.9 | 12,167,300 | 0.9 | | |
| EUROPE | | | | | | | | | | | | | | | | | | 406 | 38 |
| Population | 287,296,400 | 100.0 | 458,928,650 | 100.0 | 2,750,705 | 0 | 0 | 2,750,705 | 0.58 | 472,961,700 | 100.0 | 486,435,700 | 100.0 | 499,909,700 | 100.0 | 539,536,500 | 100.0 | | |
| Urban population | 109,172,600 | 38.0 | 303,053,000 | 66.0 | 1,885,687 | 0 | 2,345,913 | 4,231,600 | 1.31 | 324,229,000 | 68.5 | 345,369,000 | 71.0 | 367,434,000 | 73.5 | 415,443,100 | 77.0 | | |
| Rural population | 178,123,800 | 62.0 | 155,875,650 | 34.0 | 865,018 | 0 | −2,345,913 | −1,480,895 | −1.00 | 148,732,700 | 31.4 | 141,066,700 | 29.0 | 132,475,700 | 26.5 | 124,093,400 | 23.0 | | |
| Christians | 278,383,690 | 96.9 | 405,132,656 | 88.3 | 2,197,458 | −1,150,645 | 0 | 1,046,813 | 0.26 | 410,275,220 | 86.7 | 415,600,780 | 85.4 | 420,926,340 | 84.2 | 431,403,570 | 80.0 | | |
| Urban Christians | 101,740,000 | 35.4 | 255,100,000 | 55.6 | 1,421,134 | −744,142 | 1,346,308 | 2,023,300 | 0.76 | 265,332,000 | 56.1 | 275,333,000 | 56.6 | 289,526,000 | 57.9 | 308,300,000 | 57.1 | | |
| Rural Christians | 176,643,690 | 61.5 | 150,032,656 | 32.7 | 776,324 | −406,503 | −1,346,308 | −976,487 | −0.67 | 144,943,220 | 30.6 | 140,267,780 | 28.8 | 131,400,340 | 26.3 | 123,103,570 | 22.8 | | |
| LATIN AMERICA | | | | | | | | | | | | | | | | | | 202 | 21 |
| Population | 65,178,290 | 100.0 | 283,028,975 | 100.0 | 8,861,170 | 0 | 0 | 8,861,170 | 2.73 | 324,099,575 | 100.0 | 371,640,675 | 100.0 | 419,181,775 | 100.0 | 619,934,100 | 100.0 | | |
| Urban population | 8,473,200 | 13.0 | 160,647,000 | 56.8 | 5,345,935 | 0 | 2,300,065 | 7,646,000 | 3.91 | 195,529,000 | 60.3 | 237,107,000 | 63.8 | 282,109,000 | 67.3 | 514,545,300 | 83.0 | | |
| Rural population | 56,705,090 | 87.0 | 122,381,975 | 43.2 | 3,515,235 | 0 | −2,300,065 | 1,215,170 | 0.95 | 128,570,575 | 39.7 | 134,533,675 | 36.2 | 137,072,775 | 32.7 | 105,388,800 | 17.0 | | |
| Christians | 62,002,115 | 95.1 | 267,383,563 | 94.5 | 8,419,292 | −291,821 | 0 | 8,127,471 | 2.66 | 305,111,950 | 94.1 | 348,658,275 | 93.8 | 392,204,600 | 93.6 | 571,157,820 | 92.1 | | |
| Urban Christians | 7,400,000 | 11.4 | 148,500,000 | 52.5 | 4,963,489 | −172,039 | 2,099,550 | 6,891,000 | 3.83 | 179,875,000 | 55.5 | 217,410,000 | 58.5 | 257,797,000 | 61.5 | 471,120,000 | 76.0 | | |
| Rural Christians | 54,602,115 | 83.8 | 118,883,563 | 42.0 | 3,455,803 | −119,782 | −2,099,550 | 1,236,471 | 0.99 | 125,236,950 | 38.6 | 131,248,275 | 35.3 | 134,407,600 | 32.1 | 100,037,820 | 16.1 | | |
| NORTHERN AMERICA | | | | | | | | | | | | | | | | | | 194 | 30 |
| Population | 81,625,760 | 100.0 | 226,392,500 | 100.0 | 2,244,400 | 0 | 0 | 2,244,400 | 0.95 | 236,844,500 | 100.0 | 248,836,500 | 100.0 | 260,828,500 | 100.0 | 296,203,000 | 100.0 | | |
| Urban population | 35,915,330 | 44.0 | 167,872,000 | 74.2 | 1,717,635 | 0 | 1,103,465 | 2,821,100 | 1.56 | 181,257,000 | 76.5 | 196,083,000 | 78.8 | 211,271,000 | 81.0 | 254,734,600 | 86.0 | | |
| Rural population | 45,710,430 | 56.0 | 58,520,500 | 25.8 | 526,765 | 0 | −1,103,465 | −576,700 | −1.04 | 55,587,500 | 23.5 | 52,753,500 | 21.2 | 49,557,500 | 19.0 | 41,468,400 | 14.0 | | |
| Christians | 78,811,810 | 96.6 | 206,443,460 | 91.2 | 2,008,880 | −669,881 | 0 | 1,338,999 | 0.63 | 212,429,330 | 89.7 | 219,833,450 | 88.3 | 227,237,570 | 87.1 | 253,589,450 | 85.6 | | |
| Urban Christians | 33,700,000 | 41.3 | 150,843,000 | 66.7 | 1,527,524 | −509,368 | 1,241,444 | 2,259,600 | 1.40 | 161,528,000 | 68.2 | 173,439,000 | 69.7 | 185,710,000 | 71.2 | 213,089,450 | 71.9 | | |
| Rural Christians | 45,111,810 | 55.3 | 55,600,460 | 24.6 | 481,356 | −160,513 | −1,241,444 | −920,601 | −1.81 | 50,901,330 | 21.5 | 46,394,450 | 18.6 | 41,527,570 | 15.9 | 40,500,000 | 13.7 | | |
| OCEANIA | | | | | | | | | | | | | | | | | | 17 | 2 |
| Population | 6,223,400 | 100.0 | 19,323,510 | 100.0 | 415,890 | 0 | 0 | 415,890 | 1.95 | 21,307,460 | 100.0 | 23,482,410 | 100.0 | 25,657,360 | 100.0 | 32,714,700 | 100.0 | | |
| Urban population | 2,613,830 | 42.0 | 13,561,000 | 70.2 | 298,308 | 0 | 66,892 | 365,200 | 2.39 | 15,283,000 | 71.7 | 17,213,000 | 73.3 | 19,217,000 | 74.9 | 25,844,600 | 79.0 | | |
| Rural population | 3,609,570 | 58.0 | 5,762,510 | 29.8 | 117,582 | 0 | −66,892 | 50,690 | 0.84 | 6,024,460 | 28.3 | 6,269,410 | 26.7 | 6,440,360 | 25.1 | 6,870,100 | 21.0 | | |
| Christians | 4,827,450 | 77.6 | 17,851,851 | 92.3 | 372,894 | −128,200 | 0 | 244,694 | 1.28 | 19,060,096 | 89.5 | 20,298,794 | 86.4 | 21,537,492 | 83.9 | 27,741,966 | 84.8 | | |
| Urban Christians | 2,030,000 | 32.6 | 12,451,000 | 64.4 | 261,378 | −89,861 | 8,183 | 179,700 | 1.35 | 13,360,000 | 62.7 | 14,248,000 | 60.7 | 15,337,000 | 59.8 | 21,241,966 | 64.9 | | |
| Rural Christians | 2,797,450 | 45.0 | 5,400,851 | 27.9 | 111,516 | −38,339 | −8,183 | 64,994 | 1.14 | 5,700,096 | 26.8 | 6,050,794 | 25.8 | 6,200,492 | 24.2 | 6,500,000 | 19.9 | | |
| SOUTH ASIA | | | | | | | | | | | | | | | | | | 363 | 31 |
| Population | 413,361,650 | 100.0 | 1,101,370,000 | 100.0 | 32,629,300 | 0 | 0 | 32,629,300 | 2.61 | 1,250,148,000 | 100.0 | 1,427,663,000 | 100.0 | 1,605,178,000 | 100.0 | 2,269,594,000 | 100.0 | | |
| Urban population | 28,935,310 | 7.0 | 230,254,000 | 20.9 | 7,402,500 | 0 | 4,549,800 | 11,952,300 | 4.21 | 283,616,000 | 22.7 | 349,777,000 | 24.5 | 422,163,000 | 26.3 | 794,357,900 | 35.0 | | |
| Rural population | 384,426,340 | 93.0 | 871,116,000 | 79.1 | 25,226,800 | 0 | −4,549,800 | 20,677,000 | 2.14 | 966,532,000 | 77.3 | 1,077,886,000 | 75.5 | 1,183,016,000 | 73.7 | 1,475,236,100 | 65.0 | | |
| Christians | 16,920,469 | 4.1 | 78,124,616 | 7.1 | 2,645,668 | 447,043 | 0 | 3,092,711 | 3.35 | 92,188,835 | 7.4 | 109,051,740 | 7.6 | 125,914,645 | 7.8 | 192,264,050 | 8.5 | | |
| Urban Christians | 2,370,000 | 0.6 | 23,400,000 | 2.1 | 932,810 | 157,618 | 995,372 | 2,085,800 | 6.42 | 32,504,000 | 2.6 | 44,258,000 | 3.1 | 57,786,000 | 3.6 | 107,670,000 | 4.7 | | |
| Rural Christians | 14,550,469 | 3.5 | 54,724,616 | 5.0 | 1,712,858 | 289,425 | −995,372 | 1,006,911 | 1.69 | 59,684,835 | 4.8 | 64,793,740 | 4.5 | 68,128,645 | 4.2 | 84,594,050 | 3.7 | | |
| USSR | | | | | | | | | | | | | | | | | | 249 | 12 |
| Population | 125,656,000 | 100.0 | 242,768,000 | 100.0 | 2,534,700 | 0 | 0 | 2,534,700 | 0.99 | 255,038,000 | 100.0 | 268,115,000 | 100.0 | 281,192,000 | 100.0 | 315,027,000 | 100.0 | | |
| Urban population | 11,309,000 | 9.0 | 137,743,000 | 56.7 | 1,538,920 | 0 | 2,033,780 | 3,572,700 | 2.31 | 154,844,000 | 60.7 | 173,470,000 | 64.7 | 193,179,000 | 68.7 | 261,472,400 | 83.0 | | |
| Rural population | 114,347,000 | 91.0 | 105,025,000 | 43.3 | 995,780 | 0 | −2,033,780 | −1,038,000 | −1.04 | 100,194,000 | 39.3 | 94,645,000 | 35.3 | 88,013,000 | 31.3 | 53,554,600 | 17.0 | | |
| Christians | 104,993,000 | 83.6 | 86,012,300 | 35.4 | 907,238 | 164,182 | 0 | 1,071,420 | 1.17 | 91,285,000 | 35.8 | 96,726,500 | 36.1 | 102,168,000 | 36.3 | 118,101,000 | 37.5 | | |
| Urban Christians | 8,450,000 | 6.7 | 21,500,000 | 8.9 | 266,352 | 48,202 | 779,646 | 1,094,200 | 4.08 | 26,800,000 | 10.5 | 32,442,000 | 12.1 | 38,523,000 | 13.7 | 68,100,000 | 21.6 | | |
| Rural Christians | 96,543,000 | 76.8 | 64,512,300 | 26.6 | 640,886 | 115,980 | −779,646 | −22,780 | −0.04 | 64,485,000 | 25.3 | 64,284,500 | 24.0 | 63,645,000 | 22.6 | 50,001,000 | 15.9 | | |
| WORLD | | | | | | | | | | | | | | | | | | 1,969 | 181 |
| Population | 1,619,886,760 | 100.0 | 3,610,034,405 | 100.0 | 76,388,313 | 0 | 0 | 76,388,313 | 1.93 | 3,966,711,095 | 100.0 | 4,373,917,535 | 100.0 | 4,781,123,975 | 100.0 | 6,259,642,000 | 100.0 | | |
| Urban population | 232,694,940 | 14.4 | 1,354,237,000 | 37.5 | 25,757,820 | 0 | 18,566,380 | 44,324,200 | 2.84 | 1,560,309,000 | 39.3 | 1,797,479,000 | 41.1 | 2,053,544,000 | 42.9 | 3,160,381,900 | 50.5 | | |
| Rural population | 1,387,191,820 | 85.6 | 2,255,797,405 | 62.5 | 50,630,493 | 0 | −18,566,380 | 32,064,113 | 1.33 | 2,406,402,095 | 60.7 | 2,576,438,535 | 58.9 | 2,727,579,975 | 57.0 | 3,099,260,100 | 49.5 | | |
| Christians | 558,056,332 | 34.4 | 1,216,579,421 | 33.7 | 21,414,259 | 196,449 | 0 | 21,610,708 | 1.64 | 1,316,780,851 | 33.2 | 1,432,686,519 | 32.8 | 1,548,592,187 | 32.4 | 2,019,921,366 | 32.3 | | |
| Urban Christians | 159,629,000 | 9.9 | 660,757,000 | 18.3 | 11,102,053 | −638,954 | 7,916,201 | 18,379,300 | 2.46 | 746,128,000 | 18.8 | 844,550,000 | 19.3 | 953,390,000 | 19.9 | 1,404,905,416 | 22.4 | | |
| Rural Christians | 398,427,332 | 24.6 | 555,822,421 | 15.4 | 10,312,206 | 835,403 | −7,916,201 | 3,231,408 | 0.57 | 570,652,851 | 14.4 | 588,136,519 | 13.4 | 595,202,187 | 12.4 | 615,015,950 | 9.8 | | |

Global Table 22.  LITERATE AND NONLITERATE CHRISTIANS AND POPULATIONS ON 8 CONTINENTS, AD 1900-2000.

1. Literacy is measured as the number of literates in the adult population (over 15 years).
2. All percentages in this table are %s of the relevant continent's adult population, except the last 6 lines which give percentages of the world's adult population; and except also the column 'Rate' which gives annual increase as percentage per year.

| | 1900 | | mid-1970 | | Annual change, 1970–1985 | | mid-1975 | | mid-1980 | | mid-1985 | | 2000 | |
| | Adherents | % | Adherents | % | Total | Rate | Adherents | % | Adherents | % | Adherents | % | Adherents | % |
|---|---|---|---|---|---|---|---|---|---|---|---|---|---|---|
| **AFRICA** | | | | | | | | | | | | | | |
| Adult population | 61,295,498 | 100.0 | 199,581,531 | 100.0 | 6,165,619 | 2.71 | 227,594,286 | 100.0 | 261,237,716 | 100.0 | 294,881,100 | 100.0 | 460,899,200 | 100.0 |
| Literates | 2,259,949 | 3.7 | 56,481,600 | 28.3 | 2,838,727 | 4.11 | 69,145,751 | 30.4 | 84,868,869 | 32.5 | 102,028,860 | 34.6 | 207,404,640 | 45.0 |
| Nonliterates | 59,035,549 | 96.3 | 143,099,931 | 71.7 | 3,326,892 | 2.10 | 158,448,535 | 69.6 | 176,368,847 | 67.5 | 192,852,240 | 65.4 | 253,494,560 | 55.0 |
| Adult Christians | 5,639,180 | 9.2 | 81,030,100 | 40.6 | 3,443,697 | 3.56 | 96,727,570 | 42.5 | 115,467,070 | 44.2 | 133,876,020 | 45.4 | 223,075,210 | 48.4 |
| Literate Christians | 1,164,610 | 1.9 | 37,920,490 | 19.0 | 2,268,666 | 4.70 | 48,249,990 | 21.2 | 60,607,150 | 23.2 | 72,835,630 | 24.7 | 164,080,120 | 35.6 |
| Nonliterate Christians | 4,474,570 | 7.3 | 43,109,610 | 21.6 | 1,175,031 | 2.42 | 48,477,580 | 21.3 | 54,859,920 | 21.0 | 61,040,390 | 20.7 | 58,995,090 | 12.8 |
| **EAST ASIA** | | | | | | | | | | | | | | |
| Adult population | 328,166,780 | 100.0 | 571,278,260 | 100.0 | 9,829,834 | 1.59 | 619,437,260 | 100.0 | 669,576,600 | 100.0 | 719,715,900 | 100.0 | 844,946,500 | 100.0 |
| Literates | 27,575,628 | 8.4 | 335,340,300 | 58.7 | 11,286,712 | 2.90 | 389,304,720 | 62.8 | 448,207,415 | 66.9 | 510,998,290 | 71.0 | 718,204,520 | 85.0 |
| Nonliterates | 300,591,152 | 91.6 | 235,937,960 | 41.3 | −1,456,878 | −0.63 | 230,132,540 | 37.2 | 221,369,185 | 33.1 | 208,717,610 | 29.0 | 126,741,980 | 15.4 |
| Adult Christians | 1,312,670 | 0.4 | 7,997,900 | 1.4 | 405,448 | 4.09 | 9,911,000 | 1.6 | 12,052,380 | 1.8 | 13,674,600 | 1.9 | 20,278,720 | 2.0 |
| Literate Christians | 984,500 | 0.3 | 6,284,060 | 1.1 | 375,959 | 4.67 | 8,052,680 | 1.3 | 10,043,650 | 1.5 | 11,515,450 | 1.6 | 18,588,820 | 2.2 |
| Nonliterate Christians | 328,170 | 0.1 | 1,713,840 | 0.3 | 29,489 | 1.59 | 1,858,320 | 0.3 | 2,008,730 | 0.3 | 2,159,150 | 0.3 | 1,689,900 | 0.2 |
| **EUROPE** | | | | | | | | | | | | | | |
| Adult population | 212,880,638 | 100.0 | 340,118,764 | 100.0 | 1,998,189 | 0.57 | 350,335,219 | 100.0 | 360,100,654 | 100.0 | 369,866,100 | 100.0 | 399,085,500 | 100.0 |
| Literates | 153,497,802 | 72.1 | 328,894,800 | 96.7 | 1,716,034 | 0.51 | 337,630,191 | 96.4 | 346,055,141 | 96.1 | 354,331,720 | 95.8 | 379,131,220 | 95.0 |
| Nonliterates | 59,382,836 | 27.9 | 11,223,964 | 3.3 | 282,155 | 2.22 | 12,705,028 | 3.6 | 14,045,513 | 3.9 | 15,534,380 | 4.2 | 19,954,280 | 5.0 |
| Adult Christians | 206,281,340 | 96.9 | 300,324,870 | 88.3 | 720,109 | 0.24 | 303,740,630 | 86.7 | 307,525,960 | 85.4 | 311,427,260 | 84.2 | 319,268,400 | 80.0 |
| Literate Christians | 149,016,450 | 70.0 | 296,923,680 | 87.3 | 700,127 | 0.23 | 300,237,280 | 85.7 | 303,924,950 | 84.4 | 307,728,600 | 83.2 | 317,272,970 | 79.5 |
| Nonliterate Christians | 57,264,890 | 26.9 | 3,401,190 | 1.0 | 19,982 | 0.57 | 3,503,350 | 1.0 | 3,601,010 | 1.0 | 3,698,660 | 1.0 | 1,995,430 | 0.5 |
| **LATIN AMERICA** | | | | | | | | | | | | | | |
| Adult population | 37,131,436 | 100.0 | 161,777,186 | 100.0 | 4,974,491 | 2.69 | 184,853,659 | 100.0 | 211,522,099 | 100.0 | 238,190,500 | 100.0 | 352,045,600 | 100.0 |
| Literates | 10,053,878 | 27.1 | 118,582,700 | 73.3 | 4,409,640 | 3.18 | 138,882,342 | 75.1 | 162,679,101 | 76.9 | 187,455,920 | 78.7 | 288,677,390 | 82.0 |
| Nonliterates | 27,077,558 | 72.9 | 43,194,486 | 26.7 | 564,851 | 1.23 | 45,971,317 | 24.9 | 48,842,998 | 23.1 | 50,734,580 | 21.3 | 63,368,210 | 18.0 |
| Adult Christians | 35,311,990 | 95.1 | 152,879,440 | 94.5 | 4,552,829 | 2.62 | 173,947,290 | 94.1 | 198,407,730 | 93.8 | 222,946,310 | 93.6 | 324,234,000 | 92.1 |
| Literate Christians | 9,654,170 | 26.0 | 114,861,800 | 71.0 | 4,377,977 | 3.24 | 134,943,170 | 73.0 | 158,641,570 | 75.0 | 183,406,680 | 77.0 | 281,636,480 | 80.0 |
| Nonliterate Christians | 25,657,820 | 69.1 | 38,017,640 | 23.5 | 174,852 | 0.45 | 39,004,120 | 21.1 | 39,766,160 | 18.8 | 39,539,630 | 16.6 | 42,597,520 | 12.1 |
| **NORTHERN AMERICA** | | | | | | | | | | | | | | |
| Adult population | 56,151,807 | 100.0 | 155,560,050 | 100.0 | 1,538,930 | 0.95 | 162,728,950 | 100.0 | 170,949,350 | 100.0 | 179,169,800 | 100.0 | 203,357,700 | 100.0 |
| Literates | 49,892,304 | 88.9 | 153,071,090 | 98.4 | 1,631,858 | 1.01 | 161,240,144 | 99.1 | 169,389,670 | 99.1 | 177,557,270 | 99.1 | 201,324,120 | 99.0 |
| Nonliterates | 6,259,503 | 11.1 | 2,488,960 | 1.6 | −92,928 | −6.24 | 1,488,806 | 0.9 | 1,559,680 | 0.9 | 1,612,530 | 0.9 | 2,033,580 | 1.0 |
| Adult Christians | 54,242,650 | 96.6 | 141,870,760 | 91.2 | 907,752 | 0.62 | 145,967,870 | 89.7 | 150,948,280 | 88.3 | 156,056,890 | 87.1 | 174,074,190 | 85.6 |
| Literate Christians | 49,188,980 | 87.6 | 140,315,160 | 90.2 | 977,837 | 0.67 | 145,154,220 | 89.2 | 150,093,530 | 87.8 | 155,161,040 | 86.6 | 173,057,400 | 85.1 |
| Nonliterate Christians | 5,053,670 | 9.0 | 1,555,600 | 1.0 | −70,085 | −8.61 | 813,650 | 0.5 | 854,750 | 0.5 | 895,850 | 0.5 | 1,016,790 | 0.5 |
| **OCEANIA** | | | | | | | | | | | | | | |
| Adult population | 4,131,942 | 100.0 | 12,931,644 | 100.0 | 275,194 | 1.93 | 14,247,104 | 100.0 | 15,683,588 | 100.0 | 17,120,100 | 100.0 | 21,828,100 | 100.0 |
| Literates | 2,075,366 | 50.2 | 11,703,140 | 90.5 | 252,271 | 1.95 | 12,918,760 | 90.7 | 14,225,852 | 90.7 | 15,527,930 | 90.7 | 20,081,850 | 92.0 |
| Nonliterates | 2,056,576 | 49.8 | 1,228,504 | 9.5 | 22,923 | 1.73 | 1,328,344 | 9.3 | 1,457,736 | 9.3 | 1,592,170 | 9.3 | 1,746,250 | 8.0 |
| Adult Christians | 3,206,390 | 77.6 | 11,935,910 | 92.3 | 161,471 | 1.27 | 12,751,160 | 89.5 | 13,550,620 | 86.4 | 14,363,760 | 83.9 | 18,510,230 | 84.8 |
| Literate Christians | 1,983,330 | 48.0 | 11,250,530 | 87.0 | 192,368 | 1.57 | 12,252,510 | 86.0 | 13,174,210 | 84.0 | 14,038,480 | 82.0 | 18,291,950 | 83.8 |
| Nonliterate Christians | 1,223,060 | 29.6 | 685,380 | 5.3 | −30,897 | −6.20 | 498,650 | 3.5 | 376,410 | 2.4 | 325,280 | 1.9 | 218,280 | 1.0 |
| **SOUTH ASIA** | | | | | | | | | | | | | | |
| Adult population | 239,477,276 | 100.0 | 636,469,980 | 100.0 | 18,785,760 | 2.60 | 722,189,150 | 100.0 | 824,327,580 | 100.0 | 926,466,000 | 100.0 | 1,309,096,500 | 100.0 |
| Literates | 17,073,361 | 7.1 | 266,680,900 | 41.9 | 9,689,640 | 3.12 | 310,631,410 | 43.0 | 363,577,300 | 44.1 | 418,762,630 | 45.2 | 667,639,220 | 51.0 |
| Nonliterates | 222,403,915 | 92.9 | 369,789,080 | 58.1 | 9,096,120 | 2.21 | 411,557,740 | 57.0 | 460,750,280 | 55.9 | 507,703,370 | 54.8 | 641,457,280 | 49.0 |
| Adult Christians | 9,818,570 | 4.1 | 45,189,370 | 7.1 | 1,745,953 | 3.27 | 53,442,000 | 7.4 | 62,648,900 | 7.6 | 72,264,350 | 7.8 | 111,273,200 | 8.5 |
| Literate Christians | 2,394,770 | 1.0 | 31,823,500 | 5.0 | 1,763,615 | 4.44 | 39,720,400 | 5.5 | 49,459,650 | 6.0 | 60,220,290 | 6.5 | 104,727,720 | 8.0 |
| Nonliterate Christians | 7,423,800 | 3.1 | 13,365,870 | 2.1 | −17,662 | −0.13 | 13,721,600 | 1.9 | 13,189,250 | 1.6 | 12,044,060 | 1.3 | 6,545,480 | 0.5 |
| **USSR** | | | | | | | | | | | | | | |
| Adult population | 86,702,640 | 100.0 | 167,509,920 | 100.0 | 1,748,943 | 0.99 | 175,976,220 | 100.0 | 184,999,350 | 100.0 | 194,022,500 | 100.0 | 217,305,200 | 100.0 |
| Literates | 24,276,739 | 28.0 | 167,007,390 | 99.7 | 1,743,696 | 0.99 | 175,448,290 | 99.7 | 184,444,350 | 99.7 | 193,440,430 | 99.7 | 215,132,150 | 99.0 |
| Nonliterates | 62,425,901 | 72.0 | 502,530 | 0.3 | 5,247 | 0.99 | 527,930 | 0.3 | 555,000 | 0.3 | 582,070 | 0.3 | 2,173,050 | 1.0 |
| Adult Christians | 72,483,410 | 83.6 | 59,298,510 | 35.4 | 748,626 | 1.19 | 62,999,490 | 35.8 | 66,784,770 | 36.1 | 70,430,170 | 36.3 | 81,489,450 | 37.5 |
| Literate Christians | 21,675,660 | 25.0 | 59,131,000 | 35.3 | 746,877 | 1.19 | 62,823,510 | 35.7 | 66,599,770 | 36.0 | 70,236,150 | 36.2 | 81,054,840 | 37.3 |
| Nonliterate Christians | 50,807,750 | 58.6 | 167,510 | 0.1 | 1,749 | 0.99 | 175,980 | 0.1 | 185,000 | 0.1 | 194,020 | 0.1 | 434,610 | 0.2 |
| **WORLD** | | | | | | | | | | | | | | |
| Adult population | 1,025,938,017 | 100.0 | 2,245,227,335 | 100.0 | 45,316,960 | 1.84 | 2,457,361,848 | 100.0 | 2,698,396,937 | 100.0 | 2,939,432,000 | 100.0 | 3,808,564,300 | 100.0 |
| Literates | 286,705,060 | 27.9 | 1,437,761,920 | 64.0 | 33,624,078 | 2.11 | 1,595,729,538 | 64.9 | 1,774,002,702 | 65.7 | 1,960,103,050 | 66.7 | 2,697,595,110 | 70.8 |
| Nonliterates | 739,232,957 | 72.1 | 807,465,415 | 36.0 | 11,692,882 | 1.36 | 861,632,310 | 35.1 | 924,394,235 | 34.3 | 979,328,950 | 33.3 | 1,110,969,190 | 29.2 |
| Adult Christians | 388,296,200 | 37.8 | 800,526,860 | 35.7 | 12,685,885 | 1.48 | 859,487,010 | 35.0 | 927,385,710 | 34.4 | 995,039,360 | 33.9 | 1,272,203,400 | 33.4 |
| Literate Christians | 236,062,470 | 23.0 | 698,510,220 | 31.1 | 11,403,426 | 1.52 | 751,433,760 | 30.6 | 812,544,480 | 30.1 | 875,142,320 | 29.8 | 1,158,710,300 | 30.4 |
| Nonliterate Christians | 152,233,730 | 14.8 | 102,016,640 | 4.5 | 1,282,459 | 1.19 | 108,053,250 | 4.4 | 114,841,230 | 4.3 | 119,897,040 | 4.1 | 113,493,100 | 3.0 |

Global Table 23. ADHERENTS OF ALL RELIGIONS ON 8 CONTINENTS, AD 1900-2000.

1. This table is an expanded version of Global Table 4 in Part 1, adding, as a variable, continents as standardized by the United Nations. Corresponding world totals are given only in Global Table 4 and are not repeated below.
2. Indented rows are sub-divisions of the unindented names, and are included in the latter's totals.
3. The order in which all rows are listed is in descending order of total adherents in 1970. The same applies to indented listings.
4. For exact definitions of all categories, see (a) Codebook (Part 6) for brief definitions; (b) Survey Dictionary (Part 9) for expanded definitions; and (c) Methodology (Part 3) for their origination.
5. The table is derived from the 223 Tables 1 presented in Part 7 for all countries.

| Continent Year: | 1900 | | mid-1970 | | Annual change, 1970–1985 | | | | mid-1975 | | mid-1980 | | mid-1985 | | 2000 | | Countries |
|---|---|---|---|---|---|---|---|---|---|---|---|---|---|---|---|---|---|
| | *Adherents* | *%* | *Adherents* | *%* | *Natural* | *Conversion* | *Total* | *Rate* | *Adherents* | *%* | *Adherents* | *%* | *Adherents* | *%* | *Adherents* | *%* | |
| AFRICA | | | | | | | | | | | | | | | | | |
| Christians | 9,938,448 | 9.2 | 142,962,732 | 40.6 | 4,586,648 | 1,466,149 | 6,052,797 | 3.55 | 170,702,570 | 42.5 | 203,490,710 | 44.2 | 236,278,850 | 45.4 | 393,326,210 | 48.4 | 59 |
| crypto-Christians | 1,182,778 | 1.1 | 4,575,142 | 1.3 | 111,906 | 18,345 | 130,251 | 2.50 | 5,211,880 | 1.3 | 5,877,660 | 1.3 | 6,543,440 | 1.3 | 9,428,100 | 1.2 | 17 |
| professing | 8,755,670 | 8.1 | 138,387,590 | 39.3 | 4,474,742 | 1,447,804 | 5,922,546 | 3.58 | 165,490,690 | 41.2 | 197,613,050 | 42.9 | 229,735,410 | 44.1 | 383,898,110 | 47.2 | 59 |
| Roman Catholics | 2,064,270 | 1.9 | 52,813,760 | 15.0 | 1,714,145 | 683,396 | 2,397,541 | 3.75 | 63,855,920 | 15.9 | 76,789,170 | 16.7 | 89,722,420 | 17.2 | 151,972,080 | 18.7 | 59 |
| Evangelical Catholics | 0 | 0.0 | 4,900 | 0.0 | 105 | 63 | 168 | 2.98 | 5,640 | 0.0 | 6,580 | 0.0 | 7,520 | 0.0 | 13,600 | 0.0 | 3 |
| Protestants | 2,533,590 | 2.3 | 38,806,790 | 11.0 | 1,251,251 | 308,419 | 1,559,670 | 3.40 | 45,912,890 | 11.4 | 54,403,490 | 11.8 | 62,894,090 | 12.1 | 100,557,240 | 12.4 | 53 |
| Non-White indigenous | 42,400 | 0.0 | 17,829,960 | 5.1 | 627,481 | 333,319 | 960,800 | 4.33 | 22,188,340 | 5.5 | 27,437,960 | 6.0 | 32,687,580 | 6.3 | 59,808,500 | 7.4 | 31 |
| Orthodox | 3,592,950 | 3.3 | 14,937,210 | 4.2 | 401,075 | 56,887 | 457,962 | 2.68 | 17,066,740 | 4.3 | 19,516,830 | 4.2 | 21,966,920 | 4.2 | 33,711,560 | 4.1 | 26 |
| Anglicans | 521,310 | 0.5 | 12,268,730 | 3.5 | 418,684 | 52,631 | 471,315 | 3.27 | 14,393,830 | 3.6 | 16,981,885 | 3.7 | 19,569,940 | 3.8 | 31,661,110 | 3.9 | 33 |
| Marginal Protestants | 1,150 | 0.0 | 1,274,140 | 0.4 | 45,839 | 10,016 | 55,855 | 3.65 | 1,528,860 | 0.4 | 1,832,685 | 0.4 | 2,136,510 | 0.4 | 4,812,190 | 0.6 | 21 |
| Catholics (non-Roman) | 0 | 0.0 | 457,000 | 0.1 | 16,267 | 3,136 | 19,403 | 3.57 | 544,110 | 0.1 | 651,030 | 0.1 | 757,950 | 0.1 | 1,375,430 | 0.2 | 12 |
| nominal | 1,182,076 | 1.1 | 27,038,550 | 7.7 | 907,392 | 280,723 | 1,188,115 | 3.64 | 32,641,335 | 8.1 | 38,919,725 | 8.4 | 45,198,115 | 8.7 | 69,411,310 | 8.5 | 42 |
| affiliated | 8,756,372 | 8.1 | 115,924,182 | 33.0 | 3,679,256 | 1,185,426 | 4,864,682 | 3.52 | 138,061,235 | 34.4 | 164,570,985 | 35.7 | 191,080,735 | 36.7 | 323,914,900 | 39.8 | 58 |
| total practising | 7,820,490 | *89* | 90,732,243 | *78* | 2,888,195 | 924,387 | 3,812,582 | 3.53 | 108,078,775 | *78* | 128,858,055 | *78* | 149,637,335 | *78* | 234,424,080 | *72* | 58 |
| non-practising | 935,892 | *11* | 25,191,931 | *22* | 791,061 | 261,039 | 1,052,100 | 3.51 | 29,982,455 | *22* | 35,712,930 | *22* | 41,443,405 | *22* | 89,490,820 | *28* | 58 |
| Roman Catholics | 1,909,712 | 1.8 | 45,336,733 | 12.9 | 1,460,070 | 627,041 | 2,087,111 | 3.80 | 54,856,500 | 13.7 | 66,207,840 | 14.4 | 77,559,180 | 14.9 | 131,531,540 | 16.2 | 58 |
| Catholic pentecostals | 0 | 0.0 | 0 | 0.0 | 661 | 10,005 | 10,666 | 44.89 | 23,760 | 0.0 | 106,660 | 0.0 | 189,560 | 0.0 | 935,200 | 0.1 | 14 |
| Protestants | 1,836,980 | 1.7 | 27,182,284 | 7.7 | 875,227 | 204,707 | 1,079,934 | 3.37 | 32,081,905 | 8.0 | 37,981,610 | 8.2 | 43,881,315 | 8.4 | 74,466,310 | 9.2 | 56 |
| Evangelicals | 1,482,850 | 1.4 | 20,583,074 | 5.9 | 673,748 | 220,711 | 894,459 | 3.64 | 24,595,810 | 6.1 | 29,527,660 | 6.4 | 34,459,510 | 6.6 | 59,980,200 | 7.4 | 52 |
| Neo-pentecostals | 0 | 0.0 | 3,500 | 0.0 | 1,012 | 8,738 | 9,750 | 27.23 | 35,800 | 0.0 | 101,000 | 0.0 | 166,200 | 0.0 | 450,000 | 0.1 | 5 |
| Orthodox | 4,600,250 | 4.3 | 18,243,770 | 5.2 | 470,739 | 21,554 | 492,293 | 2.39 | 20,571,035 | 5.1 | 23,166,700 | 5.0 | 25,762,365 | 5.0 | 37,355,900 | 4.6 | 26 |
| Non-White indigenous | 39,200 | 0.0 | 15,971,367 | 4.5 | 557,449 | 291,211 | 848,660 | 4.29 | 19,767,330 | 4.9 | 24,457,970 | 5.3 | 29,148,610 | 5.6 | 54,355,960 | 6.7 | 43 |
| Anglicans | 369,430 | 0.3 | 7,793,170 | 2.2 | 265,467 | 22,675 | 288,142 | 3.18 | 9,069,560 | 2.3 | 10,674,585 | 2.3 | 12,279,610 | 2.4 | 20,833,460 | 2.6 | 36 |
| Evangelicals | 152,530 | 0.1 | 4,875,000 | 1.4 | 174,929 | 55,881 | 230,810 | 3.92 | 5,890,300 | 1.5 | 7,183,100 | 1.6 | 8,475,900 | 1.6 | 15,173,500 | 1.9 | 9 |
| Anglican pentecostals | 0 | 0.0 | 4,500 | 0.0 | 1,890 | 14,720 | 16,610 | 25.69 | 64,650 | 0.0 | 170,600 | 0.0 | 276,550 | 0.1 | 715,400 | 0.1 | 9 |
| Marginal Protestants | 800 | 0.0 | 994,058 | 0.3 | 35,618 | 13,870 | 49,488 | 4.05 | 1,222,775 | 0.3 | 1,488,940 | 0.3 | 1,755,105 | 0.3 | 4,093,220 | 0.5 | 45 |
| Catholics (non-Roman) | 0 | 0.0 | 402,800 | 0.1 | 14,686 | 4,368 | 19,054 | 3.87 | 492,130 | 0.1 | 593,340 | 0.1 | 694,550 | 0.1 | 1,278,510 | 0.2 | 13 |
| Muslims | 34,531,292 | 32.0 | 141,884,235 | 40.3 | 4,492,257 | 292,159 | 4,784,416 | 2.92 | 163,640,080 | 40.8 | 189,728,390 | 41.2 | 215,816,700 | 41.5 | 338,565,460 | 41.6 | 53 |
| Tribal religionists | 62,685,265 | 58.1 | 64,266,229 | 18.3 | 1,753,915 | −1,793,257 | −39,342 | −0.06 | 63,865,460 | 15.9 | 63,872,800 | 13.9 | 63,880,140 | 12.3 | 72,351,470 | 8.9 | 42 |
| Hindus | 279,320 | 0.3 | 990,330 | 0.3 | 17,381 | −1,524 | 15,857 | 1.54 | 1,027,490 | 0.3 | 1,148,900 | 0.2 | 1,270,310 | 0.2 | 1,738,720 | 0.2 | 21 |
| Baha'is | 225 | 0.0 | 695,094 | 0.2 | 24,509 | 8,425 | 32,934 | 3.88 | 847,795 | 0.2 | 1,024,440 | 0.2 | 1,201,085 | 0.2 | 2,462,610 | 0.3 | 56 |
| Non-religious | 7,210 | 0.0 | 583,170 | 0.2 | 21,732 | 24,044 | 45,776 | 5.89 | 776,545 | 0.2 | 1,040,930 | 0.2 | 1,305,315 | 0.3 | 3,751,520 | 0.5 | 40 |
| Jews | 397,900 | 0.4 | 207,090 | 0.1 | 2,862 | −297 | 2,565 | 1.20 | 213,870 | 0.1 | 232,740 | 0.1 | 251,610 | 0.0 | 364,100 | 0.0 | 19 |
| Atheists | 1,020 | 0.0 | 102,500 | 0.0 | 3,758 | 3,522 | 7,280 | 5.31 | 137,150 | 0.0 | 175,300 | 0.0 | 213,450 | 0.0 | 569,500 | 0.1 | 22 |
| Jains | 3,100 | 0.0 | 31,800 | 0.0 | 1,053 | −173 | 880 | 2.46 | 35,700 | 0.0 | 40,600 | 0.0 | 45,500 | 0.0 | 61,000 | 0.0 | 3 |
| Sikhs | 2,200 | 0.0 | 25,700 | 0.0 | −139 | −1 | −140 | −0.63 | 22,100 | 0.0 | 24,300 | 0.0 | 26,500 | 0.0 | 36,000 | 0.0 | 4 |
| Buddhists | 3,400 | 0.0 | 11,250 | 0.0 | 260 | −171 | 89 | 0.76 | 11,670 | 0.0 | 12,140 | 0.0 | 12,610 | 0.0 | 13,600 | 0.0 | 6 |
| Chinese folk-religionists | 1,900 | 0.0 | 7,240 | 0.0 | 214 | −78 | 136 | 1.72 | 7,900 | 0.0 | 8,600 | 0.0 | 9,300 | 0.0 | 13,000 | 0.0 | 3 |
| Spiritists | 1,000 | 0.0 | 2,300 | 0.0 | 78 | −8 | 70 | 2.64 | 2,650 | 0.0 | 3,000 | 0.0 | 3,350 | 0.0 | 4,600 | 0.0 | 2 |
| New-Religionists | 0 | 0.0 | 700 | 0.0 | 85 | 545 | 630 | 21.00 | 3,000 | 0.0 | 7,000 | 0.0 | 11,000 | 0.0 | 26,000 | 0.0 | 2 |
| Parsis | 200 | 0.0 | 470 | 0.0 | 1 | −1 | 0 | 0.00 | 420 | 0.0 | 470 | 0.0 | 520 | 0.0 | 700 | 0.0 | 3 |
| Other religionists | 1,780 | 0.0 | 29,930 | 0.0 | 1,034 | 666 | 1,700 | 4.42 | 38,460 | 0.0 | 46,930 | 0.0 | 55,400 | 0.0 | 106,210 | 0.0 | 20 |
| CONTINENT'S POPULATION | 107,854,260 | 100.0 | 351,800,770 | 100.0 | 10,905,648 | 0 | 10,905,648 | 2.72 | 401,332,860 | 100.0 | 460,857,250 | 100.0 | 520,381,640 | 100.0 | 813,390,700 | 100.0 | 59 |
| EAST ASIA | | | | | | | | | | | | | | | | | |
| Non-religious | 30,000 | 0.0 | 415,898,760 | 44.9 | 7,741,243 | 5,607,933 | 13,349,176 | 2.78 | 479,886,130 | 47.8 | 549,390,520 | 50.5 | 618,894,910 | 53.0 | 800,902,700 | 58.3 | 8 |
| Chinese folk-religionists | 378,889,500 | 71.1 | 207,444,730 | 22.4 | 3,251,773 | −5,029,189 | −1,777,416 | −0.89 | 200,049,590 | 19.9 | 189,670,570 | 17.5 | 179,291,550 | 15.3 | 147,716,400 | 10.8 | 5 |
| Buddhists | 97,482,800 | 18.3 | 126,481,900 | 13.7 | 1,902,942 | −765,358 | 1,137,584 | 0.86 | 132,355,910 | 13.2 | 137,857,740 | 12.7 | 143,359,570 | 12.3 | 143,811,900 | 10.5 | 8 |
| Atheists | 1,000 | 0.0 | 91,945,000 | 9.9 | 1,655,050 | 415,810 | 2,070,860 | 2.03 | 101,884,250 | 10.1 | 112,653,630 | 10.4 | 123,422,950 | 10.6 | 156,378,700 | 11.4 | 8 |
| New-Religionists | 2,030,000 | 0.4 | 26,790,000 | 2.9 | 426,514 | 323,666 | 750,180 | 2.46 | 30,434,400 | 3.0 | 34,291,800 | 3.2 | 38,149,200 | 3.3 | 51,415,000 | 3.7 | 4 |
| Muslims | 24,012,000 | 4.5 | 20,104,110 | 2.2 | 332,668 | −193,900 | 138,768 | 0.67 | 20,676,000 | 2.1 | 21,491,790 | 2.0 | 22,307,580 | 1.9 | 22,311,100 | 1.6 | 6 |
| Shamanists | 10,589,850 | 2.0 | 15,310,800 | 1.7 | 303,530 | −525,720 | −222,190 | −1.55 | 14,324,900 | 1.4 | 13,088,900 | 1.2 | 11,852,900 | 1.0 | 9,635,900 | 0.7 | 3 |
| Christians | 2,179,350 | 0.4 | 12,668,243 | 1.4 | 276,181 | 359,622 | 635,803 | 4.04 | 15,727,850 | 1.6 | 19,026,270 | 1.8 | 22,324,690 | 1.9 | 32,337,300 | 2.4 | 8 |
| crypto-Christians | 31,550 | 0.0 | 2,661,933 | 0.3 | 39,715 | −69,855 | −30,140 | −1.19 | 2,531,290 | 0.3 | 2,360,530 | 0.2 | 2,189,770 | 0.2 | 1,914,300 | 0.1 | 5 |
| professing | 2,147,800 | 0.4 | 10,006,310 | 1.1 | 236,466 | 429,477 | 665,943 | 5.05 | 13,196,560 | 1.3 | 16,665,740 | 1.5 | 20,134,920 | 1.7 | 30,423,000 | 2.2 | 7 |
| Protestants | 598,200 | 0.1 | 3,630,500 | 0.4 | 87,610 | 178,325 | 265,935 | 5.49 | 4,844,850 | 0.5 | 6,289,850 | 0.6 | 7,734,850 | 0.7 | 11,153,600 | 0.8 | 7 |
| Non-White indigenous | 24,050 | 0.0 | 3,611,000 | 0.4 | 94,544 | 204,806 | 299,350 | 5.87 | 5,098,500 | 0.5 | 6,604,500 | 0.6 | 8,110,500 | 0.7 | 12,792,300 | 0.9 | 5 |
| Roman Catholics | 1,371,700 | 0.3 | 2,304,360 | 0.2 | 46,724 | 40,400 | 87,124 | 3.20 | 2,725,500 | 0.3 | 3,175,600 | 0.3 | 3,625,700 | 0.3 | 5,426,700 | 0.4 | 7 |
| Anglicans | 60,800 | 0.0 | 242,100 | 0.0 | 3,561 | 413 | 3,974 | 1.52 | 261,760 | 0.0 | 281,840 | 0.0 | 301,920 | 0.0 | 420,200 | 0.0 | 6 |
| Marginal Protestants | 0 | 0.0 | 168,000 | 0.0 | 3,318 | 5,032 | 8,350 | 3.98 | 209,600 | 0.0 | 251,500 | 0.0 | 293,400 | 0.0 | 534,000 | 0.0 | 4 |
| Orthodox | 93,050 | 0.0 | 50,350 | 0.0 | 709 | 501 | 1,210 | 2.15 | 56,350 | 0.0 | 62,450 | 0.0 | 68,550 | 0.0 | 96,200 | 0.0 | 4 |
| nominal | 416,369 | 0.1 | 2,618,078 | 0.3 | 43,127 | −17,272 | 25,855 | 0.94 | 2,761,860 | 0.3 | 2,876,640 | 0.3 | 2,991,420 | 0.3 | 4,777,000 | 0.3 | 5 |
| affiliated | 1,762,981 | 0.3 | 10,050,165 | 1.1 | 233,054 | 376,894 | 609,948 | 4.70 | 12,965,990 | 1.3 | 16,149,630 | 1.5 | 19,333,270 | 1.7 | 27,560,300 | 2.0 | 8 |
| total practising | 1,435,690 | *81* | 6,716,450 | *67* | 168,200 | 347,617 | 515,817 | 5.62 | 9,184,830 | *71* | 11,874,620 | *74* | 14,564,410 | *75* | 20,617,540 | *75* | 8 |
| non-practising | 327,290 | *19* | 3,333,700 | *33* | 64,854 | 29,277 | 94,131 | 2.49 | 3,781,160 | *29* | 4,275,010 | *26* | 4,768,860 | *25* | 6,942,760 | *25* | 8 |
| Protestants | 451,900 | 0.1 | 3,532,236 | 0.4 | 85,122 | 156,169 | 241,291 | 5.21 | 4,633,150 | 0.5 | 5,945,150 | 0.5 | 7,257,150 | 0.6 | 9,990,600 | 0.7 | 7 |
| Evangelicals | 367,100 | 0.1 | 2,850,500 | 0.3 | 60,353 | 33,717 | 94,070 | 2.87 | 3,273,200 | 0.3 | 3,791,200 | 0.3 | 4,309,200 | 0.4 | 6,068,500 | 0.4 | 7 |
| Neo-pentecostals | 0 | 0.0 | 100,000 | 0.0 | 9,914 | 130,586 | 140,500 | 28.04 | 501,000 | 0.0 | 1,505,000 | 0.1 | 2,509,000 | 0.2 | 3,020,000 | 0.2 | 2 |
| Non-White indigenous | 11,050 | 0.0 | 3,214,305 | 0.3 | 87,174 | 221,661 | 308,835 | 6.51 | 4,741,780 | 0.5 | 6,302,660 | 0.6 | 7,863,540 | 0.7 | 11,983,400 | 0.9 | 8 |
| Roman Catholics | 1,202,790 | 0.2 | 2,996 949 | 0.3 | 54,941 | −9,160 | 45,781 | 1.43 | 3,212,550 | 0.3 | 3,454,750 | 0.3 | 3,696,950 | 0.3 | 4,744,800 | 0.3 | 8 |
| Catholic pentecostals | 0 | 0.0 | 1,000 | 0.0 | 582 | 11,618 | 12,200 | 48.80 | 25,000 | 0.0 | 123,000 | 0.0 | 221,000 | 0.0 | 800,000 | 0.1 | 4 |
| Anglicans | 41,697 | 0.0 | 147,001 | 0.0 | 2,392 | −471 | 1,921 | 1.23 | 156,800 | 0.0 | 166,200 | 0.0 | 175,600 | 0.0 | 215,700 | 0.0 | 6 |
| Marginal Protestants | 0 | 0.0 | 116,072 | 0.0 | 2,849 | 8,941 | 11,790 | 6.68 | 176,510 | 0.0 | 233,970 | 0.0 | 291,430 | 0.0 | 572,100 | 0.0 | 6 |
| Orthodox | 55,544 | 0.0 | 42,602 | 0.0 | 554 | −244 | 310 | 0.70 | 44,100 | 0.0 | 45,700 | 0.0 | 47,300 | 0.0 | 51,700 | 0.0 | 5 |
| Catholics (non-Roman) | 0 | 0.0 | 1,000 | 0.0 | 22 | −2 | 20 | 1.82 | 1,100 | 0.0 | 1,200 | 0.0 | 1,300 | 0.0 | 2,000 | 0.0 | 1 |
| Confucians | 640,000 | 0.1 | 4,516,000 | 0.5 | 94,125 | −47,725 | 46,400 | 0.98 | 4,753,000 | 0.5 | 4,980,000 | 0.5 | 5,207,000 | 0.4 | 5,356,000 | 0.4 | 1 |
| Shintoists | 6,720,000 | 1.3 | 4,173,000 | 0.5 | 46,252 | −110,914 | −64,662 | −1.66 | 3,889,200 | 0.4 | 3,526,380 | 0.3 | 3,163,560 | 0.3 | 2,658,000 | 0.2 | 1 |
| Tribal religionists | 10,110,000 | 1.9 | 1,020,000 | 0.1 | 14,844 | −35,244 | −20,400 | −2.22 | 918,000 | 0.1 | 816,000 | 0.1 | 714,000 | 0.1 | 510,000 | 0.0 | 2 |
| Baha'is | 0 | 0.0 | 27,307 | 0.0 | 544 | 348 | 892 | 2.82 | 31,620 | 0.0 | 36,230 | 0.0 | 40,840 | 0.0 | 57,400 | 0.0 | 5 |
| Hindus | 300 | 0.0 | 7,500 | 0.0 | 110 | −10 | 100 | 1.25 | 8,000 | 0.0 | 8,500 | 0.0 | 9,000 | 0.0 | 9,500 | 0.0 | 1 |
| Jews | 0 | 0.0 | 1,500 | 0.0 | 21 | −1 | 20 | 1.25 | 1,600 | 0.0 | 1,700 | 0.0 | 1,800 | 0.0 | 2,300 | 0.0 | 3 |
| Sikhs | 100 | 0.0 | 1,000 | 0.0 | 14 | −14 | 0 | 0.00 | 1,000 | 0.0 | 1,000 | 0.0 | 1,000 | 0.0 | 800 | 0.0 | 1 |
| Other religionists | 6,100 | 0.0 | 32,150 | 0.0 | 689 | 696 | 1,385 | 3.69 | 37,550 | 0.0 | 46,000 | 0.0 | 54,450 | 0.0 | 139,000 | 0.0 | 4 |
| CONTINENT'S POPULATION | 532,691,000 | 100.0 | 926,422,000 | 100.0 | 16,046,500 | 0 | 16,046,500 | 1.60 | 1,004,979,000 | 100.0 | 1,086,887,000 | 100.0 | 1,168,795,000 | 100.0 | 1,373,242,000 | 100.0 | 8 |

*Continued opposite*

| Continent Year: | 1900 Adherents | % | mid-1970 Adherents | % | Annual change, 1970–1985 Natural | Conversion | Total | Rate | mid-1975 Adherents | % | mid-1980 Adherents | % | mid-1985 Adherents | % | 2000 Adherents | % | Countries |
|---|---|---|---|---|---|---|---|---|---|---|---|---|---|---|---|---|---|
| EUROPE | | | | | | | | | | | | | | | | | |
| Christians | 278,383,690 | 96.9 | 405,132,656 | 88.3 | 2,197,458 | −1,150,645 | 1,046,813 | 0.26 | 410,275,220 | 86.7 | 415,600,780 | 85.4 | 420,926,340 | 84.2 | 431,403,570 | 80.0 | 37 |
| crypto-Christians | 0 | 0.0 | 13,984,996 | 3.0 | 103,231 | 182,883 | 286,114 | 1.86 | 15,371,370 | 3.2 | 16,846,130 | 3.5 | 18,320,890 | 3.7 | 21,533,880 | 4.0 | 8 |
| professing | 278,383,690 | 96.9 | 391,147,660 | 85.2 | 2,094,227 | −1,333,528 | 760,699 | 0.19 | 394,903,850 | 83.5 | 398,754,650 | 82.0 | 402,605,450 | 80.5 | 409,869,690 | 76.0 | 37 |
| Roman Catholics | 171,786,350 | 59.8 | 240,536,770 | 52.4 | 1,522,328 | −826,392 | 695,936 | 0.29 | 243,920,790 | 51.6 | 247,496,135 | 50.9 | 251,071,480 | 50.2 | 258,928,080 | 48.0 | 36 |
| Spiritist Catholics | 1,650,000 | 0.6 | 2,000,000 | 0.4 | 9,910 | −12,910 | −3,000 | −0.15 | 1,980,000 | 0.4 | 1,970,000 | 0.4 | 1,960,000 | 0.4 | 1,830,000 | 0.3 | 1 |
| Evangelical Catholics | 75,430 | 0.0 | 599,525 | 0.1 | 3,759 | 3,725 | 7,484 | 1.18 | 632,210 | 0.1 | 674,360 | 0.1 | 716,510 | 0.1 | 1,069,900 | 0.2 | 4 |
| Protestants | 58,360,400 | 20.3 | 82,246,270 | 17.9 | 202,897 | −421,768 | −218,871 | −0.27 | 81,128,670 | 17.2 | 80,057,560 | 16.5 | 78,986,450 | 15.8 | 74,965,460 | 13.9 | 34 |
| Orthodox | 22,626,290 | 7.9 | 33,533,900 | 7.3 | 244,356 | −89,215 | 155,141 | 0.45 | 34,360,380 | 7.3 | 35,085,310 | 7.2 | 35,810,240 | 7.2 | 37,776,100 | 7.0 | 29 |
| Anglicans | 25,470,640 | 8.9 | 31,934,000 | 7.0 | 111,489 | −5,633 | 105,856 | 0.33 | 32,479,120 | 6.9 | 32,992,560 | 6.8 | 33,506,000 | 6.7 | 34,256,520 | 6.3 | 23 |
| Catholics (non-Roman) | 118,510 | 0.0 | 1,527,220 | 0.3 | 7,348 | −7,677 | −329 | −0.02 | 1,526,780 | 0.3 | 1,523,930 | 0.3 | 1,521,080 | 0.3 | 1,559,200 | 0.3 | 15 |
| Marginal Protestants | 21,500 | 0.0 | 1,281,500 | 0.3 | 5,423 | 16,543 | 21,966 | 1.57 | 1,395,110 | 0.3 | 1,501,155 | 0.3 | 1,607,200 | 0.3 | 2,238,330 | 0.4 | 20 |
| Non-White indigenous | 0 | 0.0 | 88,000 | 0.0 | 386 | 614 | 1,000 | 1.08 | 93,000 | 0.0 | 98,000 | 0.0 | 103,000 | 0.0 | 146,000 | 0.0 | 3 |
| nominal | 4,595,280 | 1.6 | 8,023,997 | 1.7 | 42,217 | 397,702 | 439,919 | 4.33 | 10,155,015 | 2.1 | 12,423,190 | 2.6 | 14,691,365 | 2.9 | 19,954,890 | 3.7 | 32 |
| affiliated | 273,788,410 | 95.3 | 397,108,659 | 86.5 | 2,155,241 | −1,548,347 | 606,894 | 0.15 | 400,120,205 | 84.6 | 403,177,590 | 82.9 | 406,234,975 | 81.3 | 411,448,680 | 76.3 | 37 |
| doubly-affiliated | −927,310 | −0.3 | −6,510,583 | −1.4 | −40,724 | 27,927 | −12,797 | −0.19 | −6,563,070 | −1.4 | −6,638,550 | −1.4 | −6,714,030 | −1.3 | −6,711,500 | −1.2 | 12 |
| disaffiliated | −231,400 | −0.1 | −10,068,950 | −2.2 | −76,035 | −366,711 | −442,746 | −3.57 | −12,404,320 | −2.6 | −14,496,410 | −3.0 | −16,588,500 | −3.3 | −13,784,100 | −2.6 | 4 |
| total practising | 246,293,530 | *90* | 312,906,700 | *79* | 1,750,438 | −1,815,084 | −64,646 | −0.02 | 312,649,050 | *78* | 312,260,250 | *77* | 311,871,450 | *77* | 293,077,310 | *71* | 37 |
| non-practising | 27,494,880 | *10* | 84,201,940 | *21* | 404,803 | 266,737 | 671,540 | 0.77 | 87,471,150 | *22* | 90,917,340 | *23* | 94,363,530 | *23* | 118,371,400 | *29* | 37 |
| Roman Catholics | 170,627,440 | 59.4 | 254,015,061 | 55.3 | 1,634,271 | −421,486 | 1,212,785 | 0.47 | 260,061,760 | 55.0 | 266,142,915 | 54.7 | 272,224,070 | 54.5 | 278,290,170 | 51.6 | 36 |
| Catholic pentecostals | 0 | 0.0 | 13,700 | 0.0 | 1,881 | 90,029 | 91,910 | 34.19 | 268,800 | 0.1 | 932,800 | 0.2 | 1,596,800 | 0.3 | 3,926,000 | 0.7 | 13 |
| Protestants | 57,550,100 | 20.0 | 85,660,412 | 18.7 | 215,270 | −593,968 | −378,698 | −0.45 | 83,867,675 | 17.7 | 81,873,430 | 16.8 | 79,879,185 | 16.0 | 72,805,520 | 13.5 | 35 |
| Evangelicals | 17,810,050 | 6.2 | 20,572,010 | 4.5 | 59,098 | 73,663 | 132,761 | 0.62 | 21,304,570 | 4.5 | 21,899,620 | 4.5 | 22,494,670 | 4.5 | 25,259,660 | 4.7 | 30 |
| Neo-pentecostals | 0 | 0.0 | 41,500 | 0.0 | 1,123 | 56,927 | 58,050 | 24.09 | 241,000 | 0.1 | 622,000 | 0.1 | 1,003,000 | 0.2 | 2,100,000 | 0.4 | 14 |
| Orthodox | 21,595,350 | 7.5 | 40,938,818 | 8.9 | 305,703 | −74,456 | 231,247 | 0.55 | 42,122,800 | 8.9 | 43,251,280 | 8.9 | 44,379,760 | 8.9 | 47,069,360 | 8.7 | 28 |
| Orthodox pentecostals | 0 | 0.0 | 3,000 | 0.0 | 41 | 2,859 | 2,900 | 26.36 | 11,000 | 0.0 | 32,000 | 0.0 | 53,000 | 0.0 | 150,000 | 0.0 | 2 |
| Anglicans | 24,900,610 | 8.7 | 29,372,130 | 6.4 | 100,185 | −140,988 | −40,803 | −0.14 | 29,148,980 | 6.2 | 28,964,100 | 6.0 | 28,779,220 | 5.8 | 28,587,900 | 5.3 | 25 |
| Evangelicals | 13,193,880 | 4.6 | 7,654,300 | 1.7 | 28,363 | 76,307 | 104,670 | 1.28 | 8,176,800 | 1.7 | 8,701,000 | 1.8 | 9,225,200 | 1.8 | 10,794,000 | 2.0 | 4 |
| Anglican pentecostals | 0 | 0.0 | 60,100 | 0.0 | 1,022 | 53,068 | 54,090 | 18.00 | 300,500 | 0.1 | 601,000 | 0.1 | 901,500 | 0.2 | 1,205,000 | 0.2 | 2 |
| Catholics (non-Roman) | 170,220 | 0.1 | 1,877,162 | 0.4 | 8,050 | −2,182 | 5,868 | 0.31 | 1,905,940 | 0.4 | 1,935,850 | 0.4 | 1,965,760 | 0.4 | 1,937,770 | 0.4 | 23 |
| Marginal Protestants | 103,400 | 0.0 | 1,737,339 | 0.4 | 8,023 | 22,211 | 30,234 | 1.60 | 1,885,870 | 0.4 | 2,039,665 | 0.4 | 2,193,460 | 0.4 | 3,078,560 | 0.6 | 33 |
| Non-White indigenous | 0 | 0.0 | 87,270 | 0.0 | 498 | 1,306 | 1,804 | 1.91 | 94,570 | 0.0 | 105,310 | 0.0 | 116,050 | 0.0 | 175,000 | 0.0 | 7 |
| Non-religious | 1,248,180 | 0.4 | 31,920,524 | 7.0 | 224,350 | 944,769 | 1,169,119 | 3.09 | 37,800,820 | 8.0 | 43,611,720 | 9.0 | 49,422,620 | 9.9 | 69,596,600 | 12.9 | 34 |
| Atheists | 156,000 | 0.1 | 12,703,000 | 2.8 | 93,702 | 214,162 | 307,864 | 2.17 | 14,187,200 | 3.0 | 15,781,640 | 3.2 | 17,376,080 | 3.5 | 24,949,860 | 4.6 | 28 |
| Muslims | 2,772,600 | 1.0 | 6,847,690 | 1.5 | 204,130 | −25,441 | 178,689 | 2.20 | 8,109,370 | 1.7 | 8,634,580 | 1.8 | 9,159,790 | 1.8 | 9,856,500 | 1.8 | 22 |
| Jews | 4,701,980 | 1.6 | 1,439,150 | 0.3 | 6,625 | −15 | 6,610 | 0.45 | 1,470,700 | 0.3 | 1,505,250 | 0.3 | 1,539,800 | 0.3 | 1,660,190 | 0.3 | 31 |
| Hindus | 50 | 0.0 | 223,370 | 0.0 | 20,826 | 5,126 | 25,952 | 6.97 | 372,630 | 0.1 | 482,890 | 0.1 | 593,150 | 0.1 | 693,630 | 0.1 | 6 |
| Sikhs | 0 | 0.0 | 200,000 | 0.0 | 1,050 | −50 | 1,000 | 0.49 | 205,000 | 0.0 | 210,000 | 0.0 | 215,000 | 0.0 | 310,000 | 0.0 | 1 |
| Buddhists | 0 | 0.0 | 76,700 | 0.0 | 594 | 8,784 | 9,378 | 7.29 | 128,640 | 0.0 | 170,480 | 0.0 | 212,320 | 0.0 | 284,300 | 0.1 | 12 |
| Chinese folk-religionists | 0 | 0.0 | 60,000 | 0.0 | 383 | −983 | −600 | −1.05 | 57,000 | 0.0 | 54,000 | 0.0 | 51,000 | 0.0 | 40,000 | 0.0 | 3 |
| Baha'is | 0 | 0.0 | 53,810 | 0.0 | 229 | 717 | 946 | 1.61 | 58,580 | 0.0 | 63,270 | 0.0 | 67,960 | 0.0 | 105,200 | 0.0 | 26 |
| New-Religionists | 0 | 0.0 | 30,000 | 0.0 | 252 | 8 | 260 | 0.83 | 31,300 | 0.0 | 32,600 | 0.0 | 33,900 | 0.0 | 40,000 | 0.0 | 1 |
| Spiritists | 10,000 | 0.0 | 20,600 | 0.0 | 71 | −267 | −196 | −1.00 | 19,620 | 0.0 | 18,640 | 0.0 | 17,660 | 0.0 | 16,600 | 0.0 | 2 |
| Neo-pagans | 0 | 0.0 | 100 | 0.0 | 2 | 11 | 13 | 8.13 | 160 | 0.0 | 230 | 0.0 | 300 | 0.0 | 2,000 | 0.0 | 1 |
| Other religionists | 23,900 | 0.0 | 221,050 | 0.0 | 1,033 | 3,824 | 4,857 | 1.98 | 245,460 | 0.1 | 269,620 | 0.1 | 293,780 | 0.1 | 578,050 | 0.1 | 22 |
| CONTINENT'S POPULATION | 287,296,400 | 100.0 | 458,928,650 | 100.0 | 2,750,705 | 0 | 2,750,705 | 0.58 | 472,961,700 | 100.0 | 486,435,700 | 100.0 | 499,909,700 | 100.0 | 539,536,500 | 100.0 | 37 |
| LATIN AMERICA | | | | | | | | | | | | | | | | | |
| Christians | 62,002,115 | 95.1 | 267,383,563 | 94.5 | 8,419,292 | −291,821 | 8,127,471 | 2.66 | 305,111,950 | 94.1 | 348,658,275 | 93.8 | 392,204,600 | 93.6 | 571,157,820 | 92.1 | 47 |
| crypto-Christians | 0 | 0.0 | 496,808 | 0.2 | 14,800 | 32,719 | 47,519 | 6.66 | 713,000 | 0.2 | 972,000 | 0.3 | 1,231,000 | 0.3 | 1,391,000 | 0.2 | 1 |
| professing | 62,002,115 | 95.1 | 266,886,755 | 94.3 | 8,404,492 | −324,540 | 8,079,952 | 2.65 | 304,398,950 | 93.9 | 347,686,275 | 93.6 | 390,973,600 | 93.3 | 569,766,820 | 91.9 | 47 |
| Roman Catholics | 60,182,770 | 92.3 | 253,781,005 | 89.7 | 8,027,674 | −516,166 | 7,511,508 | 2.60 | 288,674,000 | 89.1 | 328,896,085 | 88.5 | 369,118,170 | 88.1 | 532,815,000 | 85.9 | 46 |
| Spiritist Catholics | 4,209,700 | 6.5 | 19,859,500 | 7.0 | 634,567 | 198,999 | 833,566 | 3.52 | 23,663,670 | 7.3 | 28,195,160 | 7.6 | 32,726,650 | 7.8 | 51,842,300 | 8.4 | 12 |
| Christo-pagans | 8,322,900 | 12.8 | 12,919,660 | 4.6 | 415,021 | −137,097 | 277,924 | 1.95 | 14,266,400 | 4.4 | 15,698,900 | 4.2 | 17,131,400 | 4.1 | 20,239,700 | 3.3 | 16 |
| Evangelical Catholics | 84,600 | 0.1 | 10,827,784 | 3.8 | 366,802 | 171,915 | 538,717 | 4.08 | 13,196,100 | 4.1 | 16,214,950 | 4.4 | 19,233,800 | 4.6 | 34,896,060 | 5.6 | 21 |
| Protestants | 957,143 | 1.5 | 8,300,935 | 2.9 | 242,065 | 98,384 | 340,449 | 3.45 | 9,877,915 | 3.0 | 11,705,425 | 3.1 | 13,532,935 | 3.2 | 22,394,090 | 3.6 | 46 |
| Non-White indigenous | 11,400 | 0.0 | 3,051,450 | 1.1 | 99,589 | 87,810 | 187,399 | 4.80 | 3,906,880 | 1.2 | 4,925,440 | 1.3 | 5,944,000 | 1.4 | 10,889,160 | 1.8 | 23 |
| Anglicans | 841,982 | 1.3 | 1,097,655 | 0.4 | 16,099 | −9,167 | 6,932 | 0.61 | 1,132,615 | 0.3 | 1,166,975 | 0.3 | 1,201,335 | 0.3 | 1,330,650 | 0.2 | 38 |
| Orthodox | 6,400 | 0.0 | 309,470 | 0.1 | 7,588 | 18 | 7,606 | 2.20 | 346,200 | 0.1 | 385,530 | 0.1 | 424,860 | 0.1 | 620,250 | 0.1 | 13 |
| Marginal Protestants | 2,420 | 0.0 | 303,340 | 0.1 | 10,921 | 14,567 | 25,488 | 6.13 | 415,690 | 0.1 | 558,220 | 0.2 | 700,750 | 0.2 | 1,651,870 | 0.3 | 29 |
| Catholics (non-Roman) | 0 | 0.0 | 42,900 | 0.0 | 556 | 14 | 570 | 1.25 | 45,650 | 0.0 | 48,600 | 0.0 | 51,550 | 0.0 | 65,800 | 0.0 | 4 |
| nominal | 1,977,055 | 3.0 | 5,355,791 | 1.9 | 168,160 | 64,223 | 232,383 | 3.63 | 6,405,495 | 2.0 | 7,679,645 | 2.1 | 8,953,795 | 2.1 | 15,671,820 | 2.5 | 39 |
| affiliated | 60,025,060 | 92.1 | 262,027,772 | 92.6 | 8,251,132 | −356,044 | 7,895,088 | 2.64 | 298,706,455 | 92.2 | 340,978,630 | 91.7 | 383,250,805 | 91.4 | 555,486,000 | 89.6 | 46 |
| doubly-affiliated | −293,100 | −0.4 | −14,819,267 | −5.2 | −479,009 | −205,338 | −684,347 | 3.82 | −17,917,850 | −5.5 | −21,662,730 | −5.8 | −25,407,610 | −6.1 | −41,238,080 | −6.7 | 20 |
| disaffiliated | −81,000 | −0.1 | −779,238 | −0.3 | −18,978 | 9,991 | −8,978 | 1.09 | −822,630 | −0.3 | −869,100 | −0.2 | −915,570 | −0.2 | −1,013,400 | −0.2 | 5 |
| total practising | 50,979,850 | *85* | 182,069,310 | *69* | 5,692,110 | −533,144 | 5,158,966 | 2.50 | 206,123,040 | *69* | 233,658,990 | *69* | 261,194,940 | *68* | 367,038,560 | *66* | 46 |
| non-practising | 9,045,210 | *15* | 79,958,446 | *31* | 2,559,022 | 177,100 | 2,736,122 | 2.96 | 92,583,420 | *31* | 107,319,640 | *31* | 122,055,860 | *32* | 188,447,440 | *34* | 46 |
| Roman Catholics | 58,696,970 | 90.1 | 254,507,787 | 89.9 | 8,016,715 | −524,816 | 7,491,899 | 2.59 | 289,398,650 | 89.3 | 329,426,760 | 88.6 | 369,454,870 | 88.1 | 526,887,180 | 85.0 | 46 |
| Catholic pentecostals | 0 | 0.0 | 14,700 | 0.0 | 8,545 | 109,775 | 118,320 | 37.29 | 317,260 | 0.1 | 1,197,900 | 0.3 | 2,078,540 | 0.5 | 10,914,800 | 1.8 | 29 |
| Protestants | 933,650 | 1.4 | 12,725,223 | 4.5 | 408,433 | 185,241 | 593,674 | 3.85 | 15,408,315 | 4.8 | 18,661,960 | 5.0 | 21,915,605 | 5.2 | 37,746,970 | 6.1 | 46 |
| Evangelicals | 759,950 | 1.2 | 10,215,600 | 3.6 | 337,663 | 211,185 | 548,848 | 4.33 | 12,686,520 | 3.9 | 15,704,080 | 4.2 | 18,721,640 | 4.5 | 34,134,540 | 5.5 | 45 |
| Neo-pentecostals | 0 | 0.0 | 66,800 | 0.0 | 6,399 | 31,521 | 37,920 | 15.35 | 247,000 | 0.1 | 446,000 | 0.1 | 645,000 | 0.2 | 1,230,000 | 0.2 | 6 |
| Non-White indigenous | 29,400 | 0.0 | 8,240,198 | 2.9 | 269,275 | 162,329 | 431,406 | 4.25 | 10,163,320 | 3.1 | 12,556,250 | 3.4 | 14,949,180 | 3.6 | 27,542,940 | 4.4 | 36 |
| Marginal Protestants | 3,820 | 0.0 | 843,897 | 0.3 | 29,418 | 23,892 | 53,310 | 4.93 | 1,080,710 | 0.3 | 1,376,980 | 0.4 | 1,673,250 | 0.4 | 3,542,750 | 0.6 | 46 |
| Anglicans | 727,920 | 1.1 | 774,259 | 0.3 | 12,118 | −7,639 | 4,479 | 0.56 | 796,610 | 0.2 | 819,040 | 0.2 | 841,470 | 0.2 | 946,860 | 0.2 | 44 |
| Evangelicals | 7,100 | 0.0 | 30,000 | 0.0 | 742 | 128 | 870 | 2.57 | 33,800 | 0.0 | 38,700 | 0.0 | 43,600 | 0.0 | 61,000 | 0.0 | 6 |
| Orthodox | 6,400 | 0.0 | 408,363 | 0.1 | 10,371 | 43 | 10,414 | 2.27 | 458,070 | 0.1 | 512,500 | 0.1 | 566,930 | 0.1 | 842,580 | 0.1 | 21 |
| Catholics (non-Roman) | 1,000 | 0.0 | 126,550 | 0.0 | 2,789 | 253 | 3,042 | 2.15 | 141,260 | 0.0 | 156,970 | 0.0 | 172,680 | 0.0 | 228,200 | 0.0 | 11 |
| Non-religious | 372,040 | 0.6 | 7,259,432 | 2.6 | 195,739 | 161,474 | 357,213 | 4.06 | 8,802,175 | 2.7 | 10,831,560 | 2.9 | 12,860,945 | 3.1 | 24,842,510 | 4.0 | 42 |
| Afro-American spiritists | 246,940 | 0.4 | 1,777,100 | 0.6 | 65,072 | 67,257 | 132,329 | 5.54 | 2,390,460 | 0.7 | 3,100,390 | 0.8 | 3,810,320 | 0.9 | 7,132,900 | 1.2 | 21 |
| Spiritists | 47,100 | 0.1 | 1,361,000 | 0.5 | 50,432 | 48,628 | 99,060 | 5.42 | 1,827,400 | 0.6 | 2,351,600 | 0.6 | 2,875,800 | 0.7 | 5,583,000 | 0.9 | 8 |
| Atheists | 9,900 | 0.0 | 1,306,000 | 0.5 | 35,877 | 36,701 | 72,578 | 4.39 | 1,654,630 | 0.5 | 2,031,780 | 0.5 | 2,408,930 | 0.6 | 4,337,460 | 0.7 | 24 |
| Tribal religionists | 2,244,540 | 3.4 | 1,148,750 | 0.4 | 34,296 | −31,846 | 2,450 | 0.21 | 1,168,300 | 0.4 | 1,173,250 | 0.3 | 1,178,200 | 0.3 | 1,190,700 | 0.2 | 20 |
| Jews | 23,110 | 0.0 | 794,780 | 0.3 | 12,574 | −132 | 12,442 | 1.46 | 853,780 | 0.3 | 919,200 | 0.2 | 984,620 | 0.2 | 1,249,040 | 0.2 | 33 |
| Hindus | 163,160 | 0.3 | 539,340 | 0.2 | 6,430 | 551 | 6,981 | 1.21 | 576,495 | 0.2 | 609,150 | 0.2 | 641,805 | 0.2 | 863,560 | 0.1 | 13 |
| Muslims | 57,710 | 0.1 | 486,850 | 0.2 | 9,257 | 215 | 9,472 | 1.78 | 532,585 | 0.2 | 581,570 | 0.2 | 630,555 | 0.2 | 909,450 | 0.1 | 25 |
| Buddhists | 5,930 | 0.0 | 386,500 | 0.1 | 11,852 | −4,359 | 7,493 | 1.77 | 431,610 | 0.1 | 461,430 | 0.1 | 501,250 | 0.1 | 591,800 | 0.1 | 23 |
| Baha'is | 0 | 0.0 | 298,350 | 0.1 | 10,080 | 6,295 | 16,375 | 4.35 | 376,070 | 0.1 | 462,100 | 0.1 | 548,130 | 0.1 | 1,005,390 | 0.2 | 45 |
| New-Religionists | 0 | 0.0 | 167,700 | 0.1 | 7,021 | 6,549 | 13,570 | 5.52 | 245,900 | 0.1 | 303,400 | 0.1 | 360,900 | 0.1 | 786,000 | 0.1 | 6 |
| Chinese folk-religionists | 1,600 | 0.0 | 64,500 | 0.0 | 1,842 | −1,542 | 300 | 0.46 | 65,950 | 0.0 | 67,500 | 0.0 | 69,050 | 0.0 | 67,700 | 0.0 | 17 |
| Other religionists | 4,145 | 0.0 | 55,110 | 0.0 | 1,406 | 2,030 | 3,436 | 4.75 | 72,270 | 0.0 | 89,470 | 0.0 | 106,670 | 0.0 | 216,770 | 0.0 | 32 |
| CONTINENT'S POPULATION | 65,178,290 | 100.0 | 283,028,975 | 100.0 | 8,861,170 | 0 | 8,861,170 | 2.73 | 324,099,575 | 100.0 | 371,640,675 | 100.0 | 419,181,775 | 100.0 | 619,934,100 | 100.0 | 47 |

*Continued overleaf*

Global Table 23. ADHERENTS OF ALL RELIGIONS ON 8 CONTINENTS, AD 1900-2000 (CONTINUED).

| Continent Year: | 1900 | | mid-1970 | | Annual change, 1970–1985 | | | | mid-1975 | | mid-1980 | | mid-1985 | | 2000 | | Countries |
|---|---|---|---|---|---|---|---|---|---|---|---|---|---|---|---|---|---|
| | *Adherents* | % | *Adherents* | % | *Natural* | *Conversion* | *Total* | *Rate* | *Adherents* | % | *Adherents* | % | *Adherents* | % | *Adherents* | % | |
| NORTHERN AMERICA | | | | | | | | | | | | | | | | | |
| Christians | 78,811,810 | 96.6 | 206,443,460 | 91.2 | 2,008,880 | −669,881 | 1,338,999 | 0.63 | 212,429,330 | 89.7 | 219,833,450 | 88.3 | 227,237,570 | 87.1 | 253,589,450 | 85.6 | 5 |
| professing | 78,811,810 | 96.6 | 206,443,460 | 91.2 | 2,008,880 | −669,881 | 1,338,999 | 0.63 | 212,429,330 | 89.7 | 219,833,450 | 88.3 | 227,237,570 | 87.1 | 253,589,450 | 86.6 | 5 |
| Protestants | 51,967,680 | 63.7 | 101,408,030 | 44.8 | 911,596 | −1,400,611 | −489,015 | −0.50 | 98,531,160 | 41.6 | 96,517,880 | 38.8 | 94,504,600 | 36.2 | 97,766,900 | 33.0 | 5 |
| Roman Catholics | 15,311,760 | 18.8 | 63,170,640 | 27.9 | 685,648 | 861,989 | 1,547,637 | 2.19 | 70,787,150 | 29.9 | 78,647,010 | 31.6 | 86,506,870 | 33.2 | 102,665,330 | 34.7 | 5 |
| Non-White indigenous | 6,083,040 | 7.5 | 20,521,440 | 9.0 | 196,824 | −51,968 | 144,856 | 0.69 | 21,061,710 | 8.9 | 21,870,000 | 8.8 | 22,678,290 | 8.7 | 25,581,840 | 8.6 | 3 |
| Anglicans | 3,768,630 | 4.6 | 8,716,730 | 3.8 | 86,531 | −159,708 | −73,177 | −0.88 | 8,354,110 | 3.5 | 7,984,960 | 3.2 | 7,615,810 | 2.9 | 8,004,880 | 2.7 | 3 |
| Marginal Protestants | 1,010,000 | 1.2 | 6,857,620 | 3.0 | 69,670 | 90,868 | 160,538 | 2.11 | 7,593,200 | 3.2 | 8,463,000 | 3.4 | 9,332,800 | 3.6 | 12,004,500 | 4.1 | 4 |
| Orthodox | 515,700 | 0.6 | 5,099,000 | 2.3 | 50,915 | −2,015 | 48,900 | 0.92 | 5,338,000 | 2.3 | 5,588,000 | 2.2 | 5,838,000 | 2.2 | 6,748,000 | 2.3 | 2 |
| Catholics (non-Roman) | 155,000 | 0.2 | 770,000 | 0.3 | 7,696 | −8,436 | −740 | −0.10 | 764,000 | 0.3 | 762,600 | 0.3 | 761,200 | 0.3 | 818,000 | 0.3 | 2 |
| nominal | 19,242,120 | 23.6 | 37,196,559 | 16.4 | 367,845 | 6,592 | 374,437 | 0.97 | 38,496,640 | 16.3 | 40,940,930 | 16.5 | 43,385,220 | 16.6 | 52,324,260 | 17.7 | 5 |
| affiliated | 59,569,690 | 73.0 | 169,246,901 | 74.8 | 1,641,035 | −676,473 | 964,562 | 0.55 | 173,932,690 | 73.4 | 178,892,520 | 71.9 | 183,852,350 | 70.5 | 201,265,190 | 67.9 | 5 |
| total practising | 56,590,947 | *95* | 152,315,625 | *90* | 1,460,391 | −950,033 | 510,358 | 0.33 | 154,793,480 | *89* | 157,419,210 | *88* | 160,044,940 | *87* | 169,961,810 | *84* | 5 |
| non-practising | 2,978,743 | *5* | 16,931,268 | *10* | 180,644 | 273,560 | 454,204 | 2.37 | 19,139,210 | *11* | 21,473,310 | *12* | 23,807,410 | *13* | 31,303,380 | *16* | 5 |
| Protestants | 37,299,590 | 45.7 | 75,208,340 | 33.2 | 713,118 | −343,921 | 369,197 | 0.48 | 77,036,350 | 32.5 | 78,900,320 | 31.7 | 80,764,290 | 31.0 | 85,248,360 | 28.8 | 4 |
| Evangelicals | 27,925,300 | 34.2 | 52,197,800 | 23.1 | 510,443 | 321,542 | 831,985 | 1.48 | 56,090,900 | 23.7 | 60,517,650 | 24.3 | 64,944,400 | 24.9 | 75,802,650 | 25.6 | 4 |
| Neo-pentecostals | 0 | 0.0 | 605,000 | 0.3 | 9,390 | 74,610 | 84,000 | 8.16 | 1,030,000 | 0.4 | 1,445,000 | 0.6 | 1,860,000 | 0.7 | 3,150,000 | 1.1 | 2 |
| Roman Catholics | 13,011,300 | 15.9 | 57,478,882 | 25.4 | 573,310 | −308,604 | 264,706 | 0.45 | 58,718,800 | 24.8 | 60,125,940 | 24.2 | 61,533,080 | 23.6 | 67,814,790 | 22.9 | 5 |
| Catholic pentecostals | 0 | 0.0 | 202,000 | 0.1 | 11,495 | 179,305 | 190,800 | 15.26 | 1,250,000 | 0.5 | 2,110,000 | 0.8 | 2,970,000 | 1.1 | 4,930,000 | 1.7 | 2 |
| Non-White indigenous | 5,752,800 | 7.1 | 19,757,819 | 8.7 | 185,803 | −19,547 | 166,256 | 0.81 | 20,580,200 | 8.7 | 21,420,380 | 8.6 | 22,260,560 | 8.5 | 25,050,940 | 8.5 | 3 |
| Evangelicals | 5,320,000 | 6.5 | 13,551,000 | 6.0 | 129,090 | 39,910 | 169,000 | 1.18 | 14,333,000 | 6.1 | 15,241,000 | 6.1 | 16,149,000 | 6.2 | 18,775,000 | 6.3 | 1 |
| Black neo-pentecostals | 0 | 0.0 | 400,000 | 0.2 | 6,500 | 23,500 | 30,000 | 5.45 | 550,000 | 0.2 | 700,000 | 0.3 | 850,000 | 0.3 | 1,600,000 | 0.5 | 1 |
| Marginal Protestants | 815,000 | 1.0 | 6,712,433 | 3.0 | 68,995 | 89,636 | 158,631 | 2.12 | 7,495,550 | 3.2 | 8,298,740 | 3.3 | 9,101,930 | 3.5 | 11,476,350 | 3.9 | 4 |
| Orthodox | 415,000 | 0.5 | 4,970,625 | 2.2 | 49,282 | −9,344 | 39,938 | 0.77 | 5,161,000 | 2.2 | 5,370,000 | 2.2 | 5,579,000 | 2.1 | 6,435,000 | 2.2 | 2 |
| Orthodox pentecostals | 0 | 0.0 | 2,000 | 0.0 | 104 | 1,996 | 2,100 | 19.09 | 11,000 | 0.0 | 23,000 | 0.0 | 35,000 | 0.0 | 120,000 | 0.0 | 2 |
| Anglicans | 2,172,000 | 2.7 | 4,433,891 | 2.0 | 43,325 | −78,510 | −35,185 | −0.83 | 4,252,690 | 1.8 | 4,082,040 | 1.6 | 3,911,390 | 1.5 | 4,463,600 | 1.5 | 3 |
| Evangelicals | 234,000 | 0.3 | 575,000 | 0.3 | 5,751 | −91 | 5,660 | 0.94 | 600,700 | 0.3 | 631,600 | 0.3 | 662,500 | 0.3 | 796,600 | 0.3 | 2 |
| Anglican pentecostals | 0 | 0.0 | 41,000 | 0.0 | 921 | 15,479 | 16,400 | 15.92 | 103,000 | 0.0 | 205,000 | 0.1 | 307,000 | 0.1 | 425,000 | 0.1 | 2 |
| Catholics (non-Roman) | 104,000 | 0.1 | 684,911 | 0.3 | 7,202 | −6,183 | 1,019 | 0.15 | 688,100 | 0.3 | 695,100 | 0.3 | 702,100 | 0.3 | 776,150 | 0.3 | 3 |
| Non-religious | 1,010,000 | 1.2 | 10,533,100 | 4.7 | 95,311 | 461,601 | 556,912 | 4.20 | 13,253,210 | 5.6 | 16,102,220 | 6.5 | 18,951,230 | 7.3 | 24,876,360 | 8.4 | 4 |
| Jews | 1,516,400 | 1.9 | 6,994,020 | 3.1 | 67,175 | −6,925 | 60,250 | 0.83 | 7,292,520 | 3.1 | 7,596,520 | 3.1 | 7,900,520 | 3.0 | 8,576,030 | 2.9 | 3 |
| Muslims | 10,050 | 0.0 | 842,000 | 0.4 | 47,090 | 75,510 | 119,600 | 8.25 | 1,450,000 | 0.6 | 2,038,000 | 0.8 | 2,626,000 | 1.0 | 3,637,000 | 1.2 | 2 |
| Atheists | 2,000 | 0.0 | 300,000 | 0.1 | 5,814 | 41,086 | 46,900 | 8.88 | 528,000 | 0.2 | 769,000 | 0.3 | 1,010,000 | 0.4 | 1,898,000 | 0.6 | 2 |
| Buddhists | 40,410 | 0.0 | 216,050 | 0.1 | 2,133 | −3,893 | −1,760 | −0.85 | 207,050 | 0.1 | 198,450 | 0.1 | 189,850 | 0.1 | 153,080 | 0.1 | 3 |
| Baha'is | 2,800 | 0.0 | 162,350 | 0.1 | 2,043 | 6,769 | 8,812 | 4.27 | 206,410 | 0.1 | 250,470 | 0.1 | 294,530 | 0.1 | 410,800 | 0.1 | 5 |
| Hindus | 1,000 | 0.0 | 120,000 | 0.1 | 5,190 | 37,310 | 42,500 | 12.50 | 340,000 | 0.1 | 545,000 | 0.2 | 750,000 | 0.3 | 753,000 | 0.3 | 2 |
| Chinese folk-religionists | 75,120 | 0.1 | 120,000 | 0.1 | 1,182 | −1,582 | −400 | −0.34 | 118,000 | 0.0 | 116,000 | 0.0 | 114,000 | 0.0 | 80,000 | 0.0 | 2 |
| New-Religionists | 0 | 0.0 | 112,000 | 0.0 | 4,056 | 55,244 | 59,300 | 14.68 | 404,000 | 0.2 | 705,000 | 0.3 | 1,006,000 | 0.4 | 1,110,000 | 0.4 | 2 |
| Tribal religionists | 144,000 | 0.2 | 82,000 | 0.0 | 750 | −1,950 | −1,200 | −1.58 | 76,000 | 0.0 | 70,000 | 0.0 | 64,000 | 0.0 | 38,000 | 0.0 | 2 |
| Sikhs | 0 | 0.0 | 7,000 | 0.0 | 102 | −2 | 100 | 1.33 | 7,500 | 0.0 | 8,000 | 0.0 | 8,500 | 0.0 | 11,000 | 0.0 | 1 |
| Shamanists | 1,170 | 0.0 | 500 | 0.0 | 10 | −23 | −13 | 2.83 | 460 | 0.0 | 370 | 0.0 | 280 | 0.0 | 230 | 0.0 | 1 |
| Other religionists | 11,000 | 0.0 | 460,020 | 0.2 | 4,664 | 9,736 | 14,400 | 2.71 | 532,020 | 0.2 | 604,020 | 0.2 | 676,020 | 0.3 | 1,070,050 | 0.4 | 3 |
| CONTINENT'S POPULATION | 81,625,760 | 100.0 | 226,392,500 | 100.0 | 2,244,400 | 0 | 2,244,400 | 0.95 | 236,844,500 | 100.0 | 248,836,500 | 100.0 | 260,828,500 | 100.0 | 296,203,000 | 100.0 | 5 |
| OCEANIA | | | | | | | | | | | | | | | | | |
| Christians | 4,827,450 | 77.6 | 17,851,851 | 92.4 | 372,894 | −128,200 | 244,694 | 1.28 | 19,060,096 | 89.5 | 20,298,794 | 86.4 | 21,537,492 | 83.9 | 27,741,966 | 84.8 | 29 |
| professing | 4,827,450 | 77.6 | 17,851,851 | 92.4 | 372,894 | −128,200 | 244,694 | 1.28 | 19,060,096 | 89.5 | 20,298,794 | 86.4 | 21,537,492 | 83.9 | 27,741,966 | 84.8 | 29 |
| Protestants | 1,858,766 | 29.9 | 6,460,746 | 33.4 | 136,928 | −61,239 | 75,689 | 1.11 | 6,846,488 | 32.1 | 7,217,641 | 30.7 | 7,588,794 | 29.6 | 9,623,624 | 29.4 | 28 |
| Anglicans | 1,861,728 | 29.9 | 5,448,056 | 28.2 | 100,608 | −91,511 | 9,097 | 0.17 | 5,512,732 | 25.9 | 5,539,024 | 23.6 | 5,565,316 | 21.7 | 6,727 882 | 20.6 | 17 |
| Roman Catholics | 1,078,946 | 17.3 | 5,310,064 | 27.5 | 119,144 | 20,699 | 139,843 | 2.34 | 5,970,411 | 28.0 | 6,708,494 | 28.6 | 7,446,577 | 29.0 | 10,002,810 | 30.6 | 28 |
| Evangelical Catholics | 300 | 0.0 | 6,276 | 0.0 | 163 | −109 | 54 | 0.84 | 6,460 | 0.0 | 6,820 | 0.0 | 7,180 | 0.0 | 7,620 | 0.0 | 2 |
| Orthodox | 5,190 | 0.1 | 357,660 | 1.8 | 9,604 | 765 | 10,369 | 2.55 | 407,130 | 1.9 | 461,350 | 2.0 | 515,570 | 2.0 | 721,800 | 2.2 | 3 |
| Marginal Protestants | 5,080 | 0.1 | 183,945 | 1.0 | 4,438 | 3,532 | 7,970 | 3.58 | 222,475 | 1.0 | 263,645 | 1.1 | 304,815 | 1.2 | 509,790 | 1.6 | 11 |
| Non-White indigenous | 17,400 | 0.3 | 81,880 | 0.4 | 1,978 | −442 | 1,536 | 1.70 | 90,410 | 0.4 | 97,240 | 0.4 | 104,070 | 0.4 | 135,160 | 0.4 | 12 |
| Catholics (non-Roman) | 340 | 0.0 | 9,500 | 0.0 | 194 | −4 | 190 | 1.82 | 10,450 | 0.0 | 11,400 | 0.0 | 12,350 | 0.0 | 20,900 | 0.1 | 2 |
| nominal | 516,001 | 8.3 | 3,182,464 | 16.5 | 70,779 | 24,791 | 95,570 | 2.62 | 3,648,223 | 17.1 | 4,138,164 | 17.6 | 4,628,105 | 18.0 | 6,380,504 | 19.5 | 28 |
| affiliated | 4,311,449 | 69.3 | 14,669,387 | 75.9 | 302,115 | −152,991 | 149,124 | 0.97 | 15,411,873 | 72.3 | 16,160,630 | 68.8 | 16,909,387 | 65.9 | 21,361,462 | 65.3 | 29 |
| doubly-affiliated | 0 | 0.0 | −6,630 | 0.0 | −176 | 39 | −137 | 1.90 | −7,200 | 0.0 | −8,000 | 0.0 | −8,800 | 0.0 | −8,300 | 0.0 | 1 |
| total practising | 3,888,665 | *90* | 12,056,576 | *82* | 247,304 | −142,836 | 104,468 | 0.83 | 12,576,338 | *82* | 13,101,252 | *81* | 13,626,166 | *81* | 15,531,927 | *73* | 29 |
| non-practising | 422,784 | *10* | 2,612,831 | *18* | 54,811 | −10,155 | 44,656 | 1.57 | 2,835,535 | *18* | 3,059,378 | *19* | 3,283,221 | *19* | 5,829,525 | *27* | 29 |
| Anglicans | 1,692,178 | 27.2 | 4,781,778 | 24.7 | 87,008 | −90,344 | −3,336 | −0.07 | 4,780,747 | 22.4 | 4,748,429 | 20.2 | 4,716,111 | 18.4 | 5,436,024 | 16.6 | 18 |
| Evangelicals | 1,102,400 | 17.7 | 1,945,600 | 10.1 | 34,797 | −34,597 | 200 | 0.01 | 1,950,100 | 9.2 | 1,947,600 | 8.3 | 1,945,100 | 7.6 | 2,214,700 | 6.8 | 2 |
| Anglican pentecostals | 0 | 0.0 | 4,000 | 0.0 | 813 | 9,787 | 10,600 | 21.20 | 50,000 | 0.2 | 110,000 | 0.5 | 170,000 | 0.7 | 310,000 | 0.9 | 2 |
| Protestants | 1,544,655 | 24.8 | 4,720,341 | 24.4 | 98,445 | −83,412 | 15,033 | 0.31 | 4,812,490 | 22.6 | 4,870,660 | 20.7 | 4,928,830 | 19.2 | 6,402,390 | 19.6 | 26 |
| Evangelicals | 1,048,150 | 16.8 | 2,103 320 | 10.9 | 48,582 | −20,777 | 27,805 | 1.24 | 2,235,270 | 10.5 | 2,381,370 | 10.1 | 2,527,470 | 9.8 | 3,576,380 | 10.9 | 18 |
| Neo-pentecostals | 0 | 0.0 | 1,100 | 0.0 | 438 | 4,252 | 4,690 | 19.54 | 24,000 | 0.1 | 48,000 | 0.2 | 72,000 | 0.3 | 235,000 | 0.7 | 3 |
| Roman Catholics | 1,048,186 | 16.8 | 4,536,887 | 23.5 | 102,282 | 16,954 | 119,236 | 2.34 | 5,105,706 | 24.0 | 5,729,236 | 24.4 | 6,352,766 | 24.8 | 8,212,608 | 25.1 | 28 |
| Catholic pentecostals | 0 | 0.0 | 2,100 | 0.0 | 371 | 3,519 | 3,890 | 18.98 | 20,500 | 0.1 | 41,000 | 0.2 | 61,500 | 0.2 | 205,000 | 0.6 | 4 |
| Orthodox | 4,190 | 0.1 | 337,500 | 1.7 | 6,952 | 853 | 7,805 | 2.10 | 372,270 | 1.7 | 415,550 | 1.8 | 458,830 | 1.8 | 559,700 | 1.7 | 3 |
| Orthodox pentecostals | 0 | 0.0 | 200 | 0.0 | 19 | 161 | 180 | 18.00 | 1,000 | 0.0 | 2,000 | 0.0 | 3,000 | 0.0 | 10,000 | 0.0 | 1 |
| Marginal Protestants | 4,280 | 0.1 | 201,356 | 1.0 | 5,213 | 3,523 | 8,736 | 3.62 | 241,030 | 1.1 | 288,725 | 1.2 | 336,420 | 1.3 | 569,540 | 1.7 | 17 |
| Non-White indigenous | 17,560 | 0.3 | 88,893 | 0.5 | 2,203 | −608 | 1,595 | 1.65 | 96,610 | 0.5 | 104,850 | 0.4 | 113,090 | 0.4 | 170,500 | 0.5 | 15 |
| Catholics (non-Roman) | 400 | 0.0 | 9,262 | 0.0 | 188 | 4 | 192 | 1.88 | 10,220 | 0.0 | 11,180 | 0.0 | 12,140 | 0.0 | 19,000 | 0.1 | 2 |
| Non-religious | 43,800 | 0.7 | 662,601 | 3.4 | 24,424 | 121,442 | 145,866 | 10.97 | 1,330,019 | 6.2 | 2,121,266 | 9.0 | 2,912,513 | 11.3 | 3,357,080 | 10.3 | 19 |
| Atheists | 900 | 0.0 | 215,000 | 1.1 | 5,701 | 14,079 | 19,780 | 6.42 | 308,200 | 1.4 | 412,800 | 1.8 | 517,400 | 2.0 | 704,000 | 2.2 | 2 |
| Hindus | 13,400 | 0.2 | 213,830 | 1.1 | 5,040 | −8 | 5,032 | 2.11 | 238,920 | 1.1 | 264,150 | 1.1 | 289,380 | 1.1 | 361,550 | 1.1 | 3 |
| Tribal religionists | 1,287,000 | 20.7 | 158,890 | 0.8 | 2,866 | −8,518 | −5,562 | −4.77 | 118,430 | 0.6 | 102,370 | 0.4 | 86,310 | 0.3 | 55,100 | 0.2 | 9 |
| Muslims | 13,372 | 0.2 | 72,047 | 0.4 | 1,566 | −27 | 1,539 | 1.93 | 79,589 | 0.4 | 87,429 | 0.4 | 95,269 | 0.4 | 179,530 | 0.5 | 6 |
| Jews | 16,800 | 0.3 | 66,600 | 0.3 | 1,357 | 1 | 1,358 | 1.85 | 73,220 | 0.3 | 80,180 | 0.3 | 87,140 | 0.3 | 106,300 | 0.3 | 3 |
| Baha'is | 0 | 0.0 | 29,355 | 0.2 | 921 | 955 | 1,876 | 4.86 | 38,640 | 0.2 | 48,115 | 0.2 | 57,590 | 0.2 | 108,310 | 0.3 | 20 |
| Chinese folk-religionists | 12,678 | 0.2 | 17,186 | 0.1 | 303 | −142 | 161 | 0.89 | 18,066 | 0.1 | 18,796 | 0.1 | 19,526 | 0.1 | 15,864 | 0.0 | 9 |
| Buddhists | 6,530 | 0.1 | 16,280 | 0.1 | 327 | −266 | 61 | 0.37 | 16,590 | 0.1 | 16,890 | 0.1 | 17,190 | 0.1 | 16,620 | 0.1 | 7 |
| Sikhs | 200 | 0.0 | 5,000 | 0.0 | 108 | 2 | 110 | 1.98 | 5,550 | 0.0 | 6,100 | 0.0 | 6,650 | 0.0 | 8,100 | 0.0 | 2 |
| Spiritists | 500 | 0.0 | 1,000 | 0.0 | 16 | 4 | 20 | 1.82 | 1,100 | 0.0 | 1,200 | 0.0 | 1,300 | 0.0 | 1,500 | 0.0 | 1 |
| Shamanists | 0 | 0.0 | 1,000 | 0.0 | 18 | −68 | −50 | −7.14 | 700 | 0.0 | 500 | 0.0 | 300 | 0.0 | 400 | 0.0 | 1 |
| Other religionists | 770 | 0.0 | 12,870 | 0.1 | 349 | 746 | 1,095 | 5.97 | 18,340 | 0.1 | 23,820 | 0.1 | 29,300 | 0.1 | 58,380 | 0.2 | 9 |
| CONTINENT'S POPULATION | 6,223,400 | 100.0 | 19,323,510 | 100.0 | 415,890 | 0 | 415,890 | 1.95 | 21,307,460 | 100.0 | 23,482,410 | 100.0 | 25,657,360 | 100.0 | 32,714,700 | 100.0 | 29 |

*Concluded opposite*

| Continent / Year | 1900 Adherents | % | mid-1970 Adherents | % | Natural | Conversion | Total | Rate | mid-1975 Adherents | % | mid-1980 Adherents | % | mid-1985 Adherents | % | 2000 Adherents | % | Countries |
|---|---|---|---|---|---|---|---|---|---|---|---|---|---|---|---|---|---|
| | | | | | | Annual change, 1970–1985 | | | | | | | | | | | |
| **SOUTH ASIA** | | | | | | | | | | | | | | | | | |
| Hindus | 202,576,100 | 49.0 | 461,690,462 | 41.9 | 12,089,767 | −289,680 | 11,800,087 | 2.29 | 515,368,840 | 41.2 | 579,691,330 | 40.6 | 644,013,820 | 40.1 | 854,832,300 | 37.7 | 23 |
| Muslims | 124,692,260 | 30.2 | 352,682,079 | 32.0 | 11,687,461 | 54,107 | 11,741,568 | 2.90 | 405,286,165 | 32.4 | 470,097,745 | 32.9 | 534,909,325 | 33.3 | 790,541,000 | 34.8 | 37 |
| Buddhists | 29,182,901 | 7.1 | 103,983,509 | 9.4 | 3,189,883 | −128,388 | 3,061,495 | 2.59 | 118,268,930 | 9.5 | 134,598,460 | 9.4 | 150,927,990 | 9.4 | 213,870,800 | 9.4 | 21 |
| Christians | 16,920,469 | 4.1 | 78,124,616 | 7.1 | 2,645,668 | 447,043 | 3,092,711 | 3.35 | 92,188,835 | 7.4 | 109,051,740 | 7.6 | 125,914,645 | 7.8 | 192,264,050 | 8.5 | 37 |
| crypto-Christians | 2,358,029 | 0.6 | 10,469,516 | 1.0 | 359,673 | 193,294 | 552,967 | 4.28 | 12,912,700 | 1.0 | 15,999,200 | 1.1 | 19,085,700 | 1.2 | 32,283,450 | 1.4 | 33 |
| professing | 14,562,440 | 3.5 | 67,655,100 | 6.1 | 2,285,995 | 253,749 | 2,539,744 | 3.20 | 79,276,135 | 6.3 | 93,052,540 | 6.5 | 106,828,945 | 6.7 | 159,980,600 | 7.0 | 33 |
| Roman Catholics | 8,606,990 | 2.1 | 46,607,230 | 4.2 | 1,630,918 | 76,813 | 1,707,731 | 3.13 | 54,528,305 | 4.4 | 63,684,535 | 4.5 | 72,840,765 | 4.5 | 103,872,660 | 4.6 | 36 |
| Evangelical Catholics | 800,100 | 0.2 | 5,209,895 | 0.5 | 216,533 | 65,777 | 282,310 | 4.28 | 6,591,000 | 0.5 | 8,033,100 | 0.6 | 9,475,300 | 0.6 | 12,065,500 | 0.5 | 1 |
| Protestants | 1,173,750 | 0.3 | 14,191,570 | 1.3 | 439,054 | 127,404 | 566,458 | 3.40 | 16,670,330 | 1.3 | 19,856,155 | 1.4 | 23,041,980 | 1.4 | 35,673,500 | 1.6 | 35 |
| Non-White indigenous | 1,062,720 | 0.3 | 3,938,700 | 0.4 | 146,977 | 68,950 | 215,927 | 4.38 | 4,926,880 | 0.4 | 6,097,970 | 0.4 | 7,269,060 | 0.5 | 15,564,300 | 0.7 | 13 |
| Orthodox | 3,217,730 | 0.8 | 2,611,000 | 0.2 | 58,963 | −20,687 | 38,276 | 1.37 | 2,787,280 | 0.2 | 2,993,760 | 0.2 | 3,200,240 | 0.2 | 4,071,900 | 0.2 | 18 |
| Anglicans | 501,250 | 0.1 | 206,600 | 0.0 | 5,812 | −460 | 5,352 | 2.29 | 233,340 | 0.0 | 260,120 | 0.0 | 286,900 | 0.0 | 398,240 | 0.0 | 23 |
| Marginal Protestants | 0 | 0.0 | 100,000 | 0.0 | 4,271 | 1,729 | 6,000 | 4.62 | 130,000 | 0.0 | 160,000 | 0.0 | 190,000 | 0.0 | 400,000 | 0.0 | 1 |
| nominal | 573,250 | 0.1 | 1,354,402 | 0.1 | 59,249 | 37,161 | 96,410 | 5.30 | 1,820,150 | 0.1 | 2,318,500 | 0.2 | 2,816,850 | 0.2 | 6,787,390 | 0.3 | 5 |
| affiliated | 16,347,219 | 4.0 | 76,770,214 | 7.0 | 2,586,419 | 409,882 | 2,996,301 | 3.32 | 90,368,685 | 7.2 | 106,733,240 | 7.5 | 123,097,795 | 7.7 | 185,476,660 | 8.2 | 37 |
| doubly-affiliated | −1,800,100 | −0.4 | −5,375,088 | −0.5 | −217,190 | −44,601 | −261,791 | 3.96 | −6,611,000 | −0.5 | −7,993,000 | −0.6 | −9,375,000 | −0.6 | −14,318,000 | −0.6 | 1 |
| total practising | 14,948,801 | 91 | 62,715,656 | 82 | 2,099,347 | 299,442 | 2,398,789 | 3.26 | 73,580,110 | 81 | 86,703,540 | 81 | 99,826,970 | 81 | 135,193,030 | 73 | 37 |
| non-practising | 1,398,419 | 9 | 14,054,581 | 18 | 487,072 | 110,440 | 597,512 | 3.56 | 16,788,575 | 19 | 20,029,700 | 19 | 23,270,825 | 19 | 50,283,630 | 27 | 37 |
| Roman Catholics | 9,923,009 | 2.4 | 49,053,263 | 4.5 | 1,718,466 | 58,461 | 1,776,927 | 3.10 | 57,301,260 | 4.6 | 66,822,515 | 4.7 | 76,343,770 | 4.8 | 109,760,420 | 4.8 | 9 |
| Catholic pentecostals | 5,000 | 0.0 | 5,000 | 0.0 | 2,599 | 22,904 | 25,503 | 28.21 | 90,410 | 0.0 | 260,030 | 0.0 | 429,650 | 0.0 | 1,390,300 | 0.1 | 37 |
| Protestants | 1,439,780 | 0.3 | 17,961,109 | 1.6 | 562,318 | 256,515 | 818,833 | 3.82 | 21,420,210 | 1.7 | 26,149,455 | 1.8 | 30,878,700 | 1.9 | 48,652,960 | 2.1 | 9 |
| Evangelicals | 942,080 | 0.2 | 9,946,970 | 0.9 | 328,425 | 222,235 | 550,660 | 4.44 | 12,403,840 | 1.0 | 15,453,570 | 1.1 | 18,503,300 | 1.2 | 32,654,900 | 1.4 | 37 |
| Neo-pentecostals | 0 | 0.0 | 6,200 | 0.0 | 906 | 10,454 | 11,360 | 33.51 | 33,900 | 0.0 | 119,800 | 0.0 | 205,700 | 0.0 | 633,000 | 0.0 | 35 |
| Non-White indigenous | 1,895,050 | 0.5 | 11,342,108 | 1.0 | 428,236 | 160,917 | 589,153 | 4.17 | 14,120,725 | 1.1 | 17,233,650 | 1.2 | 20,346,575 | 1.3 | 34,861,700 | 1.5 | 6 |
| Orthodox | 4,220,970 | 1.0 | 3,286,810 | 0.3 | 77,892 | −27,491 | 50,139 | 1.42 | 3,525,890 | 0.3 | 3,788,200 | 0.3 | 4,050,510 | 0.3 | 5,120,800 | 0.2 | 33 |
| Anglicans | 667,830 | 0.2 | 254,246 | 0.0 | 7,892 | 1,595 | 9,487 | 3.14 | 302,050 | 0.0 | 349,120 | 0.0 | 396,190 | 0.0 | 552,630 | 0.0 | 21 |
| Evangelicals | 1,000 | 0.0 | 8,800 | 0.0 | 266 | 54 | 320 | 3.08 | 10,400 | 0.0 | 12,000 | 0.0 | 13,600 | 0.0 | 22,500 | 0.0 | 32 |
| Anglican pentecostals | | | 300 | 0.0 | 26 | 304 | 330 | 22.00 | 1,500 | 0.0 | 3,600 | 0.0 | 5,700 | 0.0 | 6,800 | 0.0 | 4 |
| Marginal Protestants | 280 | 0.0 | 215,066 | 0.0 | 8,021 | 4,222 | 12,243 | 4.53 | 270,400 | 0.0 | 337,400 | 0.0 | 404,790 | 0.0 | 753,650 | 0.0 | 24 |
| Catholics (non-Roman) | 400 | 0.0 | 32,700 | 0.0 | 1,046 | 264 | 1,310 | 3.34 | 39,250 | 0.0 | 45,800 | 0.0 | 52,350 | 0.0 | 92,500 | 0.0 | 6 |
| New-Religionists | 3,880,000 | 0.9 | 49,342,720 | 4.5 | 1,392,639 | −258,711 | 1,133,928 | 2.08 | 54,607,400 | 4.4 | 60,682,000 | 4.3 | 66,756,600 | 4.2 | 84,886,800 | 3.7 | 7 |
| Tribal religionists | 29,868,790 | 7.2 | 21,401,534 | 1.9 | 567,906 | −315,156 | 252,750 | 1.12 | 22,650,330 | 1.8 | 23,929,030 | 1.7 | 25,892,240 | 1.6 | 26,390,580 | 1.2 | 18 |
| Sikhs | 2,958,100 | 0.7 | 10,373,500 | 0.9 | 332,232 | 29,914 | 362,146 | 2.99 | 12,097,680 | 1.0 | 13,994,960 | 1.0 | 15,892,240 | 1.1 | 23,465,800 | 1.0 | 10 |
| Chinese folk-religionists | 12,100 | 0.0 | 8,056,000 | 0.7 | 270,908 | 412,422 | 683,330 | 5.99 | 11,398,380 | 0.9 | 14,889,300 | 1.0 | 18,380,220 | 1.1 | 48,304,600 | 2.1 | 29 |
| Jews | 1,422,940 | 0.3 | 6,677,853 | 0.6 | 188,013 | −69,808 | 118,205 | 1.62 | 7,280,200 | 0.6 | 7,859,900 | 0.6 | 8,439,600 | 0.5 | 10,537,700 | 0.5 | 16 |
| Jains | 350,600 | 0.1 | 2,682,796 | 0.2 | 82,259 | −2,275 | 79,984 | 2.60 | 3,072,710 | 0.2 | 3,482,640 | 0.2 | 3,892,570 | 0.2 | 4,915,600 | 0.2 | 19 |
| Baha'is | 1,320,000 | 0.3 | 2,584,500 | 0.2 | 66,070 | −4,200 | 61,870 | 1.99 | 3,102,800 | 0.2 | 3,203,200 | 0.2 | 3,303,600 | 0.2 | 4,242,800 | 0.2 | 26 |
| Parsis | 108,090 | 0.0 | 120,500 | 0.0 | 3,338 | −13 | 3,325 | 2.44 | 136,220 | 0.0 | 153,750 | 0.0 | 171,280 | 0.1 | 218,000 | 0.0 | 2 |
| Mandaeans | | | 23,000 | 0.0 | 908 | −88 | 820 | 3.03 | 27,100 | 0.0 | 31,200 | 0.0 | 35,300 | 0.0 | 49,000 | 0.0 | 2 |
| Shamanists | 8,000 | 0.0 | 15,000 | 0.0 | 356 | −556 | −200 | −1.43 | 14,000 | 0.0 | 13,000 | 0.0 | 12,000 | 0.0 | 10,000 | 0.0 | 7 |
| Other religionists | 500 | 0.0 | 5,771 | 0.0 | 179 | 154 | 333 | 4.50 | 7,400 | 0.0 | 9,100 | 0.0 | 10,800 | 0.0 | 21,500 | 0.0 | 7 |
| **CONTINENT'S POPULATION** | 413,361,650 | 100.0 | 1,101,370,000 | 100.0 | 32,629,300 | 0 | 32,629,300 | 2.61 | 1,250,148,000 | 100.0 | 1,427,663,000 | 100.0 | 1,605,178,000 | 100.0 | 2,269,594,000 | 100.0 | 37 |
| **USSR** | | | | | | | | | | | | | | | | | |
| Christians | 104,993,000 | 83.6 | 86,012,300 | 35.4 | 907,238 | 164,182 | 1,071,420 | 1.17 | 91,285,000 | 35.8 | 96,726,500 | 36.1 | 102,168,000 | 36.3 | 118,101,000 | 37.5 | 1 |
| crypto-Christians | 0 | 0.0 | 23,511,300 | 9.7 | 257,060 | 225,760 | 482,820 | 1.87 | 25,865,000 | 10.1 | 28,339,500 | 10.6 | 30,814,000 | 11.0 | 39,658,000 | 12.6 | 1 |
| professing | 104,993,000 | 83.6 | 62,501,000 | 25.7 | 650,178 | −61,578 | 588,600 | 0.90 | 65,420,000 | 25.6 | 68,387,000 | 25.5 | 71,354,000 | 25.4 | 78,443,000 | 24.9 | 1 |
| Orthodox | 91,188,000 | 72.6 | 55,000,000 | 22.7 | 572,846 | −40,246 | 532,600 | 0.92 | 57,639,000 | 22.6 | 60,326,000 | 22.5 | 63,013,000 | 22.4 | 69,306,000 | 22.0 | 1 |
| Protestants | 2,213,000 | 1.8 | 4,000,000 | 1.6 | 41,245 | −11,245 | 30,000 | 0.72 | 4,150,000 | 1.6 | 4,300,000 | 1.6 | 4,450,000 | 1.6 | 5,355,000 | 1.7 | 1 |
| Roman Catholics | 11,588,000 | 9.2 | 3,500,000 | 1.4 | 36,077 | −10,077 | 26,000 | 0.72 | 3,630,000 | 1.4 | 3,760,000 | 1.4 | 3,890,000 | 1.4 | 3,780,000 | 1.2 | 1 |
| Anglicans | 4,000 | 0.0 | 1,000 | 0.0 | 10 | −10 | 0 | 0.00 | 1,000 | 0.0 | 1,000 | 0.0 | 1,000 | 0.0 | 2,000 | 0.0 | 1 |
| nominal | 7,991,000 | 6.4 | 0 | 0.0 | 0 | 0 | 0 | 0.00 | 0 | 0.0 | 0 | 0.0 | 0 | 0.0 | 0 | 0.0 | |
| affiliated | 97,002,000 | 77.2 | 86,012,300 | 35.4 | 907,238 | 164,182 | 1,071,420 | 1.17 | 91,285,000 | 35.8 | 96,726,500 | 36.1 | 102,168,000 | 36.3 | 118,101,000 | 37.5 | 1 |
| total practising | 87,301,800 | 90 | 64,509,220 | 75 | 689,500 | 307,518 | 997,018 | 1.44 | 69,376,600 | 76 | 74,479,400 | 77 | 79,582,200 | 78 | 94,480,800 | 80 | 1 |
| non-practising | 9,700,200 | 10 | 21,503,080 | 25 | 217,738 | −143,336 | 74,402 | 0.34 | 21,908,400 | 24 | 22,247,100 | 23 | 22,585,800 | 22 | 23,620,200 | 20 | 1 |
| Orthodox | 85,000,000 | 67.6 | 75,174,000 | 31.0 | 790,828 | 110,572 | 901,400 | 1.13 | 79,572,000 | 31.2 | 84,188,000 | 31.4 | 88,804,000 | 31.6 | 102,384,000 | 32.5 | 1 |
| Orthodox pentecostals | 0 | 0.0 | 10,000 | 0.0 | 497 | 8,503 | 9,000 | 18.00 | 50,000 | 0.0 | 100,000 | 0.0 | 150,000 | 0.1 | 400,000 | 0.1 | 1 |
| Protestants | 2,000,000 | 1.6 | 6,434,300 | 2.7 | 70,971 | 63,099 | 134,070 | 1.88 | 7,141,000 | 2.8 | 7,775,000 | 2.9 | 8,409,000 | 3.0 | 10,396,000 | 3.3 | 1 |
| Evangelicals | 1,800,000 | 1.4 | 6,306,000 | 2.6 | 69,551 | 61,849 | 131,400 | 1.88 | 6,998,000 | 2.7 | 7,620,000 | 2.8 | 8,242,000 | 2.9 | 10,188,000 | 3.2 | 1 |
| Roman Catholics | 10,000,000 | 8.0 | 4,393,500 | 1.8 | 45,320 | −9,670 | 35,650 | 0.78 | 4,560,000 | 1.8 | 4,750,000 | 1.8 | 4,940,000 | 1.8 | 5,300,000 | 1.7 | 1 |
| Marginal Protestants | 0 | 0.0 | 10,000 | 0.0 | 114 | 186 | 300 | 2.61 | 11,500 | 0.0 | 13,000 | 0.0 | 14,500 | 0.0 | 20,000 | 0.0 | 1 |
| Anglicans | 2,000 | 0.0 | 500 | 0.0 | 5 | −5 | 0 | 0.00 | 500 | 0.0 | 500 | 0.0 | 500 | 0.0 | 1,000 | 0.0 | 1 |
| Non-religious | 200,000 | 0.2 | 68,151,700 | 28.1 | 740,645 | 235,575 | 976,220 | 1.34 | 72,770,760 | 28.5 | 77,913,900 | 29.1 | 83,057,100 | 29.5 | 96,257,000 | 30.6 | 1 |
| Atheists | 49,800 | 0.0 | 56,500,000 | 23.3 | 575,381 | −300,081 | 275,300 | 0.48 | 57,894,000 | 22.7 | 59,253,000 | 22.1 | 60,612,000 | 21.6 | 62,060,000 | 19.7 | 1 |
| Muslims | 14,013,000 | 11.2 | 28,000,000 | 11.5 | 288,952 | −59,252 | 229,700 | 0.79 | 29,074,000 | 11.4 | 30,297,000 | 11.3 | 31,520,000 | 11.2 | 34,653,000 | 11.0 | 1 |
| Jews | 5,263,000 | 4.2 | 3,000,000 | 1.2 | 13,000 | −1,000 | 12,000 | 0.39 | 3,060,000 | 1.2 | 3,120,000 | 1.2 | 3,180,000 | 1.1 | 3,300,000 | 1.0 | 1 |
| Shamanists | 700,000 | 0.6 | 600,000 | 0.2 | 4,969 | −24,969 | −20,000 | −4.00 | 500,000 | 0.2 | 400,000 | 0.1 | 300,000 | 0.1 | 300,000 | 0.1 | 1 |
| Buddhists | 437,200 | 0.3 | 500,000 | 0.2 | 4,472 | −14,472 | −10,000 | −2.22 | 450,000 | 0.2 | 400,000 | 0.1 | 350,000 | 0.1 | 300,000 | 0.1 | 1 |
| Baha'is | 200 | 0.0 | 4,000 | 0.0 | 43 | 17 | 60 | 1.40 | 4,300 | 0.0 | 4,600 | 0.0 | 4,900 | 0.0 | 350,000 | 0.0 | 1 |
| **CONTINENT'S POPULATION** | 125,656,000 | 100.0 | 242,768,000 | 100.0 | 2,534,700 | 0 | 2,534,700 | 0.99 | 255,038,000 | 100.0 | 268,115,000 | 100.0 | 281,192,000 | 100.0 | 315,027,000 | 100.0 | 1 |

Global Table 24. WORLD POPULATION AND CHRISTIANS DIVIDED INTO 17 RACES AND 432 MAJOR ETHNOLINGUISTIC PEOPLES, AD 1900-2000.

1. This table is the source table from which Global Table 5 in Part 1 is derived. In its turn, the table is itself derived from the 223 Tables 1 presented in Part 7, by multiplying each's total population (or, its total of affiliated Christians) by its respective ethnolinguistic composition, given under each's SECULAR DATA (or, PEOPLES in Tables 2 footnotes), using the codes and classification in Part 4.
2. The codes and names of peoples in the first 2 columns are set out in exactly the same way as in our classification PEOPLES OF THE WORLD in Part 4. This classification should be consulted to see exactly how any particular group is defined. The 71 names of ethnolinguistic families are set out below in italic type, and the totals shown on each's line are the sums of (a) each's major component peoples, whose names are listed, indented, under each's family name, together with (b) in several cases, additional figures for miniscule populations too small to classify or enumerate in detail.
3. *People groups.* This column gives the total number of distinct or separate component ethnolinguistic peoples and people groups or cultures making up each people named below, and as defined in Part 4.
4. *Languages.* As defined here, the figures refer to the totals of all mother-tongue languages and/or dialects sufficiently distinct for separate translations of the Scriptures to be considered necessary or essential, whether or not such translations have yet been attempted. The totals are in many cases smaller than *People groups* in the preceding column because several culturally-distinct groups may often speak the same language for each's native or mother tongue.
5. *Translated.* The total of those languages enumerated in the preceding column which already possess translations of the Scriptures in whole or in part, as of 1980. These totals, which come from the Encyclopedia's database, are in a number of cases larger than those in the 2 major published listings, *Scriptures of the World* (UBS) and *Ethnologue* (WBT), because each of these omits numbers of languages for which the other gives translation data.
6. *Population.* The following columns, except the last two, all refer to total populations of the peoples named.
7. *Annual increase, 1970-1985.* The nett population increase per year in each group due to natural demographic increase (the 'population explosion').
8. *% Christians in 1980.* The last column but one gives affiliated Christians (church members) in each group in 1980, expressed as a percentage of each's total population.
9. *Countries.* The final column gives the number of distinct countries of the world in which each people's population is numerically significant (defined as sufficiently large to be included in the present computerized analysis). Sub-totals for ethnolinguistic families with several component peoples are not included in this table.

| *Code* | **RACE** *Family* People | *People groups* | *Lang-uages* | *Trans-lated* | Population 1900 | Population mid-1970 | Annual increase 1970–1985 | Population mid-1975 | Population mid-1980 | Population mid-1985 | Population AD 2000 | % Christian in 1980 | Coun-tries |
|---|---|---|---|---|---|---|---|---|---|---|---|---|---|
| | **AUSTRALOID** | | | | | | | | | | | | |
| | AUSTRO-ASIATIC | | | | | | | | | | | | |
| AUG01 | *Ainu/Aborigine* | 23 | 22 | 8 | 58,000 | 280,700 | 6,776 | 312,820 | 348,460 | 384,100 | 493,300 | 91.00 | 2 |
| AUG02 | *Australian Aborigine* | 260 | 260 | 22 | 41,470 | 138,072 | 2,847 | 151,899 | 166,540 | 181,181 | 222,695 | 59.64 | 1 |
| AUG03 | *Mon-Khmer* | 114 | 106 | 25 | 3,541,293 | 10,458,364 | 329,941 | 11,949,690 | 13,757,774 | 15,565,858 | 22,677,538 | 4.27 | — |
| AUG03a | Khasi | 4 | 2 | 1 | 258,573 | 610,824 | 16,829 | 686,963 | 779,112 | 871,261 | 1,203,776 | 42.40 | 2 |
| AUG03b | Khmer | 2 | 2 | 2 | 2,330,520 | 6,867,985 | 224,709 | 7,876,655 | 9,115,080 | 10,353,505 | 15,240,967 | 0.11 | 5 |
| AUG03c | Mon | 2 | 2 | 1 | 216,670 | 634,447 | 18,267 | 719,839 | 817,124 | 914,409 | 1,299,992 | 0.72 | 2 |
| AUG03d | Nicobarese | 11 | 10 | 2 | 5,000 | 16,500 | 300 | 18,000 | 19,500 | 21,000 | 32,000 | 80.95 | 1 |
| AUG03z | other Mon-Khmer | 95 | 90 | 19 | 735,530 | 2,328,608 | 69,836 | 2,648,233 | 3,026,958 | 3,405,683 | 4,900,803 | 7.92 | 5 |
| AUG04 | *Munda-Santal* | 30 | 29 | 6 | 3,507,988 | 8,289,679 | 230,384 | 9,353,958 | 10,593,530 | 11,833,102 | 16,195,144 | 5.34 | — |
| AUG04a | Ho | 2 | 1 | 1 | 459,800 | 1,086,264 | 30,235 | 1,226,434 | 1,388,618 | 1,550,802 | 2,118,858 | 0.62 | 1 |
| AUG04b | Mundari | 3 | 3 | 1 | 459,800 | 1,086,264 | 30,235 | 1,226,434 | 1,388,618 | 1,550,802 | 2,118,858 | 21.61 | 1 |
| AUG04c | Santal | 4 | 4 | 1 | 1,898,688 | 4,487,755 | 124,561 | 5,061,439 | 5,733,367 | 6,405,295 | 8,779,141 | 1.81 | 3 |
| AUG04d | Saora | 1 | 1 | 1 | 229,900 | 543,132 | 15,118 | 613,217 | 694,309 | 775,401 | 1,059,429 | 3.90 | 1 |
| AUG04z | other Munda-Santal | 20 | 20 | 2 | 459,800 | 1,086,264 | 30,235 | 1,226,434 | 1,388,618 | 1,550,802 | 2,118,858 | 9.75 | 1 |
| AUG05 | *Negrito* | 40 | 40 | 9 | 77,600 | 376,604 | 14,560 | 444,437 | 522,203 | 599,969 | 889,707 | 6.50 | 1 |
| AUG06 | *Pre-Dravidian* | 47 | 42 | 12 | 2,995,000 | 7,092,114 | 197,590 | 8,008,100 | 9,068,011 | 10,127,922 | 13,838,739 | 10.09 | — |
| AUG06a | Bhil | 21 | 21 | 3 | 1,149,500 | 2,715,660 | 75,589 | 3,066,085 | 3,471,545 | 3,877,005 | 5,297,145 | 3.90 | 1 |
| AUG06b | Gond | 12 | 12 | 5 | 1,379,400 | 3,258,792 | 90,706 | 3,679,302 | 4,165,854 | 4,652,406 | 6,356,574 | 3.90 | 1 |
| AUG06c | Oraon | 2 | 1 | 1 | 459,800 | 1,086,264 | 30,235 | 1,226,434 | 1,388,618 | 1,550,802 | 2,118,858 | 43.71 | 1 |
| AUG06z | other Pre-Dravidian | 12 | 8 | 3 | 6,300 | 31,398 | 1,060 | 36,279 | 41,994 | 47,709 | 66,162 | 24.60 | 1 |
| AUG07 | *Vedda* | 1 | 1 | 0 | 5,200 | 700 | 0 | 700 | 700 | 500 | 0 | 2.70 | 1 |
| | OCEANIC | | | | | | | | | | | | — |
| AON08 | *Fijian* | 5 | 5 | 2 | 53,991 | 232,639 | 5,132 | 258,059 | 283,958 | 309,857 | 378,923 | 83.67 | 4 |
| AON09 | *Melanesian* | 555 | 476 | 102 | 585,249 | 1,415,655 | 40,898 | 1,603,743 | 1,824,636 | 2,045,529 | 2,910,117 | 84.39 | — |
| AON09a | New Caledonian | 26 | 26 | 5 | 25,764 | 51,339 | 1,649 | 58,875 | 67,824 | 76,773 | 116,337 | 96.56 | 1 |
| AON09b | New Guinea Melanesian | 204 | 198 | 36 | 226,119 | 471,367 | 13,069 | 530,553 | 602,061 | 673,569 | 984,346 | 65.86 | 1 |
| AON09c | New Hebridean | 120 | 117 | 34 | 41,452 | 77,446 | 2,489 | 88,514 | 102,339 | 116,164 | 175,180 | 85.57 | 2 |
| AON09d | Solomoni Melanesian | 85 | 85 | 20 | 82,374 | 179,072 | 5,667 | 204,784 | 235,746 | 266,708 | 398,689 | 85.65 | 4 |
| AON09e | Western Melanesian | 120 | 50 | 7 | 209,540 | 636,431 | 18,024 | 721,017 | 816,666 | 912,315 | 1,235,565 | 96.53 | 2 |
| AON10 | *Papuan* | 878 | 703 | 129 | 1,329,483 | 3,198,454 | 91,098 | 3,617,108 | 4,109,442 | 4,601,776 | 6,541,692 | 72.56 | — |
| AON10a | Iranese Papuan | 350 | 185 | 10 | 271,600 | 836,269 | 24,781 | 952,308 | 1,084,083 | 1,215,858 | 1,662,549 | 65.00 | 1 |
| AON10b | New Guinea Papuan | 470 | 465 | 108 | 870,893 | 1,815,463 | 50,337 | 2,043,417 | 2,318,829 | 2,594,241 | 3,791,194 | 75.17 | 1 |
| AON10c | North Halmaheran | 16 | 13 | 4 | 77,600 | 238,934 | 7,080 | 272,088 | 309,738 | 347,388 | 475,014 | 27.56 | 1 |
| AON10d | Solomoni Papuan | 15 | 15 | 4 | 28,020 | 56,302 | 1,561 | 63,398 | 71,914 | 80,430 | 117,676 | 95.33 | 2 |
| AON10e | Timorese Papuan | 22 | 22 | 0 | 77,600 | 238,934 | 7,080 | 272,088 | 309,738 | 347,388 | 475,014 | 43.00 | 1 |
| AON10f | Torres Strait Islander | 5 | 3 | 3 | 3,770 | 12,552 | 259 | 13,809 | 15,140 | 16,471 | 20,245 | 65.60 | 1 |
| | **CAPOID** | | | | | | | | | | | | |
| | EARLY AFRICAN | | | | | | | | | | | | |
| BYG11 | *Khoisan* | 49 | 47 | 3 | 49,620 | 195,328 | 5,660 | 220,906 | 251,930 | 282,954 | 441,056 | 68.23 | — |
| BYG11a | Bergdama | 1 | 1 | 0 | 12,354 | 55,071 | 1,409 | 61,596 | 69,165 | 76,734 | 114,927 | 99.91 | 1 |
| BYG11b | East African Bushman | 16 | 16 | 0 | 15,200 | 53,092 | 1,912 | 61,752 | 72,208 | 82,664 | 136,180 | 79.78 | 1 |
| BYG11c | Hottentot | 4 | 3 | 1 | 6,248 | 27,852 | 713 | 31,152 | 34,980 | 38,808 | 58,124 | 97.87 | 1 |
| BYG11d | South African Bushman | 28 | 27 | 2 | 15,818 | 59,313 | 1,626 | 66,406 | 75,577 | 84,748 | 131,825 | 13.32 | 3 |
| BYG12 | *Pygmy* | 15 | 12 | 1 | 83,770 | 227,487 | 6,760 | 257,648 | 295,084 | 332,520 | 519,917 | 12.40 | 6 |
| | **CAUCASIAN** | | | | | | | | | | | | |
| | EUROPEAN | | | | | | | | | | | | |
| CEW13 | *Albanian* | 5 | 5 | 5 | 1,428,140 | 3,482,971 | 74,694 | 3,838,976 | 4,229,915 | 4,620,854 | 5,790,123 | 14.17 | 4 |
| CEW14 | *Armenian* | 6 | 4 | 4 | 2,494,726 | 5,107,698 | 70,489 | 5,440,679 | 5,812,584 | 6,184,489 | 7,390,934 | 51.02 | 18 |
| CEW15 | *Baltic* | 4 | 4 | 4 | 2,186,346 | 4,370,005 | 45,609 | 4,589,969 | 4,826,084 | 5,062,199 | 5,682,398 | 88.11 | — |
| CEW15a | Latvian | 2 | 2 | 2 | 646,548 | 1,268,393 | 13,559 | 1,333,900 | 1,403,977 | 1,474,054 | 1,656,628 | 99.57 | 4 |
| CEW15b | Lithuanian | 2 | 2 | 2 | 1,539,798 | 3,101,612 | 32,050 | 3,256,069 | 3,422,107 | 3,588,145 | 4,025,770 | 83.42 | 3 |
| CEW16 | *Basque* | 8 | 8 | 8 | 555,400 | 925,132 | 9,178 | 969,719 | 1,016,907 | 1,064,095 | 1,212,975 | 94.28 | 2 |
| CEW17 | *Caucasian* | 40 | 39 | 6 | 3,352,426 | 6,551,284 | 73,358 | 6,904,281 | 7,284,861 | 7,665,441 | 8,713,425 | 13.35 | — |
| CEW17a | Adygo-Abkhazi | 5 | 5 | 2 | 294,082 | 619,156 | 9,486 | 663,723 | 714,012 | 764,301 | 935,013 | 0.00 | 6 |
| CEW17b | Dagestani | 26 | 26 | 2 | 753,936 | 1,456,608 | 15,208 | 1,530,228 | 1,608,690 | 1,687,152 | 1,890,162 | 0.00 | 1 |
| CEW17c | Georgian | 5 | 4 | 2 | 1,801,784 | 3,504,448 | 38,525 | 3,690,178 | 3,889,699 | 4,089,220 | 4,628,142 | 25.01 | 2 |
| CEW17d | Nakh | 4 | 4 | 0 | 502,624 | 971,072 | 10,139 | 1,020,152 | 1,072,460 | 1,124,768 | 1,260,108 | 0.00 | 1 |
| CEW18 | *Celtic* | 12 | 9 | 8 | 6,618,959 | 8,734,572 | 74,545 | 9,103,345 | 9,480,007 | 9,856,669 | 11,014,439 | 82.35 | — |
| CEW18a | Breton | 5 | 3 | 3 | 984,000 | 1,216,080 | 10,639 | 1,269,912 | 1,322,472 | 1,375,032 | 1,491,144 | 80.05 | 1 |
| CEW18b | Irish | 2 | 1 | 1 | 4,818,847 | 6,316,200 | 58,944 | 6,607,944 | 6,905,634 | 7,203,324 | 8,146,913 | 82.58 | 6 |
| CEW18c | Scottish Gaelic | 1 | 1 | 1 | 76,200 | 110,960 | 408 | 112,854 | 115,038 | 117,222 | 125,588 | 73.46 | 1 |
| CEW18d | Welsh | 1 | 1 | 1 | 739,532 | 1,090,772 | 4,550 | 1,112,055 | 1,136,263 | 1,160,471 | 1,250,114 | 84.54 | 4 |
| CEW18z | other Celtic | 3 | 3 | 2 | 380 | 560 | 4 | 580 | 600 | 620 | 680 | 79.17 | 1 |
| CEW19 | *Germanic* | 63 | 57 | 54 | 163,637,061 | 343,204,948 | 2,546,848 | 355,617,908 | 368,673,359 | 381,728,814 | 424,760,747 | 79.07 | — |
| CEW19a | Afrikaner | 1 | 1 | 1 | 473,627 | 2,103,301 | 68,917 | 2,413,284 | 2,792,476 | 3,171,668 | 4,909,835 | 79.16 | 8 |
| CEW19b | Alsatian | 1 | 1 | 1 | 1,107,000 | 1,368,090 | 11,969 | 1,428,651 | 1,487,781 | 1,546,911 | 1,677,537 | 80.05 | 1 |
| CEW19c | Anglo-Australian | 1 | 1 | 1 | 3,170,424 | 10,470,719 | 214,914 | 11,514,151 | 12,619,852 | 13,725,553 | 16,872,016 | 66.75 | 11 |
| CEW19d | Anglo-Canadian | 1 | 1 | 1 | 2,412,277 | 8,889,578 | 127,211 | 9,451,677 | 10,161,684 | 10,871,691 | 12,975,821 | 75.29 | 2 |
| CEW19e | Anglo-New Zealander | 1 | 1 | 1 | 647,072 | 2,232,676 | 35,398 | 2,401,391 | 2,586,653 | 2,771,915 | 3,385,333 | 75.82 | 6 |
| CEW19f | Austrian | 2 | 1 | 1 | 6,232,254 | 8,476,712 | 29,777 | 8,624,586 | 8,774,476 | 8,924,366 | 9,499,271 | 90.19 | 8 |
| CEW19g | Danish | 1 | 1 | 1 | 2,475,559 | 5,013,760 | 18,981 | 5,117,624 | 5,203,567 | 5,289,510 | 5,494,631 | 94.55 | 8 |
| CEW19h | Dutch | 1 | 1 | 2 | 5,296,551 | 13,424,262 | 113,966 | 14,017,102 | 14,563,913 | 15,110,724 | 16,633,332 | 73.20 | 12 |
| CEW19i | English | 25 | 25 | 25 | 34,774,534 | 53,364,988 | 283,301 | 54,677,258 | 56,197,957 | 57,718,658 | 63,630,757 | 76.34 | 92 |
| CEW19j | Faeroese | 1 | 1 | 1 | 14,550 | 37,830 | 194 | 38,800 | 39,770 | 40,740 | 45,590 | 98.34 | 1 |
| CEW19k | Flemish | 1 | 1 | 1 | 4,214,998 | 6,022,203 | 28,070 | 6,160,752 | 6,302,907 | 6,445,062 | 6,777,202 | 89.54 | 5 |
| CEW19l | Frisian | 3 | 3 | 2 | 176,120 | 443,088 | 3,655 | 462,366 | 479,638 | 496,910 | 544,340 | 71.63 | 1 |
| CEW19m | German | 12 | 10 | 10 | 45,999,750 | 87,145,749 | 289,441 | 88,868,256 | 90,040,133 | 91,212,011 | 97,500,470 | 85.61 | 32 |
| CEW19n | Icelander | 1 | 1 | 1 | 82,500 | 222,550 | 2,782 | 235,777 | 250,370 | 264,963 | 305,721 | 93.90 | 2 |
| CEW19o | Luxemburger | 1 | 1 | 0 | 199,700 | 286,940 | 533 | 289,602 | 292,271 | 294,940 | 299,535 | 87.89 | 2 |
| CEW19p | Norwegian | 4 | 4 | 2 | 2,478,531 | 4,633,059 | 32,488 | 4,800,049 | 4,957,937 | 5,115,825 | 5,494,376 | 93.06 | 6 |
| CEW19q | Swedish | 2 | 1 | 1 | 5,089,666 | 8,324,226 | 53,329 | 8,585,485 | 8,857,520 | 9,129,555 | 9,778,712 | 72.60 | 6 |
| CEW19r | Ulster Irish | 1 | 1 | 1 | 718,100 | 1,028,180 | 4,014 | 1,046,996 | 1,068,322 | 1,089,648 | 1,170,312 | 74.11 | 2 |
| CEW19s | USA White | 3 | 1 | 1 | 48,073,834 | 129,716,974 | 1,227,908 | 135,484,038 | 141,996,069 | 148,508,101 | 167,765,893 | 76.24 | 48 |
| CEW20 | *Greek* | 7 | 2 | 2 | 4,016,980 | 10,889,187 | 55,986 | 11,158,801 | 11,449,022 | 11,739,243 | 12,572,701 | 94.45 | 33 |
| CEW21 | *Latin* | 73 | 49 | 46 | 112,693,627 | 184,551,040 | 1,519,797 | 192,083,051 | 199,748,914 | 207,414,777 | 229,500,285 | 85.90 | — |
| CEW21a | Catalonian | 5 | 1 | 1 | 3,271,715 | 5,847,473 | 59,810 | 6,137,381 | 6,445,571 | 6,753,761 | 7,758,816 | 96.40 | 4 |
| CEW21b | French | 10 | 9 | 9 | 35,216,299 | 45,317,147 | 406,536 | 47,365,773 | 49,382,467 | 51,399,160 | 56,142,732 | 83.94 | 42 |
| CEW21c | French-Canadian | 1 | 1 | 1 | 1,908,970 | 6,963,038 | 98,681 | 7,399,587 | 7,949,844 | 8,500,101 | 10,130,651 | 75.09 | 2 |
| CEW21d | Galician | 1 | 1 | 1 | 1,632,388 | 3,243,020 | 34,648 | 3,410,912 | 3,589,504 | 3,768,096 | 4,330,679 | 96.24 | 3 |
| CEW21e | Italian | 16 | 12 | 12 | 35,127,961 | 60,192,810 | 356,937 | 62,038,760 | 63,762,161 | 65,485,563 | 70,044,271 | 83.01 | 29 |
| CEW21f | Moldavian | 1 | 1 | 1 | 1,382,216 | 2,670,448 | 27,882 | 2,805,418 | 2,949,265 | 3,093,112 | 3,465,297 | 59.03 | 1 |
| CEW21g | Portuguese | 4 | 1 | 1 | 6,456,194 | 10,876,722 | 73,515 | 11,201,117 | 11,611,860 | 12,022,603 | 13,619,048 | 91.80 | 20 |
| CEW21h | Rhaeto-Romanian | 7 | 4 | 4 | 257,523 | 425,091 | 2,302 | 437,441 | 448,105 | 458,769 | 485,060 | 84.59 | 2 |
| CEW21i | Romanian | 5 | 2 | 2 | 9,476,891 | 17,504,446 | 157,187 | 18,312,688 | 19,076,306 | 19,839,924 | 22,275,739 | 83.87 | 8 |
| CEW21j | Sardinian | 4 | 4 | 4 | 726,000 | 1,178,430 | 6,059 | 1,210,506 | 1,239,018 | 1,267,530 | 1,339,272 | 83.64 | 1 |

*Continued opposite*

*Global Table 24 (continued)*

| Code | **RACE** *Family* People | *People groups* | *Lang-uages* | *Trans-lated* | Population 1900 | Population mid-1970 | Annual increase 1970–1985 | Population mid-1975 | Population mid-1980 | Population mid-1985 | Population AD 2000 | % Christian in 1980 | Coun-tries |
|---|---|---|---|---|---|---|---|---|---|---|---|---|---|
| CEW21k | Spanish | 6 | 2 | 2 | 14,715,267 | 26,725,344 | 278,506 | 28,069,095 | 29,510,394 | 30,951,693 | 35,823,300 | 96.11 | 27 |
| CEW21l | Walloon | 1 | 1 | 1 | 2,303,266 | 3,335,069 | 15,296 | 3,410,024 | 3,488,038 | 3,566,052 | 3,751,153 | 90.39 | 5 |
| CEW21z | other Latin | 12 | 10 | 7 | 218,372 | 270,562 | 2,349 | 282,439 | 294,051 | 305,663 | 331,177 | 80.95 | 2 |
| CEW22 | *Slav* | 35 | 21 | 17 | 142,235,223 | 256,829,327 | 2,519,200 | 269,042,844 | 282,021,281 | 294,999,720 | 328,024,138 | 54.39 | — |
| CEW22a | Bosnian | 1 | 1 | 0 | 800,440 | 1,746,396 | 17,208 | 1,830,930 | 1,918,479 | 2,006,028 | 2,227,440 | 0.00 | 2 |
| CEW22b | Bulgar | 4 | 3 | 3 | 3,274,067 | 7,381,193 | 52,627 | 7,652,149 | 7,907,467 | 8,162,785 | 8,789,274 | 70.91 | 6 |
| CEW22c | Byelorussian | 3 | 1 | 1 | 4,668,816 | 8,934,486 | 92,955 | 9,384,414 | 9,864,036 | 10,343,658 | 11,580,048 | 70.58 | 2 |
| CEW22d | Croatian | 1 | 1 | 1 | 2,048,986 | 4,445,201 | 42,130 | 4,652,448 | 4,866,498 | 5,080,548 | 5,606,292 | 90.16 | 6 |
| CEW22e | Czech | 4 | 1 | 1 | 7,810,532 | 9,508,999 | 58,671 | 9,796,296 | 10,095,711 | 10,395,127 | 11,222,580 | 79.09 | 8 |
| CEW22f | Kashubian | 1 | 1 | 0 | 145,200 | 194,838 | 1,706 | 203,046 | 211,896 | 220,746 | 239,076 | 90.43 | 1 |
| CEW22g | Macedonian | 1 | 1 | 1 | 696,187 | 1,565,056 | 13,559 | 1,632,133 | 1,700,643 | 1,769,153 | 1,937,530 | 90.67 | 4 |
| CEW22h | Montenegrin | 1 | 1 | 0 | 236,400 | 515,782 | 5,019 | 540,496 | 565,968 | 591,440 | 654,114 | 37.34 | 2 |
| CEW22i | Polish | 2 | 1 | 1 | 25,411,403 | 36,061,773 | 323,294 | 37,613,488 | 39,294,693 | 40,975,898 | 44,669,722 | 90.49 | 14 |
| CEW22j | Russian | 3 | 2 | 2 | 66,828,858 | 129,103,958 | 1,349,218 | 135,632,721 | 142,596,114 | 149,559,507 | 167,676,501 | 31.41 | 28 |
| CEW22k | Ruthenian | 1 | 1 | 0 | 412,662 | 915,665 | 9,113 | 959,248 | 1,006,795 | 1,054,342 | 1,184,567 | 91.23 | 3 |
| CEW22l | Serbian | 2 | 1 | 1 | 4,150,235 | 9,010,910 | 81,026 | 9,413,373 | 9,821,174 | 10,228,975 | 11,268,909 | 82.93 | 10 |
| CEW22m | Slovak | 3 | 1 | 1 | 3,779,504 | 4,754,689 | 30,169 | 4,902,090 | 5,056,384 | 5,210,678 | 5,635,926 | 79.87 | 7 |
| CEW22n | Slovene | 2 | 2 | 2 | 899,562 | 1,859,469 | 16,560 | 1,941,374 | 2,025,064 | 2,108,755 | 2,314,596 | 95.20 | 3 |
| CEW22o | Sorb | 2 | 2 | 2 | 184,500 | 255,870 | 450 | 257,895 | 260,370 | 262,845 | 273,495 | 63.36 | 1 |
| CEW22p | Ukrainian | 4 | 1 | 1 | 20,887,771 | 40,574,794 | 425,490 | 42,630,468 | 44,829,689 | 47,028,910 | 52,743,568 | 69.07 | 10 |
| | INDO-IRANIAN | | | | | | | | | | | | |
| CNN23 | *Dravidian* | 50 | 50 | 10 | 58,556,534 | 140,097,732 | 3,893,953 | 158,177,131 | 179,037,282 | 199,897,433 | 272,767,910 | 10.51 | — |
| CNN23a | Kanarese | 5 | 5 | 2 | 12,420,550 | 29,364,585 | 817,315 | 33,153,640 | 37,537,741 | 41,921,842 | 57,275,156 | 3.11 | 3 |
| CNN23b | Malayali | 3 | 3 | 1 | 8,983,610 | 21,280,188 | 593,688 | 24,032,879 | 27,217,084 | 30,401,289 | 41,549,842 | 31.55 | 7 |
| CNN23c | Tamil | 5 | 5 | 1 | 18,709,242 | 45,834,396 | 1,263,718 | 51,722,415 | 58,471,585 | 65,220,755 | 88,595,991 | 9.56 | 12 |
| CNN23d | Telugu | 5 | 5 | 1 | 18,208,937 | 43,057,544 | 1,198,473 | 48,613,877 | 55,042,266 | 61,470,655 | 83,987,951 | 6.32 | 5 |
| CNN23z | other Dravidian | 32 | 32 | 5 | 234,195 | 561,019 | 20,759 | 654,320 | 768,606 | 882,892 | 1,358,970 | 0.19 | 2 |
| CNT24 | *Iranian* | 131 | 48 | 10 | 17,793,682 | 51,000,332 | 1,659,550 | 58,512,596 | 67,595,802 | 76,679,008 | 114,153,330 | 0.32 | — |
| CNT24a | Afghani | 64 | 3 | 1 | 5,039,075 | 14,702,563 | 476,663 | 16,860,246 | 19,469,184 | 22,078,122 | 33,147,966 | 0.08 | 3 |
| CNT24b | Baluchi | 5 | 1 | 1 | 893,075 | 2,272,271 | 82,911 | 2,645,426 | 3,101,372 | 3,557,318 | 5,444,630 | 0.10 | 5 |
| CNT24c | Kurdish | 9 | 7 | 3 | 2,303,120 | 6,936,629 | 243,224 | 8,039,646 | 9,368,854 | 10,698,062 | 16,234,772 | 0.00 | 8 |
| CNT24d | Nuristani | 9 | 6 | 0 | 35,700 | 118,846 | 3,542 | 134,960 | 154,266 | 173,572 | 256,578 | 0.00 | 1 |
| CNT24e | Ossetian | 5 | 1 | 1 | 251,312 | 485,536 | 5,069 | 510,076 | 536,230 | 562,384 | 630,054 | 36.08 | 1 |
| CNT24f | Persian | 10 | 9 | 2 | 4,448,234 | 13,068,964 | 469,493 | 15,184,294 | 17,763,894 | 20,343,494 | 30,791,435 | 0.04 | 11 |
| CNT24g | Tadzhik | 9 | 5 | 1 | 2,819,916 | 7,452,647 | 170,575 | 8,236,741 | 9,158,397 | 10,080,053 | 13,795,010 | 0.00 | 3 |
| CNT24z | other Iranian | 20 | 16 | 1 | 2,003,250 | 5,962,876 | 208,073 | 6,901,207 | 8,043,605 | 9,186,003 | 13,843,885 | 0.00 | 3 |
| CNN25 | *North Indian* | 267 | 193 | 70 | 225,669,355 | 536,186,499 | 15,086,782 | 604,036,471 | 687,054,242 | 770,072,015 | 1,078,525,511 | 1.44 | — |
| CNN25a | Assamese | 2 | 1 | 1 | 6,021,362 | 14,272,332 | 397,088 | 16,112,862 | 18,243,214 | 20,373,566 | 27,853,074 | 3.72 | 3 |
| CNN25b | Bengali | 20 | 5 | 2 | 46,490,455 | 109,629,872 | 2,877,454 | 121,157,027 | 138,404,394 | 155,651,761 | 225,481,849 | 0.55 | 5 |
| CNN25c | Bihari | 21 | 15 | 5 | 9,538,498 | 22,683,612 | 626,134 | 25,549,151 | 28,944,939 | 32,340,727 | 44,655,436 | 0.02 | 6 |
| CNN25d | Goanese | 3 | 3 | 2 | 462,450 | 1,096,070 | 30,577 | 1,237,787 | 1,401,840 | 1,565,893 | 2,143,018 | 39.78 | 2 |
| CNN25e | Gujarati | 10 | 8 | 3 | 11,612,310 | 27,270,917 | 755,864 | 30,773,204 | 34,829,553 | 38,885,902 | 53,149,553 | 0.63 | 5 |
| CNN25f | Gypsy | 25 | 19 | 14 | 2,355,548 | 4,539,083 | 59,651 | 4,827,746 | 5,135,583 | 5,443,420 | 6,433,864 | 39.16 | 19 |
| CNN25g | Hindi | 30 | 20 | 6 | 55,792,927 | 131,758,763 | 3,656,872 | 148,710,092 | 168,327,473 | 187,944,854 | 256,702,215 | 0.54 | 12 |
| CNN25h | Jat | 6 | 5 | 2 | 1,680,030 | 3,989,634 | 148,520 | 4,656,960 | 5,474,832 | 6,292,704 | 9,696,984 | 1.35 | 1 |
| CNN25i | Kashmiri | 30 | 25 | 2 | 1,966,475 | 4,647,301 | 132,194 | 5,258,536 | 5,969,232 | 6,679,928 | 9,210,052 | 0.02 | 2 |
| CNN25j | Marathi | 12 | 9 | 1 | 20,691,000 | 48,881,880 | 1,360,593 | 55,189,530 | 62,487,810 | 69,786,090 | 95,348,610 | 2.17 | 1 |
| CNN25k | Nepalese | 22 | 19 | 8 | 3,155,442 | 7,954,276 | 213,819 | 8,918,131 | 10,092,467 | 11,266,803 | 16,216,947 | 0.03 | 4 |
| CNN25l | Oriya | 14 | 11 | 3 | 9,196,000 | 21,725,280 | 604,708 | 24,528,680 | 27,772,360 | 31,016,040 | 42,377,160 | 2.63 | 1 |
| CNN25m | Parsi | 1 | 1 | 1 | 108,290 | 120,970 | 3,325 | 136,640 | 154,220 | 171,800 | 218,700 | 0.00 | 10 |
| CNN25n | Punjabi | 8 | 6 | 4 | 25,461,248 | 60,116,931 | 2,001,906 | 69,206,200 | 80,135,997 | 91,065,794 | 134,237,379 | 1.95 | 11 |
| CNN25o | Rajasthani | 20 | 15 | 7 | 10,856,210 | 25,648,102 | 715,033 | 28,962,319 | 32,798,427 | 36.634,535 | 50,087,011 | 0.17 | 2 |
| CNN25p | Sindhi | 9 | 4 | 2 | 3,897,030 | 9,245,970 | 328,891 | 10,730,211 | 12,534,879 | 14,339,547 | 21,690,711 | 0.82 | 2 |
| CNN25q | Sinhalese | 4 | 3 | 1 | 2,591,175 | 8,930,262 | 210,444 | 9,979,011 | 11,034,693 | 12,090,375 | 15,248,790 | 2.79 | 2 |
| CNN25r | Urdu | 5 | 4 | 3 | 12,452,118 | 29,441,216 | 861,587 | 33,399,801 | 38,057,075 | 42,714,349 | 59,706,611 | 0.00 | 3 |
| CNN25z | other North Indian | 25 | 20 | 3 | 472,304 | 1,203,330 | 32,920 | 1,353,949 | 1,532,528 | 1,711,107 | 2,412,343 | 21.93 | 5 |
| | LATIN AMERICAN | | | | | | | | | | | | |
| CLT26 | *Branco (White)* | 1 | 1 | 1 | 9,552,537 | 50,547,215 | 1,654,227 | 58,252,838 | 67,089,495 | 75,926,152 | 112,762,904 | 94.56 | 6 |
| CLT27 | *Blanco (White)* | 17 | 1 | 1 | 12,101,301 | 52,694,423 | 1,218,826 | 58,415,420 | 64,882,689 | 71,349,958 | 95,763,180 | 87.04 | 27 |
| CLN28 | *Mestiço* | 6 | 1 | 1 | 2,150,000 | 11,424,400 | 374,220 | 13,167,600 | 15,166,680 | 17,165,760 | 25,500,840 | 94.82 | 1 |
| CLN29 | *Mestizo* | 20 | 2 | 2 | 23,776,431 | 86,475,670 | 2,692,039 | 98,862,494 | 113,396,063 | 127,929,632 | 191,015,375 | 92.05 | 21 |
| | MIDDLE EASTERN | | | | | | | | | | | | |
| CMT30 | *Arab* | 40 | 23 | 15 | 33,929,044 | 106,839,718 | 3,553,380 | 122,993,668 | 142,373,506 | 161,753,344 | 245,392,419 | 7.36 | 59 |
| CMT31 | *Assyrian* | 8 | 6 | 5 | 123,450 | 460,701 | 17,627 | 540,287 | 636,958 | 733,629 | 1,155,257 | 77.52 | 8 |
| CMT32 | *Berber* | 118 | 38 | 10 | 3,150,860 | 9,627,765 | 327,638 | 11,115,620 | 12,904,148 | 14,692,676 | 22,619,748 | 0.02 | — |
| CMT32a | Arabized Berber | 1 | 1 | 0 | 492,400 | 1,477,144 | 45,880 | 1,689,200 | 1,935,944 | 2,182,688 | 3,219,596 | 0.00 | 3 |
| CMT32b | Beraber | 12 | 1 | 1 | 535,600 | 1,557,978 | 54,157 | 1,802,912 | 2,099,552 | 2,396,192 | 3,698,112 | 0.00 | 1 |
| CMT32c | Kabyle | 2 | 2 | 2 | 473,800 | 1,475,990 | 56,629 | 1,729,576 | 2,042,284 | 2,354,992 | 3,776,289 | 0.19 | 1 |
| CMT32d | Oasis Berber | 12 | 8 | 0 | 161,600 | 475,133 | 16,569 | 549,327 | 640,827 | 732,327 | 1,138,287 | 0.00 | 4 |
| CMT32e | Rif | 19 | 2 | 1 | 306,800 | 892,434 | 31,022 | 1,032,736 | 1,202,656 | 1,372,576 | 2,118,336 | 0.00 | 1 |
| CMT32f | Shawiya | 1 | 1 | 0 | 193,200 | 601,860 | 23,092 | 705,264 | 832,776 | 960,288 | 1,539,846 | 0.00 | 1 |
| CMT32g | Shluh | 36 | 3 | 3 | 577,200 | 1,678,986 | 58,364 | 1,942,944 | 2,262,624 | 2,582,304 | 3,985,344 | 0.00 | 1 |
| CMT32h | Tuareg | 12 | 6 | 3 | 166,600 | 686,800 | 20,783 | 781,926 | 894,628 | 1,007,330 | 1,597,199 | 0.00 | 5 |
| CMT32i | Zenaga | 8 | 2 | 0 | 12,860 | 54,356 | 1,409 | 60,859 | 68,441 | 76,023 | 111,363 | 0.00 | 2 |
| CMT32z | other Berber | 15 | 12 | 0 | 230,800 | 727,084 | 19,733 | 820,876 | 924,416 | 1,027,956 | 1,435,376 | 0.00 | 2 |
| CMT33 | *Cushitic* | 107 | 81 | 17 | 5,823,540 | 18,395,149 | 518,979 | 20,793,046 | 23,584,952 | 26,376,858 | 40,768,361 | 27.06 | — |
| CMT33a | Agau | 15 | 11 | 2 | 40,000 | 124,275 | 3,334 | 139,875 | 157,610 | 175,345 | 268,325 | 10.74 | 1 |
| CMT33b | Galla | 16 | 12 | 6 | 3,208,700 | 9,975,741 | 268,012 | 11,229,753 | 12,655,864 | 14,081,975 | 21,559,060 | 33.44 | 2 |
| CMT33c | Iraqw | 1 | 1 | 1 | 64,600 | 225,641 | 8,124 | 262,446 | 306,884 | 351,322 | 578,765 | 13.98 | 1 |
| CMT33d | Sidamo | 35 | 35 | 4 | 720,000 | 2,236,950 | 60,003 | 2,517,750 | 2,836,980 | 3,156,210 | 4,829,850 | 72.79 | 1 |
| CMT33e | Somali | 15 | 2 | 2 | 1,362,320 | 4,552,093 | 137,271 | 5,170,727 | 5,924,815 | 6,678,903 | 10,503,434 | 0.03 | 8 |
| CMT33z | other Cushitic | 25 | 20 | 2 | 427,920 | 1,280,449 | 42,235 | 1,472,495 | 1,702,799 | 1,933,103 | 3,028,927 | 1.41 | 4 |
| CMT34 | *Ethiopic* | 16 | 13 | 4 | 2,856,120 | 8,873,805 | 238,026 | 9,987,711 | 11,254,068 | 12,520,425 | 19,159,527 | 86.42 | — |
| CMT34a | Amhara | 3 | 3 | 1 | 2,016,120 | 6,264,030 | 168,022 | 7,050,336 | 7,944,258 | 8,838,180 | 13,524,702 | 97.08 | 2 |
| CMT34b | Tigrai | 1 | 1 | 1 | 480,000 | 1,491,300 | 40,002 | 1,678,500 | 1,891,320 | 2,104,140 | 3,219,900 | 88.60 | 1 |
| CMT34c | Tigre | 1 | 1 | 1 | 160,000 | 497,100 | 13,334 | 559,500 | 630,440 | 701,380 | 1,073,300 | 3.84 | 1 |
| CMT34z | other Ethiopic | 11 | 8 | 1 | 200,000 | 621,375 | 16,668 | 699,375 | 788,050 | 876,725 | 1,341,625 | 42.96 | 1 |
| CMT35 | *Jewish* | 12 | 8 | 4 | 4,852,452 | 13,234,401 | 193,697 | 14,162,444 | 15,171,384 | 16,180,324 | 19,046,332 | 1.07 | 58 |
| CMT36 | *Maltese* | 1 | 1 | 1 | 216,431 | 369,265 | 2,108 | 378,091 | 390,354 | 402,617 | 418,122 | 91.15 | 4 |
| | **MONGOLIAN** | | | | | | | | | | | | |
| | AMERICAN INDIAN | | | | | | | | | | | | |
| MIR37 | *Central Amerindian* | 330 | 273 | 125 | 5,225,338 | 18,474,815 | 673,654 | 21,532,515 | 25,211,363 | 28,890,211 | 46,234,041 | 91.26 | — |
| MIR37a | Aztec | 20 | 16 | 8 | 892,433 | 3,223,659 | 119,837 | 3,766,165 | 4,422,033 | 5,077,901 | 8,199,070 | 92.12 | 2 |
| MIR37b | Maya | 65 | 59 | 36 | 1,298,948 | 4,327,701 | 151,836 | 5,022,101 | 5,846,063 | 6,670,025 | 10,443,756 | 89.21 | 5 |
| MIR37c | Mixtec | 40 | 36 | 20 | 272,146 | 1,006,260 | 39,304 | 1,184,080 | 1,399,300 | 1,614,520 | 2,644,880 | 93.20 | 1 |
| MIR37d | Otomí | 20 | 16 | 6 | 429,785 | 1,513,017 | 53,020 | 1,753,229 | 2,043,223 | 2,333,217 | 3,702,774 | 90.85 | 2 |
| MIR37e | Part-Indian | 5 | 1 | 0 | 1,399,547 | 5,032,898 | 184,293 | 5,867,620 | 6,875,826 | 7,884,032 | 12,671,500 | 91.83 | 6 |
| MIR37f | Zapotec | 60 | 50 | 11 | 312,968 | 1,157,199 | 45,200 | 1,361,692 | 1,609,195 | 1,856,698 | 3,041,612 | 93.20 | 1 |
| MIR37z | other Central Amerindian | 120 | 95 | 44 | 619,511 | 2,214,081 | 80,164 | 2,577,628 | 3,015,723 | 3,453,818 | 5,530,449 | 91.04 | 5 |
| MIR38 | *Northern Amerindian* | 215 | 195 | 48 | 482,933 | 1,504,508 | 17,845 | 1,585,332 | 1,682,964 | 1,780,596 | 2,069,336 | 71.16 | — |
| MIR38a | North American Indian | 195 | 185 | 48 | 306,277 | 914,321 | 10,214 | 960,989 | 1,016,463 | 1,071,937 | 1,235,872 | 70.35 | 2 |
| MIR38b | Part-Indian | 20 | 10 | 0 | 176,656 | 590,187 | 7,631 | 624,343 | 666,501 | 708,659 | 833,464 | 72.41 | 2 |
| MIR39 | *Southern Amerindian* | 1,591 | 1,238 | 151 | 4,232,657 | 15,094,662 | 480,130 | 17,326,344 | 19,895,956 | 22,465,568 | 33,486,960 | 91.30 | — |
| MIR39a | Arawak | 160 | 130 | 24 | 21,979 | 118,746 | 4,298 | 138,852 | 161,726 | 184,600 | 273,932 | 20.65 | 4 |
| MIR39b | Aymara | 7 | 5 | 1 | 621,881 | 2,085,081 | 60,439 | 2,364,111 | 2,689,475 | 3,014,839 | 4,423,236 | 93.84 | 4 |
| MIR39c | Carib | 120 | 96 | 13 | 25,541 | 95,088 | 3,017 | 109,041 | 125,253 | 141,465 | 202,947 | 37.05 | 6 |
| MIR39d | Jungle Amerindian | 530 | 420 | 56 | 127,902 | 502,265 | 17,039 | 581,536 | 672,651 | 763,766 | 1,147,686 | 16.91 | 7 |
| MIR39e | Lowland Amerindian | 310 | 210 | 36 | 165,372 | 797,934 | 23,669 | 908,377 | 1,034,618 | 1,160,859 | 1,654,983 | 50.43 | 8 |
| MIR39f | Mapuche | 9 | 1 | 1 | 103,565 | 327,915 | 6,531 | 358,855 | 393,225 | 427,595 | 537,425 | 70.08 | 1 |
| MIR39g | Quechua | 45 | 36 | 12 | 3,157,540 | 11,139,526 | 364,577 | 12,834,813 | 14,785,303 | 16,735,793 | 25,200,686 | 98.96 | 5 |
| MIR39z | other Southern Amerindian | 410 | 340 | 8 | 108,877 | 228,107 | 560 | 230,759 | 233,705 | 236,651 | 246,065 | 58.40 | 1 |
| | ARCTIC MONGOLOID | | | | | | | | | | | | |
| MRY40 | *Eskimo-Aleut* | 12 | 11 | 11 | 14,847 | 60,956 | 1,266 | 67,888 | 73,618 | 79,348 | 93,311 | 70.85 | — |
| MRY40a | Aleut | 3 | 2 | 2 | 1,000 | 1,300 | 0 | 1,300 | 1,300 | 1,300 | 2,000 | 58.40 | 1 |
| MRY40b | Eskimo | 9 | 9 | 9 | 13,847 | 59,656 | 1,266 | 66,588 | 72,318 | 78,048 | 91,311 | 70.86 | 2 |
| | ASIAN | | | | | | | | | | | | |
| MSY41 | *Altaic* | 95 | 65 | 25 | 42,668,778 | 90,731,143 | 1,807,240 | 99,169,920 | 108,803,485 | 118,437,050 | 152,625,288 | 0.81 | — |
| MSY41a | Azerbaijani | 8 | 4 | 1 | 4,190,776 | 9,635,568 | 215,357 | 10,623,478 | 11,789,135 | 12,954,792 | 17,270,447 | 0.00 | 2 |
| MSY41b | Bashkir | 3 | 1 | 1 | 628,280 | 1,213,840 | 12,674 | 1,275,190 | 1,340,575 | 1,405,960 | 1,575,135 | 7.22 | 1 |
| MSY41c | Chuvash | 1 | 1 | 1 | 879,592 | 1,699,376 | 17,743 | 1,785,266 | 1,876,805 | 1,968,344 | 2,205,189 | 20.62 | 1 |
| MSY41d | Gagauz | 1 | 1 | 1 | 129,400 | 251,258 | 2,594 | 263,831 | 277,190 | 290,549 | 325,063 | 71.90 | 2 |

*Continued overleaf*

*Global Table 24 (continued)*

| Code | **RACE** *Family* People | People groups | Languages | Translated | Population 1900 | Population mid-1970 | Annual increase 1970–1985 | Population mid-1975 | Population mid-1980 | Population mid-1985 | Population AD 2000 | % Christian in 1980 | Countries |
|---|---|---|---|---|---|---|---|---|---|---|---|---|---|
| MSY41e | Kazakh | 1 | 1 | 1 | 3,634,280 | 6,884,925 | 78,258 | 7,264,065 | 7,667,500 | 8,070,935 | 9,119,010 | 0.00 | 3 |
| MSY41f | Khalka-Mongol | 10 | 2 | 2 | 1,773,570 | 3,265,295 | 68,457 | 3,594,335 | 3,949,860 | 4,305,385 | 5,369,070 | 0.01 | 2 |
| MSY41g | Kirgiz | 1 | 1 | 1 | 889,792 | 1,733,332 | 18,755 | 1,823,826 | 1,920,881 | 2,017,936 | 2,278,497 | 0.00 | 2 |
| MSY41h | Tatar | 7 | 2 | 2 | 3,030,488 | 5,855,166 | 61,073 | 6,150,883 | 6,465,892 | 6,780,901 | 7,596,442 | 1.50 | 3 |
| MSY41i | Tungus-Manchu | 12 | 11 | 2 | 1,888,000 | 3,031,220 | 52,824 | 3,289,100 | 3,559,460 | 3,829,820 | 4,509,180 | 0.00 | 1 |
| MSY41j | Turkish | 4 | 1 | 1 | 13,836,958 | 33,994,433 | 924,634 | 38,249,070 | 43,240,757 | 48,232,444 | 68,002,243 | 0.02 | 16 |
| MSY41k | Turkmen | 4 | 1 | 1 | 1,342,798 | 2,992,535 | 55,635 | 3,250,605 | 3,548,879 | 3,847,153 | 4,929,059 | 0.00 | 7 |
| MSY41l | Uzbek | 5 | 1 | 1 | 6,301,788 | 12,552,698 | 148,484 | 13,263,664 | 14,037,534 | 14,811,404 | 17,063,958 | 0.00 | 2 |
| MSY41m | Yakut | 1 | 1 | 1 | 125,656 | 242,768 | 2,535 | 255,038 | 268,115 | 281,192 | 315,027 | 36.08 | 1 |
| MSY41y | other Mongolian | 15 | 15 | 3 | 298,292 | 615,856 | 8,858 | 658,216 | 704,440 | 750,664 | 891,144 | 0.00 | 2 |
| MSY41z | other Turkic | 22 | 22 | 6 | 3,719,108 | 6,762,873 | 139,359 | 7,423,353 | 8,156,462 | 8,889,571 | 11,175,824 | 0.00 | 6 |
| MSY42 | *Chinese* | 81 | 68 | 29 | 454,047,666 | 752,225,570 | 13,415,056 | 817,541,171 | 886,376,116 | 955,211,061 | 1,132,226,641 | 0.78 | — |
| MSY42a | Han Chinese | 75 | 65 | 28 | 451,215,666 | 747,678,740 | 13,335,820 | 812,607,521 | 881,036,926 | 949,466,331 | 1,125,462,871 | 0.79 | 61 |
| MSY42b | Hui | 6 | 3 | 1 | 2,832,000 | 4,546,830 | 79,236 | 4,933,650 | 5,339,190 | 5,744,730 | 6,763,770 | 0.00 | 1 |
| MSY43 | *Eurasian* | 25 | 15 | 0 | 53,485 | 174,694 | 4,766 | 197,114 | 222,351 | 247,588 | 333,749 | 99.04 | 5 |
| MSY44 | *Indo-Malay* | 596 | 540 | 134 | 48,806,120 | 165,162,601 | 5,268,440 | 189,774,150 | 217,847,016 | 245,919,881 | 347,014,751 | 28.92 | — |
| MSY44a | Balinese | 2 | 2 | 1 | 814,800 | 2,508,807 | 74,344 | 2,856,924 | 3,252,249 | 3,647,574 | 4,987,647 | 1.05 | 1 |
| MSY44b | Batak | 7 | 7 | 5 | 1,125,200 | 3,464,543 | 102,666 | 3,945,276 | 4,491,201 | 5,037,126 | 6,887,703 | 94.27 | 1 |
| MSY44c | Buginese | 2 | 2 | 1 | 1,090,600 | 3,366,008 | 99,832 | 3,833,418 | 4,364,328 | 4,895,238 | 6,694,304 | 0.00 | 2 |
| MSY44d | Chamorro | 1 | 1 | 1 | 3,960 | 11,110 | 374 | 12,870 | 14,850 | 16,830 | 23,980 | 93.42 | 1 |
| MSY44e | Iban | 2 | 2 | 1 | 55,037 | 275,175 | 9,245 | 317,799 | 367,628 | 417,457 | 578,372 | 30.61 | 2 |
| MSY44f | Ilocan | 1 | 1 | 1 | 966,447 | 4,615,987 | 173,058 | 5,425,924 | 6,346,574 | 7,267,224 | 10,784,069 | 89.28 | 3 |
| MSY44g | Javanese | 9 | 2 | 2 | 16,382,971 | 50,618,520 | 1,500,967 | 57,645,093 | 65,628,191 | 73,611,289 | 100,680,498 | 2.39 | 7 |
| MSY44h | Madurese | 7 | 1 | 1 | 2,716,000 | 8,362,690 | 247,814 | 9,523,080 | 10,840,830 | 12,158,580 | 16,625,490 | 1.57 | 1 |
| MSY44i | Makassarese | 4 | 3 | 1 | 465,600 | 1,433,604 | 42,482 | 1,632,528 | 1,858,428 | 2,084,328 | 2,850,084 | 0.00 | 1 |
| MSY44j | Malagasy | 12 | 11 | 2 | 2,594,852 | 6,852,742 | 234,265 | 7,916,649 | 9,195,391 | 10,474,132 | 17,436,948 | 47.10 | 5 |
| MSY44k | Malay | 10 | 8 | 4 | 2,656,302 | 10,619,883 | 339,164 | 12,194,448 | 14,011,524 | 15,828,600 | 21,989,060 | 0.02 | 11 |
| MSY44l | Minahasan | 15 | 15 | 3 | 232,800 | 716,802 | 21,241 | 816,264 | 929,214 | 1,042,164 | 1,425,042 | 99.96 | 1 |
| MSY44m | Palawan | 6 | 6 | 3 | 22,800 | 112,812 | 4,380 | 133,311 | 156,609 | 179,907 | 269,121 | 22.00 | 1 |
| MSY44n | Sundanese | 2 | 1 | 1 | 5,276,800 | 16,247,512 | 481,467 | 18,501,984 | 21,062,184 | 23,622,384 | 32,300,952 | 0.81 | 1 |
| MSY44o | Tagalog | 1 | 1 | 1 | 1,672,375 | 8,105,661 | 308,562 | 9,549,920 | 11,191,285 | 12,832,650 | 19,108,525 | 97.91 | 3 |
| MSY44p | Toraja | 27 | 25 | 4 | 349,200 | 1,075,203 | 31,862 | 1,224,396 | 1,393,821 | 1,563,246 | 2,137,563 | 45.31 | 1 |
| MSY44q | Visayan | 8 | 7 | 4 | 2,128,000 | 10,529,120 | 408,772 | 12,442,360 | 14,616,840 | 16,791,320 | 25,117,960 | 98.89 | 1 |
| MSY44x | other Filipino | 120 | 113 | 61 | 2,578,500 | 12,758,222 | 495,259 | 15,076,236 | 17,710,815 | 20,345,394 | 30,432,727 | 78.17 | 2 |
| MSY44y | other Indonesian | 290 | 270 | 23 | 7,626,071 | 23,242,479 | 684,742 | 26,443,052 | 30,089,896 | 33,736,740 | 46,179,452 | 19.20 | 5 |
| MSY44z | other Malaysian | 70 | 62 | 14 | 47,805 | 245,721 | 7,944 | 282,618 | 325,158 | 367,698 | 505,254 | 13.33 | 2 |
| MSY45 | *Japanese* | 15 | 5 | 2 | 44,877,009 | 105,020,183 | 1,345,303 | 111,915,105 | 118,473,202 | 125,031,299 | 134,640,288 | 2.33 | — |
| MSY45a | Japanese | 10 | 1 | 1 | 44,472,384 | 104,076,602 | 1,333,257 | 110,909,731 | 117,409,164 | 123,908,597 | 133,433,379 | 2.33 | 8 |
| MSY45b | Ryukyuan | 5 | 4 | 1 | 403,425 | 938,979 | 11,894 | 1,000,080 | 1,057,914 | 1,115,748 | 1,196,361 | 2.83 | 1 |
| MSY46 | *Korean* | 6 | 1 | 1 | 13,376,976 | 47,067,397 | 1,111,202 | 52,429,876 | 58,179,419 | 63,928,962 | 82,848,906 | 18.41 | 8 |
| MSY47 | *Miao-Yao* | 105 | 30 | 8 | 2,567,500 | 4,424,769 | 81,681 | 4,818,267 | 5,241,570 | 5,664,873 | 6,868,076 | 0.77 | — |
| MSY47a | Miao | 80 | 20 | 6 | 2,013,000 | 3,399,746 | 61,923 | 3,698,953 | 4,018,970 | 4,338,987 | 5,222,994 | 0.76 | 3 |
| MSY47b | Yao | 25 | 10 | 2 | 554,500 | 1,025,023 | 19,758 | 1,119,314 | 1,222,600 | 1,325,886 | 1,645,082 | 0.83 | 3 |
| MSY48 | *Paleoasiatic* | 10 | 9 | 0 | 20,000 | 26,400 | 0 | 26,400 | 26,400 | 26,000 | 20,000 | 13.33 | 1 |
| MSY49 | *Tai* | 76 | 54 | 12 | 13,209,420 | 44,049,289 | 1,413,210 | 50,622,052 | 58,181,381 | 65,740,710 | 94,054,335 | 0.80 | — |
| MSY49a | Chuang | 16 | 13 | 3 | 5,192,000 | 8,335,855 | 145,266 | 9,045,025 | 9,788,515 | 10,532,005 | 12,400,245 | 0.74 | 1 |
| MSY49b | Lao | 5 | 2 | 1 | 2,376,560 | 10,398,159 | 375,959 | 12,130,323 | 14,157,753 | 16,185,183 | 24,061,316 | 0.83 | 3 |
| MSY49c | Shan | 7 | 3 | 3 | 743,580 | 2,013,850 | 54,875 | 2,270,986 | 2,562,596 | 2,854,206 | 4,014,376 | 0.69 | 2 |
| MSY49d | Thai | 8 | 4 | 2 | 3,322,000 | 19,659,750 | 755,040 | 23,151,150 | 27,210,150 | 31,269,150 | 47,089,900 | 0.56 | 1 |
| MSY49z | other Tai | 40 | 32 | 3 | 1,533,000 | 3,391,460 | 72,460 | 3,729,917 | 4,116,056 | 4,502,195 | 5,889,172 | 2.70 | 3 |
| MSY50 | *Tibeto-Burmese* | 338 | 246 | 96 | 17,434,683 | 40,412,707 | 1,009,729 | 45,137,965 | 50,509,977 | 55,881,989 | 76,082,835 | 7.70 | — |
| MSY50a | Bhotia | 6 | 3 | 1 | 179,469 | 616,350 | 16,434 | 691,110 | 780,690 | 870,270 | 1,256,940 | 0.17 | 2 |
| MSY50b | Burmese | 9 | 6 | 2 | 7,508,196 | 19,919,708 | 534,393 | 22,421,612 | 25,263,641 | 28,105,670 | 39,433,820 | 0.17 | 2 |
| MSY50c | Chin | 45 | 37 | 20 | 198,550 | 527,212 | 14,149 | 593,560 | 668,705 | 743,850 | 1,043,138 | 54.82 | 1 |
| MSY50d | Garo | 6 | 2 | 2 | 258,573 | 610,824 | 16,829 | 686,963 | 779,112 | 871,261 | 1,203,776 | 41.39 | 2 |
| MSY50e | Gurung | 10 | 8 | 1 | 66,787 | 169,860 | 4,523 | 190,080 | 215,085 | 240,090 | 350,226 | 0.02 | 2 |
| MSY50f | Kachin | 12 | 9 | 5 | 156,750 | 416,220 | 11,171 | 468,600 | 527,925 | 587,250 | 823,530 | 42.93 | 1 |
| MSY50g | Karen | 15 | 10 | 5 | 1,121,410 | 3,056,520 | 83,685 | 3,448,572 | 3,893,367 | 4,338,162 | 6,107,182 | 23.71 | 2 |
| MSY50h | Kirati | 18 | 15 | 1 | 107,215 | 297,815 | 7,421 | 331,535 | 372,025 | 412,515 | 591,345 | 0.07 | 3 |
| MSY50i | Lahu | 30 | 25 | 5 | 31,350 | 83,244 | 2,234 | 93,720 | 105,585 | 117,450 | 164,706 | 20.00 | 1 |
| MSY50j | Lepcha | 2 | 1 | 1 | 11,322 | 43,275 | 903 | 47,595 | 52,305 | 57,015 | 77,895 | 0.62 | 2 |
| MSY50k | Limbu | 4 | 2 | 0 | 66,450 | 168,480 | 4,499 | 188,580 | 213,465 | 238,350 | 347,940 | 0.00 | 1 |
| MSY50l | Lisu | 6 | 3 | 2 | 31,350 | 83,244 | 2,234 | 93,720 | 105,585 | 117,450 | 164,706 | 10.00 | 1 |
| MSY50m | Lushai | 4 | 3 | 2 | 250,800 | 598,628 | 16,607 | 675,697 | 764,699 | 853,701 | 1,169,233 | 63.42 | 2 |
| MSY50n | Magar | 4 | 3 | 2 | 112,433 | 287,700 | 7,618 | 321,800 | 363,875 | 405,950 | 591,330 | 0.00 | 2 |
| MSY50o | Manipuri | 26 | 2 | 1 | 488,473 | 1,153,956 | 31,946 | 1,300,180 | 1,473,421 | 1,646,662 | 2,263,205 | 37.16 | 2 |
| MSY50p | Naga | 35 | 30 | 16 | 240,350 | 570,880 | 15,863 | 644,457 | 729,504 | 814,551 | 1,114,331 | 91.25 | 2 |
| MSY50q | Sherpa | 1 | 1 | 1 | 32,693 | 85,524 | 2,219 | 95,504 | 107,717 | 119,930 | 173,802 | 0.10 | 2 |
| MSY50r | Tibetan | 52 | 45 | 15 | 2,360,000 | 3,789,025 | 66,030 | 4,111,375 | 4,449,325 | 4,787,275 | 5,636,475 | 0.00 | 1 |
| MSY50s | Tripuri | 8 | 4 | 4 | 804,392 | 1,900,164 | 52,197 | 2,134,635 | 2,422,139 | 2,709,643 | 3,755,675 | 1.45 | 2 |
| MSY50z | other Tibeto-Burmese | 45 | 37 | 10 | 3,408,120 | 6,034,078 | 118,774 | 6,598,670 | 7,211,807 | 7,844,944 | 9,813,580 | 0.62 | 5 |
| MSW51 | *Uralian* | 53 | 41 | 21 | 13,337,900 | 22,388,508 | 125,922 | 23,017,293 | 23,647,761 | 24,278,230 | 25,618,431 | 76.61 | — |
| MSW51a | Estonian | 4 | 3 | 3 | 553,462 | 1,077,307 | 10,739 | 1,129,508 | 1,184,697 | 1,239,886 | 1,386,133 | 47.60 | 4 |
| MSW51b | Finnish | 2 | 1 | 1 | 2,820,459 | 4,872,140 | 12,706 | 4,938,993 | 4,999,208 | 5,059,423 | 5,153,118 | 87.17 | 5 |
| MSW51c | Karelian | 4 | 2 | 1 | 125,656 | 242,768 | 2,535 | 255,038 | 268,115 | 281,192 | 315,027 | 36.08 | 1 |
| MSW51d | Komi | 3 | 2 | 2 | 251,312 | 485,536 | 5,069 | 510,076 | 536,230 | 562,384 | 630,054 | 18.04 | 1 |
| MSW51e | Lapp | 13 | 11 | 4 | 21,174 | 35,911 | 204 | 36,985 | 37,960 | 38,935 | 41,035 | 90.48 | 3 |
| MSW51f | Livonian | 2 | 2 | 2 | 1,000 | 800 | 0 | 800 | 800 | 600 | 300 | 66.60 | 1 |
| MSW51g | Magyar | 2 | 1 | 1 | 8,309,277 | 13,247,166 | 69,322 | 13,596,313 | 13,940,401 | 14,284,490 | 14,942,794 | 80.54 | 11 |
| MSW51h | Mari | 2 | 2 | 2 | 251,312 | 485,536 | 5,069 | 510,076 | 536,230 | 562,384 | 630,054 | 90.19 | 1 |
| MSW51i | Mordvin | 3 | 2 | 2 | 628,280 | 1,213,840 | 12,674 | 1,275,190 | 1,340,575 | 1,405,960 | 1,575,135 | 64.94 | 1 |
| MSW51j | Samoyed | 7 | 6 | 0 | 20,000 | 27,000 | 200 | 28,000 | 29,000 | 30,000 | 35,000 | 6.00 | 1 |
| MSW51k | Udmurt | 1 | 1 | 1 | 376,968 | 728,304 | 7,604 | 765,114 | 804,345 | 843,576 | 945,081 | 48.10 | 1 |
| MSW51z | other Finno-Ugric | 10 | 8 | 2 | 25,000 | 30,000 | 0 | 30,000 | 30,000 | 28,000 | 20,000 | 60.00 | 1 |
| MSY52 | *Viet-Muong* | 13 | 10 | 2 | 10,227,266 | 35,130,967 | 848,218 | 39,000,377 | 43,613,142 | 48,225,907 | 67,696,678 | 7.37 | — |
| MSY52a | Muong | 4 | 1 | 1 | 154,000 | 547,484 | 13,339 | 608,314 | 680,876 | 753,438 | 1,061,228 | 5.33 | 1 |
| MSY52b | Vietnamese | 1 | 1 | 1 | 10,073,266 | 34,583,483 | 834,879 | 38,392,063 | 42,932,266 | 47,472,469 | 66,635,450 | 7.41 | 9 |
| MSY52z | other Viet-Muong | 8 | 8 | 0 | 10,000 | 20,000 | 200 | 21,000 | 22,000 | 23,000 | 30,000 | 0.00 | 1 |
| | PACIFIC | | | | | | | | | | | | |
| MPY53 | *Euronesian* | 20 | 15 | 5 | 256,759 | 1,250,354 | 47,736 | 1,473,122 | 1,727,726 | 1,982,331 | 2,958,637 | 90.40 | 17 |
| MPY54 | *Micronesian* | 25 | 18 | 9 | 53,671 | 143,945 | 4,977 | 167,647 | 193,704 | 219,762 | 310,195 | 91.53 | — |
| MPY54a | Gilbertese | 1 | 1 | 1 | 21,601 | 52,825 | 1,944 | 62,107 | 72,254 | 82,402 | 115,535 | 91.09 | 5 |
| MPY54b | Marshallese | 2 | 1 | 1 | 6,840 | 19,190 | 646 | 22,230 | 25,650 | 29,070 | 41,420 | 93.42 | 1 |
| MPY54c | Nauruan | 1 | 1 | 1 | 750 | 3,250 | 75 | 3,750 | 4,000 | 4,250 | 5,000 | 44.43 | 1 |
| MPY54d | Ponapese | 5 | 4 | 1 | 5,400 | 15,150 | 510 | 17,550 | 20,250 | 22,950 | 32,700 | 93.42 | 1 |
| MPY54e | Trukese | 1 | 1 | 1 | 10,080 | 28,280 | 952 | 32,760 | 37,800 | 42,840 | 61,040 | 93.42 | 1 |
| MPY54f | Ulithian | 3 | 2 | 0 | 1,080 | 3,030 | 102 | 3,510 | 4,050 | 4,590 | 6,540 | 93.43 | 1 |
| MPY54g | Yapese | 1 | 1 | 1 | 1,800 | 5,050 | 170 | 5,850 | 6,750 | 7,650 | 10,900 | 93.42 | 1 |
| MPY54z | other Micronesian | 11 | 7 | 3 | 6,120 | 17,170 | 578 | 19,890 | 22,950 | 26,010 | 37,060 | 93.42 | 2 |
| MPY55 | *Polynesian* | 47 | 34 | 17 | 258,630 | 842,900 | 19,446 | 931,695 | 1,037,332 | 1,142,971 | 1,545,474 | 81.31 | — |
| MPY55a | Hawaiian | 2 | 1 | 1 | 75,995 | 204,879 | 1,925 | 213,925 | 224,133 | 234,341 | 264,430 | 71.80 | 1 |
| MPY55b | Maori | 1 | 1 | 1 | 64,480 | 222,780 | 3,500 | 239,449 | 257,777 | 276,105 | 337,093 | 67.19 | 1 |
| MPY55c | Marquesan | 2 | 1 | 1 | 1,850 | 5,450 | 210 | 6,400 | 7,550 | 8,700 | 13,450 | 84.17 | 1 |
| MPY55d | Rarotongan | 6 | 2 | 1 | 10,748 | 31,417 | 848 | 35,480 | 39,892 | 44,304 | 63,611 | 85.11 | 2 |
| MPY55e | Samoan | 1 | 1 | 1 | 41,656 | 175,432 | 6,109 | 202,229 | 236,513 | 270,798 | 406,332 | 93.06 | 8 |
| MPY55f | Tahitian | 3 | 2 | 1 | 16,621 | 48,287 | 1,852 | 56,665 | 66,802 | 76,939 | 118,881 | 91.71 | 2 |
| MPY55g | Tongan | 3 | 3 | 1 | 22,400 | 93,700 | 3,402 | 109,184 | 127,709 | 146,234 | 222,837 | 95.52 | 4 |
| MPY55h | Tuamotuan | 2 | 1 | 0 | 3,330 | 9,810 | 378 | 11,520 | 13,590 | 15,660 | 24,210 | 84.17 | 1 |
| MPY55i | Uvean | 2 | 2 | 2 | 4,927 | 13,113 | 229 | 14,157 | 15,402 | 16,647 | 22,135 | 95.71 | 3 |
| MPY55z | other Polynesian | 25 | 20 | 8 | 16,214 | 36,894 | 954 | 41,366 | 46,440 | 51,515 | 70,003 | 81.58 | 10 |
| | **NEGRO** | | | | | | | | | | | | |
| | AFRICAN | | | | | | | | | | | | |
| NAB56 | *Bantoid* | 425 | 381 | 76 | 9,390,799 | 33,734,067 | 992,266 | 38,219,937 | 43,656,722 | 49,093,507 | 76,725,970 | 13.43 | — |
| NAB56a | Central Bantoid | 90 | 85 | 27 | 2,553,940 | 10,109,155 | 290,819 | 11,436,382 | 13,017,345 | 14,598,308 | 22,251,818 | 10.16 | 8 |
| NAB56b | Eastern Bantoid | 270 | 240 | 32 | 2,381,400 | 8,095,731 | 257,588 | 9,249,975 | 10,671,612 | 12,093,249 | 19,833,828 | 38.26 | 1 |
| NAB56c | Western Bantoid | 65 | 56 | 17 | 4,455,459 | 15,529,181 | 443,859 | 17,533,580 | 19,967,765 | 22,401,950 | 34,640,324 | 2.29 | 18 |
| NAB57 | *Bantu* | 649 | 538 | 212 | 31,075,975 | 102,216,604 | 3,242,637 | 116,867,867 | 134,642,967 | 152,418,065 | 242,490,030 | 63.01 | — |
| NAB57a | Cameroon Highland Bantu | 80 | 67 | 6 | 707,400 | 1,575,720 | 33,804 | 1,727,460 | 1,913,760 | 2,100,060 | 3,127,410 | 82.62 | 1 |
| NAB57b | Central Bantu | 90 | 78 | 41 | 8,259,863 | 24,554,049 | 720,776 | 27,846,176 | 31,761,814 | 35,677,452 | 56,398,716 | 65.49 | 13 |
| NAB57c | Equatorial Bantu | 104 | 93 | 23 | 2,111,210 | 4,856,464 | 123,296 | 5,415,545 | 6,089,417 | 6,763,289 | 10,277,340 | 75.69 | 8 |

*Concluded opposite*

*Global Table 24—(concluded)*

| Code | **RACE** *Family* People | *People groups* | *Lang-uages* | *Trans-lated* | Population 1900 | Population mid-1970 | Annual increase 1970–1985 | Population mid-1975 | Population mid-1980 | Population mid-1985 | Population AD 2000 | % Christian in 1980 | Coun-tries |
|---|---|---|---|---|---|---|---|---|---|---|---|---|---|
| NAB57d | Interlacustrine Bantu | 61 | 55 | 25 | 5,615,890 | 19,079,317 | 634,584 | 21,925,346 | 25,425,148 | 28,924,950 | 46,203,542 | 71.77 | 6 |
| NAB57e | Kenya Highland Bantu | 23 | 19 | 12 | 1,511,550 | 5,721,671 | 221,401 | 6,721,563 | 7,935,678 | 9,149,793 | 15,528,635 | 64.07 | 3 |
| NAB57f | Luba | 16 | 12 | 8 | 1,111,530 | 2,647,590 | 77,128 | 2,995,377 | 3,418,869 | 3,842,361 | 6,046,158 | 99.93 | 2 |
| NAB57g | Middle Zambezi Bantu | 20 | 15 | 7 | 221,078 | 1,302,535 | 47,697 | 1,520,748 | 1,779,500 | 2,038,252 | 3,488,926 | 34.38 | 4 |
| NAB57h | Mongo | 46 | 39 | 10 | 1,446,400 | 3,462,080 | 101,024 | 3,917,600 | 4,472,320 | 5,027,040 | 7,912,000 | 99.94 | 1 |
| NAB57i | Nguni | 15 | 10 | 6 | 2,314,815 | 10,784,798 | 358,192 | 12,393,282 | 14,366,719 | 16,340,156 | 25,499,925 | 59.06 | 9 |
| NAB57j | Northeast Coastal Bantu | 27 | 21 | 12 | 705,229 | 2,470,811 | 90,734 | 2 882,819 | 3,378,160 | 3,873,499 | 6,241,368 | 15.49 | 14 |
| NAB57k | Northwestern Bantu | 55 | 47 | 20 | 615,560 | 1,326,800 | 29,808 | 1,463,640 | 1,624,882 | 1,786,124 | 2,643,126 | 78.17 | 5 |
| NAB57l | Shona | 9 | 8 | 8 | 538,300 | 4,195,356 | 162,564 | 4,918,598 | 5,821,004 | 6,723,410 | 11,493,606 | 43.12 | 4 |
| NAB57m | Sotho | 6 | 4 | 3 | 1,157,250 | 4,935,250 | 154,091 | 5,624,450 | 6,476,155 | 7,327,860 | 11,218,015 | 50.15 | 5 |
| NAB57n | Southwestern Bantu | 13 | 10 | 8 | 1,384,190 | 2,856,073 | 75,746 | 3,199,388 | 3,613,533 | 4,027,678 | 6,237,937 | 70.00 | 3 |
| NAB57o | Tanganyika Bantu | 60 | 49 | 14 | 1,945,000 | 6,898,100 | 246,252 | 8,013,960 | 9,360,620 | 10,707,280 | 17,594,900 | 36.66 | 2 |
| NAB57p | Tsonga | 12 | 6 | 6 | 945,440 | 3,325,483 | 94,117 | 3,760,569 | 4,266,653 | 4,772,737 | 7,388,977 | 46.51 | 4 |
| NAB57q | Tswana | 12 | 5 | 3 | 485,270 | 2,224,507 | 71,423 | 2,541,346 | 2,938,735 | 3,336,124 | 5,189,449 | 62.09 | 4 |
| NAN58 | *Eurafrican* | 20 | 13 | 5 | 868,574 | 3,135,998 | 91,270 | 3,558,671 | 4,048,691 | 4,538,710 | 6,653,951 | 81.00 | 23 |
| NAB59 | *Guinean* | 260 | 173 | 53 | 10,178,991 | 36,562,665 | 1,157,623 | 41,747,468 | 48,138,904 | 54,530,340 | 88,216,037 | 43.93 | — |
| NAB59a | Akan | 20 | 17 | 7 | 1,384,640 | 5,544,466 | 177,084 | 6,330,946 | 7,315,306 | 8,299,666 | 13,323,898 | 53.12 | 4 |
| NAB59b | Central Togolese | 30 | 23 | 0 | 37,700 | 153,693 | 4,977 | 176,056 | 203,465 | 230,874 | 367,155 | 95.49 | 3 |
| NAB59c | Edo | 25 | 22 | 3 | 583,200 | 1,982,628 | 63,083 | 2,265,300 | 2,613,456 | 2,961,612 | 4,857,264 | 27.07 | 1 |
| NAB59d | Ewe | 4 | 1 | 1 | 438,000 | 1,718,059 | 55,883 | 1,966,825 | 2,276,888 | 2,586,951 | 4,176,892 | 54.21 | 3 |
| NAB59e | Fon | 8 | 1 | 1 | 316,560 | 1,347,258 | 42,534 | 1,541,582 | 1,772,602 | 2,003,622 | 3,002,563 | 18.86 | 3 |
| NAB59f | Ga-Adangbe | 10 | 2 | 2 | 182,600 | 716,124 | 23,389 | 819,459 | 950,018 | 1,080,577 | 1,756,612 | 55.54 | 1 |
| NAB59g | Gun | 3 | 1 | 1 | 74,400 | 322,320 | 10,176 | 368,880 | 424,080 | 479,280 | 710,520 | 37.85 | 1 |
| NAB59h | Ibo | 12 | 9 | 4 | 2,869,689 | 9,716,548 | 308,293 | 11,098,064 | 12,799,473 | 14,500,882 | 23,763,172 | 57.56 | 4 |
| NAB59i | Ijaw | 15 | 11 | 3 | 324,000 | 1,101,460 | 35,046 | 1,258,500 | 1,451,920 | 1,645,340 | 2,698,480 | 59.86 | 1 |
| NAB59j | Kru | 45 | 33 | 8 | 286,752 | 1,301,498 | 37,041 | 1,468,376 | 1,671,904 | 1,875,432 | 2,837,352 | 45.12 | 3 |
| NAB59k | Lagoon | 20 | 14 | 7 | 90,000 | 387,900 | 11,421 | 439,650 | 502,110 | 564,570 | 865,530 | 99.92 | 1 |
| NAB59l | Popo | 2 | 2 | 1 | 45,560 | 192,808 | 6,190 | 220,952 | 254,712 | 288,472 | 444,188 | 46.87 | 2 |
| NAB59m | Nupe | 20 | 9 | 2 | 324,000 | 1,101,460 | 35,046 | 1,258,500 | 1,451,920 | 1,645,340 | 2,698,480 | 2.78 | 1 |
| NAB59n | Yoruba | 21 | 10 | 3 | 3,059,890 | 10,425,713 | 329,937 | 11,905,128 | 13,725,090 | 15,545,052 | 25,364,691 | 29.85 | 8 |
| NAB59z | other Guinean | 25 | 18 | 10 | 162,000 | 550,730 | 17,523 | 629,250 | 725,960 | 822,670 | 1,349,240 | 47.33 | 1 |
| NAB60 | *Hausa-Chadic* | 205 | 176 | 30 | 4,798,550 | 15,896,926 | 489,217 | 18,095,978 | 20,789,088 | 23,482,198 | 38,066,727 | 14.14 | — |
| NAB60a | Hausa | 15 | 1 | 1 | 3,204,950 | 11,258,179 | 356,858 | 12,863,566 | 14,826,754 | 16,789,942 | 27,415,461 | 0.02 | 4 |
| NAB60b | Plateau Chadic | 190 | 175 | 29 | 959,000 | 3,174,615 | 99,709 | 3,621,795 | 4,171,700 | 4,721,605 | 7,697,300 | 68.77 | 2 |
| NAB61 | *Kanuri* | 50 | 12 | 1 | 1,094,410 | 3,529,613 | 109,166 | 4,020,909 | 4,621,270 | 5,221,631 | 8,410,486 | 0.00 | 5 |
| NAB62 | *Nilotic* | 143 | 101 | 34 | 3,801,550 | 12,590,461 | 448,394 | 14,620,870 | 17,074,386 | 19,527,902 | 31,560,684 | 38.37 | — |
| NAB62a | Acholi | 1 | 1 | 1 | 122,070 | 447,159 | 15,603 | 517,800 | 603,188 | 688,576 | 1,102,017 | 86.53 | 2 |
| NAB62b | Alur | 1 | 1 | 1 | 50,350 | 186,314 | 6,490 | 215,707 | 251,218 | 286,729 | 459,040 | 93.34 | 1 |
| NAB62c | Anuak | 2 | 1 | 1 | 37,880 | 112,490 | 3,623 | 129,022 | 148,724 | 168,426 | 263,238 | 2.61 | 2 |
| NAB62d | Barea | 1 | 1 | 0 | 24,000 | 74,565 | 2,000 | 83,925 | 94,566 | 105,207 | 160,995 | 35.80 | 1 |
| NAB62e | Bari | 4 | 1 | 1 | 152,820 | 447,294 | 16,251 | 520,380 | 609,808 | 699,236 | 1,110,042 | 20.86 | 2 |
| NAB62f | Dinka | 10 | 5 | 4 | 601,700 | 1,726,450 | 62,975 | 2,009,480 | 2,356,200 | 2,702,920 | 4,287,470 | 8.23 | 1 |
| NAB62g | Kalenjin | 8 | 6 | 3 | 292,900 | 1,135,947 | 44,854 | 1,338,351 | 1,584,488 | 1,830,625 | 3,133,020 | 51.56 | 1 |
| NAB62h | Kunama | 1 | 1 | 1 | 24,000 | 74,565 | 2,000 | 83,925 | 94,566 | 105,207 | 160,995 | 89.50 | 1 |
| NAB62i | Lango | 1 | 1 | 1 | 148,400 | 549,136 | 19,130 | 635,768 | 740,432 | 845,096 | 1,352,960 | 46.99 | 1 |
| NAB62j | Luo | 4 | 4 | 2 | 513,800 | 1,964,292 | 75,869 | 2,306,885 | 2,722,976 | 3,139,067 | 5,314,435 | 78.92 | 3 |
| NAB62k | Maasai | 7 | 4 | 1 | 112,100 | 412,788 | 15,607 | 483,339 | 568,852 | 654,365 | 1,100,055 | 12.32 | 2 |
| NAB62l | Mao | 3 | 2 | 0 | 8,000 | 24,855 | 667 | 27,975 | 31,522 | 35,069 | 53,665 | 7.90 | 1 |
| NAB62m | Nubian | 22 | 18 | 3 | 193,400 | 580,532 | 18,502 | 665,704 | 765,552 | 865,400 | 1,296,244 | 0.00 | 2 |
| NAB62n | Nuer | 10 | 4 | 2 | 297,500 | 859,315 | 30,625 | 997,325 | 1,165,566 | 1,333,807 | 2,109,845 | 4.99 | 2 |
| NAB62o | Shilluk | 5 | 2 | 1 | 109,400 | 313,900 | 11,450 | 365,360 | 428,400 | 491,440 | 779,540 | 13.58 | 1 |
| NAB62p | Suk | 5 | 2 | 1 | 34,050 | 130,641 | 5,022 | 153,318 | 180,858 | 208,398 | 351,660 | 9.56 | 2 |
| NAB62q | Teso | 3 | 3 | 1 | 264,350 | 982,322 | 34,639 | 1,139,131 | 1,328,706 | 1,518,281 | 2,446,720 | 57.42 | 2 |
| NAB62r | Turkana | 4 | 1 | 1 | 55,100 | 213,693 | 8,438 | 251,769 | 298,072 | 344,375 | 589,380 | 3.26 | 1 |
| NAB62y | other Nilotic | 24 | 20 | 7 | 345,030 | 1,078,778 | 38,922 | 1,254,151 | 1,468,002 | 1,681,853 | 2,684,668 | 40.09 | 3 |
| NAB62z | other Prenilote | 27 | 23 | 2 | 414,700 | 1,275,425 | 35,727 | 1,441,555 | 1,632,690 | 1,823,825 | 2,804,695 | 29.03 | 2 |
| NAB63 | *Nuclear Mande* | 58 | 32 | 12 | 1,683,740 | 6,584,393 | 181,913 | 7,412,029 | 8,403,514 | 9,394,999 | 14,264,360 | 0.91 | — |
| NAB63a | Bambara | 9 | 2 | 1 | 454,100 | 1,778,180 | 50,181 | 2,007,395 | 2,279,985 | 2,552,575 | 3,953,005 | 1.63 | 4 |
| NAB63b | Bozo | 1 | 1 | 0 | 22,100 | 85,799 | 2,419 | 96,849 | 109,990 | 123,131 | 191,369 | 0.00 | 1 |
| NAB63c | Dialonke | 1 | 1 | 0 | 31,680 | 125,472 | 3,498 | 141,312 | 160,448 | 179,584 | 270,560 | 0.00 | 1 |
| NAB63d | Kagoro | 1 | 1 | 0 | 10,400 | 40,376 | 1,138 | 45,576 | 51,760 | 57,944 | 90,056 | 0.00 | 1 |
| NAB63e | Kasonke | 1 | 1 | 0 | 26,000 | 100,940 | 2,846 | 113,940 | 129,400 | 144,860 | 225,140 | 1.85 | 1 |
| NAB63f | Konyanke | 3 | 1 | 0 | 19,800 | 78,420 | 2,186 | 88,320 | 100,280 | 112,240 | 169,100 | 0.00 | 1 |
| NAB63g | Koranko | 2 | 2 | 2 | 57,762 | 176,248 | 4,954 | 198,691 | 225,784 | 252,877 | 380,592 | 0.59 | 2 |
| NAB63h | Malinke | 8 | 6 | 3 | 642,108 | 2,595,132 | 71,072 | 2,916,626 | 3,305,853 | 3,695,080 | 5,555,669 | 0.04 | 11 |
| NAB63i | Nono | 2 | 1 | 0 | 2,600 | 10,094 | 285 | 11,394 | 12,940 | 14,486 | 22,514 | 0.00 | 1 |
| NAB63j | Soninke | 13 | 1 | 0 | 138,865 | 554,873 | 14,907 | 623,265 | 703,947 | 784,629 | 1,189,393 | 0.00 | 5 |
| NAB63k | Susu | 1 | 1 | 1 | 162,143 | 599,741 | 16,684 | 675,270 | 766,583 | 857,896 | 1,290,790 | 0.00 | 4 |
| NAB63l | Yalunka | 1 | 1 | 1 | 7,182 | 18,508 | 524 | 20,881 | 23,744 | 26,607 | 40,012 | 0.00 | 1 |
| NAB63z | other Nuclear Mande | 15 | 13 | 4 | 109,000 | 420,610 | 11,219 | 472,510 | 532,800 | 593,090 | 886,160 | 6.50 | 2 |
| NAB64 | *Peripheral Mande* | 27 | 16 | 15 | 749,980 | 2,595,476 | 72,987 | 2,924,956 | 3,325,358 | 3,725,760 | 5,605,442 | 8.77 | — |
| NAB64a | Dan | 3 | 3 | 3 | 94,800 | 423,540 | 12,195 | 478,590 | 545,490 | 612,390 | 930,710 | 12.99 | 2 |
| NAB64b | Gagu | 1 | 1 | 1 | 6,000 | 25,860 | 761 | 29,310 | 33,474 | 37,638 | 57,702 | 3.00 | 1 |
| NAB64c | Gbande | 4 | 1 | 1 | 9,300 | 45,690 | 1,242 | 51,240 | 58,110 | 64,980 | 96,570 | 3.47 | 1 |
| NAB64d | Guro | 3 | 2 | 1 | 30,000 | 129,300 | 3,807 | 146,550 | 167,370 | 188,190 | 288,510 | 23.92 | 1 |
| NAB64e | Kono | 1 | 1 | 1 | 49,248 | 126,912 | 3,590 | 143,184 | 162,816 | 182,448 | 274,368 | 5.68 | 1 |
| NAB64f | Kpelle | 2 | 2 | 2 | 112,620 | 508,038 | 13,940 | 570,648 | 647,442 | 724,236 | 1,081,830 | 10.43 | 2 |
| NAB64g | Loko | 1 | 1 | 1 | 29,754 | 76,676 | 2,169 | 86,507 | 98,368 | 110,229 | 165,764 | 2.15 | 1 |
| NAB64h | Loma | 2 | 2 | 2 | 50,280 | 216,852 | 5,982 | 243,792 | 276,668 | 309,544 | 463,700 | 7.73 | 2 |
| NAB64i | Mende | 4 | 1 | 1 | 317,034 | 816,996 | 23,113 | 921,747 | 1,048,128 | 1,174,509 | 1,766,244 | 7.31 | 1 |
| NAB64j | Ngere | 5 | 1 | 1 | 26,650 | 126,215 | 3,445 | 141,640 | 160,660 | 179,680 | 267,605 | 1.27 | 2 |
| NAB64k | Vai | 1 | 1 | 1 | 24,294 | 99,397 | 2,743 | 111,748 | 126,832 | 141,916 | 212,439 | 0.00 | 3 |
| NAB65 | *Songhai* | 6 | 3 | 2 | 310,700 | 1,286,936 | 38,960 | 1,465,300 | 1,676,532 | 1,887,764 | 2,988,418 | 0.03 | — |
| NAB65a | Dendi | 1 | 1 | 0 | 12,400 | 53,720 | 1,696 | 61,480 | 70,680 | 79,880 | 118,420 | 0.00 | 1 |
| NAB65b | Songhai | 4 | 1 | 1 | 225,500 | 911,936 | 27,216 | 1,036,460 | 1,184,092 | 1,331,724 | 2,104,558 | 0.05 | 4 |
| NAB65c | Zerma | 1 | 1 | 1 | 72,800 | 321,280 | 10,048 | 367,360 | 421,760 | 476,160 | 765,440 | 0.01 | 1 |
| NAB66 | *Sudanic* | 344 | 228 | 38 | 4,498,240 | 11,355,832 | 335,145 | 12,869,492 | 14,707,279 | 16,545,066 | 25,656,402 | 31.03 | — |
| NAB66a | Azande | 4 | 4 | 1 | 710,350 | 1,777,190 | 55,255 | 2,026,090 | 2,329,740 | 2,633,390 | 4,153,110 | 27.93 | 3 |
| NAB66b | Banda | 12 | 9 | 0 | 280,340 | 587,704 | 14,239 | 652,410 | 730,098 | 807,786 | 1,218,240 | 51.39 | 2 |
| NAB66c | Baya | 30 | 25 | 9 | 581,980 | 1,308,587 | 31,693 | 1,452,125 | 1,625,514 | 1,798,903 | 2,705,832 | 43.43 | 4 |
| NAB66d | Fur | 17 | 14 | 0 | 290,340 | 709,290 | 20,925 | 804,196 | 918,540 | 1,032,884 | 1,548,694 | 0.00 | 2 |
| NAB66e | Madi | 12 | 10 | 2 | 64,620 | 211,842 | 7,534 | 245,844 | 287,184 | 328,524 | 523,782 | 57.13 | 2 |
| NAB66f | Mandja | 1 | 1 | 0 | 55,440 | 116,064 | 2,822 | 128,880 | 144,288 | 159,696 | 241,920 | 59.10 | 1 |
| NAB66g | Moru-Mangbetu | 15 | 12 | 5 | 297,850 | 893,102 | 30,403 | 1,030,271 | 1,197,134 | 1,363,997 | 2,167,960 | 51.11 | 3 |
| NAB66h | Nuba | 103 | 28 | 6 | 306,320 | 878,920 | 32,060 | 1,023,008 | 1,199,520 | 1,376,032 | 2,182,712 | 8.57 | 1 |
| NAB66z | other Sudanic | 150 | 125 | 15 | 1,911,000 | 4,873,133 | 140,214 | 5,506,668 | 6,275,261 | 7,043,854 | 10,914,152 | 29.77 | 5 |
| | **AFRO-AMERICAN** | | | | | | | | | | | | |
| NFB67 | *Dutch-speaking* | 18 | 10 | 3 | 96,988 | 484,831 | 11,966 | 536,926 | 604,481 | 672,036 | 978,910 | 78.23 | — |
| NFB67a | Black | 3 | 3 | 0 | 12,208 | 62,818 | 1,901 | 70,938 | 81,823 | 92,708 | 145,621 | 92.90 | 2 |
| NFB67b | Creole | 15 | 7 | 3 | 84,780 | 422,013 | 10,065 | 465,988 | 522,658 | 579,328 | 833,289 | 75.94 | 3 |
| NFB68 | *English-speaking* | 35 | 25 | 7 | 11,378,251 | 30,085,721 | 337,953 | 31,685,202 | 33,465,220 | 35,245,238 | 40,795,656 | 73.30 | — |
| NFB68a | Black | 15 | 9 | 5 | 11,082,693 | 29,334,681 | 326,014 | 30,875,058 | 32,594,807 | 34,314,555 | 39,688,832 | 73.35 | 36 |
| NFB68b | Mulatto | 20 | 16 | 2 | 295,558 | 751,040 | 11,939 | 810,144 | 870,413 | 930,683 | 1,106,824 | 71.45 | 19 |
| NFB69 | *French-speaking* | 12 | 10 | 3 | 2,064,795 | 5,142,672 | 86,416 | 5,528,605 | 6,006,827 | 6,485,049 | 8,374,637 | 93.73 | — |
| NFB69a | Black | 5 | 4 | 0 | 1,437,962 | 4,039,867 | 68,847 | 4,342,809 | 4,728,331 | 5,113,853 | 6,717,484 | 94.35 | 4 |
| NFB69b | Creole | 7 | 6 | 3 | 626,833 | 1,102,805 | 17,569 | 1,185,796 | 1,278,496 | 1,371,196 | 1,657,153 | 91.47 | 7 |
| NFB70 | *Portuguese-speaking* | 8 | 6 | 0 | 5,940,519 | 31,446,639 | 1,029,627 | 36,242,718 | 41,742,907 | 47,243,096 | 70,172,961 | 94.60 | — |
| NFB70a | Black | 1 | 1 | 0 | 1,978,240 | 10,472,440 | 343,035 | 12,070,300 | 13,902,790 | 15,735,280 | 23,375,770 | 94.22 | 1 |
| NFB70b | Mulato | 7 | 5 | 0 | 3,958,079 | 20,950,451 | 686,260 | 24,147,034 | 27,813,053 | 31,479,072 | 46,764,330 | 94.90 | 3 |
| NFB71 | *Spanish-speaking* | 16 | 11 | 0 | 2,760,246 | 15,070,471 | 509,232 | 17,431,788 | 20,162,796 | 22,893,804 | 34,464,997 | 86.17 | — |
| NFB71a | Black | 1 | 1 | 0 | 853,889 | 4,006,131 | 124,028 | 4,582,262 | 5,246,413 | 5,910,564 | 8,630,582 | 80.43 | 11 |
| NFB71b | Mulatto | 15 | 10 | 0 | 1,906,357 | 11,064,340 | 385,204 | 12,849,526 | 14,916,383 | 16,983,240 | 25,834,415 | 88.19 | 11 |
| **GLOBAL TOTALS** | | **8,993** | **7,010** | **1,811** | **1,619,886,760** | **3,610,034,405** | **76,388,313** | **3,966,711,095** | **4,373,917,535** | **4,781,123,975** | **6,259,642,000** | **30.27** | **223** |

Global Table 25. THE WORLD'S 17 RACES AND 432 MAJOR ETHNOLINGUISTIC PEOPLES RANKED BY PERCENTAGE CHRISTIAN, AD 1980.

| Code | People | % church members |
|------|--------|------------------|
| MSY44l | Minahasan | 99.96 |
| NAB57h | Mongo | 99.94 |
| NAB57f | Luba | 99.93 |
| NAB59k | Lagoon | 99.92 |
| BYG11a | Bergdama | 99.91 |
| CEW15a | Latvian | 99.57 |
| MSY43 | Eurasian | 99.04 |
| MIR39g | Quechua | 98.96 |
| MSY44q | Visayan | 98.89 |
| CEW19j | Faeroese | 98.34 |
| MSY44o | Tagalog | 97.91 |
| BYG11c | Hottentot | 97.87 |
| CMT34a | Amhara | 97.08 |
| AON09a | New Caledonian | 96.56 |
| AON09e | Western Melanesian | 96.53 |
| CEW21a | Catalonian | 96.40 |
| CEW21d | Galician | 96.24 |
| CEW21k | Spanish | 96.11 |
| MPY55i | Uvean | 95.71 |
| MPY55g | Tongan | 95.52 |
| NAB59b | Central Togolese | 95.49 |
| AON10d | Solomoni Papuan | 95.33 |
| CEW22n | Slovene | 95.20 |
| NFB70b | Portuguese-speaking Mulato | 94.90 |
| CLN28 | Mestiço | 94.82 |
| CLT26 | Latin-American White | 94.56 |
| CEW19g | Danish | 94.55 |
| CEW20 | Greek | 94.45 |
| NFB69a | French-speaking Black | 94.35 |
| CEW16 | Basque | 94.28 |
| MSY44b | Batak | 94.27 |
| NFB70a | Portuguese-speaking Black | 94.22 |
| CEW19n | Icelander | 93.90 |
| MIR39b | Aymara | 93.84 |
| MPY54f | Ulithian | 93.43 |
| MPY54g | Yapese | 93.42 |
| MPY54b | Marshallese | 93.42 |
| MPY54d | Ponapese | 93.42 |
| MPY54e | Trukese | 93.42 |
| MSY44d | Chamorro | 93.42 |
| NAB62b | Alur | 93.34 |
| MIR37f | Zapotec | 93.20 |
| MIR37c | Mixtec | 93.20 |
| CEW19p | Norwegian | 93.06 |
| MPY55e | Samoan | 93.06 |
| NFB67a | Dutch-speaking Black | 92.90 |
| MIR37a | Aztec | 92.12 |
| CLN29 | Mestizo | 92.05 |
| MIR37e | Half-Amerindian | 91.83 |
| CEW21g | Portuguese | 91.80 |
| MPY55f | Tahitian | 91.71 |
| NFB69b | French Creole | 91.47 |
| MSY50p | Naga | 91 25 |
| CEW22k | Ruthenian | 91.23 |
| CMT36 | Maltese | 91.15 |
| MPY54a | Gilbertese | 91.09 |
| AUG01 | Ainu/Aborigine | 91.00 |
| MIR37d | Otomí | 90.85 |
| CEW22g | Macedonian | 90.67 |
| CEW22i | Polish | 90.49 |
| MSW51e | Lapp | 90.48 |
| CEW22f | Kashubian | 90.43 |
| MPY53 | Euronesian | 90.40 |
| CEW21l | Walloon | 90.39 |
| MSW51h | Mari | 90.19 |
| CEW19f | Austrian | 90.19 |
| CEW22d | Croatian | 90.16 |
| CEW19k | Flemish | 89.54 |
| NAB62h | Kunama | 89.50 |
| MSY44f | Ilocan | 89.28 |
| MIR37b | Maya | 89.21 |
| CMT34b | Tigrai | 88.60 |
| NFB71b | Spanish-speaking Mulatto | 88.19 |
| CEW19o | Luxemburger | 87.89 |
| MSW51b | Finnish | 87.17 |
| CLT27 | Spanish-American White | 87.04 |
| NAB62a | Acholi | 86.53 |
| AON09d | Solomoni Melanesian | 85.35 |
| CEW19m | German | 85.61 |
| AON09c | New Hebridean | 85.57 |
| MPY55d | Rarotongan | 85.11 |
| CEW21h | Rhaeto-Romanian | 84.59 |
| CEW18d | Welsh | 84.54 |
| MPY55c | Marquesan | 84.17 |
| MPY55h | Tuamotuan | 84.17 |
| CEW21b | French | 83.94 |
| CEW21i | Romanian | 83.87 |
| AON08 | Fijian | 83.67 |
| CEW21j | Sardinian | 83.64 |
| CEW15b | Lithuanian | 83.42 |
| CEW21e | Italian | 83.01 |
| CEW22l | Serbian | 82.93 |
| NAB57a | Cameroon Highlands Bantu | 82.62 |
| CEW18b | Irish | 82.58 |
| NAN58 | Eurafrican | 81.00 |
| AUG03d | Nicobarese | 80.95 |
| MSW51g | Magyar | 80.54 |
| NFB71a | Spanish-speaking Black | 80.43 |
| CEW19b | Alsatian | 80.05 |
| CEW18a | Breton | 80.05 |
| CEW22m | Slovak | 79.87 |
| BYG11b | East African Bushman | 79.78 |
| CEW19a | Afrikaner | 79.16 |
| CEW22e | Czech | 79.09 |
| NAB62j | Luo | 78.92 |
| NAB57k | Northwestern Bantu | 78.17 |
| CMT31 | Assyrian | 77.52 |
| CEW19i | British | 76.34 |
| CEW19s | USA White | 76.24 |
| NFB67b | Dutch-speaking Creole | 75.94 |
| CEW19e | Anglo-New Zealander | 75.82 |
| NAB57c | Equatorial Bantu | 75.69 |
| CEW19d | Anglo-Canadian | 75.29 |
| AON10b | New Guinea Papuan | 75.17 |
| CEW21c | French-Canadian | 75.09 |
| CEW19r | Ulster Irish | 74.11 |
| CEW18c | Scottish Gaelic | 73.46 |
| NFB68a | Afro-American | 73.35 |
| CEW19h | Dutch | 73.20 |
| CMT33d | Sidamo | 72.79 |
| CEW19q | Swedish | 72.60 |
| MIR38b | Part-Indian | 72.41 |
| MSY41d | Gagauz | 71.90 |

| Code | People | % church members |
|------|--------|------------------|
| MPY55a | Hawaiian | 71.80 |
| NAB57d | Interlacustrine Bantu | 71.77 |
| CEW19l | Frisian | 71.63 |
| NFB68b | English-speaking Mulatto | 71.45 |
| CEW22b | Bulgar | 70.91 |
| MRY40b | Eskimo | 70.86 |
| CEW22c | Byelorussian | 70.58 |
| MIR38a | North American Indian | 70.35 |
| MIR39f | Mapuche | 70.08 |
| NAB57n | Southwestern Bantu | 70.00 |
| CEW22p | Ukrainian | 69.07 |
| NAB60b | Plateau Chadic | 68.77 |
| MPY55b | Maori | 67.19 |
| CEW19c | Anglo-Australian | 66.75 |
| MSW51f | Livonian | 66.60 |
| AON09b | New Guinea Melanesian | 65.86 |
| AON10f | Torres Strait Islander | 65.60 |
| NAB57b | Central Bantu | 65.49 |
| AON10a | Irianese Papuan | 65.00 |
| MSW51i | Mordvin | 64.94 |
| NAB57e | Kenya Highlands Bantu | 64.07 |
| MSY50m | Lushai | 63.42 |
| CEW22o | Sorb | 63.36 |
| NAB57q | Tswana | 62.09 |
| NAB59i | Ijaw | 59.86 |
| AUG02 | Australian Aborigine | 59.64 |
| NAB66f | Mandja | 59.10 |
| NAB57i | Nguni | 59.06 |
| CEW21f | Moldavian | 59.03 |
| MRY40a | Aleut | 58.40 |
| NAB59h | Ibo | 57.56 |
| NAB62q | Teso | 57.42 |
| NAB66e | Madi | 57.13 |
| MSY50c | Chin | 54.82 |
| NAB59d | Ewe | 54.21 |
| NAB59a | Akan | 53.12 |
| NAB62g | Kalenjin | 51.56 |
| NAB66b | Banda | 51.39 |
| NAB66g | Moru-Mangbetu | 51.11 |
| CEW14 | Armenian | 51.02 |
| MIR39e | Lowland Amerindian | 50.43 |
| NAB57m | Sotho | 50.15 |

*Under 50%*

| Code | People | % church members |
|------|--------|------------------|
| MSW51k | Udmurt | 48.10 |
| MSW51a | Estonian | 47.60 |
| MSY44j | Malagasy | 47.10 |
| NAB62i | Lango | 46.99 |
| NAB59l | Popo | 46.87 |
| NAB57p | Tsonga | 46.51 |
| MSY44p | Toraja | 45.31 |
| NAB59j | Kru | 45.12 |
| MPY54c | Nauruan | 44.43 |
| AUG06c | Oraon | 43.71 |
| NAB66c | Baya | 43.43 |
| NAB57l | Shona | 43.12 |
| AON10e | Timorese Papuan | 43.00 |
| MSY50f | Kachin | 42.93 |
| AUG03a | Khasi | 42.40 |
| MSY50d | Garo | 41.39 |
| CNN25d | Goanese | 39.78 |
| CNN25f | Gypsy | 39.16 |
| NAB56b | Eastern Bantoid | 38.26 |
| NAB59g | Gun | 37.85 |
| CEW22h | Montenegrin | 37.34 |
| MSY50o | Manipuri | 37.16 |
| MIR39c | Carib | 37.05 |
| NAB57o | Tanganyika Bantu | 36.66 |
| MSW51c | Karelian | 36.08 |
| CNT24e | Ossetian | 36.08 |
| MSY41m | Yakut | 36.08 |
| NAB62d | Barea | 35.80 |
| NAB57g | Middle Zambezi Bantu | 34.38 |
| CMT33b | Galla | 33.44 |
| CNN23b | Malayali | 31.55 |
| CEW22j | Russian | 31.41 |
| MSY44e | Iban | 30.61 |
| NAB59n | Yoruba | 29.85 |
| NAB66a | Azande | 27.93 |
| AON10c | North Halmaheran | 27.56 |
| NAB59c | Edo | 27.07 |
| CEW17c | Georgian | 25.01 |
| NAB64d | Guro | 23.92 |
| MSY50g | Karen | 23.71 |
| MSY44m | Palawan | 22.00 |
| AUG04b | Mundari | 21.61 |
| NAB62e | Bari | 20.86 |
| MIR39a | Arawak | 20.65 |
| MSY41c | Chuvash | 20.62 |
| MSY50i | Lahu | 20.00 |
| NAB59e | Fon | 18.86 |
| MSY46 | Korean | 18.41 |
| MSW51d | Komi | 18.04 |
| MIR39d | Jungle Amerindian | 16.91 |
| NAB57j | Northeast Coastal Bantu | 15.49 |
| CEW13 | Albanian | 14.17 |
| CMT33c | Iraqw | 13.98 |
| NAB62o | Shilluk | 13.58 |
| MSY48 | Paleoasiatic | 13.33 |
| BYG11d | South African Bushmen | 13.32 |
| NAB64a | Dan | 12.99 |
| BYG12 | Pygmy | 12.40 |
| NAB62k | Maasai | 12.32 |
| CMT33a | Agau | 10.74 |
| NAB64f | Kpelle | 10.43 |
| NAB56a | Central Bantoid | 10.16 |

*Under 10%*

| Code | People | % church members |
|------|--------|------------------|
| MSY50l | Lisu | 10.00 |
| NAB62p | Suk | 9.56 |
| CNN23c | Tamil | 9.56 |
| NAB66h | Nuba | 8.57 |
| NAB62f | Dinka | 8.23 |
| NAB62l | Mao | 7.90 |
| NAB64h | Loma | 7.73 |
| MSY52b | Vietnamese | 7.41 |
| CMT30 | Arab | 7.36 |
| NAB64i | Mende | 7.31 |
| MSY41b | Bashkir | 7.22 |
| AUG05 | Negrito | 6.50 |
| CNN23d | Telugu | 6.32 |
| MSW51j | Samoyed | 6.00 |
| NAB64e | Kono | 5.68 |

| Code | People | % church members |
|------|--------|------------------|
| MSY52a | Muong | 5.33 |

*Under 5%*

| Code | People | % church members |
|------|--------|------------------|
| NAB62n | Nuer | 4.99 |
| AUG06b | Gond | 3.90 |
| AUG04d | Saora | 3.90 |
| AUG06a | Bhil | 3.90 |
| CMT34c | Tigre | 3.84 |
| CNN25a | Assamese | 3.72 |
| NAB64c | Gbande | 3.47 |
| NAB62r | Turkana | 3.26 |
| CNN23a | Kanarese | 3.11 |
| NAB64b | Gagu | 3.00 |
| MSY45b | Ryukyuan | 2.83 |
| CNN25q | Sinhalese | 2.79 |
| NAB59m | Nupe | 2.78 |
| AUG07 | Vedda | 2.70 |
| CNN25l | Oriya | 2.63 |
| NAB62c | Anuak | 2.61 |
| MSY44g | Javanese | 2.39 |
| MSY45a | Japanese | 2.33 |
| NAB56c | Western Bantoid | 2.29 |
| CNN25j | Marathi | 2.17 |
| NAB64g | Loko | 2.15 |
| CNN25n | Punjabi | 1.95 |
| NAB63e | Kasonke | 1.85 |
| AUG04c | Santal | 1.81 |
| NAB63a | Bambara | 1.63 |
| MSY44h | Madurese | 1.57 |
| MSY41h | Tatar | 1.50 |
| MSY50s | Tripuri | 1.45 |
| CNN25h | Jat | 1.35 |
| NAB64j | Ngere | 1.27 |
| CMT35 | Jewish | 1.07 |
| MSY44a | Balinese | 1.05 |

*Under 1%*

| Code | People | % church members |
|------|--------|------------------|
| MSY47b | Yao | 0.83 |
| MSY49b | Lao | 0.83 |
| CNN25p | Sindhi | 0.82 |
| MSY44n | Sundanese | 0.81 |
| MSY42a | Han Chinese | 0.79 |
| MSY47a | Miao | 0.76 |
| MSY49a | Chuang | 0.74 |
| AUG03c | Mon | 0.72 |
| MSY49c | Shan | 0.69 |
| CNN25e | Gujarati | 0.63 |
| AUG04a | Ho | 0.62 |
| MSY50j | Lepcha | 0.62 |
| NAB63g | Koranko | 0.59 |
| MSY49d | Thai | 0.56 |
| CNN25b | Bengali | 0.55 |
| CNN25g | Hindi | 0.54 |
| CMT32c | Kabyle | 0.19 |
| MSY50a | Bhotia | 0.17 |
| MSY50b | Burmese | 0.17 |
| CNN25o | Rajasthani | 0.17 |
| AUG03b | Khmer | 0.11 |
| CNT24b | Baluchi | 0.10 |
| MSY50q | Sherpa | 0.10 |

*Under 0.1%*

| Code | People | % church members |
|------|--------|------------------|
| CNT24a | Afghani | 0.08 |
| MSY50h | Kirati | 0.07 |
| NAB65b | Songhai | 0.05 |
| NAB63h | Malinke | 0.04 |
| CNT24f | Persian | 0.04 |
| CMT33e | Somali | 0.03 |
| CNN25k | Nepalese | 0.03 |
| MSY50e | Gurung | 0.02 |
| NAB60a | Hausa | 0.02 |
| CNN25i | Kashmiri | 0.02 |
| MSY44k | Malay | 0.02 |
| MSY41j | Turkish | 0.02 |
| CNN25c | Bihari | 0.02 |
| MSY41f | Khalka-Mongol | 0.01 |
| NAB65c | Zerma | 0.01 |

*Under 0.01%*

| Code | People | % church members |
|------|--------|------------------|
| CMT32a | Arabized Berber | 0.00 |
| CMT32b | Beraber | 0.00 |
| CMT32d | Oasis Berber | 0.00 |
| MSY41a | Azerbaijani | 0.00 |
| CMT32e | Rif | 0.00 |
| MSY50k | Limbu | 0.00 |
| CMT32f | Shawiya | 0.00 |
| CMT32g | Shluh | 0.00 |
| MSY50n | Magar | 0.00 |
| MSY41e | Kazakh | 0.00 |
| CMT32h | Tuareg | 0.00 |
| MSY41g | Kirgiz | 0.00 |
| MSY50r | Tibetan | 0.00 |
| CMT32i | Zenaga | 0.00 |
| MSY41i | Tungus-Manchu | 0.00 |
| MSY41k | Turkmen | 0.00 |
| MSY41l | Uzbek | 0.00 |
| NAB61 | Kanuri | 0.00 |
| MSW51j | Samoyed | 0.00 |
| MSY42b | Hui | 0.00 |
| NAB62m | Nubian | 0.00 |
| MSY44c | Buginese | 0.00 |
| NAB63b | Bozo | 0.00 |
| NAB63c | Dialonke | 0.00 |
| NAB63d | Kagoro | 0.00 |
| NAB63f | Konyanke | 0.00 |
| NAB63i | Nono | 0.00 |
| NAB63j | Soninke | 0.00 |
| NAB63k | Susu | 0.00 |
| NAB63l | Yalunka | 0.00 |
| MSY44i | Makassarese | 0.00 |
| CEW22a | Bosnian | 0.00 |
| CNN25m | Parsi | 0.00 |
| CEW17a | Adygo-Abkhazi | 0.00 |
| NAB64k | Vai | 0.00 |
| NAB65a | Dendi | 0.00 |
| CEW17b | Dagestani | 0.00 |
| CNN25r | Urdu | 0.00 |
| NAB66d | Fur | 0.00 |
| CNT24c | Kurdish | 0.00 |
| CNT24d | Nuristani | 0.00 |
| CEW17d | Nakh | 0.00 |
| CNT24g | Tadzhik | 0.00 |

Global Table 26. ORGANIZED CHRISTIANITY: DENOMINATIONS AND MEMBERSHIPS ON 8 CONTINENTS IN 7 ECCLESIASTICAL BLOCS, AD 1900-1985.

1. This table is an expanded version of Global Table 9 in Part 1. It is derived from the 221 Tables 2 presented in Part 7 for all countries.
2. For detailed definitions of columns and rows, see notes at the beginning of Global Table 27.
3. 'Significant' and 'total' denominations are also described and defined in Global Table 27.

| *Continent* | *Bloc* Code | Name | *Congs* 1970 | *Adults* 1970 | *Affiliated, 1900–1985* 1900 | 1970 | 1975 | 1980 | 1985 | *Denominations, 1970–1985* Significant 1970 | Total 1970 | 1975 | 1980 | 1985 | *Countries* |
|---|---|---|---|---|---|---|---|---|---|---|---|---|---|---|---|
| 1 | 2 | 3 | 4 | 5 | 6 | 7 | 8 | 9 | 10 | 11 | 12 | 13 | 14 | 15 | 16 |
| AFRICA | | | | | | | | | | | | | | | |
| | | Total | 231,580 | 57,192,008 | 8,756,372 | 115,924,182 | 138,060,650 | 164,570,376 | 191,080,131 | 1,361 | 7,321 | 7,768 | 8,265 | 8,770 | 59 |
| | A | Anglican | 23,365 | 1,902,486 | 369,430 | 7,793,170 | 9,069,553 | 10,674,573 | 12,279,603 | 40 | 40 | 42 | 43 | 45 | 36 |
| | C | Catholic (non-Roman) | 1,500 | 230,325 | 0 | 402,800 | 492,123 | 593,335 | 694,544 | 19 | 24 | 25 | 27 | 29 | 13 |
| | I | Non-White indigenous | 38,770 | 7,785,800 | 39,200 | 15,971,367 | 19,767,103 | 24,457,725 | 29,148,347 | 503 | 5,982 | 6,313 | 6,727 | 7,172 | 43 |
| | M | Marginal Protestant | 5,059 | 374,405 | 800 | 994,058 | 1,222,758 | 1,488,919 | 1,755,084 | 72 | 96 | 109 | 122 | 136 | 45 |
| | O | Orthodox | 17,441 | 10,633,405 | 4,600,250 | 18,243,770 | 20,571,020 | 23,166,682 | 25,762,353 | 52 | 55 | 56 | 57 | 60 | 26 |
| | P | Protestant | 130,094 | 10,412,327 | 1,836,980 | 27,182,284 | 32,081,605 | 37,981,313 | 43,881,032 | 617 | 1,066 | 1,165 | 1,231 | 1,270 | 56 |
| | R | Roman Catholic | 15,351 | 25,853,260 | 1,909,712 | 45,336,733 | 54,856,488 | 66,207,829 | 77,559,168 | 58 | 58 | 58 | 58 | 58 | 58 |
| | — | Doubly-affiliated | | 0 | 0 | 0 | 0 | 0 | 0 | — | — | — | — | — | 0 |
| | — | Disaffiliated | | 0 | 0 | 0 | 0 | 0 | 0 | — | — | — | — | — | 0 |
| EAST ASIA | | | | | | | | | | | | | | | |
| | | Total | 85,909 | 4,708,337 | 1,762,981 | 10,050,165 | 12,965,849 | 16,149,444 | 19,333,094 | 365 | 688 | 740 | 793 | 850 | 8 |
| | A | Anglican | 2,441 | 62,354 | 41,697 | 147,001 | 156,800 | 166,198 | 175,599 | 6 | 6 | 6 | 6 | 6 | 6 |
| | C | Catholic (non-Roman) | 0 | 500 | 0 | 1,000 | 1,100 | 1,200 | 1,300 | 1 | 1 | 1 | 1 | 1 | 1 |
| | I | Non-White indigenous | 25,966 | 1,296,420 | 11,050 | 3,214,305 | 4,741,725 | 6,302,609 | 7,863,484 | 115 | 324 | 357 | 390 | 421 | 8 |
| | M | Marginal Protestant | 831 | 49,548 | 0 | 116,072 | 176,503 | 233,963 | 291,423 | 18 | 18 | 20 | 22 | 25 | 6 |
| | O | Orthodox | 714 | 23,875 | 55,544 | 42,602 | 44,099 | 45,698 | 47,299 | 7 | 7 | 7 | 7 | 9 | 5 |
| | P | Protestant | 24,169 | 1,610,910 | 451,900 | 3,532,236 | 4,633,073 | 5,945,027 | 7,257,040 | 210 | 324 | 341 | 359 | 380 | 7 |
| | R | Roman Catholic | 31,788 | 1,664,730 | 1,202,790 | 2,996,949 | 3,212,549 | 3,454,749 | 3,696,949 | 8 | 8 | 8 | 8 | 8 | 8 |
| | — | Doubly-affiliated | | 0 | 0 | 0 | 0 | 0 | 0 | — | — | — | — | — | 0 |
| | — | Disaffiliated | | 0 | 0 | 0 | 0 | 0 | 0 | — | — | — | — | — | 0 |
| EUROPE | | | | | | | | | | | | | | | |
| | | Total | 343,124 | 274,569,089 | 273,788,410 | 397,108,659 | 400,119,738 | 403,177,090 | 406,234,493 | 1,083 | 2,577 | 2,689 | 2,811 | 2,910 | 37 |
| | A | Anglican | 21,362 | 10,290,516 | 24,900,610 | 29,372,130 | 29,148,975 | 28,964,093 | 28,779,215 | 31 | 33 | 37 | 41 | 44 | 25 |
| | C | Catholic (non-Roman) | 6,806 | 1,237,195 | 170,220 | 1,877,162 | 1,905,899 | 1,935,806 | 1,965,715 | 103 | 328 | 331 | 334 | 338 | 23 |
| | I | Non-White indigenous | 575 | 42,373 | 0 | 87,270 | 94,654 | 105,280 | 116,018 | 61 | 161 | 201 | 250 | 290 | 7 |
| | M | Marginal Protestant | 10,512 | 845,790 | 103,400 | 1,737,339 | 1,885,808 | 2,039,603 | 2,193,401 | 128 | 337 | 370 | 403 | 437 | 33 |
| | O | Orthodox | 50,544 | 29,122,813 | 21,595,350 | 40,938,818 | 42,122,751 | 43,251,219 | 44,379,711 | 129 | 149 | 152 | 155 | 160 | 28 |
| | P | Protestant | 115,330 | 57,586,132 | 57,550,100 | 85,660,412 | 83,867,389 | 81,873,143 | 79,878,898 | 593 | 1,531 | 1,560 | 1,590 | 1,603 | 35 |
| | R | Roman Catholic | 137,995 | 186,726,670 | 170,627,440 | 254,015,061 | 260,061,749 | 266,142,904 | 272,224,061 | 38 | 38 | 38 | 38 | 38 | 36 |
| | — | Doubly-affiliated | | –4,478,800 | –927,310 | –6,510,583 | –6,563,067 | –6,638,548 | –6,714,026 | — | — | — | — | — | 12 |
| | — | Disaffiliated | | –6,803,600 | –231,400 | –10,068,950 | –12,404,326 | –14,496,410 | –16,588,500 | — | — | — | — | — | 4 |
| LATIN AMERICA | | | | | | | | | | | | | | | |
| | | Total | 118,679 | 147,358,987 | 60,025,060 | 262,027,772 | 298,705,802 | 340,977,959 | 383,250,181 | 1,419 | 3,030 | 3,263 | 3,504 | 3,799 | 47 |
| | A | Anglican | 1,750 | 273,187 | 727,920 | 774,259 | 796,608 | 819,036 | 841,464 | 44 | 44 | 46 | 47 | 48 | 44 |
| | C | Catholic (non-Roman) | 302 | 68,330 | 1,000 | 126,550 | 141,259 | 156,969 | 172,679 | 13 | 13 | 15 | 17 | 19 | 11 |
| | I | Non-White indigenous | 23,254 | 3,891,644 | 29,400 | 8,240,198 | 10,163,160 | 12,556,106 | 14,949,030 | 303 | 1,059 | 1,214 | 1,346 | 1,583 | 36 |
| | M | Marginal Protestant | 4,890 | 430,212 | 3,820 | 843,897 | 1,080,669 | 1,376,939 | 1,673,211 | 96 | 161 | 168 | 175 | 181 | 46 |
| | O | Orthodox | 216 | 222,550 | 6,400 | 408,363 | 458,047 | 512,479 | 566,906 | 56 | 64 | 65 | 67 | 70 | 21 |
| | P | Protestant | 65,492 | 6,390,365 | 933,650 | 12,725,223 | 15,407,892 | 18,661,505 | 21,915,205 | 861 | 1,643 | 1,709 | 1,806 | 1,851 | 46 |
| | R | Roman Catholic | 22,775 | 145,055,470 | 58,696,970 | 254,507,787 | 289,398,642 | 329,426,750 | 369,454,862 | 46 | 46 | 46 | 46 | 47 | 47 |
| | — | Doubly-affiliated | | –8,499,971 | –293,100 | –14,819,267 | –17,917,845 | –21,662,725 | –25,407,606 | — | — | — | — | — | 20 |
| | — | Disaffiliated | | –472,800 | –81,000 | –779,230 | –822,630 | –869,100 | –915,570 | — | — | — | — | — | 5 |
| NORTHERN AMERICA | | | | | | | | | | | | | | | |
| | | Total | 386,747 | 115,829,131 | 59,569,690 | 169,246,901 | 173,932,410 | 178,892,260 | 183,852,088 | 510 | 2,035 | 2,240 | 2,465 | 2,690 | 5 |
| | A | Anglican | 11,094 | 2,838,586 | 2,172,000 | 4,433,891 | 4,252,684 | 4,082,033 | 3,911,383 | 12 | 22 | 30 | 39 | 46 | 3 |
| | C | Catholic (non-Roman) | 1,945 | 461,033 | 104,000 | 684,911 | 688,087 | 695,089 | 702,086 | 27 | 76 | 81 | 85 | 96 | 3 |
| | I | Non-White indigenous | 77,232 | 14,651,065 | 5,752,800 | 19,757,819 | 20,580,156 | 21,420,355 | 22,260,529 | 73 | 432 | 450 | 487 | 550 | 3 |
| | M | Marginal Protestant | 28,518 | 3,987,701 | 815,000 | 6,712,433 | 7,495,522 | 8,298,717 | 9,101,912 | 43 | 362 | 414 | 479 | 560 | 4 |
| | O | Orthodox | 2,297 | 3,278,800 | 415,000 | 4,970,625 | 5,160,967 | 5,369,974 | 5,578,973 | 56 | 84 | 87 | 90 | 98 | 2 |
| | P | Protestant | 242,501 | 51,226,516 | 37,299,590 | 75,208,340 | 77,036,195 | 78,900,152 | 80,764,125 | 294 | 1,054 | 1,173 | 1,280 | 1,335 | 4 |
| | R | Roman Catholic | 23,160 | 39,385,430 | 13,011,300 | 57,478,882 | 58,718,799 | 60,125,940 | 61,533,080 | 5 | 5 | 5 | 5 | 5 | 5 |
| | — | Doubly-affiliated | | 0 | 0 | 0 | 0 | 0 | 0 | — | — | — | — | — | 0 |
| | — | Disaffiliated | | 0 | 0 | 0 | 0 | 0 | 0 | — | — | — | — | — | 0 |
| OCEANIA | | | | | | | | | | | | | | | |
| | | Total | 35,409 | 6,336,078 | 4,311,449 | 14,669,387 | 15,411,710 | 16,160,484 | 16,909,231 | 370 | 598 | 653 | 716 | 780 | 29 |
| | A | Anglican | 6,853 | 898,140 | 1,692,178 | 4,781,778 | 4,780,746 | 4,748,426 | 4,716,110 | 18 | 18 | 18 | 18 | 19 | 18 |
| | C | Catholic (non-Roman) | 57 | 4,100 | 400 | 9,262 | 10,215 | 11,176 | 12,136 | 7 | 11 | 11 | 11 | 11 | 2 |
| | I | Non-White indigenous | 51 | 53,630 | 17,560 | 88,893 | 96,595 | 104,838 | 113,077 | 40 | 60 | 70 | 80 | 90 | 15 |
| | M | Marginal Protestant | 915 | 122,671 | 4,280 | 201,356 | 241,010 | 288,708 | 336,398 | 45 | 82 | 85 | 88 | 92 | 17 |
| | O | Orthodox | 245 | 227,600 | 4,190 | 337,500 | 372,257 | 415,539 | 458,816 | 27 | 36 | 37 | 38 | 40 | 3 |
| | P | Protestant | 24,312 | 2,004,417 | 1,544,655 | 4,720,341 | 4,812,384 | 4,870,566 | 4,928,732 | 205 | 363 | 404 | 453 | 500 | 26 |
| | R | Roman Catholic | 2,976 | 3,029,420 | 1,048,186 | 4,536,887 | 5,105,703 | 5,729,230 | 6,352,762 | 28 | 28 | 28 | 28 | 28 | 28 |
| | — | Doubly-affiliated | | –3,900 | 0 | –6,630 | –7,200 | –7,999 | –8,800 | — | — | — | — | — | 1 |
| | — | Disaffiliated | | 0 | 0 | 0 | 0 | 0 | 0 | — | — | — | — | — | 0 |
| SOUTH ASIA | | | | | | | | | | | | | | | |
| | | Total | 134,270 | 39,905,547 | 16,347,219 | 76,770,214 | 90,368,256 | 106,732,783 | 123,097,394 | 951 | 1,773 | 1,915 | 2,075 | 2,230 | 37 |
| | A | Anglican | 830 | 138,282 | 667,830 | 254,246 | 302,046 | 349,115 | 396,187 | 30 | 30 | 30 | 30 | 31 | 32 |
| | C | Catholic (non-Roman) | | 22,725 | 400 | 32,700 | 39,250 | 45,800 | 52,350 | 6 | 10 | 10 | 10 | 10 | 6 |
| | I | Non-White indigenous | 43,673 | 5,454,014 | 1,895,050 | 11,342,108 | 14,120,593 | 17,233,502 | 20,346,442 | 270 | 715 | 760 | 785 | 850 | 33 |
| | M | Marginal Protestant | 1,727 | 84,705 | 280 | 215,066 | 270,286 | 337,484 | 404,685 | 45 | 50 | 53 | 55 | 58 | 24 |
| | O | Orthodox | 2,780 | 1,915,790 | 4,220,970 | 3,286,810 | 3,525,856 | 3,788,169 | 4,050,476 | 72 | 83 | 84 | 86 | 88 | 21 |
| | P | Protestant | 73,187 | 7,785,521 | 1,439,780 | 17,961,109 | 21,419,974 | 26.149,210 | 30,878,490 | 490 | 847 | 940 | 1,071 | 1,155 | 37 |
| | R | Roman Catholic | 12,073 | 27,381,010 | 9,923,009 | 49,053,263 | 57,301,251 | 66,822.503 | 76,343,764 | 38 | 38 | 38 | 38 | 38 | 37 |
| | — | Doubly-affiliated | | –2,876,500 | –1,800,100 | –5,375,088 | –6,611,000 | –7,993,000 | –9,375,000 | — | — | — | — | — | 1 |
| | — | Disaffiliated | | 0 | 0 | 0 | 0 | 0 | 0 | — | — | — | — | — | 0 |
| USSR | | | | | | | | | | | | | | | |
| | | Total | 76,222 | 57,499,600 | 97,002,000 | 86,012,300 | 91,284,975 | 96,726,471 | 102,167,977 | 52 | 140 | 146 | 152 | 160 | 1 |
| | A | Anglican | 3 | 200 | 2,000 | 500 | 500 | 500 | 500 | 1 | 1 | 1 | 1 | 1 | 1 |
| | C | Catholic (non-Roman) | 0 | 0 | 0 | 0 | 0 | 0 | 0 | 0 | 0 | 0 | 0 | 0 | 0 |
| | I | Non-White indigenous | 0 | 0 | 0 | 0 | 0 | 0 | 0 | 0 | 0 | 0 | 0 | 0 | 0 |
| | M | Marginal Protestant | 0 | 5,000 | 0 | 10,000 | 11,500 | 13,000 | 14,500 | 1 | 1 | 1 | 1 | 1 | 1 |
| | O | Orthodox | 25,479 | 51,812,500 | 85,000,000 | 75,174,000 | 79,571,990 | 84,187,984 | 88,803,986 | 25 | 45 | 46 | 50 | 55 | 1 |
| | P | Protestant | 49,740 | 2,651,900 | 2,000,000 | 6,434,300 | 7,140,985 | 7,774,988 | 8,408,991 | 24 | 92 | 97 | 99 | 102 | 1 |
| | R | Roman Catholic | 1,000 | 3,030,000 | 10,000,000 | 4,393,500 | 4,560,000 | 4,749,999 | 4,940,000 | 1 | 1 | 1 | 1 | 1 | 1 |
| | — | Doubly-affiliated | | 0 | 0 | 0 | 0 | 0 | 0 | — | — | — | — | — | 0 |
| | — | Disaffiliated | | 0 | 0 | 0 | 0 | 0 | 0 | — | — | — | — | — | 0 |
| WORLD | | | | | | | | | | | | | | | |
| | | Total | 1,411,940 | 703,398,777 | 521,563,181 | 1,131,809,580 | 1,220,849,390 | 1,323,386,867 | 1,425,924,589 | 6,111 | 18,162 | 19,414 | 20,781 | 22,189 | 223 |
| | A | Anglican | 67,698 | 16,403,751 | 30,573,665 | 47,556,975 | 48,507,912 | 49,803,974 | 51,100,061 | 182 | 194 | 210 | 225 | 240 | 165 |
| | C | Catholic (non-Roman) | 10,610 | 2,024,208 | 276,020 | 3,134,385 | 3,277,933 | 3,439,375 | 3,600,810 | 176 | 463 | 474 | 485 | 504 | 59 |
| | I | Non-White indigenous | 209,521 | 33,174,946 | 7,745,060 | 58,701,960 | 69,563,886 | 82,180,415 | 94,796,927 | 1,365 | 8,733 | 9,365 | 10,065 | 10,956 | 145 |
| | M | Marginal Protestant | 52,452 | 5,900,032 | 927,580 | 10,830,221 | 12,384,056 | 14,077,333 | 15,770,614 | 448 | 1,107 | 1,220 | 1,345 | 1,490 | 176 |
| | O | Orthodox | 99,716 | 97,237,333 | 115,897,704 | 143,402,488 | 151,826,987 | 160,737,744 | 169.648,520 | 424 | 523 | 534 | 550 | 580 | 107 |
| | P | Protestant | 724,825 | 139,668,088 | 103,056,655 | 233,424,245 | 246,399,497 | 262,155,904 | 277,912,513 | 3,294 | 6,920 | 7,389 | 7,889 | 8,196 | 212 |
| | R | Roman Catholic | 247,118 | 432,125,990 | 266,419,407 | 672,319,062 | 733,215,181 | 802,659,904 | 872,104,646 | 222 | 222 | 222 | 222 | 223 | 220 |
| | — | Doubly-affiliated | | –15,859,171 | –3,020,510 | –26,711,568 | –31,099,112 | –36,302,272 | –41,505,432 | — | — | — | — | — | 34 |
| | — | Disaffiliated | | –7,276,400 | –312,400 | –10,848,188 | –13,226,950 | –15,365,510 | –17,504,070 | — | — | — | — | — | 9 |

Global Table 27. ORGANIZED CHRISTIANITY: CHURCHES AND GLOBAL MEMBERSHIPS IN 7 ECCLESIASTICAL BLOCS AND 156 TRADITIONS, AD 1970-1985.

1. This table is an expanded version of Global Table 9 in Part 1. It is derived from the 221 Tables 2 presented in Part 7 for all countries.
2. All figures are given to the last digit in order that totals here, and in all other tables, shall add up exactly. This should not be taken as implying any bogus claim to an artificial exactitude at the global level. The method of computing the totals for 1975-85 below is slightly different to that in Global Tables 2 and 4, hence some figures may differ slightly in the final 2 or 3 digits. When quoting any aggregate or global figures in these tables, therefore, they should be rounded, either to the nearest thousand, or ten thousand, or 0.1%, or 1%, as may be appropriate to the reader's requirements.

3. *Meaning of columns*
1. *Ecclesiastical bloc.* On these 7 lines are given the global statistical totals applicable to each bloc, and also, at the end of the table, for global church membership.
2-3. *Ecclesiastical tradition.* Under each of the 7 blocs are specified each's major constituent ecclesiastical traditions, listed in their codes' alphabetical order. First comes the 3-letter code as used in Tables 2, then the full name of each tradition. At the end of each listing for a bloc, the line 'Other' (whose code in Tables 2 is a blank space) then sums any smaller residual, aggregate or unspecified traditions in that bloc. Note that some 26 of the 130 distinct traditions are not unique to one bloc but occur in 2 blocs.
4-6. *Congregations* (worship centres), *adult church members*, *affiliated* or total Christian community (all referring to the year 1970). These 3 columns are totals derived directly by addition from columns 5-7 in Tables 2 for all countries.
7-9. *Affiliated* church members (total Christian community) in 1975, 1980, and 1985.
10-14. *Denominations.* A denomination is defined in this Encyclopedia as an organized aggregate of worship centres or congregations of similar ecclesiastical tradition within a specific country; i.e. as an organized Christian church or tradition or religious group or community of believers, within a specific country, whose component congregations and members are called by the same denominational name in different areas, regarding themselves as one autonomous Christian church distinct from other denominations, churches and traditions. As defined here, world Christianity consists of 7 major ecclesiastico-cultural blocs, divided into 156 major ecclesiastical traditions, composed of over 20,800 distinct denominations in 223 countries, these denominations themselves being composed of over 1,800,000 worship centres, churches or congregations.
10. *Significant.* This word refers to those denominations which are sufficiently large, important or otherwise significant in a country's context for each to have its own single line in the country's Table 2. For Roman Catholic rites (shown listed under this bloc below), column 10 has a different meaning: it enumerates the number of distinct jurisdictions which follow each rite, which add up to the total of all jurisdictions shown as J=2,606 (1980). These are not included in the totals of distinct denominations. They are shown below in italics.
11-14. *Total distinct denominations*, significant and less significant (or relatively insignificant), the latter being smaller bodies too small to each be enumerated with its own single line in Tables 2; for the years 1970, 1975, 1980 and 1985. These totals are given here only for blocs as a whole, and not for individual traditions. For the latter, rough estimates may be made by starting from column 10 and then multiplying by the ratio of its bloc's column 13 to column 10 (for 1980); etc.
15. *Countries.* Total countries in which each tradition has or had one or more significant denominations, during the 20th century.

| Bloc / Tradition / Code | Full name | Congs | Adults | Affiliated (total membership, total community) 1970 | 1975 | 1980 | 1985 | Denominations Sig 1970 | Total 1970 | 1975 | 1980 | 1985 | Coun-tries |
|---|---|---|---|---|---|---|---|---|---|---|---|---|---|
| 1 2 | 3 | 4 | 5 | 6 | 7 | 8 | 9 | 10 | 11 | 12 | 13 | 14 | 15 |
| ANGLICAN | | 67,698 | 16,403,751 | 47,556,975 | 48,507,912 | 49,803,974 | 51,100,061 | 182 | 194 | 210 | 225 | 240 | 165 |
| ACa | Anglo-Catholic | 2,658 | 368,083 | 909,553 | 1,009,237 | 1,114,591 | 1,219,948 | 37 | | | | | |
| Cen | Central (Broad Church) Anglican | 908 | 177,049 | 358,416 | 400,507 | 441,578 | 482,659 | 33 | | | | | |
| Eva | Anglican Evangelical | 9,072 | 689,763 | 2,338,551 | 2,902,210 | 3,610,370 | 4,318,535 | 10 | | | | | |
| Hig | High Church (Prayer Book Catholic) | 8,303 | 949,386 | 2,915,362 | 3,015,089 | 3,131,604 | 3,248,124 | 31 | | | | | |
| Low | Low Church (Conservative Evangelical) | 7,065 | 617,862 | 3,614,546 | 4,064,383 | 4,650,854 | 5,237,319 | 14 | | | | | |
| plu | plural (mixed) tradition Anglican | 39,139 | 13,544,976 | 37,316,303 | 37,012,655 | 36,751,370 | 36,490,086 | 41 | | | | | |
| sAC | Anglo-Catholic schismatic | 50 | 7,000 | 10,000 | 9,411 | 8,824 | 8,236 | 1 | | | | | |
| sEV | Evangelical schismatic | 343 | 43,532 | 82,044 | 82,926 | 83,991 | 85,064 | 12 | | | | | |
| smi | mixed-churchmanship schismatic | 160 | 5,000 | 10,000 | 9,411 | 8,824 | 8,236 | 1 | | | | | |
| | other Anglican | | 1,100 | 2,200 | 2,083 | 1,968 | 1,854 | 2 | | | | | |
| CATHOLIC (NON-ROMAN) | | 10,610 | 2,024,208 | 3,134,385 | 3,277,933 | 3,439,375 | 3,600,810 | 176 | 463 | 474 | 485 | 504 | 59 |
| ARo | Anglo-Roman | 352 | 10,475 | 23,000 | 25,151 | 26,855 | 28,558 | 9 | | | | | |
| CAp | Catholic Apostolic (New Apostolic) | 7,161 | 1,005,660 | 1,610,105 | 1,743,771 | 1,887,279 | 2,030,790 | 68 | | | | | |
| CCa | Conservative Catholic | 512 | 175,381 | 273,529 | 272,831 | 272,544 | 272,249 | 29 | | | | | |
| Epi | episcopi-vagantes Catholic | 2 | 2,100 | 4,200 | 4,200 | 4,202 | 4,204 | 12 | | | | | |
| Lib | Liberal Catholic | 161 | 13,597 | 25,951 | 26,149 | 26,437 | 26,722 | 19 | | | | | |
| mar | marginal Catholic | 154 | 14,000 | 55,800 | 56,244 | 56,874 | 57,504 | 3 | | | | | |
| OCa | Old Catholic | 723 | 307,145 | 445,900 | 444,686 | 443,578 | 442,471 | 20 | | | | | |
| Pro | ex-Protestant Catholic | 15 | 700 | 1,000 | 1,050 | 1,100 | 1,150 | 1 | | | | | |
| ReC | Reformed Catholic | 1,530 | 478,050 | 657,700 | 665,650 | 681,527 | 697,403 | 7 | | | | | |
| | other Catholic (non-Roman) | | 17,100 | 37,200 | 38,201 | 38,979 | 39,759 | 8 | | | | | |
| NON-WHITE INDIGENOUS | | 209,521 | 33,174,946 | 58,701,960 | 69,563,886 | 82,180,415 | 94,796,927 | 1,365 | 8,733 | 9,365 | 10,065 | 10,956 | 145 |
| ARo | Anglo-Roman | 141 | 34,735 | 60,369 | 74,136 | 92,193 | 110,245 | 9 | | | | | |
| Adv | Adventist | 224 | 20,500 | 41,150 | 54,051 | 69,333 | 84,614 | 11 | | | | | |
| Ang | ex-Anglican | 3,591 | 387,876 | 732,077 | 921,859 | 1,160,426 | 1,398,990 | 40 | | | | | |
| Bap | Baptist | 51,045 | 10,708,922 | 12,980,718 | 13,601,469 | 14,243,449 | 14,885,425 | 48 | | | | | |
| CBr | Christian Brethren (Open) | 620 | 29,730 | 144,110 | 171,617 | 206,963 | 242,307 | 15 | | | | | |
| CCa | Conservative Catholic | 1,853 | 1,192,741 | 2,457,626 | 3,062,487 | 3,794,103 | 4,525,723 | 29 | | | | | |
| Con | Congregationalist | 479 | 128,314 | 285,888 | 350,083 | 429,606 | 509,128 | 12 | | | | | |
| EBr | Exclusive Brethren | 1,764 | 75,600 | 152,300 | 179,373 | 207,250 | 235,128 | 8 | | | | | |
| Hol | Holiness (Perfectionist) | 944 | 53,759 | 143,386 | 200,798 | 262,810 | 324,829 | 22 | | | | | |
| ind | independent evangelical | 10,181 | 1,218,146 | 3,414,945 | 4,282,035 | 5,292,272 | 6,302,497 | 160 | | | | | |
| int | interdenominational | 143 | 20,359 | 47,293 | 59,297 | 72,279 | 85,256 | 14 | | | | | |
| Jeh | Jehovah's Witnesses (Russellite) schismatic | 15 | 40,500 | 91,000 | 113,359 | 140,913 | 168,467 | 6 | | | | | |
| Jew | Jewish-Christian | 217 | 38,217 | 50,000 | 52,048 | 54,101 | 56,154 | 1 | | | | | |
| Lib | Liberal Catholic | | 33,578 | 57,000 | 71,088 | 86,918 | 102,751 | 7 | | | | | |
| LuR | Lutheran/Reformed united church | 5 | 1,000 | 2,000 | 2,368 | 2,853 | 3,337 | 1 | | | | | |
| Lut | Lutheran | 2,400 | 353,700 | 764,684 | 955,647 | 1,158,229 | 1,360,811 | 23 | | | | | |
| mar | marginal | 4,688 | 948,278 | 2,427,465 | 3,276,758 | 4,182,967 | 5,089,178 | 53 | | | | | |
| Met | Methodist | 17,574 | 2,949,757 | 4,417,828 | 4,791,113 | 5,219,670 | 5,648,235 | 71 | | | | | |
| Mor | Moravian | | 70 | 200 | 250 | 300 | 350 | 1 | | | | | |
| Nes | Assyrian, Nestorian | 2 | 3,650 | 6,200 | 7,547 | 9,010 | 10,473 | 3 | | | | | |
| non | no-church (anti-church) | 903 | 50,100 | 150,300 | 184,190 | 222,215 | 260,241 | 3 | | | | | |
| pe1 | indigenous oneness-pentecostal | 7,635 | 1,119,282 | 1,693,818 | 2,075,431 | 2,485,111 | 2,894,792 | 50 | | | | | |
| pe2 | indigenous baptistic-pentecostal | 16,128 | 2,000,073 | 4,533,450 | 5,565,876 | 6,831,100 | 8,096,329 | 68 | | | | | |
| pe3 | indigenous holiness-pentecostal | 12,416 | 1,133,567 | 2,830,049 | 3,077,259 | 3,364,157 | 3,651,057 | 53 | | | | | |
| pe4 | indigenous radical-pentecostal | 71 | 5,550 | 12,000 | 14,694 | 17,922 | 21,151 | 7 | | | | | |
| peA | indigenous pentecostal-apostolic | 5,665 | 891,454 | 1,701,714 | 2,189,125 | 2,808,370 | 3,427,614 | 52 | | | | | |
| pen | indigenous charismatic/pentecostal | 24,393 | 4,813,244 | 9,375,851 | 11,356,142 | 13,750,749 | 16,145,345 | 358 | | | | | |
| rad | isolated radio-church | 34,020 | 600,670 | 1,274,730 | 1,561,357 | 1,888,552 | 2,215,746 | 58 | | | | | |
| ReC | Reformed Catholic | 3,423 | 1,877,700 | 3,551,500 | 4,446,316 | 5,453,844 | 6,461,373 | 8 | | | | | |
| Ref | Reformed (Presbyterian) | 5,817 | 820,088 | 1,760,512 | 2,523,631 | 3,342,713 | 4,161,785 | 68 | | | | | |
| ReO | Reformed Orthodox | 909 | 238,640 | 401,797 | 474,583 | 569,503 | 664,424 | 16 | | | | | |
| Sal | Salvationist (Salvation Army) | 185 | 51,477 | 114,000 | 138,011 | 167,882 | 197,753 | 8 | | | | | |
| sin | single-congregation | 210 | 17,000 | 54,000 | 67,071 | 80,868 | 94,664 | 2 | | | | | |
| Spi | spiritualist (Spiritist) | | 53,500 | 107,000 | 134,032 | 164,456 | 194,882 | 3 | | | | | |
| uni | united church | 100 | 75,000 | 150,000 | 176,545 | 207,626 | 238,706 | 2 | | | | | |
| | other Non-White indigenous | 1,760 | 1,188,169 | 2,715,000 | 3,352,240 | 4,139,702 | 4,927,167 | 75 | | | | | |
| MARGINAL PROTESTANT | | 52,452 | 5,900,032 | 10,830,221 | 12,384,056 | 14,077,333 | 15,770,614 | 448 | 1,107 | 1,220 | 1,345 | 1,490 | 176 |
| Apo | apocalyptic (eschatological) | | 10,500 | 21,000 | 22,989 | 25,054 | 27,118 | 3 | | | | | |
| BrI | British-Israelite | 551 | 104,500 | 228,000 | 253,692 | 279,918 | 306,142 | 4 | | | | | |
| Epi | episcopi-vagantes Catholic | | 1,030 | 2,050 | 2,053 | 2,058 | 2,063 | 21 | | | | | |
| Gno | Gnostic (esoteric) | 114 | 27,500 | 58,500 | 63,558 | 67,690 | 71,820 | 5 | | | | | |
| ind | independent | 7 | 735 | 1,500 | 1,675 | 1,851 | 2,027 | 1 | | | | | |
| Jeh | Jehovah's Witnesses (Russellite) | 26,268 | 1,662,719 | 4,012,405 | 4,706,291 | 5,487,303 | 6,268,327 | 181 | | | | | |
| Jew | Jewish-Christian | | 500 | 1,000 | 1,143 | 1,334 | 1,524 | 1 | | | | | |
| LdS | Latter-day Saints (Mormon) | 7,843 | 2,367,076 | 3,097,068 | 3,527,037 | 4,001,263 | 4,475,484 | 82 | | | | | |
| Lib | Liberal Catholic/Marginal Protestant | 10 | 4,500 | 5,000 | 5,718 | 6,671 | 7,624 | 1 | | | | | |
| Pe1 | Oneness (Unitarian)-Pentecostal | | 300 | 1,000 | 1,295 | 1,568 | 1,840 | 1 | | | | | |
| Sci | Divine Science (Christian Science) | 3,819 | 623,579 | 1,340,140 | 1,496,039 | 1,654,546 | 1,813,048 | 61 | | | | | |
| Spi | Spiritualist (Spiritist) | 1,471 | 216,887 | 356,522 | 393,613 | 430,910 | 468,208 | 21 | | | | | |
| Swe | Swedenborgian | 359 | 28,272 | 49,940 | 58,427 | 67,066 | 75,705 | 18 | | | | | |
| The | Theosophist | 100 | 3,776 | 6,210 | 6,722 | 7,179 | 7,635 | 3 | | | | | |
| Unt | Unitarian (Free Christian, Universalist) | 1,908 | 274,398 | 469,256 | 517,526 | 566,792 | 616,069 | 29 | | | | | |
| | other marginal Protestant | 10,002 | 573,760 | 1,180,630 | 1,326,278 | 1,476,130 | 1,625,980 | 16 | | | | | |
| ORTHODOX | | 99,716 | 97,237,333 | 143,402,488 | 151,826,987 | 160,737,744 | 169,648,520 | 424 | 523 | 534 | 550 | 580 | 107 |
| Alb | Albanian | 535 | 110,500 | 172,150 | 170,672 | 169,314 | 167,954 | 4 | | | | | |
| Ara | Arabic | 792 | 445,000 | 772,400 | 854,119 | 945,259 | 1,036,406 | 28 | | | | | |
| Arm | Armenian (Gregorian) | 874 | 1,795,540 | 2,826,198 | 2,993,983 | 3,172,309 | 3,350,626 | 37 | | | | | |
| Cop | Coptic | 2,019 | 3,491,750 | 6,027,850 | 6,643,483 | 7,281,016 | 7,918,552 | 16 | | | | | |
| Cze | Czech | 141 | 147,000 | 200,000 | 204,000 | 208,000 | 212,000 | 1 | | | | | |
| Eth | Ethiopian | 15,063 | 7,041,830 | 11,931,400 | 13,578,730 | 15,455,876 | 17,333,022 | 10 | | | | | |
| Fin | Finnish | 78 | 41,000 | 58,000 | 57,670 | 58,104 | 58,540 | 2 | | | | | |

*Concluded opposite*

| Bloc / Tradition / Code / Full name | Congs | Adults | Affiliated (total membership, total community) | | | | Denominations | | | | | Countries |
|---|---|---|---|---|---|---|---|---|---|---|---|---|
| | | | 1970 | 1975 | 1980 | 1985 | *Sig* | *Total* | | | | |
| | | | | | | | 1970 | 1970 | 1975 | 1980 | 1985 | |
| 1   2   3 | 4 | 5 | 6 | 7 | 8 | 9 | 10 | 11 | 12 | 13 | 14 | 15 |
| Geo  Georgian | 80 | 500,000 | 800,000 | 846,803 | 895,926 | 945,050 | 1 | | | | | |
| Gre  Greek | 31,112 | 8,664,873 | 12,348,972 | 12,682,054 | 13,055,760 | 13,429,465 | 71 | | | | | |
| Hun  Hungarian | 10 | 5,200 | 40,400 | 41,128 | 41,893 | 42,659 | 2 | | | | | |
| Nes  Assyrian, Nestorian | 52 | 83,240 | 144,050 | 155,322 | 167,684 | 180,049 | 16 | | | | | |
| OBe  Old Believer (Old Ritualist) | 616 | 1,596,900 | 2,274,000 | 2,405,785 | 2,543,809 | 2,681,833 | 11 | | | | | |
| OCd  Old Calendarist (Authentic Orthodox) | 188 | 105,500 | 209,000 | 211,944 | 215,364 | 218,783 | 5 | | | | | |
| Pol  Polish | 305 | 345,000 | 547,000 | 569,660 | 592,821 | 615,982 | 2 | | | | | |
| ReO  Reformed Orthodox | 47 | 11,400 | 17,000 | 17,666 | 18,359 | 19,053 | 4 | | | | | |
| Rum  Romanian | 11,873 | 11,596,050 | 16,158,850 | 16,792,312 | 17,376,315 | 17,960,324 | 19 | | | | | |
| Ser  Serbian | 2,985 | 5,031,700 | 7,405,075 | 7,632,997 | 7,868,093 | 8,103,190 | 18 | | | | | |
| Sla  Slavonic | 12,277 | 54,810,710 | 79,071,581 | 83,428,031 | 87,976,007 | 92,523,987 | 115 | | | | | |
| sub  sub-Orthodox (Russian) | 1,525 | 202,600 | 388,300 | 411,136 | 435,447 | 459,763 | 12 | | | | | |
| SyM  Syro-Malabarese/Syrian | 942 | 834,680 | 1,415,932 | 1,496,433 | 1,580,969 | 1,665,504 | 5 | | | | | |
| Syr  Syrian | 94 | 113,160 | 204,830 | 216,507 | 230,132 | 243,757 | 19 | | | | | |
| Tru  True Orthodox | 18,100 | 176,000 | 253,000 | 267,800 | 283,335 | 298,870 | 4 | | | | | |
| other Orthodox | 8 | 87,700 | 136,500 | 148,752 | 165,952 | 183,151 | 22 | | | | | |
| **PROTESTANT** | 724,825 | 139,668,088 | 233,424,245 | 246,399,497 | 262,155,904 | 277,912,513 | 3,294 | 6,920 | 7,389 | 7,889 | 8,196 | 212 |
| Ade  Christadelphian (Brothers of Christ) | 1,529 | 60,260 | 96,900 | 95,190 | 92,916 | 90,645 | 21 | | | | | |
| Adv  Adventist | 20,980 | 2,143,086 | 4,077,940 | 4,703,668 | 5,445,372 | 6,187,077 | 193 | | | | | |
| Apo  apocalyptic (eschatological) | 60 | 6,500 | 12,000 | 12,236 | 12,405 | 12,574 | 5 | | | | | |
| Bap  Baptist | 102,124 | 18,982,612 | 29,418,833 | 31,177,158 | 33,306,814 | 35,436,498 | 321 | | | | | |
| Brl  British-Israelite | 50 | 5,000 | 10,000 | 10,247 | 10,494 | 10,742 | 1 | | | | | |
| CBr  Christian Brethren (Open) | 9,720 | 534,240 | 1,255,627 | 1,357,486 | 1,484,817 | 1,612,151 | 117 | | | | | |
| com  community-church | 55 | 9,396 | 22,003 | 25,842 | 30,751 | 35,660 | 21 | | | | | |
| Con  Congregationalist | 11,495 | 1,042,950 | 2,004,792 | 2,103,500 | 2,230,023 | 2,356,553 | 91 | | | | | |
| Dis  Disciples (Restorationist) | 33,866 | 5,270,388 | 7,876,091 | 8,165,957 | 8,474,567 | 8,783,192 | 118 | | | | | |
| Dun  Dunker (German Baptist) | 2,075 | 305,436 | 513,800 | 562,182 | 619,068 | 675,958 | 10 | | | | | |
| EBr  Exclusive Brethren (Closed, Strict) | 1,704 | 91,640 | 187,800 | 182,721 | 177,195 | 171,668 | 21 | | | | | |
| Hol  Holiness (Perfectionist) | 32,430 | 1,865,090 | 4,188,938 | 4,605,748 | 5,186,276 | 5,766,841 | 300 | | | | | |
| ind  independent evangelical | 4,775 | 664,853 | 1,320,280 | 1,409,198 | 1,508,585 | 1,607,986 | 125 | | | | | |
| int  interdenominational evangelical | 12,522 | 776,942 | 2,094,117 | 2,431,231 | 2,953,705 | 3,476,191 | 199 | | | | | |
| Jeh  Jehovah's Witnesses (Russellite) schismatic | | 5,000 | 10,000 | 10,254 | 10,508 | 10,764 | 1 | | | | | |
| Jew  Jewish-Christian (Messianic) | 25 | 5,000 | 10,000 | 10,240 | 10,480 | 10,720 | 1 | | | | | |
| LuR  Lutheran/Reformed united church | 6,174 | 8,130,986 | 10,556,824 | 10,084,492 | 9,840,072 | 9,595,654 | 17 | | | | | |
| Lut  Lutheran (excluding united) | 59,994 | 23,347,633 | 39,650,970 | 40,865,277 | 42,202,147 | 43,539,026 | 217 | | | | | |
| Men  Mennonite (Anabaptist) | 5,499 | 522,011 | 947,484 | 1,032,777 | 1,141,439 | 1,250,111 | 91 | | | | | |
| Met  Methodist | 80,112 | 13,452,545 | 21,795,923 | 23,056,024 | 24,562,647 | 26,069,273 | 117 | | | | | |
| Mor  Moravian | 1,045 | 224,443 | 469,518 | 547,259 | 643,572 | 739,885 | 26 | | | | | |
| Pe1  Oneness(Unitarian)-Pentecostal | 5,715 | 474,717 | 988,430 | 1,081,724 | 1,196,176 | 1,310,636 | 60 | | | | | |
| Pe2  Baptistic-Pentecostal | 58,896 | 6,382,559 | 11,820,393 | 13,720,578 | 16,019,480 | 18,318,419 | 328 | | | | | |
| Pe3  Holiness-Pentecostal | 20,170 | 1,283,916 | 2,553,920 | 2,816,616 | 3,123,227 | 3,429,845 | 161 | | | | | |
| Pe4  Radical-Pentecostal | 2,805 | 135,560 | 265,822 | 273,839 | 284,003 | 294,165 | 32 | | | | | |
| PeA  Pentecostal Apostolic | 4,942 | 301,388 | 700,500 | 795,490 | 911,505 | 1,027,522 | 25 | | | | | |
| Pen  Pentecostal | 1,673 | 152,719 | 318,063 | 346,642 | 375,387 | 404,138 | 46 | | | | | |
| Qua  Friends (Quaker) | 3,610 | 207,710 | 377,246 | 413,268 | 457,877 | 502,486 | 50 | | | | | |
| rad  isolated radio-church | 40,248 | 1,110,750 | 1,611,500 | 1,785,533 | 1,941,672 | 2,097,807 | 9 | | | | | |
| Ref  Reformed (Presbyterian) | 77,479 | 18,989,088 | 32,434,522 | 34,449,841 | 36,866,788 | 39,283,735 | 286 | | | | | |
| Sal  Salvationist (Salvation Army) | 16,678 | 1,425,965 | 2,936,406 | 3,238,471 | 3,633,818 | 4,029,163 | 78 | | | | | |
| sin  single-congregation | 4,500 | 750,000 | 1,500,000 | 1,493,967 | 1,486,534 | 1,479,101 | 2 | | | | | |
| tel  TV(television) paradenomination | 2 | 6,000 | 20,000 | 20,494 | 20,989 | 21,484 | 1 | | | | | |
| uni  united church | 96,073 | 30,089,838 | 49,444,075 | 51,349,494 | 53,458,911 | 55,568,325 | 47 | | | | | |
| Wal  Waldensian | 144 | 25,631 | 37,358 | 40,047 | 43,112 | 46,177 | 2 | | | | | |
| other Protestant | 5,656 | 886,012 | 1,896,170 | 2,124,806 | 2,392,572 | 2,660,341 | 154 | | | | | |
| **ROMAN CATHOLIC** | 247,118 | 432,125,990 | 672,319,062 | 733,215,181 | 802,659,904 | 872,104,646 | 222 | 222 | 222 | 222 | 223 | 220 |
| Lat  Latin-rite local church | 116,236 | 203,922,320 | 337,889,866 | 379,208,614 | 427,199,552 | 475,190,504 | 194 | | | | | |
| LEr  Latin/Eastern-rite local church | 130,882 | 228,203,470 | 334,429,196 | 354,006,567 | 375,460,352 | 396,914,142 | 28 | | | | | |
| Rites of the 2,606 jurisdictions: | | | | | | | *J=*2,606 | | | | | |
| Alb  Albanian | | 2,000 | 3,000 | 3,100 | 3,200 | 3,300 | 1 | | | | | |
| Arm  Armenian | 57 | 45,870 | 76,475 | 85,153 | 95,018 | 104,883 | 14 | | | | | |
| Bul  Bulgarian | 25 | 5,000 | 7,000 | 7,245 | 7,491 | 7,736 | 1 | | | | | |
| Bye  Byelorussian (no jurisdiction) | — | — | | | | | 0 | | | | | |
| Cha  Chaldean | 177 | 152,200 | 280,456 | 312,195 | 345,680 | 379,171 | 22 | | | | | |
| Cop  Coptic | 175 | 64,150 | 109,500 | 121,769 | 133,544 | 145,320 | 5 | | | | | |
| Eth  Ethiopian | 124 | 15,600 | 87,339 | 99,291 | 113,322 | 127,351 | 3 | | | | | |
| Geo  Georgian | — | — | | | | | 1 | | | | | |
| Gre  Greek | 4 | 2,250 | 3,082 | 3,180 | 3,215 | 3,250 | 2 | | | | | |
| Hun  Hungarian | 149 | 202,100 | 269,100 | 272,731 | 276,136 | 279,542 | 2 | | | | | |
| IAb  Italo-Albanian | 40 | 50,680 | 67,588 | 69,392 | 70,957 | 72,520 | 3 | | | | | |
| Lat  Latin | 242,329 | 427,735,090 | 665,234,769 | 725,317,386 | 793,860,613 | 862,421,866 | 2,453 | | | | | |
| Mal  Syro-Malankarese | 255 | 119,000 | 201,589 | 240,409 | 280,945 | 321,482 | 3 | | | | | |
| Mar  Maronite | 889 | 653,800 | 1,130,389 | 1,258,851 | 1,417,659 | 1,576,462 | 17 | | | | | |
| Mel  Melkite | 463 | 372,350 | 650,212 | 733,642 | 830,424 | 927,202 | 20 | | | | | |
| Ori  plural Oriental rites | 30 | 134,800 | 209,000 | 228,237 | 249,173 | 270,110 | 3 | | | | | |
| Rum  Romanian (totally suppressed) | 1,794 | 600,000 | 900,000 | 910,000 | 920,000 | 930,000 | 5 | | | | | |
| Rus  Russian | | 2,000 | 3,000 | 3,113 | 3,243 | 3,373 | 2 | | | | | |
| Rut  Ruthenian | 205 | 192,400 | 279,615 | 283,126 | 286,649 | 290,170 | 4 | | | | | |
| Slo  Slovak | 201 | 128,000 | 176,000 | 179,940 | 183,899 | 187,859 | 1 | | | | | |
| SyM  Syro-Malabarese | 1,272 | 1,190,020 | 2,017,046 | 2,405,470 | 2,811,066 | 3,216,663 | 16 | | | | | |
| Syr  Syrian | 63 | 40,900 | 73,746 | 82,784 | 92,990 | 103,194 | 11 | | | | | |
| Ukr  Ukrainian (3 million suppressed) | 607 | 941,300 | 1,381,513 | 1,447,631 | 1,523,311 | 1,598,991 | 18 | | | | | |
| Yug  Yugoslav | 53 | 40,500 | 58,643 | 60,536 | 62,369 | 64,201 | 1 | | | | | |
| Total Eastern-rite Catholics | 4,789 | 4,390,900 | 7,084,293 | 7,897,795 | 8,799,291 | 9,682,780 | 153 | | | | | |
| Doubly-affiliated | | −15,859,171 | −26,711,568 | −31,099,112 | −36,302,272 | −41,505,432 | — | — | — | — | — | 34 |
| Disaffiliated | | −7,276,400 | −10,848,188 | −13,226,950 | −15,365,510 | −17,504,070 | — | — | — | — | — | 9 |
| **GLOBAL CHURCH MEMBERSHIP** | | | | | | | | | | | | |
| Total affiliated (1970) | 1,506,360 | 703,398,777 | 1,131,809,580 | — | — | — | 6,111 | 18,162 | — | — | — | 223 |
| Total affiliated (1975) | 1,599,092 | 751,393,229 | — | 1,220,849,390 | — | — | | — | 19,414 | — | — | 223 |
| Total affiliated (1980) | 1,718,404 | 806,382,134 | — | — | 1,323,386,867 | — | | — | — | 20,781 | — | 223 |
| Total affiliated (1985) | 1,840,000 | 861,371,000 | — | — | — | 1,425,924,589 | — | — | — | — | 22,189 | 223 |

## Global Table 28. ORGANIZED CHRISTIANITY BY COUNCILS AND CONCILIARISM, AD 1970-1985.

1. This table is an expanded version of Global Table 9 in Part 1. It is derived from the 221 Tables 2 presented in Part 7 for all countries.
2. For definitions of columns, see beginning of Global Table 27. Meanings and definitions of rows and codes are described in the Codebook (Part 6) and in Methodology (Part 3).
3. When looking for membership figures for a specific council, check other lines also in case of dual membership. E.g. under 'Confessional conciliarism' below, membership of WARC (World Alliance of Reformed Churches) will be found not only opposite the code 'R' alone, but as the sum of figures opposite the 4 codes F, R, r and W.

(a) *COUNCILS*

| *Code* | *Names & initials* | *Congs* | *Adults* | *Affiliated* 1970 | 1975 | 1980 | 1985 | *Sig denoms* |
|---|---|---|---|---|---|---|---|---|
| 1 | 2 | 3 | 4 | 5 | 6 | 7 | 8 | 9 |
| | CONFESSIONAL CONCILIARISM | | | | | | | |
| A | Anglican Consultative Council (ACC) | 65,708 | 16,126,278 | 46,923,432 | 47,833,301 | 49,085,501 | 50,337,707 | 63 |
| a | non-autonomous bodies in ACC | 1,437 | 220,841 | 529,299 | 570,780 | 614,866 | 658,964 | 103 |
| B | Sacred Congregation for Bishops | 179,865 | 382,398,500 | 589,365,040 | 636,701,011 | 690,151,863 | 743,602,723 | 55 |
| b | immediately subject to Holy See (under SC for Bishops) | 2,258 | 2,525,620 | 3,317,905 | 3,523,497 | 3,709,903 | 3,896,307 | 12 |
| C | related to Ecumenical Patriarchate of Constantinople (excluding P Moscow) | 46,951 | 25,902,923 | 36,913,647 | 38,194,330 | 39,483,287 | 40,772,263 | 140 |
| c | disputed relationship to EP Constantinople | 1,150 | 928,000 | 1,416,000 | 1,454,941 | 1,496,022 | 1,537,101 | 8 |
| D | related to Syrian Orthodox Patriarchate of Antioch | 1,036 | 947,840 | 1,620,762 | 1,712,940 | 1,811,101 | 1,909,261 | 24 |
| E | related to Armenian Catholicate of Echmiadzin | 404 | 1,391,700 | 2,177,400 | 2,284,799 | 2,397,354 | 2,509,905 | 28 |
| F | members of both WARC and RES | 7,190 | 1,840,568 | 3,459,104 | 3,780,425 | 4,193,110 | 4,605,799 | 22 |
| G | Mennonite World Conference (MWC) | 5,079 | 446,257 | 835,884 | 911,639 | 1,011,510 | 1,111,391 | 86 |
| H | Council for the Public Affairs of the Church (up to 1975) | 4,995 | 8,857,300 | 13,321,022 | 14,568,720 | 15,960,658 | 17,352,600 | 8 |
| I | International Association for Religious Freedom (IARF) | 3,458 | 752,098 | 1,113,806 | 1,169,548 | 1,235,873 | 1,302,210 | 33 |
| i | International New Thought Alliance (INTA) | 458 | 65,000 | 180,000 | 201,021 | 222,168 | 243,314 | 3 |
| J | Reformed Ecumenical Synod (RES) | 5,353 | 650,896 | 1,406,478 | 1,841,359 | 2,300,387 | 2,759,416 | 29 |
| K | International Federation of Free Evangelical Churches (IFFEC) | 2,531 | 205,837 | 342,210 | 347,718 | 353,702 | 359,689 | 25 |
| L | Lutheran World Federation (LWF) | 49,034 | 20,961,721 | 35,883,003 | 37,042,015 | 38,316,531 | 39,591,044 | 111 |
| l | permanent observers to LWF | 25,339 | 30,247,419 | 38,666,993 | 37,710,516 | 36,749,673 | 35,788,831 | 30 |
| M | related to Orthodox Partriarchate of Moscow (rather than to EP Constantinople) | 11,246 | 54,537,405 | 78,796,276 | 83,146,787 | 87,685,380 | 92,223,972 | 58 |
| N | related to Coptic Orthodox Patriarchate of Alexandria | 17,082 | 10,533,580 | 17,959,250 | 20,222,213 | 22,736,892 | 25,251,574 | 26 |
| O | Sacred Congregation for the Eastern Churches | 2,204 | 1,230,590 | 2,152,508 | 2,415,516 | 2,723,186 | 3,030,858 | 14 |
| P | Sacred Congregation for the Evangelization of Peoples (Propaganda) | 26,778 | 34,731,180 | 60,381,111 | 72,224,780 | 86,338,187 | 100,451,599 | 118 |
| p | immediately subject to Holy See (under Propaganda) | 365 | 720,700 | 1,237,210 | 1,334,957 | 1,429,007 | 1,523,059 | 13 |
| Q | Friends World Committee for Consultation (FWCC) | 3,587 | 206,842 | 375,746 | 411,427 | 455,622 | 499,818 | 49 |
| R | World Alliance of Reformed Churches (WARC) | 81,515 | 19,369,196 | 32,663,159 | 34,781,016 | 37,275,952 | 39,770,884 | 183 |
| r | members of both WARC and IFFEC | 2,227 | 96,397 | 223,000 | 214,634 | 205,795 | 196,955 | 2 |
| S | related to Armenian Catholicate of Cilicia (Sis) | 470 | 403,840 | 648,798 | 709,184 | 774,955 | 840,721 | 9 |
| T | Baptist World Alliance (BWA) | 125,800 | 25,018,241 | 36,436,938 | 38,630,275 | 41,113,409 | 43,596,564 | 151 |
| U | International Old Catholic Bishops Conference (IOCBC) | 4,154 | 2,177,330 | 3,962,100 | 4,846,075 | 5,841,075 | 6,836,074 | 20 |
| u | members of both IOCBC and ACC | 36 | 2,250 | 5,700 | 5,770 | 5,840 | 5,910 | 3 |
| V | World Methodist Council (WMC) | 105,420 | 16,795,978 | 26,941,800 | 28,643,990 | 30,652,721 | 32,661,463 | 204 |
| W | members of both WMC and WARC | 11,263 | 1,867,692 | 4,085,685 | 4,202,189 | 4,321,626 | 4,441,062 | 8 |
| X | Ukrainian Orthodox Church of the Free World | 514 | 226,500 | 336,475 | 356,410 | 379,598 | 402,786 | 13 |
| x | quasi-confessions (non-confessional international denominational bodies) | 242,033 | 30,909,787 | 56,908,224 | 63,591,889 | 71,556,992 | 79,522,141 | 1,949 |
| Y | related to Ancient Assyrian Patriarchate of the East | 21 | 67,240 | 119,050 | 128,700 | 139,331 | 149,963 | 14 |
| y | related to Ancient Assyrian Church of the East | 31 | 16,000 | 25,000 | 26,622 | 28,353 | 30,086 | 2 |
| Z | Pentecostal World Conference (PWC) | 94,647 | 9,524,224 | 18,661,760 | 21,626,393 | 25,155,408 | 28,684,461 | 462 |
| | Great and Holy Council of the Orthodox Church (=C + M) | 58,197 | 80,440,328 | 115,709,923 | 121,341,117 | 127,168,667 | 132,996,235 | 198 |
| | Oriental Orthodox Churches Conference (= D + E + N + S) | 18,992 | 13,276,960 | 22,406,210 | 24,929,136 | 27,720,302 | 30,511,461 | 87 |
| | Conference of Secs of Christian World Communions (CWCs/WCFs) | 840,000 | 626,700,000 | 1,008,400,000 | 1,087,800,000 | 1,179,200,000 | 1,270,500,000 | 1,770 |
| . | unrelated to any confessional council | 280,301 | 23,630,578 | 49,979,261 | 57,416,786 | 66,359,331 | 75,301,932 | 2,033 |
| | Doubly-affiliated | | −15,859,171 | −26,711,568 | −31,099,112 | −36,302,272 | −41,505,432 | — |
| | Disaffiliated | | −7,276,400 | −10,848,188 | −13,226,950 | −15,365,510 | −17,504,070 | — |
| | GLOBAL CHURCH MEMBERSHIP | 1,411,940 | 703,398,777 | 1,131,809,580 | 1,220,849,390 | 1,323,386,867 | 1,425,924,589 | 6,111 |
| | WORLD CONCILIARISM | | | | | | | |
| F | related to World Evangelical Fellowship (WEF) and EFMA | 91,639 | 8,737,038 | 16,089,827 | 18,298,546 | 21,031,837 | 23,765,179 | 559 |
| G | related to Evangelical Missionary Alliance (EMA) (UK) | 8,005 | 416,532 | 1,020,863 | 1,194,587 | 1,410,973 | 1,627,364 | 34 |
| H | related to Australian Evangelical Alliance (AEA) | 1,697 | 57,143 | 171,478 | 200,675 | 236,302 | 271,927 | 16 |
| M | related to Interdenominational Foreign Mission Association (IFMA) | 12,481 | 705,800 | 2,134,282 | 2,581,621 | 3,123,481 | 3,665,350 | 118 |
| N | related to both IFMA and EFMA | 467 | 6,539 | 19,000 | 23,236 | 29,170 | 35,103 | 5 |
| q | related to EFMA, applied to WCC | 1,167 | 89,000 | 141,000 | 159,153 | 181,628 | 204,102 | 1 |
| r | related to IFMA, applied to WCC | 582 | 46,100 | 75,000 | 92,726 | 114,617 | 136,509 | 1 |
| T | International Council of Christian Churches (ICCC) | 11,173 | 1,586,967 | 2,886,252 | 3,326,516 | 3,837,288 | 4,348,057 | 135 |
| t | former member of ICCC | 2,767 | 364,663 | 629,451 | 640,963 | 653,335 | 665,706 | 8 |
| u | associate members of WCC | 1,679 | 115,824 | 250,692 | 297,475 | 352,494 | 407,518 | 31 |
| v | applied to WCC but rejected or delayed | 17,284 | 3,018,496 | 5,901,258 | 6,846,937 | 7,901,759 | 8,956,589 | 156 |
| W | World Council of Churches (WCC) | 466,527 | 210,308,519 | 339,471,073 | 354,086,735 | 370,474,738 | 386,862,746 | 268 |
| w | related to members of WCC | 46,212 | 8,403,893 | 15,581,669 | 17,254,219 | 19,306,480 | 21,358,761 | 717 |
| | Synod of Bishops (Synodus Episcoporum), Rome (= codes x,y,z) | 247,118 | 432,125,990 | 672,319,062 | 733,215,181 | 802,659,904 | 872,104,646 | 222 |
| . | unrelated to any world or international council or synod | 503,142 | 60,551,844 | 112,678,429 | 126,956,882 | 143,740,643 | 160,524,534 | 3,840 |
| | Doubly-affiliated | | −15,859,171 | −26,711,568 | −31,099,112 | −36,302,272 | −41,505,432 | — |
| | Disaffiliated | | −7,276,400 | −10,848,188 | −13,226,950 | −15,365,510 | −17,504,070 | — |
| | GLOBAL CHURCH MEMBERSHIP | 1,411,940 | 703,398,777 | 1,131,809,580 | 1,220,849,390 | 1,323,386,867 | 1,425,924,589 | 6,111 |
| | CONTINENTAL CONCILIARISM | | | | | | | |
| A | All Africa Conference of Churches (AACC) | 86,260 | 15,865,151 | 34,397,732 | 39,578,674 | 45,680,273 | 51,781,883 | 90 |
| a | related to members of AACC | 3,570 | 370,064 | 878,922 | 1,022,868 | 1,201,537 | 1,380,211 | 67 |
| B | Council of European Bishops' Conferences (CCEE) | 132,949 | 179,934,800 | 244,726,447 | 250,591,339 | 256,491,384 | 262,391,430 | 39 |
| C | Conference of European Churches (CEC) | 127,965 | 122,378,926 | 189,783,871 | 193,352,605 | 196,966,581 | 200,580,560 | 84 |
| c | observers in CEC | 18,356 | 12,197,714 | 17,885,720 | 18,357,509 | 18,810,263 | 19,263,022 | 190 |
| D | European Evangelical Alliance (EEA) | 5,203 | 229,516 | 521,153 | 508,755 | 494,885 | 481,019 | 22 |
| E | Christian Conference of Asia (CCA) | 73,748 | 10,440,910 | 25,930,931 | 30,110,058 | 35,261,251 | 40,412,454 | 88 |
| e | related to members of CCA | 201 | 30,322 | 71,632 | 76,158 | 81,193 | 86,226 | 35 |
| F | Federation of Asian Bishops' Conferences (FABC) | 11,534 | 26,622,370 | 47,766,641 | 55,954,906 | 65,298,156 | 74,641,414 | 24 |
| G | Association of Evangelicals of Africa & Madagascar (AEAM) | 13,633 | 789,161 | 2,308,115 | 2,846,938 | 3,519,054 | 4,191,190 | 91 |
| g | associate members of AEAM | 77 | 2,567 | 4,750 | 5,400 | 6,196 | 6,990 | 5 |
| H | Evangelical Association of the Caribbean (EAC) | 3,287 | 163,881 | 331,389 | 367,283 | 410,601 | 453,914 | 30 |
| I | Organization of African Independent Churches (OAIC) | 4,952 | 716,001 | 1,561,123 | 2,049,643 | 2,667,317 | 3,284,993 | 34 |
| i | members of both OAIC and AACC | 8,059 | 2,038,050 | 3,576,100 | 4,166,176 | 4,832,422 | 5,498,667 | 8 |
| L | Latin American Episcopal Council (CELAM) | 22,072 | 143,978,300 | 252,587,024 | 287,274,595 | 327,073,793 | 366,872,995 | 22 |
| M | Caribbean Conference of Churches (CCC) | 2,909 | 450,312 | 1,187,072 | 1,232,506 | 1,283,705 | 1,334,902 | 89 |
| N | members of both CCC and CELAM | 704 | 1,071,970 | 1,909,183 | 2,112,817 | 2,342,388 | 2,571,957 | 23 |
| O | Standing Conf of Canonical Orthodox Bishops in Americas (SCOBA) | 1,423 | 2,530,800 | 3,746,350 | 3,886,360 | 4,038,365 | 4,190,368 | 19 |
| o | related to SCOBA | 140 | 198,400 | 340,863 | 377,581 | 418,088 | 458,593 | 29 |
| P | Pacific Conference of Churches (PCC) | 5,953 | 433,105 | 1,056,456 | 1,208,824 | 1,390,478 | 1,572,142 | 40 |
| p | related to members of PCC | 2,294 | 253,600 | 409,517 | 472,295 | 549,648 | 626,999 | 16 |
| Q | members of both CCC and EAC | 55 | 7,575 | 17,700 | 16,913 | 16,112 | 15,311 | 4 |
| S | Symposium of Episcopal Confs of Africa and Madagascar (SECAM) | 15,232 | 25,326,760 | 44,488,311 | 53,928,069 | 65,234,620 | 76,541,170 | 54 |
| T | ICCC-affiliated continental councils (LAACC, FECC, &c) | 5,595 | 546,638 | 1,320,988 | 1,900,240 | 2,525,560 | 3,150,877 | 71 |
| U | Latin American Council of Churches (CLAI) | 1,383 | 180,237 | 473,489 | 561,788 | 666,419 | 771,049 | 11 |
| u | related to CLAI | 20,142 | 1,595,311 | 4,409,397 | 5,373,071 | 6,527,582 | 7,682,101 | 88 |
| V | members of both CCC and CLAI | 25 | 4,460 | 9,000 | 10,300 | 11,733 | 13,166 | 4 |
| X | members of both CEC and EEA | 9,235 | 9,500,541 | 16,706,561 | 16,558,112 | 16,355,218 | 16,152,321 | 8 |
| x | members of CEC, observers in EEA | 3,091 | 147,087 | 246,000 | 246,877 | 247,020 | 247,164 | 7 |
| Y | related to both EAC and ICCC | 97 | 5,700 | 13,400 | 13,583 | 13,578 | 13,574 | 4 |
| . | unrelated to any continental council | 831,796 | 168,524,119 | 270,703,499 | 291,013,209 | 314,639,229 | 338,265,429 | 4,815 |
| | Doubly-affiliated | | −15,859,171 | −26,711,568 | −31,099,112 | −36,302,272 | −41,505,432 | — |
| | Disaffiliated | | −7,276,400 | −10,848,188 | −13,226,950 | −15,365,510 | −17,504,070 | — |
| | GLOBAL CHURCH MEMBERSHIP | 1,411,940 | 703,398,777 | 1,131,809,580 | 1,220,849,390 | 1,323,386,867 | 1,425,924,589 | 6,111 |

*Concluded opposite*

## (a)  COUNCILS (continued)

| Code | Names & initials | Congs | Adults | Affiliated 1970 | Affiliated 1975 | Affiliated 1980 | Affiliated 1985 | Sig denoms |
|---|---|---|---|---|---|---|---|---|
| 1 | 2 | 3 | 4 | 5 | 6 | 7 | 8 | 9 |
| **REGIONAL CONCILIARISM** | | | | | | | | |
| A | Council of the Church in East Asia (CCEA) | 8,376 | 2,673,396 | 7,510,805 | 8,396,850 | 9,358,286 | 10,319,731 | 15 |
| B | Assoc des Conf Episcopales du Congo/RCA/Tchad (ACECCT) | 723 | 519,800 | 908,202 | 1,102,100 | 1,340,399 | 1,578,700 | 3 |
| C | Consejo Anglicano Sud Americano (CASA) | 428 | 32,900 | 68,900 | 79,680 | 90,660 | 101,639 | 7 |
| D | Secretariado Episcopal de América Central y Panamá (SEDAC) | 1,098 | 8,000,900 | 14,860,775 | 17,141,098 | 19,801,628 | 22,462,160 | 7 |
| E | Assoc of Member Episcopal Confs in Eastern Africa (AMECEA) | 3,573 | 5,712,900 | 10,300,648 | 12,792,130 | 15,828,898 | 18,865,667 | 7 |
| F | Conf Episcopale Régionale de l'Afrique Occidentale Francophone (CERAO) | 588 | 1,239,900 | 2,176,248 | 2,680,699 | 3,306,869 | 3,933,038 | 9 |
| G | Assoc of Episcopal Confs of English-speaking West Africa (AECEWA) | 1,264 | 2,805,900 | 5,137,492 | 6,250,600 | 7,655,199 | 9,059,800 | 5 |
| H | Conférence Episcopale d'Afrique du Nord (CEAN) | 255 | 116,700 | 207,350 | 193,998 | 184,799 | 175,599 | 4 |
| I | regional councils of Black/Third-World/Non-White indigenous churches | 0 | 0 | 0 | 0 | 0 | 0 | 0 |
| J | Asociación Regional Episcopal del Norte de Sud América (ARENSA) | 2,507 | 347,318 | 565,690 | 641,050 | 734,487 | 827,920 | 11 |
| K | South Pacific Anglican Council (SPAC) | 1,041 | 77,640 | 130,230 | 154,255 | 182,738 | 211,224 | 13 |
| L | Conférence des Evêques Latins dans les Régions Arabes (CELRA) | 32 | 23,950 | 40,157 | 53,958 | 77,549 | 101,139 | 10 |
| M | Antilles Episcopal Conference (AEC) | 704 | 1,071,970 | 1,909,183 | 2,122,817 | 2,342,388 | 2,571,957 | 23 |
| N | Middle East Council of Churches (MECC) | 4,331 | 4,578,672 | 7,984,178 | 8,778,736 | 9,611,110 | 10,443,480 | 81 |
| O | regional councils of Orthodox churches | 0 | 0 | 0 | 0 | 0 | 0 | 0 |
| P | Eastern-rite Catholic Patriarchal Synods | 71 | 37,100 | 58,850 | 65,599 | 72,189 | 78,780 | 2 |
| Q | Nordic Bishops' Conference | 120 | 76,120 | 100,228 | 109,009 | 120,995 | 132,979 | 7 |
| R | Anglican Council of North America & the Caribbean (ACNAC) | 12,032 | 3,049,396 | 5,073,900 | 4,905,140 | 4,746,791 | 4,588,446 | 35 |
| S | Interterritorial Meeting of Bishops in Southern Africa (IMBISA) | 2,351 | 4,167,200 | 7,104,454 | 8,855,378 | 10,845,529 | 12,835,677 | 8 |
| T | ICCC-affiliated regional councils (MEBC, CACC, WACCC, &c) | 801 | 110,375 | 221,910 | 284,555 | 364,145 | 443,735 | 13 |
| U | members of both MECC and CAPA | 686 | 101,530 | 306,030 | 390,130 | 499,747 | 609,370 | 8 |
| V | Conference of the Anglican Provinces of Africa (CAPA) | 22,501 | 1,765,631 | 7,416,440 | 8,604,541 | 10,094,980 | 11,585,421 | 27 |
| W | members of both AMECEA and CELRA | 81 | 385,000 | 687,768 | 912,170 | 1,195,200 | 1,478,230 | 1 |
| X | Pentecostal Fellowship of North America (PFNA) | 16,984 | 1,314,864 | 2,901,877 | 2,971,792 | 3,043,596 | 3,115,403 | 20 |
| Y | Conférence des Evêques du Pacifique (CEPAC) | 242 | 137,770 | 254,886 | 297,098 | 347,051 | 397,007 | 15 |
| Z | Regional Conference of Chinese Bishops | 523 | 167,700 | 304,877 | 359,700 | 418,100 | 476,499 | 1 |
| . | unrelated to any regional council | 1,330,628 | 688,019,716 | 1,093,138,258 | 1,177,042,369 | 1,272,791,316 | 1,368,540,490 | 5,779 |
| | Doubly-affiliated | | −15,859,171 | −26,711,568 | −31,099,112 | −36,302,272 | −41,505,432 | — |
| | Disaffiliated | | −7,276,400 | −10,848,188 | −13,226,950 | −15,365,510 | −17,504,070 | — |
| | **GLOBAL CHURCH MEMBERSHIP** | 1,411,940 | 703,398,777 | 1,131,809,580 | 1,220,849,390 | 1,323,386,867 | 1,425,924,589 | 6,111 |
| **NATIONAL CONCILIARISM** | | | | | | | | |
| a | members of 2 national councils, one WCC-related, one Evangelical | 15,625 | 7,392,272 | 14,503,561 | 14,567,200 | 14,695,895 | 14,824,590 | 46 |
| b | members of 2 national councils, one WCC-related, one Non-White indigenous | 50,061 | 8,675,507 | 11,916,279 | 12,817,242 | 13,816,728 | 14,816,218 | 16 |
| C | national council with no external international affiliations | 19,935 | 2,050,006 | 3,994,536 | 4,580,173 | 5,381,209 | 6,182,247 | 302 |
| c | related to C (previous line) | 11 | 1,800 | 3,400 | 3,869 | 4,478 | 5,088 | 2 |
| d | members of 2 national councils, one WCC-related, one unaffiliated | 5,866 | 511,763 | 1,010,395 | 1,213,795 | 1,469,759 | 1,725,719 | 33 |
| E | national Evangelical alliance or council (WEF/EAC/EEA, AEAM, &c) | 39,985 | 2,846,220 | 5,701,905 | 6,000,209 | 6,436,077 | 6,871,950 | 169 |
| e | national Evangelical alliance or council, not WEF-affiliated | 1,424 | 2,783,253 | 3,776,109 | 3,890,741 | 3,992,800 | 4,094,861 | 5 |
| F | national council with RC churches but no external affiliations | 576 | 17,000 | 41,000 | 51,723 | 65,097 | 78,471 | 2 |
| f | recently withdrawn from major national councils | 2,961 | 664,787 | 1,101,551 | 1,161,059 | 1,239,032 | 1,317,007 | 17 |
| G | national Evangelical council affiliated to AEAM | 7,429 | 363,861 | 1,264,910 | 1,555,004 | 1,915,787 | 2,276,576 | 45 |
| H | Protestant national council of Pentecostal churches | 1,780 | 125,660 | 261,100 | 262,902 | 270,399 | 277,899 | 23 |
| h | miscellaneous other types of councils | 528 | 255,074 | 336,933 | 337,937 | 340,069 | 342,203 | 11 |
| I | national council of Black/Third-World/Non-White indigenous churches | 11,463 | 2,328,295 | 4,189,983 | 5,224,778 | 6,475,586 | 7,726,380 | 154 |
| i | members of I (preceding line) and also of H | 90 | 11,000 | 22,000 | 20,646 | 19,229 | 17,813 | 1 |
| J | additional national council similar to I | 7,612 | 583,504 | 1,713,500 | 1,784,502 | 1,855,909 | 1,927,316 | 7 |
| K | national council of churches, or Christian council, unofficially WCC-linked | 114,545 | 32,269,196 | 58,267,089 | 64,727,466 | 72,091,308 | 79,455,133 | 266 |
| k | associate members of K | 4,802 | 522,853 | 1,137,773 | 1,355,522 | 1,627,466 | 1,899,410 | 30 |
| L | national Evangelical council affiliated to EAC | 438 | 18,628 | 46,685 | 46,691 | 46,649 | 46,606 | 18 |
| l | members of both an EAC-linked council and ICCC | 97 | 5,700 | 13,400 | 13,583 | 13,578 | 13,574 | 4 |
| M | national council of foreign missionary societies | 0 | 0 | 0 | 0 | 0 | 0 | 0 |
| N | national council of churches, or Christian council, CWME-affiliated | 68,338 | 8,769,099 | 17,315,431 | 21,029,034 | 23,391,029 | 29,733,034 | 141 |
| n | associate members of N | 1,339 | 62,058 | 208,350 | 238,748 | 271,752 | 304,755 | 10 |
| O | national council or committee of Orthodox churches | 108 | 115,000 | 165,000 | 172,229 | 179,679 | 187,130 | 4 |
| P | plurinational Roman Catholic episcopal conference | 2,615 | 6,266,600 | 10,493,838 | 12,328,956 | 14,409,738 | 16,490,519 | 15 |
| Q | members of P and of WCC-related national council | 1,013 | 420,400 | 712,930 | 817,159 | 943,619 | 1,070,080 | 4 |
| q | as Q, but observer or associate status only | 0 | 0 | 0 | 0 | 0 | 0 | 0 |
| R | national Roman Catholic episcopal or bishops' conference | 202,207 | 362,761,270 | 573,181,486 | 627,729,714 | 689,653,719 | 751,577,736 | 68 |
| r | dioceses attached to R in another country | 362 | 1,102,540 | 1,865,526 | 2,022,416 | 2,145,625 | 2,268,838 | 14 |
| S | members of R and of WCC-related national council | 19,544 | 32,012,100 | 43,506,205 | 45,107,667 | 47,037,199 | 48,966,727 | 10 |
| s | as S, but observer or associate status only | 9,414 | 12,721,000 | 16,861,156 | 17,235,969 | 17,668,016 | 18,100,063 | 9 |
| T | national council related to ICCC | 6,854 | 672,872 | 1,602,452 | 2,243,451 | 2,941,492 | 3,639,526 | 92 |
| t | former members of T, now withdrawn | 2,922 | 357,388 | 594,700 | 609,409 | 624,131 | 638,852 | 6 |
| u | members of once-only national conference of churches | 13,763 | 55,679,000 | 82,924,000 | 87,887,786 | 93,046,670 | 98,205,558 | 19 |
| V | members of R and of non-WCC national council | 1,793 | 2,859,900 | 5,211,743 | 6,289,870 | 7,628,219 | 8,966,570 | 3 |
| v | as V, but observer or associate status only | 0 | 0 | 0 | 0 | 0 | 0 | 0 |
| W | national WCC-associate council of churches/Christian council | 291,820 | 101,457,895 | 170,769,281 | 174,245,685 | 178,697,254 | 183,148,839 | 309 |
| w | associate members of W | 4,530 | 1,429,868 | 2,564,273 | 2,984,482 | 3,497,153 | 4,009,834 | 47 |
| x | members of 2 other national councils | 5,854 | 240,804 | 583,204 | 629,942 | 696,142 | 762,345 | 25 |
| y | additional national council of Non-White indigenous churches (different to I or J) | 39 | 3,674 | 6,992 | 8,408 | 10,169 | 11,928 | 2 |
| Z | members of 3 national councils | 2,654 | 244,210 | 523,448 | 651,306 | 817,104 | 982,905 | 7 |
| z | members of 3 national councils, one WCC-related, one Evangelical | 3,836 | 175,057 | 402,300 | 402,613 | 404,906 | 407,202 | 14 |
| . | unrelated to any national council or alliance | 487,707 | 77,757,234 | 130,574,892 | 142,925,566 | 157,233,978 | 171,542,589 | 4,161 |
| | Doubly-affiliated | | −15,859,171 | −26,711,568 | −31,099,112 | −36,302,272 | −41,505,432 | — |
| | Disaffiliated | | −7,276,400 | −10,848,188 | −13,226,950 | −15,365,510 | −17,504,070 | — |
| | **GLOBAL CHURCH MEMBERSHIP** | 1,411,940 | 703,398,777 | 1,131,809,580 | 1,220,849,390 | 1,323,386,867 | 1,425,924,589 | 6,111 |

## (b)  NON-CONCILIARISM

| | Congs | Adults | 1970 | 1975 | 1980 | 1985 | Sig denoms |
|---|---|---|---|---|---|---|---|
| Denominations with no confessional conciliar ties | 280,301 | 23,630,578 | 49,979,261 | 57,416,786 | 66,359,331 | 75,301,932 | 2,033 |
| no world conciliar ties | 503,142 | 60,551,844 | 112,678,429 | 126,956,882 | 143,740,643 | 160,524,534 | 3,840 |
| no continental conciliar ties | 831,796 | 168,524,119 | 270,703,499 | 291,013,209 | 314,639,229 | 338,265,429 | 4,815 |
| no regional conciliar ties | 1,330,628 | 688,019,716 | 1,093,138,258 | 1,177,042,369 | 1,272,791,316 | 1,368,540,490 | 5,779 |
| no national conciliar ties | 487,707 | 77,757,234 | 130,574,892 | 142,925,566 | 157,233,978 | 171,542,589 | 4,161 |
| no conciliar ties of any sort | 179,695 | 14,995,243 | 30,935,614 | 36,068,660 | 42,086,086 | 48,103,578 | 1,482 |

Global Table 29. THE EXPANSION OF CHRISTIANITY AND WORLD EVANGELIZATION BY CONTINENTS, AD 30-2000.

1. This table is an expanded version of Global Tables 1 and 10 in Part 1.
2. The table is composed of 5 sections: (1) analysis by continents, (2) analysis by race, (3) analysis by colour, (4) churches, countries and languages, and (5) footnotes with documentation.
3. All figures in bold or roman type in section 1 below are, populations given in millions to the nearest 100,000 (thus '16.8' means 16,800,000). All figures in italics in section 1 are percentages of the total population shown either 3 or 4 lines above them.

| *1. CHRISTIANS AND POPULATION BY CONTINENT* Year | AD 30 | 100 | 300 | 500 | 800 | 1000 | 1200 | 1350 | 1500 | 1650 | 1750 | 1800 | 1850 | 1900 | 1970 | 1975 | 1980 | 1985 | 2000 |
|---|---|---|---|---|---|---|---|---|---|---|---|---|---|---|---|---|---|---|---|
| AFRICA | | | | | | | | | | | | | | | | | | | |
| **Population** (millions) | **16.8** | **17.2** | **18.4** | **20.0** | **25.0** | **33.0** | **37.0** | **42.0** | **46.0** | **58.0** | **65.0** | **70.0** | **81.0** | **107.9** | **351.8** | **401.3** | **460.9** | **520.4** | **813.4** |
| Christians (millions) | 0.0 | 0.4 | 6.0 | 8.0 | 8.0 | 5.0 | 2.5 | 1.3 | 1.3 | 3.0 | 2.8 | 1.0 | 2.8 | 9.9 | 143.0 | 170.7 | 203.5 | 236.3 | 393.3 |
| Evangelized (millions) | 0 | 9.0 | 10.2 | 9.0 | 9.3 | 8.1 | 3.5 | 2.5 | 3.7 | 9.5 | 11.5 | 4.0 | 15.0 | 24.9 | 245.3 | 289.7 | 344.2 | 398.7 | 695.2 |
| *% Christian* | *0.0* | *2.3* | *32.6* | *40.0* | *32.0* | *15.2* | *6.8* | *3.1* | *2.8* | *5.2* | *4.3* | *1.4* | *3.5* | *9.2* | *40.6* | *42.5* | *44.2* | *45.4* | *48.4* |
| *% evangelized* | *0* | *52.3* | *55.4* | *45.0* | *37.2* | *24.5* | *9.5* | *6.0* | *8.0* | *16.4* | *17.7* | *5.7* | *18.5* | *23.1* | *69.7* | *72.2* | *74.7* | *76.6* | *85.5* |
| EAST ASIA | | | | | | | | | | | | | | | | | | | |
| **Population** (millions) | **54.9** | **59.6** | **59.9** | **54.9** | **56.5** | **73.5** | **127.3** | **98.7** | **131.6** | **170.6** | **261.6** | **366.1** | **476.6** | **532.7** | **926.4** | **1005.0** | **1086.9** | **1168.8** | **1373.2** |
| Christians (millions) | 0 | 0 | 0 | 0 | 0.3 | 2.0 | 3.0 | 3.0 | 0.2 | 0.4 | 0.3 | 0.3 | 0.8 | 2.2 | 12.7 | 15.7 | 19.0 | 22.3 | 32.3 |
| Evangelized (millions) | 0 | 0 | 0 | 0 | 2.0 | 5.0 | 10.5 | 8.0 | 1.0 | 4.0 | 3.0 | 7.5 | 55.0 | 143.7 | 257.9 | 328.5 | 407.7 | 513.3 | 861.7 |
| *% Christian* | *0* | *0* | *0* | *0* | *0.5* | *2.7* | *2.4* | *3.0* | *0.2* | *0.2* | *0.1* | *0.1* | *0.2* | *0.4* | *1.4* | *1.6* | *1.8* | *1.9* | *2.4* |
| *% evangelized* | *0* | *0* | *0* | *0* | *3.5* | *6.8* | *8.2* | *8.1* | *0.8* | *2.3* | *1.1* | *2.0* | *11.5* | *27.0* | *27.8* | *32.7* | *37.5* | *43.9* | *62.7* |
| EUROPE | | | | | | | | | | | | | | | | | | | |
| **Population** (millions) | **30.0** | **31.8** | **30.7** | **25.5** | **25.5** | **32.0** | **49.0** | **60.5** | **69.0** | **88.0** | **114.0** | **144.0** | **205.0** | **287.3** | **458.9** | **473.0** | **486.4** | **499.9** | **539.5** |
| Christians (millions) | 0.0 | 0.3 | 7.3 | 14.0 | 17.9 | 28.2 | 44.6 | 57.8 | 67.8 | 86.9 | 113.1 | 142.1 | 201.1 | 278.4 | 405.1 | 410.3 | 415.6 | 420.9 | 431.4 |
| Evangelized (millions) | 0.1 | 15.0 | 17.0 | 20.0 | 24.0 | 32.0 | 49.0 | 60.5 | 69.0 | 88.0 | 114.0 | 144.0 | 205.0 | 286.3 | 452.3 | 466.9 | 481.3 | 495.6 | 536.8 |
| *% Christian* | *0.0* | *0.9* | *23.7* | *55.0* | *70.0* | *88.1* | *91.0* | *95.6* | *98.2* | *98.8* | *99.2* | *98.7* | *98.1* | *96.9* | *88.3* | *86.7* | *85.4* | *84.2* | *80.0* |
| *% evangelized* | *0.3* | *47.2* | *55.4* | *78.4* | *94.1* | *100.0* | *100.0* | *100.0* | *100.0* | *100.0* | *100.0* | *100.0* | *100.0* | *99.7* | *98.6* | *98.7* | *98.9* | *99.1* | *99.5* |
| LATIN AMERICA | | | | | | | | | | | | | | | | | | | |
| **Population** | **4.2** | **4.6** | **5.5** | **6.4** | **7.6** | **8.5** | **10.3** | **11.7** | **13.0** | **10.9** | **13.7** | **17.5** | **32.5** | **65.2** | **283.0** | **324.1** | **371.6** | **419.2** | **619.9** |
| Christians (millions) | 0 | 0 | 0 | 0 | 0 | 0 | 0 | 0 | 0.2 | 6.5 | 10.3 | 14.9 | 29.3 | 62.0 | 267.4 | 305.1 | 348.7 | 392.2 | 571.2 |
| Evangelized (millions) | 0 | 0 | 0 | 0 | 0 | 0 | 0 | 0 | 1.0 | 10.0 | 13.2 | 17.0 | 32.0 | 63.4 | 279.5 | 320.0 | 366.9 | 414.7 | 617.6 |
| *% Christian* | *0* | *0* | *0* | *0* | *0* | *0* | *0* | *0* | *1.5* | *60.0* | *75.0* | *85.0* | *90.0* | *95.1* | *94.5* | *94.1* | *93.8* | *93.6* | *92.1* |
| *% evangelized* | *0* | *0* | *0* | *0* | *0* | *0* | *0* | *0* | *7.7* | *91.7* | *96.4* | *97.1* | *98.5* | *97.3* | *98.7* | *98.7* | *98.7* | *98.9* | *99.6* |
| NORTHERN AMERICA | | | | | | | | | | | | | | | | | | | |
| **Population** (millions) | **0.3** | **0.3** | **0.4** | **0.4** | **0.5** | **0.5** | **0.7** | **0.9** | **1.0** | **1.1** | **2.3** | **6.5** | **26.5** | **81.6** | **226.4** | **236.8** | **248.8** | **260.8** | **296.2** |
| Christians (millions) | 0 | 0 | 0 | 0 | 0 | 0 | 0 | 0 | 0 | 0.1 | 1.4 | 5.8 | 25.0 | 78.8 | 206.4 | 212.4 | 219.8 | 227.2 | 253.6 |
| Evangelized (millions) | 0 | 0 | 0 | 0 | 0 | 0 | 0 | 0 | 0 | 0.2 | 1.9 | 6.3 | 26.0 | 81.5 | 225.6 | 236.1 | 248.4 | 260.5 | 295.9 |
| *% Christian* | *0* | *0* | *0* | *0* | *0* | *0* | *0* | *0* | *0* | *9.1* | *60.9* | *89.2* | *94.3* | *96.6* | *91.2* | *89.7* | *88.3* | *87.1* | *85.6* |
| *% evangelized* | *0* | *0* | *0* | *0* | *0* | *0* | *0* | *0* | *0* | *18.2* | *82.6* | *96.9* | *98.1* | *99.8* | *99.6* | *99.7* | *99.8* | *99.9* | *99.9* |
| OCEANIA | | | | | | | | | | | | | | | | | | | |
| **Population** (millions) | **1.0** | **1.0** | **1.1** | **1.2** | **1.4** | **1.5** | **1.7** | **1.8** | **2.0** | **2.2** | **2.3** | **2.5** | **2.2** | **6.2** | **19.3** | **21.3** | **23.5** | **25.7** | **32.7** |
| Christians (millions) | 0 | 0 | 0 | 0 | 0 | 0 | 0 | 0 | 0 | 0 | 0.0 | 0.1 | 1.0 | 4.8 | 17.9 | 19.1 | 20.3 | 21.5 | 27.7 |
| Evangelized (millions) | 0 | 0 | 0 | 0 | 0 | 0 | 0 | 0 | 0 | 0 | 0.1 | 0.4 | 1.6 | 5.1 | 19.3 | 21.3 | 23.5 | 25.6 | 32.7 |
| *% Christian* | *0* | *0* | *0* | *0* | *0* | *0* | *0* | *0* | *0* | *0* | *0.0* | *4.0* | *45.5* | *77.6* | *92.4* | *89.5* | *86.4* | *83.9* | *84.8* |
| *% evangelized* | *0* | *0* | *0* | *0* | *0* | *0* | *0* | *0* | *0* | *0* | *4.3* | *16.0* | *73.0* | *82.7* | *99.9* | *99.9* | *99.9* | *99.9* | *100.0* |
| SOUTH ASIA | | | | | | | | | | | | | | | | | | | |
| **Population** (millions) | **58.6** | **62.7** | **71.0** | **79.5** | **97.0** | **113.1** | **122.9** | **130.4** | **145.7** | **198.4** | **228.3** | **251.0** | **306.3** | **413.4** | **1101.4** | **1250.1** | **1427.7** | **1605.2** | **2269.6** |
| Christians (millions) | 0.0 | 0.3 | 6.5 | 21.2 | 23.0 | 14.8 | 18.0 | 20.0 | 3.0 | 5.0 | 7.0 | 8.0 | 11.0 | 16.9 | 78.1 | 92.2 | 109.1 | 125.9 | 192.3 |
| Evangelized (millions) | 0.2 | 26.8 | 39.5 | 51.6 | 32.1 | 21.2 | 28.1 | 21.7 | 3.2 | 7.0 | 12.3 | 25.2 | 53.3 | 105.0 | 582.9 | 739.0 | 931.0 | 1123.9 | 1894.2 |
| *% Christian* | *0.0* | *0.5* | *9.2* | *26.7* | *23.7* | *13.1* | *14.6* | *15.3* | *2.1* | *2.5* | *3.1* | *3.2* | *3.6* | *4.1* | *7.1* | *7.4* | *7.6* | *7.8* | *8.5* |
| *% evangelized* | *0.3* | *42.7* | *55.6* | *64.9* | *33.1* | *18.7* | *22.9* | *16.6* | *2.2* | *3.5* | *5.4* | *10.0* | *17.4* | *25.4* | *52.9* | *59.1* | *65.2* | *70.0* | *83.5* |
| RUSSIA | | | | | | | | | | | | | | | | | | | |
| **Population** (millions) | **3.9** | **4.3** | **5.0** | **5.5** | **6.4** | **7.1** | **13.0** | **13.7** | **17.0** | **23.0** | **33.5** | **45.0** | **73.8** | **125.7** | **242.8** | **255.0** | **268.1** | **281.2** | **315.0** |
| Christians (millions) | 0 | 0.0 | 0.1 | 0.2 | 0.3 | 0.4 | 2.0 | 4.6 | 8.5 | 15.0 | 25.1 | 36.0 | 56.8 | 105.0 | 86.0 | 91.3 | 96.7 | 102.2 | 118.1 |
| Evangelized (millions) | 0 | 0.2 | 0.5 | 0.6 | 0.8 | 1.0 | 3.0 | 8.0 | 11.4 | 17.8 | 30.0 | 41.4 | 69.4 | 121.9 | 155.4 | 172.2 | 190.4 | 213.7 | 286.7 |
| *% Christian* | *0* | *0.0* | *1.0* | *3.0* | *4.7* | *5.4* | *15.4* | *33.3* | *50.0* | *65.0* | *75.0* | *80.0* | *77.0* | *83.6* | *35.4* | *35.8* | *36.1* | *36.3* | *37.3* |
| *% evangelized* | *0* | *5.0* | *10.0* | *10.9* | *12.5* | *14.1* | *23.1* | *58.4* | *67.1* | *77.4* | *89.6* | *92.0* | *94.0* | *97.0* | *64.0* | *67.5* | *71.0* | *76.0* | *90.4* |
| WORLD TOTALS | | | | | | | | | | | | | | | | | | | |
| **Population** (millions) | **169.7** | **181.5** | **192.0** | **193.4** | **219.9** | **269.2** | **361.9** | **359.7** | **425.3** | **552.2** | **720.7** | **902.6** | **1203.9** | **1619.9** | **3610.0** | [illegible] | **4373.9** | **4781.1** | **6259.6** |
| Christians (millions) | 0.0 | 1.0 | 19.9 | 43.4 | 49.5 | 50.4 | 70.1 | 86.7 | 81.0 | 116.9 | 160.0 | 208.2 | 327.8 | 558.1 | 1216.6 | [illegible] | 1432.7 | 1548.6 | 2019.9 |
| Evangelized (millions) | 0.8 | 50.8 | 67.2 | 81.2 | 68.2 | 67.3 | 94.1 | 100.7 | 89.3 | 136.5 | 186.0 | 245.8 | 457.3 | 831.7 | 2218.1 | [illegible] | 2993.3 | 3445.9 | 5220.8 |
| *% Christian* | *0.0* | *0.6* | *10.4* | *22.4* | *22.5* | *18.7* | *19.4* | *24.1* | *19.0* | *21.2* | *22.2* | *23.1* | *27.2* | *34.4* | *33.7* | *33.2* | *32.8* | *32.4* | *32.3* |
| *% evangelized* | *0.2* | *28.0* | *35.0* | *42.0* | *31.0* | *25.0* | *26.0* | *28.0* | *21.0* | *24.7* | *25.8* | *27.2* | *38.0* | *51.3* | *61.4* | *64.9* | *68.4* | *72.1* | *83.4* |
| Ratio Evangelized/Christians | 200.0 | 50.8 | 3.4 | 1.9 | 1.4 | 1.3 | 1.3 | 1.2 | 1.1 | 1.2 | 1.2 | 1.2 | 1.4 | 1.5 | 1.8 | 2.0 | 2.1 | 2.2 | 2.6 |
| *2. CHRISTIANS BY RACE, %* | | | | | | | | | | | | | | | | | | | |
| Australoid | 0 | 0 | 0 | 0 | 0 | 0 | 0 | 0 | 0 | 0.0 | 0.0 | 0.0 | 0.0 | 0.1 | 0.4 | 0.5 | 0.5 | 0.5 | 0.6 |
| Capoid | 0 | 0 | 0 | 0 | 0 | 0 | 0 | 0 | 0 | 0 | 0.0 | 0.0 | 0.0 | 0.0 | 0.0 | 0.0 | 0.0 | 0.0 | 0.0 |
| Caucasoid | 99.9 | 99.9 | 99.9 | 97.0 | 92.0 | 90.0 | 91.0 | 94.0 | 98.7 | 86.9 | 89.2 | 91.0 | 89.8 | 88.7 | 73.5 | 71.8 | 70.0 | 68.2 | 63.0 |
| Mongoloid | 0.0 | 0.0 | 0.0 | 3.0 | 8.0 | 10.0 | 9.0 | 6.0 | 1.0 | 10.7 | 8.0 | 6.0 | 6.2 | 6.6 | 10.1 | 10.6 | 11.2 | 11.8 | 13.1 |
| Negroid | 0.0 | 0.0 | 0.0 | 0.0 | 0.0 | 0.0 | 0.0 | 0.0 | 0.3 | 2.4 | 2.8 | 3.0 | 4.0 | 4.6 | 15.9 | 17.1 | 18.3 | 19.5 | 23.2 |
| *3. CHRISTIANS BY COLOUR, %* | | | | | | | | | | | | | | | | | | | |
| Black | 0.0 | 0.0 | 0.0 | 0.0 | 0.0 | 0.0 | 0.0 | 0.0 | 0.3 | 2.4 | 2.8 | 3.0 | 4.0 | 4.5 | 15.7 | 16.8 | 18.0 | 19.3 | 22.9 |
| Brown | 0.0 | 0.5 | 1.0 | 1.4 | 2.0 | 2.4 | 2.7 | 3.0 | 1.5 | 2.5 | 2.7 | 3.0 | 3.8 | 5.1 | 9.3 | 10.0 | 10.8 | 11.6 | 13.0 |
| Grey | 0 | 0 | 0 | 0 | 0 | 0 | 0 | 0 | 0.0 | 0.0 | 0.0 | 0.0 | 0.0 | 0.1 | 0.2 | 0.2 | 0.2 | 0.2 | 0.3 |
| Red | 0 | 0 | 0 | 0 | 0 | 0 | 0 | 0 | 0.1 | 7.4 | 4.0 | 3.0 | 2.3 | 1.7 | 2.7 | 2.9 | 3.1 | 3.3 | 3.8 |
| Tan | 95.0 | 69.5 | 65.4 | 59.5 | 43.0 | 28.6 | 26.0 | 24.4 | 4.8 | 1.8 | 1.8 | 2.2 | 2.7 | 5.0 | 9.8 | 10.2 | 10.6 | 11.0 | 11.8 |
| White | 5.0 | 30.0 | 33.6 | 38.1 | 49.0 | 61.0 | 64.3 | 67.6 | 92.6 | 83.1 | 85.2 | 86.5 | 85.2 | 81.1 | 56.4 | 53.5 | 50.5 | 47.4 | 39.8 |
| Yellow | 0 | 0 | 0 | 1.0 | 6.0 | 8.0 | 7.0 | 5.0 | 0.7 | 2.8 | 3.5 | 2.3 | 2.0 | 2.5 | 5.9 | 6.4 | 6.8 | 7.2 | 8.4 |
| *4. CHURCHES, COUNTRIES AND LANGUAGES* | | | | | | | | | | | | | | | | | | | |
| Denominations (ongoing) | 1 | 33 | 50 | 70 | 80 | 92 | 109 | 117 | 150 | 290 | 390 | 510 | 840 | 1900 | 18162 | 19414 | 20781 | 22189 | 26000 |
| Countries entered | 8 | 30 | 42 | 50 | 61 | 68 | 69 | 70 | 85 | 158 | 170 | 178 | 197 | 221 | 223 | 223 | 223 | 223 | 250 |
| Languages with scriptures | *3* | *6* | *10* | *13* | *15* | *17* | *22* | *28* | 12 | 45 | 60 | 67 | 205 | 537 | 1490 | 1630 | 1811 | 2010 | 2800 |

*5. FOOTNOTES AND DOCUMENTATION*

*Continent.* The first section of the table is set out in its first column by the world's 8 continents ('major geographical regions') as recognized today by the United Nations and used in this Encyclopedia, as defined in Part 8 (Global Table 31, column 2).

*Year.* Across the page, the table sets out 19 major years or turning-points in the history of Christianity related to the 9 major epochs or pulsations in Christian history set forth in the Chronology in Part 2.

*AD 30.* This first period (2nd column) represents the world and the church at the end of its first year of existence, some months after the first Day of Pentecost. The figures for Christians and for % Christians at that time are all too small to be enumerated in this table, but their analysis by race and colour as shown reflects the composition of the early church soon after its origin. The figures for world population and continental populations shown are considerably lower than are usually quoted in the literature, because we follow here the radically new figures computed and argued persuasively by C. McEvedy & R. Jones in their *Atlas of world population history* (Harmondsworth, UK: Penguin, 1978). The Roman empire in particular has now been shown to have been much smaller than hitherto estimated, its total being 33 millions in AD 27, rising to 46 millions in AD 200, falling to 38 millions by AD 400 and to 23 millions by AD 550.

*Numbers.* All figures are in millions to the nearest 100,000, except for lines in italics introduced by '%' which are percentages. From AD 30 to 1850, population figures should be regarded as reasonably accurate only to the nearest million or even the nearest 10 million, although in the interests of consistency all are given here in millions to one decimal place.

*Zeros.* There is in this table a difference in meaning between totals of Christians or evangelized persons shown as '0' and those shown as '0.0'. The former means that no Christians or evangelized persons at all existed at the periods indicated; whereas '0.0' means that Christians or evangelized existed then but in very small numbers, less than 0.05 million (50,000).

*Evangelized.* The absolute numbers and percentages refer to all persons who had become adequately aware of Christianity, Christ and the gospel at the periods indicated, and were computed using the methodology described in Part 5.

*Ratio Evangelized/Christians.* This last line under 'World totals' gives the ratio of total evangelized persons to Christians, and serves as an indicator of Christian outreach beyond the Christian fold. The starting figure '200' for AD 30 refers to the situation at the time Jesus gave the Great Commission. Our reasoning is as follows.

As a result of Jesus' 3-year ministry, Palestine then (population 800,000) can be said to have been evangelized. Followers of Jesus then numbered at least 4,000 (500 being present at one commissioning: 1 Corinthians 15.6). This gives our ratio of 200.

*Christians by race.* The 5 rows divide up the total of Christians at each period by percentage into the 5 major races—Australoid, Capoid, Caucasoid, Mongoloid and Negroid—using the definitions and classification given in PEOPLES OF THE WORLD (in Part 4). At each period, the 5 figures shown are percentages of the total of Christians then, and add up vertically to 100%.

*Christians by colour.* The 7 rows divide up the total of Christians at each period by percentage into the 7 stylized racial colours defined in PEOPLES OF THE WORLD. At each period, the 7 figures shown are percentages of the total of Christians then, and add up vertically to 100%.

*Sources.* Figures have been extracted or computed from a large number of recent population studies. For a recent survey of the range of secular population figures over the last 20 centuries, see J.D. Durand, 'The modern expansion of world population', in *Population problems*, Proceedings of the American Philosophical Society, vol. III, 3 (22 June 1967), 136-159; and J.D. Durand, *Historical estimates of world population: an evaluation* (Population Studies Center, University of Pennsylvania, 1974). For the first 10 centuries AD, however, we follow the considerably reduced world and national totals in McEvedy & Jones, *Atlas of world population history* (1978). Our figures for Christians come from a variety of historical sources; some of the statistical evidence itself is included above in our Part 2, Chronology.

*Denominations.* The definition here is of national or nationwide organized churches and denominations which have survived as such up to the present day, and hence are reported here either as significant ones receiving each one line in our Tables 2 for countries, or are summarized in aggregate at the ends of Tables 2. This definition therefore excludes former churches or denominations which have now disappeared or been wiped out.

*Countries entered.* The total of all countries (using 1980 definition and listing) with a definitive or resident Christian presence by the end of the year indicated (derived from the data in Part 2, Chronology).

*Languages with Scriptures.* Before discovery of printing in AD 1450, these figures in italics give totals of all languages with some written portion of the Bible translated (whole Bible, New Testament, gospel or other portion); after AD 1450 (as indicated by the change from italics to roman type), totals of all languages with some printed portion published. Source: *Scriptures of the world: a compilation of 1,549 languages in which at least one Book of the Bible has been published* (United Bible Societies, 1974; revised every 2 years), et alia. In 1980, the world total of all languages was estimated at 7,010.

*Future projections.* The figures for AD 2000 are the United Nations Population Division's medium-variant estimates. Beyond that date, it is estimated by McEvedy & Jones (*op. cit.*) that world population will gradually approach a peak of 8,250 million by AD 2100, then decline, rather than increase further towards the theoretical maximum possible total of 20,000 million for our planet.

Global Table 30. EVANGELIZED, UNEVANGELIZED, AND EVANGELIZING POPULATIONS ON 8 CONTINENTS, AD 1900-2000.

1. This table is an expanded version of Global Table 11 in Part 1. Derivation, definitions and methodology for enumerating evangelization are as explained in Parts 3, 5, 6, and 9.
2. *Rows.* Each successive indentation below divides up the unindented category immediately above it. Thus, world population is divided below into 2 categories, Unevangelized and Evangelized; the latter is then divided into 2 categories, Evangelized non-Christians, and Christians; and so on.
3. *Columns.* The heading '%' in all cases throughout this table refers to the preceding absolute number as a percentage of its continent's population at that date, except for the last 7 lines which refer to total world population.
4. *Natural.* This component of annual numerical change refers, for all 7 rows, to natural (biological plus transfer) growth.
5. *Conversion.* This component of annual numerical change refers to change of allegiance or status to or from the category indicated.
6. *Total.* This column refers to the nett total of annual numerical change, equal to the sum of the 2 preceding columns.
7. *Rate.* The preceding column, divided by the following column, multiplied by 100, and hence expressed as a percent increase per year.

| Continent / Year: | 1900 | | mid-1970 | | Annual change, 1970–1985 | | | | mid-1975 | | mid-1980 | | mid-1985 | | 2000 | |
|---|---|---|---|---|---|---|---|---|---|---|---|---|---|---|---|---|
| | *Adherents* | *%* | *Adherents* | *%* | *Natural* | *Conversion* | *Total* | *Rate* | *Adherents* | *%* | *Adherents* | *%* | *Adherents* | *%* | *Adherents* | *%* |
| AFRICA | | | | | | | | | | | | | | | | |
| Total population | 107,854,260 | 100.0 | 351,800,770 | 100.0 | 10,905,648 | 0 | 10,905,648 | 2.72 | 401,332,860 | 100.0 | 460,857,250 | 100.0 | 520,381,640 | 100.0 | 813,390,700 | 100.0 |
| Unevangelized | 82,990,797 | 76.9 | 106,544,408 | 30.3 | 3,048,061 | −2,035,368 | 1,012,693 | 0.91 | 111,661,930 | 27.8 | 116,671,335 | 25.3 | 121,680,740 | 23.4 | 118,168,930 | 14.5 |
| Evangelized | 24,863,463 | 23.1 | 245,256,362 | 69.7 | 7,857,587 | 2,035,368 | 9,892,955 | 3.42 | 289,670,930 | 72.2 | 344,185,915 | 74.7 | 398,700,900 | 76.6 | 695,221,770 | 85.5 |
| Evangelized non-Christians | 14,925,015 | 13.8 | 102,293,630 | 29.1 | 3,270,939 | 569,219 | 3,840,158 | 3.23 | 118,968,360 | 29.6 | 140,695,205 | 30.5 | 162,422,050 | 31.2 | 301,895,560 | 37.1 |
| Christians | 9,938,448 | 9.2 | 142,962,732 | 40.6 | 4,586,648 | 1,466,149 | 6,052,797 | 3.55 | 170,702,570 | 42.5 | 203,490,710 | 44.2 | 236,278,850 | 45.4 | 393,326,210 | 48.4 |
| Non-evangelizing Christians | 2,117,958 | 2.0 | 52,230,489 | 14.8 | 1,698,453 | 541,762 | 2,240,215 | 3.58 | 62,623,795 | 15.6 | 74,632,655 | 16.2 | 86,641,515 | 16.6 | 158,902,130 | 19.5 |
| Evangelizing Christians | 7,820,490 | 7.2 | 90,732,243 | 25.8 | 2,888,195 | 924,387 | 3,812,582 | 3.53 | 108,078,775 | 26.9 | 128,858,055 | 28.0 | 149,637,335 | 28.8 | 234,424,080 | 28.8 |
| EAST ASIA | | | | | | | | | | | | | | | | |
| Total population | 532,691,000 | 100.0 | 926,422,000 | 100.0 | 16,046,500 | 0 | 16,046,500 | 1.60 | 1,004,979,000 | 100.0 | 1,086,887,000 | 100.0 | 1,168,795,000 | 100.0 | 1,373,242,000 | 100.0 |
| Unevangelized | 389,016,800 | 73.0 | 668,488,420 | 72.2 | 10,877,483 | −9,811,516 | 1,065,967 | 0.16 | 676,459,325 | 67.3 | 679,148,090 | 62.5 | 655,512,750 | 56.1 | 511,540,870 | 37.3 |
| Evangelized | 143,674,200 | 27.0 | 257,933,580 | 27.8 | 5,169,017 | 9,811,516 | 14,980,533 | 4.56 | 328,519,675 | 32.7 | 407,738,910 | 37.5 | 153,282,250 | 43.9 | 861,701,130 | 62.7 |
| Evangelized non-Christians | 141,494,850 | 26.6 | 245,265,337 | 26.5 | 4,892,836 | 9,451,894 | 14,344,730 | 4.59 | 312,791,825 | 31.1 | 388,712,640 | 35.8 | 490,957,560 | 42.0 | 829,363,830 | 60.4 |
| Christians | 2,179,350 | 0.4 | 12,668,243 | 1.4 | 276,181 | 359,622 | 635 803 | 4.04 | 15,727,850 | 1.6 | 19,026,270 | 1.8 | 22,324,690 | 1.9 | 32,337,300 | 2.4 |
| Non-evangelizing Christians | 743,660 | 0.1 | 5,951,793 | 0.6 | 107,981 | 12,005 | 119,986 | 1.83 | 6,543,020 | 0.7 | 7,151,650 | 0.7 | 7,760,280 | 0.7 | 11,719,760 | 0.9 |
| Evangelizing Christians | 1,435,690 | 0.3 | 6,716,450 | 0.7 | 168,200 | 347,617 | 515,817 | 5.62 | 9,184,830 | 0.9 | 11,874,620 | 1.1 | 14,564,410 | 1.2 | 20,617,540 | 1.5 |
| EUROPE | | | | | | | | | | | | | | | | |
| Total population | 287,296,400 | 100.0 | 458,928,650 | 100.0 | 2,750,705 | 0 | 2,750,705 | 0.58 | 472,961,700 | 100.0 | 486,435,700 | 100.0 | 499,909,700 | 100.0 | 539,536,500 | 100.0 |
| Unevangelized | 1,001,771 | 0.3 | 6,625,270 | 1.4 | 70,258 | −214,694 | −144,436 | −2.39 | 6,035,375 | 1.3 | 5,180,910 | 1.1 | 4,358,330 | 0.9 | 2,708,800 | 0.5 |
| Evangelized | 286,294,629 | 99.7 | 452,303,380 | 98.6 | 2,680,447 | 214,694 | 2,895,141 | 0.62 | 466,926,325 | 98.7 | 481,254,790 | 98.9 | 495,551,370 | 99.1 | 536,827,700 | 99.5 |
| Evangelized non-Christians | 7,910,939 | 2.8 | 47,170,724 | 10.3 | 482,989 | 1,365,339 | 1,848,328 | 3.26 | 56,651,105 | 12.0 | 65,654,010 | 13.5 | 74,625,030 | 14.9 | 105,424,130 | 19.5 |
| Christians | 278,383,690 | 96.9 | 405,132,656 | 88.3 | 2,197,458 | −1,150,645 | 1,046,813 | 0.26 | 410,275,220 | 86.7 | 415,600,780 | 85.4 | 420,926,340 | 84.2 | 431,403,570 | 80.0 |
| Non-evangelizing Christians | 32,090,160 | 11.2 | 92,225,956 | 20.1 | 447,020 | 664,437 | 1,111,457 | 1.14 | 97,626,170 | 20.6 | 103,340,530 | 21.2 | 109,054,890 | 21.8 | 138,326,260 | 25.6 |
| Evangelizing Christians | 246,293,530 | 85.7 | 312,906,700 | 68.2 | 1,750,438 | −1,815,084 | −64,646 | −0.02 | 312,649,050 | 66.1 | 312,260,250 | 64.2 | 311,871,450 | 62.4 | 293,077,310 | 54.3 |
| LATIN AMERICA | | | | | | | | | | | | | | | | |
| Total population | 65,178,290 | 100.0 | 283,028,975 | 100.0 | 8,861,170 | 0 | 8,861,170 | 2.73 | 324,099,575 | 100.0 | 371,640,675 | 100.0 | 419,181,775 | 100.0 | 619,934,100 | 100.0 |
| Unevangelized | 1,774,780 | 2.7 | 3,569,680 | 1.3 | 89,890 | 24,213 | 114,103 | 2.78 | 4,100,770 | 1.3 | 4,710,710 | 1.3 | 4,489,530 | 1.1 | 2,315,170 | 0.4 |
| Evangelized | 63,403,510 | 97.3 | 279,459,295 | 98.7 | 8,771,280 | −24,213 | 8,747,067 | 2.73 | 319,998,805 | 98.7 | 366,929,965 | 98.7 | 414,692,245 | 98.9 | 617,618,930 | 99.6 |
| Evangelized non-Christians | 1,401,395 | 2.2 | 12,075,732 | 4.3 | 351,988 | 267,608 | 619,596 | 4.16 | 14,886,855 | 4.6 | 18,271,690 | 4.9 | 22,487,645 | 5.4 | 46,461,110 | 7.5 |
| Christians | 62,002,115 | 95.1 | 267,383,563 | 94.5 | 8,419,292 | −291,821 | 8,127,471 | 2.66 | 305,111,950 | 94.1 | 348,658,275 | 93.8 | 392,204,600 | 93.6 | 571,157,820 | 92.1 |
| Non-evangelizing Christians | 11,022,265 | 16.9 | 85,314,253 | 30.1 | 2,727,182 | 241,323 | 2,968,505 | 3.00 | 98,988,910 | 30.5 | 114,999,285 | 30.9 | 131,009,660 | 31.3 | 204,119,260 | 32.9 |
| Evangelizing Christians | 50,979,850 | 78.2 | 182,069,310 | 64.0 | 5,692,110 | −533,144 | 5,158,966 | 2.50 | 206,123,040 | 63.6 | 233,658,990 | 62.9 | 261,194,940 | 62.3 | 367,038,560 | 59.2 |
| NORTHERN AMERICA | | | | | | | | | | | | | | | | |
| Total population | 81,625,760 | 100.0 | 226,392,500 | 100.0 | 2,244,400 | 0 | 2,244,400 | 0.95 | 236,844,500 | 100.0 | 248,836,500 | 100.0 | 260,828,500 | 100.0 | 296,203,000 | 100.0 |
| Unevangelized | 156,274 | 0.2 | 819,500 | 0.4 | 6,730 | −43,850 | −37,120 | −5.23 | 710,000 | 0.3 | 448,300 | 0.2 | 370,000 | 0.1 | 300,000 | 0.1 |
| Evangelized | 81,469,486 | 99.8 | 225,573,000 | 99.6 | 2,237,670 | 43,850 | 2,281,520 | 0.97 | 236,134,500 | 99.7 | 248,388,200 | 99.8 | 260,458,500 | 99.9 | 295,903,000 | 99.9 |
| Evangelized non-Christians | 2,657,676 | 3.2 | 19,129,540 | 8.4 | 228,790 | 713,731 | 942,521 | 3.98 | 23,705,170 | 10.0 | 28,554,750 | 11.5 | 33,220,930 | 12.7 | 42,313,550 | 14.3 |
| Christians | 78,811,810 | 96.6 | 206,443,460 | 91.2 | 2,008,880 | −669,881 | 1,338,999 | 0.63 | 212,429,330 | 89.7 | 219,833,450 | 88.3 | 227,237,570 | 87.1 | 253,589,450 | 85.6 |
| Non-evangelizing Christians | 22,220,863 | 27.2 | 54,127,835 | 23.9 | 548,489 | 280,152 | 828,641 | 1.44 | 57,635,850 | 24.3 | 62,414,240 | 25.1 | 67,192,630 | 25.8 | 83,627,640 | 28.2 |
| Evangelizing Christians | 56,590,947 | 69.3 | 152,315,625 | 67.3 | 1,460,391 | −950,033 | 510,358 | 0.33 | 154,793,480 | 65.4 | 157,419,210 | 63.3 | 160,044,940 | 61.4 | 169,961,810 | 57.4 |
| OCEANIA | | | | | | | | | | | | | | | | |
| Total population | 6,223,400 | 100.0 | 19,323,510 | 100.0 | 415,890 | 0 | 415,890 | 1.95 | 21,307,460 | 100.0 | 23,482,410 | 100.0 | 25,657,360 | 100.0 | 32,714,700 | 100.0 |
| Unevangelized | 1,076,521 | 17.3 | 28,620 | 0.1 | 478 | −1,322 | −844 | −3.37 | 25,035 | 0.1 | 20,180 | 0.1 | 14,691 | 0.1 | 0 | 0.0 |
| Evangelized | 5,146,879 | 82.7 | 19,294,890 | 99.9 | 415,412 | 1,322 | 416,734 | 1.96 | 21,282,425 | 99.9 | 23,462,230 | 99.9 | 25,642,669 | 99.9 | 32,714,700 | 100.0 |
| Evangelized non-Christians | 319,429 | 5.1 | 1,443,039 | 7.5 | 42,518 | 129,522 | 172,040 | 7.74 | 2,222,329 | 10.4 | 3,163,436 | 13.5 | 4,105,177 | 16.0 | 4,972,734 | 15.2 |
| Christians | 4,827,450 | 77.6 | 17,851,851 | 92.4 | 372,894 | −128,200 | 244,694 | 1.28 | 19,060,096 | 89.5 | 20,298,794 | 86.4 | 21,537,492 | 83.9 | 27,741,966 | 84.8 |
| Non-evangelizing Christians | 938,785 | 15.1 | 5,795,275 | 30.0 | 125,590 | 14,636 | 140,226 | 2.16 | 6,483,758 | 30.4 | 7,197,542 | 30.7 | 7,911,326 | 30.8 | 12,210,039 | 37.3 |
| Evangelizing Christians | 3,888,665 | 62.5 | 12,056,576 | 62.4 | 247,304 | −142,836 | 104,468 | 0.83 | 12,576,338 | 59.0 | 13,101,252 | 55.8 | 13,626,166 | 53.1 | 15,531,927 | 47.5 |
| SOUTH ASIA | | | | | | | | | | | | | | | | |
| Total population | 413,361,650 | 100.0 | 1,101,370,000 | 100.0 | 32,629,300 | 0 | 32,629,300 | 2.61 | 1,250,148,000 | 100.0 | 1,427,663,000 | 100.0 | 1,605,178,000 | 100.0 | 2,269,594,000 | 100.0 |
| Unevangelized | 308,372,347 | 74.6 | 518,483,610 | 47.1 | 13,427,916 | −15,611,942 | −2,184,026 | −0.43 | 511,173,815 | 40.9 | 496,643,350 | 34.8 | 481,300,030 | 30.0 | 375,432,910 | 16.5 |
| Evangelized | 104,989,303 | 25.4 | 582,886,390 | 52.9 | 19,201,384 | 15,611,942 | 34,813,326 | 4.71 | 738,974,185 | 59.1 | 931,019,650 | 65.2 | 1,123,877,970 | 70.0 | 1,894,161,090 | 83.5 |
| Evangelized non-Christians | 88,068,834 | 21.3 | 504,761,774 | 45.8 | 16,555,716 | 15,164,899 | 31,720,615 | 4.90 | 646,785,350 | 51.7 | 821,967,910 | 57.6 | 997,963,325 | 62.2 | 1,701,897,040 | 75.0 |
| Christians | 16,920,469 | 4.1 | 78,124,616 | 7.1 | 2,645,668 | 447,043 | 3,092,711 | 3.35 | 92,188,835 | 7.4 | 109,051,740 | 7.6 | 125,914,645 | 7.8 | 192,264,050 | 8.5 |
| Non-evangelizing Christians | 1,971,668 | 0.5 | 15,408,960 | 1.4 | 546,321 | 147,601 | 693,922 | 3.73 | 18,608,725 | 1.5 | 22,348,200 | 1.6 | 26,087,675 | 1.6 | 57,071,020 | 2.5 |
| Evangelizing Christians | 14,948,801 | 3.6 | 62,715,656 | 5.7 | 2,099,347 | 299,442 | 2,398,789 | 3.26 | 73,580,110 | 5.9 | 86,703,540 | 6.1 | 99,826,970 | 6.2 | 135,193,030 | 6.0 |
| USSR | | | | | | | | | | | | | | | | |
| Total population | 125,656,000 | 100.0 | 242,768,000 | 100.0 | 2,534,700 | 0 | 2,534,700 | 0.99 | 255,038,000 | 100.0 | 268,115,000 | 100.0 | 281,192,000 | 100.0 | 315,027,000 | 100.0 |
| Unevangelized | 3,769,680 | 3.0 | 87,396,480 | 36.0 | 823,778 | −1,788,091 | −964,313 | −1.16 | 82,887,350 | 32.5 | 77,753,350 | 29.0 | 67,486,080 | 24.0 | 28,352,430 | 9.6 |
| Evangelized | 121,886,320 | 97.0 | 155,371,520 | 64.0 | 1,710,922 | 1,788,091 | 3,499,013 | 2.03 | 172,150,650 | 67.5 | 190,361,650 | 71.0 | 213,705,920 | 76.0 | 286,674,570 | 90.4 |
| Evangelized non-Christians | 16,893,320 | 13.4 | 69,359,220 | 28.6 | 803,684 | 1,623,909 | 2,427,593 | 3.00 | 80,865,650 | 31.7 | 93,635,150 | 34.9 | 111,537,920 | 39.7 | 168,573,570 | 53.2 |
| Christians | 104,993,000 | 83.6 | 86,012,300 | 35.4 | 907,238 | 164,182 | 1,071,420 | 1.17 | 91,285,000 | 35.8 | 96,726,500 | 36.1 | 102,168,000 | 36.3 | 118,101,000 | 37.3 |
| Non-evangelizing Christians | 17,691,200 | 14.1 | 21,503,080 | 8.9 | 217,738 | −143,336 | 74,402 | 0.34 | 21,908,400 | 8.6 | 22,247,100 | 8.3 | 22,585,800 | 8.0 | 23,620,200 | 7.5 |
| Evangelizing Christians | 87,301,800 | 69.5 | 64,509,220 | 26.6 | 689,500 | 307,518 | 997,018 | 1.44 | 69,376,600 | 27.2 | 74,479,400 | 27.8 | 79,582,200 | 28.3 | 94,480,800 | 29.8 |
| WORLD | | | | | | | | | | | | | | | | |
| Global population | 1,619,886,760 | 100.0 | 3,610,034,405 | 100.0 | 76,388,313 | 0 | 76,388,313 | 1.93 | 3,966,711,095 | 100.0 | 4,373,917,535 | 100.0 | 4,781,123,975 | 100.0 | 6,259,642,000 | 100.0 |
| Unevangelized | 788,158,970 | 48.7 | 1,391,955,988 | 38.6 | 28,344,594 | −29,482,570 | −1,137,976 | −0.08 | 1,393,053,600 | 35.1 | 1,380,576,225 | 31.6 | 1,335,212,151 | 27.9 | 1,038,819,110 | 16.6 |
| Evangelized | 831,727,790 | 51.3 | 2,218,078,417 | 61.4 | 48,043,719 | 29,482,570 | 77,526,289 | 3.01 | 2,573,657,495 | 64.9 | 2,993,341,310 | 68.4 | 3,445,911,824 | 72.1 | 5,220,822,890 | 83.4 |
| Evangelized non-Christians | 273,671,458 | 16.9 | 1,001,498,996 | 27.7 | 26,629,460 | 29,286,121 | 55,915,581 | 4.45 | 1,256,876,644 | 31.7 | 1,560,654,791 | 35.7 | 1,897,319,637 | 39.7 | 3,200,901,524 | 51.1 |
| Christians | 558,056,332 | 34.4 | 1,216,579,431 | 33.7 | 21,414,259 | 196,449 | 21,610,708 | 1.64 | 1,316,780,851 | 33.2 | 1,432,686,519 | 32.8 | 1,548,592,187 | 32.4 | 2,019,921,366 | 32.3 |
| Non-evangelizing Christians | 88,796,559 | 5.5 | 332,557,641 | 9.2 | 6,418,774 | 1,758,582 | 8,177,356 | 2.21 | 370,418,628 | 9.3 | 414,331,202 | 9.5 | 458,243,776 | 9.6 | 689,596,309 | 11.0 |
| Evangelizing Christians | 469,259,773 | 29.0 | 884,021,780 | 24.5 | 14,995,485 | −1,562,133 | 13,433,352 | 1.42 | 946,362,223 | 23.9 | 1,018,355,317 | 23.3 | 1,090,348,411 | 22.8 | 1,330,325,057 | 21.3 |

Global Table 31.  GEOPOLITICO-RELIGIOUS DATA AND TYPOLOGIES FOR ALL COUNTRIES AND CONTINENTS, AD 1900-2000.

1. This table is the original source from which Global Table 12 in Part 1 was derived. It summarizes much of the material in this Encyclopedia's Part 7, especially in the footnotes under Tables 2, concerning Christian resources, organizations, institutions, personnel, activities and attributes in the 20th century at various points from AD 1900-2000.

2. The table is spread out over 12 pages making up 6 pairs of facing pages. Each pair lists all countries of the world, with totals for continents and for the world. Each pair then gives the statistics, codes or values for between 15 and 26 variables (in 15 to 20 columns).

3. To locate specific data for a country, the reader should use a ruler or straight edge. From the Codebook (Part 6), obtain the column number of the data you require. Locate the country (whose physical position on the pair of pages is exactly the same for all pairs), locate the column number, and read off the data.

4. *Rows.* These list all 223 countries of the world, followed by totals for the 8 continents, then totals for the world.

5. *Columns.* These give the values of 107 variables whose meaning is as set out in the Codebook. The numbers of the columns are given at the top of each page and also, for convenience, at the bottom of the second of each facing pair. Abbreviated headings are given at the top of each page; 'pmill' means total per million population. Abbreviated initials: CNR= Catholic (non-Roman), NWI=Non-White indigenous, TW= Third-World.

6. *Totals.* At the end of the listings for countries, totals are given for each continent and for the world. These are simple totals, each being the sum of the 223 figures in the column above. Many totals, for example of foreign missionaries and personnel (column 45), are clear in their meaning and so can immediately be understood and used. Other totals (of percentages) require clear thinking, interpreting, and some processing; for example, the totals in columns 4-10 will yield average values for a continent or world, if divided by 223 (for the world) or 59 for Africa, 37 for Europe, etc. For columns composed of alphabetic or alphanumeric characters, or ratios 'per million', totals are meaningless and so are omitted, being entered here as '—'. If the reader wants a global figure 'per million', he can immediately compute it by dividing the global absolute total given on the last line below by the global population for the year required.

## BRIEF MEANINGS OF COLUMNS 1–107 IN GLOBAL TABLE 31

Column *Subject*

**GEOPOLITICO-RELIGIOUS TYPOLOGIES**
**GEOGRAPHY**
1 Country
2 Continent
3 Region (UN terminology)
**POLITICO-ECONOMIC SITUATION**
4 Development, 1980
5 Economy, 1980
6 Economic system, 1980
7 Political alignment, 1970
8 — 1975
9 — 1980
10 Political freedom, 1980
11 Political freedom index, %
12 Democratic rule, 1980
**LANGUAGES**
13 Total used in country
14 Official state languages
**MODERN LIVING**
15 Urban dwellers, %
16 Cinema attendances
17 Physical quality of life index
**RELIGIO-POLITICAL SITUATION**
18 State religion or philosophy, 1900
19 — 1970
20 — 1975
21 — 1980
22 Religious liberty, 1980
**MISSION**
23 Foreign mission situation, 1970–1980

**CHURCHES**
**DENOMINATIONS**
24 Total denominations, 1975
25 Denominations per million population
26 Worship centres, 1970
27 Worship centres per million

**CHRISTIAN ORGANIZATIONS**
**INSTITUTIONS**
28 Major Christian institutions, 1973–1978
29 Institutions per million
**SERVICE AGENCIES**
30 Parachurch agencies, 1973–1978
31 Agencies per million

**CHRISTIAN PERSONNEL**
**NATIONALS AND ALIENS**
32 Total full-time workers
33 Population per worker

**NATIONALS**
34 National (citizen) personnel, 1973–1978
35 National personnel per million

**INTERNATIONAL SHARING OF PERSONNEL**
**NATIONALS SENT ABROAD (FOREIGN MISSIONARIES)**
36 Total sent abroad
37 Anglican
38 Black/Third-World indigenous
39 Catholic (non-Roman)
40 Marginal Protestant
41 Orthodox
42 Protestant
43 Roman Catholic
44 Total sent per million population
**ALIENS FROM ABROAD (FOREIGN MISSIONARIES)**
45 Total received from abroad
46 Total from Western world
47 Total from Communist world
48 Total from Third World
49 Anglican
50 Black/Third-World indigenous
51 Catholic (non-Roman)
52 Marginal Protestant
53 Orthodox
54 Protestant
55 Roman Catholic
56 Total received per million population

**CHRISTIAN LITERATURE**
**BOOKS, PERIODICALS AND LIBRARIES**
57 Annual new book titles (all subjects)
58 Annual new religious book titles
59 Religious (Christian) periodicals
60 Christian periodical titles per million
61 Major religious libraries
62 Religious libraries per million

**SCRIPTURE DISTRIBUTION**
**BIBLES PER YEAR**
63 Free distribution, 1900
64 — 1950
65 — 1960
66 — 1970
67 — 1975
68 Subsidized distribution, 1900
69 — 1950
70 — 1960
71 — 1970
72 — 1975
73 Commercial distribution, 1975
74 Total distribution, 1975
75 Total distribution per million

**NEW TESTAMENTS PER YEAR**
76 Free distribution, 1900
77 — 1950
78 — 1960
79 — 1970
80 — 1975
81 Subsidized distribution, 1900
82 — 1950
83 — 1960
84 — 1970
85 — 1975
86 Commercial distribution, 1975
87 Total distribution, 1975
88 Total distribution per million
**PORTIONS AND SELECTIONS**
89 Portions (UBS) distributed, 1975
90 Selections (UBS) distributed, 1975

**CHRISTIAN BROADCASTING**
**SETS AND LETTERS**
91 Radios and TV sets per hundred population
92 Radio letters (listeners/viewers letters), 1975
**AUDIENCE FOR CHRISTIAN BROADCASTING**
93 Regular audience (over Christian stations)
94 Regular audience (over secular stations)
95 Total regular audience (minus duplications)

**LITERACY**
**ADULT LITERACY RATE**
96 Adult literates (%) in 1900
97 — 1950
98 — 1975
99 — 1980

**EVANGELIZATION, 1900–2000**
100 Year evangelization begun
**EXTENT EVANGELIZED**
101 Individual evangelization (e %), 1970
102 Demographic evangelization (E %), 1900
103 — 1970
104 — 1980
105 — 1985
106 — 2000
**OUTREACH**
107 Total evangelized ÷ total Christians, 1980

| | GEOPOLITICO-RELIGIOUS TYPOLOGIES | | | | | | | | | | | | | | | | | | | | | | | CHURCHES | | |
|---|---|---|---|---|---|---|---|---|---|---|---|---|---|---|---|---|---|---|---|---|---|---|---|---|---|---|
| | GEOGRAPHY | | | POLITICO-ECONOMIC SITUATION | | | | | | | | | Languages | | MODERN LIVING | | | RELIGIO-POLITICAL | | | | | Mission | DENOMINATIONS | | |
| Country | No. | Cont | Region | Dev | Eco | Sys | 1970 | 1975 | 1980 | Free | Index | Rule | Total | Offic | Urban | Cinema | PQLI | 1900 | 1970 | 1975 | 1980 | Lib | Status | 1975 | pmill | Worship |
| | 1 | 2 | 3 | 4 | 5 | 6 | 7 | 8 | 9 | 10 | 11 | 12 | 13 | 14 | 15 | 16 | 17 | 18 | 19 | 20 | 21 | 22 | 23 | 24 | 25 | 26 |
| Afghanistan | 001 | 7 | 04 | 2 | 3 | 2 | 3 | 3 | 2 | 3 | 8 | 4q | 53 | *P'*N | 7 | 0.1 | 18 | RI | RI | RI | A | 9 | 1 | 8 | 0 | 17 |
| Albania | 002 | 3 | 08 | 1 | 2 | 5 | 2 | 2 | 2 | 3 | 0 | 2g | 10 | a | 37 | 4.0 | 72 | RI | A | A | A | 10 | 1 | 7 | 3 | 1000 |
| Algeria | 003 | 1 | 15 | 2 | 3 | 3 | 3 | 3 | 3 | 3 | 17 | 4q | 21 | A | 43 | 2.7 | 41 | RI | RI | RI | RI | 8 | 4 | 30 | 2 | 675 |
| American Samoa | 004 | 6 | 24 | 2 | 3 | 1 | 3 | 3 | 3 | 2 | 100 | 3i | 3 | E | 10 | 6.5 | 80 | S | S | S | S | 5 | 4 | 15 | 469 | 130 |
| Andorra | 005 | 3 | 08 | 1 | 1 | 2 | 1 | 1 | 1 | 2 | 90 | 1b | 6 | 2 | 37 | 14.0 | 90 | RC | RC | RC | RC | 3 | 1 | 3 | 130 | 10 |
| Angola | 006 | 1 | 14 | 2 | 3 | 3 | 3 | 3 | 2 | 3 | 0 | 2g | 37 | P | 14 | 0.6 | 15 | RC | RC | A | A | 7 | 4 | 29 | 5 | 2100 |
| Anguilla | 007 | 4 | 21 | 2 | 3 | 4 | 3 | 3 | 3 | 2 | 90 | 3h | 3 | E | 28 | 1.0 | 80 | S | S | S | S | 4 | 4 | 7 | 968 | 14 |
| Antigua | 008 | 4 | 21 | 2 | 3 | 4 | 3 | 3 | 3 | 1 | 90 | 1c | 4 | E | 40 | 2.0 | 80 | S | S | S | S | 5 | 4 | 17 | 233 | 170 |
| Argentina | 009 | 4 | 20 | 1 | 3 | 1 | 3 | 3 | 3 | 2 | 17 | 4r | 48 | S | 80 | 3.2 | 85 | RC | RC | RC | RC | 7 | 5 | 143 | 6 | 7744 |
| Australia | 010 | 6 | 22 | 1 | 1 | 1 | 1 | 1 | 1 | 1 | 100 | 1a | 305 | E | 84 | 5.0 | 93 | R | R | R | R | 3 | 7 | 240 | 17 | 18900 |
| Austria | 011 | 3 | 07 | 1 | 1 | 4 | 1 | 1 | 1 | 1 | 100 | 1a | 20 | G | 54 | 2.8 | 93 | R | S | S | S | 2 | 7 | 61 | 8 | 4350 |
| Bahamas | 012 | 4 | 21 | 2 | 3 | 2 | 3 | 3 | 3 | 1 | 90 | 1b | 7 | E | 72 | 3.0 | 80 | RA | RA | RA | RA | 4 | 4 | 38 | 186 | 880 |
| Bahrain | 013 | 7 | 06 | 2 | 3 | 2 | 3 | 3 | 3 | 2 | 33 | 5s | 15 | A | 64 | 8.2 | 33 | RI | RI | RI | RI | 7 | 4 | 16 | 64 | 42 |
| Bangladesh | 014 | 7 | 04 | 2 | 3 | 2 | 3 | 3 | 3 | 3 | 33 | 4r | 48 | B | 5 | 1.5 | 35 | S | RI | S | RI | 4 | 2 | 31 | 0 | 1120 |
| Barbados | 015 | 4 | 21 | 2 | 3 | 2 | 3 | 3 | 3 | 1 | 90 | 1b | 8 | E | 44 | 4.9 | 80 | RA | RA | RA | R | 2 | 4 | 49 | 200 | 400 |
| Belgium | 016 | 3 | 07 | 1 | 1 | 4 | 1 | 1 | 1 | 1 | 100 | 1b | 25 | DFG | 69 | 2.6 | 93 | R | R | R | R | 2 | 7 | 82 | 8 | 4740 |
| Belize | 017 | 4 | 19 | 2 | 3 | 4 | 3 | 3 | 3 | 1 | 80 | 3h | 15 | E | 57 | 4.0 | 70 | S | S | S | S | 4 | 4 | 32 | 229 | 340 |
| Benin | 018 | 1 | 12 | 2 | 3 | 3 | 3 | 3 | 2 | 3 | 0 | 2g | 30 | F | 13 | 0.4 | 23 | RT | S | A | A | 6 | 4 | 31 | 10 | 905 |
| Bermuda | 019 | 5 | 17 | 1 | 3 | 4 | 3 | 3 | 3 | 1 | 90 | 3h | 4 | E | 10 | 7.0 | 90 | RA | RA | R | R | 3 | 4 | 70 | 1250 | 140 |
| Bhutan | 020 | 7 | 04 | 2 | 3 | 2 | 3 | 3 | 3 | 2 | 50 | 1b | 20 | z | 4 | 0.6 | 20 | RB | RB | RB | RB | 9 | 2 | 8 | 7 | 40 |
| Bolivia | 021 | 4 | 18 | 2 | 3 | 2 | 3 | 3 | 3 | 3 | 33 | 4r | 52 | S | 34 | 0.9 | 43 | RC | RC | RC | RC | 2 | 5 | 114 | 21 | 2010 |
| Botswana | 022 | 1 | 16 | 2 | 3 | 2 | 3 | 3 | 3 | 1 | 75 | 1b | 25 | Eü | 4 | 0.2 | 45 | RR | S | S | S | 4 | 4 | 104 | 150 | 870 |
| Brazil | 023 | 4 | 18 | 2 | 3 | 2 | 3 | 3 | 3 | 2 | 42 | 4p | 250 | P | 57 | 2.6 | 67 | RC | R | R | R | 7 | 4 | 460 | 4 | 47500 |
| British Antarctic Terr | 024 | 4 | 20 | 1 | 3 | 4 | 3 | 3 | 3 | 1 | 100 | 3i | 2 | E | 0 | 5.0 | 90 | S | S | S | S | 5 | 1 | 0 | 0 | 0 |
| British Indian Ocean Terr | 025 | 1 | 13 | 2 | 3 | 4 | 3 | 3 | 3 | 2 | 90 | 3i | 3 | E | 0 | 4.0 | 80 | S | S | S | S | 5 | 1 | 2 | 1000 | 2 |
| British Virgin Is | 026 | 4 | 21 | 2 | 3 | 4 | 3 | 3 | 3 | 1 | 90 | 3i | 6 | E | 36 | 4.6 | 80 | S | S | S | S | 5 | 4 | 9 | 818 | 30 |
| Brunei | 027 | 7 | 05 | 2 | 3 | 2 | 3 | 3 | 3 | 3 | 50 | 3h | 10 | *m'*E | 46 | 17.0 | 65 | RI | RI | RI | RI | 6 | 3 | 7 | 48 | 17 |
| Bulgaria | 028 | 3 | 09 | 1 | 2 | 5 | 2 | 2 | 2 | 3 | 0 | 2g | 14 | b | 52 | 13.1 | 91 | R | A | A | A | 8 | 1 | 21 | 2 | 4310 |
| Burma | 029 | 7 | 05 | 2 | 3 | 3 | 3 | 3 | 3 | 3 | 8 | 2f | 129 | WE | 19 | 8.1 | 51 | R | S | S | S | 8 | 2 | 48 | 2 | 4970 |
| Burundi | 030 | 1 | 13 | 2 | 3 | 3 | 3 | 3 | 3 | 3 | 8 | 4r | 10 | yF | 3 | 0.0 | 22 | RT | S | S | S | 3 | 4 | 21 | 6 | 2010 |
| Cameroon | 031 | 1 | 14 | 2 | 3 | 2 | 3 | 3 | 3 | 2 | 25 | 2e | 206 | FE | 21 | 0.1 | 25 | S | S | S | S | 4 | 4 | 59 | 9 | 7730 |
| Canada | 032 | 5 | 17 | 1 | 1 | 1 | 1 | 1 | 1 | 1 | 100 | 1a | 92 | EF | 76 | 4.3 | 95 | S | S | S | S | 3 | 7 | 300 | 13 | 26900 |
| Canton & Enderbury | 033 | 6 | 24 | 2 | 3 | 4 | 3 | 3 | 3 | 2 | 90 | 3j | 4 | E | 0 | 5.0 | 80 | S | S | S | S | 5 | 1 | 1 | 5000 | 1 |
| Cape Verde | 034 | 1 | 12 | 2 | 3 | 3 | 3 | 3 | 3 | 2 | 20 | 2f | 9 | P | 8 | 1.1 | 20 | RC | RC | RC | S | 7 | 4 | 6 | 20 | 95 |
| Cayman Islands | 035 | 4 | 21 | 2 | 3 | 4 | 3 | 3 | 3 | 1 | 90 | 3i | 5 | E | 40 | 18.2 | 80 | S | S | S | S | 5 | 4 | 16 | 1454 | 45 |
| Central African Republic | 036 | 1 | 14 | 2 | 3 | 2 | 3 | 3 | 3 | 3 | 0 | 5v | 56 | Fx | 25 | 0.5 | 18 | RT | S | S | S | 4 | 4 | 20 | 11 | 1920 |
| Chad | 037 | 1 | 14 | 2 | 3 | 2 | 3 | 3 | 3 | 3 | 8 | 4r | 110 | F | 7 | 0.4 | 18 | RT | S | S | S | 6 | 4 | 23 | 6 | 1350 |
| Channel Islands | 038 | 3 | 10 | 1 | 1 | 4 | 1 | 1 | 1 | 1 | 100 | 3h | 6 | EF | 44 | 3.0 | 94 | RA | RA | RA | RA | 3 | 6 | 22 | 172 | 116 |
| Chile | 039 | 4 | 20 | 1 | 3 | 1 | 3 | 3 | 3 | 3 | 17 | 4r | 25 | S | 73 | 2.3 | 77 | RC | S | S | S | 3 | 5 | 240 | 23 | 6950 |
| China | 040 | 2 | 01 | 2 | 2 | 5 | 2 | 2 | 2 | 3 | 17 | 2g | 198 | C | 26 | 30.0 | 57 | RG | A | A | A | 9 | 1 | 14 | 0 | 52400 |
| China (Taiwan) | 041 | 2 | 01 | 2 | 3 | 1 | 3 | 3 | 3 | 3 | 42 | 2e | 24 | C | 62 | 2.0 | 86 | RG | S | S | S | 6 | 4 | 135 | 9 | 3200 |
| Christmas Island | 042 | 6 | 24 | 2 | 3 | 1 | 3 | 3 | 3 | 2 | 80 | 3i | 7 | E | 0 | 1.0 | 70 | S | S | S | S | 5 | 1 | 5 | 1515 | 5 |
| Cocos Islands | 043 | 6 | 24 | 2 | 3 | 1 | 3 | 3 | 3 | 2 | 80 | 3i | 5 | E | 0 | 1.0 | 70 | S | S | S | S | 5 | 1 | 2 | 2857 | 2 |
| Colombia | 044 | 4 | 18 | 2 | 3 | 2 | 3 | 3 | 3 | 1 | 75 | 1b | 255 | S | 60 | 4.1 | 68 | RC | RC | RC | RC | 7 | 5 | 105 | 4 | 5610 |
| Comoros | 045 | 1 | 13 | 2 | 3 | 3 | 3 | 3 | 3 | 2 | 20 | 5t | 10 | ä | 3 | 0.2 | 30 | S | S | S | S | 7 | 2 | 5 | 19 | 10 |
| Congo | 046 | 1 | 14 | 2 | 3 | 3 | 3 | 3 | 3 | 2 | 8 | 2f | 37 | F | 30 | 0.9 | 26 | S | A | A | A | 7 | 4 | 27 | 20 | 760 |
| Cook Islands | 047 | 6 | 24 | 2 | 3 | 1 | 3 | 3 | 3 | 1 | 90 | 3h | 7 | E | 10 | 4.0 | 80 | S | S | S | S | 3 | 5 | 9 | 360 | 135 |
| Costa Rica | 048 | 4 | 19 | 2 | 3 | 4 | 3 | 3 | 3 | 1 | 100 | 1b | 16 | S | 37 | 4.0 | 85 | RC | RC | RC | RC | 2 | 5 | 66 | 33 | 770 |
| Cuba | 049 | 4 | 21 | 2 | 3 | 5 | 2 | 2 | 2 | 3 | 8 | 2g | 12 | S | 56 | 14.2 | 84 | RC | A | A | A | 8 | 2 | 60 | 6 | 2170 |
| Cyprus | 050 | 7 | 06 | 2 | 3 | 2 | 3 | 3 | 3 | 2 | 75 | 1b | 10 | gT | 44 | 10.0 | 60 | R | R | R | R | 7 | 5 | 21 | 31 | 635 |
| Czechoslovakia | 051 | 3 | 09 | 1 | 2 | 5 | 2 | 2 | 2 | 3 | 8 | 2g | 12 | c*u'* | 52 | 5.8 | 93 | R | A | A | A | 9 | 1 | 26 | 2 | 8840 |
| Denmark | 052 | 3 | 10 | 1 | 1 | 4 | 1 | 1 | 1 | 1 | 100 | 1b | 21 | d | 80 | 3.7 | 96 | RL | RL | RL | RL | 2 | 5 | 51 | 10 | 3370 |
| Djibouti | 053 | 1 | 13 | 2 | 3 | 2 | 3 | 3 | 3 | 2 | 30 | 2e | 12 | F | 65 | 5.8 | 30 | S | S | S | S | 4 | 4 | 4 | 38 | 9 |
| Dominica | 054 | 4 | 21 | 2 | 3 | 4 | 3 | 3 | 3 | 1 | 90 | 1c | 8 | E | 27 | 1.0 | 80 | S | S | S | S. | 5 | 4 | 13 | 173 | 85 |
| Dominican Republic | 055 | 4 | 21 | 2 | 3 | 2 | 3 | 3 | 3 | 2 | 67 | 1b | 11 | S | 38 | 1.2 | 64 | RC | RC | RC | RC | 2 | 4 | 44 | 9 | 1870 |
| Ecuador | 056 | 4 | 18 | 2 | 3 | 2 | 3 | 3 | 3 | 2 | 33 | 4r | 23 | S | 39 | 5.6 | 67 | R | R | R | R | 3 | 4 | 120 | 17 | 1790 |
| Egypt | 057 | 1 | 15 | 2 | 3 | 3 | 3 | 3 | 3 | 2 | 42 | 2f | 20 | A | 44 | 2.0 | 42 | RI | RI | RI | RI | 8 | 2 | 58 | 1 | 3910 |
| El Salvador | 058 | 4 | 19 | 2 | 3 | 1 | 3 | 3 | 3 | 1 | 67 | 4p | 17 | S | 41 | 3.5 | 64 | RC | RC | RC | RC | 6 | 4 | 43 | 10 | 1440 |
| Equatorial Guinea | 059 | 1 | 14 | 2 | 3 | 3 | 3 | 3 | 3 | 3 | 0 | 5w | 23 | S | 30 | 1.7 | 28 | RC | A | A | S | 6 | 4 | 9 | 29 | 470 |
| Ethiopia | 060 | 1 | 13 | 2 | 3 | 3 | 3 | 3 | 2 | 3 | 0 | 4q | 103 | L | 9 | 0.1 | 19 | RO | RO | RO | A | 8 | 3 | 50 | 2 | 19950 |
| Faeroe Islands | 061 | 3 | 10 | 1 | 1 | 4 | 1 | 1 | 1 | 1 | 100 | 3h | 6 | 3 | 25 | 7.5 | 96 | RL | RL | RL | RL | 2 | 5 | 6 | 150 | 89 |
| Falkland Islands | 062 | 4 | 20 | 1 | 3 | 4 | 3 | 3 | 3 | 1 | 90 | 3i | 4 | E | 58 | 9.5 | 90 | S | S | S | S | 5 | 4 | 4 | 2041 | 18 |
| Fiji | 063 | 6 | 24 | 2 | 3 | 2 | 3 | 3 | 3 | 1 | 90 | 1b | 20 | E | 18 | 1.1 | 80 | R | R | R | R | 4 | 5 | 22 | 38 | 2370 |
| Finland | 064 | 3 | 10 | 1 | 1 | 4 | 1 | 1 | 1 | 1 | 83 | 1b | 13 | fs | 61 | 2.0 | 94 | RX | RX | RX | RX | 2 | 6 | 36 | 8 | 2060 |
| France | 065 | 3 | 07 | 1 | 1 | 2 | 1 | 1 | 1 | 1 | 100 | 1b | 48 | F | 70 | 3.3 | 94 | R | S | S | S | 4 | 7 | 294 | 6 | 44600 |
| French Guiana | 066 | 4 | 18 | 2 | 3 | 2 | 3 | 3 | 3 | 2 | 90 | 3i | 18 | F | 56 | 14.0 | 70 | S | S | S | S | 5 | 4 | 8 | 133 | 54 |
| French Polynesia | 067 | 6 | 24 | 2 | 3 | 2 | 3 | 3 | 3 | 2 | 90 | 3h | 9 | F | 28 | 3.7 | 80 | S | S | S | S | 4 | 4 | 9 | 70 | 220 |
| French Southern & Antarctic T | 068 | 1 | 16 | 2 | 3 | 2 | 3 | 3 | 3 | 1 | 90 | 3i | 2 | F | 0 | 5.0 | 90 | S | S | S | S | 5 | 1 | 0 | 0 | 0 |
| Gabon | 069 | 1 | 14 | 2 | 3 | 1 | 3 | 3 | 3 | 3 | 17 | 2e | 51 | F | 19 | 0.8 | 21 | R | R | R | R | 4 | 4 | 7 | 13 | 1562 |
| Gambia | 070 | 1 | 12 | 2 | 3 | 2 | 3 | 3 | 3 | 1 | 83 | 1b | 15 | E | 10 | 1.0 | 25 | S | S | S | S | 5 | 4 | 5 | 10 | 37 |
| German Democratic Rep | 071 | 3 | 09 | 1 | 2 | 5 | 2 | 2 | 2 | 3 | 0 | 2g | 10 | G | 81 | 4.6 | 93 | R | A | A | A | 7 | 1 | 32 | 2 | 8410 |
| Germany, Federal Rep | 072 | 3 | 07 | 1 | 1 | 4 | 1 | 1 | 1 | 1 | 100 | 1a | 40 | G | 82 | 2.1 | 93 | R | R | R | R | 2 | 7 | 250 | 4 | 43100 |
| Ghana | 073 | 1 | 12 | 2 | 3 | 2 | 3 | 3 | 3 | 3 | 25 | 4r | 112 | E | 31 | 0.1 | 34 | R | R | R | R | 4 | 4 | 520 | 53 | 11300 |
| Gibraltar | 074 | 3 | 08 | 1 | 1 | 4 | 1 | 1 | 1 | 2 | 90 | 3h | 9 | E | 93 | 11.1 | 90 | S | S | S | S | 2 | 4 | 6 | 222 | 13 |
| Greece | 075 | 3 | 08 | 1 | 1 | 1 | 1 | 1 | 1 | 1 | 83 | 1b | 17 | g | 49 | 10.0 | 88 | RO | RO | RO | RO | 2 | 3 | 53 | 6 | 30040 |
| Greenland | 076 | 5 | 17 | 1 | 3 | 4 | 1 | 1 | 1 | 1 | 90 | 3h | 4 | 4d | 10 | 7.4 | 90 | RL | RL | RL | RL | 2 | 4 | 9 | 167 | 101 |
| Grenada | 077 | 4 | 21 | 2 | 3 | 2 | 3 | 3 | 2 | 2 | 90 | 1b | 5 | E | 15 | 11.5 | 80 | R | R | R | A | 6 | 4 | 27 | 281 | 126 |
| Guadeloupe | 078 | 4 | 21 | 2 | 3 | 2 | 3 | 3 | 3 | 1 | 90 | 3i | 7 | F | 48 | 5.0 | 80 | S | S | S | S | 7 | 5 | 13 | 37 | 167 |
| Guam | 079 | 6 | 24 | 2 | 3 | 1 | 3 | 3 | 3 | 2 | 100 | 3h | 8 | E | 8 | 10.3 | 80 | R | R | R | R | 2 | 4 | 23 | 232 | 115 |
| Guatemala | 080 | 4 | 19 | 2 | 3 | 1 | 3 | 3 | 3 | 2 | 50 | 1b | 47 | S | 31 | 2.8 | 51 | RC | RC | RC | RC | 3 | 4 | 77 | 13 | 3790 |
| Guinea | 081 | 1 | 12 | 2 | 3 | 3 | 3 | 3 | 2 | 3 | 0 | 2f | 28 | F | 11 | 0.2 | 20 | S | A | A | A | 8 | 1 | 8 | 2 | 280 |
| Guinea-Bissau | 082 | 1 | 12 | 2 | 3 | 3 | 3 | 3 | 2 | 3 | 17 | 2f | 23 | P | 18 | 0.6 | 11 | RC | RC | A | A | 7 | 4 | 5 | 9 | 43 |
| Guyana | 083 | 4 | 18 | 2 | 3 | 3 | 3 | 3 | 3 | 2 | 67 | 1b | 16 | E | 35 | 10.9 | 82 | R | R | R | R | 6 | 4 | 70 | 89 | 945 |
| Haiti | 084 | 4 | 21 | 2 | 3 | 1 | 3 | 3 | 3 | 3 | 8 | 5t | 11 | F | 18 | 0.3 | 32 | RC | RC | RC | RC | 8 | 4 | 210 | 46 | 4520 |
| Holy See | 085 | 3 | 08 | 1 | 1 | 1 | 1 | 1 | 1 | 1 | 100 | 2d | 30 | 6 | 100 | 5.0 | 96 | RC | RC | RC | RC | 1 | 7 | 1 | 182 | 60 |
| Honduras | 086 | 4 | 19 | 2 | 3 | 1 | 3 | 3 | 3 | 2 | 42 | 4p | 19 | S | 26 | 3.0 | 51 | RC | RC | RC | RC | 6 | 4 | 60 | 20 | 1020 |
| Hong Kong | 087 | 2 | 03 | 2 | 3 | 4 | 3 | 3 | 3 | 2 | 90 | 3i | 25 | CE | 92 | 12.4 | 80 | S | S | S | S | 5 | 5 | 196 | 46 | 870 |
| Hungary | 088 | 3 | 09 | 1 | 2 | 5 | 2 | 2 | 2 | 3 | 25 | 2g | 15 | h | 47 | 7.0 | 91 | R | A | A | A | 8 | 1 | 25 | 2 | 6650 |
| Iceland | 089 | 3 | 10 | 1 | 1 | 2 | 1 | 1 | 1 | 1 | 100 | 1b | 6 | 5 | 72 | 10.8 | 96 | RL | RL | RL | RL | 2 | 5 | 15 | 69 | 394 |
| India | 090 | 7 | 04 | 2 | 3 | 2 | 3 | 3 | 3 | 2 | 83 | 1a | 1680 | HE | 20 | 3.8 | 43 | S | S | S | S | 5 | 2 | 306 | 0 | 69500 |
| Indonesia | 091 | 7 | 05 | 2 | 3 | 2 | 3 | 3 | 3 | 2 | 33 | 2e | 850 | X | 17 | 0.9 | 48 | RR | R | R | R | 3 | 2 | 240 | 2 | 22410 |
| Iran | 092 | 7 | 04 | 2 | 3 | 2 | 3 | 3 | 3 | 3 | 25 | 2e | 45 | N | 41 | 0.7 | 44 | RI | RI | RI | RI | 7 | 2 | 40 | 1 | 550 |
| Iraq | 093 | 7 | 06 | 2 | 3 | 3 | 3 | 3 | 3 | 3 | 0 | 2f | 22 | A | 47 | 1.3 | 39 | RI | RI | RI | RI | 8 | 1 | 21 | 2 | 690 |
| Ireland | 094 | 3 | 10 | 1 | 1 | 2 | 1 | 1 | 1 | 1 | 100 | 1b | 12 | iE | 47 | 13.0 | 93 | RC | RC | R | R | 5 | 6 | 34 | 11 | 2196 |
| Isle of Man | 095 | 3 | 10 | 1 | 1 | 4 | 1 | 1 | 1 | 1 | 100 | 3h | 5 | E | 57 | 4.0 | 94 | RA | RA | RA | RA | 3 | 6 | 21 | 362 | 114 |
| Israel | 096 | 7 | 06 | 2 | 1 | 2 | 3 | 3 | 3 | 1 | 75 | 1b | 27 | eA | 80 | 7.8 | 89 | R | RI | RJ | RJ | 6 | 4 | 65 | 19 | 280 |
| Italy | 097 | 3 | 08 | 1 | 1 | 2 | 1 | 1 | 1 | 1 | 92 | 1b | 120 | I | 53 | 9.2 | 92 | RC | RC | RC | RC | 3 | 7 | 225 | 4 | 30800 |
| Ivory Coast | 098 | 1 | 12 | 2 | 3 | 1 | 3 | 3 | 3 | 3 | 25 | 2e | 69 | F | 21 | 1.5 | 28 | S | S | S | S | 3 | 4 | 60 | 12 | 3070 |
| Jamaica | 099 | 4 | 21 | 2 | 3 | 4 | 3 | 3 | 3 | 1 | 75 | 1b | 15 | E | 38 | 0.2 | 84 | S | S | S | S | 3 | 5 | 135 | 66 | 4080 |
| Japan | 100 | 2 | 02 | 1 | 1 | 1 | 3 | 3 | 3 | 1 | 92 | 1b | 25 | J | 53 | 1.7 | 96 | RS | S | S | S | 5 | 3 | 192 | 2 | 13800 |
| Johnston Island | 101 | 6 | 24 | 2 | 3 | 1 | 3 | 3 | 3 | 2 | 100 | 3i | 2 | E | 100 | 5.0 | 90 | R | R | R | R | 2 | 1 | 2 | 2000 | 2 |
| Jordan | 102 | 7 | 06 | 2 | 3 | 1 | 3 | 3 | 3 | 3 | 17 | 5s | 9 | A | 47 | 2.0 | 47 | RI | RI | RI | RI | 4 | 3 | 26 | 13 | 301 |
| Kampuchea | 103 | 7 | 05 | 2 | 3 | 5 | 3 | 2 | 3 | 3 | 0 | 2g | 25 | k | 12 | 3.0 | 40 | RB | RB | A | A | 9 | 2 | 9 | 1 | 176 |
| Kenya | 104 | 1 | 13 | 2 | 3 | 2 | 3 | 3 | 3 | 2 | 33 | 2e | 68 | ES' | 10 | 0.4 | 39 | S | S | S | S | 4 | 4 | 246 | 19 | 18200 |
| Kiribati | 105 | 6 | 24 | 2 | 3 | 4 | 3 | 3 | 3 | 2 | 90 | 3h | 7 | E | 18 | 7.8 | 80 | S | S | S | S | 4 | 5 | 8 | 136 | 174 |
| Korea, North | 106 | 2 | 03 | 2 | 2 | 5 | 2 | 2 | 2 | 3 | 0 | 2g | 8 | K | 38 | 2.0 | 45 | RG | A | A | A | 10 | 1 | 7 | 0 | 2100 |
| Korea, South | 107 | 2 | 03 | 2 | 3 | 1 | 3 | 3 | 3 | 2 | 33 | 5u | 15 | K | 38 | 2.2 | 82 | RG | S | S | S | 6 | 3 | 173 | 5 | 16400 |
| Kuwait | 108 | 7 | 06 | 2 | 3 | 2 | 3 | 3 | 3 | 2 | 33 | 5s | 16 | A | 56 | 4.7 | 74 | RI | RI | RI | RI | 8 | 3 | 15 | 13 | 70 |
| Laos | 109 | 7 | 05 | 2 | 3 | 5 | 3 | 2 | 2 | 3 | 0 | 2g | 77 | l | 15 | 0.3 | 29 | RB | RB | A | A | 8 | 3 | 10 | 3 | 231 |
| Lebanon | 110 | 7 | 06 | 2 | 3 | 1 | 3 | 3 | 3 | 2 | 50 | 1b | 20 | A | 41 | 18.0 | 79 | RI | R | R | R | 4 | 5 | 48 | 17 | 1990 |
| Lesotho | 111 | 1 | 16 | 2 | 3 | 1 | 3 | 3 | 3 | 2 | 42 | 1b | 10 | wE | 4 | 0.3 | 48 | S | S | S | S | 6 | 4 | 293 | 255 | 1750 |
| Liberia | 112 | 1 | 12 | 2 | 3 | 1 | 3 | 3 | 3 | 2 | 33 | 4r | 39 | E | 10 | 0.6 | 26 | RX | RX | RX | RX | 4 | 4 | 130 | 76 | 2100 |
| Libya | 113 | 1 | 15 | 2 | 3 | 3 | 3 | 3 | 3 | 3 | 8 | 4q | 21 | A | 27 | 9.4 | 44 | RI | RI | RI | RI | 9 | 3 | 9 | 4 | 89 |
| Liechtenstein | 114 | 3 | 07 | 1 | 1 | 2 | 1 | 1 | 1 | 2 | 100 | 1b | 3 | G | 27 | 3.3 | 95 | RC | RC | RC | RC | 2 | 5 | 4 | 182 | 15 |
| Luxembourg | 115 | 3 | 07 | 1 | 1 | 4 | 1 | 1 | 1 | 1 | 100 | 1b | 15 | ëF | 64 | 3.2 | 95 | RC | RC | RC | RC | 2 | 6 | 27 | 79 | 330 |
| Macao | 116 | 2 | 03 | 2 | 3 | 4 | 3 | 3 | 3 | 2 | 70 | 3i | 9 | P | 100 | 81.0 | 60 | RC | RC | RC | RC | 7 | 4 | 19 | 70 | 32 |
| Madagascar | 117 | 1 | 13 | 2 | 3 | 3 | 3 | 3 | 2 | 2 | 33 | 2f | 15 | mF | 14 | 0.4 | 41 | R | R | R | A | 3 | 4 | 34 | 4 | 9490 |
| Malawi | 118 | 1 | 13 | 2 | 3 | 1 | 3 | 3 | 3 | 3 | 8 | 2e | 23 | *c'*E | 6 | 0.5 | 30 | S | S | S | S | 4 | 4 | 120 | 24 | 8160 |
| Malaysia | 119 | 7 | 05 | 2 | 3 | 2 | 3 | 3 | 3 | 2 | 58 | 1a | 182 | *m'*E | 41 | 9.1 | 62 | RI | RI | RI | RI | 8 | 3 | 50 | 4 | 1930 |

| Country | GEOPOLITICO-RELIGIOUS TYPOLOGIES: GEOGRAPHY | | | POLITICO-ECONOMIC SITUATION | | | | | | | | | Languages | | MODERN LIVING | | | RELIGIO-POLITICAL | | | | | Mission | CHURCHES: DENOMINATIONS | | |
|---|---|---|---|---|---|---|---|---|---|---|---|---|---|---|---|---|---|---|---|---|---|---|---|---|---|---|
| | No. | Cont | Region | Dev | Eco | Sys | 1970 | 1975 | 1980 | Free | Index | Rule | Total | Offic | Urban | Cinema | PQLI | 1900 | 1970 | 1975 | 1980 | Lib | Status | 1975 | pmill | Worship |
| | 1 | 2 | 3 | 4 | 5 | 6 | 7 | 8 | 9 | 10 | 11 | 12 | 13 | 14 | 15 | 16 | 17 | 18 | 19 | 20 | 21 | 22 | 23 | 24 | 25 | 26 |
| Maldives | 120 | 7 | 04 | 2 | 3 | 2 | 3 | 3 | 3 | 2 | 70 | 5t | 7 | 7 | 12 | 1.4 | 40 | RI | RI | RI | RI | 5 | 1 | 2 | 17 | 2 |
| Mali | 121 | 1 | 12 | 2 | 3 | 3 | 3 | 3 | 3 | 3 | 0 | 5v | 30 | F | 12 | 0.5 | 14 | R | S | S | S | 4 | 3 | 9 | 2 | 415 |
| Malta | 122 | 3 | 08 | 1 | 1 | 4 | 1 | 1 | 1 | 1 | 80 | 1b | 9 | ïE | 87 | 9.7 | 85 | RC | RC | RC | RC | 3 | 6 | 9 | 27 | 90 |
| Martinique | 123 | 4 | 21 | 2 | 3 | 2 | 3 | 3 | 3 | 1 | 90 | 3i | 10 | F | 50 | 6.0 | 80 | S | S | S | S | 5 | 5 | 9 | 25 | 116 |
| Mauritania | 124 | 1 | 12 | 2 | 3 | 2 | 3 | 3 | 3 | 3 | 17 | 2e | 14 | F | 7 | 0.2 | 14 | RI | RI | RI | RI | 5 | 2 | 2 | 2 | 8 |
| Mauritius | 125 | 1 | 13 | 2 | 3 | 2 | 3 | 3 | 3 | 1 | 90 | 1b | 13 | E | 42 | 18.9 | 80 | S | S | S | S | 2 | 4 | 16 | 18 | 126 |
| Mayotte | 126 | 1 | 13 | 2 | 3 | 2 | 3 | 3 | 3 | 1 | 80 | 3i | 8 | F | 3 | 0.3 | 80 | S | S | S | S | 5 | 1 | 2 | 46 | 4 |
| Mexico | 127 | 4 | 19 | 2 | 3 | 2 | 3 | 3 | 3 | 2 | 50 | 1a | 225 | S | 57 | 4.2 | 73 | S | S | S | S | 6 | 5 | 260 | 4 | 18400 |
| Midway Islands | 128 | 6 | 24 | 2 | 3 | 1 | 3 | 3 | 3 | 1 | 100 | 3i | 2 | E | 50 | 5.0 | 90 | R | R | R | R | 2 | 4 | 2 | 901 | 3 |
| Monaco | 129 | 3 | 07 | 1 | 1 | 2 | 1 | 1 | 1 | 2 | 95 | 1b | 15 | F | 100 | 4.0 | 94 | RC | RC | RC | RC | 2 | 4 | 4 | 160 | 8 |
| Mongolia | 130 | 2 | 03 | 2 | 2 | 5 | 2 | 2 | 2 | 3 | 0 | 2g | 23 | o | 37 | 2.0 | 45 | RB | A | A | A | 10 | 1 | 4 | 2 | 112 |
| Montserrat | 131 | 4 | 21 | 2 | 3 | 4 | 3 | 3 | 3 | 1 | 90 | 3h | 4 | E | 30 | 0.7 | 80 | S | S | S | S | 5 | 4 | 8 | 653 | 87 |
| Morocco | 132 | 1 | 15 | 2 | 3 | 2 | 3 | 3 | 3 | 2 | 58 | 5s | 16 | A | 33 | 1.8 | 40 | RI | RI | RI | RI | 9 | 3 | 29 | 2 | 725 |
| Mozambique | 133 | 1 | 13 | 2 | 3 | 3 | 3 | 3 | 2 | 3 | 0 | 2f | 40 | P | 6 | 0.4 | 24 | RC | RC | A | A | 8 | 4 | 138 | 15 | 4260 |
| Namibia | 134 | 1 | 16 | 2 | 3 | 1 | 3 | 3 | 3 | 2 | 25 | 3h | 20 | ME | 32 | 1.0 | 48 | R | R | R | R | 6 | 4 | 77 | 109 | 1510 |
| Nauru | 135 | 6 | 24 | 2 | 3 | 2 | 3 | 3 | 3 | 1 | 90 | 1b | 7 | E | 50 | 10.0 | 90 | R | R | R | R | 4 | 4 | 3 | 667 | 10 |
| Nepal | 136 | 7 | 04 | 2 | 3 | 2 | 3 | 3 | 3 | 3 | 25 | 5s | 78 | n | 5 | 0.5 | 25 | RH | RH | RH | RH | 8 | 2 | 12 | 1 | 77 |
| Netherlands | 137 | 3 | 07 | 1 | 1 | 4 | 1 | 1 | 1 | 1 | 100 | 1b | 31 | D | 81 | 2.1 | 96 | S | S | S | S | 3 | 7 | 235 | 17 | 8660 |
| Netherlands Antilles | 138 | 4 | 21 | 2 | 3 | 4 | 3 | 3 | 3 | 2 | 90 | 3h | 11 | D | 48 | 1.5 | 85 | S | S | S | S | 2 | 5 | 29 | 120 | 165 |
| New Caledonia | 139 | 6 | 23 | 2 | 3 | 2 | 3 | 3 | 3 | 2 | 90 | 3i | 31 | F | 41 | 5.1 | 80 | S | S | S | S | 4 | 5 | 8 | 64 | 147 |
| New Zealand | 140 | 6 | 22 | 1 | 1 | 1 | 1 | 1 | 1 | 1 | 100 | 1b | 28 | E | 79 | 3.8 | 94 | S | S | S | S | 3 | 5 | 90 | 30 | 6150 |
| Nicaragua | 141 | 4 | 19 | 2 | 3 | 1 | 3 | 3 | 3 | 2 | 33 | 4p | 19 | S | 42 | 5.0 | 53 | R | R | R | A | 6 | 4 | 81 | 35 | 1390 |
| Niger | 142 | 1 | 12 | 2 | 3 | 2 | 3 | 3 | 3 | 3 | 8 | 4r | 22 | F | 8 | 0.2 | 13 | R | S | S | S | 4 | 3 | 16 | 3 | 144 |
| Nigeria | 143 | 1 | 12 | 2 | 3 | 2 | 3 | 3 | 3 | 2 | 42 | 4p | 525 | E | 23 | 0.5 | 25 | S | S | S | S | 3 | 3 | 910 | 14 | 41000 |
| Niue Island | 144 | 6 | 24 | 2 | 3 | 1 | 3 | 3 | 3 | 1 | 90 | 3i | 4 | E | 50 | 1.2 | 90 | S | S | S | S | 3 | 4 | 6 | 1091 | 24 |
| Norfolk Island | 145 | 6 | 23 | 2 | 3 | 1 | 3 | 3 | 3 | 2 | 90 | 3i | 3 | E | 50 | 0.0 | 80 | S | S | S | S | 5 | 4 | 4 | 2353 | 4 |
| Northern Solomons | 146 | 6 | 23 | 2 | 3 | 2 | 3 | 3 | 3 | 2 | 80 | 3m | 26 | E | 10 | 1.0 | 50 | S | S | S | S | 3 | 4 | 8 | 56 | 170 |
| Norway | 147 | 3 | 10 | 1 | 1 | 4 | 1 | 1 | 1 | 1 | 100 | 1b | 15 | j | 43 | 4.6 | 96 | RL | RL | RL | RL | 2 | 7 | 43 | 11 | 4260 |
| Oman | 148 | 7 | 06 | 2 | 3 | 2 | 3 | 3 | 3 | 3 | 20 | 5s | 25 | A | 5 | 1.0 | 30 | RI | RI | RI | RI | 6 | 2 | 11 | 6 | 28 |
| Pacific Islands | 149 | 6 | 24 | 2 | 3 | 1 | 3 | 3 | 3 | 1 | 100 | 3h | 18 | E | 20 | 1.0 | 80 | S | S | S | S | 5 | 4 | 19 | 162 | 340 |
| Pakistan | 150 | 7 | 04 | 2 | 3 | 2 | 3 | 3 | 3 | 2 | 33 | 2f | 50 | UE | 23 | 0.3 | 38 | S | RI | RI | RI | 4 | 2 | 53 | 1 | 3590 |
| Palestine | 151 | 7 | 06 | 2 | 3 | 3 | 3 | 3 | 3 | 3 | 30 | 3l | 18 | A | 60 | 3.0 | 60 | RI | S | S | S | 6 | 5 | 64 | 46 | 350 |
| Panama | 152 | 4 | 19 | 2 | 3 | 1 | 3 | 3 | 3 | 3 | 25 | 4p | 19 | S | 47 | 4.8 | 80 | RC | RC | RC | RC | 7 | 5 | 52 | 31 | 1030 |
| Panama Canal Zone | 153 | 4 | 19 | 2 | 3 | 1 | 3 | 3 | 3 | 2 | 80 | 3i | 9 | E | 80 | 6.5 | 90 | S | S | S | S | 5 | 4 | 29 | 604 | 115 |
| Papua New Guinea | 154 | 6 | 23 | 2 | 3 | 2 | 3 | 3 | 3 | 2 | 83 | 1b | 960 | pE | 6 | 1.0 | 35 | S | S | S | S | 3 | 4 | 105 | 25 | 8250 |
| Paraguay | 155 | 4 | 18 | 2 | 3 | 1 | 3 | 3 | 3 | 2 | 25 | 5u | 31 | *Sg'* | 39 | 1.0 | 73 | RC | RC | RC | RC | 2 | 5 | 47 | 18 | 8010 |
| Peru | 156 | 4 | 18 | 2 | 3 | 2 | 3 | 3 | 3 | 2 | 33 | 4q | 188 | Sq | 51 | 3.0 | 59 | RC | RC | RC | RC | 2 | 4 | 100 | 6 | 5230 |
| Philippines | 157 | 7 | 05 | 2 | 3 | 1 | 3 | 3 | 3 | 2 | 33 | 4o | 160 | OES | 34 | 7.6 | 71 | R | R | R | R | 3 | 4 | 460 | 10 | 26300 |
| Pitcairn Islands | 158 | 6 | 24 | 2 | 3 | 4 | 3 | 3 | 3 | 1 | 90 | 3i | 2 | E | 50 | 2.0 | 85 | RD | RD | RD | RD | 3 | 1 | 1 | 11111 | 1 |
| Poland | 159 | 3 | 09 | 1 | 2 | 5 | 2 | 2 | 2 | 3 | 25 | 2g | 20 | Y | 51 | 4.1 | 91 | R | A | A | A | 8 | 2 | 48 | 1 | 9180 |
| Portugal | 160 | 3 | 08 | 1 | 1 | 4 | 1 | 1 | 1 | 2 | 83 | 1b | 18 | P | 37 | 4.1 | 78 | RC | RC | RC | RC | 3 | 6 | 40 | 5 | 5100 |
| Puerto Rico | 161 | 4 | 21 | 2 | 3 | 1 | 3 | 3 | 3 | 1 | 95 | 3h | 8 | SE | 48 | 2.2 | 90 | S | S | S | S | 3 | 5 | 95 | 33 | 2410 |
| Qatar | 162 | 7 | 06 | 2 | 3 | 2 | 3 | 3 | 3 | 3 | 33 | 5s | 12 | A | 69 | 0.8 | 31 | RI | RI | RI | RI | 8 | 2 | 24 | 103 | 20 |
| Reunion | 163 | 1 | 13 | 2 | 3 | 2 | 3 | 3 | 3 | 2 | 90 | 3i | 9 | F | 27 | 2.1 | 80 | S | S | S | S | 5 | 4 | 7 | 14 | 112 |
| Romania | 164 | 3 | 09 | 1 | 2 | 5 | 2 | 2 | 2 | 3 | 8 | 2g | 21 | *R'* | 42 | 8.7 | 90 | RO | A | A | A | 8 | 1 | 35 | 2 | 18250 |
| Rwanda | 165 | 1 | 13 | 2 | 3 | 2 | 3 | 3 | 3 | 3 | 17 | 4p | 10 | *Fr'* | 3 | 0.0 | 25 | RT | R | R | R | 4 | 4 | 14 | 3 | 2620 |
| Sahara | 166 | 1 | 15 | 2 | 3 | 2 | 3 | 3 | 3 | 3 | 10 | 3n | 8 | A | 32 | 6.6 | 15 | R | S | S | S | 3 | 4 | 1 | 10 | 6 |
| St Helena | 167 | 1 | 12 | 2 | 3 | 4 | 3 | 3 | 3 | 1 | 90 | 3i | 2 | E | 30 | 0.6 | 80 | RA | RA | RA | RA | 3 | 4 | 9 | 1345 | 24 |
| St Kitts-Nevis | 168 | 4 | 21 | 2 | 3 | 4 | 3 | 3 | 3 | 1 | 90 | 1c | 4 | F | 28 | 1.1 | 80 | S | S | S | S | 4 | 4 | 36 | 602 | 220 |
| St Lucia | 169 | 4 | 21 | 2 | 3 | 4 | 3 | 3 | 3 | 1 | 90 | 1c | 5 | E | 60 | 2.0 | 80 | S | S | S | S | 2 | 4 | 21 | 194 | 105 |
| St Pierre & Miquelon | 170 | 5 | 17 | 1 | 3 | 2 | 1 | 1 | 1 | 1 | 90 | 3i | 3 | F | 80 | 3.3 | 80 | S | S | S | S | 5 | 4 | 1 | 182 | 2 |
| St Vincent | 171 | 4 | 21 | 2 | 3 | 4 | 3 | 3 | 3 | 1 | 90 | 1c | 11 | E | 35 | 1.0 | 80 | S | S | S | S | 4 | 4 | 20 | 214 | 160 |
| Samoa | 172 | 6 | 24 | 2 | 3 | 2 | 3 | 3 | 3 | 2 | 90 | 1b | 8 | 8E | 24 | 1.9 | 80 | RX | RX | RX | RX | 4 | 5 | 18 | 110 | 665 |
| San Marino | 173 | 3 | 08 | 1 | 1 | 2 | 1 | 1 | 1 | 1 | 90 | 1b | 2 | I | 92 | 10.5 | 90 | S | S | S | S | 3 | 4 | 2 | 100 | 13 |
| Sao Tome & Principe | 174 | 1 | 14 | 2 | 3 | 3 | 3 | 3 | 2 | 2 | 30 | 2f | 4 | P | 21 | 1.3 | 20 | RC | RC | RC | A | 3 | 4 | 3 | 37 | 31 |
| Saudi Arabia | 175 | 7 | 06 | 2 | 3 | 2 | 3 | 3 | 3 | 3 | 17 | 5s | 40 | A | 24 | 0.5 | 28 | RI | RI | RI | RI | 9 | 1 | 20 | 2 | 320 |
| Senegal | 176 | 1 | 12 | 2 | 3 | 2 | 3 | 3 | 3 | 2 | 50 | 2e | 23 | F | 26 | 0.7 | 24 | S | S | S | S | 4 | 4 | 18 | 4 | 115 |
| Seychelles | 177 | 1 | 13 | 2 | 3 | 3 | 3 | 3 | 3 | 1 | 70 | 1b | 10 | EF | 30 | 8.6 | 80 | S | S | S | S | 4 | 4 | 6 | 102 | 33 |
| Sierra Leone | 178 | 1 | 12 | 2 | 3 | 2 | 3 | 3 | 3 | 2 | 33 | 2e | 17 | E | 14 | 0.1 | 27 | S | S | S | S | 4 | 4 | 40 | 13 | 1770 |
| Sikkim | 179 | 7 | 04 | 2 | 3 | 2 | 3 | 3 | 3 | 3 | 60 | 3n | 20 | E | 6 | 1.0 | 40 | RB | RB | RB | RB | 8 | 3 | 16 | 64 | 45 |
| Singapore | 180 | 7 | 05 | 2 | 3 | 2 | 3 | 3 | 3 | 2 | 33 | 1b | 25 | *m'*CE | 81 | 18.7 | 83 | S | S | S | S | 5 | 4 | 64 | 28 | 280 |
| Solomon Islands | 181 | 6 | 23 | 2 | 3 | 2 | 3 | 3 | 3 | 1 | 83 | 1b | 93 | E | 7 | 0.6 | 40 | S | S | S | S | 4 | 5 | 16 | 69 | 1400 |
| Somalia | 182 | 1 | 13 | 2 | 3 | 3 | 3 | 3 | 3 | 3 | 0 | 2f | 18 | vA | 20 | 1.7 | 19 | RI | RI | RI | RI | 8 | 3 | 5 | 2 | 33 |
| South Africa | 183 | 1 | 16 | 2 | 1 | 1 | 3 | 3 | 3 | 2 | 25 | 1b | 45 | ME | 51 | 5.0 | 48 | R | R | R | R | 6 | 5 | 3350 | 136 | 59500 |
| Spain | 184 | 3 | 08 | 1 | 1 | 1 | 1 | 1 | 1 | 2 | 83 | 1b | 18 | S | 61 | 7.0 | 91 | RC | RC | RC | RC | 2 | 6 | 148 | 4 | 22370 |
| Spanish North Africa | 185 | 1 | 15 | 2 | 3 | 1 | 3 | 3 | 3 | 2 | 80 | 3i | 5 | S | 85 | 5.0 | 80 | RC | RC | RC | RC | 2 | 4 | 5 | 29 | 18 |
| Sri Lanka | 186 | 7 | 04 | 2 | 3 | 2 | 3 | 3 | 3 | 2 | 83 | 1b | 12 | u | 20 | 4.0 | 82 | RB | RB | RB | RB | 6 | 2 | 37 | 3 | 1180 |
| Sudan | 187 | 1 | 15 | 2 | 3 | 2 | 3 | 3 | 3 | 3 | 25 | 2e | 145 | A | 10 | 0.7 | 35 | RI | RI | RI | RI | 8 | 2 | 21 | 1 | 1040 |
| Surinam | 188 | 4 | 18 | 2 | 3 | 4 | 3 | 3 | 3 | 1 | 83 | 1b | 19 | D | 38 | 5.0 | 83 | S | S | S | S | 2 | 4 | 25 | 59 | 270 |
| Svalbard & Jan Mayen Is | 189 | 3 | 10 | 1 | 1 | 4 | 1 | 1 | 1 | 2 | 90 | 3i | 3 | j | 90 | 5.0 | 90 | RL | RL | RL | RL | 2 | 4 | 1 | 286 | 1 |
| Swaziland | 190 | 1 | 16 | 2 | 3 | 1 | 3 | 3 | 3 | 2 | 33 | 5s | 12 | öE | 5 | 0.6 | 35 | RT | R | R | R | 4 | 5 | 87 | 186 | 1210 |
| Sweden | 191 | 3 | 10 | 1 | 1 | 2 | 1 | 1 | 1 | 1 | 100 | 1b | 28 | s | 80 | 3.1 | 97 | RL | RL | RL | RL | 2 | 6 | 107 | 13 | 11050 |
| Switzerland | 192 | 3 | 07 | 1 | 1 | 1 | 1 | 1 | 1 | 1 | 100 | 1a | 30 | GFI | 58 | 3.6 | 95 | R | R | R | R | 2 | 7 | 145 | 22 | 5620 |
| Syria | 193 | 7 | 06 | 2 | 3 | 3 | 3 | 3 | 3 | 3 | 25 | 2f | 16 | A | 44 | 5.5 | 54 | RI | RI | S | S | 7 | 2 | 27 | 4 | 780 |
| Tanzania | 194 | 1 | 13 | 2 | 3 | 3 | 3 | 3 | 3 | 3 | 17 | 2f | 130 | *S'*E | 6 | 0.2 | 27 | S | S | S | S | 5 | 4 | 77 | 5 | 9100 |
| Thailand | 195 | 7 | 05 | 2 | 3 | 1 | 3 | 3 | 3 | 1 | 25 | 4r | 48 | Z | 15 | 1.7 | 68 | RB | RB | RB | RB | 3 | 2 | 42 | 1 | 3180 |
| Timor | 196 | 7 | 05 | 2 | 3 | 2 | 3 | 3 | 3 | 3 | 20 | 3n | 19 | X | 11 | 0.3 | 30 | RC | RC | RC | RC | 3 | 4 | 5 | 7 | 70 |
| Togo | 197 | 1 | 12 | 2 | 3 | 2 | 3 | 3 | 3 | 3 | 8 | 5v | 48 | F | 13 | 0.2 | 25 | S | S | S | S | 7 | 4 | 42 | 19 | 765 |
| Tokelau | 198 | 6 | 24 | 2 | 3 | 1 | 3 | 3 | 3 | 1 | 90 | 3i | 4 | E | 60 | 2.0 | 90 | S | S | S | S | 3 | 4 | 2 | 1212 | 7 |
| Tonga | 199 | 6 | 24 | 2 | 3 | 2 | 3 | 3 | 3 | 2 | 90 | 1b | 7 | 9 | 22 | 1.0 | 80 | RM | RM | RM | RM | 2 | 5 | 13 | 129 | 680 |
| Trinidad & Tobago | 200 | 4 | 21 | 2 | 3 | 2 | 3 | 3 | 3 | 1 | 90 | 1b | 13 | E | 50 | 7.0 | 80 | R | R | R | R | 2 | 5 | 69 | 68 | 1120 |
| Tunisia | 201 | 1 | 15 | 2 | 3 | 2 | 3 | 3 | 3 | 3 | 25 | 2e | 10 | A | 44 | 2.3 | 47 | RI | RI | RI | RI | 5 | 3 | 15 | 3 | 212 |
| Turkey | 202 | 7 | 06 | 2 | 3 | 2 | 3 | 3 | 3 | 1 | 75 | 4p | 36 | T | 37 | 6.7 | 55 | RI | S | S | S | 8 | 2 | 34 | 1 | 610 |
| Turks & Caicos Islands | 203 | 4 | 21 | 2 | 3 | 4 | 3 | 3 | 3 | 1 | 90 | 3i | 3 | E | 60 | 3.8 | 80 | S | S | S | S | 5 | 4 | 14 | 1978 | 45 |
| Tuvalu | 204 | 6 | 24 | 2 | 3 | 4 | 3 | 3 | 3 | 2 | 90 | 1b | 6 | E | 10 | 3.5 | 80 | S | S | S | S | 4 | 4 | 3 | 422 | 16 |
| Uganda | 205 | 1 | 13 | 2 | 3 | 3 | 3 | 3 | 3 | 3 | 0 | 5v | 65 | E | 10 | 0.1 | 34 | S | S | S | S | 7 | 4 | 61 | 5 | 8860 |
| USSR | 206 | 8 | 11 | 1 | 2 | 5 | 2 | 2 | 2 | 3 | 8 | 2g | 150 | R | 57 | 17.7 | 91 | RO | A | A | A | 9 | 1 | 146 | 1 | 78200 |
| United Arab Emirates | 207 | 7 | 06 | 2 | 3 | 2 | 3 | 3 | 3 | 3 | 33 | 5s | 19 | A | 52 | 1.0 | 33 | RI | RI | RI | RI | 6 | 4 | 19 | 53 | 45 |
| UK of GB & NI | 208 | 3 | 10 | 1 | 1 | 4 | 1 | 1 | 1 | 1 | 100 | 1b | 60 | E | 81 | 1.9 | 94 | RA | RA | RA | RA | 3 | 7 | 500 | 9 | 63200 |
| USA | 209 | 5 | 17 | 1 | 1 | 1 | 1 | 1 | 1 | 1 | 100 | 1a | 280 | E | 74 | 2.0 | 94 | S | S | S | S | 4 | 6 | 1860 | 9 | 362200 |
| US Virgin Islands | 210 | 4 | 21 | 2 | 3 | 1 | 3 | 3 | 3 | 1 | 90 | 3h | 8 | E | 56 | 7.0 | 80 | S | S | S | S | 4 | 4 | 37 | 561 | 186 |
| Upper Volta | 211 | 1 | 12 | 2 | 3 | 2 | 3 | 3 | 3 | 2 | 42 | 4p | 50 | F | 4 | 0.2 | 16 | RT | S | S | S | 5 | 4 | 20 | 3 | 1270 |
| Uruguay | 212 | 4 | 20 | 1 | 3 | 2 | 3 | 3 | 3 | 2 | 17 | 4r | 25 | S | 78 | 5.0 | 87 | R | S | S | S | 3 | 5 | 58 | 19 | 1040 |
| Vanuatu | 213 | 6 | 23 | 2 | 3 | 2 | 3 | 3 | 3 | 2 | 90 | 1b | 120 | 1FE | 12 | 1.0 | 60 | S | S | S | RX | 3 | 4 | 16 | 167 | 510 |
| Venezuela | 214 | 4 | 18 | 2 | 3 | 4 | 3 | 3 | 3 | 1 | 92 | 1b | 105 | S | 68 | 3.4 | 79 | RC | RC | RC | RC | 2 | 5 | 93 | 8 | 3240 |
| Viet Nam | 215 | 7 | 05 | 2 | 2 | 5 | 2 | 2 | 2 | 3 | 10 | 2g | 69 | V | 21 | 3.0 | 45 | S | S | S | A | 8 | 2 | 42 | 1 | 3420 |
| Wake Island | 216 | 6 | 24 | 2 | 3 | 1 | 3 | 3 | 3 | 2 | 100 | 3i | 2 | E | 90 | 5.0 | 90 | R | R | R | R | 2 | 4 | 2 | 1250 | 4 |
| Wallis & Futuna Islands | 217 | 6 | 24 | 2 | 3 | 2 | 3 | 3 | 3 | 2 | 90 | 3i | 4 | F | 40 | 2.0 | 80 | S | S | S | S | 4 | 5 | 1 | 111 | 5 |
| Yemen, North | 218 | 7 | 06 | 2 | 3 | 2 | 3 | 3 | 3 | 3 | 25 | 4r | 12 | A | 6 | 0.5 | 27 | RI | RI | RI | RI | 8 | 2 | 5 | 1 | 36 |
| Yemen, South | 219 | 7 | 06 | 2 | 3 | 3 | 3 | 3 | 2 | 3 | 0 | 2f | 21 | A | 29 | 2.4 | 27 | S | A | A | A | 8 | 3 | 9 | 5 | 21 |
| Yugoslavia | 220 | 3 | 08 | 1 | 1 | 5 | 2 | 2 | 2 | 3 | 25 | 2g | 26 | Q*M'W'* | 37 | 3.8 | 84 | R | A | A | A | 6 | 2 | 70 | 3 | 7640 |
| Zaire | 221 | 1 | 14 | 2 | 3 | 2 | 3 | 3 | 3 | 3 | 8 | 2e | 470 | F | 16 | 0.1 | 28 | RC | R | R | R | 6 | 4 | 540 | 22 | 33100 |
| Zambia | 222 | 1 | 13 | 2 | 3 | 3 | 3 | 3 | 3 | 2 | 33 | 2e | 50 | E | 24 | 0.4 | 30 | S | S | S | S | 6 | 4 | 127 | 25 | 6620 |
| Zimbabwe | 223 | 1 | 13 | 2 | 3 | 1 | 3 | 3 | 2 | 3 | 25 | 1b | 35 | E | 20 | 0.5 | 43 | R | R | R | A | 6 | 4 | 206 | 33 | 8940 |
| Column | 1 | 2 | 3 | 4 | 5 | 6 | 7 | 8 | 9 | 10 | 11 | 12 | 13 | 14 | 15 | 16 | 17 | 18 | 19 | 20 | 21 | 22 | 23 | 24 | 25 | 26 |
| *Continent* | | | | | | | | | | | | | | | | | | | | | | | | | | |
| Africa | 6925 | 59 | 793 | 118 | 175 | 134 | 177 | 177 | 167 | 140 | 1788 | — | 3052 | — | 1157 | 102.3 | 2095 | — | — | — | — | 311 | 210 | 7768 | — | 282418 |
| East Asia | 727 | 16 | 19 | 15 | 19 | 26 | 21 | 21 | 21 | 19 | 344 | — | 327 | — | 446 | 133.3 | 551 | — | — | — | — | 58 | 22 | 740 | — | 88914 |
| Europe | 3837 | 111 | 315 | 37 | 44 | 126 | 45 | 45 | 45 | 60 | 2850 | — | 759 | — | 2293 | 217.3 | 3393 | — | — | — | — | 135 | 174 | 2689 | — | 351049 |
| Latin America | 4487 | 188 | 934 | 89 | 141 | 122 | 140 | 140 | 138 | 74 | 3214 | — | 1626 | — | 2149 | 212.7 | 3536 | — | — | — | — | 206 | 199 | 3263 | — | 130673 |
| Northern America | 506 | 25 | 85 | 5 | 11 | 12 | 7 | 7 | 7 | 5 | 470 | — | 383 | — | 250 | 24.0 | 449 | — | — | — | — | 17 | 25 | 2240 | — | 389343 |
| Oceania | 3632 | 174 | 686 | 56 | 83 | 52 | 83 | 83 | 83 | 47 | 2646 | — | 1702 | — | 947 | 96.4 | 2257 | — | — | — | — | 103 | 113 | 653 | — | 40440 |
| South Asia | 4656 | 259 | 191 | 74 | 108 | 84 | 110 | 108 | 106 | 92 | 1281 | — | 3925 | — | 1160 | 157.0 | 1743 | — | — | — | — | 239 | 98 | 1915 | — | 145323 |
| USSR | 206 | 8 | 11 | 1 | 2 | 5 | 2 | 2 | 2 | 3 | 8 | — | 150 | — | 57 | 17.7 | 91 | — | — | — | — | 9 | 1 | 146 | — | 78200 |
| **WORLD** | **24976** | **840** | **3034** | **395** | **583** | **561** | **585** | **583** | **569** | **440** | **12601** | — | **11924** | — | **8459** | **960.8** | **14115** | — | — | — | — | **1078** | **842** | **19414** | — | **1506360** |

| | | CHRISTIAN ORGANIZATIONS | | | | CHRISTIAN PERSONNEL | | | | INTERNATIONAL SHARING OF PERSONNEL | | | | | | | |
|---|---|---|---|---|---|---|---|---|---|---|---|---|---|---|---|---|---|
| | | INSTITUTIONS | | SERVICE AGENCIES | | NATIONALS & ALIENS | | Nationals only | | NATIONALS SENT ABROAD | | | | | | | |
| | pmillion | Total | pmillion | Total | pmillion | Total | Pop/pw | Total | pmillion | Total | Anglican | NWInd | CathNR | Marginal | Orthodox | Protest | RC |
| | 27 | 28 | 29 | 30 | 31 | 32 | 33 | 34 | 35 | 36 | 37 | 38 | 39 | 40 | 41 | 42 | 43 |
| Afghanistan | 1 | 0 | 0 | 12 | 1 | 88 | 192932 | 0 | 0 | 0 | 0 | 0 | 0 | 0 | 0 | 0 | 0 |
| Albania | 461 | 0 | 0 | 0 | 0 | 30 | 72300 | 30 | 14 | 0 | 0 | 0 | 0 | 0 | 0 | 0 | 0 |
| Algeria | 20 | 113 | 8 | 26 | 2 | 1816 | 7890 | 68 | 5 | 50 | 0 | 0 | 0 | 0 | 0 | 0 | 50 |
| American Samoa | 4815 | 3 | 111 | 5 | 185 | 145 | 186 | 75 | 2778 | 0 | 0 | 0 | 0 | 0 | 0 | 0 | 0 |
| Andorra | 526 | 1 | 53 | 2 | 105 | 8 | 2375 | 6 | 421 | 0 | 0 | 0 | 0 | 0 | 0 | 0 | 0 |
| Angola | 370 | 290 | 51 | 20 | 4 | 14036 | 404 | 12629 | 2227 | 100 | 0 | 4 | 0 | 0 | 0 | 42 | 54 |
| Anguilla | 2282 | 0 | 0 | 2 | 326 | 10 | 610 | 8 | 978 | 0 | 0 | 0 | 0 | 0 | 0 | 0 | 0 |
| Antigua | 2429 | 6 | 86 | 9 | 129 | 81 | 864 | 50 | 714 | 0 | 0 | 0 | 0 | 0 | 0 | 0 | 0 |
| Argentina | 326 | 1170 | 49 | 140 | 6 | 21824 | 1088 | 13000 | 547 | 991 | 0 | 6 | 5 | 20 | 0 | 45 | 915 |
| Australia | 1506 | 885 | 71 | 190 | 15 | 35270 | 356 | 32425 | 2583 | 3975 | 444 | 0 | 0 | 30 | 0 | 2157 | 1344 |
| Austria | 584 | 230 | 31 | 195 | 26 | 22267 | 334 | 21500 | 2887 | 1856 | 0 | 0 | 2 | 5 | 0 | 25 | 1824 |
| Bahamas | 4972 | 25 | 141 | 22 | 124 | 433 | 409 | 210 | 1186 | 0 | 0 | 0 | 0 | 0 | 0 | 0 | 0 |
| Bahrain | 195 | 3 | 14 | 0 | 0 | 37 | 5811 | 0 | 0 | 0 | 0 | 0 | 0 | 0 | 0 | 0 | 0 |
| Bangladesh | 17 | 182 | 3 | 40 | 1 | 1759 | 38483 | 1181 | 17 | 0 | 0 | 0 | 0 | 0 | 0 | 0 | 0 |
| Barbados | 1674 | 18 | 75 | 25 | 105 | 431 | 554 | 260 | 1088 | 6 | 2 | 2 | 0 | 0 | 0 | 0 | 2 |
| Belgium | 492 | 2210 | 229 | 330 | 34 | 53078 | 182 | 51800 | 5375 | 9340 | 0 | 0 | 0 | 0 | 0 | 40 | 9300 |
| Belize | 2833 | 27 | 225 | 13 | 108 | 520 | 231 | 296 | 2467 | 0 | 0 | 0 | 0 | 0 | 0 | 0 | 0 |
| Benin | 337 | 55 | 20 | 35 | 13 | 1382 | 1944 | 890 | 331 | 34 | 0 | 8 | 0 | 0 | 0 | 6 | 20 |
| Bermuda | 2692 | 2 | 38 | 6 | 115 | 141 | 369 | 100 | 1923 | 2 | 0 | 0 | 0 | 0 | 0 | 2 | 0 |
| Bhutan | 19 | 3 | 3 | 6 | 6 | 33 | 31667 | 0 | 0 | 0 | 0 | 0 | 0 | 0 | 0 | 0 | 0 |
| Bolivia | 421 | 300 | 63 | 90 | 19 | 4224 | 1132 | 1500 | 314 | 1610 | 0 | 0 | 0 | 0 | 0 | 0 | 1601 |
| Botswana | 1410 | 50 | 81 | 25 | 41 | 366 | 1686 | 129 | 209 | 15 | 0 | 5 | 0 | 0 | 0 | 10 | 0 |
| Brazil | 499 | 2590 | 27 | 250 | 3 | 78472 | 1213 | 63000 | 662 | 2456 | 2 | 25 | 5 | 10 | 0 | 140 | 2274 |
| British Antarctic Terr | 0 | 0 | 0 | 0 | 0 | 0 | 0 | 0 | 0 | 0 | 0 | 0 | 0 | 0 | 0 | 0 | 0 |
| British Indian Ocean Terr | 1000 | 0 | 0 | 0 | 0 | 0 | 0 | 0 | 0 | 0 | 0 | 0 | 0 | 0 | 0 | 0 | 0 |
| British Virgin Is | 3000 | 0 | 0 | 3 | 300 | 17 | 588 | 10 | 1000 | 0 | 0 | 0 | 0 | 0 | 0 | 0 | 0 |
| Brunei | 128 | 3 | 22 | 0 | 0 | 21 | 6333 | 10 | 75 | 0 | 0 | 0 | 0 | 0 | 0 | 0 | 0 |
| Bulgaria | 508 | 130 | 15 | 10 | 1 | 2604 | 3260 | 2600 | 306 | 35 | 0 | 0 | 0 | 0 | 35 | 0 | 0 |
| Burma | 179 | 41 | 1 | 20 | 1 | 4804 | 5776 | 4725 | 170 | 55 | 0 | 0 | 0 | 0 | 0 | 30 | 25 |
| Burundi | 600 | 140 | 42 | 40 | 12 | 5957 | 562 | 5139 | 1534 | 30 | 0 | 0 | 0 | 0 | 0 | 0 | 30 |
| Cameroon | 1324 | 290 | 50 | 57 | 10 | 11714 | 498 | 9813 | 1681 | 177 | 0 | 0 | 0 | 0 | 0 | 15 | 162 |
| Canada | 1257 | 750 | 35 | 350 | 16 | 84607 | 253 | 79580 | 3718 | 10173 | 27 | 0 | 30 | 140 | 0 | 2726 | 7250 |
| Canton & Enderbury | 5000 | 0 | 0 | 0 | 0 | 0 | 0 | 0 | 0 | 0 | 0 | 0 | 0 | 0 | 0 | 0 | 0 |
| Cape Verde | 354 | 7 | 26 | 8 | 30 | 128 | 2094 | 100 | 373 | 4 | 0 | 0 | 0 | 0 | 0 | 0 | 4 |
| Cayman Islands | 4091 | 1 | 91 | 0 | 0 | 39 | 282 | 25 | 2273 | 0 | 0 | 0 | 0 | 0 | 0 | 0 | 0 |
| Central African Republic | 1191 | 90 | 56 | 28 | 17 | 3029 | 532 | 2286 | 1418 | 3 | 0 | 0 | 0 | 0 | 0 | 0 | 3 |
| Chad | 371 | 55 | 15 | 26 | 7 | 4031 | 903 | 3490 | 959 | 2 | 0 | 0 | 0 | 0 | 0 | 0 | 2 |
| Channel Islands | 943 | 4 | 33 | 12 | 98 | 48 | 2542 | 40 | 328 | 10 | 10 | 0 | 0 | 0 | 0 | 0 | 0 |
| Chile | 742 | 820 | 88 | 95 | 10 | 10634 | 881 | 5100 | 544 | 649 | 0 | 53 | 0 | 14 | 0 | 32 | 550 |
| China | 68 | 1 | 0 | 0 | 0 | 1100 | 688914 | 1100 | 1 | 0 | 0 | 0 | 0 | 0 | 0 | 0 | 0 |
| China (Taiwan) | 228 | 275 | 20 | 90 | 6 | 5742 | 2444 | 3385 | 277 | 203 | 0 | 73 | 0 | 0 | 0 | 70 | 60 |
| Christmas Island | 1515 | 0 | 0 | 0 | 0 | 0 | 0 | 0 | 0 | 0 | 0 | 0 | 0 | 0 | 0 | 0 | 0 |
| Cocos Islands | 2857 | 0 | 0 | 0 | 0 | 0 | 0 | 0 | 0 | 0 | 0 | 0 | 0 | 0 | 0 | 0 | 0 |
| Colombia | 254 | 2090 | 95 | 140 | 6 | 29288 | 754 | 25000 | 1133 | 1497 | 0 | 20 | 0 | 0 | 0 | 25 | 1452 |
| Comoros | 43 | 2 | 9 | 8 | 34 | 7 | 33214 | 0 | 0 | 0 | 0 | 0 | 0 | 0 | 0 | 0 | 0 |
| Congo | 638 | 50 | 42 | 13 | 11 | 6166 | 193 | 5700 | 4786 | 8 | 0 | 2 | 0 | 0 | 0 | 0 | 6 |
| Cook Islands | 6429 | 2 | 95 | 0 | 0 | 79 | 266 | 30 | 1429 | 3 | 0 | 0 | 0 | 0 | 0 | 3 | 0 |
| Costa Rica | 443 | 65 | 37 | 76 | 44 | 2244 | 774 | 1240 | 714 | 197 | 0 | 0 | 0 | 0 | 0 | 7 | 190 |
| Cuba | 253 | 13 | 2 | 20 | 2 | 872 | 9822 | 650 | 76 | 5 | 0 | 5 | 0 | 0 | 0 | 0 | 0 |
| Cyprus | 1003 | 22 | 35 | 10 | 16 | 1089 | 581 | 970 | 1532 | 77 | 0 | 0 | 0 | 0 | 77 | 0 | 0 |
| Czechoslovakia | 616 | 14 | 1 | 20 | 1 | 12460 | 1151 | 12450 | 868 | 13 | 0 | 0 | 0 | 0 | 1 | 0 | 12 |
| Denmark | 684 | 100 | 20 | 90 | 18 | 3340 | 1476 | 2450 | 497 | 366 | 0 | 0 | 0 | 20 | 0 | 330 | 16 |
| Djibouti | 95 | 2 | 21 | 0 | 0 | 118 | 805 | 55 | 579 | 0 | 0 | 0 | 0 | 0 | 0 | 0 | 0 |
| Dominica | 1197 | 4 | 56 | 14 | 197 | 207 | 340 | 140 | 2000 | 0 | 0 | 0 | 0 | 0 | 0 | 0 | 0 |
| Dominican Republic | 417 | 180 | 41 | 40 | 9 | 2498 | 1739 | 750 | 173 | 60 | 0 | 0 | 0 | 0 | 0 | 0 | 60 |
| Ecuador | 269 | 330 | 55 | 58 | 10 | 6921 | 871 | 5010 | 831 | 150 | 0 | 10 | 0 | 0 | 0 | 20 | 120 |
| Egypt | 111 | 200 | 6 | 60 | 2 | 5303 | 6285 | 4100 | 123 | 200 | 0 | 0 | 0 | 0 | 113 | 12 | 75 |
| El Salvador | 410 | 70 | 20 | 39 | 11 | 2062 | 1705 | 970 | 276 | 80 | 0 | 0 | 0 | 0 | 0 | 0 | 80 |
| Equatorial Guinea | 1649 | 60 | 211 | 4 | 14 | 455 | 626 | 415 | 1456 | 10 | 0 | 0 | 0 | 0 | 0 | 0 | 10 |
| Ethiopia | 803 | 2610 | 105 | 69 | 3 | 161130 | 154 | 159397 | 6413 | 54 | 0 | 0 | 0 | 0 | 54 | 0 | 0 |
| Faeroe Islands | 2282 | 0 | 0 | 4 | 103 | 46 | 848 | 24 | 615 | 4 | 0 | 0 | 0 | 0 | 0 | 4 | 0 |
| Falkland Islands | 9183 | 0 | 0 | 0 | 0 | 8 | 245 | 2 | 1020 | 0 | 0 | 0 | 0 | 0 | 0 | 0 | 0 |
| Fiji | 4558 | 25 | 48 | 34 | 65 | 1171 | 444 | 828 | 1592 | 55 | 1 | 0 | 0 | 4 | 0 | 45 | 5 |
| Finland | 447 | 130 | 28 | 55 | 12 | 2574 | 1789 | 2350 | 510 | 547 | 0 | 0 | 0 | 20 | 0 | 522 | 5 |
| France | 880 | 4340 | 86 | 610 | 12 | 154772 | 327 | 141000 | 2783 | 22889 | 0 | 0 | 2 | 40 | 0 | 160 | 22687 |
| French Guiana | 1059 | 10 | 196 | 12 | 235 | 211 | 242 | 69 | 1353 | 0 | 0 | 0 | 0 | 0 | 0 | 0 | 0 |
| French Polynesia | 2018 | 18 | 165 | 12 | 110 | 322 | 339 | 117 | 1073 | 0 | 0 | 0 | 0 | 0 | 0 | 0 | 0 |
| French Southern & Antarctic T | 0 | 0 | 0 | 0 | 0 | 0 | 0 | 0 | 0 | 0 | 0 | 0 | 0 | 0 | 0 | 0 | 0 |
| Gabon | 3124 | 50 | 100 | 20 | 40 | 1758 | 284 | 1497 | 2994 | 10 | 0 | 0 | 0 | 0 | 0 | 0 | 10 |
| Gambia | 80 | 15 | 32 | 17 | 37 | 273 | 1696 | 216 | 467 | 0 | 0 | 0 | 0 | 0 | 0 | 0 | 0 |
| German Democratic Rep | 493 | 315 | 18 | 35 | 2 | 9035 | 1888 | 8900 | 521 | 0 | 0 | 0 | 0 | 0 | 0 | 0 | 0 |
| Germany, Federal Rep | 710 | 6280 | 103 | 750 | 12 | 127077 | 478 | 121000 | 1993 | 16857 | 0 | 0 | 123 | 350 | 0 | 1770 | 14614 |
| Ghana | 1310 | 250 | 29 | 65 | 8 | 9797 | 881 | 8740 | 1013 | 210 | 3 | 102 | 0 | 0 | 0 | 45 | 60 |
| Gibraltar | 500 | 1 | 38 | 3 | 115 | 49 | 531 | 17 | 654 | 0 | 0 | 0 | 0 | 0 | 0 | 0 | 0 |
| Greece | 3416 | 540 | 61 | 60 | 70 | 14007 | 628 | 13630 | 1550 | 196 | 0 | 0 | 0 | 0 | 196 | 0 | 0 |
| Greenland | 2149 | 2 | 42 | 3 | 64 | 227 | 207 | 210 | 4468 | 0 | 0 | 0 | 0 | 0 | 0 | 0 | 0 |
| Grenada | 1340 | 9 | 96 | 21 | 223 | 121 | 777 | 60 | 638 | 2 | 0 | 2 | 0 | 0 | 0 | 0 | 0 |
| Guadeloupe | 509 | 21 | 64 | 15 | 46 | 1671 | 196 | 1390 | 4238 | 112 | 0 | 0 | 0 | 0 | 0 | 0 | 112 |
| Guam | 1307 | 15 | 170 | 15 | 170 | 346 | 254 | 68 | 773 | 0 | 0 | 0 | 0 | 0 | 0 | 0 | 0 |
| Guatemala | 715 | 215 | 41 | 50 | 9 | 3985 | 1329 | 1850 | 349 | 152 | 0 | 6 | 0 | 0 | 0 | 6 | 140 |
| Guinea | 71 | 2 | 1 | 3 | 1 | 201 | 19507 | 175 | 45 | 0 | 0 | 0 | 0 | 0 | 0 | 0 | 0 |
| Guinea-Bissau | 88 | 17 | 35 | 1 | 2 | 96 | 5073 | 10 | 21 | 2 | 0 | 0 | 0 | 0 | 0 | 0 | 2 |
| Guyana | 1333 | 60 | 85 | 19 | 27 | 880 | 806 | 687 | 969 | 2 | 0 | 2 | 0 | 0 | 0 | 0 | 0 |
| Haiti | 1067 | 220 | 52 | 35 | 8 | 2745 | 1543 | 1550 | 366 | 26 | 1 | 0 | 0 | 0 | 0 | 20 | 5 |
| Holy See | 12121 | 50 | 10101 | 150 | 30303 | 1044 | 5 | 684 | 138182 | 500 | 0 | 0 | 0 | 0 | 0 | 0 | 500 |
| Honduras | 399 | 90 | 35 | 35 | 14 | 1674 | 1525 | 975 | 382 | 50 | 0 | 0 | 0 | 0 | 0 | 0 | 50 |
| Hong Kong | 221 | 250 | 63 | 110 | 28 | 2825 | 1395 | 1420 | 360 | 190 | 23 | 62 | 0 | 15 | 0 | 30 | 60 |
| Hungary | 643 | 25 | 2 | 24 | 2 | 6214 | 1664 | 6200 | 600 | 44 | 0 | 0 | 0 | 0 | 0 | 6 | 38 |
| Iceland | 1931 | 7 | 34 | 20 | 98 | 253 | 806 | 190 | 931 | 11 | 0 | 0 | 0 | 0 | 0 | 11 | 0 |
| India | 128 | 5300 | 10 | 320 | 1 | 120479 | 4508 | 114500 | 211 | 3931 | 0 | 200 | 2 | 0 | 9 | 300 | 3420 |
| Indonesia | 188 | 2800 | 23 | 105 | 1 | 32684 | 3655 | 28324 | 237 | 203 | 0 | 8 | 0 | 0 | 0 | 40 | 155 |
| Iran | 19 | 32 | 1 | 24 | 1 | 440 | 64452 | 140 | 5 | 2 | 0 | 0 | 0 | 0 | 1 | 1 | 0 |
| Iraq | 74 | 28 | 3 | 15 | 2 | 556 | 16827 | 490 | 52 | 29 | 0 | 0 | 0 | 0 | 9 | 0 | 20 |
| Ireland | 743 | 990 | 335 | 105 | 36 | 21642 | 136 | 21400 | 7244 | 9537 | 13 | 0 | 0 | 0 | 0 | 0 | 9524 |
| Isle of Man | 2036 | 0 | 0 | 8 | 143 | 93 | 602 | 90 | 1607 | 4 | 4 | 0 | 0 | 0 | 0 | 0 | 0 |
| Israel | 95 | 60 | 20 | 60 | 20 | 764 | 3872 | 230 | 78 | 8 | 0 | 0 | 0 | 0 | 0 | 0 | 8 |
| Italy | 575 | 13500 | 252 | 850 | 16 | 225888 | 237 | 216500 | 4042 | 25321 | 0 | 0 | 2 | 30 | 0 | 20 | 25269 |
| Ivory Coast | 712 | 98 | 23 | 56 | 13 | 4307 | 1001 | 3220 | 747 | 153 | 0 | 8 | 0 | 0 | 0 | 10 | 135 |
| Jamaica | 2168 | 85 | 45 | 29 | 15 | 2097 | 897 | 1500 | 797 | 376 | 44 | 187 | 0 | 0 | 0 | 105 | 40 |
| Japan | 132 | 670 | 6 | 250 | 2 | 19251 | 5420 | 13135 | 126 | 518 | 12 | 65 | 0 | 41 | 0 | 230 | 170 |
| Johnston Island | 2000 | 0 | 0 | 0 | 0 | 0 | 0 | 0 | 0 | 0 | 0 | 0 | 0 | 0 | 0 | 0 | 0 |
| Jordan | 184 | 27 | 16 | 8 | 5 | 449 | 3646 | 320 | 195 | 20 | 2 | 0 | 0 | 0 | 1 | 2 | 15 |
| Kampuchea | 25 | 7 | 1 | 4 | 1 | 218 | 32385 | 141 | 20 | 0 | 0 | 0 | 0 | 0 | 0 | 0 | 0 |
| Kenya | 1618 | 970 | 86 | 180 | 16 | 11813 | 952 | 8844 | 786 | 112 | 4 | 46 | 0 | 0 | 0 | 10 | 52 |
| Kiribati | 3480 | 13 | 260 | 4 | 80 | 392 | 127 | 341 | 6820 | 3 | 0 | 0 | 0 | 0 | 0 | 3 | 0 |
| Korea, North | 151 | 0 | 0 | 0 | 0 | 20 | 694600 | 20 | 1 | 0 | 0 | 0 | 0 | 0 | 0 | 0 | 0 |
| Korea, South | 534 | 580 | 19 | 120 | 4 | 17025 | 1804 | 15488 | 504 | 620 | 0 | 250 | 0 | 10 | 0 | 270 | 90 |
| Kuwait | 92 | 5 | 7 | 2 | 3 | 52 | 14615 | 4 | 5 | 0 | 0 | 0 | 0 | 0 | 0 | 0 | 0 |
| Laos | 78 | 80 | 27 | 15 | 5 | 493 | 6008 | 270 | 91 | 0 | 0 | 0 | 0 | 0 | 0 | 0 | 0 |
| Lebanon | 806 | 290 | 117 | 140 | 57 | 6680 | 370 | 5600 | 2268 | 173 | 0 | 0 | 0 | 0 | 19 | 4 | 150 |
| Lesotho | 1678 | 140 | 134 | 55 | 53 | 2302 | 453 | 1647 | 1579 | 18 | 0 | 4 | 0 | 0 | 0 | 4 | 10 |
| Liberia | 1379 | 125 | 82 | 35 | 23 | 2057 | 740 | 1304 | 856 | 14 | 0 | 8 | 4 | 0 | 0 | 2 | 0 |
| Libya | 46 | 0 | 0 | 0 | 0 | 179 | 10827 | 0 | 0 | 0 | 0 | 0 | 0 | 0 | 0 | 0 | 0 |
| Liechtenstein | 708 | 0 | 0 | 3 | 142 | 37 | 568 | 14 | 660 | 10 | 0 | 0 | 0 | 0 | 0 | 0 | 10 |
| Luxembourg | 973 | 25 | 74 | 45 | 133 | 2312 | 147 | 2280 | 6726 | 90 | 0 | 0 | 0 | 0 | 0 | 0 | 90 |
| Macao | 129 | 40 | 161 | 12 | 48 | 356 | 697 | 32 | 129 | 2 | 0 | 0 | 0 | 0 | 0 | 0 | 2 |
| Madagascar | 1369 | 380 | 55 | 58 | 8 | 14772 | 469 | 12900 | 1861 | 105 | 3 | 0 | 0 | 0 | 0 | 2 | 100 |
| Malawi | 1872 | 170 | 39 | 50 | 11 | 3514 | 1241 | 2520 | 578 | 92 | 7 | 10 | 0 | 10 | 0 | 35 | 30 |
| Malaysia | 184 | 185 | 18 | 41 | 4 | 2798 | 3741 | 1870 | 179 | 5 | 0 | 0 | 0 | 0 | 0 | 5 | 0 |

| | | CHRISTIAN ORGANIZATIONS | | | | CHRISTIAN PERSONNEL | | | | INTERNATIONAL SHARING OF PERSONNEL | | | | | | | |
|---|---|---|---|---|---|---|---|---|---|---|---|---|---|---|---|---|---|
| | | INSTITUTIONS | | SERVICE AGENCIES | | NATIONALS & ALIENS | | Nationals only | | NATIONALS SENT ABROAD | | | | | | | |
| | pmillion | Total | pmillion | Total | pmillion | Total | Pop/pw | Total | pmillion | Total | Anglican | NWInd | CathNR | Marginal | Orthodox | Protest | RC |
| | 27 | 28 | 29 | 30 | 31 | 32 | 33 | 34 | 35 | 36 | 37 | 38 | 39 | 40 | 41 | 42 | 43 |
| Maldives | 19 | 0 | 0 | 0 | 0 | 0 | 0 | 0 | 0 | 0 | 0 | 0 | 0 | 0 | 0 | 0 | 0 |
| Mali | 82 | 70 | 14 | 17 | 3 | 1026 | 4919 | 630 | 125 | 1 | 0 | 0 | 0 | 0 | 0 | 0 | 1 |
| Malta | 276 | 20 | 61 | 48 | 147 | 3593 | 91 | 3575 | 10966 | 746 | 0 | 0 | 0 | 0 | 0 | 0 | 746 |
| Martinique | 343 | 10 | 30 | 25 | 74 | 2087 | 162 | 1910 | 5651 | 50 | 0 | 0 | 0 | 0 | 0 | 0 | 50 |
| Mauritania | 7 | 0 | 0 | 1 | 1 | 22 | 52818 | 0 | 0 | 0 | 0 | 0 | 0 | 0 | 0 | 0 | 0 |
| Mauritius | 153 | 20 | 24 | 41 | 50 | 678 | 1215 | 527 | 640 | 31 | 0 | 0 | 0 | 0 | 0 | 0 | 31 |
| Mayotte | 107 | 0 | 0 | 0 | 0 | 0 | 0 | 0 | 0 | 0 | 0 | 0 | 0 | 0 | 0 | 0 | 0 |
| Mexico | 366 | 1260 | 25 | 205 | 4 | 43148 | 1166 | 37500 | 745 | 2086 | 0 | 66 | 0 | 0 | 0 | 30 | 1990 |
| Midway Islands | 1351 | 0 | 0 | 0 | 0 | 3 | 740 | 0 | 0 | 0 | 0 | 0 | 0 | 0 | 0 | 0 | 0 |
| Monaco | 348 | 7 | 304 | 20 | 870 | 202 | 114 | 55 | 2391 | 0 | 0 | 0 | 0 | 0 | 0 | 0 | 0 |
| Mongolia | 90 | 0 | 0 | 0 | 0 | 0 | 0 | 0 | 0 | 0 | 0 | 0 | 0 | 0 | 0 | 0 | 0 |
| Montserrat | 7250 | 0 | 0 | 4 | 333 | 9 | 1333 | 5 | 417 | 0 | 0 | 0 | 0 | 0 | 0 | 0 | 0 |
| Morocco | 48 | 50 | 3 | 31 | 2 | 1031 | 14671 | 103 | 7 | 0 | 0 | 0 | 0 | 0 | 0 | 0 | 0 |
| Mozambique | 517 | 280 | 34 | 20 | 2 | 6078 | 1355 | 4030 | 489 | 60 | 0 | 0 | 0 | 0 | 0 | 0 | 60 |
| Namibia | 2385 | 140 | 221 | 12 | 19 | 1421 | 445 | 710 | 1122 | 10 | 0 | 3 | 0 | 0 | 0 | 7 | 0 |
| Nauru | 1538 | 2 | 308 | 0 | 0 | 12 | 542 | 4 | 615 | 0 | 0 | 0 | 0 | 0 | 0 | 0 | 0 |
| Nepal | 7 | 25 | 2 | 50 | 4 | 325 | 34560 | 18 | 2 | 0 | 0 | 0 | 0 | 0 | 0 | 0 | 0 |
| Netherlands | 665 | 1800 | 138 | 340 | 26 | 43771 | 298 | 42000 | 3223 | 10381 | 0 | 0 | 4 | 20 | 0 | 349 | 10008 |
| Netherlands Antilles | 743 | 65 | 293 | 20 | 90 | 671 | 331 | 226 | 1018 | 10 | 0 | 0 | 0 | 0 | 0 | 0 | 10 |
| New Caledonia | 1349 | 38 | 349 | 12 | 110 | 522 | 209 | 275 | 2523 | 13 | 0 | 4 | 0 | 0 | 0 | 3 | 6 |
| New Zealand | 2181 | 190 | 67 | 150 | 53 | 8859 | 318 | 6800 | 2411 | 1188 | 75 | 0 | 0 | 30 | 0 | 883 | 200 |
| Nicaragua | 706 | 160 | 81 | 40 | 20 | 1910 | 1031 | 945 | 480 | 70 | 0 | 0 | 0 | 0 | 0 | 0 | 70 |
| Niger | 36 | 20 | 5 | 12 | 3 | 249 | 16129 | 32 | 8 | 0 | 0 | 0 | 0 | 0 | 0 | 0 | 0 |
| Nigeria | 744 | 730 | 13 | 105 | 2 | 21274 | 2589 | 18600 | 338 | 344 | 7 | 150 | 12 | 0 | 0 | 95 | 80 |
| Niue Island | 4800 | 0 | 0 | 0 | 0 | 21 | 238 | 14 | 2800 | 0 | 0 | 0 | 0 | 0 | 0 | 0 | 0 |
| Norfolk Island | 2353 | 0 | 0 | 0 | 0 | 1 | 1700 | 0 | 0 | 0 | 0 | 0 | 0 | 0 | 0 | 0 | 0 |
| Northern Solomons | 2138 | 20 | 252 | 4 | 50 | 624 | 127 | 444 | 5620 | 0 | 0 | 0 | 0 | 0 | 0 | 0 | 0 |
| Norway | 1099 | 70 | 18 | 110 | 28 | 3059 | 1267 | 2460 | 635 | 1458 | 0 | 0 | 0 | 10 | 0 | 1428 | 20 |
| Oman | 35 | 2 | 3 | 2 | 3 | 25 | 26280 | 0 | 0 | 0 | 0 | 0 | 0 | 0 | 0 | 0 | 0 |
| Pacific Islands | 3366 | 13 | 129 | 3 | 30 | 632 | 160 | 410 | 4059 | 0 | 0 | 0 | 0 | 0 | 0 | 0 | 0 |
| Pakistan | 59 | 210 | 3 | 45 | 1 | 2936 | 20589 | 1776 | 29 | 2 | 0 | 0 | 0 | 0 | 0 | 2 | 0 |
| Palestine | 296 | 160 | 135 | 40 | 34 | 1366 | 865 | 560 | 474 | 152 | 0 | 0 | 0 | 0 | 0 | 3 | 149 |
| Panama | 706 | 65 | 45 | 47 | 32 | 1445 | 1009 | 536 | 368 | 354 | 0 | 0 | 0 | 0 | 0 | 4 | 350 |
| Panama Canal Zone | 2602 | 3 | 68 | 10 | 226 | 52 | 850 | 15 | 339 | 0 | 0 | 0 | 0 | 0 | 0 | 0 | 0 |
| Papua New Guinea | 3419 | 570 | 236 | 130 | 54 | 11712 | 199 | 8384 | 3594 | 15 | 0 | 0 | 0 | 0 | 0 | 10 | 5 |
| Paraguay | 352 | 220 | 96 | 54 | 23 | 1949 | 1181 | 1162 | 505 | 180 | 0 | 0 | 0 | 0 | 0 | 0 | 180 |
| Peru | 395 | 450 | 34 | 130 | 10 | 10996 | 1205 | 5538 | 418 | 270 | 0 | 0 | 0 | 0 | 0 | 20 | 250 |
| Philippines | 699 | 1490 | 40 | 190 | 5 | 33090 | 1136 | 27100 | 721 | 1159 | 0 | 80 | 0 | 94 | 0 | 135 | 850 |
| Pitcairn Islands | 11111 | 0 | 0 | 0 | 0 | 3 | 30 | 3 | 33333 | 0 | 0 | 0 | 0 | 0 | 0 | 0 | 0 |
| Poland | 283 | 330 | 10 | 45 | 1 | 45215 | 718 | 45200 | 1392 | 1476 | 0 | 0 | 0 | 0 | 0 | 0 | 1476 |
| Portugal | 591 | 340 | 39 | 130 | 15 | 13455 | 641 | 13100 | 1518 | 4219 | 0 | 0 | 0 | 0 | 0 | 10 | 4209 |
| Puerto Rico | 879 | 130 | 47 | 50 | 18 | 3488 | 786 | 1510 | 550 | 615 | 0 | 25 | 0 | 0 | 0 | 70 | 520 |
| Qatar | 182 | 0 | 0 | 0 | 0 | 3 | 36667 | 0 | 0 | 0 | 0 | 0 | 0 | 0 | 0 | 0 | 0 |
| Reunion | 251 | 20 | 45 | 18 | 40 | 2610 | 171 | 2338 | 5230 | 5 | 0 | 0 | 0 | 0 | 0 | 0 | 5 |
| Romania | 901 | 205 | 10 | 20 | 1 | 14530 | 1393 | 14500 | 716 | 107 | 0 | 0 | 0 | 0 | 107 | 0 | 0 |
| Rwanda | 981 | 145 | 39 | 38 | 10 | 4605 | 799 | 3738 | 1016 | 70 | 0 | 0 | 0 | 0 | 0 | 0 | 70 |
| Sahara | 66 | 4 | 44 | 0 | 0 | 29 | 3148 | 0 | 0 | 0 | 0 | 0 | 0 | 0 | 0 | 0 | 0 |
| St Helena | 3692 | 0 | 0 | 2 | 308 | 13 | 500 | 3 | 462 | 0 | 0 | 0 | 0 | 0 | 0 | 0 | 0 |
| St Kitts-Nevis | 3735 | 0 | 0 | 8 | 136 | 74 | 796 | 46 | 781 | 2 | 0 | 2 | 0 | 0 | 0 | 0 | 0 |
| St Lucia | 1040 | 7 | 69 | 13 | 129 | 161 | 627 | 65 | 644 | 0 | 0 | 0 | 0 | 0 | 0 | 0 | 0 |
| St Pierre & Miquelon | 364 | 2 | 364 | 5 | 909 | 28 | 196 | 2 | 364 | 0 | 0 | 0 | 0 | 0 | 0 | 0 | 0 |
| St Vincent | 1818 | 6 | 68 | 7 | 80 | 90 | 989 | 35 | 398 | 0 | 0 | 0 | 0 | 0 | 0 | 0 | 0 |
| Samoa | 4716 | 18 | 128 | 12 | 85 | 1624 | 87 | 1116 | 7915 | 162 | 0 | 0 | 0 | 105 | 0 | 57 | 0 |
| San Marino | 684 | 1 | 53 | 0 | 0 | 22 | 864 | 2 | 105 | 0 | 0 | 0 | 0 | 0 | 0 | 0 | 0 |
| Sao Tome & Principe | 419 | 1 | 14 | 5 | 68 | 46 | 1604 | 10 | 135 | 0 | 0 | 0 | 0 | 0 | 0 | 0 | 0 |
| Saudi Arabia | 41 | 0 | 0 | 0 | 0 | 13 | 595385 | 0 | 0 | 0 | 0 | 0 | 0 | 0 | 0 | 0 | 0 |
| Senegal | 29 | 110 | 28 | 35 | 9 | 1869 | 2100 | 1116 | 284 | 70 | 0 | 0 | 0 | 0 | 0 | 0 | 70 |
| Seychelles | 635 | 16 | 308 | 14 | 269 | 150 | 347 | 62 | 1192 | 0 | 0 | 0 | 0 | 0 | 0 | 0 | 0 |
| Sierra Leone | 669 | 80 | 30 | 24 | 9 | 1111 | 2380 | 665 | 252 | 2 | 2 | 0 | 0 | 0 | 0 | 0 | 0 |
| Sikkim | 224 | 13 | 65 | 3 | 13 | 13 | 17692 | 0 | 0 | 0 | 0 | 0 | 0 | 0 | 0 | 0 | 0 |
| Singapore | 135 | 55 | 27 | 60 | 29 | 702 | 2956 | 240 | 116 | 12 | 0 | 0 | 0 | 0 | 0 | 10 | 2 |
| Solomon Islands | 8589 | 53 | 325 | 9 | 55 | 1331 | 122 | 1011 | 6202 | 45 | 14 | 0 | 0 | 0 | 0 | 26 | 5 |
| Somalia | 12 | 26 | 9 | 5 | 2 | 219 | 12735 | 13 | 5 | 0 | 0 | 0 | 0 | 0 | 0 | 0 | 0 |
| South Africa | 2767 | 850 | 40 | 160 | 7 | 29142 | 738 | 22635 | 1053 | 1160 | 110 | 180 | 10 | 30 | 0 | 730 | 100 |
| Spain | 662 | 4100 | 121 | 300 | 9 | 129838 | 260 | 128200 | 3795 | 27901 | 0 | 0 | 0 | 10 | 0 | 10 | 27881 |
| Spanish North Africa | 109 | 2 | 12 | 5 | 30 | 56 | 2946 | 4 | 24 | 0 | 0 | 0 | 0 | 0 | 0 | 0 | 0 |
| Sri Lanka | 94 | 130 | 10 | 45 | 4 | 4513 | 2773 | 4163 | 333 | 90 | 20 | 36 | 0 | 0 | 0 | 4 | 30 |
| Sudan | 66 | 60 | 4 | 27 | 2 | 1843 | 8516 | 1560 | 99 | 60 | 5 | 0 | 0 | 0 | 0 | 0 | 55 |
| Surinam | 728 | 35 | 94 | 24 | 65 | 494 | 751 | 164 | 442 | 10 | 0 | 0 | 0 | 0 | 0 | 4 | 6 |
| Svalbard & Jan Mayen Is | 286 | 0 | 0 | 0 | 0 | 2 | 1750 | 0 | 0 | 0 | 0 | 0 | 0 | 0 | 0 | 0 | 0 |
| Swaziland | 2958 | 50 | 122 | 18 | 14 | 1306 | 313 | 873 | 2134 | 28 | 0 | 20 | 0 | 0 | 0 | 8 | 0 |
| Sweden | 1374 | 60 | 7 | 90 | 11 | 7284 | 1104 | 6690 | 832 | 1846 | 0 | 0 | 0 | 30 | 0 | 1796 | 20 |
| Switzerland | 897 | 190 | 30 | 480 | 77 | 17574 | 357 | 16500 | 2633 | 2808 | 0 | 0 | 30 | 10 | 0 | 465 | 2303 |
| Syria | 125 | 35 | 6 | 29 | 5 | 801 | 7799 | 690 | 110 | 96 | 0 | 0 | 0 | 0 | 60 | 0 | 36 |
| Tanzania | 686 | 440 | 33 | 75 | 6 | 17381 | 764 | 14410 | 1086 | 100 | 0 | 0 | 0 | 0 | 0 | 8 | 92 |
| Thailand | 89 | 230 | 6 | 90 | 3 | 3203 | 11160 | 1870 | 52 | 15 | 0 | 0 | 0 | 0 | 0 | 10 | 5 |
| Timor | 116 | 10 | 17 | 3 | 5 | 143 | 4224 | 81 | 134 | 0 | 0 | 0 | 0 | 0 | 0 | 0 | 0 |
| Togo | 390 | 60 | 31 | 32 | 16 | 1166 | 1681 | 850 | 434 | 38 | 0 | 4 | 0 | 0 | 0 | 2 | 32 |
| Tokelau | 4118 | 0 | 0 | 0 | 0 | 43 | 40 | 40 | 23529 | 0 | 0 | 0 | 0 | 0 | 0 | 0 | 0 |
| Tonga | 7907 | 25 | 291 | 6 | 70 | 787 | 109 | 467 | 5430 | 28 | 0 | 0 | 0 | 4 | 0 | 24 | 0 |
| Trinidad & Tobago | 1173 | 80 | 84 | 30 | 31 | 876 | 1090 | 510 | 534 | 85 | 22 | 18 | 0 | 0 | 0 | 12 | 33 |
| Tunisia | 41 | 40 | 8 | 18 | 4 | 487 | 10548 | 25 | 5 | 0 | 0 | 0 | 0 | 0 | 0 | 0 | 0 |
| Turkey | 17 | 43 | 1 | 17 | 0 | 675 | 52196 | 330 | 9 | 10 | 0 | 0 | 0 | 0 | 10 | 0 | 0 |
| Turks & Caicos Islands | 8094 | 1 | 180 | 3 | 540 | 17 | 327 | 10 | 1799 | 0 | 0 | 0 | 0 | 0 | 0 | 0 | 0 |
| Tuvalu | 2667 | 1 | 167 | 0 | 0 | 28 | 214 | 25 | 4167 | 0 | 0 | 0 | 0 | 0 | 0 | 0 | 0 |
| Uganda | 904 | 230 | 23 | 59 | 6 | 13616 | 720 | 12050 | 1229 | 128 | 12 | 6 | 0 | 0 | 0 | 0 | 110 |
| USSR | 322 | 80 | 0 | 120 | 0 | 60730 | 3997 | 60700 | 250 | 157 | 0 | 0 | 0 | 0 | 157 | 0 | 0 |
| United Arab Emirates | 150 | 5 | 17 | 6 | 20 | 74 | 4054 | 0 | 0 | 0 | 0 | 0 | 0 | 0 | 0 | 0 | 0 |
| UK of GB & NI | 1139 | 2200 | 40 | 1300 | 23 | 107340 | 517 | 101600 | 1831 | 10288 | 2590 | 80 | 0 | 230 | 0 | 4900 | 2488 |
| USA | 1768 | 6900 | 34 | 2300 | 11 | 691746 | 296 | 675000 | 3294 | 57212 | 173 | 190 | 10 | 12229 | 220 | 32400 | 11990 |
| US Virgin Islands | 2976 | 10 | 160 | 10 | 160 | 141 | 447 | 50 | 800 | 0 | 0 | 0 | 0 | 0 | 0 | 0 | 0 |
| Upper Volta | 236 | 60 | 11 | 30 | 6 | 3574 | 1506 | 2680 | 498 | 56 | 0 | 0 | 0 | 0 | 0 | 0 | 56 |
| Uruguay | 352 | 130 | 44 | 68 | 23 | 3785 | 781 | 1810 | 613 | 369 | 0 | 0 | 0 | 4 | 0 | 15 | 350 |
| Vanuatu | 6071 | 15 | 179 | 8 | 95 | 425 | 198 | 225 | 2679 | 2 | 0 | 0 | 0 | 0 | 0 | 2 | 0 |
| Venezuela | 307 | 370 | 35 | 78 | 7 | 8150 | 1296 | 3630 | 344 | 480 | 0 | 0 | 0 | 0 | 0 | 0 | 480 |
| Viet Nam | 87 | 730 | 19 | 62 | 2 | 13642 | 2867 | 12836 | 328 | 360 | 0 | 0 | 0 | 0 | 0 | 20 | 340 |
| Wake Island | 2500 | 0 | 0 | 0 | 0 | 2 | 800 | 0 | 0 | 0 | 0 | 0 | 0 | 0 | 0 | 0 | 0 |
| Wallis & Futuna Islands | 556 | 2 | 222 | 6 | 667 | 83 | 108 | 61 | 6778 | 16 | 0 | 0 | 0 | 0 | 0 | 0 | 16 |
| Yemen, North | 6 | 2 | 0 | 4 | 1 | 66 | 87379 | 0 | 0 | 0 | 0 | 0 | 0 | 0 | 0 | 0 | 0 |
| Yemen, South | 15 | 4 | 3 | 1 | 1 | 68 | 21118 | 0 | 0 | 0 | 0 | 0 | 0 | 0 | 0 | 0 | 0 |
| Yugoslavia | 375 | 310 | 15 | 40 | 2 | 14979 | 1360 | 14600 | 717 | 652 | 0 | 0 | 0 | 0 | 126 | 0 | 526 |
| Zaire | 1529 | 2050 | 95 | 95 | 4 | 44985 | 481 | 36000 | 1664 | 438 | 0 | 43 | 0 | 5 | 0 | 10 | 380 |
| Zambia | 1541 | 190 | 44 | 78 | 18 | 3866 | 1111 | 1865 | 434 | 168 | 0 | 15 | 10 | 100 | 0 | 13 | 30 |
| Zimbabwe | 1684 | 360 | 68 | 58 | 11 | 4761 | 1115 | 2656 | 500 | 96 | 2 | 60 | 4 | 5 | 0 | 15 | 10 |
| Column | 27 | 28 | 29 | 30 | 31 | 32 | 33 | 34 | 35 | 36 | 37 | 38 | 39 | 40 | 41 | 42 | 43 |
| *Continent* | | | | | | | | | | | | | | | | | |
| Africa | — | 12335 | — | 1994 | — | 431321 | 249278 | 373469 | — | 4268 | 155 | 678 | 40 | 150 | 167 | 1081 | 1997 |
| East Asia | — | 1816 | — | 582 | — | 46319 | 1395274 | 35080 | — | 1533 | 35 | 450 | 0 | 66 | 0 | 600 | 382 |
| Europe | — | 38525 | — | 6304 | — | 1059742 | 105008 | 1013639 | — | 149512 | 2617 | 80 | 143 | 795 | 465 | 11846 | 133566 |
| Latin America | — | 11421 | — | 2078 | — | 257312 | 47575 | 180967 | — | 13002 | 71 | 429 | 10 | 48 | 0 | 555 | 11889 |
| Northern America | — | 7656 | — | 2664 | — | 776749 | 1321 | 754892 | — | 67387 | 200 | 190 | 40 | 12369 | 220 | 35128 | 19240 |
| Oceania | — | 1908 | — | 600 | — | 64437 | 7913 | 53163 | — | 5505 | 534 | 4 | 0 | 173 | 0 | 3213 | 1581 |
| South Asia | — | 12212 | — | 1469 | — | 235102 | 1365362 | 208439 | — | 6399 | 22 | 324 | 2 | 94 | 186 | 566 | 5205 |
| USSR | — | 80 | — | 120 | — | 60730 | 3997 | 60700 | — | 157 | 0 | 0 | 0 | 0 | 157 | 0 | 0 |
| **WORLD** | — | **85953** | — | **15811** | — | **2928112** | **3175728** | **2680349** | — | **247763** | **3634** | **2155** | **235** | **13695** | **1195** | **52989** | **173860** |

| | INTERNATIONAL SHARING OF PERSONNEL | | | | | | | | | | | | | CHRISTIAN LITERATURE | | | | | |
|---|---|---|---|---|---|---|---|---|---|---|---|---|---|---|---|---|---|---|---|
| | | ALIENS RECEIVED FROM ABROAD | | | | | | | | | | | | BOOKS, PERIODICALS & LIBRARIES | | | | | |
| | pmillion | Total | West | Comm | ThirdW | Anglican | NWInd | CathNR | Marginal | Orthodox | Protest | RC | pmillion | Titles | Religious | Periodic | pmillion | Libraries | pmillion |
| | 44 | 45 | 46 | 47 | 48 | 49 | 50 | 51 | 52 | 53 | 54 | 55 | 56 | 57 | 58 | 59 | 60 | 61 | 62 |
| Afghanistan | 0 | 88 | 82 | 0 | 6 | 1 | 0 | 0 | 0 | 0 | 77 | 10 | 5 | 33 | 5 | 0 | 0 | 0 | 0 |
| Albania | 0 | 0 | 0 | 0 | 0 | 0 | 0 | 0 | 0 | 0 | 0 | 0 | 0 | 502 | 0 | 0 | 0 | 0 | 0 |
| Algeria | 3 | 1748 | 1696 | 2 | 50 | 0 | 0 | 0 | 0 | 2 | 70 | 1676 | 122 | 100 | 20 | 15 | 1 | 10 | 1 |
| American Samoa | 0 | 70 | 50 | 0 | 20 | 0 | 0 | 0 | 50 | 0 | 18 | 2 | 2593 | 2 | 0 | 7 | 259 | 0 | 0 |
| Andorra | 0 | 0 | 0 | 0 | 0 | 0 | 0 | 0 | 0 | 0 | 0 | 0 | 0 | 4 | 0 | 1 | 53 | 1 | 53 |
| Angola | 18 | 1407 | 1344 | 1 | 62 | 0 | 10 | 0 | 0 | 0 | 104 | 1293 | 248 | 30 | 5 | 27 | 5 | 12 | 2 |
| Anguilla | 0 | 4 | 4 | 0 | 0 | 0 | 0 | 0 | 0 | 0 | 3 | 1 | 652 | 0 | 0 | 3 | 489 | 0 | 0 |
| Antigua | 0 | 31 | 21 | 0 | 10 | 9 | 0 | 0 | 0 | 0 | 16 | 6 | 443 | 7 | 1 | 7 | 100 | 0 | 0 |
| Argentina | 42 | 8824 | 7288 | 146 | 1390 | 61 | 20 | 10 | 468 | 17 | 637 | 7611 | 372 | 4578 | 63 | 120 | 5 | 90 | 4 |
| Australia | 317 | 2845 | 2692 | 58 | 95 | 270 | 5 | 2 | 220 | 26 | 329 | 1993 | 227 | 3579 | 163 | 260 | 21 | 110 | 9 |
| Austria | 249 | 767 | 751 | 6 | 10 | 1 | 0 | 2 | 70 | 7 | 257 | 430 | 103 | 5342 | 197 | 500 | 67 | 190 | 26 |
| Bahamas | 0 | 223 | 213 | 0 | 10 | 18 | 5 | 0 | 0 | 0 | 90 | 110 | 1260 | 20 | 5 | 12 | 68 | 2 | 11 |
| Bahrain | 0 | 37 | 29 | 0 | 8 | 0 | 2 | 0 | 0 | 2 | 17 | 16 | 172 | 10 | 2 | 3 | 14 | 0 | 0 |
| Bangladesh | 0 | 578 | 478 | 0 | 100 | 9 | 5 | 0 | 0 | 0 | 244 | 320 | 9 | 457 | 34 | 20 | 0 | 20 | 0 |
| Barbados | 25 | 171 | 151 | 0 | 20 | 23 | 11 | 0 | 0 | 0 | 32 | 105 | 715 | 113 | 5 | 13 | 54 | 5 | 21 |
| Belgium | 969 | 1278 | 1170 | 2 | 106 | 9 | 0 | 2 | 70 | 10 | 147 | 1040 | 133 | 8953 | 286 | 220 | 23 | 260 | 27 |
| Belize | 0 | 224 | 204 | 0 | 20 | 14 | 2 | 0 | 0 | 0 | 78 | 130 | 1867 | 10 | 2 | 8 | 67 | 0 | 0 |
| Benin | 13 | 492 | 416 | 2 | 74 | 0 | 20 | 0 | 0 | 0 | 104 | 368 | 183 | 15 | 2 | 15 | 6 | 13 | 5 |
| Bermuda | 38 | 41 | 36 | 0 | 5 | 15 | 0 | 0 | 0 | 0 | 11 | 15 | 788 | 10 | 2 | 30 | 577 | 0 | 0 |
| Bhutan | 0 | 33 | 17 | 0 | 16 | 0 | 2 | 0 | 0 | 0 | 21 | 10 | 32 | 25 | 2 | 0 | 0 | 0 | 0 |
| Bolivia | 337 | 2724 | 2378 | 9 | 337 | 2 | 14 | 0 | 80 | 0 | 728 | 1900 | 570 | 586 | 26 | 50 | 10 | 62 | 13 |
| Botswana | 24 | 237 | 142 | 0 | 95 | 7 | 40 | 0 | 0 | 0 | 128 | 62 | 384 | 52 | 1 | 20 | 32 | 5 | 8 |
| Brazil | 26 | 15472 | 13768 | 284 | 1420 | 17 | 130 | 15 | 840 | 12 | 2843 | 11615 | 162 | 9948 | 715 | 350 | 4 | 450 | 5 |
| British Antarctic Terr | 0 | 0 | 0 | 0 | 0 | 0 | 0 | 0 | 0 | 0 | 0 | 0 | 0 | 0 | 0 | 0 | 0 | 0 | 0 |
| British Indian Ocean Terr | 0 | 0 | 0 | 0 | 0 | 0 | 0 | 0 | 0 | 0 | 0 | 0 | 0 | 0 | 0 | 0 | 0 | 0 | 0 |
| British Virgin Is | 0 | 7 | 3 | 0 | 4 | 3 | 0 | 0 | 0 | 0 | 3 | 1 | 700 | 0 | 0 | 2 | 200 | 0 | 0 |
| Brunei | 0 | 11 | 7 | 0 | 4 | 2 | 0 | 0 | 0 | 0 | 2 | 7 | 83 | 19 | 3 | 2 | 15 | 0 | 0 |
| Bulgaria | 4 | 4 | 2 | 2 | 0 | 0 | 0 | 0 | 0 | 3 | 1 | 0 | 0 | 3963 | 12 | 10 | 1 | 135 | 16 |
| Burma | 2 | 79 | 50 | 1 | 28 | 0 | 0 | 0 | 0 | 0 | 8 | 71 | 3 | 1506 | 269 | 20 | 1 | 33 | 1 |
| Burundi | 9 | 818 | 770 | 24 | 24 | 33 | 0 | 0 | 0 | 2 | 141 | 642 | 244 | 17 | 2 | 13 | 4 | 17 | 5 |
| Cameroon | 30 | 1901 | 1834 | 27 | 40 | 0 | 20 | 0 | 0 | 1 | 480 | 1400 | 326 | 30 | 3 | 30 | 5 | 21 | 4 |
| Canada | 475 | 5027 | 4420 | 128 | 479 | 193 | 20 | 42 | 800 | 56 | 440 | 3476 | 235 | 6834 | 228 | 500 | 23 | 250 | 12 |
| Canton & Enderbury | 0 | 0 | 0 | 0 | 0 | 0 | 0 | 0 | 0 | 0 | 0 | 0 | 0 | 0 | 0 | 0 | 0 | 0 | 0 |
| Cape Verde | 15 | 28 | 28 | 0 | 0 | 0 | 0 | 0 | 0 | 0 | 8 | 20 | 104 | 2 | 0 | 4 | 15 | 3 | 11 |
| Cayman Islands | 0 | 14 | 10 | 0 | 4 | 0 | 2 | 0 | 0 | 0 | 10 | 2 | 1273 | 0 | 0 | 3 | 273 | 0 | 0 |
| Central African Republic | 2 | 743 | 720 | 0 | 23 | 1 | 2 | 0 | 10 | 0 | 236 | 494 | 461 | 23 | 2 | 12 | 7 | 8 | 5 |
| Chad | 1 | 541 | 507 | 2 | 32 | 0 | 0 | 0 | 4 | 0 | 157 | 380 | 149 | 10 | 2 | 10 | 3 | 8 | 2 |
| Channel Islands | 82 | 8 | 8 | 0 | 0 | 3 | 0 | 0 | 0 | 0 | 0 | 5 | 66 | 20 | 1 | 10 | 82 | 5 | 41 |
| Chile | 69 | 5534 | 5011 | 18 | 505 | 36 | 10 | 0 | 320 | 3 | 318 | 4847 | 591 | 796 | 76 | 100 | 11 | 50 | 5 |
| China | 0 | 0 | 0 | 0 | 0 | 0 | 0 | 0 | 0 | 0 | 0 | 0 | 0 | 8000 | 20 | 10 | 0 | 10 | 0 |
| China (Taiwan) | 14 | 1857 | 1742 | 15 | 100 | 9 | 48 | 0 | 145 | 0 | 820 | 835 | 132 | 252 | 100 | 56 | 4 | 60 | 4 |
| Christmas Island | 0 | 0 | 0 | 0 | 0 | 0 | 0 | 0 | 0 | 0 | 0 | 0 | 0 | 0 | 0 | 0 | 0 | 0 | 0 |
| Cocos Islands | 0 | 0 | 0 | 0 | 0 | 0 | 0 | 0 | 0 | 0 | 0 | 0 | 0 | 0 | 0 | 0 | 0 | 0 | 0 |
| Colombia | 68 | 4288 | 3316 | 11 | 961 | 5 | 35 | 2 | 60 | 1 | 874 | 3311 | 194 | 848 | 18 | 80 | 4 | 120 | 5 |
| Comoros | 0 | 7 | 6 | 0 | 1 | 0 | 0 | 0 | 0 | 0 | 1 | 6 | 30 | 2 | 0 | 0 | 0 | 0 | 0 |
| Congo | 7 | 466 | 423 | 13 | 30 | 0 | 15 | 0 | 0 | 0 | 123 | 328 | 391 | 10 | 2 | 9 | 8 | 7 | 6 |
| Cook Islands | 143 | 49 | 24 | 0 | 25 | 0 | 0 | 0 | 20 | 0 | 9 | 20 | 2333 | 2 | 0 | 3 | 143 | 2 | 95 |
| Costa Rica | 113 | 1004 | 522 | 0 | 482 | 2 | 5 | 0 | 40 | 0 | 256 | 701 | 578 | 480 | 10 | 25 | 14 | 20 | 12 |
| Cuba | 1 | 222 | 205 | 0 | 17 | 0 | 5 | 0 | 0 | 0 | 6 | 211 | 26 | 942 | 2 | 15 | 2 | 11 | 1 |
| Cyprus | 122 | 119 | 114 | 0 | 5 | 3 | 0 | 0 | 0 | 10 | 31 | 75 | 188 | 484 | 24 | 6 | 9 | 16 | 25 |
| Czechoslovakia | 1 | 10 | 10 | 0 | 0 | 0 | 0 | 0 | 0 | 0 | 10 | 0 | 1 | 9883 | 62 | 45 | 3 | 14 | 1 |
| Denmark | 74 | 890 | 814 | 76 | 0 | 1 | 0 | 2 | 200 | 0 | 10 | 677 | 181 | 6822 | 215 | 180 | 37 | 30 | 6 |
| Djibouti | 0 | 63 | 62 | 0 | 1 | 0 | 0 | 0 | 0 | 2 | 2 | 59 | 663 | 2 | 0 | 0 | 0 | 0 | 0 |
| Dominica | 0 | 67 | 57 | 0 | 10 | 0 | 2 | 0 | 0 | 0 | 19 | 46 | 944 | 4 | 1 | 6 | 85 | 1 | 14 |
| Dominican Republic | 14 | 1748 | 1647 | 1 | 100 | 6 | 30 | 0 | 0 | 0 | 151 | 1561 | 402 | 32 | 2 | 16 | 4 | 12 | 3 |
| Ecuador | 25 | 1911 | 1658 | 6 | 247 | 3 | 0 | 0 | 69 | 0 | 653 | 1186 | 317 | 32 | 2 | 50 | 8 | 45 | 7 |
| Egypt | 6 | 1203 | 1162 | 5 | 36 | 6 | 1 | 0 | 0 | 6 | 55 | 1135 | 36 | 1928 | 372 | 30 | 1 | 52 | 2 |
| El Salvador | 23 | 1092 | 591 | 1 | 500 | 1 | 10 | 0 | 200 | 0 | 52 | 829 | 311 | 27 | 2 | 20 | 6 | 12 | 3 |
| Equatorial Guinea | 35 | 40 | 26 | 0 | 14 | 0 | 0 | 10 | 0 | 0 | 4 | 26 | 140 | 2 | 0 | 6 | 21 | 6 | 21 |
| Ethiopia | 2 | 1733 | 1708 | 4 | 21 | 31 | 0 | 0 | 0 | 12 | 1423 | 267 | 70 | 150 | 20 | 30 | 1 | 60 | 2 |
| Faeroe Islands | 103 | 22 | 22 | 0 | 0 | 0 | 0 | 0 | 0 | 0 | 2 | 20 | 564 | 10 | 1 | 6 | 154 | 0 | 0 |
| Falkland Islands | 0 | 6 | 6 | 0 | 0 | 1 | 0 | 0 | 0 | 0 | 1 | 4 | 3061 | 2 | 1 | 0 | 0 | 0 | 0 |
| Fiji | 106 | 343 | 308 | 0 | 35 | 13 | 0 | 0 | 10 | 0 | 70 | 250 | 660 | 20 | 4 | 15 | 29 | 8 | 15 |
| Finland | 119 | 224 | 221 | 3 | 0 | 1 | 0 | 0 | 100 | 5 | 60 | 58 | 49 | 4245 | 233 | 105 | 23 | 60 | 13 |
| France | 448 | 13772 | 11799 | 212 | 1761 | 12 | 10 | 6 | 700 | 54 | 581 | 12409 | 272 | 26247 | 943 | 1200 | 24 | 670 | 13 |
| French Guiana | 0 | 142 | 126 | 0 | 16 | 0 | 0 | 0 | 0 | 0 | 15 | 127 | 2784 | 3 | 0 | 2 | 39 | 0 | 0 |
| French Polynesia | 0 | 205 | 181 | 3 | 21 | 0 | 0 | 0 | 70 | 0 | 22 | 113 | 1881 | 5 | 0 | 10 | 92 | 2 | 18 |
| French Southern& Antarctic T | 0 | 0 | 0 | 0 | 0 | 0 | 0 | 0 | 0 | 0 | 0 | 0 | 0 | 0 | 0 | 0 | 0 | 0 | 0 |
| Gabon | 20 | 261 | 239 | 0 | 22 | 0 | 2 | 0 | 0 | 0 | 59 | 200 | 522 | 10 | 1 | 4 | 8 | 4 | 8 |
| Gambia | 0 | 57 | 50 | 0 | 7 | 3 | 0 | 0 | 0 | 0 | 21 | 33 | 123 | 3 | 0 | 2 | 4 | 0 | 0 |
| German Democratic Rep | 0 | 135 | 132 | 3 | 0 | 0 | 0 | 0 | 100 | 5 | 10 | 20 | 8 | 5546 | 327 | 50 | 3 | 60 | 4 |
| Germany, Federal Rep | 278 | 6077 | 5508 | 134 | 435 | 10 | 10 | 0 | 1000 | 78 | 473 | 4506 | 100 | 48034 | 2288 | 2850 | 47 | 850 | 14 |
| Ghana | 24 | 1057 | 890 | 17 | 150 | 23 | 83 | 0 | 0 | 1 | 413 | 537 | 123 | 366 | 114 | 80 | 9 | 35 | 4 |
| Gibraltar | 0 | 32 | 32 | 0 | 0 | 5 | 0 | 0 | 0 | 0 | 2 | 25 | 1231 | 5 | 1 | 4 | 154 | 0 | 0 |
| Greece | 22 | 377 | 253 | 118 | 6 | 1 | 0 | 1 | 0 | 143 | 52 | 180 | 43 | 2920 | 371 | 90 | 10 | 500 | 57 |
| Greenland | 0 | 17 | 17 | 0 | 0 | 0 | 0 | 0 | 0 | 0 | 15 | 2 | 362 | 3 | 0 | 2 | 43 | 1 | 21 |
| Grenada | 21 | 61 | 53 | 0 | 8 | 0 | 0 | 0 | 0 | 0 | 16 | 45 | 649 | 10 | 1 | 12 | 128 | 0 | 0 |
| Guadeloupe | 241 | 281 | 270 | 1 | 10 | 0 | 0 | 0 | 0 | 0 | 24 | 257 | 857 | 30 | 2 | 10 | 30 | 4 | 12 |
| Guam | 0 | 278 | 245 | 0 | 33 | 1 | 2 | 0 | 20 | 0 | 35 | 220 | 3159 | 4 | 0 | 9 | 102 | 2 | 23 |
| Guatemala | 29 | 2135 | 1388 | 3 | 744 | 4 | 10 | 0 | 300 | 0 | 369 | 1452 | 403 | 166 | 9 | 40 | 8 | 60 | 11 |
| Guinea | 0 | 26 | 18 | 0 | 8 | 1 | 0 | 0 | 0 | 0 | 20 | 5 | 7 | 8 | 0 | 3 | 1 | 0 | 0 |
| Guinea-Bissau | 4 | 86 | 81 | 0 | 5 | 0 | 0 | 0 | 0 | 0 | 22 | 64 | 177 | 3 | 0 | 3 | 6 | 4 | 8 |
| Guyana | 3 | 193 | 176 | 0 | 17 | 22 | 1 | 0 | 0 | 2 | 61 | 107 | 272 | 56 | 2 | 20 | 28 | 7 | 10 |
| Haiti | 6 | 1195 | 1160 | 0 | 35 | 9 | 25 | 0 | 0 | 0 | 344 | 817 | 282 | 18 | 3 | 40 | 9 | 20 | 5 |
| Holy See | 101010 | 360 | 300 | 20 | 40 | 0 | 0 | 0 | 0 | 0 | 0 | 360 | 72727 | 417 | 213 | 100 | 20202 | 60 | 12121 |
| Honduras | 20 | 699 | 559 | 0 | 140 | 3 | 4 | 0 | 70 | 0 | 277 | 345 | 274 | 173 | 5 | 20 | 8 | 19 | 7 |
| Hong Kong | 48 | 1405 | 1279 | 2 | 124 | 23 | 51 | 0 | 114 | 0 | 543 | 674 | 356 | 806 | 41 | 220 | 56 | 50 | 13 |
| Hungary | 4 | 14 | 9 | 5 | 0 | 0 | 0 | 0 | 0 | 5 | 9 | 0 | 1 | 8050 | 67 | 27 | 3 | 45 | 4 |
| Iceland | 54 | 63 | 63 | 0 | 0 | 0 | 0 | 0 | 0 | 0 | 19 | 44 | 309 | 609 | 22 | 20 | 98 | 2 | 10 |
| India | 7 | 5979 | 5673 | 39 | 267 | 127 | 53 | 7 | 0 | 4 | 2249 | 3539 | 11 | 14064 | 841 | 650 | 1 | 580 | 1 |
| Indonesia | 2 | 4360 | 4004 | 50 | 306 | 0 | 46 | 3 | 0 | 0 | 1211 | 3100 | 36 | 1917 | 229 | 220 | 2 | 150 | 1 |
| Iran | 0 | 300 | 279 | 2 | 19 | 39 | 0 | 0 | 0 | 1 | 153 | 107 | 11 | 3353 | 582 | 18 | 1 | 5 | 0 |
| Iraq | 3 | 66 | 59 | 0 | 7 | 0 | 0 | 0 | 0 | 2 | 8 | 56 | 7 | 143 | 11 | 15 | 2 | 8 | 1 |
| Ireland | 3229 | 242 | 232 | 0 | 10 | 12 | 0 | 0 | 150 | 0 | 65 | 15 | 82 | 678 | 51 | 160 | 54 | 60 | 20 |
| Isle of Man | 71 | 3 | 3 | 0 | 0 | 2 | 0 | 0 | 0 | 0 | 1 | 0 | 54 | 10 | 1 | 15 | 268 | 0 | 0 |
| Israel | 5 | 534 | 449 | 30 | 55 | 20 | 0 | 0 | 0 | 25 | 139 | 350 | 181 | 1866 | 231 | 80 | 27 | 32 | 11 |
| Italy | 473 | 9388 | 8284 | 104 | 1000 | 9 | 0 | 4 | 0 | 9 | 271 | 9095 | 175 | 9443 | 484 | 1400 | 26 | 850 | 16 |
| Ivory Coast | 35 | 1087 | 1014 | 3 | 70 | 0 | 15 | 0 | 0 | 0 | 279 | 793 | 252 | 260 | 1 | 18 | 4 | 13 | 3 |
| Jamaica | 200 | 597 | 558 | 0 | 39 | 29 | 24 | 0 | 0 | 5 | 269 | 270 | 317 | 120 | 4 | 40 | 21 | 15 | 8 |
| Japan | 5 | 6116 | 5765 | 41 | 310 | 27 | 32 | 0 | 1060 | 5 | 2574 | 2418 | 59 | 35857 | 1770 | 280 | 3 | 120 | 1 |
| Johnston Island | 0 | 0 | 0 | 0 | 0 | 0 | 0 | 0 | 0 | 0 | 0 | 0 | .0 | 0 | 0 | 0 | 0 | 0 | 0 |
| Jordan | 12 | 129 | 109 | 0 | 20 | 4 | 0 | 0 | 0 | 1 | 54 | 70 | 79 | 89 | 10 | 8 | 5 | 0 | 0 |
| Kampuchea | 0 | 77 | 55 | 0 | 22 | 0 | 3 | 0 | 0 | 0 | 19 | 55 | 11 | 29 | 1 | 3 | 0 | 0 | 0 |
| Kenya | 10 | 2969 | 2788 | 6 | 175 | 188 | 15 | 2 | 34 | 4 | 1086 | 1640 | 264 | 224 | 91 | 120 | 11 | 28 | 2 |
| Kiribati | 60 | 51 | 49 | 0 | 2 | 0 | 0 | 0 | 0 | 0 | 5 | 46 | 1020 | 1 | 0 | 10 | 179 | 3 | 54 |
| Korea, North | 0 | 0 | 0 | 0 | 0 | 0 | 0 | 0 | 0 | 0 | 0 | 0 | 0 | 2000 | 5 | 0 | 0 | 0 | 0 |
| Korea, South | 20 | 1537 | 1423 | 2 | 112 | 8 | 22 | 0 | 320 | 1 | 544 | 642 | 50 | 7396 | 521 | 90 | 3 | 160 | 5 |
| Kuwait | 0 | 48 | 8 | 0 | 40 | 0 | 1 | 0 | 0 | 5 | 6 | 36 | 63 | 138 | 8 | 5 | 7 | 0 | 0 |
| Laos | 0 | 223 | 178 | 0 | 45 | 0 | 0 | 0 | 0 | 0 | 93 | 130 | 75 | 179 | 13 | 3 | 1 | 0 | 0 |
| Lebanon | 70 | 1080 | 966 | 10 | 104 | 3 | 0 | 0 | 0 | 26 | 272 | 779 | 437 | 427 | 120 | 60 | 24 | 55 | 22 |
| Lesotho | 17 | 655 | 482 | 2 | 171 | 38 | 40 | 0 | 0 | 0 | 135 | 442 | 628 | 63 | 19 | 20 | 19 | 14 | 13 |
| Liberia | 9 | 753 | 676 | 0 | 77 | 11 | 80 | 6 | 0 | 0 | 507 | 149 | 494 | 40 | 10 | 30 | 20 | 16 | 11 |
| Libya | 0 | 179 | 116 | 3 | 60 | 2 | 0 | 0 | 0 | 9 | 40 | 128 | 92 | 218 | 9 | 2 | 1 | 0 | 0 |
| Liechtenstein | 472 | 23 | 23 | 0 | 0 | 0 | 0 | 0 | 0 | 0 | 3 | 20 | 1085 | 4 | 0 | 3 | 142 | 0 | 0 |
| Luxembourg | 265 | 32 | 32 | 0 | 0 | 1 | 0 | 0 | 0 | 0 | 11 | 20 | 94 | 387 | 24 | 25 | 74 | 10 | 29 |
| Macao | 8 | 324 | 292 | 0 | 32 | 0 | 2 | 0 | 0 | 0 | 12 | 310 | 1306 | 2 | 0 | 2 | 8 | 1 | 4 |
| Madagascar | 15 | 1872 | 1828 | 29 | 15 | 7 | 0 | 0 | 0 | 0 | 287 | 1578 | 270 | 190 | 35 | 35 | 5 | 23 | 3 |
| Malawi | 21 | 994 | 847 | 0 | 147 | 28 | 44 | 3 | 0 | 0 | 328 | 591 | 228 | 238 | 49 | 30 | 7 | 22 | 5 |
| Malaysia | 0 | 928 | 792 | 0 | 136 | 42 | 40 | 0 | 0 | 3 | 473 | 370 | 89 | 1237 | 68 | 30 | 3 | 10 | 1 |

| | INTERNATIONAL SHARING OF PERSONNEL | | | | | | | | | | | | | CHRISTIAN LITERATURE | | | | | |
|---|---|---|---|---|---|---|---|---|---|---|---|---|---|---|---|---|---|---|---|
| | | ALIENS RECEIVED FROM ABROAD | | | | | | | | | | | | BOOKS, PERIODICALS & LIBRARIES | | | | | |
| | pmillion | Total | West | Comm | ThirdW | Anglican | NWInd | CathNR | Marginal | Orthodox | Protest | RC | pmillion | Titles | Religious | Periodic | pmillion | Libraries | pmillion |
| | 44 | 45 | 46 | 47 | 48 | 49 | 50 | 51 | 52 | 53 | 54 | 55 | 56 | 57 | 58 | 59 | 60 | 61 | 62 |
| Maldives | 0 | 0 | 0 | 0 | 0 | 0 | 0 | 0 | 0 | 0 | 0 | 0 | 0 | 24 | 1 | 0 | 0 | 0 | 0 |
| Mali | 0 | 396 | 374 | 0 | 22 | 0 | 0 | 0 | 0 | 0 | 96 | 300 | 78 | 10 | 1 | 7 | 1 | 6 | 1 |
| Malta | 2288 | 18 | 18 | 0 | 0 | 6 | 0 | 0 | 0 | 1 | 1 | 10 | 55 | 123 | 29 | 56 | 172 | 8 | 25 |
| Martinique | 148 | 177 | 119 | 0 | 58 | 0 | 0 | 0 | 0 | 0 | 10 | 167 | 524 | 15 | 2 | 4 | 12 | 2 | 6 |
| Mauritania | 0 | 22 | 22 | 0 | 0 | 0 | 0 | 0 | 0 | 0 | 0 | 22 | 19 | 5 | 1 | 1 | 1 | 0 | 0 |
| Mauritius | 38 | 151 | 126 | 0 | 25 | 10 | 0 | 0 | 0 | 0 | 11 | 130 | 183 | 86 | 3 | 4 | 5 | 2 | 2 |
| Mayotte | 0 | 0 | 0 | 0 | 0 | 0 | 0 | 0 | 0 | 0 | 0 | 0 | 0 | 0 | 0 | 0 | 0 | 0 | 0 |
| Mexico | 41 | 5648 | 4642 | 1 | 1005 | 11 | 0 | 0 | 1000 | 35 | 1431 | 3171 | 112 | 5733 | 85 | 500 | 10 | 180 | 4 |
| Midway Islands | 0 | 3 | 3 | 0 | 0 | 0 | 0 | 0 | 0 | 0 | 2 | 1 | 1351 | 0 | 0 | 0 | 0 | 0 | 0 |
| Monaco | 0 | 147 | 147 | 0 | 0 | 1 | 0 | 0 | 0 | 0 | 46 | 100 | 6391 | 114 | 1 | 6 | 261 | 1 | 43 |
| Mongolia | 0 | 0 | 0 | 0 | 0 | 0 | 0 | 0 | 0 | 0 | 0 | 0 | 0 | 587 | 2 | 0 | 0 | 0 | 0 |
| Montserrat | 0 | 4 | 2 | 0 | 2 | 2 | 0 | 0 | 0 | 0 | 1 | 1 | 333 | 0 | 0 | 3 | 250 | 0 | 0 |
| Morocco | 0 | 928 | 891 | 4 | 33 | 9 | 0 | 0 | 0 | 1 | 84 | 834 | 61 | 122 | 2 | 15 | 1 | 4 | 0 |
| Mozambique | 7 | 2048 | 1907 | 2 | 139 | 14 | 20 | 0 | 0 | 2 | 162 | 1850 | 249 | 50 | 5 | 30 | 4 | 13 | 2 |
| Namibia | 16 | 711 | 544 | 0 | 167 | 35 | 50 | 2 | 0 | 0 | 204 | 420 | 1123 | 30 | 5 | 25 | 39 | 5 | 8 |
| Nauru | 0 | 8 | 4 | 0 | 4 | 0 | 0 | 0 | 0 | 0 | 3 | 5 | 1231 | 0 | 0 | 2 | 308 | 0 | 0 |
| Nepal | 0 | 307 | 271 | 0 | 36 | 4 | 1 | 0 | 0 | 0 | 277 | 25 | 27 | 20 | 4 | 3 | 0 | 2 | 0 |
| Netherlands | 797 | 1771 | 1697 | 30 | 44 | 8 | 5 | 2 | 100 | 4 | 93 | 1559 | 136 | 11440 | 526 | 500 | 38 | 300 | 23 |
| Netherlands Antilles | 45 | 445 | 433 | 0 | 12 | 0 | 0 | 0 | 0 | 0 | 135 | 310 | 2005 | 63 | 2 | 12 | 54 | 4 | 18 |
| New Caledonia | 119 | 247 | 0 | 0 | 21 | 0 | 0 | 0 | 0 | 0 | 17 | 230 | 2266 | 5 | 1 | 7 | 64 | 4 | 37 |
| New Zealand | 421 | 2059 | 1904 | 3 | 152 | 50 | 0 | 0 | 550 | 2 | 95 | 1362 | 730 | 1598 | 58 | 155 | 55 | 30 | 11 |
| Nicaragua | 36 | 965 | 545 | 0 | 420 | 4 | 10 | 0 | 20 | 0 | 151 | 780 | 490 | 80 | 5 | 25 | 13 | 16 | 8 |
| Niger | 0 | 217 | 202 | 1 | 14 | 0 | 2 | 0 | 0 | 0 | 95 | 120 | 54 | 23 | 2 | 2 | 0 | 0 | 0 |
| Nigeria | 6 | 2674 | 2472 | 1 | 201 | 72 | 70 | 0 | 0 | 3 | 1578 | 951 | 49 | 1337 | 40 | 150 | 3 | 80 | 1 |
| Niue Island | 0 | 7 | 4 | 0 | 3 | 0 | 0 | 0 | 2 | 0 | 4 | 1 | 1400 | 0 | 0 | 2 | 400 | 0 | 0 |
| Norfolk Island | 0 | 1 | 1 | 0 | 0 | 0 | 0 | 0 | 0 | 0 | 0 | 1 | 588 | 0 | 0 | 0 | 0 | 0 | 0 |
| Northern Solomons | 0 | 180 | 160 | 0 | 20 | 0 | 0 | 0 | 0 | 0 | 20 | 160 | 2264 | 2 | 0 | 3 | 38 | 0 | 0 |
| Norway | 376 | 599 | 597 | 0 | 2 | 1 | 0 | 0 | 60 | 0 | 62 | 476 | 155 | 5694 | 319 | 90 | 23 | 30 | 8 |
| Oman | 0 | 25 | 24 | 0 | 1 | 0 | 1 | 0 | 0 | 0 | 23 | 1 | 38 | 2 | 0 | 2 | 3 | 0 | 0 |
| Pacific Islands | 0 | 222 | 190 | 0 | 32 | 0 | 0 | 0 | 26 | 0 | 66 | 130 | 2193 | 5 | 0 | 8 | 79 | 3 | 30 |
| Pakistan | 0 | 1160 | 1120 | 0 | 40 | 28 | 0 | 0 | 0 | 0 | 502 | 630 | 19 | 933 | 275 | 35 | 1 | 15 | 0 |
| Palestine | 129 | 806 | 595 | 60 | 151 | 15 | 0 | 0 | 0 | 191 | 160 | 440 | 682 | 200 | 10 | 30 | 25 | 30 | 25 |
| Panama | 243 | 909 | 566 | 0 | 343 | 10 | 8 | 0 | 20 | 0 | 181 | 690 | 623 | 171 | 2 | 20 | 14 | 20 | 14 |
| Panama Canal Zone | 0 | 37 | 27 | 0 | 10 | 3 | 2 | 0 | 0 | 0 | 16 | 16 | 837 | 2 | 0 | 10 | 226 | 0 | 0 |
| Papua New Guinea | 6 | 3328 | 3177 | 36 | 115 | 176 | 0 | 0 | 0 | 0 | 1870 | 1282 | 1379 | 50 | 10 | 30 | 12 | 34 | 14 |
| Paraguay | 78 | 787 | 624 | 17 | 146 | 25 | 6 | 0 | 10 | 2 | 244 | 500 | 342 | 100 | 5 | 20 | 9 | 16 | 7 |
| Peru | 20 | 5458 | 5145 | 23 | 290 | 8 | 20 | 0 | 270 | 2 | 795 | 4363 | 12 | 1322 | 55 | 50 | 4 | 65 | 5 |
| Philippines | 31 | 5990 | 5732 | 6 | 252 | 17 | 10 | 0 | 270 | 0 | 1307 | 4386 | 159 | 706 | 22 | 170 | 5 | 195 | 5 |
| Pitcairn Islands | 0 | 0 | 0 | 0 | 0 | 0 | 0 | 0 | 0 | 0 | 0 | 0 | 0 | 0 | 0 | 0 | 0 | 0 | 0 |
| Poland | 45 | 15 | 15 | 0 | 0 | 0 | 0 | 0 | 0 | 0 | 15 | 0 | 0 | 10744 | 173 | 75 | 2 | 76 | 2 |
| Portugal | 489 | 355 | 321 | 0 | 34 | 4 | 2 | 0 | 0 | 0 | 89 | 260 | 41 | 7326 | 323 | 220 | 25 | 35 | 4 |
| Puerto Rico | 224 | 1978 | 1538 | 0 | 440 | 12 | 10 | 0 | 30 | 1 | 275 | 1650 | 721 | 200 | 10 | 35 | 13 | 25 | 0 |
| Qatar | 0 | 3 | 2 | 0 | 1 | 0 | 0 | 0 | 0 | 1 | 0 | 2 | 27 | 152 | 38 | 0 | 0 | 0 | 0 |
| Reunion | 11 | 272 | 252 | 0 | 20 | 0 | 0 | 0 | 0 | 0 | 4 | 268 | 609 | 10 | 1 | 2 | 4 | 2 | 4 |
| Romania | 5 | 30 | 0 | 30 | 0 | 0 | 0 | 0 | 0 | 30 | 0 | 0 | 1 | 10100 | 84 | 35 | 2 | 200 | 10 |
| Rwanda | 19 | 867 | 796 | 17 | 54 | 32 | 0 | 0 | 0 | 0 | 121 | 714 | 236 | 13 | 2 | 12 | 3 | 17 | 5 |
| Sahara | 0 | 29 | 29 | 0 | 0 | 0 | 0 | 0 | 0 | 0 | 0 | 29 | 318 | 0 | 0 | 1 | 11 | 0 | 0 |
| St Helena | 0 | 10 | 5 | 0 | 5 | 7 | 0 | 0 | 0 | 0 | 2 | 1 | 1538 | 0 | 0 | 2 | 308 | 0 | 0 |
| St Kitts-Nevis | 34 | 28 | 23 | 0 | 5 | 0 | 0 | 0 | 0 | 0 | 18 | 10 | 475 | 3 | 0 | 6 | 102 | 0 | 0 |
| St Lucia | 0 | 96 | 86 | 0 | 10 | 1 | 0 | 0 | 0 | 0 | 22 | 73 | 950 | 5 | 1 | 7 | 69 | 0 | 0 |
| St Pierre & Miquelon | 0 | 26 | 26 | 0 | 0 | 0 | 0 | 0 | 0 | 0 | 0 | 26 | 4727 | 0 | 0 | 1 | 182 | 0 | 0 |
| St Vincent | 0 | 55 | 30 | 0 | 25 | 12 | 0 | 0 | 0 | 0 | 16 | 27 | 625 | 3 | 0 | 4 | 45 | 1 | 11 |
| Samoa | 1149 | 508 | 447 | 0 | 61 | 1 | 0 | 0 | 340 | 0 | 7 | 160 | 3603 | 10 | 2 | 14 | 99 | 3 | 21 |
| San Marino | 0 | 20 | 20 | 0 | 0 | 0 | 0 | 0 | 0 | 0 | 0 | 20 | 1053 | 1 | 0 | 2 | 105 | 0 | 0 |
| Sao Tome & Principe | 0 | 36 | 31 | 0 | 5 | 0 | 0 | 0 | 0 | 0 | 2 | 34 | 486 | 1 | 0 | 1 | 14 | 0 | 0 |
| Saudi Arabia | 0 | 13 | 3 | 0 | 10 | 0 | 0 | 0 | 0 | 0 | 1 | 12 | 2 | 82 | 9 | 0 | 0 | 0 | 0 |
| Senegal | 18 | 753 | 731 | 0 | 22 | 0 | 0 | 0 | 0 | 0 | 93 | 660 | 192 | 60 | 10 | 14 | 4 | 8 | 2 |
| Seychelles | 0 | 88 | 83 | 0 | 5 | 3 | 0 | 0 | 0 | 0 | 36 | 49 | 1692 | 2 | 0 | 2 | 38 | 2 | 38 |
| Sierra Leone | 1 | 446 | 415 | 0 | 31 | 11 | 14 | 0 | 0 | 0 | 246 | 175 | 169 | 73 | 10 | 15 | 6 | 8 | 3 |
| Sikkim | 0 | 13 | 3 | 0 | 10 | 0 | 2 | 0 | 0 | 0 | 6 | 5 | 65 | 0 | 0 | 0 | 0 | 0 | 0 |
| Singapore | 6 | 462 | 395 | 0 | 67 | 21 | 9 | 0 | 0 | 1 | 266 | 165 | 223 | 510 | 24 | 25 | 12 | 10 | 5 |
| Solomon Islands | 276 | 320 | 280 | 0 | 40 | 60 | 0 | 0 | 0 | 0 | 138 | 122 | 1963 | 10 | 3 | 8 | 49 | 5 | 31 |
| Somalia | 0 | 206 | 186 | 0 | 20 | 0 | 0 | 0 | 0 | 0 | 70 | 136 | 74 | 17 | 2 | 1 | 0 | 0 | 0 |
| South Africa | 54 | 6507 | 6279 | 25 | 203 | 232 | 63 | 40 | 220 | 2 | 1425 | 4525 | 303 | 3849 | 192 | 240 | 11 | 150 | 7 |
| Spain | 826 | 1638 | 1293 | 0 | 345 | 8 | 40 | 0 | 0 | 1 | 309 | 1280 | 48 | 24085 | 1411 | 910 | 27 | 300 | 9 |
| Spanish North Africa | 0 | 52 | 52 | 0 | 0 | 0 | 0 | 0 | 0 | 0 | 2 | 50 | 315 | 0 | 0 | 0 | 0 | 0 | 0 |
| Sri Lanka | 7 | 350 | 298 | 2 | 50 | 5 | 4 | 0 | 0 | 0 | 77 | 264 | 28 | 1502 | 134 | 70 | 6 | 25 | 2 |
| Sudan | 4 | 283 | 246 | 0 | 37 | 16 | 0 | 0 | 0 | 18 | 54 | 195 | 18 | 104 | 6 | 12 | 1 | 5 | 0 |
| Surinam | 27 | 330 | 310 | 0 | 20 | 0 | 0 | 0 | 0 | 0 | 104 | 226 | 889 | 10 | 1 | 5 | 13 | 2 | 5 |
| Svalbard & Jan Mayen Is | 0 | 2 | 2 | 0 | 0 | 0 | 0 | 0 | 0 | 0 | 2 | 0 | 571 | 0 | 0 | 0 | 0 | 0 | 0 |
| Swaziland | 68 | 433 | 278 | 0 | 00 | 0 | 0 | 0 | 0 | 0 | 250 | 125 | 1059 | 6 | 2 | 20 | 49 | 3 | 7 |
| Sweden | 230 | 594 | 000 | 00 | 0 | 0 | 0 | 0 | 0 | 0 | 0 | 347 | 74 | 9014 | 317 | 320 | 29 | 40 | 5 |
| Switzerland | 448 | 1074 | 961 | 33 | 80 | 11 | 0 | 8 | 100 | 10 | 100 | 845 | 171 | 9310 | 581 | 220 | 35 | 150 | 24 |
| Syria | 15 | 111 | 80 | 1 | 30 | 0 | 0 | 0 | 0 | 16 | 14 | 81 | 18 | 459 | 41 | 30 | 5 | 0 | 0 |
| Tanzania | 8 | 2971 | 2833 | 26 | 112 | 162 | 30 | 0 | 0 | 2 | 844 | 1933 | 224 | 123 | 28 | 60 | 5 | 60 | 5 |
| Thailand | 0 | 1333 | 1195 | 4 | 134 | 0 | 4 | 0 | 0 | 0 | 840 | 489 | 37 | 2255 | 302 | 20 | 1 | 15 | 0 |
| Timor | 0 | 62 | 50 | 0 | 12 | 0 | 0 | 0 | 0 | 0 | 4 | 58 | 103 | 0 | 0 | 2 | 3 | 0 | 0 |
| Togo | 19 | 316 | 231 | 8 | 77 | 0 | 35 | 0 | 0 | 0 | 68 | 213 | 161 | 30 | 5 | 10 | 5 | 5 | 3 |
| Tokelau | 0 | 3 | 1 | 0 | 2 | 0 | 0 | 0 | 0 | 0 | 2 | 1 | 1765 | 0 | 0 | 1 | 588 | 0 | 0 |
| Tonga | 326 | 320 | 260 | 0 | 60 | 0 | 0 | 0 | 250 | 0 | 21 | 49 | 3721 | 10 | 3 | 8 | 93 | 2 | 23 |
| Trinidad & Tobago | 89 | 366 | 320 | 0 | 46 | 21 | 4 | 0 | 0 | 2 | 149 | 190 | 383 | 70 | 5 | 20 | 21 | 10 | 10 |
| Tunisia | 0 | 462 | 450 | 2 | 10 | 1 | 0 | 0 | 0 | 0 | 31 | 430 | 90 | 249 | 31 | 1 | 0 | 2 | 0 |
| Turkey | 0 | 345 | 341 | 2 | 2 | 2 | 0 | 0 | 0 | 24 | 79 | 240 | 10 | 7479 | 239 | 13 | 0 | 7 | 0 |
| Turks & Caicos Islands | 0 | 7 | 4 | 0 | 3 | 0 | 0 | 0 | 0 | 0 | 6 | 1 | 1259 | 0 | 0 | 2 | 360 | 0 | 0 |
| Tuvalu | 0 | 3 | 2 | 0 | 1 | 0 | 0 | 0 | 0 | 0 | 1 | 2 | 500 | 0 | 0 | 2 | 333 | 0 | 0 |
| Uganda | 13 | 1566 | 1465 | 7 | 94 | 145 | 30 | 0 | 17 | 3 | 144 | 1227 | 160 | 373 | 19 | 28 | 3 | 28 | 3 |
| USSR | 1 | 30 | 20 | 10 | 0 | 2 | 0 | 0 | 0 | 15 | 10 | 3 | 0 | 80196 | 222 | 70 | 0 | 72 | 0 |
| United Arab Emirates | 0 | 74 | 42 | 0 | 32 | 2 | 2 | 0 | 0 | 1 | 35 | 34 | 247 | 10 | 2 | 2 | 7 | 0 | 0 |
| UK of GB & NI | 185 | 5740 | 5164 | 93 | 483 | 332 | 230 | 2 | 1830 | 70 | 202 | 3074 | 103 | 32133 | 1125 | 1400 | 25 | 480 | 9 |
| USA | 279 | 16746 | 14534 | 127 | 2085 | 244 | 185 | 22 | 320 | 151 | 5242 | 10582 | 82 | 81023 | 2041 | 5430 | 26 | 2700 | 13 |
| US Virgin Islands | 0 | 91 | 84 | 0 | 7 | 5 | 6 | 0 | 0 | 0 | 41 | 39 | 1456 | 5 | 0 | 12 | 192 | 0 | 0 |
| Upper Volta | 10 | 894 | 814 | 1 | 79 | 0 | 14 | 0 | 6 | 0 | 136 | 738 | 166 | 30 | 5 | 9 | 2 | 14 | 3 |
| Uruguay | 125 | 1975 | 1441 | 8 | 526 | 1 | 6 | 5 | 320 | 3 | 193 | 1447 | 668 | 601 | 10 | 40 | 14 | 20 | 7 |
| Vanuatu | 24 | 200 | 182 | 0 | 18 | 20 | 4 | 0 | 0 | 0 | 81 | 95 | 2381 | 2 | 0 | 6 | 71 | 2 | 24 |
| Venezuela | 45 | 4520 | 3707 | 21 | 792 | 5 | 30 | 0 | 0 | 4 | 459 | 4022 | 428 | 700 | 30 | 45 | 4 | 44 | 4 |
| Viet Nam | 9 | 806 | 731 | 0 | 75 | 0 | 10 | 0 | 0 | 0 | 326 | 470 | 21 | 729 | 31 | 30 | 1 | 65 | 2 |
| Wake Island | 0 | 2 | 2 | 0 | 0 | 0 | 0 | 0 | 0 | 0 | 1 | 1 | 1250 | 0 | 0 | 0 | 0 | 0 | 0 |
| Wallis & Futuna Islands | 1778 | 22 | 18 | 0 | 4 | 0 | 0 | 0 | 0 | 0 | 0 | 22 | 2244 | 3 | 1 | 1 | 111 | 0 | 0 |
| Yemen, North | 0 | 66 | 49 | 0 | 17 | 0 | 0 | 0 | 0 | 0 | 43 | 23 | 11 | 5 | 1 | 0 | 0 | 0 | 0 |
| Yemen, South | 0 | 68 | 38 | 0 | 30 | 0 | 0 | 0 | 0 | 0 | 31 | 37 | 47 | 4 | 0 | 0 | 0 | 0 | 0 |
| Yugoslavia | 32 | 379 | 365 | 14 | 0 | 0 | 0 | 0 | 0 | 14 | 15 | 350 | 19 | 13063 | 371 | 120 | 6 | 280 | 14 |
| Zaire | 20 | 8985 | 8566 | 47 | 372 | 6 | 20 | 0 | 0 | 6 | 1806 | 7147 | 415 | 100 | 20 | 80 | 4 | 130 | 6 |
| Zambia | 39 | 2001 | 1753 | 94 | 154 | 73 | 30 | 20 | 20 | 2 | 727 | 1129 | 466 | 39 | 5 | 40 | 9 | 33 | 8 |
| Zimbabwe | 18 | 2105 | 1742 | 2 | 361 | 115 | 50 | 15 | 0 | 3 | 1022 | 900 | 397 | 180 | 30 | 30 | 6 | 25 | 5 |
| Column | 44 | 45 | 46 | 47 | 48 | 49 | 50 | 51 | 52 | 53 | 54 | 55 | 56 | 57 | 58 | 59 | 60 | 61 | 62 |
| *Continent* | | | | | | | | | | | | | | | | | | | |
| Africa | — | 57852 | 53648 | 377 | 3827 | 1350 | 845 | 98 | 311 | 81 | 15546 | 39621 | — | 10918 | 1187 | 1382 | — | 983 | — |
| East Asia | — | 11239 | 10501 | 60 | 678 | 67 | 155 | 0 | 1639 | 6 | 4493 | 4879 | — | 54900 | 2459 | 658 | — | 401 | — |
| Europe | — | 46103 | 40813 | 931 | 4359 | 440 | 297 | 29 | 4680 | 456 | 2956 | 37245 | — | 275241 | 11059 | 10885 | — | 5702 | — |
| Latin America | — | 72745 | 60989 | 550 | 11206 | 388 | 447 | 32 | 4117 | 89 | 12392 | 55280 | — | 28084 | 1170 | 1884 | — | 1410 | — |
| Northern America | — | 21857 | 19033 | 255 | 2569 | 452 | 205 | 64 | 1120 | 207 | 5708 | 14101 | — | 87870 | 2271 | 5963 | — | 2951 | — |
| Oceania | — | 11274 | 10410 | 100 | 764 | 591 | 11 | 2 | 1558 | 28 | 2816 | 6268 | — | 5308 | 245 | 561 | — | 210 | — |
| South Asia | — | 26663 | 24318 | 207 | 2138 | 344 | 195 | 10 | 270 | 313 | 9068 | 16463 | — | 41048 | 3586 | 1575 | — | 1273 | — |
| USSR | — | 30 | 20 | 10 | 0 | 2 | 0 | 0 | 0 | 15 | 10 | 3 | — | 80196 | 222 | 70 | — | 72 | — |
| **WORLD** | — | **247763** | **219732** | **2490** | **25541** | **3634** | **2155** | **235** | **13695** | **1195** | **52989** | **173860** | — | **583565** | **22199** | **22978** | — | **13002** | — |

## SCRIPTURE DISTRIBUTION (organized)

| | BIBLES PER YEAR: (a) Free | | | | | (b) Subsidized | | | | | (c) Commercial | TOTAL | pmillion | NTs PER YEAR: (a) Free | |
|---|---|---|---|---|---|---|---|---|---|---|---|---|---|---|---|
| | 1900 | 1950 | 1960 | 1970 | 1975 | 1900 | 1950 | 1960 | 1970 | 1975 | 1975 | 1975 | 1975 | 1900 | 1950 |
| | 63 | 64 | 65 | 66 | 67 | 68 | 69 | 70 | 71 | 72 | 73 | 74 | 75 | 76 | 77 |
| Afghanistan | 0 | 0 | 0 | 0 | 0 | 0 | 0 | 0 | 0 | 30 | 0 | 30 | 2 | 0 | 0 |
| Albania | 0 | 0 | 0 | 0 | 0 | 100 | 0 | 0 | 0 | 0 | 0 | 0 | 0 | 0 | 0 |
| Algeria | 0 | 0 | 0 | 0 | 0 | 650 | 930 | 1430 | 394 | 400 | 0 | 400 | 24 | 0 | 0 |
| American Samoa | 0 | 0 | 0 | 0 | 0 | 20 | 100 | 200 | 500 | 1000 | 100 | 1100 | 34375 | 0 | 0 |
| Andorra | 0 | 0 | 0 | 0 | 0 | 0 | 0 | 0 | 0 | 0 | 0 | 0 | 0 | 0 | 0 |
| Angola | 0 | 0 | 0 | 0 | 0 | 100 | 1000 | 2000 | 6802 | 15396 | 1000 | 16396 | 2581 | 0 | 0 |
| Anguilla | 0 | 0 | 0 | 0 | 0 | 0 | 0 | 5 | 10 | 20 | 0 | 20 | 3333 | 0 | 0 |
| Antigua | 0 | 0 | 300 | 1160 | 400 | 0 | 150 | 350 | 600 | 760 | 100 | 1260 | 17260 | 0 | 0 |
| Argentina | 0 | 0 | 0 | 0 | 0 | 13000 | 37579 | 73640 | 67191 | 44159 | 60000 | 104159 | 4103 | 0 | 0 |
| Australia | 0 | 0 | 5500 | 12200 | 8060 | 20000 | 40876 | 84605 | 113146 | 170623 | 40000 | 218683 | 15836 | 0 | 200 |
| Austria | 0 | 0 | 3000 | 3100 | 3600 | 20000 | 14805 | 18972 | 28631 | 32314 | 130000 | 165914 | 22010 | 0 | 0 |
| Bahamas | 0 | 0 | 0 | 2500 | 4000 | 100 | 600 | 1400 | 2200 | 2880 | 300 | 7180 | 35196 | 0 | 0 |
| Bahrain | 0 | 0 | 0 | 0 | 0 | 5 | 0 | 0 | 0 | 0 | 0 | 0 | 0 | 0 | 0 |
| Bangladesh | 0 | 0 | 0 | 0 | 0 | 100 | 1000 | 1500 | 2041 | 8059 | 1000 | 9059 | 123 | 0 | 0 |
| Barbados | 0 | 0 | 700 | 100 | 0 | 100 | 900 | 2200 | 3300 | 4300 | 100 | 4400 | 17959 | 0 | 0 |
| Belgium | 0 | 0 | 0 | 700 | 0 | 1974 | 6724 | 7000 | 13538 | 19280 | 70000 | 89280 | 9068 | 0 | 10 |
| Belize | 0 | 0 | 0 | 180 | 120 | 0 | 10 | 50 | 100 | 300 | 100 | 520 | 3714 | 0 | 0 |
| Benin | 0 | 0 | 0 | 0 | 520 | 20 | 100 | 400 | 2440 | 1500 | 100 | 2120 | 690 | 0 | 0 |
| Bermuda | 0 | 0 | 250 | 500 | 780 | 100 | 50 | 50 | 100 | 150 | 200 | 1130 | 20179 | 0 | 0 |
| Bhutan | 0 | 0 | 0 | 0 | 0 | 0 | 0 | 0 | 0 | 0 | 0 | 0 | 0 | 0 | 0 |
| Bolivia | 0 | 0 | 0 | 0 | 0 | 0 | 8016 | 10434 | 15894 | 39401 | 10000 | 49401 | 9131 | 0 | 0 |
| Botswana | 0 | 0 | 0 | 0 | 0 | 20 | 1000 | 2000 | 4241 | 5000 | 100 | 5100 | 7381 | 0 | 0 |
| Brazil | 0 | 0 | 0 | 260 | 0 | 17782 | 77387 | 297546 | 204943 | 189005 | 486975 | 675980 | 6160 | 0 | 0 |
| British Antarctic Terr | 0 | 0 | 0 | 0 | 0 | 0 | 0 | 0 | 0 | 0 | 0 | 0 | 0 | 0 | 0 |
| British Indian Ocean Terr | 0 | 0 | 0 | 0 | 0 | 0 | 0 | 0 | 0 | 0 | 0 | 0 | 0 | 0 | 0 |
| British Virgin Is | 0 | 0 | 0 | 0 | 0 | 10 | 20 | 40 | 50 | 100 | 0 | 100 | 9091 | 0 | 0 |
| Brunei | 0 | 0 | 0 | 0 | 100 | 0 | 40 | 50 | 60 | 90 | 0 | 190 | 1293 | 0 | 0 |
| Bulgaria | 0 | 0 | 0 | 0 | 100 | 500 | 0 | 0 | 0 | 0 | 0 | 100 | 11 | 0 | 0 |
| Burma | 0 | 0 | 0 | 0 | 360 | 1244 | 5527 | 6967 | 14142 | 2018 | 0 | 2378 | 76 | 0 | 0 |
| Burundi | 0 | 0 | 0 | 0 | 0 | 0 | 200 | 500 | 1000 | 4000 | 2000 | 6000 | 1594 | 0 | 0 |
| Cameroon | 0 | 0 | 0 | 0 | 0 | 100 | 2000 | 10000 | 27515 | 12000 | 3000 | 15000 | 2344 | 0 | 0 |
| Canada | 0 | 28790 | 50030 | 30743 | 43856 | 25000 | 75845 | 101626 | 90626 | 114943 | 350000 | 508799 | 22315 | 0 | 123000 |
| Canton & Enderbury | 0 | 0 | 0 | 0 | 0 | 10 | 0 | 0 | 0 | 0 | 300 | 300 | 1017 | 0 | 0 |
| Cape Verde | 0 | 0 | 0 | 0 | 0 | 10 | 10 | 15 | 20 | 30 | 0 | 30 | 2727 | 0 | 0 |
| Cayman Islands | 0 | 0 | 0 | 0 | 0 | 0 | 100 | 600 | 6070 | 6000 | 100 | 6100 | 3408 | 0 | 0 |
| Central African Republic | 0 | 0 | 0 | 0 | 0 | 0 | 30 | 100 | 1380 | 1500 | 0 | 1500 | 373 | 0 | 0 |
| Chad | 0 | 0 | 0 | 0 | 0 | 100 | 300 | 400 | 500 | 600 | 3300 | 3900 | 30469 | 0 | 0 |
| Channel Islands | 0 | 0 | 0 | 0 | 0 | 500 | 13934 | 31338 | 34964 | 28736 | 40000 | 68736 | 6704 | 0 | 3000 |
| Chile | 0 | 0 | 0 | 0 | 0 | 14400 | 70000 | 0 | 0 | 0 | 0 | 0 | 0 | 0 | 0 |
| China | 0 | 0 | 3900 | 0 | 0 | 196 | 1500 | 25000 | 28774 | 50031 | 10000 | 60031 | 3838 | 0 | 700 |
| China (Taiwan) | 0 | 0 | 0 | 0 | 0 | 0 | 0 | 0 | 0 | 0 | 0 | 0 | 0 | 0 | 0 |
| Christmas Island | 0 | 0 | 0 | 0 | 0 | 0 | 0 | 0 | 0 | 0 | 0 | 0 | 0 | 0 | 0 |
| Cocos Islands | 0 | 0 | 0 | 0 | 0 | 0 | 0 | 0 | 0 | 0 | 0 | 0 | 0 | 0 | 0 |
| Colombia | 0 | 0 | 0 | 0 | 0 | 0 | 2721 | 25736 | 47660 | 37964 | 50000 | 87964 | 3398 | 0 | 0 |
| Comoros | 0 | 0 | 0 | 0 | 0 | 0 | 0 | 0 | 0 | 0 | 0 | 0 | 0 | 0 | 0 |
| Congo | 0 | 0 | 0 | 0 | 0 | 0 | 50 | 200 | 300 | 600 | 2000 | 2600 | 1933 | 0 | 0 |
| Cook Islands | 0 | 0 | 0 | 0 | 0 | 50 | 300 | 400 | 600 | 850 | 0 | 850 | 34000 | 0 | 0 |
| Costa Rica | 0 | 0 | 0 | 0 | 0 | 400 | 832 | 3695 | 8886 | 14222 | 20000 | 34222 | 17162 | 0 | 0 |
| Cuba | 0 | 0 | 0 | 0 | 0 | 1360 | 12206 | 40532 | 0 | 2000 | 0 | 2000 | 211 | 0 | 0 |
| Cyprus | 0 | 0 | 0 | 260 | 300 | 0 | 472 | 1013 | 674 | 462 | 700 | 1462 | 2172 | 0 | 200 |
| Czechoslovakia | 0 | 0 | 0 | 0 | 0 | 4000 | 22661 | 20000 | 31596 | 51000 | 0 | 51000 | 3456 | 0 | 0 |
| Denmark | 0 | 0 | 300 | 1500 | 500 | 1131 | 27341 | 22577 | 32059 | 28588 | 2000 | 31088 | 6185 | 0 | 0 |
| Djibouti | 0 | 0 | 0 | 0 | 0 | 0 | 0 | 0 | 0 | 0 | 0 | 0 | 0 | 0 | 0 |
| Dominica | 0 | 0 | 50 | 0 | 0 | 0 | 200 | 400 | 700 | 900 | 0 | 900 | 12000 | 0 | 0 |
| Dominican Republic | 0 | 0 | 0 | 60 | 200 | 300 | 5110 | 5396 | 17302 | 22124 | 10000 | 32324 | 6316 | 0 | 0 |
| Ecuador | 0 | 0 | 0 | 0 | 0 | 10 | 2868 | 4052 | 15972 | 21878 | 30000 | 51878 | 7317 | 0 | 0 |
| Egypt | 0 | 0 | 0 | 0 | 2300 | 30 | 7369 | 10953 | 24655 | 17893 | 1000 | 21193 | 564 | 0 | 0 |
| El Salvador | 0 | 0 | 0 | 0 | 0 | 400 | 2274 | 6103 | 9328 | 16513 | 20000 | 36513 | 8888 | 0 | 0 |
| Equatorial Guinea | 0 | 0 | 0 | 0 | 0 | 0 | 0 | 0 | 0 | 0 | 0 | 0 | 0 | 0 | 0 |
| Ethiopia | 0 | 0 | 0 | 1000 | 1000 | 10 | 2337 | 4060 | 22674 | 32865 | 3000 | 36865 | 1318 | 0 | 1000 |
| Faeroe Islands | 0 | 0 | 0 | 0 | 0 | 50 | 100 | 200 | 400 | 597 | 0 | 597 | 14925 | 0 | 0 |
| Falkland Islands | 0 | 0 | 0 | 0 | 0 | 2 | 3 | 3 | 5 | 5 | 0 | 5 | 2500 | 0 | 0 |
| Fiji | 0 | 0 | 0 | 380 | 1500 | 20 | 1000 | 2000 | 4000 | 6500 | 200 | 8200 | 14211 | 0 | 0 |
| Finland | 0 | 0 | 2090 | 0 | 1000 | 261 | 19393 | 80067 | 80207 | 76228 | 5000 | 82228 | 176676 | 0 | 700 |
| France | 0 | 0 | 0 | 5222 | 16216 | 13000 | 38836 | 41344 | 91049 | 36756 | 300000 | 352972 | 6671 | 0 | 0 |
| French Guiana | 0 | 0 | 0 | 0 | 0 | 10 | 50 | 100 | 200 | 400 | 0 | 400 | 6667 | 0 | 0 |
| French Polynesia | 0 | 0 | 0 | 0 | 0 | 677 | 800 | 1000 | 1400 | 1600 | 1000 | 2600 | 20313 | 0 | 0 |
| French Southern & Antarctic T | 0 | 0 | 0 | 0 | 0 | 0 | 0 | 0 | 0 | 0 | 0 | 0 | 0 | 0 | 0 |
| Gabon | 0 | 0 | 0 | 0 | 0 | 0 | 500 | 1000 | 2572 | 640 | 410 | 1050 | 2000 | 0 | 0 |
| Gambia | 0 | 0 | 0 | 0 | 0 | 20 | 50 | 60 | 80 | 100 | 0 | 100 | 196 | 0 | 0 |
| German Democratic Rep | 0 | 0 | 0 | 0 | 0 | 130000 | 100000 | 75673 | 27320 | 19873 | 0 | 19873 | 1156 | 0 | 0 |
| Germany, Federal Rep | 0 | 0 | 450 | 28880 | 26080 | 270000 | 200000 | 400000 | 469109 | 441036 | 500000 | 967116 | 15679 | 0 | 5 |
| Ghana | 0 | 0 | 0 | 0 | 3000 | 500 | 10000 | 20000 | 46013 | 89594 | 30000 | 122590 | 12417 | 0 | 0 |
| Gibraltar | 0 | 0 | 0 | 0 | 0 | 0 | 3 | 4 | 8 | 10 | 10 | 20 | 741 | 0 | 0 |
| Greece | 0 | 0 | 0 | 300 | 2100 | 748 | 4924 | 6285 | 17909 | 12392 | 10000 | 24492 | 2743 | 0 | 0 |
| Greenland | 0 | 0 | 0 | 0 | 0 | 20 | 70 | 100 | 150 | 170 | 0 | 170 | 3148 | 0 | 0 |
| Grenada | 0 | 0 | 150 | 150 | 300 | 10 | 200 | 500 | 800 | 950 | 0 | 1250 | 13021 | 0 | 0 |
| Guadeloupe | 0 | 0 | 0 | 0 | 0 | 50 | 1000 | 2000 | 4000 | 9000 | 1000 | 10000 | 28249 | 0 | 0 |
| Guam | 0 | 0 | 0 | 0 | 0 | 0 | 0 | 0 | 0 | 0 | 300 | 300 | 3030 | 0 | 0 |
| Guatemala | 0 | 0 | 0 | 0 | 0 | 100 | 4661 | 11096 | 24944 | 31925 | 50000 | 81925 | 13367 | 0 | 0 |
| Guinea | 0 | 0 | 0 | 0 | 0 | 0 | 0 | 0 | 153 | 0 | 0 | 0 | 0 | 0 | 0 |
| Guinea-Bissau | 0 | 0 | 0 | 0 | 0 | 0 | 0 | 0 | 0 | 0 | 100 | 100 | 190 | 0 | 0 |
| Guyana | 0 | 0 | 0 | 100 | 200 | 100 | 400 | 900 | 1500 | 2150 | 100 | 2450 | 3097 | 0 | 20 |
| Haiti | 0 | 0 | 300 | 0 | 0 | 200 | 7944 | 3846 | 24776 | 35475 | 5000 | 40475 | 8892 | 0 | 70 |
| Holy See | 0 | 0 | 0 | 0 | 500 | 0 | 0 | 0 | 0 | 0 | 500 | 1000 | 181800 | 0 | 0 |
| Honduras | 0 | 0 | 0 | 0 | 1000 | 50 | 1606 | 3666 | 9054 | 21807 | 30000 | 52807 | 17388 | 0 | 0 |
| Hong Kong | 0 | 0 | 200 | 0 | 0 | 566 | 10000 | 26572 | 35120 | 68551 | 27000 | 96551 | 22852 | 0 | 0 |
| Hungary | 0 | 0 | 0 | 0 | 0 | 10000 | 23956 | 7500 | 10000 | 19000 | 0 | 19000 | 1804 | 0 | 0 |
| Iceland | 0 | 0 | 0 | 500 | 600 | 1000 | 1650 | 1001 | 1624 | 3260 | 0 | 3860 | 17870 | 0 | 120 |
| India | 0 | 0 | 0 | 10840 | 9500 | 20000 | 30940 | 83218 | 121824 | 83246 | 30000 | 122590 | 200 | 0 | 1400 |
| Indonesia | 0 | 0 | 0 | 300 | 10540 | 200 | 5319 | 23966 | 56859 | 105163 | 40000 | 155703 | 1145 | 0 | 0 |
| Iran | 0 | 0 | 0 | 500 | 500 | 3567 | 462 | 899 | 1415 | 1581 | 100 | 2181 | 66 | 0 | 0 |
| Iraq | 0 | 0 | 0 | 0 | 0 | 1653 | 1136 | 1012 | 490 | 257 | 30 | 287 | 26 | 0 | 0 |
| Ireland | 0 | 0 | 0 | 700 | 3340 | 4000 | 7000 | 8000 | 4500 | 7000 | 15000 | 25340 | 8093 | 0 | 10 |
| Isle of Man | 0 | 0 | 0 | 0 | 1000 | 50 | 90 | 110 | 130 | 150 | 1500 | 1650 | 28448 | 0 | 0 |
| Israel | 0 | 0 | 0 | 0 | 1000 | 0 | 1597 | 10050 | 40454 | 7363 | 1000 | 9363 | 2740 | 0 | 5 |
| Italy | 0 | 0 | 0 | 0 | 1000 | 10262 | 7261 | 15079 | 25328 | 30519 | 1400000 | 1431519 | 26017 | 0 | 5 |
| Ivory Coast | 0 | 0 | 0 | 0 | 2000 | 0 | 1500 | 3000 | 5943 | 6000 | 1000 | 9000 | 1842 | 0 | 0 |
| Jamaica | 0 | 0 | 1200 | 2000 | 1000 | 2800 | 14800 | 38500 | 57000 | 74000 | 100 | 75100 | 37013 | 0 | 100 |
| Japan | 0 | 0 | 0 | 40 | 1000 | 7344 | 34892 | 90377 | 169640 | 224158 | 30000 | 255158 | 2296 | 0 | 700 |
| Johnston Island | 0 | 0 | 0 | 0 | 0 | 0 | 0 | 0 | 0 | 0 | 0 | 0 | 0 | 0 | 0 |
| Jordan | 0 | 0 | 0 | 0 | 1000 | 0 | 1498 | 4868 | 397 | 1064 | 0 | 2064 | 1070 | 0 | 0 |
| Kampuchea | 0 | 0 | 0 | 0 | 0 | 0 | 0 | 0 | 137 | 5464 | 0 | 5464 | 674 | 0 | 0 |
| Kenya | 0 | 0 | 0 | 0 | 7000 | 50 | 10000 | 25000 | 51892 | 79018 | 10000 | 96018 | 7246 | 0 | 0 |
| Kiribati | 0 | 0 | 0 | 0 | 0 | 0 | 200 | 400 | 700 | 1000 | 0 | 1000 | 15152 | 0 | 0 |
| Korea, North | 0 | 0 | 0 | 0 | 0 | 100 | 0 | 0 | 0 | 0 | 0 | 0 | 0 | 0 | 0 |
| Korea, South | 0 | 0 | 0 | 600 | 2600 | 200 | 6824 | 35615 | 142827 | 361297 | 10000 | 373897 | 11013 | 0 | 0 |
| Kuwait | 0 | 0 | 0 | 0 | 0 | 0 | 0 | 0 | 0 | 0 | 0 | 0 | 0 | 0 | 0 |
| Laos | 0 | 0 | 0 | 1000 | 400 | 0 | 0 | 0 | 453 | 1400 | 0 | 1800 | 545 | 0 | 0 |
| Lebanon | 0 | 0 | 0 | 0 | 0 | 3000 | 3000 | 4700 | 6489 | 6000 | 5000 | 11000 | 3834 | 0 | 0 |
| Lesotho | 0 | 0 | 0 | 0 | 0 | 50 | 1000 | 2000 | 4206 | 5000 | 1000 | 6000 | 5226 | 0 | 0 |
| Liberia | 0 | 0 | 0 | 0 | 2000 | 20 | 500 | 1555 | 5497 | 5366 | 0 | 7366 | 4313 | 0 | 0 |
| Libya | 0 | 0 | 0 | 0 | 0 | 30 | 50 | 100 | 35 | 30 | 0 | 30 | 13 | 0 | 0 |
| Liechtenstein | 0 | 0 | 0 | 0 | 0 | 10 | 10 | 10 | 20 | 20 | 100 | 120 | 5454 | 0 | 0 |
| Luxembourg | 0 | 0 | 0 | 0 | 0 | 100 | 100 | 100 | 150 | 150 | 1850 | 2000 | 5848 | 0 | 0 |
| Macao | 0 | 0 | 0 | 0 | 0 | 0 | 0 | 0 | 0 | 0 | 100 | 100 | 369 | 0 | 0 |
| Madagascar | 0 | 0 | 0 | 0 | 0 | 3157 | 10000 | 20326 | 15706 | 15554 | 1000 | 16554 | 2064 | 0 | 0 |
| Malawi | 0 | 0 | 0 | 1500 | 2000 | 0 | 5000 | 10000 | 19123 | 28657 | 1000 | 31657 | 6440 | 0 | 0 |
| Malaysia | 0 | 0 | 0 | 1000 | 1000 | 200 | 4120 | 6460 | 6820 | 11000 | 0 | 12000 | 992 | 0 | 0 |

## SCRIPTURE DISTRIBUTION (organized)

| | BIBLES PER YEAR: (a) Free | | | | | (b) Subsidized | | | | | (c) Commercial | TOTAL | pmillion | NTs PER YEAR: (a) Free | |
|---|---|---|---|---|---|---|---|---|---|---|---|---|---|---|---|
| | 1900 | 1950 | 1960 | 1970 | 1975 | 1900 | 1950 | 1960 | 1970 | 1975 | 1975 | 1975 | 1975 | 1900 | 1950 |
| | 63 | 64 | 65 | 66 | 67 | 68 | 69 | 70 | 71 | 72 | 73 | 74 | 75 | 76 | 77 |
| Maldives | 0 | 0 | 0 | 0 | 0 | 0 | 0 | 0 | 0 | 0 | 0 | 0 | 0 | 0 | 0 |
| Mali | 0 | 0 | 0 | 0 | 0 | 0 | 0 | 100 | 279 | 1100 | 100 | 1200 | 211 | 0 | 0 |
| Malta | 0 | 0 | 0 | 0 | 4000 | 0 | 10 | 10 | 3 | 20 | 1200 | 5220 | 15866 | 0 | 0 |
| Martinique | 0 | 0 | 0 | 0 | 1000 | 50 | 500 | 1000 | 2000 | 4000 | 1000 | 6000 | 16529 | 0 | 0 |
| Mauritania | 0 | 0 | 0 | 0 | 0 | 0 | 0 | 0 | 0 | 0 | 0 | 0 | 0 | 0 | 0 |
| Mauritius | 0 | 0 | 0 | 0 | 0 | 153 | 500 | 1000 | 1991 | 3334 | 1000 | 4334 | 4821 | 0 | 0 |
| Mayotte | 0 | 0 | 0 | 0 | 0 | 0 | 0 | 0 | 0 | 0 | 0 | 0 | 0 | 0 | 0 |
| Mexico | 0 | 0 | 0 | 0 | 10000 | 6544 | 27130 | 38579 | 93501 | 149164 | 100000 | 259164 | 4377 | 0 | 0 |
| Midway Islands | 0 | 0 | 0 | 0 | 0 | 10 | 30 | 30 | 40 | 50 | 100 | 150 | 625 | 0 | 0 |
| Monaco | 0 | 0 | 0 | 0 | 0 | 50 | 0 | 0 | 0 | 0 | 0 | 0 | 0 | 0 | 0 |
| Mongolia | 0 | 0 | 0 | 0 | 0 | 0 | 30 | 70 | 100 | 200 | 0 | 200 | 15385 | 0 | 0 |
| Montserrat | 0 | 0 | 0 | 0 | 0 | 249 | 2100 | 3200 | 654 | 750 | 100 | 850 | 49 | 0 | 0 |
| Morocco | 0 | 0 | 0 | 0 | 0 | 0 | 1000 | 3000 | 6632 | 9425 | 500 | 9925 | 1074 | 0 | 0 |
| Mozambique | 0 | 0 | 0 | 0 | 0 | 0 | 4000 | 7000 | 10000 | 15000 | 1000 | 16000 | 22599 | 0 | 0 |
| Namibia | 0 | 0 | 0 | 0 | 0 | 0 | 50 | 100 | 150 | 200 | 0 | 200 | 25000 | 0 | 0 |
| Nauru | 0 | 0 | 0 | 0 | 0 | 0 | 0 | 0 | 0 | 0 | 0 | 0 | 0 | 0 | 0 |
| Nepal | 0 | 0 | 0 | 0 | 0 | 0 | 0 | 0 | 0 | 0 | 0 | 0 | 0 | 0 | 0 |
| Netherlands | 0 | 0 | 2700 | 0 | 3000 | 35000 | 53475 | 106646 | 84415 | 114431 | 100000 | 217431 | 15989 | 0 | 20 |
| Netherlands Antilles | 0 | 0 | 1000 | 0 | 1720 | 20 | 100 | 297 | 650 | 1253 | 200 | 3173 | 13112 | 0 | 0 |
| New Caledonia | 0 | 0 | 0 | 0 | 0 | 350 | 300 | 400 | 500 | 700 | 300 | 1000 | 8000 | 0 | 0 |
| New Zealand | 0 | 0 | 2725 | 3700 | 4230 | 2438 | 13808 | 15053 | 20545 | 26588 | 6000 | 36818 | 12147 | 0 | 0 |
| Nicaragua | 0 | 0 | 0 | 0 | 0 | 400 | 992 | 3540 | 6761 | 13709 | 2000 | 15709 | 6777 | 0 | 0 |
| Niger | 0 | 0 | 0 | 0 | 0 | 0 | 100 | 200 | 370 | 300 | 0 | 300 | 65 | 0 | 0 |
| Nigeria | 0 | 0 | 0 | 1000 | 2000 | 3000 | 50000 | 200000 | 311756 | 370581 | 40000 | 412581 | 6557 | 0 | 0 |
| Niue Island | 0 | 0 | 0 | 0 | 0 | 0 | 100 | 100 | 100 | 100 | 0 | 100 | 20000 | 0 | 0 |
| Norfolk Island | 0 | 0 | 0 | 0 | 0 | 10 | 0 | 0 | 0 | 0 | 0 | 0 | 0 | 0 | 0 |
| Northern Solomons | 0 | 0 | 0 | 0 | 0 | 0 | 50 | 100 | 200 | 300 | 0 | 300 | 3330 | 0 | 0 |
| Norway | 0 | 0 | 606 | 0 | 2730 | 28000 | 26115 | 33458 | 45245 | 40265 | 5000 | 47995 | 11978 | 0 | 0 |
| Oman | 0 | 0 | 0 | 0 | 0 | 0 | 0 | 0 | 0 | 0 | 0 | 0 | 0 | 0 | 0 |
| Pacific Islands | 0 | 0 | 0 | 0 | 0 | 0 | 500 | 1000 | 2000 | 2529 | 500 | 3029 | 25889 | 0 | 0 |
| Pakistan | 0 | 0 | 0 | 0 | 100500 | 500 | 1000 | 2500 | 5001 | 7157 | 1000 | 108657 | 1540 | 0 | 0 |
| Palestine | 0 | 0 | 0 | 0 | 1000 | 2000 | 3000 | 5000 | 10000 | 15284 | 3000 | 19284 | 13804 | 0 | 0 |
| Panama | 0 | 0 | 0 | 200 | 20 | 200 | 2174 | 3210 | 10627 | 11419 | 5000 | 16439 | 9797 | 0 | 0 |
| Panama Canal Zone | 0 | 0 | 0 | 0 | 0 | 200 | 1710 | 1100 | 2000 | 3000 | 500 | 3500 | 81395 | 0 | 20 |
| Papua New Guinea | 0 | 0 | 0 | 0 | 0 | 100 | 2000 | 3000 | 4423 | 8011 | 1000 | 9011 | 3318 | 0 | 0 |
| Paraguay | 0 | 0 | 0 | 0 | 0 | 50 | 3177 | 3676 | 3117 | 7027 | 5000 | 12027 | 4544 | 0 | 0 |
| Peru | 0 | 0 | 0 | 0 | 0 | 49 | 13344 | 22117 | 46557 | 79390 | 60000 | 139390 | 9095 | 0 | 0 |
| Philippines | 0 | 0 | 1700 | 19300 | 26260 | 866 | 28984 | 33088 | 55348 | 48878 | 102000 | 177138 | 3986 | 0 | 250 |
| Pitcairn Islands | 0 | 0 | 0 | 0 | 0 | 2 | 2 | 3 | 3 | 3 | 0 | 3 | 33000 | 0 | 0 |
| Poland | 0 | 0 | 0 | 0 | 1000 | 4000 | 19503 | 14144 | 28806 | 46763 | 40000 | 87763 | 2593 | 0 | 0 |
| Portugal | 0 | 0 | 0 | 0 | 0 | 1367 | 3549 | 8052 | 22582 | 20403 | 30000 | 50403 | 5752 | 0 | 0 |
| Puerto Rico | 0 | 0 | 0 | 0 | 5000 | 486 | 6607 | 8052 | 49481 | 56774 | 20000 | 81774 | 28178 | 0 | 0 |
| Qatar | 0 | 0 | 0 | 0 | 0 | 0 | 0 | 0 | 0 | 0 | 0 | 0 | 0 | 0 | 0 |
| Reunion | 0 | 0 | 0 | 0 | 0 | 0 | 1000 | 3000 | 4000 | 6300 | 1000 | 7300 | 14570 | 0 | 0 |
| Romania | 0 | 0 | 0 | 0 | 5000 | 1000 | 450 | 400 | 50000 | 50000 | 0 | 55000 | 2597 | 0 | 0 |
| Rwanda | 0 | 0 | 0 | 0 | 0 | 0 | 500 | 1000 | 2000 | 7000 | 2000 | 9000 | 2143 | 0 | 0 |
| Sahara | 0 | 0 | 0 | 0 | 0 | 0 | 0 | 0 | 0 | 0 | 0 | 0 | 0 | 0 | 0 |
| St Helena | 0 | 0 | 0 | 0 | 0 | 5 | 10 | 15 | 20 | 20 | 0 | 20 | 4000 | 0 | 0 |
| St Kitts-Nevis | 0 | 0 | 0 | 0 | 0 | 100 | 50 | 100 | 150 | 270 | 0 | 270 | 4500 | 0 | 0 |
| St Lucia | 0 | 0 | 0 | 150 | 200 | 50 | 300 | 700 | 800 | 1250 | 100 | 1550 | 14352 | 0 | 0 |
| St Pierre & Miquelon | 0 | 0 | 0 | 0 | 0 | 0 | 0 | 0 | 0 | 20 | 0 | 20 | 4000 | 0 | 0 |
| St Vincent | 0 | 0 | 400 | 600 | 1000 | 50 | 300 | 700 | 800 | 1000 | 0 | 2000 | 21277 | 0 | 0 |
| Samoa | 0 | 0 | 0 | 0 | 0 | 100 | 2000 | 4000 | 6000 | 8000 | 0 | 8000 | 48780 | 0 | 0 |
| San Marino | 0 | 0 | 0 | 0 | 0 | 0 | 0 | 10 | 50 | 60 | 0 | 60 | 3000 | 0 | 0 |
| Sao Tome & Principe | 0 | 0 | 0 | 0 | 0 | 0 | 0 | 100 | 200 | 500 | 0 | 500 | 6250 | 0 | 0 |
| Saudi Arabia | 0 | 0 | 0 | 0 | 0 | 0 | 26 | 0 | 0 | 0 | 0 | 0 | 0 | 0 | 0 |
| Senegal | 0 | 0 | 0 | 0 | 0 | 0 | 300 | 600 | 907 | 1300 | 700 | 2000 | 453 | 0 | 0 |
| Seychelles | 0 | 0 | 0 | 0 | 0 | 0 | 500 | 1000 | 1500 | 2000 | 0 | 2000 | 33898 | 0 | 0 |
| Sierra Leone | 0 | 0 | 0 | 0 | 620 | 200 | 2000 | 5000 | 10468 | 8599 | 500 | 9719 | 3258 | 0 | 0 |
| Sikkim | 0 | 0 | 0 | 0 | 0 | 0 | 0 | 0 | 0 | 0 | 0 | 0 | 0 | 0 | 0 |
| Singapore | 0 | 0 | 0 | 1000 | 1000 | 120 | 5030 | 7870 | 8300 | 14000 | 0 | 15000 | 6673 | 0 | 0 |
| Solomon Islands | 0 | 0 | 0 | 0 | 500 | 50 | 200 | 500 | 1000 | 2000 | 0 | 2500 | 13369 | 0 | 0 |
| Somalia | 0 | 0 | 0 | 0 | 0 | 0 | 5 | 20 | 20 | 20 | 0 | 20 | 6 | 0 | 0 |
| South Africa | 0 | 0 | 0 | 10200 | 2400 | 40852 | 155000 | 250000 | 406989 | 700000 | 36000 | 738400 | 29940 | 0 | 0 |
| Spain | 0 | 0 | 0 | 0 | 1000 | 6359 | 1753 | 1852 | 9376 | 15326 | 899020 | 915346 | 25833 | 0 | 0 |
| Spanish North Africa | 0 | 0 | 0 | 0 | 0 | 0 | 0 | 0 | 0 | 0 | 1700 | 1700 | 9826 | 0 | 0 |
| Sri Lanka | 0 | 0 | 0 | 1080 | 160 | 3115 | 2000 | 5132 | 4328 | 3667 | 300 | 4127 | 295 | 0 | 0 |
| Sudan | 0 | 0 | 0 | 0 | 0 | 137 | 576 | 1023 | 804 | 1860 | 0 | 1860 | 102 | 0 | 0 |
| Surinam | 0 | 0 | 207 | 100 | 0 | 297 | 1992 | 1 | 1000 | 1064 | 0 | 1064 | 2521 | 0 | 0 |
| Svalbard & Jan Mayen Is | 0 | 0 | 0 | 0 | 0 | 0 | 0 | 0 | 0 | 0 | 0 | 0 | 0 | 0 | 0 |
| Swaziland | 0 | 0 | 0 | 0 | 300 | 0 | 1000 | 2000 | 4436 | 5000 | 0 | 5300 | 11325 | 0 | 0 |
| Sweden | 0 | 0 | 950 | 0 | 0 | 77885 | 5773 | 96188 | 101650 | 131000 | 2000 | 133000 | 16041 | 0 | 60 |
| Switzerland | 0 | 0 | 0 | 700 | 100 | 22502 | 22056 | 77427 | 13556 | 6920 | 50000 | 57020 | 8725 | 0 | 0 |
| Syria | 0 | 0 | 0 | 0 | 0 | 426 | 600 | 900 | 1007 | 581 | 0 | 581 | 80 | 0 | 0 |
| Tanzania | 0 | 0 | 0 | 0 | 0 | 10 | 5000 | 10000 | 24624 | 35340 | 2000 | 37340 | 2419 | 0 | 0 |
| Thailand | 0 | 0 | 0 | 300 | 2900 | 50 | 456 | 1431 | 2566 | 5615 | 1000 | 9515 | 226 | 0 | 0 |
| Timor | 0 | 0 | 0 | 0 | 0 | 0 | 0 | 0 | 0 | 0 | 0 | 0 | 0 | 0 | 0 |
| Togo | 0 | 0 | 0 | 0 | 0 | 0 | 50 | 100 | 115 | 1650 | 0 | 1650 | 734 | 0 | 0 |
| Tokelau | 0 | 0 | 0 | 0 | 0 | 10 | 12 | 15 | 20 | 20 | 0 | 20 | 12121 | 0 | 0 |
| Tonga | 0 | 0 | 0 | 0 | 0 | 300 | 1000 | 1500 | 2000 | 2500 | 50 | 2550 | 25248 | 0 | 0 |
| Trinidad & Tobago | 0 | 0 | 800 | 1200 | 1000 | 1285 | 1400 | 3600 | 5400 | 6900 | 100 | 8000 | 7929 | 0 | 50 |
| Tunisia | 0 | 0 | 0 | 0 | 20 | 50 | 250 | 400 | 71 | 80 | 0 | 100 | 17 | 0 | 0 |
| Turkey | 0 | 0 | 0 | 0 | 100 | 4315 | 660 | 1284 | 2350 | 1827 | 0 | 1927 | 48 | 0 | 0 |
| Turks & Caicos Islands | 0 | 0 | 0 | 0 | 0 | 50 | 30 | 20 | 20 | 20 | 0 | 20 | 3597 | 0 | 0 |
| Tuvalu | 0 | 0 | 0 | 1500 | 4000 | 0 | 10 | 20 | 100 | 100 | 0 | 100 | 16667 | 0 | 0 |
| Uganda | 0 | 0 | 0 | 0 | 0 | 1000 | 10000 | 20000 | 35844 | 46048 | 2000 | 52048 | 4585 | 0 | 0 |
| USSR | 0 | 5000 | 10000 | 20000 | 53000 | 40923 | 1000 | 62000 | 15000 | 10000 | 1000 | 64000 | 251 | 0 | 5000 |
| United Arab Emirates | 0 | 0 | 0 | 0 | 0 | 0 | 0 | 0 | 0 | 0 | 0 | 0 | 0 | 0 | 0 |
| UK of GB & NI | 0 | 0 | 12713 | 31508 | 34049 | 669017 | 297429 | 366754 | 227516 | 330360 | 1470000 | 1834409 | 32509 | 2000 | 5200 |
| USA | 5000 | 107850 | 188026 | 418063 | 893798 | 180000 | 409982 | 586066 | 691750 | 644193 | 15100000 | 16637991 | 77775 | 50000 | 1847000 |
| US Virgin Islands | 0 | 0 | 0 | 0 | 0 | 50 | 326 | 482 | 400 | 400 | 1000 | 1400 | 21212 | 0 | 0 |
| Upper Volta | 0 | 0 | 0 | 0 | 0 | 0 | 100 | 300 | 817 | 800 | 100 | 900 | 149 | 0 | 0 |
| Uruguay | 0 | 0 | 0 | 0 | 0 | 50 | 4547 | 8736 | 14974 | 10490 | 5000 | 15490 | 4984 | 0 | 0 |
| Vanuatu | 0 | 0 | 0 | 0 | 0 | 100 | 500 | 1000 | 1000 | 1000 | 0 | 1000 | 10417 | 0 | 0 |
| Venezuela | 0 | 0 | 0 | 0 | 100 | 0 | 5835 | 20998 | 45663 | 45233 | 60000 | 105333 | 8625 | 0 | 0 |
| Viet Nam | 0 | 0 | 250 | 0 | 5000 | 40 | 1824 | 2733 | 9527 | 13912 | 2000 | 20912 | 481 | 0 | 0 |
| Wake Island | 0 | 0 | 0 | 0 | 0 | 0 | 0 | 0 | 0 | 0 | 0 | 0 | 0 | 0 | 0 |
| Wallis & Futuna Islands | 0 | 0 | 0 | 0 | 0 | 0 | 0 | 0 | 0 | 0 | 50 | 50 | 5560 | 0 | 0 |
| Yemen, North | 0 | 0 | 0 | 0 | 0 | 0 | 0 | 0 | 0 | 0 | 0 | 0 | 0 | 0 | 0 |
| Yemen, South | 0 | 0 | 0 | 0 | 0 | 5 | 30 | 30 | 0 | 0 | 0 | 0 | 0 | 0 | 0 |
| Yugoslavia | 0 | 0 | 0 | 0 | 0 | 2000 | 3000 | 5335 | 9669 | 12444 | 60000 | 72444 | 3398 | 0 | 0 |
| Zaire | 0 | 0 | 0 | 0 | 0 | 10 | 15000 | 36734 | 46514 | 39000 | 15000 | 54000 | 2205 | 0 | 0 |
| Zambia | 0 | 0 | 0 | 0 | 700 | 10 | 7000 | 20000 | 47483 | 26989 | 2000 | 29689 | 5912 | 0 | 0 |
| Zimbabwe | 0 | 0 | 0 | 600 | 920 | 0 | 15000 | 30000 | 49134 | 56421 | 20000 | 77341 | 12323 | 0 | 0 |
| Column | 63 | 64 | 65 | 66 | 67 | 68 | 69 | 70 | 71 | 72 | 73 | 74 | 75 | 76 | 77 |
| *Continent* | | | | | | | | | | | | | | | |
| Africa | 0 | 0 | 0 | 15800 | 30780 | 50443 | 324702 | 711061 | 1216319 | 1666530 | 182810 | 1880120 | — | 0 | 1000 |
| East Asia | 0 | 0 | 4100 | 640 | 4600 | 22856 | 123216 | 177564 | 376361 | 704037 | 77100 | 785737 | — | 0 | 1410 |
| Europe | 0 | 0 | 22809 | 73110 | 105915 | 1314426 | 908307 | 1414628 | 1426986 | 1546815 | 5096580 | 6749310 | — | 2000 | 6130 |
| Latin America | 0 | 0 | 5107 | 8760 | 27260 | 47225 | 266025 | 680521 | 835400 | 993567 | 1073675 | 2094502 | — | 0 | 3260 |
| Northern America | 5000 | 136640 | 238306 | 449306 | 938434 | 205120 | 485947 | 687842 | 782626 | 759476 | 15450200 | 17148110 | — | 50000 | 1970000 |
| Oceania | 0 | 0 | 8225 | 16280 | 14290 | 24227 | 63808 | 115396 | 158387 | 233624 | 49500 | 297414 | — | 0 | 200 |
| South Asia | 0 | 0 | 1950 | 35580 | 161620 | 42406 | 98721 | 204671 | 350682 | 344118 | 187130 | 692868 | — | 0 | 1850 |
| USSR | 0 | 5000 | 10000 | 20000 | 53000 | 40923 | 1000 | 62000 | 15000 | 10000 | 1000 | 64000 | — | 0 | 5000 |
| WORLD | 5000 | 141640 | 290497 | 619476 | 1335899 | 1747626 | 2271726 | 4053683 | 5161761 | 6258167 | 22117995 | 29712061 | — | 52000 | 1988850 |

## SCRIPTURE DISTRIBUTION-continued

| | NTs (continued): (a) Free | | | (b) Subsidized | | | | | (c) Commercial | TOTAL | | Portions | Selections |
|---|---|---|---|---|---|---|---|---|---|---|---|---|---|
| | 1960 | 1970 | 1975 | 1900 | 1950 | 1960 | 1970 | 1975 | 1975 | 1975 | pmillion | 1975 | 1975 |
| | 78 | 79 | 80 | 81 | 82 | 83 | 84 | 85 | 86 | 87 | 88 | 89 | 90 |
| Afghanistan | 0 | 0 | 0 | 0 | 0 | 0 | 128 | 200 | 0 | 200 | 10 | 0 | 0 |
| Albania | 0 | 0 | 0 | 50 | 0 | 0 | 0 | 0 | 0 | 0 | 0 | 0 | 0 |
| Algeria | 0 | 0 | 0 | 1509 | 1800 | 2000 | 440 | 400 | 0 | 400 | 24 | 3600 | 2000 |
| American Samoa | 0 | 0 | 0 | 10 | 30 | 50 | 100 | 200 | 0 | 200 | 6250 | 200 | 1600 |
| Andorra | 0 | 0 | 0 | 0 | 10 | 20 | 30 | 50 | 0 | 50 | 2174 | 0 | 0 |
| Angola | 0 | 0 | 0 | 50 | 1000 | 2000 | 4946 | 7632 | 1000 | 8632 | 1359 | 15763 | 110520 |
| Anguilla | 0 | 0 | 0 | 0 | 0 | 5 | 10 | 20 | 0 | 20 | 3226 | 0 | 0 |
| Antigua | 2600 | 11000 | 4000 | 20 | 100 | 300 | 500 | 900 | 100 | 5000 | 68493 | 200 | 2500 |
| Argentina | 10350 | 74700 | 67190 | 15000 | 39937 | 74144 | 124604 | 116843 | 100000 | 284033 | 11189 | 506676 | 2066731 |
| Australia | 49540 | 187400 | 240800 | 10000 | 23908 | 38000 | 117433 | 165948 | 50000 | 456748 | 33076 | 555337 | -1579713 |
| Austria | 4000 | 8500 | 3000 | 60000 | 13029 | 14965 | 15428 | 22366 | 105000 | 130366 | 17295 | 39509 | 71721 |
| Bahamas | 9400 | 4400 | 9600 | 0 | 300 | 700 | 1100 | 1300 | 400 | 11300 | 55392 | 1100 | 3900 |
| Bahrain | 0 | 0 | 0 | 0 | 0 | 0 | 0 | 0 | 0 | 0 | 0 | 0 | 0 |
| Bangladesh | 0 | 0 | 129129 | 500 | 1000 | 2000 | 3482 | 43393 | 10000 | 182522 | 2475 | 271815 | 300484 |
| Barbados | 5925 | 1300 | 10000 | 20 | 200 | 500 | 800 | 1000 | 0 | 11000 | 44898 | 2000 | 43000 |
| Belgium | 789 | 0 | 8180 | 14436 | 4158 | 5500 | 6913 | 29508 | 100000 | 137688 | 13984 | 32601 | 43600 |
| Belize | 0 | 1600 | 6400 | 0 | 100 | 200 | 300 | 500 | 200 | 7100 | 50714 | 1000 | 0 |
| Benin | 0 | 0 | 5060 | 0 | 500 | 1000 | 2800 | 4000 | 100 | 9160 | 2980 | 3400 | 2000 |
| Bermuda | 0 | 800 | 1500 | 20 | 50 | 100 | 150 | 200 | 50 | 1750 | 31250 | 200 | 500 |
| Bhutan | 0 | 0 | 100 | 0 | 0 | 0 | 0 | 0 | 0 | 100 | 85 | 0 | 0 |
| Bolivia | 8000 | 0 | 552637 | 50 | 11901 | 10814 | 36649 | 45393 | 10000 | 608030 | 112390 | 84522 | 2443465 |
| Botswana | 0 | 0 | 0 | 100 | 1000 | 3000 | 5593 | 8000 | 0 | 8000 | 11577 | 10000 | 5000 |
| Brazil | 25308 | 276400 | 1611140 | 18061 | 73198 | 83499 | 79574 | 57682 | 303136 | 1971958 | 17971 | 47945 | 14090284 |
| British Antarctic Terr | 0 | 0 | 0 | 0 | 0 | 0 | 0 | 0 | 0 | 0 | 0 | 0 | 0 |
| British Indian Ocean Terr | 0 | 0 | 0 | 0 | 0 | 0 | 0 | 0 | 0 | 0 | 0 | 0 | 0 |
| British Virgin Is | 0 | 0 | 0 | 0 | 0 | 0 | 10 | 10 | 0 | 0 | 0 | 0 | 0 |
| Brunei | 0 | 0 | 4600 | 0 | 0 | 0 | 10 | 10 | 0 | 4610 | 31361 | 20 | 30 |
| Bulgaria | 0 | 0 | 1000 | 33 | 0 | 0 | 0 | 0 | 0 | 1000 | 114 | 0 | 0 |
| Burma | 0 | 300 | 28100 | 2000 | 4918 | 9194 | 9548 | 3136 | 0 | 31236 | 1000 | 37979 | 29771 |
| Burundi | 0 | 0 | 320 | 0 | 1000 | 2000 | 3840 | 5000 | 100 | 5420 | 1440 | 20000 | 4000 |
| Cameroon | 0 | 0 | 0 | 100 | 4000 | 20000 | 49056 | 21490 | 1000 | 22490 | 3515 | 22000 | 162306 |
| Canada | 205305 | 244346 | 562114 | 50000 | 73149 | 51130 | 282134 | 305136 | 430000 | 1297250 | 56894 | 586942 | 2612872 |
| Canton & Enderbury | 0 | 0 | 0 | 0 | 0 | 0 | 0 | 0 | 0 | 0 | 0 | 0 | 0 |
| Cape Verde | 0 | 0 | 18320 | 10 | 100 | 300 | 500 | 1000 | 500 | 19820 | 67186 | 0 | 0 |
| Cayman Islands | 0 | 0 | 0 | 0 | 10 | 20 | 30 | 40 | 0 | 40 | 3524 | 100 | 200 |
| Central African Republic | 0 | 0 | 0 | 0 | 5000 | 15000 | 20319 | 25000 | 0 | 25000 | 13966 | 7100 | 5600 |
| Chad | 0 | 0 | 0 | 0 | 2000 | 5000 | 10000 | 16000 | 0 | 16000 | 3977 | 20 | 0 |
| Channel Islands | 0 | 0 | 0 | 100 | 150 | 200 | 300 | 350 | 1600 | 1950 | 15234 | 2000 | 4000 |
| Chile | 30950 | 47500 | 91170 | 1000 | 22311 | 46394 | 62929 | 54158 | 40000 | 185328 | 18075 | 92524 | 2502368 |
| China | 5000 | 20000 | 63000 | 55000 | 77595 | 0 | 0 | 0 | 0 | 63000 | 75 | 0 | 0 |
| China (Taiwan) | 20200 | 39069 | 236000 | 288 | 20000 | 40000 | 83696 | 191518 | 30000 | 457518 | 29251 | 723152 | 4968482 |
| Christmas Island | 0 | 0 | 0 | 0 | 0 | 0 | 0 | 0 | 0 | 0 | 0 | 0 | 0 |
| Cocos Islands | 0 | 0 | 0 | 0 | 0 | 0 | 0 | 0 | 0 | 0 | 0 | 0 | 0 |
| Colombia | 1700 | 28100 | 109960 | 0 | 6332 | 211808 | 33801 | 45626 | 60000 | 215586 | 8327 | 433500 | 3122500 |
| Comoros | 0 | 0 | 0 | 0 | 0 | 0 | 0 | 0 | 0 | 0 | 0 | 0 | 0 |
| Congo | 0 | 0 | 0 | 0 | 150 | 600 | 1000 | 1600 | 100 | 1700 | 1264 | 0 | 0 |
| Cook Islands | 0 | 0 | 0 | 10 | 20 | 30 | 40 | 150 | 0 | 150 | 6000 | 200 | 70 |
| Costa Rica | 600 | 1500 | 29500 | 50 | 857 | 4208 | 15420 | 28788 | 20000 | 78288 | 39262 | 426542 | 916645 |
| Cuba | 1000 | 0 | 0 | 4904 | 19920 | 44258 | 0 | 1000 | 0 | 1000 | 105 | 0 | 0 |
| Cyprus | 0 | 1500 | 1500 | 20 | 1282 | 2276 | 1880 | 10240 | 100 | 11840 | 17593 | 1653 | 0 |
| Czechoslovakia | 0 | 0 | 1000 | 5000 | 12584 | 4000 | 15000 | 20000 | 0 | 21000 | 1423 | 50000 | 0 |
| Denmark | 0 | 6000 | 28500 | 811 | 45451 | 53200 | 48895 | 142003 | 8000 | 178503 | 35516 | 6585 | 26232 |
| Djibouti | 0 | 0 | 0 | 0 | 0 | 0 | 0 | 0 | 0 | 0 | 0 | 0 | 0 |
| Dominica | 600 | 0 | 0 | 0 | 200 | 500 | 800 | 1100 | 0 | 1100 | 14667 | 250 | 5600 |
| Dominican Republic | 0 | 15900 | 32510 | 100 | 5100 | 9070 | 16394 | 17748 | 5000 | 55258 | 10797 | 276169 | 2820893 |
| Ecuador | 3300 | 13100 | 72010 | 50 | 5730 | 4794 | 37496 | 40940 | 30000 | 142950 | 20162 | 357642 | 1424737 |
| Egypt | 0 | 0 | 1000 | 50 | 11463 | 22349 | 91101 | 52976 | 1000 | 54976 | 1464 | 171634 | 229435 |
| El Salvador | 3500 | 17400 | 8310 | 30 | 3053 | 7512 | 10924 | 19310 | 10000 | 37620 | 9158 | 60674 | 1305134 |
| Equatorial Guinea | 0 | 0 | 0 | 0 | 0 | 0 | 0 | 0 | 0 | 0 | 0 | 0 | 0 |
| Ethiopia | 0 | 29000 | 40980 | 100 | 892 | 2670 | 26883 | 175555 | 3000 | 219535 | 7848 | 203395 | 523434 |
| Faeroe Islands | 0 | 0 | 0 | 100 | 300 | 400 | 600 | 794 | 0 | 794 | 19850 | 0 | 0 |
| Falkland Islands | 0 | 0 | 0 | 0 | 5 | 5 | 10 | 10 | 0 | 10 | 5000 | 0 | 0 |
| Fiji | 0 | 3700 | 14000 | 3000 | 2000 | 2000 | 4000 | 7000 | 0 | 21000 | 36395 | 49000 | 160000 |
| Finland | 3000 | 20000 | 2000 | 397 | 10007 | 49406 | 69613 | 84572 | 10000 | 96572 | 20759 | 6709 | 0 |
| France | 0 | 4580 | 32370 | 57318 | 63332 | 35151 | 36488 | 100646 | 450000 | 583016 | 11018 | 612320 | 313327 |
| French Guiana | 0 | 0 | 0 | 0 | 30 | 50 | 100 | 150 | 0 | 150 | 2500 | 2800 | 16000 |
| French Polynesia | 0 | 0 | 0 | 15 | 200 | 500 | 1000 | 2000 | 0 | 2000 | 15625 | 4000 | 5000 |
| French Southern & Antarctic T | 0 | 0 | 0 | 0 | 0 | 0 | 0 | 0 | 0 | 0 | 0 | 0 | 0 |
| Gabon | 0 | 0 | 0 | 0 | 500 | 2000 | 5105 | 0 | 2000 | 2000 | 3802 | 1700 | 0 |
| Gambia | 0 | 0 | 0 | 0 | 0 | 50 | 100 | 150 | 0 | 150 | 295 | 0 | 0 |
| German Democratic Rep | 0 | 0 | 0 | 100000 | 30000 | 86105 | 37027 | 51786 | 0 | 51786 | 3012 | 24189 | 183749 |
| Germany, Federal Rep | 0 | 74800 | 158700 | 200000 | 80000 | 150000 | 163681 | 277796 | 300000 | 736496 | 11940 | 117237 | 1351114 |
| Ghana | 0 | 17900 | 51700 | 1000 | 1000 | 25000 | 46632 | 61820 | 10000 | 123520 | 12511 | 236001 | 421043 |
| Gibraltar | 0 | 0 | 0 | 0 | 5 | 10 | 30 | 10 | 50 | 60 | 2220 | 20 | 0 |
| Greece | 36245 | 16266 | 200 | 5029 | 63094 | 18751 | 166882 | 67083 | 20000 | 87283 | 9774 | 58784 | 27486 |
| Greenland | 0 | 0 | 0 | 50 | 100 | 150 | 200 | 300 | 0 | 300 | 5550 | 500 | 1000 |
| Grenada | 3300 | 0 | 0 | 0 | 100 | 200 | 400 | 500 | 0 | 500 | 5208 | 300 | 1500 |
| Guadeloupe | 0 | 0 | 0 | 10 | 50 | 100 | 150 | 200 | 1000 | 1200 | 3390 | 3700 | 18000 |
| Guam | 0 | 0 | 10500 | 0 | 100 | 300 | 500 | 1000 | 500 | 12000 | 121212 | 0 | 0 |
| Guatemala | 1000 | 14700 | 8610 | 100 | 6996 | 8296 | 31748 | 30700 | 20000 | 59310 | 9677 | 68835 | 1471526 |
| Guinea | 0 | 0 | 0 | 0 | 0 | 100 | 200 | 0 | 0 | 0 | 0 | 0 | 0 |
| Guinea-Bissau | 0 | 0 | 0 | 0 | 0 | 0 | 0 | 0 | 0 | 0 | 0 | 0 | 0 |
| Guyana | 1400 | 1300 | 17500 | 50 | 500 | 1000 | 1600 | 2800 | 0 | 20300 | 25664 | 5100 | 36700 |
| Haiti | 3700 | 30100 | 36200 | 0 | 200 | 6721 | 24585 | 28243 | 5000 | 69443 | 15255 | 232469 | 1765410 |
| Holy See | 0 | 0 | 500 | 0 | 0 | 0 | 0 | 0 | 500 | 1000 | 181800 | 4000 | 0 |
| Honduras | 0 | 14300 | 22210 | 50 | 3139 | 2315 | 18858 | 24695 | 30000 | 76905 | 25323 | 372560 | 950670 |
| Hong Kong | 3400 | 5800 | 6500 | 100 | 7000 | 15000 | 23895 | 36385 | 10000 | 52885 | 12517 | 624313 | 773364 |
| Hungary | 0 | 0 | 1000 | 50000 | 11552 | 2000 | 3000 | 4000 | 0 | 5000 | 475 | 0 | 11012 |
| Iceland | 17785 | 5999 | 5919 | 500 | 1500 | 434 | 5402 | 5319 | 0 | 11238 | 52028 | 282 | 39 |
| India | 400 | 257305 | 900000 | 10000 | 50000 | 121730 | 296050 | 464952 | 200000 | 1564952 | 2552 | 2186420 | 16854569 |
| Indonesia | 0 | 116490 | 18400 | 5000 | 82769 | 63834 | 225103 | 47890 | 20000 | 86290 | 634 | 1746796 | 16205686 |
| Iran | 0 | 25394 | 400 | 2081 | 1291 | 1642 | 3692 | 1428 | 100 | 1928 | 58 | 80934 | 512325 |
| Iraq | 0 | 0 | 0 | 50 | 765 | 786 | 2294 | 787 | 0 | 787 | 71 | 1197 | 6443 |
| Ireland | 0 | 950 | 62200 | 6000 | 12000 | 5000 | 12000 | 18160 | 30000 | 110360 | 35248 | 55000 | 4000 |
| Isle of Man | 0 | 0 | 0 | 30 | 60 | 80 | 100 | 150 | 800 | 950 | 16379 | 1000 | 2000 |
| Israel | 0 | 0 | 1000 | 50 | 1100 | 12718 | 3120 | 4359 | 1000 | 6359 | 1861 | 3240 | 23470 |
| Italy | 0 | 0 | 30254 | 23640 | 8750 | 5074 | 9064 | 21093 | 800000 | 851347 | 15473 | 500949 | 2043513 |
| Ivory Coast | 0 | 10780 | 15000 | 0 | 1000 | 3000 | 6058 | 18000 | 1000 | 34000 | 6960 | 20000 | 93000 |
| Jamaica | 11600 | 20900 | 65500 | 400 | 2000 | 5000 | 8000 | 11000 | 100 | 76600 | 37753 | 46000 | 159000 |
| Japan | 183500 | 183400 | 1005972 | 33815 | 969973 | 385017 | 491890 | 1050931 | 100000 | 2156903 | 19411 | 170123 | 5807808 |
| Johnston Island | 0 | 0 | 0 | 0 | 0 | 0 | 0 | 0 | 0 | 0 | 0 | 0 | 0 |
| Jordan | 0 | 0 | 0 | 0 | 2117 | 13254 | 5961 | 1914 | 100 | 2014 | 1044 | 10893 | 29820 |
| Kampuchea | 0 | 0 | 0 | 0 | 0 | 0 | 50 | 14920 | 0 | 14920 | 1840 | 216797 | 180302 |
| Kenya | 0 | 0 | 30500 | 100 | 20000 | 40000 | 76866 | 177880 | 10000 | 218380 | 16480 | 611818 | 1333998 |
| Kiribati | 0 | 0 | 0 | 0 | 100 | 300 | 600 | 1200 | 0 | 1200 | 18182 | 1500 | 21700 |
| Korea, North | 0 | 0 | 0 | 500 | 0 | 0 | 0 | 0 | 0 | 0 | 0 | 0 | 0 |
| Korea, South | 0 | 396500 | 903100 | 2047 | 80077 | 151002 | 826131 | 1179875 | 50000 | 2132975 | 62829 | 985673 | 17918885 |
| Kuwait | 0 | 0 | 0 | 0 | 0 | 0 | 50 | 100 | 0 | 100 | 92 | 0 | 0 |
| Laos | 0 | 2000 | 20000 | 0 | 0 | 0 | 0 | 0 | 0 | 20000 | 6055 | 700 | 25000 |
| Lebanon | 0 | 1000 | 5880 | 1000 | 10000 | 15000 | 20000 | 30000 | 10000 | 45880 | 15992 | 25000 | 255000 |
| Lesotho | 0 | 0 | 0 | 0 | 50 | 100 | 255 | 400 | 2000 | 2400 | 2091 | 1000 | 2000 |
| Liberia | 0 | 0 | 6000 | 10 | 1000 | 1791 | 8998 | 7189 | 2000 | 15189 | 8893 | 20400 | 19887 |
| Libya | 0 | 0 | 0 | 0 | 0 | 0 | 0 | 0 | 0 | 0 | 0 | 0 | 0 |
| Liechtenstein | 0 | 0 | 0 | 20 | 30 | 40 | 50 | 60 | 30 | 90 | 4091 | 100 | 0 |
| Luxembourg | 0 | 0 | 0 | 200 | 500 | 600 | 800 | 1000 | 500 | 1500 | 4386 | 1000 | 0 |
| Macao | 0 | 0 | 0 | 0 | 0 | 0 | 0 | 100 | 0 | 100 | 369 | 0 | 0 |
| Madagascar | 0 | 0 | 0 | 4000 | 7000 | 8850 | 20918 | 18704 | 2000 | 20704 | 2582 | 38002 | 252960 |
| Malawi | 0 | 17500 | 1000 | 10 | 3000 | 7000 | 14010 | 7265 | 10000 | 18265 | 3715 | 43075 | 213756 |
| Malaysia | 0 | 1000 | 167242 | 100 | 3954 | 6284 | 14693 | 16000 | 1000 | 184242 | 15235 | 92000 | 140000 |

## SCRIPTURE DISTRIBUTION-continued

| | NTs (continued): (a) Free | | | (b) Subsidized | | | | | (c) Commercial | TOTAL | | Portions | Selections |
|---|---|---|---|---|---|---|---|---|---|---|---|---|---|
| | 1960 | 1970 | 1975 | 1900 | 1950 | 1960 | 1970 | 1975 | 1975 | 1975 | pmillion | 1975 | 1975 |
| | 78 | 79 | 80 | 81 | 82 | 83 | 84 | 85 | 86 | 87 | 88 | 89 | 90 |
| Maldives | 0 | 0 | 0 | 0 | 0 | 0 | 0 | 0 | 100 | 1600 | 281 | 1500 | 5000 |
| Mali | 0 | 0 | 0 | 0 | 0 | 0 | 112 | 1500 | 1000 | 8400 | 25532 | 60 | 6000 |
| Malta | 0 | 0 | 7000 | 0 | 0 | 0 | 4 | 400 | 100 | 7464 | 20562 | 2800 | 16000 |
| Martinique | 0 | 0 | 6364 | 20 | 100 | 200 | 500 | 1000 | 100 | 7429 | 8264 | 0 | 0 |
| Mauritania | 0 | 0 | 0 | 0 | 0 | 0 | 0 | 0 | 0 | 0 | 0 | 0 | 0 |
| Mauritius | 0 | 0 | 0 | 100 | 1000 | 2000 | 4749 | 7329 | 100 | 7429 | 8264 | 39469 | 69801 |
| Mayotte | 0 | 0 | 0 | 0 | 0 | 0 | 0 | 0 | 0 | 0 | 0 | 0 | 0 |
| Mexico | 8280 | 58600 | 110242 | 10257 | 18845 | 13447 | 206030 | 75878 | 100000 | 286120 | 4833 | 332606 | 5484581 |
| Midway Islands | 0 | 0 | 0 | 0 | 0 | 0 | 0 | 0 | 0 | 0 | 0 | 0 | 0 |
| Monaco | 0 | 0 | 0 | 10 | 20 | 30 | 50 | 70 | 30 | 100 | 4167 | 100 | 0 |
| Mongolia | 0 | 0 | 0 | 0 | 0 | 0 | 0 | 0 | 0 | 600 | 461 | 0 | 2600 |
| Montserrat | 0 | 0 | 0 | 0 | 50 | 150 | 300 | 600 | 0 | 600 | 46154 | 0 | 2600 |
| Morocco | 0 | 0 | 0 | 100 | 100 | 100 | 273 | 750 | 50 | 800 | 46 | 2900 | 1200 |
| Mozambique | 0 | 0 | 39010 | 0 | 500 | 2000 | 5766 | 53273 | 300 | 92583 | 10021 | 22445 | 53855 |
| Namibia | 0 | 0 | 1000 | 0 | 2000 | 4000 | 6000 | 8000 | 5000 | 14000 | 19774 | 10000 | 20000 |
| Nauru | 0 | 0 | 0 | 0 | 40 | 60 | 80 | 100 | 0 | 100 | 12500 | 0 | 0 |
| Nepal | 0 | 0 | 5800 | 0 | 0 | 0 | 0 | 0 | 0 | 5800 | 461 | 0 | 0 |
| Netherlands | 2000 | 0 | 40565 | 18000 | 25191 | 17242 | 15672 | 148453 | 180000 | 369018 | 27136 | 93052 | 352415 |
| Netherlands Antilles | 1300 | 3050 | 12978 | 0 | 100 | 200 | 300 | 14742 | 500 | 27720 | 114545 | 740 | 24355 |
| New Caledonia | 0 | 0 | 0 | 0 | 300 | 600 | 800 | 1200 | 500 | 1700 | 13600 | 10200 | 27500 |
| New Zealand | 8400 | 46720 | 74250 | 674 | 5627 | 3990 | 29717 | 40399 | 10000 | 124649 | 41125 | 50625 | 1295930 |
| Nicaragua | 150 | 3700 | 15210 | 30 | 1280 | 2584 | 8503 | 17139 | 1000 | 33349 | 14387 | 115059 | 832572 |
| Niger | 0 | 0 | 0 | 0 | 0 | 0 | 170 | 1200 | 0 | 1200 | 261 | 1000 | 2500 |
| Nigeria | 0 | 6000 | 22000 | 1000 | 20000 | 50000 | 104646 | 68718 | 50000 | 140718 | 2236 | 117633 | 476348 |
| Niue Island | 0 | 0 | 0 | 0 | 5 | 10 | 20 | 20 | 0 | 20 | 4000 | 80 | 270 |
| Norfolk Island | 0 | 0 | 0 | 0 | 100 | 200 | 300 | 400 | 0 | 400 | 4469 | 2000 | 4000 |
| Northern Solomons | 0 | 0 | 0 | 0 | 0 | 0 | 0 | 0 | 0 | 0 | 0 | 0 | 0 |
| Norway | 855 | 20000 | 3737 | 30000 | 52975 | 96538 | 94608 | 186843 | 10000 | 200580 | 50057 | 19051 | 0 |
| Oman | 0 | 0 | 0 | 0 | 0 | 0 | 0 | 0 | 0 | 0 | 0 | 0 | 0 |
| Pacific Islands | 0 | 0 | 0 | 0 | 100 | 200 | 738 | 6945 | 1000 | 7945 | 67906 | 29600 | 110000 |
| Pakistan | 0 | 0 | 3000 | 500 | 2000 | 5000 | 10938 | 32311 | 2000 | 37311 | 529 | 228384 | 789073 |
| Palestine | 0 | 0 | 0 | 100 | 4000 | 15000 | 34558 | 19001 | 1000 | 20001 | 14317 | 16097 | 25664 |
| Panama | 3550 | 45300 | 19300 | 50 | 2974 | 1726 | 12379 | 14699 | 5000 | 38999 | 23241 | 35092 | 1063532 |
| Panama Canal Zone | 0 | 0 | 0 | 0 | 1874 | 667 | 800 | 1000 | 200 | 1200 | 27907 | 500 | 1000 |
| Papua New Guinea | 0 | 600 | 1000 | 10 | 5000 | 20000 | 43876 | 49595 | 2000 | 52595 | 19365 | 43025 | 192334 |
| Paraguay | 0 | 10300 | 11790 | 100 | 5784 | 5546 | 6447 | 16591 | 10000 | 38381 | 14500 | 34190 | 486846 |
| Peru | 0 | 21600 | 202560 | 135 | 12156 | 9895 | 99485 | 109601 | 80000 | 392161 | 25588 | 249114 | 3984743 |
| Philippines | 12200 | 300400 | 696140 | 1568 | 8363 | 26136 | 57970 | 210163 | 400000 | 1306303 | 29397 | 524418 | 11492392 |
| Pitcairn Islands | 0 | 0 | 0 | 10 | 5 | 5 | 5 | 10 | 0 | 10 | 111000 | 0 | 0 |
| Poland | 0 | 0 | 1000 | 2000 | 23704 | 4900 | 10934 | 13616 | 20000 | 34616 | 1023 | 78261 | 0 |
| Portugal | 0 | 24100 | 3000 | 2631 | 5125 | 9344 | 13098 | 11696 | 30000 | 44696 | 5101 | 54788 | 221849 |
| Puerto Rico | 0 | 13700 | 144210 | 705 | 19433 | 21795 | 43274 | 39131 | 8000 | 191341 | 65934 | 144453 | 2857850 |
| Qatar | 0 | 0 | 0 | 0 | 0 | 0 | 0 | 0 | 0 | 0 | 0 | 0 | 0 |
| Reunion | 0 | 0 | 1000 | 1000 | 900 | 800 | 30000 | 60000 | 0 | 61000 | 2880 | 2000 | 0 |
| Romania | 0 | 0 | 0 | 0 | 500 | 1000 | 3000 | 5000 | 1000 | 6000 | 1429 | 30000 | 0 |
| Rwanda | 0 | 0 | 0 | 0 | 0 | 0 | 0 | 0 | 0 | 0 | 0 | 0 | 0 |
| Sahara | 0 | 0 | 0 | 10 | 20 | 30 | 40 | 50 | 0 | 50 | 7474 | 0 | 0 |
| St Helena | 0 | 0 | 0 | 50 | 70 | 120 | 200 | 350 | 0 | 350 | 5853 | 300 | 12100 |
| St Kitts-Nevis | 0 | 0 | 0 | 100 | 700 | 1100 | 1600 | 2400 | 0 | 2400 | 22222 | 3600 | 700 |
| St Lucia | 0 | 0 | 0 | 0 | 0 | 0 | 0 | 0 | 20 | 20 | 3636 | 0 | 0 |
| St Pierre & Miquelon | 0 | 0 | 0 | 0 | 0 | 0 | 0 | 0 | 20 | 20 | 3636 | 0 | 0 |
| St Vincent | 5300 | 5200 | 0 | 50 | 300 | 500 | 700 | 900 | 100 | 1000 | 10753 | 1900 | 2700 |
| Samoa | 0 | 0 | 0 | 20 | 300 | 600 | 800 | 1100 | 100 | 1200 | 7317 | 2700 | 16700 |
| San Marino | 0 | 0 | 0 | 0 | 10 | 20 | 40 | 60 | 0 | 60 | 3000 | 0 | 0 |
| Sao Tome & Principe | 0 | 0 | 0 | 0 | 0 | 0 | 0 | 0 | 300 | 300 | 3750 | 0 | 0 |
| Saudi Arabia | 0 | 0 | 0 | 0 | 0 | 0 | 0 | 0 | 0 | 0 | 0 | 0 | 0 |
| Senegal | 0 | 0 | 4000 | 0 | 200 | 500 | 1000 | 4000 | 1000 | 9000 | 2037 | 15500 | 8600 |
| Seychelles | 0 | 0 | 0 | 0 | 0 | 10 | 30 | 0 | 200 | 200 | 3390 | 0 | 0 |
| Sierra Leone | 0 | 0 | 15500 | 100 | 1000 | 3000 | 4680 | 5139 | 1000 | 21639 | 7254 | 17825 | 11911 |
| Sikkim | 0 | 0 | 200 | 0 | 0 | 0 | 0 | 0 | 0 | 200 | 800 | 0 | 0 |
| Singapore | 0 | 0 | 123900 | 200 | 6000 | 10000 | 12000 | 20000 | 1000 | 144900 | 64457 | 162157 | 1387113 |
| Solomon Islands | 0 | 0 | 4200 | 0 | 500 | 1500 | 3000 | 5000 | 0 | 9200 | 49198 | 5000 | 10000 |
| Somalia | 0 | 0 | 0 | 0 | 0 | 0 | 0 | 30 | 0 | 30 | 9 | 180 | 170 |
| South Africa | 15350 | 178675 | 102800 | 10000 | 65000 | 100000 | 190650 | 430000 | 50000 | 582800 | 23631 | 610000 | 180000 |
| Spain | 0 | 0 | 335880 | 8755 | 2039 | 5087 | 12203 | 27351 | 795037 | 1158268 | 32689 | 66721 | 106960 |
| Spanish North Africa | 0 | 0 | 0 | 0 | 0 | 0 | 0 | 0 | 1730 | 1730 | 10000 | 0 | 0 |
| Sri Lanka | 200 | 3300 | 15600 | 1837 | 2500 | 3298 | 9400 | 8354 | 1000 | 24954 | 1784 | 87447 | 270900 |
| Sudan | 0 | 0 | 0 | 0 | 575 | 3364 | 2036 | 7706 | 0 | 7706 | 422 | 80231 | 88486 |
| Surinam | 400 | 9934 | 0 | 115 | 868 | 0 | 170 | 631 | 100 | 731 | 1732 | 40 | 14081 |
| Svalbard & Jan Mayen Is | 0 | 0 | 0 | 0 | 0 | 0 | 0 | 0 | 0 | 0 | 0 | 0 | 0 |
| Swaziland | 0 | 0 | 2500 | 0 | 300 | 500 | 861 | 2000 | 500 | 5000 | 10684 | 2000 | 3000 |
| Sweden | 1042 | 15000 | 1000 | 30000 | 18843 | 24161 | 8480 | 143000 | 2000 | 146000 | 17609 | 121500 | 0 |
| Switzerland | 0 | 22490 | 9887 | 19202 | 10213 | 53331 | 3899 | 43624 | 35000 | 88511 | 13544 | 3671 | 46266 |
| Syria | 0 | 0 | 0 | 248 | 500 | 1000 | 2694 | 1153 | 0 | 1153 | 159 | 0 | 0 |
| Tanzania | 0 | 0 | 0 | 20 | 1000 | 30000 | 43676 | 53659 | 1000 | 54659 | 3541 | 316876 | 1616602 |
| Thailand | 0 | 0 | 140000 | 59 | 789 | 3599 | 19000 | 30478 | 5000 | 175478 | 4169 | 384921 | 2664046 |
| Timor | 0 | 0 | 0 | 0 | 0 | 0 | 0 | 0 | 0 | 0 | 0 | 0 | 0 |
| Togo | 0 | 0 | 0 | 10 | 500 | 800 | 1352 | 5000 | 500 | 5500 | 2447 | 3200 | 17600 |
| Tokelau | 0 | 0 | 0 | 0 | 0 | 5 | 10 | 20 | 0 | 20 | 12121 | 0 | 0 |
| Tonga | 0 | 0 | 0 | 20 | 50 | 80 | 100 | 100 | 400 | 500 | 4950 | 400 | 1300 |
| Trinidad & Tobago | 8500 | 17500 | 36400 | 1000 | 1000 | 3000 | 5000 | 6200 | 100 | 42700 | 42319 | 14800 | 145100 |
| Tunisia | 0 | 0 | 50 | 0 | 0 | 0 | 31 | 20 | 0 | 70 | 12 | 10 | 0 |
| Turkey | 0 | 0 | 500 | 8692 | 1036 | 1142 | 1566 | 2241 | 0 | 2741 | 69 | 7933 | 43172 |
| Turks & Caicos Islands | 0 | 0 | 0 | 0 | 5 | 10 | 15 | 20 | 0 | 20 | 3597 | 0 | 0 |
| Tuvalu | 0 | 0 | 0 | 10 | 20 | 50 | 100 | 100 | 0 | 100 | 16667 | 0 | 0 |
| Uganda | 0 | 3500 | 23000 | 1000 | 10000 | 20000 | 31711 | 55284 | 1000 | 79284 | 6984 | 455474 | 37261 |
| USSR | 10000 | 30000 | 118000 | 251949 | 4000 | 4000 | 2000 | 28000 | 0 | 146000 | 572 | 2000 | 0 |
| United Arab Emirates | 0 | 0 | 0 | 0 | 0 | 0 | 0 | 0 | 0 | 0 | 0 | 0 | 0 |
| UK of GB & NI | 208761 | 454312 | 1085767 | 662410 | 129000 | 53000 | 135000 | 241555 | 710000 | 2037322 | 36105 | 1130000 | 2300000 |
| USA | 1899890 | 3060505 | 5944272 | 280000 | 726463 | 1052828 | 6168802 | 2713204 | 16600000 | 25257476 | 118067 | 4992055 | 101116329 |
| US Virgin Islands | 0 | 0 | 400 | 20 | 700 | 1000 | 2000 | 2000 | 1000 | 3400 | 51515 | 1240 | 97000 |
| Upper Volta | 0 | 0 | 0 | 0 | 100 | 500 | 1186 | 10000 | 0 | 10000 | 1658 | 4300 | 17900 |
| Uruguay | 3800 | 6500 | 26010 | 1000 | 3032 | 5277 | 11233 | 14382 | 5000 | 45392 | 14605 | 120988 | 830923 |
| Vanuatu | 0 | 0 | 0 | 0 | 100 | 500 | 1000 | 2000 | 100 | 2100 | 21875 | 7900 | 22200 |
| Venezuela | 2100 | 46800 | 380620 | 300 | 5932 | 23792 | 54392 | 50596 | 70000 | 501216 | 41040 | 757819 | 4212732 |
| Viet Nam | 12942 | 149883 | 62113 | 20 | 236 | 1150 | 25158 | 41870 | 1000 | 104983 | 2416 | 879501 | 1578572 |
| Wake Island | 0 | 0 | 0 | 0 | 0 | 0 | 0 | 0 | 0 | 0 | 0 | 0 | 0 |
| Wallis & Futuna Islands | 0 | 0 | 0 | 0 | 0 | 0 | 0 | 0 | 100 | 100 | 11110 | 0 | 0 |
| Yemen, North | 0 | 0 | 0 | 0 | 0 | 0 | 0 | 0 | 0 | 0 | 0 | 0 | 0 |
| Yemen, South | 0 | 0 | 0 | 20 | 26 | 30 | 0 | 0 | 0 | 0 | 0 | 0 | 0 |
| Yugoslavia | 0 | 0 | 0 | 1000 | 3000 | 6047 | 1764 | 4027 | 20000 | 24027 | 1127 | 6000 | 0 |
| Zaire | 0 | 10000 | 0 | 200 | 5000 | 10000 | 189253 | 54000 | 25000 | 79000 | 3226 | 52719 | 406151 |
| Zambia | 0 | 0 | 34100 | 50 | 10000 | 20000 | 32593 | 36365 | 4000 | 74465 | 14828 | 183992 | 352878 |
| Zimbabwe | 0 | 11012 | 33350 | 500 | 10000 | 15000 | 22718 | 21362 | 10000 | 64712 | 10311 | 77592 | 353061 |
| Column | 78 | 79 | 80 | 81 | 82 | 83 | 84 | 85 | 86 | 87 | 88 | 89 | 90 |
| *Continent* | | | | | | | | | | | | | |
| Africa | 15350 | 284367 | 447190 | 20129 | 199750 | 428114 | 1045103 | 1445646 | 199080 | 2091916 | — | 3511254 | 7103263 |
| East Asia | 212100 | 644769 | 2214572 | 91750 | 1154645 | 591019 | 1425612 | 2458809 | 190000 | 4863381 | — | 2503261 | 29468539 |
| Europe | 274477 | 672997 | 1823659 | 1298672 | 627532 | 701436 | 917055 | 1727441 | 3629547 | 7180647 | — | 3211818 | 7173017 |
| Latin America | 157613 | 816384 | 3720531 | 53827 | 277472 | 613422 | 960110 | 898506 | 915536 | 5534573 | — | 4837849 | 55236178 |
| Northern America | 2105195 | 3305651 | 6507886 | 330070 | 799762 | 1104208 | 6451286 | 3018840 | 17030070 | 26556796 | — | 5579697 | 103730701 |
| Oceania | 57940 | 238420 | 344750 | 13779 | 38505 | 68980 | 204219 | 284487 | 64700 | 693937 | — | 761767 | 3448317 |
| South Asia | 25742 | 858572 | 2323604 | 34045 | 184646 | 315073 | 759345 | 1004900 | 653300 | 3981804 | — | 6969973 | 52860098 |
| USSR | 10000 | 30000 | 118000 | 251949 | 4000 | 4000 | 2000 | 28000 | 0 | 146000 | — | 2000 | 0 |
| **WORLD** | **2858417** | **6851160** | **17500192** | **2094221** | **3286312** | **3826252** | **11764730** | **10866629** | **22682233** | **51049054** | **—** | **27377619** | **259020113** |

| | CHRISTIAN BROADCASTING | | | | | LITERACY | | | | EVANGELIZATION, *1900-2000* | | | | | | | |
|---|---|---|---|---|---|---|---|---|---|---|---|---|---|---|---|---|---|
| | Sets % | Letters per year | AUDIENCE, % Christian | Secular | Total | ADULT LITERACY RATE, % 1900 | 1950 | 1975 | 1980 | Year begun | EXTENT Individual | EVANGELIZED, E% 1900 | 1970 | 1980 | 1985 | 2000 | Outreach |
| | 91 | 92 | 93 | 94 | 95 | 96 | 97 | 98 | 99 | 100 | 101 | 102 | 103 | 104 | 105 | 106 | 107 |
| Afghanistan | 2 | 5 | 0.1 | 0 | 0.1 | 0 | 4 | 12 | 13 | c 300 | 5 | 3 | 14 | 17 | 20 | 28 | 401.12 |
| Albania | 8 | 2 | 0.4 | 0 | 0.4 | 27 | 46 | 80 | 83 | c 70 | 18 | 39 | 34 | 35 | 41 | 60 | 6.43 |
| Algeria | 6 | 2240 | 4.2 | 0 | 4.2 | 12 | 18 | 27 | 29 | c 100 | 17 | 15 | 24 | 25 | 33 | 55 | 32.51 |
| American Samoa | 34 | 20 | 4.4 | 70 | 74.0 | 20 | 89 | 97 | 97 | 1827 | 100 | 100 | 100 | 100 | 100 | 100 | 1.01 |
| Andorra | 46 | 0 | 5.3 | 60 | 65.0 | 30 | 80 | 90 | 91 | c 600 | 100 | 100 | 100 | 100 | 100 | 100 | 1.00 |
| Angola | 2 | 100 | 1.6 | 3 | 4.6 | 0 | 3 | 15 | 16 | 1491 | 86 | 15 | 86 | 95 | 96 | 98 | 1.06 |
| Anguilla | 50 | 2 | 2.3 | 40 | 42.0 | 5 | 70 | 80 | 81 | c1650 | 100 | 100 | 100 | 100 | 100 | 100 | 1.01 |
| Antigua | 50 | 10 | 1.0 | 50 | 51.0 | 15 | 82 | 92 | 93 | 1634 | 100 | 100 | 100 | 100 | 100 | 100 | 1.03 |
| Argentina | 53 | 16700 | 4.3 | 60 | 64.0 | 47 | 87 | 93 | 93 | 1527 | 99 | 99 | 100 | 100 | 100 | 100 | 1.05 |
| Australia | 44 | 4500 | 1.5 | 60 | 61.0 | 60 | 98 | 99 | 99 | 1788 | 100 | 100 | 100 | 100 | 100 | 100 | 1.19 |
| Austria | 52 | 3200 | 1.8 | 70 | 71.0 | 96 | 99 | 99 | 99 | 174 | 100 | 100 | 100 | 100 | 100 | 100 | 1.04 |
| Bahamas | 44 | 40 | 1.4 | 75 | 76.0 | 25 | 84 | 91 | 92 | c1670 | 100 | 100 | 100 | 100 | 100 | 100 | 1.05 |
| Bahrain | 43 | 100 | 15.5 | 0 | 15.5 | 1 | 13 | 41 | 43 | c 250 | 39 | 9 | 40 | 47 | 54 | 75 | 12.77 |
| Bangladesh | 1 | 500 | 0.4 | 0 | 0.4 | 5 | 22 | 25 | 25 | 1536 | 13 | 15 | 43 | 60 | 68 | 90 | 113.08 |
| Barbados | 60 | 10 | 0.3 | 70 | 70.0 | 20 | 91 | 98 | 98 | 1626 | 100 | 100 | 100 | 100 | 100 | 100 | 1.06 |
| Belgium | 62 | 2600 | 1.2 | 55 | 56.0 | 80 | 97 | 98 | 98 | c 200 | 99 | 100 | 100 | 100 | 100 | 100 | 1.10 |
| Belize | 52 | 50 | 3.0 | 70 | 73.0 | 5 | 81 | 88 | 89 | c1650 | 100 | 99 | 100 | 100 | 100 | 100 | 1.06 |
| Benin | 5 | 30 | 0.3 | 0 | 0.3 | 0 | 3 | 20 | 21 | 1680 | 59 | 13 | 60 | 70 | 75 | 90 | 3.03 |
| Bermuda | 108 | 20 | 1.6 | 75 | 76.0 | 70 | 97 | 99 | 99 | 1609 | 100 | 100 | 100 | 100 | 100 | 100 | 1.02 |
| Bhutan | 0 | 10 | 2.6 | 0 | 2.6 | 0 | 1 | 5 | 6 | 1865 | 11 | 0 | 12 | 16 | 19 | 29 | 249.79 |
| Bolivia | 29 | 500 | 2.1 | 40 | 42.0 | 4 | 32 | 62 | 66 | 1537 | 98 | 96 | 99 | 100 | 100 | 100 | 1.06 |
| Botswana | 1 | 200 | 5.6 | 5 | 7.0 | 5 | 22 | 35 | 37 | 1816 | 94 | 9 | 95 | 98 | 99 | 100 | 1.95 |
| Brazil | 13 | 150000 | 11.1 | 35 | 43.0 | 35 | 49 | 67 | 70 | 1500 | 100 | 98 | 100 | 100 | 100 | 100 | 1.06 |
| British Antarctic Terr | 100 | 0 | 2.0 | 0 | 2.0 | 0 | 100 | 100 | 100 | c1950 | 100 | 0 | 100 | 100 | 100 | 100 | 1.54 |
| British Indian Ocean Terr | 100 | 0 | 1.0 | 0 | 1.0 | 5 | 40 | 60 | 65 | c1850 | 85 | 50 | 90 | 95 | 96 | 100 | 2.11 |
| British Virgin Is | 70 | 5 | 3.2 | 70 | 73.0 | 20 | 84 | 93 | 93 | 1648 | 100 | 100 | 100 | 100 | 100 | 100 | 1.07 |
| Brunei | 15 | 4 | 0.6 | 0 | 0.6 | 4 | 38 | 67 | 71 | c1600 | 42 | 6 | 45 | 55 | 61 | 80 | 6.85 |
| Bulgaria | 42 | 110 | 1.1 | 0 | 1.1 | 30 | 77 | 94 | 95 | c 150 | 74 | 96 | 75 | 80 | 83 | 90 | 1.24 |
| Burma | 2 | 3950 | 1.7 | 0 | 1.7 | 30 | 55 | 68 | 69 | c 920 | 26 | 20 | 40 | 48 | 53 | 68 | 8.57 |
| Burundi | 3 | 100 | 1.7 | 7 | 8.0 | 0 | 7 | 18 | 20 | 1879 | 96 | 1 | 100 | 100 | 100 | 100 | 1.17 |
| Cameroon | 4 | 610 | 0.9 | 8 | 8.9 | 1 | 14 | 30 | 32 | 1845 | 87 | 16 | 88 | 92 | 93 | 97 | 1.66 |
| Canada | 121 | 60000 | 11.2 | 65 | 69.0 | 87 | 99 | 100 | 100 | 1534 | 100 | 99 | 100 | 100 | 100 | 100 | 1.10 |
| Canton & Enderbury | 90 | 0 | 21.0 | 0 | 21.0 | 0 | 90 | 98 | 98 | c1870 | 100 | 0 | 100 | 100 | 100 | 100 | 1.25 |
| Cape Verde | 2 | 20 | 1.6 | 2 | 3.6 | 2 | 21 | 38 | 40 | 1462 | 100 | 100 | 100 | 100 | 100 | 100 | 1.01 |
| Cayman Islands | 95 | 30 | 19.5 | 0 | 19.5 | 10 | 95 | 93 | 93 | 1670 | 100 | 100 | 100 | 100 | 100 | 100 | 1.04 |
| Central African Republic | 4 | 150 | 3.0 | 8 | 11.0 | 0 | 3 | 18 | 18 | 1894 | 99 | 0 | 99 | 100 | 100 | 100 | 1.18 |
| Chad | 2 | 25 | 0.7 | 5 | 5.7 | 0 | 3 | 10 | 11 | 1663 | 53 | 0 | 54 | 64 | 69 | 84 | 1.94 |
| Channel Islands | 73 | 100 | 3.3 | 70 | 72.0 | 90 | 100 | 100 | 100 | c 550 | 100 | 100 | 100 | 100 | 100 | 100 | 1.05 |
| Chile | 20 | 2260 | 1.6 | 40 | 41.0 | 43 | 79 | 88 | 90 | 1541 | 100 | 99 | 100 | 100 | 100 | 100 | 1.08 |
| China | 2 | 1000 | 3.0 | 0 | 3.0 | 6 | 35 | 55 | 60 | 635 | 18 | 28 | 19 | 29 | 36 | 57 | 143.37 |
| China (Taiwan) | 18 | 30000 | 14.4 | 40 | 51.0 | 5 | 50 | 85 | 88 | 1621 | 78 | 13 | 78 | 89 | 92 | 98 | 12.04 |
| Christmas Island | 30 | 0 | 10.0 | 0 | 10.0 | 6 | 60 | 70 | 72 | 1888 | 54 | 8 | 60 | 70 | 78 | 100 | 4.49 |
| Cocos Islands | 30 | 0 | 10.0 | 0 | 10.0 | 12 | 50 | 60 | 62 | 1826 | 68 | 20 | 70 | 80 | 85 | 100 | 2.20 |
| Colombia | 17 | 19000 | 6.7 | 45 | 51.0 | 29 | 62 | 82 | 84 | 1512 | 99 | 83 | 99 | 99 | 99 | 100 | 1.01 |
| Comoros | 12 | 10 | 2.0 | 0 | 2.0 | 0 | 50 | 60 | 61 | 1517 | 29 | 1 | 30 | 40 | 50 | 80 | 217.09 |
| Congo | 8 | 30 | 1.0 | 2 | 3.0 | 0 | 12 | 20 | 21 | 1491 | 99 | 14 | 99 | 99 | 99 | 100 | 1.06 |
| Cook Islands | 11 | 3 | 0.9 | 30 | 30.0 | 30 | 92 | 92 | 92 | 1823 | 100 | 100 | 100 | 100 | 100 | 100 | 1.01 |
| Costa Rica | 14 | 510 | 2.0 | 40 | 42.0 | 30 | 79 | 88 | 90 | 1514 | 100 | 100 | 100 | 100 | 100 | 100 | 1.02 |
| Cuba | 24 | 380 | 1.8 | 0 | 1.8 | 44 | 78 | 97 | 98 | 1512 | 65 | 100 | 65 | 60 | 66 | 85 | 1.43 |
| Cyprus | 37 | 100 | 1.0 | 30 | 31.0 | 20 | 62 | 78 | 80 | 46 | 92 | 94 | 94 | 97 | 98 | 99 | 1.23 |
| Czechoslovakia | 49 | 900 | 2.5 | 0 | 2.5 | 97 | 97 | 100 | 100 | 828 | 95 | 100 | 95 | 98 | 99 | 100 | 1.23 |
| Denmark | 61 | 2400 | 1.9 | 53 | 54.0 | 95 | 100 | 100 | 100 | 826 | 100 | 100 | 100 | 100 | 100 | 100 | 1.04 |
| Djibouti | 9 | 0 | 0.1 | 2 | 2.0 | 5 | 25 | 35 | 35 | 1862 | 62 | 5 | 65 | 70 | 74 | 85 | 8.01 |
| Dominica | 40 | 5 | 0.5 | 20 | 20.5 | 8 | 60 | 80 | 80 | 1642 | 100 | 100 | 100 | 100 | 100 | 100 | 1.00 |
| Dominican Republic | 8 | 6200 | 12.0 | 30 | 41.0 | 5 | 43 | 69 | 72 | 1494 | 100 | 100 | 100 | 100 | 100 | 100 | 1.02 |
| Ecuador | 30 | 25430 | 35.4 | 60 | 80.0 | 6 | 56 | 75 | 76 | 1526 | 100 | 90 | 100 | 100 | 100 | 100 | 1.02 |
| Egypt | 16 | 3800 | 2.1 | 7 | 9.0 | 6 | 21 | 43 | 45 | 30 | 43 | 34 | 48 | 58 | 63 | 78 | 3.25 |
| El Salvador | 11 | 490 | 1.4 | 30 | 31.0 | 20 | 40 | 62 | 63 | 1525 | 100 | 100 | 100 | 100 | 100 | 100 | 1.01 |
| Equatorial Guinea | 23 | 100 | 14.0 | 0 | 14.0 | 0 | 10 | 20 | 15 | 1445 | 99 | 17 | 100 | 100 | 100 | 100 | 1.13 |
| Ethiopia | 1 | 14650 | 15.0 | 0 | 15.0 | 0 | 2 | 7 | 8 | 332 | 86 | 51 | 86 | 88 | 90 | 94 | 1.54 |
| Faeroe Islands | 39 | 25 | 2.6 | 30 | 32.0 | 95 | 100 | 100 | 100 | c 750 | 100 | 100 | 100 | 100 | 100 | 100 | 1.00 |
| Falkland Islands | 52 | 1 | 3.0 | 20 | 23.0 | 70 | 98 | 98 | 98 | 1764 | 100 | 100 | 100 | 100 | 100 | 100 | 1.19 |
| Fiji | 10 | 100 | 1.3 | 21 | 22.0 | 30 | 65 | 85 | 86 | 1804 | 95 | 95 | 95 | 97 | 98 | 100 | 1.95 |
| Finland | 68 | 1150 | 1.0 | 52 | 53.0 | 39 | 99 | 100 | 100 | c1100 | 100 | 100 | 100 | 100 | 100 | 100 | 1.06 |
| France | 57 | 19170 | 1.5 | 60 | 61.0 | 83 | 97 | 99 | 99 | c 80 | 99 | 100 | 100 | 100 | 100 | 100 | 1.25 |
| French Guiana | 16 | 1 | 0.2 | 30 | 30.0 | 10 | 70 | 76 | 77 | 1598 | 97 | 97 | 99 | 100 | 100 | 100 | 1.10 |
| French Polynesia | 49 | 20 | 1.1 | 50 | 51.0 | 30 | 93 | 95 | 95 | 1659 | 98 | 100 | 100 | 100 | 100 | 100 | 1.06 |
| French Southern & Antarctic T | 100 | 0 | 1.0 | 0 | 1.0 | 0 | 100 | 100 | 100 | 1949 | 100 | 0 | 100 | 100 | 100 | 100 | 2.00 |
| Gabon | 13 | 20 | 1.1 | 20 | 21.0 | 0 | 8 | 20 | 25 | 1673 | 100 | 23 | 100 | 100 | 100 | 100 | 1.04 |
| Gambia | 16 | 2 | 0.4 | 18 | 18.0 | 0 | 3 | 10 | 11 | 1651 | 67 | 17 | 69 | 75 | 79 | 89 | 22.58 |
| German Democratic Rep | 65 | 5200 | 6.2 | 20 | 24.0 | 94 | 99 | 99 | 99 | 772 | 97 | 100 | 97 | 98 | 99 | 100 | 1.55 |
| Germany, Federal Rep | 63 | 101200 | 6.7 | 61 | 64.0 | 94 | 100 | 100 | 100 | c 90 | 99 | 100 | 100 | 100 | 100 | 100 | 1.08 |
| Ghana | 9 | 1490 | 3.9 | 17 | 20.0 | 3 | 20 | 31 | 33 | 1471 | 94 | 23 | 94 | 96 | 97 | 99 | 1.53 |
| Gibraltar | 42 | 10 | 1.6 | 20 | 22.0 | 30 | 90 | 94 | 94 | 1309 | 97 | 100 | 100 | 100 | 100 | 100 | 1.14 |
| Greece | 25 | 2000 | 1.0 | 50 | 51.0 | 33 | 74 | 86 | 87 | c 40 | 100 | 96 | 100 | 100 | 100 | 100 | 1.02 |
| Greenland | 16 | 3 | 0.4 | 10 | 10.0 | 15 | 50 | 60 | 62 | c 990 | 100 | 100 | 100 | 100 | 100 | 100 | 1.01 |
| Grenada | 21 | 8 | 0.5 | 50 | 50.0 | 10 | 77 | 93 | 93 | c1650 | 99 | 100 | 100 | 100 | 100 | 100 | 1.01 |
| Guadeloupe | 11 | 20 | 0.4 | 30 | 30.0 | 7 | 63 | 86 | 86 | 1523 | 100 | 100 | 100 | 100 | 100 | 100 | 1.03 |
| Guam | 121 | 50 | 3.6 | 80 | 83.0 | 20 | 85 | 90 | 90 | 1668 | 100 | 100 | 100 | 100 | 100 | 100 | 1.03 |
| Guatemala | 13 | 4500 | 12.8 | 32 | 44.0 | 7 | 29 | 47 | 48 | 1524 | 100 | 100 | 100 | 100 | 100 | 100 | 1.01 |
| Guinea | 2 | 2 | 0.1 | 0 | 0.1 | 0 | 6 | 10 | 11 | 1877 | 11 | 7 | 12 | 16 | 20 | 30 | 12.34 |
| Guinea-Bissau | 2 | 2 | 0.8 | 3 | 3.8 | 0 | 4 | 5 | 6 | 1445 | 24 | 8 | 30 | 36 | 42 | 60 | 3.53 |
| Guyana | 14 | 20 | 0.2 | 21 | 21.0 | 10 | 77 | 90 | 91 | 1548 | 94 | 59 | 94 | 95 | 96 | 98 | 1.83 |
| Haiti | 2 | 150 | 2.0 | 10 | 12.0 | 1 | 11 | 24 | 25 | 1493 | 100 | 100 | 100 | 100 | 100 | 100 | 1.02 |
| Holy See | 150 | 50 | 40.0 | 80 | 90.0 | 99 | 100 | 100 | 100 | c 40 | 100 | 100 | 100 | 100 | 100 | 100 | 1.00 |
| Honduras | 6 | 380 | 2.1 | 12 | 14.0 | 29 | 35 | 57 | 60 | 1524 | 100 | 99 | 100 | 100 | 100 | 100 | 1.02 |
| Hong Kong | 29 | 800 | 1.4 | 22 | 23.0 | 7 | 65 | 80 | 82 | 1841 | 98 | 16 | 98 | 99 | 99 | 100 | 5.59 |
| Hungary | 45 | 1000 | 2.0 | 50 | 52.0 | 61 | 95 | 98 | 98 | c 250 | 94 | 100 | 94 | 96 | 97 | 100 | 1.15 |
| Iceland | 53 | 50 | 1.0 | 65 | 66.0 | 96 | 100 | 100 | 100 | c 740 | 100 | 100 | 100 | 100 | 100 | 100 | 1.03 |
| India | 2 | 71000 | 2.3 | 10 | 12.0 | 6 | 18 | 36 | 37 | c 52 | 33 | 27 | 58 | 73 | 78 | 92 | 18.72 |
| Indonesia | 12 | 16700 | 3.1 | 15 | 18.0 | 9 | 30 | 63 | 64 | c 650 | 44 | 24 | 62 | 76 | 80 | 93 | 6.90 |
| Iran | 26 | 850 | 1.0 | 3 | 4.0 | 1 | 10 | 43 | 44 | c 50 | 24 | 13 | 27 | 32 | 35 | 42 | 36.96 |
| Iraq | 16 | 1340 | 4.8 | 0 | 4.8 | 3 | 14 | 40 | 41 | c 50 | 31 | 22 | 32 | 35 | 38 | 46 | 9.93 |
| Ireland | 38 | 750 | 1.0 | 82 | 83.0 | 60 | 98 | 99 | 99 | 350 | 100 | 100 | 100 | 100 | 100 | 100 | 1.01 |
| Isle of Man | 71 | 20 | 2.0 | 70 | 72.0 | 90 | 99 | 99 | 99 | 442 | 100 | 100 | 100 | 100 | 100 | 100 | 1.08 |
| Israel | 34 | 150 | 0.5 | 5 | 5.5 | 11 | 80 | 90 | 91 | 30 | 65 | 24 | 66 | 81 | 84 | 92 | 36.62 |
| Italy | 44 | 16100 | 1.3 | 65 | 66.0 | 52 | 86 | 94 | 94 | 30 | 100 | 100 | 100 | 100 | 100 | 100 | 1.20 |
| Ivory Coast | 3 | 2050 | 13.6 | 5 | 18.6 | 0 | 3 | 30 | 32 | 1637 | 79 | 5 | 79 | 84 | 87 | 95 | 2.62 |
| Jamaica | 43 | 1310 | 4.9 | 26 | 30.0 | 25 | 76 | 86 | 87 | 1509 | 100 | 100 | 100 | 100 | 100 | 100 | 1.11 |
| Japan | 88 | 164400 | 7.0 | 25 | 32.0 | 30 | 97 | 100 | 100 | 1549 | 64 | 20 | 65 | 76 | 81 | 95 | 25.33 |
| Johnston Island | 100 | 0 | 1.0 | 30 | 31.0 | 0 | 100 | 100 | 100 | c1858 | 100 | 0 | 100 | 100 | 100 | 100 | 1.25 |
| Jordan | 23 | 510 | 6.6 | 3 | 9.6 | 3 | 28 | 45 | 46 | 30 | 52 | 16 | 53 | 61 | 66 | 79 | 12.34 |
| Kampuchea | 16 | 40 | 5.5 | 0 | 5.5 | 4 | 26 | 41 | 30 | 1555 | 29 | 7 | 30 | 32 | 34 | 40 | 53.77 |
| Kenya | 4 | 3000 | 2.5 | 25 | 27.0 | 1 | 16 | 60 | 65 | 1498 | 96 | 7 | 96 | 98 | 99 | 100 | 1.34 |
| Kiribati | 21 | 5 | 0.5 | 60 | 60.0 | 20 | 90 | 95 | 95 | 1837 | 100 | 100 | 100 | 100 | 100 | 100 | 1.06 |
| Korea, North | 7 | 50 | 1.6 | 0 | 1.6 | 15 | 70 | 90 | 91 | c1600 | 23 | 19 | 23 | 25 | 28 | 35 | 27.68 |
| Korea, South | 16 | 39800 | 8.1 | 25 | 33.0 | 10 | 70 | 91 | 92 | 1592 | 90 | 16 | 90 | 94 | 96 | 100 | 4.23 |
| Kuwait | 15 | 510 | 11.2 | 0 | 11.2 | 2 | 27 | 60 | 62 | c1550 | 34 | 7 | 35 | 41 | 46 | 62 | 9.58 |
| Laos | 5 | 10 | 0.9 | 0 | 0.9 | 4 | 20 | 30 | 31 | 1630 | 38 | 4 | 38 | 42 | 45 | 55 | 23.33 |
| Lebanon | 32 | 4140 | 13.0 | 60 | 67.0 | 10 | 60 | 86 | 87 | 30 | 99 | 80 | 99 | 100 | 100 | 100 | 1.67 |
| Lesotho | 1 | 200 | 1.9 | 3 | 4.9 | 10 | 40 | 69 | 71 | 1833 | 100 | 31 | 100 | 100 | 100 | 100 | 1.08 |
| Liberia | 14 | 65900 | 51.0 | 20 | 55.0 | 1 | 7 | 10 | 11 | 1822 | 91 | 27 | 91 | 95 | 96 | 100 | 2.71 |
| Libya | 5 | 50 | 1.0 | 0 | 1.0 | 2 | 12 | 35 | 37 | 30 | 11 | 8 | 14 | 18 | 22 | 35 | 10.51 |
| Liechtenstein | 42 | 10 | 1.9 | 50 | 51.0 | 70 | 98 | 98 | 98 | c 450 | 100 | 100 | 100 | 100 | 100 | 100 | 1.01 |
| Luxembourg | 47 | 300 | 3.6 | 70 | 71.0 | 80 | 98 | 98 | 98 | c 250 | 100 | 100 | 100 | 100 | 100 | 100 | 1.06 |
| Macao | 5 | 30 | 0.9 | 19 | 19.9 | 5 | 53 | 81 | 82 | 1557 | 83 | 30 | 83 | 86 | 88 | 95 | 6.91 |
| Madagascar | 11 | 3000 | 6.2 | 25 | 31.0 | 12 | 34 | 41 | 44 | 1540 | 96 | 55 | 96 | 97 | 98 | 99 | 1.90 |
| Malawi | 2 | 220 | 1.2 | 8 | 9.0 | 0 | 7 | 25 | 26 | 1561 | 93 | 17 | 93 | 96 | 97 | 100 | 1.49 |
| Malaysia | 7 | 2400 | 6.1 | 0 | 6.1 | 4 | 39 | 57 | 59 | 1511 | 58 | 12 | 58 | 69 | 74 | 89 | 11.21 |

| | CHRISTIAN BROADCASTING | | | | | LITERACY | | | | EVANGELIZATION, *1900-2000* | | | | | | | |
|---|---|---|---|---|---|---|---|---|---|---|---|---|---|---|---|---|---|
| | Sets % | Letters per year | AUDIENCE, % Christian | Secular | Total | ADULT LITERACY RATE, % 1900 | 1950 | 1975 | 1980 | Year begun | EXTENT Individual | EVANGELIZED, E% 1900 | 1970 | 1980 | 1985 | 2000 | Outreach |
| | 91 | 92 | 93 | 94 | 95 | 96 | 97 | 98 | 99 | 100 | 101 | 102 | 103 | 104 | 105 | 106 | 107 |
| Maldives | 2 | 5 | 1.5 | 0 | 1.5 | 0 | 20 | 40 | 41 | 1887 | 4 | 0 | 11 | 12 | 19 | 40 | 93.18 |
| Mali | 1 | 50 | 2.0 | 4 | 6.0 | 0 | 2 | 10 | 11 | 1895 | 19 | 4 | 26 | 28 | 32 | 45 | 15.10 |
| Malta | 59 | 150 | 2.1 | 70 | 72.0 | 15 | 58 | 88 | 90 | 60 | 100 | 100 | 100 | 100 | 100 | 100 | 1.01 |
| Martinique | 14 | 5 | 0.1 | 30 | 30.0 | 8 | 70 | 91 | 91 | c1550 | 100 | 100 | 100 | 100 | 100 | 100 | 1.02 |
| Mauritania | 6 | 5 | 1.7 | 0 | 1.7 | 0 | 3 | 16 | 17 | 1448 | 10 | 3 | 10 | 12 | 15 | 25 | 28.26 |
| Mauritius | 16 | 125 | 1.1 | 8 | 9.0 | 10 | 51 | 80 | 82 | 1598 | 90 | 46 | 90 | 92 | 94 | 98 | 2.60 |
| Mayotte | 12 | 0 | 1.0 | 0 | 1.0 | 0 | 30 | 60 | 62 | 1517 | 25 | 1 | 35 | 45 | 56 | 90 | 36.38 |
| Mexico | 39 | 10000 | 1.5 | 80 | 81.0 | 22 | 57 | 78 | 80 | 1518 | 100 | 100 | 100 | 100 | 100 | 100 | 1.03 |
| Midway Islands | 100 | 0 | 1.0 | 50 | 51.0 | 70 | 100 | 100 | 100 | 1867 | 100 | 100 | 100 | 100 | 100 | 100 | 1.15 |
| Monaco | 92 | 20 | 3.5 | 80 | 83.0 | 80 | 99 | 99 | 99 | c 100 | 100 | 100 | 100 | 100 | 100 | 100 | 1.02 |
| Mongolia | 15 | 2 | 0.1 | 0 | 0.1 | 2 | 95 | 100 | 100 | c 650 | 16 | 10 | 19 | 23 | 27 | 38 | 130.26 |
| Montserrat | 40 | 5 | 3.0 | 50 | 53.0 | 10 | 77 | 81 | 82 | 1632 | 100 | 100 | 100 | 100 | 100 | 100 | 1.03 |
| Morocco | 9 | 2300 | 5.8 | 0 | 5.8 | 3 | 10 | 23 | 24 | c 150 | 21 | 9 | 28 | 35 | 41 | 58 | 69.74 |
| Mozambique | 1 | 40 | 0.3 | 0 | 0.3 | 0 | 2 | 21 | 24 | 1506 | 73 | 11 | 73 | 77 | 79 | 85 | 1.98 |
| Namibia | 6 | 100 | 1.8 | 20 | 21.8 | 2 | 30 | 55 | 57 | 1805 | 97 | 14 | 97 | 100 | 100 | 100 | 1.04 |
| Nauru | 60 | 2 | 1.6 | 50 | 52.0 | 20 | 100 | 100 | 100 | 1888 | 97 | 52 | 100 | 100 | 100 | 100 | 1.23 |
| Nepal | 1 | 30 | 0.2 | 0 | 0.2 | 0 | 4 | 19 | 20 | 1715 | 11 | 0 | 26 | 33 | 38 | 52 | 843.13 |
| Netherlands | 54 | 7000 | 2.1 | 52 | 54.0 | 95 | 100 | 100 | 100 | c 650 | 100 | 100 | 100 | 100 | 100 | 100 | 1.17 |
| Netherlands Antilles | 70 | 510 | 16.4 | 50 | 61.0 | 20 | 80 | 93 | 93 | c1550 | 100 | 100 | 100 | 100 | 100 | 100 | 1.03 |
| New Caledonia | 38 | 2 | 0.1 | 49 | 49.0 | 25 | 85 | 91 | 91 | 1831 | 97 | 75 | 99 | 100 | 100 | 100 | 1.10 |
| New Zealand | 122 | 910 | 1.3 | 70 | 71.0 | 80 | 98 | 98 | 98 | 1785 | 100 | 100 | 100 | 100 | 100 | 100 | 1.10 |
| Nicaragua | 9 | 430 | 2.5 | 25 | 27.5 | 15 | 38 | 61 | 61 | 1517 | 100 | 99 | 100 | 100 | 100 | 100 | 1.01 |
| Niger | 4 | 20 | 1.7 | 4 | 5.7 | 0 | 0 | 6 | 6 | c 650 | 14 | 0 | 16 | 20 | 24 | 35 | 55.15 |
| Nigeria | 8 | 26000 | 10.8 | 15 | 25.0 | 2 | 11 | 25 | 28 | 1487 | 67 | 30 | 77 | 86 | 90 | 97 | 1.76 |
| Niue Island | 17 | 1 | 1.2 | 40 | 41.0 | 20 | 93 | 96 | 96 | 1846 | 100 | 100 | 100 | 100 | 100 | 0 | 1.00 |
| Norfolk Island | 62 | 1 | 3.0 | 50 | 53.0 | 60 | 90 | 95 | 95 | 1788 | 100 | 100 | 100 | 100 | 100 | 100 | 1.15 |
| Northern Solomons | 10 | 10 | 1.3 | 30 | 31.0 | 0 | 25 | 53 | 55 | 1900 | 100 | 0 | 100 | 100 | 100 | 100 | 1.01 |
| Norway | 57 | 2450 | 2.5 | 73 | 75.0 | 95 | 100 | 100 | 100 | c 900 | 100 | 100 | 100 | 100 | 100 | 100 | 1.02 |
| Oman | 0 | 20 | 2.0 | 0 | 2.0 | 0 | 3 | 20 | 21 | 1508 | 8 | 0 | 13 | 16 | 21 | 35 | 36.75 |
| Pacific Islands | 67 | 60 | 3.8 | 90 | 92.0 | 30 | 80 | 90 | 91 | 1668 | 100 | 95 | 100 | 100 | 100 | 100 | 1.03 |
| Pakistan | 2 | 220 | 0.3 | 0 | 0.3 | 4 | 19 | 17 | 17 | c 750 | 20 | 17 | 39 | 54 | 62 | 84 | 30.36 |
| Palestine | 30 | 100 | 1.6 | 5 | 6.6 | 13 | 40 | 70 | 72 | 30 | 95 | 32 | 95 | 96 | 97 | 99 | 20.76 |
| Panama | 29 | 350 | 1.6 | 60 | 61.0 | 20 | 70 | 79 | 80 | 1513 | 99 | 99 | 100 | 100 | 100 | 100 | 1.09 |
| Panama Canal Zone | 50 | 40 | 6.5 | 80 | 86.0 | 30 | 80 | 90 | 90 | c1530 | 100 | 100 | 100 | 100 | 100 | 100 | 1.04 |
| Papua New Guinea | 5 | 200 | 1.5 | 20 | 21.5 | 0 | 10 | 33 | 35 | c1800 | 98 | 17 | 100 | 100 | 100 | 100 | 1.04 |
| Paraguay | 8 | 1300 | 4.1 | 15 | 19.0 | 10 | 66 | 81 | 81 | 1524 | 100 | 98 | 100 | 100 | 100 | 100 | 1.02 |
| Peru | 17 | 3780 | 2.7 | 30 | 32.7 | 8 | 50 | 76 | 77 | 1532 | 99 | 97 | 99 | 100 | 100 | 100 | 1.02 |
| Philippines | 6 | 30000 | 5.5 | 35 | 40.0 | 41 | 62 | 86 | 88 | 1521 | 98 | 93 | 98 | 99 | 99 | 100 | 1.05 |
| Pitcairn Islands | 70 | 0 | 10.0 | 50 | 60.0 | 40 | 80 | 90 | 90 | 1780 | 100 | 100 | 100 | 100 | 100 | 100 | 1.11 |
| Poland | 42 | 9600 | 6.0 | 60 | 66.0 | 60 | 94 | 98 | 98 | c 950 | 100 | 99 | 100 | 100 | 100 | 100 | 1.11 |
| Portugal | 24 | 2600 | 1.8 | 40 | 41.8 | 27 | 56 | 73 | 75 | c 150 | 100 | 100 | 100 | 100 | 100 | 100 | 1.05 |
| Puerto Rico | 78 | 1000 | 2.3 | 80 | 82.0 | 25 | 73 | 89 | 90 | 1509 | 100 | 100 | 100 | 100 | 100 | 100 | 1.02 |
| Qatar | 65 | 1 | 0.8 | 0 | 0.8 | 0 | 5 | 20 | 21 | c 210 | 33 | 2 | 35 | 45 | 51 | 69 | 7.59 |
| Reunion | 19 | 30 | 1.2 | 30 | 31.0 | 10 | 35 | 68 | 70 | 1649 | 99 | 48 | 100 | 100 | 100 | 100 | 1.03 |
| Romania | 25 | 7900 | 8.0 | 0 | 8.0 | 25 | 88 | 98 | 98 | c 100 | 98 | 100 | 100 | 100 | 100 | 100 | 1.21 |
| Rwanda | 1 | 100 | 1.0 | 4 | 5.0 | 0 | 6 | 20 | 22 | 1889 | 90 | 0 | 95 | 98 | 99 | 100 | 1.34 |
| Sahara | 15 | 0 | 0.1 | 0 | 0.1 | 2 | 20 | 10 | 10 | c 200 | 48 | 4 | 49 | 10 | 13 | 25 | 66.20 |
| St Helena | 12 | 0 | 3.0 | 30 | 33.0 | 60 | 95 | 98 | 98 | 1561 | 100 | 100 | 100 | 100 | 100 | 100 | 1.01 |
| St Kitts-Nevis | 50 | 10 | 1.1 | 50 | 51.0 | 20 | 82 | 90 | 90 | 1623 | 99 | 100 | 100 | 100 | 100 | 100 | 1.01 |
| St Lucia | 43 | 4 | 0.3 | 60 | 60.0 | 10 | 52 | 70 | 70 | 1648 | 100 | 100 | 100 | 100 | 100 | 100 | 1.02 |
| St Pierre & Miquelon | 63 | 1 | 1.0 | 60 | 61.0 | 50 | 97 | 99 | 99 | 1604 | 100 | 100 | 100 | 100 | 100 | 100 | 1.01 |
| St Vincent | 50 | 10 | 0.7 | 55 | 55.6 | 20 | 76 | 80 | 82 | c1650 | 100 | 100 | 100 | 100 | 100 | 100 | 1.04 |
| Samoa | 34 | 50 | 2.0 | 70 | 72.0 | 25 | 86 | 98 | 98 | 1827 | 100 | 100 | 100 | 100 | 100 | 100 | 1.02 |
| San Marino | 32 | 5 | 1.1 | 65 | 66.0 | 50 | 100 | 100 | 100 | 441 | 100 | 100 | 100 | 100 | 100 | 100 | 1.05 |
| Sao Tome & Principe | 10 | 5 | 1.5 | 15 | 16.5 | 3 | 20 | 40 | 42 | 1485 | 100 | 14 | 100 | 100 | 100 | 100 | 1.02 |
| Saudi Arabia | 1 | 350 | 3.6 | 0 | 3.6 | 0 | 2 | 12 | 13 | 100 | 4 | 3 | 18 | 32 | 39 | 60 | 39.19 |
| Senegal | 7 | 10 | 0.3 | 10 | 10.0 | 0 | 4 | 12 | 13 | 1445 | 39 | 14 | 42 | 50 | 56 | 73 | 8.73 |
| Seychelles | 14 | 10 | 1.8 | 25 | 26.8 | 10 | 28 | 60 | 62 | 1742 | 100 | 100 | 100 | 100 | 100 | 100 | 1.02 |
| Sierra Leone | 2 | 50 | 1.5 | 5 | 6.0 | 0 | 3 | 10 | 11 | 1785 | 71 | 18 | 71 | 76 | 80 | 92 | 8.44 |
| Sikkim | 1 | 1 | 0.5 | 0 | 0.5 | 0 | 2 | 10 | 10 | 1886 | 46 | 2 | 46 | 51 | 56 | 69 | 21.15 |
| Singapore | 25 | 2450 | 9.0 | 10 | 19.0 | 6 | 60 | 75 | 78 | 1511 | 85 | 21 | 85 | 91 | 93 | 99 | 10.63 |
| Solomon Islands | 7 | 20 | 1.0 | 30 | 31.0 | 3 | 40 | 70 | 72 | 1845 | 100 | 24 | 100 | 100 | 100 | 100 | 1.05 |
| Somalia | 2 | 20 | 0.2 | 0 | 0.2 | 0 | 1 | 5 | 6 | 1881 | 9 | 1 | 18 | 22 | 26 | 37 | 353.94 |
| South Africa | 11 | 3000 | 1.4 | 35 | 36.0 | 24 | 50 | 70 | 73 | 1501 | 100 | 52 | 100 | 100 | 100 | 100 | 1.26 |
| Spain | 38 | 14000 | 1.8 | 60 | 61.0 | 42 | 82 | 91 | 92 | 63 | 100 | 100 | 100 | 100 | 100 | 100 | 1.03 |
| Spanish North Africa | 25 | 30 | 1.1 | 40 | 41.0 | 30 | 70 | 92 | 92 | c 400 | 94 | 97 | 100 | 100 | 100 | 100 | 1.11 |
| Sri Lanka | 4 | 4400 | 3.5 | 5 | 8.5 | 26 | 60 | 79 | 80 | c 100 | 31 | 30 | 48 | 55 | 60 | 76 | 6.63 |
| Sudan | 8 | 380 | 1.6 | 7 | 8.6 | 1 | 11 | 18 | 20 | 34 | 24 | 8 | 30 | 35 | 39 | 49 | 3.87 |
| Surinam | 33 | 10 | 0.2 | 60 | 60.0 | 10 | 70 | 87 | 88 | 1580 | 94 | 57 | 94 | 98 | 99 | 100 | 1.34 |
| Svalbard & Jan Mayen Is | 100 | 0 | 2.0 | 20 | 22.0 | 60 | 100 | 100 | 100 | c1600 | 100 | 100 | 100 | 100 | 100 | 100 | 2.63 |
| Swaziland | 12 | 40 | 1.6 | 25 | 26.6 | 1 | 7 | 36 | 39 | 1825 | 100 | 12 | 100 | 100 | 100 | 100 | 1.30 |
| Sweden | 71 | 3300 | 1.6 | 63 | 64.6 | 95 | 100 | 100 | 100 | 829 | 100 | 100 | 100 | 100 | 100 | 100 | 1.41 |
| Switzerland | 56 | 2000 | 1.3 | 70 | 71.0 | 95 | 100 | 100 | 100 | c 200 | 100 | 100 | 100 | 100 | 100 | 100 | 1.03 |
| Syria | 40 | 500 | 1.8 | 0 | 1.8 | 8 | 32 | 42 | 44 | 30 | 42 | 42 | 48 | 57 | 63 | 82 | 6.37 |
| Tanzania | 2 | 1500 | 1.0 | 5 | 6.0 | 2 | 20 | 35 | 38 | 1502 | 80 | 19 | 80 | 88 | 91 | 99 | 2.00 |
| Thailand | 8 | 16000 | 3.2 | 10 | 13.0 | 7 | 54 | 81 | 83 | 1554 | 30 | 18 | 47 | 57 | 62 | 77 | 54.08 |
| Timor | 1 | 0 | 0.1 | 2 | 2.0 | 0 | 10 | 30 | 30 | 1511 | 34 | 21 | 42 | 50 | 56 | 75 | 1.28 |
| Togo | 2 | 10 | 0.2 | 4 | 4.0 | 0 | 3 | 17 | 18 | c1860 | 63 | 11 | 66 | 70 | 74 | 85 | 1.89 |
| Tokelau | 30 | 0 | 1.8 | 50 | 51.0 | 20 | 97 | 99 | 99 | 1861 | 100 | 100 | 100 | 100 | 100 | 100 | 1.05 |
| Tonga | 10 | 20 | 1.4 | 30 | 31.0 | 25 | 90 | 100 | 100 | 1797 | 100 | 100 | 100 | 100 | 100 | 100 | 1.01 |
| Trinidad & Tobago | 36 | 200 | 1.3 | 55 | 56.0 | 10 | 76 | 92 | 92 | 1513 | 96 | 95 | 100 | 100 | 100 | 100 | 1.51 |
| Tunisia | 9 | 430 | 1.7 | 0 | 1.7 | 3 | 14 | 38 | 40 | c 80 | 23 | 18 | 25 | 31 | 38 | 58 | 89.36 |
| Turkey | 11 | 300 | 0.2 | 0 | 0.2 | 4 | 32 | 60 | 62 | c 33 | 19 | 46 | 20 | 26 | 31 | 45 | 48.32 |
| Turks & Caicos Islands | 51 | 8 | 9.5 | 60 | 69.0 | 15 | 89 | 93 | 93 | c1750 | 100 | 100 | 100 | 100 | 100 | 100 | 1.02 |
| Tuvalu | 20 | 2 | 1.7 | 60 | 61.0 | 20 | 90 | 95 | 95 | 1861 | 100 | 100 | 100 | 100 | 100 | 100 | 1.05 |
| Uganda | 3 | 1700 | 4.6 | 7 | 11.6 | 5 | 20 | 40 | 40 | 1875 | 94 | 24 | 94 | 98 | 99 | 100 | 1.25 |
| USSR | 64 | 4800 | 8.1 | 0 | 8.1 | 28 | 96 | 100 | 100 | c 35 | 64 | 97 | 64 | 71 | 96 | 91 | 1.97 |
| United Arab Emirates | 19 | 5 | 1.1 | 0 | 1.1 | 1 | 15 | 25 | 26 | 1892 | 57 | 1 | 58 | 66 | 72 | 88 | 17.37 |
| UK of GB & NI | 99 | 72500 | 5.3 | 55 | 60.0 | 89 | 99 | 99 | 95 | 61 | 100 | 100 | 100 | 100 | 100 | 100 | 1.15 |
| USA | 230 | 3093000 | 58.0 | 80 | 85.0 | 89 | 97 | 99 | 99 | 1526 | 100 | 100 | 100 | 100 | 100 | 100 | 1.14 |
| US Virgin Islands | 63 | 15 | 1.4 | 80 | 81.0 | 30 | 90 | 95 | 95 | 1648 | 100 | 100 | 100 | 100 | 100 | 100 | 1.02 |
| Upper Volta | 2 | 10 | 0.2 | 4 | 4.0 | 0 | 1 | 11 | 12 | 1900 | 44 | 0 | 46 | 51 | 56 | 70 | 4.18 |
| Uruguay | 61 | 330 | 0.7 | 50 | 50.7 | 45 | 87 | 94 | 94 | 1616 | 100 | 90 | 100 | 100 | 100 | 100 | 1.59 |
| Vanuatu | 12 | 10 | 1.1 | 5 | 6.0 | 3 | 30 | 60 | 61 | 1830 | 100 | 39 | 100 | 100 | 100 | 100 | 1.06 |
| Venezuela | 27 | 6400 | 4.6 | 50 | 54.6 | 20 | 52 | 77 | 78 | 1513 | 99 | 97 | 99 | 99 | 99 | 100 | 1.03 |
| Viet Nam | 9 | 4150 | 1.2 | 0 | 1.2 | 7 | 35 | 50 | 55 | 1530 | 37 | 27 | 58 | 61 | 64 | 71 | 8.18 |
| Wake Island | 100 | 1 | 3.6 | 50 | 53.6 | 60 | 100 | 100 | 100 | 1899 | 100 | 90 | 100 | 100 | 100 | 100 | 1.14 |
| Wallis & Futuna Islands | 20 | 2 | 1.3 | 70 | 71.0 | 30 | 90 | 95 | 95 | 1836 | 100 | 98 | 100 | 100 | 100 | 100 | 1.01 |
| Yemen, North | 4 | 200 | 2.3 | 0 | 2.3 | 0 | 1 | 20 | 20 | c 500 | 7 | 0 | 12 | 14 | 19 | 35 | 592.21 |
| Yemen, South | 11 | 150 | 10.4 | 0 | 10.4 | 0 | 2 | 20 | 21 | c 350 | 19 | 7 | 25 | 29 | 33 | 45 | 548.16 |
| Yugoslavia | 32 | 2000 | 1.5 | 20 | 21.5 | 40 | 73 | 83 | 85 | c 60 | 88 | 100 | 94 | 98 | 99 | 100 | 1.34 |
| Zaire | 1 | 2100 | 1.6 | 3 | 4.6 | 2 | 25 | 35 | 36 | 1482 | 97 | 17 | 98 | 100 | 100 | 100 | 1.06 |
| Zambia | 3 | 500 | 1.4 | 10 | 11.0 | 2 | 35 | 48 | 50 | 1885 | 94 | 4 | 95 | 100 | 100 | 100 | 1.39 |
| Zimbabwe | 5 | 410 | 1.5 | 20 | 21.5 | 6 | 30 | 45 | 49 | 1561 | 96 | 18 | 96 | 100 | 100 | 100 | 1.72 |
| Column | 91 | 92 | 93 | 94 | 95 | 96 | 97 | 98 | 99 | 100 | 101 | 102 | 103 | 104 | 105 | 106 | 107 |
| *Continent* | | | | | | | | | | | | | | | | | |
| Africa | 608 | 136976 | 194.2 | 523 | 691.2 | 243 | 1151 | 2006 | 2098 | 78652 | 4137 | 1266 | 4255 | 4429 | 4576 | 4989 | 1109.5 |
| East Asia | 180 | 236082 | 36.5 | 131 | 163.6 | 80 | 535 | 682 | 695 | 8795 | 470 | 152 | 475 | 521 | 547 | 618 | 355.4 |
| Europe | 2023 | 279872 | 131.5 | 1861 | 1945.9 | 2489 | 3378 | 3554 | 3563 | 6185 | 3558 | 3630 | 3589 | 3605 | 3618 | 3650 | 48.0 |
| Latin America | 1726 | 252419 | 198.2 | 2026 | 2188.9 | 888 | 3223 | 3852 | 3893 | 57777 | 4637 | 4451 | 4648 | 4651 | 4659 | 4683 | 51.8 |
| Northern America | 538 | 3153024 | 72.2 | 290 | 301.0 | 311 | 440 | 457 | 459 | 6273 | 500 | 499 | 500 | 500 | 500 | 500 | 5.2 |
| Oceania | 1324 | 5989 | 94.0 | 1265 | 1351.1 | 759 | 2296 | 2544 | 2557 | 47229 | 2807 | 2113 | 2824 | 2847 | 2861 | 2900 | 36.8 |
| South Asia | 528 | 161201 | 125.7 | 193 | 311.5 | 234 | 1005 | 1663 | 1701 | 24908 | 1415 | 745 | 1670 | 1926 | 2088 | 2560 | 3400.8 |
| USSR | 64 | 4800 | 8.1 | 0 | 8.1 | 28 | 96 | 100 | 100 | 0 | 64 | 97 | 64 | 71 | 76 | 91 | 1.9 |
| **WORLD** | **6991** | **4230363** | **860.4** | **6289** | **6961.3** | **5032** | **12124** | **14858** | **15066** | **229819** | **17588** | **12953** | **18025** | **18550** | **18925** | **19991** | **5009.6** |

*NOTES ON SCRIPTURE DISTRIBUTION* (Global Table 31, columns 63-90).

(1) BIBLES.
*Free* (columns 63-67). All figures refer to Gideons International annual placements, with any additions noted below. *Subsidized* (columns 68-72). All figures refer to UBS member societies' circulation, with any additions noted below. *Commercial* (column 73). As defined in Part 3.
**Argentina.** *Commercial.* The commercial annual totals for Spanish-speaking Latin America include the 800,000 paperback copies of the (RC) Pastoral Edition (Latin American Bible) sold from 1972-76.
**Australia.** *Commercial.* 1975: including 20,602 Living Bible (Coverdale).
**Austria.** *Commercial.* 1975: including 110,000 Österreichisches Katholisches Bibelwerk, 8,000 Andreas & Andreas.
**Bangladesh.** *Free.* In 1978, 150,000 Braille Bibles were given to blind schools at government request.
**Belgium.** *Commercial.* 1975: including 15,000 Brepols.
**Bulgaria.** No production since 1945.
**Canada.** *Commercial.* 1975: including about 200,000 Living Bible (Tyndale House).
**Cuba.** *Subsidized.* In 1973, 10,000 Bibles were imported from Chile.
**Czechoslovakia.** The agency Underground Evangelism claims to have got 150,000 Bibles in by 1972 before the state's crackdown.
**France.** *Commercial.* 1975: including 50,000 Editions du Seuil, 22,094 Bible de Jérusalem (Cerf), 8,000 Editions Brepols.
**Germany, FR.** *Commercial.* 1975: including 24,000 Andreas & Andreas, 5,634 Brunnen Verlag.
**Greece.** *Commercial.* Mid-1974-mid-75: including 2,400 Bibles sold through the Zoe Brotherhood.
**Hong Kong.** *Commercial.* 1975: including 17,000 Living Bible (Tyndale House).
**Italy.** *Commercial.* 1975: mainly vast distribution of the Bible in inexpensive modern translations, through the Catholic Charismatical Renewal; also 33,000 Jerusalem Bible (EDB).
**Kenya.** *Commercial.* In 1976-77, 15,000 6-volume sets of *Pictorial Bible*, in English, were printed in Kenya.
**New Zealand.** *Commercial.* 1975: including 4,121 Living Bible (Coverdale).
**Pakistan.** *Free.* 1975: 100,000 Urdu Bible (BFTW).
**Romania.** *Subsidized.* In 1974-75, 100,000 Bibles were printed in Romania using UBS-donated paper, also 100,000 illustrated pocket Bibles for schools. In 1978 importation of 100,000 Bibles was approved.
**South Africa.** *Commercial.* 1975: including 24,633 Word of Life.
**Spain.** *Commercial.* 1975 including 73,500 Centro de Ediciones Paulinas, 70,000 Editorial Herder, 53,986 Biblia de Jerusalén (Desclee de Brouwer), 8,000 Apostolado de la Prensa.
**USSR.** *Free.* 1975-76: including 3,000 German Bibles legally imported by AUCECB. There are also sizeable print runs by the underground press in the USSR. *Subsidized.* In 1976, 50,000 copies of the pulpit-size 1876 Jubilee Bible, updated, were printed in Moscow, and a further 50,000 in 1977. In 1978 permission was given to AUCECB to import 25,000 Russian Bibles through UBS (largest import since 10,000 in 1947).
**UK.** *Subsidized.* 1975: 273,000 BFBS, 54,361 Trinitarian Bible Society (AV). *Commercial.* 1975: including 34,250 CUP, 71,268 Living Bible (Coverdale; in 1974, 149,843), 37,568 Thomas Nelson (1974), 90,000 Darton, Longman & Todd, 650,000 OUP, 28,000 Eyre & Spottiswoode, 754 Word (UK), 404,000 Collins, 4,000 Marshall, Morgan & Scott, 50,000 others. Total sales of Bibles by British publishers (in UK): 1973, £1,616,000; 1974, £1,963,000.
**USA.** Total sales of Bibles and New Testaments: 1947, 9,428,000; 1954, 11,359,000; 1958, 19,084,000 (8,903,000 Bibles); 1963, 15.3 million; 1967, 10.5 million; 1972, 29.3 million; 1975, 35 million (US Bureau of the Census). *Free.* Including 200,000 World Home Bible League (1974). There are also numerous other agencies. *Subsidized.* In addition to the ABS, there are numerous other independent agencies, including the New York Bible Society. *Commercial.* 1975: including 135,000 Darton, Longman & Todd, 1,994,000 Living Bible (Tyndale House; 2.7 million in 1973). In 1976 figures increased to 2,250,000 Living Bible, 1 million Good News Bible (TEV) in December 1976 alone, 380,000 Jerusalem Bible, 130,000 New American Standard Bible.

(2) NEW TESTAMENTS.
*Free* (columns 76-80). All figures refer to Gideons International annual placements, with any additions noted below. *Subsidized* (columns 81-85). All figures refer to UBS member societies' circulation, with any additions noted below. *Commercial* (column 86). As defined in Part 3.
**Australia.** *Free.* 1975: 7,500 Living NT (World Home Bible League). *Commercial.* 1975: including 2,126 Living NT (Coverdale).
**Austria.** *Commercial.* 1975: 105,000 Österreichisches Katholisches Bibelwerk.
**Bangladesh.** *Free.* 1973: 60,000 Living NT (Bibles For The World).
**Belgium.** *Commercial.* 1975: including 10,000 Brepols.
**Belize.** *Free.* 1975: 1,000 Living NT (WHBL).
**Bhutan.** *Free.* 1972: 165 Living NT (BFTW).
**Bolivia.** *Free.* 1975: 476,707 Living NT (WHBL).
**Brazil.** *Free.* Over 1976-78, 1,000,000 public school children ages 12-19 in Rio de Janeiro state received copies of the Living NT in Portuguese (WHBL et al).
**Burma.** *Free.* 1973: 27,000 Living NT (BFTW).
**Canada.** *Free.* 1975: including 50,000 Living NT (WHBL). *Commercial.* 1975: including about 30,000 Living NT (Tyndale House).
**China, PR.** *Free.* In 1975, including about 13,000 FEBC micro NTs in Chinese.
**Colombia.** *Free.* 1975: 10,060 Living NT (WHBL).

**Costa Rica.** *Free.* 1975: 500 Living NT (WHBL).
**Ecuador.** *Free.* 1975: 19,550 Living NT (WHBL).
**France.** *Commercial.* 1975: including 51,373 Editions du Cerf, 20,000 Editions du Seuil, 2,000 Editions Brepols.
**Germany, FR.** *Commercial.* 1975: including 30,000 Quell Verlag (Fotobibel), 4,411 Brunnen Verlag.
**Greece.** *Commercial.* From mid-1974 to mid-1975, 25,000 NT were sold through the Zoe Brotherhood.
**Guam.** *Free.* 1975: 300 Living NT (WHBL).
**India.** *Free.* 1972: 820,000 Living NT (BFTW).
**Italy.** *Commercial.* 1975: including 17,000 EDB (Bologna).
**Japan.** *Commercial.* In 1977, Kodansha sold 100,000 NTs for Roman Catholic use.
**Malaysia.** *Free.* 1974: 150,000 Living NT (BFTW).
**Mexico.** *Free.* 1975: 51,292 Living NT (WHBL).
**Nepal.** *Free.* 1972: 5,800 Living NT (BFTW).
**Nicaragua.** *Free.* 1975: 3,000 Living NT (WHBL).
**Nigeria.** *Free.* 1975: including 20,000 Living NT (WHBL).
**Peru.** *Free.* 1975: 92,000 Living NT (WHBL).
**Philippines.** *Free.* 1976-77: 309,922 Living NT (BFTW).
**Puerto Rico.** *Free.* 1975: 66,000 Living NT (WHBL).
**Romania.** *Subsidized.* In 1974-75, 200,000 NTs were printed in Romania.
**Sikkim.** *Free.* 1972: 250 Living NT (BFTW).
**Singapore.** *Free.* 1974: 120,000 Living NT (BFTW).
**South Africa.** *Commercial.* 1975: including 4,613 Word of Life.
**Spain.** *Free.* 1975: 22,000 Living NT (WHBL). *Commercial.* 1975: including 100,000 Editorial Afebe, 80,000 Editorial Herder, 45,000 Centro de Ediciones Paulinas, 30,000 Ediciones Mensajero, 12,000 Apostolado de la Prensa, 5,000 Editorial Alpha.
**Sri Lanka.** *Free.* 1973: 15,200 Living NT (BFTW, WHBL).
**Thailand.** *Free.* 1975: 65,000 Living NT (BFTW).
**USSR.** *Free.* In 1975, including about 28,000 FEBC micro NTs in Russian. *Subsidized.* In 1975-76 the Russian Orthodox Church, Moscow Patriarchate, printed 75,000 small-size NTs.
**UK.** *Free.* 1975: including 100,000 Living NT (WHBL/OM). *Subsidized.* 1975: including 32,207 Trinitarian Bible Society (AV). *Commercial.* 1975: including 17,820 CUP, 15,168 Living NT (Coverdale; in 1974, 13,080), 6,475 Marshall, Morgan & Scott, 25,000 OUP, 1,000 Word (UK), 575,000 Collins, 22,000 others.
**USA.** *Free.* Including 235,000 Living NT (WHBL) (1974; 515,321 in 1975; 550,000 in 1976). *Commercial.* 1975: including 257,000 Living NT (Tyndale House).
**Venezuela.** *Free.* 1975: 73,000 Living NT (WHBL).

(3) PORTIONS.
**China, PR.** *Portions.* In 1975, 42,000 simplified gospels entered the People's Republic.
**USSR.** *Portions.* In 1971 one mission society reported distributing 182,000 Russian gospels.

# PART 9

# DICTIONARY
Survey dictionary of world Christianity

*There are also many other things which Jesus did; were every one of them to be written, I suppose that the world itself could not contain the books that would be written.*
—John 21.25, Revised Standard Version.

This dictionary contains 2 main types of entry: (1) definitions without statistics, for which entries are shown in the singular (e.g. 'adherent', 'minister'), and (2) definitions followed by global statistical totals or surveys, for which entries are shown in the plural (e.g. 'Pentecostals', 'radio stations').

In consequence, this is not a historical dictionary, nor a theological one, nor an ecclesiastical one; rather, it is a contemporary and comparative dictionary. Firstly, it gives definitions or explanations of (a) all general and generic terms used by churches and religions in surveying their extent and influence; (b) the various categories of membership; (c) other technical terms in current use, particularly those used by one denomination or tradition alone; (d) religious and ecclesiastical concepts and terms common to surveys of Christian work and service; and (e) neologisms and other new concepts evolved in this Encyclopedia. Also included is the comparative aspect, comparing the meanings of terms like 'membership', 'minister', 'Christian', in the various major Christian traditions and blocs. Secondly, it gives overall statistical totals at the global or international level, together with brief world surveys of new data concerning the major Christian blocs and traditions, international councils and federations, ministries and activities found here in our statistical and directory sections, together with global statistics necessary for understanding the secular context (population increase, literacy, ethnolinguistic peoples and families, etc).

The dictionary deals primarily with English-language terms; however, a number of the more widely-used terms in other languages for which there are no recognized or exact English equivalents are also included, with the language of each identified in parentheses. The main entries are spelt in the form as standardized in this Encyclopedia, followed in parentheses by alternate spellings where widely in use. Separate and distinct meanings of the same word are listed as (1), (2), (3), etc. For the exact meanings, usages and etymologies of many of these words in modern English, see the *Oxford English dictionary* (12 volumes, 1933) and *Webster's third new international dictionary of the English language, unabridged* (1971). A number of our definitions below follow those of these standard works but either expand the definitions or contract them to cover only their strictly religious meanings in contemporary Christian and religious use. A few cross-references are added with entries of 2 or more words, to facilitate locating such definitions; in such cases, the main entry appears under the first letter of each's main word.

# SURVEY DICTIONARY OF WORLD CHRISTIANITY

## A

**abbé** (French). A title applied in French to clerics in general.

**abbess.** A woman who is the superior of one of certain communities of nuns following the Benedictine rule, also of orders of canonesses or of the Second Franciscan order.

**abbey.** A senior or superior monastery with a large number of monks ruled by an abbot or a convent ruled by an abbess; or an abbey church.

**abbey nullius** (Latin, abbey of no diocese; symbol AN). An abbey whose abbot is exempt from diocesan control and under direct papal jurisdiction. Total (1977) 21.

**abbot.** In the Western church, the superior of a large religious house of monks, either Benedictine (Cistercian, Trappist) or Canons Regular.

**Aboriginal.** Original indigenous inhabitant of country, of primitive culture.

**Aboriginal indigenous churches.** Churches indigenous to, because started by, Australian Aborigines.

**accessibility.** In evangelization, the quality or state or extent of a population's ability to be reached or accessible or approached or communicated with.

**accumulated enrolment.** See enrolment.

**acolyte.** In the Catholic Church, highest of the 4 minor orders conferred on candidates to the priesthood; also, a server who carries candles at mass.

**acronym.** A word formed from the initial letter or letters of each of the successive or major parts of a compound term.

**active attenders.** The most active among a group of practising Christians (qv).

**active enrolment.** See enrolment.

**active members.** Church members who are practising Christians (qv).

**actual audience.** Total persons who actually listen to or view a given radio/TV broadcast.

**Addis Ababa.** See city of Ethiopian Orthodox patriarchate and patriarch.

**adelphoi** (NT Greek). Brothers, brethren; term in use by Christian Brethren (Plymouth Brethren) and other Protestants.

**adept.** An enthusiastic adherent, well-trained devotee.

**adepte** (French). A follower, adherent.

**adequately-evangelized.** The state of evangelization or awareness of Christianity, Christ and the gospel in which persons may be described as having had an adequate opportunity to respond.

**adherent.** A follower of a particular religion, church or philosophy. As used here, the term adherents refers to followers of all kinds (professing, affiliated, practising, non-practising, etc) who are present-in-area residents: men, women, children, infants, nationals and expatriates, native- and foreign-born, immigrants, armed forces, displaced persons, refugees, nomads, et alii.

**Adivasis.** Aboriginal tribesmen in India.

**adjective of nationality.** The adjective(s) describing a national (citizen) officially sanctioned by a state for United Nations' usage.

**adult.** In law, a human male or female over a fixed age; collectively making up the working-age and old-age population. In church statistics, as often in civil law, a person over 14 years old.

**adult baptisms.** The administration of baptism to candidates over 14 years of age; in practice, the youngest age is as low as 6 years old (Anglicans, many Baptists and other Protestants, et alii).

**adult Christians.** Christians over 14 years of age.

**adult literacy.** See literacy.

**adult members.** Adult church members on average over 14 years of age and on the church's books or rolls, who are either communicants or full members, adult believers, probationary members, baptized adult non-communicants, sometimes also unbaptized attending adults.

**Adventists.** Protestant tradition begun 1844, emphasizing imminent Second Advent of Christ. Global

ADULT BAPTISM. In sea off Brighton (UK).

membership: (1970) 200 denominations with 21,200 churches and 2,163,600 adult members; total community (1970) 4,119,100, (1980) 5,514,700, (1985) 6,271,700.

**affiliated Christians.** Church members; all persons belonging to or connected with organized churches; those whose names are inscribed, written or entered on the churches' books or records, or with whom the churches are in touch, usually known by name and address to the churches at grass-roots or local parish level; i.e. all distinct individuals attached to or claimed by the institutional churches or organized Christianity and hence part of their corporate life, community and fellowship; total church membership, or total church member community or total Christian community, or inclusive membership; including full members, other attenders, their children and infants, members under discipline, and other adherents. Global total: (1970) 1,131,809,600, (1980) 1,323,389,700, (1985) 1,425,927,300.

**affiliation.** Church membership, attachment to organized Christianity; usually begun by the inscribing, writing or entering of people's names on the churches' books or records.

**affiliation, double.** See doubly-affiliated Christians.

**affiliation, legal.** Church membership in countries where the bulk of the population belongs by law to the state church or established church.

**affiliation, religious.** Membership in, or attachment to, a particular organized religion.

**African.** One of the 13 geographical races of mankind, excluding Middle Eastern (Semitic, Hamitic and Cushitic) and Early African (qv); speaking about 1,320 languages. Global population: (1970) 229,489,000, (1980) 301,084,700, (1985) 340,365,900.

**African independent churches.** African indigenous churches (qv).

**African indigenous Christianity.** Type or style of Christianity evolved and practised by African indigenous churches (qv).

**African indigenous churches.** Denominations indigenous to African peoples, begun without outside help; also termed African independent churches, African separatist churches. Global church membership: (1970) 15,971,400 in 5,980 denominations, (1980) 24,458,000, (1985) 29,148,600. Global professing adherents: (1970) 17,830,000, (1980) 27,438,000, (1985) 32,687,600.

**Afro-American.** One of the 13 geographical races of mankind, speaking over 60 languages. Global population: (1970) 82,230,300, (1980) 101,982,200, (1985) 112,539,200.

**Afro-American spiritists.** Followers of Afro-Brazilian, Afro-Cuban and other African religious survivals in the Americas; low spiritists, syncretizing Catholicism with African and Amerindian animistic religions; low spiritists as opposed to high (non-Christian) spiritists; also Afro-American syncretistic cults with Christian elements. All varieties, including

specifically Christian bodies, are detailed in G.E. Simpson, *Black religions in the New World* (New York: Columbia University Press, 1978). Global adherents: (1970) 1,777,100, (1980) 3,100,400 in 21 countries, (1985) 3,810,300.

**aggiornamento** (Italian). Updating, bringing up-to-date; used by pope John XXIII to justify convening Vatican II in 1962.

**agnosticism.** The doctrine that the existence or nature of any ultimate reality or God is unknown and unknowable.

**agnostics.** Persons professing agnosticism.

**agricultural land.** In FAO usage, arable land, land under permanent crops, permanent meadows and pastures.

**agricultural missions.** See rural missions.

**ahimsa** (Sanskrit). In Hinduism, Jainism and Buddhism, the doctrine of non-violence, or refraining from harming others including animals and insects.

AHMADIYA. Alleged tomb of Jesus, Srinagar, Kashmir.

**Ahmadis.** Followers of the Ahmadiya movement (qv). Global adherents: (1970) 2,635,200, (1980) 3,994,900 in 100 countries (46 significantly), (1985) 4,733,700.

**Ahmadiya** (Ahmadiyah, Ahmadiyya). Ex-Shia Muslim messianic movement, pronounced heretical by Pakistan, following 1889 founder Ghulam Ahmad.

**aid and relief.** At least 360 major Christian organizations are at work in this field.

**Alabaré** (Spanish: 'I will praise'). A theme song of Latin American Catholic charismatics.

**Aladura** (Yoruba: People who pray). African indigenous tradition across West Africa, with 3 million adherents.

**Alawites.** Followers of Alawiya, a sect of Shia Islam in Latakia province, Syria, Lebanon and Cilicia (Turkey), also called Nusayris. Total adherents: (1980) 1,015,000.

**Albanian.** A European ethnolinguistic family and people. Global population: (1970) 3,483,000, (1980) 4,229,900, (1985) 4,620,900.

**Albanian/Greek.** An Eastern Orthodox liturgical tradition dating back to the Apostolic era. Global membership: (1970) 4 denominations in 3 countries, with 535 churches and 110,500 adult members; total community (1970) 172,150, (1980) 169,300, (1985) 168,000.

**Alexandria.** One of the 4 earliest patriarchates in the early Church; still the see city of 4 rival patriarchates and patriarchs: Coptic Orthodox, Coptic Catholic, Melkite, and Greek Orthodox.

**Alexandrian.** The Alexandrian or Egyptian rite of the Roman Catholic Church consists of 2 sub-rites: Coptic, and Ethiopic (qv).

**alien.** A person of another family, race or place; stranger, foreigner.

**Altaic.** An Asian ethnolinguistic family, with over 40 languages. Global population: (1970) 90,731,100, (1980) 108,803,500, (1985) 118,437,100.

**altered states of consciousness.** Religious experiences of a particular intensity, especially ecstatic states, trance, or dissociation; a category of psychobiological phenomena, amenable to observation and other objective methods of study; including spirit possession, soul loss, ecstatic religious behaviour, faith-healing, mysticism, glossolalia, occult, shouting, visions, et alia.

**alternative futures.** Two or more alternative scenarios or possibilities or probable futures of a given present situation, based on current trends.

**alternative media.** In contrast to the mass media, small-scale participatory media, including drama, live theatre, dance, opera, ballet, wall newspapers (community-produced), etc.

**alternative reality tradition.** Term for the alternative view and experience of reality provided by modern Western cults of monistic/mystic/occult/shamanistic type (e.g. Theosophy, Rosicrucianism), as contrasted with the mainstream Western/European/Hebrew-Greek/normative scientific worldview of the Judeo-Christian tradition.

**amateur radio.** Operating of radio sets as a pastime rather than as a profession.

AMERICAN INDIANS. Christian market women (Bolivia).

**American Indian.** One of the 13 geographical races of mankind, speaking 1,970 languages. Global population: (1970) 35,074,000, (1980) 46,790,300, (1985) 53,136,400.

**Amerindian.** American Indian, Amerind.

**Amerindian indigenous churches.** Churches indigenous to Amerindian peoples.

**amillennialists.** Protestants who hold that the millennial reign of Christ will not be literal but occurs now in the hearts of believers.

**amplitude modulation** (AM). Broadcasting termed (in Europe) medium-wave or (in USA) standard broadcasting (employing 540-1600 kiloherz).

**Anabaptists** (from Greek: re-baptizers). Various groups in Continental Europe in the 16th century, collectively termed the Left-Wing Reformation, who refused to allow their children to be baptized and reinstituted the baptism of adult believers; represented today by Mennonites and Hutterites.

**ancestor-veneration.** A rite or cult in traditional African and other animistic religion, also in Confucianism, invoking the aid of departed ancestors; also termed ancestor-worship, and reverence for or remembrance of the living dead.

**anchorite.** One who renounces the world to live in seclusion for religious reasons; a hermit, recluse.

**Ancient Church of the East.** Also called Assyrians, Nestorians, Aramaean Christians, or East Syrians (Messihaye); Chaldean (Syriac)-speaking; the original Church of Mesopotamia, famed for its missionary expansion to 250 dioceses with 15 million adherents before its near extinction by Tamerlane around 1360. Global constituency: (1980) 176,700.

**Anglican Communion.** A worldwide family of 25 autonomous Churches and 6 other bodies in communion with the See of Canterbury and with each other, all of whom recognize the archbishop of Canterbury as the focus of unity within the Communion.

**Anglican Consultative Council** (ACC). The major advisory body of the Anglican Communion, created by the Lambeth Conference in 1969. Constituency: (1980) 49,706,200.

**Anglican Evangelicals.** Evangelicals (qv) of Anglican persuasion both within and outside the Anglican Communion; sometimes termed either Conciliar or Conservative Evangelicals, and usually including all whose churchmanship is described as either Evangelical, Conservative Evangelical or Low Church, as distinct from High Church or sacramentalist persuasion, or Central or Broad Church. Global membership: (1970) 15,088,700, (1980) 18,514,000 in 27 countries, (1985) 20,365,900. Membership in predominantly Evangelical Anglican churches: (1970) 2,338,600 total community.

ANGLICAN PENTECOSTALS. Bishops in Canterbury Cathedral.

**Anglican pentecostals.** Anglicans in the organized charismatic renewal, expressed in healings, tongues, prophesyings, etc. Active global membership: (1970) 109,900 (1980) 1,090,200 in 18 countries, (1985) 1,660,800.

**Anglican religious orders.** See religious orders in Anglicanism.

**Anglicanism.** The system of doctrine and practice upheld by those Christians in communion with the See of Canterbury.

**Anglicans.** Christians related to the Anglican Communion, tracing their origin back to the ancient British (Celtic) and English churches; including Anglican dissidents or schismatics in the Western world. Global professing adherents: (1970) 59,914,900, (1980) 65,208,400 in 144 countries, (1985) 68,048,200. Global affiliated membership: (1970) 47,557,000, (1980) 49,804,000 in 165 countries, (1985) 51,100,100.

**anglicized.** Spelt or written in a characteristically or recognizably English spelling and form.

**Anglo-Catholics.** Formerly called Tractarians or High Churchmen, that section of Anglicanism which emphasizes the dogmatic and sacramental aspects of the Catholic Faith. Global membership of 28 Anglo-Catholic dioceses: (1970) 4,079 churches with 777,100 adult members; total community (1970) 1,999,500, (1980) 2,247,600, (1985) 2,379,700.

**Anglo-Romans.** Adherents of recent schisms out of Anglicanism in a Roman Catholic direction, rejecting Anglican orders for some variant Roman succession. Global membership: (1970) 18 denominations with 493 churches and 45,200 adult members; total community (1970) 83,400, (1980) 119,000, (1985) 138,800.

**animator.** In Roman Catholic usage, an activist stimulating discussion or action groups.

**animism** (animatism). The attribution of consciousness and personality to such natural phenomena as thunder and fire, and to objects such as rocks and trees.

**animists.** Adherents of animism; sometimes termed pagans, fetishists, traditional religionists, tribal religionists (qv).

**Anno Domini** (AD, 'In the Year of the Lord'). System of dating years after the birth of Christ.

**annual attenders.** Practising Christians who attend services of public worship only once a year (usually at Christmas or Easter).

**annual baptisms.** The total number of persons baptized in any year in a given diocese, denomination or country.

**annual conference.** In Methodism, the annual convocation of the church, and its basic governing body.

**annual family income.** The average annual income earned by a family in a country; derived by multiplying the national income per person by the average household size (average number of persons living in a household or family).

**annual letters.** The total listeners' letters received in the course of a year by a radio/TV station or programme.

**anonymous Christians.** Nominal Christians (qv); unaffiliated Christians unknown to the churches, who nevertheless accept Christian beliefs and values.

**Anthroposophy.** A spiritual and mystical doctrine that grew out of Theosophy and derives mainly from the philosophy of Rudolf Steiner, an Austrian social philosopher.

**Antioch.** The third city in the ancient Roman empire where the disciples were first called Christians; in the 4th century, the 3rd patriarchal see of Christendom (after Rome and Alexandria); now the see of 5 rival patriarchs: Greek Orthodox, Syrian Orthodox, Melkite, Maronite, and Syrian Catholic (Uniate).

**Antiochene.** The Antiochene or Western Syrian rite of the Roman Catholic Church consists of 3 sub-rites: Malankarese, Maronite, and Syrian (qv).

**Antiochian.** Syro-Antiochian (qv).

**anti-conciliar.** Anti-ecumenical; opposed or hostile to the conciliar or ecumenical movements.

**anti-religious.** Opposed or militantly opposed to all religion; irreligious, hostile to religions and religious persons.

**anti-religious quasi-religionists.** Adherents of anti-religions quasi-religions (atheism, Communism, dialectical materialism, Leninism, Maoism, Marxism, scientific materialism, Stalinism, et alia).

**anti-trinitarian.** A Christian tradition openly repudiating the doctrine of the Trinity, hence unitarian.

**apartheid** (Afrikaans). The policy of segregation and political and economic discrimination against Non-Whites in the republic of South Africa.

**apartment ministry.** A pastoral type of ministry to dwellers in high-rise apartment buildings in densely-populated city areas.

**apocalyptic.** Prophetic, revelatory, predicting ultimate destiny or doom.

**apocrypha.** Quasi-scriptural non-canonical or deutero-canonical books of doubtful authorship or authority; especially, 13 books attached to versions of the Old Testament.

**apologetics.** That branch of theology devoted to the defence of the Christian faith and addressed primarily to criticisms originating from outside.

**apostasy.** The renunciation or abandonment of one's previous religious profession of faith.

**apostates.** Former church members, especially Roman Catholics, who have renounced or forsaken the Christian faith; backsliders, lapsed, disaffiliated (qv), dechristianized, post-Christians.

**apostle.** A messenger, one sent forth; one of the 12 disciples of Christ; one of certain early Christian missionaries, or (Eastern Orthodoxy) one of the 70 disciples of Jesus; first prominent Christian missionary in any part of the world; one who has extraordinary success in mission; high or highest ecclesiastical official in numerous denominations especially in African indigenous churches.

**apostolate.** In Roman Catholic usage, the service of souls and spread of the Faith, discharged by bishops, priests, religious and laity.

**apostolate, persons dedicated to the.** In Roman Catholic usage, also called the apostolic force, and consisting of all bishops, priests, permanent deacons, religious brothers, professed women religious, committed lay workers (catechists, etc), but excluding the lay apostolate. World total (1975): 1.6 million.

**apostolic administration** (symbol AA). Temporary operating of a diocese when normal operation is impossible, e.g. due to state hostility. Total (1977) 11.

**apostolic delegate.** An ecclesiastical plenipotentiary representing the Holy See (by means of an apostolic delegation) in a country without diplomatic relations with it. World total of apostolic delegations: (1974) 26.

**apostolic exhortation.** A papal document or letter published from the Vatican, hortative and pastoral in purpose rather than strictly dogmatic or legal; occasionally issued by popes since 1917.

**Apostolic Fathers.** Early Fathers who flourished and published writings in the times of the Apostles immediately following the New Testament period, and whose writings have survived: Barnabas, Clement of Rome, Hermas, Papias, Ignatius, Polycarp, et alii.

**apostolic force.** In Roman Catholic usage, the total

full-time workers dedicated to the apostolate (bishops, priests, brothers, sisters, catechists, and other lay workers) available for mission in a particular situation. World total: (1978) 1.6 million persons.
**apostolic region.** One of several areas into which a Roman Catholic country has divided itself in order to provide more meaningful pastoral areas than the traditional ecclesiastical provinces.
**apostolic succession.** The dogma that uninterrupted succession of bishops from the Apostolic era is necessary for valid sacraments and transmission of orders.
**apostolic work.** A term in use in Catholic circles for pioneer or outstanding missionary work.
**apostolicity.** The quality or character of being apostolic.
**Apostolics.** Pentecostal Apostolics (qv).
**appropriate technology.** Intermediate technology (qv).
**Arab.** A Middle Eastern ethnolinguistic family, in 59 countries. Global population: (1970) 106,840,000, (1980) 142,373,500, (1985) 161,753,300.
**Arabian Gulf.** Also termed Persian Gulf.
**Arabic/Greek.** An Eastern Orthodox liturgical tradition dating back to the Apostolic era. Global membership: (1970) 28 denominations with 792 churches and 445,000 adult members; total community (1970) 772,400, (1980) 945,300, (1985) 1,036,400.
**Aramaean Christians.** Assyrians, East Syrians (Eastern Syrians), Nestorians (qv).
**archbishop** (Greek: leading bishop). A metropolitan or primate having jurisdiction over an ecclesiastical province; occasionally an honorary title only.
**archdeacon.** In Anglican usage, a senior cleric with administrative charge over part of a diocese (archdeaconry). There are 103 archdeacons in the Church of England.
**archdiocese** (symbol AD). A diocese presided over by an archbishop.
**archetype.** In Jungian psychology, an inherited idea or mode of thought derived from the experiences of the race and present in the unconscious of each individual.
**archimandrite.** In the Eastern Church, a high administrative official next in rank after bishop.
**architecture, religious.** The art or practice of designing and building churches and temples to convey impressions and ideas basic to religion or Christianity.
**archive.** A repository for documents and other materials of historical value: diaries, photographs, correspondence, etc.
**archpriest.** In the Eastern Church, the highest title of honour given a member of the secular clergy.
**Arctic Mongoloid.** One of the 13 geographical races of mankind, with 7 languages. Global population: (1970) 61,000, (1980) 74,000, (1985) 79,000.
**areligious, a-religious.** Noncommittal or professedly neutral concerning religious matters.
**argot, religious.** A special vocabulary and idiom used by a religious group as a means of private communication within the group.
**arithmetic mean.** The sum of a number of quantities divided by their number.
**armed forces.** The combined military, naval and air forces of a nation or a group of nations; armed services.
**Armenian.** A European ethnolinguistic family, in 18 countries. Global population: (1970) 5,107,700, (1980) 5,812,600, (1985) 6,184,500.
**Armenian Apostolic.** An ancient Orthodox liturgical tradition dating back to the Apostolic era; also called Gregorians. Global membership: (1970) 37 distinct bodies with 874 churches and 1,795,500 adult members; total community (1970) 2,826,200, (1980) 3,172,300, (1985) 3,350,600.
**Armenian Catholicate of Cilicia (Sis).** Oriental Orthodox. Global constituency in canonical relationship: (1980) 775,000.
**Armenian Catholicate of Echmiadzin.** Oriental Orthodox. Global constituency in canonical relationship: (1980) 2,397,400.
**Armenian Orthodox.** Armenian Apostolic (qv).
**Armenian rite.** A rite of the Roman Catholic Church, with 14 jurisdictions and (1970) 57 parishes, 45,870 adults, 76,500 total community.
**Arminianism.** The doctrines or teachings of Arminius who opposed the absolute predestination taught by Calvin and maintained the real possibility of salvation for all.
**artificial languages.** See constructed languages.
**arts.** In the field of religion and the arts, over 70 significant Christian organizations are at work.
**Ashkenazis.** The larger of the 2 great divisions of Jews comprising the eastern European Yiddish-speaking Jews, arising in the Rhineland in the 10th century; 5.7 million exterminated by Nazis; still 84% of all world's Jews today. Global total: (1980) 14,230,000.
**ashram, asrama** (Sanskrit). A religious retreat centre for a colony of disciples, mainly in India.
**Asian.** One of the 13 geographical races of mankind; Asiatic; speaking over 840 languages. Global population: (1970) 1,306,787,800, (1980) 1,571,095,400, (1985) 1,708,567,600.

ASIAN INDIGENOUS CHURCHES. One of Indonesia's 160 bodies.

**Asian indigenous churches.** Non-White indigenous churches, indigenous to Asian peoples and begun since AD 1500. Global church membership: (1970) 14,556,400, (1980) 23,536,300, (1985) 28,210,100.
**assembly.** In some Protestant traditions (Pentecostal, Brethren, et alii), the usual term for a congregation of believers.
**assistant curate.** In Anglican usage, an assistant or unbeneficed clergyman appointed to assist an incumbent in a parish.
**assisted diocese.** In the Anglican Church of Canada, a diocese not financially self-supported, hence assisted from outside.
**Assyrian.** A Middle Eastern ethnolinguistic family. Global population: (1970) 460,700, (1980) 637,000, (1985) 733,600.
**Assyrians.** Followers of the Ancient Church of the East, who for centuries called themselves Nestorians, followers of patriarch Nestorius' theology. Global membership: (1970) 19 denominations with 54 churches and 86,900 adult members; total community (1970) 150,300, (1980) 176,700, (1985) 190,500.
**atheism.** Disbelief in the existence of God or any other deity, the doctrine that there is no God; godlessness.
**atheism, study of.** A number of universities and research centres in the Communist world profess to study atheism; what in practice they study is religion, the survival of religion, and methods of eradicating it.
**atheistic freedom.** Freedom not to believe, and freedom to oppose religion.
**atheistic states.** In 1980 some 30 nations were atheistic, their regimes being either Communist or Marxist.
**atheists.** Persons professing atheism, scepticism, impiety, disbelief or irreligion, or Marxist-Leninist Communism regarded as a political faith, or other quasi-religions, and who abstain from religious activities and have severed all religious affiliation; and others opposed, hostile or militantly opposed to all religion (anti-religious); dialectical materialists, militant non-believers, anti-religious humanists, sceptics. Global adherents: (1970) 165,288,500, (1980) 195,119,400 in 113 countries, (1985) 210,643,500.
**attendance, church.** See church attendance.
**attending non-Christians.** Non-Christians (Hindus, Muslims, pagans et alii) who, being interested in Christianity, attend church services regularly or occasionally.
**attending non-members.** Nominal Christians (unaffiliated to churches) who occasionally, or in some cases regularly, attend church services.
**attribute.** A quality, character or characteristic of a group.
**audience, radio.** See radio audience.
**audio-visuals.** Over 100 significant Christian organizations are at work in this field.
**Australian Aborigine.** An Austro-Asiatic ethnolinguistic family, with 260 languages. Global population: (1970) 138,100, (1980) 166,500, (1985) 181,200.
**Australoid.** One of the 5 races of mankind; Archaic White, Classical Australoid, Proto-Caucasoid, speaking about 1,520 languages. Global population: (1970) 31,143,300, (1980) 40,204,600, (1985) 45,109,300.
**Austro-Asiatic.** One of the 13 geographical races of mankind, speaking 440 languages. Global population: (1970) 26,296,500, (1980) 33,986,500, (1985) 38,152,100.
**authentic Christians.** See committed Christians.
**Authentic Orthodox.** Paleohemerologites or Old Calendarists (qv).
**autocephality.** The state of ecclesiastical autonomy, of a church that appoints its own chief bishop without outside sanction.
**autocephalous church.** An independent, self-governing church appointing its own chief bishop.
**autochthonous.** Indigenous, native, aboriginal; the original population of an area.
**automatic writing.** See spirit writing.
**autonomous church.** In Eastern Orthodox usage, a semi-independent and partially self-governing church; in Anglican usage, an independent and self-governing province or church.
**auto-evangelization.** Self-evangelization; the evangelization by the church of its own children and its younger generation.
**auxiliary bishop.** A titular bishop in the Roman Catholic Church who assists the ordinary of a diocese.
**average.** An arithmetical term derived by dividing the sum of a group of numbers by their total number; arithmetic mean.
**average income.** National income per person (qv).
**awakening, evangelical.** A movement of the Holy Spirit in the church bringing about a revival of New Testament Christianity.
**awareness.** In evangelization, the quality or state or extent of realization or knowledge of the gospel; perception, understanding, cognizance, consciousness, comprehension, recognition of the facts of Christianity, Christ and the gospel.
**awqaf** (Arabic: plural of *waqf*). Muslim trusts or foundations.
**ayatollah** (Persian). Shia Muslim leader or cleric of great personal accomplishment, holiness and renown.

## B

**baby.** Infant (qv).
**Babylon.** See of Chaldean Catholic patriarchate.
**backsliders.** Former church members who are falling away or have fallen away from the Christian faith; lapsed, disaffiliated, dechristianized, apostates.
**back-calls.** In Jehovah's Witnesses' terminology, return visits (qv) during house-to-house visiting work.
**Baha'i.** The doctrine and practice of a sect founded in Iran in the 19th century that emphasizes the spiritual unity of mankind and advocates peace and universal education.
**Baha'is.** Followers of the Baha'i World Faith, founded by Baha'u'llah, since 1844. In government censuses, Baha'is are usually counted as Muslims or Hindus and not shown separately. Global adherents: (1970) 2,659,400, (1980) 3,822,600 in 194 countries, (1985) 4,442,600.
**Baltic.** A European ethnolinguistic family. Global population: (1970) 4,370,000, (1980) 4,826,100, (1985) 5,062,200.
**banned churches.** In many countries, a few, some, several, many or even all denominations and religions have been banned by decree of the regime in power. Such churches rarely dissolve themselves or cease Christian worship and other activity; they usually simply disappear from public view and operate underground.
**Bantoid.** An African ethnolinguistic family, with 205 languages. Global population: (1970) 33,734,100, (1980) 43,656,700, (1985) 49,093,500.
**Bantu.** An African ethnolinguistic family, with 440 languages. Global population: (1970) 102,216,600, (1980) 134,643,000, (1985) 152,418,100.
**baptism.** The sacramental rite which admits a candidate (adult or infant) to membership in the Christian church; usually by immersion (submersion), affusion (pouring), or aspersion (sprinkling) with water.
**baptism by immersion.** (1) The rite of adult baptism through submersion in water, practised by Baptist, Pentecostal and other Protestant traditions; believer's baptism. (2) Baptism by total immersion is also universal for infant baptism among Eastern and Oriental Orthodox (e.g. Copts, at 40 days old for boys, 80 for girls).
**baptism rate.** The number of baptisms in a church or area in a given year, expressed as a percentage of the total baptized membership.
**baptismal candidate.** A catechumen (qv).
**baptisms, annual.** (1) The number of persons baptized

BAPTISM BY IMMERSION. By Archbishop Makarios (Cyprus).

in a given year. (2) The number of services of baptism held in a given year.

**baptisms, annual Roman Catholic.** (1975) 16,543,344 (15,552,617 infants up to 7 years, 990,727 adults over 7), a decline from (1972) 16,951,316 (15,886,870/1,064,446).

**Baptist World Alliance** (BWA). The major Baptist communion. Global members: (1980) 41,113,400.

**Baptist-Pentecostals.** Also termed Keswick-Pentecostals; mainline Classical Pentecostals teaching 2-crisis experience (conversion, baptism of the Spirit). Global membership, including Non-White indigenous bodies: (1970) 395 denominations with 75,020 churches and 8,382,600 adult members; total community (1970) 16,353,800, (1980) 22,850,600, (1985) 26,414,700.

**Baptists.** (1) In contrast to Pedobaptists (qv) who baptize infants, all Christian traditions which baptize adults only are termed Baptist, in its widest meaning. Global membership: (1970) 127,894,000, (1980) 149,543,000, (1985) 161,129,000; i.e. 11.3% of global church membership. (2) The specific tradition of Protestants calling themselves Baptists. Global membership: (1970) 369 denominations with 153,169 churches and 29,691,500 adult members; total community (1970) 42,399,500, (1980) 47,550,300, (1985) 50,321,900.

**baptized.** Persons who have been admitted to churches through the rite of baptism.

**basic communities.** Small ecclesial communities or groups that have sprung up in the churches, stressing community, renewal, charismatic gifts, prayer, Bible study, evangelism, et alia; spontaneous communities, underground communities, et alia.

**basic data.** Raw data, crude data, primary data.

**Basilians.** Used of Eastern monks in general.

BASILICA. Our Lady of Ireland, Knock (right).

**basilica.** In Roman Catholic and Orthodox ecclesiology, a canonical title of honour with liturgical privileges given to churches distinguished either by their antiquity, dignity, historical significance, or by their role as international centres of worship and relation to a major saint, or historical event, or (in Orthodoxy) a national patriarch. In Catholicism, they are of 2 kinds (a) major basilicas (St Peter's, St John Lateran et alia in Rome,) (b) minor basilicas (as in USA, Canada, et alia).

**Basque.** An isolated European ethnolinguistic family. Global population: (1970) 925,100 (1980) 1,017,000, (1985) 1,064,100.

**Baster.** A Eurafrican or Coloured people in Namibia.

**belief.** Statistics of personal belief have been widely investigated in public-opinion polls and surveys. Typical questions, with nation-wide adult percentage of 'Yes' responses: 'Do you believe in a God?' (1948) Brazil 96%, Australia 95%, Canada 95%, USA 94%, Norway 84%, UK 84%, Finland 83%, Netherlands 80%, Sweden 80%, Denmark 80%, France 66%; (1968) UK 74%; (1970) Netherlands 81%; (1973) Canada 67%, UK 77%; (1975) UK 72%; (1979) UK 73%. 'Do you believe Jesus Christ is the Son of God?' (1957) USA 90%, UK 71%, (1975) Spain 61%. 'Do you believe that Jesus Christ will ever return to earth?' (1960) USA 55%. 'Can a person be a Christian if he does not go to church?' (1957) UK 85%, USA 78%. 'Have you been born again through committing yourself to Christ?' (1976) USA 34%.

**believer.** One who believes or professes a religious faith; often used only of Christians, but sometimes of all religions.

**believer's baptism.** Adult baptism, by immersion, on profession of faith.

**believing Christians.** See committed Christians.

**bell-ringing.** Campanology (qv).

**Berber.** A Middle Eastern ethnolinguistic family, with 30 languages. Global population: (1970) 9,627,800, (1980) 12,904,100, (1985) 14,692,700.

**Bezirk** (German: District). An administrative region of the New Apostolic Church, which has 30 Districts across the world.

**Bible.** For Christians, the revealed Word of God, Holy Scriptures, with 66 Books (39 OT, 27 NT).

**Bible correspondence courses.** See correspondence courses.

**Bible distribution.** Global distribution (free, subsidized, commercial): (1975) 30,034,000 copies of the whole Bible per year, (1980) 36,800,000.

**Bible organizations.** There are over 370 major Christian organizations at work in this field.

**Bible schools.** Centres for the training of Christian workers usually of less than secondary education, often for the ordained ministry in Third-World countries, more usually for lay ministries. In Latin American Protestantism the term tends to be synonymous with seminaries (qv).

**Bible smuggler.** A Western tourist or courier from Europe or North America who enters Communist or non-Christian lands with numerous copies of the Bible for illegal distribution.

**Bible Student movement.** A schismatic movement out of Jehovah's Witnesses which has produced a number of new denominations.

**Bible studies.** In Jehovah's Witnesses' statistics, the number of Bible studies conducted each year by publishers in the course of house-to-house visiting. World total: (1959) 606,075, (1974) 1,351,404.

**Bible translations.** World total among UBS-related societies (1980): complete Bibles in 273 languages, New Testaments alone in another 472 languages, portions in another 940 languages; total all languages with at least one book printed, 1,685.

BIBLE-READING. In Stuntzabad (Pakistan).

**Bible-reading.** Surveys and polls have been taken in various countries. Typical questions, with nation-wide adult percentages answering 'Yes': 'Do you own a Bible or NT?' Brazil 75% of young students and workers, Spain 64% (though only 42% read it); (1973) UK 76%, (1976) UK 71%. 'Have you a Bible in your home?' (1976) UK 84%. 'Have you read the Bible all the way through?' (1939) USA 26%. 'Have you read any part of the Bible at home within the last year?' (1944) USA 62% (10% every day); (1975) USA 63% (Protestants 75%, RCs 43%), UK 38% (7% every day, 16% every week, 24% every month).

**bibliography.** A catalogue of writings and publications related to a particular subject, often with critical annotations added.

**bilaterals, bilateral conversations.** In ecumenical terminology, theological conversations undertaken by officially-appointed representatives of 2 churches, 2 traditions, or 2 confessional families, with purposes ranging from promoting mutual understanding to achieving full fellowship or eventual organic union.

**bilingual.** Used of a person knowing or speaking 2 languages.

**billion.** In British usage, a million millions; in American usage, 1,000 millions; the American billion is termed milliard in British, French and German usage.

**biological change.** Demographic change in the population of a country or body due to natural causes properly so called, i.e. the annual nett aggregate of births to members of the body minus deaths in it.

**birth rate.** The number of births per year in a population expressed as a percentage or permillage of the total population.

**bishop.** A clergyman of the highest rank or order in the Christian churches, with administrative and other duties; overseer, shepherd.

**bishop in partibus infidelium** (Latin: bishop in heathen land). A titular bishop (qv).

**bishopric.** (1) The office of a bishop. (2) The administrative area under the jurisdiction of a bishop; a diocese.

**bishops-at-large** (in Latin, *episcopi vagantes*). Bishops founding or leading miniscule unrecognized autocephalous episcopal churches, with disputed apostolic succession. 130 such churches are described here in the table Episcopal Churches with Disputed Apostolic Succession, which also lists documentation of 760 bishops-at-large.

**bishops' conferences.** Episcopal conferences (qv).

**bishop's commissary.** In Anglican usage, a clergyman appointed to represent his bishop in the latter's temporary absence abroad, or appointed by a bishop serving abroad to serve him in his home country.

**Black.** Stylized skin colour associated with the Negro (Negroid) race and the African and Afro-American geographical races. Global Black population: (1970) 308,583,300, (1980) 399,018,300, (1985) 448,366,500.

**Black Evangelicals.** Members of Black indigenous churches in the USA (but not elsewhere) who regard themselves as part of the Evangelical/Conservative Evangelical/Fundamentalist movements in the USA. Total adherents: (1970) 13,551,000, (1980) 15,241,000, (1985) 16,149,000.

**black magic.** Magic (qv) used for evil purposes, with malevolent intent.

**Black Muslims.** Followers of unorthodox Nation of Islam (since 1977, World Community of Al-Islam in the West) in the USA. Total adherents: (1970) 200,000, (1980) 800,000, (1985) 1,100,000.

**Black neo-pentecostals.** Regularly-active Black charismatics (more traditionally, 'sanctified') in the non-pentecostal Black denominations in the USA.

**Black theology.** Christian theology as interpreted from the standpoint of the oppressed Black race.

**Black/Third-World indigenous Christianity.** Type or style of Christianity evolved and practised by Non-White indigenous Christians (qv).

**Black/Third-World indigenous councils of churches.** Over 180 significant denominations of Non-White indigenous churches have banded themselves into national councils of churches, with (in 1980) 22,178,000 church members.

**Blanco** (Spanish). A White, especially in Latin America.

**blanketing.** A term used in saturation evangelism for total coverage of a target population.

**blind, the.** Global total of totally blind persons: 16 million in 1973, rising to 18.5 million by 1980, a rate or density of 422 blind persons per 100,000 population.

**bloc, ecclesiastical.** De facto ecclesiastico-cultural

grouping which has arisen during the course of Christian history. There are 7 major historico-cultural ecclesiastical blocs, coalitions or ongoing or enduring streams of Christianity: Roman Catholicism, Orthodoxy, Anglicanism, Protestant-ism, marginal Protestantism, Catholicism (non-Roman), and Non-White or Black Third-World indigenous Christianity.

**body evangelism.** Evangelism which results in visible, measurable growth of the church as the Body of Christ; extension growth, the planting of new congregations and churches.

**body life.** Life in the Body of Christ; the developing of spiritual gifts of the Body's members (fellow-Christians).

**Bohras.** Mustali Ismailis.

**Bon.** The pre-Buddhist animistic religion of Tibet.

**book.** (1) In UNESCO usage for statistical purposes, any non-periodical publication of at least 49 pages excluding covers. (2) In UBS usage, the translation of a single portion, gospel or other book of the Bible when published separate.

**book titles, annual new.** The number of non-periodical commercial publications produced each year (books and pamphlets). World total per year in 1974: 585,570. Of these, 3.6% are religious (on religion), and 2.9% on Christianity (see religious books).

**bookshops.** Global total of all Christian bookshops, bookstalls and outlets for Christian literature: (1980) 55,000.

**born-again Christians.** Those who have had, or claim to have had, an experience of new birth in Christ; committed Christians (qv). Approximate global total (1980) 420,000,000.

**Botika.** Digambara (qv).

**brackets.** In printing, square brackets [] as opposed to parentheses or curved marks ().

**Braille.** A system of writing for the blind using raised dots.

**Branco** (Portuguese). A White, especially in Brazil.

**Branhamites.** Followers of a marginal pentecostal evangelist, William Branham, and his End Time Believers.

**Brazilian indigenous churches.** Denominations indigenous to Brazilians. Membership: (1980) 220 denominations with 7,583,000 members.

**breakoff.** A schism, secession (qv).

**Brethren.** A general term for Christians, used as a proper name by several traditions, especially Christian Brethren (qv).

**Britain.** (1) A geographical term covering Great Britain, consisting of England, Wales and Scotland. (2) A political shorthand term for the United Kingdom of Great Britain and Northern Ireland.

**British Isles.** A geographical term covering England, Wales, Scotland and Ireland (both Northern Ireland and the Republic of Ireland).

**British-Israelites.** A movement holding that the British and North American peoples are part of the 10 lost tribes of Israel; not a separate sect, since members belong to many British and American denominations. Some marginal Protestant denominations, however, retain British-Israel tenets.

**Broad Church Anglicans.** See Central or Broad Church Anglicans.

**broadcast.** A radio or TV programme.

**broadcasting station.** See radio station.

**broadcasting studio.** Centre for the production or compilation (but not transmission) of radio or TV programmes, which are then sent elsewhere for broadcasting over stations.

**broadcasting, Christian.** There are over 430 organizations in this field significant at the national and wider levels.

**broadcasting, religious.** Often used as synonymous with Christian broadcasting, but incorrectly since Muslims, Hindus, Buddhists and numerous New Religions and sects make extensive use of radio and TV in many countries.

**brother.** (1) A co-religionist, especially a fellow-member of a Christian church. (2) A member of a congregation of religious men not in holy orders.

**brotherhood.** An association of Christian men, e.g. a monastic society.

**brothers.** Members of men's religious institutes or congregations not in holy orders. Roman Catholic total of Pontifical Right (1975): 67,460 perpetual vows, 6,681 temporary vows.

**Brothers of Christ.** Christadelphians (qv).

**Brown.** Stylized skin colour associated with Dravidian, North Indian, Oceanic (Melanesian, Papuan) and other peoples. Global Brown population: (1970) 782,167,100, (1980) 1,004,921,000, (1985) 1,126,560,700.

BUDDHISTS. Tibetan lamas in procession.

**Buddhists.** Followers of the Buddha, divided among (a) Mahayana (Greater Vehicle) or Northern Buddhism, or (b) Theravada (Teaching of the Elders) stigmatized by Mahayanists as Hinayana (Lesser Vehicle, i.e. the older, purer form available to less people) or Southern Buddhism, or (c) Vajra-yana (Mantrayana, Guhyamantrayana, Tantrayana (Esoteric Vehicle), Tantrism or Lamaism, Shingon), or (d) traditional Buddhist sects, but excluding neo-Buddhist new religions or religious movements. Global adherents: (1970) 231,672,200, (1980) 273,715,600, (1985) 295,570,800.

**Bulgarian rite.** A rite of the Roman Catholic Church, with (1970) 7,000 total community.

**bull.** See papal bull.

**bush telegraph.** The means whereby natives of a jungle or bush rapidly spread news from person to person; an informal but well-organized system of word-of-mouth communication.

**Byelorussian.** White-Ruthenian, a sub-rite of the Byzantine rite (qv); suppressed and with no jurisdictions (1980).

**Byzantine.** The Byzantine or Constantinopolitan rite of the Roman Catholic Church consists of 13 sub-rites: Albanian, Bulgarian, Greek, Hungarian, Italo-Albanian, Melkite, Romanian, Russian, Ruthenian, Slovak, Ukrainian, White-Ruthenian (Byelorussian), Yugoslavian (qv for separate statistics).

## C

**cadet.** In Salvation Army usage, one undergoing training for officership.

**Cafuso.** The Portuguese-speaking issue of a Negro and an Amerindian; in Spanish, Zambo.

**Calendar.** In Orthodoxy, most churches follow the Old Calendar (qv), especially the Russian Orthodox Church, although a sizeable number follow the New Calendar (qv), notably Constantinople, Greece, Romania, Finland, Cyprus.

**call sign.** A combination of identifying letters, or letters and numbers, assigned to a radio/TV station or a radio operator for use in communication.

**Calvinist.** An adherent of Calvinism, the theological doctrines that emphasize the sovereignty of God in the bestowal of grace, election or predestination, limited atonement, total depravity, irresistability of grace, and the perseverance of saints.

**campaign.** See evangelistic campaigns.

**campanology.** The art of bell ringing, or the science of making bells.

**Campbellites.** Disciples (qv).

**campus.** The grounds and buildings of a university, college or school; the university itself; the academic world.

**candidate.** In Salvationist usage, a soldier who offers to devote his or her life to officership.

**canon.** (1) A decree, decision, regulation, code or constitution made by ecclesiastical authority. (2) A relatively unchangeable part of the Catholic mass. (3) Books forming the accepted list of Holy Scripture. (4) A clergyman on the staff of a cathedral.

**canonical relationship.** In Eastern Orthodoxy, a sanctioned, orthodox, authoritative relationship of one church with another, in accordance with Orthodox canons.

**canonicity.** Canonical acceptability, authority or genuineness, based on a church's history, tradition, apostolic succession, liturgy, canons and relationships with sister churches.

**capitalism.** An economic system characterized by private or corporate ownership of capital goods, by investments on private initiative, and by prices, production and distribution in a free market.

**Capitalist world.** Nations of the Western, free or First World that practise capitalism; sometimes used of the West together with similar nations in the Third World.

**Capoid.** One of the 5 races of mankind; Archaic African, Early African (qv), speaking about 60 languages. Global population: (1970) 422,800, (1980) 547,000, (1985) 615,500.

**captain.** An officer in the Salvation Army, or Church Army (Anglican), or similar organizations with military terminology.

**cardinals.** In the Roman Catholic church, the highest ecclesiastical officials below papal rank, appointed to assist the pope in the College of Cardinals. Total: fixed at 70 from 1586-1959, then increased to 131 (1969), 145 (1973), falling to 132 (1977).

CARGO CULT. Jon Frum cult (Vanuatu).

**cargo cults.** Religio-political or nativistic (qv) movements among natives of various South Pacific islands, characterized by the messianic expectation of return of the ancestors in ships or planes carrying valuable modern cargoes.

**cassette ministry.** Evangelistic outreach through playing cassettes or tapes over recorders in outreach situations, especially in non-Christian languages in non-Christian areas.

**caste.** A social or socio-religious stratum or stratification; any hereditary and exclusive class based on socio-religious beliefs; in India, one of the 30,000 groupings, classified under 4 hereditary classes, into which society is divided in accordance with a system of rank and status fundamental to Hinduism.

**catacomb church, church of the catacombs.** See crypto-Christians.

**catechesis.** (1) The responsibility of every Christian to bear witness to the gospel and to communicate it. (2) A stage in evangelization. (3) The process of systematized instruction in the Christian faith.

**catechetical centre.** A centre for catechesis (teaching the Christian faith) and study of catechetical methods in the modern world.

**catechetics.** The technology or methodology of religious education.

**catechists.** Local teachers of catechumens. Roman Catholic totals in areas under SC Propaganda (1978): 160,000 (20,000 full-time, 50,000 part-time, 90,000 volunteer).

**catechumen.** One receiving rudimentary instruction in church doctrines, discipline and morals prior to baptism; baptismal candidate.

**cathedral.** A church that contains a cathedra (bishop's throne) and that is officially the principal church of a diocese.

**Catholic.** (1) A person belonging to or attribute of the universal Christian church. (2) A member or attribute of a Catholic or Anglican church.

**catholic.** Related to the church universal; comprehensive, universal, general.

**Catholic Apostolics.** Followers of a tradition emerging from Protestantism in 1832 and stressing Catholic features, rejecting apostolic succession and substituting government by hierarchy of living apostles; also termed Irvingites (qv), Old Apostolics, and New Apostolics (qv). Global membership: 68 denominations with 7,161 churches and 1,005,700 adult members; total community (1970) 1,610,100, (1980) 1,887,300, (1985) 2,030,800.

**Catholic charismatic.** A Roman Catholic involved in the Catholic Charismatic Renewal.

**Catholic Charismatic Renewal.** Worldwide movement begun by Catholic pentecostals (qv) in 1967 in the USA.

**Catholic charismatics.** Catholic pentecostals (qv).

**Catholic Church.** (1) The universal church begun by Christ. (2) The Church of Rome.

CATHOLIC PENTECOSTALS. Conference in Rome.

**Catholic pentecostals** (Catholic charismatics). Roman Catholics active in the organized Catholic Charismatic Renewal, expressed in healings, tongues, prophesyings, etc. Active global membership: (1970) 238,500, (1980) 4,771,400 in 75 countries, (1985) 7,547,000.

**catholicate.** The see of a catholicos.

**Catholicism.** Usually, Roman Catholicism (qv).

**catholicos.** The chief bishop of certain independent Oriental churches: Armenian, Assyrian, Georgian.

**catholicossate.** Catholicate (qv).

**Catholics (non-Roman).** Old Catholics and others in secessions from the Church of Rome since 1700 in the Western world, and other Catholic-type sacramentalist or hierarchical secessions from Protestantism or Anglicanism. Global professing adherents: (1970) 2,806,600 (1980) 2,997,600 in 35 countries, (1985) 3,104,100. Global affiliated membership: (1970) 3,134,400, (1980) 3,439,400 in 59 countries, (1985) 3,600,900.

**Caucasian.** A European ethnolinguistic family, with 35 languages in the Caucasus (though also used for Caucasoid (qv) or White person). Global population: (1970) 6,551,300, (1980) 7,284,900, (1985) 7,665,400.

**Caucasoid, Caucasian.** One of the 5 major races of mankind, speaking 630 Indo-European languages. Global population: (1970) 1,910,873,300, (1980) 2,295,080,600, (1985) 2,502,016,100.

**celebration.** An occasion or observance of public worship, especially (in Anglicanism) of Holy Communion.

**celibacy.** The state of a single, unmarried life, or the obligation (in Roman Catholicism and Orthodoxy) of bishops or priests and monks not to marry.

**Celtic.** A European ethnolinguistic family. Global population: (1970) 8,734,600, (1980) 9,480,000, (1985) 9,856,700.

**Celtic church.** The ancient Church of Britain in the 1st-6th centuries AD.

**cenobite.** A member of a religious group living in common, as contrasted with hermits.

**censorship, religious.** The practice of censoring (deleting, banning, altering, excising) letters to and from a country, especially to intercept Christian material.

**census.** A term used here solely for an official government population census (qv) usually with complete (100%) enumeration of the whole population.

**census schedule.** A form or questionnaire used for collection of information in a census.

**Central Amerindian.** An American Indian ethnolinguistic family, with 220 languages. Global population: (1970) 18,474,800, (1980) 25,211,400, (1985) 28,890,200.

**central conference.** See conference.

**Central or Broad Church Anglicans.** Prayer Book, Liberal or Comprehensive Anglicans, including (from 1976) the New Synod Group; attempting to provide a via media between Anglo-Catholics and Anglican Evangelicals. Global membership in 53 dioceses: (1980) 12,237,500.

**chaitya.** A stupa (qv).

**Chalcedonian.** Eastern Orthodox (qv).

**Chaldean.** The Chaldean or Syro-Oriental or East Syrian rite of the Roman Catholic Church consists of 2 sub-rites: Chaldean, and Syro-Malabarese.

**Chaldeans.** Chaldean-rite Catholics subordinate to Rome, with (1970) 22 jurisdictions, 152,200 adults, and 280,000 total community.

**chapel.** A Christian sanctuary other than a cathedral or parish church, sometimes private, sometimes in a school or other institution, or Nonconformist.

**chaplain.** A clergyman officially attached to a school, college or other public institution, or to the armed forces or other bodies.

**chaplaincy.** The sphere of work and office of a chaplain (qv).

**chapter.** (1) The body of canons of a cathedral. (2) The regular assembly for business of the canons of a cathedral or collegiate church or religious order or congregation.

**charisma, charismata.** Spiritual gifts or talents divinely granted as exemplified in early Christianity by the power of healing, gift of tongues, or prophesying.

**charismatic.** Gifted, instructed; a person involved in the charismatic renewal.

**charismatic communities.** See basic communities.

**charismatic renewal.** The pentecostal or neo-pentecostal renewal or revival movement within the mainline Protestant, Anglican, Catholic and Orthodox churches, characterized by healings, tongues, prophesyings, et alia.

**Chicano.** A Latin American Mestizo (Spanish/Amerindian).

**child, children.** Persons who have not yet attained puberty; defined here as ages 5-14 years, i.e. the school-age population. Often used inclusively to cover infants (defined as under 5 years old, or the pre-school population).

**children's organizations.** In this field there are over 240 significant Christian organizations.

**Chinese.** An Asian ethnolinguistic family and people. Global population: (1970) 752,225,600, (1980) 886,376,100 in 62 countries, (1985) 955,211,100.

**Chinese folk-religionists.** Followers of traditional Chinese religion (local deities including Taoist ones, ancestor veneration, Confucian ethics, Chinese universism, divination and magic, some Buddhist elements). Global adherents: (1970) 214,391,500, (1980) 197,795,400 in 55 countries, (1985) 187,994,000.

**choirmaster.** The director of a choir.

**chorepiscopus** (Greek, Latin). (1) In the Early Church, bishop of a country district. (2) In the 20th century, sub-bishop in certain Orthodox and Uniate churches, especially the Coptic Orthodox Church.

**chorten.** A stupa (qv).

**Christ Groups.** A term coined by the World Literature Crusade for the large number of congregations of converts which have emerged through WLC ministry over the last 20 years in isolated areas or towns with no existing churches. World total: (1980) 68,489 Groups.

**Christadelphians.** A premillenial Protestant group rejecting the Trinity. Global membership: (1970) 1,529 churches with 60,260 adult members; total community (1970) 96,900, (1980) 92,900, (1985) 90,600.

**Christendom.** The traditional portion of the world in which Christianity prevails or which is governed principally under Christian institutions.

**Christian.** One who believes in, or professes or confesses Jesus Christ as Lord and Saviour, or is assumed to believe in Jesus Christ; an adherent of Christianity.

**Christian approaches to other faiths.** There are over 80 significant organizations in this field worldwide.

**Christian Brethren.** Protestant tradition begun 1828 ex Church of England; also called Open Brethren; independent fundamentalist/dispensationalist. Global membership: (1970) 132 denominations with 10,340 assemblies (churches) and 563,970 adult members; total community (1970) 1,399,700, (1980) 1,691,800, (1985) 1,854,500.

**Christian cultures.** A Christian culture is defined here as a culture related to a specific ethnolinguistic people or tribe among whom affiliated church members make up a majority of the population, i.e. over 50% in number. Global total (1980): 4,047 out of 8,993 (45.0%).

**Christian education.** Organizations in this field, significant at the national or wider levels, number over 280.

**Christian Era** (CE). Used by Jehovah's Witnesses, Muslims and other non-Christians to replace Anno Domini, The Year of Our Lord (AD).

**Christian Greek Scriptures.** The Jehovah's Witnesses' term for the New Testament.

**Christian institutions.** See institutions, Christian.

**Christian literature.** In this field, organizations significant at the national or wider levels number over 300.

**Christian political parties.** In a number of countries, in Western Europe in particular, certain political parties claim to have a Christian philosophy and basis and have long had close links with Catholics or Protestants.

**Christian Scientist.** A believer in Christian Science, organized under the official name of the Church of Christ, Scientist.

**Christian socialism.** A political tradition in Europe with close links with the Roman Catholic Church.

**Christian world communions.** Official name since 1979 of what were previously termed world confessional families (WCFs), most of which are rooted primarily in Europe and North America, giving expression to the common heritages of worldwide groups of churches. Most have their own organized world confessional councils (confessional conciliarism). World total: (1980) 45.

**Christian year.** The year as it is observed by Christian churches marked by various festivals or commemorations at special seasons and on special days; the church year, church's year.

**Christianity.** The whole worldwide body of Christian believers and their religion.

**christianization.** The process of christianizing; the whole 3-fold process of church planting and growth (as outlined in the Great Commission in Matthew 28.19), namely (qv) discipling, baptizing, and perfecting.

**christianize.** To make Christian, to convert to Christianity, to imbue with Christian principles.

**Christians.** Followers of Jesus Christ of all kinds: all traditions and confessions, and all degrees of commitment. Global total: (1970) 1,216,579,400, (1980) 1,432,686,500, (1985) 1,548,592,200.

**Christmas.** The annual church festival kept on 25 December (Oriental Orthodox on 6 January) in memory of the birth of Christ.

**Christmas attenders.** The total of all persons who attend church at Christmas each year.

**christocentric.** Used of all thought, actions, or theological systems in which Christ is placed at the centre.

**Christo-paganism.** A synthesis of popular Catholicism in Latin America with traditional pre-Columbian American Indian religion.

CHRISTO-PAGANS. Altar and shamans (Guatemala).

**Christo-pagans.** Amerindian Roman Catholics in Latin America who syncretize folk-Catholicism with organized traditional Amerindian pagan religion. Global total: (1970) 12,919,700, (1980) 15,698,900 in 16 countries, (1985) 17,131,400.

**Church** (when used with a capital C). A particular denomination; or the universal Church.

**church** (when used without a capital C). A building set apart for Christian worship, or the services which go on in it; the historical institution composed of believing members, or the body of Christian believers; a local congregation or worshipping body; the visible organization to which Christ committed his mission.

**church attenders.** These can be categorized under 8 mutually-exclusive types: daily attenders, weekly (or Sunday) attenders, fortnightly attenders, monthly attenders, radio/TV service listeners, festival attenders, occasional attenders, annual attenders.

**church growth.** The study of the growth of churches

is usually divided into (a) quantitative (numerical) growth, and (b) qualitative growth, the latter including organic and spiritual growth as well as other less tangible aspects.
**church in exile.** See exiled church.
**church invisible.** The entire company of those on earth and in afterlife who whether members of the church visible or not belong to the faithful saved by Christ.
**church members.** Affiliated Christians (qv.)
**church militant.** The Christian church on earth regarded as engaged in a constant warfare against its enemies, the powers of evil.
**Church of Rome.** The Roman Catholic Church, also officially termed 'the Holy Roman and Apostolic Faith' and 'the Roman, Catholic and Apostolic Religion'.
**church of silence.** See crypto-Christians.
**church sendee.** A missionary (term coined in 1977 by Indonesian churches).
**Church Slavonic** (Old Slavic). The liturgical language of the Russian Orthodox and other churches for centuries up to the present. For global statistics of membership, see under Slavonic.
**church triumphant.** Members of the Church who have died and are regarded as enjoying eternal happiness through union with Christ.
**church union negotiations.** An attempt by 2 or more churches or denominations, through their officially-appointed representatives, to draw up a plan for organic union.
**church visible.** The whole body of professing or affiliated Christians on earth.
**church year.** See Christian year.
**Churches of Christ** (Restoration Movement). Disciples (qv).
**churches' statistics of membership.** Statistics collected and published by the churches of their own membership are defined and termed here as affiliated Christians (qv).
**churchgoer.** One who habitually attends church.
**churchmanship.** The attitude, belief or practice of a churchman.
**church-planting agencies.** Missionary societies and other organizations existing specifically for the planting of new churches and worship centres.
**church-state relations.** Nations can be categorized into a 3-fold typology, in 1980 as follows: (a) 101 countries can be termed religious countries or states, this being how they define themselves in their constitutions or other official statements, (b) 92 are secular countries or states, defining themselves as completely separate from religion, and (c) 30 states or their regimes are atheistic or anti-religious (Communist or Marxist) officially hostile to all religion.
**Cilicia,** also known as **Sis.** See of 2 rival patriarchates and patriarchs: Armenian Apostolic (catholicate). Armenian Catholic.
**cinema, religious.** See religious drama.
**circle.** In Swedenborgian and other traditions, a local church congregation.
**circuit.** In Methodist and other traditions, a group of church congregations ministered to or under the supervision of one pastor. In Jehovah's Witnesses' usage, about 20 congregations; with several circuits making up a district, and several districts a country.
**circulation, scripture.** See scripture distribution.
**circumscription.** An ecclesiastical jurisdiction.
**citadel.** In Salvationist usage, a hall used for worship and as a base for corps operations.
**cities.** Global totals: (1975) 1,969 with over 100,000 population each, 181 with over 1 million each.
**citizen.** A member of a state or nation; subject, national.
**civic attenders.** Persons who attend church services only on civic occasions or state festivals.
**civil servant.** An employee of a country's central government.
**civilian.** A resident of a country who is not on active duty in the armed services.
**clandestine Christians.** See crypto-Christians.
**Classical Pentecostals.** Blanket term for traditional types of Pentecostal (Pentecostal Apostolic, Oneness-Pentecostal, Baptistic-Pentecostal, Holiness-Pentecostal, Perfectionist-Pentecostal), as contrasted with Neo-pentecostal, Catholic pentecostal, Non-White pentecostal, etc.
**classis.** An ecclesiastical district, or the governing body of a district, in certain churches of Presbyterian polity (Dutch and German Reformed); presbytery.
**clergy.** The body of men and women duly ordained to the service of God in the Christian church: bishops, priests, deacons, ministers, deaconesses (in Anglican usage), and other ordained persons.
**clergy organizations.** There are over 200 significant bodies in this field.
**clergyman.** A member of the clergy, ordained minister, one in holy orders.
**cleric.** A clergyman.
**clerk in holy orders.** A clergyman of the Church of England.
**clines.** A number of hybrid races (Negroid-Caucasoid, Mongoloid-Caucasoid, etc) existing between the 5 major races of mankind, but only distinguished from them by a series of almost imperceptible gradations of genetic character.
**clinics.** See medical centres.
**clinical theology.** A psychiatrichal or psychological system of mental healing and mental health, derived in the Church of England in the 1950s-60s.
**Closed Brethren.** Exclusive Brethren (qv).
**closed communion.** The offering of the sacrament of communion only to those who are full members of a particular church or denomination.
**closed countries.** 16 countries across the world which are completely closed to foreign mission (not necessarily to internal mission by government policy.
**closed dioceses.** Dioceses which have been forcibly suppressed, destroyed or otherwise closed by state or other action.
**coadjutor bishop.** A bishop assisting another bishop nearing retirement, who usually has the right in due course to succeed him.
**coenobite.** See cenobite.
**collegiality.** The doctrine re-emphasized by Vatican II (1962-5) that government of the Roman Catholic Church is not by the pope alone but by the whole episcopate functioning as a college of bishops.
**colour.** A term used loosely to refer to inherited apparent pigmentation of the skin. The human race is classified, in this Encyclopedia, into 7 stylized colours (qv): Black, Brown, Grey, Red, Tan, White, Yellow.
**Coloured.** Non-White, often of mixed blood (White/Black).

COLPORTAGE. Colporteurs at work (Ghana).

**colportage.** The work of a colporteur.
**colporteur.** A peddler of Bibles, religious books and tracts.
**commercial distribution of scriptures.** Annual retail sales of scriptures published by commercial publishing houses, in which prices are not subsidized but are fixed on commercial considerations.
**commissary.** See bishop's commissary.
**committed Christians.** The inner nucleus of believing, active, practising Christians of all traditions who have, or claim to have, personal and corporate commitment to Christ and to his church; also known as believing Christians, real Christians, converted Christians, nuclear Christians, authentic Christians, born-again Christians, etc.
**Common Bible.** A modern translation of the Bible into a major language in which Protestants, Catholics and others all co-operate.
**communauté** (French: community). The term used in Zaire for Protestant denominations within the sole legal Protestant church.
**communautés de base** (French). Basic communities (qv).
**communicant, communicant member.** A church member in good standing who is entitled to partake of the sacrament of the Lord's Supper.
**communication.** The act or action of imparting or transmitting; interchange of thoughts and opinions.
**communications.** The means of communicating: equipment, systems, persons, channels, media, etc.
**communion.** (1) A body of Christians having one common faith and discipline; (2) the eucharist or Lord's Supper; (3) fellowship.
**Communism.** A system and theory advocating elimination of private ownership of property or capital; a totalitarian system of Marxist government.
**communist.** This term with a small 'c' is used in this Encyclopedia for individuals who hold Communist ideology.
**Communist bloc.** A term now in disfavour because the Communist world is, since the Sino-Soviet dispute, no longer a monolithic bloc.
**Communist world.** A term, based on political alignment, for some 30 nations in 1980 which are governed by Communist regimes, or Marxist or Marxist-Socialist regimes.
**communists.** Members of Communist Parties. Global membership: (1978) 47,000,000 members of 79 Parties (48 being illegal or semi-clandestine). 94% of these members live between the river Elbe and the Pacific in the 14 major nations governed by Communist Parties.
**community.** (1) A body of individuals organized into a local unit, with its own culture; the maximal group of persons who normally reside together in face-to-face association, with moral responsibilities towards each other as well as to the community as a whole (up to 500 persons); the principal focus of associative life, the primary unit of social participation, the distinctive culture-bearing group; with internal divisions or factors usually 2 in number. (2) A monastic body or other unified religious group. (3) A variety of smaller Christian groups: basic communities (qv), spontaneous or charismatic communities, underground communities, et alia.
**community church.** An interdenominational or non-denominational church for community use in areas under North American influence.
**comparative demographic evangelization.** An index (%) of the extent of evangelization among a population.
**comparative symbolics.** See symbolics.
**Comprehensive Anglicans.** Central or Broad Church Anglicans (qv).
**computer.** An automatic electronic machine for storing, re-arranging and retrieving information and for doing mathematical calculations, according to predesigned programmes; widely used by churches and missions.
**concelebration.** A celebration of the eucharist, Lord's Supper, or mass, in which 2 or more clergy unite in saying the words of the liturgy.
**concerts, religious.** See religious drama.
**conciliar.** Relating to conciliarism.
**conciliar Christianity.** That portion of the Christian world which co-operates through Christian councils.
**Conciliar Evangelicals.** Evangelicals in Protestant and Anglican churches that are affiliated to the Ecumenical Movement, and who generally work within and co-operate with that movement.
**conciliar fellowship.** A model of unity embraced by part of the global ecumenical movement, envisioning united local churches along primarily territorial lines, themselves united to other local churches so as to form a universal fellowship in such a way as to exclude the persistence of confessional differentiations and identities at least on the global level; in contrast to the model of 'reconciled diversity' (qv).
**conciliar movement.** The contemporary ecumenical movement, including Evangelical conciliarism.
**conciliar region.** In the Catholic Church of Italy, and other large national Catholic churches, one of a system of regions, each governed through an episcopal council, replacing the traditional but increasingly irrelevant system of dioceses attached to ecclesiastical provinces.
**conciliarism.** (1) The structuring of co-operation among differing Christian traditions into Christian councils and councils of churches at local, national, regional, continental and global levels. (2) In Roman Catholicism, the theory of church government that places final ecclesiastical authority in representative church councils instead of in the papacy.
**conciliarity.** The principle of government found in Eastern Orthodox and other churches that places final authority in representative councils (Russian, *sobornost*, qv).
**conclave.** The assembly of cardinals in the Sistine Chapel, Vatican City, to elect a new pope for the Roman Catholic Church.
**concord.** Agreement by stipulation, compact, or covenant.
**concordat.** A compact between a national government and the Holy See establishing terms of agreement on matters of mutual interest.
**conditional baptism.** A Roman Catholic and Anglican baptismal rite given when it is doubtful whether the

candidate has already previously been validly baptized.

**conference.** In Methodist, Mennonite and other churches, a stated meeting of preachers and others invested with authority to act on ecclesiastical matters. In Methodism, conferences can be annual, central or provisional.

**Conference of Secretaries of Christian World Communions.** Begun 1957 as Conference of World Confessional Families, renamed 1979. Global constituency: (1980) 1,179,200,000, i.e. 89.1% of global church membership.

**confessing Christians.** Professing Christians (qv). Sometimes used in a narrower sense for Christians who confess the faith and suffer for it in times of severe testing or persecution.

**confessing church.** A church or denomination attacked by an anti-Christian state or regime but which nevertheless retains and publicizes a clear Christian confession in highly unfavourable circumstances.

**confession.** A world confessional family or body; a large family of distinct or different autonomous churches or denominations around the world which are linked by similar ecclesiastical tradition, history, polity and name, and often by some informal or formal organization; officially known since 1979 as Christian world communions (qv).

**confessional.** (1) Denominational. (2) Adhering to a confession of faith. (3) Related to a world confessional family (qv).

**confessional Christianity.** The Christian faith as interpreted by a particular confession or Christian world communion, and emphasizing the superiority of its confessional tradition.

**confessional conciliarism.** See Christian world communions.

**confessional identities.** The recent trend emphasizing the distinctness and importance of world confessions (communions, confessional families) in contrast to the overall ecumenical movement.

**confessional pluralism.** The existence and continued persistence of some 45 Christian world communions (until 1979 termed world confessional families, WCFs) as distinct and separate identities in contrast to and hindering ecumenism and organic church union.

**confessionalism.** (1) The principle that a church should have a confession of faith. (2) Devotion or adherence to a confession of faith. (3) The contemporary movement towards re-emphasizing confessional roots in contrast to ecumenicity.

**confided.** In Roman Catholic missionary usage, given into the care and charge of a missionary society or religious order or congregation.

**confiding of a jurisdiction.** The placing (by Propaganda in Rome) of a vicariate or prefecture (and, before 1969, of a diocese) in the charge of a missionary institute.

**confirmation.** A rite of various Christian churches, supplemental to the rite of baptism, regarded as a sacrament and viewed as confirming a person in his religious faith.

**confirmations, annual.** (1) The number of persons confirmed in a given year. (2) The number of distinct services of confirmation held in a given year.

**confirmed.** Church members to whom the rite of confirmation has been administered.

**conglomerate.** A large church or denomination composed of Christians from many different peoples (tribes, castes, races), each of whom has been converted virtually singly out of a largely non-Christian people.

**confrontation.** In evangelization, the bringing of people face-to-face with the gospel of Christ; challenging, facing, facing up to them, opposing them, forcing them to consider.

**Confucians.** Non-Chinese followers of Confucius and Confucianism; mostly Koreans and in Korea. Adherents: (1970) 4,516,000, (1980) 4,980,000, (1985) 5,207,000.

**congregation.** (1) A distinct organized worship centre (qv) or group of worshippers, usually quantified by church buildings, chapels, regular worship premises, sites, stations, centres, outposts, preaching points, or (Roman Catholics) parishes and quasi-parishes. (2) In some Protestant usage, an organized self-supporting church or parish. (3) In Catholic usage, a religious institute (qv) for priests, monks, brothers or nuns living the religious life.

**Congregation for the Evangelization of Peoples.** See Sacred Congregation.

**Congregation for the Oriental Churches.** See Sacred Congregation.

**Congregation of Bishops.** Office in Roman Curia.

CONGREGATION. Methodist church in Korea.

**Congregational.** Congregationalist (qv).

**congregational publisher, congregation publisher.** See publishers (Jehovah's Witnesses).

**Congregationalism.** A Protestant tradition with a system of church government in which the local congregation has full control and final authority over church matters within its own area.

**Congregationalist.** One who belongs to a Congregational church.

**Congregationalists.** Followers of Congregational tradition still so termed (many Congregational denominations have joined united churches since 1960). Global membership: (1970) 103 denominations with 11,974 churches and 1,171,300 adult members; total community (1970) 2,290,700, (1980) 2,659,600, (1985) 2,865,700.

**congregations.** For global statistics, see worship centres, also religious institutes.

**congresses on evangelism.** National or international conferences specifically on evangelism, organized by Conservative Evangelicals. Some 45 congresses have been organized since the first, the 1966 World Congress on Evangelism (Berlin).

**conscientious objector.** One who refuses to serve, or is exempted from serving, in the armed forces, or to bear arms, as contrary to his moral or religious principles.

**conscientization** (from the Portuguese, *conscientização*). Consciousness-raising; learning collectively to perceive social, political and economic contradictions and injustices and teaching the masses to take action against the oppressive elements of reality. The movement began in Brazil in the 1950s with the teaching of illiterates under Paulo Freire.

**consecration.** The solemn dedication of a bishop or Christian monarch, or of the eucharistic elements.

**conservatism.** The tendency to accept an existing situation and to be cautious towards or suspicious of change.

**Conservative Catholics.** Followers of recent schisms ex Church of Rome in conservative or reactionary direction, rejecting authority of pope, protesting against up-dating or liberal trends; Tridentinists (qv), Traditional Catholics. Global membership: (1970) 58 denominations with 2,365 churches and 1,368,100 adult members; total community (1970) 2,731,200, (1980) 4,066,600, (1985) 4,798,000.

**Conservative Evangelicals.** Evangelicals in Protestant and Anglican churches who hold the theologically conservative doctrine of the verbal inspiration of the Bible, and all persons affiliated to denominations holding Conservative Evangelical doctrines.

**Conservative Methodists.** Holiness Christians (qv).

**Constantinople.** One of the 4 major patriarchates of the early Church, formally a patriarchate from AD 451; New Rome, or the 'Second Rome', seat of the Ecumenical Patriarchate (qv); now the see of 2 rival patriarchates and patriarchs, Eastern Orthodox and Armenian Apostolic.

**Constantinopolitan.** Byzantine (qv).

**constituency.** The body of supporters of followers of a specific church, denomination, tradition, council, confession, or religion.

**constitution.** A written instrument embodying the system of fundamental rules determining the powers and duties of official bodies and the people's guaranteed rights, and constituting the organic law of church or state. Most large churches and councils have formal constitutions for guiding procedure. Most states have constitutions which describe whether the state regards itself as religious, secular, or atheistic.

**constructed languages.** Artificial languages deliberately

invented or constructed so as to provide a global universal language; total, over 500 attempts. The most successful is Esperanto (5 million speakers), a Romance/Germanic language, since 1887; Volapük (1879; Germanic); and Interlingua (1920; primarily Romance). All have Scripture translations.

**consultations.** Discussions, conversations or bilateral or mutilateral dialogues between churches of different confessions, with a view to better mutual understanding and eventual organic union.

**consumer price index.** An index showing changes over time in the price level of goods and services, relative usually to 1970 prices (= 100) in the country concerned; the principal means for calculating the inflation rate (qv).

**contemplative.** One who practises meditation on spiritual things as a private devotion.

**contestation** (French). A method of disputation for confronting ecclesiastical authorities with the realities of a bad situation, developed in the 1970s by Roman Catholic priests in Latin Europe.

**continental conciliarism.** There are about 27 continent-wide multidenominational councils of churches, excluding confessional continental councils.

**Continental Pietists.** Moravians (qv).

**continuous evangelization.** Evangelization implemented by a constant and continual complex of evangelistic activities.

**convent.** A house or association of female recluses devoted to the religious life under a superior; a nunnery.

**conventual prior.** A prior (qv).

**conversations.** In ecumenical terminology, discussions between churches or denominations where as yet no organic union is publicly envisaged nor constitutional questions discussed.

**conversion.** The change from one belief, faith or religion to another.

**conversion change.** Change in religious allegiance in a country or body, i.e. the annual nett aggregate of conversions to the body of new adherents from other religions or religious bodies, minus defections (sometimes termed apostasies) from it of former adherents leaving to join other religions or religious bodies.

**Conversos.** Marranos (qv).

**convert.** A person converted to a religious belief, faith or religion from another religion.

**converted.** The state of having been converted to faith in Christ.

**converted Christians.** Those who have had, or claim to have had, an experience of conversion to Christ; committed Christians (qv).

**conveyors.** See decision-makers.

**conviction.** In evangelization, the state or extent of a population being convinced or persuaded or compelled to admit the truth of the gospel.

**Coptic.** Oriental Orthodox liturgical tradition dating back to Apostolic era. Global membership: (1970) 16 major churches with 2,019 congregations and 3,491,800 adult members; total community (1970) 6,027,900, (1980) 7,281,000, (1985) 7,918,500.

**Coptic Calendar.** Calendar of the Coptic Orthodox Church, and still used also by the government of Egypt for agricultural events (planting, harvesting); begun AD 284 at end of the age of martyrdom, 12 months each of 30 days each year; thus AD 1980 = Coptic 1696.

COPTS. Cairo Bible study for 7,000 led by Patriarch Shenouda.

**Coptic Orthodox Patriarchate of Alexandria.** Oriental Orthodox. Global constituency in canonical relationship: (1970) 17,959,300, (1980) 22,736,900, (1985) 25,251,600.

**Coptic rite.** Catholic rite for Egyptian Copts under Rome. Global membership: (1970) 175 parishes, 64,000 adults, 110,000 total community.

**corporately-evangelized.** A society or people who have been evangelized not individually but collectively, together with their traditions and institutions.
**corps.** In Salvation Army usage, a centre for the propagation of the gospel under one or more officers.
**correspondence courses.** In this field, there are over 320 Christian centres and organizations significant at the national or wider levels.
**council.** An assembly of ecclesiastics or church representatives convened to discuss matters of doctrine, discipline, law, morals, etc.
**Council for World Mission.** Originated as London Missionary Society in 1795; 1955, renamed Congregational Council for World Mission; 1976, renamed Council for World Mission.
**counselling.** A professional service designed to guide an individual to a better understanding of his problems and potentialities by utilizing modern psychological principles.
**country.** The land of a person's origin, birth, residence, or citizenship; motherland; a term covering both sovereign nations and non-sovereign territories.
**country's population.** Defined here as the total present-in-area resident population of a country at a given date or mid-year date.
**courier.** A person carrying messages, news or information secretly or clandestinely to, within or from underground or illegal churches in anti-Christian lands.
**co-operative** (broader than credit union). An enterprise or organization owned by and operated for the benefit of those using its services.
**co-responsible evangelization.** In Roman Catholic usage, evangelization shared among the various ranks of clergy and laity.
**co-responsibility.** In Roman Catholic usage, church government through all levels of the church, involving priests, religious personnel and laity in the whole process of consultation and decision-making.
**co-religionist.** A person having the same religion as another.
**credit unions.** Co-operative savings and credit associations that make small loans to their members at low interest rates; widespread among Roman Catholics, with 4,742 credit unions in Africa with 407,247 members (1975) and assets of US$28 million.
**creeds.** Brief authoritative doctrinal formulae beginning 'Credo' (Latin: I believe) intended to define what a Christian synod or church holds to be true and essential, and to exclude false doctrine.
**Creole.** In English usage, a Mulatto or person of mixed Black/White blood, or his language. In Spanish and French usage, a locally-born Spanish-speaking or French-speaking White (in the Antilles, Indian Ocean, etc), or his language.
**creole.** In linguistic terminology, a composite language or pidgin (qv) that has become the standard or native language of a community.
**Criollo.** A Spanish-speaking Creole or Mulatto.
**crisis theology.** Neo-orthodoxy (qv), especially in its pessimistic view of human nature.
**cross-cultural missionaries.** Full-time Christian workers sent by their churches to work among peoples of a different culture, either within their own nations or abroad.
**crown colony.** A colony of Britain over which the British crown through a governor retains some control.
**crude birth rate.** The unstandardized birth rate, not adjusted for influence of age or other variables.
**crude death rate.** The unstandardized death rate, not adjusted for influence of age or other variables.
**crusade evangelism.** Mass evangelism through organized city-wide campaigns with most denominations co-operating.
**Crusades.** Seven major military campaigns from AD 1096-1270 by the Western church to recover the Holy Land from Islam.
**crusades.** Organized evangelistic mass campaigns in large cities a week or more in length.
**crypto-Christians.** Secret believers in Christ not professing publicly, nor publicly baptized, nor enumerated or known in government census or public-opinion poll, hence unknown to the state or the public or society (but usually affiliated and known to churches), of 7 distinct types: (1) unorganized individuals secretly affiliated to or attending legal churches, including persons who choose to identify themselves publicly as non-Christians; (2) individuals or congregations permanently exiled, deported or in prison or labour camps, treated as non-religious by the state but who remain believing Christians; (3) members of unregistered denominations, and unregistered congregations in legal denominations, which are forced to operate illegally by the state's refusal to grant registration (sometimes termed churches of silence, or catacomb churches); (4) members of organized deliberately-clandestine networks of illegal underground churches; (5) members of churches or marginal bodies in certain countries opposed to the state hence refusing to divulge their affiliation to census enumerators; (6) members of organized movements of believers in Christ who choose not to regard or identify themselves as Christians (but as Hindus, Muslims, non-religious, etc); and (7) isolated radio believers (qv) in non-Christian or anti-Christian areas remote from existing legal churches. Global total: (1970) 55,699,700, (1980) 70,395,000, (1985) 78,184,800.
**crypto-Communists.** Secret sympathizers with Communism or secretly members of a Communist party.
**crypto-Evangelicals.** Secret Evangelicals or sympathizers with Evangelicalism in states or churches hostile to it.
**crypto-Jews.** Persons adhering secretly to Judaism, though professedly Christians; including Marranos (qv).
**crypto-Muslims.** Persons adhering secretly to Islam, though professedly Christians.
**cult.** A religion or minority religious group holding beliefs regarded as unorthdox or spurious; a sect.
**cultist.** A devotee or practitioner of a cult; a sectarian.
**cultural barrier.** A cultural frontier (qv).
**cultural distance.** The number of cultural frontiers or barriers that exist between persons of one culture and those of another culture; up to a maximum of 6 frontiers.
**cultural frontier.** The line of demarcation between one culture and another. As defined in this Encyclopedia (Part 4), there are up to 6 frontiers between any pair of the worlds' cultures.
**culture.** The patterned way in which a homogeneous people do things together; an integrated system of socially standardized actions, beliefs, thoughts, feelings, values, customs and institutions, all learned rather than inherited, and artifacts characteristic of a community; the total pattern of human behaviour and its products embodied in thought, speech, action and artifacts and dependent upon man's capacity for learning and transmitting knowledge to succeeding generations, which bind a society together and give it a sense of identity, dignity, security and continuity; a worldview at the centre together with values, standards of judgement and conduct, language (with proverbs, myths, folk-tales, arts), land and a common history.
**culture area, culture province.** A geographic unit in which are found similar cultures, i.e. similar patterns of cultural traits and similar modes of subsistence.
**cultures.** The exact total of cultures or peoples in particular areas depends on the exact definition used. On our definition here (see Part 4), the world has 8,993 constituent peoples or cultures, with 7,010 distinct languages.
**cultures, Christian.** See Christian cultures.
**curate.** In Anglicanism and Catholicism, (1) a clergyman who has the cure or care of souls, (2) a clergyman assisting a rector or vicar.
**cure of souls.** The spiritual charge of a parish.
**Curia.** The full body of organized congregations, tribunals and offices that aid the pope in the administration and government of the Roman Catholic Church.
**cursillistas.** Roman Catholics attending a cursillo (qv).
**cursillo** (Spanish: short course). A worldwide Roman Catholic movement emphasizing devotion to Christ and spiritual formation of Christian leadership and apostolate; a cursillo can be made only once in one's lifetime, hence is not a retreat.
**Cushitic.** A Middle Eastern ethnolinguistic family. Global population: (1970) 18,395,100, (1980) 23,584,900, (1985) 26,376,900.
**Czech/Slavonic.** Eastern Orthodox liturgical tradition using Czech and Slavonic in the liturgy. Global membership: (1970) 141 churches with 147,000 adult members; total community (1970) 200,000, (1980) 208,000, (1985) 212,000.

## D

**dagoba.** A stupa (qv).
**daily attenders.** Affiliated Christians (church members) who attend church services daily or several times a week.
**dancing.** See trumping.
**Darbyites.** Exclusive Brethren (qv).
**data.** Detailed information of any kind; experientially encountered facts or principles, upon which inferences or arguments can be built or from which an intellectual system of any sort can be constructed.
**data bank.** A collection of data and information organized for retrieval by a recall scheme.
**database.** A description of the principles of organization of a data bank; the raw data from which a survey manuscript is compiled.
**data-processing.** The use of computers for storing, sorting, re-arranging and retrieving information.
**Dataria.** An office of the Roman Curia where dates were added to papal letters, now charged with investigating the fitness of candidates for papal benefices.
**de facto** (Latin). In fact, in reality, actually, existing in fact (in contrast to de jure).
**de facto population.** The actual population, enumerated population, or present-in-area population, i.e. physically-present whether residents or non-residents, based on exactly where people have slept or spent the night; made up of all persons actually in the area on a particular day or census date, covering residents, non-residents, visitors and transients, but excluding residents temporarily absent.
**de jure** (Latin). By right, of right, by law, legal (in contrast to de facto).
**de jure population.** The population of a given area who normally inhabit and reside in the area, i.e. who are permanent, habitual, regular and legal residents or inhabitants, based on where people normally or regularly sleep or spend the night; consisting of all persons who habitually live or reside in the area, covering residents and temporarily-absent residents but excluding non-residents, visitors and transients.
**deacon.** A cleric in major orders ranking above a sub-deacon and below a priest; in Protestantism, often a ruling lay elder.
**deaconess.** In Anglicanism, an ordained woman assigned to parish work; in Protestantism, a woman in an order or sisterhood serving the church in hospitals, schools or on the mission field.
**deaf, the.** About 400 million people (10% of the world) are deaf or have hearing problems. Many denominations and service agencies across the globe minister to the deaf (e.g. Assemblies of God, USA, has 111 all-deaf congregations with 70 pastors).
**dean.** The head of the chapter of a body of canons in an Anglican cathedral; head over 10 monks in a Roman Catholic monastery.
**deanery.** The jurisdiction of a dean.
**death rate.** The number of deaths per year in a population expressed as a percentage or permillage of the total population.
**dechristianization.** The process of causing to turn from Christianity or to deprive of Christian characteristics.
**dechristianized.** See disaffiliated Christians.
**decision cards.** Printed cards filled in by enquirers or professing converts at evangelistic campaigns, giving name, address, age, and nature of decision being made.

DECISIONS. 18,916 enquirers in 1978 campaign (Bolivia).

**decisions.** During evangelistic campaigns, enquirers or seekers who make professions of faith in Christ, often for the first time, and usually by public profession and the signing of decision cards.
**decision-makers.** Those individuals, classes, groups, or elites in any society who take initiatives, act as censors, and make decisions particularly with regard to new situations or innovations arising during times of rapid social change. They are usually estimated to number from 5% to 15% of the total population.

**declared Christians.** Professing Christians (qv).

**declericalization.** The process of ridding a society of clerical influence deemed to involve dogmatic and authoritarian control of religious matters by clergy.

**deconfessionalization.** The process of ridding a society of excessive adherence to confessionalism (qv).

**defections.** Individuals lost from a religion or religious body either to other religions or religious bodies or to no religion (agnosticism, atheism).

**defections from the priesthood.** Roman Catholics leaving the priesthood: (1) secular: (1970) 1,848, (1971) 1,894, (1972) 1,964, (1973) 1,868, (1974) 1,778, (1975) 1,560; (2) religious: (1974) 1,686, (1975) 1,446.

**degrees in religious studies.** Academic degrees may be taken in (1980) over 1,500 departments of theology or religion in as many universities across the world.

**deist.** An adherent of deism, a rationalist movement based on natural religion, reason and morality, and belief in an otiose God.

**Deliverance-Pentecostals.** Perfectionist-Pentecostals (qv).

**democratic rule.** A measure of the extent to which all de facto political power is in the hands of the populace themselves.

**demographer.** A specialist in demography.

**demographic.** Relating to the dynamic balance of a population.

**demographic audience.** Total listening/viewing community including children, influenced regularly by Christian radio/TV broadcasts.

**demographic commitment profile.** A graphical presentation showing the commitment to Christianity of all sections of a particular population.

**demographic evangelization.** The extent of evangelization among a large or sizeable population, or the spreading of the gospel through all types of evangelizing activity including the church's evangelism.

**demographic increase.** An increase, or annual increase, in the size of a population due to secular or non-religious causes.

**demographic inertia.** The observable fact that large populations only change their basic characteristics, including religious characteristics, gradually or slowly over a period of years.

**demographic statistics.** The art of collecting and presenting statistical information about a population.

**demographic time series.** The values of a demographic variable over a period of time.

**demography.** The scientific and statistical study of human populations, primarily with respect to their size, structure, density, growth, distribution, development, migration and vital statistics.

**demon.** A pagan or unclean or evil spirit.

**demonology.** The systematized religious doctrine of evil spirits.

**demonstration.** In evangelization, the act of making the gospel known or evident by visible or tangible means; showing, manifesting, indicating, proving the merits of the gospel to others.

**denomination.** An organized Christian church or tradition or religious group or community of believers or aggregate of worship centres or congregations, usually within a specific country, whose component congregations and members are called by the same name in different areas, regarding themselves as an autonomous Christian church distinct from other denominations, churches and traditions. For totals, see under denominations.

**denominational.** Relating to, or controlled by, a denomination.

**denominationalism.** Devotion to denominational principles or interests; the emphasizing of denominational differences to the point of being narrowly exclusive.

**denominationally-evangelized.** Used of a people's evangelization seen only from the standpoint of a single denomination which does not acknowledge the work of other denominations.

**denominations.** For exact definition, see above under denomination. Global total: (1970) 18,162 denominations in 223 countries, (1975) 19,414, (1980) 20,781, (1985) 22,150.

**dental mission.** A foreign missionary society specializing in dentistry and dental services.

**dependant.** An economically inactive person dependent on others.

**dependency.** A territory politically dependent on another country or nation.

**depopulation.** Population decline in a specific area.

**deprogramming.** The process of forcibly changing or altering a person's religious beliefs; particularly, reversing the programmed indoctrination imparted by modern cultic organizations.

**desacralization.** The act of ceremonially divesting a taboo of supernatural qualities and rendering it non-sacred; also used for dechristianization (qv).

**desertification.** The process by which previously-valuable agricultural land or forest becomes a desert.

**development.** In Christian usage, not only a techno-economic process but primarily a process 'by which both persons and societies come to realize the full potential of human life in a context of social justice, with an emphasis on self-reliance' (Montreux Conference Report), including a more equal distribution of wealth, including gross national product, in a just and human order. In this field, there are over 220 Christian organizations significant at the national or wider levels.

**deviations, Christian.** Marginal Christian movements regarded as departures from the established body of Christian beliefs.

**devil.** The personal supreme spirit of evil and unrighteousness in Jewish and Christian theology.

**dharma** (Sanskrit). In Hinduism, social custom, the caste system, religion, the body of cosmic principles by which all things exist; in Buddhism, ideal truth, element of existence.

**diakonia** (Greek). Service to others; the witness of service.

**dialect.** A local or regional variety or variant of language.

**dialectical materialism.** The theory of reality advanced by Marx and Engels and adopted as official Soviet philosophy, maintaining the independent objective reality of matter and its priority both in time and logical importance overmind; al mostri chaterialisim.

**dialectical theology.** Neo-orthodoxy (qv), holding that man's attempts to know God by his own reasoning must give way to faith.

**dialogue.** An exchange of ideas and opinions between a group of Christians and a group of non-Christians.

**diaspora.** A people of one country dispersed into other countries; the migration, spread, scattering, exile of a people abroad; especially the dispersion of Christians isolated from their own communions.

**diaspora church.** A church or denomination formerly strongly centralized but now dispersed thinly over a wide area including abroad.

**diaspora missionaries.** Full-time Christian workers who have usually themselves been emigrants, refugees, deportees or returnees, who now serve their own ethnic communities in diaspora as civilian or military chaplains, evangelists, religious educators, et alii.

**dicastery.** A department of the Roman Curia in Vatican City. The Curia has 28 principal dicasteries.

**didache** (NT Greek). Teaching, the teaching of the Apostles.

**differential fertility.** The actual reproductive performance of one part of a population by comparison with that of another part.

**Digambara** ('Sky-clad', or Naked, or Botika). A member of a major schism (AD 83) within Jainism originally abandoning all worldly possessions including clothes, and asserting that women cannot attain salvation.

**digital computer.** A computer that operates with numbers expressed directly as digits in a decimal, binary, or other system.

**dignitaries.** A collective term for clergy and hierarchs holding positions of dignity or honour in the church.

**diocesan.** (1) A bishop having jurisdiction over a diocese. (2) Relating to a diocese.

**diocesan association.** In Anglican terminology, a loose organization of church members in Britain who raise money to support one particular Anglican diocese in a developing country. Some 25 exist in Britain.

**diocesan bishop.** A bishop having jurisdiction over a diocese.

**diocesan clergy.** In Roman Catholic usage, secular clergy serving in a diocese, as contrasted with religious or regular clergy in religious houses or monasteries. World total (1976): 259,331.

**diocesan synod.** In Roman Catholic usage since Vatican II, a one-time occasion or assembly of the whole people of God (50% of whom must be priests)

**dioceses** (symbol D). Areas over which bishops have ecclesiastical authority.

**diplomatic representation.** The Holy See, as a sovereign state, maintains diplomatic relations with 81 nations (in 1974) through 37 nunciatures with a nuncio, and 42 nunciatures headed by a pro-nuncio; and in addition maintains relations with nationwide Roman Catholic churches through 26 apostolic delegations.

**directories.** See yearbooks.

**disaffiliated Christians.** Dechristianized persons, or post-Christians: baptized Roman Catholics (or other Christians) enumerated as affiliated by a majority or state-linked church but who have recently formally withdrawn or disaffiliated themselves completely from Christianity and now profess to be non-religious (agnostics) or atheists; i.e. recent withdrawals from state or majority churches still however regarded as members by those churches, although in fact now backsliders, lapsed, or apostates. Global total: (1970) 10,848,200, (1980) 15,365,500 in 9 countries, (1985) 17,504,100.

**disaster preparedness.** Programmes organized by churches and denominations, especially the Seventh-day Adventist Church, with relief, medical-aid centres and mobile disaster-aid units around the world ready to deal with either natural or man-made disasters as they arise.

**disbelief.** Refusal to believe; withholding or rejection of belief; atheism, scepticism, irreligion.

**disciple.** A committed follower; in biblical usage, any believer in Jesus Christ (not restricted only to mature or fully-committed or dedicated followers).

**disciple** (verb). To give peoples the opportunity to become followers of Christ; to train individual believers extensively over a long period, with a view to them also becoming disciplers in multiplication evangelism (qv).

**discipler.** A Christian worker aiming to disciple a few believers with a view to making them also disciplers.

**Disciples** (Churches of Christ) (Restoration Movement). Protestant tradition also known as Restorationist, Restoration Baptist, Campbellite, or simply 'Christian'. Global membership: (1970) 118 denominations with 33,866 churches and 5,270,400 adult members; total community (1970) 7,876,100, (1980) 8,474,600, (1985) 8,783,200.

**discipline.** One of the major areas of learning in the academic world.

**discipline, church.** A body of laws and practical rules relating to conduct and church government. Church members breaking or flouting such laws may be placed temporarily under discipline (usually exclusion from communion or the Lord's Table), or even, eventually be excommunicated (qv).

**discipling.** The first of the 3 stages in church planting and growth (discipling, baptizing, perfecting, based on the Great Commission in Matthew 28.19), involving the initial or preliminary bringing of a whole people to renounce idolatry or unbelief as a group, and to a group acknowledgement of Christ as Lord; measured as the total number of all professing Christians.

**disestablishment.** The act of a state in sundering the legal relationships between it and its established church or churches.

**dispensary.** A place where medicines are dispensed to ambulant patients; see medical centres.

**dispensationalism.** Adherence to or advocacy of a futurist premillennialist system of interpreting history in terms of a series of God's dispensations, or 7 periods of history during which a particular divine revelation has predominated in the affairs of mankind; usually, futurist premillennialist and pretribulational.

**displaced person.** A person who has been moved by a public authority from his place of origin.

**disputed episcopal churches.** Autocephalous Catholic and other episcopal churches with disputed claim to apostolic succession of bishops.

**dissent.** Religious dissension or nonconformity.

**dissenter.** One who differs from an established church in the matter of doctrines, rites or government; a nonconformist.

**dissertation.** An extended systematic written treatment of a subject submitted for a doctoral degree, typically based on independent research and giving evidence of a candidate's mastery of both his own subject and of scholarly method.

**district.** An ecclesiastical division in larger denominations.

**district superintendent.** In Methodism, a minister with oversight of churches and workers in a district.

**divine.** A priest, clergyman, theologian, one skilled in divinity.

**divine healing.** Healing attributed to the direct agency of God, usually in response to faith.

**Divine Science.** See Religious Science.

**divinity.** The science of divine things; the science that deals with God, his laws and moral government, and the way of salvation; theology.

**division.** The act, process, or an instance of dividing into parts or portions; schism, breakoff, secession.
**documentation centre.** A centre for the collecting, assembling, coding and disseminating of recorded knowledge comprehensively treated, and for the processing of all kinds of documentation.
**dogma.** A doctrine or body of doctrines of theology and religion formally stated and authoritatively proclaimed by a church.
**dogmatic constitution.** The most solemn form of conciliar utterance emanating from a Roman Catholic ecumenical council. The most imposing achievement of Vatican II was 'Constitutio Dogmatica de Ecclesia', also called 'Lumen Gentium'.
**domestic church.** A term used in Roman Catholic circles for the family, or believers in a family.
**dormant Christians.** See non-practising Christians.
**double affiliation.** See doubly-affiliated Christians.

DOUBLING. Two AACJM Apostles (Zimbabwe).

**doubling.** The practice, in Africa and India, of having 2 preachers for a sermon: the first preaching a sentence at a time, the second repeating the sentence for emphasis and often (in the open air) louder or in a different direction.
**doubly-affiliated Christians.** Persons affiliated to or claimed by 2 denominations at once (especially by Evangelical and Catholic churches in Latin America and Latin Europe, and by state churches and free churches in Scandinavia). Global total: (1970) 26,711,600, (1980) 36,302,300 in 34 countries, (1985) 41,505,400.
**doubter.** An unbeliever, agnostic, sceptic.
**drama, religious.** See religious drama.
**Dravidian.** An Indo-Iranian ethnolinguistic family. Global population: (1970) 140,097,700, (1980) 179,037,300, (1985) 199,897,400.
**Druzes.** Members of an 11th-century Muslim Shia Ismaili schism with Christian and Jewish elements; strongest in Syria and Lebanon. Global adherents: (1970) 374,800, (1980) 505,100.
**dual citizenship.** Dual nationality, multiple nationality; the status of an individual who is a citizen of 2 or more states.
**dual membership.** Overlapping membership (qv).
**Dunkers.** Dippers; German Baptists practising trine immersion, love feasts and simplicity of life. Global membership: (1970) 2,075 churches with 305,400 adult members; total community (1970) 513,800, (1980) 619,100, (1985) 676,000.
**Dupka.** Karma-pa or Red Hat (Unreformed) Lamaism (qv).
**DXers.** Amateur practitioners of long-distance radio transmission.
**dynamic equivalence translation.** A translation of Scripture, as developed by the United Bible Societies, designed to be the closest natural equivalent to the source-language message, i.e. to discover what the text meant at the time of writing in order to communicate its full equivalent meaning today (e.g. in English, the NEB, JB, GNB Bibles, with the NIV halfway between formal correspondence and dynamic equivalent). By contrast, a formal correspondence translation is an exact or literal or word-for-word translation of the original.
**dynamic equivalence church.** A local church, or denomination that has an equivalent impact on or in its own society and culture to that of the original New Testament church, with particular reference to indigeneity, degree of foreign dominance, relevance, vitality, scriptural quality, decision-making patterns, self-image, community-held image, et alia.
**Dyophysites.** Eastern Orthodox, Chalcedonian.

## E

**Early African.** One of the 13 geographical races of mankind, speaking 57 languages. Global population: (1970) 422,800, (1980) 547,000, (1985) 615,500.
**Early Fathers.** The Apostolic Fathers (qv).
**East Syrians.** Assyrians, Nestorians, Syro-Chaldeans.
**Easter.** Annual church celebration commemorating Christ's resurrection.
**Easter attender.** A church member who attends church at Easter.
**Easter communicant.** A church member who receives communion at Easter.
**Eastern Church.** A collective term for Eastern Orthodox, Oriental Orthodox, Assyrian (Nestorian), Eastern-rite Catholic and other churches east of the Mediterranean.
**Eastern Orthodox.** Chalcedonian Christians, sometimes collectively referred to as Greek Orthodox, and excluding Oriental Orthodox (qv). Global membership: (1970) 121,130,000 (84.5% of all Orthodox), (1980) 132,835,000 (82.6%), (1985) 138,937,000 (81.9%).
**Eastern Syrians.** East Syrians (qv).
**Eastern-rite** (Oriental-rite) **Catholics.** All Roman Catholics or Catholics in communion with the Church of Rome who follow rites other than the Latin rite (totalling 28 rites and sub-rites). A full listing is given in Part 3. Global constituency: (1970) 7,084,300, (1980) 8,799,300, (1985) 9,682,800 (1.1% of all Roman Catholics).
**ecclesia** (NT Greek). A church; in particular, a local congregation of the Christadelphians.
**ecclesial communion.** In Roman Catholic usage, collegiality or co-responsibility (qv).
**ecclesial community.** A basic community (qv).
**ecclesiarch.** A high church official or ruling prelate.
**ecclesiastic.** A person in holy orders or consecrated to the service of the church: a clergyman.
**ecclesiastical.** Relating to the church as a formal and established institution.
**ecclesiastical name.** A new Christian name taken on election by popes, patriarchs and other high ecclesiastics, usually one in a series down the centuries.
**ecclesiastical province.** A group of dioceses, territorially contiguous, forming an ecclesiastical unit; so termed because originally coincident with the Provinces of the Roman empire. (See under province).
**ecclesiastical territories.** In Roman Catholic usage, circumscriptions or jurisdictions (qv).
**ecclesiastical tradition.** A church's or denomination's main tradition, family, rite, churchmanship, etc, with which it is most closely connected historically. Global total of all major traditions (1980): 156, including 29 Roman Catholic rites and sub-rites.
**ecclesiastical type.** A descriptive typology combining ecclesiastico-cultural major bloc, and ecclesiastical tradition.
**ecclesiastico-cultural major blocs.** A global typology of 7 basic types of Christianity: Anglican, Catholic (non-Roman), marginal Protestant, Non-White indigenous, Orthodox, Protestant, Roman Catholic.
**ecclesiography.** Descriptive analyses of churches and denominations.
**ecclesiola.** A 'church within the church', or small group of Christians living a distinct and nearly separate existence, yet remaining within the institutional church without open schism.
**ecclesiology.** The science or study of the doctrine of the church, or church policy, or the study of ecclesiastical art and antiquities.
**ecology.** The study of the relation of social organization and culture to physical environment and technology.
**ecumenical.** Worldwide, general, universal, catholic; relating to the whole of a body of churches.
**ecumenical centres.** Centres operated by the churches primarily to sponsor ecumenical or interdenominational contacts and understanding. Total centres significant at national or wider levels number over 300.
**ecumenical commission.** (1) A Roman Catholic committee set up to deal with other separated churches in a particular diocese or country. (2) An organization serving the major denominations in an area. In this field some 200 significant commissions or agencies exist.
**ecumenical councils.** Assemblies of bishops and other ecclesiastical representatives of the whole world's churches, whose decisions on doctrine liturgy, discipline, et alia, are binding on all Christians in those churches. Eastern Orthodox accept only the first 7 ecumenical councils, up to Nicea II (AD 787); Roman Catholics accept 21 councils including Vatican I and Vatican II (1962-5).
**ecumenical Evangelicals.** Conciliar Evangelicals (qv).
**ecumenical movement.** The movement to bring together all denominations and Christian bodies, for fellowship, consultation, joint action, and eventually organic union.
**ecumenical patriarch.** The patriarch of Constantinople, the acknowledged highest ecclesiastical office in the Eastern Orthodox Church by virtue of a primacy of honour.
**Ecumenical Patriarchate of Constantinople.** Leading patriarchate of the Eastern Orthodox world, since AD 451; New Rome, the 'Second Rome'. Global constituency: (1970) 117,126,000, (1980) 128,665,000, (1985) 134,533,000.
**ecumenicity.** The quality or state of being ecumenical.
**ecumenics.** The study of the nature, mission, problems, and strategy of the Christian church from the perspective of its ecumenical character as a worldwide Christian fellowship.
**ecumenism.** Ecumenical principles and practices as exemplified in the ecumenical movement.
**ecumenist.** An advocate of ecumenism.
**education rate.** The percentage of the school-age population (aged 5-24) who are enrolled in schools.
**ekistics.** The science, art, study, development of human habitation and dwellings.
**electronic data processing** (EDP). The manipulation of data by means of a computer (qv).
**eligible communicant.** A church member in good standing who is eligible to partake of the sacrament of the Lord's Supper, whether in fact he does so or not.
**emigrant.** A person who leaves a country or region to establish permanent residence elsewhere.
**emigration.** The movement of migrants out of a particular territory.
**emigre.** A person forced to emigrate by political or other circumstances beyond his control.
**encyclical.** A letter sent by a bishop or high church official, especially the Roman Catholic pope, treating a matter of grave or timely importance and intended for extensive circulation.
**encyclopedia.** A work that treats comprehensively either all the various branches of knowledge, or a particular branch of knowledge, arranged either alphabetically or topically.
**enquirers.** See decisions.
**enrolments.** The term used to enumerate the total number of persons in an area or country who have registered for postal Bible correspondence courses, either active at present, or an accumulated total over the years since courses began there.
**enthusiasm.** Originally, divine possession or frenzy; nowadays, ardent zeal or fervour, impassioned emotion, especially in religious causes.
**enumeration.** Any operation which is designed to yield a population total using a list rather than a simple count.
**enumeration, Christian.** The spelling-out, describing in detail, listing in order, counting, or numbering, of a Christian population or of some Christian entity or activity.
**enumerator.** A government employee who administers a census schedule of questions direct to the populace.
**environment.** The aggregate of social, cultural and ecological conditions (as customs, laws, language, religion, economic and political organization, climate, pollution, etc) that influence the life of an individual or community.
**eparchy.** (1) In the Eastern Orthodox Church, a diocese or ecclesiastical province, especially in the early centuries AD. (2) In Roman Catholic usage, a diocese of an Eastern rite, especially Malankara (India).
**episcopacy.** Government of the church by bishops or by a hierarchy.
**Episcopal.** Used of churches governed by bishops, especially in North American Anglicanism.
**episcopal.** Hierarchical, related to a bishop, a diocese, or a denomination or tradition governed by bishops.
**episcopal area.** In Episcopalian (Anglican) usage, a subdivision of a diocese that is placed under the episcopal authority of a suffragan or assistant bishop.
**episcopal commissariat** (symbol EC). A Roman Catholic diocese under a political regime not recognized by the Holy See, which attaches it to a diocese elsewhere.
**episcopal conferences.** Formally-constituted conferences of Roman Catholic bishops, totalling 105 national and 18 international conferences (1980).
**Episcopalians.** North American or USA usage for

the term Anglicans (qv).

**episcopate.** The whole body of bishops; office of a bishop, or the period over which a bishop is in office.

EPISCOPATE. 420 Anglican bishops (Lambeth, UK).

**episcopi vagantes** (Latin). Bishops-at-large (qv).

**erection.** In Roman Catholic usage, the formal establishment of a new diocese.

**eremite.** A hermit; a Christian living for religious reasons in solitary confinement.

**eschatological sign.** The missionary preaching of the gospel among all nations as the sign of the imminence of the End (the Second Coming of Christ), given in Matthew 24.14 and Mark 13.10.

**eschatology.** The doctrine of the Last Things; Christian doctrine of the Second Coming of Christ and the ultimate destiny or purpose of mankind and of the world.

**Eskimo-Aleut.** An Arctic Mongoloid ethnolinguistic family. Global population: (1970) 61,000, (1980) 73,600, (1985) 79,300.

**esoteric.** Used of sects whose doctrines and rites guard a mystery known only to the initiated.

**Esoteric Vehicle.** Tantrayana, or Tantrism school of Buddhists (qv).

**established church.** A church that is recognized by law as the official church of a nation, supported by civil authority; state church, national church.

**ethics, Christian.** The discipline dealing with what is good and bad or right and wrong, or with moral duty and obligation, from the Christian standpoint; the principles of conduct governing an individual or a profession.

ETHIOPIAN. Orthodox priest at Timkat festival.

**Ethiopian, Ethiopic.** Oriental Orthodox liturgical tradition, using dead language Ge'ez in its liturgy. Global membership: (1970) 10 denominations with 15,063 churches and 7,041,800 adult members; total community (1970) 11,931,400, (1980) 15,455,900, (1985) 17,333,000.

**Ethiopian Calendar.** Based on the Coptic Calendar (qv), this calendar (still used by church and state in 1980) is exactly 8 years behind the Gregorian Calendar (thus AD 1980 = Ethiopian 1972), begins its year on 11 or 12 September, and has 12 months each of 30 days each year, adjusted at leap years with a 13th month of 5 or 6 days.

**Ethiopian rite.** Rite for Ethiopian Catholics under Rome. Global membership: (1970) 124 parishes, 51,600 adults, 87,000 total community.

**Ethiopic.** (1) A Middle Eastern ethnolinguistic family. Global population: (1970) 8,873,800, (1980) 11,254,100, (1985) 12,520,400. (2) Orthodox liturgical tradition (see Ethiopian).

**ethnic.** Referring to a group distinguished by common cultural characteristics.

**ethnic group.** A group having common physical and mental traits, common heredity and cultural tradition.

**ethnic Muslims.** A term used to describe the 34 million persons (in 1970) belonging to traditionally Muslim nationalities in the USSR, of whom about 82% profess to be or regard themselves as religious Muslims.

**ethnic origin.** The racial, linguistic, tribal or cultural origin of a specific group.

**ethnic religionists.** Adherents of major world religions limited in theory or in practice to a particular ethnolinguistic group or groups; including Confucians, Hindus, Jains, Jews, Parsis, Shintoists, Sikhs, et alia.

**ethnography.** A branch of anthropology that describes the origin and filiation of races and cultures.

**ethnolinguistic composition.** The components parts of a population, with the percentage size of each, adding up to 100%.

**ethnolinguistic family.** A large family of peoples, sometimes termed a local race, or a microrace.

**ethnolinguistic families.** A total of 71 microraces or local races under which all peoples of the world can be described.

**ethnolinguistic people.** An ethnic or racial group speaking its own language or mother tongue.

**ethnology.** The study of a culture on a comparative basis; cultural anthropology.

**eucharist** (NT Greek: thanksgiving). The sacrament of the Lord's Supper.

**eucharistic congress.** A Roman Catholic series of congresses centred on the public celebration of the mass.

**eugenics.** Policies aimed at improving the quality of human populations.

**Eurafrican.** An African ethnolinguistic family; Coloured, Mulatto. Global population: (1970) 3,136,000, (1980) 4,048,700, (1985) 4,538,700.

**Eurasian.** (1) The issue of a European and an Asian. (2) An Asian ethnolinguistic family. Global population: (1970) 174,700, (1980) 222,400, (1985) 247,600.

**Euronesian.** (1) The issue of a European and an Indonesian/Melanesian/Micronesian/Polynesian. (2) A Pacific ethnolinguistic family. Global population: (1970) 1,250,400, (1980) 1,727,700, (1985) 1,982,300.

**European.** One of the 13 geographical races of mankind, with 180 languages. Global population: (1970) 824,646,200, (1980) 894,542,900, (1985) 930,336,300.

**evangelical.** (1) In Protestant and Anglican usage, of similar meaning to Evangelical. (2) In Roman Catholic usage, relating to the gospel.

**evangelical academy.** A German Protestant centre to bring church and secular world into contact; some 17 such centres flourished in West Germany from 1945-75.

**Evangelical Anglicans.** Anglican Evangelicals (qv).

**Evangelical Catholics.** In Latin countries, professing Roman Catholics who also regard themselves as Evangélicos or Evangéliques and are affiliated to churches which the state terms Evangelical (Protestant, Anglican, indigenous or marginal Protestant); in Latin America, Evangélicos who in a census are still regarded as, or profess to be, Roman Catholics. Global total: (1970) 16,648,400, (1980) 24,935,700 in 31 countries, (1985) 29,440,000.

**evangelical counsels.** The vows of the religious life: voluntary poverty, perpetual chastity, entire obedience.

**Evangelicalism.** The doctrines held by Evangelicals.

**Evangelicals.** A sub-division of Protestants consisting of affiliated church members calling themselves evangelicals, or all persons belonging to Evangelical congregations, churches or denominations; characterized by commitment to personal religion (including new birth or personal conversion experience), reliance on Holy Scripture as the only basis for faith and Christian living, emphasis on preaching and evangelism, and usually on conservatism in theology; usually divided into the 3 groupings (qv) Conservative Evangelicals, Conciliar Evangelicals, and Fundamentalists. Global membership: (1970) 124,775,300, (1980) 156,895,200 in 192 countries,

(1985) 174,202,200. Global total including Anglican and Black Evangelicals: (1970) 153,415,000, (1980) 190,650,200, (1985) 210,717,100.

**Evangélico** (Italian, Portuguese, Spanish). The term usually used for Protestant in Latin Europe and America; including also Anglican, marginal Protestant, and Non-White indigenous (Christians).

**evangelism.** The activities involved in spreading the gospel.

**Evangelism-in-Depth.** A programme and philosophy of mobilizing the total membership and resources of the churches of an area for proclamation of the gospel to non-Christians; initiated in 1960 in Latin America, later on other continents; keynote—'The expansion of any movement is in direct proportion to its success in mobilizing its total membership in continuous propagation of its beliefs'.

**evangelist.** One who offers the good news through public preaching.

**evangelistic.** Concerned with offering the good news through public preaching.

**evangelistic association.** A para-church agency formed around the evangelistic ministry of a professional evangelist (mostly in the USA), which then tends to become virtually a separate denomination.

**evangelistic campaigns.** Each year several hundred campaigns of one to ten weeks' duration are held in cities across the world, usually co-operatively by most denominations in an area, specifically for evangelistic purposes.

**evangelistic distance.** The number of distinct religious and cultural frontiers or barriers that exist between a Christian worker, evangelist or missionary, or a group of such, and their target population; measured by adding cultural distance and religious distance, up to a maximum of 11 frontiers.

**evangelistic frontier.** From the standpoint of evangelism, a religious or cultural frontier (qv) which forms a barrier or obstacle to evangelists or other Christian workers.

**evangelistic outreach.** See outreach into the world.

**evangelistic witness.** An Orthodox term used in preference to evangelism or evangelization.

**evangelistics.** The science of the propagation of Christianity.

**evangelization.** (1) The whole process of spreading the good news of the Kingdom of God. (2) The extent to which the good news has been spread. (3) The extent of awareness of Christianity, Christ and the gospel.

**evangelize.** To spread the good news of Jesus Christ, with signs following, persuading and convincing people to obey him as Lord in the fellowship of his church, and to serve him responsibly in the world.

**evangelized.** The state of having had the good news spread or offered; the state of being aware of Christianity, Christ and the gospel.

**evangelized non-Christians.** Persons who are not believers in Christ but have nevertheless become sufficiently aware of Christianity, Christ and the gospel to be regarded as evangelized. Global total: (1970) 1,001,498,000, (1980) 1,560,654,800, (1985) 1,897,319,600.

**evangelizer.** One who spreads the good news; used of (1) Christ, (2) any Christian active in evangelism, and (3) any full-time worker involved in evangelism.

**evangelizing.** Actively involved in spreading the good news.

**evangelizing Christians.** Persons who contribute definitely and consciously to the ongoing process of the evangelization of their own people or country or the world; the effective evangelizing agency among a people or in a country; the force for evangelism; measured as all practising Christians.

**examining chaplain.** In Anglican usage, an archdeacon or other learned clergyman who examines candidates for holy orders; usually 3 or more to each diocese.

**exarch.** The primate of an independent Orthodox church, or bishop with a special charge.

**exarchate** (symbol E). The jurisdiction of an exarch.

**exarchate apostolic** (symbol EA). The jurisdiction of an exarch apostolic, the title for a bishop with a special mission or commission in some Eastern churches.

**Exclusive Brethren.** Followers of Protestant tradition begun 1848 ex Christian Brethren; also termed Closed, Strict, or Plymouth Brethren; exclusive fundamentalist/dispensationalist. Global membership: (1970) 29 denominations with 3,468 assemblies (churches) and 167,200 adult members; total community (1970) 340,100, (1980) 384,400, (1985) 406,800.

**excommunicated.** Persons placed under ecclesiastical censure by competent authority for infraction of

church law or discipline, and then excluded from communion or the sacraments, often permanently. It remains relatively rare in most churches.
**exegesis.** In theology, the explanation of the original meaning of biblical texts.
**exile church.** A denomination that has largely left, or been expelled from, its original homeland by political circumstances and has begun permanent life in a foreign land; mainly from Russia, Estonia, Latvia and Eastern Europe.
**exorcism.** The act or practice of expelling evil spirits by means of prayer or set formulae and rituals; often practised in larger denominations only by professionally competent and authorized clergy.
**expatriate.** A person who resides or lives in a foreign country.
**experiential religions.** Those which lay more emphasis on religious experience than on historical dogma (e.g. mysticism, faith-healing, charismatic renewal, Eastern religions, yoga, TM, etc.)
**exposition.** In preaching or Biblical teaching, the art of interpreting the original meaning (exegesis) and then applying it to contemporary life and issues.
**exposure.** In evangelization, the act or extent of subjecting a population to the influence of the gospel; explaining, laying open, making accessible, making known, setting forth, exhibiting, revealing, disclosing, bringing to light.
**extension growth.** Visible, measureable growth of the church, especially in the planting of new congregations and churches.
**extrapolation.** The estimation of values of a series beyond or outside the range of existing known values.

## F

**faith.** Belief and trust in and loyalty to God in Christ; firm or unquestioning belief in something for which there is no proof; orthodox religious belief; also used for religion, creed, credo.
**faith missions.** A term generally applied to those non-denominational and interdenominational foreign missionary agencies since 1860 whose governing concept is to look to God alone for financial support.
**faithful, the.** The adherents of a system of religious belief, especially Eastern Orthodoxy, baptized Christians as opposed to catechumens.
**faith-healing.** A method or practice of treating diseases by prayer and exercise of faith in God.
**family.** Defined primarily by reference to relationships which pertain to or arise from reproductive processes and which are regulated by law or by custom.
**family income, average.** The total income of an average family or household in an area, computed by multiplying per capita income by average household size (qv).
**fast.** A time in the calendar of certain churches for abstaining from food as contrasted with a feast day.
**fasting.** Abstaining from food voluntarily for a time as a religious duty.
**father.** Used of ecclesiastics, i.e. of Catholic, Orthodox and some Anglican bishops, priests and monks, both in direct address and as title prefixed to the name.
**feast.** A religious festival of rejoicing as opposed to a fast; an annual holy day.
**federation.** A union of nations, states, societies, organizations, churches or denominations.
**federations of religious communities.** See religious institutes, federations of.
**fellowship.** A Christian group with intimate relationship, common purposefulness, brotherhood, partnership, and communion; in some denominations, used of a local worshipping congregation.
**Ferrette succession churches.** Autocephalous Catholic churches under bishops-at-large (qv) whose disputed episcopal orders pass through Mar Julius Ferrette (died 1889).
**fertility.** Capacity for reproducing, actual reproductive capacity, birthrate of a population.
**festival.** A Christian feast day: Christmas, Easter, Whitsuntide, Trinity Sunday, etc.
**festival attenders.** Affiliated Christians (church members) who attend church services of public worship only on the Christian festivals (Christmas, Easter, etc).
**fetishist.** A believer in magical fetishes (objects believed by primitive peoples to have preternatural power).
**field survey.** An inquiry or survey in which information is obtained by personal interview.
**Fijian.** An Oceanic ethnolinguistic family. Global population: (1970) 232,600, (1980) 284,000, (1985) 309,900.
**film.** In the field of cinema and film, there are over 170 significant Christian organizations.
**film libraries.** Many denominations, councils and para-church agencies own and operate libraries of 8mm, 16mm and 35mm movies which are hired out to churches on specific occasions.
**films, religious.** See religious drama.
**financial member.** A term used in some denominations in Africa for a full church member who has paid his annual dues.
**Finnish/Slavonic.** Eastern Orthodox liturgical tradition using Finnish and Slavonic in the liturgy. Membership: (1970) 78 churches with 41,000 adult members, 58,000 total community.
**first evangelization.** A term used in Roman Catholic mission circles for the first preaching of the gospel in a newly-entered non-Christian area.
**First World.** The Western (or Capitalist) world, as loosely contrasted with the Second (Communist) world (qv) and Third World (qv).
**fishing.** A term used in evangelistic circles for street evangelism among passers-by.
**fission.** Splitting, breaking-up into pieces, schism, secession.
**focused interview.** In sociological research, an interview with a key individual, at a late stage in the research, in which key questions are asked focused on the origins and causes of phenomena under study.
**folk media.** Small-scale or local media, indigenous media, alternative media, participatory media, group media: traditional story-telling, wandering minstrels/storytellers, drama, traditional performing arts, live theatre, dance, poetry, recitation, mime, song, et alia.
**folk religion.** Popular religion, popular religiosity (qv).
**folk-Catholicism.** Roman Catholic popular piety, religion, or religiosity (qv).
**folk-religionists.** Followers of traditional religion (qv), popular religion or religiosity (qv), or local or folk religion.
**follow-through evangelism.** Mass evangelistic campaigns in which converts or enquirers are systematically followed up, taught and trained in discipleship within local churches.
**follow-up.** A system of pursuing an initial evangelistic effort by following enquirers or converts to assist them joining churches.
**force for evangelism.** The total of all evangelizing persons and influences available in a given situation; the effective evangelizing nucleus, or the total community of all evangelizing Christians as measured by the total practising Christians.
**foreign.** Alien; situated outside a place or country.
**foreign chaplaincy.** A chaplaincy, parish or mission ministering in a foreign country to expatriate residents who are members of the home church in its own land.
**foreign evangelization.** Evangelization by foreign persons outside a particular group, people or area.
**foreign forces.** Resident military forces from outside of a country.
**foreign missionaries.** Full-time long-term Christian workers sent abroad by parent foreign missionary societies, and regularly termed and terming themselves missionaries.
**foreign missionaries and personnel.** Full-time long-term foreign missionaries and similar personnel of all churches and from all countries now serving abroad. Global total: (1973) 247,763, (1980) 249,000.
**foreign missionary councils.** Consultative or executive councils of foreign mission organizations in sending countries, to facilitate co-operation and liaison. Over 60 such councils at the national level exist.
**foreign missionary societies.** Organizations founded for and dedicated to the purpose of extending Christianity to foreign countries and their populations. Total for all traditions: (1980) about 3,100.
**foreign missionary training centres.** These number over 410 worldwide.
**foreign missions.** The enterprise of taking a religion to foreign countries and planting it there through organized, full-time workers.
**foreign personnel.** Full-time long-term Christian workers serving in a foreign country, sent abroad on behalf of their churches, but who are not described as and do not use the term missionaries.
**foreigner.** An alien, stranger, expatriate; a person belonging to or owing allegiance to a foreign country.
**formal correspondence translation.** An exact or literal or word-for-word translation of Scripture, preserving the form of the original from its original languages into contemporary languages (e.g. in English the AV (KJV), ASV, RV, NASB, RSV), in contrast to UBS policy of dynamic equivalence (qv).
**fortnightly attenders.** Affiliated Christians (church members) who attend church services of public worship on average twice a month.
**fraternal worker.** A term in use in ecumenical Protestant circles, intended in the 1960s as a replacement for 'foreign missionary'.
**Free Christians.** Unitarians (qv).
**Free churches.** Minority churches not established or under state control, specially in countries with majority state churches.
**free distribution of scriptures.** Annual statistics of placements of scriptures, donated without cost to recipients.
**Free Methodists.** Holiness Christians (qv).
**Free Pentecostals.** Perfectionist-Pentecostals (qv).
**Freemasons.** Members of the secret fraternal order of Free and Accepted Masons, the largest worldwide secret society, spread by the advance of the British empire; 5,900,000 members worldwide (4 million in USA, 1 million in British Isles, 10,000 in France, 3,400 in Kenya, also strong in Italy, Germany, Liberia, et alia. Strong hostility to the churches especially Roman Catholic Church) in France, Italy, Latin countries; banned in USSR, Hungary, Poland, Spain, Portugal, China, Indonesia, Egypt, et alia.
**freethinkers.** Agnostics, sceptics, unbelievers.
**Friends World Committee for Consultation** (FWCC). The major Quaker world communion. Global constituency: (1980) 455,600.
**Friends** (Quakers). A Protestant tradition dating from 1652. Global membership: (1970) 50 denominations with 3,610 congregations and 207,700 adult members; total community (1970) 377,200, (1980) 457,900, (1985) 502,500.
**fringe members.** Persons who are church members on the rolls, but only in a marginal sense, being irregular or occasional or casual church attenders, or rarely seen, or adherents only partly committed to church law and discipline or only partially accepting Christian faith and practice.
**frontier.** From a missionary point of view, the barrier or demarcation that exists between 2 distinct cultures or languages or types of religions, and which must be crossed before missionary contact and communication can be established.
**fulfilment.** Accomplishment, consummation, completion, e.g. of the Great Commission.
**full communion.** In Anglican usage, complete sacramental fellowship and mutual acceptance of ministries between 2 or more confessions or churches.
**full member.** An adult church member who is a baptized communicant in good standing within his church.
**full-time ministry.** Ordained persons whose primary occupation is in some form of ministry.
**full-time workers.** Persons whose primary occupation is in Christian or church work.
**fully-evangelized.** Used of an area or population in which the gospel has become universally known.
**functional literacy.** A higher level of competence than basic ability to read and write, qualifying a person to meet many of the practical needs of daily life in his culture or group.
**Fundamentalism.** A militantly conservative movement in North American Protestantism orginating around 1910 in opposition to modernist tendencies and emphasizing as fundamental to Christianity a group of 5 or 7 basic doctrines: inerrant verbal inspiration of the Bible, Virgin Birth, miracles of Christ, Resurrection, total depravity of man, substitutionary atonement, premillenial Second Coming.
**fundamentalism, structural.** A very conservative attitude to existing church structure regarded as of divine origin, or unchangeable, or otherwise sacrosanct.
**fundamentalist.** An adherent or proponent of Protestant Fundamentalism, often narrowed to premillennialism or dispensationalism.
**Fundamentalists.** Evangelicals (usually premillennialists or dispensationalists) holding the doctrine of the infallibility of the Bible, opposing modernism, liberalism and ecumenism, and stressing the 5 or 7 basic doctrines; all persons affiliated to denominations holding Fundamentalist doctrines; in the USA, estimated at 40 million persons (1980): of whom 40% (16 million) are premillennialists.
**fund-raising.** Over 1,000 organizations are devoted to to direct raising of funds for Christian use. In many countries there are Christian parachurch organizations, or branches of denominations, which specialize

in fund-raising activities on behalf of local church or development projects.

**furlough.** A leave of absence granted to a foreign missionary to return to his home country for a time for leave.

**fusion.** The union, merging, blending of 2 or more denominations into one church.

**future.** The time or period or era that is still to come.

**future research.** Futurology (qv).

**future studies.** Research studies on the probable future development of a situation, involving the producing of alternative futures (qv) or possible scenarios.

**futurist.** Relating to futurology (qv).

**futuristics.** Futurology (qv).

**futurology.** The science of the systematic study of the future.

**futurology of Christianity.** Literature discussing possible futures of Christianity and the churches has been extensive for the last 100 years, and is tabulated in Appendix C at the end of this Dictionary.

## G

**gallicanism.** The movement, or body of doctrine, which asserted the complete freedom of the Roman Catholic Church (especially in France) from the ecclesiastical authority of the papacy. Vatican I (1870) signified the end of the movement within the Roman Church, but it survives in Old Catholic and other autocephalous Catholic churches.

**gathered church.** A denomination brought into being through the influx of individuals, families or small groups, often through the mission station approach, rather than by means of a people movement (qv).

**Gelukpa.** Yellow Hat (Reformed) Lamaism (qv).

**general.** The chief of a religious order or all houses or congregations under one religious rule; superior general of the Jesuit order; supreme commander of the Salvation Army.

**general census.** A population census in which all inhabitants of a country are counted simultaneously.

**general order of magnitude.** A number or statistic or set of statistics which establishes the broad area of size of a particular situation, whether local, denominational, tribal, national, regional, racial, continental or global.

**general-order estimate.** A number or statistic indicating approximately (rounded to the nearest 10, 100, 1000 or million) the broad area of size or magnitude of a particular category or variable.

**generalate.** The headquarters of a Roman Catholic religious institute headed by a general or superior general.

**generation.** (1) A group of persons born within a specified period of time, generally taken as a calendar year. (2) The average span of time, variously computed and varying according to cultural and other conditions, between the birth of parents and that of their children; usually taken as 30 years (sometimes as 25 or 33 years).

**geographical race.** One of 13 broad, geographically-delimited races of mankind; a collection of human populations, usually rather similar physically, delimited by some natural boundary, such as an ocean, and tending to have similar heredity, skin colour, hair type, languages, etc.

**geography of religion.** The description and analysis of religious phenomena in terms of the science of geography (spatial variations in human and physical phenomena).

**geometric mean.** The square root of the product of the 2 end figures or populations in a period.

**geopolitical.** Relating to or based on geopolitics.

**geopolitico-religious.** An overall term describing the major geographical, political, sociological, socio-economic, demographic and religious characteristics of the world, or continents, or nations.

**geopolitics.** The study of the influence of physical factors such as geography, economics and demography upon the politics and foreign policy of a state; the political and geographical factors characterizing a particular state or region.

**Georgian.** Eastern Orthodox liturgical tradition (Georgian Orthodox Church). Membership: (1970) 80 churches with 500,000 adult members, 800,000 total community.

**German Baptists.** Dunkers (qv).

**Germanic.** A European ethnolinguistic family, with about 15 major languages; Teutonic. Global population: (1970) 343,204,900, (1980) 368,673,400, (1985) 381,728,800.

**gethsemane.** A mercy ground (qv).

**Ge'ez.** Ethiopic, an extinct Semitic language still used as the liturgical language of the Ethiopian Orthodox Church.

GLOSSOLALIA. High Priest Kivuli praying (Kenya).

**glossolalia** (NT Greek). The gift of tongues; ecstatic speech usually unintelligible to hearers, uttered in worship services of contemporary charismatic churches.

**Gnosticism.** The thought and practice of various cults of late pre-Christian and early Christian centuries, declared heretical by the church, characterized chiefly by pretension to mystic and esoteric religious insights, by emphasis on knowledge (*gnosis*) rather than faith, and by the conviction that matter is evil.

**Gnostics.** Followers of a complex Jewish-Christian syncretistic movement in the 2nd century AD. The only surviving Gnostics today are the 31,000 Mandaeans (qv) of Iraq and Iran.

**Goa.** See of Latin Catholic patriarchate and patriarch, since 1886.

**gospel.** The good news of salvation and new life in Jesus Christ and the coming of the Kingdom of God.

**gospelize.** To instruct in the gospel, preach the gospel, evangelize.

**Gospels.** 4 New Testament books containing narratives of the life and death of Jesus Christ, ascribed to Matthew, Mark, Luke and John.

**gospels.** See portions.

**government ministries of religion.** See state departments for religious affairs.

**government statistics of religion.** Figures of adherents of religions and churches promulgated by governments, usually derived from government censuses of population.

**graveyard evangelism.** Preaching and evangelism engaged in on the occasion of funerals or burials, especially in anti-Christian countries where preaching outside church buildings is prohibited.

**Great and Holy Council of the Orthodox Church.** Major Eastern Orthodox ecumenical council to be held shortly, the first since Nicea II in AD 787. Global total of Eastern Orthodox in canonical relationship: (1980) 127,168,700.

**Great Britain.** Geographically, the 3 countries England, Wales and Scotland; politically, often used for the whole United Kingdom of Great Britain and Northern Ireland.

**Great Church.** Official name of Santa Sophia, former cathedral church of Constantinople.

**Great Commission.** The universal or last commission delivered to his disciples by the Risen and Ascended Christ: 'Go throughout the whole world and preach the gospel to all mankind' (Mark 16.15, GNB).

**Greater Vehicle.** The Mahayana school of Buddhists (qv).

**Greek.** A European ethnolinguistic family and people. Global population: (1970) 10,889,200, (1980) 11,449,000, (1985) 11,739,200.

**Greek Catholics.** (1) Those using the Greek rite, under Rome: membership (1970) 3,082 total community. (2) Melkites (qv).

**Greek Orthodox.** (1) Christians related to the Church of Greece and the Ecumenical Patriarchate of Constantinople; often loosely used, instead of the more correct term Eastern Orthodox, to include Slavic Orthodoxy also. (2) Greek-speaking Orthodox using Greek rite. Global membership: (1970) 71 denominations with 31,112 churches and 8,664,900 adult members; total community (1970) 12,349,000, (1980) 13,055,800, (1985) 13,429,500.

**Gregorian Calendar.** New Calendar (qv).

**Gregorians.** Armenian Apostolics, or Armenian Orthodox (qv).

**Grey.** Stylized skin colour associated with the Australoid and Capoid races (Austro-Asiatic and Early African geographical races). Global Grey population: (1970) 26,719,300, (1980) 34,533,500, (1985) 38,767,600.

**gross national product.** The total value of the goods and services produced in a nation during a specific period (usually a year), and also comprising the total of expenditures by consumers and government plus gross private investment.

**gross national product per capita.** National income per person (qv).

**group dynamics.** The forces and processes of interaction operating within a relatively small human group; studied and worked out in various types of church situations.

**group ministry.** A ministry shared by several ordained and lay persons, or extended over several parishes or other ecclesiastical units.

**growth.** In church and mission circles: development, rise, emergence, evolution, expansion, size.

**growth rate.** The annual increase in a population measured as a percentage per year.

**guerrillas.** Small military forces engaged in irregular warfare or in the rear of regular forces.

**Guinean.** An African ethnolinguistic family, with about 80 languages. Global population: (1970) 36,562,700, (1980) 48,138,900, (1985) 54,530,300.

**Gypsy.** Itinerant Caucasoid people originally from India and since the 14th century scattered throughout Europe. Global total of pure or unassimilated Gypsies: (1970) 4,539,100, (1980) 5,135,600, (1985) 5,443,400.

## H

**hadith.** In Islam, the collected traditions of Mohammed.

**hajj** (hadj, haj). The pilgrimage to Mecca prescribed as a religious duty for Muslims.

**hajj pilgrims to Mecca.** Annual totals: (1912) 300,000, (1929) 90,000, (1941) 23,000, (1968) 692,784, (1975) 1,557,867, (1976) 1,456,432. Source of statistics: officially-released figures published in the Mecca newspapers soon after start of each Hajj.

**hajji** (hadji, haji). A Muslim who has made the pilgrimage to Mecca, who may then add the term to his name as a title.

**Half-Breed.** A Half-Caste (qv).

**Half-Caste.** A person of mixed blood or race.

**ham operators.** Amateur radio operators (qv).

**Hanafites.** Followers of Hanafiya, the most liberal of the 4 schools or rites of Sunni Muslim law, and by far the most widespread. Global adherents: (1980) 313,058,000.

**Hanbalites.** Followers of Hanabila, the most rigid of the 4 schools or rites of Sunni Muslim law; mainly in Central Arabia. Global adherents: (1980) 1,500,000.

**handicapped children.** Of the world's 1.6 billion children under 15 years old (1980), 80 million (5%) are severely handicapped and 192 million (12%) need special attention or rehabilitation services.

**handicapped groups, ministry to.** Special ministries exist, in most larger denominations and para-church agencies, to work with lepers, the blind, the crippled, and other groups.

**harassment.** A recognized government tactic against churches in anti-Christian societies; deliberate and repeated attempts at frustration, annoyance, impeding of rights, etc.

**Hausa-Chadic.** An African ethnolinguistic family, with over 150 languages. Global population: (1970) 15,896,900, (1980) 20,789,100, (1985) 23,482,200.

**healing.** The act or process of curing or restoring to health; a major ministry of Christ and the church. See medical centres, faith-healing.

**hearer.** (1) A catechumen (qv). (2) A person being exposed to the gospel.

**hearing.** A technical term for persons being exposed to the gospel and hence being evangelized.

**heathen.** A somewhat outdated term for non-Christians, pagans, savages, barbarians, animists, et alia.

**Hebrew-Aramaic Scriptures.** The Jehovah's Witnesses term for the Old Testament.

**helicopters.** Aircraft supported by rotors; used on mission work in about 20 countries (1980).

**heresy.** Adherence to a religious opinion that is contrary to an established dogma of a church; dissent, deviation, heterodoxy.

**heretic.** A dissenter from established Christian dogma; deviationist.

**Here's Life World.** A global series of urban and

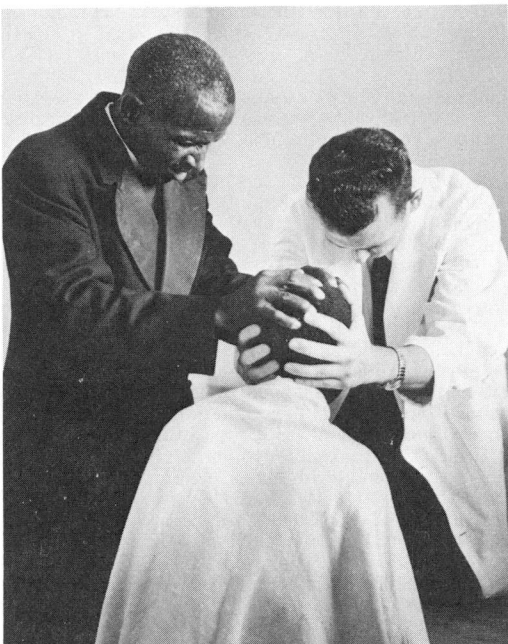

HEALING. Exorcism in Methodist hospital (Zimbabwe).

rural multimedia multiplication-evangelism campaigns, beginning in 1974 in the USA through Campus Crusade for Christ.

**hermeneutics.** The study of the general principles of biblical interpretation and explanation.

**hidden affiliation.** The situation in which Christians affiliated to minority or illegal or anti-state or persecuted churches hide this affiliation in government censuses (or whose affiliation is ignored by enumerators) and profess another type of Christianity (usually that of the majority church).

**hidden peoples.** Non-Christian peoples among whom there is no culturally relevant organized Christian church able to evangelize them.

**hierarch.** A religious leader holding high office or vested with controlling authority; chief prelate, bishop, high priest.

**hierarchical.** Relating to or controlled by the hierarchy.

**hierarchy.** In Roman Catholic usage, the episcopate or the whole body of bishops as an authoritarian body organized by rank and jurisdiction.

**hierocracy.** Government by ecclesiastics.

**hieromonk.** A monk of the Eastern Church who is also a priest.

**High Church Anglicans.** Also termed Prayer Book Catholics, or the High Church Party; Anglicans stressing the Catholic heritage. Global membership in 37 predominantly High Church dioceses: (1970) 9,100 churches with 1,938,000 adult members, 5,087,300 total community.

**high spiritism.** Mediumistic cults or religions emphasizing a synthesis of science, philosophy and religion, as contrasted with low spiritism.

**higher education.** Tertiary education; education in universities.

**higher schools.** Church- or Christian related junior and senior secondary schools, minor seminaries (secular and religious), technical schools, agricultural schools, vocational schools, teacher-training colleges, non-degree-granting colleges. Global total: (1975) 42,700.

**Hinayana.** A school of Buddhists, Theravada (qv).

**Hindu reformist movements.** These include: Arya Samaj, Shanka Acharya, Ramakrishna Mission, et alia. Global adherents: (1970) 2,320,000, (1980) 2,910,000.

**Hindus.** Followers of the main Hindu traditions: (a) Vaishnavites (Vishnaivites) (qv) numbering 70% of all Hindus; (b) Saivites (qv) numbering 25% mostly in South India; (c) Saktists (qv) or other sects (3%); (d) neo-Hindu movements and modern sects arising out of Hinduism, about 1.5%; and (e) Arya Samaj and other reformist movements, 0.5% (Brahmo Samaj, Prarthana Samaj, Swami-Narayanis, Ramakrishna Mission, but excluding Jains and Sikhs). Global adherents: (1970) 463,784,800, (1980) 582,749,900 in 69 countries with over 9 million priests and 15 million sadhus, (1985) 647,567,500.

**historic churches.** The major mainline or older churches or denominations with a long history in that part of the world under consideration.

**historic succession of the episcopate.** Apostolic succession (qv).

**historical demography.** The study of the history of population development.

**holdings.** The number of volumes and other discrete items held by a library.

**Holiness, Holiness Christians.** Protestant tradition originating in Methodism. Global membership: (1970) 322 denominations with 33,374 churches and 1,919,100 adult members; total community (1970) 4,332,300, (1980) 5,449,100, (1985) 6,091,700.

**Holiness-Pentecostals.** Pentecostals teaching 3-crisis experience (conversion, sanctification, baptism of the Spirit). Global membership: (1970) 214 denominations with 32,586 churches and 2,417,500 adult members; total community (1970) 5,383,900 (1980) 6,487,400, (1985) 7,080,900.

**holistic church growth.** The emphasis on church-planting combined with sociopolitical action.

**holistic evangelism.** Evangelism which involves sociopolitical action in some sense.

**holy cities.** Headquarters of Third-World Non-White indigenous churches, often regarded as New Jerusalem on earth. Global total: (1980) about 5,000.

**holy day of obligation.** One of the days on which Roman Catholics, Episcopalians et alii are obliged to hear mass and abstain from servile work.

**Holy Land.** Palestine; those areas of Israel and Jordan in which Christ lived and worked while on earth.

**holy orders.** Ordination; the state of being ordained.

**Holy See.** The supreme organ of the Roman Catholic Church, an international juridical entity, a sovereign state centred in Vatican City.

**Holy Spirit.** The Third Person of the Trinity.

**holy synod.** The governing body in an autocephalous church, composed of bishops and primate.

**holy war.** See jihad, Crusades.

HOLY WATER. Blessing, Aladura Church (Nigeria).

**holy water.** Water blessed by a priest and used as a purifying sacramental in church and home; especially by Roman Catholics and African indigenous churches.

**holy writing.** See spirit writing.

**Holy Year.** A jubilee year observed at Rome when proclaimed by the Holy See, in principle every 25 years. Total Holy Year pilgrims to Rome: (first Holy Year, in AD 1300) 200,000; (1950) 2.5 million; (1975) 8,370,000.

**home missionaries.** Full-time Christian workers sent by their churches to missionary areas within their own countries.

**home missions and societies.** Bodies significant at nationwide or wider levels number over 500.

**homiletics.** A branch of theology that deals with homilies or sermons; the art of preaching.

**Homo Sapiens.** The entire human race; mankind; sentient, conscious, thinking man.

**homogeneous.** Of the same kind or nature; alike, similar, congruous; of uniform nature or character throughout.

**homogeneous unit.** A population group, stratum, society or segment of society within which a number of characteristics or interests or customs (geograph-

ical, ethnic, linguistic, social, educational, cultural, vocational, economic, etc) are held in common by all members, with a common self-consciousness; a culture, sub-culture, people group, ethnolinguistic group.

**hospitals.** See medical centres.

**hours.** In Jehovah's Witnesses' statistics, the total number of hours devoted by its publishers to preaching and house-to-house literature distribution each year. Total (1959) 126,317,124 hours, rising to (1974) 371,132,570 hours.

**house church.** A group of Christians meeting as a worship centre in a private house for regular Sunday worship.

**household.** A socio-economic unit, consisting of individuals who live together sharing living quarters and principal meals.

**household size.** The average size of a household in a country or area, i.e. number of persons sharing the same unit, whether private or collective or institutional. Household size is slightly larger than average family size because it includes servants, maids, and lodgers, as well as hospitals, homes and other institutions where people live.

HOVERCRAFT. Early missionary prototype.

**hovercraft.** Land-water craft supported by cushion of air; used by Missionary Aviation Fellowship and other mission bodies.

**Huguenots.** A historical name, since 1560, for French Calvinists.

**humanism.** A philosophy based on agnosticism that rejects supernaturalism and revelation, regards man as a natural object only, and asserts the essential dignity and worth of man and his capacity to achieve self-realization and self-fulfilment through the use of reason and scientific method; naturalistic humanism, scientific humanism.

**humanism, Christian.** See religious humanism.

**humanism, religious.** See religious humanism.

**humanist.** A person who subscribes to humanism.

**Hungarian rite.** Roman Catholics following the Hungarian rite numbered (1970) 269,100 total community.

**Hungarian/Slavonic.** Eastern Orthodox liturgical tradition using Hungarian and Slavonic in the liturgy. Membership: (1970) 10 churches with 5,200 adult members, 40,400 total community.

**hybrid races.** Clines (qv).

**hymnody, hymnology.** The study of hymns (songs of praise to God) and their composition; a body of hymns of a particular period or region.

# I

**'I found it' campaigns.** A global series of evangelistic campaigns (Here's Life World) employing this deliberately-ambiguous slogan ('It' being New Life in Christ).

**Ibadis, Ibadites.** Kharijites (qv).

**icon, ikon.** A flat painted sacred picture.

**iconoclasm.** Anti-icon campaign at Constantinople, AD 726-842.

**iconography.** Art representing religious subjects by conventional images and symbols; the study of religious art and symbolism.

**iconostasis.** Screen separating nave from sanctuary, adorned with icons, in Orthodox churches.

**ideology.** The science of ideas, their origin and nature; a particular sociopolitical set of theories.

**illiterate.** A person who can neither read nor write.

**imam** (Arabic, divine guide). A Muslim religious practitioner or cleric.

**Imamis, Imamites.** Ithna-Asharis (qv), Ismailis (qv), and other Shias.

**immediately subject** (Italian, *immediate soggette alla Santa Sede*). Used of Roman Catholic jurisdictions which are not attached to any ecclesiastical province in their own country but are immediately subject to the Holy See itself.

**immigrant religion.** A religion absent from a country until brought in by recent immigrants.

**immigration.** The movement of immigrants into a particular territory.

**inclusive membership.** The total of a church's or denomination's affiliated Christians (qv) or church members, of all ages and varieties including children, infants and persons under instruction; also termed total Christian community.

**income, average.** See family income, national income per person.

**incumbent.** The holder of an ecclesiastical benefice (diocese, office, or, more usually, parish).

**Independency.** Congregationalism; a religious movement originating in England after AD 1600 asserting a congregation's independence of higher ecclesiastical authority.

**independency, religious.** A movement asserting independence of a previously recognized ecclesiastical authority, especially exemplified in the African indigenous churches (qv).

**Independent.** Congregationalist.

**independent.** Term for independent Evangelical churches with no denomination affiliation or ties.

**Index Librorum Prohibitorum.** List published at Rome of prohibited books judged dangerous to faith or morals; created 1557, abolished 1965.

**Indian indigenous churches.** Denominations indigenous to, and started by, Indians. Membership: (1980) 98 denominations with 2,650,000 members.

**indigenous.** Originating or developing or produced naturally in a particular land or region or environment; not introduced directly or indirectly from the outside.

**indigenous Christianity.** In a particular region, that type of Christianity which, in contrast to imported or foreign types, is evolved or produced by populations indigenous to that region.

**indigenous church.** A locally-founded church, i.e. one originating within a country or race or people, or produced naturally by nationals of that country or members of that race or people, as opposed to a church of foreign or alien origin imported from abroad or introduced from outside.

**indigenous churches.** As classified here, there are 3 major groupings contemporary in the world: (1) Semitic Oriental Orthodox churches indigenous to the Middle East, (2) White churches (Roman Catholic, Eastern Orthodox, Anglican, Protestant, marginal Protestant, Catholic (non-Roman)) indigenous to the White races of Europe and North America, and (3) Non-White indigenous churches begun since AD 1500.

**indigenous evangelization.** Spreading of the gospel among a non-Christian population by persons indigenous to that population.

**indigenous media.** See folk media.

**indigenous religious institutes.** In Roman Catholic usage, locally-founded religious congregations of men or women began in mission fields.

**indigenous, Third-World.** Churches and Christians indigenous to the Third World.

**individual.** A person; the fundamental statistical unit used in demography.

**Indonesian indigenous churches.** Denominations indigenous to, and started by, Indonesians. Membership: (1980) 210 denominations with 3,562,000 members.

**Indo-Iranian.** One of the 13 geographical races of mankind, with over 230 languages. Global population: (1970) 727,284,600, (1980) 933,687,300, (1985) 1,046,648,500.

**Indo-Malay.** An Asian ethnolinguistic family, with 300 languages. Global population: (1970) 165,162,600, (1980) 217,847,000, (1985) 245,919,900.

**industrial mission.** A Christian approach to industrial organizations in a particular region.

**industrialization.** The act or process of becoming industrial in a particular region or country.

**in-depth evangelism.** The strategy of united programmes of evangelism in a country or area; total mobilization evangelism, saturation evangelism, Evangelism-in-Depth, New Life for All, etc; stressing mobilization of all believers and their resources, within the framework of the church, reaching all unbelievers in the area, through every available means.

**ineligible member.** An adult church member who is not eligible to take communion, usually being under discipline for some offence.

INFANT BAPTISM. Apostolic Church AACJM (Zimbabwe).

**infant baptism.** In Catholic, Orthodox, Anglican, Lutheran, Methodist, Reformed and other pedobaptist (qv) traditions, the administration of baptism to children under 5 years old.

**infants.** Defined here as those under 5 years old, or the pre-school population, including new-born babies; although the term is often restricted to children who have not reached their first birthday.

**infilling by the Holy Spirit.** Persons baptized in the Spirit each year are enumerated in the statistics of several Pentecostal denominations (e.g. Assemblies of God, USA).

**inflation.** Annual percentage growth in consumer prices, as measured by the consumer price index (qv).

**informant.** A respondent (qv) in a census or survey; a person supplying information.

**inhabitant.** A person who dwells or resides permanently in a place as distinguished from a transient lodger or visitor, or a resident (who may be temporary or short-term).

**Injerto.** The issue of a Latin American White and a Chinese or Japanese.

**inner-city ministry.** The parish ministry adapted to inner-city dwellers in areas of urban blight.

**inquirers.** See enquirers.

**inscriptions.** A technical term in Bible correspondence course ministry for enrolments or the number of persons signing on, enrolling or writing in.

**inspectorate** (French, *inspection*). In French Lutheran usage, a large area of ecclesiastical jurisdiction equivalent to a deanery or presbytery.

**institutes, religious.** See religious institutes.

**institutional population.** Persons in correctional schools, hospitals, prisons and other institutions, who are often separately enumerated in censuses.

**institutions, Christian.** Major Christian or church-operated or -related institutions of all kinds, i.e. fixed centres with premises, plant and permanent staff, excluding church buildings, worship centres, church headquarters or offices. Global total: (1980) 91,000. For detailed statistics, see under: ecumenical centres, higher schools, medical centres, presses, radio stations, religious communities, research centres, seminaries, study centres, universities.

**interchurch aid.** Aid given by one church or denomination to another, usually as finance, personnel or other resources.

**intercommunion.** Mutual fellowship and limited sacramental and ministerial recognition between 2 or more churches or confessions, but falling short of full communion (qv).

**interconfessional.** Involving, supported by, or common to major Christian families or communions having different confessions of faith.

**interdenominational.** Occurring between or among or common to different denominations (qv).

**intermediate technology.** Technology that is sufficiently simple to directly benefit peasants and workers in developing nations.

**internal province.** In Anglicanism, a self-governing ecclesiastical province within an autonomous church.

**International Association for Religious Freedom** (IARF). Free Christian/Unitarian world communion begun 1900; since 1969, open to liberal groups in any world religion. Global constituency: (1980) 1,235,900.

**international Christian radio stations.** There are some 50 powerful radio stations under Christian auspices which beam programmes worldwide in several hundred languages.

**International Conference of Old Catholic Bishops.** See International Old Catholic Bishops Conference.

**International Congregational Council** (ICC). Confessional council begun 1891, linking all Congregationalist denominations. Merged in 1970 with World Alliance of Reformed Churches.

**International Council of Christian Churches** (ICCC). The major global Fundamentalist, anti-Ecumenical, council. Global constituency: (1980) 150 denominations with 3,837,300 members.

**international denominational bodies.** See non-confessional international denominational bodies.

**International Federation of Free Evangelical Churches** (IFFEC). A world confessional body or communion of mainly Congregationalist denominations. Global constituency: (1980) 559,500.

**International New Thought Alliance** (INTA). World communion for metaphysical Christian bodies, begun 1914.

**International Old Catholic Bishops Conference.** Also known as the Union of Utrecht, begun 1889; the major Old Catholic world communion. Global constituency: (1980) 5,846,900.

**international sharing of personnel.** The sending and receiving, between and amongst all countries of the world, and between and amongst all churches of the world, of 250,000 full-time long-term foreign missionaries and personnel.

**internuncio.** A Vatican diplomat of lower rank than nuncio.

**interpolation.** The estimation of values of a series at points intermediate between known or given values.

**interreligious.** Existing between 2 or more religions; used of activities or relationships between Christianity and one or more of the major world religions (Judaism, Islam, Hinduism, Buddhism). Interreligious organizations significant at the national or wider levels number over 150.

**inter-censal period.** The time elapsing between 2 censuses of population.

**invisible church.** In reaction to excessive denominationalism and fragmentation of the visible Church, many Christians profess to believe only in one undivided but invisible church, the Body of Christ, composed only of all true believers.

**invitation.** In evangelization, the act of inviting or challenging persons to accept Christ immediately, often at the close of an evangelistic service or meeting.

**in-depth evangelism.** See Evangelism-in-Depth.

**Iranian.** An Indo-Iranian ethnolinguistic family. Global population: (1970) 51,000,300, (1980) 67,595,800, (1985) 76,679,000.

**irregular attenders.** Persons affiliated to churches but who attend services only irregularly, infrequently or occasionally.

**irreligion.** Hostility to religion; impiety, scepticism, disbelief, atheism, anti-religious humanism.

**Irvingites.** Catholic Apostolics originating in Britain in 1832, also called Old Apostolics; marked decline since 1900 due to dying out of clergy originally ordained after 1836 by Apostles.

**Islam** (Arabic: submission to the will of God). The religious faith of Muslims (qv) who profess belief in Allah as the sole deity and in Muhammed as the prophet of Allah.

**Islamics.** The academic study of Islam.

**islamization.** The act or process of converting people, or of being converted, to Islam.

**Ismailis.** Followers of Ismailiya (also known as Seveners), second largest sect of Shia Islam, and itself divided into Nizari Ismailis (Khojas) and Mustali Ismailis (Bohras). Global adherents: (1980) 13,600,000.

**isolated radio believers.** The total community of those persons (with their dependant adults and children, and other adherents) who derive their ongoing corporate Christian life primarily from isolated radio churches or isolated Bible correspondence course student groupings. Global total: (1970) 74,300 congregations or house-churches in 67 countries with 1,711,400 adult members; total community (1970) 2,886,200, (1980) 3,830,200, (1985) 4,313,500.

**isolated radio churches.** New indigenous house churches, cells or nuclei composed of isolated radio believers (qv) brought into being solely through

Christian broadcasting and/or Bible correspondence courses by mail, who due to geographical remoteness or other reasons are isolated from existing Christian believers and are ignorant of the existence of organized denominations, hence group themselves into these new fellowships.

**Issei** (Japanese: first-generation). A Japanese immigrant to the Americas.

**Italo-Albanians.** Roman Catholics following the Italo-Albanian rite; membership (1970) 67,600 total community.

**Ithna-Asharis.** Followers of Ithna-Ashar
iya (also known as Twelvers), largest sect of Shia Islam. Global adherents: (1980) 86,027,000.

## J

**Jacobites.** Syrian Orthodox (qv), so termed after Jacob Baradaeus, bishop of Edessa (died 578).

**Jains.** Followers of the Jain reform movement from Hinduism, composed of the Svetambara and Digambara sects. Global adherents: (1970) 2,616,300, (1980) 3,243,800 in 5 countries, (1985) 3,349,100.

**Jansenists.** Dissident Roman Catholics in Holland who in 1702, 1724 et alia formed separatist churches and were later termed Old Catholics (qv).

**Japanese.** An Asian ethnolinguistic family and people. Global population: (1970) 105,020,200, (1980) 118,473,200, (1985) 125,031,300.

**Japanese indigenous churches.** Denominations indigenous to, and started by, Japanese. Membership: (1980) 69 denominations with 940,000 members.

**Jehovah's Christian witnesses.** The preferred self-appellation of Jehovah's Witnesses (qv).

**Jehovah's Witnesses.** A marginal Protestant tradition begun in 1872; also called Russellites. Global membership: (1970) 26,283 congregations with 1,708,200 adult members; total community (1970) 4,113,400, (1980) 5,638,700, (1985) 6,447,500.

**Jerusalem.** One of the 4 original partriarchates of the Apostolic Church; now the see of 4 rival patriarchs: Greek Orthodox, Armenian Apostolic, Melkite and Latin.

**Jerusalems.** See holy cities.

**Jesuits.** Members of the Society of Jesus, Roman Catholicism's largest religious order; in 1975, 29,636 members (20,604 priests, the rest brothers).

**Jesus Christ.** Founder of Christianity, Son of God, acknowledged as Lord and Saviour by 1.4 billion Christians and 21,000 denominations (1980).

**Jesus movement, people, generation.** Terms covering the widespread revival of faith in Jesus, in the 1960s and 1970s, on the part of youth and students in the Western world.

**Jesus-Only Pentecostals.** Oneness-Pentecostals (qv).

**Jew, Jews, Jewish.** (1) The secular definition: A Middle Eastern (Semitic) ethnolinguistic family. Global population: (1970) 13,234,400, (1980) 15,171,400, (1985) 16,180,300. (2) The religious definition: Followers of the Orthodox, Reformed or Liberal schools of Judaism; Ashkenazis (84% of all Jews), Orientals (10%), and Sefardis (Sephardis) (4%); and crypto-Jews. Global adherents: (1970) 15,185,900, (1980) 16,938,200, (1985) 17,838,100, in 112 countries.

**Jewish-Christians.** Also called Hebrew Christians, Messianic Christians, Messianic Jews, Jewish crypto-Christians. Total in 242 separate Jewish-Christian denominations (1970): 43,700 adult members, 61,000 total community.

**jihad** (Arabic). For Muslims, a holy war waged on behalf of Islam.

**joint action for mission.** An ecumenical programme involving (a) a joint survey by all churches in an area, (b) joint planning to secure real and effective redeployment of resources in the light of agreed goals, and (c) joint action to implement this.

**journalism, religious.** See religious journalism.

**Judaism.** The religion of the Jews (qv) characterized by belief in one God and in the mission of Jews to teach the Fatherhood of God as revealed in the Hebrew Scriptures.

**Julian Calendar.** Old Calendar (qv).

**jurisdiction.** (1) Any territory within which a bishop or other church leader exercises his authority, such as an archdiocese, diocese, vicariate, prefecture, etc. (2) In some churches, a jurisdiction (symbol J) is a specific type of territory similar to a diocese.

## K

**Kanuri.** An African ethnolinguistic family, with over 15 languages. Global population: (1970) 3,529,600, (1980) 4,621,300, (1985) 5,221,600.

**Karaites.** Readers of the Scriptures, followers of Qaraism (a Jewish sect). Total adherents: (1980) 17,100.

**Kardecism.** High spiritism (qv) or spiritualism, notably in Brazil.

**karma** (Sanskrit). In Buddhism and Hinduism, the force generated by a person's actions that is held to be the motive power for the round of rebirths and deaths endured by him until he has achieved spiritual liberation (nirvana).

**Karmatians.** See Qarmatians.

**kerygma** (NT Greek). Preaching, the preaching of the gospel; the message preached.

**Keswick-Pentecostals.** Baptistic-Pentecostals (qv).

**Kharijites** (Seceders). Followers of schism from Sunni and Shia Islam, mainly in Ibadite form. Global adherents: (1980) 1,023,500.

**Khoisan.** An Early African ethnolinguistic family, with about 50 languages. Global population: (1970) 195,300, (1980) 251,900, (1985) 283,000.

**Khojas.** Nizari Ismailis (qv), followers of the Aga Khan.

**Kibei.** A Japanese-American born of Issei parents but educated in Japan.

**kingdom hall.** In Jehovah's Witnesses' usage, a large central permanent church building and headquarters.

**Kingdom of God.** The central theme of Christ's teaching and of the New Testament, and of Christian theology subsequently.

KIRCHENTAG. Crowd of 600,000 (Germany).

**Kirchentag** (German: church congress). A series of annual mass Whitsun rallies or festivals of the German Churches (Protestant and Catholic), held approximately every 2 years since 1945; they last 4-7 days, with meetings, workshops, et alia.

**koinonia** (NT Greek). Fellowship; the witness of fellowship.

**Koran.** See Quran.

**Korean.** An Asian ethnolinguistic family and people. Global population: (1970) 47,067,400, (1980) 58,179,400, (1985) 63,929,000.

**Korean indigenous churches.** Denominations indigenous to, and started by, Koreans. Membership: (1980) 140 denominations with 4,814,000 members.

**Krio.** A Eurafrican or Coloured person, in Sierra Leone.

## L

**labour force.** In ILO usage, the economically-active population, both employed and unemployed, excluding students, women at home, retired persons, wholly-dependent persons, et alii.

**labour-intensive.** Methods of industrial or manufacturing organization which employ as many persons as possible, in developing countries.

**laicization.** The process or act of removing or nullifying priests' orders and returning clergy to the status of laity again; mainly among Roman Catholics.

**laity.** The great body of the people of a religious faith as distinguished from its clergy; in Christianity, laity number over 99.7% of the entire membership of the churches.

**lama** (Tibetan: one who is superior). A priest or monk of Tibetan Buddhism (Lamaism).

**Lamaism.** Tantrayana, or the Tantrism school of Buddhism (qv). Global adherents: (1980) 16,350,000.

**Lambeth Conference.** A conference of the bishops of the worldwide Anglican Communion called every 10 years or so by the archbishop of Canterbury; consultative only, not legislative.

**Landeskirche** (German: territorial or state church). In West Germany, the Protestant state or established church of one of the 10 Länder (states).

**land-line relay.** In large evangelistic campaigns, a campaign meeting or service which is transmitted from the host city to another city by land cable, to be heard there by another audience.

**language.** The principal means of communicating culture (the entire way of life of a people); tongue, speech, idiom, dialect.

**language phyla.** 24 major divisions under which the world's languages can be classified.

**languages.** On our classification, the world has 7,010 distinct and separate languages, excluding near variants and around 17,000 dialects.

**language, official state.** See official state languages.

**lapsed.** Former church members who have abandoned churchgoing, or the practice of Christianity, or affiliation, or Christian profession, and have deserted the faith completely; backsliders, disaffiliated, dechristianized, post-Christians, apostates.

**Last Commission.** See Great Commission.

**latent church.** A theological term (coined by P. Tillich) for nominal Christians (qv) and others not part of the organized churches which assert that Jesus is the Christ.

**latifundia** (Latin; Spanish, *latifundio;* Italian *latifondo*). A system of land concentration in vast rural estates; mainly in Latin America.

**Latin.** A European ethnolinguistic family; Romance. Global population: (1970) 184,551,000, (1980) 199,748,900, (1985) 207,414,800.

**Latin American.** One of the 13 geographical races of mankind, speaking Spanish and Portuguese. Global population: (1970) 201,141,800, (1980) 260,534,900, (1985) 292,371,500.

**Latin American indigenous churches.** Non-White indigenous churches, indigenous to Latin American peoples. Global membership: (1970) 8,240,200, (1980) 12,556,300, (1985) 14,949,200.

**Latin Europe.** A term for Belgium, France, Italy, Luxembourg, Monaco, Portugal, San Marino and Spain.

**Latin rite.** Forms of Christian worship and liturgy utilizing or based on Latin; that part of the Roman Catholic Church that employs Latin liturgies. Latin-rite Catholics numbered (in 1970) 665,235,000 (99% of the entire Church) in 242,300 parishes.

**Latter Rain.** A type of Perfectionist-Pentecostals (qv), claiming to inaugurate the Latter or Springtime Rain cited by Old Testament prophets as immediate precursor to the Second Coming of Christ.

**Latter-day Saints.** Mormons; a generic term for followers of the Church of Jesus Christ of Latter-day Saints (Salt Lake City) or of its 85 schismatic breakoff bodies; a marginal Protestant movement. Global membership: (1970) about 180 denominations with 7,843 churches and 2,367,100 adult members; total community (1970) 3,097,100, (1980) 4,001,300, (1985) 4,475,500.

**laura.** A monastery of the Eastern Church originally consisting of monks in community yet inhabiting separate cells grouped around a church.

**lay.** Belonging or relating to those church members not in holy orders; not of the clergy.

**lay ministries.** In this field, organizations significant at the national or wider levels number over 300.

**lay preachers.** Unordained unpaid but officially-accredited spare-time preachers in Protestant churches.

**lay readers.** In Anglicanism, laypersons authorized by a bishop to read parts of the public service, to preach and to assist at Holy Communion.

**lay training centres.** Study centres and other specialized centres for training the laity in their role in church and mission in the modern world.

**lay workers, layworkers.** Full-time unordained church workers.

**layman, laymen.** See laypersons.

**laypersons.** A contemporary term covering both laymen and laywomen, who together number over 99.7% of the entire membership of the churches.

**laywoman, laywomen.** See laypersons.

**Left-Wing Reformation.** See Anabaptists.

**legalism.** The principles and practices characterizing the theological doctrine of strict conformity to a code of deeds and observances.

**legate.** An ecclesiastic representing the Roman Catholic pope and invested with the authority of the Holy See.

**legislature.** The organized body having the authority to make laws for a country or state.

**lepers.** Sufferers from leprosy, still one of the most dreaded diseases and the greatest crippler of all diseases. Global total: (1980) 11,500,000.

**leprosarium, -a.** A hospital for lepers; see medical centres.

**Lesser Vehicle.** The Theravada or Hinayana school

LEGISLATURE. Council of Rulers, United Arab Emirates.

of Buddhists (qv).

**Liberal Anglicans.** Central or Broad Church Anglicans (qv).

**Liberal Catholics.** Followers of churches under bishops-at-large (qv) holding liberal or deviant Catholic views usually including Theosophical, Masonic, Gnostic, magical or occult dogmas and practices. Global membership: (1970) 27 denominations with 170 churches and 51,700 adult members; total community (1970) 87,900, (1980) 120,000, (1985) 137,100.

**Liberal Christians.** Unitarians (qv).

**Liberal Protestants.** See Unitarians.

**liberation.** The act of freeing from control or domination by a foreign party, or the state of being freed from such power.

**libraries, religious.** Major professional exclusively-theological or -religious library collections under church or Christian auspices, specializing primarily in Christianity and religion, a majority of each's holdings being religious. Global totals: (1975) 13,000. Total large Christian libraries with over 35,000 volumes each: 2,100.

**life expectancy.** The expected number of years of life of individuals in a population, based on statistical probability. World average: (1980) 59.2 years.

**life span.** The maximum possible length of human life.

**life styles.** Attitudes to money, property, discipline, moral imperatives, on the part of either denominations or individuals. During the 1970s there has been widespread discussion on what life styles (ways of living) are authentically Christian, focusing on subjects such as standard of living, waste, simplicity of dress and food, etc.

**lingua franca.** An auxiliary or compromise language used between groups having no other language in common.

**linguistics.** The study of human speech in its various aspects; linguistic science.

**Lisbon.** See of Latin Catholic patriarchate and patriarch, since 1716.

**listeners, radio.** See radio listeners.

**listeners' correspondence.** Postal mail from listeners or viewers received by a broadcasting station or programme.

**literacy.** The ability to read and write, as measured by the percentage of the adult population who can read and write their own names and a simple statement. A higher level of competence is required for functional literacy (qv). Global literacy: (1900) 27.9%, (1950) 55.0%, (1975) 64.9%, (1980) 65.7%.

**literate.** A person is defined as literate if he can, with understanding, both read and write a short, simple statement on his everyday life (United Nations).

**literature, Christian.** See Christian literature.

**Liturgical blocs.** A term for 4 of the 7 ecclesiastico-cultural major blocs (qv), which are Pedobaptist and whose worship centres on fixed or written liturgies: Roman Catholicism, Orthodoxy, Anglicanism, Catholicism (non-Roman), together with a few Protestant and indigenous Pedobaptist traditions (Lutheran, Methodist, Reformed, et alia). Global total: 92.0% of all church members. The other 3 blocs are partly Non-Liturgical (qv).

**liturgical languages.** Languages used in the liturgies of Catholic and Orthodox churches, of 2 main kinds: (1) ancient liturgical languages now no longer living (Latin, Coptic, Ge'ez, Syriac, Church Slavonic, etc), and (2) contemporary living languages into which the liturgy has been translated.

**liturgy.** A rite, series of rites, observances or procedures prescribed for public worship in Catholic, Orthodox, Anglican and other churches; the eucharist and its ceremonial and ritual. In the field of liturgy and worship, organizations significant at the national or wider levels number over 150.

**local church.** (1) In Protestant usage, the church in a particular restricted locality. (2) In Roman Catholic usage since Vatican II, either the nation-wide church, or the diocese, or the parish, or other well-defined (usually basic ecclesial) communities.

**local councils of churches.** Councils of churches and denominations in a metropolis, city, district, province or other entity smaller than a country. Global total (1980): about 2,400, in 40 countries (including 766) in Britain).

**local personnel.** Full-time church workers of local (not foreign) citizenship. Global total: (1975) 2,680,000, (1980) 2,950,000.

**local preacher.** An unordained unpaid but officially-accredited spare-time lay preacher.

**local race.** An ethnolinguistic family (qv) or microrace.

**local religionists.** Adherents of local (as contrasted with universal) religions, such as tribal religionists (qv); usually restricted to a single tribe each, and with non-missionary aims.

**locally-founded churches.** Indigenous churches (qv).

**logistics.** The science or art of planning, handling and implementation of personnel, material, facilities and other related factors.

**longitudinal study.** The study of values of a variable over a period of time.

**Lord's Supper.** The Eucharist, Communion Service, Liturgy, Holy Communion, Breaking of Bread, Mass, Agape, Love-Feast.

**Low Church Anglicans.** Conservative Evangelicals and Fundamentalists within Anglicanism, stressing the Evangelical heritage. Global membership in 25 predominantly Low Church dioceses: (1970) 7,800 churches with 1,021,800 adult members, 4,740,100 total community.

**low spiritists.** Afro-American spiritists (qv).

**Lutheran World Federation** (LWF). The major Lutheran world communion. Global constituency: (1980) 75,066,200.

**Lutheran/Reformed united churches.** Some 18 denominations, with most members being in East Germany, belong to united churches of Lutheran and Reformed composition. Global membership: (1970) 6,179 churches with 8,132,000 adult members; total community (1970) 10,558,800, (1980) 9,842,900, (1985) 9,599,000.

**Lutherans.** Followers of Martin Luther and the original German Protestant protesting tradition (16th century). Global membership: (1970) 240 denominations with 62,394 churches and 23,701,300 adult members; total community (1970) 40,415,700, (1980) 43,360,400, (1985) 44,900,000.

## M

**Macanese.** Eurasians in Macao, of Portuguese-Chinese origin.

**macroecclesiography.** The descriptive and numerical analysis of the entire Christian church in the total world context.

**macroevangelistics.** The scientific study, at the global level, of the propagation of Christianity.

**macromissiography.** The descriptive and numerical analysis of the entire Christian world mission set in and related to the total global demographic, ecological, secular and world religious, non-religious and anti-religious contexts.

**magic.** The attempt of man to govern the forces of nature directly, by means of a special lore; white magic has benevolent intent, black magic has malevolent intent.

**magisterium.** In Roman Catholic usage, the church's teaching power, function or office.

**magnetic healing.** A ministry claimed by some charismatic leaders of marginal Protestant bodies, especially Religious Science.

**magnitude, general order of.** See general order of magnitude.

**Mahayana.** The Greater Vehicle school of Buddhists (qv), or Northern Buddhism (China, Japan, et alia). Global adherents: (1980) 153,757,000 (56.2% of all Buddhists).

**mahdi.** A Muslim leader who assumes a messianic role.

**mail censorship.** See censorship, religious.

**mail evangelism.** Postal evangelism (qv).

**mail reliability.** The proportion of Christian mail, expressed as a percentage, which gets through the postal systems of sending and receiving countries; the likelihood or probability of Christian mail getting through the postal services unhindered and uncensored.

**mail survey.** A postal survey (qv).

**mail-order denomination.** A body or organization claiming to be a church or denomination which is largely concerned with the sale by post of religious articles and or alleged academic degrees in theology and related subjects.

**mainline churches.** Mainstream, orthodox Christianity as manifested in its major churches and denominations, Catholic, Protestant, Orthodox, Anglican.

**Maitreya** (Sanskrit). In Buddhism, the Buddha who is to be the next to appear on earth; a bodhisattva.

**major orders.** In Orthodox and Anglican usage: episcopate, priesthood, diaconate. In Roman Catholic usage: priesthood, diaconate, subdiaconate.

**major races.** The 5 races of mankind: Australoid, Capoid, Caucasian (Caucasoid), Mongolian (Mongoloid), Negro (Negroid).

**major seminary.** In Roman Catholic usage, a college for the training of future priests.

**majority church.** In a specific country, the dominant denomination, or largest church established in law.

**Malankara.** See Syro-Malankarese.

**Malikites.** Followers of Malikiya, one of the 4 schools or rites of Sunni Muslim law. Global adherents: (1980) 144,763,000.

**Maltese.** A Middle Eastern ethnolinguistic family. Global population: (1970) 369,300, (1980) 390,400, (1985) 402,600.

**mallam.** In West Africa, a Muslim religious practitioner or cleric.

**Mandaeans.** Gnostics (Mandaiia), followers of 2nd-century-AD syncretistic Jewish-Christian fertility religion (Christians of St John, Followers of John the Baptist, Dippers, Sabaeans, Nasoreans), regarding John the Baptist as the Messiah; found today only in Iraq and Iran. Adherents: (1970) 23,000, (1980) 31,200, (1985) 35,300.

**mandala** (Sanskrit: circle). A sacred design that represents the universe as an aid to meditation.

**mandate** (Latin: *mandatum*). An agreement whereby Propaganda in Rome grants a missionary institute the care and charge of a missionary diocese (begun in 1969).

**mandylion.** In Christian art, (1) the Mandylion of Edessa, or Icon of Christ, the only alleged actual portrait painted of Jesus; eventually lost in the Crusades (see reproduction under Czechoslovakia in Part 7); (2) the robe of Christ in glory.

**manifest church.** A theological term (coined by P. Tillich) for the organized churches who assert that Jesus is the Christ, i.e. for all affiliated Christians (qv).

**manse.** The residence of a Presbyterian clergyman.

**Mantrayana.** The Tantrism school of Buddhists; Tantrayana (qv).

**Maoism.** The teachings of Mao Tse-tung regarded as a secular quasi-religion.

**maphrian** (Syriac). The primate or catholicos of the Syrian Orthodox, or his vicar general.

**marabout.** In West Africa, a charismatic Muslim practitioner.

**marginal Catholics.** Followers of recent schisms or movements ex Church of Rome which have embraced marginal, non-christocentric or non-Christian dogmas.

**marginal churches.** Churches with doctrines deviant from mainline Christian orthodoxy, usually claiming an additional source of ongoing divine revelation and offering or experiencing altered states of consciousness (qv), including trance, dissociation, ecstasy, spirit-possession, mysticism, glossolalia, visionary experiences, faith-healing, etc; and usually drawn from the margins of society in age-distribution and in economic and social status.

**marginal Protestants.** Followers of para-Christian or quasi-Christian Western movements or deviations out of mainline Protestantism (including pseudo-Christian 'New Age' cults), not professing mainstream Protestant christocentric doctrine but claiming a second or supplementary or ongoing source of divine revelation in addition to the Bible (a new Book, angels, visions), but nevertheless centred on Jesus, Christ, the Cross and other Christian features. Global professing adherents: (1970) 10,168,500, (1980) 13,030,200 in 90 countries, (1985) 14,565,500. Global affiliated membership: (1970) 10,830,200, (1980) 14,077,500 in 176 countries, (1985) 15,770,800.

**market research.** The gathering of factual information as to consumer preferences for goods and services.

**marks of the church.** The 4 characteristic marks or 'notes of the church': One, Holy, Catholic, and Apostolic; first enumerated in the Nicene Creed.

**Maronites.** Catholics of Antiochian rite, mainly in Lebanon. Global membership: (1970) 889 parishes, 654,000 adults, 1,130,000 total community.

**Maroon.** A Mulatto (qv).

**Marranos.** Christianized Jews or Moors (Muslims) of medieval and contemporary Spain and Portugal who accepted forced conversion in the 15th century to escape persecution or death, but who still to this day secretly practise the Passover and other Jewish rites; also called Anusim, New Christians, Secret Jews, Crypto-Jews, Conversos. Total (1980): 300,000.

**marriage rate.** The rate at which marriages or other types of liaison take place within a population, measured as marriages per year for every 1,000 population (on average, 8 per 1,000 per year). For Roman Catholic marriages, the world rate has declined gradually from 6.0 per 1,000 Catholics per year (1972), to 5.9 (1973), to 5.7 (1975) or 71% of all liaisons.

**marriages, church.** The actual number of marriages or liaisons per year formally blessed in church or under Christian auspices, which can be expressed as a percentage of the local population's marriage rate (qv).

**marriages, Roman Catholic.** World totals (1975): 3,724,708 between Catholics, 353,702 mixed (between a Catholic and a non-Catholic).

**martyr.** A Christian who voluntarily suffers death as the penalty of witnessing to and refusing to renounce his faith, or a tenet, principle or practice belonging to it.

**martyrs, church of the.** A popular term for a church undergoing heavy state persecution.

**Marxist.** An adherent of Marxism, the political, economic, and social principles and policies advocated by Marx, Engels and their followers.

**Marxist-Leninist.** Related to Communism as developed by Lenin from the doctrines of Marx.

**Marxist-Leninist states.** By 1980, some 30 countries of the world were ruled by regimes espousing Marxist-Leninist principles.

**masjid** (Arabic). A mosque (qv).

MASK. Bamileke ritual dancer (Cameroon).

**mask.** A representation of a face worn in dances and rituals among primitive peoples, especially for identification with supernatural powers or beings.

**Masonic.** Belonging to or connected with Freemasons (qv) or Freemasonry.

**mass.** A celebration of the eucharist or communion.

**mass evangelism.** In this field, organizations significant at the national or wider levels number over 300.

**mass media.** The media of communication designed to reach the masses and to set their ideals, standards and aims: newspapers, radio, motion pictures, television.

**mass movement.** A vast surge of non-Christians into the churches, both by group decision in people movements (qv) and also by individuals, for a variety of motives good and bad.

**materialism.** Preoccupation with material things rather than intellectual or spiritual things.

**Mathew succession churches.** Autonomous Catholic churches under bishops-at-large (qv) whose disputed episcopal orders pass through A.H. Mathew, Archbishop of London (died 1919).

**media.** Channels, methods or systems of communication, information or entertainment.

**median.** That value of an element which divides a set of observations into 2 halves.

**mediated training package.** An instructional package based on the concept of teaching Christians how to disciple others, consisting of 16mm film, colour slides, cassette tape, student manuals, and an instructor.

**medical centres.** Church- or Christian-sponsored hospitals, leprosaria, sanatoria, clinics, dispensaries, maternity centres, et alia, have long been widespread until superseded by government services. Global total: (1975) 29,500 centres, of which 4,600 are hospitals.

**medical missions.** Foreign missionary societies whose primary purpose is medical mission, number some 400.

**medicine.** In the field of medicine and healing, Christian organizations significant at the national or wider levels number over 400.

**medium.** In spiritism, an individual through whom other persons seek to communicate with the spirits of the dead.

**medium-religionists.** Followers of medium-religions, low or high spiritism or spiritualism.

**medium-wave broadcasting.** Term used in Europe for (USA equivalents) AM or standard broadcasting, i.e. utilizing from 540-1600 kcs.

**mediumistic.** Having the qualities of a spiritualistic medium; postulated on the activities of mediums.

**Melanesian.** An Oceanic ethnolinguistic family, with 380 languages. Global population: (1970) 1,415,700, (1980) 1,824,600, (1985) 2,045,500.

**Melkites.** Byzantine Catholics of the Middle East, using Greek or Arabic. Global membership: (1970) 463 parishes, 372,000 adults, 650,000 total community.

**members, church.** Affiliated Christians (qv).

**membership, total church.** Affiliated Christians (qv).

**membership turnover.** A flow of individuals into and out of church membership.

**Memorial.** In Jehovah's Witnesses' usage, the major annual celebration of Christ's death, usually located on a single day worldwide at the beginning of Christendom's Holy Week; attenders number 100-150% more than baptized publishers; total attenders has risen from (1959) 1,283,603 persons to (1974) 4,550,457 (a 14% increase over the previous year).

**men religious.** Priests and brothers in religious orders and congregations.

**Mennonite World Conference** (MWC). The major Mennonite world communion. Global constituency: (1980) 1,011,500.

**Mennonites.** A Protestant tradition dating back to 16th-century Anabaptists and Left-Wing or Radical Reformation. Global membership: (1970) 91 denominations with 5,499 congregations and 522,000 adult members; total community (1970) 947,500, (1980) 1,141,400, (1985) 1,250,100.

**mercy ground.** In West African aladura and other indigenous churches, an open plot of ground near a church, often walled, where Christians may come for private prayer, often prostrate and for whole nights at a time; also called a gethsemane.

**messiah.** One accepted as, or claiming to be, a leader destined to bring about salvation.

**messianic Jews.** Jewish-Christians (qv).

MESSIAH. Eto, the Holy Mama, CF Church (Solomons).

**messianic movement.** A nativistic religious cult led by a prophet proclaiming salvation and the destruction of foreign culture and influence.

**messianism.** An ideological movement or system of ideas that teaches the salvation of mankind through a messiah.

**Messihaye** (Assyrian, Syriac: Christians). East Syrian or Assyrian or Syro-Chaldean Christians.

**Mestizo.** (1) The issue of a European and an Amerindian. (2) A Latin American (Spanish-speaking) ethnolinguistic family. Global population: (1970) 86,475,700, (1980) 113,396,100, (1985) 127,929,600.

**Metaphysical.** Term for movements dating from the 19th-century New Thought movement in the USA, including Spiritualism, Theosophy, Religious Science, et alia.

**Methodists.** A Protestant tradition ex Church of England in 1795. Global membership: (1970) 188 denominations with 97,686 churches and 16,402,300 adult members; total community (1970) 26,213,800, (1980) 29,782,300, (1985) 31,717,500.

**Métis.** A Half-Breed of French and Amerindian ancestry.

**metropolia.** In Eastern Orthodoxy, a metropolitan archdiocese, or diocese.

**metropolitan.** The head of an ecclesiastical province in the Eastern Orthodox Church who has his headquarters in a large city; an Anglican archbishop: a Roman Catholic archbishop with suffragan dioceses.

**metropolitan archdiocese** (symbol M). The senior diocese in an ecclesiastical province.

**metropolitan French.** French citizens born in France.

**metropolitan see.** A metropolitan archdiocese (qv).

**metropolitanate.** The see or office of a metropolitan bishop.

**Miao-Yao.** An Asian ethnolinguistic family. Global population: (1970) 4,424,800, (1980) 5,241,600, 1985) 5,664,900.

**microfilm, microfiche, microform.** An information-handling process involving photographically reducing documents to very small size on film.

**micromissiography.** The descriptive analysis in detail of a single or a local missionary situation.

**Micronesian.** A Pacific ethnolinguistic family, with 13 languages. Global population: (1970) 143,900, (1980) 193,700, (1985) 219,800.

**microrace.** An ethnolinguistic family (qv) or local race.

**micro-church.** A small, very small, miniscule or microcosmic church or fellowship.

**Middle Eastern.** One of the 13 geographical races of mankind; Afro-Asiatic, Afrasian, Hamito-Semitic. Global population: (1970) 157,800,800, (1980) 206,315,400, (1985) 232,659,900.

**migrant church.** A church made up largely or wholly of foreign immigrants from another country.

**migration.** Geographical or spatial mobility; the declared intention to reside in or leave a country for at least a year.

**migration change, migration increase.** The annual nett aggregate of Christian or religious immigration into a country or other body (arrival or transfer of members or co-religionists from other countries or areas) minus emigration out of it (departure or transfer of members or co-religionists to other countries or areas); sometimes termed transfer change.

**military chaplaincies.** Organizations specializing in ministry to military forces number over 200.

**military vicariates or ordinariates** (symbol MV). Roman Catholic jurisdictions each under a bishop serving the military forces of a particular country; vicariates castrensi. Total (1977) 27.

**millenarian.** One who believes in the millennium (the 1,000 years of Revelation 20 during which Christ will reign on earth); a chiliast.

**millennialism.** The doctrine that an earthly millennium of 1,000 years of universal peace and the triumph of righteousness will be fulfilled.

**Millerites.** Adventists (qv).

**milliard.** In British and French languages, 1,000 millions; equivalent to the American term billion.

**Milliarde** (German). A milliard or one (American) billion; 1,000 millions.

**million.** 1,000 thousands; a very large or indefinite number; the mass of common people.

**minifundia** (Latin; Spanish, *minifundio;* Italian, *minifondo*). In Latin America, a subsistence farm, or sub-family farm (too small to sustain a family) employing 2 or less workers.

**miniscule episcopal churches.** Small or minute Catholic denominations operated by bishops-at-large (qv).

**minister.** One duly authorized by ordination to conduct Christian worship, preach the gospel, and administer the sacraments.

**ministers.** In Jehovah's Witnesses' usage, all baptized members are ordained ministers; but there are also special appointed ministers who consist of (1974) 1,780 circuit overseers and 197 district overseers, directly serving the movement's 34,576 congregations.

**ministers' fraternal.** A regular but unofficial meeting for fellowship of clergy and ministers of different denominations working in the same city or area.

**ministry.** See apartment, full-time, group, part-time, team, telephone, tent-making, threefold.

**minor.** A person who has not yet attained his majority, generally a person under 21 years of age.

**minor orders.** Roman Catholic lower clerical grades: porter, lector, exorcist, acolyte.

**minor seminary.** In Roman Catholic usage, a school at secondary level for young men intending to enter the priesthood; junior seminary, preparatory seminary.

**minority.** An ethnic or linguistic group who live in a country but exhibit notable differences from the majority of the population.

**missio Dei** (Latin, the mission of God). A theological term for God's purposes in the world.

**missiography.** The descriptive analysis of the Christian world mission.

**missiology.** The science of missions, missionary history, missionary thought and missionary methods.

**mission.** The essence of mission is: Christians as servants crossing the various boundaries which empirically separate men from one another, declaring to them that in Christ all the walls that divide men from each other are already broken down.

**mission** (sui juris). In Roman Catholic missionary usage, a small territory or station independent of any other jurisdiction or diocese. Total (1977) 4.

**mission board.** A denominational board implementing a denomination's policies with regard to missionary action.

**mission church.** (1) A denomination in a missionary area or land. (2) A church not locally self-supported. (3) A daughter church of a parish church or mother church.

**mission field.** The geographical region, country, or area in which foreign mission is undertaken.

**mission station.** A place of missionary residence in or from which local missionary activity is carried on.

**missionaries, Jehovah's Witnesses'.** Full-time expatriate foreign workers paid by the organization, who are expected to put in 150 or more hours per month preaching. Total (1974): 1,105.

**missionaries on furlough.** Foreign missionaries on leave in their home countries. Since, on average, missionaries serve for 4 years abroad and then proceed on 12 months' furlough, at any given time about 20% of the entire missionary force throughout the world (or 25% of the totals on the field) are at home.

**missionary.** A Christian worker sent to propagate the faith among non-believers usually of a different culture or nation to his own; also used of a non-Christian propagating another religion.

**missionary congregation.** In Roman Catholic usage, a religious institute or congregation whose main purpose is foreign missions.

**missionary density.** See missionary occupation.

**missionary diocese.** In Anglican usage, a diocese not fully self-supporting or autonomous, hence usually directed by a province or by the archbishop of Canterbury.

**missionary district.** An area presided over by an Episcopalian missionary bishop.

**missionary institutes.** Roman Catholic religious institutes (qv) which exist to further foreign missionary work.

**missionary occupation.** An older term meaning the density with which foreign missionaries had occupied a particular area; measured as missionaries per million population.

**missionary proclamation.** The preaching of the gospel with the clear intent to definitively notify people of the gospel and to win converts; first proclamation, first evangelization.

**missionary religions.** A name given to those religions which undertake deliberate and organized missionary work in order to win converts in other countries and cultures.

**missionary societies.** Local, denominational, national or international religious organizations dedicated to the operating of missionary work.

**missionary training colleges.** Foreign missionary training centres (qv).

**missionary transportation.** Service agencies specializing in transport of missionaries by land, sea, and air,

are now numerous.

**missioner.** A home missionary, especially an evangelist in an Anglican diocese.

**missionize.** To carry on missionary work.

**missionizer.** One carrying on missionary work.

**missionization.** The act or process of conducting a mission.

**mission-receiving.** Countries, areas or churches which regularly receive foreign missionaries in their midst.

**mission-sending.** Countries, areas or churches which regularly send foreign missionaries abroad.

**mission-sharing.** Countries, areas or churches which regularly both send and receive foreign missionaries.

**mitra.** Crown worn by Byzantine Catholic bishops.

**mitre.** Hat worn by cardinals, bishops, abbots and other prelates. Styles: precious, gold and simple.

**mixed marriages.** Marriages of a Roman Catholic to a non-Catholic. Total (1975): 353,702 (8.7% of all RC marriages).

**mixed-economy states.** States combining elements of free-enterprise competition with state ownership or direction of key industries.

**mobilization evangelism.** See total mobilization evangelism.

**modality.** Part of a missiological dichotomy; see under sodality.

**moderator.** The presiding officer of various denominations or church assemblies in Protestantism, mainly Presbyterian, Methodist, Reformed.

**Modernism.** A movement in Protestantism from 1870 onwards seeking to establish the meaning and validity of the Christian faith in relation to present human experience and to reconcile traditional theological concepts with the requirements of modern knowledge.

**modernist.** An adherent of Modernism in religion.

MONASTERY. Deir El-Souriany of the Copts (Egypt).

**monastery.** A house of religious retirement or seclusion from the world for persons under religious vows; in Roman Catholic usage, a house operated by a religious monastic order for men or women and always dependent on an abbey.

**monastic order.** A religious institute dedicated to the monastic life.

**monasticism.** The monastic life, system or condition; organized asceticism as practised in a monastery.

**Mongolian, Mongoloid.** One of the 5 major races of mankind; Asiatic, Oriental, speaking over 2,900 languages. Global population: (1970) 1,344,160,000, (1980) 1,620,918,100, (1985) 1,765,128,300.

**monk.** A man who is a member of a monastic order.

**monocultural evangelism.** Evangelistic activities that take place, from evangelist to audiences, within a single culture only.

**monoethnic church.** A church or denomination whose members are entirely, or mainly, from a single ethnic group, tribe, caste or people; a one-tribe or one-people church.

**monolingual.** A person or group knowing or speaking only their own language.

**Monophysites.** Pejorative term for Oriental Orthodox (qv).

**monotheist.** One who believes in monotheism, the doctrine or belief that there exists only one God.

**monsignor, monseigneur** (mgr,msgr). A title of honour

for a non-episcopal prelate of the Roman Catholic Church.

**monthly attenders.** Affiliated Christians (church members) who attend church services of public worship on average once a month.

**monthly letters.** The total regular monthly flow of listeners' letters received by a radio or TV station or programme.

**monthly radio audience.** The average regular audience each month for a Christian radio or TV station or programme.

**Mon-Khmer.** An Austro-Asiatic ethnolinguistic family, with over 50 languages. Global population: (1970) 10,458,400, (1980) 13,757,800, (1985) 15,565,900.

**Moravians.** A Protestant tradition, also known as Unitas Fratrum (Unity of the Brethren), or Continental Pietists. Global membership: (1970) 27 denominations with 1,045 churches and 224,500 adult members; total community (1970) 469,700, (1980) 643,900, (1985) 740,200.

**more developed countries.** On UN definitions (1968), countries whose gross reproduction rate per woman is less than 2.0, or (1973) the industrialized countries of Europe, Northern America, Australia, New Zealand, Japan, USSR, and Temperate South America.

**Mormons.** Followers of the Church of Jesus Christ of Latter-day Saints and its over 90 schismatic bodies.

MOSQUE. The Great Mosque in San (Mali).

**mosque** (Arabic, *masjid*). A Muslim place of public religious worship.

**mother.** A rank or office in numerous Non-White indigenous churches.

**mother church,** Ecclesiastically (not theologically), a large central church (particularly in South American Protestantism) with a number of derived daughter churches.

**mother house, motherhouse.** The original monastery or convent of a religious community, or the one where the superior general or provincial lives.

**mother superior.** A nun who is the head of a religious house.

**mother tongue.** The first language spoken in an individual's home in his early or earliest childhood; one's first language or native language.

**motu proprio** (Latin: by one's own impulse). A rescript initiated and issued by the Roman Catholic pope of his own accord and apart from the advice of others.

**Mozarabs.** Spanish Christians living under Arab rule in Spain, AD 711-1100.

**Mulatto.** The issue of a White and a Black (Negro).

**mullah.** Among Persians, Pakistanis and North Indians, a Muslim religious practitioner or cleric.

**multiethnic church.** A church or denomination whose members come from a variety of distinct and different ethnic groups.

**multilateral conversations.** In ecumenical terminology, theological conversations undertaken by officially-appointed representatives of several churches, denominations, traditions, or confessional families.

**multimedia campaign.** An evangelistic or total mobilization campaign in which extensive, co-ordinated use is made of several of the mass media (radio, TV, film, audiovisuals, print media, et alia).

**multinational corporation.** A large centralized business organization with foreign branches whose activities outside its parent country represent a considerable percentage of its total sales, investments and profits, but whose decisions regarding production, forms of production, marketing, financing, opening of new factories, etc, are made by the parent company.

**multiplication-evangelism.** Evangelism and discipling

of small numbers of believers with a view to them also becoming disciplers (qv) and multiplying exponentially.

**multi-individual conversion** (or decision). The entry of non-Christians into the church, not through one-by-one individual conversion or decision, but at a single point in time through a corporate collective decision of the whole family/village/clan/tribe/people/nation, as a result of evangelistic methods taking into account local village or extended-family decision-making patterns.

**multi-party states.** States in which more than one genuine political party are permitted, active, and alternating occasionally in government; often termed democracies.

**multi-religious, multireligious.** An organization or activity jointly operated by 2 or more religions.

**Munda-Santal.** An Austro-Asiatic ethnolinguistic family, with 20 languages. Global population: (1970) 8,289,700, (1980) 10,593,500, (1985) 11,833,100.

**music and song.** In this field, Christian organizations significant at the national or wider levels number over 200.

**musical groups.** Amateur, semi-professional and professional groups specializing in Christian presentation through music and song have mushroomed in the Western world since 1960, and now number over 30,000.

**musicals, religious.** See religious drama.

**Muslim religious orders.** In Arabic, *tariqa* (qv).

MUSLIMS. Friday prayers, Nairobi (Kenya).

**Muslims.** Followers of Islam, in its 2 main branches (with schools of law, rites or sects): Sunnis or Sunnites (Hanafite, Hanbalite, Malikite, Shafiite), and Shias or Shiites (Ithna-Ashari, Ismaili, Alawite and Zaydi versions); also Kharijite and other orthodox sects; reform movements (Wahhabi, Sanusi, Mahdiya), also heterodox sects (Ahmadiya, Druzes, Yazidis), but excluding syncretistic religions with Muslim elements, and partially-islamized tribal religionists. Global adherents: (1970) 550,919,000, (1980) 722,956,500 in 152 countries, (1985) 817,065,200.

**mutually-exclusive categories.** A typology or series of categories each exclusive in its coverage

**mutually-unintelligible languages.** A group of languages any 2 of which are each unintelligible to the other.

**mysticism.** The experience of mystical union or direct communion with God; the doctrine or belief that direct communion with God is attainable.

**myth.** A traditional story explaining some practice, belief, institution or natural phenomenon; parable, allegory, legend, saga, fable.

**mythology.** The myths dealing with gods and demigods of a particular people.

# N

**Nasoreans.** Mandaeans (qv).

**nation.** A politically-organized nationality, ethnolinguistic group or family or people, usually with independent existence in a sovereign nation-state; state, country.

**nation, sovereign.** See sovereign territory.

**national.** (1) Relating to a nation. (2) One who owes permanent allegiance to a nation without regard to place of residence; often a citizen but not necessarily so.

**national Christian councils.** Councils of churches and denominations which also include parachurch organizations as full members.

**national church.** The church of a nation; established

church, state church, or occasionally a former state church now disestablished.

**national clergy.** Clergy who are nationals of the nation they work in.

**national conciliarism.** Nationwide councils of churches and Christian councils of all kinds number about 550.

**national councils of churches.** Councils of churches in which full membership is only open to denominations, but not to parachurch organizations.

**national income per person.** The average per capita annual income in a country at a particular date, usually derived as gross national product (qv) per capita.

**native.** An individual born or raised in the territory in which he lives.

**native speakers.** Mother-tongue speakers of a specific language.

**nativistic movement.** Among tribal or primitive peoples, a movement advocating or advancing the perpetuation or re-establishment of native culture traits and a concomitant restriction or removal of foreign culture elements often accompanied by a strong messianic or ceremonial cult.

**natural change.** Demographic change as experienced by the whole population of a country or area, including all its religious bodies, composed of biological change together with migration change. Global total: (1980) about 84 millions.

**natural growth rate.** The nett sum of crude birth rate in the populaton minus crude death rate, plus nett immigration rate.

**natural increase.** In United Nations usage, biological change or the excess of births over deaths in a population.

**naturalization.** The process by which aliens acquire the nationality of their country of residence.

**naturalized persons.** Former aliens who have now become citizens.

**negotiations.** In ecumenical terminology, church union discussions between 2 or more churches after a public commitment has been made towards eventual organic union.

**Negrito.** An Austro-Asiatic ethnolinguistic family; Asiatic Pygmy. Global population: (1970) 37,600, (1980) 52,200, (1985) 60,000.

**Negro.** One of the 5 major races of mankind; Negroid, Equatorial, Black, speaking about 1,390 languages. Global population: (1970) 311,719,300, (1980) 403,066,900, (1985) 452,905,200.

**neologism.** A new word, usage or expression; word coinage or redefinition.

**neophyte.** A recent convert, catechumen, proselyte; a newly-ordained Roman Catholic priest or novice in a convent.

**neo-Buddhist.** Relating to a new or recent Buddhist sect or movement.

**Neo-Christianity.** A reinterpretation of Christianity in terms of a current philosophy, as rationalism in the 19th century.

**Neo-Evangelicals.** A term used by Fundamentalists (qv) to describe Evangelicals willing to co-operate with non-Evangelicals and to re-examine basic Evangelical dogmas and positions.

**Neo-Fundamentalists.** A term used by extreme Fundamentalists to describe Fundamentals willing to work with other types of Evangelicals.

**Neo-Hawaiian.** The populace of the state of Hawaii, USA; Aboriginal Hawaiians (pure Polynesians) now number only 2%, the rest being Neo-Hawaiians, a highly-mixed population with (blood-group admixture) 78% Polynesian origin, 14% Mongoloid (Chinese/Japanese/Filipino/Korean), 8% Caucasoid (European).

**neo-Hindus.** Followers of new or recent Hindu sects, offshoots or movements, including Divine Light Mission. Global adherents: (1980) 9,741,000.

**neo-orthodoxy.** A 20th-century movement in Protestant theology characterized by a reaction against liberalism, re-emphasis on some orthodox Reformation doctrines, and renewed stress on classic Protestant formularies.

**neo-paganism.** Revived or new paganism, as in Iceland.

**Neo-pentecostals.** Charismatics in organized renewal groups within non-Pentecostal Protestant denominations. Global active membership: (1970) 824,100, (1980) 4,286,800 in 38 countries, (1985) 6,460,900.

**Neo-Protestants.** A term sometimes applied to newer Protestant traditions, including Adventists, Brethren, Pentecostals, etc.

**Nestorians.** Assyrians (qv).

**New Apostolics.** Christians of Catholic Apostolic origin and tradition, who belong to the New Apostolic Church (largely German in membership) or its offshoots. Global membership: (1980) 1,600,000.

**new birth.** A turning-point in life when a person commits himself or herself to Christ, experience claimed by 34% of the population in the USA.

**New Calendar.** The New Style or Gregorian Calendar, replacing the Old Style or Julian Calendar, introduced in 1582 by Pope Gregory XIII, adopted by England in 1752, and by most Orthodox in 1924 except the Churches of Jerusalem, Russia, Serbia and Bulgaria, and Old Calendarists (qv).

**New Christian** (Spanish, *cristiano nuevo*). A Marrano (qv).

**New Church.** A major branch of the Swedenborgian movement (qv).

**New Life for All** (NLFA). A saturation evangelism programme, begun in Nigeria in 1964, involving total mobilization of Christians at the local church level.

**New Reader Scriptures.** UBS-sponsored programme for producing versions of the Scriptures specially compiled for newly-literate persons. Global distribution totals: (1976) 5,623,503 New Reader portions, 38,136,399 New Reader selections.

**New Religions.** The so-called Asiatic 20th-century New Religions, New Religious movements, or radical new crisis religions (new Far Eastern or Asiatic indigenous non-Christian syncretistic mass religions, founded since 1800 and mostly since 1945), including the Japanese neo-Buddhist and neo-Shinto new religious movements, and Korean, Chinese, Vietnamese and Indonesian syncretistic religions, et alia. See New-Religionists.

**New Testament.** The covenant of God with man embodied in the coming of Christ; the printed volume of 27 books.

**New Testament distribution.** Global distribution (free, subsidized, commercial): (1975) 51,049,000 copies of the NT per year, (1980) 57,500,000.

**New Thought.** A mental healing movement embracing a number of small groups and organizations devoted to spiritual healing, the creative power of constructive thinking, and personal guidance from an inner presence.

NEW-RELIGIONISTS. Rissho-koseikai, Tokyo (Japan).

**New-Religionists.** Followers of the so-called New Religions (qv) of Asia. Global adherents: (1970) 76,443,100, (1980) 96,021,800 in 22 countries, (1985) 106,317,600.

**newspapers, daily.** In UNESCO usage, newspapers which are published at least 4 times a week.

**newspapers, general-interest.** In UNESCO terminology, publications devoted primarily to recording news of current events in public affairs, international affairs, politics, etc.

**Nilotic** (Para-Nilotic). An African ethnolinguistic family, with about 90 languages. Global population: (1970) 12,590,500, (1980) 17,074,400, (1985) 19,527,900.

**nirvana** (Sanskrit). In Hinduism, Jainism and Buddhism, the state of freedom from *karma*, extinction of desire, passion and illusion.

**Nisei** (Japanese: second-generation). A Japanese-American son or daughter of Issei (first-generation immigrants) parents, and born and educated in the Americas.

**Nizaris.** Nizari Ismailis, Khojas (qv).

**nomads.** Peoples with no fixed residence but migrating seasonally.

**nominal Christians.** Persons professing publicly to be Christians but who are not affiliated to churches, i.e. not church members; unaffiliated or unchurched; Christians not, no longer, or not yet attached to organized Christianity, or who have rejected the institutional churches whilst retaining Christian beliefs and values, who may be Christians individually but are not part of the churches' corporate life, community or fellowship. Global total: (1970) 84,769,800, (1980) 109,296,800 in 157 countries, (1985) 122,664,900.

**nominal fringe.** In countries with a Christian majority, the fringe of nominal Christians around the churches who are not church members.

**nomogram.** A figure or diagram from which calculations can be made at sight.

**Nonconformists.** Dissenters, persons who do not conform to the doctrine or discipline of an established church; especially, members of religious bodies separated from the Church of England.

**non-adherents.** Persons who are not adherents of any religion; non-religious, agnostics or atheists.

**non-affiliated.** Nominal Christians (qv).

**non-attenders.** Non-practising Christians (qv).

**non-attending Christians.** Non-practising Christians (qv).

**non-belief.** Unbelief (qv).

**non-believers.** Persons who are not adherents of or believers in any religion; non-religious, agnostics or atheists.

**Non-Chalcedonian.** Oriental Orthodox (qv).

**non-Christian attenders.** See attending non-Christians.

**non-Christian religionists.** Adherents of all religions in the world except Christianity. Global total: (1970) 1,685,101,200 (46.7% of the world), (1980) 2,030,210,200 (46.4%), (1985) 2,216,103,400 (46.3%).

**non-Christians.** All persons who are not Christian adherents of any kind, including non-believers (agnostics, or atheists).

**non-conciliar.** Unconnected with the Ecumenical Movement or with Evangelical, Indigenous or any other form of councils or conciliarism.

**Non-conciliar Evangelicals.** Evangelicals rejecting contact or co-operation with the Ecumenical Movement.

**non-confessional.** Used of a denomination or Christian activity unaligned with any confessions.

**non-confessional Christianity.** Of the world's 6,156 significant Christian denominations, 2,035 (with 67,141,800 members, i.e. total community in 1980) have no confessional allegiance (membership in world confessional councils), and a further 1,949 (with 71,557,000 members) have no confessional allegiance but themselves form quasi-confessions (qv) or non-confessional international denominational bodies.

**non-confessional international denominational bodies** (quasi-confessions). Denominations which do not belong to any of the recognized world confessional bodies or families, but which function, or regard themselves, or are often regarded, as themselves confessional bodies or world families of churches, each with organized branches and churches in 3 or more nations, although in fact each is a single worldwide or international denomination. Global membership: see quasi-confessions.

**non-denominational** (no-church groups). Churches or movements which, in reaction to Western missionary work, reject all ecclesiastical labels even including 'Christian', and all ecclesiastical practices including baptism.

**non-diocesan.** A term describing clergy and other staff in a diocese who are not on the diocesan payroll but are employed by a province, other Christian body, or a secular agency.

**non-evangelizing Christians.** Nominal Christians and non-practising Christians who, although themselves evangelized, contribute nothing to the ongoing process of the evangelization of their own people or country or of the world.

**non-historical Catholic.** Churches or Christians who regard themselves as in the Catholic tradition but who have no historical continuity supporting their claim.

**non-historical Orthodox.** Churches or Christians who regard themselves as in the Orthodox tradition but who have no historical continuity supporting their claim.

**Non-Liturgical blocs.** A term used here for 3 of the 7 ecclesiastico-cultural major blocs (qv) which are largely Baptistic or Baptists (i.e. practising adult or believer's baptism only) and whose worship is largely extempore without written liturgies: Protestantism (except for the Lutheran, Reformed, Methodist and a few other traditions), marginal Protestantism, and Non-White indigenous Christianity. Numerically, Non-Liturgical Christians number only 11.3% of global church members. The other 4 blocs are termed Liturgical (qv).

**non-participating member.** A church member or affiliated Christian who does not practise regularly; a non-practising Christian (qv).

**non-practising Christians.** Christians who are affiliated to churches but are inactive, non-attending (sometimes called dormant Christians). Global total: (1970) 247,787,800, (1980) 305,034,400, (1985) 335,578,900.

**non-receiving countries.** From the standpoint of foreign mission, countries which prohibit the receiving of foreign missionaries from other countries.

**non-religious.** Persons professing no religion, or professing unbelief or non-belief, non-believers, agnostics, freethinkers, liberal thinkers, non-religious humanists, indifference to both religion and atheism, apathetic, opposed on principle neither to religion nor to atheism; sometimes termed secularists or materialists; also post-Christian, dechristianized or de-religionized populations. Global adherents: (1970) 543,065,300, (1980) 715,901,400 in 177 countries, (1985) 805,784,900.

**non-religious Buddhists.** Persons whose family religion is Buddhism but who as individuals profess to have no personal religion.

**non-religious quasi-religionists.** Adherents of non-religious quasi-religions (some forms of agnosticism, fascism, humanism, liberal humanism, nationalism, Nazism, some forms of non-religion or secularism).

**non-Roman Catholics.** See Catholics (non-Roman).

**non-sending.** Countries, areas or churches which, for various reasons, never send, or are not permitted by the state to send, foreign missionaries abroad.

**non-sovereign territory.** A country listed in the United Nations' list of territories but not completely autonomous or independent or self-governing.

**non-trinitarian.** A Christian tradition not emphasizing the doctrine of the Trinity, hence often regarded as unitarian.

**Non-White.** A collective term referring to all races and ethnolinguistic groups distinct from the White races indigenous to Europe and North America. Global Non-White population: (1970) 2,762,999,700, (1980) 3,455,726,800, (1985) 3,826,509,500.

NON-WHITE INDIGENOUS. African Israel Church (Kenya).

**Non-White indigenous Christians.** Black/Third-World indigenous Christians in denominations, churches or movements indigenous to Black or Non-White races originating in the Third World, locally-founded and not foreign-based or Western-imported, begun since AD 1500, Black/Non-White-founded, Black/Non-White-led, forming autonomous bodies independent of Western and Eastern churches, with no Western ties, often schismatic, separatist, anti-establishment, sometimes anti-Western, anti-White or anti-European in reaction to Western influences. Global professing adherents: (1970) 49,022,400, (1980) 67,131,100 in 90 countries, (1985) 76,896,500. Global affiliated membership: (1970) 58,702,000, (1980) 82,181,100 in 145 countries, (1985) 94,797,600.

**norm.** A model, type, pattern; an authoritative rule or standard.

**normative.** Prescriptive, regulative, didactic.

**North Indian.** An Indo-Iranian ethnolinguistic family. Global population: (1970) 536,186,500, (1980) 687,054,200, (1985) 770,072,000.

**Northern Amerindian.** An American Indian ethnolinguistic family, with 200 languages. Global population: (1970) 1,504,500, (1980) 1,683,000, (1985) 1,780,600.

**Northern Buddhism.** Mahayana (qv).

**notes of the church.** Marks of the church (qv).

**notice-boards.** Since vast numbers of local church buildings carry their own detailed notice-boards, these are very useful in rapid surveys.

**novice.** One who has entered a religious house and is on probation.

**no-church.** See non-denominational.

**no-party states.** Independent nations ruled without a political party.

**nuclear Christianity.** Active, practising, committed Christianity.

**nuclear Christians.** See committed Christians.

**Nuclear Mande.** An African ethnolinguistic family, with about 30 languages. Global population: (1970) 6,584,400, (1980) 8,403,500, (1985) 9,395,000.

**Nusayris.** Alawites (qv).

**nun.** A woman belonging to a religious institute or order of women with solemn vows (moniales); a woman religious in simple vows is more properly termed a sister.

**nunciature.** The diplomatic office of the Holy See in a foreign country. World total: (1974) 79.

**nuncio.** The diplomatic envoy of the Roman Catholic pope as Sovereign of the Holy See, accredited to a foreign government in a country where Catholics are a majority, and hence accepted as diplomatic doyen. World total: (1974) 37.

**nuns, Roman Catholic.** World total (1978): 946,398; including 778,000 of Pontifical Right, a decline from 791,500 one year earlier.

## O

**obeah.** Jamaican-African word for power.

**obedience.** A sphere of jurisdiction; control, rule, spiritual authority over others; conformity to the rule of a monastic order.

**oblate.** One offered or devoted to the monastic life or to some special religious service or work; sometimes, a layman living at a monastery.

**occasional attenders.** Affiliated Christians (church members) who attend church services of public worship only occasionally or irregularly.

**occult.** The mysterious, supernatural, secret, esoteric, in religion and magic.

**Oceanic.** One of the 13 geographical races of mankind, speaking 1,083 languages. Global population: (1970) 4,846,700, (1980) 6,218,000, (1985) 6,957,200.

**offertory.** A collection of money taken at a religious service.

**office.** In liturgy, a set form of prayer or worship drawn up by church authority, usually for daily recitation by clergy.

**officer.** In Salvation Army usage, a Salvationist who has left secular employment and is engaged in full-time commissioned Army service. Global total of SA officers: 28,000 in 83 countries.

**office-holders** (German, *Amtstragern*). Officials of the New Apostolic Church, mostly Germans, and totalling 30,000.

**official languages of the United Nations.** In 1978, there were 6: Arabic, Chinese, English, French, Russian, Spanish.

**official religion.** See state religion.

**official state languages.** Languages proclaimed by states as their official or national means of communication number 76. Of these, 31 serve populations of over 20 million each, 31 serve from 1 to 20 million each, 5 from 250,000 to a million each, and 9 serve under 250,000 each.

**old age.** Usually taken to begin at the age of retirement (60-65 years).

**Old Apostolics.** Catholic Apostolics (qv), Irvingites.

**Old Believers.** Followers of AD 1666 schisms ex Russian Orthodox Church, retaining use of Old Slavonic; Old Ritualists. Global membership: (1970) 11 denominations with 616 churches and 1,596,900 adult members; total community (1970) 2,274,000, (1980) 2,543,800, (1985) 2,681,800.

**Old Calendar.** The Old Style or Julian Calendar, devised by Julius Caesar in BC 46, now 13 days behind the New or Gregorian Calendar, followed by all Orthodox churches up to 1918, and still followed in 1980 by (a) the Churches of Jerusalem, Russia, Serbia, and Bulgaria, (b) most of the monasteries on Mount Athos, and (c) various groups of Old Calendarists (qv).

**Old Calendarists.** Also called Paleohemerologites (from Greek, Palaioimerologitai), or Authentic Orthodox; Greek Orthodox who reject the Ecumenical Patriarchate's change in 1924 from the Old (Julian) Calendar to the New (Gregorian) Calendar. Global membership: (1970) 5 denominations (schisms ex Church of Greece) with 188 churches and 105,500 adult members; total community (1970) 209,000, (1980) 215,400, (1985) 218,800.

OLD CATHOLICS. Episcopal liturgy, Vienna (Austria).

**Old Catholics.** Followers of schisms ex Church of Rome retaining Old Catholic apostolic succession of bishops; especially schisms of 1702, 1724, 1870, 1897. Global membership: (1970) 20 denominations with 723 churches and 307,100 adult members; total community (1970) 445,900, (1980) 443,600, (1985) 442,500.

**Old Ritualists.** Old Believers (qv).

**Old Slavic.** Church Slavonic (qv).

**Old Testament.** The covenant of God with the Hebrews as set forth in the Bible; or, the 39 canonical books which form its record in the first part of the Bible; or a printed version or copy thereof.

**old-age population.** Persons over 65 years old.

**older churches.** A term sometimes used for the older or historical mainline denominations of Europe and North America, in contrast to the so-called younger churches of the Third World.

**on trial.** Used in Methodist and other circles for new members who are placed on trial for a period of months to demonstrate their commitment to becoming members.

**on-demand publishing of books.** Publication of material which cannot be economically handled conventionally; the production and distribution of copies of books, one or a few at a time, in response to orders rather than from a pre-printed stock of copies; usually by photocopying author-prepared copy or production from microform; a recent technique for publishers with 'excess of material worthy of publication'.

**Oneness-Pentecostals.** Also termed Unitarian-Pentecostals, Jesus-Only Pentecostals (because of baptism in name of Jesus only). Global membership, including Non-White indigenous bodies: (1970) 111 denominations with 13,350 churches and 1,594,300 adult members; total community (1970) 2,683,200, (1980) 3,682,900, (1985) 4,207,300.

**on-line database.** A large computerized data bank of information arranged for instant retrieval and in which all data can be immediately accessed.

**Open Brethren.** Christian Brethren (qv).

**open communion.** The practice of inviting all adults present at a service of worship, including those from other denominations, to participate in communion at the Lord's Table.

**operationalism.** The view that the concepts or terms used in non-analytic scientific statements must be definable in terms of identifiable and repeatable operations.

**operations research.** The application of scientific and mathematical methods to the study and analysis of complex problems not traditionally considered to fall within the field of profitable scientific enquiry.

**ophthalmic mission.** A foreign missionary society specializing in eye services.

**opinion-makers.** See decision-makers.

**opportunity.** In evangelization, the occasion, chance, time, or combinations of circumstances, times and places suitable or favourable for persons to hear and understand the gospel.

**ordained minister.** See minister.

**order, religious.** See religious orders.

**orders.** The office and dignity of a person in the Christian ministry.

**ordinand.** A person in training for ordination.

**ordinariates** (symbol O). In the Roman Catholic Church, 6 countries have country-wide jurisdictions for Eastern-rite Catholics, termed ordinariates.

**ordinary.** In canon law, an ecclesiastic in exercise of the jurisdiction permanently annexed to his office; in the RC Church, the pope and all diocesan bishops,

abbots, apostolic administrators or vicars, prelates and prefects; in Anglican usage, the bishop or archdeacon.

**ordination.** The act of admission into, or the status of being in, the Christian ministry.

**ordination of women.** See women, ordination of.

**ordinations, annual.** Total to the Roman Catholic priesthood: (1974) 4,380 secular, 2,551 religious; (1975) 4,140 secular, 2,488 religious.

**organic union.** The goal of church union negotiations whereby 2 previously separate denominations become a single organically-administered new denomination.

**organized Christianity.** Christianity as formally organized into blocs, traditions, denominations, and councils. Global membership of affiliated Christians, i.e. affiliated to organized Christianity: (1980) 1,323,389,700, (1985) 1,425,927,300.

**organized congregation.** See congregation.

**organized religion.** A religion as formally organized by subdivisions, schools, sects, denominations or other bodies or groupings requiring membership.

**Oriental Catholics.** Eastern-rite Catholics (qv) in communion with the See of Rome.

**Oriental Jews.** The third major group of Diaspora Jews, after Ashkenazis (German-rite) and Sefardis (Spanish-rite); sometimes treated as a sub-division of Sefardis; Arabic-speaking Jews from North Africa and the Middle East. Global total: (1980) 1,694,000.

**Oriental Orthodox.** Christians of Pre-Chalcedonian/ Non-Chalcedonian/Monophysite tradition, of 5 major types: Armenian, Coptic, Ethiopian, Syrian, Syro-Malabarese. Global church membership: (1970) 22,416,200 (15.6% of all Orthodox faithful), (1980) 27,735,300 (17.3%), (1985) 30,531,500 (18.0%). The percentage is rising due to rapid growth of Third-World Oriental Orthodoxy.

**Oriental Orthodox Churches Conference.** First conference of Syrian, Armenian, Coptic, Ethiopian and Syro-Malabarese Orthodox churches, held in Addis Ababa 1965. Global constituency: (1980) 27,720,300 total community.

**Oriental-rite Catholics.** Eastern-rite Catholics (qv).

**Orthodox.** In 4 traditions: Eastern (Chalcedonian), Oriental (Pre-Chalcedonian, Non-Chalcedonian, Monophysite), Nestorian (Assyrian), and non-historical Orthodox. Global professing adherents: (1970) 111,898,600, (1980) 124,419,200 in 96 countries, (1985) 130,837,400. Global affiliated membership: (1970) 143,402,500, (1980) 160,737,900 in 107 countries, (1985) 169,648,700.

**Orthodox pentecostals.** Orthodox in the organized charismatic renewal, expressed in healings, tongues, prophesying, etc. Global active membership: (1970) 15,200, (1980) 157,000 in 6 countries, (1985) 241,000.

ORTHODOXY. Throne/altar, Russian Cathedral, Nice (France).

**Orthodoxy.** The systems of faith, practice and discipline of the Eastern Orthodox and Oriental Orthodox Churches.

**orthodoxy.** Right teaching in Christian theology, as contrasted with heresy and heterodoxy.

**orthography.** A method of representing the sounds of a language by written or printed symbols; the printed letter set used.

**other religionists.** A term used here in Tables 1 for total adherents of (a) other larger non-Christian religions too few for these religions to be listed, and (b) all other smaller non-Christian religious faiths, quasi-religions, pseudo-religions, para-religions, religious systems, religious philosophies, and semi-religious brotherhoods (Gnostic, Occult, Masonic, Mystic, etc).

**otiose.** Used of God in many pagan religions: remote, aloof, uninvolved, uninterested in the human race.

**Outcastes.** Persons in India considered outside caste society. See scheduled castes.

**outreach.** In evangelization, the extent or length or whole complex of all varieties of evangelistic reaching out to the non-Christian world on the part of the Christian community.

**outreach into the world.** The act or process of the church reaching out to the world's non-Christian populations, in evangelism and in service.

**outsider.** A non-Christian, or non-affiliated.

**overlapping membership.** Membership of an individual or group, or of congregations, in 2 distinct church areas or churches or denominations.

## P

**Pacific.** One of the 13 geographical races of mankind, with 135 languages. Global population: (1970) 2,237,200, (1980) 2,958,800, (1985) 3,345,100.

**Pacific indigenous churches.** Non-White indigenous churches in Oceania, indigenous to Pacific or Oceanic peoples. Global membership: (1970) 88,900, (1980) 104,900, (1985) 113,100.

**paedobaptist.** See pedobaptist.

**pagan religionists.** See neo-paganism.

**pagans** (Latin: country-dwellers). A somewhat outdated term for non-Christians, heathen, polytheists, animists, shamanists, et alii.

**pagoda.** A stupa (qv).

**Paleoasiatic.** An Asian ethnolinguistic family. Global population: (1970) 40,000.

**Paleohomerologites.** Authentic Orthodox or Old Calendarists (qv).

**pantheism.** A doctrine that the universe conceived of as a whole is God.

**pantheist.** A follower of pantheism.

**papal bull.** A formal letter from the Roman pope, named after the lead seal (bulla) attached to it.

**Papuan.** An Oceanic ethnolinguistic family, with 700 languages. Global population: (1970) 3,198,500, (1980) 4,109,400, (1985) 4,601,800.

**parachurch.** Almost a church, resembling a church.

**parachurch agencies.** Service agencies (qv), especially those which develop a life distinct or separate from the organized churches.

**paradenomination.** A service agency which develops its own distinct and separate church life and resembles a new or separate denomination, offering its members worship facilities and other denominational perquisites.

**parallel church.** In Roman Catholic usage, suppressed but ongoing underground liberal or activist groups within the church, especially of priests (as in Portugal).

**paraphrase.** A loose translation of Scripture incorporating overt interpretation (e.g. NTME, LB).

**para-Christians.** See marginal Protestants.

**parentheses.** In printing, curved marks ( ) in contrast to square brackets [ ].

**parish.** An ecclesiastical unit of area committed to one pastor; a portion of a diocese committed to the pastoral care of one clergyman.

**Parsis** (Parsees). Descendants of Zoroastrians of Persia, worshippers of Ahura Mazda. Sects: Kadmis and Shahanshahis. Global adherents: (1970) 121,000, (1980) 154,200 in 10 countries, (1985) 171,800.

**parson.** A clergyman; rector or incumbent of a parochial church.

**partially-closed countries.** 24 countries in the world which are not fully closed to foreign mission, though strict control is exercised.

**participating member.** A practising Christian (qv) or practising church member. In Disciples (USA) usage, 'one who exercises a continuing interest in one or more of the following ways: attendance, giving, activity, spiritual concern for the fellowship of the congregation regardless of the place of residence'.

**participatory media.** See folk media.

**particular church.** In Roman Catholic usage (as e.g. in Vatican II documents), the universal church as organized in a particular diocese; the diocesan church; sometimes called the local church.

**Partners in Mission.** A scheme within the Anglican Communion whereby an autonomous church invites a number of sister churches or provinces to confer with it on discharging its mission in its own locality.

**part-time worker.** A recognized or accredited church worker whose main work is Christian ministry but who is also engaged in part-time secular work for his livelihood; in contrast to spare-time or full-time.

**pasaka, pasika** (Shona and other African languages). Passover, Easter communion service in certain African indigenous churches, attracting scores of thousands of members.
workers.

**Paschal communicants.** Roman Catholic Easter communicants (qv); all who actually take communion at Easter over a 4-week period.

**pascalisants** (French). See Paschal communicants.

**passover.** Annual Jewish religious festival commemorating deliverance from Egypt; for Christians, symbolic of Christ's atonement for sin.

**pastor.** A clergyman, priest or minister responsible for the cure of souls.

**pastoral centres.** In Roman Catholic usage, parishes, quasi-parishes, mission stations and a few other categories. World totals (1976): 322,887 centres (200,116 parishes and quasi-parishes, 83,380 mission stations, 39,391 other centres), being an increase from 297,046 in 1973.

**pastoral council.** In Roman Catholic usage, a diocesan, or a nation-wide, council of bishops, priests, religious and laity.

**pastoral region.** See apostolic region.

**pastoral reorganization.** An updating or modernizing rearrangement of traditional jurisdictions in the Roman Catholic Church in a country, in the interests of more realism, better pastoral care, new urban situations, etc.

**pastoralia.** The study of pastoral work in the church.

**pastors' conferences.** Protestant conferences for pastors and clergy in developing countries, held frequently, under sponsorship of World Vision.

**patriarch.** The supreme bishop of an autocephalous church, especially Catholic or Orthodox.

**patriarchal diocese.** A diocese administered by a patriarch.

**patriarchal exarchate** (symbol PE). The jurisdiction of an exarch under a patriarch.

**patriarchal vicariate** (symbol VP). A vicariate, usually in another city, of one of the traditional patriarchates. Total (1975): 12 Roman Catholic.

**patriarchate.** The office, dignity, jurisdiction, province, or see of a patriarch. Global total: (1980) 31 traditional Catholic (13) and Orthodox (18) patriarchates, and over 100 more of recent establishment and unsupported historical claim.

**Patristics.** Patrology (qv).

**patrology.** The science or scientific study of the teachings of the Fathers of the Church, defined as in the West all Christian writers up to Gregory the Great (died 604), and in the East to John Damascene (died 749).

**peak publishers.** In Jehovah's Witnesses' usage, the maximum number of publishers (qv) in action in any given year.

**pedobaptist.** Pedobaptist churches baptize children and infants of Christian families because they believe that in doing so they are faithful to the teaching and practice of Christ and his apostles and of the Church from the earliest times; they do not receive or give any second baptism, since baptism is by its very nature unrepeatable; they respect the convictions of fellow-Christians in the Baptist traditions (baptizing adults only) and desire fellowships and unity with them.

**Pedobaptists.** Christians in traditions that baptize infants. Global total: (1970) 1,041,265,000, (1980) 1,217,519,000, (1985) 1,311,851,000; i.e. 92% of global church membership. Some 3.3% of these are doubly-affiliated, i.e. also members of non-Pedobaptist churches and traditions.

**penetration.** The extent of evangelization into a people's or region's culture and life, usually overcoming difficulties or resistance or opposition.

**Pentecost.** Christian festival on the 7th Sunday after Easter commemorating descent of the Holy Spirit; called Pentecost by Roman Catholics, Whitsunday by Anglicans and others.

**Pentecostal.** With a capital 'P', the noun or adjective

refers here to charismatic Christians in separate or distinct Pentecostal denominations of White origin.

**pentecostal.** With a small 'p', the noun or adjective refers here to charismatic Christians (1) still within mainline non-Pentecostal denominations, and (2) those in Non-White indigenous pentecostal denominations.

**Pentecostal Apostolics.** Pentecostals differing from other Pentecostals in stress on complex hierarchy of living apostles, prophets and other charismatic officials. Global membership, including Non-White indigenous bodies: (1970) 77 denominations with 10,607 churches and 1,192,900 adult members; total community (1970) 2,402,200, (1980) 3,719,900, (1985) 4,455,100.

**Pentecostal World Conference** (PWC). The major Pentecostal world communion, mainly a triennial conference (since 1947) with minimal continuity. Global constituency: (1980) 25,155,400 total community.

**Pentecostalism.** A Christian confession or ecclesiastical tradition holding the distinctive teaching that all Christians should seek a post-conversion religious experience called the Baptism with the Holy Spirit, and that a Spirit-baptized believer may receive one or more of the supernatural gifts known in the Early Church: instantaneous sanctification, the ability to prophesy, practice divine healing, speak in tongues (glossolalia), or interpret tongues.

PENTECOSTALS. In the *orante* (praying) position (France).

**Pentecostals.** Followers of Pentecostalism (qv), a major world tradition originating around 1900. Global membership in all Pentecostal and pentecostal denominations (including Non-White indigenous): (1970) 36,794,000, (1980) 51,167,200 in 1,240 denominations, (1985) 58,999,900.

**Pentecostals: Oneness** (Jesus only). See Oneness-Pentecostals.

**Pentecostals: 2-crisis-experience.** See Baptistic-Pentecostals.

**Pentecostals: 3-crisis-experience.** See Holiness-Pentecostals.

**Pentecostals: 4-crisis-experience.** See Perfectionist-Pentecostals.

**Pentecostal-charismatics.** A blanket term for all Pentecostals, pentecostals, neo-pentecostals, and charismatics (qv). Global totals (1980): (a) active regularly-involved persons, 62,200,000; (b) all persons professing or claiming to be Pentecostal-charismatics, over 100 million worldwide.

**people.** (1) A collection of persons who are linked by a common past or a common culture, or who have a common affinity for one another. (2) An ethnolinguistic people (qv) or ethnolinguistic sub-family.

**people distance.** Cultural distance (qv).

**people group.** A people (qv).

**people movement.** A large-scale movement to Christ and into the church by a fair proportion of a people, acting as a group and with a group decision.

**people's palace.** In Salvation Army usage, a moderately-priced hotel in Australia, New Zealand or France.

**per capita.** Per head, per person; usually used of some national attribute (GNP, etc) divided by the total population (men, women, children and infants).

**per capita income.** See national income per person.

**percentage.** A proportion in a hundred.

**perfecting.** The third of the 3 stages of church planting and growth (discipling, baptizing, perfecting, based on the Great Commission in Matthew 28.19), involving the bringing of individuals to conversion and commitment to Christ, the same for their children, teaching baptized individuals the full meaning of church membership and Christian maturity, and teaching about ethical change, holiness, witness, social justice, etc.

**Perfectionist-Pentecostals.** Also termed Free Pentecostal, Deliverance-Pentecostal, Radical-Pentecostal, Revivalist-Pentecostal; Pentecostals teaching 4-crisis experience including deliverance/ecstatic confession/ascension/perfectionism/prophecy. Global membership, including Non-White indigenous bodies: (1970) 39 denominations with 2,876 churches and 141,150 adult members; total community (1970) 277,800, (1980) 301,900, (1985) 315,300.

**Perfectionists.** Holiness Christians (qv).

**periodicals, Christian.** Defined here as all Christian or church periodicals, journals, magazines, newspapers, bulletins, house organs; of popular, news, scholarly, professional or academic content; daily, semi-weekly, weekly, biweekly, monthly, quarterly, appearing at regular intervals each with 2 or more issues a year, excluding annuals and irregular serials; and in any language. Global total: (1975) 22,980 (4,500 Roman Catholic).

**Peripheral Mande.** An African ethnolinguistic family, with about 30 languages. Global population: (1970) 2,595,500, (1980) 3,325,400, (1985) 3,725,800.

**permanent deacon.** A person ordained as a deacon in an episcopal church but who remains a deacon and does not seek or receive ordination as a priest.

**permeation.** In evangelism, the act or process or state or extent of a population or culture being pervaded or saturated or fully penetrated by the gospel.

**permillage.** The rate or proportion per thousand.

**perpetual curate.** A vicar, or minister of a new church or district.

**persecuted Christians.** Christians in nations where the churches experience severe persecution, obstruction, harassment, and repression, total (1980) 200 millions.

**persecution, religious.** See religious persecution.

**personal evangelism, personal work.** Evangelistic witnessing and sharing by a Christian with other individuals.

**personnel.** Officially-recognized, officially-accredited and officially-enumerated active full-time Christian workers of all varieties, salaried or tent-making, men and women, ordained and lay, national and foreign. Global total: (1975) 2,928,100, (1980) 3,199,000.

**persuasion.** (1) A group, faction, sect or party adhering to a particular system of religious beliefs. (2) In evangelization, the act of persuading or influencing people to accept Christ by argument or reasoning.

**Phanar.** World headquarters (in Istanbul, Turkey) of the Ecumenical Patriarchate of Constantinople; the ecumenical patriarch and his curia.

**philosophy of religion.** The search for the underlying causes and principles of reality in religion through logical reasoning rather than revelation.

**phylum, phyla.** See language phyla.

**physical quality of life index.** A measure of the effectiveness of social services in a country, including measures of life expectancy, literacy and infant mortality.

**pidgin.** A contact language used for communication between groups having different native languages; when a pidgin becomes the native language of a community, it is customarily called a creole (qv).

**Pietism.** A 17th-century religious movement originating in Germany emphasizing the need for a revitalized evangelical Christianity over against an excessive formalism and intellectualism.

**Pietists** (Continental). Moravians (qv).

**pilgrim.** One who travels to visit a shrine or holy place as a devotee.

PILGRIMS. Anglicans at Glastonbury Abbey (UK).

**pilgrims.** Some 7% of all Christians (90 millions), of all traditions, are on the move as pilgrims every year, in most countries, visiting large numbers of local, national and international pilgrimage centres and shrines. (See brief listing of centres in Part 3). In addition, there are annually over 30 million Hindu, Muslim, Buddhist and other non-Christian pilgrims.

**pioneer publishers.** In Jehovah's Witnesses' terminology, unpaid part-time members who engage in pioneer preaching and house-to-house visiting, averaging 100 hours' work each per month. Total (1974): 127,135.

**placements.** Copies of the Bible or New Testament placed free of charge in a home, institution or in a recipient's hand, by free-distribution agencies. Statistics of placements published by Gideons International give not annual totals but cumulative totals since the year 1908.

**planning.** The act or process of making or carrying out plans, especially the establishment of goals, policies and procedures for a social or economic unit.

**plantatio ecclesiae** (Latin). The planting of the church; Catholic term for the aim of missions.

**pluriform church.** The contemporary church in which differences of doctrinal emphasis are accepted as inevitable but provide no basis for breaches in fellowship.

**Plymouth Brethren.** Exclusive Brethren (qv).

**pneumatography.** Spirit writing (qv).

**Polish/Slavonic.** Eastern Orthodox liturgical tradition using Polish and Slavonic in the liturgy. Membership: (1970) 305 churches with 345,000 adult members, 547,000 total community.

**political freedom index.** A measure of a nation's respect for liberty, compiled from studies of civil and political rights; up to a maximum of 100% for full respect for liberty.

**political parties.** See Christian political parties.

**political prisoners.** Persons in custody or imprisoned for alleged political offences; numbering in 1978 several millions across the world. See prisoners of conscience.

**poll.** An opinion enquiry taken at a single point in time, from a very small carefully-constructed sample (usually around 1,500-2,500 adults) representative of the entire adult population, to solicit answers to carefully-formulated questions, in order to derive information applicable to that entire population.

**polyandry.** Marriage of one wife to several husbands simultaneously.

**polygamy.** Marriage of one person to several persons simultaneously.

**polyglot.** (1) Multilingual. (2) An edition of the Bible containing parallel text in 2 or more languages.

**polygyny.** Marriage of one husband to several wives simultaneously.

**Polynesian.** A Pacific ethnolinguistic family, with over 100 languages. Global population: (1970) 842,900, (1980) 1,037,300, (1985) 1,143,000.

**polytheism.** Belief in or worship of a plurality of gods.

**polytheist.** One who believes in or worships a plurality of gods.

**pope.** The title of the spiritual head of each of several large Christian churches and non-Christian religions, including: the Bishop of Rome as head of the Roman Catholic Church; the Eastern Orthodox and Coptic patriarchs of Alexandria; the heads of Maria Legio of Africa and other ex-Catholic African indigenous churches; the head of the Cao-Daist Missionary Church; the head of Taoism; et alii.

**popular piety.** Popular expressions of Christian (especially Catholic) faith widely held by the masses, to some extent infiltrated by superstition and non-Christian values; including devotion to the Crucified Christ, devotion to the Madonna, cults of saints, etc.

**popular religion.** Term covering all widespread or popular expressions of religion held by the masses, including non-Christian expressions and folk religion as well as christianized popular religiosity (qv) and popular piety (qv).

**popular religiosity.** Christianized but deviant popular expressions of religion widely espoused by the masses, especially by the poor in Latin American countries, the most widespread groupings being Christo-pagans (qv) and Spiritist Catholics (qv).

**population.** For an area, the total of all inhabitants or residents of that area; or occasionally, the total number of persons who spend or spent the night in the area.

**population census.** A government survey to obtain information about the state of the population at a given time.

**population density.** The average population to one square mile or kilometre.

**population explosion.** A popular term for the ultra-rapid expansion of population in Third-World countries since 1950.

**population increase.** See natural increase.

**population parameter.** Any numerical value that characterizes a population.

**population projections.** Calculations showing the future development of a population based on certain assumptions and present trends.

**portions.** In UBS usage, separately-bound single gospels or other complete single books of the Bible, averaging over 48 pages in length. Global distribution per year (UBS): (1975) 27,377,600, (1980) 40,814,000.

**postal evangelism.** Evangelism carried on by post or mail.

**postal survey.** An inquiry sending questionnaires by mail.

**postconciliar.** In Roman Catholic usage, an event taking place after the Second Vatican Council of 1962-65.

**postmillenialists.** Protestants who hold that Christ will return as King after the church has established the millennium on earth through its evangelization.

**postulant.** A candidate for admission to a religious order in the stage preliminary to the novitiate.

**post-Christians.** See disaffiliated Christians.

**post-religious.** Persons or populations who have abandoned any form of religion or quasi-religion.

**potential audience.** In Christian broadcasting, all persons with access to receivers and thus able to receive and listen to or view Christian broadcasts if they wish to, and able to understand the languages employed.

**practice, religious.** See religious practice.

**practising.** Actively engaged in, as a way of life.

**practising Anglican.** An adult Anglican who fulfils the minimum obligation of attending communion 3 times each year.

**practising Christians.** Affiliated Christians of all denominations who attend public worship at least once a year, or who fulfil their churches' minimum annual attendance requirements, or who are radio/TV-service listeners; church attenders. Global total: (1970) 884,021,800, (1980) 1,018,355,300 in 221 countries, (1985) 1,090,348,400.

**practising Muslims.** Muslims who, regularly or at least annually, practise all required Muslim duties.

**practitioner.** In Christian Science usage, an authorized teacher and healer.

**praeparatio evangelica** (Latin). Preparation for the gospel; used of any major factor in a people's life which prepares them for the message of Christ.

**Prayer Book Anglicans.** Central or Broad Church Anglicans (qv).

**Prayer Book Catholics.** High Church Anglicans (qv).

**prayer group.** A term used throughout Christianity for a group of Christians regularly meeting for prayer. Catholic charismatic prayer groups vary from 2 to 1,500 members, and average 50 persons.

**prayer tower.** (1) In Muslim usage, a minaret. (2) In Christian usage, a tower specially set aside for continuous prayer.

**preaching.** The act, practice or art of delivering a sermon or exhortation.

**prediction.** An inference regarding a future event based on probability theory.

**prefect.** The supervising head of a prefecture apostolic (qv), not in episcopal orders.

**prefectures apostolic** (symbol PA). In Roman Catholic usage, districts of a missionary territory in its initial stage of ecclesiastical organization. Total (1977) 63.

**preference, religious.** See religious preference.

**prelacy.** Episcopacy (qv); prelature (qv).

**prelate.** An ecclesiastic of superior rank and authority; a dignitary.

**prelature** (prelacy) **nullius** (symbol PN). A prelatic benefice or bishopric held by a prelate exempt from diocesan control and directly under the pope. Total (1977) 102.

**premillennialism.** Doctrine expounded by premillennialists (qv); divisible into historicist and futurist premillennialism, and the later into pretribulationism, and posttribulationism.

**premillennialists.** Protestants, usually Fundamentalists or dispensationalists, who hold that Christ will return as King before the millennium in order to establish it by his own power; estimated at 16 million in the USA alone (1980).

**presbyter** (NT Greek). In episcopal churches, a priest. In the Presbyterian and Reformed churches, a lay elder.

PRAYER TOWER. (1) National Mosque minarets (Malaysia). (2) Oral Roberts University (USA) : 100,000 requests a year.

**presbyteral council.** In the Roman Catholic Church, a senate or council of all priests in a diocese or area.

**Presbyterians.** See Reformed.

**presbytery.** In Presbyterian churches, (1) the ruling body of all ministers and representative lay elders, (2) the ecclesiastical district of all congregations under the ruling body. In the Roman Catholic Church, a parish clergy house.

**presentation.** A Protestant technical term used (1) in free scripture distribution by Gideons International for a formal, publicized gift of a Bible or Testament, (2) in Campus Crusade and other Protestant evangelism for a personal explanation of the gospel through exposition of 4 spiritual laws.

**present-in-area population.** The de facto or actual population in the area, made up of all persons actually in the area on a particular day or census date, covering residents, visitors and transients, but excluding residents temporarily absent abroad.

**presidency, first.** A council of 3 in the Church of Jesus Christ of Latter-day Saints (Mormons), consisting of a president and 2 counsellors, and having jurisdiction in spiritual and temporal matters.

**president.** The presiding officer, chairman, or chief executive in a number of denominations, including the Mormon church.

**presiding bishop.** The president of the national council of the Episcopal Church in the USA who is elected by the General Convention; the chief member of the presiding bishopric of the Mormon church.

**presiding bishopric.** The chief office of the Aaronic priesthood in the Mormon church filled by 3 persons and supervised by the first presidency.

**presiding elder.** A district superintendent in Methodism, with oversight of churches and workers in a district.

**presses.** Printing presses owned and operated by churches or specifically Christian agencies number well over 1,000.

**Preto.** A Portuguese-speaking Black.

**Pre-Chalcedonian.** Oriental Orthodox (qv).

**pre-Christian.** Of, or being a time before, the beginning of the Christian era, or before the introduction of Christianity in a locality.

**Pre-Dravidian.** An Austro-Asiatic ethnolinguistic family. Global population: (1970) 7,092,100, (1980) 9,068,000, (1985) 10,127,900.

**pre-school children.** Infants, i.e. the population under 5 years old, including new-born babies.

**priest** (from NT Greek, *presbyteros*). A member of the second order of clergy in the Anglican communion, ranking below bishop and above deacon; a member of the highest order of clergy in the Roman Catholic and Eastern Orthodox churches; a professional clergyman of a religious denomination; a minister of religion.

**priests' council.** A presbyteral council (qv).

**priests, Roman Catholic.** World totals (1977): 401,168, declining from (1976) 404,783 (259,331 or 64.1% secular, 145,452 or 35.9% religious), declining from (1972) 417,774 (268,976 and 148,798). Annual increases (1975): 6,628 new ordinations, minus 355 transfers, 3,006 defections (priests leaving the ministry), 7,047 deaths, totalling 3,780 losses a year.

**priest-worker.** See worker-priest.

**primal religionists.** Original or primitive religionists in an area; animists, shamanists, spirit-worshippers, ancestor-venerators, polytheists, pantheists, tribal religionists, traditional religionists; sometimes called pagans, heathen, fetishists; usually exclusive to a particular tribe or people, hence non-missionary in emphasis; local as contrasted with universal religionists (qv).

**primary education.** Education given in primary or elementary schools.

**primary evangelization.** The first or initial or preliminary attempts at the evangelization of a people or area.

**primary religious group.** A sociological term for a denomination; defined as a social entity or group which claims the exclusive or primary religious affiliation or allegiance of its members, attempting to serve not specialized needs but the overall needs of its members, ministering to them on a regular, weekly or even daily basis.

**primate.** A bishop who has precedence in a province, group of provinces, or a nation; the ranking prelate.

**primitive religionists.** Tribal religionists (qv).

**primus.** The first in dignity of the bishops of the Episcopal Church in Scotland who has various privileges but no metropolitan authority.

**primus inter pares** (Latin). The first among equals; often used of an archbishop with no jurisdiction over his fellow bishops.

**print media.** A term covering newspapers, magazines, books, comics, and other printed literature.

**printing presses.** See presses.

**prior.** The superior of a priory.

**priory.** A religious house that ranks immediately below an abbey and is either self-sustaining or dependent upon an abbey.

**priory nullius** (Latin: priory of no diocese). A priory that is not dependent upon a diocese but on the pope.

**prisoner of war.** A person captured or interned by a belligerent power because of war with several exceptions provided by international law or agreement.

**prisoners of conscience.** Political prisoners undergoing torture, in 1980 estimated at over 700,000 across the world in over 90 countries.

**private attenders.** Persons who attend church services only for special private family occasions (baptisms, weddings, funerals).

**probability.** Something that is probable, statistically, logically or otherwise.

**probationer.** In Methodism, an intending new member who is put on probation for a period of time to demonstrate his commitment to full membership.

**proclaim.** To declare openly or publicly, make widely known in speech or in writing, announce, show, demonstrate, publish, extol; especially of the gospel and of Christ.

**proclamation.** The action of proclaiming, the condition of being proclaimed, something proclaimed; especially of the gospel.

**professed.** Monks or nuns who have taken the vows of a religious order.

**professing.** Declaring, stating, confessing, self-identifying.

**professing Christians.** Persons publicly professing (confessing, declaring, stating, self-identifying) their Christian preference or adherence in a government census or public-opinion poll, hence known as Christians to the state or society or the public. Global total: (1970) 1,160,879,700, (1980) 1,362,291,500, (1985) 1,470,407,400.

**profession, religious.** See religious profession.

**professional.** One engaging in a particular pursuit, study, or science for gain or livelihood (as contrasted with an amateur); one with authority or practical experience in an area of knowledge.

**professionals' associations.** Christian organizations for workers or professionals, significant at the national or wider levels, number over 400.

**professions.** See decisions.

**programmed learning (PL), programmed instruction (PI).** A teaching technique and device in which material to be taught is presented, the student providing his answers and immediately comparing then with correct answers; based on the concept of immediate reinforcement of correct answers as a way of impressing information on a learner.

**progressivist.** In Roman Catholicism, a progressive tendency or emphasis or attitude favouring reforms and activism, as opposed to more tradionalist attitudes.

**projection.** The carrying forward of a present trend into the future; an estimate of future possibilities based on current trends.

**Propaganda.** Sacred Congregation for the Evangelization of Peoples (qv).

**prophecy.** In modern usage in the charismatic renewal, an utterance in public by any Christian which purports to be direct speech by God concerning particular issues.

**prophesying.** Prophecy (qv).

**prophet.** (1) A Biblical, especially Old Testament, revealer, spokesman or seer. (2) An official or office-holder in some pentecostal churches. (3) A charismatic leader of a new religious movement of any sort.

**prophet movement.** An indigenous Christian movement led by a charismatic prophet figure, which usually results in a Non-White indigenous church (qv).

**proselyte.** One who has been converted from one religious faith to another, usually by questionable or dubious methods.

**proselytism.** A manner of behaving, contrary to the spirit of the gospel, which makes use of dishonest methods to attract men to a community, e.g. by exploiting their ignorance or poverty.

**protest, movements of.** See prophet movement, secession, schism.

**Protestants.** Christians in churches originating in, or reformulated at the time of, or in communion with, the Western world's 16th-century Protestant Reformation; in European languages usually called Evangéliques (French), Evangelische (German), Evangélicos (Italian, Portuguese, Spanish), though not usually Evangelicals (in English). Global professing adherents: (1970) 259,044,800, (1980) 280,348,000 in 209 countries, (1985) 292,733,700. Global affiliated membership: (1970) 233,424,200, (1980) 262,157,600 in 212 countries, (1985) 277,914,100.

**province.** In Roman Catholic usage, any of the principal ecclesiastical divisions of a country forming the jurisdiction of an archbishop or a metropolitan; a territorial division of a religious order. In Anglican usage, the term has 7 different meanings, including autonomous church, internal province within an autonomous church, or a group of dioceses which for some purposes act in association under a common constitution. Whilst provinces retain their full meaning in contemporary Anglicanism, in contemporary Roman Catholicism they have ceased to have meaning since the meaningful unit is now the nation-wide (local) church, or (in large nations) the newer apostolic regions.

**provincial.** A religious superior directing houses in a religious province.

**provisional annual conference.** A regional jurisdiction in North American Methodism.

**provost.** The head of a cathedral or cathedral chapter; in German Protestantism, a clergyman in charge of the chief church of a region.

**pro-nuncio.** The diplomatic envoy of the Roman Catholic pope to a foreign country where Catholics are in a minority. World total: (1974) 42.

**pseudo-religions.** See quasi-religions.

**psychology of religion.** The science of mind or of mental phenomena and activities with regard to religion; the psychology of religious phenomena.

**psychoneurotics.** Sufferers from psychoneuroses. Global total: (1980) 900 million.

**psychotics.** The mentally ill, or mentally abnormal; sufferers from severe mental disorders (psychoses). Global total: (1980) 44 million.

**public profession** (of religion). See professing Christians.

**publishers.** In Jehovah's Witnesses' terminology, ordinary members of congregations, who are expected to average 10-15 hours per month preaching, talking and in house-to-house visiting.

**publishing houses.** Organizations producing Christian literature member over 600.

**pupil.** A child or young person in school.

**puja, pooja** (Sanskrit). A Hindu rite, religious festival, or act of worship or propitiation.

**Pygmy.** An Early African ethnolinguistic family; Negrillo. Global population: (1970) 227,500, (1980) 295,100, (1985) 332,500.

## Q

**Qadianis.** Majority party among Ahmadis (qv).

**Qaraism.** See Karaites.

**Qarmatians, Karmatians.** A name for Muslims who are Shia Ismailis.

**Quakers.** Friends (qv).

**quality of life.** The effectiveness of social services in a country, measured by the PQLI (physical quality of life index, qv).

**quantification.** Measuring an item's quantity or number, or transforming qualitative data into quantitative.

**quasi-Christian.** Seemingly, partly, almost, in some sense, a Christian.

**quasi-confessions.** Non-confessional international denominational bodies (qv), which are partly or entirely de facto world confessional families, or world communions. Global membership: (1970) 56,908,200, (1980) 71,557,000, (1985) 79,522,100.

**quasi-continent.** Partly a continent; used of the Caribbean, Middle East and other regions.

**quasi-parish.** In Roman Catholic usage, partly or virtually a parish although not yet formally or canonically established.

**quasi-religionists.** Adherents of quasi-religions.

**quasi-religions.** Secular movements which are partly, or are virtually, religions; divided here into anti-religious quasi-religions (atheism, communism, dialectical materialism, Leninism, Maoism, Marxism, scientific materialism, Stalinism, et alia), and non-religious quasi-religions (some forms of agnosticism, fascism, humanism, liberal humanism, nationalism, Nazism, some forms of non-religion, some forms of secularism).

**Quran** (Koran). The book of writings in Arabic accepted by Muslims as revelations made to Muhammed by Allah.

**Quran translations.** Languages into which the Quran has been translated: about 130 (25 European) by 1980, including Bengali, Chinese, Dutch, English, Farsi, French, German, Gujarati, Hausa, Indonesian, Italian, Japanese, Javanese, Latin, Punjabi, Spanish, Swahili, Turkish, Urdu, Yoruba.

**Quranic schools, Koranic schools.** Elementary schools teaching only the Quran and memorizing passages.

## R

**race.** A major division of mankind with certain inherited common distinctive physical characteristics (skin colour, stature, head shape, hair type, genes, blood-group, etc) which are hereditarily-transmittable; a breeding group with gene organization differing from that of other intraspecies groups; a physical type, a racial stock; one of the subspecies of Homo Sapiens.

**racism.** A belief in the inherent superiority of one's own race and its right to domination over others.

**Radical Reformation.** The Left-Wing Reformation; Anaptists (qv).

**Radical-Pentecostals.** Perfectionist-Pentecostals (qv).

**radio audiences.** See radio listeners.

**radio believers.** See isolated radio believers.

**radio churches.** Groups or fellowships, meeting for Sunday worship, brought into being through hearing radio broadcasts.

**radio converts.** The number of converts to Christianity

RADIO CHURCH. In Kavieng (Papua New Guinea).

due to Christian broadcasting in the course of a month or a year.

**radio letters.** Annual listeners' letters or other communications received by international and national Christian radio and TV stations and programmes. Global total per year: (1975) 4,230,360.

**radio listeners.** The regular listening or viewing audience in a country is made up of (a) listeners/ viewers to Christian stations, and (b) listeners/ viewers to Christian programmes over secular, commercial or state radio/TV stations. Global total of listeners: (1980) 990,474,400.

**radio or TV denomination.** A denomination (qv), or loosely-organized grouping of churches or believers, whose existence centres on regular radio or TV broadcasts of Sunday worship services.

**radio stations.** Broadcasting centres with transmitting plant and equipment. World total of Christian radio and TV stations: (1980) 1,450.

**radiophonic school.** A broadcasting network offering basic adult education in rural areas, with local teachers or postal feedback; mostly operated by Roman Catholic dioceses in Latin American countries.

**radio/TV-service listeners.** Affiliated Christians who, for reasons of age, infirmity, sickness or absence of local churches, in place of physical church attendance instead regularly listen/view Sunday radio/TV services of worship once a week or once a month.

**Raskolniks** (Russian, Schismatics). Old Believers (qv).

**rationalist.** An advocate of rationalism, reliance on reason as the basis for the establishment of any ultimate truth including religious truth.

**reached.** The state of having had the gospel brought to one or to a people.

**reactionary.** Conservative.

**real Christians.** See committed Christians.

**receiver.** A receiving set for radio or TV broadcast programmes.

**receiving countries.** 98 countries across the world which receive far more foreign missionaries than they send out.

**receiving/sending countries.** 35 countries across the world which receive substantial numbers of foreign missionaries but which also themselves send out considerable numbers.

**reconciled diversity.** A model for the unity of the church espoused by the confessional-identities part of the ecumenical movement, in opposition to the 'conciliar fellowship' model favoured by the World Council of Churches: in order to live under the unity Christ wills, the world communions (confessions, world confessional families) must enter into a fully reconciled relationship, recognizing other confessions fully as churches of Jesus Christ, yet retaining their own confessional identities.

**recording studios.** Local broadcasting studios or soundproofed rooms under church or Christian auspices where tapes are prepared for later release over radio or TV stations.

**records, recording.** See religious drama.

**rector.** A clergyman of the Church of England who has the charge and care of a parish and owns the tithes from it; in the Roman Catholic Church, the head priest of a church, university, school, or other religious institution.

**Red.** Stylized skin colour associated with the American Indian geographical race. Global Red population: (1970) 35,074,000, (1980) 46,790,300, (1985) 53,136,400.

**Red Hat** (Unreformed) **Lamaism** (Dupka or Karmapa). That part of Tibetan Buddhism in which monasteries have resisted the 14th-century reforms of the monk Tsong-kha-pa. Red Hat Lamaism is the official religion of Bhutan.

**reduction.** In South American Catholic history, the act or process of resettlement by missionaries of Amerindians in villages or compounds for purposes of acculturation or control; or the settlement itself.

**Reformed.** A major Protestant tradition originating in continental Europe, and including the term Presbyterian originating in English-speaking countries. Global membership: (1970) 354 denominations with 83,296 churches and 19,809,200 adult members; total community (1970) 34,195,000, (1980) 40,209,500, (1985) 43,445,500.

**Reformed Catholics.** Followers of recent schisms ex Church of Rome in a Reformed or Protestant direction. Global membership: (1970) 15 denominations with 4,953 churches and 2,355,800 adult members; total community (1970) 4,209,200, (1980) 6,135,400, (1985) 7,158,800.

**Reformed Ecumenical Synod** (RES). A conservative Reformed world communion. Global constituency (1980) 6,493,500 total community in 51 denominations.

**Reformed Orthodox.** Uncanonical reform movements out of Orthodoxy, retaining Orthodox claims. Global membership: (1970) 20 denominations with 956 churches and 250,000 adult members; total community (1970) 418,700, (1980) 587,900, (1985) 683,500.

**refugee church.** A local church or congregation formed entirely by or among refugees in a particular country.

**refugees.** Persons who have migrated due to persecution, fear of persecution, or other strong pressures endangering their continued stay in their countries of origin, and who are unable or unwilling to return; excluding labour and other migrants and also returnees (qv).

**regeneration.** Spiritual rebirth, renewal, re-creation, revival, radical spiritual transformation.

**region.** In United Nations terminology, one of 24 areas into which the whole world is divided for purposes of analysis.

**region** (apostolic or conciliar). See apostolic region.

**regional conciliarism.** There are about 55 international and regional (subcontinental) councils of churches of all kinds.

**registration with government.** Legalizing the existence and status of a denomination or church in countries where registration is compulsory in law.

**regular attenders.** Church members who attend Sunday worship weekly, monthly, or at the least once annually.

**regular clergy.** Religious clergy (qv) living under a monastic or similar rule.

**regular communicant.** A communicant (qv) who takes communism weekly, monthly, or at the least annually.

**regular pioneers.** In Jehovah's Witnesses' usage, full-time workers who put in 100 hours a month on house-to-house work. Totals (1971): 81,655, including 2,326 circuit servants and 290 district servants.

**religion.** A religious faith, creed, communion, sect, cult, persuasion; a system of faith and worship, centrally concerned with the means of ultimate transformation.

**religion, comparative.** Comparative study of the origin, development, and interrelations of the religious systems of mankind.

**religion, organized.** See organized religion.

**religion, study of.** See study of religion.

**religionists.** (1) Persons professing adherence to any religion, as contrasted with non-religious or anti-religious persons or atheists. Global total: 79.1%, i.e. (1980) 3,462,897,000 (79.2% of world), (1985) 3,764,696,000 (78.7%). (2) Religious zealots, persons earnestly devoted to or attached to any religion.

**religionless Christianity.** A term coined by German theologian D. Bonhoeffer for genuine, biblical Christianity without religious trappings.

**religiosity.** Intense, excessive, or affected religiousness.

**religious.** Monks, friars, clerks regular, sisters or nuns who are bound by professed vows, sequestered from secular concerns, and devoted to lives of piety.

**religious affiliation.** See affiliation, religious.

**religious architecture.** See architecture, religious.

**religious barrier.** A religious frontier (qv).

**religious books, new.** Global total of new titles each year (in 1975): 22,200, of which 17,000 were on Christianity.

**religious Buddhists.** Buddhists who profess Buddhism as both a family religion and also a personal religion.

**religious change.** Demographic changes from one religion or religious system to another in the course of a year.

**religious clergy.** In Roman usage, clergy who are members of religious orders or institutes. World total (1975): 161,174 (decline from 162,915 a year earlier).

**religious communities.** (1) Religious institutes (qv), orders, congregations, or societies of religious personnel for the religious life, total (for Roman Catholic Church) 1,530. (2) Religious communities in the sense of buildings and centres (large monasteries, abbeys, priories, including monasteries in anti-Christian countries where their presence as legitimate or tolerated institutions is significant, mother houses of religious institutes, ashrams, and the like) number over 5,000.

**religious congregations.** Religious institutes (qv).

**religious distance.** The number of religious frontiers or barriers that exist between a Christian worker, evangelist or missionary, or a group of such, and their target population; as defined here, up to a maximum of 5 frontiers.

RELIGIOUS DRAMA. Gospel TV ballet 'Kontakion' (UK).

**religious drama.** The portrayal of Christian verities through art, literature, music, song, theatre, including live theatre, cinema, music concerts, broadcasting, recordings, etc. Worldwide annual statistical totals: each year, 3 million people attend live theatricals or musicals of this kind (e.g. 'Godspell' 3.6 million from 1971-77, 'Jesus Christ Superstar' 4 million in 15 languages and 30 countries 1971-77, Oberammergau Passion Play 500,000 every decadal year); 20 million see commercially-distributed films of Christian or biblical content; 30 million attend live concerts of Christian music; 50 million listen to religious drama by radio, and 100 million on television; 20 million LP records or cassettes of Christian music are sold.

**religious education.** Instruction in the principles of a particular religious faith.

**religious frontier.** The line of demarcation between one category of religion and another, from the Christian standpoint; up to a maximum of 5 frontiers.

**religious geography.** See geography of religion.

**religious house.** A convent or monastery.

**religious humanism.** A modern North American movement composed chiefly of non-theistic humanist churches and dedicated to achieving the ethical goals of religion without beliefs and rites resting upon supernaturalism; sometimes called Christian humanism.

**religious institutes.** In Roman Catholic usage, religious orders, congregations and societies for the religious life. World totals (1975): for men (priests, monks, brothers), 84 orders, 83 clerical religious congregations, 27 societies of common life, 30 lay religious congregations, 6 secular institutes, totalling 230 religious institutes for men using a total of 740 distinct names; for women (nuns, sisters), 1,300 religious and 21 secular institutes or congregations.

**religious institutes, federations of.** Some 190 Roman Catholic national federations of male or female religious institutes exist (for clergy, monks, priests, brothers, sisters, nuns), with 3 international federations (CLAR, UISG, USG).

**religious institutes of perfection.** Roman Catholic term for clerical and lay religious orders and congregations, societies without vows, and secular institutes. World totals (1976): 221 Pontifical Right religious institutes for men (253,903 members), 1,173 religious institutes of women of Pontifical Right (778,000 members).

**religious journalism.** Organizations and centres significant at national and wider levels number over 300.

**religious liberty.** Defined here as encompassing the following 31 categories: freedom of inner belief and conscience, freedom of public worship indoors and outdoors, freedom of assembly, freedom of self-government, freedom of association, freedom to organize religious bodies, freedom to organize Bible study circles, freedom to run Christian libraries and bookshops, freedom to collect money and to disburse it, freedom to organize credit unions for the benefit of members, freedom to offer medical care where wanted, freedom to engage in mission at home and abroad, freedom to send abroad or receive from abroad foreign missionaries, freedom of Christian political expression, freedom to teach religion and to be taught, freedom for children to join religious associations and to receive Christian instruction, freedom to change one's religion or be converted, freedom of propagation, freedom to travel on religious business within the country and abroad and to return, freedom to listen to radio religious broadcasts from any country, freedom to send and receive religious mail and literature uncensored both inland and abroad, freedom to use national press and broadcasting (radio and TV) facilities; freedom to publish, mail, broadcast, circulate scriptures, buy and sell literature, evangellize, proselytize and baptize; and freedom for minority churches and religions as well as majority religions.

**religious libraries.** See libraries, religious.

**religious life.** The life of those who aspire to perfection by retirement from the world and practice of the evangelical counsels (qv).

**religious movement.** A movement swept along by its own momentum long before it becomes organized or institutionalized.

**religious Muslims.** Ethnic Muslims (qv) who practise or profess Islam.

**religious orders.** See religious institutes.

**religious orders in Anglicanism.** There are 95 distinct Anglican religious communities (in 1978), with 395 lay religious brothers, 2,420 nuns or lay religious sisters, and about 150 ordained monks in priest's or bishop's orders.

**religious orders** (communities), **Protestant.** Total about 60 orders, brotherhoods, sisterhoods or communities especially of deaconesses, mainly Lutheran, Reformed, Church of South India, et alia.

**religious periodicals.** See periodicals, Christian.

**religious persecution.** Persecution of believers specifically on religious grounds, though this is often denied.

**religious personnel.** See religious.

**religious persuasion.** A person's religious profession or preference.

**religious pluralism.** The peaceful co-existence of completely different religions or denominations within a particular community.

**religious practice.** The actual performing of religious duties.

**religious preference.** The religion or denominational tradition which a respondee professes to adhere to when asked in a public-opinion poll.

**religious profession.** (1) the religion or denominational tradition professed or preferred in a poll or census. (2) The taking of vows in a religious order.

**religious research.** Investigation, research and experiment on any religious subject or matter.

**Religious Science.** A marginal Protestant tradition emphasizing metaphysical science, Divine Science, Christian Science, New Thought, magnetic healing and the like. Global membership: (1970) 61 denominations with 3,819 churches and 623,600 adult members; total community (1970) 1,340,100, (1980) 1,654,600, (1985) 1,813,000.

**religious sociology.** The study of religion as it affects society.

**religious state.** The situation in life of the religious vocation (persons called to the religious life).

**religious states.** States, governments or ruling regimes which identify themselves as religious, or with religion and its promotion, numbered 102 out of the world total of 223 in 1980.

**religious survival.** A religious practice or belief dating back to an earlier, outmoded, religion, which has survived into the present.

**religious toleration.** The attitude of tolerance and acceptance, on the part of a state or a majority church, towards religious minorities.

**religio-political organizations.** Bodies significant at the national or wider levels number over 200.

**renewal.** A revival (qv) in personal zeal and commitment to Christ in the churches; the charismatic renewal (qv).

**research.** Studious enquiry or examination; critical and exhaustive investigation or experimentation having for its aim the discovery of new facts and their correct interpretation, the revision of accepted conclusions, theories or laws in the light of newly-discovered facts, or the practical applications of such new or revised conclusions, theories or laws.

**research centres.** Christian-related and church-related centres producing original research and significant at the national or wider levels numbered over 930 in 1980.

**research, religious.** See religious research.

**resident.** One who resides in a place for a time, often temporary or of short duration; usually distinguished from inhabitant which implies permanent or long-term habitation.

**resident population.** The de jure population (qv).

**residential sees.** Dioceses or other jurisdictions with a resident bishop each.

**residual Christians.** Nominal Christians (qv) or post-Christians (qv) in industrialized and secularized societies.

**resistant.** A term often used to describe peoples who have been exposed to the Christian message but have not accepted it. In most cases it can be shown that they have only been inadequately evangelized, or even faultily evangelized, and that because of the absence of a culturally-adequate message they have in fact been neglected.

**respondent.** A person who answers questions in a survey or government census, in the latter case usually under a legal obligation to answer.

**Restoration Movement.** (1) The Churches of Christ, or Disciples (qv), a major USA group of denominations. (2) A neo-charismatic paradenomination splitting in 1974 from the Charismatic Renewal within the mainline Protestant and Anglican churches in UK and USA; also called Church of the Great Shepherd, Pyramid Church, House-Church Movement.

**Restorationist Baptists.** Disciples (qv).

**restricted countries.** 18 countries in the world which, although not closed or partially closed to foreign mission, restrict numbers of foreign missionaries considerably.

**Resurrection.** (1) The rising of Jesus Christ from the dead in AD 30. (2) The rising again to life of all the human dead throughout history before the Last Judgement.

**retreat.** A special centre, or period, of group withdrawal to a place of seclusion for the purpose of deepening the spiritual life of participants through prayer, meditation and study under a retreat director.

**return visits.** In Jehovah's Witnesses' statistics, back-calls or second visits in house-to-house work to speak to interested persons and to conduct Bible studies. World total: a rapid rise from 2,697,576 (1959) to 151,171,555 (1974).

**returnee.** An alien of long residence who is deported and forcibly repatriated to the country of his citizenship.

**reunion.** A union of churches or denominations after a period of separation or discord.

**reunionist.** An advocate of church reunion.

REVIVAL. East African Convention, Butere, 1961.

**revival.** A period of spontaneous religious awakening, or renewed interest in religion after indifference or decline; in some North American circles, a series of organized evangelistic meetings often characterized by emotional excitement; theologically, a great outpouring of the Spirit of God upon the churches.

**Revivalist-Pentecostals.** Perfectionist-Pentecostals (qv).

**rice Christian.** A convert to Christianity who accepts baptism not on the basis of personal conviction but out of a desire for food, medical services, or other material benefits.

**rite.** One of the historical forms of the Christian eucharistic service; a division of the Christian church as determined by liturgy.

**ritual.** The prescribed order, words and actions of a religious ceremony.

**rolls.** Written lists of names of church members of all varieties.

**roll-cleaning.** The practice of regularly updating church membership rolls, in particular working through or over rolls in order to remove former members who have now died, left the area, given up church membership, or otherwise ceased to be properly eligible for the rolls.

**Roman.** Of or relating to the Roman Catholic Church, or the Latin rite.

**Roman Catholic jurisdictions.** World totals in 1979 (followed by 1969 figures in parentheses): 2,606 (2,491) jurisdictions, consisting of 2,317 (2,142) residential sees, made up of 13 (11) patriarchates, 430 (397) metropolitan sees, 61 (62) archdioceses and 1,813 (1,672) dioceses; 1,988 (1,953) titular sees; 105 (101) prelatures, 21 (23) abbeys nullius, 9 (10) apostolic administrations, 18 (25) exarchates and ordinariates, 73 (81) vicariates apostolic, 59 (77) prefectures apostolic, 12 patriarchal vicariates, 4 (5) missions sui juris, 1 (1) priory, 27 (26) vicariates castrensi. Ecclesiastical territories by rite: 94% Latin-rite, 6% Oriental-rite.

**Roman Catholicism.** The faith, doctrine or polity of the Roman Catholic Church, or its entire system together with all its members.

**Roman Catholics.** All Christians in communion with the Church of Rome. Affiliated Roman Catholics are defined in this Encyclopedia as baptized Roman Catholics plus catechumens. Global professing adherents: (1970) 668,023,800, (1980) 809,157,000 in 218 countries, (1985) 884,222,000. Global affiliated membership: (1970) 672,319,100, (1980) 802,660,000 in 219 countries, (1985) 872,104,700.

**Roman Orthodox.** The common Arabic designation for Christians related to the 4 Byzantine (Eastern Orthodox) patriarchates in the Middle East, including Constaninople as the 'New Rome'.

ROMANIAN. One of 123 monasteries (Romania).

**Romanian.** Eastern Orthodox liturgical tradition (Romanian Orthodox Church). Global membership: (1970) 19 denominations with 11,873 churches and 11,596,000 adult members; total community (1970) 16,158,900, (1980)17,376,300, (1985) 17,960,300.

**Romanian rite.** Byzantine rite for Catholics under Rome, used in Romania; completely suppressed by state since 1948.

**Romanism.** Roman Catholicism (qv).

**Rome.** Roman Catholicism, or the capital city where its world headquarters are.

**rounding.** The expressing of a number with only a convenient degree of exactness, as by dropping decimals beyond a stated number of places or by substituting zeros for final integers or digits.

**rural area.** Defined in many countries as an administrative district with a population of under 2,000.

**rural dean.** In Anglicanism, an ecclesiastic ranking immediately under an archdeacon and appointed as a diocesan official to supervise the affairs of a group of parishes in the archdeaconry.

**rural deanery.** The area of jurisdiction under a rural dean.

**rural missions.** In the field of rural and agricultural missions, Christian organizations significant at the national or wider levels number over 250.

**Russellites.** A nickname for Jehovah's Witnesses (qv).

**Russian rite.** Byzantine rite used by Roman Catholics in USSR; only 3,000 faithful left.

**Ruthenians.** Roman Catholics using Byzantine rite of Ruthenian origin. Global membership: (1970) 279,600 total community.

## S

**sabbatarian.** A person or church which keeps the seventh day of the week (Saturday) as holy in conformity with the letter of the Decalogue (Ten

Commandments), in contrast to Christians who observe Sunday instead.

**Sabbath.** The seventh day of the week (Saturday).

**sabbath school.** A school held on the Sabbath (Saturday) for purposes of religious education.

**Sabras.** Jews born in the post-1948 State of Israel.

**sacrament.** A religious act, ceremony, or practice that is considered specially sacred as a sign or symbol of a deeper reality; in many denominations 2 in number (baptism and the eucharist), in others 7 in number.

**sacramentalist, sacramentarian.** One placing great emphasis on religious ritual and the role and function of sacraments.

**Sacred Congregation for the Evangelization of Peoples.** Founded in 1622 as SC for the Propagation of the Faith (Propaganda), the central Roman Catholic body with jurisdiction over foreign missions. Global constituency; (1980) 87,767,200 Catholics in jurisdictions.

**Sacred Congregation for the Eastern Churches.** Founded in 1862, the branch of the Roman Curia dealing with Eastern-rite and Uniate Catholic Churches. Global constituency: 14 local churches with (1970) 2,152,500 Catholics, (1980) 2,723,200, (1985) 3,030,900; or, 153 jurisdictions with (1970) 7,084,300, (1980) 8,799,300, (1985) 9,682,800.

**sadhus.** Hinduism's holy beggars. Total: 15 million.

**saints.** A theological and biblical term for the entire company of all baptized Christians; in a number of denominations, the usual term for all church members.

**Saivites, Shaivites.** Worshippers of Siva (Shiva), mainly in South India Hinduism; including these sects: Lingayats, Natha cult, Nayanars. Global adherents: (1970) 115,946,000, (1980) 145,687,000, (1985) 160,558,000.

**Saktists, Shaktites.** Worshippers of the Hindu Supreme Goddess, Sakti (Sanskrit: power, energy) or Kali/Durga/Deva/Parvati consort of Siva; strong in Bengal and Assam. Global adherents: (1970) 13,933,000, (1980) 17,447,000, (1985) 19,204,000.

**salvation.** The saving of man from the power and effects of sin; deliverance, redemption, restoration, reconciliation with God, liberation, healing, help, wholeness, preservation, etc.

**Salvation Army.** See Salvationists.

**salvation religion.** A religion offering its devotees salvation (e.g. Christianity, Omoto-kyo (Japan), etc).

SALVATIONISTS. United March of Witness (East Africa).

**Salvationists.** Soldiers or officers of the Salvation Army, a Protestant tradition begun ex Methodists in Britain, 1865. Global membership: (1970) 86 national branches with 16,863 congregations and 1,477,400 adult members; total community (1970) 3,050,400, (1980), 3,801,700 (1985) 4,226,900.

**salvific.** In Roman Catholic usage, saving or with intent to save or impart salvation.

**Samaritans.** Children of Israel (Bene-Yisrael) or Shamerim (Observant Ones), a small Jewish sect. Total adherents: (1980) 540.

**samizdat** (Russian). Self-publishing (qv).

**sample.** A small segment or quantity taken as evidence of the quality or character of the whole; a very small part of the population used for purposes of investigation and comparing properties.

**samsara** (Sanskrit). In Hinduism and Buddhism, successive reincarnations, the indefinitely-repeated cycles of birth, misery and death caused by karma.

**Sanatanists** (Sanskrit: Old Ways; or Idol-Worshippers). The vast bulk (98%) of all Hindus, consisting of Vaishnavites, Saivites, and Saktists (qv). Global adherents: (1970) 454,509,000 (1980) 571,095,000, (1985) .

**sanatorium.** A medical establishment for therapy, rest and recuperation, or for chronic illnesses; see medical centres.

**Sansei** (Japanese: third-generation). A Japanese-American of Nisei or Kibei parents, and born and educated in the Americas.

**saturated.** In evangelization, used of a population completely penetrated by the gospel.

**saturation evangelism.** See in-depth evangelism.

**saturation point.** The situation in a country or area when the markets for copies of the scriptures have become saturated, or the point at which such saturation occurs.

**scenario.** A tool for studying the future: a series of events that we imagine happening in the future.

**sceptic** (skeptic). An unbeliever, agnostic.

**scepticism.** The doctrine that any true knowledge is impossible or that all knowledge is uncertain, especially in matters of religion; agnosticism.

**schedule.** A census schedule (qv).

**scheduled castes.** Official term in India (after 1949) for low caste persons, or persons outside the traditional Indian caste system, previously called Outcastes, Untouchables, or Harijans (Children of God).

**seamen's centres.** Christian clubs or centres for seafarers exist in over 500 posts in 76 countries around the world; co-ordinated by ICMA.

**schism.** A form of division or separation in the Christian church or from a church or religious body; a division, separation, secession, split, breakoff faction, clique, etc.

**schismatic.** Used of a body or sect that has broken off or seceded from an existing Christian church or denomination.

**scholarly societies.** Total of all societies important at international and national levels: 250.

**school of evangelism.** A local course in evangelistic method sponsored by a church or parish.

**schools, Roman Catholic.** World totals (1976): 79,424 elementary schools (19,583,702 pupils), 27,542 secondary schools (9,522,274 pupils), and over 800,000 students in universities and colleges. Of all pupils, 16% are non-Catholics.

**school-age children, school-age population.** Those persons in the population who are ages 5-14 years old.

**scripture distribution.** See under Bible distribution, New Testament distribution, portions, selections.

**scriptures.** In United Bible Societies' statistical usage the sum total of all Bibles, NTs, portions and selections (qv) distributed through their auspices and agencies in a given year.

**seasonal assistants.** Short-term Christian personnel serving abroad, for periods of 6 months or less.

**seatings.** A technical term for the seating capacity of a church or of all churches in a denomination; the actual number of seats available.

**Seceders.** Kharijites (qv).

**secession.** The formal withdrawal of a body of Christians from a larger denomination; a schism, split, breakoff, separation, or faction.

**Second Coming.** The Second Advent of Christ as judge of the world on the Last Day.

**Second Rome.** Constantinople as New Rome, the successor to Rome as capital of the Christian world after the sack of Rome in AD 476 and the end of the Roman empire in the West; after 1453 replaced by Moscow claiming to be the Third Rome.

**Second World.** The 30 or so countries comprising the Communist (or Marxist Socialist) world, loosely contrasted with the First (Western or Capitalist) bloc or world, and the so-called Third World or bloc.

**secondary education.** Education in secondary or high schools.

**secret believers.** Crypto-Christians (qv).

**sect.** A comparatively small recently-organized exclusive dissenting religious body, usually considered heretical.

**sectarian.** An adherent of a particular religious sect; a dissenter, often of bigoted views.

**secular.** Relating to the worldly or temporal in contrast to the spiritual or eternal; civil, non-religious.

**secular clergy.** Diocesan clergy (qv).

**secular religions.** See quasi-religions.

**secular states.** In 1980 some 94 nations and countries out of the world total of 223 regarded themselves as secular, promoting neither religion nor irreligion, and maintaining strict separation between church and state.

**secularism.** A view of life or of any particular matter holding that religion and religious considerations should be ignored or purposely excluded.

**secularization.** The act or process of transferring matters under ecclesiastical or religious control to secular or civil or lay control; the process whereby religious thinking, practice and institutions lose social significance.

**see.** The jurisdiction of a bishop, or his rank, office, power, authority, cathedral or diocesan centre.

**seekers.** See decisions.

**Sefardis** (Sephardis). The smaller of the 2 great divisions of Jews; often loosely used to include Oriental Jews; speaking Ladino, dating from medieval Spain, now scattered from North Africa to Afghanistan, speaking Arabic, Persian, Aramaic; 14% of world's Jews today. Global total: (1980) 677,500.

**selections.** Small leaflets of 2 or 3 pages or so consisting of attractively-presented scripture passages, printed in large numbers by Bible societies usually for special occasions or needs. Global distribution per year (UBS): (1975) 259,020,100, (1979) 432,317,900.

**self-enumeration.** A census or survey method in which the questionnaire employed is completed by the respondents themselves.

**self-evangelization.** Auto-evangelization (qv).

**self-identifying Christians.** Professing Christians (qv).

**self-publishing** (in Russian, *samizdat*). Underground Christian literature (reports, descriptions, protests, et alia) typed, duplicated or handwritten, that is passed from reader to reader despite prohibition by the Soviet state; a major source of news of churches and persecution in the USSR.

**seminarian, seminarist.** A student in a seminary, a candidate for ordination to the diaconate or priesthood.

**seminarians, Roman Catholic.** World totals (1976): 201,409 (60,150 major (35.5% religious, 64.5% diocesan), 141,259 minor), a decline from (1973) 226,444 (64,647 major, 161,797 minor).

**seminaries.** Centres for the training of the ordained ministry or priesthood, equipped with premises, plant and personnel; preparing persons of secondary or higher education for ordination; covering religious and secular major seminaries, theological colleges and advanced Bible schools of all churches and also independently-run; excluding smaller Bible schools and minor seminaries. Global total: (1975) 4,150 (1980) 4,500.

**seminaries, Roman Catholic.** World totals (1976): 1,376 major (730 religious, 646 secular), 2,251 minor (1,135 religious, 1,119 secular).

**seminary, minor,** See minor seminary.

**seminary, major.** See major seminary.

**seminary, united.** See united seminary.

**Semitic indigenous churches.** Semitic initiatives or church traditions or Middle Eastern indigenous churches dating from the 1st century AD, and still completely Semitic in leadership and membership today, namely: Syrian Orthodox (later Arab), Coptic Orthodox (later Arab), Ancient Church of the East (Assyrian, later Nestorian), Ethiopian Orthodox (Amharic). Global affiliated membership: (1970) 18,038,100 (1.6% of world Christianity), (1980) 23,134,700 (1.75%).

**semi-literate.** A person who can read but not write, or read and write only with difficulty.

**sendee.** See church sendee.

**sending countries.** 10 countries across the world in which mission has traditionally been a sending operation only, and which send out far more foreign missionaries and personnel than they receive.

**seniorate.** An ecclesiastical geographical division within some Reformed denominations in Eastern Europe, corresponding to a presbytery.

**separatism.** A disposition towards secession or schism.

**separatist.** A dissenter or schismatic out of an established church; a nonconformist.

**separatist church.** A group of Christians who have separated from their parent church because of disagreement on some issue and who have formed themselves into a new and separate denomination.

**Sephardis.** See Sefardis.

**Serbian/Slavonic.** Eastern Orthodox liturgical tradition (Serbian Orthodox Church). Global membership: (1970) 18 denominations with 2,985 churches and 5,031,700 adult members; total community (1970) 7,405,100, (1980) 7,868,100, (1985) 8,103,200.

**sermon.** A religious discourse delivered in public, usually by a clergyman or minister, as part of a worship service.

**serology.** The science that treats of serums, their reactions and properties; necessary for the classification of races and peoples.

**service.** The performance of religious worship according to settled public forms or conventions.

**service agencies.** Major national, international or country-wide bodies, parachurch organizations and agencies which assist or serve the churches but are not themselves denominations or church-planting missions. Global total: (1975) 15,811, (1980) 17,500.

**session.** The ruling body of a Presbyterian congregation consisting of the elders in active service moderated by the pastor; consistory, presbytery.

**settler.** A person who settles down in a new region or colony.

**Seveners.** Ismailis (qv).

**Shafiites.** Followers of Shafiiya, one of the 4 schools or rites of Sunni Muslim law. Global adherents: (1980) 149,857,000.

**shakubuku** (Japanese). The aggressive-conversion process practised by the New Religious movement, Soka Gakkai.

**shaman.** A priest-doctor who uses magic to cure the sick, to divine the hidden, and to control events that affect people's welfare.

**shamanists.** Followers of Ural-Altaic, Amerindian, Korean and other religions which believe that the unseen world of gods, demons, and ancestral spirits is responsive only to shamans. Global adherents: (1970) 15,927,300, (1980) 13,502,800, (1985) 12,165,500.

**sharia** (Arabic). Islamic law.

**sharing countries.** 12 countries across the world which both send and receive large numbers of foreign missionaries and personnel.

**sheik, sheikh.** A Muslim religious leader or cleric or scholar; an Arab chief.

**shepherding.** In the modern charismatic movement, the practice of a leader exercising strict or extensive authority over his flock of immediate followers.

**shepherds.** Apostles in charismatic bodies.

**Shias** (Shi'is). Followers of the smaller of the 2 great divisions of Islam, rejecting the Sunna and holding that Mohammed's son-in-law Ali was the Prophet's successor; and itself divided into the Ithna-Ashari, Ismaili, Alawite and Zaydi sects. Global adherents: (1980) 105,600,000 (14.6% of all Muslims); being a majority in Iran, Iraq and North Yemen, a significant minority in 11 other countries, and a smaller minority in some 30 others.

**Shintoists.** Japanese who profess, or still profess, Shinto as their first or major religion. Global adherents: (1970) 4,173,000, (1980) 3,526,400, (1985) 3,163,600.

**shortwave broadcasting.** Wireless communication, usually over long distances, using wavelengths of 60 metres or less (frequencies of 500 kiloherz or more).

**short-service missionaries.** Foreign missionary personnel serving abroad for a single period of from 6 to 24 months only.

**short-term personnel.** Short-service missionaries (qv).

**Shroud of Christ.** See sindonology.

**sib, sibling.** A brother or sister.

**Sikhs.** Followers of the Sikh reform movement out of Hinduism, who look to the Golden Temple in Amritsar, India (sects: Akali, Khalsa, Nanapanthi, Nirmali, Sewapanthi, Udasi). Global adherents: (1970) 10,612,200, (1980) 14,244,400 in 19 countries, (1985) 16,149,900.

**silence, churches of.** See crypto-Christians.

**simpatizante** (Spanish). A sympathizer, person interested in Protestantism in Latin America but unable to make public profession or seek church membership.

SIMULTANEOUS AUDIBLE PRAYER. East African Pentecostals.

**simultaneous audible prayer.** Prayer in tongues (glossolalia) by a number of individuals, independently and on unrelated topics, aloud and at the same time during worship services.

**sindonology.** The science of the study of Christ's *sindon* (Holy Shroud) as preserved in Turin cathedral, Italy.

**single congregation.** A single autonomous worship centre, completely independent and unaffiliated to any denomination, nor claiming to be a denomination. Global total: (1980) over 5,000.

**Sis.** Cilicia (qv).

**sister.** A female church worker; a religious sister, nun; a female fellow-Christian.

**sisterhood.** A community or society of sisters.

**skeptic.** A sceptic (qv).

**Slav.** A European ethnolinguistic family. Global population: (1970) 256,829,300, (1980) 282,021,300, (1985) 295,000,000.

**Slavonic.** Eastern Orthodox liturgical tradition, followed in Russia, Bulgaria, et alia. Global membership: (1970) 115 denominations with 12,587 churches and 54,810,700 adult members; total community (1970) 79,071,600, (1980) 87,976,000, (1985) 92,524,000.

**Slovak rite.** Used by Byzantine Catholics in Czechoslovakia. Membership: (1970) 176,000 total community.

**small communities.** See basic communities.

**small-group evangelism.** Personal evangelism undertaken within the context of small study groups, house churches, et alia.

**sobor** (Russian). A synod or council.

**sobornost** (Russian). Conciliarity, ecumenicity, spiritual harmony based on freedom and unity in love.

**social communication.** Organizations co-ordinating social communications for the churches number over 200, with over 100 training centres.

**social concern.** Organizations significant at the national or wider levels number over 500.

**Social Democratic states.** States in which the party in power is of social democratic persuasion.

**Socialist countries.** States committed to the full implementation of political Socialism; often used of Marxist and Communist countries.

**society.** In several denominations, a local congregation of believers; in Christian Science, a local congregation of believers.

**sociology, religious.** See religious sociology.

**sociology of religion.** The study of religion from the standpoint of the science of society, social institutions, and social relationships.

**socio-religious.** Relating to social and religious factors.

**sodality.** In missiological use, part of the sodality/modality dichotomy. (1) A sodality is an organized society, fellowship, community, fraternity or brotherhood based on mission as the common purpose (e.g. monastic pattern, or missionary society). (2) A modality is the more normal or typical pattern for mission, i.e. the diocesan pattern of Christianity following civil-governmental patterns, church-oriented missionary outreach, parish system, family involvement, etc.

**soldier.** In Salvationist usage, converted persons at least 14 years of age who have been enrolled as members of the Salvation Army after signing its Articles of War.

**Songhai.** An African ethnolinguistic family, with about 6 languages. Global population: (1970) 1,286,900, (1980) 1,676,500, (1985) 1,887,800.

**sorcerer.** A person who practises sorcery; a wizard, magician.

**sorcery.** The use of power gained from the assistance or control of evil spirits, especially for divining; necromancy, wizardry, black magic.

**sound recordings.** Christian organizations specializing mainly in this area and significant at the national or wider levels number over 200.

**sous influence** (French). A statistical category enumerated in some Reformed denominations in Africa, covering the total membership plus non-members in the denomination's comity area or otherwise under its influence.

**Southern Amerindian.** An American Indian ethnolinguistic family, with over 1,500 languages. Global population: (1970) 15,094,700, (1980) 19,896,000, (1985) 22,465,600.

**Southern Buddhism.** Theravada or Hinayana (qv).

**sovereign territory, sovereign nation.** An independent, self-governing, autonomous state.

**spare-time worker.** A recognized or accredited church worker who nevertheless has a full-time secular job and is able to devote not part-time service but only his spare time out of work hours (e.g. Sundays or evenings) to church work; spare-time as contrasted with part-time or full-time.

**sparsely-evangelized.** A people or area is defined as sparsely evangelized when less than 20% of its population have been evangelized.

**speaking in tongues.** Glossolalia (qv).

**special pioneers.** In Jehovah's Witnesses' usage, full-time salaried workers who put in 150 or more hours per month preaching. Totals: (1971) 13,846, (1974) 14,525.

**Spirit, Spiritual.** Adjectives widely used among African indigenous churches and in their official names, referring to the element of their control by the Holy Spirit.

**spirit possession.** Possession or seizure by evil spirits.

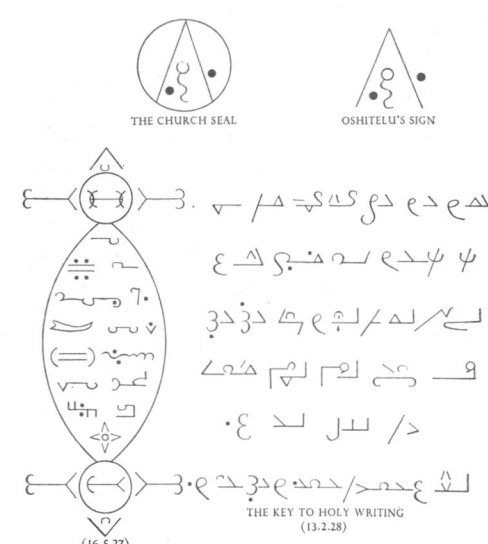

SPIRIT WRITING. Church of the Lord Aladura (Nigeria).

**spirit writing.** Automatic writing held to be produced under the action of spirits; pneumatography.

**spiritism.** Belief in the action or agency of spirits of the dead producing mediumistic phenomena. See high spiritism, low spiritism.

SPIRITIST CATHOLICS. Diablos Danzantes (Venezuela).

**Spiritist Catholics.** Roman Catholics active in organized high or low spiritism, including syncretistic spirit-possession cults. Global total: (1970) 21,859,500, (1980) 30,165,200 in 13 countries, (1985) 34,686,700.

**Spiritists.** Non-Christian spiritists or spiritualists, or thaumaturgicalists; high spiritists, as opposed to low spiritists (Afro-American syncretists); followers of medium-religions, medium-religionists. Global adherents: (1970) 1,384,900, (1980) 2,374,400, (1985) 2,898,100.

**spiritual.** Sacred, religious, ecclesiastical; influenced or controlled by the divine Spirit.

**spiritual healing.** Faith-healing (qv).

**Spiritualists.** Followers of a marginal Protestant tradition which holds that the word of God is constantly revealed to man via the mediumship of Spiritualist ministers, and which is nevertheless specifically Christian. Global membership in Christian Spiritualist churches; (1970) 24 denominations with 1,471 churches and 270,400 adult members; total community (1970) 463,500, (1980) 595,400, (1985) 663,100.

**spirituality.** Sensitivity or attachment to religious values and things of the spirit rather than material or worldly interests.

**spirit-worshippers.** See tribal religionists.

**split.** A schism, seccession (qv).

**spontaneous communities.** See basic communities.

**spontaneous expansion of the church.** See people movement.

**spreading.** In evangelization, the act or state or extent of the gospel being spread; reaching or thrusting out, expanding, extending, exposing, distributing, scattering, sowing, strewing, covering, overlaying, publishing, disseminating, making more widely known, diffusing, emitting, unfolding, circulating, propagating, radiating, et alia.

STAFFS (STAVES). During Apostles' worship (Zimbabwe).

**staff** (plural, staves). Wooden walking-sticks, symbols of discipleship and office in many African indigenous churches (qv).

**stake.** In Mormon usage, a territorial unit comprising a group of wards (qv) and governed by a stake presidency; equivalent to a diocese or jurisdiction.

**state church.** An established church (qv), national church (qv).

**state departments of religious affairs.** Over 75 countries operate government departments or ministries of religion, usually for purposes of control and surveillance of the churches.

**state religion.** An established religion, national religion recognized in law as the official religion of a country.

**stateless persons.** Persons who are citizens of no state at all.

**stations, mission.** See mission stations.

**statistical compassion.** The extending of the Christian attitude of *agape* (love, compassion) beyond one's immediate, visible circles of persons in need, to the demographically-vast but invisible multitudes beyond, and in particular to the entire world population in its totality.

**statistics.** (1) Numeral, numerical or quantitative data, or numerical facts systematically collected. (2) The science of collecting and classifying numerical data, or that branch of applied mathematics that actually arranges, describes and draws inferences from sets of numerical data. (3) A body of methods for making wise decisions in the face of uncertainty.

**stewardship.** That aspect of church life and administration which deals with individual and corporate responsibility for sharing systematically and proportionately one's time, talents and material possessions in the service of God and for the benefit of mankind.

**Sthanakavasis.** Subsect of Svetambaras (qv) in western India.

**stock.** A racial stock, race (qv).

**strategy.** In war, the overall military and psychological plans that a general (in Greek, *strategos*) makes, or the science or art of employing all the resources of a nation or coalition of nations to achieve the objects of war. In missions, the overall plans guiding the long-term evangelization of a people or territory.

**Strict Brethren.** Exclusive Brethren (qv).

**student organizations.** Christian organizations for students, significant at the national or wider levels, number over 500.

**studio.** A room or centre for the preparation (but not transmission) of Christian radio and TV programmes.

**study centres.** Church- or Christian-operated study centres and other specialized lay training centres. Global total: (1975) 1,800.

**Stupa.** A Buddhist hemispherical mound or tower, surmounted by a spire or umbrella, forming a memorial shrine of the Buddha and often containing sacred relics; also known as chaitya, tope, chorten (Tibet), dagoba (Ceylon), pagoda (Burma).

**style.** The mode of address normally used for church dignitaries.

**subject.** A citizen (qv), often of a colonial territory.

**subsidized distribution of scriptures.** Annual sales of scriptures produced by UBS-related and other Bible societies, which are subsidized to locally-realistic prices.

**sub-culture.** See homogeneous unit.

**sub-deacon.** A person in holy orders who ranks below a deacon, with duties including preparation of vessels for the eucharist.

**sub-Orthodox sects.** Formerly Russian Orthodox in the USSR who have split with their parent body to embark on total non-cooperation with the state, yet retaining elements of Orthodox ritual. Total membership: (1970) 1,525 congregations with 202,600 adult members, 388,300 total community.

**sub-population.** In any population, part of the total inhabitants, e.g. schoolchildren, persons of marriageable age, etc.

**Sudanic.** An African ethnolinguistic family, with over 255 languages. Global population: (1970) 11,355,800, (1980) 14,707,300, (1985) 16,545,100.

**suffragan bishop.** In Anglican usage, (1) an assistant to the diocesan bishop, or (2) any bishop in relation to his archbishop or metropolitan. In Roman Catholic usage, a diocesan bishop in relation to his metropolitan.

**suffragan diocese.** In Roman Catholic usage, any diocese which is part of an ecclesiastical province and therefore to some extent dependent on its metropolitan see.

**Sufism.** Islamic mysticism, including scores of millions of Sunni Muslims in 70 orders: Ahmadiya, Bektashiya, Christiya, Dargawa, Dervishes, Fakirs, Malamatiya, Mawlawiya, Naqshbandiya, Qadriya, Qalandariya, Rifaiya, Shadhiliya, Shattariya, Suhrawardiya, Tijaniya, et alia.

**Sunday attenders.** Practising Christians who attend church services of public worship on average every Sunday.

**Sunday mass attenders.** Practising Roman Catholics who attend mass on average every Sunday.

**Sunday schools.** Christian or church classes held on Sundays for the purpose of religious education; with their pupils and teachers.

**sunna.** The body of hadith, traditions of Muhammed, i.e. of Islamic custom and practice.

**Sunnis, Sunnites.** Followers of the larger of the 2 major branches of Islam, that adheres to the orthodox tradition of the sunna (qv), acknowledges the first 4 caliphs, and recognizes 4 schools of jurisprudence: Hanafite, Hanbalite, Malikite, Shafiite. Global adherents: (1980) 609,178,000 (84.3% of all Muslims).

**superintendent.** A Protestant minister charged with the general supervision of churches within a certain district.

**superior.** A head of a religious house, order or congregation.

**superior general.** The head of an entire religious order or congregation.

**supernatural change, supranatural change.** By contrast with natural change in a population (births minus deaths, plus immigrants minus emigrants), change in religious allegiance or adherence which from some points of view is unnatural, non-natural, supranatural or supernatural.

**superstock.** A language grouping or language phylum (qv).

**suppressed churches.** Churches which have been forcibly suppressed, destroyed or otherwise permanently closed by state or other action.

**suppressed dioceses.** See closed dioceses.

**surveillance.** A recognized government tactic against churches in anti-Christian states; continuous close observation for purposes of obstruction, harassment and control.

**survey.** An inquiry or operation designed to furnish information on a special subject and which has limited aims.

**suspended.** Temporarily debarred from church membership, in particular from communicant status, because of some infringement of church law.

**Svetambara.** ('white-robed'). A major Jain sect whose members clothe themselves and their sacred images in white and in contrast to the Digambaras (qv) assert that women can attain salvation.

**Swedenborgians.** Followers of a marginal Protestant tradition, the Church of the New Jerusalem/New Church. Global membership: (1980) 18 denomin-ations with 359 churches and 28,300 adult members; total community (1970) 49,900, (1980) 67,100, (1985) 75,700.

**switching.** Used of church members who change from allegiance to one denomination to allegiance to another.

**symbolics.** Historical theology dealing with Christian creeds (Latin, *symbolae*) and confessions of faith; also termed symbolic theology. Comparative symbolics (German: Konfessionskunde) is the term traditionally applied to that branch of theology or ecclesiology which deals with the various Christian churches and confessions, their doctrines, their creeds, constitutions, ways of worship, devotional life and distinctive features studied as a whole.

**sympathizer.** A term used for a person who is not a church member but who attends church services regularly.

**synagogue.** A Jewish local community or local assembly organized for public worship; or their building.

**syncretism.** The developmental process of historical growth within a religion by accretion and coalescence of different and often conflicting forms of belief and practice; as understood by Christian theology, the religious attitude which holds that there is no unique revelation in history, that there are many different ways to reach the divine reality, that all formulations of religious truth or experience are inadequate expression of that truth, and that it is necessary to harmonize all religious ideas and experiences so as to create one universal religion for mankind.

**syncretistic movement.** A religious movement incorporating conflicting or divergent beliefs, principles or practices drawn from 2 or more religious systems.

**synod.** An ecclesiastical council or church governing or advisory body, including general synod, diocesan synod (qv), holy synod (qv); either regularly-meeting, or a one-time occasion.

SYNOD OF BISHOPS. 1974, in Sistine Chapel (Holy See).

**Synod of Bishops.** Since 1965 a permanent, central, ecclesiastical institution assisting the Roman pope in the governing of the universal church. By 1980, 6 formal assemblies had been held.

**Synodus Episcoporum.** Synod of Bishops (qv).

**synthesist, synthesizer.** One who employs synthesis or follows synthetic methods with varying religious traditions.

**Syriac.** Oriental Orthodox liturgical tradition, dating back to New Testament era (Syrian Orthodox, West Syrian, Jacobite). Global membership: (1970) 19 denominations with 94 churches and 113,200 adult members; total community (1970) 204,800, (1980) 230,100, (1985) 243,800.

**Syriac/Malayalam.** Oriental Orthodox liturgical tradition, using both languages in its liturgy; Syro-Malabarese (qv).

**Syrian Orthodox Patriarchate of Antioch.** Oriental Orthodox (Jacobite). Global constituency in canonical relationship: (1980) 1,811,100.

**Syrians.** Roman Catholics using Antiochian rite. Global membership: (1970) 73,700 total community.

**Syrians, Eastern.** See Eastern Syrians.
**Syrians, Western.** See Western Syrians.
**Syro-Chaldeans.** Assyrians (qv).
**Syro-Malabarese.** (1) Orthodox St Thomas Christians of India who have remained independent of Rome but in communion with Jacobite Church (Damascus); global membership (1980) 1,581,000. (2) Catholic St Thomas Christians who submitted to Rome in 1599 and still use the East Syrian rite, with Malayalam; global membership (1980) 2,811,100.
**Syro-Malankarese.** Catholic St Thomas Christians who submitted to Rome in 1930, and who use the West Syrian rite. Global membership (1980) 280,900.
**Syro-Oriental.** A Roman Catholic rite (see Chaldean).
**systematic theology.** Constructive theology; a branch of theology that attempts to reduce all religious truth to statements forming a self-consistent and organized whole.
**systems analysis.** That approach which seeks to explain a situation or to solve a problem within the totality of its environment, seeing the situation and understanding how all of its parts are interrelated or affect one another.

# T

**tactics.** In war, the science of disposing local resources to fight particular battles. In mission, the science or art of using available resources for the immediate evangelization of a people or territory.
**Tai.** An Asian ethnolinguistic family. Global population: (1970) 44,049,300, (1980) 58,181,400, (1985) 65,740,700.
**Tan.** Stylized skin colour (olive, light brown) associated with the Middle Eastern geographical race and the Iranian and some Latin American peoples. Global Tan population: (1970) 312,042,800, (1980) 405,883,400, (1985) 456,615,000.
**Tantrayana.** Tantrism, Vajrayana, Mantrayana, Esoteric Vehicle, or Lamaism; a school of Buddhists (qv), including Shingon in Japan. Global adherents: (1980) 16,350,000 (6.0% of all Buddhists).
**Taoists.** Followers of one of the 3 major religions of China, regarded as part of Chinese folk religion. Global adherents: (1980) about 20 million Taoists.
**tariqa** (Arabic). (1) A Muslim religious brotherhood or fraternity of mystics. (2) The Sufi path of spiritual development.
**teacher.** In Christian Science usage, one authorized to teach a class of not more than 30 pupils each calender year.
**telecast.** A broadcast programme over television.
**telecentre.** A church centre equipped with a television receiver for use with classes and educational programmes.
**telephone ministries.** Christian organization in this area, significant at the national or wider levels, number over 200.
**television** (TV). See under radio, broadcasting.
**temple.** An edifice dedicated to the worship of a deity, in non-Christian religions, especially Hinduism and Buddhism; occasionally used of Christian buildings, as in Mormon usage.
**tent-making ministry.** A self-supporting ministry in which a Christian worker, often an ordained minister, earns his livelihood in some secular occupation.
**tent-making missionary.** A self-supporting foreign missionary who is not supported by a foreign missionary society or local church.
**terminology, religious.** The technical or special terms or expressions used in the descriptive study of religion.
**territory.** In Salvationist usage, a country or region in which Salvation Army work is organized under a territorial commander.
**testimony.** A brief personal account or narrative by an individual Christian concerning how Christ has worked in his life.
**thaumaturgic.** Connected with or dependent on thaumaturgy (performing of miracles or magic).
**thaumaturgicalist, thaumaturgist.** A performer of miracles, a magician.
**theatre, religious.** See religious drama.
**theist.** A believer in theism, belief in the existence of one God transcendent and immanent.
**theocracy.** Government of a state by allegedly the immediate direction or administration of God.
**theological college associations.** Associations at national or wider levels number over 80.
**theological colleges.** See seminaries.
**theological education.** An intensive and structured preparation of men and women for their participation in the ministry of Christ in the world.

**theological education by extension** (TEE). Organization specializing in this area number over 200 worldwide.
**theology.** The study of God and his relation to man and the world: apologetics, dogmatic theology, natural theology, practical theology, systematic theology, et alia.
**theophany.** A physical presentation or personal manifestation of a deity to an individual.
**Theosophists.** Persons and bodies holding to Theosophy, or synthesist views combining philosophy and religions. A small number, including Liberal Catholics (qv), are specifically Christian.
**Theosophy.** A syncretistic system following chiefly Hindu philosophies originating in the USA in 1875.
**Theravada** (Theraveda). The Teaching of the Elders, or the Hinayana school of Buddhists (qv), or Southern Buddhism (in Ceylon, India, Burma, Thailand, Cambodia, Laos). Global adherents: (1980) 103,608,000 (37.8% of all Buddhists).
**thesis.** Usually, a paper or essay submitted for a master's degree at a university.
**Third Rome.** Moscow; after the sack of Rome and the end of the Roman empire in the West in AD 476, Constantinople became known as the Second Rome, but after its fall in 1453 its claim to be the capital of the Christian world passed to Moscow with its claim to be the Third Rome.
**Third World.** A term, based on political non-alignment, for those developing nations which are non-aligned with either the Western (Capitalist) world or the Communist (Marxist) world, and so form a third bloc. For an economic and social analysis, see *The Third World: problems and perspectives*, ed. A.B. Mountjoy (London: Macmillan, 1978).
**Third-World indigenous Christians.** See Non-White indigenous Christians.
**Third-World foreign missionaries.** Citizens of Third-World nations who serve as foreign missionaries in other countries. Global total: (1975) 24,650.
**threefold ministry.** In Anglicanism, the orders of bishop, priest and deacon.
**Tibeto-Burmese.** An Asian ethnolinguistic family, with over 300 languages. Global population: (1970) 40,412,700, (1980) 50,510,000, (1985) 55,882,000.
**time lag.** In church statistics, the delay incurred between the collecting of statistics at grass-roots level and their eventual publication at denominational or nationwide level; usually 2, 3, 4, 5 or even 6 years depending upon the size and complexity of the denomination concerned.
**time level.** The exact date, year or time to which particular data, especially statistical data, apply.
**time series.** The values of a variable over a period of time.
**titular bishops.** Roman Catholic bishops each with the title of, but without jurisdiction in, a defunct see; bishops in partibus infidelium. Totals: (1969) 1,953, (1977) 1,986, (1979) 1,988.
**toleration, religious.** See religious toleration.
**tongues.** Glossolalia (qv).
**total.** Aggregate, sum, amount, whole.
**total Christian community.** The total of a church's or denomination's affiliated Christians (qv) or church members, who are part of the churches' corporate life, community and fellowship; of all ages and varieties including children, infants and persons under instruction; also called inclusive membership.
**total church member community.** Affiliated Christians (qv).
**total church membership.** Affiliated Christians (qv).
**total community.** The total of all persons affiliated to a particular denomination or religion; for the churches, affiliated Christians (qv).
**total mobilization evangelism.** See in-depth evangelism.
**totalitarian.** Authoritarian, dictatorial, despotic.
**tourism.** Travelling for recreation; touring. In this field, Christian ministries and organizations significant at the national or wider levels number over 150.
**tourists.** Persons travelling from place to place for pleasure or culture, defined as those who stay overnight usually at a hotel or inn.
**tract.** A pamphlet or leaflet containing a religious exhortation, doctrinal discussion or proselytizing appeal.
**Tractarians.** Anglo-Catholics (qv).
**tradition.** The totality of veliefs and practices (doctrine, dogmas, polity, ecclesiology, founding, origin) characterizing a particular Christian school of thought, not derived directly from the Bible but arising and handed down within the Christian community.
**Traditional Catholics.** Conservative Catholics (qv).
**tradition, ecclesiastical.** See ecclesiastical tradition.
**traditional religion.** Often used of the dominant pre-

Christian religion in a country, i.e. before the coming of Christianity.
**traditionalist.** One who adheres to tradition.
**transconfessional.** Church union negotiations between churches of 2 or more confessional families.
**transient cults.** Short-lived or ephemeral unorthodox or exotic religious movements.
**transients.** Impermanent, transitory, often homeless persons on the move.
**translations.** Total scripture translations published or available (April 1980): complete Bible in 273 languages, New Testament in 745 languages, portion in 1,811 languages.
**translation projects.** Member Bible Societies of the UBS were in 1980 engaged in a total of 695 translation projects (new translations of all or part of the scriptures).
**travel intensity.** The ratio of annual international travellers to a country or area (including tourists) divided by the size of the total resident population; or, within a country, the proportion of adults in the population who go away on holiday in a year.
**trend.** The general movement over a sufficiently long period of time of some statistical progressive change; tendency.

TRIBAL RELIGIONIST. Luo funeral mask (Nilotes).

**tribal religionists.** A collective term for primal or primitive religionists, animists, spirit-worshippers, shamanists (qv), ancestor-venerators, polytheists, pantheists, traditionalists (in Africa), local or tribal folk-religionists; including adherents of neopaganism or non-Christian local or tribal syncretistic or nativistic movements, cargo cults, witchcraft eradication cults, possession healing movements, tribal messianic movements; still occasionally termed pagans, heathen, fetishists; usually confined each to a single tribe or people, hence 'tribal' or local as opposed to 'universal' (open to any or all peoples). Global adherents including shamanists: (1970) 104,004,800, (1980) 103,466,500 in 101 countries, (1985) 103,296,200.
**tribe.** A group of persons having a common character, occupation, avocation, interest, also common language, culture, territory and traditions.
**tribunal.** A court of church law at Rome; in particular, the 3 senior courts, dating from the 13th and 14th centuries: Apostolic Penitentiary, Rota, and (the Catholic Church's supreme court) the Apostolic Signature.
**Tridentine.** Pertaining to or resulting from the Council of Trent (AD 1545-63).
**Tridentinists.** Roman Catholic traditionalists opposed to the reforms of Vatican II (1962-65) and upholding the Council of Trent (1545-63), including retention of the Latin mass and condemnation of Protestantism. In England (1977), 25% of all RCs prefer the Tridentine mass; in France, 20% support the

traditionalist archbishop M. Lefebvre suspended by the pope in 1976 (and 24% oppose him); in Switzerland 24% support him (and 39% oppose).

**trine.** Threefold, triple.

**trine immersion.** The practice of immersing a candidate for baptism 3 times in the names in turn of the Trinity.

**triumphalism.** A theology of continuous success namely that the church continually triumphs over evil, succeeds, grows numerically larger and larger. Once espoused by the Catholic Church and other large denomination, this is now rejected as unscriptural.

**True Orthodox.** Devoutly conservative Russian Orthodox in the USSR who have seceded from their parent body at various time (1900, 1927, 1944, 1956, et alia) to embark on total non-cooperation with the Soviet state. Totals: (1970) 18,100 congregations with 176,000 adult members, 253,000 total community.

**trumping.** Black religious dance from the Caribbean (especially in Revival Zion and Pocomania), known as 'dancing, trumping and labouring for the Holy Ghost', being the means whereby the Spirit or spirits are invited to take possession. Worshippers form a dancing-trumping ring and dance counter-clockwise around a centre post (symbolic of centre of the world), in a shuffling 2-step dance done to 2-2 rhythm, bending forward and up in rhythmic sequence while sucking in breath and releasing with grunting sound.

**Tukutendereza** (Luganda for 'We praise you, Jesus'). A theme song of East African Revivalists (Balokole).

**Twelvers.** Ithna-Asharis (qv).

## U

**Ukrainian Orthodox Church of the Free World.** The major Ukrainian Orthodox world communion. Global constituency: (1980) 380,000.

**Ukrainians.** Roman Catholics of the Byzantine rite using Ukrainian numbered (in 1970) 607 parishes, 941,000 adults, 1,381,000 total community, with a further 3 million suppressed by the USSR since 1945.

**ulema, ulama** (Arabic). The highest body of religious authorities in Islam; a group of Muslim theologians and scholars who are professionally occupied with the elaboration and interpretation of the Muslim legal system from a study of Quran and hadith.

**ummah** (Arabic). The community of faith embracing all Muslims, adherents of Islam.

**unaffiliated.** Nominal Christians (qv).

**unattached congregation.** An independent single congregation or worship centre with no denominational ties.

**unbaptized Christian.** A professing or believing Christian who has not, or not yet, undergone Christian baptism.

**unbelief.** Non-belief, doubt, incredulity, agnosticism, apathy in matters of religious faith.

**unbelievers.** Non-religious persons: doubters, non-believers, agnostics, freethinkers, liberal thinkers, non-religious humanists, persons indifferent to both religion and atheism.

**uncanonical.** Unsanctioned, unorthodox, not being in accord with church canons.

**unchristen.** To annul the baptism of a person.

**unchristian.** Not of the Christian faith, contrary to Christianity.

**unchristianize.** To turn people from Christianity, dechristianize.

**unchurch.** To excommunicate, expel, separate from the church, deprive of church membership.

**unchurched.** Christians unaffiliated to organized churches, not belonging to or connected with a church; nominal Christians (qv).

**under discipline.** See discipline.

**under obligation.** All baptized Roman Catholics of 7 years and older are obligated by canon law to attend Easter mass once a year.

**underground churches, underground Christians.** See crypto-Christians.

**underground communities.** See basic communities.

**unevangelized.** The state of not having had the gospel spread or offered.

**Uniate.** A Christian or a jurisdiction of an Eastern rite not belonging to a Latin patriarchate but in union with and submitting to the authority of the Roman papacy.

**union congregations.** Churches of English-speaking peoples abroad in which several denomination are present and hence an interdenomination ministry

is required.

**Union of Utrecht.** International Old Catholic Bishops Conference (qv).

**union, church.** See church unions.

**Unitarians.** Non-Trinitarians (denying the Trinity), Universalists, Free Christians, Liberal Christians: a marginal Protestant tradition in the direction of modernism. Global membership: (1970) 29 denominations with 1,908 churches and 274,400 adult members; total community (1970) 469,300, (1980) 566,800, (1985) 616,100.

**Unitarian-Pentecostals.** Oneness-Pentecostals (qv).

**united churches.** Protestant and Anglican denominations which in recent years have united to form new united denominations. Global membership excluding Lutheran/Reformed united churches: (1970) 49 denominations with 96,200 churches and 30,164,800, adult members; total community (1970) 49,594,100, (1980) 53,666,500, (1985) 55,807,000. Including Lutheran/Reformed: (1970) 60,000,900, (1980) 63,299,000, (1985) 65,164,000.

**united diocese, united dioceses.** Dioceses which were large in the past but have now shrunk numerically (especially in Ireland), hence are administered together as a single diocese.

**united seminary.** A theological college serving 2 or more denominations or confessions.

**uniting churches.** Churches or denominations that are in process of merging to form a united church.

**unity.** Oneness, singleness, accord among Christians of different traditions.

**Unity of the Brethren.** Moravians (qv).

**unity undertaking.** A Moravian jurisdiction.

**universal church.** The Christian church in its world-wide entirety down the ages; in Roman Catholic usage, the worldwide church as contrasted with local or particular churches (qv).

**Universal Commission.** The Great Commission (qv).

**universal religion.** Any religion which admits persons of any race or people; a world religion, usually missionary in emphasis.

**universal religionists.** Followers of universal religions, as contrasted with primal religionists (qv).

**universalism.** The theological doctrine that all men will eventually be saved or restored to holiness and happiness.

**Universalists.** Unitarians (qv).

**universe.** In sampling and polls, the total population to which a sample survey refers.

**universities, Christian.** Degree-granting universities and colleges teaching secular subjects, operated by churches or under Christian auspices. Global total (1980): 1,300.

**university departments of religion.** Departments significant for the study of Christianity number over 1,500 in as many universities across to world.

**unreached.** The state of not having had the gospel brought.

**unreached peoples.** Ethnic, linguistic and other groups without previous contact with Christianity, who have not or not yet had the gospel brought to them.

**unrecognized churches.** Churches or denominations whom the state refuses to legalize.

**Untouchables.** A large hereditary group in India having, in traditional Hindu belief and practice, the quality of defiling by contact the person, food, or drink of members of higher castes, and formerly being strictly segregated and restricted to menial work; the term has been illegal in India since 1949 and in Pakistan since 1953, and is now replaced by Harijans (Children of God) or Scheduled Castes. Total (1980): 96,292,000.

**untouched.** In evangelization, a population group that is not yet explored or travelled to or influenced or disturbed or reached by Christians, nor written about, but is still in its original (often primitive or aboriginal) intact state; non-evangelized.

**Uralian.** An Asian ethnolinguistic family (Whites). Global population: (1970) 22,388,500, (1980) 23,647,800, (1985) 24,278,200.

**urban area.** Defined in many countries as an administrative district with a population over 2,000.

**urban dwellers.** The population living in urban areas, usually including cities and towns with over 5,000 inhabitants. Global totals: (1900) 232,694,900 (14.4% of world), (1970) 1,354,237,000 (37.5%), (1980) 1,797,479,000 (41.1%), (2000) 3,160,381,900 (50.5%).

URBAN MISSION. Port mission in Abidjan (Ivory Coast).

**urban mission.** In the field of urban industrial mission, Christian organizations significant at the national or wider levels number over 400.

**urbanization.** The state or extent of urban areas, or the process of becoming urbanized, in a particular country.

**usual language.** The language customarily used by an individual, as distinct from his mother tongue (qv).

## V

**vagrants.** Persons of no fixed abode.

**Vaishnavites.** Worshippers of Vishnu in any of his forms or incarnations; the predominant form of Hinduism outside South India; including these sects: Alvars, Caitanya, Kapalikas, Nimbarka, Ramanandis, Tenkalai, Vadakalai, Visnuvamins, et alia. Global adherents: (1970) 324,649,000, (1980) 406,925,000, (1985) 453,398,000.

**Vajrayana.** The Tantrism school of Buddhists; Tantrayana (qv).

**variable.** A quantity that changes or varies in size; dependent variable, independent variable, etc.

**Vatican.** Official headquarters and spiritual centre of the Roman Catholic Church; in Rome.

**Vaticanism.** The dogma of absolute papal supremacy.

**Vedas.** The most ancient sacred writings of Hinduism; any of 4 Samhitas (Aranyaka, Brahmana, Sutra, Upanishad).

**Venice.** See of Latin Catholic patriarchate and patriarch, since 1451.

**vicar.** An Anglican incumbent who is not a rector; a Roman Catholic ecclesiastic who acts as the substitute or representative of another.

**vicariate** (symbol V). The office, authority, or jurisdiction of a vicar.

**vicariates apostolic** (symbol VA). Roman Catholic missionary districts over each of which a vicar apostolic exercises jurisdiction. Total (1977) 76.

**vicariates castrensi.** Military vicariates (qv).

**vicar-general.** The deputy of a Roman Catholic or Anglican bishop assisting in the jurisdiction of the diocese.

**Viet-Muong.** An Asian ethnolinguistic family. Global population: (1970) 35,131,000, (1980) 43,613,100, (1985) 48,225,900.

UNREACHED PEOPLES. Northern Turkana (Nilotes).

**village polytechnic.** A Christian programme in developing countries, offering local technical skills and intermediate technology at village level.

**Villatte succession churches.** Autocephalous Catholic churches under bishops-at-large (qv) whose disputed episcopal orders pass through J.R. Vilatte, Mar Timotheus (died 1929).

**Vishnavites.** Vaishnavites (qv).

**visible church.** See church visible.

**vital statistics.** Registration statistics of births, deaths, marriages, divorces, etc.

**vocation.** A task or function to which one is called by God.

## W

**Wahhabites.** Sunni Muslims reform movement of the most rigid school of law, Hanabila.

**Waldensians.** A Protestant tradition dating back in Italy to AD 1173. Global membership: (1970) 200 churches with 25,600 adult members, 37,400 total community.

**waqf, wakf** (Arabic; plural, *awkaf*). A Muslim religious or charitable foundation created by an endowed trust fund.

**ward.** In Mormon usage, a small territorial unit or division of a stake (qv) presided over by a bishopric and comprising branches of church auxiliary organizations and quorums of the Aaronic priesthood; equivalent to a parish.

**Watchtower, Watch Tower.** A name for Jehovah's Witnesses; part of their legal name, also of major publication.

**weddings, church.** See marriages, church.

**weekly attenders.** Affiliated Christians (church members) who attend church services of public worship at least once a week, i.e. regularly every Sunday (for sabbatarians, every Saturday).

**Wesleyans.** Holiness Christians (qv).

**West Syrians.** Syrian Orthodox (Jacobites), Orthodox Syrians (India).

**Western Church.** A collective term for the Christian Churches in the Western world, or western Europe, or the Patriarchate of the West (Rome).

**Western Syrians.** West Syrians (qv).

**Western world.** A term, based on political alignment, for the Western or Capitalist countries of Europe, North America, et alia, including capitalist and non-Marxist Socialist or Social Democratic countries.

**White.** Stylized skin colour associated with the Caucasian race and the Uralian ethnolinguistic family. Global White population: (1970)847,034,700, (1980) 918,190,700, (1985) 954,614,500.

**White indigenous churches.** Christian traditions indigenous to the White races, i.e. traditions which are predominantly White initiatives in origin. Global affiliated membership: (1970) 1,055,069,500, (93.2% of world Christianity), (1980) 1,218,073,900, (1985) 1,305,180,000.

**white magic.** Magic (qv) with benevolent intent, as opposed to black magic (qv).

**Wider Episcopal Fellowship.** An attempt to co-ordinate all churches and denominations with historic episcopacy and with some historical claim to apostolic succession.

**witch.** One supposed to possess supernatural powers in order to bewitch people inadvertently.

**witchcraft.** The inadvertent exercise of supernatural powers to harm others.

WITCHCRAFT ERADICATOR. Kajiwe in action (Kenya coast).

**witchcraft eradication movement.** A spontaneous movement, especially in Africa, attempting to eradicate witchcraft by offering holy water or other preventative magic and by denunciation of witches.

**witchdoctor.** A professional worker of magic in primitive society who by spells, charms, herbal remedies et alia seeks to cure illness, detect witches and counteract malevolent magical influences; a shaman, medicine man.

**withdrawal from church membership.** In West Germany and other European countries with state-established Protestant churches of which the whole population largely are members, legislation now provides for the possibility of persons making a formal legal withdrawal from membership, thereby avoiding church income tax.

**Witness, a witness.** A member of Jehovah's Witnesses (qv).

**witness.** Public testimony by word or deed to one's religious or Christian faith.

**wizard.** One devoted to black magic and the black arts in order deliberately to harm others; sorcerer, sorceress, magician.

**women lay workers.** See under personnel.

**women religious.** Nuns, sisters, and other full-time female religious personnel.

**women, ordained.** Organizations relating to women in the ordained ministry number over 200.

**women's organizations.** Christian organizations serving lay women and girls, and significant at the national or wider levels, number over 500.

**workers, church.** See personnel.

**workers' organizations.** Christian organizations for workers or professionals, significant at the national or wider levels, number over 400.

**worker-priest.** A French Roman Catholic priest who for missionary purposes spends part of each weekday as a worker in a secular job.

**working-age population.** All persons of 15 years of age and older, up to 65 years.

**World Alliance of Reformed Churches.** (Presbyterian and Congregational) (WARC). The major Reformed world communion. Global constituency: (1980) 45,996,000.

**world conciliarism.** Councils linking, or offering to link, or attempting to link, all denominations in the world number only 3: World Council of Churches (WCC), World Evangelical Fellowship (WEF), International Council of Christian Churches (ICCC).

**world confessional bodies, world confessional families.** Known since 1979 as Christian world communions (qv).

**World Council of Churches** (WCC). The major ecumenical body, founded 1948. Global constituency: (1970) 355,303,000, (1980) 390,134,000.

**World Evangelical Fellowship** (WEF). A loosely-organized global Conservative Evangelical alliance, which only accepts as members national alliances or councils or fellowship. Global constituency: (1980) 21,031,800.

**world evangelization.** The goal of the proclamation of the Gospel of Christ to all persons in the world; the professed goal of all Christian confessions and communions.

**World Methodist Council** (WCM). The major Methodist world communion. Global constituency: (1980) 34,974,000.

**world religion.** A universal religion (qv).

**world religions.** The major religions of the world, defined here as those with (in 1980) over 2% each of the world's population, as follows: Christianity 32.6%), Islam (16.5%), Hinduism (13.3%), Buddhism (6.3%), Chinese folk religion (4.5%), excluding (because local not universal) primal or tribal religion (2.4%), but including Asiatic New Religions (2.2%); also atheism (4.5%) and agnosticism (16.4%) regarded as worldwide quasi-religions.

**worldview.** A general understanding of the nature of the universe and of one's place in it; outlook on the world; ideology; a cosmological conception of society and institutions.

**world-religionists.** Followers of the world's major religions (see definition under world religions), numbering 96.3% of the world's population (1980), or 79.9% excluding atheists and agnostics.

**worship centres.** Distinct organized groups or congregations of Christian worshippers of any tradition or confession; usually measured by church buildings, chapels, regular worship premises, sites, stations, centres, outposts, preaching points, parishes and quasi-parishes. Global total: (1970) 1,506,400, (1975) 1,599,100, (1980) 1,718,400, (1985) 1,840,000.

## Y

**Yazidis.** Yezidis, Devil-Worshippers. Members of a 12th-century Muslim syncretistic religious sect in Iraq, also in Syria, USSR and Turkey. Global adherents: (1970) 102,000, (1980) 137,000.

**yearbooks.** Christian or church yearbooks, handbooks, directories, periodical lists, and other listings, significant at national, international, denomination and confessional levels, number over 5,000.

**Yearly Meeting.** An organizational unit of the Religious Society of Friends composed of many Quarterly Meetings (local congregations); the most comprehensive Quaker administrative body.

**Yellow.** Stylized skin colour associated with the Arctic Mongoloid, Asian and Pacific geographical races. Global Yellow population: (1970) 1,286,697,500, (1980) 1,550,480,000, (1985) 1,687,713,700.

**Yellow Hat** (Reformed). Lamaism, or Yellow Church (in Tibetan, Dge-lugs-pa, or Gelukpa, 'Model of Virtue'). That part of Tibetan Buddhism in which monasteries and monks have accepted the 14th-century reforms of the monk Tsong-Kha-pa. Its executive head is the Dalai Lama; the Panchen Lama also comes from this grouping.

**younger churches.** A term sometimes used for the newer or relatively-recent denominations of the Third World, in contrast to the older churches of Europe and North America.

**youth organizations.** Christian organizations serving youth, significant at the national or wider levels, number over 500.

**Yugoslav rite.** A Byzantine rite for Catholics in Yugoslavia. Membership: (1970) 58,600 total community.

## Z

**Zambo** (Sambo). A Spanish-speaking Latin American of mixed Negro and Amerindian origin; in Portuguese, a Cafuso.

**Zaydis** (Zaidis). A Muslim sect in Yemen that constitutes one of the 4 major branches of Shia Islam, recognizes a continuing line of imams descended through Zaid (the 5th imam), and is closest to sunna in its doctrine. Global adherents: (1980) 4,958,000.

**zionist.** An African type of charismatic indigenous movement or church; also termed spirit, spiritual, Spirit dominated, pentecostal, aladura (qv), enthusiastic, faith-healing, etc.

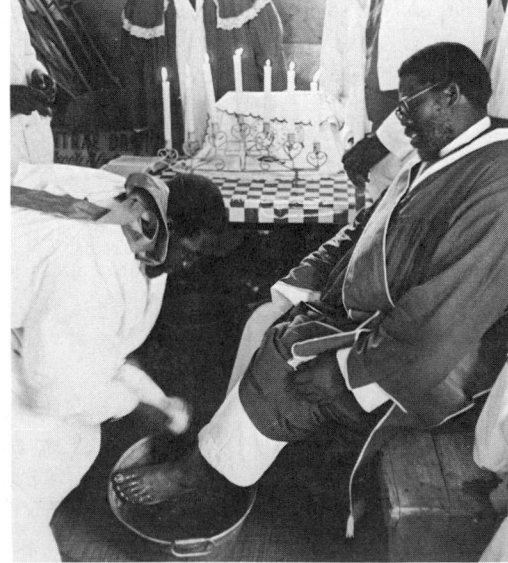

ZIONISTS. Footwashing rite (South Africa).

**Zionists.** Southern Africa charismatic Christians in Black indigenous churches, numbering 4 million in 1980.

**Zoroastrianism.** A religion founded in Persia by the prophet Zoroaster teaching the worship of Ahura Mazda, now followed only by Parsis (qv).

## DICTIONARY APPENDIXES

The following 3 tables are appended to the Survey Dictionary:

1. Terminology of church membership and Christian enumeration.
2. Episcopal churches with disputed apostolic succession, AD 1650–1980.
3. Evolution of the futurology of Christianity and religion, AD 1893–1980.

## TERMINOLOGY OF CHURCH MEMBERSHIP AND CHRISTIAN ENUMERATION

This table shows in its left-hand column the varied terminology in use concerning membership in churches across the world. Each section is arranged with the broadest or most comprehensive terms first. The table then gives across the page the definition of each term by showing what stages in Christian commitment each covers. The latter refers to the major chronological points, events, stages, steps or phases or states in the Christian life of an individual or group which are usually covered in church statistics. (The first version of this actual table was published in 1965 by D.B. Barrett, *The evangelisation of West Africa today*, p. 39). These stages are defined here to be mutually exclusive, i.e. an individual or group cannot be located at or in more than one stage at the same time. They are arranged in what we may call the average, or usual, or normal, progression of events. In practice, for many individuals and groups certain stages may overlap or be telescoped, or be bypassed, or the sequence of events may be altered or a few may even at times be reversed. Although all categories are mutually exclusive, any given category presupposes that the individual or group concerned has already passed through all the earlier stages, and has not yet reached the later stages. Also, at any stage the individual may opt completely out of the Christian world and out of this chronological sequence, by passing intermediate stages to go straight to Stage 28 or even 31. Note also that children and infants have to be treated separately from adults, with a separate scale.

Each stage begins at a point in time described by its number, and includes all persons who have got to that point and so are in that stage but have not yet reached the next stage. Stage 1 begins with the unevangelized individual or group, unaware of Christianity, Christ or the gospel. Stages 2-12 then deal with evangelization, i.e. the process of becoming evangelized. Stages 2-8 deal with the communication of the gospel to him through proclamation, confrontation and other means. Stage 10 represents the point at which the first feedback occurs, i.e. his preliminary reaction or response to the gospel, either accepting it or being open to it, rejecting it or closing himself to it, or ignoring it (this is not necessarily the point at which he accepts Christ or becomes a Christian). At stages 12-13 in a non-Christian area, decision for Christ or conversion occurs (or somewhere in the range after 11). Stages 12-23 cover progressive events in Christian commitment, with 20-23 as the most committed categories; and stages 24-31 describe those who lapse or ultimately fall away from commitment. Stage 32-41 then describe, on a separate scale, the corresponding phases that children and infants (under 15 years) move through. So for example, the term 'baptized' refers to all persons from stages 17-31 and 39-41. All individuals or groups, most societies, and many homogeneous units of population can be located somewhere along this continuum at any particular point in time.

*Quantification.* The table shows which types of membership are quantified by the various Christian traditions, and defines how each is quantified. In this Encyclopedia, we combine these various types to produce a series of standardized usages or statistical definitions, as shown in the bottom section of the table. Altogether, in this survey we quantify, wholly or in part, 26 of the 41 stages defined below (Nos. 1, 2, 9, 12, 13, 15, 16, 17, 18, 19, 20, 23, 24, 25, 29, 30, 32-41 inclusive). The remaining 15 stages are either only rarely enumerated by churches, or are virtually unknowable in practice because (as No. 11) they concern private processes within individuals or groups.

*Demographic commitment profiles.* Another, different, use for the scale 'Stages in Christian commitment' is to draw up a demographic profile of any specific population, country or ethnolinguistic group that one is interested in. Either by means of a random sample survey, or by interviewing specialists knowledgeable about the progress of Christianity among the group, we can estimate what percentage of the group's population is at or in or between each of the 41 stages. The sum of all these percentages must of course total 100%. By then setting up the scale as the vertical axis of a graph and plotting the percentages horizontally, we can obtain a 2-dimensional demographic profile of the present status of Christian commitment among the population concerned. By splitting the scale into 2 at various points we can also derive various dichotomous properties of the people concerned; e.g. we here define adult 'Christians' as those at, or between, or in, stages 12-30, and 'non-Christians' as those at or between stages 1-11, and 31. Similarly, we can split the scale at point 8 and define people at or between or in points 1-7 as 'unevangelized' (i.e. not yet evangelized) and those at or between or in 8-31 as 'evangelized'.

STAGES IN CHRISTIAN COMMITMENT

ADULTS (15 years and over)          CHILDREN (under 15s)

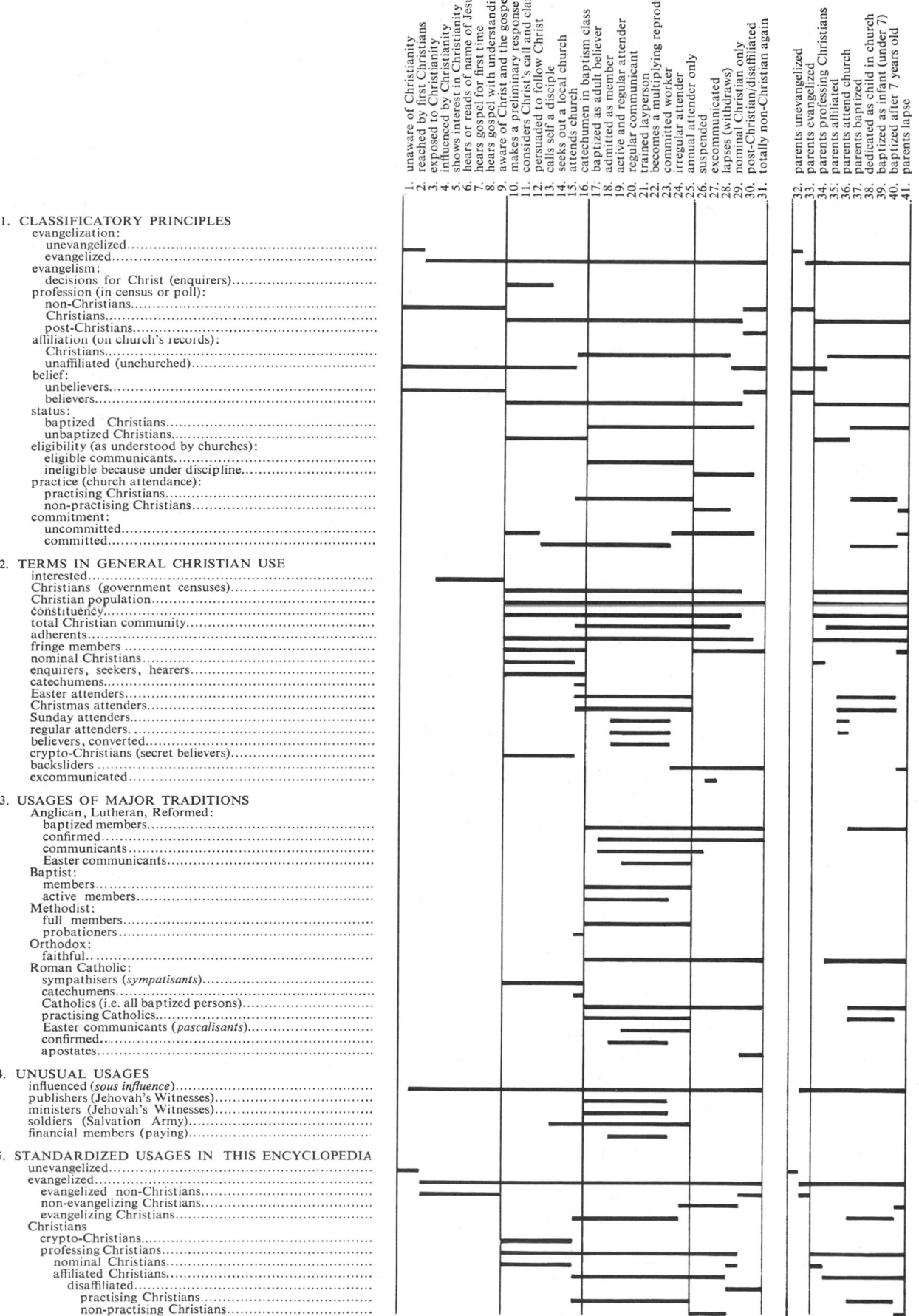

Column headings (ADULTS):
1. unaware of Christianity
2. reached by first Christians
3. exposed to Christianity
4. influenced by Christianity
5. shows interest in Christianity
6. hears or reads of name of Jesus
7. hears gospel for first time
8. hears gospel with understanding
9. aware of Christ and the gospel
10. makes a preliminary response
11. considers Christ's call and claims
12. persuaded to follow Christ
13. calls self a disciple
14. seeks out a local church
15. attends church
16. catechumen in baptism class
17. baptized as adult believer
18. admitted as member
19. active and regular attender
20. regular communicant
21. trained layperson
22. becomes a multiplying reproducer
23. committed worker
24. irregular attender
25. annual attender only
26. suspended
27. excommunicated
28. lapses (withdraws)
29. nominal Christian only
30. post-Christian/disaffiliated
31. totally non-Christian again

Column headings (CHILDREN):
32. parents unevangelized
33. parents evangelized
34. parents professing Christians
35. parents affiliated
36. parents attend church
37. parents baptized
38. dedicated as child in church
39. baptized as infant (under 7)
40. baptized after 7 years old
41. parents lapse

1. CLASSIFICATORY PRINCIPLES
    evangelization:
        unevangelized..............................
        evangelized.................................
    evangelism:
        decisions for Christ (enquirers).............
    profession (in census or poll):
        non-Christians.............................
        Christians.................................
        post-Christians............................
    affiliation (on church's records):
        Christians.................................
        unaffiliated (unchurched)...................
    belief:
        unbelievers................................
        believers..................................
    status:
        baptized Christians........................
        unbaptized Christians......................
    eligibility (as understood by churches):
        eligible communicants......................
        ineligible because under discipline.........
    practice (church attendance):
        practising Christians.......................
        non-practising Christians...................
    commitment:
        uncommitted................................
        committed..................................

2. TERMS IN GENERAL CHRISTIAN USE
    interested.....................................
    Christians (government censuses)................
    Christian population............................
    constituency...................................
    total Christian community.......................
    adherents......................................
    fringe members.................................
    nominal Christians..............................
    enquirers, seekers, hearers.....................
    catechumens....................................
    Easter attenders................................
    Christmas attenders.............................
    Sunday attenders................................
    regular attenders...............................
    believers, converted............................
    crypto-Christians (secret believers).............
    backsliders....................................
    excommunicated.................................

3. USAGES OF MAJOR TRADITIONS
    Anglican, Lutheran, Reformed:
        baptized members...........................
        confirmed..................................
        communicants...............................
        Easter communicants........................
    Baptist:
        members....................................
        active members.............................
    Methodist:
        full members...............................
        probationers...............................
    Orthodox:
        faithful...................................
    Roman Catholic:
        sympathisers (sympatisants).................
        catechumens................................
        Catholics (i.e. all baptized persons).......
        practising Catholics........................
        Easter communicants (pascalisants)..........
        confirmed..................................
        apostates..................................

4. UNUSUAL USAGES
    influenced (sous influence).....................
    publishers (Jehovah's Witnesses)................
    ministers (Jehovah's Witnesses).................
    soldiers (Salvation Army).......................
    financial members (paying)......................

5. STANDARDIZED USAGES IN THIS ENCYCLOPEDIA
    unevangelized..................................
    evangelized....................................
        evangelized non-Christians.................
        non-evangelizing Christians................
        evangelizing Christians....................
    Christians
        crypto-Christians..........................
        professing Christians......................
            nominal Christians.....................
            affiliated Christians..................
                disaffiliated......................
                    practising Christians..........
                    non-practising Christians......

## EPISCOPAL CHURCHES WITH DISPUTED APOSTOLIC SUCCESSION, 1650-1980

Most episcopal churches in the world (churches governed by a bishop or a hierarchy of bishops) have some form of recognized procedure for the selection, appointment and consecration of new bishops. This procedure can usually only take place with the consent and co-operation of one or more existing bishops. As a result, as a church's history extends over a long period of time, the succession of the episcopate becomes important. A number of large episcopal churches (e.g. United Methodist Church, USA) have maintained a succession over 200 years but are not concerned to claim that the succession goes back in unbroken line to the time of the first Apostles. Very many other major episcopal churches, however—Roman Catholic, Orthodox, Old Catholic, Anglican and Scandinavian Lutheran—do make this claim and contend that a bishop cannot have regular or valid orders unless he has been consecrated in this apostolic succession. The table below excludes all these recognized episcopal churches (such as all Old Catholics in communion with Utrecht); it also excludes the many schisms from these episcopal churches which either possess undisputed succession or which make no attempt or claim to possess apostolic succession.

In addition to these larger churches whose claim is recognized by large segments of historic Christianity, there are across the world at least 280 autocephalous episcopal churches which claim to have bishops in this historic succession of the episcopate (apostolic succession), but whose claim is disputed or contested or not recognized by any of these major historic episcopal churches, or the validity of whose succession is at present particularly opposed or contested by one or more of these churches. About half of these (150) are large or sizeable secessions from Roman Catholicism, or Orthodoxy, or Anglicanism. The other half (130) are miniscule (with only 100 or under members) autocephalous Catholic churches under bishops-at-large (episcopi vagantes) with irregular or unrecognized orders, almost all confined to the Western world, and with few or sometimes even no lay followers. A fairly complete listing (up to 1969) of 760 such bishops-at-large is given in E. Plazinski, *Mit Krummstab und Mitra* (1970, p. 239-255), which also gives a detailed list of 15 of the major disputed lines of apostolic succession (notably, Ferrette, Vilatte, Mathew). Over 700 bishops are also listed, and described with historical narrative, in P.F. Anson, *Bishops at large: some autocephalous churches of the past hundred years and their founders* (London, 1964). Biographical details of nearly 470 of them are given in H.R.T. Brandreth, 'Are they bishops? a handbook of certain episcopal sects and their founders' (London, 1972; typescript). The table below lists the majority of both these 2 types of bodies, sizeable and miniscule, and includes a variety of sizeable non-Catholic churches which nevertheless lay claim to apostolic succession in some form and have gone to considerable pains to have their bishops consecrated by bishops of other churches they regard as in that succession; many of these bodies are in Third-World countries. It also includes the fair number of miniscule bodies which once existed but were defunct by 1975. Note that the table excludes the large number of episcopal churches in the Third World (especially African indigenous churches) which, though governed by bishops, do not lay claim to any historic or apostolic succession. The table also lists only autonomous churches and denominations and excludes episcopal orders, jurisdictions, abbeys, colleges and other related types of ecclesiastical organizations.

One object of this listing is to enable the reader, who has heard of or from a specific episcopal body which is not listed in the survey's Table 2 for its country (e.g. 'British Orthodox Catholic Church'), to locate and identify it and to assess its numerical significance, if any. Each line below describes one distinct body, whether still existing (1975) or long defunct; alternative names for each body are all given on the same line. Each line also describes one distinct body together with all its organically-related international branches in other countries, if any. The meaning of the columns is as follows:

**Name.** Each official name is given here in the major European language it uses (of the 6 employed in this Encyclopedia: English, French, German, Italian, Portuguese, Spanish). Note D = Diocese, AD = Archdiocese.

**Size.** Churches with numerically large or sizeable or significant followings are also given a line each in their countries' statistical Tables 2 in this Encyclopedia, where fuller details including each's conciliar relationships will be found. Those with only small, very small, or miniscule followings are enumerated in Tables 2 only on lines at the end ('Other Catholic (non-Roman) churches') and in corresponding footnotes.

**Begun.** Year of foundation or origin.

**Type.** 1st letter: ecclesiastical bloc (A = Anglican, C = Catholic (non-Roman), I = Black/Third-World or Non-White indigenous, M = marginal Protestant, O = Orthodox).
2nd-4th letters: ecclesiastical tradition (see Codebook, Part 6). Note that the code Epi = miniscule unrecognized church under bishops-at-large (with 100 or fewer members).

**Notes.** Descriptive notes on each body, including some of the following: initials if commonly used, translation of name, alternative names, former names, title of chief bishop, line of apostolic succession adopted or claimed (about 20 distinct lines are involved), headquarters, country or countries in which present, total affiliated members if significant, and whether or not still in existence in 1975.

| Official name | Begun | Type | Descriptive notes (NB: 'ex' = schism or split from body indicated) |
|---|---|---|---|
| African Orthodox Church | 1919 | IARo | AOC. Schism ex PECUSA; Vilatte succession. West Indian Blacks. HQ New York (USA). In Bahamas, Cuba, SAfrica. |
| African Orthodox Ch of New York & Massachusetts | 1938 | IARo | Black. Large schism ex AOC. Vilatte succession. HQ New York 27 (USA). |
| Afro-American Catholic Church | 1938 | IEpi | Black. Schism ex AOC by suspended bishop. Vilatte succession. HQ USA. |
| Alexandrian Orthodox Church in America | 1963 | OSla | Former Russian and Ukrainian Orthodox now linked with American Orthodox Catholic Ch. High % Blacks. |
| All Nations Reformed Orthodox Catholic Church | c1950 | CEpi | Body set up in USA; 1954, applied to join WCC; rejected. |
| Altrömisch-Katholische Kirche von Deutschland | 1949 | CEpi | ORCC in Germany. Split ex Catholicate of the West (UK), in Vilatte succession. HQ Cologne (Germany). |
| American Catholic Church (Archdiocese of New York) | 1927 | IARo | Black. Ex African Orthodox Ch, claiming Syrian Orthodox (Jacobite) succession. HQ New York (USA). |
| American Catholic Church (Syro-Antiochian) | 1915 | CCCa | Assyrian Jacobite Apost Ch. Split ex ACC (Vilatte), in Jacobite succession. HQ Miami (USA). 1,500 members. |
| American Catholic Church (Western Orthodox) | 1914 | CCCa | Holy Cath Ch in America. Ex RCC, begun by Vilatte as primate (Jacobite succession). Virtually defunct. |
| American Episcopal Church (ACC) | 1943 | CEpi | Split ex American Catholic Ch by bishop. Vilatte succession, plus 7 other lines claimed. Short-lived. |
| American Holy Orthodox Catholic Apostolic Eastern Ch | 1932 | IARo | Ex African Orthodox Ch by bishop. Vilatte succession. HQ New York 35 (USA). Decline to 5,000 members. |
| American National Catholic Church | c1942 | CEpi | Diocese of New Jersey. HQ New Jersey (USA). |
| American Old Catholic Church | 1927 | CCCa | Split ex NAORCC by bishop in Mathew succession. Formerly 1,000 members, in Louisiana; defunct 1945. |
| American Orthodox Catholic Church | 1961 | OReO | New York Branch, Denver Branch. Rival White (Russian) and Black groups. Continuous mergers, fresh schisms. |
| American Orthodox Catholic Church (AD N&S America) | 1964 | OReO | Ex Ukrainian Orth Ch of USA. 8 bishops. Dioceses in USA, US Virgin Is, Argentina, France, Nigeria, Zaire. |
| American Orthodox Missionary Church | | CCCa | Eastern Orthodox Catholic Ch in America, under Russian Orth Ch Outside of Russia. Ex Holy Orth Ch in America. |
| Ancient Apostolic Catholic Church | 1951 | CEpi | Schism by a bishop ex Ancient Catholic Church (Chelsea, UK) and Catholicate of the West. Defunct. |
| Ancient British Church | 1874 | CARo | ABC. First British Patriarch (ex CofE) consecrated by Ferrette, in Caerleon, Wales (UK). |
| Ancient British Church (Agnostic) | 1937 | CLib | 1937 Jesuene Ch, or Free Orth Cath Ch. 1957 new name. Agnostic = rejecting Christendom. Vilatte succession. |
| Ancient Catholic Church | 1946 | CARo | Until 1950, New Pentecostal Ch of Christ. Spiritual healing, animals' services. Cathedral in Chelsea (UK). |
| Ancient Universal Orthodox Catholic Church | 1943 | CLib | Theosophical and occult religious branch of Ekklesia Agiae Sophiae (Order of Holy Wisdom). UK. |
| Anglican Orthodox Church of North America | 1963 | AsEv | Schism ex PECUSA in North Carolina (USA). Promotes Anglican Orthodox Communion in 10 nations. 4,000 in USA. |
| Anglican Orthodox Church: D Pakistan | 1968 | IAng | Episcopal Ch of Pakistan. Schism ex Anglican Ch, Sialkot. M = AOC(USA). Bishop, 18,057 members, 19 priests. |
| Antiochian Orthodox Archdiocese of Toledo | 1935 | OAra | Arabs in USA. In communion with Greek P Antioch, but not accepted as canonical. 30,000 members. |
| Apostolic Catholic Church | c1951 | CEpi | Split by bishop ex Ancient Catholic Ch. Ferrette succession. HQ London NW6 (UK). Defunct 1952. |
| Apostolic Church of St Peter | 1935 | CEpi | Dutch primate. Amalgamation of esoteric sects. HQ Kensington (UK). |
| Apostolic Episcopal Church | 1925 | CARo | Holy Eastern Cath & Apost Orth Ch. Ex PECUSA. Chaldean rite. HQ Long Island, NY. 3,000, in 5 European nations. |
| Apostolic Polish Catholic Church of Canada | c1950 | CEpi | Ex North American Old Roman Catholic Church. Attempt to create body from Polish Old Catholics. |
| Aumônerie Générale Indép Mixte Orient-Occident | | CEpi | Abbaye Missionnaire de Behême, Exarchat de Diaspora. 1968 applied to join WCC, rejected. HQ Gagny (France). |
| Authentic Old Calendar Greek Orthodox Church | 1924 | OGre | Paleohemerologites. Schism ex Ch of Greece (Greece, USA, Canada). 200,000 adherents, 250 priests. |
| Autonomous African Universal Church | 1935 | ICCa | Founded in Hornsey (UK) by a Ghanaian. Vilatte succession. HQ in Ghana. |
| Autonomous British Eastern Church | 1935 | CEpi | Orthodox-Cath Prov of Our Lady of England in Devon & Cornwall. Several lines of succession. Defunct 1940. |
| British Orthodox Catholic Church | 1935 | CEpi | Small group. 1944, united with ABC and OCOC to form Western Orthodox Catholic Ch (Catholicate of the West). |
| Brotherhood of the Blessed Sacrament | 1959 | CLib | Broederschap van het Heilig Sacrament. Schism ex Liberal Catholic Ch, in Netherlands. |
| Byelorussian Autocephalic Orthodox Church | c1945 | OSla | Refugees from White Russian church begun AD 1291, HQ Brooklyn (USA). USA 20,000; UK 1,500; Australia 1,000. |
| Byzantine American Church | 1942 | CCCa | Schism ex RCC by Melkite priest from Lebanon. Syrians. HQ San Francisco (USA). |
| Canadian Catholic Church | 1946 | CEpi | Melkite, Vilatte and 3 other successions. Canada, New Zealand, Ceylon. |
| Catholic Apostolic Church (Catholicate of the West) | 1944 | CARo | Western Orth Cath Ch. Patriarch ex CAC(Irvingite); 23 lines of succession. 1947, applied to WCC; rejected. |
| Catholic Christian Church | 1933 | CEpi | Begun in England by bishop in Vilatte succession. HQ Bournemouth (UK). Defunct c1945. |
| Catholic Church of America | 1930 | CEpi | Lithuanians. Split ex Lithuanian National Catholic Ch. Defunct c1935. |
| Catholic Tridentine Church | 1976 | CCCa | De facto schism ex Ch of Rome, supporting archbishop Lefebvre (Latin mass,&c). Also USA, NZ, Europe, LAmerica. |
| Chiesa Cattolica Nazionale | c1850 | CCCa | First attempt in Italy to set up a national church, ex RCC. Short-lived. |
| Chiesa Cattolica Nazionale d'Italia | 1882 | CCCa | Schism ex RCC by canon of Vatican Basilica. Support from Old Catholics across Europe. Defunct 1903. |
| Chiesa Cattolica Riformata d'Italia | 1881 | CReC | Schism ex RCC by 12 priests and 6 churches. Support from Swiss Old Catholics. HQ Milan (Italy). 500 members. |
| Chiesa Episcopale Nazionale Italiana | 1900 | CEpi | Old Catholic bishop of Piacenza consecrated by Vilatte (Jacobite succession). Soon defunct. |
| Christ Catholic Ch of America & Europe: D Boston | 1965 | COCa | Old Catholic teachings. Aims at total comprehensiveness. HQ New Jersey (USA). 1,000 members, 5 priests. |
| Christ Orthodox Cath Exarchate of Americas & Europe | 1959 | CCCa | Byelorussian origins. 1959 merger Old Catholic and Orthodox. 5,513 members, 21 priests. |
| Christian Community (Anthroposophical Society) | 1922 | MGno | Natural Catholicism. Theosophical, ESP. Black Templars succession. 7 sacraments. In 8 nations. |
| Church Catholic, The (The Sanctuary) | 1919 | CEpi | Mathew succession. HQ Knightsbridge (UK). Theosophical. Defunct 1940. |
| Church of the East | c1962 | INes | Assyrian schism ex Ancient Ch of the East(P Baghdad)(Iraq). 3 Dioceses, 3 bishops, 5,000 members, 11 priests. |
| Church of the Virgin Mary & Mar Gaura | | INes | Assyrian (Nestorian) schism ex P Baghdad in dispute over authority. In Iraq. 2 priests, 200 members. |
| CMS Anglican Church of India | 1966 | IAng | D Travancore & Cochin. Pulaya outcaste schism ex Ch of South India (D Madhya Kerala). 24 priests; 107,000. |
| Communion Evangelica Catholica Eucharistica | 1930 | CEpi | Cath Ev Ch of Germany. Founded by ex-RC Lutheran mystic Friedrich Heiler. Syro-Jacobite (Vilatte) succession. |
| Coptic Orthodox Church Apostolic | 1942 | IEpi | Ch of the Living God. Begun by US Black, links with Father Divine Peace Mission. HQ Manhattan (USA). |
| Croation Old Catholic Church | 1923 | COCa | Ex RCC in Croatia (Yugoslavia). 1938 repudiated by Union of Utrecht. 5,000 members, 4 priests. |
| Czechoslovak Hussite Church | 1920 | CReC | Los von Rom. Schism of 20% ex RCC (Czechoslovakia). c1935 apostolic succession (Mathew) adopted. 650,000 members. |
| Eastern Apostolic Episcopal Church | 1946 | CEpi | Begun by Missionary Bishop for Holland & Indonesia. Chaldean succession and rite. HQ Amersfoort (Holland). |
| Eastern Orthodox Catholic Church in America | 1927 | OEpi | Schism ex American Orthodox Ch. Russian Orthodox and Vilatte successions. HQ New York (USA). Defunct 1959. |
| Eglise Apostolique de Madagascar | 1968 | IAng | Apostolic Ch of Madagascar. Schism ex Eglise Episcopale (Anglican Ch). M = AOC(USA). Bishop, 15,000 adherents. |
| Eglise Catholique Apostolique de France | 1951 | CCCa | Schism ex Old Cath Mariavite Ch (Poland). HQ Nantes (France). 400 adherents. |
| Eglise Catholique Apostolique et Gallicane Autocéphale | 1950 | CEpi | Split ex Eglise Universalle Gnostique en France. Partiarch. HQ Bordeaux (France); Lyons, Cannes; Belgium. |
| Eglise Catholique Apostolique Gallicane | 1935 | CCCa | Cath Apost Gallican Ch. Ex RCC. 1975, large Synod in Bordeaux. 40,000 members. Applied to WCC, rejected. |
| Eglise Catholique Apostolique Orthodoxe de France | | CEpi | Split ex Eglise Gallicane. Linked with Eglise Catholique Ancienne. HQ Angers (France). |
| Eglise Cath Apost Primitive d'Antioche Orthodoxe | 1956 | CCCa | Egl Cath Ancienne, Syro-Byzantine. HQ Paris. 2,000 members in 19 nations: Canada, Germany, Holland, Africa, &c. |
| Eglise Catholique de France | 1951 | CCCa | Schism ex Polish Mariavite Ch. |
| Eglise Catholique du Rite Dominicain | 1947 | CCCa | Schism ex RCC (Belgium). Metropolitan. HQ Schaerbeik-Brussels. |
| Eglise Catholique Orthodoxe de France | 1924 | CLib | Eglise Cath Ev. Ex Liberal CC. HQ St-Denys, Paris. 1937, joined P Moscow, later ROCOR, later P Bucharest. |
| Eglise Catholique Française (Eglise Gallicane) | 1883 | CCCa | 1907, restored in Paris (France) by Vilatte. Attempt to revive Gnosticism. Occultism, faith-healing, magic. |
| Eglise Catholique Française (Mgr Chatel) | 1831 | CLib | Founded by Gallican RCs in France & (1837) Belgium. Suppressed by 1870. |
| Eglise Catholique Gallicane Autocéphale | 1959 | CLib | Eglise Vieille Cath Libérale, D Normandie. Succession Apost Oecuménique. Applied to WCC, rejected. 2,000. |
| Eglise Christique Primitive | 1938 | CReC | Founded by Catholic faith-healer. Sin, repentance not preached. In France, Germany, Switzerland. |
| Eglise Constitutionnelle de France | 1790 | CCCa | Ordered to adhere to civil constitution by France. 130 RC dioceses suppressed, until 1801. |
| Eglise du Christ-Roi Renovée | 1951 | CCCa | Holy Cath Apost & Roman Renewed Ch. Ex RCC(D Nancy). Papal claimant Clement XV. France 4,000, Canada 2,000. |
| Eglise Gnostique Apostolique | 1953 | CLib | Apost Gnostic Ch. Closed group protecting Gospel from world. France, Belgium, Brazil, Italy. 5,000 members. |
| Eglise Gnostique de France | 1914 | CLib | Orders through Eglise Gallicane. Vilatte succession. |
| Eglise Johannite des Chrétiens Primitifs | 1803 | CLib | Revived Templars; Masonic dogmas. Secret society. Many bishops (ex RCs). Suppressed by 1870. |
| Eglise Orthodoxe Apostolique Haïtienne | 1861 | AHig | Schism ex RCC in Haiti. Black. 1913, Missionary District of PECUSA. 38,452 members, 26 priests. |
| Eglise Orthodoxe Gallicane Autocéphale | c1952 | CEpi | Split in Belgium, related to Eglise Catholique Apostolique et Gallicane (France). Vilatte succession. |
| Eglise Primitive Catholique et Apostolique | 1937 | CCCa | Eglise Catholique Primitive. HQ Paris. Bishop a former Liberal Catholic priest; in Vilatte succession. |
| Eglise Rosicrucienne Apostolique | | MLib | Apostolic Rosicrucian Ch. Bishop in Brussels (Belgium). Gnostic teachings. Applied to join WCC, rejected. |
| Eglise Universelle Gnostique en France | 1890 | CLib | France, Switzerland. Magic, occultism. Missions in Portugal, Italy, Belgium, Brazil, NAfrica. Suppressed 1944. |
| Eglise Vieille Catholique Romaine en France | 1960 | CCCa | Old Roman Catholic Ch in France. Rapid expansion claimed since 1960. 7 priests, 1 seminary. |
| Eglise Vintrassienne | 1839 | CSpi | Oeuvre de la Miséricorde. Founder Vitras (Bayeux, France). Miracles, occultism, spiritism. |
| Eglises Catholiques Apostoliques Orthodoxes d'Occident | c1940 | CEpi | Cath Apost Orth Churches of the West. HQ Alouette-Pessac (Gironde) (France). 1947, applied to WCC, rejected. |

| | | | |
|---|---|---|---|
| English Episcopal Church | 1947 | AsEv | Ch of England (Ev). Ex Ev Ch of England. HQ Acton, London (UK). Use 1662 Book of Common Prayer. West Indians. |
| English Orthododox Church | 1950 | CEpi | Split ex Catholicate of the West. 1952, merged in Free Catholic Church. |
| English (Old Roman Catholic) Rite | 1948 | CEpi | Schism ex ORCC (Pro-Uniate Rite) by 2 deposed priests. Mathew succession. London. Elaborate rituals. |
| Episcopal Orthodox Church (Greek Communion) | c1920 | ILib | Founded in Trinidad; 1921, Cuba; 1939, New York (USA). West Indian Blacks. HQ Barbados. |
| Essene Church in the Hashemite Kingdom of Jordan | | IEpi | Small group in Jordan claiming Essene or Gnostic doctrines. Under a primate in an oriental succession. |
| Evangelical Catholic Church | 1903 | ONes | Ev Catholic Communion, Church Universal. Nestorian/Chaldean succession from South India. HQ Oxford. Defunct. |
| Evangelical Catholic Church of New York | 1927 | CEpi | Split by deposed bishop ex NAORCC. Mathew succession. Defunct 1945. |
| Evangelical Church of England | 1922 | AsEv | Anglicans opposing Anglo-Catholicism. Archbishop, in Ferrette succession. 10 churches in Lancashire (UK). |
| Free Anglo-Catholic Church | 1948 | CEpi | Order of Llanthony Brothers. 3 bishops, in Mathew succession. Extinct 1957. |
| Free Catholic Church | 1930 | CARo | Ex Church of England. Anglo-Catholic. Bishop, in Ferrette succession. HQ Forest Gate, London E7 (UK). |
| Free Catholic Church in Germany | c1950 | CEpi | Ch of the Servants of Christ. Catholic Episcopal Ch. Ex Ancient Catholic Ch (UK). Women consecrated as bishops. |
| Free Church of England | 1844 | AsEv | Linked with Reformed Episcopal Ch (USA). Ex Ch of England. 2 Dioceses. Declining. 3,194 members, 5 bishops. |
| Free Holy Catholic Church of England (D Mercia) | 1952 | CEpi | Free Protestant Catholic Communion. |
| Free Protestant Episcopal Church | 1897 | CARo | FPEC. Ecumenical Church Foundation. Ex REC(USA). Armenian succession. UK 3,000; USA, Canada, WAfrica, WIndies. |
| Gnostic Catholic Church | 1960 | CEpi | Old Cath Orth Western Primitive Rite Synod of the One Holy Cath & Apostolic Ch. Mathew succession. USA. |
| Hochkirche in Österreich | 1958 | CEpi | Ephemeral body under bishop in Vilatte succession. In Austria. |
| Holy Apostolic Catholic Church | 1963 | CEpi | Autocephalous Chaldean Rite. Nestorian succession through Catholicate of the West (UK). HQ Bremerton (USA). |
| Holy Catholic Church of the Apostles in D Louisiana | 1929 | CEpi | Split by deposed bishop ex NAORCC. Archbishop in Mathew succession. Defunct 1942. |
| Holy Orthodox Church in America | 1925 | CCCa | Begun by P Moscow as American Orthodox Ch. 1961. Western Rite Vicariate in Antiochian OC AD NY (USA). |
| Holy Orth Ch in America (Eastern Catholic & Apostolic) | 1926 | CLib | Begun as Anglican Universal Ch. Ex RCC. Vilatte succession. Rosicrucianism. 5 bishops. HQ NY (USA). |
| Hungarian Orthodox Greek Catholic Church | 1933 | OHun | Begun by P Belgrade (Serbian Orth Ch) in Hungary. 1934, Syrian (Jacobite) succession. In Hungary and USA. |
| Iglesia Católica Americana Ortodoxa | c1968 | ICCa | Schism in Argentina by RC priests, bishop. M=AOCC(USA). Maintains an Apostolic Exarchate in Rome. 30,000. |
| Iglesia Católica Apostólica Venezolana | 1946 | ICCa | Cath Apostolic Ch. Schism ex Rome by 33 RC priests. ICAB (Brazil) succession. Under Free Cath Ch in Germany. |
| Iglesia Católica Romana Antigua | 1935 | ICCa | Ecclesia Veteris Romanae Catholicae. ORCC. Ex RCC, Mexico. Mathew succession. 1965, applied to WCC, rejected. |
| Iglesia Española Reformada Episcopal | 1880 | CPro | Spanish Reformed Episcopal Ch. Split ex Spanish Ev Ch. 1894 Anglican succession. In Union of Utrecht. 1,000. |
| Iglesia Ortodoxa Católica Apostólica Mexicana | 1926 | ICCa | National Ch. State-aided schism ex RCC, Mexico. 10 bishops, Mathew succession. Decline since 1940. 60,000. |
| Igreja Brasileira | 1961 | ICCa | Schism ex Ch of Rome. 1963, 6 bishops; applied to join WCC, also to rejoin RCC; rejected. 2,000 members. |
| Igreja Católica Apostólica Brasileira | 1945 | ICCa | ICAB. Schism ex RCC in Brazil by former RC bishop of Botucatú. Clerical celibacy abolished. 2 million. |
| Igreja Católica Livre no Brasil | 1936 | ICCa | Free Catholic Ch in Brazil. Schism ex RCC. 1945, Duarte (Roman Catholic) succession adopted. 3,000 adherents. |
| Igreja Lusitana Católica Apostólica Evangélica | 1871 | CReC | Lusitanian Ch. Schism ex RCC (Portugal) by 11 priests. 1958, Anglican succession. 4,500 members. |
| Independent Catholic Church | 1922 | CEpi | Short-lived body begun by patriarch-archbishop, in Mathew succession. HQ East Molesey (UK) |
| Independent Catholic Church of Ceylon, Goa & India | 1866 | ICCa | Schism of 5,000 Latin-rite Catholics ex RCC opposing Propaganda. Jacobite (Antioch) succession. Defunct 1950. |
| Independent Church of Filipino Christians | 1946 | ILib | Schism ex Philippine Independent Ch by deposed primate Fonacier. Unitarian. HQ Baangas (Philippines). 1,700. |
| Independent Episcopal Church of the US & Canada | c1946 | CARo | Schism ex Protestant Episcopal Ch (USA), by bishop in Mathew succession in ORCC (USA). |
| Independent Syrian Church of Malabar | 1771 | IReO | Malabar Swathanthra Suriani Sabha. D Thozhiyur. Schism ex Orthodox Syrian Ch. 3,780 members, 8 priests. |
| Indian National Church | 1955 | IARo | Ex CIPBC (Anglican). Archbishop and several bishops, in Vilatte succession. HQ Delhi (India). 1,000 members. |
| Indian Orthodox Church: Patriarchate of India | 1956 | ICCa | Ex RCC. Ferrette succession. Linked with Catholicate of the West, FPEC, and American HOCAEC (USA). 2,000. |
| Katholische Kirche in Deutschland | 1845 | CCCa | Short-lived schism ex Roman Catholic Church (Germany). |
| Liberal Catholic Church | 1917 | CLib | LCC. Schism ex ORCC. Mathew succession. Theosophical, Masonic. HQ London (UK). In 18 nations. |
| Liberal Catholic Church, Order of St Germain | 1969 | CLib | Split ex LCC. In USA (Texas, Colorado, Oklahoma, California). 3,000 members, 22 priests. |
| Liberal Catholic Church (California) | 1947 | CLib | Schism ex original LCC opposing Theosophy. HQ USA. 4,000 members, 5 bishops, 62 priests. |
| Liberal Christian Episcopal Church | c1950 | CEpi | Apostolic Eastern Succession of Antioch. Archbishop. HQ USA. 1954, applied to join WCC; rejected. |
| Lutheran Episcopal Church of England | c1948 | CEpi | Schism ex English Episcopal Ch, by former minister of Reformed Presbyterian Ch in Ireland. Defunct 1956. |
| Mar Thoma Syrian Church of Malabar | 1843 | IReO | Schism ex Orthodox Syrian Ch (India). Jacobite (Antioch) succession, disputed. 5 Dioceses. 350,000 members. |
| Mariavite Church of Ancient Catholic Rite | 1936 | CCCa | Catholic Mariavite Ch. Schism ex Old Catholic Mariavite Ch of Poland. HQ Felicjanow (Poland). 4,000 members. |
| National Catholic Apostolic Church of the Philippines | 1930 | ICCa | Iglesia Catolica Apostolica Nacional. Schism ex RCC. HQ Cabanatuan City (Philippines). 35,000 members. |
| Nazarene Episcopal Ecclesia | 1873 | CEpi | British-Israelite. Ex Reformed Episcopal Ch (USA). Ferrette succession. HQ Sydenham (UK). |
| New Catholic and Free Church | c1950 | CEpi | Schism ex Catholic Apostolic Ch (Catholicate of the West). Spiritism, theosophy. HQ London N10 (UK). |
| North American Old Roman Catholic Church | 1912 | CCCa | NAORCC. ORCC in USA. Ex RCC. Mathew succession. Italians, Poles, Lithuanians. HQ Chicago. 60,098 members. |
| North American (Old Roman) Catholic Church | 1958 | CCCa | North American Catholic Ch. Schism ex original NAORCC. Mathew succession. HQ Brooklyn (USA). 1,290 members. |
| Old Catholic Archdiocese for Americas & Europe | 1940 | CEpi | Schism ex OCCA, in Mathew succession. HQ Bronx 58 (USA). |
| Old Catholic Ch in America (Catholic Ch of North A) | 1917 | CCCa | OCCA. Orth Old Cath Ch in America. Mathew succession. HQ NY (USA). 6,000; 1962, received into ROC (P Moscow). |
| Old Catholic Church in Bosnia & Herzegovina | 1965 | COCa | Founded separate from other 4 old Catholic churches in Yugoslavia. Not under Utrecht. 1,000 members. |
| Old Catholic Church in Ireland | 1916 | CEpi | Schism ex RCC and ORCC. Mathew succession, Regionary Bishop. Defunct 1960. |
| Old Catholic Church in Portugal | 1918 | CEpi | Attempt to start Old Catholic movement, by bishop in Mathew succession. Short-lived. |
| Old Catholic Church of Hungary | 1945 | CCCa | Small group ex RCC in Hungary. Close links with Mariavite Church (Poland), who provided succession. |
| Old Catholic Church of Poland | 1946 | CCCa | Schism ex RCC. Joined by Mariavite remnants. Mathew succession. Links with NAORCC (USA). |
| Old Catholic Church (Vilatte) | 1892 | CCCa | Begun by Vilatte, Jacobite (Antioch) succession. 1903, UK. 1915, dissolved into American Catholic Ch. |
| Old Catholic Evangelical Church of God | 1924 | CARo | Anglo-Saxon rite. Mathew succession. 5 bishops, 33 priests. HQ Greenwich (UK). Defunct. |
| Old Catholic Mariavite Church of Poland | 1906 | CCCa | Excommunicated by Pius X. 1906: 500,000, declining to 24,000 (1970). Women bishops. In 9 nations. |
| Old Catholic Orthodox Church | 1925 | CARo | Schism by laity after infallibility claim by primate of Old RCC (Pro-Uniate Rite). Mathew succession. In UK. |
| Old Catholic Orthodox Church (Apostolic Service Ch) | 1925 | CEpi | Formerly Independent Catholic Ch. Mathew succession. Nationalist; spiritual healing. HQ Strand, London (UK). |
| Old Holy Catholic Church (Church of the One Life) | 1955 | CARo | OHCC. Schism ex Old Catholic Evangelical Ch of God. Mathew succession. In UK. |
| Old Ritualist Ancient Orthodox Christians | c1860 | OOBe | AD Moscow. Old Believers. Beglopopovtsy (Ch of Fugitive Priests). Ex Popovtsy. 200,000 in USSR. |
| Old Ritualist Church of Belokrinitsa Concord | 1666 | OOBe | AD Moscow. Raskolniki (Schismatics), ex ROC (P Moscow). Popovtsy (Priestists). 5 dioceses. 1 million in USSR. |
| Old Roman Catholic Apostolic Church | c1965 | CCCa | Italians, ex Church of Rome, in New York state (USA). Bishop, ex RCC, in Vilatte succession. 2,500 members. |
| Old Roman Catholic Church | 1908 | CCCa | Ancient Cath Ch of England, English CC. Old CC in GB. Western Uniate CC. 1915, ORCC. Bishop AH Mathew, ex RC. |
| Old Roman Catholic Church in North America | 1958 | CCCa | Schism ex NAORCC. Mathew succession. Two rival groups using same name. |
| Old Roman Catholic Church (D Niagara Falls) | 1952 | CEpi | Ex NAORCC. HQ Niagara Falls, NY (USA). |
| Old Roman Catholic Church (English Rite) | 1950 | CCCa | Schism ex ORCC. Mathew succession. 12 churches in UK; 1963, large USA branch of 65,000 added (HQ Chicago). |
| Old Roman Catholic Church (Orthodox Orders) | c1960 | CCCa | Split ex ORCC in Canada. Ruled by a cardinal. HQ Havelock, Ontario (Canada). 1967, applied to WCC, rejected. |
| Old Roman Catholic Church (Pro-Uniate Rite) | 1915 | CARo | Western Catholic Uniate Rite. Canonical ORC Ch. Mathew succession. 2 bishops, 6 priests until 1915 LCC schism. |
| Orthodox Catholic Church in England | 1929 | CEpi | UK branch of Vilatte's American Catholic Ch (USA), with Metropolitan for the British Empire. Defunct 1938. |
| Orthodox Catholic Patriarchate of America | c1933 | CEpi | Linked with American Holy Orthodox Catholic Apostolic Eastern Ch. HQs New York, Springfield (Mass) (USA). |
| Orthodox Church of Sardinia | 1961 | CEpi | Mariavite links, claiming Russian Orthodox succession. |
| Orthodox Ecclesia | c1950 | CEpi | Short-lived attempt to found church based on Llanthony abbey, Wales. Mathew succession. Defunct. |
| Orthodox Old Catholic Church | 1964 | CEpi | OOCC, Second Movement. Primate-Bishop. HQ Philadelphia (USA). 1965, applied to join WCC; rejected. |
| Orthodox-Keltic Church of British Commonwealth of N | 1935 | CEpi | N=Nations. British Orthodox Cath Ch. British-Israelite. Vilatte succession. HQ London N7 (UK). Defunct 1942. |
| Petite Eglise (Vendéenne) | 1801 | CCCa | Little Ch. Schism of 38 bishops ex Rome, rejecting 1801 concordat with France. Declining; no clergy left. 5,000 members. |
| Philippine Church (Adarnista) | 1901 | Imar | Iglesia Filipina (Adarnistas). Followers of bishop Adarna. Rizalist (marginal Catholic) type. 15,000. |
| Philippine Independent Church | 1890 | IReC | Iglesia Filipina Independiente. Ex RCC (Philippines). 1948, Anglican succession adopted. 3,500,000 adherents. |
| Polish Catholic Church | c1920 | CCCa | Handful of Polish followers. Ex RCC before PNCC fully organized, in USA. |
| Pre-Nicene Gnostic Catholic Church | 1952 | CLib | Founded by ex-priest of Liberal Catholic Ch (Australia). Theosophical, esoteric, mystical. UK, Australia, NZ. |
| Primitive Church of Antioch | 1951 | CEpi | Set up by Primate, ex Catholicate of Austria; Vilatte succession. HQ Cologne (Germany). |
| Protestant Orthodox Western Church | 1943 | CEpi | Bishop from NAORCC in Mathew succession. USA. |
| Reformed Catholic Church (Utrecht Confession) | c1950 | CARo | Schism ex OC Ev Ch of God. Mathew succession. 2,217 members in USA; also in UK, France, Germany. |
| Reformed Episcopal Church | 1873 | AsEv | REC. Ex PECUSA opposing ritualism. 1927, communion with Free Ch of England (UK). Enquiry re joining WCC. |
| Russian Orthodox Church Outside of Russia | 1920 | OSla | ROCOR. Exiles from USSR. Ultra-conservative. 1950, world HQ moved to New York (USA). 13 Dioceses in world. |
| Russian Orthodox Living Church | 1922 | OSla | State-aided schism of 30% all parishes ex ROC (USSR). 1929: controlled 35% all ROC churches. Defunct 1943. |
| St Thomas Evangelical Church of India | 1961 | IReo | Pathiopadesa Samiti. Schism ex Mar Thoma Svrian Ch. HQ Tiruvella (India). 25,000 members, 29 priests. |
| Sainte Eglise Apostolique | 1955 | CLib | Uniate Armenian succession. Militantly Gallican. Healing, occult. HQ Colombs (Seine)(France). 1,500, members. |
| Sainte Eglise Apostolique Orth Celtique en Brétagne | 1956 | CCCa | 10 bishops, 300 Celtic-rite families. Breton nationalism (Brittany). Druidic rites, midnight sea baptism. |
| Sainte Eglise Catholique Gallicane Autocéphale | 1955 | CEpi | Begun by Primate in Vilatte succession; ex Eglise Catholique Apostolique et Gallicane Autocéphale. In France. |
| Santa Iglesia Católica Apostólica Ortodoxa de PR | 1961 | ICCa | PR=Puerto Rico. Ex RCC, aided by Polish NCC(USA). 1,000 members. HQ Bayamon. 1968 applied to WCC, rejected. |
| South African Episcopal Church | 1950 | CEpi | Ex Ch of England. Bishop, in Ferrette succession. 1662 Anglican Book of Common Prayer used. |
| True Orthodox Christian Wanderers | 1956 | OSla | IPKh, Stranniki. Underground schism ex Russian Orthodox Ch (P Moscow), across USSR. Highly-organized. |
| True Orthodox Church | 1927 | OSla | IPTS. Istinno-Pravoslavnaya Tserkov. Remnants of underground church (ex Russian OC) across USSR smashed by KGB. |
| Turkish Orthodox Church: P Istanbul | 1922 | IReO | State-aided schism in Turkey ex Ecumenical Patriarchate. Adherents: 300 in Turkey, 14,800 in USA. |
| Ukrainian Autocephalic Orthodox Church | 1947 | OSla | Ukrainian refugees in UK. Linked to UOC of the USA. 30,000 members in UK, also several other nations. |
| Ukrainian Greek-Orthodox Church of Canada | 1918 | OSla | Former Uniates; schism ex RCC in Canada. 3 Dioceses. 140,000 members 95 priests. |
| Ukrainian Orthodox Church of the USA | 1919 | OSla | From USSR. Disputed succession through hand of dead saint. 9 Dioceses in 5 nations (USA, 87,475 members). |
| Ukrainian Orthodox Church (Democratic) | 1947 | OSla | UOC (Sobornopravna). Ex UOCUSA. Bishop in Chicago (USA), also for Europe in Geneva (Switzerland). 2,000. |
| United Armenian Catholic Church in the British Isles | 1890 | CEpi | Ireland, UK. Primate, in Ferrette succession. Linked with Catholicate of the West. Defunct c1920. |
| United Episcopal Ch (Christian Cath/Church Universal) | 1959 | CEpi | Split ex Liberal Catholic Ch. Theosophical. HQ Los Angeles (USA). |
| United Old Catholic Church | 1964 | COCa | Attempt in USA to unite all Old Catholic factions. 1 monastery, 3,000 members, 28 priests. |
| United Orthodox Catholicate | 1953 | CEpi | Organization replacing temporarily-dissolved Catholicate of the West, in UK. |
| Universal Apostolic Church of Life | 1955 | CEpi | Sedes Universalis Apostolica. Universal Life Foundation. HQ North Burnaby, BC (Canada). |
| Universal Christian Communion | 1931 | CEpi | Universal Episcopal Communion. Attempt to unite all Old Catholic bodies in USA. HQ Chicago 21 (USA). |
| Vrai Eglise Catholique | 1964 | CCCa | True Catholic Ch. In Lorraine (France) and Belgium, begun by excommunicated RC priest. 1,000 members. |
| Other sizeable episcopal churches | | | At least 20 more bodies, mainly in Europe and USA. Adherents at least 10,000. |
| Other miniscule episcopal churches | | | At least 85 more bodies, mainly in Europe and USA (see list below). Adherents around 3,000. |
| Total sizeable episcopal churches (in 1975) | | | About 150 churches in 70 countries, with total adherents about 10,280,000. |
| Total miniscule episcopal churches (in 1975) | | | About 130 churches or bodies in 20 countries, with total adherents around 5,000. |
| **Total all disputed episcopal churches (in 1975)** | | | About 280 distinct churches or denominations in 80 countries, with around 10,285,000. |

NOTES. For codes, see Codebook (Part 6).
OTHER MINISCULE EPISCOPAL CHURCHES. There were in 1970 a large number of other bodies under bishops-at-large, many ephemeral or short-lived. These include such titles as: Byzantine Primitive Catholic Ch, Latin American Ecumenical Patriarchate, Orthodox Catholic Diocese of the Holy Spirit, Orthodoxe Ökumenische Cleryker, Slavonic Orthodox Ch. Totals in the 7 major nations concerned, with a selection of names, are as follows. *France*. About 10 more bodies, in addition to those listed, including: Eglise Catholique Apostolique Indépendante, Eglise Orthodoxe Française. *Germany*. About 5 more, including Evangelisch-Ökumenische Vereinigung des Augsburger Bekenntnis. *Italy*. About 10 more, including: Chiesa Cattolica Apostolica Ortodossa, Chiesa Cattolica Liberale, Chiesa Cattolica Ortodossa in Italia, Chiesa Ortodossa (D Patrasso), Chiesa Vetero-Cattolica, Pia Unione delle Chiese Cristiane. *Philippines*. At least 10 more small Aglipayan and Rizalist schisms. *Switzerland*. About 10 more. *UK*. At least 15 more, including: English Old Catholic Ch, Free Catholic Communion of the Old Catholic Ch. *USA*. At least 15 more, including: American Rite Byzantine Catholic Ch, Catholic Ch of the North American Rite, North American Orthodox Catholic Ch, Russian American Orthodox Catholic Ch.

## EVOLUTION OF THE FUTUROLOGY OF CHRISTIANITY AND RELIGION, 1893-1980.

The purpose of this table is to demonstrate the surprisingly widespread and informed involvement of Christians with concern for the future in all its aspects. The table therefore lists significant books (in italics) and articles (in quotation marks) in English (with a handful in other languages) over the last hundred years which have discussed or indicated the future prospects of religion and/or of Christianity. Items are grouped by year of publication; and within each year, alphabetically by author's surname. Columns: 1. Year of publication (each year is listed only once, covering the entry shown together with all subsequent entries without dates until the next date appears). 2. Author(s), or (ed) editor(s); the word 'Anon' signifies composite or anonymous authorship. 3. Standpoint or discipline. 4. Confession of author, editor or publisher, or origin, or background ethos. 5. Title.

| Year 1 | Author 2 | Standpoint 3 | Confession, etc. 4 | Title 5 |
|---|---|---|---|---|
| 1893 | J.T. Gracey | Religion | Protestant | 'The religion of the future'. |
| 1897 | J.M. Guyau | Sociology | French agnostic philosopher | The non-religion of the future: a sociological study. |
| 1909 | C.W. Eliot | Education | President, Harvard University | The religion of the future. |
|  | J.R. Mott | Ecumenism | Methodist ecumenist | The future leadership of the Church. |
| 1912 | P.T. Forsyth | Theology | Anglican theologian | Faith, freedom and the future. |
| 1925 | R.O. Hall | Missions | Protestant writer | 'Douglas Thornton and the future of Islam', in International review of missions (IRM). |
|  | L.W. Markley | Eschatology | Protestant | Conceptions of future punishment as developed among the Universalists. |
| 1927 | A.H. Bray | Missions | Protestant missionary | 'The future of Christianity in China', in IRM. |
|  | E.H. Hume | Missions | Medical missionary | 'The future of Christianity in China', in IRM. |
|  | J. Marchant, ed | Ecumenism | Protestant | The future of Christianity. |
|  | J.A. Vance | Religion | Protestant | America's future religion. |
| 1928 | Sigmund Freud | Psychology | Atheist psychoanalyst | The future of an illusion. |
|  | J.R. Mott | Missions | Methodist | The future of international missionary cooperation. |
| 1930 | C.E.M. Joad | Philosophy | Agnostic | The present and future of religion. |
| 1933 | F.S. Thompson | Missions | Protestant missionary | 'The future of missions', in IRM. |
| 1936 | W. Paton | Missions | Protestant missiologist | 'The International Missionary Council and the future', in IRM. |
| 1937 | H. Gulliford | Missions | Protestant missionary | 'The future of churches and missions in India', in IRM. |
| 1940 | H.A. Wilson | Theology | Anglican bishop | The Christian and the world of tomorrow. |
| 1942 | W. Paton | Missions | Protestant missiologist | 'The future of the missionary enterprise', in IRM. |
| 1943 | C.E. Raven | Theology | Anglican theologian | Science, religion and the future. |
| 1944 | G. Appleton | Missions | Anglican archbishop | 'Lessons from adversity: the future of Christian work in Burma', in IRM. |
|  | J. Rusillon | Missiology | Protestant | 'Méthodes missionnaires du passé et de l'avenir', in La lumière des nations. |
|  | W. Temple | Theology | Anglican archbishop | The Church looks forward. |
|  | H. Witschi | Missiology | Protestant | 'L'avenir de la mission: vers l'autonomie de l'Eglise indigène'. |
| 1947 | H.P. Van Dusen | Ecumenism | Presbyterian | World Christianity: yesterday, today, tomorrow. |
|  | T.O Wedel | Ecclesiology | Episcopalian | The coming Great Church: essays on church unity. |
| 1948 | K.S. Latourette | History | Baptist | The Christian outlook. |
| 1949 | L.E. Browne | Theology | Protestant | 'The religion of the world in AD 3000', in IRM. |
|  | W.M. Horton | Ecumenism | Congregationalist | Toward a reborn church: a review and forecast of the Ecumenical Movement. |
|  | K.S. Latourette | History | Baptist | The prospect for Christianity. |
| 1950 | S.M. Gibbard | Evangelism | Anglican | Tomorrow's Church: a survey of the Church's work among children with special reference to evangelism. |
|  | K.S. Latourette | History | Baptist | 'The Christian future', in Marchant 1950. |
|  | J. Marchant, ed | Ecumenism | Protestant | The coming-of-age of Christianity. |
|  | H.P. Van Dusen | Ecumenism | Presbyterian | 'The coming Great Church', in Marchant 1950. |
| 1952 | T. Houghton | Eschatology | Fundamentalist | The faith and the hope of the future. |
| 1955 | G.W. Carpenter | Missions | Ecumenical | 'The pattern of things to come in Africa'. |
|  | H.D. Dehquani-Tafti | Ecclesiology | Anglican bishop | 'Prospects for the Church in Iran', in IRM. |
|  | D. McConnell | Missions | Protestant | The pattern of things to come. |
| 1956 | V. Della Giacoma | Missiology | Roman Catholic | Il destino dell'Africa: problemi e obiettivi cristiani. |
|  | D.N. Licorish | Ecclesiology | Protestant | Tomorrow's church in today's world: a study of the 20th-century challenge to religion. |
| 1957 | J. Knox | Church history | Episcopalian | The early Church and the coming Great Church. |
|  | Pius XII | Pastoralia | Roman Catholic pope | The future of Africa: the encyclical Fidei Donum of Pope Pius XII. |
|  | C.B. Templeton | Evangelism | Protestant | Evangelism for tomorrow. |
| 1959 | E.D. Canham, ed | Philosophy | Christian Science | Man's great future. |
|  | Teilhard de Chardin | Philosophy | RC (Jesuit) | L'avenir de l'homme. |
| 1960 | P. Maury | Missions | Ecumenical | History's lessons for tomorrow's mission. |
|  | S.F. Russell | Medicine | Evangelical | Christian initiative and the future of medicine. |
|  | Christian Peace Conference | Politics | Ecumenical | The only future: documents of the 3rd Session of the CPC. |
| 1961 | G. Szczesny | Philosophy | Protestant | The future of unbelief. |
| 1962 | C. Driver | Ecclesiology | Protestant | A future for the Free Churches? |
|  | B. Findlow | Ecclesiology | Unitarian | Unitarianism: a faith with a future. |
| 1963 | Anon | Eschatology | Anglican priest | The Gospel of the future: the Christian hope in the nuclear age. |
|  | K. Haselden, et al | History | Protestant | 'What's ahead for the Church?', in The Christian Century. |
|  | J. Martin | Eschatology | Protestant | The Last Judgement in Protestant theology from orthodoxy to Ritschl. |
|  | W.Y. Milne | Youth work | Protestant | Out among youth: a contribution to the Church of the future. |
| 1964 | M.S. Bates, ed | Missions | Disciples of Christ (USA) | The prospects of Christianity throughout the world. |
|  | Teilhard de Chardin | Philosophy | RC (Jesuit) | The future of man (translation of de Chardin 1959). |
|  | K. Haselden & M.E. Marty | History | Ecumenical | What's ahead for the Churches? |
|  | A.J. Sanders | Ecclesiology | Evangelical | The evangelical ministry in the Philippines and its future. |
| 1965 | Anon. | Conciliarism | Nonconformist | The future of the Free Church Federal Council. |
|  | L.P. Barnett | Pastoralia | Methodist | Church youth leaders face their future: some reflections on the way ahead. |
|  | J.V.L. Casserley | Theology | Anglican | The Church today and tomorrow: prospects for post-Christianity. |
|  | Karl Rahner | Theology | Roman Catholic | The Christian of the future. |
|  | R.E. Sommerfeld | Ecclesiology | Lutheran | The Church of the 21st Century: prospects and proposals. |
|  | G.H. Tavard | Theology | Roman Catholic | The Church tomorrow. |
| 1966 | M. De La Bedoyere, ed | Ecclesiology | Roman Catholic | The future of Catholic Christianity. |
|  | E. Benz | Theology | Protestant | Evolution and Christian hope: man's concept of the future. |
|  | E. Carson Blake | Ecumenism | Presbyterian | The Church in the next decade. |
|  | R. De Corneille | Church history | Protestant | Christians and Jews: the tragic past and the hopeful future. |
|  | J.D. Crichton, ed | Liturgiology | Roman Catholic (SVD) | The liturgy and the future. |
|  | A.H. Dammers | Ecumenism | Anglican | AD 1980: a study in Christian unity: mission and renewal. |
|  | L. Dewart | Philosophy | Roman Catholic | The future of belief: theism in a world come of age. |
|  | N.F.S. Ferré et al | Philosophy | Protestant | Paul Tillich: retrospect and future. |
|  | H. Lindsell, ed | Missions | Evangelical | The church's worldwide mission: a strategy for future activity. |
|  | J. Lopez-Calo | Musicology | Roman Catholic | Presente y futuro de la musica sagrada: Radio Vaticana. |
|  | Overseas Missionary Fellowship | Missions | Evangelical | New century: bridge into the future. |
|  | A. Retif | Missions | Roman Catholic | Un nouvel avenir pour les missions. |
|  | R. Schackenburg | Biblical theology | Roman Catholic | Present and future: modern aspects of New Testament theology. |
|  | Paul Tillich | Philosophy | Protestant | The future of religions. |
|  | A.A. Vogel | Theology | Protestant | The next Christian epoch. |
|  | A. Wilder | Eschatology | Protestant | Kerygma, eschatology and ethics. |
| 1967 | R. Adolfs | Theology | Roman Catholic | The grave of God: has the church a future? |
|  | G. Baum, ed | Theology | Roman Catholic | The future of belief debate. |
|  | J.T. Hardyman | Missions | Congregationalist | 'The shape of things to come', in World mission. |
|  | J.I. Packer | Ecclesiology | Anglican Evangelical | Guidelines: Anglican evangelicals face the future. |
|  | K. Rahner | Theology | Roman Catholic | The Christian of the future. |
|  | R. Scarpati | Theology | Roman Catholic | Hope or hindrance? The church of the future. |
|  | E. Schillebeeckx | Theology | RC (Dominican) | 'Christian faith and the future of the world', in The Church today. |
|  | W.A. Visser't Hooft | Theology | Reformed | Christians for the future. |
| 1968 | D.B. Barrett | Sociology | Anglican | 'The future of African independency', in Christianity in Tropical Africa. |
|  | G. Briatore | Sociology | Roman Catholic | Le basi religiose e sociali del futuro. Saggio informativo per le generazioni del 2000. |
|  | J.D. Brown, ed | History | Protestant | Can Christianity survive? |
|  | Harvey Cox | Theology | Protestant | 'The future of religionless Christianity', in The Futurist. |
|  | J. Daniélou | Theology | RC cardinal (Jesuit) | L'avenir de la religion. |
|  | Encuentro Pastoral | Pastoralia | Roman Catholic | De cara al futuro de la Iglesia en Nicaragua. |
|  | W.A. Holmes | Planning | Methodist | Tomorrow's Church a cosmopolitan community: a radical experiment in church renewal. |
|  | J. Kerkhofs, et al | Missions | Roman Catholic | Dialogue d'aujourd'hui, mission de demain. |
|  | Hans Küng | Theology | Roman Catholic | Truthfulness: the future of the Church. |
|  | J. McElwain, et al | Missions | Ecumenical | 'The Christian movement in Japan: past, present and future', in Japan Christian yearbook. |
|  | M.E. Marty | Church history | Protestant | The search for a usable future. |
|  | E.L. Mascall | Theology | Anglican | Theology and the future. |
|  | M. Muckelhirn, ed | Theology | Roman Catholic | The future as the presence of a shared hope. |
|  | K. Nishitani | Philosophy | Japanese Buddhist | 'A Buddhist philosopher looks at the future of Christianity'. |
|  | Novosti | Press agency | Atheist (USSR) | The year 2017: 100 years after the October Revolution. |
|  | L.E. Schaller | Church planning | Methodist | The local Church looks to the future: a guide to church planning. |
|  | E. Schillebeeckx | Theology | RC (Dominican) | God and the future of man. |
|  | D.J. Thorman | Ecclesiology | Roman Catholic | American Catholics face the future. |
|  | T.E. Wedel | Theology | Episcopalian | The coming Great Church. |
| 1969 | M. Bergman | Theology | Protestant Taizé brother | L'avenir possible. |
|  | K. Bliss | Education | Protestant | The future of religion. |
|  | L. Boros | Theology | Roman Catholic | Living in hope: future perspectives in Christian thought. |
|  | C.E. Braaten | Theology | Lutheran | The future of God: the revolutionary dynamics of hope. |

| | | | | |
|---|---|---|---|---|
| | J.E. Carothers | Ecclesiology | Methodist | 'The Church in the year 2000', in *World outlook*. |
| | M.D. Chenu | Ecclesiology | RC (Dominican) | *L'Eglise vers l'avenir.* |
| | W.H. Cleary, ed | Ministry | Roman Catholic | *Hyphenated priests: the ministry of the future.* |
| | *Commonweal* | Science | American Academy of Arts & Science | *The Church in the year 2000.* |
| | Harvey Cox | Theology | Protestant | 'Christianity's conflicting views of the future', in *The Futurist*. |
| | D.L. Edwards | Theology | Anglican | *Religion and change.* |
| | G. Fackre | Theology | Methodist | *The Rainbow sign: Christian futurity.* |
| | A. Greeley | Sociology | Roman Catholic | *Religion in the year 2000.* |
| | J. Hoekendijk | Missiology | Reformed | 'What's ahead for the Church?', in *World outlook*. |
| | N. Hurley | Religion | Roman Catholic | 'The futurists', in *Ave Maria*. |
| | R.W. Jenson | Theology | Protestant | *God after God: the God of the past and the God of the future, seen in the work of Karl Barth.* |
| | Hans Küng, ed | Theology | Roman Catholic | *The future of ecumenism.* |
| | J.H. Leuba | Psychology | Psychologist | *A psychological study of religion: its origin, function, and future.* |
| | J. Marshall, ed | Pastoralia | Roman Catholic | *The future of Christian marriage.* |
| | G.E. Martin | Evangelism | Protestant | *The future of evangelism.* |
| | M.E. Marty | History | Protestant | *The search for a usable future.* |
| | J. Moltmann | Theology | Protestant | *Religion, revolution and the future.* |
| | L.E. Schaller | Church planning | Methodist | *The impact of the future: trends affecting the church of tomorrow.* |
| | F. Sontag | Theology | Protestant | *The future of theology.* |
| | R.W. Tapp | Publishing | Protestant | 'Prediction: the Church tomorrow', in *World call*. |
| | A. Watts | Philosophy | New-Religionist | 'The future of religion', in *Toward Century 21*. |
| 1970 | R. Aubert, ed | Church history | Roman Catholic | *Church history in future perspective.* |
| | D.B. Barrett | Missiology | Anglican | 'AD 2000: 350 million Christians in Africa', in *IRM*. |
| | W.H. Capps, ed | Theology | Lutheran | *The future of hope.* |
| | D.E. Clark | Missiology | Evangelical | *Missions in the Seventies.* |
| | *Concilium* | Theology | Roman Catholic | 'L'avenir de l'Eglise'. |
| | R.G. Cote | Theology | Protestant | 'Future prospects of the Church in Africa', in *Ministry*. |
| | Harvey Cox | Theology | Protestant | 'The future of Christianity and the Church', in *The Futurist*. |
| | *EPS Geneva* | Press service | Ecumenical (WCC) | 'Mission in the 70's'. |
| | D.L. Gelpi | Spirituality | Roman Catholic | *Discerning the spirit: foundations and futures of religious life.* |
| | L.B. Gilkey | Science | Theologian | *Religion and the scientific future: reflections on myth, science and theology.* |
| | D.M. Gill | Theology | Ecumenical (WCC) | *From here to where? technology, faith and the future of man.* |
| | T.J. Gordon | Futurology | Protestant | 'Some possible futures of American religion', in *The Futurist*. |
| | C. Kiesling | Pastoralia | Roman Catholic | *The future of the Christian Sunday.* |
| | C.A. Koob & R. Shaw | Education | Roman Catholic | *S.O.S. for Catholic schools: a strategy for future service to Church and nation.* |
| | J.M. Lee & P.C. Rooney, eds | Education | Protestant | *Toward a future for religious education.* |
| | G.A. Lindbeck | Theology | Roman Catholic | *The future of Roman Catholic theology: Vatican II, catalyst for change.* |
| | J.S. Mbiti | Theology | Anglican | 'The future of Christianity in Africa, 1970-2000', in *Communio viatorum*. |
| | M.H. Micks | Worship | Episcopalian | *The future present: the phenomenon of Christian worship.* |
| | A. Muller, ed | Catechetics | Roman Catholic | *Catechetics for the future.* |
| | R. Nyce | Sociology | Protestant | 'The Church of the future' (Singapore). |
| | T.F. O'Meara & D.M. Weisser | Theology | Roman Catholic | *Projections: shaping an American theology for the future.* |
| | M.S. Parer | Ministry | Roman Catholic | *Prophets and losses in the priesthood: in quest of the future ministry.* |
| | G. Philips | Theology | Protestant | *Le Chrétien authentique demain.* |
| | A.M. Ramsey | Theology | Anglican archbishop | *Freedom, faith, and the future.* |
| | A.M. Ramsey & L.J. Suenens | Theology | Anglican & RC primates | *The future of the Christian church.* |
| | F.A. Schaeffer | Evangelism | Evangelical | *The Church at the end of the Twentieth Century.* |
| | D.M. Schores | Sociology | Methodist | 'Ministry: year 2000', in *The Futurist*. |
| | D. Sölle | Ethics | Lutheran | *Beyond mere obedience: reflections on a Christian ethic for the future.* |
| | *The Futurist* | Futurology | Secular | 'The future of religion'. |
| | P. Toon, ed | Eschatology | Anglican | *Puritans, the Millennium and the future of Israel: Puritan eschatology, 1600 to 1660: essays.* |
| | D.E. Trueblood | Philosophy | Quaker | *The future of the Christian.* |
| | J.H. Westerhoff | Education | Protestant | *Values for tomorrow's children: an alternative future for education in the church.* |
| | H.C.N. Williams | Religious education | Anglican | *Basics and variables: the future of the Church in the modern world.* |
| 1971 | V. Brady | Theology | Protestant | *The future people: Christianity, modern culture and the future.* |
| | W.K. Cauthen | Theology | Protestant | *Christian biopolitics: a credo and strategy for the future.* |
| | Church of Ireland | Planning | Anglican | *The local church in the future.* |
| | J.A. Coriden, ed | Ecclesiology | Roman Catholic | *The once and future church: a communion of freedom: studies on unity and collegiality in the church.* |
| | D.S. Crowther | Eschatology | Evangelical | *The plan of salvation and the future in prophecy.* |
| | W.J. Danker & W.J. Kang, eds | Missions | Lutheran | *The future of the Christian world mission.* |
| | E.P. Echlin | Ministry | Roman Catholic | *The deacon in the Church: past time and future.* |
| | W.F. Groff | Theology | Protestant | *Christ the hope of the future: signals of a promised humanity.* |
| | U.T. Holmes III | Ministry | Episcopalian priest | *The future shape of ministry: a theological projection.* |
| | S. Ioane | Biography | Mystical | *Songs from the house of pilgrimage: the biography of a mystic that foretells the future of Christianity.* |
| | D. Kenny | Ecclesiology | Roman Catholic | *The Christian future: a strategy for Catholic renewal.* |
| | S. Kutb | Religion | Kuwaiti Muslim | *Islam: the religion of the future.* |
| | L.E. Lair | Ecclesiology | Disciples of Christ (USA) | *The Christian Church* (*Disciples of Christ*) *and its future.* |
| | J. Ratzinger | Theology | Roman Catholic | *Faith and the future.* |
| | L. Retif | Ecclesiology | Roman Catholic | *J'ai vu naitre l'Eglise de demain.* |
| | J.M. Robinson, ed | Theology | Protestant | *The future of our religious past: essays in honour of Rudolf Bultmann.* |
| | M. Rogness | Ecclesiology | Lutheran | *The church nobody knows: the shaping of the future church.* |
| | G. Smith | Philosophy | Roman Catholic | *Christian philosophy and its future.* |
| | A.E.C.W. Spencer | Sociology | Roman Catholic | *The future of Catholic education in England and Wales.* |
| | D.F. Wells & C.H. Pinnock | Theology | Evangelical | *Toward a theology for the future.* |
| | D.F. Wells | Church history | Evangelical | '*The future of the church*', in Wells & Pinnock 1971. |
| 1972 | K.C. Barnes | Ecclesiology | Quaker | *The future of the Society of Friends.* |
| | D.B. Barrett & J.S. Mbiti | Ecclesiology | Anglican | 'The future of Christianity in Africa'. |
| | P.A. Crow | Ministry | Protestant | 'Mission, ministry, and the future of the Church', in *Encounter*. |
| | D.A. Fox | Religion | Protestant | *Buddhism, Christianity, and the future of man.* |
| | P. Gheddo | Missions | Roman Catholic | 'C'è ancora un futuro per la missione fra i non cristiani?', in *La rivista del clero italiano*. |
| | J. Grand'maison | Theology | Roman Catholic | 'L'avenir de l'Eglise d'ici, à la lumière de l'action catholique ouvrière', in *Prêtres et laïcs*. |
| | R. Haughton | Theology | Roman Catholic | *In search of tomorrow: a future to live in.* |
| | G. Jacob | Preaching | German Protestant | *Verkündigung und Zukunft.* |
| | Karl Rahner | Theology | Roman Catholic | *Strukturwandel der Kirche als Aufgabe und Chance.* |
| | H. Schwarz | Eschatology | Lutheran | *On the way to the future: eschatology in the light of current trends in religion, philosophy, and science.* |
| | F. Sontag | Theology | Protestant | *The American religious experience: the roots, trends, and future of American theology.* |
| | K. Vaux, ed | Planning | Protestant | *To create a different future: religious hope and technological planning.* |
| | M. von Galli | Spirituality | Roman Catholic | *Living our future: Francis of Assisi and the Church tomorrow.* |
| | Pro Mundi Vita | Sociology | Roman Catholic | *The population explosion and the future of the church.* |
| 1973 | B. Besret | Ecclesiology | French RC priest | *Tomorrow: a new Church.* |
| | O. Cooper | Theology | Baptist | *The future is before us.* |
| | E.P. Echlin | Hermaneutics | Roman Catholic | *The priest as preacher, past and future.* |
| | W.P. Frost | Religion | Protestant | *The future significance of civilization, nature, and religion.* |
| | R.H. Hiers | Theology | Protestant | *The historical Jesus and the kingdom of God: present and future in the message and ministry of Jesus.* |
| | G.E. Ladd | Eschatology | Protestant | *The presence of the future: the eschatology of biblical realism.* |
| | L. Paul | Sociology | Anglican | *A church by daylight: a reappraisement of the Church of England and its future.* |
| 1974 | Teilhard de Chardin | Philosophy | RC (Jesuit) | *Toward the future.* |
| | R. Garaudy | Philosophy | French Marxist | *The alternative future: a vision of Christian Marxism.* |
| | F.C. Gérard | Theology | Protestant | *The future of the church: the theology of renewal of Willem Adolf Visser't Hooft.* |
| | P. Huizing & W. Bassett, eds | Spirituality | Anglican | *The future of the religious life.* |
| | IDOC | Missiology | Roman Catholic | *In search of mission* (Future of the Missionary Enterprise Seminar). |
| | F. Klostermann | Ecclesiology | Roman Catholic | *Gemeinde-Kirche der Zukunft.* |
| | H. McKeating | Theology | Protestant | *God and the future.* |
| | Sun Myung Moon | Theology | Korean indigenous | *The new future of Christianity.* |
| | R.B. Norris | Theology | Protestant | *God, Marx, and the future: dialogue with Roger Garaudy.* |
| | Karl Rahner | Theology | Roman Catholic | *The shape of the church to come* (translation of Rahner 1972). |
| | G. Rowell | Eschatology | Protestant | *Hell and the Victorians: theological controversies concerning eternal punishment and the future life.* |
| | B. Schlink | Eschatology | German Evangelical | *Countdown to world disaster: hope and protection for the future.* |
| | W.A. Visser't Hooft | Ecumenism | Dutch Reformed | *Has the ecumenical movement a future?* |
| | Cynthia C. Wedel | Pastoralia | Episcopalian | *Faith or fear and future shock.* |
| | J.W. White | Theology | Protestant | *Future hope.* |
| | Victoria Univ of Wellington | Religion | Interconfessional | *The future of religion in New Zealand.* |
| | Pro Mundi Vita | Sociology | Roman Catholic | *The Western family and the future of the Church.* |
| 1975 | Anon. | Theolog education | Roman Catholic | *Enchiridion clericorum: documenta ecclesiae futuris sacerdotibus formandis.* |
| | H. Babel | Religion | Philosopher | *Le secret des grandes religions: futurologie de la religion.* |
| | J.J. Gaine | Theology | Roman Catholic | *Young adults today and the future of the faith.* |
| | A.O. Hudson | Eschatology | Fundamentalist | *Future probation in Christian belief.* |
| | P.J. Jagger | Pastoralia | Anglican | *Catholic or compromise? the future of Christian initiation in the Church of England.* |
| | I. Macpherson | Eschatology | Fundamentalist | *Dial the future: a book about the second coming of Christ.* |
| | G.O'Collins | Theology | Roman Catholic | *Has dogma a future?* |
| | J.C. Policarpo | Theology | Roman Catholic | *Evangelização, anucio de liberdade: futuro do evangelho em Portugal à luz do Sínodo.* |
| | O. Riedel | Church history | Protestant | *Der Zukunft verschworen: Streifbilder aus d. Leben u. geistl. Wirken d. Jan Amos Comenius.* |
| | Christian Workers Fellowship | Mission | Protestant | *Facing the future, meeting the crisis.* |
| | Comisión Epis de Pastoral | Pastoralia | Roman Catholic | *Parroquia urbana, presente y futuro. Semana Nacional de la Parroquia.* |
| 1976 | M. Agnew | Religious education | Roman Catholic | *Future shapes of adult religious education: a Delphi study.* |

| Year | Author | Field | Denomination | Title |
|---|---|---|---|---|
| | P.L. Berger & R.J. Neuhaus | Sociology | Episcopalian et al | *Against the world for the world: the Hartford appeal and the future of American religion.* |
| | J. Broadhurst, et al | Theolog education | Anglican | *Theological training and the future of theological colleges.* |
| | W. Bühlmann | Ecclesiology | Roman Catholic | *The coming of the Third Church: an analysis of the present and future of the Church.* |
| | J.P. Clayton, ed | Theology | Protestant | *Ernst Troeltsch and the future of theology.* |
| | G. Collins, ed | Theology | Evangelical | *Facing the future: church and family together.* |
| | A.J. De Luca | Psychology | Protestant | *Freud and future religious experience.* |
| | J.A. Grau | Theology | Roman Catholic | *Morality and the human future in the thought of Teilhard de Chardin.* |
| | P. Lee | Pastoralia | Anglican | *Equipping God's people: present and future parish training schemes.* |
| | L. Lumetti | Religious education | Roman Catholic | *Educazione religiosa e futuro dell'uomo.* |
| | M. Reeves | Eschatology | Anglican | *Joachim of Fiore and the prophetic future.* |
| | D. Rössler | Religion | Protestant | *Die Verkunft der Religion.* |
| | L.E. Schaller | Pastoralia | Methodist | *Understanding tomorrow.* |
| | L.M. Xirinacs | Theology | Roman Catholic | *Futur d'esglesia: comunitat cristiana de base.* |
| | SC para la Educ Católica | Theolog education | Roman Catholic | *La formación teológica de los futuros sacerdotes.* |
| | Institute for Study of Worship | Architecture | Interdenominational | *Looking to the future: prospects for worship and religious architecture.* |
| 1977 | M. Binney & P. Burman | Pastoralia | Anglican | *Change and decay: the future of our churches.* |
| | E.M. Carlson | Education | Lutheran | *The future of church-related higher education.* |
| | J.D. Crichton | Liturgiology | Roman Catholic | *The once and the future liturgy.* |
| | C. Geffré & B. Luneau, eds | Ecclesiology | Episcopalian | *The Churches of Africa: future prospects.* |
| | A. Grumelli, et al | Theology | Roman Catholic | *Giovani e futuro della fede.* |
| | J.W. Lundin | Pastoralia | Protestant | *A church for an open future: Biblical roots and parish renewal.* |
| | L. Newbigin | Missiology | United Reformed moderator | 'The future of missions and missionaries', in *Review and expositor.* |
| | F. Sontag & J.K. Roth | Religion | Protestant | *God and America's future.* |
| | C. Thoma, ed | Theology | Protestant | *Zukunft in der Gegenwart: Wegweisungen in Judentum und Christentum.* |
| | W.J. Wolf | Theology | Protestant | *Freedom's holy light: American identity and the future of theology.* |
| | Catholic Information Services | Education | Roman Catholic | *Catechetics: the future in focus: some responses to 'Catechetics in our time'.* |
| 1978 | S.E. Ahlstrom, et al | Religion | Protestant | *American religious values and the future of America.* |
| | R.H. Bainton | Church history | Lutheran | *Yesterday, today, and what next?* |
| | W. Bühlmann | Missiology | Roman Catholic | *The missions on trial: a moral for the future from the archives of today.* |
| | H. Kline & W. Eshback | Pastoralia | Brethren | *A future with hope: aging creatively in Christian community.* |
| | Hans Küng | Theology | Roman Catholic | *Signposts for the future.* |
| | E.B. Lindaman | Theology | Baptist | *Thinking in the future tense.* |
| | H. Montefiore | Theology | Anglican | *Taking our past into our future.* |
| | T. Peters | Theology | Protestant | *Futures — human and divine.* |
| | T.P. Weber | Church history | Conservative Baptist historian | *The future explored.* |
| 1979 | Church Information Service | Industrial mission | Church of England | *Work and the future.* |
| | A.A. Hoekema | Theology | Protestant | *The Bible and the future.* |
| | J.S. Mbiti | Theology | Anglican | 'The future of Christianity in Africa', in *Cross currents.* |
| | J. Moltman | Theology | German Protestant | *The future of creation.* |
| | J.D. Whitehead, et al, eds | Sinology | Ecumenical | *China and Christianity: historical and future encounters.* |
| 1980 | B. Whyte | Sinology | Ecumenical | 'The future of religion in China', in *Religion in Communist lands.* |
| | S.H. Travis | Eschatology | Methodist | *Christian hope and the future of man.* |

# PART 10

# BIBLIOGRAPHY

Selective world bibliography of Christianity

*Men of learning—whether you be theologians, exegetes or historians—the work of evangelization needs your tireless work of research.*

—Paul VI, *Evangelii Nuntiandi*, 1975.

The Encyclopedia contains 3 major bibliographies, of different kinds, listing the main works of reference at, respectively, (1) the national level, (2) the confessional or topical level, and (3) the world or global level. These are as follows. (1) A 1,240-title *Bibliography of World Christianity* (or, *Bibliography of the Christian World*) is presented here as a series of short bibliographies appended to the descriptive texts in Part 7 for most countries, giving descriptive works significant at the national level. These list for each country the major titles describing Christianity and religions in that country (and usually restricted to only that country). (2) A 346-title *World Bibliography of Christian Directories* (at the end of Part 13) lists national, international, confessional, denominational, topical and other types of reference directory significant within their own contexts but not necessarily so at the global level. Lastly, (3) the 259-title *Selective World Bibliography of Christianity* that follows below lists the major reference works on Christianity (not only world Christianity or Christianity as a world phenomenon) which are significant at the international or world or global level.

In these bibliographies, we usually give the number of volumes or of pages of each item, so that the reader may evaluate the amount of material each contains; thus, over 300 pages is a substantial book or manuscript, whereas under 30 pages is very slim. Note that in our usage throughout the Encyclopedia, the term 'thesis' refers to work for a master's degree, whilst the term 'dissertation' is reserved for unpublished doctoral dissertations only.

The *Selective World Bibliography of Christianity* below lists a selection of the world's major works of reference, and a selection of outstanding other works, concerning Christianity and its various fields or disciplines, the non-Christian religious context, and the scientific study of religion with particular reference to Christianity. The listing has been compiled primarily with English-language users in mind, and English translations of works originally in other languages are given where available; however, a number of definitive works in other European languages, not available translated into English, are also included in order to cover all disciplines adequately. The classification under 13 heads is merely for convenience; several items could equally well go under 2 or more heads, but they are classified below only once each under whichever best describes their contents. A handful of items are secular reference works containing important listings of religious books.

Titles and sub-titles are given first, in italics, followed by any additional printed description. Titles not in the 6 languages employed in this Encyclopedia (English, French, German, Italian, Portuguese, Spanish) are given first in English in parentheses. Then follow translation of title into English (only in a few important cases, for clarification), then names of authors (or 'Ed', editor or editors) if any, then place of publication (one per title; additional places of publication are in most cases omitted), publisher, date, number of volumes (separate books) or (for a single volume) number of pages, and in several cases a brief annotation or evaluation in parentheses. Series whose publication of all volumes is completed are written thus: '2 vols, 1958–60'. Series still incomplete but with a complete publishing programme in view are written thus: 'Vols 1–9, 1920–70; in progress to 38 vols'.

# SELECTIVE WORLD BIBLIOGRAPHY OF CHRISTIANITY

## CHRISTIANITY

### 1. CONTEMPORARY STATUS OF CHRISTIANITY

*Atlas hierarchicus: descriptio geographica et statistica ecclesiae catholicae tum occidentis tum orientis*. H. Emmerich. Mödling (Austria): St Gabriel-Verlag, 1968. 76p. 1975 edition, published 1976: 107p, with *Supplement* (Vatican Press, 50p). (Contemporary survey of all Roman Catholic jurisdictions; in French, English, German, Italian, Spanish).

*Atlas zur Kirchengeschichte: Die Christlichen in Geschichte und Gegenwart*. Ed H. Jedin, K.S. Latourette & J. Martin. Freiburg im Breisgau: Herder, 1970.

*Bilan du monde: encyclopédie catholique du monde chrétien*. Ed J. Frisque et al. Louvain: Casterman. 2 vols, 1958-60. 2nd edition, 2 vols, 1964.

*Catholic encyclopedia*. An international work of reference on the constitution, doctrine, discipline and history of the Catholic church. New York: Catholic Encyclopedia Press. 17 vols, c1907-22.

(Catholic encyclopedia) *Encyklopedia Katolicka*. Ed F. Gryglewicz, R. Lukaszyk & Z. Sulowski. Lublin: Catholic University. Vols 1-12, 1973- ; in progress. (Polish).

*Constitutions of the countries of the world*. Ed A.P. Blaustein & G.H. Flanz. Dobbs Ferry, New York: Oceana Publications. Vols 1-10, 1971-72; in progress. (Updated texts, chronologies, bibliographies. Constitutional status of Christianity and religion).

*Corpus dictionary of Western Churches*. Ed T.C. O'Brien. Washington: Corpus Publications, 1970. 820p. (Primarily Roman Catholic).

*Die Kirchen der Welt*. Ed H.H. Harms, H. Krüger, G. Wagner, H.-H. Wolf et al. Stuttgart: Evangelisches Verlagswerk. Vols 1-9, 1960-71; in progress.

*Enciclopedia cattolica*. Città del Vaticano: Enciclopedia Cattolica. 12 vols, 1948-54.

*Enciclopedia ecclesiastica*. A. Bernareggi. Milano: Vallardi. Vols 1-6, 1942-55; in progress.

*Encyclopedia of modern Christian missions*. Ed B.L. Goddard. New Jersey: Nelson, 1967. 743p.

*Encyclopedia of Southern Baptists*. Nashville, Tennessee: Broadman Press. 2 vols, 1958. (Includes all Baptist denominations and movements).

*Encyclopedia of the Lutheran Church*. Ed J. Bodensieck. Minneapolis: Augsburg Publishing House. 3 vols, 1965.

*Encyclopedia of world Methodism*. Ed N.B. Harmon. Nashville, Tennessee: United Methodist Publishing House. 2 vols, 1974.

*Encyclopedic dictionary of religion*. Ed C.M. Aherne, T.C. O'Brien & P.K. Meagher. Palatine, IL: Corpus, 1977. 3 vols, 3,200p. (Primarily Roman Catholic).

*Ethnologue*. Ed B.F. Grimes. Huntington Beach (CA): Wycliffe Bible Translators. 9th edition, 1978. 417p. (Current data on 5,103 languages, including status of scripture translation).

*Guida delle missioni cattoliche 1975*. Roma: SC per l'Evangelizzazione dei Popoli, 1975 (5th edition). 1,628p. (Earlier editions 1934, 1946, 1950, 1970).

*Handbuch der Ostkirchenkunde* (Handbook of the Eastern Churches). Ed E. von Ivánka, J. Tyciak & P. Wiertz. Düsseldorf: Patmos, 1971. 839p. (The best overall reference work on the Eastern churches).

*Handbuch der Pfingstbewegung* (Handbook of Pentecostalism). W.J. Hollenweger. Geneva (duplicated). 10 vols, 1965-67. University Microfilms and ATLA Microtext Project.

*Historical catalogue of printed editions of the English Bible, 1525-1961*. A.S. Herbert. London: BFBS, 1968. (Lists 2,524 distinct editions).

*Iglesias de Oriente* (Churches of the East). A. Santos Hernández. Santander: Editorial Sal Terrae. 2 vols, 1959-63. (Including annotated bibliography of 2,250 items).

*Let the earth hear his voice: a comprehensive reference volume on world evangelization*. Ed J.D. Douglas. International Congress on World Evangelization, Lausanne 1974. Minneapolis, MN: World Wide Publications, 1975. 1,471p.

*Lexikon der christlicher Kirchen und Sekten*. J. Gründler. Wien: Herder. 2 vols, 1961. (History and description of all denominations).

*Lutheran cyclopedia*. Ed E.L. Lueker. St Louis, MO: Concordia Publishing House, 1954. 1,160p.

*New Catholic encyclopedia*. Washington: Catholic University of America. 15 vols, 1967.

*Operation World: a handbook for world intercession*. P.J. Johnstone. Bromley, Kent: STL Publications, 1978. 272p. (1st edition 1974, 208p).

*Oriente cattolico*. Cenni storici e statistiche. Città del Vaticano: SC per le Chiese Orientali, 1929, 1932, 1962, 1974. 857p.

'Religion', p.498-559 in *Propaedia* (Outline of knowledge), *New Encyclopaedia Britannica* (Chicago; 30 vols, 1975). (Complete outline of all aspects of Christianity and religion, with references to detailed articles and bibliography).

*Scriptures of the world*. A compilation of 1,549 languages in which at least one book of the Bible has been published. New York: United Bible Societies, 1965, 1968, 1970, 1972, 1974, 1976, 1978. 94p. (Computerized status of scripture translation).

'Selective bibliography on evangelism and evangelization'. D.B. Barrett. Nairobi: Centre for the Study of World Evangelization, 1980. (1,400 items).

*Seventh-day Adventist encyclopedia*. Ed D.F. Neufeld. Washington, DC: Review & Herald. 10 vols, 1966-76.

'The Anglican world in figures', D.B. Barrett, in *Lambeth Conference 1978 preparatory information* (London: CIO Publishing, 1978), p.1-37, 83-95.

*The book of a thousand tongues*. Ed E.A. Nida. 2nd edition (1st 1939). London: United Bible Societies, 1972. 536p. (Catalogue of 1,399 languages with printed scriptures, giving a scripture passage for each).

*The Mennonite encyclopedia: a comprehensive reference work on the Anabaptist-Mennonite movement*. Scottdale, PA: Mennonite Publishing House. 4 vols, 1955-59.

*The world year book of religion: the religious situation*. Ed D.R. Cutler. London: Evans Brothers. 2 vols, 1968-69 only.

*Weltkirchenlexikon*. Handbuch der Ökumene im Auftrag des Deutschen Evangelischen. Ed F.H. Littell & H.H. Walz. Stuttgart Kreuz-Verlag, 1960.

*World Christian encyclopedia: a comparative survey of churches and religions in the modern world, AD 1900-2000*. Ed D.B. Barrett. Nairobi: Oxford University Press, 1981. 1,000p.

*World Christian handbook*. Ed E.J. Bingle, K.G. Grubb & H.W. Coxill. London: World Dominion Press, 1949, 1952, 1957, 1962; Lutterworth Press, 1967. (Statistics).

*Yearbook of the Orthodox Church, 1978*. Munich: Verlag Alex Proc, 1978. 309p. Annual, alternately published in English, French and German. (Eastern Orthodox jurisdictions worldwide).

### 2. BIBLICAL STUDIES

*A bibliography of New Testament bibliographies*. J.C. Hurd. New York: Seabury, 1966. (1,300 articles and books).

*A decade of Bible bibliography*. Oxford: Blackwell, 1967. (Book lists 1957-66).

*Analytical concordance to the Bible*. R. Young. New York: Funk & Wagnalls, 1955 (1st edition 1879). 1,257p. (Hebrew and Greek originals; 311,000 references).

*Anchor Bible*. Garden City, NY: Doubleday. Vols 1-19, 1964-72; in progress to 38 vols. (Joint Protestant/Catholic/Jewish translation with extensive commentary).

*Atlas of the Bible*. L.H. Grollenberg. New York: Nelson, 1956. 165p. (Translated from 1954 Dutch 2nd edition).

*Bible bibliography, 1967-73*. Ed P.R. Ackroyd. Oxford: Blackwell, 1975. (Works in nearly 20 languages).

*Biblia Patristica: index des citations et allusions bibliques dans la littérature patristique*. I: Des origines à Clément d'Alexandrie et Tertullien. II: Auteurs du 3e siècle sauf Origène. III: Origène. Paris: CNRS. 3 vols, 1975-80. (27,000 references; computerized).

*Bibliography of New Testament literature, 1900-1950*. Ed T. Akaishi. San Anselmo: Seminary Cooperative Store, 1953. 312p. (Classified annotated bibliography of 2,400 books and some periodical articles in English).

*Concordance to the Greek Testament*. W.F. Moulton & A.S. Geden. Edinburgh: Clark (New York: Scribner), 3rd edition 1926. 1,033p.

*Das Alte Testament Deutsch*. Ed G. von Rad et al. Göttingen: Vandenhoeck & Ruprecht. 25 vols, 1949-66.

*Das Neue Testament Deutsch*. Ed G. Friedrich. Göttingen: Vandenhoeck & Ruprecht. 4 vols, 1960-68.

*Dictionary of Christ and the Gospels*. J. Hastings. New York: Scribner (Edinburgh: Clark). 2 vols, 1906-08. (Now superseded by *The interpreter's dictionary of the Bible*).

*Dictionary of the Bible*. Ed F.C. Grant & H.H. Rowley. New York: Scribner, 1963. 1,059p.

*Dictionary of the Bible*. J. Hastings. Edinburgh: Clark (New York: Scribner). 5 vols, 1898-1904.

*Dictionnaire de la Bible*. Ed F.G. Vigouroux & L. Pirot. Paris: Letouzey. 5 vols, 1895-1912. *Supplément*, ed L. Pirot el al. Vols 1-8 (letters A-P), 1928-74; in progress. (Standard French Catholic Bible dictionary).

*Elenchus bibliographicus biblicus*. P. Nober. Roma: Biblical Institute, 1970. Annual.

*Eleven years of Bible bibliography: the book lists of the Society for Old Testament Study, 1946-56*. Ed H.H. Rowley. Indian Hill, Colorado: Falcon's Wing Press, 1957. 804p. (Classified annotated lists of books in various languages).

*Encyclopaedia biblica*. Jerusalem: Hebrew University. Vols 1-3, 1950-58; in progress.

*Encyclopedia of Biblical interpretation: a millenial anthology*. M.M. Kasher. Ed H. Freedman. New York: American Biblical Encyclopedia Society. Vols 1-5, 1953-62; in progress. (Jewish interpretations of the Bible from Talmudic-Midrashic literature).

*Encyclopaedia of Biblical theology*. J.B. Bauer. London: Sheed & Ward. 3 vols, 1970. (Translation from 1959 *Bibeltheologisches Wörterbuch*).

*Encyclopedic dictionary of the Bible*. Ed L.F. Hartman. New York: McGraw-Hill, 1963. 2,600p.

*Etudes bibliques*. Ecole Biblique, Jerusalem. Paris: Lethielleux, forthcoming. (Full-length commentaries on books of Bible).

*Exhaustive concordance of the Bible*. J. Strong. London: Hodder (New York: Hunt), 1894 (Abingdon, (1963). 1,807p. (Every word of KJ(AV), RV Bibles).

*Historical catalogue of printed editions of the English Bible, 1525–1961*. A.S. Herbert. London: BFBS, 1968. (Lists 2,524 distinct editions of the Bible or parts of it).

*Index of articles on the New Testament and the early church*. B.M. Metzger. Philadelphia: Society of Biblical Literature, 1951. 182p. (Index to 2,350 articles).

*International critical commentary on the Holy Scriptures*. A critical and exegetical commentary. Ed S.R. Driver, A. Plummer & C.A. Briggs. Edinburgh: Clark (New York: Scribner). 45 vols, 1896-1937.

*International standard Bible encyclopedia*. Ed J. Orr. Chicago: Howard-Severance. 5 vols, 1930 (Eerdmans, 1960).

*Internationale Zeitschriftenschau für Bibelwissenschaft und Grenzgebiete*. Stuttgart: Verlag Katholisches Bibelwerk. Biennial since 1952 (Düsseldorf: Patmos, 1970). (Mostly German abstracts).

*Konkordanz zum hebräischen Alten Testament*. G. Lisowsky. Stuttgart: Privilegierte Württembergische Bibelanstalt, 1958. 1,672p.

*Kritisch-Exegetischer Kommentar über das Neue Testament*. Founded by H.A.W. Meyer. Göttingen: Vandenhoeck & Ruprecht, 1839- ; in progress.

*La concordance de la Bible: concordantia polyglotta*. Turnhout (Belgium): Brepols. 5 vols, 1980. (First complete Bible concordance in French with Hebrew, Greek, Latin and English parallels).

*Moffatt New Testament commentary*. Ed J. Moffatt. New York: Harper (London: Hodder & Stoughton). 17 vols, 1927-50.

*Modern New Testament concordance*. Ed M. Darton. London: Darton, Longman & Todd, 1976. (Words and 341 themes, for all modern English versions).

*Nelson's complete concordance of the Revised Standard Version*. Ed J.W. Ellison. New York: Thomas Nelson & Sons, 1957.

*New international dictionary of New Testament theology*. Ed C. Brown. London: Paternoster. Vol 1 (A-F), 1975; in progress to 3 vols. (Thematic grouping of words).

*New Testament abstracts*. Issued 3 times a year by Theological Faculty, Weston College, Weston, Massachusetts. Vol 1 (1956). (Abstracts in English from articles in many languages).

*New Testament tools and studies*. Ed B.M. Metzger. Leiden: E.J. Brill, 1966-80. Vol I: *Index to periodical literature on the Apostle Paul*. Vol VI: *Index to periodical literature on Christ and the Gospels*. (10,090 entries). Vol VII: *A classified bibliography of literature on the Acts of the Apostles* (6,645 books and articles). Vol X: *Philological, versional and patristic*.

*Table pastorale de la Bible*. Ed G. Passelecq & F. Poswick. Paris: Lethielleux, 1974. 1,214p. (Over 9,000 articles on words and themes, produced by computer).

*The Cambridge history of the Bible*. Ed P.R. Ackroyd et al. Cambridge: Cambridge University Press. 3 vols, 1963-70.

*The computer Bible*. Ed J.A. Baird & D.N. Freedman. Wooster, OH: Biblical Research Associates. Vols I-XV, 1975-78. (Word frequencies, concordances, indexes, using KWIC. Computerization to make immediately available massive amounts of critical data).

*The early versions of the New Testament*. B.M. Metzger. Oxford: Oxford University Press, 1977. (Origin, transmission, manuscripts, printed editions, for all versions up to AD 1000).

*The interpreter's Bible*. Ed G.A. Buttrick. New York, Nashville: Abingdon. 12 vols, 1951-57. (AV and RSV text, exegesis, exposition, on whole Bible).

*The interpreter's dictionary of the Bible: an illustrated encyclopedia*. Ed G.A. Buttrick. New York, Nashville: Abingdon. 4 vols, 1962. Supplementary volume, 1976 (998p.).

*Theological dictionary of the New Testament*. G. Kittel (ed & trans. G.W. Bromiley). Grand Rapids, Michigan: Eerdmans. 9 vols, 1963-74. (Translation of TWNT).

*Theologisches Wörterbuch zum Alten Testament* (TWAT). Ed G.J. Botterweck & H. Ringgren. Stuttgart: Kohlhammer, 1970- ; in progress to 4 vols. English edition (Eerdmans), Vol 1, 1974; in progress (to 12 vols).

*Theologisches Wörterbuch zum Neuen Testament* (TWNT). Ed G. Kittel, G. Friedrich et al. Stuttgart: Kohlhammer. Vols I-VIII, 1932-72; IX, forthcoming.

### 3. CHURCH HISTORY

*A Baptist bibliography*. E.C. Starr. Rochester, NY: American Baptist Historical Society. Vols 1-20, 1947-74 (letters A-R); in progress. (67,000 entries).

*Acta sanctorum quotquot toto orbe coluntur*. Paris: Palmé. 85 vols, 1863-1940. (The indispensable research work on the lives of the saints).

*Analecta Bollandiana*. Bruxelles: Société des Bollandistes (Paris: Picard). Quarterly: Vol 1(1882)- . (Current bibliography on lives of the saints).

*Ancient Christian writers: the works of the Fathers in translation*. Ed J. Quasten & W.J. Burghardt. London: Longmans, Green. 31 vols, 1946-63.

*Ante-Nicene Fathers: translations of the writings of the Fathers down to AD 325*. Ed A. Roberts & J. Donaldson. New York: Christian Literature Co. 10 vols, 1896-97 (reprint Eerdmans, 1956).

*Archiv für Reformationsgeschichte*. Vols 1-62 (1903-71); in progress.

*Atlas of the early Christian world*. F. van der Meer & C. Mohrmann. London: Nelson, 1958. 215p. (620 plates, 42 maps; first 6 centuries AD).

*Bibliographia Calviniana, 1532-1899*. D.A. Erichson. Nieuwkoop: De Graaf, 1950.

*Bibliographia Patristica*. W. Schneemelcher. Berlin: W. de Gruyter. 10 vols, 1959-65.

*Bibliographie de cartographie ecclésiastique*. Ed J.N.B. van den Brink et al. Commission International d'Histoire Ecclésiastique Comparée, CISH. Leiden: Brill. Vols 1-2, 1968-71; in progress.

*Bibliographie de la Réforme, 1450-1648*. Ed J.N.B. van den Brink et al. CISH. Leiden: Brill. 7 vols, 1958-70. (Covers 17 European countries plus USA).

*Bibliotheca Sanctorum* (Enciclopedia dei Santi). Roma: Città Nuova. 12 vols.

*Calvin-Bibliographie, 1901-1959*. W. Niesel. München: C. Kaiser, 1961. (Continuation of *Bibliographia Calviniana*).

*Catholicisme hier, aujourd'hui, demain* (encyclopédie). Ed Jacquemet & Mathon (Faculté Catholique de Lille). Paris: Letouzey. Vols 1-6 (letters A-L), 1928- ; in progress.

*Dictionary of Catholic biography*. J.J. Delaney & J.E. Tobin. Garden City, New York: Doubleday, 1961. 1,245p. (Biographies of 15,000 Catholics from beginning to 1961).

*Dictionary of Christian biography and literature to the end of the 6th century AD*. H. Wace & W.C. Piercy. London: Murray (Boston: Little), 1911. 1,028p. (Revised and abridged version of the following item).

*Dictionary of Christian biography, literature, sects, and doctrines*. Sir William Smith & H. Wace. London: Murray (Boston: Little). 4 vols, 1877-87. (Especially English, Scottish and Irish church history; subjects to the end of the 8th century AD).

*Dictionary of the Apostolic church*. J. Hastings. New York: Scribner (Edinburgh: Clark). 2 vols, 1916. (Now superseded by *Oxford dictionary of the Christian Church*).

*Dictionnaire des ordres religieux*. P. Hélyot. Paris: Migne. 4 vols, 1859-63.

*Dictionnaire d'histoire et de géographie ecclésiastiques*. Begun under A. Baudrillart; now R. Aubert & E. Van Cauwenbergh. Paris: Letouzey. Vols 1-17 (letters A-F), 1912- ; in progress.

*Dieux d'Hommes: dictionnaire des messianismes et millénarismes*

*de l'ère chrétienne*. H. Desroche. Paris: Mouton, 1969. 281p.
*Documents illustrative of the history of the church*. B.J. Kidd. London: SPCK (New York: Macmillan). 3 vols, 1920-41. (From apostolic times to AD 1500).
*Histoire de l'Eglise depuis les origines jusqu'a nos jours*. Ed J.B. Duroselle & E. Jarry. Paris: Bloud & Gay. Vols 1-14, 1948-63; in progress to 26 vols.
*History of the Christian church*. P. Schaff. New York: Scribner. 7 vols, 1889-1910.
*Nouvelle histoire de l'Eglise*. Ed L.J. Rogier, R. Aubert & M.D. Knowles. Paris: Le Seuil. 5 vols, 1963-74.
*Ostkirchliche Studien* (quarterly since 1952, Augustinus-Verlag, Würzburg). (The best bibliographical source on the Eastern churches, with about 90 pages of bibliography each year).
*Oxford dictionary of the Christian church*. Ed F.L. Cross. London: Oxford University Press, 1957. 1,492p. 2nd edition, 1974. 1,552p.
*Patrologiae cursus completus, seu bibliotheca universalis*: J.P. Migne. Paris: Migne. 221 vols, 1844-80. (Latin and Greek fathers).
*Reallexikon für Antike und Christentum*. Ed T. Klauser. Stuttgart: Hiersemann. Vols 1-7, 1950-69; in progress. (The relationship of the ancient world to Christianity up to the 6th century AD).
(Religious and ethical encyclopedia). *Thriskeutiki kai Ithiki Egyklopaidia*. Athens: A. Martinos. 12 vols, 1962-68. (Greece and Greek Orthodoxy).
*Revue d'histoire ecclésiastique*. Louvain-la-Neuve: Université Catholique de Louvain. Vols 1-67, 1900-72; in progress.
*Select library of Nicene and post-Nicene Fathers of the Christian church*. Ed P. Schaff. New York: Christian Literature Co. 28 vols, 1886-1900.
*The history of the popes, from the close of the Middle Ages*. L. Pastor (translated from the German by F.I. Anthrobus et al). London: Hodges. 40 vols, 1891-1953. (Covers the period 1305-1799).
*The new international dictionary of the Christian Church*. Ed J.D. Douglas. Exeter: Paternoster Press, 1974. 1,074p. Revised edition 1978. 1,200p. (5,000 articles).

### 4. ECUMENISM

*A history of the ecumenical movement, 1517-1948*. Vol 1. R. Rouse & S.C. Neill. London: SPCK (Philadelphia: Westminster), 1954. 822p.
(Bibliography of the Ecumenical Movement) *Bibliografia tes Oikoumenikes Kineseos, 1960-1970*. V.T. Istavridis. Athens: Theologia, 1972. 78p. (Orthodoxy and ecumenism; 1,500 titles).
*Classified catalog of the Ecumenical Movement, World Council of Churches, Geneva*. Boston: G.K. Hall. 2 vols, 1972. (20,300 entries, 967 pages).
*Commentary of the documents of Vatican II*. Ed H. Vorgrimler. New York: Herder & Herder. 5 vols, 1967-72.
*Documents on Christian unity*. G.K.A. Bell. London, New York: Oxford University Press. 4 vols, 1929-58. (Illustrates the growth of the world ecumenical movement).
*Ecumenical terminology*. Geneva: World Council of Churches, 1975. 564p. (4 languages, 1,335 words, titles, &c).
*Ecumenism around the world: a directory of ecumenical institutes, centers and organizations*. Roma: Centro pro Unione (Friars of the Atonement), n.d. (1971); 211p. 2nd edition, 1974; 169p.
*Internationale Ökumenische Bibliographie/International Ecumenical Bibliography/Bibliographie Oecuménique Internationale/Bibliografia Ecuménica Internacional*. Ed C. Graves et al. München: Chr Kaiser Verlag. Vols 1-10, 1962-75; in progress. (In English, French, German and Spanish. 55,000 titles, over half articles, on the contemporary dialogue between churches and with other religions).
*Oecumene* 1 (1977) and 2 (1978). Strasbourg: CERDIC, 1977-78. (Ecumenical bibliography; abstracts of over 1,000 journals).
'Selective bibliography of significant current ecumenical books and pamphlets', *The Ecumenical Review* (Geneva). Quarterly.
*The ecumenical advance: a history of the ecumenical movement*. Vol 2, *1948-1968*. Ed H.E. Fey. London: SPCK, 1970. 524p.

### 5. MISSIOLOGY

*A history of the expansion of Christianity*. K.S. Latourette. New York: Harper. 7 vols, 1937-45.
*Ateismo e dialogo: bolletino del Segretariato per i Non-Credenti*, Roma. Vols I-X, 1966-75; in progress. (Christian dialogue with atheism and Marxism.)
*Atlas du monde chrétien: l'expansion du Christianisme à travers les siècles*. A. Freitag et al. Paris, Bruxelles: Elsevier, 1959. 215p. (Maps and photographs).
*Bibliografia missionaria*. Roma: Pontificia Università di Propaganda Fide. Vols 1-37, 1935-74; in progress. (Annual review of previous year's literature; until 1971, some overlap with *Bibliotheca missionum*, but has now superseded it for current literature).
*Bibliography on world mission and evangelism*. At end of all issues of *International review of mission(s)*, 1912-78; in progress.
*Bibliotheca missionum*. R. Streit. Freiburg: Herder. 28 vols, 1916-71. (The major complete and retrospective Catholic bibliography of missions; discontinued 1971).
*Concise dictionary of the Christian world mission*. Ed S.C. Neill et al. London: Lutterworth, 1970. 682p.
*Critical bibliography of missiology*. L. Vriens. Nijmegen: VSKB Publ, 1960.
*Dictionary catalog of the Missionary Research Library, New York*. Boston: G.K. Hall. 17 vols, 1967. (273,000 entries, 13,039 pages).
*Histoire universelle des missions catholiques*. S. Delacroix. Paris: Librairie Grund. 4 vols, 1956-58. (Profuse illustrations and maps).
*International review of missions: index 1912-1966*. O.G. Myklebust. Geneva: IRM, 1968. (Bibliography of 1,900 articles).
*Sacrae Congregationis de Propaganda Fide Memoria Rerum*. Ed J. Metzler et al. Freiburg: Herder. 3 vols, 1972-76. 4,500p. (History of Catholic missions, 1622-1972).
*Studies in missions: an index of theses on missions*. Monrovia, CA: MARC, 1974. 73p. (200 theses and dissertations).
*The Christian-Marxist dialogue: an annotated bibliography, 1959-1969*. A.J. van der Bent. Geneva: World Council of Churches, 1969. 90p. (1,200 titles in 5 languages).
*The twentieth century atlas of the Christian world: the expansion of Christianity through the centuries*. A. Freitag. New York: Hawthorn, 1964. 199p. (Catholic pictorial atlas. French edition 1959, listed above).
*Wichtige Daten der Missionsgeschichte*. T. Ohm. Münster: Aschendorffsche Verlagsbuchhandlung, 1956. (French: *Les principaux faits de l'histoire des missions*, 1961. 162p).

### 6. SPIRITUALITY, LITURGY, MUSIC, THE ARTS

*A dictionary of hymnology*. Ed J. Julian. 1st edition 1907. New York: Dover. 2 vols, 1957.
*A dictionary of liturgy and worship*. Ed J.G. Davies. London: SCM, 1972. 385p.
*Bibliographia internationalis spiritualitatis*. Rome: Pontifical Institute of Spirituality. 3 vols, 1966-68. (6,487 titles in Vol 3).
*Dictionnaire de spiritualité, ascétique et mystique, doctrine et histoire*. Ed M. Viller. Paris: Beauchesne. Vols 1-7, 1937-71; in progress.
*Dictionnaire des églises de France, Belgique, Luxembourg, Suisse*. Ed J. Brosse et al. Paris: Robert Laffont. 5 vols, 1971. (History and architecture of church buildings).
*Dictionnaire d'archéologie chrétienne et de liturgie*. Ed F. Cabrol, H.Leclerq & H. Marrou. Paris: Letouzey. 15 vols, 1907-53.
*Encyclopédie des musiques sacrées*. Ed J. Porte. Tours (France): Labergerie-Mame. 4 vols, 1968-71 (Vol 4 consists of records).
*Iconography of Christian art*. G. Schiller. New York: NY Graphic Society, 1971. 2 vols. (3 vols in German edition).
*Lexikon der Christlichen Ikonographie*. Ed E. Kirschbaum et al. Freiburg im Breisgau: Herder. Vols 1-7, 1968-74; in progress.
*Repertorium hymnologicum*. Catalogue des chants, hymnes, proses, séquences, tropes en usage dans l'église latine depuis les origines jusqu'à nos jours. C.U.J. Chevalier. Louvain, Bruxelles: Société des Bollandistes. 6 vols, 1892-1920.

### 7. THEOLOGY

*A dictionary of Christian ethics*. J. Macquarrie. London: SCM, 1967. 366p.
*A theological book list*. London: Theological Education Fund, 1960, 1965, 1968. (Comprehensive bibliographies on all subjects, with emphasis on works available for seminaries in developing countries; 3,000 entries).
*Archiv für Katholisches Kirchenrecht*. Deutschland, Österreich, Schweiz. 121 vols, 1857-1941. Reprinted Leiden: E.J. Brill, 1973-75.
*Bilanz der Theologie im 20 Jahrhundert*. Ed H. Vorgrimler & R. Van der Gucht. Freiburg im Breisgau: Herder. 3 vols, 1970.
*Bulletin de théologie ancienne et médiévale*. Louvain: Abbey Mont César. In progress.
*Church dogmatics*. Karl Barth (translated by G.T. Thomson from *Die kirchliche Dogmatik*, 1932-59). Edinburgh: Clark. 13 vols in 4 parts, 1936-
*Concilium Vaticanum II: concordance, index verborum, liste de fréquence, tables comparatives*. Ed P. Delhaye, M. Gueret & P. Tombeur. Leuven: CETEDOC, 1974. 978p.
*Dictionnaire de théologie catholique*. Begun by Vacant & Mangenot, now E. Amann. Paris: Letouzey. 15 vols, 1909-50. Completed by *Tables générales du Dictionnaire de théologie catholique*. Ed B. Loth & A. Michel. Paris: Letouzey. 3 vols, 1951-72.
*Encyklopädie der katholischen Theologie und ihrer Hülfswissenschaften*. H.J. Wetzer. Ed F. Kaulen. Freiburg im Breisgau: Herder. 12 vols and index, 1882-1901.
*Evangelisches Kirchenlexikon: kirchlich-theologisches Handwörterbuch*. Ed H. Brunotte & O. Weber. Göttingen: Vandenhoeck & Ruprecht. 4 vols, 1955-61.
*Handbuch der Pastoraltheologie*. Ed F.X. Arnold, K. Rahner, et al. Freiburg im Breisgau: Herder. 6 vols, 1964-72.
*Institutes of the Christian religion*. Jean Calvin. H. Beveridge, 1845 (reissued 1949), 2 vols.
*Kleines Theologisches Wörterbuch*. K. Rahner & H. Vorgrimler. Freiburg im Breisgau: Herder, 1961 (7th ed 1969). (French edition 508p.)
*Lexikon für Theologie und Kirche*. Ed J. Höfer & K. Rahner. Freiburg: Herder. 10 vols, 1957-65; and 3 vols on Vatican Council plus index (1967).
*Luther's works*. Ed J. Pelikan & H.T. Lehmann. Philadelphia: Muhlenberg. Also St Louis, MO: Concordia. 56 vols, 1971-77.
*Mysterium salutis*. Dogmatique catholique de l'histoire du salut. Ed J. Feiner & M. Löhrer. Paris: Le Cerf. Vols 1-12, 1969- ; in progress to 16 vols.
*Pastorale bibliografia internazionale*. T. Stramare. Roma: Pontificia Università Lateranense, 1969. (Over 5,000 entries).
*Realencyklopädie für protestantische Theologie und Kirche*. J.J. Herzog. Leipzig, Hinrichs: Albert Hauck. 24 vols, 1896-1913.
*Religious and theological abstracts*. Meyerstown, PA. Vols 1-10, 1958-67; in progress.
*Sacramentum mundi: an encyclopedia of theology*. Ed K. Rahner et al. London: Burns, Oates. 6 vols, 1968-70.
*Systematic theology*. Paul Tillich. University of Chicago. 3 vols, 1951-63.
*The complete works of John Wesley*. Ed T. Jackson. Nashville: Abingdon. 15 vols, 1856-62.
*The creeds of Christendom: with a history and critical notes*. New York, London: Harper. 3 vols, 6th edition revised, 1919.
*The library of Christian classics*. Ed J. Baillie, J.T. McNeil & H.P. Van Dusen. London: SCM ((Philadelphia: Westminster). 26 vols, 1954-57. (A selection of the most indispensable Christian treatises written before AD 1600).
*The Summa Theologica of St Thomas Aquinas*. London: Burns, Oates & Washbourne. Vols 1-32, 1964-72; in progress.
*Theologische Realenzyklopädie* (TRE). Ed G. Fohrer et al. Berlin: Imendörffer, 1973; in progress to 25 vols.

### 8. PERIODICALS, LITERATURE AND GENERAL

*Catholic periodical and literature index*. Haverford, PA: Catholic Library Association. Vols 1-17, 1930-72; in progress.
*Christian periodical index*. Buffalo, NY: Christian Librarians' Fellowship. Quarterly. (Covers a relatively small but important number of conservative Protestant periodicals from 1956 to the present).
*Das Evangelische Schrifttum*. Gesamtausgabe 1975. Stuttgart: Vereinigung Evangelischer Buchhändler. 448p. (Protestant literature: 9,760 titles).
*Das Katholische Schrifttum*. Gesamtausgabe 1975. Stuttgart: Verband Katholischer Verleger & Buchhändler. 288p. (Catholic literature: 5,760 titles).
*Guide to atlases: world, regional, national, thematic*. G.L. Alexander. Metuchen, NJ: Scarecrow Press, 1971. (Listing of atlases published since 1950. 54 are listed under 'Bible and Christian history').
*Guide to Catholic literature, 1888-1940*. Detroit: Romig, 1940. 1,240p. Vol 2, 1940; from 1945, annually.
*Guide to religious periodicals*. (Provides an index to many denominational publications, mostly American, after 1964).
*Handbuch der Religionspädagogik*. Ed E. Feifel. 3 vols, 1973-75.
*Irregular serials and annuals: an international directory*. Ed E. Koltay. New York: R.R. Bowker. 1st edition 1967. (350 items on religion out of 14,500).
*Katholische Zeitungen und Zeitschriften*, in Streit-Dindinger, *Bibliotheca missionum* (Africa, vol XX, p.716-742; India, vol XXVIII, p.484-506; China, vol XIV, p.378-408; Oceania, vol XXI, p.711-717).
'Religion', in *Guide to reference books*, 9th Edition, E.P. Sheehy (Chicago: American Library Association, 1976), p. 252-283. (Details of 410 dictionaries, encyclopedias, directories, manuals, in English and other languages; 322 being on Christianity).
*Religious books and serials in print, 1978-79*. New York: R R. Bowker, 1978 (1st Edition). 1,259 p. (Over 47,400 entries for titles available from 1,700 publishers, under 4,600 subject headings; classified by subject, author, title).
*Religious books in print, 1974*. Religious Book Publishers Group. London: Whitaker, 1975. (Nearly 10,000 titles under 18 headings).
*RIC: Répertoire bibliographique des institutions chrétiennes*. Ed R. Metz & J. Schlick. Strasbourg: Centre de Recherche et Documentation des Institutions Chrétiennes (CERDIC). Annual since 1968. (Computer-produced indexes of Christian publications during the year; in 5 languages. 6,400 entries a year, increasing). Also RIC supplément, *Bibliographies thématiques* (several each year, each on a single theme).
*Schaff-Herzog encyclopedia*. Ed S.M. Jackson. New York: Funk & Wagnalls. 12 vols and index, 1908-12.
*Seventh-day Adventist (SDA) periodical index*. Loma Linda University Libraries, Riverside, CA (USA). 1971- ; in progress. (4,000 articles, book reviews, editorials, etc, from over 40 SDA periodicals).
*Shelf list of the Union Theological Seminary Library, New York*. Boston: G.K. Hall. 10 vols, 1960. (Worlds' largest theological library, now with 500,000 volumes; 203,000 entries, 9,685 pages).
*The dictionary of religious terms*. D.T. Kauffman. London: Marshall, Morgan & Scott, 1967. 445p. (11,000 definitions).
'Theology and religion', in M.M. Reynolds, *A guide to theses and dissertations: an annotated, international bibliography of bibliographies* (Detroit, MI: Gale Research Company, 1975), p.499-511. (54 out of 2,200 bibliographies).

## THE NON-CHRISTIAN RELIGIOUS CONTEXT

*A classical dictionary of Hindu mythology and religion, geography, history, and literature*. J. Dowson. First edition 1879. 8th edition, London: Routledge and Kegan Paul, 1953. 411p.
*A dictionary of comparative religion*. Ed S.G.F. Brandon. London: Weidenfeld & Nicolson, 1970.
*Annuaire du monde musulman*. L. Massignon. Paris: Presses Universitaires de France, 1954 (4th edition). 428p.
*Bibliographie bouddhique*. Paris: Librairie d'Amérique et d'Orient. Fasc. 1-31, 1930-61; annual.
*Bibliography on Buddhism*. S. Hanayama. Tokyo: Hokuseido Press, 1961. 869p. (15,073 numbered entries).
*Der Ursprung der Gottesidee* (The origin of the idea of God). W. Schmidt. Münster: Bornemann. 12 vols, 1926-55.
*Dictionary of comparative religion: the first comprehensive one-volume guide to the religions of the world*. Ed S.G.F. Brandon. New York: Charles Scribner's Sons, 1970. 704p.
*Dictionary of mythology, folklore and symbols*. G. Jobes. New York: Scarecrow Press, 1962. 3 parts.
*Dictionary of pagan religions*. H.E. Wedeck & W. Baskin. New York: Philosophical Library, 1971. 363p.
(Dictionary of scientific atheism) *Nauchno-ateisticheskу slovar*. Moscow: Nauka. (Standard Marxist dictionary).
*Die Religion in Geschichte und Gegenwart: Handwörterbuch für Theologie und Religionswissenschaft*. Ed K. Galling. Tübingen: J.C.B. Mohr, 3rd edition. 6 vols, 1956-62.
*Encyclopaedia Judaica: das Judentum in Geschichte und Gegenwart*. Berlin: Verlag Eschkol. 10 vols, c1928-34.
*Encyclopaedia of Buddhism*. Ed G.P. Malalasekera. Colombo: Government Press. Fasc. 1-2, 1961-63; in progress.
*Encyclopaedia of Islam*. Ed H.A.R. Gibb et al. New edition (Ed C.E. Bosworth et al). Leiden: Brill. Vols 1-3, 1954-71; in progress to 10 vols.
*Encyclopaedia of religion and ethics*. Ed J. Hastings. Edinburgh: Clark (New York: Scribner). 12 vols, 1908-27.
*Encyclopaedia of religion and religions*. E.R. Pike. London: George Allen & Unwin, 1951. 406p.
*Encyclopedia Judaica*. Ed C. Roth & G. Wigoder. Jerusalem: Keter Publishing House. 16 vols, 1972.
*Encyclopedia of Sikhism*. Ed H. Singh. Patiala (India): Punjabi University, forthcoming.
(Handbook of atheism) *Nastol'naja kniga ateista*. Moscow: Isdatelstvo Politiceskoi Literatur, 1968 (512p), 1971 (470p). (Survey of religion and atheism throughout the world).
*Histoire des religions*. Ed H.-C. Puech. Paris: Gallimard. 2 vols, 1970, 1972. 1,488p, 1,596p.
*Iconography of religions*. Ed T.P. Van Baaren, F. Leemhuis & Leertouwer. Leiden: E.J. Brill. Vols 1-24, 1973- ; in progress.
*International bibliography of the history of religions*. Leiden: E.J. Brill. Vols 1-18, 1954-73; in progress, annual. (Vol 15: 3,000 entries).
*Jewish encyclopedia*. Ed C. Adler et al. New York: Funk & Wagnalls. 12 vols, 1901-06. Revised edition: Ed I. Singer, New York: Katy Publishers. 12 vols, 1964.
*L'ateismo contemporeano*. Ed G. Girardi. Torino (Italy): SEI. 5 vols, 1967-70. (Spanish *El ateísmo contemporáneo*, 5 vols; French *L'athéisme dans la vie et la culture contemporaines*, 2 vols, incomplete).
'Marxist analysis and sociology of religions: an outline of international bibliography up to 1975', O. Maduro, *Social compass*, XXII, 3-4 (1975), 401-479. (1,215 books, 730 articles, in 7 Western languages).
*Muslim peoples: a world ethnographic survey*. Ed R.V. Weekes. Westport, CN: Greenwood Press, 1978. 547p.
*Religions, mythologies, folklores: an annotated bibliography*. K.S. Diehl. 2nd edition. New York: Scarecrow, 1962. 573p. (2,388 entries).
*The encyclopedia of witchcraft and demonology*. R.H. Robbins. New York: Crown, 1959. 571p.
*The golden bough: a study in magic and religion*. J.G. Frazer. 12 vols, 1890-1915. (Particularly detailed on animism and tribal religions).
*The sacred books of the East*. Ed F. Max Müller. Oxford: Clarendon Press. 50 vols, 1879-1910. (Includes the major books of the Vedic-Brahmanic system, Buddhism, Jainism, Islam, Confucianism, Taoism and the Parsi religion).
*Twentieth century encyclopedia of religious knowledge*. Ed L.A. Loetscher. Grand Rapids, Michigan: Baker Book House. 2 vols, 1955.
*World Communism: a handbook 1918-1965*. Ed W.S. Sworakowski. Stanford, California: Hoover Institution Press, 1973. 576p.
*World strength of the Communist Party organizations*. 30th annual report. Washington, DC: Bureau of Intelligence and Research, US Department of State, 1976. (Statistics and history for all countries).

## THE SCIENTIFIC STUDY OF RELIGION

### 1. PHILOSOPHY OF RELIGION

*Catalog of the Hoose Library of Philosophy, University of Southern California (Los Angeles)*. Boston: G.K. Hall. 6 vols, 1968. (96,000 entries, 4,577 pages).
*Encyclopedia of philosophy*. Ed P. Edwards. London: Collier-Macmillan. 4 vols, 1972.
*Philosophy in the 20th century: Catholic and Christian*. G. McLean.

Vol I: An annotated bibliography of philosophy in Catholic thought, 1900-64. Vol II: A bibliography of Christian philosophy and contemporary issues. New York: Frederick Ungar, 1967.

(Questions of scientific atheism) *Voprosy nauchnogo ateizma.* Moscow: Mysl. Vols 1-17, 1966-75; in progress.

*Répertoire bibliographique de la philosophie.* Louvain: Editions de l'Institut Supérieure de Philosophie. Vols 1-22, 1948-70; in progress.

## 2. PSYCHOLOGY OF RELIGION

*Annotated bibliography in religion and psychology.* W.W. Meissner. Academy of Religion and Health, 1961.

*Encyclopedia of psychology.* Ed H.J. Eysenck, W. Arnold & R. Meili. London: Search Press. 3 vols, 1972. ('Religion', p.136-144).

*The collected works of C.G. Jung.* Ed H. Read, M. Fordham, G. Adler, et al. Princeton University Press (Bollingen Series). Vols 1-17, 1953-72; in progress. Vol 11: *Psychology and religion: east and west* (1958).

*The handbook of social psychology.* Ed G. Lindzey & E. Aronson. 2nd edition. Reading, MA: Addison-Wesley. 5 vols, 1968-69. (Psychology of religion: V.602-659).

## 3. SOCIOLOGY OF RELIGION

(Atlas of the peoples of the world) *Atlas narodov mira.* Moscow: Akademii Nauk SSSR, 1964. 184p. (Not concerned with religion, but its ethnic maps locate ethnic minorities of religious importance).

*International bibliography of sociology of religion,* in *Social compass* (International review of socio-religious studies), Louvain, 1958-72; in progress.

*International encyclopedia of the social sciences.* Ed D.L. Sills. New York: Collier-Macmillan. 17 vols, 1968 (1972 reprinted in 8 vols).

*Social scientific studies of religion.* M.I. Berkowitz & J. Johnson. Pittsburgh: University of Pittsburgh Press, 1967.

*Sociology of Christianity: an international bibliography.* Ed H. Carrier & E. Pin. Rome: Gregorian University Press, 1964. 313p.

*Tables signalétiques, Archives de sociologie des religions* (now *Archives des sciences sociales des religions*). Paris: CNRS, 1972. 300p. (Reviews and abstracts of journal from 1956-70).

## 4. PERIODICALS, LITERATURE AND GENERAL

*A bibliography of bibliographies in religion.* J.G. Barrow. Dissertation, Yale University, 1930. Ann Arbor, Michigan: Edwards Bros, 5th edition 1955. 489p. (1,945 titles with short evaluations).

*A bibliography of modern African religious movements.* R.C. Mitchell & H.W. Turner. Evanston: Northwestern University Press, 1966. 132p. (1,300 items; updated annually in *Journal of religion in Africa*).

*Bibliography of new religious movements in primal societies.* H.W. Turner. Boston, MA: G.K. Hall. Vol 1, Black Africa, 1977 (278p, 1,900 entries); Vol 2, North America (280p); Vols. 3-4, Latin America & Caribbean, Asia with Oceania.

*Bulletin signalétique: sciences religieuses.* Paris: Centre de Documentation Sciences Humaines. Vols 1-28, 1947-74; in progress. (8,000 periodical article abstracts a year).

*Concise dictionary of religious quotations.* Ed W. Neill. London: Mowbray, 1975. 224p. (2,500 quotations by topic; Christian, Muslim, Hindu, et alia).

*Dissertation Abstracts International:* (1) *Comprehensive dissertation index, 1861-1975,* on all subjects, and (2) *Datrix II* computer retrieval system, by keywords in title, of over 500,000 North American and European university doctoral dissertations (300,000 on humanities and social sciences; about 8,000 on religion and Christianity; 950 with 'Catholic' in title, 490 with 'Protestant', 1,160 with 'Christian', 1,780 with 'church', 490 with 'God', 1,200 with 'theology' or 'theological', 2,400 with 'religion' or 'religious', etc). Annual and monthly editions and supplements, in volumes, printout or microfiche.

*Encyclopédie des sciences religieuses.* (A major French Catholic collection composed of 6 series).

'Religion', in *Guide to reference books,* E.P. Sheehy (Chicago: American Library Association, 1976; 9th edition), p.252-283. (410 dictionaries, encyclopedias, directories etc; 322 on Christianity).

*Religion index One: periodicals* (formerly *Index to religious periodical literature*), and *Religion index Two: multi-author works* (essays, conferences, etc). Ed G.F. Dickerson. Chicago: American Theological Library Association. 12 vols, 1949-77. (Vol 9, 1969-70, comprised 227p plus 75p of book reviews; since 1975, all articles are abstracted).

'Religions and theology' in *Ulrich's international periodicals directory,* Vol II (New York, London: R.R. Bowker, 14th edition, 1971), p.873-902. (Of the 35,000 periodicals currently published throughout the world, 1,000 deal with religion and theology).

*Religious books and serials in print, 1978-79.* New York: R.R. Bowker, 1978: 1st edition. 1,259p. (Classification by subject, author, title; over 47,400 entries for titles available from 1,700 publishers; 4,600 subject headings).

*The world treasury of religious quotations.* Ed R.L. Woods. New York: Hawthorn Books, 1966. (15,000 quotations, arranged by subject).

*World guide to libraries/Internationales Bibliotheks-Handbuch.* 4th edition. New York: R.R. Bowker. 2 vols, 1974. (Survey of 36,932 libraries in 157 countries, each with over 30,000 volumes; total religious and theological libraries, 2,100).

PART 11

# ATLAS

Atlas of Christianity and evangelization
in the modern world

*The light of Christ illuminates the whole world.*
　　　　　　　　　　　—Liturgy of the Presanctified, Byzantine Rite, AD 692.

## CONTENTS OF PART 11

This atlas is divided into 2 sections: a 4-page part with 8 religious maps, and a 16-page part with 18 secular maps.

### A. Global Christianity and world evangelization

The data on which Global Maps 1–8 are based come from Tables 1 and 2 in Part 7, and from Global Tables 1–31 in Parts 1 and 8. Taken in conjunction with Maps 1–18 below, they contribute to the subject known as the geography of religion, and in particular the geography of Christianity. Note that the Global Maps are meant to illustrate only the subjects in the titles; to keep them uncluttered, no names of countries are added. For these, the reader should consult Maps 1–18. Note also that the unit used on these maps is the country —every country is given a single colour in each map, corresponding to its value of the variable being depicted.

### B. The modern world: human environment and activity

The 18 maps in this section describe the modern world which forms the context for global Christianity. They are arranged not geographically but chronologically, in approximately the order of the worldwide expansion of Christianity by continents and regions, beginning with the cradle region of the Middle East. In the listing below, after each region a typical or representative country is named for illustrative purposes, followed by the date of the definitive coming of Christianity (as documented here in Part 2, Chronology).

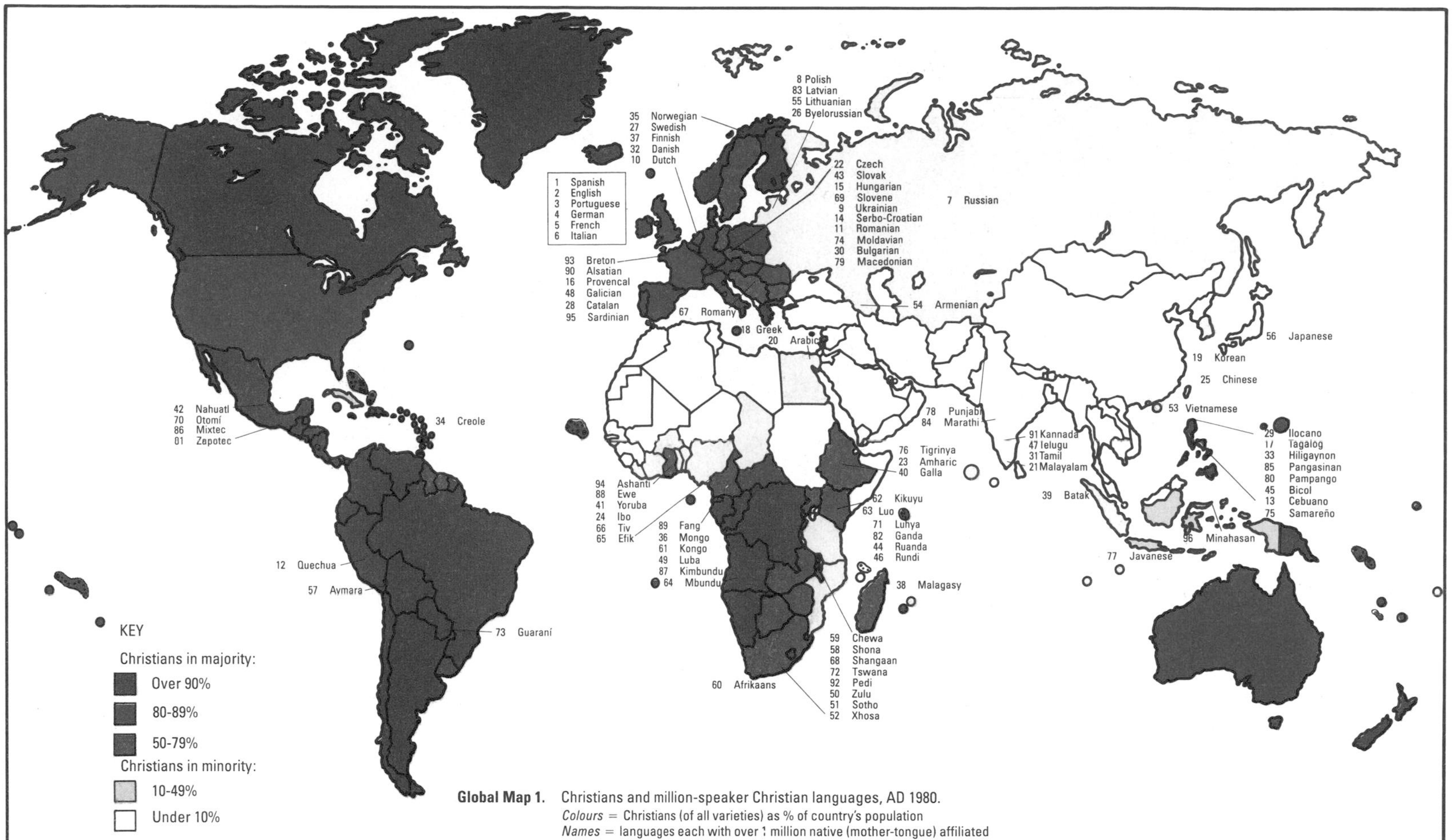

**Global Map 1.** Christians and million-speaker Christian languages, AD 1980.

*Colours* = Christians (of all varieties) as % of country's population
*Names* = languages each with over 1 million native (mother-tongue) affiliated church members, ranked 1-96 in order of size. Box = the 6 largest.
(Source of data: Tables 1 column 13 and Global Table 7).

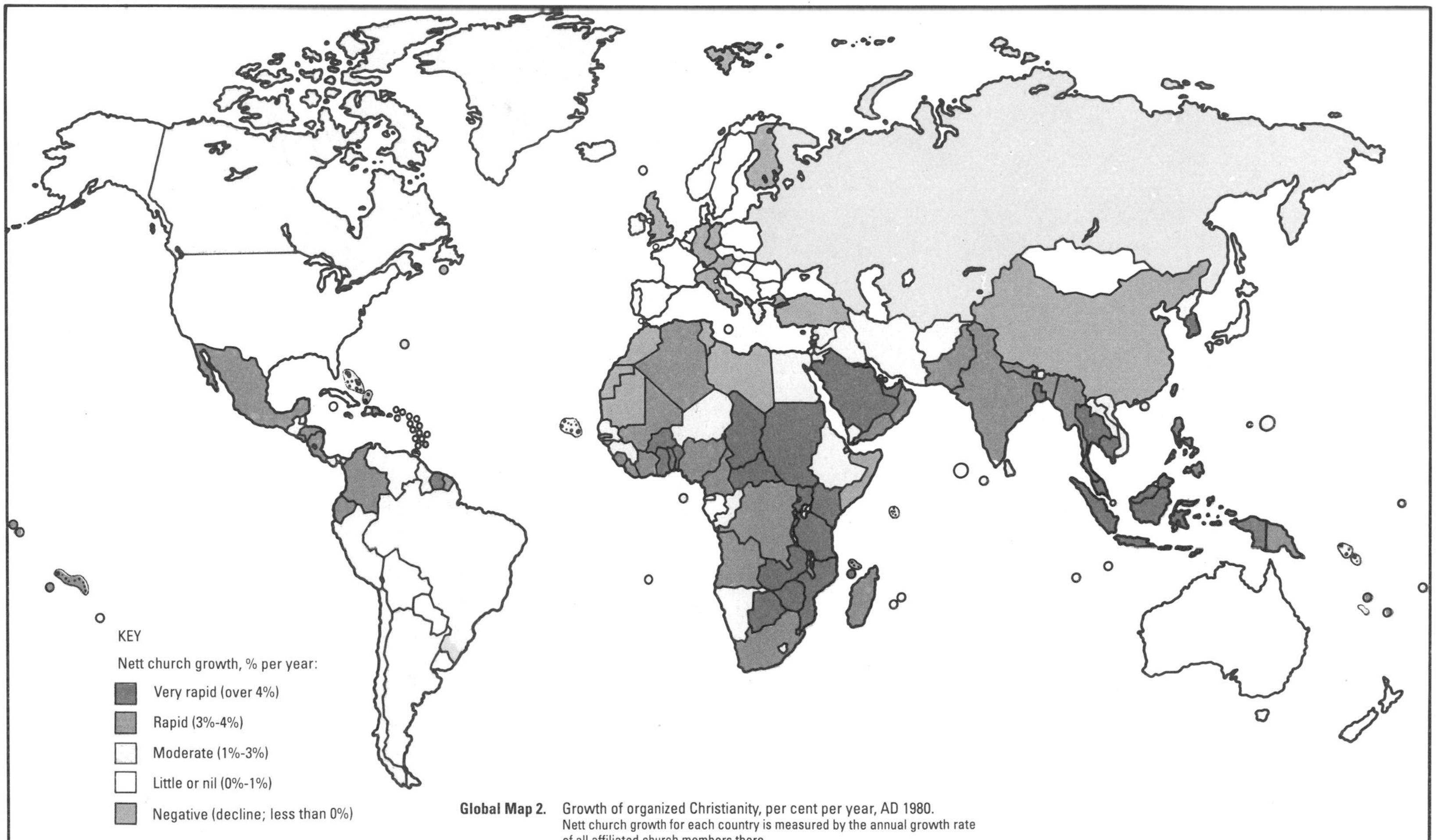

KEY

Christians in majority:

- Over 90%
- 80-89%
- 50-79%

Christians in minority:

- 10-49%
- Under 10%

Box (6 largest):
1 Spanish
2 English
3 Portuguese
4 German
5 French
6 Italian

35 Norwegian
27 Swedish
37 Finnish
32 Danish
10 Dutch

8 Polish
83 Latvian
55 Lithuanian
26 Byelorussian

93 Breton
90 Alsatian
16 Provencal
48 Galician
28 Catalan
95 Sardinian

67 Romany

22 Czech
43 Slovak
15 Hungarian
69 Slovene
9 Ukrainian
14 Serbo-Croatian
11 Romanian
74 Moldavian
30 Bulgarian
79 Macedonian

7 Russian

54 Armenian

18 Greek
20 Arabic

56 Japanese
19 Korean
25 Chinese
53 Vietnamese

78 Punjabi
84 Marathi

91 Kannada
47 Telugu
31 Tamil
21 Malayalam

76 Tigrinya
23 Amharic
40 Galla

39 Batak

29 Ilocano
17 Tagalog
33 Hiligaynon
85 Pangasinan
80 Pampango
45 Bicol
13 Cebuano
75 Samareño

96 Minahasan

77 Javanese

42 Nahuatl
70 Otomi
86 Mixtec
01 Zapotec

34 Creole

12 Quechua

57 Aymara

73 Guaraní

94 Ashanti
88 Ewe
41 Yoruba
24 Ibo
66 Tiv
65 Efik

89 Fang
36 Mongo
61 Kongo
49 Luba
87 Kimbundu
64 Mbundu

62 Kikuyu
63 Luo
71 Luhya
82 Ganda
44 Ruanda
46 Rundi

38 Malagasy

60 Afrikaans

59 Chewa
58 Shona
68 Shangaan
72 Tswana
92 Pedi
50 Zulu
51 Sotho
52 Xhosa

**Global Map 2.** Growth of organized Christianity, per cent per year, AD 1980.
Nett church growth for each country is measured by the annual growth rate of all affiliated church members there.
(Source of data: Tables 1 column 9).

KEY

Nett church growth, % per year:

- Very rapid (over 4%)
- Rapid (3%-4%)
- Moderate (1%-3%)
- Little or nil (0%-1%)
- Negative (decline; less than 0%)

KEY

State attitude to religion:

ATHEISTIC

SECULAR

RELIGIOUS

Buddhist

Hindu

Muslim

Jewish

Eastern Orthodox

Protestant or Anglican

Roman Catholic

**Global Map 3.**   Religious, secular and atheistic states, AD 1980.
● = Location of a government ministry controlling religious affairs.
*(Source of data: Global Tables 15 and 31 column 21).*

KEY

Religious liberty (de facto):

State propagates Christianity

Massive state subsidies

Limited state subsidies

School subsidies only

State non-interference

Limited restrictions

State discrimination

State obstruction

State hostility

State suppression

**Global Map 4.**   Religious liberty and persecution, AD 1970-1980.
*(Source of data: Global Tables 16 and 31 column 22).*

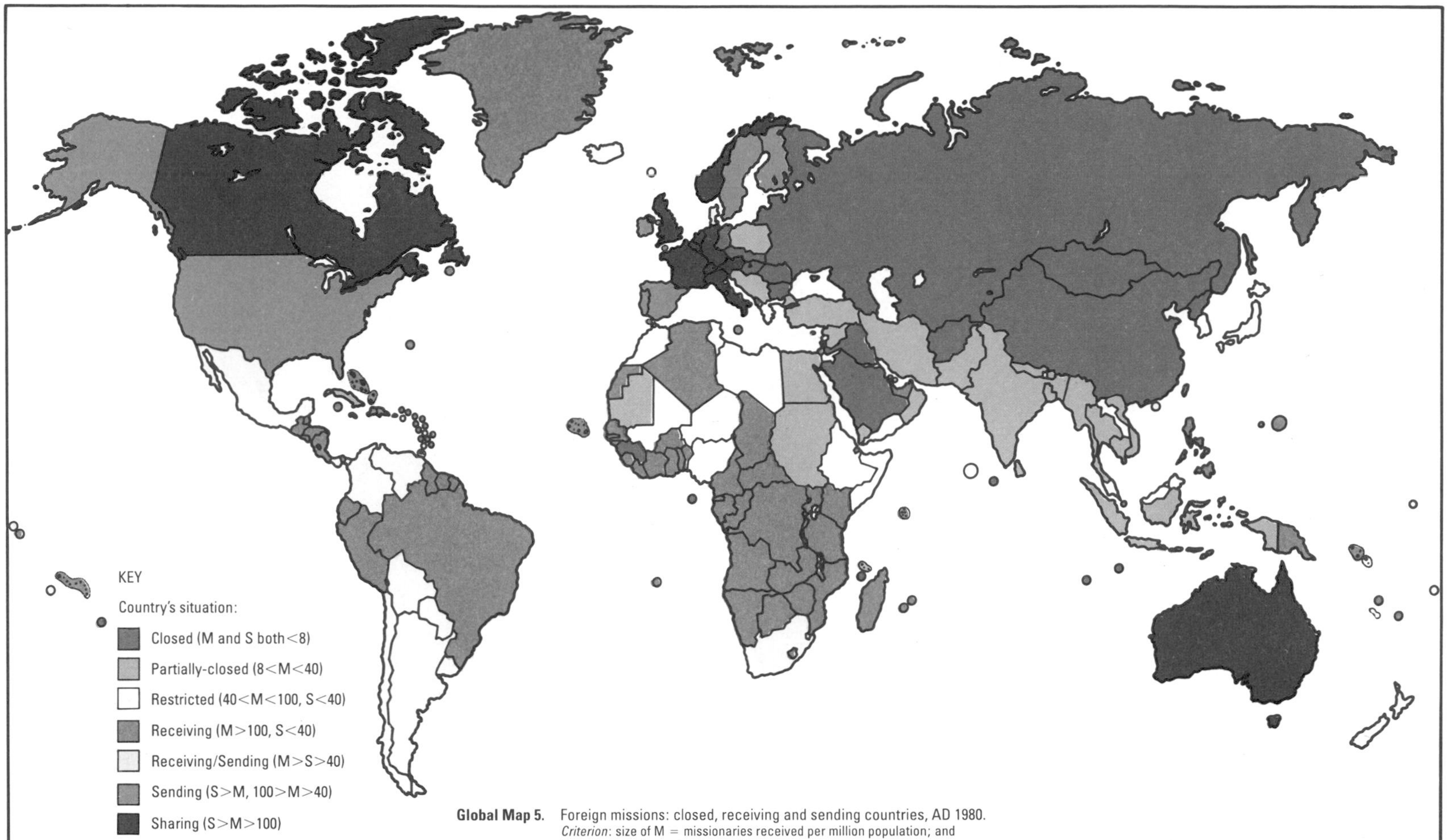

KEY

Country's situation:

- Closed (M and S both <8)
- Partially-closed (8<M<40)
- Restricted (40<M<100, S<40)
- Receiving (M>100, S<40)
- Receiving/Sending (M>S>40)
- Sending (S>M, 100>M>40)
- Sharing (S>M>100)

**Global Map 5.** Foreign missions: closed, receiving and sending countries, AD 1980.
*Criterion*: size of M = missionaries received per million population; and
S = missionaries sent out per million.
*(Source of data: Global Tables 17 and 31 column 23).*

Canada 20
Netherlands 5
Spain 46
Portugal 1
Monaco 1
Holy See 1
Italy 1
Greece 1
Cyprus 1
USA 760
South Korea 9
Japan 3
China (Taiwan) 2
Pacific Islands 2
Guam 2
Philippines 30
Mexico 2
Dominican Republic 1
Puerto Rico 2
Honduras 6
Haiti 2
Guatemala 13
El Salvador 3
Netherlands Antilles 3
Nicaragua 2
Costa Rica 3
Panama 3
Venezuela 4
Colombia 48
Liberia 2
Ecuador 27
Seychelles 1
Sri Lanka 1
Peru 20
Bolivia 10
Brazil 280
Paraguay 1
Swaziland 1
Australia 4
Chile 6
Lesotho 2
New Zealand 1

KEY

Regular audience,
% of population:

- Over 80%
- 60-79%
- 50-59%
- 30-49%
- 10-29%
- 5-9%
- Under 5%

**Global Map 6.** Christian broadcasting, AD 1980: listeners/viewers, radio/TV stations.
*Names* = countries with Christian radio/TV stations (with total stations in each shown).
*(Source of data: Global Table 31 column 95, also Part 7, Tables 2).*

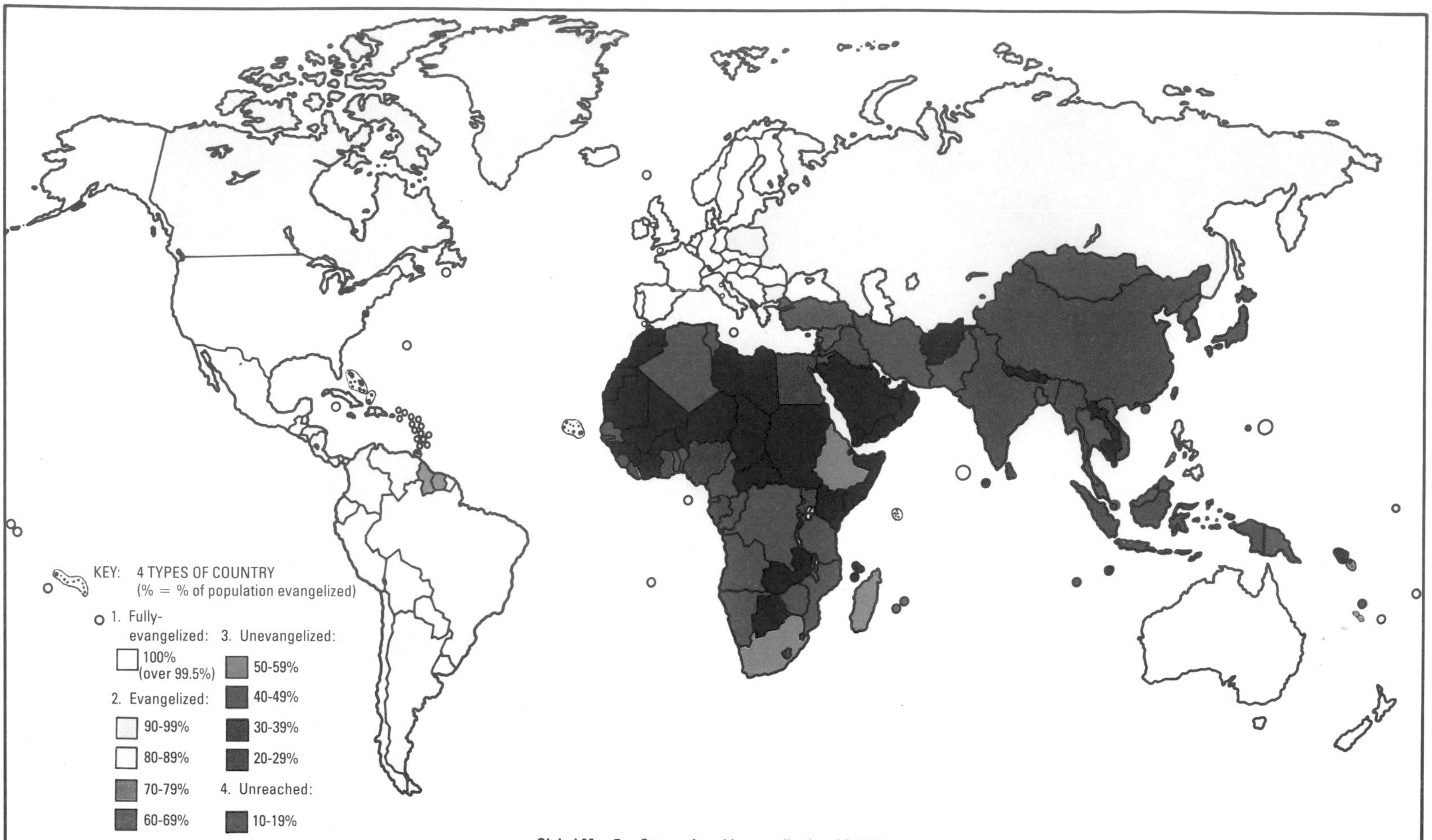

KEY:    4 TYPES OF COUNTRY
        (% = % of population evangelized)

1. Fully-
   evangelized:           3. Unevangelized:
   100%                      50-59%
   (over 99.5%)
2. Evangelized:              40-49%
   90-99%                    30-39%
   80-89%                    20-29%
   70-79%                 4. Unreached:
   60-69%                    10-19%
                             0-9%

**Global Map 7.**    Status of world evangelization, AD 1900.
*(Source of data: Global Table 31 column 102).*

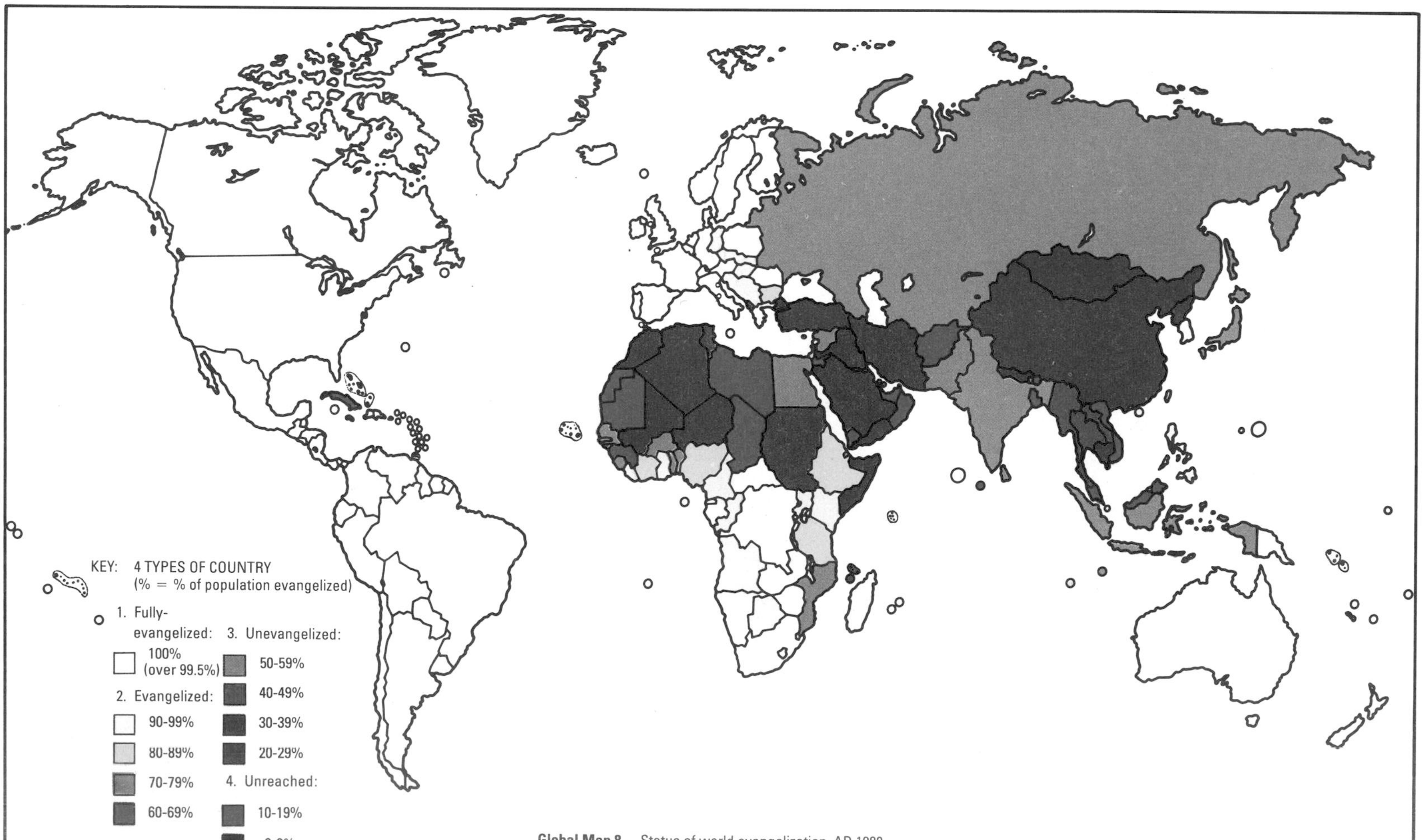

KEY:    4 TYPES OF COUNTRY
        (% = % of population evangelized)

1. Fully-
   evangelized:           3. Unevangelized:
   100%                      50-59%
   (over 99.5%)
2. Evangelized:              40-49%
   90-99%                    30-39%
   80-89%                    20-29%
   70-79%                 4. Unreached:
   60-69%                    10-19%
                             0-9%

**Global Map 8.**    Status of world evangelization, AD 1980.
*(Source of data: Global Table 31 column 104).*

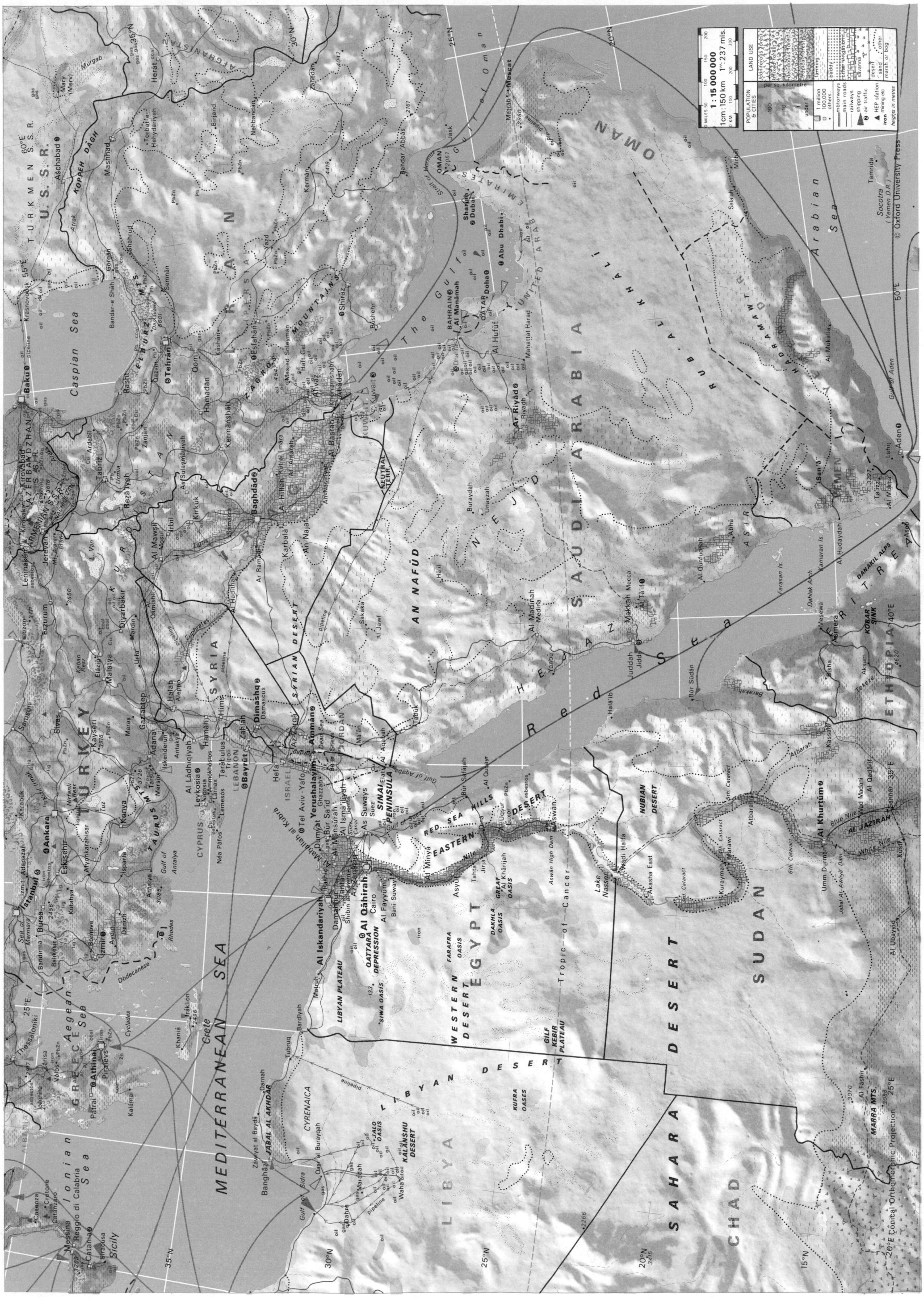

SCALE 1:15 000 000
1cm=150km   1"=237 mls.

LAND USE

POPULATION & CITIES

© Oxford University Press

**Seas and water bodies:** Caspian Sea, Mediterranean Sea, Aegean Sea, Ionian Sea, Red Sea, Arabian Sea, The Gulf, Gulf of Oman, Gulf of Aden, Black Sea, Sea of Marmara, Gulf of Antalya, Dead Sea, Gulf of Aqaba, Lake Nasser, Gulf of Sidra

**Countries/regions:** TURKMEN S.S.R., AFGHANISTAN, AZERBAYDZHAN S.S.R., ARMENIAN S.S.R., GEORGIAN S.S.R., IRAN, IRAQ, TURKEY, SYRIA, LEBANON, ISRAEL, JORDAN, CYPRUS, GREECE, SAUDI ARABIA, KUWAIT, BAHRAIN, QATAR, UNITED ARAB EMIRATES, OMAN, YEMEN, EGYPT, LIBYA, SUDAN, CHAD, ETHIOPIA, ERITREA, NEJD, HEJAZ, ASIR, HADRAMAWT, RUB' AL KHALI, SINAI PENINSULA

**Cities:** Baku, Ankara, Tehrān, Baghdād, Dimashq, Damascus, Bayrūt, Yerushalayim, Ammān, Al Qāhirah, Cairo, Al Iskandarīyah, Istanbul, İzmir, Athínai, Ar Riyāḍ, Riyadh, Abu Dhabi, Dubai, Doha, Al Manāmah, Muscat, Maṣqat, San'ā', Aden, Makkah, Mecca, Al Madīnah, Medina, Juddah, Jidda, Al Khurṭūm, Umm Durmān, Aṭbarah, Al Jazīrah, Mashhad, Aschabad, Tabrīz, Kermān, Shīrāz, Eṣfahān, Ahvāz, Al Baṣrah, Mosul, Al Mawṣil, Kirkūk, Diyarbakir, Erzurum, Konya, Adana, Al Lādhiqīyah, Halab, Aleppo, Ḥimṣ, Ḥamāh, Tarābulus, Leykosia, Nicosia, Thessaloníki, Tel Aviv-Yafo, Port Said, Būr Sa'id, As Suways, Asyūṭ, Luxor, Aswān, Al Minyā

**Deserts & physical features:** AN NAFŪD, SYRIAN DESERT, WESTERN DESERT, LIBYAN DESERT, SAHARA DESERT, NUBIAN DESERT, EASTERN DESERT, RED SEA HILLS, QATTARA DEPRESSION, LIBYAN PLATEAU, GILF KEBIR PLATEAU, KALĀNSHU DESERT, DANAKIL ALPS, KOBAR SINK, MARRA MTS., TAURUS MTS., ELBURZ MTS., ZAGROS MOUNTAINS, KOPPEH DAGH, JABAL AL AKHDAR, CYRENAICA

**Oases:** SIWA OASIS, FARAFRA OASIS, DAKHLA OASIS, KHARIJAH OASIS, GREAT OASIS, KUFRA OASES

Tropic of Cancer

Red Sea

Socotra (Yemen D.R.)

Crete, Rhodes, Cyclades, Dodecanese, Sicily, Farasan Is., Dahlak Arch., Kamaran Is.

20°E Conical Orthomorphic Projection

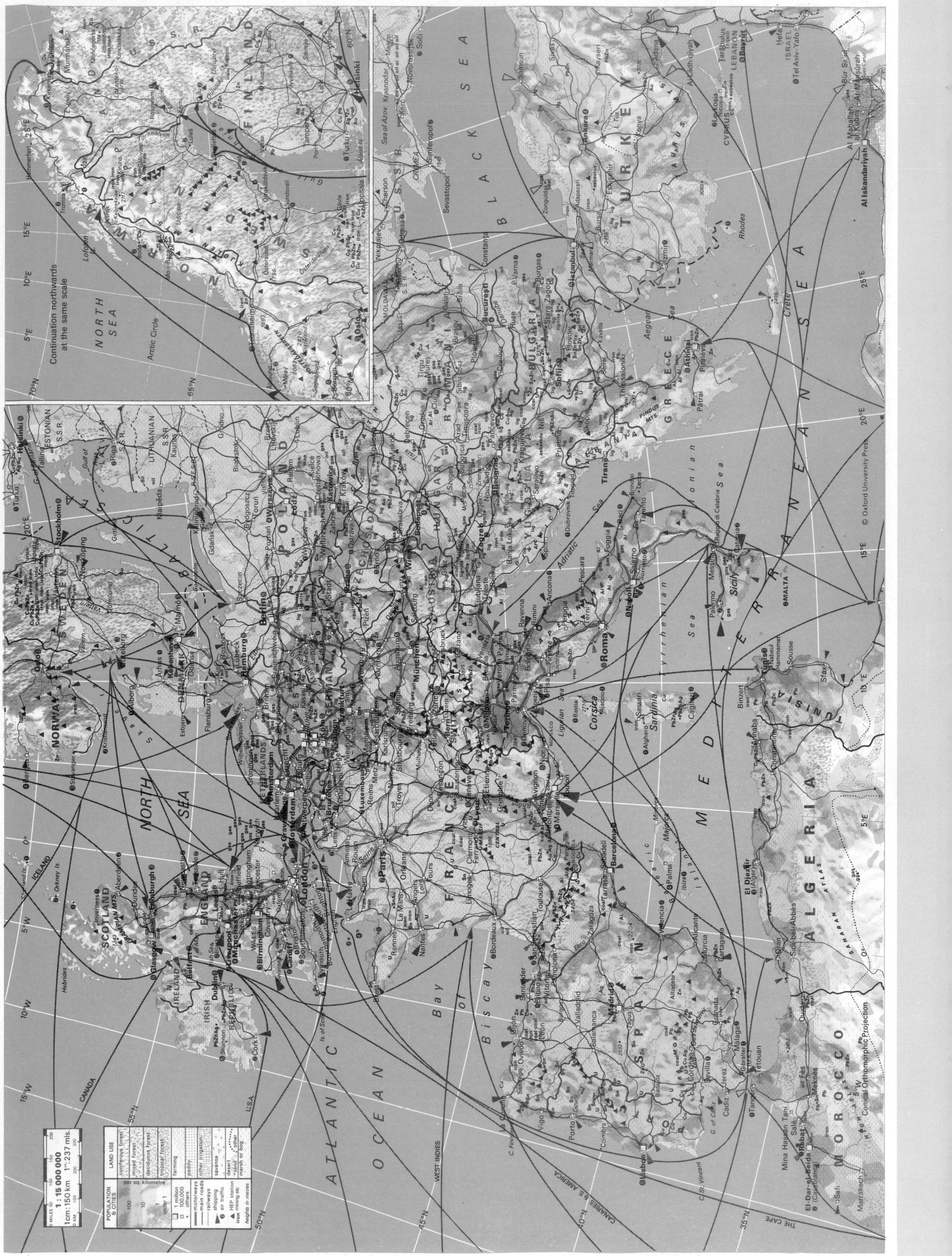
Continuation northwards at the same scale
NORTH SEA
ATLANTIC OCEAN
Bay of Biscay
MEDITERRANEAN SEA
BLACK SEA
BALTIC SEA
Tyrrhenian Sea
Ionian Sea
Aegean Sea
Adriatic Sea
Ligurian Sea
Sea of Azov
NORWAY
SWEDEN
FINLAND
SCOTLAND
ENGLAND
WALES
IRELAND
FRANCE
SPAIN
POLAND
BULGARIA
GREECE
TURKEY
ALGERIA
MOROCCO
TUNISIA
CYPRUS
LEBANON
ISRAEL
Corsica
Sardinia
Sicily
Crete
Rhodes
MALTA
London
Paris
Madrid
Roma
Berlin
München
Warszawa
Budapest
Beograd
Bucuresti
Sofija
Athinai
Istanbul
Ankara
Stockholm
Oslo
Helsinki
Lisboa
Barcelona
Marseille
Napoli
Al Iskandariyah
El Djezair (Alger)
Tunis
POPULATION & CITIES
LAND USE
1 : 15 000 000
1cm : 150 km 1": 237 mls.
coniferous forest
mixed forest
deciduous forest
tropical forest
farming
paddy
other irrigation
savanna
desert
sand
other
marsh or bog
motorways
main roads
railways
shipping
air traffic
HEP station
iron mining etc.
heights in metres
Conical Orthomorphic Projection
© Oxford University Press

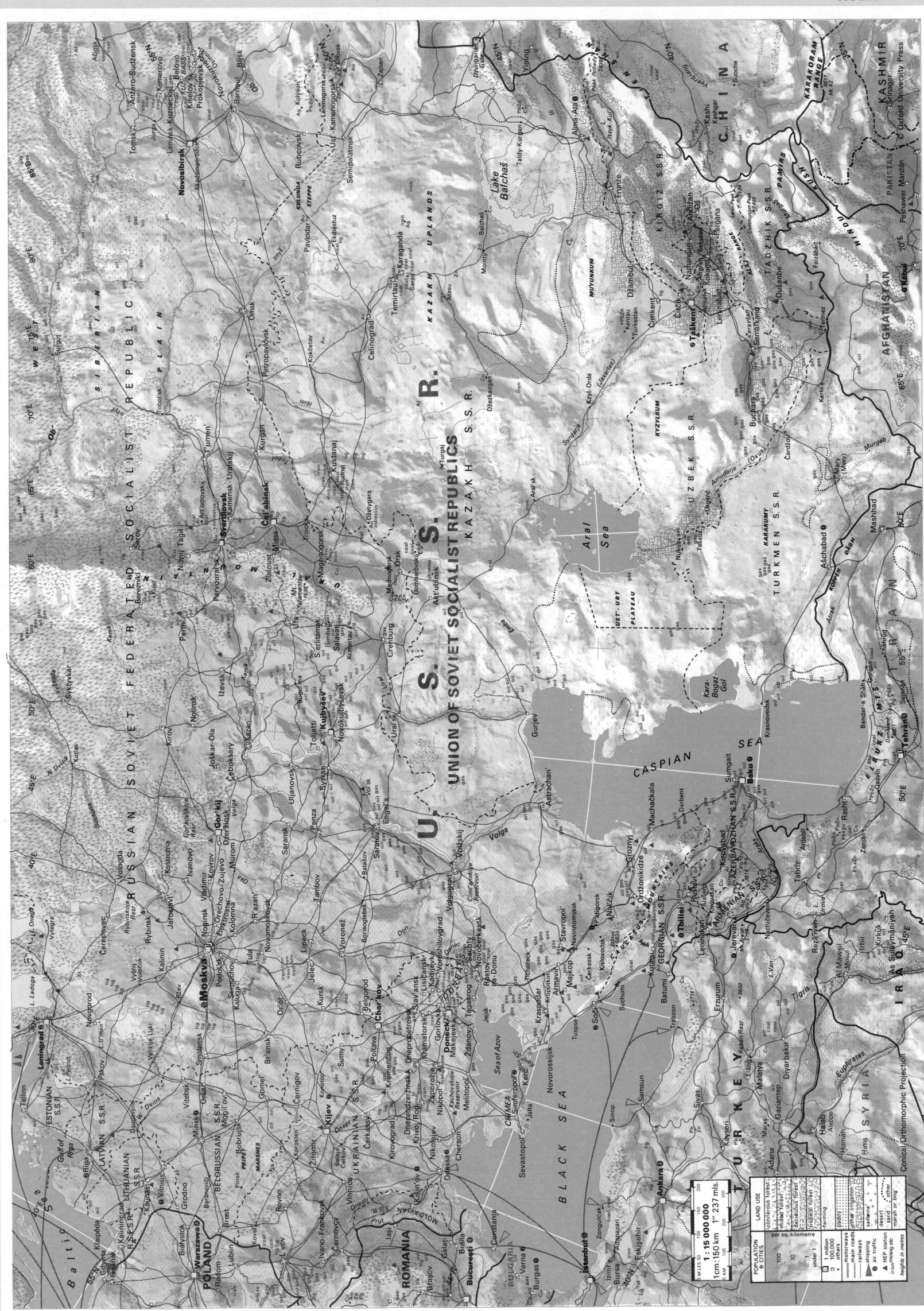

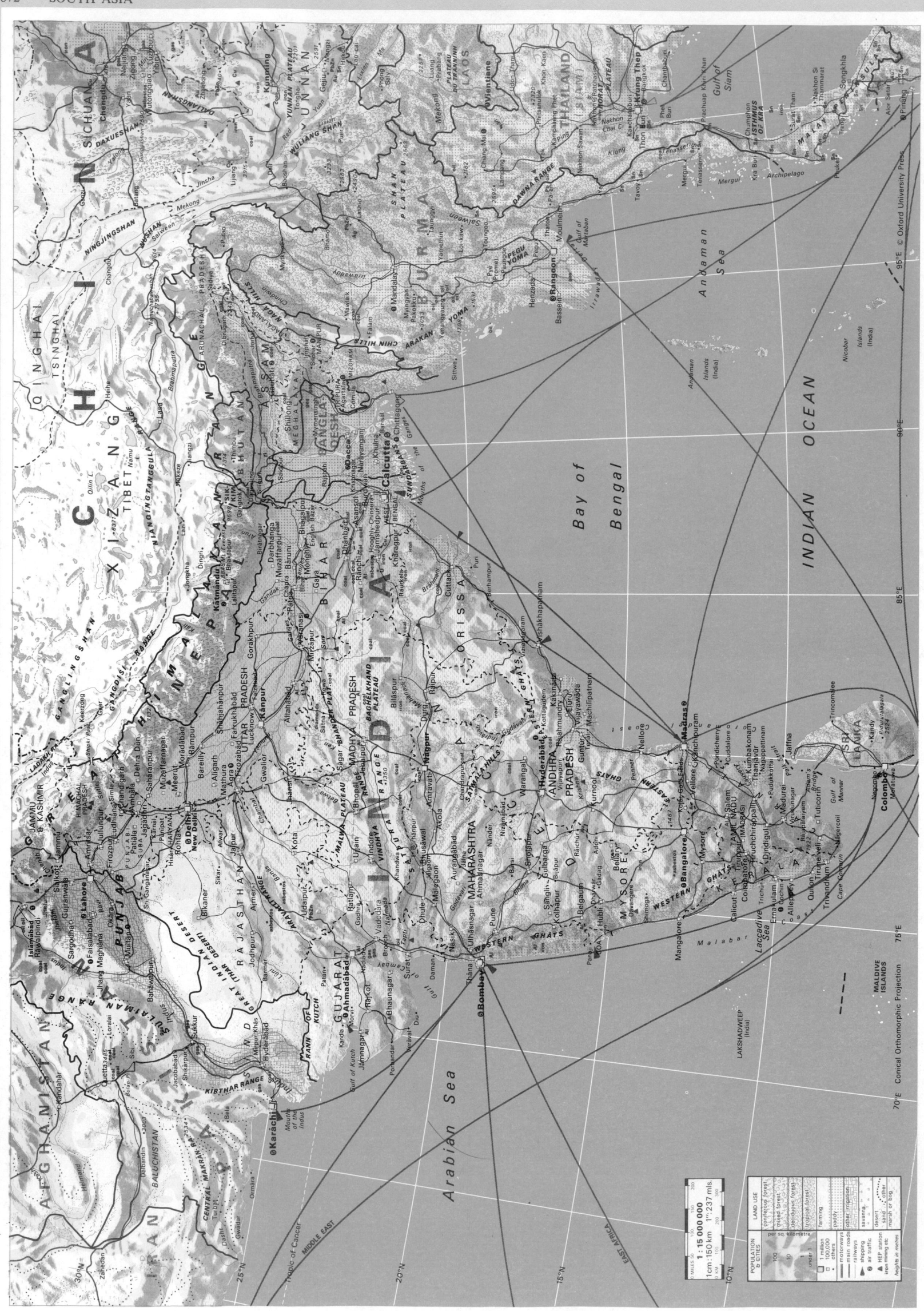

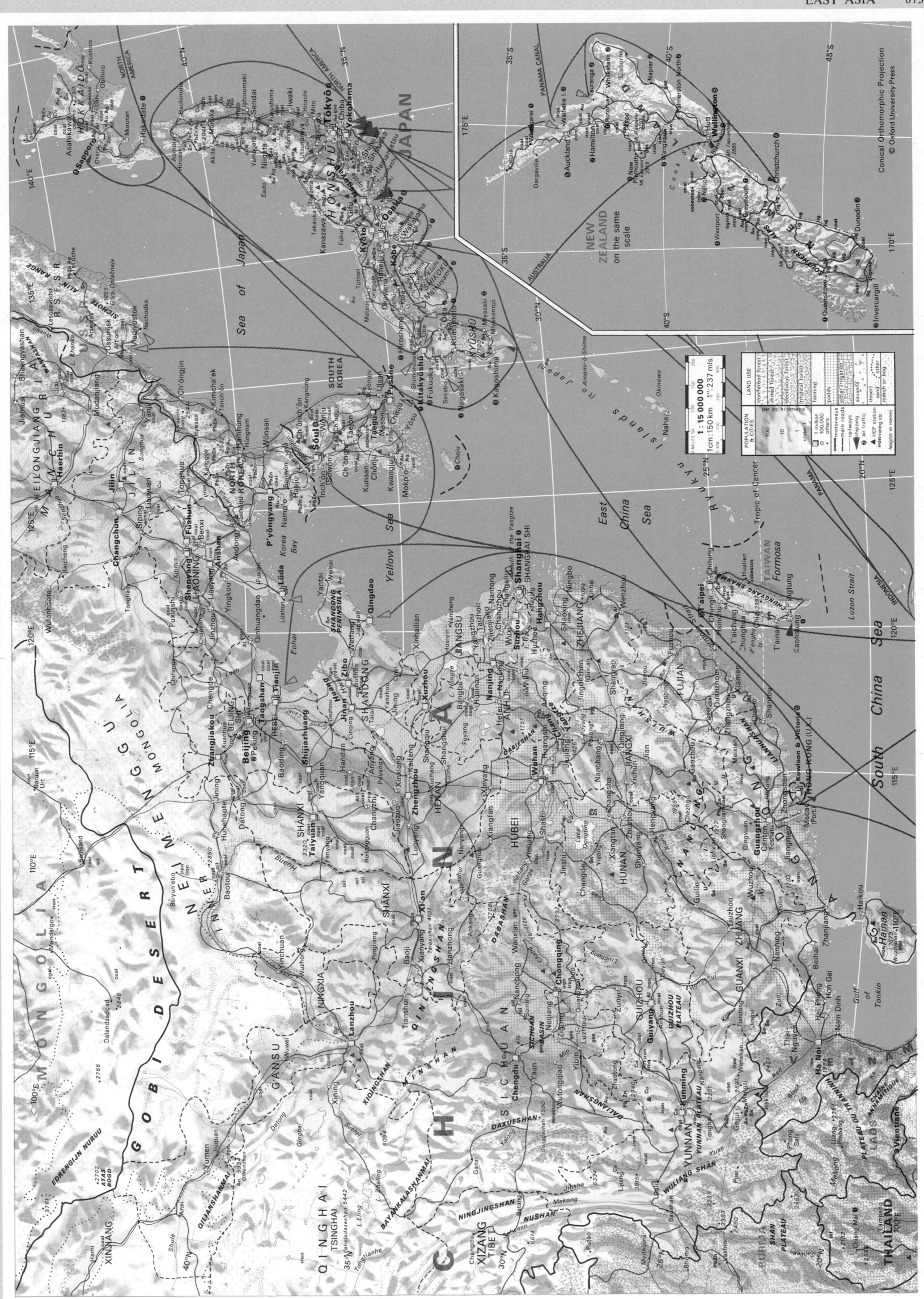

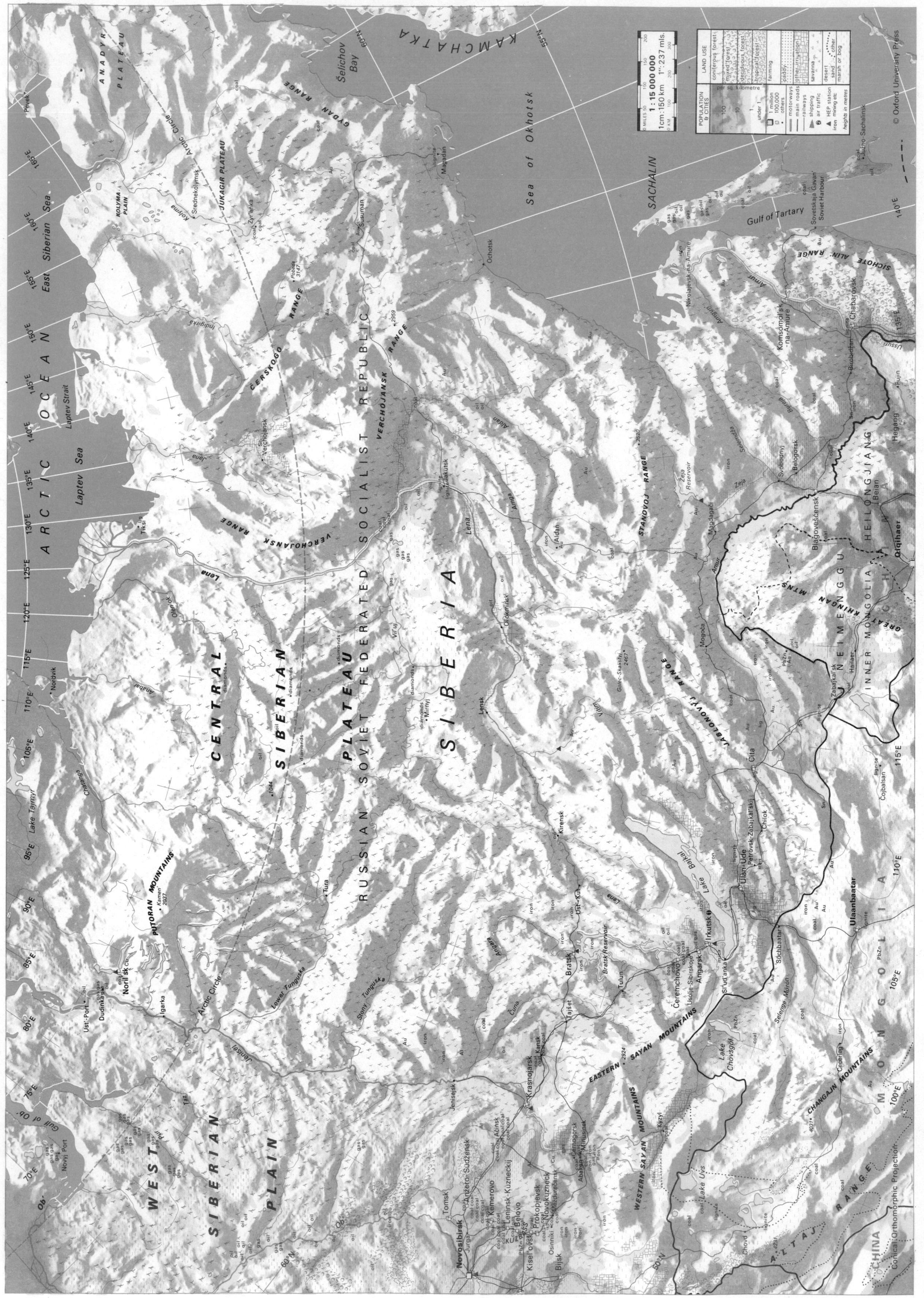
ARCTIC OCEAN
Laptev Sea
East Siberian Sea
Laptev Strait
Sea of Okhotsk
KAMCHATKA
Šelichov Bay
SACHALIN
Gulf of Tartary
Gulf of Ob'
Lake Tajmyr
WEST SIBERIAN PLAIN
CENTRAL SIBERIAN PLATEAU
PUTORAN MOUNTAINS
VERCHOJANSK RANGE
ČERSKOGO RANGE
GYDAN RANGE
ANADYR PLATEAU
KOLYMA PLAIN
JUKAGIR PLATEAU
STANOVOJ RANGE
JABLONOVYJ RANGE
EASTERN SAYAN MOUNTAINS
WESTERN SAYAN MOUNTAINS
CHANGAJN MOUNTAINS
ALTAJ RANGE
GREAT KHINGAN MTNS
SICHOTE-ALIN' RANGE
RUSSIAN SOVIET FEDERATED SOCIALIST REPUBLIC
SIBERIA
MONGOLIA
INNER MONGOLIA
HEILONGJIANG
CHINA
Lake Baikal
Lake Chövsgöl
Lake Uvs
Bratsk Reservoir
Zeja Reservoir
Lena
Jenisej
Ob'
Lower Tunguska
Stony Tunguska
Angara
Aldan
Amur
Kolyma
Indigirka
Jana
Vil'uj
Olen'ok
Novosibirsk
Tomsk
Kemerovo
Novokuzneck
Krasnojarsk
Kansk
Bratsk
Irkutsk
Angarsk
Ulan-Ude
Čita
Ulaanbaatar
Jakutsk
Magadan
Ochotsk
Chabarovsk
Komsomol'sk-na-Amure
Nikolajevsk-na-Amure
Blagoveščensk
Qiqihaer
Hailaer
Norilsk
Dudinka
Igarka
Tura
Mirnyj
Lensk
Kirensk
Tiksi
Nordvik
Verchojansk
Susuman
Pevek
Arctic Circle
Conical Orthomorphic Projection
© Oxford University Press
1 : 15 000 000
1cm : 150 km 1" : 237 mls.
POPULATION & CITIES
LAND USE
coniferous forest
mixed forest
deciduous forest
tropical forest
farming
paddy
other irrigation
savanna
desert
sand
marsh or bog
other
motorways
main roads
railways
shipping
air traffic
HEP station
iron mining etc.
heights in metres

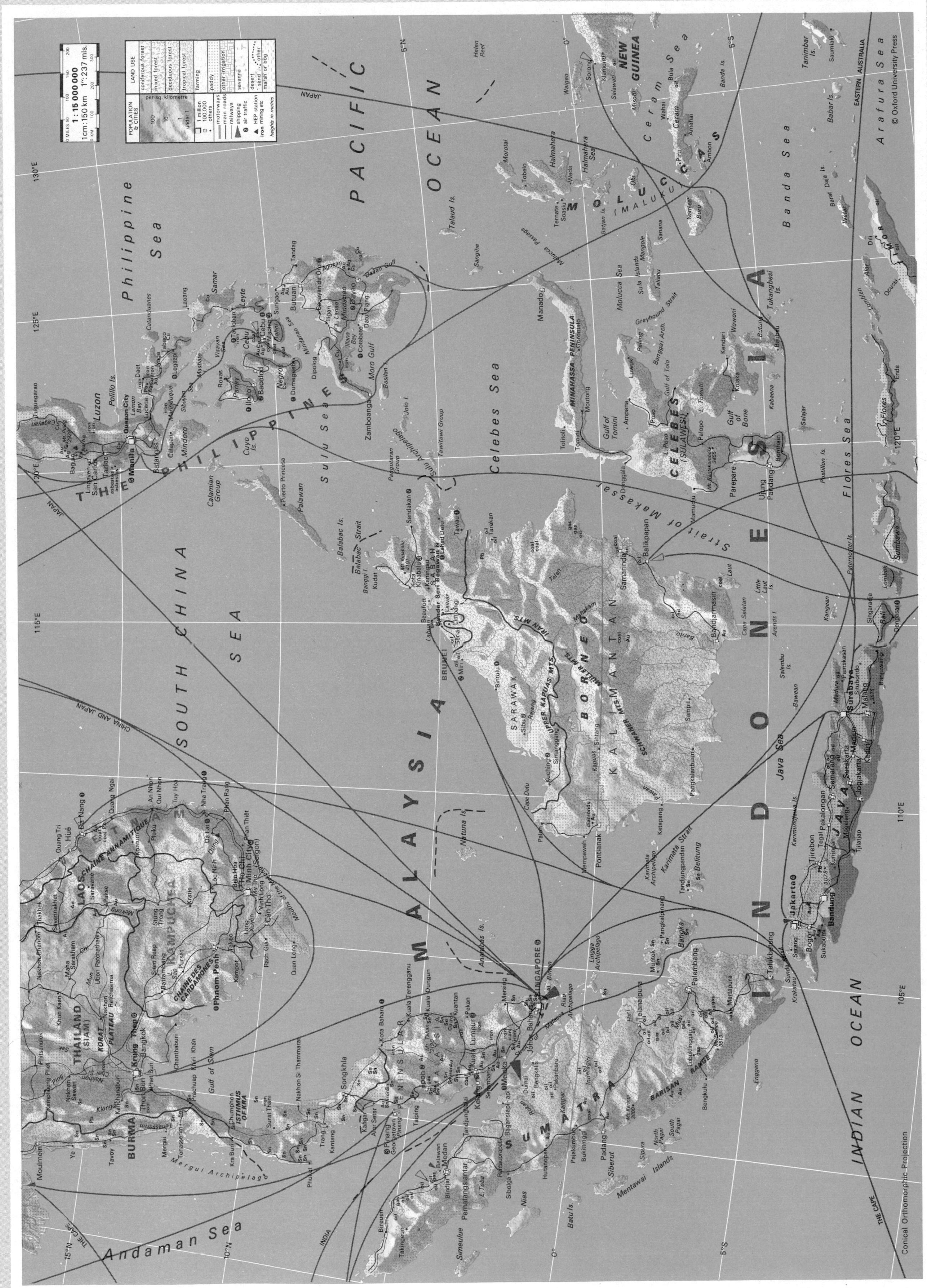

LAND USE

coniferous forest
mixed forest
deciduous forest
tropical forest
farming
other irrigation
savanna
paddy
desert
sand
marsh or bog

POPULATION & CITIES
per sq. kilometre
1 million
100,000
others
motorways
main roads
railways
air traffic
HEP station
iron mining etc.
heights in metres

1 : 15 000 000
1cm:150 km  1″:237 mls.

© Oxford University Press

PACIFIC OCEAN

JAPAN

Philippine Sea

THE PHILIPPINE

Luzon
Quezon City
Manila
San Carlos
Batangas
Mindoro
Calamian Group
Palawan
Catanduanes
Masbate
Panay
Iloilo
Bacolod
Negros
Cebu
Leyte
Samar
Bohol
Tacloban
Mindanao
Davao
Zamboanga
Cagayan de Oro
Butuan
Surigao
Davao Gulf
Moro Gulf
Jolo
Sulu Archipelago

SOUTH CHINA SEA

CHINA AND JAPAN

Balabac Strait
Balabac I.

Celebes Sea

Sulu Sea

Banggai
Kudat
Kota Kinabalu
SABAH
Bandar Seri Begawan
BRUNEI
SARAWAK
Kuching
Sibu
Miri
KALIMANTAN
BORNEO
CROCKER RANGE
IRAN MTS.
UPPER KAPUAS MTS.
SCHWANER MTS.
Pontianak
Balikpapan
Samarinda
Banjarmasin

MOLUCCAS (MALUKU)
Halmahera
Ternate
Morotai
Molucca Sea
MINAHASSA PENINSULA
Manado
Gulf of Tomini
Gorontalo
Greyhound Strait
CELEBES (SULAWESI)
Gulf of Bone
Gulf of Tolo
Banggai Arch.
Sula Islands
Kendari
Parepare
Ujung Pandang

Strait of Makassar

NEW GUINEA
Sorong
Ceram Sea
Ceram
Buru
Banda Sea
Ambon

EASTERN AUSTRALIA

Arafura Sea

Tanimbar

INDONESIA

Java Sea
Flores Sea
Flores
Bali
Lombok
Sumbawa
Sumba

JAVA
Jakarta
Bandung
Bogor
Semarang
Surabaya
Yogyakarta
Surakarta
Madura

Flores Sea

BURMA

VIETNAM
CHAINE ANNAMITIQUE
Hué
Da Nang
Quang Tri
LAOS
CHAINE DES CARDAMOMES
KAMPUCHEA
Phnom Penh
Ho Chi Minh City (Saigon)
THAILAND (SIAM)
KORAT PLATEAU
Krung Thep
Bangkok
Gulf of Siam
ISTHMUS OF KRA
Mergui Archipelago
Mekong

MALAYSIA
MALAY PENINSULA
Kota Bharu
Kuantan
Kuala Lumpur
Kuala Terengganu
SINGAPORE
Riau Archipelago
Lingga Archipelago
Bangka
Belitung
Palembang
SUMATRA
BARISAN
Padang
Medan
Pekanbaru
L. Toba
Nias
Mentawai Islands
Siberut

Andaman Sea

INDIAN OCEAN

Mergui

130°E
125°E
120°E
115°E
110°E
105°E
5°N
0°
5°S
10°S

Conical Orthomorphic Projection

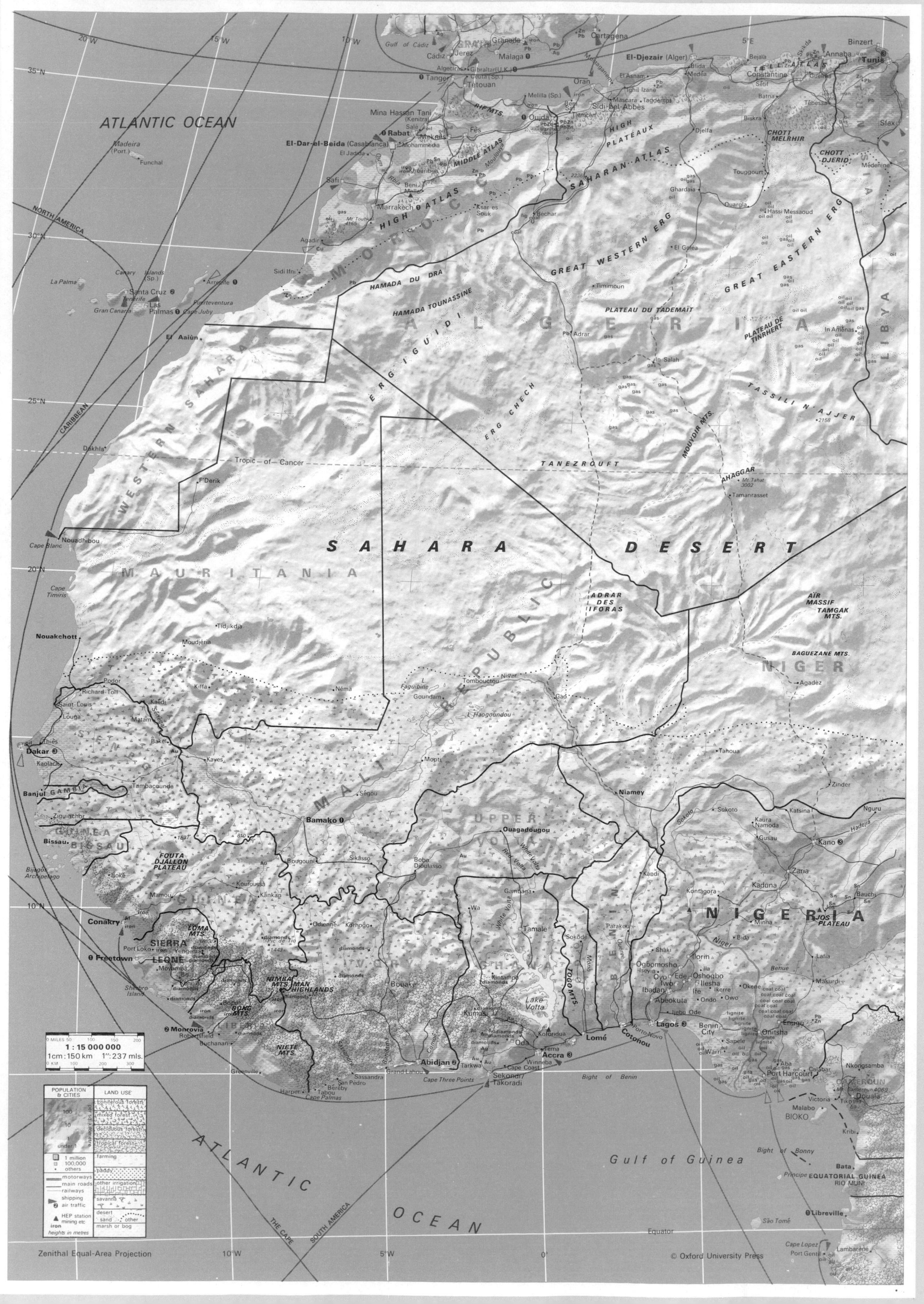

ATLANTIC OCEAN

Gulf of Cádiz
Cádiz · Jerez · Málaga · Granada · Cartagena
Algeciras · Gibraltar (U.K.) · El-Djezair (Alger) · Annaba · Bizerte · Tunis
Tanger · Tétouan · Ceuta (Sp.) · Melilla (Sp.) · Oran · Blida · Médéa · Constantine · Guelma · Souk · Sfax
RIF MTS. · Oujda · El Asnam · Sétif · Batna · Tébessa
Mina Hassan Tani (Kenitra) · Fès · Mascara · Tadempt
Madeira (Port.) · El-Dar-el-Beida (Casablanca) · Rabat · Meknès · MIDDLE ATLAS · SAHARAN ATLAS · CHOTT MELRHIR
Funchal · El Jadida · Mohammedia · HIGH PLATEAUX · CHOTT DJERID
Safi · Beni Mellal · Djelfa · Biskra · Médenine
Marrakech · HIGH ATLAS · Ksar es Souk · Béchar · Touggourt · Ghardaïa · Ouargla · Hassi Messaoud
Mt. Toubkal 4165 · GREAT WESTERN ERG · El Golea · GREAT EASTERN ERG
Agadir
Canary Islands (Sp.)
La Palma · Arrecife
Santa Cruz · Tenerife · Fuerteventura · Sidi Ifni · HAMADA DU DRA · Timimoun · PLATEAU DU TADEMAÏT · In Amenas
Gran Canaria · Las Palmas · Cape Juby · HAMADA TOUNASSINE · Reggan · In Salah · PLATEAU DE TINRHERT
El Aaiún · A L G E R I A · LIBYA
WESTERN SAHARA · ERG IGUIDI · ERG CHECH · TASSILI N'AJJER · 2158
Dakhla · Tropic of Cancer · TANEZROUFT · MOUYDIR MTS. · AHAGGAR · Mt. Tahat 3002 · Tamanrasset
F'Derik
Cape Blanc · Nouadhibou
MAURITANIA · S A H A R A   D E S E R T · ADRAR DES IFORAS · AÏR MASSIF · TAMGAK MTS.
Cape Timiris
Nouakchott · BAGUEZANE MTS. · N I G E R
Tidjikdja · Moudjéria · Niger · Tombouctou · Agadez
Kiffa · Néma · Faguibine · Gao
Podor · Kaédi · Goundam · Tahoua
Richard-Toll · Matam · Haoggoundou
Saint-Louis · Bakel · Mopti · Zinder
Louga · Kayes · M A L I   R E P U B L I C · Niamey · Sokoto · Katsina · Nguru
Thiès · Dakar · Kaolack · Ségou · Kaura Namoda · Gusau · Kano · Hadejia
Banjul · GAMBIA · Tambacounda · UPPER VOLTA · Zaria · Kaduna
Bamako · Ouagadougou · Bobo Dioulasso · Sikasso · White Volta · Kontagora · Bauchi
GUINEA BISSAU · Bougouni · Wa · Red Volta · N I G E R I A
Bissau · FOUTA DJALLON PLATEAU · Kankan · Gambaga · Minna · JOS PLATEAU
Boké · Kouroussa · Odienné · Korhogo · Tamale · Sokodé · Shaki · Ogbomosho · Ilorin · Lafia · Makurdi
Conakry · LOMA MTS. · Mamou · Bouaké · Oyo · Ede · Oshogbo · Ife · Benue
SIERRA LEONE · Port Loko · Yongoroula · Kintampo · Ibadan · Iwo · Ilesha · Ikerre · Ondo · Owo · Enugu
Freetown · NIMBA MTS. · MAN HIGHLANDS · Lake Volta · Abeokuta · Ijebu Ode
Shenge · GONG MTS. · Kumasi · Koforidua · Sapele · Onitsha
Sherbro Island · NIÉTÉ MTS. · Oda · Tema · Lagos · Benin City · Warri · Port Harcourt
Monrovia · Robertsport · Accra · Porto-Novo · Cotonou · Calabar · Nkongsamba
Buchanan · LIBERIA · Abidjan · Tarkwa · Lomé · CAMEROUN · Douala
Greenville · San Pedro · Grand-Lahou · Sekondi-Takoradi · Winneba · Cape Coast · Bight of Benin · Malabo · BIOKO
Harper · Tabou · Cape Palmas · Cape Three Points · Bata · EQUATORIAL GUINEA · RIO MUNI
Sassandra

ATLANTIC OCEAN · Gulf of Guinea · Bight of Bonny · Libreville
THE CAPE · SOUTH AMERICA
10°W · 5°W · 0° · Kribi · Principe · São Tomé · Equator · Lambaréné · Port Gentil · Cape Lopez

SCALE
0 MILES 50 · 100 · 150 · 200
1 : 15 000 000
1cm:150 km · 1″:237 mls.
0 KM · 100 · 200 · 300

POPULATION & CITIES
100
10
1
under 1
□ 1 million
□ 100,000
· others
motorways
main roads
railways
shipping
air traffic
HEP station
mining etc
iron
heights in metres

LAND USE
coniferous forest
mixed forest
deciduous forest
tropical forest
farming
paddy
other irrigation
savanna
desert
sand
marsh or bog

Zenithal Equal-Area Projection
© Oxford University Press

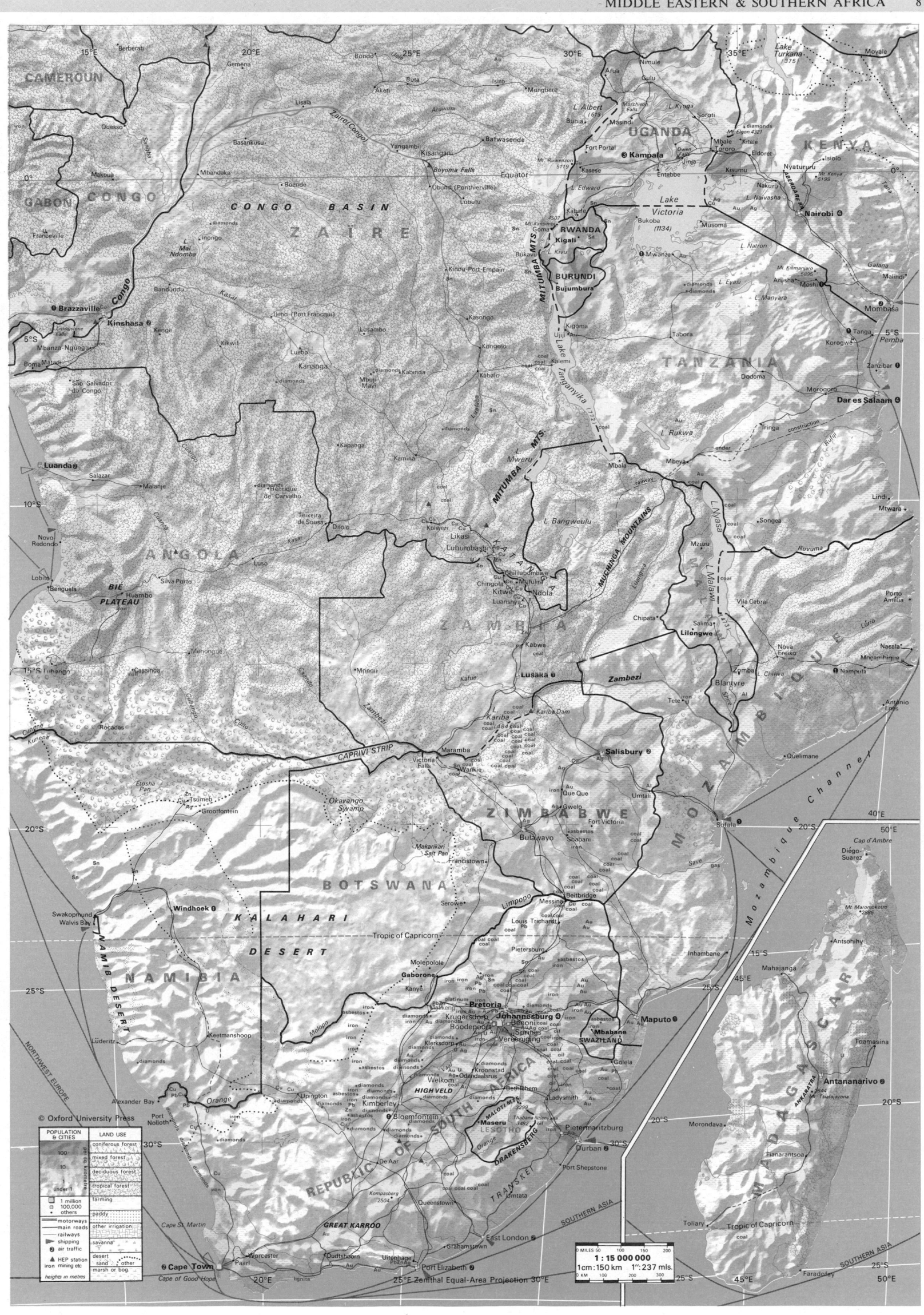

CAMEROUN

GABON

CONGO

Brazzaville

Kinshasa

ZAIRE

CONGO BASIN

Equator

Boyoma Falls

Kisangani

UGANDA

Kampala

Lake Victoria

KENYA

Nairobi

Mombasa

RWANDA
Kigali

BURUNDI
Bujumbura

TANZANIA

Dodoma

Dar es Salaam

Zanzibar

L. Tanganyika

ANGOLA

Luanda

BIE PLATEAU
Huambo

Benguela

Lobito

MITUMBA MTS

Lubumbashi

Kitwe
Ndola

ZAMBIA

Lusaka

L. Bangweulu

MUCHINGA MOUNTAINS

L. Malawi

Lilongwe

Blantyre

MOZAMBIQUE

Quelimane

Nacala

Porto Amelia

CAPRIVI STRIP

Victoria Falls

Kariba Dam

Salisbury

ZIMBABWE

Bulawayo

Mozambique Channel

MADAGASCAR

Antananarivo

Toamasina

NAMIBIA

NAMIB DESERT

Windhoek

Walvis Bay

KALAHARI DESERT

BOTSWANA

Okavango Swamp

Gaborone

Tropic of Capricorn

Limpopo

Pretoria

Johannesburg

Maputo

SWAZILAND
Mbabane

REPUBLIC OF SOUTH AFRICA

HIGHVELD

Kimberley

Bloemfontein

LESOTHO
Maseru

Durban

DRAKENSBERG

TRANSKEI

GREAT KARROO

Cape Town

Cape of Good Hope

Port Elizabeth

East London

© Oxford University Press

1:15 000 000
1cm:150 km   1":237 mls.

25°E Zenithal Equal-Area Projection 30°E

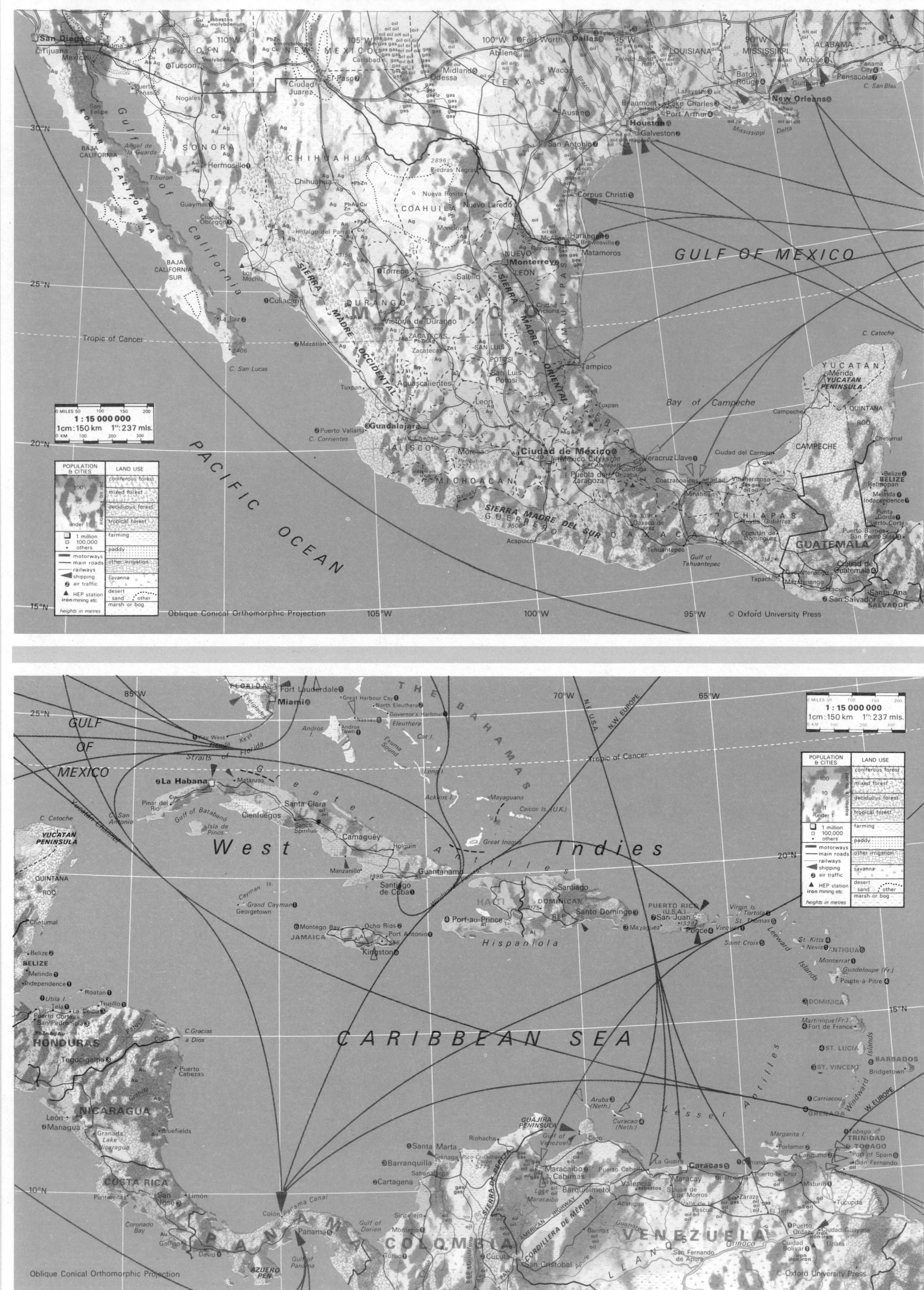

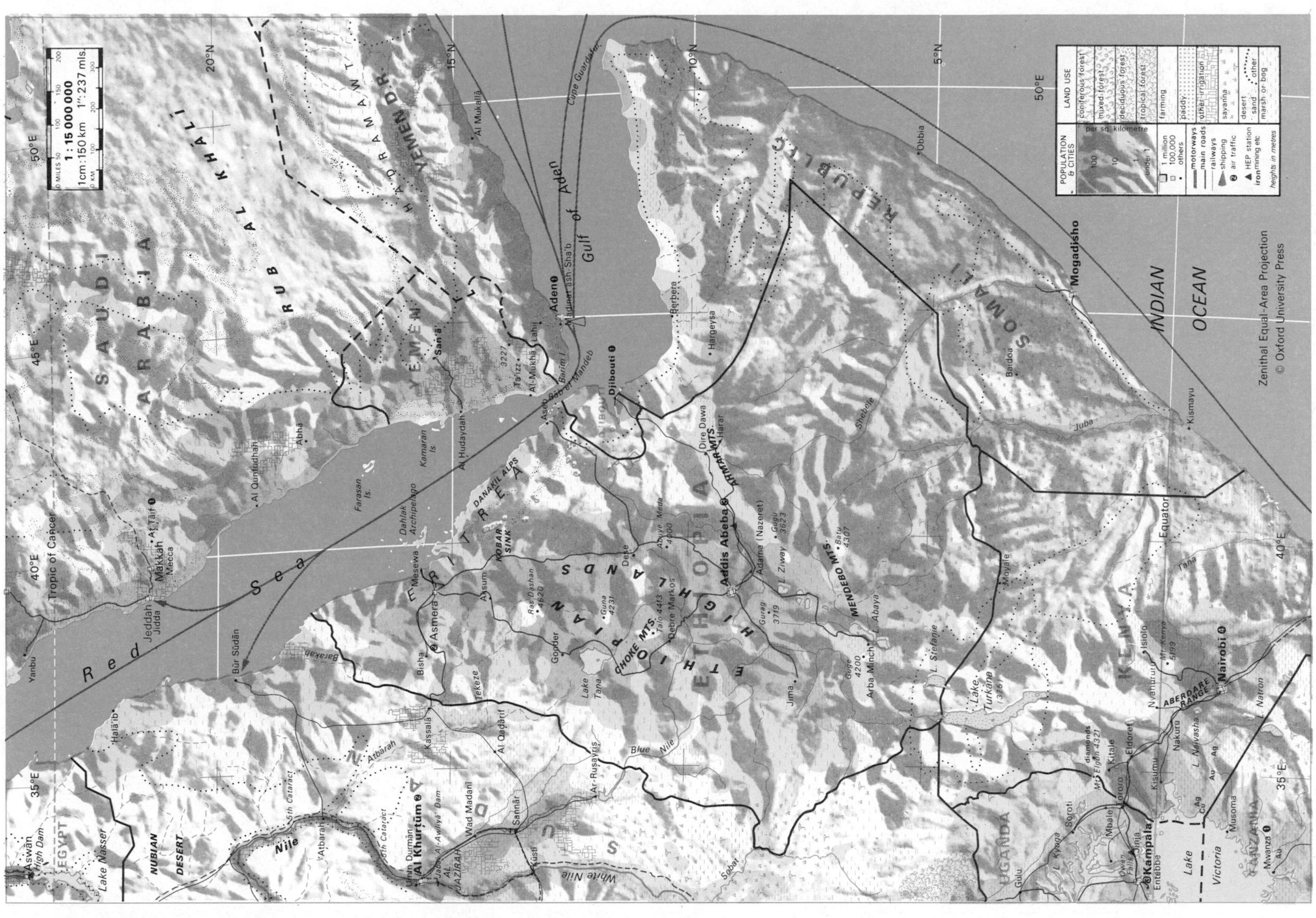

## Map 1 — Horn of Africa

1 : 15 000 000
1cm:150 km  1″:237 mls.

LAND USE
coniferous forest
mixed forest
deciduous forest
tropical forest
paddy
other irrigation
farming
savanna
desert
other
sand
marsh or bog

POPULATION & CITIES
1 million
100,000
others
motorways
main roads
railways
shipping
air traffic
HEP station
heights in metres

Zenithal Equal-Area Projection

© Oxford University Press

SAUDI ARABIA

RUB AL KHALI

YEMEN D.R.

HADRAMAWT

Tropic of Cancer

Makkah (Mecca)
Jeddah (Jidda)
At Tā'if
Al Qunfudhah
Al Mukhā
Al Hudaydah
Şan'ā'
Kamaran Is.
Farasan Is.
Dahlak Archipelago

Aden
Djibouti

Gulf of Aden

INDIAN OCEAN

Mogadishu

SOMALI REPUBLIC

Obbia

ETHIOPIA
ETHIOPIAN HIGHLANDS
Addis Ababa
ERITREA
Asmara
Massawa
DANAKIL ALPS
KOBAR SINK
ARUSSI MTS.
MENDEBO MTS.

Red Sea

Yanbu
Aswān
High Dam
Lake Nasser
EGYPT
NUBIAN DESERT
Nile
Al Khurtūm
Atbara
Kassala
AL JAZIRAH
Blue Nile
White Nile

Equator

KENYA
Nairobi
ABERDARE RANGE
L. Turkana
L. Stefanie
Lake Victoria
TANZANIA
UGANDA
Kampala
Entebbe
Mwanza

## Map 2 — Temperate South America

1 : 15 000 000
1cm:150 km  1″:237 mls.

LAND USE
coniferous forest
mixed forest
deciduous forest
tropical forest
paddy
other irrigation
farming
savanna
desert
other
sand
marsh or bog

POPULATION & CITIES
1 million
100,000
others
motorways
main roads
railways
shipping
air traffic
HEP station
iron, mining etc.
heights in metres

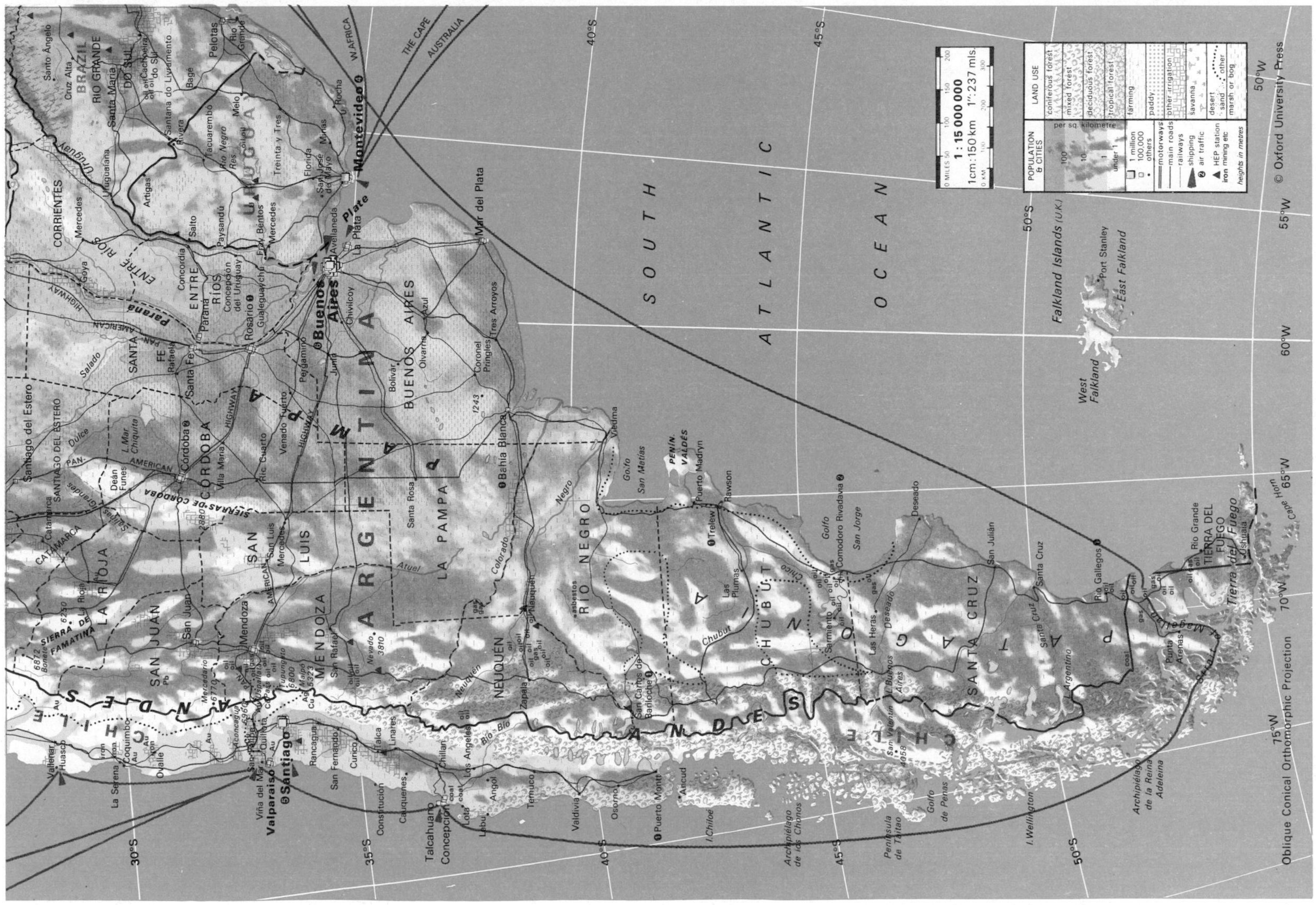

© Oxford University Press

Oblique Conical Orthomorphic Projection

BRAZIL
RIO GRANDE DO SUL
Pelotas
Porto Alegre
URUGUAY
Montevideo
Salto
Paysandú
Mercedes
R. de la Plata
Mar del Plata

ARGENTINA
BUENOS AIRES
Buenos Aires
La Plata
Rosario
Santa Fe
Paraná
CORRIENTES
ENTRE RIOS
CORDOBA
Córdoba
SANTIAGO DEL ESTERO
CATAMARCA
LA RIOJA
SAN JUAN
San Juan
SIERRA DE CORDOBA
Mendoza
MENDOZA
SAN LUIS
LA PAMPA
Bahía Blanca
NEUQUEN
RIO NEGRO
Negro
Colorado
Viedma
PENIN. VALDES
Puerto Madryn
Rawson
CHUBUT
Comodoro Rivadavia
SANTA CRUZ
PATAGONIA
Río Gallegos
TIERRA DEL FUEGO
Río Grande
Ushuaia
Cape Horn

CHILE
Santiago
Valparaíso
Viña del Mar
Concepción
Talcahuano
ANDES
Puerto Montt
Archipiélago de los Chonos
Golfo de Penas
Peninsula de Taitao

SOUTH ATLANTIC OCEAN

Falkland Islands (U.K.)
West Falkland
East Falkland
Port Stanley

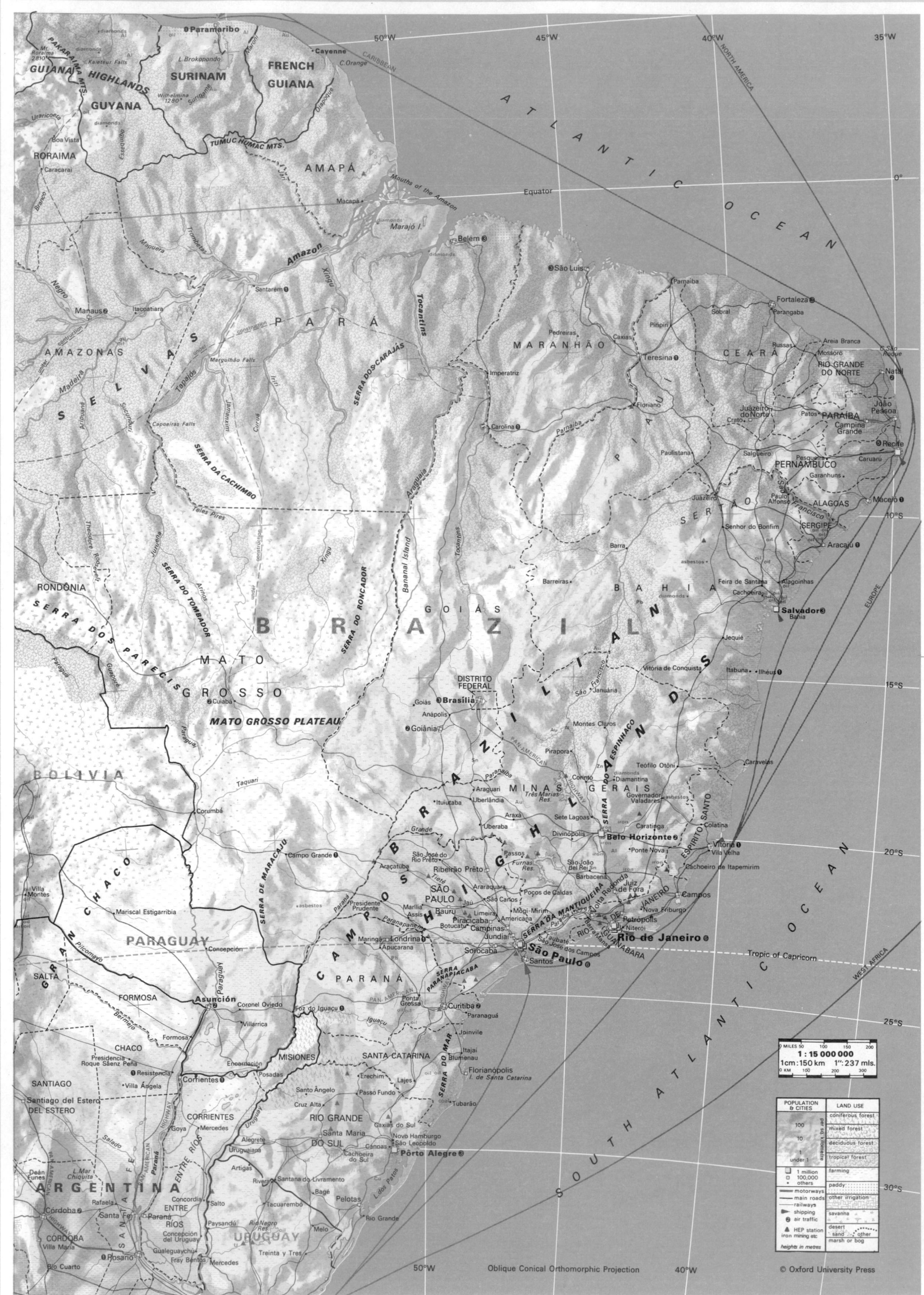

Oblique Conical Orthomorphic Projection

© Oxford University Press

1 : 15 000 000

1cm:150 km    1":237 mls.

POPULATION & CITIES

LAND USE
- coniferous forest
- mixed forest
- deciduous forest
- tropical forest
- farming
- paddy
- other irrigation
- savanna
- desert
- sand
- other
- marsh or bog

- motorways
- main roads
- railways
- shipping
- air traffic
- HEP station
- iron mining etc.

heights in metres

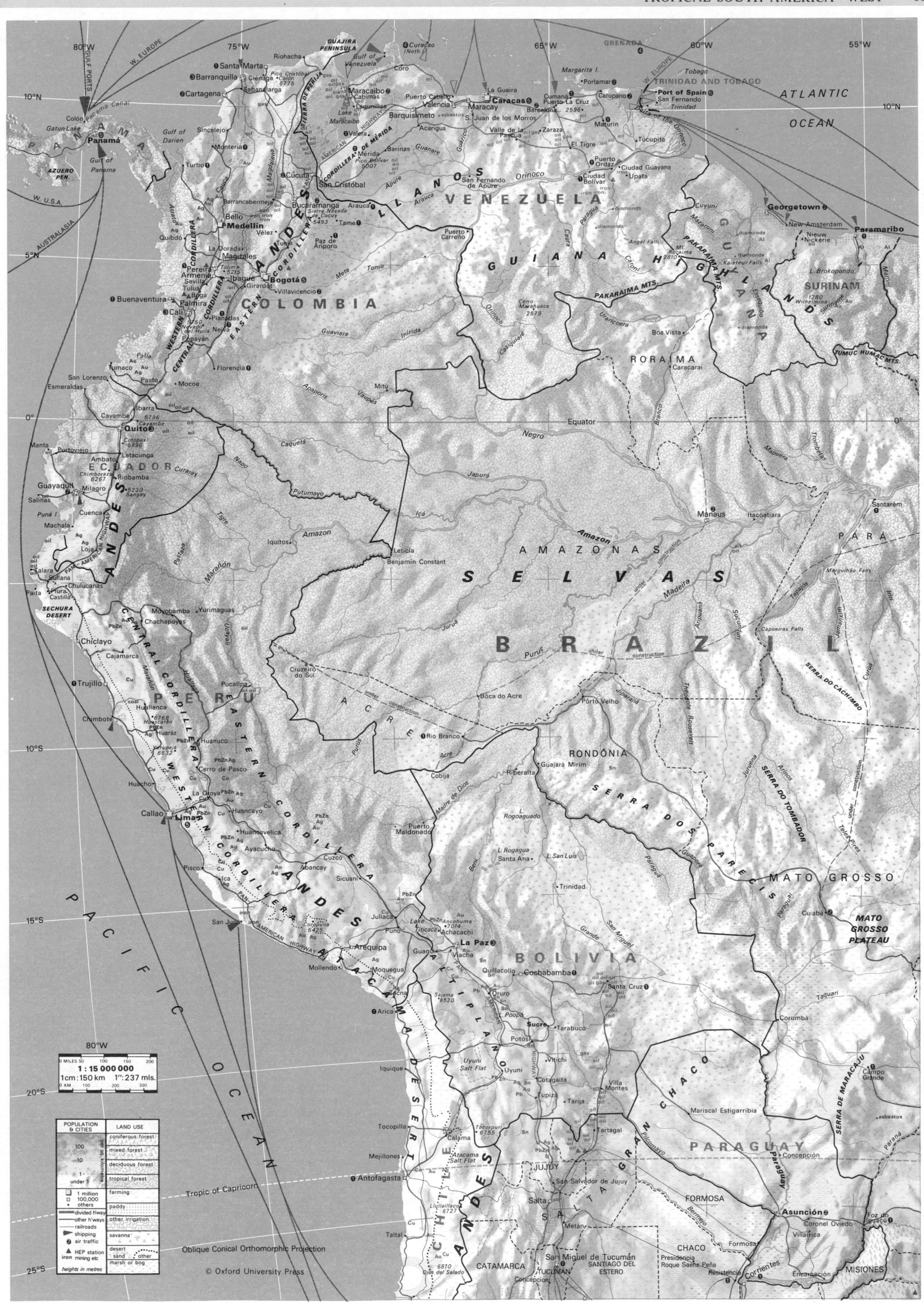

© Oxford University Press

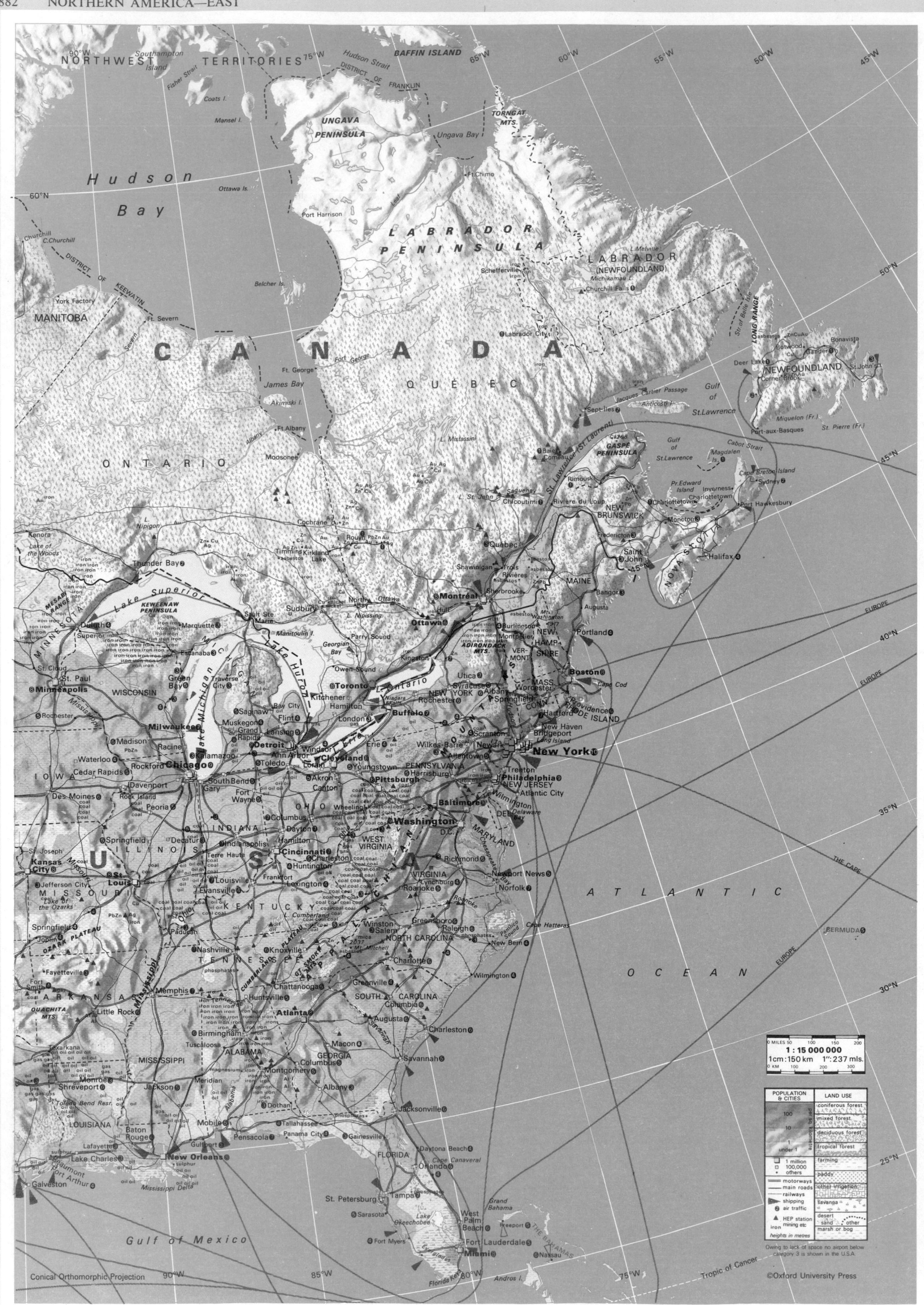

Conical Orthomorphic Projection

©Oxford University Press

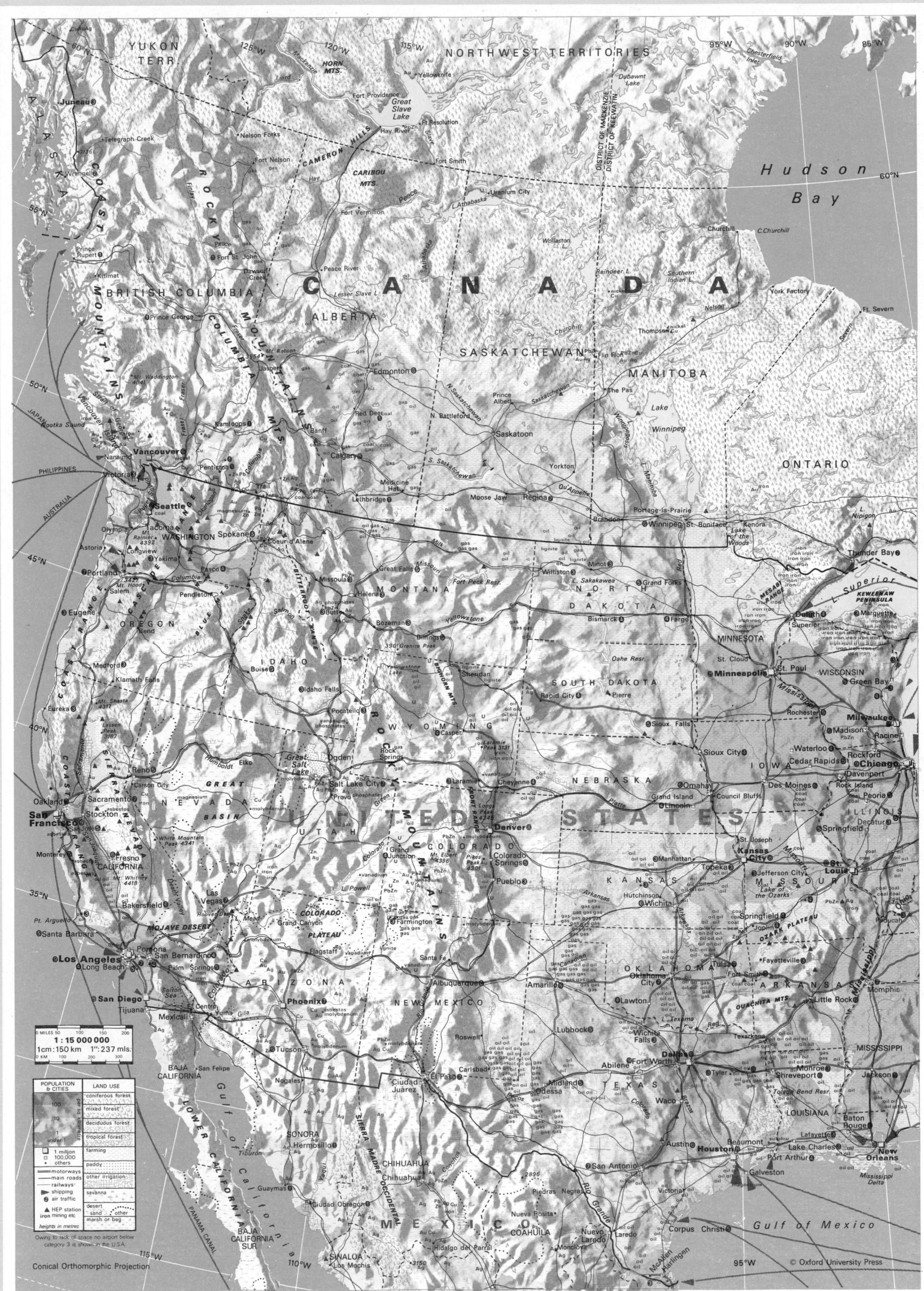

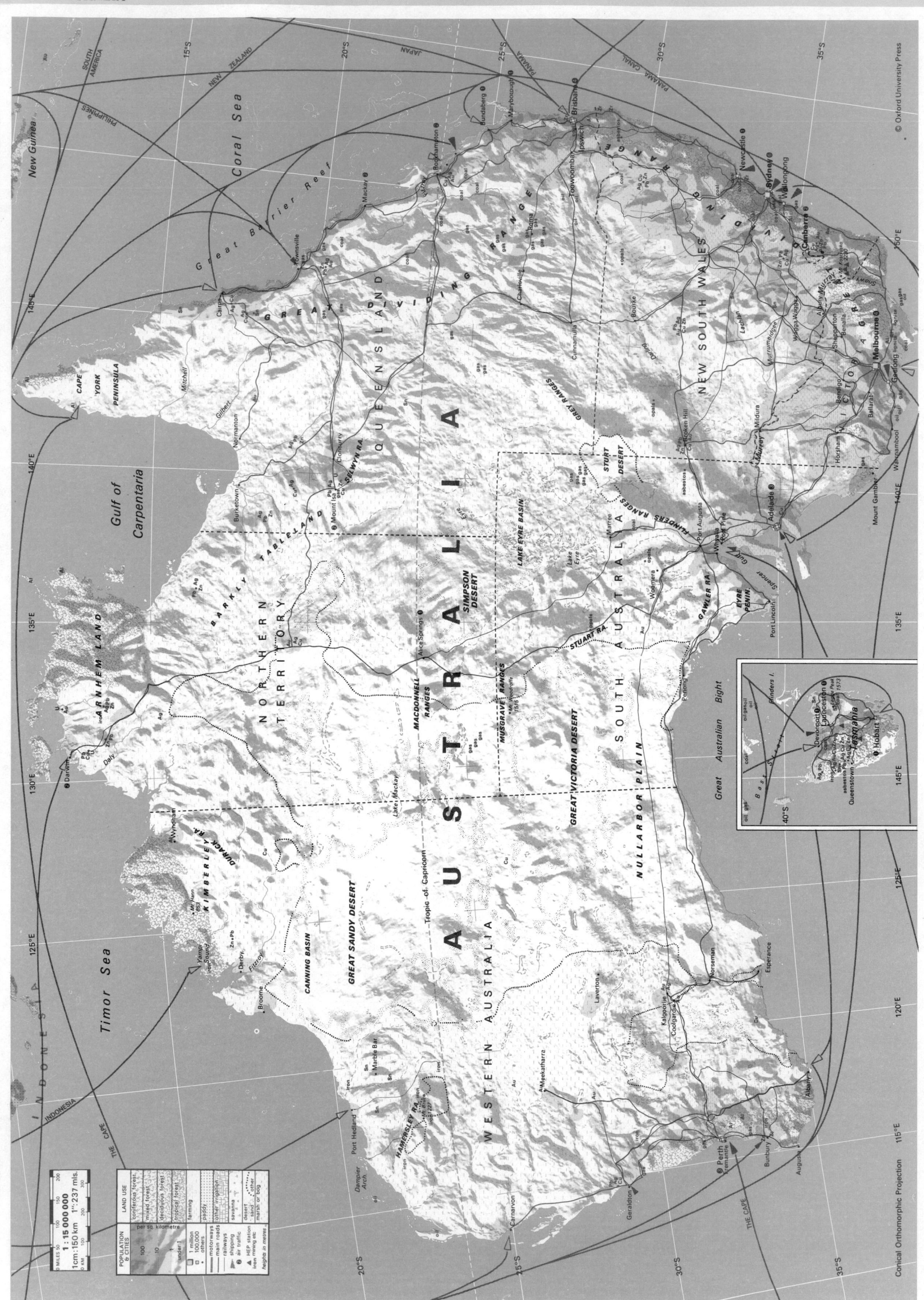

New Guinea

PHILIPPINES

JAPAN

PANAMA

PANAMA CANAL

SOUTH AMERICA

NEW ZEALAND

*Coral Sea*

New Guinea

*Great Barrier Reef*

CAPE
YORK
PENINSULA

Townsville

*Gulf of
Carpentaria*

Mitchell

Gilbert

Normanton

Burketown

Mount Isa

SELWYN RA.

A R N H E M L A N D

Daly

Darwin

Wyndham

KIMBERLEY RA.

DURACK RA.

Derby

Broome

Mt Herbert

Dampier
Arch.

Port Hedland

Marble Bar

HAMERSLEY RA.

Carnarvon

Meekatharra

Geraldton

Perth

Bunbury

Augusta

THE CAPE

Albany

Esperance

Norseman

*Great Australian Bight*

Kalgoorlie
Coolgardie

Laverton

NULLARBOR PLAIN

GREAT VICTORIA DESERT

GREAT SANDY DESERT

CANNING BASIN

*Tropic of Capricorn*

Lake Mackay

W E S T E R N   A U S T R A L I A

A U S T R A L I A

MUSGRAVE RANGES

MACDONNELL
RANGES

Alice Springs

Mt Ziel
1510

N O R T H E R N
T E R R I T O R Y

BARKLY TABLELAND

Q U E E N S L A N D

GREAT DIVIDING RANGE

Cloncurry

Charleville

Cunnamulla

Cairns

Mackay

Rockhampton

Bundaberg
Maryborough

Brisbane
Ipswich

Toowoomba

GREY RANGES

STURT DESERT

LAKE EYRE BASIN

Lake Eyre

Marree

STUART RA.

FLINDERS RANGES

SIMPSON
DESERT

S O U T H   A U S T R A L I A

Port Augusta
Port Pirie

Whyalla

GAWLER RA.

EYRE
PENIN.

Port Lincoln

Adelaide

*Great Australian Bight*

Spencer Gulf

Bourke

Broken Hill

Wilcannia

NEW SOUTH WALES

Newcastle
Sydney
Wollongong

Canberra

Murrumbidgee
Lachlan

Murray
Darling

Wagga Wagga

Albury

V I C T O R I A

Shepparton

Benalla

Bendigo

Ballarat

Mildura

Horsham

Geelong

Melbourne

Warrnambool

Mount Gambier

*Timor Sea*

INDONESIA

INDONESIA

Bass Strait

Flinders I.

Devonport

Launceston

Burnie

*Tasmania*

Queenstown

Hobart

Cradle Mt
1573

© Oxford University Press

Conical Orthomorphic Projection

1 : 15 000 000
1cm:150 km    1″:237 mls.

MILES 50  0  50  100  150  200
KM  0    100  200  300

LAND USE
coniferous forest
mixed forest
deciduous forest
tropical forest
farming
paddy
other irrigation
savanna
desert
sand
marsh or bog

POPULATION
& CITIES
1 million
100,000
others
per sq. kilometre
100
10
under 1

motorways
main roads
railways
shipping
air traffic
HEP station
iron mining etc
heights in metres

# WHO'S WHO

Who's who in the Christian world, 1970-80

*This is a true saying: If a man is eager to be a church leader, he desires an excellent work.*
—1 Timothy 3.1, Good News Bible.

This listing gives 490 names of church and council executives and other persons prominent in the contemporary Christian world in or around the period 1975–80, which may be regarded as a representative cross-section of international Christian leadership during the decade 1970–80.

The object of this Who's Who should be clearly stated. It is not to inform the reader about who the bishop or general secretary of this or that church or organization is, or was in 1970, or in 1975, or in 1980, since such appointments change too rapidly for a survey of this nature. Our object is the reverse: to inform the reader who knows a leading executive's name and wants to know what church or council or organization he directed or headed during the period 1970–80. Another purpose is to enable the reader to get a general idea of the global spread of Christian leaders and decision-makers during this period, and also an idea of the titles, ages, nationalities and denominational affiliations of the executives involved.

In the world's 20,800 distinct Christian denominations today, there are over 16,000 bishops, over 8,000 moderators and church presidents, over a million priests, pastors, ministers and clergy, some 250,000 foreign missionaries and personnel, over 3 million men and women church workers and personnel of all kinds, to say nothing of the one billion lay persons who are practising Christians. It is therefore an impossible task to draw up any concise yet balanced selection of all names of importance. So that our selection will not be too arbitrary, we need to employ and to set out certain guiding principles.

The present listing of 490 persons therefore brings together the names of individuals in the following 6 categories: (1) executive heads of all national, regional, continental, international and confessional councils or alliances of churches, Christian councils, fellowships of churches, and episcopal conferences; (2) executive heads of the 64 major Protestant, Orthodox, Anglican and other denominations with over one million affiliated members each in 1970; (3) heads of all 63 Roman Catholic local (nation-wide) churches with over one million Catholics each in 1970 (most of whom are also presidents of Catholic national episcopal conferences); (4) executive heads of a representative range of major international Christian service agencies or organizations; (5) executive heads of a representative range of major international missionary organizations; and (6) a selection of other prominent figures who are of note on the international Christian scene. On principle, for almost all organizations only one office-holder is listed, usually the main executive, and usually the one in office in or around 1975–8; if he has subsequently died, however, the year of death is added, and his successor is usually included in the listing also.

Information on each person is arranged in the standard order shown opposite. The churches and organizations listed here are mentioned only by name; further information on them is given elsewhere in this survey.

# WHO'S WHO IN THE CHRISTIAN WORLD, AD 1970–1980

1. Where an ecclesiastical name is exclusively used:
   *Ecclesiastical name*, anglicized (e.g. Paul VI, Shenouda III).
   *Alternative spelling(s)* (non-anglicized) in parentheses (Paolo VI).
   *Personal names* in parentheses, not anglicized: first names only if different from ecclesiastical name, followed by surname, then by *religious order* if any, anglicized.
   *Style* (His Holiness, His Beatitude, etc), anglicized.
   *Titles(s)* in order (active or executive only, excluding honorary), anglicized.
   *Year* title conferred, in parentheses (only added occasionally).
2. If no ecclesiastical name is normally exclusively used:
   *Surname*.
   *Style* (Most Rev., Right Rev., Rev., Dr, Bishop, Professor, Mr, Mrs, Miss, Ms, etc), anglicized. The title 'Fr' (Father) is not added for Roman Catholic priests because universally applied and understood.
   *Christian names*, not anglicized.
   *Religious order* or congregation, if any (SJ, OP, etc), anglicized.
   *Title(s)* in order (executive, not honorary), anglicized.
   *Year* main title conferred, in parentheses ('Since 1971').
   *Executive post* (if different from title), not anglicized.
   *Year* post taken up, in parentheses, or occasionally year post given up.
   *Church/denomination/council/organization* (not anglicized; in one of our 6 major languages), with initials or acronym if widely used.
   *Country* of operation or HQ (if not evident from rest of entry), in parentheses.
3. For all persons, there then follow one or more of these:
   *Year of birth* (Born 1920), and year of death if applicable (Died 1977).
   *Nationality* (country of citizenship).
   *Denomination* (confessional membership).

---

**Abainza**, Bishop Estanilao Q. General Secretary, United Church of Christ in the Philippines (UCCP). Born 1923. Nationality: Philippines. United.

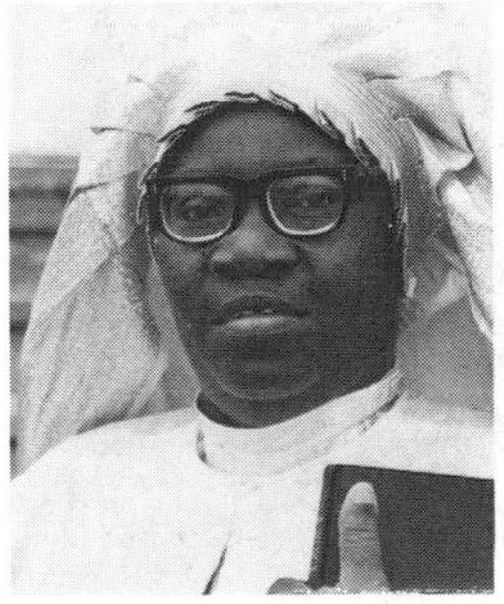

Mother ABIODUN

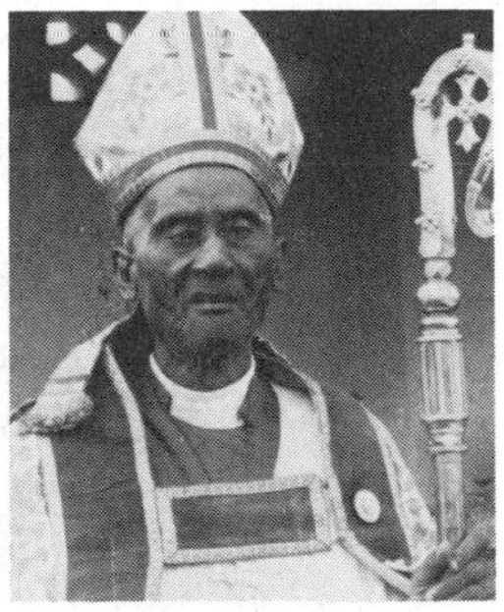

Elder Apostle ABIOLA

**Abiodun**, Most Rev. Mother Captain Christiana Emmanuel, Living Founder & Supreme Head, Sacred Order of Cherubim & Seraphim Society. Born 1908. Nationality: Nigeria. African Independent.
**Abiola**, Most Elder Apostle Adekunle Ayodele, General Superintendent & Supreme Head, Sacred Cherubim & Seraphim Society of Nigeria. Chairman-General, Nigerian Association of Aladura Churches (NAAC). Born 1899. Nationality: Nigeria. African Independent.
**Adam**, Right Rev. François Nestor, Bishop of Zion. Président: Conférence des Evêques Suisses. Born 1903. Nationality: Switzerland. Roman Catholic.
**Adejobi**, Most Rev. Dr Emmanuel Owoade Adeleke Sunday, Archbishop and Primate, Church of the Lord (Aladura). Chairman, Organization of African Independent Churches (OAIC). Born 1922. Nationality: Nigeria. African Independent.

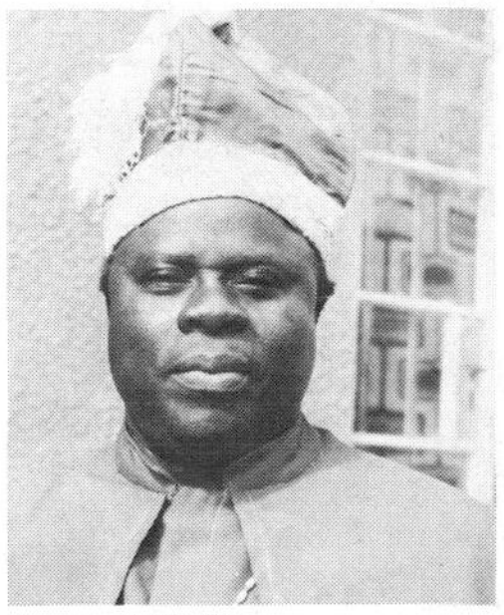

Primate ADEJOBI

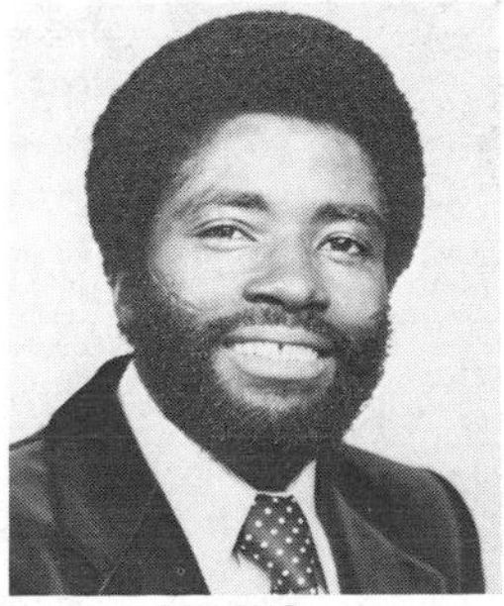

Secretary ADEYEMO

**Adeyemo**, Rev. Dr Tokunboh. General Secretary, Association of Evangelicals of Africa and Madagascar (AEAM). Born 1944. Nationality: Nigeria. Evangelical (ECWA).
**Adimou**, Most Rev. Christopher, Archbishop of Cotonou. Président, Conférence Episcopale du Benin. Born 1916. Nationality: Benin. Roman Catholic.
**Aier**, Rev K. Imotemjen. General Secretary, Council of Baptist Churches in North East India. Nationality: India. Baptist.
**Aires da Cruz**, Most Rev. José, Archbishop & Second Primate (elected 1961), Igreja Católica Apostólica Brasileira (ICAB). Nationality: Brazil. Catholic (non-Roman).
**Allin**, Right Rev. John Maury, Presiding Bishop, Episcopal Church in the USA (ECUSA). Born 1921. Nationality: USA. Episcopalian (Anglican).
**Allison**, Rev. Canon R.G. General Secretary, United Christian Council in Israel (UCCI). Nationality: UK. Anglican.
**Alton**, Bishop Ralph T. Secretary, Council of Bishops, United Methodist Church (USA). Nationality: USA. Methodist.
**Alves**, Mr J.V. President, Christian Council of St Vincent. Nationality: St Vincent.
**Andersen**, Miss Birte. Administrative Secretary, Danish Missionary Council. Nationality: Denmark. Lutheran.
**Andoh**, Right Rev. Dominic Kodwo, Bishop of Accra. President, Ghana Bishops' Conference. Born 1929. Nationality: Ghana. Roman Catholic.
**Andrews**, Rev. James E. Stated Clerk, Presbyterian Church in the US. Nationality: USA. Presbyterian.
**Anguilé**, Most Rev. André F., Archbishop of Libreville. Président, Conférence Episcopale du Gabon. Born 1922. Nationality: Gabon. Roman Catholic.
**Ansa**, Rev. Charles A. General Secretary, Christian Council of Ghana. Born 1922. Nationality: Ghana. Presbyterian.
**Aponte Martínez**, His Eminence Cardinal Luis, Arcbishop of San Juan of Puerto Rico. Presidente, Conferencia Episcopal Puertoriqueña. Born 1922. Nationality: Puerto Rico. Roman Catholic.
**Arden**, Most Rev. Donald Seymour, Archbishop of Central Africa. Secretary, Conference of Anglican Provinces in Africa (CAPA). Born 1916. Retired 1980. Nationality: UK. Anglican.
**Arlow**, Rev. William J. Secretary, Irish Council of Churches.
**Arrieta Villalobos**, Right Rev. Roman, Bishop of Tilarán. Presidente, Conferencia Episcopal de Costa Rica (CECOR). Born 1924. Nationality: Costa Rica. Roman Catholic.
**Arrupe**, Rev. Fr Pedro, SJ. General Society of Jesus; Presidente, Unione dei Superiori Generali. Born 1907. Nationality: Spain (Basque). Roman Catholic.
**Aru**, Pastor Simeon. Chairman, Vanuatu Christian Council. Nationality: Vanuatu.
**Baccino**, Right Rev. Luis, Bishop of San José de Mayo. Presidente, Conferencia Episcopal Uruguaya. Born 1905. Nationality: Uruguay. Roman Catholic.
**Baggio**, His Eminence Cardinal Sabastiano. Prefect, Sacred Congregation for Bishops, Roman Curia (Vatican City). Born 1913. Nationality: Italy. Roman Catholic.
**Bailey**, Rev. C. Evans. Executive Secretary, Jamaica Council of Churches. Nationality: Jamaica.
**Baksa**, Pastor Arpad. Secretary, Ecumenical Council of Churches in Yugoslavia. Nationality: Yugoslavia.
**Bamrungtrakul**, Right Rev. Robert Ratna, Bishop of Ratchaburi. President, Bishops' Conference of Thailand. Born 1916. Nationality: Thailand. Roman Catholic.
**Barnes**, Mr D.J. Honorary Secretary, Fiji Council of Churches.
**Barrera y Rayes**, Right Rev. Benjamin, MI, Bishop of Santa Ana. Presidente, Conferencia Episcopal del El Salvador. Born 1902. Nationality: El Salvador. Roman Catholic.
**Bartha**, Right Rev. Bishop (Fotiszteletü Püspök) Dr Tibor. Clerical President of General Synod (A Zsinat Lelkészi Elnöke) (since 1957), Reformed Church of Hungary. Born 1912. Nationality: Hungary. Reformed.
**Baselius Augen I**, His Holiness Moran Mar, Catholicos of the East & Metropolitan of Malankara (since 1962). Born 1884. Nationality: India. Syrian Orthodox.
**Batanian**, see Ignatius Peter XVI.
**Beach**, Dr Bert Beverly. Secretary, Conference of Secretaries of Christian World Communions. Born 1928. Nationality: USA. Seventh-day Adventist.
**Bekish, J.**, see Ireney.
**Bello**, Rev. I.B. Secretary, Evangelical Churches of West Africa (ECWA). Nationality: Nigeria. Evangelical.
**Beltritti**, His Beatitude Giacoma, Latin Patriarch of Jerusalem. Président, Conférence des Evêques Latins dans les Régions Arabes (CELRA). Born 1910. Nationality: Italy. Roman Catholic.
**Benech**, Mr Carlos Enrique. Executive Secretary, Federación de Iglesias Evangélicas del Uruguay (FIEU). Nationality: Uruguay.
**Benediktos I (Vassilios Papadopoulos)**, His Holiness (or His Beatitude), Patriarch of the Holy City of Jerusalem & All Palestine. Born 1892. Nationality: Israel/Greece. Greek Orthodox.
**Bengsch**, His Eminence Cardinal Alfred, Archbishop of Berlin. President, Berliner Ordinarienkonferenz (HQ German Democratic Republic). Born 1921. Nationality: German Democratic Republic. Roman Catholic.
**Benítez Avalos**, Right Rev. Felipe Santiago, Bishop of Villarrica. Presidente, Conferencia Episcopal Paraguaya. Born 1926. Nationality: Paraguay. Roman Catholic.
**Benítez Fonturvel**, Most Rev. Críspulo, Archbishop of Barquisimeto. Presidente, Conferencia Episcopal de Venezuela. Born 1905. Nationality: Venezuela. Roman Catholic.
**Beras Rojas**, Most Rev. Octavio Antonio, Archbishop of Santo Domingo. Presidente, Conferencia del Episcopado Dominicano. Born 1906. Nationality: Dominican Republic. Roman Catholic.
**Biayenda**, His Eminence Cardinal Emile, Archbishop of Brazzaville. Président, Conférence Episcopale du Congo (Brazzaville). Born 1927. Murdered 1977. Nationality: Congo. Roman Catholic.
**Bjerno**, Mr Aage. President, Evangelical Alliance of Denmark. Nationality: Denmark.
**Blanch**, Most Rev. & Right Hon. Stuart Yarworth, Archbishop of York & Primate of England & Metropolitan. Born 1918. Nationality: UK. Anglican.
**Bokeleale**, Rev. Dr Itofo Bokambanza. Président, Eglise du Christ au Zaïre (ECZ). Born 1919. Nationality: Zaire. Disciples.
**Boseto**, Rev. Leslie. Moderator, United Church in Papua New Guinea & the Solomon Islands. Born 1933. Nationality: Papua New Guinea. United.
**Bright**, Dr William R. Founder and President, Campus Crusade for Christ International (CCCI). Born 1925. Nationality: USA. Presbyterian.
**Brosnahan**, Most Rev. Thomas J., CSSp, Archbishop of Freetown and Bo. President, Inter-territorial Episcopal Conference of Gambia, Liberia and Sierra Leone. Born 1905. Nationality: Sierra Leone. Roman Catholic.

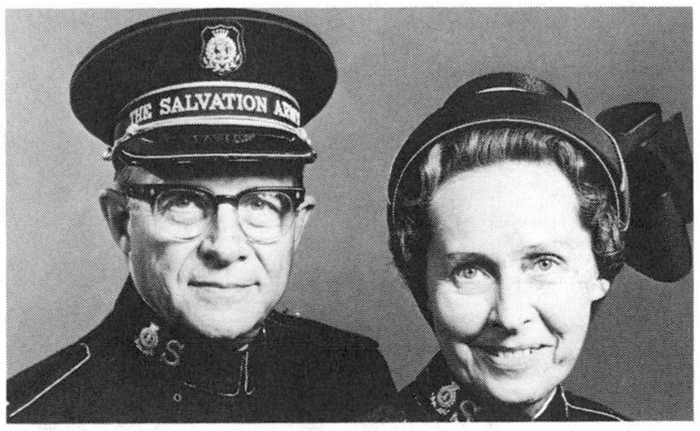

General & Mrs General BROWN

**Brown**, General Arnold. Eleventh General of the Salvation Army (1977). Born 1913. Nationality: Canada. Salvationist.
**Burnett**, Most Rev. Bill Bendyshe, Archbishop of Cape Town & Metropolitan of South Africa, Church of the Province of South Africa (CPSA). Born 1917. Nationality: South Africa. Anglican.
**Buttler**, Pastor P.G. Secretary, Deutscher Evangelischer Missions-Rat. Nationality: FR Germany.
**Bychkov**, Rev. Alexei M. General Secretary, Union of Evangelical Christians-Baptists of USSR (AUCECB). Born 1928. Nationality: USSR. Baptist.
**Câmara**, see Pessoa Câmara.
**Campbell**, Rev. Robert C. General Secretary, American Baptist Churches in the USA. Nationality: USA. Baptist.
**Campi**, Rev. Dr Emidio. General Secretary, World Student Christian Federation (WSCF). Born 1943. Nationality: Italy. Waldensian.
**Carr**, Rev. Canon Burgess. General Secretary, All Africa Conference of Churches (AACC) (until 1979). Born 1935. Nationality: Liberia. Episcopalian.
**Carter**, Most Rev. Samuel Emmanuel, SJ, Archbishop of Kingston in Jamaica. President, Antilles Episcopal Conference (AEC). Born 1919. Nationality: Jamaica. Roman Catholic.
**Castrén**, Miss Inga-Brita. General Secretary, Ecumenical Council of Finland. Born 1919. Nationality: Finland. Lutheran.
**Cheikho**, see Paul II.
**Chiona**, Most Rev. James, Archbishop of Blantyre. President, Episcopal Conference of Malawi. Born 1924. Nationality: Malawi. Roman Catholic.
**Class**, Bishop Helmut, Landesbischof, Evangelische Landeskirche in Württemberg; Vorsitzender, Rat der Evangelischen Kirche in Deutschland (Chairman, EKD Council of Bishops). Nationality: FR Germany.
**Coggan**, Most Rev. & Right Hon. Frederick Donald, Archbishop of Canterbury and Primate of All England (retired 1980). Born 1909. Nationality: UK. Anglican.
**Coggins**, Dr Wade T. Executive Director, Evangelical Foreign Missions Association (EFMA). Nationality: USA.
**Comba**, Rev. Pastor Aldo. Secretary, Federazione delle Chiese Evangeliche in Italia (FCEI). Born 1924. Nationality: Italy.
**Constant**, Right Rev. Emmanuel, Bishop of Les Gonaïves. Président, Conférence Episcopale de Haiti. Born 1928. Nationality: Haiti. Roman Catholic.
**Conway**, His Eminence Cardinal William, Archbishop of Armagh. President, Episcopal Conference of Ireland. Born 1913. Died 1977. Nationality: Ireland. Roman Catholic.
**Cooray**, His Eminence Cardinal Thomas B., OMI, Archbishop of Colombo. President, Bishops' Conference of Sri Lanka. Born 1901. Nationality: Sri Lanka. Roman Catholic.
**Cordeiro**, His Eminence Cardinal Joseph, Archbishop of Karachi. President, Pakistan Episcopal Conference. Born 1918. Nationality: Pakistan. Roman Catholic.
**Cruz**, Rev. Orestes Gonzales. Executive Secretary, Consejo de Iglesias Evangélicas de Cuba. Nationality: Cuba.
**Cunha**, Rev. Ireneu da Silva. General Secretary, Conselho Português de Igrejas Cristãs. Nationality: Portugal.
**Dalmais**, Most Rev. Paul, SJ, Archbishop of N'Djamena. Président, Association des Conférences Episcopales du Congo, de la République Centrafricaine, et du Tchad (ACECCT). Born 1917. Nationality: Chad. Roman Catholic.
**Damaris**, Rev. Stephanus. Secretary General, Indonesia Evangelical Fellowship.
**Damien**, Most Rev., Archbishop of Tirana. Died 1973. Nationality: Albania. Greek Orthodox.
**Darmojuwono**, His Eminence Cardinal Justinus, Archbishop of Semarang. President, General Conference of Ordinaries of Indonesia (MAWI). Born 1914. Nationality: Indonesia. Roman Catholic.

**David V (Gregory Sidamonidze),** His Beatitude, Archbishop of Mtzkheta, Metropolitan of Tiflis and Catholicos-Patriarch of All Georgia. Born 1896. Died 1977. Nationality: USSR. Georgian Orthodox.
**Davies,** Mr J.E.(Ted). Honorary Secretary, New Zealand Evangelical Alliance. Nationality: New Zealand.
**Davies,** Rev. Meirion Lloyd. General Secretary, Council of Churches for Wales. Nationality: UK.
**Davies,** Mrs P.W. Secretary, Isle of Man Council of Churches. Nationality: UK.
**Daws,** Rev. C.K. President General, Methodist Church of Australia. Nationality: Australia. Methodist.

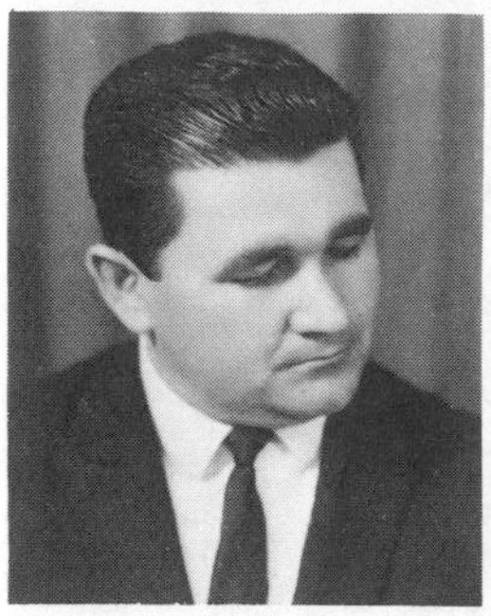
Missionário DE MELLO

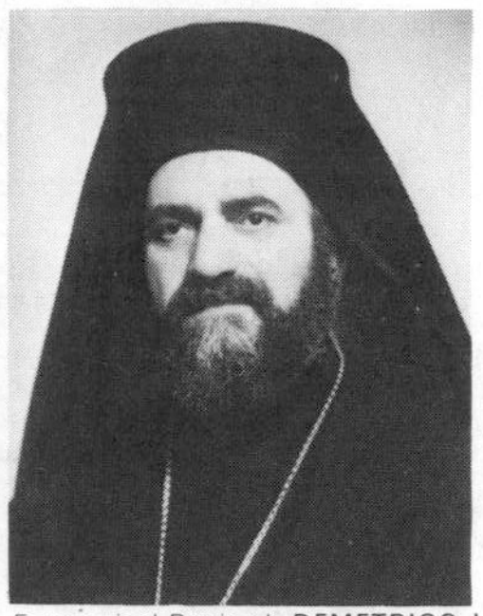
Ecumenical Patriarch DEMETRIOS I

**de Mello Silva,** Pastor Manoel. President, Evangelical Pentecostal Church 'Brazil for Christ' (OBPC). Born 1929. Nationality: Brazil. Indigenous pentecostal.
**de Run,** Rev. Lloyd B. Chairman, National Evangelical Fellowship of Malaysia. Nationality: Malaysia.
**Demetrios I (Dimitrios Papadopoulos),** His All-Holiness, Archbishop of Constantinople, New Rome & Ecumenical Patriarch (elected 1971). Born 1914. Nationality: Turkey. Greek Orthodox.
**Deng,** Right Rev. Pio Yukwan, Bishop of Malakal. President, Sudan Episcopal Conference. Nationality: Sudan. Roman Catholic.
**Denisenko,** see Filaret.
**Denny,** Dr Robert S. General Secretary, Baptist World Alliance (BWA). Nationality: USA. Baptist.
**Dharmaraj,** Mr Alfred Clarke. General Secretary, Church of North India (CNI). Born 1912. Nationality: India. United.

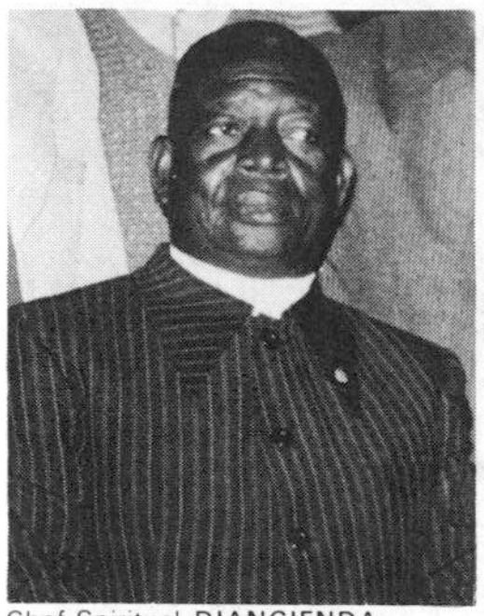
Chef Spirituel DIANGIENDA

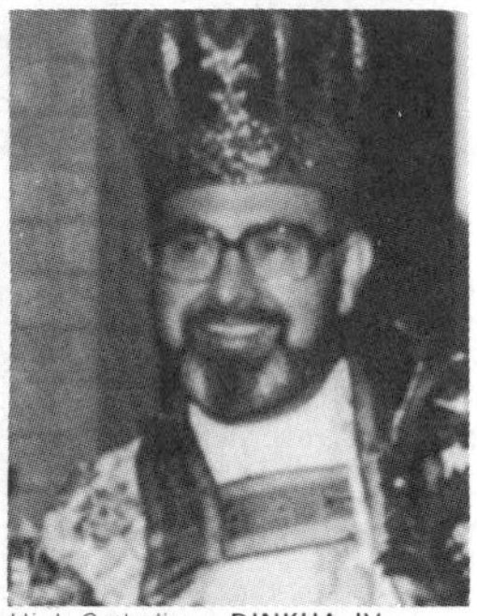
High Catholicos DINKHA IV

**Diangienda,** His Eminence Joseph Ku Ntima. Chef Spirituel, Eglise de Jésus-Christ sur la Terre par le Prophète Simon Kimbangu (EJCSK). Born 1918. Nationality: Zaire. African Independent.
**Dinkha IV,** His Holiness Mar (Dinkha Khananyia), High Catholicos Patriarch of the East, Ancient Assyrian Church of the East, elected 1977. Born 1936. Nationality: Iran. Assyrian.
**Dombrava,** Rev. Mother Florina Jana. Mother Superior, Pasarea Monastery, Romanian Orthodox Church. Born 1930. Nationality: Romania. Orthodox.
**Domínguez y Rodríguez,** Right Rev. José Maximino Eusebio, Bishop of Matanzas. Presidente, Conferencia Episcopal de Cuba. Born 1915. Nationality: Cuba. Roman Catholic.
**Döpfner,** His Eminence Cardinal Julius, Archbishop of Munich and Friesing. President, Deutsche Bischofskonferenz, and Bayerische Bischofskonferenz. Born 1913. Nationality: FR Germany. Roman Catholic.
**Dorotey (Filipp),** His Beatitude, Metropolitan of Prague & All Czechoslovakia. Born 1913. Nationality: Czechoslovakia. Greek Orthodox.
**Dositey (Stoykovsky),** His Beatitude, Archbishop of Ochrid & Macedonia, Metropolitan of the Macedonian Orthodox Church. Born 1906. Nationality: Yugoslavia. Orthodox.
**Dosseh Anyron,** Most Rev. Robert, Archbishop of Lomé. Président, Conférence Plénière des Ordinaires de l'Afrique Occidentale; Président, Conférence Episcopale du Togo. Born 1925. Nationality: Togo. Roman Catholic.
**Du Plessis,** Rev. David Johannes. Ecumenical Pentecostal evangelist. Born 1905. Nationality: USA. Assemblies of God.
**Dube,** Rev. Joseph James. Secretary, Christian Apostolic Church in Zion; Secretary, League of Independent Churches of Swaziland. Born 1915. Nationality: Swaziland. African Independent.
**Dutta,** Mr Dilip Kumar. Executive Secretary, National Council of Churches of Bangladesh. Born 1942. Nationality: Bangladesh. Baptist.
**Dutton,** Rev. Denis C. Honorary General Secretary, Council of Churches of Malaysia.
**Duval,** His Eminence Cardinal Léon-Etienne, Archbishop of Algiers. Président, Conférence Episcopale d'Afrique du Nord. Born 1903. Nationality: Algeria. Roman Catholic.
**D'Almeida Trindade,** Right Rev. Manuel, Bishop of Aveiro. Presidente, Conferência Episcopal Portuguesa da Metrópole. Born 1918. Nationality: Portugal. Roman Catholic.
**Echeverria Ruiz,** Most Rev. Bernardino, OFM, Archbishop of Guayaquil. Presidente, Conferencia Episcopal Ecuatoriana. Born 1912. Nationality: Ecuador. Roman Catholic.
**Ekandem,** His Eminence Cardinal Dominic, Bishop of Ikot Ekpene. President, National Episcopal Conference of Nigeria. Born 1917. Nationality: Nigeria. Roman Catholic.
**Elias IV (Mo'awad),** His Holiness (or His Beatitude), Patriarch of Antioch and All the East. Born 1914. Died 1979. Nationality: Syria. Greek Orthodox.
**Elisha (Yeghishe) II (Derderian),** His Beatitude, Armenian Patriarch of Jerusalem. Born 1910. Armenian Apostolic.
**Ellison,** Rev. Father R. Secretary, Gambia Christian Council.
**Engel,** Rev. Frank Graham. General Secretary, Australian Council of Churches (ACC). Nationality: Australia. Presbyterian.
**Enrique y Tarancón,** His Eminence Cardinal Vicente, Archbishop of Madrid. Presidente, Conferencia Episcopal Española. Born 1907. Nationality: Spain. Roman Catholic.
**Etchegaray,** Most Rev. Roger, Archbishop of Marseilles. President, Consilium Conferentiarum Episcopalium Europae (CCEE). Born 1922. Nationality: France. Roman Catholic.
**Faichney,** Right Rev. N. Moderator-General, Presbyterian Church of Australia. Nationality: Australia. Presbyterian.
**Feller,** Mr A.E. Secretary General, Fédération des Eglises Protestantes de la Suisse (FEPS). Nationality: Switzerland. Reformed.
**Fen,** Mr Li Shih. President, China Evangelical Fellowship, Taiwan. Nationality: Taiwan.
**Ferraz,** Rev. José Coelho. Executive Secretary, Confederação Evangélica do Brasil. Nationality: Brazil.
**Fick,** Rev. Ulrich. General Secretary, United Bible Societies (UBS). Born 1922. Nationality: FR Germany. Lutheran.
**Filaret (Michail Antonovic Denisenko),** Exarch of the Ukraine, Archbishop of Kiev and Galicia, Russian Orthodox Church. Born 1929. Nationality: USSR. Orthodox.
**Filaret (Voznessenskiy),** His Eminence, Metropolitan of East America and New York. Primate, Russian Orthodox Church Outside of Russia. Born 1903. Nationality: USA. Russian Orthodox.
**Fiolet,** Dr H.A.M. Secretary, Council of Churches in the Netherlands. Nationality: Netherlands.
**Fitzgerald,** Most Rev. Joseph P., OMI, Archbishop of Bloemfontein. President (1975), Southern Africa Catholic Bishops' Conference. Born 1914. Nationality: South Africa. Roman Catholic.
**Forck,** Rev. Dr Gottfried. General Superintendent, Federation of Evangelical Churches in the GDR. Born 1923. Nationality: German Democratic Republic. Lutheran.
**Fortier,** Most Rev. Jean-Marie, Archbishop of Sherbrooke. President, Canadian Catholic Conference (CCC). Born 1920. Nationality: Canada. Roman Catholic.
**Franklin,** Mr Fredrik. Secretary General. World Alliance of YMCAs.
**Fraser,** Rev. Wilfred. Secretary, Guyana Council of Churches. Nationality: Guyana.
**Freeman,** His Eminence Cardinal James Darcy, Archbishop of Sydney. President, Australian Episcopal Conference. Born 1907. Nationality: Australia. Roman Catholic.
**Frizen,** Mr Edwin L., Jr. Executive Director, Interdenominational Foreign Mission Association (IFMA). Nationality: USA.
**Ga,** Right Rev. Macario V., Obispo Maximo, Iglesia Filipina Independiente (Philippine Independent Church). Nationality: Philippines. Independent Catholic.
**Gaillard,** Mr Yves. Secretary, Swiss Evangelical Fellowship. Nationality: Switzerland.
**Galvin,** Right Rev. Anthony Denis, MHM, Vicar Apostolic of Miri. President, Catholic Bishops' Conference of Malaysia-Singapore. Born 1919. Roman Catholic.
**Ganguli,** Most Rev. Theotonius A., CSC, Archbishop of Dacca. President, Catholic Bishops' Conference of Bangladesh. Born 1920. Nationality: Bangladesh. Roman Catholic.
**Garrone,** His Eminence Cardinal Gabriel-Marie. Prefect, Sacred Congregation for Catholic Education, Roman Curia (Vatican City). Born 1901. Nationality: Holy See. Roman Catholic.
**Gatu,** Rev. John G. Chairman, All Africa Conference of Churches (AACC). Born 1925. Nationality: Kenya. Presbyterian.
**Gaxiola,** Rev. Manuel J. Bishop, Apostolic Church of the Faith in Christ Jesus. Nationality: Mexico. Independent pentecostal.
**Gegeyo,** Rev. Kingsley. Executive Secretary, Melanesian Council of Churches. Nationality: Papua New Guinea.
**Genheimer,** Rev. Don. Chairman, Association of Evangelicals of South Africa. Nationality: South Africa.
**Gerardi Conedera,** Right Rev. Juan, Bishop of Santa Cruz del Quiché. Presidente, Conferencia Episcopal de Guatemala. Born 1922. Nationality: Guatemala. Roman Catholic.

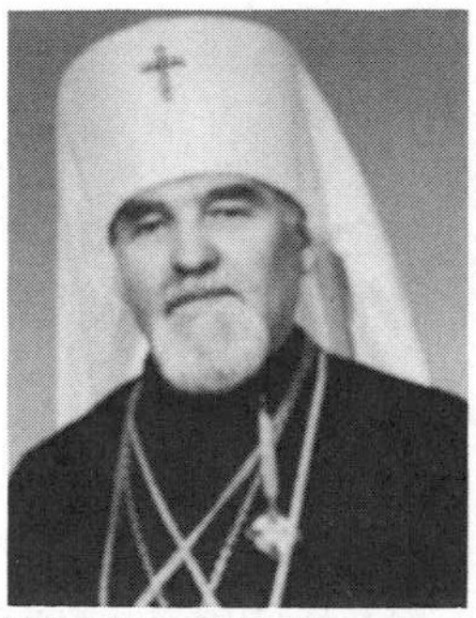
Metropolitan DOROTEY

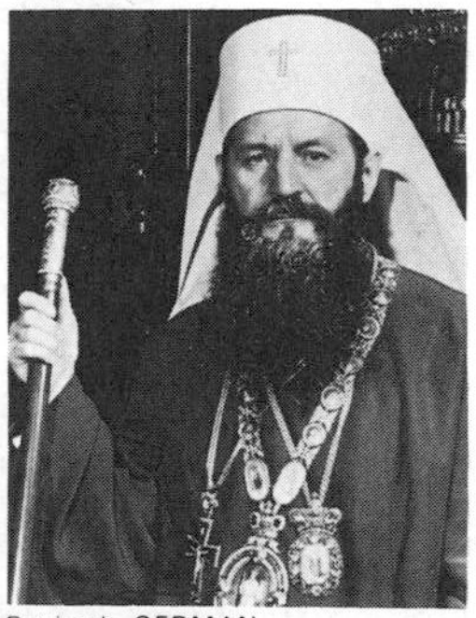
Patriarch GERMAN

**German (Djorich),** His Holiness, Archbishop of Pec, Metropolitan of Belgrade & Karlovitz, Patriarch of Serbia. Born 1899. Nationality: Yugoslavia. Serbian Orthodox.
**Gill,** Rev. William. Chairman, Evangelical Fellowship of Pakistan. Nationality: Pakistan.
**Gilson-Rome,** Mme C. Secretary, Fédération des Eglises Protestantes de Belgique. Nationality: Belgium.
**Gjerding,** Mr Uffe. General Secretary, Ecumenical Council of Denmark. Nationality: Denmark. Lutheran.
**Goncalves,** Most Rev. Raul Nicolau, Archbishop of Goa & Damao, Patriarch of the East Indies. Born 1927. Nationality: India. Roman Catholic.
**Gonzi,** Most Rev. Michael, Archbishop of Malta. President, Maltese Episcopal Conference. Born 1885. Nationality: Malta. Roman Catholic.
**Gottschald,** Rev. K. President, Evangelical Federation of Brazil. Nationality: Brazil.
**Graham,** Rev. Dr William Franklin (Billy). World evangelist. Born 1918. Nationality: USA. Southern Baptist.
**Gray,** His Eminence Cardinal Gordon J., Archbishop of St Andrews and Edinburgh. President, Bishops' Conference of Scotland. Born 1910. Nationality: UK. Roman Catholic.
**Greet,** Rev. Kenneth Gerald. Secretary of the Conference (since 1971), Methodist Church of Great Britain. Nationality: UK. Methodist.
**Gregory,** Archbishop-Abbot, Church of Sinai, St Catherine's Monastery, Mount Sinai (Egypt). Greek Orthodox.
**Gruhn,** Dr Klaus. Executive Secretary, Deutscher Evangelischer Missionsrat. Nationality: FR Germany.
**Guelly,** Mr Joseph. General Secretary, Sudan Council of Churches Born 1938. Died 1978. Nationality: Sudan. Anglican.
**Haddad,** Mr Fuad. General Secretary, United Christian Council of Israel (UCCI). Nationality: Israel.
**Hadley,** Mr Herbert M. Secretary, Friends World Committee for Consultation (FWCC). Nationality: USA. Quaker.
**Hakim,** see Maximos V.
**Hale,** Rev. Joe. General Secretary, World Methodist Council (WMC). Nationality: USA. Methodist.
**Hallencreutz,** Dr Carl-Fredrik. Assistant General Secretary, Svenska Missionsradet. Born 1934. Nationality: Sweden. Lutheran (Church of Sweden).
**Hand,** Most Rev. Geoffrey David, Archbishop of Papua New Guinea. Chairman, South Pacific Anglican Council (SPAC). Born 1918. Nationality: Papua New Guinea. Anglican.
**Hayek (Haik),** Ignace Antony II, Syrian Catholic Patriarch of Antioch of the Syrians. Head, Syrian Patriarchal Synod. Born 1910. Roman Catholic.
**Hermaniuk,** Most Rev. Maxim, CSSR, Archbishop of Winnipeg. President, Conference of the Ukrainian Catholic Hierarchy. Born 1911. Nationality: Canada. Roman Catholic.
**Hian,** Mr Chua Wee. General Secretary, International Fellowship of Evangelical Students (IFES).
**Hmyin,** Rev. U Ba. General Secretary, Burma Baptist Convention. Nationality: Burma. Baptist.
**Honey,** Dr T.E. Floyd. General Secretary, Canadian Council of Churches (until 1976). Nationality: Canada.
**Howe,** Right Rev. John William Alexander. Secretary General, Anglican Consultative Council (ACC); Secretary, Lambeth Conference. Born 1920. Nationality: UK. Anglican.
**Hoyois,** Pastor M. Wilfred. Président, Departement Missionnaire Protestant de Belgique. Nationality: Belgium.
**Hughes,** Dr Ray H. General Overseer, Church of God (Cleveland); Chairperson, Pentecostal Fellowship of North America (PFNA). Nationality: USA. Pentecostal.
**Hume,** His Eminence Cardinal George Basil, Archbishop of Westminster. President, Bishops' Conference of England & Wales. Born 1923. Nationality: UK. Roman Catholic.
**Humphries,** Rev. M. Secretary-Treasurer, New Hebrides Christian Council.
**Iakovos (James Coucouzis),** His Eminence Archbishop, Exarch of the Ecumenical Patriarch and Primate of the Greek Orthodox Church in North and South America. Chairperson, Standing Conference of Canonical Orthodox Bishops in the Americas (SCOBA). Born 1911. Nationality: USA. Greek Orthodox.
**Ibrahim,** Rev. Simon A., General Secretary, Evangelical Churches of West Africa (ECWA). Born 1942. Nationality: Nigeria. Evangelical.

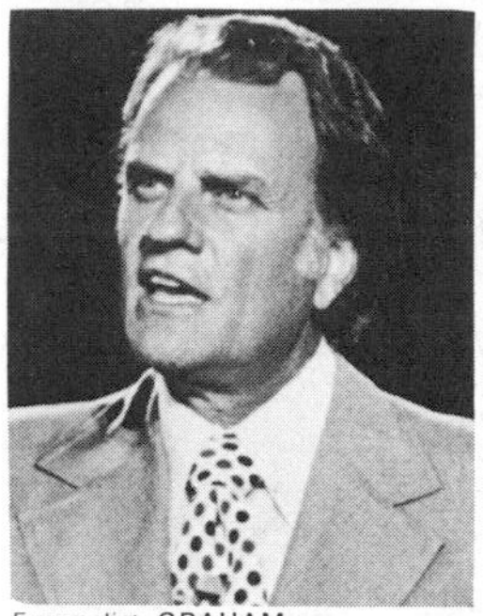
Evangelist GRAHAM

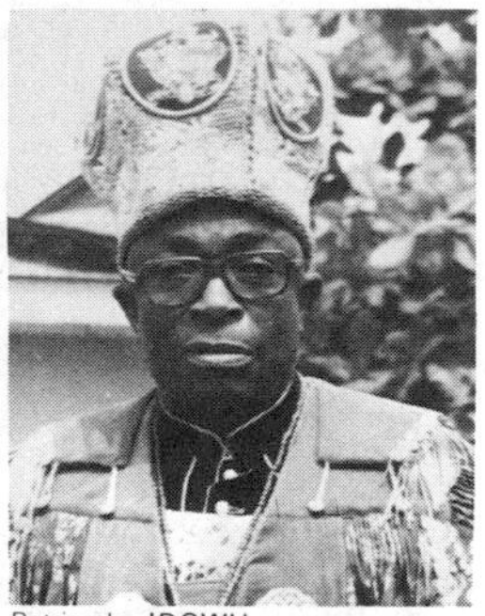
Patriarch IDOWU

**Idowu,** His Pre-Eminence Rev. Prof Emmanuel Bolaji. Archbishop & Patriarch, Patriarchate Conference, Methodist Church Nigeria. Born 1913. Nationality: Nigeria. Methodist.
**Ignatius IV (Habeeb Hazim),** His Holiness (or, His Beatitude), Patriarch of Antioch and All the East. Born 1920. Nationality: Syria. Greek Orthodox.
**Ignatius Yacub III (Severios Jacob Tuma),** His Holiness Moran Mar, Patriarch of Antioch & All the East (since 1957), Supreme Head of the Orthodox Syrian Church. Born 1912. Died 1980. Nationality: Syria. Syrian Orthodox.
**Ignatius Peter XVI (Batanian),** His Beatitude, Patriarch of Cilicia of the Armenians; Head, Armenian Patriarchal Synod. Born 1899. Nationality: Lebanon. Roman Catholic.
**Ijjas,** Most Rev. Jozsef, Archbishop of Kalocsa. President, Magyar Puspoki Kar. Born 1901. Nationality: Hungary. Roman Catholic.

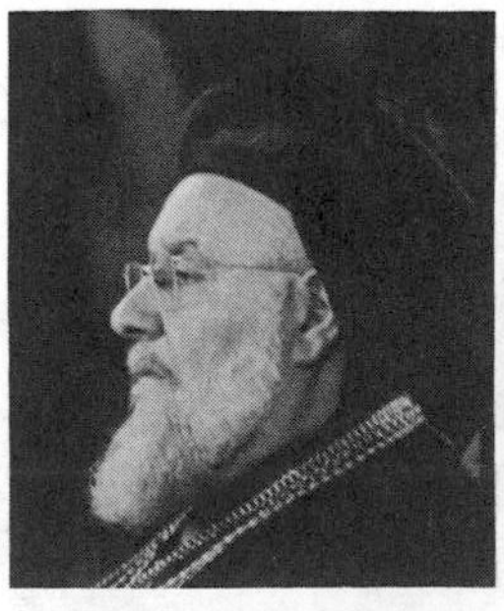
Patriarch IGNATIUS YACUB III

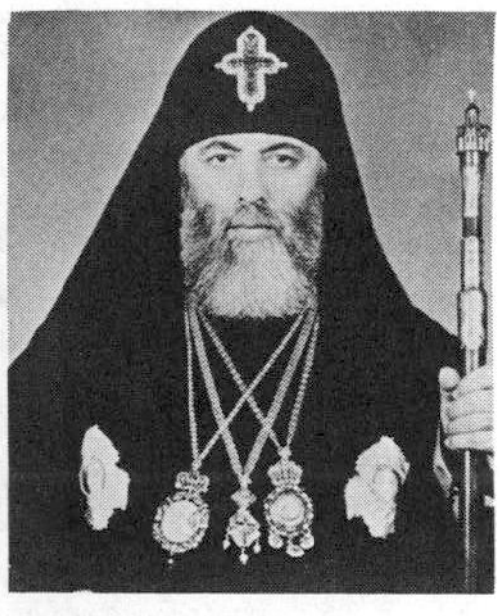
Catholicos ILIYA II

**Ilya II (Shiolashvili),** His Beatitude, Archbishop of Mcheta, Metropolitan of Tiflis, Catholicos-Patriarch of All Georgia, since 1977. Born 1933. Nationality: USSR. Georgian Orthodox.
**Ireney (John Bekish),** His Beatitude, Archbishop of New York, Metropolitan of All America & Canada, Primate, Orthodox Church in America, until 1977. Born 1892. Nationality: USA. Russian Orthodox.
**Ishai (Jesse) Shimun XXIII,** Mar, Patriarch-Catholicos of the Assyrians, Ancient Church of the East (resigned 1973; assassinated 1975). Nationality: Iraq, then naturalized USA citizen. Assyrian.
**Isteero,** Rev. Albert. General Secretary, Middle East Council of Churches (MECC). Born 1930. Nationality: Egypt. Coptic Evangelical.
**Izvekov,** see Pimen.
**Jackson,** Rev. Dr Joseph H. President, National Baptist Convention, USA. Nationality: USA. Baptist.

**Jacob,** Very Rev. W. Ungoed. President, Council of Churches for Wales (UK). Nationality: UK. Anglican.
**Jaime,** Rev. Angel Luis. Coordinator, UNELAM (Movimiento Pro Unidad Evangélica Latinoamericana). Nationality: Puerto Rico.
**Jegasothy,** Mr J.S. General Secretary, National Christian Council of Sri Lanka. Nationality: Sri Lanka.
**Jimenez-Perez,** Mrs Alda de. Secretary, Christian Council of Trinidad and Tobago. Nationality: Trinidad & Tobago.

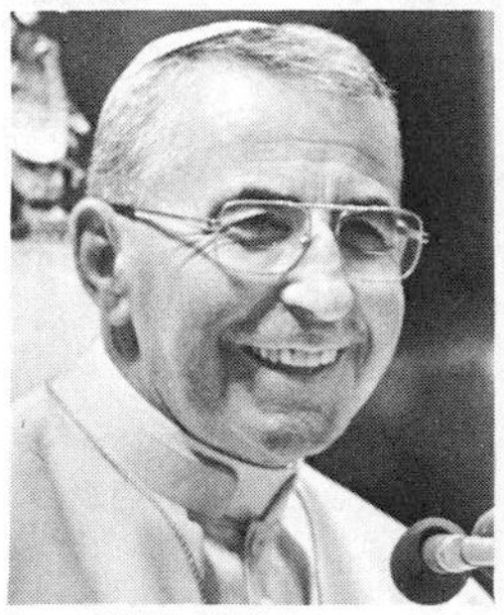
Pope JOHN PAUL I

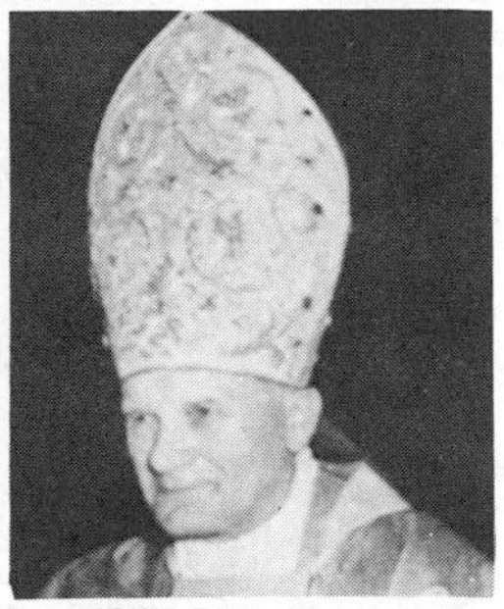
Pope JOHN PAUL II

**John Paul I (Albino Luciani),** His Holiness the Pope (elected 1978), Bishop of Rome, Sovereign of Vatican City State. Born 1912. Died 1978. Nationality: Holy See, and Italy. Roman Catholic.
**John Paul II (Karol Wojtyla),** His Holiness the Pope (elected 1978), Bishop of Rome, Vicar of Jesus Christ, Successor of the Prince of the Apostles, Supreme Pontifex of the Universal Church, Patriarch of the West, Primate of Italy, Sovereign of Vatican City State. Born 1920. Nationality: Holy See, and Poland. Roman Catholic.
**Johnson,** Rev. E.H. Moderator, Presbyterian Church in Canada. Nationality: Canada. Presbyterian.
**Johnston,** Most Rev. Allen Howard. Archbishop, Church of the Province of New Zealand (CPNZ). Born 1912. Nationality: New Zealand. Anglican.
**Juhanon Mar Thoma,** Most Rev. Dr, Metropolitan of Mar Thoma Syrian Church of Malabar (since 1947). Died 1976. Nationality: India. Independent Orthodox.
**Justin (Moisescu),** His Holiness (or His Beatitude), Archbishop of Bucharest, Metropolitan of Ungrovalacia, Patriarch of Romania from 1977. Born 1910. Nationality: Romania. Romanian Orthodox.
**Justinian (Ioan Marina),** His Holiness (or His Beatitude), Archbishop of Bucharest, Metropolitan of Ungrovalacia, Patriarch of Romania. Born 1901. Died 1977. Nationality: Romania. Romanian Orthodox.
**Kachaje,** Rev. Gibiel Adam. General Secretary, Christian Council of Malawi. Born 1930. Nationality: Malawi. Anglican.
**Kahihia,** Right Rev. Benjamin. Bishop, African Independent Pentecostal Church of Africa. Nationality: Kenya. African Independent.
**Kaldy,** Bishop Zoltan. Lutheran Church in Hungary. Born 1919. Nationality: Hungary. Lutheran.
**Kale,** Right Rev. Seth Irunsewe, Bishop of Lagos (since 1963), Anglican Church in Nigeria. Nationality: Nigeria. Anglican.
**Kalustian (Shnork),** His Beatitude, Armenian Patriarch of Constantinople. Born 1907. Nationality: Turkey. Armenian Apostolic.
**Kamau,** Mr John C. General Secretary, National Christian Council of Kenya (NCCK). Born 1923. Nationality: Kenya. Presbyterian.
**Kanyonza,** Rev. Fr Vincent. Executive Secretary, Uganda Joint Christian Council. Born 1930. Nationality: Uganda. Roman Catholic.
**Kao,** Rev. Dr Chun-Ming. General Secretary, Presbyterian Church of Taiwan. Born 1929. Nationality: Taiwan. Presbyterian.
**Kavanagh,** Right Rev. John Patrick, Bishop of Dunedin. President, New Zealand Episcopal Conference. Born 1913. Nationality: New Zealand. Roman Catholic.
**Kayuwa-Tshibumbu wa Kahinga,** Patriarch. President, Church of Christ in Zaire, Community Christ the Light. Born 1931. Nationality: Zaire. African Independent.
**Keijer,** Magister Augustinus. General Secretary, International Federation of Free Evangelical Churches (IFFEC). Nationality: Sweden.
**Khin,** Rev. U Aungh. General Secretary, Burma Council of Churches. Nationality: Burma.
**Khoabane,** Mr Jubilee Tseliso. General Secretary, Christian Council of Lesotho. Nationality: Lesotho.
**Khoren I (Paroján),** His Holiness, Catholicos of the Great House of Cilicia (Sis) (since 1963). Born 1914. Nationality: Cyprus and Lebanon. Armenian Apostolic.
**Kibira,** Right Rev. Dr Josiah M. Bishop of North West Tanzania, Evangelical Lutheran Church in Tanzania (ELCT). Born 1925. Nationality: Tanzania. Lutheran.
**Kim,** Rev. Kwan Suk. General Secretary, National Council of Churches in Korea. Born 1918. Nationality: Korea. Presbyterian.
**Kim,** His Eminence Cardinal Stephen Sou Hwan, Archbishop of Seoul. President, Catholic Conference of Korea; President, Federation of Asian Bishops' Conferences. Born 1922. Nationality: Korea. Roman Catholic.
**Kimball,** Mr Spencer. 12th President of the Church (elected 1973), Church of Jesus Christ of Latter-day Saints. Born 1895. Nationality: USA. Mormon.
**Kipe,** Rev. H. Frank. Chairman, Evangelical Fellowship of Zambia. Nationality: Zambia.
**Kivuli,** Baba M.P.D. Zakayo, High Priest, African Israel Church Nineveh (AICN). Chairman, Kenya Independent Churches Fellowship. Born 1896. Died 1974. Nationality: Kenya. African Independent.
**Kjaer,** Mr Karlo. Secretary, Ecumenical Council of Denmark. Nationality: Denmark. Lutheran.
**Knight,** Rev. Howard. Executive Secretary, Australian Evangelical Alliance. Nationality: Australia.
**Knight,** Rev. S. President, Antigua Christian Council. Nationality: Antigua.
**Knorr,** Brother Nathan H. President, 1942-77, Watch Tower Bible & Tract Societies of Pennsylvania and New York; President of International Bible Students Association (Jehovah's Christian witnesses). Born 1905. Died 1977. Nationality: USA. Jehovah's Witnesses.
**Knox,** His Eminence Cardinal James Robert. Prefect, Sacred Congregation for the Sacraments and Divine Worship, Roman Curia (Vatican City). Born 1914. Nationality: Australia. Roman Catholic.
**Kok,** Most Rev. Professor Marinus, Archbishop of Utrecht & Metropolitan of the Church Province of the Netherlands. President, International Conference of Old Catholic Bishops. Born 1916. Nationality: Netherlands. Old Catholic.
**Kolowa,** Bishop Sabastian. Bishop of the North-Eastern Diocese and Presiding Bishop of the Evangelical Lutheran Church in Tanzania (ELCT). Born 1933. Nationality: Tanzania. Lutheran.
**König,** His Eminence Cardinal Franz, Archbishop of Vienna. President, Österreichische Bischofskonferenz. Born 1905. Nationality: Austria. Roman Catholic.
**Kotto,** Pastor Jean. President, Fédération des Eglises et Missions Evangéliques du Cameroun (FEMEC). Born 1918. Nationality: Cameroon. Evangelical Church of Cameroon.
**Kraybill,** Rev. Paul N. Executive Secretary, Mennonite World Conference. Nationality: USA. Mennonite.
**Kreuzeder,** Dr Ernest. Chairman, Ecumenical Council of Churches in Austria. Nationality: Austria. Old Catholic.
**Kristensen,** Dr Invar. Chairman, Curaçao Council of Churches. Nationality: Netherlands Antilles.
**Krüger,** Oberkirchenrat D Dr H. Secretary, Arbeitsgemeinschaft Christlicher Kirchen in der BRD und Berlin. Born 1914. Nationality: FR Germany. Lutheran.

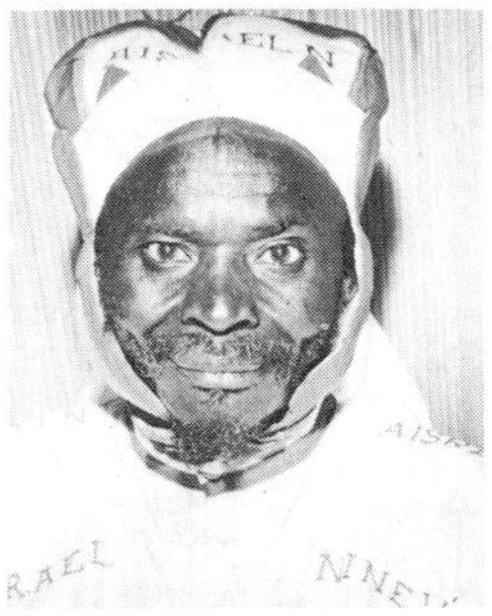
High Priest KIVULI

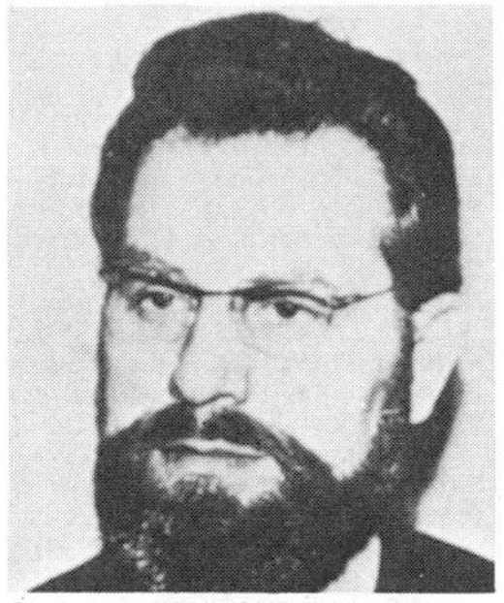
Chairman KRYUCHKOV

**Kryuchkov,** Gennadi Konstantinovich. Chairman, Council of Churches of Evangelical Christians and Baptists, USSR. Born 1926. Nationality: USSR. Baptist.
**Kuharic,** Most Rev. Franjo, Archbishop of Zagreb. President, Biskupska Konferencija Jugoslavija. Born 1919. Nationality: Yugoslavia. Roman Catholic.
**Kujok,** Rev. Ezekiel. General Secretary, Sudan Council of Churches. Born 1938. Nationality: Sudan. Presbyterian.
**Kunene,** Rev. Z. President, Swaziland Conference of Churches. Nationality: Swaziland.
**Kuria,** Most Rev. Manasses, Archbishop of Kenya and Bishop of Nairobi, Church of the Province of Kenya (CPK). Born 1927. Nationality: Kenya. Anglican.
**Lagos,** Rev. Sepulveda. General Secretary, Unión de Misiones Pentecostales Libres de Chile. Nationality: Chile. Independent pentecostal.
**Lanarès,** Dr Pierre. Secrétaire général, Association Internationale pour la Défense de la Liberté Religieuse.
**Landázuri Ricketts,** His Eminence Cardinal Juan, OFM, Archbishop of Lima. Presidente, Conferencia Episcopal Peruana. Born 1913. Nationality: Peru. Roman Catholic.
**Landreth,** Mr Gordon. General Secretary, Evangelical Alliance of Great Britain (EAGB). Nationality: UK. Anglican.
**Latyshev,** see Nikodim.
**Laws,** Rev. W.R. Secretary, Methodist Church of New Zealand. Nationality: New Zealand. Methodist.
**Lee,** Dr Allan W. General Secretary, World Convention of Churches of Christ. Born 1924. Nationality: USA. Disciples.
**Lichtenberger,** Ms Ruth, General Director, Nurses Christian Fellowship International.
**Linscott,** Sister Mary. Superior General, Sisters of Our Lady of Namur; Presidente, Unione Internazionale delle Superiore Generali (UISG). Roman Catholic.
**Lissy,** Pfarrer Rudolf. General Secretary, Österreichischer Missionsrat. Nationality: Austria.
**Livingston,** Elder F.L. President, National Convention, National Primitive Baptist Convention. Nationality: USA. Baptist.
**Loosdregt,** Right Rev. Etienne Auguste Germain, OMI, Vicar Apostolic of Vientiane. Président, Conférence Episcopale du Laos et de la République Khmère. Born 1908. Roman Catholic.
**Lorscheider,** Most Rev. Aloisio, OFM, Archbishop of Fortaleza. Presidente, Conferência Nacional dos Bispos do Brasil. Born 1924. Nationality: Brazil. Roman Catholic.
**Luciani,** A., see John Paul I.
**Lunga,** Mr M. Secretary, Evangelical Alliance of the South Pacific Islands.

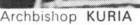

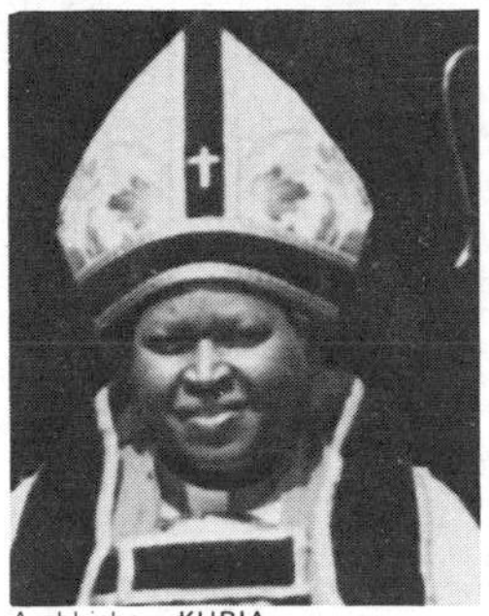
Archbishop KURIA

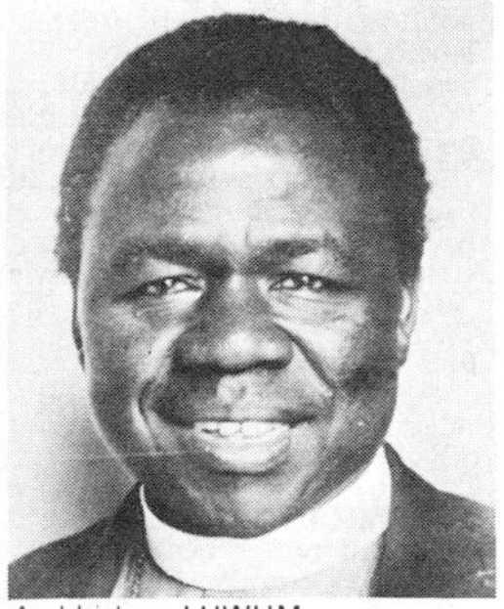
Archbishop LUWUM

**Luwum,** Most Rev. Janani, Archbishop of Uganda & Bishop of Kampala, Church of Uganda, Rwanda, Burundi & Boga-Zaire. Born 1925. Murdered 1977. Nationality: Uganda. Anglican.
**Maasdorp,** Pastor Albertus. Administrative Secretary, Evangelical Lutheran Church of South West Africa. Nationality: South Africa. Lutheran.
**Machunga,** Rev. A.W. General Secretary, Fellowship of Churches of Christ in Nigeria (TEKAN). Nationality: Nigeria. Evangelical.
**MacLeod,** Rev. Angus Hamilton. General Secretary, National Council of Churches in New Zealand (NCCZ). Born 1926. Nationality: UK. Baptist.
**Maillis,** Mr Alexander P. Secretary, Bahamas Christian Council. Nationality: Bahamas. Greek Orthodox.
**Makarakiza,** Most Rev. André, Archbishop of Gitega. Président, Conférence des Ordinaires du Rwanda et du Burundi (COREB). Born 1919. Nationality: Burundi. Roman Catholic.
**Makarios III (Mihail Christodoulou Mouskos),** His Beatitude, Archbishop of New Justiniana & All Cyprus; President of the Republic of Cyprus. Born 1913. Died 1977. Nationality: Cyprus. Greek Orthodox.
**Makokwe,** Rev. J.W. General Secretary, Protestant Alliance of Burundi. Nationality: Burundi.
**Mall,** Mr William K. Executive Secretary, National Council of Churches in Pakistan. Born 1912. Nationality: Pakistan. United Presbyterian.
**Malula,** His Eminence Cardinal Joseph, Archbishop of Kinshasa, former Président, Conférence Plénière des Ordinaires du Zaïre. Born 1917. Nationality: Zaïre. Roman Catholic.

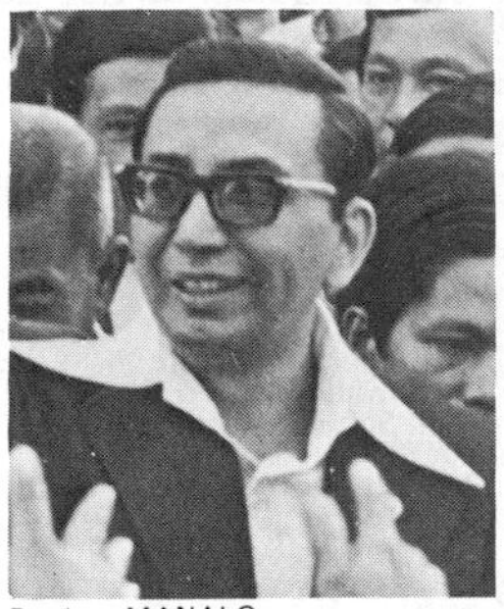
Brother MANALO

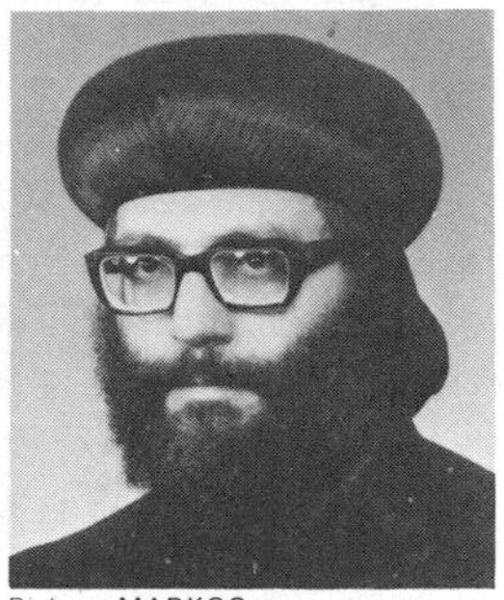
Bishop MARKOS

**Manalo,** Brother Eraño G. Executive Minister, Iglesia ni Cristo (INC). Nationality: Philippines. Independent.
**Mans,** Rev. Sedu Joseph. President, Evangelical Fellowship of Sierra Leone. Nationality: Sierra Leone.
**Maqina,** Rev. E.V.M. National President, African Independent Churches Association (AICA). Nationality: South Africa. African Independent.
**Marina,** I., see Justinian.
**Markos,** His Grace Anba Antonious (Magdy Sobhy Mikhail), Bishop of African Affairs, Coptic Orthodox Church. Organizing Secretary, Organization of African Independent Churches (OAIC). Born 1936. Nationality: Egypt. Coptic Orthodox.
**Marsh,** Rev. Dr Clinton M. Stated Clerk, United Presbyterian Church in the USA. Born 1916. Nationality: USA. Presbyterian.
**Marshall,** Rev. Dr Robert James. President, Lutheran Church in America (LCA). Born 1918. Nationality: USA. Lutheran.
**Martin,** Most Rev. Pierre, former Archbishop of Nouméa. Président, Conférence des Evêques du Pacifique. Born 1910. Roman Catholic.
**Marton,** Right Rev. Aaron, Bishop of Alba Julia. President, Romanian Catholic Episcopal Conference. Born 1896. Nationality: Romania. Roman Catholic.
**Marty,** His Eminence Cardinal François, Archbishop of Paris. Président, Conférence Episcopale Française. Born 1904. Nationality: France. Roman Catholic.

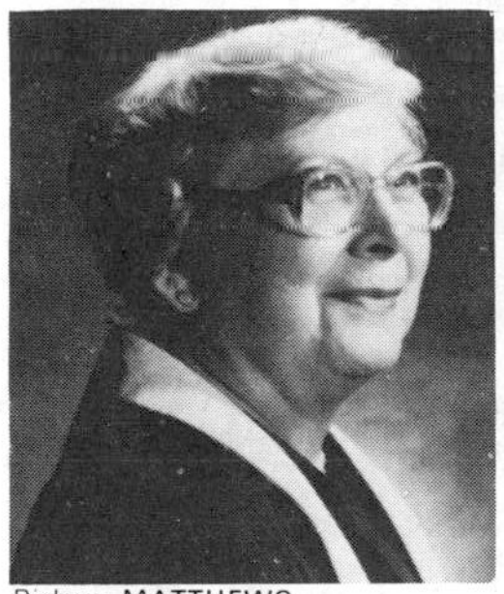
Bishop MATTHEWS

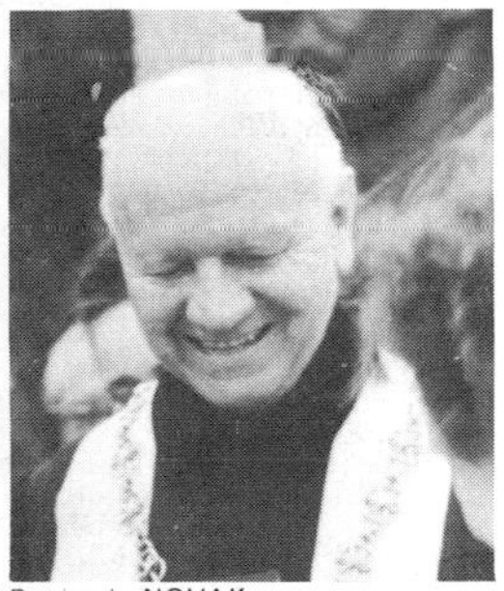
Patriarch NOVAK

**Matthews,** Bishop Marjorie Swank. Area Bishop for Wisconsin, North Central Jurisdictional Conference, United Methodist Church, USA. Born 1916. Nationality: USA. Methodist.
**Matulaitis-Labukas,** Right Rev. Giuseppe, Apostolic Administrator of Kaunas and Vilkaviskis. President, Catholic Bishops' Conference of Lithuania. Born 1894. Nationality: USSR. Roman Catholic.
**Mau,** Dr Carl Henning. General Secretary, Lutheran World Federation (LWF). Born 1922. Nationality: USA. American Lutheran.
**Maurer,** His Eminence Cardinal José Clemente, CSSR, Archbishop of Sucre. Presidente, Conferencia Episcopal de Bolivia. Born 1900. Nationality: Bolivia. Roman Catholic.
**Maury,** Pastor Jacques. Président, Eglise Réformée de France. Born 1920. Nationality: France. Reformed.
**Maxim (Neidenov-Minkov),** His Holiness, Patriarch of Bulgaria & Metropolitan of Sofia. Born 1914. Nationality: Bulgaria. Orthodox.
**Maximos V Hakim,** His Beatitude, Greek Catholic Patriarch of Antioch and All the East, Alexandria and Jerusalem. President, Assembly of Bishops of Syria, and Melkite Patriarchal Synod. Born 1908. Nationality: Syria. Roman Catholic.
**Mazombwe,** Right Rev. Médard Joseph, Bishop of Chipata. President, Zambia Episcopal Conference. Born 1931. Nationality: Zambia. Roman Catholic.
**Mbiti,** Rev. Professor John Samuel. Director, Ecumenical Institute, Bossey (Switzerland). Born 1931. Nationality: Kenya. Anglican.
**McCann,** His Eminence Cardinal Owen, Archbishop of Cape Town. President (1974), Southern Africa Catholic Bishops' Conference. Born 1907. Nationality: South Africa. Roman Catholic.
**McCauley,** Most Rev. Vincent, CSC, former Bishop of Fort Portal. Executive Secretary, Association of Member Episcopal Conferences in Eastern Africa (AMECEA). Born 1906. Nationality: USA. Roman Catholic.
**McClure,** Dr Robert B. Moderator, United Church of Canada. Nationality: Canada. United.
**McIntire,** Rev. Dr Carl. President, International Council of Christian Churches (ICCC). Born 1906. Nationality: USA. Presbyterian.
**McLean,** Mr Ralph. Editor, Directory of the Ministry, Christian Churches & Churches of Christ (no central organization). Nationality: USA. Churches of Christ.

**Meeking,** Rev. Basil. Executive Secretary, Secretariat for Christian Unity (Vatican). Born 1929. Nationality: New Zealand. Roman Catholic.
**Melaku,** see Tekle-Haimonot.
**Melvin,** Dr Billy. Executive Director, National Association of Evangelicals (NAE). Nationality: USA.
**Méouchi,** His Eminence Cardinal Paul Pierre, Maronite Patriarch of Antioch. President, Assembly of Catholic Patriarchs and Bishops of Lebanon, and Maronite Patriarchal Synod. Born 1894. Roman Catholic.
**Mercado,** Rev. LaVerne Diwa. General Secretary, National Council of Churches in the Philippines (NCCP). Born 1921. Nationality: Philippines. United Methodist.
**Mercier,** Pastor Henri. Secretary, Conseil Suisse des Missions Evangéliques/Schweizerischer Evangelischer Missionsrat. Nationality: Switzerland.
**Mickelson,** Dr Arnold R. General Secretary, American Lutheran Church (ALC). Born 1922. Nationality: USA. Lutheran.
**Montini,** G.B., see Paul VI.
**Moon,** Rev. Sun Myung. Prophet & Founder (1954), Unification Church International (Holy Spirit Association for the Unification of World Christianity). Born 1920. Nationality: Korea. Independent.
**Mooneyham,** Dr W. Stanley. President, World Vision (USA). Born 1926. Nationality: USA. Baptist.
**Morapeli,** Most Rev. Alfonso Liguori, OMI, Archbishop of Maseru. President, Episcopal Conference of Lesotho. Born 1929. Nationality: Lesotho. Roman Catholic.
**Morton,** Rev. Harry Osborne. General Secretary, British Council of Churches (BCC). Born 1925. Nationality: UK. Methodist.
**Moshi,** Right Rev. Dr Stefano R. President, Evangelical Lutheran Church in Tanzania (ELCT). Born 1906. Died 1976. Nationality: Tanzania. Lutheran.
**Moss,** Rev. Dr Robert V. President, United Church of Christ. Born 1922. Nationality: USA. United.
**Mouskos,** M. C., see Makarios III.
**Mo'awad,** see Elias IV.
**Mugambe,** Rev. Father Francis Xavier. Joint Secretary, Uganda Joint Christian Council. Nationality: Uganda. Roman Catholic.
**Murrieta,** Rev. Israel Ortiz. Executive Secretary, Federación Evangélica de México. Nationality: Mexico.
**Musu,** Rev. Posenai. General Secretary, Pacific Conference of Churches (PCC). Died 1976.
**Mwenda,** Rev. Kingsley C. General Secretary, Christian Council of Zambia (CCZ). Born 1930. Nationality: Zambia. United Church of Zambia.
**Nababan,** Rev. Dr Soritua A. E. General Secretary, Council of Churches in Indonesia (DGI). Born 1933. Nationality: Indonesia. Lutheran (HKBP).
**Nakajima,** Rev. John Masaaki. General Secretary, National Christian Council of Japan (NCCJ). Born 1928. Nationality: Japan. United (UCCJ).
**Nasir,** Bishop Dr Eric Samuel, Bishop in Delhi. Moderator, Church of North India (CNI). Nationality: India. United.
**Ndandali,** Right Rev. Justin, Bishop of Butare. Secretary, Conseil Protestant du Rwanda. Born 1942. Nationality: Rwanda. Anglican.
**Ndebele,** Rev. P.J.M. General Secretary, Christian Council of Botswana. Nationality: Botswana.
**Neehall,** Rev. Dr Roy Gilbert. General Secretary, Caribbean Conference of Churches (CCC). Born 1928. Nationality: Trinidad & Tobago. Presbyterian.
**Ngomberume,** Abel. High Priest, African Apostolic Church of Johane Maranke (AACJM). Born 1925 Nationality: Zimbabwe. African Independent.
**Nguyên van Binh,** Most Rev. Paul, Archbishop of Saigon. Président, Conférence Episcopale du Viêtnam. Born 1910. Nationality: Viet Nam. Roman Catholic.
**Nicolas,** Pastor Albert Jean. General Secretary, Fédération Protestante de France (FPF). Born 1918. Nationality: France. Reformed.
**Nicole,** Dr Jules-Marcel. Secretary, French Evangelical Alliance. Nationality: France.
**Nikodim (Boris Georgievic Rotov),** Metropolitan of Leningrad & Ladoga. Chairman of Holy Synod, Russian Orthodox Church. Born 1929. Died 1978. Nationality: USSR. Russian Orthodox.
**Nikodim (Latyshev),** Archbishop of Moscow & All Russia (since 1971), Old Ritualist Church of the Belokrinitsa Concord (Old Believers). Nationality: USSR. Old Believer.
**Nikolaos VI (Varelopoulo),** His Beatitude, Pope & Patriarch of Alexandria, All Egypt & All Africa. Born 1915. Nationality: Greece. Greek Orthodox.
**Nku,** Mother Christina Mokutudu (Ma Nku). Founder, Head, & Life General President, St John's Apostolic Faith Mission of South Africa. Born 1894. Nationality: South Africa. African Independent.
**Noel,** Rev. Claude. General Secretary, Concile des Eglises Evangéliques d'Haiti. Nationality: Haiti.
**Norniella,** Rev. Francisco. President, Presbyterian Reformed Church in Cuba. Born 1914. Nationality: Cuba. Presbyterian.

Secretary OSEI-MENSAH

Evangelist PALAU

**Novak,** Patriarch Dr Miroslav. President, Czechoslovak Hussite Church. Born 1907. Nationality: Czechoslovakia. Catholic (non-Roman).
**Nsubuga,** His Eminence Cardinal Emmanuel, Archbishop of Kampala. President, Uganda Episcopal Conference. Born 1914. Nationality: Uganda. Roman Catholic.
**Nunes Gabriel,** Most Rev. Manuel, Archbishop of Luanda. Presidente, Conferência Episcopal de Angola e São Tomé (CEAST). Born 1912. Nationality: Angola. Roman Catholic.
**Nunes Teixeira,** Right Rev. Francisco, Bishop of Quelimane. Presidente, Conferência Episcopal de Moçambique. Born 1910. Nationality: Mozambique. Roman Catholic.
**Nuñez,** Right Rev. Daniel Enrique, Bishop of David. Presidente, Conferencia Episcopal de Panamá (CEP). Born 1927. Nationality: Panama. Roman Catholic.
**Nyangor,** Rev. Albert Boaz Ogadason. General Secretary, African Israel Church Ninevah (AICN). Born 1923. Nationality: Kenya. African Independent.
**N'Dayen,** Most Rev. Joachim, Archbishop of Bangui. Président, Conférence Episcopale de la République Centrafricaine. Born 1934. Nationality: CAR. Roman Catholic.
**Obando Bravo,** Most Rev. Miguel, SDB, Archbishop of Managua. Presidente, Conferencia Episcopal de Nicaragua. Born 1926. Nationality: Nicaragua. Roman Catholic.
**Oliver,** Mr Ernest. Secretary, Evangelical Missionary Alliance of Great Britain. Nationality: UK.
**Olufusoye,** Most Rev. Timothy Omotayo, Archbishop of Nigeria, Church of Nigeria. Born 1918. Nationality: Nigeria. Anglican.
**Ondeto,** Holy Father (Baba Mtakatifu) Simeon, Maria Legio of Africa. Born 1910. Nationality: Kenya. African Independent.
**Osborne,** Mr Charles. Président, Fraternité Evangélique du Sénégal. Nationality: Senegal.
**Osei-Mensah,** Rev. Gottfried. Executive Secretary, Lausanne Committee for World Evangelization (LCWE), Nairobi, Kenya. Born 1934. Nationality: Ghana. Baptist.
**Otunga,** His Eminence Cardinal Maurice M., Archbishop of Nairobi. President, Kenya Episcopal Conference (KEC). Born 1923. Nationality: Kenya. Roman Catholic.
**Paavali Olmari,** Most Rev., Archbishop of Karelia & All Finland. Born 1914. Nationality: Finland. Greek Orthodox.
**Pabst,** Oberkirchenrat Dr Walter. Geschäftsführer, Arbeitsgemeinschaft Christlicher Kirchen in der DDR. Born 1912. Nationality: German Democratic Republic. Lutheran.
**Palau,** Rev. Dr Luis. International evangelist. Born 1934. Nationality:Argentina & USA. Evangelical.
**Palchian,** see Vasken I.
**Palmer,** Ms Elizabeth. General Secretary, World Young Women's Christian Association (YWCA).
**Papadopoulos,** D., see Demetrios I.
**Papadopoulos,** V., see Benediktos I.
**Parecattil,** His Eminence Cardinal Joseph, Archbishop of Ernakulam. President, Catholic Bishops' Conference of India (CBCI). Born 1912. Nationality: India. Roman Catholic.
**Patterson,** Bishop J.O., Sr. Presiding Bishop, Church of God in Christ. Nationality: USA. Black pentecostal.
**Patterson,** Rev. Thomas Carlisle. General Secretary, Conference of Missionary Societies in Great Britain and Ireland (CBMS). Born 1922. Nationality: UK. Presbyterian Church in Ireland.
**Paul II,** His Beatitude Mar Cheikho. Patriarch of Babylon of the Chaldeans (since 1958), Chaldean Catholic Church. Head of the Chaldean Patriarchal Synod. Born 1906. Nationality: Iraq. Roman Catholic.
**Paul VI (Paolo VI) (Giovanni Battista Montini),** His Holiness the Pope (elected 1963), Bishop of Rome, Sovereign of Vatican City State. Born 1897. Died August 1978. Nationality: Holy See and Italy. Roman Catholic.
**Pawlik,** Rev. Pastor Zdzislaw. General Secretary, Polish Ecumenical Council. Nationality: Poland.
**Perret,** Rev. Dr Edmond Jean. General Secretary, World Alliance of Reformed Churches (WARC). Born 1925. Nationality: Switzerland. Reformed.
**Pessoa Câmara,** Most Rev. Dom Helder, Archbishop of Olinda & Recife. Born 1909. Nationality: Brazil. Roman Catholic.
**Philippe,** His Eminence Cardinal Paul, OP. Prefect, Sacred Congregation for the Oriental Churches, Roman Curia (Vatican City). Born 1905. Nationality: France. Roman Catholic.
**Pierson,** Mr Robert H. President, General Conference of Seventh-day Adventists, until 1978. Nationality: USA. Adventist.
**Pignedoli,** His Eminence Cardinal Sergio. President, Secretariat for Non-Christians, Roman Curia (Vatican City). Born 1910. Died 1980. Nationality: Italy. Roman Catholic.

Patriarch PIMEN

Secretary POTTER

**Pimen (Sergij Izvekov),** His Holiness, Patriarch of Moscow & All Russia (elected 1971). Born 1910. Nationality: USSR. Russian Orthodox.
**Pimiento Rodríguez,** Right Rev. José de Jesús, Bishop of Garzón. Presidente, Conferencia Episcopal de Colombia. Born 1919. Nationality: Colombia. Roman Catholic.
**Pironio,** Right Rev. Eduardo, Bishop of Mar del Plata. Presidente, Consejo Episcopal Latinoamericano (CELAM). Born 1920. Nationality: Argentina. Roman Catholic.
**Pitts,** Rev. S.G. President, Methodist Church of South Africa. Nationality: South Africa. Methodist.
**Poma,** His Eminence Cardinal Antonio, Archbishop of Bologna. Presidente, Conferenza Episcopale Italiana. Born 1910. Nationality: Italy. Roman Catholic.
**Pong,** Right Rev. James, Bishop of Taiwan. Chairman, Council of the Church in East Asia (CCEA). Born 1911. Nationality: Taiwan. Episcopalian (Anglican).
**Pont,** Pastor Maurice Paul. General Secretary, Departement Evangélique Français d'Action Apostolique (DEFAP). Born 1919. Nationality: France. Reformed Church of France.
**Potter,** Rev. Dr Philip Alford. General Secretary, World Council of Churches (WCC). Born 1921 (Dominica, West Indies). Nationality: UK. Methodist.
**Preus,** Rev. Dr David W. General President, American Lutheran Church (ALC). Born 1922. Nationality: USA. Lutheran.
**Preus,** Rev. Dr Jacob Aall O. President, Lutheran Church—Missouri Synod. Born 1920. Nationality: USA. Lutheran.
**Prieto Vega,** Right Rev. Ignacio, Bishop of Wankie. President, Rhodesia Catholic Bishops' Conference. Born 1923. Nationality: Spain. Roman Catholic.
**Pröhle,** Professor Dr Karoly. General Secretary, Ecumenical Council of Hungarian Churches. Born 1911. Nationality: Hungary. Lutheran.
**Quinn,** Most Rev. John Raphael, Archbishop of San Francisco. President, National Conference of Catholic Bishops (NCCB), USA. Born 1929. Nationality: USA. Roman Catholic.

Secretary RAFRANSOA

Primate RAMSEY

**Rafransoa,** Rev. Dr Maxime Victor. General Secretary, All Africa Conference of Churches (AACC). Born 1934. Nationality: Madagascar. Reformed.
**Raimondi,** His Eminence Cardinal Luigi. Prefect, Sacred Congregation for the Causes of Saints, Roman Curia (Vatican City). Born 1912. Nationality: Italy. Roman Catholic.
**Rairi,** Mr Nga. General Secretary, Cook Islands Christian Church. Born 1932. Nationality: New Zealand. Congregationalist.
**Rakotoarimanana,** Pastor Victor. Secretary General, Communauté Evangélique d'Action Apostolique (CEVAA). Nationality: Madagascar. United (FJKM).
**Ramambasoa,** Pastor Joseph Joelson. President, Eglise du Jésus-Christ à Madagascar. Born 1925. Nationality: Madagascar. United (FJKM).
**Ramsey,** Most Rev. & Right Hon. Arthur Michael, Archbishop of Canterbury and Primate of All England (retired 1974). Born: 1904. Nationality: UK. Anglican.
**Randall,** Dr Claire. General Secretary, National Council of Churches of Christ in the USA (NCCCUSA). Born 1919. Nationality: USA. United Presbyterian.
**Ratanabutra,** Rev. Charan. President, Evangelical Fellowship of Thailand. Nationality: Thailand. Evangelical.
**Ratéfy,** Rev. Pastor Daniel. General Secretary, Christian Council of Madagascar (FFPM). Born 1913. Nationality: Madagascar. United (FJKM).
**Razafimahatratra,** His Eminence Cardinal Victor, SJ, Bishop of Farafangana. Président, Conférence Episcopale de Madagascar. Born 1921. Nationality: Madagascar. Roman Catholic.
**Reed,** Dr Roy M. President, American Baptist Association (ABA). Nationality: USA. Baptist.
**Rees,** Mr John Charles. General Secretary (until 1977), South African Council of Churches (SACC). Born 1937. Nationality: South Africa. Methodist.
**Ribeiro,** His Eminence Cardinal Antonio, Patriarch of Lisbon. Born 1928. Nationality: Portugal. Roman Catholic.
**Ricciardi,** Rev. Salvatore. Secretary, Federazione delle Chiese Evangeliche in Italia (FCEI). Nationality: Italy.
**Robinson,** Bishop Hubert N. President, Bishops' Council, African Methodist Episcopal Church. Nationality: USA. Methodist.
**Rocchietti,** Mr Marcos. Executive Secretary, Federación de Iglesias Evangélicas del Uruguay (FIEU). Nationality: Uruguay.
**Rodriguez,** Rev. Antonio Rivera. Presidente, Concilio Evangélico de Puerto Rico. Nationality: Puerto Rico.
**Rolston,** Rev. M.A.Z. General Secretary, National Christian Council of India (NCCI). Nationality: India.
**Rompas,** Rev. Paul Hein. Moderator, Protestant Church in Indonesia. Born 1921. Nationality: Indonesia. Reformed.
**Rosales,** His Eminence Cardinal Julio, Archbishop of Cebu. President, Catholic Bishops' Conference of the Philippines. Born 1906. Nationality: Philippines. Roman Catholic.
**Rossi,** His Eminence Cardinal Agnelo. Prefect, Sacred Congregation for the Evangelization of Peoples (Propaganda Fide), Roman Curia (Vatican City). Born 1913. Nationality: Brazil. Roman Catholic.
**Rotov,** see Nikodim.
**Routh,** Mr Porter Wroe. Executive Secretary-Treasurer, Southern Baptist Convention. Nationality: USA. Southern Baptist.
**Rowell,** Right Rev. Kevin William, OFM, Bishop of Aitape. President, Bishop's Conference of Papua New Guinea & the Solomon Islands. Born 1927. Nationality: Australia. Roman Catholic.
**Roy,** His Eminence Cardinal Maurice, Archbishop of Quebec, President, Consilium de Laicis (HQ Vatican City). Born 1905. Nationality: Canada. Roman Catholic.

Cardinal RUGAMBWA

Primate RUNCIE

**Rugambwa,** His Eminence Cardinal Laurean, Archbishop of Dar es Salaam. Former President, Tanzania Episcopal Conference. Born 1912. Nationality: Tanzania. Roman Catholic.
**Ruivivar,** Mr Faustino Jr. Chairman, Philippine Council of Evangelical Churches. Nationality: Philippines.
**Runcie,** Most Rev. & Right Hon. Robert, Archbishop of Canterbury and Primate of All England. Born 1921. Nationality: UK. Anglican.
**Russell,** Rev. Dr David Syme. General Secretary, Baptist Union of Great Britain and Ireland. Born 1916. Nationality: UK. Baptist.
**Salajka,** Professor Dr Milan. Secretary, Ecumenical Council of Churches in the CSR. Nationality: Czechoslovakia.
**Salazar López,** His Eminence Cardinal José, Archbishop of Guadalajara. Presidente, Conferencia del Episcopado Mexicano. Born 1910. Nationality: Mexico. Roman Catholic.
**Sams,** Dr James C. President, National Baptist Convention of

America. Nationality: USA. Baptist.
**Samuel**, His Grace Anba, Bishop for Public, Ecumenical and Social Services, Coptic Orthodox Church; Chairman, Ecumenical Advisory Council for Church Services in Egypt. Born 1920. Nationality: Egypt. Coptic Orthodox.
**Samuel**, Most Rev. Ananda Rao, Bishop in Krishna-Godavari. Moderator, Church of South India. Nationality: India. United.
**Samuel**, Right Rev. John Victor. Moderator, Church of Pakistan. Born 1930. Nationality: Pakistan. United.
**Sangaré**, Most Rev. Luc Auguste, Archbishop of Bamako. Président, Conférence Episcopale du Mali. Born 1925. Nationality: Mali. Roman Catholic.
**Santos Hernández**, Most Rev. Hector Enrique, SDB, Archbishop of Tegucigalpa. Presidente, Conferencia Episcopal de Honduras. Born 1917. Nationality: Honduras. Roman Catholic.
**Sarli**, Rev. Feliciano A. Presidente, Federación Argentina de Iglesias Evangélicas (FAIE). Nationality: Argentina.
**Schmale**, Pastor K.H. Secretary, Federation of Evangelical Lutheran Churches in South Africa (FELCSA). Nationality: South Africa. Lutheran.
**Schmidt**, Chief Apostle Walter. Stammapostel (elected 1960), New Apostolic Church (Neuapostolische Kirche). Born 1891. Nationality: FR Germany. New Apostolic.
**Schneider**, Mr Peter. General Secretary, Germany Evangelical Alliance. Nationality: FR Germany. Evangelical.
**Schrotenboer**, Rev. Dr Paul Gerard. General Secretary, Christian Reformed Church USA. Born 1922. Nationality: USA. Reformed.
**Scott**, Most Rev. Archbishop Edward Walter. Primate, Anglican Church of Canada (Eglise Episcopale du Canada). Born 1919. Nationality: Canada. Anglican.
**Scott**, Most Rev. Moses Nathaniel Christopher Omobiala, Archbishop of West Africa & Bishop of Sierra Leone, Church of the Province of West Africa (CPWA). Born 1911. Nationality Sierra Leone. Anglican.
**Seidenspinner**, Dr Charles. President, Evangelical Fellowship of Canada. Nationality: Canada.
**Seper**, His Eminence Cardinal Franjo. Prefect, Sacred Congregation for the Doctrine of the Faith, Roman Curia (Vatican City). Born 1905. Nationality: Yugoslavia. Roman Catholic.
**Seraphim (Tikas)**, His Beatitude, Archbishop of Athens & Primate of All Greece. Born 1913. Nationality: Greece. Greek Orthodox.
**Shauri**, Mr Stanford Abraham. General Secretary, Christian Council of Tanzania (CCT). Born 1929. Nationality: Tanzania. Anglican.
**Shenk**, Rev. Jacob. Chairman, Evangelical Fellowship of Zimbabwe-Rhodesia. Nationality: USA. Mennonite.

Pope SHENOUDA III

Patriarch SIDAROUSS

**Shenouda III (Nazeer Gayed)**, His Holiness Anba, Pope and Patriarch of Alexandria, All Egypt & All Africa (elected 1971). Born 1923. Nationality: Egypt. Coptic Orthodox.
**Shiolashvili**, see Iliya.
**Shnork**, see Kalustian.
**Sianipar**, Rev. Professor Frans Hanaehan. General Secretary, Batak Protestant Christian Church (HKBP). Born 1929. Nationality: Indonesia. Lutheran.
**Sidamonidze**, G., see David V.
**Sidarouss**, His Eminence Cardinal Stephanos I., CM, Coptic Patriarch of Alexandria. Head, Coptic Patriarchal Synod; President, Assembly of Bishops of Egypt. Born 1904. Nationality: Egypt. Roman Catholic.
**Sigrist**, Dr Walter. Président, Fédération des Eglises Protestantes de la Suisse (FEPS). Nationality: Switzerland. Reformed.
**Sikakane**, Rev. Enos. Programme Director, Interdenominational African Ministers Association of Southern Africa (IDAMASA). Nationality: South Africa.
**Silva Henríquez**, His Eminence Cardinal Raúl, SDB, Archbishop of Santiago de Chile. Presidente, Conferencia Episcopal de Chile (CECH). Born 1907. Nationality: Chile. Roman Catholic.
**Simojoki**, Most Rev. Martti I., Archbishop of Turku (Abo) & Primate, Evangelical Lutheran Church of Finland. Born 1908. Nationality: Finland. Lutheran.
**Sindamuka**, Mr Samuel. General Secretary, Alliance des Eglises Protestantes du Burundi. Nationality: Burundi.
**Sintim-Misa**, Right Rev. Gottfried Kwadwo. Moderator, Presbyterian Church of Ghana. Born 1912. Nationality: Ghana. Presbyterian.
**Sipilä**, Miss Annikki. Secretary, Finnish Missionary Council. Nationality: Finland. Lutheran.
**Skrypnyk**, His Eminence Mstyslav, Metropolitan of the Ukrainian Autocephalous Orthodox Church in Exile & in the USA. Born 1898. Nationality: USA. Ukrainian Orthodox.
**Slack**, Rev. Dr Kenneth. Director, Christian Aid. Born 1917. Nationality: UK. United Reformed.
**Smail**, Rev. Thomas A. Director, Fountain Trust (charismatic). Nationality: UK. Presbyterian (Church of Scotland).
**Smith**, Dr Nelson Henry. President, Progressive National Baptist Convention. Born 1930. Nationality: USA. Baptist.
**Solzhenitsyn**, Mr Alexandr. Writer. Born 1918. Nationality: USSR (deprived 1974). Russian Orthodox.
**Spae**, Rev. Dr Joseph J., CICM. General Secretary, SODEPAX; author. Born 1913. Nationality: Belgium. Roman Catholic.
**Srisang**, Dr Koson. General Secretary, Church of Christ in Thailand. Born 1938. Nationality: Thailand. United.
**Stewart**, Rev. W. Chairman, Scottish Churches Council. Nationality: UK.
**Stratiew**, Msgr Metodio Dimitrow, Exarch of Sofia. President, Bulgarian Catholic Bishops' Conference. Born 1916. Nationality: Bulgaria. Roman Catholic.
**Stöylen**, Right Rev. Kaare, Bishop of Oslo. Chairman of Bishops' Conference, Church of Norway. Born 1909. Nationality: Norway. Lutheran.
**Suenens**, His Eminence Cardinal Leo Jozef, Archbishop of Malines-Brussels & Primate of Belgium. Président, Conférence Episcopale de Belgique. Born 1904. Nationality: Belgium. Roman Catholic.
**Sundby**, Most Rev. Olof Carl, Archbishop of Uppsala & Primate, Church of Sweden. Born 1917. Nationality: Sweden. Lutheran.
**Sundholm**, Mr Nils. Secretary, Swedish Ecumenical Council. Nationality: Sweden. Lutheran.
**Tabera**, His Eminence Cardinal Araoz Arturo, CMF. Prefect, Sacred Congregation for Religious and Secular Institutes, Roman Curia (Vatican City). Born 1903. Nationality: Spain. Roman Catholic.
**Taguchi**, His Eminence Cardinal Paul Yoshigoro, Archbishop of Osaka. President, Japan Catholic Bishops' Conference. Born 1902. Died 1978. Nationality: Japan. Roman Catholic.
**Tan**, Rev. Stephen. Honorary General Secretary, National Council of Churches of Singapore. Nationality: Singapore.
**Tchidimbo**, Most Rev. Raymond-Marie, CSSp, Archbishop of Conakry. Président, Conférence Episcopale de la Guinée. Born 1920. Nationality: Guinea. Roman Catholic.
**Teegarden**, Dr Kenneth L. General Minister & President, Christian Church (Disciples of Christ). Nationality: USA. Disciples.
**Tekle-Haimanot**, His Holiness Abuna (Abba Wolde-Mikael Melaku), Patriarch, Ethiopian Orthodox Church. Born 1918. Nationality: Ethiopia. Orthodox.
**Theodosius (Lazor)**, His Beatitude, Archbishop of New York, Metropolitan of All America and Canada, Primate, Orthodox Church in America, since 1977. Born 1933. Nationality: USA. Orthodox.
**Theophilus I (Tewoflos)**, His Holiness Abuna (Anba, Abba), Patriarch of Ethiopia 1971-76. Deposed by military regime 1976. Nationality: Ethiopian. Ethiopian Orthodox.
**Thevabalasingham**, Mr Sam. Secretary, Evangelical Alliance of Ceylon. Nationality: Sri Lanka.
**Thiandoum**, His Eminence Cardinal Hyacinthe, Archbishop of Dakar. Président, Conférence Episcopale du Sénégal-Mauritanie. Nationality: Senegal. Roman Catholic.
**Thohey**, Most Rev. Gabriel, Archbishop of Rangoon. President, Burma Catholic Bishops' Conference. Born 1927. Nationality: Burma. Roman Catholic.
**Thompson**, Mr William P. Stated Clerk, United Presbyterian Church in the USA. Nationality: USA. Presbyterian.
**Thorne**, Rev. John Francis. General Secretary, United Congregational Church of Southern Africa. Born 1926. Nationality: South Africa. Congregationalist.
**Ting**, Bishop Kuang-Hsun (Ding Guangxun). President, China Christian Council (1980); and Chairperson, Chinese Christian Three-Self Patriotic Movement. Born 1915. Nationality: PR China. Anglican, now Post-denominational.
**Tomasek**, His Eminence Cardinal Frantisek, Archbishop of Prague. Born 1899. Nationality: Czechoslovakia. Roman Catholic.
**Torrance**, Right Rev. Professor Thomas F. Moderator (1976-77), Church of Scotland. Nationality: UK. Presbyterian.
**Tortolo**, Most Rev. Adolfo Servando, Archbishop of Paraná. Presidente, Conferencia Episcopal Argentina. Born 1911. Nationality: Argentina. Roman Catholic.
**Toth**, Rev. Dr Karoly. General Secretary, Christian Peace Conference (CPC). Born 1931. Nationality: Hungary. Reformed Church in Hungary.
**Tuboku-Metzger**, Rev. Dr C.E. General Secretary, United Christian Council of Sierra Leone. Nationality: Sierra Leone.
**Tucci**, Rev. Roberto. Director, Vatican Radio. Born 1921. Nationality: Italy. Roman Catholic.
**Tung**, Rev. William C. General Secretary, Hong Kong Christian Council (HKCC). Born 1936. Nationality: Hong Kong/UK. Methodist.
**Tutu**, Right Rev. Desmond, former Bishop of Lesotho. General Secretary, South African Council of Churches (SACC). Born 1935. Nationality: South Africa. Anglican.
**Vaivods**, Right Rev. Giuliano, Apostolic Administrator of Riga & Leipaja. President, Catholic Bishops' Conference of Latvia. Born 1895. Nationality: USSR. Roman Catholic.
**van den Heuvel**, Rev. Dr Albert Hendrik. General Secretary, Netherlands Reformed Church (NHK). Born 1932. Nationality: Netherlands. Reformed.
**van der Merwe**, Ds. (Rev.) Dr Willem Jacobus. Moderator, Federal Council of Dutch Reformed Churches. Born 1907. Nationality: South Africa. Reformed.
**van der Veen**, Rev. Rein Jan. General Secretary, Netherlands Missionary Council. Born 1921. Nationality: Netherlands. Reformed Churches in the Netherlands.
**Van Meing**, Rev. Doan. Chairman, Evangelical Fellowship of Viet Nam. Nationality: Viet Nam.
**Varthalitis**, Most Rev. Antonio, AA, Archbishop of Corfù, Zante and Cefalonia. President, Catholic Episcopal Conference of Greece. Born 1924. Nationality: Greece. Roman Catholic.
**Vasken I (Palchian)**, His Holiness, Supreme Patriarch, Catholicos & Chief Bishop of All the Armenians (since 1955), Echmiadzin. Born 1908. Died 1978. Nationality: USSR. Armenian Apostolic.
**Vassiliy (Basil Doroshkevich)**, His Beatitude, Metropolitan of Warsaw & All Poland. Born 1914. Nationality: Poland. Eastern Orthodox.
**Vazgen**, see Vasken I.
**Verschuren**, Right Rev. Paul, SCI, Bishop of Helsinki. President, Scandinavian Episcopal Conference. Born 1925. Nationality: Finland. Roman Catholic.
**Villot**, His Eminence Cardinal Jean. Secretary of State, Holy See; Prefect, Council for the Public Affairs of the Church, Roman Curia (Vatican City). Born 1905. Died 1980. Nationality: Holy See and France. Roman Catholic.
**von Heyl**, Rechtsanwalt Cornelius A. Präses, Präsidium der Synode, Evangelische Kirche in Deutschland (EKD). Nationality: FR Germany. Lutheran.

Patriarch TEKLE-HAIMANOT

Catholicos VASKEN I

**Vorster**, Dominie (Rev.) Dr Jacobus Daniel. Moderator, Algemene Synode van die Nederduitse Gereformeerde Kerk (Moederkerk)/General Synod of the Dutch Reformed Church (Mother Church) of South Africa. Born 1910. Nationality: South Africa. Reformed.
**Wasikye**, Rev. Canon J. Joint Secretary, Uganda Joint Christian Council. Nationality: Uganda. Anglican.
**Wati**, Dr I. Ben. Executive Secretary, Evangelical Fellowship of India (EFI). Nationality: India.
**Watyoka**, Mr Cornelius Dick. General Secretary, Christian Council of Rhodesia. Born 1934. Nationality: UK. Methodist.
**Westergard-Madsen**, Right Rev. Willy, Bishop of Copenhagen & Primate, National Church of Denmark. Born 1907. Nationality: Denmark. Lutheran.
**Wickham**, Mr D. Pablo. Secretary, Alianza Evangélica Espanõla. Nationality: Spain.
**Willebrands**, His Eminence Cardinal Johannes Gerardus Maria, Archbishop of Utrecht & Primate of the Netherlands. President, Netherlands Bishops' Conference; President, Secretariat for Christian Unity (Vatican City). Born 1909. Nationality: Netherlands. Roman Catholic.
**Williams**, Mr C.O. General Secretary, Christian Council of Nigeria. Nationality: Nigeria.
**Williams**, Dr Glen Garfield. General Secretary, Conference of European Churches (CEC).
**Williams**, Most Rev. Gwilym Owen, Archbishop of Wales & Bishop of Bangor, Church in Wales. Born 1913. Nationality: UK. Anglican.
**Wiseman**, General Clarence. Tenth General (1974), Salvation Army International. Born 1907, retired 1977. Nationality: Canada. Salvationist.
**Wojtyla**, see John Paul II.
**Wong**, Rev. Dr Peter. General Secretary, Church of Christ in China (Hong Kong Council). Born 1913. Nationality: Hong Kong/UK. United.
**Woods**, Most Rev. Frank, Archbishop of Melbourne, Metropolitan of the Province of Victoria & Primate of Australia, Church of England in Australia. Born 1907, retired 1977. Nationality: Australia. Anglican.
**Wright**, His Eminence Cardinal John Joseph. Prefect, Sacred Congregation for the Clergy, Roman Curia (Vatican City). Born 1909. Nationality: USA and Holy See. Roman Catholic.
**Wyszynski**, His Eminence Cardinal Stefan, Archbishop of Gniezno and Warsaw. President, Polish Episcopal Conference. Born 1901. Nationality: Poland. Roman Catholic.
**Yago**, Most Rev. Bernard, Archbishop of Abidjan. Président, Conférence Episcopale de la Côte d'Ivoire. Born 1916. Nationality: Ivory Coast. Roman Catholic.
**Yap** Kim-Hao, Bishop Dr. Methodist Church in Malaysia & Singapore. General Secretary, Christian Conference of Asia (CCA). Born 1929. Nationality: Malaysia. Methodist.
**Yemmeru**, Most Rev. Asrate M., Archbishop-Metropolitan of Addis Ababa. Presidente, Conferenza Episcopale di Etiopia. Born 1904. Nationality: Ethiopian. Roman Catholic.
**Yü Pin**, His Eminence Cardinal Paul, Archbishop of Nanking. President, Regional Episcopal Conference of China (Taiwan). Born 1901. Nationality: China. Roman Catholic.
**Zimmerman**, Rev. Dr Thomas F. General Superintendent, Assemblies of God; Chairman, World Pentecostal Conference. Nationality: USA. Pentecostal.
**Zoa**, His Eminence Cardinal Jean, Archbishop of Yaoundé. Président, Conférence Episcopale du Cameroun. Born 1924. Nationality: Cameroon. Roman Catholic.

Bishop YAP

Cardinal ZOUNGRANA

**Zoungrana**, His Eminence Cardinal Paul, WF, Archbishop of Ouagadougou. Président, Conférence des Evêques de la Haute Volta et du Niger; Président, Symposium des Conférences Episcopales d'Afrique et de Madagascar (SCEAM). Born 1917. Nationality: Upper Volta. Roman Catholic.
**Zurenuo**, Right Rev. Zurewe K. Bishop, Evangelical Lutheran Church of Papua New Guinea. Nationality: Papua New Guinea. Lutheran.

# PART 13

# DIRECTORY
Topical directory of world Christianity

*Almost incidentally the great world fellowship has arisen; it is the great new fact of our era.*
—Archbishop William Temple (1881–1944).

This directory illustrates Temple's 'great new fact of our era' by giving for every country in the world, and for 76 different topics, the names, addresses and telephone numbers through which this 'great world fellowship' operated during the decade 1970–80 and to a large extent still operates today.

# DIRECTORY TOPICS

*Page*

TOPICAL DIRECTORY OF WORLD CHRISTIANITY

This survey directory of the Christian enterprise in the modern world is not offered here as, in the first instance, a corrected or completely up-to-date address list suitable for immediate mass mailings. Instead, it is primarily a survey listing of names and addresses as existing during the decade 1970-80, compiled to give a complete panorama of the extraordinary complexity of the total Christian enterprise. It should be regarded therefore as a listing that is selective and illustrative, or suggestive, rather than as exhaustive. Its primary purpose is to give an idea or an overview of the total situation during 1970-80, and to provide leads to the enquirer and user. For 64 topics covering the range of Christian activity and its context, it gives the major significant organizations within each country, where such exist, for the 223 countries of the world. For a further 12 topics, brief guides are given. The directory also illustrates the survey articles on each country in Part 7; all major organizations mentioned in the articles will be found below.

Although the listing represents the period 1970-80 and some 5% of all its addresses have probably changed by 1980, the vast majority of entries here were still up-to-date in 1980. A regularly-updated version of the directory is held and periodically published by the Centre for the Study of World Evangelization, Nairobi.

The layout by topic employed here attempts to reduce to intelligible, manageable, and yet stimulating shape, the vast diversity of Christian organizations across the world. It portrays the immense dynamism and diversity of world Christianity and its multifold ministries, and the links, cohesion and co-operation that exist for a large variety of topics. The user interested in a particular topic (e.g. BIBLE AND SCRIPTURE ORGANIZATIONS, or MEDICINE AND HEALING, or RESEARCH CENTRES) can therefore immediately see a sketch of the whole extent of such organizations throughout the world. At the same time, the directory has also been planned to assist the day-to-day user looking for either an organization whose exact name he knows, or one whose approximate name is known, or whose country only is known, or whose approximate function only is known.

## LAYOUT

*How information is set out.* The directory is divided into 4 main sections; (a) BASIC CHURCH STRUCTURES (churches and denominations), (b) CHRISTIAN LIFE, SERVICE & OUTREACH, (c) DIRECTORIES, and (d) NON-CHRISTIAN RELIGIOUS ORGANIZATIONS. The largest of these is (b), which sets out 71 topics arranged in alphabetical order. Under each topic, countries are listed in alphabetical order; and under each country individual organizations are listed, also in alphabetical order.

*Only one entry per organization.* Each organization is given only one entry and appears only once in this directory, at a single point, namely under that topic which best describes its primary function, purpose or activity. This may involve the reader wanting a specific organization in a short search under 2 or 3 possible topics.

*Listing by country.* All entries are filed under the country in which their headquarters is situated. Apparent exceptions are official Vatican offices located physically outside the City of the Vatican, in Italy; but since most have extraterritorial status, they are filed here under the Holy See. Sometimes a headquarters is in a country different to what one would expect from the organization's title; this applies to various groups in exile from their home countries.

*Items included for each entry.* Each entry for an organization is filed under its country and consists of most or all of the following elements: *official name* in bold type, in the national language (if this is English, French, German, Italian, Portuguese or Spanish; if not, the name is given in English, followed by that in the national language in parentheses); if there are 1, 2 or more other official names e.g. in other major languages, these are given separated by a slash /; *alternative names,* if any; *initials* of name, where widely known or used; *title* of responsible executive officer (but not name of present encumbent, unless essential for full postal identification); *street address* (physical location of office or headquarters); *postal address* (if different from street address), with postal zip code if any; *telephone,* with in brackets area code if any; if no area code or exchange is given, the exchange is the same as the city or town of the address. Lastly, additional information describing the body may appear in parentheses, including denominational affiliation (Protestant, RC, etc, unless evident from the title itself), statistics of members or library holdings, alternative addresses, etc.

*How to find what you want.* To find the address of an organization whose full name you know, first look under the topic which best describes the organization, then under its country, then alphabetically. If an organization you want is not under the topic you would expect, see under any cross-referenced topics; if it is not there either, find it in the World Index of Christian and Religious Organizations at the end. Similarly, if you want to know what bodies exist under a particular topic in a particular country, locate the topic first and then the country.

## TOPICS

*Definitions of topics.* The directory classifies all Christian bodies, churches, missions, societies, institutions, agencies, centres, ministries, programmes, groupings, and other kinds of organization, by a *topic,* namely the major function or purpose of each. The 76 topics are listed under DIRECTORY TOPICS below, and are expanded to show what subjects each covers under DEFINITIONS OF TOPICS below. In most cases entries exemplifying all these topics and subjects are given. Although for most topics a majority of the significant bodies at the national and international levels are recorded here, for a few topics the coverage is thinner or more selective. It is for this reason that the directory as a whole should be treated as suggestive, or illustrative, rather than as exhaustive in its listings.

*No topic is watertight.* These topics or categories are not (and cannot be) entirely logical and mutually exclusive because (1) a great many organizations have multiple purposes and overlapping functions, concerns, objectives, interests and clienteles; and (2) in the course of Christian activity, discrete categories related to a single word or activity tend to arise and crystallize out by themselves to meet the working needs of the community. The directory therefore tends to use these latter natural clusters as its categories, and to recognize topics thrust up in this way.

*Overlapping topics.* Although clearly defined here, these topics cannot always be mutually exclusive. Most topics tend to shade off into other topics in various directions. Research centres may also be information centres, monasteries may also be ecumenical centres, a religious publisher may also be a literature distributor, radio stations may also operate Bible correspondence courses. Most of the organizations in the directory have several overlapping functions in this way. The directory therefore classifies each by the major topic which describes it, i.e. by its *primary* description or function. In cases where an organization could be said to have its major significance under more than one topic, it is listed here under its primary topic and can be located through the World Index.

*Few topics are all-inclusive.* Only a few topics include almost all organizations significant at the national and international levels and therefore classifiable under the topic concerned. For most topics, there are numerous other organizations of similar function which are however classified here under some other topic because that better describes their primary role.

*Cross-referencing of topics.* Since many topics overlap, several definitions (given below) end with a cross-reference 'see also...' to other topics where a number of similar subjects may be found. Individual organizations however are not cross-referenced in this way because far too numerous.

*Surveys of each topic.* A very brief survey of each topic, describing its extent and influence across the world, is given in Part 9, Survey Dictionary.

*Statistical totals.* In each such survey in the Dictionary are given such statistics as are relevant and available concerning the extent of Christian activity under the topic. These statistics should be regarded as minimal, covering as they do only known organizations; it is likely that the full numerical extent of almost all of these activities is somewhat larger.

*Recourse to quantification.* During the data-gathering stage for this directory, entries were compiled for a number of topics for which later the total of entries became excessive and eventually too large for complete inclusion here. Among these topics were: Bible schools and colleges, Christian universities, church or mission hospitals, church-operated secular schools and colleges, foreign missionary societies, lay training centres, local councils of churches, medical centres, monasteries, periodicals, radio and television stations, religious communities, religious libraries with under 30,000 volumes each, seminaries and theological colleges, student and youth organizations, smaller service agencies of all kinds, and other varieties of institution. Our solution was therefore to omit the full, detailed listing from the directory (except for placing any directories concerning them under topic 73 here) and instead to quantify the data on each category and, for each country, to place them in the footnotes under all Tables 2. Likewise, although our topic 1, CHURCHES AND DENOMINATIONS, contains a selection of the major bodies, a complete enumeration or quantification is given only in the last 3 statistical rows of all Tables 2 for all countries.

*Catholic and Protestant specialization.* Because of particular emphases in the two best-organized Christian blocs, Roman Catholicism and Protestantism, certain topics feature entries from predominantly one or the other of the 2 traditions. Thus entries under URBAN INDUSTRIAL MISSION are largely Protestant, while those under DIPLOMATIC REPRESENTATION and FEDERATIONS OF RELIGIOUS COMMUNITIES are almost entirely Catholic.

## KINDS OF BODY INCLUDED

*A specifically Christian directory.* This is primarily a directory of Christian or religious organizations, i.e. of organizations under Christian or religious auspices, ending with a section (Nos. 74-76) on secular or non-Christian organizations included in order to assist in setting the context. In respect of a certain number of topics, for example AID AND RELIEF, the churches have no monopoly of activity, and numbers of non-religious organizations are also at work, often co-operating closely with their Christian counterparts. Such non-religious or secular bodies are excluded here by virtue of the directory's specifically Christian nature. However, there are also countless borderline cases of secular organizations just sufficiently Christian or pro-Christian to warrant their inclusion in this directory. In general, such bodies have been included only if their name, objectives, orientation, constitution or programmes identify them as specifically church or Christian or religious organizations.

This restriction must be remembered when searching for bodies in subjects where secular activity is much greater or better organized than specifically Christian activity. For example, the reader looking for photographic libraries will find few listed here; he needs then to know that valuable collections of religious photographs are often held in the archives of both local secular newspapers and also international newsmagazines and related agencies (AP, UPI, *Life, Newsweek, Time,* etc).

*Spontaneity versus institutionalization.* By its very nature, a directory of agencies can record only relatively permanent institutionalized expressions of Christianity. It must not be forgotten that in almost all categories of Christian enterprise spontaneous unorganized activity takes place, often on a massive scale, long before institutionalized expressions of it arise. Again, an organization in an adjacent country may supply a country's needs before its own organization is formed. Absence of an organization in any country—e.g. an organized Bible distribution society—must not therefore be taken to mean absence of interest or activity. At the same time, this directory can be seen to record the degree of institutionalization reached in each country during the period 1970-80.

*International organizations.* For many topics, there exist international co-ordinating organizations, which serve several countries, or many, or all. Although such entries are arranged alphabetically within other entries for each country, they can usually be spotted from the content of their names.

*Headquarters but not branches.* Where large international Christian organizations are concerned, this directory gives the international headquarters addresses but not those of all national or regional branches, since these are often far to numerous to list. In several cases, e.g. under AID AND RELIEF, national branches which are headquarters for the sending out of large quantities of aid are included whereas national branches for receiving and distributing this aid are omitted. In most cases a full printed directory of all branches can be obtained from each organization's international headquarters. In cases where no official headquarters exists, or where it changes its location annually, a contact address is given here.

*Minor sub-divisions.* Under the major denominations and parachurch organizations listed here, there are a vast number of commissions, divisions, committees and sub-committees dealing with many of the topics in this directory. A large denomination may have a committee for virtually each and every topic. Each Roman Catholic episcopal conference may have a commission on many topics such as liturgy. National councils of churches have divisions of inter-church aid, research, lay training, and so on. Rather than attempt to list all these, many of which are ephemeral or short-lived, this directory lists the parent bodies only, from whom the reader can seek further details.

## NAMES

*Names and languages used.* Names of organizations are given throughout in each's major language in use, if this is one of the 6 major European languages (English, French, German, Italian, Portuguese or Spanish). In such cases no translation into English is given here unless in the interests of clarifying the organization's function, or if English is one of the body's official languages. If any other language is the major one used, this is given in parentheses but is preceded by its English translation, except in a few cases where the names are so similar that in the interests of brevity the English translation can be dispensed with. Note that some international organizations have titles in a different language to that of their host country (e.g. a French name for a religious order whose headquarters is in Italy).

*Official names are used.* Entries are alphabetized here under the official name, which may be different from the popular or abbreviated names in use. When trying to locate a certain body, therefore, the reader may have to look for it under any variations that might be possible.

*Most names are self-explanatory.* The names of most organizations are self-descriptive and explain what their role and function are, and so no further explanation is provided after each's entry. Where this is not so, a brief explanatory note has been added in parentheses after the address. Similarly, if the denominational affiliation of an organization is important but is not clear from its title, this has been added in parentheses.

*Some names are misleading.* Some bodies are not what they appear to be from their titles. Thus the Council for World Mission (CWM) is not, as one might expect, a council of churches or missionary societies, but is a single denominational or confessional missionary society (formerly the LMS, then the CCWM, now supported by Congregational churches in the UK, Australia and elsewhere). It should therefore be classified, not under CONCILIARISM, but under FOREIGN MISSIONARY SOCIETIES.

*Classification by key word in title.* In cases where an organization could equally well be classified under 2 or more categories, priority has been given to the main key word or words in its title when classifying it.

*Legal incorporation.* Many organizations are legally incorporated in their own countries or have legal status or a legal personality entitling them to hold property, etc, and so include in their titles such abbreviations as: Ltd (UK), & Co (UK), Inc (USA), Cie (France), Pty (Australia), Ltda and SA (Latin America), GmbH and eV (West Germany), etc. In the interests of brevity all such abbreviations are omitted in this directory, except for a handful of cases where the full title is advisable for purposes of identification or to avoid confusion with similar bodies.

## ADDRESSES

*Executive officers.* For many organizations the title of the main executive officer is given, if significant. In all other cases, the secretary should be addressed. The following abbreviations are used:

| | |
|---|---|
| Abp | archbishop |
| Bp | bishop |
| Dir | director |
| Dir Gen | director general |
| Exec Sec | executive secretary |
| Gen Dir | general director |
| Gen Sec | general secretary |
| Hon Sec | honorary secretary |
| Pres | president |
| Sec | secretary |
| Sec Gen | secretary general |
| Sek | sekretar |

*Postal addresses.* Where postal boxes or bags (PO Box, PB, IPO, Apdo, CP, BP, Postfach, Fah, etc) are given, they should always be used on envelopes in correspondence; in such cases the street address should not be added. In many countries (e.g. Bolivia, Kenya) there is no postal delivery to street addresses but only to boxes in central post offices. Where the postal (zip) code of the postal address is different from that of the street address, we give that of the former only. With regard to addresses of dioceses, these can mostly be found in national directories, for Roman Catholic, Anglican and similar jurisdictions. For Orthodox dioceses in traditionally-Orthodox countries, including in the Communist world, it often suffices to use as address 'The Bishop/Metropolitan/&c of....' followed only by the name of his see city.

*Abbreviations in addresses.* The following are used throughout the directory:

| | |
|---|---|
| Apdo | apartado postal |
| Av | avenue, avenida |
| Bldg(s) | building(s) |
| Blvd | boulevard |
| BP | boite postale (PO Box) |
| CP | casa postal (PO Box) |
| GPO | general post office |
| IPO | international post office |
| PA | postal agency |
| PB | post bag, private bag |
| PMB | private mail bag |
| PO | post office |
| Rd | road |
| St | street |
| Str | strasse (German) |
| T | telephone |

*International addressing procedures.* Postal addresses are written here in one standard format (house, street, post box, town, city, province), there being as yet no agreed internationalized format. Certain countries utilize a different format (e.g. in Germany, envelopes are typed with town or city before street and house number), but in this directory one standard procedure is followed throughout. There is however international agreement that city names should be spelt as in the country being written to: e.g. Roma, El Djezair/Alger, Moskva, instead of Rome, Algiers, Moscow; and that the country's name should be written or typed in capital letters (Universal Postal Union, 1970).

*Zip and other postal codes.* From 1959-1974, 25 nations introduced their own individual alphanumeric postal codes to speed up sorting, routeing and distribution of mail. By 1980, a number more had followed suit. These codes differ in length and composition from one country to another. The codes are not always used or given by organizations, although not to use them may involve lengthy delays in delivery. The countries by 1974 were: Australia, Austria, Belgium, Canada, Denmark, Finland, France, FR Germany, German DR, Hungary, India, Italy, Japan, Nepal, Netherlands, Norway, Peru, Philippines, Poland, Sweden, Switzerland, Yugoslavia, UK, USA, USSR.

*Alternative addresses.* In a few cases, 2 or more addresses for an organization are extant, either additional or alternative or a contact address, or one is a former address still in use. These additional addresses are given in parentheses, thus: (Also:        ).

*Use of out-of-date addresses.* Although the addresses and telephone numbers given here go out of date at a rate around 3% per year, an out-of-date address or telephone number can still be useful in tracking down changed locations.

*Individual letters versus mass mailing.* A caution should be sounded here concerning the proliferation of correspondence. Most of the organizations listed below have clearly-defined areas of concern and interest, and they can be expected to answer individual personally-signed or -addressed letters within those areas. However, most also have limited resources and are fully committed in terms of time and personnel. It becomes increasingly unlikely therefore that they will answer impersonal mass mailings, mass questionnaires, printed or duplicated letters and so on, unless these latter are clearly within their areas of concern and interest and contain some incentive or inducement to answer.

*Telephones.* The custom in many countries is to break up the writing of long numbers with fullstops, periods or dashes, thus: 28.12.35 or 28-12-35. However, since this custom is seldom standardized even within a single country, the practice in this directory is to remove all punctuation marks and print the digits together, thus: 281235. If there is an area code used for long-distance calls, this is usually given here at the beginning in parentheses. The only exceptions to this are the UK, USA, Canada and one or 2 other countries who use 7-digit numbers always separated by a dash: 281-2351. If a body has more than one number, these are separated by a comma(s). The symbol / indicates a second number differing from the first by the number shown (thus 216/7 means 216 & 217). In certain countries, the numbering system is continually being updated; hence, as explained in the first sentence of this Part 13, the phone numbers given here for certain countries (e.g. Belgium) do not pretend to be up-to-date. For the latest, exact, telephone directories, the reader must use current official directories. The object of the present Topical Directory is simply to alert him to the existence of a whole range of Christian organizations of which he may not otherwise have been aware.

## UPDATING

*Updating procedures.* The names, addresses and telephone numbers in this directory date from the period 1969-80. They can be expected to change at a rate around 3% per year, and so the directory should remain useful as a working tool until after 1980. Updated versions of the directory will be issued from time to time.

# DEFINITIONS OF TOPICS

## Basic Church Structures

1. **CHURCHES AND DENOMINATIONS.** Headquarters addresses of a selection of 2,600 of the larger or more significant (in each country) of the world's 20,000 denominations (primary religious groups), using the same names as occur in our Tables 2 (where translations, sub-titles, jurisdictions, etc, will be found). The cut-off point below which smaller bodies are excluded below varies from country to country; it can be small, in small countries, but it usually varies here from a total community of 1,000 in many countries, or below 10,000 (in UK) or below 200,000 (in USA).

## Christian Life, Service & Outreach

2. **AID AND RELIEF.** Specifically Christian voluntary agencies dealing with programmes of inter-church aid, Christian aid, relief, emergency action, disasters, refugees, population problems, minority groups, migrants, migration; inter-church service agencies; charities, charitable societies. See also DEVELOPMENT, JUSTICE AND PEACE.

3. **ARTS (RELIGION AND THE ARTS).** Christian involvement in the arts; the artistic aspects of the mass media, speech, drama, theatre, opera, cinema, performing arts, circus, literature, festivals; renowned centres of Christian artistic presentation (Oberammergau, Forest Lawn, Einsiedeln); unusual types of Christian exhibition (Holy Land museum, Nijmegen); Christian museums of major importance; Christian art centres; church architecture, church buildings, historical monuments.

4. **AUDIOVISUAL AIDS.** Agencies, programmes and centres specializing in the production or dissemination of all kinds of audiovisual aids except movie films (see CINEMA AND FILM): slides, filmstrips, posters, pictures, drawings, cartoons, videotape materials; audiovisual training centres oriented towards education, catechesis, evangelization, development; microform materials; microfilm, microfiche libraries, computerized micrographics. See also SOCIAL COMMUNICATIONS CO-ORDINATION.

5. **BIBLE AND SCRIPTURE ORGANIZATIONS.** Bible societies and publishing houses, Bible translation and distribution agencies, scripture distribution agencies, colportage agencies, Christian linguistic organizations and centres, Bible-reading organizations, Bible study associations, Bible-memorizing programmes, Bible text societies (literature, posters), the biblical apostolate. See also PUBLISHING for commercial publishers specializing (but not exclusively) in Bible production.

6. **BIBLE SCHOOLS AND COLLEGES.** Centres for the training of Christian workers: (a) in Western countries, degree- or diploma-granting bodies sometimes for the ordained ministry but more usually not; and (b) in Third-World countries, often for the ordained ministry, also for lay ministries, both for candidates of less than secondary education.

7. **BROADCASTING.** Organizations and centres (excluding radio/TV stations) specializing in Christian religious broadcasting, commissions, radio/TV programming, programme production, production of materials, cable TV, spots, major production studios; programme distribution agencies (distributing to stations); radio/TV training schools and centres; educational or mass-education radio and TV, teleclubs, mass education by satellite (without postal feedback); listeners' and viewers' associations. See also RADIO & TELEVISION STATIONS.

8. **CATECHESIS AND CHRISTIAN EDUCATION.** Sunday schools, vacation schools, religious education, councils of religious education; Christian schools or colleges of national importance, school or college chaplaincies of national importance, Christian technical or training schools (industrial, rural, vocational); secular education under Christian auspices, schools managements; catechetics.

9. **CHILDREN'S ORGANIZATIONS.** Agencies specializing in work with or for children, children's missions, child evangelism, child welfare, children's societies, children's homes, orphanages. For education and Sunday schools, see CATECHESIS AND CHRISTIAN EDUCATION.

10. **CHRISTIAN APPROACHES TO OTHER FAITHS.** Christian missionary or evangelistic initiatives directed primarily towards the other major world religions (especially Judaism, Islam, Hinduism, Buddhism), including agnosticism and atheism, primarily concerned with mission and evangelism, or with interfaith dialogue or mutual understanding; activities, information and study centres. See also RESEARCH CENTRES. For joint activity between Christians and non-Christians, see INTERRELIGIOUS ORGANIZATIONS.

11. **CHRISTIAN UNIVERSITIES.** Church- or Christian-operated, -owned, -controlled, -sponsored, or -linked universities granting academic degrees mainly in secular subjects.

12. **CINEMA AND FILM.** Christian involvement in the cinema, films, motion pictures; video-cassette ministries; cinema and film training schools and centres; film libraries; film festivals, weeks, seminars.

13. **CLERGY-LAY AND CLERGY ORGANIZATIONS.** Organizations of individuals for consultation and co-operation between clergy (priests, pastors, ministers), or clergy and laity, or clergy/laity/religious personnel, or missionary personnel; either within a single church or denomination, or interdenominational or ecumenical; priests' councils or senates, national priests' organizations, ministerial or clergy fellowships, ministers' fraternals, pastoral councils, pastoral consultative bodies, fellowships of foreign missionary personnel, Catholic national and diocesan synods; clergy recruitment organizations, clergy or lay employment bureaux. For women, see WOMEN IN THE ORDAINED MINISTRY. For religious personnel, see FEDERATIONS OF RELIGIOUS COMMUNITIES.

14. **CONFESSIONAL CONCILIARISM.** Councils of churches or denominations belonging to a world confessional family (world family of churches) of one particular ecclesiastical tradition; international councils, federations, alliances; Roman Catholic world-wide congregations of dioceses; confessional conciliarism, collegiality and consultation.

15. **CONTINENTAL CONCILIARISM.** Interdenominational or ecumenical councils of churches or denominations and dioceses of different ecclesiastical traditions, for a single continent, sub-continent or quasi-continent; councils, federations, alliances; continent-wide conciliarism, collegiality and consultation.

16. **CORRESPONDENCE AND RADIOPHONIC SCHOOLS.** Christian mass educational courses with individual postal feedback; instructional courses by post, or by radio/TV with enrolment and local instructors or postal feedback; radio (radiophonic) schools, TV schools (teleschools, telecentres), radio/TV correspondence courses, radio literacy courses; Bible instruction, evangelistic, theological, vocational, educational. religious teaching; Sunday-school by post.

17. **DEVELOPMENT, JUSTICE AND PEACE.** The churches' involvement in the areas of development, justice and peace: economic development, international development, multinationals (transnational corporations), overseas development, poverty, problems of underdevelopment, socio-economic promotion; ecology, environment, pollution, desertification; citizenship, civil rights, religious liberty, legal and other relations with governments, canon law, injustice, racism, torture, political prisoners; pacifism, peace or anti-war groups, conscientious objectors; Christian involvement in revolution, liberation movements, guerrilla movements; co-ordinating bodies; development education, conscientization. For local development and community projects, see SOCIAL AND PASTORAL CONCERN. See also AID AND RELIEF.

18. **DIPLOMATIC REPRESENTATION.** Diplomatic representatives of the Holy See across the world, to nations and to the major international organizations; nunciatures, apostolic delegations, permanent observers.

19. **ECUMENICAL CENTRES.** Centres primarily for interdenominational or ecumenical meeting, study, dialogue and training, for both clergy and laity. For centres or institutes primarily concerned with ecumenical research, see RESEARCH CENTRES. See also LAY TRAINING CENTRES.

20. **ECUMENICAL COMMISSIONS AND AGENCIES.** Organizations for Christian unity or understanding either set up by large churches, or independent of any denomination, for the fostering of relations between the churches, ecumenical meeting, dialogue, study, fellowship, joint action; interconfessional groups; faith and order commissions; church union negotiating bodies and commissions for churches negotiating towards organic union.

21. **EVANGELIZATION AND MASS EVANGELISM.** International evangelistic organizations, evangelistic societies, evangelistic associations, professional evangelists, revival campaigns, tent campaigns, crusades, missions, long-term campaigns (Evangelism-in-Depth, New Life for All), saturation evangelism (total mobilization evangelism), multiplication evangelism; evangelistic centres, radio and TV evangelistic enterprises, film evangelism; annual or regular mass rallies (e.g. Cliff College, UK); national and international congresses of evangelism and evangelization; world evangelization agencies, councils, congresses, institutions, programmes.

22. **FEDERATIONS OF RELIGIOUS COMMUNITIES.** Federations or groupings of religious communities or congregations, or of religious personnel (priests, brothers and sisters).

23. **FINANCE, PROPERTY AND STEWARDSHIP.** Organizations primarily concerned with church finance and/or property, financial services, Christian stewardship organizations, insurance bodies, co-operatives, savings societies, credit unions; foundations, trusts, funding agencies, fund-raising agencies, fund-transmitting agencies, pension schemes, ministerial funding societies, charitable societies; new church construction or building societies; management consulting, business methods for churches. See also AID AND RELIEF, and DEVELOPMENT, JUSTICE AND PEACE. Also, most denominational HQs listed under CHURCHES AND DENOMINATIONS deal also with finance and property.

24. **FOREIGN MISSIONARY COUNCILS.** Councils of foreign missionary societies of different denominations and/or dioceses set up in parent sending countries to facilitate co-ordination, joint discussion, co-operation and missionary action to overseas or foreign countries (but not themselves sending money or personnel); committees, commissions.

25. **FOREIGN MISSIONARY SOCIETIES.** Societies and agencies primarily and principally concerned with the sending abroad of foreign missionary personnel and resources, including international missionary societies, denominational mission boards, orders primarily formed for foreign missions, and Catholic missionary congregations or institutes under SC Propaganda; international headquarters only (not national branches, nor field addresses). Small societies with under 10 personnel serving abroad are usually excluded here. Women's societies are found under WOMEN'S LAY ORGANIZATIONS.

26. **FOREIGN MISSIONARY TRAINING.** Training colleges at home or abroad primarily or solely for foreign missionaries or persons proceeding overseas in secular employment, orientation schools, language schools, refresher courses, graduate schools of mission specializing in training, seminaries primarily for foreign missionaries; not primarily academic or degree-granting. For primarily the academic study of mission and missiology, see UNIVERSITY DEPARTMENTS OF RELIGION.

27. **FOREIGN MISSIONS SUPPORT ORGANIZATIONS.** Agencies for support of foreign missions and missionary

societies, but not themselves founding missions or churches or (usually) sending personnel; service organizations, co-ordinating agencies; fund-raising, recruiting in home (sending) countries; technical aid, missionary aviation and transport, missionary equipment services; Anglican diocesan associations (funds for overseas dioceses). For prayer support, see PRAYER SOCIETIES.

28. **HOME AND FAMILY LIFE.** Family movements, the family apostolate; marriage guidance and conselling, family planning, abortion, adoption services.

29. **HOME MISSIONS, SOCIETIES AND RENEWAL.** Home or domestic missionary societies, agencies, congregations or orders in a nation formed for work only or primarily within that nation; home evangelistic societies, inner missions, city missions (except those classified under CHURCHES AND DENOMINATIONS), renewal movements within the churches, charismatic movements, charismatic services and communication centres; societies for lobbying particular viewpoints, pressure groups. See also: RURAL AGRICULTURAL MISSION, URBAN INDUSTRIAL MISSION.

30. **JOURNALISM, THE PRESS AND INFORMATION.** The religious press, newspapers, radio and TV religious news offices, news services, clippings services, religious editors of international newspapers and secular radio and TV networks; press agencies of major denominations, church information agencies and centres, agencies publishing news bulletins, church publicity centres, church advertising and public relations; photographic libraries, agencies and services; journalism training centres, schools of journalism.

31. **LAY MINISTRIES.** Organizations for laity only (men and women), specifically emphasizing the lay contribution; laymen's associations, the lay apostolate, lay movements, unstructured movements, businessmen's committees, non-ordained ministries, lay preachers, lay readers, laymen overseas, lay missionary societies; lay ministries for men only; personal evangelism, small-group evangelism. See also WOMEN'S LAY ORGANIZATIONS.

32. **LAY TRAINING CENTRES.** Centres primarily for general training of the laity, in almost all cases with physical plant for conferences or residential activities; study centres, evangelical academies, colleges of evangelism, retreat centres, Catholic pastoral centres and institutes, major Catholic catechetical centres, lay seminaries, pastoral orientation centres, conference centres, fellowship centres, renewal centres, retreat centres; social, economic and development training; leadership training, discipleship training, charismatic training, training programmes, study programmes, conference organizations, large-scale organizations for lay training through conferences, institutes, teach-ins, discipleship groups, evening classes. Specialized training centres are listed not here but under their respective categories (see: audiovisual, cinema and film, broadcasting, charismatic renewal, ecumenical, foreign missionary, industrial mission, journalism and information, literature, liturgy, medicine, research, rural mission, social communications, student, theological, university departments of religion, urban mission, youth).

33. **LIBRARIES.** The world's major religious book library collections (only those with over 35,000 volumes in 1966): theological, religious, missiological, biblical. The figure in parentheses after the address is the number of volumes held (1966). For non-book libraries (photographic libraries, film libraries, record libraries, recorded music libraries, tape libraries, microfilm or microfiche libraries), see CINEMA AND FILM, JOURNALISM, SOUND RECORDINGS, MUSIC AND SONG, etc.

34. **LITERATURE.** International and national organizations for Christian literature, publications programmes, literature distribution, bookshop chains and headquarters; tract societies; literature training centres; religious book clubs; writers' courses; literacy materials, campaigns, courses, programmes, agencies, co-ordinating bodies.

35. **LITURGY AND WORSHIP.** Liturgical centres, organizations, major supply agencies for liturgical equipment, literature, vestments; liturgical training centres; ritual, rites, sacraments, doctrines; wholesale and retail supply houses for religious articles. See also MUSIC AND SONG.

36. **LOCAL (SUB-NATIONAL) CONCILIARISM.** Interdenominational or ecumenical councils of churches or denominations and dioceses of different ecclesiastical traditions, for a province, area of city within a single nation; local conciliarism, collegiality and consultation.

37. **MEDICAL CENTRES.** Church- or Christian-sponsored hospitals, leprosaria, sanatoria, clinics, dispensaries, mobile units, maternity centres, et alia.

38. **MEDICINE AND HEALING.** Medical missions, fellowship and witness in the medical world, major Christian medical centres, associations of hospitals (or clinics or dispensaries), medical missionary institutes, nursing training centres, dental missions, ophthalmic missions, leprosy missions, other specialist missions, medical missions support organizations, public health, hospital chaplaincy organizations, medical services, medical supply agencies, pharmacists, ministries to handicapped groups (the deaf, the blind, cripples, epileptics, incurables, lepers, mental institutions), suicides, religion and psychiatry, religion and health, mental health, Christian psychologists, clinical theology, spiritual healing, faith-healing groups and centres; training centres and courses. See also RESEARCH CENTRES.

39. **MILITARY CHAPLAINCIES.** Major organizations ministering to armed services at home or overseas (armies, navies, air forces, police forces, paramilitary units); military jurisdictions, bishops for armed services.

40. **MONASTERIES AND RELIGIOUS HOUSES.** Catholic, Orthodox, Anglican, Protestant and other monasteries, abbeys, priories, convents, mother houses of religious orders

and congregations, retreat centres, ashrams, spiritual life centres, religious communities, brotherhoods, sisterhoods, et alia.

41. **MUSIC AND SONG.** Choirs, evangelistic groups, singing groups, Christian pop groups, discotheques, coffee houses, libraries of religious music, Christian recording organizations, church music training centres, musicals (shows), opera, rock opera, festivals; campanology, bell-ringing. See also LITURGY AND WORSHIP.

42. **NATIONAL CONCILIARISM.** Interdenominational or ecumenical councils of churches or denominations and dioceses of different ecclesiastical traditions, occasionally including foreign missionary societies, either (NATIONAL) for a single nation, or (PLURINATIONAL) for a small grouping of 2 or 3 adjacent nations included in the council's title; councils, federations, alliances, fellowships; Roman Catholic national episcopal or bishops' conferences, national inter-rite assemblies; national conciliarism, collegiality and consultation; including the remaining 3 or 4 missionary councils (councils of foreign missions at work in a nation), but excluding interreligious national councils open to non-Christian bodies (for these, see INTERRELIGIOUS ORGANIZATIONS).

43. **PRAYER SOCIETIES.** Societies and fellowships concerned primarily with prayer, the prayer life, intercession, meditation, days of prayer. There are countless other prayer fellowships and societies praying for specific areas or subjects, and in a sense all types of Christian organizations, and the denominations themselves, can be considered as prayer societies.

44. **PUBLISHING.** Publishing houses producing religious or Christian literature (usually church- or Christian-owned, -operated, -controlled, -sponsored or -linked), church printing presses; including secular houses which give major importance to publishing books on religion. For publications and programmes, see LITERATURE. For agencies exclusively publishing scriptures, see BIBLE AND SCRIPTURE ORGANIZATIONS.

45. **RADIO AND TELEVISION STATIONS.** Church- or Christian-owned, -operated, -controlled, or -sponsored radio or TV broadcasting stations (defined as organized centres with transmitting equipment); with both their call signs and their programme names; national associations of stations.

46. **REGIONAL CONCILIARISM.** Interdenominational or ecumenical councils of churches or denominations and dioceses of different ecclesiastical traditions, for a region covering a number of nations; councils, federations, alliances; regional conciliarism, collegiality and consultation; Roman Catholic regional episcopal conferences and multinational episcopal conferences.

47. **RELIGIOUS COMMUNITIES.** Religious orders, congregations, societies, communities, brotherhoods, sisterhoods, mixed communities, communers, and other communities following a religious rule (regular) or the religious life, with a permanent centre, permanent membership and permanent residential community, for men and/or women, with either ordained, religious, lay or mixed personnel; usually or often with religious vows of poverty, chastity and obedience; not primarily concerned with foreign missionary work; Catholic congregations of pontifical status (directly under Rome); and indigenous communities and local congregations (clerical or lay) begun in the Third World. For deaconesses orders, see WOMEN IN THE ORDAINED MINISTRY. For congregations primarily devoted to foreign missionary work, see FOREIGN MISSIONARY SOCIETIES.

48. **RELIGIOUS PERIODICALS.** Christian or church periodicals, journals, magazines, newspapers, bulletins, house organs, and other regular serials; of popular, news, scholarly, professional or academic content; daily, semi-weekly, weekly, biweekly, monthly, quarterly, excluding irregular serials and annuals. See also under DIRECTORIES.

49. **RELIGIO-POLITICAL ORGANIZATIONS.** Christian political parties (e.g. Christian Democrats), church groups with a political or ideological emphasis, especially progressivist or traditionalist groups; church organizations dealing with international political affairs or public affairs; polemical groups, radical groups, front organizations, rightist organizations; counter-revolutionary organizations, reactionary groups, movements of religious conservatism; non-violent groups, paramilitary organizations; pressure groups or lobbies working on governments or the United Nations.

50. **RESEARCH CENTRES.** Centres, institutes and institutions undertaking original research related to Christianity and religions — religious, socio-religious, anthropological, historical, biblical, theological, communications, information, missiological, missiographical, micromissiographical, macromissiographical, ecclesiological, ecclesiographical, macroecclesiographical, futurological; ecumenical centres and institutes at university level; experimental institutes, think tanks; Christian or church-related centres for study and research in non-Christian religions or atheism; documentation centres and services, resource centres, research archives, library research centres; public opinion polls, survey organizations, market research, radio/TV audience research centres, statistical services, pastoral research services, planning agencies, management research services; information management, computerized data banks, data processing organizations, computer bureaux, survey archives, research publications agencies. (Note: other research centres in specialized topics, e.g. LITURGY AND WORSHIP, BROADCASTING, will be found under those topics only if the research function is not their major one).

51. **RURAL AGRICULTURAL MISSION.** Agricultural missions, agricultural assistance, Christian rural or farming communities

or centres, village polytechnics, rural transformation, rural development aid, ministry to rural situations, agricultural co-operatives, farmers' trade unions; rural and agricultural training centres. (Note: many centres included under LAY TRAINING CENTRES specialize in rural courses).

52. **SCHOLARLY SOCIETIES.** National and international associations, learned societies and commissions (as contrasted with institutes or centres) : biblical studies, theology, missiology, church history, religion sociology, anthropology, ethnology, psychology, archeology, religion and science, religion and philosophy, religion and futurology; scholarly lecture series; associations of scholars; Catholic pontifical commissions in scholarly disciplines.

53. **SCHOOLS AND COLLEGES.** Schools under church or Christian auspices or sponsorship : junior and senior secondary schools teaching secular subjects, minor seminaries (secular or religious), technical schools, agricultural schools, vocational schools, junior colleges, technical colleges, teacher-training colleges.

54. **SOCIAL AND PASTORAL CONCERN.** Organizations concerned primarily with local Christian social, pastoral and community action and service in the secular world; voluntary service, pastoral concern and action, pastoralia, social action and service centres and ministries, social welfare, moral welfare, community development, unemployment, housing, population control, eugenics, the underprivileged, the elderly and aged, almshouses, delinquency, alcoholism, temperance, drug addiction, gambling, pornography, crime, prisons and prison chaplaincies, rehabilitation of released prisoners; counselling services.

55. **SOCIAL COMMUNICATIONS CO-ORDINATION.** Agencies and centres co-ordinating social cummunications, i.e. several or all types of mass media and communications (often including audiovisuals, cinema, recordings, radio, TV, literature, newspapers, public opinion media); group media, alternate media; Christian production of social communications material, multimedia production centres and studios; the technical aspects of communication, mass communication, and instant communication; photography, mass-circulation newspapers, satellite communications; Christian centres and other agencies engaged in social communications outreach; public opinion agencies and centres. See also RESEARCH CENTRES.

56. **SOCIAL COMMUNICATIONS TRAINING.** Training centres covering all aspects of social communications, the mass media and communication arts (excluding specialized centres for one of the mass media only), and public opinion, including centres at university level; application to education, catechesis, evangelization, development.

57. **SOUND RECORDINGS.** Centres or organizations involved in tape, cassette or disc recordings and their preparation; tape or cassette ministries, audio ministries, videotape cassette ministries; record, tape, cassette or disc libraries, recorded music libraries.

58. **SPIRITUAL LIFE CONVENTIONS, RALLIES, RETREATS.** Annual or limited-duration movements or meetings not primarily for evangelism but for the deepening of the spiritual life; annual mass conventions, mass rallies, the retreat movement, retreat organizations, retreat centres (for temporary residence only). The majority of such activities are not listed here but are operated by organizations under RELIGIOUS COMMUNITIES and LAY TRAINING CENTRES.

59. **STATE DEPARTMENTS FOR RELIGIOUS AFFAIRS.** State or government ministries or departments responsible for or charged with religious or ecclesiastical affairs, or other government ministries whose formal or legal responsibilities include religious affairs (controlling registration, worship, propaganda, proselytism, education, relations between religions); state religious organizations, state co-ordinating bodies, state legal agencies, state bodies for surveillance and control of churches. Whilst some of these bodies are Christian in sympathies or activities, others are hostile to Christianity and the churches.

60. **STUDENT ORGANIZATION FEDERATIONS.** Inter-university Christian groups, campus organizations, major university chaplaincies and related national organizations, major student centres, student leadership training centres, scholarship-awarding bodies.

61. **TELEPHONE MINISTRIES.** Centres and agencies in large cities offering specialized public counselling facilities by telephone, taped messages, taped Bible readings, sometime in conjunction with radio programmes; telephone missionars news and prayer information services.

62. **THEOLOGICAL COLLEGE ASSOCIATIONS.** Regional or wider groupings of theological colleges for co-operation in accrediting, syllabuses, curricula, higher studies, research, and conferences; international co-ordinating bodies.

63. **THEOLOGICAL COLLEGES AND SEMINARIES.** Centres for the training of the ordained ministry or priesthood : major seminaries (religious or secular), theological colleges, advanced Bible schools.

64. **THEOLOGICAL EDUCATION BY EXTENSION.** Institutionalized courses and programmes utilizing TEE principles of theological training by outreach at a number of selected centres.

65. **TOURISM, RECREATION AND TRAVEL.** Christian tour organizations, travel agencies, charter companies, holiday organizations, package tours, travel service and advice centres; pilgrimage organizations; associations of camping sites, summer camps, holiday centres and/or houseparty centres; ministries to tourism, leisure, recreation, athletics

and sport. For missionary air travel, see also FOREIGN MISSIONS SUPPORT ORGANIZATIONS.

66. **UNIVERSITY DEPARTMENTS OF RELIGION.** Faculties or departments specializing in the academic degree-level teaching of, and granting degrees in, religious studies, divinity, theology, mission, missiology, church history, philosophy of religion, sociology or psychology of religion, or related subjects (but not specifically training persons for the ordained ministry). See also RESEARCH CENTRES.

67. **URBAN INDUSTRIAL MISSION.** Industrial missions and projects, urban ministry; urban-industrial ecumenical parishes, experimental parishes, inner-city parishes; team ministries, ministries to urban structures and institutions, experimental ministries, new or exploratory ministries in specialized areas; urban industrial mission training centres; intermediate technology, appropriate technology, labour-intensive projects; factory evangelism, occupational evangelism.

68. **WOMEN IN THE ORDAINED MINISTRY.** Organizations for women in the ordained ministry, diaconate or priesthood; associations, training schools, Bible and theological colleges for women only; deaconesses, deaconess orders, deaconess homes or houses, deaconess training institutions.

69. **WOMEN'S LAY ORGANIZATIONS.** Groups for laywomen and girls only, emphasizing the role or lay ministry of women, the place of women in church and society; women's lay orders, mothers' and wives' groups, women's rights, women's liberation movements, feminist movements, women's caucuses, task forces, co-ordinating agencies; YWCA and organizations serving women and girls; women's home or foreign missionary societies; and other movements either radical or conservative.

70. **WORKERS' AND PROFESSIONALS' ASSOCIATIONS.** Organizations and movements bringing together or uniting Christians who are labourers or workers (labour, industry) or Christians working in the various secular professions (arts, journalism, legal, medical, scientific, teaching, business, social service, welfare workers); Christian (mainly Catholic) workers' movements and labour or trade unions; secular trade unions retaining Christian names, principles or other ties; young workers' associations; federations or unions of workers' or professionals' associations; professional associations. For religious professionals, see CLERGY-LAY AND CLERGY ORGANIZATIONS, SCHOLARLY SOCIETIES, etc.

71. **WORLD CONCILIARISM.** Interdenominational or ecumenical councils of churches or denominations of different ecclesiastical traditions, at the international or world level; councils, federations, alliances, fellowships; world conciliarism, collegiality and consultation.

72. **YOUTH ORGANIZATIONS.** Groups and activities for young people (boys and girls together), teenagers; youth work, hostels, camps, work camps, Bible camps, houseparties, YMCA; youth evangelism. For young workers, see WORKERS' AND PROFESSIONALS' ASSOCIATIONS. For rural youth, see RURAL AGRICULTURAL MISSION.

## Directories

73. **DIRECTORIES, YEARBOOKS, HANDBOOKS, AND INDEXES.** In each country, the major current directories, yearbooks and reference handbooks (containing names, addresses, statistics, listings, descriptive materials, but not usually histories, surveys or descriptive texts) of churches at the national level (usually excluding dioceses and other sub-divisions), denominations, councils and Christian organizations, agencies, institutions, personnel and periodicals; both denominational, interdenominational, local, national, plurinational, international, and topical; and the publishing addresses from which they may be obtained. *Periodicals.* As described in this Encyclopedia, the total number of current periodicals concerned with Christianity and religion is over 3,000 scholarly journals in the various disciplines, together with over 20,000 Christian magazines and newspapers of less academic and more popular content. A majority of these are listed in denominational and other directories, but a small selection of significant directories dealing only with periodicals is also included here.

## Non-Christian Religious Organizations

74. **ATHEISTIC, HUMANIST AND ANTI-RELIGIOUS ORGANIZATIONS.** Atheistic or non-theistic humanistic (or anti-supernaturalist) movements, freethinkers' organizations, societies or groups, committed to active or militant opposition to Christianity or to all religion; organizations for the promotion or propagation of atheism or non-theistic humanism; centres for the study of atheism; atheism research centres, research centres dealing with religion but under anti-religious auspices, university faculties of atheism.

75. **INTERRELIGIOUS ORGANIZATIONS.** Commissions, councils or organizations not primarily or exclusively Christian but run jointly by all or several major religions including Christianity, i.e. run by Christians and one or more non-Christian religions. for some joint non-missionary inter-faith activity other than mission; including national councils of religious bodies open to Christians and non-Christians alike.

76. **NON-CHRISTIAN RELIGIONS.** A selection of major headquarters and organizations, world federations, missionary organizations, study centres operated by or for these religions, non-Christian research centres, universities, institutes and institutions.

## TOPICAL DIRECTORY SUBJECT INDEX

This index lists 790 subjects, contained in the
Topical Directory (Part 13), relating to the Christian
enterprise and its context in the secular and religious
worlds. It then gives a number or numbers, these being
those of the Directory's 76 topics under which each
subject may be found. The index enables the reader
wanting a particular subject to find the number or
numbers (1-76) of the topic or topics under which it
is classified in this Directory. Usually, the bulk of the
entries for a particular subject are found under one
topic only. A few entries below are general: thus
'parachurch agencies' are shown as '2–73', which
means that all topics from 2 to 73 inclusive refer
to this subject.

# 1
# Churches and Denominations

*Definition of topic.* Headquarters addresses of a selection of 2,600 of the larger or more significant (in each country) of the world's 20,000 denominations (primary religious groups), using the same names as occur in our Tables 2 (where translations, sub-titles, jurisdictions, etc. will be found). The cut-off point below which smaller bodies are excluded below varies from country to country; it can be small, in small countries, but it usually varies from a total community of 1,000 in many countries, or below 10,000 (in UK), or below 200,000 (in USA).

For complete and up-to-date listings in any country, or for any confession, communion or denomination, consult the latest editions of any relevant yearbooks (listed here under Topic 73, DIRECTORIES).

*AFGHANISTAN*

**Catholic Ch,** Embassy of Italy, Kabul. T: 24247.
**Community Christian Ch of Kabul,** PO Box 0, Kabul. T: 42224.

*ALGERIA*

**Armée du Salut,** 11 Rue Tirman, El Djezair (Alger).
**Eglise Adventiste du Septième Jour,** Sec, 3 Rue du Sacré-Coeur, El Djezair (Alger). T: 602675.
**Eglise Catholique en Algérie,** Archevêché, 13 Rue Khelifa-Boukhalfa, El Djezair (Alger). T: 634244.
**Eglise Protestante d'Algérie,** 78 Chemin Beaurepaire, El-Biar, El Djezair (Alger). T: 783291.
**Mission d'Afrique du Nord,** 3 Rue du Xacear, Hydra, El Djezair (Alger).

*AMERICAN SAMOA*

**Assemblies of God in Samoa,** Central Office, Mission House, PO Box 218, Pago Pago.
**Seventh-day Adventist Ch,** Dir, PO Box 146, Pago Pago.

*ANGOLA*

**Igreja Adventista do Sétimo Dia,** Pres, Rua Teixeira da Silva, CP 3, Nova Lisboa. T: 23803.
**Igreja Católica em Angola,** Arcebispado, CP 87, Luanda. T: 34640.
**Igreja de Deus,** CP 230, Nova Lisboa.
**Igreja Ev de Angola,** Sec, CP 19, Cabinda.
**Igreja Ev de Angola Central,** CP 28, Bela Vista.
**Igreja Ev do Sudoeste de Angola,** CP 29, Caluquembe.
**Igreja Ev do Sul de Angola,** CP 33, Sá da Bandeira.
**Igreja Ev dos Irmãos,** CP 107, Luso.
**Igreja Lusitana Católica Apóstolica Ev,** D João 11 St 36-38, PO Box 2072 C, Luanda.
**Igreja Metodista Unida de Angola,** Bp, CP 68, Luanda.

*ANTIGUA*

**Anglican Ch,** Bp, Diocese of Antigua, PO Box 23, Saint John's.
**Catholic Ch,** Catholic Offices, PO Box 836, Saint John's. T: 21135.
**Jehovah's Witnesses,** PO Box 119, Saint John's.
**Methodist Ch, in the Caribbean and the Americas,** Pres, Conference HQ, PO Box 9, Saint John's.
**Salvation Army,** 36 Long St, PO Box 2, Saint John's. T: 115.

*ARGENTINA*

**Alianza Cristiana y Misionera,** Pampa 2975, Buenos Aires.
**Asamblea Cristiana Cultural,** Salvador Maria del Carril 5069, Buenos Aires.
**Asamblea Cristiana de Argentina,** Salvador Maria del Carril 5069, Buenos Aires.
**Asamblea de Dios,** Juan B. Alberdi 2260, Buenos Aires.
**Congregación Cristiana Católica Apóstolica,** 1 de C Rey, Apdo de Correos 1855, Buenos Aires.
**Convención Ev Bautista de Argentina,** Tucuman 358/6, Buenos Aires.
**Ejército de Salvación,** Av Rivadavia 3257, Sucursal 3, Casilla 194, Buenos Aires. T: 890621/2/3.
**Iglesia Adventista del Séptimo Día,** Pres, Suc 25 (Palermo), Casilla 39, Buenos Aires. T: 7409955.
**Iglesia Anglicana,** Diocese of Northern Argentina, Bp, Casilla 187, Salta.
**Iglesia Católica en la Argentina,** CEA, Calle Paraguay 1867, Buenos Aires. T: 313317.
**Iglesia Congregacionalista en la República Argentina,** San Martín 119, Concordia, Entre Rios.
**Iglesia de Dios Cristiana Pentecostal,** Villa Ballester, Cordoba 626, Malaver, Buenos Aires.
**Iglesia de los Hermanos Libres,** Pico 1641, Buenos Aires.
**Iglesia del Nazareno,** Pirán 5978, Buenos Aires.
**Iglesia del Río de la Plata,** Pres, Esmeralda 162, Buenos Aires. T: 457520.
**Iglesia Ev Luterana Unida,** Pres, Cuenca 3285, Buenos Aires. T: 506483.
**Iglesia Ev Pentecostal Argentina,** Rivadavia 3133 (& Ricardo Güiraldes 114, Villa Diehl, San Martín), Buenos Aires.
**Iglesia Ev Valdense,** Camacuá 282, Buenos Aires. (also: Colonia Belgrano, Santa Fe).
**Iglesia Luterana Argentina (LCMS),** Combet 46, Villa Ballester, Buenos Aires.
**Iglesia Metodista Argentina,** José Maria Moreno 240-10, Buenos Aires 24.
**Iglesia Ortodoxa Griega,** Av Figueroa Alcorta 3187, Buenos Aires. T: 833204.
**Iglesia Ortodoxa Russa,** Calle Nunez 3541, Buenos Aires. T: 7012691. (ROCOR).
**Iglesia Ortodoxa Russa (P Mosca),** Calle Conesa 1925, 5 Piso B, Buenos Aires.
**Movimiento Cristiano y Misionero,** La Plata, Provincia de Buenos Aires.
**Testigos de Jehová,** Calle Honduras 5646, Buenos Aires 14.
**Unión Misionera Neotestamentaria,** Estevez Correa 139, Temperley, Pcia de Buenos Aires.
**Unión Nacional de las Asambleas de Dios,** Hidalgo 353, Casilla de Correo 4669, Buenos Aires.

*AUSTRALIA*

**Aborigines Inland Mission Fellowship Ch,** Gen Sec, 9 Carramarr Rd, Castle Hill 2154.
**Apostolic Ch of Australia & NZ,** 89 Livingstone Rd, Marrickville, Sydney, NSW 2204.
**Armenian Apostolic Ch,** 372 Miller St, GPO Box 4866, Sydney, NSW 2001.
**Assemblies of God in Australia,** 79 Moray St, New Farm, Brisbane, Queensland. (Also: National Super, Stafford, Queensland 4053).
**Australian Aborigines Ev Mission,** Cundeelee via Zanthus, Trans-Australian Railway, Western Australia. (Also: 8 Victory, Asquith).
**Catholic Ch in Australia,** AEC, 12 Kennedy St, PO Box 297, Kingston, ACT 2604. T: 283539.
**Christadelphian Ecclesias,** Sec, PO Box 40, Seven Hills, NSW 2147.
**Christian Brethren,** Emmaus Bible School, PO Box 343, Camberwell, Victoria 3124.
**Christian Revival Crusade,** Sunrise House, 95 Wattle St, Fullarton, South Australia 5063. T: 710486.
**Ch of Christ, Scientist,** First Church, Macquarie and Bligh Sts, Canberra.
**Ch of England in Australia,** General Synod Office, 1st Floor, St Andrew's House, Sydney Square, NSW 2000. T: (02)20642.
**Ch of Jesus Christ of Latter-day Saints,** 5 Russel St, Wollstonecraft, NSW.
**Ch of the Nazarene,** Nazarene Bible College, 235 Pennant Hills Rd, Thornleigh, NSW.
**Chs of Christ in Australia,** Federal Conference, Pres, 1 Buttrose St, Glenelg East, South Australia 5045.
**Congregational Union of Australia,** Pres, 25 Nicholson St, Burwood, NSW 2134. (Also: Sec, 15 Russell St, Eastwood, NSW 2122).
**Fellowship of Ev Chs in Australia,** 247 Gertrude St, Fitzroy, Victoria.
**Full Gospel Ch in Australia,** 15 Fromm St Grange, GPO Box 1708 V, Brisbane, Queensland 4051.
**Greek Orthodox Ch,** Archdiocese of Australia, Archbp, 242 Cleveland St, Sydney-Redfern, NSW 2016. T: (02)695811.
**International Ch of the Foursquare Gospel,** LIFE Bible College, 2 Margaret St, Strathfield, NSW.
**Jehovah's Witnesses,** 11 Beresford Rd, Strathfield, NSW 2135.
**Latvian Ev Lutheran Ch in Exile,** Dean, 42 Cameron St, Regent, Victoria 3073. T: 474620.
**Lutheran Ch of Australia,** Pres-Gen, Lutheran Church House, 58 O'Connell St, North Adelaide, South Australia. T: 68151.
**Macedonian Orthodox Ch,** St George's Church, 52 Young St, Fitzroy, Victoria.
**Methodist Ch of Australasia,** 130 Little Collins Av, Melbourne C1, Victoria.
**Presbyterian Ch of Australia,** Clerk of Assembly, Assembly Hall, 156 Collins St, Melbourne, Victoria 3000.
**Reformed Chs of Australia,** Marsten Rd, St Mary's, Sydney, NSW.
**Romanian Orthodox Ch,** Church of St Irene, Grattan and Rathdown Sts, Carlton, Victoria.
**Russian Orthodox Ch Outside of Russia,** Archbishop's House, 18 Chelmsford Av, Croydon, NSW 2132. T: (2)747-5892.
**Salvation Army,** Territorial Commander, 140 Elizabeth St, PO Box 6, Brickfield Hill, Sydney, NSW 2000. T: 261711.
**Serbian Orthodox Ch,** Archpriest, 9 Freedman Rd, Mount Lawley 6050.
**Seventh-day Adventist Ch,** Sec, 3 Norfolk Rd, PO Box 41, Surrey Hills, Victoria 3127. T: 835782.
**Ukrainian Autocephalous Orthodox Ch,** 45 Wheatsheaf Rd, Glenroy, Victoria 3046. (Also: Metropolitan Diocese, Bp, 2a Bloom St, Church Court, Moonie Ponds, Victoria).
**Ukrainian Autocephalous Orthodox Ch (Council Led),** Administrator, 80 Suspension St, Ardeer, Victoria.
**Unitarian and Liberal Christian Chs,** Sec, 123 Mt Pleasant Rd, Belmont, Geelong, Victoria 3216.
**United Pentecostal Ch,** 172b Burwood Rd, Belmore, NSW.

*AUSTRIA*

**Alt-katholische Kirche in Österreich,** Schottenring 17/1, Wien 1/1.
**Bund der Baptisten-Gemeinden in Österreich,** Margaretenguertel 24-34/4/4, Wien V.
**Ev Kirche AB in Österreich,** Bp, Schellinggasse 12, A-1015 Wien.
**Ev Kirche HB,** Dorotheergasse 16, A-1010 Wien.
**Ev-Methodistenkirche,** Bennogasse 11, Wien VIII. T: 429371.
**Freie Christengemeinden in Österreich,** Halbgasse 17, A-1070 Wien VII.
**Griechrisch-Orthodoxe Kirche,** Metropolitan, Fleischmarkt 13, A-1010 Wien.
**Heilsarmee,** Richtergasse 3/11/8, A-1070 Wien. T: 9319163.
**Katholische Kirche Österreichs,** Wollzeile 2, A-1010 Wien. T: (0222)529511.
**Mennonitengemeinde,** Cottagegasse 16, Wien XVIII. T: 340167.
**Orthodoxe Kirche von Rumänien,** Löwelstr 8, Wien 1.
**Siebenten-Tags-Adventisten,** Nussdorferstr 5, A-1090 Wien. T: (0222)345179.
**Zeugen Jehovas,** Gallgasse 44, A-1130 Wien.

*BAHAMAS*

**Anglican Ch,** Diocese of Nassau & the Bahamas, PO Box 656, Nassau.
**Assemblies of Brethren,** PO Box 4059, Nassau.
**Assemblies of God in the Bahamas,** Super, PO Box 5123 MS, Nassau.
**Bahamas Baptist Union,** PO Box 516, Nassau.
**Catholic Ch,** Hermitage, PO Box 8187, Nassau. T: 28919.
**Ch of God in the Bahamas,** PO Box 4446 & 1708, Nassau.
**Ch of God of Prophecy,** PO Box 1467, Nassau.
**Greek Orthodox Ch,** PO Box 4014, Nassau.
**Jehovah's Witnesses,** PO Box 1247, Nassau.
**Lutheran Ch of Nassau,** PO Box 4794, Nassau.
**Methodist Ch in the Carribbean & the Americas,** PO Box 497, Nassau.
**Presbyterian Ch,** PO Box 1099, Nassau.
**Salvation Army,** PO Box 205, Ivanhoe Rd, Nassau. T: 22445.
**Seventh-day Adventist Ch,** Pres, East Shirley St, PO Box N-356, Nassau. T: 23011, 28921.

*BAHRAIN*

**Anglican Ch,** PO Box 36, Al Manamah.
**Catholic Ch,** Sacred Heart Convent, Al Manamah.
**Interdenominational Ch,** PO Box 401, Awali.
**Malayalee Christian Congregation,** PO Box 588, Al Manamah.
**Mar Thoma Syrian Ch,** c/o Gray Mackenzie Ltd, Al Manamah.
**National Ev Ch of Bahrain,** American Mission, PO Box 1, Al Manamah.
**Orthodox Syrian Ch of India,** PO Box 36, Al Manamah.

*BANGLADESH*

**All One In Christ Fellowship,** Fellowship Home, Toot Para Main Rd, Khulna.
**Assemblies of God,** PO Box 277, Dacca. (Also: Super, West Rupsa, Khulna).
**Association of Baptists for World Evangelism,** Field Council Chairman, PO Box 78, Chittagong.
**Bangladesh Baptist Union,** Mission House, PO Chandpur, District Comilla.
**Bangladesh Ev Lutheran Ch,** Gen Super, Amnura Mission, PO, Rajshahi District.
**Baptist Union of Bangladesh,** Baptist Mission, 1 Liaquat Av, PO Sadar Ghat, Dacca 1.
**Catholic Ch in Bangladesh,** Archbishop's House, PO Box 3, Ramna, Dacca 2. T: 242379.
**Church of Bangladesh,** Bp, St Thomas's Ch, Dacca.
**Ch of God (Anderson),** Mission House, Lalmanirhat, Rangpur.
**Ch of Sylhet,** Orange Tilla, Moulovibazar, Sylhet.
**Mymensingh Garo Baptist Convention,** PO Birisiri, District Mymensingh.
**Seventh-day Adventist Ch,** Gordon Rd, Shah Ali Bagh, Mirput, PO Box 80, Ramna, Dacca 2. T: 256015.
**United Christian Ch,** Lakma Mission House, PO Dholohor via Panchbibi, Bogra.

*BARBADOS*

**African Methodist Episcopal Ch,** AME Manse, Upper Collymore Rock, St Michael.
**Anglican Ch,** Diocese of Barbados, Bp, Bishopscourt, St Michael.
**Bible Missionary Ch,** Bermouth, 3rd Av, Strathclyde.
**Catholic Ch,** St Patrick's Cathedral, Jemmott's Lane, Bridgetown. T: 62325.
**Ch of God (Anderson),** General Office, Chapman St, Bridgetown.
**Ch of the Nazarene,** Super, Bresee Eagle Hall, Bridgetown.
**Jehovah's Witnesses,** Fontabelle Rd, Bridgetown.
**Methodist Ch in the Caribbean & the Americas,** James St, Bridgetown.
**Moravian Ch,** Eastern WI Province, Super, Moravian Manse, Welches Terrace, St Michael.
**New Testament Ch of God,** Island Supervisor, River Rd, St Michael.
**Pentecostal Assemblies of the West Indies,** Pastor, Evangel Temple, Bishop's Court Hill, Bridgetown.
**Salvation Army,** Provisional HQ, Reed St, PO Box 57, Bridgetown. T: 62467.
**Seventh-day Adventist Ch,** Pres, Brittons Cross Rd, Box 223, Bridgetown. T: 77987/8.
**United Holy Ch of America,** Barbados District, Baycroft Rd, Carrington Village, St Michael.
**Wesleyan Ch,** HQ, Bank Hill, Bridgetown.

*BELGIUM*

**Armée du Salut,** Chef du Territoire, Nouveau Marché aux Grains 34, B-1000 Brussel. T: (02)133904.
**Assemblée Chrétienne Ev,** Prés, Av des Statuaires 90, B-1180 Brussel.
**Assemblées de Dieu de Belgique,** Prés, Rue de Mérode 229 (& Prudent Blvd 83), B-1060 Brussel.
**Eglise Adventiste du Septième Jour,** Prés, Rue Ernest Allard 11-13, B-1000 Brussel. T: 113680.
**Eglise Anglicane,** Rue Crespel 29, B-1050 Brussel.
**Eglise Catholique de Belgique,** Aartsbisdom, Wollemarkt 15, B-2800 Mechelen. T: (015)16501.
**Eglise Ev Luthérienne Belge,** Prés, Rue de la Loi 46, Brussel 1. T: 217568.
**Eglise Ev Teniel,** Rue de Serment 29, Anderlecht, Brussel.
**Eglise Orthodoxe Grecque,** Rue de Stassart 92, B-1050 Brussel.
**Eglise Protestante de Belgique,** Prés, Rue Champ-de-Mars 5, B-1050 Brussel.
**Eglise Réformée de Belgique,** Prés, Rue Royale 193, B-1030 Brussel.
**Eglise Pentecôtistes,** Rue Langveld 179, Uccle, Brussel.
**Gereformeerde Kerken in België,** Sek, Pater Hilarionlaan 30, B-1150 Brussel.
**Témoins de Jéhovah,** Rue d'Argile 60, Kraainem, Brabant.
**Union des Eglises Ev Baptistes de Belgique,** Prés, Rue de l'Académie 51, B-4000 Liège.
**Union des Eglises Ev Libres de Belgique,** Prés, Av du Cimetière 19, B-5700 Auvelais.

*BELIZE*

**Anglican Ch,** Diocese of Belize, Bishopthorpe PO Box 535, Southern Foreshore, Belize City.
**Assemblies of God,** PO Box 158, Belize City.
**Baptist Chs in Belize,** PO Box 508, Belize City.
**Catholic Ch,** Bishop's House, 144 North Front St, Belize City. T: 2122.
**Ch of God (Cleveland),** PO Box 201, Belize City.
**Jehovah's Witnesses,** PO Box 257, Belize City.
**Salvation Army,** 9 Glynn St, PO Box 64, Belize City. T: 3365.
**Seventh-day Adventist Ch,** Pres, 26 corner of Regent & Kings Sts, PO Box 90, Belize City. T: 2115.

*BENIN*

**Assemblées de Dieu,** National Super, BP 903, Cotonou.
**Eglise Apostolique du Nigérie,** Pastor, BP 335, Porto-Novo.
**Eglise Catholique au Bénin,** Archevêché, BP 491, Cotonou. T: 313145.
**Eglise Ev Chrétienne de l'Ouest-Africain,** SIM/ECWA, Parakou.
**Eglise Protestant Méthodiste au Bénin,** Sec, 54 Av Steinmetz, BP 34, Cotonou.
**Témoins de Jéhovah,** BP 874, Cotonou.

*BERMUDA*

**African Methodist Episcopal Ch,** Presiding Elder, Harris Bay, Smith's Parish. T: 20505. (Also: St Paul's, Hamilton).
**Anglican Ch of Bermuda,** Bp, Bishop's Lodge, PO Box 769, Hamilton.
**Catholic Ch,** St Theresa's Cathedral, PO Box 1191, Hamilton 5. T: 27730.
**Christian Brethren,** Paget Gospel Chapel, Paget. T: 22254.
**Ch of the Nazarene,** PO Box Smith's Parish. T: 13974.
**Lutheran Ch,** Pastor, Peace Lutheran Church, South Shore Rd, Paget. T: 25330.
**Methodist Ch (Wesley),** Church St, Hamilton. T: 20418.
**New Testament Ch of God,** Pastor, Curving Av, Pembroke. T: 23149.
**Portuguese Ev Church,** Pastor, Parsonage, White Sands Rd, Paget.
**Presbyterian Ch,** Manse Rd, Paget. T: 20400, 11313.
**Salvation Army,** Court St, PO Box 412, Hamilton. T: 20601.
**Seventh-day Adventist Ch,** Pres, PO Box 1170, Hamilton. T: 24110.
**United Ch of Canada,** Methodist Parsonage, Rosemont Av, Pembroke Parish.

*BOLIVIA*

**Asambleas de Dios de Bolivia,** Casilla 181, Santa Cruz. (Also: Super, Casilla 4462, La Paz).
**Convención Bautista Boliviana,** Instituto Bíblico Bautista, Casilla 181, Santa Cruz.
**Ejército de Salvación,** Cañada Strongost 1878, Casilla 926, La Paz. T: 28372.
**Hermanos Libres,** Casilla 680, Cochabamba.
**Iglesia Adventista del Séptimo Día,** Pres, Rosengo Villalobos 1592, Casilla 355, La Paz. T: 27244.
**Iglesia Boliviana de Santidad,** Casilla 1119, La Paz.
**Iglesia Católica en Bolivia,** CEB, Arzobispado, Casilla 205, Sucre. T: 1109.
**Iglesia de Dios Boliviana,** Casilla 2371, La Paz.
**Iglesia del Evangelio Cuadrangular,** Casilla 6, Trinidad.
**Iglesia del Nazareno,** Casilla 1056, La Paz.
**Iglesia Ev Boliviana,** Casilla de Correo 1690, La Paz.
**Iglesia Ev Los Amigos,** Casilla 922, La Paz.
**Iglesia Ev Luterana Boliviana,** Casilla 3809, La Paz.
**Iglesia Ev Luterana de habla Alemana,** Casilla 2851, La Paz. T: 12063.
**Iglesia Ev Metodista en Bolivia,** Exec Sec, 423 Landaeta, Casilla 356, La Paz.
**Iglesia Ev Mundial,** Field Super, Casilla 55, Santa Cruz.
**Iglesia Ev Nacional,** Casilla 578, Santa Cruz.
**Iglesia Ev Pentecostal de Chile,** Casilla 822, Cochabamba.
**Iglesia Nacional Bethesda,** Casilla 290, Santa Cruz.
**Iglesia Nacional Ev de Los Amigos (INELA),** Casilla 544, La Paz.
**Iglesia Pentecostal Nacional,** Casilla 51, Trinidad.
**Iglesia Pentecostal Sueca,** Casilla 1692, Cochabamba.
**Misión Neuvas Tribus,** Casilla 1422, La Paz.
**Testigos de Jehová,** Casilla 1440, La Paz.
**Unión Bautista Boliviana,** Casilla 86, Cochabamba.
**Unión Cristiana Ev,** Casilla 1196, Cochabamba.

*BOTSWANA*

**Anglican Ch,** Diocese of Botswana, Bp, PO Box 573, Gaborone.
**Assemblies of God in Botswana,** Gen Super, PO Box 533, Gaborone.
**Catholic Ch,** Bishop's House, PO Box 218, Gaborone. T: 52928.
**Ch of God in Christ,** State Bp, PO Box 97, Lobatse.
**Dutch Reformed Church Mission,** PO Box 24, Mochudi.
**Ev Lutheran Ch in SA,** Tswana Region, PO Box 365, Gaborone.
**Full Gospel Ch of God in Southern Africa,** PO Box 159, Gaborone.
**Methodist Ch of South Africa,** PO Box 92, Lobatse.
**St John's Apostolic Faith Mission of South Africa,** PO Box 173, Mochudi.
**St Paul's Apostolic Faith Mission,** PO Box 1, Sikwane.
**St Peters Apostolic Faith Healing Ch,** PO Box 173, Mahalapye.
**Seventh-day Adventist Ch,** Pres, PO Box 86, Francistown. T: 330.
**United Congregational Ch of Southern Africa,** Sec, PO Box 18, Maun.
**Zion Christian Ch of South Africa,** PO Box 209, Mochudi.

*BRAZIL*

**Assembleias de Deus,** CP 3274 (& CP 19), Rio de Janeiro, GB. (Also: Rua Henrique Fleiuss 420, 20000 Tijuca, GB).

**Associação das Igrejas dos Irmãos Menonitas,** CP 1559, Curitiba, Paraná.
**Associação dos Batistas Evangelismo Mundial,** CP 30045, São Paulo, SP.
**Associação Ev Menonita,** CP 1013, Campinas, SP.
**Associação Geral das Igrejas Batistas Regulares do Brasil,** Instituto Bíblico Batista, CP 51, Juazeiro, Ceará.
**Congregação Cristã do Brasil,** Rua Visconde de Parnaiba 1616, Brás Quarter, São Paulo, SP. T: 934395.
**Congregação dos Missionários Discipulos da Santíssima Trinidade,** Séde, Av Deputado Aloisio, Souto Pinto 17, Caetés, Pernambuco.
**Convenção Batista Brasileira,** Rua Senador Furtade 56, CP 320, ZC-00 Rio de Janeiro, GB.
**Cruzada Nacional de Evangelização,** CP 3870, São Paulo, SP.
**Exército de Salvação,** Av Brigadeiro Luiz Antônio 1573, CP 8631, São Paulo, SP, T: 371014.
**Igreja Adventista do Sétimo Dia,** Travessa Mauriti 2881, CP 822, 66000 Belém, Pará. T: 9174, 9925.
**Igreja Batista Bethel,** CP 638, Pôrto Alegre.
**Igreja Católica no Brasil,** CNBB, Av L3 Sul, ES 801, Lt 1-A, CP 13-2067, 70000 Brasília, DF. T: 2422404.
**Igreja Cristã Batista Bíblica,** Rua Muniz de Souza 615, Bairro de Cambuci, CP 9198, São Paulo, SP.
**Igreja Cristã Reformada Latinoamericana,** CP 1251, São Paulo, SP.
**Igreja de Cristo Jesus,** Rua Amarel Girgel 276, São Paulo, SP.
**Igreja de Deus do Brasil (Cleveland),** CP 5409, 20000 Cidade Nova, GB.
**Igreja de Deus Pentecostal do Brasil,** CP 23, Belo Horizonte, MG.
**Igreja de Jesucristo dos Santos dos Ultimos Dias,** CP 20809, São Paulo, SP.
**Igreja Episcopal do Brasil,** Diocese of South Central Brazil, CP 30928, 01000 São Paulo, SP.
**Igreja Ev Congregaçional Cristã,** Rua do Costa 60, Rio de Janeiro, GB.
**Igreja Ev da Confissão Luterana no Brasil,** CP 2876, 90000 Pôrto Alegre, RS. T: 45011.
**Igreja Ev Holiness do Brasil,** CP 3919, São Paulo, SP.
**Igreja Ev Luterana do Brasil,** CP 166, Canoas, RS. T: 26875.
**Igreja Ev Pentecostal Elim,** Rua Acri 372, Santo Amaro, São Paulo 18, SP.
**Igreja Ev Pentecostal Unida 'O Brasil para Cristo',** Missionário, Rua Carlos Vícari 124, Largo de Pompeia, CP 4054, São Paulo, SP. T: 657007.
**Igreja Ev Reformada do Brasil,** CP 33, Carambei, via Castro, Paraná.
**Igreja Metodista do Brasil,** Bp, CP 2009, Campinas, 01000 São Paulo, SP.
**Igreja Metodista Livre do Brasil,** CP 18027, São Paulo, SP.
**Igreja Ortodoxa Russa,** Bp, Rua Tamandare 710, São Paulo 01525. T: (5511)2781004.
**Igreja Pentecostal da Nova Vida,** CP 2734, 20000 Rio de Janeiro, GB.
**Igreja Pentecostal Unida do Brasil,** CP 5151, São Paulo, SP.
**Igreja Presbiteriana Conservadora do Brasil,** Rua Pedroso 351, São Paulo, SP.
**Igreja Presbiteriana do Brasil,** Rua Barata Ribeiro 335, Rio de Janeiro.
**Igreja Presbiteriana Independente do Brasil,** Damião, CP 76, Mzambinho, CK.
**Irmãos Cristãos,** CP 901, ZC-00, 20000 Rio de Janeiro, GB.
**Missão Novas Tribos do Brasil,** CP 29, Jacutinga, MG.
**Testemunhas de Jeová,** Rua Guaíra 216, Bosque da Saúde, São Paulo 8, SP.
**União Batista Ev,** CP 572, São Paulo, SP.

*BULGARIA*

**Baptist Union of Bulgaria,** 63 Pelo Pelovsky St, Sofija 3.
**Bulgarian Orthodox Ch,** Holy Synod, Oborishte 4, Sofija.
**Catholic Ch in Bulgaria,** Près de l'Eglise, Rua Liliana Dimitrova 3, Plovdiv.
**Romanian Orthodox Ch,** 152 Str Tzar Boris 1, Sofija.
**Seventh-day Adventist Ch,** V Kolarov 10, Sofija. T: 881218.

*BURMA*

**Assemblies of God,** Pastor, 128 Civil Station Rd, Rangoon.
**Burma Baptist Convention,** 143 St John's Rd, Rangoon.
**Catholic Ch in Burma,** Archbishop's House, 289 Theinbyu St, Rangoon. T: 12752.
**Church of the Province of Burma,** Diocese of Rangoon, Bishopscourt, 140 Pyidaungsu Yeiktha Rd, Dagon PO, Rangoon.
**Independent Anglican Ch,** Sec, Mohnyin, Kachin State.
**Independent Ch of Burma,** Sec, Tahan, PO Tahan, Kalemyo, Mawlaik District.
**Independent Methodist Ch of Burma,** Sec, 256 Creek St, Rangoon.
**Jehovah's Witnesses,** PO Box 62, Rangoon.
**Mara Christian Ch,** Sec, Sabawngpi, Matupi PO, Mindat District.
**Methodist Ch of the Union of Burma,** Bp, 22 Signal Pagoda Rd, Rangoon.
**Methodist Ch,** Upper Burma, Chairman, Civil Lines, PO Box 82, Mandalay.
**Presbyterian Ch of Burma,** Synod Office, Falam, Chin Hills.
**St Gabriel's Church Union,** CIB, Pastor, Bogyoke Market, E Wing, Rangoon.
**Salvation Army,** 176/8 Anawrahta St, Bigandet, Rangoon. T: 16760.
**Self-Supporting Karen Baptist Mission Society,** 82 Sinyegan Lan, Ahlone, Rangoon.
**Seventh-day Adventist Ch,** Sec, 68 U Wisara Rd, PO Box 977, Rangoon. T: 15248.
**Seventh-day Baptist Ch,** Tahan PO Kalemyo, Upper Chindwin.

*BURUNDI*

**Eglise Adventiste du Septième Jour,** BP 1710, Bujumbura. T: 3130.
**Eglise Catholique au Burundi,** Archevêché, BP 118, Gitega. T: 2149.
**Eglise Ev des Amis,** BP 120 & 76, Gitega.
**Eglise Ev Mondiale,** BP 113, Gitega.
**Eglise Libre Méthodiste au Burundi,** BP 73, Gitega.
**Eglise Protestante Episcopale du Burundi,** Ibuye, BP 58, Ngozi. (Also: BP 17, Bujumbura).
**Eglise de Pentecôte,** Sec, Mission Libre Suédoise, BP 239, Bujumbura.
**Union des Eglises Baptistes du Burundi,** Museme DS 106, Bujumbura 1.

*CAMEROON*

**Cameroon Baptist Convention,** Exec Sec, PO Box 1, Bamenda, West Cameroon. T: 63.
**Confédération Baptiste du Cameroun,** BP 917, Bali, Douala.
**Congrégation Baptiste du Cameroun,** BP 72, Douala-Deido.
**Eglise Adventiste du Septième Jour,** Prés, BP 401, Yaoundé. T: 224301.
**Eglise Baptiste Camerounaise (EBC),** BP 437, Douala.
**Eglise Catholique au Cameroun,** Archevêché, BP 207, Yaoundé. T: 224083.
**Eglise Ev du Cameroun,** BP 89, Douala.
**Eglise Ev Luthérienne du Cameroun,** BP 27, Meiganga. (Also: BP 9, Tibati).
**Eglise Fraternelle Luthérienne au Cameroun,** BP 12, Guider.
**Eglise Presbytérienne Camerounaise,** BP 519, Yaoundé.
**Eglise Protestante Africaine,** BP 26, Lolodorf. (Also: BP 2260, Messa Yaoundé).
**Mission Baptiste Européenne,** BP 82, Maroua.
**Mission Unie du Soudan,** BP 31, Mokolo.
**Presbyterian Ch in Cameroon,** Synod Clerk, PO Box 19, Buea, West Cameroon.
**Témoins de Jéhovah,** BP 5428, Douala-Akwa.
**Union des Eglises Baptistes du Cameroun,** BP 7, New-Bell, Douala. T: 4964.

*CANADA*

**African Methodist Episcopal Ch in Canada,** 765 Lawrence au West, Toronto, Ontario.
**Anglican Ch of Canada,** 600 Jarvis St, Toronto 285, Ontario. T: 924-9192.
**Antiochian Orthodox Christian AD New York & All North America,** St George's Orthodox Ch, 555-575 Jean Talon St East, Montréal, Québec.
**Apostolic Ch of Pentecost,** 1612 Adelaide St East, Saskatoon, Saskatchewan.
**Armenian Apostolic Church: D Canada,** St Gregory the Illuminator Cathedral, 615 Stuart Av, Montréal, Québec. T: 279-3066.
**Associated Gospel Chs,** 280 Plains Rd West, Burlington, Ontario.
**Association of Regular Baptist Chs of Canada,** 337 Jarvis St (or 130 Gerrard St), Toronto 2, Ontario. T: (416)925-3261.
**Baptist Federation of Canada,** 91 Queen St, PO Box 1298, Brantford, Ontario. T: (519)752-9114.
**Baptist General Conference,** 5011-122A St, Edmonton, Alberta. T: (403)435-4974.
**Brethren in Christ Ch,** PO Box 65, Sherkston, Ontario. T: (416)894-3602.
**Bulgarian Orthodox Ch,** Sec, Cathedral, 237 Sackville, Toronto, Ontario.
**Catholic Ch of Canada,** Canadian Catholic Conference, 90 Parent Av, Ottawa, Ontario K1N 7B1. T: (613)237-4540.
**Christian Ch (Disciples of Christ),** Suite 301, 130 Merton St, Toronto 7, Ontario. T: (416)488-1412.
**Christian Reformed Chs in Canada,** Stated Clerk, RR 8, London, Ontario.
**Christian & Missionary Alliance in Canada,** Sec, 2026 Yonge St, Toronto 295, Ontario. T: (416) 489-1659.
**Ch of Christ, Scientist,** 696 Yonge St, Suite 403, Toronto 285, Ontario. T: (416)922-7473.
**Ch of Jesus Christ of Latter-day Saints,** Ontario-Quebec Mission, Suite 205, 338 Queen St East, Brampton, Ontario.
**Ch of the Nazarene,** Sec, 2236 Capital Hill Crescent, NW, Calgary 44, Alberta.
**Coptic Orthodox Ch in Canada,** 176 Windermere Av, Toronto 9, Ontario.
**Ev Ch in Canada,** 164-5th St, SE, Medicine Hat, Alberta T1A 0M3. T: (403)527-2754.
**Ev Lutheran Ch of Canada,** Pres, 212 Wiggins Av N, Saskatoon, Saskatchewan S7N 1K4. T: (306) 653-0133.
**Ev Mennonite Conference,** PO Box 1268, Steinbach, Manitoba.
**Fellowship of Ev Baptist Chs in Canada,** Gen Sec, 74 Sheppard Av West, Willowdale, Ontario. T: (416)223-8696.
**Free Methodist Ch in Canada,** Pres, 11 Kingsview Blvd, Weston, Ontario.
**Greek Orthodox Archdiocese of North & South America,** Ninth Archdiocesan District, 27 Teddington Park Av, Toronto 12, Ontario. T: (416)481-4643.
**Independent Assemblies of God, Canada,** 15 Beecher St, St Catherines, Ontario. T: (416)685-5392.
**International Ch of the Foursquare Gospel,** District Office, 3628 Edinburgh, Burnaby, Vancouver, BC.
**Italian Pentecostal Ch of Canada,** 6724 Fabre St, Montréal 35, Québec. T: (514)721-5614.
**Jehovah's Witnesses,** 150 Bridgeland Av, Toronto, Ontario.
**Latvian Ev Lutheran Ch Outside Latvia,** Archbp, 5 Valleymede Rd, Toronto 3, Ontario.
**Lutheran Ch in America,** Canada Section, 509-251 King St West, Kitchener, Ontario. T: (519)741-1461.
**Lutheran Ch - Canada,** Pres, 7205 Sharon Av, Niagara Falls, Ontario.
**Mennonite Brethren Chs of North America,** HQ, 159 Henderson Highway, Winnipeg, Manitoba.
**Mennonite Ch (Canada),** 117 King St, West, Kitchener, Ontario. T: (519)743-2673.
**Orthodox Ch in America,** Archdiocese of Canada, Archbp, 1175 Champlain St, Montréal, Québec.
**Pentecostal Assemblies of Canada,** Gen Super, 10 Overlea Blvd, Toronto 17, Ontario. T: (416) 425-1010.
**Pentecostal Assemblies of Newfoundland,** 444 Waler St, St John, Newfoundland.
**People's Church,** Pastor, 374 Sheppard Av East, Toronto, Ontario.
**Polish National Catholic Ch,** Sec, St John's Cathedral, 186 Cowan Av, Toronto 146, Ontario.
**Presbyterian Ch in Canada,** 50 Wynford Drive, Don Mills 403, Ontario. T: (416)429-0110.
**Primitive Baptist Conference of New Brunswick,** Conference Clerk, Bath, New Brunswick. T: (506)375-6673.
**Reformed Ch in America,** 405 Rossland Rd West, Whitby, Ontario.
**Reorganized Ch of Jesus Christ of Latter-day Saints,** Sec, Box 38, Guelph, Ontario.
**Romanian Orthodox Ch in America,** St George's Cathedral, 1960 Tecumeseh Rd East, Windsor, Ontario.
**Romanian Orthodox Episcopate of America,** Vicar, 421 Victoria Av, Regina, Saskatchewan. T: (306)523-3501.
**Russian Orthodox Ch in Canada,** Administrator, 10630-83rd Av, Edmonton, Alberta.
**Salvation Army in Canada,** Commissioner, Territorial HQ, 20 Albert St, Toronto 102, Ontario. T: (416)362-1071.
**Serbian Orthodox Ch,** Sec, 212 Delaware, Toronto, Ontario.
**Seventh-day Adventist Ch in Canada,** 1148 King St, Oshawa, Ontario. T: (416)723-3409.
**Standard Chs of America,** 243 Perth St, Brockville, Ontario.
**Ukrainian Greek-Orthodox Ch of Canada,** Consistory, 7 St John's Av, Winnipeg, Manitoba R2W 1G8. T: (204)568-3095.
**Union of Spiritual Communities of Christ,** USCC Central Office, Box 670, Grand Forks, BC. T: (604)442-3757.
**Unitarian Universalist Association,** Pres, 3415 Simpson St, Montréal 25, Québec.
**United Ch of Canada,** United Church House, 85 St Clair Av East, Toronto 7, Ontario. T: (416)925-5931.
**United Pentecostal Ch in Canada,** Sec, PO Box 801, Picton, Ontario.
**Wesleyan Methodist Ch of America in Canada,** 25 Dixon Drive, Trenton, Ontario.
**Worldwide Ch of God,** 1365 Boundary, Vancouver, BC.

*CAPE VERDE*

**Igreja Adventista do Sétimo Dia,** Apdo 6, Praia.
**Igreja Católica,** Bp, CP 46, Cidade de Praia. T: 203.

*CAYMAN ISLANDS*

**Seventh-day Adventist Ch,** Cayman Islands Mission, Pres, PO Box 515, Georgetown, Grand Cayman. T: 92647.

*CENTRAL AFRICAN REPUBLIC*

**Christianisme Prophétique en Afrique,** BP 1117, Bangui.
**Eglise Adventiste du Septième Jour,** Dir, BP 274, Bangui.
**Eglise Catholique au RCA,** Archevêché, BP 1518, Bangui. T: 614621.
**Eglise Ev Centrafricaine,** Mission Protestante, Obo via Bangassou.
**Eglise Ev des Frères,** Rue Languedoc et Missions, BP 240, Bangui.
**Eglise Ev du Réveil,** Alindao.
**Eglise Protestante du Bangui,** Rue des Missions, BP 608, Bangui. T: 2487.
**Eglises Baptistes du RCA,** Field Dir, Baptist Mid-Missions, Sibut.
**Témoins de Jéhovah,** BP 662, Bangui.
**Union des Eglises Baptistes,** Mission Baptiste Suédoise, Bania, Berberati.

*CHAD*

**Assemblées Chrétiennes du Tchad,** BP 116, N'Djamena (Fort Lamy). (Also: BP 10, Doba par Moundou).
**Eglise Catholique au Tchad,** Archevêché, BP 456, N'Djamena (Fort Lamy). T: 2711.
**Eglise Ev des Frères,** BP 16, Baibokoum.
**Eglise Fraternelle Luthérienne au Tchad,** BP 7, Pala.
**Eglise Baptistes du Tchad,** BP 89, Fort Archambault.
**Eglise Ev au Tchad,** Field Dir SUM, Bebalem, BP 15 & 123, Moundou, Logone.

*CHILE*

**Asambleas de Dios,** Alto de la Alianza 100, Casilla 13189, Santiago. T: 23673.
**Asambleas de Dios Autónomos,** Cisterna, Casilla 56, Santiago.
**Congregación Ev de la Fe Apostólica del Séptimo Día,** Villa Mora, Coronel, Concepción.
**Convención Ev Bautista de Chile,** Casilla 9941, Santiago.
**Corporación Ev de Vitacura,** Rozas 1546, Santiago
**Corporación Ev Pentecostal (Nuevo Amanecer),** Cumming 793, Santiago.
**Corporación Iglesia del Señor,** Casilla 921, Temuco.
**Ejército de Salvación,** Agustinas 3074, Casilla 3225, Santiago 1. T: 94073,90877.
**Ejército Ev de Chile,** Eyzaguirre 1149, Santiago.
**Iglesia Adventista del Séptimo Día,** Americo Vespucio Norte 134, Casilla 2317, Santiago. T: 281725,281801,281915.
**Iglesia Aliancista Nacional de Sostén y Gobierno Proprió,** Almirante La Torre 140, Casilla 853, Valdivia.
**Iglesia Alianza Cristiana y Misionera,** Casilla 711, Concepción.
**Iglesia Anglicana,** Casilla 566, Valparaiso.
**Iglesia Católica en Chile,** Casilla 30-D, Santiago de Chile. T: 63275.
**Iglesia de Dios Pentecostal,** Calle Tres Antonios, Casilla 53, Nuña, Santiago.
**Iglesia de Jesucristo de los Santos de los Altimos Dias,** Alcantara 360, Casilla 28, Las Condes.
**Iglesia del Evangelio Cuadrangular,** Clasificador 880, Casilla 14586, Santiago.
**Iglesia Ev Luterana en Chile,** Calle Obispo Cardenas 1483, Casilla 2000, Santiago. T: 20370.
**Iglesia Ev Pentecostal de Chile (IEP),** Casilla 7008, Santiago.
**Iglesia Metodista Nacional de Chile,** Bp, Casilla 67, Santiago.
**Iglesia Metodista Pentecostal de Chile (IMP),** Jotabeche 36, Casilla 4581, Santiago.
**Iglesia Pentecostal Apostólica,** Casilla 12025, Santiago.
**Iglesia Pentecostal de Chile,** Gen Super, Casilla 2, Curico.
**Iglesia Pentecostal de Chile Austral,** Valdivia.
**Iglesia Pentecostal de la Trinidad,** Obispo, Casilla 744, Temuco.
**Iglesia Pentecostal Unida de Chile,** Clasificador 1124, Santiago.
**Iglesia Presbiteriana en Chile,** Maciver 142, Of 602, Casilla 14025, Santiago. T: 393796.
**Iglesia Unión de Centros Bíblicos,** Casilla 15199, Santiago.
**Iglesia Wesleyana Nacional,** Casilla 131446, Santiago.
**Misión Iglesia Pentecostal,** Pres, CP 7033, Santiago.
**Testigos de Jehová,** Av Sanchez Lima 2146, Casilla 261-V, Correo 15, Santiago.

*CHINA (TAIWAN)*

**Baptist Bible Fellowship,** 102D Morrison Rd, PO Box 116, Taichung.
**Catholic Ch in Taiwan,** Archbishop's House, PO Box 7-91, Taipei. T: 7071311.
**China Assemblies of God,** 95 Hang Chow South Rd, Section 2, PO Box 385, Taipei.
**China Ev Lutheran Ch,** 52 Sinsheng North Rd, PO Box 543, Taipei. T: 26045.
**Christian & Missionary Alliance,** 63 Fu Heng 1st Rd, PO Box 480, Kaohsiung.
**Christian Ch of Salvation,** 10 Shang Hsia Hsiang, 2nd Ku Shan Rd, Kaohsiung.
**Ch of the Nazarene,** 100 Shengching Rd, Kuantou Peitou, Taipei. T: 892784.
**Conservative Baptist Association,** 38 Wu Lang St, Taichung.
**Elim Foursquare Gospel Alliance,** 3-19-186 T'ung Hwa, Taipei.
**Ev Alliance Mission,** 8 Lane, 11 Tsingtien St, Taipei. T: 22879.
**Full Gospel Assemblies,** 116 Ming Hu-li Ta-Hu, Mialoi-hsien.
**Gospelaires Missionary Ch,** PO Box 1200, Taipei.
**Jehovah's Witnesses,** 5 Lane 99, Yun-Ho St, Taipei.
**Mennonite Ch in Taiwan,** PO Box 508, Taipei. T: 541378.
**Methodist Ch of the ROC,** Bp, 4 Jen Ai Rd, Section 4, Taipei. T: 72017. (Also: 113 Sinsheng S Rd, Section 1, Taipei).
**Norwegian Pentecostal Mission,** PO Box 67, Taichung.
**Presbyterian Ch in Taiwan,** 89-5 Chang Chun Rd, PO Box 2119, Taipei 104.
**Quemoy Christian Ch of Christ,** Huo Pu, Quemoy Island.
**Seventh-day Adventist Ch,** Pres, 424 Pa Te Rd, Section 2, Taipei 105. T: 772855.
**Taiwan Baptist Convention,** PO Box 427, Taipei.
**Taiwan Episcopal Ch,** Diocese of Taiwan, Bp, 12 Lane 101, South Hangchow Rd, Section 1, Taipei.
**Taiwan Lutheran Ch,** Pres, 144-3 Hsin Sheng South Rd, Section 1, Taipei. T: 20720.

*COLOMBIA*

**Alianza Cristiana y Misionera,** Dir, Apdo Aéreo 4583, Cali, Valle.
**Asambleas de Dios de Colombia,** Super, Apdo 51314, Bogotá 2, DE.
**Asociación de Iglesias Ev de Colombia del Oriente,** Apdo Aéreo 576, Nal 64, Cúcuta, Norte de Santander. T: 79-87.
**Asociación de Iglesias Ev del Caribe,** Dir, Apdo Aéreo 335, Sincelejo, Sucre.
**Asociación de Iglesias Ev del Magdalena,** Apdo Aéreo 786, Santa Marta, Magdalena.
**Asociación de Iglesias Ev Interamericanas,** Pres, Diagonal No 49-13, Of 301, Apdo Aéreo 4788, Medellín, Antioquia. T: 451292.
**Convención Bautista Colombiana,** Apdo Aéreo 1809, Barranquilla.
**Embajadores Cristianos de Colombia,** Dir, Apdo Aéreo 315, Cartagena.
**Hermanos en Cristo,** Carrera 22 No 20-81, Apdo Aéreo 209 & 379, Pasto, Nariño. T: 2413.
**Iglesia Adventista del Séptimo Día,** Carrera 84 No 33B/47, Apdo Nacional 39, Correo Aéreo 609, Medellín. T: 481176,480030.
**Iglesia Católica en Colombia,** Arzobispado, Carrera 7 No 10-20, Bogotá, DE. T: 2437700.
**Iglesia Cristiana del Norte,** Dir, Carrera 32 No 65-46/54, Apdo Aéreo 8703, Bogotá. T: 403681.
**Iglesia de Dios en Colombia,** Calle 45 No 27-36, Bogotá.
**Iglesia del Evangelio Cuadrangular,** Dir, Apdo Aéreo 650, Bucaramanga, Santander. T: 77806.
**Iglesia Episcopal en Colombia,** Dir, Apdo Aéreo 21464, Bogotá 2, DE.
**Iglesia Ev Luterana,** Apdo Aéreo 20038 & 53005, Bogotá 2, DE. T: 495137.
**Iglesia Ev Pentecostal Unida,** Apdo Aéreo 1006, Barranquilla.
**Iglesia Metodista Wesleyana de Colombia,** Pres, Apdos Aéreo 964, Nal 233, Medellín. T: 454272.
**Iglesia Presbiteriana Cumberland,** Sec, Apdo Aéreo 173, Cali, Valle.
**Iglesia Presbiteriana de Colombia,** Pres, Calle 91 No 13A-44, Apdo Aéreo 6876, Bogotá, DE. T: 430230. (Also: Apdo Nacional 26, Girardot, Cundinamarca).

**Misión Nuevas Tribus de Colombia,** Dir, Apdo Aéreo 16569, Bogotá, DE. T: 393988.
**Misión Panamericana de Colombia,** Dir, Calle 67A No 51C-23, Apdo Aéreo 51762, Medellín, Antioquia. T: 442861.
**Testigos de Jehová,** Apdo Aéreo 2687, Barranquilla.
**Unión Misionera Ev,** Dir, Apdo Aéreo 4342, Cali, Valle. T: 511590.

*CONGO*
**Armée de Salut,** Rue de Reims (Rue Alfonse Fondere), BP 20, Brazzaville. T: 2610.
**Eglise Apostolique Unie en Afrique (EAUA),** BP 389, Brazzaville.
**Eglise Baptiste du Congo Populaire,** BP 23, Ouésso.
**Eglise Catholique au Congo,** Archevêché, BP 2301, Brazzaville. T: 811793.
**Eglise de Jesus-Christ sur la Terre par le Prophète Simon Kimbangu (EJCSK),** BP 3011, Poto-Poto-Brazzaville.
**Eglise Ev de la Likouala,** BP 12, Impfondo.
**Eglise Ev du Congo (EEC),** BP 3205, Bacongo-Brazzaville.
**Témoins de Jéhovah,** BP 2114, Brazzaville.

*COOK ISLANDS*
**Catholic Ch,** Catholic Mission, PO Box 147, Rarotonga. T: 2137.
**Cook Islands Christian Ch (CICC),** PO Box 93, Rarotonga.
**Seventh-day Adventist Ch,** Pres, PO Box 31, Rarotonga.

*COSTA RICA*
**Asambleas de Dios,** Super, Apdo 840, San José.
**Asociación Bautista Costarricense,** Apdo 1883, San José.
**Asociación de Iglesias Bíblicas Costarricenses (LAM),** Apdo 1307, San José.
**Ejército de Salvación,** Av 37, Apdo 316, Port Limon.
**Iglesia Adventista del Séptimo Día,** Calle 33, Av 13, Apdo 10113 No 3178, Barrio Escalante, San José. T: 250665.
**Iglesia Católica en Costa Rica,** Arzobispado, Apdo 497, San José. T: 218048.
**Iglesia de Dios de Costa Rica (Anderson),** Sec, Apdo 5080, San José.
**Iglesia de Dios de Costa Rica (Cleveland),** Apdo 2875, San José.
**Iglesia de Dios de la Profecía,** Apdo 2903, San José.
**Iglesia de Jesucristo de los Santos de los Ultimos Dias,** Central America Mission, Apdo 2339, San José.
**Iglesia del Evangelio Cuadrangular,** Apdo 4492, San José.
**Iglesia Episcopal,** Diocese of Costa Rica, Obispo, Apdo 2773, San José.
**Iglesia Metodista,** Apdo 78, Alajuela.
**Iglesia Santa Pentecostés,** Apdo 1209, San José.
**Testigos de Jehová,** Apdo 10043, San José.

*CUBA*
**Asambleas de Dios,** Instituto Bíblico, Manacas, Las Villas. (Also: Apdo 548, Camagüey).
**Asociación Ev de Cuba,** Paseo de las Paz, 61 Santa Clara, LV.
**Convención Bautista de Cuba Occidental,** Zulueta No 520 Esq Dragones, La Habana.
**Convención Bautista de Cuba Oriental,** Calle 1 No 101, Apdo 893, Santiago de Cuba.
**Convención Bautista Libres de Cuba,** Apdo 27, Pinar del Rio.
**Iglesia Adventista del Séptimo Día,** Pres, Calle 168 No 31504, Rancho Boyeros, Santiago de las Vegas, Apdo 50, General Peraza, La Habana. T: Santiago de la Vegas 3729,2656.
**Iglesia Apostólica de Jesucristo,** Apdo 144, Marianao, La Habana.
**Iglesia Católica en Cuba,** Calle Havana 152, Apdo 594, La Habana 1. T: 68463.
**Iglesia Cristiana Pentecostal,** Julio Sanguily 278, Camagüey.
**Iglesia de Dios de la Profecía,** Apdo 13, Güines, La Habana.
**Iglesia Episcopal de Cuba,** Obispo, Calle 13 No 874, Vedado, La Habana.
**Iglesia Metodista en Cuba,** Bp, Calle 58 No. 4305, Marianao, La Habana.
**Iglesia Ortodoxa de Cuba,** Apdo 6081, La Habana.
**Iglesia Presbiteriana Reformada en Cuba,** Milanes y 24 de Febrero, Apdo 205 & 154, Matanzas.
**Testigos de Jehová,** Av 15 Núm 4608, Almendares, Marianao, La Habana.

*CYPRUS*
**Catholic Ch in Cyprus,** Vicariate General, Latin Patriarchate of Jerusalem, PO Box 164, Levkosia (Nicosia).
**Ch of God of Prophecy,** 13 Trachana Rd, Neapolis, Levkosia (Nicosia).
**Jehovah's Witnesses,** PO Box 1590, Levkosia (Nicosia).
**Orthodox Ch of Cyprus,** Iera Archiepiscopi Kyprou, Archbp, Palace, Levkosia (Nicosia). T: 74411.
**Seventh-day Adventist Ch,** Pres, PO Box 1984, Levkosia (Nicosia). T: 76142.

*CZECHOSLOVAKIA*
**Baptist Unity of Brethren,** Vinohradská 68, Praha 3. T: 251286.
**Catholic Ch in Czechoslovakia,** Arcibiskupsky Ordinariat, Hradcanske nam 16, 119 02 Praha 1. T: 539548.
**Ch of Brethren (Congregational Ch),** Chairman, Konevova 24, Praha II.
**Czechoslovak Hussite Ch,** Patriarch, V.V. Kujbyseva 5, Praha 6.
**Czechoslovak Unitarian Association,** Karlova 8/186, Praha 1.
**Ev Ch of Czech Brethren,** Jungmannova 9, Praha 1.
**Old Catholic Ch in Czechoslovakia,** Leninova 503, Warnsdorf.
**Orthodox Ch of Czechoslovakia,** V Jáme 6, Praha 1. T: 225200,225139,227934.
**Reformed Christian Ch in Slovakia,** Alesovo nbr 7, Kosice.
**Seventh-day Adventist Ch,** Londynska 30, Vinohrady, Praha 2. T: 257863.
**Silesian Ev Ch of the Augsburg Confession,** Bp, Na Nivách 7, Cesky Tesín. T: 6656.
**Slovak Ch of the Augsburg Confession,** Generalbischof, Palisády 52, Bratislava. T: 32842.
**United Methodist Ch in Czechoslovakia,** Jecná 19, Praha 2.
**Unity of Brethren,** Halkova 5, Praha 2. (Also: Usti nad Orlici).

*DENMARK*
**Apostolic Ch in Denmark,** Lykkegardsvej 100, DK-6000 Kolding. T: (05)524765.
**Baptist Union of Denmark,** Marsalavej 14, DK-2300 Kobenhavn S. T: (01)555325.
**Catholic Ch,** Catolsk Bispekontor, Bredgade 69A, DK-1260 Kobenhavn K. T: (01)116080.
**Ch of England,** Rosenvaengets Hovedvej 21A, DK-2100 Kobenhavn O.
**Ch of Jesus Christ of Latter-day Saints,** Denmark Mission, 164 Dalgas Blvd, DK-2000 Kobenhavn F.
**Elim Ch,** Kronprinsengade 7, Kobenhavn.
**Free Church Union,** 30 Dag Hammarsköld Alle, DK-2100 Kobenhavn Q.
**Jehovah's Witnesses,** Kongevejen 207, DK-2830 Virum.
**Methodist Ch in Denmark,** Stokhusgade 2/1, DK-1317 Kobenhavn K.
**National Ch of Denmark,** BP, Norregade 11, Kobenhavn K.
**Pentecostal Movement in Denmark,** Lyngbyvej 67, DK-2100 Kobenhavn O.
**Reformed Church Synod in Denmark,** Gothersgade 109, DK-1123 Kobenhavn K.
**Salvation Army,** Frederiksberg Alle 9, DK-1820 Kobenhavn V. T: (01)314192.
**Seventh-day Adventist Ch,** Suomisvej 5, DK-1927 Kobenhavn V. T: (01)398800.

*DJIBOUTI*
**Eglise Catholique,** Evêché, Blvd de la République, BP 94, Djibouti. T: 350140.
**Eglise Protestante de Djibouti,** Pasteur, BP 416, Djibouti.

*DOMINICA*
**Catholic Ch,** Bishop's House, Roseau. T: 2837.

*DOMINICAN REPUBLIC*
**Asambleas de Dios,** Apdo 153, Ciudad Trujillo. (Also: Super, Apdo 605, Santo Domingo).
**Asociación Adventista del Séptimo Día,** Pres, Calle Juan Sanchez Ramirez 46, Apdo 1500, Santo Domingo. T: (682)2020,2373.
**Asociación de Templos Ev,** Apdo 235, La Vega.
**Hermanos Libros,** Apdo 44, Santo Domingo.
**Iglesia Católica en la República Dominicana,** Arzobispado, Apdo 186, Santo Domingo. T: 6853141.
**Iglesia Cristiana Bíblica,** Apdo 334, San Pedro de Macorís.
**Iglesia de Dios de la Profecía,** Apdo 22, San Pedro de Macorís.
**Iglesia de Dios (Cleveland),** Apdo 574, Ciudad Trujillo.
**Iglesia Episcopal Dominicana,** Bp, Av Indepencia 61, Apdo 764, Santo Domingo.
**Iglesias de la Fe Apostólica,** Calle Presidente Horicia 40, La Romana.
**Testigos de Jehová,** Av Francia 33, Santo Domingo.

*ECUADOR*
**Asambleas de Dios en el Ecuador,** Super, Casilla 3404, Guayaquil.
**Asociación de Iglesias Ev Interamericanas,** Casilla 860, Guayaquil.
**Asociación de Iglesias Misioneras,** Casilla 187, Esmeraldas.
**Hermanos Libres,** Casilla 2424, Quito.
**Iglesia Adventista del Séptimo Día,** Pres, Calle Tulcan 901 y Hurtado, Casilla 1140, Guayaquil. T: 361205.
**Iglesia Alianza Cristiana y Misionera,** Casilla 137, Quito.
**Iglesia Bautista,** Casilla 503, Quito.
**Iglesia Católica en el Ecuador,** Arzobispado, Apdo 106, Quito. T: 210703.
**Iglesia de Cristo Jesús,** Mision Evangélica, Casilla 5288, Guayaquil.
**Iglesia del Evangelio Cuadrangular,** Casilla 3252, Quito.
**Iglesia del Pacto Ev en el Ecuador,** Casilla 166, Quito.
**Iglesia Episcopal,** Diocese of Ecuador, Apdo 3108, Quito.
**Iglesia Ev Bereana,** Casilla 54, Guaranda.
**Iglesia Ev Luterana,** Casilla 3255, Quito. T: 34391.
**Iglesia Ev Unida del Ecuador,** Casilla 3023, Quito.
**Iglesia Pentecostal Unida del Ecuador,** Casilla 5208, Guayaquil.
**Iglesia Unión Misionera Ev en el Ecuador,** Casilla 698, Guayaquil.
**Testigos de Jehová,** Casilla 4512, Guayaquil.
**World Radio Missionary Fellowship,** HCJB, Casilla 691, Quito.

*EGYPT*
**Armenian Ev Ch,** Sec, 14 Bustan al-Kafuri, Faggala, Al-Qahirah.
**Assemblies of God in Egypt,** Sec, 86 23rd July St, Bur Said.
**Catholic Ch in Egypt,** Coptic Catholic Patriarchate, 34 Rue Ibn Sandar, Pont de Koubbeh, Al-Qahirah. T: 821740.
**Christian Brethren,** Ruqui al-Ma'arif, Geziret Bodran, Shubra, Al-Qahirah.
**Ch of Sinai,** Archbp, St Catarina Monastery, Mount Sinai.
**Coptic Ev Ch,** Pres, PO Box 50, Minia.
**Coptic Orthodox Ch,** Patriarchate of Alexandria, Pope of Africa, Anba Rueis Bldg, Ramses St, Abbasiya, Al-Qahirah.
**Episcopal Ch in Jerusalem & Middle East,** All Saints Cathedral, Box 1427, Al-Qahirah.
**Greek Orthodox Patriarchate of Alexandria,** Pope and Patriarch, Box 2006, Al Iskandariyah.
**Pentecostal Ch of God,** 8 Ahmed Pacha Kamal, Gayerit Badran, Shubra, Al Qahirah.
**Seventh-day Adventist Ch,** Pres, 16 Av de Koubbeh, PO Box 12, Heliopolis. T: 860292,861596.

*EL SALVADOR*
**Asambleas de Dios,** Super, Apdo 840, Santa Ana. T: 252064.
**Asociación Bautista del El Salvador,** Primera Iglesia Bautista, Av Cuscatlan 528, Apdo 1641, San Salvador.
**Consejo de Iglesias Luteranas,** Apdo Postal 985, San Salvador.
**Iglesia Adventista del Séptimo Día,** Pres, Av Espana 1257, San Salvador. T: 252721,250880.
**Iglesia Apostólica de la Fe en Cristo Jesús,** Apdo 929, San Salvador.
**Iglesia Católica en El Salvador,** Arzobispado, 1 Calle Pte 3402, San Salvador. T: 234124.
**Iglesia de Dios (Cleveland),** 16th Av, Sur Santa Tecla.
**Iglesia del Nazareno,** Sec, Calle Concepción 1201, San Salvador.
**Iglesia Episcopal,** Diocese of El Salvador, Apdo 1706, San Salvador.
**Testigos de Jehová,** Apdo 401, San Salvador.

*EQUATORIAL GUINEA*
**Iglesia Adventista del Séptimo Día,** Pres, Apdo 423, Malabo, Fernando Poo.
**Iglesia Católica en la Guinea Ecuatorial,** Obispado, Apdo 82 Mbini. T: 181.
**Iglesia Ev en la Guinea Ecuatorial,** Apdo 25, Ebebiyin, Rio Muni. (Also: Apdo 195, Bata).
**Iglesia Metodista,** Apdo 15, Malabo, Fernando Poo. T: 249.

*ETHIOPIA*
**Anglican Ch,** PO Box 109 & 503, Addis Abeba.
**Armenian Apostolic Ch,** PO Box 116, Addis Abeba.
**Baptist Bible Fellowship,** PO Box 128, Addis Abeba. T: 15011.
**Baptist Ev Ch,** PO Box 2323, Addis Abeba. T: 47594.
**Baptist Mission of Ethiopia,** PO Box 131, Addis Abeba. T: 43444,49209.
**Bethel Ev Ch of Ethiopia,** PO Box 1111, Addis Abeba. T: 13285.
**Catholic Ch in Ethiopia,** PO Box 21903, Addis Abeba. T: 111667.
**Christ Foundation Ch,** PO Box 1165, Addis Abeba. T: 12323.
**Christian Brethren,** PO Bati, Wallo.
**Chs of Christ,** PO Box 40001 & 3147, Addis Abeba. T: 45142.
**Ethiopian Orthodox Ch,** Patriarch, Secretariat, Haile Selassie I Av, PO Box 31090, Addis Abeba. T: 16616. (Also: PO Box 1283 & 1337, Addis Abeba).
**Ev Ch Mekane Jesus,** Exec Sec, PO Box 2087, Addis Abeba. T: 17220.
**Ev Ch of Eritrea,** Sec, Massawa Rd, PO Box 905, Asmera. T: 10711.
**Faith Ch of Christ,** PO Box 796, Asmera.
**Greek Orthodox Patriarchate of Alexandria,** Diocese of Aksum, PO Box 571, Addis Abeba. T: 12440.
**Lutheran Ch of Bible-true Friends in Ethiopia,** PO Box 1002, Addis Abeba.
**Lutheran Ch of Eritrea,** Pres, PO Box 99, Asmera. T: 11214.
**Seventh-day Adventist Ch,** Pres, PO Box 145, Addis Abeba. T: 47220/1.
**Sidamo Free Chs,** PO Box 529, Addis Abeba. T: 45287.
**United Pentecostal Ch of Ethiopia,** PO Box 350, Addis Abeba. T: 17071.
**Word of Life Ev Ch,** PO Box 127, Addis Abeba. T: 47679.

*FALKLAND ISLANDS*
**Catholic Ch,** Port Stanley. T: Stanley 204.

*FIJI*
**Anglican Ch,** Diocese of Polynesia, 7 Disraeli Rd, GPO Box 35, Suva.
**Assemblies of God of Fiji,** Calvary Temple, 83 Robertson Rd, PO Box 3697, Samabula, Suva.
**Catholic Ch,** Archdiocesan Office, Pratt St, PO Box 109, Suva. T: 22851.
**Christian Brethren,** Gospel Chapel, 28 Belo St, Samabula, Suva.
**Ch of Jesus Christ of Latter-day Saints,** Berry & Des Voeux Rds, Suva.
**Methodist Church in Fiji,** GPO Box 357, Suva.
**Seventh-day Adventist Ch in Fiji,** Pres, PO Box 297, Suva. T: 361022,361295,361451.

*FINLAND*
**Baptist Union of Finland,** Oikokatu 10A, Jyväskylä.
**Catholic Ch in Finland,** Rehbinderintie 21, 00150 Helsinki 15. T: (90)637907.
**Ch of Jesus Christ of Latter-day Saints,** Finland Mission, Neitsytpolku 3A3, Helsinki 14.
**Ev Lutheran Ch of Finland,** Kaisaniemenkatu 13A/Vuorikatu 17B, Helsinki 10. (Also: Agricolankatu 2, Turku. T: 15300).
**Free Ch of Finland,** Sec, Annankatu 1, 00120 Helsinki.
**Free Mission Covenant Ch,** Högbergsgatan 22, Helsinki 13.
**Free Pentecostal Revival of Finland,** Ulvilartie 10A, Helsinki.
**Jehovah's Witnesses,** Kuismatie 58, Tikkurila.
**Methodist Ch in Finland,** Eerikink 27, Turku. (Also: Punavuorenkatu 2, Helsinki 12).
**Orthodox Ch of Finland,** Archbp, Puistokatu 35, Kuopio 30. (Also: Soukatu 41A26).
**Pentecostal Revival of Finland,** Pengerkatu 9, Helsinki.
**Salvation Army,** Territorial HQ, Undenmaankatu 40, PB 161, Helsinki 12. T: (90)174844.
**Seventh-day Adventist Ch of Finland,** Pres, Vuorikatu 8a 24, 2070 Turku 70. T: (921)10550.
**Swedish Baptist Ch of Finland,** Radhusgatan 44, Vasa. T: 11559.

*FRANCE*
**Amis de l'Homme,** Sec, 91 Av Ledon-Rollin, F-75011 Paris.
**Armée du Salut,** Sec, 76 Rue de Rome, F-75008 Paris. T: 387-4119.
**Assemblées de Dieu en France,** Sec, 29 Rue des Capucins, Les Andelys, Eure.
**Assemblées des Frères,** Sec, 32 Villa Wagram-Saint-Honoré, Paris.
**Association Culturelle Antoiniste,** Sec, 34 Rue Vergniaud, F-75013 Paris.
**Association des Etudiants de la Bible Aurore,** Sec, Villa Maranatha, Av du Docteur Ménard, Nice.
**Eglise Adventiste du Septième Jour,** Pres, 130 Blvd de l'Hospital, F-75013 Paris. T: 331-6176/7.
**Eglise Apostolique,** 4 Rue Kitchener, Sanvic, SI.
**Eglise Catholique de France,** 8 Rue de la Ville-l'Evêque, F-75008 Paris. T: 2669015.
**Eglise Catholique Gallicane Autocéphale,** Diocèse de Normandie, 6 Rue de la Vatine, Mont-St-Aignan, S Mar.
**Eglise Catholique Orthodoxe de France,** 26 Rue Friant, F-75014 Paris. T: (1)707-2453.
**Eglise de Jésus-Christ des Saints des Derniers Jours,** Sec, 7 Av Franco-Russe, F-75007 Paris.
**Eglise de la Confession d'Augsberg d'Alsace et de Lorraine,** Prés, 1a Quai St-Thomas, Strasbourg, Bas-Rhin. T: 324586/7.
**Eglise Ev Luthérienne de France,** Prés, 16 Rue Chauchat, F-75009 Paris. T: 770-8030.
**Eglise Luthérienne Libres,** Prés, 16 Rue Jacques-Peirotes, Strasbourg, Bas-Rhin.
**Eglise Néo-Apostolique,** Sec, 17 Villa de Wils, Vanves, Seine.
**Eglise Orthodoxe Grecque en France,** 7 Rue Georges-Bizet, F-75116 Paris. T: (1)720-8235.
**Eglise Orthodoxe Roumaine en Europe Occidentale,** Evêché, 133 Rue Saint-Dominique, F-75007 Paris.
**Eglise Orthodoxe Russe,** 12 Rue Daru, F-75008 Paris. T: 2273734.
**Eglise Orthodoxe Russe Hors-Frontières,** Synode, 46 Rue Abel Vacher, F-92170 Meudon. T: (1)027-1916.
**Eglise Orthodoxe Serbe,** 23 Rue Simplon, F-75018 Paris. T: 255-3105.
**Eglise Réformée de France,** Prés, 47 Rue de Clichy, F-75009 Paris. T: 874-9092.
**Eglise Réformée d'Alsace et de Lorraine,** Prés, 2 Rue du Bouclier, Strasbourg, Bas-Rhin. T: 321617.
**Enfants de Dieu/Children of God,** BP 12, F-91230 Montgeron, Paris. T: 272-3881.
**Fédération des Eglises Ev Baptistes de France,** Prés, 48 Rue de Lille, F-75007 Paris. T: 548-7096.
**Témoins de Jéhovah,** Sec, 81 Rue du Point-du-Jour, Boulogne-Billancourt, Seine.
**Unión des Eglises Ev Libres de France,** Prés, Montalivet, Annonay, Ardèche.
**Union Nationale des Eglises Armeniennes de France,** Prés, 37 Rue Faillebin, Villeurbanne, Rhône.

*FRENCH GUIANA*
**Courants de Puissance,** Maison Carrée, 9 Rue Lt Cl Tourte, Saint-Laurent-du-Maroni.
**Eglise Adventiste du Septième Jour,** Prés, 39 Rue Schoelcher, BP 169, Cayenne. T: 366.
**Eglise Catholique,** Evêché, BP 378, 97302 Cayenne. T: 310118.

*FRENCH POLYNESIA*
**Eglise Adventiste du Septième Jour,** Prés, Av Prince Hinoi & Cours de l'Union Sacrée, BP 95, Papeete, Tahiti.
**Eglise Catholique de Polynésie Française,** Archevêché, BP 94, Papeete. T: 20251.
**Eglise Ev de Polynésie Française,** Prés, BP 113, Papeete, Tahiti.
**Eglise de Jésus-Christ des Saints des Derniers Jours,** Prés, Av du Commandante Chesse, Papeete, Tahiti.

*GABON*
**Eglise Catholique au Gabon,** Archevêché, BP 2146, Libreville. T: 722073.
**Eglise Ev de Pentecôte,** Elim, Médouneu, par Libreville.
**Eglise Ev du Gabon,** Prés, BP 80, Libreville.
**Eglise Ev du Sud Gabon,** Prés, BP 85 & 113, Mouila.

*GAMBIA*
**Anglican Ch,** Diocese of Gambia & the Rio Pongas, Bp, Bishop's House, Box 51 & 136, Banjul.
**Catholic Ch,** Bishop's House, PO Box 165, Banjul. T: 638.
**Methodist Ch in the Gambia,** Dobson St, PO Box 288, Banjul.

*GERMAN DEMOCRATIC REPUBLIC*
**Alt-Katholische Kirche in der DDR,** Wilhelm-Pieck-Str 31, DDR-1054 Berlin.
**Bund der Ev Kirchen in der DDR,** Auguststr 80, DDR-104 Berlin. T: 425186.
**Bund Ev-Freikirchlicher Gemeinden,** Generalsek, Gubener Str, DDR-1034 Berlin. T: 581832.
**Bund Freier Ev Gemeinden in der DDR,** Bandelowstr 42, DDR-154 Falkensee.
**Ev Brüder-Unität,** Unitätsdir, Vogtshof, DDR-8709 Herrnhut.
**Ev Kirche der Kirchenprovinz Sachsen,** Evangelisches Konsistorium, Am Dom 2, DDR-301 Magdeburg. T: 31881.
**Ev Kirche des Görlitzer Kirchengebietes,** Evangelisches Konsistorium, Berliner Str, DDR-89 Görlitz. T: 5485.
**Ev Kirche in Berlin-Brandenburg,** Neue Grunstr 19, DDR-1025 Berlin.
**Ev Landeskirche Anhalts,** Landeskirchenrat, Otto-Grotewohl-Str 22, Schliessfach 174, DDR-45 Dessau.
**Ev Landeskirche Greifswald,** Str der Nationalen Einheit 3, DDR-22 Greifswald. T: 2286.
**Ev-Lutherische Kirche in Thüringen,** Stadtparksstr 2, Pflugensberg, DDR-59 Eisenach. T: 2824.

**Ev-Lutherische Landeskirche Mecklenburgs,** Münzstr 8, DDR-27 Schwerin. T: 4165.
**Ev-Lutherische Landeskirche Sachsens,** Lukassre 6, DDR-8032 Dresden A27. T: 49841.
**Ev-Lutherische (Altlutherische) Kirche,** Kirchenrat Schröter, Annenstr 42, DDR-102 Berlin.
**Ev-Methodistische Kirche in der DDR,** Bischof, Wiener Str 56, DDR-8020 Dresden.
**Katholische Kirche Deutschlands,** Berliner Ordinarienkonferenz, Französische Str 34, DDR-108 Berlin. T: 200281.
**Mennonitengemeinde in der DDR,** Schwedter Str 262, DDR-1054 Berlin.
**Russisch-Orthodoxe Kirche,** Mitteleuropäisches Exarchet des Moskauer Patriarchats, Erzbischof, Wildensteiner Str 10, DDR-1157 Berlin-Karlshorst.
**Siebenten-Tags-Adventisten in der DDR,** Pres, Edisonstr 37, DDR-116 Berlin-Oberschoeneweide. T: 631320.

*GERMANY, Federal Republic of*
**Alt-Katholische Kirche in Deutschland,** Gregor-Mendel-Str 28, D-53 Bonn.
**Altreformierte Kirchen in Deutschland,** Grafschaft Bentheim, D-4459 Veldhausen.
**Arbeitsgemeinschaft der Christengemeinden in Deutschland,** Liegnitzerstr 11, D-6000 Frankfurt am Main.
**Bremische Ev Kirche,** Kirchenausschuss, Franziuseck 2/4, D-28 Bremen 1. T: 204241.
**Bund Ev-Freikirchlicher Gemeinden in Deutschland,** Louisenstr 121, D-6380 Bad Homburg, v d H. T: 23051.
**Bund Freier Ev Gemeinden in Deutschland,** Schumannstr 4, D-62 Wiesbaden.
**Christlicher Gemeinschaftverband,** Mollerstr 40, D-61 Darmstadt.
**Ev Brüder-Unität in Deutschland,** Unitätshaus, D-7325 Bad Boll über Göppingen.
**Ev Kirche im Rheinland,** Landeskirchenamt, Hans-Böckler-Str 7, Postfach 10182, D-4 Düsseldorf. T. 444057.
**Ev Kirche in Berlin-Brandenburg,** Evangelisches Konistorium, Bachstr 1-2, Postfach 79, D-1 Berlin 12. T: 310201.
**Ev Kirche in Deutschland (EKD),** Kirchliches Aussenamt, Bockenheimer Landstr 109, Postfach 174025, D-6 Frankfurt am Main 1.
**Ev Kirche in Hessen und Nassau,** Kirchenversaltung, Paulusplatz 1, Postfach 669, D-61 Darmstadt. T: 26041.
**Ev Kirche von Kurhessen-Waldeck,** Landekirchenamt, Heinrich-Wimmer-Str 4, D-3500 Kassel-Wilhelmshöhe. T: (0561)30021.
**Ev Kirche von Westfalen,** Landeskirchenamt, Altstadter Kirchplatz 5, Postfach 2740, D-48 Bielefeld. T: 64711.
**Ev Landeskirche in Baden,** Overkirchenrat, Blumenstr 1, Postfach 2269, D-75 Karlsruhe 1. T: (0721)25961).
**Ev Landeskirche in Württemberg,** Ev Oberkirchenrat, Gänsheidestr 2 u4, Postfach 92, D-7 Stuttgart 1. T: (0711)240351.
**Ev-Lutherische Kirche in Bayern,** Landeskirchenrat, Meiserstr 13, Schliessfach 37, D-8 München 37. T: (0811)55951.
**Ev-Lutherische Kirche in Oldenburg,** Oberkirchenrat, Huntestr 14, Postfach 269, D-2900 Oldenburg. T: (0441)22211,24323.
**Ev-Lutherische Landeskirche Eutin,** Landeskirchenrat, Schlossstr 13, Postfach 209, D-242 Eutin (Holstein).
**Ev-Lutherische Landeskirche Schamburg-lippe,** Landeskirchenamt, Schloss-Westflügel, Postfach 1307, D-4967 Böckeburg. T: (05722)4244.
**Ev-Lutherische Landeskirche Schleswig-Holsteins,** Landeskirchenamt, Dänische Str 27-35, D-23 Kiel. T: 47850.
**Ev-lutherische Bekenntniskirche,** Pres, Braunchweigerstr 38, Bremen.
**Ev-lutherische Kirche im Hamburgischen Staate,** Landeskirchenamt, Neue Burg 1, Postfach 111240, D-2 Hamburg 11. T: 321831.
**Ev-lutherische Kirche in Lübeck,** Kirchenkanzlei, Bäckerstr 3-5, D-24 Lübeck. T: 597526.
**Ev-lutherische Kirche Lettlands in Exil,** Tannenbergstr 6 II, D-73 Esslingen/Neckar.
**Ev-lutherische Landeskirche Hannovers,** Landeskirchenamt, Rote Reihe 6, D-3 Hannover. T: (0511) 15312.
**Ev-lutherische Landeskirche in Braunschweig,** Landeskirchenamt, Neuer Weg 88-90, Postfach 420, D-334 Wolfenbüttel.
**Ev-methodistische Kirche in Deutschland,** Wilhelm-Leuschner-Str 8, D-6 Frankfurt/Main.
**Ev-reformierte Kirche in Nordwestdeutschland,** Landeskirchenrat, Saarstr 6, D-295 Leer/Ostfriesland.
**Freier Brüderkreis,** Martin-Luther-Str 4, D-5240 Betzdorf/Sieg.
**Gemeinde der Christen Ecclesia,** Schlossbleiche 12, Postfach 3014, Solingen-Ohligs.
**Griechisch-Orthodoxe Metropolie von Deutschland,** Niebuhrstr 61, D-53 Bonn.
**Heilsarmee,** Salierring 23-27, D-5000 Köln. T: 234747.
**Katholische Apostolische Kirche (Urkirche),** Neheim-Hustem 1.
**Katholische Kirche Deutschlands,** Plenarkonferenz der Bischöfe, Kaiserstr 163, D-5300 Bonn. T: (02221)220095/7.
**Kirche Jesu Christi der Heiligen der Letzten Tage,** Germany West Mission, Ditmarstr 9, D-6 Frankfurt am Main 90.
**Lippische Landeskirche,** Landeskirchenamt, Leopoldstr 27, Postfach 132, D-493 Detmold.
**Litauische Ev-Lutherische Exilkirche,** Ferdinand-Lassalle-Str 20, D-28 Bremen 20. T: 461018.
**Neuapostolische Kirche,** Stammapostel, 88 Westfalendamn, D-46 Dortmund
**Orthodoxe Kirche von Rumänien,** Michaelstr 2, D-757 Baden-Baden.
**Russisch-Orthodoxe Kirche ausserhalb Russlands,** Erzbischof, Hagenbeckstr 10, D-2000 Hamburg 54. T: (040)404060,403444.
**Selbständige Ev-Lutherische Kirche (SELK),** Funckstr 43, D-56 Wuppertal 1.
**Serbische Orthodoxe Kirche,** Infanterierstr 12, D-8 München 13.
**Siebenten-Tags-Adventisten,** Pres, Schlaegerstr 5, D-3 Hannover. T: 880831,880606.
**Ukrainische Autokephale Orthodoxe Kirche,** Achatstr 2, D-8000 München 50. T(089)1504833. (Also: Vikarbischof, Schneidemühler Str 12, D-75 Karlsruhe-Waldstadt).
**Vereinigung der Deutschen Mennonitengemeinden,** Brückstr 74, D-297 Emden.
**Vereinigte Protestantisch-Ev-Christliche Kirche der Pfalz,** Landeskirchenrat, Domplatz 5, D-672 Speyer (Rhein). T: 2421.
**Volksmission Entschiedener Christen,** Rosenstr 45, Schorndorf.
**Zeugen Jehovas,** Am Kohlheck, Postfach 13025, D-62 Wiesbaden-Dortzheim.

*GHANA*
**African Faith Tabernacle Ch,** PO Box 50, Anyinam, Akim Abuakwa.
**African Methodist Episcopal Ch,** PO Box 239, Sekondi.
**African Methodist Episcopal Zion Ch,** PO Box 111, Sekondi.
**Anglican Ch,** PO Box 8, Accra.
**Apostles Revelation Society (ARS),** Spiritual Head, New Tadzewu, PO Box 1, Tadzewu, Volta Region.
**Apostolic Ch,** Ghana, Sec, PO Box 633, Accra.
**Apostolic Divine Ch of Ghana,** PO Box 5149, Accra.
**Army of the Cross of Christ Ch (MDCC),** General Head Prophet, Mozano, PO Box 3, Gomoa Eshiem, via Agona Swedru.
**Assemblies of God in Ghana,** PO Box 3363, Kumasi.
**Bethesda Church Mission,** PO Box 290, Kumasi.
**Catholic Ch in Ghana,** Archbishop's House, PO Box 112, Cape Coast. T: 2593.
**Christ Apostolic Ch,** PO Box 6298, Accra.
**Ch of Pentecost,** PO Box 2194, Accra.
**Ch of the Lord (Aladura),** PO Box 3725, Accra.
**Divine Healer's Ch,** A 764/1 Crowther Av, PO Box 3017, Accra. T: 64747.
**Eden Revival (F'Eden) Ch,** International HQ, PO Box 6757, Accra North. T: 23830,63525.
**Ev Presbyterian Ch,** Synod Clerk, PO Box 18, Ho, Volta Region.
**Jehovah's Witnesses,** PO Box 760, Accra.
**Methodist Ch,** Ghana, PO Box 403, Accra.
**Nazarene Healing Ch,** Prophet, PO Box 6683, Accra.
**Presbyterian Ch of Ghana,** PO Box 1800, Accra.
**Salvation Army,** 132 Osu Av, PO Box 320, Accra. T: 24705.
**Saviour Ch of Ghana,** Sec, PO Box 552, Sekondi.
**Seventh-day Adventist Ch,** Pres, PO Box 1016, Accra. T: 23720,24805.
**United Pentecostal Ch of Ghana,** PO Box 300, Accra.

*GIBRALTAR*
**Catholic Ch,** Bishop's House, 215 Main St, PO Box 21, Gibraltar. T: 4688.

*GREECE*
**Armenian Apostolic Ch,** 10 Kriezi St, Athínai. T: 524884.
**Assemblies of God,** Andreou Miaouli 8, Katerina. (Also: PO Box 24, Athínai).
**Catholic Ch in Greece,** Archevêché Catholique, Corfù. T: 30277.
**Ch of Crete,** Archbp of Crete, Iráklion. T: 282632.
**Ch of God of Pentecost,** Ag Apostolon 28, Athínai 513.
**Ch of God of Prophecy,** Thessalonika 136, Athínai. T: 364912.
**Ch of Greece,** I Gennadiou 14, Athínai 140. T: (021)3237654/6,3248731/7. (Also: Hodos Agias Philotheis 19-21, Athínai 117. T: 237654).
**Ch of the Dodecanese,** Bp, Ródhos. T: (0241)22314.
**Free Apostolic Ch of Pentecost,** Elpolidos 8, Athínai.
**Free Evangelical Chs of Greece,** 3 Alkiviadou St, Athínai.
**Greek Ev Ch,** 50 Amalias Av, Athínai. T: 231079. (Also: 20A Miaoulis St, Korydallos, Piraiévs).
**Jehovah's Witnesses,** 4 Kartali St, Athínai 611.
**Oriental Apostolic Ch,** Laskaridou 112B, Athínai. T: 960384.
**Seventh-day Adventist Ch,** Pres, Keramikou 18, Athínai 107. T: 524962.
**Union of Armenian Ev Chs in the Near East,** 30 Lamias St, Pal Kokkinia, Athínai. T: 493603.

*GREENLAND*
**Lutheran Ch of Greenland,** Dean, Godthaab.
**Pentecostal Chs,** PO Box 320, Laxa, Julianehab.
**Seventh-day Adventist Ch,** PO Box 34, Godthaab.

*GRENADA*
**Anglican Ch,** Rectory, Church St, St George's.
**Catholic Ch,** Bishop's House, PO Box 375, St George's. T: 2999.
**Ch of God,** Pearls, St Andrew's.
**Methodist Ch in the Caribbean & the Americas,** Wesley Manse, Church St, St George's.
**Presbyterian Ch in Trinidad & Grenada,** Knox House, St George's.
**Salvation Army,** Grenville St, St George's.
**Seventh-day Adventist Ch,** Mt Parnasus, St George's.

*GUADELOUPE*
**Eglise Adventiste du Septième Jour,** Prés, 5e Rue de l'Assainissement, BP 19, Pointe-à-Pitre. T: 821121.
**Eglise Catholique,** BP 50, 97101 Basse-Terre. T: 813669.
**Témoins de Jéhovah,** BP 239, Pointe-à-Pitre.

*GUAM*
**Assemblies of God,** PO Box 1948, Agaña.
**Catholic Ch,** Chancery Office, PO Box 125, Agaña. T: 4726116.
**Ch of Christ, Scientist,** Agaña Heights Society, opposite Naval Hospital, PO Box 2826, Agaña. T: 96910.
**Ch of God,** PO Box 801, Agaña.
**Seventh-day Adventist Ch,** PO Box EA, Agaña. T: 776618.

*GUATEMALA*
**Asambleas de Dios,** Super, Instituto Bíblico, 28 Calle y Av Elena, Zona 3, Apdo 103, Ciudad Guatemala.
**Asambleas de Hermanos,** 24 Calle 8-37, Zona 11, Ciudad Guatemala.
**Asociación de Iglesias Ev Hispanoamericas de Guatemala,** Super, 2a Calle 0-04, Zona 9, Ciudad Guatemala.
**Convención Bautista de Guatemala,** 11 Av 11-72, Zona 1, Apdo 1135 & 372, Ciudad Guatemala.
**Iglesia Adventista del Séptimo Día,** 1 Calle 18-24, Vista Hermosa 11, Zona 15, Apdo 770, Ciudad Guatemala. T: 690573.
**Iglesia Apostólica de la Fe en Cristo Jesús,** Apdo 737, Ciudad Guatemala.
**Iglesia Católica en Guatemala,** Arzobispado, Apdo 723, Ciudad Guatemala. T: 29707.
**Iglesia Centroamericana en Guatemala,** 4a Av 6-36, Zona 11, Ciudad Guatemala.
**Iglesia de Dios de la Profecía,** 16 Calle 4-26, Zona 3, Ciudad Guatemala.
**Iglesia de Dios Misionera,** Supervisor Gen, Av Centro America 15-67, Zona 1, Ciudad Guatemala.
**Iglesia de Jesucristo de los Santos de los Altimos Días,** 3a Calle 16-91, 18 Av A 2-09, Zona 1, Ciudad Guatemala.
**Iglesia Defensores de la Fe,** Dir, 19 Av 30-44, Zona 5, Ciudad Guatemala.
**Iglesia del Evangelio Cuadrangular,** Av Amatitlan y El Trebal, Zona 11, Ciudad Guatemala.
**Iglesia del Principe de Paz,** Dir Gen, 12 Calle B 35-01, Zona 5, Ciudad Guatemala.
**Iglesia Ev del Nazareno de Guatemala,** Super, Apdo Postal 11, Cobán.
**Iglesia Episcopal,** Diocese of Guatemala, Bp, Apdo 58-A, Ciudad Guatemala.
**Iglesia Nacional Presbiteriana de Guatemala,** 21 Calle 1-48, Zona 3, Apdo 655, Ciudad Guatemala.
**Iglesia Ev Amigos de Centroamerica,** Apdo Postal 8, Chiquimula.
**Testigos de Jehová,** 11 Av 5-67, Zona 1, Ciudad Guatemala.

*GUINEA*
**Eglise Anglicaine,** BP 105, Conakry.
**Eglise Catholique au Guinée,** Archevêché, BP 1006 Bis, Conakry. T: 43627.
**Eglise de la Bible Ouverte,** BP 101, Kindia.
**Eglise Ev Protestante,** BP 438, Conakry.
**Eglise Libre Pentecôtiste,** Voriyama, BP 50, Macenta.

*GUINEA-BISSAU*
**Igreja Católica,** CP 20, Bissau. T: 2469.
**Igreja Ev da Guiné,** Missão Evangélica, CP 49, Bissau.

*GUYANA*
**African Methodist Episcopal Ch,** 209 New Garden St, Georgetown 6.
**African Methodist Episcopal Zion Ch,** 150 Regent St, Lacytown.
**Anglican Ch,** Austin House, Georgetown.
**Assemblies of God in Guyana,** Super, 330 Church and East Sts, Box 610, Georgetown.
**Catholic Ch,** Bishop's House, 27 Brickdam, Georgetown. T: (02)64469.
**Christian Brethren,** 193 Camp St, Georgetown.
**Ch of God (Anderson),** Sec, PO Box 158, Georgetown.
**Ch of the Nazarene,** 230 Almond St, Georgetown 6.
**Elim Foursquare Gospel,** 147 Albert St, PO Box 497, Georgetown.
**Ethiopian Orthodox Ch,** 26 Princess St, Georgetown.
**Guyana Baptist Mission,** 65 Brickdam, Georgetown.
**Guyana Congregational Union,** Sec, Congregational Manse, Bagotville, WB Demerara.
**Jehovah's Witnesses,** 50 Brickdam, Georgetown 11.
**Lutheran Ch in Guyana,** Pres, Lutheran Courts, New Amsterdam, Berbice. T: 2068.
**Methodist Ch in the Caribbean & the Americas,** Trinity Manse, High St, Georgetown.
**Moravian Ch,** 53 New Garden St, Georgetown 6.
**Presbytery of Guyana,** Moderator, 82 Albert St, Bourda, Georgetown.
**Salvation Army,** 5 Church St, PO Box 259, Georgetown. T: 61638.
**Seventh-day Adventist Ch,** Pres, 222 Peter Rose & Armond Sts, PO Box 78, Queenstown, Georgetown. T: 3313.
**Unevangelized Fields Mission,** PO Box 109, Georgetown.
**Wesleyan Ch in Guyana,** Interior 60 Hadfield St, Wortmanville.

*HAITI*
**Armée du Salut,** BP 301, Port-au-Prince. T: 24502.
**Assemblées de Dieu,** Super, BP 127, Port-au-Prince.
**Convention Baptiste d'Haïti,** BP 20, Cap-Haïtien.
**Eglise Adventiste du Septième Jour,** Ruelle Ganot 78, BP 1325, Port-au-Prince. T: 23452.
**Eglise Catholique au Haïti,** Archevêché, Port-au-Prince. T: 22043.
**Eglise de Dieu en Christ,** 165 Rue des Front-Forts, Port-au-Prince.
**Eglise de Dieu Pentecôtiste,** BP 562, Port-au-Prince.
**Eglise de Dieu (Cleveland),** BP 592, Port-au-Prince.
**Eglise Episcopale d'Haïti,** Bp, BP 1309, Port-au-Prince.
**Eglise Evangélique d'Haïti,** Cap Haïtien.
**Eglise Méthodiste d'Haïti,** Gen Super, BP 6, Port-au-Prince.
**Eglise Méthodiste Libre,** Sec, BP 994, Port-au-Prince.
**Mission Baptiste Conservatrice,** BP 673, Port-au-Prince.
**Mission Ev Baptiste du Sud-Haïti,** BP 1051, Port-au-Prince.
**Témoins de Jéhovah,** BP 185, Port-au-Prince.

*HOLY SEE*
**Curia Romana (Roman Curia),** Palazzo Apostolico Vaticano, I-00120 Città del Vaticano. T: 698-3954.
**Vicariato della Città del Vaticano,** Palazzo Apostolico Vaticano, I-00120 Città del Vaticano. T: 698-3145.

*HONDURAS*
**Asambleas de Dios,** Super, Apdo 117, San Pedro Sula.
**Convención Bautista Hondureña,** Apdo 100, San Pedro Sula.
**Iglesia Adventista del Séptimo Día,** Apdo 121, Tegucigalpa. T: 23781.
**Iglesia Católica en Honduras,** Arzobispado, Apdo 106, Tegucigalpa. T: 220335.
**Iglesia Centroamericana,** Apdo 30, Choluteca.
**Iglesia de Dios (Cleveland),** Barrio Alvarado, La Ceiba.
**Iglesia de los Hermanos Unidos en Cristo,** Apdo 47, La Ceiba.
**Iglesia del Evangelio Cuadrangular,** Apdo 421, Tegucigalpa.
**Iglesia Ev Menonita,** Tocoa, Colón.
**Iglesia Morava,** Brus Laguna, La Mosquitia.
**Misión Ev Mundial,** Apdo 331, Tegucigalpa.
**Sinodo Ev y Reformada,** Cincuenenario 1921-1971, Apdo 17, San Pedro Sula.
**Testigos de Jehová,** Apdo 14, Tegucigalpa.

*HONG KONG*
**Anglican Ch in China,** Diocese of Hong Kong & Macau, Bishop's House, 1 Lower Albert Rd, Hong Kong. T: H-225753.
**Assemblies of God,** PO Box 4, Shatin, NT. (Also: PO Box 5049 & 9550, Kowloon).
**Catholic Ch,** 16 Caine Rd, Hong Kong. T: 5241633.
**China Peniel Missionary Society,** 90 Portland St, Kowloon.
**Chinese Full Gospel Ch,** 22 Hennessy Rd, PO Box 5683, Kowloon. T: 890440.
**Chinese Methodist Ch,** 22 Hennessy Rd, Kowloon.
**Chinese Rhenish Ch,** Hong Kong Synod, Tat Chee Av, Yau Yat Chuen, Kowloon.
**Christian and Missionary Alliance,** 31 Chatham Rd 5/F, E Block, Kowloon.
**Christian Nationals' Evangelism Commission,** 305 Prince Edward Rd 2/F, PO Box 5307, Kowloon.
**Ch of Christ in China,** Hong Kong Council, Gen Sec, Morrison Memorial Centre, 191 Prince Edward Rd, Kowloon. T: K-802371/3.
**Ev Hakka Ch,** Sec, 59 Hong Kong St 2/F, San Po Kong, Kowloon. (Also: Kau Yan Church, 87 High St, Kowloon).
**Ev Lutheran Ch of Hong Kong,** 50A Waterloo Rd, Hong Kong.
**Evangelize China Fellowship,** 51 Bun Hoi St, North Point, Hong Kong.
**Hong Kong Ev Chs,** 9 Tong Yam St, Tai Hang Tung, Kowloon.
**Hong Kong Methodist Ch,** Metropole Bldg 7/F, 57 Peking Rd, Kowloon. T: K-670041.
**Hong Kong Swatow Christian Ch,** 20 Shelly St, Hong Kong.
**Jehovah's Witnesses,** 312 Prince Edward Rd 2/F, Kowloon.
**Lock Tao Christian Chs Association,** D 1 Mirador Mansion 11/F, 45-65 Nathan Rd, Kowloon. T: K-668697.
**Lutheran Ch—Missouri Synod,** 68 Begonia Rd, Yau Yat Chuen, Kowloon.
**Pentecostal Holiness Ch,** 6 Dorset Crescent G/F, Kowloon.
**Salvation Army,** 547-555 Nathan Rd, Kowloon. T: 3884141.
**Seventh-day Adventist Ch,** Pres, 17 Ventries Rd, PO Box 310, Hong Kong. T: 773838/9,770436.
**Spiritual Food Worldwide Evangelistic Mission,** 1 Grampion, Kowloon.
**United Hong Kong Christian Baptist Chs Association,** 73 Waterloo Rd 1/F, Kowloon.

*HUNGARY*
**Apostolic Ch (Primitive Christian Brethren),** Balso Bela u 75, Miskcolc.
**Baptist Ch in Hungary,** Orszagos Kozpont, Aradi-Utca 48, Budapest VI.
**Catholic Ch in Hungary,** Berenyi Zsigmond u.2, Pf25, H-2501 Esztergom.
**Ev Lutheran Ch in Hungary,** Bp, Ulloi utca 24, Budapest VIII.
**Ev Christian Pentecostal Ch,** Aray Janos u 60, Pilis.
**Hungarian Methodist Ch,** Felso Erdo sor 5, Budapest VI.
**Orthodox Ch in Hungary,** Bp, Galamb VY4, Budapest.
**Reformed Ch of Hungary,** Abonyi utca 21, Budapest XIV.
**Seventh-day Adventist Ch,** Szekely Bertalan u 13, Budapest VI. T: 125980.
**Unitarian Ch in Hungary,** Consistory, Högyes Endre-u 3, Budapest IX.

*ICELAND*
**Catholic Ch,** Egilsgötu 18, 101 Reykjavík. T: (91)11423.
**Jehovah's Witnesses,** PO Box 251, Reykjavík.
**National Ch of Iceland,** Bp, Reykjavík.
**Pentecostal Movement in Iceland,** Hverfisgatan 44, Reykjavík.
**Salvation Army,** PO Box 372, Reykjavík. T: 13203.
**Seventh-day Adventist Ch,** Pres, PO Box 262, Reykjavík. T: 13899,19442.

*INDIA*
**Advent Christian Conference,** 2 Mount Rd, Madras, Tamil Nadu 600015.
**Andhra Evangelical Lutheran Ch,** Gunn Bungalow, PO Box 205 & 231, Guntur, AP.

**Apostolic Ch of Pentecost in India,** Muttambalam PO, Kottayam, Kerala.
**Arcot Lutheran Ch,** Sec, Siloam, Tirukoilur, South Arcot District, Tamil Nadu.
**Armenian Apostolic Ch,** Diocese of India, Armenian College, Park St, Calcutta 16.
**Assemblies of God,** Ashti, Beed District, via Ahmednagar.
**Assemblies of God,** North India, 789 Napier Town, Jabalpur, MP. (Also: 177 Faizabad Rd, Lucknow 7, UP).
**Assemblies of God,** South India, Sec, Bethel Bible School, Punalur, District Quailon, Kerala.
**Assemblies (Jehova Shammah),** Brother Bakht Singh, PO Box 217, Hyderabad, AP.
**Association of Oriya Baptist Chs,** Raygada PO, via Parlakhemundi, District Ganjam, Orissa.
**Baptist Ch of Mizo District,** Gen Sec, Lughleh, Mizo District, Assam.
**Bengal-Orissa-Bihar Baptist Convention,** Sec, Jamda, District Midnapur, West Bengal.
**Bible Mission,** Bethel House, Railpet, District Guntur, AP.
**Catholic Ch in India,** CBCI Centre, 1 Ashok Place, New Delhi 110001. T: 46466.
**Ceylon Pentecostal Mission,** Gen Sec, 48 Main Rd, Royapuram, Madras 13, Tamil Nadu.
**Chaldean Syrian Ch,** Metropolitan, Cathedral, Trichur, Kerala.
**Christian Assemblies in India,** Rajahmundry, East Godavari District, AP.
**Christian & Missionary Alliance of India,** Gujerati Field, No 20 Camp, Ahmedabad, Gujarat.
**CMS Anglican Ch of India,** Bp, Kottayam, Kerala.
**Ch of God (Full Gospel) in India,** Sec, Malakuzha, Chengannur, District Alleppey, Kerala.
**Ch of North India (CNI),** Gen Sec, 19 August Kranti Marg, Bombay 7.
**Ch of South India (CSI),** Synod Office, Cathedral, PO Madras 6, Tamil Nadu.
**Convention of Baptist Chs in the Northern Circars,** Luthergiri, Rajahmundry 1, East Godavari District, AP.
**Convention of Telugu Baptist Chs,** CAM High School Compound, Nellore 3, AP.
**Council of Baptist Chs in NE India,** Gen Sec, Pan Bazar, Gauhati 1, Assam.
**Ev Free Ch of India,** Pres, Gen HQ, Sielmat, PO Churachandpur South District, Manipur.
**Federation of Ev Lutheran Chs in India (FELC),** Bp, Allithurai Rd, Puthur, Tiruchirapalli-1, Tamil Nadu.
**Goalpara Boro Baptist Church Union,** Sec, PO Tukrajhar, via Bongaigaon, District Goalpara, Assam.
**Gossner Ev Lutheran Ch,** Pres, Ranchi, Bihar.
**Independent Christian Bible Believers Gospel Fellowship,** Ramachandrapuram, EG District, AP.
**Independent Ch of India,** Sielmat, Churachandpur PO, Manipur.
**Independent Full Gospel Ch,** National School Compound, By-Pass Rd, Rajahmundry, 533 103 AP.
**Independent Syrian Ch of Malabar,** Thozhiyur, Tolur PO, District Trichur, Kerala.
**India Christian Assemblies,** Chilakalapudi PO, District Krishna, AP.
**India Christian Mission,** Eluru PO, District West Godavari, AP.
**India Ev Lutheran Ch,** Gen Sec, Ambur, North Arcot District, Tamil Nadu.
**India Mennonite Brethren Ch,** Sec, AMB Mission, Mahbubnagar, AP.
**India Mission,** Good News Literature Centre, PO Box 114 & 144, Secunderabad, AP.
**Indian Orthodox Ch,** Patriarchate of India, 1592 Faiz Ganj, Daryaganj, Delhi 6.
**Indian Pentecostal Ch of God,** Hebron, Kumbanad, District Alleppey, Kerala.
**Jehovah's Witnesses,** South Av, Santa Cruz, Bombay 400054.
**Jeypore Ev Lutheran Ch,** Pres, Jeypore, District Koraput, Orissa.
**Lakher Independent Ev Ch,** Sec, Lorrainville, PO Serkawr, South Mizo District, Assam.
**London Mission Ch,** Nagercoil, PO Dennis St, Kanyakumari District.
**Madhya Pradesh Ev Lutheran Ch,** Pres, PB 1, Chhindwara, MP.
**Mar Thoma Syrian Ch of Malabar,** Metropolitan, Sabha Office, Tiruvalla, District Alleppey, Kerala.
**Methodist Ch in Southern Asia (MCSA),** Sec, Robinson Memorial Church, Byculla, Bombay 8.
**Metropolitan Church Association,** PO Siwait, Allahabad District, UP.
**North Bank Baptist Association,** Sec, Baptist Christian Hospital, Tezpur, District Darrang, Assam.
**Northern Ev Lutheran Ch,** Koroya Mission, PO Dumka, Santal Parganas, Bihar.
**Norwegian Free Ev Ch,** Sec, Banda, UP.
**Orthodox Syrian Ch of the East,** Catholicate Palace, Kottayam-4, Kerala. T: 8499.
**St Thomas Ev Ch of India,** Bp, PO Tiruvella, Kerala.
**Salvation Army,** Veturinimadam SO, Nagercoil, 3, Kanyakumari District, Tamil Nadu 629003. T: Nagercoil 836.
**Saora Association of Baptist Chs,** Serango, via Gumma, District Ganjam, Orissa.
**Seventh-day Adventist Ch,** Pres, 11 Hailey Rd, New Delhi 1. T: 42309.
**South Andhra Lutheran Ch,** Sec, Centenary High School, Naidupet, District Nellore, AP.
**Tamil Ev Lutheran Ch,** Pres, Tranquebar House, Tiruchirapalli, Tamil Nadu.
**TEAM Christian Chs,** Amalner, District Jalgaon, Maharashtra.
**Theistic Ch of India,** Goldmine, Kench's Trace, Shillong 4, Assam.
**Tripura Baptist Christian Union,** Gen Sec, PO Arundhutinagar, Agartala, Tripura.
**United Pentecostal Ch in India,** Sec, Mission Bungalow, Adur, District Quilon, Kerala.

*INDONESIA*
**Assemblies of God,** Jalan Krembangan Barat 55, Kotakpos 2156, Jakarta.
**Bali Christian Protestant Ch (GKPB),** Rao Pasikian, Jalan Dedes No 6, Penjobekan, Kotakpos 220, Denpasar-Bali.
**Baptist Gospel Association of Indonesia (PIBI),** Sungai Betung, Bengkajong, Kalimantan Barat.
**Batak Christian Protestant Ch (HKBP),** Ephorus, Pearaja-Tarutung, Sumatera Utara.
**Batak Christian Community Ch (PKB),** Jalan HOS Cokroaminoto 96, Jakarta.
**Batak Ev Lutheran Christian Ch,** Kp Lumban Siagian, Taratung.
**Bethel Full Gospel Ch (GBIS),** Jalan KH Wahid Hasjim 67, Jakarta. (Also: Jalan Baladewa 10, Jakarta Pusat).
**Bethel Tabernacle Ch (GBT),** Jalan Mahoni 21, Jakarta.
**Catholic Ch in Indonesia,** Jalan Kathedraal 7, Jakarta V/6. T: 362392.
**Christian Ch in Central Sulawesi (GKST),** Pres, Tentena, Poso, Central Sulawesi.
**Christian Ch in Luwuk Banggai (GKLB),** Kantor Synode, Luwuk, Sulawesi Tengah.
**Christian Ch in South Sulawesi (GKSS),** Badan Pengurus Synode, Jalan Lasinrang 21, Makassar, Sulawesi Selatan.
**Christian Ch of North Central Java (GKJTU),** Jalan Indraprasta 100, Semarang.
**Christian Ch of Sumba (GKS),** Kantor, Pajeti VII-93, Pos Waingapu, Sumba.
**Christian Chs of Java (GKJ),** Exec Sec, Jalan Dr Sumardi 5, Salatiga, Mid Java.
**Christian Ev Ch in Minahasa (GMIM),** Pres, Tomohon, Minahasa, Sulawesi Utara.
**Ch of Christ (GK),** Badan Pekerja Synode, Jalan K.H. Zainul Arifin 9, Jakarta Pusat. (Also: Jalan Palmerah, Jakarta).
**Ch of Jesus Christ (the Messiah) (GIA),** Majelis Pusat Harian, Jalan Pringgading 13, Semarang.
**Ch of the Lord Jesus Christ (GKT),** Synode, Jalan Argopuro 6, Malang.
**East Java Christian Ch (GKJW),** Majelis Agung, Jalan Kelud 10, Malang, East Java.
**Ev Christian Ch in Bolaang-Mongondow (GMIBM),** Badan Pekerja Synode, Kotamodagu, Bolaang-Mongondow.
**Ev Christian Ch in Halmahera (GMIH),** Badang Pekerja Synode, Tobelo, Halmahera, Maluku Utara.
**Ev Christian Ch in Java (GITJ),** Sek, Jalan Ronggowongso 37, Pati Jateng.
**Ev Christian Ch in Sangihe-Talaud (GMIST),** Badan Pekerja Synode, Tahuna, Sangihe, Sulawesi Utara.
**Ev Christian Ch in Timor (GMIT),** Pres, Jalan Merdeka 46, Kupang, Timor.
**Ev Christian Ch in West Irian (GKI Ir-jay),** Badan Pekerja Synode Umum (BPSU Jalan Argapura Kotakpus 14, Jayapura, Irian Barat.
**Ev Ch in Kalimantan (GKE),** Jalan Jenderal Sudirman 8, Banjarmasin, South Kalimantan.
**Holy Spirit Ch of Indonesia (GSRKI),** Jalan Wahid Hasjim 56, Medan, Sumatera.
**Indonesia Protestant Christian Ch (GKPI),** Ephorus, Jalan Abdullah Lubis 48, Medan, Sumatera. T: 445.
**Indonesian Christian Ch (HKI),** Kantor Putjuk Pimpinan, Jalan Marihat 109-111, Pematangsiantar, Sumatera Utara.
**Indonesian Christian Ch in Central Java (GKI Ja-Teng),** Badan Pekerja, Jalan Ngupasan 21, Jogjakarta.
**Indonesian Christian Ch in East Java (GKI Ja-Tim),** Sekr Badan Pekerja, Jalan Greges 14, Surabaja.
**Indonesian Christian Ch of West Java (GKI Ja-Bar),** Jalan Ir H Djvanda 102E, Bandung.
**Jehovah's Witnesses,** Jalan Batutjeper 25, Jakarta.
**Karo Batak Protestant Ch (GBKP),** Gen Sec, Jalan Kapt Pala Bangun, Kabanjahe, North Sumatera.
**Methodist Ch in Indonesia (GMI),** Bp, Jalan Hang Tuah 8, Medan, Sumatera Utara.
**Minahasa Protestant Church Association (KGPM),** Jalan Gereja Inggris 5, Jakarta.
**Moluccan Protestant Ch (GPM),** Gen Sec, Jalan Imam Bondjol, Ambon, Maluku.
**Muria Christian Ch in Indonesia (GKMI),** Synode Muria, Jalan Pemuda 75, Delakang, Semarang.
**Nias Christian Protestant Ch (BNKP),** Gen Sec, Gunungsitoli, Nias, North Sumatera.
**Pesundan Christian Ch (GKP),** Pres, Jalan HOS Cokroaminoto 93, PO Box 178, Bandung.
**Pentecostal Ch of God,** Calvary Mission, Ternate.
**Pentecostal Ch of Indonesia (GPdI),** PO Box 2633, Jakarta. (Also: Jalan Gunung Merapi 106, Makassar).
**Pentecostal Movement Ch (GGP),** Jalan Waja I/16 Par, Galur Tanah Tinggi, Jakarta Pusat.
**Protestant Ch in Indonesia (GPI),** Pres, Jalan Merdeka Timur 10, Jakarta.
**Protestant Ch in South East Sulawesi (GEP-SULTRA),** Badan Pekerja Synode, Jalan Gereja 1, Kendari, Sulawesi Tenggara.
**Ray of the Gospel Christian Ch (GKPI),** Majelis Synode, Tanjung Lapang, Malinau, Tanah Tidung, Kaop Bulongan, Kalimantan Timur.
**Salvation Army,** Jalan Jawa 16, Bangung. T: 2029.
**Seventh-day Adventist Ch,** Pres, Jalan MH Thamrin 22, PO Box 221, Jakarta. T: 46657.
**Simalungun Protestant Christian Ch (GKPS),** Jalan Jenderal Sudirman 24, Pematangsiantar, Sumatera Utara.
**Spiritual Food Ch of Indonesia (GSRI),** Jalan Taman Sari 79, Jakarta.
**Surabaya Pentecostal Ch (GPPS),** Majelis Besar, Jalan Arjuno 90, Surabaja.
**Toraja Christian Ch,** Gen Sec, Jalan Taman Bahagia 30, Rantepao, Sulawesi Selatan.
**Toraja Ch in Mamasa (GTM),** Badan Pekerja Synode, Perwakilan Makassar, Jalan Sungai Sa'dang Lorong 32 9A, Makassar, Sulawesi Selatan.
**United Pentecostal Ch (GPS),** Jalan Mataram 970, Semarang, Java.

*IRAN*
**Catholic Ch in Iran,** Archevêché, Av Forsat 91, Shah Reza, Tehran 15. T: 823549.
**Episcopal Ch of Iran,** Bp, Abbas-Abad, PO Box 12, Isfahan.
**Ev Ch of Iran,** Synod Exec Sec, PO Box 1505, Tehran.
**Seventh-day Adventist Ch,** 111 Pahlavi Av, Tehran. T: 44525

*IRAQ*
**Catholic Ch in Iraq,** Patriarch, Chaldean Catholic Patriarchate, Baghdad. T: 8880689.
**Seventh-day Adventist Ch,** Pres, PO Box 2077, Baghdad. T: 84971.

*IRELAND*
**Catholic Ch in Ireland,** Archbishop's House, Dublin 9. T: 373732/6.
**Ch of Ireland,** Representative Body, Chief Officer and Sec, Church of Ireland House, Church Av, Rathmines, Dublin 6.
**Lutheran Ch in Ireland,** 21 Merlyn Park, Dublin 4.
**Methodist Ch in Ireland,** 11 Elgin Rd, Dublin 4.

*ISRAEL*
**Association of Baptist Chs in Israel,** PO Box 20, Nazareth.
**Baptist Convention in Israel,** PO Box 154, Jerusalem.
**Catholic Ch in Israel,** Patriarch, Latin Patriarchate, Old City, PO Box 14152, Jerusalem. T: (02)282323.
**Coptic Orthodox Ch,** Convent, 4 Pestalucci, Tel Aviv. T: TA 823300.
**Greek Orthodox Patriarchate of Jerusalem,** Myrsiades, Nazareth, PO Box 19632, Jerusalem.
**Jehovah's Witnesses,** PO Box 44520, Hefa.
**Scandinavian Seamen's Ch,** 43 Hagefen St, Hefa. T: 521422.

*ITALY*
**Assemblee di Dio in Italia,** Gen Super, Via dei Bruzi 11, I-00185 Roma.
**Associazione Missionaria Ev Italiana (AMEI),** Via Curtatone 10, Roma. T: 482396.
**Chiesa Anglicana,** Via del Babuino 153B, Roma.
**Chiesa Apostolica in Italia,** Via Oberdan 39, Grosseto.
**Chiesa Cattolica in Italia,** Conferenza Episcopal Italiana, Circonvallazione Aurelia 50, I-00165 Roma. T: 6982 int 6197. (Vicariato di Roma).
**Chiesa Cristiana Avventista del 7 Giorno,** Pres, Lungotevere Michelangelo 7, I-00192 Roma. T: 315936.
**Chiesa Cristiana Ev dei Fratelli in Italia,** Via della Vigna Vecchia 15-17, CP 5/13035, Firenze.
**Chiesa di Gesù Cristo dei Santi degli Ultimi Giorni,** Piazza Vescovio 3, Roma.
**Chiesa Ev del Nazarene,** Sovrintendente, Via Miccinesi 5D, Firenze. T: 410291.
**Chiesa Ev Internazionale,** Via Chiovenda 57, Piazza Cavalieri del Lavoro, I-00173 Roma.
**Chiesa Ev Luterana in Italia,** Vio Toscana 7, Roma. (Also: Dean, Via Tasso 470, I-80127 Napoli. T: 385354).
**Chiesa Ev Metodista d'Italia,** Via Firenze 38, Roma.
**Chiesa Ev Valdese,** Via IV Novembre 107, I-00187 Roma.
**Chiesa Universale Giuio Davidica,** Via Tevere 21/5, Roma.
**Comunità Cattolica dei SS Andrea Ap e di Caffa,** Comunità Ecclesiale Ecumenica, Via Anassimandro 47, I-00176 Roma. T: 274845.
**Esercito della Salvezza,** Via Ariosto 32, I-00185 Roma. T: (06)734214.
**Testimoni di Geova,** Via Monte Maloia 32, Roma.
**Unione Cristiana Ev Battista d'Italia,** Piazza in Lucina 35, I-00186 Roma.

*IVORY COAST*
**Assemblées de Dieu,** BP 4266, Abidjan.
**Association des Eglises Baptistes du Nord,** BP 111, Ferkessedougou.
**Convention Baptiste Nigérienne,** BP 20812, Abidjan.
**Eglise Adventiste du Septième Jour,** Prés, Route du Lycée Technique, Cocody, BP 335, Abidjan. T: 311655.
**Eglise Baptiste Libre,** Mission Protestante, BP 112, Bondoukou.
**Eglise Catholique en Côte d'Ivoire,** Archevêché, BP 1287, Abidjan. T: 222007.
**Eglise Harriste,** Comité National Harris de Côte d'Ivoire, Sec Gén & Prédicateur-Episcopal, BP 20710, Abidjan. (Also: Bregbo, BP 25, Bingerville; Temple Biblique No 1 de Grand-Lahou).
**Eglise Protestante du Centre,** BP 5, Zuenoula.
**Eglise Protestante Ev du Centre,** Prés, BP 585, Bouaké.
**Eglise Protestante Libre,** Akradjo, Dabou.
**Eglise Protestante Méthodiste en Côte d'Ivoire,** Prés, BP 1282, Abidjan.
**Union des Eglises Ev du Sud-Ouest de CI,** BP 25, Gagnoa. (Also: BP 8020, Abidjan).

*JAMAICA*
**African Methodist Episcopal Ch,** PO Oracabessa
**Anglican Ch,** Church House, 2 Caledonia Av, Kingston 5.
**Assemblies of God,** Super, PO Box 7-8, Kingston 5.
**Catholic Ch in Jamaica,** Archbishop's Residence, 21 Hopefield Av, PO Box 43, Kingston 6. T: 9279915.
**Ch of God in Christ,** 4 Daguilor Rd, Kingston.
**Ch of God in Jamaica,** 35 Hope Rd, Kingston 10.
**Ch of God of Prophecy,** 36 Maxfield Av, Whitfield Town.
**Disciples of Christ in Jamaica,** 24 Hagley Park Plaza, Kingston 10.
**Ethiopian Orthodox Ch,** Holy Trinity Church, Wareika P A, Kingston.
**International Ch of the Foursquare Gospel,** PO Box 22, Hagley Park.
**Jamaica Baptist Union,** Pres, 6 Hope Rd, Kingston 10.
**Jehovah's Witnesses,** 41 Trafalgar Rd, Kingston 10.
**Methodist Ch in Jamaica,** 2B Braemar Av, Kingston 10.
**Moravian Ch in Jamaica,** Pres, 3 Hector St, Kingston 5.
**Open Bible Standard Chs of Jamaica,** Field Super, Box 142, HWT, Kingston 10.
**Pentecostal Ch of God,** PO Box 177, Mandeville.
**Religious Society of Friends,** Jamaica Yearly Meeting of Friends, 11 Caledonia Av, Kingston 5.
**Salvation Army,** Corner King St & North Parade, PO Box 153, Kingston. T: 932-3351.
**Seventh-day Adventist Ch,** Pres, PO Box 22, Mandeville. T: 962-2284.
**United Ch of Jamaica & Grand Cayman,** Moderator, 24 Hagley Park Plaza, Kingston 10.

*JAPAN*
**Catholic Ch in Japan,** Archbishop's House, Sekiguchi, 3-chome, 16-15, Bunkyo-ku, Tokyo 112. T: (03)943-2301.
**Christian Brotherhood Ch,** Dir, 448, Tabata-cho, Kita-ku, Tokyo 114. T: (03)821-0210.
**Christian Canaan Ch,** Dir, 1-36 Higashi, Kushiyamachi, Sakai-shi, Osaka 590. T: (0722)23345.
**Christian Ch of the Glorious Gospel,** Dir, Uchinomaki, Asomachi, Agogun, Kumamoto-ken 869-12. T: Aso 20303.
**Christian Chs & Chs of Christ,** 7-8, 3-chome, Higashi-Nakano, Nakano-ku, Tokyo. T: (03)361-0533.
**Ch of Christ in Japan (Presbyterian and Reformed),** Moderator, 14-10, 3-chome, Tsurumaki, Setagaya-ku, Tokyo 154. T: (03)420-7047.
**Ch of Jesus Christ of Latter-day Saints,** Japan Mission, 5-8-10 Minami Azabu, Minato-ku, Tokyo 106. T: (03)442-7438.
**Conservative Baptist Association of Chs,** Moderator, 3-26, 2-chome, Higashihara-cho, Yamagata-shi 990. T: (02362)24789.
**Ev Alliance Mission,** Dir, 15-15, 3-chome, Daisawa, Setagaya-ku, Tokyo 155. T: (03)413-2345.
**Free Methodist Ch of Japan,** Moderator, 3-61, 1-chome, Maruyama-dori, Abendo-ku, Osaka-shi 545. T: (06)652-2091.
**Holy Jesus Society,** Dir, 3-880 Totsuka-machi, Shinjuku-ku, Tokyo 160. T: (03)368-8278.
**Holy Orthodox Ch of Japan,** Nikorai-Do, 1-3, 4-chome, Surugadai, Kanda, Chiyoda-ku, Tokyo. T: (03)291-1885.
**Holy Spirit Association for the Unification of World Christianity,** 1-1-2 Shoto, Shibuya-ku, Tokyo. T: (03)467-6161.
**Immanuel General Mission,** Shin Kokusai Bldg, 3-4 Marunouchi, Chiyoda-ku, Tokyo 10. T: (03) 211-2789.
**Japan Alliance Ch,** 255 Itsukaichi-cho, Saekigun, PO Box 70, Hiroshima-ken 738. T: (0829)212514.
**Japan Apostolic Mission,** Tawaraguchi, Ikoma-cho, Nara-ken. T: (907437)3821.
**Japan Assemblies of God,** 20-15-3 San chome, Komagome, Toshima-ku, Tokyo 170. T: (03)918-5935.
**Japan Baptist Convention,** 350, 2-chome, Nishi Okubo, Shinjuku-ku, Tokyo 160. T: (03)351-2166.
**Japan Ch of Jesus Christ,** 1-22, 1-chome, Takamaru, Tarumi-ku, Kobe-shi 655. T: (078)765689.
**Japan Ch of the Nazarene,** 237 Oyama-cho, Tamagawa, Setagaya-ku, Tokyo. T: (03)466-2416.
**Japan Free Religious Association,** Seisoku High School, 21 Shiba Park, Minato-ku, Tokyo 105. T: (03)431-0914.
**Japan Holiness Ch,** Megurit, Higashimurayama-shi, Tokyo.
**Japan Holy Catholic Ch (NSKK),** 1-4-21 Higashi, Shibuya-ku, Tokyo. T: (03)400-2314.
**Japan Jesus Christ Ch,** 130 Aio Machi 1 chome, Akashi-shi.
**Japan Lutheran Ch (Missouri Synod),** Super, 2-32, 1-chome, Fujimi-cho, Chiyoda-ku, Tokyo. T: (03)261-5266/7.
**Japan Union Mission of Seventh-day Adventists,** Pres, 846 Kami Kawai-cho, Hodogaya-ku, Yokohama-shi 241. T: (045)951-2421.
**Japan United Pentecostal Ch,** Super, 365 Kamigamo Honzan, Kita-ku, Kyoto-shi 603. T: (075)791-4887.
**Jehovah's Witnesses,** 5-5-8 Mita Minato-ku, Tokyo 108.
**Kinki Ev Lutheran Ch,** 420 Kamisumiyoshi-cho, Sumiyoshi-ku, Manato PO Box 32, Osaka 552. T: (06)691-4398.
**Korea Christian Ch in Japan,** 24 Wakamiya-cho, Shinjuku-ku, Tokyo 162. T: (03)269-2909.
**Living Water Christian Ch,** Sawai 406, 2-chome, Odawara-shi, Kanagawa-ken.
**Original Gospel (Tabernacle Movement),** Dir, 5-35 Yoyogi, Shibuya-ku, Tokyo 151. T: (03)466-1558.
**Reformed Ch in Japan,** Moderator, 5-20 Shimo-dori, Shibuya-ku, Tokyo 150. T: (03)461-4614.
**Salvation Army in Japan,** 13 Ichigaya, Honmuracho, Shinjuku-ku, Tokyo 162. T: (03)260-4941/5.
**Spirit of Jesus Ch,** 3-152 Ogikubo, Suginami-ku, Tokyo 167. T: (03)391-5925.
**Swedish Free Mission,** 2-122 Iwama-cho, Hodogaya-ku, Yokohama-shi 240. T: (045)331-0643.
**True Jesus Ch in Japan,** Gen Sec 1-15 Naka Kagaya-cho, Sumiyoshi-ku, Osaka-shi 558.
**United Ch of Christ in Japan (UCCJ),** Moderatori Japan Christian Centre, Room 31, 551 Totsukamach, 1-chome, Shinjuku-ku, Tokyo 160. T: (03)561-6131.

*JORDAN*
**Catholic Ch in Jordan,** Archevêché Melkite, PO Box 2435, Jabal-Amman. T: 24757.
**Episcopal Ch in Jerusalem & the Middle East,** PO Box 598, Amman.
**Jordan Baptist Convention,** PO Box 10, Ajloun.
**Seventh-day Adventist Ch,** Pres, PO Box 2404, Amman. T: 25345.

*KAMPUCHEA*
**Eglise Catholique au Cambodge,** Evêché, 69 Blvd Prachea Thippatei, Phnom-Penh. T: 24904.
**Eglise Ev Khmère,** 72 Preah Bat Norodom, BP 545, Phnom Penh. T: 24319.

*KENYA*
**Africa Gospel Ch (AGC),** PO Box 123, Kericho. T: 123.
**Africa Inland Ch (AIC),** Ziwani Church Office, PO Box 13024, Nairobi. T: 25149.

**African Brotherhood Ch (ABC),** Bp, HQ Mitaboni, PO Box 32, Machakos.
**African Christian Ch & Schools (ACCS),** Gen Sec, ACC & S Church, Gituru, PO Box 291, Thika.
**African Independent Pentecostal Ch of Africa (AIPCA),** Bp, PO Box 28133, Nairobi. (Also: PO Box 255, Ruiru).
**African Interior Ch,** Ebunangwe, Bunyore, PO Box 106, Maragoli.
**African Israel Ch Nineveh (AICN),** HQ Nineveh (17 miles north of Kisumu), PO Box 701, Kisumu.
**African Orthodox Ch of Kenya,** Archbp, Valley Rd, PO Box 46119, Nairobi. T: 28804.
**Assemblies of God,** Kenya District Council, PO Box 492, Kakamega.
**Baptist Convention of Kenya,** Kariobangi Baptist Church, PO Box 20312, Nairobi.
**Catholic Ch in Kenya,** Catholic Secretariat, Westlands Shopping Centre, PO Box 48062, Nairobi. T: 44302
**Ch of Christ in Africa (CCA),** Bp, Dala Hera, Kibos Rd, PO Box 782, Kisumu. T: 2536.
**Ch of God in East Africa,** Kima Station, PO Box 160, Maseno.
**Ch of the Province of Kenya (CPK),** Archbp, Imani House, St John's Gate, PO Box 40502, Nairobi. T: 28146.
**Deliverance Ch,** Penguin House, Tom Mboya St, PO Box 28600, Nairobi. T: 20500.
**East Africa Pentecostal Chs,** PO Box 245, Meru.
**East Africa Yearly Meeting of Friends (EAYM),** Kaimosi Mission, PO Box 10035, Tiriki. T: RN 2047.
**Episcopal Ch of Africa,** Bp, Ondiek Estate, PO Box 1573, Kisumu.
**Ev Lutheran Ch in Tanzania (Kenya Synod),** PO Box 72772, Nairobi.
**Full Gospel Chs of Kenya (FGCK),** PO Box 5, Koru. T: 11.
**Good News Ch of Africa,** PO Box 72708, Nairobi.
**Holy Trinity Ch in Africa,** Bp, PO Box 160, Kisumu.
**Jehovah's Witnesses,** Kingdom Hall, Woodlands Rd, PO Box 47788, Nairobi. T: 24905.
**Kenya Foundation of the Prophets Ch,** Ithiru, Gatanga Location, Kandara Division, PO Box 223, Thika.
**Lost Israelites of Kenya,** Prophet of God, Kimilili Kamalewa, Bondeni, PO Box 699, Kitale.
**Lutheran Ch in Kenya,** Itierio Mission, PO Box 50, Kisii.
**Maria Legio of Africa,** Holy Father, Mount Zion, Kalafari (Calvary), Got Kwer, Suna Location, PO Box 70, Kisii.
**Methodist Ch in Kenya,** Presiding Bp, St Andrew's Church, St Andrew's Rd, PO Box 47633, Nairobi. T: 24841.
**Nomiya Luo Ch (NLC),** Archbp, Diocese of Oboch, PO Box 1283, Kisumu.
**Norwegian Pentecostal Mission in Kenya,** Nyambare Hill, PO Box 15, Ukwala.
**Pentecostal Assemblies of God (PAG),** Nyang'ori, PO Box 671, Kisumu. T: Nyang'ori Y4.
**Pentecostal Evangelistic Fellowship of Africa (PEFA),** Elim Church, Jomo Kenyatta Av, PO Box 82627, Mombasa. T: 26132.
**Power of Jesus Around the World Ch,** PO Box 1588, Kisumu.
**Presbyterian Ch of East Africa (PCEA),** St Andrew's Church, Nyerere Rd, PO Box 48268, Nairobi. T: 25095.
**Salvation Army,** Moi Av, PO Box 40575, Nairobi. T: 27541/2.
**Seventh-day Adventist Ch,** Pres, Invergara Grove, off Bernard Rd, PO Box 42276, Nairobi. T: 66025.
**Spirit Ch of God of Israel,** Ibwali Mission, Jemuguni Village, Tiriki, PO Box 246, Kisumu.

*KIRIBATI*
**Catholic Ch,** Bishop's House, PO Box 79, Tarawa.
**Ch of God,** Eita Village, Tarawa.
**Gilbert Islands Protestant Ch,** Church Office, Antebuka, Tarawa.
**Seventh-day Adventist Ch,** Super, Bairiki, Tarawa.

*KOREA, South*
**Bible Presbyterian Ch of Korea,** Moderator, Tondong 1-Ga 22, Soul.
**Catholic Ch in Korea,** Archbishop's House, 2Ka-1 Myeong Dong, Jung Ku, Soul 100. T: 7764083.
**Ch of Jesus Christ of Latter-day Saints,** Korea Mission, 7 Chongun Dong, Chongno Ku, PO Box 210, Kwang Hwa Moon, Soul.
**Ev Alliance Mission in Korea,** 24-3 Yunhi Dong, Sudaimoon Ku, IPO Box 2673, Soul 100. T: 327190.
**Holy Spirit Association for the Unification of World Christianity,** 71-3, 1-GA Chungpa-Dong, Yongsam-Gu, Soul.
**Jehovah's Witnesses,** 65-19, 2-Ka Ch'ungchong, Sudaimoon, Soul.
**Jesus Korean Holiness Ch,** 12 Mukyo Dong, Chung Ku, Soul.
**Jesus Korean Methodist Ch,** 1-64 Chong-P'a Dong 1-Ka, Yonsan Ku, Soul.
**Korea Baptist Bible Fellowship,** 267-9 Haengdang Dong, Songdong Ku, Soul.
**Korea Baptist Convention,** Dong Ja Dong 18-7, Soul. (Also: 55-5 Ka Choong Moo Ro, Soul).
**Korea Ch of Christ (Instrumental),** 5-198, Hyo-ch'ang Dong, Yongsan Ku, Soul.
**Korean Christian Assemblies of God,** 90-21 Ch'ung Chongno 1-Ka, Sudaimoon Ku, Soul.
**Korean Methodist Ch,** 64-8 Chung-Ku, Taepyongno 1-Ka, KPO Box 285, Soul.
**Korean Nazarene Ch,** 7-2 Hyonjo Dong, Sudaimoon Ku, Soul.
**Koryo Presbyterian Ch,** 34 Amnam Dong, So-Ku, Pusan.
**Presbyterian Ch in the ROK,** 69-23 Chung Chongno 2-Ka, Sudaimoon Ku, Soul.
**Presbyterian Ch of Korea,** 136-46 Yunji Dong, Chongno Ku, PO Box 335, Soul.
**Salvation Army,** 1-23 Chong Dong, Sudaemon Ku, Soul. T: 756986.
**Seventh-day Adventist Church,** Pres, 66 Hoiki-dong, Tong-dai-moon-ku, PO Box 1243, Soul. T: 960071/2.
**True Jesus Ch,** Korea Assembly, 95-14 Hoiki Dong, Tongdaimoon Ku, Soul.

*KUWAIT*
**Catholic Ch,** Bishop's House, PO Box 266, Kuwait. T: 434637.

*LAOS*
**Eglise Catholique au Laos,** Mission Catholique, Vientiane. T: 3229.
**Eglise Ev du Laos,** BP 615, Saphangmo, Vientiane. T: 3552.
**Mission Ev,** BP 3, Vientiane.

*LEBANON*
**Ancient Ch of the East,** Diocese of Beirut, PO Box 3625, Bayrut. T: 263362.
**Armenian Apostolic Ch,** Catholicos, Catholicate of Cilicia, Antelias. T: 410003. (Winter residence) (Summer: Couvent Arménien Apostolique, Bikfaya (Amrieh). T: 980060).
**Assemblies of God,** PO Box 3204 & 5724, Bayrut.
**Catholic Ch in Lebanon,** Maronite Patriarch, Rue Collège de la Sagesse, Bayrut. T: 334829. (Winter residence: Bkerké. T: 390011; summer residence: Diman, Liban Nord. T: Hasroun 7).
**Coptic Orthodox Ch,** Furn el Chebbak, Bayrut. T: 284948.
**Ch of God,** Pres, Rue Madraset el Salam (Achrafieh), Bayrut. T: 321566.
**Episcopal Ch in Jerusalem & Middle East,** All Saints Ch, Av des Français, Zeitouné, PO Box 2211 & 4008, Bayrut. T: 255233,342598.
**Ev Ch of the Nazarene,** Super, Achrafieh, Sioufi, PO Box 2328, Bayrut. T: 328342.
**Greek Orthodox Patriarchate of Antioch,** Archevêché, Rue Sursock, PO Box 186, Bayrut. T: 226281. (Winter residence) (Summer residence: Souk El-Gharb. T: 675013).
**Jehovah's Witnesses,** PO Box 1122, Bayrut.
**Lebanese Baptist Convention,** PO Box 4014, Bayrut. T: 342542.
**National Ev Christian Alliance Ch,** Rue Abdel Aziz, Ras Beyrouth, PO Box 3276, Bayrut. T: 304829.
**National Ev Ch of Beirut,** Sec Gen, Rue l'Eglise Evangélique (Zkak el Blat), PO Box 5224, Bayrut. T: 227175.
**National Ev Synod of Syria & Lebanon,** Pres, Rue Zkak el Blat, PO Box 235, Bayrut. T: 229503, 232563,770026.
**Seventh-day Adventist Ch,** Pres, Sayar, Hotel Dieu St, PO Box 3715 (also 2020), Bayrut. T: 226535, 264356.
**Syrian Orthodox Ch,** Archevêché, Moussaitbé 246, Bayrut. T: 303373. (Winter residence) (Summer residence: Couvent St Georges des Syriens Orthodoxes, Rue Midane, Zahle. T: 820588).
**Union of Armenian Ev Chs in the Near East,** Rue Zkak el Blat, PO Box 235 & 377, Bayrut. T: 227101.

*LESOTHO*
**African Methodist Episcopal Ch,** Bishop's Mission, PO Box 223 & 98, Maseru.
**Anglican Ch in Lesotho,** Bp, Bishop's House, PO Box 87 & 127, Maseru.
**Assemblies of God in Lesotho,** PO Box 130, Maseru.
**Catholic Ch in Lesotho,** Archbishop's House, PO Box 267, Maseru. T:22565.
**Lesotho Ev Ch,** Gen Sec, PO Box 260, Maseru.
**Methodist Ch of South Africa,** PO Box 81, Maseru.
**St Paul's Ch of Africa,** Cardinal, Lefihlile Mission, PO Box 436, Maseru.
**Seventh-day Adventist Ch,** Pres, PO Box 714, Maseru.

*LIBERIA*
**African Methodist Episcopal Ch,** St Mark's Church, Newport St, PO Box 161, Monrovia.
**African Methodist Episcopal Zion Ch,** Bp, PO Box 169, Monrovia.
**Bafu Bay Ch,** Sinoe County, Juarzon.
**Catholic Ch in Liberia,** Catholic Mission, PO Box 297, Monrovia. T: 21399.
**Ch of the Lord (Aladura),** Bp, 22 Center St, PO Box 467, Monrovia.
**ELWA Chapels,** SIM, Radio ELWA, PO Box 192, Monrovia.
**Episcopal Ch of Liberia,** Bp, Chase Manhattan Bldg, Rendall St, PO Box 277, Monrovia. T: 21065.
**Free Protestant Episcopal Ch (Ecumenical Church Foundation),** Diocese of West Africa, Gen Synod Sec, 28 Perry St, PO Box 361, Monrovia.
**Jehovah's Witnesses,** PO Box 171, Monrovia.
**Liberia Assemblies of God,** Brewerville, PO Box 37, Monrovia.
**Liberian Baptist Convention,** PO Box 390 & 1416, Monrovia.
**Lighthouse Fellowship of Chs,** Mother Blatch, Benson St, Monrovia.
**Lutheran Ch in Liberia,** Bp, PO Box 1046, Monrovia. T: 26058.
**Pentecostal Assemblies of the World,** PO Box 1073, Monrovia.
**Presbytery of Liberia in West Africa,** Stated Clerk, PO Box 1957, Monrovia.
**Seventh-day Adventist Ch,** Pres, PO Box 52, Monrovia. T: 21057,26041.
**United Liberia Inland Ch,** PO Box 26, Monrovia. T: 21839.
**United Methodist Ch of Liberia,** Bp, 57 Ashmun St, PO Box 1010, Monrovia.
**United Pentecostal Ch of Liberia,** Sec, Corner Tubman Blvd & Spriggs Payne Rd, PO Box 44, Monrovia.

*LIBYA*
**Catholic Ch in Libya,** PO Box 365, Tarabulus. T: 31863.
**Seventh-day Adventist Ch,** PO Box 240, Banghazi.

*LIECHTENSTEIN*
**Ev-Lutherische Kirche,** Pastor, 9490 Vaduz-Barte-grosch. T: (075)22515.

*LUXEMBOURG*
**Communauté des Protestants** CECA, Pfarrer, Av Gaston-Diderich 35, Luxembourg-ville.
**Eglise Catholique,** Evêché, CP 419, Luxembourg. T: 42023.
**Eglise Néo-Apostolique,** 200 Rue de Rollingergrund, Luxembourg. T: 29402.
**Eglise Protestante du Canton d'Esch,** Esch-sur Alzette. T: 52384.
**Eglise Protestante du Grand-Duché de Luxembourg,** Consistoire, Rue de la Congrégation, Luxembourg-ville. T: 29670.
**Mission Intérieure au Luxembourg,** Prés, 105 Rue Ernest Beres, Luxembourg-ville.
**Témoins de Jéhovah,** 15 Rue de l'Egalité, Luxembourg-Bonnevoie.

*MACAO*
**Igreja Católica,** Bispado, Largo da Sé, CP 324, Macau. T: 3058.

*MADAGASCAR*
**Eglise Adventiste du Septième Jour,** Prés, Soamanadrariny, Canton Ambohimangakely, BP 700, Tananarive. T: 40465.
**Eglise Apostolique de Madagascar,** Prés, Andohatapenaka, Tananarive.
**Eglise Baptiste Biblique à Madagascar (FBMB),** Prés, Lot 11 L 10 bis, BP 351, Tananarive.
**Eglise Catholique au Madagascar,** Conférence Episcopale, 102 bis Av Maréchal Joffre, BP 667, Antanimena, Tananarive. T: 20726.
**Eglise de Jésus-Christ à Madagascar (FJKM),** Prés, Imarivolanitra, BP 623, Tananarive.
**Eglise du Réveil des Disciples du Seigneur,** Prés, Soatanana, Canton Isandra, BP 1072, Fianarantsoa.
**Eglise Episcopale de Madagascar,** Evêché Anglican, Ambohimanoro, Tananarive.
**Eglise Luthérienne Malgache (FLM),** Prés, BP 1061, Fianarantsoa. T: 149.
**Eglise Pentecôtiste en Madagascar (FPM),** BP 1113, Tananarive.
**Eglise Protestante Malgache (FMTA),** Dir, VB-48 Lalana Amiral Pierre, Tananarive. T: 21124.
**Eglise Réformée Ev de Madagascar (MET),** 25 VK Ambohimanobo, Tananarive.
**Témoins de Jéhovah,** 11 M 78 A Antsakaviro, Tananarive.

*MALAWI*
**Africa Ev Ch of Malawi,** Chididi, PO Box 14, Nsanje. (Also: Box 136, Blantyre).
**African Methodist Episcopal Ch,** Box 29, Kasungu. T: 200243.
**Anglican Ch in Malawi,** Malosa, P/A Chilema, Zomba.
**Apostolic Ch of Pentecost of Malawi,** PO Box 2, Mponela. (Also: Box 929, Blantyre. T: 33675).
**Assemblies of God in Malawi,** PO Box 5749, Limbe. (Also: Box 30064, Chichiri, Blantyre 3. T: 31003).
**Baptist Mission of Central Africa,** PO Box 94, Limbe.
**Catholic Ch in Malawi,** Catholic Secretariat, PO Box 5368, Limbe. T: 33905.
**Ch of Central Africa Presbyterian,** Blantyre Synod, PO Box 413, Blantyre. T: 30977.
**Ch of the Nazarene in Malawi,** Field Sec, PO Box 566, Limbe.
**Chs of Christ,** Gowa, PO Mlangeni (PO Ntcheu).
**Ev Ch of Malawi,** PO Box 13, Cholo.
**Pentecostal Holiness Association,** PO Box 30, Chitipa. (Also: Box 557, Blantyre. T: 33367,34115).
**Providence Industrial Mission,** PO Box 6, Chiradzulu.
**Seventh Day Baptist Ch,** Central Africa Conference, Gen Sec, PO Box 337, Blantyre. T: 33653.
**Seventh-day Adventist Ch,** Pres, Robins Rd, Kabula Hill, PO Box 926, Blantyre. T: 33522.
**Zambezi Ev Ch,** PO Box 216, Blantyre.

*MALAYSIA*
**Anglican Ch of Malaysia,** Diocese of West Malaysia, Bp, 14 Pesiaran Stonor, Kuala Lumpur.
**Assemblies of God,** 99 Jalan Gasing, Petaling Jaya, Kuala Lumpur, Selangor.
**Catholic Ch in Malaysia,** Bishop's House, N528 Bukit Nanas, Kuala Lumpur 0401. T: (03)85089.
**Ev Ch of Borneo,** Lawas, Sarawak, via Labuan, East Malaysia.
**Ev Lutheran Ch in Malaysia,** Bp, No 1 Rd 11/4, Petaling Jaya, Kuala Lumpur, Selangor.
**Lutheran Ch in Malaysia & Singapore,** PO Box 747, Kuala Lumpur, Selangor.
**Malaysia-Singapore Baptist Convention,** 86 Lim Lean Teng Rd, Penang.
**Presbyterian Ch in Malaysia,** 50 Jalan Junid, Muar.
**Presbyterian Ch in Singapore & Malaysia,** Parit Java, Muar, Johor, West Malaysia.
**Protestant Ch in Sabah,** PO Box 378, Kota Kinabalu, Sabah.
**Seventh-day Adventist Ch,** Pres, 166-A Jalan Bukit Bintang, Kuala Lumpur, Selangor.

*MALI*
**Eglise Catholique au Mali,** Archevêché, BP 298, Bamako. T: 225499.
**Eglise Chrétienne Ev du Mali,** BP 19, Koutiala.
**Eglise Ev Protestante au Mali,** Mission Protestante, Av de la Nation, BP 158, Bamako.
**Eglise Protestante de Kayes,** Mission Protestante, BP 51, Kayes.

*MALTA*
**Catholic Ch in Malta,** Archbishop's Curia, Palace, Valetta. T: 625943.
**Ch of Scotland,** St Andrew's Church, South St, Valetta.
**Gospel Hall,** 6 Filippo Sceberras Square, Floriana.
**Greek Orthodox Ch,** St George's Church, 83 Merchants St, Valetta.

*MARTINIQUE*
**Eglise Adventiste du Septième Jour,** Route de Schoelcher 2 Km 100, BP 580, Fort-de-France. T: 3289.
**Eglise Catholique,** Archevêché, Route Didier, BP 586, 97207 Fort-de-France. T: 717070.

*MAURITANIA*
**Eglise Catholique,** Evêché, BP 353, Nouakchott. T: 2515.

*MAURITIUS*
**Anglican Ch,** Diocese of Mauritius, Bp, Bishop's House, Phoenix.
**Catholic Ch,** Evêché, Rue Mgr Gonin, Port-Louis. T: 23068.
**Jehovah's Witnesses,** 106A Prince of Wales St, Rose Hill.
**Seventh-day Adventist Ch,** Pres, 10 Salisbury St, PO Box 18, Rose Hill. T: 42167.

*MEXICO*
**Asambleas de Dios de México,** Calle Nicolas Leon No 118, Colonia Jardin Balvuena, México 8, DF.
**Asociación de Iglesias Cristianas Ev en México (Discipulos de Cristo),** Sec, Hospitalidad 137, Apdo 351, Aguascalientes.
**Bando Evangelistico Gedeón,** Calle San Antonio, Manzana 513, lote 5, Colonia Santa Ursula, México 22, DF.
**Concilio Latino-Americano de Iglesias Cristianas,** Promiente 94-B No 26, San Francisco Xocotitla, México 4, DF.
**Convención Nacional Bautista de México,** Pres, 16 de Septiembre No 6-401, México 1, DF.
**Ejército de Salvación,** Sec Divisional, Bucareli 53-22, Apdo 5-410, México 6, DF. T: 5356248, 5351862.
**Iglesia Adventista del Séptimo Día,** Pres, Uxmal 365, Colonia Narvarte, Apdo 12-710, México 12, DF. T: 5237973,5430993.
**Iglesia Apostólica de la Fe en Cristo Jesús,** Obispo Pres, Apdo 18-1000, México 2, DF.
**Iglesia Católica en México,** Arzobispado, Apdo Postal 1-331, Guadalajara, Jalisco. T: 257101.
**Iglesia Cristiana Interdenominacional,** Reform y Libertad 27, Esq con Reforma, Col San Simon, Portales, México 13, DF.
**Iglesia Cristiana Unida,** Super, Prol Matias Romero 218, México 12, DF.
**Iglesia de Dios de la Profecía,** Manuel Jose Othron 98, Col Obrera, México 8, DF.
**Iglesia de Dios en la República Mexicana,** Obispo, Calzada de Guadalupe 214, México 14, DF. T: 5371834.
**Iglesia de Dios (Evangelio Completo),** Super Nacional, Apdo 67-566, México 2, DF.
**Iglesia de Jesucristo de los Santos de los Altimos Dias,** Monte Caucaso 1110, Lomas de Chatulpepec, México 10, DF.
**Iglesia del Evangelio Cuadrangular,** Canamea No 1443 Nte, Col Pablo de la Garza, Apdo 425, Monterrey, NL.
**Iglesia del Nazareno en México,** Apdo 1077, Guadalajara, Jalisco.
**Iglesia Episcopal Mexicana,** Obispo, Av San Jeronimo 117, México 20, DF.
**Iglesia Ev de los Hermanos Libres,** Sec, Centro Evangélico, Calle Rojas 5, Col San Simon Tolnahuac, México 3, DF.
**Iglesia Ev de los Peregrinos,** Apdo 144, Cd Valles, San Luis Potosí.
**Iglesia Menonita,** Correo No 256-2, México 13, DF.
**Iglesia Metodista de México,** Obispo, Calzada México-Coyoacan 349, México 13, DF.
**Iglesia Nacional Presbiteriana de México,** Sec Perm, Apdo 20430, Arenal 40, México 20, DF.
**Iglesia Ortodoxa Católica Apostólica Mexicana,** Archbp, San Antonio Abad 18, México 8, DF.
**Iglesia Presbiteriana Asociada Reformada,** Pres, Fes 1 Madero No 43, Nte Cd Valles, Apdo 25, San Luis Potosí.
**Iglesias de Cristo,** 13 de Septiembre No 26 Col Condesa, Apdo 32482, México 7, DF.
**Misión Evangelistica Mexicana,** Apdo 647, Chihuahua.
**Movimiento Iglesias Ev Pentecostales Independientes (MIEPI),** Pres, Carretones 123, Apdo 9304, México 1, DF.
**Testigos de Jehová,** Calzada Melchor Ocampo 71, México 4, DF.
**Union de Iglesias Ev Independientes (Iglesia Cristana Independiente Pentecostés),** Pedro Ma Anaya 10, Pachuac, Hidalgo.
**Unión de Iglesias Ev Mexicanas,** Gen Dir, Apdo 18, Tamazunchole, San Luis Potosí.

*MONACO*
**Eglise Catholique,** Evêché, 1 Rue de l'Abbaye, Monaco. T: (93)308813.

*MOROCCO*
**Assemblées de Dieu,** Calle 7, Rue Josafat 110, Dpt 14, BP 391, Tanger.
**Eglise Catholique au Maroc,** Archevêché, 1 Rue Abou Inane, BP 258, Rabat. T: 22534.
**Eglise Chrétienne de Réveil,** Mission Ev, 24bis Av de Pont-à-Mousson, El-Dar-el-Beida (Casablanca).
**Eglise Ev au Maroc,** 33 Rue d'Azilal, El-Dar-el-Beida (Casablanca).
**Mission d'Afrique du Nord** (Mr. S. Smithwaite), BP 75, Tétouan.

*MOZAMBIQUE*
**Assembleias de Deus Pentecostales,** 1680 Qu Pinheiro Chegas (& 29a Av Latino Coelho), Maputo.
**Igreja Adventista do Setima Dia,** CP 1468, 453 Av 24 Julho, Maputo. T: 742868.
**Igreja Anglicana,** Diocese of Lebombo, Bp, CP 120, Maputo.
**Igreja Católica em Moçambique,** Paço Arquiepiscopal, Av Eduardo Mondlane 1448, CP 258, Maputo. T: 26240.
**Igreja Congregacional Unida de Moçambique,** Chamanculo, CP 930, Maputo.
**Igreja de Cristo em Manica e Sofala,** CP 396, Beira.

**Igreja de Nazareno,** 4 Rua Dr Angelo Fereira, CP 410, Maputo.
**Igreja Metodista Livre,** Nyamchafu Mission, Inharrime.
**Igreja Metodista Unida,** Bispo, CP 45, Inhambane.
**Igreja Presbiteriana de Moçambique,** Sec, Mission Suisse, CP 21, Maputo.
**Missão Baptista Escandinava,** CP 599, Maputo.
**Missão Metodista Wesleyana,** CP 724, Maputo.

*NAMIBIA*
**Anglican Ch,** Diocese of Damaraland, Bp, PO Box 57, Windhoek.
**Catholic Ch in Namibia,** PO Box 272, Windhoek 9100. T: 22220.
**Christian Reformed Ch (NHK),** Sek, 62 Bismarck St, PO Box 1318, Windhoek.
**Dutch Reformed Church Mission in SWA,** 44 Trift St, PO Box 389, Windhoek.
**Ev Lutheran Ch in SWA,** Präs, PO Box 21 & 5069, Windhoek. T: 6775.
**Ev Lutheran Ovambokavango Ch,** Bp, Oniipa, PB 2015, Ondangwa, Ovamboland.
**German Ev Lutheran Ch in SWA,** Sek, PO Box 233, Windhoek.
**Methodist Ch of South Africa,** Minister, PO Box 143, Windhoek.
**Reformed Ch,** Sek, 6 Hügelstrasse, PO Box 981, Windhoek.

*NEPAL*
**Unitarian Universalist Association of Kathmandu,** Organizer, 18/55 Maharaj Gunj, Panipokhari, Kathmandu.

*NETHERLANDS*
**Assemblies of God,** Scheveningseweg 11, 's-Gravenhage. T: (070)642540.
**Association of Free Ev Congregations,** Vogelkersstraat 44, Leeuwarden. T: (05100)25535.
**Catholic Ch in the Netherlands,** Nederlandse Bisschoppen Konferentie, Biltstraat 121, Postbus 13049, Utrecht. T: (030)316956.
**Christian Reformed Chs in the Netherlands,** Anna Paulownalaan 17, Apeldoorn.
**Ev Lutheran Ch in the Netherlands,** Sec, Velperweg 156, Arnhem. T: (085)437426.
**Greek Orthodox Ch,** Stadhoudersplein 140b, Rotterdam. T: (010)248010.
**Jehovah's Witnesses,** Voorburgstraat 250, Amsterdam 17.
**Mennonite Brotherhood,** Bureau ADS, Singel 454, Amsterdam-C. T: (020)230914.
**Moluccan Protestant Ch in the Netherlands,** Bazarstraat 50, 's-Gravenhage.
**Moravian Ch in the Netherlands,** Broederplein 33, Zeist. T: (03404)12213.
**Netherlands Reformed Ch,** Sec-Gen, Carnegielaan 9, 's-Gravenhage-3A. T: (070)653915.
**New Apostolic Ch in the Netherlands,** Sec, Henri Polakstraat 36, Amsterdam.
**Old Catholic Ch in the Netherlands,** Sec, Bagijnhof 25, Delft.
**Old Reformed Chs,** Scriba, Heereweg 4, Lisse. T: (02530)3158.
**Protestant Union of the Netherlands,** Nieuwe Gracht 27, Utrecht 2501. T: (030)25228.
**Reformed Chs in the Netherlands,** Dir, Koningslaan 11, Utrecht. T: (030)510441.
**Reformed Chs (Liberated),** Sec, Wilhelminastraat 9, Assen.
**Reformed Communities in the Netherlands,** Sec, Prins Mauritsstraat 6, Gouda.
**Remonstrant Brotherhood,** Nieuwe Gracht 23, Utrecht. T: (030)316970.
**Restored Apostolic Missionary Ch,** Blauwburgwal 20, Amsterdam.
**Russian Orthodox Ch in the Netherlands,** Pastorie Sweelinckstraat 54, 's-Gravenhage. T: (070)320435.
**Salvation Army,** Damstraat 13, Amsterdam-C. T: (020)241703.
**Seventh-day Adventist Ch,** Biltseweg 14, Bosch en Duin, Postbus 61, 's-Gravenhage. T: (030)784280.
**Streams of Power Movement,** Eemnesserweg 44a, Baarn.
**Union of Baptist Chs in the Netherlands,** Biltseweg 10, Bilthoven. T: (030)784823,(08300) 23007.

*NETHERLANDS ANTILLES*
**Catholic Ch,** Breedestraat 31, Willemstad, Curaçao. T: 25876.
**Jehovah's Witnesses,** Oosterbeekstraat 11, Willemstad, Curaçao.
**Salvation Army,** Hoogstr 18, PO Box 2143 Otrabauda, Willemstad, Curaçao. T: 23450.
**Seventh-day Adventist Ch,** Pres, De Ruyterkade No 60, PO Box 300, Willemstad, Curaçao. T: 12917.
**United Protestant Ch of Curaçao,** Fort Amsterdam, Barentslaan 11, Willemstad, Curaçao.

*NEW CALEDONIA*
**Assemblées de Dieu de Nouméa,** PO Box 296, Nouméa.
**Eglise Adventiste du Septième Jour,** Prés, 17 Rue RP Gaudet, Vallée des Colons, BP 149, Nouméa. T: 4779.
**Eglise Catholique,** Archevêché, BP 3, Nouméa. T: 273149.
**Eglise Ev en Nouvelle Caledonie et aux Iles Loyauté,** Blvd Vauban, BP 277, Nouméa.

*NEW ZEALAND*
**Apostolic Ch of Australia & NZ,** Apostolic House, 72 Webb St, Wellington.
**Assemblies of God in New Zealand,** PO Box 91, Kumeu. T: Auckland 412-8832.
**Associated Chs of Christ in New Zealand,** Gen Sec, PO Box 30516, Lower Hutt.
**Baptist Union of New Zealand,** Gen Sec, PO Box 6212, Wellington.
**Catholic Ch in New Zealand,** Chancery Office, 152 Brougham St, PO Box 198, Wellington 1. T: 721189.
**Ch of Jesus Christ of Latter-day Saints,** New Zealand North Mission, 48 Arney Rd, PO Box 72, Auckland 1.
**Ch of the Province of New Zealand,** Provincial Sec, PO Box 800, Christchurch.
**Congregational Christian Ch of Samoa in New Zealand,** Sec, 75 Preston Rd, Otara.
**Congregational Union of New Zealand,** Sec, 28 Wright St, Wellington.
**Greek Orthodox Archdiocese of New Zealand,** Metropolitan, Courtenay Place, PO Box 9361, Wellington.
**Jehovah's Witnesses,** NZ Watchtower Society, 621 New North Rd, Auckland 3.
**Lutheran Ch of NZ,** Sec, 7 Holdsworthy Rd, New Plymouth.
**Methodist Ch in New Zealand,** Gen Sec, PO Box 931, Christchurch.
**Presbyterian Ch of New Zealand,** Convenor, 116 St John's Rd, Meadowbank, Auckland 5.
**Ratana Ch,** Sec, Temple, Ratana Pa.
**Reformed Chs of New Zealand,** Stated Clerk, 141 Wallace Rd, Mangere Bridge, Auckland.
**Ringatu Ch,** PO Omaio, East Coast.
**Russian Orthodox Ch Outside of Russia,** 38 Park Av, Waikanae.
**Salvation Army,** Territorial HQ, 204 Cuba St, PO Box 6015, Wellington. T: 555649.
**Seventh-day Adventist Ch,** Pres, 591 Dominion Rd, Mt Eden, PO Box 10018, Balmoral, Auckland. T: 689038.

*NICARAGUA*
**Asambleas de Dios,** Super, Apdo 1225, Managua.
**Convención Centroamericana,** Gasolinera San Luis 1, cuadra al sur, Barrio San Luis, Managua.
**Convención Nacional Bautista de Nicaragua,** Apdo 2593, Managua.
**Iglesia Adventista del Séptimo Día,** Pres, 9a Av SO entre 3a y 4a Calle No 406, Apdo 92, Managua. T: 25691.
**Iglesia Apostólica de la Fe en Cristo Jesús,** Apdo 855, Managua.
**Iglesia Católica en Nicaragua,** Arzobispado, Apdo 3058, Managua. T: 97094.
**Iglesia de Cristo,** Napoleon Tapia, Masatepe.
**Iglesia de Dios (Cleveland),** 5a Av SO No 901, Apdo 2330, Managua.
**Iglesia del Evangelio Cuadrangular,** Apdo 922, Managua.
**Iglesia del Nazareno,** Apdo 38, Granada.
**Iglesia de Príncipe de Paz,** Apdo 2220, Managua.
**Iglesia Episcopal,** Diocese of Nicaragua, Obispo, Apdo 1207, Managua.
**Iglesia Ev Misión Centroamericana,** Apdo 109, Managua.
**Iglesia Morava de Nicaragua,** Puerto Cabezas.
**Misión Bautista Internacional,** Apdo 1127, Managua.
**Testigos de Jehová,** Apdo 183, Managua.

*NIGER*
**Eglise Catholique,** Evêché, BP 10270, Niamey. T: 733079.
**Eglises Ev du Niger,** Sudan Interior Mission, BP 121, Maradi.
**Union des Eglises Ev Baptistes,** BP 519 & 69, Niamey.

*NIGERIA*
**African Apostolic Ch of Nigeria & Benin,** PO Box 89, Ibadan, Oyo State. (Also: PO Box 26, Surulere, Lagos).
**Anglican Ch in Nigeria,** Clerical Sec, PO Box 515, Ibadan.
**Apostolic Ch of Nigeria,** PO Box 8, Ilesha.
**Assemblies of God,** National Super, PO Box 875, Ibadan.
**Catholic Ch in Nigeria,** National Episcopal Conference of Nigeria, 6 Force Rd, PO Box 951, Lagos. T: 25339.
**Christ Apostolic Ch (CAC),** N/4 2489 Yemetu Adeoyo, PO Box 530, Ibadan.
**Christ Army Ch,** Bp, Ikot Idem St, Ede Obom PA, Uyo SES.
**Ch of the Lord (Aladura),** Primate, PO Box 377, Mushin, (also: PO Box 308, Ikeja), Lagos.
**Chs of Christ,** PO Box 614, Aba.
**Divine Healing Ch of Israel,** Supreme Head, Adefala Layout, Ring Rd Area, PO Box 1378, Ibadan.
**Eternal Sacred Order of Cherubim & Seraphim,** Spiritual Head, 88-90 Okesuna St, Ebute-Meta, Lagos.
**Ev Chs of West Africa,** PO Box 63, Jos.
**Ev Lutheran Ch of Nigeria,** Pres, Obot Idim, PO Uyo.
**Fellowship of Chs of Christ in the Sudan (Tekas),** PO Box 495 & 88, Jos.
**International Ch of the Foursquare Gospel,** PO Box 100 & 239, Yaba, Lagos.
**Methodist Ch, Nigeria,** Wesley House, 21/22 Marina, PO Box 2011, Lagos.
**Nigerian Baptist Convention,** Gen Sec, PMB 5113, Ibadan.
**Nigerian Christian Fellowship,** PO Box 36, Uyo, Calabar.
**Pentecostal Holiness Ch,** PO Box 370, Mushin, Lagos.
**Pilgrim Baptist Mission,** PO Box 1, Issele-Uku, Mid-Western Region.
**Presbyterian Ch of Nigeria,** PO Box 251, Ebute Metta, Lagos.
**Qua Iboe Ch,** Field Sec, PO Box 42, Etinan via Uyo.
**Salvation Army,** Territorial Commander, 11 Odunlamy St, PO Box 125, Lagos. T: 51346.
**Seventh-day Adventist Ch,** Pres, PO Box 19, Ibadan. T: 21146.
**United Missionary Ch of Africa,** Field Sec, PO Box 172, Ilorin.
**Zion Methodist Ch,** Mbieri, Owerri, East Central State.

*NIUE ISLAND*
**Niue Christian Ch,** PO Box 25, Alofi.

*NORTHERN SOLOMONS*
**Catholic Ch,** Diocese of Bougainville, PO Box 106, Kieta. T: 956021.

*NORWAY*
**Catholic Ch in Norway,** Bishop's House, Akersveien 5, PB 8270 Hammersborg, Oslo 11. T: (02)207226.
**Ch of Jesus Christ of Latter-day Saints,** Pres, Drammensveien 96g, Oslo 2.
**Ch of Norway,** St Halvards Pl 3, Oslo.
**Congregation of God at Vegarshei,** 4930 Vegarshei.
**Ev Lutheran Free Ch of Norway,** Synodeformann, Josefinesgt 5, Oslo 3.
**Jehovah's Witnesses,** Inkognitogaten 28b, Oslo 2.
**Methodist Ch of Norway,** St Olavsgt 28, Oslo 1.
**Mission Covenant Ch of Norway,** Misjonsforstander, Mollergt 26, Oslo 1.
**Norwegian Baptist Union,** Gen Sec, Hausmannsgt 22, Oslo 1.
**Norwegian Pentecostal Assemblies,** 24 St Olavsgt, Oslo 1.
**Salvation Army,** Kommandor, Pilestredet 22, Oslo 1. T: 200405.
**Seventh-day Adventist Ch,** Pres, Holmenkollveien 31, Oslo 3. T: 144592.

*OMAN*
**Protestant Ch in Oman,** PO Box 790, Masquat.

*PACIFIC ISLANDS*
**Assemblies of God,** Dir, Laura, Majuro, Marshall Islands, US Trust Territory 96960.
**Catholic Ch,** Chancery Office, PO Box 125, Agaña, US Trust Territory 96910. T: 4726116.
**Protestant Ch in the Caroline Islands,** Liebenzell Mission, Koror, Palau District, Western Caroline Islands, US Trust Territory 96940. (Also: PO Box 339, Yap).
**Protestant Ch of East Truk,** Dublon, Truk District, US Trust Territory 96942.
**Saipan Community Ch,** PO Box 5, Saipan, Mariana Islands, US Trust Territory 96950.
**Seventh-day Adventist Ch,** Kolonia, Ponape District, US Trust Territory 96941.
**United Ch of Christ in Ponape,** Kolonia, Ponape District, PO Box 7, Caroline Islands, US Trust Territory 96941.
**United Ch of Christ in the Marshall Is,** Ebeye, Kwajalein, Marshall Islands, US Trust Territory 96970.

*PAKISTAN*
**Anglican Orthodox Ch,** Bp, Narowal, District Sialkot.
**Associate Reformed Presbyterian Ch,** Mission House, Sahiwal, District Sahiwal.
**Bhai Mission (Brethren Missionary Fellowship),** 96-D Model Town, Lahore.
**Catholic Ch in Pakistan,** St Patrick's Cathedral, Karachi 3. T: 515870.
**Ch of Pakistan,** Bp, PO Box 3939, Karachi 4.
**Full Gospel Assemblies of Pakistan,** Fern Cottage, Jhika Gali Rd, Murree.
**International Missions,** Mohalla Islamabad, Leiah, District Muzzafargarh.
**Jehovah's Witnesses,** 8-E Habibullah Rd, Lahore.
**National Ch of Pakistan,** Clarkabad, District Lahore.
**National Virgin Ch of Pakistan,** Moderator, Pasrur, Sialkot.
**Pakistan Christian Fellowship,** Bible Training Institute, 27 Liaquat Rd, Hyderabad, Sindh.
**Salvation Army,** 35 Shara-e-Fatima Jinnah, PO Box 242, Lahore 4. T: 53422.
**Seventh-day Adventist Ch,** Pres, Adventpura, Multan Rd, PO Box 32, Lahore. T: 53910.
**United Presbyterian Ch in Pakistan,** Civil Lines, PO Box 68, Gujranwala.
**United Presbyterian Ch of Pakistan,** 2-A Empress Rd, Lahore 2.

*PALESTINE*
**Apostolic Ch of Pentecost,** PO Box 77, Bethlehem.
**Armenian Apostolic Ch,** Patriarchate of Jerusalem, Monastery of St James, 8 Shelom Zion Hamalka St, Jerusalem. T: 28607.
**Catholic Ch,** Latin Patriarchate, Old City, PO Box 14152, Jerusalem. T: (02)282323.
**Ch of God,** Mt of Olives, PO Box 568, East Jerusalem.
**Coptic Orthodox Ch,** Archbp, Old City, Jerusalem. T: 84405.
**Episcopal Ch in Jerusalem & the Middle East,** St George's Close, Salah el Din St, PO Box 1248, Jerusalem. T: 82146,87708.
**Ethiopian Orthodox Ch,** Harat el Nazara (or Ethiopian St), Jerusalem. T: 82848,86871.
**Ev Lutheran Ch in Jordan,** Old City, PO Box 4076, East Jerusalem. T: 82543.
**Free Pentecostal Ch,** PO Box 129, Beit Jala.
**Greek Orthodox Patriarchate of Jerusalem,** Patriarch, David Hamelekh St, Old City, PO Box 190632, Jerusalem. T: 27846.
**Native Ch of God,** PO Box 10, Bir Zeit.
**Romanian Orthodox Ch,** Archimandrite, 46 Shivtei Israel, Jerusalem. T: 87355.
**Russian Orthodox Ch,** Russian Compound, PO Box 1042, Jerusalem. T: 22565.
**Syrian Orthodox Patriarchate of Antioch,** St Mark's Convent, Old City, Jerusalem. T: 83304.

*PANAMA*
**Convención Bautista de Panamá,** Sec, Apdo 6942 & 6212, Panamá 5.
**Ejército de Salvación,** Apdo 8407, Panamá. T: 41545.
**Iglesia Adventista del Séptimo Día,** Apdo 3244, Panamá 5.
**Iglesia Apostólica Pentecostal Nacional,** Sec, Apdo 1362, Panamá.
**Iglesia Católica en Panamá,** Arzobispado, Apdo 6386, Panamá 5. T: 627400.
**Iglesia Centroamericana,** Sec, Apdo 6420, Panamá 5.
**Iglesia de Dios (Anderson),** Apdo 6064, Panamá. T: 43198.
**Iglesia del Evangelio Cuadrangular,** Apdo 1772, Panamá.
**Iglesia del Nazareno,** Apdo 8378, Panamá.
**Iglesia Episcopal,** Obispo, Apdo 7103, Panamá.
**Iglesia Metodista Unida,** Apdo 6424, Panamá 5.
**Misión Ev de Panamá,** Apdo 7258, Panamá.
**Testigos de Jehová,** Apdo 1386, Panamá 1.

*PANAMA CANAL ZONE*
**Iglesia Adventista del Séptimo Día,** 844 Gavilan Rd, PO Box 2006, Balboa. T: 525859,526531, 526283.
**Iglesia Episcopal,** Diocese of Panamá, Bp, PO Box R, Balboa.

*PAPUA NEW GUINEA*
**Anglican Ch,** Diocese of Papua New Guinea, Bp, Bishop's House, PO Box 806, Port Moresby.
**Apostolic Christian Ch,** Tilibia, via Mt Hagen, SHD. (Also: Laiagam, WHD).
**Apostolic Church Mission (New Zealand),** Kandep, via Mt. Hagen, SHD.
**Assemblies of God in Australia,** Maprik, via Wewak.
**Baptist Union Western Highlands,** Baiyer River Free Mail Bag, via Mt Hagen, SHD.
**Bible Missionary Ch,** Kagua, via Mt Hagen, SHD.
**Catholic Ch in Papua New Guinea,** Bishops' Conference of PNG & the SI, PO Box 69, Mendi, Southern Highlands. T: 591002.
**Christian Brethren,** Koroba, via Mt. Hagen, SHD.
**Ch of the Nazarene,** PO Box 70, Banz.
**Chs of Christ Mission,** Free Mail Bag, Tung, via Wewak.
**Ev Ch of Papua,** Balimo, WD.
**Ev Lutheran Ch of New Guinea (ELCONG),** Bp, PO Box 80, Lae. T: 2901.
**Faith Mission,** PO Box 23, Goroka.
**International Ch of the Foursquare Gospel,** PO Box 139, Goroka.
**Jehovah's Witnesses,** PO Box 113, Port Moresby.
**Manus Ev Ch,** Lugos, Manus Island.
**New Tribes Mission,** Goroka.
**Salvation Army,** Moyon St, Koki. T: Port Moresby 55507.
**Seventh-day Adventist Ch,** Pres, Memorial Av, PO Box 86, Lae. T: 2361. (Also: PO Box 391, Rabaul).
**South Sea Ev Ch,** Brugam Free Bag, Wewak.
**Sovereign Grace Baptist Mission,** Tanggi, Koroba, via Mt Hagen, SHD.
**Swiss Brotherhood Mission,** 6-Mile, Markham Rd, PO Box 324, Lae 2399.
**United Ch in PNG & the SI,** PO Box 3401, Port Moresby.
**Wabag Lutheran Ch (Missouri),** Wabag.

*PARAGUAY*
**Asambleas de Dios en el Paraguay,** Super, Sede Central, Choferes del Chaco, Barrio Previsión Social, Casilla 514, Asunción.
**Convención Bautista del Paraguay,** Pres, Casilla 1194, Asunción.
**Ejército de Salvación en el Paraguay,** Haster y Mayor Casianoff, Casilla 92, Asunción. T: 60291.
**Hermanos Menonitas,** Casilla de Correo 1154, Asunción.
**Iglesia Adventista del Séptimo Día,** Pres, Yegros 861, Asunción. T: 45134.
**Iglesia Anglicana en el Paraguay,** Obispo, Casilla 1124, Asunción.
**Iglesia Católica en el Paraguay,** Arzobispado, CC 654, Asunción. T: 44150.
**Iglesia de Dios en el Paraguay,** Casilla 1001, Asunción.
**Iglesia Ev del Río de la Plata,** General Dias 429, Asunción.
**Iglesia Ev Filadelfia,** Pres, Av Acuña de Figueroa esquina Iturbe, Casilla 583, Asunción.
**Iglesia Ev Gracia y Gloria,** Calle Pitiantuta 456, Asunción.
**Iglesia Ev Menonita en el Paraguay,** República de Colombia 1050, Casilla 166, Asunción.
**Iglesia Ev Plenitud,** Pastor, Casilla 547, Asunción.
**Testigos de Jehová,** Casilla de Correo 482, Asunción.
**Unión Misionera Neotestamentaria,** Mariscall Estigarribia 1427, Asunción.

*PERU*
**Asambleas de Dios del Perú,** Super, Apdo 4550, Lima.
**Asociación de Iglesias Ev del Nor-Oriente Peruano,** Casilla 122, Tarapoto, San Martín.
**Asociación Misionera Ev Nacional (AMEN),** Huancas 533, Apdo 657, Huancayo. T: 3446.
**Ejército de Salvación,** Jirón Huancayo 245, Apdo 690, Lima. T: 239838.
**Hermanos Libres,** Apdo 5755, Lima.
**Iglesia Adventista del Séptimo Día,** Av Comandante Espinar 610 & 730, Miraflores, Casilla 1002, Lima. T: 256639,458297.
**Iglesia Alianza Cristiana y Misionera,** Av Arequipa 2356, Apdo 2178, Lima.
**Iglesia Anglicana,** Church of the Good Shepherd, 491 Av Santa Cruz, Miraflores, Lima. T: 227719.
**Iglesia Católica en el Perú,** Arzobispado, Plaza de Armas, Apdo 1512, Lima. T: 275980.
**Iglesia de Dios del Perú,** Fuente y Cortez 312, Pueblo Libre.
**Iglesia de Jesucristo de los Santos de los Ultimos Dias,** Los Cedros 388, Miraflores.
**Iglesia de los Peregrinos del Perú,** Dir, Apdo 86, Chiclayo.
**Iglesia del Nazareno,** Dir, Apdo 209, Chiclayo.
**Iglesia Ev Luterana en el Perú,** Las Magnolias 495, Urb el Jardín, Lima-San Isidro. T: 24452.
**Iglesia Ev Pentecostal de Chile,** Casilla 2, Curico.
**Iglesia Ev Peruana (IEP),** Sec, Apdo 1277, Lima.
**Iglesia Metodista Peruana,** Recuay 152, Breña.
**Testigos de Jehová,** Gervasio Santillana 370, Miraflores, Lima.

*PHILIPPINES*
**Alaph Divine Temple,** Colonia Divina, Sagay, Occidental.
**Assemblies of God,** Philippine General Council, 1404 General Luna, Ermita, PO Box 3549, Manila.
**Association of Baptist Chs in Luzon, Visayan & Mindanao,** 1301 Leon Guinto Sr St, Ermita, Manila.
**Association of Fundamental Baptist Chs in the Philippines,** PO Box 2800, Manila.

**Banner of the Race Ch,** Lecheria, Calamba, Laguna.

**Baptist Bible Fellowship of the Philippines,** 3970 Sociego St, PO Box 2395, Manila.

**Catholic Ch in the Philippines,** Archbishop's House, 1000 General Solano, PO Box 132, San Miguel, Mandaluyong, Metro-Manila. T: 481867.

**Christian and Missionary Alliance Chs,** PO Box 127 & 290, Zamboanga City N-329.

**Christian Ev Mission,** Corner Jacinto & Ponce Gomez Sts, Davao City.

**Christian Mission in the Far East,** 74 Leyte, Singalong, PO Box 3076, Manila.

**Christian Spiritist Union of the Philippines,** Niugan, Malabon, Rizal.

**Ch of Christ (Iglesia ni Cristo, INC),** Corner Central & Commonwealth Avs, Dil, Quezon City D-505. T: 980611. (Also termed Manalista).

**Ch of God in Christ Jesus,** 1991 Juan Luna, Tondo, Manila.

**Ch of Jesus Christ New Jerusalem,** Templo de Caridad, Dagupan Extension, Solis, Tondo, Manila.

**Ch of Jesus Christ of Latter-day Saints,** Philippines Mission, Commercial Centre, PO Box 801, Makati, Rizal D-708. (Also: 2680-C Taft Av Extension, Pasay City)

**Chs of Christ,** Philippine Mission, 34-B Cruzada, PO Box 2774, Manila.

**Convention of Philippine Baptist Chs,** PO Box 263, Iloilo City K-421. T: 73874.

**Crusaders of the Divine Ch of Christ,** Nibaliw West, San Fabian, Pangasinan.

**Edified Ch of Jesus Christ,** MH del Pilar St, Maysilo, Malabon, Rizal.

**Ev Methodist Ch in the Philippines,** 640 Penaloza, Tondo, Manila. T: 216776.

**God, Mysterious Mother,** Mambangan, San Leonardo, Nueva Ecija.

**International Ch of the Foursquare Gospel,** 3975 Magsaysay Blvd, Manila.

**Jehovah's Witnesses,** 186 Roosevelt Av, San Francisco del Monte, Quezon City D-503.

**Lutheran Ch in the Philippines,** 441 Old St Mesa, PO Box 507, Manila. T: 605041.

**New Testament Ch of God,** 2304 FB Harrison St, Pasay City, PO Box 2971, Manila.

**Patriotic Ch of our Lord Jesus Christ,** 194-A Washington St, Davao City.

**Philippine Baptist Mission,** PO Box 7, Baguio City.

**Philippine Ch (Adarnista),** Bangar, La Union.

**Philippine Episcopal Ch,** Diocese of Central Philippines, Bp, 281 E Rodriguez Sr Blvd, PO Box 655, Manila 12105. T: 702143.

**Philippine Independent Ch,** 1500 Taft Av, Ermita, PO Box 2065, Manila. T: 505724. (Also: 1327 Alfredo St, Santa Cruz, Manila).

**Sacred Ch of the Race,** 1534 Sta Maria St, Tondo, Manila.

**Salvation Army,** 1414-1416 Leon Guinto Sr, Ermita, PO Box 1100, Makati, Rizal D-708. T: 597759.

**Seventh-day Adventist Ch,** Pres, 2059 Donada St, Pasay, PO Box 401, Manila. T: 500061,801682.

**United Ch of Christ in the Philippines (UCCP),** 939 Epifanio de los Santos Av, Quezon City, PO Box 718, Manila. T: 996241.

**United Ev Ch of Christ,** 634 Moriones, Tondo, Manila. T: 219511.

**United Filipino Ch,** Labazon, Zamboanga del Norte.

**United Methodist Ch in the Philippines,** 640 Menalosa, Tondo, PO Box 756, Manila. T: 592406.

**United Pentecostal Ch (Philippines),** Balibago, Angeles, Pampanga.

*PITCAIRN ISLANDS*

**Seventh-day Adventist Ch,** Pitcairn Island Mission, Adamstown.

*POLAND*

**Catholic Ch in Poland,** Ul Miodowa 17-19, 00-246 Warszawa. T: 315231.

**Ev Ch of the Augsburg Confession in Poland,** Bp, Ul Miodowa 21, Warszawa. T: 315187.

**Methodist Ch in the Polish Republic,** Super, Wokotowska 12, Warszawa.

**Old Catholic Mariavite Ch of Poland,** Ul J Wieczorka 27, Plock.

**Orthodox Ch of Poland,** Metropolitan, Gen Swierczewskiego 52, Warszawa 4.

**Polish Baptist Union,** Pres, Apartment 16, Spasowskiego 13, Warszawa 18. (Also: Ul Walicöw 25).

**Polish National Catholic Ch,** Ul Wilcza 31, Warszawa.

**Reformed Ev Ch in Poland,** Präses, 2-4 Kredytowa, Warszawa. (Also: 76a Al Swierczewskiego, Warszawa).

**Seventh-day Adventist Ch,** Pres, Foksal 8, Warszawa. T: 277611/3,278619.

**United Ev Ch of the Gospel,** Al Jerozolimskie 99/37, Warszawa.

*PORTUGAL*

**Assembleias de Deus em Portugal,** Dirigente, Rua Neves Ferreira 13-3, Calcada do Poco dos Mouros, Lisboa 1.

**Associação de Igrejas Batistas Portuguesas,** Pres, R Elias Garcia 281 F, Amadora.

**Congregação Cristã em Portugal,** Sec, Rua do Bonjardim 961, Porto.

**Convenção Batista Portuguesa,** Pres, Rua Filipe Folque 36-1 E, Lisboa 1.

**Igreja Adventista do Sétimo Dia,** Pres, Rua Joaquin Bonifacio 17, Lisboa 1. T: 42169.

**Igreja Católica em Portugal,** Patriarch, Campo dos Mártires da Pátria 45, Lisboa 1. T: 563901.

**Igreja Ev Congregacional,** Estrada de Chelas 145, Lisboa 6.

**Igreja Ev Metodista Portuguesa,** Rua do Molhe 555, Foz do Douro, Porto.

**Igreja Ev Presbiteriana de Portugal,** Sec, Rua Carlos da Maia 26-2 E, Lisboa 3.

**Igreja Lusitana Católica Apostólica,** Bispo, Quinta do Bacalhau, Vila Franca de Xira. (Also: 1 de Maio 54-2, Villa Nova de Gaia).

**Movimento Ev Cigano de Portugal,** Pres, Rua de Beneditina 115, Foz do Douro, Porto.

*PUERTO RICO*

**Iglesia Adventista del Séptimo Día,** Pres, Verona 1188, Villa Capri, PO Box 20455, Rio Piedras, PR 00924. T: 7651323.

**Iglesia Alianza Cristiana y Misionera,** Av Magnolia Gardens L-29, Magnolia Gardens.

**Iglesia Católica en Puerto Rico,** Arzobispado, Apdo 1967, San Juan, PR 00903. T: 7277373.

**Iglesia de Dios de la Profecía,** PO Box 1066, Rio Piedras.

**Iglesia de Dios Pentecostal,** Calle América 1473, Parada 22, Santurce.

**Iglesia de Dios (Cleveland),** PO Box 8212, Santurce.

**Iglesia Defensores de la Fe,** Calle Progreso 357, Villa Palmares, Santurce.

**Iglesia del Evangelio Cuadrangular,** PO Box 1267, Ponce.

**Iglesia Episcopal,** Diocese of Puerto Rico, Obispo, Centro Diocesano San Justo, PO Box C, Saint Justo, PR 00750.

**Iglesia Luterana Puertorriqueña,** 148 Calle del Parque, San Juan, PR 00911.

**Santa Iglesia Católica Apostólica Ortodoxa de Puerto Rico,** El Centre y Seminario, PO Box 2789, Bayamon, PR 00619. T: 7860730.

**Testigos de Jehová,** Calle Onix 23, Urb Bucaré, Rio Piedras, PR 00927.

*REUNION*

**Eglise Adventiste du Septième Jour,** Prés, BP 227, Saint-Denis. T: 212769.

**Eglise Catholique,** Evêché, 42 Rue de Paris, BP 55, 97462 Saint-Denis. T: 212849.

*ROMANIA*

**Baptist Union of Romania,** Strada Nicolai Titulescu 56/A, Raion Stalin-Bucuresti.

**Catholic Ch in Romania,** Strada Nuferilor 19, Bucuresti. T: 133936.

**Christian Brethren (Ch of the Gospel),** 7 Noiemerie 60A, Bucuresti. T: 354347.

**Ev Ch of the Augsburg Confession,** Strada General Magheru Nr 4, Sibiu (Hermannstadt). T: 11780.

**Ev Lutheran Synodal Presbyterial Ch,** Strada Kossuth Lajos 1 (& Bulevardul Lenin Nr 1), Kolozsvár, Cluj. T: 13637.

**Pentecostal Chs in the PRR,** Strada Carol Davila Nr 81, Bucuresti.

**Reformed Ch of Romania,** Strada 23 August 51, Cluj.

**Romanian Orthodox Ch,** Patriarch, Palatul Patriarhiei, Intrarea Patriarhiei Nr 9, Sectorul 5, Bucuresti. (Also: Aleea Marii Adunari Nationale, and Strada Patriarhiei 21).

**Seventh-day Adventist Ch,** Pres, Strada Labirint 116, Bucuresti IV. T: 215960.

**Unitarian Chs in Romania,** Bulevardul Lenin Nr 9, Cluj.

*RWANDA*

**Eglise Adventiste du Septième Jour,** BP 247, Kigali.

**Eglise Anglicane du Rwanda (EAR),** Evêqué, EAR Gahini, BP 61, Kigali.

**Eglise Catholique au Rwanda,** Archevêché, BP 715, Kigali. T: 5769.

**Eglise Libre Méthodiste au Rwanda,** BP 31, Cyangugu.

**Eglise Presbytérienne au Rwanda,** BP 56, Kigali.

**Eglises de Pentecôte,** BP 99, Gisenyi.

**Union des Eglises Baptistes du Rwanda,** BP 59, Nyatanga Butare.

*SAHARA*

**Iglesia Católica,** Misión Católica, Aaiún.

*ST HELENA*

**Anglican Ch,** Diocese of St Helena, Bp, Bishopsholme, St Helena Island, South Atlantic.

*ST KITTS-NEVIS*

**Antioch Baptist Ch,** Minister, Basseterre, St Kitts.

**Jehovah's Witnesses,** Kingdom Hall, Sandy Point, St Kitts.

**Methodist Ch in the Caribbean & the Americas,** Basseterre, St Kitts.

**Moravian Ch,** Basseterre, St Kitts.

**Seventh-day Adventist Ch,** Basseterre, St Kitts.

**Wesleyan Ch,** Minister, Basseterre, St Kitts.

*ST LUCIA*

**Catholic Ch,** PO Box 267, Castries. T: 2416.

**Salvation Army,** High St, PO Box 56, Castries.

*ST PIERRE & MIQUELON*

**Eglise Catholique,** Evêché, St-Pierre, via Newfoundland, Canada. T: 35.

*ST VINCENT*

**Anglican Ch,** Diocese of the Windward Islands, Bp, PO Box 128, Kingstown.

**Salvation Army,** Middle St, Kingstown.

*SAMOA*

**Catholic Ch,** Bishop's House, PO Box 532, Apia. T: 20400.

**Ch of Jesus Christ of Latter-day Saints,** Samoa Mission, PO Box 197, Apia.

**Congregational Christian Ch in Samoa,** Gen Sec, PO Box 468, Apia.

**Methodist Ch in Samoa,** Pres, PO Box 199, Apia.

**Seventh-day Adventist Ch,** Samoa Mission, Pres, Lalovaea, PO Box 600, Apia. T: 820/1.

*SAO TOME & PRINCIPE*

**Igreja Adventista do Sétimo Dia,** Pres, CP 120, São Tomé.

**Igreja Católica,** Centro Diocesano, CP 146, São Tomé. T: 308.

*SENEGAL*

**Assemblées de Dieu,** BP 3130, Dakar.

**Eglise Adventiste du Septième Jour,** 31 Rue de Denain, BP 1013, Dakar. T: 37273.

**Eglise Catholique au Sénégal,** Archevêché, BP 1908, Dakar. T: 225918.

**Eglise Protestante du Sénégal,** 44 Rue Dial Diop, BP 847, Dakar.

**Mission Ev de l'Afrique Occidentale,** BP 179, Saint Louis. (Also: BP 75, Ziguinchor).

**Mission Mundiale Unie,** BP 3103, Dakar.

**Témoins de Jéhovah,** BP 3107, Dakar.

*SEYCHELLES*

**Anglican Ch,** Diocese of the Seychelles, Bp, PO Box 44, Victoria, Mahé.

**Catholic Ch,** Bishop's House, PO Box 43, Port Victoria, Mahé. T: 2152.

**Seventh-day Adventist Ch,** Pres, PO Box 28, Victoria, Mahé.

*SIERRA LEONE*

**African Methodist Episcopal Ch,** 1A Elliott St, Freetown.

**Assemblies of God,** PO Box 265 & 522, Freetown.

**Catholic Ch in Sierra Leone,** Archbishop's House, Brookfields, PO Box 893, Freetown. T: 24590.

**Ch of God of Prophecy,** PO Box 570, Freetown.

**Countess of Huntingdon's Connexion,** c/o Fourah Bay College, Freetown.

**God is Our Light Ch (GIOL),** Pastor, PO Kaema.

**Jehovah's Witnesses,** PO Box 136, Freetown.

**Methodist Ch, Sierra Leone,** PO Box 64, Freetown.

**Nigerian Baptist Convention,** PO Box 46, Magburaka.

**Seventh-day Adventist Ch,** Pres, PO Box 26, Bo. T: 659.

**Sierra Leone Ch (CPWA),** Bishopscourt, PO Box 128 & 537, Freetown.

**Sierra Leone Missionary Ch,** PO Box 32, Magburaka.

**Sierra Leone Wesleyan Ch,** 39 Waterloo St, PO Box 33, Freetown.

**United Brethren in Christ,** PO Box 102, Bumpe via Bo. (Also: PO Box 19, Mattru).

**United Methodist Ch,** Bp, 146 Circular Rd, PO Box 843, Freetown.

**United Pentecostal Ch,** PO Box 5, Magburaka.

**West African Methodist Ch,** 39 Waterloo St, Freetown.

*SINGAPORE*

**Anglican Ch,** Diocese of Singapore, Bp, St Andrew's Cathedral, Coleman St, Singapore 12.

**Assemblies of God,** 1079 Serangoon Rd, Singapore 12.

**Bible Presbyterian Ch of Malaysia,** 9A Gilstead Rd, Singapore 11.

**Catholic Ch,** Archbishop's House, 31 Victoria St, Singapore 7. T: 328818.

**Christian Brethren Assemblies,** Sec, Bethesda Gospel Hall, 77 Bras Basah Rd, Singapore 7.

**Ch of Christ of Malaya (Independent),** 54 Sophia Rd, Singapore 9.

**Fishermen of Christ Ch,** 84A Robinson Rd, Singapore 1. (Also: 38 Prinsep St, Singapore 7).

**Jehovah's Witnesses,** 8 Exeter Rd, Singapore 9. (Also: 11 Jalan Sejarah, Singapore 11).

**Mar Thoma Syrian Ch in Singapore,** St Thomas Church, 25 Mar Thoma Rd, Singapore 12. T: 884145.

**Methodist Ch, Malaysia and Singapore,** Bp, 23-B Coleman St, PO Box 483, Singapore 6.

**Pentecostal Ev Ch,** Glad Tidings Church, 1 Valley Rd, Singapore 19. T: 82883.

**Presbyterian Ch in Singapore,** 102 Lorong M, Telak Kurau, Singapore 15.

**Salvation Army,** 207 Clemenceau Av, PO Box 545, Singapore 9. T: 379122.

**Seventh-day Adventist Ch,** Pres, 251 Upper Serangoon Rd, Singapore 13. T: 89292/3. (Also: PO Box 226, Singapore 11. T: 531155,531221).

**True Jesus Ch,** Sec, 32 Lorong H, Telok Kurau, Singapore 15. (Also: 339-A Beach Rd, Singapore 7).

*SOLOMON ISLANDS*

**Catholic Ch in the Solomon Islands,** Catholic Mission, PO Box 237, Honiara. T: 387.

**Christian Fellowship Ch,** Silas Eto, Paradise, New Georgia.

**Ch of the Province of Melanesia,** Archbp, PO Box 113, Honiara.

**Seventh-day Adventist Ch,** PO Box 63, Honiara.

**South Sea Ev Ch (SSEC),** Auki, Malaita.

**United Ch in the PNG & the Solomon Islands,** Sec, Munda.

*SOMALIA*

**Catholic Ch,** CP 273, Mogadisho. T: 22013.

**Somalia Mennonite Mission,** PO Box 2, Mogadisho.

**Sudan Interior Mission,** PO Box 29, Mogadisho.

*SOUTH AFRICA*

**African Ev Ch,** PO Box 988, Cape Town.

**African Methodist Episcopal Ch,** PO Box 56, Batho Village, Bloemfontein.

**Apostolic Faith Mission of South Africa,** PO Box 197, Lyndhurst, Transvaal.

**Bantu Presbyterian Ch of South Africa,** 48 Eagle St, Umtata, Transkei.

**Baptist Union of South Africa,** 210 Transafrica Bldg, 21 Wolmarans St, Johannesburg.

**Catholic Ch in South Africa,** SACBC, Standard Bank Bldgs, Paul Kruger St, Pretoria 0001. T: 728048.

**Christian Brethren,** Elim Mission, PO Box 13, Nqaboni, Natal.

**Ch of Christ, Scientist,** First Church, Orange St at Grey's Pass, Cape Town, CP.

**Ch of England in South Africa,** Balfour House, St Georges St, PO Box 1530, Cape Town, CP.

**Ch of God in Christ,** 328 Fortuin St, Lady Selborne, Pretoria.

**Ch of Jesus Christ of Latter-day Saints,** South Africa Mission, Cumorah, 4 Fifth Av, Lower Houghton, Johannesburg.

**Ch of the Nazarene,** PO Box 48 & 92, Florida, Transvaal.

**Ch of the Province of Southern Africa (CPSA),** Archbp, Bishopscourt, Claremont, 7700 Cape Town, CP. (Also: Church House, Queen Victoria St, Cape Town. T: 20558).

**Chs of Christ,** PO Box 17, Cape Town, CP.

**Dutch Reformed Ch in Africa (Bantu Ch),** PO Box 1004, Bloemfontein.

**Dutch Reformed Ch in SA (NHK),** PO Box 2368, Pretoria. (Also: Sek, Posbus 171, Krugersdorp).

**Dutch Reformed Mission Ch (Coloured),** PO Box 14, Kakamas, CP.

**Ev Lutheran Ch in South Africa,** PO Box 15196, Lynn, East Pretoria.

**Free Ch of Scotland,** 14 Frere St, King William's Town. T: 3129.

**Free Methodist Ch in South Africa,** PO Box 8, Izingolweni, Natal.

**Full Gospel Ch of God in Southern Africa,** Sec Gen, 8 Jan Smuts Av, PO Box 14, Irene, Transvaal.

**International Ch of the Foursquare Gospel,** Willowvale, Transkei.

**Jehovah's Witnesses,** Private Bag, 2 Elandsfontein, Transvaal.

**Latter Rain Assemblies of South Africa,** PO Box 416, Benoni.

**Methodist Ch in South Africa,** PO Box 708, Cape Town.

**Moravian Ch,** Eastern Cape Province, Mvenyane Mission, P Bag 524, Cedarville, East Griqualand.

**Moravian Ch,** Western Cape Province, PO Box 11, Landsdowne, Cape.

**Nazarite Baptist Ch,** Phoenix, PO Inanda, Natal.

**Pentecostal Assemblies of God,** PO Box 101, Florida, Transvaal. (Also: National Super, PO Box 505, Roodepoort, Transvaal).

**Pentecostal Holiness Ch in South Africa,** PO Box 36, Krugersdorp, Transvaal.

**Presbyterian Ch of Africa,** 7058 NU3, Mdantsane, East London.

**Presbyterian Ch of Southern Africa,** PO Box 11347, Johannesburg.

**Reformed Ch in South Africa,** PO Box 20004, North Bridge, Pochefstroom. T: 5269. (Also: Posbus 20031, Pk Noordbrug, Transvaal).

**St John's Apostolic Faith Mission,** 5759 Orlando East, Johannesburg.

**Salvation Army,** 119 Rissik St, Wanderers' View, PO Box 1018, Johannesburg. T: 725-2220,2270/1.

**Scandinavian Independent Baptist Union,** Sec, 108 Landdrost St, Vryheid, Natal.

**Seventh-day Adventist Ch,** Pres, 17 Louis Rd, PO Box 46061, Orange Grove Orchards, Johannesburg. T: 452231/2/3.

**Swazi Christian Ch in Zion of South Africa,** PB Moroka, Johannesburg.

**Swedish Alliance Mission,** PO Box 263, Cleveland, Johannesburg.

**Swedish Holiness Union Mission,** South African Field, PO Bothas Hill, Natal.

**Tsonga Presbyterian Ch,** PO Box 6, Elim, Northern Transvaal.

**United Congregational Ch of Southern Africa,** PO Box 31083, Braamfontein, Johannesburg.

**United Ev Lutheran Ch of South Africa (UELCSA),** Geluk, 46 Buxton Av, Oranjezicht, Cape Town.

**United Methodist Ch,** 76 Leicester Rd, Kensington, Johannesburg.

**Zion Christian Ch (ZCC),** Zion City, Morija, Boyne, Transvaal.

**Zion Mission Ch of South Africa,** 10143 Orlando West 2, PO Phirima, Johannesburg.

*SPAIN*

**Asambleas de Dios de España,** c Rodriguez Aris 55, 5 D, Bilbas 11. T: 415244 (Also: Dir, Apdo 59, Ronda, Malaga).

**Asociación de Iglesias Ev Bautistas Independientes de España,** Place Federico Soler 6, Barcelona 6. T: 2479769.

**Comunión Bautista Independiente,** Calle Leizarán 29, Apdo Postal 2098, Madrid 2.

**Congregaciones Ev Neotestamentarias,** Cercado Bajo de Cartuja 16, Granada.

**Federación de Iglesias Ev Independientes de España (FIEIDE),** Calle Verdi 189 1, Barcelona 12.

**Iglesia Adventista del Sétimo Día,** Pres, Calle Alenza 6, Apdo 3106, Madrid 3. T: 2531220,2347037.

**Iglesia Católica en España,** Arzobispado, Bailén 8, Madrid 13. T: 2414804

**Iglesia de Dios Pentecostal,** Calle Florencio García 4, Apdo Postal 50452, Madrid 17.

**Iglesia de Jesucristo de los Santos de los Ultimos Dias de España,** Spain Mission, Calle San Telmo 26, Madrid 16.

**Iglesia Española Reformada Episcopal,** Calle Isaac Peral 52, Madrid 3. T: 2439231.

**Iglesia Ev Española,** Sec, Calle Bravo Murillo 85, Madrid 3.

**Iglesia Ev Filadelfia,** Chalet Ferrer, Av Paris, Puerto de Pollensa, Mallorca.

**Iglesia Ev Pentecostal de España,** Calle Tortosa 3 (also Calle Corazon de Maria 53), Madrid 7. T: 2891323.

**Iglesia Ortodoxa Griega en España,** Calle Luis Diaz Dobena 20, Madrid.

**Iglesias de Cristo en España,** Apdo 2029, Madrid.

**Iglesias Ev de Hermanos,** Calle Esteban Mora 24, Madrid 17. T: 2460368.

**Unión Ev Bautista Española (UEBE),** Calle Ciudad de Balaguer 40, Barcelona 6.

*SRI LANKA*

**Assemblies of God in Sri Lanka,** 108 Rosemead Place, Colombo 7.

**Catholic Ch in Sri Lanka,** Archbishop's House, 976 Granarthapradeepaya Mawatha, Colombo 8. T: 95471.

**Ceylon Pentecostal Mission,** 41 Greenpath, Colombo 3.

**Ch of Ceylon,** Diocese of Colombo, Bp, Bishop's House, 370 Bauddhaloka Mawatha, Colombo 7.

**Ch of South India (CSI),** Diocese of Jaffna, Bp, Bishop's House, Vaddukoddai.

**Jehovah's Witnesses,** 7 Alfred House Rd, Colombo 3.

**Methodist Ch of Ceylon,** Galle Rd, Colombo 3.

**Presbytery of Ceylon,** Moderator, General Consistory Office, 363 Galle Rd, Colombo 6.

**Presbytery of Lanka,** Moderator, 171 Maya Av, Colombo 6.

**Salvation Army,** 2 Union Place, PO Box 193, Colombo 2. T: 24660.
**Seventh-day Adventist Ch,** Pres, 7 Alfred House Gardens, PO Box 1253, Colombo. T: 85851.
**Sri Lanka Baptist Union,** Carey College, 46 Kynsey Rd, Colombo 8.
**Swedish Pentecostal Mission,** Calvary Devastanaya, 33 Siebel Av, Colombo 6.
**United Pentecostal Ch,** 101 Galle Rd, Dehiwala.

*SUDAN*

**Armenian Apostolic Ch,** PO Box 932, Al Khurtum.
**Catholic Ch in the Sudan,** PO Box 49, Al Khurtum. T: 72677.
**Ch in the East Central Sudan,** SIM, PO Box 220, Al Khurtum.
**Ch of Christ in the Nuba Mountains,** Sec, PO Box 40, Malakal.
**Ch of Christ in the Upper Nile,** Moderator, PO Box 40, Malakal.
**Ch of the Province of the Sudan,** Archbp, Clergy House, PO Box 135, Al Khurtum. T: 72121. (Also: PO Box 110, Juba).
**Coptic Orthodox Ch in the Sudan,** Archbp, Bishop's House, PO Box 4, Al Khurtum.
**Ethiopian Orthodox Ch in the Sudan,** 44 Africa St, PO Box 1482, Al Khurtum.
**Ev Ch in the Sudan,** PO Box 1928, Al Khurtum.
**Greek Orthodox Ch,** PO Box 47, Al Khurtum.

*SURINAM*

**Catholic Ch,** Bisschopshuis, Gravenstraat 12, POB 1230, Paramaribo. T: 73306.
**Ev Lutheran Ch in Surinam,** PO Box 585, Paramaribo.
**Ev Methodist Ch in Guiana,** PO Box 478, Paramaribo.
**Jehovah's Witnesses,** Wicherstraat 8, PO Box 49, Paramaribo.
**Moravian Ch in Surinam,** Provincial Board, PO Box 219, Paramaribo.
**Salvation Army,** Gravenstraat 172, PO Box 317, Paramaribo. T: 3310.
**Seventh-day Adventist Ch,** Pres, Madelieffesstraat 8, PO Box 1909, Paramaribo. T: 97071.

*SWAZILAND*

**Africa Ev Ch,** PO Box 13 & 204, Mbabane.
**African Methodist Episcopal Ch,** PO Box 276, Mbabane.
**Anglican Ch,** Bp, Bishop's House, PO Box 118, Mbabane.
**Bantu Swedish Free Ch,** PO Box 579, Mbabane.
**Catholic Ch,** Bishop's House, PO Box 19, Manzini. T:52348.
**Ch of the Nazarene,** RFM Hospital, PO Box 14, Manzini.
**Evangelical Ch of Swaziland,** PO Box 611, Mbabane. T: 2907.
**Ev Lutheran Ch,** Southeast Region, PO Box 117, Mbabane.
**Free Ev Assemblies,** PO Hlatikulu.
**Methodist Ch of South Africa,** PO Box 272, Mbabane.
**Seventh-day Adventist Ch,** Pres, Louw St, PO Box 562, Manzini. T: 2617.
**Swazi Christian Ch in Zion,** Bp, Boyane Tribal School, PO Box 42, Kwaluseni.
**United Christian Ch of Africa,** PO Box 6, Mbabane.

*SWEDEN*

**Baptist Union of Sweden,** Norrtullsgatan 10, S-113 27 Stockholm. T: (08)235245.
**Catholic Ch in Sweden,** Valhallavägen 132, Fack, S-102 40 Stockholm 5. T: (08)618034.
**Ch of Christ, Scientist,** Eriksbergsgatan 10, S-114 30 Stockholm.
**Ch of Jesus Christ of Latter-day Saints,** Botkyrka, Fack, S-147 00 Tumba.
**Ch of Sweden,** Arkebiskop, Box 640, S-751 27 Uppsala. T: (018)155340.
**Estonian Ev Lutheran Ch in Exile,** Wallingatan 32, S-111 24 Stockholm. T: (08)213277.
**Estonian Orthodox Ch in Exile,** Sec of the Synod, Sturegatan 14, S-172 31 Sundbyberg.
**Finnish Orthodox Ch,** Enspännargatan 64 II, S-162 33 Väallingby.
**Free Baptist Union,** Järnvägsgatan 32, S-294 00 Sölvesborg. T: (0456)10175.
**Jehovah's Witnesses,** Folkungavagen 8, Jakobsberg.
**Maranatha Revival Ch,** Missionsvägen 24, S-161 35 Bromma. T: (08)802935.
**Methodist Ch in Sweden,** Sibyllegatan 18, S-114 42 Stockholm. T: (08)670155.
**Örebro Mission Society,** Järnvägsgatan 28A, Box 330, S-701 05 Örebro. T: (019)119360.
**Orthodox Ch in Sweden,** Metropolitan, Wallingatan 37, S-111 24 Stockholm. T: (08)117682.
**Pentecostal Revival Movement of Sweden,** Filadelfia, Rörstrandsgatan 5-7, Box 21055, S-100 31 Stockholm. T: (08)349850.
**Russian Orthodox Ch,** Birger Jarlsgatan 98, S-114 20 Stockholm.
**Salvation Army,** Östermalmsgatan 71, Box 5090, S-102 42 Stockholm. T: (08)631700.
**Serbian Orthodox Ch,** Näsby Chausseen, S-291 00 Kristianstad.
**Seventh-day Adventist Ch,** Tunnelgatan 25, S-111 22 Stockholm. T: (08)140365.
**Swedish Alliance Mission,** Box 1293, S-551 02 Jönköping 1.
**Swedish Holiness Union,** Gotabro, Box 67, S-692 01 Kumla. T: (019)70940.
**Sweden Mission Covenant Ch,** Tegnergatan 8, Box 6302, S-113 81 Stockholm. T: (08)151830.
**Swedish Salvation Army,** Sibyllegatan 18, S-114 42 Stockholm. T: (08)634501.

*SWITZERLAND*

**Bund der Baptistengemeinden in der Schweiz,** Bahnhofstr 13, CH-8803 Ruschlikon-Zürich.
**Christkatholische Kirche der Schweiz,** Bischof, Willadingweg 39, CH-3000 Bern.
**Eglise Adventiste du Septième Jour,** Gubelstr 23, CH-8050 Zürich. T: (051)464702.
**Eglise de Jésus-Christ des Saints des Derniers Jours,** Switzerland Mission, Pilatusstr 11, CH-8032 Zürich.
**Eglise Ev Libre de Genève,** Sec, Rue Tabazan 7, CH-1204 Genève.
**Eglise Ev Reformée Vaudoise,** Secretariat, 31 Rue de l'Ale, CH-1000 Lausanne.
**Eglise Nationale Protestante de Genève,** CP 252, CH-1211 Genève 3.
**Eglise Orthodoxe Russe de Genève (ROCOR),** Rue Toepffer 3, CH-1206 Genève. T: (022)464709.
**Eglise Orthodoxe Russe (Patriachat de Moscou),** Rue Beaumont 6, Genève.
**Ev Gesellschaft des Kantons Bern,** Sek, 16 Lehrer, CH-2722 Mont-Tramelan.
**Ev-Methodistische Kirche,** Bischof, Badenerstr 69, CH-8004 Zürich.
**Ev-Reformierte Kirche des Kantons Aargau,** Bureau des Kirchenrates, Augustin-Keller-Str 3, CH-5000 Aarau. T: (064)222912.
**Ev-Reformierte Kirche des Kantons Appenzell AR,** Präs des Kirchenrates, CH-9100 Herisau. T:(071)512430.
**Ev-Reformierte Kirche des Kantons Basel-Landschaft,** Sekretariat, Rosengasse 1, CH-1410 Liestal. T: (061)912251.
**Ev-Reformierte Kirche des Kantons Basel-Stadt,** Sekretariat, Rittergasse 1, CH-4000 Basel. T: (061)238995.
**Ev-Reformierte Kirche des Kantons Bern,** Sekretariat, Bürenstr 12, CH-3007 Bern. T: (031) 453623.
**Ev-Reformierte Kirche des Kantons Glarus,** Präs, Landstr 44, CH-8750 Glarus. T: (058)614392.
**Ev-Reformierte Kirche des Kantons Graubünden,** Präs des Kirchenrates, CH-7017 Flims. T: (081)391274.
**Ev-Reformierte Kirche des Kantons St Gallen,** Präs des Kirchenrates, Museumstr 45, CH-9000 St Gallen. T: (071)242874.
**Ev-Reformierte Kirche des Kantons Schaffhausen,** Sekretariat, Albulastr 4a, CH-8200 Schaffhausen. T: (053)44862.
**Ev-Reformierte Kirche des Kantons Thurgau,** Präs des Kirchenrates, Schulstr 9, CH-9542 Münchwilen. T: (073)262997.
**Ev-Reformierte Kirche des Kantons Zürich,** Sekretariat, Hirschengraben 40, CH-8001 Zürich. T: (01)322520.
**Ev-Reformierte Kirche im Kanton Solothurn,** Präs des Synodalrates, CH-4658 Daniken. T: (062)651223.
**Freie Christengemeinden,** Au, Kappel, SG.
**Gemeinde für Urchristentum,** Pfr Oberhofen am Thunersee.
**Heilsarmee,** Laupenstr 5, Postfach 2659, CH-3001 Bern. T: (031)250591/3.
**Katholische Kirche in der Schweiz,** Conférence des Evêques Suisses, Av Moléson 30, CH-1700 Fribourg 1. T: (037)224794.
**Neuapostolische Kirche,** Rue Liotard 14, Genève.
**Pilgermission St-Chrischona,** Direktion, 22 St-Christchona, CH-4126 Bettingen.
**Schweizerische Pfingstmission,** Seehofstr 16, Zürich.
**Schweizerischer Verein für Freies Christentum,** Hofstattstr 5, CH-8280 Kreuzlingen.
**Témoins de Jéhovah,** Allmendstr 39, CH-3000 Bern 22.

*SYRIA*

**Catholic Ch in Syria,** Archevêché Syrien Catholique, Bab Charki, Dimashq. T: 110882.
**Greek Orthodox Ch,** Patriarch, Patriarchate, PO Box 9, Dimashq. T: 110329,116329.
**Syrian Orthodox Ch,** Patriarch, Bab Touma, PO Box 914, Dimashq. T: 117810.

*TANZANIA*

**Africa Inland Ch,** Bp, PO Box 125 & 905, Mwanza. T: 2177.
**African Greek Orthodox Ch,** Bp, PO Box 1090, Dar es Salaam.
**Baptist Convention of Tanzania,** Baptist Seminary of EA, PO Box 739, Arusha.
**Bible Ch,** CMML, PO Box 524, Mtwara. T: 15.
**Catholic Ch in Tanzania,** Archbishop's House, PO Box 167, Dar es Salaam. T: 22031.
**Christian Brethren,** Admin Sec, PO Box 2596, Dar es Salaam. T: 63654.
**Christian Witness Ch,** Ibanda-Geita, PO Box 7, Geita.
**Ch of the Province of Tanzania (CPT),** Archbp, PO Box 35161, Dar es Salaam. T: 63151.
**Chs of Christ,** PO Box 258, Dar es Salaam.
**Ev Lutheran Ch of Tanzania (ELCT),** Askofu Mkuu, PO Box 3033, Arusha. T: 2426,2134.
**Moravian Ch,** Bp, PO Box 29, Tabora. T: 214,230. (Also: PO Box 32, Tukuyu. T: 30).
**Pentecostal Assemblies of God,** Gen Sec, PO Box 732, Mwanza.
**Pentecostal Chs in Tanzania,** PCSAT, PO Box 6, Kigoma.
**Pentecostal Holiness Association Mission,** Sec, PO Box 77, Mbeya. (Also: PO Box 65, Tukuyu).
**Salvation Army,** PO Box 1273, Dar es Salaam. T: 50395.
**Seventh-day Adventist Ch,** Pres, PO Box 26, Musoma.
**Tanganyika Mennonite Ch,** Bp, PO Box 7, Musoma.
**Tanzania Assemblies of God,** PO Box 2292, Dar es Salaam. T: 67403.

*THAILAND*

**Catholic Ch in Thailand,** Assumption Cathedral, Bangrak, Bangkok 5. T: 2338712.
**Ch of Christ in Thailand (CCT),** Gen Sec, 14 Pramuan Rd, Bangkok.
**Ch of God in Thailand,** 119/26-27 Soi Poomchit, Rama Four St, PO Box 11-121, Bangkok 11. T: 3925408.
**Ev Gospel Ch of Thailand,** 1483 Usdang Rd, PO Box 1, Korat.
**Jehovah's Witnesses,** 69/1 Soi 2, Sukhumwit Rd, Bangkok 11.
**Overseas Missionary Fellowship,** Field Sec, 135 Pan Rd, Silom, Bangkok 5. T: 33133.
**Seventh-day Adventist Ch,** Pres, Soi Charoen, Suk 90/23, Klongton Prakanong, PO Box 11-234, Bangkok. T: 913595.
**Thai Full Gospel Ch,** 70/7 Soi Areesampan 10, PO Box 247, Bangkok. T: 58345,76209.
**Thailand Baptist Chs Association,** 133/15 Raja Damri Rd, PO Box 832, Bangkok. T: 57078.

*TOGO*

**Assemblées de Dieu,** National Super, BP 252, Lomé.
**Association Baptiste Togolaise,** 124 Blvd Circulaire, BP 640, Lomé.
**Cherubin et Seraphin du Mont Zion du Togo,** BP 6083, Lomé.
**Eglise Adventiste du Septième Jour,** Prés, Mission Adventiste, 3 Rue Curie, BP 1222, Lomé. T: 3141.
**Eglise Apostolique du Togo et Benin,** 18 Rue d'Italie, Lomé.
**Eglise Catholique au Togo,** Archevêché, BP 348, Lomé. T: 2272.
**Eglise de Pentecôte Apostolique,** BP 361, Lomé.
**Eglise du Christianisme Céleste,** BP 1970, Lomé.
**Eglise du Seigneur (Aladura),** Cocoterrain, Agbetsiafa, Lomé.
**Eglise Ev du Togo,** BP 2, Lomé.
**Société Révélation Apostolique,** BP 957, Lomé.
**Témoins de Jéhovah,** BP 1237, Lomé.

*TONGA*

**Assemblies of God of Tonga,** Central Office, PO Box 218, Nukualofa.
**Catholic Ch,** Bishop's House, PO Box 1, Nukualofa. T: 433.
**Ch of Jesus Christ of Latter-day Saints,** Pres, PO Box 58, Nukualofa.
**Free Wesleyan Ch of Tonga,** PO Box 57, Nukualofa.
**Seventh-day Adventist Ch,** Pres, PO Box 15, Nukualofa.

*TIMOR*

**Igreja Católica,** Bispado, Dili. T: 2351.

*TRINIDAD & TOBAGO*

**African Methodist Episcopal Ch,** 20 Woodford St, Newtown, Port of Spain.
**Anglican Ch,** Diocese of Trinidad, Bp, 21 Maraval Rd, Port of Spain.
**Assembly of God,** Sec, Piarco Village, Trinidad.
**Baptist Union of Trinidad & Tobago,** 11 Phillip St, Port of Spain. (Also: High St, Princes Town).
**Catholic Ch,** 27 Maraval Rd, Port of Spain. T: (62) 21103
**Ch of God,** 15 Carlos St, Woodbrook, Port of Spain.
**Ch of God (Anderson),** 15 Carlos St, Port of Spain.
**Ch of the Nazarene,** 5 Angelina St, St James, Port of Spain.
**Jehovah's Witnesses,** 21 Taylor St, Woodbrook, Port of Spain.
**Methodist Ch in the Caribbean & the Americas,** 2 Victoria Av, Port of Spain.
**Moravian Ch,** 129 Laventill Rd, Port of Spain.
**New Testament Ch of God,** Plaisance Main Rd, Pointe-à-Pierre.
**Open Bible Standard Chs,** 8/14 Ruth Av, San Fernando.
**Pentecostal Assemblies of the West Indies,** 85 Tunapuna Rd, Tunapuna.
**Presbyterian Ch in Trinidad & Grenada,** Moderator, 5 Carib St, San Fernando.
**Salvation Army,** 27 Edward St, PO Box 248 Port of Spain. T: 54120.
**Seventh-day Adventist Ch,** Pres, 7 Rookery Nook, PO Box 221, Port of Spain. T: 22514,22543.
**United Holy Ch of America,** Bp, 9 Whitney St, Laventille.
**Wesleyan Ch,** 2 Queen St, St Joseph.

*TUNISIA*

**Eglise Catholique,** Prélature, 4 Rue d'Alger, Tunis. T: 245225.

*TURKEY*

**Armenian Apostolic Patriarchate of Constantinople,** Sirapnel sok 20-22, Kumkapi, Istanbul.
**Armenian Ev Union,** Balipasa Yokusu 27, Gedikpasa, Istanbul.
**Bulgarian Orthodox Exarchate,** Halaskar Gazi Caddesi 319, Sisli, Istanbul.
**Catholic Ch in Turkey,** Ataturk Caddesi 210/6, PK 267, Izmir. T: 24017.
**Ch of England,** Crimean Memorial Church, Ingilterre Bas Konsoloslugu, Beyoglu, Istanbul.
**Ecumenical Patriarchate of Constantinople (Rum Patrikhanesi),** Sadrazam Ali Pasha Caddesi 35, Fener (Phanar), Istanbul. T: 239850.
**German Protestant Ch,** Emin Cami Sokak 42, Aynalicesme, Istanbul.
**Syrian Orthodox Ch,** Metropolitan, PK 16, Mardin.
**Turkish Orthodox Ch,** Patriarch, Karaköy, Istanbul. T: 442810. (Also in Galata).

*TURKS & CAICOS ISLANDS*

**Anglican Ch,** Diocese of Nassau and the Bahamas, PO Box 24, Grand Turk.
**Seventh-day Adventist Ch,** Pres, PO Box 7, Grand Turk.

*TUVALU*

**Tuvalu Ch,** Funafuti.

*UGANDA*

**African Greek Orthodox Ch (AGOC),** Bp, Namungona, PO Box 508, Kampala.
**Association of Baptist Chs,** PO Box 93, Masaka.
**Catholic Ch in Uganda,** Catholic Secretariat, PO Box 2886, Kampala. T: 43042,63206,54507,54541.
**Ch of Uganda (CURBZ),** Archbp, Namirembe Hill, PO Box 14123, Kampala.
**Elim Pentecostal Fellowship of Uganda,** PO Box 2613, Kampala.
**Full Gospel Chs of Uganda,** PO Box 2560, Kampala.
**Pentecostal Assemblies of God,** PO Box 252, Mbale.
**Salvation Army,** PO Box 1186, Kampala.
**Seventh-day Adventist Ch,** Pres, PO Box 22, Kampala. T: 60222.

*USSR*

**Armenian Apostolic Ch,** Catholicos, Holy Echmiadzin, Erevan, Armenian SSR.
**Catholic Ch in the USSR,** Vilniaus Gatve 4, Kaunas, Lietuva, Lithuanian SSR. T: 22097.
**Ev Lutheran Ch of Estonia,** Archiepiszkop, Raamatukognstr 8, Quartier K, Tallinn, Estonian SSR.
**Ev Lutheran Ch of Latvia,** Archbp, Kirov-Str 37-5, Riga, Latvian SSR.
**Ev Lutheran Ch of Lithuania,** Lietuviu gatve 10, Kaunas, Lithuanian SSR.
**Ev Reformed Ch of Lithuania,** Wilnastr 44, Birzai, Lithuanian SSR.
**Georgian Orthodox Ch,** Catholicos-Patriarch, 4 Sionskayastr, Tbilisi, Georgian SSR.
**Reformed Ch in Carpatho-Ukraine,** Selo Strumnovka, Ushgorov Raion, 20 Karpathian Oblast, Ukrainian SSR.
**Russian Orthodox Ch,** Exarchate of the Ukraine, Exarch & Metropolitan, Pushkinskaya 36, Kijev, Ukrainian SSR. T: 49000,58118.
**Russian Orthodox Ch,** Patriarchate of Moscow, Patriarch, Chisty Pereulok 5, Moskva G-34. (Also: Dept of External Affairs, Ryleev St 18/2, Moskva G-34. T: 2022954,2023043).
**Union of Ev Christians-Baptists,** Gen Sec, Pokrousky Blvd, Malyi Vusoksky 3, PO Box 520, Moskva. T: 227-8947.

*UK OF GB & NI*

(Denominations with 10,000 or more adherents).
**Apostolic Ch of Great Britain,** General HQ, Penygroes, Lanelli, South Wales.
**Assemblies of God in GB & Ireland,** 106-114 Talbot St, Nottingham, Notts NG1 5GW.
**Baptist Union of GB & Ireland,** Baptist Church House, 4 Southampton Row, London WC1B 4AB.
**Baptist Union of Ireland,** Gen Sec, 3 Fitzwilliam St, Belfast 9. T: 22303.
**Baptist Union of Scotland,** 14 Aytoun Rd, Glasgow S1.
**Baptist Union of Wales & Monmouthshire,** Ilston House, 94 Munnsel St, Swansea.
**Catholic Ch in England and Wales,** Archbishop's House, Westminster, London SW1P 1QJ. T: (01) 834-4717.
**Catholic Ch in Ireland,** Archbishop's House, Ara Coehli, Armagh, Northern Ireland. T: 2045.
**Catholic Ch in Scotland,** Press Office, 86 St Vincents St, Glasgow G2 5UP.
**Christian Brethren (Open),** 1 Widcombe Crescent, Bath, Avon.
**Ch in Wales,** Representative Body, Sec, 39 Cathedral Rd, Cardiff CF1 9XF.
**Ch of Christ, Scientist,** First Church, Ingersoll House, 9 Kingsway, London WC2.
**Ch of England,** General Synod, Church House, Dean's Yard, Westminster, London SW1P 3NZ. T: (01)222 9011.
**Ch of God of Prophecy,** 27 Drewstead Rd, London SW16.
**Ch of Jesus Christ of Latter-day Saints,** England East Mission, 64 Exhibition Rd, London SW7 2PA.
**Ch of Scotland,** Principal Clerk, 121 George St, Edinburgh EH2 4YN.
**Ch of the Nazarene,** 6 Blencairne Rd, London SW11.
**Chs of Christ in GB & Ireland,** Gen Sec, 59 Vicarage Rd, King's Heath, Birmingham B14 7QA.
**Congregational Federation,** 28a Fredrick St, Loughborough, Leics.
**Cooneyites (Gospel Preachers),** Sec, County Fermanagh, Northern Ireland.
**Elim Pentecostal Ch,** St Georges Rd, Cheltenham, Glos. T: (0422)59904/6
**Episcopal Ch in Scotland,** Representative Church Council, Gen Sec, 21 Grosvenor Crescent, Edinburgh EH12 5EE. T: (031)225-6357.
**Fellowship of Independent Ev Chs (FIEC),** 136 Rosendale Rd, West Dulwich, London SE21 8LG.
**Free Ch of England,** 16 North Bank St, Edinburgh 1.
**Free Presbyterian Ch of Ulster,** Moderator, 128 Ravenhill Rd, Belfast 6.
**Greater World Christian Spiritualist League,** 3 Landsdowne Rd, London W11.
**Greek Orthodox Ch,** Archdiocese of Thyateira and GB, 5 Craven Hill, London W2. T: (01)723-4787.
**Holy Spirit Association for the Unification of World Christianity,** Cleeve House, Seend, nr Devizes, Wilts.
**Independent Methodist Connexion,** 55 Toothill Rd, Loughborough, Leics LE11 1PN.
**Jehovah's Witnesses,** Watch Tower House, The Ridgeway, London NW7.
**Lutheran Council of Great Britain,** Lutheran Church House, 8 Collingham Gardens, London SW5.
**Methodist Ch in Ireland,** 3 Upper Malone Rd, Belfast BT9 6TD, N Ireland.
**Methodist Ch of Great Britain,** 1 Central Bldgs, London SW1H 9NH.
**New Testament Ch of God,** Wolverhampton Rd, Sedgley, nr Dudley, Worcs.
**Polish Orthodox Ch Abroad,** 5 Penywern Rd, London SW5.
**Presbyterian Ch in Ireland,** Church House, Fisherwich Place, Belfast, BT1 6DW, N Ireland. T: 665627.
**Presbyterian Ch of Wales,** 9 Camden Rd, Brecon, Breconshire LD3 7BU, South Wales.
**Religious Society of Friends,** Friends House, Euston Rd, London NW1 2BJ.
**Russian Orthodox Ch,** Metropolitan, Ennismore Gardens, London SW7.
**Russian Orthodox Ch Outside of Russia,** Bp, 14 St Dunstan Rd, London W6.
**Salvation Army,** International HQ, 101 Queen Victoria St, PO Box 249, London EC4P 4EP. T: (01)236-5222.
**Serbian Orthodox Ch,** Bp, St Sava's Church,

Lancaster Rd, London W11.
**Seventh-day Adventist Ch,** Pres, 119 St Peter's St, St Albans, Herts. T: 60331.
**Spiritualist Association of Great Britain,** 33 Belgrave Square, London SW1. T: Belgravia 3351.
**Spiritualists National Union (SNU),** Kelvedon Rd, London SW6. T: (01)736-3031.
**Strict and Particular Baptist Chs,** Taylors Farm House, Battisford, Stowmarket, Suffolk IP14 2BN.
**Ukrainian Autocephalic Orthodox Ch,** 70 Lansdowne Rd, London W11.
**Union of Welsh Independents,** 11 St Helen's Rd, Swansea, Glamorgan SA1 4AL.
**Unitarian and Free Christian Chs,** Essex Hall, 1-6 Essex St, Strand, London WC2R 3HY. T: (01) 240-2384/5.
**United Apostolic Faith Ch,** Wightman Rd, London N8.
**United Free Ch of Scotland,** 11 Newton Place, Glasgow G3 7PR.
**United Reformed Ch,** 86 Tavistock Place, London WC1H 9RT.
**Wesleyan Reform Union,** 123 Queens St, Sheffield S1 2DU.

*USA*
(Denominations with 200,000 or more adherents).
**African Methodist Episcopal Ch,** Senior Bp, 2295 Seventh Av, New York, NY 10030. T: (212)926-4259.
**African Methodist Episcopal Zion Ch,** 1200 Windermere Drive, Pittsburgh, PA 15218.
**American Baptist Association,** Pres, 4605 North State Line Av, Texarkana, AR 75501. T: (214)792-2783.
**American Baptist Chs in the USA,** Gen Sec, Valley Forge, PA 19481. T: (215)768-2000.
**American Lutheran Ch,** Pres, 422 South 5th St, Minneapolis, MN 55415. T: (612)338-3821.
**Armenian Ch of North America,** Primate, St Vartan's Cathedral, 630 Second Av, New York, NY 10016. T: (212)686-0710.
**Assemblies of God,** General Conference, Gen Super, 1445 Boonville Av, Springfield, MO 65802 T: (417)862-2781.
**Baptist Bible Fellowship International,** Pres, PO Box 191, 730 East Kearney, Springfield, MO 65801. T: (417)862-5001.
**Baptist Missionary Association of America,** PO Box 2866, Texarkana, AR 75501.
**Catholic Ch in the USA,** National Conference of Catholic Bishops, 1312 Massachusetts Av, NW, Washington, DC 20005. T: (202)659-6600.
**Christian Ch (Disciples of Christ),** Pres, 222 South Downey Av, PO Box 1986, Indianapolis, IN 46206. T: (317)353-1491.
**Christian Methodist Episcopal Ch,** Sec, 664 Vance Av, Memphis, TN 38126.
**Christian Reformed Ch,** Clerk, 2850 Kalamazoo Av, SE, Grand Rapids, MI 49508. T: (616)241-1691.
**Ch of Christ, Scientist,** Mother Church, Christian Science Center, Boston, MA 02115. T: (617)262-2300.
**Ch of God in Christ,** National HQ, 938 Mason St, Memphis, TN 38126.
**Ch of God (Anderson),** Exec Sec, PO Box 2420, Anderson, IN 46011. T: (317)642-0256.
**Ch of God (Cleveland),** Gen Overseer, Keith St at 25th NW, Cleveland, TN 37311. T: (615)472-3361.
**Ch of Jesus Christ of Latter-day Saints,** Church HQ, 47 East South Temple St, Salt Lake City, UT 84111. T: (801)531-2238.
**Ch of the Brethren,** Gen Sec, 1451 Dundee Av, Elgin, IL 60120. T: (312)742-5100
**Ch of the Nazarene,** Gen Sec, 6401 The Paseo, Kansas City, MO 64131. T: (816)333-7000.
**Conservative Baptist Association of America,** Gen Dir, Geneva Rd, PO Box 66, Wheaton, IL 60187. T: (312)653-5350.
**Episcopal Ch in the USA,** Presiding Bp, 815 Second Av, New York, NY 10017. T: (212)867-8400.
**Free Methodist Ch of North America,** 901 College Av, Winona Lake, IN 46590. T: (219)267-7161.
**General Association of Regular Baptist Chs,** 1800 Oakton Blvd, Des Plaines, IL 60018. T: (312)827-7105.
**General Conference, Mennonite Ch,** 722 Main, Newton, KS 67114. T: (316)283-5100.
**Greek Orthodox Archdiocese of North & South America,** Primate, 8-10 East 79th St, New York, NY 10021. T: (212)628-2500.
**Independent Fundamental Chs of America,** National Exec Dir, 1860 Mannheim Rd, Westchester, IL 60153. T: (312)562-0234.
**International Ch of the Foursquare Gospel,** Angelus Temple, 1100 Glendale Blvd, Los Angeles, CA 90026. T: (213)484-1100.
**Jehovah's Witnesses,** 124 Columbia Heights, Brooklyn, NY 11201. T: (212)625-1240.
**Lutheran Ch in America,** 231 Madison Av, New York, NY 10016. T: (212)532-3410.
**Lutheran Ch—Missouri Synod,** Pres, 500 North Broadway, St Louis, MO 63102. T: (314)231-6969.
**National Association of Free Will Baptists,** 1134 Murfreeboro Rd, Nashville, TN 37217. T: (615)244-3470.
**National Baptist Convention of America,** 2620 South Marsallis Av, Dallas, TX 75216.
**National Baptist Covention, USA,** Sec, 915 Spain St, Baton Rouge, LA 70802.
**National Council of Community Chs,** Pres, 89 East Wilson Bridge Rd, Worthington, OH 43085. T: (614)888-4501.
**National Primitive Baptist Convention,** 1525 South Bronough St, PO Box 2355, Tallahassee, FL 32301.
**Native American Ch,** Pres, c/o Omaha Tribal Office, Macy, NE 68039.
**Orthodox Ch in America,** Primate Chancery, Route 25A, PO Box 675, Syosset, NY 11791. T: (516)922-0550.
**Pentecostal Holiness Ch,** Gen Super, PO Box 295, Franklin Springs, GA 30639. T: (404)245-6111.
**Polish National Catholic Ch of North America,** Prime Bp, 529 East Locust St, Scranton, PA 18505.
**Presbyterian Ch in the US,** 341 Ponce de Leon Av NE, Atlanta, GA 30308. T: (404)875-8921.
**Progressive National Baptist Convention,** Exec Sec, 3907 Georgia Av, NW, Washington, DC 20011. T: (202)291-2050.
**Reformed Ch in America,** 475 Riverside Drive, New York, NY 10027.
**Reorganized Ch of Jesus Christ of Latter-day Saints,** Pres, Auditorium, Independence, MO 64051. T: (816)833-1000.
**Salvation Army,** 120 West 14th St, New York, NY 10011. T: (212)243-8700.
**Seventh-day Adventist Ch,** General Conference, 6840 Eastern Av, NW, Washington, DC 20012. T: (202)723-0800.
**Southern Baptist Convention,** 460 James Robertson Parkway, Nashville, TN 37219. T: (615)244-2355.
**Unitarian Universalist Association,** 25 Beacon St, Boston, MA 02108.
**United Ch of Christ,** 297 Park Av South, New York, NY 10010. T: (212)475-2121.
**United Methodist Ch,** Council on Finance and Administration, 1200 Davis St, Evanston, IL 60201. T: (312)869-3345.
**United Pentecostal Ch,** Gen Sec, 8855 Dunn Rd, Hazelwood, MO 63042. T: (314)837-7300.
**United Presbyterian Ch in the USA,** Stated Clerk, 475 Riverside Drive, New York, NY 10027. T: (212)870-2664.
**Wisconsin Ev Lutheran Synod,** 3512 West North Av, Milwaukee, WI 53208. T: (414)445-4022.
**Worldwide Ch of God,** Ambassador College, PO Box 111, Pasadena, CA 91109.

*US VIRGIN ISLANDS*
**Catholic Ch,** Bishop's Residence, PO Box 1825, St Thomas, VI 00801. T: (809)774-1102.
**Ch of God of Prophecy,** Levkoi C17, St Thomas.
**Ch of God (Cleveland),** PO Box 787, St Thomas.
**Episcopal Ch,** Bp, PO Box 1589, St Thomas 00801.
**Metropolitan Church Association,** PO Box 105, Christiansted, St Croix.
**Moravian Ch,** PO Box 617, Frederiksted, St Croix.
**Salvation Army,** 2 Torvets Gade Back St, PO Box 74, St Thomas 00801. T: 774-1151.

*UPPER VOLTA*
**Assemblées de Dieu en Haute-Volta,** National Super, BP 29 & 121, Ouagadougou.
**Association des Eglises Ev en Haute-Volta,** Sudan Interior Mission, Fada N'Gourma.
**Eglise Apostolique de Haute-Volta,** BP 550, Ouagadougou.
**Eglise Catholique en Haute-Volta,** Archevêché, BP 1471, Ouagadougou. T: 35180.
**Eglise Chrétienne Ev en Haute-Volta,** BP 128, Bobo-Dioulasso.
**Eglises Ev de Pentecôte en Haute-Volta,** BP 1, Léo.
**Mission Ev de l'Afrique Occidentale,** Mission Evangélique, Gaoua.

*URUGUAY*
**Asambleas de Dios (Sueca),** Nerdi 4665, Casilla 50, Montevideo.
**Asambleas de Dios (USA),** Teodoro García 3238, Casilla de Correo 1617, Montevideo.
**Convención Ev Bautista del Uruguay,** Agraciada 3452, Montevideo.
**Ejército de Salvación,** Hocquart 1886, Montevideo. T: 47581.
**Iglesia Adventista del Séptimo Día,** Av Larranaga 2738, Casilla 286, Montevideo. T: 584083,587720.
**Iglesia Católica en el Uruguay,** Arzobispado, Calle Treinta y Tres 1368, Montevideo. T: 901642.
**Iglesia de Dios (Cleveland),** Nancy 4264, Montevideo.
**Iglesia Ev Metodista en el Uruguay,** San José 1457, Montevideo.
**Iglesia Ev Pentecostal de Chile,** Las Piedras, Población El Obelisco, Montevideo.

*VANUATU*
**Apostolic Ch,** Pastor, Walaha, Aoba via Santo.
**Assemblies of God,** Pastor, Vila.
**Catholic Ch,** Evêché, BP 59, Port Vila. T: 2640.
**Chs of Christ in the New Hebrides,** Duindui, Aoba via Santo.
**Presbyterian Ch of the New Hebrides,** PO Box 150, Vila.
**Seventh-day Adventist Ch,** Pres, PO Box 14, Santo. T: 427.

*VENEZUELA*
**Asambleas de Dios en Venezuela,** Apdo 2169, Caracas.
**Asociación de Iglesias Ev del Oriente (ASIGEO),** Apdo 4258, Puerto La Cruz, Anzoátegui.
**Convención Nacional Bautista de Venezuela,** Apdo 14190, Caracas. (Also: Apdo 9190, Candelaria, Caracas).
**Hermanos Unidos,** Apdo 646, Valencia, Carabobo.
**Iglesia Adventista del Séptimo Día,** Pres, Carcel a Pilita 2, Apdo 986, Caracas. T: 413877.
**Iglesia Anglicana,** Diocese of Venezuela, Obispo, Apdo 68733, ZP 106, Caracas.
**Iglesia Católica en Venezuela,** Arzobispado, Apdo 954, Caracas 101. T: 813252.
**Iglesia del Evangelio Cuadrangular,** Apdo 270, San Cristobal, Pachira.
**Iglesia Pentecostal Unida de Venezuela,** Apdo 197, Barquisimeto, Edo Lara.
**Iglesia Presbiteriana de Venezuela,** Apdo 212, Caracas.
**Iglesias Bautistas de Delta,** Monagas y Guayana Apdo 46, Puerto Ordaz, Edo Bolivar.
**Iglesias Ev Independientes y Nacionales de Venezuela,** Apdo 161, Maturín, Edo Mlonagas.
**Iglesias Ev Libres de Venezuela (IELV),** Apdo 8380, Caracas.
**Iglesias Nativas Venezolanas de Apure,** Calle Diamante 41, San Fernando de Apure, Edo Apure.
**Misión Nuevas Tribus de Venezuela,** Misión Evangélica, Puerto Ayacucho, TF Amazonas.
**Organización Venezolana de Iglesias Cristianas Ev (OVICE),** Apdo 74, Barinas, Edo Barinas.
**Testigos de Jehová,** Av Honduras, Quinta Luz, Urb Las Acacias, Caracas.
**Unión Pentecostal Venezolana,** Apdo 311, Barquisimeto, Edo Lara.

*VIET NAM*
**Catholic Ch in Viet-Nam,** Archevêché, 40 Phô Nhà Chung, Hanoi.
**Ev Ch of Viet-Nam,** 2 Su Van Hanh, Cholon District, PO Box 923, Saigon. T: 38136.
**Mennonite Ch of Viet-Nam,** 336 Phan Thanh Gian, Saigon.
**Seventh-day Adventist Ch,** Pres, 230 Chi-Long, Phu-Nhuan, PO Box 453, Saigon.
**Vietnam Christ's Church,** Pres, 376 Tram Quy Cap St, Saigon.

*WALLIS & FUTUNA ISLANDS*
**Eglise Catholique,** Evêché, Lano, Ile Wallis, via Nouméa. T: 83.

*YEMEN, South*
**Catholic Ch,** Vicariate of Arabia, Steamer Point, PO Box 1155, Aden. T: 22900.

*YUGOSLAVIA*
**Catholic Ch in Yugoslavia,** Biskupska Konferencija Jugoslavije, Kaptol 31, PB 02-406, 41000 Zagreb. T: (041)34156.
**Christian Adventist Ch in Yugoslavia,** Pres, Bozidara Adzije br 4, 11000 Beograd. T: 453842/866, 4441285.
**Ch of God in Yugoslavia,** Glavno Staresinsivo, Lenjinova br 66A, Vintovci.
**Ch of the Spirit (Foot-washing),** Praninska 43, Srem Mitrovica.
**Ch of the Spirit (Infant-baptizing),** Radonovac 53/a, Subotica.
**Ev Christian Ch in Slovenia,** Murska Sobota.
**Ev Ch in Croatia, Bosnia, Herzegovina D Vojvodina,** Gunduliceva 28, Zagreb.
**Ev Ch in the People's Republic of Serbia,** P Kujundrica 17, Subaotica.
**Free Brethren Congregations,** Ulica Aleksandra Glisica 6, Beograd. (Also: Kosovska Ulica br 17, Novi Sad).
**Macedonia Orthodox Ch,** Archbp, Makedonska Arhiepiskopija, 91000 Skopje, Macedonian PR. T: 32408,33880.
**Pentecostal Ch of Christ in Yugoslavia,** Boze Jankovica 74, Beograd.
**Reformed Christian Ch in Yugoslavia,** Dobracina 33, Beograd. T: 622079.
**Serbian Orthodox Ch,** Patriarch, Serbian Patriarchate, Holy Synod, Ulica 7 Jula br 5, Fah 182, 11000 Beograd.
**Slovak Ev Christian Ch,** Bp, Karadziceva 2, Novi Sad.
**Union of Baptist Chs in Yugoslavia,** Pres, Brace Ribnikara 41, Novi Sad.
**United Jehovah's Witnesses in Yugoslavia,** Kula Strazara, Kamaufovr 11, Zagreb.

*ZAIRE*
**Eglise Catholique au Zaire,** Archevêché, BP 8431, Kinshasa 1. T: 69221.
**Eglise Chrétienne Ev en Afrique (ECEA),** BP 302, Kisangani.
**Eglise de Jésus-Christ sur la Terre par le Prophète Simon Kimbangu (EJCSK),** Chef Spirituel, 87 Rue Monkoto, BP 7069, Kinshasa 1. T: 68944.
**Eglise de Jésus-Christ sur la Terre par le Saint-Esprit,** BP 3523, Kinshasa-Kalina.
**Eglise de la Foi par Messie Jésus-Christ,** Sec Gen, BP 1090, Kinshasa.
**Eglise des Noirs en Afrique Centrale (ENAC),** Patriarche, Ntendesi, BP 8029, Kinshasa.
**Eglise Dieu-Donné au Zaire,** Fondateur, 95 Av Mawanga, Quartier III, Commune de Ngaba, Kinshasa.
**Eglise du Christ au Zaire (ECZ),** Sec, BP 3094, Kinshasa-Kalina.
**Eglise Ev du Haut-Uélé,** BP 81, Isiro.
**Eglise Ev Zairoise au Mayombe,** Paroisse de Kisenso, BP 380 Limete, Kinshasa.
**Eglise Orthodoxe,** BP 5007, Kinshasa. (Also: BP 719, Lubumbashi. T: 4252,2060).
**Eglise Sabbatique du Saint-Esprit,** BP 160, Kinshasa-Limete.
**Eglise Unie du Saint-Esprit (EUSE),** 195 Rue Movenda, Ngiri-Ngiri, BP 6, Kinshasa I.
**Témoins de Jéhovah,** BP 634, Kinshasa-Limete.

*ZAMBIA*
**African Methodist Episcopal Ch,** Sec, PO Box 7, Buchi, Kitwe.
**Anglican Ch in Zambia,** Bp, Bishop's Lodge, PO Box 183, Lusaka.
**Apostolic Faith Mission of Zambia,** PO Box 709, Lusaka.
**Baptist Mission of Zambia,** PO Box RW 500 (& Box 1945), Lusaka.
**Baptist Union of Central Africa,** Field Sec, PO Box 730, Ndola.
**Brethren in Christ Ch,** Bp, PO Box 115, Choma.
**Catholic Ch in Zambia,** Archdiocese, PO Box 2764, Lusaka. T: (012)81607.
**Christian Brethren,** Kalene Hill Mission, PO Ikelenge.
**Ch of Jesus Christ on Earth through the Prophet Simon Kimbangu,** PO Box 2702, Lusaka.
**Chs of Christ,** PO Box 22, Kalome.
**Dutch Reformed Ch (Mother Ch),** PO Box 1922, Lusaka.
**Ev Ch in Zambia,** PO Box 1395, Ndola.
**Jehovah's Witnesses,** Bethel, PO Box 1598, Kitwe.
**Lambaland Baptist Ch,** Field Super, PO Box 248, Ndola.
**Pentecostal Assemblies of God of Zambia,** PO Box 297, Chingola.
**Presbyterian Ch in Zambia,** PO Box 1004, Lusaka.
**Reformed Ch in Zambia,** Synod Clerk, PO Box 18 & 100, Katete.
**Salvation Army,** PO Box RW 193, Lusaka. T: 74761.
**Scandinavian Independent Baptist Union,** Sec, Mpongwe Mission, PO Box 96, Luknshya.
**Seventh-day Adventist Ch,** Pres, PO Box 1309, Lusaka. T: Monze 2712. (Also: PO Box 13, Chisekesi).
**United Ch of Zambia,** Synod Clerk, PO Box RW 122, Lusaka.
**Wesleyan Ch,** Field Super, PO Box 103, Choma.

*ZIMBABWE*
**Africa Evangelical Ch,** Biriiri Mission Station, PB M7295, Umtali.
**African Apostolic Ch of Johane Maranke (AACJM),** High Priest, Maranke Reserve, PO Umtali.
**African Methodist Ch in Zimbabwe,** Gen Super, PO Box 67, Umvuma.
**African Methodist Episcopal Ch,** 48 Beatrice Cottages, PO Harare, Salisbury.
**African Reformed Ch in Zimbabwe,** Field Sec, PO Morgenster.
**Anglican Ch in Zimbabwe,** Diocese of Mashonaland, Bp, Bishop's Mount, PO Box UA 7, Salisbury.
**Apostolic Faith Mission of South Africa,** Sec, 163 Sinoia St, Salisbury.
**Assemblies of God in Zimbabwe,** 55 Central Av, PO Box 302, Salisbury.
**Baptist Convention of Zimbabwe,** 152 Fourth Av, Parktown, Salisbury.
**Baptist Union of Central Africa,** Gen Sec, PO Box 280, Salisbury.
**Brethren in Christ Ch in Africa,** PO Box 711, Bulawayo.
**Catholic Ch in Zimbabwe,** Catholic Secretariat, PO Box 8060, Causeway, Salisbury. T: 27386.
**Christian Marching Ch of Central Africa,** PO Box 10016, Mabvuku, Salisbury. T: 81619. (Also: Gen Sec, PO Box 9038, Harare, Salisbury).
**Ch of Central Africa Presbyterian (CCAP),** PO Box 533, Salisbury.
**Chs of Christ (NZ),** Dadaya Mission, PO Dadaya.
**Chs of Christ (USA),** PO Box 108, Shabani
**Dutch Reformed Ch (Mother Church),** Sec, Jameson Av & Moffatt St, PO Box 967, Salisbury.
**Ev Ch of Zimbabwe,** PO Box H-60, Hatfield, Salisbury.
**Ev Lutheran Ch in Zimbabwe,** Bp, Mnene Mission, Belingwe. T: 0202.
**Free Methodist Ch,** Sec, PO Box 9030, Fort Victoria.
**Full Gospel Ch of God in Southern Africa,** Sec, Speke Av & Salisbury St, Salisbury.
**Greek Orthodox Archbishopric of Zimbabwe,** Moffatt St & Montagu Av, PO Box 2832, Salisbury.
**Independent African Ch,** PO Box 9027, Harare, Salisbury.
**Jehovah's Witnesses,** PO Box 1462, Salisbury.
**Methodist Ch in Zimbabwe,** Gen Super, 7 Central Av, PO Box 8298 & 3566, Causeway, Salisbury. T: 24069.
**Pentecostal Assemblies of God in Zimbabwe,** 35 Divine Rd, Milton Park, Salisbury.
**Presbyterian Ch of Southern Africa,** PO Box 106, Bulawayo.
**Salvation Army,** 45 Montagu Av, PO Box 14, Salisbury. T: 27717/8/9.
**Seventh-day Adventist Ch,** Pres, 114 Jameson St, PO Box 573, Bulawayo. T: 63937.
**United Apostolic Faith Ch,** Sec, 7 Ward Rd, Braeside, Salisbury.
**United Ch of Christ,** Chikore Mission, PO Craigmore.
**United Methodist Ch,** Bp, PO Box 8293 & 3408, Causeway, Salisbury.

# 2
# Aid and Relief

*Definition.* Specifically Christian voluntary agencies dealing with programmes of inter-church aid, Christian aid, relief, emergency action, disasters, refugees, population problems, minority groups, migrants, migration; inter-church service agencies; charities, charitable societies. See also DEVELOPMENT, JUSTICE AND PEACE.

This section omits national branches which are mainly on the receiving and distributing ends, of Caritas, CRS-USCC, ICMC, WVI, et alia (which are found in most countries). It includes international branches of largely sending nature, and a representative selection of receiving bodies in smaller countries.

*ALGERIA*
**Christian Committee for Service in Algeria,** Dir, 33 Av Ali-Khodja, Alger-El Biar.
**Service Quaker,** Arbaa des Ouacifs, Tizi Ouzou. T: Ouacif 19.

*ARGENTINA*
**Comisión Católica Argentina de Inmigración (CCAI),** Gen Sec, Laprida 930, Buenos Aires. T: 842683.
**Comisión Católica Argentina de la Lucha contra el Hambre,** Montevideo 850, Piso 1, Buenos Aires.
**Conferencias Vicentinas de Hombres,** Combate de los Pozos 347, Buenos Aires.
**Conferencias Vicentinas de Mujeres,** Riobamba 258, Buenos Aires.
**Emaus,** Sarandí 1139, Buenos Aires.

*AUSTRALIA*
**Australian Catholic Relief,** PO Box C360, Clarence St, Sydney, NSW 2000. T: 297896.
**Australian Council for Overseas Aid,** 241 King St, Melbourne, Victoria 3000.
**Bush Church Aid Society for Australia and Tasmania,** BCA House, 135 Bathurst St, Sydney. T: 263164.
**Division of Inter-Church Aid,** Australian Council of Churches, Gen Sec, 3rd Floor, 511 Kent St, Sydney, NSW 2000.

**Federal Catholic Immigration Committee (FCIC),** National Dir, 355 Kent St, Sydney, NSW 2000. T: 297884,292441.
**National Catholic Welfare Committee,** 582 Victoria Rd, Ryde, NSW. T: 804022.
**Quaker Service Council,** Friends House, 631 Orrong Rd, Toorak, Victoria 3142. T: 243592.
**World Vision of Australia,** Dir, 343 Little Collins, 7th Floor, Melbourne, Victoria 3000, and Box 399-C, Melbourne, Victoria 3001.

*AUSTRIA*
**Bauorde,** Postfach 5, A-1033 Wien. T: 735254. (Builds houses and churches).
**Komitee zur Betreuung Serbisch-Orthodoxer Gastarbeiter in Österreich,** Christian Coulinstr 24, A-4020 Linz.
**Österpriesterhilfe,** Nibelungengasse 1/4 Stg/III, A-1010 Wien. T: 571577.
**Österreichische Caritas-Zentrale,** Gen Sec, Nibelungengasse 1/4, Postfach 114, A-1010 Wien. T: (0222)571577. (Member, BICE).
**SOS Gemeinschaft,** Wahringer Gürtel 104, A-1090 Wien.

*BANGLADESH*
**Bangladesh Ecumenical Relief & Rehabilitation Service (BERRS),** 9 New Eskaton Road, Ramna, PO Box 220, Dacca 2. T: 282869.
**Christian Organization for Relief and Rehabilitation (CORR),** 23 New Eskaton Rd, PO Box 994, Dacca 2.

*BELGIUM*
**Association Internationale des Charités de Saint-Vincent de Paul (AIC),** Chaussée d'Ixelles 144, B-1050 Brussel. T: (02)5130881.
**Caritas Catholica Belgica,** Rue Guimard 5, B-1040 Brussel. T: (02)5123379,111006. (Member, BICE).
**Entraide Educative et Sociale (EES),** Rue Capouillet 10, Brussel 6. T: (02)374797.
**Entr'aide et Fraternité (Broederlijk Delen),** Rue de Commerce 70-72, B-1040 Brussel. T: (02) 5114255.
**Secours International de Caritas Catholica,** Rue Guimard 5, B-1040 Brussel.
**Service National d'Emigration (SNE),** National Dir, Rue Guimard 5, B-1040 Brussel. T: (02)114255.

*BRAZIL*
**Banco da Providência,** Ladeira da Gloria 99, ZC-01 Rio de Janeiro, GB.
**Federação de Orgãos para Assistência Social e Educational (FASE),** Exec Dir, Rua Mena Barreto 161, Andar 3, Botafogo-Guanabara, Rio de Janeiro. T: 463230.
**Secretariado Latinoamericano de Caritas,** c/o Caritas Brasileira, Ladeira da Gloria 67, CP 16094, ZC-01 Rio de Janeiro, GB. T: 2454021.

*BURMA*
**Burma National ECLOF Committee,** Pres, State Commercial Bank, Rangoon.

*CANADA*
**Canadian Friends Service Committee,** 60 Lowther Av, Toronto 180, Ontario. T: 920-5213.
**Catholic Charities Council of Canada,** 90 Av Parent, Ottawa, Ontario K1N 7B1.
**Catholic Immigrant Service (CIS),** Gen Sec, 637 Craig St West, Montréal 101, Québec. T: 861-8581.
**Comité d'Accueil Interconfessionnel,** 2000 Sherbrooke Ouest, Montréal 109, Québec. T: 931-7311 poste 224.
**Conseil des Oeuvres et du Bien-être du Diocèse de Québec,** 625 Grande-Allée Est, CP 730, Québec 4, Québec.
**Office des Néo-Canadiens,** 2000 Sherbrooke Ouest, Montréal 109, Québec. T: 931-7311 postes 126 et 110.
**Office National du Bien-être et de la Santé,** 1225 est, Boul Saint-Joseph, Montréal 176, Québec. T: 274-3658.
**Service d'Accueil aux Voyageurs et aux Immigrants (SAVI),** 750 Côte de la Place d'Armes, Montréal 126, Québec. T: jour 842-2971, soir 877-4291.
**Services pour Immigrants Catholiques/Catholic Immigrant Services,** 637 Craig Ouest, Montréal 101, Québec. T: 861-8581.
**World Vision of Canada,** Pres, 410 Consumers Rd, PO Box 781, Station B, Willowdale, Ontario. T: (416)487-2183.

*CENTRAL AFRICAN REPUBLIC*
**Secours Catholique Centrafricain,** BP 710, Bangui.

*CHAD*
**Secours Catholique National Tchadien,** BP 654, N'Djamena.

*CHILE*
**Ayuda Cristiana Evangélica,** Bombero Salas 1351, Of 250, Casilla 14066, Correo 15, Santiago.
**Instituto Católico Chileno de Migración (INCAMI),** Exec Dir, Erasmo Escala 1822, Piso 2, Casilla 468, Santiago. T: 89495.

*CHINA (TAIWAN)*
**Taiwan Christian Service (Church World Service),** Exec Dir, Jen Ai Rd, Sec 4 No 6, Taipei. T: 773171.

*COLOMBIA*
**Minuto de Dios,** c/o Padres Eudistas, Carrera 73 No 82A-05, Bogotá.
**Sociedad de San Vincente de Paul,** Calle 16 No 8-22, Bogotá.

*CONGO*
**Secours Catholique,** BP 117, Brazzaville. T: 3093.

*CYPRUS*
**Quaker Service,** PO Box 7, Kyrenia. T: 08152591.

*CZECHOSLOVAKIA*
**Caritas Catholique Slovaque (Ustredná Charita na Slovensku),** Heydukova 20, 80000 Bratislava. T: 50566.
**Caritas Catholique Tcheque (Ceská Katoliká Charita),** Vladislavova 12, 111 37 Praha 1. T: 249165.

*DENMARK*
**Danish Committee for Algeria (Danske Algierkomite),** Granbakken 13, Hillerod.
**Danish Refugee Council,** Frederiksborgvej 5, DK-2400 Kobenhavn NV.

*ECUADOR*
**Conferencias de San Vicente de Paul,** Quito.
**Instituto Vivenda Caritas (INVICA),** Quito.

*EGYPT*
**Comité Conjoint pour la Coordination des Services et de l'Aide aux Personnes déplacées et Victimes de l'Agression,** EACCS, Anba Rueis Bldg, Ramses St, Abbasiya, Al Qahirah.

*ETHIOPIA*
**Christian Relief and Development Association,** Addis Abeba.
**Christian Relief Committee,** PO Box 5674, Addis Abeba.
**Ethiopian Catholic Welfare Organization,** Catholic Secretariat, PO Box 2454, Addis Abeba.
**Ethiopian Committee for Aid to Refugees,** c/o Faculty of Law, Haile Selassie I University, PO Box 1176, Addis Abeba.
**Inter-Church Aid Office,** Ethiopian Orthodox Church, PO Box 503, Addis Abeba.

*FRANCE*
**Action Chrétienne en Orient,** Sec, 7 Rue Général-Offenstein, Strasbourg-Meinau (B-Rhin). T: 341155.
**Aide aux Missions d'Afrique,** 82 Rue Dutot, F-75015 Paris. T: (01)532-8749.
**Aumônerie des Etrangers Protestants en France,** 176 Rue de Grenelle, F-75007 Paris. T: 705-9399.
**BIP-SNOP,** 47 Rue de Clichy, F-75009 Paris. (Aid).
**Comité de Liaison des Oeuvres Bénévoles travaillant pour les Réfugiés en France,** 47-49 Rue de la Glacière, F-75013 Paris.
**Comité Inter-Mouvements auprès des Evacués (CIMADE),** Sec-gén, 176 Rue de Grenelle, F-75007 Paris. T: 705-9399.
**Commission Episcopale pour les Migrations,** Sec Gén, 106 Rue du Bac, F-75341 Paris. T: 222-5708.
**Conférence Mondiale des Chrétiens pour la Palestine/World Conference of Christians for Palestine,** Sec, 49 Rue du Faubourg Poissonnière, F-75009 Paris. T: (01)824-9764.
**Entraide Missionnaire Internationale (EMI)/ International Missionary Benefit Society,** 119 Rue du Président-Wilson, F-92 Levallois. T: 2708752, 2708753.
**Entraide Protestante,** Pres, 84 Av Niel, F-75017 Paris.
**Faim et Soif,** 6 Rue du Faubourg Poissonnière, F-75009 Paris.
**Oeuvre Apostolique,** 8 Rue Daniel Lesueur, F-75007 Paris. T: (01)306-4437.
**Orthodox Advisory Committee,** 11 Rue Mongagne-Ste-Geneviève, F-75005 Paris. T: ODE 7446.
**Propagation de la Foix,** 5 Rue Monsieur, F-75007 Paris. T: (01)783-6795. (Also: 12 Rue Sala, F-69287 Lyon. T: (78)371382).
**Secours Catholique,** Gen Sec, 106 Rue du Bac, F-75007 Paris. T: (01)222-2119.
**Société de Saint-Vincent de Paul,** Sec, 5 Rue du Pré-aux-Clercs, F-75007 Paris. T: (01)548-6220.

*GABON*
**Secours Catholique Gabon,** Maison des Oeuvres, BP 134, Libreville.

*GERMAN DEMOCRATIC REPUBLIC*
**Caritas,** Deutscher Caritasverband, Zentralstelle Berlin, Grosse Hamburgerstr 18-19, DDR-104 Berlin. T: 425026.

*GERMANY, Federal Republic of*
**American Fund for Czechoslovak Refugees,** Possartstr 9, D-8 München 27.
**Arbeitsgemeinschaft Ev Auswandererfürsorge,** Am Dobben 112, Postfach 450, D-28 Bremen. (For German emigrants).
**Arbeitsgemeinschaft für Weltmission,** Gen Sek, Mittelweg 143, D-2000 Hamburg 13. T: 456424.
**Arbeitsstelle für Soziale Arbeit in Ubersee,** International Social Services, Wintererstr 19, D-78 Freiburg im Breisgau. T: (0761)31497.
**Brot für die Welt,** Geschäftsstelle, Gerokstr 17, D-7 Stuttgart 1.
**Christlicher Missionsdienst (Christian Mission Service),** Schulstr 17, D-7251 Hirschlanden.
**Deutscher Caritasverband,** Lorenz-Werthmannhaus, Karlstr 40, Postfach 420, D-78 Freiburg im Breisgau. T: (0761)2001. (Member, BICE).
**Deutscher Hilfsbund für Christliches Liebeswerk im Orient,** Im Rosengarten 4, D-6380 Bad Homburg 1. T: (06172)29447. (German Association for Christian Charity in the Near East; 1896).
**Dienste in Ubersee,** Gerokstr 17, D-7 Stuttgart 1.
**Gustav-Adolf-Werk (West) der EKD,** Zentrale, Kirchweg 68, Postfach 351, D-35 Kassel. (Financial aid to any Protestant minority churches abroad).
**Innere Mission und Hilfswerk der EKD (IMHEKD),** Hauptgeschäftstelle, Alexanderstr 23, Postfach 476, D-7000 Stuttgart 1. T: 246951.
**Kirchliches Aussenamt der EKD,** Bochenheimer Landstr 109, Postfach 174025, D-6 Frankfurt/Main. (For overseas German congregations).
**Konvent der Zerstreuten Evangelischen Ostkirchen,** Geschäftsstelle, Andreastr 2A, D-3 Hannover. (Aid society for assisting refugee Protestant churches in eastern Europe).
**Martin-Luther-Bund,** Diasporawerk Evangelisch-Lutherischer Kirchen, Fahrstr 15, D-852 Erlangen. (Financial aid to Lutheran minority churches in Austria and South America).
**Misereor,** Mozartstr 9, D-5100 Aachen. T: (0241) 25851/4. (Catholic Bishops fund for overseas development).
**MISSIO (Internationales Katholisches Missionswerk),** Hirtenstr 26, D-8000 München 2. T: (0811) 555981. (Pastoral work projects).
**Ostkirchenausschuss (Kirchlicher Hilfsausschuss für die Ostvertriebenen),** Andreastr 2A, D-3 Hannover. (For Protestant refugees from eastern Europe).
**St Raphaels-Verein,** Gen Sec, Grosse Allee 41, D-2000 Hamburg 1. T: 242239,246155.
**Verband Zur Förderung des Evangeliums in Spanien,** Egidienplatz 37, D-85 Nürnberg. (Aid (money, materials) to minority churches in Spain).

*GREECE*
**Divine Providence,** Greek Catholic Exarchate, 246 Acharnon St, Athínai 815. T: 870170,872723.

*GRENADA*
**Madonna Houses,** Victoria (Grenada) and Carriacou (Grenadines).

*GUATEMALA*
**Comité de Servicio de los Amigos,** 38 Av 4-89, Zona 7, Ciudad de Guatemala. T: 45103.
**Comité Evangélica Permanente Ayuda (CEPA),** Ciudad de Guatemala. (Begun 1974).

*HAITI*
**Secours Protestant/Service Chrétienne,** Exec Sec, Methodist Church, BP 6, Port-au-Prince.

*HONDURAS*
**Comité Evangélica (CEDEN),** Tegucigalpa.

*HONG KONG*
**Asbury Village,** Tai Wo Hau, Tsuen Wan, NT. T: NT-201073.
**Hong Kong Christian Service,** Metropole Bldg, 57 Peking Rd 4/F, Kowloon. T: K-678031.
**Hong Kong Christian Welfare and Relief Council,** Sec, 23 Waterloo Rd, Kowloon. T: K-55255.
**Methodist Committee for Overseas Relief (CORE),** 54 Waterloo Rd, Kowloon. T: K-887174.
**Wesley Village,** Tai Hang Rd, Hong Kong. T: H-760444.
**World Council of Churches Service to Refugees,** 33 Granville Rd, Kowloon. T: K-670071.

*INDIA*
**Action for Food Production Office (AFPRO),** C-52, ND South Extension II, New Delhi 49. T: 621651.
**Caritas India,** Dir, CBCI Centre, Alexandra Place, New Delhi 1. T: 45462.
**Central Relief Committee (India),** Lok Kalyan Bhavan, 11A Rouse Av, New Delhi.
**Christian Agency for Social Action,** Relief and Development (CASA). 16 Ring Rd, Lajpat Nagar IV, New Delhi 24.
**Committee on Relief and Gift Supplies,** Dir, 4 Mathura Rd, Jungpura, Delhi. T: 618234.

*INDONESIA*
**Soegijapranata Social Foundation,** Jalan Pandanaran 13, Semarang. (RC. Aiding slumdwellers to migrate).

*IRELAND*
**Catholic Social Service Conference,** 75 Merrion Square, Dublin 2. T: 65608.
**Catholic Social Welfare Bureau,** 35 Harcourt St, Dublin 2. T: 780866.
**Emigrants Section,** Catholic Social Welfare Bureau, 18 Westland Row, Dublin 2. T: 654189.

*ISRAEL*
**Caritas Jerusalem,** Social Centre, PO Box 19653, Jerusalem. T: 87574.
**Catholic Relief Service,** c/o Ratisbonne Monastery, PO Box 768, Jerusalem. T: 23837.
**Pontifical Mission for Palestine,** Administrator, PO Box 19642, East Jerusalem (Old City).

*ITALY*
**Aide au Développement Intégral (ADI),** Via Nomentana 118, I-00161 Roma.
**Aiuto alla Chiesa che Soffre,** Via Ulpiano 47/18, Roma. (Aid to the church in distress).
**Caritas Internationalis (International Confederation of Catholic Charities, CICC),** Secretariat, Piazza San Calisto 16, I-00153 Roma. T: 6984635, 6984695,6984597,6984578. (Branches in 95 countries).
**Caritas Italiana,** Viale Ferdinando Baldelli 41, I-00146 Roma. T: 552251,553251.
**Caritas Trieste,** Dir, Via Baciocchi 1A, PO Box 1345-TS3, I-34123 Trieste. T: 38173.
**Catholic Relief Services (UCSS),** Regional Office, Dir, Via Boezio 21, I-00192 Roma. T: 318051.
**Mani Tese (Hands Extended),** Via dei Carracci 2 (also Via Pagliano 2), I-20149 Milano. T: 4697188.
**Opera Assistenza Spirituale Nomadi in Italia,** Via della Scrofa 70, I-00186 Roma. T: 305794. (Member, BICE) (Aid to nomads).
**Pontificia Opera di Assistenza,** Dir, Piazza Benedetto Cairoli 117, I-00146 Roma. T: 650563.
**Società di S Vincenzo de Paoli,** Via della Pigna 13/A, I-00186 Roma. T: 687393.
**Ufficio Centrale per l'Emigrazione Italiana (UCEI),** Dir, Via della Scrofa 70, I-00186 Roma. T: 6568048.
**Unione Nazionale fra gli Enti di Beneficenza e di Assistenza (UNEBA),** Piazza Missori 3, I-20123 Milano. T: 898657.

*JAPAN*
**American Friends Service Committee,** 12-7 4-chome, Minami Azabu, Minato-ku, Tokyo 106.
**Japan Catholic Migration Commission (JCMC),** Sec, 10 Rokubancho, Chiyoda-ku, Tokyo. T: 262-2663.
**Japan ECLOF Committee (NCCJ),** Sec Gen, 22 Midorigaoka Shibuya-ku, Tokyo.
**Japan Friends Service Committee,** Friends Center, 8-19 4-chome, Mita,Minato-ku, Tokyo 108.

*KENYA*
**Joint Refugee Services of Kenya (JRSK),** Exec Officer, Diamond Trust Bldg, Ronald Ngala St, Moi Av, PO Box 45627, Nairobi. T: 26595.

*KOREA, South*
**Korean Catholic Migration Commission (KCMC),** Pres, 1 Myong-Dong, 2-ka Chung Ku, c/o IPO Box 1035, Soul. T: 754381.

*LEBANON*
**Conférence Mondiale des Chrétiens pour la Palestine,** Sec, Rue Mak'houl (Abdel-Aziz), BP 1375, Bayrut. T: 341902/3.
**Near East Ecumenical Committee for Palestinian Refugees (NEECPR),** Bayrut. T: 223091.
**Pontifical Mission for Palestine,** Exec Dir, Souheil Farah Bldg, Sidani St, PO Box 3264, Bayrut. T: 226928,344508. (Aid to refugees).

*LIECHTENSTEIN*
**Association for the Study of the World Refugee Problem (AWR),** Postfach 34706, FL-9490 Vaduz.

*LUXEMBOURG*
**Bridderlech Delen,** 23 Blvd du Prince Henri, Luxembourg-ville. T: 472172,23698.
**Caritas Luxembourg,** 23 Blvd du Prince Henri, CP 138, Luxembourg-ville. T: 23698,472172.

*MACAO*
**Secretariado dos Serviços Diocesanos de Assistência Social (USCC),** Centro Católico, Dir, Rua da Praia Grande, Macau. T: 4486.

*MADAGASCAR*
**Friends Service Council,** Mission FFMA, Faravohitra, Tananarive.

*MALAWI*
**Catholic Secretariat of Malawi,** PO Box 5368, Limbe. T: Blantyre 50866.
**Christian Service Committee,** PO Box 949, Blantyre.

*MALAYSIA*
**Sabah Catholic Welfare,** PO Box 684, Jesselton, Sabah. T: 2038. (Formerly Catholic Social Welfare Association of North Borneo).

*MALI*
**Secours Catholique Malien,** BP 298, Bamako.

*MALTA*
**Malta Emigrants' Commission,** Exec Dir, Palazzo Carafa, 94 Old Bakery St, Valletta. T: 22644.
**National Caritas Council (Kunsill Nazzionali Caritas),** Archbishop's Residence, Valletta. T: 27755.

*MAURITIUS*
**Bureau Catholique d'Emigration,** Dir, Centre Miséreor, Rue d'Estaing, Port-Louis. T: 22342.

*MEXICO*
**Acción Católica Mexicana,** Serapio Randon 43, México 4, DF.
**Ayuda Social Católica de México,** Liverpool 143-305, México 6, DF. T: 251307.
**Comité de Servicio de los Amigos,** Ignacio Mariscal 132, México 1, DF. T: 5352752.

*NETHERLANDS*
**Aid for Algeria (Hulpactie voor Algerie),** Quaker Centrum, Vossiusstraat 20, Amsterdam Z. T: (020) 794238.
**Bisschopelijk Gedelegeerde voor Emigratie en Immigratie,** Nieuwe Gracht 80, NL-Haarlem. T: (023)321650.
**Christelijke Emigratie Centrale,** Heulstraat 3, 's-Gravenhage.
**International Reformed Agency for Migration (IRAM),** Sec Gen, 42 Eperweg, 't Harde. T: 05255550.
**Katholiek Landelijk Centrum voor Maatschappelijke Dienstverlening,** Luybenstraat 19, 's-Hertogenbosch. T: (04100)34134,37513.
**Katholieke Centrale Emigratiestichting (KCES),** Dir, Laan van Meerdervoort 150, 's-Gravenhage. T: (070)333472.
**Katholieke Stichting voor Vluchtelingen en Ontheemden,** Jacob Catsstraat 19, 's-Hertogenbosch. T: (04100)31623. (For refugees and stateless).
**Mensen in Nood-Caritas Neerlandica,** Hekellaan 6, Postbus 1041, 's-Hertogenbosch. T: (073)144544.
**Vincentius Vereniging,** Westeinde 99, 's-Gravenhage. T: (070)392387.

*NEW ZEALAND*
**Inter-Church Committee on Immigration,** PO Box 297, Christchurch.
**New Zealand Catholic Overseas Aid Committee,** Liston House, St Patrick's Square, PO Box 780, Auckland 1.
**NZ Council of Organizations for Relief Service Overseas (CORSO),** 303 Willis St, PO Box 2500, Wellington.
**New Zealand Friends Service Committee,** Clerk, 24 Turere Place, Wanganui. T: 6388.
**St Vincent de Paul Society,** Catholic Immigration Committee, National Sec, 181 High St, PO Box 30602, Lower Hutt. T: 699812.
**World Vision of New Zealand,** Dir, 6 High St, PO Box 1923, Auckland 1.

*NICARAGUA*
**Evangelical Committee for Development (CEPAD),** Managua. (Recent survey of 550 Protestants).

*NORWAY*
**Friends Service Committee (Kvekerhjelp),** Meltzersgt 1, Oslo 2. T: (02)562518.
**Norwegian Church Relief (Kirkens Nodhjelp),** Sec, Kirkegaten 5, Oslo 1.

**Norwegian Refugee Council,** Prof Dahls Gt 1, Oslo 3.

*PANAMA*

**Fe y Alegría,** Apdo B-3, Panamá 9-A. T: 235820.

*PERU*

**Comisión Católica Peruana de Migración (CCPM),** Dir, Jirón Chancay 725, Lima 1.

*PHILIPPINES*

**Catholic Charities of Archdiocese of Manila,** Catholic Charities Bldg, 1499 Otis Pandacan, Manila. T: 505829,505645.
**Church World Service (CWS),** c/o NCCP, 941 Epifanio de los Santos Av, Quezon City.

*POLAND*

**Caritas Committee,** 62 ul Krakowskie Przedmiescie, Warszawa.
**Secrétariat de Pastorale Charitable,** ul Kanonicza 5, 31 002 Kraków.

*PORTUGAL*

**União de Caridade Portuguesa (Caritas),** Commissão Central, Av da Republica 84/2, Lisboa 1. T: 767736.

*RWANDA*

**Bureau Rwandais pour les Migrants,** Dir, BP 124, Kigali.

*SENEGAL*

**CIMADE,** Centre de Bopp, Dispensaire Foyer, BP 5070, Dakar. T: 32607.
**Secours Catholique du Sénégal,** 3 Rue Paul Holle, BP 439, Dakar. T: 22077.

*SEYCHELLES*

**Union Chrétienne Seychelloise,** PO Box 32, Victoria, Mahé.

*SPAIN*

**Campaña Contra el Hambre en el Mundo,** Madrid.
**Caritas Española,** Cuesta de Santo Domingo 5, Madrid. T: 2489405. (Member, BICE).
**Comisión Católica Española de Migración (CCEM),** National Dir, Guadiana 10—El Viso, Madrid 2. T: 2617200.
**Edificio Migrans,** Chief of Information, San Roman del Valle s/n, Gran San Blas, Madrid 17. T: 2060241. (Information only).

*SURINAM*

**Jepie Makandra,** Aide Mutuelle, Paramaribo.
**Pater Ahlbrinckstichting (PAS) (Father Ahlbrinck Association),** Marowijnestraat 2, Postbus 2075, Paramaribo.

*SWITZERLAND*

**American Friends Service Committee,** 12 Rue Adrien Lachenal, CH-1207 Genève.
**Brethren Service Commission,** 150 Route de Ferney, CH-1211 Genève 20.
**Brot für Brüder (Bread for Brothers),** Missionsstr 21, CH-4003 Basel. T: (061)243350.
**Caritas Internationalis,** 6 Rue du Conseil-Général, CH-1205 Genève.
**Catholic Relief Services (CRS-USCC),** 11 Rue Cornavin, CH-1201 Genève. T: 314654.
**Christkatholisches Hilfswerk,** Willadingweg 39, Bern. (Old Catholic).
**Churches Committee on Migrant Workers in Western Europe,** 150 Route de Ferney, CH-1211 Genève 20. T: (022)333400.
**Division of Inter-Church Aid,** Refugee and World Service (DICARWS), 150 Route de Ferney, CH-1211 Genève 20.
**Evangelische Arbeitsgemeinschaft für das Gastgewerbe,** Pres, Anton Graffstr 19, CH-8400 Winterthur.
**International Catholic Migration Commission (ICMC) (Commission Internationale Catholique pour les Migrations, CICM),** Gen Sec, 65 Rue de Lausanne, CH-1202 Genève. T: (022)314750.
**International Council of Voluntary Agencies (ICVA) (Conseil International des Agences Bénévoles),** 7 Av de la Paix, CH-1202 Genève. T: 332025.
**Inter-Church Aid,** WCC, 150 Route de Ferney, CH-1211 Genève 20.
**Katholische Arbeitnehmer-Bewegung (KAB),** Ausstellungstr 21, CH-8005 Zürich. T: (01)420030/31.
**Pestalozzi Children's Village Foundation,** CH-9043 Trogen. (Secretariat: Hoschgasse 83, CH-8008 Zürich).
**Protestantisch-Kirchliche Hilfsvereine,** Sek, Chrischonastr 62, CH-4000 Basel. T: (061)333370.
**Schweizer Hilfsbund für Christliches Liebeswerk im Orient,** Präs, CH-8635 Dürnten/ZH. T: (055)43463.
**Schweizerische Evangelische Freundeskreis für die Araber in Israel (SEFAI),** Präs, Ref Pfarramt, CH-6260 Reiden. T: (062)811173.
**Schweizerische Katholische Arbeitsgemeinschaft für Fremdarbeiter (SKAF) (Communauté de Travail Catholique Suisse pour les Travailleurs Etrangers),** Löwenstr 3, CH-6002 Luzern. T: (041)222960.
**Schweizerischer Caritasverband/Union Suisse de Charité/Unione Svizzera di Carità,** Löwenstr 3, CH-6002 Luzern. T: (041)231144. (Member, BICE).
**Swiss Aid to Tibetans,** Kauffmannsweg 8, CP 234, CH-6000 Luzern 2. (Geneva Office: 1228 Plan-les-Ouates, CP 31).
**Swiss Central Office for Aid to Refugees,** Kinkelstr 2, CH-8035 Zürich.
**Waldenserhilfe,** Präs, Sempacherstr 41, CH-8032 Zürich.

*SYRIA*

**Oeuvres Sociales Al Kalimat,** BP 107, Halab. T: 10506,13261,13262. (Greek Catholics).

*THAILAND*

**Asian Christian Service,** Dir, 14/2 Pramuan Rd, Bangkok.
**Cama Services,** 28/2 Pracha Utit Lane, Pradipa Rd, Bangkok 4. T: 279-7752. (C & MA).

*TUNISIA*

**Service Social de la Prélature de Tunis,** 4 Rue d'Alger, Tunis. T: 242235,245832.

*TURKEY*

**Association des Amis des Pauvres (Fakirlerin Dostu Cemiyeti),** Satirci Sok No 2, Pangalti, Istanbul.

*UGANDA*

**Comboni Charity Fund,** Kampala.

*UK OF GB & NI*

**Aid to European Refugees,** 40 Windsor·House, 46 Victoria St, London SW1.
**Aid to the Church in Need (ACN),** 3-5 North St, Chichester, West Sussex PO19 1LB. (RC).
**Aid to the Russian Church,** 25 Aldermay Rd, Bromley, Kent BR1 3PH.
**British Council for Aid to Refugees,** 35 Great Peter St, London SW1.
**Christian Aid,** 240-250 Ferndale Rd, London SW9 8BH. T: (01)733-5500. (A division of British Council of Churches).
**Churches Committee on Migrant Workers in Western Europe,** 1 Rivercourt Rd, Hammersmith, London W6 9LD. T: (01)748-3575.
**Churches Main Committee,** Fielden House, Little College St, London SW1P 3JZ. T: (01)930-4984. (Charity).
**Committee on International Affairs and Migration,** Church of England, Church House, Dean's Yard, Westminster, London SW1P 3NZ. T: (01)222-9011.
**Compassion of Great Britain,** 48 Kerr St, Kirkintilloch, Glasgow G66 1JZ. T: (041)776-6046.
**Disasters Emergency Committee,** Co-ordinator, London. (To co-ordinate relief work of OXFAM, War on Want, Save the Children Fund, Christian Aid, Red Cross).
**Friends Service Council (FSC),** Friends House, Euston Rd, London NW1 2BJ. T: (01)387-3601.
**Indian Church Aid Association,** 2 Eaton Gate, London SW1. T: (01)730-9611.
**International Refugee Missionary Fellowship,** Gen Sec, Well House, Dean Row Rd, Wilmslow, Cheshire SK9 2BU. T: 22062.
**Ladies of Charity and Companions of St Vincent,** 39 Blakehall Rd, London E11 2QQ. T: (01)989-1336.
**OXFAM,** 274 Banbury Rd, Oxford OX2 7DZ. (Secular but with many Christian agencies assisting).
**Relief and Refugee Committee,** Catholic Women's League, Gen Sec, 21b Soho Square, London W1V 6NR. T: (01)437-4509.
**St Vincent de Paul Society,** 546 Sauchiehall St, Glasgow C2. T: (041)332-7752.
**Scottish Catholic International Aid Fund,** St Columbkille's, Rutherglen, Glasgow G73 2SL, Scotland.
**Society of St Vincent de Paul,** 2 Iddesleigh House, Caxton St, London SW1H 0PS. T: (01)799-1342.
**Spanish and Portuguese Church Aid Society,** Hon Sec, 4 Stone Bldgs, London WC2. T: Chancery 5716.
**Standing Conference of British Organizations for Aid to Refugees,** 26 Bedford Square, London WC1.
**TEAR Fund (The Evangelical Alliance Relief Fund),** Dir, 19 Draycott Place, London SW3 2SJ. T: (01)584-0114/5.
**War on Want,** 3 Madeley Rd, Ealing, London W5.

*USA*

**American Baptist Relief,** Sec, 1628 16th St NW, Washington, DC 20009. T: (202)265-5027.
**American Council for Emigres in the Professions,** Room 800, 345 East 46th St, New York, NY 10017.
**American Friends Service Committee,** 160 North 15th St, Philadelphia, PA 19102. T: (215)LO3-9372.
**American Fund for Czechoslovak Refugees,** Room 430, 1775 Broadway, New York, NY 10019.
**American Waldensian Aid Society,** Room 1850, 475 Riverside Drive, New York, NY 10027.
**Brethren Service,** Church of the Brethren, 1451 Dendee Av, Elgin, IL 60120.
**CARE Inc,** 660 First Av, New York, NY 10016. (Cooperative for American Relief Everywhere).
**Catholic Near East Welfare Association (CNEWA),** 330 Madison Av, New York, NY 10017.
**Catholic Relief Services (CRS),** United States Catholic Conference, Exec Dir, 350 5th Av, New York, NY 10001. T: (212)954-9300.
**Christian Reformed World Relief Committee,** Exec Dir, 2850 Kalamazoo Av SE, Grand Rapids, MI 49508. T: (616)452-8681.
**Christian Services Corps,** 1501 11th St NW, Washington, DC 20001.
**Church World Service,** DOM-NCCCUSA, Chairman, 475 Riverside Drive, New York, NY 10027. T: (212)870-2257.
**Compassion,** 7774 West Irving Park Rd, Chicago, IL 60634.
**Dept of Immigration and Refugee Service,** Lutheran Council in the USA, 315 Park Av South, New York, NY 10010.
**Direct Relief Foundation,** 27 East Canon Perdido St, Santa Barbara, CA 93101.
**Food for the Hungary,** Vice-Pres, 1115 Colorado Blvd, Los Angeles, CA 90041.
**Home of Onesiphorus,** Pres, 3939 North Hamlin Av, Chicago, IL 60618.
**International Christian Relief,** Dir, 801 Haddon Av, Collingswood, NJ 08108. T: (609)858-0700
**Lutheran World Relief,** Pres, Suite 1940, 315 Park Av, New York, NY 10010. T: (212)677-3950.
**Meals for Millions Foundation,** 1800 Olympic Blvd, PO Box 1666, Santa Monica, CA 90406.

**Mennonite Church Board of Missions and Charities,** Chairman, 1711 Prairie St, Elkhart, IN 46514. T: (219)522-2630.
**Methodist Committee for Overseas Relief (UMCOR),** Gen Sec, 475 Riverside Drive, New York, NY 10027. T: (212)749-0700.
**Migration and Refugee Services,** USCC, National Office, Dir, 1312 Massachusetts Av NW, Washington, DC 20005. T: (202)659-6625. (Northeast Area Office: 201 Park Av South, New York, NY 10003).
**Mission to the Migrants,** 2007 West 78th Place, Los Angeles, CA 90047.
**Mustard Seed,** 1377 Colorado St, Glendale CA 91205.
**National Conference of Catholic Charities (NCCC),** 1346 Connecticut Av, Washington, DC 20036. T: DE2-2730.
**Self Help,** 116 Sixth St, SE Waverly, IA 50677. (Machinery for overseas).
**Seventh-day Adventist Welfare Service,** 6840 Eastern Av, Washington, DC.
**Society of St Vincent de Paul,** 611 Olive St, St Louis, MO 63101.
**Unitarian Universalist Ministry to Migrant Farm Workers,** Minister, 1148 Cragmont Av, Berkeley, CA 94708. T: (415)848-6304.
**Unitarian Universalist Service Committee,** 78 Beacon St, Boston, MA 02108. T: (617)742-2100.
**United States Committee for Refugees,** 20 West 40th St, New York, NY 10018.
**Volunteers for International Technical Assistance Inc (VITA),** College Campus, Schenectady, NY 12308.
**World Neighbors,** Pres, 5116 North Portland Av, Oklahoma City, OK 73112.
**World Vision International,** Pres, PO Box 0, Pasadena, CA 91109. T: (213)357-1111. (919 West Huntington Drive, Monrovia, CA 91016).

*URUGUAY*

**Castores de Emmaus,** Soriano 1472, Montevideo.
**Emmaus,** Soriano 1465, Montevideo.
**Instituto Católico Uruguayo de Inmigración (ICUI),** Pres, Yaguarón 1448, Piso 6, Apdo 601, Montevideo.

*VENEZUELA*

**Comisión Católica Venezolana de Migración (CCVM),** National Dir, Av Negrin, Calle El Apartado, La Florida, Apdo 2301, Caracas.
**Instituto de Vivienda Cáritas (INVICA),** Edf América, Piso 4, Av Urdaneta Esq Veroes, Caracas 101. T: 812272.
**Sociedad de San Vicente de Paul,** Edf San Luis Ap 8, 2a Avda Santa Eduvigis, Caracas 107. T: 416542.

*VIET NAM*

**Asian Christian Service of the East,** 215/36/1A Chi-Lang, Phu-Nhuan, Saigon.

*YUGOSLAVIA*

**Bureau de Liaison entre la Conférence Episcopale Yougoslave et Caritas Internationalis (Ured Za Vezu Sa Caritas Internationalis),** Biskupska Konferencija Yugoslavije, Archevêché, Kaptol 31, PB 02-406, 41000 Zagreb. T: 38446.

*ZAIRE*

**Entraide et Développement/Zaire Protestant Relief Agency,** ECZ, BP 3094, Kinshasa-Gombe. T: 59829.

*ZAMBIA*

**Socio-Economic Department,** Zambia Catholic Secretariat, Unity House, Corner Stanley/Jameson Rds, PO Box 1965, Lusaka. T: 73467,73470.
**Zambia Christian Refugee Service,** Dir, PO Box 2778, Lusaka. T: 51358.

# 3
# Arts, Religion & the

**Definition.** Christian involvement in the arts; the artistic aspects of the mass media, speech, drama, theatre, opera, cinema, performing arts, circus, literature, festivals; renowned centres of Christian artistic presentation (Oberammergau, Forest Lawn, Einsiedeln); unusual types of Christian exhibition (Holy Land museum, Nijmegen); Christian museums of major importance; Christian art centres; church artchitecture, church buildings, historical monuments.

*CANADA*

**Christian Drama Society of Canada,** Toronto.

*FRANCE*

**Musée Calvin,** Sec, Place Aristide-Briand, Noyon (Oise). T: 359.
**Musée de la France Protestante de l'Ouest,** Prés, Le Bois-Tiffrais, Monsireigne (Vendee). T: 3.
**Musée Huguenot de l'Eglise de la Rochelle,** 2 Rue Saint-Michel, La Rochelle. T: 348628.
**Société d'Exportation d'Art Religieux (SEAR),** Prés, 5 Faubourg St Honore, F-75008 Paris. T: 265-2260.

*GERMANY, Federal Republic of*

**Oberammergau 1960,** Ammergebirge, Bayerische Alpen. (Passion play; south of Munich near Austrian border).
**Religionskundliche Sammlung der Universität Marburg,** Schloss 1, Eingang Innenhof, D-3550 Marburg. T: (06421)6912480. (Collection of religious exhibits).

*GREECE*

**Christian Drama Society of Greece,** Athínai.

*HOLY SEE*

**Pontificia Commissione Centrale per l'Arte Sacra in Italia,** Segretario, Palazzo della Cancellaria Apostolica, Piazza della Cancellaria 1, I-00186 Roma, Italy. T: 6527226

*ITALY*

**Centro Cattolico Teatrale (CCT),** Ente dello Spettacolo, Via della Conciliazione 2c, I-00193 Roma. T: 561775,564132.
**Museo Storico Valdese,** Via Beckwith, Torre Pellice (To).

*NORWAY*

**Institute for Christian Drama (Institutt for Kristen Dramatikk),** Holsteinvn 22, Oslo 8.

*SWEDEN*

**Society for Liturgy and Drama (FLOD),** Stockholm.

*SWITZERLAND*

**Commission Suisse d'Art Religieux,** CH-1041 Poliez-le-Grand. T: (021)811274.
**International Society of Christian Artists,** Pres, Hevelstr 21, CH-8032 Zürich.
**Schweizerische Kommission für Biblische Wandbilder,** Präs, General Guisan-Str 1 5, CH-4000 Basel.
**Schweizerische Kommission für Gute Religiöse Bilder,** 3123 Belp BE T: (031)810142.

*UK OF GB & NI*

**Actors Church Union,** Senior Chaplain, St Paul's, Church, Covent Garden, London WC2.
**Arts Centre Group,** Batailes, Great Easton, near Dunmow, Essex. T: Great Easton 246. (Jesus Movement. Also 19 Draycott Place, London SW3 2SJ).
**Arts Media Workshop,** 35 Albany Rd, New Malden, Surrey. T: (01)949-4609.
**Cathedrals Advisory Committee,** Sec, 83 London Wall, London EC2M 5NA. T: (01)638-0971.
**Catholic Stage Guild,** Sec, 39/42 New Bond St, London W1Y 9HB
**Chichester Diocesan Buildings Study Group,** Diocesan Church House, 9 Brunswick Square, Hove, Sussex BN3 1EN. T: (0273)73571.
**Council for Places of Worship,** Sec, 83 London Wall, London EC2M 5NA. T: (01)638-0971.
**Council for the Church in the Circus,** Gen Sec, Chideock Vicarage, Bridport, Dorset.
**Fellowship of Christians in the Arts,** London.
**Historic Churches Preservation Trust,** Fulham Palace, London SW6. T: (01)736-3054.
**Institute for the Study of Worship & Religious Architecture,** The University, Birmingham 15.
**International Society of Christian Artists (Société Internationale des Artistes Chrétiens, SIAC),** Glasspools, Gillsman's Hill, St Leonards-on-Sea. (World congresses: Bologne 1967, Salzburg 1969).
**New Christian Arts Centre Group,** Sec, 17 Wansford Close, Brentwood, Essex.
**New Churches Research Groups (NCRG),** 11 Parkway, Wilmslow, Cheshire. (5a Lancaster Rd, Wimbledon, London SW19). (Affiliated to Institute of Advanced Architectural Studies, University of York).
**Religious Drama Society of Great Britain (RADIUS),** Administrative Sec, George Bell House, Ayres St, London SE1 1ES. T: (01)407-4374.
**Scottish Guild of Catholic Artists,** 14 Newton Place, Glasgow C3.
**Society of Catholic Artists (SCA),** 3 St Oswalds Studios, Sedlescombe Rd, London SW6. T: (01)385-3734.
**Society of Church Craftsmen,** 26 Conduit St, London W1. T: (01)629-8300.
**Superstar Ventures Ltd,** 118/120 Wardour St, London W1V 4BT. T: (01)437-3224/5. (Producers of play Jesus Christ Superstar).

*USA*

**American National Orthodox Museum,** PO Box 238, Elberton, Alberta, GA 30635.
**American Society for Church Architecture,** New York.
**Armenian Museum & Cultural Center,** 630 2nd Av, New York, NY 10016.
**Associated Church Builders,** PO Box 187, Palate, IL 60067.
**Bible History Wax Museum,** 3rd, 4th & E Sts SW, Washington, DC 20001. T: (202)628-2994.
**Bible World,** Orlanda, Florida. (Vast area of Bible scenes; 10 million tourists annually).
**Bibletown USA,** Box A, Boca Raton, FL 33432.
**Catholic Art Association,** Washington DC.
**Church Architectural Guild of America,** Washington DC.
**Churches as Indoor Pavilions,** Suite 1527, Action Theatre Inc, 250 West 57th St, New York, NY 10019.
**Commission on Church Architecture,** Lutheran Church in America, Exec Dir, 231 Madison Av, New York, NY 10016.
**Committee on Religious Architecture,** American Institute of Architects, Washington DC.
**Community Arts Foundation,** 615 Wellington Av, Chicago, IL 60657.
**Department of Church Building and Architecture,** NCCCUSA, 475 Riverside Drive, New York, NY 10027.
**Department of Speech and Drama,** Catholic University of America, Washington, DC 20017.
**Department of Speech,** John Carroll University, University Heights, Cleveland, OH 4418. T: (216)491-4438.
**Department of Speech,** St Louis University, 221 North Grand Blvd, St Louis, MO 63103.
**Guild of Church Architects,** Washington DC.
**Index of Christian Art,** Princeton University, McCormick Hall, Princeton, NJ. T: WA1-6600.
**Ministry of Music to All Churches,** Kauai Evangelical Association, PO Box 636, Kalaheo, HA 96741.

**Ministry To and With the Fine and Performing Arts,** Spencer Memorial Church, Clinton and Remsen Sts, Brooklyn Heights, New York.
**Religious Arts Guild,** Exec Sec, 25 Beacon St, Boston, MA 02108. T: (617)742-2100,395-2572.
**St Mary's Museum & Cultural Center,** 3256 Warren Rd, Cleveland, OH 44111.
**School of Speech,** Marquette University, 625 North 15th St, Milwaukee, WI 53233.
**Theatre of Involvement,** UCCF Center, 331 17th Av SE, Minneapolis, MN 55414.
**Traveling Theater Troupe,** Department of Adult Education, Board of Christian Education, PO Box 1176, Richmond, VA 23209.
**Unified Church Structures,** 47925 North Gratiot Av, Mt Clemens, MI 48043.
**Universal Pictures,** 100 Universal Plaza, Universal City, CA 91609. (Producers of film Jesus Christ Superstar).

# 4
# Audiovisual Aids

*Definition.* Agencies, programmes and centres specializing in the production or dissemination of all kinds of audiovisual aids except movie films (see CINEMA AND FILM): slides, filmstrips, posters, pictures, drawings, cartoons, videotape ministries; audiovisual training centres oriented towards education, catechesis, evangelization, development; microform materials; microfilm, microfiche libraries, computerized micrographics. See also SOCIAL COMMUNICATIONS CO-ORDINATION.

*ARGENTINA*
**Centro Audio-Visual Evangélico de la Argentina (CAVEA),** O'Higgins 3162/68, Buenos Aires 29.
**Centro Audio-Visual Evangélico Rioplatense,** Camacua 282, Buenos Aires 6. (Member of WACC).

*AUSTRIA*
**Bild und Ton,** Stephansplatz 6, A-1010 Wien. (Audio-visual aids for catechists).
**SHB Film (Audiovisuelle Medien in Unterricht und Bildung),** Bundestaatliche Hauptstelle für Lichtbild und Bildungsfilm, Sensengasse 3, A-1090 Wien 9. T: 432147,432148.

*BELGIUM*
**Diafrica,** Celestijnenlaan 70, B-3030 Heverlee. T: (016)23349. (Slides for catechesis).
**Edelweiss,** Mutsaerstraat 32, B-2000 Antwerpen. T: (033)10339. (Slides. Flemish).
**Office Scolaire Belge d'Etudes par le Film,** 15 Av Ernest Masoin, B-1090 Brussel. T: (02)783706. (Posters, slides, films).
**Uitgeverscentrum Patmos,** Kapelsestraat 222, B-2080 Kapellen. T: (03)654320. (Posters. Flemish).

*BENIN*
**Centre Audio-Visuel,** BP 714, Cotonou.

*BRAZIL*
**Centro Audio-Visual Evangélico (CAVE),** Dir, CP 943, Campinas, São Paulo, SP. (Sponsors Radio Jaguariaiva).
**Federación de Organizaciones para la Asistencia Social y Educational (FASE),** Rua Mena Barréto 161, Piso 3, Botafogo, Rio de Janeiro, GB. T: 2464559,2433230. (Production of audio-visual aids and press; Catholic).
**Instituto de Sistemas Audio-Visuais,** Pontificia Universidade Católica de Pôrto Alegre, Pôrto Alegre, RS.

*BURMA*
**Christian Audio-Visual Centre (CAVE),** Dir, 82nd St, Mandalay.

*CAMEROON*
**Audio-Visual Committee, Fédération Evangélique,** BP 1133, Yaoundé.
**Centre des Techniques Audio-Visuelles de l'Eglise Presbytérienne Camerounaise,** BP 187, Yaoundé.

*CANADA*
**Novalis,** Université Saint Paul, 1 Rue Stewart, Ottawa 2, Ontario. T: (613)236-0807. (Slides, tapes).
**Novalis,** 3826 Rue Saint Hubert, Montréal 132, Québec. T: (514)844-7996. (Slides, tapes).
**Raema Communications,** 249 Battleford, Saskatchewan. T: (306)937-2131. (Slides, filmstrips, tapes, printed matter).
**Service Audio-Visuel pour le Développement,** Maison Bellarmin, 25 Rue Jarry Ouest, Montréal 351, Québec.

*CHILE*
**Centre for Audio-Visual Instruction via Satellite (CAVISAT),** Almirante Barroso 24, Casilla de Correos 10445, Santiago de Chile T: 68442.
**Centro Audio Visual Evangélico (CAVE-CHILE),** Casilla 9558, Santiago.

*CHINA (TAIWAN)*
**Taiwan Christian Audio-Visual Association,** Exec Sec, 105 Chung Shan Pei Rd Sec 2, Taipei. T: 556755.

*COLOMBIA*
**CAVECOL (CAVE-Colombia),** Apdo Aéreo 51092, Bogotá. (Member of WACC).
**Departamento de Medios de Communicación Social (DEMECOS),** Carrera 9a No 13-33, Apdo 6290, Bogotá. T: 414096,466866. (Audio-Visual aids).
**Instituto de Sistemas Audiovisuales (ISAV),** Instituto Colombiano de Desarrollo Social, Calle 16 No 4-75, Apdo Aéreo 11966, Bogotá.

*EGYPT*
**Christian Centre for Audio-Visual Services,** PO Box 1422, Al Qahirah T: 913590.

*FRANCE*
**Association Catéchétique Nationale pour l'Audio-Visuel (ACNAV),** 6 Av Vavin, F-75006 Paris. T: (01)633-2160.
**Bonne Presse Audio-Visuel,** 22 Cours Albert-Ier, F-75008 Paris. T: (01)225-7305. (Slides, film-records).
**Centrale d'Editions et de Diffusion de Matériel Audio-Visuel (CEDIMA),** 59 bis Rue Bonaparte, F-75006 Paris T: (01)633-8076. (Slides).
**Centre Audiovisuel Recherche et Communication (CREC),** 19 Rue de Chavril, F-69 Ste-Foy-lès-Lyon. T: (78)256817.
**Centre International de Documentation Audio-Visuelle (CIDAL),** Maison de la Radio-Télévision Catholique, Centre d'Etudes, L'Hôtellerie, Firfol, F-14100 Lisieux. T: Firfol 7.
**Editions CEFAG,** 153 Rue de Grenelle, F-75007 Paris. (Slides, posters).
**Editions des Nouvelles Images,** F-45 Lombreuil. (Records, slides, posters).
**Editions du Berger,** 4 Rue Cassette, F-75006 Paris. (Slides, records).
**Editions du Chalet,** 8 Rue Madame, F-75006 Paris. T: (01)222-4121. (Posters).
**Editions du Sénevé,** 34 Rue Le Brun, F-75013 Paris. (Posters, slides).
**Editions Internationales de Radio-Télévision,** 121 Av de Villiers, F-75017 Paris. T: (01)380-3056. (Slides).
**Encyclopédie Oecuménique Audio-Visuelle,** 121 Av de Villiers, F-75017 Paris. (Slides).
**Enseignement par l'Image et par le Son (EPIS),** 4 Rue Hénocque, F-95 Enghien-les-Bains. (Slides).
**Filmens,** 8A Rue des Heros-Nogentais, F-94 Nogent-sur-Marne. (Slides, film-recordings).
**Société pour l'Evangélisation par des Moyens Audio-Visuels (SEMA),** Dir, BP 232, Vichy (Allier). T: (70)983721. (Recordings, cassettes).

*GERMANY, Federal Republic of*
**Christophorus Verlag,** Freiburg/Breisgau.
**OCIC Audio-Visual Service,** Sprollstr 20, D-7407 Rottenburg/Neckar. T: (07472)791.
**Ton Bild (TB),** Benediktiner Missionare, D-8711 Münsterscwarzach. T: (09324)217. (Slides with sound track for Korea &c).

*HONG KONG*
**Audio Visual Evangelism Committee,** Hong Kong Christian Council, Metropole Bldg, 57 Peking Rd, 3/F, Kowloon. T: K-678031. (Member of WACC. Also 373 Ma Tam Wei Rd, Kowloon).

*INDIA*
**Audio-Visual Service,** Catholic Centre, St Mary's Town, Bangalore 5. T: 50369.
**Christian Association for Radio and Audio-Visual Service (CARAVS),** 15 Civil Lines, Jabalpur, MP. T: 942. (Protestant — RC; member of WACC).
**Tamilnadu Audio Visual Education Service (TAVES),** Catholic Centre Tindivanam, PO Tindivanam, South Arcot, Tamil Nadu.

*ITALY*
**Editrice Elle Di Ci,** Centro Catechistico Salesiano, I-10096 Torino-Leimann. (Slides, filmstrips).
**Editrice La Scuola di Brescia,** Sede Centrale e Officine Grafiche, Via Luiji Cadorna 11, I-25100 Brescia.

*JAPAN*
**Audio-Visual Aids Commission (AVACO),** Exec Dir, NCCJ, 4-13 Shibuya 4-chome, Shibuya-ku, Tokyo 150. (Member of WACC).
**Audio-Visual Department,** Sophia University, 7 Kioi-cho, Chiyoda-ku, Tokyo. T: 032659211. (Slides and films with tapes).
**Christian Audio-Visual Center,** 4-13 Shibuya 4-chome, Shibuya-ku, Tokyo 150.
**Evangelical Alliance Mission Audio-Visual Education Dept (TEAM-AVED),** 10-8 3-chome, Umegaoka, Setagaya-ku, Tokyo 154.
**Jiyu Christian Crusade Beyond The Sunset,** 25-22 2-chome, Tahara, Fukui-shi 910.
**Kinki Christian Audio-Visual Center,** Osaka Christian Center, 5151 Niemon-cho, Higashi-ku, Osaka 540.

*KOREA, South*
**Audio-Visual Catechetical Centre,** Kimchon. (RC).
**Korea Audio-Visual Aids Committee,** Soul. (Member of WACC).

*LEBANON*
**Paraboles et Symbôles pour Aujourd'hui (PSA),** BP 7002, Bayrut. (Audio-visual catechesis; ecumenical).

*MAURITIUS*
**Studio d'Art Sonore,** c/o Paroisse N-D de Lourdes, Route Royale, Rose Hill. T: 41279

*MEXICO*
**Centro Audio-Visual Evangélico (CAVE de México),** Gerente, Apdo M-9223 z1, 1 Liverpool 65-206 z6, México, DF. T: 148352. (Member of WACC).
**Sociedad Audio-Visual Educativa Sistema Todd,** Apdo 23, Cuautla, Morelos.

*NEW ZEALAND*
**Christian Audio-Visual Society of NZ,** PO Box 8727, Auckland.

*NIGERIA*
**Churches Audio-Visual Centre,** PO Box 67, Ilesha.

*PERU*
**Cine para el Desarrollo (CIDE/COC),** Paseo de Colón 378, Apdo 44, Lima. (Mass education in slums through audio-visuals).
**Sonoviso del Perú,** Oficina Nacional de Catequesis Lima. (Slides).

*PHILIPPINES*
**National Office of Mass Media Production Centre,** 2307 Herran, Sta Ana, PO Box 2722, Manila. T: 597081.

*SPAIN*
**Centro de Communicación Aplicada,** C Muntaner 270, IV B, Barcelona 6.

*SRI LANKA*
**Catechetical and Audio-Visual Centre,** Archbishop's House, Colombo 8.

*SWITZERLAND*
**Centrale Protestante des Moyens Audio-Visuels,** 8 Chemin des Crettets, CH-1211 Conches, Genève. T: 470525.
**Flanellbilder für Sonntagschulen,** Verlag A Tobler, CH-8038 Zürich. T: (051)452050.
**Graphoson,** 7 Av de Crousaz, CH-1010 Lausanne.
**Sonolux (Vita Series),** Centre pour Aides Audio-Visuelles, Prés, Grand-Rue 34, BP 45, CH-1700 Fribourg 2. T: (037)225778. (Sound-slide programme for adult Christians in Africa).

*THAILAND*
**National Catholic Office for Cinema and Audio-Visual Aids,** 251/1 Suranari Rd, Nakhon Ratchasima.

*UK OF GB & NI*
**Audio-Visual Aid Department,** 185 Marylebone Rd, PO Box 67, London NW1. T: (01)262-3211.
**Audio-Visual Department,** Corpus Christi College, 13-15 Denbigh Rd, London W11.
**Carwal Audio-Visual-Aids,** 250 Woodcote Rd, Wallington, Surrey. T: (01)647-5161.
**Christian Visual Aids Team,** Sec, 68 Church Crescent, Muswell Hill Rd, London N10 3NE. T: (01)883-4590.
**Vigilanti Audio-Visual Library,** 15 Victoria Crescent, Glasgow G12.
**Vision Screen Services,** Dir, Riversdale House, North Farmbridge, Chelmsford, Essex CM3 6NT. T: Maldon 740755.

*USA*
**Audio-Visual Services (Seventh-day Adventist),** 6840 Eastern Av NW, Washington, DC 20012.
**Catholic Audio-Visual Educators Association,** PO Box 618, New York, NY 10008.
**Dept of Audio-Visual Communication,** Booking Clerk, Brigham Young University, Provo, Utah.
**Mark-IV Presentations,** La Salette Center, Attleboro, MA 02703. T: (617)222-5410. (Slides, Tapes, Films).
**National Institute of Biblical Studies (NIBS),** 4001 North Dixie Highway No. 204, Pompano Beach, FL 33064. T: (305)781-4650. (Videotape programmes).
**Sights and Sounds,** Alba House Communications, Canfield, OH 44406. T: (216)533-5503. (Distribution house for filmstrips, records).
**Visual Evangels Publishers,** 1401 Ohio St Michigan City, IN 46370.

# 5
# Bible & Scripture Organizations

*Definition.* Bible societies and publishing houses, Bible translation and distribution agencies, scripture distribution agencies, colportage agencies, Christian linguistic organizations and centres, Bible-reading organizations, Bible study associations, Bible-memorizing programmes, Bible text societies (literature, posters), the biblical apostolate. See also PUBLISHING for commercial publishers specializing (but not exclusively) in Bible production. In addition to Bible societies related to the United Bible Societies, given below, most countries have branches of Scripture Union, Gideons, PTL, WBT, SGM, BRF, et alia (given here for only a handful of major countries).

*ALGERIA*
**Société Biblique en Afrique du Nord,** Chaplain's Apt, Villa Gardner, 64 Av Souidani Bou djemna, Alger. T: 633996.

*ANGOLA*
**Sociedade Bíblica,** Sec, Av Combatentes 114-A, 4 Andar, Apt 10, CP 10238 BG, Luanda. T: 45023.

*ARGENTINA*
**Sociedad Bíblica Argentina,** Sec, Casa de la Biblia, Tucumán 352-358, 1049 Buenos Aires. T: 328558,325787,323400.

*AUSTRALIA*
**Bible Society in Australia,** Sec, Memorial Bible House, Garema Place, PO Box 507, Canberra City, ACT 2601. T: 485118
**Bible Union of Australia,** 2 Swindon Grove, McKinnon, SE 14, Victoria. (Upholding inspiration of the Bible).
**Catholic Biblical Association of Australia,** Holy Cross Retreat, Serpells Rd, Templestowe, Victoria 3106.
**Gideons International in Australia,** 511 Kent, Sydney, NSW. T: 616470.
**Pocket Testament League of Australia (PTL),** 24 Westminster Av, Dee Why, NSW 2099. T: 988854.
**Scripture Union Anzea Council (SU),** Sec, 1 Lee St, Sydney, NSW 2000. T: 612598.
**Wycliffe Bible Translators,** 315 Collins St, Melbourne C1.

*AUSTRIA*
**Bibellesebund in Österreich (Scripture Union),** Sek, Fach 237, A-5021 Salzburg.
**Österreichische Bibelgesellschaft,** Bibelhaus, Breite Gasse 8, A-1070 Wien. T: 938240.
**Österreichische Katholische Bibelwerk (OKB),** Stiftsplatz 8, A-3400 Klosterneuburg.

*BANGLADESH*
**Bangladesh Bible Society,** Sec, 38 Hatkhola Rd, PO Box 360, Ramna, Dacca 2. T: 246442.

*BARBADOS*
**Bible Society in the East Caribbean,** PO Box 36B, Brittons Hill, St Michael.

*BELGIUM*
**Europe Regional Centre,** United Bible Societies, Rue de Trône 160, B-1050 Brussel. T: (02)647-0102.
**Flemish Biblical Association (Vlaamse Bijbelstichting),** Sint-Michielsstraat 2, B-3000 Leuven.
**Société Biblique Belge,** Sec, Rue de Trône 160, B-1050 Brussel. T: (02)640-1575.

*BENIN*
**Société Biblique du Benin,** Sec, BP 34, Cotonou.

*BOLIVIA*
**Sociedad Bíblica en Bolivia,** Sec, Bolivar 3685, Casilla 329, Cochabamba. T: 1745.

*BOTSWANA*
**Bible Society in Botswana,** PO Box 251, Gaberone.

*BRAZIL*
**Liga de Estudio Bíblicos,** Dir, Rua Pio XII 205, São Paulo, SP.
**Memorizadores da Bíblia Internacional,** CP 7966, 01.000 São Paulo, SP.
**Sociedade Bíblica do Brasil,** Edificio da Biblia, CP 10-2371, 70.000 Brasília, DF.
**União Bíblica (Scripture Union),** Sec, CP 907, 01.000 São Paulo, SP.

*BURMA*
**Bible Society of Burma,** Sec, 262 Sule Pagoda Rd, PB 106, Rangoon. T: 14638.

*BURUNDI*
**Société Biblique au Burundi,** Sec, Blvd d'Uprona 33, BP 2100, Bujumbura. T: 3688.

*CAMEROON*
**Société Biblique,** Sec, Maison de la Bible, Av Foch, BP 1133, Yaoundé. T: 224276.

*CANADA*
**Bible Centre of the Archdiocese of Montréal (Services de l'Education de la Foi des Adultes, Section Bible),** 2000 Sherbrooke West, Montréal 109, Québec.
**Bible Club Movement,** Box 1052, Station D, Hamilton, Ontario.
**Canadian Bible Society/Société Canadienne de la Bible,** Suite 200, 1835 Yonge St, Toronto 295, Ontario M4S 1Y1. T: (416)481-1312.
**Canadian Home Bible League,** 734 Wilson Av, Downsview, Ontario.
**Catholic Bible Society/Société Catholique de la Bible,** Dir, 5221 De Gaspé Av, Montréal 151, Québec.
**Gideons International,** 90 Thorncliffe Park Drive, Toronto M4H 1L8, Ontario.
**Pocket Testament League (PTL),** Internat Dir, 74 Crescent Rd, Toronto 5, Ontario.
**Scripture Gift Mission (SGM),** 21 Spadina Rd, Toronto 4, Ontario.
**Scripture Union Americas Council,** Sec, 114 Pricefield Rd, Toronto 5, Ontario. T: 925-5616.
**Scripture Union (Ligue pour la Lecture de la Bible),** Gen Dir, 2100 Lawrence Av East, Scarborough, Ontario M1R 2Z7. T: 759-4181.
**Trinitarian Bible Society,** Pres, 26 Gracey Blvd, Weston, Ontario M9R 1Z9. T: (416)249-0718.
**Wycliffe Bible Translators,** 3431 19th St, NW, Box 833, Calgary, Alberta.

*CENTRAL AFRICAN REPUBLIC*
**Société Biblique,** Foyer de la Bible, BP 1127, Bangui. T: 3035.

*CHAD*
**Ligue pour la Lecture de la Bible (Scripture Union),** Rep, BP 127, Ndjamena (Fort Lamy).

*CHILE*
**Sociedad Bíblica Chilena,** Sec, San Francisco 54, Casilla 784, Santiago. T: 383139.

*CHINA*
**China Bible Society,** Bible House, 58 Hong Kong Rd, Shanghai.

*CHINA (TAIWAN)*
**Bible Society in the Republic of China,** Sec, 116 Jen Ai Rd, Sec 3, PO Box 3401, Taipei. T: (02) 7718445,7719258.
**Reformation Translation Fellowship,** Nanking East Rd, Sec 4, Lane 144, Alley 8, No. 1, Taipei. T: 711278.

*COLOMBIA*
**Movimiento Bíblico Católico,** Pres, Calle 36, No 64/A 10, Medellín.
**Sociedad Bíblica Colombiana,** Sec, Carrera 5a, No 15-95, Apdo Aéreo 4931, Nacional 159, Bogotá 1, DE. T: 814671,814635,417427.

*COSTA RICA*
**Sociedad Bíblica en Costa Rica,** Sec, Av 6, Calles 6-8, Apdo 5672, San José. T: 219770.

*CUBA*
**Bible Society in Cuba,** Sec, Neptuno 629, La Habana 2. (Work closed 1968).

*CYPRUS*
**Cyprus Bible House,** Sec, Isaakiou Komninou St 12-14, PO Box 1066, Levkosia (Nicosia). T: 62876.

*CZECHOSLOVAKIA*
**Bible Work of the Czech Ecumenical Council of Churches (Biblické Dílo Ekumenické Rady Církví v CSR),** Sec, Jungmannova 9, 11513 Praha 1, Nové Mesto 22. T: 247101/2.

*DENMARK*
**Danish Bible Society (Danske Bibelselskab),** Gen Sec, Kobmagergade 67, DK-1150 Kobenhavn K. T: (01)127835.

*DOMINICAN REPUBLIC*
**Sociedad Bíblica en República Dominicana,** Agency Sec, Calle El Conde 29, Box 1767, Santo Domingo. T: (682)9528.

*ECUADOR*
**Acción Bíblica Católica,** Av América 1886, Apdo de Correos 3008, Quito.
**Sociedad Bíblica en el Ecuador,** Sec, Av Eloy Alfaro 171, Casilla 1030, Quito. T: 527912,527942.

*EGYPT*
**Bible Society in Egypt,** Sec, 70 Gomhouria St, PO Box 724, Al Qahirah, T: 922255.

*EL SALVADOR*
**Sociedad Bíblica en El Salvador,** Apdo (06) 1014, San Salvador. T: 219712.

*ETHIOPIA*
**Bible Society of Ethiopia,** 39 Haile Selassie I Av, Box 30750, Addis Abeba. T: 122033.

*FIJI*
**Bible Society in the South Pacific,** Sec, Suite 1A and 1B Victoria Arcade, PO 5173, Raiwaga, Suva. T: 24803,26270,26119.

*FINLAND*
**Finnish Bible Society (Suomen Pipliaseura),** Gen Sec, Yliopistonkatu 29a, 20100 Turku 10. T: (921)17622.

*FRANCE*
**Alliance Biblique Française/French Bible Society,** BP 31, F-93380 Pierrefitte.
**Association Catholique Française Etude de la Bible (ACFEB),** Dir, 21 Rue d'Assas, F-75006 Paris.
**Equipes de Recherche Biblique,** Sec, 47 Rue de Clichy, F-75009 Paris. T: 874-1508.

*GABON*
**Société Biblique au Caméroun-Gabon,** Sec, Librairie Evangélique, BP 171, Oyem.

*GERMAN DEMOCRATIC REPUBLIC*
**Arbeitsgemeinschaft der Evangelischen Bibelgesellschaften in der DDR,** Sek, Stiftsgraben 20, DDR-7400 Altenburg.

*GERMANY, Federal Republic of*
**Bibellesebund in Deutschland (Scripture Union)** Gen Sek, In der Fleute 33, Postfach 220152, D-5600 Wuppertal 22. T: (02121)602306.
**Bibelmission in Deutschland,** Wittensteinstr 114, D-5600 Wuppertal 2. T: (02121)555655. (Bible distribution in hotels, &c).
**Evangelisches Bibelwerk in der Bundesrepublik,** Sek, Hauptstätterstr 51, Postfach 755, D-700 Stuttgart 1. T: (0711)247341. (Verband der Ev Bibelgesellschaften in Deutschland/German Bible Societies; 1948).
**Katholisches Bibelwerk,** Dir, Silberburgstr 121, D-7000 Stuttgart 1.
**Ökumenische Arbeitsgemeinschaft für Bibellesen,** Fröbelstr 26, D-843 Gütersloh.
**United Bible Societies,** Bible House, Balinger Strasse 31, PO Box 810340, D-7000 Stuttgart 80. T: (0711)720030.
**World Catholic Federation for the Biblical Apostolate (WCFBA),** Sek, Silberburgstr 121A, D-700 Stuttgart 1.
**Wycliff Bibelübersetzer,** Deutscher Zweig, Siegenweg 32, D-5909 Burbach-Holzhausen. T:(02779)395. (Wycliffe Bible Translators; 1962).

*GHANA*
**Bible Society of Ghana,** Sec, Bible House, High St, James Town, PO Box 761, Accra. T: 63803.

*GREECE*
**Bible Society in Greece (Biblicke Etaireia),** Sec, 3 Nicodemou St, Athínai 118. T: 322800, 3241324.

*GUATEMALA*
**Sociedad Bíblica en Guatemala,** Sec, 8a Av 12-31, Zona 1, Apdo 1369, Guatemala City. T: 28460,28590.

*HAITI*
**La Chambre Haute,** Office de l'Edition Française, Petit Goave.
**Maison Haitienne de la Bible/Haiti Bible House,** Sec, 138 Rue du Centre, BP 253, Port-au-Prince. T: 22655.

*HONDURAS*
**Sociedade Bíblica en Honduras,** Sec, Av Jerez No 1011, Apdo Postal 747, Tegucigalpa, DF. T: 226555.

*HONG KONG*
**Asia Pacific Regional Centre,** United Bible Societies, 24-34 Hennessy Rd, 25th Floor, Hong Kong. T: 5283654/6.
**Bible Society in Hong Kong,** Sec, 67-71 Chatham Rd, Oriental Centre (9th Floor), Kowloon.
**Scripture Gift Mission (SGM),** PO Box 9152, Kowloon. T: K-829844.
**The Upper Room Chinese Publication Committee,** 57 Peking Rd, 7th Floor, Kowloon.

*HUNGARY*
**Hungarian Bible Council (Magyar Bibliatanács),** Superintendant, Abonyi utca 21, Pf 5, H-1440 Budapest XIV. T: 227870,227879.

*ICELAND*
**Icelandic Bible Society (Hid Islen ka Bibíufélag),** Gen Sec, Gudbrandsstofa, Hallgrimskirkja, PO Box 1016, Reykjavík. T: 17805.

*INDIA*
**Bible Society of India,** Sec, 20 Mahatma Gandhi Rd, Bangalore 560 001, South India. T: 54617, 52257,51567,53657.
**Catholic Biblical Association of India (CBAI),** Sec, St Johns Regional Seminary, Ramanthapur Uppal PO, Hyderabad 39 (AP).
**National Biblical Centre of India (NBCLC),** Dir, Mary Town, Post Bag No 577, Bangalore 560005.

*INDONESIA*
**Bible Society (Lembaga Biblika),** Kotak Pos 29, Jogjakarta.
**Indonesian Bible Society (Lembaga Alkitab Indonesia),** Gen Sec, Salemba Raya 12, PO Box 255/DKT, Jakarta. T: 82890.

*IRAN*
**Bible Society in Iran (Anjomane Kotobe Moghadasseh),** Sec, 7/3-4 Av, Gharam-ol-Saltaneh, PO Box 1412, Tehran. T: 311987.

*IRAQ*
**Bible Society in Iraq,** Sec, 321/1 Rashid St, PO Box 337, Baghdad. T: 80969.

*IRELAND*
**Hibernian Bible Society,** Sec, 41 Dawson St, Dublin 2. (Also: 27 Howard St, Belfast BTI 6NB, UK).
**Irish Catholic Biblical Association,** Maynooth College.

*ISRAEL*
**Bible Society in Israel,** Bible Society Bookshop, PO Box 19627, Jerusalem.
**World Jewish Bible Society,** PO Box 024, Jerusalem. T: 62536.

*ITALY*
**Abbey of St Jerome for Revision of the Vulgate,** Via di Torre Rossa 21, I-00165 Roma. T: 620173.
**Bible Society in Italy, Libreria Sacre Scritture,** Sec, Via Dell'Umilta 33, I-00187 Roma. T: 6794254.
**Casa della Bibbia,** Via Balbi 132r, Genova. T: 67948.
**Commission for the New Vulgate,** Palazzo San Calisto, Piazza San Calisto 16, I-00153 Roma.
**Missione Evangelica per l'Europa (Gideon's International),** Via Terme di Traiano 5, Roma.
**World Catholic Federation for the Biblical Apostolate,** Via del Plebiscito 107-2, I-00186 Roma. T: 686675. (3 Piazza Madonna delle Salette, I-00152 Roma).

*IVORY COAST*
**Maison de la Bible,** BP 2559, Abidjan.
**Société Biblique en Côte d'Ivoire,** Sec, 30 Blvd Angoulevant, PO Box 1529, Abidjan. T: 229366.

*JAMAICA*
**Bible Society of the West Indies,** Exec Sec, Bible House, 24 Hagley Park Plaza, Kingston 10. T: 9362772.

*JAPAN*
**Gideons International in Japan,** Toko Bldg, 12 Tomoe-cho, Shiba Nishikubo, Minato-ku, Tokyo 105.
**Japan Bible Society (Nippon Seisho Kyokai),** 5-1, 4-chome, Ginza, Chuo-ku, Kyobashi, PO Box 6, Tokyo. T: (03)567-1986.
**Oriental Bible Study Fellowship,** 3704, Karuizawa-machi, Nagano-ken 389-01.
**The Upper Room,** 7-5,4-chome, Sakai Mianami-cho, Musashino-shi, Tokyo 180.

*JORDAN*
**Bible Society in Jordan,** Sec, PO Box 627, Amman.

*KAMPUCHEA*
**Bible Society in Kampuchea,** Agency Sec, 72 Moha Vithei 9, PO Box 2133, Phnom Penh. T: 24319.

*KENYA*
**Africa Regional Centre,** United Bible Societies, Regional Sec for Africa, KNUT Bldg, Mfangano St, PO Box 42726, Nairobi. T: 26117,20567.
**Bible Society of Kenya,** Exec Sec, Bible House, Mfangano St, PO Box 72983, Nairobi. T: 25587, 27338.
**Scripture Union of Kenya (SU),** Sec, Church House, Moi Av, PO Box 40717, Nairobi. T: 29841, 28248.

*KOREA, South*
**Korean Bible Society (Daihan Sungsuh Kong Hoi),** Gen Sec, 84-9, 2-Ka, Chongo, IPO Box 1030, Soul. T: 742792.
**Korean Catholic Biblical Commission,** 100 Hwa Seo Dong, PO Box 2, Suwon.

*LAOS*
**American Bible Society,** PO Vientane.

*LEBANON*
**Bible Society in Lebanon,** Sec, Bible House, Place de l'Etoile, PO Box 11-747, Bayrut. T: 226678, 253899.

*LESOTHO*
**Bible Society in Lesotho,** Machache House, PO Box 660, Maseru.

*LIBERIA*
**Bible Society in Liberia,** Sec, Bible House, Tubman Blvd, Sinkor, PO Box 39, Monrovia. T: 26175,26024.

*LUXEMBOURG*
**Swiss Bible Society,** Av de la Liberté 6, Luxembourg. T: 22193.

*MADAGASCAR*
**Société Biblique Malgache (Fikambanana Mampiely Baiboly),** Sec, 12 Làlana Jeneraly Rabehevitra, BP 922, Tananarive. T: 25135.

*MALAWI*
**Bible Society in Malawi,** Exec Sec, Victoria Av, PO Box 740, Blantyre. T: 35443/4.

*MALTA*
**Malta Bible Society,** 8 St Mary's St, Tarzien. (Also Catholic Institute, Floriana).

*MAURITIUS*
**Bible Society in Mauritius,** Local Sec, 39b Royal Rd, Eau Coulée, Curepipe Rd. T: 42157.

*MEXICO*
**Americas Regional Centre,** United Bible Societies, Liverpool No 65, Apdo 61-281, México 6, DF. T: (905)592-1577.
**Gedeones (Gideons),** Pres, México, DF. T: 242107.
**Instituto de Santa Escritura,** Dir, Universidad 1700, México 21, DF.
**Instituto Penzotti,** Liverpool 65, Apdo 6-820, México 6, DF. T: 288801. (Bible distribution training).
**Liga del Testamento de Bolsillo (PTL),** Apdo 29, Cd Satélite, Edo de México. T: 602460.
**Misión Bíblica Católica,** Sec, Apdo Postal 157, Naucalpan de Juarez.
**Sociedad Bíblica Católica de México,** Dir, Mos, México.
**Sociedad Bíblica de México,** Sec, Liverpool No 65, Apdo 6-820, México 6, DF. T: (905)533-5570.
**Wycliffe Bible Translators,** Apdo 22-067, México 22, DF.

*MOROCCO*
**Maison de la Bible,** 5 bd Tahar el Alaoui, El-Dar-el-Beida (Casablanca).

*MOZAMBIQUE*
**Casa da Biblia,** Sec, Av Eduardo Mondlane 2678, Maputo. T: 28698.

*NETHERLANDS*
**Bijbel Kiosk Vereniging,** Hoofdstraat 55, Driebergen. T: (03438)3455.
**Catholic Bible Society (Katholieke Bijbelstichting) (KBS),** Dir, Baroniestraat 43, Postbox 27, Boxtel.
**Christian Esperanto International Association,** Slijpkruikweg 17, Ede (Gld). T: (08380)11223.
**Netherlands Bible Society (Nederlandsch Bijbelgenootschap),** Gen Sec, PO Box 620, 2003 RP Haarlem.
**Society for Spreading the Holy Scriptures (Vereiniging tot Verspreiding der Heilige Schrift),** NZ Kolk 19-21, Amsterdam.

*NETHERLANDS ANTILLES*
**Antillean Bible Society (Sosydat Bibliko Antiyano Antilliaans Bijbel Genootschap),** Sec, Maishiweg 39, PO Box 786, Willemstad, Curaçao. T: 93922.

*NEW ZEALAND*
**Bible Society in New Zealand,** Sec, 183 Willis St, PO Box 27-244, Wellington 1. T: 844119. (Covers NZ, New Hebrides, New Caledonia, French Polynesia, Cook Is).
**Scripture Gift Mission,** NZ Council, Sec, 427 Queen St, Auckland 1.
**Scripture Union (SU),** Gen Sec, PO Box 760, Wellington. T: 50782.
**Wycliffe Bible Translators,** NZ Council, Dir, 11 Grant St, Mt Albert, Auckland 3.

*NICARAGUA*
**Sociedad Bíblica en Nicaragua,** Sec, Apdo 2597, Managua.

*NIGERIA*
**Bible Society of Nigeria,** Sec, 18 Wharf Rd, PO Box 68, Apapa, Lagos. T: 42403.
**Scripture Union Africa Council,** Sec, PO Box 643, Jos. T: 2109.

*NORWAY*
**Norwegian Bible Society (Norske Bibelselskap),** Sec, Munchs Gate 2, PO Box 7062, Homansbyen, Oslo 3. T: (02)203477.

*PACIFIC ISLANDS*
**Bible Society in Micronesia,** PO Box 338, Agaña, Guam 96910.

*PAKISTAN*
**Pakistan Bible Society,** Sec, Bible House, Anarkali, Lahore 2. T: 53421.

*PANAMA*
**Sociedad Bíblica de Panamá,** Calle Santa Rita, Urb Obarrio, Edif Valladolid, Apdo 3316, Panamá 4. T: 611510.

*PANAMA CANAL ZONE*
**Sociedad Bíblica en Costa Rica y Panamá,** Sec, Box 5065, Cristobal.

*PAPUA NEW GUINEA*
**Bible Society of Papua New Guinea,** Sec, Bible House, Hubert Murray Highway, Koke, PO Box 18, Port Moresby. T: 54668.

*PARAGUAY*
**Sociedad Bíblica en el Paraguay,** Sec, 15 de Agosto 652, Casilla de Correo 167, Asunción. T: 48975.

*PERU*
**Sociedad Bíblica Peruana,** Sec, Av Petit Thouars 991, Santa Beatriz, Apdo 448, Lima 1. T: 319555, 317247.

*PHILIPPINES*
**Asia Pacific Regional Centre,** United Bible Societies, PO Box 1730, Makati, Rizal 3117. T: 504470.
**Catholic Bible Centre,** Dir, PO Box 3992, Manila.
**Christian Translators Fellowship,** Box 4174, Manila.
**Philippine Bible Society,** Sec, 890 United Nations Av, Ermita, PO Box 755, Manila. T: 597076,505032.

*POLAND*
**British and Foreign Bible Society (Brytyjskie i Zagraniczne Towarzystwo Biblijne),** Sec, Nowy Swiat 40, 00-363 Warszawa. T: 264986.

*PORTUGAL*
**Sociedade Bíblica Escocesa (Scottish Bible Society),** Sec, Rua Arriaga 11, Lisboa 3. T: 662640.
**Sociedade Bíblica,** Sec, Rua Passos Manuel 1B, Lisboa 1100. T: 45534.

*PUERTO RICO*
**Bible Society in Puerto Rico & the Virgin Is (Sociedad Bíblica de Puerto Rico e Islas Virgenes),** Sec, Calle El Roble 54, PO Box 20821, Rio Piedras, PR 00928. T: 7674165.

*RWANDA*
**Société Biblique au Rwanda,** BP 788 Kigali.

*SIERRA LEONE*
**Bible Society in Sierra Leone,** Sec, 37a Westmoreland St, PO Box 1169, Freetown. T: 4644.

*SINGAPORE*
**Bible Society of Singapore, Malaysia & Brunei,** Sec, 7 Armenian St, Singapore 6. T: 321498,321502.
**Gideons International,** 7 Claymore Rd, Singapore 9.

*SOUTH AFRICA*
**Bible Society of South Africa,** Sec, Bible House, Anton Anreith Arcade Foreshore, PO Box 6215, Roggebaai, Cape Town 8012. T: 22554.

*SPAIN*
**Sociedad Bíblica en España,** Sec, Casa de la Biblia, Joaquín García Morato 133, Madrid 3. T: 2545298.

*SRI LANKA*
**Ceylon Bible Society(Sri Lanka Bible Samagama),** Sec, Bible House, 293 Galle Rd, Colombo 3. T: 24483.

*SUDAN*
**Bible Society in the Sudan,** Sec, Bible House, Sharia Khalifia 15, PO Box 532, Al Khurtum. T: 80023.

*SURINAM*
**Surinam Bible Society (Surinaams Bijbel-Genootschap),** Heerenstraat 19, PO Box 2154-Zd, Paramaribo. T: 76676.

*SWAZILAND*
**Bible Society,** Sec, PO Box 550, Manzini.

*SWEDEN*
**Institute for Bible Translation (IBT),** Box 20100, 5-104 60 Stockholm. T: 08945414. (Non-Slavic languages in Slavic countries).
**Swedish Bible Society (Svenska Bibelsällskapet),** Sec, Kammakargatan 13, S-11140 Stockholm. T: (08)205495.
**Wycliffe Bible Translators,** Anggatan 24, Box 394, Örebro.

*SWITZERLAND*
**Bibellesebund (Scripture Union),** Römerstr 151, CH-8404 Winterthur. T: (052)274801.
**Geneva Bible Society,** Le Roc, Cologny, Genève. (Linked with Action Biblique).
**Heimstätte der Vereinigten Bibelgruppen,** CH-6612 Moscia-Ascona/TI.
**Ligue pour la Lecture de la Bible (Scripture Union),** Gen Sec, Route de Berne 90, CH-1010 Lausanne. T: (021)321538.
**Portfolio for Biblical Studies,** World Council of Churches, 150 Route de Ferney, CH-1211, Genève 20.
**Schweizerische Bibelgesellschaft (Swiss Bible Society),** Sek, Waffengasse 20, CH-2501 Biel. (German-speaking).
**Scripture Union European Council,** Talackerstr 15, CH-8404 Winterthur. T: (052)274801.
**Scripture Union International Council,** Internat Sec, Talackerstr 15, CH-8404 Winterthur. T: (052) 274801.
**Société Biblique Suisse (Swiss Bible Society),** Sec, 29 Av de la Gare, CH-2000 Neuchâtel. T:41500. (French-speaking).
**Swiss Catholic Biblical Works,** Ch de Bethléem 76, CH-1700 Fribourg.
**Vereinigte Bibelgruppen in Schule, Universität & Beruf (VBG),** Gen Sek, Angelrain 6, CH-5600 Lenzburg. T: (064)514440.
**Wycliffe Bibelübersetzer,** Postfach 2, Basel 1.

*SYRIA*
**Bible Society in Syria,** Pennsylvania St, PO Box 1305, Halab.

*TANZANIA*
**Bible Society of Tanzania,** Sec, PO Box 175, Dodoma. T: 229.

*THAILAND*
**Bible Society in Thailand and Laos,** Sec, 150 North Sathorn Rd, Bangkok 5. T: 2342271.

**Catholic Biblical Commission of Thailand,** PO Box 4, Khon Kaen.

*TOGO*
**Bible Society in Togo (Biblia Habobo),** BP 3014, Lomé.

*TURKEY*
**British and Foreign Bible Society (Ingiliz ve Ecnebi Kitab Mukaddes),** Sec, Istiklal Cad No 481, Geyoglu, PO Box 186 (Merkez), Istanbul. T: 278100.

*UGANDA*
**Bible Society of Uganda,** Sec, 15 Obote Av, PO Box 3621, Kampala. T: 54248.

*UK OF GB & NI*
**Association for the Free Distribution of the Scriptures,** Sec, 10 Grange Rd, Bushey, Herts. T: Watford 28055.
**Bible Club Movement,** Room 404, 157 Waterloo Rd, London SE1 8UU. T: (01)928-8876.
**Bible Fellowship Union,** 11 Lyncroft Gardens, Hounslow, Middlesex.
**Bible Reading Fellowship (BRF),** Dir, 148 Buckingham Palace Rd, London SW1. T: (01) 730-9181/2. (Work in over 60 nations).
**Bible Spreading Union,** 1 Donald Way, Gloucester Av, Chelmsford, Essex.
**Bible Text Publicity Mission,** Metropolitan Tabernacle, Elephant & Castle, London SE1 6SD.
**British & Foreign Bible Society (BFBS),** Gen Sec, 146 Queen Victoria St, London EC4V 4BX. T: (01)248-4751.
**Catholic Biblical Association of GB,** 24 Golden Square, London W1R 3PA. (Also: St Joseph's College, Mill Hill, London NW7).
**Christian Colportage Association,** 53 High St, Cobham, Surrey. (Also: 3 Grange Rd, Egham. Formed 1874).
**Gideons International,** Sec, Western House, George St, Lutterworth, Leics, LE17 4EE. T: (04555) 4241.
**Hibernian Bible Society,** Sec, 24 Howard St, Belfast BT1 6NB, Northern Ireland. T: 26577.
**International Bible Reading Association (IBRA),** Gen Sec, Robert Denholm House, Nutfield, Surrey. T: Nutfield Ridge 2411. (Begun 1882. Under NSSU, now National Christian Educational Council. 200,000 readers in English worldwide).
**National Bible Society of Scotland,** Gen Sec, 7 Hampton Terrace, Edinburgh EH12 5XU.
**Pocket Testament League (PTL),** Gen Sec, 16 Holwood Rd, Bromley, Kent BR1 3EB. T: (01) 460-5317.
**Scripture Gift Mission (SGM),** Sec, Radstock House, 3 Eccleston St, London SW1W 9LZ. T: (01)730-2155/6/7.
**Scripture Union Council for GB & NI,** Sec, 5 Wigmore St, London W1H 0AD. T: (01)486-2561.
**Scripture Union (SU),** Gen Dir, 47 Marylebone Lane, London W1M 6AX. T: (01)486-2561.
**Society for Distributing the Holy Scriptures to the Jews,** Gen Sec, 1 Rectory Lane, Edgware, Middlesex HA8 7LF. T: (01)952-9892.
**Trinitarian Bible Society,** Sec, 217 Kingston Rd, London SW19 3NN T: (01)540-3021.
**World Service Centre,** United Bible Societies, 146 Queen Victoria St, London EC4V 4BX. T: (01)248-4751.
**Wycliffe Bible Translators (Summer Institute of Linguistics),** Bletchingley Rd, Merstham, Surrey T: Merstham 2395.

*USA*
**Air Mail from God Mission,** PO Box 2013, Los Angeles, CA 90054. (Air service dropping scriptures over Latin America).
**American Bible Society (ABS),** Gen Sec, 1865 Broadway, New York, NY 10023. T: (212)581-7400.
**American Biblical Encyclopedia Society,** 210 West 91st, New York, NY 10024. T: (212)SU7-4085.
**American Scripture Gift Mission,** Pres, 1211 Arch St, Philadelphia, PA 19107. T: (215)561-3232. (441 Bourse Bldg, 5th St at Ludlow).
**Association for Final Advance of Scripture Translation (FAST),** Pres, 1740 Westminster Drive, Denton, TX 76201. T: (817)387-9531.
**Audio Bible Studies,** Founder, 6430 Sunset Blvd, Hollywood, CA 90028. T: (213)466-6121.
**B.B. Kirkbridge Bible Co,** K of P Bldg, Indianapolis, IN 46200.
**Back to the Bible Missionary Agency,** Dir, 301 South 11th St, Box 233, Lincoln, NE 68501. T: (402)435-2171.
**Bible Club Movement,** Pres, 237 Fairfield Av, Upper Darby, PA 19082. T: (215)352-7177.
**Bible Crusaders,** Box 777, Westminster, CA 92683.
**Bible Literature International,** Internat Pres, 625 E North Broadway, PO Box 477, Columbus, OH 43216. T: (614)267-3116.
**Bible Meditation League,** PO Box 477, Columbus, OH 43216.
**Bible Memory Association,** Chairman, 6341 Easton, Box 516, Wellston Station, St Louis, MO 63112. T: (314)726-1323.
**Bible Translations on Tape,** Pres, PO Box 2500, Orange, CA 92669. T: (714)558-1027.
**Bibles for the World,** 1415 Hill Av, PO Box 805, Wheaton, IL 60187. T: (312)668-7733.
**Catholic Bible Society of America,** Pres, PO Box 2206, Dallas, TX 75221.
**Catholic Biblical Association of America (CBA),** Exec Sec, 620 Michigan Av NE, Washington, DC 20017. T: (202)LA9-6000 ext 425.
**Cicero Bible Press,** 2301 Roosevelt Rd, Broadview, IL 60153.
**Dake Bible Sales,** Station A, Box 11110, Atlanta, GA 30310.
**Gideons International,** Pres, 2900 Lebanon Rd, Nashville, TN 27314. T: (615)883-8533.
**International Society of Bible Collectors (ISBC),** Pres, Rose Memorial Library, 13800 Biola Av, La Mirada, CA 90638.
**Language Institute for Evangelism,** Dir, 21 North Olive, Alhambra, CA 91801.
**Lutheran Bible Translators,** Exec Dir, PO Box 885, Orange, CA 92666. T: (714)639-2850.
**Million Testaments Campaigns,** Exec Dir, 1505 Race St, Philadelphia, PA 19102. T. (215)567-1747.
**Miracle Press Bible Memory Association,** PO Box 516, Wellston Station, St Louis, MO 63112.
**National Center for the Catholic Biblical Apostolate,** USCC, 1312 Massachusetts Av NW, Washington, DC 20005.
**New Tribes Mission,** Gen Sec, Woodworth, WI 53194. T: (414)857-2861. (Linguistics, literacy and Bible translation).
**New York International Bible Society,** Pres, 144 Tices Lane, East Brunswick, NJ 08816. (Publisher of NIV Bible).
**Pocket Testament League (PTL),** Internat Dir, 49 Honeck St, Englewood, NJ 07631. T: (201) 567-2332.
**Reformation Translation Fellowship,** 1031 Glenrose Av, Phoenix, AZ 85014.
**Scripture Union (SU),** Exec Dir, 1716 Spruce St, Philadelphia, PA 19103. T: K16-1160.
**Summer Institute of Linguistics (SIL),** 219 West Walnut, PO Box 1960, Santa Ana, CA 92701.
**The Living Bible,** Tyndale House Foundation, Wheaton, Illinois.
**The Upper Room Publishing House,** 1908 Grand Av, Nashville, TN 37203. (Bible study notes, United Methodist Church. Circulation 2.6 million in USA, 37 languages worldwide).
**Tokyo Bible Centre,** Beth Eden Baptist Church, 2600 Wadsworth Blvd, Denver, CO 80215.
**US Catholic Biblical Apostolate,** 1312 Massachusetts Av, NW, Washington, DC 20005.
**Watchtower Bible and Tract Society of New York,** IBSA, 124 Columbia Heights, Brooklyn, NY 11201. (Jehovah's Witnesses).
**World Bible Translation Center,** Coor, 344 Cambridge St, Burlington, MA 01801. T: (214)263-8179.
**World Home Bible League,** Dir, 425 West 107th St, Chicago, IL 60628. T: (312)928-7022.
**World Service Center,** United Bible Societies, 1865 Broadway, New York, NY 10023. T: (212) 581-7400.
**Wycliffe Bible Translators (WBT),** Gen Dir, 219 West Walnut, PO Box 1960, Santa Ana, CA 92702. T: (714)547-6526.

*URUGUAY*
**Sociedad Bíblica del Uruguay,** Sec, Calle Constituyente 1540, Montevideo. T: 410034.

*VENEZUELA*
**Sociedad Bíblica de Venezuela,** Sec, Av Jose A Páez, Qta Casa de la Biblia, El Paraiso, Apdo 222, Caracas 101, DF. T: 427784,410928.

*VIET NAM*
**Bible Society in Vietnam (Thanh-Kinh Hoi Viet-Nam),** Sec, 5 Suong nguyet Anh, PO Box 716, Saigon 2. T: 23802.

*YUGOSLAVIA*
**British & Foreign Bible Society in Yugoslavia (Britansko i Inostrano Biblijsko Drustvo),** Sec, Marsala Tita 26, 11000 Beograd. T: (011) 656779.

*ZAIRE*
**Centre pour l'Apostolat Biblique,** Dir, BP 19, Bandundu.
**Société Biblique du Zaire,** Sec, 17 Av Strauch, BP 8911, Kinshasa-Est.

*ZAMBIA*
**Bible Society of Zambia,** Sec, 1566 Freedom Way, PO Box 1316, Lusaka. T: 73563.

*ZIMBABWE*
**Bible Society in Rhodesia,** Sec, Bible House, 99 Victoria St, PO Box 1081, Salisbury C1. T: 24583.

# 6
# Bible Schools & Colleges

*Definition.* Centres for the training of Christian workers: (a) in Western countries, degree- or diploma-granting bodies sometimes for the ordained ministry but more usually not; and (b) in Third-World countries, often for the ordained ministry, also for lay ministries, both for candidates of less than secondary education.

No names and addresses are given here because such institutions number in the thousands. See under DIRECTORIES for listings in particular continents, countries, confessions, or denominations.

# 7
# Broadcasting

*Definition.* Organizations and centres (excluding radio/TV stations) specializing in Christian religious broadcasting, commissions, radio/TV programming, programme production, production of materials, cable TV, spots, major production studios; programme distribution agencies (distributing to stations); radio/TV training schools and centres; educational or mass-education radio and TV, teleclubs, mass education by satellite (without postal feedback); listeners' and viewers' associations. See also RADIO & TELEVISION STATIONS.

There are over 430 organizations in this field significant at national, continental, international, or confessional levels.

*ANDORRA*
**Emissions Catholiques,** Radio Andorra, BP 1, Andorra. T: (61)20100,20104.

*ARGENTINA*
**Comisión de Radio y Televisión,** Convención Evangélica Bautista, Tucuman 358, 6K, Buenos Aires.
**Escuela de Radio y Televisión Educativa,** Don Bosco 4002, Buenos Aires. T: 869352.
**Ministerio de la Canción,** Sarandi 65, Buenos Aires. (Ministry of Song; records).
**Stacy Recording Studio,** Venezuela 452, Buenos Aires.

*AUSTRALIA*
**Australian Broadcasting Commission,** Box 487, Sydney, NSW. (Member of WACC).
**Back to the Bible Broadcast,** Dir, PO Box 45, Stanmore, NSW 2048.
**Bible Radio and Television Productions,** Box 412F, GPO, Brisbane, Queensland.
**Catholic Radio and TV,** 143 A'Beckett St, Melbourne, Victoria 3000.
**Christian Broadcasting Association,** Managing Dir, 420 Lyons Rd, Five Dock, Sydney, NSW 2046.
**Christian Radio Missionary Fellowship,** Box 5271, GPO, Sydney, NSW. T: 417283.
**Christian TV Association of South Australia,** PO Box 518E, GPO, Adelaide, South Australia. (Member of WACC).
**Christian TV Association of Victoria,** 130 Little Collins St, Melbourne 3000. (Member of WACC).
**Gospel Broadcasters,** 4 Verona St, Box Hill, Victoria.
**National Catholic Radio/TV Centre,** Dir, 50 Abbotsford Rd, Homebush, NSW 2140. T: 760459, 760450. (Under Episcopal Conference).

*AUSTRIA*
**Katholische Funk- und Fernsehschau,** Singerstr 7-IV-II, A-1010 Wien. T: 524386.

*BAHAMAS*
**Bahamas Catholic Hour,** PO Box 187, Nassau. (Begun 1947).

*BELGIUM*
**Emissions Missionnaires,** Radio de Belgique, Dir, Hemelaerstraat 58, Sint-Niklaas, Wass.
**Global Gospel Broadcasters,** 69 Av Devoer, Vilvorde.
**Hoger Sint-Lucasinstituut,** Paleizenstraat 70, B-1030 Brussel. (Catholic radio-TV training).
**Katholiek Televisie en Radio Centrum (KTRC),** Sec Gen, De Vergniestraat 41, B-1050 Brussel. T: (02)489008. (Flemish).
**Radio-Télévision Catholique Belge (RTCB),** Pres, 3 Av des Nerviens, B-1040 Brussel. T: (02) 352800. (French).
**UNDA/Association Catholique Internationale pour la Radiodiffusion et la Télévision,** Rue de l'Orme 12, B-1050 Brussel.

*BENIN*
**Emissions Catholiques,** Paroisse St-Michel, Cotonou.

*BOLIVIA*
**Southern Cross Studio,** Cajon 1408, La Paz. (Canadian Baptists OMB. Sponsors CP-27, CP-75, CP3FM).

*BOTSWANA*
**Catholic Broadcasting Secretary,** PO Box 13, Gaberone.

*BRAZIL*
**CEPROL,** Rua de Mocoa 3.758, São Paulo, SP.
**Evangelical Studio,** Missão Presbiteriana, CP 435, Recife, Pernambuco.
**Fundação Centro Brasileiro de TV Educativa,** Av NSenhora de Copacabana 928.10.0, Rio de Janeiro, GB.
**Fundação Educativa Padre Landel de Moura,** Av Bastian 285, Pôrto Alegre, RS.
**Movimento de Educação de Base (MEB),** Rua São Clemente 385, Rio de Janeiro ZC-02-GB.
**Pia Società di San Paolo,** CP 7200, São Paulo, SP. (Radio and TV production).
**Radio Clube de Ribeirão Preto,** Rua Barão do Amazonas 35, SP.
**Radio-TV Difusora Portoalegrense,** Rua Delfino Riet 183, Pôrto Alegre, Rio Grande do Sul. (Regional branch, SERPAL).

*BURMA*
**Broadcast Network,** National Council of Churches, Production Studio, 82nd St, Mandalay.

*BURUNDI*
**Emissions Catholiques,** Collège du Saint-Esprit, BP 825, Bujumbura.

*CAMEROON*
**Emissions Catholiques Hebdomadaires,** BP 75, Garoua.
**Fédération Radio Studio (CENTAVEP),** BP 187, Yaoundé. (Protestant).
**Literature and Radio Department,** Presbyterian Church in West Cameroon, Sec, PO Box 19, Buea.
**Responsable des Emissions Catholiques,** BP 4164, Yaoundé.
**Studio Sawtu Linjiila,** Dir, BP 2, Ngaoundere.

*CANADA*
**Arabic Radio Mission,** Chairman, 95 Stratford Crescent, Toronto, Ontario. T: (416)487-0720.
**Canadian Broadcasting Corporation,** 354 Jarvis St, Toronto, Ontario. (Member of WACC).
**Commission de la Radio et de la Télévision,** Office des Communications Sociales, 4635 De Lorimier, Montréal, Québec.
**Emissions Témoignages,** 25 Ouest, Rue Jarry, Montréal 351, Québec. T: (514)387-2541. (Jesuit studio).
**Interchurch Broadcasting,** National Catholic Communications Center, 21 Grenville St, Toronto 189, Ontario. (Ecumenical. Member of WACC).
**La Bonne Nouvelle Recording Studio,** 249/253 St George St, Moncton, NB.
**People's Gospel Hour,** Box 1660, Halifax.
**Sacred Heart Program,** 2 Hawthorn Gardens, Toronto 287, Ontario.
**Service des Emissions Religieuses,** Dir, Radio-Canada, CP 6000, Montréal, Québec.
**World Radio Missionary Fellowship,** Gen Sec, Box 128, Station D, Toronto, Ontario.

*CENTRAL AFRICAN REPUBLIC*
**Emissions Catholiques,** Archevêché, BP 789, Bangui.

*CHAD*
**Emissions Catholiques,** Mission Catholique, BP 456, Fort-Lamy.

*CHILE*
**Asociación de Radiodifusoras de Chile,** Casilla 10476, Santiago.
**Instituto Nacional de Acción Poblacional (INAP),** Principe de Gales 87, Casilla 13508, Correo 15, Santiago. (Catholic educational TV programmes).
**Responsable TV,** Universidad Católica de Santiago, Santiago.

*CHINA (TAIWAN)*
**Kuangchi Program Service for Radio and TV,** Tun-hua, South Rd, Lane 451, No 8, PO Box 24042, Taipei. T: 772136/37.
**Lutheran Voice,** Taipei. (Member of WACC).
**Overseas Radio & Television Inc,** Pei An Rd, Lane 501, No 55, PO Box 37003, Taipei. T: 559144. (Production studios).
**Southern Baptist Mission Radio Studio,** 47-1 Hwaining St, Taipei. T: 39887.
**TEAM/Far East Broadcasting Company,** PO Box 153, Taichung.

*COLOMBIA*
**Cine,** Radio-TV Centro de Producción y Formación (CENPRO), Carrera 23, No 39-69, Bogotá, DE 1. T: 444675,445154.
**OSAL Centro,** Técnicas de Comunicación para el Desarrollo, Calle 20 No 9-45, Apdo Aéreo 12-721 Bogotá, DE. (Regional branch, SEAPAL).

*CONGO*
**Emissions Catholiques,** Séminaire Libermann, BP 210, Brazzaville.

*COSTA RICA*
**Asociación de Radio Faro del Caribe,** Apdo 2710, San José.
**Catholic Broadcasting,** Radio Fides, Calle Ier, Av IIa, San José.
**Difusiones Inter Americanas (DIA),** Apdo 2470, San José.

*DENMARK*
**Association Catholique des Auditeurs,** Pres, Teglbrandertoften 8, DK-2890 Hareskov. T: 987675.
**Catholic Broadcasting,** Askelkkevej 9, DK-2770 Kastrup. T: 513061.

*DJIBOUTI*
**Emissions Catholiques,** Paroisse de la Cathédrale, BP 94, Djibouti.

*ECUADOR*
**All Ecuador Gospel Network,** 'Vozandes, Establon del Guayas', Casilla 5383, Guayaquil.
**La Biblia Dice,** Casilla 37-15, Quito.
**World Radio Missionary Fellowship,** Pres, Villalengua 278, Casilla 691, Quito. T: 241550. (HCJB).

*EGYPT*
**Catholic Broadcasting,** Rue Adly Pasha 9, Ap 8, Al Qahirah.

*EL SALVADOR*
**Latin American Radio Evangelism,** San Salvador.

*EQUATORIAL GUINEA*
**Catholic Broadcasting,** Apdo 82, Bata, Rio Muni.

*ETHIOPIA*
**Catholic Broadcasting,** PO Box 21903, Addis Abeba.
**Yemissrach Dimts Studio,** Dir, PO Box 1153, Addis Abeba.

*FINLAND*
**Finnish Broadcasting Company,** Helsinki. (Member of WACC).
**Helsingen Ev Lut Seurakuntien Elokuva — Ja TV-Palvelu,** Helsinki. (Member of WACC).
**Radio and Television Department,** Catholic Information Centre (KATT), Kotipolku 18, Helsinki 60. T: (90)794197.

*FRANCE*
**Association Evangélique de Radio,** 109 Rue de l'Aiguillette, F-13012 Marseille. T: 488240.
**Comité de Coordination Interorthodoxe,** 4 Rue de Ursuliness, F-75005 Paris. T: 633-9315.
**Comission Education Religieuse Radio-TV,** UNDA, Responsable, 121 Av de Villiers, F-75017 Paris.
**Les Amis de la Radio-Télévision Protestante,** Sec, 47 Rue de Clichy, F-75009 Paris. T: 874-1508.
**L'Heure de la Décision,** BP 345, F-75365 Paris-Cédex 08. T: 225-8051. (Billy Graham Evangelistic Association).
**Maison de la Radio-Télévision Catholique,** 121 Av de Villiers, F-75017 Paris. T: (01)380-3056.

**Office Catholique Français de Radio-Télévision (OCFRT),** 193 Rue de l'Université, F-75007 Paris. T: (01)705-4358,551-9462.
**Radio Evangile (Monte-Carlo),** Dir, BP 360/R9, F-67009 Strasbourg. T: (88)311625. (French branch of Trans World Radio).
**Radio Réveil,** Au Port, 74 Saint-Jorioz, Toulouse.
**Service de la Radio-Télévision,** FPF, Responsable, 47 Rue de Clichy, F-75009 Paris. T: 874-1508.
**Télérama,** Dir Gen, 10 Rue Laborde, F-75008 Paris. T: 522-9185. (4 Place de Breteuil, F-75006 Paris).
**Voix de l'Evangile,** 109 Rue de l'Aiguillette, F-13012 Marseille, BP 45 Marseille RP (B-du-Rh). T: 488240.

*FRENCH GUIANA*
**Emissions Catholiques,** Evêché, BP 122, Cayenne.

*GABON*
**Emissions Catholiques,** Archevêché, BP 1146, Libreville.

*GAMBIA*
**Catholic Radio Broadcasts,** Sec, PO Box 165, Bathurst.

*GERMANY, Federal Republic of*
**Arbeitsgemeinschaft der Offentlichrechtlichen Rundfunkanstalten der BRD (ARD),** Vorsitzender, Bertramstr 8, D-6 Frankfurt 1. (Co-ordination of religious TV programmes).
**Arbeitsgemeinschaft Evangelischer Radiomission 'Christus Lebt',** Pressehaus, PO Box 2640, D-4813 Bethel bei Bielefeld. T: (0521)44861. (Christ Lives).
**Die Stimme der Heimat,** Evangelist Werner, Heukelbach, D-5281 Wiedenest. (Voice of the Homeland; Brethren).
**Evangelisches Rundfunk und Fernsehreferat der Norddeutschen Landeskirchen,** Hamburg. (Member of WACC).
**Evangeliums-Rundfunk,** Berliner Ring 62, Box 1444, D-6330 Wetzlar. T: (06441)6079. (German branch of Trans World Radio).
**Katholische Fernseharbeit in Deutschland (KFD),** Grillparzerstr 30, D-6 Frankfurt 1. T: (0611) 727097,561088. (TV).
**Katholische Rundfunk Arbeit in Deutschland,** Wittelsbacherring 9, Postfach 290, D-53 Bonn. T: (02221)51414.
**Katholisches Rundfunkinstitut eV,** Am Hof 28, 5 Köln. T: (0511)231600.
**Kirchenfunk, Bayerischer Rundfunk,** Rundfunkplatz 1, D-8 München 2.
**Kirchenfunk, Deutsche Welle,** Hohenzollernring 62, D-5 Köln.
**Kirchenfunk, Deutschlandfunk,** Lindenallee 7, D-5 Köln-Marienburg.
**Kirchenfunk, Hessischer Rundfunk,** Bertramstr 8, D-6 Frankfurt 1.
**Kirchenfunk, Norddeutscher Rundfunk,** Rothenbaum Chaussee 132-4, D-2 Hamburg 13.
**Kirchenfunk, Radio Bremun,** Heinrich Hertz Str 13, D-28 Bremen.
**Kirchenfunk, Saarländischer Rundfunk,** Funkhaus Halberg, D-66 Saarbrücken.
**Kirchenfunk, Sender Freies Berlin,** Masuren Allee 8-14, D-1 Berlin 19.
**Kirchenfunk, Süddeutscher Rundfunk,** Neckarstr 145, D-7 Stuttgart 1. (Member of WACC).
**Kirchenfunk, Südwestfunk,** Hans Bredow Str, D-757 Baden-Baden.
**Kirchenfunk, Westdeutscher Rundfunk,** Wallrafplatz 5, D-5 Köln. (Member of WACC).
**Kirchenfunk, Zweites Deutsches Fernsehen,** Grosse Bleiche/Ecke Flachsmarkstr, D-65 Mainz.
**Konferenz für Evangelische Rundfunk- und Fernseharbeit,** Haus der Ev Publizistik, Friedrichstr 34, D-6 Frankfurt am Main.
**Lutherische Stunde,** Wessenburger Str 36, D-28 Bremen. (Lutheran Hour. Member of WACC).
**Radiodienst Vox Christiana,** Bonner Platz 1/III, D-8 München 2. (Radio programmes for Latin American stations).
**Tellux-Film GmbH,** Leopoldstr 20, D-8 München 23. T: 340724. (TV production).

*GHANA*
**Broadcasting and Audio-Visual Services (BRAVS),** Dir, Box 919, Accra.
**Department of Press & Broadcasting,** National Catholic Secretariat, PO Box 7530, Accra. T: 22871.

*GREECE*
**Catholic Broadcasting,** 246 Rue Acharnon, Athínai 8.

*GUADELOUPE*
**Emissions Catholiques,** Maison des Oeuvres, 28 Rue Peynier, BP 414, Pointe à Pitre 971.

*GUAM*
**Catholic Broadcasting,** Chancery Office, Agaña.

*GUATEMALA*
**Radio Metropolitana,** Palacio Arzobispol, Guatemala City.

*GUINEA-BISSAU*
**Catholic Broadcasting,** Prefecture Apostolic, CP 20, Bissau.

*GUYANA*
**Christian Association of Broadcasters,** 293 Oronoque St, Georgetown. T: 4893.

*HAITI*
**Emissions Catholiques,** Radio Manrèse, Poste 4 VM, CP 525, Port-au-Prince.

*HOLY SEE*
**Radio Vatican, Radiovaticana,** Production Studios, Direzione Generale, I-00120 Città del Vaticano. T: (06) 6983045.

*HONG KONG*
**Catholic Broadcasting,** Wah Yan College, Queen's Rd East, HK.
**Chinese Provincial Broadcast,** PO Box 13225, HK.
**LWF Broadcasting Service,** Dir, Room 408, Yu To Sang Bldg, Queen's Rd Central, HK.

*INDIA*
**Adventist World Radio Asia,** PO Box 15, Poona 411001.
**Christian Association for Radio Audio-Visual Services (CARAVS),** Exec Sec, 15 New Civil Lines, Jabalpur, MP.
**Evangelical Radio Fellowship of India,** Jhansi, UP.
**Far East Broadcasting Associates of India,** Bangalore-Moody-Studios, 7 Commissariat Rd, Bangalore 560025, Mysore State.
**Living Waters Gospel Broadcasts,** PO Box 6654, Bandra, Bombay 50.
**Nazarene Radio Service,** Dhamdary Mission House, Buldana, Maharashtra.
**St Xavier's Centre,** Chaibasa, Singhbhum-District.
**Sound Recording Studio,** Gyan Ashram, Andheri, Bombay. (Catholic).
**Suvartha Vani,** Andhra Christian Council Recording Studio, Dir, Box 379, Vijayawada 2, AP. (Production. Member of WACC).

*INDONESIA*
**Catholic Broadcasting,** Jalan Kemiri 15, Jakarta 11/16.
**DGI Broadcast Network,** Production Studio, 10 Salemba Raya, Jakarta IV/3.
**Educational Radio and TV Centre for Development,** Jalan Kamiri 15/a, Jakarta 11/16.

*IRAN*
**Near East Council of Churches Radio Program Centre for Iran,** Exec Sec, Box 2995, Tehran.

*IRELAND*
**Oblate Conference Library,** Oblate Fathers, Inchicore, Dublin 8. (Videotape recording).

*ITALY*
**Centro Cattolico Televisivo (CCTV),** Ente dello Spettacolo, Via della Conciliazione 2c, I-00193 Roma. T: 561775,564132.
**Gospel Missionary Union,** Voce della Biblia, CP 580, 41100 Modena.
**Radio Réveil,** 51 Via Tesserete, Lugano.
**Studio Radio per l'Evangelo in Italia,** Via Trieste 45, Florence.

*IVORY COAST*
**Emissions Catholiques,** BP 1287, Abidjan (radio); and BP 8016, Abidjan (TV).

*JAPAN*
**Baptist Evangelical Broadcasting Center,** Sapporo CPO Box 201, Sapporo-shi 060-91.
**Baptist Hour,** Japan Baptist Convention, 2-350 Nishi Okubo, Shinjuku-ku, Tokyo 160.
**Broadcasting and Audio-Visual Aids Committee (BAVACO),** Sec, 1-551 Totsuka-Machi, Shinjuku-ku, Tokyo 160. (EACC, now CCA).
**Christian Broadcasting Association,** 6-14 Nakamiya-cho, Asahi-ku, Osaka 535.
**Far East Broadcasting Company (FEBC),** Dir, CPO Box 55, Naha, Ryukyu Islands. T: 78208.
**Hokkaido Radio Evangelism Mass Communications (HOREMCO),** Gen Dir, Box 202, Sapporo, Hokkaido.
**Japan Mission Broadcasting Evangelism,** 242-3 Hanyuno, Habikino-shi, Osaka 583.
**Joint Broadcasting Committee,** United Church of Christ in Japan, 5-1, 4-chome, Ginza, Chuo-ku, Tokyo 104.
**Lutheran Hour,** 2-32, 1-chome, Fujimi-cho, Chiyoda-ku, Tokyo 102.
**LWF Broadcasting Service,** Tokyo Office, Room 624, Nikkatsu Hotel, 1-1 Yurakucho, Chiyoda-ku, Tokyo 100.
**National Catholic Broadcasting Committee,** Taishido-2 chome 15-3, Setagaya-ku, Tokyo.
**Nazarene Hour,** 8-589 Kami Meguro, Meguro-ku, Tokyo 153.
**Pacific Broadcasting Association,** 10-8 Umegaoka 3-chome, Setagaya-ku, CPO Box 1000, Tokyo 100-91. T: 4203166.
**St Paul Film and Radio Centre,** 1-5 Wakaba, Shinjuku-ku, Tokyo 160. (Catholic).
**Time for Christ,** Minami Presbyterian Church Radio Evangelism Dept, 4-33 Chikara-cho, Higashi-ku, Nagoya-shi 461.
**Voice of Life,** Missions to Japan, 10-6 Hamadamachi, Kure-shi, Hiroshima-ken 737.

*KENYA*
**Afromedia,** PO Box 21028, Nairobi. T: 25149. (TV film production).
**Communications and Radio Centre,** Baptist Convention of Kenya, PO Box 20312, Nairobi.
**Department of Communications,** Kenya Catholic Secretariat, PO Box 48062, Nairobi.
**Kenya Christian Broadcasting Advisory Committee (KCBAC),** Sec, PO Box 45009, Nairobi. (1974; joint NCCK-Catholic).
**Religious Department, Voice of Kenya (VOK),** Broadcasting House, Harry Thuku Rd, PO Box 30456, Nairobi. T: 34567 ext 209.

*KOREA, South*
**Christian Broadcasting System of Korea,** Christian Bldg, 136 Yun Chi Dong, Soul. (HLKY, 5 stations. Member of WACC)
**KAVACO (Korea AV-TV Centre),** 91 Chong No 2, Ka, Soul.
**National Office for Radio and Television Broadcasting,** Catholic Conference of Korea, 52-15 2 Ka, Chung Mu Ro, Jung Ku, CPO Box 16, Soul. T: 23-8789.

*LEBANON*
**Baptist Recording Studio,** PO Box 5232, Bayrut. (Member of WACC).
**Catholic Broadcasting,** Université St Joseph, PO Box 293, Bayrut.
**Christian Recording Society,** Box 5269, Bayrut.
**Division for Radio Broadcasting (DORBNECC),** PO Box 5376, Bayrut. (Member of WACC).
**Lissan-ul-Hal,** Bayrut. (Member of WACC).
**Path of Light (ELWA) Recording Studio,** PO Box 5485, Bayrut. (SIM, Liberia).
**Trans World Radio,** PO Box 6442 & 141, Bayrut.

*LIBERIA*
**Catholic Broadcasting,** Apostolic Internunciature, Monrovia.

*MADAGASCAR*
**Radio Feon'Ny Filazantsara,** BP 95, Antsirabe.

*MALAWI*
**Catholic Broadcasting,** Catholic Secretariat of Malawi, Zomba Rd, PO Box 5368, Limbe.
**Gospel Broadcasting Committee,** PO Box 162, Lilongwe.

*MALI*
**Emissions Catholiques,** Archevêché, BP 298, Bamako.

*MALTA*
**Religious Broadcasting Advisor,** 12 Old Treasury St, Valletta. (Catholic).

*MARTINIQUE*
**Emissions Catholiques,** 1 Rue Le Cornu, Fort-de-France.

*MEXICO*
**Asociación Nacional de Radio-Escuchas,** ACM, Serapio Rendon 43, México 4, DF. (Listeners' association).
**Asociación Nacional de Tele-clubs,** Medellín 33, México 7, DF.
**Audición Luz y Verdad,** Apdo 30, México 1, DF. T: 496711.
**Circulo Radiomundial,** Apdo 12750, México 12, DF.
**Hora de Hermandad Cristiana,** Apdo 53-114, México 17, DF.

*MONACO*
**Centre National Catholique Radio-TV,** Evêché, Monte Carlo.
**Eurofilm,** Monte Carlo. (Distribution agency, from programmers to transmitters).
**Trans World Radio (TWR),** Field Dir, 5 Rue de la Poste, Box 141, Monte Carlo. T: 203233.

*MONTSERRAT*
**Catholic Broadcasting,** Bishop's House, Plymouth.

*MOROCCO*
**IBRA,** Tanger. (Swedish Pentecostal).
**Trans World Radio (TWR),** Box 92, Tanger.

*NAMIBIA*
**Catholic Broadcasting,** Vicariate Apostolic, Keetmanshoop.

*NETHERLANDS*
**Kabelvisie,** Antwoordnummer 18, Culemborg. (Publication on cable TV).
**KRO-schoolradio en -televisie,** Emmastraat 52, NL Hilversum. T: (02150)49141.
**NCRV-schoolradio en -televisie,** Schuttersweg 8-10, Hilversum. T: (02150)13651.
**NET,** Box 75, Kampen.
**Stichting de Evangelische Omroep,** BP 565, Hilversum. T: (02150)12500
**Stichting Katholieke Radio-Omroep (KRO),** Emmastraat 52, NL-Hilversum. T: (02150)49141. (Under Episcopal Conference).
**Trans World Radio,** Box 141, Baarn.
**VPRO,** Hilversum. (Member of WACC).

*NETHERLANDS ANTILLES*
**Catholic Broadcasting,** PO Box 220, Curaçao.
**New Testament Baptist Enterprises,** PO Box 147, St Maarten. (PJD-2).

*NEW CALEDONIA*
**Emissions Catholiques,** Archevêché, BP 3, Nouméa.

*NEW ZEALAND*
**Catholic Broadcasting Training Centre,** National Catholic Broadcasting Committee, 154 Brougham St, Wellington C4. T: 50936,76131.
**Evangelical Radio Witness,** Birkdale, Auckland.
**International Radio Crusades,** PO Box 157, Paeroa, NI.
**New Zealand Broadcasting Corporation,** PO Box 98, Wellington. (Member of WACC).
**New Zealand Churches TV Commission,** PO Box 10000, Wellington Cl. (Member of WACC).

*NIGERIA*
**Broadcasting and AV Services (BRAVS),** Dir, Box 67, Ilesha.
**Centre for Production of Radio & TV Programmes,** Kaduna. (Catholic).
**Christian Radio Studio,** Box 795, Enugu, Eastern Nigeria.
**Christian Radio Studio,** Dir, Box 351, Jos.
**ELWA Recording Studio,** Igbaja via Ilorin.
**Muryar Bishara,** Dir, Box 287, Jos.
**National Catholic Broadcasting Committee,** Catholic Secretariat, PO Box 951, Lagos.
**Nigerian Broadcasting Corporation,** Broadcasting House, PMB 12504, Lagos. (Member of WACC).

*NORWAY*
**Norsk Rikskringkasting,** Oslo. (Member of WACC).
**Norwegian Christian Radio/TV Association (Norges Kristelige Radio-og Fjernsynslag),** Sec, Thorvald Meyers Gate 48, Oslo 5.
**Radio Norea (Nordic Radio Evangelistic Association),** Gransen 19, Oslo 1. T: 332525. (Programmes for Norway transmitted by TWR Monte Carlo).
**Television Mission (Telefunksjonaerers Misjonsforbund),** Grünersgt 6, Oslo 5.

*PAPUA NEW GUINEA*
**Catholic Broadcasting,** Catholic Mission, Alexishafen-Madang.
**Christian Radio Missionary Fellowship (CRMF),** Rugli, PO Box 345, Mt Hagen, WHD.

*PHILIPPINES*
**Back to the Bible Broadcast,** PO Box 1750, Manila.
**Call of the Orient,** Box 2041, Manila. (DZAS & 12 others. Far East Broadcasting Company).
**Centre for Educational Television,** Ateneo of Manila, PO Box 154, Loyola Heights, Quezon City, Manila. (Catholic).
**Far East Broadcasting Company (FEBC),** Dir, Box 2041, Manila. T: 233357. (DXKI Marvel, Cotabato. FEBC beams into central Siberia).
**Mascom Network Interchurch,** 1648 Taft Av, Manila. (Member of WACC).
**Mountain Province Broadcasting Corporation,** St Louis University Campus, Bonifacio St, PO Box 71, Baguio City .T: 2582,2453,3874. (CICM).
**National Council of Churches Broadcasting Network,** Dir Gen, Box 4147, Manila.
**Philippine Federation of Catholic Broadcasters (National Federation),** 2307 Herran St, PO Box 2722, Santa Ana, Manila. T: 597081. (Also Box 280, Cebu City).
**Philippine Radio Education and Information Center,** Radio Veritas, PO Box 132, Manila. T: 971158.
**South East Asia Radio Voice (SEARV),** Exec Dir, Box 4148, Manila. (Member of WACC).
**Tagum Community Development Radio Corporation,** Davao del Norte.
**UNDA (International Catholic Association for Radio and Television),** Gen Sec, Secretariat for Asia, National Office of Mass Media, PO Box 1061, Manila.
**Visayan Educational Radio and TV Association (VERTA),** Bishop's House, Bacolod City 70501.
**Voice of Christian Brotherhood,** Dumaguete City, Box 4148, Manila. (DZCH & 4 others. RAVEMCCO/Intermedia).

*POLAND*
**Biuro do Spraw Srodków Oddzialywania Spolecznego,** Dir, Aleja 1, Armii Wojska Polskiego 12, Warszawa. T: 212337. (Radio/TV).

*PORTUGAL*
**Adventist World Radio (AWR),** CP 2590, Lisboa 2.
**IBRA (Radio Trans-Europe),** IFAP Secção 5, Rua Braamcamp 84, 60, Esq, Lisboa. (Pentecostal. Reaches European Russia, Ukraine).
**Radio Renascença,** Dir, Rua Capelo 5-2 Esq, Lisboa 2. T: 30172.

*PUERTO RICO*
**Luz y Verdad (MBI),** Apdo 25, Albonito.

*REUNION*
**Association Réunionnaise d'Education Populaire (AREP),** Rue la Bourdonnais, St-Denis. (Educational radio).
**Emissions Catholiques,** Cure du Tampon.

*ST LUCIA*
**Catholic Broadcasting,** Bishop's House, Castries.

*SENEGAL*
**Emissions Catholiques,** BP 5098, Dakar-Fann.

*SEYCHELLES*
**Catholic Broadcasting,** Evêché, Victoria.
**Far East Broadcasting Association (FEBA),** Field Dir, Box 234, Victoria, Mahé. T: 749.

*SIERRA LEONE*
**American Wesleyan Mission Studio,** Box 33, Bendumbu, via Makeni.
**Catholic Broadcasting,** Catholic Mission, St Edward's Secondary School, PO Box 673, Freetown.

*SINGAPORE*
**Singapore Recording Centre,** Far East Broadcasting Company, 338 Jalan Minyek (York Hill), Singapore 3.

*SOUTH AFRICA*
**Christian Action by Radio in Africa (CARA),** Box 269, Stellenbosch.
**Christian Radio Fellowship,** Box 69, Roodepoort Transvaal.
**LEMIK (Let's Make it Known),** PO Box 11131, Vlaeberg, Capetown. T: 430679.
**Lutheran Production Studios,** PO Box 59, Roodepoort, Transvaal.
**Olga Weiss Memorial Studio,** Africa Evangelical Fellowship (SAGM), PO Box 97, Roodepoort, Transvaal.
**Trans World Radio (TWR),** PO Box 825, Roodepoort, Transvaal.

*SPAIN*
**Cadena de Ondas Populares Españolas (COPE),** Montesa 27, Madrid 6.

*SRI LANKA*
**Back to the Bible Broadcast,** Box 1012, Colombo.
**Catholic Broadcasting,** St Joseph's College, Colombo 10. T: 78491.
**Jeevithalokaya Studio (Back to the Bible Broadcast),** Dir, 15 Melbourne Ave, Bambalapitiya, PO Box 1021, Colombo 4.
**Technical Personnel for Broadcasting Stations,** Radio and Electronics Ltd, 55 St Lucia's St, Colombo 13. T: 5015. (Catholic training courses).

*SUDAN*
**Catholic Broadcasting,** Bishop's House, Al Khurtum.

*SWAZILAND*
**Catholic Broadcasting,** Bishop's House, PO Box 19, Manzini.

**Christian Radio Fellowship,** Box 244, Mbabane.
**Trans World Radio,** Field Dir, Box 64, Manzini.

*SWEDEN*
**Catholic Broadcasting,** Katolska Biskopämbetet, Fack S-102, 40 Stockholm 5.
**Church of Sweden Mission,** Uppsala. (Member of WACC).
**IBRA Radio Mission,** Box 396, S-101-25 Stockholm. (Swedish Pentecostal Radio Mission, begun 1955, producing 150 hours a week programmes for use over 20 stations worldwide, in 48 languages to 75 countries).

*SWITZERLAND*
**Arbeitsgemeinschaft Radio-TV,** Habsburgerstr 44, CH-6000 Luzern. T: (041)235645. (German-speaking).
**Association Catholique Internationale pour la Radiodiffusion et la Télévision (UNDA),** Sec-Gen, 5 Rue de Romont, CP 211, CH-1701 Fribourg. T: (037)223012.
**Baptist Recording Studio,** Baptist Theological Seminary, Rüschlikon-ZH.
**Catholic Broadcasting Secretary,** Borghetto 2, CH-6901 Lugano. T: (091)21097. (Italian-speaking).
**Centre Catholique de Radio et Télévision (CCRT),** Dir, Chemin du Boisy 19, CP 2824, CH-1004 Lausanne 22. T: (021)248737
**Commission Radio-TV-Education,** UNDA, 5 Rue de Romont, CP 211, CH-1701 Fribourg. T: (037) 223012.
**Dept of Communication,** WCC, Sec for Radio & TV, 150 Route de Ferney, CH-1211 Genève 20.
**Equipe Protestante Génévoise,** Prés, 16 Av des Arpillières, CH-1224 Chêne-Bourgeries. T: 355242.
**Janz Brothers Studio,** PO Box 2831, Zürich 23.
**Lutheran World Federation Broadcasting Service,** 150 Route de Ferney, CH-1211 Genève 20. T: 333400. (Member of WACC).
**L'Heure de la Grâce,** 66 Rue de la Côte, CH-2000 Neuchâtel.
**Missionswerk Mitternachtsruf,** PO Box 2831, Zürich 23.
**Radio Messias,** PO Box 1204, CH-6002 Luzern.
**Radio Réveil et Paroles de Vie,** Action Chrétienne par la Radio et la Presse, CH-2022 Bevaix (NE). (Also BP 77, Genève 6).
**Radio- und Fernsehkommission,** Christkatholische Kirche, Dufourstr 105, CH-2500 Biel. T: (032)42179.
**Worte des Lebens (MBI),** Bienenberg, CH-4410 Liestal.

*TANZANIA*
**Catholic Broadcasting,** Catholic Secretariat, PO Box 2133, Dar es Salaam.
**Joint Christian Religious Broadcasting Committee,** Sec, PO Box 2133 & 2537, Dar es Salaam. (Joint Catholic/Protestant).
**Sauti ya Injili (Radio Voice of the Gospel) (RVOG),** Lutheran Radio Centre, Dir, Box 777, Moshi.

*THAILAND*
**Catholic Office MCS,** Marivithaya School, Nakhornrajasima.
**National Catholic Office for Radio and TV,** 251/1 Surinari Rd, Nakhon Ratchasima.
**Programme Production Center (B-RAVA),** Dir, 14 Pramuan Rd, Bangkok.
**Radio-TV and Visual Aids Dept,** Southern Baptist Mission, GPO Box 832, Bangkok.
**Voice of Peace,** PO Box 131, Chiang Mai.

*TOGO*
**Emissions Catholiques (Collège St Joseph),** BP 63, Lomé.

*TRINIDAD & TOBAGO*
**Caribbean Committee for Joint Christian Action (CCJCA),** Trinidad and Tobago Television, Dir, Television House, Maraval Rd, Port of Spain.
**Catholic Broadcasting,** Catholic Centre, 52A Jerningham Av, Port of Spain.

*UGANDA*
**Catholic Broadcasting,** Catholic Secretariat, PO Box 2886, Kampala.
**Literature and Radio Centre,** Church of Uganda, Box 4, Mukono. T: 644. (Member of WACC).

*UK OF GB & NI*
**Back to the Bible Broadcast,** Dir, 18 Upper Redlands Rd, Reading, Berkshire RG1 5JR. T: 64039.
**Baptist Radio Crusade,** 2 Liberia Rd, Highbury, London N5. T: (01)226-2805.
**Calvary Radio Ministry Trust,** PO Box 8, Fishponds, Bristol.
**Catholic Broadcasting Secretary (NI),** St Teresa's Presbytery, Glen Rd, Belfast, NI.
**Catholic Radio & TV Centre,** St Gabriel's House, Oakleigh Rd, Hatch End, Middlesex HA5 4HB. T: (01)428-1198,1154. (Training, production).
**Central Religious Advisory Committee (CRAC),** BBC and Independent Broadcasting Authority (IBA), Dir, Broadcasting House, London.
**Christian Broadcasting Commission,** Hawkley Studios, near Liss, Hants. T: Blackmoor 351.
**Christian Newsletter,** British Broadcasting Corporation, PO Box 76, Bush House, London.
**Church's Broadcasting Panel,** Church Information Office, Church House, Dean's Yard, London SWIP 3NZ. T: (01)222-9011.
**Churches Advisory Committee on Local Broadcasting (CACLB),** Sec, 9 Porchester Gardens, London W2 4DB.
**Churches' Television and Radio Centre (CTVC),** Dir, Hillside, Merry Hill Rd, Bushey, Watford WD2 1DR. T: (01)950-4426. (Member of WACC).
**Ecumenical Satellite Commission (ECUSAT),** 7 St James St, London SW1.
**Far East Broadcasting Association,** Skywaves, St Paul's Rd, Woking, Surrey. T: 66733.
**Gospel Broadcasting System,** Sec, 67 Meadow Lane, Liverpool L12 5EB. T: (051)226-4212.
**Gospel by Radio to Spain,** Sec, c/o Temple Gothard & Co, 33/34 Chancery Lane, London WC2A 1EN. T: (01)836-7932.
**Hour of Revival Association,** 13 Lismore Rd, Eastbourne, East Sussex. T: 25231.
**IBA Panel of Religious Advisors,** Independent Broadcasting Authority, 70 Brompton Rd, London SW3 1EY. T: (01)584-7011. (Formerly ITV. IBA is a member of WACC).
**IBRA Radio,** The Haven, Barnfield Av, Luton, Bedfordshire. (Swedish pentecostal).
**Independent Television Companies Association (ITCA),** 52-66 Mortimer St, London W1N 8AN. T: (01)636-6866. (Member of WACC).
**Irish Gospel Broadcasting Fellowship,** Evangelical Outreach Ltd, Belfast, NI.
**Lifeline Recording and Broadcasting Fellowship,** Drumgask, Lurgan, NI.
**Radio Committee,** Evangelical Missionary Alliance, 19 Draycott Place, London SW3 2SJ. T: (01)581-0051.
**Radio Council,** Assemblies of God in GB & I, Producer, 106/114 Talbot St, Nottingham NG1 5GH.
**Radio ELWA (SIM),** 84 Beulah Hill, London SE19. T: (01)653-3953.
**Radio Worldwide (WEC),** Dir, 13 Harold Rd, London SE19 3PU. T: (01)653-4753.
**Religious Broadcasting Department,** BBC, Broadcasting House, London W1A 1AA. T: (01)580-4468. (BBC is a member of WACC).
**Television & Radio Dept,** Church Information Office, Church House, Dean's Yard, London SW1. (Member of WACC).
**Trans World Radio (TWR),** Pres, 175 Tower Bridge Rd, London SE1 2AB. T: (01)407-3614.
**Way to Life Hour,** Hailsham, East Sussex. T: 390.
**Wondrous Story Radio Mission,** Woking Baptist Church, Percy St, Woking, Surrey. T: Brookwood 2871.
**World Association for Christian Communication,** 122 Kings Rd, London SW3 4TR.
**World Association of Methodist Radio Amateurs & Clubs (WAMRAC),** The Manse, Kendal Rd, Tebay, Penrith, Cumbria. T: Orton 275.
**World Radio Missionary Fellowship,** Pres, Brecklands, North Pickenham, Swaffham, Norfolk. T: Holme Hale 562.

*USA*
**Amateur Radio Missionary Service,** 560 Main St, Chatham, NJ 07928.
**Archdiocese of Los Angeles Instructional Television System,** 1520 West Ninth St, Los Angeles, CA 90015.
**Arctic Broadcasting Association,** 5101 North Francisco Av, Chicago 25, Ilinois. (KICY, Nome, Alaska).
**Ave Maria Hour,** St Christopher's Inn, Graymoor, Garrison, New York, NY 10524. T: (914)424-3671.
**Back to God Hour,** 10858 South Michigan Av, Chicago, IL 60628. T: (312)468-8700.
**Back to the Bible Missionary Agency,** 12th and M Sts, Box 82808, Lincoln, NE 68501.
**Bauman Bible Telecasts,** 4214 Wehawken Rd, Washington, DC 20016. T: (301)652-3154.
**Broadcast & Film Commission,** NCCCUSA, 475 Riverside Drive, New York, NY 10027. T: (212)870-2251. (Member of WACC).
**Brooklyn Diocesan TV Centre,** 500 19th St, Brooklyn, NY 11215. (RC).
**Catholic Broadcasters Association of America,** 320 Cathedral St, Baltimore, MD 21201.
**Catholic Broadcasting Association (CBA),** 135 West Georgia St, Indianapolis, IN 46225.
**Central Africa Broadcasting Company,** Dir, 309 Laurel, Box A, Friendswood, TX 77546. (Radio Cordac in Burundi).
**Christ Truth Radio Crusade,** Pres, 189 Wagner Drive, Claremont, CA 91711. T: (714)624-8875.
**Christian Amateur Radio Fellowship (CARF),** Pres, Route 3, Box 234, Worthington, MN 56187. (World missionary communication for Churches of Christ, USA).
**Christian Broadcasters Inc (KSEW),** Box 258, Sitka, Alaska.
**Christian Broadcasting Association,** 3555 Harding Av, Honolulu, HA 96816. T: 734-1985.
**Christian Broadcasting Network (CBN),** International Headquarters, Virginia Beach, Virginia.
**Christian Radio Mission (Korea),** 306 East Gerald, San Antonio, TX 78214.
**Christian Television & Film Productions,** 604 NE 20th Av, Portland, OR 97232.
**Christian Television Mission,** PO Box 3411, Springfield, MO 65804. T: (417)881-6303. (Begun 1955).
**Christian Viewpoint,** 175 Floridahaven Drive, Maitland, FL 32751.
**Christian Voice,** Maynard Waters Family, Box 488, Eden, NC 27288. (TV including cable).
**Christians' Hour,** PO Box 1001, Cincinnati, OH 45201. T: (513)661-4240. (15-minute weekly national radio broadcast).
**Commission on Press, Radio & TV,** Lutheran, Church in America, 231 Madison Av, New York, NY 10016. T: (212)532-3410.
**Contact Teleministries USA,** Exec Dir, Room 125, 900 South Arlington Av, Harrisburg, PA 17109. T: (717)652-3410.
**Cultural and Religious Broadcasts,** Dir, CBS News, New York, NY.
**Division of Mass Media,** United Presbyterian Church USA, Room 1920, 475 Riverside Drive, New York, NY 10027. T: (212)870-2027.
**Division of Radio-TV,** Episcopal Church, 815 Second Av, New York, NY 10017. T: (212)867-8400.
**Episcopal Radio TV Foundation,** Exec Dir, 15 16th St NE, Atlanta, GA 30309. T: (404)892-0141.
**Family Theater Productions,** 7201 Sunset Blvd, Hollywood, CA 90046. T: (213)874-6633. (Broadcast by over 300 radio and TV stations).
**Far East Broadcasting Company,** Chairman, 12724 Whittier Blvd, PO Box 1, Whittier, CA 90608. T: (213)698-0438. (World HQ).
**Franciscan Communications Center (St Francis Productions),** 1229 South Santee St, Los Angeles, CA 90015. T: (213)748-2191. (Radio, TV).
**Global Gospel Broadcasts,** Pres, 3 Martins Lane, Berwyn, PA 19312. T: (215)644-8741.
**Gospel of Christ TV Mission,** Evangelist, Box 111, Carthage, MO 64836. (Begun 1954).
**Hermano Pablo Radio-TV Evangelism,** Box 100, Costa Mesa, CA 92626. T: (714)645-0676.
**Hour of the Crucified,** West Springfield, Massachusetts.
**Insight Paulist Productions,** 17575 Pacific Coast Highway, Pacific Palisades, CA 90272. T: (213)454-0688.
**International Christian Broadcasters (ICB),** Exec Dir, 101 North Cascade, Colorado Springs, CO 80902. T: (303)473-8358. (Till 1964, World Conference on Missionary Radio).
**International Mission Radio Association (IMRA),** Exec Sec, WIHWK, Western Observatory, Weston, MA 02193. (Thousands of priests and missionaries across the world are amateur (ham) radio operators).
**Lutheran Church Television Production,** 210 North Broadway, St Louis, MO 63102. T: (314)231-6969.
**Lutheran Hour 'Bringing Christ to the Nations',** Exec Dir, 2185 Hampton Av, St Louis, MO 63139. (Programme-producing; heard on 1,400 stations worldwide).
**Lutheran Laymens League,** 2185 Hampton Av, St Louis, MO 63139. (Member of WACC).
**Marienschwester (Darmstadt),** Fairbanks, Alaska. (30-60 hours monthly).
**Marketing Services Department,** Southern Baptist Radio-TV Commission, PO Box 12157, Fort Worth, TX 76116. T: (817)737-4011.
**Mary Immaculate School,** 14032 Dennis Lane, Dallas, TX 75234. T: (214)247-2964.
**Mary Productions Airtime,** 58 Lenison Av, Belford, NJ 07718.
**Maryknoll Media Relations,** Walsh Bldg, Maryknoll, NY 10545. T: (914)941-7590.
**Mennonite Broadcasts,** Mennonite Board of Missions, Pres, 1251 Edom Rd, Box 472, Harrisonburg, VA 22801. T: (713)434-6701. (Member of WACC).
**National Association of Council Broadcast Executives,** 65 Columbia East, Detroit, MI 48201. (Member of WACC).
**National Catholic Office for Radio and Television (NCORT),** Suite 4200, Chrysler Bldg, 405 Lexington Av, New York, NY 10017. T: (212)867-8460.
**National Religious Broadcasters (NRB),** Pres, 2 Green Village Rd, Box 308, Madison, NJ 07940. T: (201)377-4400.
**Old-Fashioned Revival Hour,** 44 South Mentor Av, Pasadena, CA 91101.
**Overseas Radio and Television,** Dir, Box 118, Seattle, WA 98111. T: (206)784-4339.
**Pacific Broadcasting Association,** Pres, 106 North Dorchester, PO Box 941, Wheaton, IL 60187. T: (312)653-4164.
**Pan American Broadcasting Company,** 380 Lexington Av, New York, NY 10017. (Distribution agency from programmers to transmitters).
**Passionist Radio and TV Apostolate 'Crossroads',** 1089 Elm St, West Springfield, MA 01089. T: (413)732-4546.
**Paulist Productions,** Box 1057, Pacific Palisades, CA 90272. T: (213)454-0688.
**Protestant Radio and TV Center,** 1727 Clifton Rd NE, Atlanta, GA 30329. T: (404)634-3324.
**Radio & Audio-Film Commission,** American Council of Christian Churches, Dir, Valley Forge, PA 19481. T: (215)933-8904.
**Radio & Television Commission,** Southern Baptist Convention, 6350 Ridgmar Square, PO Box 12157, Fort Worth, TX 76116.
**Radio Bible Class,** PO Box 22, Grand Rapids, MI 49507.
**Radio Revival,** Box 1928, Birmingham, AL 35200.
**Radio-TV,** Greek Orthodox Archdiocese of N&S America, Dir, 8-10 East 79th St, New York, NY 10021. T: (212)628-2500.
**Radio/TV,** United Church Board for Homeland Ministries, 287 Park Av South, New York, NY 10010. T: (212)475-2121.
**Revival Fires (Christian Evangelizers Association),** Box 747, Joplin, MO 64801.
**Rio Grande Family Radio Fellowship,** PO Box 16, Pharr, TX 78577.
**Sacred Heart Program (TV),** 3900 Westminster Place, St Louis, MO 63108. T: (314)533-0320.
**Seventh-day Adventist Radio TV and Film Center,** 1000 Lawrence Drive, Newbury Park, Box 0, Thousand Oaks, CA 91360. T: (805)498-6661,6677.
**Shrine of Our Lady of San Juan de los Lagos,** 216 West First St, PO Box 747, San Juan, TX 78589. T: (512)787-2532.
**Spanish World Gospel Broadcasting,** Pres, PO Box 335, Winona Lake, IN 46590. T: (219)267-8821.
**Tele-Missions,** 132 Linwood Av, Bogota, NJ 07603.
**The Christophers,** 12 East 48th St, New York, NY 10017. (Radio TV).
**TRAFCO,** United Methodist Church, Suite 420, 475 Riverside Drive, New York, NY 10027. T: (212)663-8900.
**Trans World Radio,** Pres, 560 Main St, Box 98, Chatham, NJ 07928. T: (201)635-5775. (World HQ).
**TRAV,** Presbyterian Church in the US, 341 Ponce de Leon Av NE, Atlanta, GA 30308. T: (404)875-8921.
**TV and Studio Services,** University of Detroit, 3800 Puritan Av, Detroit, MI 48238. T: (313)862-6313.
**TV Radio Films,** American Lutheran Church, 1568 Eustis St, St Paul, MN 55113. T: (612)645-9173.
**Twentieth Century Reformation Hour Broadcast,** PO Box 190, Collingswood, NJ 08108.
**Vida Abundante Mensaje por Radio,** Box 22, Sierra Vista, AZ 85635.
**Voces del Seminario,** Oblate College of the Southwest, 285 Oblate Drive, San Antonio, TX 78216. T: (512)341-1366. (TV studio).
**West Indies Mission,** Route 1, Homer City, Pennsylvania. (Radio Lumière, Cayes, Haiti).
**World Radio Missionary Fellowship, Inc,** Box 691, Miami, FL 33147. (World HQ).
**World Religious News,** National Religious Broadcasters, PO Box 512, Madison, NJ 07940. (Weekly news broadcast syndicated news service).

*UPPER VOLTA*
**Emissions Catholiques,** BP 149 Bobo-Dioulasso.

*URUGUAY*
**Centro Nacional de MCS,** Cerrito 475, Montevideo. T: 85903,91905. (Under Episcopal Conference).
**Servicio de Radio y TV,** Cerrito 485, Montevideo.
**UNDA/Association Catholique Internationale pour la Radiodiffusion et la Télévision,** Latin American Secretariat (UNDA-AL), Cerrito 475, Montevideo.

*VENEZUELA*
**TEAM Recording Studio,** Apdo 355, San Cristobal, Tachira.

*VIET NAM*
**Television Service Centre for Community Development (THDL),** 161 Yen-do, PO Box 2094, Saigon. T: 98427.

*ZAIRE*
**RENAPEC,** Service Technique Africain de Radio-TV (TELESTAR), BP 1698, Kinshasa. T: 25812. (Name changed to RENAPEC 1973. Member of WACC).
**Studiproka,** BP 700, Luluabourg.

*ZAMBIA*
**Catholic Broadcasting,** Zambia Catholic Secretariat, PO Box 1965, Lusaka.
**Educational TV Service,** PO Box 1106, Kitwe.
**Zambia Studio,** Box 244, Lusaka.

*ZIMBABWE*
**Radio and Television Apostolate,** Zimbabwe Catholic Bishops' Conference, PO Box 1221, Salisbury.
**Sound Studio Driefontein Mission,** P Bag 9001, Gwelo.

# 8
# Catechesis & Christian Education

*Definition.* Sunday schools, vacation schools, religious education, councils of religious education; Christian schools or colleges of national importance, school or college chaplaincies of national importance, Christian technical or training schools (industrial, rural, vocational); secular education under Christian auspices, schools managements; catechetics.

Organizations in this field, of major significance at the national or wider levels, number over 280.

*ALGERIA*
**Commission d'Enseignement Religieux d'Afrique du Nord,** La Palmeraie, El-Biar, El Djezair (Alger).
**Secrétariat National des Ecoles Diocésaines,** 6 Rue Tagore, El Djezair (Alger).

*ARGENTINA*
**Consejo Superior de Educación Católica,** Cordoba 1439, Buenos Aires.
**Unión Cristiana Americana de Educadores (UCADE),** Brasil 721, Buenos Aires.

*AUSTRALIA*
**Catholic Education Office,** 18 Brunswick St, Fitzroy, Victoria 3065. T: 416657.
**Division of Christian Education,** Australian Council of Churches, 100 Flinders St, Melbourne C1, Victoria.
**Federal Catholic Education Office,** PO Box 1213, Canberra, ACT 2601.
**Universities Catholic Federation of Australia,** 36 Cochrane St, Brighton, Victoria 3186.

*AUSTRIA*
**Erzbischöfliches Amt für Unterricht und Erziehung,** Kathechetisches Institut, Stephanplatz 3/IV, A-1010 Wien. T: 526448,526473.

*BANGLADESH*
**Diocesan Board of Education,** Bishop's House, PO Box 152, Chittagong. (RC).

*BARBADOS*
**Education (Renewal) Agency (ERA),** Christian Action for Development in the Caribbean (CADEC), PO Box 616, Bridgetown.

*BELGIUM*
**Centre International d'Etudes de la Formation Religieuse 'Lumen Vitae',** Rue Washington 184-186, B-1050 Brussel. T: (02)3435023.
**Office International de l'Enseignement Catholique (OIEC)/Catholic International Education Office (CIEO),** Sec Gén, Rue des Ebucons 60, B-1040 Brussel. T: (02)736341.
**OIEC Bureau de Recrutement de Professeurs,** Dir, Rue des Ebucons 60, B-1040 Brussel. T: (02) 7363041.
**OIEC Section Europe,** Dir, Rue des Ebucons, Brussel. T: (02)7363041.
**Secrétariat National de l'Enseignement Catholique (SNEC)/National Secretariat van het Katholiek Onderwijs (NSKO),** Rue Guimard 5, B-1040 Brussel. T: (02)5136880.

*BENIN*

**Direction National de l'Enseignement Catholique,** BP 153, Cotonou. T: 4009.

*BOLIVIA*

**Alfalit Boliviano,** Junin 6305, Casilla 1466, Cochabamba. T: 4953.

**Asociación Boliviana de Educación Católica (ABEC),** Colegio San Calixto, Casilla 283, La Paz.

*BRAZIL*

**Alfabetização de Adultos,** Campinas, SP.

**Associação Educação Católica (AEC),** Rua Martins Ferreira 23, Rio de Janeiro.

**Comisión Evangélica Latino-americana de Educación Cristiana (CELADEC)/Evangelical Latin American Commission on Christian Education,** Sala 1203, Av Campos Salles 890, CP 1440, Campinas, SP. (Also: Apdo 3994, Lima, Peru).

**Secretariado Nacional de Educação e Cultura,** Ladeira da Glória 99, ZC-01 Rio de Janeiro, GB. T: 2253290.

*BURUNDI*

**Secrétariat National de l'Enseignement Catholique (SNEC),** BP 690, Bujumbura. T: 2942.

*CAMEROON*

**Direction Nationale de l'Enseignement Catholique,** BP 297, Yaoundé. T: 3331.

**Equipes Enseignantes Africaines et Malgaches,** BP 815, Yaoundé.

*CANADA*

**Canadian Sunday School Mission,** Room 24, 177 Lombard Av, Winnipeg, Manitoba.

**Department of Christian Education,** Canadian Council of Churches, 40 St Clair Av East, Toronto 7, Ontario.

**National Education Office,** Canadian Catholic Conference, 90 Parent Av, Ottawa 2, Ontario. T: (613)236-9461.

*CENTRAL AFRICAN REPUBLIC*

**Bureau National de l'Enseignement Catholique,** BP 798, Bangui.

*CHAD*

**Direction Nationale l'Enseignement Privé,** Archevêché, BP 456, Ndjamena (Fort Lamy). T: 2711.

*CHILE*

**Federación Nacional Colegios Católicos,** Alonso Ovalle 1546, Casilla 13305, Santiago.

**Oficio Central de Educación Católica (OCEC),** Erasmo Escala 1822, 6 piso, Casilla 723, Santiago. (Member, BICE).

*CHINA (TAIWAN)*

**China Sunday School Association,** Chung Shan North Rd, Section 2, No 105, Taipei. T: 545518.

**Christian Education Commission,** Catholic Central Bureau, 34 Lane 32, Kuang Fu Rd, PO Box 1723, Taipei. T: 771295.

**United Board for Christian Higher Education in Asia,** Pres, Tunghai University, Taichung.

*COLOMBIA*

**Comité Latinoamericana de la Fe (CLAF),** Sección Catequística, Apdo Aéreo 20621, Bogotá, DE.

**Confederación Colegios Cubanos Católicos (CCCC),** Calle 36, No 13A-09, Bogotá. (Cubans in exile).

**Confederación Interamericana de Educación Católica (CIEC),** Sec Ejecutivo, Calle 78, 12-16, Apdo Aéreo 7478, Apdo National 401, Bogotá. T: 411189. (Branch of OIEC in Brussels).

**Conferencia Nacional de Colegios Católicos (Federación Nacional de Centros Docentos),** Carrera 13A No 23-80, Bogotá.

**Departemento de Educación (DEC),** Apdo 21437, Bogotá, DE.

*COSTA RICA*

**Asociación de Establecimientos Privados de Ensenañza (AEPE),** Colegio Calasanz, Apdo 3187 (and 6141), San José.

*DENMARK*

**Danish Free Church Sunday School Association,** Pilealle 7, DK-9460 Brovst.

**Danish Sunday School Committee,** Radman Steinsalle 202, DK-2000 Kobenhavn F.

*DJIBOUTI*

**Secrétariat Diocesain de l'Enseignement Catholique,** c/o Evêché Djibouti.

*DOMINICAN REPUBLIC*

**Unión Nacional de Colegios Católicos (UNCC),** Residencia Universitaria San José de Calasanz, Av Independencia, Santo Domingo.

*ECUADOR*

**Confederación Ecuatoriana de Establecimientos de Educación Católica,** Secretariado Nacional Educación Católica, Casilla de Correos A-126, Quito.

*EGYPT*

**Board of Christian Education and Sunday Schools,** Coptic Orthodox Church, 28 Khalifa-el-Mansour, Heliopolis, Al Qahirah.

**Collège de la Sainte Famille,** Al Qahirah. T: 900411,900892.

**Egypt and Sudan Sunday School Union,** 4 Samuel Morcos St, Terra El Boulakia, Shubra, PO Box 1422, Al Qahirah.

*EL SALVADOR*

**Federación Nacional de Colegios Católicos,** Av Espana 312, altos, Apdo 1617, San Salvador. T: 215584.

**Secretariado Nacional de Educación,** Arzobispado, 1c Pte 3402, San Salvador. T: 234124.

*ETHIOPIA*

**Catholic Education Office,** PO Box 2454, Addis Abeba.

**Christian Education Centre,** Central Synod EC-MY, PO Box 24, Nakamte.

*FIJI*

**Pacific Islands Christian Education Council (PICEC),** PO Box 208, Suva.

*FINLAND*

**Finnish Sunday School Association,** Uudenmaankatu 4, Helsinki.

**Swedish Sunday School Association in Finland,** Lutherinstitutet, Helsinki 32.

*FRANCE*

**Catholic International Federation for Physical and Sports Education,** Secretariat, 5 Rue Cernuschi, F-75017 Paris. T: 924-3112.

**Centre National de l'Enseignement Religieux,** 6 Av Vavin, F-75006 Paris. T: (01)633-2160.

**Dialogue et Coopération/Equipes Enseignantes,** 140 Av Daumesnil, F-75012 Paris. T: (01)344-0506. (Teacher exchanges worldwide).

**Organisation Mondiale des Ancines et Anciennes Elèves de l'Ensignement Catholique/World Organization of Former Students of Catholic Schools,** Secretariat, 17 Rue Michel Charles, F-75012 Paris. T: (01)343-7629.

**Secrétariat Générale de l'Enseignement Catholique,** 277 Rue Saint Jacques, F-75005 Paris. T: (01)633-9450.

**Service Technique pour l'Education (STE),** 19 bd Poissonnière, F-75002 Paris.

**Société des Ecoles du Dimanche,** 15 Rue de Buci, F-75006 Paris.

**Syndicat National de l'Enseignement Chrétien (SNEC),** 58 Rue Custine, F-75018 Paris.

*GABON*

**Direction de l'Enseignement Catholique,** BP 1179, Libreville. T: 3054.

*GAMBIA*

**Education Secretariat,** Catholic Mission, Bathurst.

*GERMANY, Federal Republic of*

**Arbeitsgemeinschaft Evangelischer Schulbünde** Paul-Gerhardt-Schule, D-3354 Dassel (Solling). (Voluntary groups in secondary schools).

**Arbeitsgemeinschaft für Evangelische Unterweisung,** Karl-Ludwig-Str 18, D-6992 Weikersheim. (Official curricula in primary and secondary schools).

**Bischöfliche Hauptstelle für Schule und Erziehung,** Rubensstr 25-27, D-5000 Köln 1. T: (0221) 230692.

**Bund Katholischer Erzieher Deutschlands (BKED),** Goldenbrunnengasse 4, D-65 Mainz.

**Bundesarbeitsgemeinschaft für Katholische Erwachsenenbildung,** Dransdorfer Weg 15, D-5300 Bonn. T: (02221)655969. (Catholic adult education).

**Commission on Education,** National Council of the Lutheran Churches in Germany, Am alten Kirchof 10, D-235 Neumunster.

**Europäische Föderation für Katholische Erwachsenenbildung (FEECA)/European Association for Catholic Adult Education,** Secretariat, Drandsdorfer Weg 15/IV, D-5300 Bonn. T: (02221)655969.

**Evangelischer Schulbund in Bayern,** Wilhelm-Löhe-Schule, Rollnerstr 15, D-85 Nürnberg.

**Evangelischer Schulbund in Nordwestdeutschland,** Paul-Gerhardt-Schule, D-3354 Dassel (Solling).

**Evangelischer Schulbund in Südwestdeutschland,** Zinzendorfgymnasium, D-7744 Königsfeld (Schwarzwald).

**German Free Church Sunday School Board,** Gruneburgweg 51, D-6 Frankfurt 1. (Also: Jahnstr 2, D-6344 Ewarsbach).

**Katholisches Schulkommissariat Bayern I und Bayern II,** Maxburgstr 2, D-8000 München. T: (0811)213267/8.

**Kirchliche Zentrale für Katholische Freie Schulen und Internate,** Breite Str 106, D-5000 Köln 1. T: (0221)235480,277771.

**Verband Bildung und Erziehung (VBE),** Theodor-Heuss-Ring 36, D-5 Köln.

*GHANA*

**Catholic Schools Secretariat,** PO Box 54, Accra. T: 22871.

*GREECE*

**Comité des Ecoles Catholiques de Grèce,** 10 Charilaou, Tricoupi, Athínai. T: 631684.

*GUATEMALA*

**Asociación Nacional Colegios Católicos,** 12 Av 4-30, Zona 1, Guatemala.

*HAITI*

**Association d'Enseignement Catholique,** c/o Commission Nationale de Pastorale, Archevêché, Port-au-Prince. T: 22043.

*HOLY SEE*

**Sacred Congregation for Catholic Instruction SC per l'Educazione Cattolica,** Cardinal Prefect, Palazzo delle Congregazioni, Piazza Pio XII 3, I-00193 Roma. T: 6984569.

*HONDURAS*

**Federación Colegios Católicos,** Instituto San Francisco, Apdo Postal 367, Tegucigalpa.

*HONG KONG*

**China Sunday School Association,** 6 Granville Rd, 3/F, Kowloon. T: K-672099.

**Hongkong Catholic Education Council(HKCED),** St Francis Xavier's College, Maple St, Shum Shui Po, Kowloon.

**Hongkong Council for Christian Education,** c/o Hip Woh Primary School, 191B Prince Edward Rd, Kowloon. T: K-801752.

*INDIA*

**All India Association for Christian Higher Education,** Y Raj Niwas Marg, Delhi 6.

**All-India Association of Christian Schools,** NCCI, Nagpur.

**India Sunday School Union,** Keswick, Coonor, Nilgiris, South India.

**Karnataka Christian Education Society,** Karnataka Theological College, Balmatta, Mangalore 1, Mysore State.

**Orthodox Syrian Sunday School Association,** Kottayam 4, Kerala.

**Xavier Association Secondary Schools,** St Peter's College, Wazirpura Rd, Agra 3, UP. T: 73671.

*INDONESIA*

**Catholic Education Association (Persatuan Guru Katholik, PGK),** Jalan Pos 2, Jakarta.

**Department of Education(Bagian B Pendidikan),** Kantor Waligeredja Indonesia (KWI), Taman Tjut Mutiah 10, Jakarta 11/14. T: 47548.

*IRELAND*

**Catholic Schools Secretariat,** Milltown Park, Dublin 6. T: (01)960343.

**Council of Managers of Catholic Secondary Schools (CMCSS),** Sacred Heart College, The Crescent, Limerick.

*ITALY*

**Federazione Istituti Dipendenti della Autorità Ecclesiastica (FIDAE),** Via della Pigna 13, I-00186 Roma. T: 6791341,6791097.

**Federazione Universitaria Catholica Italiana (FUCI),** Via della Conciliazione 4d, I-00193 Roma. T: 655621,581948.

**Italian National Sunday School Council,** Via della Signora 6, I-20122 Milano. (Also: Via T Grossi 17, I-22100 Como).

**Katholischer Sudtiroler Lehrerbund (KLS),** Haus der Kultur, Wlater v. da Vogelweide, Crispistrasse 4/3, I-39100 Bolzano.

**Pontificia Facoltà di Scienze dell Educazione,** Via S Maria, Mazzarello 102, I-10142 Torino. T: 702911.

*IVORY COAST*

**Direction Nationale de l'Enseignement Catholique,** BP 4119, Abidjan. T: 22968.

**Direction Nationale de l'Enseignement Protestant,** BP 8840, Abidjan.

*JAMAICA*

**Jamaica Catholic Education Association (JCEA),** Archdiocesan Education Secretariat, 2 Emerald Rd, Kingston 4.

*JAPAN*

**Catholic Education Council of Japan,** 10-1 Rokubancho, Chiyoda-ku, Tokyo 102. T: (03) 262-2662. (Member, BICE).

**Education Association of Christian Schools in Japan,** 5-1 4-chome, Ginza, Chuo-ku, Tokyo 104.

**Japan Sunday School Union,** 21-3 5-chome, Mita, Minato-ku, Tokyo 108.

*KENYA*

**Christian Churches' Educational Association (CCEA),** Sec Gen, Church House (3rd floor), Moi Av, PO Box 45009, Nairobi. T: 22312.

**Christian Learning Materials Centre (CLMC),** AEAM, Ralph Bunche Rd, PO Box 49332, Nairobi. T: 21894.

**East Africa Religious Education Committee (EAREC),** PO Box 45009, Nairobi. T: 22312.

**Education Department,** Kenya Catholic Secretariat, Westlands, PO Box 48062, Nairobi. T: 21613.

**National Association of Religious Education Teachers (NARET),** Sec, Alliance High School, PO Box 7, Kikuyu. T: 2026.

**Nyanza Christian College,** Church of Christ in Africa (CCA), Dala Hera (City of Love), Kibos Rd, PO Box 782, Kisumu. T: 2536. (Extensive African indigenous church schools).

*KOREA, South*

**Korean Council of Christian Education,** 136-46 Yunji-Dong, Chongno-ku, Soul.

*LEBANON*

**Bible Lands Union for Christian Education,** PO Box 235, Bayrut.

**Catéchese Harmonisée/Joint Catechesis,** BP 7002, Bayrut. (Ecumenical).

**Commission Episcopale pour l'Ecole Catholique (CEEC),** BP 4413, Bayrut. T: 241554.

**Division of Christian Education,** NECC, PO Box 5376, Bayrut.

**OIEC,** Secrétariat Régional pour le Proche et Moyen Orient, BP 4413, Bayrut. T: 241554.

**Sunday Schools Directorate,** Armenian Catholicossate of the Great House of Cilicia, Dir Gen, Antelias.

*LESOTHO*

**Catholic Education Secretariat,** PO Box 80, Maseru.

*LIBERIA*

**National Secretariat of Catholic Education,** Catholic Mission, PO Box 297, Monrovia.

*LUXEMBOURG*

**Centre de Pedagogie Catholique (CPC),** Av Gaston Diderich 110 (et 243), Luxembourg. T: 25049.

*MADAGASCAR*

**Direction Nationale de l'Enseignement Catholique,** BP 667, Tananarive. T: 20478.

*MALAWI*

**Education Department,** Catholic Secretariat of Malawi, PO Box 5368, Limbe. T: Blantyre 50866.

*MALAYSIA*

**Guild of Assisted Catholic Schools,** Butik Nanas Convent, Kuala Lumpur, Selangor.

*MALI*

**Direction Nationale de l'Enseignement Privé Catholique,** Archevêché, BP 298, Bamako. T: 4439.

*MALTA*

**Malta Private Secondary Schools' Association,** De la Salle College, Cottonera.

*MAURITIUS*

**Fédération des Enseignements Catholique (EEC),** Morcellement Lamusse, Rue Malartic, Rose Hill.

*MEXICO*

**Confederación Nacional Escuelas Particulares (CNEP),** Madero 39-215, México 1, DF.

*MOROCCO*

**Enseignement Catholique au Maroc (ECAM),** BP 258, Rabat. T: 31430.

*MOZAMBIQUE*

**Comissão Episcopal da Educação Cristã e do Ensino,** Maputo (Lourenço Marques).

*NETHERLANDS*

**Central Office for Catholic Education (Centraal Bureau voor het Katholiek Onderwisj),** Bezuidenhoutseweg 275, NL-2000 's-Gravenhage. T: (070)814491.

**Netherlands Sunday School Union (Nederlandse Zondagsschool Vereniging),** Bloemgracht 65, Amsterdam C.

**Reformed Sunday School Association (Jachin),** Amsterdijk 85, Amsterdam 2.

*NETHERLANDS ANTILLES*

**Catholic Teachers' Union (RK Vereniging voor Onderwijzend),** St Thomas, Kashustraat 8, PO Box 582, Oranjestadt, Aruba.

*NEW ZEALAND*

**Catholic Education Council,** 152 Brougham St, Wellington 1.

**New Zealand Council for Christian Education,** Gen Sec, PO Box 228, Wellington.

**New Zealand Sunday School Union,** 323 Queen St, PO Box 5166, Auckland E1.

*NICARAGUA*

**Federación Nicaraguense Educación Católica (FENEC),** 5a Calle No 614, Apdo 2934, Managua.

*NIGERIA*

**Catholic Education Office,** Federal District, PO Box 48, Abeokuta.

**Centre for Applied Religion and Education,** PO Box 9270, Ibadan.

**Education Department,** Catholic Secretariat, PO Box 951, Lagos. T: 25339.

**Interdiocesan Religious Education Training Institute (IRETI),** PO Box 11, Iperu-Remo.

**National Institute of Moral and Religious Education,** Project TIME, PMB 1140, Yaba, Lagos.

*NORWAY*

**Norwegian Sunday School Council,** Gronlandsleret, Oslo 1.

**Norwegian Sunday-school Association (Norsk Sondagsskoleforbund),** Kr Augusts gt 19, Oslo 1.

*PAKISTAN*

**Adult Basic Education Office,** Civil Lines, Gujranwala.

**Catholic Board of Education,** St Patrick's Cathedral, Karachi 3.

**Department of Christian Education,** Pakistan Christian Council, Christian High School, Raja Bazar Rawalpindi.

*PANAMA*

**Federación National Colegios Católicos,** Apdo 6925, Panamá.

*PAPUA NEW GUINEA*

**Churches' Education Council,** PO Box 1323, Boroko.

**National Catholic Education Office,** Boroko.

*PARAGUAY*

**Asociación Paraguaya Enseñanza Católica (APEC),** Curia Vice-provincial, Casilla 346, Asunción.

**Comité Lationoamericano de la Fe (CLAF),** Eligio Ayala 907, Asunción. T: 47976. (Catechetics).

*PERU*

**Consorcio de Centros Educacionales de la Iglesia,** Oficina Nacional de Educación Católica, Palacio Arzobispal, Oficina 22, Plaza de Armas, Lima. T: 75094.

*PHILIPPINES*

**Catholic Educational Association of the Philippines (CEAP),** Social Communications Center Bldg, R Magsaysay Blvd, corner Santol St, Santa Mesa, Manila, PO Box 1214, Manila. T: 612185,605226, 605118.

**Office of Education and Student Chaplains (FABC),** PO Box EA-12, Manila.

**OIEC Regional Secretariat for Asia,** 2401 Taft Av, Manila. T: 54592.

*PORTUGAL*

**Centro de Orientação e Documentação do Ensino Particular (CODEPA),** Duque de Loulé 75, 6D, Lisboa.

**Liga Escolar Católica (LEC),** Campo dos Martires de Patria 48, Lisboa.

**Secretariado Nacional do Ensine Religioso Médie,** Rua de Santa Catarina 428, Porto.

**União das Escolas Dominicais do Norte de Portugal (UEDNOP),** Rua do Molhe 555, Foz do Douro, Porto.

*PUERTO RICO*

**Archdiocesan Office of Education,** Box 1967, San Juan, PR 00903.

*RWANDA*
**Secrétariat National de l'Enseignement Catholique (SNEC),** BP 36, Kigali.

*SENEGAL*
**Direction Nationale de l'Enseignement Catholique,** 2 Rue Paul Holle, BP 3164, Dakar. T: 23478.

*SIERRA LEONE*
**Catholic Education Office,** PO Box 588, Freetown. T: 4011.

*SOUTH AFRICA*
**Department of Education,** South African Bishops' Conference, PO Box 941, Pretoria.
**South African National Sunday School Association,** Grace St, PO Box 17, Port Elizabeth.

*SPAIN*
**Federación Española Comunidades Universitarias (FECUN),** Hermosilla 20, Madrid 1.
**FERE,** Conde de Penalver 45, 4a Planta, Madrid 6.
**Instituto Juan XXIII de Pedagogia Sacerdotal,** Colegio Mayor Pio XI, Limite 3, Madrid 3. T: 2534007, 2335200.

*SUDAN*
**Secretary for Catholic Schools,** PO Box 356, Wad Medani. T: 2396.

*SURINAM*
**Catholic Teachers' Union (Katholieke Onderwijzers Bond, KOB),** Burenstraat 38, Paramaribo.

*SWEDEN*
**Church of Sweden Sunday School Committee,** PO Box 7034, S-10381 Stockholm 7.
**Swedish Sunday School Council (Svenska Södangsskolradet),** PO Box 6302, S-11381 Stockholm.

*SWITZERLAND*
**Aumônerie des Foyers d'Education,** 124 Chemin de la Montagne, CH-1224 Chêne-Bougeries. T: 359571.
**Education Renewal Fund (ERF),** 150 Route de Ferney, CH-1211 Genève 20. (WCC/WCCE).
**Katholische Kommission für Erziehung und Unterricht der Schweiz,** Löwenstr 5, CH-6000 Luzern.
**Schweizerischer Sonntagsschulverband,** Bahnofstr, CH-6460 Altdorf, UR.
**Verband Freier Evangelischer Schulen der Schweiz,** Sek, Muristr 8a, CH-3000 Bern. T: (031) 447155.
**World Council of Christian Education (WCCE),** 150 Route de Ferney, CH-1211 Genève 20.

*SYRIA*
**Commission Episcopale pour les Ecoles Catholiques,** Archevêché des Arméniens Catholiques, Halab (Aleppo). T: 13946.
**Société du Catechisme,** Rue Al Tall, Halab.

*TANZANIA*
**Education Secretary General,** Tanzania Episcopal Conference, PO Box 2133, Dar es Salaam. T: 20477.

*THAILAND*
**Catholic Education Council of Thailand,** St Gabriel's College, 565 Samsen Rd, Bangkok 3.
**Office of Christian Education and Literature,** Church of Christ in Thailand, 14 Pramuan Rd, Bangkok.

*TRINIDAD & TOBAGO*
**Trinidad and Tobago Council of Christian Education,** 20 Warner St, St Augustine.

*TUNISIA*
**Service de l'Enseignement,** Prélature de Tunis, 4 Rue d'Alger, Tunis. T: 245831.

*UGANDA*
**Interdiocesan Secretariat of Catholic Education,** PO Box 2886, Kampala. T: 3042.

*UK OF GB & NI*
**Association for Religious Education,** Sec, Highcroft House, Crown Lane, Four Oaks, Sutton Coldfield, Warwick. T: (021)353-5956.
**Board of Education,** General Synod of the Church of England, Gen Sec, Church House, Dean's Yard, Westminster, London SW1P 3NZ. T: (01)222-9011.
**British Lessons Council,** Sec, 27 Rosemont Rd, Acton, London, W3. T: (01)992-2062. (Sunday-school curricula).
**Catholic Education Commission,** 43 Greenhill Rd, Rutherglen, Glasgow G73.
**Catholic Education Council for England and Wales,** 41 Cromwell Rd, London SW7 2DJ. T: (01) 584-7491/5
**Christian Education Fellowship,** 39 Bedford Square, London WC1B 3EY.
**Christian Education Movement,** Annandale, North End Rd, London NW11 7QX. T: (01)458-4366. (In schools throughout UK; formerly SCM).
**Church Education Corporation,** Sec, 100 Brook Green, London W6. (Public schools for girls) (Also: 35 Denison House, London SW1. T: (01)834-3319).
**Church in Wales Provincial Council of Education** 8 Hickman Rd, Penarth, South Glamorgan CF6 2YQ. T: (708)234)8234.
**Church Schools Company,** Sec, 29 Euston Rd, London NW1 2SL. T: (01)837-2979. (Anglican).
**Corporation of SS Mary and Nicolas (The Woodard Schools),** Registrar, The Manor House, Grinshill, near Shrewsbury, Salop. T: Clive 293.
**Institute of Religious Education,** Corpus Christi College, 17-23 Denbigh Rd, London W11 2SL. T: (01)229-4461.
**Methodist Education Committee,** Gen Sec, 25 Marylebone Rd, London NW1. T: (01)935-3723.
**National Christian Education Council,** Robert Denholm House, Nutfield, Redhill, Surrey RH1 4HW. T: Nutfield Ridge 2411. (Formerly National Study School Union, NSSU. Incorporating IBRA, and Denholm House Press).
**National Institute of Religious Education,** Corpus Christi College, 17 Denbigh Rd, London W11 2SL. T: (01)229-0725.
**National Society for Promoting Religious Education,** Gen Sec, Church House, Dean's Yard, Westminster, London SW1P 3NZ. T: (01)222-1672. (Operates Anglican schools with nearly 1 million pupils in England and Wales).
**Sabbath School Society for Ireland,** Hon Sec, The Manse, 19 Castlehill Rd, Belfast 4, NI.
**Schools Lecturers' Association,** Hon Sec, 4 Banton Lodge Av, Newcastle-upon-Tyne NE7 7LU. (Providing lectures for schools).
**Scottish Sunday School Union for Religious Education,** 70 Bothwell St, Glasgow C2.
**Vacation Bible School Fellowship,** 14 Cherry Walk, Grays, Essex RM16 4UN. T: (0375)822602.
**World Council of Christian Education (WCCE),** Hillside, Merry Hill Rd, Bushey, Herts. T: (01)950-4488/9.

*USA*
**American Association of Christian Schools of Higher Learning,** Box 35139, Greenville, SC 29614.
**American Baptist Education Association (ABEA),** Valley Forge, PA 19481. T: (215)768-2065.
**American Committee For KEEP (Kiyosato Educational Experimental Project),** Room 906, 343 South Dearborn St, Chicago, IL 60604. T: (312) 939-4324.
**American Sunday School Union,** Gen Dir, 1816 Chestnut St, Philadelphia, PA 19103.
**Association for Ministries in Higher Education,** 4864 Woodward Av, Detroit, MI 48201.
**California Association of Christian Schools,** Exec Sec, 14408 East Whittier, Whittier, CA 90607. T: (714)698-5153.
**Christian Released Time Education Inc,** 1346 North Highland Av, Hollywood, CA 90028.
**Church Society for College Work,** 99 Brattle St, Cambridge, MA 02138. T: (617)491-3373. (Also: 2 Brewer St, Cambridge).
**Division of Christian Education, NCCCUSA,** 475 Riverside Drive, New York, NY 10027.
**Evangelical International Schools,** 1720 Oakland Blvd, Walnut Creek, CA 94596.
**Evangelical Sunday Schools Service,** Dir, 3145 NE 59th St, Portland, OR 97213.
**Evangelical Teacher Training Association,** 499 Gundersen, Box 327, Wheaton, IL 60187.
**Greater Los Angeles Sunday School Association (GLASS),** 110 West Broadway, Glendale, CA 91204.
**Liberal Religious Education Directors' Association,** Sec, First Parish Church, Needham, Massachusetts.
**National Association of Christian Schools,** 131 West 6th St, PO Box 28, Wheaton, IL 60187. T: (312) 653-5595.
**National Catholic Educational Association (NCEA),** Suite 350, 1 Dupont Circle, NW, Washington, DC 20036.
**National Sunday School Association,** Exec Dir, PO Box 685, Wheaton, IL 90187. T: (312)653-3090.
**National Union of Christian Schools,** 865 25th St, SE, Grand Rapids, MI 49508. T: (616)245-8618.
**Program of Advanced Christian Education,** 9405 NE Park Drive, Miami, FL 33138.
**Religious Education Association,** 545 West 111th St, New York, NY 10025. T: (212)865-7408.
**Unitarian Sunday School Society,** c/o First Parish, 3 Church St, Cambridge, MA 02138.
**United Board for Christian Higher Education in Asia,** Gen Sec, 475 Riverside Drive, New York, NY 10027. T: (212)870-2601.
**United Ministries in Higher Education,** Witherspoon Bldg, Philadelphia, PA 19107. T: (215)735-6722.
**Weekday Religious Education of Greater Indianapolis,** Exec Dir, 3544 Central Av, Indianapolis, IN 46205.
**World Association of Daily Vacation Bible Schools (VBS),** Room 3202, 551 5th Av, New York, NY 10017.
**World Council of Christian Education and Sunday School Association,** 475 Riverside Drive, New York, NY 10027.
**Worldwide Christian Education Ministries,** 5500 West Division St, Chicago, IL 60651. T: (312) 626-5050.

*UPPER VOLTA*
**Union Nationale des Etablissements Catholiques (UNEC),** BP 90, Ougadougou.

*URUGUAY*
**Consejo Metodista de Educación Cristiana,** Constituyente 1462, Montevideo.
**Unión Nacional Educación Católica (UNEC),** Palacio Arzobispal, Treinta y tres 1360, Montevideo.

*VENEZUELA*
**Asociación de Promoción de la Educación Popular (APEP),** Av La Salle, frente a 4 Transversal, Sebucan, Apdo Postal 70045, Caracas 107. T: 340110.
**Asociación Venezolana de Educación Católica (AVEC),** Adif San Mauricio, Apdo 44, Mijares a Sta Capilla, Caracas. T: 828426.

*VIET NAM*
**Office National de l'Enseignement Catholique (Institution Taberd),** Box H-1, Saigon.

*ZAIRE*
**Bureau National de l'Enseignement Catholique,** Av Adjudant Cassart, BP 3258, Kalina-Kinshasa. T: 30082.
**OIEC Secrétariat Régional pour l'Afrique et Madagascar (CRAM),** BP 3258, Kinshasa Kalina. T: 30082.

*ZAMBIA*
**Education Department,** Catholic Secretariat, PO Box 1965, Lusaka. T: 73467,73470.

*ZIMBABWE*
**General Secretariat for Catholic Education,** Catholic Bishops' Conference, PO Box 2591, Salisbury.

# 9
# Children's Organizations

*Definition.* Agencies specializing in work with or for children, children's missions, child evangelism, child welfare, children's societies, children's homes, orphanages. For education and Sunday schools, see CATECHESIS AND CHRISTIAN EDUCATION.

In this field, there are over 240 organizations of major significance.

*ARGENTINA*
**Acción Católica de la Infancia,** Montevideo 850, 1 piso, Buenos Aires. (Member, BICE).

*AUSTRALIA*
**Child Evangelism Fellowship (CEF),** National Dir, 148 Ryde Rd, West Pymble, NSW 2073. T: (02)498-4775.

*AUSTRIA*
**Katholische Jungschar Österreiches,** Johannesgasse 16, A-1010 Wien.
**Österreichisches Nationalkomitee des BICE,** Nibelungengasse 1 III/50, A-1010 Wien.

*BELGIUM*
**Croisade Eucharistique,** Service de Documentation et d'Action pour l'Enfance, Rue Brialmont 11, B-1030 Brussel.
**Croisade Eucharistique Pie X,** Abbaye d'Averbode, B-3281 Averbode.

*BRAZIL*
**Associação de Educação de Brasil,** Rua Martin Ferreira 23, Rio de Janeiro. (Member, BICE).

*CANADA*
**Association Canadienne des Educateurs de Langue Française,** 3 Place Jean Talon, Québec. (Member, BICE).
**Association d'Education du Québec,** Ste Foy, CP 518, Québec 10. (Member, BICE).
**Child Evangelism Fellowship (CEF),** National Office, Box 201K, Toronto 12, Ontario.
**Children's Special Service Mission (CSSM),** Scripture Union, 3 Rowanwood Av, Toronto 5, Ontario.
**Christian Children's Fund of Canada (CCF),** 1407 Yonge St, Toronto, Ontario, M4T 1Y8.
**Conseil du Québec de l'Enfance Exceptionnelle,** 2765 Chemin de la Côte Ste Catherine, Montréal 250, Québec. (Member, BICE).
**Frank Wellington Children's Crusades,** 298 Hillcrest Av, Willowdale, Ontario.
**Mission to Orphans,** Gen Sec, Box 625, Three Hills, Alberta.
**Office Catéchistique Provincial,** 1845 Blvd Pie IX, Montréal 4, Québec. (Member, BICE).

*CHILE*
**Federación Nacional de Instituciones Privadas de Protección de Menores,** Erasmo Escala 1822, 2 piso, Santiago. (Member, BICE).

*CHINA (TAIWAN)*
**Child Evangelism Fellowship International,** 1-7 Chin Hsi St, 2nd floor, Taipei.

*COLOMBIA*
**Instituto Cristiano de San Pablo,** Calle 13 No 12-42, Bogotá. (Member, BICE).

*DENMARK*
**Danish Organization for the Protection of Children (Landorganisationen Red Barnet),** Nialsgade 19/2, Kobenhavn S.
**Friends of Padre Pire in Denmark (Pater Pire Kredsen i Danmark),** Gronnevei 254, Virum. (Education of refugee children).

*EGYPT*
**Scouts Wadi El Nil,** 15 Rue Emad El Dine, Al Qahirah. (Member, BICE).

*FIJI*
**Child Evangelism Fellowship (CEF),** 12 Matuku St, Samabula.

*FRANCE*
**Action Féminine pour une Pastorale de l'Enfance et de la Jeunesse,** 43 Rue de Turbigo, F-75003 Paris. T: (01)887-0935. (Traditionalist).
**Coeurs Vaillants Ames Vaillantes,** 6 Rue Duguay-Trouin, F-75006 Paris. (Member, BICE).
**Comité Catholique de l'Enfance,** 106 Rue du Bac, F-75007 Paris. (Member, BICE).
**Commission de la Presse et Littérature Enfantines,** BICE, 31 Rue de Fleurus, F-75006 Paris.
**Commission des Institutions et Mouvements Internationaux Apostoliques des Enfants (CIMIADE),** 8 Rue Duguay-Trouin, F-75006 Paris. (Member, BICE).
**Fédération Internationale des Associations d'Enfants de Marie-Immaculée/International Association of Children of Mary,** Secrétariat, 67 Rue de Sèvres, F-75006 Paris. T: (01)222-3390.
**Groupe des Ecoles d'Educateurs et d'Educatrices Spécialisés (Groupe AMCE),** 145 Av Parmentier, F-75010 Paris. (Member, BICE).
**Les Nids de Paris,** 83 Av de St Mandé, F-75012 Paris. (Member, BICE).
**Mouvement International d'Apostolat des Enfants (MIDADE)/International Movement of Apostolate of Children,** 8 Rue Duguay-Trouin, F-75007 Paris. T: (01)222-8481.
**Movement pour les Villages d'Enfants,** 67 Rue Anatole France, F-92 Levallois-Perret. (Member, BICE).
**Pontificia Opera della Santa Infanzia,** 277 Rue Saint-Jacques, F-75005 Paris. T: 325-8028.
**Secrétariat Catholique de l'Enfance et de la Jeunesse Inadaptées,** 23 Av Bosquet, F-75007 Paris. (Member, BICE).
**Union des Oeuvres Catholiques de France,** 31 Rue de Fleurus, F-75006 Paris. (Member, BICE).
**Union Nationale des Assistants et Educateurs de l'Enfance (UNAEDE),** 47 Blvd Montparnasse, F-75006 Paris. (Member, BICE).

*GERMANY, Federal Republic of*
**Arbeitsgemeinschaft für Ev Kinderpflege Deutschlands,** Lenaustr 41, D-4 Düsseldorf.
**Berufsgemeinschaft Katholischer Jugendleiterinnen und Kindergärtenerinnen,** Karlstr 40, D-78 Freiburg im Breisgau. (Member, BICE).
**Bonifatius der Kinder,** Burgunder Weg 1, D-4790 Paderborn.
**Bund Katholischer Erzieher Deutschlands,** Goldenbrunnengasse 4, D-65 Mainz. (Member, BICE).
**Evangelischer Verein für das Syrische Waisenhaus,** Im Oberiddelsfeld 1, D-5000 Köln 80. T: (0221)682160. (Orphanage support).
**Gesamtverband für Kindergottesdienst in der EKD,** Am Alten Kirchhof 10, D-235 Neumünster.
**Hilfsbund für das Lillian Trasher Waisenhaus Assiout,** Im Stahlbühl 3, D-7100 Heilbronn. T: (07131)87860. (Orphanage in Egypt).
**Katholische Diasporakinderhilfe,** Burgunder Weg 1, D-4790 Paderborn.
**Kindernothilfe Duisburg-Rhurort,** Kanalstr 5a, D-41 Duisburg-Meiderich.
**Kindernothilfe (Aid for Children in Need),** 28 Kufsteinerstr 100, D-4100 Duisburg. T: (02131) 700064.
**Päpstliches Missionswerk der Kinder in Deutschland,** Stephanstr 35, D-5100 Aachen.
**Verband Ev Kinderpflegerinnen,** Alsterdorfer Str 140, D-2 Hamburg 39.
**Vereinigung Ev Kinderpflegeverbände Deutschlands,** Reinsburgstr 50, D-7 Stuttgart-W.
**Zentralverband Katholischer Kindergärten und Kinderhorte Deutschlands,** Weissenburgstr 14, D-5000 Köln 1. T: (0221)732231. (Member, BICE).

*GREECE*
**Oeuvre Charitable pour l'Enfance du Diocèse d'Athènes,** 9 Rue Homere, Athínai 135. (Member, BICE).

*HONG KONG*
**Christian Children's Fund (CCF),** 21 Chatham Rd, 6F, Kowloon. T: K-667271/2.

*INDIA*
**Dohnavur Fellowship,** Dohnavur, Tirunelveli, South India.
**Dr Graham's Homes,** Kalimpong, West Bengal.

*ISRAEL*
**Child Evangelism Fellowship (CEF),** PO Box 292, Nazareth.

*ITALY*
**Azione Cattolica dei Ragazzi,** Via della Conciliazione 1, I-00193 Roma. (Member, BICE).
**Child Evangelism Fellowship (CEF),** Via Picco dei Tre Signori 20, I-00141 Roma.
**Comitato Nazionale Italiano del BICE,** Via della Conciliazione 1, I-00193 Roma.
**Opera Nazionale Città dei Ragazzi,** Lungotevere Marzio 12, I-00186 Roma. (Member, BICE).
**Unione Italiana Stampa Periodica Educativa per Ragazzi (UISPER),** Via della Conciliazione 1, I-00193 Roma. (Member, BICE).

*JAPAN*
**Child Care,** 10-37 Kugenuma Kaigan, 2-chome, Fujisawa-shi, Kanagawa-ken 251.
**Child Evangelism Fellowship of Japan (CEF),** 1599 Higashikubo, Kamiarai, Tokorozawa-shi, Saitama-ken 359.
**Christian Children's Fund,** Shibuya Chiyoda Bldg 13, Nanpeidai, Shibuya-ku, Tokyo 150.
**Christian Federation of Childhood Education,** 17-11, 3-chome, Mejiro, Toshima-ku, Tokyo 171.
**World Missions to Children,** 850 Tenjin-cho, Sasebo-shi, Nagasaki-ken 857-11.

*LIBERIA*
**Child Evangelism Fellowship of Liberia (CEF),** Dir, Box 50, Monrovia. T: 22059.

*LUXEMBOURG*
**Action Catholique de l'Enfance,** 105A Rue d'Eich, Luxembourg. (Member, BICE).

*MALTA*
**Children's Homes,** 84 Old Mint St, Valetta. (Member, BICE).

*MEXICO*
**Centro Cultural Pro la Ninez,** Dir, 16 de Septiembre 6-611, Zona 1, Apdo M 7571, México, DF. T: 102673.
**Departamento Nacional de Infancia y Adolescencia de la Acción Católica Mexicana,** Apdo Postal 1647, México 1, DF. (Member, BICE).

*NETHERLANDS*
**Catholic Alliance for the Protection of Children (Katholiek Verbond voor Kinderbescherming),** Buitenhaven 5, 's-Hertogenbosch. T: (04100)39661. (Member, BICE).
**Catholic Parents Association (Katholieke Oudervereniging voor het Zorgenkind),** Woonark

Oude Leidseweg t/o Zwembad, NL-Den Hommel (Oog in Al). T: (030)936823.
**Dutch Federation of Institutions for Unmarried Mothers and Children (Nederlandes Federatie van Instellingen voor Ongehuwde Moeder en Haar Kind, FIOM),** Nieuwe Schoolstraat 28, NL-'s-Gravenhage. T: (070)645848.

*NEW ZEALAND*
**Child Evangelism Fellowship,** New Zealand Council, Sec, 375 Cambridge Terrace, Lower Hutt.

*PAKISTAN*
**Child Evangelism Fellowship,** 36 Ferozepur Rd, Lahore.

*PHILIPPINES*
**Children's Mission,** PO Box 3349, Manila.
**International Child Evangelism Fellowship (CEF),** PO Box 1205, Manila.
**Philippine Children's Mission,** PO Box 1897, Manila.

*PORTUGAL*
**Aliança Pró-Evangelização das Crianças de Portugal,** Rua Santos Rocha 20, 3 Esq, Coimbra.
**National Co-ordinating Commission of Children's Movements in Portugal,** Av Duque de Loule 83/2, Lisboa. (Member, BICE).

*SPAIN*
**Colegio de Huérfanos de Ferroviarios,** Atocha 83, Madrid 12. (Railway orphans. Member, BICE).
**Comisión Nacional Católica Española de la Infancia (Acción Católica),** Calle Alfonso XI 4/4, Madrid 14. (Member, BICE)
**Commission Juridique (BICE),** Cea Bermúdez 46, Madrid 3.
**Consejo Superior de Protección de Menores,** Cea Bermúdez 48, Madrid 3. (Member, BICE).
**Delegación Nacional de Juventudes,** José Ortega y Gasset 71, Madrid 6. (Member, BICE).
**Delegación Nacional de la Sección Femenina,** BICE, Almagro 36, Madrid 4.
**Escuelas Profesionales de la Sagrada Familia,** Apdo 5, Ubeda, Jaén. (Member, BICE).
**Instituto Municipal de Educación de Madrid,** Mejia Lequerica 21, Madrid 4. (Member, BICE).
**Mutualidad Nacional de Enseñanza Primaria,** Fernández de la Hoz 64, Madrid 3. (Member, BICE).
**Secretariado Categuistico Nacional,** Alfonso XI 4/1, Madrid 14. (Member, BICE).
**Servicio Español del Magesterio,** Alcalá 44, Madrid 14. (Member, BICE).

*SWITZERLAND*
**Bois-Soleil,** Dir, Route du Signal 25-27,CH-1018 Lausanne. T: (021)224568. (Home for sick children).
**Bureau International Catholique de l'Enfance (BICE)/International Catholic Child Bureau (ICCB),** Sec, 65 Rue de Lausanne, CH-1202 Genève. T: (022)313248.
**Direktion des Seraphischen Liebeswerkes Pro-Infante et Familia,** Antoniushaus, CH-4500 Solothurn. (Member, BICE).
**Kinderdorf Pestalozzi,** CH-9043 Trogen.
**Komitee der Deutschsprahigen Länder im Internationalen Katholischen Büro des Kindes,** Gurzelngasse 14, CH-4500 Solothurn. (Member, BICE).

*UGANDA*
**Child Evangelism Fellowship (CEF),** PO Box 2089, Kampala.

*UK OF GB & NI*
**Child Evangelism Fellowship (CEF),** Dir, 31 Lampton Rd, Hounslow, Middx. T: (01)572-2656.
**Child Welfare Office,** 18 Park Circus, Glasgow G3.
**Children's Council,** Church of England Board of Education, Church House, Dean's Yard, London SWIP 3NZ. T: (01)222-9011.
**Children's Relief International,** Sec, Overstream House, Victoria Av, Cambridge, CB4 1EQ.
**Children's Special Service Mission (CSSM),** Gen Dir, 5 Wigmore St, London W1. T: (01)486-2561.
**Church of England Children's Society,** Gen Sec, Old Town Hall, Kennington, London SE11. T: (01)735-2441.
**Commission for Social Welfare,** BICE, 1A Stert St, Abingdon, Berkshire.
**Dr Barnado's Homes,** Dir Gen, Tanner's Lane, Barkingside, Essex. T: (01)550-8822. (Begun 1866).
**Dr Graham's Homes (Kalimpong),** 9 Brackendale Gardens, Upminster, Essex. T: 5011.
**Fellowship of St Nicholas,** Sec, Christ Church Rectory, St Leonards-on-Sea, East Sussex. T: (0424)3683. (Homeless children aged 3-18).
**Good Templar and Temperance Children's Home,** Crondall Lodge, Crondall, nr Farnham, Surrey.
**Gorakhpur Nurseries Fellowship,** 27 Motspur Park, New Malden, Surrey. T: (01)942-0270. (Mission near Nepal border).
**Homeless Children's Aid and Adoption Society,** Gen Sec, 54 Grove Av, London N10. T: (01)883-4896.
**Mr Fegan's Homes,** Headquarters, 372 Wandsworth Rd, London SW8. (Begun 1870).
**National Children's Homes,** 85 Highbury Park, London N5 1UD.
**Our Lady's Catechists,** 48 Lowndes Square, London SW1. (Member, BICE).
**St Dominic Savio Guild,** 30 Orbel St, London SW11. (Member, BICE).
**Shaftesbury Society,** Sec, Shaftesbury House, 112 Regency St, London SW1P 4AX. T: (01)834-2656.
**UK Band of Hope Union,** Gen Sec, 45 Great Peter St, London SW1. T: (01)222-6809. (Children's temperance movement).

*USA*
**Child Care,** 610 East Lime St, Box 1342, Lakeland, FL 33802.
**Child Evangelism Fellowship International (CEF),** Exec Dir, 44 Ionia Av, SW, PO Box 1156, Grand Rapids, MI 49501. T: (616)459-4291.
**Children's Bible Mission,** Box 1137, Lakeland, FL 33802.
**Children's Sand and Surf Ministry,** PO Box 11710, Pittsburgh, PA 15228.
**Christian Children's Fund (CCF),** Exec Dir, 203 East Carey St, PO Box 511, Richmond, VA 23204. T: (703)644-2375.
**Department of Child Care,** Catholic Charities of the Archdiocese of New York, 112 East 22nd St, New York, NY 10010. (Member, BICE).
**Holt Adoption Program,** PO Box 95, Cresswell, OR 97426. T: (503)895-2202.
**National Christ Child Society,** 5151 Winscosin Av, NW, Washington, DC 20016.
**Pan Pacific Centres,** 881 Via de la Paz, Pacific Palisades, CA 90272. (Orphanages).
**Pre-Kindergarten Program,** Berkeley Area Council of Churches, 1942 Virgia Av, Berkeley, CA 94709.
**Refugee Children,** Dir, PO Box 106, Stamford, CT 06904.
**World Missions to Children,** Gen Dir, PO Box 1048, Grants Pass, OR 97526. T: (503)479-3731.

# 10
# Christian Approaches to Other Faiths

*Definition.* Christian missionary or evangelistic initiatives directed primarily towards the other major world religions (especially Judaism, Islam, Hinduism, Buddhism), including agnosticism and atheism, primarily concerned with mission and evangelism, or with interfaith dialogue or mutual understanding; activities, information and study centres. See also RESEARCH CENTRES. For joint activity between Christians and non-Christians, see INTERRELIGIOUS ORGANIZATIONS.

There are over 80 organizations of major significance in this field worldwide.

*AUSTRALIA*
**Jewish Evangelical Witness (JEW),** Dir, 4 David Court, 67 Murrumbeena Rd, Murrumbeena, Victoria 3163. T: 562961.

*BRAZIL*
**Centro Yoga Cristão,** Av Lauro Sodré 83, ZC 82, Tunel Novo, Rio de Janeiro, GB.
**Esperanca de Israel,** Rua General Rondon 49, CP 9040, São Paulo, SP. T: 629055.

*CANADA*
**Centre MI-CA-EL,** 4661 Queen Mary Rd, Montréal 247, Québec. T: 7396048. (RC. Until 1965, Centre Ratisbonne. Dialogue with Judaism).
**Fellowship of Faith for the Muslims,** Exec Sec, Room 25, 205 Yonge St, Toronto 1, Ontario M5B 1N2. T: (416)364-5054.
**Hebrew Evangelization Society,** Gen Sec, 55 East 18th Av, Vancouver 10, BC.
**Service Incroyance et Foi,** 2930 Rue Lacombe, Montréal H3T 1LA. T: (514)735-1565/6.

*CHINA (TAIWAN)*
**Association of Friends for the Study of Chinese Culture (Tsung chiao Wen-hua Yu-i shih),** Chung-hua Rd, 2nd section, 404-1, Taipei.

*DENMARK*
**Danske Israelsmission,** Lipkesgade 5, DK-2100 Kobenhavn O.
**Scandinavian Buddhist Mission (Nordiske Kristne Buddhistmission),** Bernstorffvej 65A, DK-2900 Hellerup. T: (01)HELrup 8405.

*FINLAND*
**Friends of Israel,** Pikku Robertinkatu 5/17, Helsinki.

*FRANCE*
**Amitié Judéo-Chrétienne de France (AJCF),** 68 Rue de Babylone, F-75007 Paris.
**Comité Episcopal pour les Relations avec les Juifs,** Secrétariat Général de l'Episcopat, 106 Rue du Bac, F-75341 Paris. T: 222-5708.
**Commission Inter-Africaine des Religions,** Société Africaine de Culture, 25bis Rue des Ecoles, F-75005 Paris. T: 033-1374.
**Eglise et Monde Juif,** 13 Rue de Poissy, F-75005 Paris. T: 033-3241.
**Encounter Today,** 11 Rue Jules Guesde, F-92 Issy-les-Moulineaux. T: 6422170.
**Foiet Cultures/Ad Lucem,** 12 Rue Guy de la Brosse, F-75005 Paris. T: 331-7955.
**Rencontres entre Chrétiens et Juifs,** 62 Blvd Montparnasse, F-75015 Paris.
**Secrétariat pour la Rencontre avec les Musulmans,** 24 Quai Fernand Saguet, F-94 Maisons-Alforet. T: 368-3464.
**Service Incroyance-Foi (SIF),** 127 Rue Notre Dame des Champs, F-75006 Paris. T: 633-5938.
**Service International de Documentation Judéo-Chrétienne (SIDIC),** 73 Rue Notre Dame des Champs, F-75006 Paris. T: 325-5620.
**SILOE,** 61 Rue du Cherche-Midi, F-75006 Paris.

*GERMANY, Federal Republic of*
**Arbeitsgemeinschaft für Dienst an Israel,** Koblenzer Str 306, D-4972 Löhne 1. T: (05732)2258.
**Evangelisch-lutherischer Zentralverein für Mission unter Israel,** Motterstr 1, D-8500 Nürnberg. T: (0911)634774.
**Jerusalemsverein,** Handjerystr 19/20, D-1000 Berlin 41. T: (030)8513061. (Begun 1852).
**Nazarethwerk,** Hamburger Str 57, D-2057 Reinbek. T: (040)7226855. (Begun 1966).
**Studienkommission Kirche und Judentum der EKD,** Herrenhaüserstr 2A, Postfach 2, D-3000 Hannover 21.

*HOLY SEE*
**Secretariat for Non-Believers/Segretariato per i Non Credenti/Secretariatus pro Non Credentibus,** Pres, Piazza San Calisto 16, I-00120 Città del Vaticano. T: 6984393,6984004,6984773,6984577. (Catholic approaches to agnostics and atheists).
**Secretariat for Non-Christians/Segretariato per i Non Cristiani,** Pres, Piazza San Calisto 16, I-00120 Città del Vaticano. T: 6982 int 4321,4593. (Catholic approaches to believers in non-Christian religions).

*HONG KONG*
**Christian Mission to Buddhists,** Tao Fong Shan, Shating, NT. T: NT-61450.

*INDIA*
**CBCI Commission for Dialogue,** St Mary's Cathedral Church, 66 Varanasi Cantt, UP.
**Christian Literature for Muslims Committee,** Henry Martyn Institute, 15 Nehru Rd, Lucknow 2, UP.

*ISRAEL*
**American Association for Jewish Evangelism,** PO Box 376, Ramt Gan.
**Maison St-Isaïe (Beit Yeshayaou),** 20 Rue Gershon Agron, BP 1332, Jerusalem. T: (02)29763.
**Oasis de Paix (Nevé Shalom),** Rue Ha'neviim, Jerusalem. T: (02)87250.

*LAOS*
**Bureau du Bouddhisme,** Mission Catholique, Vientiane. T: 3257.

*LEBANON*
**Muslim World Evangelical Literature Service,** Araya, Kehale PO.

*NEW ZEALAND*
**International Jews Society,** New Zealand Council, Sec, PO Box 6455, Auckland.

*NIGERIA*
**Islam in Africa Project Council,** Gen Adviser, 5 Awosika Av, Bodija, PO Box 4045, Ibadan. T: 23884.

*NORWAY*
**Norwegian Mission to Buddhists (Nordiske Kristne Buddhistmisjon),** Elisenbergveien 6, Oslo 2.
**Norwegian Mission to Israel (Norske Israelmisjon),** Colletggt 43, Oslo 4.
**Norwegian Mission to Muslims (Norske Muhammedanermisjon),** Storgt 38, Oslo 1.

*PAKISTAN*
**Loyola Hall,** 28 Warris Rd, Lahore.

*SOUTH AFRICA*
**Cape Town Diocesan Mission to Moslems,** Rectory, Pinelands, CP.

*SWEDEN*
**Church and Judaism (Riksorganisationen Kyrkan och Judendomen),** Idungatan 4, Box 230 57, S-104 35 Stockholm. T: (08)339250.
**Northern Christian Buddhist Mission (Nordiska Kristna Buddhistmissionen),** Box 297, S-751 05 Uppsala.
**Swedish Jerusalem Society (Svenska Jerusalemsföreningen),** Fredrikshovsgatan 3A, S-115 22 Stockholm.

*SWITZERLAND*
**Schweizerische Evangelische Judenmission,** Sekretariat, Rötelstr 96, CH-8057 Zürich. T: (051) 601310.
**The Church and the Jewish People,** WCC, 150 Route de Ferney, CH-1211 Genève 20. T: 333400.

*UK OF GB & NI*
**Christian Mission to the Communist World (Jesus to the Communist World),** PO Box 19, Bromley, Kent BR1 1DJ. T: (01)460-9319.
**Christian Witness to Israel,** 44 Lubbock Rd, Chislehurst, Kent BR7 5JX. T: (01)467-2296. (Formerly Barbican Mission to the Jews).
**Church's Ministry Among the Jews (CMJ),** Vincent House, Vincent Square, London SW1P 2PX. T: (01)834-4527/8.
**Fellowship of Faith for the Muslims Publications,** Librarian, 14 Tudor Close, Hove, East Sussex BN3 7NR.
**Fellowship of Faith for the Muslims,** Sec, The Manse, Hatch Beauchamp, Taunton, Somerset T: (082348)335. (Also: The Manse, Great Sampford, Saffron Walden, Essex).
**Hebrew Christian Alliance of Great Britain,** Exec Sec, 8 Brockenhurst Rd, Ramsgate, Kent. T: (843)52669.
**Hebrew Christian Testimony to Israel,** 139 Whitechapel Rd, London E1 1DN. T: (01)247-5270.
**Hebrew Evangelization Society,** 92-94 Amhurst Park, London N16. T: (01)800-7315.
**International Hebrew Christian Alliance (IHCA),** Exec Sec, Shalom, 8 Brockenhurst Rd, Ramsgate, Kent. T: (843)52669.
**International Society for the Evangelization of the Jews,** Gen Sec, 45 Gildredge Rd, Eastbourne, East Sussex BN21 4RZ. T: 30617/8.
**Jerusalem and the East Mission (JEM),** 12 Warwick Square, London SW1V 2AA. T: (01)834-9588. (Anglican).
**Mildmay Mission to the Jews,** Mildmay Hall, 214 Mile End Rd, Stepney, London E1 4LJ. T: (01) 790-2079.
**Pentecostal Jewish Mission,** Sec, 23 John Campbell Rd, Stoke Newington, London N16. T: (01)254-3039.

*USA*
**American Association for Jewish Evangelism,** 5860 North Lincoln Av, Chicago, IL 60645.
**American Board of Missions to the Jews,** 236 West 72nd St, New York, NY 10023.
**Cleveland Hebrew Mission,** PO Box 18056, Cleveland, OH 44118.
**Evangelical Islamics Committee,** IFMA, PO Box 395, Wheaton, IL 60187.
**Evangelism to Communist Lands,** PO Box 303, Glendale, CA 91209. T: (213)243-7973.
**Fellowship of Christian Testimonies to the Jews,** Pres, 7448 North Damen Av, Chicago, IL 60645.
**Hebrew Christian Alliance of America,** 100 West Chicago Av, Chicago, IL 60610.
**Hebrew Christian Center,** 862 North Fairfax Av, PO Box 46040, Los Angeles, CA 90046.
**Hebrew Evangelization Society,** PO Box 707, Los Angeles, CA 90022.
**International Hebrew Christian Alliance,** Sec, PO Box 506, Clearwater, FL 33517.
**Israel's Hope,** 2107 East 9th St, Brooklyn, NY 11223. T: (212)339-4556. (Bible correspondence course to Jews in 16 nations).
**Jesus to The Communist World,** Gen Dir, 1109 East Chevy Chase, Box 11, Glendale, CA 91205. T: (213)243-5558. (Christian Mission to the Communist World).
**Los Angeles Hebrew Mission,** Exec Sec, 850 Echo Park Av, Los Angeles, CA 90026.
**Messengers of the New Covenant,** 109 Treacy Av, Newark, NJ 07108.
**Ministry to the Jewish People,** American Lutheran Church, 422 South Fifth St, Minneapolis, MI 55415.
**Minneapolis Friends of Israel,** 4932 Xerxes Av South, Minneapolis, MI 55410.
**Operation Connection,** Exec Dir, Room 860, 1120 Connecticut Av, NW, Washington, DC 20036. T: (202)659-4140.
**Russia for Christ,** Pres, 3009A De La Vina, PO Box 30000, Santa Barbara, CA 93105. T: (805)687-7696. (Ministry in communist lands).
**Underground Evangelism,** 1222 South Glendale Av, Glendale, PO Box 808, Los Angeles, CA 90053. T: (213)247-6060. (In communist countries).

# 11
# Christian Universities

*Definition.* Church- or Christian-operated, -owned, -controlled, -sponsored, or -linked universities granting academic degrees mainly in secular subjects.

Many denominations operate or sponsor universities. The largest number are Roman Catholic (640 universities, 47 directly founded by the Holy See); another large operator is the Seventh-day Adventist Church, with 71 universities worldwide. The total of all such Christian universities is around 1,300. Because of this large number, they are not listed here, but will be found in a number of national and denominational yearbooks listed here under DIRECTORIES.

# 12
# Cinema & Film

*Definition.* Christian involvement in the cinema, films, motion pictures; video-cassette ministries; cinema and film training schools and centres; film libraries; film festivals, weeks, seminars.

*ARGENTINA*
**Comisión Episcopal del Cine,** Departmento de CEA, Rodriguez Pena 834, Buenos Aires.
**Festival de Cine Experimental y Documental,** Calle Obispo Trejo 323, Cordoba. T: 48080,26671. (RC).

*AUSTRALIA*
**Australian Religious Film Society (ARFS),** 162 Russell St, Melbourne, Victoria 3000. T: 6632061. (Also: 44 Margaret St, Sydney, NSW 2000. T: 296134).
**Fact and Faith Films,** Lido House, 400 Kent St, Sydney, NSW 2000. T: 2901600.

*AUSTRIA*
**Katholische Filmkommission fur Österreich,** Goldschmiedgasse 6, A-1010 Wien. T: 639100.

*BELGIUM*
**Africa Films,** PB, Rue Guillaume Leke 13, B-4802 Heusy, Verviers.
**Cedoc-Film (Cinéma Educatif, Documentaire et Culturel)/Filmvormingscentrum van het Nationaal Secretariaat v/h Katholiek Onderwijs,** Rue Cornet de Grez 14, B-1030 Brussel. T: (02) 172498. (Catholic education by film).
**Centre Catholique d'Action Cinématographique (CCAC)/Middenbestuur van de Katholieke Filmactie (KFA),** Rue de l'Orme 10, B-1040 Brussel. T: (02)340880,343438.
**Films and Youth Service,** OCIC, Rue de l'Orme 10, B-1040 Brussel.
**OCIC Secretariat for Children's Cinema,** Rue de l'Orme 10, B-1040 Brussel. T: (02)348150.
**Office Catholique International Cinéma (OCIC)/International Catholic Film Organization,** Gen Sec, Rue de l'Orme 8, B-1040 Brussel. T: (02) 7348150.

*BOLIVIA*
**Centro de Orientación Cinematográfica,** Av Ecuador 595, Casilla 2283, La Paz. T: 24797.

*BRAZIL*

**Central Católica do Cinema,** Rua do Russel 76, CP 16085, Rio de Janeiro, GB. T: 523541.
**Cineduc,** Rua do Russel 76, 5 andar, CP 16085, Rio de Janeiro, GB. T: 523541.
**Escola Superior de Cinema,** Faculdade São Luis, Av Paulista 2324, São Paulo, SP.
**Escola Superior de Cinema,** Universidade Católica de Minas Gerais, Av Brasil 2023, 6 andar, Belo Horizonte, MG. T: 40486.

*CHILE*

**Centro de Educación Cinemagográfica,** Depto 42, de la Olleria 966, Santiago. T: 34470.
**Instituto Filmico,** Universidad Católica de Chile, Bernardo O'Higgins 1801, Casilla 10445, Santiago. T: 36958.

*COLOMBIA*

**Centro Católico de Orientación Cinematográfica,** Oficina 402, Carrera 10, No 19-64, Bogotá. T: 494985.

*CUBA*

**Centro Católico de Orientación Cinematográfica (CCOC),** Apdo 594, La Habana.

*DENMARK*

**Catholic Film Group (Katolsk Film Gruppe),** 9 HC Orstedvej, DK Kobenhavn V.

*DOMINICAN REPUBLIC*

**Centro Católico de Orientación Cinematográfica,** Apdo Postal 841, Santo Domingo. T: 27665.

*ECUADOR*

**Centro de Orientación Cinematográfica (COC),** Apdo 2296, Quito.
**Instituto de Antropologia Filmica,** Centro de Educación Cinematográfica (CEDUCI), Calle Benalcazar 615, Tercer piso, Oficina 3, Casilla 2296, Quito. T: 513070.

*EGYPT*

**Centrale Catholique Egyptienne du Cinéma,** 9 Rue Adly Pacha, Al Qahirah. T: 59892,74568.

*EL SALVADOR*

**Oficina Católica de Cine,** Av Espana 312, Altos, Apdo Postal 1236, San Salvador. T: 215584.

*FRANCE*

**Cinéma et Télécinéma,** 129 Fg St-Honore, F-75008 Paris.
**Decision (Films de l'Association d'Evangélisation Billy Graham),** BP 345, F-75365 Paris. T: 225-8051.
**Expression,** Association Culturelle de Diffusion Cinematographique, 10 Place de la Libération, Dijon. T: (80)303430. (Production).
**Films et Vie,** 24 Rue de Milan, F-75009 Paris.
**Missions par le Cinéma et la Radio-Télévision,** Dir, 222 Rue du Faubourg St-Honoré, F-75008 Paris.
**OCIC Département Professionnel & Secrétariat** à l'Information, BP 1106, F-75008 Paris.
**OCIC Secrétariat Culturel,** 10 Place de l'Abbaye, F-42 Saint Etienne, Loire.
**OCIC Service d'Education,** 21 Rue de la Paix, F-42 Saint-Etienne, Loire. T: (77)322640.
**OCIC Service Scolaire,** 21 Rue de la Paix, F-42 Saint-Etienne, Loire. T: (77)322640.
**Office Catholique Français du Cinéma (OCFC),** 193 Rue de l'Université, F-75007 Paris. T: (01)705-4358,551-9462. (Under Episcopal Conference).
**Organisation Internationale Catholique du Cinéma (OCIC),** Service Scolaire, 10 Place de l'Abbaye, F-42 St Etienne.
**Production du Parvis,** 121 Av de Villiers, F-75017 Paris. T: (01)380-3056.

*GERMANY, Federal Republic of*

**Brücken Film,** Kaulbaschtr 85, D-8 München 23.
**Calig-Verlag,** Renatastr 71, D-8000 München 2.
**Deutscher Katecheten-Verein,** Preysingstr 83c, D-8000 München 2.
**Eikon Gemeinnützige Gesellschaft für Fernsehen und Film,** Lachnerstr 20, D-8 Müchen 19.
**Evangelische Filmgilde,** Gottfried-Keller-Str, D-6 Frankfurt (Main) 50.
**Evangelischer Arbeitskreis Lichtbild (EAL),** Geschädtsstelle, Querallee 50-52, D-35 Kassel.
**Evangelisches Filmwerk,** Haus der Ev Publizistik, Friedrichstr 34, 6 Frankfurt am Main.
**Film und Bildverlag,** Renatastr 71, Postfach 146, D-8000 München 19. T: (0811)5163476.
**Ichtys-Film,** Goethestr 24, D-8 München.
**Katholisches Filmwerk,** Karmeliterstr 9, Postfach 5, D-7407 Rottenburg-Neckar. T: (07472)373. (Also Kaiserstr 67/III, Postfach 16.502, D-6 Frankfurt/Main. T: (0611)233526).
**Kirchliche Haupstelle für Bild- und Filmarbeit,** Ursulaplatz 1, D-5 Köln. T: (0221)212782.
**Matthias-Film,** Diemershaldenstr 45, D-7 Stuttgart.
**OCIC Audio-Visual Service for Development (SAV),** Sprollstr 20, D-7407 Rottenburg/Neckar. T: 7412241.
**Provobis, Gesellschaft für Film und Fersehen,** Charlottenburger Chaussee 51-55, D-1 Berlin 20 (Spandau). T: 3047948,3048347.
**Steyl SVD Film und Ton,** Dauthendeystr 25, D-8000 München 55. T: (0811)741522.
**Tellux,** Leopoldstr 20, D-8000 München 2.
**Werner Junger Verlag,** Eppstreiner Str 36, D-6 Frankfurt am Main.

*GREECE*

**OCIC Middle East Service,** Eglise Catholique, Saint-François, Rhodes.

*HOLY SEE*

**OCIC Filmis,** Secretariat for Africa, Asia and Oceania, Piazza San Calisto 16, Scala 4, Piano 3, I-00120 Città del Vaticano. T: 5806216,6984755.
**Vatican Film Library (Filmoteca Vaticana),** Palazzo San Carlo, I-00120 Città del Vaticano. T: 6983197,6983597.

*HONDURAS*

**Oficina Nacional de Cine,** Gimnasio de Choluteca, Choluteca.

*INDIA*

**Sunil Studio,** Manvila, Kulathur, Trivandrum (Films).

*IRELAND*

**National Film Institute of Ireland,** 65 Harcourt St, Dublin. T: 53638.
**Redharc Films,** Booterstown Av, Blackrock, County Dublin. T: 881939.

*ITALY*

**Centro Cattolico Cinematografico (CCC),** Ente dello Spettacolo, Via dello Conciliazione 2c, I-00193 Roma. T: 561775,564132.
**Centro Italiano Addestramento Cinematografico (CIAC),** Via Camillucia 12 (for men), & Via Cimone 145 (for women), Roma.
**Centro Italiano Documentari Educativi Religiosi (CIDER),** Via Donatello 16, I-35100 Padova. T: 5144. (Films).
**Edizioni Missionarie Italiane (EMI),** c/o Oltremare Film, Viale Vaticano 90, I-00165 Roma. T: 315949. (Films on missions).
**Filmine Don Bosco,** Via Maria Ausiliatrice 32, I-10152 Torino.
**Instituto Luce,** Piazza Cineccitta 11, I-00174 Roma.
**Instituto Superiore di Scienze Tecniche dell'Opinione,** Specializzazione Cinematografica, Università Internazionali degli Studi 'Pro Deo', Viale Pola 12, Roma.
**Oltremare Film,** Centro Saveriano d'Azione Missionario, Viale Vaticano 90, I-00165 Roma. T: 315949.
**Pontificio Istituto Missioni Estere,** Via S Teresa 12, I-00198 Roma. (Films).
**San Paolo Films,** Film Distribution Centre, Via Castro Pretorio 16, I-00185 Roma. T: 4957276.
**San Paolo Films,** Via Portuense 746, CP 5033, I-00148 Roma. T: 5230292,5230207. (24 agencies in Italy).
**Vita-Film,** Via Briosco 3, I-35100 Padova.

*JAMAICA*

**Catholic Film Centre,** St George's College, Winchester Park, Kingston.

*JAPAN*

**Saint Paul Film and Radio Centre,** 1-5 Wakapa, Shinjuku-ku, Tokyo.

*KENYA*

**East African Religious Films Library,** Sec, NCCK Film Library, PO Box 45009, Nairobi. T: 22264.
**NCCK Film Library,** Librarian, Church House (1st floor), Moi Av, PO Box 45009, Nairobi. T: 22264.

*LEBANON*

**Centrale Catholique Libanaise du Cinéma,** Université St-Joseph, BP 293, Bayrut. T: 249766.

*LUXEMBOURG*

**Office Catholique du Cinéma, de la Radio et de la Télévision,** 5 Rue Bourbon, Luxembourg. T: 485181.

*MALAYSIA*

**LCMS Film Library,** Audiovisual Centre, Jalan Semangat, PO Box 1068, Petaling Jaya, Selangor. (Lutheran Ch of Malaysia & Singapore).

*MALTA*

**Film Section,** Catholic Institute, Floriana.

*MAURITIUS*

**Comité Catholique du Cinéma,** 20 Rue Rope Hennessy, Port-Louis.

*MEXICO*

**Cinematográfica Interamericana,** Porfirio Diaz 195, Zona 12, México, DF.
**Instituto de Cultura Cinematográfica,** Universidad Iberoamericana, Cerro de las Torres 395, Churubusco-Campestre, México 21, DF.
**Oficina Nacional de Cine,** Apdo Postal 61-166, México 6, DF.
**Peliculas Cientificas,** Sara 4508, Col Guadaloupe Tepeyac, Zona 14, México, DF. T: 340755.
**Peliculas Rodriguez,** México 13, DF.

*NETHERLANDS*

**International Inter-Church Film Centre (INTERFILM),** Steynlaan 8, Postbus 515, Hilversum. T: 42222.
**Katholieke Film Actie,** Nieuwe Schoolstraat 85, 's-Gravenhage. T: 112211.
**Office National Catholique du Cinema en Hollande,** Amersfoortsestraat 10, Huis Ter Heide.

*NICARAGUA*

**Oficina Nacional de Cine,** Apdo 2183, Managua.

*NORWAY*

**Christian Film Society (Kristen Filmtjeneste),** Munchsgt 2, Oslo 1.

*PANAMA*

**Oficina Nacional de Cine (CENCOS),** Apdo 386, Panamá 1.

*PARAGUAY*

**Oficina Nacional de Cine,** Casilla de Correos 587, Asunción. T: 8422.

*PERU*

**Centro de Orientación Cinematográfica (CEOC),** Av 9 de Diciembre 378, Paseo Colón, Apdo 44, Lima. T: 312339.
**Imágenes para el Desarrollo,** Jirón Chancay 716, Apdo 10226, Lima. T: 238944. (Films, slides).
**OCIC Centro Latinoamericano de Lenguaje Total (SAL),** Av 9 de Diciembre 378, Paseo Colón, Apdo 44, Lima. T: 312339.
**OCIC Secretariado para América Latina,** Av 9 de Diciembre 378, Paseo Colón, Apdo 44, Lima. T: 312339.
**Servicio de Educación Cinematográfica (SEC),** Av 9 de Diciembre 378, Paseo Colón, Apdo 44, Lima. T: 312339.

*POLAND*

**Catholic Episcopal Commission for Film, Radio, TV and Theatre (Biuro Komisji Episkopatu Polski dla spraw Filmu, Radia, Telewizji i Teatru),** Aleja I Armii Wojska Polskiego 12, Warszawa X.

*PORTUGAL*

**Secretariado do Cinema,** Rua de Serpa Pinto 10D, Lisboa 2. T: 30172.

*PUERTO RICO*

**Sección de Cine,** Centro de MCS, Barro Obrero Station, Apdo 14125, Santurce, PR 00916. T: 7246471.

*SOUTH AFRICA*

**Billy Graham Evangelistic Films,** 835 Maritime House, 26 Loveday St, PO Box 4134, Johannesburg. T: 8382859,8366326.
**World Wide Pictures,** 835 Maritime House, 26 Loveday St, PO Box 4134, Johannesburg. T: 8382859, 8366326.

*SPAIN*

**Audifilm,** Albareda 15, Gerona. T: 203297.
**Bosco Films,** Fuencarral 13, Madrid 4.
**Catéfilms,** Condal 27, Barcelona 02.
**Departemento de Cine,** Secretariado de MCS, 4 Alfonso XI, Madrid 14. T: 2315400.
**Sallem-Films,** Victor Pradera, Madrid.
**San Pablo Films (PSSP),** Mayor 11, Madrid 13.
**Semana Internacional de Cine Religioso y de Valores Humanos (SEMINCI),** Edif Caja de Ahorros Provincial, Plaza de Madrid 1, Valladolid. T: 229493. (RC film festival).

*SWITZERLAND*

**Schweizer Film-Mission,** Leitung, CH-7299 Valzeina. T: (081)521166.
**Schweizerischer Protestant Film- und Radio-Verband,** Saatweisenstr 22, CH-8600 Dübendorf. T: (051)852070.
**Schweizerisches Katholisches Filmburo,** Wilfriedstr 15, Zürich 7. T: (051)320208.
**Vereinigung Ev-ref Kirchen der deutschsprachigen Schweiz fur kirchl Film-Radio- und Fernseharbeit,** Sulgenauweg 26, CH-3000 Bern 7. T: (031)461676/7.

*SYRIA*

**Office Catholique Syrien du Cinéma,** 10 Haret el Bagdadi, Kassaa, Dimashq.

*THAILAND*

**Catholic Film Office,** MCS Catholic National Committee, 251/1 Surahari Rd, Nakhon Ratchasima.

*UK OF GB & NI*

**Catholic Film Institute,** 14 Newton Place, Glasgow C3, Scotland. T: (041)3323701.
**Christian Cinema and Religious Film Society,** Sec, 6 Eaton Gate, London SW1. T: (01)730-2143. (Member of WACC).
**Concord Films Council,** Nacton, Ipswich, Suffolk. T: (0473)76012.
**Don Summers National Film Crusade,** PO Box 8, 37 Grove Rd, Fishponds, PO Box 4, Bristol BS99 7TF. T: (0272)654714.
**Fact & Faith Films,** Sec, Falcon Court, 32 Fleet St, London EC4Y 1NA. T: (01)351-6147. (Long-standing evangelistic series originated by Moody Institute of Science, introducing Christianity through scientific subjects or phenomena).
**His Paper Film Department,** PO Box 166, London SE19 3TG. (Charismatic films).
**International Christian Films,** 545 Harrow Rd, London W10 4RH. T: (01)969-3000.
**International Films,** Central London Christian Film Library, 235 Shaftesbury Av, London WC2H 8EL. T: (01)836-2254/5.
**Light and Life Films,** 13 Donegal Rd, Belfast BT12 5JJ, NI. T: 31550. (Also: 42 Fountainhall Rd, Edinburgh EH9 2LW).
**Midlands Evangelistic Film Unit,** 22 Westfield Rd, Hurst Green, Halesowen, Hereford and Worcester. T: (021)422-6158.
**Vision Screen Services,** Riverside House, N Farmbridge, Chelmsford, Essex.

*USA*

**Asian Screen,** Pres, PO Box 1432, Hollywood, CA 90028. T: (213)466-7187.
**Association Films,** 347 Madison Av, New York, NY 10017.
**Billy Graham Evangelistic Association,** 1300 Harmon Place, Minneapolis, MN 55403. T: (612)332-8081. (Numerous feature films, documentaries, etc, on subjects of evangelism, evangelistic crusades, evangelistic methods).
**Broadman Press & Films** 127 Ninth Av North, Nashville, TN 37203.
**Cathedral Films,** 2921 West Alameda Av, Burbank, CA 91505.
**Century Gospel Film Library,** PO Box 101, Souderton, PA 18964.
**Christian Films,** Box 565, La Habra, CA 90633.
**Christian Youth Cinema,** 279 Keswick Av, Glenside, PA 19038.
**Church-Craft Pictures,** 4222 Utah St, St Louis, MO 63116.
**Concordia Publishing House & Films,** 3558 South Jefferson Av, St Louis, MO 63118.(Conservative Lutheran).
**Family Films,** 582 Santa Monica Blvd, Hollywood, CA 90038.
**Films Department,** Augsburg Publishing House, 425 South Fourth St, Minneapolis 15, Minnesota. (Lutheran tradition).
**Films for Christ Association,** 1204 North Elmwood Av, Peoria, IL 61606.
**Good News Production,** Chester Springs, PA 19425.
**Gospel Films,** 2735 East Apple Av, PO Box 455, Muskegon, MI 49443. T: (616)773-3361. (Film of evangelistic content).
**Ideal Pictures Inc,** 58 East South Water St, Chicago, IL 60601.
**Insight Paulist Productions,** 17575 Pacific Coast Highway, Pacific Palisades, CA 90272. T: (213)454-0688. (Roman Catholic film production centre under Paulists).
**International Films,** Dir, (1021 East Winona Av, Warsaw, IN 46580), PO Box 618, Winona Lake, IL 46590. T: (219)267-5774. (Interdenominational; mainly films for youth evangelism).
**Ken Anderson Films,** Pres, PO Box 618, Winona Lake, IN 46590.
**Kent Films,** 511 West 2nd St, Dayton, OH 45402.
**Light & Life Films,** Box 271, Mt Prospect, IL 60057.
**Living Language Films,** 11040 Santa Monica Blvd, Los Angeles, CA 90025. T: (213)472-9511.
**National Catholic Office for Motion Pictures,** Suite 4200, 405 Lexington Av, New York, NY 10017. (All aspects of film).
**North African Crusades,** 741 Center Rd, Pittsburgh, PA 15239. (Film services).
**Religious Film Library,** 17 Park Place, New York.
**Roa's Films (Audio-visuals for Catholic education),** 1696 North Astor St, Milwaukee, WI 53202. T: (414)271-0861.
**Sacred Cinema/Valley Forge Films,** Chester Springs, PA 19425.
**Unusual Films,** Bob Jones University, Greenville, SC 29614. T: (803)242-5100
**World Horizon Films,** Maryknoll, Walsh Bldg, New York, NY 10545. (Catholic Foreign Mission Society of America).
**World Wide Pictures,** 2520 West Olive, Burbank, CA 91505. T: (213)843-1200.

*URUGUAY*

**Centro Católico del Espectaculo,** Cerrito 475, Montevideo. T: 85903.
**Centro de Cultura Filmica (CCF),** Torre a Madrices, Edf Juan XXIII, Apdo del Este 4310, Caracas. T: 815208.

*ZAIRE*

**Centre Catholique d'Action Cinématographique Zairois (CCACZ),** BP 936, Kinshasa. T: 2248 (Production and other aspects of feature and documentary films, under Roman Catholic auspices).
**Luluafilm,** BP 21, Kananga (Luluabourg).
**Service d'Images Chrétiennes Africaines (SICA),** Av des Huileries 478, BP 936, Kinshasa. T: 22248. (Specialized material on Africa).

# 13

# Clergy-lay & Clergy Organizations

*Definition.* Organizations of individuals for consultation and co-operation between clergy (priests, pastors, ministers), or clergy and laity, or clergy/laity/religious personnel, or missionary personnel; either within a single church or denomination, or interdenominational or ecumenical; priests' councils or senates, national priests' organizations, ministerial or clergy fellowships, ministers' fraternals, pastoral councils, pastoral consultative bodies, fellowships of foreign missionary personnel, Catholic national and diocesan synods; clergy recruitment organizations, clergy or lay employment bureaux. For women, see WOMEN IN THE ORDAINED MINISTRY. For religious personnel, see FEDERATIONS OF RELIGIOUS COMMUNITIES.

*ARGENTINA*

**Consejo Pastoral Nacional (CPN),** CEA, Paraguay 1867, Buenos Aires. (RC).
**Cruzada Sacerdotal Argentina,** Jujuy 1241, Buenos Aires. (Traditionalist).

*AUSTRALIA*

**Priests' Forum,** 10 Hamilton St, Bentheigh, Victoria 3204. (Progressivist).

*AUSTRIA*

**Arbeitsgemeinschaft Österreichischer Priesterräte,** Stephansplatz 6, A-1010 Wien. T: 524644. (National presbyteral council).
**Pastoralkommission Österreichs,** Stephansplatz 3, A-1010 Wien.

*BAHAMAS*

**Diocesan Pastoral Council,** PO Box 187, Nassau. (RC).
**Senate of Priests,** Our Lady of the Holy Souls, Deveaux St, South Youngtown. (RC).

*BELGIUM*

**Amitiés Sacerdotales,** Ry de Brabant 5, B-6358 Manage-Longsart. T: (064)552268.
**Bureau Européen des Délégués des Conseils Presbytéraux,** c/o Abbé Dhanis, Rue Joseph II 34, B-1040 Brussel. T: (02)511-1259,513-7796.
**Centre National des Vocations,** Rue Belliard 26, B-1040 Brussel. T: (02)512-1300.
**Flemish Interdiocesan Pastoral Council (Interdiocesaan Pastoraal Beraad, IPB),** Guimardstraat 5, B-1040 Brussel. T: (02)511-0585,512-3379.
**Ghent Informal Priests Group (Informele Priestergroep Gent),** Maisstraat 12, B-9000 Gent.

*BERMUDA*

**Bermuda Ministerial Association,** The Manse, Paget.

*BURUNDI*

**Union Apostolique et Culturelle des Prêtres Burundais (UACPB),** Grand Séminaire, BP 850, Bujumbura.

*CAMEROON*

**Association Interdiocésaine des Prêtres Indigènes (AIPI),** BP 93, Deschang.

*CANADA*

**National Federation of Senates of Priests,** English Sector, PO Box 1689, Charlottetown, PEI. (RC).

*CHILE*

**Comité Pastoral,** CECH, Cienfuegos 47, Casilla 13191 Correo 21, Santiago. T: 717733. (RC).
**Consejo Pastoral Nacional,** CECH, Cienfuegos 47, Casilla 13191 Correo 21, Santiago. T: 717733. (RC).

*CHINA (TAIWAN)*

**Taiwan Missionary Fellowship,** 272 Nanking East Rd, Section 3, PO Box 555, Taipei. T: 772521/2.

*COLOMBIA*

**Asociación Ministerial de Bogotá,** Calle 69 No 5-33, Apdo Aéreo 20236, Bogotá. T: 496997.
**Departemento de Ministerios Jerárquicos,** Av 39 No. 13-61 Apdo Aéreo 11086, Bogotá, DE. T: 453193. (RC).
**Federation of Evangelical Ministries of Colombia,** Apdo Aéreo 190, Sincelejo.
**Secretaria del Clero,** Depto de Ministerios Jerárquicos, Apdo Aéreo 51086, Bogotá, DE. (RC).
**Secretaria del Diaconado,** Depto de Ministerios Jerárquicos, Apdo Aéreo 51086. Bogotá, DE. (RC).

*CZECHOSLOVAKIA*

**Pacem in Terris Association of Catholic Priests (Sdruzení Katolickych Duchovních Pacem in Terris CSR),** Czech Secretariat, Spálená 8, 110 00 Praha 1. T: 293985. (Progressivist).
**Pacem in Terris Association of Catholic Priests (Sdruzení Katolickych Duchonvních Pacem in Terris, Federální Sekretariát),** Federal Secretariat, Spálená 8, 110 10 Praha 1. T: 293985. (Progressivist).
**Pacem in Terris Association of Catholic Priests (Sdruzení Katolickych Duchovních Pacem in Terris),** Slovak Secretariat, Kapitulská 1, 886 10 Bratislava. T: 30266. (Progressivist).

*DENMARK*

**Pastoral Council,** c/o Katolsk Bispekontor, Bredgade 69A, DK-1260 Kobenhavn K. T: (01)116080. (RC).
**Presbyteral Council,** c/o Katolsk Bispekontor, Bredgade 69A, DK-1260 Kobenhavn K. (01)116080. (RC).

*ECUADOR*

**Consejo Nacional de Presbiteros del Ecuador,** Apdo 2876, Quito.

*FIJI*

**Senate of Priests,** c/o Catholic Presbytery, PO Box 160, Ba.

*FRANCE*

**Association des Pasteurs de France (APF),** 47 Rue de Clichy, F-75009 Paris.

*FRENCH GUIANA*

**Conseil Presbytéral,** c/o Evêché, BP 378. Cayenne.

*GAMBIA*

**Pastoral Council,** PO Box 165, Bathurst. (RC).

*GERMANY, Federal Republic of*

**Arbeitsgemeinschaft der Priesterräten der Diözesen der BRD und West Berlins (AGPR),** An der Stadtkirche 8, D-4440. T: (02531)3288.
**Arbeitsgemeinschaft der Social-, Industrie- und Arbeiterpfarrer,** Ev Sozialakademie, D-5241 Friedewald über Betzborf (Sieg).
**Arbeitsgemeinschaft lutherischer Konferenzen und Konvente,** Berlinstr 2, D-31 Celle. (Lutheran groups).
**Arbeitsgemeinschaft von Priester- und Solidaritätsgruppen in der BRD (AGP),** Beethovenstr 28, D-6 Frankfurt.
**Bekenntnisbewegung 'Kein anderes Evangelium',** Worthstr 49, D-588 Lüdenscheid. (Clergy-lay, very conservative).
**Bensheimer Kreis (Kreis ehemaliger röm-kath Priester, die heute im evang Pfarr-oder Lehramt stehen),** Bahnhofstr 59, D-588 Lüdenscheid. (Ex-RC priests now Protestant pastors).
**Bruderrat Evangelischer Kirchen,** Geschäftsstelle, Marktplatz 8, D-714 Ludwigsburg. (Pastors).
**Bund Evangelischer Missionare,** Vogelsangstr 62, D-7000 Stuttgart 1. T: (0711)638131. (Association of Protestant Missionaries; begun 1921).
**Evangelische Michaelsbruderschaft,** Koppel 55, D-2 Hamburg 1. (Fraternity of high-church Protestant pastors and laity).
**Evangelischer Bund,** Hauptgeschäftsstelle und Konfessions-kindliches Institut, Eifelstr 35, D-614 Bensheim (Bergstrasse). (Mainly pastors. Conservative evangelical, anti-Catholic).
**Kirchliche Sammlung um Bibel und Bekenntnis (innerhalb der BRD),** D-2418 Ratzeburg. (Clergy-lay, conservative).
**Notgemeinschaft Evangelischer Deutscher,** Ludwigstr 8, Postfach 1107, D-7024 Bernhausen. (Clergy-lay, conservative, opposing modernism and the social gospel).
**Pfarrer-Gebets-Bruderschaft,** Postfach 80, D-3551 Wehrda bei Marburg. (Pastors' fraternal).
**Priesterkreise für Konziliare Erneuerung (PKE),** Untergasse 27, D-6374 Steinbach. (For conciliar renewal).
**Priester-Missionsbund,** Hermannstr 14, D-5100 Aachen. T: (0241)35321.

*GUADELOUPE*

**Conseil Pastoral,** c/o Evêché, BP 50, F-97-1 Basse-Terre. T: 811169. (RC).
**Conseil Presbytéral,** c/o Evêché, BP 50, F-97-1 Basse-Terre. T: 811169. (RC).

*GUATEMALA*

**Asociación Nacional de Pastores y Ministros Evangélicos,** Iglesia Presbiteriana El Mesías, 15 Calle A 13-06, Zona 1, Guatemala.
**Confederación de Sacerdotes y Seglares Diocesanos en Guatemala (COSDEGUA),** 15 Calle 34-24, Zona 5, Guatemala-Ciudad. (Progressivist).

*GUYANA*

**Pastoral Council,** Bishop's House, 27 Brickdam, Georgetown. (RC).
**Senate of Priests,** Bishop's House, 27 Brickdam, Georgetown. (RC).

*HOLY SEE*

**Pontifical Missionary Union of the Clergy & Religious (MPU),** International Secretariat, Propaganda Fide, 1 Via di Propaganda, I-00187 Roma.
**Sacred Congregation for Priests/SC per il Clero,** Cardinal Prefect, Palazzo delle Congregazioni, Piazza Pio XII 10, I-00193 Roma. T: 6982 int 4151.
**Sacred Congregation for Religious and Secular Institutes,** Cardinal Prefect, Palazzo Congregazioni, Piazzo Pio XII 10, I-00193 Roma. T: 6982 int 4128.

*HONG KONG*

**Pastoral Council,** c/o Catholic Mission, 16 Caine Rd, Hong Kong. T: H-232487.
**Senate of Priests,** c/o Catholic Mission, 16 Caine Rd, Hong Kong. T: H-232487.

*IRAQ*

**Alliance Sacerdotale Chaldéenne (Al Rabita al Kahnoutiya al Caldaniya),** Archevêché Chaldéen, Al Mawsil (Mosul).
**Prêtres du Christ-Roi,** Eglise Saint Thomas des Syriens Catholiques, Al Mawsil (Mosul).

*IRELAND*

**Irish Missionary Fellowship,** 95 Meadow Grove, Dundrum, Dublin 14.
**St Joseph's Young Priest Society,** 23 Merrion Square, Dublin 2. (RC).

*IVORY COAST*

**Secretariat Permanent du Clergé Africain (SPCA),** Centre Mgr Chappoulie, Yopoungon, Abidjan.

*JAMAICA*

**Pastoral Council,** PO Box 43, Kingston 6. (RC).
**Senate of Priests,** PO Box 43, Kingston 6. (RC).

*JAPAN*

**Fellowship of Christian Missionaries,** Kyobunkwan, 2 4-chome, Ginza, Chuo-ku, Tokyo 104. T: 11357.
**Japan Evangelical Missionary Association (JEMA),** 1 2-chome, Surugadai, Kanda, Chiyoda-ku, Tokyo.
**National Catholic Committee of Japan,** Rokubancho 10-1, Chiyoda-ku, Tokyo 102.
**Tokyo Pastoral Synod,** c/o Archbishop's House, 16-15 Sekiguchi 3-chome, Bunkyo-ku, Tokyo. (RC).

*KENYA*

**Priests' Association of Kenya,** Office: Jericho Parish, PO Box 48069, Nairobi. (RC).

*LEBANON*

**Association Sacerdotale Interrituelle,** Séminaire Mar Maroun, Ghazir. T: 955004.
**Prêtres du Christ-Roi,** Curé de la Paroisse St-Jean-Baptiste, Boochyriyé, Bayrut. (RC, Maronite).

*LUXEMBOURG*

**Conseil Presbytéral,** c/o Evêché, 4 Rue Génistre, BP 419, Luxembourg. T: 22069. (RC).

*MACAO*

**Conseil Presbytéral,** c/o Bispado, Macau. T: 3058. (RC).
**Macao Ministers' Fellowship,** 89-100 Av Hortae Costa, Macau.

*MALAWI*

**National Council of Priests,** Archbishop's House, PO Box 385, Blantyre. T: 8523. (RC).

*MALTA*

**Diocese of Gozo Pastoral Council,** Bishop's Curia, Rabat, Gozo. (RC).
**Diocese of Gozo Presbyteral Council,** Bishop's Curia, Rabat, Gozo. (RC).
**Malta Pastoral Council (Kunsill Pastorali),** Archbishop's Curia, Valletta. (RC).
**Malta Presbyteral Council (Kunsill Presbiterali),** Archbishop's Curia, Valletta. (RC).

*MARTINIQUE*

**Conseil Presbytéral,** c/o Archevêché, Route de Didier, Fort-de-France. T: 2070. (RC).

*MAURITIUS*

**Conseil Pastoral,** c/o Evêché, Rue Mgr Gonin, Port-Louis. T: 23068. (RC).
**Conseil Presbyteral,** c/o Evêché, Rue Mgr Gonin, Port-Louis. T: 23068,23360. (RC).

*MEXICO*

**Ministerios Jerárquicos,** Secretaria de Seminarios, c/o Seminario Palafoxiano, 44 Nte y JM Morelos—Col El Porvenir, Puebla. T: 23707. (RC).
**Sacerdotes para el Pueblo,** Apdo Postal 61-128, México 6, DF. (Progressivist).

*MONACO*

**Conseil Pastoral,** c/o Evêché de Monaco, 1 Rue de l'Abbaye, Monte Carlo. (RC).
**Conseil Presbytéral,** c/o Evêché de Monaco, 1 Rue de l'Abbaye, Monte Carlo. (RC).

*MOROCCO*

**Conseil Pastoral,** Archevêché Rabat, BP 258, Rabat. (RC).
**Conseil Presbytéral,** Archevêché Rabat, BP 258, Rabat. (RC).

*NETHERLANDS*

**Dutch Association for Religious Priests (Stichting Nederlandse Priester-Religieuzen, SNPR),** van Alkemadelaan 1, 's-Gravenhage. T: (070)244594.
**Hospitium Oecumenicum San Luchesio,** Waldeck Pyrmontlaan 9, Amsterdam-Zuid. T: (020)716861. (Clergy hostel).
**Institute for Aid to Clergy in Europe (Instituut voor Europese Priesterhulp),** Stokstraat 47, Maastricht. T: (0400)14244.
**Limburg Priests Group (Priestergroep Limburg),** Vrijthof 21, Echt (L). T: (04754)1659.
**National Pastoral Conference (Landelijk Pastoraal Overleg),** Biltstraat 121, Utrecht.

*NEW ZEALAND*

**National Association of Priests,** Catholic Presbytery, Nelson.

*PAPUA NEW GUINEA*

**Catholic Indigenous Priests' Conference,** Catholic Mission, Wewak, New Guinea.
**Conference of Indigenous Priests,** Bomana Seminary, PO Box 1717, Boroko.
**Missionary Association of Papua and New Guinea,** PO Box 1627, Boroko.

*PERU*

**Comisión Episcopal del Clero (CEC),** c/o Arzobispado, Plaza de Armas, Apdo Postal 1512, Lima. T: 271252.
**Movimiento ONIS Sacerdotal/Oficina Nacional de Información Social (ONIS),** c/o Parroquia de San Juan Apostol, Aragón 280, Pueblo Libre, Lima. (Progressivist).

*PHILIPPINES*

**Philippine Priests Incorporated (PPI),** Sta Mesa, Magsaysay Blvd, PO Box 1525, Manila. T: 618272. (Progressivist).
**Philippines Missionary Fellowship,** PO Box 3349, Manila.

*PUERTO RICO*

**Asociación Puertorriquena de Sacerdotes,** Proyecto La Perla, Calle Hemetrio (Daly), Country Club, Rio Pedras.

*REUNION*

**Conseil Presbytéral,** c/o Evêché, 42 Rue de Paris, BP 55, St Denis. T: 212849. (RC).

*RWANDA*

**Conseil Pastoral,** Université Nationale du Rwanda, BP 117, Butare. (RC).

*ST LUCIA*

**Council of Priests,** c/o Bishop's House, Castries. (RC).
**Pastoral Council,** c/o Bishop's House, Castries. (RC).

*SAMOA*

**Senate of Priests,** Diocese of Apia, PO Box 532, Apia. (RC).

*SEYCHELLES*

**Conseil Presbytéral,** c/o Evêché de Port-Victoria, PO Box 43, Port-Victoria, Mahé. (RC).

*SINGAPORE*

**Senate of Priests,** c/o Archbishop's House, 31 Victoria St, Singapore 7. T: 28818. (RC).

*SOLOMON ISLANDS*

**National Presbyteral Council,** PO Box 237, Honiara. (RC).
**Pastoral Council of the Church in the Solomon Islands,** PO Box 237, Honiara. (RC).

*SOMALIA*

**Pastoral Council,** c/o Vicariato Apostolico, CP 273, Mogadisho. (RC).
**Presbyteral Council,** c/o Vicariato Apostolico, CP 273, Mogadisho. (RC).

*SOUTH AFRICA*

**Interdenominational African Ministers' Association of Southern Africa (IDAMASA),** PO Box 39, Johannesburg, Transvaal.
**Southern African Council of Priests (SACP),** PO Box 17054, Hillbrow, Transvaal. T: 419059. (RC).

*SPAIN*

**Asamblea Conjunta de Obispos y Sacerdotes,** Secretariado Nacional del Clero, Cuesta de Santo Domingo 5, Madrid 13. (RC).
**Hermandad Sacerdotal Española,** San Marcos 3, Madrid. T: 2224572. (Traditionalist).
**Obra de Cooperación Sacerdotal Hispanoamericana (OCSHA),** Bosque 9, Apdo 14133, Madrid 3. (RC).
**Synod of the Diocese of Seville,** Palacio Arzobispal, Sevilla. (RC).

*SURINAM*

**Presbyteral Council (Priesters Raad),** c/o Bisschopshuis, Gravenstraat 12, POB 1230, Paramaribo. T: 73306. (RC).

*SWEDEN*

**Presbyteral Council,** Valhallavägen 132, Fack 102, 40 Stockholm 5. T: (08)618034. (RC).

*SWITZERLAND*

**Fraternité Sacerdotale Saint Pie X,** CH-1908 Econe-par-Riddes.
**Schweizerische Verband Evangelischer Arbeiter und Angestellter (SVEA),** Zentralsekretariat, Höhenring 29, CH-8052 Zürich-Seebach. T: (051) 466424. (Evangelists, lay preachers and workers).
**Schweizerischer Reformierter Pfarrverein,** Zentralpräsident, CH-3645 Gwatt bei Thun. T: (033) 363131. (Association of pastors).
**Synode des Catholiques Suisses,** Secrétariat Central, Baselstr 58, CH-4500 Solothurn.
**Synode des Catholiques Suisses,** Secrétariat Romand, Rue des Alpes 49, CH-1700 Fribourg.
**Vereinigung Reformierter Schweizer Auslandspfarrer,** Sek, Aemtlerstr 23, CH-8003 Zürich. T: (051)334488.

*TANZANIA*

**Association of Diocesan Priests of Tanzania (UMAWATA),** PO Box 640, Morogoro.

*TRINIDAD & TOBAGO*

**Council of Priests,** 27 Maraval Rd, St Clair, Trinidad. (RC).

*TUNISIA*

**Conseil Pastoral,** Prélature de Tunis, 4 Rue d'Alger, Tunis. (RC).

*UK OF GB & NI*

**Additional Curates Society,** Sec, 14 Rothamsted Av, Harpenden, Herts. T: 3512.
**Advisory Council for the Church's Ministry (ACCM),** Chief Sec, Church House, Dean's Yard, London SW1P 3NZ. T: (01)222-9011. (Church of England recruitment).
**Association of Church Fellowships,** Sec, ACF Office, 12 Abbey Square, Chester. T: 20711. (Clergy-laity).
**Catholic Priests' Association,** St George Presbytery, Eastbourne Rd, Polegate, East Sussex.
**Church Patronage Trust,** Sec, 3 Amen Court, London EC4M 7BU. T: (01)248-1817.
**Church Vacancies,** 17 Denmark St, Diss, Norfolk. T: 3419. (Regular printed lists of vacant Church of England benefices).
**Clergy Appointments Advisor,** Fielden House, Little College St, London SW1P 3SH. T: (01) 839-7544/5.
**Evangelical Churchmen's Ordination Council (ECOC),** Greyfriars Vicarage, Reading, Berks RG1 1EH.
**Evangelical Fellowship of the Anglican Communion (EFAC),** Gen Sec, 12 Weymouth St, London W1N 3FB. T:(01)580-1867. (Founded 1961).
**Fellowship of Evangelical Churchman,** Sec, St John's Vicarage, London SE8. T: (01)692-2857.
**Islington Clerical Conference,** Pres, St Mary's Vicarage, Upper St, London N1. T: (01)226-3400. (Begun 1827. Originally clergy, now clergy-laity).
**National Conference of Priests,** St Therese's Presbytery, Southdown Rd, Port Talbot, Glamorgan, South Wales.
**Ordination Candidates' Exhibition Fund,** 8 Victoria Rd, Chingfield, London E4.
**Parochial Clergy Association,** Sec, Minal Rectory, Marlborough, Wilts. T: (06725)2096.
**Peache Trustees,** Sec, West Field, Southern Rd, Thame, Oxon. T: (084421)2026. (Benefices).
**Simeon's Trustees,** Hon Sec, 1 Selwyn Gardens, Cambridge CB3 9AX, T: (0223)54774. (Benefices).
**Southport Evangelical Conference,** Sec, St Helen's Vicarage, Lancs. T: 22067.

*USA*

**Academy of Parish Clergy (APC),** PO Box 86, Princeton, NJ 08540.
**Alaskan Native Brotherhood (ANB),** Grand Camp President, c/o Mount Edgecumbe Hospital, Sitka, AL 99839. (Amerindians).
**American Ministerial Association,** PO Box 1252, York, PA 17405.
**Black Ecumenical Commission of Massachusetts,** Dir, Room 302, 14 Beacon St, Boston, MA 02108.
**Christian Hope Indian Eskimo Fellowship (CHIEF),** PO Box 2600, Orange, CA 92669. T: (714) 997-3920.
**Council of Black Clergy,** 2200 Locust St, Philadelphia, PA 19103.
**Evangelical Ministers Fellowship International,** 105 West Madison St, Chicago, IL 60602
**International Ministerial Federation,** Exec Sec, 5290 North Sherman Av, Fresno, CA 93726. T: (209)222-9338. (Also: Box 8000, St Petersburg, FL 33738).
**National Committee of Black Churchmen,** Exec Dir, 110 East 125th St, New York. NY 10035.
**National Conference of Black Churchmen (NCBC),** Suite 1005, 200 West 57th St, New York, NY 10019. T: (212)581-3860. (Also: 671 Beckwith St, SW, Atlanta, Georgia).
**National Federation of Priests' Councils(NFPC),** 1307 South Wabash Av, Chicago, IL 60605. T: (312)427-0115. (RC).
**National Fellowship of Indian Workers,** 3025 Fir St, San Diego, CA 92102. (For Amerindians).
**National Office for Black Catholics (NOBC),** 734 15th St, NW, Washington, DC 20005.
**Self-Supporting Priesthood Project,** Idaho Lay Ministry Project, 107 East Fort St, Boise, ID 83702.
**Serra International,** 22 West Monroe St, Chicago, IL 60603.
**Union of Black Episcopalians,** 729 8th SE, Washington, DC 20003.
**United Indians of Nebraska,** 11924 Poppleton Plaza, Omaha, NE 68114. T: (402)334-9477/8. (Amerindians).
**US Catholic Institutions for the Training of Candidates for the Priesthood,** 1717 Massachusetts Av, NW, Washington, DC 20036.

*URUGUAY*

**Mesa Nacional de Presbiteros,** c/o Arzobispado, Treinta y Tres 1368, Montevideo. (RC).

*WALLIS & FUTUNA ISLANDS*

**Conseil Presbytéral,** c/o Evêché, Lano, via Nouméa. (RC).

*YUGOSLAVIA*
**Association of Officers of the Slovak Evangelical Church,** Novi Sad. (Government-controlled).
**Association of Reformed Christian Priests,** Novi Sad. (Begun 1959 ; government-controlled).
**Cyrillo-Methodian Association of Priests,** Pazin. (One of 6 government-controlled associations of Roman Catholic priests).
**Federation of Associations of Orthodox Priests of Yugoslavia,** Beograd. (Begun 1946 ; 23 diocesan associations, with 1,700 priests ; government-controlled).

# 14
# Confessional Conciliarism

*Definition.* Councils of churches or denominations belonging to a world confessional family (world family of churches) of one particular ecclesiastical tradition ; international councils, federations, alliances ; Roman Catholic world-wide congregations of dioceses ; confessional conciliarism, collegiality and consultation.
World confessional families, renamed Christian world communions since 1979, number at least 45.

*ARGENTINA*
**Consejo Luterano Rioplatense (Lutheran Council of the River Plate),** Esmeralda 162, Buenos Aires. T : 457520.

*CANADA*
**Lutheran Council in Canada,** Gen Sec, 500-365 Hargrave St, Winnipeg, Manitoba R3B 2K3. T : (204)942-0096.

*EGYPT*
**Coptic Patriarchal Synod,** 34 Rue Ibn Sandar, 14 Port de Koubbeh, Al Qahirah. T : 821740. (RC).

*ETHIOPIA*
**Oriental Orthodox Churches Conference (Conference of the Heads of the Oriental Orthodox Churches),** PO Box 2717, Addis Abeba. (Armenian, Syrian, Coptic, Ethiopian).

*GERMAN DEMOCRATIC REPUBLIC*
**Vereinigte Ev-Lutherische Kirche in der DDR,** Pfludensberg, Postfach 139, DDR-59 Eisenach. T : 5226.

*GERMANY, Federal Republic of*
**Vereinigte Ev-Lutherische Kirche Deutschlands (VELKD),** Postfach 1060, D 3 Hannover 1. T : (0511)623061/4.

*HOLY SEE*
**Council for the Public Affairs of the Church/ Consiglio per gli Affari Pubblici della Chiesa,** Palazzo Apostolico, I-00120 Città del Vaticano. T : 6983274. (Deals with Portuguese territories).
**Sacred Congregation for Bishops/SC per i Vescovi/SC pro Episcopis,** Palazzo delle Congregazioni 10, Piazza Pio XII, I-00193 Roma, Italy. T : 6983311.
**Sacred Congregation for the Oriental Churches/ SC per le Chiese Orientali/SC pro Ecclesiis Orientalibus,** Palazzo dei Convertendi, Via della Conciliazione 34, I-00193 Roma, Italy. T : 6982 int 4293. (Eastern-rite Catholics).

*IRAQ*
**Chaldean Patriarchal Synod,** Chaldean Catholic Patriarchate, Baghdad. T : 8880689. (RC).

*LEBANON*
**Armenian Patriarchal Synod,** Jeitaoui, 2400 Bayrut. T : 329391. (RC).
**Maronite Patriarchal Synod,** Dimane. T : 675107. (RC).
**Syrian Patriarchal Synod,** Rue Damas, BP 118879, Bayrut. T : 381532. (RC).

*NETHERLANDS*
**International Association for Liberal Christianity and Religious Freedom (IARF),** 40 Laan Copes Van Cattenburch, 's-Gravenhage. (Begun 1900).

*SWEDEN*
**International Federation of Free Evangelical Churches/Internationaler Bund Freier Evangelischer Gemeinden,** Sek, Tegnergatan 8, Box 6302, S-113 81 Stockholm. T : (08)349680.

*SWITZERLAND*
**Bund Ev-Lutherischer Kirchen in der Schweiz und im Fürstentum Liechtenstein,** Sec, Hirschwiesenstr 9, CH-8057 Zürich. T : (01)281162.
**International Conference of Old Catholic Bishops,** Sec, Willadingweg 39, CH-3000 Bern.
**Interorthodox Preparatory Commission,** Gen Sec, Great & Holy Council of the Orthodox Church, Orthodox Centre of the Ecumenical Patriarchate. 37 Chemin de Chambésy, CH-1292 Chambésy, Genève.
**Lutheran World Federation (LWF),** Gen Sec, 150 Route de Ferney, CH-1211 Genève 20. T : 333400.
**World Alliance of Reformed Churches (Presbyterian & Congregational) (WARC),** Gen Sec, 150 Route de Ferney, CH-1211 Genève 20. T : 333400. (Including former World Presbyterian Alliance, and International Congregational Council).

*SYRIA*
**Greek-Melkite Patriarchal Synod,** BP 22249, Bab-Charki, Dimashq. T : 223129. (RC).

*TURKEY*
**Ecumenical Patriarchate of Constantinople (Rum Ortodoks Patrikhanesi),** Sadrazam Ali Pasha Caddesi 35, Fener (Phanar), Istanbul.

*UK OF GB & NI*
**Anglican Consultative Council (ACC),** Sec Gen, 14 Great Peter St, London SW1P 3NQ. T : (01)222-2851/2.
**Baptist World Alliance (BWA),** 4 Southampton Row, London WC1B 4AB.
**Friends World Committee for Consultation (FWCC),** Gen Sec, Drayton House, 30 Gordon St, London WC1H 0AX. T : (01)388-0497.
**Lambeth Conference of Bishops of the Anglican Communion,** Archbishop of Canterbury, Lambeth Palace, London SE1 7JU. T : (01)928-8282.
**Lutheran Council of Great Britain,** Sec, 8 Collingham Gardens, London SW5. T : (01)373-9604.

*USA*
**Ancient Church of the East,** Catholicos Patriarch, 554 Argallo Drive, San Francisco, CA 94132. (Assyrian, Nestorian).
**Anglican Orthodox Communion,** Presiding Bishop, 323 East Walnut St, PO Box 128, Statesville, NC 28677. T : (704)873-8365.
**Baptist World Alliance (BWA),** Gen Sec, 1628 16th St, NW, Washington, DC 20009.
**Council of Christian Communions,** Dir, 1836 Fairmont, Cincinnati, OH 45214.
**Free Methodist World Fellowship,** Exec Sec, Winona Lake, IN 46950. T : (615)256-1424. (A single denomination).
**International Convention of Christian Churches,** Exec Sec, Box 19136, Indianapolis, IN 46219. (Disciples of Christ).
**International New Thought Alliance (INTA),** 7015 Sunset Blvd, Hollywood, CA 90028. (Begun 1914).
**Lutheran Council in the USA,** Gen Sec, 315 Park Av South, New York, NY 10010. T : (212)677-3950.
**Mennonite World Conference,** Pres, 3003 Benham Av, Elkart, IN 46514. T : (219)523-1385.
**Pentecostal World Conference,** Chairman, 1445 Boonville Av, Springfield, MO 65802.
**Reformed Ecumenical Synod (RES),** Gen Sec, 1677 Gentian Drive SE, Grand Rapids, MI 49508.
**World Methodist Council (WMC),** Gen Sec, PO Box 518, Lake Junaluska, NC 28745.

# 15
# Continental Conciliarism

*Definition.* Interdenominational or ecumenical councils of churches or denominations and dioceses of different ecclesiastical traditions, for a single continent, sub-continent or quasi-continent ; councils, federations, alliances ; continent-wide conciliarism, collegiality and consultation.
There are about 27 continent-wide multidenominational councils of churches.

*BARBADOS*
**Caribbean Conference of Churches (CCC),** Gen Sec, PO Box 616, Bridgetown.

*CHILE*
**Alianza Latinoamericana de Iglesias Cristianas (Latin American Alliance of Christian Churches),** Arauco 890, Chillán.

*COLOMBIA*
**Consejo Episcopal Latinoamericano (CELAM),** Calle 78 No 11-17, Apdo Aéreo 5278, Bogotá, DE. T : 357041.

*FIJI*
**Pacific Conference of Churches (PCC),** Gen Sec, 4 Thurston St, PO Box 208, Suva. T : 311335.

*GHANA*
**Symposium of Episcopal Conferences of Africa and Madagascar (SECAM)/Symposium des Conférences Episcopales d'Afrique et de Madagascar (SECAM),** PO Box 7530, Accra-North. (Also : PO Box 9156, Airport, Accra. T : 27347).

*HONG KONG*
**Federation of Asian Bishops' Conferences (FABC),** Central Secretariat, PO Box 2984, Hong Kong. T : H-221071.

*KENYA*
**All Africa Conference of Churches (AACC),** Gen Sec, Waiyaki Way, PO Box 14205, Nairobi. T : 62601/2/3/4/5.
**Association of Evangelicals of Africa and Madagascar (AEAM),** Ralph Bunche Rd, PO Box 49332, Nairobi. T : 21894.
**Organization of African Independent Churches (OAIC),** Organizing Sec, PO Box 21570, Nairobi. T : 567849,23649.

*LEBANON*
**Middle East Council of Churches (MECC),** Rue Makhoul, Immeuble Dib, BP 5376, Bayrut. T : 344894. (Formerly Near East CC).

*NETHERLANDS*
**ICCC European Alliance,** c/o Frederiksplein 24, Amsterdam 1002. T : 248271.

*PUERTO RICO*
**Latin American Council of Churches in Formation/Movimiento pro Unidad Evangélica Lati-** noamerica **(UNELAM),** Apdo Aéreo 5491, Puerta-de-Tiera, San Juan, PR 00906. (Ecumenical ; created 1978).

*SINGAPORE*
**Christian Conference of Asia (CCA),** Gen Sec, 480 Lorong 2, Toa-Payoh, Singapore 12.
**Far Eastern Council of Christian Churches (FECCC),** Zion Bldg, 5 Tavistock Av, Singapore 19.

*SURINAM*
**Caribbean Council of Christian Churches,** PO Box 478, Paramaribo.

*SWITZERLAND*
**Conference of European Churches (CEC),** 150 Route de Ferney, CH-1211 Genève 20. T : 333400.
**Consilium Conferentiarum Episcopalium Europae (CCEE) (Conseil des Conférences Episcopales Européennes),** Klosterhof 6b, CH-9000 St Gallen.

*TOGO*
**Conférence des Eglises de Toute l'Afrique (CETA/AACC),** Secrétariat Ouest-Africain, Rue Seth Harlley-Kodjoviakope, BP 2268, Lomé.

*UK OF GB & NI*
**European Evangelical Alliance,** 19 Draycott Place, London SW3 2SJ. T : (01)584-9333.

*USA*
**Standing Conference of Canonical Orthodox Bishops in the Americas,** Chairman, 8005 Ridge Blvd, Brooklyn, NY 11209. T : (212)745-8481.

# 16
# Correspondence & Radiophonic Schools

*Definition.* Christian mass educational courses with individual postal feedback ; instructional courses by post, or by radio/TV with enrolment and local instructors or postal feedback : radio (radiophonic) schools, TV schools (teleschools, telecentres), radio/ TV correspondence courses, radio literacy courses ; Bible instruction, evangelistic, theological, vocational, educational, religious teaching ; Sunday-school by post.
In this field, there are over 320 centres and organizations of major significance.
In addition to those shown below, there are in most countries branches of the major Protestant organizations specializing in Bible correspondence courses.

*ALGERIA*
**Cercles Bibliques,** Centre Diocésain, Section Théologie, 5 Chemin des Glycines, El Djezair (Alger). (Roman Catholic).

*ANGOLA*
**Escola Bíblica de Emaus (Emmaus BCC Centre),** CP 107, Luso.

*ARGENTINA*
**Asociación Latinoamericana de Educación Radiofónica (ALER),** Buenos Aires.
**Centro de Promoción Humana del Nordeste (CEPRHU),** Reconquista, Prov de Santa Fe. (RC radiophonic school for northeast Argentina's uneducated farmers).
**Instituto de Cultura Popular (INCUPO),** Casilla 30, Reconquista, Prov de Santa Fe. (RC radiophonic school, NE Argentina, for uneducated farmers).

*AUSTRALIA*
**Living Word Correspondence Courses,** World Outreach, PO Box 10, Tabulam, NSW 2470. (Work with Aborigines. Also : PO Box 105, Carlingford, NSW 2118).
**Postal Sunday School,** 6 Orchid St, Guildford, NSW.
**Voice of Melody and Bible School of the Air,** 25 Ray Rd, Epping, NSW.

*AUSTRIA*
**Light of Life BCC Centre,** Beckmanngasse 66/48, Wien 15.

*BAHAMAS*
**Emmaus BCC Centre,** PO Box 436, Marsh Harbour, Abaco.

*BANGLADESH*
**Bangladesh BCC Centre,** Principal, PO Manikganj, Dacca District.

*BARBADOS*
**Light of Life BCC Centre,** Ebenezer Manse, St Philip 2.

*BELGIUM*
**Le Monde à Venir,** BP 31, B-6000 Charleroi. (Worldwide Church of God).

*BERMUDA*
**Emmaus BCC Centre,** PO Box 659, Hamilton.

*BOLIVIA*
**Acción Cultural Loyola (ACLO),** Casilla 155, Sucre. T : 2230. (RC radiophonic school in Quechua language ; 10,000 audience).
**Centro Teórico de Capacitación de Adultos** (CETCAR), Emisoras Bolivia, Calle Potosí 421, Casilla 525, Oruro. T : 52110. (RC).
**Departamento de Investigación y Promoción Social San Rafael,** Radio San Rafael, Casilla 546, Cochabamba. T : 4495. (RC radiophonic school).
**Escuelas Radiofónicas de Bolivia (ERBOL),** Oficina de MCS, Casilla 4064, La Paz. T : 41920. (RC radiophonic school ; 1,320 telecentres, 18,000 enrolled).
**Escuelas Radiofónicas de Radioemisoras Juan XXIII,** Vicariato de Chiquitos, Correo Central, San Ignacio de Velasco. (44 groups, 1,000 peasants. RC).
**Escuelas Radiofónicas Fides,** Radio Fides, Casilla 5782, La Paz. T : 24422. (RC ; La Paz suburbs).
**Escuelas Radiofónicas Pío XII,** Radio Pío XII, Casillo 434, Oruro. (RC).
**Escuelas Radiofónicas San Gabriel,** Radio San Gabriel, Casilla 4792, Peñas, La Paz. (RC ; 25 telecentres, 161 schools, 2,000 students).
**Escuelas Radiofónicas San Miguel,** Radio San Miguel, Casilla 9, Riberalta-Beni. T : 5. (Educational programming ; RC).
**Estudios Bíblicos per Correspondencia,** Cajón 514, Cochabamba.

*BRAZIL*
**Escolas Radiofônicas,** Uruguaiana, RS, (RC).
**Movimento de Educação de Base (MEB),** Rua São Clemente 385, ZC-02 Rio de Janeiro, GB. (RC mass-education radiophonic school, 1,798 centres, 31,083 enrolled).
**Sistema Educativo Radiofônico de Bragança (SERB),** Av Barão do Rio Branco s/n, Bragança (Guamá), PA.
**Sistema Radioeducativo de Santarém (SIRESEME),** Trav dos Mártires s/n, Santarém, PA.

*BURUNDI*
**Light of Life BCC Centre,** PO Box 122, Bujumbura.

*CANADA*
**BCC Department,** Latin American Mission, Box 33, Station F, Toronto 5, Ontario.
**Light of Life,** Ukrainian Missionary & Bible Society, PO Box 126, Saskatoon, Saskatchewan.
**Salvation Army Bible Studies,** Education Dept, 37 Dundas St E, Toronto 2, Ontario.

*CHAD*
**Emmaus BCC Centre,** Mission Evangélique, Doba, par Moundou.

*CHILE*
**Escuelas Radiofónicas Santa Clara,** Radio La Voz de la Costa, Casilla 5, Osorno.
**Fundación Radio Escuela para el Desarrollo Rural (La Voz de la Costa),** Misión de Rahue, Casilla Postal 5-0, Osorno. T : 3518.
**Instituto Nacional de Acción Poblacional (INAP),** Principe de Gales 87, Casilla 13508, Correo 15, Santiago. (Teleclubs, educational TV programmes).
**Pontificia Universidad de Chile (Channel 13, TV),** Avda Bernardo O'Higgins 340, Casilla 114D, Santiago de Chile. (12,000 enrolled).
**Secretariado de Communicación Social (SEDECOS),** Cienfuegos 15, CP 9990, Santiago 1. T : 713217. (Mass education ; RC).

*CHINA (TAIWAN)*
**Living World Bible Correspondence School,** c/o Overseas Radio & Television, Inc, PO Box 37003, Taipei.

*COLOMBIA*
**Acción Cultural Popular (ACPO),** Calle 20, No 9-45, Apdo Aéreo 7170, Bogotá, DE. T : 420543. (22,212 RC radiophonic schools, with 169,696 enrolled, over 4 stations).
**Cursos de Correspondencia,** Emmaus BCC Centre, Apdo Aéreo 14818, Bogotá 1, DE.

*COSTA RICA*
**Curso de Correspondencia,** Apdo 1307, San José.

*DOMINICA*
**Emmaus BCC Centre,** PO Box 103, Roseau.

*DOMINICAN REPUBLIC*
**Radio ABC Radio Schools,** Arzobispado de Santo Domingo, Casilla 186, Santo Domingo. T : 99203. (150,000 enrolled).
**Radio Santa María,** Casa Curial, Santo Cerro, La Vega. (RC radiophonic schools).

*ECUADOR*
**Academia Christiana del Aire,** Dir, Casilla 691, Quito.
**Escuelas Radiofónicas de Pichincha,** Pichincha, Tabacundo. (RC).
**Escuelas Radiofónicas Populares (formerly Escuelas Radiofónicas de Rio Bamba),** Rio Bamba. (RC).
**Radio Federación de Centros Shuaras,** Sucúa. (RC radiophonic schools ; 14,000 members).

*EL SALVADOR*
**Bible Correspondence Department,** Apdo 557, San Salvador.
**Escuelas Radiofónicas de El Salvador,** Radio YSAX, 2a Av Sur 102, Altos, San Salvador. T : 218011/2. (RC).

*ETHIOPIA*
**Light of Life BCC Centre,** Emmaus Centre, SIM, Box 127, Addis Abeba.

*FAEROE ISLANDS*
**Emmaus BCC Centre,** Tórshavn.

*FIJI*
**Living Word Correspondence Courses,** World Outreach, PO Box 29, Tavua, Fiji.

*FRANCE*
**Cours Bibliques par Correspondance,** Centre de Formation Chrétienne, 8 Villa du Parc Montsouris,

F-75 Paris. (Evangelical Alliance).
**Etudes Agricoles par Correspondance,** 271 Av de Grande-Bretagne, F-31 Toulouse 03 (Haute Garonne). T: 61423387.
**Formation Oecuménique Interconfessionelle (FOI),** Dir, 2 Place Gailleton, F-69002 Lyon. (Correspondence courses).
**La Chaine (Association Radiophonique pour l'Eglise du Silence),** BP 79, F-92405 Courbevoie.
**Les Cours Legendre,** 5 Blvd Morland, Paris 4. T: 272-3365,3147. (Correspondence).
**L'Eau Vive BCC Department,** Principal, 63 Rue St Gabriel, 51 Lille.

*FRENCH GUIANA*
**Emmaus BCC Centre,** BP 127, Cayenne.

*GERMANY, Federal Republic of*
**Servicio Radiofónico para Latina América (SERPAL),** Bonner Platz 1/III, D-8000 München 23. T: 3001316. (Formerly Radiodienst Vox Christiana. Films and radiophonic programmes for Latin America).

*GHANA*
**BCC Department,** WEC Mission, PO Box 5, Kpandai, via Yendi.
**Radio Bible School,** Emmaus BCC Centre, PO Box 1958, Kumasi.

*GRENADA*
**Emmaus BCC Centre,** PO Box 68, St George's.

*GUATEMALA*
**Escuelas Radiofónicas,** Radio Chortis, Jocotan, Dpto Chiquimula. (RC).
**Escuelas Radiofónicas La Voz del Hogar,** 13 Calle 2-52, Zona 1, Guatemala City. T: 85592. (RC).
**Federación Guatemalteca de Escuelas Radiofónicas (FGER),** Edificio Recinos, 8a Calle 11-13, Z 1 of 303, Guatemala. T: 20650 ext 50. (Also: 2a Calle, 4-80, Zona 9, Apdo Postal 13-29, Guatemala City. T: 67982). (RC).

*HONDURAS*
**Escuelas Radiofónicas Suyapa y Acción Cultural Popular Hondureña,** Av República de Chile 516, Barrio San Rafaél, Apdo Postal C-24, Tegucigalpa, DC. T: 21401. (RC).

*HONG KONG*
**Living Word BCC,** World Outreach, Dir, 9th Floor, 102 Macdonnell Rd, PO Box 13448, GPO.

*ICELAND*
**Light of Life BCC Centre,** Asvallagata 13, Box 243, Reykjavík.

*INDIA*
**BCC Department,** India Every Home Crusade, Principal, Q-3 Green Park Extension, New Delhi 16.
**Bible Correspondence Centre,** Principal, Mission Compound, Vellore, North Arcot District, Tamil Nadu.
**Bible Correspondence Department,** Box 66, Vellore, North Arcot District, Tamil Nadu.
**Christian Life Correspondence Course,** Good News Centre, Post Box 168, 37 Cantonment Rd, Lucknow, UP.
**Emmaus BCC Centre,** Principal, 25A Rundall Rd, Veprey PO, Madras 7.
**Institute for Home Studies,** De Nobili College, Poona 14. (Courses in Christianity in English and Indian languages).
**Nepali BCC Centre,** Principal, PO Box 39, Ranchi 1, Bihar.
**Southern Asia Bible Institute BCC Department,** Dir, PO Box 36, Bangalore 1, Mysore State.
**U-Search-U-Find BCC Centre,** Principal, Graceville, Observatory Lane, Trivandrum 1, Kerala.
**Way of Truth BCC Centre,** Principal, Box 26, Baramati, Poona District, Maharashtra State.

*INDONESIA*
**Living Word Bible Correspondence School,** World Outreach, PO Box 171, Bandung.
**Terang Hidup BCC Centre,** Kotak Pos 156, Bandung.

*IRAN*
**Good News Ministries,** PO Box 2276, Tehran.

*IRELAND*
**Emmaus BCC Centre,** 6 Ashdale Park, South Douglas Rd, Cork.

*ITALY*
**Centro Cattolico Radiofonico (CCR),** Ente dello Spettacolo, Via della Conciliazione 2c, I-00193 Roma. T: 561775,564132.
**Corso Biblico per Corrispondenza,** Centro di Cultura Biblica 'La Voce della Speranza' (The Voice of Hope), Lungotevere Michelangelo 7, I-00192 Roma. (Seventh-day Adventist).
**Corso Biblico Superiore 'La Via della Salvezza'** (The Way of Salvation), Ecumenical Centre 'Ut unum sint', Via Antonino Pio 75, I-00145 Roma. (RC; Sisters of St Paul).
**Corso Quadriennale,** Istituto di Teologia per Corrispondenza, Ecumenical Centre 'Ut unum sint', Via Antonio Pio 75, I-00145 Roma.
**La Via Della Vita (The Way of Life),** Crociata dell'Evangelo per Ogni Casa, Via Palestro 30, I-00185 Roma.

*IVORY COAST*
**Light of Life BCC Centre,** Mission Protestante, BP 585, Bouaké.

*JAMAICA*
**Emmaus BCC Centre,** Jamaica Bible School, Box 141, Manelville.

*JAPAN*
**Good Shepherd Movement,** Kawaramchi-Sanjo, Kyoto 604. (Correspondence courses in religion on national radio/TV; Maryknoll).
**Voice of Prophecy,** 846 Kami Kawai-cho, Hodogaya-ku, Yokohama-shi 241.

*KENYA*
**Correspondence Course Department,** Nairobi Pentecostal Bible College, Garden Estate, Thika Rd, PO Box 30202, Nairobi. T: Ruaraka 2391. (Pentecostal; 7,400 enrolled).
**Living Word Correspondence Courses,** World Outreach, PO Box 30791, Nairobi.

*KOREA, South*
**Living Word Correspondence Courses,** World Outreach, IPO Box 1442, Soul.

*LEBANON*
**BCC,** Middle East Lutheran Ministry, PO Box 2496, Bayrut.
**Light of Life BCC Centre,** PO Box 3276, Bayrut.

*LIBERIA*
**Emmaus BCC Centre,** ELWA, PO Box 192, Monrovia.

*MADAGASCAR*
**Emmaus BCC Centre,** BP 351, Tananarive.

*MALAWI*
**Emmaus BCC Centre,** PO Box 688, Blantyre.

*MALAYSIA*
**Light of Life BCC Centre,** North Borneo Mission, Principal, Box 108, Kuching, Sarawak.

*MEXICO*
**Asociación Nacional de Radio-escuelas,** ACM, Serapio Rendon 43, México 4, DF. (RC).
**El Camino de la Vida Cursos por Correspondencia,** Apdo 1608, Guadalajara, Jalisco.
**Escuelas Radiofónicas de la Tarahumara,** Sisoguichi, Chiti. (RC; 60 radio schools, 1,512 enrolled).
**Estudios Bíblicos por Correspondencia,** Aniceto Ortega No 841-1, z12, México, DF. T: 750407.
**Instituto Bíblico por Correspondencia,** Dir, Apdo 3, Pob Anahuac, Tamps.
**Sistema Educativo Radiofónico de México (SER),** México, DF.

*MOROCCO*
**BCC Department,** Gospel Missionary Union, Principal, BP 10, Khemisset.

*NEW ZEALAND*
**Light of Life BCC Centre,** United Maori Mission, 32 Shackleton Rd, Mt Eden, Auckland SE.

*NICARAGUA*
**Asociación Cultural Nicaraguense,** Box 607, Managua, DN.
**Escuelas Radiofónicas de Nicaragua,** c/o Radio Católica, Apdo 11.30, Managua. T: 72260. (294 schools, 6,000 enrolled).

*NIGER*
**Emmaus BCC Centre,** BP 620, Niamey.

*NIGERIA*
**Courses on Islam and Christianity,** Islam in Africa Project Council, Study Centre for Islam and Christianity, 5 Awosika Av, Bodija, Ibadan.
**Light of Life BCC School,** Principal, UMS, Jebba.

*PAKISTAN*
**BCC School,** Principal, 214-B Chandni Chowk, Satellite Town, PO Box 104, Rawalpindi.
**Bible Correspondence School,** Principal, c/o Indus Christian Fellowship, Baker Bldg, Larkana.
**Pakistan BCC School,** Principal, Jail Rd, Campbellpur.
**Pakistan Bible Correspondence School (PBCS),** 33-A People's Colony, PO Box 117, Lyallpur. (100,002 enrolled by 1976).

*PANAMA CANAL ZONE*
**Emmaus BCC Centre,** Box 1081, Balboa.

*PAPUA NEW GUINEA*
**Living Word Correspondence Courses,** World Outreach, PO Box 67, Goroka.

*PARAGUAY*
**Centro Experimental de TV Educativa (CETE),** Universidad Católica, Asunción. (TV mass education).

*PERU*
**Escuelas Radiofónicas del Perú,** Radio Onda Azul, Casilla 112, Puno. (RC).
**Radio San José,** Apdo 216, Iquitos. (RC; 72 radio schools, 1,023 enrolled).
**Tele-Escuela Popular Americana (TEPA),** Calle Don Bosco 129, Casilla 891, Arequipa. T: 4786. (Many Catholic mass-education radio/TV stations).

*PHILIPPINES*
**Back to the Bible,** Light of Life BCC Centre, Box 1750, Manila.
**Good News BCC Centre,** Dir, PO Box 1417, Manila.

*PORTUGAL*
**Light of Life BCC Centre,** Rua do Almirante Pessanha, 16-3E Lisboa.

*PUERTO RICO*
**Emmaus BCC Centre,** PO Box 10913, Caparra Heights, Puerto Rico 00922.

*RWANDA*
**Université Radiophonique de Gitarama,** BP 13, Gitarama. (RC).

*SIERRA LEONE*
**Emmaus BCC Centre,** c/o Christian Literature Crusade, PO Box 1465, Freetown.

*SINGAPORE*
**Living Word BCC,** Christian Literature Centre, PO Box 3038, Singapore 1.

*SOUTH AFRICA*
**AICA Theological Correspondence Course,** 603 Pharmacy House, 80 Jorissen St, Braamfontein, Johannesburg.
**All Africa School of Theology,** Box 263, Witbank, Transvaal. (For over 200 African independent churches).
**Light of Life BCC Centre,** PO Box 208, Roodepoort, Transvaal.
**Living Word Correspondence Courses,** World Outreach, PO Box 180, Halfway House, Johannesburg.

*SPAIN*
**Gospel Missionary Union,** Apdo 570, Malaga. (Radio courses in Moroccan Arabic).
**Radio ECCA,** Emisora Cultural Canaria, Av de Mesa y Lopes, Apdo 994, Las Palmas de Gran Canaria, Islas Canarias. T: 261212. (RC radiophonic schools).
**Radio Popular de Córdoba,** Radio Ensenañza Sección, Plaza Cardenal Toledo 2, Córdoba. T: 221814,222738. (RC radiophonic school).
**Radio Popular de Granada,** Gran Via 26 II, Granada. T: 221539. (RC radiophonic school).

*SUDAN*
**Emmaus BCC Centre,** American Mission, PO Box 112, Was Medani.

*SWAZILAND*
**BCC Department,** Every Home Crusade, Principal, Box 379, Mbabane.

*SWEDEN*
**Emmaus BCC Centre,** Kindbovagen 16, Mölnlycke.

*SWITZERLAND*
**Biblischer Fernkurs,** Apollos Verlag, Teufen/AR. (Ev Reformed Church).
**Cours Bibliques par Correspondance,** Evangile et Culture, 7 Chemin des Cedres, Lausanne. (Formerly Eglise Evangélique Libre du Canton de Vaud).

*TANZANIA*
**Acts of the Apostles (Kitabu cha Matendo ya Mitume),** Diocese of Central Tanzania, St Philip's College, Kongwa.
**Life of Jesus (Swahili),** Mennonite Church, PO Box 7, Musoma.
**Read the New Testament (Soma Agano Jipya),** Tarime Bible School, PO Box 26, Tarime.
**Word of Life BCC,** PO Box 2572, Dar es Salaam.

*THAILAND*
**Lamp of Thailand (CCT),** PO Box 111, Chieng Mai.
**Light of Life BCC Centres,** 201 Hicks Lane, North Sathorn Rd, Bangkok.
**Living Word BCC School,** World Outreach Literature Centre, New Life Centre, GPO Box 1864, Bangkok.

*TRINIDAD & TOBAGO*
**TEAM,** Bible Correspondence Department, PO Box 77, Port of Spain, Trinidad.

*TUNISIA*
**BCC Centre,** Principal, 28 Av Bap Djebid, Tunis.

*UGANDA*
**Emmaus BCC Centre,** PO Box 14180, Mengo, Kampala.

*USSR*
**ECB Correspondence Courses,** AUCECB, PO Box 520, Moskva. (For ECB members).

*UK OF GB & NI*
**BCC Department,** Bientôt (Soon Magazine), Principal, 49 Offington Av, Worthing, West Sussex.
**Christian Witness (Outreach Ministry),** Sec, Slough Gospel Tabernacle, Pitts Rd, Slough, Bucks. (Pentecostal correspondence course).
**Sunday School by Post,** Sec, Sleepy Hollow, Swinmore, Ledbury, Herefordshire. T: Trumpet 313.
**Swedenborg Society,** 20-21 Bloomsbury Way, London WC1A 2TH. T: (01)405-7986.
**World Outreach,** Living Word Correspondence Courses, Sec, 13 Wollaston Rd, Dorchester, Dorset DT1 1EH. (Tracts, courses; Pentecostal).

*USA*
**Alaska Radio Mission of Northern Alaska,** Box 101, Nome, AK 99762. T: (907)443-2675. (RC radiophonic school; 52 towns).
**Baumann Bible Telecast,** 5214 Wehawken Rd, Washington, DC 20016. (Colour TV Bible studies).
**Bethel Series,** Adult Christian Education Foundation, 313 Price Place, Box 5305, Madison, WI 53705. (Lutheran).
**Bible Study Hour Cassettes,** 1617 Spruce St, Philadelphia, PA 19103.
**BCC Department,** Campus Crusade for Christ, Arrowhead Springs, San Bernardino, California.
**BCC Department,** Dallas Bible College, 8733 La Prada Drive, Dallas, TX 75228.
**BCC Department,** Every Home Crusade Headquarters, Principal, Box 1313, Studio City, CA 91604.
**BCC Department,** Source of Light Mission, Principal, Box 8, Madison, GA 30650. T: (404)342-0397.
**Capuchin Correspondence Course,** 4121 Harewood Rd, NE, Washington, DC 20017.
**CCD Correspondence Courses for Catechists and Parent-Educators,** 424 N Broadway, Wichita, KS 67202. (RC; 1,500 enrolled).
**Christian Outreach BCC Centre,** Principal, Box 115, Huntingdon Valley, PA 19006.
**Confraternity of Christian Doctrine Course,** PO Box 179, Aledo, IL 61231. (For Catholics attending public schools; 75,000 enrolled).
**Emmaus Bible School,** Home Study Division, 156 North Oak Park Av, Oak Park, IL 60301.
**Home Bible Studies,** Mennonite Broadcasting, Harrisonburg, VA 22801.
**Home Study Service,** Religious Information Bureau, 3473 South Grand, St Louis, Missouri. (RC).
**International Correspondence Institute,** 1445 Boonville Av, Springfield, MO 65802. (Assemblies of God).
**International Institute,** Exec Dir, 5661 N Northcott Av, Chicago, IL 60631. T: (312)823-1852. (Also: PO Box 66053, Chicago, IL 60666).
**Israel's Hope BCC Center,** 2107 East Ninth St, Brooklyn, NY 11223. T: (212)339-4556.
**Layman's Bible Study Programme,** Roa's Films, 1696 North Astor St, Milwaukee, WI 53202.
**LCA/ALC Augsburg Bible Studies,** Board of Publication, LCA, 2900 Queen Lane, Philadelphia, PA 19129.
**Leadership Instruction & Training,** 13521 Deluxe St, Houston, TX 77047.
**Light of Life BCC Centre,** Christian Education Foundation, PO Box 1557, Honolulu, HA 96806.
**Living Word Correspondence Courses,** World Outreach, Sec, PO Box 12, South Bend, IN 46624.
**Moody Bible Institute,** Correspondence Course Division, Dir, 820 North La Salle St, Chicago, IL 60610. T: (312)642-1570.
**Paulist Home Study School,** Paulist Fathers, 21 East Van Buren St, Chicago, IL 61231.
**Religious Correspondence School,** 1165 South West Blvd, Wichita, Kansas. (One of over 20 Catholic courses in USA).
**Salzmann Correspondence Courses,** 3257 South Lake Drive, Milwaukee, Wisconsin. (RC).
**The World to Come,** Ambassador College, PO Box 111, Pasadena, CA 91123. (Worldwide Church of God).
**University Correspondence Study,** Tennessee School of Religion, University of Tennessee, Knoxville, TN 37916.
**Voice of Prophecy,** 1500 East Chevy Chase Drive, PO Box 1519, Glendale, CA 91206. T: (213)245-2349. (Seventh-day Adventist).
**World Gospel Crusades,** PO Box 3, Upland, CA 91786.

*US VIRGIN ISLANDS*
**Emmaus BCC Center,** PO Box 2244, Charlotte Amalie, St Thomas, VI 00802.

*URUGUAY*
**Asociación pro Emisiones Culturales (APEC),** Agraciada 2974, Montevideo. T: 593778.

*VENEZUELA*
**Acción Cultural Popular Venezolana (ACPOVEN),** Edificio Don Miguel, 7 piso, Ap 71 Esquina de Cipreses, Casilla 13437, Caracas. T: 454216. (500 RC radio schools, 6,000 enrolled).

*VIET NAM*
**Living Word BCC School,** Christian Literature Distribution Centre, PO Box 1262, Saigon.

*ZAIRE*
**Ndinga ya Moto Ecole Biblique Emmaus,** Principal, AMBM, BP 4714, Kinshasa II.

*ZAMBIA*
**BCC Department,** Dorothea Mission, Principal, Box 2696, Lusaka.
**BCC Department,** Every Home Crusade, Principal, Box 2211, Lusaka.
**Bible Way in English,** Nyamja (Malawi) South Baptist Mission, Principal, Box 2262, Lusaka.
**Correspondence Course Department (CMML),** Principal, 59 Zenobia Av, Luanshya.

*ZIMBABWE*
**BCC Department,** Source of Light Mission, Principal, 19 Alexandra Drive, Hatfield, Salisbury.
**Light of Life BCC Centre,** Principal, PB 2, PO Karoi.

# 17

# Development, Justice & Peace

*Definition.* The churches' involvement in the areas of development, justice and peace: economic development, international development, multinationals (transnational corporations), overseas development, poverty, problems of underdevelopment, labour-intensive schemes, socio-economic promotion; ecology, environment, pollution, desertification; citizenship, civil rights, religious liberty, legal and other relations with governments, canon law, injustice, racism, torture, political prisoners; pacifism, peace or anti-war groups, conscientious objectors; Christian involvement in revolution, liberation movements, guerrilla movements; co-ordinating bodies; development education, conscientization. For local development and community projects, see SOCIAL AND PASTORAL CONCERN. See also AID AND RELIEF.

In this field, there are over 220 Christian organizations of major significance.

*ALGERIA*
**COPRODEV,** 5 Rue Cne Mennani, El Djezair (Alger). (Centre for village development projects. Ecumenical).

*AUSTRALIA*
**Action for World Development,** CIDSE, PO Box 124, Brickfield Hill, NSW 2000.
**Joint Secretariat on Action for World Development in Australia,** Exec Sec, ACC, PO Box 111, Brickfield Hill, NSW 2001. T: 262901.

*AUSTRIA*
**CIDSE,** Türkenstr 3, Wien 9.
**Institut für Internationale Zusammenarbeit,**

Österreichische Setkion, Pax Christi, Annagasse 20, Wien 1.
**MIVA,** Zentrale Österreich, A-4651 Stadl Paura.
**Mouvement International de la Reconciliation (MIR),** Schottengasse 3/a, Wien 1.
**Österreichischen Bischofskonferenz,** Österreichischer Entwicklungshilferdienst, Türkenstr 3, A-1090 Wien.

*BARBADOS*
**Christian Action for Development in the Caribbean (CADEC),** PO Box 616, Bridgetown.

*BELGIUM*
**Centre de Recherche des Pays en Développement,** E Van Evenstraat 2A, B-3000 Leuven. T: (016)228597.
**International Co-operation for Socio-Economic Development (CIDSE),** Secretariat, Av Adolphe Lacomblé 59-61, B-1040 Brussel. T: (01)7365798, 7365801.
**Mouvement Chrétien pour la Paix (MCP),** Secrétariat Européen, Rue Louvrex 36, B-4000 Liège. T: (041)230741.

*BENIN*
**Comité pour le Développement des Investissements Intellectuels en Afrique et à Madagascar (CODIAM),** BP 249, Cotonou. T: 3888.
**Développement et Culture,** BP 262, Cotonou. T: 2604.

*BOLIVIA*
**Acción Cultural Loyola (ACLO),** Casilla 155, Sucre. T: 1885,1677. (Rural conscientization).
**Comisión Boliviana de Acción Social Evangélica (COMBASE),** Av 9 de Abril, Casilla 869, Cochabamba.
**Departamento de Investigación y Promoción Social San Rafael,** Casilla 546, Cochabamba. T: 4495.
**Equipo Chapare,** Villa Tunari, Chapare, Casilla 770, Cochabamba. (Ecumenical).

*BRAZIL*
**Comissão de Desenvolvimento da Mata Sul de Pernambuco (CODEMAS),** c/o Arcebispado, Residência Episcopal, Palmares, PE.
**Comissão Ecumenica de Serviço,** Pres, Rua Artur Azevedo 32, Apt 8, 05404 São Paulo, SP.
**Instituto de Desenvolvimento Integral (IDI),** Praça da Sé 1, 2 andar, Salvador, BA. T: 32979.
**Movimento de Educação de Base (MEB),** Rua S Clemente 385, Botafogo ZC 02, 20.000 Rio de Janeiro, GB. T: 2221698. (Rural conscientization).
**Operação Esperança,** Recife, PE.

*CAMEROON*
**Commission pour le Développement,** FEMEC, BP 491, Yaoundé. T: 222821.

*CANADA*
**Canadian Catholic Organization for Development and Peace (CCODP)/Organisation Catholique Canadienne pour le Développement et la Paix,** 1452 Rue Drummond, ch 218, Montréal H3G 1W2, Québec. T: (514)845-7141.
**Canadian Coalition for Development,** 90 Parent, Ottawa 2.
**Canadian Coalition for Development/Ligue des Canadiens pour le Développement,** 4824 Chemin Côte des Neiges, Montréal 247, Québec.
**Conseil de Développement Social du Montréal Metropolitain,** 445 Rue St-François-Xavier, Montréal 125, Québec.
**Inter-Church Association to Promote Justice in Canada,** c/o Vancouver & District Council of Christian Churches, 1708 West 16th Av, Vancouver, BC V6J 2M1. T: 733-3131. (Focus on poverty).
**Joint CCC-CCC Steering Committee on Poverty Strategy/Comité Mixte CCC-CCC pour la Pauvreté,** 40 St Clair Av East, Toronto, Ontario M4T 1M9. T: (416)921-4152.

*CHAD*
**Centre d'Etudes et de Formation pour le Développement (CEFOD),** BP 456, Ndjamena (Fort-Lamy). T: 3916.

*CHILE*
**Centro para el Desarrollo Económico y Social de América Latina (DESAL),** Carmen Silva 2542, Casilla 9990, Santiago. T: 499269.
**Hogar de Cristo Viviendas,** Chorrillos 3808, Santiago. (RC. Low-cost housing).
**Instituto de Viviendas Populares (INVICA),** Erasmo Escala 1835, Santiago. (RC. Low-cost housing).

*COLOMBIA*
**Acción Cultural Popular (ACPO),** Calle 20 No 9-45, Bogotá. (Rural conscientization).
**Centro para el Desarrollo Económico y Social de América Latina (DESAL),** Carrera 10 No 65-48, Bogatá.

*COSTA RICA*
**Exodo,** Calle 9, Av 14 bis, Apdo Postal 3771, San José. (Ecumenical. Conscientization).

*CZECHOSLOVAKIA*
**Christian Peace Conference (CPC)/Conference Chrétienne pour la Paix (CCP) (Krest'anskã Mírová),** Jungmannova 9, PO Box 192, 11121 Praha 1. T: 248866,248536.

*DENMARK*
**Nordic Catholic Development Aid (Nordisk Katolsk Udviklingshjaelp),** Griffenfeldsgade 44, DK-2200 Kobenhavn N. T: (01)353085.

*ETHIOPIA*
**Ethiopia Orthodox Church Development Commission,** Exec Dir, Haile Selassie Av, PO Box 503 Addis Abeba. T: 119661,123642.

*FRANCE*
**Assemblée Internationale des Chrétiens Solidaires des Peuples Vietnamien, Laotien et Cambodgien/International Assembly of Christians in Solidarity with the Vietnamese, Laotian and Cambodian Peoples (Dai Hôi Quôc Tê Nhung Nguòl Ki Tô Giaó Doàn Kêt Vói Cac Dân Tôc Viêt Nam, Laò Và Campuchia),** 18 Rue de Cardinal Lemoine, F-75005 Paris. T: 033-5295.
**Association des Amis de Croissance des Jeunes Nations,** 19 Rue du Plat, Lyon 2.
**Association du Tiers-Monde (IEDES),** 58 Blvd Arago, F-75013 Paris.
**Association Française des Volontaires du Progrès (AFVP),** 9 Rue Lincoln, F-75008 Paris.
**Association Internationale de Développement,** 7 Av de Jena, F-75016 Paris.
**Centre Catholique pour l'UNESCO,** 9 Rue Cler, F-75007 Paris. T: 551-1759.
**Centre de Coopération pour Développement Economique et Humain,** 82 Rue Sain-Lazare, F-75009 Paris.
**Centre de Formation des Experts de la Coopération Technique Internationale,** 27 Rue Saint-Guillaume, F-75007 Paris.
**Centre de Formation pour le Développement,** 3 Rue St-Léon, F-67082 Strasbourg.
**Centre de Reflexion et d'Information sur la Coopération (CRIC),** 30 Rue Voltaire, Grenoble 12.
**Centre d'Information sur le Développement (CIDEV),** 47 Quai des Grands-Augustins, F-75006 Paris. T: (01)325-3102.
**Centre LJ Lebret/Foi et Développement,** 9 Rue Guénégaud, F-75006 Paris. T: (01)033-2502.
**Comité Catholique National contre la Faim et pour le Développement (CCFD),** 47 Quai des Grands-Augustins, F-75262 Paris. T: (01)325-3102.
**Délégation Catholique pour la Coopération (DCC),** 277 Rue Saint-Jacques, F-75005 Paris. T: (01)326-1250.
**Entraide pour le Développement Intégral,** 6 Rue Boissac, F-69002 Lyon.
**Foi et Cultures (Ad Lucem),** 12 Rue Guy-de-la-Brosse, F-75005 Paris. T: (01)331-7955. (RC. International co-operation and Third-World development).
**Fraternités Terre-Nouvelle,** 12 Rue du 11 Novembre, F-92110 Clichy.
**Institut de Recherche et d'Application des Méthodes de Développement (IRAM),** 97 Rue Reamur, F-75002 Paris.
**Institut International de Recherches et de Formation en vue du Développement (IRFED),** 47 Rue de la Glacière, F-75013 Paris.
**Institut Oecuménique au Service du Développement des Peuples (INODEP)/Ecumenical Institute for the Development of Peoples,** 34 Av Reille, F-75014 Paris. T: (01)589-1321.
**Mouvement Chrétien pour la Paix (MCP),** 46 Rue de Vaugirard, F-75006 Paris. T: 325-4970. (Also: 9 Rue de Versailles, Ville d'Avray).
**Mouvement International de la Réconciliation (MIR),** Sec Gén, 9 Place d'Allemagne, Massy (Essonne).
**Secrétariat du Comité Episcopal France-Amerique Latine,** 2 Rue Abbé Patureau, F-75018 Paris. T: (01)252-0789.
**Service et Développement,** 42 Montée St-Barthélémy, F-69005 Lyon. (Ex Inter-Service).

*GERMAN DEMOCRATIC REPUBLIC*
**Aktion für die Hungerden,** Auguststr 82, DDR-104 Berlin.

*GERMANY, Federal Republic of*
**Aktion Sühnezeichen Friedensdienste,** Jebensstr 1, D-1000 Berlin 12. T: (030)316701. (Reparation and peace).
**Arbeitsgemeinschaft Ev Seminare für Gemeindedienst,** Graf-Recke-Str 209, D-4 Düsseldorf.
**Arbeitsgemeinschaft für Entwicklungshilfe (AGEH),** Franzstr 107/109, Postfach 23, D-5100 Aachen. T: (0241)29894/5. (Also: Mittelstr 16, D-5100 Aachen).
**Arbeitsgemeinschaft Missionarische Dienste,** Stafflenbergstr 78, Postfach 476, D-7 Stuttgart 1. (Foreign missionary council for development aid; DiU, EZE, BrotfdW, EA GWM).
**Arbeitskreise Dritte Welt,** Lorettostr 2a, Freiburg.
**Christlicher Friedensdienst (CFD),** Freiheit 4, D-637 Oberursel. (Peace service).
**Deutsche Landjugend Akademie Klausenhof,** D-4293 Dingden/Westfalen.
**Eirene (International Christian Service for Peace),** Maltegerhof, D-5332 Romlinghoven bei Bonn. T: Königswinter 5255.
**Evangelische Zentralstelle für Entwicklungshilfe,** Poppelsdorfer Allee 29, D-53 Bonn.
**Institut für Entwicklungshilfe,** Theodor Hurth Str 2-6, D-5 Köln-Deutz.
**Institut für Vorbereitung von Akademischen Mitarbeitern für Entwicklungsländer,** Overathers Str 21/23, D-506 Bensberg-Köln.
**Institut St Michel/Vorbereittungsstätte für Entwicklungshelfer,** Kuhlendahl 63, D-433 Mülheim/Ruhr.
**Kirchenrechtliches Institut der EKD,** Prof-Huber-Platz 2/III, D-8 München 22. (Legal questions relating to EKD).
**Konferenz der Ev Pfarrer an den Justizvollzugsanstalten der BDR und in West-Berlin,** Postfach 600, D-325 Hameln.
**Misereor,** Mozartstr 9, D-51 Aachen.
**MISSIO,** Dir, Hirtenstr 26, D-8 München 2. T: 555981/2. (Documentation, information and funding centre for development in Third World).
**Seminar für Socialarbeit in Ubersee,** 19 Winterstr, D-78 Freiburg/Breisgau.
**Weltbund für Religiöse Freiheit/Association Internationale pour la Liberté Religieuse,** Frankfurt/Main.
**Wirtschaftsgilde Ev Arbeitskreis für Wirtschaftsethik und Sozialgestaltung,** Blumenstr 7, D-75 Karlsruhe 1. (Ethics in economic and social relations).

*GHANA*
**Department of Socio-Economic Development,** National Catholic Secretariat, PO Box 7530, Accra North.

*GUATEMALA*
**Centro de Desarrollo Integral,** Apdo 6, Huehuetenango.
**Instituto para el Desarrollo Económico Social de América Central (IDESAC),** 1a Av 8-16, Zona 1, Apdo Postal 10-A Reforma, Ciudad de Guatemala. T: 29991.
**Proyecto de Colonización Juan XXIII,** San Juan Acul, Sayaxche, Petén.

*HAITI*
**Commission Haïtienne des Eglises pour le Développement (CHED),** Angle Rue Camp-de-Mars et Magasin de l'Etat, BP 285, Port-au-Prince.

*HOLY SEE*
**Pontifical Commission for Preparation of the Code of Oriental Canon Law,** Palazzo dei Convertendi, Via della Conciliazione 34, I-00193 Roma, Italy. T: (698)4295.
**Pontifical Commission for the Revision of the Code of Canon Law,** Palazzo dei Convertendi, Via dell'Erba 1, I-00193 Roma, Italy. T: 6982 int 3933.
**Pontificia Commissione Iustitia et Pax,** Palazzo San Calisto, Piazza San Calisto 16, Roma, I-00120 Città del Vaticano. T: (698)4776,4491.
**Pontificio Consiglio Cor Unum,** Sec, Palazzo Apostolico, I-00120 Città del Vaticano. T: 6984556, 6984831. (Development fund co-ordination).

*HONG KONG*
**Hong Kong Sodepax Committee,** c/o 57 Peking Rd, 5/f, Kowloon.
**Joint Development Committee,** HKCC/Catholic Church, 57 Peking Rd, 5/f, Kowloon.

*INDIA*
**Alliance for Development,** St Joseph's Club, Purulia Rd, Ranchi. (Catholics & others).
**Christian Agency for Social Action, Relief and Development (CASA),** 16 Ring Rd, Lajpat Nagar IV, New Delhi 24.
**Home for All Housing Society,** Syro-Malankara Archbishop's House, Trivandrum-4, Kerala.

*INDONESIA*
**Episcopal Commission for Socio-Economic Development,** Jalan Kemiri 15 (belakang), Jakarta. (RC)
**SODEPAXI (Sodepax Indonesia),** DGI, Jalan Salemba Raya 10, Jakarta IV/3.

*IRELAND*
**Irish Commission for Justice & Peace,** Veritas House, 7-8 Lower Abbey St, Dublin 1. (Also: TROCAIRE).
**Trocaire,** 130 Booterstown Av, Dublin. T: 885043, 887190.

*ITALY*
**Centro d'Azione Culturale (CENDAC),** c/o IDAC, 27 Chemin des Crâts, CH-1218 Grand Saconnex, Genève, Switzerland. (Conscientization and education for development).
**Commission for Justice and Peace,** Pres, Piazza San Calisto 16, I-00153 Roma. T: 6984697, 6984521.
**MIVA,** St Joseph's Missionshaus, Postfach 185, I-39042 Brixen, BZ.
**Movement for a Better World,** Secretariat, Centro Internationale Pio XII, Via dei Laghi Km 10, I-00040 Rocca di Papa. T: 949010,949122.
**Movimento Internazionale della Riconciliazione (MIR),** Via Rasella 155, Roma. T: 463206.

*IVORY COAST*
**Commission du Synode Eglise et Développement,** c/o Archevêché, 23 Blvd Clozel, BP 1287, Abidjan. T: 222007.
**Institut Africain pour le Développement Economique et Social (INADES),** 15 Av Jean-Mermoz, Cocody, BP 8008, Abidjan-Cocody. T: 49292.

*JAPAN*
**Sodepax Japan,** Co-Chairman, 24 Japan Christian Center, 551 Totsuka-cho, 1-chome, Shinjuku-ku, Tokyo 160. (Also: 10-1 Rokubancho, Chiyoda-ku, Tokyo 102).

*KENYA*
**African Independent Churches Service (AICS),** PO Box 59969, Nairobi. T: 26894,23649.
**Socio-Economic Development Department,** Kenya Catholic Secretariat, PO Box 48062, Nairobi. T: 21613.

*KOREA, South*
**Justice and Peace Commission of Korea,** c/o CPO Box 16, Soul 100. T: 238789.
**Sodepax Korea Committee,** Sec Gen, 52-15, 2KA, Chung Mu Ro Jung-ku, Soul.

*LEBANON*
**Ecumenical Commission for Development, Justice & Peace,** PO Box 1375, Bayrut.

*LESOTHO*
**LESODEPAX (Lesotho Sodepax Commission),** PO Box 929, Maseru.

*MADAGASCAR*
**Centre d'Etudes et d'Animation du Développement,** Lot IV-G 199, Antanimena, Tananarive.

*MALAWI*
**Christian Service Committee of the Churches of Malawi (CSC),** Chileka Rd, PO Box 949, Blantyre. T: 30671.
**Movement for Ecumenical Action in National Development (MEND),** PO Box 949, Blantyre.

*MAURITIUS*
**Institut pour le Développement et le Progrès,** 42 Rue Pope Hennessy, Port-Louis. T: 20975.

*NETHERLANDS*
**Apostolate of Reconciliation (Apostolaat der Hereniging),** Prins Hendrikstraat 47, Boxtel. T: (04116)3040.
**Association Internationale pour le Christianisme Libéral et la Liberté Religieuse,** Sec Gén, 26 Riouwstraat, Amsterdam.
**Bishops Advent Fund (Bisschoppelijk Adventsactie),** Laan van Meerdervoort 148, 's-Gravenhage.
**Developing Countries Foundation (Stichting Laden in Ontwikkeling),** Laan van Meerdervoort 148, 's-Gravenhage. T: (070)655207.
**Dutch Bishops Lenten Campaign (Bisschoppeljke Vastenaktie Nederland),** Utrechtseweg 29a, Zeist. T: (03404)17887,23404. (Also: Zamenhoflaan 17, Zeist). (For development overseas).
**Ecumenical Development Corporative Society,** Amsterdam. (Loans to churches in Third World).
**Interchurch Advent Fund for Latin America (Interkerkelijke Adventsactie voor Latijns Amerika),** Laan van Meerdervoort 148, 's-Gravenhage. T: (070)655207.
**Interchurch Council for Peace (Interkerkeljk Vredesberaad, IKV),** Celebesstraat 60, 's-Gravenhage. T: (070)656823.
**International Fellowship of Reconciliation (IFOR),** Admin Sec, Prins Hendriklaan 9, Driebergen. T: 3620.
**Pax Christi,** Secretariat, Celebesstraat 60, 's-Gravenhage.

*NEW ZEALAND*
**Amnesty International (NZ),** PO Box 3597, Wellington.
**Christian Pacifist Society of New Zealand,** 19 Head St, Christchurch 8.
**Citizen's Association for Racial Equality (CARE),** PO Box 2794, Auckland.

*NICARAGUA*
**Comité Evangélico pro Ayuda al Desarrollo (CEPAD),** Apdo Postal 3091, Managua.

*NORWAY*
**Christian Institute for Project Aid (Kristen Innsats for Ulöste Oppgaver),** Munchsgate 2, Oslo 1.

*PAPUA NEW GUINEA*
**Sodepang (Sodepax Papua New Guinea)** c/o Box 1015, Boroko, Port Moresby.

*PHILIPPINES*
**National Christian Peace Federation,** 1519 Craig St, Sampaloc, Manila.
**Office for Human Development,** Federation of Asian Bishops' Conferences (FABC), 2325 Agno St (off Taft Av, near La Salle), Malate, PO Box EA-12 Ermita, Manila.
**Philippine Peace Federation of Christian Churches,** 1908 Taft Av, Pasay City.

*POLAND*
**Pax Association (Stowarzyszenie Pax),** Ul Mokotowska 43, Warszawa. (Progressivist).

*SOUTH AFRICA*
**Catholic Action for Racial Education (CARE),** PO Box 31135, Braamfontein, Transvaal.
**Study Project on Christianity in Apartheid Society (SPROCAS),** SACC, PO Box 31134, Braamfontein, Transvaal.

*SPAIN*
**Secretariado de Cooperación al Desarrollo,** Paseo de Juan XXIII 3, Madrid-3. T: (01)2534007.

*SRI LANKA*
**Social and Economic Development Centre** 976 Gnanartha Pradipaya Mawata, Colombo 8.
**Sodepax Sri Lanka Committee,** 61 Sir James Peiris Mawata, Colombo 2.

*SWEDEN*
**Swedish Ecumenical Committee for Development (SEKURF), Justice and Peace,** Bellmansgatan 100, S-75428 Uppsala.

*SWITZERLAND*
**Christian Movement for Peace/Christlicher Friedensdienst,** Dittlingerweg 4, CH-3000 Bern. T: (031)430474.
**Church Alert on Development Decade II,** Sodepax, 150 Route de Ferney, CH-1211 Genève 20. (A documentation service).
**Church and Society,** WCC, 150 Route de Ferney, CH-1211 Genève 20.
**Department of Missions and Development Aid,** Habsburgerstr 44, CH-6002 Luzern.
**Fastenopfer der Schweiz Katholischen/Action de Carême des Catholiques Suisses (Swiss Lenten Projects),** Zentralstelle, Habsburgerstr 44, Postfach 754, CH-6000 Luzern. T: (041)227538.
**Institut d'Action Culturelle (IDAC)/Institute of Cultural Action,** 27 Chemin des Crêts, CH-1218 Grand Saconnex, Genève. (Conscientization and education for development).
**Interteam (Entwicklungsdienst durch Freiwilligen Einsatz),** Zürichstr 68, CH-6000 Luzern. T: (041)366768.
**Kirchlicher Friedensbund/La Réconciliation,** Zentralpräs, Reinacherstr 18, CH-8032 Zürich. T: (051)471824.
**La Suisse et le Tiers-Monde,** Commission des Eglises en Suisse, Institut d'Etudes Oecuméniques, 262 Rue de Morat, CH-1700 Fribourg. T: (037) 234744.
**MIVA,** Catholic Parish, CH-9499 Altenrhein.
**Programme Unit of Justice and Service,** WCC 150 Route de Ferney, CH-1211 Genève 20.
**Service Social International/International Social Service,** 24 Blvd des Philosophes, Genève.

**Sodepax (Commission de Recherche du COE et de l'Eglise Catholique sur la Société, le Développement et la Paix),** 150 Route de Ferney, CH-1211 Genève 20. T: (22)333400.
**Swiss Bishops Lenten Fund,** CP 40, CH-1700 Fribourg 3. T: (037)244794.
**Theologische Konkordatsprüfungsbehörde,** Sek, Sandackerstr 1, CH-8200 Schaffhausen. (Catholic legal committee to examine concordat).

*THAILAND*
**Baptist Church Development Division,** 84 Soi 2, Sukhumvit Rd, Bangkok. T: 2525057.
**Catholic Council of Thailand for Development (CCTD)(Sapha Khatholik Heng Pratet Thai Phua Karn Phrathana),** National Catholic Centre, 25/2 Soi Sunklangtheva, Prachasongkhroh St, Bangkok 10. T: 770108.

*USSR*
**Council of Evangelical Christian & Baptist Prisoners' Relatives,** Krasnodon 1, Podgornaya 30, Voroshilovgrad Region.

*UK OF GB & NI*
**Anglican Pacifist Fellowship,** Gen Sec, 29 Great James St, London WC1N 3ES. T: (01)242-7476.
**Baptist Union Christian Citizenship Department,** Baptist Church House, 4 Southampton Row, London WC1B 4AB.
**Catholic Commission for Racial Justice,** 1 Cambridge Terrace, London NW1. T: (01)935-0568.
**Catholic Fund for Overseas Development (CAFOD),** Dir, 75 Kinnerton St, (and 3 Lyall St), London SW1W 8EU. T: (01)235 or 231-4931,1924. (Also: 21A Soho Square, London W1V 6NR. T: (01)734-4188).
**Catholic Institute for International Relations,** 1 Cambridge Terrace, London NW1. T: (01)487-4431.
**Christian Movement for Peace,** Stowford House, Bayswater Rd, Oxford.
**Christian Solidarity International (CSI),** 24 Gilbert St, London W1Y 2EQ. T: (01)493-8561. (Assistance on human rights).
**Churches' Action for World Development (CAWD),** 2 Sloane Gardens, PO Box 1, London SW1.
**Congregational Pacifist Fellowship,** Hon Sec, 9 Coombe Rd, New Malden, Surrey. T: 942-6521.
**Fellowship of Reconciliation (FOR),** 29 Great James St, London WC1. T: (01)242-7130.
**Friends' Peace and International Relations Committee,** Gen Sec, Friends House, Euston Rd, London NW1.
**Intermediate Technology Development Group,** Dir, 9 King St, Covent Garden, London WC2E 8HN. T: (01)836-5211. (Labour-intensive methods in the Third World).
**Methodist Christian Citizenship Department,** 1 Central Bldgs, Matthew Parker St, London SW1.
**Overseas Development Institute,** 160 Piccadilly, London W1. T: (01)493-2654.
**Pace,** 1 Claremont St, Belfast BT9 6AP, NI.
**Scottish Catholic International Aid Fund,** 156 King's Gate, Aberdeen AB2, Scotland.
**Scottish Churches Action for World Development,** 41 George IV Bridge, Edinburgh EH1 1EI, Scotland.
**War on Want,** 9 Madeley Rd, London W5. T: (01)567-1429.

*USA*
**Action for Interracial Understanding (AIU),** Exec Dir, 575 Neponset St, Norwood, MA 02062. T: (617)762-4139. (RC).
**American Pax Association,** Box 139, Murray Hill, NY 10016.
**Association for International Development,** 374 Grand St, Paterson 1, New Jersey.
**Campaign for Human Development,** 1312 Massachusetts Av, NW, Washington, DC 20005.
**Catholic Inter-American Cooperation Program (CICOP),** 1312 Massachusetts Av, NW, Washington, DC 20005. (Sponsored by USCC).
**Christian Freedom Foundation,** 7960 Cresent Av, Buena Park, CA 90602.
**Clergy and Laity Concerned,** 535 Schenectady St, Schenectady, NY 12307. T: (518)374-3561. (Anti-war).
**Commission for Racial Justice,** United Church of Christ, Exec Dir, 287 Park Av South, New York, NY 10010.
**Cooperation in Development (CODEL),** 79 Madison Av, New York, NY 10016.
**Federation for World Peace and Unification,** 723 South Broadway, Tarrytown, NY 10591. T: (914) 631-3630. (Begun 1970 by HSAUWC, Korea).
**Fellowship of Reconciliation (FOR),** Box 271, Nyack, NY 10960. T: (914)358-4601.
**International Association for Religious Freedom (IARF),** Pres, Concord, Massachusetts.
**International Development Assistance Commission (IDAC),** 100 Western Union Bldg, Washington, DC 20005.
**Inter-American Technical Assistance Foundation,** PO Box 3146, Mansfield, Ohio.
**Joint Strategy and Action Committee,** Exec Dir, Room 1700A, 475 Riverside Drive, New York, NY 10027. (Development).
**Liberal Religious Peace Fellowship,** 15 Dixon St, Tarrytown, NY 10591.
**MIVA,** South Rd, Wurtsboro, NY 12790.
**National Catholic Conference for Interracial Justice (NCCIJ),** 1307 South Wabash Av, Chicago, IL 69605.
**Orthodox Peace Fellowship (OPF)/Alliance Orthodoxe pour la Paix,** 132 West 4th St, New York, NY 10012.
**People Against Racism,** 212 McKerchy Bldg, 2361 Woodward Av, Detroit, MI 48201.
**Secretariat for World Justice and Peace,** National Conference of Catholic Bishops, 1312 Massachusetts Av, Washington, DC 20005.
**United States Interreligious Committee on Peace (USICOP),** 100 Maryland Av, NE, Washington, DC 20002.

*URUGUAY*
**Instituto de Promoción Económico-Socio del Uruguay (IPRU),** Cerrito 475, 1 piso, Montevideo.
**Sodepax-Uruguay,** c/o Arzobispado, Treinta y Tres 1368, Montevideo.

*ZAIRE*
**Bureau pour le Développement,** BP 3258, Kinshasa. T: 30082.

# 18 Diplomatic Representation

*Definition.* Diplomatic representatives of the Holy See across the world, to some 90 nations and to the major international organizations; nunciatures, apostolic delegations, permanent observers.
This listing omits countries whose Vatican representatives reside in other nations or who have no offices there.

*ALGERIA*
**Délégation Apostolique de l'Afrique Septentrionale,** Délégué, 1 Rue de la Basilique, Bologhine-Alger. T: 578430. (Serves Northern Africa).
**Nonciature Apostolique,** Pro-Nonce, 1 Rue de la Basilique, Bologhine-Alger. T: 623430.

*ANGOLA*
**Apostolic Delegation,** Irmas NS de Muxima 29, CP 1030, Luanda. T: 30532.

*ARGENTINA*
**Nunciatura Apostólica,** Nuncio, Av Alvear 1605, 1014 Buenos Aires. T: 429697.

*AUSTRALIA*
**Apostolic Nunciature,** Pro-Nuncio, 2 Vancouver St, Red Hill, ACT 2603. T: (062)953876.

*AUSTRIA*
**Agence Internationale de l'Energie Atomique (AIEA),** Délégué Apostolique, Theresianumgasse 31, A-1040 Wien IV. T: 651327.
**Apostolische Nunziatur,** Nunzius, Theresianumgasse 31, A-1040 Wien IV. T: 651327.

*BANGLADESH*
**Apostolic Nunciature,** Pro-Nuncio, House No 9, Rd 50, PB 361, Gulhsan, Dacca 12. T: 300218, 302446.

*BELGIUM*
**Comitato Internazionale di Medicina e Farmacia Militare,** Delegate. Rue de Louvain 84, Tirlemont.
**Communauté Européenne (Ceca, CEE, Euratom),** Nonce, Av des Franciscains 5-9, B-1150 Brussel. T: 7622005.
**Nonciature Apostolique de Belgique,** Nonce, Av des Franciscains 5-9, B-1150 Brussel. T: 7622005. (Also serves Luxembourg)

*BOLIVIA*
**Nunciatura Apostólica,** Nuncio, Av Arce 2990, CP 136, La Paz. T: (02)375007.

*BRAZIL*
**Nunciatura Apostólica,** Nuncio, Av das Nações, lote No 1, CP 07-0153, 70.000 Brasília-DF. T: 2230794,2231794.

*BURUNDI*
**Nonciature Apostolique,** Nonce, BP 1068, Bujumbura. T: 2326.

*CAMEROON*
**Nonciature Apostolique,** Pro-Nonce, Rue du Vatican, BP 210, Yaoundé. T: 220475. (Also serves Gabon and Equatorial Guinea).

*CANADA*
**Apostolic Nunciature,** Pro-Nuncio, 724 Manor Av, Ottawa K1M 0E3. T: (613)746-4914.

*CENTRAL AFRICAN REPUBLIC*
**Nonciature Apostolique,** Pro-Nonce, Av Boganda, angle Av Bokassa, BP 1447, Bangui. T: 612654. (Also serves Chad and Congo).

*CHILE*
**Nunciatura Apostólica,** Nuncio, Calle Nuncio Sotero Sanz 200, Casilla 507, Santiago. T: 41229, 498176.

*CHINA (TAIWAN)*
**Apostolic Nunciature,** Pro-Nuncio, Chin Shan St, Lane 63 No 6, Taipei. T: 3216847.

*COLOMBIA*
**Nunciatura Apostólica,** Nuncio, Carrera 15 No 36-33, Apdo Aéreo 3740, Bogotá. T: 454260.

*COSTA RICA*
**Nunciatura Apostólica,** Nuncio, Sabana Oeste, Apdo Postal 10254, San José de Costa Rica. T: 322128.

*CUBA*
**Nunciatura Apostólica,** Nuncio, Calle 12 No 514, Miramar Marianao 13, La Habana. T: 295700,25296.

*CYPRUS*
**Apostolic Nunciature,** Pro-Nuncio, Holy Cross Catholic Church, PO Box 1964, Nicosia.

*DENMARK*
**Apostolic Delegation to Scandinavia,** Delegate, Immortellevej 11, DK-2950 Vedbaek, Kobenhavn. T: 891550. (Serves Iceland, Denmark, Norway, Sweden).

*DOMINICAN REPUBLIC*
**Nunciatura Apostólica,** Nuncio, Av Máximo Gómez 27, Apdo Postal 312, Santo Domingo. T: 6823773.

*ECUADOR*
**Nunciatura Apostólica,** Nuncio, Av Orellana 692, Apdo Postal N.4543-A-Norte, Quito. T: 528783, 232056.

*EGYPT*
**Apostolic Nunciature,** Pro-Nuncio, Safarat Al-Vatican, 5 Sharia Mohamed Mazhar, Zamalek, Al Qahirah. T: 805152.

*EL SALVADOR*
**Nunciatura Apostólica,** Nuncio, 87 Av Norte y 7 Calle Ponente, Colonia Excalón, Apdo Postal 359, San Salvador. T: 232454,237607.

*ETHIOPIA*
**Apostolic Nunciature,** Pro-Nuncio, Makanissa Rd, PO Box 588, Addis Abeba. T: 448095.

*FINLAND*
**Apostolic Nunciature,** Pro-Nuncio, Bulevardi 5 as 12, Helsinki 12. T: 644664.

*FRANCE*
**Conseil de l'Europe,** 2 Rue Le-Nôtre, F-67000 Strasbourg. T: (88)350244.
**Nonciature Apostolique,** Nonce, 10 Av du Président Wilson, F-75116 Paris. T: 7235834.
**UNESCO,** Observateur Permanent, 10 Av du Président Wilson, F-75116 Paris. T: 7236229.

*GERMANY, Federal Republic of*
**Apostolic Nunciature,** Nuncio, Turmstr 29, Plittersdorf, D-5300 Bonn-Bad Godesberg. T: (00492221) 376901.

*GHANA*
**Apostolic Nunciature,** Nuncio, 2 Akosombo St, Airport Residential Area, PO Box 9675, Accra. T: 75972. (Also serves Benin and Togo).

*GUATEMALA*
**Nunciatura Apostólica,** Nuncio, 10 Calle 4/47, Zona 9, Guatemala City. T: 61918,324274.

*HAITI*
**Nonciature Apostolique,** Nonce, Av John Brown, BP 326, Port-au-Prince. T: 20315. (Also serves the Antilles and Caribbean).

*HOLY SEE*
**Consiglio per gli Affari Pubblici della Chiesa/Consilium pro Publicis Ecclesiae Negotiis,** Palazzo Apostolico Vaticano, I-00120 Città del Vaticano. T: 6983274. (Controls Vatican diplomatic service).
**World Tourist Organization,** Permanent Observer, I-00120 Città del Vaticano. T: 6984663.
**Istituto Internazionale per l'Unificazione del Diritto Privato,** Delegate. I-001200 Città del Vaticano. T: 6983068.
**Secretariat of State (Papal Secretariat),** Cardinal Prefect, Palazzo Apostolico, I-00120 Città del Vaticano. T: 6983126. (Policy for Vatican diplomatic service).

*HONDURAS*
**Nunciatura Apostólica,** Nuncio, Apdo Postal 324, Tegucigalpa. T: 328280.

*HONG KONG*
**Apostolic Nunciature of China,** Hong Kong Office, 133 Waterloo Rd, Kowloon. T: 821566. (Pro-Nuncio in Taiwan).

*INDIA*
**Apostolic Nunciature,** Pro-Nuncio, 50-C Niti Marg, Chanakyapuri, New Delhi 110021. T: 616522.

*INDONESIA*
**Apostolic Nunciature,** Pro-Nuncio, Jalan Merdeka Timur 18, PO Box 4227, Jakarta. T: 341142/3.

*IRAN*
**Apostolic Nunciature,** Pro-Nuncio, Carrefour Av de France 97, BP 47, Tehran. T: 643574.

*IRAQ*
**Apostolic Nunciature,** Pro-Nuncio, Abu Nawas St 207/1, PO Box 2090, Alwyiah, Baghdad. T: 92426. (Also servies Kuwait).

*IRELAND*
**Apostolic Nunciature,** Nuncio, 183 Navan Rd, Dublin 7. T: 309344.

*ISRAEL*
**Apostolic Delegation to Jerusalem & Palestine,** Delegate, PO Box 19-199, Jerusalem. T: 282298. (Also serves Jordan and Israel).

*ITALY*
**Food & Agriculture Organization (FAO),** Permanent Observer, Piazza San Calisto 16, I-00153, Roma. T: 6984634.
**Nunziatura Apostolica,** Nunzio, Via PO 27-29, I-00198 Roma. T: 866287,862092.

*IVORY COAST*
**Nonciature Apostolique,** Pro-Nonce, BP 1347, Abidjan 08. T: 443835, (Also serves Upper Volta and Niger).

*JAPAN*
**Apostolic Nunciature,** Pro-Nuncio, 9-2 Sanban-Cho, Chiyoda-ku, Tokyo. T: 2636851.

*KENYA*
**Apostolic Nunciature,** Pro-Nuncio, Manyani Rd, PO Box 14326, Nairobi. T: 48468,48583.

*KOREA, South*
**Apostolic Nunciature,** Pro-Nuncio, Kwang Hwa Moon, PO Box 393, Soul. T: 725725.

*LEBANON*
**Nonciature Apostolique,** Nonce, Rue Georges Picot, BP 1882, Bayrut. T: 361766/7.

*LIBERIA*
**Apostolic Nunciature,** Pro-Nuncio, PO Box 297, Monrovia. (Also serves Gambia, Guinea and Sierra Leone).

*MADAGASCAR*
**Nonciature Apostolique,** Pro-Nonce, Villa Roma II, Route d'Ivandry, BP 650, Tananarive-Ambonilοha. T: 42376. (Also serves Mauritius).

*MALTA*
**Apostolic Nunciature,** Nuncio, Villa Cor Jesu, Pitkali Rd, Attard. T: 41543.

*MEXICO*
**Delegación Apostólica,** Delegado, Guadalupe Inn, Calle Felipe Villanueva 118, Apdo Postal 19-106, México 19, DF. T: 5244050,5346591.

*MOZAMBIQUE*
**Délégation Apostolique,** Av Julius Nyerere 882, Maputo. T: 741144.

*NETHERLANDS*
**Apostolic Nunciature,** Pro-Nuncio, Carnegielaan 5, 's-Gravenhage. T: (070)468966/7.

*NEW ZEALAND*
**Apostolic Delegation to the Pacific Ocean,** Delegate, 112 Queen's Drive, Wellington 3. T: 873470.
**Apostolic Nunciature,** Pro-Nuncio, 112 Queen's Drive, Wellington 3. T: 873470.

*NICARAGUA*
**Nunciatura Apostólica,** Nuncio, Carretera Sur, Km 10.8, Apdo Postal 506, Managua. T: 58657.

*NIGERIA*
**Apostolic Delegation to Nigeria,** Delegate, 9 Anifowoshe St, Victoria Island, PO Box 2470, Lagos. T: 21411,22984.

*PAKISTAN*
**Apostolic Nunciature,** Pro-Nuncio, Diplomatic Enclave N.1, 5th St, PO Box 1106, Islamabad. T: 28287/8.

*PANAMA*
**Nunciatura Apostólica,** Nuncio, Punta Paitilla, Apdo 4251, Zona 5, Panamá. T: 234847,237123.

*PAPUA NEW GUINEA*
**Apostolic Nunciature,** Pro-Nuncio, PO Box 98, Port Moresby. T: 256021. (Also serves Solomon Islands).

*PARAGUAY*
**Nunciatura Apostólica,** Nuncio, Av Mariscal Lopez 1750, CP 83, Asunción. T: 200750.

*PERU*
**Nunciatura Apostólica,** Nuncio, Av Salaverry, Esquina Nazca, Apdo 397, Lima. T: 236063/4.

*PHILIPPINES*
**Apostolic Nunciature,** Nuncio, 2140 Taft Av, PO Box 3604, Manila. T: 593515,583072.

*PORTUGAL*
**Nunciatura Apostólica,** Nuncio, Av Luis Bivar 18, Lisboa 1. T: 547186.

*RWANDA*
**Nonciature Apostolique,** Nonce, BP 261, Kigali. T: 5293.

*SENEGAL*
**Nonciature Apostolique,** Pro-Nonce, BP 5076, Dakar. T: 212674. (Also serves Cape Verde, Guinea Bissau, Mali, Mauritania).

*SOUTH AFRICA*
**Apostolic Delegation to Southern Africa,** Delegate, 800 Pretorius St, Pretoria 0002. T: 742489. (For several countries in Southern Africa).

*SPAIN*
**Nunciatura Apostólica,** Nuncio, Av Pio XII 46, Apdo 19041, Madrid 16. T: 2020840.

*SRI LANKA*
**Apostolic Delegation,** Delegate, 1 Gower St, Colombo 5. T: 82554,86099.

*SUDAN*
**Apostolic Delegation for the Red Sea,** Delegate, PO Box 623, Al Khurtum.
**Apostolic Nunciature,** Pro-Nuncio, New Bridge St, Al Safia City, Shambat, PO Box 623, Al Khurtum. T: 32792.

*SWITZERLAND*
**Nonciature Apostolique/Apostolische Nunziatur,** Nonce/Nunzius, Thunstr 60, CH-3000 Bern. T: 446040.
**United Nations (ONU, OMS, OIT),** Observateur Permanent, Chemin Colladon 24, CH-1209 Genève. T: 985111/2. (Representative of the Holy See to the UN).

*SYRIA*
**Nonciature Apostolique,** Pro-Nonce, 82 Rue Masr, BP 2271, Dimashq. T: 332601.

*TANZANIA*
**Apostolic Nunciature,** Pro-Nuncio, Plot No 462, Msasani Peninsula, PO Box 480, Dar es Salaam. T: 68403.

*THAILAND*
**Apostolic Delegation to Laos, Malaysia & Singapore,** Delegate, 217-1 Sathorn Tai Rd, Bangkok. T: 31804.
**Apostolic Nunciature,** Pro-Nuncio, 217 Sathorn Tai Rd, Bangkok. T: 2339109.

*TRINIDAD & TOBAGO*
**Apostolic Nunciature,** Pro-Nuncio, 146 Belmont Circular Rd, PO Box 86, Port of Spain. T: (62)44606.

*TURKEY*
**Apostolic Nunciature (Vatikan Sefareti),** Pro-Nuncio, Koroglu Sokak 6, Gazi Osman Pasa, Ankara. T: 275188.

*UGANDA*
**Apostolic Nunciature,** Pro-Nuncio, PO Box 7177, Kampala. T: 61167.

*UK OF GB & NI*
**Apostolic Delegation to Great Britain,** Delegate, 54 Parkside, Wimbledon, London SW19 5NF. T: (01)946-1410.

*USA*
**Apostolic Delegation to the United States,** Delegate, 3339 Massachusetts Av, NW, Washington, DC 20008. T: (202)333-7121.
**Organization of American States (OAS),** Permanent Observer, 3339 Massachusetts Av, NW, Washington, DC 20008. T: (202)333-7121.
**United Nations (UN, ONU),** Permanent Observer, 20 East 72nd St, New York, NY 10021. T: (212)734-2900.

*URUGUAY*
**Nunciatura Apostólica,** Nuncio, Bulevar Artigas 1270, CP 1503, Montevideo. T: 411410,411947.

*VENEZUELA*
**Nunciatura Apostólica,** Nuncio, Urb Los Caobos Av La Salle, Apdo 29, Caracas. T: 7818939,7813101.

*VIET NAM*
**Délégation Apostolique au Vietnam et Cambodge,** Délégué, 173 Hai Bà Trung, PO Box 592, Saigon. T: 96876. (Until 1975).

*YUGOSLAVIA*
**Apostolic Nunciature,** Pro-Nuncio, Svetog Save 24, Beograd. T: 432822.

*ZAIRE*
**Nonciature Apostolique,** Pro-Nonce, Av Goma 81, BP 3091, Kinshasa-Gombe. T: 31419.

*ZAMBIA*
**Apostolic Nunciature,** Pro-Nuncio, Brentwood Drive, PO Box 1445, Lusaka. T: 50786. (Also serves Malawi).

# 19
# Ecumenical Centres

*Definition.* Centres primarily for interdenominational or ecumenical meeting, study, dialogue and training, for both clergy and laity. For centres or institutes primarily concerned with ecumenical research, see RESEARCH CENTRES. See also LAY TRAINING CENTRES.
The total centres of major significance number over 300.

*AUSTRIA*
**Pro Orient Centres,** In der Burg, Saulenstiege II-54, A-1010 Wien.

*BELGIUM*
**Brussels Ecumenical Centre,** Av Charles Thielemans 110, Brussel 15.
**Centre Oecuménique des Frères Carmes,** Galerie Porte Luise 221, Brussel 5.
**Centre Oecuménique pour Eglise et Société,** Av d'Auderghem 23, B-1040 Brussel. T: (02) 7331131.
**Foyer Oriental Chrétien,** Av de la Couronne 206, B-1050 Brussel. T: (02)477106.
**Monastère Bénédictin,** Dom Olivier Rousseau, B-5395 Chevetogne.

*BRAZIL*
**Centro de Ecumenismo do Rio de Janeiro (CERJ),** Rua Cosme Velho 98, Laranjeiras, Rio de Janeiro, GB. T: 2251547.

*CANADA*
**Centre Mi-ca-el,** 4661 Queen Mary Rd, Montréal 247, Québec. T: (514)739-6048.
**Centre Monchanin,** 4917 Rue St Urbain, Montréal 151, Québec H2T 2W1.
**Centre Oecuménique Diocésain/Ecumenical Centre,** 1444 Rue Drummond, Montréal 107, Québec. T: (514)845-7141.
**Ecumenical Institute of Canada,** 11 Madison Av, Toronto, Ontario M5R 232. T: (416)924-9351.

*DENMARK*
**Ecumenical Centre,** Klovermarksvej 4, DK-8200 Arhus N. T: 06136711.

*ETHIOPIA*
**Saint Frumentius Ecumenical Centre,** PO Box 3, Adi-Ugri.

*FINLAND*
**Ecumenical Centre of Myllyjärvi (Myllyjärvi Ekumeeninen Keskus),** Myllyjärvi, 00950 Kunnarla. T: (90)857148.
**Orthodox Institute (Ortodoksinen Laitos),** Helsingin Yliopiston Ekumeeninen Arkisto, Helsinki.

*FRANCE*
**Abbaye de Notre-Dame du Bec,** F-27800 Le Bec, Hellouin.
**Abbaye St Martin,** F-86240 Ligugé.
**Centre de Villemétrie,** Orgemont, 91 La Ferte Alais.
**Centre d'Etudes Istina,** 45 Rue de la Glacière, F-75013 Paris. T: 587-3735.
**Centre d'Etudes Oecuméniques,** 8 Rue Gustave Klotz, F-67 Strasbourg. T: (88)362926.
**Centre Oecuménique,** 12 Rue Fénélon, 36 Lyon.
**Centre Oecuménique de Liaisons Internationales (COELI),** 68 Rue de Babylone, F-75007 Paris. T: 555-2554.
**Centre Oecuménique Enotikon,** 43 du Fer-à-Moulin, F-75005 Paris. T: 535-8098.
**Centre Oecuménique Unité Chrétienne,** 2 Rue Jean Carriès, F-69005 Lyon. T: (78)421167.
**Centre Protestant de l'Ouest,** Celles-sur-Belle, Deux-Sèvres.
**Centre Saint-Irénée,** 2 Place Gailleton, F-69002 Lyon. T: (78)374982.
**Formation Oecuménique Interconfessionnelle (FOI),** 2 Place Gailleton, F-69002 Lyon. T: (78) 374982.
**Liebfrauenberg,** Pasteur, Maison de l'Eglise, Goersdorf (Bas-Rhin).
**L'Accueil Fraternel,** Le Chambon-sur-Lignon, Loire.
**Monastère Invisible de l'Unité Chrétienne,** 6 Rue Jean-Ferrandi, F-75006 Paris.
**Orthodox Patriarchal Centre,** F-71460 Taizé. (Greek Orthodox).

*GERMAN DEMOCRATIC REPUBLIC*
**Okumenisches Institut beim Ökumenisch-Missionarischen Amt,** Georgenkirchstr 70, DDR-1017 Berlin. T: 5383271.
**Ökumenisches Seminar,** Kirchliche Hochschule Berlin, Teltower Damm 118/122, DDR-1000 Berlin 37. (Protestant).

*GERMANY, Federal Republic of*
**Anglikanisches Institut der Abtei St Matthias,** D-55 Trier.
**Lebenzentrum für die Einheit der Christen,** Schloss Craheim, D-8721 Wetzhausen. (Charismatic).
**Ökumenisches Institut,** Abtei Niederaltaich, D-8351 Niederaltaich bei Deggendorf. T: (0991)318/224.
**Ökumenisches Lebenszentrum Ottmaring (OLZ),** Am Wasserturm 5-13, D-8901 Ottmaring bei Augsberg. T: (0821)602114/5/6/7,59911,599116.

*GUYANA*
**David Rose Centre,** 274 Front Rd, West Ruimveldt, South Georgetown. T: 71209,68899. (Under Guyana Council of Churches).

*INDIA*
**Christian Ecumenical Centre,** 20 Ramakrishnappa Rd, Whitefield PO, Bangalore 5. T: Bangalore 50113.
**Ecumenical Centre,** Sneha Sena Office, PO Box 1774, Cochin-16, Kerala. T: 32056.
**Ecumenical Christian Centre,** Whitfield, Bangalore 562136.

*INDONESIA*
**Christian Ecumenical Centre (Madjelis Pemunda Kristen Oikumenis),** Jalan Teuku Umar 17, Jakarta.
**Wisma Oikumene,** 13-B Jalan Gudang, Sukabumi.

*IRELAND*
**Irish School of Ecumenics,** Sandford Rd, Milltown Park, Dublin 6. T: 977544.

*ISRAEL*
**Ecumenical Institute of Jerusalem,** c/o St George's Close, Jerusalem.
**St Isaiah's House,** 20 Rehov, Gershon Agron, PO Box 1332, Jerusalem. T: (02)29763.

*ITALY*
**Abazia Greza di Grottaferrata,** I-00046 Roma.
**Centro Anglicano,** Palazzo Doria, Via del Corso 303, I-00186 Roma. T: 6780302.
**Centro di Orientamento Ecumenico e Missionario,** Corso Ticinese 15, Milano.
**Centro Ecumenico Cremonese,** Via Cavallotti 25, I-26100 Cremona.
**Centro Ecumenico Nordico (Nordiskt Ekumeniskt Centrum),** US Pietro Campagna 154, I-06081 Assisi (Perugia). T: 821379.
**Centro Ecumenico Pastorale,** Curia Vescoville di Lungro, I-87010 Lungro (Cosenza). T: 27233.
**Centro Ecumenico Santa Nicola,** Padri Domenicani, Basilica S Nicola, I-70122 Bari. T: 211269.
**Centro Ecumenico Santa Rita,** Via Montanara 8, I-00186 Roma. T: 659648.
**Centro Ecumenico Universitario San Martino,** Via del Verzaro 23, I-06100 Perugia.
**Centro Evangelico,** Via Provinciale 17, San Fedele d'Intelvi (Como).
**Centro Evangelico di Cultura,** Via Pietro Cossa 42, Roma.
**Centro Francescano d'Azione Ecumenica,** Chiesa Nouvá, I-06081 Assisi (Perugia).
**Centro Pro Unione (Foyer Unitas),** Frati dell'Atonement, Via S Maria dell'Anima 30 (Piazza Navona), I-00186 Roma. T: 659552,6540657.
**Centro Uno per l'Unità dei Cristiani,** Piazza Tor Sanguigna 13-2, I-00186 Roma. T: 6569598.
**Centro Ut Unum Sint,** Via Antonino Pio 75, I-00145 Roma. T: (06)5138898,5132941.
**Comunità Ecumenica di Rose,** I-13050 Magnano (VC). T: (015)679185.
**Comunità Evangelica Ecumica di Ispra-Varese,** Chiesa Evangelica di San Giovanni, I-21034 Cocquio-Caldana (Varese). T: 79371.
**Foyer & Casa Unitas,** Via Santa Maria dell'Anima 30, I-00186 Roma. T: 565951,651618.
**Hospitium Oecumenicum di San Damiano,** I-06081 Assisi, Perugia.
**St Anthony's Ecumenical Hospice,** Suore dell'Atonement, Via Galeazzo Alessi 10, I-06081 Assisi (Perugia).
**Studi Ecumenici/Centro Internazionale della Pace,** Via Goffredo Casalis 35, I-10143 Torino. T: 745819.

*LEBANON*
**Monastère Notre-Dame de l'Unité,** Yarzé-Baabda, BP 4077, Bayrut. T: 420095. (Clarisse nuns).

*NETHERLANDS*
**Ecumenical Training Centre (Oecumenisch Vormingscentrum Oud Poelgeest),** Oegstgeest.
**Hospitium Oecumenicum,** Waldeck Pyrmontlaan 9, Amsterdam Zuid. T: (020)716861,717631.
**Provincial Training Centre (Provinciaal Vormingscentrum De Haaf),** Natteweg 9, Bergen.

*NORWAY*
**Centre for Ecumenical Theology (Centrum for Okumenisk Teologi),** PO Box 1046, N-5001 Bergen.
**Institute for Ecumenical Meeting (Institutt for Ekumenisk Kontakt),** Gemlevn 17, Oslo.

*PHILIPPINES*
**John XXIII Ecumenical Center (JEC),** Loyola House of Students, PO Box 4082, Manila. T: 991561.

*PORTUGAL*
**Centro Ecumênico Reconciliação,** Apdo 88, Buarcos, Figueira da Foz.

*SOUTH AFRICA*
**Bureau of African Churches,** Christ the King Theological School, Durban.
**Edendale Lay Ecumenical Centre,** PO Box 63, Plessislaer, Natal.
**Stellenbosch Ecumenical Centre,** 81 Brich St, Stellenbosch, CP.
**Wilgespruit Ecumenical Centre,** PO Box 81, Roodepoort, Transvaal. T: (763)1270,2650.

*SPAIN*
**Centro Ecumenico,** Delegación Diocesana de Ecumenismo, Palacio Episcopal, Córdoba.
**Centro Ecumenico,** Lersundi 13, Bilbao 9.
**Centro Ecumenico,** Via Layetana 32, Barcelona 3.
**Centro Ecumenico El Salvador,** Playa del Inglés, Gran Canaria.
**Centro Ecumenico Interconfessional,** Taquígrafo Martí 3-7, Valencia 5.
**Instituto Ecumenico Juan XXIII,** Ramon y Cajal 7, Salamanca.

*SWEDEN*
**Nordic Ecumenical Institute (Nordiska Ekumeniska Institutet),** Stora gatan 65, Box 68,S-190-30 Sigtuna. T: (0760)50330.

*SWITZERLAND*
**Centre Orthodoxe du Patriarcat Oecuménique,** 37 Chemin de Chambésy, CH-1292 Chambésy, Genève. T: (022)581629,581768.
**Ecumenical Institute (WCC),** Dir, Château de Bossey, CH-1298 Céligny (Genève). T: (022) 762531.

*TRINIDAD & TOBAGO*
**Ecumenical Centre,** Deane St, St Augustine.

*UK of GB & NI*
**Audenshaw Foundation,** Muher, Richmond, Yorkshire DL11 6QQ.
**Blaendulais Ecumenical Centre,** Tanyswynfa, Neath, Glamorgan, Wales. (Also: Bryncarnau, Alltwen Chwith, Pontardawe. T: Pontardawe 862388).
**Catholic Ecumenical Centre,** Wood Hall, Linton near Wetherby, Yorks.
**Christian Unity Centre of Charlton,** Assumption Convent, 151 Charlton Rd, London SE7.
**Delaney Centre for Ecumenical Co-operation,** Froddle Crook, Armsthwaite, Cumbria.
**Ecumenical Commission,** Diocese of Westminster, 47 Francis St, London SW1P 1QR.
**Farnecombe Community,** 5 Wolseley Rd, Farnecombe, Godalming, Surrey. T: Godalming 7255.
**Iona Community,** Community House, 214 Clyde St, Glasgow C1, Scotland. (Summer address: Isle of Iona, by Oban, Argyll).
**London Ecumenical Centre,** 35 Jermyn St, London SW1. T: (01)437-0235.
**Scottish Churches' House,** Dunblane, Perthshire, Scotland. T: Dunblane 3588.

*USA*
**Boston Ecumenical Institute,** Box 171, Merrimac, MA 01860.
**Eastlake Ecumenical Center,** Kennydale United Methodist Church, 9321 104th Av, SE, Renton, Washington, DC.
**Ecumenical Continuing Education Center,** Yale University, 363 St Ronan St, New Haven, CT 06511.
**Ecumenical House,** 190 Denslowe Drive, San Francisco, CA 94132.
**Ecumenical Institute,** Wake Forest University, Winston-Salem, NC 27109.
**Ecumenical Institute,** 3444 Congress Parkway, Chicago, IL 60624. T: (312)769-5635.
**Ecumenical Institute,** 4750 North Sheridan, Chicago, IL 60640.
**Graymoor Ecumenical Institute,** Friars of the Atonement, Graymoor Garrison, NY 10524. T: (914) 424-3209,3671.
**John LaFarge Institute,** 106 West 56th St, New York, NY 10019.
**John XXIII Ecumenical Center,** Fordham University, Bronx, NY 10458.
**Laymen's Academy for Oecumenical Studies (LAOS),** 14 Boltwood Av, Box 452, Amherst, MA 01002.
**Metropolitan Ecumenical Training Center,** 2015 Allen Place, NW, Washington, DC 20009.
**North American Academy of Ecumenists,** c/o New York Theological Seminary, 235 East 49 St, New York, NY 10017.
**Packard Manse Ecumenical Center,** Stoughton, MA 02072.
**Parishfield,** Brighton, Michigan.
**Training for Ecumenical Action in Mission (TEAM),** Kansas City, Kansas.
**Wilton Ecumenical Center,** Box 74, Wilton, CT 06897.

*URUGUAY*
**Instituto Ecuménico,** 8 de Octubre 3324, Casilla de Correo 2123, Distrito 5, Montevideo. T: 586818.

*ZAMBIA*
**Mindolo Ecumenical Centre (Foundation),** Principal, Box 1192, Kitwe. T: 84712/3. (Also: PO Box 1493).

*ZIMBABWE*
**Bureau of African Churches,** Lobengula St, Bulawayo.

# 20
# Ecumenical Commissions & Agencies

*Definition.* Organizations for Christian unity or understanding either set up by large churches, or independent of any denomination, for the fostering of relations between the churches, ecumenical meeting, dialogue, study, fellowship, joint action; interconfessional groups; faith and order commissions; church union negotiating bodies and commissions for churches negotiating towards organic union.

*ALGERIA*
**Commission pour l'Oecuménisme,** c/o Archêveché, 13 Rue Khelifa-Boukhalfa, El Djezair (Alger). T: 634244.

*ARGENTINA*
**Catholica Unio,** National Sec, Abadia de Niño Dios, Victoria, ER.
**Comisión Episcopal de Fe y Ecumenismo,** CEA, Paraguay 1867, Buenos Aires.
**Departmento de Ecumenismo (CELAM),** c/o Seminario de Villa de Voto, José Cubas 35-43, Buenos Aires
**Departmento de Ecumenismo,** Arzobispado de Buenos Aires, Suipacha 1034, Buenos Aires.
**Secretariado Nacional de Ecumenismo,** CEA, Paraguay 1867, Buenos Aires.

*AUSTRALIA*
**Committee for Ecumenism,** Australian Episcopal Conference, GPO Box 42, Canberra, ACT 2600.
**Ecumenical Office,** Archdiocese of Melbourne, Sacred Heart Presbytery, 199 Rathdowne St, Carlton 3053. T: 3471644.
**Joint Secretariat RCEC-ACC,** c/o 401A Pitt St, PO Box 111, Brickfield Hill, NSW 20001.

*AUSTRIA*
**Altkatholisch-römisch-katholische Konsultationen,** Sek der Österreichischen Bischofskonferenz, Rotenturmstr 2, A-1010 Wien.
**Catholica Unio,** Zentrale fur Österreich, Landessekretär, p/A Dreifaltigkeitsgasse 14, Postfach 66, A-5024 Salzburg. (Also: Kolster Maria Plain, A-5028 Salzburg-Kasern).
**Diözesankommission für Ökumenische Fragen,** Wollzeille 3, A-1010 Wien.
**Katholischer Arbeitskreis für die Weltgebetswoche in Deutschland, Österreich und der Schweiz** Catholica Unio, Maria Plain, A-5028 Salzburg-Kasern.
**Katholischer Ökumenischer Arbeitskreis in Österreich,** CM v Weber-Grasse 3, Graz.
**Kommission der Katholischen und Evangelischen Kirche Österreichs (Gemischte Katholisch-Evangelische Kommission Österreichs),** Rotenthurmstr 1/2 (& Schellinggasse 12), A-1010 Wien.
**Stiftungsfonds Pro Oriente/Foundation Pro Oriente,** Generalsek, In der Burg, Säulenstiege II/54, A-1010 Wien.

*BAHAMAS*
**Ecumenical Commission,** Diocese of Nassau, PO Box 187, Nassau.

*BELGIUM*
**Commission pour l'Oecuménisme (Conférence Episcopale Catholique),** Rue Guimard 5, B-1040 Brussel. T: (02)5118256.

*BELIZE*
**Planning Commission of Churches,** Regent St, Belize City.

*BENIN*
**Commission Episcopale pour l'Islam et l'Oecuménisme,** BP 491, Cotonou.

*BRAZIL*
**Catholica Unio,** National Sec, Priorado San Ana, Jundiaí, SP.

**Equipe Fraterna,** CP 2013, Recife, PE.

**Fraternidade de Reconciliação,** Rua São Bento 44, CP 975 Recife, PE.

**Secretaria de Ecumenismo da CNBB e Regionais,** Ladeira da Glória 99, Rio de Janeiro GB.

**Serviço Interconfessional de Aconselhamento (SICA),** AV Alberto Bins 1008, Pôrto Alegre, Rio Grande do Sul. T: 247877.

*CAMEROON*

**Comité de l'Union des Eglises au Cameroun,** Sec, Bibia, BP 10, Lolodorf.

**Oeuvre Sociale Oecuménique,** BP 913, Douala.

*CANADA*

**General Commission on Church Union,** Room 312, 85 St Clair Av East, Toronto 290, Ontario. T: (416)920-4030.

**Groupe de Travail des Eglises de Montréal (Joint Working Group of Montreal Churches),** Montréal, Québec.

**Joint Working Group CCC-CCC/Groupe Mixte de Travail du CCC-CCC,** 40 St Clair Av East, Toronto 290, Ontario. T: (416)921-4152. (Catholic/Protestant).

**National Office of Ecumenism,** CCC, 830 Bathurst St, Toronto 179, Ontario.

**National Secretariat for Ecumenism,** 830 Bathurst St, Toronto 179, Ontario. T: (416)534-2326.

**Office National d'Oecuménisme,** CCC, 1444/1452 Rue Drummond, ch 214, Montréal 107, Québec. T: (514)845-7141.

**People's Opportunities in Ecumenical Mission (POEM),** Co-Ordinator, 1708 West 16th Av, Vancouver, BC, V6J 2M1. T: 733-3131.

*CHANNEL ISLANDS*

**St Brelade Group of Churches,** Rectory, La Marquanderie, St Brelade, Jersey. T: (0534)42302.

*CHILE*

**Departamento Nacional de Ecumenismo,** Las Ramadas 716, Dpto 23, Classificador 11, Casilla 9194 (& 13861), Santiago.

*COLOMBIA*

**Comité Nacional de Ecumenismo del Secretariado Permanente del Episcopado,** Carrera 10 No 19-42, of 410, Bogotá. T: 414642.

*CUBA*

**Comisión Episcopal Nacional de Ecumenismo,** Apdo 594, La Habana 1. T: 68463.

*CZECHOSLOVAKIA*

**Catholic Diocesan Ecumenical Commission,** c/o Archdiocese of Prague, Hradcanské nám 16, 119 02 Praha 1. T: 536022.

*FINLAND*

**Ecumenical Secretariat of the Diocese of Helsinki (Helsingin hiippakunnan ekumeeninen sihteeristö),** Stadium Catholicum, Helsinki.

**Ecumenical Society in Finland (Suomen Ekumenninen Seura),** Temppelikatu 21 C 13, 00100 Helsinki 10.

*FRANCE*

**Association Oecuménique (BOSEB),** 67 Rue St Dominique 75, F-75007 Paris.

**Comité Mixte Catholique-Protestant,** 8 Villa du Parc Montsouris, F-75014 Paris. T: (01)589-5569. (Also: 17 Rue de l'Assomption, F-75016 Paris. T: (01)647-7357).

**Groupe Interconfessionnel des Dombes,** Côté Catholique, 6 Rue Jean Ferrandi, F-75006 Paris.

**Groupe Interconfessionnel des Dombes,** Côté Protestant, 12 Rue Fénelon, F-69 Lyon

**Groupe Mixte Anglican-Catholique Romain,** 17 Rue de l'Assomption F-75016 Paris. T: (01) 288-2185.

**Recherche Theologique et Relations Oecuméniques,** FPF, Sec, 47 Rue de Clichy, F-75009 Paris. T: 874-1508.

**Secrétariat Français pour l'Unité des Chrétiens,** 17 Rue de l'Assomption, F-75016 Paris. T: (01) 647-7357.

**Unité Chrétienne (Association Interconfessionnelle),** 2 Rue Jean-Carries, F-69005 Lyon. T: (78)421167. (Catholic-Protestant).

*GERMAN DEMOCRATIC REPUBLIC*

**Konfessionskundliches Arbeitwerk der Ev Kirche in DDR,** Mauerstr 9, DDR-15 Postdam.

**Ökumenische Arbeitstelle der Diözese Meissen,** Karl Heine Str 110, DDR-7031 Leipzig.

**Referent für Ökumenische Fragen der Ordinarienkonferenz der Bistumer und Kommissariate der DDR,** Karl Heine Str 110, DDR-7031 Leipzig.

*GERMANY, Federal Republic of*

**Ausschuss der EKD für des Gespräch mit der Russischen Orthodoxen Kirche,** Bockenheimer Landstr 109, D-6 Frankfurt/Main.

**Bund für Evangelisch-Katholische Wiedervereinigung,** Postfach 15, D-6393 Wehreheim (Taunus).

**Catholica Unio,** Zentrale für Deutschland, Nationalsek, Dominikanerplatz 4, D-87 Wurzburg. (Begun 1923, working for reunion with Orthodoxy).

**Catholica-Ausschuss der EKD,** Meiserstr 13, D-8 München 37.

**Evang Kath Okumenischer Arbeitkreis,** Herzog-Wilhelm Str 24, D-8000 München 2.

**Evangelische Arbeitsgruppe für die Ökumenische Gebetswoche in Deutschland, Österreich und der Schweiz,** Ökumenische Centrale, Bockenheimer Landstr 109, D-6 Frankfurt/M.

**Gemeinsame Kommission der Konferenz der Katholischen Bischofe Deutschlands und der Alt-katholischen Kirche in Deutschland,** Arndtstr 23, D-53 Bonn. (Also: Abtei St Mathias, D-55 Trier).

**Gemeinsame Kommission des Rates der EKD und der Konferencz der Katholischen Bischöfe Deutschlands,** Meiserstr 13, D-8 München 37. (Also: Domplatz 3, D-479 Paderborn).

**Kommission für Ökumenische Fragen der Katholischen Bischöf Deutschland,** Beringstr 30, D-5300 Bonn. T: (02221)631661/65.

**Ökumenische Centrale,** Arbeitsgemeinschaft Christlicher Kirchen in Deutschland, Bochenheimer Landstr 109, Postfach 4025, D-6 Frankfurt/Main. T: 770521.

**Ökumenische Kommission der Konferenz der Katholischen Bischöfe Deutschlands,** Domplatz 3, D-479 Paderborn.

**Ökumenische Kommission für die Unterstützung Orthodoxer Priester in der BRD,** Geschäftsführer, Possartstr 9, D-8 München 27.

**Ökumenische Verenigung des Augsburgischen Bekenntnisses,** Geschäftsführung, Postfach 594, D-44 Münster. (Ecumenical Lutheran/Catholic).

**Ökumenischer Arbeitskreis der Evangelischen Michaels-brüderschaft,** Sek, Wiesenstr 26, D-477 Soest.

**Ökumenischer Leiterkreis der Akademien und Laieninstitute in Europa,** Ev Akademie, D-7325 Bad Boll über Göppingen. T: (07164)351.

**Ökumenisches Referat des Kirchlichen Aussenamites der EKD,** Bochenheimer Landstr 109, D-6000 Frankfurt/Main.

*GHANA*

**Committee of Co-operation,** c/o National Catholic Secretariat, PO Box 5730, Accra. T: 22871.

**Ghana Church Union Committee,** PO Box 1434, Accra.

*HAITI*

**Groupe Oecuménique de Recherches,** BP 117, Port-au-Prince.

*HOLY SEE*

**Secretariat for Christian Unity/Segretariato per l'Unione dei Cristiani,** I-00120 Città del Vaticano. T: 6982 int 3071,4271. (Also: Via dell-'Erba 1, I-00193 Roma, Italy).

*HONG KONG*

**Diocesan Ecumenical Commission,** c/o Catholic Centre.

*INDIA*

**All India Liaison Body,** c/o CBCI, Ashok Place, New Delhi 110001. (Catholic/Protestant).

**Commission for Ecumenism,** CBCI, Ashok Place, New Delhi 110001.

**Fellowship of St Thomas and St Paul,** Sec, Adur PO, Travancore. (Syrian Orthodox and other churches).

**Joint Faith and Order Study Project,** Catholic Bishop of Poona, Poona 411001, Maharashtra. (Also: CSI Bishop of Madras, San Thome, Mylapore, Madras 600004).

**United Christmas Celebration Committee in Trivandrum Area,** Syro-Malankara Archbishop's House, Trivandrum 4, Kerala.

*INDONESIA*

**Ecumenical Commission,** MAWI, PWI Ekumene, Jalan Jend Achmad Yani 25, Bogor. (RC).

*ISRAEL*

**Ecumenical Commission,** Latin Patriachate, Old City, POB 14152, Jerusalem. T: 0282323.

*ITALY*

**Associazione Cattolica Italiana per l'Oriente Cristiano (ACIOC),** Piazza Bellini 3, I-90133 Palermo.

**Associazione Internazionale Unitas,** Via del Corso 306, I-00186 Roma.

**Azione Ecumenica Europea,** Largo Chigi 19, I-00187 Roma.

**Circolo Ecumenico Koinonia,** Via dei Greci 3, I-00187 Roma.

**Gruppo Ecumenico Genovese,** Gall Mazzini 7/5A, I-16121 Genova.

**Interconfessional Ecumenical Training,** Via Statuto 4, I-20121 Milano.

**Segretariato Attivita Ecumeniche,** Via della Cava Aurelia 8, I-00165 Roma. T: 635049. (Also: Via A De Gasperi 2, I-00165 Roma).

*JAMAICA*

**Commission on Ecumenism,** Archbishop's Residence, 21 Hopefield Av, PO Box 43, Kingston 6.

*JAPAN*

**Episcopal Commission for Ecumenism,** c/o National Catholic Committee of Japan, 10-1 Rokubancho, Chiyoda-ku, Tokyo 102. T: 26236913.

**Japan Ecumenical Association (JEA),** 2-28-5 Matsubara, Setagaya-ku, Tokyo 156. T: 3227601.

*KENYA*

**Inter-Christian Churches Denomination,** Sec, Nyeri Parish PCEA, Hospital Rd, PO Box 182, Nyeri. T: 251.

*KOREA, South*

**Ecumenical Commission,** 90-2 Hye Hwa Dong, Jong Ro Ku, Soul. T: 736781.

*LEBANON*

**Comité de Coordination des Mouvements Chrétiens,** Pres, BP 1375, Bayrut. T: 341902.

**Commission du Catholicossat Arménien de Cilicie pour les Relations Ecuméniques,** Catholicossat Arménien, Antélias.

**Groupe Oecuménique de Pastorale (GOP),** BP 7002 or 1375, Bayrut. T: 300425,341902.

*LIBERIA*

**United Ecumenical Organization (UEO),** Monrovia.

*LUXEMBOURG*

**Oekumenische Heimstätte,** Lorochette. T: 87081.

*MADAGASCAR*

**Commission pour l'Oecuménisme,** Conférence Episcopale de Madagascar, BP 3846, Tananarive. T: 20763.

*MALAWI*

**National Catholic Commission for Ecumenism,** PO Box 385, Blantyre.

*MALTA*

**Ecumenical Commission,** Episcopal Conference, Archbishop's House, Valletta.

**Ecumenical Group,** 1 Victory St, Valletta.

*MEXICO*

**Secretariado Nacional de Ecumenismo,** Av Universidad 1700, Apdo Postal 21-984, México 21, DF. T: 5348245.

*MOZAMBIQUE*

**Comissão Episcopal do Ecumenismo,** CP 21, Maputo (Lourenço Marques).

*NAMIBIA*

**Christian Foundation of South West Africa (Christelike Stigting van Suidwes-Afrika),** PO Box 8090, Bachbrecht, Windhoek.

*NETHERLANDS*

**Ecumenical Action Centre (Oekumenisch Actie Centrum),** Di Horst 1, Driebergen.

*NEW ZEALAND*

**Ecumenical Affairs Committee,** Convenor, 272a Te Atatu Rd, Auckland 8.

**Joint Commission on Church Union in NZ,** Sec, PO Box 87, Wellington.

**Joint Working Committee (NCCNZ-RCC),** PO Box 297, Christchurch.

**National Commission of Ecumenism,** 140 Austin St, Wellington 1. T: 58518.

*NORWAY*

**Church of Norway Council on Foreign Relations (Mellomkirkelig Rad for den Norske Kirke),** Geitmyrsveien 7D, Oslo 1. T: 463416.

**Contact Circle for Churches (Kontaktkretsen for Kirkesamfunn),** Kragsvei 1, Oslo 3.

*PAKISTAN*

**Commission for Ecumenism,** Catholic Bishops' Conference, St Patrick's Cathedral, Karachi 3.

*PANAMA*

**Departamento Arquidiocesano de Ecumenismo,** Apdo 6386, Panamá 5. T: 627400 ext 13.

*PARAGUAY*

**Departamento de Ecumenismo,** CEP, Coronel Bogado 884, Casilla de Correo 654, Asunción. T: 41946.

*PERU*

**Secretariado para la Unión de los Cristianos,** Malecon Armendariz 211, Dpto 142, Miraflores, Lima.

*PHILIPPINES*

**Bishops' Commission for Promoting Christian Unity (BCPCU),** Loyola House of Studies, PO Box 4082, Manila. T: 981441,991561/4.

*POLAND*

**Episcopal Ecumenical Commission,** ul Miodowa 17, Warszawa.

**Section Oecuménique,** Université Catholique de Lublin, 7 ul Nowotki, Lublin.

*RWANDA*

**Fraternité Oecuménique,** BP 528, Kigali.

**Secrétariat pour l'Unité des Chrétiens,** BP 405, Kigali.

*SEYCHELLES*

**Comité Oecuménique,** Evêché, PO Box 43, Port Victoria, Mahé. T: 2152.

*SINGAPORE*

**Toa Payoh Ecumenical Community Service,** 127 Block 4, Lorong 7, Toa Payoh, Singapore 12.

*SOUTH AFRICA*

**Church Unity Commission,** PO Box 31083, Braamfontein, Transvaal.

**Commission for Ecumenism and Afrikaans Affairs,** PO Box 941, Pretoria. T: 36230,30322.

*SPAIN*

**Misioneras de la Unidad,** Los Arfe 43, Madrid 17. T: 4073798.

**Secretariado Nacional de Ecumenismo,** CEE, Calle Alfonso XI 4-1, Madrid 14.

*SRI LANKA*

**Ecumenical Commission,** Archbishop's House, Colombo 8.

**Secretariat for Christian Unity,** 976 Marandana Rd, Colombo 8.

*SWEDEN*

**Swedish Ecumenical Association (Svenska Ekumeniska Föreningen),** Sec, Box 6302, 113 81 Stockholm 6.

*SWITZERLAND*

**Catholica Unio Internationalis,** Generalsek, Charrière, CH-1700 Fribourg.

**Commission de Dialogue entre les Eglises Réformées et l'Eglise Catholique Romaine,** Rue de Morat 262, CH-1700 Fribourg. T: (037)234744.

**Commission de Dialogue entre l'Eglise Catholique Romaine et l'Eglise Vieille Catholique,** Fellenbergstr 1, CH-3012 Bern. T: (031)238144.

**Commission pour l'Oecuménisme,** Conférence des Evêques Suisses, Chemin Eaux-Vives 21, CP 40, CH-1700 Fribourg 3. T: (037)2444794.

**Department of Church Co-operation,** Lutheran World Federation, 150 Route de Ferney, CH-1211 Genève 20.

**Ev Katholische Gesprachskommission des Schweizerischen Evangelischen Kirchenbundes und der Schweizerischen Katholischen Bischofskonferenz,** Murtengasse 262, CH-1700 Fribourg. (Also: Romerweg 26, CH-4450 Sissach).

**Gesprachskommission der Christkatholischen und Romisch-Katholischen Kirchen in der Schweiz,** Shylerstr 24 & Schwarztorstr 35, CH-3000 Bern.

**Katholische Kommission für Ökumenische Fragen in der Schweiz,** Rue de Lausanne 86, CH-1700 Fribourg.

**Ligue Oecuménique pour l'Unité Chrétienne,** Rue du Stand 64, CH-2500 Biel.

**Ökumenische Kommission des Schweizerischen Evangelischen Kirchenbundes,** Zeltweg, CH-8032 Zürich.

**Schweizerische Ostkirchenwerk Catholica Unio,** Sek, Adligenswilerstr 13, CH-6000 Luzern. T: (041)226657. (RC body working for reunion with Orthodoxy).

**Solidaritätsgruppen Schweiz,** Postfach 613, CH-8050 Zürich.

*TANZANIA*

**Commission for Ecumenism,** Tanzania Episcopal Conference, Mission Bldg, Mansfield St, PO Box 2133, Dar es Salaam. T: 20430,20477.

*TUNISIA*

**Service Oecuménique en Tunisie,** 10 Rue Eve Nohelle, Tunis. T: 245592.

*TURKEY*

**Commission pour les Affaires Oecuméniques,** Vicariat Apostolique, Satirci sok 2, Pangalti, Istanbul.

*USSR*

**Department of International Church Relations,** Moscow Patriarchate, Chairman, Ryleev St 18/2, Moskva G-34. T: 467405.

*UK of GB & NI*

**Amitié,** Organizing Sec, 67 Cranford Av, London, N13. (Teachers for Christian unity).

**Anglican and Eastern Churches Association,** Sec, 85 Mortimer Rd, London NI. T: (01)254-7945. (Also: 88 Farlington Av, Drayton, Portsmouth).

**Catholic Episcopal Commission for Ecumenism,** Ara Coeli, Armagh, NI.

**Church of England Council on Foreign Relations,** Gen Sec, Palace Court, 222 Lambeth Rd, London SE1. T: (01)928-4880.

**Church Union,** 199 Uxbridge Rd, London W12. T: (01)743-0726.

**Churches Unity Commission,** Church House, Dean's Yard, London SW1P 3NZ. T: (01)222-9011.

**Consultative Committee for Local Ecumenical Projects England & Wales (CCLEPE),** Sec, 10 Eaton Gate, London SW1.

**Ecumenical Society of the Blessed Virgin Mary,** 237 Fulham Palace Rd, London SW6 6UB. T: (01)381-1615.

**English Catholic-Methodist Committee,** c/o RC Bishops Conference and Methodist Headquarters, London.

**Fellowship of St Alban & St Sergius,** Sec, St Basil's House, 52 Ladbroke Grove, London W11 2PB. T: (01)727-7713. (Anglican-Orthodox).

**Fellowship of St Andrew,** Canmore, 24 The Scores, St Andrews, Fife. T: 3133.

**ICC-RCC Joint Working Group,** c/o Irish Council of Churches, 1 Meadow Grove, Crawfordburn, County Down, NI.

**International Ecumenical Fellowship (IEF),** Gen Sec, 42 Crutched Friars, London EC3N 2AL. (Also: Effingham Park, Copthorne, Sussex) (RC/Anglican/Protestant/Old Catholic).

**Joint Commission between Church of England and RC Church in England,** c/o RC Bishops' Conference and Church of England Headquarters, London.

**One for Christian Renewal,** Sec, 300 Granville Rd, Sheffield S2 2RT. T: (0742)21020. (Incorporating Parish & People, Friends of Reunion).

**Order of Christian Unity,** Sec, 39 Victoria St, London SW1. T: (01)222-6331.

**Roman Catholic Ecumenical Commissions of England and Wales,** Sacred Heart Convent, Woldingham, Nr Caterham, Surrey CR3 7YA. T: Caterham 46703.

**Roman Catholic Ecumenical Commission of Scotland,** Convent of Notre Dame, 7 Victoria Circus, Dowanhill, Glasgow G12 9LA.

**Society of St John Chrysostom,** 40 Therlmere Rd, London N10 2DN. T: (01)888-6144.

**Vita et Pax Foundation for Unity.** (For monks: Christus Rex Priory, 29 Bramly Rd, London N14. T: (01)449-6648. For nuns: Benedictine Priory, 1 Priory Close, Southgate, London N14 4AT. T: (01) 449-8336.

*USA*

**American-European Fellowship for Christian Oneness,** Pres, 15 Philips Place, Yonkers, NY 10701.

**Consultation on Church Union (COCU),** Gen Sec, 228 Alexander St, Princeton, NJ 08540. T: (609) 921-7866.

**Council on Christian Unity,** 222 South Downey Av, PO Box 1986, Indianapolis, IN 46207.

**Ecumenical Associates,** 84 Michigan National Tower, Lansing, MI 48933.

**Ecumenical Program for Inter-American Communication and Action (EPICA),** 2201 P St, NW, Washington, DC 10037.

**Ecumenical Training Council,** 107 East Forst St, Boise, ID 83702.

**Joint Commission on Ecumenical Relations,** 815 Second Av, New York, NY 10017. (Episcpal Church).

**North American Academy of Ecumenists,** New York, NY 10017.

**Packard Manse,** 583 Plain St, Stoughton, MA 02072. (Also: 41 Winthrop St, Roxbury, Massachusetts).

*VENEZUELA*
**Comisión Arquidiocesana de Ecumenismo,** Apdo 954, Caracas 101. T: 811189.
**Comisión de la Fe, Moral y Ecumenismo,** Edf Juan XXIII, piso 6, Torre a Madrices, Caracas 101.
**Segretriado de la Fe,** Edf Juan XXIII, piso 6, Torre a Madrices, Caracas 101.

*YUGOSLAVIA*
**Commission for Ecumenism,** Biskupska Konferencija Jugoslavije, Kaptol 31, YU-41000 Zagreb.

*ZAIRE*
**Secrétariat pour l'Unité,** Conférence Episcopale du Zaïre, BP 3258, Kinshasa-Gombe.

*ZAMBIA*
**National Ecumenical Commission,** ZEC, Unity House, Stanley Rd, Jameson St, PO Box 1965, Lusaka. T: 73470.

*ZIMBABWE*
**Episcopal Commisison for Ecumenism,** PO Box 2591, Salisbury.

# 21
# Evangelization & Mass Evangelism

*Definition.* International evangelistic organizations, evangelistic societies, evangelistic associations, professional evangelists, revival campaigns, tent campaigns, crusades, missions, long-term campaigns (Evangelism-in-Depth, New Life for All), saturation evangelism (total mobilization evangelism), multiplication evangelism; evangelistic centres, radio and TV evangelistic enterprises, film evangelism; annual or regular mass rallies (e.g. Cliff College, UK); national and international congresses of evangelism and evangelization; world evangelization agencies, councils, congresses, institutions, programmes.

*AUSTRALIA*
**Campaigners for Christ,** 379 Kent St, PO Box A87, Sydney South, NSW 2000. T: 2901592.
**Church Army in Australia,** Wyatt Av, Belrose, Sydney. T: 4518395.
**Key 75,** c/o Diocesan Church House, George St, Sydney, NSW 2000. T. 262371.
**Open Air Campaigners,** National Office and Training Department, 20 Minnie St, Belmore, NSW 2192. T: 7508646.
**Oral Roberts Evangelistic Association,** PO Box 17, Rockdale. NSW 2216.
**United Churches Evangelistic Crusades,** CENEF Memorial Centre, Bathurst & Kent Sts. Sydney. T: 617788.

*BRAZIL*
**Associação Brasileira de Evangelização/Brazilian Evangelistic Association,** CP 19.010, 01000 São Paulo, ZP-15, SP.
**T.L.Osborn Evangelistic Association,** CP 2, Penha, ZC-22, 20.000 Rio de Janeiro, GB.

*BURUNDI*
**New Life for All,** BP 120, Gitega.

*CAMEROON*
**New Life for All,** BP 4092, Yaoundé.

*CANADA*
**Campbell Reese Evangelistic Association,** Box 10, Milton, Ontario.
**Church Army in Canada,** 397 Brunswick Av, Toronto 4, Ontario.
**Crusade Evangelism,** Barry Moore and Team, Box 2, London, Ontario.
**Invitation to Live Crusades,** Marney Patterson and Team, 36 Shady Lane Crescent, Thornhill, Ontario.
**Janz Brothers Gospel Association,** Pres, 144 Westview Drive, Box 400, Calgary, Alberta. T: 249-2073.
**Leighton Ford Evangelistic Association,** 96 Rexdale Blvd, Rexdale, Ontario.
**Mission La Bonne Nouvelle,** 249-253 St George St, Moncton, New Brunswick.
**Oral Roberts Evangelistic Association,** Canada Rep, Station K, Box 8, Toronto, Ontario.
**Terry Winter Evangelistic Association,** 416 West 28th Av, Box 7307, Vancouver 15, BC.

*CENTRAL AFRICAN REPUBLIC*
**New Life for All,** Life in Christ, BP 240, Bangui.

*CHAD*
**New Life for All,** c/o Mission SUM, Ndjamena (Fort Lamy).

*CHINA (TAIWAN)*
**Every Home Crusade,** Dir, Hsin Sheng S Rd, Sec 1, Lane 146, No 7-1, Box 4020, Taipei. T: 20084.
**Overseas Crusades,** Nanking East Rd, Sec 3, No 272, Box 555, Taipei. T: 772522. (Also: Nanking East Rd, Lane 405, No 6, Taipei. T: 42122/3).

*COSTA RICA*
**Comunidad Latinoamericana de Ministerios Evangélicos (CLAME),** Pres, Apdo 1307, San José. T: 215622. (Latin American Mission).

*ETHIOPIA*
**New Life for All,** MEGM, PO Box 1092, Asmera.
**New Life for All,** Sudan Interior Mission, PO Box 127, Addis Abeba.

*GERMANY, Federal Republic of*
**Deutsche Zeltmission,** Sohlbacher Str 152, Postfach 1, D-593 Hüttental-Geisweid.
**Deutscher Evangelischer Kirchentag,** Leitung, Magdeburger Str 59, D-6400 Fulda. T: (0661)71091.
**MV Doulos,** Postfach 2808, D-7100 Heilbronn. (Evangelistic ship).

*GHANA*
**New Life for All,** Box 919, Accra.

*HOLY SEE*
**Mouvement International d'Apostolat des Milieux Sociaux Indépendants (MIAMSI),** Piazza San Calisto 16, I-00120 Città del Vaticano. T: 6894683. (Evangelization of the middle and upper classes).
**Sacred Congregation for the Evangelization of Peoples/SC pro Gentium Evangelizatione (De Propaganda Fide),** Palazzo di Propaganda Fide, Piazza di Spagna 48, I-00187 Roma, Italy. T: 686941.

*HONG KONG*
**Chinese Coordination Center of World Evangelism (CCCWE),** 12-14 Hart Av 17/F, PO Box 6127, Tsim Sha Tsui, Kowloon.

*INDIA*
**All Kerala United Evangelistic Movement,** Convenor, PO Box 16, Tiruvalla, Kerala.
**Oral Roberts Evangelistic Association,** South India Rep, Sunbeam, Plammoodu, Trivandrum 4, Kerala.

*INDONESIA*
**Malachi Evangelistic Foundation,** Evangelist, Martadinata 75, Bandung.

*ITALY*
**Crociata dell'Evangelo per Ogni Casa,** Via Curtatone 10, Roma.

*IVORY COAST*
**New Life for All,** BP 585, Bouaké.

*JAPAN*
**Tokyo Evangelistic Center,** 2-30 6-chome, Higashi Fushimi, Hoya-shi, Tokyo.

*KENYA*
**African Evangelistic Enterprise (AEE),** Convenor, Bible House, Mfangano St, PO Box 47596, Nairobi. T: 28023.
**Every Home Evangelism,** National Dir, Leslander House, Haile Selassie Av, PO Box 72933, Nairobi. T: 25702.

*KOREA, South*
**International Fellowship for World Evangelization,** OMS International, CPO Box 1261, Soul 100. (Uniting 17 OMS denominations across world).

*LEBANON*
**Equipes d'Evangelisation,** BP 7002, Bayrut. (Roman Catholic).

*MALAWI*
**New Life for All,** PO Box 450, Lilongwe.

*MALAYSIA*
**Malaysia Evangelistic Fellowship (MEF),** Pres, 35 Jalan Munshi Abdullah, Melaka (Malacca).

*MALI*
**New Life for All,** BP 158, Bamako.

*MEXICO*
**Asociación Billy Graham,** Bucareli No 42-303, Zona 1, México, DF. T. 133014.

*NEW ZEALAND*
**Open Air Campaigners (NZ),** PO Box 2160 Auckland 1.
**Oral Roberts Evangelistic Association,** New Zealand Rep, PO Box 6288, Te Aro, Wellington.

*NIGER*
**New Life for All,** Sudan Interior Mission, Maradi.

*NIGERIA*
**National Congress on Evangelisation,** PO Box 500, Jos.
**New Life for All,** Gen Sec, PO Box 77, Jos, Northern Nigeria.

*PERU*
**Evangelismo a Fondo,** Jr Unión 521, Of 205, Apdo 3997, Lima. T: 31888.

*PHILIPPINES*
**A.A. Allen Revivals,** Lauan and Molave Sts, Quirnio District, Project III, Quezon City.
**Asian Evangelists Commission,** PO Box 2799, Manila.
**Christ for Greater Manila,** 989 Fermin St, Malate, Manila.
**Christian Laymen's Evangelistic Crusade,** 949 East de los Santos Av, Quezon City.
**Gospel Harvestors Evangelistic Association,** PO Box 2002, Manila.
**Harvest Fields Evangelistic Association,** PO Box 4142, Manila.
**National Fellowship for Philippines Evangelism (NAFE),** PO Box 2557, Manila.
**Open Air Campaigners,** 259-B Kanlaon, Mandaluyong, Rizal, PO Box 2772, Manila.
**Philippine Crusades,** Field Dir, 210 A Martinez, Mandaluyong, Rizal, PO Box 1416, Manila. T: 704061.
**Philippine Evangelical Enterprises,** 3111 Nagtahan, Manila.

*PORTUGAL*
**Comissão Nacional para a Evangelização da Ilha do Príncipe,** Alameda das Linhas de Torres 122, Lisboa-5.
**Cruzada Pró-Evangelização de Portugal,** Dirigente, Apdo 32, Leiria.
**Movimento Promotor de Evangelização,** Dir, Rua da Mãe d'Agua, 13, 2 Dto, Lisboa-2.

*SIERRA LEONE*
**New Life for All,** PO Box 86, Bo.

*SINGAPORE*
**Asia Evangelistic Fellowship,** Founder, 120 Upper Serangoon Rd, GPO Box 579, Singapore 13. T: 81542. (Malaysia Ev Fellowship).
**Asia South Pacific Congress on Evangelism,** 65 Wishart Rd, Singapore 4.
**Asian Leadership Conference on Evangelism (ALCOE),** PO Box 337, Tanglin, Singapore 10. T: 2356525.
**Asian Office of Evangelism-in-Depth,** 9 Bassein Rd, Singapore 11.
**Co-ordinating Office for Asian Evangelism (COFAE) (Christ Seeks Asia),** Exec Dir, 6 Mount Sophia, Singapore 9. T: 24918.

*SOUTH AFRICA*
**Africa Enterprise,** 202 Longmarket St, PO Box 647, Pietermaritzburg, Natal. T: 24904.
**Dorothea Mission in South Africa,** PO Box 219, Pretoria, Transvaal.
**Lay Institute for Evangelism (LIFE),** PO Box 13046, Northmead, Benoni, Transvaal. T: 8493612.
**Modern Evangelistic Methods in Africa (MEMA),** 12 Ninth St, Menlopark, Pretoria.
**Oral Roberts Evangelistic Association,** South Africa Rep, PO Box 345, Johannesburg, Transvaal.

*SWAZILAND*
**New Life for All,** PO Box 333, Mbabane.

*SWITZERLAND*
**Commission on World Mission and Evangelism (CWME),** World Council of Churches, 150 Route de Ferney, CH-1211 Genève 20. T: (0104122)333400.
**Eurovangelism,** 30 Ch des Passereaux, CH-1225 Chêne-Bourg, Genève.
**International Congress on World Evangelization,** Continuation Committee, Palais de Beaulieu, Av de Jomini, CP 225, CH-1001 Lausanne. T: (021)213270. (16-25 July 1974, and followup).
**Schweizerische Zeltmission,** Sek, Gossetstr 64, CH-3084 Wabern. T: (031)543672.

*TANZANIA*
**New Life for All,** Diocese of Morogoro, Berega, PO Kilosa.

*UGANDA*
**African Enterprise,** PO Box 114, Kabale.

*UK OF GB & NI*
**Ambassadors for Christ Britain,** 63 Ivybridge Rd, Coventry CU3 5PF. T: 411577.
**Archbishops' Council on Evangelism,** Exec Sec, Diocesan House, Quarry St, Guildford, Surrey GU1 3XG. T: (0483)32237.
**Billy Graham Evangelistic Association,** Dir, Shirley House, 27 Camden Rd, London NW1 9LN. T: (01)267-0065.
**Church Army,** Chief Sec, CSC House, North Circular Rd, London NW10 7UG. T: (01)903-3763.
**Church of England Council on Evangelism,** Exec Sec, The Vicarage, Crawley Green Rd, Luton, Beds. T: 28925.
**Countries Evangelistic Work,** 221 Kings Rd, Reading RG1 4LS, Berks. T: 65299.
**Crusade for World Revival,** PO Box 11, Walton-on-Thames, Surrey.
**Deo Gloria Trust,** 5 London Rd, Bromley, Kent. (Outreach for Jesus; Jesus Movement).
**Don Summers Evangelistic Association & Crusades,** 37 Grove Rd, Fishponds, PO Box 4, Bristol BS99 7TF. T: 654714. (Also: PO Box 10, Weston-super-Mare, Avon. T: 20836,21916.
**Eurovangelism Trust,** Dir, PO Box 123, Bristol BS99 7EL. T: 20350.
**Evangelism International,** Pres, Venture House, 70 Pavilion Way, Eastcote, Ruislip, Middx. T: (01)868-5990.
**Filey Christian Holiday Crusade,** Filey, North Yorkshire.
**Fishers Fellowship,** 96 Plaistow Lane, Bromley, Kent BR1 3AS. T: (01)460-7306.
**Hour of Revival Association,** 13 Lismore Rd, Eastbourne, East Sussex.
**Intercessors for Britain,** 100 Broadwater St West, Worthing, West Sussex.
**Irish Evangelistic Band (IEB),** 39 Belmore St, Enniskillen, Country Fermanagh, NI. T: 2400.
**Irish Evangelistic Treks,** Cloverley Hall, Whitchurch, Salop. T: Calverhall 217.
**Lausanne Committee for World Evangelization (LCWE),** Exec Sec, 186 Kennington Park Rd, London SE11 4BT. T: (01)582-0408.
**Movement for World Evangelization (MWE),** 102 Coles Lane, Sutton Coldfield, West Midlands B72 1NL. T: (021)354-9937/8.
**MV Logos,** Box 17, Bromley, Kent. (Evangelistic ship).
**Open Air Mission,** Sec, 19 John St, Bedford Row, London WC1. T: (01)405-6135.
**Oral Roberts Evangelistic Association,** British Isles Rep, 42 Baldwin St. Bristol BS1 1PN.
**POWER,** 19 Draycott Place, London SW3 2SJ. T: (01)584-9333.
**SPRE-E 73,** c/o 19 Draycott Place, London SW3 2SJ.
**Training for Evangelism,** 5 Alpins Close, Harpenden, Herts.
**Underground Evangelism,** Box BM 7001, London WC1V 6KX.
**United Beach Missions,** 44 Headingley Mount, Leeds LS6 3CW. T: 53006.
**Village Evangelists,** Firstwood, Colehill, Wimborne, Dorset.
**World Revival Crusade,** 10 Clarence Av, London SW4. T: (01)674-3175.
**World Vision for Christ,** 70 Sixth Av, London E12 5PR. T: (01)478-7908/1073. (Evangelistic team).
**You Need Christ Crusade,** Dir, 181 Hercules Rd, London SE1 7LD. T: (01)261-1808. (Also: 50 Grays Inn Rd, WC1X 8LT. T: (01)242-7566).

*USA*
**African Enterprise,** Exec Dir, 465 East Union, PO Box 988, Pasadena, CA 91102. T: (213)796-5830.
**Al Croker Evangelistic Association,** Bangor, ME 04401.
**Alaska Evangelization Society,** Walworth, WI 53184.
**Allen Revivals,** Miracle Valley, AZ 85635. (A A Allen).
**Ambassadors for Christ,** Dir, 5711 16th St, NW, Washington, DC 20011.
**America Back to God,** PO Box 717, Detroit, MI 48121.
**American Crusade,** Pres, Box 7, Montrose, CA 91020.
**American Evangelistic Association,** Box 2413, Baltimore, MD 21203.
**American-European Fellowship for Christian Oneness and Evangelization,** 15 Philips Place, Yonkers, NY 10701.
**Anchor Bay Evangelistic Association,** Box 188, New Baltimore, MI 48047.
**Appleman Campaigns,** 7339 Broadway, Kansas City, MO 64114.
**Arthur Blessitt Evangelistic Association,** Pres, PO Box 46216, Los Angeles, CA 90046. (Jesus Movement).
**Back-Country Evangelism,** Box 36, Pasadena, CA 91102.
**Barry Evangelistic Association,** Brownsburg, IN 46112.
**Bill Glass Evangelistic Association,** Pres, PO Box 356, Dallas, TX 75221.
**Billy Graham Evangelistic Association,** 1300 Harmon Place, Minneapolis, MN 55403.
**Billy Walker Evangelistic Association,** Southgate, MI 48192.
**Bluefield College of Evangelism,** Christian Acres, PO Box 1601, Bluefield, VA 24701. T: (304)589-6223.
**Bob Watters Evangelistic Association,** PO Box 1330, Minneapolis, MN 55440.
**California Evangelistic Association,** 1800 East Anaheim, Long Beach, CA 90813.
**Campus Crusade for Christ International,** Arrowhead Springs, San Bernardino, CA 92400. T: (714)886-5224.
**Charles Correl Evangelistic Association,** Somerset, KY 42501.
**Church Army,** Sec, 815 Second Av, New York, NY 10021. T: (212)687-1365.
**Church Centred Evangelism,** Dir, Valley Forge, PA 19481.
**Consultation on World Evangelization 1980 (COWE),** Box 1179, Wheaton, IL 60187.
**Crusaders for Christ,** Exec Dir, PO Box 11092, Pittsburgh, PA 15237.
**Dave Grant Evangelistic Association,** 6039 Elba Place, Woodland Hills, CA 91364.
**David Wilkerson Youth Crusades,** PO Box 34451, Dallas, TX 75234.
**Douds Evangelistic Ministry,** Box 5040, Dallas, TX 78422.
**Echo Park Evangelistic Association,** 1100 Glendale Blvd, Los Angeles, CA 90026. (International Ch of the Foursquare Gospel).
**European Evangelistic Crusade,** 811 Westview St, Philadelphia, PA 19119.
**Eurovangelism,** World Evangelism Foundation, Box 85, Abington, PA 19001.
**Evangelism for Christ Association,** PO Box 8, Eliot, ME 03903.
**Evangelism in Depth,** Box 735, Coconut Grove Stations, Miami, FL 33133.
**Evangelism International,** 1645 Tullie Circle, NE, PO Box 13, Atlanta, GA 30301. T: (404)633-9553.
**Evangelistic Association of New England,** Exec Dir, 88 Tremont St, Boston, MA 02108.
**Evangelistic Campaign for Christ,** PO Box 8086, Philadelphia, PA 19401.
**F Gonzalez Evangelistic Association,** Box M, South Gate, CA 90280.
**Florida Evangelistic Association,** Hobe Sound, FL 33455.
**Full Gospel Evangelistic Association,** Pres, 415 Second St, PO Box D, Anderson, MO 64831. T: (417)845-3359.
**Fuller Evangelistic Association,** Exec Dir, 44 South Mentor Av, Box 99, Pasadena, CA 91102. T: (213)449-0425.
**Great Commission Evangelistic Association,** PO Box 677, Smartville, CA 95977.
**Guido Evangelistic Association,** Metter, GA 30439.
**Haggai Evangelistic Association,** Pres, PO Box 13, Atlanta, GA 30301.
**Hal Webb Evangelistic Association,** Ridley Park, PA 19078.
**Hermano Pablo Evangelismo por Radio y Television,** 2080 Placentia St, PO Box 100, Costa Mesa, CA 92626.
**International Evangelism Crusades,** 7970 Woodman Av, Van Nuys, CA 91402.
**Inter-Church Evangelism,** Atglen, PA 19310.
**Ivan Lee Sisk Evangelistic Association,** 4327 Moraga, San Diego, CA 92117.
**Jack Van Impe Crusades,** Washington Square Plaza, Royal Oaks, MI 48067.
**Jesus People Inc,** Dir, Box 1949, Hollywood, CA 90028.
**Language Institute for Evangelism,** 21 North Olive Av, Alhambra, CA 91801.
**Lay Evangelism,** Box 565, Wheaton, IL 60188.
**Lay Involvement for Evangelism (LIFE),** Campus Crusade for Christ, Arrowhead Springs, San Bernardino, CA 92414. T: (714)886-5224
**Les Rawlins Evangelistic Association,** Pratt, VA 25162.
**Lester Sumrall Evangelistic Association,** 19440 Ireland Rd, PO Box 12, South Bend, IN 46624. T: (219)291-3292.
**Letourneau Evangelistic Center,** PO Box 2307, Longview, TX 75601.
**Literacy and Evangelism,** 4202 East 59th Place,

Tulsa, OK 74135. T: (918)627-4288.
**New England Christian Evangelizing Mission,** Bedford, NH 03102.
**North American Key 73,** California.
**Open Air Campaigners,** 108 North Main St, PO Box 469, Wheaton, IL 60187. T: (312)665-0313. (Also: 166 Berkeley Place, Glen Rock, NJ 07452).
**Oral Roberts Evangelistic Association,** Exec Dir, 1720 South Boulder, Tulsa, OK 74102. (Also: 7777 South Lewis, Tulsa, OK 74102).
**Oregon Evangelistic Fellowship,** Yamhill, OR 97148.
**Ralph Neighbor Evangelistic Association,** Elyria, OH 44035.
**RE Jeffery Evangelistic Association,** 3517 West Rancho Drive, Phoenix, AZ 85019.
**Sam Dalton Lay Evangelism Association,** 1331 West Evans, Denver, CO 80223.
**Spanish Evangelistic Crusades,** PO Box 1002, Greensboro, NC 27402.
**Teen Chalenge,** 5445 Chicago Av, PO Box 5652, Riverside, CA 92507.
**TL Osborn Evangelistic Association,** Box 10, Tulsa, OK 74102.
**Tokyo Evangelistic Center (Tokyo Fukuin Senta),** 6001 South California Av, Chicago, IL 60629.
**Tom Skinner Associates,** Pres, 521 Hopkinson Av, PO Box C, Brooklyn, NY 11212. T: (212)596-2480.
**Trans World Missions,** Exec Dir, 4205 Santa Monica Blvd, PO Box 2013, Los Angeles, California. (Formerly Air Mail from God).
**Tri-State Evangelistic Association,** Fayette, OH 43521.
**Underground Evangelism,** 1222 South Glendale Av, Glendale, CA 91205.
**Velmer Gardner Evangelistic Association,** Box 2253, Springfield, MO 65801.
**Winning The Nations Crusade,** Pres, PO Box 8658, Dallas, Texas.
**Word of Life Fellowship,** 91 Main St, Orange, NJ 07050. T: (518)532-7115. (HQ: Schroon Lake, NY 12870). (Youth evangelism).
**World Evangelism,** 4665 Mercury St, PO Box 9525, San Diego, CA 92109. T: (714)278-4160.

*UPPER VOLTA*
**New Life for All,** BP 128, Bobo-Dioulasso.

*ZAIRE*
**Christ Pour Tous,** BP 3691, Kinshasa-Kalina.
**New Life for All,** BP 3366, Kinshasa.

*ZAMBIA*
**Every Home Crusade,** PO Box 2211, Lusaka
**New Life for All,** Box 172, Ndola.

*ZIMBABWE*
**New Life for All,** 99 Victoria St (& 68 Third Av, Parktown), PO Box 925, Salisbury.

# 22
# Federations of Religious Communities

*Definition.* Federations or groupings of religious communities or congregations, or of religious personnel (priests, brothers and sisters). In 1980, Roman Catholic federations numbered 187 (4 being international: USG, UISG, CLAR, CMIS).

*ALGERIA*
**Union des Supérieures Majeures Diocèsaines,** Maison Provinciale des Soeurs Blanches, BP 29, Birmandreis, El Djezair (Alger).

*ANGOLA*
**Conferenza dei Superiori Maggiori (CIRMA),** CP 1230, Luanda.

*ARGENTINA*
**Conferencia Argentina de Religiosas (CONFER),** Callao 289, 3 Piso, Buenos Aires. T: 408615. (Erected 1955).
**Conferencia Argentina de Religiosos (CAR),** Callao 289, 3 Piso, Buenos Aires. T: 408615,464393. (Erected 1955).

*AUSTRALIA*
**Association of Major Clerical Religious Superiors,** Sacred Heart Monastery, Kensington, NSW 2033.
**Conference of Major Religious Superiors of Women's Institutes (CMRSWI),** St Vincent's Convent, Potts Point, NSW 2011. (Erected 1967).
**Provincials Conference of Religious Brothers,** Holy Cross College, Victoria Rd, Ryde 2112.

*AUSTRIA*
**Superiorenkonferenz der Männlichen Ordensgemeinschaften Österreichs,** Schotternabtei, Freyung 6, A-1010 Wien. (Erected 1958).
**Vereinigung der Frauenorden und Kongregationen Österreichs (VFKO),** Stephansplatz 6, A-1010 Wien. (Erected 1966).

*BANGLADESH*
**Conference of Major Religious Superiors (BCR),** Mary House, Tejgaon, Dacca 8.

*BELGIUM*
**Assemblée des Supérieurs Majeurs de Belgique (ASBL)/Vereniging der Mannelijke Hogere Oversten van Belgie,** Chaussée de Haacht 3, B-1030 Brussel. T: (02)2181713. (Erected 1959).
**Concile des Frères Enseignants de Belgique,** Rue du Strop 125, Gand.
**Union des Supérieures Majeures de Belgique/Vereniging van de Vrouwelijke Hogere Oversten,** Rue de la Senne 20, B-1000 Brussel. T: (02)5111440. (Erected 1958).

*BOLIVIA*
**Conferencia Nacional de Religiosos de Bolivia (CONFER),** Arzobispado, Casilla 283, La Paz. T: 41920. (Erected 1955).
**Conferencia Nacional de Religiosas,** Casilla 5805, La Paz. T: 41920. (Erected 1956).

*BRAZIL*
**Conferência dos Religiosos do Brasil (CRB),** Rua Alcindo Guanabara 24/4, 20.000 Rio de Janeiro, RJ. T: (021)224-3004. (Men and women. Erected 1955).

*BURMA*
**Conference of Religious Sisters of Burma (CRSB),** 133 Kyaikasan Rd, Tamwe, Rangoon. (Erected 1962).

*BURUNDI*
**Conférence des Supérieurs Majeurs du Burundi et du Rwanda (COSUMA),** BP 825, Bujumbura. (Erected 1969).
**Union des Supérieures Majeures,** BP 1390, Bujumbura. (Erected 1963).

*CAMEROON*
**Conférence des Supérieurs Majeurs du Cameroun,** BP 185, Yaoundé. (Erected 1972).
**Union des Supérieures Majeures et Déléguées du Cameroun (USMDC),** BP 185, Yaoundé.

*CANADA*
**Canadian Religious Conference/Conférence Religieuse Canadienne (CRC),** 324-est Av Laurier, Ottawa K1N 6P6. (Erected 1954).
**Fédération des Frères Enseignants du Canada,** Cap Rouge, Québec.

*CHILE*
**Conferencia de Superiores Mayores Religiosos de Chile (CONFERRE),** Erasmo Escala 822, of 302, Casilla 9501, Santiago. T: 87832. (Men and women. Erected 1954).

*CHINA (TAIWAN)*
**Association of Major Superiours of Religious Men,** 25 Mingsheng Rd, Taipei. (Erected 1965).
**Association of Major Superiors of Religious Women,** Regina Mundi Convent, 121 Hsinsheng St, RD Section 1, Taipei. (Erected 1964).

*COLOMBIA*
**Confederación Latino Americana de Religiosos (CLAR),** Calle 78 No 12-16, Apto 101, Apdo Aéreo 90710, Bogotá 2, DE. T: 550504. (Erected 1959).
**Conferencia de Superiores Mayores,** Calle 71A No. 11-20, Apdo Aéreo 52332, Chapinero, Bogotá 2. T: 498674. (Erected 1953).

*COSTA RICA*
**Conferencia Costarricense de Religiosos (CONCOR),** Apdo 6377, San José. (Erected 1960).
**Conferencia de Religiosas de Costa Rica (CONFEREC),** Apdo 2819, San José. (Erected 1961).

*CUBA*
**Confederación Cubana de Religiosas (CONCUR)** Reina 463, La Habana 2, T: 622480. (United 1974 with men's conference).
**Conferencia Cubana de Religiosos (CONCUR),** Calle San Lázaro 885, La Habana 3. (Erected 1974).

*DENMARK*
**Catholic Council of Religious Women (Katolske Sostres Faellesrad).** Jens Jessensvej 7, DK-2000 Kobenhavn F. T: (01)714872.
**Union of Superiors of Women Religious of Denmark,** Collegievej 2, Charlottenlund, Kobenhavn.

*DOMINICAN REPUBLIC*
**Confederación Dominicana de Religiosos (CONDOR),** Calle Ramón Santana 16, Apart 76, Santo Domingo. T: 682820. (Men and women. Erected 1959).

*ECUADOR*
**Conferencia Ecuatoriana de Religiosos (CER),** Av América 1866, Apdo 3904, Quito. T: 522436. (Men and women. Erected 1954).

*EGYPT*
**Assemblée des Supérieurs Majeurs des Instituts,** Sekket El Daher 29, Al Qahirah. (Erected 1968).
**Union des Supérieures Majeures,** 194 Rue Ramsès Ghamra, Al Qahirah. (Erected 1968).

*EL SALVADOR*
**Confederación de Religiosos de El Salvador (CONFRES),** Apdo 06971, San Salvador. T: 221070. (Men and women. Erected 1966).
**Secretariado para Religiosos de Centroamérica y Panamá (SERCAP),** 1a C Poniente 1148, Apdo 1095, San Salvador. T: 221070.

*ETHIOPIA*
**Conference of Religious Superiors of North Ethiopia,** Strada 317, Campo Polo, Asmera.
**Conference of Religious Superiors of Southern Ethiopia,** PO Box 30220, Addis Abeba.

*FRANCE*
**Religieuses dans les Professions de Santé (REPSE),** 106 Rue du Bac, F-75007 Paris.
**Union des Frères Enseignants (UFE),** 277 Rue St Jacques, F-75005 Paris.
**Union des Religieuses Educatrices Paroissiales (UREP),** 106 Rue Jean-Bart, F-75006 Paris. (Erected 1968).
**Union des Religieuses Enseignantes (URE),** 10 Rue Jean-Bart, F-75006 Paris. (Erected 1960).
**Union des Supérieures Majeures de France (USMF),** 10 Rue Jean-Bart, F-75006 Paris. T: (01)548-1832/3. (Erected 1957)
**Union des Supérieurs Majeurs de France,** 95 Rue de Sèvres, F-75006 Paris. T: 222-7784. (Erected 1958).

*GERMANY, Federal Republic of*
**Arbeitskreis Kirchlicher Brüderschaften,** An der Thomaskirche, D-4 Düsseldorf-Nord. (Federation of Evangelical orders).
**Frankfurter Gespräche, Arbeitskreis Verschiedener Kreise und Brüderschaften,** Geleitstr 104, D-605 Offenbach (Main). (Loose federation of Evangelical religious orders).
**Vereinigung Deutscher Ordensoberen (VDO),** Kielstr 35, D-5000 Köln 80. (Founded 1898, erected 1957).
**Vereinigung Höherer Ordensoberen der Brüderorden und Kongregationen Deutschlands (VHOB),** Rütscherstr 182, D-5100 Aachen. T: 32033. (Erected 1958).
**Vereinigung Höherer Ordensoberinnen Deutschlands (VHOD),** Bonner Talweg 135, D-53 Bonn. (Erected 1957).

*GHANA*
**Conference of Major Superiors of Religious Men of Ghana,** POB 492, Sekondi. (Erected 1971).
**Conference of Major Superiors of Religious Women,** PO Box 306, Nsawam. (Erected 1971).

*GREECE*
**Union des Religieux de Grèce (URG),** 28 Rue Michel Voda, Athínai. (Erected 1974).

*GUATEMALA*
**Conferencia de Religiosos y Religiosas de Guatemala (CONFREGUA),** 4a Calle 5.52, Zona 1, Apdo 1698, Guatemala. T: 29816. (Erected 1963).

*HAITI*
**Conférence Haïtienne des Religieux (CHR),** Angle Rue Lamarre et Champ-de-Mars, Port-au-Prince. (Men and women. Erected 1973).

*HONDURAS*
**Conferencia de Institututos Religiososde Honduras (CIRH),** Calle 25 de Enero, Bo Morazón, Apdo 307, Tegucigalpa. T: 221765. (Erected 1956)

*HONG KONG*
**Association of Major Religious Superiors of Men in Hong Kong,** c/o Ricci Hall, 93 Polnfulam Rd, HK.

**Association of Major Religious Superiors of Women in Hong Kong,** c/o Maryknoll Convent, Boundary St, Kowloon Tong.

*INDIA*
**Ceylon Conference of Major Religious Superiors,** Brother's Subsection, St Andrew's House, 24 Palmgrove, Bangalore 7. (Erected 1960).
**Conference of Religious of India (CRI),** 4 Rajniwas Marg, Delhi 110006. (Men and women. Erected 1963).

*INDONESIA*
**Association of Sisters of All Indonesia (Ikatan Biarawati Seluruh Indonesia, IBSI),** Jalan Supratman 1, Bandung.
**National Association of Brothers Institutes (Madjelis Bruder Indonesia, MABRI),** Jalan Dr Sutomo 4, Semarang. (Erected 1970).
**National Association of Clerical Institutes (Madjelis Serikat Imam, MASRI),** Kolese Kanisius, Jalan Menteng Raya 64, Jakarta-Pusat. (Erected 1969).

*IRELAND*
**Conference of Major Religious Superiours,** Milltown Park, Dublin 6. (Men and women. Erected 1960).

*ISRAEL*
**Union des Religieuses d'Israël (URI),** Pensionnat St-Joseph, Rehov Yafo 25, Yafo.

*ITALY*
**Conferenza Italiana dei Superiori Maggiori (CISM),** Via degli Scipioni 256/B, I-00192 Roma. T: (06)314254. (Erected 1960).
**Conferenza Mondiale degli Istituti Secolari (CMIS),** Via Florida 20, I-00186 Roma. T: (06) 657489. (Erected 1974).
**Federazione Nazionale delle Congregazioni Marianae (CCMM),** Via Serchio 7, I-00198 Roma. T: 864578.
**Unione dei Superiori Generali (USG),** Via dei Penitenzieri 19, I-00193 Roma. T: (06)6568229. (Erected 1957).
**Unione Internazionale delle Superiore Generali (UISG),** Piazza Ponte San Angelo 28, I-00186 Roma. T: (06)655921. (Erected 1965).
**Unione Superiore Maggiori d'Italia (USMI),** Via Zanardelli 32, I-00186, Roma. (Erected 1956).
**World Federation of Christian Life Communities,** Secretariat, Borgo Santo Spirito 8, CP 9048, I-00198 Roma. T: 6568079.

*JAMAICA*
**Conference of Major Superiors of the Antilles,** Mount Alvernia, PO Box 124, Montego Bay. (Erected 1970).

*JAPAN*
**Association of Religious Congregations of Sisters in Japan,** 1966-chome, Gotanda Shinagawa-ku, Tokyo.
**National Conference of Major Superiors of Women Religious,** 10-1 Rokuban-cho, Chiyoda-ku, Tokyo 102. (Erected 1965).
**Superiors Conference of Japan,** National Catholic Committee of Japan, 10-1 Rokuban-cho, Chiyoda-ku, Tokyo 102. T: (03)2623691. (Erected 1970).

*KENYA*
**Association of Sisterhoods of Kenya (AOSK),** Sec, PO Box 48062, Nairobi. (Erected 1969).
**Religious Superiors' Association of Kenya (RSAK),** Sec, PO Box 1913, Kisumu. (Erected 1969).

*KOREA, South*
**Association of Major Superiors of Religious Women in Korea,** CPO Box 16, Soul. T: 271161/3. (Erected 1969).
**Conference of Major Superiors of Men in Korea,** CPO Box 16, Soul. T: 271161/3. (Erected 1968).

*LEBANON*
**Assemblée des Supérieurs Majeures,** BP 3744, Bayrut. (Erected 1963).
**Assemblée des Supérieures Majeurs,** Couvent St-Roch, Decouané près de Bayrut. (Erected 1963).
**Union Interrituelle des Religieuses Enseignantes,** BP 472, Bayrut.

*LESOTHO*
**Lesotho Conference of Major Religious Superiors,** PO Box MH 134, Mohale's Hoek. (Erected 1977).

*LUXEMBOURG*
**Union des Instituts Religieux Féminins,** 50 Av Gaston Diderich, BP 1181, Luxembourg. (Erected 1967).

*MADAGASCAR*
**Union des Supérieures Majeures Féminines de Madagascar,** ND du Cénacle, Rue Albert Picquié 33, Tananarive. (Erected 1966).
**Union des Supérieurs Majeurs de Madagascar (USMM),** BP 34, Maintirano. (Erected 1966).

*MALAWI*
**Association of Men Religious Institutes in Malawi (AMRIM),** PO Box 133, Lilongwe. (Erected 1968).
**Association of Religious Institutes of Malawi (ARIMA),** PO Box 477, Lilongwe. (Erected 1968).

*MALAYSIA*
**Association of Major Superiors of Women,** c/o Convent of the Infant Jesus, Bukit Nanas, Kuala Lumpur. (Erected 1969).
**Superiors' Conference of Malaysia and Singapore,** Montfort Boys Town, PO Box 211, Batutiga, Subang Salangor. (Erected 1971).

*MALI*
**Union des Supérieures Majeures des Congrégations Autochtones d'Afrique de l'Ouest Francophone,** BP 298, Bamako

*MALTA*
**Consilium Nationale Religiosorum Melitensium,** St Benild School, Church St, Sliema. (Erected 1959).
**Malta Sisters Conference (KSSM),** Catholic Institute, Floriana. (Erected 1968).

*MARTINIQUE*
**Conseil des Religieuses,** Cité Godissard Z5 C16, 97-2 Fort-de-France. T: 2070.

*MAURITIUS*
**Union des Supérieures Majeures,** Couvent de Marie Réparatrice, Route Royale 232, Rose-Hill. T: 43723.

*MEXICO*
**Conferencia de Institutos Religiosos de México (CIRM),** Av Amores 13-18, Apdo Postal 44-051 (ZP 12), México 12, DF. T: 5752700. (Men and women. Erected 1959).
**Federación de Religiosas Enfermeras Mexicanas (FREM),** Av Ejército Nacional 613, México 17, DF. (Erected 1956).

*MOROCCO*
**Conseil des Religieuses,** c/o Archevêché, BP 258, Rabat.

*MOZAMBIQUE*
**Federação dos Institutos Religiosos Maculinos de Moçambique,** Paroquia NS de Fátima, CP 1233, Beira. (Erected 1975).
**Federação Nacional dos Institutos Religiosos Femininos,** Casa de Maria Imaculada, CP 39, Matola, Maputo (Lourenço Marques). (Erected 1975).

*NETHERLANDS*
**Association Council for Monks (Stichting Monialen Beraad, SMB),** Hollende Wagenweg 20, Werkhoven. T: (03437)330.
**Association of Dutch Congregations of Brothers (Stichting Broedercongregaties in Nederland, SBCN),** Zwanenveld 25-40, Nijmegen. T: (08800) 32918. (Erected 1958).
**Association of Dutch Religious Priests (Stichting der Nederlandse Priester-Religieuzen, SNPR),** Postbus 3170, 5003 DD Tilburg. (Erected 1958).
**Association of Dutch Sisters (Stichting Nederlandse Vrouwelijke Religieuzen, SNVR),** Carmelweg 1, Nijmegen. T: (08800)32642. (Erected 1956).
**Central Missionary Council for Brothers and Sisters (Centraal Missionair Beraad Religieuzen, CMBR),** van Alkemadelaan 1, Den Haag. T: (070) 244594. (RC).
**Union des Congrégations des Religieuses Infirmières (St. Canisiusbond),** Curaçaoweg 1, Nijmegen.

*NEW ZEALAND*
**Conference of Major Superiors of Women Religious,** St Mary's Convent, PO Box 7025, Auckland 1. (Erected 1967).
**New Zealand Conference of Major Superiors of**

**Men,** 30 Bassett Rd, Remuera, Auckland 5. (Erected 1969).

*NICARAGUA*

**Conferencia Nacional Nicaragüense de Institutos Religiosos (CONFER),** Apdo 3796, Managua. T: 25168. (Erected 1956).

*NIGER*

**Comité des Religieuses,** c/o Evêché, BP 208, Niamey.

*NIGERIA*

**Conference of Major Women Religious Superiors,** PO Box 5245, Ibadan. (Erected 1971).
**Nigerian National Conference of Major Superiors,** 6 Awolowo Av, PO Box 1784, Ibadan. (Erected 1971).

*PAKISTAN*

**Association of Major Religious Superiors of Men in Pakistan,** c/o St Patrick's Cathedral, Karachi 3, Sind. (Erected 1970).
**Association of Major Religious Superiors of Women,** St Joseph's Convent, PO Box 7260, Karachi. (Erected 1962)

*PALESTINE*

**Union des Religieuses de Jordanie (URJ),** PO Box 11, Bethlehem.

*PANAMA*

**Federación de Religiosos y Religiosas de Panamá (FEDEPAR),** Parroquia del Carmen-Pasadena, Apdo 4980, Panamá 5. T: 230360,238204. (Men and women. Erected 1959).

*PAPUA NEW GUINEA*

**Association of Religious Superiors,** Catholic Mission, PO Alexishafen, Madang. (Erected 1968). (Also covers Solomon Islands).
**Conference of Religious Brothers,** PO Box 760, Goroka, EHD. (Erected 1974).
**National Conference of Major Women Superiors,** PO Box 1321, Boroko. (Erected 1968. Also covers Solomon Islands).

*PARAGUAY*

**Federación de Religiosos del Paraguay (FERELPAR),** Calle Alberdi 782, CC 1847, Asunción. T: 41122. (Men and women. Erected 1959).

*PERU*

**Conferencia Peruana de Religiosos (CPR),** Jirón Cuzco 376, Apdo Postal 5016, Lima 100. T: 273485. (Men and women. Erected 1969)

*PHILIPPINES*

**Association of Major Religious Superiors of Men in the Philippines (AMRSMP),** 214 N. Domingo St, PO Box 2156, Quezon City, Manila. (Erected 1956).
**Association of Major Religious Superiors of Women in the Philippines (AMRSWP),** PO Box 3553, Manila. (Erected 1956).

*POLAND*

**Conference of Major Superiors of Religious Women of Poland (Konferencja Przelozonych Wyzszych Zenskich Unstytutów Zakonnych w Polsce),** ul Dziekania 1, 00-279 Warszawa 40. (Erected 1970).
**Conference of Religious Major Superiors of Poland (Konferencja Przelozonych Wyzszych Zakonow Meskich w Polsce),** ul Dziekania 1, 00-279 Warszawa 40. (Erected 1970).

*PORTUGAL*

**Conferência Nacional dos Institutos Religiosos (CNIR),** Praça Prof. Santos Andrea 18, 1 Dto, Lisboa 4. T: 707987. (Erected 1954).
**Federação Nacional dos Institutos Religiosos Femininos (FNIRF),** Praça Prof. Santos Andrea 18, 1 Dto, Lisboa 4. (Erected 1954. Member, BICE).

*PUERTO RICO*

**Conferencia de Religiosas de Puerto Rico (CORPORI),** Apdo 2204 or 4201, San Juan, PR 00903. T: 7257053,7230476.
**Conferencia de Religiosos de Puerto Rico (COR de Puerto Rico),** Av Ponce de León 265, parada 5, San Juan, PR 00906. T: 7224289. (Erected 1972)

*RWANDA*

**Conférence des Supérieurs Majeurs du Burundi et du Rwanda (COSUMA),** BP 69, Kigali.
**Union des Supérieures Majeures du Rwanda,** BP 130, Butare. (Erected 1969).

*SENEGAL*

**Conférence des Supérieures Majeures,** BP 5082, Dakar (Erected 1971).
**Conférence des Supérieurs Majeurs des Instituts Masculins du Sénégal,** Monastère Bénédictin, Keur-Moussa. (Erected 1970).

*SINGAPORE*

**Superiors' Conference of Malaysia and Singapore,** 300 Thomson Rd, Singapore 11.

*SOUTH AFRICA*

**Association of Religious Women,** Cathedral Place, PO Box 32, Johannesburg 2000. (Erected 1956).
**Association of Teaching Brothers,** Corner 3 Av & 3 Rd, Victory Park, Johannesburg 2001.
**Conference of Clerical Major Superiors in Southern Africa,** St John Vianney Seminary, 191 Main St, Waterkloof, Pretoria. (Erected 1959).

*SPAIN*

**Conferencia Española de Religiosas,** Calle Núñez de Balboa 99-3C, Madrid 6. T: 2627696. (Erected 1969).
**Conferencia Española de Religiosos (CONFER),** Calle Núñez de Balboa 115 bis, Madrid 6. T: 2624612. (Erected 1969).
**Federación Española de Religiosos de Enseñanza (FERE),** Conde de Peñalver 45, Madrid 6. (Erected 1957).
**Federación Española de Religiosas Sanitarias (FERS),** Martínez Campos 18, Madrid 10. (Erected 1970).

*SRI LANKA*

**Conference of Major Religious Superiors of Sri Lanka,** 130 de la Salle St, Colombo 15. (Erected 1960).

*SWITZERLAND*

**Union des Supérieures Majeures de Suisse Romande (USMSR),** Av de la Tour, CH-1950 Sion. T: (027)21448. (Erected 1965).
**Vereinigung Christikatholischer Schwestern und Fürsorgerinnen,** Leiterin, Taubblindenheim, Sudstr 10, CH-8008 Zürich. (Old Catholic).
**Vereinigung der Höhern Ordensobern der Schweiz/Union des Supérieurs Majeurs Religieux de Suisse (USM),** Grand'rue 34, CP 20, CH-1702 Fribourg.
**Vereinigung Höherer Oberinnen Ordensgemeinschaften der Deutschsprachigen Schweiz/Union des Supérieures Majeures de Suisse Alémanique,** CH-6440 Ingenbohl. (Erected 1967)

*TANZANIA*

**Association of Religious Superiors in Tanzania,** PO Box 5124, Dar es Salaam.
**Association of Women Religious Superiors of Tanzania,** PO Box 2133, Dar es Salaam. (Erected 1966).

*THAILAND*

**Association of Major Religious Superiors of Men in Thailand,** 123/19 Ruam Rudi Lane, Wireless Rd, Bangkok 5. (Erected 1969).
**Association of Major Religious Superiors of Women in Thailand,** c/o St Joseph's Convent, 7 Convent Rd, Bangkok 5. (Erected 1960).

*TUNISIA*

**Union des Congrégations (Féminines) en Tunisie (UDTC),** c/o Maison Provinciale des Soeurs Blanches, 9 Rue Raspail, Tunis.

*TURKEY*

**Union des Religieux et des Religieuses de Turquie (URT),** Eglise St Louis, PK 280, Beyoglu.

*UGANDA*

**Association of Religious Women of Uganda (Associatio Religiosarum Ugandae) (ARU),** PO Box 1587, Kampala. T: 64251,46251. (Erected 1972).
**Conference of Major Superiors of Men's Institutes in Uganda (COMSIU),** PO Box 2912, Kampala. (Erected 1970).

*UK OF GB & NI*

**Council of Major Religious Superiors of England and Wales (CMRS),** 114 Mount St, London W1Y 6AH. (Men and women. Erected 1958).
**Council of Major Superiors of Scotland,** St David's, Glasgow. (Erected 1958).

*USA*

**Association of Contemplative Sisters,** Esopus, NY 12429.
**Conference of Major Superiors of Men's Institutes (CMSM),** 1302 18th St, NW, Suite 601, Washington, DC 20036. T: (202)785-1343. (Erected 1957).
**Conference of Major Superiors of Women's Institutes (Leadership Conference of Women Religious),** 1302 18th St, NW, Suite 601, Washington, DC 20036. (Erected 1959).
**Leadership Conference of Women Religious in the USA (LCWR),** 1325 Massachusetts Av, NW, Washington, DC 20005.
**National Association of Religious Brothers,** 11601 Georgia Av, Wheaton, MD 20902.
**National Association of Women Religious (NAWR),** 720 North Rush St, Chicago, IL 60611. (Members: individual nuns, sisters councils, organizations of women religious).
**National Black Sisters' Conference (NBSC),** 3508 Fifth Av, Pittsburgh, PA 15213.
**National Coalition of American Nuns (NCAN),** 1307 South Wabash Av, Chicago, IL 60605. (Members: RC women religious).
**National Sister Formation Conference (NSFC),** 1325 Massachusetts Av, NW, Washington, DC 20005.
**National Sisters Vocation Conference (NSVC),** 1307 South Wabash Av, Chicago, IL 60605.
**Sisters Uniting,** 700 North Seventh St Memphis, TN 38107. (Member: all organizations of sisters and superiors).

*UPPER VOLTA*

**Association des Supérieurs Majeurs des Instituts Masculins en Haute-Volta,** BP 630, Ouagadougou. (Erected 1969).
**Union des Supérieures Majeures en Haute-Volta (USMHV),** BP 630, Ouagadougou. (Erected 1976).

*URUGUAY*

**Federación de Religiosos del Uruguay (FRU),** Canelones, 1164 Montevideo. T: 44157. (Erected 1961).

*VENEZUELA*

**Conferencia Venezolana de Religiosos (CONVER),** Torre a Madrices, Apdo 4582, Caracas 101. T: 814437. (Erected 1960).
**Federación de Religiosas de Venezuela (FERVE),** Torre a Madrices, Apdo 4582, Caracas 101. T: 814437. (Erected 1959).

*VIET NAM*

**Comité Permanent des Religieux du Vietnam (Hiệp-Hội Tu-Sĩ Việt-Nam),** 38 Ky-Dông, Saigon.
**Union des Supérieures Majeures,** 4 Cu'o'ng-Dê, Saigon. T: 20455. (Erected 1965).
**Union des Supérieurs Majeurs,** 4 Cuong-De, Ho Chi Minh Ville. (Erected 1965).

*YUGOSLAVIA*

**Higher Council of Religious (Vijece Visih Redovnickih Poglavara, VIJECE VRP),** Palmoticeva 33, YU-41001 Zagreb. T: (041)441604.
**Union of Major Superiors of Religious Women in Yugoslavia (Unija Visih Redovnickih Poglavarica Jugoslavije),** Frankopanska 17, pp 702, YU-41001 Zagreb. T: (041)572319. (Erected 1968).

*ZAIRE*

**Assemblée des Supérieurs Majeurs (ASUMA),** BP 180, Kinshasa 1. (Erected 1960).
**Union des Supérieures Majeures du Zaïre (USUMA),** BP 3276, Kinshasa-Gombe. (Erected 1963).

*ZAMBIA*

**Association of Religious Superiors in Zambia (Male),** PO Box 2494, Lusaka. (Erected 1964).
**Association of Sisterhoods of Zambia,** PO Box 162, Kitwe. (Erected 1960).

*ZIMBABWE*

**Conference of Major Religious Superiors of Zimbabwe (Men),** 1 Sawley Close, Marlborough, Salisbury. (Erected 1970).
**Conference of Major Superiors of Women Religious of Zimbabwe,** PB 804, Marandellas. (Erected 1970).

# 23

# Finance, Property & Stewardship

*Definition.* Organizations primarily concerned with church finance and/or property, financial services, Christian stewardship organizations, insurance bodies, co-operatives, savings societies, credit unions; foundations, trusts, funding agencies, fund-raising agencies, fund-transmitting agencies, pension schemes, ministerial funding societies, charitable societies; new church construction or building societies; management consulting, business methods for churches. See also AID AND RELIEF, and DEVELOPMENT, JUSTICE AND PEACE. Also, most denominational HQs listed under CHURCHES AND DENOMINATIONS deal also with finance and property.

*AUSTRALIA*

**Wells Organization Pty,** Box A248, PO Sydney South. T: 618569.

*BRAZIL*

**Movimento Cooperativista,** Barra, BA.

*CANADA*

**Anglican Association of Credit Unions,** 135 Adelaide St East, Toronto 1.
**Ecclesiastical Insurance Office Ltd,** 123 Eglinton Av East, Toronto, Ontario M4P 1J2. T: (416)484-4555. (Founded 1887).
**Pentecostal Benevolent Association of Ontario,** 3760 Sheppard Av East, Box 70, Agincourt, Ontario. (Pentecostal Assemblies of Canada).
**Pentecostal Benevolent Association of Quebec,** Suite 1007, 1280 Rue St Marc, Montréal 108, Québec. (PAoC).

*EL SALVADOR*

**Fundación Promotora de Cooperativas,** Av Espana 312, 3 piso, San Salvador. T: 216468,217200.

*FRANCE*

**Caisse Auxiliaire de Retraites des Ministres du Culte Protestant (CARP),** Sec Gén, 47 Rue de Clichy, F-75009 Paris.
**Entraide Missionnaire Internationale (EMI)/International Missionary Benefit Society,** 119 Rue du Président-Wilson, F-92 Levallois. T: 2708752, 2708753.

*GERMANY, Federal Republic of*

**Evangelisches Studienwerk,** D-5845 Haus Villigst, bei Schwete (Ruhr). (University scholarships).
**Kirchenkanzlei der EKD,** Herrenhäuser Str 2A, Postfach 210220, D-3 Hannover-Herrenhausen. (Financial office).

*GREECE*

**Organization for Finances and Property of the Church of Greece (Organimos Dioikiseos kai Diacheiriseos tis Ekklisiastikis Periousias, ODDEP),** Holy Synod, I Gennadiou 14, Athínai 140.

*HOLY SEE*

**Administration of the Patrimony of the Apostolic See,** Pres, I-00120 Città del Vaticano. T: 6982 int 4306.
**Prefecture of the Economy of the Holy See,** Pres, Palazzo delle Congregazioni, Largo del Colonnato 3, I-00193 Roma, Italy. T: 69282 int 4263.

*INDIA*

**Biblical Library Fund (BLF),** 105 Savitri Building, Greater Kailash II, New Delhi 110048.
**Catholic Co-operative Society,** BP 2, Ranchi.
**Fellowship of the Least Coin,** St Stephen House, 4 Rajpur Rd, Delhi 11006.

*INDONESIA*

**Institute for the Education and Counselling of Credit Union Leaders,** Biro Sosial, Jalan Jend A Yan 13, Semarang, Surabaja.

*JAMAICA*

**Church Credit Union,** Moravian Church in Jamaica, 3 Hector St, Kingston 5.

*KENYA*

**Church Commissioners for Kenya (CPK),** Sec, Church House (5th floor), Moi Av, PO Box 30422, Nairobi. T: 25004. (Anglican property and finances).
**Co-operative Savings and Credit Society,** Field Officer, Kenya House, Koinange St, PO Box 49539, Nairobi. T: 23455 ext 2.

*LESOTHO*

**Lesotho Credit Union League,** c/o PO Box 267, Maseru.

*MALAWI*

**Faith Christian Services,** Box 5436, Limbe. (Channels overseas finance).

*NEW ZEALAND*

**Zealandia Associates,** Brandon House, Corner of Featherston & Brandon Sts, GPO Box 2808, Wellington 1. T: 51794. (Fund-raising).

*NORWAY*

**Christian Institute for Project Aid (Kristen Innsats for Uløste Oppgaver),** Munchsgate 2, Oslo 1. (Financing new church projects).

*PANAMA*

**Fondo de Apostolado Arquidiocesano,** Apdo 6386, Panamá 5. T: 627400 ext 17.

*SWITZERLAND*

**Ecumenical Church Loan Fund (ECLOF),** Exec Sec, 150 Route de Ferney, CH-1211 Genève 20.
**Stiftungsrat der Schweizerischen Reformationsstiftung,** Sek, CH-3000 Bern. (Finance).

*TANZANIA*

**New Life Crusade,** Sec, Mr M.P. Nyagwaswa, PO Box 2679, Dar es Salaam. (Official banking account for East African Revival Movement).

*UK OF GB & NI*

**Aged Pilgrims' Friendly Society,** 26-30 Holborn Viaduct, London EC1. T: (01)583-8116/1. (Life pensions and flats).
**Anglican Stewardship Association,** 157 Waterloo Rd, London, SE1 8UU.
**Apprenticeship Society,** Sec, Livingstone House, 11 Carteret St, London SW1. (Grants to children of Protestant clergy).
**Assemblies of God Property Trust,** Sec, 242 Big Barn Lane, Mansfield, Notts. T: 28568.
**Baptist Building Fund,** 4 Southampton Row, London WC1B 4AB.
**Baptist Men's Movement Housing Association,** 4 Southampton Row, London WC1B 4AB.
**Booker's Bounty,** Sec, 37 Gay St, Bath, Somerset T: (0225)25229.
**Came's Charity for Clergymen's Widows,** 7 New Square, Lincoln's Inn, London WC2. T: (01)405-6789.
**Catholic Housing Aid Society,** 189a Old Brompton Rd, London SW5. T: (01)373-4961.
**Catholic National Building Office,** 3 Great James St, London WC1. T: (01)242-5096.
**Central Board of Finance of the Church of England,** Sec, Investment office, Winchester House, 77 London Wall, London EC2N 1DB. T: (01)588-1815.
**Central Finance Board of the Methodist Church (Covenant Department),** Iddesleigh House, Caxton St, London SW1.
**Christian Economic & Social Research Foundation,** 12 Caxton St, London SW1. T: (01)222-4001.
**Christian Witness Fund,** Sec, 120 Leamington Rd, Coventry CV3 6JY. (Grants to retired Protestant clergy).
**Church Benefit Society,** Chief Sec, 45 Sheen Lane, London SW14. T: (01)876-6242.
**Church Commissioners for England,** Sec, 1 Millbank, Westminster, London SW1P 3JZ. T: (01)930-5444. (Annual income £26 million).
**Church Duty Money Movement,** Sec, 138A Durham Rc, Wimbledon, London, SW20 0DG. T: (01)946-3034.
**Church Extensions Association,** Hon Sec, St Michael's Convent, Ham Common, Richmond, Surrey.
**Church Finance Supplies Ltd,** Radley Rd Industrial Estate, Abingdon-on-Thames, Berks. T: 4488.
**Church of England Clergy Stipend Trust,** 5 New Square, Lincoln's Inn, London WC2A 3RP. T: (01)405-3613.
**Church of England Pensions Board/Clergy Pensions Institution,** Sec, 53 Tufton St, London SW1. T: (01)222-1568.
**Church Schoolmasters' and Schoolmistresses' Benevolent Institution,** Sec, 9 Athelstan Way, Horsham, West Sussex. T: (0403)3881. (Financial relief).
**Community Counselling Service,** 27 Grosvenor St, London W1. T: (01)629-1715. (RC. Fund-raising consultants).
**Congregational Fund Board,** Sec, Livingstone House, 11 Carteret St, London SW1. (Begun 1695; grants to colleged and aged clergy).
**Congregational Insurance Co Ltd,** 21-22 Apsley Crescent, Bradford, West Yorkshire. T: (0274)41351.
**Congregational Ministers' Friendly Society,** 11 Carteret St, London SW1.
**Congregational Ministers' Pension Fund,** Pensions Officer, Livingstone House, 11 Carteret St, London SW1.
**Congregational Pastors' Insurance Aid Society,** 11 Carteret St, London SW1.
**Congregational Pastors' Superannuation Fund,** 11 Carteret St, London SW1.
**Congregational Pastors' Widows' Fund,** 11 Carteret St, London SW1.

**Congregational Welfare Fund,** Welfare Dept, 11 Carteret St, London SW1.
**Council for Christian Stewardship,** Dir, St Michael, Mark St, London EC2.
**Curates' Augmentation Fund,** Sec, East Wing, Fulham Palace, London SW6. T: (01)736-7141.
**Ecclesiastical Insurance Office,** Dir, Aldwych House, Aldwych, London WC2. T: (01)242-9790. (Also: Personal Insurances Consultant, Wood Sorrel Cottage, Nursery Lane, Nutley, Uckfield, Sussex. T: Nutley 2764.
**Fidelity Trust,** Sec, 41 Tothill St, London SW1H 9LG. T: (01)930-6524/7203. (Property trustees).
**Hooker Craigmyle & Co,** 11 Old Burlington St, London W1. (Fund-raising). (Also: The Grove, Harpenden, Herts).
**Incorporated Church Building Society,** Sec, 7 Queen Anne's Gate, London SW1H 9BX. T: (01)930-8889. (Grants).
**Management Study Group (MSG),** 39 Bedford Square, London WC1B 3EY. T: (01)636-5113. (Professional group in GF, IVF).
**Martyrs' Memorial and Church of England Trust,** CPAS, Falcon Court, 32 Fleet St, London EC4Y 1DB. T: (01)353-4821.
**Memorial Hall Trust,** Manager, Lown Hall, Howard Rd, Cricklewood, London NW2. T: (01)452-4174. (Congregationalist).
**Methodist Insurance Company,** Sec, 51 Spring Gardens, Manchester M60 2AR. T: (061)236-1818/6801.
**Methodist Stewardship Organization,** 165 Wokingham Rd, Reading RG6 1LS.
**Milton Mount College,** Sec, Livingstone House, 11 Carteret St, London SW1. (Educational trust for girls; Congregationalist).
**Moorhill Charity,** Sec, 17 Greenacres, Branksome Park, Poole, Dorset. (Holiday grants for Protestant clergy).
**New Life Foundation Trust,** PO Box 20, Bromley BR1 1DW, Kent. T: (01)460-0500. (Finances for drug addict ministry).
**Overseas Bishoprics Fund,** Hon Sec, Church House, Dean's Yard, Westminster, London SW1P 3NZ. T: (01)222-9011.
**Planned Giving Ltd,** Boardman House, Chestergate, Stockport, Cheshire.
**Poor Clergy Relief Corporation,** Sec, 27 Medway St, London SW1.
**Protestant Union,** Sec, Livingstone House, 11 Carteret St, London SW1. (Begun 1798; mutual insurance society for clergy).
**Reliance Bank Ltd,** Salvation Army, 101 Queen Victoria St, London EC4P 4EP. T: (01)236-5222, 248-4128.
**Robinson's Relief Fund,** Clerk, 22 St Andrew St, Holborn Circus, London EC4. (Grants to married Independent or Baptist clergy).
**Salvation Army General Insurance Corporation Ltd,** 4 Holywell Hill, St Albans, Herts. T: (55634) 64567.
**Salvation Army Trustee Company,** 101 Queen Victoria St, London EC4P 4EP. T: (01)236-5222.
**Society for the Relief of Poor Clergymen,** 86 Wickham Rd, Beckenham BR3 2QH.
**Southwark Christian Stewardship Department,** 112 Kennington Rd, London SE11 6RE. (Diocese of Southwark).
**Templeton Foundation,** 2 Bristow Park, Upper Malone Rd, Belfast BT9 6TH, NI.
**Wells International Advisory Services/Wells Management Consultants,** 1-11 Hay Hill, London W1. T: (01)629-1061. (Fund-raising).
**Wells Organization,** 87 Marylebone High St, London W1. (Fund-raising).
**Widows' Fund for Widows of Protestant Dissenting Ministers of the Three Denominations,** Sec, 92 Great North Way, Hendon, London NW4. T: (01)203-3282. (Begun 1733; Congregational, Baptist, Unitarian).
**Woodward Trusts,** Sec, 9 Hillside Av, Bromley Cross, near Bolton, Lancs. T: 52597. (Clergy grants for life insurance).

*USA*
**Association for Benevolent Care,** Pres, 430 Cleveland Av, SW, Canton, OH 44702.
**Association of Privately Owned Seventh-day Adventist Services and Industries,** 6840 Eastern Av NW, Washington, DC 20012. T: (202)723-0800.
**Church Mutual Insurance Company,** Merrill, WI 54452.
**Church Records Management,** 11752 Coral Hills Pl, Dallas, TX 75229.
**Commission on Church Family Financial Planning,** 1701 K St, NW, Washington, DC. T: (202)638-0850.
**D M Stearns Missionary Fund,** 147 West School House Lane, Philadelphia, PA 19144.
**Evangelical Foundation,** 1716 Spruce St, Philadelphia, PA 19103.
**General Conference Insurance Service,** 6930 Carroll Av, Takoma Park, MD 20012. T: (202)723-0800. (Seventh-day Adventists).
**Indiana Christian Benevolent Association,** Dir, 7860 Lafayette Rd, Indianapolis, IN 46278.
**Interfaith Committee on Social Responsibility in Investments,** New York, NY.
**Kings Garden, Inc,** 19303 Fremont AvN orth, Seattle, WA 98133. (Transmission of funds for missions).
**Massachusetts Congregational Charitable Society,** 10 Broad St, Salem, MA 01970.
**Narramore Christian Foundation,** 1409 North Walnut Grove Av, Rosemead, CA 91770. T: (213)288-7000.
**National Association of Church Business Administrators (NACBA),** Sec, 122 West Franklin Av, Glen Ellyn, IL 60137. T: (612)332-2571. (Also: 2302 Malcolm Av, Los Angeles, CA 90064).
**Native Preacher Company,** 1780 Broadway, New York, NY 10019. (Transmission of funds for national pastors overseas).
**OMI Brotherhood Foundation of America,** 33 Oxford Av, Dayton, OH 45407. (Fund-raising for OMI Brotherhood, Japan).
**Pension Trust (Church of Christ),** Field Rep, Box 851, Mount Vernon, IL 62864. T: (618)244-1636.
**Security Church Finance,** Suite 115, 2050 North Loop West, Houston, TX 77081. T: 231-6068. (Serving Churches of Christ).
**Society for Ministerial Relief,** Treasurer, 10 Broad St, Salem, MA 01970. (Congregational).
**Southern Baptist Foundation (SBF),** Exec Sec, 460 James Robertson Parkway, Nashville, TN 37219. T: (615)254-8823.
**Unitarian Service Pension Society,** 78 Mt Vernon St, Boston, Massachusetts.

*ZIMBABWE*
**National Co-ordinating Council for the Credit Union Movement in Zimbabwe,** PO Box 8409, Causeway, Salisbury.

# 24
# Foreign Missionary Councils

*Definition.* Councils of foreign missionary societies and agencies of different denominations and/or dioceses set up in parent sending countries to facilitate co-ordination, joint discussion, co-operation and missionary action to overseas or foreign countries (but not themselves sending money or personnel); committees, commissions, associations, boards, secretariats.

At the national and wider levels, over 70 such councils exist.

*AUSTRALIA*
**Division of Missions,** Australian Council of Churches, 511 Kent St, Sydney, NSW.
**Evangelical Missionary Alliance (NSW),** 9 Carramarr Rd, Castle Hill, 2154.

*AUSTRIA*
**Österreichischer Missionsrat,** Sek, Seilerstätte 12, A-1010 Wien. T: 523275. (Also: Gumpendorfer Str 129, Wien VI). (Affiliated to CWME).

*BELGIUM*
**Comité des Instituts Missionnaires (CIM)/Comité van de Missionerende Instituten (CMI),** Rue François Gay 276, B-1150 Brussel. T: (02) 7704869.
**Conseil Missionnaire National (CMN)/Nationaal Missieraad,** Blvd du Souverain 199, B-1160 Brussel. T: (02)6736040.
**Département Missionnaire Protestante de Belgique,** Sec, Chaussée de Haecht 32, B-1030 Brussel. (Affiliated to CWME).

*CANADA*
**Commission on World Concerns (CCC-CWC),** Canadian Council of Churches, Chairman, 40 St Clair Av East, Toronto, Ontario M4T 1M9. T: (416)921-4152.
**Conseil National Missionnaire (CNM),** 1145 Chemin de la Canardirèe, Québec 3, Québec. T: (418) 529-4924. (RC)
**National Missionary Council (NMC),** 2661 Kingston Rd, Scarboro 713, Ontario. T: (416)266-9704. (RC).

*CHINA (TAIWAN)*
**Taiwan Missionary Fellowship,** PO Box 555, Taipei 100.

*DENMARK*
**Danish Missionary Council (Danske Missionsraad),** Sec, Vendersgade 28, DK-1363 Kobenhavn K. T: (01)145949,146349. (Affiliated to CWME).
**Scandinavian (Nordic) Missionary Council (Nordiska Missionsradet),** Strandagervej 24, Hellerup. (Founded 1923. Links the 4 Scandinavian missionary councils).

*ETHIOPIA*
**Ethiopian Inter-Mission Council,** Sec, PO Box 2642, Addis Abeba.

*FINLAND*
**Finnish Missionary Council (Suomen Lähetysneuvosto),** Sec, Tahtitornikatu 18, Helsinki 14. T: 13305.

*FRANCE*
**Comité Episcopal des Missions à l'Extérieur (CEME),** 128 Rue du Bac, F-75341 Paris. T: (01)222-8123.
**Département Evangélique Française d'Action Apostolique,** Dir, 102 Blvd Arago, F-75015 Paris. (Affiliated to CWME).
**Groupe d'Organismes de Coopération Missionnaire (OCM),** 128 Rue du Bac, F-75007 (& F-75341) Paris. T: (01)222-8123.
**Secrétariat du Comité Episcopal France/Amérique Latine,** 2 Rue Abbé Patureau, F-75018 Paris. T: (01)252-0789.

*GERMAN DEMOCRATIC REPUBLIC*
**Ökumenisch-Missionarischer Rat,** Georgenkirchstr 70, DDR-1017 Berlin. (Begun 1960).

*GERMANY, Federal Republic of*
**Arbeitsgemeinschaft Evangeliker Missionen,** Postfach 21, D-7263 Bad Liebenzell. T: (07052)2031. (Formerly Konferenz Evangelikaler Missionen, Olperstr 10, D-5275 Bergneustadt 2 — Wiedenest, also D-6920 Buchenauerhof. Several fundamentalist and Pentecostal missionary societies).
**Conference of Evangelical Missions,** Sek, Ganzenstr 13, D-7 Stuttgart-Mohringer.
**Deutscher Evangelischer Missionsrat,** Sek, Mittelweg 143, D-2000 Hamburg 13. T: (040)417021. (Affiliated to CWME).
**Deutscher Katholischer Missionsrat,** Gen Sek, Kieler Str 35, D-5000 Köln 80. (Also: Hermannstr 14, D-5100 Aachen).
**Evangelisches Missionswerk in Südwestdeutschland e V,** Vogelsangstr 62, D-7000 Stuttgart 1. T: (0711)638131. (ELK Württenburg, EK Baden, Moravian Ch, Basel Mission, et alia).
**Katholisches Auslandssekretariat,** Kaiser-Friedrich-Str 9, D-5300 Bonn 3. T: (02221)225991.
**Verband Evangelischer Missionskonferenzen,** Peiner Weg 57, D-2080 Pinneberg. T: (04101)22625. (Begun 1906). (Board of several faith missions).

*GREECE*
**Inter-Orthodox Missionary Centre,** 30 Sina St, Athínai 135.

*IRELAND*
**Association of Irish Missionary Societies,** 35 Molesworth St, Dublin. T: 790939.
**Irish Missionary Union (Federation of Missionary Institutes),** 54 Wellington Rd, Dublin 4. T: (01)689674.

*HONG KONG*
**Evangelical Missions Fellowship,** PO Box 6605, Kowloon.
**Hong Kong Association of Christian Missions,** 310 King's Rd, North Point.

*ITALY*
**Commissione Episcopale de la Cooperazione tra le Chiese,** Via della Conciliazione 1, I-00193 Roma.
**Conférence des Supérieurs Majeurs des Instituts Missionnaires d'Origine Italienne,** Via Luigi Lilio 80, I-00143 Roma.
**Consiglio Missionario Nazionale,** Segreteria Generale, Via Levico 14, I-00198 Roma. T: 867080.
**Secrétariat Unitaire des Instituts Missionnaires,** Via Guerrazzi 11, I-00152 Roma.

*NETHERLANDS*
**Central Missions Commissariat (Centraal Missie Commissariat, CMC),** van Alkemadelaan 1, 's-Gravenhage. T: (070)244594.
**Dutch Missionary Council (Nederlandse Missieraad, NMR),** Halve Maanstraat 7, 5211 VV 's-Hertogenbosch. T: (073)142748.
**Evangelical Missionary Alliance (Stichting Evangelische Zendings Alliantie, EZA),** Postbus 156, Doorn. T: (03438)4434. (Formerly Box 134, Driebergen. Faith missions and Pentecostals).
**Netherlands Missionary Council (Nederlandse Zendingsraad),** Gen Sec, 37 Prins Hendriklaan, Amsterdam 7. T: (020)717654. (Affiliated to CWME).

*NEW ZEALAND*
**Commission Overseas Missions and Inter-Church Aid,** National Council of Churches of New Zealand, PO Box 291, Christchurch.
**New Zealand Evangelical Missionary Alliance,** Chairman, 427 Queen St, PO Box 8140, Auckland.

*NORWAY*
**Norwegian Missionary Council (Norsk Misjonsrad),** Geitmyrsvn 7 D, Oslo 1.

*PANAMA*
**Departamento de Misiones,** Apdo 18, Bocas del Toro. T: 59258.

*POLAND*
**Commission Missionnaire de l'Episcopat de Pologne,** Secrétariat de la Commission (Komisja Episkopatu Polski do Spraw Misji, Sekretariat Komisji), Ul Dziekania 1, 00 279 Warszawa. T: 319662.

*PORTUGAL*
**Liga Evangélica de Accão Missionaria,** Alameda das Linhas de Torres 122, Lisboa 5. T: 790039.

*SPAIN*
**Comisión Episcopal de Misiones y Cooperación entre las Iglesias,** Calle del Bosque 9, Madrid 3. T: 2332003.

*SWEDEN*
**Swedish Missionary Council (Svenska Missionsradet),** Sec, Kungsgatan 28, S-751 05 Uppsala. T: (018)120240. (Affiliated to CWME).

*SWITZERLAND*
**Alliance Missionnaire Evangélique (AME),** Siège Central, 7 Av de Cour, CH-1007 Lausanne.
**Commission on World Mission and Evangelism (CWME),** Dir, World Council of Churches, Ecumenical Centre, 150 Route de Ferney, CH-1211 Genève 20. T: (0104122)333400.
**Département Missionnaire des Eglises Protestantes de la Suisse Romande,** Chemin des Cèdres 5, CP 136, CH-1000 Lausanne 9.
**Kooperation Evangelischer Kirchen und Missionen in der Deutschsprachigen Schweiz (KEM),** Gen Sek, Missionsstr 21, CH-4003 Basel. T: (061) 253725.
**Schweizerischer Evangelischer Missionsrat (SEMR)/Conseil Suisse des Missions Evangéliques,** Sek, 29 Av Vinet, CH-1004 Lausanne. T: (021)242438. (Also: 5 Chemin des Cèdres, CP 136, CH-1000 Lausanne 9). (Swiss Missionary Council. Affiliated to CWME).
**Schweizerischer Katholischer Missionsrat/Conseil Missionnaire Catholique Suisse,** Grandrue 34, CH-1700 Fribourg 2.

*UK OF GB & NI*
**Conference for World Mission (CFWM),** Gen Sec, Edinburgh House, 2 Eaton Gate, London SW1W 9BL. T: (01)730-9611. (Up to 1978 named Conference of Missionary Societies in GB & I/Conference of British Missionary Societies, CBMS).
**Evangelical Missionary Alliance (EMA),** 19 Draycott Place, London SW3 2SG. T: (01)584-9333/4. (Co-ordinates British Evangelical missions worldwide).
**National Missionary Council of England and Wales,** St Joseph's College, Lawrence St, London NW7 4JX. T: (01)959-8125. (RC).

*USA*
**Associated Missions,** International Council of Christian Churches (TAM-ICCC), 756 Haddon Av, Collingswood, NJ 08108. T: (609)858-0700.
**Association of Church Missions Committees (ACMC),** Suite 202, 1021 East Walnut St, Pasadena, CA 91106.
**Division of Overseas Ministries (DOM-NCCCUSA),** 475 Riverside Drive, New York, NY 10027. T: (212)870-2175.
**Evangelical Foreign Missions Association (EFMA),** 100 Western Union Bldg, 1405 G St, NW, Washington, DC 20005. T: (202)628-7911. (Co-ordinates USA Conservative Evangelical missions worldwide).
**Fellowship of Missions (FOM),** 4205 Chester Av, Cleveland, OH 44103. T: (216)431-5222. (11 mission agencies, 1,850 missionaries).
**Interdenominational Foreign Mission Association (IFMA),** PO Box 395, Wheaton, IL 60187. T: (312)682-9270. (Co-ordinates USA Fundamentalist missions worldwide).
**United States Catholic Mission Council,** Room 500, 1325 Massachusetts Av, NW, Washington, DC 20005.

*YUGOSLAVIA*
**Missions Office (Misijska Centrala),** R Lacic 7, pp 155, YU-71001 Sarajevo.
**National Missionary Council,** Biskupska Konferencija Jugoslavije, Kaptol 31, YU-41000 Zagreb.

# 25
# Foreign Missionary Societies

*Definition.* Societies and agencies primarily and principally concerned with the sending abroad of foreign missionary personnel and resources, including international missionary societies, denominational mission boards, orders primarily formed for foreign missions, and Catholic missionary congregations or institutes under SC Propaganda. Small societies with under 10 personnel serving abroad are usually excluded in most directories. Women's societies are found under WOMEN'S LAY ORGANIZATIONS.

The total of foreign missionary societies of all traditions numbers about 3,100 (1980). For this reason, no listing is given here, but lists at various levels, and for Catholic, Protestant, Orthodox and other confessions, can be found here under DIRECTORIES.

# 26
# Foreign Missionary Training

*Definition.* Training colleges at home or abroad primarily or solely for foreign missionaries or persons proceeding overseas in secular employment, orientation schools, language schools, refresher courses, graduate schools of mission specializing in training, seminaries primarily for foreign missionaries; not primarily academic or degree-granting. For primarily the academic study of mission and missiology, see UNIVERSITY DEPARTMENTS OF RELIGION.

Such centres number over 410 worldwide.

*ALGERIA*
**Centre de Langues et de Pastorale,** Dir, Grand Séminaire, Komba.

*AUSTRALIA*
**Missionary Training College,** St Leonards, Tasmania.
**Summer Institute of Linguistics (SIL),** Gumbalanya, Barnawarth South, Victoria.

*AUSTRIA*
**Missiologisches Institut der Päpstlichen Missionswerke,** Seilerstätte 12, A-1010 Wien. T: 523275.
**Salzburger Missionsschule,** Brauhausstr 22, Salzburg-Maxglan.

*BELGIUM*
**CIM Service de Formation,** Chaussée de Mont-Saint-Jean 95, B-3030 Heverlee.
**CIM Service de Formation Permanente,** Rue François Gay 276, B-1150 Brussel.
**Collège pour l'Amérique Latine (COPAL)/College voor Latijns-Amerika,** Tervuursestraat 56, B-3000 Leuven. T: (016)225845,226415.
**Compagni Costruttori,** Naamsesteenweg 537, Haverlee. T: (016)279,20523. (RC lay missionaries).
**La Rocca,** Av Gounod 98, Brussel 7. T: (02)234861.
**LOFC-KAV,** Rue de la Poste 111, Brussel 3. T: (02)192650.
**Semaine de Missiologie de Louvain,** Chaussée de Mont-Saint-Jean 95, B-3030 Heverlee.

*BOLIVIA*
**Instituto Internacional de Idiomas,** Av Simon-Lopez s/n, Casilla 550, Cochabamba. T: 7521.
**Instituto Linguistico de Verano,** Casilla 64, Riberalta, Beni.
**Instituto Linguistico de Verano,** Casilla 1415, Cochabamba.

*BRAZIL*
**Centro de Orientação Missionária (COM),** CFP, Rua Sinimbu 1756, CP 59, Caxias, MA. T: 211183.
**Instituto Evangélico Missionário Peniel,** CP 29, Jacutinga, MG.
**Summer Institute of Linguistics (Wycliffe),** CP 43, ZC-09 Rio de Janeiro. (Also CP 4216).

*CANADA*
**Canadian School of Missions and Ecumenical Institute,** 97 St George St, Toronto 5, Ontario.
**Madonna House Apostolat,** Combernere via Barry's Bay, Ontario.
**Missionary Health Institute,** Pres, 4000 Leslie St, Willowdale, Ontario. T: (416)444-1131.

*CHINA (TAIWAN)*
**Taichung Language Institute,** Wei Tao Rd, Lane Chiu Tso No 69, Taichung. T: 8842.
**Taipei Language Institute,** Chunghsiao Rd, Sec 1 No 5, Taipei. T: 330022. (Also: 1559 Chung Cheng Rd, Taipei).

*COLOMBIA*
**Instituto Linguistico de Verano,** Apdo Nac 5787, Bogotá.

*COSTA RICA*
**Spanish Language Institute,** Apdo 2240, San José.

*ECUADOR*
**Instituto Linguistico de Verano,** Casilla 1007, Quito.

*EL SALVADOR*
**Centro de Animación Misionera,** c/o Hogar Santa Teresita, Apulo.

*FRANCE*
**Bureau Central d'Etude pour les Equipements d'Outre-Mer (BCEOM),** 15 Square Moyse-Hymens, Paris.
**Centre de Formation Missionnaire,** Dir, 50 Rue des Galibouds, Albertville (Savoie). (Also: 5 Rue Monsieur, Paris 7 and 24 Rue du Maréchal-Joffre, F-78000 Versailles. T: 950-2771). (French courses for missionaries).
**Centre d'Enseignement des Monitrices de la Jeunesse (CEMJ),** 44 Rue des Rochettes, Nantes 16.
**Centro di Formazione e Scambi Internazionali,** 73 Rue des Heros Nogentais, F-94 Nogent-sur-Marne. T: 071 2020. (RC lay missionaries).
**Ecole Technique d'Outre-Mer,** 1 Rue Dume d'Aplemont, Le Havre.
**Missionary Orientation Centre,** Dir, 156 Rue de Longchamp, Paris 16.
**Prévoyance des Techniciens Missionnaires de la Coopération Internationale (PRETEMIC),** 77 Rue du Président Herriot, Lyon 2.

*GERMAN DEMOCRATIC REPUBLIC*
**Friedensau Missionary Seminary,** Bez Magdeburg, DDR-3271 Friedensau bei Burg. (SDA).

*GERMANY, Federal Republic of*
**Arbeitsgemeinschaft für Entwicklungshilfe,** Leonhardstr 4, Aachen. (Recruitment and training of technicians).
**Arbeitskreis für Mission und Ökumenische Beziehungen in der Evangelischen Studentengemeinde,** Mercedesstr 5-7, D-7 Stuttgart 50. T: 562303/04.
**Bibelschule,** Bergstr, Postfach 9, D-6101 Seeheim. T: (06257)2000.
**Breklumer Seminar für Missionarischen und Kirchlichen Dienst,** D-2257 Bredstedt-Land.
**Frauenmission Malche,** Bad Freienwalde/Oder. (Women's missionary training).
**Missionsakademie an der Universität Hamburg,** Rupertistr 67, Hamburg-Nienstedten. (Also: Mittelweg 143, D-2 Hamburg 13).
**Missionshaus Bibelschule Wiedenest,** Olperstr 10, D-5275 Bergneustadt 2, Wiedenest. T: (02261) 4777.
**Missionspädagogische Arbeitsgemeinschaft,** Mittelweg 143, D-2000 Hamburg 13. T: (040)417021.
**Nordelbisches Zentrum für Weltmission und Kirchlichen Weltdienst,** Agathe-Lasch-Weg 16, D-2000 Hamburg 52. T: (0411)880183. (Centre for World Mission).
**Seminar Marienhoehe/Marienhoehe Missionary Seminary,** Auf der Marienhoehe 32, D-61 Darmstadt. T: 55055/6. (SDA).

*GHANA*
**Summer Institute of Linguistics (SIL),** PO Box 47, Achimota.

*GUATEMALA*
**Instituto de Capacitación Missionera (ICM),** 4a Calle 5-52, Zona 1, Guatemala.

*HONG KONG*
**Hong Kong Language Institute,** Principal, Hong Kong.

*ITALY*
**Centro Assistenza Laici Missionari (CALM),** Via Vittorio Veneto 197, I-19100 La Spezia.
**Centro Collegamenti Tecnici per le Missioni (CCTM),** Via Belvedere 11, I-80127 Napoli.
**Centro Educazione Missionario (CEM),** Via San Martino 8, Parma.
**Centro Laici Italiani per le Missioni (CLIM),** Piazza Fontana 2, I-20122 Milano. T: 806184. (Lay missionary centre).
**International Centre for Missionary Animation,** St Peter's College, Viale delle Mura Aurelie 4, I-00152 Roma. T: 582228.
**Piccoli Operai Missionari Ecumenici,** Città della Ecumenica, Via Taddeide 24, I-00060 Riano (Roma).
**Pontificio Instituto Missioni Estere (PIME),** Via Santa Terese 12, I-00198 Roma.

*JAPAN*
**Hayama Missionary Seminar,** Lacy-kan, Hayama, Kanagawa-ken.
**Japan Missionary Language Institute,** Tokyo.

*KENYA*
**Baptist Language School,** Principal, Brackenhurst Baptist Assembly, Tigoni, PO Box 137, Limuru. T: Tigoni 256.
**CPK Language & Orientation School,** Principal, Bishops Rd, PO Box 49849, Nairobi. T: 20992. (Anglican).

*KOREA, South*
**International School of Missions,** 238 Hooam-dong, Yonsaku, PO Box 3476, Soul.

*MALAWI*
**Katete Language Centre,** PO Box 7, Champira. (Citumbuka. RC).
**Language Centre,** PO Box 274, Lilongwe. (Chichewa. RC).

*MEXICO*
**Instituto Linguistico de Verano,** Apdo 2975, México 1, DF.
**Seminario de Missiones Extranjeras,** Apdo 22009, México 22, DF.
**Spanish Language School,** 12 de Diciembre 25, Apdo 1616, Guadalajara, Jalisco. T: 57663.

*NETHERLANDS*
**Contact Training School (Vormingscentrum Kotakt der Kontinenten),** Amersfoortstraat 20, Soesterberg.
**Hendrik Kraemer Institute,** Postbus 12, 2340AA Oegstgeest. (Training workers for overseas).
**Mission School of the Netherlands Reformed Church (Zendingshogeschool der Nederlandse Hervormde Kerk),** Leidsestraatweg 11, Oegstgeest.
**Missionary Seminary of the Refomed Churches in the Netherlands,** Wilhelminalaan 3, Baarn.
**Missionary Training Centre,** Ubbergen-bij Nijmegen.

*NORWAY*
**Missionary College of the Norwegian Mission Society,** Stavanger.

*PAPUA NEW GUINEA*
**Melanesian Institute for Pastoral and Socio Economic Service,** PO Box 571, Goroka, EHD. (Missionary orientation RC/Angl/Luth/UCPN & SI).
**Summer Institute of Linguistics (SIL),** PO Ukarumpa, EHD.

*PERU*
**Centro Latinoamericano de Lenguaje Total,** Av 9 de Diciembre (Paseo Colón) 378, Lima. T: 31239.
**Instituto Linguistico de Verano,** Casilla 2492, Lima.

*PHILIPPINES*
**Interchurch Language School,** PO Box 3096, Manila.
**Philippine Missionary Institute,** Biga, Silang Cavite D-318.
**Summer Institute of Linguistics (SIL),** Nasuli, Malaybalay, Bukidnon, PO Box 2270, Manila.

*POLAND*
**Missionary Centre of the Verbist Priests (Seminarium Misyjne Ksiezy Werbistów),** ul Kolonia 19, 14 500 Pieniezno.

*PORTUGAL*
**Centro de Estudos Missionários,** Lisboa.

*PUERTO RICO*
**College of World Mission,** Pres, Box 66, Catano, PR 00632. T: (809)784-4903. (Churches of Christ USA).

*SPAIN*
**Centro Missionero de Adaptación Pastoral,** Colegio Vasco de Quiroga, Ciudad Universitaria, Madrid 3.

*SWITZERLAND*
**Frères sans Frontières,** Grand Rue 34, CH-1700 Fribourg. T: (037)231432. (Laymen trained for overseas).

*TANZANIA*
**Maryknoll Language School,** PO Box 298, (RC). (Swahili).

*UGANDA*
**Mushanga Language Centre,** PO Box 187, Mbarara. (White Fathers).

*UK OF GB & NI*
**Ad Lucem,** c/o CIIR, Hinsley House, 38 King St, London WC2.
**All Nations Christian College,** Easneye, Ware, Herts SG12 0LX. T: Ware 61243. (1971 Union of Mount Hermon Missionary Training College and 2 others).
**Catholic Institute for International Relations (CIIR),** 38 King St, London WC2E 8JT.
**Catholic Overseas Appointments Bureau,** 38 King St, London WC2E 8JT.
**Centre for International Briefing,** Dir, The Castel, Farnham, Surrey. T: (02513)21194. (Formerly Overseas Service College).
**Christian Overseas Information Service,** 38 King St, London WC2E 8JT.
**Christian Preparation for Work Abroad,** 2 Eaton Gate, London SW1. T: (01)730-9611.
**Christians Abroad,** 15 Tufton St, London SW1P 3QQ. T: (01)222-2165. (Information, appointments and briefing for work in developing countries).
**College of the Ascension,** Principal, Weoley Park Rd, Selly Oak, Birmingham B29 6RD. T: (021) 472-1667. (USPG; Anglican).
**Crowther Hall,** Principal, Selly Oak, Birmingham B29 6LE. (CMS; Anglican).
**Emmanuel Bible College and Missions,** Dir, 1 Palm Grove, Birkenhead, Cheshire L43 1TE.
**Group on Education for Mission (GEM),** 2 Eaton Gate, London SW1. T: (01)730-9611.
**Kingsmead,** Bristol Rd, Selly Oak, Birmingham B29 6LE. (Methodist Missionary Society).
**Lebanon Missionary Bible College,** Castle Terrace, Berwick-on-Tweed. T: 6190.
**Missionary Education Centre,** 23 Eccleston Square, London SW1.
**Missionary Horticultural Training College,** Arkley Manor, Arkley, Nr Barnet, Herts. T: (01) 449-3131.
**Missionary Institute,** Oak Lodge, Totteridge Lane, London N20 8NB. T: (01)959-1968.
**Missionary Orientation Centre,** WEC, Bulstrode, Gerrards Cross, Bucks SL9 8SZ.
**Missionary Training College,** 10 Prince Albert Rd, Glasgow W2.
**National Lay Missionary Centre,** All Saints Pastoral Centre, Colney, Herts. (RC. Volunteer Missionary Movement, VMM).
**Overdale College,** Bristol Rd, Selly Oak, Birmingham B29 6LE. (Churches of Christ in Great Britain).
**Redcliffe Missionary Training College,** 66 Grove Park Rd, Chiswick, London W4 3QB. T: (01)994-3408.
**Ridgelands Bible College,** Dartford Rd, Bexley, Kent. T: Crayford 21842.
**St Andrew's Hall,** Selly Oak, Birmingham B29 6LE. (BMS, CCWM, Presbyterian Ch of England).
**Selly Oak Colleges,** Pres, Weoley Park Rd, Selly Oak, Birmingham B29 6LE. T: (021)472-4231.
**Woodbrooke College,** Bristol Rd, Selly Oak, Birmingham B29 6LE. (Religious Society of Friends).

*USA*
**Note.** Missionary training in the USA is largely given by means of courses in missions at seminaries, theological colleges and Bible schools and institutes; and also at university departments of mission and missiology. A total of 285 such institutions offering courses are listed in *Mission handbook 10th edition* (1973); of these, 101 offer graduate courses. Others are listed in *An American directory of schools & colleges offering missionary courses,* ed G. Schwartz (South Pasadena: William Carey Library, 1973). The list that follows below gives only a handful of centres primarily concerned with foreign missionary training.
**Baptist Missionary Association Theological Seminary,** PO Box 1797, Jacksonville, TX 75766.
**Bethany Fellowship Missionary Training Center,** 6820 Auto Club Rd, Minneapolis, MN 55431.
**Bible Missionary Institute,** 3501 46th Av, Rock Island, IL 61201.
**Center for World Christian Interaction,** 6148 McPherson Av, St Louis, MO 63112.
**Central American Mission Practical Missionary Training,** 216 East Commonwealth Av, PO Box 628, Fullerton, CA 92631. T: (714)526-5139.
**Committee to Assist Missionary Education Overseas (CAMEO),** Coordinator, 5010 West Sixth Av, Denver, CO 80204.
**Department of World Mission,** Andrew University, Berrien Springs, MI 49104. (Seventh-day Adventist).
**Jaffray School of Missions,** Nyack College, Nyack, NY 10960. T: (914)358-1710. (Christian & Missionary Alliance).
**Kennedy School of Missions,** 55 Elizabeth St, Hartford, CT 06105.
**Koinonia Foundation,** Pikesville, Box 5744, Baltimore, MD 21208. (Training for laymen overseas).
**Laos Team,** 4920 Piney Branch Rd, NW, Washington, DC 20011. (Recruiting laymen for overseas).
**Mission Training and Resource Center (MTRC),** 221 East Walnut St, Suite 271, Pasadena, CA 91101. T: (213)577-1733.
**Missionary Orientation Center,** Exec Sec, Cricket-town Rd, Stony Point, NY 10980. T: (914)886-2752.
**Overseas Ministries Study Center,** Pres, 6315 Ocean Av, PO Box 2057, Ventnor, NJ 08406. T: (609)822-2194,(201)635-7466.
**Practical Missionary Training,** Box 28005, Dallas, TX 75228.
**Practical Missionary Training,** Gen Dir, PO Box 628, Fullerton, CA 92632.
**School of World Mission and Institute of Church Growth,** Fuller Theological Seminary, 135 North Oakland Av, Pasadena, CA 91101.
**Southern Missionary College,** Pres, Collegedale, TN 37315. T: (615)356-2111.
**Summer Institute of Linguistics (SIL),** 219 West Walnut St, Box 1960, Santa Ana, California.
**Summer Institute of Missions,** Wheaton College, Wheaton, IL 60188.
**Summer Mission Institute,** University of San Francisco, 2131 Fulton St, San Francisco, CA 95053.
**United Presbyterian Center for Mission Studies,** Pres, PO Box 2613, Fullerton, CA 92633. T: (714) 870-4481.

*VIET NAM*
**Summer Institute of Linguistics (SIL),** PO Box L11, Saigon.

*ZAMBIA*
**Language Training Centre,** Ilondola, PO Chinsali. (Bemba).

# 27 Foreign Missions Support Organizations

*Definition.* Agencies for support of foreign missions and missionary societies, but not themselves founding missions or churches or (usually) sending personnel; service organizations, co-ordinating agencies; fund-raising, recruiting in home (sending) countries; technical aid, missionary aviation and transport, missionary equipment services; Anglican diocesan associations (funds for overseas dioceses). For prayer support, see PRAYER SOCIETIES.

*ARGENTINA*
**Agencia de Promoción Misiologica (APOYO),** Casilla 3, 1602 Suc, Puente Saavedra, Buenos Aires.

*AUSTRALIA*
**Mission Enterprises Limited (MEL),** Gen Manager, 685 Burwood Rd, Hawthorn, Victoria 3122. T: 822110. (Service, support).
**Missionary Aviation Fellowship (Australia) (MAF),** Dir, PO Box 52, Box Hill, Victoria 3128. T: 894009.

*AUSTRIA*
**Evangelisches Arbeitskreis für Aussere Mission in Österreich,** Kaiser-Josef Platz 9, Graz.
**Gruppo Austriaco di Lavoro per i Transporti nelle Missioni (MIVA),** Gmundnerstr 21, A-4651 Stadl-Paura. (RC).
**Institut für Internationale Zusammenarbeit (IZA),** Singerstr 7, A-1010 Wien.
**MIVA,** Zentrale Österreichs, Mivagasse 2, A-4651 Stadl-Paura. T: (07245)545.
**Päpstliche Missionswerk in Österreich,** Seilerstätte 12, A-1010 Wien. T: (0222)523275.

*BELGIUM*
**Amis du Père Damien,** Rue Stévin 16, B-1040 Brussel. T: (02)2192996.
**Catholic Co-ordinating Committee for the Sending of Technicians (CCET),** Rue de la Limite 6, B-1030 Brussel.
**Fraternités Terre Nouvelle (FNT),** Rue du Moulin 98, B-1030 Brussel. T: (02)2185402. (For Africa).
**ITECO,** Rue Traversière 32, B-1030 Brussel. T: (02)2171046.
**Les Amis des Missions,** Chaussée de Haecht 32, B-1030 Brussel. T: (02)179885. (Protestant; cheap air fares overseas).
**RAPTIM-Belgium,** Rue Royale 179, Brussel 3. T: 193235. (Reduced air fares).

*CANADA*
**Entr'aide Missionnaire,** 1215 Rue Visitation, Montréal 133, Québec. T: (514)521-1011.
**Japan Missionary Fellowship,** 237 McKee Av, Willowdale, Ontario.
**RAPTIM-Canada,** 1652 Rue St Hubert, Montréal 132, Québec. T: 849-5323.

*CHAD*
**Service Missionnaire Aérien (Missionary Aviation Fellowship),** BP 275, Ndjamena (Fort-Lamy).

*ECUADOR*
**Alas de Socorro,** Casilla 137, Quito. (MAF).

*FRANCE*
**Aide aux Missions d'Afrique,** 82 Rue Dutot, F-75015 Paris. T: (01)532-8749.
**Centre de Formation pour la Coopération Internationale,** BP 14, Saint-Ilan, F-22120 Yffiniac.
**Cercle St-Jean-Baptiste,** 3 Rue de l'Abbaye, F-75006 Paris. T: 633-2414.
**European Student Missionary Association (ESMA),** European Bible Institute, Paris. (Founded 1955).
**Foi et Cultures Ad Lucem,** 12 Rue Guy-de-la-Brosse, F-75005 Paris. T: (01)331-7955.
**Groupe d'Organismes de Coopération Missionnaire (OCM),** 128 Rue du Bac, F-75007 Paris. T: (01)222-8123. (RC).
**International Missionary Benefit Society,** Paris.
**Oeuvre Apostolique,** 8 Rue Daniel Lesueur, F-75007 Paris. T: (01)306-4437. (Aid to missions, RC).

*GERMANY, Federal Republic of*
**Deutsche Evangelische Missionshilfe (1913),** Mittelweg 143, D-2000 Hamburg 13. T: (040)417021.
**Evangelisches Missionswerk im Bereich der BRD und Berlin (West),** Berlin. (Protestant missionary co-operation centre).
**MBK Mission,** Mission der Evangelischen Schülerinnen- und Frauen- Bibelkreise, Hermann-Lons-Str 14, D-4902 Bad Salzuflen. T: (05222)50088. (Mission of Protestant Girl Students' and Women's Bible Circles; 1925).
**MISSIO Internationales Katholisches Missionswerk,** Hermannstr 14, Postfach 1110, D-5100 Aachen. T: (0241)32441.
**RAPTIM-Deutschland,** Hermannstr 14, D-51 Aachen. T: 32757.
**Vereinigte Deutsche Missionshilfe,** Postfach 93, D-7016 Gerlingen. T: (07156)22890.
**Vereinigte Missionsfreunde,** Bismarckstr 44, D-5930 Hüttental-Weidenau. T: (0271)44122. (Also: Oranienstr 18, D-5905 Freudenberg. T: (02734)7930). (Begun 1931).
**Wirtschaftsstelle Ev Missionsgesellschaften Ubersee-Warenversorgung und Passagen GmbH,** Mittelweg 143, D-2000 Hamburg 13. T: (040)440151. (Protestant missionary societies' supply company for goods and passages overseas).

*IRELAND*
**Irish Missionary Union,** 54 Wellington Rd, Dublin 4.

*ITALY*
**Associazione di Laici in Aiuto alle Missioni,** Via Kramer 5, Milano. (RC).
**Associazione Laici Pro-Missioni,** c/o Scuola del Cristo, Cannaregio 1723, I-30121 Venezia. (RC).
**Centro di Collegamento Tecnica-Missioni,** Via Belvedere 11, Napoli.
**Centro Internazionale per l'Aviazione e la Motorizzazione Missionaria (CIAMM),** Via Magenta 12bis, I-10128 Torino. T: 531441. (RC). (Also: Via Francesco Duodo 49/12, I-00136 Roma).
**Cooperatori Salesiani,** Ufficio Centrale Cooperatori Salesiani, Via Maria Ausiliatrice 32, I-10152 Torino. (Also: Via della Pisana III, I-00163 Roma).
**Gruppi Appoggio Missionario (GAM),** Piazza Tripoli 22, Milano. (RC).
**Gruppi di Appoggio Alle Missioni,** Via Arquata 23/74, Torino. (RC).
**Oeuvres Pontificales Missionnaires,** Via di Propaganda 1c, I-00187 Roma. T: 6795183,6780508, 6795007,681568.
**Opera Apostolica per il Corredo Missionario,** Via Levico 14, Roma. (RC).
**Servizio Missionario per l'Africa e l'Asia,** Consiglio Missionario Nazionale, Via Levico 14, I-00198 Roma.
**Società Tecnica Aiuto Missioni (STAM),** Ufficio Missionario Diocesano, Via Arcivescovado 12, Torino.

*MEXICO*
**Alas de Socorro,** Apdo 17, San Cristobal las Casas, Chiapas. T: 470. (MAF).
**Mexico Missionary Services,** Suc K, 12 de Diciembre No 365, Col Chapalita, Apdo 3115, Guadalajara, Jalisco.

*NETHERLANDS*
**Aid to Dutch Missions (Curatorium Week voor de Nederlandse Missionaris),** Van Alkemadelaan 1, 's-Gravenhage. T: (070)244594.
**Carosi,** Groot Haesebroekseweg 12, Wassenaar.
**Continents Contact Centre (Centrum Kontakt der Kontinenten),** Amersfoortsestraat 20, Soesterberg. T: (03463)1755.
**Group for Mission Support Agencies (Werkgroep Missieprocuratoren),** Amersfoortsestraat 20a, Soesterberg. T: (03463)1536.
**MIVA (Stichting Missie Verkeersmiddelen Actie),** Keizergracht 252, Amsterdam.
**Pontifical Missionary Works (Pauselijke Missiewerken, PMW),** Laan Copes van Cattenburgh 127, 's-Gravenhage. T: (070)112343.
**Society for the Interests of Active Missionaries in Asia (SIAMA),** 105 Gerard Brandtstraat, Leiden. T: (01710)40584. (Travel agents for missionary groups).
**RAPTIM-Nederland,** Anna Paulownastraat 45A, 's-Gravenhage. T: 605925. (Also: Heuvelring 31, Tilburg. T: (04250)35085).

*NEW ZEALAND*
**Consiglio Neozelandese delle Organizzazioni di Assistenza d'Oltremare (CORSO),** 63 Abel Smith St, PO Box 2500, Wellington.
**Missionary Aviation Fellowship (MAF),** NZ Council, PO Box 1760, Auckland.

*PAPUA NEW GUINEA*
**Missionary Aviation Fellowship (MAF),** Operations Manager, Wewak 82, New Guinea.

*PHILIPPINES*
**Missionary Aviation Fellowship (MAF),** 1300 M De Comillas, PO Box 4198, Manila.

*SWITZERLAND*
**Associazione Internazionale dei Soci Costruttori (IBO),** Postfach 28, CH-9658 Vildhaus.
**Associazione Svizzera di Assistenza Tecnica (HELVETIAS),** CH-1950 Sion.
**Comité Auxiliaire Suisse de l'Eglise Chrétienne Missionnaire Belge,** Prés, Rue de St-Jean 86, CH-1201 Genève.
**Groupes Missionnaires,** 2 Av des Pléiades, CH-1800 Vevey. (Missions service agency).
**Heli Mission,** CH-9043 Trogen. (Helicopters for missionary field transport).

*UK OF GB & NI*
**Accra Diocesan Association,** Sec, 128 Harbord St, London SW6 6PH. T: (01)385-7942.
**Association of the Dioceses of Singapore and West Malaysia,** Sec, 57 Balcombe Rd, Haywards Heath, West Sussex. T: (0444)2188.
**Belize Church Association,** Sec, Moorcroft, Cassington, Oxford. T: (08678)288.
**Board for Mission and Unity,** Church of England, Church House, Dean's Yard, London SW1P 3NT. T: (01)222-9011.
**Borneo Mission Association,** Sec, Alcester Rectory, Alcester, Warwick. T: (078971)2639.
**Carpentaria Association,** Sec, St Mary's, Holy Lane, Rushmere St Andrew, Ipswich, Suffolk.
**Catholic Overseas Appointments,** 38 King St, London WC2E 8JT. T: (01)836-8792.
**Church of Burma Association,** Sec, St John's Vicarage, Felixstowe, Suffolk. T: (03942)4226.
**Church of South India Council in Great Britain,** Sec, 25 Marylebone Rd, London NW1 5JR. T: (01)935-2541
**Church of Sri Lanka Association,** Sec, 41 Greencroft Gardens, London NW6 3LN. T: (01)624-5639.
**Fellowship of the Arctic,** Sec, 11 Hamilton House, Belgrave Rd, Seaford, Sussex.
**Friends of Vellore,** Gen Sec, 36 St George's St, Winchester, Hants. T: 66239.
**Hong Kong Diocesan Association,** Hon Sec, 61A Furze Croft, Hove BN3 1PD, East Sussex. T: (0273) 773648.
**House of Rest for Christian Workers,** 10 Finchley Rd, St John's Wood, London NW8 6D5. T: (01)722-3536. (Guesthouse for foreign missionaries).
**Iran Diocesan Association,** Sec, Flat 1, Hershell Court, Upper Richmond Rd West, London SW14 7DH.
**London Association in Aid of Moravian Missions,** Sec, Moravian Church House, 5-7 Muswell Hill, London N10 3TJ. T: (01)883-3409.
**Ludhiana British Fellowship,** Dir, 157 Waterloo Rd, London SE1 8UU. T: (01)928-1173.
**Missionary Aviation Fellowship (MAF),** Gen Dir, 3 Beechcroft Rd, South Woodford, London E18 1BJ. T: (01)989-0838.
**Nassau Association,** Sec, 13 Docklands Av, Ingatestone, Essex CM4 9DS. T: (02775)2902.
**Polynesia Diocesan Association,** Sec, 21 Chayne Close, Ware, Herts.
**Scottish National Council of the Pontifical Society for the Propagation of the Faith,** 21 Whitevale St, Glasgow E1. T: (041)554-0285.
**South Asia Church Aid Association,** Sec, 2 Eaton Gate, London SW1W 9BL. T: (01)730-9611.

*USA*
**Air Team,** Pres, PO Box 304, Lexington, MA 02173.
**Amazing Grace Missions,** 600 Richmond Av, San Antonio, TX 78215. (Fund transmitting agency).
**American Council of Voluntary Agencies for Foreign Service,** 9th Floor, 44 East 23 St, New York NY 10010.
**Assistance in Missions (AIM),** Pres, 9003 Terhune Av, Sun Valley, CA 91352. T: (213)767-9767.
**Christ for the Nations,** PO Box 8658, Dallas, TX 75216. (Construction funds, literature for overseas).
**Christian Missions Recruiting Service,** PO Box 339, Salida, CO 81201. T: (303)539-4079.
**Commission on Voluntary Service & Action,** Room 830, 475 Riverside Drive, New York, NY 10017.
**Council for Cooperation with the Dominican Evangelical Church,** 475 Riverside Drive, New York, NY 10027. T: (212)749-0700. (Formerly Board for Christian Work in Santo Domingo).
**Co-laborers Inc,** Pres, 6110 Radford Av, North Hollywood, CA 91606. T: (213)980-4293. (Encouraging self-supporting missionaries).
**Evangelical Latin League (TELL),** Box 816, Alamo, TX 78516.
**Friends of Indonesia Fellowship,** 1485 Monte Verde Av, Upland, CA 91786.
**Friends of Mexico,** PO Box 694, Downey, CA 90241.
**Friends of Turkey and Postal Evangelism,** 2601 Arcadia Drive, Miramar, FL 33023. T: (305)983-7555.
**Interlink,** Exec Dir, PO Box 832, Wheaton, IL 60187. (Matching men and resources).
**International Christian Organization (Intercristo),** PO Box 9323, Seattle, WA 98109. T: (206)623-0715. (Computerized missions personnel information).
**Japan North American Commission on Cooperative Mission,** Room 618, 475 Riverside Drive, New York, NY 10027. T: (212)870-2021.
**Jungle Aviation and Radio Service (JARS),** Wycliffe Bible Translators, Exec Dir, PO Box 248, Waxhaw, NC 28173. T: (704)843-2185.
**Lafricasia Mission Advance Fellowship (LAMAF),** 135 North Oakland Av, Pasadena, CA 91106. (Third-World missionaries).
**LAOS,** 4920 Piney Branch Rd, Washington, DC 20011.
**Lay Mission-Helpers Association,** 1531 West 9th St, Los Angeles, CA 90015.
**Lutheran Council in the USA Division of Mission and Ministry,** 315 Park Av South, New York, NY 10010. T: (212)677-3950.
**Mission Aviation Fellowship (MAF),** Pres, 3519 West Commonwealth, PO Box 2828, Fullerton, CA 92633. T: (714)525-8206.
**Mission Engineering,** Box 278, Hiawatha, IA 52233.
**Mission Services Association,** Exec Dir, County Rd, 400 North at 900 West, Tipton County, PO Box 177, Kempton, IN 46049. T: (317)947-3781.
**Missionary Electronics,** Room 511, 110 East Wilshire, PO Box 27, Fullerton, CA 92632. T: (714) 526-5881.
**Missionary Equipment Fund,** 7654 West Berwyn Av, Chicago, IL 60656.
**Missionary Flights International,** Pres, PO Box 6213, West Palm Beach, FL 33462. T: (305)967-3682.
**Missionary Service Organization,** Pres, 207 North Broadway, Santa Ana, CA 92701. T: (714)547-6451.
**Missionary Services,** 327 Gundersen Drive, Carol Stream, PO Box 853, Wheaton, IL 60187. T: (312) 653-3770. (Formerly Missionary Equipment Service. 80-page catalogue).
**Missionary Strategy Agency,** Gen Dir, 1054 North Saint Andrew Place, Los Angeles, CA 90038. T: (213)465-2267.
**Missionary Tech Team,** 1418 Mary Jane Drive, Longview, TX 75601. T: (214)758-9492.
**Missionary Vehicle Association,** 102 Kinggold St, Peekskill, NY 10566.
**New Life League,** 7654 West Berwyn Av, Chicago, IL 60656. (Tracts, missions service agency).
**Procurement Service,** Pres, 1115 Colorado Blvd, Los Angeles, CA 90041. T: (213)256-3141.
**REAP Mission,** Dir, PO Box 185, Arlington Heights, IL 60006. T: (312)392-6047. (Reinforcing Evangelists and Aiding Pastors).
**Seventh-day Adventist Transportation Bureau,** 6840 Eastern Av, NW, Washington, DC 20012. T: (202)723-0800.
**Short Terms Abroad,** Pres, 1604 Jefferson, PO Box 575, Downers Grove, IL 60515. T: (312)969-6103. (Recruiting agency).
**Society for the Propagation of the Faith,** 366 Fifth Av, New York, NY 10001.
**Technoserve,** 309 Greenwich Av, Greenwich, CT 06830. T: (203)661-4150.
**United Missionary Services,** Dir, 5114 Beechnut, Houston, TX 77035.
**Wings of Mercy Missions,** Pres, 2125 South Main St, Santa Ana, CA 92702. T: (714)545-5308. (Relief, medicine, support).

*ZAIRE*
**Missionary Aviation Fellowship (MAF),** BP 393 & 3160, Kinshasa.

# 28
# Home & Family Life

*Definition.* Family movements, the family apostolate, marriage guidance and counselling, family planning, abortion, adoption services.

*ARGENTINA*
**Fundación Hogares Argentinos,** Av Antártida Argentina y Ramos Mejia, Buenos Aires. (Member, BICE).
**Liga de Madres de Familia,** Aráoz 2972, Buenos Aires.
**Liga de Padres de Familia,** Comisión Central, Paraguay 1931, Buenos Aires. (Member, BICE).

*AUSTRALIA*
**Australian Federation of Christian Family and Social Apostolate Organizations (AFCFSAO),** 222 Victoria Square, Adelaide, SA 500. (Member, WMCW).
**Salvation Army Adoption Service,** Principal Officer, 140 Elizabeth St, Sydney. T: (02)261711.

*AUSTRIA*
**Katholische Familienverband Österreichs,** Wollzeile 2, A-1010 Wien.
**Katholische Familienwerk Österreichs,** Stephansplatz 6, A-1010 Wien.

*BARBADOS*
**Home and Family Life Programme,** CADEC, Coordinator, PO Box 616, Bridgetown.

*BELGIUM*
**Centre d'Education à la Famille et à l'Amour (CEFA),** Rue de la Prévoyance 58, B-1000 Brussel. T: (02)5131749.
**Groupe International Femmes et Hommes dans l'Eglise,** Rue de la Prévoyance 58, B-1000 Brussel. T: (02)5131749.

*BENIN*
**Action Catholique des Familles (ACF),** BP 1590, Cotonou. (Member, WMCW).

*BRAZIL*
**Movimiento Familiar Cristiano (MFC),** Secretariado para Latino America, CP 480, Belo Horizonte, MG.

*BURUNDI*
**Mouvement d'Action Catholique des Familles,** BP 690, Bujumbura. (Related to WMCW).

*CAMEROON*
**Association Chrétienne des Foyers (ACF),** BP 550, Yaoundé. (Member, WMCW).

*CENTRAL AFRICAN REPUBLIC*
**Action Catholique des Familles,** BP 855, Bangui. (Related to WMCW).

*CHILE*
**Federación de Asociaciones de Padres de Familia de Establecimientos Educacionales Particulares (FEDAP),** Bellavista 67, Santiago. (Member, BICE).
**Hogar de Cristo,** Calle Alonso Ovalle 1479, Casilla 4594 Correo 2, Santiago. (Member, BICE).

*COSTA RICA*
**Federación Centro-Americana de Centros de Integración Familiar,** Av 7 No 358, San José.

*FRANCE*
**Associations Familiales Protestantes (AFP),** Sec, 47 Rue de Clichy, F-75009 Paris. T: 874-1508.

*GERMANY, Federal Republic of*
**Bundesvereinigung Evangelischer Eltern und Erzieher,** Goldlackstr 6, D-56 Wuppertal-Ronsdorf.
**Evangelishe Aktionsgemeinschaft fur Familienfragen,** Bundesgeschäftsstelle, Meckenheimer Allee 162, D-53 Bonn.
**Evangelische Konferenz fur Familien- und Lebensberatung,** Stafflenbergstr 78, Postfach 476, D-7 Stuttgart 1.
**Katholisches Zentralinstitut für Ehe- und Familienfragen,** Hohenzollernring 38-40. T: (0221) 210931.

*GHANA*
**Christian Marriage and Family Life Committee,** Christian Council of Ghana, PO Box 919, Accra.

*HOLY SEE*
**Comitato per la Famiglia/Secretariat for Family Life,** Concilium de Laicis, Piazza San Calisto 16, I-00153 Roma, Italy. (I-00129 Città del Vaticano). T: 698-4322,4441,4843. (Begun 1973. Pastoral study and research).
**Commissione Speciale di Dispensa dal Matrimonio,** Palazzo delle Congregazioni, Piazza Pio XII 10, I-10093 Roma, Italy. T: 6982 int 4005,4416.

*HONG KONG*
**Christian Family Service Centre,** 3 Tsui Ping Rd, Kwun Tong, Kowloon. T: K-891242.

*INDIA*
**Commission for the Family and Laity,** 21 Museum Rd, Bangalore 25.

*ITALY*
**Associazione Nazionale Famiglie degli Emigrati,** Via Federico Cesi 44, I-00193 Roma. T: 317764.
**Centro Cattolico di Preparazione al Matrimonio,** Via dei Prefetti 26, I-00186 Roma. T: 6794653.
**Centro di Preparazione alla Famiglia,** Via Casalis 72, I-10138 Torino.

*IVORY COAST*
**Action Catholique des Familles (ACF),** BP 1993, Abidjan. (Member, WMCW).

*LUXEMBOURG*
**Action Catholique des Hommes et Pères de Famille (ACHPF),** 3 Rue Bourbon, Luxembourg. (Member, WMCW).

*MALAYSIA*
**Christian Family and Social Movement,** 528 Bukit Nanas, Kuala Lumpur. (Related to WMCW).

*MALI*
**Action Catholique des Familles,** BP 298, Bamako. (Related to WMCW).

*MAURITIUS*
**Action Familiale,** Route Royale, Rose Hill. T: 43512.

*NETHERLANDS*
**National Catholic Association for Family Social Service (Stichting Nationale Katholieke Gezinszorg),** Fred Hendrikstraat 77, Utrecht. T: (030) 514471.
**National Catholic Organization for Family and Youth (Katholiek Nationale Stichting voor Bijzonder Gezins-en Jeugdwerk),** Niewe Gracht 85, Utrecht. T: (030)10649.

*NORWAY*
**Church Families Association (Kirkens Familieradgivning),** Mollergt 43, Oslo 1.

*RWANDA*
**Mouvement Familial Chrétien,** BP 425, Kigali. (Related to WMCW).

*SINGAPORE*
**Christian Family and Social Movement (CFSM),** 73 Bras Basah Rd, Singapore 15. (Member WMCW).

*SPAIN*
**Confederación Católica Nacional de Padres de Familia,** Relatores 22, Madrid 12. (Traditionalist).
**Movimiento Familiar Cristiano (MFC),** Velásquez 92, Madrid 6. (Member, BICE).

*SWITZERLAND*
**Commission pour la Pastorale des Foyers Mixtes,** Institut d'Etudes Oecuméniques, Rue de Morat 262, CH-1700 Fribourg. T: (037)234744. (Mixed marriages).
**Evangelische Eheanbahnungsstellen,** Kinkelstr 28, CH-8006 Zürich. T: (051)280185. (Marriage bureau).
**Mutter- und Familienerholungsheime,** Präs, CH-1823 Glion.

*UK OF GB & NI*
**Board for Social Responsibility,** Church of England, Sec, Church House, Dean's Yard, Westminster, London SW1P 3NZ. T: (01)222-9011. (Family, social and industrial affairs).
**Catholic Adoption Society,** 5 Brandon St, Edinburgh EH3 5DX. T: (031)556-8221.
**Catholic Introductions Bureau,** 9 Belgrave Rd, London SW1.
**Catholic Marriage Advisory Council,** 33 Willow Place, Francis St, London SW1P 1JH. T: (01)828-8307. (Also: 15 Lansdowne Rd, W11).
**Company of Compassion,** Sec, Mary Sumner House, 24 Tufton St, London SW1P 3RB. (Assisting women after marriage breakdown).
**Family and Social Action (FSA),** 106 Clapham Rd, London SW19. (Member, WMCW).
**Joint Commission RCC/Church of Scotland on Marriage,** Dunblane, Perthshire.
**St Margaret of Scotland Adoption Society,** 274 Bath St, Glasgow C2. T: (041)332-8371.

*USA*
**Family Life Bureau,** US Catholic Conference, 1312 Massachusetts Av, NW, Washington, DC 20005. (Member, BICE).
**International Confederation of Christian Family Movements (ICCFM),** 1655 West Jackson Blvd, Chicago, IL 60612. T: (312)829-6101.

*URUGUAY*
**Centro de Investigationes y Estudios Familiares (CIEF),** Calle Lavalleja 2115, Montevideo. T: 400681.
**Movimiento Familiar Cristiano (MFC),** Juan Benito Blanco 614, Montevideo. T: 793616.

*ZAIRE*
**Mouvement Familial Chrétien (MFC),** BP 7213, Kinshasa. (Member, WMCW).

# 29
# Home Missions, Societies & Renewal

*Definition.* Home or domestic missionary societies, agencies, congregations or orders in a nation formed for work only or primarily within that nation; home evangelistic societies, inner missions, city missions (except those classified under CHURCHES AND

DENOMINATIONS), renewal movements within the churches, charismatic movements, charismatic services and communication centres; societies for lobbying particular viewpoints, pressure groups. See also: RURAL AGRICULTURAL MISSION, URBAN INDUSTRIAL MISSION.

Bodies of major significance at national or wider levels number over 500.

*AUSTRALIA*

**Aborigines Inland Mission,** Gen Sec, 135 Wentworth Rd, Enfield, NSW 2136.

**Evangelization Society of Australia (ESA),** Box 122, East Bentleigh, Victoria 3165. T: 573456. (For rural areas).

**New Life Foundation (Australia),** PO Box 225, Fairy Meadow, NSW 2519.

**Temple Trust,** PO Box 63, Waverley, NSW 2024. T: 3997444. (Charismatic renewal).

**United Aborigines Mission,** 262 Flinders Lane, Melbourne C1, Victoria. T: 632506.

*BELGIUM*

**International Communication Office,** Boulevard de Smet de Naeyer 570A, B-1020 Brussel. T: (02) 4798565. (Catholic Charismatic Renewal).

*BOLIVIA*

**Misioneras Cruzadas de la Iglesia,** Cala-Cala, Casilla 698, Cochabamba. T: 2763. (RC).

**Misioneras de María Madre de la Iglesia,** Av Final 20 Octobre 2656, La Paz. T: 24137. (RC).

*BRAZIL*

**Congregação da Missionáiras Brasileiras,** Campinas, SP.

**Congregação das Irmãs Missionárias da Imaculada Conceição da Mãe de Deus,** Casa Geral, Travessa Humaita 700, Pedreira, 66000 Belém, Para.

**Conselho Indigenista Missionário,** CP No. 10-2382, SQN 403-B1F—Apto 203, 7000 Brasília, DF.

**Conselho Missionário Nacional (COMINA),** Rua do Russel 76, ZC 01, CP 16085, 20.000 Rio de Janeiro, GB.

**Instituto Estrêla Missionária,** CP 258, Nova Iguaçu, RJ.

**Sociedade das Missionárias de Santa Terezinha,** Casa Generalicia, Praça da Bandeira s/n, 68600 Bragança, Para.

*CANADA*

**Canadian Revival Fellowship,** Box 584, Regina, Saskatchewan. T: 584-0999.

**North American Indian Mission,** 2205 Fir St, Vancouver, BC.

**Quebec Gospel Fellowship,** Gen Dir, PO Box 12, Montréal, Québec.

**Scarboro Foreign Mission Society (SFM),** 2685 Kingston Rd, Scarboro, Ontario. (RC).

**Société des Sants-Apôtres,** 3719-est Blvd Gouin, Montréal 459, Québec. T: (514)322-0560.

**Soeurs de Charité de la Providence,** 12055 Rue Grenet, Montréal 390, Québec. T: (514)334-9090.

**Soeurs de la Charité d'Ottawa,** 9 Rue Bruyère, Ottawa, Ontario K1N 5C9. T: (613)237-2710.

**Soeurs Grises de Montréal,** 9409-ouest Blvd Guoin, Pierrefonds, Roxboro 910, Québec. T: (514) 683-3083.

**Soeurs Missionnaires de l'Immaculée-Conception,** 121 Maplewood, Montréal 153, Québec. T: (514)274-5691.

**Soeurs Missionnaires de N-D des Anges,** CP 1060, Lennoxville, Québec. T: (819)567-8011.

**Soeurs Missionnaires du Christ-Roi,** 4730-ouest Blvd Lévesque, Chomedey, Laval, Québec. T: (514) 681-5821.

**United Church Renewal Fellowship,** Box 41, New Lowell, Ontario. (UCC; conservative evangelical).

*COLOMBIA*

**Departemento de Misiones (DMC),** Calle 37 No 13-A-09, Apdo 5258, Bogotá, DE. T: 455992.

**Escuela de Servidores,** Centro Carismatico El Minuto de Dios, Apdo Aéreo 56437, Bogotá, DE. (Leadership training).

**Federación Colombiana de Ministerios Evangélicos,** Apdo aéreo 190, Sincelejo.

*ECUADOR*

**Evangelical Ecuadorian Missionary Association,** Casilla 3787, Quito.

*FINLAND*

**Lutheran Evangelical Association of Finland,** Malminkatu 12, 00100 Helsinki 10.

*FRANCE*

**Centre de Formation des Pothières,** 49 Montée du Chemin-Neuf, F-69005 Lyon. (Catholic Charismatic Renewal; leadership training).

**Jean Paul II International Centre,** 222 Rue du Fanbourg St-Honoré, F-75008 Paris. (Emmanuel Community; Catholic Charismatic Renewal).

**Mission Populaire Evangélique de France (Mission MacAll),** Sec, 47 Rue de Clichy, F-75009 Paris. T: 874-9858.

*GERMANY, Federal Republic of*

**Arbeitsgemeinschaft Evangelischer Stadtmissionen,** Stafflenbergstr 78, Postfach 476, D-7 Stuttgart 1. (City mission social work).

**Deutscher Verband für Gemeinschaftspflege und Evangelisation (Gnadauer Verband),** Löfflerstr 4, D-2 Hamburg-Altona. (Also: Melancthonstr 32, D-56 Wuppertal-Barmen).

**Diakonischer Werk der EKD,** Stafflenbergstr 76, D-7000 Stuttgart 1.

**Gesellschaft zur Ausbreitung des Evangeliums,** Dilsheimerstr 4, D-875 Aschaffenberg.

**Innere Mission und Hilfswerk der EKD,** Hauptgeschäftsstelle, Stafflenbergstr 78, Postfach 476, D-7 Stuttgart 1.

**Internationales Diakonatezentrum,** Freiburg.

**Missionarischer Dienst im Hotel- und Gaststättengewerbe,** Im Trierischen Hof 7, D-6 Frankfurt/Main. (Restaurants, hotel workers).

**Ökumenische Begegnungsstätte,** Schloss Craheim, D-8721 Wetzhausen. T: (09724)741. (Charismatic renewal).

**Verband der Deutschen Evangelischen Bahnhofsmission,** Bödkerstr 74, D-3 Hannover. (Railway station offices).

**Verband der Evangelischen Binnenschiffergemeinden in Deutschland,** Stafflenbergstr 78, D-7 Stuttgart 1. (Workers on rivers and canals. Has boats).

*GREECE*

**Orthodox Missionary Society of Crete,** Chania.

*INDIA*

**All India Prayer Fellowship,** Q-3 Green Park Extension, New Delhi 16.

**Evangelize India Fellowship,** PO Box 16, Tiruvalla, Kerala.

**India Every Home Crusade,** All India Dir, L-2 Green Park, New Delhi, 110016.

**Indian Missionary Society (IMS),** Gen Sec, 11-A Trivandrum Rd, Tirunelveli-2, Tamil Nadu.

**Missionary Society of St Thomas the Apostle (SST),** Deeptinagar, Melampara, Bharananganam.

**National Missionary Society of India,** NMS House, 102-3 Peter's Rd, Royappettah, Madras 14.

**Servants of the Cross,** Mulanthuruthi, Cochin.

*INDONESIA*

**Indonesian Missionary Fellowship (JPPII),** Institut Indjil Indonesia, Batu Malang, East Java.

*IRELAND*

**Holy Rosary Sisters,** Killeshandra, Country Cavan.

**National Service Committee of the Catholic Charismatic Renewal in Ireland,** 5 Pembroke Park, Dublin 4. (Also: St Albans, Bewsey St, Warrington, Cheshire, UK. T: (0925)30927).

*KENYA*

**Africa Inland Church Missionary Society,** Sec, AIC Mukaa, PO Kilome, Machakos.

**Church Army in Eastern Africa (CA),** Gen Sec, Jogoo Rd (opposite St Stephen's Church), PO Box 72584, Nairobi. T: 558253.

**Kufufuka (Re-Awakened Ones).** (Revival movement within the older churches. No organization or officers, no central office or address).

**Maseno South Diocesan Missionary Association (DMA),** Church House, Dhanwant Singh Rd, PO Box 380, Kisumu. T: 2131.

**Mount Kenya Diocesan Missionary Association (DMA),** Martyrs' Memorial Cathedral, PO Box 121, Murang'a. T: 53.

**Nairobi Diocesan Missionary Association (DMA),** PO Box 40502, Nairobi. T: 28146.

**Nakuru Diocesan Missionary Association (DMA),** PO Box 56, Nakuru.

**Trinity Fellowship (TF),** Gen Sec, Siriba Teachers College, PO Box 192, Maseno. T: 4. (Charismatic renewal).

*MADAGASCAR*

**Malagasy Missionary Society (Ny Isan-Enim-Bolana),** Tranon'd Rasalama, Andravoahangy, Tananarive.

*MALAYSIA*

**Malaysia Renewal Fellowship,** 11 Jalan Padang Midah, Taman Midah, Kuala Lumpur 20-17.

*MEXICO*

**Centro Nacional de Ayuda a las Misiones Indigenas (CENAMI),** Gomez Palacio 142, México 11, DF. T: 5164293.

**Consejo Nacional de Misiones,** Av Juarez 64-206, Apdo M-1915, México 1, DF. T: 5186348,5214813.

**Cruzada Mexicana en Cada Hogar,** Apdo 55, Zona 1, México, DF. T: 754112.

**Misioneras del Sagrado Corazón y Sta Maria de Guadalupe,** Ceylan 279, México 15, DF. T: 5672893.

**Misioneros del Espirito Santo (MSpS),** Madero 11, México 1, DF.

**Misioneros del Sagrado Corazón y Sta Maria de Guadalupe (MSC),** Aldama 27, México 15, DF. T: 5672816.

**Misioneros Josefinos de México,** Zempoala 496, México 13, DF. T: 5391987.

*NETHERLANDS*

**Dutch Pentecostal Charismatic Action Community (Penningmeester Charismatische Werkgemeenschap Nederland),** Abeelweg 238, Box 286.41.71, Rotterdam 3012. T: (010)182908. (Sec: Scandinavielaan 78, Emmeloord. T: (05270) 4488). (RC/Old Catholic/Protestant inter-church revival).

*NEW ZEALAND*

**Christian Advance Ministries,** PO Box 6549, Wellington. T: 46698. (Charismatic renewal).

**United Maori Mission,** Sec, 358 Hillsborough Rd, Auckland 4.

*NORWAY*

**Agape,** Boks 5105, Majorstuen, Oslo 3. T: (02) 461448. (Charismatic renewal).

**Oslo Mission (Oslo Indremisjon),** Maridalsp 33, Oslo 1.

*PANAMA*

**Departamento de Misiones,** Apdo 18, Bocas del Toro. T: 59258.

**Fondo de Apostolado Arquidiocesano,** Apdo 6386, Panamá 5. T: 627400 ext 17.

*PHILIPPINES*

**Faith Venture in Missions,** Tay Tay, Cainta, Rizal, Box 4530, Manila.

**Mission Society of the Philippines (FIL Mission),** Patria de Cebu, Cebu City.

*POLAND*

**Dominican Missionary Sisters of Jesus and Mary (Zgromadzenie Siόstr Dominikanek Misjonarek Jezusa i Maryi),** ul Sienkiewicza 27, 05 220 Zielonka k/Warszawa.

**Sisters of the Holy Family (Zgromadzenie Siόstr Misjonarek Sw Rodziny),** ul Dabrowskiego 1, 15 872 Bialystok.

**Sisters of the BVM of the Immaculate Conception (Sluzebniczki Najswietszej Maryi Panny ze Starej Wsi),** woj Rzeszowskie, 23 104 Stara Wies, pt Brzozów.

**Society of Christ for Polish Emigrants (Towarzystwo Chrystusowe dla Wychodców),** ul Lubranskiego 1a, 01 108 Poznan.

*PORTUGAL*

**Movimento Evangélico Cigano de Portugal,** Rua da Beneditina 115, Foz do Douro, Porto.

*SOUTH AFRICA*

**Christian Interdenominational Fellowship of South Africa,** 10 St Luke's Rd, East London. T: 26003,20495. (Charismatic renewal).

*SPAIN*

**Cristo en Casa,** Secretariado Nacional Fe Católica, C Maldonado 1, Madrid 6. (Under bishops, in many dioceses).

*SWEDEN*

**Alliance for the Service of the Church to Finnish-speaking People in Sweden (Riksförbundent för Finskspraķigt Församlingsarbete i Sverige),** Humlegardsgatan 17, S102 40 Stockholm. T: (08)601393.

**Eastern Smaland Missionary Society (Östra Smalands Missionsförening),** c/o E Eklund, Bestorp, S-590 54 Sturefors. (Low-church).

**Movement of L.L. Laestadius (Laestadianismen),** Editor, Hugleiksvägen 6, S-161 54 Bromma. (Low Church revivalist group, particularly among Lapps of Sweden and Finland).

**National Evangelical Association (Evangeliska Fosterlandsstiftelsen, EFS),** Tegnérgatan 34, S-113 59 Stockholm. T: (08)340290. (Independent inner-mission organization).

*SWITZERLAND*

**Diasporaverband,** Präs, Libellenstr 36, CH-6000 Luzern. T: (04)367909.

**Evangelische Gesellschaft der Kantons St Gallen und Appenzell,** Präs, Katharimingasse 21, CH-9000 St Gallen.

**Evangelische Gesellschaft des Kantons Zürich,** Sek, Augustinerhof 2, CH-8001 Zürich. (Also: Brauerstr 60, CH-8004 Zürich).

**Evangelische Stadtmission,** 7 Rue Bergalonne, CH-1205 Genève. T: 264460.

**Evangelische Stadtmission Basel,** Präs, St Alban-Ring 176, Ch-4000 Basel.

**Freunde der Erweckung,** Chalet Ebenezer, Biel.

**Inländische Mission (IM)/Missions Intérieures,** Zug.

**Internationale Vereinigung Christlicher Geschaftsleute,** Box 110, CH-8024 Zürich.

**Mission Intérieure de l'Eglise Nationale Protestante de Genève,** Rue de la Madeleine 10, 2 étage, CH-1204 Genève.

**Missionswerk Strassen- und Haus-Mission,** H Federer-Str 5, CH-8038 Zürich. T: (051)452059.

**Schweizerische Erweckungsgemeinschaft,** Viktoriastr 32, Zürich.

**Schweizerische Zigeuner-Mission (SZM),** Kleiner Adlergarten, CH-8400 Winterthur. T: (052) 232279. (Gypsy work).

**Schweizerischer Verband für Innere Mission und Evangelische Liebestätigkeit,** Secretariat, Sihlstr 33, Postfach 384, CH-8021 Zürich. T: (051) 238899.

**Union pour le Réveil,** Allées 34, La Chaux-de-Fonds.

**Vereinigung für Evangelisation und Erweckung,** Zürich.

*UK OF GB & NI*

**Anglican Society,** Gen Sec, 1 Harcourt Villas, London Rd, Sittingbourne, Kent.

**Anglo-French Christian Fellowship,** Hon Sec, 31 Strathearn Av, Whitton, Middx.

**Barnabas Fellowship,** Whatcombe House, Winterborne, Whitechurch, Blandford, Dorset DT11 0PB. T: Milton Abbas 280. (Charismatic renewal).

**Birmingham City Mission,** 36 Bromsgrove St, Birmingham B5 6NU. T: (021)692-1915.

**British Sailors' Society,** Chaplain, 680 Commercial Rd, London E14 7HF. T: (01)987-4191.

**Capernwray Missionary Fellowship,** Gen Dir, Capernwray Hall, Carnforth, Lancs. T: 2785.

**Catholic Renewal Movement,** 12 Laburnum Grove, New Malden, Surrey.

**Catholic Truth Society (CTS),** 38-40 Eccleston Square, PO Box 422, London SW1 1PD. T: (01)834-4392.

**Christian Renewal Centre,** Shore Rd, Rostrevor, County Down, NI. T: (069)373492. (Charismatic).

**Church Army,** Sec, 185 Marylebone Rd, London NW1 5QL. T: (01)262-3211. (Anglican; evangelism).

**Church of England Evangelical Council,** Sec, Bebington Rectory, Wirral, Cheshire L63 3EX. T: (01)645-6478.

**Church Pastoral-Aid Society (CPAS),** Sec, Falcon Court, 32 Fleet St, London EC4. T: (01) 353-4821.

**Church Society,** Sec, 7 Wine Office Court, London EC4. T: (01)583-1484.

**Church Union,** Gen Sec, 199 Uxbridge Rd, London W12. T: (01)743-0726/7.

**Community of Celebration Christian Trust,** Yeldall Manor, Hare Hatch, Twyford, Berks RG10 9XR. T: Wargrave 2272. (Charismatic renewal).

**Congregational Evangelical Revival Fellowship,** Sec, The Manse, Hoestock Rd, Sawbridgeworth, Herts. T: 2373.

**Fountain Trust,** Central Hall, Durnsford Rd, London SW19 8EG. T: (01)947-4313. (Also: 3a High St, Esher, Surrey KT10 9RP. T: 67331). (Charismatic renewal).

**Good News Trailer Missionary Fellowship,** Gen Sec, Jersey Gardens, Wickford, Essex. T: 3729.

**Irish Evangelistic Band,** 3 Belmore St, Enniskillen, Country Fermanagh, NI. T: 2400.

**Irish Evangelistic Treks,** Dir, Woodlands Conference Centre, Wellington St, Matlock, Derby DE4 3GU. T: 2258.

**Jesus Family,** The Living Room, 41 Westow St, Upper Norwood, London SE19. T: (01)653-6413. (Commune: 56 Beulah Hill Rd, Upper Norwood).

**Jesus Liberation Front,** Sunnyhill, Hemel Hempstead, Herts. T: 59817. (Publications).

**Mission House,** 175 Tower Bridge Rd, London SE1 4TR. T: (01)407-7585.

**London Embankment Mission,** Webber St, Waterloo, London SE1. T: (01)928-1677.

**Lord's Day Observance Society (LDOS),** Gen Sec, 55 Fleet St, London EC4Y 1DR. (Sunday observance).

**Churchyard,** Manchester 2.

**Mayflower Family Centre,** Warden, Cooper St, Canning Town, London E16 1PT. T: (01)475-1171.

**Mersey Mission to Seamen,** Gen Sec, Kingston House, James St, Liverpool 2. T: (051)236-2432.

**Metropolitan Visiting and Relief Association,** Hon Sec, 501-5 Kingsland Rd, Dalston, London E8 4AA. T: (01)254-6251.

**Missions to Seamen,** St Andrew's Waterside Church Mission for Sailors, Gen Sec, St Michael Paternoster Royal, College Hill, London EC4R 2RL. T: (01)248-5202.

**Modern Churchmen's Union (MCU),** Hon Sec, Cayham Vicarage, Ludlow, Salop SY8 3BN. T: (0584)2701. (Formed 1898).

**One for Christian Renewal,** 300 Granville Rd, Sheffield S2 2RT. T: 21020.

**Open-Air Mission,** Sec, 19 John St, Bedford Row, London WC1. T: (01)405-6135.

**Order of Christian Unity,** 39 Victoria St, London SW1. (Campaigns for Christian standards in society).

**Protestant Reformation Society (PRS),** Sec, 1 Lawn Mansions, 7f High St, Barnet, Herts. T: (01) 449-6252.

**Protestant Truth Society (PTS),** Sec, 194 Fleet St, London EC4.

**Railway Mission,** 12 Instow Drive, Sunnyhill, Derby DE3 7LS. T: Derby 24801. (Begun 1881: for railway workers).

**Royal National Mission to Deep Sea Fishermen (RNMDSF),** Sec, 43 Nottingham Place, London W1M 4BX. T: (01)935-6823/4.

**Scottish Churches Renewal** 30 Faskally Rd, Bishopbriggs, Glasgow. T: (041)772-2966.

**Scottish Renewal Group,** 17 Broom Rd, Glasgow G43.

**Seamen's Christian Friend Society,** Sec, 87 Brigstock Rd, Thornton Heath, Surrey CR4 7JL. T: (01)684-2244/5. (In 11 UK ports).

**Seamen's Mission,** Gen Sec, Queen Victoria Seamen's Rest, 121-131 East India Dock Rd, Poplar, London E14. T: (01)987-4622.

**Shaftesbury Society,** Sec, 112 Regency St, London SW1. T: (01)834-2656. (A number of mission centres in London).

**Society of St David (Cymdeithas Dewi Sant),** 22 Park Av, Porthcawl, Mid Glamorgan, Wales.

**Southwark Diocesan Charismatic Fellowship,** 17 Stradella Rd, Herne Hill SE24 9HN. T: (01) 274-6677.

**Union of Modern Free Churchmen,** Sec, 79 Friern Watch Av, North Finchley, London N12. (Also: 61 Oakroyd Av, Potters Bar, Herts).

**Whatcombe House,** near Dorchester, Dorset. (Charismatic training).

**World Revival Crusade,** 10 Clarence Av, London SW4.

*USA*

**American Baptist Home Mission Societies,** Exec Sec, Valley Forge, PA 19481. T: (215)768-2390.

**American Indian Liberation Crusades,** 4009 South Halldale Av, Los Angeles, CA 90062.

**American Indian Missions,** Custer, PO Box 84 Rapid City, SD 57701. T: (605)343-0554.

**American Mission to the Greeks,** 801 Broad Av, Ridgefield, NJ 07657. T: (201)943-4733.

**Arctic Missions,** PO Box 512, Gresham, OR 97030. (Also: Box 756, Anchorage, AK 9951). (52 missionaries in Alaska).

**Back-Country Evangelism,** PO Box 36, Pasadena, CA 91102.

**Brethren Service Commission,** Church of the Brethren, 1451 Dundee Av, Elgin, Illinois.

**Catholic Church Extension Society of the USA,** 1307 South Wabash Av, Chicago, IL 60695. T: (312) 939-5338. (Aids Black and Latin church building projects).

**Central Alaskan Missions,** Box 5, Glennallen, AK 99588.

**Charismatic Educational Centres,** 1730 SW 22n Av, PO Box 9387, Fort Lauderdale, FL 33312.

**Charismatic Renewal Conferences,** PO Drawer A, Notre Dame, IN 465566. T: (219)234-6021.

**Christian Echoes National Ministry,** 2808 South Sheridan Rd, PO Box 977, Tulsa, OK 74102. T: (918) 836-1692.

**Christian Reformed Church,** Board of Home Missions, 2850 Kalamazoo Av, SE, Grand Rapids, MI 49508. T: (616)241-1691.

**Christian Service Corps,** Pres, 1509 16th St, St, NW, Washington, DC 20036. T: (202)462-8822.

**Community Renewal Society,** 235 East 49th St, New York, NY 10017.

**Conservative Baptist Home Mission Society (CBHMS),** Gen Dir, 25 West Geneva Rd, PO Box 828, Wheaton, IL 60187. T: (312)665-1200.

**Crossfire Ministries,** 25 East 59th St, Jacksonville, FL 32208. (Methodist charismatic renewal).

**Division of National Missions,** Board of Missions of the United Methodist Church, 475 Riverside Drive, New York, NY 10027.

**Domestic & Foreign Missionary Society,** Protestant Episcopal Church, 815 Second Av, New York, NY 10017. T: (212)867-8400.

**Episcopal Charismatic Fellowship (ECF),** 100 Colorado Blvd, Denver, CO 80206. (Charismatic renewal in the Episcopal Church).

**Faith at Work Inc,** 279 Fifth Av, New York, NY

10016. T: (212)683-9444.
**Foundation for Christian Renewal,** Dir, 7610 4th St, SE, Everett, WA 98201.
**Grand Old Gospel Fellowship,** 6701 Cresheim Rd, PO Box 8081, Philadelphia, PA 19101. T: (215) 848-9561.
**Haven of Rest (Crew of the Good Ship Grace),** 2400 Hyperion, Hollywood, CA 90028.
**Holy Spirit Teaching Mission,** 2310 SW 40th Av, Ft Lauderdale, FL 33314. T: (305)587-8997.
**Immanuel Mission to Seamen,** 7443 Stockton Av, El Cerrito, CA 94530.
**Inter-Church Ministries,** Dir, 77 West Washington, Chicago, IL 62220.
**Inter-Religious Foundation,** 475 Riverside Drive, New York, NY 10027. (Black, militant, ministry).
**Jesus People Incorporated,** Dir, Box 1949, Hollywood, CA 90028.
**Logos International Fellowship,** 185 North Av, Plainfield, NJ 07060. (Linked to Fountain Trust, UK).
**Logos Ministry for Orthodox Renewal,** 2133 Embassy Drive, Fort Wayne, IN 46806. T: (219) 447-1255. (Formerly Logos Foundation; also 2707 South Calhoun St, Fort Wayne).
**Lord's Day Alliance of the US,** 71 West 23rd St, New York, NY 10010.
**National Holiness Association,** National Headquarters, Winona Lake, IN 46590.
**Navajo Gospel Mission,** Field Dir, Oraibi, AZ 86039. T: (602)283-5476.
**Oklahoma Indian Ministries,** 701 NW 8th St, Oklahoma City, OK 73012. T: (405)232-3695. (Amerindians).
**Personal Christianity,** 14952 East Pacific Av, PO Box 157, Baldwin Park, CA 91706. T: (213) 338-7333.
**Presbyterian Charismatic Communion,** 428 NW 34th, Oklahoma City, OK 73118. T: (405)525-2711.
**Society for Propagating the Gospel among the Indians and Others in North America,** Sec, 8 Orne Square, Salem, Massachusetts.
**Society of Domestic Missionaries,** Orthodox Working Priests, PO Box 238, Elberton, GA 30635.
**Southern Baptist Convention Home Mission Board,** 161 Spring St, NW, Atlanta, GA 30303.
**United Indian Missions,** Gen Dir, 2920 North 4th St, PO Box U, Flagstaff, AZ 86001. T: (602)774-0651.
**Wings of Healing,** 6615 Allston St, PO Box 22290, Los Angeles, CA 90022. T: (213)724-3873. (Pentecostal).
**World Charismatic Renewal Fellowship,** 342 West Pearl St, Coldwater, MI 49036. T: (517) 278-5244.

# 30

# Journalism, The Press & Information

*Definition.* The religious press, newspapers, radio and TV religious news offices, news services, clippings services, religious editors of international newspapers and secular radio and TV networks; press agencies of major denominations, church information agencies and centres, agencies publishing news bulletins, church publicity centres, church advertising and public relations; photographic libraries, agencies and services; journalism training centres, schools of journalism.

Organizations of major significance in this field number over 300.

*ARGENTINA*
**Agencia Informativa Católica Argentina (AICA),** Rodríguez Peña 846, 4P, Buenos Aires. T: Central 2886. (Press).
**Escuela de Periodismo y Ciencias de la Información,** Facultad Católica de Humanidades, Maipú 1369, Rosario, Santa Fe.

*AUSTRALIA*
**Catholic Press Association of Australia and New Zealand (CPA),** 143 a'Becket St, Melbourne C1.
**Charismatic Information Centre,** Temple Trust, PO Box 63, Waverley, NSW 2024. T: 3997444.
**National Catholic Press Association Standard Publishing Company,** Box 393 D, Hobart, Tasmania.

*AUSTRIA*
**Katholische Presse-Agentur (Kathpress),** Wollzeile 2, A-1010 Wien. T: 525283.
**Verband Katholischer Publizisten Österreichs,** Wollzeile 2, Wien 1. (Press).

*BELGIUM*
**Association des Journalistes Catholiques de Belgique,** Blvd de Smet de Naeyer 613, B-1020 Brussel.
**Centre d'Information de Presse (CIP),** Dir, 38 Av des Arts, Brussel. T: 100636,119243.
**Centre d'Information et d'Education Populaire,** Rue de la Loi 121, B-1040 Brussel. T: (02)735-6050.
**Fédération Internationale des Agences Catholiques de Presse (FIAC)/International Federation of Catholic Press Agencies,** Rue Guimard 9, B-1040 Brussel.
**Office Catholique d'Information sur les Problèmes Européens (OCIPE),** Av de Tervuren 60, B-1040 Brussel. T: (02)733-8770.
**Photos Service,** Chaussée de Charleroi 14, B-5000 Namur.
**Union des Journaux Catholiques de Belgique,** Av des Arts 38, B-1000 Brussel.

*BOLIVIA*
**Agencia de Noticias Fides (ANF),** CP 5782, La Paz. T: 24422.
**Sección Periodismo,** Escuela Normal Católica, Cochabamba.

*BRAZIL*
**Centro Ecumênico de Informações (CEI),** Av Princesa Isabel 323/1012, Copacabana, Rio de Janeiro, GB. T: 2367088.
**Centro Informativo Católico (CIC),** CP 23, Petropólis, RJ.
**Curso de Jornalismo,** Instituto Nuestra Señora de Lourdes, Epitacio Pessoa 208, João Pessoa, Paraíba.
**Curso de Jornalismo,** Universidade Católica de Pelotas, Av Rui Barbosa 412, Pelotas, Rio Grande do Sul.
**Curso de Jornalismo,** Universidade Católica de Pernambuco, Rua do Príncipe 526, Recife, Pernambuco. (Communication and information research).
**Departemento de Jornalismo,** Pontificia Universidade Católica, Rua Marquês de São Vicente 209/223, Rio de Janeiro, ZC-20, GB.
**Escola de Jornalismo Jackson de Figueiredo,** Rua Euclides da Cunha 247, Santos, SP.
**Facultade de Jornalismo Casper Libero,** Pontificia Universidade Católica de São Paulo, Av Paulista 900, São Paulo, SP.
**Missionary Information Bureau (MIB),** CP 1498, 01 000 São Paulo, SP.

*CANADA*
**Association Canadienne des Périodiques Catholiques (ACPC),** 5875 Est Rue Sherbrooke, Montréal, Québec.
**Catholic Association of the Ukrainian Press,** 278 Bathurst St, Toronto, Ontario.
**Catholic Information Centre,** 830 Bathurst St, Toronto 179, Ontario. T: (416)534-2326.
**Dialogue,** Centre d'Information et d'Oecumenisme, 2185 Rue Bishop, Montréal 107, Québec. T: (514) 288-5960.
**Paulist Information Centre,** 830 Bathurst St, Toronto 4, Ontario.

*CHILE*
**Escuela de Periodismo,** Universidad Católica de Chile, Calle San Isidro 560, Casilla 114-D, Santiago. T: 383018,31913.

*CHINA (TAIWAN)*
**Catholic I-Shi News Agency,** 120 Yun-Ho St, Taipei.

*FINLAND*
**Catholic Information Centre (Katolsk Upplysningscentrum),** Kotipolku 18, Helsinki 60. T: (90)794197.
**Information Centre of the Church of Finland (Kirkon Tiedotuskeskus),** Mannerheimintie 18A, Helsinki 10.

*FRANCE*
**Agence Française d'Articles et de Reportages (AFAR),** 153 Rue de Granelle, F-75007 Paris. T: 705-9875.
**Association Française des Journalistes Catholiques,** 14 Rue St Benoît, F-75006 Paris. T: 548-6916.
**Association Nationale des Periodiques Catholiques de Province (ANPCP),** 43 Rue de Trevise, F-75009 Paris.
**Bureau d'Information Missionnaire (BIM),** 5 Rue Monsieur, F-75007 Paris. T: (01)783-6795.
**Bureau d'Information Protestant (BIP),** Dir, 47 Rue de Clichy, F-75009 Paris. T: 744-7126.
**Centrale Technique d'Information Catholique (CTIC),** 31 Rue Croulebarbe, F-75013 Paris. T: 535-8860.
**Centre National de Presse Catholique (CNPC),** 14 Rue St Benoît, F-75006 Paris. T: 548-6916.
**Documentation et Information sur l'Amerique Latine (DIAL),** 170 Blvd du Montparnasse, F-75014 Paris.
**Fédération Internationale des Agences Catholiques de Presse (FIAC),** Sec, 43 Rue St Augustin, F-75002 Paris. T: 742-9216.
**Fédération Internationale des Directeurs de Journaux Catholiques (FIDJC)/International Federation of Directors of Catholic Publications,** 22 Cours Albert I, F-75008 Paris. T: (01)359-9111.
**Fédération Internationale des Journalistes Catholiques (FIDJC)/International Federation of Catholic Journalists,** 43 Rue St Augustin, F-75002 Paris. T: (01)742-9216.
**Federation Internationale des Quotidiens et Périodiques/International Federation of Catholic Dailies & Periodicals,** Sec, 43 Rue St Augustin, F-75002 Paris. T: 742-9216.
**Institut de Presse Missionnaire,** 52 Av de Breteuil, F-75327 Paris. T: (01)734-0804.
**Oeuvre d'Orient,** 20 Rue du Regard, F-75006 Paris. (Information about Oriental churches).
**Office Catholique d'Information sur les Problèmes Européens (OCIPE),** Sec, 6 Rue Wencker, Strasbourg. T: 366325.
**Union Catholique International de la Presse (UCIP)/International Catholic Press Union (ICPU),** Sec, 43 Rue St Augustin, F-75002 Paris. T: (01)742-9216.

*GERMAN DEMOCRATIC REPUBLIC*
**Evangelischer Nachrichtendienst in der DDR (ENA),** Krautstr 52, DDR-1017 Berlin.

*GERMANY, Federal Republic of*
**Altkatholischer Internationaler Informationsdienst (AKID),** Vater-Jahn-Str 11, D-4150 Krefeld. T: (02151)61941
**Arbeitsgemeinschaft Katholische Presse,** Stiftsgasse 13, D-53 Bonn.
**Evangelischer Pressedienst,** Zentralredaktion, Friedrichstr 34, D-6 Frankfurt am Main.
**Evangelischer Presseverband für Deutschland,** Haus der Ev Publizistik, Friedrichstr 34, D-6 Frankfurt am Main. (Member of WACC).
**Gemeinschaftswerk der Ev Presse (Zusammenschluss Kirchlicher Zeitungen und Zeitschriften),** Haus der Ev Publizistik, Friedrichstr 34, D-6 Frankfurt am Main.
**Gesellschaft Katholischer Publizisten Deutschlands,** Breitestr 110, D-Köln.
**Informationsdienst Konzil-Kirche-Welt der Katholischen Nachrichten Agentur,** Kaiser-Friedrich-Str 9, D-53 Bonn.
**Institut zur Forderung Publizistischen Nachwuchses,** Koniginstr 29, D-8000 München 2. T: 285811.
**Katholische Nachrichten Agentur (KNA),** Pressebild, Eyssenstr 25, D-6 Frankfurt am Main. T: 551252.
**Katholische Nachrichten Agentur (KNA),** Wesselstr 8, D-5300 Bonn 1. T: (02221)653561.
**Kommission für Publizistik der Deutschen Bischofskonferenz,** Beringstr 30, D-53 Bonn.

*GREECE*
**Typos-Bonne Presse,** Agence Catholique d'Information, 246 Rue Acharnon, Athínai 815. T: 626091, 878363.

*HONG KONG*
**Catholic Centre Press Bureau,** PO Box 2964, Hong Kong.
**China News Analysis,** Wise Mansion, 52 Robinson Rd, PO Box 13225, Hong Kong.

*HUNGARY*
**Magyar Kurir,** Karolyi w 4-8, Postafiok 41, Budapest V. T: 180442.
**Press Department,** Reformed Church in Hungary, Synodal Office, Abonyi u 21, Budapest XIV.

*ICELAND*
**Centre for Information and Ecumenism (Centrum for Kontakt og Ekumenisme),** Stigahlio 63, Reykjavik. T: 9184740.

*INDIA*
**Catholic Charismatic Information Centre (CCIC),** St Mary's High School (ISC), Nesbit Rd, Mazagon, Bombay 400 010. T: 378294.
**Catholic Information Centre,** Dir, PO Box 1588, Secunderabad 3, AP.
**Catholic News Service of India (CNI),** 4 Raj Niwas Marg, Delhi 6.
**Catholic Press Ranchi,** PO Box 8, Ranchi 1.
**Christian Information Centre,** Thoburn Methodist Church, 151 Dharamtalla St, Calcutta 13, Bengal.
**Indian Catholic Press Association,** 4 Ludlow Castle Rd, Delhi 6.

*INDONESIA*
**Agence Pax,** Jalan Kramat Raya 134, Jakarta IV/5.
**Documentation and Information Dept (Bagian Dokumentasi-Penerangan),** Taman Tjut Mutiah 10, Jakarta II/14. (Member of IAMS).

*IRELAND*
**Information Office,** Catholic Church in Ireland, St Dominics, 130 Booters Town Av, Blackrock, County Dublin.

*ISRAEL*
**Christian Information Centre (CIC),** Omar Ibn el-Khattab Square, Jaffa Gate, PO Box 14308, Jerusalem. T: 287647. (Ecumenical).
**Christian News from Israel,** 23 Shlomo Hamelech, PO Box 1167, Jerusalem.

*ITALY*
**Agenzia Internazionale Fides,** Via di Propaganda 1c, I-00187 Roma. T: 672414,6792414.
**Agenzia Stampa Cattolica Associata (ASCA),** Via Uffici del Vicario 30, I-00186 Roma. T: 6794442/3/4/5.
**CSEO Documentazione (Centro Studi Europa Orientale),** CP 210, I-40100 Bologna.
**Centrum Informationis Catholicum (CIC),** Via Domenico Silveri 30, I-00165 Roma. T: 632952/3.
**Pontificia Fotografia Felici,** Via del Babuino 75, I-00187 Roma. T: 6790836. (Papal photographer).
**Servizio Informazioni per le Chiese Orientali (SICO),** Via della Conciliazione 34, I-00193 Roma. (News bulletin).
**Servizio Informazioni Romano Cattolico (SIRC),** Piazza San Silvestro 13, I-00165 Roma.
**Servizio Informazioni Stampa Evangelica,** Via Curtatone 10, Roma.
**SJ Ufficio Stampa e Informazione/SJ Press and Information Office/SJ Oficina de Prensa y Información,** Borgho Santo Spirito 8, I-00193 Roma. T: 659283,657032.
**Unione Cattolica della Stampa Italiana (UCSI),** Piazza Montecitorio 115 int 6, I-00186 Roma. T: 6790847,673344. (Also: Via Uffici del Vicario 30, Roma).
**Unione Cattolica Pubblicità (UCP),** Corso Vittorio Emanuele II 326, I-00186 Roma. (Under Episcopal Conference).

*JAPAN*
**Catholic Press Center,** Yotsuya 1-5, Shinjuku-ku, Tokyo. T: 3595427.
**Journalism and Education Department,** Sophia University, 7 Kioicho, Chiyoda-ku, Tokyo. (Courses in TV).
**To-Sei News,** Dir, 10 6-Brancho, Chiyoda-ku, Tokyo. T: 331323,334874,334763.

*KENYA*
**Africa Acts Feature Service,** Dir, AACC, Waiyaki Way, PO Box 20390, Nairobi. T: 33510. (Until 1978).
**Africa Church Information Service (ACIS),** AACC, Waiyaki Way, PO Box 14205, Nairobi. T: 62601. (Ecumenical).

*LEBANON*
**Near East Ecumenical Bureau Information Interpretation (NEEBII)/Bureau Oecuménique du Proche-Orient pour l'Information-Interprétation,** Dir, Immeuble Anis Daouk, Rue Abdel Aziz, BP 5376, Bayrut. T: 349584.

*LUXEMBOURG*
**Association des Journalistes Catholiques du Luxembourg,** 5 Rue Bourbon, Luxembourg.

*MADAGASCAR*
**Bureau de Liaison de l'Information Religieuse dans l'Océan Indien (BLIROI),** BP 3920, Tananarive. (Ecumenical; WACC/UNDA/UCIP).

*MALAWI*
**CAPA Information Service,** P/A Chilema, Zomba. (Anglican).

*MEXICO*
**Comité Nacional de Publicidad Evangélica,** Priv de Agustin Gutierrez 67, Zona 1, México, DF. T: 346603.
**Documentación y Información Católica,** Dir, Aristoteles 239, México 1.
**Escuela de Periodismo,** Instituto de Humanidades Pio XII, Av La Paz 275, Guadalajara, Jalisco.
**Escuela de Periodismo Carlos Septién García,** Durando 341, México 7, DF. T: 286679.
**Facultad de Ciencias y Técnicas de la Información,** Universidad Iberoamericana, Cerro de las Torres 395, México 21, DF. T: 493500.

*NETHERLANDS*
**Netherlands Catholic Journalists' Association (Katholieke Nederlandse Journalistenkring),** Koninginstraat 22b, Hilversum. (Also: van Alpherstraat 18, Utrecht).
**Press and Publicity Commission (Commissie Pers en Publiciteit),** Biltstraat 119, Utrecht.

*NEW ZEALAND*
**Catholic Enquiry Centre,** 140 Austin St, Wellington.

*NIGERIA*
**Catholic News and Photo Service,** Press Department, National Catholic Secretariat, PO Box 951, Lagos.

*NORWAY*
**Christian Press Office (Kristelig Pressekontor),** Holbergs Plass 4, Oslo 1.
**Church Information Office (Kirkens Informasjonstjeneste),** Munchsgt 2, Oslo 1.

*PAKISTAN*
**Catholic News Service of Pakistan (CNSP),** III Depot Lines, Karachi 3.

*PERU*
**Centro de Información Católica,** Ucayali 259, 8 piso, Casilla 5594, Lima. T: 272839.
**Escuela de Periodismo,** Pontificia Universidad Católica del Perú, Plaza Francia 1164, Apdo 1761, Lima. T: 41716.

*PHILIPPINES*
**Institute of Journalism and Communication Arts,** University of Santo Tomas, Espana, Manila. T: 32231.

*SINGAPORE*
**Malaysian Catholic News,** Kingsmead Hall, 8 Victoria Park Rd, Singapore 10.

*SOUTH AFRICA*
**Ecumenical Press Agency,** South Africa Council of Churches, PO Box 21190, Braamfontein, Transvaal.
**Information Bureau of the Dutch Reformed Church,** 119 De Korte St, Braamfontein, Transvaal. T: 7245158,442037.

*SPAIN*
**Centro de Información y Orientación (CIO),** Paseo de la Habana 44, Madrid 16. T: 2595381. (Traditionalist).
**Escuela de Periodismo de la Iglesia,** Paseo Juan XXIII 3, Ciudad Universitaria, Madrid 3. T: 2534007, 2335200.
**Información Católica Ibero-americana (ICIA),** OCSHA Centro de Información y Sociología, Ciudad Universitaria, Madrid 3.
**Instituto de Periodismo,** Universidad de Navarra, Ciudad Universitaria, Pamplona. T: 221650.
**LOGOS,** Mateo Inurria 15, Madrid 16.
**Officina General de Información y Estatistica de la Iglesia en España,** Alfonso XI 4, Madrid 14.
**Prensa Asociada (PA),** Alfonso XI 4, Apdo 14530 Madrid 14. T: 221090.
**Servicio de Información Prensa y Espectáculos (SIPE),** Calle Pintor J Pinazo 15, Apdo 1677, Valencia 10. T: 693700. (Under Episcopal Conference).

*SWITZERLAND*
**Association de la Presse Catholique Romaine,** 33 Av de Pérolles, Genève.
**Association des Editeurs de Journaux Catholiques,** 1 Route du Jura, CH-1700 Fribourg.
**Centre International de Reportages et d'Information Culturelle (CIRIC),** Av de la Gare des Eaux-Vives 10, CH-1207 Genève. T: (022)369877. (Photos, slides).
**Ecumenical Press Service (EPS),** WCC, 150 Route de Ferney, CH-1211 Genève 20.
**Information Missionnaire pour Laïcs,** Sion, Valais.
**Institut de Journalisme,** Université de Fribourg, 1 Route du Jura, CH-1700 Fribourg. T: (037)224051.
**Katholische Internationale Press-Agentur (KIPA),** Université de Fribourg, BP 443 and CP 1054, CH-1700 Fribourg. T: 222888.
**Lutheran World Federation News Service,** 150 Route de Ferney, CH-1211 Genève 20. T: (022) 333400.
**Pressekomitee,** Christkatholische Kirche, Präs, Hegaustr 25, CH-8200 Schaffhausen. T: (053)52231. (Old Catholic).
**Reformed Press Service (RPS),** WARC, 150 Route de Ferney, CH-1211 Genève 20. T: 333400.
**Schweizer Seelsorgen Zentrum/Centre Suisse d'Information et de Documentation pour la Pastorale,** Holdermattstr 34, CH-4632 Trimbach/

Olten. T: (062)222525.
**Schweizerischer Evangelischer Pressedienst,** Röschibachstr 27, Postfach, CH-8037 Zürich. T (051)444877.
**Service de Presse Protestant,** Pres, Evole 2, CH-2000 Neuchâtel.
**Union Catholique Internationale de la Presse (UCIP),** 10 Av de la Gare des Eaux Vives, CP 313, CH-2111 Genève 6. T: (022)350909.

*TANZANIA*
**All-Africa Lutheran Information & Coordination Centre (ALICE),** ELCT Building, PO Box 3033, Arusha.

*THAILAND*
**Catholic Information Bureau,** National Catholic Committee for the Mass Media, 251/1 Suranari Rd, Nakhon Ratchasima.
**Christian Information Service,** PO Box 1405, Bangkok.

*UGANDA*
**Uganda Catholic Press Association,** Catholic Secretariat, PO Box 2886, Kampala.

*USSR*
**Information Service of the Pentecostal Movement in the USSR,** PO Box 520, Moskva. T: 2278947.

*UK OF GB & NI*
**Catholic Information Office for England and Wales (CIOEW),** Dir, Avante House, 9 Bridge St, Pinner, Middx. T: (01)866-2278. (Also: 14 Howick Place, London SW1. T: (01)834-8700).
**Catholic Press Office,** 86 St Vincent St, Glasgow C2, Scotland. T: (041)221-7600.
**Christian Intelligence Service,** Evangelical Alliance, 19 Draycott Place, London SW3 2SJ. T: (01)584-9333/4.
**Christian Publicity Organization,** Gen Sec, Ivy Arch Rd, Worthing, West Sussex BN14 8BU. T: 30852.
**Christian Weekly Newspapers (CWN),** 146 Queen Victoria St, London EC4V 4BX. T: (01)248-4751.
**Church Information Office,** Press Officer, Church House, Dean's Yard, Westminster, London SW1P 3NZ. T: (01)222-9011.
**Church News Service,** 11 Ludgate Square, London EC4. T: (01)248-2872.
**Church of Scotland Department of Publicity and Publication,** 121 George St, Edinburgh EH2 4YN. T: (031)225-5722.
**Koinonia Information Service,** WEC, Bulstrode, Gerrards Cross, Bucks SL9 8SZ. T: 84631.
**Methodist Press and Information Service,** Press and Information Officer, 1 Central Bldgs, Westminster, London SW1. T: (01)930-1751.
**Overseas Christian Communication Centre,** Denholm House, Nutfield, near Redhill, Surrey.
**Overseas Information Service,** Graduates' Fellowship, 39 Bedford Square, London WC1B 3EY. T: (01)636 6113.
**Press Office,** General Synod of the Church of England, Press Officer, Church House, Dean's Yard, Westminster, London SW1P 3NZ. T: (01)222-9011.
**Sociology of Religion in Britain Information Service,** Department of Sociology, University of York, York. T: 59861.

*USA*
**American Lutheran Publicity Bureau,** 155 East 22nd St, New York, NY 10010.
**Associated Church Press,** Exec Sec, 875 North Dearborn St, Chicago, IL 60610. (Also: 27 East 39th St, New York, NY 10016. Largely Protestant).
**Association for the Development of Religious Information Systems (ADRIS),** Coordinator, Marquette University, Milwaukee, WI 53233.
**Catholic Information Society,** 310 Westfield St, Middletown, CT 06457.
**Catholic Institute of the Press,** Dir, 315 East 47th St, New York, NY 10017.
**Catholic Press Association (CPA),** 432 Park Av South, New York, NY 10016.
**CBS News,** Religion Editor, 524 West 57th St, New York, NY 10019. T: (212)765-4321. (Radio/TV).
**Center for Study of the American Press,** College of Journalism, Marquette University, Milwaukee, WI 53233.
**Chicago Tribune,** Religion Editor, 435 North Michigan Av, Chicago, IL 60611.
**Christian Information Service,** Sec, 1712 West Greenleaf, Chicago, IL 60626. T: (312)763-6374.
**College of Journalism,** Marquette University, 1135 West Kilbourn Av, Milwaukee, WI 52233.
**Department of Journalism,** Texas Christian University, Fort Worth, TX 76129.
**Detroit Free Press,** Religion Editor, Detroit, MI 48231.
**Eastern Rite Information Service,** 2203 West Chicago Av, Chicago, IL 60622.
**Ecumedia News Service,** Suite 1920, 475 Riverside Drive, New York, NY 10027. T: (212)870-3101. (Protestant, also Jews and Catholics).
**Evangelical Missions Information Service (EMIS),** Exec Dir, Geneva and Gary Rds, PO Box 794, Wheaton, IL 60187. T: (312)653-2158.
**Evangelical Press Association/News Service,** Exec Sec, PO Box 707, La Canada, CA 91011. T: (213)790-2272.
**Evening Star,** Religion Editor, 225 Virginia Av, SE, Washington, DC 20003.
**Greek Orthodox Information Center,** 6638 South Marshfield Av, Chicago, IL 60636.
**Inter-Catholic Press Agency,** 118 West 16th St, New York, NY 10011.
**LADOC (Documentation Service of the Latin America Bureau),** USCC, 1401 K St, NW, Washington, DC 20005.
**Liberation News Service,** 160 Claremont Av, New York, NY 10027.
**Los Angeles Times,** Religion Editor, Times-Mirror Square, Los Angeles, CA 90053.
**Miami Herald,** Religion Editor, 1 Herald Plaza, Miami, FL 33100.
**Missionary Information Exchange,** Dir, 23401 Grove, St Clair Shores, PO Box 664, Warren, MI 48090. T: (313)779-1043.
**Missionary News Service (MNS),** Box 794, Wheaton, IL 60187.
**National Catholic News Service,** 1312 Massachusetts Av, NW, Washington, DC 20005. T: RF7-3553.
**National Information Service,** Salvation Army, 120-130 West 14th St, New York, NY 10011. T: (212)243-8700. (Includes radio/TV services).
**National Newspaper Syndicate of America,** Syndicated Columnist, 20 North Wacker Drive, Chicago, IL 60606.
**National Observer,** Religion Editor, 11501 Columbia Pike, Silver Springs, MD 20904.
**National Religious Public Relations Council,** Indianapolis.
**New York Times,** Religion Editor. 229 West 43rd St, New York, NY 10036.
**Newsweek,** Religion Editor, 444 Madison Av, New York, NY 10022.
**Public Communications,** Church of Jesus Christ of Latter-day Saints, 50 East North Temple St, Salt Lake City, UT 84150.
**Religious News Service,** Managing Editor, 43 West 57th St, New York, NY 10019. T: (212)688-7094.
**Religious Newswriters Association (RNA),** Detroit Free Press, Detroit, MI 48231. T: (313)222-6600. (Also: (216)623-1111, and c/o major newspapers).
**Religious Public Relations Council,** Room 1031, 475 Riverside Drive, New York, NY 10027. T: (212)870-2014.
**Washington Post,** Religion Editors, 1515 L St, NW, Washington, DC 20005.
**Western Rite Information Center,** 333 Reed St, Philadelphia, PA 19147. (Orthodox).

*URUGUAY*
**Unión Latinoamericana de Prensa Católica (UCLAP),** 25 de Mayo 617, Casilla de Correo 1052 Sub-Central, Montevideo.

*VENEZUELA*
**Escuela de Periodismo y Ciencias de la Comunicación Social,** Universidad Católica Andrés Bello, Esquina de Jesuitas a Tienda Honda 37, Apdo 422, Caracas. T: 817731.

*VIET NAM*
**Centre de Presse et d'Information Catholique du Viêt-Nam,** 72/12 Nguyên-dinh-Chiêu, Saigon. T: 41366.
**Office of Missionary Information,** PO Box 410 Saigon. (Protestant).

*ZAIRE*
**Agence de Presse DIA (Documentation et Information Africaine),** BP 2598, Kinshasa. T: 3805.

*ZAMBIA*
**Africa Literature Centre,** Art Studio and Journalism Courses, PO Box 1319, Kitwe. (Training).

# 31 Lay Ministries

*Definition.* Organizations for laity only (men and women), specifically emphasizing the lay contribution; laymen's associations, the lay apostolate, lay movements, unstructured movements, businessmen's committees, non-ordained ministries, lay preachers, lay readers, laymen overseas, lay missionary societies; lay ministries for men only; personal evangelism, small-group evangelism. See also WOMEN'S LAY ORGANIZATIONS.

Ministries of major significance number over 300.

*ALGERIA*
**Union des Croyants,** BP 5, Boufarik, El Djezair.

*ARGENTINA*
**Acción Misionera Argentina (AMA),** Rodríguez Peña 881, Buenos Aires. (RC lay evangelism in the interior).
**Subsecretariado de Apostolado de los Laicos,** CEA, Paraguay 1867, Buenos Aires.

*AUSTRALIA*
**Navigators,** Box 17, Haberfield, NSW 2045.
**Paulian Association Lay Missionary Secretariat (PALMS),** 175 Elisabeth St, Sidney, NSW 2000.

*AUSTRIA*
**Arbeitsgemeinschaft der Katholischen Aktion Österreichs,** Türkenstr 3/II/225, A-1090 Wien IX. T: 340321/2.
**Arbeitsgemeinschaft Katholischer Verbände,** Postgasse 4a, A-1010 Wien.
**Cursillo-Europäischen Arbeitsgemeinschaft,** Wickenburggasse 16/18, Postfach 52, A-1081 Wien. T: 428358.
**Institut für Internationale Zusammenarbeit (IZA),** Singerstr 7, A-1010 Wien.
**Kanaa-Gemeinschaft,** Viriotgasse 4, A-1090 Wien.
**Kartellverband Katholischer Nichtfarbentragen der Akademischer Vereiniging Österreichs,** Ebendorferstr 6, A-1010 Wien.
**Katholischer Männerbewegung Österreichs,** Türkenstr 3, A-1090 Wien.
**Legio Mariae,** Rennweg 10, A-1030 Wien.
**Österreichischer Laiensrat,** Türkenstr 3, A-1090 Wien.
**Salzburger Hochschulwochen,** Mönchsberg 2, Postfach 219 (5010), A-5020 Salzburg. T: (06222) 81788.

*BENIN*
**Union Dahoméenne d'Apostolat des Laïcs (UDAL),** c/o Centrale des Oeuvres Catholiques, BP 519, Cotonou. T: 3592.

*BELGIUM*
**Aide Educative et Sociale (Opvoedkundige en Sociale Hulp),** Capouilletstraat 10, B-1060 Brussel.
**Association Internationale des Compagnons Bâtisseurs,** Internationale Bouworde Naamsesteenweg 573, B-3030 Heverlee. T: (016)227979,220523.
**Bureau de Recruitement de l'Office International de l'Enseignement Catholique,** Rue Guimard 5, B-1040 Brussel.
**Centre International de Formation des Compagnons Bâtisseurs (Internationaal Vormingcentrum van de Bouworde),** Kapelstraat 71, Heusden (Limburg).
**Collaboration des Laïcas en Amérique Latine (Samenwerking van de Leken in Latijns-Amerika),** Tervuursestraat 56, B-3000 Leuven.
**Compagnons Bâtisseurs Internationaux,** Internationale Bouworde, Naamsesteenweg 573, B-3030 Heverlee. T: (016)227979.
**Conférence des Organisations Internationales Catholiques (OIC),** Sec, Av Molière 248, B-1060 Brussel. T: (02)345-4848.
**Conseil Général de l'Apostolat des Laïcs (CGAL),** Rue Guimard 5, B-1040 Brussel.
**Coopération des Laïcs en Amérique Latine,** Tervuursestraat 56, B-3000 Leuven. T: (016)226415.
**Coopération Technique Internationale (ITECO),** Rue du Moulin 32, B-1030 Brussel.
**European Forum of National Committees of the Laity,** Secretariat, Mutsaerstraat 32, B-2000 Antwerpen. T: (031)317835.
**Fraternités Africaines,** Av Adolphe Lacomblé 46, B-1040 Brussel.
**La Maison Blanche,** Institut de Marie Vierge Immaculée, Hundelgemsesteenweg 1, B-9220 Merelbeke.
**La Rocca,** Tiers Monde, Av Gounod, B-1070 Brussel.
**Volontaires de l'Enseignement,** Rue Guimard 5, B-1040 Brussel. T: (02)513-6880.

*BRAZIL*
**Navegadores,** CP 2925, Curitiba, Paraná. T: 227769.

*BURUNDI*
**Coordination des Mouvements d'Apostolat Laïcs,** BP 2010, Bujumbura.

*CAMEROON*
**Conseil National de l'Apostolat des Laïcs,** c/o Archevèché, BP 207, Yaoundé. T: 222478.

*CANADA*
**Canadian Lay Missioners,** Box 200, Wawa, Ontario.
**Centre d'Etudes et de Coopération International (CECI),** 1961 Est Rue Rachel, Montréal.
**Latin American Institute,** Box 310, St Mary's, Ontario.
**Madonna House,** Combermere, via Berry's Bay, Ontario.
**Missionnaires Laïques de Notre-Dame,** 150 Ouest Blvd Gouin, Montréal, Québec.
**Navigators,** 5 Redcastle Crescent, Agincourt, Ontario.
**Office of Lay Apostolate,** 90 Av Parent, Ottawa. T: 236-9461.

*CENTRAL AFRICAN REPUBLIC*
**Direction Nationale des Oeuvres,** Centre Jean XXIII, BP 855, Bangui. T: 2984.

*CHILE*
**Secretariado Nacional de Acción Católica Especializada,** Carrera 94, Santiago.

*COLOMBIA*
**Acción Católica Colombiana,** Carrera 13 No 68-50, Bogotá.

*COSTA RICA*
**Instituto de Teología para Seglares,** Apdo 4562, San José.
**Navegantos,** Apdo 2927, San José.

*CUBA*
**Apostolado Seglar Organizado (ASO),** Apdo 594, La Habana 1.

*DENMARK*
**Navigators (Navigatorerne),** PO Box 1423, DK-2000 Kobenhavn F. T: 348730.

*EGYPT*
**Action Catholique,** Assemblée Interrituelle Catholique, 5 Sharia Mohamed Mazhar, Zamalek, Al Qahirah.

*ETHIOPIA*
**Christian Business Men's Association,** PO Box 6, Addis Abeba.

*FINLAND*
**Navigators,** Haapasaarentie 9B 318, Helsinki 96.

*FRANCE*
**Ad Lucem,** Association Catholique de Coopération Internationale, 12 Rue Guy-de-la-Brósse, F-75005 Paris.
**Auxiliaires Missionnaires de l'Assomption (AMA),** 17 Rue de l'Assomption, F-75016 Paris.
**Centre Chrétien de Formation pour Laïcs au Service des Pays en Dévelopement,** 5 Rue St-Léon, F-69 Strasbourg.
**Centre de Formation et d'Echanges Internationaux,** 73 Rue des Héros-Nogentais, F-94130 Nogent/Marine.
**Conférence des OIC,** Centre Catholique pour l'UNESCO, 9 Rue Cler, F-75007 Paris. T: 551-1759.
**Délégation Catholique pour la Coopération,** 277 Rue St Jacques, F-75005 Paris.
**Equipes Notre-Dame,** 49 Rue de la Glacière, F-75013 Paris. T: (01)587-0588. (Advancement of spirituality).
**Fédération Internationale Catholique d'Education Physique,** Sec, 5 Rue Cernuschi, F-75017 Paris. T: 924-3112.
**Fédération Internationale des Associations d'Enfants de Marie Immaculée,** 67 Rue de Sèvres, F-75006 Paris. T: (01)222-3390.
**Groupe International Laïcat et Communauté Chrétienne/Laity and Christian Community,** Sec, 98 Rue de l'Université, F-75007 Paris.
**Institut International de Recherche et de Formation en Vue du Dévelopement Harmonisé (IRFED),** 47 Rue de la Glacière, F-75013 Paris.
**Le Graal/The Grail,** Secrétariat International, 22 Rue du Dr Germain Sée, F-75015 Paris.
**Organisation Mondiale des Missionnaires Laïcs/World Organization of Lay Missionaries,** 17 Rue de l'Assomption, F-75016 Paris.
**Secrétariat Général pour l'Apostolat des Laïcs,** 106 Rue du Bac, F-75341 Paris. T: (01)222-5639.
**Service du Laïcat Missionnaire,** 12 Rue Sala. Lyon 2.

*FRENCH GUIANA*
**Association des Hommes Indiens de la Guyane,** c/o Evêché, BP 378, Cayenne.

*GAMBIA*
**Lay Apostolate Council,** PO Box 165, Banjul (Bathurst).

*GERMAN DEMOCRATIC REPUBLIC*
**Arbeitsgemeinschaft für Volksmission,** Schönhauser Allee 59, DDR-1058 Berlin.
**Mannerarbeit der EKD,** Waisenstr 28, DDR-102 Berlin.
**Quäkerburo,** Planckstr 20, DDR-108 Berlin.

*GERMANY, Federal Republic of*
**Action 365,** Ökumenische Laienbewegung, Kennedyallee 111a, D-6000 Frankfurt 70.
**Arbeitsgemeinschaft für Volksmission,** Alexanderstr 23, 7 Stuttgart 1.
**Männerarbeit der EKD,** Hauptgeschäftsstelle, Kanstr 9, D-605 Offenbach (Main).
**Navigators,** Am Bahnhof 70, D-6541 Niederschren. T: (06543)2141. (US servicemen. Also: Hohe St 18, D-46 Dortmund).
**Sozialdienst Katholischer Männer,** Ulmesnst 32, D-4000 Düsseldorf-Nord. T: (0211)441592.
**Unio Internationalis Laicorum in Servitio Ecclesiae,** Secretariat, Breite Str 106-110, Postfach 102068, D-5 Köln. T: (0221)218817.
**Zentralkomitee der Deutschen Katholiken (Zdk),** Hochkreuzalle 246, D-5300 Bonn-Bad Godesberg. T: (02221)738190.

*GREECE*
**Zoe Brotherhood of Theologians (Zoe Movement),** Hippocratous St 189, Athínai 708. (1,200 Bible study groups with 15,000 members).

*GUADELOUPE*
**Direction des Oeuvres et des Mouvements,** 28 Rue Peynier, BP 414, F-97-1 Pointe-à-Pitre. T: 820967.

*HOLY SEE*
**Consilium de Laicis/Council for the Laity,** Palazzo San Calisto, Piazza San Callisto 16, I-00120 Città del Vaticano. T: 5890141,5890851,4322.
**Fédération Internationale des Hommes Catholiques (FIHC) (Unum Omnes),** Piazza San Calisto 16, I-00153 Roma, Italy, I-00120 Città del Vaticano.

*HONDURAS*
**Fomento Cooperativo (Educación de Adultos por Acción en Grupo),** Centro Loyola, Apdo 676, Colonia Palmira, Tegucigalpa. T: 25467.

*HONG KONG*
**Lay Apostolate Central Council Diocesan Office,** Grand Bldg, 16th Floor, 15-18 Connaught Rd, Hong Kong.
**Navigators,** Distribution Center, PO Box 5966, Kowloon. T: 897656.

*INDIA*
**Cherupusha (Little Flower) Mission League,** League Central Office, Bharananganam PO, Kerala. (Lay movement).

**Quaker International Affairs Program in South Asia,** Quaker House, 224 Jor Bagh, New Delhi 3. T: 617657.
**Teaching Teams,** Regional Secretariat for Asia, 69 Perumal Koil St, Karaikal, Madras State.

*INDONESIA*
**Navigators,** Jalan Rangga Malela 22, Bandung. T: 50957.

*IRELAND*
**Legion of Mary,** Secretariat, De Montfort House, North Brunswick St, Dublin 7. T: 776011/2.
**National Council for the Apostolate of the Laity,** 7 Lower Abbey St, Dublin 1. T: 48750,48759.

*ITALY*
**Association Laïque Pro-Missions,** c/o Scuola del Cristo, Cannaregio 1723. I-30121 Venezia.
**Associazione Italiana Volontarie per l'Africa e il Sud-America,** Via e Filiberto 8, I-12100 Cueno.
**Ausilarii Laichi della Missioni,** Via Trullo 300, Roma.
**Azione Cattolica Italiana (ACI),** Via della Conciliazione 1, I-00193 Roma. T: 6568751.
**Centro Laici Italiani per le Missioni (CELIM),** Via Garibaldi 10, I-24100 Bergamo.
**Conférence des OIC,** Permanence de Rome, Piazza San Calisto 16, I-00153 Roma. T: 6984842.
**Cooperazione Internationale,** CP 977, I-20100 Milano.
**Francescane Ausiliarie Laiche Missionarie Immacolata (FALMI),** Via Bibbona 79 (Trullo), I-00148 Roma.

**Gruppo Laici Attività Missionaria (GLAM),** Via Galepina 14, I-38100 Trento.
**Gruppo Laici di Appogio alle Missioni,** Via Tosio I, I-25100 Brescia.
**International Pen Friend Service,** Bellavista, I-10015 Ivrea. (Lay Catholics, ecumenical).
**Legio Mariae,** Via Ruggero Bonghi 11/B, I-00184 Roma. T: 7579276. (One million active members worldwide, none salaried).
**Movimento Laici per l'America Latina (CEIAL),** Via Rusticucci 14, I-00193 Roma.
**Pia Unione Santa Caterina de Genove,** Sol San Bartelomeo del Carmine 4-1, Genova.
**Segretario Triveneto Laici Missionari,** Fundamenta Nuova 4885, Venezia.
**Tecnici Volontari Cristiani,** Via Roentgen 20, I-20136 Milano.

*IVORY COAST*
**Conseil National de l'Apostolat des Laïcs,** BP 1287, Abidjan.
**Direction Nationale des Oeuvres,** BP 1287, Abidjan. T: 222968.

*JAPAN*
**Navigators,** 1-31 Higashi-Kiebukuro, PO Box 121, Toshima-ku, Tokyo 170-91. T: 9828649 (Also: Box 73, Koza, Okinawa. T: (077)4709).
**Quaker International Affairs Program in East Asia,** Sendagaya Apts, Room 606, 9-9 Sendagaya 1-chome, Shibuya-ku, Tokyo 151. T: (402)4656.

*KENYA*
**Catholic Lay Council of Kenya,** Catholic Secretariat, Westlands, PO Box 48062, Nairobi. T: 21613.

*KOREA, South*
**Korean Association of Voluntary Agencies (KAVA),** IPO Box 1641, Soul. T: 233797.
**National Council for the Lay Apostolate,** 52-15, 2 Ka, Chung Mu Ro, Jung Ku, Soul. T: 271161/3, 267951.
**Navigators,** IPO Box 1952, Soul.

*LEBANON*
**Comité de Coordination des Mouvements d'Apostolat des Laïcs,** BP 5690, Bayrut. T: 252054.
**Navigators,** BP 235, Bayrut. T: 253940.

*LUXEMBOURG*
**Conseil National pour l'Apostolat des Laïcs,** 5 Rue Bourbon, Luxembourg-ville.

*MALAWI*
**National Council of the Laity,** PO Box 5368, Limbe.

*MALAYSIA*
**Navigators,** 10 Jalan 3, Petaling Jaya, Selangor. T: 59046,563549.

*MALTA*
**Archdiocese of Malta Council for the Lay Apostolate (Kunsill Djocezan ta' l-Apostolat tal Lajci, KDAL),** Archbishop's Curia, Valletta.
**Diocese of Gozo Commission for the Lay Apostolate (Kummissjoni Djocezana ghall-Apostolat tal-Lajci),** 37 Racecourse St, Nadur, Gozo.

*MARTINIQUE*
**Direction de l'Apostolat des Laïcs,** Rue Martin Luther King, Voie 7, F-97200 Fort-de-France. T: 716268.

*MAURITIUS*
**Centrale des Oeuvres,** 42 Rue Pope Hennessy, Port-Louis. T: 20975.

*MEXICO*
**Comisión Episcopal de Apostolado de los Laicos,** Apdo 331, Guadalajara, Jalisco.
**Navegantes,** Apdo 805, Guadalajara, Jalisco.

*MONACO*
**Direction des Oeuvres Diocésaines,** Paroisse St Charles, 8 Av St-Charles, Monaco. T: 300345.

*NETHERLANDS*
**Academic Lay Missionary Action (Academische Leken Missie Actie),** Raamweg 32, 's-Gravenhage.
**Centrum Kontakt der Kontinenten,** Amersfontsestraat 20, Soesterberg.
**Navigators,** 4 Van Limburg Stirumstraat, Utrecht. T: (030)14125.
**St John Crusades (Kruisvaarders van St Jan),** Vogelenzangseweg 77, Vogelzang.
**Sekulier Instituut Unitas,** Priorij Gods Werkhof, Hollende Wagenweg 16, Werkhoven.
**Sekulier Instituut Maria Annuntiatie,** Glorieuxlaan 2, Vught.
**The Grail International Centre (De Graal International Centrum),** Rijksstraatweg 50, Ubbergen.
**Werkgroep Landen in Ontwikkeling,** Laan van Meerdervoort 150, 's-Gravenhage.

*NEW ZEALAND*
**Navigators,** PO Box 1951, Christchurch. T: 67156.

*NORWAY*
**Navigators (Navigatorene),** Postboks 122, Sentrum, Oslo 1. T: 604183.
**Oslo Diocese Lay Council (Legmannsradet),** Akersveien 5, N-Oslo 1. T: 207268.

*PARAGUAY*
**Consejo Nacional de Coordinación de los Movimientos Laicos,** Independencia Nacional y Communeros, Asunción.
**Departmento de Laicos,** Coronel Bogado 884, Casilla Correo 1170, Asunción. T: 47130.

*PERU*
**Acción Católica Peruana,** Junta Nacional, Maximo Abril 608, Lima. T: 33392.

*PHILIPPINES*
**Asian Working Group on Cursillos de Cristiandad,** Pius XII Catholic Center, United Nations Av, Manila.
**Chinese Catholic Apostolate in the Phillippines,** PO Box 113, Manila.

**National Catholic Action,** Pius XII Catholic Center, United Nations Av, Manila.
**Navigators,** 65 West Av, PO Box 63, Quezon City.

*PORTUGAL*
**Junta Central da Acção Católica Portuguesa,** Campo de Santana 43, Lisboa 1. T: 536108.
**Liga Evangélica de Acção Missionária e Educacional,** Alameda das Linhas de Torres 122, Lisboa 5. T: 790039.

*SENEGAL*
**Direction Nationale des Oeuvres Catholiques,** 4 Rue Sandiniéry, BP 1354, Dakar. T: 26005.

*SINGAPORE*
**Christian Business Men's Committee,** Nanyang Bldg, 63 Robinson Rd, Singapore 1.
**Navigators,** 1 Jalan Naga Sari, Singapore 11. T: 663284. (Also: 408-B Upper East Coast Rd, Singapore 16).
**Quaker International Seminars in South East Asia,** 203-B Thomson Rd, Singapore 11. T: 530288.

*SOUTH AFRICA*
**Commission for the Lay Apostolate,** Standard Bank Bldgs, Paul Kruger St, PO Box 941, Pretoria. T: 36230,30322.
**Executive Ministry Seminar,** Campus Crusade for Christ, PO Box 91015, Auckland Park, Johannesburg 2006.
**Southern Africa Council of Catholic Laity,** PO Box 3336, Pretoria.

*SPAIN*
**Asociación de Misionerismo Seglar (AMS),** Ercilla 48, Apdo 623, Madrid 5.
**Junta Nacional de AC Española,** Alfonso XI 4, Madrid 14.
**Misiones de las Dioceses Vascongadas,** Sancho el Sabio 15, Vitoria.
**Navigators,** Joaquin Garcia Morato 147, 7-C, Madrid 3. T: 2545510.
**Obra de Cooperción Apostólica Seglar Hispanoamericana (OCASHA),** Belisana 2, Madrid 17. T: 2000146.
**Seglares Missioneros de Sun Pablo,** Avda de los Toreros 9, Madrid 2.
**Unión Nacional de Apostolado Seglar (UNAS),** Cuesta Santo Domingo 5/1, Madrid 13. T: 2489405.
**Voluntarias del Sagrado Corazón,** Santa Magdalena Sofia 12, Madrid 16. T: 2021943.

*SWEDEN*
**Navigators (Navigatorerna),** Box 433, S-751 06 Uppsala.

*SWITZERLAND*
**Comité de Coordination Catholique pour les Technicians Envoyés dans les Pays en Voie de Développement/International Catholic Migration Commission (ICMC),** 65 Rue de Lausanne, Genève.
**Comité National de l'Apostolat des Laïcs,** Chemin Eaux-Vives 21, CP 40, CH-1700 Fribourg 3. T: (037)244794.
**Communauté Romande de l'Apostolat des Laïcs (CRAL),** CP 836, CH-1000 Lausanne.
**Conférence des OIC,** Secretariat Permanent, 1 Route du Jura, BP 365, CH-1700 Fribourg. T: (037) 26782.
**Deutscheschweizerisches Katolisches Laienhelferwerk,** 34 Grand Rue, Fribourg.
**Informations Missionnaires pour Laïcs (IMPL),** 34 Grand Rue, CH-1700 Fribourg.
**International Conferences and Seminars,** Centre Quaker International, 12 Rue Adrien-Lachenal, CH-1207 Genève. T: 368876/7.
**Oeuvres des Missionnaires Laïques de Fribourg,** Villa Beata, 8 Rue Fries, Fribourg.
**Schweizerisches Katholisches Laienhelferwerk (SKLW),** Reichengasse 34, CH-1700 Fribourg.

*TANZANIA*
**Council of Catholic Laity in Tanzania (Baraza la Waumini Katoliki Tanzania),** PO Box 9361, Dar es Salaam. T: 20430,20477.

*TOGO*
**Dialogues Internationaux en Afrique Occidentale,** BP 971, Lomé. T: 5329. (Quakers).

*TRINIDAD & TOBAGO*
**Catholic Action,** 27 Maraval Rd, St Clair, Trinidad.

*UGANDA*
**National Council of the Lay Apostolate,** UEC, PO Box 2886, Kampala. T: 54521,43042.

*UK OF GB & NI*
**Catholic Overseas Appointments,** 38 King St, London WC2 8JS. T: (01)836-1701.
**Catholic People's Weeks,** 66 Orchard Av, Parkstone, Poole, Dorset BH14 9AJ.
**Catholic Union,** 18 The Boltons, London SW10 9SY. T: (01)373-3515.
**Central Readers Conference, Church of England,** Church House, Dean's Yard, London SW1P 3NZ. T: (01)222-9011. (Lay readers. Under ACCM).
**Christian Action,** Exec Officer, 2 Amen Court, London EC4. T: (01)606-6123.
**Christian Teamwork Trust,** Dir, 1 Whitehall Place, London SW1. T: (01)930-6364.
**Church of England Guild of Vergers,** The Verger's Lodge, Coventry Cathedral, Warwickshire CV1 5ES. T: (0203)27597.
**Church of England Men's Society (CEMS),** Gen Sec, Central Office, 24 Tufton St, London SWIP 3RA. T: (01)222-0611.
**Knights of St Columba,** 54 Berkeley St, Glasgow C3.
**Legion of Mary,** 32 Derby Lane, Liverpool L13 3DL. T: (051)228-1451.
**National Council for Lay Apostolate in Scotland,** 17 Marlborough Av, Glasgow G11.
**National Council for the Lay Apostolate,** c/o 44 Grays Inn Rd, London WC1X 8LR.
**Navigators,** Dir, 88a Coombe Rd, New Malden, Surrey. T: (01)942-2211,7788.
**One By One Band,** Evangelical Publications, 56 Orchard St, Weston-super-Mare, Somerset.
**St Louise de Marillac Association,** 24 Blandford St, London WI.
**Serra Club,** 14 Sheldon Av, London N6 4JT. T: (01)340-5642.
**Sword of the Spirit,** 38 King St, London WC2. T: Temple 1973. (Lay international apostolate).
**Toc H,** Gen Sec, 42 Crutched Friars, London EC3. T: (01)709-0472.
**Volunteer Missionary Movement,** 1 Victoria Rd, Mill Hill, London NW7 4SA. T: (01)959-2491.
**William Temple Association,** Sec, Liddon House, 24 South Audley St, London W1Y 5DL. T: (01) 493-2782.

*USA*
**American Laymen Overseas,** NCCCUSA, 475 Riverside Drive, New York, NY 10027. T: (212) 870-2200. (Catering for the 1% of US citizens living overseas, and US tourists).
**Amigos Internacionales,** Box 1068, Athens, TX 75751.
**Boston College Lay Apostolate,** Cosnut Hill, MA 02167.
**Catholics for Latin America (CELA),** PO Box 101, Yonkers, NY 10702.
**Chaminade's Auxiliaries from North America (CANA),** Front Line, University of Dayton, Dayton, Ohio.
**Churchmen Overseas Program,** NCCCUSA, 475 Riverside Drive, New York, NY 10027. T: (212) 870-2200. (English-language and union churches).
**Committee of Christian Laymen,** Box 285, Woodland Hills, California.
**Friends in the Orient Committee,** Clerk, Friends Meeting House, 2151 Vine St, Berkeley, CA 94709.
**Full Gospel Business Men's Fellowship International (FGBMFI),** 836 South Figueroa St, Los Angeles, CA 90017. (300,000 members in 700 chapters worldwide).
**Interamerican Cooperative Institute (ICI),** Room 803, 21 East van Buren St, Chicago, IL 60605.
**International Christian Leadership,** Exec Dir, Suite 614, 1028 Connecticut Av, NW, Washington, DC 20036. T: (202)296-5830.
**International Consultation on Simple Life-Style,** Box 12236, Philadelphia, PA 19144.
**International Fellowship of Christians,** Box 404, Grand Haven, MI 49417. T: (616)846-5352. (Evangelicals).
**Jesuit Volunteer Corps,** PO Box 4408, Portland, OR 97208.
**Knights of Columbus,** Supreme Council, New Haven, Connecticut. (International fraternal benefit society of Roman Catholic men; begun 1882; now 1,150,000 members in over 5,600 councils).
**Lay Mission-Helpers Association,** 1531 West Ninth St, Los Angeles, CA 900015.
**Layman's Home Missionary Movement,** Chester Springs, PA 19455.
**Laymen's Christian Council,** 312 Woodlawn Drive, Lexington, NC 27292.
**Laymen s League,** 7908 Orchid St, NW, Washington, DC 20012.
**Laymen's Movement,** International HQ, Wainwright House, 250 Stuyvesant Av, Milton Point, Rye, NY 10580.
**Lutheran Layman's League,** The Lutheran Hour, 2185 Hampton Av, St Louis, MO 63139. T: (314) 647-4900.
**National Association of Laity (NAL),** 15770 Heyden, Detroit, MI 48223.
**National Council of Catholic Men,** 1312 Massachusetts Av, NW, Washington, DC 20005.
**National Council of the Catholic Laity (NCCL),** 1312 Massachusetts Av, NW, Washington, DC 20005.
**Navigators,** International HQ, Glen Eyres, Box 1659, Colorado Springs, CO 80901. T: (303)634-2861.
**Papal Volunteers for Latin America (PAVLA),** Tower Bldg Mezzanine, 1410 K St, NW, Washington, DC 20005.
**Religion in American Life,** 475 Fifth Av, New York, NY 10017. T: (212)683-5464.
**Techo Foundation,** Scarborough Rd, PO Box 1200, Briarcliff Manor, NY 10510.
**United Methodists for Methodism,** Chairman, Box 17, Bellwood, IL 60104.
**World Brotherhood Exchange,** 315 Park Av South, New York, NY 10010.

*UPPER VOLTA*
**Secrétariat de l'Apostolat des Laïcs,** BP 90, Ouagadougou. T: 2993.

*VENEZUELA*
**Junta Nacional de Apostolado Seglar,** CEV, Edif Juan XXIII, piso 2, Torre a Madrices, Apdo 954, Caracas 101, DF. T: 815922.
**Latin American Office of the International Council of Catholic Men,** Edificio Juan XXIII, 4 Piso, Torre a Madrices, Apdo de Correos 1352, Caracas. T: 818716/7.
**Oficina Latinoamericana de Cursillos de Cristiandad,** Mosen Sol, Av Sorocaina, El Marques, Apdo 70489, Caracas 107. T: 217722.

*YUGOSLAVIA*
**Commission pour l'Apostolat des Laïcs,** Biskupska Konferencija, Kaptol 31, YU-41000 Zagreb.

*ZAMBIA*
**Association of Christian Lay Centres in Africa (ACLCA),** Sec, Mindolo Ecumenical Centre, PO Box 1192 or 1493, Kitwe. T: 3389,84712/3.
**National Council for the Lay Apostolate,** ZEC, Stanley Rd, PO Box 1965, Lusaka. T: 73467,73470.

*ZIMBABWE*
**Roman Catholic Council of the Laity,** PO Box 512, Que Que.

# 32
# Lay Training Centres

*Definition.* Centres primarily for general training of the laity, in almost all cases with physical plant for conferences or residential activities: study centres, evangelical academies, colleges of evangelism, retreat centres, Catholic pastoral centres and institutes, major Catholic catechetical centres, lay seminaries, pastoral orientation centres, conference centres, fellowship centres, renewal centres, retreat centres; social, economic and development training; leadership training, discipleship training, charismatic training, training programmes, study programmes, conference organizations, large-scale organizations for lay training through conferences, institutes, teach-ins, discipleship groups, evening classes. Specialized training centres are listed not here but under their respective categories (see: audiovisual, cinema and film, broadcasting, charismatic renewal, ecumenical, foreign missionary, industrial mission, journalism and information, literature, liturgy, medicine, research, rural mission, social communications, student, theological, university departments of religion, urban mission, youth).

Because these centres are so numerous, no listing is attempted here. Extensive lists are given in many national and denominational yearbooks listed here under DIRECTORIES.

# 33
# Libraries

*Definition.* The world's major religious book library collections (only those with over 35,000 volumes in 1966): theological, religious, missiological, biblical. The figure in parentheses after any address is the number of volumes held (in the year 1966). For non-book libraries (photographic libraries, film libraries, record libraries, recorded music libraries, tape libraries, microfilm or microfiche libraries), see CINEMA AND FILM, JOURNALISM, SOUND RECORDINGS, MUSIC AND SONG, etc.

On the global scene, there are some 2,100 large Christian libraries with over 35,000 volumes each, and around 11,000 smaller Christian libraries.

*ARGENTINA*
**Pontificia Universidad Católica Argentina 'Santa Maria de los Buenos Aires',** Facultad de Teología, José Cubas 3543, Buenos Aires 19. (RC. Founded 1899; 35,000).

*AUSTRALIA*
**St Patrick's Ecclesiastical College,** Manly, NSW. (RC. Founded 1834; 51,000).
**Society of the Sacred Mission,** Australian Province, St Michael's House, Crafers, South Australia. (Anglican. Founded 1947; 35,000).

*AUSTRIA*
**Jesuitenkollegs,** Sillgasse 6, Postfach 569, A-6021 Innsbruck. (RC. Founded 1562; 100,000).

*BELGIUM*
**Groot Seminarie Mechelen-Brussel,** 18 de Merodestraat, Mechelen (.RC. Founded 1808; 100,000).
**Ruusbroec-Genootschap,** Printsstraat 17, Antwerpen 1. (Founded 1925; 60,000).
**Saint-Albert,** 95 St Jansbergsteenweg, Leuven. (RC/SJ. Founded 1940; 350,000).
**Séminaire Episcopal,** Rue des Jésuites 28, Tournai. (RC. Founded 1808; 50,000).
**Sint Jan Berchmanscollege,** Waversebaan 220, Heverlee. (RC/SJ. Founded 1839; 350,000).

*BRAZIL*
**Alfonsianum,** Via Raposo Tavares KN 20, CP 11.170, São Paulo 9. (RC. Founded 1950; 52,000).
**Colegio Cristo Rei,** São Leopoldo, Rio Grande do Sul. (RC/SJ. Founded 1942; 54,000).

*CANADA*
**Abbaye Saint-Benoît du Lac,** Province de Québec. (RC/OSB. Founded 1912; 75,000).
**Grand Séminaire de Montréal,** 2065 Ouest, Rue Sherbrooke, Montréal 25, Québec. (RC. Founded 1840; 82,000).
**Holy Redeemer College,** Windsor, Ontario. (RC. Founded 1958; 36,000).
**Huron College,** London, Ontario. (Anglican. Founded 1863; 58,000).
**McGill University,** Faculty of Divinity, 3520 University St, Montréal 2, Québec. (Interdenominational. Founded 1948; 60,000).
**St Basil's Seminary,** 95 St Joseph St, Toronto 5, Ontario. (RC. Founded 1894; 35,000).
**Scholasticate St Joseph,** Av des Oblates, Ottawa 1, Ontario. (RC/OMI. Founded 1885; 75,000).
**Séminaire des Sainte Thérèse,** Sainte Thérèse de Blainville, Québec. (RC. Founded 1825; 70,000).

**Séminaire Saint Antoine**, 3351 Blvd des Forges, Trois Rivières, Québec. (RC. Founded 1960; 59,000).
**University of King's College**, Coburg Rd, Halifax, Nova Scotia. (Anglican. Founded 1802; 50,000).

*COLOMBIA*
**Universidad Javeriana**, Faculdades Eclesiasticas, Carrera 10, No 65-48, Bogotá 2. (RC/SJ. Founded 1940; 110,000).

*EGYPT*
**Library of the Greek Orthodox Patriarchate of Alexandria**, 166 Rue Port Said, Al-Iskandariyah (Alexandria). (Founded 952; 42,000).

*FRANCE*
**Collegium Wilhelmitanum**, Séminaire Protestant, 1 bis Quai St-Thomas, Strasbourg 67, Bas-Rhin. (Lutheran/Reformed. Founded 1544; 60,000).
**Faculté de Théologie**, 4 Montée de Fourvière, F-69 Lyon 5. (RC/SJ. Founded 1858; 150,000).
**Faculté Théologie Protestante**, Rue Louis Perrier, Montpellier, Herault. (Eglise Réformée de France. Founded 1809; 60,000).
**Facultés Catholiques de Lyon**, 25 Rue du Plat, F-69 Lyon 2. (RC. Founded 1875; 120,000).
**Facultés Dominicaines**, Le Saulchoir-Etoilles, Soissy-sur-Seine. (RC. Founded 1905; 250,000).
**Grand Séminaire**, Montée de Tresum, Annecy 74, Haute-Savoie. (RC. Founded 1660; 50,000).
**Grande Séminaire**, 147 Rue de Brest, F-35 Rennes. (RC. Founded 1907; 35,000).
**Grand Séminaire de Besançon**, 20 Rue Megevand, F-25 Besançon. (RC. Founded 1680; 40,000).
**Grand Séminaire de Bordeaux**, 135 Rue Saint Genes, Bordeaux. (RC. Founded 1804; 40,000).
**Grand Séminaire de Nancy**, 54 Villars-les-Nancy. (RC. Founded 1805; 80,000).
**Institut Catholique**, 31 Rue de la Fonderie, F-31 Toulouse. (RC. Founded 1876; 200,000).
**Institut Catholique de Paris**, 21 Rue d'Assas, Paris 6. (RC. Founded 1875; 600,000).

*GERMAN DEMOCRATIC REPUBLIC*
**Humboldt-Universität**, Theologischer Institut, Marx-Engels-Platz, DDR-10 Berlin. (Lutheran. Founded 1810; 70,000).
**Kirchlichen Hochschule Berlin**, Teltower Damm 118, DDR-37 Berlin. (Lutheran. Founded 1946; 120,000).

*GERMANY, Federal Republic of*
**Bischofliches Priesterseminars Mainz**, Augustinerstr 34, D-6500 Mainz. (RC. Founded 1654; 145,000).
**Bischofliche-Philosophie-Theologische Hochschule**, Am Hofgarten 1, D-8833 Eichstatt/Bayern. (RC. Founded 19th century; 150,000).
**Caritasbibliothek**, Werthmannplatz 4, D-78 Freiburg im Breisgau. (Founded 1896; 100,000).
**Diozesanbibliothek**, Mozartstr 7, Postfach 233, D-5100 Aachen. (RC. Founded 1938; 90,100).
**Erzbischofliche Akademische**, Papstlichen Facultät, Leostr 21, D-4790 Paderborn. (RC. Founded 1615; 160,000).
**Erzbischofliche Diozesan-Bibliothek Köln**, Gereonstr 2-4, D-5 Köln. (RC. Founded 1737; 125,000).
**Katholisch-Theologisches Seminar**, Liebermeisterstr 12, D-74 Tübingen. (RC. Founded 1817; 60,000).
**Kirchlichen Hochschule**, Friedhofsweg 67, D-4813 Bethel. (Founded 1905; 60,000).
**Priesterseminars Trier**, Jesuits-str 13, Postfach 320, D-55 Trier. (RC. Founded 1805; 125,000).
**Seminar der Abteilung für Ev Theologie**, Buscheystr, Gebäude 1A 1/40, D-463 Bochum-Querenburg. (Founded 1963; 35,000).
**Universität Bochum**, Im Lottental, Zeche Klosterbusch, D-4630 Bochum-Querenburg. (Founded 1965; 80,000).
**Universität Heidelberg**, Wissenschaftliche Theologische Seminar, Klingerteichstr 2 und Karlstr 4, D-6900 Heidelberg. (Founded 1895; 38,000).
**Universität Marburg**, Theologischen Seminare, Lahntor 3, Marburg/Lahn. (Founded 1527; 40,000).
**Universität Wurzburg**, Theologischen Facultät, Sanderring 2, D-8700 Wurzburg. (Founded 1803; 70,000).
**Universität-Hamburg-Ev-Theologische Facultät**, Von-Melle-Park 6, D-2 Hamburg 13. (Founded 1954; 50,000).
**Vereinigte Theologische Seminare**, Nikolausberger Weg 5v, D-34 Göttingen. (Founded 1878; 35,000).
**Westfallischen-Wilhelms-Universität**, Seminare und Institute der Ev-Theologischen Facultät, Universitätsstr 13-17, D-4400 Münster. (Founded 1914; 72,000).

*HOLY SEE*
**Biblioteca Apostolica Vaticana/Vatican Library**, I-00120 Città del Vaticano. T: 6982,3323. (900,000 vols, 61,700 mss, 100,000 maps).
**Pontificia Biblioteca Missionaria della SC per l'Evangelizzazione dei Popoli (Biblioteca Missionum)**, Pontificia Università Urbaniana, I-00120 Città del Vaticano.

*HONG KONG*
**Chung Chi College**, Shatin, NT. (United. Founded 1951; 84,700).

*HUNGARY*
**Library of the Lutheran Church in Hungary (Orszagos Evangelikus Konyvtar)**, Ulloi ut 24, Budapest VIII. (Founded 1923; 110,000).
**Reformed Academy of Theology**, Raday-utca 28, sz, Budapest. (Founded 1711; 125,000).

*INDIA*
**Pontifical Athenaeum Poona**, Poona 14, Maharashtra (RC/SJ. Founded 1955; 50,000).
**St Joseph's Pontifical Seminary**, Alwaye, Kerala. (RC. Founded 1692; 52,000).
**St Mary's Theological College**, St Mary's Hill, PO Kurseong, Darjeeling District, West Bengal. (RC/SJ. Founded 1889; 63,000).

*IRELAND*
**St Patrick's College**, Maynooth, County Kildare. (RC. Founded 1800; 60,000.
**Trinity College**, University of Dublin, Dublin. (Founded 1732).

*ITALY*
**Collegio Alberoni**, Via Emilia Parmense 77, Piacenza. (Vincentians. Founded 1751; 69,000).
**Facultà Teologica dell'Italia Meridionale (San Luigi)**, Via Petrarca 115, I-80122 Napoli. (RC/SJ. Founded 1898; 45,000).
**Facultà Valdese di Teologia**, Via Pietro Cossa 42, I-00193 Roma. (Waldensian. 45,000).
**Pontificia Facultà Teologica Marianum**, Viale Trenta Aprile 6, I-00153 Roma. T: 5890441. (RC. 80,500 vols, 400 mss).
**Pontificia Facultà Teologica San Bonaventura**, Via del Serafico 1, I-00142 Roma. T: 5911651. (RC. 85,000).
**Pontificia Università Gregoriana**, Piazza della Pilotta 4, I-00187 Roma. T: 6701. (RC. 600,000 vols, 3,000 mss).
**Pontificia Università Lateranense**, Piazza San Giovanni in Laterano 4, I-00184 Roma. T: 754385. (RC. Founded 1773; 25,000 vols, 400 mss).
**Pontificia Università Salesiana**, Piazza dell'Ateneo Salesiano 1, I-00139 Roma. T: 884641. (RC. 300,000).
**Pontificia Università San Tommaso d'Aquino**, Largo Angelicum 1, I-00184 Roma. T: 6793400. (RC/OP. Founded 1577; 800,000).
**Pontificia Università Urbaniana de Propaganda Fide**, Via Urbano VIII 16, I-00165 Roma. T: 655992. (RC. 100,000).
**Pontificio Ateneo Antonianum**, Via Merulana 124/B, I-00185 Roma. T: 7574551. (RC/OFM. Founded 1890; 360,000 vols, 200 mss).
**Pontificio Ateneo San Anselmo**, Piazza dei Cavalieri di Malta 5, I-00153 Roma. T: 570073. (Benedictine. 55,000).
**Pontificio Istitutio Biblico**, Via della Pilotta 25, I-00187 Roma. T: 6799147. (RC. 180,000).
**Pontificio Istituto di Studi Orientali**, Piazza Maria Maggiore 7, I-00185 Roma. T: 7312254. (RC. 103,500).
**Pontificium Institutum Archeologia Christiana**, Via Napoleone III 1, I-00185 Roma. T: 735824. (RC. 35,000).
**Seminario Arcivescovile Santa Caterina**, Piazza Santa Caterina 4, Pisa. (RC. Founded 1759; 35,000).
**Seminario Maggiore della Diocesi de Faenza**, Stradone 30, Faenza. (RC. Founded 1948; 55,000).
**Seminario Vescovile di Novara**, Via Monte San Gabriele 60, Novara. (RC. Founded 1650; 70,000).

*JAPAN*
**Doshisha University**, School of Theology, Nishijin, Kyoto. (Founded 1875; 65,200).
**Tokyo Union Theological Seminary**, 264 Iguchi, Mitaka-shi, Tokyo (UCCJ). (Founded 1963; 50,000).

*KOREA, South*
**Presbyterian Theological Seminary**, Kwangjangdong, Sungdong-ku, Soul. (Presbyterian Church in Korea. Founded 1960; 50,000).

*LEBANON*
**Université Saint-Joseph**, Bibliothèque Orientale, PO Box 293, Bayrut. (RC. 145,000).

*NETHERLANDS*
**Bibliotheek Canisianum**, Tongersestraat 53, Maastricht. (RC/SJ. Founded 1852; 250,000).
**Doopsgezinde Gemeente**, Singel 452, Amsterdam (C). (Mennonite. Founded 1680; 50,000).
**Free University**, De Boelelaan 1115, Amsterdam-Buitenveldert. (Reformed Churches of the Netherlands. Founded 1880; 100,000).
**Groot Seminarie**, Ryksweg 9, Haaren, NB. (RC. Founded 1498; 100,000).
**Theologische Hogeschool**, Keizersgracht 105, Amsterdam. (RC/SJ. Founded 1852; 300,000).

*PALESTINE*
**Armenian Patriarchal Library**, Old City, Jerusalem. (Armenian Apostolic. Founded 1929; 50,000).

*PHILIPPINES*
**University of Santo Tomas**, Espana, Manila. (RC. Founded 1611; 200,000).

*SPAIN*
**Abodía de Montserrat**, Catalonia. (200,000).
**Facultad de Filosofía**, Apdo 10, Alcala de Henares, Madrid. (RC/SJ. Founded 1932; 50,000).
**Facultad de Teología**, Apdo 32, Paseo de Cartuja, Granada. (RC/SJ. Founded 1939; 83,700).
**San Francisco de Borja Facultad Teologica**, San Cugat del Valles, Barcelona. (RC. Founded 1898; 300,000).

*SWITZERLAND*
**Priesterseminar St Luzi**, CH-700 Chur. (RC. Founded 1800; 42,000).
**World Council of Churches**, 150 Route de Ferney, CH-1211 Genève 20. (Founded 1946; 62,000).

*UGANDA*
**Makerere University**, Department of Religion and Philosophy, PO Box 7062, Kampala. (Founded 1922; 97,000).

*UK OF GB & NI*
**Chapter Library**, Archivist, The Precincts, Canterbury, Kent. T: (0227)63510. (Anglican. 40,000 vols, many mss).
**Durham Cathedral Library**, Durham. (Anglican. 50,000).
**Friends House**, Euston Rd, London NWI. (Quaker. Founded 1673; 100,000).
**House of the Sacred Mission (SSM)**, Kelham, Newark, Notts. (Anglican. Founded 1893; 35,500).
**Oscott College**, Sutton Coldfield, Warwick. (RC. Founded 1794; 40,000).
**St Deiniol's Library**, Warden, Hawarden, Deeside, Clwyd CH5 3DF. T: (0244)523350. (100,000).
**Sion College Library**, Victoria Embankment, Blackfriars, London EC4Y 0DN. T: (01)799-7983. (100,000).

*USA*
**Alma College**, PO Box 1258, Los Gatos, CA 95030. (RC/SJ. Founded 1934; 66,000).
**Andover Newton Theological School**, 169 Herrick Rd, Newton Center, MA 02159. (ABC, UCC. Founded 1807; 95,000).
**Andrews University**, Berrien Springs, MI 49104. (SDA. Founded 1937; 165,000).
**Archabbey Library**, St Meinrad, IN 47577. (RC/OSB. Founded 1854; 70,000).
**Asbury Theological Seminary**, Wilmore, KY 40390. (Founded 1973; 61,000).
**Austin Presbyterian Theological Seminary**, 100 West 27th St, Austin, TX 78705. (PCUS. Founded 1884; 79,400).
**Bellarmine School of Theology**, 230 South Lincoln Way, North Aurora, IL 60542. (RC/SJ. Founded 1934; 107,500).
**Berkeley Baptist Divinity School**, 2606 Dwight Way, Berkeley 4, CA 94704. (ABC. Founded 1871; 60,000).
**Bloomfield College**, Bloomfield, NJ 07003. (Presbyterian. Founded 1869; 35,000).
**Boston University School of Theology**, 745 Commonwealth Av, Boston, MA 02215. (Methodist. Founded 1839; 78,700).
**Brite Divinity School**, Texas Christian University, Fort Worth, TX 76129. (Disciples of Christ. Founded 1914; 62,100).
**California Baptist Theological Seminary**, Seminary Knolls, Covina, CA 91722. (ABC. Founded 1946; 55,100).
**Capuchin Library**, Glenclyffe, Garrison, NY 10524. (RC. Founded 1932; 35,000).
**Catholic University of America**, Washington, DC 20017. (RC. Founded 1887; 83,000).
**Central Baptist Theological Seminary**, 2915 Minnesota Av, Kansas City, KS 66102. (ABC. Founded 1901; 52,000).
**Christian Theological Seminary**, 1000 West 42nd St, Box 88267, Indianapolis, IN 46208. (Disciples of Christ. Founded 1924; 70,300).
**Columbia Theological Seminary**, Decatur, GA 30031. (PCUS. Founded 1828; 75,000).
**Conception Seminary**, Conception, MO 64433. (RC. Founded 1873; 51,000).
**Concordia Seminary**, 801 DeMun Av, St Louis, MO 63105. (Lutheran Church - Missouri Synod. Founded 1839; 120,000).
**Concordia Theological Seminary**, Springfield, IL 62702. (Lutheran Church - Missouri Synod. Founded 1875; 48,600).
**Congregational Library**, 14 Beacon St, Boston, MA 02108. (Founded 1853; 200,000).
**Crozer Theological Seminary**, 21st and Upland Sts, Chester, PA 19013. (ABC. Founded 1867; 07,000).
**Dallas Theological Seminary and Graduate School of Theology**, 3909 Swiss Av, Dallas, TX 75204. (Independent. Founded 1924; 55,000).
**Darlington Seminary**, Ramsey, NJ 07446. (RC. Founded 1860; 50,000).
**Dominican House of Studies**, 487 Michigan Av, NE, Washington, DC 20017. (RC/OP. Founded 1905; 38,000).
**Drew University**, Madison, NJ 07940. (Methodist. Founded 1866; 302,000).
**Eastern Baptist Theological Seminary**, City Line and Lancaster Av, Philadelphia, PA 19151. (Founded 1925; 67,000).
**Eden Theological Seminary**, 475 East Lockwood Webster Groves, MO 63119. (UCC. Founded 1850; 48,700).
**Emory University**, Atlanta, GA 30322. (Methodist. Founded 1914; 80,000).
**Episcopal Theological Seminary of the Southwest**, PO 2247, Austin, TX 78767. (Episcopalian. Founded 1959; 42,000).
**Evangelical Lutheran Theological Seminary**, 2199 East Main St, Columbus, OH 43209. (ALC. Founded 1830; 40,600).
**Franciscan Monastery**, 1400 Quincy St, NE, Washington, DC 20017. (RC. Founded 1897; 35,000).
**Fuller Theological Seminary**, 135 North Oakland Av, Pasadena, CA 91101. (Evangelical. Founded 1947; 101,000).
**Garrett Theological Seminary**, 2121 Sheridan Rd, Evanston, IL 60201. (Methodist. Founded 1855; 175,000).
**General Theological Seminary**, 175 Ninth Av, New York, NY 10011. (Episcopalian. Founded 1817; 150,000).
**Golden Gate Baptist Theological Seminary**, Mill Valley, CA 94941. (Southern Baptist. Founded 1944; 64,300.
**Gordon Divinity School**, 225 Grapevine Rd, Wenham, MA 01984. (Independent. Founded 1945; 35,000).
**Goshen College Biblical Seminary**, Goshen, IN 46526. (Mennonite. Founded 1958; 36,400).
**H. Orton Wiley Library**, 1539 East Howard Av, Pasadena, CA 91104. (Nazarene. Founded 1910; 100,000).
**Hamma School of Theology**, Springfield, OH 45504. (LCA. Founded 1845; 36,000).
**Hartford Seminary Foundation**, 55 Elizabeth St, Hartford, CT 06105. (Interdenominational. Founded 1834; 194,000).
**Harvard Divinity School**, 45 Francis Av, Cambridge, MA 02138. (Non-denominational. Founded 1910; 280,000).
**Holy Cross College**, 40001 Harewood Rd, NE, Washington, DC 20017. (RC. Founded 1897; 35,000).
**Holy Name College**, 14th and Shepherd Sts, NE, Washington, DC 20017. (RC/OFM. Founded 1930; 35,000).
**Howard University**, School of Religion, Washington, DC 20001. (Founded 1940; 57,000).
**Iliff School of Theology**, Denver, CO 80210. (Methodist. Founded 1892; 70,000).
**Lancaster Theological Seminary**, West James and Pine Sts, Lancaster, PA 17603. (UCC. Founded 1825; 80,000).
**Lexington Theological Seminary**, South Limestone, Lexington, KY 40508. (Disciples of Christ. Founded 1865; 60,000).
**Louisville Presbyterian Theological Seminary**, 1044 Alta Vista Rd, Louisville, KY 40205. (PCUS, UPUSA. Founded 1853; 44,200).
**Luther Theological Seminary**, 2375 Como Av West, St Paul, MN 55108. (ALC. Founded 1869; 85,000).
**Lutheran School of Theology at Chicago**, 1100 East 55th St, Chicago, IL 60615. (LCA. Founded 1962; 90,000).
**Lutheran Theological Seminary at Philadelphia**, 7301 Germantown Av, Philadelphia, PA 19119. (LCA. Founded 1864; 92,000).
**McCormick Theological Seminary**, 800 West Belden Av, Chicago, IL 60614. (UPUSA. Founded 1829; 144,000).
**Maryknoll Seminary**, Maryknoll, MY 10545. (RC. Founded 1912; 42,700).
**Meadville Theological School**, 5701 Woodlawn Av, Chicago, IL 60637. (Unitarian Universalist. Founded 1844; 72,000).
**Midwestern Baptist Theological Seminary**, 5001 North Oak St Trafficway, Kansas City, MO 65118. (Southern Baptist. Founded 1958; 50,000).
**Missionary Research Library (MRL)**, Union Theological Seminary, 3041 Broadway, New York, NY 10027. T: (212)662-7100. (Interdenominational. 110,000).
**Montezuma Seminary**, Montezuma, NM 87731. (RC/SJ and Mexican hierarchy. Founded 1937; 43,000).
**Moody Bible Institute**, 820 North LaSalle St, Chicago, IL 60610. Non-denominational. Founded 1890; 65,000).
**Mount Saint Alphonsus Seminary**, Esopus, NY 12429. (RC. Founded 1907; 42,000).
**Mount Saint Mary's Seminary**, 5440 Moeller Av, Norwood, OH 45212. (RC. Founded 1831; 54,000).
**Nashotah House**, Nashotah, WI 53058. (Episcopalian. Founded 1842; 40,000).
**New Brunswick Theological Seminary**, 21 Seminary Place, New Brunswick, NJ 08901. (RCA. Founded 1784; 115,000).
**New Orleans Baptist Theological Seminary**, 4110 Seminary Place, New Orleans, LA 70126. (Southern Baptist. Founded 1917; 112,000).
**Northern Baptist Theological Seminary**, Oak Brook, IL 60521. (ABC. Founded 1913; 62,400).
**Northwestern Lutheran Theological Seminary**, 1501 Fulham St, St Paul, MN 55108. (LCA. Founded 1920; 40,000).
**Notre Dame Seminary**, 2901 South Carrollton Av, New Orleans, LA 70118. (RC. Founded 1923; 42,900).
**Pacific School of Religion**, 1798 Scenic Av, Berkeley, CA 94709. (Interdenominational. Founded 1866; 133,000).
**Perkins School of Theology**, Southern Methodist University, Dallas, TX 75222. (Methodist. Founded 1950; 104,000).
**Philadelphia Divinity School**, 4205 Spruce St, Philadelphia, PA 19104. (Episcopalian. Founded 1860; 72,000).
**Philips University**, Box 2035, University Station, Enid, OK 73701. (Disciples of Christ. Founded 1950; 52,000).
**Pontifical College Josephinum**, North High St, Worthington, OH 43085. (RC. Founded 1888; 51,200).
**Princeton Theological Seminary**, Mercer St at Library Place, Box 111, Princeton, NJ 08540. (UPUSA. Founded 1812; 282,900).
**St Albert's College**, 6172 Chabot Rd, Oakland, CA 94618. (RC. Founded 1932; 100,000).
**St Anthony-on-Hudson**, Rensselaer, NY 12144. (RC/OFMConv. Founded 1912; 46,000).
**St Bernard's Seminary**, 2260 Lake Av, Rochester, NY 14612. (RC. Founded 1893; 70,000).
**St Charles Seminary**, Carthagena Station, Celina, OH 45822. (RC. Founded 1861; 40,000).
**St Francis Seminary**, 3257 South Lake Drive, Milwaukee, WI 53207. (Founded 1856; 46,000).
**St John's Seminary**, Lake St, Brighton, MA 02135. (RC. Founded 1884; 777,200).
**St John's Seminary**, 5012 East Seminary Rd, Camarillo, CA 93010. (RC. Founded 1939; 40,000).
**St John's University**, Collegeville, MN 56321. (RC/OSB. Founded 1875; 160,000).
**St Leonard College**, 8100 Clyo Rd, Dayton, OH 45459. (RC. Founded 1930; 36,000).
**St Louis University School of Divinity**, Room 0616, 3655 West Pine Blvd, St Louis, MO 63108. (Founded 1899; 90,000).
**St Mary of the Lake Seminary**, Mundelein, IL 60060. (RC. Founded 1925; 123,300).
**St Mary's Seminary and University**, 5400 Roland Av, Roland Park, Baltimore, MD 21210. (RC. Founded 1891; 85,000).
**St Patrick's Seminary**, 320 Middlefield Rd, Menlo Park, CA 94025. (RC. Founded 1898; 40,000).
**Saint Paul School of Theology**, 5123 Truman Rd, Kansas City, MO 65127. (Methodist. Founded 1958; 47,000).
**St Paul's College**, 3015 Fourth St, NE, Washington, DC 20017. (RC. Founded 1889; 38,000).
**St Vincent College**, Latrobe, PA 15650. (RC. Founded 1846. 198,900).
**San Francisco Theological Seminary**, San Anselmo, CA 94960. (UPUSA. Founded 1871; 140,000).
**Seabury-Western Theological Seminary**, Sheridan Rd, Evanston, IL 60201. (Episcopalian. Founded 1858; 175,000).
**Southern Baptist Theological Seminary**, 2825 Lexington Rd, Louisville, KY 40206. (Founded 1859; 138,000).
**Talbot Theological Seminary**, 13800 Biola Av, La Mirada, CA 90638. (Founded 1936; 80,000).

**Union Theological Seminary in the City of New York,** 3041 Broadway, New York, NY 10027. (Interdenominational. Founded 1836; 393,100).
**University of Chicago Divinity School,** 5801 South Ellis Av, Chicago, IL 60637. Founded (1890; 153,000).
**University of the South School of Theology,** Sewanee, TN 37375. (Episcopalian. Founded 1878; 39,000).
**Vanderbilt University Divinity School,** Nashville, TN 37203. (Independent. Founded 1875; 82,500).
**Virginia Theological Seminary,** 3737 Seminary Rd, Alexandria, VA 22304. (Episcopalian. Founded 1823; 80,000).
**Virginia Union University,** 1500 North Lombardy St, Richmond, VA 23220; (ABC. Founded 1865; 70,000).
**Wadhams Hall Seminary,** Riverside Drive, Ogdensburg, NY 13669. (RC. Founded 1924; 35,000).
**Wartburg Seminary,** Dubuque, IA 52001. (ALC. Founded 1854; 65,000).
**Wesley Theological Seminary,** 4400 Massachusetts Av, NW, Washington, DC 20016. (Methodist. Founded 1890; 60,000).
**Western Theological Seminary,** 86 East 12th St, Holland, MI 49423. (RCA. Founded 1895; 46,600).
**Weston College,** Weston, MA 02193. (RC/SJ. Founded 1922; 110,000).
**Yale University Divinity School,** 409 Prospect St, New Haven, CT 06510. (Founded 1932; 246,300).

# 34

# Literature

*Definition.* International and national organizations for Christian literature, publications programmes, literature distribution, bookshop chains and headquarters; tract societies; literature training centres; religious book clubs; writers's courses; literacy materials, campaigns, courses, programmes, agencies, co-ordinating bodies.

Organizations of major significance number over 300.

This listing omits most branches, found in most nations, of SPCK, CLC, EHC(WLC), and also bookshops and bookstores.

*AUSTRALIA*
**Canterbury Book Depot,** 22 Leigh St, Adelaide, SA 5000.
**Church of England Book Depot,** Mayfair Arcade, 124 Adelaide St, Brisbane, Queensland 4000
**Diocesan Book Depot,** 27 Murray St, Hobart, Tasmania 7001.
**Methodist Book Depot,** Box 2036-S, GPO, Melbourne, Victoria 3001.
**Pacific Christian Literature Society,** 511 Kent St, Sydney, NSW.

*BOLIVIA*
**Alfalit Boliviano,** Junín 6305, Casilla 1466, Cochabamba. T: 4953.

*BRAZIL*
**Association for Christian Literature,** Rua Licinio Cardoso 330, 20.000 Rio de Janeiro, GB.
**Camara de Literatura Evangélica do Brasil,** CP 1061-ZC-00, Rio de Janeiro, GB.
**Christian Literature Advance,** CP 2600, São Paulo, SP.
**Periodicos da Igreja Metodista,** CP 8816, 01000 São Paulo, SP.
**Publicações Cristãs Brasil,** CP 403, 74.000 Goinia, Goiás.

*BURMA*
**Burma Christian Literature Society,** Rangoon.

*BURUNDI*
**Burundi Literature Fellowship,** BP 76, Gitega.

*CAMEROON*
**Centre de Littérature Evangélique,** BP 4048, Yaoundé.

*CANADA*
**Anglican Book Centre,** 600 Jarvis St, Toronto 5, Ontario.
**Arabic Literature Mission,** 205 Yonge St, Toronto 1, Ontario. T: 3645054.
**Canadian Tract Society,** 67 Harbord St, Toronto 4, Ontario. T: (416)923-5888.
**Everyday Publications,** 1915-43 Thorncliffe Park Drive, Toronto 17, Ontario. T: 425-4185.
**Quiet Moments,** Box 31, Mount Brydges, Ontario.

*CHANNEL ISLANDS*
**Christian Bookshop Mission,** 78 Central Market, St Helier, Jersey. T: Central 33380.

*CENTRAL AFRICAN REPUBLIC*
**Ligue Evangélique de Littérature de l'Afrique Centrale,** BP 13, Bozoum.

*COSTA RICA*
**Alfalit,** HQ, Apdo 292, Alajnela. (Church-related literacy programmes in 12 Latin American countries).
**Literatura Evangélica para América Latina,** Apdo 3813, San José.

*EGYPT*
**Literature and Sunday School Centre,** Shubra, Al Qahirah.
**SPCK Depot,** CMS Bldg, Boulac, Al Qahirah.

*ETHIOPIA*
**Ethiopia Literature Fellowship,** PO Box 1087, Addis Abeba.
**Light & Life Book Fellowship,** PO Box 131, Addis Abeba.
**Lutheran Publications,** PO Box 658, Addis Abeba.
**Yemissrach Dimts Literature Programme,** PO Box 658, Addis Abeba.

*FIJI*
**Lotu Pasifika Productions (LPP),** PO Box 208, Suva.

*FRANCE*
**Office Chrétien du Livre (OCL),** 193 Rue de l'Université, F-75007 Paris. T: (01)705-4358,551-9462. (Under Episcopal Conference).

*GERMANY, Federal Republic of*
**Evangelische Buchhilfe,** Geschäftstelle, Falkensteinstr 5A, D-35 Kassel-Oberzwehren. (Literature, reviews for lay people).

*GHANA*
**Sudan Interior Bookshops (SIM),** PO Box 402, Accra.

*GREECE*
**O Logos Publications,** Athínai.

*HONG KONG*
**Chinese Christian Book Giving Association,** 22B The Peak, Cheung Chau, NT.
**Chinese Christian Literature Council,** Metropole Bldg, 2/F, 57 Peking Rd, Kowloon. T: K-678031. (Also: 2 Upper Albert Rd, Hong Kong).
**Lutheran Literature Society,** 50 Waterloo Rd, Kowloon. T: K-844806,887061.

*INDIA*
**Bombay Tract & Book Society,** 21 Waudby Rd, Bombay 1.
**Christian Literature Centre,** NEICC Office, Pan Bazar, Gauhati, Assam.
**Christian Literature Service Association (CLSA),** NCCI, N-21, Greater Kailash, New Delhi.
**Christian Literature Society (CLS),** PO Box 501, Park Town, Madras 3.
**Christian Writing Institute,** Nasik, Maharashtra.
**CSI Madura-Ramnad Diocesan Depot,** PO Box 37, Tallakulam, Madurai-2, Tamil Nadu.
**Evangelical Literature Depot,** 11/1 Mission Row, Calcutta 1.
**Evangelical Literature Fellowship of India (ELFI),** 17 Sundar Nagar, New Delhi 3. T: 73560. (Literature arm of EFI, with 66 agencies).
**Evangelical Literature Service,** Vespery, Madras 7.
**ISPCK,** All Saints' Cathedral Compound, Nagpur 1. (Also: 51 Chowringhee Rd, Calcutta 16).
**Literature Mission,** PO Kalimpong, West Bengal.
**Methodist Church Mobile Bookshop,** Bengal Christian Literature Centre, 6 Riverside Rd, Barrackpore, West Bengal.
**Taraporevala (DB) Sons & Co,** Treasure House of Books, 210 Dr Dadbhai Naoroji Rd, Bombay. T: 261433.

*IRAN*
**Literature Committee,** Iran Council of Churches, PO Box 1505, Tehran.

*IRELAND*
**Fallon (CJ),** 77 Marlboro St, Dublin 1. T: 46191.

*ITALY*
**Crociata del Libro Cristiano (CLC),** Via Ricasoli 97r, Firenze. T: 283205.
**Libreria Editrice Claudiana,** Via Principe Tommaso 1D, Torino. T: 682458.

*IVORY COAST*
**Centre de Publications Evangéliques,** BP 8900, Abidjan.
**Croisade du Livre Chrétien,** BP 4494, Abidjan.
**Editions Africaines,** BP 4142, Abidjan.

*JAPAN*
**Christian Literature Crusade (CLC),** 2-1 Surugadai Kanda, Chiyoda-ku, Tokyo 101.
**Concordia-Sha,** 2-32 1-chome, Fujimi-cho, Chiyoda-ku, Tokyo 102.
**Japan Assemblies of God Literature Dept,** 3-430 Komagome, Toshima-ku, Tokyo 170.
**Nippon Seikokai Publications Division,** 4-21 1-chome, Higashi, Shibuya-ku, Tokyo 150. (Anglican).
**Omi Brotherhood Kosei-Sha,** Moto Uoyamachi, Omi Hachiman-shi, Shiga-ken 523.
**United Church of Christ in Japan Board of Publications,** 5-1 4-chome, Ginza, Chuo-ku, Tokyo 104.

*KENYA*
**Baptist Publications,** Editor, Likoni Rd, PO Box 30370, Nairobi. T: 558744.
**Catholic Bookshop,** Manager, Kaunda St (behind Holy Family Cathedral), PO Box 30249, Nairobi. T: 25172.
**Evangelical Literature Fellowship of East Africa (ELFEA),** PO Box 36351, Nairobi.
**Kenya Pastors' Book Club,** PO Box 665, Nakuru.

*KOREA, South*
**Christian Literature Society of Korea,** PO Box 170, Soul.

*LEBANON*
**Arabic Literature Mission,** PO Box 5039, Bayrut.
**Christian Arabic Literature League,** PO Box 166, Bayrut.
**Gospel Lietrature Service,** PO Box 5269, Bayrut.
**Muslim World Evangelical Literature Service (MWELS),** Kehale PO.

*LESOTHO*
**Lesotho Book Centre,** PO Box 608, Maseru.
**Sesuto Book Depot,** PO Box 4, Morija.

*LIBERIA*
**Christian Literature Crusade,** Mission Dir, Box 26, Monrovia. T: 22728.

*MALAWI*
**Christian Literature Association in Malawi (CLAIM),** PO Box 503, Blantyre.
**Emmanuel Tract Fellowship,** PO Box 135, Zomba. T: 2465.

*MEXICO*
**Alfalit,** Comite Nacional en México, Calz México-Coyoacan 349, Zona 13, México, DF. T: 244792.
**Cruzada de Literatura,** Anicerto Ortego 845-1, Zona 12, México, DF. 750407.

*NEW ZEALAND*
**Anglican Book Centre,** PO Box 800, Christchurch.
**Arabic Literature Mission,** New Zealand Council, PO Box 380, Auckland 1.
**Christian Literature Crusade (CLC),** New Zealand Council, Sec, 10 Currie Av, Hillsborough, Auckland 4.
**Evidence Book Depot,** PO Box 6288, Te Aro, Wellington.
**Kell's Christian Book Centre,** PO Box 994, Hastings.

*NIGERIA*
**Baptist Publications and Bookstore,** PM Bag 5070, Ibadan.
**Baraka Publications,** PM Bag 2086 (and Box 171), Kaduna.
**Daystar Publications,** PO Box 1261, Ibadan.
**ELFON Publications,** ELWA/SIM Publications, PM Bag 9, Jos.
**Niger Challenge Publications,** Editor, PM Bag 12067, Lagos.
**SUM/CRC Publications,** PO Box 24, Makurdi, Benue-Plateau State.
**SUM/EKAS Publications,** PO Box 643, Jos.

*NORWAY*
**Andaktsbokselskapet,** Munchs Gate 2, Oslo 1. (Devotional books; affiliated to Norwegian Bible Society).

*PAKISTAN*
**Christian Literature Crusade (CLC),** Christian Bookshop, Bonus Rd, Karachi.
**Punjab Religious Book Society,** Anarkali, Lahore.

*PANAMA*
**Publicaciones El Escudo,** Apdo 808, Panamá.

*PAPUA NEW GUINEA*
**Christian Literature Crusade (CLC),** Okari St, Port Moresby. T: 53059. (Also: Box 1136, Boroko).
**NAMASU Bookshop,** 4th St, PO Box 615, Lae. T: 53732.

*PHILIPPINES*
**Board of Publication and Literature,** Philippine Central Conference of the Methodist Church, 900 UN Av, Manila.
**Christian Literature Crusade,** 104 Karuhatan, PO Box 513, Valenzuela, Manila.
**Committee on World Literacy and Christian Literature (Lit-Lit),** NCCP, 941 Epifanio de los Santos Av, Quezon City.
**Literature Crusades,** PO Box 3627, Manila.
**Mindanao Christian Literature,** Legaspi St, Davao City.
**Philippines Every Home Crusade,** PO Box 2650, Manila. (World Literature Crusade).

*PORTUGAL*
**Centro de Literatura Ev do Norte,** Av Afonso Henriques, Fontainhas, S João de Madeira.
**Comissão de Literatura Cristã,** Apdo 5, Queluz.
**Depósito de Literatura Cristã,** Rua de Infantaria 16, 77-r/c-Esq, Lisboa 3.
**Espada do Senhor,** Apdo 1, Barreiro.
**Junta Presbiteriana de Publicações,** RD Vasco da Câmara Belmonte 8, Carcavelos.
**Liga de Publicações Ev Portugueses,** Apdo 12, Amadora.
**Nucleo de Distribuição de Literatura Cristã,** Dir, Rua Higino de Sousa 6-3 Dt, Apdo 1, Queluz.

*SINGAPORE*
**Christian Literature Distribution Centre,** 2-F Ban Hoe Bldg, 115 Beach Rd, Singapore 7.

*SOUTH AFRICA*
**Christian Booksellers Association,** 229 Nicolson Rd, Durban, Natal.
**Christian Literature Centre (NGK),** PO Box 217, Umtata, CP.
**Church of Christ Literature Service,** 11 Jasmay Place, Nahoon Valley, East London, CP
**Sunday School Centre Bookshop,** PO Box 3020, Cape Town, CP.
**Wycliffe Booksellers,** PO Box 2130, Pretoria, Transvaal.

*SPAIN*
**Propaganda Popular Católica (PPC),** Apdo 116, Salamanca.

*SRI LANKA*
**Christian Literature Society of Sri Lanka,** Front St, Colombo 11.

*SWEDEN*
**Christian Science Committee on Publications (Kristen Vetenskaps Publikationskommitte),** Stenbackstigen 5, S-181 62 Lidingö. T: (08)766-3937.

*TANZANIA*
**Christian Literature Distribution,** PO Box 113, Morogoro.
**Literature & Christian Education Centre,** PO Box 15, Dodoma.
**Msalato Literature Centre,** PO Box 15, Dodoma. (Anglican).
**Swedish Free Tract Centre,** PO Box 838, Dar es Salaam.

*THAILAND*
**Alliance Literature Department,** 28/2 Soi Pracha Utit, Pradipat Rd, Bangkok 4. T: 2791523.

*UGANDA*
**Evangelical Literature Centre,** 9 Bambo Rd, PO Box 4607, Kampala.

*UK OF GB & NI*
**Agency for Christian Literature Development (ACLD),** 7 St James's St, London SW1A 1EF. T: (01)839-5776. (Formerly Christian Literature Fund).
**Arabic Literature Mission,** Gen Sec, 22 Culverden Park Rd, Tunbridge Wells, Kent. T: 21541.
**Associates of the Late Dr Bray (Dr Bray's Libraries),** Sec, SPCK, Holy Trinity Church, Marylebone Rd, London NW1 4DU. T: (01)387-5282. (61 libraries in UK, 15 overseas).
**Buzz,** 10 Seaforth Av, New Malden, Surrey. T: (01)942-8847.
**Catholic Truth Society (CTS),** 40 Eccleston Square, London SW1. T: (01)834-4392.
**Central Church Reading Union,** Sec, 6 Amen Court, London EC4. T: (01)248-1943. (Book grants).
**Challenge Literature Fellowship,** Gen Sec, Revenue Bldgs, Chapel Rd, Worthing, West Sussex. T: 200775.
**Christian Book Club,** 3 The Common, Parbold, Wigan WN8 7DD.
**Christian Book Development Society,** SPCK, Holy Trinity Church, Marylebone Rd, London NW1 4DU.
**Christian Literature Council,** 2 Eaton Gate, London SW1.
**Christian Literature Crusade (CLC),** Gen Sec, The Dean, Alresford, Hants. T: 3141. (Also: 210 Church Rd, London SE19).
**Christian Literature Development Agency,** 20 Warwick St, London W1.
**Church House Bookshop,** Manager, Great Smith St, London SW1P 3BN. T: (01)222-9011.
**Crusade Book Club,** 19 Draycott Place, London SW3 3SJ.
**Feed the Minds,** Sec, Edinburgh House, 2 Eaton Gate, PO Box 461, London SW1W 9BL. T: (01) 730-9611.
**Gospel Healing Tract Depot and Divine Healing Centre,** 2 Arch Rd, Coventry.
**Gospel Light Publications,** 27 Camden Rd, London NW1. T: (01)267-0065.
**Gospel Literature Worldwide,** CEDO, WEC, Bulstrode, Gerrards Cross, Bucks.
**Harrison Trust,** Sec, 1 Lawn Mansions, 7F High St, Barnet, Herts. T: (01)449-6252.
**Latimer Literature Trust,** Trustee Dir, Capernwray Hall, Carnforth, Lancs. T: 2785.
**Overcomer Literature Trust,** 3 Munster Rd, Parkstone, Poole, Dorset BH14 9PS. T: Parkstone 744551.
**St Thomas More Society,** 19 Waterloo St, Glasgow C2.
**Society for Promoting Christian Knowledge (SPCK),** Gen Sec, Holy Trinity Church, Marylebone Rd, London NW1 4DU. T: (01)387-5282. (Founded 1698).
**Stirling Tract Enterprise (Drummond Press) and Drummond Tract Depot,** 41 The Craigs, Stirling. T: 3384.
**United Society for Christian Literature (USCL),** Gen Sec, Luke House, Farnham Rd, Guildford, Surrey GU1 4XD. T: (0483)77536.
**Victory Tract Club,** 189 Brighton Rd, South Croydon, Surrey. T: (01)688-4986.

*USA*
**All Nations Literacy Movement,** Santa Ana, CA 92711.
**American Baptist Board of Education & Publication,** Valley Forge, PA 19481.
**American Book & Church Supplies,** 248 Huguenot St, New Rochelle, NY 10801.
**American Church Growth Book Club,** 305 Pasadena Av, South Pasadena, CA 91030. T: (213) 799-4559.
**American Tract Society,** Gen Dir, 660 Kinderkamack Rd, Oradell, NJ 07649. T: (201)261-6900.
**Association for Christian Literature,** Dir, PO Box 20594, Dallas, TX 75220. T: (214)352-1467. (Also: Box 2141, Dallas).
**Baptist Publication Committee,** 716 Main St, Little Rock, AR 72201.
**Bible Literature International,** International Press, PO Box 477, Columbus, OH 43216. T: (614) 267-3116.
**Board of Publication,** Lutheran Church in America, 2900 Queen Lane, Philadelphia, PA 19129.
**Bookmates International,** 3905 Rolling Hills Rd, St Paul, MN 55112. T: (612)633-6948.
**Books Inc,** 1250 Connecticut Av, NW, Washington, DC 20036.
**Chinese Evangelical Literature Committee,** 199 Bridge St, South Hamilton, MA 01982.
**Christian Booksellers Association (CBA),** Dir, 2031 West Cheyenne Rd, Colorado Springs, CO 80906. (1,700 bookshops (45% of all Christian ones) are members in USA and Canada, 100 more overseas).
**Christian Life Publications,** Gundersen Drive/Schmale Rd, Wheaton, IL 60187. T: (312)653-4200.
**Christian Literature,** PO Box 388, Midway City, CA 92655.
**Christian Literature and Bible Center,** 3840 Oakley Av, Memphis, TN 38111.
**Christian Literature Crusade (CLC),** 701 Pennsylvania Av, PO Box 356, Fort Washington, PA 19034. T: (215)643-1556.
**Christian Publications,** Third & Reily Sts, Harrisburg, PA 17102.
**Church Growth Book Club,** 305 Pasadena Av, South Pasadena, CA 91030. T: (213)799-4559.
**Committee on Christian Literature for Women and Children in Mission Fields,** 475 Riverside Drive, New York, NY 10027. T: (212)870-2378.
**Committee on Publication,** Christian Science Center, Boston, MA 02115.
**Committee on World Literacy and Christian**

**Literature,** 475 Riverside Drive, New York, NY 10027.
**Concordia Tract Mission,** Dir, PO Box 201, St Louis, MO 63166. T: (314)664-7000.
**David C. Cook Foundation,** Cook Square, Elgin, IL 60120.
**Evangelical Literature League,** 941 Wealthy St, PO Box 6219, Grand Rapids, MI 49506. T: (616) 454-3196.
**Evangelical Literature Overseas (ELO),** 491 Gundersen Drive, PO Box 725, Wheaton, IL 60187. T: (312)668-4747.
**Evangelical Reprint Library,** College Press, Box 1132, Joplin, MO 64801.
**Forward Movement Publications,** 412 Sycamore St, Cincinnati, OH 45202. (Episcopalian).
**Free Tracts,** PO Box 1264, Covina, CA 91722.
**Friends Book & Supply House,** 101 Quaker Hill Drive, Richmond, IN 47374.
**Gospel Light Publications,** 725 East Colorado Blvd, Glendale, CA 91205.
**Great Commission Publications,** 7401 Old York Rd, Philadelphia, PA 19126.
**Immanuel Tract Society,** 220 Second St, SW, Orange City, IA 51041.
**Independent Baptist Publications,** 8321 Ballard Rd, Niles, IL 60648.
**Kregel's Bookstore,** Kregel Publications, 525 Eastern Av, SE, PO Box 2607, Grand Rapids, MI 49501. (Largest US supplier of out-of-print theological and religious books.)
**Laubach Literacy Fund (Afrolit),** 1011 Harrison St, Box 131, Syracuse, NY 13210. T: (315)476-2101.
**Liga de Tratados Fe y Oración,** 1016 Eleventh St, NW, Grand Rapids, MI 49500.
**Lighthouse Gospel Distribution,** 517 West Thomas St, Toulon, IL 61483.
**Literacy and Evangelism,** Dir, 4202 East 59th Place, Tulsa, OK 74135. T: (918)627-4288.
**Literature Crusade,** 515 Schoenbeck Rd, PO Box 203, Prospect Heights, IL 60070. T: (312)253-8811.
**Lutheran Literature Society for China,** 1120 Forest Av, Northfield, MN 55057.
**Mariners Literature Fellowship,** Dir, 386 West 5th St, San Pedro, CA 90731.
**Maryknoll Publications,** Maryknoll, NY. (RC).
**Missionary Literature Foundation,** PO Box 374, Burbank, CA 91503. T: (213)845-7931.
**Missionary Prayer and Literature Fellowship,** 453 King St, Redwood City, CA 94062.
**Moody Literature Mission,** 820 North Lasalle St, Chicago, IL 60610. T: (312)642-1570.
**Osborn Foundation International (OSFO),** Box 7572, Tulsa, OK 74105.
**Pan American Literature Mission,** Dir, 5215 East Fort Lowell Rd, Tucson, AZ 85716. T: (602) 326-1787.
**Reformation Translation Fellowship,** 1031 East Glenrosa, Phoenix, AZ 85014.
**Religious Book Discount House,** PO Box 2455, Grand Rapids, MI 49501. T: (616)949-9500.
**Rusthoi Soul Winning Publications,** Box 595, Montrose, CA 91020.
**Scripture Press Ministries,** Box 513, Glen Ellyn, IL 60137. T: (312)668-6002.
**World Literature Crusade,** 10545 Burbank Blvd, North Hollywood, Box 1313, Studio City, CA 91604. T: (213)877-0366.
**World Wide Tract Ministry,** West End, PO Box 3625, Birmingham, AL 35211.
**World-Wide Missionary Crusader,** Exec Dir, 4606 Av H, Lubbock, TX 79404. T: (806)747-5417. (Literature in 60 languages).

*ZAMBIA*
**African Literature Centre,** Mindolo Ecumenical Centre, Box 1319, Kitwe.
**Copperbelt Christian Publications,** PO Box 959, Ndola.
**Lunda Ndembu Publications,** CMML, PO Ikelenge.
**Message of Victory Evangelism (Zambian Christian Book Crusade),** PO Box 783, Luanshya.

# 35
# Liturgy & Worship

***Definition.*** Liturgical centres, organizations; major supply agencies for liturgical equipment, literature, vestments; liturgical training centres; ritual, rites, sacraments, doctrines; wholesale and retail supply houses for religious articles. See also MUSIC AND SONG.

Organizations of major significance in this field number over 150.

*ARGENTINA*
**Centro Litúrgico Nacional,** CEA, Paraguay 1867, Buenos Aires. T: 425708.
**Una Voce Argentina,** Reconquista 165, Oficina 622, Buenos Aires.

*AUSTRALIA*
**Australian Episcopal Liturgical Commission,** c/o Catholic Presbytery, 33 Howard St, West Melbourne, Victoria 3033. T: 303474.
**Church Stores,** Daking House, Rawson Place, Sydney, NSW 2000.
**Institute of Pastoral Liturgy,** St Patrick's College, Manly, NSW 2095. T: 974870.
**Latin Mass Society,** GPO Box 2773, Sydney, NSW. (Member of Una Voce).

*AUSTRIA*
**Liturgisches Institut (Institutum Liturgicum),** Erzabtei St Peters, Postfach 113, A-5010 Salzburg. T: (06222)42166.
**Una Voce Austria,** An der Furt 2, A-6020 Innsbruck.

*BELGIUM*
**Apostolate for Church Life (Apostolaat voor Kerkelijk Leven),** Norbertijneabdij, B-3190 Tongerlo. T: (014)55041. (Liturgical records; Flemish-language).
**Commission Interdiocésaine de Pastorale Liturgique (CIPL),** Av Reine Astrid 10, B-7000 Mons. T: (065)331278.
**Interdiocesan Commission for Pastoral Liturgy (Interdiocesane Commissie voor Liturgische Zielzorg),** ICLZ, Guimardstraat 5, B-1040 Brussel. T: (02)123379,125203. (Flemish-speaking). (Also: Hoogstraat 41, B-9000 Gent).
**Liturgical Institute (Liturgisch Instituut),** Abdij Keizersberg, Mechelsestraat 202, B-3000 Leuven. T: (016)224174.
**Liturgisch Centrum De Wijngaard,** Begijnhof, B-8000 Brugge. T: (050)330011.
**Madrigaal (Het Madrigaal),** Herestraat 51, B-3000 Leuven. T: (016)33967. (Liturgical records; Flemish-language).
**Una Voce Belgique,** Rue de la Montagne 52a, B-1000 Brussel.

*BRAZIL*
**Centro Catequético e Litúrgico Lumen Christi,** c/o Secretariado Arquidiocesano de Pastoral, Rua Ir Serafina 88, Campinas, SP. T: 25316,89784, 92742.
**Centro Litúrgico Nacional,** Comissão Nacional de Litúrgia, Rua do Russel 76, 5 andar, CP 16085, 20000 Rio de Janeiro, GB, ZC-01-Gloria. T: 2252761.
**Instituto Nacional de Pastoral,** Rua Cosme Velho 120, 20000 Rio de Janeiro, GB, ZC-01-Cosme Velho.

*CANADA*
**Canadian Council on Liturgy,** 1070 Waterloo St, London 11, Ontario. T: (519)433-0658.
**National Liturgical Office,** Dir, 90 Parent Av, Ottawa 2, Ontario K1N 7B1. T: (613)236-9461.
**Office National de Liturgie,** Dir, 1215 est, Blvd Saint-Joseph, Montréal 176, Québec. T: (204) 247-9851. (French-speaking).
**Studio RM,** 12 Rue St Denis, Cap-de-la-Madeleine, Québec. T: 374-2441. (Recordings for use in catechism and liturgy).
**Una Voce Canada,** Box 5093, Station F, Ottawa 5.

*CHILE*
**Magnificat,** Morandé 322, Of 210, Santiago (Member of Una Voce).

*COLOMBIA*
**Departamento de Litúrgia,** CELAM, Apdo Aéreo 1931, Medellín, Ant.
**Departamento de Litúrgia,** Secretariado Permenente del Episcopado Colombiano, Calle 26 No 27-48, Apdo Aéreo 7448, Apdo Nacional 4553, Bogotá. T: 414186,414642.
**Instituto Latinoamericano de Litúrgia Pastoral (ILP),** Calle 19, No 81-83, Apdo Aéreo 1931, Medellín, Ant. T: 381626,381728.

*DENMARK*
**Una Voce Dacia,** Maglekildevej 6, DK-1853 Kobenhavn V.

*EL SALVADOR*
**Comisión Nacional de Litúrgia,** Equipo de Reflexión, Arzobispado, San Salvador. T: 257041, 257042,257082.

*FRANCE*
**Association des Amis de Kuer-Moussa,** Abbaye Saint-Pierre de Solesmes, F-72 Sablé-sur-Sarthe. (Liturgical records in Wolof (Senegal) and French).
**Association Una Voce,** BP 174, F-75017 Paris.
**Centre National de Pastorale Liturgique (CNPL),** Institut Supérieur de Liturgie, 4 Av Vavin, F-75006 Paris. T: (01)325-4000.
**Editions Ouvrières,** Disques DMO, 12 Av Soeur Rosalie, F-75013 Paris. (Liturgical records).
**Institut Supérieur de Liturgie,** 4 Av Vavin, F-75006 Paris. T: (01)325-4000.

*GERMANY, Federal Republic of*
**Berneuchener Dienst,** Geschäftsstelle, über Hob aN, D-7241 Kloster Kirchberg. (Liturgical movement).
**Liturgisches Institut,** Jesuitenstr 13c, Postfach 371, D-5500 Trier. T: (0651)48106/7.
**Lutherische Liturgische Konferenz Deutschlands,** Am Markt 7, D-2418 Ratzeburg.
**Societas Liturgica/International Society for Liturgical Study & Renewal,** Sec, Jesuitenstr 13c, Postfach 2628, D-5500 Trier. T: (0651)48106/7.
**Una Voce in Deutschland,** Akazienhof 1, D-414 Rheinhausen.

*HOLY SEE*
**Sacred Congregation for the Causes of Saints/SC per le Cause dei Santi,** Cardinal Prefect, Palazzo delle Congregazioni, Piazza Pio XII 10, I-00193 Roma, Italy. T: (6982)4247.
**Sacred Congregation for the Discipline of the Sacraments/SC per la Disciplina dei Sacramenti,** Cardinal Prefect, Palazzo delle Congregazioni, Piazza Pio XII 10, I-00193, Roma, Italy. T: (6982)4005,4416.
**Sacred Congregation for the Divine Worship/SC per il Culto Divino,** Cardinal Prefect, Palazzo delle Congregazioni, Piazza Pio XII 10, I-00193 Roma, Italy. T: (6982)4316/8.
**Sacred Congregation for the Doctrine of the Faith/SC per la Dottrina della Fede/SC pro Doctrina Fidei,** Palazzo della stessa S. Congregazione, Piazza del S. Uffizio 11, I-00193 Roma, Italy. T: (6982)3357.

*INDIA*
**National Biblical Catechetical and Liturgical Centre (NBCLC),** St Mary's Town, PB 577, Bangalore 560005. T: 52369.
**Tamil Nadu Biblical, Catechetical and Liturgical Centre (TNBCLC),** Tindivanam PO, Tamil Nadu.

*INDONESIA*
**Pastoral Research and Service Centre (Pusat Pastoral Solo),** Jalan Jendral Sundirman 3, Surakarta, Central Java. T: 3904.

*IRAQ*
**Latin Church,** Karadat Mariam, Baghdad. T: 33643

*IRELAND*
**Coetus Consultorum Commissionis Liturgicae,** St Patrick's College, Maynooth, Country Kildare. T: 286261.
**International Society for Liturgical Study and Renewal (Societas Liturgica),** The Deanery, Lismore, County Waterford.

*ITALY*
**Centro di Azione Liturgica,** Via Liberiana 17, I-00185 Roma. T: 481870.
**Istituto di Liturgia Pastorale per le Tre Venezie,** Via Giuseppe Ferrari 2A, I-35100 Padova.
**Pontificio Istituto Liturgico di San Anselmo,** Via di Porta Lavernale 19, I-00153 Roma. T: 5745127.
**Standing Committee for International Eucharistic Congresses,** Via del Pozzetto 160, Roma. T: 6790310.
**Una Voce Italia,** Corso Vittorio Emanuele 21, I-00186 Roma.
**Union of Adorers of the Blessed Sacrament,** Largo dei Monti Parioli 3, I-00197 Roma.

*JAPAN*
**Liturgical Institute (Institutum Liturgicum),** Sophia University, 1-710 Kamishakujii, Nerima-ku, Tokyo 102. T: (03)264-0875.

*KENYA*
**Kenya Association for Liturgical Music (KALM),** Sec, St Thomas Aquinas Seminary, Langata, PO Box 30517, Nairobi. T: Langata 405.

*LEBANON*
**Institut Supérieur de Liturgie,** Université St-Esprit, Kaslik.

*NETHERLANDS*
**Ecumenical Liturgical Centre (Liturgisch Oecumenisch Centrum),** Mathenesserlaan 301c, NL-3003 Rotterdam. T: (010)252759.
**National Liturgical Council (Nationale Raad voor Liturgie),** Biltstraat 119, Utrecht. T: (030) 334244.
**Netherlands Liturgical Centre (Nederlands Liturgisch Centrum),** Biltstraat 119, Utrecht. T: (030)12950.
**Netherlands Society for Religious Articles (Nederlandse Katholieke Vereniging van Detailhandelaren in Religieuze Artikelen),** Haarlemmerstraat 123, Leiden. T: (01710)22889.
**St Gregory Association of the Netherlands (Nederlandse St-Gregoriusvereniging),** Biltstraat 119, Utrecht. T: (030)334244.
**Society for the Study of Liturgy (Genootschap voor Liturgiestudie),** Biltstraat 119, Utrecht. T: (030)12950.

*NEW ZEALAND*
**National Liturgical Commission,** St Joseph's Parish House, 7 Paterson St, Wellington 1. T: 50914.

*NIGERIA*
**Pastoral Department,** Catholic Secretariat of Nigeria, 6 Force Rd, PO Box 951, Lagos. T: 25339.
**Pastoral Institute,** Bodija, PO Box 1784, Ibadan. T: 24328.

*NORWAY*
**Una Voce Norvegia,** Majorstuveien 8, Oslo 3.

*PAPUA NEW GUINEA*
**National Liturgical Centre,** PO Box 1101, Port Moresby, Boroko. T: 81347.
**National Subcommission for Christian Initiation,** Catholic Mission Yobai, PO Gumine via Goroka.
**National Subcommission for General Liturgy,** Catholic Mission Mapua, Tabar Island, PO Kavieng, New Ireland.

*PARAGUAY*
**Departamento Nacional de Litúrgia,** Coronel Bogado 884, Casi Tucuari, CP 1436, Asunción. T: 41122.

*PERU*
**Officina Nacional de Litúrgia,** Dir, Azangaro 260, Oficina 309, Apdo 1512, Lima. T: 280137.

*PHILIPPINES*
**East Asian Pastoral Institute,** Ateneo de Manila Campus, Loyola Heights, Quezon City, PO Box 1815, Manila. T: 903182.

*POLAND*
**Department of Liturgics,** Catholics University of Lublin (Katedra Liturgiki, Instytut Teologii Pastoralnej, Katolicki Uniwersytet Lubelski), Aleje Raclawickie 14, skr p 279, 20 950 Lublin 1. T: 30426.
**Liturgical Institute (Instytut Liturgiczny przy Papieskim Wydziale Teologicznym Krakowie),** ul sw Marka 10, Kraków.
**Liturgical Section,** Pastoral Institute (Papieski Instytut Pastoralny, Sekcja Liturgi zna), KUL, Aleje Raclawickie 14, Lublin.

*PORTUGAL*
**Grémio Concelho dos Comerciantes de Antiguidades,** Artigos Religiosos e Funerários de Lisboa (Corporation of Distributors of Religious & Funerary Articles), Lisboa.
**Liga dos Amigos do Canto Gregoriano,** Campo Martires da Patria 96-2, Lisboa. (Member of Una Voce).

*RWANDA*
**Centre de Pastorale Liturgique et Catéchétique,** Dir, BP 49, Butare. T: 3032.

*SAMOA*
**Liturgical Translations Committee,** Catholic Cathedral, Apia. T: 58.

*SENEGAL*
**Monastère de Keur-Moussa,** Keur-Moussa, par Pout. (Association des Amis de Keur-Moussa, France; liturgical records in Wolof and French).

*SOMALIA*
**Commissione Liturgica del Vicariato,** Centro Laicato Cattolico, Via Tomaso Carletti, PO Box 273, Mogadisho.

*SPAIN*
**Centro de Pastoral Litúrgica,** Dir, Canuda 45, Barcelona 2.
**Departamento de Litúrgia,** Instituto Superior de Pastoral, Instituto León XIII, Límite 3, Madrid 3.
**Secretariado Nacional de Litúrgia,** Plaza del Conde Barajas 1, Madrid 12. T: 2664834.
**Una Voce España,** Fundación Pastor, Serrano 107, Madrid.

*SRI LANKA*
**National Liturgy Centre,** Archbishop's House, Colombo 8. T: 95471.

*SWEDEN*
**Una Voce Suecia,** Skomakarg 13 III, S-111 29 Stockholm.

*SWITZERLAND*
**Centre Romand de Liturgie,** Petit Séminaire du St-Sacrement, CH-1723 Marly-le-Petit. T: (037) 221666. (French-speaking).
**Centro di Liturgia,** CP 26, CH-6901 Lugano. T: (093)334762. (Italian-speaking).
**Fédération Internationale Una Voce,** St Georges 18, CH-1815 Clarens. (Militant right-wing federation defending the Latin mass and Gregorian chant).
**Liturgische Konsultativkommission,** Christkatholische Kirche der Schweiz, Willadingweg 39, CH-3000 Bern.
**Liturgisches Institut,** Gartenstr 36, CH-8002 Zürich. T: (05)361146. (German-speaking).

*USSR*
**Episcopal Liturgical Commission of Lithuania (Lietuvos Vyskupiju Liturgine Komisija),** Kretingos 16, 232024 Vilnius, Lithuanian SSR. T: 26455.

*UK OF GB & NI*
**Alcuin Club,** Editorial Sec, 5 St Andrew's St, London EC4A 3AB. (Studies of Book of Common Prayer).
**Association for Latin Liturgy,** 11 Barton Close, Cambridge. T: (0223)57255.
**Baptismal Reform Movement,** Sec, 5 Meadway, Epsom, Surrey. (Opposing indiscriminate baptism).
**Church of England Liturgical Commission,** Sec, Church House, Dean's Yard, Westminster, London SW1P 3NZ. T: (01)222-9011.
**Gregorian Association,** Gen Sec, Rosedale, Petersham Rd, Richmond, Surrey TW10 7AD.
**J. Wippell & Co,** 11 Tufton St, Westminister, London SW1. T: (01)222-4528. (Clerical tailors and robemakers).
**Latin Mass Society of England & Wales,** 43 Blandford St, London W1. (Member of Una Voce).
**League of Anglican Loyalists,** Sec, 11 Cumberland Mansions, Hampstead, London NW6. T: (01) 435-1614. (Anglican; defence of Catholic churchmanship).
**Liturgy Commission,** General Synod of the Church of England, Church House, Dean's Yard, London SW1P 3NZ. T: (01)222-9011.
**Pax House,** Liturgical Church Furnishers, 29 Lower Brook St, Ipswich, Suffolk. T: 56832. (RC).
**Society of St Gregory,** 14 Ellenborough Park South, Weston-super-Mare, Somerset BS23 1XW. T: (0934)21929.
**Una Voce Scottish Branch,** 6 Belford Park, Edinburgh 4.

*USA*
**Bishop's Committee on the Liturgy,** Dir, 1312 Massachusetts Av, NW, Washington, DC 20005. T: (202)659-6850.
**Gregorian Institute of America,** 7404 South Madison Av, Chicago, IL 60638.
**Liturgical Art Manufacturing Company,** 644 Broadway, New York, NY. T: 228-6100.
**Liturgical Arts Society of New York,** New York, NY. (Catholic).
**Liturgical Conference,** 1330 Massachusetts Av, NW, Washington, DC 20005.
**Liturgical Prayer Publications,** 1860 Broadway, New York, NY. T: 541-7667.
**Murphy Center for Liturgical Research,** University of Notre Dame, Notre Dame, IN 46556.
**New Patterns in Worship,** William Penn College, Oskaloosa, IA 52577.
**Notre Dame Liturgical Center,** University of Notre Dame, Notre Dame, IN 46556. T: (219) 283-6662.
**St John's Liturgical Center,** St John's Abbey, Collegeville, MN 56321. T: (612)363-7761.
**Shared Worship Facilities,** St Mark's Church, 1101 Euclid St, Kansas City, MO 64127.
**Una Voce in the United States,** PO Box 446, Grand Central Station, New York, NY 10017.
**Woodstock Center for Religion and Worship,** Room 240, 475 Riverside Drive, New York, NY 10027. T: (212)866-7646.
**World Center for Liturgical Studies,** PO Box DD, Boyton Beach, FL 33435.

*URUGUAY*
**Instituto Nacional de Estudios Litúrgicos (INEL),** Secretariado Nacional de Litúrgia, Rio Branco 1430, Montevideo. T: 84404.
**Una Voce Uruguay,** Casilla 12, Montevideo.

*YEMEN, South*
**Liturgical Commission,** Catholic Mission, Steamer Point, PO Box 1155, Aden. T: 22900.

*YUGOSLAVIA*
**Centre Présent Chrétien (Krscanska Sadasnjost),** Zagreb. (Liturgical records, books, journals).

# 36
# Local (Sub-National) Conciliarism

*Definition.* Interdenominational or ecumenical councils of churches or denominations and dioceses of different ecclesiastical traditions, for a province, area or city within a single nation; local conciliarism, collegiality and consultation.

Organized local councils of this nature number some 2,400, in 40 countries. They are too numerous to list here, but listings can be located under DIRECTORIES mainly in national yearbooks.

# 37
# Medical Centres

*Definition.* Church- or Christian-sponsored hospitals, leprosaria, sanatoria, clinics, dispensaries, mobile units, maternity centres, et alia.

Vast numbers of centres exist. The global total (1975) is 29,500, of which 4,600 are hospitals. No listing of names or addresses is given here, but listings at national, international and confessional levels are included under DIRECTORIES, mainly in confessional or national yearbooks.

# 38
# Medicine & Healing

*Definition.* Medical missions, fellowship and witness in the medical world, major Christian medical centres, associations of hospitals (or clinics or dispensaries), medical missionary institutes, nursing training centres, dental missions, ophthalmic missions, leprosy missions, other specialist missions, medical missions support organizations, public health, hospital chaplaincy organizations, medical services, medical supply agencies, pharmacists, ministries to handicapped groups (the deaf, the blind, cripples, epileptics, incurables, lepers, mental institutions), suicides, religion and psychiatry, religion and health, mental health, Christian psychologists, clinical theology, spiritual healing, faith-healing groups and centres; training centres and courses. See also RESEARCH CENTRES.

In this field, Christian organizations of major significance number over 400.

*AFGHANISTAN*
**International Afghan Mission,** Medical Assistance Program (MAP), Exec Sec, Box 625, Kabul.
**National Organization for Ophthalmic Rehabilitation (NOOR),** Box 625, Kabul.

*ALGERIA*
**Union Nationale des Religieuses d'Action Hospitalière et Sociale,** El-Djezair.

*AUSTRALIA*
**Christian Medical Fellowships,** 7a Drummoyne Av, Drummoyne, NSW 2047.
**Mission to Lepers,** 174 Collins St, Melbourne.
**Mission to the Blind Overseas,** United Insurance Bldgs, 52 Queen St, Melbourne C1, Victoria.
**Nurses' Christian Fellowship (NCF),** 63 Orchard St, PO Box 168, Chatswood, NSW 2067. T: 412-1197.

*BELGIUM*
**Aid for Maternity Hospitals and Dispensaries in Central Africa/Assistance aux Maternités et Dispensaries d'Afrique Centrale (AMDAC),** Rue Brialmont 11, B-1030 Brussel. T: (02)2170497.
**Fédération des Institutions Hospitalières (FIH),** Rue Guimard 5, B-1040 Brussel.
**Fédération des Services Médico-Sociaux (FSMS),** Rue Guimard 5, B-1040 Brussel.
**International Committee of Catholic Nurses/Comité International Catholique des Infirmières et Assistantes Médico-Sociales (CICIAMS),** Sec, Square Vergote 43, B-1040 Brussel. T: (02)2170631.
**International Federation of Associations of Catholic Doctors (FIAMC),** Sec, Rue des Deux-Eglises 38, B-1040 Brussel. T: 176517.
**International Medical Missionary Association/Association Internationale Médico-Missionnaire,** Av Brugman 300, Brussel 18.
**Medical Aid to Central Africa/Assistance Médicale à l'Afrique Centrale (AMAC),** Blvd Louis Schmidt 111, B-1040 Brussel. T: (02)7347377
**Medicus Mundi,** Dwarsstraat 32, B-1030 Brussel. T: (02)2171046.
**Volontaires du Service Médical, Educatif et Social,** Rue Capouillet 10, Brussel 6.

*BOTSWANA*
**Medical Missionary Association of Botswana,** Sec, Scottish Livingstone Hospital, Molepolole.

*BRAZIL*
**Comunhão Dental Amazonica/Amazon Dental Fellowship,** CP 302, 69.000 Manaus, Amazonas.

*CAMEROON*
**Secrétariat Médical et Scolaire,** BP 790, Yaoundé.

*CANADA*
**Bible & Medical Missionary Fellowship Canada (BMFF),** 4805 Yonge St, Willowdale, Toronto 7, Ontario. T: 223-7515.
**Christian Medical Society,** 131 Delhi St, Guelph, Ontario.
**Evangelical Medical Missionary Aid Society,** 4805 Yonge St, Willowdale, Toronto 7, Ontario. T: 223-7515.
**International Christian Leprosy Mission,** Gen Dir, 954 Wentworth Av, North Vancouver, BC.
**International Grenfell Association,** St Anthony, Newfoundland.
**Missionary Health Institute (International Health Institute),** Pres, 400 Leslie St, Willowdale, Ontario. T: (416)444-1131.
**Ontario Mission to the Deaf,** Evangelical Church of the Deaf, Toronto.

*CHINA (TAIWAN)*
**Taiwan Leprosy Relief Association,** Superintendent, Jen Ai Lu, 4th Sec, No 6, Taipei T: 77958.

*DENMARK*
**Missionary Association of Nurses (Sygeplejerskernes Missionsforbund),** Lyshojgardsvej 43, Valdy.

*ECUADOR*
**Asociación de Dentistas Misioneros,** Casilla 691, Quito.

*ETHIOPIA*
**All-Africa Leprosy & Rehabilitation Training Centre,** PO Box 165, Addis Abeba.

*FRANCE*
**Association Médico-Sociale Protestante,** Secrétariat Général, 1 Rue Michelet, F-75006 Paris.
**Commission Médico-Pédagogique et Psycho-Sociale,** 53 Rue de Babylone, F-75007 Paris. (Member BICE).
**Croisade des Aveugles/International Crusade for the Blind,** Sec, 15 Rue Mayet, F-75006 Paris. T: (01)734-9732.
**Fraternité Catholique des Malades et Infirmes/Catholic Fraternity of the Sick and Infirm,** Sec, Foyer des Malades, 49 Rue St-Sauveur, F-55100 Verdun.
**International Federation of Catholic Pharmacists/Fédération Internationale des Pharmaciens Catholiques (FIPC),** Secrétariat, 60 Av des Pages, F-78110 Le Vesinet.
**Medicus Mundi,** Faculté de Médecine Pitié-Salpétrière, 91 Blvd de l'Hôpital, F-75013 Paris.
**Secrétariat National des Oeuvres Catholiques Sanitaires et Sociales,** 103 Faubourg St-Honoré, F-75008 Paris. T: (01)225-1676.
**Union Evangélique Médicale et Para-Médicale,** 463 Rue de l'Eglise, Bois-Guillaume (Seine-Mar). T: Rouen 705003.
**Union Nationale Interfédérale des Oeuvres et Organismes Privés Sanitaires et Sociaux (UNIOPSS),** 103 Faubourg St-Honoré, F-75008 Paris. T: (01)225-1676.

*GERMANY, Federal Republic of*
**Arbeitsgemeinschaft Deutscher Evangelischer Seelsorger für Gemüts- und Nervenkranke,** D-4813 Bethel.
**Arbeitsgemeinschaft Ev Gehörlosenseelsorger Deutschlands,** D-68 Mannheim.
**Arbeitsgemeinschaft für Ev Schwerhörigenseelsorge,** Felnnerstr 12, D-6 Frankfurt/Main 1.
**Christlicher Blindendienst,** Postfach 630, D-355 Marburg/Lahn.
**Christoffel-Blindenmission im Orient,** Nibelungenstr 124, D-6140 Bensheim-Schönberg T: (06251) 6043. (Begun 1908).
**Deutscher Evangelischer Krankenhausverband,** Stafflenbergstr 78, Postfach 476, D-7 Stuttgart 1.
**Deutsches Institut für Arztliche Mission/German Institute for Medical Missions,** Paul-Lechler-Str 24, D-7400 Tubingen. T: (07122)4687. (Begun 1918).
**Evangelische Arbeitsgemeinschaft für Müttergenesung,** Deutenbacher Str 1, D-8504 Stein bei Nurnberg.
**Hildesheimer Blindenmission,** Neustädter Markt 37, D-3200 Hildesheim. T: (05121)34594.
**Konferenz der Evang Kur- und Erholungseinrichtungen,** Alexanderstr 23, Postfach 476, D-7 Stuttgart 1.
**Medicus Mundi,** Secretariat, Mozartstr 9, D-51 Aachen.
**Medicus Mundi International,** Hauptstr 10, Bensberg-Köln.
**Missionsärzliches Institut/Medical Missionary Institute,** Salvatorstr 7, D-8700 Wurzburg.
**Verband der Evangelischen Einrichtungen für dei Rehabilitation Behinderter,** Stafflenbergstr 78, D-7 Stuttgart 1.
**Verband Evangelischer Einrichtungen für Geistig und Seelische Behinderte,** D-4971 Wittekindshof bei Bad Oeynhausen.
**Verein für Errichtung Deutsche-Evangelischer Gottesdienste in Kurorten,** Feyerleinstr 11, D-6 Frankfurt/Main. (Ministry to spas and health resorts).
**Verein zur Errichtung Evangelischer Krankenhäuser,** Teutonenstr 9, Postfach 101, D-1 Berlin 38.

*GHANA*
**Catholic Nurses Guide of Ghana,** St Patrick's Hospital, PO Box 17, Maase-Offinso.
**Christian Hospital Association of Ghana (CHAG),** Accra.
**Christian Medical Workers' Fellowship (CMWF),** PO Box M-77, Accra.
**Ghana Society for Sick, Destitutes & Deviants,** PO Box 846, Kumasi.

*HONG KONG*
**Junk Bay Medical Relief Council,** Po Lam Rd, Junk Bay, NT, PO Box 9072, Kowloon.

*INDIA*
**Catholic Hospital Association (CHA),** CBCI Centre, Ashok Place, New Delhi 1.
**Christian Medical Association of India,** Gen Sec, Christian Council Lodge, Nagpur 1.
**Christian Medical College & Brown Memorial Hospital,** Principal, Brown Rd, Ludhiana, Punjab.
**Christian Medical College & Hospital,** Vellore, North Arcot, Madras State.
**Co-ordinating Agency for Health and Planning (CAHP),** c/45 South Extension, Part II, New Delhi 49.
**CSI School for the Deaf,** Mylapore, South India.
**Emmanuel Hospital Association,** E-32 Panch Shila Park, New Delhi 110017. (15 hospitals).
**Kerala Ecumenical Mental Hospital,** Syro-Malankara Archbishop's House, Trivandrum 4, Kerala.
**Kotagiri Medical Fellowship,** Kotagiri PO, Nilgiris.
**St John's Medical College,** Robert Koch Bhavan, Sarjapur Rd, Bangalore 34.

*INDONESIA*
**Indonesian Christian Medical Workers' Association,** DGI, Jalan Salemba Raya 10, Jakarta IV/3.

*IRELAND*
**Damian Medico-Missionary Society,** 47 Fitzwilliam Square, Dublin.
**Irish International Medical Service,** 9 Harcourt Terrace, Dublin 2.
**Medical Missionaries of Mary,** Rosemount, Booterstown Av, Dublin. T: 882722.
**Medical Missionary Society,** University College, Cork. (RC).

*ISRAEL*
**Helen Keller Vocational Training Centre (Bible Lands Society),** Jerusalem. (For blind girls).
**Social Orthodox Committee for the Sick,** Harat el Nazara, Jerusalem. T: 82076.

*ITALY*
**Associazione Femminile Medico-Missionaria (AFMM)/Medico-Missionary Association for Women,** Via delle Terme Deciane 5/A, I-00153 Roma. T: 573482.
**Centro Italiano di Sessuologia,** Instituto di Psicologia, Città Universitaria, I-00100 Roma. T: (4991)550212.
**Collegio Universitario Aspiranti Medici Missionaria (CUAMM)/University College for Medical Missionary Aspirants,** Via Galileo Galilei 18, I-35100 Padova. (Also: Via Acquetta 12, Padova, and Via Napoleone III 1, I-00185 Roma. T: 735824).
**Ente Nazionale per la Protezione e d'Assistenza di Sordomuti,** Via Gregorio VII 120, I-00165 Roma. T: 6377041.
**Medical Mission Sisters/Society of Catholic Medical Missionaries,** Via di Villa Troili 32, I-00163 Roma. T: 80847. (Under Propaganda).
**Unione Medici Missionaria Italiana (UMMI),** Ospedale San Cuore/Civile, I-37024 Negrar (Verona). T: 650044.

*JAMAICA*
**Caribbean Christian Centre for the Deaf,** Kingston.

*JAPAN*
**Association for the Relief of Leprosy in Asia (Ajia Kyurai Kyokai),** No 7 Yuraka-cho 1-chome, Chiyoda-ku, Tokyo.
**Japan Christian Medical Association (JCMA),** National YMCA Bldg, 1-2 Nishi Kanda, Chiyoda-ku, Tokyo. (735 doctors, nurses and paramedical workers).
**Japan Council of Christian Evangelism for the Blind (Mojin Dendo Kyogikai),** 4-8-11 Miyamae, Suginami-ku, Tokyo 167.
**Japan Mission for Hospital Evangelism,** 242-3 Hanyuno, Habikino-shi, Osaka-fu 583.
**Japan Overseas Christian Medical Cooperative Service (Nippon Kiristokyo Kaigai Iryo Kyoryokukai),** National YMCA Bldg, 1-2 Nishi Kanda, Chiyoda-ku, Tokyo. (Also: 551-23 1-chome Tetsukache, Shinjuku-ku, Tokyo).

*JORDAN*
**Society of the Mission to the Blind in Bible Lands,** PO Box 265, Jerusalem.

*KENYA*
**East African Braille Press,** Manager, Sikri, PO Box 285, Kisii. (Catholic).
**Hospitals Chaplaincy of Kenya,** Sec, Westlands, PO Box 14424, Nairobi. T: 60803.
**Kenya Hospitals Christian Fellowship (KHCF),** PO Box 30024, Nairobi.
**Kenya Mental Health Association,** Gen Sec, Health Education Division, PO Box 30562, Nairobi. T: 23973,20651.
**Northern Frontier Medical Fellowship,** PO Box 56, Nakuru. T: 2810.
**Protestant Churches Medical Association (PCMA),** Flat 3, Lenana Rd/Woodlands Rd, PO Box 30690, Nairobi. T: 20695.

*KOREA, South*
**Catholic Leprosy Workers Association,** Eub Nae 5 Dong, Chil Kok Myeon, Chil Kok Kun, Kyeong Buk.
**Korean Christian Medical Society,** IPO Box 1010, Soul.
**National Catholic Hospitals Association,** 2, 1 Ka, Jeo Dong, Jung Ku, Soul. T: 261046.

*LEBANON*
**Christian Medical Association of the Near East,** CMC Hospital, Bayrut.

*LIBERIA*
**Gospel Witness to the Deaf,** Mail Bag 9038, Monrovia.

*MALAWI*
**Private Hospital Association of Malawi (PHAM),** PO Box 948, Blantyre. T: 8581.

*MEXICO*
**Centro Psiquiatrico Infantil,** 437 Col Del Valle, Zona 12, México, DF. T: 231412.
**Clinica Dental/International Dental Institute,** Calle 4a No 1524, Tijuana, BC.

*NETHERLANDS*
**Catholic Study Centre for Mental Health (Katholiek Studiecentrum voor Geestelijke Volksge zondheio),** Wilhelminapark 26, Utrecht. T: (030)510421.
**Catholic Union for the Sick and Hospitalized (Katholieke Unie van Verplegenden en Verzorgenden),** Koningslaan 6, Utrecht. T: (030)512321.
**Central Office for Catholic Hospitals and Clinics (Centraal Bureau voor het Katholieke Ziekendhuiswezen),** Badhuisweg 72, 's-Gravenhage. T: (070)512581.
**Foundation MEMISA (Stichting Medische Missie Actie),** Eendrachtsweg 49, Rotterdam.
**International Catholic Confederation of Hospitals/Confédération Internationale Catholique des Institutions Hospitalières (CICIH),** Secretariat, Van Schaek Mathonsingel 4, Nijmegen. T: 58711.
**Medical Missionary Action (Medische Missie Actie),** Duinweg 21b, 's-Gravenhage. (Also: Eendrachtsweg 49 & Heemraadssingel 334, Rotterdam.
**Medicus Mundi,** Prof Van Weliestraat 8, Nijmegen. (Also: Van Schaeck Mathonsingel 4, Nijmegen).
**Protestant Medica! Organization (Protestants Christelijke Artsen Organisatie),** Reeweg 0 151, Dordrecht.
**Volunteers for Medical and Social Aid to the Third World (Unie van Vrijwilligers voor Medische, Sociale Hulp en Onderwijs in Ontwikkelinges Landen),** A Nobellan 122, De Bilt.
**Yellow & White Cross National Federation (Nationale Federatie Het Wit-Gele Kruis),** Herenstraat 35, Utrecht. T: (030)13546. (Polyclinics and dispensaries).

*NEW ZEALAND*
**Bible & Medical Missionary Fellowship (BMMF),** New Zealand Council, 427 Queen St, Auckland 1.
**Christian Medical Fellowship of New Zealand,** 876 New North Rd, Auckland 3.
**Inter-Church Advisory Council on Hospital Chaplaincy,** Sec, PO Box 800, Christchurch.
**Lepers' Trust Board,** Private Bag, Christchurch.
**Leprosy Mission (NZ),** 43 Mt Eden Rd, PO Box 8579, Auckland 3.

*NIGERIA*
**Christian Mission for the Deaf,** PO Box 808, Ibadan.

*NORWAY*
**Christian Medical Association (Kristelig Laegeforening),** Theresesgt 51 B, Oslo 3.
**Nurses' Missionary Association (Skykepleiernes Misjonsring),** PA Munchs vei 3, Oslo 8.

*PAKISTAN*
**Christian Caravan Hospital,** Integrated Community Health Care Centre, Mirpur Khas.

*PALESTINE*
**Pontifical Mission Centre for the Blind,** Gaza City, Gaza Strip.

*PHILIPPINES*
**Philippine Leprosy Mission,** NCCP, 941 Epifanio de los Santos Av, Quezon City.

*PORTUGAL*
**Comissão Portuguese Pró-Leprosos,** Alameda das Linhas de Torres 122, Lisboa-5.
**União Médica Cristã Evangélica,** Pres Apdo 32, Leiria.

*SINGAPORE*
**Singapore Nurses Christian Fellowship,** c/o Vicker's House, General Hospital, Singapore 3.

*SOUTH AFRICA*
**International Hospital Christian Fellowship (IHCF),** 25 Oak Park Av, PO Box 353, Kempton Park, Transvaal.
**Medical Christian Fellowship of South Africa/Christen-Geneesheersbond van Suid-Afrika,** c/o 27 Silwood Rd, Rondebosch, CP.

*SPAIN*
**Escuela Española de Medicina para Misioneros,** Raimundo Lulio, Colegio Vasco de Quiroga, Ciudad Universitaria, Madrid 3.
**Medicus Mundi en España,** Secretariado de Misiones y Propaganda, Lauria 13, Barcelona 10.
**Organización Nacional de Ciegos Espanoles,** José Ortega y Gasset 18, Madrid 6. (For the blind. Member BICE).

*SWEDEN*
**African Mission of the Deaf,** c/o Evangeliska Fosterlands-Stiftelsen, Tegnergatan 34, Stockholm VA.
**Catholic Nurses' Association,** Framnasgatan 14, Goteborg S.

*SWITZERLAND*
**Arbeitsgemeinschaft Evangelischer Artze der Schweiz,** Sek, Eichstr 51, CH-8712 Stäfa.

**Association des Infirmières Catholiques,** Batiment UBS, Av de la Gare, Martigny (Valais).
**Christian Medical Commission,** 150 Route de Ferney, CH-1211 Genève 20. (0104122)333400.
**Communauté Protestante de l'Hôpital,** 5 Chemin Venel, Genève. T: 465114.
**Ev Aussätzigen-Mission/Mission Evangélique contre la Lèpre,** Schweizerische Sekretariat, Schönenwerderstr 35a, CH-5000 Aarau. T: (064)245051.
**Evangelische Krankenpflegerschule Chur,** Schulleiter, Loestr 117, CH-7000 Chur.
**Fédération Européenne d'Associations de Médecins Catholiques,** Secrétariat du Bulletin, Petit Schönberg 505, CH-1700 Fribourg.
**Ministère auprès des Mentalement Handicapés,** Conseil, 10 Chemin Buisson, Genève. T: 334801.
**Schaffhauser Verein für Arztliche Mission,** Präs, Stauffacherstr 22, CH-8200 Schaffhausen.
**Schweizerische Anstalt für Epileptische,** Südstr 120, CH-8008 Zürich. T: (051)536060.
**Semaines de Médecine de la Personne,** Le Grain de Blé, Chemin J Ormond, CH-1256 Troinex, Genève.
**Union des Médicins Catholiques,** Emmen(Luzern).
**Vereinigung der Deutschschweizerischen Spitalpfarrel,** Präs, Alle Kantonsspital, Zürich.

*TANZANIA*
**Adventist Seminary of Health Evangelism,** Heri Mission Hospital, SLP Kigoma.

*THAILAND*
**Asian Ecumenical Conference on the Role of Health in the Development of Nations,** c/o 315 Silom Rd, Bangkok 5.
**Asian Regional Executive Committee (AREC),** Federation of Catholic Medical Associations (FIAMC), Gen Sec, 315 Silom Rd, Bangkok 5. T: 37090/9.

*UK OF GB & NI*
**Aged and Infirm Protestant Dissenting Ministers' Society,** Sec, Baptist Church House, 4 Southampton Row, London WC1.
**Apostolate of the Sick,** National Dir, 81 Parkway, Welwyn Garden City, Herts.
**Association for Clinical Theological Training & Care,** Lingdale, Weston Av, Mount Hooton Rd, Nottingham NG7 4BA. T: (0602)75475.
**Association of Religious Nursing Sisters of Great Britain,** National Centre, St Vincents, Carlisle Place, London SW1. T: (01)834-4759 (RC).
**Bible and Medical Missionary Fellowship (BMMF),** Gen Sec, 352 Kennington Rd, London SE11 4LF. T: (01)735-8228.
**Bible Lands Society,** The Old Kiln, Hazlemere, High Wycombe, Bucks. (Centres for the blind in Palestine).
**Calix Society,** National Sec, 60 Lamington Rd, Glasgow SW2. T: (041)882-1941. (RC; alcoholics)
**Catholic Nurses Guild of England and Wales,** National Hon Sec, St Lawrence, Dunstanburgh Rd, Newcastle upon Tyne NE6 2PT.
**Catholic Nursing Institute,** 80 Lambeth Rd, London SE1. T: (01)928-6526.
**Catholic Overseas Appointments,** Sec, Hinsley House, 38 King St, London WC2. T: (01)8361-1701. (Appoints doctors, etc.).
**Catholic Pharmaceutical Guild,** Sec Gen, c/o 33 Carshalton Park Rd, Carshalton, Surrey.
**Catholic Psychology Group,** Sec, Spode House, Hawkesyard Priory, Rugeley, Staffs.
**Christian Healing Fellowship,** Sec, The Manse, Cokeham Lane, Sompting, Sussex. (Congregationalist, Baptist, Presbyterian).
**Christian Medical Fellowship (CMF),** Sec, 56 Kingsway, London WC2. T: (01)242-2361. (Also: 39 Bedford Square, London WC1B 3EY. T: (01) 636-5113. Profesional group in GF, UCCF).
**Church of England Hospital Chaplains' Fellowship,** Sec, Addenbrooke's Hospital, Hills Rd, Cambridge CB2 2QQ. T: (0223)45151.
**Churches' Council for Health and Healing,** Dir, St Peter's Vestry, Eaton Square, London SW1W 0HH. T: (01)235-3305.
**Council for the Deaf,** General Synod of the Church of England, Church House, Dean's Yard, London SWIP 3NZ. T: (01)222-9011.
**Council of Church Missioners to the Deaf and Dumb,** Hon Sec, 24 Beacon Close, Farnham, Surrey. T: 54579.
**Deaf Evangelical Fellowship,** Missioner, 6 Mill Hills, Todwick, Sheffield S31 0HT. T: Kiveton 771175.
**Disabled Christians' Fellowship,** Prince's Hall, Prince St, Bristol 1.
**Divine Healing Mission,** Crowhurst Home of Healing, Old Rectory, Crowhurst, near Battle, East Sussex. T: (042483)204.
**Edinburgh Medical Missionary Society,** Sec, 12 Mayfield Terrace, Edinburgh EH9 1SA. T: (031) 667-2518.
**Frickers Healing Centre,** 40 Howard Rd, London N15. T: STA 6668. (Also: 15 Wyndham Place, London W1. T: PAD 1150).
**Friends of Vellore,** 36 St George's St, Winchester, Hants. T: (0962)66239.
**Glasgow Catholic Medical Society,** 7 Victoria Rd, Paisley, Scotland.
**Guild of Health,** Sec, Edward Wilson House, 26 Queen Anne St, Harley St, London W1M 9LB. T: (01)580-2492. (Co-operation between doctors and churches).
**Guild of Pastoral Psychology,** Sec, 41 Redcliffe Gardens, London SW10. T: (01)352-6903. (C of E).
**Guild of St Luke, SS Cosmas and Domian,** Hon Sec, 228 Cranbrook Rd, Ilford, Essex. T: (01)554-7255. (Also: 7 Webster Coates Rd, Edinburgh 12). (Catholic doctors).
**Guild of St Raphael for the Ministry of Healing,** All Saints Vicarage, 7 Margaret St, London W1N 8JQ.
**Hospital Chaplaincies Council,** General Synod of the Church of England, Church House, Dean's Yard, London SW1P 3NZ. T: (01)222-9011.
**Hospitaller Order of St John of God,** St John of God Hospital, Scorton, Richmond, Yorks. T: (074) 881-5356.
**Institute of Religion and Medicine,** Organizing Sec, St Mary Abchurch Vestry, Abchurch Lane, London EC4N 7BA. T: (01)626-0306. (Formerly: 58a Wimpole St, W1M 7DE) (Psychology).
**Islington Medical Centre,** 303 Upper St, Islington, London N1. T: (01)226-3651.(Interdenominational medical mission).
**Japan Mission for Hospital Evangelism,** Sec, 18 Frensham Rd, New Eltham, London SE9 3RQ. T: (01)300-5859.
**Joint Mission Hospital Equipment Board,** 5 Robin Hood Lane, Sutton, Surrey. T: (01)643-8101. (Also: 124 Spa Rd, London SE16).
**Leprosy Mission International,** 50 Portland Place, W1N 3DG. T: (01)637-2611.
**Lingfield Hospital School,** Medical Dir, Lingfield, Surrey RH7 6PN. T: 2243. (320 epileptic boys and girls).
**London Healing Mission,** Chaplain, 20 Dawson Place, London W2. T: (01)229-3349.
**Ludhiana British Fellowship,** 157 Waterloo Rd, London SE1 8UU. T: (01)928-1173.
**Medical Missionary Association (MMA),** Sec, 6 Canonbury Place, London N1 2NJ. T:(01)359-1313.
**Mental After Care Association,** Sec, 110 Jermyn St, London SW1Y 6HB. T: (01)839-5953.
**Mental Health Trust and Research Fund,** 8 Wimpole St, London W1M 8HY. T: (01)580-0145.
**Mildmay Mission Hospital,** Hackney Rd, London E2 7NA. T: (01)739-2331.
**Missionary School of Medicine,** 2 Powis Place, Great Ormond St, London WC1N 3HT. T: (01) 837-5832.
**National Association for Mental Health (MIND),** 22 Harley St, London W1N 2ED.
**National Federation of Spiritual Healers,** Administrator, 12 Gloucester Place, London W1. (2,000 practitioners).
**Nurses Christian Fellowship International,** 157 Waterloo Rd, London SE1 8UU.
**Nurses Christian Fellowship (NCF),** Central Dir, 277a Ewell Rd, Surbiton, Surrey KT6 7AX. T: (01) 390-2626.
**Nurses' Christian Movement,** 5 St Martin's Place, London WC2.
**Richmond Fellowship,** Dir, 8 Addison Rd, Kensington, London W14 8DL. T: (01)603-6373/4/5. (Clergy education in mental health; therapeutic communities).
**Royal Association in Aid of the Deaf and Dumb,** 7/11 Armstrong Rd, Acton, London W3 7JL. T: (01) 743-6187. (In Diocese of London and 5 others).
**St Cecilia's Guild for the Catholic Blind,** Sec, 21 Elvin Crescent, Rottingdean, Brighton BN2 7EF.
**St Christopher's Hospice,** Laurie Park Rd, London SE16. (Incurables).
**St Francis Leprosy Guild,** Sec, FMM, 20 The Boltons, London SW10. T: (01)370-4388. (RC).
**St John's Guild for the Blind,** Gen Sec, 44 Abingdon Rd, Luton, Beds. T: (0582)57824.
**St Joseph's Hospice Association,** Dir, Metropolitan Cathedral Bldgs, Brownlow Hill, Liverpool L3 5RQ. (RC; incurables).
**St Luke's Nursing Home for the Clergy,** Sec, 14 Fitzroy Square, London W1P 0AH. T: (01) 387-1382.
**Scottish Pastoral Association,** Joint Sec, St Mary's College, St Andrews.(Psychology and religion).
**Seamen's Christian Friend Society Hospital Trust,** 46 Denison House, Vauxhall Bridge Rd, London SW1. (King George V Hospital, Malta).
**Sheffield School of Christian Psychotherapy,** 12 Marden Rd, Sheffield S7 1RE.
**Society of Our Lady of Lourdes,** Hon Sec, 110 Horseferry Rd, London SW1. T: (01)222-2286. (RC. Pilgrimages for the sick).
**Torch Trust for the Blind,** Torch House, 4 Hassocks Rd, Hurstpierpoint, Sussex BN6 9QN. T: 2282.
**World Federation for Mental Health,** Department of Psychiatry, Royal Edinburgh Hospital, Morningside Park, Edinburgh 10. (Also: 10 Av des Amazones, CH-1224 Chêne-Bougeries, Genève, Switzerland).

*USA*
**American Baptist Homes and Hospitals Association,** Sec, Valley Forge, PA 19481.
**American Committee for IME,** c/o Africa Committee DOM, NCCUSA, 475 Riverside Drive, New York, NY 10027. (Institut Médical Evangélique, Kimpese, Zaire).
**American Federation of Catholic Workers for the Blind and Visually Handicapped,** 106 East 41st St, New York, NY 10017.
**American Foundation of Religion and Psychiatry,** Dir, 3 West 29th St, New York, NY 10001. T: (212)685-6138.
**American Leprosy Missions,** 297 Park Av South, New York, NY 10010. T: (212)475-5854.
**Apostolate of Suffering,** 1551 North 34th St, Milwaukee, WI 53208.
**Association for Clinical Pastoral Education,** Exec Dir, 475 Riverside Drive, New York, NY 10027. T: (212)870-2558.
**Association of Mental Hospital Chaplains (AMHC),** Hudson River State Hospital, Poughkeepsie, New York.
**Baker Palace,** 730 Baker St, San Francisco, California. (Mental Health).
**Bible & Medical Missionary Fellowship USA (BMMF),** 38 Garrett Rd, Upper Darby, PA 19082. T: (215)352-0581.
**Biola School of Missionary Medicine,** 558 South Hope St, Los Angeles, CA 90017.
**Broadcast Service for the Blind,** Dir of Broadcasting, St John's University, Collegeville, MN 56321.
**Carrol Rehabilitation Center for the Visually Impaired,** 770 Centre St, Newton, MA 02158.
**Catholic Hospital Association,** 1438 South Grand Blvd, St Louis, MO 63104.
**Catholic Medical Mission Board,** 10 West 17th St, New York, NY 10011.
**Christian Dental Society,** Pres, 868 North University Av, Provo, UT 84601. T: (801)375-3797.
**Christian Medical Council,** DOM, NCCCUSA, 475 Riverside Drive, New York, NY 10027. T: (212) 870-2454/5.
**Christian Mission for Deaf Africans,** PO Box 1452, Detroit, MI 48231.
**Christian Record Braille Foundation,** 4444 South 52nd St, PO Box 6097, Lincoln, NE 68506. T: (402)488-0981. (Seventh-day Adventist).
**Conference of Catholic Schools of Nursing,** 1438 South Grand Blvd, St Louis, MO 63104.
**Deaf Missions,** Route 2, Council Bluffs, IA 51501.
**Episcopal Conference of the Deaf,** 4 St Martin's Rd, Baltimore, MD 21218.
**Episcopal Guide for the Blind,** 157 Montague, Brooklyn, NY 11201. T: (212)625-4886.
**Evangelical Deaf Mission,** 3231 SE 150th, Portland, OR 97236. (Founded 1959 in Puerto Rico).
**Gospel Association for the Blind,** 15-16 122nd St, College Point, NY 11356. T: (212)353-7577.
**Group Ministry for Parents,** 8915 Timberside Drive, Houston, TX 77025. (Family mental health).
**Guild of Catholic Psychiatrists (GCP),** 1703 Rhode Island Av, NW, Washington, DC.
**Hospital Chaplains Ministry,** PO Box 1006, North Downey Station, Downey, CA 90240.
**Hospital Ministry,** Institute of Religion, Texas Medical Center, Houston, TX 77025.
**Institutional Ministry,** PO Box 774, Butner, NC 27509. (Mental health).
**International Catholic Deaf Association,** St John's School for the Deaf, Milwaukee, WI 53207.
**International Christian Leprosy Mission,** 6917 SW Oak St, PO Box 8164, Portland, OR 97207.
**International Dental Institute,** PO Box 1858, San Ysidro, CA 92073.
**International Federation of Catholic Medical Associations/Fédération Internationale des Associations Médicales Catholiques (FIAMC),** 7 Englewood Rd, Upper Darby, PA 19082. T: (215) 789-9525.
**John Milton Society for the Blind,** 475 Riverside Drive, New York, NY 10027.
**Kathryn Kuhlman Foundation,** Pres, 603 Carlton House, Pittsburgh, PA 15219. (Healing campaigns).
**Ludhiana Christian Medical College Board,** 475 Riverside Drive, New York, NY 10027. T: (212) 870-2641.
**Lutheran Institute of Human Ecology,** Medical Mission Program, 1800 West Dempster St, Park Ridge, IL 60068. T: (312)696-2210.
**Medical Amateur Radio Council,** Exec Sec, PO Box 229, Manchester, CT 06040.
**Medical Assistance Programs (MAP),** 327 Gundersen Drive, Carol Stream, Box 50, Wheaton, IL 60187. T: (312)653-6010. (Formerly Missionary Equipment Service).
**Medical Center Ministry,** 4 South Dunlap St, Memphis, TN 38103.
**Medical Mission Sisters,** 8400 Pine Rd, Philadelphia, PA 19111. T: (215)742-6100.
**Medical Supplies for Missions,** Pres, 612 South K St, Tacoma, WA 98405. T: (206)272-0244.
**Mexican Medical Mission,** 4636 Niagara St, San Diego, CA 92109.
**Misión Medica Independiente,** 6822 East 42nd St, Tucson, AZ 85701.
**Missionary Dentist,** PO Box 7002, Seattle, WA 98133. T: (206)546-1200.
**Missions to the Deaf,** PO Box 1031, San Jose, CA 95108. T: (408)243-7000.
**Narramore Christian Foundation,** 1409 North Walnut Grove Av, Rosemead, CA 91770. (Psychological testing, counselling etc).
**North American Committee for IME (Institut Médical Evangélique),** Apt 6, 3063 Virginia Av South, Minneapolis, MN 55426.
**Nurses Christian Fellowship (NCF),** 233 Langdon St, Madison, WI 53703.
**Sons of Mary, Health of the Sick (FMS),** 567 Salem End Rd, Framingham, MA 01701.
**Tainan Special Skin Clinic,** 4606 Av H, Lubbock, TX 79404. T: (806)742-5948.
**University Hospital Chaplains,** UCLA Center for Health Science, 10833 Le Conte Av, Los Angeles, CA 90024.
**Vellore Christian Medical College Board,** 475 Riverside Drive, New York, NY 10027. T: (212) 870-2642.
**Welfare of the Blind,** 4706 Bethesda Av, Bethesda, MD 20014. (Also: 4813 Woodway Lane, NW, Washington, DC 20016).
**Xavier Society for the Blind,** 154 East 23rd St, New York, NY 10010.

*ZAIRE*
**Bureau des Oeuvres Médicales,** BP 3258, Kinshasa-Gombe. T: 30057 ext 57.
**Institut Médical Evangélique (IME),** Mission Baptiste, Kimpese. (Interdenominational; hospital school & leprosarium).
**Union Missionnaire Hospitalière,** BP 3094, Kinshasa-Kalina.

*ZAMBIA*
**Churches' Medical Association of Zambia (CMAZ),** Unity House, Freedom Way, PO Box 1965, Lusaka. T: 73467,73470.
**Medical Assistance Service/Servico de Assistencia Medical (SAM-MPLA),** PO Box 1595, Lusaka. (Medical work in Angola).

*ZIMBABWE*
**Homeopathy Surgery,** Bureau of African Churches, Lobengula St, Bulawayo.

# 39 Military Chaplaincies

***Definition.*** Major organizations ministering to armed services at home or overseas (armies, navies, air forces, police forces, paramilitary units); military jurisdictions, bishops for armed services.

Over 200 significant organizations specialize primarily in ministry to armed services.

*ARGENTINA*
**Military Vicariate of Argentina,** Arzobispado, Suipacha 1034, Buenos Aires. (Catholic; 67 military chaplains, 112 auxiliaries).

*AUSTRALIA*
**Catholic Military Vicariate of Australia,** 3 Coral Place, Campbell, Canberra, ACT 2601.

*AUSTRIA*
**International Military Apostolate,** Kaiseralle 23, A-2100 Korneuburg. (Also: Militärvikariat, Mariahilferstr 24, A-1070 Wien. T: (0222)939666).
**Military Vicariate of Austria,** Domplatz 1, A-3100 Sankt Pölten. T: (02742)2101. (Catholic; 18 churches, 18 military chaplains).

*BELGIUM*
**Military Vicariate of Belgium,** Place de Jamblinne de Meux 38, B-1040 Brussel. T: (02)343498. (Catholic; 134 chapels, 108 military chaplains).

*BOLIVIA*
**Military Vicariate of Bolivia,** Calle Ingavi 44, Casilla 25, La Paz. (Catholic; 40 military chaplains).

*BRAZIL*
**Military Vicariate of Brazil,** CP 07-561, Brasília, DF. (Catholic; 23 churches, 97 military chaplains).

*CANADA*
**Catholic Military Vicariate of Canada/Division de l'Aumônier Général Catholique,** Quartiers Généraux des Forces Canadiennes, Ottowa K1A 0K2. T: (612)992-6025. (120 military chaplains, 60 auxiliaries).
**Officers Christian Union (OCU),** Royal Military College, Kingston, Ontario. (Protestant).

*CHILE*
**Military Vicariate of Chile,** Vicaría Castrense, Correo 8, Santiago. (Catholic; 18 churches, 23 military chaplains, 60 auxiliaries).

*CHINA (TAIWAN)*
**Overseas Christian Servicemen's Centres,** PO Box 332, Taichung. T: 91603.
**World Military Missions Crusade,** 91 Chien Yeh Village, Tsoying.

*COLOMBIA*
**Military Vicariate of Colombia,** Arzobispado, Correo 7 N 10-20, Bogotá, DE. (Catholic; 1 church, 7 military chaplains, 60 auxiliaries).

*DOMINICAN REPUBLIC*
**Military Vicariate of the Dominican Republic,** Arzobispado, Apdo 186, Santo Domingo. (Catholic).

*EL SALVADOR*
**Military Vicariate of El Savador,** Obispado, Apdo Postal 43, San Miguel. (Catholic).

*FRANCE*
**Aumônerie Militaire,** Aumônier Général, FPF, 47 Rue de Clichy, F-75009 Paris. T: 874-7742. (Protestant).
**Military Vicariate of France,** 20 Rue Notre-Dame-des-Champs, F-75006 Paris. T: 222-4130. (Catholic; 256 churches, 227 chaplains, 225 auxiliaries).

*GERMANY, Federal Republic of*
**Catholic Military Vicariate of Germany,** Zwölfling 16, Postfach 1428, D-4300 Essen. (114 military chaplains, 39 auxiliaries).
**Evangelisches Kirchenamt (EKD) für die Bundeswehr,** Kölner Str 107a, D-53 Bonn-Bad Godesberg. (German Army).

*INDONESIA*
**Catholic Military Vicariate of Indonesia,** Jalan Pandanaran 13, Semarang, Java. (15 military chaplains, 114 auxiliaries).

*ITALY*
**Accademia Allievi Cappellani Militari (Castrense Collegio),** Vicario Generale Militare, Rettore, Salita del Grillo 37, I-00184 Roma. T: 675100.
**Military Vicariate of Italy,** Salita del Grillo 37, I-000184 Roma. T: (06)6795100. (Catholic; 210 churches & chapels, 319 chaplains).

*KENYA*
**Catholic Military Vicariate of Kenya,** PO Box 14231, Nairobi.
**Officers' Christian Fellowship (OCU),** PO Box 40668, Nairobi. T: 27411. (Protestant).

*KOREA South*
**World Military Missions Crusade,** Armed Forces Service Center, 35 Hwa-Chung Dong, Chinhae.

*MADAGASCAR*
**Aumônerie Protestante de l'Armée Nationale,** College Soamiandry, Ampasampito, Tananarive.

*NETHERLANDS*
**Catholic Military Vicariate of the Netherlands,** Aartbisdom, Maliedaan 40, Utrecht. (60 churches, 105 chaplains).

*OMAN*
**Mission to Military Garrisons,** Royal Air Force, Mazirah.

*PACIFIC ISLANDS*
**Island Memorial Chapel,** Kwajalein, Marshall Islands, Protestant Chaplain, Box 1711, APO San Francisco, USA 96555.

*PARAGUAY*
**Military Vicariate of Paraguay,** Av Mariscal

López y Pai Pérez 410, Asunción. T: 23329. (Catholic; 24 chaplains).

*PERU*
**Military Vicariate of Peru,** Av Tacna 482, Lima. T: 249395. (Catholic; 66 chaplains).

*PHILIPPINES*
**Military Vicariate of the Philippines,** 1000 General Solano St, San Miguel, Manila. (Catholic; 44 military chaplains).
**Overseas Christian Servicemen's Centers,** Subic Service Center, Olongapo City, Zambales.

*PORTUGAL*
**Military Vicariate of Portugal,** Rua da Cova da Moura 1, Lisboa 3. (Catholic; 206 chaplains).

*SOUTH AFRICA*
**Catholic Military Vicariate of South Africa,** Archbishop's House, Main St, Pretoria.

*SPAIN*
**Military Vicariate of Spain,** Calle Nuncio 13, Madrid 5. T: 2653654. (Catholic; 15 churches, 150 chapels, 341 chaplains, 66 auxiliaries).

*SWITZERLAND*
**Armeeseelsorge,** Feldpredigerchef, Herrengasse 22, CH-3000 Bern.

*UGANDA*
**Catholic Military Vicariate of Uganda,** Bishop's House, PO Box 200, Gulu.

*UK OF GB & NI*
**Bishopric of the Forces,** 54 Ennismore Gardens, London SW7. T: (01)589-1273. (RC).
**Catholic Military Vicariate of Great Britain,** 54 Ennismore Gardens, London SW7. (34 churches, 225 chapels, 116 military chaplains, 488 auxiliaries).
**Royal Navy Chaplain of the Fleet,** Ministry of Defence, Lacon House, Theobalds Rd, London WC1X 8RY. T: (01)242-0222.
**Church of England Soldiers', Sailors, & Airmen's Clubs (CESSAC),** Central Office, 1 Shakespeare Terrace, High St, Portsmouth, Hants PO1 2RH. T: (0705)29319. (Begun 1891).
**Guild of St Helena,** Chief Sec, Duke of York's Headquarters, Kings Rd, Chelsea, London SW3. T: (01)730-3477 ext 154. (Aid to soldiers' families).
**Mission to Mediterranean Garrisons,** Ashfield House, 402 Sauchiehall St, Glasgow G2 3JH, Scotland. T: (041)332-2438.
**Mission to Military Garrisons,** Sec, Ashfield House, 402 Sauchiehall St, Glasgow G2 3JH, Scotland. T: (041)332-2438.
**Naval Military & Air Force Bible Society,** Radstock House, Eccleston St, London SW1.
**Officers' Christian Union (OCU),** 35 Catherine Place, London SW1. (Protestant, Anglican).
**Royal Air Force Chaplains Branch,** Chaplain-in-Chief, Ministry of Defence (RAF), Adastral House, Theobalds Rd, London WC1X 8RU. T: (01)405-3434 ext 7268.
**Royal Army Chaplains' Department,** Chaplain General, Ministry of Defence (Army), Landsdowne House, Berkeley Square, London W1X 6AA. T: (01) 499-8040. (Chaplains' Centre: Bagshot Park, Surrey GU19 5PL. T: (0276)71717).
**Royal Naval Lay Readers' Society,** Sec, Ministry of Defence, Lacon House, Theobalds Rd, London WCIX 8RY. T: (01)242-0222 ext 847.
**Sandes Soldiers' & Airmens' Homes,** Gen Sec, 508 Scottish Provident Bldg, 7 Donegall Square West, Belfast BT1 6JG, NI. T: 25724.
**Soldiers' and Airmen's Scripture Readers' Association (SASRA),** Gen Sec, Havelock House, 35 Catherine Place, London SW1E 6ER. T: (01) 834-1314/5.
**Toc H,** Gen Sec, 15 Trinity St, London SW1. T: (01) 222-1033.

*USA*
**Catholic Military Vicariate of the USA,** 451 Madison Av, New York, NY 10022. (3,000 chapels, 835 chaplains, 715 auxiliaries).
**Chaplaincy Endorsement Commission,** Christian Churches & Churches of Christ, Box 637, Johnson City, TN 37601.
**Charlie Brown Coffee House,** 6217th Combat Support Group, CMR Box 3585, APO San Francisco 96319.
**Christian Churches & Churches of Christ Military Fellowship,** Box 177, Kempton, IN 46049. (Also: 802 W Delaware, Fairfield, IL 62837).
**Christian Servicemen's Fellowship,** Exec Sec, 1405 G St, NW, Washington, DC 20005. (Evangelical).
**Commission of Chaplains,** United Methodist Church, 475 Riverside Drive, New York, NY 10027.
**General Commission on Chaplains and Armed Forces Personnel,** Exec Sec, 122 Maryland Av, NE, Washington, DC 20002. T: (202)L17-8310.
**Military Chaplains Association of the USA (MCA),** Sec, Suite 235, 2300 Connecticut Av, NW, Washington, DC 20008.
**Officers Christian Fellowship,** Exec Dir, 3100 South Sheridan, Box 19398, Denver, CO 80219.
**Overseas Christian Servicemen's Centers,** 2100 South Lincoln St, PO Box 19188 & 10308, Denver, CO 80219.
**Summer Ministry to Off-Duty Servicemen,** US Naval Chaplain School, Newport, RI 02840.
**Travis International Hospitality (TIHI),** Dir, PO Box 1223, Travis Air Force Base, CA 94535. T: (707)422-8600. (East Tabor & Solano Av, Fairfield, CA 94533).
**World Military Missions Crusade,** Exec Dir, 846 Fifth Av, PO Box 2001, San Diego, CA 91212. T: (714)234-1300.

*VIET NAM*
**Vietnamese Military Evangelism,** PO Box 410, Saigon. (Until 1975).

# 40
# Monasteries & Religious Houses

***Definition.*** Catholic, Orthodox, Anglican, Protestant and other monasteries, abbeys, priories, convents, mother houses of religious orders and congregations, retreat centres, ashrams, spiritual life centres, religious communities, brotherhoods, sisterhoods, et alia.

These centres for the religious life number many thousands, hence cannot be listed here. Listings will be found in various yearbooks listed under DIRECTORIES.

# 41
# Music & Song

***Definition.*** Choirs, evangelistic groups, singing groups, Christian pop groups, discotheques, coffee houses, libraries of religious music, Christian recording organizations, church music training centres, musicals (shows), opera, rock opera, festivals; campanology, bell-ringing. See also LITURGY AND WORSHIP.

In this field, organizations of major significance number over 200.

*AUSTRALIA*
**Music Advisory Committee,** Australian Episcopal Liturgical Commission, Catholic Presbytery, 33 Howard St, West Melbourne, Victoria 3033. T: 303474.

*FRANCE*
**Association des Choeurs d'Eglise Protestantes d'Alsace-Lorraine,** Sec, 4 Cem de la Holzmatt, Strasbourg 3. T: 300088.
**Fédération Musique et Chant du Protestantisme Français,** Prés, 8 Villa du Parc Montsouris, F-75014 Paris. T: 5895569.
**Institut de Musique Liturgique,** 21 Rue d'Assas, F-75006 Paris. T: (01)222-1027.
**Union Fédérale Français de Musique Sacrée (UFFMS),** 16 Rue du Regard, F-75006 Paris. T: (01)222-4233.

*GERMANY, Federal Republic of*
**Deutsche Arbeitsgemeinschaft für Gesangbuchreform,** Rumannstr 10, D-3 Hannover.
**Direktorenkonferenz der Ev Kirchenmusikalischen Ausbildungsstätten Deutschlands,** Friedrich-Ebert-Anlage 62, D-69 Heidelberg.
**Institut für Kirchenmusik der Universität Erlangen-Nürnberg,** Kochstr 6, D-8520. T: (09131) 8512226.
**International Association of Music Libraries (IAML),** Standeplatz 16, D-35 Kassel. T: 12277.
**Verband Evangelischer Kirchenchöre Deutschlands,** Reitwallstr 8, D-3 Hannover.
**Verband Evangelischer Kirchenmusiker Deutschlands,** Domplatz 5, D-672 Speyer.
**Zentralstelle für Evangelische Kirchenmusik,** Jebensstr 1, D-1 Berlin 12.

*HOLY SEE*
**Pontificio Instituto di Musica Sacra,** Piazza San Agostino 20A, I-00186 Roma, Italy. T: 6540422. (RC).

*HUNGARY*
**Hungarian Association of St Cecilia (Országos Magyar Cecilia Egyesület),** Mártirok ut ja 64/b, 1027 Budapest.

*ITALY*
**Consociatio Internationalis Musicae Sacrae (CIMS),** Piazza San Agostino 20A, I-00139 Roma. T: 6540422.
**International Federation of Pueri Cantores,** Piazza Augusto Imperatore 6, I-00186 Roma. T: 680619.

*JAPAN*
**Japan Church Music Publishing Society,** 2-193 Ogikubo, Suginami-ku, Tokyo 167.

*KENYA*
**Kenya Church Music Society (KCMS),** Sec, PO Box 41482, Nairobi.
**Nairobi Youth Christian Choirs Association,** Sec, St Stephen's Church, Jogoo Rd, PO Box 50005, Nairobi. T: 55168.

*MEXICO*
**Comisión Episcopal de Litúrgia, Música y Arte de México,** Apdo M-2181, México. T: 5355589.
**Conjunto Bethel,** Pesos No 32, Zona 9, México, DF. T: 346303.
**Coro Amen,** Pino No 68, Zona 20, México.

*NEW ZEALAND*
**Contemporary Hymns (NZ),** PO Box 2437, Christchurch.

*NORWAY*
**Musica Sacra,** Prof Dahlsgt 7, Oslo 3.
**Norwegian Society of Organists (Norges Organistforbund),** Bleikerfaret 63, Asker.

*SWITZERLAND*
**Arbeitskreis für Evangelische Kirchenmusik,** Sek, Zollikerstr 233, CH-8008 Zürich. T: (051)534545.
**Cantate Domino,** CH-1870 Monthey/VD.
**Christliche Sängerbund der Schweiz (CSS),** Präs, Muristr 70, CH-3000 Bern. T: (031)447807.
**Evangelische Singgemeinde,** Leimenstr 4, CH-4000 Basel. T: (061)247062.
**Institut für Kirchenmusik in Zürich,** Leitung, Brühlbergstr 47, CH-8400 Winterthur. T: (052) 234507.
**Schweizerische Kirchengesangsbund,** Präs, Bernstr 85, CH-3018 Bern.
**Société de Chant Sacré,** Prés, 22 Av de Châtelaine, Genève. T: 452421.

*UK OF GB & NI*
**Ancient Society of College Youths,** Hon Sec, 21A Fieldhouse Rd, London SW12 0HL. T: (01) 673-2720. (Bell-ringers. Founded 1637).
**Archbisho of Canterbury's Certificate in Church Music,** Registrar, IGCM, 16 The Cloisters, Windsor Castle, Berks.
**Cathedral Organists' Association,** Addington Palace, Croydon CR9 5AD. T: (01)654-7676.
**Celebration Services,** Yeldall Manor, Hare Hatch, Twyford, Berks RG10 9XR. T: (073522)2272. (Charismatic renewal).
**Central Council of Church Bell-Ringers,** Sec, 19 Ravensgate Rd, Charlton Kings, Cheltenham, Glos GL53 8NR. T: (0242)32454.
**Choir Benevolent Fund,** Sec, Foxearth Cottage, Frittenden, Cranbrook, Kent. T: (05809)225.
**Choir Schools Association,** Sec, Cathedral Choir School, Ripon, Yorks. T: (0765)2134.
**Christian Development Service,** St Mark's Church Chambers, Kennington Park Rd, London SE11 4PW. T: (01)582-9335. (Produces musicals: 'Come Together', 'If My People').
**Church Music Association (CMA),** 171 Victoria St, London SW1E 5LR. T: (01)828-5775. (Also 24 Ashley Place, London SW1). (Formed 1955).
**Church Music Society,** 4 The Rookery, Blasham, Cambridge CB1 6EV. T: (022)029259. (Formed 1906).
**Come Together,** 7 Oxshott Way, Cobham, Surrey. T: 3522,5426. (Charismatic musical worship).
**Friends of Cathedral Music,** The Wardenry, Farley, Salisbury. (Also: 7 Tufton St, London SW1).
**Gregorian Association,** Gen Sec, 67 Grange Crescent, Grange Hill, Chigwell, Essex. T: (01) 500-3457.
**Guild of Congregational Organists and Choirmasters,** Sec, 6 The Lees, Malvern, Worcs.
**Hymn Society of Great Britain & Ireland,** 12 St John's Rd, Knutsford, Cheshire.
**Incorporated Guild of Church Musicians,** Sec, 7 Tufton St, London, SW1.
**International Music Editorial Department,** Salvationist Publishing and Supplies Ltd, 117-121 Judd St, King's Cross, London, WC1. T: (01)387-1656.
**International Organ Festival Society,** Artistic Dir, 31 Abbey Mill Lane, St Albans AL1 1BY. T: 64738. (Biennial festival since 1961; 1975 in St Albans Cathedral).
**Livingston Organs & Church Furnishings Ltd,** Greycaines House, Greycaines Rd, North Watford, Herts, T: 27378.
**Los Picaflores (The Humming Birds),** Sec, SAMS, 157 Waterloo Rd, London SE1. T: (01) 928-3188.
**Methodist Church Music Society,** 1 Central Bldgs, Westminster, London SW1. T: (01)930-7608.
**Musical Gospel Outreach,** 10 Seaforth Av, New Malden, Surrey KT3 6JP. T: (01)942-8847.
**Psalms & Hymns Trust,** Sec, 4 Southampton Row, London WC1B 4AB.
**Royal School of Church Music (RSCM),** Sec, Addington Palace, Croydon, Surrey CR9 5AD. T: (01)654-7676.
**St Mary-of-the-Angels Song School Trust,** Principal, 79 Ashacre Lane, Offington, Worthing, West Sussex BN13 2DE. T: (0903)60927.
**Scope,** Park Lane, Hemel Hempstead, Herts HP2 4TD.
**Walker Organs,** JW Walker & Sons, Braintree Rd, Ruislip, Middx. T: (01)845-6501.

*USA*
**Atrec Productions,** 1688 Meridian Av, Miami, FL 33139.
**Bullseye Music Inc,** 6525 Selma Av, Hollywood, CA 90028.
**Chimes Record & Music Co,** 34816 Yucaipa Blvd, Yucaipa CA 92399.
**Christian Music Association,** Route 1, Box 349, Croton-on-Hudson, NY 10520.
**Composers' Forum for Catholic Worship,** PO Box 8554, Sugar Creek, MO 64054.
**Diadem Productions Inc,** 1553 Plainfield Av, NE, Grand Rapids, MI 49505.
**Fiesta Music Inc,** Box 2471, Hollywood, CA 90028.
**Gospel Artists Unlimited,** MPO Box 766, Springfield, MO 65801.
**Gospel Music Association,** Exec Sec, 817 18th Av South, Nashville, TN 37203.
**Grand Rapids School of the Bible and Music,** 110 Crescent St, NE, Grand Rapids, MI 49503.
**Hamblen Music Co,** Box 46-294, Los Angeles, CA 90046.
**Manna Music Inc,** 1328 North Highland Av, Hollywood, CA 90028.
**Mieir Choir Clinic,** 1328 North Highland Av, Hollywood, CA 90028.
**Mills Music Inc,** 1619 Broadway, New York, NY 10019.
**Music Enterprises,** Jeffers, MN 56145.
**RE Winsett Music Co,** Box 327, Dayton, TN 37321.
**Westminister Choir College,** Pres Hamilton at Walnut, Princeton, NJ 08540.
**World Library of Sacred Music (WLSM),** 2145 Central Parkway, Cincinnati, OH 45214. (Publishers, distributors for music, records, etc, Catholic & Protestant).

*ZIMBABWE*
**Kwanongoma College of Music,** United College of Education, Old Falls Rd, PB T 5392, Bulawayo. T: 62990.

# 42
# National Conciliarism

***Definition.*** Interdenominational or ecumenical councils of churches or denominations and dioceses of different ecclesiastical traditions, occasionally including foreign missionary societies, either (NATIONAL) for a single nation, or (PLURINATIONAL) for a small grouping of 2 or 3 adjacent nations included in the council's title; councils, federations, alliances, fellowships; Roman Catholic national episcopal or bishops' conferences, national inter-rite assemblies; national conciliarism, collegiality and consultation; including the remaining 3 or 4 missionary councils (councils of foreign missions at work in a nation), but excluding interreligious national councils open to non-Christian bodies (for these, see INTERRELIGIOUS ORGANIZATIONS).

Nationwide councils or fellowships of churches of all kinds number some 550.

*ALGERIA*
**Association des Eglises et Oeuvres Protestantes en Algérie,** Sec, c/o 78 Chemin Beaurepaire, El-Biar, El Djezair. T: 783291.

*AMERICAN SAMOA*
**Interdenominational Committee of American Samoa,** PO Box 468, Apia, Western Samoa.

*ANGOLA*
**Alianca Evangélica de Angola,** CP 230, Nova Lisboa. (Also CP 29, Caluquembe).
**Conferência Episcopal de Angola e São Tomé (CEAST),** Largo de Palacio 9, CP 1230, Luanda. T: 25791.

*ANTIGUA*
**Antigua Christian Council,** Pres, PO Box 863, St John's.

*ARGENTINA*
**Confederación de Iglesias Evangélicas del Río de la Plata,** Tucumán 358, 60L, Buenos Aires.
**Conferencia Episcopal Argentina (CEA),** Calle Paraguay 1867, Buenos Aires. T: 313317.
**Federación Argentina de Iglesias Evangélicas (FAIE),** Pres, Tucumán 358, Piso 6 L, Buenos Aires 6. T: 317432.

*AUSTRALIA*
**Australian Consultative Council of the ICCC,** 22 Angwin Av, Blair Athol, South Australia.
**Australian Council of Churches (ACC),** Gen Sec, 401A Pitt St, Sydney, PO Box 111, Brickfield Hill, NSW 2001. T: 262901.
**Australian Episcopal Conference (AEC),** 12 Kennedy St, PO Box 297, Kingston, ACT 2604. T: 283539.
**Australian Evangelical Alliance,** 4 Wellesley St, Mont Albert, Victoria 3127. T: (03)836-6079.

*AUSTRIA*
**Evangelische Allianz Österreichs,** c/o Richtergasse 3/11/8, A-1070 Wien. T: 9319163.
**Ökumenischer Rat der Kirchen in Österreich,** Schottenring 17, A-1010 Wien. (Also: Kolonitzgasse 11, A-1030 Wien).
**Österreichische Bischofskonferenz,** Rotenturmstr 2, A-1010 Wien. T: (0222)529511.

*BAHAMAS*
**Bahamas Christian Council,** Sec, PO Box 4014, Nassau.

*BANGLADESH*
**Bangladesh National Council of Churches (Jatio Church Parishad),** Exec Sec, 9 New Eskaton Rd, Ramna, PO Box 220, Dacca 2. T: 282869.
**Catholic Bishops' Conference of Bangladesh (CBCB),** Archbishop's House, PO Box 3, Ramna, Dacca 2. T: 242379.

*BARBADOS*
**Barbados Council of Evangelical Churches (BCEC),** PO Box 818E, Eagle Hall, St Michael.
**Barbados Ministerial Association,** Exec Sec, Belmont Manse, Welches Territory.

*BELGIUM*
**Conférence Episcopale de Belgique/Bisschoppenconferentie van België,** Aartsbisdom Mechelen, Wollemarkt 15, B-2800 Mechelen. T: (015)16501. (Also: Rue Guimard 5, B-1040 Brussel. T: (02)511-8256).
**Fédération des Eglises Protestantes de Belgique/ Federatie der Protestantse Kerken van België,** Sec, Rue du Champs de Mars 5, B-1050 Brussel. T: (02)743154.

*BELIZE*
**Belize Christian Social Council,** Sec, 149 Allenby St, PO Box 508, Belize City. T: 2077.

*BENIN*
**Conférence Episcopale du Benin,** Archevêché, BP 491, Cotonou. T: 313145.

*BOLIVIA*
**Asociación Nacional de Evangélicos de Bolivia (ANDEB),** Casilla 4810, La Paz.
**Confederation of Fundamental Evangelical Churches of Bolivia,** Casilla 953, Cochabamba.
**Conferencia Episcopal de Bolivia (CEB),** Casilla 129, Cochabamba.

*BOTSWANA*
**Botswana Association of Inter Spiritual Churches,** Gen Sec, PO Box 374, Gaberone.

**Botswana Spiritual Christian Churches,** PO Box 183, Francistown.
**Christian Council of Botswana,** Gen Sec, PO Box 355, Gaberone.
**Evangelical Fellowship of Botswana,** PO Box 59, Francistown.

*BRAZIL*
**Confederação das Igrejas Evangélicas Fundamentalistas (CIEF),** Rua 14 de Julho 285, São Paulo, SP.
**Confederação Evangélica Brasileira (or, CE do Brasil),** Exec Sec, Rua Braulio Gomes 25, 4 andar, s/405, 01047 São Paulo, SP.
**Conferência Nacional dos Bispos do Brasil (CNBB),** Av L3 Sul, ES801, Lt 1-A, CP 13-2067, 70000 Brasília, DF. T: 2422404.

*BRITISH VIRGIN ISLANDS*
**Tortola Inter-Church Council,** PO Box 33, Road Town, Tortola.

*BULGARIA*
**Bulgarian Catholic Bishops' Conference,** Ul Pashovi 10B, Sofiya VI.

*BURMA*
**Burma Catholic Bishops' Conference (BCBC),** 292 Prome Rd, Sanchaung PO, Rangoon. T: 12752.
**Burma Council of Churches,** Gen Sec, Central YMCA Building, 263 Maha Bandoola St, Rangoon. T:13290.

*BURUNDI*
**Alliance des Eglises Protestantes du Burundi (AEPB),** Gen Sec, BP 17, Bujumbura.
**Conférence des Ordinaires du Rwanda et du Burundi (COREB),** 5 Av de l'Uprona, BP 690, Bujumbura. T: 3263.

*CAMEROON*
**Episcopal Conference of Cameroon/Conférence Episcopale Nationale du Cameroun,** BP 207, Yaoundé/PO Box 82, Mankon-Bamenda.
**Fédération des Eglises et Missions Evangéliques du Cameroun (FEMEC),** Gen Sec, BP 491, Yaoundé. T: 222821.

*CANADA*
**Canadian Anglican Evangelical Fellowship,** Box 731, Station F, Toronto, Ontario.
**Canadian Catholic Conference/Conférence Catholique Canadienne (CCC),** 90 Parent Av, Ottawa, Ontario K1N 7B1. T: (613)236-9461.
**Canadian Council of Churches/Conseil Chrétien des Eglises (CCC),** Gen Sec, 40 St Clair Av East, Toronto, Ontario M4T 1M9. T: (416)921-4152.
**Canadian Council of Evangelical Protestant Churches,** 130 Gerrard St East, Toronto 2, Ontario.
**Canadian Unitarian Council,** 175 St Clair Av, W Toronto 195, Ontario.
**Evangelical Fellowship of Canada,** Pres, Box 8800, Station B, Willowdale, Ontario M2K 2R6. T: (416)499-1937.
**Lutheran Council in Canada,** 500-365 Hargrave St, Winnipeg, Manitoba R3B 2K3. T: (204)942-0096.
**Ukrainian Catholic Metropolitan Conference,** Archbishop's House, 235 Scotie St, Winnipeg 17, Manitoba R2V IV7. T: (204)339-7457.

*CENTRAL AFRICAN REPUBLIC*
**Association des Eglises Evangéliques Centrafricaines,** Sec, BP 240, Bangui.
**Conférence des Evêques de la République Centrafricaine (CERCA),** BP 798, Bangui. T: 2188.

*CHAD*
**Conférence Episcopale du Tchad,** Archevêché, BP 456, Ndjamena (Fort Lamy). T: 2711.
**Fédération des Eglises Evangéliques du Tchad,** BP 127, Ndjamena.

*CHILE*
**Concilio Evangélico de Chile (CEC),** Exec Sec, Bombero Salas 1351, Of 250, Casilla 14025 Correo 15, Santiago. T: 83715.
**Confederación Fundamentalista de Iglesias Evangélicas de Chile (CFEC, or CIEF),** (Confederation of Ev Fundamentalist Churches of Chile), Aranco 890, Chillán.
**Conferencia Episcopal de Chile (CECH),** Cienfuegos 47, Casilla 13191 Correo 21, Santiago. T: 717733,81416.
**Unión de Misiones Pentecostales Libres,** Obispo Presidente, Casilla 14727, Correo 21, Santiago. T: 375680. (35 affiliated member bodies).

*CHINA*
**Catholic Patriotic Association,** Beijing.
**National Christian Council of China,** Missions Bldg, 169 Yuan Ming Yuan Rd, Shanghai. (Defunct since 1950 but still listed as a CWME-affiliated council by WCC).
**Protestant Three-Self Movement,** Beijing.

*CHINA (TAIWAN)*
**Evangelical Fellowship of Taiwan,** 4-2 Chin Hsi St, PO Box 2102, Taipei.
**Republic of China Council of Christian Churches,** PO Box 1200, Taipei.
**Taiwan Ecumenical Co-operative Committee,** Sec, c/o YMCA, 19 Hsu Chang St, Taipei.

*COLOMBIA*
**Asociación Evangélica pro-Indigena de Colombia (Evangelical Association for the Indians of Colombia),** Apdo Aéreo 29225, Bogotá, DE.
**Confederación Evangélica de Colombia (CEDEC),** Exec Sec, Apdo Aéreo 3604, Bogotá, DE.
**Conferencia Episcopal de Colombia,** Apdo 7448, Bogotá, DE. T: 414186,2437700.

*CONGO*
**Conférence Episcopale du Congo,** BP 2301, Brazzaville.
**Fédération des Eglises Chrétiennes du Congo,** BP 3205, Bacongo-Brazzaville. (Began 1970).

*COSTA RICA*
**Alianza Evangélica Costarricense,** Apdo 5134, San José.
**Alianza Evangélica de Costa Rica,** Apdo 901, San José.
**Conferencia Episcopal de Costa Rica (CECOR),** Arzobispado, Apdo 497, San José. T: 218048.

*CUBA*
**Conferencia Episcopal de Cuba (CEC),** Arzobispado, Apdo 26, Santiago de Cuba. T: 54801.
**Consejo de Iglesias Evangélicas de Cuba,** Exec Sec, Calle 6 No 273 E/11 y 13, Vedado, Apdo 4179, La Habana 4.

*CZECHOSLOVAKIA*
**Ecumenical Council of Churches in the Czech Socialist Republic, ECCC (Ekumenická Rada Církví v Ceske Socialisticke Republice),** Sec, Jungmannova 9, Praha 1. T: 248866.

*DENMARK*
**Council of Free Churches (Evangelisk Frikirkerad),** Chairman, Toftefaeksvej 15, DK-2800, Lyngby.
**Ecumenical Council of Denmark (Okumeniske Faellesrad i Danmark),** Sec, Norregade 11, DK-1165 Kobenhavn K. T: (01)145949.
**Evangelical Alliance of Denmark (Evangelisk Alliance i Danmark),** Skansebjerg 12, DK-2700 Kobenhavn-Bronshoj.

*DOMINICA*
**Dominica Christian Council,** Sec, PO Box 92, Roseau.

*DOMINICAN REPUBLIC*
**Conferencia del Episcopado Dominicano (CED),** Arzobispado, Apdo 186, Santo Domingo, DN. (Also: Av García Godoy 32, La Vega).
**Servicio Social de Iglesias Dominicanas (SSID),** c/o Unelam, 19 de Marco No 62, Santo Domingo.

*ECUADOR*
**Conferencia Episcopal Ecuatoriana,** Av America 1866 y La Gasca, Apdo 1081, Quito. T: 38221,39596.
**Confraternidad Evangélica Ecuatoriana (CEE),** Casilla 455 & 2990, Quito.

*EGYPT*
**Bishops' Assembly of Egypt (Assemblée des Ordinaires de la RAU),** Patriarcat Grec-Catholique, Daher St, Faggalah, Al Qahirah.
**Catholic Inter-Rite Assembly (Assemblée Interrituelle Catholique),** Apostolic Nunciature, Safarat Al-Vatican, 5 Sharia Mohamed Mazhar, Zamalek, Al Qahirah. T: 805152.
**Ecumenical Advisory Council for Church Services in Egypt,** Chairman, Amba Rueis Bldg, Ramses St, Abbasiya, Al Qahirah.
**Evangelical Fellowship of Egypt,** Sec, 3 Sharia Tafish El Misaha, Asyut.

*EL SALVADOR*
**Conferencia Episcopal de El Salvador (CEDES),** Arzobispado, 8a Av Nte 913, Apdo Postal 78, San Salvador. T: 217734.

*ETHIOPIA*
**Conference of the Catholic Bishops of Ethiopia,** PO Box 21903, Addis Ababa. T: 11667.
**Council for Co-operation of Churches in Ethiopia (CCCE),** Sec, PO Box 1283, Addis Ababa.

*FIJI*
**Fiji Council of Churches,** Hon Sec, Epworth House, PO Box 35, Suva.

*FINLAND*
**Council of Free Christians and Churches in Finland (Association of Free Evangelical Congregations in Finland) (Suomen Vapaitten Kristittyjen ja Kirkkokuntien Neuvosto),** Nynasg 4, 68620 Jakobstad 20. (Also: Hämeenkatu 4 A 1, 20500 Turku 50).
**Ecumenical Council of Finland (Suomen Ekumeeninen Neuvosto),** Gen Sec, Vuorikatu 22A (or Aleksanterinkatu 15 B4), 00100 Helsinki 10. T: 9015211.

*FRANCE*
**Alliance Evangélique Française,** 47 Rue de Clichy, F-75009 Paris. T: 874-2572.
**Conférence Episcopale de France (CEF),** 106 Rue du Bac, F-75341 Paris Cedex 07. T: (01)222-5708.
**Fédération Evangélique de France,** Sec Gen, 163 bis Rue Belliard, Paris 18.
**Fédération Protestante de France (FPF),** Sec Gen, 47 Rue de Clichy, F-75009 Paris.

*GABON*
**Conférence Episcopale du Gabon,** Archevêché Sanctae Mariae, BP 2146, Libreville.

*GAMBIA*
**Gambia Christian Council,** Sec, c/o RC Mission House, 73 Hagan St, Banjul (Bathurst).

*GERMAN DEMOCRATIC REPUBLIC*
**Arbeitsgemeinschaft Christlicher Kirchen in der DDR (Council of Christian Churches in the GDR),** Auguststr 80, DDR-104 Berlin. T: 425186.
**Berliner Ordinarienkonferenz,** Französische Str 34, DDR-108 Berlin. (RC).

*GERMANY, Federal Republic of*
**Arbeitsgemeinschaft Christlicher Kirchen in Deutschland,** Ökumenische Centrale, Friedrichstr 2-4, Postfach 174025, D-6000 Frankfurt/Main.
**Bund Evangelisch-Reformierter Kirchen Deutschlands,** Untere Karspüle 11a, D-34 Göttingen.
**Deutsche Evangelische Allianz (DEA),** Geschäftsführer, Altenberger Str 6, D-633 Wetzlar. T: (06441) 45261. (Also: Albestr 4, D-1 Berlin 41).
**Deutsches Nationalkomitee des Lutherischen Weltbundes,** Richard-Wagner-Str 26, D-3 Hannover.
**Evangelische Kirche des Union (EKU),** Kirchenkanzlei, Jebensstr 3, D-1 Berlin 12.
**Lutherischer Weltbund,** Deutscher Hauptausschuss, Diemershaldenstr 45, D-7 Stuttgart-0.
**Plenarkonferenz der Bischöfe der Diözesen Deutschlands (Deutsche Bischofskonferenz),** Kaiserstr 163, D-5300 Bonn. T: (02221)631661/65. (RC).
**Reformierter Bund,** Generalsekretariat, Bleichstr 40, D-6 Frankfurt/Main. (Also: Bockenheimer Landstr 109).
**Vereinigte Ev-Lutherische Kirche Deutschlands (VELKD),** Lutherisches Kirchenamt, Richard-Wagner-Str 26, Postfach 1860, D-3 Hannover.

*GHANA*
**Christian Council of Ghana (CCG),** Gen Sec, PO Box 919, Accra.
**Ghana Bishops' Conference,** Bishop's House, PO Box 247, Accra. T: 22728.
**Ghana Evangelical Fellowship,** Sec, PO Box 3110, Kumasi.
**National Council of Spiritual Churches,** Bikhazi House, Liberty Av, PO Box 446, Accra. (Before 1972 known as Ghana Council of Liberal Churches, Sec, PO Box 446, Accra).
**National Pentecostal Council of Spiritual Churches of Ghana,** Bikhazi House, Liberty Av, PO Box X-118 or 446, James Town, Accra. (Formerly Ghana Council for Liberal Churches).
**Pentecostal Association of Ghana,** Sec, PO Box 23, Bibiani, WR. (Founded 1962).

*GREECE*
**Catholic Episcopal Conference of Greece (Synodos Katholikis Ierarchias Ellados),** Catholic Archbishop's House, Kérkira (Corfu). T: 8277.

*GRENADA*
**Grenada Christian Council,** Gen Sec, Lucas St, Box 104, St George's. (Formerly Grenada Inter-Church Council for Social Welfare).

*GUATEMALA*
**Alianza Evangélica de Guatemala,** Iglesia Evangélica Emanuel, Jalapa.
**Conferencia Episcopal de Guatemala (CEG),** Secretariado Católico Nacional, 4a calle 9-45, Zona 1, Apdo Postal 1698, Ciudad de Guatemala. T: 26831. 84571.

*GUINEA*
**Conférence Episcopale Nationale de la République de Guinée,** BP 1006 bis, Conakry.

*GUYANA*
**Guyana Council of Churches,** Sec, 71 Murray St, Georgetown.
**Guyana Council of the ICCC,** 256 New Garden St, Georgetown.

*HAITI*
**Concile des Eglises Evangéliques d'Haïti,** BP 592 ou 458, Port-au-Prince.
**Conférence Episcopale d'Haïti (CEH),** Archevêché, Port-au-Prince. T: 22043.

*HONDURAS*
**Alianza Evangélica Hondureña,** Apdo 17, San Pedro de Sula.
**Conferencia Episcopal de Honduras (CEH),** Palacio Arzobispal, 3a Calle No 11-13, Apdo Postal 106, Tegucigalpa. T: 20353.

*HONG KONG*
**Hong Kong Chinese Christian Churches Union,** Gen Sec, 6th Floor, Metropole Bldg, 57 Peking Rd, Kowloon. T: K-666467.
**Hong Kong Christian Council (HKCC),** Christian Centre, 5th Floor, Metropole Bldg, 57 Peking Rd, Kowloon. T: 6780317.
**Hong Kong Consultative Council of the ICCC,** Room 17, 10/F, Liu Chong Hing Bank Mongkok Bldg, Kowloon.

*HUNGARY*
**Council of Free Churches in Hungary (Magyarországi Szabadegyházak Tanácsa),** Aradi-utca 48, Budapest VI. T: 310194. (Member of Ecumenical Council of Hungarian Churches).
**Ecumenical Council of Hungarian Churches, ECHC (Magyarországi Egyházak Ökumenikus Tanácsa),** Gen Sec, Szbadság-tér 2.I, Budapest V. T: 114862.
**Hungarian Episcopal Assembly (Magyar Püspöki Kar),** Erseki Szekhaz, Szabadság-tér 1, Kalocsa. T: 155. (Also: Berenyi Zsigmond u.2, Pf 25, H-2501 Esztergom).

*INDIA*
**Catholic Bishops' Conference of India (CBCI),** CBCI Centre, 1 Ashok Place, New Delhi 110001. T: 46466,43176/7.
**Evangelical Fellowship of India (EFI),** Exec Sec, M-96 Greater Kailash 1, New Delhi 110048. T: 73560.
**Federation of Evangelical Churches of India (FECI),** c/o Christian Community Church, Sector 6, Bhilai-1, MP. (Inaugurated 1974).
**India Bible Christian Council (IBCC),** 3-6-209 Himayatnagar, Hyderabad 500029, AP.
**National Christian Council of India (NCCI),** Sec, N-21, Greater Kailash, New Delhi.

*INDONESIA*
**Association of Evangelical Churches of Indonesia,** Sec, Inter-Mission Business Office (IMBO), Jalan Fachruddin 9, Jakarta. (Also: Martadinata 75, Bandung).
**Bishops' Conference of Indonesia (Majelis Agung Para Waligereja Indonesia, MAWI),** Taman Cut Mutiah 10, Jakarta II/14. T: 41194.
**Council of Churches in Indonesia (Dewan Gereja-Gereja di Indonesia, DGI),** Gen Sec, Jalan Salemba Raya 10, Jakarta IV/3. T: 82317.
**United Pentecostal Full Gospel Churches of Indonesia (UPFGCI),** Jalan KHA Wahid Hasjim 67, Jakarta.

*IRAN*
**Inter-Rite Episcopal Conference (Conseil Episcopal Interrituel),** c/o Arquidiocèse de Isfahan, Khiabane Djamshid Abad 100, Tehran. T: 69203.
**Iran Council of Churches (ICC),** Sec, PO Box 1505, Tehran. T: 311868.

*IRAQ*
**Inter-Rite Bishops' Meeting of Iraq (Réunion Interrituelle des Evêques d'Irak),** Baghdad.

*IRELAND*
**Episcopal Meetings,** Ara Coeli, Armagh, Northern Ireland. T: (0861)522045.

*ISLE OF MAN*
**Isle of Man Council of Churches,** Sec, 35-37 Athol St, Douglas. (Also: May Bank, The Crescent, Baldrine).

*ISRAEL*
**United Christian Council in Israel (UCCI),** Gen Sec, 82 Prophets Rd, PO Box 116, Jerusalem. T: 25184.

*ITALY*
**Conferenza Episcopale Italiana (CEI),** Circonvallazione Aurelia 50, I-00165 Roma. T: 6982 int 6197.
**Federazione delle Chiese Evangeliche in Italia,** Sec, Via Firenze 38, I-00184, Roma. T: 481095.

*IVORY COAST*
**Conférence Episcopale de la Côte d'Ivoire,** BP 1287, Abidjan. T: 312041.
**Fédération Evangélique de Côte d'Ivoire (FECI),** Sec, BP 40, Toulépleu.

*JAMAICA*
**Jamaica Association of Evangelical Churches (National Council of Fundamentalist Churches in Jamaica),** 7 West Av, PO Box 18, Kingston 14. (Also: 77 Constant Spring Rd, Kingston 10).
**Jamaica Council of Churches (JCC),** Exec Sec, 6 Hope Rd, Kingston 10. T: 9265636.

*JAPAN*
**Catholic Bishops' Conference of Japan,** Catholic Center, 10-34 Uenomachi, Nagasaki-shi. T: (0958) 464246.
**Japan Bible Christian Council,** 4-5-15 Azuma-cho, Iruma-shi, Saitama-ken 358.
**Japan Evangelical Fellowship (Council),** Zenpuhuju Suginami-ku 1-16-17, Tokyo.
**National Christian Council of Japan (NCCJ),** Gen Sec, Japan Christian Center, 551 Totsuka-machi, 1-chome, Shinjuku-ku, Tokyo 160. T: (03)203-0372.

*KENYA*
**East Africa Christian Alliance (EACA),** Gen Sec, Mercury House, Tom Mboya St, PO Box 72681, Nairobi. T: 28280.
**East African United Churches (Eastern Orthodox Churches and the Coptic Communion),** Bishop, PO Box 9217, Nairobi.
**Ethiopian Orthodox Holy Spirit & United Churches of East Africa,** PO Box 47909, Nairobi. (Indigenous).
**Evangelical Fellowship of Kenya (EFK),** Chairman, PO Box 13024, Nairobi. T: 25149.
**Kenya African United Christian Churches,** Chairman, PO Box 521, Kisumu. (Indigenous).
**Kenya Episcopal Conference (KEC),** Catholic Secretariat, Waumini House, Westlands, PO Box 48062, Nairobi. T: 44302/3/4/5. (RC).
**Kenya Independent Churches Fellowship,** Chairman, HQ: AICN Nineveh, PO Box 701, Kisumu. (Indigenous).
**National Christian Council of Kenya (NCCK) (Jumuiya ya Wakristo wa Kenya),** Gen Sec, Church House (4th floor), Moi Av, PO Box 45009, Nairobi. T: 22264/5,27360,24652.
**United Churches of Africa,** Chairman, Olympic House, Koinange St, PO Box 16362, Nairobi. (Indigenous).
**United Orthodox Independent Churches of East Africa,** Gen Sec, Penguin House, Tom Mboya St, PO Box 28919, Nairobi. (Indigenous).
**United Orthodox Independent (Zion) Churches of Kenya,** PO Box 28159, Nairobi. (Indigenous).

*KOREA, South*
**Bishops' Conference of Korea (Hanguk Jukyo Hweoi),** 52-15 2 Ka, Chung Mu Ro, Jung Ku, CPO Box 16, Soul 100. T: 238789.
**Korea Evangelical Council of Christian Churches,** Choong Ang Holiness Church, 12 Moo Kyo-Dong, Soul.
**National Council of Churches in Korea,** Gen Sec, Christian Bldg, 136-46 Yun'chi'dong, Chong'ro, Kwang-Wha-Moon, PO Box 143, Soul.

*KUWAIT*
**Council of Churches in Kuwait,** Bishop's House, PO Box 266. T: 434637. (Begun 1960).

*LAOS*
**Conférence Episcopale du Laos et Cambodge (CELAC) (Sapha (Sangharat) Lao-Kmen),** Centre Catholique, Vientiane. T: 3229.

*LEBANON*
**Assembly of Catholic Patriarchs and Bishops of Lebanon/Assemblée des Patriarches et Evêques Catholiques du Liban,** Archevêché Grec-Catholique, Rue de Damas, BP 901, Bayrut.
**Supreme Council of Evangelical Churches in Syria & Lebanon/Conseil Suprème des Eglises Evangéliques au Liban et en Syrié,** Sec, Rue de l'Eglise Evangélique (Zkak el Blat), BP 5224, Bayrut. T: 227175.

*LESOTHO*

**Christian Council of Lesotho (CCL) (Lekhotla la Likereke la Lesotho)**, Sec, PO Box 547, Maseru.
**Episcopal Conference of Lesotho**, Archbishop's House, PO Box 267, Maseru. T: 22565.
**Federation of African Independent Churches**, Maseru.

*LIBERIA*

**Liberia Evangelical Fundamental Fellowship (LEFF)**, Sec, PO Box 393, Monrovia 1.
**National Interdenominational Conference of Bishops**, Monrovia.
**United Pentecostal Assemblies of the World in Liberia & Sierra Leone**, Gen Sec, PO Box 9038, Monrovia.

*MADAGASCAR*

**Conférence Episcopale de Madagascar**, 102 bis Av du Maréchal Joffre, BP 667, Antanimena, Tananarive. T: 20478.
**Fédération de Eglises Protestantes de Madagascar (Fiombonan' Ny Fiangonana Protestanta Eto Madagasikara)**, Gen Sec, Prezidà, 50 Rue George V, Mpitandrina, Faravohitra, Tananarive. T: 21368,24786.

*MALAWI*

**Christian Council of Malawi (CCM)**, Gen Sec, PO Box 30068, Lilongwe 3. T: 30499.
**Episcopal Conference of Malawi (ECM)**, Catholic Secretariat, Zomba Rd, PO Box 5368, Limbe. T: 50866.
**Evangelical Association of Malawi (EAM)**, PO Box 136, Blantyre.

*MALAYSIA*

**Catholic Bishops' Conference of Malaysia-Singapore**, PO Box 108, Miri, Sarawak via Singapore.
**Council of Churches of Malaysia and Singapore**, Gen Sec, 21 Jalan Abdul Samad, Brickfields, Kuala Lumpur, West Malaysia. T: 204273.

*MALI*

**Association des Groupements d'Eglises et Missions Protestantes Evangéliques au Mali**, Pres, BP 4, Markala.
**Conférence Episcopale du Mali**, Archevêché, BP 298, Bamako.

*MALTA*

**Malta Episcopal Conference**, Palazzo Arcivescovile, Valletta. T: 625943.

*MEXICO*

**Asociación Fraternal de Iglesias Pentecostales en la República de México**, Sec, Calle Nicolás León 118, Colonia Jardín Balbuena, México 8, DF. T: 5716531.
**Conferencia del Episcopado Mexicano (CEM)**, Apdo 32-661, México 1, DF. T: 5468811. (Also: Apdo Postal 1-331, Guadalajara, Jalisco. T: 145504).
**Federación Evangélica de México**, Exec Sec, Motolinia No 8-107, México 1, DF. T: 51307001.

*MONTSERRAT*

**Montserrat Council for Social Action**, PO Box 226, Plymouth.

*MOZAMBIQUE*

**Conferência Episcopal de Moçambique (CEM)**, Secretariado Geral da CEM, CP 286, Maputo. T: 26240.
**Conselho Cristão de Moçambique (Christian Council of Mozambique)**, CP 108, Maputo.

*NEPAL*

**Nepal Christian Fellowship**, c/o United Mission to Nepal, Box 126, Kathmandu.

*NETHERLANDS*

**Council of Churches in the Netherlands (Raad van Kerken in Nederland)**, Sec, Kon Wilhelminalaan 5, Amersfoort. T: (03490)33844. (Formerly Maliebaan 88, Utrecht. T: (030)22779).
**Netherlands Bishops' Conference (Nederlandse Bisschoppen Konferentie)**, Pres, Biltstraat 121, Postbus 13049, Utrecht. T: (030)316956.

*NETHERLANDS ANTILLES*

**Curaçao Ecumenical Council of Churches**, Chairman, Fort Church, Willemstad, Curaçao. (Also Kinjanweg 15).

*NEW ZEALAND*

**National Council of Churches in New Zealand (NCCNZ)**, Gen Sec, 176 Hereford St, PO Box 297, Christchurch C1. T: 69274.
**New Zealand Consultative Council of the ICCC**, 59 Kent Lodge Av, Christchurch 4. (Also PO Box 622, Nelson).
**New Zealand Episcopal Conference**, PO Box 198, Wellington 1. (Also: 277 Rattray St, Dunedin C2).
**New Zealand Evangelical Alliance**, Sec, 427 Queen St, PO Box 8140, Auckland.

*NICARAGUA*

**Conferencia Episcopal de Nicaragua**, Palacio Arzobispal, Av del SCentenario 502, Apdo 20.08, Managua. T: 4413.

*NIGERIA*

**Christian Council of Nigeria (CCN)**, Gen Sec, 139 Ogunluna Drive, Surulere, PO Box 2838, Lagos.
**Communion of Aladura Churches of Nigeria (Isokan Ijo Aladura Nigeria)**, HQ Office, PO Box 1693, Ibadan.
**National Episcopal Conference of Nigeria**, 6 Force Rd, PO Box 951, Lagos. T: 25339.
**Nigeria Evangelical Fellowship**, Sec, Box 63, Jos, BP State.

*NORWAY*

**Norwegian Free Church Council (Norske Frikirkerad)**, c/o St Olavsgt 28, Oslo 1.

*PAKISTAN*

**Catholic Bishops' Conference of Pakistan**, St Patrick's Cathedral, Karachi 3. T: 515870.
**Evangelical Fellowship of Pakistan**, Gordon College, Rawalpindi. (Also Chak 190/9, Al Dist, Sahiwal).
**Pakistan Christian Council**, Exec Sec, 32-B Shahrah-e-Fatima Jinnah, PO Box 357, Lahore 4. T: 67307.

*PANAMA*

**Alianza Evangélica de Panamá**, Apdo 7453, Panamá 5.
**Conferencia Episcopal de Panamá (CEP)**, Centro Católico, Av México y Calle 20, Apdo 386, Panamá 1.

*PAPUA NEW GUINEA*

**Bishops' Conference of Papua New Guinea and the Solomon Islands**, PO Box 69, Mendi, Southern Highlands. T: 591002.
**Evangelical Alliance of the South Pacific Islands (EASPI)**, Sec, Asia Pacific Christian Mission, Balimo, WD.
**Melanesian Council of Churches (MCC)**, Sec, Box 1015, Boroko, Port Moresby. T: 55632.

*PARAGUAY*

**Comisión Coordinadora Evangélica de Paraguay**, Casilla de Correo 167, Asunción.
**Conferencia Episcopal Paraguaya (CEP)**, Calle Alberdi 782, Casilla Correo 1436, Asunción. T: 41946.

*PERU*

**Concilio Nacional Evangélico del Perú**, Sec Gen, Apdo 2566, Lima. T: 81754.
**Conferencia Episcopal Peruana**, Azángaro 254 y 260, Apdo 310, Lima 1.

*PHILIPPINES*

**Catholic Bishops' Conference of the Philippines (CBCP)**, 2655 FB Harrison, Pasay City, PO Box 1160, Manila.
**National Council of Churches in the Philippines (NCCP) (Sangguniang Pambansa ng mga Simbahan sa Pilipinas)**, 941 Epifano de los Santos Av, Quezon City, Box 1767, Manila. T: 998636.
**Philippine Council of Fundamental Evangelical Churches**, PO Box 1886, Manila.

*POLAND*

**Polish Ecumenical Council (Polska Rada Ekumeniczna)**, Gen Sec, ul Swierczewskiego 76a, Warszawa.
**Polish Episcopal Conference (Konferencja Episkopatu Polski)**, ul Miodowa 17, 00-246 Warszawa. T: 312157.

*PORTUGAL*

**Aliança Evangélica Portuguesa**, Avenida Conselheiro Barjona De Freitas 16-B/C, 1500 Lisboa.
**Comissão Inter-eclesiástica Portuguesa**, Pres, Praça Coronel Pacheco, Porto.
**Conferência Episcopal Portuguesa da Metrópole (CEPM)**, Campo dos Mártires da Pátria 43-1 Esq, Lisboa-1. T: 42123.
**Conselho Português de Igrejas Cristãs (COPIC)**, Gen Sec, Rua Dr Henriques Seco 14, Coimbra.

*PUERTO RICO*

**Concilio Evangélico de Puerto Rico/Evangelical Council of Puerto Rico**, Exec Sec, 54 Robles St, PO Box 'C', Río Piedras, PR 00928. T: (809)766-2189.
**Conferencia Episcopal Puertorriqueña (CEP)**, Calle Cristo 50, Apdo 1967, San Juan, PR 00903. T: 722903. (RC).

*ROMANIA*

**Romanian Catholic Episcopal Conference**, Palatul Episcopiei, Alba-Julia. (RC).

*RWANDA*

**Conseil Protestant du Rwanda**, Sec, BP 79, Kigali. T: 5741.

*ST KITTS-NEVIS*

**Christian Council of St Kitts**, PO Box 141, West Square St, Basse Terre, St Kitts.

*ST LUCIA*

**St Lucia Inter-Church Council**, c/o Jnsurance & Agencies, Castries.

*ST VINCENT*

**Christian Council of St Vincent**, Sec, PO Box 126 or 445, Kingstown.

*SAMOA*

**Fellowship of Christian Churches in Samoa**, PO Box 468, Apia.

*SENEGAL*

**Conférence Episcopale de Sénégal-Mauritanie**, BP 5082, Dakar. T: 225918.
**Fraternité Evangélique du Sénégal**, Pres, BP 2961, Dakar.

*SIERRA LEONE*

**Inter-Territorial Episcopal Conference of the Gambia, Liberia & Sierra Leone**, Santanno House, PO Box 893, Freetown. T: 24590.
**Sierra Leone Evangelical Fellowship**, PO Box 300, Freetown. T: 6573.
**United Christian Council of Sierra Leone (UCCSL)**, Gec Sec, PO Box 404, Freetown. T: 3268.

*SINGAPORE*

**Council of Churches of Malaysia and Singapore**, Gen Sec, 6 Mount Sophia, Singapore 9.
**Malaysia Council of Christian Churches**, 9a Gilstead Rd, Singapore 11.

*SOLOMON ISLANDS*

**Solomon Islands Christian Association (SICA)**, Box A173, Honiara.

*SOUTH AFRICA*

**African Independent Churches Association (AICA)**, 35 Jorissen St, PO Box 31190, Braamfontein, Transvaal. (Indigenous).
**African Independent Churches' Ecumenical Movement**, Johnson Rd, Veeplaats, Port Elizabeth.
**African Independent Churches' Movement (AICM)**, V560 Umlazi Township, 4066 Ntokozweni, near Durban, Natal. (Indigenous).
**Assembly of Zionist and Apostolic Churches**, Box 97, Johannesburg.
**Bureau of African Churches**, Dir, PO Box 11, Rossburgh, Durban, Natal.
**South African Council of Christian Churches (SACCC)**, Spesbonalaan, Parow, CP.
**South African Council of Churches (SACC)/ Suid-Afrikaanse Raad van Kerke**, Gen Sec, 112 Dunwell, 35 Jorissen St, PO Box 31190, Braamfontein, Transvaal. T: 7244459.

*SPAIN*

**Alianza Evangélica Española**, Sec, Calle Verdi 189, Barcelona 12.
**Conferencia Episcopal Española (CEE)**, Alfonso XI 4-1, Madrid 14.
**Consejo Evangélico Español**, Bravo Murillo 85, Madrid. T: 2547145.

*SRI LANKA*

**Bishops' Conference of Sri Lanka (Lanka Raja Guru Sammelanaya)**, Archbishop's House, Borella, Colombo 8.
**Evangelical Alliance of Sri Lanka**, PO Box 66, Colombo.
**National Christian Council of Sri Lanka**, Gen Sec, 490 Havelock Rd, Colombo 6. (Also: 61 Sir James Peiris Mawata, Colombo 2).

*SUDAN*

**Sudan Council of Churches (Maglis al Kanayis fi Sudan)**, Gen Sec, PO Box 469, Al Khurtum.
**Sudan Episcopal Conference (SEC)**, Catholic Secretariat, PO Box 49, Al Khurtum. T: 72677.

*SURINAM*

**Surinam Christian Council of Churches (Comite Christelijke Kerken)**, Chairman, PO Box 219, Paramaribo.

*SWAZILAND*

**Swaziland Conference of Churches**, Pres, PO Box 333, Mbabane. T: 2440.

*SWEDEN*

**Swedish Ecumenical Council (Svenska Ekumeniska Nämnden)**, Sec, Akeshovsvägen 29, 161 51 Bromma. T: (08)266399.
**Swedish Free Church Council (Sveriges Frikyrkorad)**, Sec, Box 1205, 111 82 Stockholm.

*SWITZERLAND*

**Commission de Travail des Eglises Chrétiennes en Suisse/Schweizerischen Evangelischen Kirchebunder**, Sulgenauweg 26, CH-3007 Bern. T: (031)462511. (Arbeitsgemeinschaft Christlicher Kirchen in der Schweiz).
**Conférence des Evêques Suisses/Conferenza dei Vescovi Svizzeri/Schweizerische Bischofskonferenz**, Secrétariat, Av Moléson 30, CH-1700 Fribourg 1. T: (037)224794.
**Fédération des Eglises Protestantes de la Suisse/Schweizerischer Evangelischer Kirchenbund**, Pres, Sulgenauweg 26, CH-3007 Bern.
**Römisch-Katholische Zentralkonferenz der Landeskirchen (RKZ) (Conférence Centrale Catholique Romaine des Eglises Nationales)**, Gartenstr 36, CH-8002 Zürich.
**Schweizerische Evangelische Allianz**, Exec Sec, Zentralkomitee, Bienenberg, CH-4410 Liestal.
**Verband Unabhängiger Evangelischer Kirchen und Körperschaften (Aarauer Verband)**, Sek, Konkordiastr 27, CH-9000 St Gallen.

*SYRIA*

**Assemblée de la Hiérarchie Catholique en Syrie**, Archevâché Maronite, Rue Azizié, Halab.

*TANZANIA*

**Christian Council of Tanzania (CCT)**, Gen Sec, PO Box 2537, Dar es Salaam.
**Tanzania Episcopal Conference (TEC)**, Catholic Secretariat, Mission Bldg, Mansfield St, PO Box 2133, Dar es Salaam. T: 20430,20477.

*THAILAND*

**Church of Christ in Thailand**, Sec, 14 Pramuan Rd, Bangkok. T: 37976/7. (Formerly National Council of Churches in Thailand).
**Episcopal Conference of Thailand (Sapa Sangkharat Heng Prathet Thai)**, Archbishop's House, Assumption Cathedral, Oriental Av, Bangrak, Bangkok 5. T: 2338712.
**Evangelical Fellowship of Thailand (EFT)**, 487 Silon Rd, GPO Box 1200, Bangkok 5. T: 2342382.

*TOGO*

**Conférence Episcopale du Togo**, BP 348, Lomé. T: 2272.

*TRINIDAD & TOBAGO*

**Christian Council of Trinidad and Tobago**, Sec, Catholic Centre, 52a Jerningham Av, Port of Spain.
**Federal Council of Evangelical Churches of Trinidad and Tobago**, Pres, Box 248, Port of Spain.

*TURKEY*

**Episcopal Conference of Turkey**, Olcek Sokak 83, Harbiya, Istanbul. (RC).
**Union of Evangelical Churches**, Chairman, Box 142, Istanbul.

*TURKS & CAICOS ISLANDS*

**Turks and Caicos Inter-Church Committee**, Pres, The Rectory, Grand Turk.

*UGANDA*

**Evangelical Fellowship of Uganda**, Sec, PO Box 2307, Kampala.
**Uganda Episcopal Conference (UEC)**, Catholic Secretariat, PO Box 2886, Kampala. T: 54521,43042.
**Uganda Joint Christian Council (UJCC)**, Joint Secs, PO Box 14284 or 2886, Kampala.

*USSR*

**Bishops' Conference of Latvia**, Pils Jela 2, Riga, Latvian SSR.
**Bishops' Conference of Lithuania**, Vilniaus Gatve 4, 233000 Kaunas, Lithuanian SSR. T: 22097.

*UK OF GB & NI*

**Bishops' Conference of England and Wales**, Archbishop's House, Westminster, London SW1P 1QJ. T: (01)834-4717. (RC).
**Bishop's Conference of Scotland**, Archbishop's House, 42 Greenhill Gardens, Edinburgh EH10 4BJ. T: (031)447-3337. (RC).
**British Council of Churches (BCC)**, Gen Sec, 10 Eaton Gate, London SW1W 9BT. T: (01)730-9611.
**British Council of Protestant Christian Churches**, 9 Milnthorpe Rd, Chiswick, London W4.
**British Evangelical Council (BEC)**, Gen Sec, 21 Woodstock Rd North, St Albans, Herts AL1 4QB. T: 55655.
**British Pentecostal Fellowship**, 23 John Campbell Rd, Stoke Newington, London N17. (Also: 51 Newington Causeway, London SE1).
**Council of African & Allied Churches in the UK**, 99 Strathville Rd, London SW18 4QR.
**Episcopal Conference of Ireland**, Ara Coeli, Armagh, NI. T: 2045.
**Evangelical Alliance of Great Britain (EAGB)**, Gen Sec, 19 Draycott Place, London SW3 2SJ. T: (01)581-0051.
**Evangelical Fellowship of Ireland**, The Manse, 11 Waterloo Gardens, Belfast, NI BT15 4EX.
**Free Church Federal Council (FCFC)**, 27 Tavistock Square, London WC1. T: (01)387-8413.
**Irish Council of Churches**, Sec, Inter-Church Centre, 48 Elmwood Av, Belfast, BT9 6AZ. T: (0232) 663145.

*USA*

**American Council of Christian Churches (ACCC)**, Valley Forge, PA 19481. T: (215)933-8903/4.
**Christian Holiness Association**, Exec Dir, 21 Beachway Drive, Indianapolis, IN 46224. T: (317)241-8281. (Co-ordinating Wesleyan-Arminian religious bodies).
**Lutheran Council in the USA**, Gen Sec, 315 Park Av South, New York, NY 10010. T: (212)677-3950.
**National Association of Evangelicals (NAE)**, Pres, 350 South Main Place, PO Box 28, Wheaton, IL 60187. T: (312)665-0500.
**National Association of State Catholic Conferences**, 1312 Massachusetts Av, NW, Washington, DC 20005.
**National Black Evangelical Association (NBAE)**, Pres, PO Box 193, Pasadena, CA 91101. (Formerly NNAE).
**National Committee of the Lutheran World Federation**, Pres, 315 Park Av South, New York, NY 10010. T: (212)677-3950.
**National Conference of Catholic Bishops (NCCB)**, 1312 Massachusetts Av, NW, Washington, DC 20005. T: (202)659-6600.
**National Council of Churches of Christ in the USA (NCCCUSA)**, Gen Sec, 475 Riverside Drive, New York, NY 10027. T: (212)870-2200.
**National Federation of Pentecostal Churches**, Pres, Washington, DC. (Black; social action by ghetto churches).
**National Fraternal Council of Churches (NFCC)**, AMEC, 475 Riverside Drive, New York NY 10027. (Black).
**Pan-Indian Ecumenical Association**, 4753 North Broadway Av, Chicago, IL 50540. T: (312)275-0619. (Also: Cree Reservation, Montana; and other reservations).
**United States Catholic Conference (USCC)**, 1312 Massachusetts Av, NW, Washington, DC 20005. T: (202)659-6600. (Operational arm of NCCB).

*US VIRGIN ISLANDS*

**St Thomas Inter-Church Council**, PO Box 1827, Charlotte Amalie, St Thomas.

*UPPER VOLTA*

**Fédération des Missions et Eglises Evangéliques en Haute-Volta**, BP 121, Ouagadougou.
**Conférence des Evêques de la Haute-Volta et du Niger**, BP 90, Ouagadougou. T: 2993.

*URUGUAY*

**Conferencia Episcopal del Uruguay (CEU)**, Av Uruguay 1319, Montevideo.
**Federación de Iglesias Evangélicas del Uruguay (FIEU)**, Exec Sec, San José 1457, Casilla 445, Montevideo.

*VANUATU*

**Vanuatu Christian Council**, Sec-Treasurer, Lolowai, Aoba via Santo.

*VENEZUELA*

**Alianza de Evangélicos**, Apdo 402, Maracaibo.
**Conferencia Episcopal Venezolana (CEV)**, Edif Juan XXIII, piso 2, Torre a Madrices, Apdo 954, Caracas 101, DF. T: 815922.
**Consejo Evangélico de Venezuela (Venezuela Council of Churches)**, Apdo 222, Caracas 101, DF.

*VIET NAM*

**Conférence Episcopale du Viêtnam**, 180 Phan-Dinh-Phung, Ho Chi Minh Ville 180. (RC).
**Evangelical Fellowship of Viet-Nam (Hoi Tin Lanh Tong Cong Vietnam)**, 30 Huynh Quang Tien, Ho Chi Minh Ville.
**National Liaison Committee of Patriotic and Peace-loving Catholics**, 34 Rue Ngo Quyen, Hanoi. (Government-organized).

**Vietnamese Association of Churches,** Hanoi. (Government-sponsored).

*YUGOSLAVIA*
**Ecumenical Council of Churches in Yugoslavia (Ekumenski Savet Crkava u Jugoslaviji),** Secretariat, Fah 182, Beograd.
**Yugoslav Bishops' Conference (Biskupska Konferencija Jugoslavije),** Pres, Kaptol 31, PB 02-406, YU-41000 Zagreb. T: (041)36446.

*ZAIRE*
**Alliance Evangélique du Zaire,** BP 757, Bukavu-Kivu.
**Conférence Episcopale du Zaire (Conférence Plénière des Ordinaires du Zaire),** Evêché, BP 3258, Kinshasa-Gombe. T: 30082/3.
**Conseil Supérieur des Sacrificateurs pour l'Unité des Eglises Indépendantes du Congo,** BP 985, Kananga (Luluabourg). (Also known as COSSEUJCA).
**Eglise du Christ au Zaire, ECZ (Church of Christ in Zaire),** Sec Gen, 1A Av Pumbu, BP 3094, Kinshasat Gombe. T: 30493. (Formerly Congo Protestan-Council).

*ZAMBIA*
**Christian Council of Zambia (CCZ),** Sec, PO Box 315, Lusaka. T: 73287.
**Evangelical Fellowship of Zambia (EFZ),** Chairman, PO Box 115, Choma.
**Zambia Christian Commission for Development (ZCCD),** Sec, Mindolo Ecumenical Centre, PO Box 1493, Kitwe. T: 84712/3.
**Zambia Episcopal Conference (ZEC),** Catholic Secretariat, Unity House, Stanley Rd, Jameson St, PO Box 1965, Lusaka. T: 73467,73470.
**Zambian Anglican Council,** PO Box 8100, Lusaka.

*ZIMBABWE*
**African Independent Churches' Conference (AICC) (Fambidzano Yamakereke Avatema),** Gen Sec, 22 Fitzgerald Av, PO Box 127, Fort Victoria. T: 2787. (Indigenous).
**Bureau of African Churches,** Dir, PO Box 50, Mpopoma, Bulawayo. (Indigenous).
**Christian Council of Zimbabwe (CCZ),** Gen Sec, Box 3566, Salisbury. T: 28500.
**Evangelical Fellowship of Zimbabwe (EFZ),** Chairman, Box H-60, Hatfield, Salisbury.
**Zimbabwe Catholic Bishops' Conference (ZCBC),** PO Box 8135, Causeway, Salisbury. T: 27386.
**Zimbabwe Christian Conference (ZCC),** Gen Sec, PO Box 904, Causeway, Salisbury.

## 43
## Prayer Societies

*Definition.* Societies and fellowships concerned primarily with prayer, the prayer life, intercession, meditation, days of prayer. There are countless other prayer fellowships and societies praying for specific areas or subjects, and in a sense all types of Christian organizations, and the denominations themselves, can be considered as prayer societies

*BOLIVIA*
**Liga de Oración en Misión Mundial,** ANDEB, Casilla 266, La Paz.

*GERMANY, Federal Republic of*
**Evangelische Arbeitsgruppe für die Ökumenische Gebetswoche,** Bockemheimer Landstr 109, D-6000 Frankfurt/Main 1.
**Katholischer Arbeitskreis für die Veltgebetswoche,** D-8351 Niederaltaich b Deggendorf/Ndb. T: (09901)318,224.

*HOLY SEE*
**Apostleship of Prayer,** Secretariat, Borgo Santo Spirito 5, I-00193 Roma. T: 650933.

*INDIA*
**All India Prayer Fellowship,** D-3, Green Park Extension, New Delhi 16. (Operates also in Nepal, Sikkim).

*JAPAN*
**Kyoto Overseas Missionary Intercessory Prayer Fellowship,** c/o CLC, Teramachi Imadegawa Sagaru, Kamigyoku, Kyoto-shi.

*KENYA*
**Kenya Christian Teachers' Prayer Fellowship (KCTPF),** Sec, PO Box 21352, Nairobi. T: 22312.

*LEBANON*
**Prière Commune,** BP 7002, Bayrut.

*NEW ZEALAND*
**Latin American Prayer Fellowship (LAPF),** Hon Sec, 1719 Great North Rd, Auckland 7.

*PHILIPPINES*
**World-Wide Christian Prayer Fellowship,** 544-546 Asuncion, San Nicolas, Manila.

*UK OF GB & NI*
**Guild of Prayer and Spiritual Healing,** Addington Park, Near Maidstone, Kent. T: West Malling 3589.
**Intercessors for Britain,** 100 Broadwater St West, Worthing, West Sussex.
**Nilgiri Prayer Fellowship,** Sec, Merrymickle, Burney Rd, Westhumble, Dorking, Surrey. T: (0306) 5175.
**Prayer Fellowship for South Asia,** 1 Kings Av, Carshalton, Surrey. T: (01)643-5611. (Also: Christ Church Vicarage, Cancell Rd, London SW9. T: (01) 735-1343).
**Society for Spreading the Knowledge of True Prayer,** 14a Eccleston St, London SW1. T: (01) 730-4635.
**Teachers' Prayer Fellowship,** 47 Maryblebone Lane, London W1M 6AX.
**Universal Prayer Group (UPG),** St Saviour's Church, Chalk Farm, London NW.
**Women's World Day of Prayer,** 3A Grenville Place, South Kensington, London SW7 4RU. T: (01)373-9245.
**World Movement for United Prayer,** Glen Rossal House, Nash Court, Marnhull, Dorset.

*USA*
**International Committee on the World Day of Prayer,** Sec, Room 806, 475 Riverside Drive, New York, NY 10027. T: (212)870-3035.
**Latin American Prayer Fellowship (LAPF),** PO Box 323 M, Pasadena, CA 91102.
**Missionary Prayer and Literature Fellowship,** PO Box 6288, Los Angeles, CA 90055.
**Missionary Prayer League,** 89 Quincy St, Brooklyn, NY 11238.
**World Mission Prayer League,** Press, 232 Clifton Av, Minneapolis, MN 55403. T: (612)338-7843.
**World-Wide Prayer and Missionary Union,** 6821 North Ottawa Av, Chicago, IL 60631. T: (312) 763-2553.

## 44
## Publishing

*Definition.* Publishing houses producing religious or Christian literature (usually church- or Christian-owned, -operated, -controlled, -sponsored or -linked), church printing presses; including secular houses which give major importance to publishing books on religion. For publications and programmes, see LITERATURE. For agencies exclusively publishing Scriptures, see BIBLE AND SCRIPTURE ORGANIZATIONS.

Religious publishing houses and secular publishers specializing in religion are extremely numerous (around 200 in Britain, over 400 in USA, et alia). Only a selection are given here. For Britain, see the directory *Publishers in the UK*.

*ANGOLA*
**Angola Publishing House,** CP 3, Nova Lisboa. (Seventh-day Adventist).

*ARGENTINA*
**Buenos Aires Publishing House,** Av San Martin 4555, Florida, Buenos Aires. T: 7412426,7400415. (Seventh-day Adventist).

*AUSTRALIA*
**Signs Publishing Co,** Warburton, Victoria 3799. T: 662501/2/3. (Seventh-day Adventist).

*AUSTRIA*
**Austrian Publishing House,** Nussdorferstr 5, A-1090 Wien. T: (0222)345297. (Seventh-day Adventist).

*BELGIUM*
**Belgian-Flemish Publishing House,** Rue Ernest Allard 11-13, B-1000 Brussel. T: 113680. (Seventh-day Adventist).

*BRAZIL*
**Brazil Publishing House,** Av Pereira Barreto 42, CP 34, 09000 Santo Andre, São Paulo, SP. T: 445333. (Seventh-day Adventist).

*BURMA*
**Kinsaung Press,** 206 Shwe Thitsa Rd, Knabe, PO Box 977, Rangoon. (Seventh-day Adventist).

*BURUNDI*
**Grace Memorial Press,** WGM, PB 59, Gitega.

*CAMEROON*
**Centre de Littérature Evangélique,** Editions CLE, BP 1501 (& 4048), Yaoundé. T: 4673. (Publisher. Member of WACC).
**Equatorial African Publishing House,** BP 61, Yaoundé. T: 4437. (Seventh-day Adventist).

*CANADA*
**Maracle Press,** PO Box 400, Oshawa, Ontario. (Seventh-day Adventist).

*CENTRAL AFRICAN REPUBLIC*
**Presse Biblique Baptiste,** BP 6, Fort Sibut.

*CHINA (TAIWAN)*
**Christian Witness Press,** 63 Chung Shan Rd, PO Box 210, Taipei.
**Signs of the Times Publishing Association,** 424 Pa Te Rd, Section 2, Taipei. T: 777006. (Seventh-day Adventist).

*COSTA RICA*
**Centro de Publicaciones Cristianas,** Apdo 2773, San José.

*CZECHOSLOVAKIA*
**Czechoslovakian Publishing House,** Londynska 30, Vinohrady, Praha 2. T: 257863. (Seventh-day Adventist).
**Society of St Adalbert (Spolok Svätého Vojdecha),** Divadelná 4, 917 85 Trnava. T: 21745. (RC publishing house).

*DENMARK*
**Danish Publishing House,** Borstenbindervej 4, PB 550, DK-5100 Odense. T: (09)139843. (Seventh-day Adventist).

*ETHIOPIA*
**Ethiopian Advent Press,** Addis Abeba. T: 14218. (Seventh-day Adventist).
**Globe Publishing House,** PO Box 4798, Addis Abeba.
**Tenzae Zugubae Printing Press,** Dir, PO Box 1563, Addis Abeba. T: 12296. (Ethiopian Orthodox Church's press).

*FIJI*
**Rarama Publishing House,** Queen's Rd, PO Box 3083, Lami, Suva. T: 361727. (Seventh-day Adventist).

*FINLAND*
**Finland Publishing House,** Kirjatoimi, PO Box 94, 33100 Tampere 10. T: 93167000. (Seventh-day Adventist).

*FRANCE*
**French Publishing House,** 60 Av Emile-Zola, F-77 Dammarie-les-Lys. T: (437)0521. (Seventh-day Adventist).
**Société Nouvelle de Publications Protestantes,** 33 Rue Puits-Gaillot, Lyon 1.

*GERMAN DEMOCRATIC REPUBLIC*
**Publishing Association of the Union of Seventh-day Adventists in the GDR,** Edisonstr 37, DDR-116 Berlin-Oberschöneweide.
**St Benno Verlag,** Thüringerstr 1-3, Postfach 98, DDR-7033 Leipzig.

*GERMANY, Federal Republic of*
**Christliches Verlagshaus,** Senefelderstr 109, D-7 Stuttgart 1.
**Hamburg Publishing House,** Grindelberg 13-17, D-2 Hamburg 13. T: (0411)441391. (Seventh-day Adventist).
**Vereinigung Evangelischer Buchhändler,** Silberburgstr 58/1, Postfach 721, D-7 Stuttgart-W.

*GHANA*
**Advent Publishing House,** PO Box 0102, Christiansborg, Accra. T: 77861. (Seventh-day Adventist).
**Africa Christian Press,** PO Box 30, Achimota.

*GREECE*
**Bureau de la Bonne Presse,** 246 Acharnon, 815 Athínai. T: 878363,626091,872723. (RC publishing house).
**Greek Publishing House,** Keramikou 18, Athínai 107. T: 520796. (Seventh-day Adventist).

*HOLY SEE*
**Tipografia Poliglotta Vaticana,** Dir, I-00120 Città del Vaticano. T: 6982 int 4649.

*HONG KONG*
**Assemblies of God Press,** 102 East Argyle St, Victory Av, Kowloon. T: K 016601.
**Baptist Press,** 322 Prince Edward Rd, Kowloon. T: K-820716
**China Alliance Press,** 31 Chatham Rd, 5/F, Kowloon. T: K-667654.
**Christian Witness Press,** 144 Boundary St, Kowloon. T: K-822205.
**Evangel Press & Bookstore,** 110 Prince Edward Rd, Kowloon. T: K-801106.
**Morning Light Press,** 17 Cumberland Rd, Kowloon. T: K-823002.
**Rock House Publishers,** PO Box 6138, Kowloon. (Baptist).
**Sheng Tao Press,** 893 King's Rd, 2/F, North Point, Hong Kong. T: H-612538.
**Taosheng Publishing House,** 50A Waterloo Rd, Kowloon. T: K-844806,887061.

*HUNGARY*
**Ecclesia Szövetkezet,** Károlyi Mihály u 4/8, 1053 Budapest.
**Szent István Társulat (St Stephen's Society),** Kossuth Lajos u 1, 1053 Budapest.

*ICELAND*
**Iceland Publishing House,** PO Box 262, Reykjavík. (Seventh-day Adventist).

*INDIA*
**Benagaria Mission Press,** PO Benagaria, SP.
**Christian Literature Society Press,** 1 Dickenson Rd, Bangalore 42.
**Christian Publishing House,** Vidbyangar, Rajahmundry-3, East Godavari District, AP.
**CMS Press and Book Depot,** Kottayam, Kerala.
**ISPCK,** Post Box 1585, Kashmere Gate, Delhi 6.
**Lucknow Publishing House,** 37 Cantonment Rd, Lucknow, UP.
**Oriental Watchman Publishing House,** Salisbury Park, Post Box 35, Poona 1. T: 24164. (Seventh-day Adventist).
**Tranquebar Publishing House,** Purasawalkam, Madras 7.
**YMCA Publishing House,** Massey Hall, Jai Singh Rd, New Delhi 1.

*INDONESIA*
**Indonesia Publishing House,** Post Box 85, Bandung, Java. T: 52395. (Seventh-day Adventist).

*ITALY*
**Centro Editoriale Studi Islamici (CESI),** Via Riboty 1, I-00195 Roma. T: 373306.
**Editrice Missionaria Italiana (EMI),** Via Meloncello 3/3, Bologna. (Also: Corso Ferrucci 14, Torino; Via Mosè Bianchi 94, Milano; Via S Matrino 8, Parma).
**IRADES Edizioni Pastorali,** Centro Stampa IRADES, Via Paisiello 6, 1-00198 Roma.
**Italian Publishing House,** Via Trieste 23, I-50139 Firenze. T: 493406. (Seventh-day Adventist).
**Libreria Editrice Claudiana,** Via S Pio Quinto 18 bis, I-10125 Torino. (Waldensian).
**Unione Editori Cattolici Italiani,** Via Doménico Silveri 9, I-00165 Roma.

*IVORY COAST*
**Centre d'Edition et Diffusion Africaine (CEDA),** BP 4541, Abidjan.

*JAPAN*
**Evangelical Publishing Depot,** 1-15 Kagurazaka, Shinjuku-ku, Tokyo 162.
**Fukuin Dendo Kyodan Publishing Department,** 4-4 2-chome, Hiyoshi-cho, Maebashi-shi, Gunma-ken 371.
**Japan Alliance Church Publishing Department,** 12-2 5-chome, Sanban-cho, Matsuyama-shi, Ehime-ken 790.
**Japan Publishing House,** 1966 Kamikawai-cho, Asahi-ku, Yokohama 241. T: (045)951-1385. (Seventh-day Adventist).
**Jordan Press,** 2-350 Nishi Okubo, Shinjuku-ku, Tokyo 160.
**Protestant Publishing Company,** 3-1 Shin Ogawamachi, Shinjuku-ku, Tokyo 162.
**Salesian Press (Shinjiko-ku),** Wakaba, Tokyo 122.
**Salvationist Publishing and Supplies,** 2-17 Kanda Jinbo-cho, Chiyoda-ku, Tokyo 101.
**Tamagawa University Press,** 1-1 6-chome, Tamagawa Gakuen, Machida-shi, Tokyo 194.
**Word of Life Press,** 6 Shinano-machi, Shinjuku-ku, Tokyo 160.
**YMCA Press,** 2nd Kosuga Bldg, 6/F, 30 Ryogoku, Nihonbashi, Chuo-ku, Tokyo 103.

*KENYA*
**African Herald Publishing House,** PO Box 5049, Kendu Bay. T: Radiocall Nairobi 2153. (Seventh-day Adventist).
**African Inland Church Press,** AIC Kijabe Station, PO Box 40, Kijabe. T: 12Y7.
**Church of God Press,** Editor, Kima Mission, PO Box 160, Maseno.
**Evangel Publishing House (EPH),** PO Box 969, Kisumu. T: Nyang'ori 1Y5.
**Uzima Press,** Imani House, PO Box 48127, Nairobi. T: 20239. (Anglican).

*KOREA, South*
**Korean Publishing House,** Chung Yang Ri, c/o SDA Mission, IPO Box 1243, Soul. T: 960071.

*LEBANON*
**Middle East Press,** PO Box 2345, Bayrut. T: 260932. (Seventh-day Adventist).

*LESOTHO*
**Morija Printing Works,** PO Box 5, Morija.

*MADAGASCAR*
**Imprimerie Luthérienne (Trano Printy Loterana),** BP 538, Tananarive.
**Malagasy Publishing House,** BP 1134, Tananarive. T: 40365. (Seventh-day Adventist).

*MALAWI*
**Assemblies of God Press,** PO Box 5749, Limbe.
**Malamulo Publishing House,** PO Makwasa. T: 206. (Seventh-day Adventist).
**Petro Printing Press,** Nkhoma.

*MOZAMBIQUE*
**Mozambique Publishing House,** Av 24 de Julho 453, CP 1468, Maputo. (Seventh-day Adventist).

*NETHERLANDS*
**Netherlands Publishing House,** Van Weede van Dijkveldstr 77, 's-Gravenhage. T: (70)554140. (Seventh-day Adventist).

*NORWAY*
**Norwegian Publishing House,** Akersgaten 74, Oslo. T: 204179. (Seventh-day Adventist).
**Unges Forlag,** NKRO, Hausmannsgate 22, Oslo. (Mission Alliance. One of many smaller publishing houses).

*PAKISTAN*
**Christian Publishing House (MIK Press),** 36 Ferozepur Rd, Lahore 4.

*PHILIPPINES*
**Philippine Publishing House,** Baesa, Caloocan City, PO Box 813, Manila, P D-406. (Seventh-day Adventist).

*POLAND*
**Polish Publishing House,** Foksal 8, Warszawa. T: 277611/3,262506. (Seventh-day Adventist).

*PORTUGAL*
**Casa Publicadora das Assembleias de Deus,** Av Al Reis 97-1, Lisboa-1.
**Centro Baptista de Publicações,** Rua Marechal Gomes da Costa 2-3, Dt, Apdo 8, Queluz.
**Edições Palavras de Vida (TEAM),** Rua da Prata 156, Lisboa-2.
**Edições Vida Nova,** Apdo 10, Marinha Grande.
**Portuguese Publishing House,** Rua Joaquim Bonifacio 17, Lisboa 1. T: 2510844. (Seventh-day Adventist).

*SOUTH AFRICA*
**Advocate Press,** PO Box 627, Krugersdorp, Transvall.
**Christian Publishing Company,** PO Box 132, Roodepoort, Transvaal.
**Emmanuel Press,** PO Box 7, Nelspruit, Tranvaal.
**Gospel Publishing House,** Book Deport, PO Box 505, Roodepoort, Transvaal.
**Hart Publishers,** PO Box 353, Kempton Park, Transvaal.
**LIFE Publishers,** PO Box 47, Nelspruit, Transvaal.
**Lovedale Press,** Lovedale, CP.
**Lutheran Publishing House,** 220 West St, Durban, Natal.
**Methodist Publishing House and Press,** PO Box 708, Cape Town, CP.

**Nazarene Publishing House and Press,** PO Box 5, Florida, Transvaal.
**Sentinel Publishing Association,** Rosmead Av, Kenilworth, Cape Town. T: 779141. (Seventh-day Adventist).
**Word of Life Publishers (TEAM),** PO Box 595, Durban, Natal.

*SPAIN*
**Ediciones Don Bosco,** Paseo San Juan Bosco 62, Barcelona 17. (Member, BICE).
**Spanish Publishing House,** Paseo San Francisco de Sales 11, Madrid 3. T: 2436544,2438832. (Seventh-day Adventist).

*SWEDEN*
**Swedish Publishing House,** Satrahojden 14, S-803 60 Gavle. T: (026)187298. (Seventh-day Adventists).

*SWITZERLAND*
**CVN Buch & Druck,** Badenerstr 69, CH-8026 Zürich. (Methodist publishing house).
**Schweizerische Evangelische Verlagsgesellschaft,** CH-3177 Laupen.
**Swiss Publishing House,** Wylerhalde, CH-3704 Krattigen. T: (033)541065. (Seventh-day Adventist).

*TANZANIA*
**Central Tanganyika Press,** Msalato, PO Box 15, Dodoma. (Anglican).
**Evangelical Press (CMML),** PO Box 524, Mtwara.
**Inland Publishers,** PO Box 125, Mwanza. (African Inland Mission).
**Ndanda Mission Press,** PO Ndanda via Lindi.
**Mennonite Press,** PO Box 7, Musoma.
**Vuga Press (ELCT),** PO Box 25, Soni. (Lutheran).

*THAILAND*
**Gospel Printing Press,** Mass Communication Building, 1st Floor, PO Box 11/1293, Bangkok.
**Kingdom Development (Gospel Press),** 10 Soi 6, Sukhumvit Rd, Bangkok 11. T: 2525418,3920756.
**OMF Publishers,** 111/0 Pan Rd, Silom, Bangkok 5. T: 2348258.
**Suriyaban Publishers (Church of Christ in Thailand),** 14 Pramuan Rd, Bangkok 5. T: 2347991/2.
**Thailand Publishing House,** 9/23 Soi Chareon Suk, PO Box 11/234, Bangkok. T: 913594. (Seventh-day Adventist).

*UGANDA*
**Uganda Church Press,** Georgiadis Chambers, 6A Kampala Rd, PO Box 2776, Kampala. T: 41599.

*UK OF GB & NI*
**Ambassador College Press,** St Albans. (Worldwide Church of God).
**Aquin Press,** Bloomsbury Publishing Co, Woodchester Lodge, Woodchester, Stroud, Gloucs GL5 5PB. T: Amberley 2591/2.
**Assemblies of God Publishing House,** 106/114 Talbot St, Nottingham NG1 5GH. T: (0602)44525/6.
**Associated Christian Publishers,** Lottbridge Drove, Eastbourne, East Sussex BN23 6NT.
**Bagster (Samuel) & Sons,** 72 Marylebone Lane, London W1M 6BS. T: (01)486-1420.
**Banner of Truth Trust,** 78b Chiltern St, London W1E 2EZ. (Puritan works).
**Campfield Press,** St Albans, Herts. T: 5651162.
**Chapman (Geoffrey) Publishers,** 18 High St, Wimbledon, London SW19. T: (01)946-3047.
**Church Book Room Press,** 7 Wine Office Court, Fleet St, London EC4. T: (01)583-1484.
**Clark (T & T),** 38 George St, Edinburgh EH2 2LQ. T: (031)225-4703.
**Collins (William) Sons & Company,** 14 St James' Place, London SW1A 1TS. T: (01)493-5321.
**Darton, Longman & Todd,** 85 Gloucester Rd, London SW7 4SU. T: (01)370-5031.
**Drummond Press,** Gen Manager, Drummond House, 41 The Craigs, Stirling. T: 3384. (Stirling Tract, Enterprise).
**Edinburgh House Press,** 2 Eaton Gate, London SW1. T: (01)730-9611.
**Epworth Press & Methodist Publishing House,** 27 Marylebone Rd, London NW1. T: (01)935-2549.
**Faber & Faber,** 3 Queen Square, London WC1N 3AU. T: (01)278-6881.
**Faith Press,** 7 Tufton St, London SW1P 3QD. T: (01)222-3940. (Anglican).
**Falcon Books,** Church Pastoral-Aid Society, Falcon Court, London EC4. T: (01)353-4821.
**Fellowship of Faith for the Muslims Publications,** 14 Tudor Close, Hove, East Sussex BN3 7NR.
**Foundational Book Company,** 77 Beckwith Rd, Herne Hill, London SE24. T: (01)274-5874.
**Gospel Printing Mission,** Hon Dir, 91 Auckland Rd, Ilford, Essex. T: (01)554-0968.
**Highway Press (CMS),** 157 Waterloo Rd, London SE1 8UU. T: (01)928-2902.
**Hodder Religious Books,** Hodder & Stoughton, St Paul's House, Warwick Lane, London EC4. T: (01)248-5797.
**Home Words Printing & Publishing Company,** 11 Ludgate Square, London EC4. T: (01)248-2872.
**Inter-Varsity Press (IVP),** 39 Bedford Square, London WC1B 3EY. T: (01)737-5113. (IVF).
**James (Arthur),** The Drift, Evesham, Worcs WR11 4NW. T: 6566.
**Lutterworth Press,** Gen Manager, Albion House, Woking, Surrey. T: 64765/8.
**Marshall, Morgan & Scott Publications** 1-5 Portpool Lane, Holborn, London EC1. T: (01) 405-7011/6.
**Mowbray (AR) & Company,** Alden Press, Osney Mead, Oxford OX2 0EG. T: (0865)42507.
**Nelson (Thomas) & Sons,** 36 Park St, London W1Y 4DE. T: (01)493-8351.
**Oxford University Press,** Walton St, Oxford OX2 6DP. T: (0865)56767.
**Paternoster Press,** Paternoster House, 3 Mount Radford Crescent, Exeter, Devon EX2 4JW. T: 58977.
**Pickering & Inglis,** 29 Ludgate Hill, London EC4. T: (01)248-2246. (Also: 26 Bothwell St, Glasgow C2. T: (041)552-5044.
**Religious Book Publishers Group,** Publishers Association, 19 Bedford Square, London WC1B 3HJ. T: (01)580-6321.
**Religious Education Press (REP),** Headington Hill Hall, Oxford OX3 0BW. T: 64881.
**Saint Andrew Press,** 121 George St, Edinburgh EH2 4YN. T: (031)225-5722.
**Salvationist Publishing and Supplies,** 117-121 Judd St, London WC1H 9NN. T: (01)387-1656.
**Sheed and Ward,** 33 Maiden Lane, London WC2E 7LA. T: (01)240-1777/8.
**Society for Promoting Christian Knowledge (SPCK),** Holy Trinity Church, Marylebone Rd, London NW1 4DU. T: (01)387-5282.
**Stanborough Press,** Alma Park, Grantham, Lincs. T: 4284. (Seventh-day Adventist).
**Student Christian Movement Press,** 56-58 Bloomsbury St, London WC1B 3QX. T: (01)636-3841.
**Sumner Press,** 24 Tufton St, London SW1P 3RB. T: (01)222-5533.
**Tufton Press,** 15 Tufton St, London SW1P 3QQ. T: (01)222-4222.
**Tyndale Press,** 39 Bedford Square, London WC1B 3EY. T: (01)636-5113. (IVF).
**Victory Press (Evangelical Publishers),** Lottbridge Drove, Eastbourne, East Sussex. T: (0323) 27454.
**WEC Press,** Worldwide Evangelization Crusade, Kilcreggan Lodge, Barbour Rd, Kilcreggan, Dunbartonshire G84 0HG.
**World's Work Ltd,** The Press at Kingswood, Tadworth, Surrey. T: Mogador 3511.

*USA*
**Abingdon Press,** 201 Eighth Av South, Nashville, TN 37203.
**Advocate Press,** PO Box 98, Franklin Springs, GA 30639. (Pentecostal Holiness Church).
**American Christian Press (The Way Inc),** New Knoxville, OH 45871.
**Associated Church Press,** 343 South Dearborn St, Chicago, IL 60604. T: (312)922-5444.
**Augsburg Publishing House,** 426 South 5th St, Minneapolis, MN 55415.
**Baker Book House,** 1019 Wealthy St SE, Grand Rapids, MI 49506.
**Baptist Press,** Nashville, TN 37102.
**Beacon Press,** 25 Beacon St, Boston, MA 02108. T: (617)742-2100.
**Berean Publishers,** PO Box 1091, Indianapolis, IN 46206.
**Bethany Press,** Box 179, St Louis, MO 63166.
**Bethel Publishing Company,** 1819 South Main St, Elkhart, IN 46514.
**Brethren Press,** 1451 Dundee Av, Elgin, IL 60120.
**Christian Missions Press,** PO Box 545, Waynesbord, GA 30830.
**Christian Victory Publishing Company,** 2909 Umatilla St, Denver, CO 80211.
**Church Press Printing,** Glendale, CA 91209.
**Concordia Publishing House,** 3558 South Jefferson Av, St Louis, MO 63118. T: (314)664-7000. (Lutheran).
**Congregational Holiness Publishing House,** Griffin, GA 30223.
**Cook (David C) Publishing Company,** 850 North Grove Av, Cook Square, Elgin, IL 60120. T: (312) 741-2400.
**Covenant Press,** 5101 North Francisco Av, Chicago, IL 60625.
**Cowman Publishing Company,** 1415 Lake Drive SE, Grand Rapids, MI 49506.
**Cross Publishing Company,** 290 Monroe Av, Kenilworth, NJ 07033.
**Eerdmans (Wm B) Publishing Company,** 225 Jefferson Av, Grand Rapids, MI 49506.
**Evangel Press,** 301-305 North Elm, Nappanee, IN 46550.
**Fortress Press,** 2900 Queen Lane, Philadelphia, PA 19129.
**Free Church Publications,** PO Box 9177, Berkeley, CA 94709. T: (415)549-0649. (Directories of 900 radical task-oriented groups across USA).
**Friendship Press,** Box 37844, Cincinnati, OH 45237.
**Golden Press,** 850 Third Av, New York, NY 10022.
**Gospel Folio Press,** 817 North Av NE, Grand Rapids, MI 49501.
**Gospel Publishing Company,** Burlington, WI 53105.
**Gospel Publishing House,** 1445 Boonville Av, Springfield, MO 65802. (Assemblies of God).
**Herald Press,** Scottdale, PA 15683.
**Herald Publishing House,** 3225 South Noland, Box 1019, Independence, MO 64051.
**Hope Publishing Company,** 5707 West Lake St, Chicago, IL 60644.
**Inter-Varsity Press,** 130 North Wells, Chicago, IL 60606.
**Judson Press,** Valley Forge, PA 19481.
**Knox (John) Press,** Box 1176, Richmond, VA 23209.
**Light & Life Press,** Winona Lake, IN 46590.
**Logos International,** 185 N Av, Plainfield, NJ 07060.
**Macmillan Publishing Company,** 866 Third Av, New York, NY 10022.
**Methodist Publishing House,** 201 Eighth Av South, Nashville 2, Tennessee.
**Moody Press,** 820 North Lasalle, Chicago, IL 60610. T: (312)642-1570.
**Morehouse-Barlow Company,** 14 East 41st St, New York, NY 10017. T: (212)532-4370.
**Nazarene Publishing (Beacon Hill),** PO Box 527, Kansas City, MO 64141.
**Nelson (Thomas) & Sons,** Copewood & Davis Sts, Camden, NJ 08103. T: (609)365-6550.
**Oxford University Press,** 200 Madison Av (417 Fifth Av), New York, NY 10016. T: (212)679-7300.
**Pacific Press Publishing Association,** 1350 Villa St, Mountain View, CA 94040. T: (415)961-2323. (Seventh-day Adventist).
**Pathway Press,** 1080 Montgomery Av, Cleveland, TN 37311. (Ch of God).
**Pentecostal Publishing House,** 3645 S Grand Blvd, St Louis, MO 63418. (United Pentecostal Church).
**Practical Press,** Box 111, Bible School Park, NY 13737.
**Presbyterian & Reformed Publishing Company,** Box 185, Nutley, NJ 07110.
**Protestant Church Owned Publishers Association,** Bryn Mawr, PA 19010.
**Rapids Christian Press,** PO Box 467, Wisconsin Rapids, WI 54494.
**Regular Baptist Press,** 1800 Oakton, Des Plaines, IL 60018.
**Religious Herald Publishing Association,** PO Box 8377, Richmond, VA 23226.
**Revell (Fleming H) Company,** Old Tappan, NJ 07675. T: (201)768-8060.
**Review & Herald Publishing Association,** 6800 Eastern Av NE, Washington, DC 20012. T: (202) 723-3700. (Seventh-day Adventist).
**Scripture Press Publications,** 1825 College Av, Wheaton, IL 60187.
**Seabury Press,** 815 Second Av, New York, NY 10017. T: (212)TN7-8282.
**Sheed & Ward,** 64 University Place, New York, NY 1003. T: (212)OR4-8807.
**Southern Publishing Association,** 2119 Twenty-fourth Av, North Nashville, TN 37208. T: (615) 254-0636. (Seventh-day Adventist).
**Sovereign Grace Publishers,** 1242 Centerville Rd, Wilmington, DE 19808.
**Spearhead Press,** 1218 Chestnut St, Philadelphia, PA 19107.
**Standard Publishing Company,** 8100 Hamilton Av, Cincinnati, OH 45231.
**Tabernacle Publishing Company,** 5707 West Lake St, Chicago, IL 60644.
**Through the Bible Publishers,** 4032 Swiss Av, Dallas, TX 75204.
**Tyndale House Publishers,** 336 Gundersen Drive, Box 80, Wheaton, IL 60187. T: (312)668-8300. (Also: 133 North Washington St, Wheaton, IL 60187. *Living Bible*, et alia).
**Union Gospel Press,** 2000 Brookpark Rd, PO Box 6059, Cleveland, OH 44101.
**United Church Press,** 1505 Race St, Philadelphia, PA 19102.
**Voice Christian Publishers,** PO Box 672, Northridge, CA 91324.
**Voice of Healing Publishing Company,** PO Box 8658, Dallas, TX 75216. (Christ for the Nations).
**Westminster Press,** Witherspoon Bldg, Philadelphia, PA 19107.
**White Wing Publishing House,** Keith St, Cleveland, TN 37311. (Church of God of Prophecy).
**Word Inc,** PO Box 1790, Waco, TX 76703.
**World Publishing Company,** 2231 West 110th St, Cleveland, OH 44102.
**Zondervan Publishing House,** 1415 Lake Drive, Grand Rapids, MI 49506.

*VENEZUELA*
**Tipografía Evangélica Asociada,** Apdo 402, Maracaibo.

*VIET NAM*
**Vietnam Signs Press,** 373 Dai-lo Vo di Nguy, PO Box 453, Phu-Nhuan, Saigon. T: 41604. (Seventh-day Adventist).

*YUGOSLAVIA*
**Yugoslavian Publishing House,** Bozidara Adzije, 11000 Beograd. T: 441286. (Seventh-day Adventist).

*ZAIRE*
**Editions du Léopard,** BP 2244, Kinshasa 1.
**Editions Evangéliques,** Nyankunde par Bunia, Province Orientale.
**Librairie Evangélique au Zaire (LEZA),** BP 123, Kinshasa 1. (Protestant publishing).

*ZAMBIA*
**African Christian Books,** PO Box 376, Luanshya.
**Baptist Publishing House,** PO Box 1995, Lusaka.

*ZIMBABWE*
**Mambo Press,** PO Box 779, Gwelo. T: 2293. (RC).
**Rhodesian Christian Press,** PO Box 2146, Bulawayo.

# 45

# Radio & Television Stations

***Definition.*** Church- or Christian-owned, -operated, -controlled, or -sponsored radio or TV broadcasting stations (defined as organized centres with transmitting equipment); national associations of stations.

The world total of Christian radio and TV stations is about 1,450 (1980). They are too numerous to be listed here, but listings of stations together with their call signs and programme names are given under DIRECTORIES.

# 46

# Regional Conciliarism

***Definition.*** Interdenominational or ecumenical councils of churches or denominations and dioceses of different ecclesiastical traditions, for a region covering a number of nations; councils, federations, alliances; regional conciliarism, collegiality and consultation; Roman Catholic regional episcopal conferences and multinational episcopal conferences.

There are around 55 international and regional (subcontinental) councils of churches across the world.

*ALGERIA*
**Conférence Episcopale d'Afrique du Nord,** Rue Khelifa Boukhalfa 13, El Djezair (Alger). T: 634244, 640582

*AUSTRALIA*
**Australasian Alliance of Bible Believing Christian Churches,** PO Box 8, St Agnes 5091.

*CENTRAL AFRICAN REPUBLIC*
**Association des Conférences Episcopales du Congo, de la RCA et du Tchad (ACECCT),** Secretariat, BP 1518, Bangui. T: 614621.

*CHINA (TAIWAN)*
**Regional Episcopal Conference of China/ Regional Conference of Chinese Bishops (Chung Kuo Chu-chiao T'uan),** 34 Lane, 32 Kuangfu Rd, PO Box 1723, Taipei. T: 771295.

*COLOMBIA*
**Comisión de Cooperación Presbiteriano en Latinoamérica (Commission for Presbyterian Co-operation in Latin America),** Apdo Aéreo 14-650, Bogotá.
**Consejo Anglicano Latinoamericano (CALA) (Anglican Council of Latin America),** Cra 13 63-39, Of 407, Apdo Aéreo 52964, Bogotá 2.

*COSTA RICA*
**Communidad Latinoamericana de Ministerios Evangélicos,** Pres, Apdo 1307, San José. T: 215622.

*DENMARK*
**Nordic Bishops Conference (Conferentia Episcopalis Scandiae),** Bredgade 69A, DK-1260 Kobenhavn K. T: (01)116080.

*EL SALVADOR*
**Secretariado Episcopal de América Central y Panamá (SEDAC),** Junto al Seminario, Apdo Postal 78, San Salvador. T: 236690.

*FIJI*
**Conférence des Evêques du Pacifique (CEPAC) (Episcopal Conference of the Pacific),** PO Box 1200, Suva. T: 22851.

*FRANCE*
**Commission des Eglises Evangéliques d'Expression Française à l'Exterieur (CEEEFE),** Sec, 47 Rue de Clichy, F-75009 Paris. T: 874-1508.

*INDIA*
**Syro-Malabar Bishops' Synod,** Catholic Bishops' House, Kottayam-1, Kerala. T: 3527.

*ISRAEL*
**Conférence des Evêques Latins dans les Régions Arabes (CELRA),** Patriarcat Latin, PO Box 14152, Jerusalem (Old City). T: (02)282323.

*KENYA*
**Association of Member Episcopal Conferences in Eastern Africa (AMECEA),** Sec, Gen, AMECEA Office, 49 Gitanga Rd, PO Box 21191, Nairobi. T: 566506.
**Central Africa Christian Council (CACC),** Chairman, Dala Hera, Kibos Rd, PO Box 782, Kisumu.

*LEBANON*
**Middle East Bible Council,** Pres, Box 2165, Bayrut.
**Middle East Council of Churches (MECC),** Sec, Rue Makhoul, Immeub'e Dib, BP 5376, Bayrut. T: 344894.

*MALAWI*
**Conference of the Anglican Provinces of Africa (CAPA),** PO Box 19, Chilema.

*NIGERIA*
**Association of the Episcopal Conferences of Anglophone West Africa (AECAWA),** PO Box 951, Lagos. (Also: AECEWA, using 'English-speaking' instead of Anglophone).
**West African Council of Christian Churches,** P.O. Box 53, Abak, South Eastern State.

*PERU*
**Consejo Anglicano Sud Americano (CASA) (Anglican Council of South America),** Apdo 10266, Correo Colmena, Lima.

*SINGAPORE*
**Council of the Church of South-East Asia (CCSEA),** Chairman, Bishopsbourne, 4 Bishopsgate, Singapore 10.

*SOLOMON ISLANDS*
**South Pacific Anglican Council (SPAC),** Chairman, Bishopdale, Mendana Av, PO Box C13, Honiara.

*SOUTH AFRICA*
**Conference of Archbishops of Anglican Provinces in Africa (Anglican African Archbishops' Conference),** Sec, Bishopscourt, Claremont, CP. (Succeeded by CAPA).
**Inter-Regional Meeting of Bishops of Southern Africa (IMBISA),** PO Box 17054, Hillbrow 2038, Johannesburg. T: (011)725-3244. (RC).
**Southern African Catholic Bishops' Conference (SACBC) (Beraadsliggaam van die Suid-Afrikaanse Katolieke Biskoppe),** Standard Bank Bldgs/Geboue, Paul Kruger St, PO Box 941, Pretoria 001. T: 36230,30322.

*SWEDEN*
**Scandinavian Evangelical Council,** Källparksgatan 10a, Uppsala. (Also c/o Frederiksplein 24, Amsterdam 1002, Netherlands).

*TRINIDAD & TOBAGO*
**Antilles Episcopal Conference (AEC),** 27 Maraval Rd, Port of Spain. T: (62)21103.

*UK OF GB & NI*
**European Baptist Federation,** Gen Sec, Baptist Church House, 4 Southampton Row, London WC1 T: Holborn 3939.

*USA*
**Pentecostal Fellowship of North America (PFNA),** Chairman, 1445 Boonville, Springfield, MO 65802.

*UPPER VOLTA*
**Conférence Episcopale Régionale de l'Afrique de l'Ouest Francophone (CERAO),** BP 1471, Ouagadougou. T: 35180.

*ZAIRE*
**Africa Inter-Mennonite Mission,** CIM Hostel, BP 4081, Kinshasa II.

# 47 Religious Communities

*Definition.* Religious orders, congregations, societies, communities, brotherhoods, sisterhoods, mixed communities, and other communities following a religious rule (regular) or the religious life, with a permanent centre, permanent membership and permanent residential community, for men and/or women, with either ordained, religious, lay or mixed personnel; usually or often with religious vows of poverty, chastity and obedience; not primarily concerned with foreign missionary work; Catholic congregations of pontifical status (directly under Rome); and indigenous communities and local congregations (clerical or lay) begun in the Third World. For deaconess orders, see WOMEN IN THE ORDAINED MINISTRY. For congregations primarily devoted to foreign missionary work, see FOREIGN MISSIONARY SOCIETIES.

These communities number 1,530 for the Roman Catholic Church, with several hundred more for other churches, hence are too numerous to list below. Listings will be found described here under DIRECTORIES.

# 48 Religious Periodicals

*Definition.* Christian or church periodicals, journals, magazines, newspapers, bulletins, house organs, and other regular serials; of popular, news, scholarly, professional or academic content; daily, semi-weekly, weekly, biweekly, monthly, quarterly, excluding irregular serials and annuals.

As decribed in this Encyclopedia, the total number of current periodicals concerned with Christianity and religion is over 3,000 scholarly journals in the various disciplines, together with over 20,000 Christian magazines and newspapers of less academic and more popular content. Because of these vast numbers, no attempt is made here to list them. A small selection of significant directories and yearbooks dealing with periodicals will be found here under DIRECTORIES.

# 49 Religio-Political Organizations

*Definition.* Christian political parties (e.g. Christian Democrats), church groups with a political or ideological emphasis, especially progressivist or traditionalist groups; church organizations dealing with international political affairs or public affairs; polemical groups, radical groups, front organizations, rightist organizations; counter-revolutionary organizations, reactionary groups, movements of religious conservatism; non-violent groups, paramilitary organizations; pressure groups or lobbies working on governments or the United Nations.

Organizations of major significance in this field number over 200.

*ARGENTINA*
**Ciudad Católica,** Córdova 679, 5 piso, of 504, Buenos Aires. (Traditionalist).
**Macabeos Siglo XX,** José Hernández 2535, Buenos Aires. (Traditionalist).
**Movimiento de Sacerdotes para el Tercer Mundo (MSTM),** P Genesio 630, Santa Fe. (Progressivist).
**Sociedad Argentina de Defensa de la Tradición, Familia y Propiedad (TFP),** Avda Figueroa Alcorta 3260, Suc 25, Buenos Aires. (Traditionalist).

*AUSTRALIA*
**Catholic Lay Association of Melbourne,** Alfred St, Kew, Victoria. (Progressivist).
**Catholic Worker,** c/o Dept of Mathematics, University of Melbourne, Parkville, Victoria. (Progressivist).
**Latin Mass Society,** Box 2773, GPO, Sydney, NSW. (Traditionalist).
**Non-Violent Power,** c/o Catholic Presbytery, Harbord, Sydney, NSW. (Progressivist).
**Pax/Catholics for Peace,** Dept of Philosophy, University of Melbourne, Parkville, Victoria. (Progressivist).

*AUSTRIA*
**Arbeitskreis Kritisches Christentum (AKC),** Kärtnerstr 25, A-1010 Wien. T: (02222)521681. (Progressivist).
**Pax Christi,** Seelsorge Institut, Stephansplatz 6/6/51, A-1010 Wien. T: 524646/73.
**SOG-Österreich (Solidaritätsgemeinschaft Engagierter Christen),** Postfach 170, A-5010 Salzburg.

*BELGIUM*
**Alternative Ecclésiastique Eliker-Ik/Kerkelijk Alternatief Eliker-Ik,** Hoogstraat 9, B-9000 Gent.
**Assemblée pour un Concile des Wallons et des Bruxellois (ACWB),** Rue Agimont 5, B-4000 Liège. T: (041)230486. (Progressivist).
**Chrétien pour le Socialisme/Christenen voor het Socialisme,** Rue Agimont 5, B-4000 Liège. T: (041)230486. (Also: Consciencestraat 46, B-2000 Antwerpen). (Progressivist).
**European Christian Democratic Union,** Rue de Deux Eglises 41, B-1040 Brussel.
**Groupe d'Action, Co-responsabitité Diocèses de Gand/Aktiegroep Inspraak Bisdom Gent,** Chaussée de Gand 85, B-9411 Erondegem. (Progressivist).
**Inspraak,** Voornitgangstraat 245, B-1000 Brussel. (Progressivist).
**Les Fraternités Jean XXIII,** Les Rameaux, B-1340 Ottignies. T: (010)416225. (Progressivist).
**Pax Christi,** Rue de la Poste 111, B-1030 Brussel. T: 190589.
**Présence et Témoignage,** Rue des Frères Taymans 202, B-1360 Tubize. (Progressivist).
**Rassemblement des Silencieux de l'Eglise,** Clos des Peuplieurs 58, B-1200 Brussel. (Traditionalist).
**Thomas More Genootschap,** O.I. Vrouwdrey 8, B-9040 Oostakker. (Traditionalist).

*BOLIVIA*
**Legión Boliviana Social Nacionalista,** Cochabamba. (Traditionalist).

*BRAZIL*
**Hora Presente,** Rua Sete de Abril 125, 3 andar, conj 307, São Pauló, SP. (Traditionalist).
**Permanência,** Rua da Laranjeiras 540, CP 88, Rio de Janeiro, GB. (Traditionalist).
**Sociedade Brasileira de Defesa da Tradicão, Familia e Propiedade (TFP),** Rua Alagoas 344, Sao Pauló, SP. (Traditionalist).

*CAMEROON*
**Servir et Libérer,** Mission Catholique Bipindi, par Kribi.

*CHILE*
**Christian Democratic Organization of America,** Av Bernardo O'Higgins 1460, Casilla 1448, Santiago.
**Sociedad Chilena para la Defensa de la Tradición y Propiedad (Fiducia),** Casilla 85-12 Correo 12, Santiago. (Traditionalist).

*COLOMBIA*
**Grupo Tradicionalista de Jóvenes Cristianos de Colombia,** Apdo Aéreo 51918, Medellín. (Traditionalist).
**Juventud de Colombia Pro-Civilización Cristiana,** Apdo Aéreo 52885, Bogotá. (Traditionalist).

*COSTA RICA*
**Exodo,** Calle 9 Av 14 bis, Apdo Postal 3771, San José. (Progressivist).
**Juventud Obrera Cristiana,** Apdo Postal 5271, San José. (Progressivist).
**Juventud Universitaria Cristiana,** Centro Universitario Cultural, San Pedro de Montes de Oca. (Progressivist).
**Movimiento Estudiantil Cristiano,** Apdo Postal 5271, San José. (Progressivist)
**Movimiento Iglesia Joven,** Apdo Postal 5271, San José. (Progressivist).
**Movimiento Juvenil Cristiano,** Departamento de Vida Estudiantil, Universidad Nacional Heredia. (Progressivist).

*CZECHOSLOVAKIA*
**Pacem in Terris Association of Catholic Priests (Sdruzeni Katolickych Duchovnich Pacem in Terris),** Federální Sekretariat, Spálená 8, 110 10 Praha 1. T: 293985. (Also: Czech Secretariat, Spálená 8, 110 10 Praha 1. T: 293985; Slovak Secretariat, Kapitulská 1, 886 10 Bratislava. T: 30266). (Progressivist).

*FRANCE*
**Action Féminine pour une Pastorale de l'Enfance et de la Jeunesse,** 43 Rue de Turbigo, F-75003 Paris. T: (01)887-0935. (Traditionalist).
**Alliance Saint-Michel,** BP 58, F-75012 Paris. T: (01)344-5874. (Traditionalist).
**Assemblée Internationale des Chrétiens Solidaires des Peuples Vietnamien, Laotien et Cambodgien/International Assembly of Christians in Solidarity with the Vietnamese, Laotian and Cambodian Peoples/Dai Hôi Quôc Te Nhung Nguòi Ki Tò Giáo Doàn Vói Các Dân Tôc Viêt Nam, Lào Và Campuchia,** 18 Rue de Cardinal Lemoine, F-75005 Paris. T: 0335295.
**Boquen,** 118 Le Gouray par Lamballe, F-22 Plénee-Jugon. T: 96381111. (Progressivist).
**Centre Albert le Grand,** La Tourette, F-69210 L'Arbresle. T: 43. (Progressivist).
**Cercle Jean XXIII,** 51 Route de St-Joseph, F-44 Nantes. T: (40)748848. (Progressivist).
**Chrétiens pour le Socialisme,** Comité International, Centre Oecuménique de Liaisons Internationales (COELI), 68 Rue de Babylone, F-75007 Paris. T: 5552554. (Also for the Spanish diaspora, 6 Rue St-Severin, F-75007 Paris).
**Cité Nouvelle Midi,** 26 Blvd des Dames, F-13001 Marseille. (Progressivist).
**Cité Nouvelle/Chrétiens Marxistes,** 46 Rue Vaugirard, F-75006, Paris. T: 0333149. (Progressivist).
**Collectif 'Pour une Société Nouvelle'/Collectif St-VBenoît,** 14 Rue St Benoît, F-75006 Paris. (Progressivist).
**Concertation,** 25 Quai de Bondy, F-69005 Lyon. (Progressivist).
**Conférence Mondiale des Chrétiens pour la Palestine/World Conference of Christians for Palestine,** Secretariat Général, 49 Rue du Faubourg Poissonnière, F-75009 Paris. T: (01)824-9764.
**Echanges,** Centre International d'Echanges Religieux, Culturels et Sociaux (CIDERCS), 72 Rue de Sèvres, F-75007 Paris. T: (01)566-9166. (Progressivist).
**Echanges et Dialogue,** 86 bis Rue du Château, F-75014 Paris. (Progressivist).
**Esprit,** 19 Rue Jacob, F-75006 Paris. T: (01)033-9970. (Progressivist).
**Frères du Monde,** 208 Rue de Pessac, F-33000 Bordeaux. T: 929612. (Progressivist).
**La France Catholique/Ecclésia,** 12 Rue Edmond-Valentin, F-75007 Paris. T: (01)705-4331. (Traditionalist).
**La Lettre,** 68 Rue de Babylone, F-75007 Paris. T: (01)551-5713. (Progressivist).
**Le Combat de la Foi,** F-37150 Bléré. T: (47) 297247. (Traditionalist).
**Ligue de la Contre-Réforme Catholique,** Maison St-Joseph, F-10 Parres-les-Vaudes. (Traditionalist).
**L'Homme Nouveau,** Place Saint Sulpice 1, F-75006 Paris. (Traditionalist).
**Mouvement du Christianisme Social,** Sec Gén, 36 Rue de l'Université, Strasbourg (B-Rhin). T: 362098. (Also: 20 Rue de la Michodière, F-75002 Paris).
**Notre Combat (Chrétiens pour le Socialisme),** 49 Rue du Faubourg-Poissonnière, F-75009 Paris. T: 8249764. (Progressivist).
**Opus Sacerdotale (L'Oeuvre Sacerdotale placée sous le Patronage de Marie, Mère de l'Eglise),** 28 Rue Joachim du Bellay, F-49 Angers. (Traditionalist).
**Pax Christi,** 5 Rue de l'Abbaye, F-75006 Paris.
**Pro Fide et Ecclesia,** 43 Rue de Turbigo, F-75003 Paris. T: (01)887-0935. (Traditionalist).
**Rassemblement des Silencieux de l'Eglise (Pro Fide et Ecclesia),** 43 Rue de Turbigo, F-75003 Paris. T: (01)887-0935. (Traditionalist).
**Témoignage Chrétien (TC),** 49 Rue du Faubourg-Poissonnière, F-75009 Paris. T: (01)824-9764. (Progressivist).
**Vie Nouvelle,** 73 Rue Ste-Anne, F-75002 Paris. T: (01)742-7367. (Progressivist).

*GERMANY, Federal Republic of*
**Christen für des Sozialismus,** Wiesbadenstr 98, Konigstein TS. T: (06174)3234. (Progressivist).
**Pax Christi,** Exchanges and Correspondences Dept, Postfach 462, D-663 Saarlouis.
**Pax Christi,** Windmühlstr 2, D-6 Frankfurt/Main. T: 252398.

*GUATEMALA*
**Confederación de Sacerdotes y Seglares Diocesanos en Guatemala (COSDEGUA),** 15 Calle 34-24, Zona 5, Ciudad de Guatemala. (Progressivist).

*HUNGARY*
**Opus Pacis,** Dezsö u 3, Budapest I. (Progressivist).

*INDIA*
**Blue Army of Our Lady of Fatima,** Indian National Secretariat, 92 Acharya Jagadish Bose Rd, Calcutta 70014. (Traditionalist).

*IRELAND*
**Pax Christi,** 11 Sandymount Castle Drive, Dublin 4.

*ITALY*
**Christian Democratic Union of Central Europe (CDUCE),** Piazza del Gesu 46, Roma. T: 684541.
**Christian Democratic World Union,** Palazzo Doria, Via del Plebiscito 107, I-00186 Roma. T: 688583.
**Comitato Civico Nazionale,** Via della Conciliazione 1, I-00198 Roma. T: 6569551. (Traditionalist).
**Cristiani per il Socialismo,** Via Poggio Bracciolini 40, I-50126 Firenze. T: 689630 (Progressivist).
**European Christian Democratic Union,** Palazzo Doria, Via del Plebiscito 107, I-00186 Roma. T: 688583.
**Movimento Nazionale 7 Novembre,** Via Allessandro Severo 105/A, I-00145 Roma. T: (06)5139694. (Progressivist).
**Pax Christi,** Piazza Adriana 21, Roma.

*LEBANON*
**Conférence Mondiale des Chrétiens pour la Palestine,** Secrétariat pour les Pays Arabes, Rue Mak'houl (Abdel-Aziz), Immeuble Tanios Rebeiz, BP 1375, Bayrut. T: 341902/3.
**Eglise pour Notre Temps (Maronite),** BP 1145 Bayrut. (Progressivist).

*LUXEMBOURG*
**Pax Christi,** 5 Rue Bourbon, Luxembourg.

*MALTA*
**Ghaqda Christus Rex,** c/o Archbishop's Seminary, Florina.

*MEXICO*
**Cristianos para el Socialismo,** Apdo Postal 27-533, México, DF. T: 5743982. (Progressivist).

*NETHERLANDS*
**Action Committee For Pope and Church (Aktie Comité Voor Paux en Kerk),** Haydnlaan 21, Enschede. T: (05420)20108. (Traditionalist).
**Association for the Preservation of Roman Catholic Life in the Netherlands (Stichting tot Behoud van het Rooms-Katholieke Leven in Nederland),** Röntgenstraat 11, Tilburg. T: (013) 422831. (Traditionalist).
**Catholic Life Association (Stichting Katholiek Leven),** Postbus 214, Heerlen. (Traditionalist).
**Christians for Socialism (Christenen voor het Socialisme),** Woudschoten, Zeist. T: (03439)226. (Progressivist).
**Confrontation (Confrontatie),** Ververstraat 10, Heerlen. T: (045)714703. (Traditionalist).
**Dutch Roman Catholic Centre Pro Fide et Ecclesia (Rooms Katholiek Nederlands Centrum Pro Fide et Ecclesia),** Brouwerstraat 10, Helmond. T: (04920)36073. (Traditionalist).
**Ekklesia Den Haag,** 's-Gravenhage. (Progressivist).
**For Pope and Church (Voor Paus en Kerk),** St Jorisstraat 2, Venlo. T: (077)10012. (Traditionalist).
**International League of Religious Socialists,** Pres, Bentweldweg 5, Bentveld. T: (02500)41301.
**Jongerenkerk Venlo,** Grote Kerkstraat 36, Venlo. (Progressivist).
**Kritische Gemeente Ijmond,** Zwaansmeerstraat 8, Beverwijk. (Progressivist).
**Michael Legioen,** Le van Swindenstraat 31, Amsterdam. T: (020)356094. (Traditionalist).
**Open Kerk,** Postbus 2, Heemstede. (Progressivist).
**Pax Christi International,** Celebesstraat 60, 's-Gravenhage. T: (070)656823,65356,110536.
**Pax Christi 'Routes Internationales',** Postbus 444, Den Bosh. T: (04100)35140.
**Rooms Katholiek Partij Nederland (RKPN),** Agippinastraat 7, Postbus 100, NL-2119 Voorburg. T: (070)909275.
**Septuagint,** De Wetstein Pfisterlaan 55, Driebergen. T: (03438)3204. (Progressivist).
**Sint Willibrord Stichting,** St Janssingel 21, 's-Hertogenbosch. T: (073)136471. (Traditionalist).
**Stichting Sint Willibrord Omroep,** Minstreelaan 5, Utrecht. (Traditionalist).
**Werkplaats Kritische Gemeente Gooi,** Bussum. (Progressivist).

*NEW ZEALAND*
**New Zealand Inter-Church Council on Public Affairs,** 1 Randwick St, Northland, Wellington 5.

*POLAND*
**Catholic Intellectuals' Club (Klub inteligencji Katolickiej),** Secretariat of Co-ordination of Clubs, Rue Kopernika 34, Warszawa. (Progressivist).
**Christian and Social Association (Chrzescijanskie Stowarzyszenie Spoleczne, ChSS),** Marszalkowska 4, 00 590 Warszawa. T: 299251. (Progressivist).
**Social Publishing Institute 'The Sign' (Spoleczny Instytut Wydawniczy 'Znak')/The Sign Movement (Ruch Znak),** Rue Wislna 12, Kraków. (Progressivist).

*PORTUGAL*
**Christians for Socialism,** Rua Rodriguez Sampaio 79/3, Lisboa 5. T: 763097. (Progressivist).

*SPAIN*
**Alianza del Credo por la Iglesia Perseguida,** Balmes 87/4, Barcelona 8. (Traditionalist).
**Christians for Socialism,** Begonia 4, bajos 3, Ciudad Satellite San Idelfonso, Cornell (Barcelona). (Progressivist).
**Cristiandad,** Lauria 15, Barcelona. (Traditionaist).
**Cruzado Español,** Via Layetana 103/3, Barcelona 9. (Traditionalist).
**El Ciervo (Le Cerf),** Calvet 56, Apdo 12121, Barcelona 6. T: 2284265. (Progressivist).
**Fuerza Nueva,** Nuñez de Balboa 31, Madrid 1. T: 2769352. (Traditionalist).
**Iglesia Mundo,** Santa Teresa 6, Madrid 4. T: 4199465. (Traditionalist).
**Iglesia Viva,** c/o Desclée de Brower, Henao 6, Bilbao 9. (Progressivist).
**Pax Christi,** Duque de Mandas 43/4 centro, San Sebastian.
**Qué pasa?,** Lagasca 121, Madrid 6. T: 2613797. (Traditionalist).

*SWEDEN*
**Christian Group,** Swedish Parliament, Stockholm (100 members in parliament).
**Pax Christi,** Valhallavägen 132, Stockholm.
**Thursday Group (Parliament Bible Class),** Swedish Parliament, Stockholm. (Free and Low church members in parliament).

*SWITZERLAND*
**Armée Bleue de N-D de Fatima,** Secrétariat Mondial, 25 Beim Buremichelskopf, CP 9, CH-4024 Basel. T: (061)345919.
**Chrétiens du Mouvement,** Rue Rothschild 52, CP 25, CH-1211 Genève. T: (022)327977. (Progressivist).
**Commission of the Churches on International Affairs (CCIA),** Ecumenical Centre, 150 Route de Ferney, CH-1211 Genève 20.
**Communione et Liberazione,** Chemin de Béthléem 3, CH-1700 Fribourg. (Progressivist).
**Dialoghi,** Via del Tiglio, CH-6605 Locarno. (Progressivist).
**Für eine Offene Kirche,** Informationsdienst Kritischer Gruppen, Postfach 286, CH-8053 Zürich. (Progressivist).
**Pax Christi,** 3 Pré du Marché, CH-1004 Lausanne. (Also: Feld, CH-9606 Bütschwil).
**Solidaritätsgruppen Schweiz (SOG),** Postfach 613, CH-8050 Zürich. (Progressivist).
**Una Voce Helvetica (UVA),** Postfach 2120, CH-8023 Zürich. (Also: Postfach 523, CH-1701 Fribourg). (Traditionalist).
**Union Protestante Libérale,** Prés, 11 Chemin Monplaisir, Chêne-Bougeries. T: 351411.

*UK OF GB & NI*

**Alliance Mondiale et Politique Sainte-Jeanne d'Arc,** 15 Carlisle St, London W1. T: (01)437-4564.

**Catholic Institute for International Relations,** 38 King St, London WC2.

**Christian Socialist Movement (CSM),** Kingsway Hall, Kingsway, London WC2. T: (01)405-3246.

**Christians for Socialism,** CIIR, 1 Cambridge Terrace, London NW1. (Progressivist).

**Commission of the Churches on International Affairs (CCIA),** 34 Brook St, London SW1.

**Evangelical Parliamentary Group,** Sec, 17 Wansford Close, Brentwood, Essex.

**Latin Mass Society,** Hon Sec, 43 Blandford St, London W1H 3AE. (Traditionalist).

**Pax Christi,** 168 Homefield Rd, Sibely, Loughborough, Leics.

**Pro Fide Movement,** 92 Cheyne Walk, London SW10. (Also: 1 Waverley Place, Saltcoats, Ayrshire). (Traditionalist).

*USA*

**Blue Army of Our Lady of Fatima,** Secretariat, Ave Maria Institute, Washington, NJ 07882. (Traditionalist).

**Catholic Traditionalist Movement,** 200 Park Av, New York, NY 10017.

**Church League of America,** Exec Sec, 422 North Prospect St, Wheaton, IL 60187. T: (312)653-6100.

**Citizens United for Faith (CUF),** 222 North Av, New Rochelle, NY 10801. (Conservative).

**Commission of the Churches on International Affairs (CCIA),** 777 United Nations Plaza, New York, NY 10017.

**Council on Religion and International Affairs,** Press, 170 East 64th St, New York, NY 10021. T: (212)TE8-4120.

**Federated Russian Orthodox Clubs,** Sec, 84 East Market St, Wilkes-Barre, PA 18701.

**Friends Committee on National Legislation (FCNL),** 245 Second St NE, Washington DC 20002. T: (202)547-4343. (Registered lobbying group).

**Lutherans Alert,** 409 North Tacoma Av, Tacoma, WA 98403.

**National Association for Christian Political Action,** Pres, Box 185, Sioux Centre, IA 51250. T: (712)722-8641.

**Peoples Christian Coalition,** Editor, Box 132, Deerfield, IL 60015.

**Protestants and Other Americans United for Separation of Church and State,** 1633 Massachusetts Av, NW, Washington, DC 20036.

**Quaker Office at the United Nations,** Room 206, 345 East 46th St, New York, NY 10017. T: (212) 682-2745.

**Southern Christian Leadership Conference (SCLC),** Pres, 334 Auburn Av, NE, Atlanta, GA 30303.

**Thomas More Association,** 180 North Wabash Av, Chicago, IL 60601.

**Una Voce America,** PO Box 446, Grand Central Station, New York, NY 10017. (Traditionalist).

**Unitarian Universalist United Nations Office,** 777 United Nations Plaza, New York, NY 10017. T: (212)986-5165.

# 50

# Research Centres

*Definition.* Centres, institutes and institutions undertaking original research related to Christianity and religions — religious, socio-religious, anthropological, historical, biblical, theological, communications, information, missiological, missiographical, micromissiographical, macromissiographical, ecclesiological, ecclesiographical, macroecclesiographical, futurological; ecumenical centres and institutes at university level; experimental institutes, think tanks; Christian or church-related centres for study and research in non-Christian religions or atheism; documentation centres and services, resource centres, research archives, library research centres; public opinion polls, survey organizations, market research, radio/TV audience research centres, statistical services, pastoral research services; planning agencies, management research services; information management, computerized data banks, data processing organizations, computer bureaux, survey archives, research publications agencies. (Note: other research centres in specialized topics, e.g. LITURGY AND WORSHIP, BROADCASTING, will be found under those topics only if the research function is not their major one).

Christian- and church-related centres producing original research and significant at the national or wider levels numbered over 930 in 1980.

*ALGERIA*

**Centre Chrétien d'Etudes Maghrébines,** 36 Chemin Cheikh Bachir Brahimi (Beaurepaire), El-Biar, El Djezair. (Suppressed 1970).

**Centre de Langues et de Pastorale d'El Biar,** El Djezair.

**Centre d'Etudes Berbères (CEB),** Dir, 20 Rue des Fusillés, El Djezair.

**Centre d'Etudes Interdiocésaïn,** 5 Chemin des Glycines, El Djezair.

**Centre Pédagogique Arabe,** 70 Av Souidàni Boudjemaa, El Djezair.

*ARGENTINA*

**Centro de Estudios Cristianos (CEC),** Paraná 489, piso 2, Of 9, Buenos Aires. T: 494996. (Centre for Christian Studies of the River Plate).

**Centro de Investigación y Acción Social (CIAS),** O'Higgins 1331 (also Palpa 2440), Buenos Aires 26. (A chain of 6 CIAS centres in Latin America, run by Jesuits. In ICRA).

**Centro de Investigación y Estudio (CIE),** Centro Eclesiástico de Documentación y Estadistica (CEDE), Av La Plata 50, Buenos Aires.

**Centro de Investigación y Orientación Social (CIOS),** 9 de Julio 1643, Santa Fe. (Socio-religious).

**Centro de Investigaciones Motivacionales y Sociales (CIMS),** Aguero 2306, Buenos Aires.

**Centro de Investigaciones Sociales,** Lavalle 106, 5 piso, Buenos Aires.

**Centro de Investigaciones Sociales y Religiosas,** 1054 Rodriguez Pena, Buenos Aires. T: 418393.

**Centro de Investigaciones y Estudio de Servicio Social,** Sarandi 65, Buenos Aires.

**Equipo Coordinador de Investigaciones sobre Sociedad y Religión (ECOISYR),** Ntra Sra del Buen Viaje 936, Mrorón, Buenos Aires.

**Escuela de Ciencias Sagradas,** Rodriguez Pena 1054, Buenos Aires. T: 420256.

**Escuela de Periodismo y Ciencias de la Información,** Facultad Católica de Humanidades, Maipù 1369, Rosario. (Communication and information research).

**Instituto de Ciencias Sagradas,** Colegio Champagnat, Montevideo 1050, Buenos Aires.

**Instituto de Estudios e Investigaciones,** Fundación FAPES, Méjico 1880, Buenos Aires.

**Instituto de Teologia,** Junta Catequistica Central, La Plata 15-51 y 53, Buenos Aires. T: 26672.

**Secretaria Tecnica del Arzobispado de Santa Fe,** Gral López 2720, Santa Fe. (Socio-religiuos).

*AUSTRALIA*

**Australian Frontier,** 10 Floor, Room 18, 422 Collins St, Melbourne, Victoria 3000. (Formerly Institute for the Study of Man and Society).

**Division of Studies and Communication,** Australian Council of Churches, 511 Kent St, Sydney, NSW 2000.

*AUSTRIA*

**Erstes Philosophisches Institut der Universität,** Liebiggasse 5, Wien I.

**Institut für Dogmengeschichte und Ökumenische Theologie,** Universität Graz, Universitätsplatz 3, A-8010 Graz. T: (03122)31581/338. (Catholic).

**Institut für Kirchliche Sozialforschung (IKS),** Grillparzerstr 5, A-1010 Wien. T: 434284. (In FERES).

**Institut für Kirchliche Zeitgeschichte (IKZ),** Mönchsberg 2a, A-5020 Salzburg.

**Institut für Ökumenische Theologie,** Universität Salzburg, Sigmund-Haffnergasse 20, A-5020 Salzburg. T: (06222)86111247.

**Institut für Religionswissenschaft und Theologie,** Internationales Forschungszentrum für Grundfagen der Wissenschaften, Mönchsberg 2a, Salzburg.

**Internationales Forschungszentrum für Grundfagen der Wissenschaften Salzburg,** Mönchsberg 2a, A-5020 Salzburg. T: (06222)854467. (Science of religions, theology, church history).

**Katholische Sozialakademie,** Schottenring 35, A-1010 Wien.

**Ökumenisches Institut der Universität Graz,** A-8010 Graz.

**Pastoraltheologisches Institut der Universität Innsbruck,** Universitätsstr 4b, A-6020 Innsbruck.

**Philosophisches Institut,** Universität Salzburg, St-Peter-Bezirk 8/9, I Stock, Z20, A-5020 Salzburg. T: (06222)84285.

**Ungarisches Kirchensoziologischen Institut (UKI),** Grillparzerstr 5/10, A-1010 Wien. T: (0222) 942189. (Also: Linzerstr 263/18, A-1140 Wien).

**Wiener Katholische Akademie,** Freyung 6, 1 Stiege, A-1010 Wien. T: 6374927.

*BANGLADESH*

**Henry Martin Institute of Islamic Studies,** Baptist Mission House, Sadarghat, Dacca 1.

*BARBADOS*

**Department of Documentation and Research,** Christian Action for Development in the Caribbean (CADEC), PO Box 616, Bridgetown.

*BELGIUM*

**Académie Internationale des Sciences Religieuses,** Av de Tervuren 221, B-1150 Brussel. T: (02)733-2311.

**Bureau de Documentation Pastorale,** Chaussée de Wavre 216, B-1040 Brussel

**Centre Chrétien Flamand d'Etude et de Documentation (Christelijk-Vlaams Studi en Documentiecentrum),** St-Pietersnieunstraat 79, B-9000 Gent.

**Centre de Psychologie Religieuse,** Tiensestraat 127, B-3000 Leuven. T: (016)232448.

**Centre de Recherches Missiologiques,** Redingeustraat 16, B-3000 Leuven. T: (016)224975. (Also: B-1348 Louvain-la-Neuve).

**Centre de Recherches Socio-Religieuses (CRSR),** Place Montesquieu 1, bôite 21, B-1348 Ottignies-Louvain-la-Neuve. T: (010)418181. (French-speaking). (In FERES).

**Centre de Traitement Electronique des Documents (CETEDOC),** Université Catholique de Louvain, Tiensevest 156, B-3000 Leuven. T: (016) 235375.

**Centre des Techniques de Diffusion et Relations Publiques (CETEDI),** Université Catholique de Louvain, Van Evenstraat 2a, B-3000 Leuven. T: (016)28751. (Communication and information research).

**Centre d'Etudes des Problèms du Monde Musulman,** Université de Bruxelles, Brussel.

**Centre d'Etudes des Religions,** Université Libre de Bruxelles, Av Franklin Roosevelt 50, Brussel.

**Centre for Sociological Research (Centrum voor Sociologish Onderzoekinstituut),** Afdeling Godsdienstsociologie, Van Evenstraat 2a, B-3000 Leuven. T: (016)25601.

**Centre for Socio-Religious Research (Centrum voor Socio-Religieus Onderzoek),** de Beriotstraat 34, B-3000 Leuven. T: (016)225244. (Flemish-speaking). (In FERES).

**Centre International d'Etudes de la Formation Religieuse (Lumen Vitae),** Sec, Rue Washington 186, B-1050 Brussel. T: (02)343-5023.

**Centre National des Hautes Etudes Juives,** Institut de Sociologie, Université Libre de Bruxelles, Brussel.

**Centre pour les Sciences de la Communication (Centrum voor Communicatiewetenschappen, CECOWF),** Katholiek Universiteit Leuven, Van Evenstraat 2a, B-3000 Leuven. T: (016)21070. (Flemish-speaking).

**Centrum voor Socio-Religieus Onderzoek,** De Beriotstraat 34, B-3000 Leuven. T: (016)225244.

**CMN Centre de Documentation,** Blvd du Souverain 199, B-1160 Brussel.

**Fédération Internationale des Instituts de Recherches Socio-Religieuses (FERES)/International Federation of Institutes for Socio-Religious Research,** Secrétariat Général, Place Montesquieu 1, boîte 21, B-1348 Ottignies-Louvain-la-Neuve. T: (010)418181.

**Institut des Hautes Etudes des Communciations Sociales (IHECS),** Chaussée de Tournai 26b, B-7721 Ramegnies-Chin.

**Institut d'Histoire du Christianisme,** Faculté de Philosophie et Lettres, Université Libre de Bruxelles, Av F.D. Roosevelt 50, B-1050 Brussel. T: (02)649-0030 ext 2405.

**Institut Supérieur de Sciences Religieuses,** Redingenstraat 16, B-3000 Leuven. T: (016)224915. (Also: B-1348 Louvain-la-Neuve).

**International Centre for Studies in Religious Education,** Sec Gen, Rue Washington 186, B-1050 Brussel. T: 435023.

**International Congress on the Communication of Culture (ICCC),** Secretariat, Rue Washington 29, B-1050 Brussel.

**Irénikon,** Monastère Bénédictin, Prior, B-5395 Chevetogne. T: (083)21763.

**Pro Mundi Vita,** Gen Sec, Rue de la Limite 6, Brussel 3. T: (02)25136880.

**Prospective (Centre Internationale de Recherche et de Communication pour l'Eglise à Venir),** Pres, Av Armand Huysmans 77, B-1050 Brussel. T: 474261. (Also: Rue E Cattoir 16, B-1050 Brussel. T: (02)648-2766).

*BOLIVIA*

**Centro de Investigación Socio-Religiosa,** Yanacacha 545, Casilla 3077, La Paz.

**Centro de Investigación y Acción Social (CIAS),** Av Buenos Aires 588, Casilla 283, La Paz.

**Centro de Investigación y Promoción del Campesinado (CIPCA),** Illampu 733, Casilla 5458, La Paz. T: 21176.

**Iglesia y Sociedad en America Latina (ISAL),** c/o Icthus, Casilla 356, La Paz.

**Instituto Boliviano de Estudio y Acción Social,** Depto de Estudios Socio-Religiosos, Casilla 3277, La Paz. T: 25667. (In FERES).

**Instituto de Investigación Cultural para Educación Popular (INDICEP),** Calle Potosí 421, Casilla 525, Oruro. T: 52110. (RC; radiophonic school research).

**Instituto Superior de Estudios Teológicos (ISET),** Av Peru 3901, Casilla 2118, Cochabamba.

*BRAZIL*

**Centro Brasiliero de Informação Missionária (CEBIMI),** Rua Dr Gradim 365 fundos, 24400 São Goncalo, RJ.

**Centro de Estatística Religiosa e Investigações Sociais (CERIS),** Rua Dr Julio Ottoni 571, Santa Tereza, 20.000 Rio de Janeiro, ZC 45, GB. T: (245) 1464,(265)5177/8. (In FERES).

**Centro de Estudos Bíblicos e Ecumênicos,** Rua Almirante Alexandrino 3286, Sta Tereza, Rio de Janeiro, GB. T: (245)2780.

**Centro de Estudos pro Evangelismo (CEPE)/Centre for Advanced Studies in Evangelism (CASE),** Dir, CP 30.548, 01000 São Paulo, SP. (Church growth research).

**Centro de Orientação Missionária (COM),** 95 100 Caxias do Sul, RS.

**Centro Latinoamericano de Parapsicologia (CLAP),** Via Anhanguera Km 26, CP 11587, São Paulo, SP.

**Conselho Indigentista Missionário (CIMI),** 79 100 Campo Grande, MT.

**Faculdade dos Meios de Comunicação Social,** Pontificía Universidade Católica do Rio Grande, Av Ipiranga 6681, CP 1429, Pôrto Alegre, Rio Grande do Sul. (Communication and information research).

**FERES Regional Secretariat for Latin America,** Rua Dr Julio Ottoni 571, Rio de Janeiro, ZC 45, GB. T: 451464.

**Instituto Brasiliero de Desenvolvimento (IBRADES),** Rua Bambina 115, Botafogo, 20 000 Rio de Janeiro, ZC 02, GB. T: (226)8137,5866,6335.

**Instituto de Evangelização em Profundade (INDEP)/Institute of In-Depth Evangelism (INDEPTH, INDEF),** Coordinador General, CP 18.961 (Aeroporto), 01000 São Paulo, SP. T: 619602. (Linked with INDEF in Costa Rica).

**Instituto de Teologia do Recife (ITER),** Faculdade de Filosofia do Recife, Conde da Boa Vista s/n, Recife, PE.

**Instituto Evangélico de Pesquisas,** Rua Régo Freitas 530, Apto F.13, São Paulo, SP.

**Missionary Information Bureau (MIB),** Exec Sec, Rua São Bento 290, 1s 1, s/14, CP 1498, São Paulo, SP.

**Operação Anchieta,** Av Alberto Bins 1026, 90 000 Pôrto Alegre, RS. (Missiology).

**Sepal do Brasil,** Dir, Rua Princesa Isabel 109, 2 Andar, CP 30.548, São Paulo, SP. T: (61)9084.

**Serviço de Cooperação Apostólica Internacional (SCAI),** CP 133, 20 000 Rio de Janeiro, GB.

**Voluntários Internacionais e Brasileiros para a Amazôniz,** Rua Dr Assis 834, Arsenal, 66 000 Belém, Pará. (Missiology).

*BULGARIA*

**Institute of Christian Culture,** Sophia University, Sofija.

*BURMA*

**Centre for the Study of Buddhism,** Commission on Buddhism, 104c Inya Rd, University PO, Rangoon.

*BURUNDI*

**Centre de Coopération au Développement et de Recherches Sociologiques,** BP 1390, Bujumbura. T: 3263.

**Centre de Recherches et d'Animation Sociale (CERAS),** BP Bujumbura. T: 3236.

**Centre de Recherches Socio-Religieuses (CERES),** BP 1390, Bujumbura.

*CANADA*

**Canadian Church Growth Centre,** 4400-4th Av, Regina S4T 0H8. T: (306)545-1515.

**Centre de Recherches en Sociologie Religieuse (CRSR),** Grand Séminaire, Université Laval, Cité Universitaire, Québec G1K 7P4. T: 656-3207. (In FERES).

**Centre de Recherches Sociologiques et Religieuses,** Université Laval, Cité Universitaire, Québec G1K 7P4.

**Centre Diocésain de Recherches Pastorales,** 725 Rue Brassard, CP 1268, Nicolet, PQ.

**Centre for Ecumenical Studies,** St Michael's College, University of Toronto, Toronto, Ontario.

**Centre for the Study of Institutions and Theology,** 215 Cottingham St, Toronto 7, Ontario.

**Institut des Sciences Missionnaires de l'Université St-Paul/Institute of Mission Studies,** 233 Rue Main, Ottawa, Ontario K1S 1C4. T: (613)235-1421 local 37.

**Institute for Behavioural Research,** York University, 4700 Keele St, Downsview 463, Ontario. (Includes religion).

**Institute of Christian Studies,** Regent College, Vancouver, BC.

**Institute of Islamic Studies,** McGill University, 1345 Redpath Crescent, Montréal, Québec. T: VI4-6311. (Also: 805 West Sherbrooke, Montréal 25).

**Institute of Mediaeval Studies,** 59 Queen's Park Crescent, Toronto, Ontario.

**Office National des Techniques de Diffusion,** 4635 de Lorimier, Montréal 34, Québec. (Communication research).

**Research Committee of the Sociology of Religion,** International Sociological Association, Sec, 60 Oak Av, Dundas, Ontario.

**School of Communication,** St Paul University, 223 Main St, Ottawa 1, Ontario. (Communication and information research).

**Sermons from Science,** Gen Manager, PO Box 602, Station B, Montréal 2, Québec.

**Toronto Institute of Linguistics,** Principal, 16 Spadina Rd, Toronto, Ontario M5R 2S8. T: (416) 924-7167.

*CHILE*

**Centro de Investigación y Acción Social (CIAS),** Centro Bellarmino, Casilla 10445, Santiago. T: 68442. (In FERES).

**CIDE,** Almirante Barroso 22, Santiago. (Applied research, educational materials).

**DEC,** Sección Planeamiento, Erasmo Escala 1822, Oficina 415, Casilla 13383, Santiago.

**Oficina de Sociologia Religiosa,** Cienfuegos 47, Clas 197, Santiago. T: 713126.

*CHINA*

**Centre for the Study of Religion,** Nanjing University, Nanjing. (Formerly Protestant Theological Seminary).

*CHINA (TAIWAN)*

**Taiwan Church Growth Society,** 11 Lane 241, No 16, Ta-ya Rd, Taichung 400.

*COLOMBIA*

**Centro Antropológico de Misiones (ETHNIA),** Carrera 10 No 9-64, Bogotá.

**Centro de Investigación y Acción Social (CIAS),** Carrera 5a No 11-43, Bogotá. T: 435581.

**Escuelo de Ciencias de la Comunicación,** Pontifícia Universidad Bolivariana, Calle 48, No 27.05, Apdo 14-16, Medellín, Antioqiua. (Communication research).

**Instituto Colombiano de Desarollo Social (ICODES),** Calle 37 No 13A-09, Apdo Aéreo 11966, Bogotá. T: 435581. (In FERES).

**Instituto de Doctrina y Estudios Sociales (IDES),** Calle 26 No 27-48, 6 piso, Apdo Aéreo 12309, Bogotá. T: 328821,328841.

*COSTA RICA*

**Instituto de Evangelización a Fondo (INDEF)/Institute of In-Depth Evangelism (INDEPTH),** Secretariado, Apdo 1307, San José. T: 227188.

**Latin American Evangelical Center for Pastoral Studies,** San José.

*CUBA*

**Centro de Estudios Ecumenicos (CENDESEC),** Seminario San Carlos y San Ambrosio, Av del Puerto Esquina a Chacón, Apdo 594, La Habana 1. T: 613735.

**Study Centre,** Dir, Apdo 4179, La Habana 4.

*CZECHOSLOVAKIA*

**Ecumenical Section,** John Hus Theological Faculty (Joannis Hus Facultas Theologica Pragae, Sectio Oecumenica), VV kujbyseva 5, Dejvice, Praha 6. T: 320569.

*DENMARK*

**Academy of Futures Research,** Pres, Society for Futures Research, Skovfaldet 2S, DK-8200 Arhus N. (Secular).

**Church History Institute (Institut for Kirkhistotie),** Kobmagergade 44-46, DK-1150 Kobenhavn K.

**Ecumenical Institute (Okumeniske Institut),** Copenhagen University, Kobenhavn.

**IDOC,** Cathrinebjergvej 95, DK-8200 Arhus N.

**Institute of Church and Mission History (Institut for Praktisk Teologi og Religionsvidenskab),** University of Copenhagen, Lille Kirkestraede 1, DK-1072 Kobenhavn K. (Also: Kobmagergade 44-46, DK-1150 Kobenhavn K).

**Institute of Ecumenical Theology and Missionary Science (Okumeniske Theologi og Missionsvedenskab),** Faculty of Theology, Arhus Universitet, DK-8000 Arhus C. T: (06)136711.

**New Religious Movements in Western Societies Study Centre,** Ecumenical Centre, Arhus Universitet, DK-8000 Arhus C.

*DOMINICAN REPUBLIC*

**Centre for Ecumenical Planning and Action (CEPAE),** Benigno F Rojas 67 (Altos), Santo Domingo. (Serving slum areas, peasants).

**Centro de Investigación y Acción Social (CIAS),** Apdo 1004, Santo Domingo, DN.

*ECUADOR*

**Centro de Investigación y Acción Social (CIAS),** Benalcázar 562, Apdo 2876, Quito.

**Instituto de Ciencias Sagradas,** Pontificia Universidad Católica del Ecuador, 12 de Octubro No 1076, Apdo 2184, Quito.

*EGYPT*

**Centre d'Etudes Arabes,** Collège La Salle, 6 Rue Sekket el Bechnine, Daher, Al Qahirah. T: 904322, 904740.

**Centre d'Etudes Dar El-Salam,** 4 Midan Cheikh Youssef, Garden City, Al Qahirah.

**Centro Francescano di Studi Orientali Cristiani (Franciscan Centre of Christian Oriental Studies),** 12 Bendâqah St, POB 381, Muski, Al Qahirah. T: 909906.

**Institut Dominicain d'Etudes Orientales (IDEO),** Dir, 1 Rue Masna Al-Tarabich, Abassiyah, Al Qahirah. T: 825509.

**Institute for Coptic Studies,** St Peter's Church, Abbassiyah, Al Qahirah.

**Institute for Oriental Studies of the Library of the Greek Orthodox Patriarchate of Alexandria,** Al Iskandariyah (Alexandria).

*EL SALVADOR*

**Centro de Estudios Sociales y Promoción Popular (CESPROP),** Centro Universitario Católico, Apdo Postal 723, San Salvador. T: 258979.

*ETHIOPIA*

**Department of Audience Research & Planning,** RVOG, PO Box 654, Addis Abeba. T: 448190.

**Department of History, Research, Mission and Publications,** Ethiopian Orthodox Church, Miazia 27, PO Box 30066, Addis Abeba.

*FINLAND*

**Ecumenical Institute of the University of Helsinki (Helsingin Yliopiston Ekumeeninen Arkisto),** Fabianinkatu 33, Helsinki 17. T: 15211. (Also: Aleksanterinkatu 15 B4, 00100 Helsinki 10).

**Institute for Ecumenics and Social Ethics (Institutet för Ekumenik och Socialetik vid Abo Akademi),** Biskopsgatan 16, Abo 2. T: 18968.

**Research Institute of the Lutheran Church of Finland,** Satakunnankatu 11 B 21, Box 239, SF-33100 Tampere 10.

**Studium Catholicum,** Dominikaainien Kulttuurikeskus, Ritarikatu 3bA, Helsinki 17. T: 634221.

*FRANCE*

**Action Populaire,** Centre de Recherche et d'Action Sociales (CERAS), 15 Rue Raymond Marcheron, 92 Vanves.

**Association Internationale Futuribles,** Pres, 52 Rue des Saints-Pères, Paris 7. (Secular).

**Centre Catholique de Socialogie Religieuse,** 99 Quai Clémenceau, F-69 Caluire, Rhône.

**Centre de Documentation Oecuménique et Judéo-Chrétienne,** 43 bis Rue du Port, F-59 Lille.

**Centre de Recherche et de Documentation des Institutions Chrétiennes (CERDIC),** Palais Universitaire, Place de l'Université, F-67084 Strasbourg. T: (88)355940.

**Centre de Recherche et d'Echange sur la Diffusion et l'Inculturation du Christianisme (CREDIC),** Faculté de Théologie, Université de Lyon III, Château de Mannevieux, F-69700 Givors.

**Centre de Recherche Théologique Missionnaire (CRTM),** 5 Rue Monsieur, F-75007 Paris. T: (01)783-6795.

**Centre de Sociologie du Protestantisme,** Dir, Université de Strasbourg, Palais Universitaire, F-67084 Strasbourg.

**Centre de Sociologie Religieuse de l'Eglise Réformée de France,** 10 Rue du Maire Kuss, F-67 Strasbourg.

**Centre Diocésain d'Etudes Sociologiques,** c/o 25 Rue Sylvabelle, F-13006 Marseille. T: (91)376863.

**Centre d'Analyse et de Documentation Patristiques,** Université de Strasbourg, F-67084 Strasbourg.

**Centre d'Etudes et de Recherches Interdisciplinaires en Théologie (CERIT),** Palais Universitaire, F-67084 Strasbourg.

**Centre d'Etudes et de Recherches Missionnaires (CRTM),** 128 Rue du Bac, F-75341 Paris.

**Centre d'Etudes et de Recherches Philosophiques (CERP),** 128 Rue Blomet, F-75015 Paris.

**Centre d'Etudes Istina,** 45 Rue de la Glacière, F-75013 Paris. T: 587-3735.

**Centre d'Etudes Oecuméniques (Ecumenical Research Institute),** 8 Rue Gustav Klotz, F-67 Strasbourg. T: (88)362926.

**Centre d'Etudes Orthodoxes,** Institut de Théologie Orthodoxe St-Serge, 93 Rue de Crimée, Paris. T: 208-1293.

**Centre d'Histoire des Religions,** Université de Liège, Place du Vingt-Aout 16, Liège. T: (041)235-5129.

**Centre L.J. Lebret 'Foi et Developpement',** 6-9 Rue Guénégaud, F-75006 Paris. T: 0332502.

**Centre pour l'Intelligence de la Foi (CIF),** 76 Rue des Saints-Pères, F-75007 Paris.

**Centre Protestant de Rencontres et de Recherches de Villemétrie,** Orgemont, F-91 La Ferté-Alais, Essonne.

**Centre Protestant d'Etudes et de Documentation (CPED),** Dir, 8 Villa du Parc-Montsouris, F-75014 Paris. T: 589-5569.

**Centre Régional d'Etudes Socio-Religieuses,** 39 Rue de la Monnaie, F-59042 Lille. T: (20)553026. (In FERES).

**Centre Régional Protestant de Recherche et de Formation,** 15 Rue Jeanne-d'Arc, Lille.

**Centre Saint-Irénée,** 2 Place Gailleton, F-69002 Lyon. T: (78)374982.

**Centre Thomas More,** La Tourette-Eveux, F-69210 L'Arbresle. T: (78)019111.

**Commission de Sociologie de la Fédération Protestante de France,** 47 Rue de Clichy, F-75009 Paris.

**Conférence Internationale de Sociologie Religieuse/International Conference for Sociology of Religion (CISR),** Secrétariat Général, 39 Rue de la Monnaie, F-59042 Lille. T: 553026.

**Documentation et Information sur l'Amérique Latine (DIAL),** 170 Blvd du Montparnasse, F-75014 Paris.

**Economie et Humanisme,** 99 Quai Clémenceau, F-69300 Caluire. T: (78)232178. (Research on humane society).

**Groupe de Sociologie des Religions,** 82 Rue Cardinet, Paris. T: (01)924-2624.

**Institut de Langage Total, Recherches Educatives et Culturelle (REC),** 21 Rue de la Paix, F-42 Saint-Etienne. T: (77)331621. (Catholic. Communications research).

**Institut de Science et de Théologie des Religions (ISTR),** Institut Catholique, 5 Rue Roger Verlomme, F-75003 Paris. (Also: 128 Rue du Bac, F-75007 Paris). T: (01)548-1992.

**Institut de Sciences Sociales des Religions (ISSR),** c/o Groupe de Sociologie des Religions (CNRS), 22 Rue d'Athènes, F-75009 Paris. T: (01)526-1512.

**Institut de Théologie Orthodoxe,** Saint Serge, 93 Rue de Crimée, F-75019 Paris.

**Institut des Sciences Religieuses de Nancy,** 35 Cours Léopold, F-54000 Nancy.

**Institut d'Etudes Sémitiques (IES),** 16 Rue de la Sorbonne, F-75005 Paris. T: ODE-2413 ext 287.

**Institut Français d'Etudes Byzantines,** 8 Rue François ler, F-75008 Paris. T: 256-0321.

**Institut Supérieur d'Etudes Oecuméniques,** 21 Rue d'Assas, F-75006 Paris. T: (01)222-0651,4180.

**Les Fontaines,** BP 53, F-60500 Chantilly. T: 457-2460. (Research and reflection).

**Lutheran Foundation for Inter-Confessional Research,** Institute for Ecumenical Research, 8 Rue Gustav Klotz, F-67000 Strasbourg. T: (88)362926.

**Maison des Sciences de l'Homme,** 54 Blvd Raspail, F-75006 Paris.

**Semaines Sociales de France,** 9 Rue Guénégaud, F-75006 Paris. T: (01)033-2501. (Colloquia on social action).

**Service Documentation Sectes,** Ligue Cathlioque de l'Evangile, 2 Rue de la Planche, F-75007 Paris. (Research on sects).

*GERMAN DEMOCRATIC REPUBLIC*

**Emil-Fuchs Institut für Religionssoziologie,** Karl Marx Universität, Peterssteinweg 2-8, Leipzig C1.

**Konfessionskundliche Forschungsstelle und Geschäftsstelle des Evangelischen Bundes in der DDR,** Mauerstr 9, 15 Potsdam.

*GERMANY, Federal Republic of*

**Altkatholisches Ökumenisches Forum,** Universität Bonn, Arndstr 23, D-5300 Bonn.

**Amtliche Zentralstelle für Kirchliche Statistik,** Antwerpenerstr 35, D-5000 Köln. T: (0221)523800. (Catholic).

**Anglicanisches Institut der Abtei St Mathias Abbaye St Mathieu,** OSB, Trier.

**Anthropos-Institut,** Arnold-Janssen-Str 20, D-5205 St Augustin.

**Bucer-Institut,** Arbeitsstelle für Reformationsgeschichtliche Editionen der Universität Münster, Universitätsstr 13-17, D-4400 Münster. T: (0251)49012540. (Research on the 16th-century Reformation).

**Bysantinisches Institut der Abtei Scheyern,** D-8069 Scheyern. T: (08441)2244.

**Bysantinisches Institut Ettal,** D-8101 Ettal.

**Evangelische Zentralstelle für Weltanschauungsfraten,** Hölderlinplatz 2A, D-7 Stuttgart 1.

**Forschungsstätte der Evangelischen Studiengemeinschaft Christiphorus Stift (FEST),** Schmeilweg 5, D-6900 Heidelberg. T: (06221)25317.

**Gesellschaft für Zukunftsfragen,** Chairman, c/o Hamburgisches Weltwirtschaftsarchiv, Karl-Muck-Platz 1, D-2 Hamburg 36. (Secular).

**Institut der Orden für missionarische Seelsorge und Spiritualität (IMS),** Waldschmidstr 42a, D-6 Frankfurt I.

**Institut für Christliche Gesellschaftslehre,** Universität Tübingen, Olgastr 8, D-7400 Tübingen.

**Institut für Christliche Gesellschaftwissenschaften,** Universität Münster, Universitätsstr 13-17, D-44 Münster. T: (0251)4902550.

**Institut für Christliche Sozialwissenschaften der Universität Münster,** Pferdegasse 3, D-4400 Münster.

**Institut für Christliche Weltanschauung und Religionsphilosophie der Universität München,** Kaulbachstr 31/I, D-8000 München 22.

**Institut für Europäische Geschichte,** Abteilung für Abendländische Religionsgeschichte, Dir, Alte Universitätstr 19, D-6500 Mainz. (Catholic).

**Institut für Gesellschaftspolitic,** Kaulbachstr 33, D-8000 München 22. T: (089)286077.

**Institut für Gesellschaftswissenschaft,** Dominikanerkloster, D-5301 Walberberg.

**Institut für Kirchenbau and Kirchliche Kunst der Gegenwart,** Am Plan 3, D-355 Marburg. (Research on modern church architecture and art).

**Institut für Kirchliche Sozialforschung des Bistum Essen (IKSE),** Zwölfling 2, D-4300 Essen. T: (02141)2204210.

**Institut für Konfessionskunde der Orthodoxie,** Evangelisch-Theologische Fakultät, Grosse Steinstr 16, 401 Halle/Saale.

**Institut für Missionswissenschaft und Ökumenische Theologie der Universität,** Dir, Hausserstr 43, D-74 Tübingen. T: 712592.

**Institut für Ökumenische Forschung,** Dir, Universität Tübingen, Nauklerstr 37a, D-7400 Tübingen. T: (07122)712871.

**Institut für Ökumenische Theologie an der Ev-theologische Fakultät,** Münster.

**Institut für Ökumenische Theologie an der Katholisch-Theologische Fakultät,** Leopoldstr 101, D-8000 München 23.

**Institut für Staatskirchenrecht der Diözesen Deutschlands,** Lennistr 25, D-5300 Bonn 1. T: (02221)633633.

**Institut Kirche und Judentum,** Kirchlichen Hochschule Berlin, Teltower Damm 120-122, D-1000 Berlin 37 (Zehlendorf). T: (0311)8151067.

**Institutum Judaicum Delitzschianum,** Wilmergasse 1-4, D-4400 Münster. T: (0251)49014400.

**Institutum Judaicum der Universität Tübingen,** Liebermeisterstr 12, D-7400 Tübingen. T: (07122) 292590.

**Internationales Institut für Missionswissenschaftliche Forschungen,** Johannisstr 8-10, D-4400 Münster. (Also: Franziskaner Missionszentrale, Albertus-Magnus Str 39, POB 200443, D-5300 Bonn).

**Johann-Adam-Möhler-Institut für Konfessions- und Diasporakunde,** Prälat, Leostr 19a, D-4790 Paderborn. T: (05251)24644.

**Katholisches Institut für Sozialforschung,** Bischof-Kallerstr 3, Königstein/Tanua. T: 3297,2851.

**Katholische-Ökumenisches Institut,** Westfälische Wilhelms-Universität, Johannisstr 8-10, D-44 Münster /Westf.

**Kirchensgeschichtliches Seminar,** Evangelisch-Theologische Facultät, Universität Marburg, Lahnstr 3, D-355 Marburg.

**Kirchliche Gemeinschaftsstelle für Elektronische Datenverarbeitung,** Hanauer Landstr 126, D-6 Frankfurt am Main. T: (0611)443006/7.

**Konfessionskundliche Forschungstelle des Evangelischen Bundes,** Gen Sek, Eifelstr 35, D-6140 Bensheim.

**Konfessionskundliches Seminar,** Evangelisch-Theologische Fakultät, Universität Heidelberg, Plock 66, D-69 Heidelberg.

**Korean New Religions Research Centre,** Hamburg.

**Lenenszentrum für Einheit der Christen,** Schloss Craheim, D-8721 Wetzhausen.

**Missionswissenschaftliches Institut Missio,** Hermannstr 14, Postfach 1110, D-5100 Aachen. (RC).

**Ökumenisches Archiv der EKD,** Jebensstr 3, D-1000 Berlin 12. T: (030)310491.

**Ökumenisches Institut,** Abteilung fur Evangelische Theologie, Universität Bochum, Overbergstr 16, D-463 Bochum-Querenburg.

**Ökumenisches Institut,** Evangelisch-Theologische Fakultät, Universität Bonn, Liebfrauenweg 1, D-5300 Bonn. T: (0227)6034510.

**Ökumenisches Institut,** Evangelisch-theologische Fakultät, Universität Bonn, Am Hof 1, Hauptgebaude, II Stock, D-5300 Bonn.

**Ökumenisches Institut,** Evangelisch-theologische Fakultät, Universität Heidelberg, Plankengasse 1, D-6900 Heidelberg.

**Ökumenisches Institut,** Katholisch-theologische Fakultät, Universität Münster, Johannisstr 8-10, D-44 Münster.

**Ökumenisches Seminar,** Theologische Fakultät, Universität Marburg, Lahntor 3, D-355 Marburg.

**Ökumenisches Seminar,** Universität Hamburg, Dir, Von-Melle-Park 6, 2 Hamburg 13. T: 441972560.

**Ostkirchen-Institut,** Evangelisch-theologische Fakultät, Universität Münster, Am Stadtgraben 13/15, 44 Münster.

**Ostkirchliches Institut der Augustiner,** Augustinerkloster St Bruno, Steinbachtal 2a, D-8700 Würzburg. T: (0931)74607.

**Religionssoziologisches Institut an der Kirchlichen Hochschule Berlin,** Teltower Damm 120-122, D-1000 Berlin 37 (Zehlendorf). T: (0311) 8151067/9.

**Religionswissenschaftliches Institut der Freien Universität Berlin,** Boltzmannstr 4, D-1000 Berlin 33.

**Seminar für Geschichte und Theologie des Christlichen Ostens,** Evangelisch-Theologische Fakultät, Universität Erlangen, Kochstr 6, D-852 Erlangen.

**Seminar für Missionstheologie und Religionswissenschaft,** Johs Gutenberg Universität, Saarstr 21, D-6500 Mainz.

**Seminar für Ostkirchenkunde,** Katholisch-Theologische Fakultät, Universität Würzburg, Sanderring 2, D-87 Würzburg.

**Seminar für Theologie des Christlichen Ostens,** Evangelisch-theologische Fakultät, Universität Erlangen-Nürnberg, Kochstr 6, Erlangen.

**Sozialinstitut des Bistums Essen,** Zwölfling 2, D-43 Essen. T: (22)04210.

**Sozialteam für Sozialschulung und Sozialforschung,** Danzigerstr 6, D-679 Landstuhl-Süd.

**Steyler Missionswissenschaftliche Institut,** Arnold Janssenstr 12/24, D-5205 St Augustin über Siegburg. (Member IAMS).

**Südasien-Institut der Universität Heidelberg,** Im Neuerheimer Feld 13, D-6900 Heidelberg.

**Theological Information and Documentation Centre (THEODOK),** Universitätsbibliothek, D-7400 Tübingen 1. (Depository Library for theology and religious sciences for West Germany).

**Ungarisches Kirchensocialogischen Institut (ULI),** Rosenheimerstr 141, D-8 München. T: 448610.

**Zentrum Berlin für Zukunftsforschung eV (Berlin Centre for Future Research),** Dir, Höhenzollerndamm 170, D-1 Berlin 31. (Secular).

*GREECE*

**Athens Centre of Ekistics,** Athens Technological Organization, Dir, 24 Strat Syadesmou St, Athínai 136. (Ekistics=development of human settlement. Secular, with religious application).

**Byzantine Institute,** 11 Vassileos Konstantinou St, Psychiko, Athínai.

**Inter-Orthodox Missionary Centre' Porefthendes',** 30 Sina St, Athínai 135.

**National Centre of Social Research (Ethnikon Kentron Koinonikon Ereynon),** Athínai.

**Patriarchal Institute for Patristic Studies,** Hiera Patriarchiki Moni Vlatadon, Thessaloniki. (Ecumenical Patriarchate of Constantinople).

**Scientific Conference Centre of Denys the Areopagite (Kentron Epistimonikon Omilion Dionysios Areopagitis),** Michel Voda St 28, Athínai. T: 813570. (Latin-rite Catholic; Jesuit).

*GUADELOUPE*

**Centre d'Etude et d'Action Sociale (CEAS),** 28 Rue Peynier, BP 414, F-97-1 Pointe-à-Pitre. T: 820967.

*GUYANA*

**Guyana Institute for Social Research and Action (GISRA),** Dir, 1 Brickdam, PO Box 528, Georgetown. T: 61789. (Under Guyana Council of Churches, & Catholic Church)

*HAITI*

**Centre d'Information et de Statistique Evangélique (CISE),** BP 458, Port-au-Prince.

**Haitian Research Centre in Social Sciences (CHISS),** Rue Bonne Foi 23, BP 1294, Port-au-Prince. (Secular, some church officers).

*HOLY SEE*

**Archivio del Concilio Vaticano II,** Via P Pancrazio Pfeiffer 10, I-00193 Roma, Italy. T: 69282 int 4236.

**Archivio Secreto Vaticano,** I-00120 Città del Vaticano. T: 6982 int 3314.

**Istituto Superiore di Scienze Religiose 'Ecclesia Mater',** Piazza San Giovanni in Laterano 4, I-00184 Roma, Italy. T: 750892.

**Pontificia Commissione per gli Archivi Ecclesiastici d'Italia,** Palazzo Apostolico, I-00120 Città del Vaticano. T: 6982 int 3314.

**Scuola Vaticana di Biblioteconomia,** Palazzo Apostolico, I-00120, Città del Vaticano. T: 6983323.

**Superior Institute for the Study of Atheism,** Pontifical Urbanian University, Città del Vaticano.

**Ufficio Centrale di Statistica della Chiesa/ Central Office of Statistics of the Church,** Palazzo Apostolico, I-00120 Città del Vaticano. T: 6983046. (Edits *Annuario Pontificio*).

*HONG KONG*

**Chinese Church Research Center,** China Graduate School of Theology, Hong Kong.

**Christian Study Center on Chinese Religion & Culture,** Co-Dir, Tao Fong Shan, PO Box 33, Shatin, NT. T: 061490.

**FEBC Communication Research Centre,** 423-427 J Hotung House, Hankow Rd, Box 6789, Kowloon.

*INDIA*

**Catholic Family Social Welfare Centre,** Indian Social Institute, South Ext 11d-25-D, New Delhi 49. T: 622379. (Jesuit).

**Christian Association for Socio-Religious Research of India,** 17 Miller's Rd, PO Box 1504, Bangalore 6. T: 75181.

**Christian Institute for Sikh Studies,** Dir, Baring Union Christian College, Batala, District Gurdaspur, Punjab.

**Christian Institute for the Study of Religion and Society (CISRS),** Devanandan House, 17 Miller's Rd, PO Box 604, Bangalore 6. T: 75181.

**Church Growth Research Centre,** 109 Secretariat Colony 6th St, Post Bag 768, Kilpauk, Madras 600-010. T: 663972.

**Henry Martin Institute of Islamic Studies (HMI),** Dir, St Luke's Compound, Nampalli Station Rd, PO Box 153, Hyderabad 500001 (AP). T: 45957.

**Henry Martyn Institute of Islamic Studies,** Leonard Theological College, Jabalpur, MP.

**Henry Martyn Institute of Islamic Studies,** PO Box 134, Lucknow 1, UP.

**Indian Social Institute,** South Ext 11d-25-D, New Delhi 49. T: 622379.

**Institute for Social Studies and Community Development (Seva Sadan),** Department of Socio-Religious Studies, 1250 Quarters, TT Nagar South, Bhopal, MP. T: 432.

**Islamic Research Association,** 8 Shepherd Rd, Bombay 8. T: 373574.

**Lumen Institute,** PB 1769, Ernakulam, Cochin 682016, Kerala. T: 32056.

**Theological Research and Communication Institute (TRACI),** Union Biblical Seminary, Dir, Yeotmal, Maharashtra 445 001.

**Xavier Centre of Historical Research,** Goa. (Jesuit).

*INDONESIA*

**Atma Jaya Research Centre,** Jalan Jenderal Sudirman 49A, PO Box 2639, Jakarta. T: 586491. (RC. Begun 1972).

**Drijarkara Philosophical Institute (Sekolah Tinggi Filsafat Drijarkara),** Jalan Menteng Raya 64, Jakarta. T: 47278. (Philosophical enquiry).

**Institute for Research and Study (Lembaga Penelitian Dan Studi, DGI),** Dir, Council of Churches in Indonesia, Jalan Salemba Raya 10, Jakarta-Pusat. T: 82317.

**Institute of Social Research and Development (Lembaga Penelitian dan Pembangunan Sosial),** Jalan Kemiri 15 pav, Jakarta. (Also: Jalan Kramat Raya 134, Jakarta IV/5).

**Pastoral Research and Service Centre (Pusat Pastoral Solo),** Dir, Jalan Jendral Sudirman 3, Surakarta, Central Java. T: 3904.

**Research Centre,** Satya Wacana Christian University, Salatiga, Central Java.

**Research Institute (HKBP),** Nommensen University, P Siantar, North Sumatra.

*IRELAND*

**Mater Dei Institute,** Clonliffe Rd, Dublin 3. T: 40854.

**Research and Development Unit/Commission,** Catholic Communications Institute of Ireland, Veritas House, 7/8 Lower Abbey St, Dublin 1. T: 48502. (Socio-religious).

*ISRAEL*

**American Institute of Holy Land Studies,** PO Box 1276, Mt Zion, Jerusalem.

**Ecole Biblique et Ecole Archéologique Française,**

Jerusalem. (Founded 1890 by OP; 50,000-volume library).
**CARTA,** Dir. Beit Hadar, Mazie St, Jerusalem. (Map research).
**Centre of Jewish Studies and Jewish-Christian Dialogue,** Dominican Fathers, Jerusalem.
**Ecole Biblique et Ecole Archéologique Française,** Couvent Dominicain St-Etienne, PO Box 19055, Jerusalem. T: 82213.
**Ecumenical Institute for Advanced Theological Studies in Jerusalem (EIATS),** PO Box 19556, Tantur (on the main road to Bethlehem), Jerusalem.
**Ecumenical Theological Research Fraternity in Israel,** PO Box 249, Jerusalem. T: (02)66308.
**German Evangelical Institution for Archaeology of the Holy Land,** Sheikh Jarah, Jerusalem. T: 84792.
**Institut Biblique Franciscain,** PO Box 190 & 424, Old City, Jerusalem.
**Institute of Contemporary Jewry,** Hebrew University of Jerusalem, Jerusalem.
**Near East Christian Centre/Proche-Orient Chrétien,** Saint Anne, PO Box 19079, Jerusalem. T: (02)83285. (Begun 1951; White Fathers; 30,000-volume library).
**Pontifical Biblical Institute,** 3 Paul Emil Botta St, PO Box 497, Jerusalem. T: 22843.

*ITALY*
**Centro di Previsione Sociale,** Dir. Via Carlo Alberto 57, I-10123 Turin. (Secular, futurology).
**Centro di Studi Ecumenici Giovanni XXIII,** Priorato di Santo Egidio, I-24039 Sotto il Monte (Bergamo).
**Centro Diocesano di Ricerche Sociali,** Via Altabella 6, Bologna. T: 231944.
**Centro Ecclesiale Italiano per l'America Latina (CEIAL),** Séminaire N-D de Guadelupe, San Massimo, I-37100 Verona. T: 49485.
**Centro Internazionale di Recherche Sociali (CIRIS),** Piazza della Pilotta 4, I-00187 Roma. T: 6791446. (In FERES).
**Centro Internazionale di Studi Umanistici,** Istituto di Studi Filosofici, Università de Roma, Via Lagrarege 1, Roma.
**Centro Studi Asiatici,** Centro Missionario PIME, Via Mosè Bianchi 94, I-20149 Milano.
**Centro Studi Emigrazione Roma (CSER),** Via della Pisana 1301, I-00163 Roma. T: 6740074.
**Ente dello Spettacolo,** Via della Conciliazione 2c, I-00193 Roma. T: 561775,564132. (Communication and information research).
**IDOC International (International Documentation on the Contemporary Church),** Via Santa Maria dell'Anima 30, I-00186 Roma. T: 6568332.
**International Centre of Sindonology,** Archdiocese of Turin, Torino. (Scientific study of the Holy Shroud of Turin).
**International Conference of Religious Sociology,** Piazza della Pilotta 4, I-00187 Roma. T: 681443.
**Istituto di Ricerche Applicata Documentazione e Studi (IRADES),** Via Paisiello 3, I-00198 Roma. T: 866346. (Socio-religious).
**Istituto di Scienze Missionaria,** Pontificia Università Urbaniana, Via Urbano VIII 16, I-00165 Roma. T: 655992,6568640.
**Istituto di Scienze Religiose,** Pontificia Università Gregoriana, Piazza della Pilotta 3, Roma. T: 671446.
**Istituto di Studi e Ricerche Carlo Cattaneo,** Via Santo Stefano 6, Bologna.
**Istituto per le Scienze Religiose,** Via SC Vitale 114, Bologna. T: 239532.
**Istituto Superiore di Scienze Religiose 'Mater Ecclesiae',** Largo Angelicum 1, I-00184 Roma. T: 673400.
**Laboratorio di Sociologia Religiosa,** Facoltà di Scienze Politiche, Università di Padova, Padova.
**Pontificio Istituto Biblico,** Piazza della Pilotta 4, I-00187 Roma. T: 6701.
**Pontificio Istituto di Studi Arabi/Pontifical Institute of Arab Studies (PIAS),** Rector, Piazza di San Apollinare 49, I-00186 Roma. T: 561131, 561592. (White Fathers. Member of IAMS).
**Pontificio Istituto di Studi Orientale,** Piazza Santa Maria Maggiore 7, I-00185 Roma. T: 7312254, 7312255. (Jesuit).
**Pontificio Istituto 'Jesus Magister',** Piazza San Giovanni in Laterano 4, I-00184 Roma.
**Pontificio Seminario per gli Studi Giuridici,** Piazza Santo Apollinare 49, I-00186 Roma. T: 561103.
**Pontificium Institutum Biblicum de Urge,** Via della Pilotta 25, I-00187 Roma. T: 672778.
**Scuola Superiore delle Communicazioni Sociali,** Università Cattolica del S Cuore, Via Sant'Agnese 2, I-20123 Milano. (Communication research).
**Servizio di Documentazione e Studi (SEDOS),** Via dei Verbiti 1, CP 5080, I-00100 Roma. T: 571350. (Central office of religious orders and congregations for mass media).

*IVORY COAST*
**Centre des Sciences Humaines,** Abidjan.
**Institut Supérieur de Culture Religieuse (ISCR),** BP 8022, Abidjan-Cocody. T: 340325.

*JAPAN*
**Catholic Social Research Institute,** Tokyo-to, Shijuku-ku, Kita, Shinjuku 1-33-20.
**Christian Center for the Study of Japanese Religions,** Shugakuin (10 Daido-cho), Sakya-ku, Kyoto.
**Department of Communications,** Sophia (Jochi) University, Chiyoda-ku 7, Kioicho, Tokyo. (Communications research).
**Institute for Taoistic Research,** Tokyo. T: (203)4111.
**Institute of Oriental Culture,** University of Tokyo, Hongo Bunkyo-ku, Tokyo. T: (812)2111.
**International Institute for the Study of Religions (Kokusai Shukyo Kenkyu Sho),** Sophia University, 7 Kioicho, Chyoda-ku, Tokyo. T: 2636267.
**Japan Church Growth Research Association,** 448-3 Hosono, Kobayashi City, Miyazaki.
**Japan Society of Christian Studies,** College of Theology, Kanto-Gaskuin University, Kanagawa-ku, Mutsuura-cho 4834.
**Japanese Institute of Religious Sociology,** Shinseikaikan, 33 Shinano machi Shinjuku-ku, Tokyo. (In FERES).
**NCCJ Center for the Study of Japanese Religions,** Dir, School of Theology, Doshisha University, Karasuma-Shimotachiuri, Kamikyo-ku, Kyoto. T: 4321945.
**Oriens Institute for Religious Research,** Dir, Chitose, PO Box 14, Tokyo 156. T: 3227601/2.
**Nanzan Institute for Religion and Culture,** Nanzan University, Nagoya. (RC/SVD).
**Research Institute on Mission,** United Church of Christ in Japan, 551 Totsukamachi 1-chome, Shinjuku-ku, Tokyo 160. T: 2020541.
**St Thomas Aquinas Institute,** Research Center for Christian Philosophy, Kyoto-fu, Kyoto-shi, Kamikyo-kui, Kawara-machi, Hirokogi, Kajii-cho 461.
**Studium Biblicum Franciscanum,** Dir. 4-16-1 Seta, Setagaya-ku, Tokyo 158.

*KENYA*
**AMECEA Research Department,** Gaba Pastoral Institute, Kisumu Rd, PO Box 908, Eldoret. T: 2634.
**Centre for the Study of World Evangelization (CSWE),** PO Box 40230, Nairobi. T: 23649. (World Christian Encyclopedia).
**Daystar Communications,** Valley Rd & Ngong Rd, PO Box 44400, Nairobi. T: 26894,337600.
**Great Commission Research & Strategy Centre,** PO Box 21417, Nairobi. T: 336110.
**Kenya Beliefs Systems Project,** Institute of African Studies (near National Museum), University of Nairobi, PO Box 30197, Nairobi. T: 28631/2.
**Kenya Church History Archives,** Librarian, St Paul's United Theological College, Redhill Rd, Private Bag, Limuru. T: Tigoni 338.

*KOREA, South*
**East-West Center for Missions Research & Development,** CPO Box 2732, Soul. T: 792-5542.
**Institute for Church Growth,** Soul.
**Institute for Ecumenical and Inter-Religious Studies,** Hanguk Jongkyo Munje Yonku-so, International PO Box 3251, Soul. T: 746712.
**Institute of Korean Culture,** CPO 206, Soul.
**Institute of Socio-Religious Research,** Korean Union College (Sam Yuk Tai Hak), IPO Box 1243, Soul. T: 964287. (Seventh-day Adventist).
**Korean Church History Institute,** 187, 1 Ka, Han Kang Ro, Yong San Ku, Soul. T: 422821.
**New Religious Research Institute,** Dir, c/o NCCK, PO Box 143, Soul.
**Social Research Institute,** Sogang University, IPO Box 1142, Seoul.

*LAOS*
**Bureau d'Etudes Buddhiques,** Mission Catholique, BP 130, Vientiane. (Also in Lam Prabang).

*LEBANON*
**Centre de Recherches et d'Etudes Arabes,** Université St-Joseph, BP 293, Bayrut. T: 326636. (Formerly CREA, founded 1945).
**Centre de Sociologie Religieuse,** Archevêché Grec-Catholique, Rue de Damas, BP 901, Bayrut. T: 231612,222375,236066.
**Centre d'Etudes pour le Monde Arabe Moderne (CEMAM),** St Joseph's University, BP 8664, Bayrut. (Jesuit).
**Centre for Religious Studies,** PO Box 901, Bayrut.
**Institut Supérieur de Formation Religieuse (ISFR),** c/o Université St-Joseph, Bayrut.
**Institute for Oriental Studies,** St Joseph's University, Bayrut.

*MALAWI*
**Pastoral Service,** Catholic Secretariat, PO Box 368, Limbe. T: 5866.

*MALTA*
**Catholic Institute (Istitut Kattoliku),** Floriana. T: 239.
**Pastoral Research Services,** 65 Old Mint St, Valletta. T: 22360.

*MEXICO*
**Centro de Estudios Ecuménicos,** Guty Cárdenas 131, México 20, DF. T: 5480820,5488489.
**Centro de Investigación y Acción Social (CIAS),** Zaragoza 78 (Coyoacan), México 21, DF.
**Centro de Investigación y Communicación de México (CINCOMEX),** Campo Florida No 79, z.18, Apdo 84, z.1, México 6, DF. T: 104434.
**Centro Intercultural de Documentación (CIDOC),** Dir, 7 Calle Principal, Rancho Tetela, Apdo Postal 479, Cuernavaca, Morelos. T: 24590.
**Escuela de Ciencias y Tecnicas de Información,** Universidad Iberoamericana, Cerro de las Torres 395, México 21, DF. T: 493500. (Communication and information research).
**Iglesia y Sociedad en América Latina (ISAL),** Apdo 71-343, México 3, DF.
**Instituto Mexicano de Estudios Sociales (IMES),** Av Cuauhtémoc 1486-501, Piso 5, Apdo Postal 549, México 13, DF. T: 5242448,5244941. (RC. In FERES).
**Instituto Superior de Estudios Eclesiásticos,** Seminario Conciliar de México, Tlalpan, Calle Victoria 21, México 22, DF. T: 5732222,5732225,5732918.
**Secretariado Regional para América Latina (FERES),** c/o IMES, Av Cuauhtémoc 1486, Piso 5, México 13, DF. T: 5242448,5244941.

*NETHERLANDS*
**Catholic Documentation Centre (Katholiek Documentatie Centrum, KDC),** Erasmuslaan 36, 6525GG Nijmegen. T: (08800)58711.
**Catholic Institute for Mass Media (Stichting Katholiek Instituut voor Massamedia),** Universiteit Nijmegen, Verlengde Grone Straat, Nijmegen. (Communication research).
**Catholic Institute for Socio-Ecclesiastical Research (Katholek Sociaal Kerkelijk Instituut, KASKI),** Paul Gabriëlstraat 28-30, 's-Gravenhage. T: (070)245415. (In FERES).
**De Horstink,** Koningin Wilhelminalaan 17, Amersfoort. T: (03490)17958.
**Ecumenical Research Exchange (ERE)/Echange Oecuménique de Recherches,** Oostmaaslaan 950, 3063 DM Rotterdam. T: (010)139485.
**Europe 2000,** Central Administration, European Cultural Foundation, Emmastraat 30, Amsterdam. (Secular; futurology).
**European Cultural Foundation,** Sec Gen, Emmastraat 30, Amsterdam. (Secular; futurology).
**Hendrik Kraemer Instituut,** Leidsestraatweg 11, 2341 GR Oegstgeest. (Member of IAMS).
**Institute for Byzantine and Ecumenical Studies (Instituut voor Byzantijnse se Oecumenische Studies),** Louisweg 12, Nijmegen. T: (08800)24061.
**Institute of Applied Sociology (Instituut voor Toegepaste Sociologie, ITS),** Verlengde Groenestraat 55, Nijmegen. T: (080)512460.
**Institute of Religious Iconography,** State University, Groningen.
**Instituut voor Godsdiensthistorische Beelddokumentatie (IGB),** Niewe Kijk in 't Jantstraat 104, Groningen. T: (050)114791.
**Interuniversity Institute for Missiological and Ecumenical Research (Interuniversitair Instituut voor Missiologie en Oecumenica, IIMO),** Dir, Boerhaavelaan 43, Leiden. T: (01710)51925. (Dept of Ecumenics: Heidelberglaan 2, Utrecht. T: (030) 539111).
**Labour Institute (Instituut voor Arbeidsvraagstukken, IVA),** Prof Verbernelaan 121a, Tilburg. T: (04250)70960.
**Netherlands Institute for Public Opinion (Nederlands Instituut voor de Publieke Opinie en het Marktonderzoek, NIPO),** Westerdokhuis, Barentzplein 7, Amsterdam. T: 248844. (Gallup polls, including on religion).
**Peshitta Institute,** Leiden University, Leiden. (Study of the Old Testament in Syriac).
**Sociology of Religion Working Group (Werkgroep voor Godsdienstsociologie),** Prins Hendriklaan 27-29, Amsterdam. T: (020)723677.
**Titus Brandsma Instituut,** Groesbeekseweg 147, Nijmegen. T: (08800)58711 toestel 2162.

*NICARAGUA*
**Instituto de Cultura Religiosa Mater Ecclesiae,** Colegio de la Asunción, Managua. T: 4801.

*NIGERIA*
**Institute of Church and Society,** Oyo Rd, PO Box 4020, Ibadan. T: 22078.
**National Institute for Religious Studies,** Lagos.
**Pastoral Institute,** Bodija, PO Box 1784, Ibadan. T: 24328.
**Religious Studies Unit,** Polytechnic University, Ibadan.
**Study Centre for Islam and Christianity,** Islam in Africa Project Council, General Advisor, 5 Awosika Av, Bodija, PO Box 4045, Ibadan. T: 23884. (Pierre Benignus Study Centre).

*NORWAY*
**Centre for Development Research (Sentrum for Utviklingsforskning),** Herman Foss gate 9, PO Box 1046, N-5001 Bergen. T: 30994. (Socio-religious).
**Centre for the Study of Ideologies (Sentrum for Idiologisforskning, formerly Sentrum fur Kultur-og Religionsforskning),** Christiesgate 16, Bergen.
**Ecumenical Institute,** Oslo University, Krags Vei 1, Oslo 3.
**Egede Institute for Missionary Study and Research (Egede Institutet for Misjonskunnskap og Misjonsgransking),** Theresesgt 51 B, Oslo 3. T: 466800. (Member of IAMS).

*PAKISTAN*
**Christian Study Centre,** Dir, 126B Murree Rd, Rawalpindi Cantt. T: 67412. (Also 128 Saifullah Lodhi Rd (Burton Rd), Rawalpindi). (Member of IAMS).
**Institute for Religious and Social Studies (IRSS),** Franciscan Friary, St Patrick's Cathedral, Karachi 0328. T: 417978.
**Islamic Research Institute,** 692-E, G-VI-4, PO Box No 1035, Islamabad.

*PANAMA*
**Centro de Investigaciones Socio-Religiosas de la Arquidiócesis de Panamá (CISRAP),** Apdo 6386, Panamá 5.
**Instituto de Estudios Religiosos Avanzados (IDERA),** Apdo 6386, Panamá 5. T: 625693.

*PAPUA NEW GUINEA*
**Institute of Social Order,** Box 1897, Boroko.

*PARAGUAY*
**Centro de Estudios Antropológicos de la Universidad Católica (CEADUC),** Universidad Católica, Independencia Nacional y Comuneros, Asunción. (Missiology).
**Centro de Estudios Socio-Religiosos (CESR),** Coronel Bogado 367, Asunción. T: 45598,41009.
**Instituto Superior de Teologia y Ciencias Religiosas,** Universidad Católica Nuestra Señora de la Asunción, Independencia Nacional y Comuneros, Asunción. T: 41044.

*PERU*
**Centro de Investigaciones Sociales, Economicas, Politicas y Antropológicas,** Sección de Investigaciones Socio-Religiosas, Pontificia Universidad Católica del Perú, Camaná 459, Apdo 1761, Lima. T: 39824.
**Centro Latinoamericano de Lenguaje Total (SEC-SAL-OCIC),** Av 9 de Diciembre, Paseo Colon 378, Apdo 44, Lima. T: 312339. (Communication research).
**Departamento de Investigación y Pleneamento Parroquial,** c/o Arzobispado, Apdo 1512, Lima.
**Oficina Arquidiocesana de Investigación y Planeamiento,** Arzbispado de Lima, Plaza de Armas, Apdo 1512, Lima.

*PHILIPPINES*
**Bureau of Economic Research,** St Louis University, Box 71, Baguio City 20801. T: 3043.
**Cardinal Bea Institute for Ecumenical Studies,** PO Box 4082, Manila. T: 981441.
**Christian Institute for Ethnic Studies in Asia,** Dir, PO Box 1767/3167, Manila. T: 72907.
**Dansalan Research Center,** Dansalan College, PO Box 5430, Iligan City 8801. (United Church: Muslim/Christian relations).
**Department of Communication,** Ateneo de Manila University, Loyola Heights, Quezon City, PO Box 154, Manila. T: 998721. (Communication research).
**Institute of Philippine Culture,** Ateneo de Manila University, Loyola Heights, Quezon City. T: 91721.
**Research Department,** Far East Broadcasting Company (FEBC), Box 2041, Manila. T: 233357.
**Research Institute on Sulu Culture,** Ateneo University, Loyola Heights, Quezon City, PO Box 154, Manila T: 998721. (RC).

*POLAND*
**Centre for Religious Documentation and Studies (Orsodek Dokumentacji i Studiów Religijnych Stowarzyszenie Pax),** Ul Mokotowska 43, Skr poctz 79, Warszawa. T: 291758. (Progressivist).
**Centre for Social Documentation and Studies (Osrodek Dokumentacji i Studiów Spolecznych, ODiSS),** Ul Mokotowska 45, Skr poctz 79, Warszawa. T: 291758. (Progressivist).
**Department of Religious Sociology,** Institute of Pastoral Theology, Catholic University of Lublin (Katedra Socjologii Religii, Instytut Teologii Pastoralnej, Katolicki Uniwersytet Lubelski), Aleje Raclawickie 14, skr p 279, 20 950 Lublin. T: 30426.
**Institute for Socio-Religious Research (Instytut Badan Socialno-Religijny),** Oftzerzew, Kilingskiego 20, Ozanow Mazowiecki.
**Missiology Department,** Catholic Faculty of Theology (Akademia Teologii Katolickiej Warszawie, ATK), ul Dewajtis 3, 01 653 Warszawa.

*PORTUGAL*
**Centro de Cultural Católica (CCC),** Casa da Torre da Marca, Rua D Manuel II 286, Porto. T: 29691.
**Centro de Estudos Missionários,** Rua de Junqueira 86, Lisboa.
**Escola de Ciencias Socio-Empresariais,** Universidade Católica, Lisboa.
**Instituto Superior de Psicologia Aplicada,** Rua da Emenda 40, Lisboa.
**Liga Intensificadora de Acção Missionária (LIAM),** Rua Santo Amaro à Estrela 51, Lisboa 2. T: 661424.

*SINGAPORE*
**Church Growth Study Centre,** 2 Dundee Rd, Singapore 3.
**Institute for the Study of Religions and Society in Singapore and Malaysia (ISRS),** Dir, 7 Mount Sophia, Singapore 9. T: 321013.

*SOLOMON ISLANDS*
**Pacific Research Unit,** Pacific Conference of Churches (PCC), PO Box 19, Honiara. (History, oral tradition, indigenous theology, primal world views).

*SOUTH AFRICA*
**Bureau of African Churches Information and Research Institute,** Christ the King Theological School, Durban.
**Christian Institute of Southern Africa (Christelike Instituut van Suidelike Afrika),** 305 Dunwell, 35 Jorissen St, PO Box 31134, Braamfontein, Transvaal. T: 7240346/7.
**Ecumenical Research Unit (Ekumeniese Navorsingseenheid),** Dir, St John Vianney Seminary, 1911 Main St, Waterkloof, PO Box 17128, Groenkloof, Pretoria. T: 789011.
**Institute for Social Research,** King George V Av, Durban.
**Institute for Theological Research,** University of South Africa (UNISA), PO Box 392, Pretoria 0001. T: 4402171. (Computer bank on *New Testament abstracts*).
**Institute of Islamic Studies,** University of Stellenbosch, Stellenbosch, CP.
**Missiological Institute,** Lutheran Theological College, Private Bag 206, Mapumulo, Natal 4470.
**Missiological Research and Training Institute,** PO Box 11, Lady Frere, CP.
**Research Centre for Church and Industry,** UNISA, PO Box 392, Pretoria 0001.

*SPAIN*
**Barriada y Vida,** Centro de Investigaciones Sociales y Religiosas, Calle Claudio Coello 141, Madrid 6.
**Centro de Estudios Orientales,** Calle Claudio Coello 129, Madrid 6.
**Centro de Estudios Universitarios (CEU),** Julian Romea 2, Madrid 3.
**Centro de Información y Sociología,** Instituto de Adaptación Pastoral Latino-Americano, Colegio Vasco de Quiroga, Ciudad Universitaria, Madrid 3.
**Cento de Pastoral Litúrgica,** Canuda 45, Barcelona.
**Centro Ecumenico Juan XXIII,** Universidad Pontificia, Ramon y Cajal 7, Salamanca.
**Departamento de Misionología Española,** Serrano 123, Madrid 6. T: 2619800.
**Instituto Católico de Estudios Sociales de Barcelona,** Rivadeneyra 6, 3, Barcelona 2. T:2315220,2222110.
**Instituto de Ciencias Sociales,** Universidad de Deusto, Av Dr Morcillo 28, Apdo 1, Bilboa. (Socio-religious).
**Instituto de Cultura Religiosa Superior,** Cuesta de Santo Domingo 5, Madrid 13.
**Instituto de Estudios Sociales Fomento Social,** Pablo Aranda 3, Madrid 6. T: 2624930/38/39. (Socio-religious).
**Instituto de Formación Superior en Ciencias Religiosas,** Universidad de Deusto, Av Dr Morcillo 28, Apdo 1, Bilbao.

**Instituto de Sociología Aplicada de Madrid (ISAMA),** Claudio Coello 141, Madrid 6. T: 2620239. (Socio-religious).
**Instituto de Sociología y Pastoral Aplicadas (ISPA),** Calle Amigo 17-19, Barcelona 6. T: 2275167. (In FERES: socio-religious).
**Instituto de Teología,** Disputación 231, Barcelona 7. T: 2541600.
**Instituto Fe y Secularidad (FEYSEC),** Diego de Leon 33, 3 Dcha, Madrid 6.
**Obra del Oriente Cristiano y Centro de Estudios Orientales,** Claudio Coello 129, Madrid 6. T: 2750698.
**Oficina General de Sociología Religiosa y Estadística de la Iglesia,** Alfonso XI 4, 2, Madrid 14. T: 2324887.

*SRI LANKA*
**Centre for Social and Economic Development,** 916 Gnartha Pradipaya Mawata, Colombo 8.
**Christian Institute for the Study of Religion and Society,** Christa Seva Ashram, Chunnakam, Jaffna. (Also Jaffna College, Vaddukoddai).
**Study Centre for Religion and Society,** Dir, 490/5 Havelock Rd, Colombo 6. T: 86998.

*SWEDEN*
**Institute for Ethnics and Work (Institut för Arbeitsetik),** Mälartorget 15, Stockholm C.
**Nordic International Institute of Missionary and Ecumenical Research (NIME),** Ostra Agatan 9, PO Box 297, S-75105 Uppsala.
**Stockholm Institute of Sociology of Religion (Religionssociologiska Institutet i Stockholm),** Blasieholmasgatan 4B, 111 48 Stockholm. T: 215464, 212290.
**Stockholm Theological Institute (Stockholms Teologiska Institut),** Värdshusbacken 1, 11265 Stockholm K.
**Swedish Institute of Missionary Research (Svenska Institutet för Missionsforskning),** Domkyrkoplan 1/2, S-75220 Uppsala. (Member of IAMS).

*SWITZERLAND*
**Apologetisches Institut,** Scheideggstr 45, CH-Zürich 2.
**Centre de Recherches et d'Etudes des Institutions Religieuses,** Dir, 3 Route de Suisse, CH-1290 Versoix, Genève.
**Centre Protestant d'Etudes,** 7 Rue Tabazan, CH-1204 Genève. T: 255660.
**Glaube in der 2 Welt,** Zürichstr 155, CH-8700 Kusnacht. (Research on religion in communist lands).
**Humanum Studies,** World Council of Churches, 150 Route de Ferney, CH-1211 Genève 20.
**Institut de Missiologie et de Science des Religions,** Université/Misericorde, CH-1701 Fribourg.
**Institut d'Ethique Social,** Fédération des Eglises Protestantes de la Suisse, Sulgenauweg 26, CH-3007 Bern.
**Institut d'Etudes Missionnaires,** Faculté de Théologie, Salle 1019, Université de Fribourg, CH-1700 Fribourg. (Member of IAMS).
**Institut d'Etudes Oecuméniques de l'Université de Fribourg,** Dir, 262 Rue de Morat, CH-1700 Fribourg. T: (037)297744.
**Institut für Weltanschauliche Frägen,** Scheideggstr 45, CH-8002 Zürich. T: 360760.
**Kirchensoziologische Forschung und Beratung (KFB),** Ackerstr 57, CH-8005 Zürich. T: (051) 428466,443380. (Also: Hadlaubstr 121, CH-80006 Zürich). (Socio-religious).
**Schweizerisches Pastoralsoziologisches Institut (SPI),** Webergasse 5, CH-9001 St Gallen.
**Study on Christians in Changing Institutions,** WCC, 150 Route de Ferney, CH-1211 Genève 20.
**Swiss Society for Futures Research,** Pres, Ecole Polytechnique Fédérale, Léonhardstr 27, Zürich. (Secular).

*TANZANIA*
**Tanzania Pastoral and Research Institute (TAPRI),** PO Box 325, Tabora. T: 2532.

*THAILAND*
**Thailand Church Growth Committee,** 120 Kasemkit Building, Room 702, 7th Floor, Silom Rd, GPO Box 432, Bangkok. T: 2339560.

*TOGO*
**Groupe de Recherches Culturelles et Religieuses dans le Sud Togo (GREST),** c/o Père Prieur, Monastère de Dzogbégan, Par Palimé.

*TUNISIA*
**Centre Protestant d'Etudes,** Dir, 39 Av des Felibres, Tunis.
**Institut des Belles Lettres Arabes (IBLA),** 12 Rue Djemaa-El-Haoua, Tunis. T: 260133. (White Fathers).

*UGANDA*
**Church of Uganda Research Unit,** Planning and Development Advisory Office, Provincial Secretariat, Bishop Willis Rd, Namirembe, PO Box 14123, Kampala. T: 46218/9.

*UK of GB & NI*
**Catholic Institute for International Relations (CIIR),** 41 Holland Park, London W11. T: (01)727-3195.
**Centre for the Study of Islam and Christian-Muslim Relations,** Selly Oak Colleges, Birmingham 29.
**Centre for the Study of Religion and Communism (CSRC),** Dir, Keston College, Heathfield Rd, Keston, Kent BR2 6BA. T: Farnborough (Kent) 50116.
**Christian Organizations Research and Advisory Trust (CORAT),** 15 Dover St, Canterbury, Kent CT1 3HD. T: (0227)62102.
**Christian Studies Unit,** 94 Kennington Av, Bishopston, Bristol 7.
**Christian Study Centre,** Sec, St Margaret Pattens Church, Eastcheap, London EC3. T: (01)623-6630.
**Churches' Fellowship for Psychical and Spiritual Studies,** 5/6 Denison House, Vauxhall Bridge Rd, London SW1. T: (01)834-4329.
**Department of Educational and Socio-Religious Research,** 4 Gerard Rd, Harrow, Middlesex. T: 907-1816.
**Gallup,** 211 Regent St, London W1A 3AU. T: (01)734-3671. (Regular polls on religious questions).
**Grubb Institute of Behavioural Studies,** Dir, 1 Whitehall Place, London SW1 2HD. T: (01)930-6364. (Formerly Christian Teamwork Institute of Education).
**Institute for Strategic Studies,** 18 Adam St, London WC2. (Military; Christian origin).
**Institute for the Study of Worship and Religious Architecture,** University of Birmingham, PO Box 363, Edgbaston, Birmingham 15.
**Institute of Religion and Medicine,** 58a Wimpole St, London W1M 7DE. T: (01)935-4687. (Also: St Mary Abchurch, Abchurch Lane, London EC4N 7BA).
**Institute of the Science of Religion,** 15 Edge St, London W8. T: (01)229-6618.
**Library for Charismatic Studies,** Fountain Trust, Central Hall, Durnsford Rd, London SW19 8ED. T: (01)947-4314. (Research).
**Liverpool Institute of Social-Religious Studies,** Christ's College, Woolton Rd, Liverpool L16 8DN. T: Childwall 3121.
**Mankind 2000,** Exec Dir, c/o Bank of Scotland, 30 Bishopsgate, London EC2. (Secular; futurology).
**Methodist Archives & Research Centre,** Connexional Archivist, 1 Central Bldg, Westminster, London SW1 T: (01)930-7608.
**New Churches Research Group (NCRG),** Hon Sec, 5a Lancaster Rd, Wimbledon, London SW19. T: (01)946-9855. (Also: 11 Parkway, Wilmslow, Cheshire. Affiliated to Institute of Advanced Architectural Studies, University of York).
**Oxford Institute for Church and Society,** Dir, St Margaret's Vicarage, Oxford. (Begun 1974).
**Oxford Institute of Methodist Theological Studies,** Co-Chairman, 2 College House, Richmond College, Surrey.
**Pastoral Research Centre (PRC),** 16 Osborne Gardens, Malone, Belfast 9, NI. T: 667127.
**Project for the Study of New Religious Movements (PRONERM),** Department of Religious Studies, King's College, Aberdeen AB9 2UB.
**Religious Experience Research Unit (RERU),** Dir, Manchester College, Holywell St/Mansfield Rd, Oxford. (Begun 1970).
**Research Department,** Worldwide Evangelization Crusade, Bulstrode, Gerrards Cross, Bucks. T: 84631.
**Scottish Institute of Missionary Studies,** Sec, Department of Religious Studies, Taylor Building, Kings College, University of Aberdeen, Aberdeen, Scotland AB9 2UB. T: (0224)40241 ext 6263.
**Southwark Diocesan Department of Religious Sociology,** 94 Lambeth Rd, London SE1.
**SSRC Data Bank,** Dir Social Science Research Council, University of Essex, Wivenhoe Park, Colchester, Essex. (Includes religion).
**Statistical Unit,** Central Board of Finance of the Church of England, Church House, Dean's Yard, Westminster, London SW1. T: (01)222-9011. (Parish and diocesan statistics, for England only).
**Teilhard Centre for the Future of Man,** Pres, 3 Cromwell Place, London SW7.
**Urban Theology Unit (UTU),** Dir, 210 Abbeyfield Rd, Sheffield S4 7AZ.

*USA*
**Alverno Research Center on Women,** Alverno College, 3401 South 39th St, Milwaukee, WI 53215. (Interdenominational, academic).
**American Institute of Holy Land Studies,** 460 Central Av, PO Box 456, Highland Park, IL 60035. T: (315)433-4060.
**American Institute of Public Opinion,** Gallup International, Pres, 53 Bank St, Princeton, NJ 08540. T: (609)924-9600. (Regular polls on religious questions. Also a centre for religious research, archives, etc; see below under PRRC).
**Amistad Research Center,** Fisk University, Nashville. (Missions).
**Biblical Research Associates,** College of Wooster, Wooster, OH 44691. (Produces *The computer Bibles*).
**Bureau of Community Research,** Pacific School of Religion, Berkeley, California.
**Bureau of Research and Survey,** NCCCUSA, 475 Riverside Drive, New York, NY 10027.
**Cambridge Center for Social Studies,** Dir, 42 Kirkland St, Cambridge, MA 02138. T: (617)868-1210.
**Center for Advanced Study in Theology and the Sciences,** Meadville Theological School, Lombard College, 5750 Ellis Av, Chicago, IL 60637.
**Center for Applied Research in the Apostolate (CARA),** 1717 Massachusetts Av NW, Washington, DC 20036. T: (202)265-3900. (In FERES).
**Centre for Human Communications,** Fairfield University, Fairfield, CT 06433.
**Center for Pastoral Studies,** 501 Caldwell Hall, Catholic University of America, Washington, DC 20017.
**Center for Social Research in the Church,** Dir, Concordia Teachers College, River Forest, Illinois.
**Center for the Advancement of Human Communication,** Fairfield University, North Benson Rd, Fairfield, CT 06430. T: (203)255-5411.
**Center for the Study of Development and Social Change,** Dir, 1430 Massachussetts Av, Cambridge, MA 01238.
**Center for the Study of Man,** University of Notre Dame, Notre Dame, Indiana.
**Center for the Study of the Future,** Exec Dir, 4110 NE Alameda, Portland, OR 97212. (Research on future and relation of Body of Christ to it).
**Center for the Study of World Religions,** Harvard University, 42 Francis Av, Cambridge, MA 02138.
**Center for Understanding Media,** Fordham University, Bronx, NY 10458. (RC).
**Center for Urban Church Studies,** 127 Ninth Av North, Nashville, TN 37234. T:(615)251-2920. (Southern Baptist).
**Center of Interreligious Research,** 105 West Adams St, Chicago, IL 60603.
**Christian Data Systems,** PO Box 954, Wheaton, IL 60187.
**Christian Research Inc,** Dir, 2624 First Av South, Minneapolis, MN 55408. T: (612)822-4428.
**Christian Research Institute,** Pres, 116 Surrey Drive, Wayne, NJ 07470.
**Christian Resource Associates (CRA),** PO Box 2100, Orange, CA 92669. (Management courses).
**Christian Theological Seminary Program in Church Research and Planning,** Box 88257, Indianapolis, IN 46208. T: (317)924-1331.
**Church Data Systems,** 6705 NE 38th Av, Portland, OR 97211.
**Church Surveys,** Department of Sociology and Social Ethics, Boston University, 745 Commonwealth Av, Boston, MA 02215. T: 353-3064.
**Church Youth Research,** 122 West Franklin, Minneapolis, MN 55404. T: (612)332-2571.
**Combined Motivation Education Systems,** 6300 River Rd, Rosemont, IL 60018.
**Committee to Assist Missionary Education Overseas (CAMEO),** Co-Chairman, 8210 W 16th Place, Lakewood, CO 80215. T: (303)237-7154.
**Computer Consultants for the Christian Community,** Pres, Suite 1418, One Wilshire Bldg, Los Angeles, CA 90017. T: (213)627-6451.
**Conference on Religion and The Future,** Crozer Theological Seminary, Chester, PA 19031. (1969 conference in King of Prussia (PA), and followup).
**Cooperation in Documentation and Communication (CoDoC),** 1500 Farragut St, NW, Washington, DC 20011.
**Creation Science Research Center,** Dir, 2716 Madison Av, San Diego, CA 92116. T: (714)283-2164.
**Daystar Communications,** 1432 Orchard St, PC Box 1717, Eugene, OR 97405. T: (503)342-6712.
**Department of Research,** Office of Planning and Program, NCCCUSA, 475 Riverside Drive, New York, NY 10027. T: (212)870-2562.
**Department of Research and Statistics,** Lutheran Church - Missouri Synod, 500 North Broadway, St Louis, MO 63102.
**Department of Research and Survey,** Board of Missions of the Methodist Church, 475 Riverside Drive, New York, NY 10027. T: (212)749-700.
**Duncan Black Macdonald Center for the Study of Islam and Christian/Muslim Relations,** Hartford Seminary Foundation, 55 Elizabeth St, Hartford, Connecticut.
**Dynasty Church Systems,** 1011 N Broadway, Los Angeles, CA 90052.
**Ecumenical Center of Renewal and Planning,** Merom Institute, Merom, IN 47861. (Also: PO Box 88377, Indianapolis, IN 46208. T: (317)924-1331. For non-metropolitan areas).
**Ecumenical Consultants,** 1829 Post Rd, Darien, CT 06820. T: (203)655-2307.
**Ecumenical Institute of Religious Studies,** Assumption College, 500 Salisbury St, Worcester, MA 01609.
**Ecumenism Research Agency,** Dir, 11040 Windsor Drive, Sun City, AR 85351.
**Evangelical Communications Research Foundation,** Pres, Box 28539, Dallas, TX 75228. T: (214)279-6995.
**FEBC Research Department,** Far East Broadcasting Company, Box 1, Whittier, CA 90608. T: (213)698-0438.
**Foundation for Reformation Research,** 6477 San Bonita Av, St Louis, MO 63105. T: PA 7-6655.
**Geoscience Institute,** 600 College Av, PO Box 161, Andrews Rural Station, Berrien Springs, MI 49104. T: (616)471-7751. (Seventh-day Adventist).
**Glenmary Research Center,** 4606 East-West Highway, Washington, DC 20014. T: (301)654-7501. (Roman Catholic; rural apostolate).
**IDOC North America,** 637 West 125 St, New York, NY 10027.
**Institute for Advanced Pastoral Studies,** 380 Lone Pine Rd, Bloomfield Hills, MI 48013.
**Institute for Advanced Religious Studies,** University of Notre Dame, Notre Dame, IN 46556.
**Institute for American Church Growth,** 1857 Highland Oaks, Arcadia, California.
**Institute for Antiquity and Christianity,** Claremont Graduate School, 880 North College Av, Claremont, CA 91711.
**Institute for Cross-Cultural Research,** 4000 Albermarle St NW, Washington, DC 20016. T: (202)362-6668.
**Institute for Ecumenical and Cultural Research,** Exec Dir, St John's University, Collegeville, MN 56321. T: (612)363-7761. (Main centre for Catholic pentecostal studies).
**Institute for Religious and Social Studies,** 3080 Broadway, New York, NY 10027. T: (212)RI9-8000.
**Institute for Socio-Religious Research,** University of San Francisco, San Francisco, CA 94117. T: 752-1000.
**Institute for the Future,** Riverview Centre, Middletown, CT 06457. (Secular).
**Institute for the Study of American Religion (ISAR),** Dir, 2121 Sheridan Rd, Evanston, IL 60201 T: (812)328-1852.
**Institute for Thomistic and Ecumenical Studies,** 1740 Arch St, Berkeley, CA 94709.
**Institute for Thomistic and Ecumenical Studies'** 2570 Asbury St, Dubuque, IA 52002.
**Institute of Christian Oriental Research,** Washington, DC 20017.
**Institute of Church Growth (ICG),** Dean, Fuller Theological Seminary, 135 North Oakland Av, Pasadena, CA 91101. T: (213)449-1745.
**Institute of Ethics and Society,** San Francisco Theological Seminary, San Anselmo, CA 94960. T: 453-2280.
**Institute of Judaico-Christian Studies,** Seton Hall University, South Orange, NJ 07079.
**Institute of Strategic Studies,** Board of National Missions, UPUSA, 475 Riverside Drive, New York, NY. T: (212)870-2914.
**Institute on Religion in an Age of Science (Zygon),** 5700 Woodlawn Av, Chicago, IL 60637.
**Institute on the Church in Urban Industrial Society,** 800 West Belden Av, Chicago, IL 60614. T: (312)549-3700.
**International Research Associates,** 1270 Av of the Americas, New York, NY 10020. T: (212)581-2010. (Secular, but undertakes religion polls).
**International Workshop on Mass Media and Religious Education,** 6815 South Zarzamora St, PO Box 28240, San Antonio, TX 78228.
**John XXIII Center for Eastern Christian Studies,** Fordham University, 2546 Belmont Av, Bronx, NY 10458. T: (212)933-2233. (Also: Fordham Rd and 3rd Av, New York, NY 10458).
**Lutheran Institute of Human Ecology,** Coordinator, 1800 West Dempster St, Park Ridge, IL 60068. T: (312)696-2210.
**Maryknoll Center for Mission Research,** Maryknoll PO, NY 10545. T: (914)941-7590.
**Mediaeval Institute,** University of Notre Dame, Notre Dame, Indiana. T: (219)284-6604.
**Membership Information Systems for Churches,** 608 N St Paul, Dallas, TX 75210.
**Membership Services Inc,** Pres, PO Box 217, Irving, TX 75060.
**Mental Health Research Institute,** University of Michigan, Dir, Ann Arbor, MI 48104.
**Ministry Studies Board,** 608 Dupont Circle Bldg, 1717 Massachusetts Av NW, Washington, DC 20036. T: (202)232-3432.
**Missions Advanced Research and Communication Center (MARC),** Dir, 919 West Huntington Drive, Monrovia, CA 91016. T: (213)357-1111.
**Moody Institute of Science,** Moody Bible Institute, 12000 E Washington Blvd, Whittier, CA 90606. T: (213)698-8256. (Science films in 18 languages).
**National Church Growth Research Center,** Dir, Box 3760, Washington, DC 20007.
**National Institute for Mental Health,** Washington, DC. (Secular).
**Office of Pastoral Research,** Archdiocese of New York, 1011 First Av, New York, NY 10022.
**Office of Research, Statistics and Archives of the Lutheran Council in the USA,** 315 Park Av South, New York, NY 10010. T: (212)577-3950.
**Overseas Ministries Study Center (OMSC),** Ventnor, NJ 08406.
**Paulist Institute for Religious Research,** 415 West 59th St, New York, NY 10019.
**Pentecostal Research Center,** Oral Roberts University Library, 7777 South Lewis, PO Box 2187, Tulsa, OK 74102.
**Princeton Religion Research Center (PRRC),** 53 Bank St, Princeton, NJ 08540. T: (609)924-9600. (Gallup polls).
**Regional Church Planning Office,** 2230 Euclid Av, Cleveland, OH 44115.
**Religion Analysis Service,** Pres, Minneapolis, MN 55440.
**Religious Heritage of the Black World,** Project Dir, 671 Beckwith St SW, Atlanta, Georgia.
**Religious Research Center,** Candler School of Theology, Emory University, Atlanta, GA 30303. T: (414)377-2411 ext 7633.
**Research Center for Religion & Human Rights in Closed Societies,** RCDA, 475 Riverside Drive, New York, NY 10027. T: (212)870-2481,2440.
**Research Office,** Episcopal Church in the USA, 815 Second Av, New York, NY 10017. T: (212)867-8400. (Formerly General Division of Research and Field Study).
**Research Office of the Presbytery of Chicago,** 800 W Belden Av, Chicago, IL 60614. T: (312) 549-3700 ext 35.
**Research Publications,** PO Box 3903, Amity Station, New Haven, CT 06525.
**Resources for the Future Inc,** Pres, 1755 Massachusetts Av, NW, Washington, DC 20036. (Secular).
**Roper Public Opinion Research Center,** Dir, Williams College, Box 624, Williamstown, MA 01267. (Includes religion).
**Samuel Zwemer Institute (SZI),** Dir, Box 365, Altadena, CA 91001. T: (213)794-1121/2. (Evangelization among Muslims).
**Society for the Study of Religion under Communism,** PO Box 171, Wheaton, IL 60187.
**Studies in Church and State,** Box 380, Baylor University, Waco, TX 76703.
**Study Centre on Religion and Society,** 2880 Oahu Av, Honolulu, Hawaii 96822.
**Survey Research Centre,** University of California, 2220 Piedmont Av, Berkeley, CA 94720. T: 845-6000 ext 4044. (Includes religion).
**Unitarian Universalist Futures Program,** Department of Development, Unitarian Universalist Association, 25 Beacon St, Boston, MA 02108.
**United Presbyterian Center for Mission Studies,** Dir, PO Box 2612, Fullerton, CA 92633.
**United States Center for World Mission (USCWM),** 1605 E. Elizabeth St, Pasadena, CA 91104. T: (213)794-7155.
**Western Church Records Management Inc,** 2034 Glenview Terrace, Altadena, CA 91001. T: (213)798-4616.
**William Carey Institute for Evangelism and Church Growth (WCI),** Exec Dir, 1021 East Walnut St, Suite 202, Pasadena, CA 91106. T: (213)796-0237.
**World Future Society,** Secretariat, 5501 Lincoln St, Bethesda, PO Box 19285, 20th St Station, Washington, DC 20036. (Secular).
**Xerox University Microfilms,** 300 North Zeeb Rd, Ann Arbor, MI 48106. (500,000 university dissertations with 8,000 on Christianity or religion, accessible via Datrix II computer retrieval system).

*UPPER VOLTA*
**Centre de Recherche et d'Action Sociale (CERAS),** BP 90, Ouagadougou. T: 2674.
**Centre d'Etudes Economiques et Sociales d'Afrique Occidentale (CESAO),** BP 305, Bobo-Dioulasso. T: 9551.

*URUGUAY*
**Centro de Estudios Cristianos del Rio de la Plata,** Casillo Correo 445, Montevideo.
**Centro de Estudios Religiosos (CER),** Av Agraciada 2974, Montevideo.

**Centro de Investigación y Acción Social (CIAS),** Av Agraciada 2974, Montevideo.
**Centro Nacional de Sociología Religiosa,** Treinta y Tres 1368, Montevideo.
**Iglesia y Sociedad en América Latina (ISAL),** Pza Cagancha 1342, 1 Piso, Of 6, Casilla Correo 179, Montevideo.
**Instituto Filosófico del Uruguay,** Av 8 de Octubre 3060, Montevideo.
**Instituto Teológico del Uruguay,** Av 8 de Octubre 3060, Montevideo.

*VANUATU*
**Pacific Churches Research Centre,** Box 551, Port Vila.

*VENEZUELA*
**Centro de Desarrollo Indigena (CEDI),** Apdo 8150, Caracas 101.
**Centro de Estudios del Futuro de Venezuela,** Universidad Católica Andrés Bello, Urb Montalban, Apdo 13228, Caracas. (Futurology).
**Centro de Investigaciones en Ciencias Sociales (CISOR),** Apdo 1283, Caracas 101.
**Centro de Investigación y Acción Social (CIAS),** Apdo 638, Esquina de Pajaritos, Caracas.
**Centro de Investigaciones Sociales y Socio-Religiosas (CISOR),** Edificio Juan XXIII, Piso 3, Torre a Madrices, Apdo 12863 Coliseo, Caracas 101. T: 816181. (In FERES).
**Centro Gumilla,** Av Berrizbeitia 14, El Paraiso, Apdo Postal 29056, Caracas 102. T: 423482.
**Fundación La Salle de Ciencias Naturales,** CAS, Apdo 8150, Caracas 101. T: 729612. (Missiology).
**Instituto Caribe de Antropología y Sociología (ICAS),** Apdo 8150, Caracas 101. T: 729612.
**Instituto de Estudios Teológicos,** Universidad Católica Andrés Bello, Caracas.
**Instituto Venezolano de Lenguas Indígenas,** UCAB, Apdo 13228, Caracas 101. T: 496721.

*YUGOSLAVIA*
**Espicopal Centre for Socio-Pastoral Research (KRSOL) (Skofijski svet za Pastoralno Socioloska Raziskovanjo, SPSS),** Cirkulane Pri Ptuju, Slomskov trg 19, Maribor. T: 21341.

*ZAIRE*
**Centre de Communications Sociales,** Université Nationale du Zaire, BP 832, Kinshasa XI.
**Centre de Recherches Socio-Religieuses,** c/o Conférence Episcopale, BP 3258, Kinshasa-Gombe. T: 5457 ext 40.
**Centre d'Etudes Bibliques et de Réflexion Chrétienne,** Centre St Irenée, Dir, BP 144, Kikwit.
**Centre d'Etudes de Sciences Humaines (CESH),** Université Nationale du Zaire, Kinsagani.
**Centre d'Etudes des Religions Africaines (CERA),** Faculté de Théologie, Université Nationale du Zaire, BP 756, Kinshasa XI.
**Centre d'Etudes Ethnologiques de Bandundu (CEEB),** Collège St-Paul, Bandundu.
**Centre d'Etudes Pastorales,** BP 724, Limete-Kinshasa. T: 77418.
**Institut Supérieur des Sciences Religieuses,** Université Nationale du Zaïre (ex-Lovanium), Campus de Kinshasa, BP 832, Kinshasa XI.

*ZAMBIA*
**Institute for Social Research,** University of Zambia, PO Box 900, Lusaka. T: 74721.
**Pastoral Service,** Catholic Secretariat, PO Box 8002, Lusaka. T: 62180.

*ZIMBABWE*
**Pastoral Service,** Catholic Secretariat, Salisbury.

# 51 Rural Agricultural Mission

***Definition.*** Agricultural missions, agricultural assistance, Christian rural or farming communities or centres, village polytechnics, rural transformation, rural development aid, ministry to rural situations; agricultural co-operatives, farmers' trade unions; rural and agricultural training centres. (Note: many centres included under LAY TRAINING CENTRES specialize in rural courses).

Christian organizations of major significance in this field number over 250.

*ARGENTINA*
**Misiones Rurales Argentinas,** Santa Fe 1005, Buenos Aires.
**Movimiento Rural de Acción Católica,** Montevideo 850, Buenos Aires.
**Secretariado del Movimiento Rural,** Rodriguez Pena 846, 1 Piso, Buenos Aires. (Member, MIJARC).

*AUSTRALIA*
**National Catholic Rural Movement,** PO Box 125, Camberwell. (In ICRA).
**Steer Inc,** PO Box 21, Armadale, Victoria 3143. T: 203236. (Gifts of stock and crops to missions).

*AUSTRIA*
**KLJ/O und KLJM/O,** Generalsekretariat, Johannesgasse 16, A-1010 Wien 1. (Member, MIJARC).

*BELGIUM*
**Alliance Agricole Belge,** Rue Joseph II 82, B-1040 Brussel. T: (02)2186979.
**Fédération Internationale des Mouvements d'Adultes Ruraux Catholiques (FIMARC)/International Federation of Catholic Rural Movements,** Secretariat, Rue Africaine 92, B-1050 Brussel. T: (02)5187842.
**KLJ Centrale,** Diestsevest 26, B-3000 Leuven (Member, MIJARC).
**KLJM,** Diestsevest 18, B-3000 Leuven. (Member, MIJARC).
**Mouvement International de la Jeunesse Agricole et Rurale Catholique (MIJARC)/International Movement of Catholic Agricultural & Rural Youth,** Sec Gén, Diestsevest 24, B-3000 Leuven. T: (016)228312. (Member of OIC).
**Secrétariat de la JRC et JRCF,** Rue du Sémanaire 11, B-5000 Namur (Member, MIJARC).
**Union Catholique Internationale de Service Social (UCISS)/Catholic International Union for Social Service,** Rue de la Poste 111, B-1030 Brussel. T: (02)172858.

*BELIZE*
**Lynam Agricultural College,** Belize. (Catholic).

*BENIN*
**JAC/F,** Secrétariat National, Mission Catholique, Dangbo via Porto-Novo. (Member, MIJARC).

*BOLIVIA*
**Departmento de Fomento Cooperativo,** Yanococha 545, Casilla Correo 3077, La Paz. (In ICRA).
**Hermanas Franciscanas Misioneras Rurales,** Casilla 3848, La Paz. T: 43049. (RC).
**Instituto de Educación Rural (IER),** Casilla 731, Cochabamba. T: 9084.
**Secretariado JAC/F,** Casilla 353, Santa Cruz. (Member, MIJARC).
**Secretariado JAC y JACF,** Casilla 731, Cochabamba. (Member, MIJARC).

*BRAZIL*
**Associação Diocesana de Assistência Rural,** Maringá, PR.
**Celio Bonetti,** Rua 13 de Maio, Sorocaba, São Paulo, SP. (Member, MIJARC).
**Centro de Formação de Líderes Rurais (CFLR),** Casa Sagrada Família, Av João XXIII s/n, CP 37, São Mateus, ES.
**Cooperativa de Colonização Agro-Pecuária de Penedo,** Penedo, AL.
**Cooperativa de Colonização Agro-Pecuária de Pindorama,** Penedo, AL.
**Cooperativa Mista Agrícola do Araguaia,** São Felix, MT.
**Escola de Formação Categuista e Líderes Rurais,** Roraima, RR.
**Escola de Formação de Líderes Rurais,** Av 1 de Julho 110, Divinópolis, MG.
**Frente Agrária Gaúcha,** Rua Dr Flôres 105, 4 andar, s/412, Pôrto Alegre, RS.
**Frente Agrária Gaúcha,** Rua João Cardoso, s/n, Cêrro Largo, RS. T: 29.
**Frente Agrária Gaúcha,** Rua Marechal Deodoro 582, CP 86, Santa Cruz do Sul, RS. T: 2078.
**Frente Agrária Gaúcha,** Vacaria, RS.
**Frente Agrária Paranaense,** Residência Episcopal, CP 152, 87 100 Maringá, PR. T: 21700.
**Servico de Orientação Rural de Pernambuco (SORPE),** Rua do Giriquiti 48, 50 000 Recife, PE.

*CAMEROON*
**JAC et JACF,** Secrétariat, BP 4272, Yaoundé. (Member, MIJARC).
**MIJARC,** Sécretariat Panafricain, BP 859, Yaoundé.

*CANADA*
**Fédération des Caisses Populaires des Jardins,** 59 Av Bégin, Levis, Québec. (In ICRA).
**JRC,** Secrétariat, Apt 1, 1225 Jean Talon Est, Montréal 328, Québec. (Member, MIJARC).
**Rural Life Mission,** 41 Main St N, Hagersville, Ontario.

*CENTRAL AFRICA REPUBLIC*
**Animation Rurale Féminine (ARF),** Central Jean XXIII, Bangui.

*CHAD*
**JAC,** Secrétariat, BP 14, Koumra. (Member, MIJARC).
**JACF,** Secrétariat, BP 857, Ndjamena (Fort-Lamy). (Member, MIJARC).
**Jeunesse Agricole pour le Développement (JAD),** BP 8, Mongo, Guera. (Member, MIJARC).
**Société Chrétienne Agricole,** BP 2162, Ndjamena (Fort-Lamy).

*CHILE*
**ACR,** Secretariado, Classificador 515, Santiago. (Member, MIJARC).
**Instituto de Educación Rural,** Casilla 10397, Santiago. (In ICRA).

*CHINA (TAIWAN)*
**Association for Social-Economic Development in China (ASEDROC),** 279-1 3rd Floor, Roosevelt Rd, Section 3, Taipei. (In ICRA).

*COLOMBIA*
**Acción Cultural Popular (ACPO),** Escuelas Radiofónicas, Calle 20 No 9-45, Bogotá. (In ICRA).
**Granjas del Padre Luna,** Carrera 7 No 26-37, Bogotá. (Farm houses).
**JAC y JACF,** Secretariado, Calle 8 No 23-20, Ocana, Norte de Santander. (Member, MIJARC).

*ECUADOR*
**Central Ecuatoriana de Servicios Agricolas (CESA),** c/o Apdo 36, Riobamba, Chimborazo.
**JAC/F,** Apdo 36, Riobamba, Chimborazo. (Member, MIJARC).

*EL SALVADOR*
**Coordinación Centroamericana de Centros Campesinos Cristianos,** Centro La Providencia, Apdo 1941, Santa Ana. T: 413110.
**Juventud Agrária Católica (JAC) & JACF,** Secretariado, Colegio Pio X, Cujutepeque, Dpto Cuscatlan. T: 320308. (Member, MIJARC).

*ETHIOPIA*
**Agri-Service Ethiopia,** PO Box 3406, Soddo-Wolloam.

*FRANCE*
**Centri d'Istruzione Agricola Nord-Africana,** 33 Rue Rabelais, Angers.
**Donation Rurale,** F-59232 Vieux-Berquin. (In ICRA).
**Ecole Supérieure d'Agriculture de Purpan,** 271 Av de Grande-Bretagne, F-31300 Toulouse. (In ICRA).
**Institut Social d'Action Populaire,** 15 Rue Raymond Marcheron, F-92170 Vanves. (In ICRA).
**Mouvement d'Action Rurale,** FPF, Sec-gén, 47 Rue de Clichy, F-75009 Paris.
**MRJC,** Secrétariat, 42 Rue la Bruyère, F-75009 Paris. (Member, MIJARC).

*GABON*
**JAC et JACF,** Secrétariat, BP 100, Oyem. (Member, MIJARC).

*GAMBIA*
**Agricultural, Technical & Community Development Centre,** PO Box 165, Bathurst.

*GERMANY, Federal Republic of*
**Arbeitsgemeinschaft für Dorfkirchlichen Dienst innerhalb der EKD,** In Weidergarten 12, D-35 Kassel-K. (Church work in rural areas — youth, families, social).
**Bauernschule Gamburg,** Ländliche Heimvolkshochschule, D-6981 Gamburg (Tauber). (Farmers' training).
**Ev-Lutherische Ländvolk-Hochschule,** D-2321 Koppelsberg über Plön. (Rural training).
**Internationale Föderation Katholische Ländlicher Heimvolkshochschulen,** Adrianstr 141, D-5300 Bonn-Oberkassel. T: (02221)440323.
**Katholische Landvolkbewegung Deutschlands,** Kriemhildenstr 14, D-8000 München 38. (In ICRA).
**KLJB,** Bundestelle, Klausenhofstr 38, D-4203 Dingden, Westfalen. (Member, MIJARC).
**Ländliche Heimvolkshochschule,** D-7112 Hohebuch-Waldenburg. (Rural training).
**Ländvolkshochschule Rheinland,** Diepersbergweg 13-17, D-523 Altenkirchen (Westerwald). (Farmers' training).
**Ostfriesische Evangelische Ländvolkshochschule,** D-2919 Potshausen (Ostfriesland). (Rural training).
**Schwäbische Bauernschule Bad Waldsee,** Döchbuhl, D-7967 Waldsee.

*GREECE*
**Union des Cooperatives Agricoles de Syra,** Place Héroou 7, Hermoupolis, Syra. (In ICRA).

*HOLY SEE*
**Agrimission,** Secretariat, Piazza San Calisto 16, I-00120 Città del Vaticano. T: 6984443.

*INDIA*
**Agricultural Development Society,** Gen Manager, PO Naini, Allahabad, UP.
**Catholic Social Action,** Latin Archbishop's House, Ernakulam, Cochin 11, Kerala. (In ICRA).
**Chota Nagpur Catholic Mission Co-operative Credit Society,** PB 2, Ranchi. (In ICRA).
**Chowpatta Agricultural & Industrial Mission,** PO Berenag District, Pithoragarh, Kumaon, UP.
**Indian Social Institute,** Lodi Rd, New Delhi 110003. (In ICRA).
**Maharastra Prabodan Seva Mandal,** St Francis Av, Santa Cruz, Bombay 54. (In ICRA).
**Rural Training Centre,** United Christian School, PO Box 57, Jullundur City, Punjab.
**St Joseph's Co-operative Farming Society,** Isanagar, Meerut.

*INDONESIA*
**Ikatan Petani Pancasila,** Jalan Gunung Sahari III/7, Jakarta. (In ICRA).

*IRELAND*
**Ferns Diocesan Youth Service,** Bunclody, Wexford. (Member, MIJARC).
**Irish Creamery Milk Suppliers' Association,** John Feely House, 15 Upper Mallow St, Limerick. (In ICRA).
**National Farmers' Association,** 27 Earlscourt Terrace, Dublin 2. (In ICRA).
**People of the Country (Muintir na Tire),** Tipperary. (RC. Improvement of rural conditions. In ICRA).

*ITALY*
**Centro Sociale e Cooperativa Agricola di Villa S Sebastiano,** Via S Barbara 23, Villa S Sebastiano (Aq).
**Communità dei Braccianti,** Viale Ferdinando Baldelli 41, I-00146 Roma. T: 552251.
**Confederazione Cooperativa Italiana,** 78 Borgo S Spirito, Roma. (In ICRA).
**Confederazione Nazionale Coltivatori Diretti,** Via XXIV Maggio 43, Roma. (In ICRA).
**Federazione Italiana Clubs 3P,** Via XXIV Maggio 43, Roma. (In ICRA).
**International Catholic Rural Association (ICRA),** Secretariat, Piazza San Calisto 16, I-00153 Roma. T: 6984723.

*IVORY COAST*
**JAC/F,** Secretariat, BP 4119, Abidjan. (Member, MIJARC).

*JAPAN*
**Japan Rural Evangelism Fellowship,** Field Chairman, Tachi West Court W-145, Nakagami-Machi, Akishima-shi, Tokyo 196.
**Japan Rural Mission,** PO 16, Saiki-shi, Oita-ken 876.
**Rural and Printing Evangelism in Japan,** 1014 Kuge/Yana Cho, Ono City, Hyogo-ken.
**Tsurukawa Rural Institute,** 2024 Nozuta-cho, Machida-shi, Tokyo. T: (0427)35-2430. (Training Christian rural workers; UCCJ).

*KENYA*
**Christian Rural Fellowship of East Africa (CRFEA),** Sec, Lugari Farmers Training Centre, PO Box 30, Turbo.
**Christian Rural Service (CRS),** PO Box 79, Eldoret. T: 2051.
**Kataboi Fishing Village,** Dir, Kataboi Catholic Mission, Private Bag, Kitale.
**Loarengak Fishing Village,** Dir, Catholic Mission, PO Box Lokitaung, Kitale.
**Maasai Rural Development Centre (PCEA),** Dir, Olooseos, Magadi Rd, PO Box 24860, Nairobi.
**Maasai Rural Training Centre (CPK),** Manager, Isinya, PO Box 24, Kajiado.

*KOREA, South*
**Catholic Rural Youth,** 6 Ku Wonpyung Kumi, Kyongbuk. (Member, MIJARC).
**Isidore Development Association (Dae Rim Ri, Han Rim Eub, Cheju-Do),** PO Box 50, Cheju Do. T: Cheju City 4635. (In ICRA).

*LESOTHO*
**Machobane Rural Training Centre,** Machobane.
**Roma Valley Agricultural Project,** Archbishop's House, PO Box 267, Maseru. T: 2565.

*LUXEMBOURG*
**JACF,** Secrétariat, 3 Place du Théâtre, Luxembourg-ville. (Member, MIJARC).
**JBJW,** Secrétariat, 3 Rue Borgen, Luxembourg. (Member, MIJARC).

*MADAGASCAR*
**Centre Artisanal de Promotion Rurale,** BP 1170, Fianarantsoa.
**Centre d'Apprentissage Agricole,** Bevalala, Tananarive.
**Centre d'Education Familiale et Rurale,** BP 98, Antsiramandroso, Tamatave.
**Centre Ménager Rural,** PB 1782, Tananarive.
**Ferme-Ecole,** Andriamboasary par Fianarantsoa.
**Ferme-Ecole,** Betomba par Belo-sur-Tsiribihina.
**Madagascar Catholic Rural Youth Movement (Fivondronan'ny Tanora Malagasy Tantsaha Katolika, FTMTK),** Evêché, BP 100, Antsirabe. (Member, MIJARC).

*MEXICO*
**Acción Católica Mexicana,** Consejo Nacional de Campesinos, Minerva 104, 5 piso, México 20, DF. (In ICRA).
**ACJM,** Secretariado, Jalapa 35-c, México 7, DF. (Member, MIJARC).
**Heifer Project,** Apdo 390, Celaya, Gto.
**Ingenieros Agrónomos,** Antonio Vélez 24, Apdo 15, Atlacomulco.
**JAC,** Secretariado, 20 de Noviembre 9, Morelia Mich. (Member, MIJARC).

*NETHERLANDS*
**Agromisa (Bureau voor Landvouwkindige Adviezen aan Missionarissen),** Postbus 41, Wageningen.
**KPJM,** Sekretariat, Scheveningseweg 46, 's-Gravenhage. (Member, MIJARC).

*NIGERIA*
**Rural Consultation Mission (RUCOM),** Faith and Farm, PO Vom, via Jos. (Sudan United Mission).

*PARAGUAY*
**Instituto de Educación Rural (IDER),** Mariscal Estigarribia 629, Tavá arroyo.
**JAC y JACF,** Secretariado, Oliva 476, Asunción. (Member, MIJARC).
**Ligas Agrarias Cristianas,** c/o Oliva 476, Asunción.

*PERU*
**Movimiento Sindical Cristiano del Perú,** Jiron Ucayali 332, Apdo 1321, Lima. (In ICRA).

*PHILIPPINES*
**Agricultural Missions,** 941 Epifanio de los Santos Av, Quezon City.
**College of Agriculture,** Xavier University, Cagayan de Oro City. (In ICRA).
**Farm Workers for an Enlightened Republic,** PO Box 1767, Manila. T: 998636.
**Free Farmers' Federation (FFF),** 39 Highland Drive, Blue Ridge, Quezon City D504. (RC). (In ICRA).
**Junior Free Farmers,** 39 Highland Drive, Blue Ridge, Quezon City D504. (Member, MIJARC).
**South East Asian Rural Social Leadership Institute (SEARSOLIN),** c/o Xavier University, Cagayan de Oro City L-305. (In ICRA).

*PORTUGAL*
**JARC,** Secretariado, Campo Martires da Patria 43, Lisboa 1. (Member, MIJARC).
**JARCF,** Secretariado, Av Duque de Loulé 90, r-c dto, Lisboa 1. (Member, MIJARC).

*RWANDA*
**JAC et JACF,** Sécretariat, BP 87, Gisenyi. (Member, MIJARC).

*SENEGAL*
**Union des Jeunesses Catholiques Rurales du Sénégal,** BP 24, Thies. (Member, MIJARC).

*SOUTH AFRICA*
**Church Agricultural Projects,** Manager, Maria Ratschitz, Northern Natal.

*SPAIN*
**Comisión Nacional JARCF,** República Argentina 72-20, Benicarlo, Castellon. (Member, MIJARC).

*SWAZILAND*
**Lutheran Farmers Training Centre,** Pigg's Peak.

*SWITZERLAND*

**JRC et JRCF,** Grand Rue 48, CH-1680 Romont. (Member, MIJARC).

*THAILAND*

**Co-operative Farm,** Chiengmai.

*TOGO*

**JAC et JACF,** Secrétariat, BP 55, Sokode. (Member, MIJARC).
**Société Civile et Agricole de Dzoghégan (SCAD),** Dzoghégan. (Beneditine).

*TUNISIA*

**Association pour le Développement et l'Animation Rurale poursuivant les Activités du Service Oecuménique en Tunisie (ASDEAR),** Dir, 10 Rue Eve Nohelle, Tunis. T: 245592. (Reformed Church).

*UGANDA*

**Agricultural and Animal Husbandry School,** Diocesan Development Department, PO Box 1103, Mbale. T: 2570. (RC).
**Buswale Agricultural Scheme,** PO Box 673, Jinja. (RC).
**Christian Rural Service (CRS),** PO Box 7046, Kampala.
**Mugalibe Tea and Dairy Scheme,** PO Box 34 Hoima. (RC).

*UK OF GB & NI*

**Agricultural Christian Fellowship,** Sec, 39 Bedford Square, London WC1B 3EY.
**Institute of Rural Life at Home and Overseas,** 3 Hendon Av, Finchley, London N3. (Also: 27 Northumberland Rd, New Barnet).

*USA*

**Agricultural Aids Foundation,** 5241 Santa Monica Blvd, Los Angeles, CA 90029.
**Agricultural Missions,** 475 Riverside Drive, New York, NY 10027. T: (212)870-2553.
**Agropolitan Ministries,** Exec Dir, PO Box 145, Merom, IN 47861. T: (812)356-4681. (Ecumenical).
**American Committee for KEEP,** 343 South Dearborn St, Chicago, IL 60604.
**Christian Rural Fellowship (CRF),** 475 Riverside Drive, New York, NY 10027.
**Christian Rural Overseas Program (CROP),** 117 West Lexington Av, Box 227, Elkhart, IN 46514. (Church World Service community hunger appeal). (Also: 475 Riverside Drive, New York, NY 10027).
**Commission on Agricultural Missions,** NCCCUSA, 475 Riverside Drive, New York, NY 10027.
**Commission on Religion in Appalachia,** Exec Dir, 864 Weisgarber Rd, NW, Knoxville, TN 37919. T: (615)584-6133.
**Co-Laborers,** Pres, 6110 Radford Av North, Hollywood, CA 91606. T: (213)980-4293.
**Farms Inc,** Pres, 123 West 57th St, New York, NY 10019. T: (212)246-9692.
**Good Shepherd Agricultural Mission,** Pres, 822 Main St, Box 116, Fontanelle, IA 50846. T: (515) 745-4041.
**Harvesters International,** Dir, 3409 Gumwood, Box 1986, McAllen, TX 78501.
**Heifer Project,** 111/202 West Main St, PO Box 269, North Manchester, IN 46962. (Also: 1720 Chouteau Av, St Louis, MO 63103. T: (314)436-2442).
**Hinton Rural Life Centre,** PO Box 27, Hayesville, NC 28904.
**National Catholic Rural Life Conference,** 3801 Grand Av, Des Moines, IA 50312. (In ICRA).
**National Farm Worker Ministry,** Dir, Suite 511, 1411 West Olympic Blvd, Los Angeles, CA 90015. T: (213)286-8130).
**Rural Gospel and Medical Missions of India,** 945 South Euclid Av, Pasadena, CA 91106. T: (213) 799-2022.
**Rural Missions,** Route 1, Box 454, Johns Island, SC 29455.
**Rural Urban Nexus,** Agricultural Missions, 475 Riverside Drive, New York, NY 10027.
**Self Help Inc,** 116 6th St, SE, Waverly, IA 50677. T: (319)352-4483. (Farm machinery overseas).
**Wisconsin Indian Resource Council (WIRC),** Room 142, Old Main Building, University of Wisconsin, Stevens Point, WI 54481. T: (715) 346-2746. (For Amerindians).

*URUGUAY*

**JAC y JACF,** Secretariado, 25 de Mayo 493, Casilla 61, San José. (Member, MIJARC).
**MIJARC,** Secretariado Latinoamericano, Cerrito 475, Casilla Postal 1811 (Correo Central), Montevideo.

*VENEZUELA*

**Instituto Venezolano de Acción Comunitaria,** Av Libertador, Edif La Linea, 3er piso No 34-A, Caracas. (In ICRA).

*VIET NAM*

**Secrétariat Social,** 86 Nguyen Du, Ho Chi Minh Ville. (In ICRA).

*ZAIRE*

**JAC,** Secretariat National, BP 31, Bunia, Province Orientale. (Member, MIJARC).
**JACF,** Secrétariat, BP 50, Goma. (Member, MIJARC).
**JACF/F,** Secrétariat, BP 70, Kananga (Luluabourg). (Member, MIJARC).

# 52
# Scholarly Societies

*Definition.* National and international associations, learned societies and commissions (as contrasted with institutes or centres): biblical studies, theology, missiology, church history, religion, sociology, anthropology, ethnology, psychology, archeology, religion and science, religion and philosophy, religion and futurology; scholarly lecture series; associations of scholars; Catholic pontifical commissions in scholarly disciplines.

Scholarly societies significant at national or wider levels number over 250.

*AUSTRIA*

**Société du Droit de Eglises Orientales,** Karl Luerger Ring I, A-1010 Wien.
**World Union of Catholic Philosophical Societies /Union Mondiale des Sociétés Catholiques de Philosophie,** Secretariat, Aignerstr 25, A-5026 Salzburg.

*BELGIUM*

**International Association for the History of Religions,** Rue Ducale 1, Brussel.

*CANADA*

**Canadian Church History Society,** c/o Scarborough College, 1265 Military Trail, West Hill, Ontario.
**Evangelical Theological Society of Canada,** Ontario Bible College, 16 Spadina Rd, Toronto 4, Ontario.

*DENMARK*

**Nordic Society for Studies in Church History,** Nordic Missionary Council, Strandagervej 24, Hellerup.

*FRANCE*

**Association Française de Sociologie Religieuse,** 32 bis Rue du Bois, F-75019 Paris. T: 2037414.
**Conférence Internationale de Sociologie Religieuse (CISR)/International Conference for the Sociology of Religion,** Exec Sec, Rue de la Monnaie 39, F-59042 Lille. T: (20)553026.
**International Association for Patristic Studies/ Association Internationale d'Etudes Patristiques,** IC Quai Saint Thomas, F-67000 Strasbourg.
**Société Calviniste de France,** Sec, 10 Rue de Villars, St-Germain-en-Laye (Yvelines).
**Société de l'Histoire du Protestantisme Français (SHPF),** Sec Gén, 54 Rue des Saints-Pères, F-75007 Paris. T: LIT 7845,6207.

*GERMANY, Federal Republic of*

**Deutsche Gesellschaft für Missionswissenschaft/German Society for the Study of Missions,** Eckenerstr 1, D-6900 Heidelberg. T: (06221)40935. (Member of IAMS. Begun 1918).
**Gesellschaft für Geistegeschichte,** Kuchstr 4, D-8520 Erlangen.
**Görres-Gesellschaft zur Pflege der Wissenschaft,** Postfach 100905, D-5000 Köln 1. T: (0221) 237774. (Scientific culture).
**Internationale Gesellschaft für Religionsychologie/Association Internationale pour la Psychologie Religieuse,** Hiltenspergerstr 107/I, D-8000 Munchen 40. T: (089)3002800.
**Konvent Ev Theologinnen in der DDR und Westberlin,** Goethestr 26-30, D-1 Berlin 12. (Women theologians).
**Luther-Gesellschaft,** Geschäftsstelle, Grindel-Allee 7, D-2 Hamburg 13. (Lutheranism).

*HOLY SEE*

**Pontificia Accademia delle Scienze/Pontifical Academy of Sciences,** Cancelleria, Casina di Pio IV, Città del Vaticano. T: 6982 int 3195,3451.
**Pontificia Commissione Biblica/Pontifical Commission for Biblical Studies,** Palazzo della SCDF, Piazza del Santo Uffizio 11, I-00193 Roma, Italy. T: 6983357.
**Pontificia Commissione di Archeologia Sacra,** Palazzo del PIA, Via Napoleone III 1, I-00185 Roma, Italy. T: 735824.
**Pontificia Commissione per gli Archivi Ecclesiastici d'Italia,** Palazzo Apostolico, I-00120 Città del Vaticano. T: 6982 int 3314.

*INDIA*

**Church Growth Society of India.**
**Church History Association of India,** Serampore College, Serampore, West Bengal.

*ITALY*

**Commission for Latin America,** Palazzo delle Congregazioni, Piazza Pio XII 10, I-00193 Roma. T: 6982 int 3311,4465,4738.
**Commission for the Revision of Canon Law,** Palazzo dei Convertendi, Via dell'Erba, I-00193 Roma. T: 6982 int 3933,3934,3994.
**Commission for the Revision of Oriental Canon Law,** Palazzo dei Convertendi, Via della Conciliazione 34, Roma. T: 698 int 4295.
**Consociatio Internationalis Studio Iuris Canonici Promovendo,** Prof Cesare Mirabelli, Via Cicerone 49, I-00193 Roma.
**International Society for the Study of Prehistoric and Ethnological Religions,** Roma.
**Società di Studi Valdesi,** Via Massimo d'Azeglio, I-10066 Torre Pellice (To). (Waldensian).

*LUXEMBOURG*

**Association Catholique Internationale d'Etudes Médico-Psychologiques (ACIEMP),** 31 Blvd Jacquemart, Luxembourg. T: 483860.

*MEXICO*

**Commission of Studies for Latin American Church History (CEHILA),** Apdo 22-278, México 22, DF.

*NETHERLANDS*

**International Association for Mission Studies (IAMS),** Sec, Interuniversity Institute, Boerhaavelaan 43, Leiden.

*NIGERIA*

**Nigerian Association for the Study of Religions,** Department of Religious Studies, University of Ibadan, Ibadan.

*SOUTH AFRICA*

**South African Missiological Society,** Gen Sec, 31 Veertiende (14th) St, Menlo Park, Pretoria 0081.
**South African Society for the Study of Mission,** PO Box 213, Umtata, Transkei.

*SWEDEN*

**International Association for the Study of the Old Testament (IASOT),** Dekanhuset, The University, Uppsala.

*SWITZERLAND*

**Verband Schweizerischer Theologinnen,** Präs, CH-4125 Riehen/BS. (Lay women theologians).

*UK OF GB & NI*

**Alcuin Club,** Hon Sec, c/o Canon Gate House, Chichester. (Study of history and use of Book of Common Prayer, and liturgies).
**Bampton Lectures (Oxford University),** Sec, University Registry, Clarendon Bldgs, Broad St, Oxford. T: 48491.
**Baptist Historical Society,** Baptist Church House, 4 Southampton Row, London WC1.
**Canterbury & York Society,** 79 Whitwell Way, Coton, Cambridge. T: (095)43204. (Prints ecclesiastical records).
**Catholic Record Society,** Hon Sec, 114 Mount St, London W1. (Publishes documents on Roman Catholicism in England & Wales).
**Church Historical Society,** Holy Trinity Church, Marylebone Rd, London NW1. T: (01)387-5282. (Anglican).
**Churches' Fellowship for Psychical & Spiritual Studies,** Gen Sec, 5-6 Denison House, 296 Vauxhall Bridge Rd, London, SW1. T: (01)834-4329.
**Congregational Historical Society,** Hon Sec, 9 Priory Way, Hitchin, Herts. T: 3580. (Founded 1899; annual lecture).
**Ecclesiastical History Society,** Westfield College, London NW3. T: (01)435-7601.
**Ecclesiological Society,** Hon Sec, 1 Burghley Rd, Wimbledon, London SW19. T: (01)946-4340. (Study of architecture, crafts, music, worship).
**English Church History,** 68 Irby Rd, Heswall, Liverpool. T: (051)342-4476.
**Evangelical Fellowship for Missionary Studies,** 19 Draycott Place, London SW3 2SJ.
**Friends Historical Society,** Library, Friends House, Euston Rd, London NW1. T: Euston 3601. (Study of Quaker history).
**Historical Society of the Church in Wales,** Trinity College, Carmarthen. T: (0267)7971.
**Hulsean Lectures (Cambridge University),** University Marshal, 1a Rose Crescent, Cambridge. T: 58933/296.
**Hymn Society of Great Britain and Ireland,** Sec, 85 Lord Haddon Rd, Ilkeston, Derbyshire. T: 5850. (Study and research on hymns and hymnbooks).
**International Association for the History of Religions (IAHR),** Department of Religious Studies, Cartmel College, University of Lancaster, Bailrigg, Lancaster.
**International Methodist Historical Society,** The Manse, St Keverne, Helston, Cornwall.
**International Organization for the Study of the Old Testament (IOSOT),** St John's College, Cambridge CB2 1TP. T: (23)63219.
**Philosophical Society of England,** Gen Sec, 7 Cholmley Gardens, Aldren Rd, London NW6. T: (01)435-7691. (Also: 233 Chester Rd, Hartford, Cheshire).
**Royal Institute of Philosophy,** 14 Gordon Square, London WC1. T: Euston 4130.
**Scottish Catholic Historical Association,** c/o John S Burns & Sons, 25 Finlas St, Glasgow G22.
**Scottish Ecclesiological Society,** 16 Heriot Row, Edinburgh 3. T: 26188.
**Society for African Church History,** Sec, Department of Religious Studies, University of Aberdeen AB9 2UB.
**Society for Physical Research,** 1 Adam and Eve Mews, London W8. T: Western 8984.
**Society for the Christian Religion in Publications and Transmission,** All Souls College, Oxford.
**Society for the Study of Medical Ethics,** Sec, 103 Gower St, London WC1.
**Society for the Study of the New Testament,** Sec, King's College, Old Aberdeen AB9 2UB. T: (0224)40241 ext 308.
**Studiorum Nove Testamenti Societas (SNTS),** Pres, The University, Nottingham.
**Unitarian Historical Society,** Hon Sec, Unitarian College, Victoria Park, Manchester 14. T: Rusholme 2849.
**Victoria Institute (Philosophical Society of Great Britain),** Sec, 38 Jennings Rd, St Albans, Herts. (Relation between the Christian revelation and modern scientific research).
**Wesley Historical Society,** Sec, The Manse, St Keverne, Helston, Cornwall. T: 399.

*USA*

**Academy of Religion and Mental Health,** 16 East 34th St, New York, NY 10016.
**American Academy of Religion (AAR),** Department of Religious Thought, University of Pennsylvania, Philadelphia, PA 19104. (Also: AAR National Office, Wilson College, Chambersburg, PA 17201).
**American Baptist Historical Society (ABHS),** Sec, 1106 South Goodman St, Rochester, NY 14620. T: (716)473-1740. (Also: 50 Round Hill Rd, Henrietta, NY 14467).
**American Catholic Historical Association,** Catholic University of America, Washington, DC 20017.
**American Catholic Philosophical Association,** Catholic University of America, Washington, DC 20017.
**American Foundation of Religion and Psychiatry,** 3 West 29th St, New York, NY 10001.
**American Society of Christian Ethics (ASCE),** Candler School of Theology, Emory University, Atlanta, GA 30322. (Also: Bucknell University, Lewisburg, PA 17837).
**American Society of Missiology** Sec, PO Box 2057, Ventnor, NJ 08406.
**Association for Social-Economics (ASE),** 2323 North Seminary Av, Chicago, IL 60614.
**Association for the Development of Religious Information Systems (ADRIS),** Dept of Sociology & Anthropology, Marquette University, Milwaukee, WI 53233. T: (414)224-6838.
**Association for the Sociology of Religion,** 1403 North St Mary's St, San Antonio, TX 78215. (Also: Loyola Marymount University, Los Angeles, CA 90045).
**Association of Evangelical Professors of Missions,** Pres, Fuller Theological Seminary, 135 North Oakland Av, Pasadena, CA 91101.
**Association of Professors of Missions,** Pres, 5401 S Cornell Av, Chicago, IL 60615.
**Association of Statisticians of American Religious Bodies (ASARB),** Sec-Treas, 120 West 14th St, New York, NY 10011. T: (212)243-8700.
**Biblical Research Associates,** College of Wooster, Box 3182, Wooster, OH 44691.
**Biblical Research Society,** Pres, 4005 Verdugo Rd, Los Angeles, CA 90065.
**Canon Law Society of America (CLSA),** Exec Co-ordinator, 134 Farmington Av, Hartford, CT 06105. T: (203)527-4201. (Also: Toledo, Ohio). (RC).
**Catholic Biblical Association (CBA),** Catholic University of America, Washington, DC 20017.
**Catholic Commission on Intellectual and Cultural Affairs (CCICA),** Dir, 620 Michigan Av, Washington, DC 20017.
**Catholic Theological Society of America (CTSA),** St Mary of the Lake Seminary, Mundelein, IL 60060.
**College Theology Society (CTS),** Manhattan College, Bronx, NY 10471.
**Conference on Science and Religion,** 1090 South La Brea Av, Los Angeles 19, California.
**Council on the Study of Religion,** 314 Murphey Hall, University of North Carolina, Chapel Hill, NC 27514. (Also: Department of Religion Studies, Wilson College, Chambersburg, PA 17201). (Federation co-ordinating USA learned societies in religion; members AAR, ASCE, CBA, CTSA, CTS, SBL, SSSR).
**Historical Commission,** Southern Baptist Convention, Exec Sec, 127 9th Av, North Nashville, TN 37203. T: (615)254-1631.
**Mormon History Association (MHA),** Brigham Young University, Provo, UT 84601.
**Presbyterian Historical Society,** Sec, 425 Lombard St, Philadelphia, PA 19147.
**Religious Research Association,** PO Box 228, Cathedral Station, New York, NY 10025.
**Seventh Day Baptist Historical Society,** 510 Watchung Av, PO Box 868, Plainfield, NJ 07061. T: (201)754-3404.
**Sociedad Teológical Mexicana/Mexican Theological Society,** Montezuma Seminary, Montezuma, NM 87731.
**Society for Pentecostal Studies,** Sec, Lee College, Cleveland, TN 37311.
**Society for Religion in Higher Education,** 400 Prospect St, New Haven, CT 06511. T: (203) 865-8839.
**Society for the Scientific Study of Religion (SSSR),** 1200 17th St NW, Washington, DC 20036. (Also: Department of Sociology, University of Notre Dame, Notre Dame, IN 46556).
**Society of Biblical Literature (SBL),** Exec Sec, Department of Religious Studies, University of Montana, Missoula, MT 59801. (406)243-2632.
**Society of Biblical Literature and Exegesis (SBLE),** Divinity Quadrangle, Vanderbilt University, Nashville 5, Tennessee.
**Unitarian Historical Society,** Sec, First Church of Boston, 66 Marlborough St, Boston, MA 02116.
**Universalist Historical Society,** Pres, 2425 Sierra Blvd, Sacramento, CA 95825.
**World Association for Public Opinion Research,** Roper Public Opinion Research Centre, Williams College, Williamstown, Massachusetts. (Wide holdings on religion).
**World Methodist Historical Society,** Exec Sec, Cambridge Apartment, 402 Alden Park, PA 19144.
**World Union of Catholic Philosophical Societies,** Catholic University of America, Washington, DC 20017.
**Zygon,** Journal of Religion and Science, 5700 South Woodlawn Av, Chicago, IL 60637. T: (312) 643-0800 ext 3163.

# 53
# Schools & Colleges

*Definition.* Schools under church or Christian auspices or sponsorship: junior and senior secondary schools teaching secular subjects, minor seminaries (secular or religious), technical schools, agricultural schools, vocational schools, junior colleges, technical colleges, teacher-training colleges.

These institutions are too numerous and widespread to list here. In 1980, global totals (all denominations) are: about 140,000 elementary or primary schools, 40,000 secondary schools. Many listings of schools are contained in yearbooks given here under DIRECTORIES.

# 54
# Social & Pastoral Concern

*Definition.* Organizations concerned primarily with local Christian social, pastoral and community action and service in the secular world; voluntary service, pastoral concern and action, pastoralia, social action and service centres and ministries, social welfare, moral welfare, community development, unemployment, housing, population control, eugenics, the underprivileged, the elderly and aged, almshouses, delinquency, alcoholism, temperance, drug addiction, gambling, pornography, crime, prisons and prison chaplaincies, rehabilitation of released prisoners; counselling services.

Organizations of major significance in this field number over 500.

This section lists only some 300 out of many thousands of possible entries on this subject.

*ALGERIA*

**Secrétariat Social d'Alger,** 5 Rue Mennani, El Djezair. (RC).

*ARGENTINA*

**Catholic International Union for Social Service,** Latin American Secretariat, Uruguay 1176-7, Buenos Aires.

*AUSTRALIA*

**Alcoholic & Drug Dependent Rehabilitation Service,** Programme Dir, Salvation Army, PO Box A229, Sydney, NSW. T: 261711.

*AUSTRIA*

**Arbeitsgemeinschaft Freiwilliger Sozialer Dienst,** Steinergasse 3, A-1170 Wien.

*BELGIUM*

**Confédération des Institutions d'Aide Sociale,** Rue Guimard 5, B-1040 Brussel.
**Mouvement Chrétien des Indépendants et des Cadres (MIC),** Rue Mercelis 88, B-1050 Brussel. T: (02)6488933.
**National Christelijk Middenstandsverbond,** Rue de Spa 8, B-1040 Brussel. T: (02)2183140.
**Nationaale Raad voor Gezinspastoraal (NRGP),** Vlamingenstraat 80, B-8000 Brugge. T: (050) 334187.
**Oeuvre d'Assistance Sociale au Zaire,** Rue de la Poste 111, Brussel 3.
**Union Catholique Internationale de Service Social (UCISS),** Rue de la Poste 111, B-1030 Brussel. T: (02)2172858.

*BENIN*

**Secrétariat Social,** BP 1, Lokossa. (RC).

*BOLIVIA*

**Comisión Boliviana de Acción Social Evangliéca (COMBASE),** Av 9 de Abril, Casilla 869, Cochabamba.

*BRAZIL*

**Departamento de Ação Social,** Rio de Janeiro, GB.
**Federação de Orgços para Assistência Social e Educational (FASE),** Rua das Palmeiras 90, ZC-02 Rio de Janeirô, GB. T: 2464559,2661265.
**Movimento de Organização Comunitária,** Feira de Santana, BA.

*CAMEROON*

**Oeuvre Social Oecuménique de Douala,** Dir, BP 914, Douala.

*CANADA*

**Christian Counselling Services,** Suite 210, 455 Spadina Av, Toronto.
**National Office for Social Action & Family Life Bureau/Office National de l'Action Sociale,** 90 Av Parent, Ottawa, Ontario K1N 7B1.
**Ray of Hope,** Box 313, Fergus, Ontario. (Mission to prisoners).

*CHINA (TAIWAN)*

**Institute for Social Action in China (ISAC),** 267 Chi-Loien, 2nd Rd, Kaohsiung, Taiwan 800.
**Kuangchi Program Service,** 8 Lane 451, Tunhua South Rd, PO Box 24042, Taipei 105. T: 772136, 772137.
**Taiwan Christian Service,** Exec Dir, Jen Ai Rd, Section 4, No 486, Taipei.
**Tribal Service Centre,** Dir, 24-5 Wu-shun St, Taipei. T: 554508

*COLOMBIA*

**Departamento de Pastoral de Conjunto,** Calle 37 No 13-A-09, Apdo Aéreo 5278, Bogotá, DE. T: 457963.
**Instituto Colombiano de Desarrollo Social (ICODES),** Calle 16 No 4-75, Apdo Aéreo 28195, Bogotá 1.

*COSTA RICA*

**Comisión Arquidiocesana de Pastoral,** Curia Metropolitana, San José.

*DOMINICAN REPUBLIC*

**Secretariado Nacional de Pastoral de Conjunto,** Abraham Lincoln 78, Apdo 186, Santo Domingo, DN. T: 5657070.

*ECUADOR*

**Centro Ximena,** Apdo 5250, Guayaquil.

*EGYPT*

**As-Sanabel Association,** 13 Rue Hefny Bey Nassef, Koubbeh Gardens, Al Qahirah. T: 821790.
**Coptic Evangelical Organization for Social Services,** Dir, PO Box 1304, Al Qahirah. T: 906683.

*EL SALVADOR*

**Secretariado Social Interdiocesano,** Arzobispado, 8a Av Nte 913, San Salvador. T: 257082.

*FRANCE*

**Aumônerie des Prisons,** Aumônier Gén, 47 Rue de Clichy, F-75009 Paris.
**Organisation Protestante pour le Logement,** Prés, 47 Rue de Clichy, F-75009 Paris. T: 8749092/9757.

*GERMANY, Federal Repulic of*

**Arbeitsgemeinschaft Evangelischer Höherer Fachschulen für Sozialarbeit und Sozialpädagogik,** Heimchenstr 10, D-3 Hannover-Kleefeld. (Federation of social workers' training schools).
**Arbeitsgemeinschaft Katholisch-Sozialer Bildungswerke in der BRD,** Dransdorfer Weg 15, D-5300 Bonn. T: (02221)654592.
**Blaues Kreuz in der Evangelischen Kirche,** Mathiasstr 1, D-463 Bochum-Linden.
**Blaues Kreuz in Deutschland,** Freiligrathstr 27, D-56 Wuppertal-Barmen.
**Bund Abstinenter Pfarrer in Deutschland,** Uhlandstr 9, D-7142 Marbach (Neckar).
**Committee for Society Related Services,** Gerokstr 17, D-7 Stuttgart 1.
**Deutscher Evangelischer Verband für Altenhilfe,** Stafflenbergstr 78, Postfach 476, D-7 Stuttgart 1.
**Diakonisches Werk,** Alexanderstr 23,D-7 Stuttgart 1.
**Evangelische Konferenz für Gefährdetenfürsorge,** Stafflenbergstr 78, D-7 Stuttgart 1. (Care of alcoholics and drug addicts).
**Evangelische Konferenz für Straffälligenpflege,** Stafflenbergstr 78, D-7 Stuttgart 1. (Care of released prisoners).
**Evangelischer Fachverband für Nichtsesshaftenhilfe,** Postfach 3, D-4813 Bethel. (Vagrants).
**Evangelischer Gesamtverband zur Abwehr der Suchtgefahren,** Brüder-Grimm-Platz 4, D-35 Kassel. (Combatting drugs and alcoholism).
**Katholische Sozialwissenschaftliche Zentralstelle (KSZ),** Viktoriastr 76, D-4050 Mönchengladbach. T: (02161)26883.
**Liga Catholica Internationalis Sobrietas,** Secretariat, Lorenz-Werthmannhaus, Karlstr 40, D-7800 Freiburg/Breisgau. T: (0761)2001.
**Sozialamt der Evangelischen Kirche von Westfalen,** Haus Villigst, D-5840 Villigst bei Schwerte/Ruhr.
**Spangenberg-Sozial-Werk,** Magdenburger Tor 15, D-3330 Helmstedt. (Moravian).
**Verband Christlicher Hospize und Erholungsheime,** Schützenhofstr 9, D-62 Wiesbaden. (Rest homes).
**Verband der Mitternachtsmission in Deutschland,** Stafflenbergstr 78, Postfach 476, D-7 Stuttgart 1. (Social work similar to Salvation Army).
**Verband Ev Ausbildungsstätten für Sozialpädagogik,** Am Kleianskreuz 23, D-4 Düsseldorf-Kaiserwerth. (Controls social workers' training centres).
**Weisses Kreuz,** am Rain 1, D-35 Kassel-Harleshausen. (Opposing smoking; Fundamentalist).

*GHANA*

**Department of Pastoral and Social Action,** National Catholic Secretariat, PO Box 7530, Accra.

*GREECE*

**Pastoral Commission (Pimantiki Epitropi),** Catholic Episcopal Conference, Catholic Archbishop's House, Kérkire (Corfu).

*GUYANA*

**Community Development Project,** GCC, 71 Murray St, Georgetown.

*HONDURAS*

**Acción Cultural Popular Hondureña (ACPOH),** Av República de Chile 516, Barrio San Rafael, Apdo Postal C-24, Tegucigalpa, DC. T: 21401.
**Asociación de Promoción Humana,** Altos de Almacén La Urbana, Apdo Postal 786, Tegucigalpa. T: 28657,25621.

*HONG KONG*

**Hong Kong Christian Mutual Improvement Society,** Pak Lee Mansion, 6B King's Rd, 2/F, Hong Kong. T: H-709395,709073.
**Hong Kong Christian Welfare & Relief Council,** Morrison Memorial Centre, 191 Prince Edward Rd, Kowloon. T: K-846692.
**Hong Kong Council of Social Service,** Anne Black Red Cross Bldg, 2/f, Harcourt Rd, PO Box 474, Hong Kong.
**Society for Community Organization,** Room 310, Sun Hing Bldg, 607 Nathan Rd, Kowloon.
**Tai Wan Shan Community Organization Project,** c/o Holy Carpenter Community Centre, 1 Dyer Av, Hung Hom, Kowloon. T: K-625137.

*INDIA*

**Action for Food Production Office (AFPRO),** C-52 ND South Extension II, New Delhi 49. T: 621651.
**Christian Agency for Social Action (CASA),** Dir, 16 Ring Rd, Lajpat Nagar IV, New Delhi 24.
**Home for All Housing Society,** Syro-Malankara Archbishop's House, Trivandrum 4, Kerala.
**Madras Community Service Centre,** CSI Camp, Belfour Rd, Kilpauk.

*INDONESIA*

**Biro Sosial,** Jalan Jend A Yani 13, Semarang, Surabaja.
**Bureau for Juridical Assistance,** c/o Keuskupan Semarang, Jalan Jend A Yani 13, Jogjakarta.
**Community Organization Committee,** c/o Keuskupan Agung Jakarta, Jalan Katedral 7, Jakarta V/6.

*IRELAND*

**Catholic Social Service Conference,** 75 Merrion Square, Dublin 2.
**Catholic Social Welfare Bureau,** 18 Westland Row, Dublin 2. T: 65418.

*ITALY*

**Associazione Volontari Italiani del Sangue,** Via Imperia 2, I-00161 Roma. T: 862440. (Blood donors).
**Centro Servizio Cristiano di Riesi,** Via 1 Maggio 69, Riesi (C1). T: 123.
**Ente Italiano di Servizio Sociale (EISS),** Via Colossi 50, I-00146 Roma. T: 5571396.
**Federazione Italiana Centri e Istituti per la Riabilitazione (FICIR),** Viale Ferdinando Baldelli 41, I-00146 Roma. T: 553251.
**Federazione Organismi Cristiani di Servizio Internazionale Volontario (FOCSIV),** Via Pordenone 1/D, I-20132 Milano. T: (02)2152386.
**Mouvement International d'Apostolat des Milieux Sociaux Indépendants,** Sec, Piazza San Calisto 16, I-00153 Roma. T: 6984683.
**Opera Divino Redentore per la Redenzione Sociale dei Liberati del Carcere Casa dell Amore Fraterno,** Via Ardeatina 930, I-00179 Roma. T: 5918454. (Aid to ex-prisoners).
**Patronato ACLI per i Servizi Sociali dei Lavoratori,** Monte de'Cenci 8, I-00186 Roma. T: 651186.
**Ufficio per la Pastorale Scolastica in Italia,** Via della Conciliazione 1, I-00193 Roma.

*IVORY COAST*

**Centre d'Etudes et d'Action Sociales,** c/o Archevêché, 23 Blvd Clozel, BP 1287, Abidjan. T: 222007.

*JAMAICA*

**Social Action Centre (SAC),** Dir, 2 Olivier Rd, Kingston 8. (Catholic-related; interdenominational action).

*JAPAN*

**Japan Christian Social Work League,** c/o Naigai Kyoryoku Kai, 5-1 4-chome, Ginza, Chuo-ku, Tokyo 104.
**Nishi Chugoku Christian Social Work Association,** 1438 Minami Sanjomachi, Hiroshima-shi 733.
**Pillar of Cloud Foundation,** 8-19 3-chome, Kami Kitazawa, Setagaya-ku, Tokyo 156.

*KENYA*

**Amani Counselling Society (ACS),** Waumini House, Westlands, PO Box 41738, Nairobi. T: 743897. (Ecumenical).
**Catholic Prisons Chaplaincy,** Senior Chaplain, Dept of Prisons, Bishop's Rd, PO Box 30175, Nairobi. T: 29001 ext 11.
**Kenya Prisons Chaplaincy,** Sec, Chaplains' Office, Dept of Prisons, Bishop's Rd, PO Box 30175, Nairobi. T: 29001 ext 11.
**Mji wa Huruma (Village of Mercy),** Superintendent, Kiambu Rd, PO Box 27058, Nairobi. T: 512292. (Town for beggars and destitutes; Salvation Army).

*LEBANON*

**Centre de Catéchèse et de Pastorale ND des Dons,** Rue Achrafieh, Bayrut. T: 321615.
**Groupe Oecuménique de Pastorale (GOP),** PB 7002, Bayrut. T: 300425. (Also: PB 1375, Bayrut. T: 341902).
**Secrétariat des Instituts Religieux Libanais pour les Affaires Sociales (SIRLAS),** Sec Gen, BP 293, Bayrut. T: 220535. (RC).

*MADAGASCAR*

**Bureau de Liaison d'Action Sociale et Caritative (BLASC),** Lot IV-G 199, Antanimena, Tananarive.
**Centre Culturel et Social,** BP 98, Salazamay, Tamatave.
**Ecole de Service Social,** Av Maréchal Joffre 129 bis, Tananarive.

*MEXICO*

**Secretariado Social Mexicana (SESOMEX),** Roma 1, México 7, DF. T: 5477016,5467031.

*NETHERLANDS*

**Catholic Association for Rehabilitation of Criminals (Katholieke Reclasseringvereniging),** Zuid Willemvaart 167, 's-Hertogenbosch. T: (04100) 43991.
**Catholic Association of Old People's Homes (Katholieke Vereniging van Bejaardentehuizen),** Wassenaarseweg 22, 's-Gravenhage. T: (070) 652804.
**Catholic Social Council Foundation (Stichting Katholiek Maatschappelijk Beraad),** Laan van Meerdervoort 150, 's-Gravenhage. T: (070)333472.
**Dutch Federation of Cathoilc Enterprises (Nederlands Katholiek Oudernemersverbond, NKOV),** Treubstraat 25, Rijswijk. T: (070)992722.
**National Association of Clubs (Stichting Samenwerkende Landelijke Centrale Organen voor Wijk-, buurt-en clubhuiswerk, SALCO),** Maliebaan 20, Utrecht. T: (030)26845.
**National Catholic Social Service Centre (Katholiek Landelijk Centrum voor Maatschappelijke Dienstverlening, KLCMD),** Luybenstraat 19, 's-Hertogenbosch. T: (04100)34134.

*NEW ZEALAND*

**Catholic Social Services,** Diocese of Wellington, 5 Dufferin St, Wellington 1.
**National Society on Alcoholism and Drug Dependence,** PO Box 1642, Wellington.
**NZ Inter-Church Council on Public Affairs,** Sec, 1 Randwick Rd, Wellington 5.

*NIGERIA*

**Community Development Group (CDG),** c/o Pastoral Institute, PO Box 1784, Ibadan.
**Pastoral Department,** Catholic Secretariat of Nigeria, 6 Force Rd, PO Box 951, Lagos. T: 25339.

*NORWAY*

**Diaconal Service Council (Diakonirad for den Norske Kirke),** Munchsgate 2, Oslo 1.

*PANAMA*

**Fe y Alegria,** Apdo B-3, Panamá 9-A. T: 235820.

*PAPUA NEW GUINEA*

**Institute of Social Order (ISO),** PO Box 1897, Boroko, New Guinea.
**Port Moresby Community Development Group,** PO Box 8083, Waigani.

*PHILIPPINES*

**Christ Mission for Unfortunates,** Buenavista, Agusan.
**Institute of Social Order (ISO),** 509 P Faura, Manila.
**Interchurch Committee on Urban Squatter Resettlement (ICUSR),** National Council of Churches, 941 E de los Santos Av, Quezon City.
**National Secretariat for Social Action (NASSA),** 2655 FB Harrison, Pasay City.
**Philippine Ecumenical Committee on Community Organization,** Holy Spirit Social Centre, PO Box 3553, Manila.
**Priests' Institute for Social Action (PISA),** Bureau of Asian Affairs, PO Box 4132, Manila.

*REUNION*

**Union des Oeuvres Sociales Réunionnaises (UOSR),** BP 58, Saint-Denis. T: 2276.

*SINGAPORE*

**Bukit Ho Swee Community Service Project,** Nazareth Centre, Block 44, Bukit Ho Swee, Singapore 3.

*SOUTH AFRICA*

**Unemployment Challenges the Churches,** PO Box 8079, Pietermaritzburg 3200. T: (0331)54821. (SACC).

*SWITZERLAND*

**Arbeitsstelle für Bildungsfragen (KAGEB)/Office de Travail pour les Questions Culturelles,** Löwenstr 5, CH-6000 Luzern.
**Bildungsrat der Schweizer Katholiken/Secrétariat du Conseil Culturel des Catholiques Suisses,** Löwenstr 5, CH-6000 Luzern.
**Centre Social Protestant (CSP),** Promenade Saint-Antoine 20 (res-de-chaussée), Genève. T: 260350.
**Hilfswerk der Evangelischen Kirchen der Schweiz,** Stampfenbachstr 123, CH-8006 Zürich. T: (051)266600.
**International Catholic League Sobrietas,** Sec Gen, Löwenstr 3, CH-6002 Luzern. (Begun 1897).
**Schweizerische Katholische Arbeitsgemeinschaft für Elternschulung (SAKES),** Postfach 248, CH-9004 St Gallen.
**Schweizerisches Soziales Seminar (SSS)/Séminaire Social Suisse,** Löwenstr 5, CH 5000 Luzern. T: (041)225775.
**Société Suisse pour l'Observation du Dimanche,** Sihlstr 33, Postfach 384, CH-8021 Zürich. T: (051) 238899.
**World Christian Temperance Federation,** Sec Gen, Weiherhofstr 50, CH-4054 Basel.

*SYRIA*

**Oeuvres Sociales Al-Kalimat,** Archevêché Grec-Catholique, Place Mgr Farhat, Halab.

*TANZANIA*

**Pentecostal Churches Social Association in Tanganyika,** PO Box 2, Bukene.
**Social Development Institute,** Social Training Centre, PO Box 307, Mwanza. T: 2218 ext 2.

*UK OF GB & NI*

**Advisory Committee on Pastoral Care and Counselling,** Diocese of Southwark, 94 Lambeth Rd, London SE1. T: (01)928-6637.
**Age Concern (National Old People's Welfare Council),** Dir, 55 Gower St, London WC1E 6HJ. T: (01)637-2886/7.
**Association for Pastoral Care and Counselling,** Sec, The Rectory, Skibbs Lane, Chelsfield, Kent.
**Association of Interchurch Families,** 18 South Grove, Barton, Preston, PR3 5AP. T: Brock 40605. (For interchurch or mixed marriages).
**Board for Social Responsibility of the Church of England,** Church House, Dean's Yard, Westminster, London SW1.
**British Churches Housing Trust,** 10 Eaton Gate, London SW1.
**Career Plan Ltd,** 7 Wine Office Court, London EC4A 3BY. (Christian employment agency for banking, insurance, law, secretarial).
**Catholic Commission for Social Welfare,** 1a Stert St, Abingdon, Berks.
**Catholic Housing Aid Society,** 137 Holland Rd, London W14. (Also: 189a Old Brompton Rd, London SW5 0AN. T: (01)373-4961,370-4885).
**Catholic Prisoners' Social Service (CPSS),** 84 Uxbridge Rd, Shepherd's Bush, London W12 8LR. T: (01)743-8606.
**Catholic Social Service for Prisoners,** 497a King's Rd, London SW10. T: (01)352-9711.
**Catholic Social Service Centre,** 5 Brandon St, Edinburgh EH3 5DX. T: (031)556-8221.
**Christian Action,** 2 Amen Court, London EC4. T: (01)606-6123.
**Christian Action (Enfield) Housing Association Ltd,** 6 Avenue Parade, London N21. T: (01)360-9145.
**Christian Enterprise Housing Association,** 24 Torrington Park, London N12. T: (01)445-1030.
**Christian Road Safety League (CRSL),** 136 Old Christchurch Rd, Bournemouth, Dorset. T: (0202) 25920.
**Christians in Action,** 67 Melfort Rd, Thornton Heath, Surrey.
**Church in Wales Provincial Council for Moral Welfare Work,** The Vicarage, Newton, Swansea, West Glamorgan.
**Church Moral Aid Association,** Sec, 2 Gray's Inn Square, London WC1.
**Church of England Committee for Social Work and the Social Services,** Sec, Church House, Dean's Yard, Westminster, London SW1P 3NZ. T: (01)222-9011.
**Church of England Council for Social Aid,** Sec, Church House, Dean's Yard, Westminster, London SW1P 3NZ. T: (01)222-9011.
**Church of Scotland Department of Social and Moral Welfare,** 121 George St, Edinburgh EH2 4YN.
**Church's' Council on Gambling,** Sec, 19 Abbey House, Victoria St, London SW1. T: (01)222-4252. (Also: 10 Eaton Gate, London SW1. T: (01) 730-9611).
**Committee for Social Work and Social Services,** Church of England, Sec, Church House, Deans' Yard,

Westminster, London SW1P 3NZ. T: (01)222-9011.
**Congregational Homes for the Elderly,** Hon Gen Sec, 5 Acland Av, Colchester, Essex. T: 73454.
**Friends Service Council,** Friends House, Euston Rd, London NW1.
**Friends Social Witness Committee,** Friends House, Euston Rd, London NW1.
**Guild of Pastoral Psychology,** 9 Phoenix House, 5 Waverley Rd, London N8.
**Interservice,** 19 Draycott Place, London SW3. (Employment agency for Christians).
**Josephine Butler Society,** Hon Sec, 83 Denison House, 296 Vauxhall Bridge Rd, London SW1. T: (01)824-5193. (Morals, anti-vice, legislation).
**Life for the World Trust,** Dir, Northwick Park Mansion, Blockley, Moreton-in-Marsh, Gloucs GL56 9RG. T: Blockley 440. (Christian social ministry amongst drug addicts).
**Lord's Day Observance Society (LDOS),** Sec, 55 Fleet St, London EC4. T: (01)353-3157.
**Men's Social Services in Great Britain & Ireland (Salvation Army),** 110-112 Middlesex St, Bishopsgate, London E1 7HZ. T: (01)247-6831/4.
**National and London United Temperance Councils,** Sec, 165 Clapham Rd, London SW9. T: RELiance 3454.
**National Association of Almshouses,** Gen Sec, Billingbear Lodge, Wokingham, Berks. T: (0434) 4177.
**National Council for Social Welfare,** 18 Park Circus, Glasgow G3.
**National Temperance Federation,** Hon Gen Sec, 12 Caxton St, London SW1.
**New Life Foundations Ministry to Addicts,** PO Box 20, Bromley BR1 1DW, Kent. T: (01) 460-0500.
**Pastoral Development Group (PDG),** 54 Mayfield Rd, South Croydon, Surrey CR2 0BF.
**Prison and Borstal Chaplaincy Service,** Chaplain General of Prisons, Home Office Prisons Department, 89 Eccleston Square, London SW1V 1PU. T: (01) 828-9848.
**Roman Catholic Commission for Social Welfare,** 1a Stert St, Abingdon, Berks.
**St George's Crypt,** St George's Parish Church, Great George St, Leeds 2, West Yorkshire. T: (0532) 459061. (For vagrants).
**St Vincent's Family Housing Association,** 2 Iddlesleigh House, Caxton St, London SW1H 0PS. T: (01)222-5011.
**Shaftesbury Society,** Sec, Shaftesbury House, 112 Regency St, London SW1. T: (01)834-2656.
**Spitalfields Crypt Trust,** Spitalfields Rectory, 2 Fournier St, London E1. T: (01)247-7766.
**Spurgeon's Homes,** Park Rd, Birchington, Kent.
**Temperance Council for the Christian Churches,** Drayton House, Gordon St, London WC1. T: (01) 387-3030.
**Toc H,** Administrative Padre, 15 Trinity Square, London EC3. T: (01)709-0472. (For community service; army origins, begun 1915).
**Unitarian Social Service Department,** Essex Hall, 1-6 Essex St, Strand, London WC2R 3HY.
**Westminster Pastoral Foundation,** Dir, Central Hall, London SW1. T: (01)930-6676/7.

*USA*

**Action,** Exec Dir, PO Box 25040, Los Angeles, CA 90025. T: (213)670-0644.
**Adventist Community Task-Force,** Dir, 503 East H St, Ontario, CA 91762. T: (714)983-8264.
**American Friends Service Committee Penal Ministry,** 2160 Lake St, San Francisco, CA 94121.
**Bowery Mission,** Dir, 27 East 39th St, New York, NY 10016. (Vagrants).
**Capitol Hill Association of Christian Churches (CHOICE: Churches Organized in Common Effort),** 1710 11th Av, Seattle, WA 98122.
**Catholic Civics Clubs of America (CCCA),** Dir, Catholic University of America, Washington, DC 20017. T: (202)LA9-6000 ext 228.
**Catholic Interracial Council of New York,** 55 Liberty St, New York, NY 10005.
**Center for Civic Initiative,** 2218 North 3rd St, Milwaukee, WI 53212.
**Christian Action Ministry,** 3932 West Madison, Chicago, IL 60624.
**Christian Church Homes of Kentucky,** Exec Sec, 942 South 4th St, Louisville, KY 40203.
**Christian Community Service Agency Ministry to Cuban Refugees,** Box 752, Miami, FL 33143.
**Christian Counselling & Educational Foundation (CCEF),** 1790 East Willow Grove Av, Laverock, PA 19118.
**Christian Jail Workers Inc,** PO Box 5, Los Angeles, CA 90051.
**Christian Social Ministry Program,** Lancaster County Council of Churches, 129 East Orange St, Lancaster, PA 17602.
**Columbia Cooperative Ministry,** Suite 316, Teachers Bldg, 10221 Wincopin Circle, Columbia, MD 21043.
**Commission on Community Action,** 1027 Superior Av, Cleveland, OH 44114.
**Commission on Religion in Appalachia,** 114 West Clinch Av, SW, Knoxville, TN 37916.
**Connecticut Project Equality,** Suite 606, 750 Main St, Hartford, Connecticut.
**Council on Religion and the Homosexual,** 330 Ellis St, San Francisco, CA 94102.
**Day Care for the Disadvantaged,** First Presbyterian Church, North El Street, Greensboro, NC 27410.
**Evangelical Welfare Agency,** 6354 South Painter Av, Whittier, CA 90601.
**Experimental Study of Religion and Society,** 27 Horne St, Raleigh, NC 27607.
**FORCE Community Organization,** 6177 Southampton Drive, Dayton, OH 45459.
**Genesee-Orleans Ministry of Concern,** 114 Platt St, Albion, NY 14411.
**Homes of Oakridge,** 216 Securities Bldg, Des Moines, IA 50309.
**Human Design,** Suite 2-E, 212 West Franklin Av, Minneapolis, Minnesota.
**Interracial Ministry,** Lakeview Presbyterian Church, 1310 Lakeview Av, St Petersburg, FL 33705.
**Joint Diaconate of Kalamazoo,** 321 West South St, Kalamazoo, MI 49006.
**Joint Strategy and Action Committee (JASC),** Dir, Room 510, 475 Riverside Drive, New York, NY 10027.
**Lake Texoma United Ministry,** 1501 West Munson, Denison, TX 75020.
**Lift Foundation (Housing),** 912 North Burdick St, Kalamazoo, MI 49007.
**Long Range Educational Ministry,** 711 South Seventh St, Nashville, TN 37206.
**Lord's Day Alliance of the United States,** Room 518, 475 Riverside Drive, New York, NY 10027. T: (212)870-2058.
**Martin Luther King Memorial Centre,** Co-Chairmen, 87 Chestnut St, SW, Atlanta, GA 30314.
**Ministry to Alcoholics,** Box 907, Helena, MT 59601.
**Missouri Delta Ecumenical Ministry,** Kennett, MO 63857.
**Multiple Ministries,** Highland Av Baptist Church, 87-10 162nd St, Jamaica, NY 11432.
**National Catholic Resettlement Council,** 1312 Massachusetts Av, NW, Washington, DC 20005.
**Neighborhood Involvement Program,** 6911 Olivia Av South, Minneapolis, Minnesota.
**New Church Development and Special Ministries,** Northminster United Presbyterian Church, 9400 Plano Rd, Dallas, TX 75238.
**Operation Outreach,** PO Box 247, Beaumont, TX 77704.
**Outreach Ministries,** First Presbyterian Church, 2407 Dana St, Berkeley, California.
**Parish Ministries Commission,** Church of the Brethren General Board, 1451 Dundee Av, Elgin, IL 60120.
**Pastoral Counselling Institute,** Willowynde, Beech Haven, Athens, GA 30601.
**Prison Mission Association,** PO Box 11186, Phoenix, AZ 85107.
**Project Amigos,** Bishops College, 3837 Simpson-Stuart Rd, Dallas, TX 75241.
**Project for Progress,** Peoria Area Council of Churches, 2508 North Sheridan Rd, Peoria, IL 61604.
**Project Response (Prison Pre-Parolee Ministry),** 15050 Hubbell Av, Detroit, MI 48227.
**Saturday Enrichment Program,** 304 Burns Av, Bartonville, IL 61607.
**Service Within The Congregation,** Meadowlawn Presbyterian Church, 1770 62nd St North, St Petersbourg, FL 33714.
**Skid Row Ministry,** First Avenue Service Center, 8400 46th SW, Seattle, WA 98116.
**Smith Haven Ministries,** 3207 Jericho Turnpike, Lake Grove, NY 11755.
**Social Action Ministry,** Lynchburg Christian Fellowship, Lynchburg, Virginia.
**Southern California Council on Religion and the Homophile,** 3330 West Adams Blvd, Los Angeles, CA 90018.
**Spanish Speaking Social Action,** 565 Adams St, Gary, Indiana.
**Special Ministry to Vocations,** 1917 Arch St, Little Rock, AR 72206.
**Synod of Oklahoma Tent Making Ministry,** Suite B, 4540 NW 10th St, Oklahoma City, OK 73127.
**Unitarian Universalist Black Affairs Council,** Admin Sec, Room 1101, 18 West Chelten Av, Philadelphia, PA 19144. T: (215)438-7878.
**Unitarian Universalist Service Committee (UUSC),** 78 Deacon St, Boston, MA 02108. T: (617) 742-2120.
**Unitarian Universalist Society for Alcohol Education,** Room 612, 88 Tremont St, Boston, MA 02108.
**Unitarian Universalists for Black and White Action,** 66 Marlborough St, Boston, MA 02116.
**Vocations for Social Change,** 2010 B St, Hayward, CA 94541.
**Wesleyan Service Guild,** Room 1414, 475 Riverside Drive, New York, NY 10027.

*URUGUAY*

**Economia Humana,** Cerrito 475, Montevideo.

*VENEZUELA*

**Fe y Algeria,** Edf Galipan, Apto B2, Chacao, Apdo Postal 61207, Caracas 106. T: 330802.

*ZAIRE*

**Centre de Formation Socio-Pastorale (CENFO),** BP 215, Kinshasa XI. T: 30123.
**Centre d'Etudes Pastorales (CPE),** BP 724, Kinshasa-Limete. T: 77418.

*ZAMBIA*

**Cooperbelt Christian Service Council,** PO Box 274, Kitwe.

*ZIMBABWE*

**Christian Care,** Box MP 167, Mount Pleasant, Salisbury.
**Salisbury Churches' Joint Action,** Sec, PO Box 3566, Salisbury.
**School of Social Work,** P Bag 22, PO Kopje, Salisbury.

# 55 Social Communications Co-ordination

*Definition.* Agencies and centres co-ordinating social communications, i.e. several or all types of mass media and communications (often including audio-visuals, cinema, recordings, radio, TV, literature, newspapers, public opinion media); group media, alternate media; Christian production of social communications material, multimedia production centres and studios; the technical aspects of communication, mass communication, and instant communication; photography, mass-circulation newspapers, satellite communications; Christian centres and other agencies engaged in social communications outreach; public opinion agencies and centres. See also RESEARCH CENTRES.

Organizations of major significance in this field number over 200. Most are given in yearbooks listed here under DIRECTORIES.

*ARGENTINA*

**Oficina Coordinadora de los Medios de Comunicación Social (OCMCS),** Paraguay 1867, Buenos Aires. T: 869352. (Under Episcopal Conference).

*AUSTRALIA*

**Episcopal Committee for Mass Media,** AEC, St Mary's Cathedral, Sydney, NSW 2000.

*AUSTRIA*

**Katholisches Zentrum für Film, Funk und Fernsehen in Österreich,** Singerstr 7, A-1010 Wien. T: 524386. (Under Episcopal Conference).

*BAHAMAS*

**Templeton Foundation,** New Providence. (Member of WACC).

*BARBADOS*

**Caribbean Christian Communications Network,** Diocesan House, St Michael's Row, Bridgetown. (Member of WACC).

*BELGIUM*

**Conseil Interdiocésain des Moyens de Communication Sociale,** Prés, Rue Guimard 5, B-1040 Brussel. (Under Episcopal Conference).

*BOLIVIA*

**Oficina de Medios de Comunicación Social,** Casilla 4064, La Paz. T: 41920. (Under Episcopal Conference).

*BRAZIL*

**Secretariado Nacional de Opinião Publica,** Rua do Russel 76, 5 andar, CP 16085, Rio de Janeiro, ZC-01, GB. T: 2252761. (Under Episcopal Conference).

*CANADA*

**Communications Division,** Anglican Church of Canada, 600 Jarvis St, Toronto 285, Ontario. T: 924-9192. (Member of WACC).
**Ecumenical Satellite Commission (ECUSAT),** Pres, Toronto.
**National Catholic Communication Services,** 830 Bathurst St, Toronto, Ontario.
**National Catholic Communications Centre (NCCC),** Dir, 21 Grenville St, Toronto 189, Ontario. T: (416)929-3125. (Under Episcopal Conference. Member of WACC).
**Office National des Communications Sociales (ONCS),** 4635 Rue de Lorimier, Montréal, Québec. T: (514)526-9165. (Under Episcopal Conference; French-speaking).

*CHILE*

**Departamento de Opinión Publica del Arzobispado de Santiago (DOPAS),** Erasmo Escala 1822, Oficina 401, Casilla 1540, Santiago. T: 85581. (Under Episcopal Conference; co-ordination).

*COLOMBIA*

**Centro Nacional de MCS,** Carrera 10 No 19-64, Oficina 402, Apdo Aéreo 14453, Bogotá, DE. T: 428008.
**Servicio Colombiano de Communicación Social,** Apdo Aéreo 24910, Bogotá, DE 1.

*COSTA RICA*

**Co-ordination Offices for Press, Radio, TV and Cinema,** c/o Av 2-4 Calle I, Apdo 10-64, San José. T: 225903. (Under Episcopal Conference).
**Interamerican Gospel Communication,** Apdo 2470, San José.

*DOMINICAN REPUBLIC*

**Centro Nacional de MCS (CENICOS),** Calle Mercedes 17, Altos, Apdo 841, Santo Domingo. T: 23848. (Under Episcopal Conference).

*ECUADOR*

**Oficina Nacional de Medios de Comunicación Sociale (OMECO),** Av América 1866 y la Gasca, Casilla 1081, Quito. T: 520926. (Under Episcopal Conference).

*ETHIOPIA*

**SIM Communications Centre,** PO Box 127, Addis Abeba.
**Voice of Good News (Yemissrach Dimts),** PO Box 658, Addis Abeba.

*FIJI*

**Lotu Pasifika,** PCC, PO Box 357, Suva. (Communications materials, Pacific Conference of Churches).

*FRANCE*

**Fédération des Organismes de Communication Sociale (FOCS),** Sec, Gen, 193 Rue de l'Université, F-75007 Paris. T: (01)705-4358,551-9462. (Unde, Episcopal Conference; cinema, radio, TV, recordingsr books).
**Secrétariat National de l'Opinion Publique et des Moyens de Communications Sociales,** 106 Rue du Bac, F-75007 Paris. T: (01)222-6170. (Under Episcopal Conference).

*GERMANY, Federal Republic of*

**Catholic Media Council (CMC),** Exec Sec, Hermannstr 12, Postfach 1912, D-51 Aachen. T: (0241)21741. (Media planning for developing countries).
**Evangelische Konferenz für Kommunikation,** Geschäftsstelle, Friedrichstr 34, D-6 Frankfurt/Main.
**Vereinigung für Christliche Publizistik,** Frankfurt-am-Main. (Member of WACC).

*GHANA*

**Department of Social Communications,** PO Box 1989, Accra.

*GUATEMALA*

**Departamento de Communicaciones Sociales,** Secretariado Católico Nacional, 4a Av 9-35, Zona 1, Apdo 1698, Guatemala. T: 26831.

*HOLY SEE*

**Pontificia Commissione per le Comunicazioni Sociali/Pontifical Commission for Social Communications,** Pres, Palazzo San Carlo, I-00120 Città del Vaticano. T: (698)3197,3597.

*HONG KONG*

**Asia Christian Communications Fellowship (ACCF),** CCL Box 5364, Tsim Sha Tsui PO, Hong Kong.
**Christian Communications Foundations,** 144 Boundary St, Kowloon.
**Communications Department,** Hong Kong Baptist College, 224 Waterloo Rd, Kowloon.

*INDIA*

**Christian Arts & Communication Centre,** 3 Eldam's Rd, Teynampet, Madras 18. (Member of WACC).
**Communications Co-ordination Centre,** CBCI Centre, Alexandra Place, New Delhi 1. T: 43176. (Under Episcopal Conference).
**Communications Co-ordination Centre,** Golmuri PO, Jamshedpur 3, Bihar.
**Social Communications Service (SCS),** St Xavier's College, 30 Park St, Calcutta 16. (Under Episcopal Conference).

*INDONESIA*

**DGI Communications Commission (Komisi Komonikasi Masa, Kokoma),** Jalan Salemba Raya 10, Jakarta IV/3. (Member of WACC).

*IRELAND*

**Catholic Communications Institute of Ireland,** Veritas House, 7/8 Lower Abbey St, Dublin 1. T: 886144,48502.

*ITALY*

**Department of Social Communications,** SVD Generalate, 1 Via dei Verbiti, CP 5080, I-00154 Roma. T: 570059,575000.
**Ente dello Spettacolo,** Via della Conciliazione 2c, I-00193 Roma. T: 561775,564132. (Radiophonic schools, TV, theatre, cinema).
**International Jesuit Centre for Social Communication (JESCOM),** Borgho Santo Spirito 5, CP 9040, I-00100 Roma. T: (06)650-0041.
**Multimedia International,** Pres, Borgho Santo Spirito 5, CP 9048, I-00100 Roma. (Interdenominational).
**Office of Social Communication,** White Fathers, General Secretariat, Via Aurelia 269, I-00165 Roma. T: 632314,632318.
**Secretariat for Social Communications,** Missionary Oblates of Mary Immaculate (OMI), Via Aurelia 290, I-00165 Roma. T: 6370251.
**Social Communications Office,** Casa Generalizia della Pia Società Figlie di San Paolo, Via Antonino Pio 75, I-00145 Roma.

*JAMAICA*

**National Office of Cinema, Radio and Television,** 126 Red Hills Rd, Kingston 8. T: 9242337. (Under Episcopal Conference).

*JAPAN*

**Episcopal Commission for Social Communications,** 10-1 Rokuban-cho, Chiyoda-ku, Tokyo 102.

*KENYA*

**AMECEA Office of Social Communications,** Secretariat, PO Box 21191, Nairobi. T: 66506.
**Baptist Communications Centre,** Dir, Likoni Rd, PO Box 30370, Nairobi. T: 557392,559076.
**Communications Department,** Kenya Catholic Secretariat, Westlands, PO Box 48062, Nairobi. T: 21613/4.
**Daystar Communications,** Valley Rd & Ngong Rd, PO Box 44400, Nairobi.
**Department of Christian Communications,** NCCK, PO Box 45009, Nairobi. T: 22264.

*LESOTHO*

**Lesotho Communications Centre,** Box 80, Maseru. T. 2525.

*LUXEMBOURG*

**Office Catholique du Cinéma, de la Radio et de la Télévision,** 5 Rue de Bourbon. T: 485181.

*MALAWI*

**Mass Media Office,** Catholic Secretariat of Malawi, PO Box 5368, Limbe. T: 50866.

*MALAYSIA*

**Commission for Mass Media,** 5 Jalan Bukit Nanas, Kuala Lumpur. (Under Episcopal Conference).

*MALTA*

**National Commission for Means of Social Communications,** Catholic Institute, Floriana. (Under Episcopal Conference).

*MEXICO*

**Centro de Comunicaciones,** Puente de Alvarado 14, México 1, DF.
**Centro Nacional de Comunicación Social (CENCOS),** Medellín 33, México 7, DF. T: 286898, 256541. (Under Episcopal Conference).

*NETHERLANDS*

**Convent van Kerken,** Hilversum. (Member of WACC).

**Stem van Afrika,** Wassenaar. (Member of WACC).

*NORWAY*

**Mass Media Commission (Massemediakommisjonen),** Oslo Katolske Bispedömme, Liavn, 7 Lysaker.

*PANAMA*

**Comisión Nacional de MCS y Centro de Comunicaciones Sociales del Arzobispado,** Av México y Calle 20, Apdo 386, Panamá City. T: 255270.

*PERU*

**Consejo Nacional de MSC (CONAMCOS),** Azangaro 451, Apdo 387, Lima. T: 30010.

**Departamento de Comunicación Social (DECOS),** CELAM, Av 9 de Diciembre, Pasco Colón 378, Apdo 44, Lima 1.

*PHILIPPINES*

**National Office of Mass Media,** Sec, PO Box 2061, Manila.

**Social Communications Centre,** Ramon Magsaysay Blvd Corner Santol Rd, PO Box 2156, Santa Mesa, Manila. T: 608917.

*POLAND*

**Episcopal Commission for Film, Radio, TV & Theatre (Biuro Komisji Episkopatu Polski dla spraw Filmu, Radia, Telewizji i Teatru),** Aleja I Armii Wojska Polskiego 12, Warszawa X. (Under Episcopal Conference).

*PORTUGAL*

**Secretariado do Cinema e da Radio,** 5 Rua Capelo, 2 Esq, Lisboa 2. T: 30172. (Under Episcopal Conference).

*PUERTO RICO*

**Centro Nacional de MCS,** Obrero Station, Apdo 14125, Santurce, PR. T: 7246471. (Under Episcopal Conference).

*RWANDA*

**Office National Catholique des Moyens de Communication Sociale (ONCMCS),** BP 69, Butare. (Under Episcopal Conference).

*SOUTH AFRICA*

**Director of Communications and Studies,** SACC, PO Box 31190, Braamfontein, Transvaal.

**Go-Tell Communications,** PO Box 4134, Johannesburg, Transvaal.

**Lutheran Productions,** PO Box 59, Roodepoort, Transvaal.

**Radio and Cinema Department,** SABC, PO Box 941, Pretoria, Transvaal.

*SPAIN*

**Secretariado Nacional de Medios de Communicaciones Sociales,** Alfonso XI 4-2, Madrid 14. T: 2320446,2213508. (Under Episcopal Conference).

*SRI LANKA*

**Office of Social Communications,** Archbishop's House, Colombo 8.

*SWEDEN*

**Catholic Bishop's Commission (Katolska Biskopsämbetet),** Valhallavägen 132, S-102 40 Stockholm 5.

*SWITZERLAND*

**Department of Communication,** World Council of Churches, 150 Route de Ferney, CH-1211 Genève 20.

*THAILAND*

**Baptist Mass Communications,** PO Box 11-1007, Bangkok 11. T: 2528473.

**Department of Mass Communications,** Church of Christ in Thailand, 14 Pramuan Rd, Bangkok 5.

**ECCE (Encouraging Contemporary Communications Enterprises),** GPO Box 127, Bangkok.

**Thailand Full Gospel Mass Communication,** 10-12 Soi 6, Sukhumvit Rd, GPO Box 1825, Bangkok T: 2525418.

*UK OF GB & NI*

**Christian Communications Ltd,** 17 Gannett's Park, Swanage, Dorset. T: 3122. (Trust fund).

**Division of Communications Studies,** Head, Trinity & All Saints' Colleges (TASC), Leeds. (Member of WACC).

**Ecumenical Satellite Commission (ECUSAT)/ Commission Oecuménique pour les Satellites,** Sec Gen, 7 St James's St, London SW1. T: (01)839-5776.

**Network,** 26 Tresco Gardens, Seven Kings, Ilford, Essex. T: (01)599-0506.

**Overseas Christian Communication Centre,** Exec Dir, Reeth, Langley Marsh, Wiveliscombe, near Taunton, Somerset. T: (09842)793.

**World Association for Christian Communication (WACC),** Exec Dir, 7 St James's St, London SW1. T: (01)839-5776.

*USA*

**Catholic Communications Foundation (CCF),** Chrysler Bldg, 405 Lexington Av, New York, NY 10017. T: (212)867-8460.

**Christian Communication Specialities,** Dir, 6944 Indianapolis Blvd, Hammond, IN 46324. T: (219)845-1700.

**Christian Communications Council,** 491 Gundersen Drive, Carol Stream, IL 60187.

**Community Now (New Life Communications Foundation),** 2045 Main St, Kansas City, MO 64108.

**Daystar Communications,** 392 East Third Av, PO Box 10123, Eugene, OR 97401. T: (503)342-6712.

**Department of Communications,** Maryknoll Fathers, Maryknoll, NY 10545. T: (914)WI1-7590.

**Division of Mass Media,** United Presbyterian Church USA, 475 Riverside Drive, New York, NY 10027. (Member of WACC)

**Interamerican Gospel Communications,** PO Box 6050, Philadelphia, PA 19114.

**Intermedia,** DOM-NCCCUSA, 475 Riverside Drive, New York, NY 10027. T: (212)870-2376. (Formerly RAVEMCCO. Member of WACC).

**Mass Media Newsletter,** Editor, 2116 North Charles St, Baltimore, MD 21218.

**Mennonite Media Services,** Box 1018, 1251 Edom Rd, Harrisonburg, VA 22801. T: (703)434-2026.

**Office of Communication,** United Church of Christ, 289 Park Av South, New York, NY 10010. T: (212)475-2121. (Member of WACC).

**TRAFCO,** United Methodist Church, 1908 Grand Av, PO Box 840, Nashville, TN 37202. T: (615)327-2727. (Member of WACC).

**TRAV,** Presbyterian Church in the US, 341 Ponce de Leon Av NE, Atlanta, GA 30308. T: (404)875-8921. (Member of WACC).

**United Communications Mission,** Pres, Route 3, Box 399, Orlando, FL 32811. T: (305)241-9632.

**WACC Los Angeles Group,** Los Angeles, California. (Member of WACC).

*VENEZUELA*

**Secretariado de Opinión Publica,** Torre a Madrices, Edf Juan XXIII, Apdo 954, Caracas. T: 818715. (Under Episcopal Conference).

**Servicio de Communicación Social (SERCOS),** Jesuítas a Tierra Honda 37, Apdo 422, Caracas. T: 817731/35.

*ZAMBIA*

**Multimedia Zambia (and Multimedia Publications),** Woodlands, PO Box 1965, 8199 & 1373, Lusaka. T: 73467,73470. (CCZ & Zambia Episcopal Conference).

# 56

# Social Communications Training

*Definition.* Training centres covering all aspects of social communications, the mass media and communication arts (excluding specialized centres for one of the mass media only), and public opinion, including centres at university level; application to education, catechesis, evangelization, development.

Over 100 centres worldwide are devoted specifically to this subject.

*BARBADOS*

**CADEC Communications Network (CCN),** Dir, PO Box 616, Bridgetown. (Training in communications techniques).

*BELGIUM*

**Centre des Techniques de Diffusion et Relations Publiques (CETEDI),** Université Catholique de Louvain, Van Evenstraat 2A, B-3000 Leuven. T: (016)28751.

**Centre for Social Communications (Centrum voor Communicatiewetenschappen, CECOWE),** Katholieke Universiteit Leuven, Van Evenstraat 2A, B-3000 Leuven. T: (016)21070.

**Département de Communications Sociales,** Université Catholique de Louvain, Van Evenstraat 2A, B-3000 Leuven. T: (016)28751. (Cinema training).

**Institut des Arts et Diffusion (IAD),** Av de Tervueren 15, B-1040 Brussel. (Radio/TV/cine/theatre training).

**Institut des Hautes Etudes des Communications Sociales (IHECS),** Chaussée de Tournai 26b, B-7721 Ramagnies-Chin. (Including cinema training).

*BOLIVIA*

**Instituto Superior de Ciencias y Tecnicas de la Opinion Pública,** Universidad Católica Boliviana, Casilla 892, La Paz.

*BRAZIL*

**Centro Educativo de Comunicações do Nordeste (CECOSNE),** Av Conde da Boa Vista 921, Recife, PE. T: 234029. (Training in mass education).

**Departamento de Comunicação Social,** Centro de Ciências Sociais da Pontifícia Universidade Católica, Rua Marquês de São Vicente 209/223, Rio de Janeiro, GB, ZC-20.

**Departamento de Comunicação Social,** Universidade Católica de Minas Gerais, Av do Contorno 7919, Belo Horizonte, MG.

**Departamento de Comunicação Social,** Universidade Católica de Paraná, Rua 15 de Novembro 1004, CP 670, Curitiba, Paraná.

**Faculdade dos Meios de Comunicação Social,** Pontifícia Universidade Católica do Rio Grande do Sul, Av Ipiranga 6681, CP 1429, Pôrto Alegre, Rio Grande do Sul.

*CANADA*

**Department of Communication Arts,** Loyola College, 7141 Sherbrooke St North, Montréal 262, Québec. T: (514)482-0320.

**School of Social Communications,** St Paul University, 223 Main St, Ottawa 1, Ontario. T: (613) 235-1421.

*CHILE*

**Escuela de Comunicación Social de la Universidad del Norte,** Av Angamos 6010, Casilla 1282, Antofagasta. T: 22686,23077.

*COLOMBIA*

**Escuela de Ciencias de la Comunicación Social,** Pontifícia Universidad Javariana, Carrera 7a No 40-62, of 307, Apdo Aéreo 5315, Bogotá, DE.

**Escuela de Humanidades y Ciencias de la Comunicación Social,** Pontifícia Universidad Bolivariana, Calle 48 No 27.05, Apdo 14-16, Medellín, Antioquia.

**Técnicas de Comunicación Social para el Desarrollo (OSAL),** Calle 20 No 9-45, Apdo Aéreo 12721, Bogotá, DE.

*INDIA*

**Institute of Communication Arts,** St Xavier's College, Bombay 1. T: 266661.

**Lumen Institute,** Tamil Nadu Catholic Centre, PO Tindivanam, South Arcot, Tamil Nadu.

*IRELAND*

**Catholic Communications Institute of Ireland (CCII),** 7-8 Lower Abbey St, Dublin 1.

*ITALY*

**Istituto Superiore di Scienze e Techiche del'Opinione Pubblica,** Università Internazionale degli Studi Sociali Pro Deo, Vilae Pola 12, I-00198 Roma. (Radio/TV training).

**Scuola Superiore delle Communicazioni Sociali,** Università Cattolica del S Cuore, Piazza Vecchia 8, Palazzo del Podestà, Bergamo. (Also: Via Sant' Agnese 2, I-20123 Milano). (Radio/TV training).

*KENYA*

**AACC Communications Training Centre,** Dir, Waiyaki Rd, PO Box 14206, Nairobi. T: 61166. (Radio/TV; residential. WACC/UNDA).

*KOREA, South*

**Department of Mass Communications,** Sogang University, CPO Box 1142, Soul. T: (73)5201/2/3/4.

*MEXICO*

**Communications Institute of the Americas (CITA),** Hacienda Vista Hermosa, Apdo Postal 127, Cuernavaca, Morelos.

**Escuela de Ciencias de la Communicación,** Instituto Tecnológico y Estudios Superiore de Occidente (ITESO), Av Lopez Mateos 2352, Cd del Sol, Guadalajara, Jalisco. T: 152334/5/6.

*NETHERLANDS*

**Catholic Mass Media Institute (Stichting Katholiek Instituut voor Massamedia),** Universiteit Nijmegen, Verlengde Grone Straat 43, Nijmegen.

*PARAGUAY*

**Departmento de Ciencias de la Comunicación,** Universidad Católica de Asunción, Av 25 de Diciembre, Casilla 346, Asunción.

*PERU*

**Facultad de Ciencias de la Comunicación Social,** Universidad Católica Santa Maria, Casilla 491, Arequipa.

*PHILIPPINES*

**Programmes in Communication,** Ateneo Graduate School of Arts and Sciences, Ateneo de Manila University, Loyola Heights, Quezon City, PO Box 154, Manila. T: 998721.

*PUERTO RICO*

**Intercultural Communication Institute/Instituto Intercultural para Comunicaciones,** Universidad Católica de Puerto Rico, Ponce, PR 00731. T: (809) 842-4150.

*TANZANIA*

**Publicity Media Institute,** Social Training Centre, PO Box 307, Mwanza. T: 2218.

*UK OF GB AND NI*

**Centre for Overseas Communications Students,** Westbourne Park Baptist Church, Bayswater, London. (WACC courses).

**Overseas Communication Courses (COVAT),** Selly Oak Colleges, Birmingham B29 6LE. T: (021) 472-4231.

*USA*

**Communication Arts Department,** Fordham University, Bronx, New York, NY 10458.

**Communication Arts Department,** Loyola University, 7101 West 80th St, Los Angeles, CA 90045.

**Communication Arts Department,** Xavier University, Victory Parkway, Cincinnati, OH 45207.

**Communication Arts Division,** Creighton University, 2500 California St, Omaha, NE 68131. T: (402) 536-2817.

**Department of Arts and Communication,** Detroit University, 4001 West McNichols Rd, Detroit, MI 48221.

**Department of Communication Art,** University of Notre-Dame, Indiana. T: 284-7316.

**Department of Communications,** Loyola University, 6363 St Charles Av, New Orleans, LA 70118.

**Department of Communications Arts and Instructional Aids,** Loyola University, 6525 Sheridan Rd, Chicago, IL 60626.

*ZAIRE*

**Département de Communications Sociales,** Université de Kinshasa, BP 832, Kinshasa XI.

# 57

# Sound Recordings

*Definition.* Centres or organizations involved in tape, cassette or disc recordings and their preparation; tape or cassette ministries, audio ministries, videotape cassette ministries, record, tape, cassette or disc libraries, recorded music libraries.

Organizations of significance at national levels number over 200.

*AUSTRALIA*

**Gospel Extension Ministry (GEM),** Dir, 144 Albany Rd, Petersham, NSW 2049. T: 594174. (Recordings, tapes, cassettes).

*BELGIUM*

**Centre Catholique d'Information Discographique (CCID),** Rue Cornet de Grez 14, Brussel 3. T: 176815.

*BRAZIL*

**Sonoviso do Brasil,** Av Paulo de Frontin 568, ZC-10 Rio de Janeiro, GB.

*CANADA*

**Gospel Recordings,** 2 Audley St, Toronto 530, Ontario.

*FRANCE*

**Editions de Casettes,** Studio d'Enregistrement, Centre Missionnaire, 50 Rue des Galibouds, F-73200 Albertville T: 396.

**Evangélisation par la Chanson,** BP 2002, F-68058 Mulhouse-Cédex (H-Rhin). (Bible recordings, hymns).

**Jéricho,** 31 Blvd de la Tour-Maubourg, F-75 Paris 7. T: (01)468-3053. (Records).

**La Dikakhè,** 310 Rue des Vaugirard, F-75 Paris 15. T: (01)532-2274. (Recordings).

**OCD (Pastorale & Musique, Unidisc-Clarté),** 33 Rue de Fleurus, F-75 Paris 6. T: (01)548-4995.

**Office Chrétien de l'Enregistrement Sonore (OCES),** 193 Rue de l'Université, F-75 Paris 7. T: (01)705-4358,551-9462.

**Studio SM,** 54 Rue Michel-Ange, F-75 Paris 16. T: (01)224-5060. (Records).

*GERMANY, Federal Republic of*

**Evangelische Arbeitskreis Schallplatte,** Falkensteinstr 16, D-35 Kassel.

*INDIA*

**Gospel Recording Association,** 8 Commissariat Rd, Bangalore 560025, Mysore State.

*ITALY*

**Angelicum,** Piazza Sant'Angelo 2, I-20121 Milano. (Records, theatrical).

**Antomianum Centre,** Via Guinizeli 3, I-40125 Bologna. T: 391484. (Records, theatrical).

**Casa Editrice Apes,** Via anzio 32, I-00178 Roma. T: (06)945-9542. (Record production).

**Edizioni Paoline Musicali e Discografiche,** Via 4 Novembre, I-0041 Albano Laziale. T: 930396. (Recordings).

**Pro Civitate Christiana,** Cittadella Cristiana, CP 46, I-06081 Assisi. T: 812234,812410. (Records, slides).

*LIBERIA*

**Bible Teaching Cassette Program,** ELWA, Box 192, Monrovia. (Literacy and vernaculars).

*NETHERLANDS*

**BmG-Grammofoonplaten (BmG-Records),** Postbus 34, Bloemendaal. (Religious records).

**Gooi en Sticht,** Vaartweg 51, Postbus 17, Hilversum. (Religious records).

*NEW ZEALAND*

**Gospel Recordings,** New Zealand Council, 19 Coates Av, Orakei, Auckland 5.

*PAPUA NEW GUINEA*

**Gospel Recordings,** Banz.

*SOUTH AFRICA*

**Christian Video Network,** 288 25th Av, Villieria, Pretoria 0186.

*SPAIN*

**Central Catequística Salesiana,** Alcala 164, Madrid 2. (Records).

**Discoteca Pax,** Centro Propaganda Popular Católica (PPP), Calle Acebo 54, Madrid 16. (Records).

**Ediciones Instituto Pontificio S Pio X,** Tejares, Salamanca. Records).

**Ediciones Paulistas,** Protasio Goméz 15, Madrid 17. (Recordings).

**Enciclopedia Sonora de Enseñanza,** Claudio Coelho 32, Madrid 1.

*TANZANIA*

**Bible Courses on Cassette,** Msalato Centre (DCT) P.O. Box 15 Dodoma.

*THAILAND*

**Voice of Peace,** PO Box 131, Chieng Mai. T: 235654 (Cassette and radio ministry).

*UK OF GB & NI*

**Celebration Records,** Yeldall Manor, Hare Hatch, Twyford, Berks RG10 9XR. T: (073522)2272. (Charismatic renewal).

**Christadelphian Recordings Library Committee,** Librarian for Tape Recordings, 159 Lazy Hill, Kings Norton, Birmingham 30.

**Christian Recording Associates,** Hon Sec, 120 Chipstead Valley Rd, Coulsdon, Surrey.

**Evangelical Recordings,** 141 Richmond Rd, Kingston, Surrey.

**Gospel Recordings Fellowship,** Exec Sec, Morelands Trading Estate, Bristol Rd, Gloucester GL1 5RZ.

**Gospel Sound and Vision,** 44 Georgia Rd, Thornton Heath, Surrey CR4 8DW. T: (01)764-1520.

**International Christian Communications,** ICC Studios, 4 Regency Mews, Silverdale Rd, Eastbourne, East Sussex BN20 7AB. T: (0323)26134. (Recordings, studios).

**Key Records,** 10 Seaforth Av, New Malden, Surrey. T: (01)942-8847.

**Pilgrim Recordings**, Blundell House, Goodwood Rd, London SE14.
**Sacred Heart Publications**, Southchurch Rd, Southend-on-Sea, Essex. T: 265238. (Records).
**World Records and Tapes**, Park Lane, Hemel Hempstead, Herts HP2 4TD.
**Word (UK)**, Greycaines House, Greycaine Rd, North Watford, Herts WD2 4UN.
**World Record Club**, Park Lane, Hemel Hempstead, Herts HP1 3YB.

*USA*
**Argus Communications**, 3505 North Ashland, Chicago, IL 60657. (Records, tapes).
**Audio Bible Studies**, Founder, 6430 Sunset Blvd, Hollywood, CA 90028. T: (213)466-6121.
**Charismatic Renewal Services**, Communication Center, PO Drawer A, Notre Dame, IN 46556. T: (219)282-2508. (Books, records, cassettes).
**Christian Faith Recordings**, 18108 Parthenia, PO Drawer I, Northridge, CA 91326.
**Christian Tape Center**, PO Box 6011, Glendale, CA 91502.
**Creative Sound Productions**, 911 Diamond St, Los Angeles, CA 90012.
**Gospel Recordings**, Pres, 122 Glendale Blvd, Los Angeles, CA 90026. T: (213)624-7461.
**Missionary Tapes**, Dir, 1721 North Lake Av, Pasadena, CA 91104. T: (213)798-8318. (Also: 173 West Mountain View, Altadena, CA 91102).
**Portable Recording Ministries**, Pres, 222 South River Av (or 681 Windcrest Drive), Holland, MI 49423. T: (616)396-5291.
**Supreme Recordings**, Box 352, Glendale, CA 91209.
**Tape of the Month Club**, Bethany Fellowship, 6820 Auto Club Rd, Bloomington, MN 55438. (Charismatic renewal).
**Weaver Audio Studios**, Park View, Harrisonburg, Virginia.

# 58

# Spiritual Life Conventions, Rallies, Retreats

*Definition.* Annual or limited-duration movements or meetings not primarily for evangelism but for the deepening of the spiritual life: annual mass conventions, mass rallies, the retreat movement, retreat organizations, retreat centres (for temporary residence only). The majority of such activities are not listed here but are operated by organizations under RELIGIOUS COMMUNITIES and LAY TRAINING CENTRES.

*AUSTRALIA*
**Belgrave Heights Convention**, Sec, 237 Flinders Lane, Melbourne, Victoria 3000. T: 635955.

*GERMANY, Federal Republic of*
**Arbeitsgemeinschaft Lutherischer Konferenzen und Konvente**, Sek, Berlinstr 2, D-31 Celle. T: (05141)7730.
**Deutscher Evangelischer Kirchentag**, Leitung, Magdeburgerstr 59, D-64 Fulda. T: 891. (Annual Protestant mass rally).

*INDIA*
**Maramon Convention**, Diocese of Maramon, Mar Thoma Syrian Church, Maramon, Kerala. (Mass convention annually since 1896).

*ITALY*
**Better World Movement**, Pope John XIII Centre, Roma. (Revitalizing spiritual life through retreats, seminars, institutes).

*KENYA*
**Kenya Keswick Convention**, Sec, PO Box 45942, Nairobi. (Annual, similar to UK convention).

*MEXICO*
**Annual Spiritual Life Conference**, Apdo 1114, Puebla, Puebla. T: 11601.

*SWITZERLAND*
**Association des Retraites Spirituelles de Presinge**, CH-1253 Vandoeuvres.

*UK OF GB & NI*
**Association for Promoting Retreats**, Sec, Aldwych House, Aldwych, London WC2. T: (01) 242-9790 ext 28. (Anglican Communion).
**Keswick Convention**, 12 Skiddaw St, Keswick, Cumbria. T: 72589. (Sec: 231 Mereside Way North, Solihull, Warwick. T: (021706)7536. (Annually in Lake District since 1875).
**Nationwide Festival of Light (NFOL)**, 37 Eastwood Rd, South Woodford, London E18 1BN. (Interdenominational).
**Society of Retreat Conductors**, Stacklands Retreat House, West Kingsdown, Sevenoaks, Kent. T: (04)7485-2247.
**SPRE-E 73 (Spiritual Re-Emphasis)**, Shirley House, 27 Camden Rd, London NW1 9YG. T: (01) 267-0065. (Mass rallies; interdenominational).

*USA*
**Americas' Keswick Inc**, Route 530, Whiting, NJ 08759.
**Inter-Church Holiness Convention**, Exec Sec, 375 West State St, Salem, OH 44460. T: (216) 337-7377.

# 59

# State Departments for Religious Affairs

*Definition.* State or government ministries or departments responsible for or charged with religious or ecclesiastical affairs, or other government ministries whose formal or legal responsibilities include religious affairs (controlling registration, worship, propaganda, proselytism, education, relations between religions); state religious organizations, state co-ordinating bodies, state legal agencies, state bodies for surveillance and control of churches. Whilst some of these bodies are Christian in sympathies or activities, others are hostile to Christianity and the churches.
Government departments or ministries of religion are operated by over 75 countries, most for the purpose of control and surveillance over the churches.

*ALGERIA*
**Ministère de l'Enseignement Original et des Affaires Religieuses/Ministère des Habous (Wizarat al-Ta'alim al-'Asli wa al-Su'un al-diniyya)**, 4 Rue de Timgad, Hydra, El Djezair. T: 600290,600293,600936.

*ANGOLA*
**Direcção dos Serviços de Educação**, Repartição de Cultos, Luanda. (Directorate of Education, Churches Dept).

*ARGENTINA*
**Subsecretaria de Culto**, Ministerio de Relaciones Exteriores y Culto, Calle Arenales 761, Buenos Aires.

*AUSTRIA*
**Kultursektion der Bundesministeriums für Unterreicht und Kunst**, Minoriterplatz 5, A-1010 Wien.

*BARBADOS*
**Ministry of Ecclesiastical Affairs**, Ministry of Education, Hon Minister, Bridgetown.

*BELGIUM*
**Administration des Cultes**, Ministère de la Justice, 58 Rue aux Laines, B-1000 Brussel. T: (02)51142000.

*BENIN*
**Ministère des Affaires Intérieures**, Cotonou.

*BOLIVIA*
**Ministerio de Relaciones Exteriores y Culto**, Calle Ingavi Esq. Plaza Murillo 1099, La Paz. T: 2428.

*BOTSWANA*
**Ministry of Health, Labour and Home Affairs**, Private Bag 2, Gaborone.

*BRAZIL*
**Serviço de Estatística Demográfica, Moral e Política**, Dir, 128 Rua Mexico, 2 Floor, Rio de Janeiro, Guanabara.

*BURMA*
**Ministry of Religious Affairs**, Old Secretariat, Rangoon.

*CHAD*
**Ministère de l'Intérieur**, BP 742, Ndjamena.

*CHINA*
**Bureau of Religious Affairs**, State Council, Peking. (Functions at national, provincial and city level).

*CHINA (TAIWAN)*
**Bureau of Social Affairs**, Ministry of Interior (Min-Cheng-Sse, Nei-Cheng-Pu), 107 Roosevelt Rd, Sec IV, Taipei.

*COMOROS*
**Chargé de l'Intérieur et de la Justice Musulmane**, Prés, Moroni.

*CZECHOSLOVAKIA*
**Federal State Office for Ecclesiastical Affairs**, Federal Ministry of Culture (Ministerstvo Kultury, Urad Predsednictva Vlády, Sekretariát pro Vec Církevní), Nábr kpt Jarose 4, 125 09 Praha 1. T: 2102.
**Secretariat for Ecclesiastical Affairs (Czech Section)**, Ministry of Culture (Ministerstvo Kultury, Sekretariát pro Veci Církevní, Církevní Urad v Praze), Valdstejnská 10, 110 00 Praha 1 Malá Strana. T: 513.
**Secretariat for Ecclesiastical Affairs (Slovak Section)**, Ministry of Culture (Ministerstvo Kultury, Sekretariát pre Cirkevné Veci, Cirkevné Urad v Bratislava), Suvorovova 16, 800 00 Bratislava. T: 59862.

*DENMARK*
**Ministry for Church Affairs (Kirkeministeriet)**, Staldmestergarden, Frederiksholms Kanal 21, DK-1220 Kobenhavn K. T: (01)146263.

*DOMINICAN REPUBLIC*
**Secretaría de Estado de Educación**, Bellas Artes y Culto, Av Máximo Gómez, Santo Domingo, DN.

*ECUADOR*
**Ministerio de Gobierno y Cultos**, Quito.

*EGYPT*
**Ministry for Azhar and Waqfs**, Bab-el-Louk, Al Qahirah. (Al-Azhar Muslim University; Muslim endowments and foundations; all mosques; propagation of Islam).

*ETHIOPIA*
**Department of Security**, Ministry of Interior, Ethiopian Government, Addis Abeba.

*FINLAND*
**Ministry of Education (Opetusministeriö)**, Rauhankatu 4, Helsinki 17.

*FRANCE*
**Bureau des Cultes**, Ministère de l'Intérieur, 1 Place des Saussaies, Paris 8. T: 2652830.

*GERMAN DEMOCRATIC REPUBLIC*
**Staatssekretariat für Kirchenfragen bei der Regierung der DDR**, Herman-Matern Str 56, DDR-104 Berlin. (Public Office for Church Questions).

*GERMANY, Federal Republic of*
**Ministry of Religious Affairs**, Wiesbaden.

*GREECE*
**Ministry of Foreign Affairs (Hypourgeion Exoterikon)**, Hodos Zalokosta 2, Athínai. (Handles Ecumenical Patriarchate's affairs).
**Ministry of National Instruction and Religions (Hypourgeion Ethnikis Paideias kai Thriskevmaton)**, Office for Religions (Geniki Dievthynsis Thriskevmaton), Hodos Mitropoleos, Athínai. T: 32079.

*GREENLAND*
**Greenland Ecclesiastical Commission (Gronlandske Kirkenaevn)**, PO Box 63, DK-3900 Godthab. T: 1134.

*HAITI*
**Département des Affairs Etrangères et des Cultes**, Cité de l'Exposition, Port-au-Prince.

*HOLY SEE*
**Segretaria di Stato/Secretaria Status seu Papalis**, Segretario di Stato, Palazza Apostolico Vaticano, I-00120 Città del Vaticano. T: 6983126.

*HUNGARY*
**State Office for Church Affairs (Allami Egyhàzügyi Hivatal)**, Sec of State for Church Affairs, Lendvay u 28, 1062 Budapest VI.

*ICELAND*
**Ministry of Justice and Ecclesiastical Affairs (Dóms -og Kirkjumálaráduneytid)**, Arnarhvoli, Reykjavík.

*INDONESIA*
**Department of Religious Affairs (Kementerian Agama, Departemen Agama RI)**, JI HM Thamrin, Jakarta.
**Directorate for Christian Religious Affairs (Direktorat Urusan Agama Kristen)**, Dir, Departemen Agama RI, JI Siah 6, Jakarta. T: 49962 ext 54.

*IRAQ*
**Ministry of Waqfs (Riaasat Al Awkaf Alaamma)**, Baghdad.

*ISRAEL*
**Department of Christian Affairs**, Ministry of Religious Affairs, 23 Rue Shlomo Hamelekh, Jerusalem.
**Ministry of Religious Affairs (Misrad Hadatoth)**, 30 Rue Yafo, Jerusalem. T: 25206.
**Section for Ecclesiastical Affairs**, Ministry for Foreign Affairs (Misrad Hahutz), Jerusalem.

*ITALY*
**Camera dei Deputati, Affari Interni e di Culto**, Pres, Piazza di Montecitorio, Roma. T: Centr 6760.
**Direzione Generale degli Affari di Culto (General Department of Religious Affairs)**, Ministero dell'Interno, Palazzo Viminale, Roma. T: Centr 4667.
**Direzione Generale del Fondo per Il Culto**, Dir, Gen, Ministero dell'Interno, Palazzo Viminale, Roma. T: Centr 4667.
**Divisione Culti Acattolici**, Direzione Generale degli Affari di Culto, Dir, Palazzo Viminale, Roma.

*JAPAN*
**Department of Religious Affairs**, Bureau of Culture, Ministry of Education (Shukyo-Hojin Bunkacho, Mombusho), 3-2-2 Kasumigaseki, Chiyoda-ku, Tokyo 100.

*KAMPUCHEA*
**Ministry of Religious Affairs (Krasuong Thommaka)**, Terak vithei Phaatarak Pheap (ex Preap Sisovath), Phnom Penh. T: 25151.

*KOREA, South*
**Ministry of Culture and Public Information (Munhwa Kongbo-bu)**, 1 Sejong-ro, Chongro-ku, Soul. (For registration).
**Ministry of Education (Munkyo-bu)**, Soul. (Supervises lands, buildings, and finances of religions).

*KUWAIT*
**Ministry of Waqfs and Islamic Affairs**, Dir, PO Box 13, Kuwait.

*LAOS*
**Département de l'Administration Religieuse**, Ministère des Cultes (Kom Pokkhong Satsana), Vientiane.

*LIBERIA*
**Department of Education**, Monrovia.

*LIBYA*
**Ministry of Unity and Foreign Affairs (Wizaret al-Wihda wa al-Kharijia)**, Tripoli. T: 41302,34060.

*LUXEMBOURG*
**Ministère des Affaires Culturelles et des Cultes**, 19 Côte d'Eich, Luxembourg-Ville.

*MADAGASCAR*
**Ministère de l'Intérieur**, Tananarive. (Deals with churches, authorization, closure, cte.)

*MALAYSIA*
**National Council for Islamic Affairs**, Religious Affairs Department (Jabatan Hal Ehwal Ugama Islam), Prime Minister's Office, Kuala Lumpur. (No national ministry — each state has its own department).

*MAURITIUS*
**Prime Minister's Office**, Government House, Port-Louis.

*MEXICO*
**Comité Nacional Evangélico de Defensa**, Isabel la Católica No 13-308, Zona 1, Apdo 7665, México, DF. T: 215553.
**Secretaria de Gobernación (Interior Department, Government Office)**, Dirección Generale de Gobierno, México, DF. (For religious affairs).

*MONACO*
**Ministère d'Etat, Département de l'Intérieur**, Monaco-Ville.

*MOROCCO*
**Ministère des Habbous**, Ministre des Habbous, Palais Royal, Rabat.

*NETHERLANDS*
**Ministerie van Justitie**, Secretaris-Generaal, 's-Gravenhage.

*NICARAGUA*
**Ministerio de Gobernación**, Palacio Nacional, Managua, DN. (Handles church affiars).

*NORWAY*
**Royal Ministry of Church Affairs and Education (Kongelige Kirke og Undervisningsdepartement)**, Akersgaten 42, Oslo 1 (Deals with Church of Norway.)
**Royal Ministry of Police and Justice (Kongelige Politi og Justisdepartement)**, Akersgaten 42, Oslo 1. (Deals with the free churches).

*PARAGUAY*
**Ministerio de Educación y Culto**, Chile, el Humasta y Piribeby, Asunción.

*PERU*
**Sub-Dirección de Culto**, Palacio de Gobierno, Calle Pescaderia, Lima 1.

*POLAND*
**Office for Religious Affairs (Urzad do Spraw Wysnan)**, Al Ujardowskie 5, Warszawa.

*ROMANIA*
**Department of Cults/Religious Affairs (Departamentul Cultelor)**, Str Snagov 40, Buçuresti 6.

*SAUDI ARABIA*
**Ministry of Pilgrimage and Religious Foundations**, Riyadh.

*SOMALIA*
**Ministerio di Grazia, Giustizia ed Affari Religiosi**, Dir-Gen, Central Government Offices (Governo), Mogadisho. (Ministry of Justice, Religious Affairs and Labour).

*SPAIN*
**Comisión de Libertad Religiosa**, Ministerio de Justicia, San Bernardo 47, Madrid 8.

*SRI LANKA*
**Ministry of Cultural and Religious Affairs (Sanskruthika Amathyansaya)**, 212 Bauddhaloka Mawatha, Colombo 7.

*SUDAN*
**Office for Christian Education (Maktab Taftish deen al Maseeh)**, Ministry of Education, Al Khurtum.

*SWAZILAND*
**Ministry of Education**, PO Box 39, Mbabane. (Responsible for church affairs).

*SWEDEN*
**Ministry of Education (Utbildningsdepartementat)**, Fack, 103 10 Stockholm 2. (Handles affairs of Church of Sweden).
**Office for Religious Affairs (Byran för kyrkokameralee fragor)**, Ministry of Education (Utbildningsdepartementat), Mynttorget 1, Fack, 103 10 Stockholm 2. (Handles affairs of the free churches).

*SYRIA*
**Ministère des Biens-Dédiés (Wizarat Al-'Awkaf)**, Charch Al-Nassr, Dimashq.

*THAILAND*
**Department of Religious Affairs**, Ministry of Education (Kromkarn Satsana), Dir Gen, Ratchadamnoen Av, Bangkok. T: 46411.

*TUNISIA*
**Ministry of Foreign Affairs (Ouizaratou-I-Oumouri-I-Kharijiya)**, Place du Gouvernement, Tunis.

*TURKEY*
**Presidency/Office of Religious Affairs (Diyanet Isleri Baskanligi)**, Pres, Olgunlar Sok, Kocatepe, Ankara. (Responsible for Muslim affairs only).

*UGANDA*
**Department of Religious Affairs**, Dir, Office of the President, PO Box 7168, Kampala.

*USSR*
**Council for Religious Affairs (Sovet po Delam Religii)**, Smolensky Bulvar 11/2, Moskva. T: 2438565,2438515.

*UPPER VOLTA*
**Ministère de l'Intérieur et de la Sécurité,** Ouagadougou.

*VENEZUELA*
**Dirección de Cultos y Asuntos Indígenas,** Ministerio de Justicia, Edf Lincoln, piso 11, Av Lincoln, Sabana Grande, Caracas 105. T: 724461, 723018,726500,727013.

*VIET NAM*
**Comité pour les Questions Religieuses auprès du Bureau de la Présidence du Conseil (Ban Ton Giao Phu Thu Tuong),** Hanoi.

*YUGOSLAVIA*
**Commission for Relations with Religious Communities (Komisija za Vjerska Pitanja),** Jezuitski Trg 4, 41000 Zagreb. (Also in each other republic, with a federal commission in Belgrade).

*ZAIRE*
**Direction des Cultes et Associations,** Ministère de la Justice, Palais de la Justice, BP 3137, Kinshasa 1. T: 30850.

# 60
# Student Organization Federations

*Definition.* Federations of inter-university Christian groups, campus organizations, major university chaplaincies and related national organizations, major student centres, student leadership training centres, scholarship-awarding bodies.

Organizations of major significance in this field number over 500. In the following listing only a selection of headquarters are given, omitting national branches (present in most nations) of IFES, IVF (UCCF), JEC, JUC, MEC, MIEC, SCM, WSCF (FUACE), et alia.

*BELGIUM*
**Fondation Catholique des Bourses pour Etudiants Africains (FONCABA),** Rue du Mulin 29, B-1030, Brussel. T: (02)179516. (Also: Rue de la Prévoyance 60, B-1000 Brussel. T: (02)5116943).

*FRANCE*
**Association Chrétienne des Etudiants Africains Protestants,** Centre International Protestant, 8/16 Villa du Parc Mountsouris, F-75014 Paris. T: 5895569, 7078969.
**Fédération Antillo-Guyannaise des Etudiants Catholiques en France (FAGEC),** 277 Rue St Jacques, F-75005 Paris. T: (01)326-1330. (Pax Romana).
**Fédération des Etudiants Catholiques Vietnamiens de France,** 15 Rue Boissonade, F-75014 Paris. (Pax Romana).
**Jeunesse Etudiante Catholique Internationale (JECI)/International Young Catholic Students,** Secrétariat, 171 Rue de Rennes, F-75006 Paris. T: (01)551-1472.
**Russian Orthodox Student Christian Movement,** 91 Rue Olivier de Serres, F-75015 Paris. T: 2505366.
**Union des Etudiants Catholiques Africains (UECA),** 6 Rue Thibaud, F-75014 Paris. T: (01)734-9628. (Pax Romana).

*ITALY*
**Associazione Studentesca Euro-Afro-Asiatica,** S Marcuola 1723, I-30121 Venezia.
**Comitato Borse di Studio per Studenti Afro-Asiatici,** Corso Umberto 26, I-10128 Torino.
**Federazione delle Istituzioni per Studenti Esteri in Italia (FISEI),** Piazza Duse 2, I-20122 Milano. T: 791447.

*LEBANON*
**Ecumenical Youth and Students Office for the Middle East/Secrétariat Oecuménique pour la Jeunesse et les Etudiants du Moyen-Orient (SOJEMO),** Rue Mak'houl (Abdel-Aziz), Immeuble Tanios Rebeiz, 1375, Bayrut. T: 341902/3.

*NETHERLANDS*
**Liberal Christian Student Movement (Vryzinning Christelyke Studentenbond),** Nieuwe Gracht 27, Utrecht.

*SWITZERLAND*
**European Student Missionary Association,** Mission 76, CP 387, CH-1000 Lausanne 17.
**International Fellowship of Evangelical Students (IFES),** Gen Sec, Chemin de Chandolin 8, CP 6, CH-1000 Lausanne 5. T: (021)233250.
**International Movement of Catholic Students (Mouvement International des Etudiants Catholiques, MIEC) (Pax Romana),** 1 Route du Jura, BP 1062, CH-1701 Fribourg. T: (037)222649/53.
**World Student Christian Federation (WSCF),** 37 Quai Wilson, CH-1201 Genève.

*UK OF GB & NI*
**Christian Education Movement,** Annandale, North End Rd, London, NW11 7QX. T: (01)458-4366. (Formerly Student Christian Movement).
**International Students Club (Church of England),** Sec, 29/31 Trebovir Rd, Earl's Court, London SW5. T: (01)373-6962.
**Students Pentecostal Fellowship,** 1 Brishing Close, Park Rd, Maidstone, Kent.
**Universities and Colleges Christian Fellowship of Evangelical Unions (UCCF),** Gen Sec, 38 De Montfort St, Leicester LE1 7GP. T: (0533)536771. (Name changed 1973 from IVF).
**University Chaplaincies in England and Wales,** 111 Gower St, London WC1E 6AR. T: (01)387-6370.

*USA*
**Federation of Associations of Ukrainian Catholic Students (OBNOVA),** 2315 West Superior St, Chicago 12, Illinois. (Ukrainians in exile).
**Inter Varsity Christian Fellowship (IVCF),** 233 Langdon St (620 North Carroll St), Madison, WI 53703. T: (608)257-0263.
**National Association of Christian Student Foundations,** Pres, 101 N Calver, Muncie, IN 47303. (Also: Box 1456, Bloomington, IN 47401).
**National Campus Ministry Association,** Admin Sec, PO Box 92, King of Prussia, PA 19406. T: (215)768-2050.
**Student Foreign Missions Fellowship (IVCF),** Dir, 233 Langdon St, Madison, WI 53703. T: (608) 257-0263.

# 61
# Telephone Ministries

*Definition.* Centres and agencies in large cities offering specialized public counselling facilities by telephone, taped messages, taped Bible readings, sometimes in conjunction with radio programmes; telephone missionary news and prayer information services.

Organizations significant in this field number over 200.

*AUSTRALIA*
**Life Line International,** Wesley Centre, 210 Pitt St, Sydney, NSW 2000.

*AUSTRIA*
**Telephonsseelsorge,** Goldschmiedgasse 6, A-1010 Wien. T: (0222)639100. (Catholic and Protestant).

*FRANCE*
**Eglise du Tabernacle Bonne Nouvelle par Téléphone,** 163 bis Rue Belliard, F-75018 Paris. T: 627-4719.
**SOS Amitié France,** 5 Rue de Laborde, F-75008 Paris. T: 825-7050 (and in 16 other cities). (Psychological and moral help by phone. Non-denominational).

*GERMANY, Federal Republic of*
**Evangelische Konferenz für Telefonseelsorge,** Stafflenbergstr 78, Postfach 476, D-7 Stuttgart 1.
**Priesternotruf,** Königstr 64, D-85 Nürnberg 2.

*ITALY*
**La Voce Amica,** Roma. T: 7310354/5 (3 lines). (RC; spiritual aid and comfort; begun 1956; 24 hours a day; 35,000 calls a year).
**Telefono Amico,** Angelicum, Piazza Sant 'Angelo 2, I-20121 Milano. T: 6882153.
**Tele-Bibbia,** Roma. T: (06)7311344. (Service of La Voce Amica. Brief commentaries on biblical passages 24 hours a day).
**Tele-Soccorso Spirituale.** (Under different names, in Bologna, Cagliari, Firenze, Genova, Mestre, Milano, Napoli, Palermo, Roma, Torino, Verona).

*JAPAN*
**Life Phone (Inochi no Denwa),** Phone Center, Lutheran Center, Tokyo. T: (03)264-4343. (Begun 1971).
**Tokyo English Life Line (TELL-a-phone),** Tokyo. T: 264-4347. (Anonymous, ecumenical; begun 1973).

*NORWAY*
**Lutheran Telegraph and Telephone Mission (Telegraf og Telefonfunks jonaerers Lutherske Misjonsforening),** Televerket, 5500 Haugesund.
**Telephone Mission (Telefunksjonaerers Misjonsforbund),** Grunersgt 6, Oslo 5.

*SPAIN*
**Teléfono de Dios,** Radio Nacional de España, Madrid. T: 2794600 ext 293. (Begun 1970; including Catholic radio programme 'Extension 293').

*SWITZERLAND*
**Schweizerische Verband für Telephonseelsorge,** Schützengasse 19, CH-2500 Biel. T: (032)28733.

*UK OF GB & NI*
**Bristol Telephone Ministry,** 1 Unity St, Bristol 1. T: 298787.
**Christian Counsel Telephone Service,** 102 Bramshot Av, London SE7. T: (01)858-1212.
**Christian Message.** T: Barnet (01)440-7277, Redbridge (01)553-0828, Merton (01)648-8639, Eltham (01)850-5511.
**Lifeline Birmingham,** 47 Newhall St, Birmingham B3 3RB. T: (021)233-1641. (Pregnancy advisory service).
**Message,** 47 The Drive, Sevenoaks, Kent. T: (0732) 53164. (2-minute telephone messages; 20 centres across UK).
**Samaritans Incorporated,** Gen Sec, 17 Uxbridge Rd, Slough, Bucks. T: 32713. (24-hour telephone counselling and referral. Branches across GB and N Ireland).
**The Samaritans,** 17 Hungate, Lincoln. T: (0522) 28282 (24 hours), Grantham 67616. (To help suicidal and despairing).

*USA*
**Dial a Priest,** Kansas City. (Begun 1968; 17% of calls deal with marriage and family. Also Chicago and other cities).
**Lifeline Telephone Ministry,** 36 Puritan Rd, Springfield, MA 01129.
**Telephone Bible Reading,** New York Bible Society, New York, NY. T: (212)PL5-5500.

# 62
# Theological College Associations

*Definition.* Regional or wider groupings of theological colleges for co-operation in accrediting, syllabuses, curricula, higher studies, research, and conferences; international co-ordinating bodies.

Associations at national or wider levels number over 80.

*ARGENTINA*
**Asociación Sudamericana de Instituciones Teólogicas (ASIT),** Camacua 282, Buenos Aires.

*AUSTRALIA*
**Australian and New Zealand Association of Theological Schools (ANZATS),** Queen's College, University of Melbourne, Parkville, Victoria 3052.

*BOLIVIA*
**Asociación Andina de Educación Teólogica (AADET),** CP 266 La Paz. (Bolivia and Peru).

*BRAZIL*
**Associação de Seminarios Teólogicos Evangélicos (ASTE),** Rua Rêgo Freitas 530, F-B, São Paulo, SP. T: 2569896.

*CAMEROON*
**Association of Theological Schools in French-speaking Africa (ATSFA),** Centre de Littérature Evangélique, BP 4048, Yaoundé.

*CANADA*
**Association of Canadian Bible Colleges,** Winnipeg Bible College, Box 99, Station C, Winnipeg, Manitoba.

*CHINA (TAIWAN)*
**Commission of Theological Education in Taiwan (COTE),** Central Taiwan Theological College, PO Box 74, Taichung.

*COLOMBIA*
**Union of Bible Institutions of Colombia (UNICO),** Apdo Aéreo 5945, Cali.

*COSTA RICA*
**Asociación Latinoamericana de Escuelas Teólogicas (ALET),** Región del Norte, Apdo 2053, San José. (Mexico, Caribbean, North Latin America).
**Asociación Latinoamericana de Instituciones Bíblico-Teólogicas (Región del Norte),** Apdo 288, Alajiela.

*EGYPT*
**Association for Theological Education in the Near East (ATENE),** Faculté de Théologie Copte Orthodoxe, Terrains Anba Roueiss, Rue Ramsés, Al Qahirah. T: 827954.

*FIJI*
**South Pacific Association of Theological Schools (SPATS),** Methodist Theological Institution, Davuilevu, Box 8, Naussori.

*HOLY SEE*
**Sacra Congregazione per l'Educazione Cattolica,** Palazzo delle Congregazioni, Piazza Pio XII 3, I-00193 Roma, Italy. T: 6984569. (Catholic seminaries).

*HONG KONG*
**Association for the Promotion of Chinese Theological Education (APCTE),** Room 604, 310 King's Rd, 6/F, Hong Kong.

*INDIA*
**Board of Theological Education of the NCCI (BTE),** Exec Sec, Union Biblical Seminary, Yeotmal, Maharashtra.

*INDONESIA*
**Association of Theological Schools in Indonesia (PERSETHIA),** Sekolah Tinggin Theologia, Jalan Pegangsaan Timor 27, Jakarta III/20.

*JAPAN*
**Japan Association for Theological Education,** Japan Lutheran Theological College, 3-10-30, Osawa, Mitaka, Tokyo

*KENYA*
**Association of Theological Institutions in Eastern Africa (ATIEA),** Sec, AACC, PO Box 50784, Nairobi. T: 62601.
**Conference of African Theological Institutions (CATI),** Sec, PO Box 50784, Nairobi. T: 62601.
**Council on Higher Studies in Religion,** University of Nairobi, Harry Thuku Rd, PO Box 30197, Nairobi. T: 34244.

*KOREA, South*
**Korean Association of Accredited Theological Schools (KAATS),** Methodist Theological Seminary, PO Box 45, West Gate PO, Soul.
**North East Asia Association of Theological Schools (NEAATS),** Methodist Theological Seminary, PO Box 45, West Gate PO, Soul.

*LEBANON*
**Association for Theological Education in the Near East (ATENE)/Association pour la Formation Théologique au Proche-Orient,** Northern Region, Rue Alfred Naccache, BP 7424, Ras Bayrut. T: 341788.

*MADAGASCAR*
**Association of Theological Teachers of Madagascar (ATTM),** 29 Rue George V, Tananarive.

*MEXICO*
**Organización de Seminarios Latinoamericanos (OSLAM),** Departamento de Ministerios, CELAM, Apdo Postal M-8877, México 1, DF T: 5331520.

*NIGERIA*
**Accrediting Council for Theological Education in Africa (ACTEA),** PMB 2009, Jos.
**Council for Theological Education in Nigeria (CTEN),** PO Box 171, Ilorin, Kwara State.
**West African Association of Theological Institutes (WAATI),** Department of Religion, University of Nigeria, Nsukka.

*PAPUA NEW GUINEA*
**Melanesian Association of Theological Schools (MATS),** Holy Spirit Regional Seminary, PO Box 1101 and 5768, Boroko.

*PERU*
**Asociación Evangélica de Educación Teológica,** Apdo 664, Lima.

*PHILIPPINES*
**Foundation for Theological Education in South-east Asia,** 941 Epifanio de los Santos Av, Quezon City, Manila.
**Philippine Association of Bible and Theological Schools (PABATS),** PO Box 1416, Manila. (Also: PO Box 99, Davao City).
**Philippines Association of Theological Schools (PATS),** Union Theological Seminary, Dasmariñas, Cavite.

*SINGAPORE*
**Association of Theological Schools in South East Asia (ATSSEA),** 6 Mount Sophia, Singapore 9.
**Foundation for Theological Education in South East Asia,** 6 Mount Sophia, Singapore 9.
**Theological Assistance Program (TAP) Asia,** SE Asia Coordinator, 33A Chancery Lane, Singapore 11.

*SOUTH AFRICA*
**Association of Southern African Theological Institutions (ASATI),** St Peter's College, Private Bag 308, Alice, CP.

*SWITZERLAND*
**Programme on Theological Education (PTE),** Unit 1, WCC, 150 Route de Ferney, CH-1211 Genève 20. (Formerly TEF).

*USA*
**American Association of Theological Schools in the USA & Canada (AATS),** PO Box 396, Vandalia, OH 45377.
**Theological Assistance Programs (TAP),** 100 Western Union Bldg, Washington, DC 20005.

*ZAMBIA*
**Association of Evangelical Bible Institutes and Colleges of Africa and Madagascar (AEBICAM),** PO Box 131, Choma.

# 63
# Theological Colleges

*Definition.* Centres for the training of the ordained ministry or priesthood: major seminaries (religious or secular), theological colleges, advanced Bible schools.

Such colleges are too numerous to list here, totalling as they do some 4,500 in 1980, of all denominations. Listings of them will be found in national and confessional yearbooks listed here under DIRECTORIES.

# 64
# Theological Education By Extension (TEE)

*Definition.* Institutionalized courses and programmes utilizing TEE principles of theological training by outreach at a number of selected centres.

Organizations specializing in this area number over 200 worldwide.

*ARGENTINA*
**Seminario por Extensión Anglicano,** Santiago 1862, San Migueld e Tucumán.

*AUSTRALIA*
**Armidale Diocesan Theological Education by Extension,** Box W73, West Tamworth, NSW 2340.

*BRAZIL*
**Asociación Evangélica de Textos Teológicos de Extensión (AETTE)/Evangelical Theological Association for Training by Extension,** CP 5938, 01000 São Paulo, SP.
**Extension Course of the Presbytery of Cuiaba,** CP 41, 78000 Cuiaba, MT.
**Instituto Batista de Educação Teológica por Extensão (IBETE),** Rua João Ramalho 466, São Paulo, SP.

*CHILE*
**Seminario Bíblico por Extensión,** Moneda 1898, Santiago

*COLOMBIA*
**Estudios Teológicos por Extensión,** Apdo Aéreo 786, Santa Marta, Magdalena.
**Instituto Bíblico Betel,** División-Extensión, Apdo Aéreo 516, Armenia, Quindío.
**Latin American Association of Institutions and Theological Seminaries by Extension (ALISTE),** Treasurer, Apdo Aéreo 3041, Medellín. (1973 successor to CATA (Advisory Committee on Self-Teaching Texts) and CLATT (Latin American Committee on Theological texts)).

*ECUADOR*
**Seminario Luterano de Extensión,** Casilla 1334, Cuenca.

*FRANCE*
**Centre d'Enseignement Théologique à Distance (CETAD),** 22 Rue Cassette, F-75006 Paris. (Catholic).
**Ecole Théologique du Soir,** Salle Pasteur, Palais Universitaire, F-67 Strasbourg.

*GUATEMALA*
**Extension seminary,** Apdo 1881, Guatemala. (Periodical, English and Spanish).

*HAITI*
**Ecole Biblique par Extension,** BP 458, Port-au-Prince.
**Extension Bible School of Eastern Haiti,** BP 1096, Port-au-Prince.

*HONDURAS*
**Instituto Bíblico de Extensión,** Apdo 164, La Ceiba.
**Instituto Bíblico de Extensión,** Misión Bautista, Olancho, Horo.

*INDIA*
**Association for Theological Education by Extension (TAFTEE),** 9/15 Lloyd Rd Extn, Bangalore 560006.

*INDONESIA*
**Western Indonesia Theological Education (Lembaga Pembinaan Jemaat GPIB),** 10 Medan Merdeka Timur, Jakarta. (Lay and ministerial training by extension).

*IRAN*
**Iran Extension of the Near East School of Theology,** PO Box 1505, Tehran.

*ITALY*
**Instituto Biblico Evangelico,** Via Cimone 100, I-00141 Roma. (Theological training by extension, 1973).

*KENYA*
**Organization of African Independent Churches, OAIC/TEE,** PO Box 21570, Nairobi. T: 26894,567849

*LEBANON*
**TEE,** PO Box 126, Tarabulus (Tripoli).

*MEXICO*
**Departamento de Extensión,** La Buena Tierra, Apdo 407, Saltillo, Coahuila.
**Departamento de Extensión,** Seminario Lutereno Augsburgo, Apdo Postal 20-416, México 20, DF.
**Seminario Teológico por Extensión del Sureste,** Calle 61/529, Mérida, Yucatán.

*PAKISTAN*
**Extension Seminary of Theology,** 27-B Satellite Town, Rahim Yar Khan.
**Pakistan Committee on Theological Education by Extension (PACTEE),** Co-ordinator, PO Box 13, Gujranwala.

*PERU*
**Seminario de Extensión Teológico,** Iglesia del Nazareno, Apdo 85, Chiclayo.

*PHILIPPINES*
**Conservative Baptist Bible College,** Extension Dept, PO Box 1882, Manila.
**Philippine Committee on Theological Education by Extension (PAFTEE),** PO Box 1416, Manila.

*SOUTH AFRICA*
**Free Methodist Extension Bible School,** PO Box 1263, Witbank.
**Theological Education by Extension College (TEEC),** Dir, Cathedral Place, 3 Saratoga Av, Berea, PO Box 23923, Joubert Park, Johannesburg 2044. T: 724-5429.

*THAILAND*
**Thai CoCoTEE,** 422/3 Suan Plu Bangkok.
**Thailand Theological Education by Extension Committee,** 7th Floor, Sirinee Building, Pleonchit Rd, Bangkok. T: 2527703.

*USA*
**Extension,** 135 North Oakland Av, Pasadena, CA 91101. (Monthly airmail newsletter, summarizing theological education by extension worldwide).
**Extension Dept,** American Baptist Theological Seminary, Dir of Extension, Nashville, TN 37207.
**Extension Dept,** Fuller Theological Seminary, Dir of Extension, 135 North Oakland Av, Pasadena, CA 91101.
**Extension Dept,** Pittsburgh Theological Seminary, Pittsburgh, PA 15206.
**Extension Dept,** San Francisco Theological Seminary, San Anselmo, CA 94960.
**Los Angeles Christian Training Center,** 8219 Florence Av, Downey, CA 90240. (Extension programmes).
**Melodyland Schools,** PO Box 6000, Anaheim, CA 92806. (Theological education by extension).

*ZIMBABWE*
**Rusitu Bible Institute,** Extension Dept, PO Box 576, Umtali.

# 65
# Tourism, Recreation & Travel

*Definition.* Christian tour organizations, travel agencies, charter companies, holiday organizations, package tours, travel service and advice centres; pilgrimage organizations; associations of camping sites, summer camps, holiday centres and/or houseparty centres; ministries to tourism, leisure, recreation, athletics and sport. For missionary air travel, see also FOREIGN MISSIONS SUPPORT ORGANIZATIONS.
In this field, ministries and organizations of major significance number over 150.

*AUSTRALIA*
**Centenary Travel Service,** 213 Victoria Rd, Gladesville, NSW 2111.

*AUSTRIA*
**Österreichische Turn-und Sport-Union,** Falkestr 1, A-1010 Wien.

*BELGIUM*
**Commission du Plein Air et des Loisirs,** Av Zénobe Gramme 58, B-1050 Brussel. (Member, BICE, Leisure, open-air).
**Commission pour la Pastorale du Tourisme de l'Eglise Catholique en Belgique,** Rue de l'Enseignement 7, Blankenberge.

*CANADA*
**Aide Olympique Chrétienne,** Room 600, 455 Craig St West, Montréal, Québec H2Z 1JL. T: (514) 866-2787.
**Canadian Churchman Tours,** 600 Jarvis St, Toronto, Ontario M4Y 2J6. (Anglican).
**Christian Camping International (Canada),** 745 Mount Pleasant Rd, Toronto, Ontario.
**Christian Transportation,** Rear 512 Yonge St, Toronto, Ontario.
**In-Church Travel Tours,** Suite 214, 6 Lansing Square, Willowdale, Ontario M2J 1T8.
**Menno Travel Service,** Henderson Highway, Manitoba 851, Winnipeg. T: (204)334-1868. (Also: South Fraser Way, Clearbrook, BC.T: (604)859-9753).
**Transport for Christ,** Box 371, Rexdale, Ontario.

*EGYPT*
**Commission du Tourisme Religieux Chrétien,** EACCS, Anba Rueis Bldg, Ramses St, Abbasiya, Al Qahirah.

*FRANCE*
**Centre d'Accuil et de Recherches Touristiques,** 31 Rue Emilien Dumas, 30 Sommières.
**Comité Protestant des Centres de Vacances (CPCV),** FPF, 47 Rue de Clichy, F-75009 Paris. T: 874-5500,874-5533.
**Commission Catholique des Centres de Vacances,** 4 Rue Fondary, F-75015 Paris (Member, BICE).
**Fédération Internationale Catholique d'Education Physique et Sportive (FICEP),** 5 Rue Cernuschi, F-75017 Paris. T: (01)924-3112/14.

*GERMANY, Federal Republic of*
**Evangelische Arbeitskreis für Freizeit und Erholung,** Oberkirchenrat, Evangelische Kirchenkanzlei, Hannover-Herrenhausen. (Protestant commission for leisure & tourism).
**Ökumenische Studienreise Gesellschaft,** Bahnhofstr 4/II, D-6 Frankfurt. (Study & travel).
**Studienkreis für Tourismus,** Joseph Jagerhuberstr 28, D-813 Starnberg.

*GREECE*
**Commission de Tourisme,** 246 Acharnon, 815 Athínai.

*HOLY SEE*
**Pontificia Commissione per la Pastorale delle Migrazioni e del Turismo (Apostolatus Maris),** Palazzo San Calisto, Piazza San Calisto 16, I-00153 Roma, Italy. T: (698)4693-4775.

*ISRAEL*
**Sharon Tours,** 39 Bialik St, Ramat-Gan. T: 728193. (Menno Travel Service, USA).

*ITALY*
**Centro Sportivo Italiano (CSI),** Via Conciliazione 3, I-00193 Roma. T: 6567941.
**Istituto di Patronato per l'Assistenza Sociale (IPAS),** Viale Ferdinando Baldelli 41, I-00146 Roma. T: 552251. (Aid to travellers).
**Peregrinatio Romana ad Petri Sedem,** Via della Conciliazione 10, I-00193 Roma.

*KENYA*
**Menno Travel Service,** Lullington House, Kaunda Lane, PO Box 40444, Nairobi. T: 33051,29487.

*NETHERLANDS*
**Commission for Recreation (Commissie van Overleg in Recreatiezaken),** PO Box 38, Driebergen.
**National Catholic Secretariat for Church and Recreation (Kerk en Recreatie),** Brinkstraat 85, Putten (Geld)

*SWEDEN*
**Church of Sweden Committee for Tourist & Church Activities in Foreign Countries,** Kyrkoherde i St Petri, Själbodgatan 4B, Malmö C.

*SWITZERLAND*
**Commission Eglise et Tourisme de la Fédération des Eglises Protestantes de la Suisse,** Pres, CH-1885 Chesières/VD.
**European Christian Service Camp and Retreat,** Bethel Chapel, Via Dufour 13, Lugano. (Camping: Campo San Salvatore, CH-6911 Noranco/Lugano).
**Fédération des Colonies de Vacances Protestantes,** Sec, Centre Protestant de Vacances, 20 Promenade Saint-Antoine, CH-1204 Genève. T: 260350.

*UK OF GB & NI*
**Baptist Holiday Fellowship,** 4 Southampton Row, London WC1B 4AF.
**Catholic Association,** 26 Ashley Place, London SW1. T: (01)834-5122. (Travel agents, pilgrimages).
**Catholic Touring Association,** 110 Coombe Lane, London SW20. T: (01)947-6991. (Travel agents).
**Catholic Travel Association,** 21 Fleet St, London EC4. T: (01)353-2428.
**CE Holiday Homes,** Dept O, 24 Berwick Av, Heaton Mersey, Stockport SK4 3AA.
**Christian Holiday Crusade,** 10 Cuthbert Rd, Croydon, CR0 3RB. T: (01)688-7458.
**Christian International Travel Club (CITC),** 31 Oxford St, Barnsley, South Yorkshire. (Also: Gelderd Rd, Leeds LS12 6DH. T: (0532)636181).
**Christian Mountain Centre (Snowdonia),** Warden, Gorffwysfa, Tremadoc, Gwynedd.
**Christian Sailing Centre,** Dodnor Creek, Newport, Isle of Wight. T: Newport 2195.
**Christian Travel International,** 111 Oxford St, Box 4RH London W1A. T: (01)437-9151,4136. (Formerly Christian Friendship International).
**Church Pilgrimage Association,** 23 Great Smith St, London SW1. T: (01)799-7461.
**Church Travel Club,** Normanhurst, Godalming, Surrey. T: 21516. (Charismatic pilgrimage to Holy Land).
**Cruisair,** Warmwell House, 113 George St, Edinburgh EH2 5JN. T: (031)225-8335,4429.
**European Holiday Evangelism,** Hook Place, Burgess Hill, East Sussex RH15 8RF.
**Filey Christian Holiday Crusade,** Butlin's Holiday Camp, Filey, Yorks. T: 2241.
**Highway Holidays,** 1a Snow Hill Court, London EC1A 2DJ. T: (01)248-2352.
**Holy Land Advice Service,** 6 Borrowdale Av, Ipswich, Suffolk. T: 51152.
**Holy Land Travel (CWN),** 30 Sackville Gardens, Hove, East Sussex BN3 4GH.
**Inter-Church Travel,** 125 Pall Mall, London SW1Y 5EN. T: (01)930-2241.
**Lighthouse Christian Travel,** 4 Priory Way, Southall UB2 JEU. T: (01)574-1267.
**Methodist Travel Bureau,** 25 Marylebone Rd, London NW1 5JR. T: (01)539-2541.
**Migration and Travel Service (Salvation Army),** 101 Queen Victoria St, London EC4P 4EP. T: (01) 236-5222.
**Missionair,** 17 Meadow Rd, Southall, UB1 2JE. T: (01)571-3355. (Travel agents).
**Outreach to Visitors,** 24 Elm Grove, London N8 9AL. T: (01)348-1908. (Ministry to 1 million tourists a month).
**Spes Travel,** 31 Ashley Place, London SW1. T: (01)834-3631. (Catholic travel agents, pilgrimages).
**Summer Isles Adventure Centre (SIAC),** Dir, Tanera, Achiltibuie by Ullapool, Wester Ross.
**Westminster Pilgrimages,** Westminster Touring Association, 38/39 Parliament St, Whitehall, London SW1. T: (01)839-1151. (RC).
**World Friends Travel,** 52 Shaftesbury Av, London, W1V 7DE. T: (01)734-1768/9.

*USA*
**Air West Clergy Bureau,** San Francisco International Airport, San Francisco, CA 94128.
**Airlines Clergy Bureau,** Clergy Bldg, 3030 Mayhew Rd, Sacramento, CA 95827. (50% discount on 24 airlines).
**Am-ur-asia Christian Tours,** 515 North Harbor City Blvd, Melbourne, FL 32935. T: (305)254-6366. (Ship cruises).
**Athletes in Action (AIA),** Suite 12, 1451 East Irvine Blvd, Tustin, CA 92680. T: (714)832-3260. (A ministry of Campus Crusade for Christ).
**Central Clergy Bureau,** 505 South Wabash Av, Chicago, IL 60605. (Discounts on motor coach lines).
**Christian Camp & Conference Association International,** Pres, PO Box 3727, Van Nuys, CA 91407.
**Christian Camping International,** Exec Dir, Box 400, Somonauk, IL 60552.
**Christian Ministry in the National Parks,** Dir, 745 Riverside Drive, New York, NY 10027. T: (212) 870-2155.
**Courier Travel,** 536 Crescent Blvd, Glen Ellyn, IL 60137.
**Eastern Clergy Bureau,** Room 1268, 222 South Riverside Plaza, Chicago, IL 60606. (Reduced airline fares).
**Enquire,** 3400 Galt Ocean Drive, Ft Lauderdale, FL 33308.
**Evangelical Travel Service,** Pres, 642 East Colorado Blvd, Pasadena, CA 91101. T: (213) 793-3103.
**Guild of Catholic Travel,** 500 5th Av, New York, NY. T: (212)OX5-4460.
**Lake Monroe Summer Ministry,** 1156 East 57th St, Chicago.
**Menno Travel Service (MTS),** 800 Second Av, New York, NY 10017. T: (212)490-1160/1/2/3. (Mennonite. Also: 301 South Main, Goshen, IN 46526. T: (219)533-8497).
**Professional Athletes Outreach (PAO),** 4110 North 70th St, Scottsdale, AZ 85251. T: (602) 947-7557.
**US Clergy Bureaus,** Room 1268,222 South Riverside Plaza, Chicago, IL 60606. (Reduced travel fares).
**Western Railroad Clergy Bureau,** Room 1268, 222 South Riverside Plaza, Chicago, IL 60606. (Reduced fares).
**Wheaton Tours,** Box 468, Wheaton, IL 60187.

*ZAIRE*
**Zaire Travel Service,** 11 Blvd du 30 Juin, BP 15812, Kinshasa. T: 23288,24875. (Formerly Menno Travel Service).

# 66
# University Departments of Religion

*Definition.* Faculties or departments specializing in the academic degree-level teaching of, and granting degrees in, religious studies, divinity, theology, mission, missiology, church history, philosophy of religion, or related subjects (but not specifically training persons for the ordained ministry). See also RESEARCH CENTRES.
Departments significant for the study of Christianity number over 1,500 in as many universities across the world.

*ARGENTINA*
**Departamento de Pastoral,** Facultad de Teología, Universidad Católica Argentina, José Cubas 3543, Buenos Aires.
**Departamento de Teología,** Universidad Católica de Mar del Plata, Jujuy 3750, Mar del Plata.
**Escuela de Teología,** Universidad del Norte Santo Tomás de Aquino, Casilla de Correo 32, San Miguel de Tucuman.
**Facultad de Teología,** Pontificia Universidad Católica Argentina Santa Maria de los Buenos Aires, Rio Bamba 1227, Buenos Aires.
**Facultad de Teología,** Universidad Católica de Córdoba, Obispo Trejo 323, Cordoba.
**Facultad de Teología,** Universidad Católica de Santa Fé, San Martin 1966, Santa Fé.
**Facultad de Teología,** Universidad del Salvador, Calle 542, Buenos Aires.
**Facultad de Teología y Filosofía San Miguel,** Mitre 3236, Casilla 10, San Miguel, B7. (SJ).

*AUSTRALIA*
**Department of Religious Studies,** Australian National University, Canberra.
**Faculty of Theology,** St Patrick's College, Manly, Sydney, NSW 2095.
**Joint Theological Faculty,** King's College, Upland Rd, St Lucia, Brisbane, Queensland 4067.
**Joint Theological Faculty,** 55 Hereford St, Glebe, NSW 2037.
**United Faculty of Theology,** Ormond Theological Hall, Parkville, Victoria 3052.

*AUSTRIA*
**Evangelisch-Theologische Fakultät,** Universtät Wien, Wien.
**Katholisch-Theologische Fakultät,** Universität Wien, Dr-Karl-Lueger-Ring 1, A-1010 Wien. T: (427611)244/5.
**Theologische Fakultät der Leopold-Franzens-Universität,** Universitätstr 4b/1, A-6021 Innsbruck.
**Theologische Fakultät der Universität Graz,** Universitätsplatz 3, A-8010 Graz.
**Theologische Fakultät der Universität Salzburg,** Hofstallgasse 4, A-5020 Salzburg. T: (06222) 86111245.

*BELGIUM*
**Faculté de Théologie,** Université Catholique de Louvain, Place Croix du Sud 1, B-1348 Louvain-la-Neuve. T: (010)416201.
**Faculté de Théologie Protestante (Protestantse Theologische Faculteit),** Bollandistenstraat 40, Brussel 4.
**Faculté Internationale de Droit Canon (UCL),** B-1348 Louvain-la-Neuve.
**Faculté Universitaire de Mons,** Chaussée de Binche 151, B-7000 Mons. T: (065)312113.
**Facultés Universitaires N-D de la Paix,** Rue de Bruxelles 61, B-5000 Namur. T: (081)229061.
**Facultés Universitaires St-Louis,** Blvd du Jardin Botanique 43, B-1000 Brussel. T: (02)2177651, 2177653.
**Religious Sociology Dept (Afdeling Godsdienstsociologie aan het Sociologisch Onderzoekinstituut),** Katholieke Universiteit te Leuven, E Van Evenstraat 2B, B-3000 Leuven. T: (016)226335.
**Universitaire Faculteiten St Aloysius,** Av de la Liberté 17, B-1080 Brussel. T: (02)4289113.

**Universitaire Faculteiten St Ignacius,** Prinsstraat 13, B-2000 Antwerpen. T: (031)316660.

*BRAZIL*

**Departamento de Ciências Religiosas,** Universidad Federal de Juiz de Fora, Juiz de Fora, MG.

**Departamento de Teologia,** Centro de Teologia e Ciências Humanas (CTCH), PUCRJ, Rua Marquês de S Vicente 225, Ed Cardeal Leme, Bl II, sl, Cavea, ZC 20, 20000 Rio de Janeiro, GB. T: 2476030.

**Escola Superior de Teologia S. Lourenço de Brindes,** Rua Paulino Chaves 291, Partenon, Pôrto Alegre, RS. T: 232283. (OFM Corp).

**Faculdade de Teologia,** Pontifícia Universidade Católica de São Paulo, Rua Monte Alegre 984, Perdizeo, SP.

**Instituto Central de Filosofia e Teologia,** UCMG, Av Augusto de Lima 1705, Belo Horizonte, MG. T: 355873,355899.

**Instituto de Ciências Religiosas,** Av D Manoel 3, Fortaleza, CE. T: 211300.

**Instituto de Teologia,** Universidade Católica de Salvador, Pça Pe Anchieta 1, Salvador, BA.

**Instituto de Teologia de Recife (ITER),** Av Conde da Boa Vista 971, Recife, PE. T: 222036.

**Instituto de Teologia e de Ciências de Comportamento Humano (ITECIC),** Av Constantino Nery 1667, Manaus, AM.

**Instituto de Teologia, Filosofia e Ciências Humanas,** Universidade Católica de Petrópolis, Petrópolis.

**Instituto Superior de Teologia Pastoral (ISTEP),** Pça Sta Helena, CP 174, Goiânia, GO. T: 61854.

*BULGARIA*

**Theological Academy of St Clement of Ochrida,** Lenin Square 19, Sofija. (Orthodox).

*CAMEROON*

**Faculté de Théologie Protestante,** BP 4011, Yaoundé.

*CANADA*

**Acadia University School of Theology,** Wolfville, Nova Scotia.

**College of Theology,** Saint Mary's University, Halifax, Nova Scotia. T: 4226421.

**Département de Théologie,** Université du Québec, CP 500, Trois Rivières, Québec. T: 3765011.

**Emmanuel College of Victoria University,** 75 Queen's Park Crescent, Toronto 5, Ontario.

**Faculté de Théologie,** Université de Montréal, 3034 Blvd Edouard-Montpetit, CP 6128, Montréal 101, Québec. T: 3436840.

**Faculté de Théologie,** Université de Sherbrooke, Chemin Ste Catherine, Cité Universitaire, Sherbrooke, Québec.

**Faculté de Théologie,** Université Laval, Cité Universitaire, CP 460, Québec.

**Faculté de Théologie,** University of St Michael's College, Toronto 181, Ontario.

**Faculté des Arts,** Mount St Vincent University, Halifax, Nova Scotia. (Religious studies).

**Faculté des Arts,** St Francis Xavier University, Antigonish, Nova Scotia. (Religious studies).

**Faculty of Divinity,** McGill University, 3520 University St, Montréal 2, Québec.

**Faculty of Divinity,** Trinity College, Toronto 5, Ontario.

**Faculty of Theology,** St Paul University, 223 Main St, Ottawa 1, Ontario.

**Faculty of Theology,** University of Winnipeg, Winnipeg 2.

**Institute of Missiology,** St Paul's University, Ottawa. (RC: Propaganda Fide).

**McMaster Divinity College,** McMaster University, Hamilton, Ontario.

*CHILE*

**Facultad de Teología,** Universidad Católica de Chile, Av Bernardo O'Higgins 340, Casilla 114-D, Santiago. T: 224450.

*COLOMBIA*

**Facultad de Ciencias Religiosas,** Universidad de Santo Tomás, Carrera 9a No 51-23, Apdo Aéreo 21019, Bogatá.

**Facultad de Ciencias Religiosas,** Universidad Social Católica de La Salle, Calle 11 No 47, Apdo Aéreo 28638, Bogotá, DE.

**Facultad de Teología,** Pontificia Universidad Javeriana, Carrera 10 No 65-48, Apdo Aéreo 5315, Bogotá, DE.

**Instituto de Teología,** Colegio Mayor de San Buenaventura, Calle 72 No 10-88, Bogotá.

**Instituto de Teología,** Pontificia Universidad Bolivariana, Av La Playa 40-102, Medellín.

*CZECHOSLOVAKIA*

**Ecumenical Institute of the Comenius Theological Faculty (Ekumenicky Institut),** Jungmannova 9, Praha 1. T: 233259,233250.

**Ecumenical Institute of the Protestant Theological Faculty (Slovenska Evanjelicka Bohoslovecká, SEBF),** Konventna 11, Bratislava. (Lutheran).

**Faculty of SS Cyril and Methodius of Prague (Rímskokatolická Cyrilometodejská Bohoslovecká Fakulta v Praze),** Domské nam 10, 412 82 Litomerice T: 2747.

**John Hus Theological Faculty (Joannis Hus Facultas Theologica Pragae, Sectio Oecumenica),** Kujibysevova 5, Praha 6, Dejvice.

**Orthodox Theological Faculty (Pravoslavna Bohoslovecka Fakulta),** Sladkovicova 23, Presov.

*DENMARK*

**Institute of Church and Mission History,** University of Kobenhavn, Lille Kirkestraede 1, DK-1072 Kobenhavn K.

**Theological Faculty,** Arhus University (Teologisk Fakutet, Arhus Universitet), Ndr Ringgade 1, DK-8000 Arhus C.

**Theological Faculty,** University of Kobenhavn (Teologisk Fakultet, Kobenhavns Universitet), Frue Plads, DK-1168 Kobenhavn K.

*EGYPT*

**Coptic Orthodox Theological and Clerical University College,** Anba Rueis Bldg, Ramses St, Abbasiah, Al Qahirah.

*ETHIOPIA*

**Theological College of the Holy Trinity,** Haile Selassie University, PO Box 665, Addis Abeba.

*FINLAND*

**Theological Faculty (Abo Akademi),** Biskopsgatan 16, Abo, Turku. (Swedish-language).

**Theological Faculty,** Helsinki University, Fabianinkatu, 33, Helsinki 17.

*FRANCE*

**Comité International de Liaison des Facultés Catholiques de Théologie,** 21 Rue d'Assas, F-75006 Paris. T: (01)222-4180.

**Faculté de Théologie,** Facultés Catholiques de Lille, 41 Rue du Port, F-59 Lille.

**Faculté de Théologie,** Facultés Catholiques de Lyon, 25 du Plat, F-69002 Lyon. T: (78)426630.

**Faculté de Théologie,** Institut Catholique de Paris, 21 Rue d'Assas, F-75006 Paris. T: (01)222-4180.

**Faculté de Théologie,** Institut Catholique de Toulouse, 31 Rue de la Fondarie, F-31068 Toulouse. T: (61)526235.

**Faculté de Théologie,** Université Catholique de l'Ouest, Place André-Leroy, BP 858, F-49 Angers. T: (41)882222.

**Faculté de Théologie BMV Immaculatae in Foro Vetero,** Fourvière, F-69 Lyon. (SJ).

**Faculté de Théologie Catholique de Strasbourg,** Palais Universitaire, 9 Place de l'Université, F-67084 Strasbourg. T: (88)355940.

**Faculté de Théologie Protestante de Montpellier,** 26 Blvd Berthelot, Rue Louis-Perrier, F-34 Montpellier (Hérault). T: 67926128. (Eglise Réformée de France).

**Faculté de Théologie Protestante de Strasbourg,** Palais de l'Université, F-67 Strasbourg (B-Rhin). T: 355940.

**Faculté Libre de Théologie Evangélique de Vaux-sur-Seine,** 85 Av de Cherbourg, Vaux-sur-Seine (Yvelines). T: 4740986.

**Faculté Libre de Théologie Protestante de Paris,** 83 Blvd Arago, F-75014 Paris. T: 3316164.

**Faculté Libre de Théologie Protestante d'Aix-en-Provence,** 33 Av Jules-Ferry, F-13 Aix-en-Provence (B-du-Rh). T: 261355.

**Facultés Catholiques de Lille,** 60 Blvd Vauban, F-59 Lille T: (20)572800.

**Facultés Dominicaines de Philosophie et de Théologie,** Le Saulchoir, Etiolles, F-91 Sousy-sur-Seine.

**Institut de Théologie Orthodoxe St Serge,** 93 Rue de Crimée, F-75019 Paris.

*GERMAN DEMOCRATIC REPUBLIC*

**Theologische Fakultät,** Ernst-Moritz-Arndit-Universität, Rubenowstr 1, DDR-22 Greifswald.

**Theologische Fakultät,** Friedrich-Schiller-Universität, Weigelstr 1, DDR-69 Jena.

**Theologische Fakultät,** Humboldt-Universität, Unter den Linden 6, DDR-108 Berlin.

**Theologische Fakultät,** Karl-Marx-Universität, Zimmer 234, Peterssteinweg 8, DDR-701 Leipzig.

**Theologische Fakultät,** Martin-Luther-Universität, Universitätsplatz 8/9, DDR-402 Halle/Saale.

**Theologische Fakultät,** Universität Rostock, Universitätsplatz, DDR-25 Rostock.

*GERMANY, Federal Republic of*

**Abteilung für Ev Theologie der Ruhr-Universität Bochum,** Buscheystr 132, Postfach 2148, D-4630 Bochum. T: (02321)7112500.

**Alttestamentliches Seminar der Universität Hamburg,** Sedanstr 19, D-2000 Hamburg 13, T: (0411)441973788.

**Alttestamentliches Seminar der Universität Heidelberg,** Klingenteichstr 2, D-6900 Heidelberg. T: (06221)541270.

**Alttestamentliches Seminar der Universität Mainz,** Saarstr 21, Forum Universitatis 5, D-6500 Mainz. T: (06131)1712652.

**Alttestamentliches Seminar der Universität München,** Veterinärstr 1/III (Geschäftszimmer), D-8000 München 22. T: (0811)218013479.

**Alttestamentliches Seminar der Universität Münster,** Universitätsstr 13-17, D-4400 Münster. T: (0251)49012533/4.

**Alt-Katholisches Seminar der Universität Bonn,** Hauptgebäude, Am Hof 3-5, D-53 Bonn.

**Anerkannter Sonderforschungsbereich (DFG-SFB Nr 1) Patristik an der Universität Bonn,** Am Hof 1, D-5300 Bonn. T: (02221)7314414.

**Arbeitsstelle der Historischen Kommission zur Erforschung des Pietismus an der Universität Münster,** Universitätsstr 13-17, D-4400 Münster. T: (0251)49012572.

**Biblisch-Archäologisches Institut an der Universität Tübingen,** Liebermeisterstr 12 und Gartenstr 18, D-7400 Tübingen. T: (07122)7112879.

**Christlich-Archäologisches Seminar der Universität Bonn,** Liebfrauenweg 3, D-5300 Bonn. T: (02221)7314454.

**Christlich-Archäologisches Seminar der Universität Heidelberg,** Karlstr 2, D-6900 Heidelberg. T: (06221)541486.

**Christlich-Archäologisches Seminar der Universität Marburg,** Ernst-von-Hülsen Haus, Biegenstr 11, D-3550 Marburg T: (06421)6912347.

**Deutsches Ev Institut für Altertumswissenschaft des Heiligen Landes,** Bockenheimer Landstr 109, Postfach 4025, D-6000 Frankfurt/Main. T: (0611)770521.

**Diakoniewissenchaftliches Institut der Universität Heidelberg,** Hauptstr 126, D-6000 Heidelberg. T: (06221)541267. (Social church work studies).

**Ev-Theologische Facultät der Eberhard-Karls-Universität,** Wilhelmstr 7, D-74 Tübingen.

**Ev-Theologische Facultät der Johannes-Gutenberg-Universität,** Saarstr 21, D-65 Mainz.

**Ev-Theologische Facultät der Rheinischen Friedrich-Wilhelm-Universität,** Am Hof 1, D-53 Bonn.

**Ev-Theologische Facultät der Universität Hamburg,** Edmund-Siemers-Allee 1, D-2 Hamburg 13

**Ev-Theologische Facultät der Universität München,** Veterinärstr 1, D-8 München 22.

**Ev-Theologische Facultät der Westfälischen Wilhelms-Universität,** Universitätsstr 13-17, D-44 Münster/Westfalen.

**Ev-Theologisches Seminar der Universität Bonn,** Am Hof 1, D-5300 Bonn. T: (02221)7314414.

**Ev-Theologisches Seminar der Universität Tübingen,** Liebermeisterstr 12, D-7400 Tübingen. T: (07122)7112540.

**Fachbereich Ev Theologie Alttestamentlisches Seminar der Universität Marburg,** Lahntor 3, D-3550 Marburg T: (06421)6912451.

**Fachbereich Ev Theologie der Universität Marburg,** Lahntor 3, D-3550 Marburg. T: (06421) 6912441.

**Fachbereich Ev Theologie Institut für Hermeneutik der Universität Marburg,** Am Plan 3, D-3550 Marburg. T: (06421)6913931.

**Institut für Biblische Archäologie der Universität Mainz,** Saarstr 21, Forum Universitatis 4, D-6500 Mainz. T: (06131)1712685.

**Institut für Christliche Gesellschaftslehre der Universität Tübingen,** Olgastr 8, D-7400 Tübingen. T: (07122)7112591.

**Institut für Christliche Gesellschaftswissenschaften der Universität Münster,** Universitätsstr 13-17, D-4400 Münster T: (0251)49012550.

**Institut für Christliche Sozialethik der Universität Erlangen-Nürnberg,** Kochstr 6, D-8520 Erlangen. T: (09131)8512216.

**Institut für Ev Theologie der Universität des Saarlandes,** Bau 11 2 OG, D-6600 Saarbrücken 11. T: (0681)30212349.

**Institut für Hermeneutik der Universität Tübingen,** Wildermutstr 10, D-7400 Tübingen. T: (07122)7112066.

**Institut für Kirchenbau und Kirchliche Kunst der Gegenwart an der Universität Marburg,** Am Plan 3, D-3550 Marburg. T: (06421)23143.

**Institut für Missionswissenschaft und Ökumenische Theologie der Universität Tübingen,** Hausserstr 43, D-7400 Tübingen. T: (06122)7112592.

**Institut für Neutestamentliche Textforschung der Universität Münster,** Am Stadtgraben 13-15, D-4400 Münster. T: (0251)49012581/2.

**Institut für Ökumenische Theologie der Universität Münster,** Am Stadtgraben 13-15, D-4400 Münster. T: (0251)49012576.

**Institut für Spätmittelalter und Reformation der Universität Tübingen,** Hölderlinstr 17, D-7400 Tübingen. T: (07122)7112886.

**Institut für Westfälische Kirchengeschichte an der Universität Münster,** Universitätsstr 13-17, D-4400 Münster. T: (0251)49012571.

**Institut für Wissenschaftliche Irenik der Universität Frankfurt,** Mertonstr 17, D-6000 Frankfurt. T: (0611)79813179.

**Institutum Judaicum Delitzschianum an der Universität, Münster,** Wilmergasse 1-4, D-4400 Münster. T:(0251)49012561.

**Institutum Judaicum der Universität Erlangen-Nürnberg,** Kochstr 6, D-8520 Erlangen. T: (09131) 8512206.

**Institutum Judaicum der Universität Tübingen,** Liebermeisterstr 12, D-7400 Tübingen. T: (07122) 7112590

**Kirchengeschichtliches Seminar der Universität Heidelberg,** Karlstr 2, D-6900 Heidelberg. T: (06221)541486/7.

**Kirchengeschichtliches Seminar der Universität Mainz,** Saarstr 21, Forum Universitatis 5, D-6500 Mainz. T: (06131)1712686 bzw 2749.

**Kirchengeschichtliches Seminar der Universität Marburg,** Lahntor 3, D-3550 Marburg. T: (06421) 6914280.

**Kirchengeschichtliches Seminar der Universität München,** Gorgenstr 7, D-8000 München 13. T: (0811)218013481.

**Kirchen- und Dogmengeschichtliches Seminar der Universität Hamburg,** Sedanstr 19, D-2000 Hamburg 13. T: (0411)4419713818.

**Kirchlich-Archäologisches Institut der Universität Kiel,** Neue Universität, Haus 14, Olshausenstr 40-60, D-2300 Kiel. T: (0431)53112394.

**Konfessionskundliches Institut des Evangelischen Bundes,** Eifelstr 35, D-6140 Bensheim/Bergstrasse. T: (06251)270077732.

**Konfessionskundliches Seminar der Universität Heidelberg,** Karlstr 2, D-6900 Heidelberg. T: (06221)541486/7.

**Lehrstuhl für Grundfragen der Ev Theologie der Universität Regensburg,** Universitätsstr 31, D-8400 Regensburg. T: (0941)94312325.

**Missionsakademie an der Universität Hamburg,** Rupertistr 67, D-2000 Hamburg 52. T: (040)828642.

**Missionswissenschaftliches Seminar der Universität Hamburg,** Sedanstr 19, D-2000 Hamburg 13. T: (0411)4419713775.

**Neutestamentliches Seminar der Universität Hamburg,** Sedanstr 19, D-2000 Hamburg 13. T: (0411)4419173795.

**Neutestamentliches Seminar der Universität Mainz,** Saarstr 21, Forum Universitatis 5, D-6500 Mainz. T: (06131)1712603 bzw 2285.

**Neutestamentliches Seminar der Universität Marburg,** Lahntor 23, D-3550 Marburg. T: (06421) 6912443.

**Neutestamentliches Seminar der Universität München (Ev-Theol Fakultät),** Veterinärstr 1/III, D-8000 München 22. T: (0811)218013480.

**Neutestamentliches Seminar der Universität Münster,** Universitätsstr 13-17, D-4400 Münster. T: (0251)49012542/43.

**Neutestamentliches Seminar und Jüdisch-Hellenistsche Abteilung der Universität Heidelberg,** Klingenteichstr 2, D-6900 Heidelberg. T: (06221)541270.

**Ökumenisches Institut der Ev Theol Fakultät der Universität München,** Veterinärstr 1, D-8000 München 22. T: (0811)21813482,3489.

**Ökumenisches Institut der Universität Bochum,** Buscheystr 132, Gebäude GA, D-4630 Bochum. T: (02321)7114793.

**Ökumenisches Institut der Universität Bonn,** Am Hof 1c D-5300 Bonn. T: (02221)7314510.

**Ökumenisches Institut der Universität Heidelberg,** Plankengasse 1, D-6900 Heidelberg. T: (06221)541217.

**Ökumenisches Seminar der Universität Hamburg,** Sedanstr 19, D-2000 Hamburg 13. T: (0411) 4419713775.

**Ökumenisches Seminar der Universität Marburg,** Lahntor 3, D-3500 Marburg. T: (06421) 6914280.

**Patristische Arbeitsstelle an der Universität Münster,** Universitätsstr 13-17, D-4400 Münster. T: (0251)49012572.

**Patristisches Seminar der Universität Marburg,** Lahntor 3, D-3550 Marburg. T: (06421)6912446.

**Praktisch-Theologisches Seminar der Universität Kiel,** Neue Universität, Olshausenstr 40-60, D-2300 Kiel. T: (0431)59312389.

**Praktisch-Theologisches Seminar (mit Abteilung Ev Kirchenmusik) der Universität Mainz,** Saarstr 21, Forum Universitatis 5, D-6500 Mainz. T: (06131)1712653.

**Religions Kundliche Sammlung der Universität Marburg,** Schloss 1, D-3550 Marburg.

**Religionswissenschaftliches Seminar der Universität Bonn,** Am Hof 34, D-5300 Bonn.

**Seminar für Allgemeine Kirchengeschichte der Universität Erlangen-Nürnberg,** Kochstr 6, D-8520 Erlangen. T: (09131)85187071.

**Seminar für Alte Kirchengeschichte der Universität Münster,** Universitätsstr 13-17, D-4400 Münster T: (0251)4912536.

**Seminar für Alttestamentliche Theologie der Universität Erlangen-Nürnberg,** Kochstr 6, D-8520 Erlangen. T: (09131)8512204.

**Seminar für Apologetik der Universität Erlangen-Nürnberg,** Kochstr 6, D-8520 Erlangen. T: (09131) 8512217.

**Seminar für Christliche Archäologie und Kunstgeschischte der Universität Erlangen-Nürnberg,** Kochstr 6, D-8520 Erlangen. T: (09131) 8512213.

**Seminar für Christliche Religionsphilosophie der Universität Freiburg,** Belfortstr 11, D-7800 Freiburg.

**Seminar für Christliche Soziallehre und Allgemeine Religionssoziologie der Universität München,** Geschwister-School-Platz 1, D-8000 München 22.

**Seminar für Ev Theologie der Freien Universität Berlin,** Ihnestr 56, D-1000 Berlin 33. T: (0311) 769013669.

**Seminar für Ev Theologie der Universität Frankfurt,** Fachbereich Religionswissenschaften' Gräfstr 69, D-6000 Frankfurt/M. T: (0611)79813179.

**Seminar für Ev Theologie und Didaktik der Glaubenslehre Fachbereich Religionswissenschaften der Universität Frankfurt,** Farrentrappstr 47, D-6000 Frankfurt/M. T: (0611)79813538.

**Seminar für Ev Theologie (Aussenstelle der Ev-Theol Fakultät der Universität Bonn),** Repgowstr 9, D-5000 Köln-Lindenthal. T: (0221) 47012511.

**Seminar für Geschichte des Urchristentums der Universität Erlangen-Nürnberg,** Kochstr 6, D-8520 Erlangen. T: (09131)8512208.

**Seminar für Geschichte und Exegese des Alten Testaments der Universität Erlangen-Nürnberg,** Kochstr 6, D-8520 Erlangen. T: (09131)8512206.

**Seminar für Geschichte und Theologie des Christlichen Ostens der Universität Erlangen-Nürnberg,** Kochstr 6, D-8520 Erlangen. T: (09131) 8512217.

**Seminar für Homiletik der Universität Erlangen-Nürnberg,** Kochstr 6, D-8520 Erlangen. T: (09131) 851.

**Seminar für Katechetik der Universität Erlangen-Nürnberg,** Kochstr 6, D-8520 Erlangen. T: (09131) 851.

**Seminar für Katholische Religionsphilosophie der Universitüt Frankfurt,** Geog-Viogt-Str 8, D-6000 Frankfurt/M.

**Seminar für Missionswissenschaft,** Sanderring 2, D-8700 Würzburg. T: (0931)31258.

**Seminar für Missionswissenschaft der Universität Erlangen-Nürnberg,** Kochstr 6, D-8520 Erlangen. T: (09131)8512220.

**Seminar für Missions- und Religionswissenschaft der Universität München,** Veterinärstr 1, D-8000 München 22. T: (0811)218013484.

**Seminar für Mittlere und Neuere Kirchengeschichte der Universität Münster,** Universitätsstr 13-17, D-4400 Münster. T: (0251)49012539.

**Seminar für Neutestamentliche Theologie der Universität Erlangen-Nürnberg,** Kochstr 6, D-8520 Erlangen. T: (09131)8512207.

**Seminar für Ostkirchenkunde am der Katholische Theologische Facultät,** Sanderring 2, D-8700 Würzburg.

**Seminar für Praktische Theologie,** Fachbereich Ev Theologie der Universität Marburg, Lahntor 3, D-3550 Marburg. T: (06421)6914284 bzw 4282.

**Seminar für Praktische Theologie der Universität Hamburg,** Sedanstr 19, D-2000 Hamburg 13. T: (0411)4419713797.

**Seminar für Praktische Theologie der Universität Heidelberg,** Schulgasse 2, D-6900 Heidelberg. T: (06221)541272.

**Seminar für Praktische Theologie der Universität München,** Veterinärstr 1, D-8000 München. T: (0811)218013483.

**Seminar fur Praktische Theologie und Religionspädagogik der Universität Münster,** Universitätsstr 13-17, D-4400 Münster. T: (0251)49012551.

**Seminar für Reformationsgeschichte der Universität Erlangen-Nürnberg,** Kochstr 6, D-8520 Erlangen. T: (09131)85187071.

**Seminar für Reformierte Theologie der Universität Erlangen-Nürnberg,** Kochstr 6, D-8520 Erlangen. T: (09131)8512202.

**Seminar für Reformierte Theologie im Fachereich Ev Theologie der Universität Münster,** Universitätsstr 13-17, D-4400 Münster. T: (0251) 49012548.

**Seminar für Religionsgeschichte der Universität**

**Freiburg,** Belfortstr 11, D-7800 Freiburg.

**Seminar für Religionsgeschichte der Universität Marburg,** Lahntor 3, D-3550 Marburg. T: (06421)6914287.

**Seminar für Religionsgeschichte und Missionswissenschaft der Universität Heidelberg,** Karlstr 2, D-6900 Heidelberg. T: (06221)541586/7.

**Seminar für Religionspädagogik der Universität Erlangen-Nürnberg,** Kochstr 6, D-8520 Erlangen. T: (09131)8512221.

**Seminar für Religionsphilosophie und Geschichte der Theologie der Universität Marburg,** Lahntor 3, D-3550 Marburg. T: (06421)6914288.

**Seminar für Religionswissenschaft,** Pferdegasse 3, D-4400 Münster.

**Seminar für Religions- und Geistesgeschichte der Universität Erlangen-Nürnberg,** Kochstr 6, D-8520 Erlangen.

**Seminar für Religions- und Missionswissenschaft der Universität Mainz,** Saarstr 21, Forum Universitatis 4, D-6500 Mainz. T: (06131)172539.

**Seminar für Religions- und Missionswissenschaft der Universität Münster,** Universitätsstr 17-17, D-4400 Münster. T: (0251)49012531.

**Seminar für Sozialethik der Universität Marburg,** Lahntor 3, D-3550 Marburg. T: (06421) 6914276.

**Seminar für Systematische Theologie der Ev-Theol Fakultät der Universität München,** Veterinärstr 1/II, D-8000 München 22. T: (0811) 218013482.

**Seminar für Systematische Theologie der Universität Erlangen-Nürnberg,** Kochstr 6, D-8520 Erlangen. T: (09131)8512215.

**Seminar für Systematische Theologie der Universität Hamburg,** Sedanstr 19, D-2000 Hamburg 13. T: (0411)4419713801.

**Seminar für Systematische Theologie der Universität Münster,** Universitätsstr 13-17, D-4400 Münster. T: (0251)49012547,2531.

**Seminar für Systematische Theologie und Apologetik der Universität Marburg,** Lahntor 3, D-3550 Marburg. T: (06421)6912444.

**Seminar für Territorialkirchengeschichte der Universität Mainz,** Saarstr 21, Forum Universitatis 5, D-6500 Mainz. T: (06131)1713284.

**Seminar für Theologie der Christlichen Ostens an der Ev-Theologische Fakultät,** Kochstr 6, D-8520 Erlangen.

**Seminar für Wissenschaft vom Judentum der Universität Mainz,** Saarstr 31, Forum Universitatis 5, D-6500 Mainz. T: (06131)1712545.

**Socialethisches Institut der Universität Kiel,** Neue Universität, Haus 14, Olshausenstr 40-60, D-2300 Kiel. T: (0431)59312395.

**Systematisches Seminar der Universität Heidelberg,** Karlstr 4, D-6900 Heidelberg. T: (06221)541.

**Theologische Fakultät der Christian-Albrechts-Universität,** Neue Universität, Olshausenstr 40-60, D-2300 Kiel.

**Theologische Fakultät der Friedrich-Alexander-Universität,** Kochstr 6, D-8520 Erlangen.

**Theologische Fakultät der Georg-August-Universität,** Nikolausberger Weg 5b, D-34 Göttingen.

**Theologische Fakultät der Philipps Universität,** Lahntor, D-3550 Marburg/Lahn.

**Theologische Fakultät der Ruprecht-Karl-Universität,** Schulgasse 2 und 4, D-6900 Heidelberg.

**Theologische Fakultät Paderborn,** Kamp 6, D-4790 Paderborn. T: (05251)25619.

**Theologische Fakultät SJ,** Offenbacher Landstr 224, D-8000 Frankfurt. T: (0611)651047.

**Theologische Fakultät Trier,** Jesuitenstr 13, D-5500 Trier. T: (0651)75011.

**Theologisches Institut (im Aufbau) der Universität Bielefeld (Arbeitsstelle Theologie),** Schulstr 9, D-4400 Münster. T: (0251)23022.

**Theologisches Seminar der Universität Kiel,** Neue Universität, Haus 14/16, Olshausenstr 40-60, D-2300 Kiel. T: (0431)59312352.

**Vereinigte Theologische Seminar der Universität Göttingen,** Nikolausberger Weg 5b, D-3400 Göttingen. T: (0551)5241.

*GHANA*

**Department for the Study of Religions,** University of Ghana, PO Box 66, Legon, Accra.

*GREECE*

**Faculty of Theology,** University of Athens, Odos Ivannou Gennadiou 14, Athínai 140. T: (021)7795177.

**Faculty of Theology,** University of Salonica, Thessaloníki. T: (031)23922260.

*HONG KONG*

**Chung Chi College Theology Division,** Chinese University of Hong Kong, Shatin, NT. T: 61431.

**Dept of Religious Knowledge and Philosophy,** Chung Chi College, Chinese University of Hong Kong, Shatin, NT. T: 61431.

*HUNGARY*

**Academy of Theology (Hittudomànyi Akadémia)** Eötvös Lorand u 7, 1053 Budapest.

**Reformatus Theologiai Akademia,** Kalvin tér 16, Debrecen.

**Reformatus Theologiai Akademia,** Rakay u 28, Budapest.

**Theological Academy (Magyarorszagi Evangélikus Rgyhaz, Teologiai Akadémiaja),** Ullöi u 24, Budapest VIII. (Lutheran).

*INDIA*

**Pontifical Athenaeum (Papal Seminary),** Poona 6.

**Pontifical Theological Institute,** St Joseph's Pontifical Seminary, Alwaye 683103, Kerala.

**Theology Dept,** Serampore College, Serampore, Hooghly, West Bengal.

*INDONESIA*

**Fakultas Theologia,** Universitas HKBP Normmensen, Jalan Asahan 4, Pematangsiantar, Sumatera.

**Fakultas Theologia Satya Watjana,** Satya Watjana Christian University, Jl Diponagosla 54-58, Salatiga, Jateng.

**Fakultas Theologia UKIT,** Tomohon, Sultara, Sulawesi.

*IRELAND*

**Faculty of Divinity,** Trinity College, Dublin University, Dublin 2.

**Faculty of Theology,** College of St Joseph, Milltown Park, Dublin 6.

**Faculty of Theology,** St Patrick's College, Maynooth, County Kildare. T: Celbridge 286261.

**Milltown Institute of Theology and Philosphy,** Milltown Park, Dublin 6, T: (01)976731.

*ITALY*

**Facoltà di Missionologia,** Pontificia Università Gregoriana, Piazza della Pilotta 4, I-00187 Roma.

**Facoltà Teologica Napoletana,** Viale Colli Aminei Capodimonte, I-80131 Napoli. (Also: Via Petrarca 115).

**Facoltà Valdese di Teologia,** Via Pietro Cossa 42, I-00193 Roma. T: 374266.

**Instituto Missionario Scientifica,** Pontificia Università Urbaniana, Via Urbano VIII 16, I-00165 Roma. T: 655992.

**Pontificia Facoltà Teologica dei Santi di Gesù e Giovanni della Crose,** Piazza San Pancrazio 5-A, 1-00152 Roma.

**Pontificia Facoltà Teologica del SS Cuore di Gesù,** Pontificio Seminario Regionale Sardo, I-08100 Cuglieri, Nuoro.

**Pontificio Ateneo Antonianum,** Via Merulana 124, I-00184 Roma.

**Pontificio Ateneo Salesiano,** Piazza dell'Ateneo Salesiano 1, I-00139 Roma.

**Pontificio Ateneo San Anselmo,** Piazza de, Cavalieri di Malta 5, I-00153 Roma.

**Pontificio Facoltà Teologica San Bonaventura,** Via dei Serafico 1, I-00142 Roma. T: 5911651.

**Pontificio Istituto Superiore di Latinita,** Ateneo Salesiano, Piazza dell'Ateneo Salesiano 1, I-00139 Roma. T: 884641.

*JAPAN*

**College of Theology,** Kanto Gakuin University, 4834 Mutsuura-cho, Kanazawa-ku, Yokohama 236.

**Department of Theology,** Aoyama Gakuin University, 4-4-25 Shibuya, Shibuya-ku, Tokyo.

**Department of Theology,** Kwansei Gakuin University, 1-155 Ichiban-cho, Uegahara Nishinomiya-shi 662.

**Department of Theology,** Seinan Gakuin University, 420 Hoshiguma, Oaza, Nishi-ku, Fukuoka City 814.

**Faculty of Theology,** Sophia University, 1-710 Kamishakujii, Nerima-ku, Tokyo 177.

**St Paul's (Rikkyo) University,** Christian Studies Department, Nishi-Ikebukuro 3-chome, Toshima-ku, Tokyo.

**School of Theology,** Doshisha University, Karasuma-Imadegawa, Kamikyo-ku, Kyoto.

**Tohoku Gakuin University,** Tsuchidoi 3-1, Sendai City Miyagi Pref 982.

*KENYA*

**Department of Philosophy and Religious Studies,** University of Nairobi, Harry Thuku Rd, PO Box 30197, Nairobi. T: 34244.

**Department of Religious Studies,** Kenyatta University College, PO Box 43844, Nairobi. T: Templer 356.

*KOREA, South*

**College of Theology,** Yonsei University, 134 Shinchen-dong, Sudaemoon-ku, Soul.

**Department of Christian Studies,** College of Liberal Arts, Ewha Womans University, Soul.

**United Graduate School of Theology,** Yonsei University, 134 Shin-Chong Dong, Soul.

*LEBANON*

**Department of Religious Studies,** American University of Beirut, PO Box 1428, Bayrut.

**Faculté de Théologie,** Université St Joseph en Beirut, Rue de l'Université St Joseph, BP 293, Bayrut. (Maronite Catholic).

**Facultés de Théologie et de Philosophie de l'Université Saint-Esprit,** Kaslik-Jounieh.

*LESOTHO*

**Department of Theology,** University of Botswana, Lesotho and Swaziland (UBLS), PO Box Roma, via Maseru.

*LIBERIA*

**Cuttington College and Divinity School,** PO Box 277, Monrovia.

*MADAGASCAR*

**Institut Supérieur de Théologie,** Ambatoroka, Tananarive. T: 20763.

*MALAWI*

**Department of Religious Studies,** Chancellor College, University of Malawi.

*MALTA*

**Faculty of Theology,** Royal University of Malta, Msida, Valletta. T: 36451.

*NETHERLANDS*

**Faculty of Religion (Faculteit der Godgeleerdheid),** Gemeentelijke Universiteit, Kloveniersburgwal 89, Amsterdam.

**Faculty of Religion (Faculteit der Godgeleerdheid),** Rijksuniversiteit te Utrecht, Heidelberglaan 2, Utrecht. T: (030)531853. (Also: Rapenburg 59, Leiden. T: (01710)23773).

**Faculty of Religion (Faculteit der Godgeleerdheid),** Rijksuniversiteit, Oude Kyk in't Jotstraat 9, Groningen.

**Faculty of Religion (Faculteit der Godgeleerdheid),** Vrije Universiteit, De Boelelaan 1115, Amsterdam.

**Hogeschool voor Theologie en Pastoraat te Heerlen,** Oliemolenstraat 60, Heerlen. T: (045) 717851.

**Katholieke Theologische Hogeschool te Amsterdam,** Keizergracht 105, Amsterdam. T: (020)242752.

**Katholieke Theologische Hogeschool Utrecht,** Rijksuniversiteit Utrecht, Heidelberglaan 2, Utrecht. T: (030)539111 toestel 2149.

**Sektie Missiologie van de Theologische Faculteit van de RK Universiteit te Nijmegen,** Nijmegen.

**Theologische Akademie,** Johannes Calvijn Stiching, Oudestraat 5, Kampen.

**Theologische Faculteit te Tilburg,** Hoteschoollaan 225, Tilburg. T: (013)669111.

**Theologische Faculteit van de Katholieke Universiteit te Nijmegen,** Erasmuslaan 4, Nijmegen. T: (08800)58711.

*NEW ZEALAND*

**Department of Religion,** University of Otago.

**Department of Religion,** University of Wellington.

*NIGERIA*

**Department of Religion,** University of Nigeria, Nsukka, East Central State.

**Department of Religious Studies,** University of Ibadan, Ibadan.

**Department of Religious Studies and Philosophy,** University of Ife, PMB 27, Ile-Ife.

*NORWAY*

**Faculty of Theology,** University of Oslo (Teologiske Fakultet, Universitetet i Oslo), Blindern, Oslo.

**Teologiske Menighedsfakultet,** St Olavsgatan 29, Oslo. (Lutheran).

*PAPUA NEW GUINEA*

**Department of Religious Studies,** University of Papua New Guinea, PO Box 1144, Boroko.

*PERU*

**Facultad de Teología Pontificia y Civil,** Av Sucre 1200, Pueblo Libre, Apdo 1838, Lima 21. T: 618531.

*PHILIPPINES*

**College of Theology,** Central Philippine University, PO Box 231, Iloilo City.

**College of Theology,** Northern Christian College, PO Box 105, Laoag, Ilocos Norte, Luzon.

**Department of Theology,** Ateneo de Manila Loyola Heights, Quezon City, PO Box 4082, Manila.

**Faculty of Theology,** Pontifical University of Santo Tomás, Espana St Manila.

**Faculty of Theology,** University of San Carlos, PO Box 182, Cebu City. T: 72419. (RC).

*POLAND*

**Christian Theological Academy (Chrzescijanska Akedemia Teologiczna),** Ul Miodowa 21, Warszawa. (United).

**Faculty of Theology,** Katolicki Uniwersytet Lubelski, Aleje Raclawickie 14, Lublin.

**Faculty of Theology, Law and Christian Philosophy,** Catholic Theological Academy (Akademia Teologii Katolockiej, ATK), Gwiazdzista 81, Warszawa 45.

**Faculty of Theology and Law (Wydzial Teologiczhy),** ul Podzamcze 8, 31-003 Kraków.

**Higher School of Theology,** 52/54 ul Krakowskie Przedmiéscie, 00-322 Warszawa.

**Pontifical Faculty of Theology,** 2 ul Wiezowa, Poznan.

**Pontifical Faculty of Theology (Papieski Wydzial Teologiczny we Wroclawin),** 14 Plac Katedralny, 50-329 Wroclaw.

*PORTUGAL*

**Faculdade de Filosofia,** Universidade Católica Portuguesa, Instituto Superior de Filosofia Beato Miguel de Carvalho, Rua de S Barnabé 42, Braga. T: 22528.

**Faculdade de Teologia,** Universidade Católica Portuguesa, Palma de Cima, Lisboa 4. T: 781817.

*PUERTO RICO*

**Faculdad de Teología,** Universidad Católica de Porto Rico, Ponce, PR 00731. T: (809)842-4150.

*ROMANIA*

**Orthodox Theological Institute (Institutul Teologic Ortodox de Grad Universitar),** Strada Sfinta Ecaterina 2, Sectorul 5, Oficiul Postol 53, Buçuresti.

**Orthodox Theological Institute (Institutul Teologic Ortodox de Grad Universitar),** Strada 1 Mai 20, Sibiu, Judetul Sibiu.

**Protestant Theological Institute (Institutul Teologic Protestant de Grad Universitar),** Sectiile reformata, sinodala-prezbiteriana si unitariana (limba maghiara), Piata Victoriei 13, Cluj. (Also: Str General Magheru 4, Sibiu).

*SIERRA LEONE*

**Department of Theology,** Fourah Bay College, University of Sierra Leone, Mount Aureol, Freetown.

*SOUTH AFRICA*

**Dept of Missiology,** Faculty of Divinity, University of South Africa (UNISA), Pretoria.

**Faculty and Department of Divinity,** Rhodes University, PO Box 94, Grahamstown, CP.

**Faculty of Theology,** University of Durban/Westville, PB 4001, Durban.

**Faculty of Theology,** University of Fort Hare, PB 314, Alice, CP.

**Faculty of Theology,** University of Natal, Pietermaritzburg.

**Faculty of Theology,** University of the North, PO Sovenga, Dist Pietersburg.

**Faculty of Theology (Fakulteit van Godgeleerdheid) Universiteit van Stellenbosch,** Dorp St, Stellenbosch. (NGK).

*SPAIN*

**Facultad de Sagrada Teología, de Derecho Canónico y de Filosofía,** Universidad Pontificia Comillas, Maldonado 1-B, Madrid 6.

**Facultad de Sagrada Teología,** Universidad de Deusto, Av de las Universidades, Apdo 1, Bilbao.

**Facultad de Sagrada Telogía y de Derecho Canónico,** Universidad de Navarra, Ciudad Universitaria, Pamplona.

**Facultad de Teología y de Derecho Canónico,** Universidad Pontificia de Salamanca, Compañia 1, Apdo 23, Salamanca.

**Facultad Teológica de Barcelona,** Sección San Pacianó, Seminario Conciliar, Calle Disputación 231, Barcelona 7.

**Facultad Teológica del Norte,** Seminario Metropolitano, Calle 5 Tomas de Zumarraga, Apdo 48, Burgos.

*SWEDEN*

**Faculty of Theology,** Lund University (Teologiska Fakulteten, Lunds Universitet), Sandgatan 1, Lund.

**Faculty of Theology,** Uppsala University (Teologiska Fakulteten, Uppsala Universitet), Uppsala.

*SWITZERLAND*

**Christkatholisch-Theologische Fakultät,** Universität Bern, Hochschulstr 4, CH-3000 Bern.

**Evangelisch-theologische Fakultät,** Universität Bern, Hochschulstr 4, CH-3000 Bern.

**Faculté Autonome de Théologie Protestante,** Université de Genève, CH-1205 Genève.

**Faculté de Théologie,** Université Neuchâtel, CH-2000 Neuchâtel.

**Faculté de Théologie Catholique,** Université de Fribourg, Rue du Botzet 8, CH-1700 Fribourg. T: (037)221124.

**Faculté de Théologie Protestante,** Université de Lausanne, CH-1005 Lausanne.

**Theologische Fakultät,** Universität Zürich, Rämistr 71, CH-8006 Zürich.

**Theologische Fakultät der Universität Basel,** Nadelberg 10, CH-4000 Basel.

*TURKEY*

**Faculty of Theology,** University of Ankara (Ankara Universitesi, Ilâhiyat Falkütesi), Yldirim Beyazit Meydani. T: 113176.

*UGANDA*

**Department of Religious Studies and Philosophy,** Makerere University, PO Box 7062, Kampala.

*USSR*

**Leningrad Theological Academy,** Obvodny Kanal 17, Leningrad C-167. T: 779068, (Russian Orthodox).

**Moscow Theological Academy,** Zagorsk, Moskva. (Russian Orthodox).

*UK OF GB & NI*

**Department of Biblical History and Literature,** University of Sheffield, Sheffield 10.

**Department of Divinity,** University of Newcastle-upon-Tyne.

**Department of Principles of Religion,** University of Glasgow G12 8QQ.

**Department of Religious Studies,** Universiy of Aberdeen, Aberdeen.

**Department of Religious Studies,** University of Lancaster, Cartmel College, Bailrigg, Lancaster, Lancs.

**Department of Religious Studies,** University of Sussex, Brighton, East Sussex.

**Department of Theology,** University of Birmingham, Birmingham 15.

**Department of Theology,** University of Bristol, Bristol.

**Department of Theology,** University of Exeter, Exeter, Devon.

**Department of Theology,** University of Hull, Hull, Humberside.

**Department of Theology,** University of Kent, Canterbury, Kent.

**Department of Theology,** University of Leeds, Leeds.

**Department of Theology,** University of Nottingham, University Park, Nottingham.

**Department of Theology and the Study of Religion,** University of Southampton, Southampton SO9 5NH.

**Faculty of Divinity,** New College, University of Edinburgh, The Mound, Edinburgh.

**Faculty of Divinity,** University of Cambridge, Cambridge.

**Faculty of Divinity,** University of Durham, Durham.

**Faculty of Theology,** Christ's College, University of Aberdeen, Aberdeen.

**Faculty of Theology,** King's College, University of London, Strand, London WC2.

**Faculty of Theology,** Queen's University, Belfast, NI.

**Faculty of Theology,** St Mary's College, University of St Andrew's, St Andrew's.

**Faculty of Theology,** Trinity College, University of Glasgow, Glasgow.

**Faculty of Theology,** University of Manchester, Manchester.

**Faculty of Theology,** University of Oxford, Oxford.

**School of Theology,** St David's University College, University of Wales, Lampeter.

**School of Theology,** University College, University of Wales, Bangor.

**School of Theology,** University College, University of Wales, Cardiff.

*USA*

(A small selection only).

**Boston University School of Theology,** 745 Commonwealth Av, Boston, MA 02215.

**Brite Divinity School,** Texas Christian University, Fort Worth, TX 76129.

**Candler School of Theology,** Emory University, Atlanta, GA 30322.

**Council on the Study of Religion,** Department of Religious Thought, University of Pennsylvania, Philadelphia, PA 19104 (Members 11,500)

**Department of Religion,** Columbia University, New York, NY 10027.

**Department of Religion,** University of Hawaii, 2560 Campus Rd, Honolulu, HA 96822.

**Department of Theology,** Fordham University, Fordham Rd & Third Av, New York, NY 10458.

**Department of Theology,** Marquette University, 615 North 11th St, Milwaukee, WI 53233.

**Department of Theology,** University of Notre Dame, Notre Dame, IN 46556.

**Division of Religion and Philosophy,** Bishop

College, 3837 Simpson Stuart Rd, Dallas, TX 75241.
**Division of Religion and Philosophy,** Marion College, 4301 S Selby, Marion, IN 46952.
**Division of Theology and Christian Education,** Houghton College, Houghton, NY 14744. T: (716) 567-8776.
**Drew University Theological School,** Madison, NJ 07940.
**Duke University Divinity School,** Durham, NC 27706.
**Graduate School of Theology,** Oberlin College, Oberlin, OH 44074.
**Hamma School of Theology,** Wittenberg University, Springfield, OH 45501 T: (513)327-6121.
**Hartford Seminary Foundation,** 55 Elizabeth St, Hartford, CT 06105.
**Harvard Divinity School,** Harvard University, 45 Francis Av, Cambridge, MA 02138.
**Howard University School of Religion,** Washington, DC 20001.
**Kennedy School of Missions,** Hartford Seminary Foundation, 55 Elizabeth St, Hartford, CT 06105.
**Lampon School of Religion,** J P Cambell College, PO Box 1526, Jackson, MS 39205.
**Meadville Theological School,** Lombard College, 5701 Woodlawn Av, Chicago, IL 60637. T: (312) 493-7531.
**Perkins School of Theology,** Southern Methodist University, Dallas, TX 75222. T: (214)363-5611.
**Phillips University Graduate Seminary,** University Station, Enid, OK 73701.
**St John's School of Divinity,** St John's University, Collegeville, MN 56321.
**St Louis University School of Divinity,** 220 North Spring Av, St Louis, MO 63108.
**School of Theology,** University of the South, Sewanee, TN 37375.
**School of World Mission (SWM),** Fuller Theological Seminary, 135 N Oakland Av, Pasadena, CA 91101. T: (213)449-1745.
**University of Chicago Divinity School,** Chicago, IL 60637.
**Vanderbilt University Divinity School,** Nashville, TN 37205.
**Yale University Divinity School,** 409 Prospect St, New Haven, CT 06510.

*VIET NAM*
**Faculté de Théologie Université de Dalat,** Collège Pontifical St Pie X, BP 88, Dalat.
**Faculté de Théologie Université Minh Duc,** Ho Chi Minh Ville.

*YUGOSLAVIA*
**Catholic Theological Faculty (Katolicki Bogoslovni Fakuetet u Zagrebu),** Kaptol 29, 4100 Zagreb.
**Theological Faculty (Teoloska Fakulteta Ljubljana),** Dolnicargeva 5, 61001 Ljubljana. (Catholic).

*ZAIRE*
**Faculté de Théologie,** Université Nationale du Zaïre, Campus de Kinshasa, BP 122, Kinshasa XI. (Catholic).
**Faculté de Théologie Protestante au Congo,** Université National du Zaïre, BP 2012, Kisangani.

*ZIMBABWE*
**Department of Theology,** University of Rhodesia, PO Box MP167, Salisbury.

# 67

# Urban Industrial Mission

*Definition.* Industrial missions and projects, urban ministry; urban-industrial ecumenical parishes, experimental parishes, inner-city parishes; team ministries, ministries to urban structures and institutions, experimental ministries, new or exploratory ministries in specialized areas; urban industrial mission training centres; intermediate technology, appropriate technology, labour-intensive projects; factory evangelism, occupational evangelism.

In this field there are over 400 organizations of major significance.

This section presents only a small selection from several hundred possible entries.

*ARGENTINA*
**Centro de Estudios Urbanos y Regionales,** Virrey del Pino 3230, Buenos Aires.
**Centro Urbano Nueva Parroquia,** Viamonte 2445, Valentin Alsina, Lanus, Buenos Aires.

*AUSTRALIA*
**Inter-Church Trade & Industry Mission,** ACC, GPO Box 3582, NSW 2001. T: 278889.

*BOTSWANA*
**Shashi Complex Urban and Industrial Mission,** c/o Botswana Christian Council, PO Box 94, Francistown.

*BURMA*
**UIM Initiatives,** Burma Christian Council, 20 Signal Pagoda Rd, Rangoon. T: 13290.

*CAMEROON*
**Evangélisation Urbaine et Industrielle Edéa,** BP 4, Edéa.
**Western Africa Urban Industrial Mission Committee,** AACC/Comité Ouest-Africain pour les Villes et l'Industrie, CETA, BP, 4 Edéa.

*CANADA*
**Canadian Urban Training Project for Christian Service,** 51 Bond St (& 875 Queen St East), Toronto, Ontario M5B 1X1.

*CHINA (TAIWAN)*
**Taiwan Ecumenical Industrial Ministry,** 26 Shanhsia Lane, Kaohsiung 800. T: 554994.
**YMCA Industrial Projects,** 19 Hsu-chuan St, Taipei. T: 24431.

*DENMARK*
**Industrial Mission in Armenia (Industrimissionen i Armenien),** Mejlgade 101, 8000 Arhus C. T: (06)122240.

*FRANCE*
**Mission dans l'Industrie de la Région Parisienne (MIRP),** Groupe de Coordination des Enterprises d'Evangélisation, Conseiller, 47 Rue de Clichy, F-75009 Paris. T: 874-9092.

*GERMANY, Federal Republic of*
**Ev Aktionsgemeinschaft für Arbeitnehmerfragen in Deutschland,** Blumenstr 1, Postfach 4, D-7325 Bad Boll (Wttbg). (Employee problems).

*GHANA*
**Tema Industrial Mission,** PO Box 25, Tema.

*HONG KONG*
**Caritas Urban Community Development,** Caritas House, PO Box 13522, Kowloon. T: H-242071.
**Hong Kong Christian Industrial Committee,** HKCC, Metropole Bldg, 57 Peking Rd, Kowloon. T: K-678031.
**Motor Mechanics Training Class,** 14 Lun Chang St, To Kwa Wan, Kowloon. T: K-829983.
**Tao Fong Shan Porcelain Workshop,** Tao Fong Shan, Shatin, NT. T: NT-61450.

*INDIA*
**Calcutta Urban Service,** 16 Sudder St, Calcutta 16.
**Chowpatta Agricultural & Industrial Mission,** PO Berenag, via Almora, Kumaon, UP.
**Christian Service to Industrial Society,** Balfour Rd, Kilpauk, Madras 10 T: 664979.
**Coimbatore Industrial Service,** 100 Race Course, Coimbatore 641018, South India.
**CSI Industrial Training Centre,** Kodiannoorkonam, Nellimood PO, Trivandrum, Kerala.
**CSI School of Industries,** PB 1, Station Rd, Tumkur.
**Durgapur Industrial Service (ESII),** Bidhan Nagar, Durgapur 1.
**Ecumenical Social & Industrial Institute (ESII),** St Michael's Centre, Bidhan Nagar, Durgapur 1, West Bengal. T: 5817.
**India Industrial Mission,** 5A Seal's Garden Lane, Cossipore, Calcutta 2.
**Industrial Service Institute,** 1840 Church Hall, Kingsway, Nagpur 1, Maharashtra. T: 33455.
**Industrial Team Service,** St Mark's Cathedral, 1 Mahatma Gandhi Rd, Bangalore 560001.
**Mar Baselios Industrial Training Centre,** Mavelikara PO, Alleppey District, Kerala.
**Mar Thoma Industrial Training Centre,** Kozhencherry, Kerala.
**National Commission on Urban Industrial Mission,** 1 Mahatma Gandhi Rd, Bangalore 560001
**NCCI Urban Industrial Mission Committee,** N-21, Greater Kailash, New Delhi.
**St Xavier's Industrial School,** PO Eluru, West Godavari District, AP.
**UIM Initiatives in Bombay,** St Stephen's Church, Mount Mary Rd, Bandra, Bombay 400050 T: 263904
**United Christian Institute,** Suranussi, Jullundur City, Punjab. (Industrial training).

*INDONESIA*
**Industrial Evangelism Institute,** Jalan Guntur 43, Jakarta III/10.
**UIM Committee,** DGI, Jalan Salemba Raya 10, Jakarta IV/3. T: 82317.

*IVORY COAST*
**Abidjan Industrial Mission,** BP 1282, Abidjan.

*JAPAN*
**Ikoi no Ie Labour Centre,** 79-1 Sakura-machi, Toyota-shi, Aichi Prefecture. (Lutheran. Financed by Toyota Motor Co).
**Kansai Industrial Mission Committee,** Japan Institute for International Study, 2nd Ashike Bldg, 3-40 Andojibashi-dori, Minami-ku, Osaka. T: (06) 252-8236.
**Kansai Labour Evangelism,** c/o Naniwa Church, 3-20 Koraibashi, Higashi-ku, Osaka. T: 2314951.
**Kitakyushu Urban Industrial Mission,** 1-2-35 Saburomaru-cho, Kokura-ku, Kitakyushu-shi 802.
**Labor Traffic Welfare Center,** 112 Takahata, Hiraoka-cho, Kakogawa-shi, Hyogo-ken 675-01.
**Mining Mission in Northern Kyushu,** c/o Miyata Church, 73 Miyata, Miyata-cho, Kurate-gun, Fukuoka Prefecture. T: Miyata 20733.
**Poor Little Church in the Day Labourers District,** Tmahime Hotel, 2-21-20 Kiyokawa, Daito-ku, Tokyo.
**Student Labor Seminar,** 3-20 Koraibashi, Higashi-ku, Osaka-shi 541.
**Tokyo Labour School (Tokyo Industrial Mission Committee),** 4-5 Ginza, Chuoku, Tokyo. T: 5679069.
**Traffic Workers' Welfare Centre (Trucker Mission),** 115 Takaha-take, Hiraoka-cho, Kakogawa-shi. T: 26768.
**UIM Committee,** NCCJ, 1-551-24 Totsuka, Shinjuku-ku, Tokyo 160. T: (03)203-0372.
**Urban Mission for Slum Area,** c/o Nishinari Church, 6-14 Nankai, Nishinari-ku, Osaka. T: 5621450.

*KENYA*
**Christian Industrial Training Centre (CITC),** Principal, Meru Rd, Pumwani, PO Box 72935, Nairobi. T: 24763. (Anglican).
**CITC Secretarial College,** Principal, Bonyo Rd, PO Box 1437, Kisumu. T: 3046. (Anglican).
**Eastern Africa Committee for Urban Industrial & Rural Mission,** AACC, Pioneer Hourse, PO Box 20301, Nairobi. T: 33510.

*KOREA, South*
**Dong Inchon Labour Centre,** 72-11 Mansuk Dong, Dong-ku, Inchon. T: 20181.
**Industrial Welfare Centre,** 58-76 Moonraedong 3-ka, Yongdongpo, Soul. T: 623436.
**Institute of Labor and Management (ILM),** Sogang University, 1 Sin Su Dong, Ma Po Ku, Soul. T: 320141.
**Institute of Urban Studies and Development,** Yonsei University, Sudaemoon-ku, Soul. T: 330131/41.
**Korea Christian Action Organizations for UIM,** IPO Box 3668, Soul. T: 746076.
**Korean United Committee of UIM,** 70-7 St, Yongdongpo Dong, Soul. T: 627972.
**Mission to Labour & Industry,** 183 Wha Soo Dong, Dong-ku, Inchon.
**Yongdongpo Industrial Mission,** 70-7 St, Yongdongpo Dong, Soul. T: 627972.

*LIBERIA*
**Bendoo Industrial Mission,** Lake Piso, Grand Cape Mount Country. T: 26008.
**Bong Mining Parish,** PO Box 1538, Monrovia.

*MADAGASCAR*
**Centre d'Initiation Technique,** Frères de la Doctrine Chrétienne, Mananjary.

*MALAYSIA*
**Committee for Selangor UIM,** 6 Jalan 11/4A, Petaling Jaya, Selangor.

*NETHERLANDS*
**Churches Industrial Service (Dienst in de Industriele Samenleving Vanwege de Kerken),** Noordermarkt 26, Amsterdam-C.
**Europe Urban Industrial Mission,** De Horst 1, Driebergen.
**X-Y Action Groups,** Van Blankenburgstr 6, 's-Gravenhage.

*NEW ZEALAND*
**Inter-church Trade & Industry Mission,** 26 Charles Upham Av, PO Box 297, Christchurch. T: 69274.

*NIGERIA*
**Lagos Industrial Mission,** PO Box 78, Lagos.

*PAKISTAN*
**Pakistan Christian Industrial Service,** Exec Sec, 74 Garden Rd, Karachi 3. T: 74607.
**Technical Services Association,** 3 Empress Rd, Lahore.

*PHILIPPINES*
**Committee on Industrial Life and Vocations,** PO Box 718, Manila. T: 96241.
**Division of UIM,** NCCP, PO Box 1767, Manila. T: 998636.
**Interchurch Committee on Urban Squatter Resettlement (ICUSR),** NCCP, PO Box 1767, Manila. T: 998636.
**Workers' Institute for Social Enlightenment,** NCCP, PO Box 1767, Manila. T: 998636.

*PUERTO RICO*
**Puerto Rico Industrial Mission Project,** Apdo 9002, Santurce, PR 00908.

*SIERRA LEONE*
**Industrial Ministry,** UCCSL, PO Box 404, Freetown. T: 3268.

*SINGAPORE*
**Jurong Industrial Mission,** Jurong Christian Church and Civic Centre, 4-J Block 111, Ho Ching Rd, Jurong Town. T: 21539.

*SOUTH AFRICA*
**South African Intermediate Technology Group,** PO Box 31190, Braamfontein, Transvaal.
**Witwatersrand Committee for Industrial Mission,** PO Box 81, Roodepoort, Transvaal.

*SWITZERLAND*
**Advisory Committee on Technical Services (ACTS),** WCC, 150 Route de Ferney, CH-1211 Genève 20.
**Arbeiterseelsorger,** Kapuzinerhospiz, Rebbergstr 16, CH-5400 Ennetbaden. T: (056)24130.
**Churches' Committee on Migrant Workers,** 150 Route de Ferney, CH-1211 Genève 20.
**European Contact Group on Church and Industry,** 150 Route de Ferney, CH-1211 Genève 20.
**Foi et Cité,** 5 Route des Acacias, CH-1227 Genève. T: 429952.
**Institut Kirche und Industrie,** Zeltweg 21, CH-8032 Zürich.
**Ministère Protestant dans l'Industrie,** 5 Route des Acacias, CH-1227 Genève. T: 429952.
**Schweizerische Katholische Arbeitsgemeinschaft Kirche und Industrie,** Ackerstr 57, CH-8005 Zürich. T: (01)429582.
**Schweizerische Reformierte Arbeitsgemeinschaft Kirche und Industrie,** Vorsitzender, Guggenbühlstr 41, CH-8404 Winterthur.
**Urban Industrial Mission Desk,** WCC, 150 Route de Ferney, CH-1211 Genève 20.

*TANZANIA*
**Urban Project,** Christian Council of Tanzania, PO Box 2537, Dar es Salaam.

*THAILAND*
**Urban Industrial Life Division,** Church of Christ in Thailand, 14/2 Pramuan Rd, Bangkok. T: 37976/7.

*UK OF GB & NI*
**Christian Teamwork Trust,** Grubb Institute of Behavioural Studies, 1 Whitehall Place, London SW1A 2HD. T: (01)930-6364.
**Church of England Industrial Committee,** Sec, Church House, Dean's Yard, Westminster, London SW1P 3NZ. T: (01)222-9011.
**Coventry Industrial Mission,** Senior Industrial Chaplain, Cathedral Offices, Priory Row, Coventry.
**Deanery of Priest-Workers,** Diocese of Southwark, Dean, 73 Woodbrook Rd, London SE2 0PB. T: (01)854-4509.
**Evangelical Urban Training Project,** Project Officer, St John's Church, Everton, Liverpool.
**French Protestant Industrial Mission (British Committee),** 22 The Gallop, Sutton, Surrey.
**Gateshead Team Ministry,** St Mary's Rectory, 347 Durham Rd, Gateshead, Tyne and Wear NE9 5AJ.
**Industrial Christian Fellowship (ICF),** Gen Sec, St Katharine Cree Church, Leadenhall St, London EC3. T: (01)283-5733/4.
**Sheffield Industrial Mission,** Senior Missioner, 2 Old Vicarage, Highgate, Sheffield S9 1WN. T: 42879. (Also: 19 Division St, Sheffield. T: 79452).
**South London Industrial Mission (SLIM),** Industrial Centre, Christ Church, 27 Blackfriars Rd, London SE1.

*USA*
**Apartment House Ministry,** 163-47 103rd Av, Queens, New York, NY.
**Board for Urban Ministry,** Rochester Area Council of Churches, 657 Main St, Rochester, NY 14604.
**Board of Metropolitan Strategy and Christian Social Relations,** 105 West Monument St, Baltimore, MD 21201.
**Boston Industrial Mission,** 56 Boylston St, Cambridge, MA 02138.
**Broadway Inner City Project,** 1654 Broadway, Indianapolis, IN 46202.
**Business Industrial Ministry,** Suite 301, 6804 Windsor Av, Berwyn, IL 60402.
**Catholic Committee on Urban Ministry,** PO Box 606, Notre Dame, IN 46556.
**Catholic Council on Working Life (CCWL),** 1307 South Wabash Av, Chicago, IL 60605.
**Center for Urban Encounter,** 2200 University Av, St Paul, MN 55114.
**Center of Metropolitan Mission in Service Training (COMMIT),** 817 West 34th St, Los Angeles, CA 90007.
**Chicago Business Project,** 19 South La Salle St, Chicago, IL 60603.
**Christian Associates of Metropolitan Erie (CAME),** Room 200, YMCA Bldg, Erie, PA 16501.
**Church and Industry Institute,** Wake Forest University, Box 7223, Winston-Salem, NC 27109.
**Church on the Dyke Ministry to Fishermen,** Box 2188, Texas City, TX 77591.
**Church on the East Side for Social Action (CESSA),** 3840 Fairview Av, Detroit, MI 48214.
**Cicero Industrial Ministry,** 247 Home, Oak Park, Illinois.
**Cincinnati Indiustrial Mission,** 1717 Section Rd, Cincinnati, OH 45237.
**Cleveland Inner City Protestant Parish,** 2230 Euclid Av, Cleveland, OH 44115.
**Cleveland Metropolitan Ministry,** 505 Hanna Bldg, Cleveland, OH 44115.
**Commission for Metropolitan Mission,** Northern California Council of Churches, San Francisco, California. (Also: Oakland-Berkeley, San José).
**Community Human and Resources Training,** 6 West 14th St, Cincinnati, OH 45210.
**Comprehensive Suburban Training Program,** 778 Sherman St, Denver, CO 80203.
**Cooperating Churches of East Harlem,** 2050 Second Av, New York, NY 10029.
**Core City Ministries,** 861 Galapago St, Denver, CO 80204.
**Denver Inner City Protestant Parish,** 910 Galapago St, Denver, CO 80204.
**Department of Urban Ministries,** United Methodist Church, 475 Riverside Drive, New York, NY 10027.
**Downtown Neighborhood Council,** Exec Dir, 303 East Spring St, New Albany, IN 47150. T: (812) 948-9248.
**East St Louis Metropolitan Ministry,** 6901 State St, East St, Louis, IL 62203.
**Ecumenical Metropolitan Ministry,** Puget Sound Region, 1551 10th Av East, Seattle, WA 98102.
**Evangelical Committee for Urban Ministries,** Back Bay Annex, 387 Shawmut Av, PO Box 606, Boston, MA 02117.
**Flint Industrial Mission,** 140 East Second St, Flint, MI 48502.
**Fresno Metropolitan Ministry,** Exec Dir, PO Box 2452, Fresno, CA 93723.
**Grand Rapids Area Council of Churches Night Ministry,** Federal Square Bldg, 29 Pearl St, Grand Rapids, MI 49502.
**Hawaii Interfaith Urban Coalition,** Catholic Social Services Bldg, Honolulu, Hawaii.
**House-Church Structure in Congregation,** Trinity Presbyterian Church, South High and Maryland Av, Harrisburg, Pennsylvania.
**Houston Metropolitan Ministries,** Exec Dir, 900 Lovett Blvd, Houston, TX 77006. T: (713)522-3955.
**HUB-CAP,** Greater Portland Council of Churches, 0245 SW Bancroft, Portland, OR 97204.
**Indianapolis Industrial Mission,** 4072 North Park Av, Indianapolis, Indiana.
**Inner City Indian Ministry,** 4540 NW 10th, Oklahoma City, OK 73127.
**Institute for Clergymen in Urban Ministry,** Case Western Reserve University, Cleveland, Ohio. T: (216)368-2140.
**Institute on the Church in Urban-Industrial Society (ICUIS),** Dir, 800 West Belden Av, Chicago, IL 60614.
**Inter Church Board for Metropolitan Affairs,** 209 South High St, Columbus, OH 43215.
**Interdenominational Directors of Urban Missions (IDUM),** 202 West Rittenhouse Square, Philadelphia, PA 19103.
**Internship for Clergymen in Urban Ministry,** 9606 Euclid, Cleveland, OH 44106.
**Joint Office of Urban & Industrial Ministries,** UPUSA, 475 Riverside Drive, New York, NY 10027.
**Joint Urban Ministry (JUM),** 1213 Delaware Av, Wilmington, DE 19806.
**Joint Urban Mission Program,** 122 West Franklin, Minneapolis, MN 55402.

**Lutheran Inner City Ministry,** 322 Ohio St, Racine, WI 53405.
**Market Place Ministries,** 5725 Duke St, Alexandria, Virginia.
**Metro North,** 105 East 22nd St, New York, NY 10010.
**Metropolitan Area Church Board,** 209 South High St, Columbus, OH 43215.
**Metropolitan Area Religious Coalition of Cincinnati (MARCC),** Room 920, 632 Vine St, Cincinnati, OH 45202. T: (513)721-4843. (Cable TV etc).
**Metropolitan Associates of Philadelphia,** Urban Study-Action Group, 101 South 13th St, Philadelphia, Pennsylvania.
**Metropolitan Churches United,** Exec Dir, 212 Belmonte Park E, PO Box 3, Dayton, OH 45402. T: (513)222-8654.
**Metropolitan Community Action Corporation,** Syracuse Area Council of Churches, 3049 East Genesee St, Syracuse, NY 13224.
**Metropolitan Corporation Mission,** 510 Broad St, Newark, New Jersey.
**Metropolitan Ecumenical Consultation on Christian Action (MECCA),** 601 Fifth Av, Watervliet, NY 12189.
**Metropolitan Ecumenical Ministry,** Exec Dir, 969 McCarter Highway, Newark, NJ 07102. T: (201) 623-9224.
**Metropolitan Interchurch Ministries,** 282 West Bowery St, Akron, OH 44307. T: (216)535-3112.
**Metropolitan Sacramento Urban Ministry,** PO Box 9368, Sacramento, CA 95816.
**Metropolitan Transaction Center,** Syracuse Area Council of Churches, 3049 East Genesee St, Syracuse, NY 13224.
**Metropolitan Urban Service Training Facility (MUST),** 235 East 49th St, New York, NY 10017.
**Miami Experimental Ministry,** 2600 NW 112th St, Miami, FL 33167.
**Ministry of the Protestant Chapel to the Christian Transient,** JFK International Airport, Jamaica, NY 11430.
**Ministry to Low Income Areas,** 120 Sigourney St, Hartford, CT 06105.
**Ministry to Night Workers,** 130 East Oak St, Chicago, IL 60611.
**Ministry to Seamen in Houston,** Trinity Presbyterian Church, 7000 Lawndale, Houston, TX 77023.
**Ministry to Single Women on Manhattan,** Ten Eyck Troughton, 145 East 39th St, New York, NY 10016.
**Mobile Home Ministry,** Box 15066, Broadview Station, Baton Rouge, LA 70815.
**National Center for Urban Ethnic Affairs,** 702 Lawrence St, NE, Washington, DC 20017.
**National Committee on Industrial Missions,** 10600 Puritan Av, Detroit, MI 48238.
**Native American Urban Transition Program,** 548 South Lincoln, Denver, CO 80209. (Amerindians).
**Near North Side Cooperative Ministry,** 2105 North Hudson, Chicago, Illinois.
**Near North Side Team Ministry,** Apt 102, 2231 Dickson Ct, St Louis, MO 63106.
**Night Ministry Project,** United Community Church, 4690 Weiss Rd, Saginaw, MI 48602.
**Northside Christian Ministry,** 1216 Brighton Rd, Pittsburgh, PA 15233.
**Northside Ecumenical Ministry,** 1004 Queen Av, Minneapolis, MN 55411.
**Pittsburgh Experiment,** Benedum-Trees Bldgs, Pittsburgh, PA 15222. T: (412)281-9578.
**Portland Action Committee Together,** 1925 SE Taylor St, Portland, OR 97214.
**Protestant Community Services,** Exec Dir, 304 North Church St, Rockford, IL 61101. T: (815) 965-8769.
**Racine Urban Ministry,** Exec Dir, 815 Silver St, Racine, WI 53404. T: (414)637-1341.
**Richmond Industrial Ministry,** 920 Earlham Drive, Richmond, IN 47374.
**Rochester Neighborhood Ministries,** 175 Genesee St, Rochester, NY 14611.
**St Paul's Urban Center,** 15th and J Sts, Sacramento, California.
**South Providence Neighborhood Ministry,** 747 Broad St, Providence, RI 02907.
**Stockton Metropolitan Ministry,** Exec Dir, PO Box 6201, Stockton, CA 95206.
**Street Ministry,** 715 West State St, Rockford, IL 61101.
**Taos Area Ecumenical Ministry,** Box 845, Taos, NM 87571.
**Taskforce for Research,** Urban Strategy Training (TRUST), Box 1313, Richmond, VA 23210.
**Tulsa Metropolitan Ministry,** 222 East Fifth St, Tulsa, OK 74103. T: (918)582-3147.
**UIM Documentation,** ICUS, 800 West Balden Av, Chicago, IL 60614.
**United Methodist Church Night Ministry,** 485 Appleton St, Holyoke, MA 01040.
**Urban Ministry,** PO Box 195, Holyoke, MA 01040.
**Urban Ministry,** 321 West South St, Kalamazoo, Michigan.
**Urban Training Centre for Christian Mission,** 21 East Van Buren St, Chicago, IL 60605. T: (312) 939-2762. (Also 40 North Ashland Av).
**Urban Training Organization of Atlanta,** 1026 Ponce de Leon Av, NE, Atlanta, Georgia.
**Urban Young Adult Action,** 74 Trinity Place, New York, NY 10006.
**Value Analysis Linkage with Urban Educational Systems (VALUES),** Center for Urban Affairs, 740 DeMun, St Louis, MO 63105.
**Wall Street Ministry,** 55 Liberty St, New York, NY 10005.
**Watertown Urban Mission,** 327 Franklin St, Watertown, NY 13601.
**West St Louis Ecumenical Parish,** Union Memorial Methodist Church, 1141 Belt, St Louis, MO 63112.
**Westside Cooperative Ministry,** Rockford, Illinois.
**Winder City Parish,** 48 Howe St, New Haven, Connecticut.
**Yokefellow Institute,** 920 Earlham Drive, Richmond, IN 47374.

*ZAMBIA*
**Church and Industry on the Copperbelt,** Christian Council of Zambia, PO Box 555, Kitwe.
**Commerce and Industry Programme,** Mindolo Ecumenical Foundation, PO Box 4093, Kitwe.

*ZIMBABWE*
**Christian Urban Programme,** Urban Sec, Christian Council of Rhodesia, PO Box 3566, Salisbury. T: 28500.

# 68
# Women in the Ordained Ministry

*Definition.* Organizations for women in the ordained ministry, diaconate or priesthood; associations, training schools, Bible and theological colleges for women only; deaconesses, deaconess orders, deaconess homes or houses, deaconess training institutions.
There are over 200 organizations of major significance in this field.

*AUSTRALIA*
**All Australia Anglican Deaconess Conference,** Deaconess House, 28 Carillon Av, Newton, NSW 2042. T: 511172. (Member, Diakonia).
**Methodist Deaconess Association,** Wesley House, Box 674 GPO, Brisbane, Q-4001. (Member, Diakonia).
**Presbyterian Deaconess Association of NSW,** Sec, Pittwood Home for Aged Ladies, 23 Charlotte St, Ashfield, NSW 2131. (Member, Diakonia).
**Presbyterian Deaconess Association of Victoria,** Sec, 130 Belford Rd, North Kew, Victoria 3102. (Member, Diakonia).

*AUSTRIA*
**Evangelische Diakonissenanstalt Gallneukirchen,** Ev Diakoniewerk, Hauptstr 3, A-4210 Gallneukirchen/Linz. (Member, Diakonia).

*BAHAMAS*
**Deaconess Order of the Methodist Church in the Caribbean & the Americas,** Box 497, Nassau. (Member, Diakonia).

*CANADA*
**Fellowship of Deaconesses and Other Professional Women Workers,** United Church of Canada, 6060 Côte Saint Luc Rd, Apt 206, Montréal 253, Québec. (Member, Diakonia).
**Order of Deaconesses of the Presbyterian Church in Canada,** Box 400, Harriston, Ontario. (Member, Diakonia).

*DENMARK*
**Association of Danish Deaconess Houses (Verband der Dänischen Diakonissenhäuser),** Danske Diakonissestiftelse, Kobenhavn F. (Member, Diakonia).

*FINLAND*
**Association of Deaconess Houses in Finland,** Büro, Diakonissalaitos, Alppikatu 2, Helsinki 53. (Member, Diakonia).

*FRANCE*
**Communauté des Diaconesses de Reuilly,** 95 Rue de Reuilly, F-75571 Paris. T: 343-5433, 345-7000.
**Fédération Nationale des Communautés de Diaconesses de France,** 10 Rue Porte de Buc, F-5800 Versailles. (Member, Diakonia).

*GERMAN DEMOCRATIC REPUBLIC*
**Konferenz Kaiserswerther Diakonissenhäuser in der DDR,** Diakonissen-Mutterhaus, DDR-59 Eisenach. (Member, Diakonia).

*GERMANY, Federal Republic of*
**Bund Deutscher Gemeinschafts-Diakonissen-Mutterhäuser,** Dir, Hildesheimer Str 8, Postfach 226, D-3353 Bad Gandersheim. (Member, Diakonia).
**Deaconess Community,** Escherheimerlandstr 122, D-6 Frankfurt/Main.
**Deaconess Community,** Wichernstr 4-8, D-44 Münster/Westf.
**Deaconess Community,** D-8806 Neuensdettelsau über Ansbach.
**Deaconess Community of Sarepta,** Bethal bei Bielfield.
**Diakonia (World Federation of Deaconess Associations/Ökumenischer Bund der Verbände von Diakonissen - Gemeinschaften/Alliance Oecuménique des Communautés et Associations de Diaconesses),** Sek, Glockenstr 8, D-1000 Berlin 37 (Zehlendorf). T: 846707.
**Diakonissen-Mutterhaus Aidlingen,** D-7031 Aidlingen. T: (07034)651. (1951; overseas sisters).
**Kaiserwerther Verband Deutscher Diakonissen-Mutterhäuser,** Hofstr 3, D-532 Bad Godesberg. (Member, Diakonia).
**Verband der Ev-Freikirchlichen Diakonissen-Mutterhäuser,** Diakonissenhaus Bethel, Clayallee 18-23, D-1000 Berlin 33. (Member, Diakonia).
**Verband der Ev-Freikirchlichen Diakonissen-Mutterhäuser in Deutschland, der Schweiz und Frankreich,** Martinistr 41-49, D-2 Hamburg 20.
**Zehlendorfer Verband für Evangelische Diakonie,** Dir, Glockenstr 8, D-1000 Berlin 37 (Zehlendorf). T: 846707. (Member, Diakonia).

*GHANA*
**Deaconess Order of the Methodist Church,** Ghana, PO Box 522, Kumasi. (Member, Diakonia).

*INDIA*
**Order for Women in the Church of South India,** PO Box 3, Erode, South India. (Member, Diakonia).
**Tamil Evangelical Lutheran Church Deaconesses,** Bethania Deaconess Home, 1084 Mission Church Rd, Thanjavur-613001. (Member, Diakonia).

*ITALY*
**Casa Valdese delle Diaconesse,** I-10066 Torre Pellice, Torino. (Member, Diakonia).

*JAMAICA*
**Deaconess Order of the Methodist Church in the Caribbean and the Americas,** UTCWC, Kingston. (Member, Diakonia).

*JAPAN*
**Bethsda Deaconess Mother House,** UCCJ, 526 Oizumigakuen-cho, Nerima-ku, Tokyo 177. (Member, Diakonia).
**Deaconess House,** Hamamatsu-Shi, Nikatabara-cho 3015, Juji No Sono. (Member, Diakonia).

*LEBANON*
**Deaconesses of Hülfsbund (Germany),** Armenian Evangelical High School, Bayrut. T: Anjar 4. (Evangelical).
**Deaconesses of Richen (Switzerland),** Institute for the Deaf, PO Box 4623, Bayrut. T: 420735. (Evangelical).

*MALAYSIA*
**Deaconesses of the Evangelical Lutheran Church in Malaysia,** 21 Djalan Abdul Samad, Kuala Lumpur. (Member, Diakonia).

*MEXICO*
**Escuela Metodista para Diaconisas,** Sedi Carnot 73, México 4, DF. T: 356570.

*NETHERLANDS*
**Verband Christlicher Krankernhäuser und Diakonissenmutterhäuser,** Ziekenhuiscentrum, Oudlaan 4, Utrecht. (Member, Diakonia).

*NEW ZEALAND*
**Anglican Deaconesses,** Diocese of Christchurch, 124 Elisabeth St, Christchurch 4. (Member, Diakonia)
**Deaconess Association,** Methodist Church of New Zealand, Box 931, Christchurch.
**Diakonia,** South East Asia and Pacific Regional Conference (1973), Chairman, Flat 9, 48 Carton Mill Rd, Christchurch 1. (Member, Diakonia).
**Presbyterian Deaconess Association,** 23a Frederick St, Lower Hutt. (Member, Diakonia).

*NIGERIA*
**Church Sisters of the Presbyterian Church of Nigeria,** Nigerian Deaconesses, Creektown, Calabar, SE State. (Member, Diakonia).

*NORWAY*
**Norwegian Deaconesses Association of the Methodist Church,** Sosterhjemmet Betanien, Akersbakken 35, Oslo 1. (Member, Diakonia).
**Norwegian Lutheran Diaconesses Association,** Loviesnberggt 15, Oslo. (Member, Diakonia).

*PAKISTAN*
**United Biblical Training Centre,** Gujranwala. (Short term and residential courses for women).

*PHILIPPINES*
**Central Conference Commission on Deaconess Work of the United Methodist Church,** Harris Memorial College, PO Box 1174, Manila D-406. (Member, Diakonia).

*SOUTH AFRICA*
**Deaconess Order of the Methodist Church of South Africa,** 120 de Korte St, Clifton, Johannesburg. (Member, Diakonia).

*SURINAM*
**Surinam Deaconess Order (Surinaamse Stichting Diakonessenarbeid),** Madeliefjesstraat 32, Paramaribo. (Member, Diakonia).

*SWEDEN*
**Church of Sweden Deaconess Board (Svenska Kyrkans Diakoni-NAMND),** Gen Sec, Erstagatan 1, S-11636 Stockholm SÖ. (Member, Diakonia).

*SWITZERLAND*
**Arbeitsgemeinschaft für den Diakonischen Einsatz,** Präs, Sihlstr 33, Postfach 384, CH-8021 Zürich. T: (051)238899
**Deaconess Community of Bern,** Schanzlistr 43, Bern.
**Deaconess House of Saint-Loup,** par Pompaple's Vaud.
**Diakonenhaus St Stephanus,** CH-8803 Rüschlikon. T: (051)927183.
**Konferenz der Schweizerischen Diakonissenhäuser,** Diakonissenwerk Neumünster, CH-8125 Zollikerberg. (Member, Diakonia).
**Schweizerische Reformierte Diakonenhaus,** CH-8606 Greifensee. T: (051)871682.

*UK OF GB & NI*
**Anglican Group for the Ordination of Women to the Historic Ministry of the Church,** 29 Thurloe Court, Fulham Rd, London SW3. (Also: Hon Sec, Guillard's Oak House, Midhurst, West Sussex).
**Church of Scotland Deaconess Board,** Room 306, 121 George St, Edinburgh 2. (Member, Diakonia).
**Church Sisters of the Presbyterian Church in Ireland,** Women's Home Mission, Church House, Belfast 1, NI. (Member, Diakonia).
**Council for Women's Ministry in the Church,** Gen Sec, Church House, Dean's Yard, Westminster, London SW1. T: (01)222-9011.
**Deaconess Association of the United Reformed Church of England,** 373 Andover St, Sheffield S3 9ER, South Yorkshire. (Member, Diakonia).
**Deaconess Community of St Andrew,** Mother Superior, St Andrew's House, 12 Tavistock Crescent, London W11. T: (01)229-2662. (Anglican).
**Deaconess Order of Anglican Accredited Lay Workers Federation,** Church of England, St Wilfreds' House, Brayton, Selby, North Yorkshire. (Member, Diakonia).
**Deaconess Order of the United Reformed Church of England,** Church Cottage, Manaton, Newton Abbot, Devon. (Member, Diakonia).
**Gilmore House,** Head Deaconess, 113 North Side, Clapham Common, London SW4. T: (01)228-2130.
**Order of Baptist Deaconesses,** Baptist Church House, 4 Southampton Rd, London WC1B 4AB. (Also: 4 Ash Tree Walk, Leeds LS14 5NG. T: 649436). (Member, Diakonia).
**Society for the Ministry of Women in the Church,** Sec, 93 Hatherley Court, Hatherley Grove, London W2. T: (01)229-3197.
**Wesley Deaconess Order of the Methodist Church,** Ilkley House, 7 Pritchatts Rd, Birmingham B15 2QU. (Member, Diakonia).

*USA*
**American Lutheran Church Deaconesses,** Deaconess House, 2224 W Kilbourn Av, Milwaukee, WI 53233. (Member, Diakonia).
**Deaconess Association of the Lutheran Church Missouri Synod,** Deaconess Hall, Union St, Valparaiso, IN 46383. (Member, Diakonia).
**Deaconess Home Missionary Service of the United Methodist Church,** Exec Sec, Room 326, 475 Riverside Drive, New York, NY 10027. (Member, Diakonia).
**Deaconesses of the Episcopal Church in the USA,** Central Home for Deaconesses, 1914 Orrington Av, Evanston, IL 60201. (Member, Diakonia).
**Deaconesses of the United Church of Christ,** 6150 Oakland Av, St Louis, MO 63139. (Member, Diakonia).
**International Association of Women Ministers,** Gen Sec, 4116 South Landes St, Marion, IN 46952.
**LCA Deaconess Community,** Lutheran Church in America, Exec Sec, 2900 Queen Lane, Philadelphia, PA 19129 (Member, Diakonia).
**Women's Institute of the Boston Theological Institute,** 99 Brattle St, Cambridge, MA 02138.

# 69
# Women's Lay Organizations

*Definition.* Groups for lay women and girls only, emphasizing the role or lay ministry of women, the place of women in church and society; women's lay orders, mothers' and wives' groups, women's rights, women's liberation movements, feminist movements, women's caucuses, task forces, co-ordinating agencies; YWCA and organizations serving women and girls; women's home or foreign missionary societies; and other movements either radical or conservative.
Christian organizations of major significance in this field number over 500.
This listing omits most of the multifold national branches of the YWCA and ACISJF except major international headquarters.

*ARGENTINA*
**Organismo Latinoamericano de la Unión Mundial de Organizaicones Femeninas Católicas (UMOFC),** Gelly y Obes 2213, Buenos Aires.
**Orientación para la Joven,** Montevideo 1440, Buenos Aires. (RC. Member, ACISJF).

*AUSTRALIA*
**Vocational Centre for Girls,** 15 Jephson St, Toowong, Queensland 4066. T: Brisbane (072) 217526.

*AUSTRIA*
**ACISJF,** Katholische Frauenwerk in Österriech, Stephansplatz 6, A-1010 Wien.
**Katholische Frauenbewegung Österreiche (Austrian Catholic Women's Movement),** Stephansplatz 6/V, A-1010 Wien.
**Katholische Frauenwerk Österreichenentwicklungshilfe,** Stephansplatz 6, A-1010 Wien. T: 525531,524646/48.
**Ökumenischer Arbeitkreis der Frauen,** Schweglerstr 39, A-1150 Wien.
**Seminar für Kirchliche Frauen Berufe,** Wolfrathplatz 2, Wien 13.

*BARBADOS*
**Caribbean Church Women (CCW),** CADEC, PO Box 616, Bridgetown.

*BELGIUM*
**ACISJF,** Accueil et Orientation, Av des Ormeaux 26, B-1180 Brussel.
**Auxilaires Féminines Internationales (AFI),** Rue Gachard 13 & 84, Brussel 5. T: (02)472039. (RC).
**Fédération des Foyer Belges de l'YWCA,** Rue St Bernard 43, B-1060 Brussel. T: 372876.
**Fédération Nationale des Patros de Jeunes Fillets (FNPF),** Chausée de Châtelet 48, B-6060 Gilly. T: (071)412026.
**Groupe International 'Femmes et Hommes dans l'Eglise',** Rue de la Prévoyance 58, B-1000 Brussel. T: (02)131749.
**St Joan's International Alliance,** Belgian Section, Av Brugmann 213, B-18 Brussel.
**Vie Féminine (VF),** Rue de la Poste 111, B-1030 Brussel. T: (02)2172952. (Member, WMCW).

*BOLIVIA*
**Orientación para la Joven,** Casilla 2573, La Paz. (RC. Member, ACISJF).

*BRAZIL*

**ACISJF**, Orientação da Joven, Rua Pereira da Silva 251, Laranjeiras, Rio de Janeiro, GB. (RC).

**Associação Feminina do Rio de Janeiro**, Av Franklin Roosevelt 84, 10 andar, Rio de Janeiro, GB. T: 2425358,2426786.

**Confédération Internationale du Guidisme (GISC)**, Av Maréchal Camara 186, 20000 Rio de Janeiro.

*BURMA*

**Burmese Women's Bible School**, Seminary Hill, Insein.

**Karen Women Bible School**, Seminary Hill, Insein.

*CANADA*

**Baptist Women's Missionary Society of Ontario and Quebec**, Exec Sec, 188-190 St George St, Toronto 5, Ontario.

**Christian Women's Clubs**, 25 Blue Ridge, Willowdale, Ontario.

**National Council of the YWCA**, 571 Jarvis St, Toronto 285, Ontario. T: 921-2117.

**Pioneer Girls**, 2320 Fairview St, Burlington, Ontario.

**Women Missionary Society Regular Baptists of Canada**, 75 Lowther Av, Toronto 5, Ontario.

**Women's Inter-Church Council**, 77 Charles St West, Toronto 181, Ontario. T: (416) 922-6177.

*CHILE*

**Orientación para la Joven**, Erasmo Escala 1822, Santiago. (RC. Member, ACISJF).

*CHINA*

**YWCA**, 123 Tibet Rd, Shanghai.

*CHINA (TAIWAN)*

**Tribal Girls Bible School**, 1-3 Tieh Shan Rd, Puli, Hantou Hsien.

*COLOMBIA*

**Orientación para la Joven**, Carrera 15 No 42-45, Bogotá. (RC. Member, ACISJF).

*DOMINICAN REPUBLIC*

**Comité de Orientación a la Joven**, Santomé 94, Santo Domingo. (RC. Member, ACISJF).

*FRANCE*

**Auxiliaires Missionnaires de l'Assomption (AMA)**, 17 Rue de l'Assomption, F-75016 Paris.

**Conférence Internationale Catholique du Guidisme (CICD)/International Catholic Conference of Guiding**, Sec, 65 Rue de la Glacière, F-75013 Paris. T: (01)707-8559.

**Fédération Française des Mouvements et Services Féminins (YWCA)**, Jeunes Femmes, 8 Villa du Parc Montsouris, F-75014 Paris. T: 5895569.

**Groupe International 'Femmes et Hommes dans l'Eglise'**, Section Parisienne, 72 Rue de Sèvres, F-75006 Paris.

**International Grail Movement**, Secretariat, 22 Rue du Dr Germain Sée, F-75016 Paris.

**Salésiennes Auxiliaires des Missions (SADM)**, 50 Rue de Bourgogne, F-75007 Paris.

**Services de la Jeunesse Féminine**, 70 Av Denfert-Rochereau, F-75014 Paris. (RC. Member, ACISJF).

**Union Mondiale des Organisations Féminines Catholiques/World Union of Catholic Women's Organizations (WUCWO)**, Secretariat, 20 Rue Notre-Dame-des-Champs, F-75006 Paris. T: (01) 705-2221. (Also: 98 Rue de l'Université, Paris 7).

*GERMAN DEMOCRATIC REPUBLIC*

**Frauenhilfe der EKD**, Behlertstr 1A, DDR-15 Potsdam.

*GERMANY, Federal Republic of*

**Aktionsgemeinschaft für Verantwortliche Mitarbeit der Frau in der Katholischen Kirche/Working Group for Responsible Co-operation of Women in the Catholic Church**, Weihergartenstr 20, D-65 Mainz.

**Arbeitsgemeinschaft für Ev Schülerinnen- und Frauen-Bibel-Kreise (MBK Mission)**, Hermann-Löns-Str 14, D-4902 Bad Salzuflen. (Girls secondary school and women's Bible groups).

**Bayerischer Mutterdienst der Ev-Lutherischen Kirche**, Deutenbacherstr 1, D-8504 Stein über Nürnberg.

**Bischöflichen Diozesanstelle für die Frauenseelsorge und Frauenarbeit**, Willigstr 4, Mainz.

**Bund Altkatholischen Frauen**, Gregor-Mendel-Str 28, D-53 Bonn. T: 232285. (Old Catholic).

**Bund Christlicher Pfadfinderinnen**, Post Rödelsee, D-8711 Schloss Schwanberg.

**Deutscher Evangelischer Frauenbund**, Bodekerstr 59, D-3 Hannover. (Also: Unterlindau 80, D-6 Frankfurt).

**Deutscher Frauen - Missions - Gebetsbund-Arbeitsgruppe West**, Heisterkamp 18 (and Kleekamd 3), D-2000 Hamburg 63. T: (040)5385478.

**Deutscher Verband Katholischer Mädchensozialarbeit**, Werthmannhaus, Karlstr 40, Postfach 420, D-78 Freiburg. T: (0761)2001. (Member, ACISJF).

**Evangelische Frauenarbeit in Deutschland**, Geschäftsstelle, Unterlindau 80 (and Westendstr 89), D-6 Frankfurt/Main.

**Evangelische Frauenhilfe in Deutschland**, Geschäftsstelle, Bahnhofstr 24, D-44 Münster. (Also: Unterlindau 80, D-6 Frankfurt).

**Evangelische Weibliche Jugend Deutschlands (YWCA)**, Burckhardthaus, Herzbachweg 3, D-6460 Gelnhausen. T: (06051)5021/3.

**Frauenmission Malche**, Portastr 8, D-4954 Barkhausen a.d. Porta. T: (0571)7552. (Begun 1898).

**Frauenseminar für Entwicklungshilfe**, Robert-schumannstr 25, D-51 Aachen.

**Haus der Katholischen Frauen**, Prinz Georgstr 44, D-4 Düsseldorf.

**International Grail Movement**, German Centre, 470 Duisburgstr, D-Mülheim.

**Katholischer Deutscher Frauenbund**, Kaessenstr 18, D-5 Köln.

**Mission der Ev Schulerinnen- und Frauen-Bibelkreise (MBK)**, Hermann-Löns-Str 14, Postfach 560, D-4902 Bad Salzuflen. T: 50088/9.

**Morgenländische Frauenmission**, Finckensteinallee 21-27, D-1000 Berlin 45. T: (030)8337031. (Begun 1842).

**Päpstliches Werk der Missionsvereinigung Katholischen Frauen und Jungfrauen**, Raven-steynstr 26, D-5400 Koblenz-Pfarrendorf.

**Pfarrfrauenbund**, Melittastr 10, D-7 Stuttgart-Degerloch. (Pastors' wives).

**St Joan's International Alliance**, German Section, Burgstr 3, Viersen. (RC).

**Sozialdienst Katholischer Frauen**, Agnes-Neuhaus-Str 5, D-4600 Dortmund. T: (0231) 528126/7.

**Zentralverband der Katholischen Frauen und Muttergemeinschaften Deutschland**, Haus 21b, D-7801 Wittnau.

*GREECE*

**Foyer International Divine Providence**, 52 Rue Capodistriou, Athínai 102. (Member, ACISJF; Catholic).

*HOLY SEE*

**Ecumenical Women's Liaison Group**, Consilium de Laicis, Piazza San Callisto 16, I-00120 Città del Vaticano.

*INDIA*

**Asian Church Women's Conference**, St Stephen House, 4 Rajpur Rd, New Delhi 1106.

**Tabita Bible School for Girls**, Govindpur, Bihar.

**Training Institute for Women**, Tamil Evangelical Lutheran Church, Mayuram, Tanjore Dt, Tamil Nadu.

**YWCA of India**, Parliament St, New Delhi 1. T: 45294,43561.

*INDONESIA*

**HKBP Women's Bible School (Sekolah Bijbel Vrouw HKBP)**, Laguboti, Tapanuli Utara.

*IRELAND*

**International Catholic Girls' Society (ACISJF)**, 91 Lower Baggot St, Dublin.

*ISRAEL*

**YWCA of Jerusalem**, Sheikh Jarrah Quarter, Wadil Joz St, Jerusalem. T: 82593.

*ITALY*

**Associazione Guida Italiane**, Via Alpi 30, I-00198 Roma. (Member, BICE).

**Ausiliarie Femminili Internazionali (AFI)**, Via Filipo Lippi 45, I-20131 Milano. T: 225828. (Also: Via di Villa Albani 20, I-00198 Roma).

**Centro Italiano Femminile (CIF)**, Via Carlo Zucchi 25, I-00165 Roma. T: 6221167,6221436, 6221507.

**Collegio Universitario Missionario Internazionale Femminile (CUMIF)**, Via Santa Brigida 8, I-35100 Padova. T: 35175. (Also: Via Acquetta 12, Padova).

**Comitato Nazionale Italiano AC Servizio della Giovane**, Via Urbana 158, I-00184 Roma. (RC. Member, ACISJF).

**Gruppo Femminile Missionarie**, Via Trino 24, I-15033 Casale Monferrato (Alessandria).

**Scuola Biblica Femminile/Istituto Betania**, Via Antelao 14, Monte Sacro, Roma. T: 890941.

**Unione Cristiana delle Giovani (YWCA)**, Via Balbo 4, I-00184 Roma. T: 474525.

*JAPAN*

**Woman's Union Missionary Society**, 221 Yamate, Naka-ku, Yokohama-shi 231.

*KENYA*

**National Council of Catholic Women**, PO Box 48437 or 48062, Nairobi. T: 21613.

*KOREA, South*

**Hanil Women's Seminary**, Wha San Dong 149, Chulla Pukto, Chonju.

**Taejon Women's Biblical Seminary**, 347 Sunwha Dong, Taejon-shi.

*MEXICO*

**Association Catholique Internationale des Services de la Jeunesse Féminine**, Secrétariat Latino-Américain, 89 Av Oaxaca, México 7, DF.

**Asociación Cristiana Femenina (ACF) (YWCA)**, Humboldt 62, México 1, DF. T: 5850655.

**Bolletin Documental sobre la Mujer**, CIDAL, Rio Fuerte 3, Cuernevaca, Morelos.

**Federación Mundial de la Juventud Femenina Católica (FMJFC)**, Secretariado Regional para América Latina, Apdo Postal 1143, México 1, DF.

**Juventud Católica Femenina Mexicana (Movimiento Estudiantil y Professional)**, Tabasco 264, México.

**Orientación a la Joven**, International Catholic Girls' Society (ACISJF), Latin American Secretariat, Av Oaxaca 89, México 7, DF.

**Unión Nacional Interdenominacional de Sociedades Femeniles Cristianas**, Apdo 1415, Zona 1, México, DF.

*NETHERLANDS*

**Catholic Women's Guild (Katholiek Vrouwengilde)**, Heusdenhoutseweg 13, Breda.

**Catholic Women's Society (Katholiek Vrouwendispuut)**, Kameelstraat 6, Nijmegen.

**Co-operation of Men and Women in the Church (Werkgroep Samenwerking Man-Vrouw in de Kerk)**, de Horst 1, Driebergen. T: (03438)2241.

**International Grail Movement (De Graal)**, International Secretariat, Koningslaan 30, Amsterdam.

**International Union of Liberal Christian Women (IULCW)**, 40 Laan Copes van Cattenburch, 's-Gravenhage. T: 558360.

**Netherlands Union of Reformed Women's Movements (Nederlandse Bond van Gereformeerde Vrouwenverenigingen)**, Steynlaan 8, Baarn.

**Reformed Women's Service (Hervormde Vrouwen Dienst)**, Oude Arnhemseqweg 281, Zeist.

**YWCA (Christen Jonge Vrouwen Federatie, CJVF)**, FC Dondersstraat 23, Utrecht. T: (030) 715525.

*NEW ZEALAND*

**Girl's Brigade (NZ)**, PO Box 5141, Wellesley St, Auckland.

**YWCA**, 33 Tory St, Courtenay Place, PO Box 9315, Wellington C1. T: 558363.

*NORWAY*

**Norwegian Catholic Women's Federation**, PO Box 281, N-1371 Asker.

**St Catherine's (Sankta Katarinajhemmet)**, Dominican Sisters, 8 Gjorstads Gate, N-Oslo. (Member, ACISJF).

**Sisters Missionary Guild (Skepleierskeres Misjonsring)**, Johs Brungst 12c, Oppgang B, Oslo.

**Women Missionary Workers (Kvinnelige Misjonsarbeidere)**, Storgt 38, Oslo 1.

**YWCA (Norges KFUK)**, Holbergspl 1, Oslo 1. T: 204475.

*PAKISTAN*

**Women's Union Missionary Society**, Women's Christian Hospital, 85 Nusrat Rd, Multan.

*PANAMA*

**Federación Nacional de Mujeres Católicas**, Apdo 8714, Panamá. (Member, ACISJF).

*PARAGUAY*

**Orientación para la Joven**, Independencia Nacional 1060, Asunción. (RC. Member, ACISJF).

*PERU*

**Asociación de Orientación para la Joven**, Calle Roma 452, San Isidro, Lima. (RC. Member, ACISJF).

*PORTUGAL*

**ACISJF**, Travessa do Ferragial 1, Lisboa. (RC. Member, ACISJF).

**Senhoras Evangélicas Unidas de Portugal**, Rua da Bela Vista 5-1, Cascais.

**União Cristã da Mocidade Feminina**, Rua Santana a Lapa 157/2D, Lisboa-3.

**União Cristã Feminina**, Rua do Arco a S Mamede 9/3D, Lisboa-2.

*SRI LANKA*

**Asian Church Women's Conference**, 28 Hotel Rd, Mt Lavinia, Colombo.

*SWEDEN*

**Girls' Association**, Dominican Sisters, 21 Villagatan, S-Stockholm. (Member, ACISJF).

**Missionary Society of Swedish Women (Svenska Kvinnors Missionsförenining)**, Kungsgatan 28, S-751 05 Uppsala. T: (018)120240.

**Swedish Ecumenical Women's Council (Sveriges Ekumeniska Kvinnorad)**, Kungsholms Kyrkoplan 4, S-111 24 Stockholm. T: (08)522142.

**Women Missionary Workers (Kvinnliga Missionsarketare)**, Birger Jarlsgatan 67, S-113 56 Stockholm. T: (08)304884.

**Women Teachers' Missionary Association (Lärarinnornas Missionsförening)**, Vasaplatsen 4, S-411 34 Göteborg. T: (031)112440.

*SWITZERLAND*

**Alliance Mondiale des Unions Chrétiennes Féminine (YWCA)**, 37 Quai Wilson, CH-1201 Genève. T: 323100.

**Alliance Nationale Suisse des Unions Chrétiennes Féminines (UCF)/Schweizerischer Nationalverband Christliche Vereine Junger Frauen (CVJF)**, 15 Av Virgile-Rossel, CH-1012 Lausanne. T: (021)324334. (YWCA).

**Association Catholique Internationale des Services de la Jeunesse Féminine (ACISJF)/International Catholic Girls Society**, International Secretariat, 1 Route du Jura, CH-1700 Fribourg. T: (037)223727. (Protection of girls isolated from families).

**Association des Femmes de Pasteurs de Genève**, 9 Rue des Alpes, CH-1201 Genève. T: (022)324898.

**Auxilaires Feminines Internationales (AFI)**, 31/91 Rue de la Servette, CH-1202 Genève. T: 330907.

**Co-operation of Men and Women in Church, Family and Society**, WCC, 150 Route de Ferney, CH-1211 Genève 20.

**Evangelischer Frauenbund der Schweiz**, Schönaustr 27, CH-5430 Wettingen. T: (056)66668.

**Schweizerische Evangelische Verband Frauenhilfe**, Gryphenhübeliweg 45, CH-3000 Bern. T: (031) 447782.

**Schweizerische Pfarrfrauenvereiniqung**, CH-8303 Bassersdorf/ZH.

*UK OF GB & NI*

**British League of Unitarian & Other Liberal Christian Women**, Essex Hall, 1/6 Essex St, London, WC2R 3HY.

**Catholic Guide Advisory Council**, 17 Buckingham Palace Rd, London SW1.

**Catholic Women's League**, Scottish National Council, 53 Greenock Rd, Largs. T: (046)57-3442.

**Catholic Women's League**, 23 Eccleston St, London SW1W 9LX. T: (01)730-6157.

**Girls Friendly Society and Townsend Fellowship**, Gen Sec, Townsend House, Greycoat Place, London SW1. T: (01)834-3524.

**Girls' Brigade**, International Council, Brigade House, 8 Parsons Green, London SW6 4TH. T: (01) 736-8481.

**International Catholic Girls' Society (ACISJF)**, Rooms 16-17, 1st Floor, 39 Victoria St, London SW1H 0EE. T: (01)799-4588.

**International Union of Liberal Christian Women (IULCW)**, Sec, 86 Chatsworth Rd, Croydon CR0 1HB, Surrey. T: 7803.

**Ladies of Charity and Companions of St Vincent**, 39 Blakehall Rd, London E11 2QQ. T: (01)989-1336.

**Missionary Settlement for University Women (Bombay)**, Annandale, North End Rd, Golders Green, London NW11 7QX. T: (01)455-0510.

**Mothers' Union**, Central Sec, Mary Sumner House, 24 Tufton St, London SW1P 3RB. T: (01)222-5533.

**National Board of Catholic Women**, 67 Bodley Rd, New Malden, Surrey KT3 5QJ. T: (01)942-3738.

**Relief and Refugee Committee**, Catholic Women's League, 21b Soho Square, London W1V 6NR. T: (01)437-4509.

**St Joan's International Alliance**, International Secretariat, Newman House, 15 Carlisle St, London W1. T: (01)437-4564. (RC).

**Scottish Catholic Guiders' Advisory Committee**, 16 Coates Crescent, Edinburgh 3. T: (031)225-3455.

**Union of Catholic Mothers**, 47 Oakdene Drive, Surbiton, Surrey KT5 9NH. T: (01)337-2196.

**Women Together**, 1 Claremont St, Belfast BT9 6AP, N Ireland. T: 26446. (Peace movement among women).

**Womens' Missionary Association**, 86 Tavistock Place, London WC1. (Formerly Presbyterian Church of England).

**Women's Protestant Union**, Sec, Clive Court, Ashdown Av, Saltdean, East Sussex. T: Brighton 31145. (From 1891-1969, World Protestant Union).

**Womens' Social Services in Gt Britain & Ireland (Salvation Army)**, 280 Mare St, Hackney, London E8 1HE. T: (01)985-1181,1801.

**World Women's Christian Temperance Union (WWCTU)**, Pres, 62 Becmead Av, London SW16 1UP. T: (01)769-6649.

**Young Women's Christian Association (YWCA)**, Gen Sec, National HQ, 2 Weymouth St, London W1N 4AX. T: (01)636-9722/6.

**YWCA for Ireland**, 3-5 Malone Rd, Belfast BT9 6RT, NI.

*USA*

**Archconfraternity of Christian Mothers**, Exec Sec, 220 37th St, Pittsburgh, PA 15201. T: (412) 683-2400.

**Board of American Lutheran Church Women**, Pres, 422 South 5th St, Minneapolis, MN 55415.

**Board of Missions Women's Division**, United Methodist Church, 475 Riverside Drive, New York, NY 10027. T: (212)749-0700.

**Board of Women's Work**, Baptist General Conference, 5750 North Ashland Av, Chicago, IL 60626.

**Christian Women's Benevolent Association**, 6600 Washington Av, St Louis, MO 63130.

**Church Women United**, 475 Riverside Drive, New York, NY 10027. T: (212)870-2347.

**Committee on Christian Literature for Women and Children in Mission Fields**, 475 Riverside Drive, New York, NY 10027.

**Eastern Orthodox Women's Guild**, 3256 Warren Rd, Cleveland, OH 44111.

**Freedom for Women Project**, National Association of the Laity, Suite 21-D, 7 East 14th St, New York, NY 10003. (RC).

**Grail Movement**, Grailville, Loveland, OH 45140. T: (513)683-2340. (RC, now ecumenical. Married and single women).

**International Union of Liberal Christian Women**, Center Lovell, ME 04016.

**Joint Committee of Organizations Concerned with the Status of Women in the Church**, Apt 115, 1600 Sunset Av, Waukegan, IL 60085. (Also: 3901 Livingston St, NW, Washington, DC 20015). (Mostly RC).

**Lutheran Church Women**, 231 Madison Av, New York, NY 10016. T: (212)532-3410.

**Lutheran Women's Missionary League Missouri Synod**, Sec, 3558 South Jefferson Av, St Louis, MO 63118.

**National Council of American Baptist Women**, Exec Dir, Valley Forge, PA 19481.

**National Council of Catholic Women**, 1312 Massachusetts Av, NW Washington, DC 20005. T: (202)659-6810. (Member, ACISJF).

**National Organization for Women (NOW)**, Ecumenical Task Force on Women and Religion, 1942 El Dorado Av, Berkeley, CA 94707.

**National Women's Christian Temperance Union**, 1730 Chicago Av, Evanston, IL 60201.

**National Women's Missionary Society**, Church of God (Anderson), 1303 East 5th St, PO Box 2328, Anderson, IN 46011.

**National YWCA Resource Center on Women**, 600 Lexington Av, New York, NY 10022.

**Nazarene World Missionary Society**, Sec, 6401 The Paseo, Kansas City, MO 64131. T: (816) 333-7000. (Formerly Women's Foreign Missionary Society).

**New York Task Force on Women in Changing Institutions**, 99 Claremont Av, NY 10027. (Interdenominational).

**Office of Women's Affairs**, Graduate Theological Union, 2465 LeConte Av, Berkeley, CA 94709. (Ecumenical).

**Philadelphia Task Force on Women in Religion (PTFWR)**, PO Box 24003, Philadelphia, PA 19139.

**Pioneer Girls**, 11 North Cross St, Box 788, Wheaton, IL 60187.

**St Joan's International Alliance**, US Branch, 435 West 119th St, New York, NY 10027. (RC).

**Senior Women's Auxiliary**, National Baptist Convention of America, 2315 Harlem Av, Baltimore, MD 21216.

**Task Force on Women in Church and Society**, United Church of Christ, 297 Park Av South, New York, NY 1001.

**Task Force on Women**, United Presbyterian Church USA, Board of Christian Education, 730 Witherspoon Bldg, Philadelphia, PA 19107.

**Unitarian Universalist Women's Federation**, 25 Beacon St, Boston, MA 02108.

**United Fellowship for Christian Service**, 72 County Rd, Tenafly, NJ 07670. T: (212)929-3575. (Formerly Women's Union Missionary Society).

**United Foursquare Women**, Angelus Temple, 1100 Glendale Blvd, Los Angeles, CA 90026.

**United Presbyterian Women**, UPUSA, 475 Riverside Drive, New York, NY 10027.

**United Society of Friends Women**, Friends United Meeting, RR 2, Marshalltown, IA 50158.

**Woman Volunteers Association,** 1671 Madison St, NW, Washington, DC 20011.
**Women's Auxiliary Church of God,** Keith St at 25th, NW, Cleveland,. TN 37311. T: (615)472-3361.
**Women's Auxiliary Convention Free-Will Baptists,** 1134 Murfreesbord Rd, Nashville, TN 37217.
**Women's Auxiliary,** National Baptist Convention of USA, 584 Arden Park, Detroit, MI 48202.
**Women's Congress National Primitive Baptist Convention,** 2112 Russell St, Charlotte, NC 28208.
**Women's Home & Foreign Mission Society,** AME Zion Church, 7405 Monticello St, Pittsburg, PA 15208.
**Women's Home and Foreign Mission Society,** Advent Christian Church, Box 117, Arlington, MA 02174.
**Women's Missionary Association,** General Conference Mennonite Church, 722 Main St, Newton, KS 67114.
**Women's Missionary Association,** United Brethren in Christ, Exec Sec, 411 UB Bldg, Huntington, IN 46750.
**Women's Missionary Council,** Assemblies of God, 1445 Boonville Av, Springfield, MO 65802.
**Women's Missionary Society,** AME Church, 1541 14th St, NW, Washington, DC 20005.
**Women's Missionary Society,** Wesleyan Church, Swayzee Rd at Highway 37, PO Box 2000, Marion, IN 46952. T: (317)674-3301.
**Women's Missionary Union,** Southern Baptist Convention, 600 North 20th St, Birmingham, AL 35203.
**Women's Rights Committee,** National Association of the Laity, 2303 Canterbury Rd, University Heights, OH 44118. (RC).
**World Federation of Methodist Women (WFMW),** 475 Riverside Drive, New York, NY 10027.
**YWCA of the USA,** 600 Lexington Av, New York, NY 10022. T: (212)753-4700.

*URUGUAY*
**Orientación para la Joven,** Palmar 2519, Montevideo. (RC. Member, ACISJF).

*ZAMBIA*
**Women's Training Centre,** Mindolo Ecumenical Centre, PO Box 1493, Kitwe.

# 70
# Workers' & Professionals' Associations

*Definition.* Organizations and movements bringing together or uniting Christians who are labourers or workers (labour, industry) or Christians working in the various secular professions (arts, journalism, legal, medical, scientific, teaching, business, social service, welfare workers); Christian (mainly Catholic) workers' movements and labour or trade unions; secular trade unions retaining Christian names, principles or other ties; young workers' associations; federations or unions of workers' or professionals' associations; professional associations. For religious professionals, see CLERGY-LAY AND CLERGY ORGANIZATIONS, SCHOLARLY SOCIETIES, etc.

Christian organizations for workers or professionals, significant at the national or wider levels, number over 400.

*ARGENTINA*
**Confederación Argentina Católica de Educadores (CACE),** Brasil 721, Buenos Aires.
**Federación de Circulos Católicos de Obreros,** Junin 1063, Buenos Aires. (Workmen's clubs).

*AUSTRIA*
**Berufsgruppe Fürsorgerinnen in der Katholische Frauenbewegung,** Stephansplatz 6, A-1010 Wien. (Member, UCISS. Women welfare officers).
**Fraktion Christlicher Gewerkschaftler im OGB,** Hohenstaufengasse 10-12, A-Wien 1. T: 633711. (Member, WCL).
**KAJ (JOC),** Klappe 78, A-56 Tür.
**Katholischer Akademikerverbard,** Währingerstr 2-4, A-1090 Wien IX. T: 346165.
**Katholische Arbeiterbewegung Österreichs (KAB),** Stephansplatz 6/5, A-1010 Wien. (Member, WMCW).
**Katholische Lehrerschaft Österreichs (KLO),** Stephansplatz 5, II Stiege, IV Stock, A-1010 Wien 1.

*BELGIUM*
**Association des Dirigeants et Cadres Chrétiens (ADIC),** Blvd Lambermont 140, B-1030 Brussel. T: (02)2418677.
**Catholic Workers Union (Katolieke Werkliedenbonden, KWB),** Rue de la Lo i135, B-1040 Brussel. (Member, WMCW).
**Christian Women Workers Union (Kristelijke Arbeiders Vrouwengilden, KAV),** Poststaat 111, B-1030 Brussel. (Member, WMCW).
**Confédération des Syndicats Chrétiens de Belgique (CSC) (Algemeen Christelijk Vakverbond, ACV),** Rue de la Loi 121 & 135, B-1040 Brussel. T: (02)7356090. (Links with Catholic Church; 965,000 members, 18 trade unions. Member, WCL).
**Confédération Mondiale du Travail (CMT)/World Confederation of Labour (WCL),** Rue Joseph II 50, B-1040 Brussel. T: (02)2176367. (Formerly Confédération Internationale des Syndicats Chrétiens (CISC)/International Federation of Christian Trade Unions (IFCTU), 1968 deconfessionalized and name changed. 1971: 14,345,340 members in 81 national organizations, 23 being confessional).
**Equipes Populaires (EP),** Rue de la Loi 127, B-1040 Brussel. (Member, WMCW).
**Fédération des Instituteurs Chrétiens de Belgique (FIC),** Rue Belliard 159, B-1040 Brussel.
**Fédération Internationale Chrétienne de Dirigeants d'Entreprise/Union Internationale des Patrons Chrétiens (UNIAPAC)/International Christian Union of Business Executives/Christian Managers and Businessmen's Union,** Sec, Av d'Auderghem 49, B-1040 Brussel. T: (02)354178.
**Institut Supérieur de Culture Ouvrière (ISCO),** Rue de la Loi 121, B-1040 Brussel. T: (02)7356050.
**International Federation of Christian Agricultural Workers Unions (FISCOA),** Rue Joseph II 50, B-1040 Brussel. T: 176387.
**International Federation of Christian Factory Workers Unions,** Av d'Auderghem 26, B-1040 Brussel.
**International Federation of Christian Metalworkers Unions,** Av Julien Hanssens 23, B-1020 Brussel. T: 258141.
**International Federation of Christian Miners Unions,** Av d'Auderghem 26, B-1040 Brussel. T: 361100.
**International Federation of Christian Trade Unions of Transport Workers,** Av d'Auderghem 26, B-1040 Brussel. T: 361100.
**Jeunesse Ouvrière Chrétienne Internationale (JOCI)/International Young Christian Workers (YCW),** International Secretariat, Rue Juste-Lipse 26, B-1040 Brussel. T: (02)7361134.
**Mouvement Mondial des Travailleurs Chrétienne (MMTC)/World Movement of Christian Workers (WMCW),** Sec Gén, Rue des Palais 90, B-1030 Brussel. T: (02)2419552.
**Mouvement Ouvrier Chrétien (MOC)/Algemeen Christelijk Werkeraverbond (ACW),** Rue de la Loi 121, B-1040 Brussel. T: (02)7356050.
**National Teachers Service (Nationale Dienst voor Monitors en Monitricen),** Biekorfstraat 46, B-1030 Brussel. (Member, BICE).
**Union Catholique des Groupements d'Action Sociale,** Av R Vandendriessche, B-1150 Brussel. (Member, UCISS).
**Union Catholique Internationale de Service Social (UCISS)/Catholic International Union for Social Service (CIUSS),** Sec, Rue de la Poste 111, B-1030 Brussel. T: (02)172858. (Members: national unions of social workers).
**Union Internationale Chrétienne des Dirigeants d'Enterprise (UNIAPAC),** Av d'Auderghem 49, B-1040 Brussel. T: (02)7354178.
**Verbond van Christelijke Werkgevers (VKW),** Av Lambermont 140, B-1030 Brussel.T: (02)2418677.

*BRAZIL*
**Associação Brasileira de Assistentes Sociais,** Av F Roosevelt 137, 5 andar, Rio de Janeiro, GB.
**Movimento Sindical,** Barra, BA.
**Sindicatos de Trabalhadores Rurais,** R Jaime Coelho 444, Campo Mourão, PR.

*CAMEROON*
**Ecumenical Association of African Theologians (EAAT),** BP 1539, Yaoundé.
**Syndicat des Enseignants Catholiques du Diocèse de Douala (SECDD),** BP 1138, Douala.

*CANADA*
**Association Canadiennes des Educateurs de Langue Française,** Suite 338, 3 Place Jean Talon, Québec, PQ.
**Canadian Scientific and Christian Affiliation,** Box 234, Perth, Ontario K7H 3E4. (Evangelical; for scientists).
**Christian Business Men's Committee,** 180 Duncan Mill Drive, Don Mills 405, Ontario.
**Christian Labour Association of Canada,** 100 Rexdale Blvd, Toronto, Ontario.
**Christian Writers Association,** 411 Balliol St, Toronto, Ontario.
**Christian Writers of Canada,** 84A Rosevear Av, Toronto 368, Ontario.
**Corporation des Enseignants du Québec (CEQ),** 2336 Chemin Ste Foy, Québec 10, PQ.
**International Young Christian Workers/Jeunesse Ouvrière Chrétienne Internationale (JOCI),** North American Secretariat/Secrétariat Nord Américain, 685 Blvd Décarie, Ville St Laurent, Québec. (JOC/YCW).
**Mouvement des Travailleurs Chrétiens (MTC),** 7559 Blvd St Laurent, Montréal 327, Québec. (Member, WMCW).
**Ontario English Catholic Teachers' Association,** 1260 Bay St, Toronto 5, Ontario.
**Police Christian Fellowship,** 14 Sonmore Drive, Agincourt, Ontario.

*CHILE*
**Academia de Asistentes Sociales San Vicente de Paul,** Villavicencio 337. (Member, UCISS).
**Asociación de Visitadoras Sociales de Chile,** c/o Escuela de Servicio Social, 360 Avda Vicuna Mackena, Santiago. (Member, UCISS).
**Movimiento de Profesores de Acción Católica (MOPAC),** 2 Sur No 870, Talca.
**Movimiento Obrero de Acción Católica (MOAC),** Catedral 1893, Clasificador G 249, Santiago. (Member, WMCW).

*CHINA (TAIWAN)*
**Adult Movement,** Pei Ta Lu 263, Hsinchu. (Related to WMCW).

*COLOMBIA*
**Federación Nacional de Trabajadores Sociales,** Apdo Aéreo 16434, Bogotá, DE. (Member, UCISS).
**Juventud Trabajadora Colombiana (JTC),** Bogotá, DE.

*COSTA RICA*
**Confederación de Obreros y Campesinos Cristianos (COCC),** Calle 6, 4 y 6 No 449, Apdo 4137, San José. T: 217701. (Member, WCL).

*DENMARK*
**Catholic Teachers' Society of Denmark (Danmarks Katolske Laererforbund, DKL),** Dag-Hammarskjolds Alle 17, DK-2000 Kobenhavn.
**Catholic Workers Action (Katolsk Arbejderaktion),** Westend 9/I, Kobenhavn V. (Related to WMCW).
**Women Teachers' Missionary Association (Laerernes Missionsforbund),** V Ostensgade, DK-2791 Dragor.

*DOMINICAN REPUBLIC*
**Confederación Autonoma de Sindicatos Cristianos (CASC),** Juan Pablo Pina, 27 altos, Apdo 309, Santo Domingo. T: 28454. (Member, WCL).
**Movimiento de los Trabajadores Cristianos,** Apdo 487, Santo Domingo. (Related to WMCW).

*ECUADOR*
**Confederación Ecuatoriana de Organizaciones Sindicales Cristianas (CEDOC),** Edificio Cedoc, 4 Piso Flores No 846, Quito. T: 214267. (Member, WCL).

*EGYPT*
**Soeurs Scolaires Franciscaines,** 9 Rue el Haras, Garden City, Al Qahirah. (Member, ACISJF).

*EL SALVADOR*
**Movimiento Obrero de Acción Católica,** Iglesia El Rosario, San Salvador. (Related to WMCW).

*FRANCE*
**Académie Internationale des Ecrivains Catholiques,** 21/23 Rue Cap de Castel, Domaine de l'Immaculée-Conception, F-81700 Puylaurens.
**Action Catholique Ouvrière (ACO),** 7 Rue Paul Lelong, F-75002 Paris. (Member, WMCW).
**Association Catholique Internationale des Enseignants et Chercheurs en Sciences et Techniques de l'Information,** Sec, 43 Rue Saint-Augustin, F-75002 Paris. T: 7429216.
**Confédération Française des Travailleurs Chrétiens (CFTC),** Sec Gen, 13 Rue des Ecluses St-Martin, F-75010 Paris. T: 205-7966. (Based on social doctrines of Catholic Church; 100,000 members, 24 trade unions).
**Fédération des Syndicats Chrétiens de la Metallurgie et Parties Similaires,** 8 Rue Drouot, F-75009 Paris. T: 770-3315.
**Fédération des Syndicats Chrétiens des Finances et des Affairs Economiques et Assimilés,** 13 Rue des Ecluses St-Martin, F-75010 Paris. T: 205-7966. (Member, CFTC).
**Fédération des Syndicats Chrétiens du Textile, du Cuir et de l'Habillement,** 3 Rue Notre-Dame, F-59300 Valenciennes. T: 462942.
**Fédération Générale des Syndicats Chrétiens des Fonctionnaires de l'Etat, des Collectivités Locales et Assimilés,** 56 Rue du Faubourg Poissonnière, F-75010 Paris. T: 523-3022. (Civil servants).
**Fédération Internationale des Pharmaciens Catholiques (FIPC),** 60 Av des Pages, F-78110 Le Vésinet. T: 966-0016.
**Fédération Nationale des Syndicats Chrétiens des Services de Santé et des Services Sociaux,** 13 Rue des Ecluses St-Martin, F-75010 Paris. T: 205-7966.
**Fédération Syndicale Chrétienne des Travailleurs des PTT,** 56 Rue du Faubourg Poissonnière, F-7510 Paris. T: 523-3377. (Posts & telecommunications).
**Jeunes Travailleurs en Service,** Copainville, F-10 Troyes.
**Organisation Mondiale des Anciens et Anciennes,** Eleves de l'Enseignement Catholique, 17 Rue Michel Charles, F-75012 Paris. T: (01) 343-7629.
**Secrétariat International des Elèves Ingénieurs Catholiques (SIEIC),** 18 Rue de Varenne, F-75007 Paris. T: (01)222-1856. (Pax Romana).
**Secrétariat International des Ingénieurs, des Agronomes et des Cadres Economiques Catholiques (SIIAEC),** 18 Rue de Varenne, F-75007 Paris. T: (01)222-1856.
**Section des Assistantes Sociales de l'UCSS,** 16 Rue Tiphaine, F-75015 Paris. (Member, UCISS).
**Syndicat National de l'Enseignement Chrétien,** Siège, 359 Rue Herbeuse, F-76230 Bois-Guillaume. T: 709923.
**Union Departmentale des Syndicats Chrétiens de Moselle,** 38 Rue Mazelle. F-5700 Metz. T: 742857.
**Union des Frères Enseignants,** Secrétariat National, 277 Rue St-Jacques, F-75005 Paris. (Member, BICE).
**Union des Religieuses Educatrices Paroissiales,** 10 bis Rue Jean Bart, F-75006 Paris. (Member, BICE).
**Union des Syndicats Chrétiens d'Ile de France,** 8 Rue Drouot, F-75009 Paris. T: 770-3315.
**Union Nationale des Congrégations d'Action Hospitalière et Sociale (UNCAHS),** 106 Rue du Bac, F-75007 Paris. (UCISS member).
**Verband der Renaissance (Gesellschaften Katholischer Akademiker an Schweizerischen Hochschulen),** 10 Rue du Centre, F-1723 Marly le Petit.

*FRENCH GUIANA*
**Centrale des Travailleurs Chrétiens de la Guyane (CTCG),** 113 Rue Christophe Colomb, BP 383, F-973 Cayenne. T: 232. (Member, WCL).

*GERMANY, Federal Republic of*
**Arbeitgemeinschaft für Ev Schulerinnen und Frauen-Bibel-Kreise,** PO Box 560, D-4902 Bad Salzuflen. T: 50088.
**Berufsverband Katholischer Sozialarbeiterinnen und Sozialarbeiter,** 2 Hedwig Dransfeld Platz, D-Essen West. (Member, UCISS).
**Christlicher Gewerkschaftsbund Deutschlands (CGBD),** Rheinweg 97, D-53 Bonn. T: 225937. (Christian Trade Union Federation. Member, WCL. 188,000 white collar members).
**Evangelische Akademikerschaft Deutschlands,** Generalsekretariat, Mercedesstr 5-7, D-7 Stuttgart 50.
**Evangelische Arbeiterbewegung,** Geschäftsstelle, Brunostr 12, D-43 Essen.
**Evangelische Arbeitnehmerbewegung in Deutschland (EAB),** Landesverband Rheinland-Westfalen, Seidlstr 2, D-43 Essen.
**Junge Christliche Arbeitnehmer (CAJ),** Hüttmannstr 52, D-4300 Essen. T: (02141)671065
**Katholische Arbeiterbewegung (KAB),** Bernhard Letterhausstr 26, Köln. (Member, MWCW).
**Verband Evangelischen Sozialpädagogen,** Bismarckstr 140, D-662 Völklingen (Saar). (Protestant social workers).
**Verband Evangelischer Handwerker,** Auf Böhlingerhof 15, D-465 Gelsenkirchen.
**Verein Katholischer Deutscher Lehrerinnen (VKDL),** Hedwig-Dransfeld-Platz 4, D-43 Essen.
**Werkvolk,** Pettenkoferstr 8, München 15. (Member, WMCW).

*GREECE*
**Christian Union of Professional Men,** Athínai.

*GRENADA*
**Grenada Catholic Teachers Association,** Calvigny Rd, Woburn PO, St George's.

*GUADELOUPE*
**Centrale Démocratique des Travailleurs Chrétiens de Guadeloupe (CDTGG),** 15 Rue Victor Hugo, BP 369, Pointe-à-Pitre. T: 821168. (Member, WCL).

*HAITI*
**Action Catholique Ouvrière (ACO),** BP 160B, Port-au-Prince. (Member, WMCW).
**Fédération Haïtienne des Syndicats Chrétiens (FHSC),** Apdo Postal 6681, Caracas, Venezuela. T: 728961. (Member, WCL. In exile, based in Venezuela).

*HONG KONG*
**Christian Workers' Association,** Caritas House, 2 Caine Rd, Hong Kong. (Related to WMCW).

*HUNGARY*
**Actio Catholica,** Kárólyi u 4-8 III I-8, Budapest V. (Related to WMCW).

*INDIA*
**All India Federation of Catholic Teachers Guilds (AIFCTG),** 70 Gauthan Lane No 1, Andheri, Bombay 58.
**Christian Workers' Movement (CWM),** 5 Naudidroog Rd, Bangalore 6. (Member, WMCW).

*INDONESIA*
**Federation of Pancasila Unions,** c/o Taman Cut Mutiali 10, Jakarta II/14. T: 41194. (Catholic. 'Five-Principle' trade unions).
**Indonesian Federation of Christian Workers' Associations (KESPEKRI),** Jalan Jenderal Sudirman 1, Jakarta. (Member, WCL).

*ITALY*
**Associazione Insegnanti Cristiani Evangelici,** Viale Romagna 53, Milano.
**Associazione Italiana Maestri Cattolici (AIMC),** Clivo Monte del Gallo 48, I-00165 Roma.
**Associazione Nazionale della Comunità di Lavoro (ANCOL),** Via Ferdinando Baldelli 41, I-00146 Roma. T: 552251.
**Associazioni Cristiani Lavoratori Italiana (ACLI),** Via Monte della Farina 64 I-00186 Roma T: 655351/2,655251. (Member, WMCW, WCL).
**Confederazione Italiana Sindacati Lavoratori (CISL),** Sec Gen, Via PO 21, I-00198 Roma. (Italian Confederation of Labour Unions. Catholic; 2.45 million members).
**Confederazione Nazionale Coltivatori Diretti,** Via XXIV Maggio 43, I-00187 Roma. T: 462908.
**Federazione Italiana Religiose Assistenza Sociale (FIRAS),** Via Zanardelli 32, I-00186 Roma. (Member UCISS).
**Mouvement International des Intellectuels Catholiques (MIIC),** Secrétariat Professionnel SIJC (Juristes), Via della Conciliazione 4d, I-00193 Roma.
**Movimento Maestri di Azione Cattolica (MMAC),** Via della Conciliazione 3, I-00193 Roma.
**Unione Cattolica Assistenti Sociali Italiane (UCASI),** Via della Conciliazione 4d, I-00100 Roma, (Member, UCISS).
**World Union of Catholic Teachers (WUCT)/Union Mondiale des Enseignants Catholiques (UMEC)/Weltunion Katholischer Lehrer/Unión Mundial de Educadores Católicos,** Sec, Piazza San Calisto 16, I-00153 Roma. T: 6984786. (Also: Via della Conciliazione 3-4d, I-00193 Roma. T: 564978).

*JAPAN*
**Christian Workers' Movement,** Kita Kyushu-shi, Kokura-ku, Kurobaru Honmachi 11. (Related to WMCW).
**Fellowship of Small and Middle-sized Industry Workers,** 473 Kita-hosoe, Shikama-ku, Himeji-shi. T: 354718.
**Fellowship of Young Workers,** St Messiah Church, 6 Fuyuki-cho, Fukagawa, Koto-ku, Tokyo. T: 6413886.
**Fellowship of Young Workers of Small Stores,** Shitaya Church, 3-37-10 Higashi-ueno, Daito-ku, Tokyo. T: 8319310.

*KENYA*
**Kenya Christian Graduates' Fellowship (KCGF),** Sec, PO Box 48789, Nairobi.

*KOREA, South*
**Korea Catholic Workers Movement (KCWM),** 221-41 Sinkildong Yougdongpo-ku, Soul. (Member, WMCW).

*LESOTHO*
**Lesotho Catholic Teachers Federation (LCTF),** Sacred Heart High School, St Monica, PO Leribe.

*LUXEMBOURG*
**Confédération des Syndicats Chrétiens du**

**Luxembourg (Letzeburger Chrechtleche Gewerkschafts Verband, LCGV),** 13 Rue Bourbon, Luxembourg. T: 21342,489797. (Member, WCL. 15,000 Members; 9 trade unions).
**Union Catholique Luxembourgeoise des Infirmières et Assistantes Sociales,** 23 Blvd du Prince, Luxembourg-ville.

*MADAGASCAR*
**Confédération Chrétienne des Syndicats Malgaches (CCSM),** Route de Majunga, BP 1035, Tananarive. T: 23174. (Member, WCL).
**Mouvement d'Adultes,** 6 Rue Rainizanabololona, Antanimena, Tananarive. (Related to WMCW).

*MALTA*
**Malta Catholic Action Teachers' Movement (MCATM),** Catholic Institute, Floriana.
**Malta Union of Teachers (MUT),** Teachers Institute, 7/3 Merchants St, PO Box 525, Valletta.
**Social Action Movement Azjoni Socjali),** 15 Old Mint St, Valletta. (Related to WMCW).
**YCW Adults,** Piazza Filippo Sciberras, Floriana. (Related to WMCW).

*MAURITIUS*
**Ligue Ouvrière d'Action Catholique (LOAC),** 42 Rue Pope Hennessy, Port-Louis. (Member, WMCW).

*MEXICO*
**Acción Cristiana Obrera (ACO),** Patricio Sanz 449, México 12, DF. (Member, WMCW).
**Unión Mexicana de Trabajadores Sociales,** Liverpool 69-102, México 6, DF. (Member, UCISS).

*NETHERLANDS*
**Christian National Federation of Trade Unions in the Netherlands (Christelijk Nationaal Vakverbond in Nederland, CNV),** Revellaan 1, Postbus 2475, Utrecht. T: (030)941041. (Member, WCL. Protestant; 240,000 members in 26 unions).
**Confédération Catholique Néerlandaise des Agriculteurs et Maraîchers/Katholieke Nederlandse Boeren en Tuindersbond (KNBTN),** Scheveningseweg 46, 's-Gravenhage. T: (070) 514191.
**Confédération des Patrons Chrétiens aux Pays-Bas/Nederlands Christlijk Werkgeversverbond (NCW),** Scheveningseweg 52, 's-Gravenhage. T: (060)514071.
**Mouvement International des Intellectuels Catholiques (MIIC),** Secrétariat Professionels SIAC (Artistes), Stadhouderskade 86, Amsterdam.
**Mouvement International des Intellectuels Catholiques (MIIC),** Secrétariat Professionels SIESC (Enseignants), Biesseltsebaan 40, Nijmegen.
**Netherlands Federation of Catholic Trade Unions (Nederlands Katholiek Vakverbond,** NKV), Oudenoord 12, Utrecht. T: (030)333316. (Member, WCL. 400,000 members in 19 trade unions).
**Netherlands Protestants Union of Civil Servants (Nederlandse Christelijke Bond van Overheidspersoneel),** Postbus 1804, 's-Gravenhage. T: (070)514051. (53,000 members).
**Netherlands Union of Catholic Teachers (Katholieke Onderwijzerverbond, KOV),** Koninginnergracht 70-71, 's-Gravenhage. T: (070)557193.
**Secrétariat International des Enseignants Secondaires Catholiques (SIESC),** Sous-Secrétariat de Pax Romana (MIIC), Biesseltsebaa 40, Nijmegan.

*NETHERLANDS ANTILLES*
**Catholic Teachers' Council (RK Onderwijsraad),** Juliana Plein 5, Willemstad, Curaçao.
**Catholic Union for Teaching Personnel (RK Vereniging voor Onderwijzend Personeel),** Don Bosco, Kantoor Nijweg 1, PB 2038, Curaçao.
**Christian Trade Union of Curaçao (Curacaosch Cristelijk Vakverbond),** Emmastraat esq Ijserstraat 2, PO Box 154, Willemstad, Curaçao. T: 24405. (Member, WCL).

*NICARAGUA*
**Central de Trabajadores Nicaragüenses,** Apdo Postal 1863, Managua.
**Movimiento Obrero de Acción Católica,** Apdo 2183, Managua. (Related to WMCW).

*NIGERIA*
**Catholic Teachers' Association,** Lagos Branch, PO Box 262, Surrulere, Lagos.
**Nigerian Movement of Christian Workers,** 45 Ikorodu Rd, Yaba, Lagos. (Related to WMCW).

*NORWAY*
**Women Teachers' Missionary Association (Laererinnenes Misjonsforbund),** Theresesgt 51B, Oslo 3.

*PANAMA*
**Federación Istmena de Trabajadores Cristianos,** Via España 16, Of 3, Apdo 6308, Panamá 5. T: 235813. (Member, WCL).

*PARAGUAY*
**Confederación Cristiana de Trabajadores (CTC),** Calle John F Kennedy 1038, Asunción. T: 235813. (Member, WCL).
**Movimiento International de Intelectuales Católicos (MIIC),** Secretariado Latinoamericano, Quinta Ykuá Satí, Barrio Isla de Francia, Asunción. T: 60058.
**Movimiento Obrero Católica,** Oliva 472, Asunción. (Related to WMCW).

*PERU*
**Asociación de Asistentes Sociales del Perú,** Casilla 635, Lima. (Member, UCISS).
**Juventud Obrero Católica Internacional (JOC-YCW International),** Secretariado para Latina América, Apdo de Correo 1494, Lima. (JOC/YCW).
**Movimiento Sindical Cristiano del Perú (MOSICP) (Movimiento de los Trabajadores Cristianos),** Ucayali 332, Apdo 1321, Lima. T: 71671. (Member, WCL and WMCW).

*PHILIPPINES*
**Catholic Teachers' Guild of the Philippines,** Pius XII Catholic Center, United Nations Av, Manila.
**Christian Workers' Movement,** 2661 Mercedes St, Singalong, Manila. (Related to WMCW).
**Federation of Free Workers (FFW),** 1845-E Taft Av, Manila.
**Ozanam Guild,** PO Box 1329, Manila. (Member, UCISS).
**Young Christian Socialists (YCS),** Manila.

*PORTUGAL*
**Liga Operária Católica (LOC),** Rua Manuel Bernardes 30/1, Lisboa 2. (Member, WMCW).
**Liga Operária Católica Feminina (LOCF),** Rua do Salvador 2a, Lisboa 2. (Member, WMCW).
**Movimento dos Homens Cristãos de Negócios,** Rua Dr António Martins 2, Estoril.
**Sindicato National das Profissionais SS,** Rua Luciano Cordeiro 18, 3 dto, Lisboa 1. (Member, UCISS).

*ST LUCIA*
**St Lucia Catholic Teachers' Association,** 36 Coral St, Castries.

*ST VINCENT*
**Catholic Teachers' Association,** New Montrose.

*SEYCHELLES*
**Union Seychelloise des Travailleurs Chrétiens (USTC),** Victoria, Mahé. (Member, WCL).

*SINGAPORE*
**International Young Christian Workers,** Asian Secretariat, 73 Bras Basah Rd, Singapore 7. (JOC/YCW).

*SOUTH AFRICA*
**Catholic African Teachers' Federation of South Africa (CATF),** PO Box 941, Pretoria, Transvaal.

*SPAIN*
**Asociación Cultural de Asistentes Sociales Españolas (ACASE),** Lagasca 79, Madrid 6. (Member, UCISS).
**Asociación de Asistentes Sociales,** Puerta Ferrisa 18-1/1, Barcelona 2. (Member, UCISS).
**Federación Católica de los Maestros Españoles (FCME),** Calle San Marcos 3, Madrid. (Also: Alfonso XI 4-6, Madrid 14).
**Federación Española de Asociaciones de Asistentes Sociales (FEDAAS),** Diluvio 10, Barcelona 12. (Member, UCISS).
**Federación Española de Regiosos de Enseñanza (FERE),** Claudio Coello 32, Madrid 1. (Member, BICE).
**Hermandad Obrera de Acción Católica Femenina (HOACF),** Alfonso XI 4, Madrid 14. (Member, WMCW).
**Hermandad Obrera de Acción Católica Masculina (HOACM),** Alfonso XI 4, Madrid 14. (Member, WMCW).
**Hermandades del Trabajo,** 1 Juan de Austria 6, Madrid 10. (Related to WMCW).
**Junta Superior de las Hermandades dos Ingenieros,** Calle San Marcos 3, Madrid.
**Movimiento de Apostolado Seglar Maestros de Acción Católica,** Alfonso XI 4-6, Madrid 14.
**Unión de Graduados de la ACE (Juristas, Farmaceuticos, Tacnicos, Medicos, Cientificos),** Luchana 21, Madrid.
**Unión Española de Hermandades Professionales,** Calle San Marcos 3, Madrid. (Union of Professional Guilds).

*SRI LANKA*
**Christian Workers' Fellowship,** YMCA Bldg, PO Box 381, Colombo 1. T: 25252.
**Christian Workers' Movement (CWM),** 108 Minuwangoda, Negombo. (Member, WMCW).

*SURINAM*
**Catholic Teachers (Katholiek Onderwijs),** Gravenstraat 21, Paramaribo.

*SWEDEN*
**Christian Workers (Kristna Arbetare),** Järnvägsgatan 35/IV, Landskrona. (Related to WMCW).
**United Christian Teachers' Association of Sweden (Sveriges Förenade Kristliga Lärarförbund),** Box 5, S-610 60 Tystberga. T: (0155)60500.

*SWITZERLAND*
**Action Catholique Ouvrière (ACO),** 4 Av Crozet, CH-1211 Genève. (Member, WMCW).
**Christlich-Nationaler Gewerkschaftbund der Schweiz (CNG),** Hopfenweg 21, CH-Bern. T: 235442. (Member, WCL).
**Katholische Arbeiter- und Angestellten-bewegung (KAB),** Ausstellungsstr 21, CH-8005 Zürich. (Member, WMCW).
**Katholischer Lehreverein der Schweiz (KLS),** Postfach 70, Zug. (Also: Fluelen (Uri)).
**Mouvement International des Intellectuels Catholiques (MIIC) (Pax Romana),** 1 Route de Jura, Fribourg. T: (037)222649,222653.
**Schweizerischer Verband Evangelischer Arbeiter und Angestellter (SVEA),** Höhenring 29, Zürich 52. T: 466424. (Member, WCL).
**Verband Renaissance,** Thurfirsten, CH-7320 Sargens. (Catholic graduates).
**Verein Katholischer Lehrinnen der Schweiz (VKLS),** Amlehstr 33, CH-6010 Kriens. (Also: Heinrich-Federer-Str 9, St Gallen).

*THAILAND*
**Catholic Teachers' Association of Thailand,** St Gabriel's College, 565 Samsen Rd, Bangkok 3.

*TOGO*
**Association Togolaise des Volontaires Chrétiens au Travail (ASTOVOCT),** Eglise Evangélique, BP 97, Palime.

*TRINIDAD & TOBAGO*
**Catholic Teachers' Association of Trinidad and Tobago,** Busby St, Marabella, Trinidad.

*UK OF GB & NI*
**Accountants' Christian Fellowship,** 53 Downsview Drive, Wivelsfield Green, Haywards Heath, West Sussex RH17 7RN.
**Association of Christian Teachers,** 47 Marylebone Lane, London W1M 6AX.
**Catholic Pharmaceutical Guild,** 1191 Dumbarton Rd, Glasgow W4.
**Catholic Railway Guild,** 114 Liberton St, Glasgow E3.
**Catholic Teachers' Federation of England and Wales (CTF),** 12 Queens Rd, Hendon, London NW4.
**Christian Education Fellowship,** 39 Bedford Square, London WC1B 3EY. T: (01)636-5935. (Teachers).
**Christian Golfers' Association (CGA),** 10 Cuthbert Rd, Croydon CR0 3RB. T: (01)688-7458.
**Civil Service Christian Union (CSCU),** 27 Jacqueline Gardens, Billericay, Essex CM12 0PL. (British civil servants).
**Graduates' Fellowship (GF),** 39 Bedford Square, London WC1B 3EY. T: (01)636-5113. (Linked with IVF).
**Guild of Catholic Professional Social Workers,** 18 Falmouth Rd, Springfield, Chelmsford, Essex. (Member, UCISS).
**Guild of Catholic Teachers,** Scottish National Council, 13 Kenmuir Av, Mount Vernon, Glasgow E2.
**International Society of Christian Artists/Société Internationale des Artistes Chrétiens (SIAC),** Glasspools, Gillsman's Hill, St Leonards-on-Sea. (World Congresses: Bologna 1967, Salzburg 1969).
**Librarians' Christian Fellowship,** Sec, 94 Church Way, Iffley, Oxford OX4 4EF.
**Merchant Navy Christian Fellowship,** Gen Sec, 180 Hope St, Glasgow G2 2UE. T: (041)331-5456.
**National Union of Funeral Service Operatives,** Sec, 16 Woolwich New Rd, London SE18 6DH. T: (01)854-5870. (1,075 members).
**Post Office Christian Association,** Gen Sec, Drayton House, Gordon St, London WC1H 0AN. T: (01)387-3350.
**Research Scientists' Christian Fellowship,** 39 Bedford Square, London WC1B 3EY. T: (01) 636-5113.
**Teachers' Prayer Fellowship,** Hon Gen Sec, 45 Old Bisley Rd, Frimley, Surrey.
**Workers Christian Fellowship (WCF),** Gen Sec, 113 Whitchurch Gardens, Edgware, Middlesex HA8 6PG. T: (01)952-0068.
**Young Christian Workers (YCW),** 106 Clapham Rd, London SW9 0JX. T: (01)735-7031.

*USA*
**America Association of Christians in Behavioral Sciences,** PO Box 14188, Oklahoma City.
**American Scientific Affiliation (ASA),** 5 Douglas Av, Elgin, IL 60120. (Begun 1941; 2,000 scientists who are evangelicals).
**Association of Catholic Teachers (AST),** De La Salle College, La Salle Rd, NE, Washington, DC 20018. T: (212)548-1400.
**Association of Professors of Missions,** 5401 South Cornell, Chicago, IL 60615.
**Catholic Accountants Guild,** Sec, 611 Eighth Av, Brooklyn, NY 11215.
**Catholic Central Union of America (CCUA),** Dir, 3835 Westminster Place, St Louis, MO 63108.
**Catholic Social Workers Association of the Middle Atlantic,** 1200 North Broom St, Wilmington, Delaware. (Member, UCISS).
**Christian Accountants Association,** Dir, Box 782, Wheaton, IL 60187.
**Christian Business and Professional Women of America,** 10121 Grandview Rd, Kansas City, MO 64137.
**Christian Business Men's Committee International,** Exec Sec, 799 Roosevelt Rd, Glen Ellyn, IL 60137. T: (312)858-1660.
**Christian Legal Society,** PO Box 2069, Oak Park, IL 60303.
**Christian Librarians' Fellowship,** Library, Wheaton College, Wheaton, IL 60187.
**Christian Medical Society,** 1122 Westgate Av, Oak Park, IL 60301. T: (312)848-9510. (Founded 1946; doctors, dentists, et alii).
**Christian Pilots Association,** Pres, 4373 Santa Anita, El Monte, CA 91731. T: (213)444-5358.
**Christian Writers Guild,** Dir, La Canada, CA 91011.
**Christian Writers Institute,** Gundersen Drive & Schmale Rd, Wheaton, IL 60187.
**Fellowship of Christian Athletes (FCA),** 1125 Grand Av, Kansas City, MO 64106.
**Fellowship of Christian Composers,** PO Box 6181, Fort Worth, TX 76115. (Music).
**Guild of Catholic Lawyers,** 350 5th Av, New York, NY. T: (212)563-4242.
**National Association of Ecumenical Staff (NAES),** 475 Riverside Drive, New York, NY 10027. T: (212)870-2157. (Professionals in ecumenical work. Formerly Association of Council Secretaries).
**National Educators Fellowship,** Pres, PO Box 243, South Pasadena, CA 91030.
**National Federation of Catholic Physicians,** 2825 North Mayfair Rd, Milwaukee, WI 53222.
**National Guild of Catholic Psychiatrists,** 3225 Garfield St, NW, Washington, DC 20008.
**Religious Newswriters Association (RNA),** 422 South Fifth St, Minneapolis, MN 55415.

*URUGUAY*
**Asociación de Asistentes Sociales del Uruguay,** Lavalleja 1824, Montevideo. (Member, UCISS).
**Movimiento Obrero de Acción Católica (MOAC),** Arenal Grande 2564, Montevideo. (Member, WMCW).

*VENEZUELA*
**Asociación de Ex-Alumnas de la Escuela de SS,** Calle de la Iglesia 6, Sabana Grande, Caracas. (Member, UCISS).
**Association Catholique Internationale des Enseignants et des Chercheurs en Sciences et Techniques de l'Information,** Sec Gén, Apdo 422, Caracas.
**Comité Unitario de los Sindicalistas Cristianos (CUSIC),** Av Paez, Quinta Granada, Apdo 6058, El Paraiso, Caracas. T: 425981. (Member, WCL).
**Movimiento Obrero de Acción Católica,** Casa Parroquial, Urbanización Gil Fortoul, Barquisimeto. (Related to WMCW).

*VIET NAM*
**Association des Professionnelles du Service Social,** 38 Rue Tu'Xuong, Saigon. (Member, UCISS).
**Association Enseignants Catholiques du Vietnam,** 53 Nguyen-Du, Saigon.
**Mouvement des Travailleurs Chrétiens,** 370 Le Van Duyêt, Saigon. (Related to WMCW).

*ZAIRE*
**Jeunesse Ouvrière Chrétienne Internationale,** Sec Panafricain, BP 8314, Kinshasa. (JOC/YCW).

*ZIMBABWE*
**Christian Writers' Club,** Bulawayo. (Founded 1969).

# 71
# World Conciliarism

*Definition.* Interdenominational or ecumenical councils of churches or denominations of different ecclesiastical traditions, at the international or world level; councils, federations, alliances, fellowships; world conciliarism, collegiality and consultation.

*HOLY SEE*
**Synodus Episcoporum/Synod of Bishops/Synode des Evêques/Sinodo dei Vescovi,** Segreteria Generale, Piazza Pio XII 3, I-00193 Roma, Italy. T: 6984821,6984324.

*NETHERLANDS*
**International Council of Christian Churches (ICCC),** IHQ, 2 Groenekanseweg, PO Box 80, De Bilt-2664. T: (030)764344.

*SWITZERLAND*
**Conference of Secretaries of Christian World Communions (CWCs),** Sec, 150 Route de Ferney, CH-1211 Genève 20. T: 333400. (Until 1979, World Confessional Families, WCFs).
**World Council of Churches (WCC)/Conseil Oecuménique des Eglises (COE)/Ökumenischer Rat der Kirchen (ORK),** Gen Sec, 150 Route de Ferney, CH-1211 Genève 20. T: (0104122)333400.

*USA*
**World Evangelical Fellowship (WEF),** International Sec, PO Box 670, Colorado Springs, CO 80901.

# 72
# Youth Organizations

*Definition.* Groups and activities for young people (boys and girls together), teenagers; youth work, hostels, camps, work camps, Bible camps, houseparties, YMCA; youth evangelism. For young workers, see WORKERS' AND PROFESSIONALS' ASSOCIATIONS. For rural youth, see RURAL AGRICULTURAL MISSION.

Christian organizations ministering to youth, and of major significance at the national or wider levels, number over 500. Ministries to or from youth are legion. In almost every country there are branches of the major organizations, YMCA (Young Men's Christian Association), YFCI (Youth for Christ International), et alia; but all these branches are omitted below, leaving only the HQs in Switzerland, UK and USA, from which global directories can be obtained.

*AUSTRIA*
**Arbeitsgemeinschaft Katholische Jugend Österreichs,** Johannesgasse 16, A-1010 Wien. T: 561621.
**Evangelical Youth Work Association in Austria,** Welzergasse 23 aM, Baden bei Wien.
**Internationaler Christlicher Jugendaustausch (ICJ)/International Christian Youth Exchange,** p/A Grillparzerstr 29, A-4840 Vöcklabruck.
**Katholische Hochschuljugend Österreichs,** Ebendorferstr 8, A-1010 Wien.
**Katholische Jungschar Österreichs,** Johannesgasse 16, A-1010 Wien. T: 561621.
**Katholisches Landjugendwerk für Entwicklungshilfe,** Seiberstätte 14, Linz.
**Mittelschüler-Kartellverband,** Neubaugasse 25, A-1070 Wien.
**Ökumenischer Jugendrat in Österreich (ÖJRiÖ),** Johannesgasse 16, A-1010 Wien. T: 561621.
**Pfadfinder Österreichs,** Mahlerstr 7, A-1010 Wien.

*BARBADOS*
**Caribbean Ecumenical Youth Action (CEYA),** CADEC, PO Box 616, Bridgetown.

*BELGIUM*
**Chirojeugd-Jongens,** Kipdorp 30, B-2000 Antwerpen. T: (031)316795.
**Conférence Internationale du Scoutisme**

**Catholique/Fédération des Scouts Catholiques (FSC)/International Catholic Scouters Conference,** Sec, 21 Rue de Dublin, B-1050 Brussel. T: (02)5118453,5124691.
**Conseil de la Jeunesse Catholique (CJC),** Rue Guimard 5, B-1040 Brussel.
**Ecumenical Youth Council in Europe,** Sec, Leuvensesteenweg 135, B-2980 Boortmeerbeek. T: (015)53376.
**Fédération des Institutions Spécialisées d'Aide à la Jeunesse,** Rue Guimard 4, B-1040 Brussel.
**Fédération Internationale des Communautés de Jeunesse Catholique Paroissiales (FIMCAP),** Kipdorp 30, B-2000 Antwerpen. T: (031)310795.
**Fédération Mondiale de Jeunesse Catholique (FMJC)/World Federation of Catholic Youth,** Sec, Av de l'Hôpital Français 31, B-1080 Brussel. T: (02)4280682.
**Fédération Nationale des Patros Masculins de Belgique (FNP Jeunes Gens),** Rue de l'Hôpital 17, B-6060 Gilly. T: (071)412026.
**International Federation of Catholic Parochial Youth Communities (FIMCAP),** Secretariat, Kipdorp 30, Antwerpen. T: (03)310795.
**Katholieke Jeugdraad (KJR),** Rue Guimard 5, B-1040 Brussel.

*BRAZIL*
**União Brasileira de Juventudes Ecumênicas (UBRAJE),** CP 2969, Curitiba, PR.

*CANADA*
**Christian Service Brigade,** Box 246, Burlington, Ontario. (Boys).
**Teen Challenge,** 5 East Broadway, Vancouver 10, BC.
**Youth Ventures,** Box 4774, Vancouver 10, BC.

*CHILE*
**Instituto Superior de Pastoral de la Juventud,** Av Salvador 2549, Santiago.

*COLOMBIA*
**Instituto de Pastoral Latinoamericano de la Juventud (IPLAJ),** Carrera 5 No 8-36, Apdo Aéreo 25681, Bogotá, DE. T: 420973,814109.

*COSTA RICA*
**Movimiento Iglesia Joven,** Apdo Postal 5271, San José. (Progressivist).
**Movimiento Juvenil Cristiano,** Departamento de Vide Estudiantil, Universidad Nacional, Heredia. (Progressivist)

*DENMARK*
**Boys and Girls Brigade (FDFs og FPFs Missionsudvalg),** Hjalmar Brantingsplads 6, DK-2100 Kobenhavn O. T: (01)353926.
**Ecumenical Youth Council,** Vendersgade 28, Kobenhavn K.
**International Hostel,** Ecumenical Centre, Klovermarksveij 4, DK-8200 Aarhus N. T: (06)162645.

*ECUADOR*
**Asociación Cristiana de Jóvenes,** 9 de Octubre No 100 y Paria, Casilla 1177, Quito. T: 238220, 239890.

*FRANCE*
**Association du Foyer du Jeune Libéré,** Sec, 47 Rue de Clichy, F-75009 Paris.
**Echanges Internationaux de Jeunesse Chrétienne (ICYWE France),** Pres, 13 Av Raymond-Poincaré, F-75016 Paris. T: 727-9296.
**Interservice Jeunes et Monde,** 42 Montée St Barthélémy, Lyon 5.
**Jeunes Travailleurs en Service,** Copainville, F-10 Troyes.
**Jeunesse et Reconstruction,** 10 Rue de Tevise, F-75009 Paris.
**Mission Française de la Jeunesse Orthodoxe auprès des Disséminés,** 14 Rue Victor-Hugo, F-92400 Courbevoie.
**Scouts de France (SDF),** 10 Rue Dantzig, F-75015 Paris.

*GABON*
**Jeunesse Chrétienne,** Dir, Eglise Evangélique du Gabon, BP 80, Libreville.

*GERMAN DEMOCRATIC REPUBLIC*
**Jugendkammer der EKD,** Schönhauser Allee 141 DDR-1058 Berlin.

*GERMANY, Federal Republic of*
**Arbeitsgemeinschaft der Ev Jugend Deutschlands,** Gerokstr 21, D-7 Stuttgart 1.
**Bund der Deutschen Katholischen Jugend (BDKJ),** Aschattenburger Str 82, D-6050 Offenbach.
**Bundesarbeitsgemeinschaft Jugendaufbaudienst,** Diemershaldenstr 48, D-7 Stuttgart 1.
**Christliche Pfadfinderschaft Deutschlands,** Herzbachweg 2, D-646 Gelnhausen.
**Deutscher Verband der Jugenbünde für Entschiedenes Christentum,** Frankfurter Str 180, D-35 Kassel.
**Evangelische Bundesarbeitskreis für Jugendschutz,** Stafflenbergstr 78, Postfach 476, D-7 Stuttgart 1.
**Evangelische Erziehungs-Verband,** Cellerstr 102, D-3 Hannover.
**Evangelische Jugend Deutschlands Schülerbibelkreise,** Föhrenstr 35, Postfach 217, D-56 Wuppertal-Barmen. T: (02121)594209.
**Evangelischer Arbeitskreis für Jugendführung (EAFJ),** Links der Alb 23, D-75 Karlstruhbe 51.
**Internationales Katholisches Jugendwerk für Ost- und Mitteleuropa,** Beichstr 1, Postfach 149, D-8000 München 44. T: (0811)398160.
**Katholische Landjugendbewegung (KLJB),** Kalusenhofstr 38, Postfach 23, D-4293 Dingden. T: (02852)2091/2.
**Ökumenischer Jugendienste (OJD),** Gerokstr 21, D-7000 Stuttgart 0. (Also: Reinsburgengerstr 46, D-7000 Stuttgart 1).
**Verein für Internationale Jugendarbeit,** Poppelsdorfer Allee 27, D-53 Bonn.

*INDIA*
**Christian Youth Service Committee,** Valakom, Kerala.
**Commission for Youth,** Archbishop's House, 33 Ahmendabad, Palace Rd, Bhopal. (RC).
**International Youth Centre,** Dir, E-45 NDSE-1, New Delhi 49.

*ITALY*
**Agape,** Centro Ecumenico per la Gioventù, Prali (To). T: 8514.
**Associationes Juventutis Salesianae,** Secretariat, Via Maria Ausiliatrice 32, I-10152 Torino.
**Associazione Cattolica Nazionale delle Opera per la Protezione della Giovane,** Via Urbana 158, I-00184 Roma. T: 460056,471989.
**Associazione Scouts Cattolici Italiani (ASCI),** Piazza Pasquale Paoli 18, I-00186 Roma. T: 650207, 657711. (Member, BICE).
**Casa CARES (Comitato Assistenza Ragazzi e Studenti),** Via Pisana, Firenze.
**Centro Salesiano di Pastorale Giovanile (CPG),** Viale dei Salesiani 9, I-00175 Roma.
**Ecumene,** Centro Giovanile, Località Cigliolo-Velletri, Via Firenze 38, Roma.
**General Union of Pastoral Work for Youth,** Secretariat, Via Palestro 26, I-00185 Roma.
**Instituto per Ragazzi E Gould,** Palazzo Salviata, Via dei Serragli 49, Firenze. T: 272576.
**Jeunesse Indépendante Catholique Internationale (JICI),** Piazza San Calisto 16, I-00153 Roma. T: 6984645.
**Organizzazione Gioventù d'Azione Biblica,** Via Balbi 132r, Genova.
**Union Générale des Oeuvres Pastorales pour la Jeunesse,** Via Palestro 26, I-00185 Roma.
**Villagigo della Gioventù Battista,** Viale Jonio 84, San Severa-Roma, Catania.

*JAMAICA*
**Jamaica Christian Boys' Home,** PO Box 5, Half Way Tree.

*JAPAN*
**High School Evangelism Fellowship,** Hi-BA Center, 22-16 Shibuya 2-chome, Shibuya-ku, Tokyo 150.
**Young Life Crusade of Japan,** 17 4-chome, Dumano-cho, Hyogo-ku, Kobe-shi.

*KENYA*
**Christian Hostels Fellowship (CHF),** Boys Hostel, St John's Church, Pumwani, PO Box 72636, Nairobi.
**Orthodox Christian Youth Association of Kenya (OCYAK),** Valley Rd, PO Box 47008, Nairobi. T: 28804.

*LEBANON*
**Armenian Evangelical Christian Endeavour Union,** Exec Sec, BP 235, Bayrut. T: 225553.
**Ecumenical Youth and Student Secretariat of the Middle East,** Rue Makhoul, Imm Ianios Rubeiz, BP 1375, Bayrut. T: 341902,341903.
**Mouvement de la Jeunesse Orthodoxe (Harakat al-Shabibat al-Orthodoxia),** Sec Gén, Furn el Hayek St, Achrafieh, BP 2966, Bayrut. T: 238063. (Greek Orthodox).
**World Fellowship of Orthodox Youth Organizations (SYNDESMOS),** Gen Secretariat, PO Box 1375, Bayrut. (Founded 1953).

*LESOTHO*
**Evangelize Youth (Mophato oa Morija),** Lesotho Ecumenical Youth Centre, PO Box 6, Morija.

*MEXICO*
**Adelante Juventud,** Apdo 45-641, Argentina No 29, Zona 1, México, DF. T: 212003.
**Clubes Biblicos Juveniles,** 21 Pte No 1501-A, Apdo 1011, Puebla. T: 28536.
**Desafío Juvenil,** Apdo 1190, Ensenada, BC.

*NETHERLANDS*
**Netherlands Youth Information and Counselling Centre (Nederlands Informatie en Adviescentrum Jonge Mensen),** Herengracht 162, Amsterdam C. (RC. Member ACISJF).
**Roman Catholic Youth Contact (Rooms Katholiek Jongeren Contact),** Geert Teisstraat 14, Stads Kanaal. T: (05990)3671.

*NETHERLANDS ANTILLES*
**Jeugd Centrale,** c/o Bisdom, Willemstad, Curaçao.

*NICARAGUA*
**Consejo de la Pastoral Juvenil,** Av del Centenario 502, Apdo 2008, Managua.

*PERU*
**Asociación Cristiana de Jóvenes de Lima,** Las Camelias 789, San Isidro, Apdo 2411, Lima. T: 405140, 405190.
**Christian Democratic Youth of Latin America (JUDCA),** Apdo 4361, Lima. T: 231717.

*SWEDEN*
**Christian Youth Council of Sweden (Sveriges Kristna Ungdomsrad),** Sec, L Nygatan 16, S-111 28 Stockholm.
**Free SCM in High Schools (Frikyrkliga Gymnasistrorelsen, FKG),** Malartorget 15, Stockholm. T: (08)214584.
**Swedish Christian Youth Council (Sveriges Kristna Ungdomsrad),** Regeringsgatan 80, S-111 39 Stockholm. T: (08)115721.

*SWITZERLAND*
**Christkatholische Jugend der Schweiz,** Zentralpräsident, Judengasslein 23, CH-4123 Allschwill. T: (061)393892. (Old Catholic).
**Evangelische Jugendheimstätte,** CH-6983 Magliaso/TI.
**Interkantonaler Verein für Ev Jugendberatung,** Präs, Hans Haller-Gasse 7, CH-8180 Bülach. T: (051) 961391.
**International Christian Youth Exchange (ICYE),** 150 Route de Ferney, CH-1211 Genève 20. T: (022) 333400.
**Junge Kirche,** Zeltweg 9, CH-8032 Zürich. T: (051) 471957.
**Schweizerische Zentrakomitee der Ev Jugendverbande,** Sek, 63 Av des Alpes, CH-1820 Montreux.
**World Alliance of YMCAs/Alliance Universelle des Unions Chrétiennes de Jeunes Gens (UCJG),** 37 Quai Wilson, CH-1201 Genève. T: (022)323100.

*TOGO*
**Comité de Coordination des Mouvements des Jeunes (CCAC),** CET, BP 348, Lomé.

*UK OF GB & NI*
**Anglican Young Peoples' Association (AYPA),** Sec, Chi Rho House, All Saints Vicarage, Compton, Leek, Staffs. T: (0538)382588.
**Boys' Brigade (BB),** Brigade House, 8 Parsons Green, London SW6 4TH. T: (01)736-8481.
**British Christian Pen Pal Club,** Sec, 17 Heyburn Rd, Tuebrook, Liverpool L13 8BT. T: (051)226-6018.
**British Youth for Christ,** Dir, 131 Lewes Rd, Brighton BN2 3LG. T: 687400.
**Campaigners,** Clan's Chief, 2a Portman Mansions, Chiltern St, London W1. T: (01)935-9012. (Evangelical youth movement).
**Capernwray Missionary Fellowship of Torchbearers,** Capernwray Hall, Carnforth, Lancashire.
**Catholic Scout Advisory Council,** 5 Wayside Rd, Southbourne, Bournemouth.
**Catholic Youth Council,** Catholic Youth Office, 14 Newton Place, Glasgow C3. T: (041)332-6103.
**Christian Endeavour Union of Great Britain & Ireland,** Sec, 31 Lampton Rd, Hounslow, Middx TW3 1JD. T: (01)570-9215.
**Christian Mountain Centre,** Warden, Gorffwysfa, Tremadoc, Gywnedd.
**Church Lads' and Church Girls' Brigade,** National HQ, Claude Hardy House, 15 Etchinglam Park Rd, Finchley, London N3 2DU. T: (01)349-2616.
**Church Youth Fellowship Association (CYFA),** 7 Wine Office Court, Fleet St, London EC4. T: (01) 583-1484.
**Congregational Youth,** Sec, Livingstone House, 11 Carteret St, London SW1.
**Conservative & Christian Democratic Youth Community (COCDYC),** Sec Gen, Young Conservatives Organization, 32 Smith Square, London SW1P 3HH.
**Crusaders' Union,** 1 Ludgate Hill, London EC4 T: (01)248-5983. (Also: 280 St Vincent St, Glasgow. T: (041)221-7200).
**Evangelical Youth Movement,** Dir, Inch Abbey House, Downpatrick, Country Down, NI. T: 2392.
**Frontier Youth Trust (SU),** Sec, 47 Marylebone Lane, London W1M 6AX. T: (01)486-2561.
**IEB Youth Movement,** Dir, Portadown, Craigavon, Country Armagh, NI.
**Inter-School Christian Fellowship (ISCF),** 47 Marylebone Lane, London W1M 6AX. T: (01) 486-2561.
**Methodist Youth Department,** 2 Chester House, Pages Lane, Muswell Hill, London N10 1PZ. T: (01) 444-9845.
**National Catholic Youth Association,** 41 Cromwell Rd, London SW7.
**National Council of YMCAs,** National HQ, 640 Forest Rd, London E17 3DZ. T: (01)520-5599.
**National Young Life Campaign (NYLC),** 10 Fairfield West, Kingston-upon-Thames, Surrey. T: (01)546-9718.
**National Youth Camp,** Assemblies of God in GB & I, 47 Fortescue Rd, Parkstone, Poole, Dorset.
**National Youth Council of Assemblies of God in GB & I,** 2 Thornridge, Brentwood, Essex.
**Operation Youth (Soho London Teams),** All Souls Church, All Souls Place, London W1. T: (01) 794-7450.
**Scottish National Council of YMCAs,** 10 Palmerston Place, Edinburgh EH12 5AD. T: (031) 225-5022.
**Seaside Camps for London Boys and Girls,** Warden, Hawkshill Camp, Walmer, Deal, Kent. T: 5090.
**Teen Challenge in Great Britain and Ireland,** Dir, 4 York Rd, Tunbridge Wells, Kent. (Assemblies of God in GB & I; ministry to drug addicts).

*USA*
**Catholic Central Youth Union of America (CCYUA),** 3835 Westminster Place, St Louis, MO 63108.
**Christian Service Brigade,** Box 150, 2525 North Main St, Wheaton, IL 60187. (Boys' clubs).
**Christian Youth Cinema,** 279 Keswick Av, Glenside, PA 19038.
**Christian Youth Publications,** 4466 West Pine 15F, St Louis, MO 63108.
**Church Youth Research,** 122 West Franklin, Minneapolis, MN 55404.
**Council of Eastern Orthodox Youth Leaders of America,** 3256 Warren Rd, Cleveland, OH 44111.
**Hawaii Activist Youth,** 250 South Vineyard St, Honolulu, HA 96813.
**High School Evangelistic Fellowship,** Gen Dir, 46 West Clinton Av, Tenafly, PO Box 234, South Hackensack, NJ 07670. T: (201)871-3414.
**Huckleberry House for Runaways,** 1 Broderick St, San Francisco, CA 94117.
**Institute in Basic Youth Conflicts,** Chairman, 1027 Arlington Av, Lagrange, IL 60525. T: (312) 323-3593.
**International Christian Youth Exchange (ICYE),** Exec Dir, 475 Riverside Drive, New York, NY 10027. T: (212)666-9445.
**International Youth Development Organization,** 1113 Metropolitan Savings Bldg, Dallas, TX 75202. T: (214)748-7287.
**Liberal Religious Youth (LRY),** 25 Beacon St, Boston, MA 02108.
**National Council of YMCAs of the USA,** Pres, 291 Broadway, New York, NY 10007. T: (212) 349-0700.
**National Young Adult Project,** 1908 Grand Av, Nashville, TN 37203.
**New Life Youth Camps,** Eugene, OR 97400.
**Protestant Youth Council,** 1515 52nd St, Kenosha, WI 53140.
**Teen Challenge,** Dir, PO Box 161, New York, NY 10001.
**Teen Mission, USA,** 371 Hill'n'dale, Lexington, KY 40503. T: (606)277-1150.
**The Interlude Coffee House for Teenagers,** Box 2188, Texas City, TX 77591.
**The Mustard Seed Coffee House,** Washington, DC. (Guidance for runaway teenagers).
**World Christian Endeavor Union (WCEU)/International Society of Christian Endeavor,** 1221 East Broad St, Box 1110, Columbus, OH 43216. T: (614)253-8541.
**World Youth Crusades,** Exec Dir, Box 2, Upland, California.
**Youth Enterprises,** Gen Dir, Box 95, Chula Vista (Box 1001, Imperial Beach), CA 92032.
**Youth for Christ International (YFCI),** North Main St, PO Box 419, Wheaton, IL 60187. T: (312) 668-6600.
**Youth Missions International,** Dir, PO Box 1888, Calexico, CA 92231.
**Youth Unlimited Gospel Outreach (YUGO),** 13115 Silver Bow, Norwalk, CA 90650.
**Youth with a Mission (YWAM),** International Dir, PO Box 4044, Burbank, CA 91503. T: (213) 845-8462.

*URUGUAY*
**Unión Latinoamericana de Juventud Evangélica (ULAJE),** San José 991, Montevideo.

*VENEZUELA*
**Movimiento Juvenil Jóvenes de Acción,** Pasaje Gradillas, local 5c, Torre a Madrices, Caracas 101. T: 813885.

*VIET NAM*
**Association de la Jeunesse Catholique (Thanh Niem Cong Ciao),** Eglise Catholique, Hanoi.

*ZAIRE*
**Fédération Nationale de la Jeunesse Protestante,** BP 3094, Kinshasa-Kalina.

# 73
# Directories, Yearbooks, Handbooks & Indexes

**(World Bibliography of Christian Directories)**

*Definition.* In each country, the major current directories, yearbooks, reference handbooks, and indexes (containing names, addresses, statistics, listings, descriptive material, but not usually histories, surveys or descriptive texts) of churches at the national level (usually here excluding dioceses and other subdivisions), denominations, councils and Christian organizations, agencies, institutions, personnel and periodicals; both confessional, denominational, interdenominational, local, national, plurinational, international, and topical; and the publishing addresses from which they may be obtained.

Christian or church yearbooks, handbooks, directories and indexes of significance at national or wider levels number over 5,000.

**Notes.** (1) Many of these publications are annual, biennial or triennial. This listing does not attempt systematically to give the latest editions, which in most cases may be assumed to date from 1975-81. Addresses are the publishing addresses from which they may be obtained. These date from the year of publication; if subsequently changed, the latest addresses are available from the organizations as listed elsewhere in this Topical Directory. (2) In addition to the international and national-level directories given below, there are large numbers of others (not given here) at diocesan, congregational and other local levels; these should be consulted for names of clergy, places of worship, times of services and languages used, etc. Further, a large number of the organizations listed in this Topical Directory of World Christianity have lists of foreign branches, directories, address lists, mailing lists, or lists of personnel and programmes. (3) Note that all country-wide directories are listed under the country of the church in their titles, even though they may be published in a different country as shown in the address. (4) After many items, the number of pages is given. Thus '239p.' means '239 pages in length'.

*ANGOLA*
**Boletim ecclesiástico de Angola e São Tomé, 1963-1964.** Tipografia da Missão Católica, CP 1230, Luanda. T: 34640. 239p.

*ARGENTINA*
**Panorama estadístico de la Iglesia Argentina.** 1976. N. Rosato. Arzobispado, Suipacha 1034, Buenos Aires. T: 313317. 24p.

*AUSTRALIA*
**Australian charismatic directory.** Temple Trust, PO Box 63, Waverley, NSW 2024.
**Australian Evangelical Alliance: directory of missions, 1973.** 4 Wellesley St, Mont Albert,

Victoria 3127. T: (03)836-6079. 1st edition 1973. 45p.
**Official year book of the Catholic Church of Australia, Papua New Guinea, New Zealand and the Pacific Islands, 1971.** Cusa House, 175 Elizabeth St, PO Box 3592, GPO, Sydney 2001. 544p.
**Orthodox and other Eastern churches in Australia.** Church of England in Australia, Flinders St, Townsville, Queensland. (First edition 1963, revised 1978).
**Year book of the Diocese of Sydney, 1970.** Diocesan Church House, George St, Sydney, NSW.
**Year book of the Presbyterian Church of Australia, 1970-71.** 147 Collins St, Melbourne.

*AUSTRIA*
**Alt-katholisches Jahrbuch 1964.** Alt-katholischen Kirche Österreichs, Schottenring 17/1, Wien 1/1. (Old Catholic).
**Jahrbuch für die Kirche von Wien 1970.** Erzbischöflichen Pastoralamt im Wiener-Dom Verlag, Stephensplatz 6/VI, A-1010 Wien. (Catholic)

*BANGLADESH*
**Catholic directory of Bangladesh, 1973.** Catholic Bishops' Conference, Archbishop's House, Ramna, PO Box 3, Dacca 2.
**Directory of Christian work in East Pakistan.** c1960. Literature Committee, East Pakistan Christian Council, Dacca.

*BARBADOS*
**Handbook of churches in the Caribbean.** 1st edition, 1973. Ed Joan Brathwaite. CADEC, Caribbean Conference of Churches, PO Box 616, Bridgetown. 234p.

*BELGIUM*
**Annuaire mondial de la radio et de la télévision catholiques, 1970-71.** UNDA, Rue de l'Orme 12, B-1050 Brussel.
**Christian teacher training institutions: register of Christian church-related teacher training institutions in Africa, Asia and Latin America, 1964-5.** FERES, Vlamingenstraat 116, Louvain.
**Directory of centers for religious research and study, 1968.** Vlamingenstraat 116, Louvain. T: (016)20809.
**Katholiek Jaarboek voor België/Annuaire Catholique de Belgique, 1971-72.** Centre Interdiocésain, Rue Guimard 5, B-1040 Brussel.

*BOLIVIA*
**Guia de la Iglesia, Bolivia, 1970.** Secretariado Nacional de Estudios Sociales, Casilla 2309, La Paz. (Catholic).

*BRAZIL*
**Anuário Católico do Brasil, 1970/1971.** CERIS, Rua Dr Julio Ottoni 571, Santa Tereza, ZC-45, 20000 Rio de Janeiro, GB. 2292p.
**Brazil 1980: the Protestant handbook.** W.R. Read & F.A. Ineson. MARC, 919 West Huntington Drive, Monrovia, CA 91016, USA.

*BURMA*
**Catholic directory of Burma, 1969.** Archdiocese of Rangoon, 289 Theinbyu St, Rangoon. T: 12752. (Duplicated).

*BURUNDI*
**Annuaire ecclésiastique, Burundi et Rwanda 1970-1971.** SECOREB, BP 1390, Bujumbura. (Catholic).

*CANADA*
**Anglican year book 1972.** Anglican Church of Canada, Anglican Book Centre, 600 Jarvis St, Toronto 285. 207p.
**Directory of the Ukrainian Catholic Church (except USSR), 1971.** Redeemer's Voice Press, Yorkton, Saskatchewan. (Ukrainian-rite; RC).
**Le Canada ecclésiastique/Catholic directory of Canada, 1971-72.** Librairie Beauchemin Limitée, 450 Av Beaumont, Montréal 303, Québec.
**Missions étrangères: annuaire 1970.** Centre d'Animation Missionnaire, 59 Rue Desnoyers, Pont-Viau, Ville de Laval, Québec.
**Official directory of ministers and churches: Pentecostal Assemblies of Canada, 1971.** International Offices, 10 Overlea Blvd, Toronto 354, Ontario. T: (416)425-1010.
**Report volume of the Baptist Federation of Canada, 1967-1970.** 91 Queen St, Box 901, Brantford, Ontario.
**The church overseas 1972: Kenya, Zaire, India, Bolivia.** Canadian Baptist Overseas Mission Board, 217 St George St, Toronto 5, Ontario.
**United Church of Canada year book 1974.** 2 vols (volume I Statistics). 85 St Clair Av East, Toronto 290, Ontario.

*CHILE*
**Guia Eclesiástica y parroquial de Chile, 1972.** Arzobispado de Santiago, Erasmo Escala 1822, 6 piso, Casilla 30-D, Santiago. T: 63275. (Catholic).

*CHINA (TAIWAN)*
**Church directory of the Republic of China, 1969.** China Evangelical Fellowship, 4-2 Chin Hsi St, PO Box 2102, Taipei. 94p. (In Chinese).
**Taiwan Catholic directory, 1970.** Catholic Central Bureau, 34 Lane 32 Kuangfu Rd, Taipei 105.
**Taiwan Missionary Fellowship directory 1972.** Dixon Press, 48-50 Po Al Rd, Taipei. T: 29449. 159p.

*COLOMBIA*
**Anuario del Instituto de Missione de Yarumal, 1970.** Oficina de Relaciones Publicas de Imey, Calle 49 (Ayacucho) 38-33, Medellín.
**Directorio Católico Latino-Americano, 1968.** CELAM, Secretariado General, Apdo Aéreo 5278, Bogotá, DE.
**Directorio de la Iglesia en Colombia, 1969.** Departamento de Sociología de Varios Servicios Ltda, Edificio Banco Central Hipotecario, Apdo Aéreo 14784, Bogotá. (Catholic).
**Directorio Evangélico y calendario de oración de Colombia, 1975-76.** Tipografia Union, Apdo Aéreo 964, Medellín.
**Guia de las Iglesias Evangélicas de Colombia.** 1971. Retiro Nacional de Pastores, Medellín.

*COSTA RICA*
**Directorio de institutos y seminarios teológicos en America Latina.** Difusiones Interamericanas, Apdo 2470, San José.
**Estado del Clero de la Provincia de Costa Rica, 1972.** EXODO, Apdo 3771, San José. (Catholic).

*CUBA*
**Directorio Eclesiástico de Cuba, 1971.** Conferencia Episcopal de Cuba, Apdo 594, La Habana 1 (Catholic).

*DOMINICAN REPUBLIC*
**Directorio de la Iglesia Católica en República Dominicana, 1972.** Conferencia del Episcopado Dominicano, Secretariado Nacional de Pastoral de Conjunto, Apdo 186, Santo Domingo.

*EGYPT*
**Annuaire Catholique d'Egypte, 1973.** Nonciature Apostolique, Safarat Al-Vatican, 5 Sharia Mohamed Mazhar, Zamalek, Al Qahirah. T: 805152.

*EL SALVADOR*
**Anuario Eclesiástico de El Salvador, 1970.** Secretariado Social Interdiocesano, Arzobispado, 1C Pte 3402, San Salvador. T: 234124. (Catholic).

*ETHIOPIA*
**Catholic directory of Ethiopia, 1968.** PO Box 1000, Addis Abeba.

*FIJI*
**Directory: Archdiocese of Suva, Fiji, 1973.** Catholic Supply Store, Box 1260, Suva.

*FRANCE*
**Annuaire Catholique de France, 1973.** Publicat, 17 Blvd Poissonnière, F-75002 Paris.
**Annuaire de l'Eglise Catholique en Afrique francophone, Iles de l'Océan Indien, Départementes et Territoires Français d'Outre-mer, 1972-1973.** Office National de Publications Culturelles, 3 bis, Cité d'Hauteville, F-75011 Paris.
**Annuaire des églises, associations et institutions orthodoxes.** 1966. CIMADE, 1766 Rue de Grenelle, F-75007 Paris. T: 705-9399.
**Annuaire évangélique 1970.** DEFI, BP 544, 38-Grenoble.
**Annuaire 1971 des Assemblés de Dieu de France, 1971.** Viens et Vois, 10 Rue du Sentier, Paris 2.
**La France protestante 1974.** Fédération Protestante de France, 47 Rue de Clichy, F-75009 Paris. 544p.

*GERMANY, Federal Republic of*
**Adressbuch für das katholische Deutschland, 1972.** Zentralkomitee der Deutschen Katholiken, Hochkreuzallee 246, D-53 Bonn-Bad Godesberg.
**Kirchliches Handbuch: Amtliches statistisches Jahrbuch der katholischen Kirche Deutschlands, 1968.** Amtlichen Zentralstelle für kirchliche Statistik des Katholischen Deutschlands, Antwerpener Str 35, D-Köln.
**Handbuch der Pfingstbewegung.** W.J. Hollenweger. 1965. UNI-Druck, Amalienstr 85, 8 München 13. (Pentecostalism).
**Kirchliches Jahrbuch für die Alt-Katholiken in Deutschland, 1970.** Gregor-Mendel-Str 28, Bonn.
**Scriptures of the world: a compilation of 1.549 languages in which at least one Book of the Bible has been published, 1974.** United Bible Societies, PO Box 755, D-7000 Stuttgart 1.
**Taschenbuch der Evangelischen Kirchen in Deutschland, 1974.** Okumenische Centrale, Bockenheimer Landstr 109, 6 Frankfurt/Main. 924p.
**United Bible Societies directory, 1975.** PO Box 755, D-7000 Stuttgart 1. (Earlier editions 1965, 1970).
**Who's who in the Catholic world, 1967-1968.** Volume I, Europe. L. Schwann Verlag, Postfach 7640, D-4 Düsseldorf 1.
**Yearbook of the Orthodox Church, 1978 edition.** Buchverlag Alex Proc, Athos-Verlog, POB 801425, D-8000 München 80. 309p. (Annual, alternately in German, English, French).

*GHANA*
**Ghana Catholic diary, 1970.** Accra Catholic Press, PO Box 765, Accra.

*GREECE*
**Hemerologion of the Church of Greece.** 1975. Church of Greece, I Gennadiou 14, Athínai 40. T: 237654. 540p. (In Greek).

*GUATEMALA*
**Directorio de la Arquidiócesis de Guatemala, 1971.** Arzobispado, Palacio Arzobispal, 7a Av 6-21, Zona 1, Guatemala Ciudad. (Catholic).
**Estadistica de la obra religioso-cristiana en Guatemala.** Iglesia Luterana, 8a Av 10-43, Zona 1, Altos 5 piso, Guatemala. 235p.

*HAITI*
**Annuaire de l'Eglise d'Haïti. Numéro spécial 1972.** Archevêché, Port-au-Prince. T: 22043. (Catholic).
**Annuaire Protestant 1971-1972.** Centre d'Information et de Statistique Evangélique, BP 458, Port-au-Prince.
**Protestant yearbook of foreign missions, 1971-1972.** Concile des Eglises Evangéliques d'Haïti, BP 458, Port-au-Prince.

*HOLY SEE*
**Annuario Pontificio 1978.** Tipografia Poliglotta Vaticana, Città del Vaticano.
**Annuarium statisticum ecclesiae/Statistical yearbook of the Church, 1977.** Rationarium Generale Ecclesiae, Secretaria Status, Città del Vaticano. (Annual). 350p.
**Catholic international organizations (CIO). The laity today.** Bulletin of the Consilium de Laicis, No 13-14 (1973), Piazza San Calisto 16, I-00153 Roma, Italy.
**Guida alla Catechesi nel mondo.** 1971. SC per il Clero, Piazza Pio XII 10, I-00193 Roma, Italy. T: 6982 int 4151. (Catechetical centres, bibliographies on countries).
**Guida delle Mission Cattoliche, 1975.** 5th edition. SC per l'Evangelizzazione dei Popoli, Palazzo di Propaganda Fide, I-00187 Roma, Italy. T: 686941. 1628p.
**Sacra Congregazione per il Culto Divino. Elenco dei membri e consultori. Commissioni, Centri, Instituti, Periodici di Liturgia, 1972.** Piazza Pio XII 10, IV piano, I-00193 Roma, Italy.
**Seminaria Ecclesiae Catholicae, MCMLXIII (1963).** SC de Seminariis et Studiorum Universitatibus, I-00120 Città del Vaticano. (Seminaries).

*HONDURAS*
**Anuario de la Iglesia en Honduras, 1970.** Arzobispado, Apdo 106, Tegucigalpa. (Catholic).

*HONG KONG*
**Hong Kong Catholic directory and yearbook, 1972.** Catholic Truth Society of China, Catholic Centre, Grand Bldg, Hong Kong.
**Hong Kong church directory, 1969.** Chinese Christian Literature Council, 57 Peking Rd, 2nd Floor, Kowloon. 312p.

*HUNGARY*
**Handbuch des ungarischen Katholizismus, 1975.** UKI, Grillparzerstr 5/10, A-1010 Wien, Austria. 208p.

*INDIA*
**Catholic directory of India, 1972.** St Paul International Book Centre, H-30 Connaught Circus, New Delhi 1.
**Christian handbook of addresses of heads of churches and Christian agencies in India, 1970.** Literature Dept, National Christian Council, Nagpur 1. 74p.
**Christian handbook of India, 1959.** National Christian Council of India, Nagpur 1.
**Directory of information for Christian colleges in India, 1967.** R. & N. Dickinson. Christian Literature Society, Madras.

*INDONESIA*
**Buku Petundjuk Geredja Katolik Indonesia, 1970/Directory of the Catholic Church in Indonesia.** Kantor Waligereja Indonesia, Taman Tjut Mutiah 10, Jakarta.

*IRELAND*
**Church of Ireland directory 1971.** Irish Church Publications, 59 Merrion Square, Dublin 2. T: 63581/2/3. 258p.
**Irish Catholic directory, 1971.** James Duffy & Co, 21 Shaw St, Pearse St, Dublin 2. 878p.
**Methodist Church in Ireland, Minutes of Conference 1970.** Mayo House, 61 Rathdown Park, Dublin 6.

*ISRAEL*
**Annuaire de l'Eglise Catholique en Terre Sainte, 1972.** Franciscan Printing Press, Jerusalem. (Holy Land).

*ITALY*
**Addresses: White Fathers Generaleat, 1966.** Padri Bianchi, Via Aurelia 269, I-00165 Roma.
**Annuario Cattolico d'Italia, 1972/73.** CNEC, Via Vigliena 10, I-00192, Roma.
**Annuario del PIME, 1970.** Pontificio Istituto Missioni Estere, Casa Generalizia, Via San Erasmo 2, I-00184, Roma.
**Annuario Evangelico 1972-73: indirizzi e orari di tutte le chiese et opere evangeliche in Italia.** Editrice Claudiana, Via Principe Tommaso 1, Torino. 346p.
**Caritas Internationalis. Annuaire 1970-1972.** General Secretariat, Palazzo San Calisto, Piazza San Calisto 16, I-00153 Roma. 273p.
**Catalogus Generalis Ordinis Praedicatorum, 1967.** Curia Generalitia Santa Sabina, Piazza Pietro d'Illiria 1, Aventino, I-00153 Roma. (Dominican).
**Catholic media: world directory 1971.** R. Aquilo. IRADES Edizioni Pastorali, Via Paisiello 6, I-00198 Roma.
**Catholic newspapers and periodicals in Africa, 1970.** Rome: Development Commission, International Catholic Press Union, Piazza Montecitorio 115 int 6, I-00186 Roma. T: 6790847. 117p.
**Catholic newspapers and periodicals in Asia, 1970: a preliminary listing.** F.-J. Eilers. CP 5080, I-00153 Roma. 232p.
**Conspectus Ordinis Carmelitarum Discalceatorum, 1971.** Casa Generalizia Carmelitani Scalzi, Corso d'Italia 38, I-00198 Roma. (Carmelites).
**Cristianesimo Evangelico, 1967-68.** Editrice Claudiana, Via Principe Tommaso 1, Torino. 219p.
**Ecumenism around the world: a directory of ecumenical institutes, centers and organizations.** 2nd edition, 1974. Centro Pro Unione, Via Santa Maria dell'Anima 30, I-00186 Roma.
**Elenchus Sodalium. Official membership list of the Missionhurst Fathers and Brothers, 1971.** Casa Generalizia CICM, Via de Villa Trioli 26, I-00163 Roma.
**Elenco alfabetico ed elenco per residenza attuale dei Membri Novizi e Professi e delle Case e Centri Missionary IMC con indirizzi postali. 1970.** Instituto Missioni Consolata, Corso Ferrucci 14, I-10138 Torino.
**Missionari Comboniani. Catalogo. Congregazione dei Figli del Sacro Cuore di Gesù. 1971.** Via San Pancrazio 17, I-00152 Roma.
**Personnel OMI, 1967.** Administration Générale, Via Aurelia 290, Roma 6.
**SS Patriarchae Benedicti Familiae Confoederatae. Catalogus Monasteriorum OSB, 1970.** Secretariatus Abbatis Primatis, Badia Primaziale Sant'Anselmo, Piazza Cavalieri di Malta 5, I-00153 Roma.
**Stato del Personale con prospetto alfabetico dei Saveriani, 1970.** Numero speciale del Bolletino interno Notiziario Saveriano. Pia Società San Francesco Saverio per le Missioni Estere, Viale San Martino 8, I-43100 Parma. (Xaverians).
**The Jesuits: yearbook of the Society of Jesus, 1972-1973.** Casa Generalizia, Borgo Santo Spirito 5, I-00193 Roma. T: 6569841.

*IVORY COAST*
**Annuaire du clergé, des religieux et religieuses de Côte d'Ivoire, 1971.** Secrétariat de l'Episcopat, BP 8016, Abidjan. (Catholic).

*JAMAICA*
**Caribbean Catholic directory, 1977.** Antilles Episcopal Conference, Secretariat, PO Box 43, Kingston 6.
**1973 Journal of the One Hundred and Third Annual Synod of the Church in Jamaica in the Province of the West Indies.** The Herald Ltd., 43 East St, Kingston.

*JAPAN*
**Japan Catholic directory, 1972.** National Catholic Committee of Japan, 10 RoKubancho, Chiyoda-ku, Tokyo.
**Japan Christian yearbook 1969-1970.** Christian Literature Society of Japan, 5 4-chome, Ginza, Tokyo. T: 567-1986. 429p.
**Japan's religions — directory of Buddhist denominations.** No 3, 1957. International Institute for the Study of Religions, National YMCA Bldg, 2-1 Nishi Kanda, Chiyoda-ku, Tokyo. T: 40838.
**Kirisutokyo Nenkan** (Christian yearbook). 1972. Tokyo.
**Shukyo Nenkan** (Religious yearbook in Japanese) 1970. Agency for Cultural Affairs, Tokyo.

*KENYA*
**Christian literature in Kenya and Tanzania: a survey.** 1966. Christian Council of Kenya, PO Box 5009, Nairobi.
**Directory of Bible training institutions in Africa.** Association of Evangelicals of Africa & Madagascar, Ralph Bunche Rd, PO Box 49332, Nairobi. T: 21894.
**Kenya Churches handbook 1973.** Ed D.B. Barrett et al. PO Box 40230, Nairobi. T: 23649. 349p.
**Who's who in the African independent churches, 1973.** D.B. Barrett. Unit of Research, PO Box 40230, Nairobi. (56 biographies, with addresses).

*KOREA, South*
**Catholic address book, 1971.** Catholic Conference of Korea, CPO Box 16, Soul.
**Christian yearbook 1970.** National Council of Churches in Korea, 136-46 Yun'chi'dong, Chong'ro, Kwang-Wha-Moon, PO Box 143, Soul. 688p. (In Korean language only).
**Prayer calendar of Christian mission and general directory 1974.** Christian Literature Society of Korea, Christian Center Bldg, 136-146 Yun ji Dong, Chongno Ku, Soul. T: 350076.

*LEBANON*
**Directory: Syndesmos.** World Fellowship of Orthodox Youth Organizations, Gen Secretariat, PO Box 1375, Bayrut.

*LUXEMBOURG*
**Annuaire diocésain de Luxembourg, 1971.** Evêché, 4 Rue Génistre, CP 419, Luxembourg-Ville. (Catholic).

*MADAGASCAR*
**Agenda 1973: annuaire de l'Eglise Catholique à Madagascar.** Archevêché, Andohalo, Antananarivo. T: 20726.
**Diary Malagasy, 1966.** Imprimerie Luthérienne, Antsahamanitra, Tananarive.

*MALAWI*
**Catholic directory of Malawi, 1970.** Catholic Secretariat, PO Box 5368, Limbe.

*MALAYSIA*
**Catholic directory & diary 1973, Malaysia and Singapore.** Bishop's House, 528 Bukit Nanas, Kuala Lumpur.

*MALTA*
**Catholic directory of Malta and Gozo, 1963.** Empire Press, Floriana.

*MARTINIQUE*
**Annuaire ecclésiastique 1971, Martinique, Guadeloupe, Guyane.** Imprimerie Antillaise Saint-Paul, 90 Rue de la République, Fort-de-France. (Catholic).

*MAURITIUS*
**Annuaire du Diocèse de Port-Louis, 1971.** Evêché, Rue Mgr Gonin, Port-Louis. (Catholic).

*MEXICO*
**Anuario de la Iglesia en México, 1970.** Secretariado General del Episcopado, Apdo 32-661, México 1, DF. (Catholic).
**Directorio Evangélico de la Ciudad de México, 1969-70.** Federación Evangélica de México, Motolinia 8-107, Apdo Postal 1830, México 1, DF. 72p.
**Directorio Evangélico de México 1970.** Mexico Missionary Services, Apdo 333, México, DF.

*MOROCCO*
**Anuario 1970, Archidiocesis de Tanger.** Curia Pastoral, San Francisco 55, Tanger. (Catholic).

*MOZAMBIQUE*
**Anuario Católico de Moçambique, 1971.** Conferência Episcopal de Moçambique, Secretariado Geral, CP 292, Quelimane. 465p.

*NETHERLANDS*
**Naamlijst. Commissies en Organen van Bijstand in de Nederlands Hervormde Kerk, 1971.** Carnegielaan 9, 's-Gravenhage-3A. T: (070)653915.
**Nieuw Kerkelijk Handboek (Van Alphen), 1972-73.** NV Drukkerij Koch & Knuttel, Gouda. 613p.
**Pius Almanak: Jaarboek van Katholiek Nederland, 1971.** NV Drukkerij De Tijd, Nieuwezijds Voorburgwal 65-73, Amsterdam.

*NICARAGUA*
**Anuario Eclesiástico de Nicaragua, 1967.** Conferencia Episcopal de Nicaragua, Apdo 20-08, Managua. (Catholic).

*NIGERIA*
**African Church lectionary, 1965.** The African Church, 58 Broad St, PO Box 2846, Lagos.
**Official Nigeria Catholic directory, 1973.** Catholic Secretariat of Nigeria, PO Box 951, Lagos. 163p.
**West African Churchman's calendar, 1967.** Immanuel College, PO Box 515, Ibadan.
**Year book of Nigerian churches, 1969/70.** Department of Religious Publication, Akin Akinniola Associates, PO Box 883, Ibadan. 169p.

*NORWAY*
**Arbok for den Norske Kirke, 1970.** Forlaget Land og Kirke, Norske Kirke, St Halvards Place 3, Oslo.
**Oversikt over den Katolske Kirke i Norden (Nordic Catholic Church directory), 1971.** Nordiske Bispekonferanse, Akersveien 5, Oslo 1.

*PAKISTAN*
**Pakistan Catholic directory, 1966.** Archbishop's House, St Patrick's Cathedral, Shahrah Iraq, Karachi 3.

*PANAMA*
**Anuario Eclesiástico de Panamá, 1965.** Curia Arzobispal, Apdo 386, Ciudad de Panamá (Catholic).

*PAPUA NEW GUINEA*
**United Church directory, 1975.** UCPNGSI, PO Box 3401, Port Moresby.

*PARAGUAY*
**Anuario Eclesiástico del Paraguay, 1972.** Centro de Estudios Socio Religiosos, Coronel Bogado 130, Asunción. (Catholic).
**Guía de las iglesias evangélicas en el Paraguay.** 3rd edition, 1964. Asociación de Obreros, Pastores y Misioneros del Paraguay, Asunción. 20p.

*PERU*
**Anuario Eclesiástico del Perú, 1969.** Secretariado del Episcopado Nacional, Arzobispado. Apdo 1512, Lima. (Catholic).

*PHILIPPINES*
**Catholic directory of the Philippines, 1971.** Catholic Trade School, PO Box 2036, Manila.
**Churches and sects in the Philippines.** D.J. Elwood, 1968. Silliman University, Dumaguete City. 213p.
**Philippine missionary directory, 1968.** Philippine Crusades, Box 1416, Manila.

*PORTUGAL*
**Anuário Católico de Portugal, 1968.** Secretariado de Informação Religiosa, Edifício de São Vincente, Lisboa 2.
**Prontuário de igrejas, organismos e obreiros evangélicos em Portugal, 1967.** Movimento Promoter de Evangelização, Rua da Mae d'Agua 13-2, Lisboa 2. 176p.

*REUNION*
**Annuaire ecclésiastique du Diocèse de la Réunion, 1971.** Evêché, 42 Rue de Paris, Saint-Denis. (Catholic).

*SENEGAL*
**Annuaire Catholique du Sénégal pour l'année 1972.** Archevêché de Dakar, BP 1908, Dakar.

*SINGAPORE*
**A handbook of churches and Christian organizations in Singapore.** J. Wong, 1971. SU Christian Book Centre, 36H Prinsep St, Singapore 7. 69p.
**Directory of Singapore Churches 1969.** Council of Churches, 6 Mt Sophia, Singapore 9. 43p.
**Directory of urban industrial mission projects in the EACC area, 1970.** Stamford College Press, 340-342 Joo Chiat Rd, Singapore 15.
**Guide to Chinese Catholic diaspora, 1971.** Singapore Catholic Central Bureau, 225-B Queen St, Singapore 7.

*SOUTH AFRICA*
**Almanak van die Gereformeerde Kerk 1971.** Posbus 20004, Pk Noordbrug, Potchefstroom.
**Almanak van die Gereformeerde Kerk onder Nie-Blankes, 1967.** Posbus 20004, Pk Noordbrug, Potchefstroom.
**Catholic directory of Southern Africa, 1971.** Somerset Rd, PO Box 870, Cape Town.
**Lutheran almanak 1973.** Lutheran Publishing House, 176 West St, Durban.
**Jaarboek van die Nederduitse Gereformeerde Kerke (Moeder-, Sending- en Bantoekerke). 124 Jaargang, 1973.** 119 de Korte St, Braamfontein, Johannesburg. T: 442037.
**Minutes of the Annual Conference of the Methodist Church of South Africa, 1965.** Methodist Publishing House and Book Depot, Cape Town.
**Year book and clerical directory 1969/70.** Publications Department, Church of the Province of South Africa, PO Box 1932, Cape Town.
**Year book 1972 of the United Congregational Church of Southern Africa.** 75 de Korte St, Braamfontein, Johannesburg.
**Zulu Almanac, 1966.** Lutheran Publishing House, 220 West St, Durban.

*SPAIN*
**Anuario Evangélico Español 1973.** Tipografía Artística, Alameda 12, Madrid 14. 272p.
**Guía de la Iglesia en España, 1970.** Oficina General de Información y Estadística de la Iglesia, Secretariado del Episcopado Español, Alfonso XI 4, Madrid 14. (Catholic).

*SRI LANKA*
**National Catholic directory of Sri Lanka, 1978.** Ed J.B.C. Anandappa. Archbishop's House, Colombo 8. 520p.

*SUDAN*
**Directory of the Christian Churches in the Sudan, 1967.** Sudan Council of Churches, PO Box 1928, Al Khurtum. 45p.

*SWEDEN*
**Metodistkyrkans i Sverige Arsbok, 1969.** Sibyllegatan 18, S-114 42 Stockholm. T: (08)670155.
**Svenska Kyrkans Arsbok, 1970.** AB Verbum, Kyrkliga Centralförlaget, Stockholm. 323p.
**Where is the Baptist Church? Directory of the European Baptist Churches: headquarters, theological seminaries and holiday centres, 1967.** E. Rudén. Westerbergs Forlag, Hässleholm, Stockholm 6. 52p.

*SWITZERLAND*
**Agenda pastoral de Eglises protestantes de Suisse, 1970.** Rittergasse 3, CH-4000 Basel. 332p.
**Annuaire du diocèse de Lausanne, Genève et Fribourg 1971.** Evêché, CP 77, CH-1700 Fribourg. (Catholic).
**Annuaire protestant du Canton de Genève. 1970-71.** Consistoire, Eglise Nationale Protestante de Genève, Rue de Cloître 2, Genève.
**Association Internationale pour la Défense de la Liberté Religieuse.** Schosshaldenstr 17, CH-3006 Bern.
**Centres of renewal for study and lay training.** Department of the Laity, WCC, 150 Route de Ferney, CH-1211 Genève 20.
**Die Heilsarmee: Disposition der Truppen in der Schweiz und Österreich 1970.** Nationales Hauptquartier, Laupenstr 5, Postfach 2659, CH-3001 Bern.
**Directory of Christian councils.** 2nd edition, 1975. World Council of Churches, 150 Route de Ferney, CH-1211 Genève 20. 256p.
**Directory of theological training institutions in Europe (Non-Roman Catholic).** Conference of European Churches, 150 Route de Ferney, CH-1211 Genève 20. 57p.
**Directory, World Alliance of YMCAs, 1972.** YMCA, 37 Quai Wilson, CH-1201 Genève. 140p.
**Directory/Liste d'adresses/Anschriftenliste/ Guía de direcciones (1972).** YWCA/UCF/CVJF/ACFM, 37 Quai Wilson, CH-1201 Genève. T: 323100.
**Ecumenical prayer cycle,** WCC, 150 Route de Ferney, CH-1211 Genève 20.
**Handbook of member churches, World Alliance of Reformed Churches, 1974.** WARC, 150 Route Ferney, CH-1211 Genève 20. 75p.
**Jahrbuch 1971 der Christkatholischen Kirche der Schweiz.** Christkatholischer Schriftenverlag, CH-4123 Allschwil/Basel. 124p.
**Jahresbericht 1971, Bistum Chur, Dienst der römisch-katholischen Kirke in der deutschen Schweiz.** Bistum Chur, Hof 19, CH-7000 Chur.
**'Lutheran Churches in the world: a handbook',** *Lutheran world* (Geneva) (vol. 24, 2-3, 1977, p.113-352). LWF, 150 Route de Ferney, CH-1211 Genève 20.
**Lutheran communication directory,** LWF, 150 Route de Ferney, CH-1211 Genève 20.
**Lutheran directory: 1973 supplement to 1971 edition.** Lutheran World Federation, 150 Route de Ferney, CH-1211 Genève 20.
**Mennonites around the world/Mennoniten in aller Welt.** Agape-Verlag, Basel.
**Survey of Church Union negotiations 1975-77,** WCC, 150 Route de Ferney, CH-1211 Genève 20.
**World Alliance of Reformed Churches.** 1964. WARC, 150 Route de Ferney, CH-1211 Genève 20.
**World Student Christian Federation directory, 1971.** CP 5, CH-1211 Genève 2.

*TANZANIA*
**Catholic directory of Eastern Africa, 1977-79.** T.M.P. Book Dept, PO Box 399, Tabora. 241p. (Previous editions 1965, 1968, 1971, 1974-76).
**Christian Council of Tanzania directory, 1972.** CCT, Box 2537, Dar es Salaam. 31p.
**Kalenda, Kanisa la Kiinjili la Kilutheri.** 1972. ELCT, PO Box 3033, Arusha. T: 2426,2134.

*THAILAND*
**Catholic directory o f Thailand 1967.** Xavier Hall 70/9 Rajavithi Rd, Bangkok.
**Christian directory to Thailand, Vietnam, Laos, Khmer Republic and Malaysia, 1974.** Suthep Chaviwan, Box 1405, Bangkok.
**1972 Mission directory of Thailand, Cambodia and Laos.** Ed B. Bray. Newsasia, Bangkok.

*TUNISIA*
**Ordo et annuaire de la prélature de Tunis pour l'année 1970.** 4 Rue d'Alger, Tunis. (Catholic).

*USSR*
**Church handbook for the USSR: a handbook for the Christian tourist in the USSR.** J. Innes. Keston College, Heathfield Rd, Keston, Kent BR2 6BA, UK. (Loose-leaf, in progress 1967-75).

*UK OF GB & NI*
**A Christian year book 1950.** SCM Press, 56 Bloomsbury St, London, WC1.
**A directory of missionary training in the United Kingdom.** 1972. Evangelical Fellowship for Missionary Studies, EAGB, 19 Draycott Place, London SW3 2SJ.
**Baptist handbook 1971.** Baptist Union of Great Britain and Ireland, 4 Southampton Row, London WC1B 4AB.
**Assemblies of God in GB & Ireland year book 1972-73.** Assemblies of God Publishing House, 106/114 Talbot St, Nottingham NG1 5GH.
**Anglican religious communities: a directory of principles and practice, 1977.** SLG Press, Convent of the Incarnation, Fairacres, Oxford OX4 1TB.
**Catholic directory for Scotland, 1972.** John S. Burns & Sons, 25 Finlas St, Glasgow G22 5DS.
**Catholic directory of England and Wales, 1974.** Associated Catholic Newspapers, London.
**CBMS handbook 1973.** Conference of Missionary Societies in GB and Ireland, Edinburgh House, 2 Eaton Gate, London SW1W 9BL. T: (01)730-9611.
**Charismatic directory.** 2nd edition, 1976. Fountain Trust, 3a High St, Esher, Surrey KT10 9RP. T: 67331.
**Christian directory 76/77.** Buzz, 99a Burlington Rd, New Malden, Surrey KT3 4LR. (470 societies).
**Church of England year book, 1978.** Church Information Office, Church House, Dean's Yard, London SW1P 3NZ. 432p.
**Church of Scotland year-book 1974.** Department of Publicity and Publication, 119 George St, Edinburgh. 430p.
**Congregational year book 1970-71.** Congregational Church in England and Wales, Livingstone House, 11 Carteret St, London SW1.
**Crockford's clerical directory 1977-78.** 87th issue. Oxford University Press, Walton St, Oxford OX2 6DP. Tel: (0865)56767. (Directory of all Anglican clergy).
**Directory of St Joseph's Society, Mill Hill.** 1971. St Joseph's College, Mill Hill, London NW7.
**Directory of theological schools and related institutions, 1974.** 8th edition. Theological Education Fund, 13 London Rd, Bromley, Kent BR1 1DE.
**Directory 1971-72, General Assembly of Unitarian and Free Christian Churches.** Essex Hall, 1-6 Essex St, Strand, London WC2R 3HY. T: (01)240-2384.
**Echoes daily prayer guide, 1969.** Echoes of Service, 1 Widcombe Crescent, Bath. (Brethren).
**Elim Pentecostal Church year book, 1972/3.** PO Box 38, Cheltenham GL50 3ED. T: 59904/5/6.
**Fellowship of Independent Evangelical Churches handbook 1974.** Fellowship House, 136 Rosendale Rd, West Dulwich, London SE21 8LG. T: (01)670-5815/6.
**Free Church directory 1970-71.** Ed J. McNicol. Crown House Publications, Crown House, Morden, Surrey. T: (01)540-1101.
**Free Church of Scotland year book, 1973.** Knox Press, 15 North Bank St, Edinburgh EH1 2LS.
**General Conference of the New Church: year book 1973-74.** 20 Bloomsbury Way, London WC1A 2TH.
**Handbook of the General Assembly of Unitarian and Free Christian Churches, 1970-73.** Unitarian Headquarters, Essex Hall, 1-6 Essex St, Strand, London WC2R 3HY. T: (01)240-2384.
**Handbook of the Religious Society of Friends, 1972.** Friends World Committee for Consultation, Drayton House, 30 Gordon St, London WC1H 0AX.
**Handbook of the United Free Church of Scotland 1971-72.** 11 Newton Place, Glasgow C3.
**Local councils of churches today, 1971.** British Council of Churches, 10 Eaton Gate, London SW1. 117p. (Directory of 700 councils).
**London Diocese book 1974.** Starling Press, Risca, Newport, Monmouth NP1 6YB.
**Membership, manpower and money in the Anglican Communion: a survey of 27 Churches and 360 Dioceses.** 1973. Anglican Consultative Council, 32 Eccleston St, London SW1W 9PY. Tel: (01)730-5271.
**Minutes and yearbook of the Methodist Conference 1971.** 25 Marylebone Rd, London NW1. T: (01)935-2541.
**Minutes of the General Assembly and directory of the Presbyterian Church in Ireland.** 1973. Church House, Fisherwick Place, Belfast BT1 6DW, Northern Ireland. T: 665627.
**Moravian almanack 1968 revision.** Moravian Book Room, 5 Muswell Hill, London N10.
**Mothers' Union official handbook, 1971.** Mary Sumner House, Westminster, London SW1P 3RB.
**Praying always, 1972-1973.** Worldwide Evangelization Crusade, Bulstrode, Gerrards Cross, Bucks.
**Salvation Army yearbook 1978.** Salvationist Publishing and Supplies, Judd St, King's Cross, London WC1H 9NN.
**Scottish Baptist year book 1971.** Union Office, Baptist House, 14 Aytoun Rd, Glasgow S1.
**Scottish Episcopal Church year book and directory 1971/72.** Representative Church Council, 21 Grosvenor Crescent, Edinburgh EH12 5EE.
**Strict Baptist directory 1966.** National Strict Baptist Federation, 5 Swiss Av, Watford, Herts.
**'The Anglican world in figures',** in *Lambeth Conference 1978: preparatory information.* Anglican Consultative Council, 14 Great Peter St, London SW1P 3NQ.
**UK Protestant missions handbook.** Vol. 1: Overseas (1977), Vol. 2: Home (1978). Evangelical Alliance, 19 Draycott Place, London SW3 2SJ. 80p,56p. (Earlier editions: 1969, 1973).
**Who's Who at Lambeth '68.** 1968. Church Information Office, Church House, Dean's Yard, Westminster, London SW1.
**Who's Who at Lambeth 1978.** ACC, 32 Eccleston St, London SW1W 9PY.
**Year book of the Congregational Union of Scotland 1970-71.** 217 West George St, Glasgow C2.
**Your English-speaking churches: a directory of churches in Europe, North Africa and the Near East.** Commonwealth and Continental Church Society, 7 York Bldgs, London WC2. T: (01)930-1563.

*USA*
**A directory of religious bodies in the United States.** J.G. Melton, 1977. ISAR, PO Box 1311, Evanston, IL 60201. 305p. (1,200 Christian denominations and non-Christian groups).
**A directory of the ministry of the undenominational fellowship of Christian Churches and Churches of Christ, 1974.** 1525 Cherry Rd, Springfield, IL 62704. T: (217)546-3566. (CCCC (Instrumental) USA).
**Acts and reports of the Reformed Ecumenical Synod.** 1677 Gentian Drive SE, Grand Rapids, MI 49508.
**AME Zion handbook.** 1968-1972. 1326-28 You St, NW, Washington, DC 20009.
**Annual report, American Bible Society.** 1865 Broadway, New York, NY 10023. T: (212)581-7400.
**Assembly minutes of the Church of God of Prophecy 1970.** Bible Place, Cleveland, TN 37311.
**Baptist General Conference annual 1970.** 1233 Central, Evanston, IL 60201.
**Calendar of prayer and directory of the United Church Board for World Ministries.** 1967-1968. 475 Riverside Drive, New York, NY 10027.
**Calendarul Solia 1969.** Romanian Orthodox Episcopate of America, Route 7, Jackson, MI 49201.
**Catholic almanac.** 1978. Our Sunday Visitor, Noll Plaza, Huntington, IN 46750. 700p.
**Catholic press directory, 1977: United States and Canada newspapers, magazines and general publishers.** Catholic Press Association, 432 Park Av South, New York, NY 10016. Tel: (212)684-2550. (Total 435 newspapers and magazines).
**Catholic religious orders, 1957.** St John's Abbey Press, Collegeville, Minnesota.
**Christian and Missionary Alliance: report for 1971.** CMA, 260 West 44th St, New York, NY 10036.
**Christian Reformed Church yearbook 1971.** 2850 Kalamazoo Av, Grand Rapids, MI 49508.
**Church directory 1972-1974.** Church of God. General Offices, Keith at 25th NW, Cleveland, TN 37311.
**Church directory of the General Association of Regular Baptist Churches 1970-1971.** GARB, 1800 Oakton Blvd, Des Plaines, IL 60018.
**Church of the Brethren 1973 directory.** 1451 Dundee Av, Elgin, IL 60120. T: (312)742-5100.
**Conservative Baptist Association of America directory, 1971.** Box 66, Wheaton, IL 60187.
**Deseret News 1974: Church almanac.** PO Box 838, Salt Lake City, UT 84110. (Mormon. 225p).
**Directory of churches in Europe.** 1968-69. Executive Council of the Episcopal Church, 815 Second Av, New York, NY 10017.
**Directory of churches in Latin America and the West Indies, 1965-66.** Executive Council of the Episcopal Church, 815 Second Av, New York, NY 10017.
**Directory of Oriental Catholic churches in the USA.** PO Box 83, West Newton, MA 02165.
**Directory of programs in religion in universities and colleges in the United States and Canada.** 1966. Journal for the Scientific Study of Religion, 1200 17th St, NW, Washington, DC 20036.
**Directory of Protestant church-related hospitals outside Europe and North America.** 1963. Missionary Research Library, Broadway & 120th St, New York, NY 10027.
**Directory of Protestant medical missions.** 1959. Missionary Research Library, Broadway & 120th St, New York, NY 10027.
**Directory of Sabbath-observing groups.** Bible Sabbath Association, Fairview, OK 73737.
**Directory of the African Orthodox Church 1968.** 122 West 129th St, New York, NY 10027.
**Directory of the American Baptist Churches in the USA, 1973.** Judson Book Store, Valley Forge, PA 19481.
**Directory of the Liberated Church in America.** PO Box 9177, Berkeley, CA 94709. T: (415)549-0649.
**Directory of the Moravian Church in America 1971.** 69 West Church St, Bethlehem, PA 18018.
**Directory of theological schools in the US and Canada.** Ed L. Carr. American Association of Theological Schools, PO Box 396, Vandalia, OH 45377.
**Directory, English-speaking congregations around the world.** International Fellowship of Christians, Box 404, Grand Haven, MI 49417. T: (616)846-5352. (Evangelicals).
**Eastern Orthodox world directory.** 1968. Ed J. Kuzmission. 200 South 6th St, Terre Haute, IN 47801. 305p. (Unofficial).
**Encyclopedia of modern Christian missions.** B.L. Goddard, 1967. Gordon College, Wenham, MA 01984. Tel: (617)927-2300. 743p.
**Episcopal Church annual 1977.** 815 Second Av, New York, NY 10017. T: (212)867-8400.
**Evangelical Covenant Church of America yearbook 1972.** 5101 North Francisco Av, Chicago, IL 60625.
**Evangelical Free Church of America yearbook 1970.** 1515 East 66th St, Minneapolis, MN 55423.
**Evangelization of the Chinese: a survey of Protestant agencies and Chinese unreached peoples.** 1976. MARC, 919 West Huntington Drive, Monrovia, CA 91016. 108p.
**General Conference Mennonite Church handbook of information 1972-1973.** 722 Main, Newton, KS 67114.
**General minutes of the Annual Conferences of the United Methodist Church, 1975.** 1200 Davis St, Evanston, IL 60201.
**Greek Orthodox Archdiocese of North and South America yearbook 1969.** 8-10 East 79th St, New York, NY 10021.
**Handbook for United Presbyterians.** 1969. 475 Riverside Drive, New York, NY 10027.
**Handbook of American Orthodoxy.** Council on Relations with the Eastern Churches, PECUSA, 185 Second Av, New York, NY 10017.
**Handbook of denominations in the United States.** 1970 (5th edition). F.S. Mead. Abingdon Press, Nashville, Tennessee.
**Handbook of missions, Brethren in Christ.** 1970. PO Box 149, Elizabethtown, PA 17022.
**Independent Fundamental Churches of America directory 1971-1972.** 145 North Washington St, Wheaton, IL 60187.
**International directory of religious information systems, 1971.** Ed D.O. Moberg. Department of Sociology and Anthropology, Marquette University, Milwaukee, WI 53233. 88p.

**International directory: Catholic charismatic prayer groups, 1975-1976.** PO Box 363, Ann Arbor, MI 48107. T: (313)761-8505. (Annual since 1968).
**Jesuit schools: Jesuit international school survey and directory, 1969.** W.J. Mehok. Cambridge Center for Social Studies, Cambridge, Massachusetts.
**Lutheran annual 1973.** Dept of Statistics & Research, Lutheran Church - Missouri Synod, 3558 South Jefferson Av, St Louis, MO 63118. T: (314)664-7000.
**Lutheran Church in America yearbook 1973.** Board of Publications, LCA, 2900 Queen Lane, Philadelphia, PA 19129.
**Mennonite yearbook and directory.** 1969. Mennonite Publishing House, Scottdale, Pennsylvania.
**Minutes of the National Association of Free Will Baptists 1970.** Box 1088, Nashville, TN 37202.
**Minutes, 54th General Assembly of the Church of God, 1972.** Church of God Publishing House, Cleveland, Tennessee.
**Mission handbook: North American Protestant ministries overseas.** 11th edition, 1976. Ed E.R Dayton. MARC, 919 West Huntington Drive, Monrovia, CA 91016. 589p. (Triennial. 620 agencies).
**Mission yearbook of prayer, 1971.** United Presbyterian Church, 475 Riverside Drive, New York, NY 10027.
**Missionary atlas: a manual of the foreign work of the Christian and Missionary Alliance.** 1964. Christian Publications, Harrisburg, Pennsylvania.
**Missionary prayer handbook, 1971.** The Fields Inc, 16 Hudson St, New York, NY 10013.
**Official Catholic directory, 1978.** P.J. Kenedy & Sons, 866 Third Av, New York, NY 10022. T: (212) 935-5640.
**Official guide to Catholic educational institutions and religious communities in the US, 1972-73.** Ed Doris B. Gray. US Catholic Conference, Washington, DC.
**Official list of the foreign missionaries affiliated with the General Council of the Assemblies of God.** Foreign Missions Dept, 1445 Boonville Av, Springfield, MO 65802.
**Orthodox Church in America 1973 year book and church directory.** 59 East 2nd St, New York, NY 10003. T: (212)475-6320,477-7836.
**Parishes and clergy of the Orthodox and other Eastern Churches in North and South America, together with the parishes and clergy of the Polish National Catholic Church, 1970-71.** Episcopal Church in the USA, 815 Second Av, New York, NY 10017. 208p. (Illustrated).
**Partnership in missions.** Board of Missions of the United Methodist Church, 475 Riverside Drive, New York, NY 10027.
**Prayer directory.** 1970. Wycliffe Bible Translators, Box 1960, Santa Ana, CA 92702.
**Protestant and Orthodox Church directory, 1969.** Council of Churches of the City of New York, 475 Riverside Drive, New York, NY 10027.
**Scriptures of the world, 1974.** American Bible Society, 1865 Broadway, New York, NY 10019.
**SDA (Seventh-day Adventist) periodical index.** Loma Linda University Libraries, Riverside, CA 92505.
**Seventh-day Adventist yearbook, 1977.** Review and Herald Publishing Association, Takoma Park, Washington, DC 20012.
**Southern Baptist Convention 1976 annual.** 460 James Robertson Parkway, Nashville, TN 37219.
**Statistical yearbook 1972.** Lutheran Church - Missouri Synod. Dept of Research and Statistics, 500 North Broadway, St Louis, MO 63102.
**Translation prayer directory, 1972.** Wycliffe Bible Translators, PO Box 1960, Santa Ana, CA 92702.
**United Methodist directory.** 475 Riverside Drive, New York, NY 10027.
**United Pentecostal Church directory, 1970-1971.** Hollywood, MO 63042.
**Unreached peoples directory.** 1974. MARC, 919 West Huntington Drive, Monrovia, CA 91016. 117p.
**Where the Saints meet.** Churches of Christ Firm Foundation Publisher, 3110 Guadalupe St, Box 610, Austin, TX 78767. T: (512)452-7651.
**World directory of mission-related educational institutions.** Eds R.B. Buker & T. Ward. William Carey Library, 533 Hermosa St, South Pasadena, CA 91030.
**World directory of theological education by extension.** 1973. W.C. Weld. William Carey Library, 533 Hermosa St, South Pasadena, CA 91030. T: (213)682-2047.
**World directory of theological libraries.** 1968. C.M. Ruoss. Scarecrow Press, Metuchen, New Jersey.
**World Methodist Council handbook of information, 1971-76.** PO Box 518, Lake Junaluska, NC 28745.
**Yearbook and directory of the Christian Church (Disciples of Christ), 1973.** 222 South Downey Av, Box 1986, Indianapolis, IN 46206. T: (317)353-1491.
**Yearbook of American and Canadian churches, 1978.** Ed C.H. Jacquet. NCCCUSA, 475 Riverside Drive, New York, NY 10027. 280p.
**Yearbook of the American Lutheran Church 1973.** 422 South 5th St, Minneapolis, MN 55415.
**Yearbook of the Free Methodist Church.** Winona Lake, IN 46590.
**Yearbook of Wisconsin Evangelical Lutheran Synod 1971.** 3512 West North Av, Milwaukee, WI 53208.
**1978 directory, Unitarian Universalist Association.** 25 Beacon St, Boston, MA 02108. T: (617) 742-2100.
**1978 yearbook of Jehovah's Witnesses.** Watch Tower Bible & Tract Society of Pennsylvania, 124 Columbia Heights, Brooklyn, NY 11201.
**1978 yearbook of the Church of God: United States and Canada.** Division of Church Service, PO Box 2420, Anderson, IN 46011.

*URUGUAY*
**Guia de la Iglesia Uruguaya 1971.** Curia Eclesiástica de Montevideo, Oficina de Prensa, Treinta y Tres 1368, Montevideo. (Catholic).

*VENEZUELA*
**Directorio de la Iglesia Católica en Venezuela, 1972-1973.** Centro de Investigaciones Sociales y Socio-Religiosas, Apdo 12863, Caracas.

*VIET NAM*
**Protestant directory of churches, missions and organizations in South Vietnam, 1973.** Office of Missionary Information, Saigon. 50p.
**Viet-Nam Cong-Giao Niên-Gian 1964** (Annuaire catholique du Vietnam). Archevêché, 180 Rue Phan-dinh-Phung, BP 2371, Saigon 3. T: 20828.

*ZAIRE*
**Annuaire de l'Eglise du Congo, 1969.** Centre de Recherches Sociologiques, Service des Statistiques, BP 3258, Kalina, Kinshasa. 17p. (Catholic).

*ZIMBABWE*
**Catholic directory of Rhodesia, 1972.** Mambo Press, Senga Rd, PO Box 779, Gwelo. T: 2293. 75p.

# 74

# Atheistic, Humanist & Anti-Religious Organizations

*Definition.* Atheistic or non-theistic humanistic (or anti-supernaturalist) movements, freethinkers' organizations, societies or groups, committed to active or militant opposition to Christianity or to all religion; organizations for the promotion or propagation of atheism or non-theistic humanism; centres for the study of atheism; atheism research centres, research centres dealing with religion but under anti-religious auspices, university faculties of atheism.

Of the very wide range of such agencies, a small representative listing is given here.

*BULGARIA*
**Institute of Philosophy of the Academy of Sciences,** 6 Rue P. Evtimi, Sofiya.

*CHINA*
**Chinese Association for Atheism,** Peking.
**Society for the Study of Tibetan Buddhism,** Peking.
**World Religion Research Institute (Institute of World Religions),** Academy of Social Sciences, Peking. (Communist. Closed 1966, refounded 1978).

*CZECHOSLOVAKIA*
**Institute of Scientific Atheism,** Brno.

*FRANCE*
**World Union of Freethinkers,** Pres, 4 Rue Vitelu, F-94 Saint-Mandé.

*GERMAN DEMOCRATIC REPUBLIC*
**Chair of Atheism,** Jena University, Jena

*NETHERLANDS*
**International Humanist & Ethical Union (IHEU),** Oudegracht 152, Utrecht. T: 312155.

*USSR*
**All-Union Society for the Dissemination of Political and Scientific Knowledge,** Moskva. (Successor to League of Militant Godless. Controls all anti-religious propaganda).
**Department for the Study of Atheism,** Institute of Philosophy, Academy of Sciences, Kijev, Ukrainian SSR.
**Division of Atheism,** Institute of Philosophy, USSR Academy of Sciences, Moskva.
**Institute of Scientific Atheism (Institut Nauchnogo Ateizma),** Academy of Social Sciences of the Central Committee of the Communist Party of the Soviet Union (Akademii Obshchestvennykh Nauk Pri TsK KPSS), Sadovaya-Kudrinskaya 9, Moskva. T: 2448806.
**Museum of Atheism,** 74 Gorky St, Vilnius, Lithuanian SSR. (Opened 1966; formerly St Casimir's Church).
**Museum of the History of Atheism,** Dir, St Sophia Cathedral, Polotsk, Byelorussian SSR. (One of 4 museums in SSR; for atheistic propaganda and training).
**Museum of the History of Religion and Atheism/ Anti-Religious Museum,** Dir, Leningrad Academy of Sciences, Nevsky Prospekt, Leningrad, RSFSR. (Reopened 1946; over 150,000 titles; formerly Kazan Cathedral).
**University for Atheism,** Ashhabad, Turkmen SSR.

*UK OF GB & NI*
**British Humanist Association,** 13 Prince of Wales Terrace, London W8. T: (01)937-2341.
**Communist Party (UK),** National HQ, 16 King St, London WC2. T: (01)836-2151.
**National Secular Society,** 698 Holloway Rd, London N19. T: (01)272-1266. (Also: 103 Borough High St, London SE1. T: (01)407-2717).
**Rationalist Press Association,** 88 Islington High St, London N1 8EN. T: (01)226-7251 (Also: 40 Drury Lane, London WC2. T: Covent Garden 2077/8).

*USA*
**American Association for the Advancement of Atheism,** Pres, Box 2831, San Diego, CA 92110. (Also: 38 Park Row, New York, NY 10008).

*YUGOSLAVIA*
**Institut de Recherches Sociales,** Section de Recherches sur l'Athéisme et les Religions, Jezuitski trg 4, Zagreb.

# 75

# Interreligious Organizations

*Definition.* Commissions, councils or organizations not primarily or exclusively Christian but run jointly by all or several major religions including Christianity, i.e. run by Christians and one or more non-Christian religions, for some joint non-missionary inter-faith activity other than mission; including national councils of religious bodies open to Christians and non-Christians alike.

In this field there are numerous organizations of major significance. A selection are listed here.

*ARGENTINA*
**Confraternidad Judeo-Cristiana,** Florida 681, 7 piso, of 63, Buenos Aires. T: 3929135.

*AUSTRIA*
**Aktion gegen den Antisemitismus in Österreich,** Bachenbrümgasse 7, Postfach 458, A-1011 Wien. T: 4725662.
**Informationszentrum im Dienste der Christliche-Jüdischen Verständigung (IDCIV),** Burggasse 37, A-1070 Wien. T: 932657. (Bibliothek: Lassingleithnerplatz 3/6, A-1020 Wien. T: 246235).
**Koordinierungsausschuss für Christlich-Jüdische Zusammenarbeit,** Stephansplatz 6/VI/51, A-1010 Wien. T: 524646.

*BELGIUM*
**Bureau de Documentation sur les Relations Judéo-Chrétiennes,** Rue Felix Delharse 2, B-1060 Brussel.

*BRAZIL*
**Conselho da Fraternidade Cristão-Judaica (CFCJ),** Rua Maranhão 990, São Paulo, SP.

*CANADA*
**Alberta Inter-Faith Community Action Committee,** 9901-107 St, Edmonton, Alberta T5K 1G4.
**Canadian Council of Christians and Jews,** National Office, Room 506-8, 229 Yonge St, Toronto, Ontario M5B 1N9. T: 368-8026.
**Centre Monchanin,** 4917 Rue St-Urbain, Montréal 151, Québec. T: (514)288-7229. (Non-confessional; encounter between the religions).
**Continuing Committee on Muslim-Christian Cooperation,** 29 Eastbourne Av, Toronto 7, Ontario.
**Manitoba Inter-Faith Council,** 50 Stafford Av, Winnipeg, Manitoba R3M 2V7.

*CHILE*
**Confraternidad Judeo-Cristiana de Chile,** Casilla 4106, Santiago.

*CHINA (TAIWAN)*
**Office of Ecumenical and Inter-religious Affairs (FABC),** PO Box 7-91, Taipei.

*GERMANY, Federal Republic of*
**Arbeitsgruppe Juden und Christen beim Deutschen Evangelischen Kirchentag,** Magdeburgerstr 59, D-6400 Fulda.
**Arbeitsgemeinschaft der Kirchen und Religionsgesellschaften in Berlin,** Bonhoefferufer 3, D-1 Berlin 10. (Christians, Jews and Muslims).
**Deutscher Koordinierungsrat der Gesellschäften für Christlich-Jüdische Zusammenarbeit (DKR),** Lindenstr 45, D-5000 Köln.
**Freiburger Rundbrief (FR),** Arbeitskreis für Christlich-Jüdische Begegnung, Postfach 420, D-7800 Freiburg Breisgau.
**Ständiger Gesprächskreis Juden und Christen beim Zentralkomitee der Deutschen Katholiken,** Hochkreuzallee 246, D-5300 Bonn-Bad Godesberg. T: (022221)376904.

*INDIA*
**World Conference on Religion and Peace,** Indian Committee, Sec, 221 Deen Dyal Upadhyaya Marg, New Delhi 1.
**World Fellowship of Religions,** 12 Lady Hardinge Rd, New Delhi 1. T: 48437. (Begun 1957).

*ISRAEL*
**Interfaith,** Israeli Committee for Religious Understanding (Ha'vad lehavana bein-datith), 9 Ethiopia St, BP 2028, Jerusalem. T: (02)233551.
**Interreligious Group (Ha'houg bein dati),** 64 Rue Bilou, Tel-Aviv. T: (03)248560.
**United Religions Organization,** Pres, 16 Shumel Hanagid, Jerusalem.

*ITALY*
**Amicizia Ebraico-Cristiana di Firenze,** CP 282, I-50100 Firenze.
**International Information Service for Jewish-Christian Relations/Service International de Documentation Judéo-Chrétienne (SIDIC),** Via del Plebiscito 112, I-00186 Roma. T: 5810465.

*JAPAN*
**Japan Religions League,** Sec, 2-7 Motoyoyogi-machi, Shibuya-ku, Tokyo 151.
**Japan Religions League (Nihon Shukyo Remmei),** c/o Nishihongan-ji Betsuin, 3-15-1 Tsukiji, Chuo-ku, Tokyo 104.
**Organization for Industrial, Spiritual and Cultural Advancement International (OISCA),** 105-1 Yochomachi, Shinjuku-ku, Tokyo. T: 3598555.
**World Conference on Religion and Peace,** Japan Committee, Sec, 2-7 Motoyoyogi-machi, Shibuya-ku, Tokyo 151.

*LEBANON*
**Christian-Muslim Dialogue Group,** Ibn Roshd-Zaidania, Bayrut.

*LUXEMBOURG*
**Association Interconfessionnelle du Luxembourg,** c/o Rue Jules Wilhelm 1, Luxembourg. T: 431619. (Begun 1965).

*MAURITIUS*
**Inter-Religious Committee of Mauritius,** c/o Evêché, Rue Mgr Gonin, Port Louis. T: 23068.
**Solidarité Fraternelle Mondiale (Comité Inter-religieux Mauricien),** 20 Rue Pope Hennessy, BP 278, Port-Louis. T: 43420,23318.

*NETHERLANDS*
**Catholic Council for Israel (Katholieke Raad voor Israel, KRI),** St-Janssingel 21, 's-Hertogenbosch.
**Christian/Muslim Understanding (Begrip-Christentom/Islam),** Wüstelaan 76, Santpoort.
**Interkerkelijk Contact Israel (ICI),** Jacob van Ruisdaelstraat 62, Utrecht. T: (030)510942.
**Interreligio Institute for Religious Communication (Instituut voor Godsdienstcommunicatie Interreligio,** Postbus 52005, Weena Paviljoen 9, Rotterdam.
**Permanent Committee for Jews, Christians and Muslims in Europe (Permanent Comité van Joden, Christenen en Moslims in Europa),** p/a Instituut voor Godsdienstwetenschap, Vrije Universiteit, Amsterdam.
**Reformed Council for Church-Israel Relations (Hervormde Raad voor de Verhouding van Kerk en Israel),** Jacob van Ruisdaelstraat 62, Utrecht. T: (030)510942.

*RWANDA*
**Groupe Islamo-Chrétien,** c/o Université Nationale, Butare.

*SINGAPORE*
**Inter-Religious Organizations Council,** Singapore.

*SPAIN*
**Amistad Islamo-Cristiana,** Alcala 41, 3 Izda, Madrid 14.
**Amistad Judeo-Cristiana,** Residencia de Nuestra Señora de Sion, Calle Hilarion Eslava 50, Madrid 15.

*SRI LANKA*
**Congress of Religions,** 118 Rosmead Place, Colombo 7.

*SWITZERLAND*
**Christlich-Jüdische Arbeitsgemeinschaft in der Schweiz (CJA)/Amitié Judéo-Chrétienne en Suisse/Amicitia Ebraico-Christiana Ticino,** Amselstr 25, CH-4000 Basel. T: (061)344234.
**World Assembly for Moral Re-armament (MRA),** Mountain House, CH-1824 Caux. T: 614241. (Formed 1938. Also: Winkerlriedstr 14, CH-6000 Luzern).

*TRINIDAD & TOBAGO*
**Inter-Religious Organization of Trinidad and Tobago (IRO),** Archbishop's House, 27 Maraval Rd, Port-of-Spain. T: 21103.

*UK OF GB & NI*
**Commission to Implement the Vatican Declaration on the Jews,** 17 Chepstow Villas, London W11 3DZ. T: (01)727-2597.
**Council of Christians and Jews,** Gen Sec, 41 Cadogan Gardens, London SW3 2TD. T: (01) 730-5010,8333.
**International Consultative Committee of Organizations for Christian-Jewish Co-operation,** 41 Cadogan Gardens, London SW3 2TD. T: (01)730-5010,8333.
**London Diocesan Council for Christian-Jewish Understanding,** Sec, Deanery of St Pauls, Dean's Court, London EC4V 5AA.
**London Society of Jews and Christians,** 28 St John's Wood Rd, London NW8. (Joint conferring on common ideals).
**Spiritual Unity of Nations Association (SUN),** International Pres, Sun House, 49 Portland Rd, Hove, East Sussex.
**Standing Conference of Jews, Christians and Muslims in Europe (JCM),** British Branch, 17 Chepstow Villas, London W11 3DZ. T: (01)727-3597.
**Study Centre for Christian-Jewish Relations,** 17 Chepstow Villas, London W11 3DZ. T: (01) 727-3597.
**World Congress of Faiths (WCF),** Sec Gen, Younghusband House, 23 Norfolk Square, London W2. T: (01)723-9820. (Begun 1936).
**World Spiritual Council,** Chairman, Monks Horton, Sellindge, Ashford, Kent. T: Sellindge 2138. (Begun 1946).

*USA*
**Berkeley Area Interfaith Council,** Dir, Room 206, 2340 Durant Av, Berkeley, CA 94704. T: (415) 841-0881.
**Bishops' Committee for Ecumenical and Interreligious Affairs,** NCCB, Exec Dir, 1312 Massachusetts Av, NW, Washington, DC 20005. T: (202) 659-6855.
**Coalition of New Jersey State Religious Leaders,** 800 West State St, Trenton, New Jersey.
**Council of Hyde Park & Kenwood Churches & Synagogues,** Pres, 1400 East 53rd St, Chicago, IL 60615. T: (312)324-5300.
**Detroit Interfaith Action Council,** 10600 Puritan Av, Detroit, Michigan.
**Ecumenical Media Services (ECUMEDIA),** 320 Cathedral St, Baltimore, MD 21201. T: (301)

727-5510. (Protestants, Catholics, Jews).
**Edgewater Association of Clergy and Rabbis,** 1449 Edgewater Av, Chicago, Ilinois.
**Fellowship of Religious Humanists,** 105 West North College St, PO Box 278, Yellow Springs, OH 45387.
**Great Plains Inter-Religious Commission,** 3380 Bellair St, Denver, CO 80207.
**Indiana Interreligious Commission on Human Equity,** Exec Dir, 1100 West 42nd St, Indianapolis, IN 46208. T: (317)924-4226
**Interfaith Action Centres,** 10600 Puritan Av, Detroit, MI 48235.
**Interfaith Action Council of Great Flint,** Interfaith Center, 900 Chippewa, Flint, MI 48503.
**Interfaith Housing Council,** 3110 Winchell Av, Kalamazoo, MI 49001.
**International Inter-Faith Fellowship,** Church Centre for the United Nations, 777 UN Plaza, New York, NY 10017. T: (212)661-1762.
**International Religious Fellowship,** North American IRF Committee, 25 Beacon St, Boston, MA 02108.
**Interreligious Council of Southern California,** Pres, 1901 South San Gabriel Blvd, San Gabriel, CA 91776.
**Inter-Religious Center for Urban Affairs,** Suite 811, Shell Bldg, 1211 Locust St, St Louis, MO 63103.
**Inter-Religious Committee,** Los Angeles Region Goals Project, 817 West 34th St, Los Angeles, CA 90007. (Metropolitan planning).
**Inter-Religious Foundation for Community Organization (IFCO),** Exec Dir, 475 Riverside Drive, New York, NY 10027. (Black; militant ministry).
**Listen (Interfaith Ministry),** 6620 Arlesworth, Lincoln, NE 68505.
**Memphis Metro Interfaith Association,** 692 Poplar Av, Memphis, TN 38105.
**Metropolitan Inter Faith Association,** 1254 Lamar Av, Memphis, Tennessee.
**National Conference of Christians and Jews (NCCJ),** Sec, 43 West 57th St, New York, NY 10019. T: (212)MU8-7530.
**National Interreligious Affairs, American Jewish Committee,** 165 East 56th St, New York, NY 10022.
**National Interreligious Service Board for Conscientious Objectors,** Washington Bldg, Room 550, 15th & New York Av, NW, Washington, DC 20005. T: (202)393-4868.
**Religion in American Life,** 475 Fifth Av, New York, NY 10017. T: (212)683-5464.
**Stamford-Darien Council of Churches and Synagogues,** Exec Dir, 58 Church St, Stamford, CT 06906. T: (203)348-2800.
**Temple of Understanding,** Washington DC. (Founded 1960; interreligious; 10-religion congresses in 1968, 1970, 1975).
**Tri-State Inter-Faith Development Enterprise,** Exec Dir, 122 West Franklin Av, Minneapolis, MN 55404.
**US Inter-Religious Committee on Peace,** Sec, United Methodist Church, 100 Maryland Av, NE, Washington, DC 20002.
**World Conference on Religion and Peace (WCRP),** Sec Gen, 777 United Nations Plaza, New York, NY 10017. (Founded at 1970 Kyoto Conference, Japan).
**World Interfaith Relations Committee (Disciples),** Chairman, 1156 East 57th St, Chicago, IL 60637.

*URUGUAY*
**Confraternidad Judeo-Cristiana,** Montevideo 1806/10.

*ZIMBABWE*
**People-to-People Congress of Zimbabwe,** c/o Dept of Theology, PO Box MP 167, Mount Pleasant, Salisbury. (Affiliated to World Congress of Faiths founded in 1936).

# 76

# Non-Christian Religions

*Definition.* A selection of major headquarters and organizations, world federations, missionary organizations, study centres operated by or for non-Christian religions of all kinds, non-Christian research centres, universities, institutes and institutions.

*ALGERIA*
**Institut al-Hayat (La Vie),** Guerara (Oasis).

*ARGENTINA*
**Arab Islamic Society,** San Nigel 1650, La Heras, Mendoza.
**Centro de Estudios Islamicos,** Rojas 6, Piso 2, Of 1, Buenos Aires.
**Centro Islamico,** San Juan 3053, Buenos Aires.
**Club Honor y Patria,** Unión de los Pueblos Arabes Americanos, Juncal 857, Buenos Aires. (Muslim).
**Confederación Espíritista Argentina (CEA),** Buenos Aires.
**El Diario Sirio Libanés,** Reconquista 1040, Buenos Aires.
**International Council of Jewish Women,** Rio Bamba 1020, Buenos Aires. T: 414557.
**Seminario Rabinico Latinoamericano,** 11 de Setiembre 1669, Buenos Aires.
**World Union of Jewish Students,** Luca 2280, Buenos Aires 23.

*AUSTRALIA*
**Australian Federation of Islamic Societies,** 90 Cramer St, Preston, Victoria 3072. T: 472424. (Also: 11 Thomas St, Thomastown, Victoria, 3074. (Imams in every state capital).
**Baha'i National Spiritual Assembly,** 2 Lang Rd, Paddington. T: 313696.
**Blavatsky Lodge of the Theosophical Society,** 25 Bligh, Sydney. T: 289270.
**'I Am' Religious Sanctuary of Sydney,** 55 Manson Rd, Strathfield. T: 769109.
**L.A. Falk Library and F.L. Cohen Memorial Library,** 69 Cook Rd, Centennial Park, Sydney, NSW. (Jewish).

*AUSTRIA*
**Institut für Judaistik,** Universität Wien, Landesgerichtsstr 18, A-1010 Wien.
**Muslimische Sozialdienst,** Werdertorgasse 4/13, A-1010 Wien. (Also: Munzgasse 3/I, A-1030 Wien).
**Verband der Österreichischen Israelitischen Kultusgemeinden,** Bauernfeldgasse 4, Wien 19.
**Verein Österreichisches Jüdisches Museum Eisenstadt,** Universität Wien, Landesgerichtsstr 18, A-1010 Wien.

*BELGIUM*
**Centre Islamique,** Imam, Av Damien 17, B-1150 Brussel.
**Centre Islamique et Culturel de Belgique,** Parc du Cinquantenaire 14, B-1040 Brussel. T: (02) 7353071.
**Centre National des Hautes Etudes Juives,** Av Jeanne 14, B-1050 Brussel. T: (02)6488158.
**Consistoire Central Israélite de Belgique,** Rue J Dupont 2, B-1000 Brussel. T: (02)5122190.
**Service Social Juif,** Av Ducpétiaux 68, St Gilels, Brussel 6.

*BERMUDA*
**Baha'i World Faith,** Court St, Hamilton. T: 21141.

*BRAZIL*
**Centro Budista Theravada,** Rua Princesa Leopoldina 8, Rio de Janeiro, GB.
**Centro Hinduista Samadhi,** Rua Visconde de Pirajá, Rio de Janeiro, GB.
**Federação Espírita Brasileira (FEB) (Brazilian Spiritualist Federation),** São Paulo. (Founded 1884; 5,000 associations).
**Federação Espírita do Estado de São Paulo,** Rua Maria Paula 158, São Paulo, SP. T: 333742. (Separate organization from União SE).
**Tenda de Umbanda,** Caboclo Inco, Av Pacaembó, São Paulo SP.
**União Sociedades Espíritas do Estado do São Paulo,** 158 Rua Maria Paula, São Paulo, SP. T: 333742.

*BURMA*
**All Burma Council of Young Monks Association,** Rangoon.
**International Institute of Advanced Buddhistic Studies,** Rangoon.
**Pâli Buddhist University,** Rangoon.

*CAMEROON*
**Association Culturelle Islamique,** BP 594, Yaoundé.

*CANADA*
**Buddhist Center,** 5250 Saint-Urbain, Montéal 14, Québec.
**Buddhist Churches of Canada,** Bishop, 918 Bathurst St, Toronto, Ontario, MSR 3G5. T: (416) 534-4302.
**Canadian Jewish Congress,** 1590 McGregor Av, Montréal 109, Québec.
**Council of Muslim Communities of Canada,** Box 400, Station D, Toronto 9, Ontario.
**Islamic Foundation of Toronto,** 182 Rhodes Av, Toronto, Ontario. T: (416)465-2525.
**National Spiritual Assembly of Baha'is in Canada,** 7290 Leslie St, Willowdale, Ontario.
**The Sound of India,** 3702 Mountain, Montréal 7, Québec.
**World Union of Progressive Judaism,** Rabbi, 1950 Bathurst St at Ava Rd, Toronto 10, Ontario.
**Yoga Vedanta Sivananda Centre,** 5178 Blvd Saint-Laurent, Montréal 14, Québec.

*CHILE*
**Comunidad Israelita,** Calle Canada Strongest 1846, Santiago. T: 28052.
**Departamento de Cultura Judaica,** Instituto Pedagogico, Universidad de Chile, Av Bernardo O'Higgins 1058, Casilla 10-D, Santiago.

*CHINA*
**Dege Buddhist Scripture Publishing House,** Sichuan.

*CHINA (TAIWAN)*
**Chinese Muslim Association,** Pres, 62 Sin Sheng S Rd, Sec 2, Taipei.
**Chinese Muslim Youth League,** Taipei.
**National Taoist Association of the Republic of China,** Taipei.

*CZECHOSLOVAKIA*
**Council of Jewish Religious Communities in Bohemia and Moravia,** Maislova 18, Staré Mesto, Praha 1.
**Jewish State Museum,** Jachmova 3, Praha.
**Union of Jewish Religious Communities in Slovakia,** Smeralova 29, Bratislava.

*DENMARK*
**Ahmadiya Mosque (Nursat Djahan Moske),** Eriksmunde Alle 2, Hvidovre, Kobenhavn.
**Islamic Cultural Centre,** Norre Sogade 43, DK-1370 Kobenhavn.

*EGYPT*
**Académie des Recherches Islamiques (Majma' al-buhuth al-islamiyya),** Administration Générale de l'Azhar, Al Qahirah. T: 909922.
**Al Azhar Islamic University (Djami' a Al-Azhar),** Rector, Administration General, Al-Azhar, Al Qahirah. T: 905914.
**Cairo Radio,** Box 325, Al Qahirah. (Regular Muslim information).
**City of Muslim Missions (Madinat al-Bu'uth al-Islamiya),** Al Qahirah.
**Council for Islamic Studies,** Al Qahirah.
**Cultural Contacts Department,** Dir, Al-Azhar University, Al Qahirah.
**Grand Mufti of Egypt,** Rector, Al-Azhar University, Al Qahirah.
**Halabi Press,** 5 Khan Jaafar, Al Hussein, Al Qahirah. T: 905871.
**Higher Council of Islamic Affairs (al-Majlis al-a'la li-l shu'un al-Islamiya),** 11 Rue Hassan Sabri, Zemalek, Al Qahirah. T: 802665.
**House of the Qu'ran (Maison du Coran/Dar al-Qur'an),** Midan el Azhar, Al Qahirah.

*FIJI*
**Ahmadiyya Islamic Centre,** 82 Kings Rd, Samabula.
**Baha'i World Faith,** 68 Pender St, Suva.
**Hindu Temple (Shree Sanatan Dharm Ramayan Mandali),** Mandir St, Samabula.
**Sikh Temple,** Samabula.
**Suva Muslim League,** Jame Mosque, Amy St, Suva.

*FRANCE*
**Aga Khan Foundation,** HH The Aga Khan, Aiglemont, F-60270 Gouvieux. T: (4)4574022. (Khoja Ismaili world HQ).
**Alliance Israélite Universelle (AIU),** 45 Rue La Bruyère, F-75425 Paris. T: 7447584.
**Bureau d'Animation des Centres Communautaires (BACC),** 19 Rue de Téhéren, F-75008 Paris. (Jewish).
**Centre Universitaire d'Etudes Juives (CUEJ),** 30 Blvd du Port-Royal, F-75005 Paris.
**Conseil Représentatif des Israélites de France (CRIF)/Consultative Council of Jewish Organizations,** Delegation for Europe, 45 Rue La Bruyère, F-75009 Paris.
**Consistoire Israélite de France,** 17 Rue Saint-Georges, F-75009 Paris.
**European Council of Jewish Community Services,** 14 Rue Georges Berger, F-75017 Paris. T: 6225351.
**Fonds Social Juif Unifié (FSJU),** 19 Rue de Téhéran, F-75008 Paris.
**Fraternité d'Abraham,** 20 Blvd Poissonière, F-75009 Paris. T: 770-2369.
**Grande Famille Amana,** 123 Rue Pelleport, Paris 20. T: 636-8456.
**Union Musulmane Internationale,** Institut Musulman de Paris, Grande Mosquée de Paris, Place du Puits-de-l'Ermite, F-75005 Paris.
**World Union of Jewish Students,** HQ, 17 Rue Fortuny, F-75017 Paris.

*GERMAN DEMOCRATIC REPUBLIC*
**Verband der Judischen Gemeinden in der DDR,** Bautznerstr 20, Dresden.

*GHANA*
**African Herbalist Healing Union,** Sec, PO Box 1380, Kumasi.
**Akonnedi's Healing Shrine,** Nana, PO Box 37, Larteh.
**Muslim Representative Council of Ghana,** PO Box 642, Accra.
**Spiritual Assembly of the Baha'is of Ghana,** PO Box 2582, Accra.
**Theosophical Society in Ghana,** Sec, PO Box 720, Accra.

*GREECE*
**Central Board of the Jewish Communities of Greece,** 8 Melidoni St, Athínai.
**Organization for Muslim Unity in Greece (Itihad Islam),** 35 Antigonou St, Komotiny.

*HONG KONG*
**World Fellowship of Confucianists,** Hong Kong and Macao Regional Centre, Hong Kong. (4 schools of thought; begun 1909).

*HUNGARY*
**Jewish Theological Seminary of Hungary,** Jozsef-Korut 17, Budapest. (Begun 1877; 60,000 volumes).

*INDIA*
**Aligarh Muslim University,** Aligarh, UP. T: 20.
**Anjuman Tanzim-ul-Muslamin,** Calcutta.
**Benaras Hindu University,** Varanasi 5, UP. T: 64491.
**Bharat Sevak Samaj,** 9-A Theatre Communication Bldg, Con Place, New Delhi 1.
**Bharatiya Vidya Bhavan,** Chowpatty Rd, Bombay 7.
**Chavara Library and Cultural Centre,** Karikamurry Rd, Cochin 682011, Kerala. T: 33227.
**Chief Khalsa Diwan,** GT Rd, Amritsar, Punjab. (Sikh reform movement).
**Dar ul 'ulum Seminary,** Deoband, UP. (Great Muslim seminary, ranking next to Al-Azhar, Cairo).
**Darul-Musannifin,** Shibly Academy, Azamgarh, UP.
**Department of Adi Granth Studies,** Punjabi University, Patiala. (Preparing Encyclopedia of Sikhism).
**Department of Religious Studies (Guru Gobind Singh Bhavan),** Punjabi University, Patiala. (Sikh renaissance emphasis).
**Gandhi Smarak Sangrahalaya,** Harijan Ashram, Ahmedabad 13.
**Gandhi Smarak Sangrahalaya,** Raighat, New Delhi 1.
**HH Shankaracharya Ashrams,** Dwarka/Badrinath/Mysore/Puri/Bhanpur. There are in India 5 Shankaracharyas (leading exponents of Saivite (Siva) Hinduism), at four maths (ashrams or monasteries established by HH Shankaracharya in the 8th century AD): Dwarka (west), Badrinath (north), Mysore (south), Jagannath Puri (east), and (more recently) Bhanpur (Ujjain, central India).
**Indian Institute of Islamic Studies,** Panchkuin Rd, New Delhi 110001. (Also: Kalka Tughlaq Rd, Tughlaqabad, New Delhi. Proposed computerized library of 1.5 million volumes and 3,000 periodicals. Edits *Studies in Islam*).
**Indo-Muslim Cultural Institute,** Hyderabad.
**Institute of Islamic Studies,** Muslim University of Aligarh, Aligarh.
**Islam and Modern Age Society,** Jamia Nagar, New Delhi 110025.
**Islamic Research Association,** 8 Shephard Rd, Bombay 8.
**Islamic Research Circle,** Islamic Library, Shamshad Bldg, Aligarh.
**Kerala Philosophical Congress,** 66 Varanasi Cantt, UP, Kerala.
**Lumen Institute,** Davis Rd, Cochin 682016, Kerala. T: 32056.
**Mahabodhi Society of India,** Kalimpong. (Also: 4A Bankim Chatterjee St, Calcutta 12).
**Masih Vidya Bhavan,** 87 Muncipal Office Rd, Indore 452003.
**Muslim Community of India (Jamaate Islami Al-Hind),** Chitli Qabar, Jama Masjid, Delhi 6.
**Muslim University,** Vice-Chancellor, Aligarh.
**Nadwa Arabic College,** Lucknow. (Nadwat-ul-Ulama).
**Osmania Oriental Publication Bureau (Dairatu'l Ma'arif'l-Osmania),** Osmania University, Hyderabad, AP. (Muslim. Founded 1889).
**Quran Foundation,** 128 Dr Ambedkar Rd, Meerut, UP. (Correspondence course on learning Quran).
**Ramakrishna Institute of Culture,** Gol Park, Calcutta 29.
**Santi-Sadan,** 34/4 Telipara Lane, Calcutta 700004.
**Shanti-Bhavan,** 1/32B Prince Golam Mohamed Rd, Calcutta 26. T: 467300.
**Shriomani Gurdwara Prabandhak Committee (SGPC),** Golden Temple, Amritsar, Punjab. (Supreme Sikh governing body).
**Signasu Kendra,** Kamala Nehru Rd, Allahabad 1, UP.
**Sufi Hamsaya,** Bara Bazar Rd, Shillong 1.
**Theosophical Society,** Pres, Adyar, Madras 20. T: 73915,71904.
**United Lodge of Theosophists,** Theosophy Hall, 40 New Marine Lines, Bombay 20. T: 299024.
**Urdu University (Jami's Millia),** Delhi.

*INDONESIA*
**International Islamic Organization,** Jakarta. (Founded 1970 by Afro-Asian Islamic Organization).
**Perisada Hindu Dharma,** Jakarta.

*IRAN*
**Faculty of Islamic Theology,** Tehran University, Tehran.
**Radio Naft-E Melli Shoru Mishavad,** National Iranian Oil Company, Abadan. (Private station heard during Ramadan).
**Zoroastrian Anjuman,** Pres, Bimeh Iran, Saadi Av, Tehran.

*IRAQ*
**Institute of Higher Learning in Iraq,** Shari'ah College, Baghdad.
**Shari'ah College,** Baghdad.
**Shi'ah Theological Academy,** Najaf.

*ISRAEL*
**Agudas Israel World Organization,** POB 326, Jerusalem. (Solving, in the spirit of the Torah, Jewish world problems).
**Department of Arabic Language & Literature, and History of the Islamic Peoples,** University of Haifa, Hefa.
**Universal House of Justice,** Supreme Administrative Body, Baha'i World Centre, Hefa.
**World Union of Jewish Students,** NUIS, POB 1184, Jerusalem.

*ITALY*
**Assemblea Spirituale Nazionale,** La Fede Baha'i, Sec, via Astoppani 10, Roma.
**Centro di Documentazione Ebraica Contemporanea,** Via Guastalla 19, Milano. (Jewish).
**Centro Islamico Culturale d'Italia,** Via Sebastiano Conca 6, Roma. (Also: Via Salaria 290, I-00199 Roma).
**Unione delle Communità Israelitiche Italiane,** Lungotevere Sanzio 9, Roma.
**Unione Islamica in Occidente,** Via Poggio Moiano 55, I-00199 Roma.

*JAPAN*
**Association of Shinto Shrines (Jinja Honcho),** 4-12-26 Higashi, Shibuya-ku, Tokyo.
**Buddha Adoration Association in Japan,** 3-2-24 Akabanedai, Kita-ku, Tokyo 115.
**Church of Perfect Liberty,** Patriarch, PO Box 1, Tondabayashi-shi, Osaka 584.
**Federation of Sectarian Shinto (Kyoba Shinto Rengokai),** 7-18-5 Roppongi, Minato-ku, Tokyo.
**Institute of Theology and Applied Education,** Church of Perfect Liberty, 1-14-1 Ebisu, Shibuya-ku, Tokyo 150.
**Japan Buddhist Council for World Federation,** c/o Engakuji Temple, Yamanouchi, Kamakura-shi, Kanagawa-ken 247.
**Japan Buddhist Federation (Zen-Nihon Bukkyo-kai),** c/o Tsukiji Honganji Temple, Chuo-ku, Tokyo. T: 5422969.
**Japan Free Religious Association,** Pres, 26 Shiba Nishikubo Hiro-machi, Minato-ku, Tokyo 105.
**Japan Muslim Association,** 1-24-4 Yoyogi Shibuya-ku, Tokyo. (Also: 2-22 Naka, Kunitachi, Tokyo 186).
**Shinto University (Kokugakuin Daigaku),** 10-28 Higashi 4-chome, Shibuya-ku, Tokyo.
**Shrine Work Department,** Association of Shinto Shrines, Yutenji Apartment House, 4-31-11 Kamimeguro, Meguro-ku, Tokyo 153.
**Union of New Religious Organizations in Japan (Shin Nippon Shukyo Dantai Rengo Kai),** Exec Dir, 2-1 Nishi Kanda, Chiyoda-ku, Tokyo. T: (291)4231. (Buddhist, Shinto sects; new religions. Begun 1951. Also: 2-7 Moto Yoyogimachi, Shibuya-ku, Tokyo).
**World Peace Prayer Society,** Pres, 3-20-17 Yawata, Ichikawa-shi, Chiba-ken 272.

*JORDAN*

**Grand Mufti of Jordan,** Amman.

*KENYA*

**Arya Samaj (Vedic Churches of East Africa),** Vedic House, Mama Ngina St, PO Box 40243, Nairobi. T: 21573.

**HH The Aga Khan Ismailia Supreme Council for Africa,** Jamatkhana Bldg, Moi Av, PO Box 40555, Nairobi, T: 25114.

**Hindu Council of Kenya (HCK),** Sec, PO Box 49012, Nairobi. T: 27054. (1969 union of all Hindu, Jain and Sikh bodies in Kenya).

**Khoja Shia Ithnasheri Jamaats of Africa,** Supreme Council of the Federation, Nehru Rd, PO Box 81085, Mombasa. T: 5856.

**Medicine Men's Society (Waganga wa Miti Shamba),** Plot 909/123, PO Box 334, Machakos. (Organization of over 110 traditional healers or witchdoctors).

**Sanatan Dharma Sabha,** Chairman, PO Box 40032, Nairobi. ('Idol-worshipping' Hindus).

**Shree Sthanakvasi Jain Mandal,** Chairman, Keekorok Rd, PO Box 46469, Nairobi. T: 25831.

**Siri Guru Singh Sabba,** Uyoma Rd, PO Box 40496, Nairobi. T: 25340. (Largest Sikh temple in Kenya).

**Wakf Commissioners for Kenya,** White Fathers Rd, PO Box 80272, Mombasa.

*KOREA, South*

**Korea Muslim Federation,** IPO Box 2865, Soul.

*LEBANON*

**Grand Mufti of the Lebanon,** Bayrut.

**World Muslim Congress/Congrès du Monde Islamique,** Bureaux Régionaux Moyen Orient, PB 883, Bayrut.

*LESOTHO*

**Basotho Medicine Men and Herbalist Association (Unification of Basotho Medicine Men),** PO Box 320, Maseru. (Traditionalist).

**Lesotho Muslim Congregation,** Mosque, Butha Buthe.

*LIBERIA*

**Ahmadiyya Muslim Mission,** 116 Carey St, Monrovia.

**Muslim Community of Liberia,** Vai Town, Bushrod Island.

*LIBYA*

**Association de la Vocation Islamique (Jamiat Al-Dawah Al-Islamiah),** Tarabulus.

*MALAWI*

**Nuru Muslim Association,** Islamic Education HQ, PO Box 5742, Limbe.

**Shree Hindu Seva Mandal,** PO Box 676, Blantyre.

**Wochiritsa African Traditional Medicine,** Proprietor, Blantyre.

*MALAYSIA*

**All Malayan Muslim Welfare Organization,** 32 Jalan Othman, Petaling Jaya, Selangor.

**Malayan Muslim Welfare Association,** Kuala Lumpur. (Established 1960).

**Muslim College of Malaya,** Pres, Petaling Jaya, Kuala Lumpur.

**Penang Chinese Muslim Association,** Penang. (Founded 1969).

*MOROCCO*

**Université al Qarawiyin,** Rabat. (Campuses also at Fès and Marrakech). (Muslim theological university).

**Université Ben Youssef,** Cité Universitaire, Marrakech.

*NETHERLANDS*

**Dutch Muslim Association (Ahle Soenat Djamaat),** BP 9070 Utrecht.

**Islam Foundation Holland,** Nierkerkstraat 87 II, Amsterdam.

**Islamic Centre Foundation (Islam Morkezi Vakfi),** Ottersstraat 82, Utrecht.

**Islamic Society (Islamitisch Genootschap),** Oostduinlaan 79, 's-Gravenhage.

**Netherlands Islamic Society (Nederlands Islamitische Societeit/Islamitische Societeit van Nederlanders),** Actsveld 30, Vinkeveen.

**Portuguese Israelite Community of Amsterdam (Ets Hain),** Rapenburger St 197, Amsterdam. (Begun 1637. Library of 25,000).

*NETHERLANDS ANTILLES*

**Association of Curaçao Muslims (Vereiniging van de Moslem Gemeente op Curaçao),** Curaçao.

*NIGERIA*

**Grand Qadi,** Sharia Court of Appeal, Kaduna, Northern Nigeria.

**Muslim International Relief Organization (MIRO),** 60a Campbell St, Lagos. (Large relief programme).

**United Muslim Council of Nigeria,** Lagos. (Begun 1958).

*PAKISTAN*

**Ahimia Institute of Islamic Studies,** Islamic Centre, B Block, North Nazimabad, Karachi.

**Ahmadiyya Muslim Mission (Tahrik-i-Jadid Anjuman Ahmadiyya),** Headquarters, Rabwah, Lyallpur District. T: 573. (Missionaries in 80 countries).

**Al-Ahibba (Friends of the Muslim World),** Pres, 92 Gulberg, Lahore.

**Begun Aisha Bawany Wakf,** PO Box 4178, Karachi 2.

**Central Institute of Islamic Research,** PO Box 1035, Islamabad. (Government).

**Holy Quran Society of Karachi,** Karachi.

**Iqbal Academy,** Karachi.

**Islamic Publications,** Sha Alam Market, Lahore.

**Muslim World,** Sec Gen, PO Box 5030, Karachi 2. (Publisher).

**Muslimnews International,** 3 Bonus Rd, PO Box 3955, Karachi 4.

**Shah Wali Ullah Academy,** Hyderabad, Sind.

**Society for the Protection of Islam (Anjuman-i-Himayati-i-Islam),** Islamiya High School, Islamiya College, Lahore. (Founded about 1885).

**Umma Publication House,** Bahadurabad Commercial Area, Karachi 5.

**World Federation of Islamic Missions,** Islamic Centre, B Block, North Nazimabad, Karachi 5.

**World Muslim Congress (Motamar al-alam al-Islami),** Sec Gen, 171-B Block 3, Pechs, PO Box 5030, Karachi 29. T: 412822,414047.

*PHILIPPINES*

**Agama Islamic Society,** Majliso Shoora Pacasum St, Marawi City.

**Muslim Association of the Philippines,** Headquarters, BP 4221, Manila.

**Sulu Muslim Association,** Pres, Sarentes St, Jolo, Sulu.

*PORTUGAL*

**Comunidade Islâmica de Lisboa,** Rua Luis de Camões 100, 3 Esq, Lisboa 3. T: 635203.

*RWANDA*

**Association Islamique du Rwanda,** BP 594, Kigali.

**Ismaili Community,** BP 31, Kigali.

*SAUDI ARABIA*

**Grand Mufti of Saudi Arabia,** Riyadh.

**Hajj Research Centre,** King Abdulaziz University, POB 1540, Jeddah.

**Islamic University of Medina,** Vice Chancellor, Medina.

**Muslim World League (Rabita Al-Alam Al-Islami),** Mecca Almukarramah.

**World Muslim Secretariat,** Islamic Secretariat, Sec Gen, Kilo 6, Mecca Rd, PO Box 178, Jeddah. T: 23880,25848,24848.

*SENEGAL*

**Shaikhul Islam,** PO Box 1, Madina, Kaolack.

**Union Culturelle Musulmane,** Dakar.

*SIERRA LEONE*

**Supreme Islamic Council,** 62 Kissy Rd, Freetown.

*SIKKIM*

**Namgyal Institute of Tibetology,** Gangtok.

*SINGAPORE*

**Islamic World,** Semenanjog Press Ltd, Singapore.

**Jamiat al-dawah,** c/o Room AD, 14th Floor, Asia Insurance Bldg, Finlayson Green, Singapore.

**Muslim Religious Council (Majlis Ugama Islam),** Singapore.

**Ramakrishna Mission,** 9 Norris Rd, Singapore 8.

**Sikh Missionary Society (Malaya),** 35 Medeiros Bldg, 18 Cecil St, Singapore.

**Singapore Buddhist Federation,** Yan Kit Rd, Singapore.

**Singapore Buddhist Sangha Organization,** Pho Kark See, Bright Hill Drive, Thomson Rd, Singapore-20.

**Singapore Regional Centre of World Fellowship of Buddhists,** 387 Guillemard Rd, Singapore.

**World Red Swastika Society,** Singapore Branch Association HQ, Hill St, Singapore.

*SOMALIA*

**Islamic Assembly,** PO Box 179, Mogadisho.

*SOUTH AFRICA*

**Al Jihaad Propagation Department,** 72 Aspeling St, Cape Town. (Publishers).

**Islamic Bureau,** PO Box 17, Athlone, Cape.

**Islamic Propagation Centre,** 47-48 Madressa Arcade, PO Box 2349, Durban, Natal.

**South African Jewish Board of Deputies,** POB 1180, Johannesburg.

**World Union of Jewish Students,** Sixth Av, Lower Houghton, Johannesburg, Transvaal.

*SPAIN*

**Asociación Musulmana en España,** Calle Aguilar de Campoo 25/5D, Madrid.

**Centro Islamico,** Apdo de Correos 2024, Granada.

**Congress of Arab and Islamic Studies,** Ciudad Universitaria, Madrid 3.

**Instituto de Estudios Sephardies,** Duque de Medinaceli 4, Madrid.

**Instituto Egipcio de Estudios Islamicos,** Mendez Casariego 10, Madrid.

**Islamic Institute,** Arriza 3, 5 dch, Madrid.

**Islamic Spanish Institute,** Dir, Hous Bacquer 4, Madrid 6. (1,500 students).

**Misión Ahmadia del Islam en España,** Calle Cuidad Real 12 1 izda, Madrid.

*SPANISH NORTH AFRICA*

**Asociación Musulmana de Melilla,** Calle García Cabrelles 31, Melilla (Málaga), North Africa.

**Zauia Musulmana de Mohamadia Mahoma (Ceuta),** Arroyo Paneque A, Cádiz, Spain.

*SRI LANKA*

**All Sri Lanka Buddhist Congress,** 380 Bullers Rd, Colombo 7. T: 91695.

**All Sri Lanka Muslim League,** Colombo.

**Al-Ilm,** 211 Dematagoda Rd, Maradana, Colombo 9.

**Buddhist Publication Society,** PO Box 61, Kandy.

**Buddhist Theosophical Society,** Colombo.

**Buddhist Training Centre for Missionaries,** Maharagama. (Also: c/o Buddhist Academy of Ceylon, 29 Rosmead Place, Colombo 7).

**Islamic Study Circle,** Khalafat House, 1 Poonagala Rd, Bandarawela.

**Maha Bodhi Society of Sri Lanka,** 130 Maligakande Rd, Maradana, Colombo 10.

**Muslim Ladies' Arabic College,** Colombo.

**Ramakrishna Mission,** Colombo.

**Sri Lanka Assembly of Muslim Youth,** 41 Dematagode Rd, Colombo 9.

**World Buddhist Sangha Council,** Sec Gen, Pirivena Teachers Training College, Pirivena Rd, Mount Lavinia.

*SUDAN*

**African Islamic Institute,** Wadmedani, Rd, Al Khurtum. (Begun 1977; government college, training Muslim missionaries from all over Africa).

**Broadcasting Service of the Democratic Republic of the Sudan,** Dir, PO Box 572, Umm Durman. (Muslim programmes, in Arabic).

**College for Arabic and Islamic Studies,** PO Box 238, Umm Durman.

**Islamic University,** Morada, Umm Durman.

*SURINAM*

**Arya Dewaker,** Wanicastraat 210, Paramaribo.

**Islamic Movement of Surinam (Surinamase Islamitische Vereniging),** Keizerstraat 88A, Paramaribo.

**Surinam Muslim Association,** PO Box 912, Jadenbreestraat 51, Paramaribo.

*SWEDEN*

**Baha'i Centre,** Matilda Jungstedts Väg 27, S-122 35 Stockholm-Enskede. (Begun 1920).

**Jewish Congregation in Stockholm (Mosaiska Församlingen i Stockholm),** Box 7057, S-103 82 Stockholm.

**Theosophical Society** (Teosofiska Samfundet), Östermalmsgatan 12, S-114 26 Stockholm. (Begun 1889).

*SWITZERLAND*

**Ahmadiyya Mission des Islams,** Imam Mushtag Bajwa, Mahumud Moschee, Forchstr 323, CH-8008 Zürich. T: (01)325577.

**Bahai-Sekretariat,** Dufourstr 13, CH-3000 Bern.

**Buddhistische Informationsstelle der Schweiz,** Postfach 681, CH-8021 Zürich.

**B'nai B'rith International Council,** 94 Rue des Eaux-Vives, CH-1207 Genève.

**Centre Védantique,** Swami Nityabodhânanda, Av Peschier 20, CH-1200 Genève. T: (022)461248.

**Co-ordinating Board of Jewish Organizations for Consultation with ECOSOC,** 94 Rue des Eaux-Vives, CH-1207 Genève.

**Divine Light Zentrum,** Anton-Graff-Str 65, CH-8400 Winterthur. T: (052)221903.

**European Council of Jewish Community Services,** 75 Rue de Lyon, CH-1211 Genève 13.

**Groupement Bouddhique,** Place Pépinet 4, CH-1000 Lausanne. T: (021)227136.

**International Association for the Advancement of the Science of Creative Intelligence (IAASCI),** Hotel Seeblick, CH-6353 Weggis. (Transcendental Meditation, TM).

**International Council on Jewish Social and Welfare Services,** 75 Rue de Lyon, CH-1211 Genève 13. T: 449000.

**International Islamic Publications,** Manager, Genève-Cornavin 253.

**Jewish Agency for Israel,** 26 Route de Malagnou, CH-1211 Genève 17.

**Krishnamurti-Freunde der Schweiz,** Herrn Edgar Graff, CH-6986 Novaggio-TI.

**Maharishi European Research University (MERU),** World Plan Administrative Centre, Seelisberg. (Transcendental Meditation, TM).

**Tibet-Institut,** Herrn P Lindegger-Stauffer, CH-8486 Rikon/ZH. T: (052)351729.

**World Jewish Congress (WJC)/Congrès Juif Mondial (CJM),** Sec Gen, 1 Rue de Varembé, CH-1211 Genève 20. T: 341325.

*TANZANIA*

**Ahmadiyya Muslim Association,** PO Box 376, Dar es Salaam.

**Comorian Mosque,** PO Box 181, Dar es Salaam.

**National Spiritual Assembly of Baha'is,** PO Box 585, Dar es Salaam.

**Shia Imami Ismaili Provincial Council,** PO Box 460, Dar es Salaam.

*THAILAND*

**Buddhist University,** Bangkok.

**World Fellowship of Buddhist (WFB),** 41 Phra Athit Rd (Also 33 Sukhumvit Rd), Bangkok. T: 819564,511188/90. (Begun 1950).

*TOGO*

**Conseil Suprême pour les Affairs Islamiques du Togo,** BP 64, Lomé.

*TRINIDAD & TOBAGO*

**Anjuman Sunnatul Jamat Association,** 16 Farah St, PO Box 97, San Fernando.

**Islamic Missionaries Guild of the Caribbean and and South America,** 1 Mucurapo Rd, PO Box 800, Port of Spain.

*TUNISIA*

**Grand Mufti,** Tunis.

**Quranic Zaitunah University,** Tunis.

*TURKEY*

**Higher Institute for Islamic Studies (Yüksek Islâm Enstitüsü),** Baglarbasi, Istanbul.

**Higher Institute for Islamic Studies (Yüksek Islâm Enstitüsü),** Konya.

**Imam ve Hatip School,** Istanbul. (A first modern medrese).

**Islamic Institute,** Imam ve Haliji School, Istanbul.

**Université d'Ankara,** Faculté de Théologie (Ankara Universitesi, Ilâhiyat Falkütesi), Yldirim Beyazit Meydani, Ankara. T: 113176.

*UGANDA*

**National Association for the Advancement of Muslims (NAAM),** Kampala.

**National Muslim Secretariat,** Kadhi of Uganda, PO Box 30380, Kampala.

*USSR*

**Congress of Community Representatives,** Mufti (Sheikh-ul-Islam), Tashkent. (Supreme Muslim body in USSR).

**Department of International Ties of Muslim Organization of the USSR,** Tashkent.

**Jama Masjid,** Imam, Moskva. (5,000 Muslims at Friday prayers).

**Leningrad Mosque,** Imam, Lengingrad.

**Mir-i-Arab Medresseh,** Bokhara.

**Muslim Theological Administration for Central Asia and Kazakhstan,** Pres, Tashkent, Uzbekistan SSR.

**Muslim Theological Administration for European USSR and Siberia,** Pres, Ufa, Bashkir SSR.

**Muslim Theological Administration for North Caucasus and Daghestan,** Pres, Buynaksk, Daghestan SSR.

**Muslim Theological Administration for the Transcaucasus,** Pres, Baku, Azerbaijan SSR.

*UK OF GB & NI*

**Baha'i Centre,** 27 Rutland Gate, London SW7.

**Belfast Hebrew Synagogue,** 49 Somerton Rd, Belfast 15.

**Bhagawan Soaham World Peace Meditation Centre,** Soaham Yogashram, 90 Alma Rd, London SW18. T: (01)870-3602.

**British-Israel World Federation,** Sec, 6 Buckingham Gate, London SW1.

**Buddhist Society,** Sec, 58 Eccleston Square, London SW1V 1PH. T: (01)828-1313.

**Conference of European Rabbis & Associated Religious Organizations,** Sec, Adler House, Tavistock Square, London WC1. T: (01)387-1066.

**Hindu Centre,** 39 Grafton Terrace, London NW5.

**Institute of Ismaili Studies,** 14-15 Great James St, London WC1. T: (01)405-5328/9.

**Institute of Jewish Affairs (IJA),** 13-16 Jacob's Well Mews, George St, London W1H 5PD. T: (01) 935-1436.

**International Society for Krishna Consciousness,** 7 Bury Place, London WC1A 2LA.

**International Spiritualist Federation (ISF),** Sec Gen, 14 Fielding St, Faversham, Kent. T: 3528. (Also: 82 Sydney Rd, Muswell Hill, London N10).

**Islamic Bookshop,** 148 Liverpool Rd, London N1.

**Islamic Council of Europe,** 38 Mapesbury Rd, London NW2 4JD.

**Islamic Cultural Centre,** Regent's Lodge, 146 Park Rd, London NW8.

**Islamic Foundation,** 223 London Rd, Leicester LE2 1ZE. (Research centre).

**Jewish Chronicle Publications,** 25 Furnival St, London EC4. T: (01)405-9252.

**Jewish Historical Society of England,** 33 Seymour Place, London W1. T: PAD 4404. (Library of 20,000 vols).

**Muslim Students Society,** 86 Stapleton Hall Rd, London N4 4QA.

**Reform Synagogues of Great Britain,** 33 Seymour Place, London W1. T: (01)723-8118.

**Standing Conferences of Organization in the Welfare of the Falashas of Ethiopia,** Woburn House, Upper Woburn Place, London WC1. T: (01)387-5849. ('Black Jews').

**Theosophical Society in England,** 50 Gloucester Place, London W1. T: WEL 9261.

**Theosophical Society in Europe/Société Nationale Théosophique en Europe,** 2 Tekels Park, Camberley, Surrey.

**Union of Muslim Organizations of UK and Eire,** 30 Baker St, London W1M 2DS.

**White Eagle Lodge,** White Temple, Brewells Lane, Rake, Liss, Hants GU33 7HY. T: (073082)3300. (Spiritualist).

**World Jewish Congress,** British Section, Gen Sec, 55 New Cavendish St, London W1.

**World Sephardi Federation,** Sec Gen, New House 67/8 Hatton Garden, London EC1N 8JY. T: (01) 242-4556.

**World Union for Progressive Judaism,** 34 Upper Berkeley St, London W1. T: (01)262-0999.

**World Union of Jewish Students,** 247 Gray's Inn Rd, London WC1. T: (01)837-3070.

**World Zionist Organization,** 4 Regent St, London SW1. T: (01)930-5152.

*USA*

**American Buddhist Association,** Pres, 1151 West Leland Av, Chicago, IL 60640. T: (312) 334-4461.

**American Jewish Committee,** Interreligious Affairs Department, 165 East 56th St, New York, NY 10022.

**American Jewish History Center,** Jewish Theological Seminary of America, 3080 Broadway, New York, NY 10027. T: (212)R19-8000.

**Anti-Defamation League of B'nai B'rith,** 315 Lexington Av, New York, NY 10016.

**Baha'i International Community (BIC),** 866 United Nations Plaza, New York, NY 10017. T: (212) 752-0510.

**Baha'i World Faith,** National Spiritual Assembly, HQ, Baha'i Temple, 536 Sheridan Rd, Wilmette, IL 60091. T: (312)256-4400.

**Buddhist Center of the USA,** PO Box 193, Fredericksburg, VA 22401.

**Buddhist Churches of America,** Headquarters, 1710 Octavia St, San Francisco, CA 94109. (Jodo Shinsu sect. Begun 1899).

**B'nai B'rith International Council,** 1640 Rhode Island Av, NW, Washington, DC 20036. T: EX3-5284. (Jewish fraternal organization uniting all schools of religious thought).

**California House of Israel,** 5365 Wilshire Blvd, Los Angeles, CA 90036.

**Church of All Worlds,** PO Box 2953, St Louis, MO 63130.

**Church of Light,** PO Box 1525, Los Angeles, CA 90053.

**Church of Satan,** 6114 California St, San Francisco, CA 94121.

**Church of the Eternal Source,** PO Box 7091, Burbank, CA 91505.

**Church Universal & Triumphant,**

**College of Jewish Studies,** 72 East 11th St, Chicago, IL 60605.

**Conference on Jewish Social Studies (CJSS),** 1814 Broadway, New York, NY 10023. T: (212) C15-7826.

**Consultative Council of Jewish Organizations,** Suite 1711, 61 Broadway, New York, NY 10006.
**Federation of Islamic Associations in the USA and Canada,** Cedar Rapids, Iowa. (Founded 1952).
**Hebrew Theological College,** 7135 Carpenter Rd, Skokie, IL 60076.
**Hebrew Union College,** Jewish Institute of Religion, 40 West 68th St, New York, NY 10023.
**Hongwanji Buddhist Mission of Hawaii,** 1727 Fort St, Honolulu, Hawaii.
**International Society for Krishna Consciousness (ISKCON),** 61 Second Av, New York, NY 10003.
**Islamic Centre,** 2551 Massachusetts Av, NW, Washington, DC 20008.
**Islamic Centers in USA,** East 97th St, New York, NY. (Also : Ricker College, Maine).
**Jewish Chautauqua Society of the Union of American Hebrew Congregations,** 538 Fifth Av, New York, NY 10021.
**Jewish Teachers Seminary and People's University,** 515 Park Av, New York, NY 10022.
**Jewish Theological Seminary,** 3080 Broadway, New York, NY 10027.

**Mosque of the Faithful,** Gary, Indiana. (500 Muslims).
**Muslim Brotherhood,** 5312 West Girard Av, Philadelphia 31, Pennsylvania. (The Black Muslims. Also : 2618 East MacDougall St, Detroit, Michigan).
**Muslim Students Association of the USA and Canada,** University Station, Minneapolis, MN 55414. (Also : 3702 West 11th Av, Gary, IN 46404).
**National Federation of Buddhist Women's Associations,** Buddhist Churches of America, 1710 Octavia St, San Francisco, CA 94109.
**National Young Buddhist Association (NYBA),** Buddhist Churches of America, 1710 Octavia St, San Francisco, CA 94109.
**Nichiren Shoshu of America (NSA),** 1351 Ocean Front, Santa Monica, CA 90401.
**Overseas Buddhist Association,** Sec Gen, c/o Fellowship of Reconciliation, Box 271, Nyack, NY 10960.
**Rosicrucian Order (AMORC),** Supreme Sec, Rosicrucian Park, San José, CA 95114.
**School of Islamic and African Studies,** 307 West 125 St, New York, NY 10027.

**Self-Realization Fellowship,** IHQ, 3880 San Rafael Av, Los Angeles, CA 90065.
**Subud North American Inquiry Section,** PO Box 453, Cooper Station, New York, NY 10003.
**Synagogue Council of America,** 432 Park Av South, New York, NY 10016.
**Talmudical Academy of Baltimore,** 3701 Cottage Av, Baltimore, MD 21215. (Jewish).
**Theosophical Society in America,** Box 270, Wheaton, IL 60187.
**United Lodge of Theosophists,** 245 West 33rd St, Los Angeles, CA 90007.
**World Conference of Jewish Organizations (COJO),** 515 Park Av, New York, NY 10022.
**World Council of Synagogues (Conservative),** Pres, 3080 Broadway, New York, NY 10027. T: (212) R19-8000.
**World Union for Progressive Judaism,** Exec Dir, 838 Fifth Av, New York, NY 10021. T: (212) 249-0100.

### UPPER VOLTA
**Communauté Musulmane,** Ouagadougou.

### VENEZUELA
**Culto Aborigen de Maria Lionza,** Apdo 10980, Caracas 101.

### VIET NAM
**Cao Daist Missionary Church (Dai Dao Tam Ky Pho Do Doctrine of the Third Revelation of God),** Sa Saintété Pham-Cong-Tac, Gaio-Tong (Pope), Saint-Siège de Tayninh.
**Cham and Vietnam Muslim Association,** 23 TK 10 Ben Choung Doung, Saigon.
**Unified Buddhist Association of Viet-Nam,** Hanoi.
**Unified Buddhist Church (UBC),** Supreme Patriarchate, HQ, Vietnam Quoc Tu (National Pagoda of Vietnam), 243 Su Van Hanh, Ho Chi Minh City/Saigon 10.

### YUGOSLAVIA
**League of Jewish Communities of Yugoslavia,** 7 Jula 71 a/III, Beograd.
**Muslim Religious Union,** Reis-ul-Ulema, Sarajevo. (Seats : Sarajevo and Skopje).
**Supreme Council of Islam in Yugoslavia,** Mufti, Sarajevo.

PART 14

# INDEXES

Quick-reference indexes

*The end of the survey is the beginning of action.*
—Samuel Marinus Zwemer, Apostle to Islam (1867–1952).

# POLYGLOT GLOSSARY OF RELIGIOUS TERMINOLOGY

| English | Chinese | French | German | Italian | Portuguese | Russian | Spanish |
|---|---|---|---|---|---|---|---|
| apostle | shitu | apôtre | Apostel | apostolo | apóstolo | apostol | apóstol |
| baptism | jinli | baptême | Taufe | battesimo | baptismo | kreshchenie | bautismo |
| baptize, to | shoujin | baptizer | taufen | battezzare | baptizar | krestit | bautizar |
| Bible | Shengjing | Bible | Bibel | Bibbia | Bíblia | Biblia | Biblia |
| bishop | zhujiao | evêque | Bischof | vescovo | bispo | episkop | obispo |
| blessing | zhufu | bénédiction | Segen | benedizione | bênção | blagoslovenie | bendición |
| Christ | Jidu | Christ | Christus | Cristo | Cristo | Khristos | Cristo |
| Christian | jidujiaotu | Chrétien/Chrétienne | Christ/Christin | Cristiano | Cristão | khristianin | Cristiano |
| Christianity | Jidujiao | Christianisme | Christentum | Cristianesimo | Cristianismo | Khristianstvo | Cristianismo |
| church | jiaotang | église | Kirche | chiesa | igreja | tserkov | iglesia |
| commandment | jielü | commandement | Gebot | comandamento | mandamento | zapoved | mandamiento |
| communion | shengcan | communion | Kommunion | comunione | comunhão | prichastie | comunión |
| community | shequ | communauté | Gemeinschaft | comunità | comunidad | soobshchestvo | comunidad |
| confession | renzui | confession | Bekenntnis | confessione | confissão | ispoved | confesión |
| congregation | huizhong | congrégation | Kongregation | congregazione | congregação | sobranie | congregación |
| conversion | zhuanbian | conversion | Bekehrung | conversione | conversação | obrashchenie | conversión |
| council | juhui | conseil | Rat | concilio | concelho | soviet | consejo |
| cross | shizijia | croix | Kreuz | croce | cruz | krest | cruz |
| denomination | jiaopai | dénomination | Denomination | denominazione | denominação | veroispovedanie | denominación |
| devil | mogui | diable | Teufel | diavolo | diablo | dyavol | diablo |
| evangelist | chuanjiaoshi | évangéliste | evangelist | evangelista | evangelista | evangelist | evangelista |
| faith | xinxin | foi | Glaube | fede | religião | vera | fe |
| fasting | zhaijie | jeûne | Fasten | digiuno | jejum | post | vigilia |
| fellowship | zhunei | communauté | Gemeinschaft | compagnia | comunhão | bratstvo | comunidad |
| God | Shen | Dieu | Gott | Dio | Deus | Bog | Dios |
| gospel | fuyin | évangile | Evangelium | vangelo | evangelho | evangelie | evangelio |
| grace | renci | grâce | Gnade | grazia | graçia | milost | gracia |
| heaven | tiantang | ciel | Himmel | cielo | céu | nebesa | cielo |
| hell | diyu | enfer | Hölle | inferno | inferno | ad | infierno |
| Holy Spirit | shengling | Saint-Esprit | Heilige Geist | Spirito Santo | Espírito Santo | svyatoy dukh | Santo Espíritu |
| hymn | zanmeishi | hymne | Hymne | inno | hino | tserkovny gimn | himno |
| independent | zizhude | indépendant | selbstandig | indipendente | independente | nezavisimy | indipendiente |
| Jesus | Yesu | Jésus | Jesus | Gesù | Jesus | Iisus | Jesús |
| Lord | Zhu | Seigneur | der Herr | Signore | Senhor | Gospod | Señor |
| love | ci ai | aimer | Liebe | amore | amor | lyubov | amor |
| man/men | ren | homme/hommes | Mann | uomo/uomini | homen | chelovek | hombre |
| minister, a | mushi | pasteur | Pfarrer | pastore | pastor | svyashchennik | pastor |
| missionary | chuanjiaoshi | missionnaire | Missionar | missionario | missionário | missioner | misionario |
| New Testament | Xinyuequanshu | Nouveau Testament | Neue Testament | Nuovo Testamento | Novo Testamento | Novy Zavet | Nuevo Testamento |
| offering | fengxian | offrande | Opfer | offerta | offranda | pozhertvovanie | oblación |
| Old Testament | Jiuyuequanshu | Ancien Testament | Alte Testament | Antico Testamento | Antigo Testamento | Vetkhy Zavet | Antiguo Testamento |
| prayer | daogao | prière | Gebet | preghiera | oração | molitva | rezo |
| preacher | mushi | prédicateur | Prediger | predicatore | pregador | propovednik | predicador |
| preaching | jiangdao | prédication | Predigt | predicatione | pregar | propovedovanie | predicación |
| priest | shenfu | prêtre | Priester | prete | sacerdote | svyashchennik | sacerdote |
| prophet | xianzhi | prophète | Prophet | profeta | profeta | prorok | profeta |
| religion | zongjiao | religion | Religion | religione | religião | religia | religión |
| repentance | chanhui | repentir | Reue | pentimento | arrependimento | raskayanié | arrepentimiento |
| resurrection | fuhuo | résurrection | Auferstehung | risurrezione | ressurreição | voskresenie | resurrección |
| sacrament | shengcan | sacrement | Sakramént | sacramento | sacramento | prichastie | sacramento |
| sacrifice | xisheng | sacrifice | Opfer | sacrificio | sacrifício | zhertva | sacrificio |
| saint | shengren | saint | Sankt | santo | santo | svatoy | santo |
| salvation | jiushi | salut | Heil | salvazione | salvação | spacenie | salvación |
| sermon | jiangdao | sermon | Predigt | predica | sermão | propved | sermón |
| service (worship) | zhurichongbai | office divin | Gottsdienst | servizio | cerimonia | sluzhba | servicio |
| sin | zui-e | péché | Sünde | peccato | pecado | grekh | pecado |
| soul | linghun | âme | Seele | anima | alma | dusha | alma |
| spirit | shengling | esprit | Geist | spirito | espírito | dukh | espíritu |
| testimony | jiansheng | témoignage | Zeugnis | attestazione | testamunho | svidetelstvo | testimonio |
| traditions | chuantong | traditions | Traditions | tradizioni | tradição | traditsii | tradicións |
| Trinity | Sanweiyiti | Trinité | Dreieinigkeit | Trinità | Trindade | Troitsa | Trinidad |
| witness, a | jianzhengren | témoin | Zeuge | teste | testamunha | svidetel | testigo |
| worship | chongbai | adoration | Anbeten | adorare | adoração | poklonenie | adorar |

# NAMES OF COUNTRIES IN 6 MAJOR LANGUAGES

| English | French | German | Italian | Portuguese | Spanish |
|---|---|---|---|---|---|
| Afghanistan | Afghanistan | Afghanistan | Afghanistan | Afeganistão | Afganistán |
| Albania | Albanie | Albanien | Albania | Albania | Albania |
| Algeria | Algérie | Algerien | Algeria | Algélia | Argelia |
| American Samoa | Samoa Américaine | Amerikanisch-Samoa | Samoa Americane | Samoa Americana | Samoa Americana |
| Andorra | Andorre | Andorra | Andorra | Andorra | Andorra |
| Angola | Angola | Angola | Angola | Angola | Angola |
| Anguilla | Anguilla | Anguilla | Anguilla | Anguilla | Anguila |
| Antigua | Antigua | Antigua | Antigua | Antigua | Antigua |
| Argentina | Argentine | Argentinien | Argentina | Argentina | Argentina |
| Australia | Australie | Australien | Australia | Austrália | Australia |
| Austria | Autriche | Österreich | Austria | Austria | Austria |
| Bahamas | Bahamas | Bahamainseln | Bahama | Baamas | Bahamas |
| Bahrain | Bahrein | Bahrein | Bahrein | Barhein | Bahrain |
| Bangladesh | Bangladesh | Bangladesch | Bangladesh | Bangladesh | Bangladesh |
| Barbados | Barbade | Barbados | Barbados | Barbados | Barbados |
| Belgium | Belgique | Belgien | Belgio | Bélgica | Bélgica |
| Belize | Belize | Belize | Belize | Belize | Belice |
| Benin | Bénin | Benin | Benin | Benin | Benin |
| Bermuda | Bermudes | Bermudsinseln | Bermuda | Bermudas | Bermudas |
| Bhutan | Bhoutan | Bhutan | Bhutan | Bhután | Bután (Bhután) |
| Bolivia | Bolivie | Bolivien | Bolivia | Bolívia | Bolivia |
| Botswana | Botswana | Botswana | Botswana | Botswana | Botswana |
| Brazil | Brésil | Brasilien | Brasile | Brasil | Brasil |
| British Antarctic Territory | Terre Antarctique Britannique | Britisches Antarktis-Territorium | Antartide Britannica | Território Antártico Británico | Territorio Antártico Británico |
| British Indian Ocean Territory | Territoire Britannique de l'Océan Indien | Britisches Indischer Ozean-Territorium | Territorio Britannico dell'Oceano I | Território Británico do Oceano Indico | Territorio Británico del Océano Indico |
| British Virgin Islands | Iles Vierges Britanniques | Britisch Jungferninseln | Vergini Isole (GB) | Ilhas Virgens Británicas | Islas Vírgenes Británicas |
| Brunei | Brunéi | Brunei | Brunei | Brunei | Brunei |
| Bulgaria | Bulgarie | Bulgarien | Bulgaria | Bulgaria | Bulgaria |
| Burma | Birmanie | Birma | Birmania | Birmania | Birmania |
| Burundi | Burundi | Burundi | Burundi | Burundi | Burundi |
| Cameroon | Cameroun | Kamerun | Camerun | Camarões | Camerún |
| Canada | Canada | Kanada | Canadà | Canadá | Canadá |
| Canton & Enderbury Islands | Iles Canton et Enderbury | Canton und Enderbury | Isole Canton e Enderbury | Ilhas de Cantão e Enderbury | Islas Canton y Enderbury |
| Cape Verde | Cap-Vert | Kap-verdische Inseln | Isole del Capo Verde | Cabo Verde | Cabo Verde |
| Cayman Islands | Iles Caïmanes | Kaiman Inseln | Isole Caiman | Ilhas Caiman | Islas Caimán |
| Central African Republic | République Centrafricaine | Zentralafrikanisches Republik | Repubblica Centrafricana | República Centro-Africana | República Centroafricana |
| Chad | Tchad | Tschad | Ciad | Chade | Chad |
| Channel Islands | Iles Anglo-Normandes | Kanal Inseln | Isole del Canel | Ilhas Canal | Islas del Canal |
| Chile | Chili | Chile | Cile | Chile | Chile |
| China | Chine | China | Cina | China | China |
| China (Taiwan) | Chine (Taïwan) | China (Taiwan) | Cina (Taiwan) | China (Taiwan) | China (Taiwán) |
| Christmas Island | Ile Christmas | Weihnachtinsel | Isola Christmas | Ilha Natal | Isla Christmas |
| Cocos (Keeling) Islands | Iles des Cocos (Keeling) | Kokos-Inseln | Isole Cocos (Keeling) | Ilhas Cocos (Keeling) | Islas Cocos (Keeling) |
| Colombia | Colombie | Kolombien | Colombia | Colômbia | Colombia |
| Comoros | Comores | Komoren | Comore | Comores | Comores |
| Congo | Congo | Kongo | Congo | Congo | Congo |
| Cook Islands | Iles Cook | Cook-Inseln | Isole Cook | Ilhas Cook | Islas Cook |
| Costa Rica | Costa Rica | Costerica | Costa Rica | Costa Rica | Costa Rica |
| Cuba | Cuba | Cuba | Cuba | Cuba | Cuba |
| Cyprus | Chypre | Zypern | Cipro | Chipre | Chipre |
| Czechoslovakia | Tchécoslovaquie | Tschechoslovakei | Cecoslovacchia | Checoslováquia | Checoslovaquia |
| Denmark | Danemark | Dänemark | Danimarca | Danamarca | Dinamarca |
| Djibouti | Djibouti | Dschibuti | Djibouti | Djibouti | Djibouti |
| Dominica | Dominique | Dominica | Dominica | Dominica | Dominica |
| Dominican Republic | République Dominicaine | Dominikanische Republik | Repubblica Dominicana | República Dominicana | República Dominicana |
| Ecuador | Equateur | Equador | Ecuador | Ecuador | Ecuador |
| Egypt | Egypte | Agypten | Egitto | Egito | Egipto |
| El Salvador | El Salvador | El Salvador | El Salvador | El Salvador | El Salvador |
| Equatorial Guinea | Guinée Equatoriale | Aquatorial-Guinea | Guinea Equatoriale | Guiné Equatorial | Guinea Ecuatorial |
| Ethiopia | Ethiopie | Athiopien | Etiopia | Etiopia | Etiopía |
| Faeroe Islands | Iles Féroé | Färöer Inseln | Isole Faroë | Ilhas Feroe | Islas Feroe |
| Falkland Islands | Iles Falkland | Falklandinseln | Isole Falkland | Ilhas Malvinas | Islas Malvinas |
| Fiji | Fidji | Fidschi | Figi | Fiji | Fiji |
| Finland | Finlande | Finnland | Finlandia | Finlândia | Finlandia |
| France | France | Frankreich | Francia | França | Francia |
| French Guiana | Guyane Française | Französisch-Guayana | Guyana Francese | Guyana Francesa | Guayana Francesa |
| French Polynesia | Polynésie Française | Französisch-Polynesien | Polinesia Francese | Polinésia Francesa | Polinesia Francesa |
| French Southern & Antarctic Territories | Terres Australes et Antarctiques Fr | Französische Sud-und Antarktis-Gebiete | Terre Australi e Antartico Francese | Terras Austrais e Antarticas Francesas | Tierras Australes y Antárticas Francesas |
| Gabon | Gabon | Gabun | Gabon | Gabão | Gabón |
| Gambia | Gambie | Gambia | Gambia | Gambia | Gambia |
| German Democratic Republic | Allemagne Oriental | Deutsche Demokratische Republik | Repubblica Democratica Tedesca | Alemanha Oriental | Alemania Oriental |
| Germany, Federal Republic of | Allemagne Occidentale | Bundesrepublik Deutschland | Repubblica Federale di Germania | Alemanha Occidental | Alemania Occidental |
| Ghana | Ghana | Ghana | Ghana | Gana | Ghana |
| Gibraltar | Gibraltar | Gibraltar | Gibilterra | Gibraltar | Gibraltar |
| Greece | Grèce | Griechenland | Grecia | Grécia | Grecia |
| Greenland | Groenland | Grönland | Groenlandia | Gronelândia | Groenlandia |
| Grenada | Grenade | Grenada | Grenada | Grenada | Granada |
| Guadeloupe | Guadeloupe | Guadeloupe | Guadalupa | Guadalupe | Guadalupe |
| Guam | Guam | Guam | Guam | Guam | Guam |
| Guatemala | Guatemala | Guatemala | Guatemala | Guatemala | Guatemala |
| Guinea | Guinée | Guinea | Guinea | Guiné | Guinea |
| Guinea-Bissau | Guinée-Bissau | Guinea-Bissau | Guinea-Bissau | Guiné-Bissau | Guinea-Bissau |
| Guyana | Guyane | Guayana | Guyana | Guiana | Guayana |
| Haiti | Haiti | Haiti | Haiti | Haití | Haití |
| Holy See | Saint-Siège | Heilige Stuhl | Santa Sede | Santa Sé | Santa Sede |
| Honduras | Honduras | Honduras | Honduras | Honduras | Honduras |
| Hong Kong | Hong-Kong | Hongkong | Hong Kong | Hong-Kong | Hong Kong |
| Hungary | Hongrie | Ungarn | Ungheria | Hungria | Hungría |
| Iceland | Islande | Island | Islanda | Islândia | Islandia |
| India | Inde | Indien | India | India | India |
| Indonesia | Indonésie | Indonesien | Indonesia | Indonésia | Indonesia |
| Iran | Iran | Iran | Iran | Irã | Irán |
| Iraq | Irak | Irak | Iraq | Iraque | Iraq |
| Ireland | Irlande | Irland | Irlanda | Irlanda | Irlanda |
| Isle of Man | Ile de Man | Insel Man | Isola Man | Ilha de Man | Isla de Man |
| Israel | Israël | Israel | Israele | Israel | Israel |
| Italy | Italie | Italien | Italia | Itália | Italia |
| Ivory Coast | Côte d'Ivoire | Elfenbeinküste | Costa d'Avorio | Costa do Marfim | Costa de Marfil |
| Jamaica | Jamaique | Jamaika | Giamaica | Jamaica | Jamaica |
| Japan | Japon | Japan | Giappone | Japão | Japón |
| Johnston Island | Ile Johnston | Johnston Insel | Isola Johnston | Ilha Johnston | Isla Johnston |
| Jordan | Jordanie | Jordanien | Giordania | Jordania | Jordania |
| Kampuchea | Cambodge | Kambodscha | Cambodia | Camboja | Camboya |
| Kenya | Kenya | Kenia | Kenya | Quênia | Kenia (Kenya) |
| Kiribati | Iles Gilbert | Gilbert Inseln | Isole Gilbert | Ilhas Gilbert | Islas Gilbert |
| Korea, North | Corée du Nord | Nord-Korea | Corea del Nord | Coréia do Norte | Corea del Norte |
| Korea, South | Corée du Sud | Süd-Korea | Corea del Sud | Coréia do Sul | Corea del Sur |
| Kuwait | Koweit | Kuwait | Kuwait | Coveite | Kuwait |
| Laos | Laos | Laos | Laos | Laos | Laos |
| Lebanon | Liban | Libanon | Libano | Líbano | Líbano |
| Lesotho | Lesotho | Lesotho | Lesotho | Lesoto | Lesotho |
| Liberia | Libéria | Liberia | Liberia | Liberia | Liberia |
| Libya | Libye | Libyen | Libia | Líbia | Libia |
| Liechtenstein | Liechtenstein | Liechtenstein | Liechtenstein | Liechtenstein | Liechtenstein |
| Luxembourg | Luxembourg | Luxemburg | Lussemburgo | Luxemburgo | Luxemburgo |
| Macao | Macao | Macau | Macao | Macau | Macao |
| Madagascar | Madagascar | Madagaskar | Madagascar | Madagascar | Madagascar |
| Malawi | Malawi | Malawi | Malawi | Malawi | Malawi |
| Malaysia | Malaisie | Malaysia | Malaysia | Malásia | Malasia |

# NAMES FOR GOD IN 900 LANGUAGES

This index is in 2 parts. The first index (1) is an alphabetical listing of names for God used in translations of the Scriptures in some 900 languages, based on a listing prepared by the British and Foreign Bible Society, each followed by the name or names of all languages using the name; names which are normally in non-roman script are here transliterated into roman characters. The second index (2) is the same but arranged alphabetically by language. Orthographies used in these 2 listings differ in places from those adopted in our classification PEOPLES OF THE WORLD (Part 4). For full identification and details of languages, see *The book of a thousand tongues* (revised edition) (London: United Bible Societies, 1972).

## (1) Names for God followed (after comma) by languages

Aabi, Gio
Abece, Ibembe
Abradu,
 Nuba
 Nyimang
Ade, Mer
Aê Diê, Radé
Agwatana,
 Bassa
 Kwomu
Ahi, Paama
Ahogbre, Eggon
Aitu, Rotuma
Akôtesieti, Lifu
Akua, Hawaiian
Akuj,
 Karamajong
 Turkana
Ala,
 Kambera
 Koalib
 Krongo
 Nirere
 Nuba
 Wajewa
Alatalla,
 Dayak
 Manyan
Alauna, Masana
Alhou,
 Naga
 Sema
Alla,
 Bambara
 Eggon
 Kuranko
 Madurese
 Maltese
 Mandingo
 Meninka
 Soso
 Yalunka
Allach,
 Gagauzi
 Turkish
Allah,
 Algerian Arabic
 Arabic
 Balantian
 Bentuni
 Bisaya
 Eggon
 Fulani
 Goulei
 Hausa
 Javanese
 Judeo-Arabic
 Kabba Laka
 Kabyle
 Kazan
 Kumuk
 Macina
 Madjingai
 Malay
 Mbai
 Murut
 Ngambai
 Nogai
 Palestinian Arabic
 Pashto
 Sara
 Sasak
 Shilha
 Sundanese
 Syriac
 Transcaucasian
 Turkish
Allah Taala,
 Land Dayak
 Sea Dayak
Allaha,
 Fula
 Futa-Jalon
 Macina
Allahi,
 Egyptian Arabic
 Tunisian Arabic
Allahu,
 Hebrew
 Moorish
Alla-taâla,
 Bugis
 Macassar
Altjira, Aranda
Ama, Habbe
Anatumi, Kyaka
Andriamanitra, Malagasy
Anna, Kunama
Anôtô, Jabim
Anut,
 Amele
 Graged
Anutu,
 Adzera
 Kate
 Kuman
 Melpa
 Sinasina
Anyambe, Benga
Anyambie,
 Galwa
 Kele
 Omyene

Anyambye, Omyene
Anyame, Fang
Aôndo, Tiv
Apajuí, Aguaruna
Apistotokiua, Blackfoot
Arnam, Mikir
Asapavan, Anal
Asdulaz, Armenian
Asila, Dakkarkari
Atemit, Diola
Atua,
 Aneityum
 Aniwa
 Aulua
 Baki
 Bieria
 Efate
 Ellice Islander
 Epi
 Gilbertese
 Kwamera
 Malekula
 Maori
 Marquesan
 Nguna
 Niuean
 Nogugu
 Pangkumu
 Rarotongan
 Samoan
 Santo
 Tahitian
 Tanna
 Uripiv
Aualari, Orokolo
Augad,
 Mabuiag
 Saibai
Ayeba, Ijo
A-pa Li Boi,
 Asho
 Chin

Ba, Iregwe
Bali, Gouro
Banara,
 Bambatana
 Vella Lavella
Bao, Houailou
Bari, Ogoni
Bhagawan,
 Bhili
 Chhattisgarhi
 Gurmukhi
 Punjabi
 Sindhi
 Valvi
Bhagwan, Kurku
Bhogana,
 Bhili
 Dehwali
Bhogawan, Bhili
Blei, Khasi
Bog,
 Bulgarian
 Byelorussian
 Croatian
 Hungaro
 Macedonian
 Polish
 Russian
 Serbian
 Slavonic
 Slovenian
 Wendish
 White Russian
Bôh, Slovak
Boi ogoda, Mailu
Bok Kei-Dei, Bahnar
Bon Diê, Dominican
Bondié, Mauritius Creole
Bondiu, Carib
Borgan,
 Kalmuk
 Mongolian
Borhan, Mongolian
Bozymy, Ukrainian
Buh, Czech

Chido,
 Jukun
 Wukari
Chihowa, Choctaw
Chineke, Ibo
Chios, Igorot
Chiuta, Tonga
Ciong-Di,
 Chinese
 Kienning
Ciuta, Tumbuka
Cuku, Ibo

Dagwi, Burum
Dagwonom, Jarawa
De,
 Epi
 Lewo
 Tasiko
Debata,
 Angkola-Mandailing
 Batak
 Toba Batak
Deews, Latvian
Deis, Romansh
Del i Luma,
 German Romany
 Romany

Demenu, Bobo
Dén-did,
 Dinka
 Kyec
Deos, Indo-Portuguese
Deovel,
 Finnish Romany
 Romany
Déu, Catalan
Deus,
 Brazilian
 Latin
 Portuguese
 Romansch
 Sardinian
Devac, Konkani
Devadu, Telugu
Devam, Malayalam
Devan,
 Konkani
 Tamil
Devaru,
 Badaga
 Kannada
Devel,
 German Romany
 Latvian Romany
 Moravian Romany
 Romany
Dever, Tulu
Deviyanwahansay,
 Sinhalese
Devlehêe,
 Romany
 Yugoslav Romany
Devléskere, Romany
Devudu,
 Gondi
 Koi
Dévuni,
 Gondi
 Koi
Dewa,
 Marathi
 Pali
Dia, Gaelic
Día, Irish
Dieu,
 French
 Provençal
 Romansh
Dievas, Lithuanian
Dievs, Latvian
Diewas, Samogit
Diews, Lithuanian
Dio,
 Corsican
 Esperanto
 Italian
Dios,
 Ancash
 Ayacucho
 Aymara
 Bicol
 Cakchiquel
 Cebuano
 Cuzco
 Huanuco
 Ibanag
 Ilocano
 Judeo-Spanish
 Junín
 Lengua
 Mataco
 Mexican
 Pampangan
 Panayan
 Pangasinan
 Quechua
 Quiché
 Samareño
 Shipibo
 Spanish
 Toba
 Visayan
Diou, Vaudois
Dioz, Maya
Dirava,
 Motu
 Police Motu
Diws, Latgalian
Diyos, Tagalog
Dkon-mchhog, Tibetan
Dkon-mjog, Ladakhi
Dok, Kim
Doue, Breton
Droué, Pénérihouen
Duata, Sangir
Duc Chua Troi,
 Vietnamese
Duc Chua Pha, Tho
Dumendelu, Macedonian
Dumnezeu, Rumanian
Duw, Welsh

Eaubada,
 Bwaidoga
 Dobu
 Kiriwina
 Suau
 Tavara
 Tubetube
Edeke, Teso
Efile Mukulu,
 Kalebwe
 Luba
 Songi

Efozu, Avikam
Elo,
 Nuba
 Otoro
Eloba, Nama
Elohim,
 Hebrew
 Moorish
Eloi, Namau
engÄi, Maasai
Eso, Kabre

Foy, Bullom

Gaddel, Sora
Gado, Negro-English
Gala, Loma
Gedepo, Bassa
Gnallaeh,
 Nancowry
 Nicobarese
God,
 Afrikaans
 Ahamb
 Anganiwei
 Arosi
 Bamu
 Binandere
 Bislama
 Bugotu
 Dutch
 English
 Epi
 Fanting
 Fiu
 Flemish
 Frisian
 Gogodala
 Guadalcanar
 Gunwingu
 Kiwai
 Kuliviu
 Kunini
 Kusaiean
 Kwagutl
 Kwara'ae
 Lau
 Lewo
 Mabuiag
 Malekula
 Malo
 Malu
 Marovo
 Moskito
 Mota
 Mukawa
 Mwala
 Navajo
 Neo-Melanesian
 Notu
 Nunggubuyu
 Opa
 Orokaiva
 Pitjantjatjara
 Raga
 Rennellese
 Saa
 Santo
 Suki
 Tangoa
 Tasiko
 Tasiriki
 Tawarafa
 Ubir
 Ulawa
 Wedau
 Worrora
 Yahgan
Goda, Dieri
Godebo, Foe
Godim, Eskimo (Western Arctic)
Godimli, Eskimo (Copper)
Godku, Gupapuynu
Gosanyith, Malto
Gospod,
 Perm
 Zyryan
Got,
 Yapese
 Yiddish
Gotega, Gawigh
Goteme, Kewa
Gott,
 German
 Nauruan
Goyakalu, Piro
Gud,
 Danish
 Icelandic
 Norwegian
 Swedish
Gûdib,
 Eskimo
 Labrador Eskimo
Guisha, Lahu
Gusune, Bariba
Gûtip,
 Eskimo
 Greenlandic
Gvray Gvsvng, Rawang
G'mert'man, Georgian
G't'n, Georgian

Hadayun, Khasi
Hananim, Korean

Hatalla,
 Dayak
 Ngaju
Hera,
 Naga
 Zeme
Hinegbau, Igbira
Hollum, Latuka
Hudha, Balochi
Hunavan, Teop
Hven, Mbum
Hyalatamwa, Higi
Hyel, Bura

Ibmel,
 Lapp
 Norwegian Lapp
Iddio, Italian
Iddiou, Piedmontese
Iehova,
 Goaribari
 Kiwai
 Panaieti
Igziabiheir,
 Amharic
 Tigrinya
Iju, Margi
Ikkegon,
 Kunuzi
 Nubian
Ilahey, Somali
Imana,
 Ha
 Hangaza
 Ruanda
 Rundi
Immlja,
 Lapp
 Russian Lapp
Inallah, Shilha
Inan, Yergum
Inmar, Votiak
Iricouei, Dyerma
Iruva,
 Chagga
 Machame
Isawr, Riang
Ishal,
 Achik
 Garo
Ishor,
 Abor Miri
 Diamasa
Ishôra, Boro
Ishwar,
 Assamese
 Bagheli
 Bengali
 Bhatneri
 Bhojpuri
 Bihari
 Bikaneri
 Chhindwara
 Dogri
 Gonda
 Gujarati
 Harauti
 Hindi
 Ho
 Jaunsari
 Kanauji
 Kanauri
 Kashmiri
 Kharia
 Kumaoni
 Magahi
 Malvi
 Mandla
 Manipuri
 Marwari
 Nagpuria
 Nepali
 Palpa
 Panjabi
 Parsi
 Rabha
 Sanskrit
Isol, Garo
Isor, Santali
Issur,
 Garhwali
 Tehri
Isten, Hungarian
Izuwa, Taveta

Jainkoak,
 Basque
 Labourdin
Jañahary, Tsimihety
Jaungoicoac,
 Basque
 Guipuzcoan
Jee, Manx
Jehoba, Kipsigis
Jehova,
 Manus Islander
 Nandi
Jehovah,
 Nandi-Kipsigis
 Narrinyeri
Jen, Zyryan
Jihova,
 Konyak
 Mao
 Naga
Jihova-a,
 Angami

Naga
Jincouac,
 Basque
 Souletin
Jing-ming,
 Chinese
 Ningpo
Jiwheyewhe, Gu
Joo, Murle
Jueng, Maban
Juma,
 Buryat
 Mongolian
Jumahlto, Livonian
Jumal,
 Estonian
 Finnish
 Karel
 Reval
Jumala, Finnish
Jummal,
 Dorpat
 Estonian
 Setu
Jupmel, Swedish Lapp
Jwok, Shilluk

Kabeshyampungu,
 Kalanga
 Luba
Kalaga, Lega
Kalo,
 Heiban
 Nuba
Kalou,
 Fijian
 Patpatar
Kalunga,
 Kuanyama
 Luimbe
 Ndonga
 Nyemba
Kami, Japanese
Kamisama, Bunun
Kamui, Ainu
Kanu, Limba
Karai Kasang,
 Atsi
 Kachin
Karunga, Kwangali
Katonda,
 Ganda
 Haya
Kavangi,
 Naga
 Phom
Kawas, Ami
Khaien, Chuvash
Khazopa, Lakher
Khoda,
 Bengali
 Kurdish
 Kurmanji
 Musalmani
Khong, Uvea
Khozai,
 Bashkir
 Turkish
Khuda,
 Balti
 Brahui
 Dakhini
 Gurezi
 Hindko
 Kachchhi
 Kashgar
 Kashmiri
 Kazan
 Kermanshahi
 Kirgiz
 Kurdish
 Lahnda
 Mukri
 Persian
 Shina
 Sindhi
 Tamil
 Turkish
 Urdu
 Uzbek
Khudadin, Kirgiz
Khudai, Kirgiz
Khutzau, Ossete
Khwedê,
 Kurdish
 Kurmanji
Kibumba, Soga
Kinerehingan, Dusun
Kinikhawma,
 Chin
Khumi Awa
Kinorohingan,
 Dusan
 Ranau
Kishemanito, Chippewa
Kon-chhog,
 Bunan
 Lahuli
Kon-chok,
 Lahuli
 Tinan
Kot,
 Mortlock
 Tanna
Kuma, Nanjeri
Kumno, Lele

**(2) Languages followed (after comma) by names for God**

# INDEX OF PEOPLES AND LANGUAGES

This is a comprehensive index to all names of peoples, languages, geographical races, ethnolinguistic families, tribes, cultures and other ethnolinguistic groups which occur in our anglicized classification PEOPLES OF THE WORLD (in Part 4) or elsewhere in this survey. The total listed here is 2,200, out of the grand total of 8,990 described in that classification. To assist the reader who comes across a name which he cannot classify or locate, the index gives the code under which each name will be found in the classification. Using the codes given in Part 4, the reader can then immediately identify the people's race, geographical race, and colour: and, from the classification itself, its context among other peoples. Names in capitals are the 13 geographical races in our classification.

We omit here the adjectives 'North', 'South', 'East', 'West', 'Central', etc, except where they are part of the name of a family or major people, and in 2 or 3 other important cases. Prefixes for Bantu peoples (A-, Aba-, Ama-, Ba-, Ma-, Wa-, etc) and others are omitted.

In a few cases, the same term (eg Ho) may apply to 2 or more widely-separated and totally-unrelated peoples. In such cases all the references are given at the same point but are clearly distinguished by differing numbers in parentheses.

Aakwo, NAB59c
Ababda, CMT33z
Abazinian, CEW17a
Abe, NAB59k
Abkhazian, CEW17a
Aboriginal Siberian, MSY48
Abraka, NAB59z
Abriba, NAB59n
Abure, NAB59k
Abyssinian, CMT34a
Achinese, MSY44y
Acholi, NAB62a
Achuale, MIR39d
Adamawa, NAB66
Adangbe, NAB59f
Adangme, NAB59f
Adarawa, NAB60a
Adda, NAB59h
Adele, NAB59b
Adere, CMT34a
Adilabad, AUG06b
Adja, NAB59e
Adyghe, CEW17a
Adygo-Abkhazi, CEW17a
Adzerma, NAB65c
Aeta, AUG05
Afar, CMT33z
Afenmai, NAB59c
Afghani, CNT24a
Afrasian, CMT
AFRICAN, NAB, NAN
African Semitic, CMT34
Afridi, CNT24a
Afrikaans, CEW19a
Afrikaner, CEW19a
AFRO-AMERICAN, NFB
Afro-Asian, NFB68b
Afro-Asiatic, CMT
Afro-Chinese, NFB68b
Afshar, MSY41z
Afuno, NAB60a
Agar, NAB62f
Agau, CMT33a
Agbon, NAB59z
Aghbar, CMT32g
Aguly, CEW17b
Ahaggaren, CMT32h
Ahirwati, CNN25o
Ahom, MSY49c
Ainu, AUG01
Aiome, AUG05
Air, CMT32h
Airym, MSY41a
Aissor, CMT31
Aizo, NAB59e
Ajukru, NAB59k
Aka, BYG12
Akan, NAB59a
Akebu, NAB59a
Akha, MSY50z
Akim, NAB59a
Akposo, NAB59b
Akre, CNT24c
Aku, NAN58
Akwapim, NAB59a
Akyem, NAB59a
Alagya, NAB59k
Albanian, CEW13
Aleut, MRY40a
Algonkian, MIR38a
Alladian, NAB59k
Allush, CMT32i
Almaguero, MIR39g
Alorese, AON10e
Alpine, CEW
Alsatian, CEW19b
Altai, MSY41y
Altaic, MSY41
Altayan, MSY41
Alua, NAB62b
Alur, NAB62b
Amadiyah, CNT24c
Amam, NAB62l
Amami, MSY45b
Amarar, CMT33z
Amba, NAB57c
Ambo, NAB57n
Ambonese, AON09e
Amer, CMT33z
AMERICAN INDIAN, MIR
Americo-Liberian, NAN58
Amerind, MIR
Amerindian, MIR
Amhara, CMT34a
Amharic, CMT34a
Ami, AUG01
Amoy-Swatow, MSY42a
Amur, MSY41i
Amuzgo, MIR37c
Ana, NAB59n
Anag, NAB62m
Anatolian Turk, MSY41j
Anatri, MSY41c
Ancash, MIR39g
Andalusian, CEW21j
Andamanese, AUG05
Andhra, CNN23d
Andi-Tsezi, CEW17b
Andorran, CEW21a
Anecho, NAB59l

Anfillo, NAB62l
Angami, MSY50p
Angas, NAB60b
Angkola, MSY44b
Anglo, NAB59d
Anglo-Australian, CEW19c
Anglo-Burmese, MSY43
Anglo-Canadian, CEW19d
Anglo-Chinese, MSY43
Anglo-Indian, CNN25z
Anglo-New Zealander, CEW19e
Angoni NAB57i
Anima, NAB59f
Annamese, MSY52b
Antaisaka, MSY44j
Antandroy, MSY44j
Antessar, CMT32h
Antillean, NFB67b, NFB69b
Antillese, NFB67b, NFB69b
Anuak, NAB62c
Anyang, NAB56b
Anyi-Baule, NAB59a
Ao, MSY50p
Apache, MIR38a
Arab, CMT30
Arabic, CMT30
Arabized Berber, CMT32a
Arain, CNN25z
Arakan, MSY50b
Aramaean, CMT31
Aramaic, CMT31
Araucanian, MIR39f
Arawak, MIR39a
Arawakan, MIR39
ARCTIC MONGOLOID, MRY
Arem, MSY52z
Argobba, CMT34a
Argonese, CEW21j
Ari, NAB59k
Armenian, CEW14
Armin, CEW22g
Aromanian, CEW21i
Arowak, MIR39a
Arunta, AUG02
Arusha, NAB62k
Arusi, CMT33b
Arzal, CNN25b
Asa, (1) BYG11b
(2) CMT33c
Asben, CMT34a
Aser, NAB63j
Ashanti, NAB59a
Ashkenazi, CMT35
Ashksarhik, CEW14
Ashkun, CNT24d
Asho, MSY50c
Ashraf, CNN25b
ASIAN, MSY, MSW
Asian Turk, MSY41j
Asiatic, MSY
Asiatic Pygmoid, AUG05
Aslian, AUG05
Asmat, AON10a
Assamese, CNN25a
Assamese Bengali, CNN25a
Assini, NAB59k
Assuran, CEW21j
Asturan, CEW21j
Asu, NAB57e
Asuri, AUG04z
Aswanik, NAB63j
Atayal, AUG01
Athabaskan, MIR38a
Athpare, MSY50h
Atka, MIR40a
Atta, CMT32z
Attie, NAB59a
Attuan, MRY40a
Atwot, NAB62n
Atzi, MSY50f
Auca, MIR39d
Aulliminden, CMT32h
Australian Aborigine, AUG02
Austrian, CEW19f
AUSTRO-ASIATIC, AUG
Avar, CEW17b
Avatime, NAB59b
Avikam, NAB59k
Awa, AON10b
Awadhi, CNN25g
Awan, CNN25h
Awiya, CMT33a
Awngi, CMT33a
Awutu, NAB59f
Ayacucho, MIR39g
Aymara, MIR39b
Aynallu, MSY41a
Azande, NAB66a
Azerbaijani, MSY41a
Azeri, MSY41a
Azjer, CMT32h
Azna, NAB60a

Aztec, MIR37a
Azteco-Tanoan, MIR37

Baba Malay, MSY44k
Babuyan, MSY44m
Babwa, NAB57c
Bacha, BYG11b
Badaga, CNN23a
Bafut, NAB57a
Bagane, NAB63d
Baggara, CMT30
Bagheli, CNN25g
Bagirmi, NAB66z
Bahasa Indonesia, MSY44k
Bahasa Malay, MSY44k
Bahnar, AUG03z
Bajau, NAB66c
Bajau, MSY44z
Bajun, NAB57j
Bakairi, MIR39c
Bakedi, NAB62q
Bakhtiari, CNT24z
Bako, CMT33d
Bakwe, NAB59j
Balante, NAB56c
Balcarce, CEW21a
Bali, NAB57a
Balinese, MSY44a
Baloch, CNT24b
Balt, CEW15
Balti, MSY50r
Baltic, CEW15
Balu, NAB64h
Baluchi, CNT24b
Baluga, AUG05
Baluva, NAB57f
Bama, MSY50b
Bambara, NAB63a
Bambatana, AON09d
Bambugu, NAB63h
Bamileke, NAB57a
Bamum, NAB57a
Banaban, MPY54z
Banakal, NAB66b
Bande, NAB64c
Bandya, NAB66a
Bangaru, CNN25r
Bangi, NAB57c
Bangkalan, MSY44h
Banjarese, MSY44y
Banjuri, CNN25f
Banjuwangi, MSY44g
Bankoti, CNN25d
Banmana, NAB63a
Banso, NAB57a
Banten, MSY44n
Bantoid, NAB56
Bantu, NAB57
Banziri, NAB66z
Bara, MSY44j
Baraba, MSY41h
Barabra, NAB62m
Bararetta, CMT33b
Barea, NAB62d
Bargu, MSY41f
Bari, (1) MIR39e
(2) NAB62e
Baria, CNN25e
Bariba, NAB56a
Barotse, NAB57g
Barr, NAB62n
Bartang, CNT24g
Barya, NAB62d
Basa Kedatan, MSY44g
Basakomo, NAB56b
Bashkir, MSY41b
Basila, NAB59b
Basque, CEW16
Bassa, NAB59j
Bassange, NAB59m
Baster, NAN58
Bat, CEW17d
Batache, NAB59m
Batah, MSY44m
Batak, MSY44b
Bauan, AON08
Baule, NAB59a
Bauré, MIR39a
Bavarian, CEW19m
Bawean, MSY44h
Bawm, MSY50z
Baya, NAB66c
Bayat, MSY41y
Baygo, NAB66d
Bazen, NAB62h
Be, MSY49z
Bedda, AUG07
Bedouin, CMT30
Beja, CMT33z
Belingo, NAB66b
Belle, NAB64c
Belorussian, CEW22c
Bemba, NAB57b
Bena, NAB59f
Bena Kalundwe, NAB57f
Bena Kanioka, NAB57f
Bena Lulua, NAB57f
Bengali, CNN25b
Beni, NAB59m
Bentoeni, AON10a
Benue, NAB56b
Benue-Congo, NAB57

Beraber, CMT32b
Berber, CMT32
Berbero-Libyan, CMT32
Bergdama, BYG11a
Bergus, CMT32c
Beriberi, NAB61
Berta, NAB62z
Berti, NAB61
Bessarabian, CEW21f
Bete, NAB59j
Betsileo, MSY44j
Betsimisaraka, MSY44j
Betul, AUG06b
Bghai, MSY50g
Bhatri, CNN25l
Bhil, AUG06a
Bhili, AUG06a
Bhojpuri, CNN25c
Bhote, MSY50a
Bhotia, MSY50a
Bhumij, AUG04z
Bhutanese, MSY50a
Bhutia, MSY50a
Bicol, MSY44x
Bideyat, NAB61
Bidjandjara, AUG02
Bihari, CNN25c
Bijogo, NAB56c
Bilin, CMT33a
Bilua, AON10d
Binga, BYG12
Bini, NAB59c
Bira, NAB57c
Birhor, AUG04b
Birifor, NAB59a
Birked, NAB62m
Birom, NAB56b
Bisaya, MSY44z
Bisayan, MSY44q
Bisharin, CMT33z
Bislama, MPY53
Bisonhorn Maria, AUG06b
Bitin, CMT33a
Black Carib, NFB68b
Black Lisu, MSY50l
Black Meo, MSY47a
Black Sea Turk, MSY41j
Black Tai, MSY49z
Blanco, CLT27
Blue Meo, MSY47a
Bo, AUG03z
Bobo, NAB56a
Bod, MSY50r
Bodic, MSY50r
Bodo, MSY50d
Bodpa, MSY50r
Boer, CEW19a
Bogo, CMT33z
Bogos, CMT33a
Bogoto, NAB66c
Bohemian, CEW22e
Bokmal, CEW19p
Boloven, AUG03z
Bompaka, AUG03d
Bonggo, AON09e
Bongo, (1) BYG12
(2) NAB66e
Boni, (1) BYG11b
(2) NFB69a
Bontoc, NAB54x
Bor, NAB62f
Boran, CMT33b
Bornu, NAB61
Bosaka, NAB57h
Bosnian, CEW22a
Bougainvillian, AON10d
Boumpe, NAB64i
Bourbonnais, CEW21b
Bozo, NAB63b
Brahui, CNN23z
Braj Bhasa, CNN25g
Branco, CLT26
Brao, AUG03z
Brass, NAB59i
Bre, MSY50g
Breton, CEW18a
British, CEW19i
British Irish, CEW19r
Briton, CEW19i
Broad Bantu, NAB56
Brong, NAB59a
Brythonic, CEW18
Bubi, NAB57k
Budjga, NAB57i
Budu, NAB57c
Budukh, CEW17b
Buem, NAB59b
Buginese, MSY44c
Bugotu, AON09d
Bulgar, CEW22b
Bulgarian Macedonian, CEW22z
Bulgeda, NAB61
Bullom, NAB56c
Bundeli, CNN25g
Bunu, NAB59n
Bunun, AUG01
Bura, NAB60b
Burji, NAB62z
Burman, MSY50b
Burmese, MSY50b
Burun, NAB62z

Burungi, CMT33z
Burusho, CNN25z
Buryat, MSY41b
Burzhan, MSY41b
Busa, NAB56a
Busansi, NAB63z
Busasi, NAB62l
Bush Negro, NFB67a, NFB68a, NFB69a
Bushmanoid, BYG11
Buzi, NAB64h
Bwaidoga, AON09b
Bwaka, NAB66z
Bwe, MSY50g
Bwodho, NAB62o
By, NAB64k
Byelorussian, CEW22c

Caboclo, CLN28
Caboverdian, NAN58
Cafuso, NFB70b
Cajamarca, MIR39g
Cakavian, CEW22d
Cakchiquel, MIR37b
Calit-Bhasa, CNN25b
Cambodian, AUG03b
Cameroon Highland Bantu, NAB57a
Camorta, AUG03d
Camóvia, CEW13
Campa, MIR39a
Campidanian, CEW21j
Cannibal, MIR39c
Cantonese, MSY42a
Cape Coloured, NAN58
Cape Hottentot, BYG11c
Car, AUG03d
Carib, MIR39c
Cariban, MIR39c
Caribbean East Indian, CNN25
Carolinian, MPY54z
Carpathian, CEW22p
Carpatho-Russian, CEW22k
Carpatho-Ukrainian, CEW22k
Castellano, CEW21k
Castilian, CEW21k
Catalán, CEW21
Catalonian, CEW21a
Caucasian, CEW17
Cauqui, MIR39b
Cayapa, MIR39e
Cebuano, MSY44q
Celtic, CEW18
Central Amerindian, MIR37
Central Bantoid, NAB56a
Central Bantu, NAB57b
Central Togolese, NAB59b
Central Twa, BYG12
Cepleng, NAB62p
Ceramese, AON09e
Ceylon Burgher, CNN25z
Ceylon Moor, CNN23z
Chadic, NAB60
Chagga, NAB57e
Chakhar, MSY41f
Chakesang, MSY50p
Chakma, MSY50s
Chakru, MSY50p
Chaldean, CMT31
Cham, MSY44z
Cham Re, AUG03z
Chamba, NAB66c
Chambiali, CNN25k
Chamic, MSY44
Chamling, MSY50h
Chamoror, MSY44d
Cham-Malay, MSY44k
Chan, CEW17c
Chang, (1) MSY50k
(2) MSY50p
Chaouyah, CMT32f
Chapacura, MIR39d
Chatino, MIR37e
Chechen, CEW17d
Cheju-do, MSY46
Chenchu, AUG04z
Cheremis, MSW51h
Cheribon, MSY44g
Cherkess, CEW17a
Cherokee, MIR38a
Chewa, NAB57b
Chhattisgarhi, CNN25g
Chhindwara, AUG06b
Chibcha, MIR39e
Chicano, CLN29
Chichimec, MIR37d
Chiga, NAB57d
Chilote, CLN29
Chimbu, AON10b
Chin, MSY50c
Chinese, MSY42
Chinese Nung, MSY49a
Ching, MSY52b
Chingpo, MSY50f
Chinocholo, NFB71b

Chi-lao, MSY47a
Chleuch, CMT32z
Choapán, MIR37f
Chocó, MIR39c
Chokwe, NAB57b
Chol, MIR37b
Cholo, CLN29
Chon, MIR39e
Chontal, MIR37b
Chopi, NAB57p
Chorti, MIR37b
Choson Muntcha, MSY46
Chowa, AUG03d
Chuang, MSY49a
Chukchi, MSY48
Chungcha, MSY49a
Chutiya, MSY50d
Chuvash, MSY41c
Cingalese, CNN25q
Circassian, CEW17a
Classical Mongoloid, MSY
Cochinchinese, MSY52b
Coloured, (1) NAN58
(2) NFB68b
Comende, NAB64i
Comorian, NAB57j
Congoid, NAB
Constantino, MSY44q
Cook Islander, MPY55d
Cook Islands Maori, MPY55d
Coorg, CNN23z
Copt, CMT30
Cornish, CEW18z
Cornouaille, CEW18a
Corsican, CEW21z
Crau, NAB59j
Creek, MIR38a
Creole, MIR38b, NAN58, NFB67b, NFB68b, NFB69b
Cretan, CEW20
Criollo, NFB71b
Crioulo, NFB70b
Croat, CEW22d
Croatian, CEW22d
Csango, MSW51g
Cuicatec, MIR37c
Cuna, MIR39e
Cunama, NAB62h
Cushitic, CMT33
Cymraeg, CEW18d
Czech, CEW22e

Da, NAB64a
Daco-Rumanian, CEW21i
Dafla, MSY50z
Dagari, NAB56a
Dagestani, CEW17b
Dagu, NAB66d
Dagur, MSY41y
Dahomean, NAB59e
Dahuk, CNT24c
Dahur, MSY41y
Daic, MSY49
Dair, NAB62m
Dairi, MSY44b
Daju, NAB66d
Dakhini, CNN25r
Dakpwa, NAB66b
Dalinga, NAB66d
Dama, NAB62j
Damal, AON10a
Damara, BYG11a
Damot, CMT33a
Dan, NAB64a
Danagla, NAB62m
Danakil, CMT33z
Dandawa, NAB65a
Dane, CEW19g
Dani, AON10a
Danish, CEW19g
Dano-Norwegian, CEW19p
Darasa, CMT33d
Dard, CNN25i
Dardic, CNN25i
Dargin, CEW17b
Dargwa, CEW17b
Dari, CNT24f
Dariganga, MSY41f
Darkhat, MSY41y
Darod, CMT33e
Dayak, MSY44y
Daza, NAB61
De, CLN29
Deccani, CNN25r
Degema, NAB59c
Dekini, CNN25j
Dembo, NAB62o
Demotic Greek, CEW20
Dendi, NAB65a
Denkawi, NAB62f
Deori, MSY50d
Desi, CNN25j
Deswali, CNN25r
Dholuo, NAB62j
Dialonke, NAB63c
Diawara, NAB63j
Dibo, NAB59m

# CHRISTIAN ABBREVIATIONS, ACRONYMS AND INITIALS

Something like 7,000 sets of initials are widely in use for Christian organizations across the world. This index lists, alphabetically by initials, a representative selection of them. First, (a) are all recognized and widely-used abbreviations used in this Encyclopedia (excluding codes designed only for this Encyclopedia, which are given in the Codebook). Second, (b) are acronyms (names as words formed from the initial letters of other words) ; and third, (c) are initials of Christian and religious bodies in widespread or international use. The vast majority relate to Christian organizations, with a few widely-used secular abbreviations. In the interests of brevity, no translation into English nor additional identification or explanation is given, except for international bodies with names in English and also other languages, such as Roman Catholic religious orders and

congregations (whose initials are usually derived from their names in Latin) ; in such cases, non-English names are only added if necessary to exactly amplify the abbreviations. In the latter cases also, it should be noted that there are usually initials in use in each of the non-English languages also, although most of these latter are excluded here. Most bodies may be identified further from the various parts and indexes in this Encyclopedia, in particular the Topical Directory, Part 13. In general, initials of denominations within one country, and of organizations or small centres whose influence is confined to a single country, are not listed here (except for national Christian councils of churches, and denominations extending under the same name and initials over a number of nations) but are listed, together with the full names they stand for, only in that country's text,

tables and directory. In cases where the same initials are used by 2 different bodies, both usages are given. Although this index deals predominantly with the abbreviations of names and titles in the main European language they are used in, in a number of cases their counterpart initials in other international languages are also given, with equivalents (e.g. WCC=COE=OKR). Most of the organizations given here are still in existence today under the names shown, but a small proportion are bodies no longer in existence under the names shown but are given here for historical interest and ease of identification.

This listing thus omits (1) initials of denominations within a country, except major plurinational or global ones, (2) most organizations at the subnational level, and (3) a number at the national level, too.

## A

| | |
|---|---|
| AA | apostolic administration |
| AA | Assumptionists (Augustinians of the Assumption) |
| AACC | All Africa Conference of Churches |
| AAM | American Advent Mission |
| AB | Augsburg Bekenntnis/Confession |
| ABCFM | American Board of Commissioners for Foreign Missions |
| ABCIM | American Baptist Churches in the USA, International Ministries |
| ABFMS | American Baptist Foreign Mission Society |
| ABHMS | American Baptist Home Mission Societies |
| ABM | Australian Board of Missions |
| ABMS | Australian Baptist Missionary Society |
| ABS | American Bible Society |
| ABWE | Association of Baptists for World Evangelism |
| AC | Apostolic Church (Great Britain) |
| ACAC | American Christian Action Council |
| ACC | Advent Christian Church |
| ACC | Anglican Consultative Council |
| ACC | Australian Council of Churches |
| ACCC | American Council of Christian Churches |
| ACE | Ayuda Cristiana Evangélica (Christian Aid) |
| ACE | Action Catholique de l'Enfance |
| ACEACCAM | Association des Conférences Episcopales de l'Afrique Centrale et du Cameroun |
| ACECCT | Association des Conférences Episcopales du Congo/RCA/Tchad |
| ACF | Action Catholique Familiale |
| ACF | Asociación Cristiana Femenina (YWCA) |
| ACGF | Action Catholique Générale des Femmes |
| ACGH | Action Catholique Générale des Hommes |
| ACI | Action Catholique des Milieux Indépendants |
| ACISJF | Association Catholique Internationale des Services de la Jeunesse Féminine |
| ACJ | Asociación Cristiana de Jovenes (YMCA) |
| ACKD | Arbeitsgemeinschaft Christlicher Kirchen in der BRD |
| ACKDDR | Arbeitsgemeinschaft Christlicher Kirchen in der DDR |
| ACKS | Arbeitsgemeinschaft Christlicher Kirchen in der Schweiz |
| ACM | Alliance Chrétienne Missionnaire |
| ACMM | Apostolic Church Missionary Movement |
| ACNAC | Anglican Council of North America & the Caribbean |
| ACO | Action Catholique Ouvrière |
| ACP | Apostolic Church of Pentecost |
| ACROSS | Africa Committee for the Rehabilitation of the Southern Sudan |
| ACTS | Asia Centre for Theological Studies and Mission |
| ACU | Action Catholique Universitaire |
| AD | archdiocese |
| AD | Anno Domini (In the Year of Our Lord) |
| AdD | Asambleas de Dios |
| AdD | Assemblées de Dieu |
| ADEOPA | Association des Eglises et Oeuvres Protestants en Algérie |
| AEA | Australian Evangelical Alliance |
| AEAM | Association of Evangelicals of Africa and Madagascar |
| AEBET | Asociación Evangélica Boliviana de Educación Teológica |
| AEBG | Asociación Evangelistica de Billy Graham |
| AEC | Alianza Evangélica Costarricense |
| AEC | Antilles Episcopal Conference |
| AEC | Association des Eglises Chrétiennes |
| AECEWA | Association of Episcopal Conferences of English-speaking West Africa |
| AEE | African Evangelistic Enterprise |
| AEEC | Association des Eglises Evangéliques Centrafricaines |
| AEET | Asociación Evangélica de Educación Teológica |
| AEF | Africa Evangelical Fellowship |
| AEGM | Anglican Evangelical Group Movement |
| AEH | Alianza Evangélica Hondureña |
| AEP | Alianza Evangélica de Panamá |
| AEP | Aliança Evangélica Portuguesa |
| AEPB | Alliance des Eglises Protestantes du Burundi |
| AETTE | Associação Evangélica Teológica para Treinamonto por Extensão |
| AFI | Auxiliaires Féminines Internationales |
| AFM | Apostolic Faith Mission |
| AFPRO | Action for Food Production Office |
| AFREC | Africa Regional Centre, UBS |
| AICA | African Independent Churches Association |
| AICA | Agencia Informativa Católica Argentina |
| AICC | Aboriginal and Islander Catholic Council |
| AICM | African Independent Churches Movement |
| AICS | African Independent Churches Service |
| AICs | African Indigenous/Independent Churches |
| AIM | Africa Inland Mission |
| AIPF | All-India Pentecostal Fellowship |
| AKC | Arbeitskreis Kritisches Christentum |
| ALC | American Lutheran Church |
| ALCOE | Asian Leadership Conference on Evangelism |
| ALER | Asociación Latinoamericana de Educación Radiofónica |
| ALET | Asociación Latinoamericana de Escuelas Teológicas |
| ALFALIT | Alfabetización y Literatura |
| AM | audio modulation, amplitude modulation |
| AMAA | Armenian Missionary Association of America |
| AMAC | Medical Aid to Central Africa |
| AMDAC | Aid to Maternity Dispensaries of Central Africa |
| AMEC | African Methodist Episcopal Church |
| AMECEA | Association of Member Episcopal Conferences in Eastern Africa |
| AMEZC | African Methodist Episcopal Zion Church |
| AMG | American Mission to Greeks |
| AMORC | Ancient Mystical Order Rosae Crucis |
| AMREC | Americas Regional Centre, UBS |
| AN | abbey nullius |
| ANDEB | Asociación Nacional de Evangélicos de Bolivia |
| AO | autonomous oblast |
| AoG | Assemblies of God |
| AP | Annuario Pontificio |

| | |
|---|---|
| APCTE | Association for the Promotion of Chinese Theological Education |
| ARCIC | Anglican/Roman Catholic International Commission |
| ARENSA | Asociación Regional Episcopal del Norte del Sud América |
| ARMS | Amateur Radio Missionary Service |
| ARPC | Associate Reformed Presbyterian Church |
| ASIT | Asociación Sudamericana de Instituciones Teológicas |
| ASO | Apostolado Seglar Organizado |
| ASPREC | Asia Pacific Regional Centre, UBS |
| ASSR | autonomous soviet socialist republic |
| ASTE | Asociação de Seminarios Teológicos Evangélicos |
| ASV | American Standard Version (of the Bible) |
| ATENE | Association for Theological Education in the Near East |
| AV | Augsburg Confession |
| AV | Authorised Version (of the Bible) |
| AZASA | Assembly of Zionist & Apostolic Churches of South Africa |

## B

| | |
|---|---|
| B | Barnabites (Clerics Regular of St Paul) |
| BAVACO | Broadcasting and Audio-Visual Aids Committee |
| BB | Boys' Brigade |
| BB | Bush Brotherhood |
| BBFI | Baptist Bible Fellowship International |
| BCAS | Bush Church Aid Society |
| BCC | Bible correspondence course |
| BCC | Botswana Christian Council |
| BCC | British Council of Churches |
| BCE | Before Christian Era (Jehovah's Witnesses usage) |
| BCEC | Barbados Council of Evangelical Churches |
| BCEOM | Bureau Central d'Etude pour les Equipements d'Outre Mer |
| BCF | Bangladesh Christian Fellowship |
| BCMC | Belgian Christian Missionary Church |
| BCMS | Bible Churchmen's Missionary Society |
| BCOQ | Baptist Churches of Ontario and Quebec |
| BCPCU | Bishops' Commission for Promoting Christian Unity |
| BCSC | Belize Christian Social Council |
| BCSL | Bishops' Conference of Sri Lanka |
| BCU | Bible Christian Union |
| BCWM | Brethren in Christ World Missions |
| BD | bachelor of divinity |
| BDKJ | Bund der Deutschen Katholischen Jugend |
| BEC | British Evangelical Council |
| BEM | Borneo Evangelical Mission |
| BERRS | Bangladesh Ecumenical Relief & Rehabilitation Service |
| BFBS | British & Foreign Bible Society |
| BGC | Baptist General Conference |
| BGEA | Billy Graham Evangelistic Association |
| BiCC | Brethren in Christ Church |
| BICE | Bureau International Catholique de l'Enfance |
| BIM | Baptist International Missions |
| BIM | Bureau d'Information Missionnaire |
| BIP | Bureau d'Information Protestant |
| BKED | Bund Katholischer Erzieher Deutschlands |
| BLASC | Bureau de Liaison d'Action Sociale et Caritative |
| BLIROI | Bureau de Liaison de l'Information Religieuse dans l'Océan Indien |
| BLUCE | Bible Lands Union for Christian Education |
| BM | Basel Mission |
| BMAA | Baptist Missionary Association of America |
| BMC | Bible Missionary Church |
| BMM | Baptist Mid-Missions |
| BMMF | Bible and Medical Missionary Fellowship |
| BMS | Baptist Missionary Society |
| BNCC | Bangladesh National Council of Churches |
| BP | boîte postale/post box |
| BPT | Bethel Pentecostal Temple |
| BRAVS | Broadcasting and Audio-Visual Services |
| BRF | Bible Reading Fellowship |
| BS | Bible School |
| BUGBI | Baptist Union of GB & Ireland |
| BVM | Bibeltrogner Vänner (Bible True Friends) |
| BWA | Baptist World Alliance |

## C

| | |
|---|---|
| C | catholicate, diocese of catholicos |
| C | central |
| c | circa (approximately) |
| C&S | Cherubim & Seraphim |
| CA | Church Army |
| CAC | Christ Apostolic Church |
| CACC | Central Africa Christian Council |
| CACE | Confederación Argentina Católica de Educadores |
| CADEC | Christian Action for Development in the Caribbean |
| CAF | Church of the Apostolic Faith |
| CAFOD | Catholic Fund for Overseas Development |
| CAHP | Co-ordinating Agency for Health and Planning |
| CAJ | Christliche Arbeitjugen |
| CALA | Consejo Anglicano Latinoamericano |
| CALM | Centro Assistenza Laici Missionari |
| CAM | Central American Mission |
| CAMEO | Committee to Assist Missionary Education Overseas |
| CAN | Christian Association of Nigeria |
| CAPA | Council of Anglican Provinces of Africa |
| CAR | Conferencia Argentina de Religiosos |
| CARA | Christian Action by Radio in Africa |
| CARAVS | Christian Association for Radio Audio-Visual Services |
| CARE | Catholic Action for Racial Education |
| CARE | Citizen's Association for Racial Equality |
| CARF | Christian Amateur Radio Fellowship |
| CARITAS | Catholic Relief Services |
| CARP | Caisse Auxiliaire de Retraites des Ministres du Culte Protestant |

| | |
|---|---|
| CASA | Christian Agency for Social Action, Relief and Development |
| CASA | Consejo Anglicano Sud Americano |
| CASC | Confederación Autonome de Sindicatos Cristianos |
| CATA | Comité Acesor de Textos Autodidacticos |
| CATF | Catholic African Teachers' Federation of South Africa |
| CAVE | Centro Audio-Visual Evangélico |
| CAVEA | Centro Audio-Visual Evangélico de la Argentina |
| CAVISAT | Centre for Audio-Visual Instruction via Satellite |
| CAWD | Churches' Action for World Development |
| CBA | Catholic Biblical Association |
| CBA | Catholic Broadcasting Association |
| CBAI | Catholic Biblical Association of India |
| CBCB | Catholic Bishops' Conference of Bangladesh |
| CBCI | Catholic Bishops' Conference of India |
| CBCJ | Catholic Bishops' Conference of Japan |
| CBCP | Catholic Bishops' Conference of the Philippines |
| CBFMS | Conservative Baptist Foreign Mission Society |
| CBHMS | Conservative Baptist Home Mission Society |
| CBM | Christadelphian Bible Mission |
| CBMEC | Comité Belge de Mission Evangélique au Congo |
| CBN | Christian Broadcasting Network |
| CBOMB | Canadian Baptist Overseas Mission Board |
| CBS | Christian Broadcasting System |
| CC | Churches of Christ |
| CCA | Christian Conference of Asia |
| CCAC | Comité de Coordination des Mouvements des Jeunes |
| CCAI | Comisión Católica Argentina de Immigración |
| CCAP | Church of Central Africa Presbyterian |
| CCB | Christian Council of Botswana |
| CCC | Canadian Catholic Conference/Conférence Catholique Canadienne |
| CCC | Canadian Council of Churches |
| CCC | Caribbean Conference of Churches |
| CCC | Christian Catholic Church |
| CCC | Congregational Christian Churches |
| CCC | Centro Cattolico Cinematografico |
| CCCA | Catholic Civics Clubs of America |
| CCCC | Caribbean Council of Christian Churches |
| CCCC | Christian Churches & Churches of Christ |
| CCCC | Confederación Colegios Cubanos Católicos |
| CCCE | Council for Co-operation of Churches in Ethiopia |
| CCCI | Campus Crusade for Christ International |
| CCCS | Commonwealth and Continental Church Society |
| CCEA | Christian Churches' Educational Association |
| CCEA | Council of the Church in East Asia |
| CCEE | Consilium Conferentiarum Episcopalium Europae |
| CCEM | Comisión Católica Española de Migración |
| CCEP | Comisión Coordinadora Evangélica de Paraguay |
| CCF | Centro de Cultura Filmica |
| CCF | Catholic Communications Foundation |
| CCF | Christian Children's Fund |
| CCFD | Comité Catholique National contre la Faim et pour le Développement |
| CCG | Christian Council of Ghana |
| CCH | Collegium Catholicum Holmiense |
| CCIA | Commission of the Churches on International Affairs |
| CCIC | Catholic Charismatic Information Centre |
| CCID | Centre Catholique d'Information Discographique |
| CCII | Catholic Communications Institute of Ireland |
| CCJCA | Caribbean Committee for Joint Christian Action |
| CCJP | Consultation of the Church and the Jewish People |
| CCL | Christian Council of Lesotho |
| CCM | Christian Council of Malawi |
| CCM | Conselho Cristão de Moçambique |
| CCM | Council of Churches of Malaysia |
| CCMA | Catholic Campus Ministry Association |
| CCMIE | Comité Catholique pour les Migrations Intra-Européennes de la CICM |
| CCN | Christian Council of Nigeria |
| CCN | Council of Churches in the Netherlands |
| CCNA | Christian Church of North America |
| CCOC | Centro Católico de Orientación Cinematográfica |
| CCODP | Canadian Catholic Organization for Development and Peace |
| CCOWE | Chinese Congress on World Evangelization |
| CCPD | Commission on the Churches' Participation in Development |
| CCPM | Comisión Católica Peruana de Migración |
| CCR | Catholic Charismatic Renewal |
| CCR | Centro Cattolico Radiofonico |
| CCR | Christian Council of Rhodesia |
| CCRT | Centre Catholique de Radio et Télévision |
| CCS | Church of Christ, Scientist |
| CCSA | Christian Committee for Service in Algeria |
| CCSEA | Council of the Church in South East Asia |
| CCSM | Confédération Chrétienne des Syndicats Malgaches |
| CCSV | Christian Council of St Vincent |
| CCT | Centro Cattolico Teatrale |
| CCT | Christian Council of Tanzania |
| CCTD | Catholic Council of Thailand for Development |
| CCTM | Centro Collegamenti Tecnici per le Missioni |
| CCTT | Christian Council of Trinidad & Tobago |
| CCTV | Centro Cattolico Televisivo |
| CCUA | Catholic Central Union of America |
| CCVM | Comisión Católica Venezolana de Migración |
| CCW | Caribbean Church Women |
| CCW | Council of Churches for Wales |
| CCWL | Catholic Council on Working Life |
| CCWM | Congregational Council for World Mission |
| CCYUA | Catholic Central Youth Union of America |
| CCZ | Christian Council of Zambia |
| CDG | Community Development Group |
| CDTCG | Centrale Démocratique des Travailleurs Chrétiens de Guadeloupe |
| CDUCE | Christian Democratic Union of Central Europe |
| CE | Christian Era (similar to AD, but used by Jehovah's Witnesses and non-Christians) |

| | |
|---|---|
| CEA | Confederación Espíritista Argentina |
| CEA | Conferencia Episcopal Argentina |
| CEAP | Catholic Educational Association of the Philippines |
| CEAST | Conferência Episcopal de Angola e São Tomé |
| CEB | Confederação Evangélica do Brasil |
| CEB | Conferencia Episcopal de Bolivia |
| CEC | Centro de Estudios Cristianos |
| CEC | Comisión Episcopal del Clero |
| CEC | Concilio Evangélico de Chile |
| CEC | Conference of European Churches |
| CEC | Conferencia Episcopal de Cuba |
| CEC | Cruzada Estudiantil para Cristo (Campus Crusade) |
| CECH | Conferencia Episcopal de Chile |
| CECI | Centre d'Etudes et de Coopération International |
| CECOR | Conferencia Episcopal de Costa Rica |
| CECOSNE | Centro Educativo de Comunicações do Nordeste |
| CECOWE | Centrum voor Communicatiewetenschappen |
| CECVN | Confédération des Etudiants Catholiques du Vietnam |
| CED | Conferencia del Episcopado Dominicano |
| CEDA | Centre d'Edition et Diffusion Africaine |
| CEDEC | Confederación Evangélica de Colombia |
| CEDES | Conferencia Episcopal de El Salvador |
| CEDIMA | Centrale d'Editions et de Diffusion de Matériel Audio-Visuel |
| CEDOC | Confederación Ecuatoriana de Organizaciones Sindicales Cristianas |
| CEDUCI | Centro de Educación Cinematográfica |
| CEE | Conferencia Episcopal Española |
| CEE | Consejo Evangélico Español |
| CEE | Confraternidad Evangélica Ecuatoriana |
| CEEC | Commission Episcopale pour l'Ecole Catholique |
| CEECA | Conférence des Evêques de l'Empire Centrafricaine |
| CEEEFE | Commission des Eglises Evangéliques d'Expression Française a l'Extérieur |
| CEEH | Conseil des Eglises Evangéliques d'Haïti |
| CEEP | Comité Central Evangélico en el Paraguay |
| CEF | Child Evangelism Fellowship |
| CEF | Conférence Episcopale de France |
| CEFOD | Centre d'Etudes et de Formation pour le Développement |
| CEG | Conferencia Episcopal de Guatemala |
| CEH | Conférence Episcopale d'Haïti |
| CEH | Conferencia Episcopal de Honduras |
| CEHVN | Conférence Episcople de Haute-Volta et Niger |
| CEI | Centro Ecuménico de Informações |
| CEI | Conferenza Episcopale Italiana |
| CEIAL | Movimento Laici per l'America Latina |
| CELA | Catholics for Latin America |
| CELA | Conferencia Evangélica Latinoamericana |
| CELAC | Conférence Episcopale du Laos et Cambodge |
| CELADEC | Comisión Evangélica Latinoamericana de Educación Cristiana |
| CELAM | Consejo Episcopal Latinoamericano |
| CELIM | Centro Laici Italiani per le Missioni |
| CELRA | Conférence des Evêques Latins dans les Régions Arabes |
| CEM | Centro Educazione Missionario |
| CEM | Confederación Evangélico Mundial |
| CEM | Conferencia del Episcopado Mexicano |
| CEM | Conferência Episcopal de Moçambique |
| CEME | Comité Episcopal des Missions à l'Extérieur |
| CEMJ | Centre d'Enseignement des Monitrices de la Jeunesse |
| CEMS | Church of England Men's Society |
| CENAMI | Centro Nacional de Ayuda a las Misiones Indigenas |
| CENCOS | Centro Nacional de Comunicación Social |
| CENDAC | Centro d'Azione Culturale |
| CENFO | Centre de Formation Socio-Pastorale |
| CENPRO | Centro de Producción y Formación |
| CEOC | Centro de Orientación Cinematográfica |
| CEOSS | Coptic Evangelical Organization for Social Services |
| CEP | Centre d'Etudes Pastorales |
| CEP | Conferencia Episcopal de Panamá |
| CEP | Conferencia Episcopal Paraguaya |
| CEP | Conferencia Episcopal Puertorriqueña |
| CEPA | Comité Evangélico Permanente Ayuda |
| CEPAC | Conférence des Evêques du Pacifique |
| CEPAD | Comité Evangélico pro Ayuda al Desarrollo |
| CEPM | Conferência Episcopal Portuguese da Metrópole |
| CEPR | Concilio Evangélico de Puerto Rico |
| CEPRHU | Centro de Promoción Humana del Nordeste |
| CEPZA | Conseil des Eglises Protestantes du Zaïre |
| CEQ | Corporation des Enseignants du Québec |
| CER | Conferencia Ecuatoriana de Religiosos |
| CERAO | Conférence Episcopale Régionale de l'Afrique Occidentale Francophone |
| CERCA | Conférence des Evêques de la RCA |
| CERJ | Centro de Ecumenismo do Rio de Janeiro |
| CESI | Centro Editoriale Studi |
| CESM | Conférence Episcopale de Sénégal—Mauritanie |
| CESSAC | Church of England Soldiers', Sailors' & Airmen's Clubs |
| CETA | Conférence des Eglises de Toute l'Afrique (AACC) |
| CETAD | Centre d'Enseignement Théologique à Distance |
| CETE | Centro Experimental de TV Educación |
| CETEDI | Centre des Techniques de Diffusion et Relations Publiques |
| CETMI | Comité des Eglises auprès des Travailleurs Migrants |
| CEU | Conferencia Episcopal del Uruguay |
| CEV | Consejo Evangélico de Venezuela |
| CEV | Conferencia Episcopal Venezolana |
| CEVAA | Communauté Evangélique d'Action Apostolique |
| CEYA | Caribbean Ecumenical Youth Action |
| CEZ | Conférence Episcopale du Zaïre |
| CFA | Congregation of Alexian Brothers |
| CFC | Fratelli Cristiani |
| CFC | Council of Free Churches |
| CFCCF | Council of Free Christians & Churches in Finland |
| CFCH | Council of Free Churches in Hungary |
| CFCJ | Conselho da Fraternidade Cristão-Judaica |
| CFD | Christlicher Friedensdienst |
| CFM | Christian Family Movement |
| CFMMA | Fratelli della Misericordia di Santa Maria Ausiliatrice |
| CFP | Fratelli Poveri di San Francesco Serafico |
| CFS | Congregation of the Priestly Fraternity |
| CFSM | Christian Family and Social Movement |
| CFTC | Confédération Française des Travailleurs Chrétiens |
| CFX | Brothers of St Francis Xavier |
| CGAL | Conseil Général de l'Apostolat des Laïcs |
| CGBD | Christlicher Gewerkschaftsbund Deutschlands |
| CGH | Church of God Holiness |
| CGNA | Churches of God in North America (General Eldership) |
| CGP | Church of God of Prophecy |
| CHA | Catholic Hospital Association |
| CHA | Christian Holiness Association |
| CHAG | Christian Hospital Association of Ghana |
| CHC | Calvary Holiness Church |
| CHED | Commission Haïtienne des Eglises pour le Développement |
| CHIEF | Christian Hope Indian Eskimo Fellowship |
| CHR | Conférence Haïtienne des Religieux |
| CIAC | Centro Italiano Addestramento Cinematografico |
| CIAE | Conselho das Igrejas Angolanas Evangélicas |
| CIC | Centrum Informationis Catholicum |
| CIC | Christian Information Centre |
| CICC | Cook Islands Christian Church |
| CICM | Commission Internationale Catholique pour les Migrations |
| CICM | Missionaries of Scheut (Immaculate Heart of Mary Mission Society) (Scheutists) |
| CICOP | Catholic Inter-American Cooperation Program |
| CIDAL | Centre International de Documentation Audio-Visuelle |
| CIDER | Centro Italiano Documentari Educativi Religiosi |
| CIDEV | Centre d'Information sur le Développement |
| CIDSE | Coopération Internationale pour le Développement Socio-Economique |
| CIEC | Confederación Interamericana de Educación Católica |
| CIEF | Centro de Investigaciones y Estudios Familiares |
| CIEF | Confederação das Igrejas Evangélicas Fundamentalistas |
| CIEMAL | Council of Evangelical Methodist Churches in Latin America |
| CIIC | Concilio Internacional de Iglesias Cristianas (ICCC) |
| CIIR | Catholic Institute for International Relations |
| CIM | China Inland Mission |
| CIM | Comité des Instituts Missionnaires |
| CIMADE | Comité Inter-Mouvements auprès des Evacués |
| CIMIADE | Commission des Institutions et Mouvements Internationaux Apostoliques des Enfants |
| CIMS | Consociatio Internationalis Musicae Sacrae |
| CIO | Centro de Información y Orientación |
| CIO | Church Information Office |
| CIOEW | Catholic Information Office for England and Wales |
| CIP | Centre d'Information de Presse |
| CIPBC | Church of India, Pakistan, Burma and Ceylon |
| CIPL | Commission Interdiocésaine de Pastorale Liturgique |
| CIRH | Conferencia de Institutos Religiosos de Honduras |
| CIRIC | Centre International de Reportages et d'Information Culturelle |
| CIRMA | Conferencia de Institutos Religiosos de México |
| CIS | Catholic Immigrant Service |
| CISL | Confederazione Italiana Sindacati Lavoratori |
| CISM | Conferenza Italiana dei Superiori Maggiori |
| CISR | Conférence Internationale de Sociologie Religieuse |
| CITA | Communications Institute of the Americas |
| CITC | Christian Industrial Training Centre |
| CITC | Christian International Travel Club |
| CJ | Josephite Fathers (Congregation of St Joseph) |
| CJA | Christlich-Judische Arbeitsgemeinschaft in der Schweiz |
| CJC | Conseil de la Jeunesse Catholique |
| CJCLdS | Church of Jesus Christ of Latter-day Saints (Mormons) |
| CJM | Eudists (Congregation of Jesus and Mary) |
| CJPM | Central Japan Pioneer Mission |
| CJSS | Conference on Jewish Social Studies |
| CLADE | Congreso Latinoamericano de Evangelización |
| CLAF | Comité Latinoamericano de la Fé |
| CLAI | Concilio Latinoamericano de Iglesias |
| CLAIM | Christian Literature Association in Malawi |
| CLAL | Coopération des Laïques en Amérique Latine |
| CLAME | Comunidad Latinoamericana de Ministerios Evangélicos |
| CLAR | Confederación Latino Americana de Religiosos |
| CLAST | Latin American Federation of Christian Trade Unions |
| CLAT | Latin American Federation of Workers |
| CLATT | Comité Latinoamericano de Textos Teológicos |
| CLB | Church of the Lutheran Brethren |
| CLC | Christian Literature Crusade/Crociata del Libro Cristiano |
| CLIM | Centro Laici Italiani per le Missioni |
| CLS | Christian Literature Society |
| CLSA | Canon Law Society of America |
| CLSA | Christian Literature Service Association |
| CM | Lazzarists (Congregation of the Mission), Vincentians |
| CMA | Church Music Association |
| CMC | Catholic Media Council |
| CMC | Central Missions Commissariat |
| CMC | Christian Medical Commission |
| CMCSS | Council of Managers of Catholic Secondary Schools |
| CMCW | Christian Mission to the Communist World |
| CMEC | Christian Methodist Episcopal Church |
| CMF | Christian Missionary Fellowship |
| CMF | Claretians (Missionary Sons of the Immaculate Heart of Mary) |
| CMI | Carmelitani della BV Maria Immacolata |
| CMI | Consejo Mundial de Iglesias (WCC) |
| CMJ | Church's Ministry among the Jews |
| CMM | Congregation of Mariannhill Missionaries |
| CMML | Christian Missions in Many Lands |
| CMN | Conseil Missionnaire National |
| CMRSWI | Conference of Major Religious Superiors of Women's Institutes |
| CMS | Catholic Mission Society |
| CMS | Christian Medical Society |
| CMS | Church Missionary Society |
| CMSF | Missionary Congregation of St Francis of Assisi |
| CMSM | Conference of Major Superiors of Men's Institutes |
| CMT | Confédération Mondiale du Travail |
| CMWF | Christian Medical Workers' Fellowship |
| CNBB | Conferência Nacional dos Bispos do Brasil |
| CNEC | Christian Nationals Evangelism Commission |
| CNEP | Concilio Nacional Evangélico del Peru |
| CNEP | Confederación Nacional Escuelas Particulares |
| CNEWA | Catholic Near East Welfare Association |
| CNG | Christlich-Nationaler Gewerkschaftsbund der Schweiz |
| CNI | Catholic News Service of India |
| CNIR | Conferencia Nacional dos Institutos Religiosos |
| CNM | Conseil National Missionnaire |
| CNPC | Centre National de Presse Catholique |
| CNPL | Centre National de Pastorale Liturgique |
| CNSP | Catholic News Service of Pakistan |
| CoB | Church of the Brethren |
| COC | Centro de Orientación Cinematográfica |
| CoC | Church of Christ |
| COCC | Confederación de Obreros y Campesinos Cristianos |
| COCDYC | Conservative & Christian Democratic Youth Community |
| COCU | Church of Christ Uniting |
| COCU | Consultation on Church Union |
| COCU | Council on Christian Unity |
| CODEL | Cooperation in Development |
| CODEPA | Centro de Orientação e Documentação do Ensino Particular |
| CODIAM | Committee for the Development of Intellectual Investments in Africa & Madagascar |
| COE | Conseil Oecuménique des Eglises (WCC) |
| COEM | Comité Oecuménique d'Entr'aide au Maroc |
| COEMAR | Commission on Ecumenical Mission and Relations |
| COEMAS | Congress on Evangelism for Malaysia and Singapore |
| COFAE | Co-ordinating Office for Asian Evangelism |
| CofE | Church of England |
| CoG | Church of God |
| CoGiC | Church of God in Christ |
| COJO | World Conference of Jewish Organizations |
| COLJCB | Church of Our Lord Jesus Christ (Bickertonites) |
| COM | Centro de Orientação Missionária |
| COMBASE | Comisión Boliviana de Acción Social Evangélica |
| COMINA | Conselho Missionário Nacional |
| CoN | Church of the Nazarene |
| CONCUR | Confederación Cubana de Religiosos |
| CONDOR | Confederación Dominicana de Religiosos |
| CONELCO | Conseil des Eglises Libres du Congo |
| Conf | conference |
| CONFER | Conferencia Argentina de Religiosas |
| CONFER | Conferencia de Religiosos |
| CONFER | Conferencia Española de Religiosos |
| CONFER | Conferencia Nacional Nicaraguense de Institutos Religiosos |
| CONFERRE | Conferencia de Religiosos de Chile |
| CONFREGUA | Conferencia de Religiosos y Religiosas de Guatemala |
| CONFRES | Confederación de Religiosos de El Salvador |
| CONVER | Conferencia Venezolana de Religiosos |
| COp | Calasantini (Congregation of St Joseph Calasanctius for Christian Works) |
| COPAL | Collège pour l'Amérique Latine |
| COPE | Cadena de Ondas Populares Españolas |
| COPIC | Conselho Português de Igrejas Cristãs |
| CORDAC | Central Africa Broadcasting Company |
| CORE | Committee for Overseas Relief |
| COREB | Conférence des Ordinaires du Rwanda et du Burundi |
| CORPORI | Conferencia de Religiosas de Puerto Rico |
| CORR | Christian Organization for Relief and Rehabilitation |
| CORSO | Council of Organizations for Relief Services Overseas |
| COSEI | Consiglio degli Organismi per Studenti Esteri in Italia |
| COSSEUJCA | Conseil Supérieur des Sacrificateurs pour les Eglises-Unies de Jésus-Christ en Afrique |
| COSUMA | Conférence des Supérieurs Majeurs du Burundi et du Rwanda |
| COTE | Commission of Theological Education in Taiwan |
| COWE | Consultation on World Evangelization |
| CP | casella postale/post box |
| CP | Passionists (Congregation of the Passion) |
| CPA | Catholic Press Association |
| CPAS | Church Pastoral-Aid Society |
| CPB | Confederação Pentecostal do Brasil |
| CPC | Centre de Pédagogie Catholique |
| CPC | Christian Peace Conference |
| CPCV | Comité Protestant des Centres de Vacances |
| CPG | Centro Salesiano di Pastorale Giovanile |
| CPM | Ceylon Pentecostal Mission |
| CPM | Congregation of Priests of Mercy |
| CPN | Consejo Pastoral Nacional |
| CPPS | Precious Blood Fathers (Society of the Precious Blood) |
| CPR | Conseil Protestant du Rwanda |
| CPSS | Catholic Prisoners' Social Service |
| CR(1) | Resurrectionists (Congregation of the Resurrection) |
| CR(2) | Theatine Fathers (Order of Regular Clerics) |
| CRAC | Central Religious Advisory Committee |
| CRAL | Communauté Romande de l'Apostolat des Laïcs |
| CRB | Conferência dos Religiosos do Brasil |
| CRC | Christian Revival Crusade |
| CRC | Conferencia de Religiosos de Colombia |
| CREC | Centre Audiovisuel Recherche et Communication |
| CRFEA | Christian Rural Fellowship of East Africa |
| CRI | Conference of Religious of India |
| CRIC | Congregation of Canons Regular of the Immaculate Conception |
| CRIF | Conseil Représentatif des Israelites de France |
| CRL | Congregation of Canons Regular of the Lateran (Augustinian) |
| CRMF | Christian Radio Missionary Fellowship |
| CRP | Conferencia de Religiosos del Peru |
| CRP | Premonstratensians (Order of Canons Regular of Prémontré), Norbertines (OPraem) |
| CRS | Catholic Relief Services |
| CRS | Christian Rural Service |
| CRS | Order of Clerks Regular of Somascha |
| CRSA | Canonesses of St Augustine |
| CRSB | Conference of Religious Sisters, Burma |
| CRSL | Christian Road Safety League |
| CRU | Centre Religieux Universitaire |
| CS | Scalabrinians (Congregation of the Missionary Fathers of St Charles) |
| CSB | Basilians (Congregation of St Basil) |
| CSC | Christian Service Committee of the Churches of Malawi |
| CSC | Christian Students Council |
| CSC | Confédération des Syndicats Chrétiens de Belgique |
| CSC | Council of Swaziland Churches |
| CSC | Holy Cross Fathers (Congregation of the Holy Cross) |
| CSCU | Civil Service Christian Union |
| CSCW | Church Society for College Work |
| CSF | Congregazione della Sacra Famiglia di Bergamo |
| CSI | Centro Sportivo Italiano |
| CSJ | Josephites of Murialdo (Congregation of St Joseph) |
| CSM | Christian Socialist Movement |
| CSM | Church of Scotland Mission |
| CSP | Centre Social Protestant |
| CSP | Paulists (Congregation of Missionary Priests of St Paul the Apostle) |
| CSS | Stigmatines (Congregation of the Sacred Stigmata) |
| CSSM | Children's Special Service Mission |
| CSSp | Spiritans (Congregation of the Holy Ghost and the Immaculate Heart of Mary) |
| CSsR | Redemptorists (Congregation of the Most Holy Redeemer) |
| CSsS | Brigittines (Congregation of the Most Holy Saviour) |
| CSV | Clerics of St Viator |
| CSWE | Centre for the Study of World Evangelization |
| CT | Christusträger |
| CTCG | Centrale des Travailleurs Chrétiens de la Guyane |
| CTCH | Centro de Teología e Ciencias Humanas |
| CTEN | Council for Theological Education in Nigeria |
| CTF | Catholic Teachers' Federation of England and Wales |
| CTIC | Centrale Technique d'Information Catholique |
| CTS | Catholic Truth Society |
| CTS | College Theology Society |
| CTSA | Catholic Theological Society of America |
| CUAMM | Collegio Universitario Aspiranti Medici Missionaria |
| CUC | Church Unity Commission |
| CUC | Churches' Unity Commission |
| CUEJ | Centre Universitaire d'Etudes Juives |
| CUF | Citizens United for Faith |
| CUFF | Catholics United for the Faith |
| CUMIF | Collegio Universitario Missionario Internazionale Femminile |
| CURBZ | Church of Uganda, Ruanda, Burundi and Zaire |
| CUSIC | Comité Unitario de los Sindicalistas Cristianos |
| CVM | Vincentian Congregation of Malabar (Congregazione |

| | |
|---|---|
| | Vincenziana Malabarese) |
| CVUOSB | Congregazione Benedettina Vallombrosana |
| CV/AV | Coeurs Vaillants (boys)/Ames Vaillantes (girls) |
| CWC | Commission on World Concerns |
| CWCs | Christian World Communions |
| CWM | Christian Workers' Movement |
| CWM | Council for World Mission |
| CWME | Commission on World Mission and Evangelism |
| CWN | Christian Weekly Newspapers |
| CWS | Church World Service |
| CYFA | Church Youth Fellowship Association |

## D

| | |
|---|---|
| D | diocese, eparchy |
| DCC | Délégation Catholique pour la Coopération |
| DCL | doctor of canon law |
| DD | doctor of divinity |
| DEA | Deutsche Evangelische Allianz |
| DEC | Departamento de Educación |
| DECOS | Departamento de Comunicación Social |
| DEFAP | Départment Evangélique Français d'Action Apostolique |
| DEMECOS | Departamento de Medios de Comunicación Social |
| DESAL | Centro para la Desarrollo Económico y Social de América Latina |
| DFI | Dialogue with People of Living Faiths and Ideologies |
| DGI | Council of Churches in Indonesia |
| DIA | Difusiones Interamericanas |
| DIAL | Documentation et Information sur l'Amérique Latine |
| DICARWS | Division of Inter-Church Aid, Refugee and World Service |
| DKR | Deutscher Koordinierungsrat der Gesellschaften für Christlich-Jüdische Zusammenarbeit |
| DLM | Danish Lutheran Mission |
| DM | Dorothea Mission |
| DMA | Diocesan Missionary Association |
| DMC | Departamento de Misiones |
| DMiss | doctor of missiology |
| DMS | Danish Missionary Society |
| DNR | David Nunn Revivals, USA |
| DOM | Division of Overseas Ministries, NCCCUSA |
| DOPAS | Departamento de Opinión Publica del Arzobispado de Santiago |
| DRC | Dutch Reformed Church |
| DRCM | Dutch Reformed Church Mission |
| DSS | doctor of sacred scripture |
| DTLM | Door to Life Ministries |
| DU | Dienste in Ubersee |
| DW | Diakonisches Werk |
| DWME | Division of World Mission and Evangelism |
| DZINTARS | Latvian Catholic Student Association |

## E

| | |
|---|---|
| E | east, eastern |
| E | exarchate |
| EA | exarchate apostolic |
| EAB | Evangelische Arbeitnehmerbewegung in Deutschland |
| EAC | Evangelical Association of the Caribbean |
| EACA | East Africa Christian Alliance |
| EACC | East Asia Christian Conference |
| EACCSE | Ecumenical Advisory Council for Church Service in Egypt |
| EAD | Evangelical Alliance of Denmark |
| EAF | Evangelismo a Fondo (Evangelism-in-Depth) |
| EAFJ | Evangelischer Arbeitskreis für Jugendführung |
| EAGB | Evangelical Alliance of Great Britain |
| EAGWM | Evangelische Arbeitsgemeinschaft für Weltmission |
| EAL | Evangelischer Arbeitskreis Lichtbild |
| EAM | Evangelical Association of Malawi |
| EAREC | East Africa Religious Education Committee |
| EASPI | Evangelical Alliance of the South Pacific Islands |
| EBF | European Baptist Federation |
| EBM | Evangelical Baptist Mission |
| ECAM | Enseignement Catholique au Maroc |
| ECC | Evangelical Covenant Church |
| ECCA | Evangelical Covenant Church of America |
| ECCLA | Latin American Catholic Charismatic Renewal Leaders Conference |
| ECCY | Ecumenical Council of Churches in Yugoslavia |
| ECD | Ecumenical Council of Denmark |
| ECF | Episcopal Charismatic Fellowship |
| ECF | Evangelize China Fellowship |
| ECHL | Ecumenical Council of Hungarian Churches |
| ECI | Episcopal Conference of Ireland |
| ECJME | Episcopal Church in Jerusalem & the Middle East |
| ECL | Episcopal Conference of Lesotho |
| ECLA | Evangelical Committee for Latin America |
| ECLOF | Ecumenical Church Loan Fund |
| ECM | Episcopal Conference of Malawi |
| ECM | European Christian Mission |
| ECOC | Evangelical Churchmen's Ordination Council |
| ECUMEDIA | Ecumenical Media Services |
| ECUSA | Episcopal Church in the USA |
| ECUSAT | Ecumenical Satellite Commission |
| ECWA | Evangelical Churches of West Africa |
| ECZ | Eglise du Christ au Zaïre |
| ed | editor, edited by |
| EEA | European Evangelical Alliance |
| EES | Entr'aide Educative et Sociale |
| EES | European Evangelistic Society |
| EFAC | Evangelical Fellowship of the Anglican Communion |
| EFB | Evangelical Fellowship of Botswana |
| EFCA | Evangelical Free Church of America |
| EFE | Evangelical Fellowship of Egypt |
| EFGA | Elim Foursquare Gospel Alliance |
| EFI | Evangelical Fellowship of India |
| EFK | Evangelical Fellowship of Kenya |
| EFMA | Evangelical Foreign Missions Association |
| EFP | Evangelical Fellowship of Pakistan |
| EFR | Evangelical Fellowship of Rhodesia |
| EFS | Swedish Evangelical Mission |
| EFT | Evangelical Fellowship of Thailand |
| EFV | Evangelical Fellowship of Viet-Nam |
| EFZ | Evangelical Fellowship of Zambia |
| EHC | Every Home Crusade |
| EID | Evangelism-in-Depth |
| EIRENE | International Christian Service for Peace |
| EJCSK | Eglise de Jésus-Christ sur la Terre par le Prophète Simon Kimbangu |
| EKD | Evangelische Kirche in Deutschland |
| EKU | Evangelische Kirche der Union |
| ELC | Evangelical Lutheran Church |
| ELFEA | Evangelical Literature Fellowship of East Africa |
| ELFI | Evangelical Literature Fellowship of India |
| ELK | Evangelisch-Lutherische Kirche |
| ELO | Evangelical Literature Overseas |
| ELWA | Eternal Love Winning Africa |
| EMA | Elim Missionary Assemblies |
| EMA | Evangelical Missionary Alliance |
| EMBMC | Eastern Mennonite Board of Missions and Charities |
| EMI | Editrice Missionaria Italiana |
| EMI | Edizioni Missionarie Italiane |
| EMI | Ent'raide Missionnaire Internationale |
| EMIS | Evangelical Missions Information Service |
| EMS | Evangelical Missionary Society |
| ENA | Evangelischer Nachrichtendienst in der DDR |
| EP | Ecumenical Patriarchate |
| EP | Equipes Populaires |
| EPF | European Pentecostal Fellowship |
| EPIS | Enseignment par l'Image et par le Son |
| EPS | Ecumenical Press Service |
| ERA | Educational (Renewal) Agency |
| ERBOL | Escuelas Radiofónicas de Bolivia |
| ERF | Education Renewal Fund |
| ERV | English Revised Version (of the Bible) |
| ESA | Evangelization Society of Australia |
| ESCEAL | Estudios Sociológicos del Cristianismo Evangélico en América Latina |
| ESG | Evangelische Studentengemeinde in Österreich |
| ESII | Ecumenical Social & Industrial Institute |
| ESP | Ecumenical Sharing of Personnel |
| ESP | extra-sensory perception (telepathy) |
| esp | especially |
| ESYSME | Ecumenical Secretariat for Youth and Students of the Middle East |
| et al | & others |
| et alia | & other things |
| et alii | & other people |
| EUREC | Europe Regional Centre, UBS |
| EUSA | Evangelical Union of South America |
| eV | eingetragener Verein (registered society) (Germany) |
| EVAF | Evangelismo a Fondo (Evangelism-in-Depth) |
| Ev-L | Evangelisch-Lutherische |
| Ev-l | Evangelisch-lutherische |
| EWIBM | East & West Indies Bible Mission |
| ex | out of, from (used in this Encyclopedia exclusively of schisms or secessions) |
| EYCE | Ecumenical Youth Council in Europe |
| EYS | Ecumenical Youth Service |
| EZE | Evangelische Zentralstelle für Entwicklungshilfe |

## F

| | |
|---|---|
| FABC | Federation of Asian Bishops' Conferences |
| FAIE | Federación Argentina de Iglesias Evangélicas |
| FALMI | Francescane Ausiliarie Laiche Missionarie Immacolata |
| FASE | Federação de Orgãos para Assistencia Social e Educacional |
| FAST | Association for Final Advance of Scripture Translation |
| FBF | see OH |
| FBM | French Bible Mission |
| FC | Figli della Carità |
| FCA | Fellowship of Christian Athletes |
| FCAC | Federal Council of African Churches |
| FCC | Fiji Council of Churches |
| FCCS | Fellowship of Christian Churches in Samoa |
| FCEI | Federazione delle Chiese Evangeliche in Italia |
| FCFC | Free Church Federal Council |
| FCIC | Federal Catholic Immigration Committee |
| FCME | Federación Católica de los Maestros Españoles |
| FdCC | Canossians (Congregation of Sons of Charity) |
| FDM | Brothers of Mercy |
| FDP | Brothers of Divine Providence |
| FDPMM | Father Divine Peace Mission Movement |
| FEAM | Far East Apostolic Mission |
| FEB | Federação Espírita Brasileira |
| FEBA | Far East Broadcasting Association |
| FEBC | Far East Broadcasting Company |
| FEBC | Fellowship of Evangelical Baptist Churches |
| FEBEC | Federación Boliviana de Educación Católica |
| FEC | Fédération des Enseignements Catholiques |
| FECC | Fédération des Eglises Chrétiennes du Congo |
| FECCC | Far Eastern Council of Christian Churches |
| FECI | Fédération Evangélique de Côte d'Ivoire |
| FECI | Federation of Evangelical Churches of India |
| FECOR | Federación Costarricense de Religiosos |
| FECUN | Federación Española Comunidades Universitarias |
| FEDAAS | Federación Española de Asociaciones de Asistentes Sociales |
| FEDEPAR | Federación de Religiosos y Religiosas de Panamá |
| FEECA | Europäische Föderation für Katholische Erwachsensbildung |
| FEET | Fédération des Eglises Evangéliques du Tchad |
| FEGC | Far Eastern Gospel Crusade |
| FELCSA | Federation of Evangelical Lutheran Churches in Southern Africa |
| FEM | Federación Evangélica de México |
| FEME | Fédération des Eglises et Missions Evangéliques en Haute-Volta |
| FEMEC | Fédération des Eglises et Missions Evangéliques du Cameroun |
| FENEC | Federación Nicaraguense Educación Católica |
| FEPS | Fédération des Eglises Protestantes de la Suisse |
| FERE | Federación Española de Religiosos de Enseñanza |
| FEREC | Federación de Religiosas de Costa Rica |
| FERELPAR | Federación de Religiosos del Paraguay |
| FERES | Fédération Internationale des Instituts de Recherches Socio-Religieuses |
| FERVE | Federación de Religiosas de Venezuela |
| FES | Fraternité Evangélique du Sénégal |
| FFF | Free Farmers' Federation |
| FFFM | Finnish Free Foreign Mission |
| FFKM | Fédération Chrétien de Madagascar |
| FFPM | Christian Council of Madagascar |
| FFSC | Fratelli Francescani della Santa Croce (Treviri) |
| FFSI | Fratelli Figli di San Giuseppe del Rwanda (Bayozefiti) |
| FFW | Federation of Free Workers |
| FGBMFI | Full Gospel Business Men's Fellowship International |
| FGC | Friends General Conference |
| FGER | Federación Guatemalteca de Escuelas Radiofónicas |
| FHSC | Fédération Haitienne des Syndicats Chrétiens |
| FIAC | Fédération Internationale des Agences Catholiques de Presse |
| FIAMC | International Federation of Associations of Catholic Doctors |
| FIC | Brothers of the Immaculate Conception (Fratelli dell' Immacolata Concezione di Maastricht) |
| FIC | Fédération des Instituteurs Chrétiens de Belgique |
| FICEP | Fédération Internationale Catholique d'Education Physique et Sportive |
| FICIR | Federazione Italiana Centri e Instituti per la Riabilitazione |
| FICP | Institute of Brothers of Christian Instruction of Ploërmel |
| FEDAE | Federazione Instituti Dipendenti della Autorita Ecclesiastica |
| FIDJC | Fédération Internationale des Journalistes Catholiques |
| FIDJC | Fédération Internationale des Directeurs de Journaux Catholiques |
| FIEC | Fellowship of Independent Evangelical Churches |
| FIEU | Federación de Iglesias Evangélicas del Uruguay |
| FIH | Fédération des Institutions Hospitalières |
| FIHC | Fédération Internationale des Hommes Catholiques |
| FIMCAP | Fédération Internationale des Communautés de Jeunesse Catholique Paroissiales |
| FIPC | Fédération Internationale des Pharmaciens Catholiques |
| FIRAS | Federazione Italiana Religiose Asistenza Sociale |
| FIUC | Fédération Internationale des Universités Catholiques |
| FKG | Frikyrkliga Gymnasistrorelsen |
| FLOD | Society for Liturgy and Drama |
| FM | frequency modulation |
| FMC | Free Methodist Church |
| FMI | Sons of Mary Immaculate (Chavagne Fathers) |
| FMJC | Fédération Mondiale de Jeunesse Catholique |
| FMJFC | Federación Mundial de la Juventud Femenina Católica |
| FMM | Fratelli della Misericordia |
| FMM | Franciscan Missionaries of Mary |
| FMS | Finnish Missionary Society |
| FMS | Marist Brothers |
| FMS | Sons of Mary, Health of the Sick |
| FMSI | Figli di Santa Maria Immacolata |
| FNIRF | Federação Nacional dos Institutos Religiosos Femininos |
| FNP | Fédération Nationale des Patros Masculins de Belgique |
| FNPF | Fédération Nationale des Patros de Jeunes Filles |
| FOCSIV | Federazione Organizzazioni Cristiane di Servizio Internazionale Volontario |
| FOCUS | Fellowship of Christian Unions |
| FOI | Formation Oecuménique Interconfessionnelle |
| FOM | Fellowship of Missions |
| FONCABA | Fondation Catholique des Bourses pour Etudiants Africains |
| FOR | Fellowship of Reconciliation |
| FPC | Free Protestant Church |
| FPF | Fédération Protestante de France |
| FR | Freiburger Rundbrief |
| FRU | Federación de Religiosos del Uruguay |
| FS | Fathers of Sion |
| FSA | Family and Social Action |
| FSC | Brothers of Christian Schools (de la Salle Brothers) |
| FSC | Fédération des Scouts Catholiques |
| FSCJ | Verona Fathers, Combonians (Sons of the Sacred Heart) |
| FSF | Brothers of the Holy Family of Belley |
| FSG | Brothers of St Gabriel |
| FSJU | Fonds Social Juif Unifié |
| FSMI | Congregation of Sons of Mary Immaculate |
| FSMS | Fédération des Services Médico-Sociaux |
| FUACE | Fédération Universelle des Associations Chrétiennes d'Etudiants |
| FUCI | Federazione Universitaria Cattolica Italiana |
| FUM | Friends United Mission |
| FWCC | Friends World Committee for Consultation |

## G

| | |
|---|---|
| GAM | Gruppi Appoggio Missionario |
| GARB | General Association of Regular Baptists |
| GBC | Ghana Bishops' Conference |
| GBU | Gruppi Biblici Universitari (IFES) |
| GBUAF | Groupes Bibliques Universitaires d'Afrique Francophone |
| GCC | Guyana Council of Churches |
| GCF | Graduates Christian Fellowship |
| GCP | Guild of Catholic Psychiatrists |
| GCUC | Ghana Church Union Committee |
| GEF | Ghana Evangelical Fellowship |
| GEM | Gospel Extension Ministry |
| GEM | Group on Education for Mission |
| GF | Graduates' Fellowship |
| GFS | Girls Friendly Society |
| GHM | German Hermannsburg Mission |
| GISC | Confédération Internationale du Guidisme |
| GKN | Gereformeerde Kerken in Nederland |
| GLAM | Gruppo Laici Attività Missionaria |
| GmbH | Gesellschaft mit beschränkter Haftung (= Limited, Incorporated) (Germany) |
| GMF | German Missionary Fellowship |
| GMU | Gospel Missionary Union |
| GMWA | Gospel Multimedia Workers Association |
| GNB | Good News Bible |
| GOC | Greek Orthodox Church |
| GOP | Groupe Oecuménique de Pastorale |
| GFF | Gospel Furthering Fellowship |

## H

| | |
|---|---|
| HAESA | Haimanote Abew Ethiopian Students Association |
| HANSEA | Student Christian Movement of Ethiopia |
| HB | Helvetische Bekenntnis/Confession |
| HCJB | Heralding Christ Jesus' Blessings |
| HCMS | Hibernian Church Missionary Society |
| HEKS | Hilfswerk der Evangelischen Kirchen der Schweiz |
| HELVETIAS | Associazione Svizzera di Asistenza Tecnica |
| HKBP | Batak Protestant Christian Church |
| HKCC | Hong Kong Christian Council |
| HKCCCU | Hong Kong Chinese Christian Churches Union |
| HKCEC | Hong Kong Catholic Education Council |
| HKFCS | Hong Kong Federation of Catholic Students |
| HOACF | Hermandad Obrero de Acción Católica Femenina |
| HOACM | Hermandad Obrero de Acción Católica Masculina |
| HOREMCO | Hokkaido Radio Evangelism Mass Communications |
| HQ | headquarters |

## I

| | |
|---|---|
| IAD | Institut des Arts et Diffusion |
| IAHR | International Association for the History of Religions |
| IAM | International Afghan Mission |
| IAML | International Association of Music Libraries |
| IAMS | International Association for Mission Studies |

| | |
|---|---|
| MSpS | Missionaries of the Holy Ghost |
| MSsCc | Congregation of Missionaries of the Sacred Hearts of Jesus and Mary |
| MSSP | Società Missionaria di San Paolo |
| MSSST | Congregation of Missionary Servants of the Most Holy Trinity |
| MSTM | Movimiento de Sacerdotes para el Tercer Mundo |
| MTC | Mouvement des Travailleurs Chrétiens |
| MTh | master of theology |
| MTS | Menno Travel Service |
| MU | Mothers' Union |
| MUST | Metropolitan Urban Service Training Facility |
| MUT | Malta Union of Teachers |
| MW | medium-wave |
| MWC | Mennonite World Conference |
| MXY | Foreign Missions Institute of Yarumal (Xaverian Missionaries of Yarumal) |

# N

| | |
|---|---|
| N | north, northern |
| NAAC | Nigeria Association of Aladura Churches |
| NAAM | National Association for the Advancement of Muslims |
| NACLA | National Christian Leadership Assembly |
| NAE | National Association of Evangelicals |
| NAES | National Association of Ecumenical Staff |
| NAFWB | National Association of Free Will Baptists |
| NAL | National Association of Laity |
| NAM | North Africa Mission |
| NAPARC | North American Presbyterian and Reformed Council |
| NARET | National Association of Religious Education Teachers |
| NASSA | National Secretariat for Social Action |
| NAWR | National Association of Women Religious |
| NBCLC | National Biblical Catechetical and Liturgical Centre |
| NBEA | National Black Evanglical Association |
| NBSC | National Black Sisters' Conference |
| NCAN | National Coalition of American Nuns |
| NCBC | National Conference of Black Churchmen |
| NCC | National Christian Council |
| NCC | National Council of Churches |
| NCCB | National Conference of Catholic Bishops |
| NCCC | National Catholic Communications Centre |
| NCCC | National Conference of Catholic Charities |
| NCCCUSA | National Council of Churches of Christ in the USA |
| NCCI | National Christian Council of India |
| NCCIJ | National Catholic Conference for Interracial Justice |
| NCCJ | National Christian Council of Japan |
| NCCJ | National Conference of Christians and Jews |
| NCCK | National Christian Council of Kenya |
| NCCK | National Council of Churches in Korea |
| NCCL | National Council of Catholic Laity |
| NCCNZ | National Council of Churches in New Zealand |
| NCCP | National Council of Churches in Pakistan |
| NCCP | National Council of Churches in the Philippines |
| NCCSL | National Christian Council of Sri Lanka |
| NCEA | National Catholic Educational Association |
| NCF | Nurses Christian Fellowship |
| NCORT | National Catholic Office for Radio and Television |
| NCRG | New Churches Research Groups |
| NCRMA | Netherlands Christian Reformed Missionary Association |
| NCRMS | Netherlands Christian Reformed Missionary Society |
| NCRV | Netherlands Christian Broadcasting Corporation |
| NCW | Nederlands Christlijk Wekgeversverbond |
| N-D | Notre-Dame |
| n.d. | no date (undated book or publication) |
| NE | northeast, northeastern |
| NEA | Norwegian Evangelical Alliance |
| NEAATS | North East Asia Association of Theological Schools |
| NEB | New English Bible |
| NECC | Near East Council of Churches |
| NEEBII | Near East Ecumenical Bureau Information Interpretation |
| NEECPR | Near East Ecumenical Committee for Palestinian Refugees |
| NEFM | National Evangelical Fellowship of Malaysia |
| NEOM | Norwegian Evangelical Orient Mission |
| NFCC | Norwegian Free Church Council |
| NFCC | National Fraternal Council of Churches |
| NFPC | National Federation of Priests' Councils |
| NGGM | New Guinea Gospel Mission |
| NGK | Dutch Reformed Church (South Africa) |
| NHA | National Holiness Association |
| NHK | Netherlands Reformed Church (Nederduits Hervormde Kerk) |
| NKV | Nederlandse Christlijke Bond van Overheidspersoneel |
| NLFA | New Life For All |
| NLM | Norwegian Lutheran Mission |
| NMA | Norwegian Missionary Alliance |
| NMC | National Missionary Council |
| NMR | Nederlandse Missieraad |
| NMS | National Missionary Society |
| NMS | Norwegian Missionary Society |
| NMZ | Nordelbisches Zentrum für Weltmission und Kirchlichen Weltdienst |
| NNAE | National Negro Evangelical Association |
| NOBC | National Office for Black Catholics |
| NOOR | National Organization for Ophthalmic Rehabilitation |
| NOW | National Organization for Women |
| NPY | Norwegian Pentecostal Mission |
| NRB | National Religious Broadcasters |
| NRC | Netherlands Reformed Church |
| NRGP | Nationaale Raad voor Gezinspastoraal |
| NRP | New Reader Scripture Portions |
| NRS | New Reader Scripture Selections |
| NS | Nossa Senhora, Nuestra Señora |
| NSFC | National Sister Formation Conference |
| NSVC | National Sisters Vocation Conference |
| NT | New Testament |
| NTM | New Tribes Mission |
| NTMU | New Testament Missionary Union |
| NW | northwest, northwestern |
| NYBA | National Young Buddhist Association |
| NYLC | National Young Life Campaign |
| NZBFMS | New Zealand Baptist Foreign Mission Society |
| NZEC | New Zealand Episcopal Conference |
| NZG | Netherlands Missionary Society (Nederlandsch Zendeling-Genootschap) |

# O

| | |
|---|---|
| O | ordinariate |
| OAIC | Organization of African Independent Churches |
| OBNOVA | Federation of Associations of Ukrainian Catholic Students |
| OBSC | Open Bible Standard Churches |
| OC | Carmelites (Order of Our Lady of Mt Carmel) |
| OCart | Carthusian Order |
| OCASEI | Obra Católica de Asistencia a Estudiantes Iberoamericano |
| OCASHA | Obra de Cooperación Apostólica Seglar Hispano-americana |
| OCD | Order of Discalced Carmelites |
| OCEC | Oficio Central de Educación Católica |
| OCES | Office Chrétien de l'Enregistrement Sonore |
| OCFC | Office Catholique Français du Cinéma |
| OCFRT | Office Catholique Français de Radio-Télévision |
| OCIC | Office Catholique International Cinéma |
| OCIPE | Office Catholique d'Information sur les Problèmes Européens |
| OCist | Cistercians |
| OCL | Office Chrétien du Livre |
| OCM | Groupe d'Organismes de Coopération Missionnaire |
| OCMCS | Oficina Coordinadora de los Medios de Comunicación Social |
| OCR | Cistercian Order, Reformed (Trappists) |
| OCSHA | Obra de Cooperación Sacerdotal Hispanoamericana |
| OCSO | Trappists (Order of Cistercians of the Strict Observance) |
| OCU | Officers Christian Union |
| OCYAK | Orthodox Christian Youth Association of Kenya |
| OdeM | Mercedarians (Order of Our Lady of Mercy for the Ransom of Captives) |
| ODUCAL | Organización de Universidades Católicas de América Latina |
| OESA | Hermit Augustinians (Order of Hermits of St Augustine) |
| OFM | Franciscans (Order of Friars Minor) |
| OFMCap | Capuchins (Order of Friars Minor Capuchin) |
| OFMConv | Conventuals (Order of Friars Minor Conventual) |
| OH | Order of Brothers Hospitallers of St John of God |
| OHC | Order of the Holy Cross |
| OIC | Organisations Internationales Catholiques |
| OIEC | Office International de l'Enseignement Catholique |
| OJD | Ökumenischer Jugenddienste |
| OJRiO | Ökumenischer Jugendrat in Österreich |
| OKB | Österreichische Katholische Bibelwerk |
| OKR | Ökumenischer Rat der Kirchen (WCC) |
| OM | Operation Mobilization |
| OM | Minim Hermits of St Francis of Paola |
| OMECO | Oficina Nacional de Medios de Comunicación Social |
| OMF | Overseas Missionary Fellowship |
| OMI | Missionaries Oblates of Mary Immaculate |
| OMS | Oriental Missionary Society |
| OMV | Oblates of the Blessed Virgin Mary |
| ONCS | Office National des Communications Sociales |
| OP | Dominicans (Order of Preachers) |
| OPC | Orthodox Presbyterian Church |
| OPraem | Premonstratensians, or Norbertines (Canons Regular of Prémontré) |
| ORSA | Recollect Augustinians (Order of Augustinian Recollects) |
| OSA | Augustinian Friars (Order of St Augustine) |
| OSB | Confederate Benedictines (Order of St Benedict) |
| OSBM | Basilians (Order of St Basil the Great) |
| OSC | Crosier Fathers (Canons Regular of the Order of the Holy Cross) |
| OSC | Orthodox Syrian Church |
| OSCam | Camillians (Ministers of the Sick, Clerics Regular) |
| OSCO | Overseas Students Coordination |
| OSFO | Osborn Foundation International |
| OSFS | Oblates of St Francis de Sales |
| OSLAM | Organización de Seminarios Latinoamericanos |
| OSM | Servites (Order of the Servants of Mary) |
| OSsT | Trinitarian Fathers (Order of the Most Holy Trinity) |
| OSU | Ursuline Sisters of the Roman Union |
| OT | Old Testament |
| OW | Operation World |
| OYM | Orthodox Youth Movement |

# P

| | |
|---|---|
| P | patriarchate, patriarchal diocese |
| p. | number of pages in book, article or periodical |
| PA | Patres Albi, Pères d'Afrique (WF) |
| PA | prefecture apostolic |
| PABATS | Philippine Association of Bible and Theological Schools |
| PACLA | Pan-African Christian Leadership Assembly |
| PACTEE | Pakistan Committee on Theological Education by Extension |
| PAFES | Pan-African Fellowship of Evangelical Students |
| PAFTEE | Philippine Committee on Theological Education by Extension |
| PAG | Pentecostal Assemblies of God |
| PALMS | Paulian Association Lay Missionary Secretariat |
| PAO | Professional Athletes Outreach |
| PAoC | Pentecostal Assemblies of Canada |
| PAoW | Pentecostal Assemblies of the World |
| PAoWI | Pentecostal Assemblies of the West Indies |
| PAS | Pater Ahlbrinckstichting |
| PATS | Philippines Association of Theological Schools |
| PAVLA | Papal Volunteers for Latin America |
| PAW | Pentecostal Assemblies of the World |
| PBCS | Pakistan Bible Correspondence School |
| PCA | Presbyterian Church of Australia |
| PCC | Pacific Conference of Churches |
| PCC | Pentecostal Church of Christ |
| PCE | Presbyterian Church of England |
| PCEC | Philippine Council of Evanglical Churches |
| PCG | Pentecostal Church of God |
| PCJ | Prêtres du Sacré-Coeur de Jésus de Bétharram |
| PCMA | Protestant Churches Medical Association |
| PCR | Programme to Combat Racism |
| PCUS | Presbyterian Church in the US |
| PCW | Presbyterian Church of Wales |
| PDC | Partido Democrata Cristiano |
| PDG | Pastoral Development Group |
| PE | patriarchal exarchate |
| PECUSA | Protestant Episcopal Church in the USA |
| PEMS | Paris Evangelical Missionary Society |
| PERSETHIA | Association of Theological Schools in Indonesia |
| PFES | Pakistan Fellowship of Evangelical Students |
| PFM | Marist Brothers (Little Brothers of Mary) |
| PFNA | Pentecostal Fellowship of North America |
| PHAM | Private Hospital Association of Malawi |
| PHC | Pentecostal Holiness Church |
| PhD | doctor of philosophy |
| PI | Programmed Instruction |
| PICEC | Pacific Islands Christian Education Council |
| PIME | Pontifical Institute for Foreign Missions (Pontificio Istituto Missioni Estere) |
| PISA | Priests' Institute for Social Action |
| PKE | Priesterkreise für Konziliare Erneuerung |
| PMCA | Pentecostal Mission Churches Association |
| PME | Foreign Missions Society, Province of Quebec |
| PMU | Pontifical Missionary Union |
| PMV | Pro Mundi Vita |
| PMW | Pontifical Missionary Works |
| PN | prelature (prelacy) nullius |
| PNCC | Polish National Catholic Church |
| PPC | Propaganda Popular Católica |
| PPP | Discoteca Pax, Centro Propaganda Popular Católica |
| PRE | Polish Ecumenical Council |
| PSA | Paraboles et Symbôles pour Aujourd'hui |
| PSS | Sulpicians (Society of the Priests of St Sulpice) |
| PSSC | Missionari di San Carlo (Scalabrinians) |
| PTFWR | Philadelphia Task Force on Women in Religion |
| PTL | Pocket Testament League |
| PTS | Protestant Truth Society |
| PUCRGS | Pontificia Universidade Católica do Rio Grande do Sul |
| PUCRJ | Pontificia Universidade Católica do Rio de Janeiro |
| PUCSP | Pontificia Universidade Católica de São Paulo |

# Q

| | |
|---|---|
| qv | quod vide (which see; i.e. refer to previous item) |

# R

| | |
|---|---|
| RADIUS | Religious Drama Society of Great Britain |
| RBMU | Regions Beyond Missionary Union |
| RC | Reformed Church |
| RC | Roman Catholic |
| RCA | Reformed Church in America |
| RCBC | Rhodesia Catholic Bishops' Conference |
| RCC | Rhodesia Christian Conference |
| RCC | Roman Catholic Church |
| RCI | Congregation of Rogationist Fathers of the Heart of Jesus |
| RCJCLdS | Reorganized Church of Jesus Christ of Latter-day Saints |
| RCMS | Church Missionary Society (Ruanda Mission) |
| REC | Reformed Episcopal Church |
| REP | Religious Education Press |
| RES | Reformed Ecumenical Synod |
| RICA | Reformed Independent Churches Association |
| RKPN | Rooms Katholiek Partij Nederland |
| RKZ | Romisch-Katholische Zentralkonferenz der Landeskirchen |
| RM | Rhenish Mission |
| RN | priory nullius |
| RNA | Religious Newswriters Association |
| RNMDSF | Royal National Mission to Deep Sea Fishermen |
| ROC | Russian Orthodox Church |
| ROCOR | Russian Orthodox Church Outside of Russia |
| ROEG | Rassemblement Oecuménique des Eglises de Genève |
| RPCES | Reformed Presbyterian Church, Evangelical Synod |
| RPCNA | Reformed Presbyterian Church of North America |
| RPS | Reformed Press Service |
| RSAK | Religious Superiors' Association of Kenya |
| RSB | Radio School of the Bible |
| RSCM | Royal Society for Church Music |
| RSMT | Red Sea Mission Team |
| RSV | Religiosi di San Vicenzo de' Paoli, Padri e Fratelli |
| RSV | Revised Standard Version (of the Bible) |
| RTCB | Radio-Télévision Catholique Belge |
| RUCOM | Rural Consultation Mission |
| RV | Revised Version (of the Bible) |
| RVat | Radio Vatican |
| RVOG | Radio Voice of the Gospel |

# S

| | |
|---|---|
| S | south, southern |
| SA | Franciscan Friars of the Atonement (Graymoor) |
| SA | Soeurs d'Afrique (White Sisters) |
| SA | Salvation Army |
| SABMS | South African Baptist Missionary Society |
| SAC | Pallottines (Society of the Catholic Apostolate) |
| SAC | Social Action Centre |
| SACBC | Southern Africa Catholic Bishops' Conference |
| SACC | South African Council of Churches |
| SACCC | South African Council of Christian Churches |
| SACLA | South Africa Christian Leadership Assembly |
| SACP | Southern African Council of Priests |
| SADM | Saléssiennes Auxiliaires des Missions |
| SAGM | South Africa General Mission |
| SAIM | South America Indian Mission |
| SAM | Swedish Alliance Mission |
| SAM | South America Mission |
| SAMS | South American Missionary Society |
| SASRA | Soldiers' and Airmen's Scripture Readers' Association |
| SAVI | Service d'Accueil aux Voyageurs et aux Immigrants |
| SBC | Southern Baptist Convention |
| SBF | Southern Baptist Foundation |
| SBL | Society of Biblical Literature |
| SBLE | Society of Biblical Literature and Exegesis |
| SBU | Sociedades Biblicas Unidas (UBS) |
| SC | Sacred Congregation (in Rome) |
| SC | Sacré-Coeur |
| SC | Brothers of the Sacred Heart (Fratelli del Sacro Cuore) |
| SCA | Student Christian Association |
| SCAD | Société Civile et Agricole de Dzoghégan |
| SCC | Scottish Churches Council |
| SCC | Swaziland Conference of Churches |
| SCJ | Congregation of the Priests of the Sacred Heart |
| SCJ | Priests of the Sacred Heart (Betharram) |
| SCJ | Society of the Sacred Heart of the Infant Jesus |
| SCLC | Southern Christian Leadership Conference |
| SCM | Student Christian Movement |
| SCOBA | Standing Conference of Canonical Orthodox Bishops in the Americas |
| SCS | Social Communications Service |
| SDA | Seventh-day Adventists |
| SDB | Salesians of St John Bosco (Society of St Francis de Sales) |
| SDB | Seventh Day Baptists |
| SDBC | Seventh Day Baptist Church |
| SDF | Scouts de France |
| SDS | Salvatorians (Society of the Divine Saviour) |
| SDV | Società Divine Vocazioni (Padri Vocazionisti) |
| SE | southeast, southeastern |
| SEA | Swedish Evangelical Alliance |

# PHOTOGRAPHIC INDEX

Listed here are all subjects and topics illustrated in the photographs and diagrams contained in this volume, or described in their accompanying captions. In particular, the index lists their countries, places, occasions, events, persons, peoples, languages, cultures, ethnolinguistic groups, races, religions, types of Christian, ecclesiastical blocs and traditions, types of denomination, types of Christian organization, councils, church growth or decline, trends, beliefs, activities, evangelism, religious practices, resources, buildings, projects, rituals, liturgies, uniforms, vestments, robes, headgear, other details of religious equipment, representations (images,

icons, paintings, statues), and the range of phenomena of religion and Christianity in general. It also lists illustrations of the methods of description, enumeration and analysis evolved in this Encyclopedia. On the other hand, the index does not record the smaller details of all photographs. In general, it omits names of small towns and villages, also names of denominations and individual churches or congregations.
The index omits certain widely-applicable terms that would otherwise occur too frequently. 'Roman Catholics' and 'Protestants', for instance, occur in every other illustration. Terms thus omitted include :

Christian, Christians, church, churches, church buildings, missions, mission stations, Protestants, Roman Catholics, Catholics, Evangelicals (partially included), priests, ministers, clergy, preachers.
The notation 'et alia' is added to a few cases where there are numbers of other secondary illustrations of subjects but which are too frequent to detail.
The listing follows its own type of alphabetization, varying slightly from that used elsewhere in the book : it alphabetizes on first letters irrespective of whether these are in capitals or in lowercase.

# STANDARD AND DEFINITIVE LOCATIONS INDEX

This is primarily an index of general subjects, major categories of data, and types of information.

KEY
1. Numbers standing alone (1-999) = page numbers of major or definitive locations.
2. Entries without page numbers = standard locations, repeated for all countries.
3. The word 'total' = global total of category shown.

There is no need in this Encyclopedia for a general subject index because (a) most significant material has already been presented throughout under several alphabetical listings (countries, denominations, service agencies, directory entries), and (b) most specific categories of data or information are placed in standardized locations within the overall framework. As a

result, comparative data from one country to the next can rapidly be found. This final index attempts to facilitate the whole process of locating specific data.

There are 2 types of entry below: those with page numbers, and those with Part numbers. These will now be described.

(1) All numbers (1-999) standing alone below are *page numbers* unless otherwise clearly stated. These give the definitive or major or unique location or locations of specific categories — items of data or information or definition, or directory of addresses; they also indicate pages with global maps where relevant. Hence, if you wish to find the total number of Methodists, or Maronites, in the world for a particular year, this index refers you to its definitive location. Sometimes 2 or more locations are given, placing the required total in different contexts. This represents the quickest way of finding herein an exact total or figure or definition that you require for any clearly-defined category.

(2) Locations with *Part numbers* (e.g. 'Part 7, SECULAR DATA') give the regular or standardized or repeated location or locations in which may be found information on any category existing in a large number of countries. The locations are repeated in exactly the same position and sequence from one country to the next, especially throughout Part 7. Hence, in cases where a specific statistical category or other item of data occurs frequently for a large number of countries, or denominations, or religions, the index refers the reader to any standard position or location that it occupies in a country's survey article or other position, at which the data may immediately be found. These locations are given here mainly by parts (Part 1, Part 2, etc), with further internal position where simple to describe. Thus the reference 'Part 7, SECULAR DATA, STATE' tells the reader that the items he wants will be found throughout Part 7 for all countries under the heading SECULAR DATA, and under the sub-heading STATE at that location.

# ACKNOWLEDGEMENTS

The editor wishes to acknowledge his indebtedness not only to the contributors and collaborators listed at the beginning of the book, but also to the very large number of other persons and organizations who supplied information each about their own activities. Most of the denominations listed in each country, and many other agencies and bodies mentioned or described, supplied this information to us either directly by mail or in person in interviews. The 4 associate editors should also be credited with the bringing together and making sense of this vast mass of information. François Houtart interpreted the major movements of the era and worked out how to document them, Georges Deroy produced pioneering surveys of the Catholic world in all countries, and Malcolm McVeigh collated these with those of the Protestant and other worlds; whilst John Padwick, a specialist in the African indigenous churches, fitted these disparate materials together.

We also express gratitude to a number of church-related organizations which contributed grants towards the operating of this project. Grants and assistance small or large were received from the following: Adveniat (Germany), American Baptist Churches, Anglican Church of Canada, Anglican Consultative Council (UK), Bishops' Conference of Germany, Campus Crusade for Christ International, Christian Church (Disciples of Christ), Church Missionary Society (UK), Church of the Province of Kenya, Commission on World Mission and Evangelism/WCC, Division of Overseas Ministries/NCCCUSA, Sacred Congregation for the Evangelization of Peoples, Episcopal Church in the USA, FERES (Belgium), Humanum (Germany), Lausanne Committee for World Evangelization, Lutheran Church Missouri Synod, Lutheran World Federation, Maryknoll Mission, Missio (Germany), Mission Training and Resource Center (Pasadena), Missions Advanced Research and Communication Centre (Monrovia, USA), National Council of Churches of Christ in the USA, Survey Application Trust (Grubb Institute for World Studies, UK), United Church of Christ (USA), United Methodist Church (World Division, Board of Global Ministries), United Presbyterian Church in the USA, World Council of Churches, World Vision International. Among donors of smaller grants were: Abbaye d'Orval (Belgium), American Baptist Foreign Missionary Society, Assemblies of God (USA), Christian Reformed Church, Conservative Baptist Association of America, Department of Philosophy & Religious Studies/University of Nairobi, Lutheran Church in America, Netherlands Reformed Church, Reformed Church in America, Sudan Interior Mission, United Church Board for World Mission, United Reformed Church (UK), West Indies Mission, World Radio Missionary Fellowship, et alia.

## Maps and flags

The editor is especially grateful to 3 organizations who supplied maps. Firstly, Reader's Digest Almanac allowed us to use their maps and flags for 180 countries as locating symbols on the mastheads of the articles in Part 7. Secondly, W.H. Allen & Co. Ltd. granted permission for us to reproduce 180 small maps from their Book of the World, by T.C.G. Stacey; these are our quick-reference locating maps which highlight the boundaries and cities of some 180 countries in the narrative text of Part 7. Thirdly, Oxford University Press has permitted us to reproduce in our Part 11 their 18 Human Environment maps from the Oxford World Atlas/Penguin World Atlas.

## Photographs

We further acknowledge with gratitude the assistance of a number of photographic libraries and agencies, as well as individual experts and specialists, in the assembling of a collection of illustrations which would do justice to the complexity of contemporary global Christianity and its context in the modern world. Half of the photographs in this encyclopedia are the editor's own; the other half were supplied from or are owned by the organizations and persons listed alphabetically below (with individuals included alphabetically by surname), whose co-operation and permission to reproduce has been much appreciated. In a number of cases, the denominations illustrated in photographs sent us copies waiving credit or charges. Their illustrations have made our survey that much more complete. Special thanks are due to John Taylor and the staff of the various World Council of Churches photo departments, whose extensive holdings on world Christianity were invaluable to the editor's search for representative coverage; as a result, 50 of our illustrations are WCC/COE/ORK photographs. Lastly, a few professional photographic libraries searched their collections for our categories; for these, the relevant page numbers of their photographs are added below in parentheses.

Every effort has been made to trace and contact copyright owners. If there are any inadvertent omissions in these acknowledgements, we apologize to those concerned and invite them to apply for redress.